Income Tax Regulations

Including Proposed Regulations

As of January 10, 2002

Volume 4
§1.871-1–§1.1563-4

CCH Editorial Staff Publication

CCH INCORPORATED
Chicago

This publication is designed to provide accurate and authoritative information in regard to the subject matter covered. It is sold with the understanding that the publisher is not engaged in rendering legal, accounting, or other professional service. If legal advice or other expert assistance is required, the services of a competent professional person should be sought.

ISBN 0-8080-0761-0

©2002, **CCH** INCORPORATED

4025 W. Peterson Ave.
Chicago, IL 60646-6085
1 800 248 3248
http://tax.cchgroup.com

No claim is made to original government works; however, within this Product or Publication, the following are subject to CCH's copyright: (1) the gathering, compilation, and arrangement of such government materials; (2) the magnetic translation and digital conversion of data, if applicable; (3) the historical, statutory and other notes and references; and (4) the commentary and other materials.

All Rights Reserved
Printed in the United States of America

Nonresident Aliens and Foreign Corporations

[Reg. § 1.871-1]

§ 1.871-1. Classification and manner of taxing alien individuals.—(a) *Classes of aliens.* For purposes of the income tax, alien individuals are divided generally into two classes, namely, resident aliens and nonresident aliens. Resident alien individuals are, in general, taxable the same as citizens of the United States; that is, a resident alien is taxable on income derived from all sources, including sources without the United States. See § 1.1-1(b). Nonresident alien individuals are taxable only on certain income from sources within the United States and on the income described in section 864(c)(4) from sources without the United States which is effectively connected for the taxable year with the conduct of a trade or business in the United States. However, nonresident alien individuals may elect, under section 6013(g) or (h), to be treated as U.S. residents for purposes of determining their income tax liability under chapters 1, 5, and 24 of the Code. Accordingly, any reference in §§ 1.1-1 through 1.1388-1 and §§ 1.1491-1 through 1.1494-1 of this part to nonresident alien individuals does not include those with respect to whom an election under section 6013(g) or (h) is in effect, unless otherwise specifically provided. Similarly, any reference to resident aliens or U.S. residents includes those with respect to whom an election is in effect, unless otherwise specifically provided.

(b) *Classes of nonresident aliens*—(1) *In general.* For purposes of the income tax, nonresident alien individuals are divided into the following three classes:

(i) Nonresident alien individuals who at no time during the taxable year are engaged in a trade or business in the United States,

(ii) Nonresident alien individuals who at any time during the taxable year are, or are deemed under § 1.871-9 to be, engaged in a trade or business in the United States, and

(iii) Nonresident alien individuals who are bona fide residents of Puerto Rico during the entire taxable year.

An individual described in subdivision (i) or (ii) of this subparagraph is subject to tax pursuant to the provisions of subpart A (section 871 and following), part II, subchapter N, chapter 1 of the Code, and the regulations thereunder. See §§ 1.871-7 and 1.871-8. The provisions of subpart A do not apply to individuals described in subdivision (iii) of this subparagraph, but such individuals, except as provided in section 933 with respect to Puerto Rican source income, are subject to the tax imposed by section 1 or section 1201(b). See § 1.876-1.

(2) *Treaty income.* If the gross income of a nonresident alien individual described in subparagraph (1)(i) or (ii) of this paragraph includes income on which the tax is limited by tax convention, see § 1.871-12.

(3) *Exclusions from gross income.* For rules relating to the exclusion of certain items from the gross income of a nonresident alien individual, including annuities excluded under section 871(f), see §§ 1.872-2 and 1.894-1.

(4) *Expatriation to avoid tax.* For special rules applicable in determining the tax of a nonresident alien individual who has lost United States citizenship with a principal purpose of avoiding certain taxes, see section 877.

(5) *Adjustment of tax of certain nonresident aliens.* For the application of pre-1967 income tax provisions to residents of a foreign country which imposes a more burdensome income tax than the United States, and for the adjustment of the income tax of a national or resident of a foreign country which imposes a discriminatory income tax on the income of citizens of the United States or domestic corporations, see section 896.

(6) *Citizens of certain United States possessions.* For rules for treating as nonresident alien individuals certain citizens of possessions of the United States who are not otherwise citizens of the United States, see section 932 and § 1.932-1.

(7) *Conduit financing arrangements.* For rules regarding conduit financing arrangements, see §§ 881-3 and 1.881-4.

(c) Reserved.

(d) *Effective date.* This section shall apply for taxable years beginning after December 31, 1966. For corresponding rules applicable to taxable years beginning before January 1, 1967, see 26 CFR 1.871-1 and 1.871-7(a) (Rev. as of Jan. 1, 1971). [Reg. § 1.871-1.]

☐ [T.D. 6258, 10-23-57. Amended by T.D. 7332, 12-20-74, T.D. 7670, 1-30-80 and T.D. 8611, 8-10-95.]

[Reg. § 1.871-2]

§ 1.871-2. Determining residence of alien individuals.—(a) *General.* The term "nonresident alien individual" means an individual whose residence is not within the United States, and who is not a citizen of the United States. The term includes a nonresident alien fiduciary. For such purpose the term "fiduciary" shall have the meaning assigned to it by section 7701(a)(6) and the regulations in Part 301 of this chapter (Regulations on Procedure and Administration). For presumption as to an alien's nonresidence, see paragraph (b) of § 1.871-4.

(b) *Residence defined.* An alien actually present in the United States who is not a mere transient or sojourner is a resident of the United States for purposes of the income tax. Whether he is a transient is determined by his intentions with regard to the length and nature of his stay. A mere floating intention, indefinite as to time, to return to another country is not sufficient to constitute him a transient. If he lives in the United States and has no definite intention as to his stay, he is a resident. One who comes to the United States for a definite purpose which in its nature may be promptly accomplished is a transient; but, if his purpose is of such a nature that an extended stay may be necessary for its accomplishment, and to that end the alien makes his home temporarily in the United States, he becomes a resident, though it may be his intention at all times to return to his domicile abroad when the purpose for which he came has been consummated or abandoned. An alien whose stay in the United States is limited to a definite period by the immigration laws is not a resident of the United States within the meaning of this section, in the absence of exceptional circumstances.

(c) *Application and effective dates.* Unless the context indicates otherwise, §§ 1.871-2 through 1.871-5 apply to determine the residence of aliens for taxable years beginning before January 1, 1985. To determine the residence of aliens for taxable years beginning after December 31, 1984, see section 7701(b) and §§ 301.7701(b)-1 through 301.7701(b)-9 of this chapter. However, for purposes of determining whether an individual is a qualified individual under section 911(d)(1)(A), the rules of §§ 1.871-2 and 1.871-5 shall continue to apply for taxable years beginning after December 31, 1984. For purposes of determining whether an individual is a resident of the United States for estate and gift tax purposes, see § 20.0-1(b)(1) and (2) and § 25.2501-1(b) of this chapter, respectively. [Reg. § 1.871-2.]

☐ [*T.D.* 6258, 10-23-57. *Amended by T.D.* 8411, 4-24-92.]

[Reg. § 1.871-3]

§ 1.871-3. **Residence of alien seamen.**—In order to determine whether an alien seaman is a resident of the United States for purposes of the income tax, it is necessary to decide whether the presumption of nonresidence (as prescribed by paragraph (b) of § 1.871-4) is overcome by facts showing that he has established a residence in the United States. Residence may be established on a vessel regularly engaged in coastwise trade, but the mere fact that a sailor makes his home on a vessel which is flying the United States flag and is engaged in foreign trade is not sufficient to establish residence in the United States, even though the vessel, while carrying on foreign trade, touches at American ports. An alien seaman may acquire an actual residence in the United States within the rules laid down in § 1.871-4, although the nature of his calling requires him to be absent for a long period from the place where his residence is established. An alien seaman may acquire such a residence at a sailors' boarding house or hotel, but such a claim should be carefully scrutinized in order to make sure that such residence is bona fide. The filing of Form 1078 or taking out first citizenship papers is proof of residence in the United States from the time the form is filed or the papers taken out, unless rebutted by other evidence showing an intention to be a transient. [Reg. § 1.871-3.]

☐ [*T.D.* 6258, 10-23-57.]

[Reg. § 1.871-4]

§ 1.871-4. **Proof of residence of aliens.**—(a) *Rules of evidence.* The following rules of evidence shall govern in determining whether or not an alien within the United States has acquired residence therein for purposes of the income tax.

(b) *Nonresidence presumed.* An alien, by reason of his alienage, is presumed to be a nonresident alien.

(c) *Presumption rebutted* —(1) *Departing alien.* In the case of an alien who presents himself for determination of tax liability before departure from the United States, the presumption as to the alien's nonresidence may be overcome by proof—

(i) That the alien, at least six months before the date he so presents himself, has filed a declaration of his intention to become a citizen of the United States under the naturalization laws; or

(ii) That the alien, at least six months before the date he so presents himself, has filed Form 1078 or its equivalent; or

(iii) Of acts and statements of the alien showing a definite intention to acquire residence in the United States or showing that his stay in the United States has been of such an extended nature as to constitute him a resident.

(2) *Other aliens.* In the case of other aliens, the presumption as to the alien's nonresidence may be overcome by proof—

(i) That the alien has filed a declaration of his intention to become a citizen of the United States under the naturalization laws; or

Reg. § 1.871-3

(ii) That the alien has filed Form 1078 or its equivalent; or

(iii) Of acts and statements of the alien showing definite intention to acquire residence in the United States or showing that his stay in the United States has been of such an extended nature as to constitute him a resident.

(d) *Certificate.* If, in the application of paragraphs (c)(1)(iii) or (2)(iii) of this section, the internal revenue officer or employee who examines the alien is in doubt as to the facts, such officer or employee may, to assist him in determining the facts, require a certificate or certificates setting forth the facts relied upon by the alien seeking to overcome the presumption. Each such certificate, which shall contain, or be verified by, a written declaration that it is made under the penalties of perjury, shall be executed by some credible person or persons, other than the alien and members of his family, who have known the alien at least six months before the date of execution of the certificate or certificates. [Reg. § 1.871-4.]

☐ [*T.D.* 6258, 10-23-57.]

[Reg. § 1.871-5]

§ 1.871-5. Loss of residence by an alien.—An alien who has acquired residence in the United States retains his status as a resident until he abandons the same and actually departs from the United States. An intention to change his residence does not change his status as a resident alien to that of a nonresident alien. Thus, an alien who has acquired a residence in the United States is taxable as a resident for the remainder of his stay in the United States. [Reg. § 1.871-5.]

☐ [*T.D.* 6258, 10-23-57.]

[Reg. § 1.871-6]

§ 1.871-6. Duty of withholding agent to determine status of alien payees.—For the obligation of a withholding agent to withhold the tax imposed by this section, see chapter 3 of the Internal Revenue Code and the regulations thereunder. [Reg. § 1.871-6.]

☐ [*T.D.* 6258, 10-23-57. *Amended by T.D.* 7332, 12-20-74; *T.D.* 7977, 9-19-84 *and T.D.* 8734, 10-6-97 (T.D. 8804 delayed the effective date of T.D. 8734 from January 1, 1999, to January 1, 2000; T.D. 8856 further delayed the effective date of T.D. 8734 until January 1, 2001).]

[Reg. § 1.871-7]

§ 1.871-7. Taxation of nonresident alien individuals not engaged in U.S. business.—(a) *Imposition of tax.*—(1) This section applies for purposes of determining the tax of a nonresident alien individual who at no time during the taxable year is engaged in trade or business in the United States. However, see also § 1.871-8 where such individual is a student or trainee deemed to be engaged in trade or business in the United States or where he has an election in effect for the taxable year in respect to real property income. Except as otherwise provided in § 1.871-12, a nonresident alien individual to whom this section applies is not subject to the tax imposed by section 1 or section 1201(b) but, pursuant to the provisions of section 871(a), is liable to a flat tax of 30 percent upon the aggregate of the amounts determined under paragraphs (b), (c), and (d) of this section which are received during the taxable year from sources within the United States. Except as specifically provided in such paragraphs, such amounts do not include gains from the sale or exchange of property. To determine the source of such amounts, see sections 861 through 863, and the regulations thereunder.

(2) The tax of 30 percent is imposed by section 871(a) upon an amount only to the extent the amount constitutes gross income. Thus, for example, the amount of an annuity which is subject to such tax shall be determined in accordance with section 72.

(3) Deductions shall not be allowed in determining the amount subject to tax under this section except that losses from sales or exchanges of capital assets shall be allowed to the extent provided in section 871(a)(2) and paragraph (d) of this section.

(4) Except as provided in §§ 1.871-9 and 1.871-10, a nonresident alien individual not engaged in trade or business in the United States during the taxable year has no income, gain, or loss for the taxable year which is effectively connected for the taxable year with the conduct of a trade or business in the United States. See section 864(c)(1)(B) and § 1.864-3.

(5) Gains and losses which, by reason of section 871(d) and § 1.871-10, are treated as gains or losses which are effectively connected for the taxable year with the conduct of a trade or business in the United States by the nonresident alien individual shall not be taken into account in determining the tax under this section. See, for example, paragraph (c)(2) of § 1.871-10.

(6) For special rules applicable in determining the tax of certain nonresident alien individuals, see paragraph (b) of § 1.871-1.

(b) *Fixed or determinable annual or periodical income*—(1) *General rule.* The tax of 30 percent imposed by section 871(a)(1) applies to the gross amount received from sources within the United States as fixed or determinable annual or periodical gains, profits, or income. Specific items of fixed or determinable annual or periodical income are enumerated in section 871(a)(1)(A) as interest, dividends, rents, salaries, wages, premiums, annuities, compensations, remunerations, and emoluments, but other items of fixed or determinable annual or periodical gains, profits, or income are also subject to the tax, as, for instance, royalties, including royalties for the use of patents, copyrights, secret processes and formulas, and other like property. As to the determination of fixed or determinable annual or periodical income, see § 1.1441-2(b). For special rules treating gain on the disposition of section 306 stock as fixed or determinable annual or periodical income for purposes of section 871(a), see section 306(f) and paragraph (h) of § 1.306-3.

(2) *Substitute payments.* For purposes of this section, a substitute interest payment (as defined in § 1.861-2(a)(7)) received by a foreign person pursuant to a securities lending transaction or a sale-repurchase transaction (as defined in § 1.861-2(a)(7)) shall have the same character as interest income paid or accrued with respect to the terms of the transferred security. Similarly, for purposes of this section, a substitute dividend payment (as defined in § 1.861-3(a)(6)) received by a foreign person pursuant to a securities lending transaction or a sale-repurchase transaction (as defined in § 1.861-3(a)(6)) shall have the same character as a distribution received with respect to the transferred security. Where, pursuant to a securities lending transaction or a sale-repurchase transaction, a foreign person transfers to another person a security the interest on which would qualify as portfolio interest under section 871(h) in the hands of the lender, substitute interest payments made with respect to the transferred security will be treated as portfolio interest, provided that in the case of interest on an obligation in registered form (as defined in § 1.871-14(c)(1)(i)), the transferor complies with the documentation requirement described in § 1.871-14(c)(1)(ii)(C) with respect to the payment of the substitute interest and none of the exceptions to the portfolio interest exemption in sections 871(h)(3) and (4) apply. See also §§ 1.861-2(b)(2) and 1.894-1(c).

(c) *Other income and gains*—(1) *Items subject to tax.* The tax of 30 percent imposed by section 871(a)(1) also applies to the following gains received during the taxable year from sources within the United States:

(i) Gains described in section 402(a)(2), relating to the treatment of total distributions from certain employees' trusts; section 403(a)(2), relating to treatment of certain payments under certain employee annuity plans; and section 631(b) or (c), relating to treatment of gain on the disposal of timber, coal, or iron ore with a retained economic interest;

(ii) [Reserved]

(iii) Gains on transfers described in section 1235, relating to certain transfers of patent rights, made on or before October 4, 1966; and

(iv) Gains from the sale or exchange after October 4, 1966, of patents, copyrights, secret processes and formulas, good will, trademarks, trade brands, franchises, or other like property, or of any interest in any such property, to the extent the gains are from payments (whether in a lump sum or in installments) which are contingent on the productivity, use, or disposition of the property or interest sold or exchanged, or from payments which are treated under section 871(e) and § 1.871-11 as being so contingent.

(2) *Nonapplication of 183-day rule.* The provisions of section 871(a)(2), relating to gains from the sale or exchange of capital assets, and paragraph (d)(2) of this section do not apply to the gains described in this paragraph; as a consequence, the taxpayer receiving gains described in subparagraph (1) of this paragraph during a taxable year is subject to the tax of 30 percent thereon without regard to the 183-day rule contained in such provisions.

(3) *Determination of amount of gain.* The tax of 30 percent imposed upon the gains described in subparagraph (1) of this paragraph applies to the full amount of the gains and is determined (i) without regard to the alternative tax imposed by section 1201(b) upon the excess of the net long-term capital gain over the net short-term capital loss; (ii) without regard to the deduction allowed by section 1202 in respect of capital gains; (iii) without regard to section 1231, relating to property used in the trade or business and involuntary conversions; and (iv), except in the case of gains described in subparagraph (1)(ii) of this paragraph, whether or not the gains are considered to be gains from the sale or exchange of property which is a capital asset.

(d) *Gains from sale or exchange of capital assets*—(1) *Gains subject to tax.* The tax of 30 percent imposed by section 871(a)(2) applies to the excess of gains derived from sources within the United States over losses allocable to sources within the United States, which are derived from the sale or exchange of capital assets, determined in accordance with the provisions of subparagraphs (2) through (4) of this paragraph.

(2) *Presence in the United States 183 days or more.* (i) If the nonresident alien individual has been present in the United States for a period or

Reg. § 1.871-7(b)(2)

periods aggregating 183 days or more during the taxable year, he is liable to a tax of 30 percent upon the amount by which his gains, derived from sources within the United States, from sales or exchanges of capital assets effected at any time during the year exceed his losses, allocable to sources within the United States, from sales or exchanges of capital assets effected at any time during that year. Gains and losses from sales or exchanges effected at any time during such taxable year are to be taken into account for this purpose even though the nonresident alien individual is not present in the United States at the time the sales or exchanges are effected. In addition, if the nonresident alien individual has been present in the United States for a period or periods aggregating 183 days or more during the taxable year, gains and losses for such taxable year from sales or exchanges of capital assets effected during a previous taxable year beginning after December 31, 1966, are to be taken into account, but only if he was also present in the United States during such previous taxable year for a period or periods aggregating 183 days or more.

(ii) If the nonresident alien individual has not been present in the United States during the taxable year, or if he has been present in the United States for a period or periods aggregating less than 183 days during the taxable year, gains and losses from sales or exchanges of capital assets effected during the year are not to be taken into account, except as required by paragraph (c) of this section, in determining the tax of such individual even though the sales or exchanges are effected during his presence in the United States. Moreover, gains and losses for such taxable year from sales or exchanges of capital assets effected during a previous taxable year beginning after December 31, 1966, are not to be taken into account, even though the nonresident alien individual was present in the United States during such previous year for a period or periods aggregating 183 days or more.

(iii) For purposes of this subparagraph, a nonresident alien individual is not considered to be present in the United States by reason of the presence in the United States of a person who is an agent or partner of such individual or who is a fiduciary of an estate or trust of which such individual is a beneficiary or a grantor-owner to whom section 671 applies.

(iv) The application of this subparagraph may be illustrated by the following examples:

Example (1). B, a nonresident alien individual not engaged in trade or business in the United States and using the calendar year as the taxable year, is present in the United States from May 1, 1971, to November 15, 1971, a period of more than 182 days. While present in the United States, B effects for his own account on various dates a number of transactions in stocks and securities on the stock exchange, as a result of which he has recognized capital gains of $10,000. During the period from January 1, 1971, to April 30, 1971, he carries out similar transactions through an agent in the United States, as a result of which B has recognized capital gains of $5,000. On December 15, 1971, through an agent in the United States B sells a capital asset on the installment plan, no payments being made by the purchaser in 1971. During 1972, B receives installment payments of $50,000 on the installment sale made in 1971, and the capital gain from sources within the United States for 1972 attributable to such payments is $12,500. In addition, during the period from January 1, 1972, to May 31, 1972, B effects for his own account, through an agent in the United States, a number of transactions in stocks and securities on the stock exchange, as a result of which B has recognized capital gains of $20,000. At no time during 1972 is B present in the United States or engaged in trade or business in the United States. Accordingly, for 1971, B is subject to tax under section 871(a)(2) on his capital gains of $15,000 from the transactions in that year on the stock exchange. For 1972, B is not subject to tax on the capital gain of $12,500 from the installment sale in 1971 or on the capital gains of $20,000 from the transactions in 1972 on the stock exchange.

Example (2). The facts are the same as in example (1) except that B is present in the United States from June 15, 1972, to December 31, 1972, a period of more than 182 days. Accordingly, B is subject to tax under section 871(a)(2) for 1971 on his capital gains of $15,000 from the transactions in that year on the stock exchange. He is also subject to tax under section 871(a)(2) for 1972 on his capital gains of $32,500 ($12,500 from the installment sale in 1971 plus $20,000 from the transactions in 1972 on the stock exchange).

Example (3). D, a nonresident alien individual not engaged in trade or business in the United States and using the calendar year as the taxable year, is present in the United States from April 1, 1971, to August 31, 1971, a period of less than 183 days. While present in the United States, D effects for his own account on various dates a number of transactions in stocks and securities on the stock exchange, as a result of which he has recognized capital gains of $15,000. During the period from January 1, 1971, to March 31, 1971, he carries out similar transactions through an agent in the United States, as a result of which

Reg. § 1.871-7(d)(2)

D has recognized capital gains of $8,000. On December 20, 1971, through an agent in the United States, D sells a capital asset on the installment plan, no payments being made by the purchaser in 1971. During 1972, D receives installment payments of $200,000 on the installment sale made in 1971, and the capital gain from sources within the United States for 1972 attributable to such payments is $50,000. In addition, during the period from February 1, 1972, to August 15, 1972, a period of more than 182 days, D effects for his own account, through an agent in the United States, a number of transactions in stocks and securities on the stock exchange, as a result of which D has recognized capital gains of $25,000. At no time during 1972 is D present in the United States or engaged in trade or business in the United States. Accordingly, D is not subject to tax for 1971 or 1972 on any of his recognized capital gains.

Example (4). The facts are the same as in example (3) except that D is present in the United States from February 1, 1972, to August 15, 1972, a period of more than 182 days. Accordingly, D is not subject to tax for 1971 on his capital gains of $23,000 from the transactions in that year on the stock exchange. For 1972 he is subject to tax under section 871(a)(2) on his capital gains of $25,000 from the transactions in that year on the stock exchange, but he is not subject to the tax on the capital gain of $50,000 from the installment sale in 1971.

(3) *Determination of 183-day period* —(i) *In general.* In determining the total period of presence in the United States for a taxable year for purposes of subparagraph (2) of this paragraph, all separate periods of presence in the United States during the taxable year are to be aggregated. If the nonresident alien individual has not previously established a taxable year, as defined in section 441(b), he shall be treated as having a taxable year which is the calendar year, as defined in section 441(d). Subsequent adoption by such individual of a fiscal year as the taxable year will be treated as a change in the taxpayer's annual accounting period to which section 442 applies, and the change must be authorized under this part (Income Tax Regulations) or prior approval must be obtained by filing an application on Form 1128 in accordance with paragraph (b) of § 1.442-1. If in the course of his taxable year the nonresident alien individual changes his status from that of a citizen or resident of the United States to that of a nonresident alien individual, or vice versa, the determination of whether the individual has been present in the United States for 183 days or more during the taxable year shall be made by taking into account the entire taxable year, and not just that part of the taxable year during which he has the status of a nonresident alien individual.

(ii) *Definition of "day".* The term "day", as used in subparagraph (2) of this paragraph, means a calendar day during any portion of which the nonresident alien individual is physically present in the United States (within the meaning of sections 7701(a)(9) and 638) except that, in the case of an individual who is a resident of Canada or Mexico and, in the normal course of his employment in transportation service touching points within both Canada or Mexico and the United States, performs personal services in both the foreign country and the United States, the following rules shall apply:

(a) The performance of labor or personal services during eight hours or more in any one day within the United States shall be considered as one day in the United States, except that if a period of more or less than eight hours is considered a full work day in the transportation job involved, such period shall be considered as one day within the United States.

(b) The performance of labor or personal services during less than eight hours in any day in the United States shall, except as provided in (a), be considered as a fractional part of a day in the United States. The total number of hours during which such services are performed in the United States during the taxable year, when divided by eight, shall be the number of days during which such individual shall be considered present in the United States during the taxable year.

(c) The aggregate number of days determined under (a) and (b) shall be considered the total number of days during which such individual is present in the United States during the taxable year.

(4) *Determination of amount of excess gains*—(i) *In general.* For the purpose of determining the excess of gains over losses subject to tax under this paragraph, gains and losses shall be taken into account only if, and to the extent that, they would be recognized and taken into account if the nonresident alien individual were engaged in trade or business in the United States during the taxable year and such gains and losses were effectively connected for such year with the conduct of a trade or business in the United States by such individual. However, in determining such excess of gains over losses no deduction may be taken under section 1202, relating to the deduction for capital gains, or section 1212, relating to the capital loss carryover. Thus, for example, in determining such excess gains all amounts considered under chapter 1 of the Code as gains or losses

Reg. § 1.871-7(d)(3)

from the sale or exchange of capital assets shall be taken into account, except those gains which are described in section 871(a)(1)(B) or (D) and taken into account under paragraph (c) of this section and are considered to be gains from the sale or exchange of capital assets. Also, for example, a loss described in section 631(b) or (c) which is considered to be a loss from the sale of a capital asset shall be taken into account in determining the excess gains which are subject to tax under this paragraph. In further illustration, in determining such excess gains no deduction shall be allowed, pursuant to the provisions of section 267, for losses from sales or exchanges of property between related taxpayers. Any gains which are taken into account under section 871(a)(1) and paragraph (c) of this section shall not be taken into account in applying section 1231 for purposes of this paragraph. Gains and losses are to be taken into account under this paragraph whether they are short-term or long-term capital gains or losses within the meaning of section 1222.

(ii) *Gains not included.* The provisions of this paragraph do not apply to any gains described in section 871(a)(1)(B) or (D), and in subdivision (i), (iii), or (iv) of paragraph (c)(1) of this section, which are considered to be gains from the sale or exchange of capital assets.

(iii) *Allowance of losses.* In determining the excess of gains over losses subject to tax under this paragraph losses shall be allowed only to the extent provided by section 165(c). Losses from sales or exchanges of capital assets in excess of gains from sales or exchanges of capital assets shall not be taken into account.

(e) *Credits against tax.* The credits allowed by section 31 (relating to tax withheld on wages), by section 32 (relating to tax withheld at source on nonresident aliens), by section 39 (relating to certain uses of gasoline and lubricating oil), and by section 6402 (relating to overpayments of tax) shall be allowed against the tax of a nonresident alien individual determined in accordance with this section.

(f) *Effective date.* Except as otherwise provided in this paragraph, this section shall apply for taxable years beginning after December 31, 1966. Paragraph (b)(2) of this section is applicable to payments made after November 13, 1997. For corresponding rules applicable to taxable years beginning before January 1, 1967, see 26 CFR 1.871-7(b) and (c) (Rev. as of Jan. 1, 1971). [Reg. § 1.871-7.]

☐ [T.D. 6258, 10-23-57. Amended by T.D. 6464, 5-11-60; T.D. 6782, 12-23-64; T.D. 6823, 5-5-65; T.D. 6841, 7-26-65; T.D. 7332, 12-20-74; T.D. 8734, 10-6-97 (T.D. 8804 delayed the effective date of T.D. 8734 from January 1, 1999, to January 1, 2000; T.D. 8856 further delayed the effective date of T.D. 8734 until January 1, 2001) and T.D. 8735, 10-6-97.]

[Reg. § 1.871-8]

§ 1.871-8. **Taxation of nonresident alien individuals engaged in U.S. business or treated as having effectively connected income.**—(a) *Segregation of income.* This section applies for purposes of determining the tax of a nonresident alien individual who at any time during the taxable year is engaged in trade or business in the United States. It also applies for purposes of determining the tax of a nonresident alien student or trainee who is deemed under section 871(c) and § 1.871-9 to be engaged in trade or business in the United States or of a nonresident alien individual who at no time during the taxable year is engaged in trade or business in the United States but has an election in effect for the taxable year under section 871(d) and § 1.871-10 in respect to real property income. A nonresident alien individual to whom this section applies must segregate his gross income for the taxable year into two categories, namely, (1) the income which is effectively connected for the taxable year with the conduct of a trade or business in the United States by that individual and (2) the income which is not effectively connected for the taxable year with the conduct of a trade or business in the United States by that individual. A separate tax shall then be determined upon each such category of income, as provided in paragraph (b) of this section. The determination of whether income or gain is or is not effectively connected for the taxable year with the conduct of a trade or business in the United States by the nonresident alien individual shall be made in accordance with section 864(c) and §§ 1.864-3 through 1.864-7. For purposes of this section income which is effectively connected for the taxable year with the conduct of a trade or business in the United States includes all income which is treated under section 871(c) or (d) and § 1.871-9 or § 1.871-10 as income which is effectively connected for such year with the conduct of a trade or business in the United States by the nonresident alien individual.

(b) *Imposition of tax*—(1) *Income not effectively connected with the conduct of a trade or business in the United States.* If a nonresident alien individual who is engaged in trade or business in the United States at any time during the taxable year derives during such year from sources within the United States income or gains described in section 871(a)(1) and paragraph (b) or (c) of § 1.871-7 or gains from the sale or exchange of capital assets determined as provided in

Reg. § 1.871-8(b)(1)

section 871(a)(2) and paragraph (d) of § 1.871-7, which are not effectively connected for the taxable year with the conduct of a trade or business in the United States by that individual, such income or gains shall be subject to a flat tax of 30 percent of the aggregate amount of such items. This tax shall be determined in the manner, and subject to the same conditions, set forth in § 1.871-7 as though the income or gains were derived by a nonresident alien individual not engaged in trade or business in the United States during the taxable year, except that (i) the rule in paragraph (d)(3) of such section for treating the calendar year as the taxable year shall not apply and (ii) in applying paragraph (c) and (d)(4) of such section, there shall not be taken into account any gains or losses which are taken into account in determining the tax under section 871(b) and subparagraph (2) of this paragraph. A nonresident alien individual who has an election in effect for the taxable year under section 871(d) and § 1.871-10 and who at no time during the taxable year is engaged in trade or business in the United States must determine his tax under § 1.871-7 on his income which is not treated as effectively connected with the conduct of a trade or business in the United States, subject to the exception contained in subdivision (ii) of this subparagraph.

(2) *Income effectively connected with the conduct of a trade or business in the United States*—(i) *In general.* If a nonresident alien to whom this section applies derives income or gains which are effectively connected for the taxable year with the conduct of a trade or business in the United States by that individual, the taxable income or gains shall, except as provided in § 1.871-12, be taxed in accordance with section 1 or, in the alternative, section 1201(b). See section 871(b)(1). Any income of the nonresident alien individual which is not effectively connected for the taxable year with the conduct of a trade or business in the United States by that individual shall not be taken into account in determining either the rate or amount of such tax. See paragraph (b) of § 1.872-1.

(ii) *Determination of taxable income.* The taxable income for any taxable year for purposes of this subparagraph consists only of the nonresident alien individual's taxable income which is effectively connected for the taxable year with the conduct of a trade or business in the United States by that individual; and, for this purpose, it is immaterial that the trade or business with which that income is effectively connected is not the same as the trade or business carried on in the United States by that individual during the taxable year. See example (2) in § 1.864-4(b). In determining such taxable income all amounts constituting, or considered to be, gains or losses for the taxable year from the sale or exchange of capital assets shall be taken into account if such gains or losses are effectively connected for the taxable year with the conduct of a trade or business in the United States by that individual, and, for such purpose, the 183-day rule set forth in section 871(a)(2) and paragraph (d)(2) of § 1.871-7 shall not apply. Losses which are not effectively connected for the taxable year with the conduct of a trade or business in the United States by that individual shall not be taken into account in determining taxable income under this subdivision, except as provided in section 873(b)(1).

(iii) *Cross references.* For rules for determining the gross income and deductions for the taxable year, see sections 872 and 873, and the regulations thereunder.

(c) *Change in trade or business status*—(1) *In general.* The determination as to whether a nonresident alien individual is engaged in trade or business within the United States during the taxable year is to be made for each taxable year. If at any time during the taxable year he is engaged in a trade or business in the United States, he is considered to be engaged in trade or business within the United States during the taxable year for purposes of sections 864(c)(1) and 871(b), and the regulations thereunder. Income, gain, or loss of a nonresident alien individual is not treated as being effectively connected for the taxable year with the conduct of a trade or business in the United States if he is not engaged in trade or business within the United States during such year, even though such income, gain, or loss may have been effectively connected for a previous taxable year with the conduct of a trade or business in the United States. See § 1.864-3. However, income, gain, or loss which is treated as effectively connected for the taxable year with the conduct of a trade or business in the United States by a nonresident alien individual will generally be treated as effectively connected for a subsequent taxable year if he is engaged in a trade or business in the United States during such subsequent year, even though such income, gain, or loss is not effectively connected with the conduct of the trade or business carried on in the United States during such subsequent year. This subparagraph does not apply to income described in section 871(c) or (d). It may not apply to a nonresident alien individual who for the taxable year uses an accrual method of accounting or to income which is constructively received in the taxable year within the meaning of § 1.451-2.

Reg. § 1.871-8(b)(2)

(2) *Illustrations.* The application of this paragraph may be illustrated by the following examples:

Example (1). B, a nonresident alien individual using the calendar year as the taxable year and the cash receipts and disbursements method of accounting, is engaged in business (business R) in the United States from January 1, 1971, to August 31, 1971. During the period of September 1, 1971, to December 31, 1971, B receives installment payments of $30,000 on sales made in the United States by business R during that year, and the income from sources within the United States for that year attributable to such payments is $7,500. On September 15, 1971, another business (business S) which is carried on by B only in a foreign country sells to U.S. customers on the installment plan several pieces of equipment from inventory. During the period of September 16, 1971, to December 31, 1971, B receives installment payments of $50,000 on these sales by business S, and the income from sources within the United States for that year attributable to such payments is $10,000. Under section 864(c)(3) and paragraph (b) of § 1.864-4 the entire income of $17,500 is effectively connected for 1971 with the conduct of a business in the United States by B. Accordingly, such income is taxable to B under paragraph (b)(2) of this section.

Example (2). Assume the same facts as in Example (1), except that during 1972 B receives installment payments of $20,000 from the sales made during 1971 in the United States by business R, and of $80,000 from the sales made in 1971 to U.S. customers by business S, the total income from sources within the United States for 1972 attributable to such payments being $13,000. At no time during 1972 is B engaged in a trade or business in the United States. Under section 864(c)(1)(B) the income of $13,000 for 1972 is not effectively connected with the conduct of a trade or business in the United States by B. Moreover, such income is not fixed or determinable annual or periodical income. Accordingly, no amount of such income is taxable to B under section 871.

Example (3). Assume the same facts as in Example (2), except that during 1972 B is engaged in a new business (business T) in the United States from July 1, 1972, to December 31, 1972. Under section 864(c)(3) and paragraph (b) of § 1.864-4, the income of $13,000 is effectively connected for 1972 with the conduct of a business in the United States by B. Accordingly, such income is taxable to B under paragraph (b)(2) of this section.

Example (4). Assume the same facts as in Example (2), except that the installment payments of $20,000 from the sales made during 1971 in the United States by business R and not received by B until 1972 could have been received by B in 1971 if he had so desired. Under § 1.451-2, B is deemed to have constructively received the payments of $20,000 in 1971. Accordingly, the income attributable to such payments is effectively connected for 1971 with the conduct of a business in the United States by B and is taxable to B in 1971 under paragraph (b)(2) of this section.

(d) *Credits against tax.* The credits allowed by section 31 (relating to tax withheld on wages), section 32 (relating to tax withheld at source on nonresident aliens), section 33 (relating to the foreign tax credit), section 35 (relating to partially tax-exempt interest), section 38 (relating to investment in certain depreciable property), section 39 (relating to certain uses of gasoline and lubricating oil), section 40 (relating to expenses of work incentive programs), and section 6402 (relating to overpayments of tax) shall be allowed against the tax determined in accordance with this section. However, the credits allowed by sections 33, 38 and 40 shall not be allowed against the flat tax of 30 percent imposed by section 871(a) and paragraph (b)(1) of this section. Moreover, no credit shall be allowed under section 35 to a nonresident alien individual with respect to whom a tax is imposed for the taxable year under section 871(a) and paragraph (b)(1) of this section, even though such individual has income for such year upon which tax is imposed under section 871(b) and paragraph (b)(2) of this section. For special rules applicable in determining the foreign tax credit, see section 906(b) and the regulations thereunder. For the disallowance of certain credits where a return is not filed for the taxable year, see section 874 and § 1.874-1.

(e) *Effective date.* This section shall apply for taxable years beginning after December 31, 1966. For corresponding rules applicable to taxable years beginning before January 1, 1967, see 26 CFR 1.871-7(d) (Rev. as of Jan. 1, 1971). [Reg. § 1.871-8.]

☐ [T.D. 6258, 10-23-57. Amended by T.D. 6782, 12-23-64 and T.D. 7332, 12-20-74.]

[Reg. § 1.871-9]

§ 1.871-9. **Nonresident alien students or trainees deemed to be engaged in U.S. business.**—(a) *Participants in certain exchange or training programs.* For purposes of §§ 1.871-7 and 1.871-8 a nonresident alien individual who is temporarily present in the United States during the taxable year as a nonimmigrant under subpar-

Reg. § 1.871-9(a)

agraph (F) (relating to the admission of students into the United States) or subparagraph (J) (relating to the admission of teachers, trainees, specialists, etc., into the United States) of section 101(a)(15) of the Immigration and Nationality Act (8 U.S.C. 1101(a)(15)(F) or (J)), and who without regard to this paragraph is not engaged in trade or business in the United States during such year, shall be deemed to be engaged in trade or business in the United States during the taxable year. For purposes of determining whether an alien who is present in the United States on an F visa or a J visa is a resident of the United States, see §§ 301.7701(b)-1 through 301.7701(b)-9 of this chapter.

(b) *Income treated as effectively connected with U.S. business.* Any income described in paragraph (1) (relating to the nonexcluded portion of certain scholarship or fellowship grants) or paragraph (2) (relating to certain nonexcluded expenses incident to such grants) of section 1441(b) which is received during the taxable year from sources within the United States by a nonresident alien individual described in paragraph (a) of this section is to be treated for purposes of §§ 1.871-7, 1.871-8, 1.872-1, and 1.873-1 as income which is effectively connected for the taxable year with the conduct of a trade or business in the United States by that individual. However, such income is not to be treated as effectively connected for the taxable year with the conduct of a trade or business in the United States for purposes of section 1441(c)(1) and paragraph (a) of § 1.1441-4. For exclusion relating to compensation paid to such individual by a foreign employer, see paragraph (b) of § 1.872-2.

(c) *Exchange visitors.* For purposes of paragraph (a) of this section a nonresident alien individual who is temporarily present in the United States during the taxable year as a nonimmigrant under subparagraph (J) of section 101(a)(15) of the Immigration and Nationality Act includes a nonresident alien individual admitted to the United States as an "exchange visitor" under section 201 of the United States Information and Educational Exchange Act of 1948 (22 U.S.C. 1446), which section was repealed by section 111 of the Mutual Educational and Cultural Exchange Act of 1961 (75 Stat. 538).

(d) *Mandatory application of rule.* The application of this section is mandatory and not subject to an election by the taxpayer.

(e) *Effective date.* This section shall apply for taxable years beginning after December 31, 1966. For corresponding rules applicable to taxable years beginning before January 1, 1967, see 26 CFR 1.871-7(a)(3) (Rev. as of Jan. 1, 1971). [Reg. § 1.871-9.]

☐ [T.D. 7332, 12-20-74. Amended by T.D. 8411, 4-24-92.]

[Reg. § 1.871-10]

§ 1.871-10. **Election to treat real property income as effectively connected with U.S. business.**—(a) *When election may be made.* A nonresident alien individual or foreign corporation which during the taxable year derives any income from real property which is located in the United States and, in the case of a nonresident alien individual, held for the production of income, or derives income from any interest in any such property, may elect, pursuant to section 871(d) or 882(d) and this section, to treat all such income as income which is effectively connected for the taxable year with the conduct of a trade or business in the United States by that taxpayer. The election may be made whether or not the taxpayer is engaged in trade or business in the United States during the taxable year for which the election is made or whether or not the taxpayer has income from real property which for the taxable year is effectively connected with the conduct of a trade or business in the United States, but it may be made only with respect to that income from sources within the United States which, without regard to this section, is not effectively connected for the taxable year with the conduct of a trade or business in the United States by the taxpayer. If for the taxable year the taxpayer has no income from real property located in the United States, or from any interest in such property, which is subject to the tax imposed by section 871(a) or 881(a), the election may not be made. But if an election has been properly made under this section for a taxable year, the election remains in effect, unless properly revoked, for subsequent taxable years even though during any such subsequent taxable year there is no income from the real property, or interest therein, in respect of which the election applies.

(b) *Income to which the election applies*—(1) *Included income.* An election under this section shall apply to all income from real property which is located in the United States and, in the case of a nonresident alien individual, held for the production of income, and to all income derived from any interest in such property, including (i) gains from the sale or exchange of such property or an interest therein, (ii) rents or royalties from mines, oil or gas wells, or other natural resources, and (iii) gains described in section 631(b) or (c), relating to treatment of gain on the disposal of timber, coal, or iron ore with a retained economic interest. The election may not be made with respect to

Reg. § 1.871-10(a)

only one class of such income. For purposes of the election, income from real property, or from any interest in real property, includes any amount included under section 652 or 662 in the gross income of a nonresident alien individual or foreign corporation that is the beneficiary of an estate or trust if, by reason of the application of section 652(b) or 662(b), and the regulations thereunder, such amount has the character in the hands of that beneficiary of income from real property, or from any interest in real property. It is immaterial that no tax would be imposed on the income by section 871(a) and paragraph (a) of § 1.871-7, or by section 881(a) and paragraph (a) of § 1.881-2, if the election were not in effect. Thus, for example, if an election under this section has been made by a nonresident alien individual not engaged in trade or business in the United States during the taxable year, the tax imposed by section 871(b)(1) and paragraph (b)(2) of § 1.871-8 applies to his gains derived from the sale of real property located in the United States and held for the production of income, even though such income would not be subject to tax under section 871(a) if the election had not been made. In further illustration, assume that a nonresident alien individual not engaged in trade or business, or present, in the United States during the taxable year has income from sources within the United States consisting of oil royalties, rentals from a former personal residence, and capital gain from the sale of another residence held for the production of income. If he makes an election under this section, it will apply with respect to his royalties, rentals, and capital gain, even though such capital gain would not be subject to tax under section 871(a) if the election had not been made.

(2) *Income not included.* For purposes of subparagraph (1) of this paragraph, income from real property, or from any interest in real property, does not include (i) interest on a debt obligation secured by a mortgage of real property, (ii) any portion of a dividend, within the meaning of section 316, which is paid by a corporation or a trust, such as a real estate investment trust described in section 857, which derives income from real property, (iii) in the case of a nonresident alien individual, income from real property, such as a personal residence, which is not held for the production of income or from any transaction in such property which was not entered into for profit, (iv) rentals from personal property, or royalties from intangible personal property, within the meaning of subparagraph (3) of this paragraph, or (v) income which, without regard to section 871(d) or 882(d) and this section, is treated as income which is effectively connected for the taxable year with the conduct of a trade or business in the United States.

(3) *Rules applicable to personal property.* For purposes of subparagraph (2) of this paragraph, in the case of a sales agreement, or rental or royalty agreement, affecting both real and personal property, the income from the transaction is to be allocated between the real property and the personal property in proportion to their respective fair market values unless the agreement specifically provides otherwise. In the case of such a rental or royalty agreement, the respective fair market values are to be determined as of the time the agreement is signed. In making determinations under this subparagraph, the principles of paragraph (c) of § 1.48-1, relating to the definition of "section 38 property", apply for purposes of determining whether property is tangible or intangible personal property and of paragraph (a)(5) of § 1.1245-1 apply for purposes of making the allocation of income between real and personal property.

(c) *Effect of the election*—(1) *Determination of tax.* The income to which, in accordance with paragraph (b) of this section, an election under this section applies shall be subject to tax in the manner, and subject to the same conditions, provided by section 871(b)(1) and paragraph (b)(2) of § 1.871-8, or by section 882(a)(1) and paragraph (b)(2) of § 1.882-1. For purposes of determining such tax for the taxable year, income to which the election applies shall be aggregated with all other income of the nonresident alien individual or foreign corporation which is effectively connected for the taxable year with the conduct of a trade or business in the United States by that taxpayer. To the extent that deductions are connected with income from real property to which the election applies, they shall be treated for purposes of section 873(a) or section 882(c)(1) as connected with income which is effectively connected for the taxable year with the conduct of a trade or business in the United States by the nonresident alien individual or foreign corporation. An election under this section does not cause a nonresident alien individual or foreign corporation, which is not engaged in trade or business in the United States during the taxable year, to be treated as though such taxpayer were engaged in trade or business in the United States during the taxable year. Thus, for example, the compensation received during the taxable year for services performed in the United States in a previous taxable year by a nonresident alien individual, who has an election in effect for the taxable year under this section but is engaged in trade or business in the United States at no time during the taxable year, is not effectively connected for the taxable year

Reg. § 1.871-10(c)(1)

with the conduct of a trade or business in the United States. In further illustration, gain for the taxable year from the casual sale of personal property described in section 1221(1) derived by a nonresident alien individual who is not engaged in trade or business in the United States during the taxable year but has an election in effect for such year under this section is not effectively connected with the conduct of a trade or business in the United States. See § 1.864-3. If an election under this section is in effect for the taxable year, the income to which the election applies shall be treated, for purposes of section 871(b)(1) or section 882(a)(1), section 1441(c)(1), and paragraph (a) of § 1.441-4, as income which is effectively connected for the taxable year with the conduct of a trade or business in the United States by the taxpayer.

(2) *Treatment of property to which election applies.* Any real property, or interest in real property, with respect to which an election under this section applies shall be treated as a capital asset which, if depreciable, is subject to the allowance for depreciation provided in section 167 and the regulations thereunder. Such property, or interest in property, shall be treated as property not used in a trade or business for purposes of applying any provisions of the Code, such as section 172(d)(4)(A), relating to gain or loss attributable to a trade or business for purposes of determining a net operating loss; section 1221(2), relating to property not constituting a capital asset; or section 1231(b), relating to special rules for treatment of gains and losses. For example, if a nonresident alien individual makes the election under this section and, while the election is in effect, sells unimproved land which is located in the United States and held for investment purposes, any gain or loss from the sale shall be considered gain or loss from the sale of a capital asset and shall be treated, for purposes of determining the tax under section 871(b)(1) and paragraph (b)(2) of § 1.871-8, as a gain or loss which is effectively connected for the taxable year with the conduct of a trade or business in the United States.

(d) *Manner of making or revoking an election*— (1) *Election, or revocation, without consent of Commissioner*—(i) *In general.* A nonresident alien individual or foreign corporation may, for the first taxable year for which the election under this section is to apply, make the initial election at any time before the expiration of the period prescribed by section 6511(a), or by section 6511(c) if the period for assessment is extended by agreement, for filing a claim for credit or refund of the tax imposed by chapter 1 of the Code for such taxable year. This election may be made without the consent of the Commissioner. Having made the initial election, the taxpayer may, within the time prescribed for making the election for such taxable year, revoke the election without the consent of the Commissioner. If the revocation is timely and properly made, the taxpayer may make his initial election under this section for a later taxable year without the consent of the Commissioner. If the taxpayer revokes the initial election without the consent of the Commissioner, he must file amended income tax returns, or claims for credit or refund, where applicable, for the taxable years to which the revocation applies.

(ii) *Statement to be filed with return.* An election made under this section without the consent of the Commissioner shall be made for a taxable year by filing with the income tax return required under section 6012 and the regulations thereunder for such taxable year a statement to the effect that the election is being made. This statement shall include (*a*) a complete schedule of all real property, or any interest in real property, of which the taxpayer is titular or beneficial owner, which is located in the United States, (*b*) an indication of the extent to which the taxpayer has direct or beneficial ownership in each such item of real property, or interest in real property, (*c*) the location of the real property or interest therein, (*d*) a description of any substantial improvements on any such property, and (*e*) an identification of any taxable year or years in respect of which a revocation or new election under this section has previously occurred. This statement may not be filed with any return under section 6851 and the regulations thereunder.

(iii) *Exemption from withholding of tax.* For statement to be filed with a withholding agent at the beginning of a taxable year in respect of which an election under this section is to be made, see paragraph (a) of § 1.1441-4.

(2) *Revocation, or election, with consent of Commissioner*—(i) *In general.* If the nonresident alien individual or foreign corporation makes the initial election under this section for any taxable year and the period prescribed by subparagraph (1)(i) of this paragraph for making the election for such taxable year has expired, the election shall remain in effect for all subsequent taxable years, including taxable years for which the taxpayer realizes no income from real property, or from any interest therein, or for which he is not required under section 6012 and the regulations thereunder to file an income tax return. However, the election may be revoked in accordance with subdivision (iii) of this subparagraph for any subsequent taxable year with the consent of the Commissioner. If the election for any such taxable year is revoked

with the consent of the Commissioner, the taxpayer may not make a new election before his fifth taxable year which begins after the first taxable year for which the revocation is effective unless consent is given to such new election by the Commissioner in accordance with subdivision (iii) of this subparagraph.

(ii) *Effect of new election.* A new election made for the fifth taxable year, or taxable year thereafter, without the consent of the Commissioner, and a new election made with the consent of the Commissioner, shall be treated as an initial election to which subparagraph (1) of this paragraph applies.

(iii) *Written request required.* A request to revoke an election made under this section when such revocation requires the consent of the Commissioner, or to make a new election when such election requires the consent of the Commissioner, shall be made in writing and shall be addressesd to the Director of International Operations, Internal Revenue Service, Washington, D.C. 20225. The request shall include the name and address of the taxpayer and shall be signed by the taxpayer or his duly authorized representative. It must specify the taxable year for which the revocation or new election is to be effective and shall be filed within 75 days after the close of the first taxable year for which it is desired to make the change. The request must specify the grounds which are considered to justify the revocation or new election. The Director of International Operations may require such other information as may be necessary in order to determine whether the proposed change will be permitted. A copy of the consent by the Director of International Operations shall be attached to the taxpayer's return required under section 6012 and the regulations thereunder for the taxable year for which the revocation or new election is effective. A copy of such consent may not be filed with any return under section 6851 and the regulations thereunder.

(3) *Election by partnership.* If a nonresident alien individual or foreign corporation is a member of a partnership which has income described in paragraph (b)(1) of this section from real property, any election to be made under this section in respect of such income shall be made by the partners and not by the partnership.

(e) *Effective date.* This section shall apply for taxable years beginning after December 31, 1966. There are no corresponding rules in this part for taxable years beginning before January 1, 1967. [Reg. § 1.871-10.]

☐ [T.D. 7332, 12-20-74.]

[Reg. § 1.871-11]

§ 1.871-11. **Gains from sale or exchange of patents, copyrights, or similar property.**—(a) *Contingent payment defined.* For purposes of section 871(a)(1)(D), section 881(a)(4), § 1.871-7(c)(1)(iv), § 1.881-2(c)(1)(iii), and this section, payments which are contingent on the productivity, use, or disposition of property or of an interest therein include continuing payments measured by a percentage of the selling price of the products marketed, or based on the number of units manufactured or sold, or based in a similar manner upon production, sale or use, or disposition of the property or interest transferred. A payment which is certain as to the amount to be received, but contingent as to the time of payment, or an installment payment of a principal sum agreed upon in a transfer agreement, shall not be treated as a contingent payment for purposes of this paragraph. For the inapplication of section 1253 to certain amounts described in this paragraph, see paragraph (a) of § 1.1253-1.

(b) *Payments treated as contingent on use.* Pursuant to section 871(e), if more than 50 percent of the gain of a nonresident alien individual or foreign corporation for any taxable year from the sale or exchange after October 4, 1966, of any patent, copyright, secret process or formula, goodwill, trademark, trade brand, franchise, or other like property, or of any interest in any such property, is from payments which are contingent on the productivity, use, or disposition of such property or interest, all of the gain of such individual or corporation for the taxable year from the sale or exchange of such property or interest are, for purposes of section 871(a)(1)(D), section 881(a)(4), section 1441(b), or section 1442(a), and the regulations thereunder, to be treated as being from payments which are contingent on the productivity, use, or disposition of such property or interest. This paragraph does not apply for purposes of determining under section 871(b)(1) or 882(a)(1) the tax of a nonresident alien individual or foreign corporation on income which is effectively connected for the taxable year with the conduct of a trade or business in the United States.

(c) *Sale or exchange.* A sale or exchange for purposes of this section includes, but is not limited to, a transfer by an individual which by reason of section 1235, relating to the sale or exchange of patents, is considered the sale or exchange of a capital asset. The provisions of section 1253, relating to transfers of franchises, trademarks, and trade names, do not apply in determining whether a transfer is a sale or exchange for purposes of this section.

(d) *Recovery of adjusted basis.* For purposes of determining for any taxable year the amount of gains which are subject to tax under section 871(a)(1)(D) or 881(a)(4), payments received by the nonresident alien individual or foreign corporation during such year must be reduced by amounts representing recovery of the taxpayer's adjusted basis of the property or interest which is sold or exchanged. Where the taxpayer receives in the same taxable year payments which, without reference to section 871(e) and this section, are not contingent on the productivity, use, or disposition of the property or interest which is sold or exchanged and payments which are contingent on the productivity, use, or disposition of the property or interest which is sold or exchanged, the taxpayer's unrecovered adjusted basis in the property or interest which is sold or exchanged must be allocated for the taxable year between such payments on the basis of the gross amount of each such type of payments. Where the taxpayer receives in the taxable year only payments which are not so contingent or only payments which are so contingent, the taxpayer's unrecovered basis must be allocated in its entirety to such payments for the taxable year.

(e) *Source rule.* In determining whether gains described in section 871(a)(1)(D) or 881(a)(4) and paragraph (b) of this section are received from sources within the United States, such gains shall be treated, for purposes of section 871(a)(1)(D), section 881(a)(4), section 1441(b), and section 1442(a), as rentals or royalties for the use of, or privilege of using, property or an interest in property. See section 861(a)(4), § 1.861-5, and paragraph (a) of § 1.862-1.

(f) *Illustrations.* The application of this section may be illustrated by the following examples:

Example (1). (a) A, a nonresident alien individual who uses the cash receipts and disbursements method of accounting and the calendar year as the taxable year, holds a United States patent which he developed through his own effort. On December 15, 1967, A enters into an agreement of sale with M Corporation, a domestic corporation, whereby A assigns to M Corporation all of his United States rights in the patent. In consideration of the sale, M Corporation is obligated to pay a fixed sum of $60,000, $20,000 being payable on execution of the contract and the balance payable in four annual installments of $10,000 each. As additional consideration, M Corporation agrees to pay to A a royalty in the amount of 2 percent of the gross sales of the products manufactured by M Corporation under the patent. A is not engaged in trade or business in the United States at any time during 1967 and 1968. His adjusted basis in the patent at the time of sale is $28,800.

(b) In 1967, A receives only the $20,000 paid by M Corporation on the execution of the contract of sale. No gain is realized by A upon receipt of this amount, and his unrecovered adjusted basis in the patent is reduced to $8,800 ($28,800 less $20,000).

(c) In 1968, M Corporation has gross sales of $600,000 from products manufactured under the patent. Consequently, for 1968, M Corporation pays $22,000 to A, $10,000 being the annual installment on the fixed payment and $12,000 being payments under the terms of the royalty provision. A's recognized gain for 1968 is $13,200 ($22,000 reduced by the unrecovered adjusted basis of $8,800). Of the total gain of $13,200, gain in the amount of $6,000 ($10,000 − [$8,800 × $10,000/$22,000]) is considered to be from the fixed installment payment and of $7,200 ($12,000 − [$8,800 × $12,000/$22,000]) is considered to be from the royalty payment. Since 54.5 percent ($7,200/$13,200) of the gain recognized in 1968 from the sale of the patent is from payments which are contingent on the productivity, use, or disposition of the patent, all of the $13,200 gain recognized in 1968 is treated, for purposes of section 871(a)(1)(D) and section 1441(b), as being from payments which are contingent on the productivity, use, or disposition of the patent.

Example (2). (a) F, a foreign corporation using the calendar year as the taxable year and not engaged in trade or business in the United States, holds a U.S. patent on certain property which it developed through its own efforts. Corporation F uses the cash receipts and disbursements method of accounting. On December 1, 1966, F Corporation enters into an agreement of sale with D Corporation, a domestic corporation, whereby D Corporation purchases the exclusive right and license, and the right to sublicense to others, to manufacture, use, and/or sell certain devices under the patent in the United States during the term of the patent. The agreement grants D Corporation the right to dispose, anywhere in the world, of machinery manufactured in the United States and equipped with such devices. Corporation D is granted the right, at its own expense, to prosecute infringers in its own name or in the name of F Corporation, or both, and to retain any damages recovered.

(b) Corporation D agrees to pay to F Corporation annually $5 for each device manufactured under the patent during the year but in no case less than $5,000 per year. In 1967, D Corporation manufactures 2,500 devices under the patent; and, in 1968, 1,500 devices. Under the terms of

Reg. § 1.871-11(d)

the contract D Corporation pays to F Corporation in 1967 $12,500 with respect to production in that year and $7,500 in 1968 with respect to production in that year. F Corporation's basis in the patent at the time of the sale is $17,000.

(c) With respect to the payments received by F Corporation in 1967, no gain is realized by that corporation and its unrecovered adjusted basis in the patent is reduced to $4,500 ($17,000 less $12,500).

(d) With respect to the payments received by F Corporation in 1968, such corporation has recognized gain of $3,000 ($7,500 reduced by unrecovered adjusted basis of $4,500). Of the total gain of $3,000, gain in the amount of $2,000 ($5,000 − [$4,500 × $5,000/$7,500]) is considered to be from the fixed installment payment and of $1,000 ($2,500 − [$4,500 × $2,500/$7,500]) is considered to be from payments which are contingent on the productivity, use, or disposition of the patent. Since 33.3 percent ($1,000/$3,000) of the gain recognized in 1968 from the sale of the patent is from payments which are contingent on the productivity, use, or disposition of the patent, only $1,000 of the $3,000 gain for that year constitutes gains which, for purposes of section 881(a)(4) and section 1442(a), are from payments which are contingent on the productivity, use, or disposition of the patent. The balance of $2,000 is gain from the sale of property and is not subject to tax under section 881(a).

(g) *Effective date.* This section shall apply for taxable years beginning after December 31, 1966, but only in respect of gains from sales or exchanges occurring after October 4, 1966. There are no corresponding rules in this part for taxable years beginning before January 1, 1967. [Reg. § 1.871-11.]

☐ [*T.D.* 7332, 12-20-74.]

[Reg. § 1.871-12]

§ 1.871-12. **Determination of tax on treaty income.**—(a) *In general.* This section applies for purposes of determining under § 1.871-7 or § 1.871-8 the tax on a nonresident alien individual, or under § 1.881-2 or § 1.882-1 the tax of a foreign corporation, which for the taxable year has income described in section 872(a) or 882(b) upon which the tax is limited by an income tax convention to which the United States is a party. Income for such purposes does not include income of any kind which is exempt from tax under the provisions of an income tax convention to which the United States is a party. See § § 1.872-2(c) and 1.883-1(b). This section shall not apply to a nonresident alien individual who is a bona fide resident of Puerto Rico during the entire taxable year.

(b) *Definition of treaty and nontreaty income*—(1) *In general.* (i) For purposes of this section the term "treaty income" shall be construed to mean the gross income of a nonresident alien individual or foreign corporation, as the case may be, the tax on which is limited by a tax convention. The term "nontreaty income" shall be construed, for such purposes, to mean the gross income of the nonresident alien individual or foreign corporation other than the treaty income. Neither term includes income of any kind which is exempt from the tax imposed by chapter 1 of the Code.

(ii) In determining either the treaty or nontreaty income the gross income shall be determined in accordance with § § 1.872-1 and 1.872-2, or with § § 1.882-3 and 1.883-1, except that in determining the treaty income the exclusion granted by section 116(a) for dividends shall not be taken into account. Thus, for example, treaty income includes the total amount of dividends paid by a domestic corporation not disqualified by section 116(b) and received from sources within the United States if, in accordance with a tax convention, the dividends are subject to the income tax at a rate not to exceed 15 percent but does not include interest which, in accordance with a tax convention, is exempt from the income tax. In further illustration, neither the treaty nor the nontreaty income includes interest on certain governmental obligations which by reason of section 103 is excluded from gross income, or interest which by reason of a tax convention is exempt from the tax imposed by chapter 1 of the Code.

(iii) For purposes of applying any income tax convention to which the United States is a party, original issue discount which is subject to tax under section 871(a)(1)(C) or 881 (a)(3) is to be treated as interest, and gains which are subject to tax under section 871(a)(1)(D) or 881(a)(4) are to be treated as royalty income. This subdivision shall not apply, however, where its application would be contrary to any treaty obligation of the United States.

(2) *Application of permanent establishment rule of treaties.* In applying this section with respect to income which is not effectively connected for the taxable year with the conduct of a trade or business in the United States by a nonresident alien individual or foreign corporation, see section 894(b), which provides that with respect to such income the nonresident alien individual or foreign corporation shall be deemed not to have a permanent establishment in the United States at any time during the taxable year for purposes of

Reg. § 1.871-12(b)(2)

applying any exemption from, or reduction in rate of, tax provided by any tax convention.

(c) *Determination of tax*—(1) *In general.* If the gross income of a nonresident alien individual or foreign corporation, as the case may be, consists of both treaty and nontreaty income, the tax liability for the taxable year shall be the sum of the amounts determined in accordance with subparagraphs (2) and (3) of this paragraph. In no case, however, may the tax liability so determined exceed the tax liability (tax reduced by allowable credits) with respect to the taxpayer's entire income, determined in accordance with § 1.871-7 or § 1.871-8, or with § 1.881-2 or § 1.882-1, as though the tax convention had not come into effect and without reference to the provisions of this section. Determinations under this paragraph shall be made without taking into account any credits allowed by sections 31, 32, 39, and 6402, but such credits shall be allowed against the tax liability determined in accordance with this subparagraph.

(2) *Tax on nontreaty income.* For purposes of subparagraph (1) of this paragraph, compute a partial tax (determined without the allowance of any credit) upon only the nontreaty income in accordance with § 1.871-7 or § 1.871-8, or with § 1.881-2 or § 1.882-1, whichever applies, as though the tax convention had not come into effect. To the extent allowed by paragraph (d) of § 1.871-8, or paragraph (c) of § 1.882-1, the credits allowed by sections 33, 35, 38, and 40 shall then be allowed, without taking into account any item included in the treaty income, against the tax determined under this subparagraph.

(3) *Tax on treaty income.* For purposes of subparagraph (1) of this paragraph, compute a tax upon the gross amount, determined without the allowance of any deduction, of each separate item of treaty income at the reduced rate applicable to that item under the tax convention. No credits shall be allowed against the tax determined under this subparagraph.

(d) *Illustration.* The application of this section may be illustrated by the following example:

Example. (a) A nonresident alien individual who is a resident of a foreign country with which the United States has entered into a tax convention receives during the taxable year 1967 from sources within the United States total gross income of $22,000, consisting of the following items:

Compensation for personal services the tax on which is not limited by the tax convention (effectively connected income under § 1.864-4(c)(6)(ii)) $20,000

Oil royalties the tax on which is limited by the tax convention to 15 percent of the gross amount thereof (effectively connected income by reason of election under § 1.871-10) 2,000

Total gross income $22,000

(b) The taxpayer is engaged in business in the United States during the taxable year but does not have a permanent establishment therein. There are no allowable deductions, other than the deductions allowed by sections 613 and 873(b)(3).

(c) The tax liability for the taxable year is $6,100, determined as follows:

Nontreaty gross income $20,000
Less: Deduction for personal exemption . . . 600

Nontreaty taxable income $19,400

Tax under section 1 of the Code on
 nontreaty taxable income ($5,170 plus
 45% of $1,400) . . . . $ 5,800
Plus: Tax on treaty income (Gross oil
 royalties) ($2,000 × 15%) 300

Total tax (determined as provided
 in paragraph (c)(2) and (3) of this
 section) . . . . $ 6,100

(d) If the tax had been determined under paragraph (b)(2) of § 1.871-8 as though the tax convention had not come into effect, the tax liability would have been $6,478, determined as follows and by taking into account the election under § 1.871-10:

Total gross income $22,000
Less: Deduction under section 613
 for percentage depletion
 ($2,000 × 27½%) $550
  Deduction for personal
   exemption 600   1,150

Taxable income $20,850

Tax under section 1 of the Code on taxable
 income ($6,070 plus 48% of $850) . . . $ 6,478

(e) *Effective date.* This section shall apply for taxable years beginning after December 31, 1966. For corresponding rules applicable to taxable years beginning before January 1, 1967, see 26 CFR 1.871-7(e) (Rev. as of Jan. 1, 1971). [Reg. § 1.871-12.]

☐ [T.D. 7332, 12-20-74. Amended by T.D. 8657, 3-5-96.]

[Reg. § 1.871-13]

§ 1.871-13. Taxation of individuals for taxable year of change of U.S. citizenship or residence.—(a) *In general.* (1) An individual who is a citizen or resident of the United States at the beginning of the taxable year but a nonresident

Nonresident Aliens and Foreign Corporations

alien at the end of the taxable year, or a nonresident alien at the beginning of the taxable year but a citizen or resident of the United States at the end of the taxable year, is taxable for such year as though his taxable year were comprised of two separate periods, one consisting of the time during which he is a citizen or resident of the United States and the other consisting of the time during which he is not a citizen or resident of the United States. Thus, for example, the income tax liability of an alien individual under chapter 1 of the Code for the taxable year in which he changes his residence will be computed under two different sets of rules, one relating to resident aliens for the period of residence and the other relating to nonresident aliens for the period of nonresidence. However, in determining the taxable income for such year which is subject to the graduated rate of tax imposed by section 1 or 1201 of the Code, all income for the period of U.S. citizenship or residence must be aggregated with the income for the period of nonresidence which is effectively connected for such year with the conduct of a trade or business in the United States. This section does not apply to alien individuals treated as residents for the entire taxable year under section 6013(g) or (h). These individuals are taxed under the rules in § 1.1-1(b).

(2) For purposes of this section, an individual is deemed to be a citizen or resident of the United States for the day on which he becomes a citizen or resident of the United States, a nonresident of the United States for the day on which he abandons his U.S. residence, and an alien for the day on which he gives up his U.S. citizenship.

(b) *Acquisition of U.S. citizenship or residence.* Income from sources without the United States which is not effectively connected with the conduct by the taxpayer of a trade or business in the United States is not taxable if received by an alien individual while he is not a resident of the United States even though he becomes a citizen or resident of the United States after its receipt and before the close of the taxable year. However, income from sources without the United States which is not effectively connected with the conduct by the taxpayer of a trade or business in the United States is taxable if received by an individual while he is a citizen or resident of the United States, even though he earns the income earlier in the taxable year while he is neither a citizen nor resident of the United States.

(c) *Abandonment of U.S. citizenship or residence.* Income from sources without the United States which is not effectively connected with the conduct by the taxpayer of a trade or business in the United States is not taxable if received by an alien individual while he is not a resident of the United States, even though he earns the income earlier in the taxable year while he is a citizen or resident of the United States. However, income from sources without the United States which is not effectively connected with the conduct by the taxpayer of a trade or business in the United States is taxable if received by an individual while he is a citizen or resident of the United States, even though he abandons his U.S. citizenship or residence after its receipt and before the close of the taxable year.

(d) *Special rules*—(1) *Method of accounting.* Paragraphs (b) and (c) of this section may not apply to an individual who for the taxable year uses an accrual method of accounting.

(2) *Deductions for personal exemptions.* An alien individual to whom this section applies is entitled to deduct one personal exemption for the taxable year under section 151. In addition, he is entitled to such additional exemptions as are allowed as a deduction under section 151 but only to the extent the amount of such additional exemptions do not exceed his taxable income (determined without regard to any deduction for personal exemptions) for the period in the taxable year during which he is a citizen or resident of the United States. This subparagraph does not apply to the extent it is inconsistent with section 873, and the regulations thereunder, or with the provisions of an income tax convention to which the United States is a party.

(3) *Exclusion of dividends received.* In determining the $100 exclusion for the taxable year provided by section 116 in respect of certain dividends, only those dividends for the period during which the individual is neither a citizen nor resident of the United States may be taken into account as are effectively connected for the taxable year with the conduct of a trade or business in the United States. See § 1.116-1(e)(1).

(e) *Illustrations.* The application of this section may be illustrated by the following examples:

Example (1). A, a married alien individual who uses the calendar year as the taxable year and the cash receipts and disbursements method of accounting, becomes a resident of the United States on June 1, 1971. During the period of nonresidence from January 1, 1971, to May 31, 1971, inclusive, A receives $15,000 income from sources without the United States which is not effectively connected with the conduct of a trade or business in the United States. During the period of residence from June 1, 1971, to December 31, 1971, A receives wages of $10,000, dividends of $200 from a foreign corporation, and dividends of $75 from a domestic corporation qualifying under section

Reg. § 1.871-13(e)

116(a). Of the amount of wages so received, $2,000 is for services performed by A outside the United States during the period of nonresidence. Total allowable deductions (other than for personal exemptions) amount to $700, none of which are deductible under section 62 in computing adjusted gross income. For 1971 A's spouse has no gross income and is not the dependent of another taxpayer. For 1971, A's taxable income is $8,200, all of which is subject to tax under section 1, as follows:

Wages		$10,000
Dividends from foreign corporation		200
Dividends from domestic corporation ($75 less $75 exclusion)		0
Adjusted gross income		$10,200
Less deductions:		
Personal exemptions (2 × $650)	$1,300	
Other allowable deductions	700	2,000
Taxable income		$ 8,200

Example (2). The facts are the same as in example (1) except that during the period of nonresidence from January 1, 1971, to May 31, 1971, A receives from sources within the United States income of $1,850 which is effectively connected with the conduct by A of a business in the United States and $350 in dividends from domestic corporations qualifying under section 116(a). Only $50 of these dividends are effectively connected with the conduct by A of a business in the United States. The assumption is made that there are no allowable deductions connected with such effectively connected income. For 1971, A has taxable income of $10,075 subject to tax under section 1 and $300 income subject to tax under section 871(a)(1)(A), as follows:

Wages		$10,000
Business income		1,850
Dividends from foreign corporation		200
Dividends from domestic corporation ($125 less $100 exclusion)		25
Adjusted gross income		$12,075
Less deductions:		
Personal exemptions (2 × $650)	$1,300	
Other allowable deductions	700	2,000
Taxable income subject to tax under section 1		$10,075
Income subject to tax under section 871(a)(1)(A)		$ 300

Example (3). A, a married alien individual with three children, uses the calendar year as the taxable year and the cash receipts and disbursements method of accounting. On October 1, 1971, A and his family become residents of the United States. During the period of nonresidence from January 1, 1971, to September 30, 1971, A receives income of $18,000 from sources without the United States which is not effectively connected with the conduct of a trade or business in the United States and of $2,500 from sources within the United States which is effectively connected with the conduct of a business in the United States. It is assumed there are no allowable deductions connected with such effectively connected income. During the period of residence from October 1, 1971, to December 31, 1971, A receives wages of $2,000, of which $400 is for services performed outside the United States during the period of nonresidence. Total allowable deductions (other than for personal exemptions) amount to $250, none of which are deductible under section 62 in computing adjusted gross income. Neither the spouse nor any of the children has any gross income for 1971, and the spouse is not the dependent of another taxpayer for such year. For 1971, A's taxable income is $1,850, all of which is subject to tax under section 1, as follows:

Wages (residence period)		$2,000
Less: Allowable deductions		250
Taxable income (without deduction for personal exemptions) (residence period)		$1,750
Business income (nonresidence period)		2,500
Total taxable income (without deduction for personal exemptions)		$4,250
Less deduction for personal exemptions:		
Taxpayer	$ 650	
Wife and 3 children (4 × $650, but not to exceed $1,750)	1,750	2,400
Taxable income		$1,850

(f) *Effective date.* This section shall apply for taxable years beginning after December 31, 1966. There are no corresponding rules in this part for taxable years beginning before January 1, 1967. [Reg. § 1.871-13.]

☐ [T.D. 7332, 12-20-74. Amended by T.D. 7670, 1-30-80.]

[Reg. § 1.871-14]

§ 1.871-14. Rules relating to repeal of tax on interest of nonresident alien individuals and foreign corporations received from certain portfolio debt investments.—(a) *General rule.* No tax shall be imposed under section 871(a)(1)(A), 871(a)(1)(C), 881(a)(1) or 881(a)(3)

Reg. § 1.871-14(a)

on any portfolio interest as defined in sections 871(h)(2) and 881(c)(2) received by a foreign person. But see section 871(b) or 882(a) if such interest is effectively connected with the conduct of a trade or business within the United States.

(b) *Rules concerning obligations in bearer form*—(1) *In general.* Interest (including original issue discount) with respect to an obligation in bearer form is portfolio interest within the meaning of section 871(h)(2)(A) or 881(c)(2)(A) only if it is paid with respect to an obligation issued after July 18, 1984, that is described in section 163(f)(2)(B) and the regulations under that section and an exception under section 871(h) or 881(c) does not apply. Any obligation that is not in registered form as defined in paragraph (c)(1)(i) of this section is an obligation in bearer form.

(2) *Coordination with withholding and reporting rules.* For an exemption from withholding under section 1441 with respect to obligations described in this paragraph (b), see § 1.1441-1(b)(4)(i). For rules relating to an exemption from Form 1099 reporting and backup withholding under section 3406, see section 6049 and § 1.6049-5(b)(8) for the payment of interest and § 1.6045-1(g)(1)(ii) for the redemption, retirement, or sale of an obligation in bearer form.

(c) *Rules concerning obligations in registered form*—(1) *In general*—(i) *Obligation in registered form.* For purposes of this section, an obligation is in registered form only as provided in this paragraph (c)(1)(i). The conditions for an obligation to be considered in registered form are identical to the conditions described in § 5f.103-1 of this chapter. Therefore, an obligation that would be an obligation in registered form except for the fact that it can be converted at any time in the future into an obligation that is not in registered form shall not be an obligation in registered form. An obligation that is not in registered form by reason of the preceding sentence may nevertheless be in registered form, but only after the possibility of conversion is terminated. An obligation that is not in registered form and can be converted into an obligation that would meet the requirements of this paragraph (c)(1)(i) for being in registered form shall be considered in registered form only after the conversion is effected. For purposes of this section, an obligation is convertible if the obligation can be transferred by any means not described in § 5f.103-1(c) of this chapter. An obligation is treated as an obligation in registered form if—

(A) The obligation is registered as to both principal and any stated interest with the issuer (or its agent) and transfer of the obligation may be effected only by surrender of the old instrument, and either the reissuance by the issuer of the old instrument to the new holder or the issuance by the issuer of a new instrument to the new holder;

(B) The right to the principal of, and stated interest on, the obligation may be transferred only through a book entry system maintained by the issuer (or its agent) described in this paragraph (c)(1)(i)(B). An obligation shall be considered transferable through a book entry system if the ownership of an interest in the obligation, is required to be reflected in a book entry, whether or not physical securities are issued. A book entry is a record of ownership that identifies the owner of an interest in the obligation; or

(C) It is registered as to both principal and any stated interest with the issuer (or its agent) and may be transferred by way of either of the methods described in paragraph (c)(1)(i)(A) or (B) of this section.

(ii) *Requirements for portfolio interest qualification in the case of an obligation in registered form.* Interest (including original issue discount) received on an obligation that is in registered form qualifies as portfolio interest only if—

(A) The interest is paid on an obligation issued after July 18, 1984;

(B) The interest would be subject to tax under section 871(a)(1)(A), 871(a)(1)(C), 881(a)(1) or 881(a)(3) but for section 871(h) or 881(c);

(C) A United States (U.S.) person otherwise required to deduct and withhold tax under chapter 3 of the Internal Revenue Code (Code) receives a statement that meets the requirements of section 871(h)(5) that the beneficial owner of the obligation is not a U.S. person; and

(D) An exception under section 871(h) or 881(c) does not apply.

(2) *Required statement.* For purposes of paragraph (c)(1)(ii)(C) of this section, a U.S. person will be considered to have received a statement that meets the requirements of section 871(h)(5) if either it complies with one of the procedures described in this paragraph (c)(2) and does not have actual knowledge or reason to know that the beneficial owner is a U.S. person or it complies with the procedures described in paragraph (d) or (e) of this section.

(i) The U.S. person (or its authorized foreign agent described in § 1.1441-7(c)(2)) can reliably associate the payment with documentation upon which it can rely to treat the payment as made to a foreign beneficial owner in accordance

Reg. § 1.871-14(c)(2)

with § 1.1441-1(e)(1)(ii). See § 1.1441-1(b)(2)(vii) for rules regarding reliable association with documentation.

(ii) The U.S. person (or its authorized foreign agent described in § 1.1441-7(c)(2)) can reliably associate the payment with a withholding certificate described in § 1.1441-5(c)(2)(iv) from a person claiming to be withholding foreign partnership and the foreign partnership can reliably associate the payment with documentation upon which it can rely to treat the payment as made to a foreign beneficial owner in accordance with § 1.1441-1(e)(1)(ii).

(iii) The U.S. person (or its authorized foreign agent described in § 1.1441-7(c)(2)) can reliably associate the payment with a withholding certificate described in § 1.1441-1(e)(3)(ii) from a person representing to be a qualified intermediary that has assumed primary withholding responsibility in accordance with § 1.1441-1(e)(5)(iv) and the qualified intermediary can reliably associate the payment with documentation upon which it can rely to treat the payment as made to a foreign beneficial owner in accordance with its agreement with the Internal Revenue Service (IRS).

(iv) The U.S. person (or its authorized foreign agent described in § 1.1441-7(c)(2)) can reliably associate the payment with a withholding certificate described in § 1.1441-1(e)(3)(v) from a person claiming to be a U.S. branch of a foreign bank or of a foreign insurance company that is described in § 1.1441-1(b)(2)(iv)(A) or a U.S. branch designated in accordance with § 1.1441-1(b)(2)(iv)(E) and the U.S. branch can reliably associate the payment with documentation upon which it can rely to treat the payment as made to a foreign beneficial owner in accordance with § 1.1441-1(e)(1)(ii).

(v) The U.S. person receives a statement from a securities clearing organization, a bank, or another financial institution that holds customers' securities in the ordinary course of its trade or business. In such case the statement must be signed under penalties of perjury by an authorized representative of the financial institution and must state that the institution has received from the beneficial owner a withholding certificate described in § 1.1441-1(e)(2)(i) (a Form W-8 or an acceptable substitute form as defined § 1.1441-1(e)(4)(vi)) or that it has received from another financial institution a similar statement that it, or another financial institution acting on behalf of the beneficial owner, has received the Form W-8 from the beneficial owner. In the case of multiple financial institutions between the beneficial owner and the U.S. person, this statement must be given by each financial institution to the one above it in the chain. No particular form is required for the statement provided by the financial institutions. However, the statement must provide the name and address of the beneficial owner, and a copy of the Form W-8 provided by the beneficial owner must be attached. The statement is subject to the same rules described in § 1.1441-1(e)(4) that apply to intermediary Forms W-8 described in § 1.1441-1(e)(3)(iii). If the information on the Form W-8 changes, the beneficial owner must so notify the financial institution acting on its behalf within 30 days of such changes, and the financial institution must promptly so inform the U.S. person. This notice also must be given if the financial institution has actual knowledge that the information has changed but has not been so informed by the beneficial owner. In the case of multiple financial institutions between the beneficial owner and the U.S. person, this notice must be given by each financial institution to the institution above it in the chain.

(vi) The U.S. person complies with procedures that the U.S. competent authority may agree to with the competent authority of a country with which the United States has an income tax treaty in effect.

(3) *Time for providing certificate or documentary evidence*—(i) *General rule.* Interest on a registered obligation shall qualify as portfolio interest if the withholding certificate or documentary evidence that must be provided is furnished before expiration of the beneficial owner's period of limitation for claiming a refund of tax with respect to such interest. See, however, § 1.1441-1(b)(7) for consequences to a withholding agent that makes a payment without withholding even though it cannot reliably associate the payment with the documentation prior to the payment. If a withholding agent withholds an amount under chapter 3 of the Code because it cannot reliably associate the payment with the documentation for the beneficial owner on the date of payment, the beneficial owner may nevertheless claim the benefit of an exemption from tax under this section by claiming a refund or credit for the amount withheld based upon the procedures described in §§ 1.1464-1 and 301.6402-3(e) of this chapter. For this purpose, the taxpayer must attach a withholding certificate described in § 1.1441-1(e)(2)(i) to the income tax filed for claiming a refund of tax. In the alternative, adjustments to any amount of overwithheld tax may be made under the procedures described in § 1.1461-2(a) (for example, if the beneficial owner furnishes documentation to the withholding agent before the due date for filing the return required under § 1.1461-1(b) with respect to that payment).

Reg. § 1.871-14(c)(3)

Nonresident Aliens and Foreign Corporations

See p. 20,601 for regulations not amended to reflect law changes

(ii) *Example.* The following example illustrates the rules of this paragraph (c)(3) and their coordination with § 1.1441-1(b)(7):

Example. A is a withholding agent who, on October 12, 2001, pays interest on a registered obligation to B, a foreign corporation. B is a calendar year taxpayer, engaged in the conduct of a trade or business in the United States, and is, therefore, required to file an annual income tax return on Form 1120F. The interest, however, is not effectively connected with B's U.S. trade or business. On the date of payment, B has not furnished, and A cannot associate the payment with documentation for B. However, A does not withhold under section 1442, even though, under § 1.1441-1(b)(3)(iii)(A), A should presume that B is a foreign person, because A's communications with B are mailed to an address in a foreign country. Assuming that B files a return for its taxable year ending December 31, 2001, and that its statute of limitations period with regard to that year expires on June 15, 2005, the interest paid on October 12, 2001, may qualify as portfolio interest only if B provides appropriate documentation to A on or before June 15, 2005. If B does not provide the documentation on or before June 15, 2005, and does not pay the tax, A is liable for the tax under section 1463, even if B provides the documentation to A after June 15, 2005. Therefore, the provisions in § 1.1441-1(b)(7), regarding late-received documentation would not help A avoid liability for tax under section 1463 even if the documentation is furnished within the statute of limitations period of A. This is because, in a case involving interest, the documentation received within the limitations period of the beneficial owner serves as a condition for the interest to qualify as portfolio interest. When documentation is received after the expiration of the beneficial owner's limitations period, the interest can no longer qualify as portfolio interest. On the other hand, A could rely on documentation that it receives after the expiration of B's limitations period to establish B's right to a reduced rate of withholding under an applicable income tax treaty (since, in such a case, a claim of treaty benefits is not conditioned upon providing documentation prior to the expiration of the beneficial owner's limitations period).

(4) *Coordination with withholding and reporting rules.* For an exemption from withholding under section 1441 with respect to obligations described in this paragraph (c), see § 1.1441-1(b)(4)(i). For rules applicable to withholding certificates, see § 1.1441-1(e)(4). For rules regarding documentary evidence, see § 1.6049-5(c)(1). For application of presumptions when the U.S. person cannot reliably associate the payment with documentation, see § 1.1441-1(b)(3). For standards of knowledge applicable to withholding agents, see § 1.1441-7(b). For rules relating to an exemption from Form 1099 reporting and backup withholding under section 3406, see section 6049 and § 1.6049-5(b)(8) for the payment of interest and § 1.6045-1(g)(1)(i) for the redemption, retirement, or sale of an obligation in registered form. For rules relating to reporting on Forms 1042 and 1042-S, see § 1.1461-1(b) and (c).

(d) *Application of repeal of 30-percent withholding to pass-through certificates*—(1) *In general.* Interest received on a pass-through certificate qualifies as portfolio interest under section 871(h)(2) or 881(c)(2) if the interest satisfies the conditions described in paragraph (b)(1), (c)(1), or (e) of this section without regard to whether any obligation held by the fund or trust to which the pass-through certificate relates is described in paragraph (b)(1), (c)(1)(ii), or (e) of this section. This paragraph (d)(1) applies only to payments made to the holder of the pass-through certificate from the trustee of the pass-through trust and does not apply to payments made to the trustee of the pass-through trust. For example, a mortgage pass-through certificate in bearer form must meet the requirements set forth in paragraph (b)(1) of this section, but the obligations held by the fund or trust to which the mortgage pass-through certificate relates need not meet the requirements set forth in paragraph (b)(1), (c)(1)(ii), or (e) of this section. However, for purposes of paragraphs (b)(1), (c)(1)(ii), and (e) of this section and section 127 of the Tax Reform Act of 1984, a pass-through certificate will be considered as issued after July 18, 1984, only to the extent that the obligations held by the fund or trust to which the pass-through certificate relates are issued after July 18, 1984.

(2) *Interest in REMICs.* Interest received on a regular or residual interest in a REMIC qualifies as portfolio interest under section 871(h)(2) or 881(c)(2) if the interest satisfies the conditions described in paragraph (b)(1), (c)(1)(ii), or (e) of this section. For purposes of paragraph (b)(1), (c)(1)(ii), or (e) of this section, interest on a regular interest in a REMIC is not considered interest on any mortgage obligations held by the REMIC. The foregoing rule, however, applies only to payments made to the holder of the regular interest from the REMIC and does not apply to payments made to the REMIC. For purposes of paragraph (b)(1), (c)(1)(ii), or (e) of this section, interest on a residual interest in a REMIC is considered to be interest on or with respect to the obligations held by the REMIC, and not on or with respect to the residual interest. For purposes of paragraphs

Reg. § 1.871-14(d)(2)

(b)(1), (c)(1)(ii), and (e) of this section and section 127 of the Tax Reform Act of 1984, a residual interest in a REMIC will be considered as issued after July 18, 1984, only to the extent that the obligations held by the REMIC are issued after July 18, 1984, but a regular interest in a REMIC will be considered as issued after July 18, 1984, if the regular interest was issued after July 18, 1984, without regard to the date on which the mortgage obligations held by the REMIC were issued.

(3) *Date of issuance.* In general, a mortgage pass-through certificate will be considered to have been issued after July 18, 1984, if all of the mortgages held by the fund or trust were issued after July 18, 1984. If some of the mortgages held by the fund or trust were issued before July 19, 1984, then the portion of any interest payment which represents interest on those mortgages shall not be considered to be portfolio interest. The preceding sentence shall not apply, however, if all of the following conditions are satisfied:

(i) The mortgage pass-through certificate is issued after December 31, 1986;

(ii) Payment of the mortgage pass-through certificate is guaranteed by, and a guarantee commitment has been issued by, an entity that is independent from the issuer of the underlying obligation;

(iii) The guarantee commitment with respect to the mortgage pass-through certificate cannot have been issued more than 14 months prior to the date on which the mortgage pass-through certificate is issued; and

(iv) The fund or trust to which the mortgage pass-through certificate relates cannot contain mortgage obligations on which the first scheduled monthly payment of principal and interest was made more than twelve months before the date on which the guarantee commitment was made.

(e) *Foreign-targeted registered obligations*—(1) *General rule.* The statement described in paragraph (c)(1)(ii)(C) of this section is not required with respect to interest paid on a registered obligation that is targeted to foreign markets in accordance with the provisions of paragraph (e)(2) of this section if the interest is paid by a U.S. person, a withholding foreign partnership, or a U.S. branch described in § 1.1441-1(b)(2)(iv)(A) or (E) to a registered owner at an address outside the United States, provided that the registered owner is a financial institution described in section 871(h)(5)(B). In that case, the U.S. person otherwise required to deduct and withhold tax may treat the interest as portfolio interest if it does not have actual knowledge that the beneficial owner is a United States person and if it receives the certificate described in paragraph (e)(3)(i) of this section from a financial institution or member of a clearing organization, which member is the beneficial owner of the obligation, or the documentary evidence or statement described in paragraph (e)(3)(ii) of this section from the beneficial owner, in accordance with the procedures described in paragraph (e)(4) of this section.

(2) *Definition of a foreign-targeted registered obligation.* An obligation is considered to be targeted to foreign markets for purposes of paragraph (e)(1) of this section if it is sold (or resold in connection with its original issuance) only to foreign persons (or to foreign branches of United States financial institutions described in section 871(h)(5)(B)) in accordance with procedures similar to those prescribed in § 1.163-5(c)(2)(i)(A), (B), or (D). However, the provisions of that section that require an obligation to be offered for sale or resale in connection with its original issuance only outside the United States do not apply with respect to registered obligations offered for sale through a public auction. Similarly, the provisions of that section that require delivery to be made outside the United States do not apply to registered obligations offered for sale through a public auction if the obligations are considered to be in registered form by virtue of the fact that they may be transferred only through a book entry system. The obligation, if evidenced by a physical document other than a confirmation receipt, must contain on its face a legend indicating that it has been sold (or resold in connection with its original issuance) in accordance with those procedures.

(3) *Documentation.* A certificate described in paragraph (e)(3)(i) of this section is required if the United States person otherwise required to deduct and withhold tax (the withholding agent) pays interest to a financial institution described in section 871(h)(5)(B) or to a member of a clearing organization, which member is the beneficial owner of the obligation. The documentation described in paragraph (e)(3)(ii) of this section is required if a withholding agent pays interest to a beneficial owner that is neither a financial institution described in section 871(h)(5)(B) nor a member of a clearing organization.

(i) *Interest paid to a financial institution or a member of a clearing organization*—(A) *Requirement of a certificate*—(*1*) If the withholding agent pays interest to a financial institution described in section 871(h)(5)(B) or to a member of a clearing organization, which member is the beneficial owner of the obligation, the withholding agent must receive a certificate which states that,

Reg. § 1.871-14(d)(3)

beginning at the time the last preceding certificate under this paragraph (e)(3)(i) was provided and while the financial institution or clearing organization member has held the obligation, with respect to each foreign-targeted registered obligation which has been held by the person providing the certificate at any time since the provision of such last preceding certificate, either—

(*i*) The beneficial owner of the obligation has not been a United States person on each interest payment date; or

(*ii*) If the person providing the certificate is a financial institution which is holding or has held an obligation on behalf of the beneficial owner, the beneficial owner of the obligation has been a United States person on one or more interest payment dates (identifying such date or dates), and the person making the certification has forwarded or will forward the appropriate United States beneficial ownership notification to the withholding agent in accordance with the provisions of paragraph (e)(4) of this section.

(*2*) The person providing the certificate need not state the foregoing where no previous certificate has been required to be provided by the payee to the withholding agent under this paragraph (e)(3)(i).

(B) *Additional representations.* Whether or not a previous certificate has been required to be provided with respect to the obligation, each certificate furnished pursuant to the provisions in this paragraph (e)(3)(i) must further state that, for each foreign-targeted registered obligation held and every other such obligation to be acquired and held by the person providing the certificate during the period beginning on the date of the certificate and ending on the date the next certificate is required to be provided, the beneficial owner of the obligation will not be a United States person on each interest payment date while the financial institution or clearing organization member holds the obligation and that, if the person providing the certificate is a financial institution which is holding or will be holding the obligation on behalf of a beneficial owner, such person will provide a United States beneficial ownership notification to the withholding agent (and a clearing organization that is not a withholding agent where a member organization is required by this paragraph (e)(3) to furnish the clearing organization with a statement) in accordance with paragraph (e)(4) of this section in the event such certificate (or statement in the case of a statement provided by a member organization to a clearing organization that is not a withholding agent) is or becomes untrue with respect to any obligation. A clearing organization is an entity which is in the business of holding obligations for member organizations and transferring obligations among such members by credit or debit to the account of a member without the necessity of physical delivery of the obligation.

(C) *Obligation must be identified.* The certificate described in paragraph (e)(3)(ii)(A) of this section must identify the obligation or obligations with respect to which it is given, except where the certification is given with respect to an obligation that has not been acquired at the time the certification is made. An obligation is identified if it or the larger issuance of which it is a part is described on a list (e.g., $5 million principal amount of 12% debentures of ABC Savings and Loan Association due February 25, 1995, $3 million principal amount of 10% U.S. Treasury notes due May 28, 1990) of all registered obligations targeted to foreign markets held by or on behalf of the person providing the certificate and the list is attached to, and incorporated by reference into, the certificate. The certificate must identify and provide the address of the person furnishing the certificate.

(D) *Payment to a depository of a clearing organization.* If the withholding agent pays interest to a depository of a clearing organization, then the clearing organization must provide the certificate described in this paragraph (e)(3)(i) to the withholding agent. Any certificate that is provided by a clearing organization must state that the clearing organization has received a statement from each member which complies with the provisions of this paragraph (e)(3)(i) and of paragraph (e)(4) of this section (as if the clearing organization were the withholding agent and regardless of whether the member is a financial institution described in section 871(h)(5)(B)).

(E) *Statement in lieu of Form W-8.* Subject to the requirements set out in paragraph (e)(4) of this section, a certificate or statement in the form described in this paragraph (e)(3)(i), in conjunction with the next annual certificate or statement, will serve as the certificate that may be provided in lieu of a Form W-8 with respect to interest on all foreign-targeted registered obligations held by the person making the certification or statement and which is paid to such person within the period beginning on the date of the certificate and ending on the date the next certificate is required to be provided.

(F) *Electronic transmission.* The certificate described in this paragraph (e)(3)(i) may be provided electronically under the terms and conditions of § 1.163-5(c)(2)(i)(D)(*3*)(*ii*).

(ii) *Payment to a person other than a financial institution or member of a clearing or-*

Reg. § 1.871-14(e)(3)

ganization. If the withholding agent pays interest to the beneficial owner of an obligation that is neither a financial institution described in section 871(h)(5)(B) nor a member of a clearing organization, then such owner must provide the withholding agent a statement described in paragraph (c)(1)(ii)(C) of this section.

(4) *Applicable procedures regarding documentation*—(i) *Procedures applicable to certificates required under paragraph (e)(3)(i) of this section*—(A) *Time for providing certificate.* Where no previous certificate for foreign-targeted registered obligations has been provided to the withholding agent by the person providing the certificate under paragraph (e)(3)(i) of this section, such certificate must be provided within the period beginning 90 days prior to the first interest payment date on which the person holds a foreign-targeted registered obligation. The withholding agent may, in its discretion, withhold under section 1441(a), 1442(a), or 1443 if the certificate is not received by the date 30 days prior to the interest payment. Thereafter the certificate must be filed within the period beginning on January 15 and ending January 31 of each year. If a certificate provided pursuant to the first sentence of this paragraph (e)(4)(i)(A) is provided during the period beginning on January 15 and ending on January 31 of any year, then no other certificate need be provided during such period in such year.

(B) *Change of status notification on Form W-9.* If, on any interest payment date after the obligation was acquired by the person making the certification, the beneficial owner of the obligation is a U.S. person, then the person to whom the withholding agent pays interest must furnish the withholding agent with a U.S. beneficial ownership notification within 30 days after such interest payment date. A U.S. beneficial ownership notification must include a statement that the beneficial owner of the obligation has been a U.S. person on an interest payment date (identifying such date), that such owner has provided to the person providing the notification a Form W-9 (or a substitute form that is substantially similar to Form W-9 and completed under penalties of perjury), and that the person providing the notification has been and will be complying with the information reporting requirements of section 6049, if applicable.

(C) *Alternative notification statement.* Where the person providing the notification described in paragraph (e)(4)(i)(B) of this section is neither a controlled foreign corporation within the meaning of section 957(a), nor a foreign corporation 50-percent or more of the gross income of which from all sources for the three-year period ending with the close of the taxable year preceding the date of the statement was effectively connected with the conduct of trade or business in the United States, such person must attach to the notification a copy of the Form W-9 (or substitute form that is substantially similar to Form W-9 and completed under penalties of perjury) provided by the beneficial owner. When a person that provides the U.S. beneficial ownership notification does not attach to it a copy of such Form W-9 (or substitute form that is substantially similar to Form W-9 and completed under penalties of perjury), such person must state that it is either a controlled foreign corporation within the meaning of section 957(a), or a foreign corporation 50-percent or more of the gross income of which from all sources for the three-year period ending with the close of its taxable year preceding the date of the statement was effectively connected with the conduct of a trade or business in the United States. A withholding agent that receives a Form W-9 (or a substitute form that is substantially similar to Form W-9 and completed under penalties of perjury) must send a copy of such form to the IRS, at such address as the IRS shall indicate, within 30 days after receiving it and must attach a statement that the Form W-9 or substitute form was provided pursuant to this paragraph (e)(4) with respect to a U.S. person that has owned a foreign-targeted registered obligation on one or more interest payment dates.

(D) *Failure to provide notification.* If either a Form W-9 (or a substitute form that is substantially similar to a Form W-9 and completed under penalties of perjury) or the statement described in paragraph (e)(4)(i)(C) of this section is not attached to the U.S. beneficial ownership notification provided pursuant to paragraph (e)(4)(i)(B) of this section, the withholding agent is required to withhold under section 1441, 1442, or 1443 on a payment of interest made after the withholding agent has received the notification unless such form or statement (or a statement that the beneficial owner of the obligation is no longer a U.S. person) is received before the interest payment date from the person who provided the notification (or transferee). If, during the period beginning on the next January 15 and ending on the next January 31, such person certifies as set out in paragraph (e)(3)(i) of this section (subject to paragraph (e)(3)(i)(A)(*2*) of this section) then the withholding agent is not required to withhold during the year following such certification (unless such person again provides a U.S. beneficial ownership notification without attaching a Form W-9 or substitute form that is substantially similar to Form W-9 and completed under penalties of perjury or the statement described in paragraph (e)(4)(i)(C) of this section).

(E) *Procedures for clearing organizations.* Within the period beginning 10 days before the end of the calendar quarter and ending on the last day of each calendar quarter, any clearing organization (including a clearing organization that is a withholding agent) relying on annual certificates or statements from its member organizations, as set forth in paragraph (e)(3)(i) of this section, must send each member organization having submitted such certificate or statement a reminder that the member organization must give the clearing organization a U.S. beneficial ownership notification in the circumstances described in paragraph (e)(4)(i)(B) of this section.

(F) *Retention of certificates.* The certificate described in paragraph (e)(3)(i) of this section must be retained in the records of the withholding agent for four years from the end of the calendar year in which it was received. The statement described in paragraph (e)(3)(i) of this section that is received by a clearing organization from a member organization must be retained in the records of the clearing organization for four years from the end of the calendar year in which it was received.

(G) *No reporting requirement.* The withholding agent who receives the certificate described in paragraph (e)(3)(i) of this section is not required to file Form 1042S to report payments under § 1.1461-1(b) or (c) of interest that are made with respect to foreign-targeted registered obligations held by the person providing the certificate and are made within the period beginning with the certificate date and ending on the last date for filing the next certificate.

(ii) *Procedures regarding certificates required under paragraph (e)(3)(ii) of this section*—
(A) *Time for providing certificate.* The statement described in paragraph (e)(3)(ii) of this section must be provided to the withholding agent within the period beginning 90 days prior to and ending on the first interest payment date on which the withholding agent pays interest to the beneficial owner. The withholding agent may, in its discretion, withhold under section 1441(a), 1442(a), or 1443 if the statement is not received by the date 30 days prior to the interest payment. The beneficial owner must confirm to the withholding agent the continuing validity of the documentary evidence within the period beginning 90 days prior to the first day of the third calendar year following the provision of such evidence and during the same period every three years thereafter while the owner still owns the obligation. The withholding agent who receives the statement described in paragraph (e)(3)(ii) of this section is not required to report payments of interest under § 1.1461-1(b) or (c) if the payments are made with respect to foreign-targeted registered obligations held by the person who provides the statement and are made within the period beginning with the date on which the statement is provided and ending on the last date for confirming the validity of the statement. The statement received for purposes of paragraph (e)(3)(ii) of this section is subject to the applicable procedures set forth in § 1.1441-1(e)(4).

(B) *Change of status notification on Form W-9.* If on any interest payment date after the obligation was acquired by the person providing the statement described in paragraph (e)(3)(ii) of this section, the beneficial owner of the obligation is a U.S. person, then the beneficial owner must so inform the withholding agent within 30 days after such interest payment date and must provide a Form W-9 (or substitute form that is substantially similar completed under penalties of perjury) to the withholding agent. However, the beneficial owner is not required to provide another Form W-9 (or substitute form that is substantially similar and completed under penalties of perjury) if such person has already provided it to the withholding agent within the same calendar year.

(iii) *Disqualification of documentation.* In accordance with the provisions of section 871(h)(4), the Secretary may make a determination in appropriate cases that a certificate or statement by any person, or class of persons, does not satisfy the requirements of that section. Should that determination be made, all payments of interest that otherwise qualify as portfolio interest to that person would become subject to 30-percent withholding under section 1441(a), 1442(a), or 1443.

(iv) *Special effective date.* Notwithstanding the foregoing requirements of this section—

(A) Any certificate that is required to be filed with the withholding agent during the period beginning on January 15 and ending on January 31, 1986, is not required to state that the beneficial owner of an obligation, prior to the date of the certificate, either was not a United States person or was a United States person if the obligation was acquired by the person providing the certificate on or before September 19, 1985; and

(B) All of the requirements of this paragraph (e), as in effect prior to the effective date of these amendments, shall remain effective with respect to each interest payment prior to the filing of the certificate described in paragraph (e)(4)(iv)(A) of this section, except that the provi-

Reg. § 1.871-14(e)(4)

sions of paragraph (e)(3) of this section relating to which persons are required to receive certificates or statements and paragraph (e)(3)(ii) or (4)(ii) of this section shall become effective with respect to each interest payment after September 20, 1985.

(5) *Information reporting.* See § 1.6049-5(b)(7) for special information reporting rules applicable to interest on foreign-targeted registered obligations. See § 1.6045-1(g)(1)(ii) for information reporting rules applicable to the redemption, retirement, or sale of foreign-targeted registered obligations.

(f) *Securities lending transactions.* For applicable rules regarding substitute interest payments received pursuant to a securities lending transaction or a sale-repurchase transaction, see §§ 1.871-7(b)(2) and 1.881-2(b)(2).

(g) *Definitions.* For purposes of this section, the terms *U.S. person* and *foreign person* have the meaning set forth in § 1.1441-1(c)(2), the term *beneficial owner* has the meaning set forth in § 1.1441-1(c)(6), the term *withholding agent* has the meaning set forth in § 1.1441-7(a); the term *payee* has the meaning set forth in § 1.1441-1(b)(2); and the term *payment* has the meaning set forth in § 1.1441-2(e).

(h) *Effective date*—(1) *In general.* This section shall apply to payments of interest made after December 31, 2000.

(2) *Transition rule.* For purposes of this section, the validity of a Form W-8 that was valid on January 1, 1998, under the regulations in effect prior to January 1, 2001 (see 26 CFR parts 1 and 35a, revised April 1, 1999) and expired, or will expire, at any time during 1998, is extended until December 31, 1998. The validity of a Form W-8 that is valid on or after January 1, 1999 remains valid until its validity expires under the regualtions in effect prior to January 1, 2001 (see 26 CFR parts 1 and 35a, revised April 1, 1999) but in no event will such a form remain valid after December 31, 2000. The rule in this paragraph (h)(2), however, does not apply to extend the validity period of a Form W-8 that expired solely by reason of changes in the circumstances of the person whose name is on the certificate. Notwithstanding the first three sentences of this paragraph (h)(2), a withholding agent or payor may choose to not take advantage of the transition rule in this paragraph (h)(2) with respect to one or more withholding certificates valid under the regulations in effect prior to January 1, 2001 (see 26 CFR parts 1 and 35a, revised April 1, 1999) and, therefore, may choose to obtain withholding certificates conforming to the requirements described in this section (new withholding certificates). For purposes of this section, a new withholding certificate is deemed to satisfy the documentation requirement under the regulations in effect prior to January 1, 2001 (see 26 CFR parts 1 and 35a, revised April 1, 1999). Further, a new withholding certificate remains valid for the period specified in § 1.1441-1(e)(4)(ii), regardless of when the certificate is obtained. [Reg. § 1.871-14.]

☐ [*T.D. 8734, 10-6-97. Amended by T.D. 8804, 12-30-98 and T.D. 8856, 12-29-99.*]

[Reg. § 1.872-1]

§ 1.872-1. **Gross income of nonresident alien individuals.**—(a) *In general*—(1) *Inclusions.* The gross income of a nonresident alien individual for any taxable year includes only (i) the gross income which is derived from sources within the United States and which is not effectively connected for the taxable year with the conduct of a trade or business in the United States by that individual and (ii) the gross income, irrespective of whether such income is derived from sources within or without the United States, which is effectively connected for the taxable year with the conduct of a trade or business in the United States by that individual. For the determination of the sources of income, see sections 861 through 863 and the regulations thereunder. For the determination of whether income from sources within or without the United States is effectively connected for the taxable year with the conduct of a trade or business in the United States, see sections 864(c) and 871(c) and (d), §§ 1.864-3 through 1.864-7, and §§ 1.871-9 and 1.871-10. For special rules for determining the income of an alien individual who changes his residence during the taxable year, see § 1.871-13.

(2) *Exchange transactions.* Even though a nonresident alien individual who effects certain transactions in the United States in stocks, securities, or commodities during the taxable year may not, by reason of section 864(b)(2) and paragraph (c) or (d) of § 1.864-2, be engaged in trade or business in the United States during the taxable year through the effecting of such transactions, nevertheless he shall be required to include in gross income for the taxable year the gains and profits from those transactions to the extent required by § 1.871-7 or § 1.871-8.

(3) *Exclusions.* For exclusions from gross income, see § 1.872-2.

(b) *Individuals not engaged in U.S. business.* In the case of a nonresident alien individual who at no time during the taxable year is engaged in trade or business in the United States, the gross income shall include only (1) the gross income from sources within the United States which is described in section 871(a) and paragraphs (b),

Reg. § 1.872-1(a)(1)

(c), and (d) of § 1.871-7 and (2) the gross income from sources within the United States which, by reason of section 871(c) or (d) and § 1.871-9 or § 1.871-10, is treated as effectively connected for the taxable year with the conduct of a trade or business in the United States by that individual.

(c) *Individuals engaged in U.S. business.* In the case of a nonresident alien individual who is engaged in trade or business in the United States at any time during the taxable year, the gross income shall include (1) the gross income from sources within and without the United States which is effectively connected for the taxable year with the conduct of a trade or business in the United States by that individual, (2) the gross income from sources within the United States which, by reason of the election provided in section 871(d) and § 1.871-10, is treated as effectively connected for the taxable year with the conduct of a trade or business in the United States by that individual, and (3) the gross income from sources within the United States which is described in section 871(a) and paragraphs (b), (c), and (d) of § 1.871-7 and is not effectively connected for the taxable year with the conduct of a trade or business in the United States by the individual.

(d) *Special rules applicable to certain expatriates.* For special rules for determining the gross income of a nonresident alien individual who has lost United States citizenship with a principal purpose of avoiding certain taxes, see section 877(b)(1).

(e) *Alien resident of Puerto Rico.* This section shall not apply in the case of a nonresident alien individual who is a bona fide resident of Puerto Rico during the entire taxable year. See section 876 and § 1.876-1.

(f) *Effective date.* This section shall apply for taxable years beginning after December 31, 1966. For corresponding rules applicable to taxable years beginning before January 1, 1967, see 26 CFR 1.872-1 (Rev. as of Jan. 1, 1971). [Reg. § 1.872-1.]

☐ [*T.D.* 6528, 10-23-57. *Amended by T.D.* 7332, 12-20-74.]

[Reg. § 1.872-2]

§ 1.872-2. **Exclusions from gross income of nonresident alien individuals.**—(a) *Earnings of foreign ships or aircraft* —(1) *Basic rule.* So much of the income from sources within the United States of a nonresident alien individual as consists of earnings derived from the operation of a ship or ships documented, or of aircraft registered, under the laws of a foreign country which grants an equivalent exemption to citizens of the United States nonresident in that foreign country and to corporations organized in the United States shall not be included in gross income.

(2) *Equivalent exemption*—(i) *Ships.* A foreign country which either imposes no income tax, or, in imposing an income tax, exempts from taxation so much of the income of a citizen of the United States nonresident in that foreign country and of a corporation organized in the United States as consists of earnings derived from the operation of a ship or ships documented under the laws of the United States is considered as granting an equivalent exemption for purposes of the exclusion from gross income of the earnings of a foreign ship or ships.

(ii) *Aircraft.* A foreign country which either imposes no income tax, or, in imposing an income tax, exempts from taxation so much of the income of a citizen of the United States nonresident in that foreign country and of a corporation organized in the United States as consists of earnings derived from the operation of aircraft registered under the laws of the United States is considered as granting an equivalent exemption for purposes of the exclusion from gross income of the earnings of foreign aircraft.

(3) *Definition of earnings.* For purposes of subparagraphs (1) and (2) of this paragraph, compensation for personal services performed by an individual aboard a ship or aircraft does not constitute earnings derived by such individual from the operation of ships or aircraft.

(b) *Compensation paid by foreign employer to participants in certain exchange or training programs*—(1) *Exclusion from income.* Compensation paid to a nonresident alien individual for the period that the nonresident alien individual is temporarily present in the United States as a nonimmigrant under subparagraph (F) (relating to the admission of students into the United States) or subparagraph (J) (relating to the admission of teachers, trainees, specialists, etc., into the United States) of section 101(a)(15) of the Immigration and Nationality Act (8 U.S.C. 1101(a)(15)(F) or (J)) shall be excluded from gross income if the compensation is paid to such alien by his foreign employer. Compensation paid to a nonresident alien individual by the United States office of a domestic bank which is acting as paymaster on behalf of a foreign employer constitutes compensation paid by a foreign employer for purposes of this paragraph if the domestic bank is reimbursed by the foreign employer for such payment. A nonresident alien individual who is temporarily present in the United States as a nonimmigrant under such subparagraph (J) includes a nonresident alien individual admitted to

Reg. § 1.872-2(b)

the United States as an "exchange visitor" under section 201 of the United States Information and Educational Exchange Act of 1948 (22 U.S.C. 1446), which section was repealed by section 111 of the Mutual Education and Cultural Exchange Act of 1961 (75 Stat. 538).

(2) *Definition of foreign employer.* For purposes of this paragraph, the term "foreign employer" means a nonresident alien individual, a foreign partnership, a foreign corporation, or an office or place of business maintained in a foreign country or in a possession of the United States by a domestic corporation, a domestic partnership, or an individual who is a citizen or resident of the United States. The term does not include a foreign government. However, see section 893 and § 1.893-1. Thus, if a French citizen employed in the Paris branch of a banking company incorporated in the State of New York were admitted to the United States under section 101(a)(15)(J) of the Immigration and Nationality Act to study monetary theory and continued to receive a salary from such foreign branch while studying in the United States, such salary would not be includible in his gross income.

(c) *Tax convention.* Income of any kind which is exempt from tax under the provisions of a tax convention or treaty to which the United States is a party shall not be included in the gross income of a nonresident alien individual. Income on which tax is limited by tax convention shall be included in the gross income of a nonresident alien individual if it is not otherwise excluded from gross income. See §§ 1.871-12 and 1.894-1.

(d) *Certain bond income of residents of the Ryukyu Islands or the Trust Territory of the Pacific Islands.* Income derived by a nonresident alien individual from a series E or series H United States savings bond shall not be included in gross income if such individual acquired the bond while he was a resident of the Ryukyu Islands or the Trust Territory of the Pacific Islands. It is not necessary that the individual continue to be a resident of such Islands or Trust Territory for the period when, without regard to section 872(b)(4) and this paragraph, the income from the bond would otherwise be includible in his gross income under the provisions of section 446 or 454.

(e) *Certain annuities received under qualified plans.* Pursuant to section 871(f), income received by a nonresident alien individual as an annuity under a qualified annuity plan described in section 403(a)(1) (relating to taxation of employee annuities), or from a qualified trust described in section 401(a) (relating to qualified pension, profit-sharing, and stock bonus plans) which is exempt from tax under section 501(a) (relating to exemption from tax on corporations, certain trusts, etc.), shall not be included in gross income, and shall be exempt from tax, for purposes of section 871 and §§ 1.871-7 and 1.871-8, if—

(1) All of the personal services by reason of which the annuity is payable were either—

(i) Personal services performed outside the United States by an individual (whether or not the annuitant) who, at the time of performance of the services, was a nonresident alien individual, or

(ii) Personal services performed in the United States by a nonresident alien individual (whether or not the annuitant) which, by reason of section 864(b)(1) (or corresponding provision of any prior law), were not personal services causing such individual to be engaged in trade or business in the United States during the taxable year, and

(2) At the time the first amount is paid (even though paid in a taxable year beginning before January 1, 1967) as such annuity under such annuity plan, or by such trust, to (i) the individual described in subparagraph (1) of this paragraph, or (ii) his nonresident alien beneficiary if such beneficiary is entitled to receive such first amount, 90 percent or more of the employees or annuitants for whom contributions or benefits are provided under the annuity plan, or under the plan or plans of which the trust is a part, are citizens or residents of the United States.

This paragraph shall apply whether or not the taxpayer is engaged in trade or business in the United States at any time during the taxable year in which the annuity is received. This paragraph shall not apply to distributions by an employees' trust or from an annuity plan which give rise to gains described in section 402(a)(2) or 403(a)(2), whichever applies. See section 871(a)(1)(B) and paragraph (c)(1)(i) of § 1.871-7. For exemption from withholding of tax at source on an annuity which is exempt from tax under section 871(f) and this paragraph, see paragraph (g) of § 1.1441-4.

(f) *Other exclusions.* Income which is from sources without the United States, as determined under the provisions of sections 861 through 863, and the regulations thereunder, is not included in the gross income of a nonresident alien individual unless such income is effectively connected for the taxable year with the conduct of a trade or business in the United States by that individual. To determine specific exclusions in the case of other items which are from sources within the United States, see the applicable sections of the Code. For special rules under a tax convention for determining the sources of income and for excluding, from gross income, income from sources without the United States which is effectively connected with the conduct of a trade or business in the United

Reg. § 1.872-2(b)(2)

States, see the applicable tax convention. For determining which income from sources without the United States is effectively connected with the conduct of a trade or business in the United States, see section 864(c)(4) and § 1.864-5.

(g) *Effective date.* This section shall apply for taxable years beginning after December 31, 1966. For corresponding rules applicable to taxable years beginning before January 1, 1967, see 26 CFR 1.872-2 (Rev. as of Jan. 1, 1971). [Reg. § 1.872-2.]

☐ [T.D. 6258, 10-23-57. Amended by T.D. 6782, 12-12-64 and T.D. 7332, 12-20-74.]

[Reg. § 1.873-1]

§ 1.873-1. Deductions allowed nonresident alien individuals.—(a) *General provisions*—(1) *Allocation of deductions.* In computing the taxable income of a nonresident alien individual the deductions otherwise allowable shall be allowed only if, and to the extent that, they are connected with income from sources within the United States. No deduction shall be allowed in respect of any item, or portion thereof, which is not connected with income from such sources. For this purpose, the proper apportionment and allocation of the deductions with respect to sources of income within and without the United States shall be determined as provided in Part I (section 861 and following), subchapter N, chapter 1 of the Code, and the regulations thereunder, except as may otherwise be provided by tax convention. Thus, from the items of gross income specifically from sources within the United States and from the items allocated thereto under the provisions of section 863(a), there shall be deducted (i) the expenses, losses, and other deductions which are connected with those items of income and are properly apportioned or allocated thereto, and (ii) a ratable part of any other expenses, losses, or deductions which are connected with those items of income but cannot definitely be allocated to some item or class of gross income. The ratable part shall be based upon the ratio of gross income from sources within the United States to the total gross income. See §§ 1.861-8 and 1.863-1. In the case of income partly from within and partly from without the United States the expenses, losses, and other deductions connected with income from sources within the United States shall also be deducted in the manner prescribed by §§ 1.863-2 through 1.863-5 in order to ascertain under section 863 the portion of the taxable income attributable to sources within the United States.

(2) *Personal exemptions.* The deductions for the personal exemptions allowed by section 151 or 642(b) shall not be taken into account for purposes of subparagraph (1) of this paragraph but shall be allowed to the extent provided by paragraphs (b) and (c) of this section.

(3) *Adjusted gross income.* The adjusted gross income of a nonresident alien individual shall be the gross income from sources within the United States, determined in accordance with § 1.871-7, minus the deductions prescribed by section 62 to the extent such deductions are allowed under this section in computing taxable income.

(4) *Standard deduction.* The standard deduction shall not be allowed in computing the taxable income of a nonresident alien individual. See section 142(b)(1) and the regulations thereunder.

(5) *Exempt income.* No deduction shall be allowed under this section for the amount of any item or part thereof allocable to a class or classes of exempt income, including income exempt by tax convention. See section 265 and the regulations thereunder.

(b) *No United States business*—(1) *Income of not more than $15,400*—(i) *Deduction for losses only.* A nonresident alien individual within class 1 shall not be allowed any deductions other than the deduction for losses from sales or exchanges of capital assets determined in the manner prescribed by paragraph (b)(4)(vii) of § 1.871-7. Thus, an individual within this class shall not be allowed any deductions for the personal exemptions otherwise allowed by section 151 or 642(b).

(ii) *Source of losses.* Notwithstanding the provisions of section 873(b)(1), losses from sales or exchanges of capital assets shall be allowed under this subparagraph only if allocable to sources within the United States. See paragraph (b)(4)(i) of § 1.871-7.

(2) *Aggregate more than $15,400*—(i) *Deductions allowed.* In computing the income subject to tax under section 1 or section 1201(b), a nonresident alien individual within class 2 shall be allowed deductions to the extent prescribed by paragraph (c)(3) of § 1.871-7, but subject to the limitations of this section. For this purpose, the deduction for the personal exemptions shall be allowed in accordance with subdivision (iii) of this subparagraph.

(ii) *Deductions disallowed.* In computing the minimum tax prescribed by section 871(b)(3), that individual shall not be allowed any deductions other than the deduction for losses from sales or exchanges of capital assets determined in the manner prescribed by paragraph (b)(4)(vii) of § 1.871-7. For this purpose, the deductions for the personal exemptions shall not be allowed. See paragraph (c)(4) of § 1.871-7.

(iii) *Personal exemptions.* When the deductions for personal exemptions are allowed under

Reg. § 1.873-1(b)(2)

this subparagraph, only one exemption under section 151 shall be allowed in the case of an individual who is not a resident of Canada or Mexico. A resident of either of those countries shall be allowed all the exemptions granted by section 151 to the extent prescribed therein. An estate or trust, whether or not a resident of Canada or Mexico, shall determine its deduction for the personal exemption in accordance with section 642(b) and the regulations thereunder.

(iv) *Source of losses.* Notwithstanding the provisions of section 873(b), losses from sales or exchanges of capital assets shall be allowed under this subparagraph only if allocable to sources within the United States. See paragraph (c)(3)(i) of § 1.871-7.

(3) *Election to be taxed on a net basis.* Notwithstanding the other provisions of this paragraph, a nonresident alien individual within class 1 or 2 shall be allowed the deductions allowed by paragraph (c) of this section, if pursuant to a tax convention he is entitled, and does elect, to be subject to United States tax on a net basis as though he were engaged in trade or business within the United States through a permanent establishment situated therein.

(c) *United States business*—(1) *Deductions in general.* For purposes of computing the income subject to tax, a nonresident alien individual within class 3 shall be allowed deductions to the extent prescribed by paragraph (d) of § 1.871-7, but subject to the limitations of this section. For this purpose, the deductions for the personal exemptions shall be allowed in accordance with subparagraph (3) of this paragraph.

(2) *Special deductions.* Notwithstanding the rule of source prescribed in paragraph (a) of this section, an individual within class 3 shall be allowed the following deductions whether or not they are connected with income from sources within the United States:

(i) *Losses on transactions for profit.* Any loss sustained during the taxable year and not compensated for by insurance or otherwise, if incurred in any transaction entered into for profit, though not connected with a trade or business, shall be allowed to the extent allowed by section 165(c)(2), but only if and to the extent that the profit, if the transaction had resulted in a profit, would be taxable to such individual. Losses allowed under this subdivision shall be deducted in full, as provided in §§ 1.861-8 and 1.863-1, when the profit from the transaction, if it had resulted in a profit, would, under the provisions of section 861(a) or 863(a), have been taxable in full as income from sources within the United States; but shall be deducted under the provisions of § 1.863-3 when the profit from the transaction, if it had resulted in profit, would have been taxable only in part.

(ii) *Casualty losses.* Any loss of property not connected with a trade or business, sustained during the taxable year and not compensated for by insurance or otherwise, if the loss arises from fire, storm, shipwreck, or other casualty, or from theft, shall be allowed to the extent allowed by section 165(c)(3), but only if the loss is of property within the United States. Losses allowed under this subdivision shall be deducted in full, as provided in §§ 1.861-8 and 1.863-1, from the items of gross income specified under sections 861(a) and 863(a) as being derived in full from sources within the United States; but, if greater than the sum of those items, the unabsorbed loss shall be deducted from the income apportioned under the provisions of § 1.863-3 to sources within the United States.

(iii) *Charitable contributions.* The deduction for charitable contributions and gifts, to the extent allowed by section 170, shall be allowed under this subparagraph, but only as to contributions or gifts made to domestic corporations, or to community chests, funds, or foundations, created in the United States.

(3) *Personal exemptions.* Only one exemption under section 151 shall be allowed in the case of an individual who is not a resident of Canada or Mexico. A resident of either of those countries shall be allowed all the exemptions granted by section 151 to the extent prescribed therein. An estate or trust, whether or not a resident of Canada or Mexico, shall determine its deduction for the personal exemption in accordance with section 642(b) and the regulations thereunder. [Reg. § 1.873-1.]

☐ [*T.D. 6258, 10-23-57.*]

[Reg. § 1.874-1]

§ 1.874-1. **Allowance of deductions and credits to nonresident alien individuals.**—(a) *Return required.* A nonresident alien individual shall receive the benefit of the deductions and credits otherwise allowable with respect to the income tax, only if the nonresident alien individual timely files or causes to be filed with the Philadelphia Service Center, in the manner prescribed in subtitle F, a true and accurate return of the income which is effectively connected, or treated as effectively connected, with the conduct of a trade or business within the United States by the nonresident alien individual. No provision of this section (other than paragraph (c)(2)) shall be construed, however, to deny the credits provided by sections 31, 32, 33, 34 and 852(b)(3)(D)(ii). In addition, notwithstanding the requirement that a nonresident alien must file a timely return in order to receive the benefit of the deductions and credits otherwise allowable with respect to the income tax, the nonresident alien individual may, for purposes of determining the amount of tax to be withheld under section 1441 from remuneration paid for labor or personal services performed within the United States, receive the benefit of the deduction for personal exemptions provided in section 151, to the extent allowable under section 873(b)(3) and paragraph (c)(3) of § 1.873-1, or any applicable tax convention, by filing a claim therefor with the withholding agent. The amount of the deduction for the personal exemptions and the amount of the tax to be withheld under those circumstances shall be determined in accordance with paragraph (e)(2) of § 1.1441-3. The deductions and credits allowed such a nonresident alien individual electing under a tax convention to be subject to tax on a net basis may be obtained by filing a return of income in the manner prescribed in the regulations (if any) under the tax convention or under any other guidance issued by the Commissioner.

(b) *Filing deadline for return*—(1) *General rule.* As provided in paragraph (a) of this section, for purposes of computing the nonresident alien individual's taxable income for any taxable year, otherwise allowable deductions and credits will be allowed only if a true and accurate return for that taxable year is filed by the nonresident alien individual on a timely basis. For taxable years of a nonresident alien individual ending after July 31, 1990, whether a return for the current taxable year has been filed on a timely basis is dependent upon whether the nonresident alien individual filed a return for the taxable year immediately preceding the current taxable year. If a return was filed for that immediately preceding taxable year, or if the current taxable year is the first taxable year of the nonresident alien individual for which a return is required to be filed, the required return for the current taxable year must be filed within 16 months of the due date, as set forth in section 6072 and the regulations under that section, for filing the return for the current taxable year. If no return for the taxable year immediately preceding the current taxable year has been filed, the required return for the current taxable year (other than the first taxable year of the nonresident alien individual for which a return is required to be filed) must have been filed no later than the earlier of the date which is 16 months after the due date, as set forth in section 6072, for filing the return for the current taxable year or the date the Internal Revenue Service mails a notice to the nonresident alien individual advising the nonresident alien individual that the current year tax return has not been filed and that no deductions or credits (other than those provided in sections 31, 32, 33, 34 and 852(b)(3)(D)(ii)) may be claimed by the nonresident alien individual.

(2) *Waiver.* The filing deadlines set forth in paragraph (b)(1) of this section may be waived by the District Director or Assistant Commissioner (International) in rare and unusual circumstances if good cause for such waiver, based on the facts and circumstances, is established by the nonresident alien individual.

(3) *Income tax treaties.* A nonresident alien individual who has a permanent establishment or fixed base, as defined in an income tax treaty between the United States and the country of residence of the nonresident alien individual, in the United States is subject to the filing deadlines as set forth in paragraph (b)(1) of this section.

(4) *Protective return.* If a nonresident alien individual conducts limited activities in the United States in a taxable year which the nonresident alien individual determines does not give rise to gross income which is effectively connected with the conduct of a trade or business within the United States as defined in sections 871(b) and 864(b) and (c) and the regulations under those sections, the nonresident alien individual may nonetheless file a return for that taxable year on a timely basis under paragraph (b)(1) of this section and thereby protect the right to receive the benefit of the deductions and credits attributable to that gross income if it is later determined, after the return was filed, that the original determination was incorrect. On that timely filed return, the nonresident alien individual is not required to report any gross income as effectively connected with a United States trade or business or any deductions or credits but should attach a statement indicating that the return is being filed for the reason set forth in this paragraph (b)(4). If the nonresident alien individual determines that part of the activities which he or she conducts in the United States in a taxable year gives rise to gross income which is effectively connected with the conduct of a trade or business and part does not, the nonresident alien individual must timely file a return for that taxable year to report the gross income determined to be effectively connected, or treated as effectively connected, with the conduct of that trade or business within the United States and the deductions and credits attributable to the gross income. In addition, the nonresident alien individual should attach to that return the statement described in this paragraph (b)(4) with regard to the other activities. The nonresident alien individual may follow the same

Reg. § 1.874-1(b)(4)

procedure if the nonresident alien individual determines initially that he or she has no United States tax liability under the provisions of an applicable income tax treaty. In the event the nonresident alien individual relies on the provisions of an income tax treaty to reduce or eliminate the income subject to taxation, or to reduce the rate of tax to which that income is subject, disclosure may be required pursuant to section 6114.

(c) *Allowed deductions and credits*—(1) *In general.* Except for losses of property located within the United States, charitable contributions and personal exemptions (see section 873(b)), deductions are allowed to a nonresident alien individual only to the extent they are connected with gross income which is effectively connected, or treated as effectively connected, with the conduct of the nonresident alien individual's trade or business in the United States. Other than credits allowed by sections 31, 32, 33, 34 and 852(b)(3)(D)(ii), the nonresident alien individual is entitled to credits only if they are attributable to effectively connected income. See paragraph (a) of this section for the requirement that a return be timely filed. Except as provided by section 906, a nonresident alien individual shall not be allowed the credit against the tax for taxes of foreign countries and possessions of the United States allowed by section 901.

(2) *Verification.* At the request of the Internal Revenue Service, a nonresident alien individual claiming deductions from gross income which is effectively connected or treated as effectively connected with the conduct of a trade or business in the United States and credits attributable to that income must furnish at the place designated pursuant to § 301.7605-1(a) information sufficient to establish that the nonresident alien individual is entitled to the deductions and credits in the amounts claimed. All information must be furnished in a form suitable to permit verification of the claimed deductions and credits. The Internal Revenue Service may require, as appropriate, that an English translation be provided with any information in a foreign language. If a nonresident alien individual fails to furnish sufficient information, the Internal Revenue Service may in its discretion disallow any claimed deductions and credits in full or in part.

(d) *Return by Internal Revenue Service.* If a nonresident alien individual has various sources of income within the United States, so that from any one source, or from all sources combined, the amount of income shall call for the assessment of a tax greater than that withheld at the source in the case of that individual, and a return of income has not been filed in the manner prescribed by subtitle F, including the filing deadlines set forth in paragraph (b)(1) of this section, the Internal Revenue Service shall:

(1) Cause a return of income to be made,

(2) Include on the return the income described in § 1.871-7 or § 1.871-8 of that individual from all sources concerning which it has information, and

(3) *Assess the tax.* If the nonresident alien individual is not engaged in, or does not receive income that is treated as being effectively connected with, a United States trade or business and § 1.871-7 is applicable, the tax shall be assessed on the basis of gross income without allowance for deductions or credits (other than the credits provided by sections 31, 32, 33, 34 and 852(b)(3)(D)(ii)) and collected from one or more sources of income within the United States. If the nonresident alien individual is engaged in a United States trade or business or is treated as having effectively connected income and § 1.871-8 applies, the tax on the income of the nonresident alien individual that is not effectively connected, or treated as effectively connected with the conduct of a United States trade or business shall be assessed on the basis of gross income, determined in accordance with the rules of § 1.871-7, without allowance for deductions or credits (other than the credits provided by sections 31, 32, 33, 34 and 852(b)(3)(D)(ii)) and collected from one or more of the sources of income within the United States. Tax on income that is effectively connected, or treated as effectively connected, with the conduct of a United States trade or business shall be assessed in accordance with either section 1, 55 or 402(e)(1) without allowance for deductions or credits (other than the credits provided by sections 31, 32, 33, 34 and 852(b)(3)(D)(ii)) and collected from one or more of the sources of income within the United States.

(e) *Alien resident of Puerto Rico, Guam, American Samoa, or the Commonwealth of the Northern Mariana Islands.* This section shall not apply to a nonresident alien individual who is a bona fide resident of Puerto Rico, Guam, American Samoa, or the Commonwealth of the Northern Mariana Islands during the entire taxable year. *See* section 876 and § 1.876-1. [Reg. § 1.874-1.]

☐ [T.D. 6258, 10-23-57. Amended by T.D. 6462, 5-5-60; T.D. 6669, 8-26-63 *and* T.D. 8322, 12-10-90.]

[Reg. § 1.875-1]

§ 1.875-1. Partnerships.—Whether a nonresident alien individual who is a member of a partnership is taxable in accordance with subsection (a), (b), or (c) of section 871 may depend on the status of the partnership. A nonresident alien individual who is a member of a partnership which is not engaged in trade or business within the United States is subject to the provisions of section 871(a) or (b), as the case may be, depending on whether or not he receives during the taxable year an aggregate of more than $15,400 gross income described in section 871(a), if he is not otherwise engaged in trade or business within the United States. A nonresident alien individual who is a member of a partnership which at any time within the taxable year is engaged in trade or business within the United States is considered as being engaged in trade or business within the United States and is therefore taxable under section 871(c). For definition of what the term "partnership" includes, see section 7701(a)(2) and the regulations in Part 301 of this chapter (Regulations on Procedure and Administration). The test of whether a partnership is engaged in trade or business within the United States is the same as in the case of a nonresident alien individual. See § 1.871-8. [Reg. § 1.875-1.]

☐ [T.D. 7332, 12-20-74.]

[Reg. § 1.875-2]

§ 1.875-2. **Beneficiaries of estates or trusts.**—(a) [Reserved]

(b) *Exception for certain taxable years.* Notwithstanding paragraph (a) of this section, for any taxable year beginning before January 1, 1975, the grantor of a trust, whether revocable or irrevocable, is not deemed to be engaged in trade or business within the United States merely because the trustee is engaged in trade or business within the United States.

(c) [Reserved] [Reg. § 1.875-2.]

☐ [T.D. 7332, 12-20-74.]

[Reg. § 1.876-1]

§ 1.876-1. **Alien residents of Puerto Rico.**—(a) *General.* A nonresident alien individual who is a bona fide resident of Puerto Rico during the entire taxable year is, in accordance with the provisions of section 876, subject to tax under section 1 or, in the alternative, under section 1201(b) in generally the same manner as in the case of an alien resident of the United States. See paragraph (b) of § 1.1-1 and § 1.871-1. The tax is imposed upon the taxable income of such a resident of Puerto Rico, determined in accordance with section 63(a) and the regulations thereunder, from sources both within and without the United States, except that under the provisions of section 933 income derived from sources within Puerto Rico (other than amounts received for services performed as an employee of the United States or any agency thereof) is excluded from gross income. For determining the form of return to be used by such an individual, see section 6012 and the regulations thereunder.

(b) *Exceptions.* Though subject to the tax imposed by section 1, a nonresident alien individual who is a bona fide resident of Puerto Rico during his entire taxable year shall nevertheless be treated as a nonresident alien individual for the purpose of many provisions of the Code relating to nonresident alien individuals. Thus, for example, such a resident of Puerto Rico is not allowed to determine his tax in accordance with the optional tax table (section 4(d)(1)); is not allowed the standard deduction (section 142(b)(1)); is not allowed a deduction for a "dependent" who is a resident of Puerto Rico unless the dependent is a citizen of the United States (section 152(b)(3)); is subject to withholding of tax at source under chapter 3 of the Code (sections 1441(e) and 1451(e)); is generally excepted from the collection of income tax at source on wages (paragraph (d)(1) of § 31.3401(a)(6)-1 of this chapter (Employment Tax Regulations)); is not allowed to make a joint return or a joint declaration of estimated tax (sections 6013(a)(1) and 6015(b)); must pay his estimated income tax on or before the 15th day of the 4th month of the taxable year (sections 6015(i)(3), 6073(a), and 6153(a)(1)); and generally must pay his income tax on or before the 15th day of the 6th month following the close of the taxable year (sections 6072(c) and 6151(a)).

(c) *Credits against tax.* The credits allowed by section 31 (relating to tax withheld on wages), section 32 (relating to tax withheld at source on nonresident aliens), section 33 (relating to taxes of foreign countries), section 35 (relating to partially tax-exempt interest), section 38 (relating to investment in certain depreciable property), section 39 (relating to certain uses of gasoline and lubricating oil), and section 40 (relating to expenses of work incentive programs) shall be allowed against the tax determined in accordance with this section. No credit shall be allowed under section 37 in respect of retirement income.

(d) *Effective date.* This section shall apply for taxable years beginning after December 31, 1966. For corresponding rules applicable to taxable years beginning before January 1, 1967, see 26 CFR 1.876-1 (Rev. as of Jan. 1, 1971). [Reg. § 1.876-1.]

☐ [T.D. 6258, 10-23-57. Amended by T.D. 6777, 12-15-64 and T.D. 7322, 12-20-74.]

Reg. § 1.876-1(d)

[Reg. § 1.879-1]

§ 1.879-1. Treatment of community income.—(a) *Treatment of community income*—1) *In general.* For taxable years beginning after December 31, 1976, community income of a citizen or resident of the United States who is married to a nonresident alien individual, and the deductions properly allocable to that income, shall be divided between the U.S. citizen or resident spouse and the nonresident alien spouse in accordance with the rules in section 879 and paragraph (a)(2) through (a)(6) of this section. This section does not apply for any taxable year with respect to which an election under section 6013(g) or (h) is in effect. Community income for this purpose includes all gross income, whether derived from sources within or without the United States, which is treated as community income of the spouses under the community property laws of the State, foreign country, or possession of the United States in which the recipient of the income is domiciled. Income from real property also may be community income if so treated under the laws of the jurisdiction in which the real property is located.

(2) *Earned income.* Wages, salaries, or professional fees, and other amounts received as compensation for personal services actually performed, which are community income for the taxable year, shall be treated as the income of the spouse who actually performed the personal services. This paragraph (a)(2) does not apply, however, to the following items of community income:

(i) Community income from any trade or business carried on by the husband or the wife.

(ii) Community income attributable to a spouse's distributive share of the income of a partnership to which paragraph (a)(4) of this section applies.

(iii) Community income consisting of compensation for personal services rendered to a corporation which represents a distribution of the earnings and profits of the corporation rather than a reasonable allowance as compensation for the personal services actually performed, but not including any income that would be treated as earned income under the second sentence of section 911(b).

(iv) Community income derived from property which is acquired as consideration for personal services performed.

These items of community income are divided in accordance with the rules in paragraph (a)(3) through (a)(6) of this section.

(3) *Trade or business income.* If any income derived from a trade or business carried on by the husband or wife is community income for the taxable year, all of the gross income, and the deductions attributable to that income, shall be treated as the gross income and deductions of the husband. However, if the wife exercises substantially all of the management and control of the trade or business, all of the gross income and deductions shall be treated as the gross income and deductions of the wife. This paragraph (a)(3) does not apply to any income derived from a trade or business carried on by a partnership of which both or one of the spouses is a member (see paragraph (a)(4) of this section). For purposes of this paragraph (a)(3), income derived from a trade or business includes any income derived from a trade or business in which both personal services and capital are material income producing factors. The term "management and control" means management and control in fact, not the management and control imputed to the husband under the community property laws of a state, foreign country, or possession of the United States. For example, a wife who operates a pharmacy without any appreciable collaboration on the part of a husband is considered as having substantially all of the management and control of the business despite the provisions of any community property laws of a state, foreign country, or possession of the United States vesting in the husband the right of management and control of community property. The income and deductions attributable to the operation of the pharmacy are considered the income and deductions of the wife.

(4) *Partnership income.* If any portion of a spouse's distributive share of the income of a partnership, of which the spouse is a member, is community income for the taxable year, all of that distributive share shall be treated as the income of that spouse and shall not be taken into account in determining the income of the other spouse. If both spouses are members of the same partnership, the distributive share of the income of each spouse which is community income shall be treated as the income of that spouse. A spouse's distributive share of the income of a partnership that is community income shall be determined as provided in section 704 and the regulations thereunder.

(5) *Income from separate property.* Any community income for the taxable year, other than income described in section 879(a)(1) or (2) and paragraph (a)(2), (3), or (4) of this section, which is derived from the separate property of one of the spouses shall be treated as the income of that spouse. The determination of what property is separate property for this purpose shall be made in accordance with the laws of the State, foreign country, or possession of the United States in

which, in accordance with paragraph (a)(1) of this section, the recipient of the income is domiciled or, in the case of income from real property, in which the real property is located.

(6) *Other community income.* Any community income for the taxable year, other than income described in section 879(a)(1), (2), or (3), and paragraph (a)(2), (3), (4), or (5) of this section, shall be treated as income of that spouse who has a proprietary vested interest in that income under the laws of the State, foreign country, or possession of the United States in which, in accordance with paragraph (a)(1) of this section, the recipient of the income is domiciled or, in the case of income from real property, in which the real property is located. Thus, for example, this paragraph (a)(6) applies to community income not described in paragraph (a)(2), (3), (4), or (5) of this section which consists of dividends, interest, rents, royalties, or gains, from community property or of the earnings of unemancipated minor children.

(7) *Illustrations.* The application of this paragraph may be illustrated by the following examples:

Example (1). H, a U.S. citizen, and W, a nonresident alien individual, each of whose taxable years is the calendar year, were married throughout 1977. H and W were residents of, and domiciled in, foreign country Z during the entire taxable year. No election under section 6013(g) or (h) is in effect for 1977. During 1977, H earned $10,000 from the performance of personal services as an employee. H also received $500 in dividend income from stock which under the community property laws of country Z is considered to be the separate property of H. W had no separate income for 1977. Under the community property laws of country Z all income earned by either spouse is considrd to be community income, and one-half of this income is considered to belong to the other spouse. In additon, the laws of country Z provide that all income derived from property held separately by either spouse is to be treated as community income and treated as belonging one-half to each spouse. Thus, under the community property laws of country Z, H and W are both considered to have realized income of $5,250 during 1977, even though Z's laws recognize the stock as the separate property of H. Under the rules of paragraph (a)(2) and (5) of this section all of the income of $10,500 derived during 1977 is treated, for U.S. income tax purposes, as the income of H.

Example (2). (a) The facts are the same as in example (1), except that H is the sole proprietor of a retail merchandising company, which has a $10,000 profit during 1977. W exercises no management and control over the business. In addition, H is a partner in a wholesale distributing company, and his distributive share of the partnership profit is $5,000. Both of these amounts of income are treated as community income under the community property laws of country Z, and under these laws both H and W are treated as realizing $7,500 of the income. Under the rule of paragraph (a)(3) and (4) of this section all $15,000 of the income is treated as the income of H for U.S. income tax purposes.

(b) If W exercises substantially all of the management and control over the retail merchandising company, then for U.S. income tax purposes the $10,000 profit is treated as the income of W.

Example (3). The facts are the same as in example (1), except that H also received $1,000 in dividends on stock held separately in his name. Under the community property laws of country Z the stock is considered to be community property, the dividends to be community income, and one-half of the income to be the income of each spouse. Under the rule of paragraph (a)(6) of this section, $500 of the dividend income is treated, for U.S. income tax purposes, as the income of each spouse.

(b) *Definitions and other special rules*—(1) *Spouses with different taxable years.* A special rule applies if the nonresident alien and the United States citizen or resident spouse of the alien do not have the same taxable years, as defined in section 441(b) and the regulations thereunder. The special rule is as follows. With respect to the United States citizen or resident spouse, section 879 and this section shall apply to each taxable year of the United States citizen or resident spouse for which no election under section 6013(g) or (h) is in effect. With respect to the nonresident alien spouse, section 879 and this section apply to each period falling within the consecutive taxable years of the nonresident alien spouse which coincides with a taxable year of the United States citizen or resident spouse to which section 879 and this section apply.

(2) *Determination of marital status.* For purposes of this section, marital status shall be determined under section 143(a). [Reg. § 1.879-1.]

☐ [T.D. 7670, 1-30-80.]

[Reg. § 1.881-0]

§ 1.881-0. **Table of contents.**—This section lists the major headings for §§ 1.881-1 through 1.881-4.

§ 1.881-1. *Manner of taxing foreign corporations.*

(a) Classes of foreign corporations.

(b) Manner of taxing.

Reg. § 1.881-0

48,336 Nonresident Aliens and Foreign Corporations

See p. 20,601 for regulations not amended to reflect law changes

(1) Foreign corporations not engaged in U.S. business.

(2) Foreign corporations engaged in U.S. business.

(c) Meaning of terms.

(d) Rules applicable to foreign insurance companies.

(1) Corporations qualifying under subchapter L.

(2) Corporations not qualifying under subchapter L.

(e) Other provisions applicable to foreign corporations.

(1) Accumulated earnings tax.

(2) Personal holding company tax.

(3) Foreign personal holding companies.

(4) Controlled foreign corporations.

(i) Subpart F income and increase of earnings invested in U.S. property.

(ii) Certain accumulations of earnings and profits.

(5) Changes in tax rate.

(6) Consolidated returns.

(7) Adjustment of tax of certain foreign corporations.

(f) Effective date.

§ 1.881-2. Taxation of foreign corporations not engaged in U.S. business.

(a) Imposition of tax.

(b) Fixed or determinable annual or periodical income.

(c) Other income and gains.

(1) Items subject to tax.

(2) Determination of amount of gain.

(d) Credits against tax.

(e) Effective date.

§ 1.881-3. Conduit financing arrangements.

(a) General rules and definitions.

(1) Purpose and scope.

(2) Definitions.

(i) Financing arrangement.

(A) In general.

(B) Special rule for related parties.

(ii) Financing transaction.

(A) In general.

(B) Limitation on inclusion of stock or similar interests.

(iii) Conduit entity.

(iv) Conduit financing arrangement.

(v) Related.

(3) Disregard of participation of conduit entity.

(i) Authority of district director.

(ii) Effect of disregarding conduit entity.

(A) In general.

(B) Character of payments made by the financed entity.

(C) Effect of income tax treaties.

(D) Effect on withholding tax.

(E) Special rule for a financing entity that is unrelated to both intermediate entity and financed entity.

(iii) Limitation on taxpayers's use of this section.

(4) Standard for treatment as a conduit entity.

(i) In general.

(ii) Multiple intermediate entities.

(A) In general.

(B) Special rule for related persons.

(b) Determination of whether participation of intermediate entity is pursuant to a tax avoidance plan.

(1) In general.

(2) Factors taken into account in determining the presence or absence of a tax avoidance purpose.

(i) Significant reduction in tax.

(ii) Ability to make the advance.

(iii) Time period between financing transactions.

(iv) Financing transactions in the ordinary course of business.

(3) Presumption if significant financing activities performed by a related intermediate entity.

(i) General rule.

(ii) Significant financing activities.

(A) Active rents or royalties.

(B) Active risk management.

(c) Determination of whether an unrelated intermediate entity would not have participated in financing arrangement on substantially same terms.

(1) In general.

(2) Effect of guarantee.

(i) In general.

(ii) Definition of guarantee.

(d) Determination of amount of tax liability.

(1) Amount of payment subject to recharacterization.

Reg. § 1.881-0

(i) In general.
(ii) Determination of principal amount.
(A) In general.
(B) Debt instruments and certain stock.
(C) Partnership and trust interests.
(D) Leases and licenses.
(2) Rate of tax.
(e) Examples.
(f) Effective date.

1.881-4. Recordkeeping requirements concerning conduit financing arrangements.
(a) Scope.
(b) Recordkeeping requirements.
(1) In general.
(2) Application of sections 6038 and 6038A.
(c) Records to be maintained.
(1) In general.
(2) Additional documents.
(3) Effect of record maintenance requirement.
(d) Effective date.
[Reg. § 1.881-0.]

☐ [T.D. 8611, 8-10-95.]

[Reg. § 1.881-1]

§ 1.881-1. Manner of taxing foreign corporations.—(a) *Classes of foreign corporations.* For purposes of the income tax, foreign corporations are divided into two classes, namely, foreign corporations which at no time during the taxable year are engaged in trade or business in the United States and foreign corporations which, at any time during the taxable year, are engaged in trade or business in the United States.

(b) *Manner of taxing*—(1) *Foreign corporations not engaged in U.S. business.* A foreign corporation which at no time during the taxable year is engaged in trade or business in the United States is taxable, as provided in § 1.881-2, on all income received from sources within the United States which is fixed or determinable annual or periodical income and on other items of income enumerated under section 881(a). Such a foreign corporation is also taxable on certain income from sources within the United States which, pursuant to § 1.882-2, is treated as effectively connected for the taxable year with the conduct of a trade or business in the United States.

(2) *Foreign corporations engaged in U.S. business.* A foreign corporation which at any time during the taxable year is engaged in trade or business in the United States is taxable, as provided in § 1.882-1, on all income from whatever source derived, whether or not fixed or determinable annual or periodical income, which is effectively connected for the taxable year with the conduct of a trade or business in the United States. Such a foreign corporation is also taxable, as provided in § 1.882-1, on income received from sources within the United States which is not effectively connected for the taxable year with the conduct of a trade or business in the United States and consists of (i) fixed or determinable annual or periodical income, or (ii) other items of income enumerated in section 881(a). A foreign corporation which at any time during the taxable year is engaged in trade or business in the United States is also taxable on certain income from sources within the United States which, pursuant to § 1.882-2, is treated as effectively connected for the taxable year with the conduct of a trade or business in the United States.

(c) *Meaning of terms.* For the meaning of the term "engaged in trade or business within the United States," as used in section 881 and this section, see section 864(b) and the regulations thereunder. For determining when income, gain, or loss of a foreign corporation for a taxable year is effectively connected for that year with the conduct of a trade or business in the United States, see section 864(c), the regulations thereunder, and § 1.882-2. The term "foreign corporation" has the meaning assigned to it by section 7701(a)(3) and (5) and § 301.7701-5 of this chapter (Regulations on Procedure and Administration), except that, for purposes of section 881 and § 1.881-2, in the case of taxable years beginning after December 31, 1971, the term "foreign corporation" does not include a corporation created or organized in Guam or under the law of Guam. Thus, for example, for such a taxable year the first sentence of paragraph (b)(1), and the second sentence of paragraph (b)(2), of this section do not apply to a Guamanian corporation.

(d) *Rules applicable to foreign insurance companies*—(1) *Corporations qualifying under subchapter L.* A foreign corporation carrying on an insurance business in the United States at any time during the taxable year, which, without taking into account its income not effectively connected for the taxable year with the conduct of a trade or business in the United States, would qualify for the taxable year under part I, II, or III of subchapter L if it were a domestic corporation, shall be taxable for such year under that part on its entire taxable income (whether derived from sources within or without the United States) which is, or which pursuant to section 882(d) or (e) and § 1.882-2 is treated as, effectively connected for the taxable year with the conduct of a trade or business (whether or not its insurance business) in the United States. Any income derived by that foreign corporation from sources within the United States which is not effectively connected for the taxable year with the conduct of a trade or business in the United States is taxable as provided in section 881(a) an § 1.882-1. See sections 842 and 861 through 864, and the regulations thereunder.

(2) *Corporations not qualifying under subchapter L.* A foreign corporation which carries on an insurance business in the United States at any time during the taxable year, and which, without taking into account its income not effectively connected for the taxable year with the conduct of a trade or business in the United States, would not qualify for the taxable year under part I, II, or III of subchapter L if it were a domestic corporation, and a foreign insurance company which does not carry on an insurance business in the United States at any time during the taxable year, shall be taxable—

(i) Under section 881(a) and § 1.881-2 or § 1.882-1 on its income from sources within the United States which is not effectively connected for the taxable year with the conduct of a trade or business in the United States,

(ii) Under section 882(a)(1) and § 1.882-1 on its income (whether derived from sources within or without the United States) which is effectively connected for the taxable year with the conduct of a trade or business in the United States, and

(iii) Under section 882(a)(1) and § 1.882-1 on its income from sources within the United States which pursuant to section 882(d) or (e) and § 1.882-2, is treated as effectively connected for the taxable year with the conduct of a trade or business in the United States.

(e) *Other provisions applicable to foreign corporations.*—(1) *Accumulated earnings tax.* For the imposition of the accumulated earnings tax upon the accumulated taxable income of a foreign corporation formed or availed of for tax avoidance purposes, whether or not such corporation is engaged in trade or business in the United States, see section 532 and the regulations thereunder.

(2) *Personal holding company tax.* For the imposition of the personal holding company tax upon the undistributed personal holding company income of a foreign corporation which is a personal holding company, whether or not such corporation is engaged in trade or business in the United States, see sections 541 through 547, and the regulations thereunder. Except in the case of a foreign corporation having personal service contract income to which section 543(a)(7) applies, a foreign corporation is not a personal holding company if all of its stock outstanding during the last half of the taxable year is owned by nonresident alien individuals, whether directly or indirectly through foreign estates, foreign trusts, foreign partnerships, or other foreign corporations. See section 542(c)(7).

(3) *Foreign personal holding companies.* For the mandatory inclusion in the gross income of the United States shareholders of the undistributed foreign personal holding company income of a foreign personal holding company, see section 551 and the regulations thereunder.

(4) *Controlled foreign corporations*—(i) *Subpart F income and increase of earnings invested in U.S. property.* For the mandatory inclusion in the gross income of the U.S. shareholders of the subpart F income, of the previously excluded subpart F income withdrawn from investment in less developed countries, of the previously excluded subpart F income withdrawn from investment in foreign base company shipping operations, and of the increase in earnings invested in U.S. property, of a controlled foreign corporation, see sections 951 through 964, and the regulations thereunder.

(ii) *Certain accumulations of earnings and profits.* For the inclusion in the gross income of U.S. persons as a dividend of the gain recognized on certain sales or exchanges of stock in a foreign corporation, to the extent of certain earnings and profits attributable to the stock which were accumulated while the corporation was a controlled foreign corporation, see section 1248 and the regulations thereunder.

(5) *Changes in tax rate.* For provisions respecting the effect of any change in rate of tax during the taxable year on the income of a foreign corporation, see section 21 and the regulations thereunder.

(6) *Consolidated returns.* Except in the case of certain corporations organized under the laws of Canada or Mexico and maintained solely for the purpose of complying with the laws of that country as to title and operation of property, a foreign corporation is not an includible corporation for purposes of the privilege of making a consolidated return by an affiliated group of corporations. See section 1504 and the regulations thereunder.

(7) *Adjustment of tax of certain foreign corporations.* For the application of pre-1967 income tax provisions to corporations of a foreign country which imposes a more burdensome income tax than the United States, and for the adjustment of the income tax of a corporation of a foreign country which imposes a discriminatory income tax on the income of citizens of the United States or domestic corporations, see section 896.

Reg. § 1.881-1(d)(2)

(f) *Effective date.* This section applies for taxable years beginning after December 31, 1966. For corresponding rules applicable to taxable years beginning before January 1, 1967, see 26 CFR 1.881-1 (Rev. as of Jan. 1, 1971). [Reg. § 1.881-1.]

☐ [T.D. 6258, 10-23-57. Amended by T.D. 7293, 11-27-23, *T.D.* 7385, 10-28-75 *and T.D.* 7893, 5-11-83.]

[Reg. § 1.881-2]

§ 1.881-2. Taxation of foreign corporations not engaged in U.S. business.—(a) *Imposition of tax.*—(1) This section applies for purposes of determining the tax of a foreign corporation which at no time during the taxable year is engaged in trade or business in the United States. However, see also § 1.882-2 where such corporation has an election in effect for the taxable year in respect to real property income or receives interest on obligations of the United States. Except as otherwise provided in § 1.871-12, a foreign corporation to which this section applies is not subject to the tax imposed by section 11 or section 1201(a) but, pursuant to the provisions of section 881(a), is liable to a flat tax of 30 percent upon the aggregate of the amounts determined under paragraphs (b) and (c) of this section which are received during the taxable year from sources within the United States. Except as specifically provided in such paragraphs, such amounts do not include gains from the sale or exchange of property. To determine the source of such amounts, see sections 861 through 863, and the regulations thereunder.

(2) The tax of 30 percent is imposed by section 881(a) upon an amount only to the extent the amount constitutes gross income.

(3) Deductions shall not be allowed in determining the amount subject to tax under this section.

(4) Except as provided in § 1.882-2, a foreign corporation which at no time during the taxable year is engaged in trade or business in the United States has no income, gain, or loss for the taxable year which is effectively connected for the taxable year with the conduct of a trade or business in the United States. See section 864(c)(1)(B) and § 1.864-3.

(5) Gains and losses which, by reason of section 882(d) and § 1.882-2, are treated as gains or losses which are effectively connected for the taxable year with the conduct of a trade or business in the United States by such a foreign corporation shall not be taken into account in determining the tax under this section. See, for example, paragraph (c)(2) of § 1.871-10.

(b) *Fixed or determinable annual or periodical income*—(1) *General rule.* The tax of 30 percent imposed by section 881(a) applies to the gross amount received from sources within the United States as fixed or determinable annual or periodical gains, profits, or income. Specific items of fixed or determinable annual or periodical income are enumerated in section 881(a)(1) as interest, dividends, rents, salaries, wages, premiums, annuities, compensations, remunerations, and emoluments, but other items of fixed or determinable annual or periodical gains, profits, or income are also subject to the tax as, for instance, royalties, including royalties for the use of patents, copyrights, secret processes and formulas, and other like property. As to the determination of fixed or determinable annual or periodical income, see paragraph (a) of § 1.441-2. For special rules treating gain on the disposition of section 306 stock as fixed or determinable annual or periodical income for purposes of section 881(a), see section 306(f) and paragraph (h) of § 1.306-3.

(2) *Substitute payments.* For purposes of this section, a substitute interest payment (as defined in § 1.861-2(a)(7)) received by a foreign person pursuant to a securities lending transaction or a sale-repurchase transaction (as defined in § 1.861-2(a)(7)) shall have the same character as interest income received pursuant to the terms of the transferred security. Similarly, for purposes of this section, a substitute dividend payment (as defined in § 1.861-3(a)(6)) received by a foreign person pursuant to a securities lending transaction or a sale-repurchase transaction (as defined in § 1.861-2(a)(7)) shall have the same character as a distribution received with respect to the transferred security. Where, pursuant to a securities lending transaction or a sale-repurchase transaction, a foreign person transfers to another person a security the interest on which would qualify as portfolio interest under section 881(c) in the hands of the lender, substitute interest payments made with respect to the transferred security will be treated as portfolio interest, provided that in the case of interest on an obligation in registered form (as defined in § 1.871-14(c)(1)(i)), the transferor complies with the documentation requirement described in § 1.871-14(c)(1)(ii)(C) with respect to the payment of substitute interest and none of the exceptions to the portfolio interest exemption in sections 881(c)(3) and (4) apply. See also §§ 1.871-7(b)(2) and 1.894-1(c).

(c) *Other income and gains*—(1) *Items subject to tax.* The tax of 30 percent imposed by section 881(a) also applies to the following gains received during the taxable year from sources within the United States:

(i) Gains described in section 631(b) or (c), relating to the treatment of gain on the disposal of timber, coal, or iron ore with a retained economic interest;

(ii) [Reserved]

(iii) Gains from the sale or exchange after October 4, 1966, of patents, copyrights, secret processes and formulas, goodwill, trademarks, trade brands, franchises, or other like property, or of any interest in any such property, to the extent the gains are from payments (whether in a lump sum or in installments) which are contingent on the productivity, use, or disposition of the property or interest sold or exchanged, or from payments which are treated under section 871(e) and § 1.871-11 as being so contingent.

(2) *Determination of amount of gain.* The tax of 30 percent imposed upon the gains described in subparagraph (1) of this paragraph applies to the full amount of the gains and is determined (i) without regard to the alternative tax imposed by section 1201(a) upon the excess of net long-term capital gain over the net short-term capital loss; (ii) without regard to section 1231, relating to property used in the trade or business and involuntary conversions; and (iii) except in the case of gains described in subparagraph (1)(ii) of this paragraph, whether or not the gains are considered to be gains from the sale or exchange of property which is a capital asset.

(d) *Credits against tax.* The credits allowed by section 32 (relating to tax withheld at source on foreign corporations), by section 39 (relating to certain uses of gasoline and lubricating oil), and by section 6402 (relating to overpayments of tax) shall be allowed against the tax of a foreign corporation determined in accordance with this section.

(e) *Effective date.* Except as otherwise provide[d] in this paragraph, this section applies for taxable years beginning after December 31, 1966. Paragraph (b)(2) of this section is applicable to payments made after November 13, 1997. For corresponding rules applicable to taxable years beginning before January 1, 1967, see 26 CFR 1.881-2 (Rev. as of Jan. 1, 1971). [Reg. § 1.881-2.]

☐ [T.D. 6258, 10-23-57. Amended by T.D. 6841, 7-26-65; T.D. 7293, 11-27-73 and T.D. 8735, 10-6-97.]

[Reg. § 1.881-3]

§ 1.881-3. Conduit financing arrangements.—(a) *General rules and definitions*—(1) *Purpose and scope.* Pursuant to the authority of section 7701(l), this section provides rules that permit the district director to disregard, for purposes of section 881, the participation of one or more intermediate entities in a financing arrangement where such entities are acting as conduit entities. For purposes of this section, any reference to tax imposed under section 881 includes, except as otherwise provided and as the context may require, a reference to tax imposed under sections 871 or 884(f)(1)(A) or required to be withheld under section 1441 or 1442. See § 1.881-4 for recordkeeping requirements concerning financing arrangements. See §§ 1.1441-3(j) and 1.1441-7(d) for withholding rules applicable to conduit financing arrangements.

(2) *Definitions.* The following definitions apply for purposes of this section and §§ 1.881-4, 1.1441-3(j) and 1.1441-7(d).

(i) *Financing arrangement*—(A) *In general.* Financing arrangement means a series of transactions by which one person (the financing entity) advances money or other property, or grants rights to use property, and another person (the financed entity) receives money or other property, or rights to use property, if the advance and receipt are effected through one or more other persons (intermediate entities) and, except in cases to which paragraph (a)(2)(i)(B) of this section applies, there are financing transactions linking the financing entity, each of the intermediate entities, and the financed entity. A transfer of money or other property in satisfaction of a repayment obligation is not an advance of money or other property. A financing arrangement exists regardless of the order in which the transactions are entered into, but only for the period during which all of the financing transactions coexist. See *Examples 1, 2,* and *3* of paragraph (e) of this section for illustrations of the term financing arrangement.

(B) *Special rule for related parties.* If two (or more) financing transactions involving two (or more) related persons would form part of a financing arrangement but for the absence of a financing transaction between the related persons, the district director may treat the related persons as a single intermediate entity if he determines that one of the principal purposes for the structure of the financing transactions is to prevent the characterization of such arrangement as a financing arrangement. This determination shall be based upon all of the facts and circumstances, including, without limitation, the factors set forth in paragraph (b)(2) of this section. See *Examples 4* and *5* of paragraph (e) of this section for illustrations of this paragraph (a)(2)(i)(B).

(ii) *Financing transaction*—(A) *In general.* Financing transaction means—

(*1*) Debt;

(*2*) Stock in a corporation (or a similar interest in a partnership or trust) that meets the requirements of paragraph (a)(2)(ii)(B) of this section;

(*3*) Any lease or license; or

(*4*) Any other transaction (including an interest in a trust described in sections 671 through 679) pursuant to which a person makes an advance of money or other property or grants rights to use property to a transferee who is obligated to repay or return a substantial portion of the money or other property advanced, or the equivalent in value. This paragraph (a)(2)(ii)(A)(*4*) shall not apply to the posting of collateral unless the collateral consists of cash or the person holding the collateral is permitted to reduce the collateral to cash (through a transfer, grant of a security interest or similar transaction) prior to default on the financing transaction secured by the collateral.

(B) *Limitation on inclusion of stock or similar interests*—(*1*) *In general.* Stock in a corporation (or a similar interest in a partnership or trust) will constitute a financing transaction only if one of the following conditions is satisfied—

(*i*) The issuer is required to redeem the stock or similar interest at a specified time or the holder has the right to require the issuer to redeem the stock or similar interest or to make any other payment with respect to the stock or similar interest;

(*ii*) The issuer has the right to redeem the stock or similar interest, but only if, based on all of the facts and circumstances as of the issue date, redemption pursuant to that right is more likely than not to occur; or

(*iii*) The owner of the stock or similar interest has the right to require a person related to the issuer (or any other person who is acting pursuant to a plan or arrangement with the issuer) to acquire the stock or similar interest or make a payment with respect to the stock or similar interest.

(*2*) *Rules of special application*—(*i*) *Existence of a right.* For purposes of this paragraph (a)(2)(ii)(B), a person will be considered to have a right to cause a redemption or payment if the person has the right (other than rights arising, in the ordinary course, between the date that a payment is declared and the date that a payment is made) to enforce the payment through a legal proceeding or to cause the issuer to be liquidated if it fails to redeem the interest or to make a payment. A person will not be considered to have a right to force a redemption or a payment if the right is derived solely from ownership of a controlling interest in the issuer in cases where the control does not arise from a default or similar contingency under the instrument. The person is considered to have such a right if the person has the right as of the issue date or, as of the issue date, it is more likely than not that the person will receive such a right, whether through the occurrence of a contingency or otherwise.

(*ii*) *Restrictions on payment.* The fact that the issuer does not have the legally available funds to redeem the stock or similar interest, or that the payments are to be made in a blocked currency, will not affect the determinations made pursuant to this paragraph (a)(2)(ii)(B).

(iii) *Conduit entity* means an intermediate entity whose participation in the financing arrangement may be disregarded in whole or in part pursuant to this section, whether or not the district director has made a determination that the intermediate entity should be disregarded under paragraph (a)(3)(i) of this section.

(iv) *Conduit financing arrangement* means a financing arrangement that is effected through one or more conduit entities.

(v) *Related* means related within the meaning of sections 267(b) or 707(b)(1), or controlled within the meaning of section 482, and the regulations under those sections. For purposes of determining whether a person is related to another person, the constructive ownership rules of section 318 shall apply, and the attribution rules of section 267(c) also shall apply to the extent they attribute ownership to persons to whom section 318 does not attribute ownership.

(3) *Disregard of participation of conduit entity*—(i) *Authority of district director.* The district director may determine that the participation of a conduit entity in a conduit financing arrangement should be disregarded for purposes of section 881. For this purpose, an intermediate entity will constitute a conduit entity if it meets the standards of paragraph (a)(4) of this section. The district director has discretion to determine the manner in which the standards of paragraph (a)(4) of this section apply, including the financing transactions and parties composing the financing arrangement.

(ii) *Effect of disregarding conduit entity*—(A) *In general.* If the district director determines that the participation of a conduit entity in a financing arrangement should be disregarded, the financing arrangement is recharacterized as a transaction directly between the remaining parties to the financing arrangement (in most cases, the financed entity and the financing entity) for purposes of section 881. To the extent that a disregarded conduit entity actually receives or makes payments pursuant to a conduit financing arrangement, it is treated as an agent of the

Reg. § 1.881-3(a)(3)

financing entity. Except as otherwise provided, the recharacterization of the conduit financing arrangement also applies for purposes of sections 871, 884(f)(1)(A), 1441, and 1442 and other procedural provisions relating to those sections. This recharacterization will not otherwise affect a taxpayer's Federal income tax liability under any substantive provisions of the Internal Revenue Code. Thus, for example, the recharacterization generally applies for purposes of section 1461, in order to impose liability on a withholding agent who fails to withhold as required under § 1.1441-3(j), but not for purposes of § 1.882-5.

(B) *Character of payments made by the financed entity.* If the participation of a conduit financing arrangement is disregarded under this paragraph (a)(3), payments made by the financed entity generally shall be characterized by reference to the character (e.g., interest or rent) of the payments made to the financing entity. However, if the financing transaction to which the financing entity is a party is a transaction described in paragraph (a)(2)(ii)(A)(*2*) or (*4*) of this section that gives rise to payments that would not be deductible if paid by the financed entity, the character of the payments made by the financed entity will not be affected by the disregard of the participation of a conduit entity. The characterization provided by this paragraph (a)(3)(ii)(B) does not, however, extend to qualification of a payment for any exemption from withholding tax under the Internal Revenue Code or a provision of any applicable tax treaty if such qualification depends on the terms of, or other similar facts or circumstances relating to, the financing transaction to which the financing entity is a party that do not apply to the financing transaction to which the financed entity is a party. Thus, for example, payments made by a financed entity that is not a bank cannot qualify for the exemption provided by section 881(i) of the Code even if the loan between the financed entity and the conduit entity is a bank deposit.

(C) *Effect of income tax treaties.* Where the participation of a conduit entity in a conduit financing arrangement is disregarded pursuant to this section, it is disregarded for all purposes of section 881, including for purposes of applying any relevant income tax treaties. Accordingly, the conduit entity may not claim the benefits of a tax treaty between its country of residence and the United States to reduce the amount of tax due under section 881 with respect to payments made pursuant to the conduit financing arrangement. The financing entity may, however, claim the benefits of any income tax treaty under which it is entitled to benefits in order to reduce the rate of tax on payments made pursuant to the conduit financing arrangement that are recharacterized in accordance with paragraph (a)(3)(ii)(B) of this section.

(D) *Effect on withholding tax.* For the effect of recharacterization on withholding obligations, see §§ 1.1441-3(j) and 1.1441-7(d).

(E) *Special rule for a financing entity that is unrelated to both intermediate entity and financed entity*—(*1*) Liability of financing entity. Notwithstanding the fact that a financing arrangement is a conduit financing arrangement, a financing entity that is unrelated to the financed entity and the conduit entity (or entities) shall not itself be liable for tax under section 881 unless the financing entity knows or has reason to know that the financing arrangement is a conduit financing arrangement. But see § 1.1441-3(j) for the withholding agent's withholding obligations.

(*2*) *Financing entity's knowledge*—(*i*) *In general.* A financing entity knows or has reason to know that the financing arrangement is a conduit financing arrangement only if the financing entity knows or has reason to know of facts sufficient to establish that the financing arrangement is a conduit financing arrangement, including facts sufficient to establish that the participation of the intermediate entity in the financing arrangement is pursuant to a tax avoidance plan. A person that knows only of the financing transactions that comprise the financing arrangement will not be considered to know or have reason to know of facts sufficient to establish that the financing arrangement is a conduit financing arrangement.

(*ii*) *Presumption regarding financing entity's knowledge.* It shall be presumed that the financing entity does not know or have reason to know that the financing arrangement is a conduit financing arrangement if the financing entity is unrelated to all other parties to the financing arrangement and the financing entity establishes that the intermediate entity who is a party to the financing transaction with the financing entity is actively engaged in a substantial trade or business. An intermediate entity will not be considered to be engaged in a trade or business if its business is making or managing investments, unless the intermediate entity is actively engaged in a banking, insurance, financing or similar trade or business and such business consists predominantly of transactions with customers who are not related persons. An intermediate entity's trade or business is substantial if it is reasonable for the financing entity to expect that the intermediate entity will be able to make payments under the financing transaction out of the cash flow of that trade or business. This presumption may be rebut-

Reg. § 1.881-3(a)(3)

ted if the district director establishes that the financing entity knew or had reason to know that the financing arrangement is a conduit financing arrangement. See *Example 6* of paragraph (e) of this section for an illustration of the rules of this paragraph (a)(3)(ii)(E).

(iii) *Limitation on taxpayer's use of this section.* A taxpayer may not apply this section to reduce the amount of its Federal income tax liability by disregarding the form of its financing transactions for Federal income tax purposes or by compelling the district director to do so. See, however, paragraph (b)(2)(i) of this section for rules regarding the taxpayer's ability to show that the participation of one or more intermediate entities results in no significant reduction in tax.

(4) *Standard for treatment as a conduit entity*—(i) *In general.* An intermediate entity is a conduit entity with respect to a financing arrangement if—

(A) The participation of the intermediate entity (or entities) in the financing arrangement reduces the tax imposed by section 881 (determined by comparing the aggregate tax imposed under section 881 on payments made on financing transactions making up the financing arrangement with the tax that would have been imposed under paragraph (d) of this section);

(B) The participation of the intermediate entity in the financing arrangement is pursuant to a tax avoidance plan; and

(C) Either—

(*1*) The intermediate entity is related to the financing entity or the financed entity; or

(*2*) The intermediate entity would not have participated in the financing arrangement on substantially the same terms but for the fact that the financing entity engaged in the financing transaction with the intermediate entity.

(ii) *Multiple intermediate entities*—(A) *In general.* If a financing arrangement involves multiple intermediate entities, the district director will determine whether each of the intermediate entities is a conduit entity. The district director will make the determination by applying the special rules for multiple intermediate entities provided in this section or, if no special rules are provided, applying principles consistent with those of paragraph (a)(4)(i) of this section to each of the intermediate entities in the financing arrangement.

(B) *Special rule for related persons.* The district director may treat related intermediate entities as a single intermediate entity if he determines that one of the principal purposes for the involvement of multiple intermediate entities in the financing arrangement is to prevent the characterization of an intermediate entity as a conduit entity, to reduce the portion of a payment that is subject to withholding tax or otherwise to circumvent the provisions of this section. This determination shall be based upon all of the facts and circumstances, including, but not limited to, the factors set forth in paragraph (b)(2) of this section. If a district director determines that related persons are to be treated as a single intermediate entity, financing transactions between such related parties that are part of the conduit financing arrangement shall be disregarded for purposes of applying this section. See *Examples 7* and *8* of paragraph (e) of this section for illustrations of the rules of this paragraph (a)(4)(ii).

(b) *Determination of whether participation of intermediate entity is pursuant to a tax avoidance plan*—(1) *In general.* A tax avoidance plan is a plan one of the principal purposes of which is the avoidance of tax imposed by section 881. Avoidance of the tax imposed by section 881 may be one of the principal purposes for such a plan even though it is outweighed by other purposes (taken together or separately). In this regard, the only relevant purposes are those pertaining to the participation of the intermediate entity in the financing arrangement and not those pertaining to the existence of a financing arrangement as a whole. The plan may be formal or informal, written or oral, and may involve any one or more of the parties to the financing arrangement. The plan must be in existence no later than the last date that any of the financing transactions comprising the financing arrangement is entered into. The district director may infer the existence of a tax avoidance plan from the facts and circumstances. In determining whether there is a tax avoidance plan, the district director will weigh all relevant evidence regarding the purposes for the intermediate entity's participation in the financing arrangement. See *Examples 11* and *12* of paragraph (e) of this section for illustrations of the rule of this paragraph (b)(1).

(2) *Factors taken into account in determining the presence or absence of a tax avoidance purpose.* The factors described in paragraphs (b)(2)(i) through (iv) of this section are among the facts and circumstances taken into account in determining whether the participation of an intermediate entity in a financing arrangement has as one of its principal purposes the avoidance of tax imposed by section 881.

(i) *Significant reduction in tax.* The district director will consider whether the participation of the intermediate entity (or entities) in the financing arrangement significantly reduces the

Reg. § 1.881-3(b)(2)

tax that otherwise would have been imposed under section 881. The fact that an intermediate entity is a resident of a country that has an income tax treaty with the United States that significantly reduces the tax that otherwise would have been imposed under section 881 is not sufficient, by itself, to establish the existence of a tax avoidance plan. The determination of whether the participation of an intermediate entity significantly reduces the tax generally is made by comparing the aggregate tax imposed under section 881 on payments made on financing transactions making up the financing arrangement with the tax that would be imposed under paragraph (d) of this section. However, the taxpayer is not barred from presenting evidence that the financing entity, as determined by the district director, was itself an intermediate entity and another entity should be treated as the financing entity for purposes of applying this test. A reduction in the absolute amount of tax may be significant even if the reduction in rate is not. A reduction in the amount of tax may be significant if the reduction is large in absolute terms or in relative terms. See Examples 13, 14 and 15 of paragraph (e) of this section for illustrations of this factor.

(ii) *Ability to make the advance.* The district director will consider whether the intermediate entity had sufficient available money or other property of its own to have made the advance to the financed entity without the advance of money or other property to it by the financing entity (or in the case of multiple intermediate entities, whether each of the intermediate entities had sufficient available money or other property of its own to have made the advance to either the financed entity or another intermediate entity without the advance of money or other property to it by either the financing entity or another intermediate entity).

(iii) *Time period between financing transactions.* The district director will consider the length of the period of time that separates the advances of money or other property, or the grants of rights to use property, by the financing entity to the intermediate entity (in the case of multiple intermediate entities, from one intermediate entity to another), and ultimately by the intermediate entity to the financed entity. A short period of time is evidence of the existence of a tax avoidance plan while a long period of time is evidence that there is not a tax avoidance plan. See Example 16 of paragraph (e) of this section for an illustration of this factor.

(iv) *Financing transactions in the ordinary course of business.* If the parties to the financing transaction are related, the district director will consider whether the financing transaction occurs in the ordinary course of the active conduct of complementary or integrated trades or businesses engaged in by these entities. The fact that a financing transaction is described in this paragraph (b)(2)(iv) is evidence that the participation of the parties to that transaction in the financing arrangement is not pursuant to a tax avoidance plan. A loan will not be considered to occur in the ordinary course of the active conduct of complementary or integrated trades or businesses unless the loan is a trade receivable or the parties to the transaction are actively engaged in a banking, insurance, financing or similar trade or business and such business consists predominantly of transactions with customers who are not related persons. See *Example 17* of paragraph (e) of this section for an illustration of this factor.

(3) *Presumption if significant financing activities performed by a related intermediate entity*—(i) *General rule.* It shall be presumed that the participation of an intermediate entity (or entities) in a financing arrangement is not pursuant to a tax avoidance plan if the intermediate entity is related to either or both the financing entity or the financed entity and the intermediate entity performs significant financing activities with respect to the financing transactions forming part of the financing arrangement to which it is a party. This presumption may be rebutted if the district director establishes that the participation of the intermediate entity in the financing arrangement is pursuant to a tax avoidance plan. See *Examples 21, 22* and *23* of paragraph (e) of this section for illustrations of this presumption.

(ii) *Significant financing activities.* For purposes of this paragraph (b)(3), an intermediate entity performs significant financing activities with respect to such financing transactions only if the financing transactions satisfy the requirements of either paragraph (b)(3)(ii)(A) or (B) of this section.

(A) *Active rents or royalties.* An intermediate entity performs significant financing activities with respect to leases or licenses if rents or royalties earned with respect to such leases or licenses are derived in the active conduct of a trade or business within the meaning of section 954(c)(2)(A), to be applied by substituting the term *intermediate entity* for the term *controlled foreign corporation.*

(B) *Active risk management*—(1) *In general.* An intermediate entity is considered to perform significant financing activities with respect to financing transactions only if officers and employees of the intermediate entity participate actively and materially in arranging the interme-

Reg. § 1.881-3(b)(3)

diate entity's participation in such financing transactions (other than financing transactions described in paragraph (b)(3)(ii)(B)(3) of this section) and perform the business activity and risk management activities described in paragraph (b)(3)(ii)(B)(2) of this section with respect to such financing transactions, and the participation of the intermediate entity in the financing transactions produces (or reasonably can be expected to produce) efficiency savings by reducing transaction costs and overhead and other fixed costs.

(2) *Business activity and risk management requirements.* An intermediate entity will be considered to perform significant financing activities only if, within the country in which the intermediate entity is organized (or, if different, within the country with respect to which the intermediate entity is claiming the benefits of a tax treaty), its officers and employees—

(*i*) Exercise management over, and actively conduct, the day-to-day operations of the intermediate entity. Such operations must consist of a substantial trade or business or the supervision, administration and financing for a substantial group of related persons; and

(*ii*) Actively manage, on an ongoing basis, material market risks arising from such financing transactions as an integral part of the management of the intermediate entity's financial and capital requirements (including management of risks of currency and interest rate fluctuations) and management of the intermediate entity's short-term investments of working capital by entering into transactions with unrelated persons.

(3) *Special rule for trade receivables and payables entered into in the ordinary course of business.* If the activities of the intermediate entity consist in whole or in part of cash management for a controlled group of which the intermediate entity is a member, then employees of the intermediate entity need not have participated in arranging any such financing transactions that arise in the ordinary course of a substantial trade or business of either the financed entity or the financing entity. Officers or employees of the financing entity or financed entity, however, must have participated actively and materially in arranging the transaction that gave rise to the trade receivable or trade payable. Cash management includes the operation of a sweep account whereby the intermediate entity nets intercompany trade payables and receivables arising from transactions among the other members of the controlled group and between members of the controlled group and unrelated persons.

(*4*) *Activities of officers and employees of related persons.* Except as provided in paragraph (b)(3)(ii)(B)(3) of this section, in applying this paragraph (b)(3)(ii)(B), the activities of an officer or employee of an intermediate entity will not constitute significant financing activities if any officer or employee of a related person participated materially in any of the activities described in this paragraph, other than to approve any guarantee of a financing transaction or to exercise general supervision and control over the policies of the intermediate entity.

(c) *Determination of whether an unrelated intermediate entity would not have participated in financing arrangement on substantially the same terms*—(1) *In general.* The determination of whether an intermediate entity would not have participated in a financing arrangement on substantially the same terms but for the financing transaction between the financing entity and the intermediate entity shall be based upon all of the facts and circumstances.

(2) *Effect of guarantee*—(i) *In general.* The district director may presume that the intermediate entity would not have participated in the financing arrangement on substantially the same terms if there is a guarantee of the financed entity's liability to the intermediate entity (or in the case of multiple intermediate entities, a guarantee of the intermediate entity's liability to the intermediate entity that advanced money or property, or granted rights to use other property). However, a guarantee that was neither in existence nor contemplated on the last date that any of the financing transactions comprising the financing arrangement is entered into does not give rise to this presumption. A taxpayer may rebut this presumption by producing clear and convincing evidence that the intermediate entity would have participated in the financing transaction with the financed entity on substantially the same terms even if the financing entity had not entered into a financing transaction with the intermediate entity.

(ii) *Definition of guarantee.* For the purposes of this paragraph (c)(2), a guarantee is any arrangement under which a person, directly or indirectly, assures, on a conditional or unconditional basis, the payment of another person's obligation with respect to a financing transaction. The term shall be interpreted in accordance with the definition of the term in section 163(j)(6)(D)(iii).

(d) *Determination of amount of tax liability*— (1) *Amount of payment subject to recharacterization*—(i) *In general.* If a financing arrangement is a conduit financing arrangement, a portion of

Reg. § 1.881-3(d)(1)

each payment made by the financed entity with respect to the financing transactions that comprise the conduit financing arrangement shall be recharacterized as a transaction directly between the financed entity and the financing entity. If the aggregate principal amount of the financing transaction(s) to which the financed entity is a party is less than or equal to the aggregate principal amount of the financing transaction(s) linking any of the parties to the financing arrangement, the entire amount of the payment shall be so recharacterized. If the aggregate principal amount of the financing transaction(s) to which the financed entity is a party is greater than the aggregate principal amount of the financing transaction(s) linking any of the parties to the financing arrangement, then the recharacterized portion shall be determined by multiplying the payment by a fraction the numerator of which is equal to the lowest aggregate principal amount of the financing transaction(s) linking any of the parties to the financing arrangement (other than financing transactions that are disregarded pursuant to paragraphs (a)(2)(i)(B) and (a)(4)(ii)(B) of this section) and the denominator of which is the aggregate principal amount of the financing transaction(s) to which the financed entity is a party. In the case of financing transactions the principal amount of which is subject to adjustment, the fraction shall be determined using the average outstanding principal amounts for the period to which the payment relates. The average principal amount may be computed using any method applied consistently that reflects with reasonable accuracy the amount outstanding for the period. See *Example 24* of paragraph (e) of this section for an illustration of the calculation of the amount of tax liability.

(ii) *Determination of principal amount*—(A) *In general.* Unless otherwise provided in this paragraph (d)(1)(ii), the principal amount equals the amount of money advanced, or the fair market value of other property advanced or subject to a lease or license, in the financing transaction. In general, fair market value is calculated in U.S. dollars as of the close of business on the day on which the financing transaction is entered into. However, if the property advanced, or the right to use property granted, by the financing entity is the same as the property or rights received by the financed entity, the fair market value of the property or right shall be determined as of the close of business on the last date that any of the financing transactions comprising the financing arrangement is entered into. In the case of fungible property, property of the same type shall be considered to be the same property. See *Example 25* of paragraph (e) for an illustration of the calculation of the principal amount in the case of financing transactions involving fungible property. The principal amount of a financing transaction shall be subject to adjustments, as set forth in this paragraph (d)(1)(ii).

(B) *Debt instruments and certain stock.* In the case of a debt instrument or of stock that is subject to the current inclusion rules of sections 305(c)(3) or (e), the principal amount generally will be equal to the issue price. However, if the fair market value on the issue date differs materially from the issue price, the fair market value of the debt instrument shall be used in lieu of the instrument's issue price. Appropriate adjustments will be made for accruals of original issue discount and repayments of principal (including accrued original issue discount).

(C) *Partnership and trust interests.* In the case of a partnership interest or an interest in a trust, the principal amount is equal to the fair market value of the money or property contributed to the partnership or trust in return for that partnership or trust interest.

(D) *Leases or licenses.* In the case of a lease or license, the principal amount is equal to the fair market value of the property subject to the lease or license on the date on which the lease or license is entered into. The principal amount shall be adjusted for depreciation or amortization, calculated on a basis that accurately reflects the anticipated decline in the value of the property over its life.

(2) *Rate of tax.* The rate at which tax is imposed under section 881 on the portion of the payment that is recharacterized pursuant to paragraph (d)(1) of this section is determined by reference to the nature of the recharacterized transaction, as determined under paragraphs (a)(3)(ii)(B) and (C) of this section.

(e) *Examples.* The following examples illustrate this section. For purposes of these examples, unless otherwise indicated, it is assumed that FP, a corporation organized in country N, owns all of the stock of FS, a corporation organized in country T, and DS, a corporation organized in the United States. Country T, but not country N, has an income tax treaty with the United States. The treaty exempts interest, rents and royalties paid by a resident of one state (the source state) to a resident of the other state from tax in the source state.

Example 1. Financing arrangement. (i) On January 1, 1996, BK, a bank organized in country T, lends $1,000,000 to DS in exchange for a note issued by DS. FP guarantees to BK that DS will satisfy its repayment obligation on the loan.

Reg. § 1.881-3(d)(2)

There are no other transactions between FP and BK.

(ii) BK's loan to DS is a financing transaction within the meaning of paragraph (a)(4)(ii)(A)(*1*) of this section. FP's guarantee of DS's repayment obligation is not a financing transaction as described in paragraphs (a)(2)(ii)(A)(*1*) through (*4*) of this section. Therefore, these transactions do not constitute a financing arrangement as defined in paragraph (a)(2)(i) of this section.

Example 2. Financing arrangement. (i) On January 1, 1996, FP lends $1,000,000 to DS in exchange for a note issued by DS. On January 1, 1997, FP assigns the DS note to FS in exchange for a note issued by FS. After receiving notice of the assignment, DS remits payments due under its note to FS.

(ii) The DS note held by FS and the FS note held by FP are financing transactions within the meaning of paragraph (a)(2)(ii)(A)(*1*) of this section, and together constitute a financing arrangement within the meaning of paragraph (a)(2)(i) of this section.

Example 3. Financing arrangement. (i) On December 1, 1994 FP creates a special purposes subsidiary, FS. On that date FP capitalizes FS with $1,000,000 in cash and $10,000,000 in debt from BK, a Country N bank. On January 1, 1995, C, a U.S. person, purchases an automobile from DS in return for an installment note. On August 1, 1995, DS sells a number of installment notes, including C's, to FS in exchange for $10,000,000. DS continues to service the installment notes for FS.

(ii) The C installment note now held by FS (as well as all of the other installment notes now held by FS) and the FS note held by BK are financing transactions within the meaning of paragraph (a)(2)(ii)(A)(*1*) of this section, and together constitute a financing arrangement within the meaning of paragraph (a)(2)(i) of this section.

Example 4. Related persons treated as a single intermediate entity. (i) On January 1, 1996, FP deposits $1,000,000 with BK, a bank that is organized in country N and is unrelated to FP and its subsidiaries. M, a corporation also organized in country N, is wholly-owned by the sole shareholder of BK but is not a bank within the meaning of section 881(c)(3)(A). On July 1, 1996, M lends $1,000,000 to DS in exchange for a note maturing on July 1, 2006. The note is in registered form within the meaning of section 881(c)(2)(B)(i) and DS has received from M the statement required by section 881(c)(2)(B)(ii). One of the principal purposes for the absence of a financing transaction between BK and M is the avoidance of the application of this section.

(ii) The transactions described above would form a financing arrangement but for the absence of a financing transaction between BK and M. However, because one of the principal purposes for the structuring of these financing transactions is to prevent characterization of such arrangement as a financing arrangement, the district director may treat the financing transactions between FP and BK, and between M and DS as a financing arrangement under paragraphs (a)(2)(i)(B) of this section. In such a case, BK and M would be considered a single intermediate entity for purposes of this section. See also paragraph (a)(4)(ii)(B) of this section for the authority to treat BK and M as a single intermediate entity.

Example 5. Related persons treated as a single intermediate entity. (i) On January 1, 1995, FP lends $10,000,000 to FS in exchange for a 10-year note that pays interest annually at a rate of 8 percent per annum. On January 2, 1995, FS contributes $10,000,000 to FS2, a wholly-owned subsidiary of FS organized in country T, in exchange for common stock of FS2. On January 1, 1996, FS2 lends $10,000,000 to DS in exchange for an 8-year note that pays interest annually at a rate of 10 percent per annum. FS is a holding company whose most significant asset is the stock of FS2. Throughout the period that the FP-FS loan is outstanding, FS causes FS2 to make distributions to FS, most of which are used to make interest and principal payments on the FP-FS loan. Without the distributions from FS2, FS would not have had the funds with which to make payments on the FP-FS loan. One of the principal purposes for the absence of a financing transaction between FS and FS2 is the avoidance of the application of this section.

(ii) The conditions of paragraph (a)(4)(i)(A) of this section would be satisfied with respect to the financing transactions between FP, FS, FS2 and DS but for the absence of a financing transaction between FS and FS2. However, because one of the principal purposes for the structuring of these financing transactions is to prevent characterization of an entity as a conduit, the district director may treat the financing transactions between FP and FS, and between FS2 and DS as a financing arrangement. See paragraph (a)(4)(ii)(B) of this section. In such a case, FS and FS2 would be considered a single intermediate entity for purposes of this section. See also paragraph (a)(2)(i)(B) of this section for the authority to treat FS and FS2 as a single intermediate entity.

Example 6. Presumption with respect to unrelated financing entity. (i) FP is a corporation organized in country T that is actively engaged in a substantial manufacturing business. FP has a

Reg. § 1.881-3(e)

revolving credit facility with a syndicate of banks, none of which is related to FP and FP's subsidiaries, which provides that FP may borrow up to a maximum of $100,000,000 at a time. The revolving credit facility provides that DS and certain other subsidiaries of FP may borrow directly from the syndicate at the same interest rates as FP, but each subsidiary is required to indemnify the syndicate banks for any withholding taxes imposed on interest payments by the country in which the subsidiary is organized. BK, a bank that is organized in country N, is the agent for the syndicate. Some of the syndicate banks are organized in country N, but others are residents of country O, a country that has an income tax treaty with the United States which allows the United States to impose a tax on interest at a maximum rate of 10 percent. It is reasonable for BK and the syndicate banks to have determined that FP will be able to meet its payment obligations on a maximum principal amount of $100,000,000 out of the cash flow of its manufacturing business. At various times throughout 1995, FP borrows under the revolving credit facility until the outstanding principal amount reaches the maximum amount of $100,000,000. On December 31, 1995, FP receives $100,000,000 from a public offering of its equity. On January 1, 1996, FP pays BK $90,000,000 to reduce the outstanding principal amount under the revolving credit facility and lends $10,000,000 to DS. FP would have repaid the entire principal amount, and DS would have borrowed directly from the syndicate, but for the fact that DS did not want to incur the U.S. withholding tax that would have applied to payments made directly by DS to the syndicate banks.

(ii) Pursuant to paragraph (a)(3)(ii)(E)(*1*) of this section, even though the financing arrangement is a conduit financing arrangement (because the financing arrangement meets the standards for recharacterization in paragraph (a)(4)(i)), BK and the other syndicate banks have no section 881 liability unless they know or have reason to know that the financing arrangement is a conduit financing arrangement. Moreover, pursuant to paragraph (a)(3)(ii)(E)(*2*)(*ii*) of this section, BK and the syndicate banks are presumed not to know that the financing arrangement is a conduit financing arrangement. The syndicate banks are unrelated to both FP and DS, and FP is actively engaged in a substantial trade or business—that is, the cash flow from FP's manufacturing business is sufficient for the banks to expect that FP will be able to make the payments required under the financing transaction. See § 1.1441-3(j) for the withholding obligations of the withholding agents.

Example 7. Multiple intermediate entities—special rule for related persons. (i) On January 1, 1995, FP lends $10,000,000 to FS in exchange for a 10-year note that pays interest annually at a rate of 8 percent per annum. On January 2, 1995, FS contributes $9,900,000 to FS2, a wholly-owned subsidiary of FS organized in country T, in exchange for common stock and lends $100,000 to FS2. On January 1, 1996, FS2 lends $10,000,000 to DS in exchange for an 8-year note that pays interest annually at a rate of 10 percent per annum. FS is a holding company that has no significant assets other than the stock of FS2. Throughout the period that the FP-FS loan is outstanding, FS causes FS2 to make distributions to FS, most of which are used to make interest and principal payments on the FP-FS loan. Without the distributions from FS2, FS would not have had the funds with which to make payments on the FP-FS loan. One of the principal purposes for structuring the transactions between FS and FS2 as primarily a contribution of capital is to the amount of the payment that would be recharacterized under paragraph (d) of this section.

(ii) Pursuant to paragraph (a)(4)(ii)(B) of this section, the district director may treat FS and FS2 as a single intermediate entity for purposes of this section since one of the principal purposes for the participation of multiple intermediate entities is to reduce the amount of the tax liability on any recharacterized payment by inserting a financing transaction with a low principal amount.

Example 8. Multiple intermediate entities. (i) On January 1, 1995, FP deposits $1,000,000 with BK, a bank that is organized in country T and is unrelated to FP and its subsidiaries, FS and DS. On January 1, 1996, at a time when the FP-BK deposit is still outstanding, BK lends $500,000 to BK2, a bank that is wholly-owned by BK and is organized in country T. On the same date, BK2 lends $500,000 to FS. On July 1, 1996, FS lends $500,000 to DS. FP pledges its deposit with BK to BK2 in support of FS' obligation to repay the BK2 loan. FS', BK's and BK2's participation in the financing arrangement is pursuant to a tax avoidance plan.

(ii) The conditions of paragraphs (a)(4)(i)(A) and (B) of this section are satisfied because the participation of BK, BK2 and FS in the financing arrangement reduces the tax imposed by section 881, and FS', BK's and BK2's participation in the financing arrangement is pursuant to a tax avoidance plan. However, since BK and BK2 are unrelated to FP and DS, under paragraph (a)(4)(i)(C)(*2*) of this section, BK and BK2 will be treated as conduit entities only if BK and BK2

Reg. § 1.881-3(e)

would not have participated in the financing arrangement on substantially the same terms but for the financing transaction between FP and BK.

(iii) It is presumed that BK2 would not have participated in the financing arrangement on substantially the same terms but for the BK-BK2 financing transaction because FP's pledge of an asset in support of FS' obligation to repay the BK2 loan is a guarantee within the meaning of paragraph (c)(2)(ii) of this section. If the taxpayer does not rebut this presumption by clear and convincing evidence, then BK2 will be a conduit entity.

(iv) Because BK and BK2 are related intermediate entities, the district director must determine whether one of the principal purposes for the involvement of multiple intermediate entities was to prevent characterization of an entity as a conduit entity. In making this determination, the district director may consider the fact that the involvement of two related intermediate entities prevents the presumption regarding guarantees from applying to BK. In the absence of evidence showing a business purpose for the involvement of both BK and BK2, the district director may treat BK and BK2 as a single intermediate entity for purposes of determining whether they would have participated in the financing arrangement on substantially the same terms but for the financing transaction between FP and BK. The presumption that applies to BK2 therefore will apply to BK. If the taxpayer does not rebut this presumption by clear and convincing evidence, then BK will be a conduit entity.

Example 9. Reduction of tax. (i) On February 1, 1995, FP issues debt to the public that would satisfy the requirements of section 871(h)(2)(A) (relating to obligations that are not in registered form) if issued by a U.S. person. FP lends the proceeds of the debt offering to DS in exchange for a note.

(ii) The debt issued by FP and the DS note are financing transactions within the meaning of paragraph (a)(2)(ii)(A)(*1*) of this section and together constitute a financing arrangement within the meaning of paragraph (a)(2)(i) of this section. The holders of the FP debt are the financing entities, FP is the intermediate entity and DS is the financed entity. Because interest payments on the debt issued by FP would not have been subject to withholding tax if the debt had been issued by DS, there is no reduction in tax under paragraph (a)(4)(i)(A) of this section. Accordingly, FP is not a conduit entity.

Example 10. Reduction of tax. (i) On January 1, 1995, FP licenses to FS the rights to use a patent in the United States to manufacture product A. FS agrees to pay FP a fixed amount in royalties each year under the license. On January 1, 1996, FS sublicenses to DS the rights to use the patent in the United States. Under the sublicense, DS agrees to pay FS royalties based upon the units of product A manufactured by DS each year. Although the formula for computing the amount of royalties paid by DS to FS differs from the formula for computing the amount of royalties paid by FS to FP, each represents an arm's length rate.

(ii) Although the royalties paid by DS to FS are exempt from U.S. withholding tax, the royalty payments between FS and FP are income from U.S. sources under section 861(a)(4) subject to the 30 percent gross tax imposed by § 1.881-2(b) and subject to withholding under § 1.1441-2(a). Because the rate of tax imposed on royalties paid by FS to FP is the same as the rate that would have been imposed on royalties paid by DS to FP, the participation of FS in the FP-FS-DS financing arrangement does not reduce the tax imposed by section 881 within the meaning of paragraph (a)(4)(i)(A) of this section. Accordingly, FP is not a conduit entity.

Example 11. A principal purpose. (i) On January 1, 1995, FS lends $10,000,000 to DS in exchange for a 10-year note that pays interest annually at a rate of 8 percent per annum. As was intended at the time of the loan from FS to DS, on July 1, 1995, FP makes an interest-free demand loan of $10,000,000 to FS. A principal purpose for FS' participation in the FP-FS-DS financing arrangement is that FS generally coordinates the financing for all of FP's subsidiaries (although FS does not engage in significant financing activities with respect to such financing transactions). However, another principal purpose for FS' participation is to allow the parties to benefit from the lower withholding tax rate provided under the income tax treaty between country T and the United States.

(ii) The financing arrangement satisfies the tax avoidance purpose requirement of paragraph (a)(4)(i)(B) of this section because FS participated in the financing arrangement pursuant to a plan one of the principal purposes of which is to allow the parties to benefit from the country T-U.S. treaty.

Example 12. A principal purpose. (i) DX is a U.S. corporation that intends to purchase property to use in its manufacturing business. FX is a partnership organized in country N that is owned in equal parts by LC1 and LC2, leasing companies that are unrelated to DX. BK, a bank organized in country N and unrelated to DX, LC1 and LC2, lends $100,000,000 to FX to enable FX to

Reg. § 1.881-3(e)

purchase the property. On the same day, FX purchases the property and engages in a transaction with DX which is treated as a lease of the property for country N tax purposes but a loan for U.S. tax purposes. Accordingly, DX is treated as the owner of the property for U.S. tax purposes. The parties comply with the requirements of section 881(c) with respect to the debt obligation of DX to FX. FX and DX structured these transactions in this manner so that LC1 and LC2 would be entitled to accelerated depreciation deductions with respect to the property in country N and DX would be entitled to accelerated depreciation deductions in the United States. None of the parties would have participated in the transaction if the payments made by DX were subject to U.S. withholding tax.

(ii) The loan[s] from BK to FX and from FX to DX are financing transactions and, together constitute a financing arrangement. The participation of FX in the financing arrangement reduces the tax imposed by section 881 because payments made to FX, but not BK, qualify for the portfolio interest exemption of section 881(c) because BK is a bank making an extension of credit in the ordinary course of its trade or business within the meaning of section 881(c)(3)(A). Moreover, because DX borrowed the money from FX instead of borrowing the money directly from BK to avoid the tax imposed by section 881, one of the principal purposes of the participation of FX was to avoid that tax (even though another principal purpose of the participation of FX was to allow LC1 and LC2 to take advantage of accelerated depreciation deductions in country N). Assuming that FX would not have participated in the financing arrangement on substantially the same terms but for the fact that BK loaned it $100,000,000, FX is a conduit entity and the financing arrangement is a conduit financing arrangement.

Example 13. Significant reduction of tax. (i) FS owns all of the stock of FS1, which also is a resident of country T. FS1 owns all of the stock of DS. On January 1, 1995, FP contributes $10,000,000 to the capital of FS in return for perpetual preferred stock. On July 1, 1995, FS lends $10,000,000 to FS1. On January 1, 1996, FS1 lends $10,000,000 to DS. Under the terms of the country T-U.S. income tax treaty, a country T resident is not entitled to the reduced withholding rate on interest income provided by the treaty if the resident is entitled to specified tax benefits under country T law. Although FS1 may deduct interest paid on the loan from FS, these deductions are not pursuant to any special tax benefits provided by country T law. However, FS qualifies for one of the enumerated tax benefits pursuant to which it may deduct dividends paid with respect to the stock held by FP. Therefore, if FS had made a loan directly to DS, FS would not have been entitled to the benefits of the country T-U.S. tax treaty with respect to payments it received from DS, and such payments would have been subject to tax under section 881 at a 30 percent rate.

(ii) The FS-FS1 loan and the FS1-DS loan are financing transactions within the meaning of paragraph (a)(2)(ii)(A)(*1*) of this section and together constitute a financing arrangement within the meaning of paragraph (a)(2)(i) of this section. Pursuant to paragraph (b)(2)(i) of this section, the significant reduction in tax resulting from the participation of FS1 in the financing arrangement is evidence that the participation of FS1 in the financing arrangement is pursuant to a tax avoidance plan. However, other facts relevant to the presence of such a plan must also be taken into account.

Example 14. Significant reduction of tax. (i) FP owns 90 percent of the voting stock of FX, an unlimited liability company organized in country T. The other 10 percent of the common stock of FX is owned by FP1, a subsidiary of FP that is organized in country N. Although FX is a partnership for U.S. tax purposes, FX is entitled to the benefits of the U.S.-country T income tax treaty because FX is subject to tax in country T as a resident corporation. On January 1, 1996, FP contributes $10,000,000 to FX in exchange for an instrument denominated as preferred stock that pays a dividend of 7 percent and that must be redeemed by FX in seven years. For U.S. tax purposes, the preferred stock is a partnership interest. On July 1, 1996, FX makes a loan of $10,000,000 to DS in exchange for a 7-year note paying interest at 6 percent.

(ii) Because FX is required to redeem the partnership interest at a specified time, the partnership interest constitutes a financing transaction within the meaning of paragraph (a)(2)(ii)(A)(*2*) of this section. Moreover, because the FX-DS note is a financing transaction within the meaning of paragraph (a)(2)(ii)(A)(*1*) of this section, together the transactions constitute a financing arrangement within the meaning of (a)(2)(i) of this section. Payments of interest made directly by DS to FP and FP1 would not be eligible for the portfolio interest exemption and would not be entitled to a reduction in withholding tax pursuant to a tax treaty. Therefore, there is a significant reduction in tax resulting from the participation of FX in the financing arrangement, which is evidence that the participation of FX in the financing arrangement is pursuant to a tax avoidance plan. However, other facts relevant to the existence of such a plan must also be taken into account.

Example 15. Significant reduction of tax. (i) FP owns a 10 percent interest in the profits and capital of FX, a partnership organized in country N. The other 90 percent interest in FX is owned by G, an unrelated corporation that is organized in country T. FX is not engaged in business in the United States. On January 1, 1996, FP contributes $10,000,000 to FX in exchange for an instrument documented as perpetual subordinated debt that provides for quarterly interest payments at 9 percent per annum. Under the terms of the instrument, payments on the perpetual subordinated debt do not otherwise affect the allocation of income between the partners. FP has the right to require the liquidation of FX if FX fails to make an interest payment. For U.S. tax purposes, the perpetual subordinated debt is treated as a partnership interest in FX and the payments on the perpetual subordinated debt constitute guaranteed payments within the meaning of section 707(c). On July 1, 1996, FX makes a loan of $10,000,000 to DS in exchange for a 7-year note paying interest at 8 percent per annum.

(ii) Because FP has the effective right to force payment of the "interest" on the perpetual subordinated debt, the instrument constitutes a financing transaction within the meaning of paragraph (a)(2)(ii)(A)(*2*) of this section. Moreover, because the note between FX and DS is a financing transaction within the meaning of paragraph (a)(2)(ii)(A)(*1*) of this section, together the transactions are a financing arrangement within the meaning of (a)(2)(i) of this section. Without regard to this section, 90 percent of each interest payment received by FX would be treated as exempt from U.S. withholding tax because it is beneficially owned by G, while 10 percent would be subject to a 30 percent withholding tax because beneficially owned by FP. If FP held directly the note issued by DS, 100 percent of the interest payments on the note would have been subject to the 30 percent withholding tax. The significant reduction in the tax imposed by section 881 resulting from the participation of FX in the financing arrangement is evidence that the participation of FX in the financing arrangement is pursuant to a tax avoidance plan. However, other facts relevant to the presence of such a plan must also be taken into account.

Example 16. Time period between transactions. (i) On January 1, 1995, FP lends $10,000,000 to FS in exchange for a 10-year note that pays no interest annually. When the note matures, FS is obligated to pay $24,000,000 to FP. On January 1, 1996, FS lends $10,000,000 to DS in exchange for a 10-year note that pays interest annually at a rate of 10 percent per annum.

(ii) The FS note held by FP and the DS note held by FS are financing transactions within the meaning of paragraph (a)(2)(ii)(A)(*1*) of this section and together constitute a financing arrangement within the meaning of (a)(2)(i) of this section. Pursuant to paragraph (b)(2)(iii) of this section, the short period of time (twelve months) between the loan by FP to FS and the loan by FS to DS is evidence that the participation of FS in the financing arrangement is pursuant to a tax avoidance plan. However, other facts relevant to the presence of such a plan must also be taken into account.

Example 17. Financing transactions in the ordinary course of business. (i) FP is a holding company. FS is actively engaged in country T in the business of manufacturing and selling product A. DS manufactures product B, a principal component in which is product A. FS' business activity is substantial. On January 1, 1995, FP lends $100,000,000 to FS to finance FS' business operations. On January 1, 1996, FS ships $30,000,000 of product A to DS. In return, FS creates an interest-bearing account receivable on its books. FS' shipment is in the ordinary course of the active conduct of its trade or business (which is complementary to DS' trade or business.)

(ii) The loan from FP to FS and the accounts receivable opened by FS for a payment owed by DS are financing transactions within the meaning of paragraph (a)(2)(ii)(A)(*1*) of this section and together constitute a financing arrangement within the meaning of paragraph (a)(2)(i) of this section. Pursuant to paragraph (b)(2)(iv) of this section, the fact that DS' liability to FS is created in the ordinary course of the active conduct of DS' trade or business that is complementary to a business actively engaged in by DS is evidence that the participation of FS in the financing arrangement is not pursuant to a tax avoidance plan. However, other facts relevant to the presence of such a plan must also be taken into account.

Example 18. Tax avoidance plan—other factors. (i) On February 1, 1995, FP issues debt in Country N that is in registered form within the meaning of section 881(c)(3)(A). The FP debt would satisfy the requirements of section 881(c) if the debt were issued by a U.S. person and the withholding agent received the certification required by section 871(h)(2)(B)(ii). The purchasers of the debt are financial institutions and there is no reason to believe that they would not furnish Forms W-8. On March 1, 1995, FP lends a portion of the proceeds of the offering to DS.

Reg. § 1.881-3(e)

(ii) The FP debt and the loan to DS are financing transactions within the meaning of paragraph (a)(2)(ii)(A)(1) of this section and together constitute a financing arrangement within the meaning of paragraph (a)(2)(i) of this section. The owners of the FP debt are the financing entities, FP is the intermediate entity and DS is the financed entity. Interest payments on the debt issued by FP would be subject to withholding tax if the debt were issued by DS, unless DS received all necessary Forms W-8. Therefore, the participation of FP in the financing arrangement potentially reduces the tax imposed by section 881(a). However, because it is reasonable to assume that the purchasers of the FP debt would have provided certifications in order to avoid the withholding tax imposed by section 881, there is not a tax avoidance plan. Accordingly, FP is not a conduit entity.

Example 19. Tax avoidance plan—other factors. (i) Over a period of years, FP has maintained a deposit with BK, a bank organized in the United States, that is unrelated to FP and its subsidiaries. FP often sells goods and purchases raw materials in the United States. FP opened the bank account with BK in order to facilitate this business and the amounts it maintains in the account are reasonably related to its dollar-denominated working capital needs. On January 1, 1995, BK lends $5,000,000 to DS. After the loan is made, the balance in FP's bank account remains within a range appropriate to meet FP's working capital needs.

(ii) FP's deposit with BK and BK's loan to DS are financing transactions within the meaning of paragraph (a)(2)(ii)(A)(1) of this section and together constitute a financing arrangement within the meaning of paragraph (a)(2)(i) of this section. Pursuant to section 881(i), interest paid by BK to FP with respect to the bank deposit is exempt from withholding tax. Interest paid directly by DS to FP would not be exempt from withholding tax under section 881(i) and therefore would be subject to a 30% withholding tax. Accordingly, there is a significant reduction in the tax imposed by section 881, which is evidence of the existence of a tax avoidance plan. See paragraph (b)(2)(i) of this section. However, the district director also will consider the fact that FP historically has maintained an account with BK to meet its working capital needs and that, prior to and after BK's loan to DS, the balance within the account remains within a range appropriate to meet those business needs as evidence that the participation of BK in the FP-BK-DS financing arrangement is not pursuant to a tax avoidance plan. In determining the presence or absence of a tax avoidance plan, all relevant facts will be taken into account.

Example 20. Tax avoidance plan—other factors. (i) Assume the same facts as in *Example 19*, except that on January 1, 2000, FP's deposit with BK substantially exceeds FP's expected working capital needs and on January 2, 2000, BK lends additional funds to DS. Assume also that BK's loan to DS provides BK with a right of offset against FP's deposit. Finally, assume that FP would have lent the funds to DS directly but for the imposition of the withholding tax on payments made directly to FP by DS.

(ii) As in *Example 19,* the transactions in paragraph (i) of this *Example 20* are a financing arrangement within the meaning of paragraph (a)(2)(i) and the participation of the BK reduces the section 881 tax. In this case, the presence of funds substantially in excess of FP's working capital needs and the fact that FP would have been willing to lend funds directly to DS if not for the withholding tax are evidence that the participation of BK in the FP-BK-FS financing arrangement is pursuant to a tax avoidance plan. However, other facts relevant to the presence of such a plan must also be taken into account. Even if the district director determines that the participation of BK in the financing arrangement is pursuant to a tax avoidance plan, BK may not be treated as a conduit entity unless BK would not have participated in the financing arrangement on substantially the same terms in the absence of FP's deposit with BK. BK's right of offset against FP's deposit (a form of guarantee of BK's loan to DS) creates a presumption that BK would not have made the loan to DS on substantially the same terms in the absence of FP's deposit with BK. If the taxpayer overcomes the presumption by clear and convincing evidence, BK will not be a conduit entity.

Example 21. Significant financing activities. (i) FS is responsible for coordinating the financing of all of the subsidiaries of FP, which are engaged in substantial trades or businesses and are located in country T, country N, and the United States. FS maintains a centralized cash management accounting system for FP and its subsidiaries in which it records all intercompany payables and receivables; these payables and receivables ultimately are reduced to a single balance either due from or owing to FS and each of FP's subsidiaries. FS is responsible for disbursing or receiving any cash payments required by transactions between its affiliates and unrelated parties. FS must borrow any cash necessary to meet those external obligations and invests any excess cash for the benefit of the FP group. FS enters into interest rate and foreign exchange contracts as necessary to manage the risks arising from mismatches in incoming and outgoing cash flows. The activities

Reg. § 1.881-3(e)

of FS are intended (and reasonably can be expected) to reduce transaction costs and overhead and other fixed costs. FS has 50 employees, including clerical and other back office personnel, located in country T. At the request of DS, on January 1, 1995, FS pays a supplier $1,000,000 for materials delivered to DS and charges DS an open account receivable for this amount. On February 3, 1995, FS reverses the account receivable from DS to FS when DS delivers to FP goods with a value of $1,000,000.

(ii) The accounts payable from DS to FS and from FS to other subsidiaries of FP constitute financing transactions within the meaning of paragraph (a)(2)(ii)(A)(1) of this section, and the transactions together constitute a financing arrangement within the meaning of paragraph (a)(2)(i) of this section. FS's activities constitute significant financing activities with respect to the financing transactions even though FS did not actively and materially participate in arranging the financing transactions because the financing transactions consisted of trade receivables and trade payables that were ordinary and necessary to carry on the trades or businesses of DS and the other subsidiaries of FP. Accordingly, pursuant to paragraph (b)(3)(i) of this section, FS' participation in the financing arrangement is presumed not to be pursuant to a tax avoidance plan.

Example 22. Significant financing activities—active risk management. (i) The facts are the same as in *Example 21*, except that, in addition to its short-term funding needs, DS needs long-term financing to fund an acquisition of another U.S. company; the acquisition is scheduled to close on January 15, 1995. FS has a revolving credit agreement with a syndicate of banks located in Country N. On January 14, 1995, FS borrows ¥10 billion for 10 years under the revolving credit agreement, paying yen LIBOR plus 50 basis points on a quarterly basis. FS enters into a currency swap with BK, an unrelated bank that is not a member of the syndicate, under which FS will pay BK ¥10 billion and will receive $100 million on January 15, 1995; these payments will be reversed on January 15, 2004. FS will pay BK U.S. dollar LIBOR plus 50 basis points on a notional principal amount of $100 million semi-annually and will receive yen LIBOR plus 50 basis points on a notional principal amount of ¥10 billion quarterly. Upon the closing of the acquisition on January 15, 1995, DS borrows $100 million from FS for 10 years, paying U.S. dollar LIBOR plus 50 basis points semiannually.

(ii) Although FS performs significant financing activities with respect to certain financing transactions to which it is a party, FS does not perform significant financing activities with respect to the financing transactions between FS and the syndicate of banks and between FS and DS because FS has eliminated all material market risks arising from those financing transactions through its currency swap with BK. Accordingly, the financing arrangement does not benefit from the presumption of paragraph (b)(3)(i) of this section and the district director must determine whether the participation of FS in the financing arrangement is pursuant to a tax avoidance plan on the basis of all the facts and circumstances. However, if additional facts indicated that FS reviews its currency swaps daily to determine whether they are the most cost efficient way of managing their currency risk and, as a result, frequently terminates swaps in favor of entering into more cost efficient hedging arrangements with unrelated parties, FS would be considered to perform significant financing activities and FS' participation in the financing arrangements would not be pursuant to a tax avoidance plan.

Example 23. Significant financing activities—presumption rebutted. (i) The facts are the same as in *Example 21*, except that, on January 1, 1995, FP lends to FS DM 15,000,000 (worth $10,000,000) in exchange for a 10 year note that pays interest annually at a rate of 5 percent per annum. Also, on March 15, 1995, FS lends $10,000,000 to DS in exchange for a 10-year note that pays interest annually at a rate of 8 percent per annum. FS would not have had sufficient funds to make the loan to DS without the loan from FP. FS does not enter into any long-term hedging transaction with respect to these financing transactions, but manages the interest rate and currency risk arising from the transactions on a daily, weekly or quarterly basis by entering into forward currency contracts.

(ii) Because FS performs significant financing activities with respect to the financing transactions between FS, DS and FP, the participation of FS in the financing arrangement is presumed not to be pursuant to a tax avoidance plan. The district director may rebut this presumption by establishing that the participation of FS is pursuant to a tax avoidance plan, based on all the facts and circumstances. The mere fact that FS is a resident of country T is not sufficient to establish the existence of a tax avoidance plan. However, the existence of a plan can be inferred from other factors in addition to the fact that FS is a resident of country T. For example, the loans are made within a short time period and FS would not have been able to make the loan to DS without the loan from FP.

Reg. § 1.881-3(e)

Example 24. Determination of amount of tax liability. (i) On January 1, 1996, FP makes two three-year installment loans of $250,000 each to FS that pay interest at a rate of 9 percent per annum. The loans are self-amortizing with payments on each loan of $7,950 per month. On the same date, FS lends $1,000,000 to DS in exchange for a two-year note that pays interest semi-annually at a rate of 10 percent per annum, beginning on June 30, 1996. The FS-DS loan is not self-amortizing. Assume that for the period of January 1, 1996 through June 30, 1996, the average principal amount of the financing transactions between FP and FS that comprise the financing arrangement is $469,319. Further, assume that for the period of July 1, 1996 through December 31, 1996, the average principal amount of the financing transactions between FP and FS is $393,632. The average principal amount of the financing transaction between FS and DS for the same periods is $1,000,000. The district director determines that the financing transactions between FP and FS, and FS and DS, are a conduit financing arrangement.

(ii) Pursuant to paragraph (d)(1)(i) of this section, the portion of the $50,000 interest payment made by DS to FS on June 30, 1996, that is recharacterized as a payment to FP is $23,450 computed as follows: ($50,000 x $469,319/$1,000,000) = $23,450. The portion of the interest payment made on December 31, 1996 that is recharacterized as a payment to FP is $19,650, computed as follows: ($50,000 x $393,632/$1,000,000) = $19,650. Furthermore, under § 1.1441-3(j), DS is liable for withholding tax at a 30 percent rate on the portion of the $50,000 payment to FS that is recharacterized as a payment to FP, i.e., $7,035 with respect to the June 30, 1996 payment and $5,895 with respect to the December 31, 1996 payment.

Example 25. Determination of principal amount. (i) FP lends DM 5,000,000 to FS in exchange for a ten year note that pays interest semi-annually at a rate of 8 percent per annum. Six months later, pursuant to a tax avoidance plan, FS lends DM 10,000,000 to DS in exchange for a 10 year note that pays interest semi-annually at a rate of 10 percent per annum. At the time FP make its loan to FS, the exchange rate is DM 1.5/$1. At the time FS makes its loan to DS the exchange rate is DM 1.4/$1.

(ii) FP's loan to FS and FS' loan to DS are financing transactions and together constitute a financing arrangement. Furthermore, because the participation of FS reduces the tax imposed under section 881 and FS' participation is pursuant to a tax avoidance plan, the financing arrangement is a conduit financing arrangement.

(iii) Pursuant to paragraph (d)(1)(i) of this section, the amount subject to recharacterization is a fraction the numerator of which is the lowest aggregate principal amount advanced and the denominator of which is the principal amount advanced from FS to DS. Because the property advanced in these financing transactions is the same type of fungible property, under paragraph (d)(1)(ii)(A) of this section, both are valued on the date of the last financing transaction. Accordingly, the portion of the payments of interest that is recharacterized is ((DM 5,000,000 × DM 1.4/$1)/(DM 10,000,000 × DM 1.4/$1) or 0.5.

(f) *Effective date.* This section is effective for payments made by financed entities on or after September 11, 1995. This section shall not apply to interest payments covered by section 127(g)(3) of the Tax Reform Act of 1984, and to interest payments with respect to other debt obligations issued prior to October 15, 1984 (whether or not such debt was issued by a Netherlands Antilles corporation). [Reg. § 1.1881-3.]

☐ [*T.D.* 8611, 8-10-95.]

[Reg. § 1.881-4]

§ 1.881-4. Recordkeeping requirements concerning conduit financing arrangements.—(a) *Scope.* This section provides rules for the maintenance of records concerning certain financing arrangements to which the provisions of § 1.881-3 apply.

(b) *Recordkeeping requirements*—(1) *In general.* Any person subject to the general recordkeeping requirements of section 6001 must keep the permanent books of account or records, as required by section 6001, that may be relevant to determining whether that person is a party to a financing arrangement and whether that financing arrangement is a conduit financing arrangement.

(2) *Application of Sections 6038 and 6038A.* A financed entity that is a reporting corporation within the meaning of section 6038A(a) and the regulations under that section, and any other person that is subject to the recordkeeping requirements of § 1.6038A-3, must comply with those recordkeeping requirements with respect to records that may be relevant to determining whether the financed entity is a party to a financing arrangement and whether that financing arrangement is a conduit financing arrangement. Such records, including records that a person is required to maintain pursuant to paragraph (c) of this section, shall be considered records that are required to be maintained pursuant to section

Reg. § 1.881-4(a)

6038 or 6038A. Accordingly, the provisions of sections 6038 and 6038A (including, without limitation, the penalty provisions thereof), and the regulations under those sections, shall apply to any records required to be maintained pursuant to this section.

(c) *Records to be maintained*—(1) *In general.* An entity described in paragraph (b) of this section shall be required to retain any records containing the following information concerning each financing transaction that the entity knows or has reason to know comprises the financing arrangement—

(i) The nature (e.g., loan, stock, lease, license) of each financing transaction;

(ii) The name, address, taxpayer identification number (if any) and country of residence of—

(A) Each person that advanced money or other property, or granted rights to use property;

(B) Each person that was the recipient of the advance or rights; and

(C) Each person to whom a payment was made pursuant to the financing transaction (to the extent that person is a different person than the person who made the advance or granted the rights);

(iii) The date and amount of—

(A) Each advance of money or other property or grant of rights; and

(B) Each payment made in return for the advance or grant of rights;

(iv) The terms of any guarantee provided in conjunction with a financing transaction, including the name of the guarantor; and

(v) In cases where one or both of the parties to a financing transaction are related to each other or another entity in the financing arrangement, the manner in which these persons are related.

(2) *Additional documents.* An entity described in paragraph (b) of this section must also retain all records relating to the circumstances surrounding its participation in the financing transactions and financing arrangements. Such documents may include, but are not limited to—

(i) Minutes of board of directors meetings;

(ii) Board resolutions or other authorizations for the financing transactions;

(iii) Private letter rulings;

(iv) Financial reports (audited or unaudited);

(v) Notes to financial statements;

(vi) Bank statements;

(vii) Copies of wire transfers;

(viii) Offering documents;

(ix) Materials from investment advisors, bankers and tax advisors; and

(x) Evidences of indebtedness.

(3) *Effect of record maintenance requirement.* Record maintenance in accordance with paragraph (b) of this section generally does not require the original creation of records that are ordinarily not created by affected entities. If, however, a document that is actually created is described in this paragraph (c), it is to be retained even if the document is not of a type ordinarily created by the affected entity.

(d) *Effective date.* This section is effective September 11, 1995. This section shall not apply to interest payments covered by section 127(g)(3) of the Tax Reform Act of 1984, and to interest payments with respect to other debt obligations issued prior to October 15, 1984 (whether or not such debt was issued by a Netherlands Antilles corporation). [Reg. § 1.881-4.]

☐ [T.D. 8611, 8-10-95].

[Reg. § 1.882-0]

§ 1.882-0. Table of contents.—This section lists captions contained in §§ 1.882-1, 1.882-2, 1.882-3, 1.882-4 and 1.882-5.

§ 1.882-1. Taxation of foreign corporations engaged in U.S. business or of foreign corporations treated as having effectively connected income.

(a) Segregation of income.

(b) Imposition of tax.

(1) Income not effectively connected with the conduct of a trade or business in the United States.

(2) Income effectively connected with the conduct of a trade or business in the United States.

(i) In general.

(ii) Determination of taxable income.

(iii) Cross references.

(c) Change in trade or business status.

(d) Credits against tax.

(e) Payment of estimated tax.

(f) Effective date.

§ 1.882-2. Income of foreign corporation treated as effectively connected with U.S. business.

(a) Election as to real property income.

(b) Interest on U.S. obligations received by banks organized in possessions.

(c) Treatment of income.

(d) Effective date.

§ 1.882-3. Gross income of a foreign corporation.

(a) In general.

(1) Inclusions.

(2) Exchange transactions.

(3) Exclusions.

(b) Foreign corporations not engaged in U.S. business.

(c) Foreign corporations engaged in U.S. business.

(d) Effective date.

§ 1.882-4. Allowance of deductions and credits to foreign corporations.

(a) Foreign corporations.

(1) In general.

(2) Return necessary.

(3) Filing deadline for return.

(4) Return by Internal Revenue Service.

(b) Allowed deductions and credits.

(1) In general.

(2) Verification.

§ 1.882-5. Determination of interest deduction.

(a) Rules of general application.

(1) Overview.

(i) In general.

(ii) Direct allocations.

(A) In general.

(B) Partnership interest.

(2) Coordination with tax treaties.

(3) Limitation on interest expense.

(4) Translation convention for foreign currency.

(5) Coordination with other sections.

(6) Special rule for foreign governments.

(7) Elections under § 1.882-5.

(i) In general.

(ii) Failure to make the proper election.

(8) Examples.

(b) Step 1: Determination of total value of U.S. assets for the taxable year.

(1) Classification of an asset as a U.S. asset.

(i) General rule.

(ii) Items excluded from the definition of U.S. asset.

(iii) Items included in the definition of U.S. asset.

(iv) Interbranch transactions.

(v) Assets acquired to increase U.S. assets artificially.

(2) Determination of the value of a U.S. asset.

(i) General rule.

(ii) Fair-market value election.

(A) In general.

(B) Adjustment to partnership basis.

(iii) Reduction of total value of U.S. assets by amount of bad debt reserves under section 585.

(A) In general.

(B) Example.

(iv) Adjustment to basis of financial instruments.

(3) Computation of total value of U.S. assets.

(c) Step 2: Determination of total amount of U.S.-connected liabilities for the taxable year.

(1) General rule.

(2) Computation of the actual ratio.

(i) In general.

(ii) Classification of items.

(iii) Determination of amount of worldwide liabilities.

(iv) Determination of value of worldwide assets.

(v) Hedging transactions.

(vi) Treatment of partnership interests and liabilities.

(vii) Computation of actual ratio of insurance companies.

(viii) Interbranch transactions.

(ix) Amounts must be expressed in a single currency.

(3) Adjustments.

(4) Elective fixed ratio method of determining U.S. liabilities.

(5) Examples.

(d) Step 3: Determination of amount of interest expense allocable to ECI under the adjusted U.S. booked liabilities method.

(1) General rule.

(2) U.S. booked liabilities.

(i) In general.

(ii) Properly reflected on the books of the U.S. trade or business of a foreign corporation that is not a bank.

(A) In general.

(B) Identified liabilities not properly reflected.

(iii) Properly reflected on the books of the U.S. trade or business of a foreign corporation that is a bank.

(A) In general.

Reg. § 1.882-0

(B) Inadvertent error.

(iv) Liabilities of insurance companies.

(v) Liabilities used to increase artificially interest expense on U.S. booked liabilities.

(vi) Hedging transactions.

(vii) Amount of U.S. booked liabilities of a partner.

(viii) Interbranch transactions.

(3) Average total amount of U.S. booked liabilities.

(4) Interest expense where U.S. booked liabilities equal or exceed U.S. liabilities.

(i) In general.

(ii) Scaling ratio.

(iii) Special rules for insurance companies.

(5) U.S.-connected interest rate where U.S. booked liabilities are less than U.S.-connected liabilities.

(i) In general.

(ii) Interest rate on excess U.S.-connected liabilities.

(6) Examples.

(e) Separate currency pools method.

(1) General rule.

(i) Determine the value of U.S. assets in each currency pool.

(ii) Determine the U.S.-connected liabilities in each currency pool.

(iii) Determine the interest expense attributable to each currency pool.

(2) Prescribed interest rate.

(3) Hedging transactions.

(4) Election not available if excessive hyperinflationary assets.

(5) Examples.

(f) Effective date.

(1) General rule.

(2) Special rules for financial products.

[Reg. § 1.882-0.]

☐ [T.D. 8658, 3-5-96.]

[Reg. § 1.882-1]

§ 1.882-1. Taxation of foreign corporations engaged in U.S. business or of foreign corporations treated as having effectively connected income.—(a) *Segregation of income.* This section applies for purposes of determining the tax of a foreign corporation which at any time during the taxable year is engaged in trade or business in the United States. It also applies for purposes of determining the tax of a foreign corporation which at no time during the taxable year is engaged in trade or business in the United States but has for the taxable year real property income or interest on obligations of the United States which, by reason of section 882(d) or (e) and § 1.882-2, is treated as effectively connected for the taxable year with the conduct of a trade or business in the United States by that corporation. A foreign corporation to which this section applies must segregate its gross income for the taxable year into two categories, namely, the income which is effectively connected for the taxable year with the conduct of a trade or business in the United States by that corporation and the income which is not effectively connected for the taxable year with the conduct of a trade or business in the United States by that corporation. A separate tax shall then be determined upon each such category of income, as provided in paragraph (b) of this section. The determination of whether income or gain is or is not effectively connected for the taxable year with the conduct of a trade or business in the United States by the foreign corporation shall be made in accordance with section 864(c) and §§ 1.864-3 through 1.864-7. For purposes of this section income which is effectively connected for the taxable year with the conduct of a trade or business in the United States includes all income which is treated under section 882(d) or (e) and § 1.882-2 as income which is effectively connected for the taxable year with the conduct of a trade or business in the United States by the foreign corporation.

(b) *Imposition of tax*—(1) *Income not effectively connected with the conduct of a trade or business in the United States.* If a foreign corporation to which this section applies derives during the taxable year from sources within the United States income or gains described in section 881(a) and paragraph (b) or (c) of § 1.881-2 which are not effectively connected for the taxable year with the conduct of a trade or business in the United States by that corporation, such income or gains shall be subject to a flat tax of 30 percent of the aggregate amount of such items. This tax shall be determined in the manner, and subject to the same conditions, set forth in § 1.881-2 as though the income or gains were derived by a foreign corporation not engaged in trade or business in the United States during the taxable year, except that in applying paragraph (c) of such section there shall not be taken into account any gains which are taken into account in determining the tax under section 882(a)(1) and subparagraph (2) of this paragraph.

(2) *Income effectively connected with the conduct of a trade or business in the United States*—(i) *In general.* If a foreign corporation to which this section applies derives income or gains

Reg. § 1.882-1(b)(2)

which are effectively connected for the taxable year with the conduct of a trade or business in the United States by that corporation, the taxable income or gains shall, except as provided in § 1.871-12, be taxed in accordance with section 11 or, in the alternative, section 1201(a). See sections 11(f) and 882(a)(1). Any income of the foreign corporation which is not effectively connected for the taxable year with the conduct of a trade or business in the United States by that corporation shall not be taken into account in determining either the rate or amount of such tax.

(ii) *Determination of taxable income.* The taxable income for any taxable year for purposes of this subparagraph consists only of the foreign corporation's taxable income which is effectively connected for the taxable year with the conduct of a trade or business in the United States by that corporation; and, for this purpose, it is immaterial that the trade or business with which that income is effectively connected is not the same as the trade or business carried on in the United States by that corporation during the taxable year. See example (2) in § 1.864-4(b). In determining such taxable income all amounts constituting, or considered to be, gains or losses for the taxable year from the sale or exchange of capital assets shall be taken into account if such gains or losses are effectively connected for the taxable year with the conduct of a trade or business in the United States by that corporation.

(iii) *Cross references.* For rules for determining the gross income and deductions for the taxable year, see section 882(b) and (c)(1) and the regulations thereunder.

(c) *Change in trade or business status.* The principles of paragraph (c) of § 1.871-8 shall apply to cases where there has been a change in the trade or business status of a foreign corporation.

(d) *Credits against tax.* The credits allowed by section 32 (relating to tax withheld at source on foreign corporations), section 33 (relating to the foreign tax credit), section 38 (relating to investment in certain depreciable property), section 39 (relating to certain uses of gasoline and lubricating oil), section 40 (relating to expenses of work incentive programs), and section 6042 (relating to overpayments of a tax) shall be allowed against the tax determined in accordance with this section. However, the credits allowed by sections 33, 38, and 40 shall not be allowed against the flat tax of 30 percent imposed by section 881(a) and paragraph (b)(1) of this section. For special rules applicable in determining the foreign tax credit, see section 906(b) and the regulations thereunder. For the disallowance of certain credits where a return is not filed for the taxable year see section 882(c)(2) and the regulations thereunder.

(e) *Payment of estimated tax.* Every foreign corporation which for the taxable year is subject to tax under section 11 or 1201(a) and this section must make payment of its estimated tax in accordance with section 6154 and the regulations thereunder. In determining the amount of the estimated tax the foreign corporation must treat the tax imposed by section 881(a) and paragraph (b)(1) of this section as though it were a tax imposed by section 11.

(f) *Effective date.* This section applies for taxable years beginning after December 31, 1966. For corresponding rules applicable to taxable years beginning before January 1, 1967, see 26 CFR 1.882-1 (Rev. as of Jan. 1, 1971). [Reg. § 1.882-1.]

☐ [*T.D. 6258, 10-23-57. Amended by T.D. 7244, 12-29-72 and T.D. 7293, 11-27-73.*]

[Reg. § 1.882-2]

§ 1.882-2. **Income of foreign corporation treated as effectively connected with U.S. business.**—(a) *Election as to real property income.* A foreign corporation which during the taxable year derives any income from real property which is located in the United States, or derives income from any interest in any such real property, may elect, pursuant to section 882(d) and § 1.871-10, to treat all such income as income which is effectively connected for the taxable year with the conduct of a trade or business in the United States by that corporation. The election may be made whether or not the foreign corporation is engaged in trade or business in the United States during the taxable year for which the election is made or whether or not the corporation has income from real property which for the taxable year is effectively connected with the conduct of a trade or business in the United States, but it may be made only with respect to income from sources within the United States which, without regard to section 882(d) and § 1.871-10, is not effectively connected for the taxable year with the conduct of a trade or business in the United States by that corporation. The income to which the election applies shall be determined as provided in paragraph (b) of § 1.871-10 and shall be subject to tax in the manner, and subject to the same conditions, provided by section 882(a)(1) and paragraph (b)(2) of § 1.882-1. Section 871(d)(2) and (3) and the provisions of § 1.871-10 thereunder shall apply in respect of an election under section 882(d) in the same manner and to the same extent as they apply in respect of elections under section 871(d).

(b) *Interest on U.S. obligations received by banks organized in possessions.* Interest received from sources within the United States during the taxable year on obligations of the United States by a foreign corporation created or organized in, or under the law of, a possession of the United States and carrying on the banking business in a possession of the United States during the taxable year shall be treated, pursuant to section 882(e) and this paragraph, as income which is effectively connected for the taxable year with the conduct of a trade or business in the United States by that corporation. This paragraph applies whether or not the foreign corporation is engaged in trade or business in the United States at any time during the taxable year but only with respect to income which, without regard to this paragraph, is not effectively connected for the taxable year with the conduct of a trade or business in the United States by that corporation. Any interest to which this paragraph applies shall be subject to tax in the manner, and subject to the same conditions, provided by section 882(a)(1) and paragraph (b)(2) of § 1.882-1. To the extent that deductions are connected with interest to which this paragraph applies, they shall be treated for purposes of section 882(c)(1) and the regulations thereunder as connected with income which is effectively connected for the taxable year with the conduct of a trade or business in the United States by the foreign corporation. An election by the taxpayer is not required in respect of the income to which this paragraph applies. For purposes of this paragraph the term "possession of the United States" includes Guam, the Midway Islands, the Panama Canal Zone, the Commonwealth of Puerto Rico, American Samoa, the Virgin Islands, and Wake Island.

(c) *Treatment of income.* Any income in respect of which an election described in paragraph (a) of this section is in effect, and any interest to which paragraph (b) of this section applies, shall be treated, for purposes of paragraph (b)(2) of § 1.882-1 and paragraph (a) of § 1.441-4, as income which is effectively connected for the taxable year with the conduct of a trade or business in the United States by the foreign corporation. A foreign corporation shall not be treated as being engaged in trade or business in the United States merely by reason of having such income for the taxable year.

(d) *Effective date.* This section applies for taxable years beginning after December 31, 1966. There are no corresponding rules in this part for taxable years beginning before January 1, 1967. [Reg. § 1.882-2.]

☐ [T.D. 6258, 10-23-57. Amended by T.D. 7293, 11-27-73.]

[Reg. § 1.882-3]

§ 1.882-3. Gross income of a foreign corporation.—(a) *In general*—(1) *Inclusions.* The gross income of a foreign corporation for any taxable year includes only (i) the gross income which is derived from sources within the United States and which is not effectively connected for the taxable year with the conduct of a trade or business in the United States by that corporation, and (ii) the gross income, irrespective of whether such income is derived from sources within or without the United States, which is effectively connected for the taxable year with the conduct of a trade or business in the United States by that corporation. For the determination of the sources of income, see sections 861 through 863, and the regulations thereunder. For the determination of whether income from sources within or without the United States is effectively connected for the taxable year with the conduct of a trade or business in the United States, see sections 864(c) and 882(d) and (e), §§ 1.864-3 through 1.864-7, and § 1.882-2.

(2) *Exchange transactions.* Even though a foreign corporation which effects certain transactions in the United States in stocks, securities, or commodities during the taxable year may not, by reason of section 864(b)(2) and paragraph (c) or (d) of § 1.864-2, be engaged in trade or business in the United States during the taxable year through the effecting of such transactions, nevertheless it shall be required to include in gross income for the taxable year the gains and profits from those transactions to the extent required by paragraph (c) of § 1.881-2 or by paragraph (a) of § 1.882-1.

(3) *Exclusions.* For exclusions from gross income of a foreign corporation, see § 1.883-1.

(b) *Foreign corporations not engaged in U.S. business.* In the case of a foreign corporation which at no time during the taxable year is engaged in trade or business in the United States the gross income shall include only (1) the gross income from sources within the United States which is described in section 881(a) and paragraphs (b) and (c) of § 1.881-2, and (2) the gross income from sources within the United States which, by reason of section 882(d) or (e) and § 1.882-2, is treated as effectively connected for the taxable year with the conduct of a trade or business in the United States by that corporation.

(c) *Foreign corporations engaged in U.S. business.* In the case of a foreign corporation which is engaged in trade or business in the United States at any time during the taxable year, the gross income shall include (1) the gross income from sources within and without the United States which is effectively connected for the taxable year with the conduct of a trade or business in the

Reg. § 1.882-3(c)

United States by that corporation, (2) the gross income from sources within the United States which, by reason of section 882(d) or (e) and § 1.882-2, is treated as effectively connected for the taxable year with the conduct of a trade or business in the United States by that corporation, and (3) the gross income from sources within the United States which is described in section 881(a) and paragraphs (b) and (c) of § 1.881-2 and is not effectively connected for the taxable year with the conduct of a trade or business in the United States by that corporation.

(d) *Effective date.* This section applies for taxable years beginning after December 31, 1966. For corresponding rules applicable to taxable years beginning before January 1, 1967, see 26 CFR 1.882-2 (Rev. as of Jan. 1, 1971). [Reg. § 1.882-3.]

☐ [T.D. 6258, 10-23-57. Amended by T.D. 7293, 11-27-73.]

[Reg. § 1.882-4]

§ 1.882-4. **Allowance of deductions and credits to foreign corporations.**—(a) *Foreign corporations*—(1) *In general.* A foreign corporation that is engaged in, or receives income treated as effectively connected with, a trade or business within the United States is allowed the deductions which are properly allocated and apportioned to the foreign corporation's gross income which is effectively connected, or treated as effectively connected, with its conduct of a trade or business within the United States. The foreign corporation is entitled to credits which are attributable to that effectively connected income. No provision of this section (other than paragraph (b)(2)) shall be construed to deny the credits provided by sections 33, 34 and 852(b)(3)(D)(ii) or the deduction allowed by section 170.

(2) *Return necessary.* A foreign corporation shall receive the benefit of the deductions and credits otherwise allowed to it with respect to the income tax, only if it timely files or causes to be filed with the Philadelphia Service Center, in the manner prescribed in subtitle F, a true and accurate return of its taxable income which is effectively connected, or treated as effectively connected, for the taxable year with the conduct of a trade or business in the United States by that corporation. The deductions and credits allowed such a corporation electing under a tax convention to be subject to tax on a net basis may be obtained by filing a return of income in the manner prescribed in the regulations (if any) under the tax convention or under any other guidance issued by the Commissioner.

(3) *Filing deadline for return.* (i) As provided in paragraph (a)(2) of this section, for purposes of computing the foreign corporation's taxable income for any taxable year, otherwise allowable deductions (other than that allowed by section 170) and credits (other than those allowed by sections 33, 34 and 852(b)(3)(D)(ii)) will be allowed only if a return for that taxable year is filed by the foreign corporation on a timely basis. For taxable years of a foreign corporation ending after July 31, 1990, whether a return for the current taxable year has been filed on a timely basis is dependent upon whether the foreign corporation filed a return for the taxable year immediately preceding the current taxable year. If a return was filed for that immediately preceding taxable year, or if the current taxable year is the first taxable year of the foreign corporation for which a return is required to be filed, the required return for the current taxable year must be filed within 18 months of the due date as set forth in section 6072 and the regulations under that section, for filing the return for the current taxable year. If no return for the taxable year immediately preceding the current taxable year has been filed, the required return for the current taxable year (other than the first taxable year of the foreign corporation for which a return is required to be filed) must have been filed no later than the earlier of the date which is 18 months after the due date, as set forth in section 6072, for filing the return for the current taxable year or the date the Internal Revenue Service mails a notice to the foreign corporation advising the corporation that the current year tax return has not been filed and that no deductions (other than that allowed under section 170) or credits (other than those allowed under sections 33, 34 and 852(b)(3)(D)(ii)) may be claimed by the taxpayer.

(ii) The filing deadlines set forth in paragraph (a)(3)(i) of this section may be waived by the District Director or Assistant Commissioner (International), in rare and unusual circumstances if good cause for such waiver, based on the facts and circumstances, is established by the foreign corporation.

(iii) A foreign corporation which has a permanent establishment, as defined in an income tax treaty between the United States and the foreign corporation's country of residence, in the United States is subject to the filing deadlines set forth in paragraph (a)(3)(i) of this section.

(iv) If a foreign corporation conducts limited activities in the United States in a taxable year which the foreign corporation determines does not give rise to gross income which is effectively connected with the conduct of a trade or business within the United States as defined in sections 882(b) and 864(b) and (c) and the regulations under those sections, the foreign corporation may nonetheless file a return for that taxable year on a timely basis under paragraph (a)(3)(i) of this section and thereby protect the right to receive the benefit of the deductions and credits attributable to that gross income if it is later determined, after the return was filed, that the original determination was incorrect. On that timely filed return, the foreign corporation is not required to report any gross income as effectively connected with a United States trade or business or any deductions or credits but should attach a statement indicating that the return is being filed for the reason set forth in this paragraph (a)(3). If the foreign corporation determines that part of the activities which it conducts in the United States in a taxable year gives rise to gross income which is effectively connected with the conduct of a trade or business and part does not, the foreign corporation must timely file a return for that taxable year to report the gross income determined to be effectively connected, or treated as effectively connected, with the conduct of the trade or business within the United States and the deductions and credits attributable to the gross income. In addition, the foreign corporation should attach to that return the statement described in this paragraph (b)(3) with regard to the other activities. The foreign corporation may follow the same procedure if it determines initially that it has no United States tax liability under the provisions of an applicable income tax treaty. In the event the foreign corporation relies on the provisions of an income tax treaty to reduce or eliminate the income subject to taxation, or to reduce the rate of tax, disclosure may be required pursuant to section 6114.

(v) In order to be eligible for any deductions and credits for purposes of computing the accumulated earnings tax of section 531, a foreign corporation must file a true and accurate return; on a timely basis, in the manner as set forth in paragraph (a)(2) and (3) of this section.

(4) *Return by Internal Revenue Service.* If a foreign corporation has various sources of income within the United States and a return of income has not been filed, in the manner prescribed by subtitle F, including the filing deadlines set forth in paragraph (a)(3) of this section, the Internal Revenue Service shall:

(i) Cause a return of income to be made,

(ii) Include on the return the income described in § 1.882-1 of that corporation from all sources concerning which it has information, and

(iii) Assess the tax and collect it from one or more of those sources of income within the United States, without allowance for any deductions (other than that allowed by section 170) or credits (other than those allowed by sections 33, 34 and 852(b)(3)(D)(ii)).

If the income of the corporation is not effectively connected with, or if the corporation did not receive income that is treated as being effectively connected with, the conduct of a United States trade or business, the tax will be assessed under § 1.882-1(b)(1) on a gross basis, without allowance for any deduction (other than that allowed by section 170) or credit (other than the credits allowed by sections 33, 34 and 852(b)(3)(d)(ii)). If the income is effectively connected, or treated as effectively connected, with the conduct of a United States trade or business, tax will be assessed in accordance with either section 11, 55 or 1201(a) without allowance for any deduction (other than that allowed by section 170) or credit (other than the credits allowed by sections 33, 34 and 852(b)(3)(D)(ii)).

(b) *Allowed deductions and credits*—(1) *In general.* Except for the deduction allowed under section 170 for charitable contributions and gifts (see section 882(c)(1)(B)), deductions are allowed to a foreign corporation only to the extent they are connected with gross income which is effectively connected, or treated as effectively connected, with the conduct of a trade or business in the United States. Deductible expenses (other than interest expense) are properly allocated and apportioned to effectively connected gross income in accordance with the rules of § 1.861-8. For the method of determining the interest deduction allowed to a foreign corporation, see § 1.882-5. Other than the credits allowed by sections 33, 34 and 852(b)(3)(D)(ii), the foreign corporation is entitled to credits only if they are attributable to effectively connected income. See paragraph (a)(2) of this section for the requirement that a return be filed. Except as provided by section 906, a foreign corporation shall not be allowed the credit against the tax for taxes of foreign countries and possessions of the United States allowed by section 901.

(2) *Verification.* At the request of the Internal Revenue Service, a foreign corporation claiming deductions from gross income which is effectively connected, or treated as effectively connected, with the conduct of a trade or business in the United States or credits which are attributable to that income must furnish at the place designated pursuant to § 301.7605-1(a) information sufficient to establish that the corporation is entitled to the deductions and credits in the amounts claimed. All information must be furnished in a form suitable to permit verification of claimed deductions and credits. The Internal Rev-

Reg. § 1.882-4(b)(2)

enue Service may require, as appropriate, that an English translation be provided with any information in a foreign language. If a foreign corporation fails to furnish sufficient information, the Internal Revenue Service may in its discretion disallow any claimed deductions and credits in full or in part. For additional filing requirements and for penalties for failure to provide information, see also section 6038A. [Reg. § 1.882-4.]

☐ [T.D. 6258, 10-23-57. Amended by T.D. 7749, 12-30-80 and T.D. 8322, 12-10-90.]

[Reg. § 1.882-5]

§ 1.882-5. Determination of interest deduction.—(a) *Rules of general application*—(1) *Overview*—(i) *In general.* The amount of interest expense of a foreign corporation that is allocable under section 882(c) to income which is (or is treated as) effectively connected with the conduct of a trade or business within the United States (ECI) is the sum of the interest paid or accrued by the foreign corporation on its liabilities booked in the United States, as adjusted under the three-step process set forth in paragraphs (b), (c) and (d) of this section and the specially allocated interest expense determined under section (a)(1)(ii) of this section. The provisions of this section provide the exclusive rules for allocating interest expense to the ECI of a foreign corporation. Under the three-step process, the total value of the U.S. assets of a foreign corporation is first determined under paragraph (b) of this section (Step 1). Next, the amount of U.S.-connected liabilities is determined under paragraph (c) of this section (Step 2). Finally, the amount of interest paid or accrued on liabilities booked in the United States, as determined under paragraph (d)(2) of this section, is adjusted for interest expense attributable to the difference between U.S.-connected liabilities and U.S. booked liabilities (Step 3). Alternatively, a foreign corporation may elect to determine its interest rate on U.S.-connected liabilities by reference to its U.S. assets, using the separate currency pools method described in paragraph (e) of this section.

(ii) *Direct allocations*—(A) *In general.* A foreign corporation that has a U.S. asset and indebtedness that meet the requirements of § 1.861-10T(b) and (c), as limited by § 1.861-10T(d)(1), may directly allocate interest expense from such indebtedness to income from such asset in the manner and to the extent provided in § 1.861-10T. For purposes of paragraphs (b)(1) or (c)(2) of this section, a foreign corporation that allocates its interest expense under the direct allocation rule of this paragraph (a)(1)(ii)(A) shall reduce the basis of the asset that meets the requirements of § 1.861-10T(b) and (c) by the principal amount of the indebtedness that meets the requirements of § 1.861-10T(b) and (c). The foreign corporation shall also disregard any indebtedness that meets the requirements of § 1.861-10T(b) and (c) in determining the amount of the foreign corporation's liabilities under paragraphs (c)(2) and (d)(2) of this section, and shall not take into account any interest expense paid or accrued with respect to such a liability for purposes of paragraphs (d) or (e) of this section.

(B) *Partnership interest.* A foreign corporation that is a partner in a partnership that has a U.S. asset and indebtedness that meet the requirements of § 1.861-10T(b) and (c), as limited by § 1.861-10T(d)(1), may directly allocate its distributive share of interest expense from that indebtedness to its distributive share of income from that asset in the manner and to the extent provided in § 1.861-10T. A foreign corporation that allocates its distributive share of interest expense under the direct allocation rule of this paragraph (a)(1)(ii)(B) shall disregard any partnership indebtedness that meets the requirements of § 1.861-10T(b) and (c) in determining the amount of its distributive share of partnership liabilities for purposes of paragraphs (b)(1), (c)(2)(vi), and (d)(2)(vii) or (e)(1)(ii) of this section, and shall not take into account any partnership interest expense paid or accrued with respect to such a liability for purposes of paragraph (d) or (e) of this section. For purposes of paragraph (b)(1) of this section, a foreign corporation that directly allocates its distributive share of interest expense under this paragraph (a)(1)(ii)(B) shall—

(*1*) Reduce the partnership's basis in such asset by the amount of such indebtedness in allocating its basis in the partnership under § 1.884-1(d)(3)(ii); or

(*2*) Reduce the partnership's income from such asset by the partnership's interest expense from such indebtedness under § 1.884-1(d)(3)(iii).

(2) *Coordination with tax treaties.* The provisions of this section provide the exclusive rules for determining the interest expense attributable to the business profits of a permanent establishment under a U.S. income tax treaty.

(3) *Limitation on interest expense.* In no event may the amount of interest expense computed under this section exceed the amount of interest on indebtedness paid or accrued by the taxpayer within the taxable year (translated into U.S. dollars at the weighted average exchange rate for each currency prescribed by § 1.989(b)-1 for the taxable year).

Reg. § 1.882-5(a)(1)

(4) *Translation convention for foreign currency.* For each computation required by this section, the taxpayer shall translate values and amounts into the relevant currency at a spot rate or a weighted average exchange rate consistent with the method such taxpayer uses for financial reporting purposes, provided such method is applied consistently from year to year. Interest expense paid or accrued, however, shall be translated under the rules of § 1.988-2. The district director or the Assistant Commissioner (International) may require that any or all computations required by this section be made in U.S. dollars if the functional currency of the taxpayer's home office is a hyperinflationary currency, as defined in § 1.985-1, and the computation in U.S. dollars is necessary to prevent distortions.

(5) *Coordination with other sections.* Any provision that disallows, defers, or capitalizes interest expense applies after determining the amount of interest expense allocated to ECI under this section. For example, in determining the amount of interest expense that is disallowed as a deduction under section 265 or 163(j), deferred under section 163(e)(3) or 267(a)(3), or capitalized under section 263A with respect to a United States trade or business, a taxpayer takes into account only the amount of interest expense allocable to ECI under this section.

(6) *Special rule for foreign governments.* The amount of interest expense of a foreign government, as defined in § 1.892-2T(a), that is allocable to ECI is the total amount of interest paid or accrued within the taxable year by the United States trade or business on U.S. booked liabilities (as defined in paragraph (d)(2) of this section). Interest expense of a foreign government, however, is not allocable to ECI to the extent that it is incurred with respect to U.S. booked liabilities that exceed 80 percent of the total value of U.S. assets for the taxable year (determined under paragraph (b) of this section). This paragraph (a)(6) does not apply to controlled commercial entities within the meaning of § 1.892-5T.

(7) *Elections under § 1.882-5*—(i) *In general.* A corporation must make each election provided in this section on the corporation's federal income tax return for the first taxable year beginning on or after the effective date of this section. An amended return does not qualify for this purpose, nor shall the provisions of § 301.9100-1 of this chapter and any guidance promulgated thereunder apply. Each election under this section, whether an election for the first taxable year or a subsequent change of election, shall be made by the corporation calculating its interest expense deduction in accordance with the methods elected. An elected method must be used for a minimum period of five years before the taxpayer may elect a different method. To change an election before the end of the requisite five-year period, a taxpayer must obtain the consent of the Commissioner or her delegate. The Commissioner or her delegate will generally consent to a taxpayer's request to change its election only in rare and unusual circumstances.

(ii) *Failure to make the proper election.* If a taxpayer, for any reason, fails to make an election provided in this section in a timely fashion, the district director or the Assistant Commissioner (International) may make any or all of the elections provided in this section on behalf of the taxpayer, and such elections shall be binding as if made by the taxpayer.

(8) *Examples.* The following examples illustrate the application of paragraph (a) of this section:

Example 1. Direct allocations. (i) *Facts*: FC is a foreign corporation that conducts business through a branch, B, in the United States. Among B's U.S. assets is an interest in a partnership, P, that is engaged in airplane leasing solely in the U.S. FC contributes 200x to P in exchange for its partnership interest. P incurs qualified nonrecourse indebtedness within the meaning of § 1.861-10T to purchase an airplane. FC's share of the liability of P, as determined under section 752, is 800x.

(ii) *Analysis*: Pursuant to paragraph (a)(1)(ii)(B) of this section, FC is permitted to directly allocate its distributive share of the interest incurred with respect to the qualified nonrecourse indebtedness to FC's distributive share of the rental income generated by the airplane. A liability the interest on which is allocated directly to the income from a particular asset under paragraph (a)(1)(ii)(B) of this section is disregarded for purposes of paragraphs (b)(1), (c)(2)(vi), and (d)(2)(vii) or (e)(1)(ii) of this section. Consequently, for purposes of determining the value of FC's assets under paragraphs (b)(1) and (c)(2)(vi) of this section, FC's basis in P is reduced by the 800x liability as determined under section 752, but is not increased by the 800x liability that is directly allocated under paragraph (a)(1)(ii)(B) of this section. Similarly, pursuant to paragraph (a)(1)(ii)(B) of this section, the 800x liability is disregarded for purposes of determining FC's liabilities under paragraphs (c)(2)(vi) and (d)(2)(vii) of this section.

Example 2. Limitation on interest expense— (i) FC is a foreign corporation that conducts a real estate business in the United States. In its 1997

Reg. § 1.882-5(a)(8)

tax year, *FC* has no outstanding indebtedness, and therefore incurs no interest expense. *FC* elects to use the 50% fixed ratio under paragraph (c)(4) of this section.

(ii) Under paragraph (a)(3) of this section, *FC* is not allowed to deduct any interest expense that exceeds the amount of interest on indebtedness paid or accrued in that taxable year. Since *FC* incurred no interest expense in taxable year 1997, *FC* will not be entitled to any interest deduction for that year under § 1.882-5, notwithstanding the fact that *FC* has elected to use the 50% fixed ratio.

Example 3. Coordination with other sections—(i) *FC* is a foreign corporation that is a bank under section 585(a)(2) and a financial institution under section 265(b)(5). *FC* is a calendar year taxpayer, and operates a U.S. branch, *B*. Throughout its taxable year 1997, *B* holds only two assets that are U.S. assets within the meaning of paragraph (b)(1) of this section. *FC* does not make a fair-market value election under paragraph (b)(2)(ii) of this section, and, therefore, values its U.S. assets according to their bases under paragraph (b)(2)(i) of this section. The first asset is a taxable security with an adjusted basis of $100. The second asset is an obligation the interest on which is exempt from federal taxation under section 103, with an adjusted basis of $50. The tax-exempt obligation is not a qualified tax-exempt obligation as defined by section 265(b)(3)(B).

(ii) *FC* calculates its interest expense under § 1.882-5 to be $12. Under paragraph (a)(5) of this section, however, a portion of the interest expense that is allocated to *FC*'s effectively connected income under § 1.882-5 is disallowed in accordance with the provisions of section 265(b). Using the methodology prescribed under section 265, the amount of disallowed interest expense is $4, calculated as follows:

$$\$12 \times \frac{\$50 \text{ Tax-exempt U.S. assets}}{\$150 \text{ Total U.S. assets}} = \$4$$

(iii) Therefore, *FC* deducts a total of $8 ($12 - $4) of interest expense attributable to its effectively connected income in 1997.

Example 4. Treaty exempt asset—(i) *FC* is a foreign corporation, resident in Country X, that is actively engaged in the banking business in the United States through a permanent establishment, *B*. The income tax treaty in effect between Country X and the United States provides that *FC* is not taxable on foreign source income earned by its U.S. permanent establishment. In its 1997 tax year, *B* earns $90 of U.S. source income from U.S. assets with an adjusted tax basis of $900, and $12 of foreign source interest income from U.S. assets with an adjusted tax basis of $100. *FC*'s U.S. interest expense deduction, computed in accordance with § 1.882-5, is $500.

(ii) Under paragraph (a)(5) of this section, *FC* is required to apply any provision that disallows, defers, or capitalizes interest expense after determining the interest expense allocated to ECI under § 1.882-5. Section 265(a)(2) disallows interest expense that is allocable to one or more classes of income that are wholly exempt from taxation under subtitle A of the Internal Revenue Code. Section 1.265-1(b) provides that income wholly exempt from taxes includes both income excluded from tax under any provision of subtitle A and income wholly exempt from taxes under any other law. Section 894 specifies that the provisions of subtitle A are applied with due regard to any relevant treaty obligation of the United States. Because the treaty between the United States and Country X exempts foreign source income earned by *B* from U.S. tax, *FC* has assets that produce income wholly exempt from taxes under subtitle A, and must therefore allocate a portion of its § 1.882-5 interest expense to its exempt income. Using the methodology prescribed under section 265, the amount of disallowed interest expense is $50, calculated as follows:

$$\$500 \times \frac{\$100 \text{ Treaty-exempt U.S. assets}}{\$1000 \text{ Total U.S. assets}} = \$50$$

(iii) Therefore, *FC* deducts a total of $450 ($500 $50) of interest expense attributable to its effectively connected income in 1997.

(b) *Step 1: Determination of total value of U.S. assets for the taxable year*—(1) *Classification of an asset as a U.S. asset*—(i) *General rule*. Except as otherwise provided in this paragraph (b)(1), an asset is a U.S. asset for purposes of this section to the extent that it is a U.S. asset under § 1.884-1(d). For purposes of this section, the term *determination date*, as used in § 1.884-1(d), means each day for which the total value of U.S. assets is computed under paragraph (b)(3) of this section.

(ii) *Items excluded from the definition of U.S. asset*. For purposes of this section, the term U.S. asset excludes an asset to the extent it produces income or gain described in sections 883(a)(3) and (b).

(iii) *Items included in the definition of U.S. asset*. For purposes of this section, the term U.S. asset includes—

(A) U.S. real property held in a wholly-owned domestic subsidiary of a foreign corporation that qualifies as a bank under section 585(a)(2)(B) (without regard to the second sen-

Reg. § 1.882-5(b)(1)

tence thereof), provided that the real property would qualify as used in the foreign corporation's trade or business within the meaning of § 1.864-4(c)(2) or (3) if held directly by the foreign corporation and either was initially acquired through foreclosure or similar proceedings or is U.S. real property occupied by the foreign corporation (the value of which shall be adjusted by the amount of any indebtedness that is reflected in the value of the property);

(B) An asset that produces income treated as ECI under section 921(d) or 926(b) (relating to certain income of a FSC and certain dividends paid by a FSC to a foreign corporation);

(C) An asset that produces income treated as ECI under section 953(c)(3)(C) (relating to certain income of a captive insurance company that a corporation elects to treat as ECI) that is not otherwise ECI; and

(D) An asset that produces income treated as ECI under section 882(e) (relating to certain interest income of possessions banks).

(iv) *Interbranch transactions.* A transaction of any type between separate offices or branches of the same taxpayer does not create a U.S. asset.

(v) *Assets acquired to increase U.S. assets artificially.* An asset shall not be treated as a U.S. asset if one of the principal purposes for acquiring or using that asset is to increase artificially the U.S. assets of a foreign corporation on the determination date. Whether an asset is acquired or used for such purpose will depend upon all the facts and circumstances of each case. Factors to be considered in determining whether one of the principal purposes in acquiring or using an asset is to increase artificially the U.S. assets of a foreign corporation include the length of time during which the asset was used in a U.S. trade or business, whether the asset was acquired from a related person, and whether the aggregate value of the U.S. assets of the foreign corporation increased temporarily on or around the determination date. A purpose may be a principal purpose even though it is outweighed by other purposes (taken together or separately).

(2) *Determination of the value of a U.S. asset*—(i) *General rule.* The value of a U.S. asset is the adjusted basis of the asset for determining gain or loss from the sale or other disposition of that item, further adjusted as provided in paragraph (b)(2)(iii) of this section.

(ii) *Fair-market value election*—(A) *In general.* A taxpayer may elect to value all of its U.S. assets on the basis of fair market value, subject to the requirements of § 1.861-9T(g)(1)(iii), and provided the taxpayer uses the methodology prescribed in § 1.861-9T(h). Once elected, the fair market value must be used by the taxpayer for both Step 1 and Step 2 described in paragraphs (b) and (c) of this section, and must be used in all subsequent taxable years unless the Commissioner or her delegate consents to a change.

(B) *Adjustment to partnership basis.* If a partner makes a fair market value election under paragraph (b)(2)(ii) of this section, the value of the partner's interest in a partnership that is treated as an asset shall be the fair market value of his partnership interest, increased by the fair market value of the partner's share of the liabilities determined under paragraph (c)(2)(vi) of this section. See § 1.884-1(d)(3).

(iii) *Reduction of total value of U.S. assets by amount of bad debt reserves under section 585*—(A) *In general.* The total value of loans that qualify as U.S. assets shall be reduced by the amount of any reserve for bad debts additions to which are allowed as deductions under section 585.

(B) *Example.* The following example illustrates the provisions of paragraph (b)(2)(iii)(A) of this section:

Example. Foreign banks; bad debt reserves. FC is a foreign corporation that qualifies as a bank under section 585(a)(2)(B) (without regard to the second sentence thereof), but is not a large bank as defined in section 585(c)(2). FC conducts business through a branch, B, in the United States. Among B's U.S. assets are a portfolio of loans with an adjusted basis of $500. FC accounts for its bad debts for U.S. federal income tax purposes under the reserve method, and B maintains a deductible reserve for bad debts of $50. Under paragraph (b)(2)(iii) of this section, the total value of FC's portfolio of loans is $450 ($500 $50).

(iv) *Adjustment to basis of financial instruments.* [Reserved]

(3) *Computation of total value of U.S. assets.* The total value of U.S. assets for the taxable year is the average of the sums of the values (determined under paragraph (b)(2) of this section) of U.S. assets. For each U.S. asset, value shall be computed at the most frequent, regular intervals for which data are reasonably available. In no event shall the value of any U.S. asset be computed less frequently than monthly (beginning of taxable year and monthly thereafter) by a large bank (as defined in section 585(c)(2)) and semiannually (beginning, middle and end of taxable year) by any other taxpayer.

(c) *Step 2: Determination of total amount of U.S.-connected liabilities for the taxable year*—(1)

Reg. § 1.882-5(c)(1)

General rule. The amount of U.S.-connected liabilities for the taxable year equals the total value of U.S. assets for the taxable year (as determined under paragraph (b)(3) of this section) multiplied by the actual ratio for the taxable year (as determined under paragraph (c)(2) of this section) or, if the taxpayer has made an election in accordance with paragraph (c)(4) of this section, by the fixed ratio.

(2) *Computation of the actual ratio*—(i) *In general.* A taxpayer's actual ratio for the taxable year is the total amount of its worldwide liabilities for the taxable year divided by the total value of its worldwide assets for the taxable year. The total amount of worldwide liabilities and the total value of worldwide assets for the taxable year is the average of the sums of the amounts of the taxpayer's worldwide liabilities and the values of its worldwide assets (determined under paragraphs (c)(2)(iii) and (iv) of this section). In each case, the sums must be computed semi-annually (beginning, middle and end of taxable year) by a large bank (as defined in section 585(c)(2)) and annually (beginning and end of taxable year) by any other taxpayer.

(ii) *Classification of items.* The classification of an item as a liability or an asset must be consistent from year to year and in accordance with U.S. tax principles.

(iii) *Determination of amount of worldwide liabilities.* The amount of a liability must be determined consistently from year to year and must be substantially in accordance with U.S. tax principles. To be substantially in accordance with U.S. tax principles, the principles used to determine the amount of a liability must not differ from U.S. tax principles to a degree that will materially affect the value of taxpayer's worldwide liabilities or the taxpayer's actual ratio.

(iv) *Determination of value of worldwide assets.* The value of an asset must be determined consistently from year to year and must be substantially in accordance with U.S. tax principles. To be substantially in accordance with U.S. tax principles, the principles used to determine the value of an asset must not differ from U.S. tax principles to a degree that will materially affect the value of the taxpayer's worldwide assets or the taxpayer's actual ratio. The value of an asset is the adjusted basis of that asset for determining the gain or loss from the sale or other disposition of that asset, adjusted in the same manner as the basis of U.S. assets are adjusted under paragraphs (b)(2)(ii) through (iv) of this section.

(v) *Hedging transactions.* [Reserved]

(vi) *Treatment of partnership interests and liabilities.* For purposes of computing the actual ratio, the value of a partner's interest in a partnership that will be treated as an asset is the partner's adjusted basis in its partnership interest, reduced by the partner's share of liabilities of the partnership as determined under section 752 and increased by the partner's share of liabilities determined under this paragraph (c)(2)(vi). If the partner has made a fair market value election under paragraph (b)(2)(ii) of this section, the value of its interest in the partnership shall be increased by the fair market value of the partner's share of the liabilities determined under this paragraph (c)(2)(vi). For purposes of this section a partner shares in any liability of a partnership in the same proportion that it shares, for income tax purposes, in the expense attributable to that liability for the taxable year. A partner's adjusted basis in a partnership interest cannot be less than zero.

(vii) *Computation of actual ratio of insurance companies.* [Reserved]

(viii) *Interbranch transactions.* A transaction of any type between separate offices or branches of the same taxpayer does not create an asset or a liability.

(ix) *Amounts must be expressed in a single currency.* The actual ratio must be computed in either U.S. dollars or the functional currency of the home office of the taxpayer, and that currency must be used consistently from year to year. For example, a taxpayer that determines the actual ratio annually using British pounds converted at the spot rate for financial reporting purposes must translate the U.S. dollar values of assets and amounts of liabilities of the U.S. trade or business into pounds using the spot rate on the last day of its taxable year. The district director or the Assistant Commissioner (International) may require that the actual ratio be computed in dollars if the functional currency of the taxpayer's home office is a hyperinflationary currency, as defined in § 1.985-1, that materially distorts the actual ratio.

(3) *Adjustments.* The district director or the Assistant Commissioner (International) may make appropriate adjustments to prevent a foreign corporation from intentionally and artificially increasing its actual ratio. For example, the district director or the Assistant Commissioner (International) may offset a loan made from or to one person with a loan made to or from another person if any of the parties to the loans are related persons, within the meaning of section 267(b) or 707(b)(1), and one of the principal purposes for entering into the loans was to increase artificially the actual ratio of a foreign corporation. A purpose may be a principal purpose even though it is

Reg. § 1.882-5(c)(2)

outweighed by other purposes (taken together or separately).

(4) *Elective fixed ratio method of determining U.S. liabilities.* A taxpayer that is a bank as defined in section 585(a)(2)(B)(without regard to the second sentence thereof) may elect to use a fixed ratio of 93 percent in lieu of the actual ratio. A taxpayer that is neither a bank nor an insurance company may elect to use a fixed ratio of 50 percent in lieu of the actual ratio.

(5) *Examples.* The following examples illustrate the application of paragraph (c) of this section:

Example 1. Classification of item not in accordance with U.S. tax principles. Bank Z, a resident of country X, has a branch in the United States through which it conducts its banking business. In preparing its financial statements in country X, Z treats an instrument documented as perpetual subordinated debt as a liability. Under U.S. tax principles, however, this instrument is treated as equity. Consequently, the classification of this instrument as a liability for purposes of paragraph (c)(2)(iii) of this section is not in accordance with U.S. tax principles.

Example 2. Valuation of item not substantially in accordance with U.S. tax principles. Bank Z, a resident of country X, has a branch in the United States through which it conducts its banking business. Bank Z is a large bank as defined in section 585(c)(2). The tax rules of country X allow Bank Z to take deductions for additions to certain reserves. Bank Z decreases the value of the assets on its financial statements by the amounts of the reserves. The additions to the reserves under country X tax rules cause the value of Bank Z's assets to differ from the value of those assets determined under U.S. tax principles to a degree that materially affects the value of taxpayer's worldwide assets. Consequently, the valuation of Bank Z's worldwide assets under country X tax principles is not substantially in accordance with U.S. tax principles. Bank Z must increase the value of its worldwide assets under paragraph (c)(2)(iii) of this section by the amount of its country X reserves.

Example 3. Valuation of item substantially in accordance with U.S. tax principles. Bank Z, a resident of country X, has a branch in the United States through which it conducts its banking business. In determining the value of its worldwide assets, Bank Z computes the adjusted basis of certain non-U.S. assets according to the depreciation methodology provided under country X tax laws, which is different than the depreciation methodology provided under U.S. tax law. If the depreciation methodology provided under country X tax laws does not differ from U.S. tax principles to a degree that materially affects the value of Bank Z's worldwide assets or Bank Z's actual ratio as computed under paragraph (c)(2) of this section, then the valuation of Bank Z's worldwide assets under paragraph (c)(2)(iv) of this section is substantially in accordance with U.S. tax principles.

Example 4. [Reserved]

Example 5. Adjustments. FC is a foreign corporation engaged in the active conduct of a banking business through a branch, B, in the United States. P, an unrelated foreign corporation, deposits $100,000 in the home office of FC. Shortly thereafter, in a transaction arranged by the home office of FC, B lends $80,000 bearing interest at an arm's length rate to S, a wholly owned U.S. subsidiary of P. The district director or the Assistant Commissioner (International) determines that one of the principal purposes for making and incurring such loans is to increase FC's actual ratio. For purposes of this section, therefore, P is treated as having directly lent $80,000 to S. Thus, for purposes of paragraph (c) of this section (Step 2), the district director or the Assistant Commissioner (International) may offset FC's liability and asset arising from this transaction, resulting in a net liability of $20,000 that is not a booked liability of B. Because the loan to S from B was initiated and arranged by the home office of FC, with no material participation by B, the loan to S will not be treated as a U.S. asset.

(d) *Step 3: Determination of amount of interest expense allocable to ECI under the adjusted U.S. booked liabilities method*—(1) *General rule.* The adjustment to the amount of interest expense paid or accrued on U.S. booked liabilities is determined by comparing the amount of U.S.-connected liabilities for the taxable year, as determined under paragraph (c) of this section, with the average total amount of U.S. booked liabilities, as determined under paragraphs (d)(2) and (3) of this section. If the average total amount of U.S. booked liabilities equals or exceeds the amount of U.S.-connected liabilities, the adjustment to the interest expense on U.S. booked liabilities is determined under paragraph (d)(4) of this section. If the amount of U.S.-connected liabilities exceeds the average total amount of U.S. booked liabilities, the adjustment to the amount of interest expense paid or accrued on U.S. booked liabilities is determined under paragraph (d)(5) of this section.

(2) *U.S. booked liabilities*—(i) *In general.* A liability is a *U.S. booked liability* if it is properly reflected on the books of the U.S. trade or busi-

Reg. § 1.882-5(d)(2)

ness, within the meaning of paragraph (d)(2)(ii) or (iii) of this section.

(ii) *Properly reflected on the books of the U.S. trade or business of a foreign corporation that is not a bank*—(A) *In general.* A liability, whether interest bearing or non-interest bearing, is properly reflected on the books of the U.S. trade or business of a foreign corporation that is not a bank as described in section 585(a)(2)(B) (without regard to the second sentence thereof) if—

(*1*) The liability is secured predominantly by a U.S. asset of the foreign corporation;

(*2*) The foreign corporation enters the liability on a set of books relating to an activity that produces ECI at a time reasonably contemporaneous with the time at which the liability is incurred; or

(*3*) The foreign corporation maintains a set of books and records relating to an activity that produces ECI and the District Director or Assistant Commissioner (International) determines that there is a direct connection or relationship between the liability and that activity. Whether there is a direct connection between the liability and an activity that produces ECI depends on the facts and circumstances of each case.

(B) *Identified liabilities not properly reflected.* A liability is not properly reflected on the books of the U.S. trade or business merely because a foreign corporation identifies the liability pursuant to § 1.884-4(b)(1)(ii) and (b)(3).

(iii) *Properly reflected on the books of the U.S. trade or business of a foreign corporation that is a bank*—(A) *In general.* A liability, whether interest bearing or non-interest bearing, is properly reflected on the books of the U.S. trade or business of a foreign corporation that is a bank as described in section 585(a)(2)(B) (without regard to the second sentence thereof) if—

(*1*) The bank enters the liability on a set of books relating to an activity that produces ECI before the close of the day on which the liability is incurred; and

(*2*) There is a direct connection or relationship between the liability and that activity. Whether there is a direct connection between the liability and an activity that produces ECI depends on the facts and circumstances of each case.

(B) *Inadvertent error.* If a bank fails to enter a liability in the books of the activity that produces ECI before the close of the day on which the liability was incurred, the liability may be treated as a U.S. booked liability only if, under the facts and circumstances, the taxpayer demonstrates a direct connection or relationship between the liability and the activity that produces ECI and the failure to enter the liability in those books was due to inadvertent error.

(iv) *Liabilities of insurance companies.* [Reserved]

(v) *Liabilities used to increase artificially interest expense on U.S. booked liabilities.* U.S. booked liabilities shall not include a liability if one of the principal purposes for incurring or holding the liability is to increase artificially the interest expense on the U.S. booked liabilities of a foreign corporation. Whether a liability is incurred or held for the purpose of artificially increasing interest expense will depend upon all the facts and circumstances of each case. Factors to be considered in determining whether one of the principal purposes for incurring or holding a liability is to increase artificially the interest expense on U.S. booked liabilities of a foreign corporation include whether the interest expense on the liability is excessive when compared to other liabilities of the foreign corporation denominated in the same currency and whether the currency denomination of the liabilities of the U.S. branch substantially matches the currency denomination of the U.S. branch's assets. A purpose may be a principal purpose even though it is outweighed by other purposes (taken together or separately).

(vi) *Hedging transactions.* [Reserved]

(vii) *Amount of U.S. booked liabilities of a partner.* A partner's share of liabilities of a partnership is considered a booked liability of the partner provided that it is properly reflected on the books (within the meaning of paragraph (d)(2)(ii) of this section) of the U.S. trade or business of the partnership.

(viii) *Interbranch transactions.* A transaction of any type between separate offices or branches of the same taxpayer does not result in the creation of a liability.

(3) *Average total amount of U.S. booked liabilities.* The *average total amount* of U.S. booked liabilities for the taxable year is the average of the sums of the amounts (determined under paragraph (d)(2) of this section) of U.S. booked liabilities. The amount of U.S. booked liabilities shall be computed at the most frequent, regular intervals for which data are reasonably available. In no event shall the amount of U.S. booked liabilities be computed less frequently than monthly by a large bank (as defined in section 585(c)(2)) and semi-annually by any other taxpayer.

(4) *Interest expense where U.S. booked liabilities equal or exceed U.S. liabilities*—(i) *In general.* If the average total amount of U.S. booked liabilities (as determined in paragraphs (d)(2) and (3) of this section) exceeds the amount of U.S.-

Reg. § 1.882-5(d)(3)

connected liabilities (as determined under paragraph (c) of this section (Step 2)), the interest expense allocable to ECI is the product of the total amount of interest paid or accrued within the taxable year by the U.S. trade or business on U.S. booked liabilities and the scaling ratio set out in paragraph (d)(4)(ii) of this section. For purposes of this section, the reduction resulting from the application of the scaling ratio is applied prorata to all interest expense paid or accrued by the foreign corporation. A similar reduction in income, expense, gain, or loss from a hedging transaction (as described in paragraph (d)(2)(vi) of this section) must also be determined by multiplying such income, expense, gain, or loss by the scaling ratio. If the average total amount of U.S. booked liabilities (as determined in paragraph (d)(3) of this section) equals the amount of U.S.-connected liabilities (as determined under Step 2), the interest expense allocable to ECI is the total amount of interest paid or accrued within the taxable year by the U.S. trade or business on U.S. booked liabilities.

(ii) *Scaling ratio.* For purposes of this section, the scaling ratio is a fraction the numerator of which is the amount of U.S.-connected liabilities and the denominator of which is the average total amount of U.S. booked liabilities.

(iii) *Special rules for insurance companies.* [Reserved]

(5) *U.S.-connected interest rate where U.S. booked liabilities are less than U.S.-connected liabilities*—(i) *In general.* If the amount of U.S.-connected liabilities (as determined under paragraph (c) of this section (Step 2)) exceeds the average total amount of U.S. booked liabilities, the interest expense allocable to ECI is the total amount of interest paid or accrued within the taxable year by the U.S. trade or business on U.S. booked liabilities, plus the excess of the amount of U.S.-connected liabilities over the average total amount of U.S. booked liabilities multiplied by the interest rate determined under paragraph (d)(5)(ii) of this section.

(ii) *Interest rate on excess U.S.-connected liabilities.* The applicable interest rate on excess U.S.-connected liabilities is determined by dividing the total interest expense paid or accrued for the taxable year on U.S.-dollar liabilities shown on the books of the offices or branches of the foreign corporation outside the United States by the average U.S.-dollar denominated liabilities (whether interest-bearing or not) shown on the books of the offices or branches of the foreign corporation outside the United States for the taxable year.

(6) *Examples.* The following examples illustrate the rules of this section:

Example 1. Computation of interest expense; actual ratio—(i) *Facts.* (A) *FC* is a foreign corporation that is not a bank and that actively conducts a real estate business through a branch, *B*, in the United States. For the taxable year, *FC*'s balance sheet and income statement is as follows (assume amounts are in U.S. dollars and computed in accordance with paragraphs (b)(2) and (b)(3) of this section):

	Value
Asset 1	$2,000
Asset 2	$2,500
Asset 3	$5,500

	Amount	Interest Expense
Liability 1	$ 800	56
Liability 2	$3,200	256
Capital	$6,000	0

(B) Asset 1 is the stock of *FC*'s wholly-owned domestic subsidiary that is also actively engaged in the real estate business. Asset 2 is a building in the United States producing rental income that is entirely ECI to *FC*. Asset 3 is a building in the home country of *FC* that produces rental income. Liabilities 1 and 2 are loans that bear interest at the rates of 7% and 8%, respectively. Liability 1 is a booked liability of B, and Liability 2 is booked in *FC*'s home country. Assume that *FC* has not elected to use the fixed ratio in Step 2.

(ii) *Step 1.* Under paragraph (b)(1) of this section, Assets 1 and 3 are not U.S. assets, while Asset 2 qualifies as a U.S. asset. Thus, under paragraph (b)(3) of this section, the total value of U.S. assets for the taxable year is $2,500, the value of Asset 2.

(iii) *Step 2.* Under paragraph (c)(1) of this section, the amount of *FC*'s U.S.-connected liabilities for the taxable year is determined by multiplying $2,500 (the value of U.S. assets determined under Step 1) by the actual ratio for the taxable year. The actual ratio is the average amount of *FC*'s worldwide liabilities divided by the average value of *FC*'s worldwide assets. The amount of Liability 1 is $800, and the amount of Liability 2 is $3,200. Thus, the numerator of the actual ratio is $4,000. The average value of worldwide assets is $10,000 (Asset 1 + Asset 2 + Asset 3). The actual ratio, therefore, is 40% ($4,000/$10,000), and the amount of U.S.-connected liabilities for the taxable year is $1,000 ($2,500 U.S. assets x 40%).

(iv) *Step 3.* Because the amount of *FC*'s U.S.-connected liabilities ($1,000) exceeds the average total amount of U.S. booked liabilities of *B* ($800), *FC* determines its interest expense in accordance with paragraph (d)(5) of this section by adding the interest paid or accrued on U.S. booked liabili-

Reg. § 1.882-5(d)(6)

ties, and the interest expense associated with the excess of its U.S.-connected liabilities over its average total amount of U.S. booked liabilities. Under paragraph (d)(5)(ii) of this section, FC determines the interest rate attributable to its excess U.S.-connected liabilities by dividing the interest expense paid or accrued by the average amount of U.S.-dollar denominated liabilities, which produces an interest rate of 8% ($256/$3200). Therefore, FC's allocable interest expense is $72 ($56 of interest expense from U.S. booked liabilities plus $16 ($200 x 8%) of interest expense attributable to its excess U.S.-connected liabilities).

Example 2. Computation of interest expense; fixed ratio—(i) The facts are the same as in Example 1, except that FC makes a fixed ratio election under paragraph (c)(4) of this section. The conclusions under Step 1 are the same as in Example 1.

(ii) *Step 2.* Under paragraph (c)(1) of this section, the amount of U.S.-connected liabilities for the taxable year is determined by multiplying $2,500 (the value of U.S. assets determined under Step 1) by the fixed ratio for the taxable year, which, under paragraph (c)(4) of this section is 50 percent. Thus, the amount of U.S.-connected liabilities for the taxable year is $1,250 ($2,500 U.S. assets x 50%).

(iii) *Step 3.* As in Example 1, the amount of FC's U.S.-connected liabilities exceed the average total amount of U.S. booked liabilities of B, requiring FC to determine its interest expense under paragraph (d)(5) of this section. In this case, however, FC has excess U.S.-connected liabilities of $450 ($1,250 of U.S.-connected liabilities $800 U.S. booked liabilities). FC therefore has allocable interest expense of $92 ($56 of interest expense from U.S. booked liabilities plus $36 ($450 x 8%) of interest expense attributable to its excess U.S.-connected liabilities).

Example 3. Scaling ratio.—(i) *Facts.* Bank Z, a resident of country X, has a branch in the United States through which it conducts its banking business. For the taxable year, Z has U.S.-connected liabilities, determined under paragraph (c) of this section, equal to $300. Z, however, has U.S. booked liabilities of $300 and U500. Therefore, assuming an exchange rate of the U to the U.S. dollar of 5:1, Z has U.S. booked liabilities of $400 ($300 + (U500 ÷ 5)).

(ii) *U.S.-connected liabilities.* Because Z's U.S. booked liabilities of $400 exceed its U.S.-connected liabilities by $100, all of Z's interest expense allocable to its U.S. trade or business must be scaled back pro-rata. To determine the scaling ratio, Z divides its U.S.-connected liabilities by its U.S. booked liabilities, as required by paragraph (d)(4) of this section. Z's interest expense is scaled back pro rata by the resulting ratio of 3/4 ($300 ÷ $400). Z's income, expense, gain or loss from hedging transactions described in paragraph (d)(2)(vi) of this section must be similarly reduced.

Example 4. [Reserved]

(e) *Separate currency pools method*—(1) *General rule.* If a foreign corporation elects to use the method in this paragraph, its total interest expense allocable to ECI is the sum of the separate interest deductions for each of the currencies in which the foreign corporation has U.S. assets. The separate interest deductions are determined under the following three-step process.

(i) *Determine the value of U.S. assets in each currency pool.* First, the foreign corporation must determine the amount of its U.S. assets, using the methodology in paragraph (b) of this section, in each currency pool. The foreign corporation may convert into U.S. dollars any currency pool in which the foreign corporation holds less than 3% of its U.S. assets. A transaction (or transactions) that hedges a U.S. asset shall be taken into account for purposes of determining the currency denomination and the value of the U.S. asset.

(ii) *Determine the U.S.-connected liabilities in each currency pool.* Second, the foreign corporation must determine the amount of its U.S.-connected liabilities in each currency pool by multiplying the amount of U.S. assets (as determined under paragraph (b)(3) of this section) in the currency pool by the foreign corporation's actual ratio (as determined under paragraph (c)(2) of this section) for the taxable year or, if the taxpayer has made an election in accordance with paragraph (c)(4) of this section, by the fixed ratio.

(iii) *Determine the interest expense attributable to each currency pool.* Third, the foreign corporation must determine the interest expense attributable to each currency pool by multiplying the U.S.-connected liabilities in each currency pool by the prescribed interest rate as defined in paragraph (e)(2) of this section.

(2) *Prescribed interest rate.* For each currency pool, the prescribed interest rate is determined by dividing the total interest expense that is paid or accrued for the taxable year with respect to the foreign corporation's worldwide liabilities denominated in that currency, by the foreign corporation's average worldwide liabilities (whether interest bearing or not) denominated in that currency. The interest expense and liabilities are to be stated in that currency.

(3) *Hedging transactions.* [Reserved]

Reg. § 1.882-5(e)(1)

(4) *Election not available if excessive hyperinflationary assets.* The election to use the separate currency pools method of this paragraph (e) is not available if the value of the foreign corporation's U.S. assets denominated in a hyperinflationary currency, as defined in § 1.985-1, exceeds ten percent of the value of the foreign corporation's total U.S. assets. If a foreign corporation made a valid election to use the separate currency pools method in a prior year but no longer qualifies to use such method pursuant to this paragraph (e)(4), the taxpayer must use the method provided by paragraphs (b) through (d) of this section.

(5) *Examples.* The separate currency pools method of this paragraph (e) is illustrated by the following examples:

Example 1. Separate currency pools method—(i) *Facts.* (A) Bank Z, a resident of country X, has a branch in the United States through which it conducts its banking business. For its 1997 taxable year, Z has U.S. assets, as defined in paragraph (b) of this section, that are denominated in U.S. dollars and in U, the country X currency. Accordingly, Z's U.S. assets are as follows:

	Average Value
U.S. Dollar Assets	$20,000
U Assets	U 5,000

(B) Z's worldwide liabilities are also denominated in U.S. Dollars and in U. The average interest rates on Z's worldwide liabilities, including those in the United States, are 6% on its U.S. dollar liabilities, and 12% on its liabilities denominated in U. Assume that Z has properly elected to use its actual ratio of 95% to determine its U.S.-connected liabilities in Step 2, and has also properly elected to use the separate currency pools method provided in paragraph (e) of this section.

(ii) *Determination of interest expense.* Z determines the interest expense attributable to its U.S.-connected liabilities according to the steps described below.

(A) First, Z separates its U.S. assets into two currency pools, one denominated in U.S. dollars ($20,000) and the other denominated in U (U5,000).

(B) Second, Z multiplies each pool of assets by the applicable ratio of worldwide liabilities to assets, which in this case is 95%. Thus, Z has U.S.-connected liabilities of $19,000 ($20,000 x 95%), and U4750 (U5000 x 95%).

(C) Third, Z calculates its interest expense by multiplying each pool of its U.S.-connected liabilities by the relevant interest rates. Accordingly, Z's allocable interest expense for the year is $1140 ($19,000 x 6%), the sum of the expense associated with its U.S. dollar liabilities, plus U570 (U4750 x 12%), the interest expense associated with its liabilities denominated in U. Z must translate its interest expense denominated in U in accordance with the rules provided in section 988, and then must determine whether it is subject to any other provision of the Code that would disallow or defer any portion of its interest expense so determined.

Example 2. [Reserved]

(f) *Effective date*—(1) *General rule.* This section is effective for taxable years beginning on or after June 6, 1996.

(2) *Special rules for financial products.* [Reserved] [Reg. § 1.882-5.]

☐ [T.D. 7749, 12-30-80. Amended by T.D. 7939, 2-2-84 and T.D. 8658, 3-5-96.]

[Reg. § 1.883-1]

§ 1.883-1. Exclusions from gross income of foreign corporations.—(a) *Earnings of foreign ships or aircraft*—(1) *Basic rule.* So much of the income from sources within the United States of a foreign corporation as consists of earnings derived from the operation of a ship or ships documented, or of aircraft registered, under the laws of a foreign country which grants an equivalent exemption to citizens of the United States nonresident in that foreign country and to corporations organized in the United States shall not be included in gross income.

(2) *Equivalent exemption*—(i) *Ships.* A foreign country which either imposes no income tax, or, in imposing that tax, exempts from taxation so much of the income of a citizen of the United States nonresident in that foreign country and of a corporation organized in the United States as consists of earnings derived from the operation of a ship or ships documented under the laws of the United States is considered as granting an equivalent exemption for purposes of the exclusion from gross income of the earnings of a foreign ship or ships.

(ii) *Aircraft.* A foreign country which either imposes no income tax, or, in imposing that tax, exempts from taxation so much of the income of a citizen of the United States nonresident in that foreign country and of a corporation organized in the United States as consists of earnings derived from the operation of aircraft registered under the laws of the United States is considered as granting an equivalent exemption for purposes of the exclusion from gross income of the earnings of foreign aircraft.

(b) *Income tax conventions.* Generally, income of any kind which is exempt, under the provisions

Reg. § 1.883-1(b)

of an income tax convention to which the United States is a party, from any tax imposed by subtitle A (relating to income taxes) is not included in the gross income of a foreign corporation. However, see paragraph (a) of § 1.894-1 for certain exceptions to this rule. Income on which any tax imposed by such subtitle is limited by an income tax convention is included in the gross income of a foreign corporation if it is not otherwise excluded from gross income. For the determination of the tax when the taxpayer has income upon which the tax is limited by an income tax convention, see § 1.871-12.

(c) *Other exclusions.* Income which is from sources without the United States, as determined under the provisions of sections 861 through 863 and the regulations thereunder, is not included in the gross income of a foreign corporation unless such income is effectively connected for the taxable year with the conduct of a trade or business in the United States by that corporation. To determine specific exclusions in the case of other items which are from sources within the United States, see the applicable sections of the Code. For special rules under a tax convention for determining the sources of income and for excluding, from gross income, income from sources without the United States which is effectively connected with the conduct of a trade or business in the United States, see the applicable tax convention. For determining which income from sources without the United States is effectively connected with the conduct of a trade or business within the United States see section 864(c)(4) and § 1.864-5.

(d) *Effective date.* This section applies for taxable years beginning after December 31, 1966. For corresponding rules applicable to taxable years beginning before January 1, 1967, see 26 CFR 1.883-1 (Rev. as of Jan. 1, 1971). [Reg. § 1.883-1.]

☐ [T.D. 6258, 10-23-57. Amended by T.D. 7293, 11-27-73.]

[Reg. § 1.884-0]

§ 1.884-0. **Overview of regulation provisions for section 884.**—(a) *Introduction.* Section 884 consists of three main parts: a branch profits tax on certain earnings of a foreign corporation's U.S. trade or business; a branch-level interest tax on interest paid, or deemed paid, by a foreign corporation's U.S. trade or business; and an anti-treaty shopping rule. A foreign corporation is subject to section 884 by virtue of owning an interest in a partnership, trust, or estate that is engaged in a U.S. trade or business or has income treated as effectively connected with the conduct of a trade or business in the United States. An international organization (as defined in section 7701(a)(18)) is not subject to the branch profits tax by reason of section 884(e)(5). A foreign government treated as a corporate resident of its country of residence under section 892(a)(3) shall be treated as a corporation for purposes of section 884. The preceding sentence shall be effective for taxable years ending on or after September 11, 1992, except that, for the first taxable year ending on or after that date, the branch profits tax shall not apply to effectively connected earnings and profits of the foreign government earned prior to that date nor to decreases in the U.S. net equity of a foreign government occurring after the close of the preceding taxable year and before that date. Similarly, § 1.884-4 shall apply, in the case of branch interest, only with respect to amounts of interest accrued and paid by a foreign government on or after that date, or, in the case of excess interest, only with respect to amounts attributable to interest accrued by a foreign government on or after that date and apportioned to ECI, as defined in § 1.884-1(d)(1)(iii). Except as otherwise provided, for purposes of the regulations under section 884, the term "U.S. trade or business" includes all the U.S. trades or businesses of a foreign corporation.

(1) *The branch profits tax.* Section 1.884-1 provides rules for computing the branch profits tax and defines various terms that affect the computation of the tax. In general, section 884(a) imposes a 30-percent branch profits tax on the after-tax earnings of a foreign corporation's U.S. trade or business that are not reinvested in a U.S. trade or business by the close of the taxable year, or are disinvested in a later taxable year. Changes in the value of the equity of the foreign corporation's U.S. trade or business are used as the measure of whether earnings have been reinvested in, or disinvested from, a U.S. trade or business. An increase in the equity during the taxable year is generally treated as a reinvestment of the earnings for the current taxable year; a decrease in the equity during the taxable year is generally treated as a disinvestment of prior years' earnings that have not previously been subject to the branch profits tax. The amount subject to the branch profits tax for the taxable year is the dividend equivalent amount. Section 1.884-2T contains special rules relating to the effect on the branch profits tax of the termination or incorporation of a U.S. trade or business or the liquidation or reorganization of a foreign corporation or its domestic subsidiary.

(2) *The branch-level interest tax.* Section 1.884-4 provides rules for computing the branch-level interest tax. In general, interest paid by a U.S. trade or business of a foreign corporation ("branch interest", as defined in § 1.884-4(b)) is treated as if it were paid by a domestic corpora-

Reg. § 1.884-0(a)(1)

tion and may be subject to tax under section 871(a) or 881, and to withholding under section 1441 or 1442. In addition, if the interest apportioned to ECI exceeds branch interest, the excess is treated as interest paid to the foreign corporation by a wholly-owned domestic corporation and is subject to tax under section 881(a).

(3) *Qualified resident.* Section 1.884-5 provides rules for determining whether a foreign corporation is a qualified resident of a foreign country. In general, a foreign corporation must be a qualified resident of a foreign country with which the United States has an income tax treaty in order to claim an exemption or rate reduction with respect to the branch profits tax, the branch-level interest tax, and the tax on dividends paid by the foreign corporation.

(b) *Outline of major topics in §§ 1.884-1 through 1.884-5.*

§ 1.884-1. Branch profits tax.

(a) General rule.

(b) Dividend equivalent amount.

(1) Definition.

(2) Adjustment for increase in U.S. net equity.

(3) Adjustment for decrease in U.S. net equity.

(4) Examples.

(c) U.S. net equity.

(1) Definition.

(2) Definition of amount of a U.S. asset.

(3) Definition of determination date.

(d) U.S. assets.

(1) Definition of a U.S. asset.

(2) Special rules for certain assets.

(3) Interest in a partnership.

(4) Interest in a trust or estate.

(5) Property that is not a U.S. asset.

(6) E&P basis of a U.S. asset.

(e) U.S. liabilities.

(1) Liabilities based on § 1.882-5.

(2) Insurance reserves.

(3) Election to reduce liabilities.

(4) Artificial decrease in U.S. liabilities.

(5) Examples.

(f) Effectively connected earnings and profits.

(1) In general.

(2) Income that does not produce ECEP.

(3) Allocation of deductions attributable to income that does not produce ECEP.

(4) Examples.

(g) Corporations resident in countries with which the United States has an income tax treaty.

(1) General rule.

(2) Special rules for foreign corporations that are qualified residents on the basis of their ownership.

(3) Exemptions for foreign corporations resident in certain countries with income tax treaties in effect on January 1, 1987.

(4) Modifications with respect to other income tax treaties.

(5) Benefits under treaties other than income tax treaties.

(h) Stapled entities.

(i) Effective date.

(1) General rule.

(2) Election to reduce liabilities.

(3) Separate election for installment obligations.

(4) Special rule for certain U.S. assets and liabilities.

(j) Transition rules.

(1) General rule.

(2) Installment obligations.

§ 1.884-2T. *Special rules for termination or incorporation of a U.S. trade or business or liquidation or reorganization of a foreign corporation or its domestic subsidiary (temporary).*

(a) Complete termination of a U.S. trade or business.

(1) General rule.

(2) Operating rules.

(3) Complete termination in the case of a section 338 election.

(4) Complete termination in the case of a foreign corporation with income under section 864(c) (6) or 864(c)(7).

(5) Special rule if a foreign corporation terminates an interest in a trust. [Reserved]

(6) Coordination with second-level withholding tax.

(b) Election to remain engaged in a U.S. trade or business.

(1) General rule.

(2) Marketable security.

(3) Identification requirements.

(4) Treatment of income from deemed U.S. assets.

(5) Method of election.

(6) Effective date.

(c) Liquidation, reorganization, etc. of a foreign corporation.

Reg. § 1.884-0(b)

(1) Inapplicability of paragraph (a)(1) to section 381(a) transactions.

(2) Transferor's dividend equivalent amount for the taxable year in which a section 381(a) transaction occurs.

(3) Transferor's dividend equivalent amount for any taxable year succeeding the taxable year in which the section 381(a) transaction occurs.

(4) Earnings and profits of the transferor carried over to the transferee pursuant to the section 381(a) transaction.

(5) Determination of U.S. net equity of a transferee that is a foreign corporation.

(6) Special rules in the case of the disposition of stock or securities in a domestic transferee or in the transferor.

(d) Incorporation under section 351.

(1) In general.

(2) Inapplicability of paragraph (a)(1) of this section to section 351 transactions.

(3) Transferor's dividend equivalent amount for the taxable year in which a section 351 transaction occurs.

(4) Election to increase earnings and profits.

(5) Dispositions of stock or securities of the transferee by the transferor.

(6) Example.

(e) Certain transactions with respect to a domestic subsidiary.

(f) Effective date.

§ 1.884-3T. Coordination of branch profits tax with second-tier withholding (temporary). [Reserved]

§ 1.884-4. Branch-level interest tax.

(a) General rule.

(1) Tax on branch interest.

(2) Tax on excess interest.

(3) Original issue discount.

(4) Examples.

(b) Branch interest.

(1) Definition of branch interest.

(2) [Reserved]

(3) Requirements relating to specifically identified liabilities.

(4) [Reserved]

(5) Increase in branch interest where U.S. assets constitute 80 percent or more of a foreign corporation's assets.

(6) Special rule where branch interest exceeds interest apportioned to ECI of a foreign corporation.

(7) Effect of election under paragraph (c)(1) of this section to treat interest as if paid in year of accrual.

(8) Effect of treaties.

(c) Rules relating to excess interest.

(1) Election to compute excess interest by treating branch interest that is paid and accrued in different years as if paid in year of accrual.

(2) Interest paid by a partnership.

(3) Effect of treaties.

(4) Example.

(d) Stapled entities.

(e) Effective dates.

(1) General rule.

(2) Special rule.

(f) Transition rules.

(1) Election under paragraph (c)(1) of this section.

(2) Waiver of notification requirement for non-banks under Notice 89-80.

(3) Waiver of legending requirement for certain debt issued prior to January 3, 1989.

§ 1.884-5. Qualified resident.

(a) Definition of qualified resident.

(b) Stock ownership requirement.

(1) General rule.

(2) Rules for determining constructive ownership.

(3) Required documentation.

(4) Ownership statements from qualifying shareholders.

(5) Certificate of residency.

(6) Intermediary ownership statement.

(7) Intermediary verification statement.

(8) Special rules for pension funds.

(9) Availability of documents for inspection.

(10) Examples.

(c) Base erosion.

(d) Publicly-traded corporations.

(1) General rule.

(2) Established securities market.

(3) Primarily traded.

(4) Regularly traded.

(5) Burden of proof for publicly-traded corporations.

(e) Active trade or business.

(1) General rule.

(2) Active conduct of a trade or business.

(3) Substantial presence test.

Reg. § 1.884-0(b)

(4) Integral part of an active trade or business in the foreign corporation's country of residence.

(f) Qualified resident ruling.

(1) Basis for ruling.

(2) Factors.

(3) Procedural requirements.

(g) Effective dates.

(h) Transition rule.

[Reg. § 1.884-0.]

☐ [T.D. 8432, 9-10-92. Amended by T.D. 8657, 3-5-96.]

[Reg. § 1.884-1]

§ 1.884-1. Branch profits tax.—(a) *General rule.* A foreign corporation shall be liable for a branch profits tax in an amount equal to 30 percent of the foreign corporation's dividend equivalent amount for the taxable year. The branch profits tax shall be in addition to the tax imposed by section 882 and shall be reported on a foreign corporation's income tax return for the taxable year. The tax shall be due and payable as provided in section 6151 and such other provisions of Subtitle F of the Internal Revenue Code as apply to the income tax liability of corporations. However, no estimated tax payments shall be due with respect to a foreign corporation's liability for the branch profits tax. See paragraph (g) of this section for the application of the branch profits tax to corporations that are residents of countries with which the United States has an income tax treaty, and § 1.884-2T for the effect on the branch profits tax of the termination or incorporation of a U.S. trade or business, or the liquidation or reorganization of a foreign corporation or its domestic subsidiary.

(b) *Dividend equivalent amount*—(1) *Definition.* The term "dividend equivalent amount" means a foreign corporation's effectively connected earnings and profits ("ECEP", as defined in paragraph (f)(1) of this section) for the taxable year, adjusted pursuant to paragraph (b)(2) or (3) of this section, as applicable. The dividend equivalent amount cannot be less than zero.

(2) *Adjustment for increase in U.S. net equity.* If a foreign corporation's U.S. net equity (as defined in paragraph (c) of this section) as of the close of the taxable year exceeds the foreign corporation's U.S. net equity as of the close of the preceding taxable year, then, for purposes of computing the foreign corporation's dividend equivalent amount for the taxable year, the foreign corporation's ECEP for the taxable year shall be reduced (but not below zero) by the amount of such excess.

(3) *Adjustment for decrease in U.S. net equity*—(i) *In general.* Except as provided in paragraph (b)(3)(ii) of this section, if a foreign corporation's U.S. net equity as of the close of the taxable year is less than the foreign corporation's U.S. net equity as of the close of the preceding taxable year, then, for purposes of computing the foreign corporation's dividend equivalent amount for the taxable year, the foreign corporation's ECEP for the taxable year shall be increased by the amount of such difference.

(ii) *Limitation based on accumulated ECEP.* The increase of a foreign corporation's ECEP under paragraph (b)(3)(i) of this section shall not exceed the accumulated ECEP of the foreign corporation as of the beginning of the taxable year. The term "accumulated ECEP" means the aggregate amount of ECEP of a foreign corporation for preceding taxable years beginning after December 31, 1986, minus the aggregate dividend equivalent amounts for such preceding taxable years. Accumulated ECEP may be less than zero.

(4) *Examples.* The principles of paragraph (b)(2) and (3) of this section are illustrated by the following examples.

Example 1. Reinvestment of all ECEP. Foreign corporation A, a calendar year taxpayer, had $1,000 U.S. net equity as of the close of 1986 and $100 of ECEP for 1987. A acquires $100 of additional U.S. assets during 1987 and its U.S. net equity as of the close of 1987 is $1,100. In computing A's dividend equivalent amount for 1987, A's ECEP of $100 is reduced under paragraph (b)(2) of this section by the $100 increase in U.S. net equity between the close of 1986 and the close of 1987. A has no dividend equivalent amount for 1987.

Example 2. Partial reinvestment of ECEP. Assume the same facts as in *Example 1* except that A acquires $40 (rather than $100) of U.S. assets during 1987 and its U.S. net equity as of the close of 1987 is $1,040. In computing A's dividend equivalent amount for 1987, A's ECEP of $100 is reduced under paragraph (b)(2) of this section by the $40 increase in U.S. net equity between the close of 1986 and the close of 1987. A has a dividend equivalent amount of $60 for 1987.

Example 3. Disinvestment of prior year's ECEP. Assume the same facts as in *Example 1* for 1987. A has no ECEP for 1988. A's U.S. net equity decreases by $40 (to $1,060) as of the close of 1988. A has a dividend equivalent amount of $40 for 1988, even though it has no ECEP for 1988. A's ECEP of $0 for 1988 is increased under paragraph (b)(3)(i) of this section by the $40 reduction in U.S. net equity (subject to the limita-

Reg. § 1.884-1(b)(4)

tion in paragraph (b)(3)(ii) of this section of $100 of accumulated ECEP).

Example 4. Accumulated ECEP limitation. Assume the same facts as in *Example 2* for 1987. For 1988, A has $125 of ECEP and its U.S. net equity decreases by $50. A's U.S. net equity as of the close of 1988 is $990 ($1,040-$50). In computing A's dividend equivalent amount for 1988, the $125 of ECEP for 1988 is not increased under paragraph (b)(3)(i) of this section by the full amount of the $50 decrease in U.S. net equity during 1988. Rather, the increase in ECEP resulting from the decrease in U.S. net equity is limited to A's accumulated ECEP as of the beginning of 1988. A had $100 of ECEP for 1987 and a dividend equivalent amount of $60 for that year, so A had $40 of accumulated ECEP as of the beginning of 1988. The increase in ECEP resulting from a decrease in U.S. net equity is thus limited to $40, and the dividend equivalent amount for 1988 is $165 ($125 ECEP + $40 decrease in U.S. net equity).

Example 5. Effect of deficits in ECEP. Foreign corporation A, a calendar year taxpayer, has $150 of accumulated ECEP as of the beginning of 1991 ($200 aggregate ECEP less $50 aggregate dividend equivalent amounts for years preceding 1991). A has U.S. net equity of $450 as of the close of 1990, U.S. net equity of $350 as of the close of 1991 (*i.e.,* a $100 decrease in U.S. net equity) and a $90 deficit in ECEP for 1991. A's dividend equivalent amount is $10 for 1991, *i.e.,* A's deficit of $90 in ECEP for 1991 increased by $100, the decrease in A's U.S. net equity during 1991. A portion of the reduction in U.S. net equity in 1991 ($90) is attributable to A's deficit in ECEP for that year. The reduction in U.S. net equity in 1991 ($100) triggers a dividend equivalent amount only to the extent it exceeds the $90 current year deficit in ECEP for 1991. As of the beginning of 1992, A has $50 of accumulated ECEP (*i.e.,* $110 aggregate ECEP less $60 aggregate dividend equivalent amounts for years preceding 1992).

Example 6. Nimble dividend equivalent amount. Foreign corporation A, a calendar year taxpayer, had a deficit in ECEP of $100 for 1987 and $100 for 1988, and has $90 of ECEP for 1989. A had $2,000 U.S. net equity as of the close of 1988 and has $2,000 U.S. net equity as of the close of 1989. A has a dividend equivalent amount of $90 for 1989, its ECEP for the year, even though it has a net deficit of $110 in ECEP for the period 1987-1989.

(c) *U.S. net equity*—(1) *Definition.* The term "U.S. net equity" means the aggregate amount of the U.S. assets (as defined in paragraphs (c)(2) and (d)(1) of this section) of a foreign corporation as of the determination date (as defined in paragraph (c)(3) of this section), reduced (including below zero) by the U.S. liabilities (as defined in paragraph (e) of this section) of the foreign corporation as of the determination date.

(2) *Definition of the amount of a U.S. asset*— (i) *In general.* For purposes of this section, the term "amount of a U.S. asset" means the U.S. asset's adjusted basis for purposes of computing earnings and profits ("E&P basis") multiplied by the proportion of the asset that is treated as a U.S. asset under paragraphs (d)(1) through (4) of this section. The amount of a U.S. asset that is money shall be its face value. See paragraph (d)(6) of this section for rules concerning the computation of the E&P basis of a U.S. asset.

(ii) *Bad debt reserves.* A bank described in section 585(a)(2)(B) (without regard to the second sentence thereof) that uses the reserve method of accounting for bad debts for U.S. federal income tax purposes shall decrease the amount of loans that qualify as U.S. assets by any reserve that is permitted under section 585.

(3) *Definition of determination date.* For purposes of this section, the term "determination date" means the close of the day on which the amount of U.S. net equity is required to be determined. Unless otherwise provided, the U.S. net equity of a foreign corporation is required to be determined as of the close of the foreign corporation's taxable year.

(d) *U.S. assets*—(1) *Definition of a U.S. asset*— (i) *General rule.* Except as provided in paragraph (d)(5) of this section, the term "U.S. asset" means an asset of a foreign corporation (other than an interest in a partnership, trust, or estate) that is held by the corporation as of the determination date if—

(A) All income produced by the asset on the determination date is ECI (as defined in paragraph (d)(1)(iii) of this section) (or would be ECI if the asset produced income on that date); and

(B) All gain from the disposition of the asset would be ECI if the asset were disposed of on that date and the disposition produced gain.

For purposes of determining whether income or gain from an asset would be ECI under this paragraph (d)(1)(i), it is immaterial whether the asset is of a type that is unlikely to, or cannot, produce income or gain. For example, money may be a U.S. asset although it does not produce income or gain. In the case of an asset that does not produce income, however, the determination of whether income from the asset would be ECI shall be made under the principles of section 864 and the regulations thereunder, but without regard to

Reg. § 1.884-1(c)(1)

§ 1.864-4(c)(2)(iii)(b). For purposes of determining whether an asset is a U.S. asset under this paragraph (d)(1), a foreign corporation may presume, unless it has reason to know otherwise, that gain from the sale of personal property (including inventory property) would be U.S. source if gain from the sale of that type of property would ordinarily be attributable to an office or other fixed place of business of the foreign corporation within the United States (within the meaning of section 865(e)(2)).

(ii) *Special rules for assets not described in paragraph (d)(1)(i) of this section.* An asset of a foreign corporation that is held by the corporation as of the determination date and is not described in paragraph (d)(1)(i) of this section shall be treated as a U.S. asset to the extent provided in paragraph (d)(2) of this section (relating to special rules for certain assets, including assets that produce income or gain at least a portion of which is ECI), and in paragraphs (d)(3) and (4) of this section (relating to special rules for interests in a partnership, trust, and estate).

(iii) *Definition of ECI.* For purposes of the regulations under section 884, the term "ECI" means income that is effectively connected with the conduct of a trade or business in the United States and income that is treated as effectively connected with the conduct of a trade or business in the United States under any provision of the Code. The term "ECI" also includes all income that is or is treated as effectively connected with the conduct of a U.S. trade or business whether or not the income is included in gross income (for example, interest income earned with respect to tax-exempt bonds).

(2) *Special rules for certain assets*—(i) *Depreciable and amortizable property.* An item of depreciable personal property or an item of amortizable intangible property shall be treated as a U.S. asset of a foreign corporation in the same proportion that the amount of the depreciation or amortization with respect to the item of property that is allowable as a deduction, or is includible in cost of goods sold, for the taxable year in computing the effectively connected taxable income of the foreign corporation bears to the total amount of depreciation or amortization computed for the taxable year with respect to the item of property.

(ii) *Inventory.* An item or pool of inventory property (as defined in section 865(i)(1)) shall be treated as a U.S. asset in the same proportion as the amount of gross receipts from the sale or exchange of such property for the three preceding taxable years (or for such part of the three-year period as the corporation has been in existence) that is effectively connected with the conduct of a U.S. trade or business bears to the total amount of gross receipts from the sale or exchange of such property during such period (or part thereof). If a foreign corporation has not sold or exchanged such property during such three-year period (or part thereof), then the property shall be treated as a U.S. asset in the same proportion that the anticipated amount of gross receipts from the sale or exchange of the property that is reasonably anticipated to be ECI bears to the anticipated total amount of gross receipts from the sale or exchange of the property.

(iii) *Installment obligations.* An installment obligation received in connection with an installment sale (as defined in section 453(b)) for which an election under section 453(d) has not been made shall be treated as a U.S. asset to the extent that it is received in connection with the sale of a U.S. asset. If an obligation is received in connection with the sale of an asset that is wholly a U.S. asset, it shall be treated as a U.S. asset in its entirety. If a single obligation is received in connection with the sale of an asset that is in part a U.S. asset under the rules of paragraphs (d)(2) through (4) of this section, or in connection with the sale of several assets including one or more non-U.S. assets, the obligation shall be treated as U.S. asset in the same proportion as—

(A) The sum of the amount of gain from the installment sale that would be ECI if the obligation were satisfied in full on the determination date and the adjusted basis of the obligation on such date (as determined under section 453B) attributable to the amount of gain that would be ECI bears to

(B) The sum of the total amount of gain from the sale if the obligation were satisfied in full and the adjusted basis of the obligation on such date (as determined under section 453B).

However, the obligation will only be treated as a U.S. asset if the interest income or original issue discount with respect to the obligation is ECI or the foreign corporation elects to treat the interest or original issue discount as ECI in the same proportion that the obligation is treated as a U.S. asset. A foreign corporation may elect to treat interest income or original issue discount as ECI by reporting such interest income or original issue discount as ECI on its income tax return or an amended return for the taxable year. See paragraph (d)(6)(ii) of this section to determine the E&P basis of an installment obligation for purposes of this paragraph (d)(2)(iii).

(iv) *Receivables*—(A) *Receivables arising from the sale or exchange of inventory property.* An account or note receivable (whether or not bearing stated interest) with a maturity not ex-

Reg. § 1.884-1(d)(2)

ceeding six months that arises from the sale or exchange of inventory property (as defined in section 865(i)(1)) shall be treated as a U.S. asset in the proportion determined under paragraph (d)(2)(iii) of this section as if the receivable were an installment obligation.

(B) *Receivables arising from the performance of services or leasing of property.* An account or note receivable (whether or not bearing stated interest) with a maturity not exceeding six months that arises from the performance of services or the leasing of property in the ordinary course of a foreign corporation's trade or business shall be treated as a U.S. asset in the same proportion that the amount of gross income represented by the receivable that is ECI bears to the total amount of gross income represented by the receivable. For purposes of this paragraph (d)(2)(iv)(B), the amount of income represented by a receivable shall not include interest income or original issue discount.

(v) *Bank and other deposits.* A deposit or credit balance with a person described in section 871(i)(3) or a Federal Reserve Bank that is interest-bearing shall be treated as a U.S. asset if all income derived by the foreign corporation with respect to the deposit or credit balance during the taxable year is ECI. Any other deposit or credit balance shall only be treated as a U.S. asset if the deposit or credit balance is needed in a U.S. trade or business within the meaning of § 1.864-4(c)(2)(iii)(a).

(vi) *Debt instruments.* A debt instrument, as defined in section 1275(a)(1) (other than an asset treated as a U.S. asset under any other subdivision of this paragraph (d)) shall be treated as a U.S. asset, notwithstanding the fact that gain from the sale or exchange of the obligation on the determination date would not be ECI, if—

(A) All income derived by the foreign corporation from such obligation during the taxable year is ECI; and

(B) The yield for the period that the instrument was held during the taxable year equals or exceeds the Applicable Federal Rate for instruments of similar type and maturity.

Shares in a regulated investment company that purchases solely instruments that, under this paragraph (d)(2)(vi), would be U.S. assets if held directly by the foreign corporation shall also be treated as a U.S. asset.

(vii) *Securities held by a foreign corporation engaged in a banking, financing or similar business.* Securities described in § 1.864-4(c)(5)(ii)(*b*)(*3*) held by a foreign corporation engaged in the active conduct of a banking, financing, or similar business in the United States during the taxable year shall be treated as U.S. assets in the same proportion that income, gain, or loss from such securities is ECI for the taxable year under § 1.864-4(c)(5)(ii).

(viii) *Federal income taxes.* An overpayment of Federal income taxes shall be treated as a U.S. asset to the extent that the tax would reduce a foreign corporation's ECEP for the taxable year but for the fact that the tax does not accrue during the taxable year.

(ix) *Losses involving U.S. assets.* A foreign corporation that sustains, with respect to a U.S. asset, a loss for which a deduction is not allowed under section 165 (in whole or in part) because there exists a reasonable prospect of recovering compensation for the loss shall be treated as having a U.S. asset ("loss property") from the date of the loss in the same proportion that the asset was treated as a U.S. asset immediately before the loss. See paragraph (d)(6)(iv) of this section to determine the E&P basis of the loss property.

(x) *Ruling for involuntary conversion.* If property that is a U.S. asset of a foreign corporation is compulsorily or involuntarily converted into property not similar or related in service or use (within the meaning of section 1033), the foreign corporation may apply to the Commissioner for a ruling to determine its U.S. assets for the taxable year of the involuntary conversion.

(xi) *Examples.* The principles of paragraphs (c) and (d)(1) and (2) of this section are illustrated by the following examples.

Example 1. Depreciable property. Foreign corporation A, a calendar year taxpayer, is engaged in a trade or business in the United States. A owns equipment that is used in its manufacturing business in country X and in the United States. Under § 1.861-8, A's depreciation deduction with respect to the equipment is allocated to sales income and is apportioned 70 percent to ECI and 30 percent to income that is not ECI. Under paragraph (d)(2)(ii) of this section, the equipment is 70 percent a U.S. asset. The equipment has an E&P basis of $100 at the beginning of 1993. A's depreciation deduction (for purposes of computing earnings and profits) with respect to the equipment is $10 for 1993. To determine the amount of A's U.S. asset at the close of 1993, the equipment's $90 E&P basis at the close of 1993 is multiplied by 70 percent (the proportion of the asset that is a U.S. asset). The amount of the U.S. asset as of the close of 1993 is $63.

Example 2. U.S. real property interest connected to a U.S. business. FC is a foreign corporation that is a bank, within the meaning of section 585(a)(2)(B) (without regard to the second sentence thereof), and is engaged in the business of

Reg. § 1.884-1(d)(2)

taking deposits and making loans through its branch in the United States. In 1996, FC makes a loan in the ordinary course of its lending business in the United States, securing the loan with a mortgage on the U.S. real property being financed by the borrower. In 1997, after the borrower has defaulted on the loan, FC takes title to the real property that secures the loan. On December 31, 1997, FC continues to hold the property, classifying it on its financial statement as *Other Real Estate Owned*. Because all income and gain from the property would be ECI to FC under the principles of section 864(c)(2), the U.S. real property constitutes a U.S. asset within the meaning of paragraph (d) of this section.

Example 3. U.S. real property interest not connected to a U.S. business. Foreign corporation A owns a condominium apartment in the United States. Assume that holding the apartment does not constitute a U.S. trade or business and the foreign corporation has not made an election under section 882(d) to treat income with respect to the property as ECI. The condominium apartment is not a U.S. asset of A because the income, if any, from the asset would not be ECI. However, the disposition by A of the condominium apartment at a gain will give rise to ECEP.

Example 4. Stock in a domestically-controlled REIT. As an investment, foreign corporation A owns stock in a domestically-controlled REIT, within the meaning of section 897(h)(4)(B). Under section 897(h)(2), gain on disposition of stock in the REIT is not treated as ECI. For this reason the stock does not qualify as a U.S. asset under paragraph (d)(1) of this section even if dividend distributions from the REIT are treated as ECI. Thus, A will have a dividend equivalent amount based on the ECEP attributable to a distribution of ECI from the REIT, even if A invests the proceeds from the dividend in additional stock of the REIT. (Stock in a REIT that is not a domestically-controlled REIT is also not a U.S. asset. See § 1.884-1(d)(5)).

Example 5. Section 864(c)(7) property. Foreign corporation A is engaged in the equipment leasing business in the United States and Canada. A transfers the equipment leased by its U.S. trade or business to its Canadian business after the equipment is fully depreciated in the United States. The Canadian business sells the equipment two years later. Section 864(c)(7) would treat the gain on the disposition of the equipment by A as taxable under section 882 as if the sale occurred immediately before the equipment was transferred to the Canadian business. The equipment would not be treated as a U.S. asset even if the gain was ECI because the income from the equipment in the year of the sale in Canada would not be ECI.

(3) *Interest in a partnership*—(i) *In general.* A foreign corporation that is a partner in a partnership must take into account its interest in the partnership (and not the partnership assets) in determining its U.S. assets. For purposes of determining the proportion of the partnership interest that is a U.S. asset, a foreign corporation may elect to use either the asset method described in paragraph (d)(3)(ii) of this section or the income method described in paragraph (d)(3)(iii) of this section.

(ii) *Asset method*—(A) *In general.* A partner's interest in a partnership shall be treated as a U.S. asset in the same proportion that the sum of the partner's proportionate share of the adjusted bases of all partnership assets as of the determination date, to the extent that the assets would be treated as U.S. assets if the partnership were a foreign corporation, bears to the sum of the partner's proportionate share of the adjusted bases of all partnership assets as of the determination date. Generally a partner's proportionate share of a partnership asset is the same as its proportionate share of all items of income, gain, loss, and deduction that may be generated by the asset.

(B) *Non-uniform proportionate shares.* If a partner's proportionate share of all items of income, gain, loss, and deduction that may be generated by a single asset of the partnership throughout the period that includes the taxable year of the partner is not uniform, then, for purposes of determining the partner's proportionate share of the adjusted basis of that asset, a partner must take into account the portion of the adjusted basis of the asset that reflects the partner's economic interest in that asset. A partner's economic interest in an asset of the partnership must be determined by applying the following presumptions. These presumptions may, however, be rebutted if the partner or the Internal Revenue Service shows that the presumption is inconsistent with the partner's true economic interest in the asset during the corporation's taxable year.

(*1*) If a partnership asset ordinarily generates directly identifiable income, a partner's economic interest in the asset is determined by reference to its proportionate share of income that may be generated by the asset for the partnership's taxable year ending with or within the partner's taxable year.

(*2*) If a partnership asset ordinarily generates current deductions and ordinarily generates no directly identifiable income, for example because the asset contributes equally to the generation of all the income of the partnership (such as

Reg. § 1.884-1(d)(3)

an asset used in general and administrative functions), a partner's economic interest in the asset is determined by reference to its proportionate share of the total deductions that may be generated by the asset for the partnership's taxable year ending with or within the partner's taxable year.

(3) For other partnership assets not described in paragraph (d)(3)(ii)(B)(*1*) or (*2*) of this section, a partner's economic interest in the asset is determined by reference to its proportionate share of the total gain or loss to which it would be entitled if the asset were sold at a gain or loss in the partnership's taxable year ending with or within the partner's taxable year.

(C) *Partnership election under section 754.* If a partnership files an election in accordance with section 754, then for purposes of this paragraph (d)(3)(ii), the basis of partnership property shall reflect adjustments made pursuant to sections 734 (relating to distributions of property to a partner) and 743 (relating to the transfer of an interest in a partnership). However, adjustments made pursuant to section 743 may be made with respect to a transferee partner only.

(iii) *Income method.* Under the income method, a partner's interest in a partnership shall be treated as a U.S. asset in the same proportion that its distributive share of partnership ECI for the partnership's taxable year that ends with or within the partner's taxable year bears to its distributive share of all partnership income for that taxable year.

(iv) *Manner of election*—(A) *In general.* In determining the proportion of a foreign corporation's interest in a partnership that is a U.S. asset, a foreign corporation must elect one of the methods described in paragraph (d)(3) of this section on a timely filed return for the first taxable year beginning on or after the effective date of this section. An amended return does not qualify for this purpose, nor shall the provisions of § 301.9100-1 of this chapter and any guidance promulgated thereunder apply. An election shall be made by the foreign corporation calculating its U.S. assets in accordance with the method elected. An elected method must be used for a minimum period of five years before the foreign corporation may elect a different method. To change an election before the end of the requisite five-year period, a foreign corporation must obtain the consent of the Commissioner or her delegate. The Commissioner or her delegate will generally consent to a foreign corporation's request to change its election only in rare and unusual circumstances. A foreign corporation that is a partner in more than one partnership is not required to elect to use the same method for each partnership interest.

(B) *Elections with tiered partnerships.* If a foreign corporation elects to use the asset method with respect to an interest in a partnership, and that partnership is a partner in a lower-tier partnership, the foreign corporation may apply either the asset method or the income method to determine the proportion of the upper-tier partnership's interest in the lower-tier partnership that is a U.S. asset.

(v) *Failure to make proper election.* If a foreign corporation, for any reason, fails to make an election to use one of the methods required by paragraph (d)(3) of this section in a timely fashion, the district director or the Assistant Commissioner (International) may make the election on behalf of the foreign corporation and such election shall be binding as if made by that corporation.

(vi) *Special rule for determining a partner's adjusted basis in a partnership interest.* For purposes of paragraphs (d)(3) and (6) of this section, a partner's adjusted basis in a partnership interest shall be the partner's basis in such interest (determined under section 705) reduced by the partner's share of the liabilities of the partnership determined under section 752 and increased by a proportionate share of each liability of the partnership equal to the partner's proportionate share of the expense, for income tax purposes, attributable to such liability for the taxable year. A partner's adjusted basis in a partnership interest cannot be less than zero.

(vii) *E&P basis of a partnership interest.* See paragraph (d)(6)(iii) of this section for special rules governing the calculation of a foreign corporation's E&P basis in a partnership interest.

(viii) The application of this paragraph (d)(3) is illustrated by the following examples:

Example 1. General rule—(i) *Facts.* Foreign corporation, FC, is a partner in partnership ABC, which is engaged in a trade or business within the United States. FC and ABC are both calendar year taxpayers. ABC owns and manages two office buildings located in the United States, each with an adjusted basis of $50. ABC also owns a non-U.S. asset with an adjusted basis of $100. ABC has no liabilities. Under the partnership agreement, FC has a 50 percent interest in the capital of ABC and a 50 percent interest in all items of income, gain, loss, and deduction that may be generated by the partnership's assets. FC's adjusted basis in ABC is $100. In determining the proportion of its interest in ABC that is a U.S. asset, FC elects to use the asset method described in paragraph (d)(3)(ii) of this section.

Reg. § 1.884-1(d)(3)

(ii) *Analysis.* FC's interest in ABC is treated as a U.S. asset in the same proportion that the sum of FC's proportionate share of the adjusted bases of all ABC's U.S. assets (50% of $100), bears to the sum of FC's proportionate share of the adjusted bases of all of ABC's assets (50% of $200). Under the asset method, the amount of FC's interest in ABC that is a U.S. asset is $50 ($100 × $50/$100).

Example 2. Special allocation of gain with respect to real property—(i) *Facts.* The facts are the same as in *Example 1*, except that under the partnership agreement, FC is allocated 20 percent of the income from the partnership property but 80 percent of the gain on disposition of the partnership property.

(ii) *Analysis.* Assuming that the buildings ordinarily generate directly identifiable income, there is a rebuttable presumption under paragraph (d)(3)(ii)(B)(*1*) of this section that FC's proportionate share of the adjusted basis of the buildings is FC's proportionate share of the income generated by the buildings (20%) rather than the total gain that it would be entitled to under the partnership agreement (80%) if the buildings were sold at a gain on the determination date. Thus, the sum of FC's proportionate share of the adjusted bases in ABC's U.S. assets (the buildings) is presumed to be $20 [(20% of $50) + (20% of $50)]. Assuming that the non-U.S. asset is not income-producing and does not generate current deductions, there is a rebuttable presumption under paragraph (d)(3)(ii)(B)(*3*) of this section that FC's proportionate share of the adjusted basis of that asset is FC's interest in the gain on the disposition of the asset (80%) rather than its proportionate share of the income that may be generated by the asset (20%). Thus, FC's proportionate share of the adjusted basis of ABC's non-U.S. asset is presumed to be $80 (80% of $100). FC's proportionate share of the adjusted bases of all of the assets of ABC is $100 ($20 + $80). The amount of FC's interest in ABC that is a U.S. asset is $20 ($100 x $20/$100).

Example 3. Tiered partnerships (asset method)—(i) *Facts.* The facts are the same as in *Example 1*, except that FC's adjusted basis in ABC is $175 and ABC also has a 50 percent interest in the capital of partnership DEF. DEF owns and operates a commercial shopping center in the United States with an adjusted basis of $200 and also owns non-U.S. assets with an adjusted basis of $100. DEF has no liabilities. ABC's adjusted basis in its interest in DEF is $150 and ABC has a 50 percent interest in all the items of income, gain, loss and deduction that may be generated by the assets of DEF.

(ii) *Analysis.* Because FC has elected to use the asset method described in paragraph (d)(3)(ii) of this section, it must determine what proportion of ABC's partnership interest in DEF is a U.S. asset. As permitted by paragraph (d)(3)(iv)(B) of this section, FC also elects to use the asset method with respect to ABC's interest in DEF. ABC's interest in DEF is treated as a U.S. asset in the same proportion that the sum of ABC's proportionate share of the adjusted bases of all DEF's U.S. assets (50% of $200), bears to the sum of ABC's proportionate share of the adjusted bases of all of DEF's assets (50% of $300). Thus, the amount of ABC's interest in DEF that is a U.S. asset is $100 ($150 × $100/$150). FC must then apply the rules of paragraph (d)(3)(ii) of this section to all the assets of ABC, including ABC's interest in DEF that is treated in part as a U.S. asset ($100) and in part as a non-U.S. asset ($50). FC's interest in ABC is treated as a U.S. asset in the same proportion that the sum of FC's proportionate share of the adjusted bases of the U.S. assets of ABC (including ABC's interest in DEF), bears to the sum of FC's proportionate share of the adjusted bases of all ABC's assets (including ABC's interest in DEF). Thus, the amount of FC's interest in ABC that is a U.S. asset is $100 (FC's adjusted basis in ABC ($175) multiplied by FC's proportionate share of the sum of the adjusted bases of ABC's U.S. assets ($100)) over FC's proportionate share of the sum of the adjusted bases of ABC's assets ($175)).

Example 4. Tiered partnerships (income method)—(i) *Facts.* The facts are the same as in *Example 3*, except that FC has elected to use the income method described in paragraph (d)(3)(iii) of this section to determine the proportion of its interest in ABC that is a U.S. asset. The two office buildings located in the United States generate $60 of income that is ECI for the taxable year. The non-U.S. asset is not-income producing. In addition ABC's distributive share of income from DEF consists of $40 of income that is ECI and $140 of income that is not ECI.

(ii) *Analysis.* Because FC has elected to use the income method it does need to determine what proportion of ABC's partnership interest in DEF is a U.S. asset. FC's interest in ABC is treated as a U.S. asset in the same proportion that its distributive share of ABC's income for the taxable year that is ECI ($50) ($30 earned directly by ABC + $20 distributive share from DEF) bears to its distributive share of all ABC's income for the taxable year ($55) ($30 earned directly by ABC + $25 distributive share from DEF). Thus, FC's interest in ABC that is a U.S. asset is $159 ($175 × $50/$55).

Reg. § 1.884-1(d)(3)

(4) *Interest in a trust or estate*—(i) *Estates and non-grantor trusts.* A foreign corporation that is a beneficiary of a trust or estate shall not be treated as having a U.S. asset by virtue of its interest in the trust or estate.

(ii) *Grantor trusts.* If, under sections 671 through 678, a foreign corporation is treated as owning a portion of a trust that includes all the income and gain that may be generated by a trust asset (or pro rata portion of a trust asset), the foreign corporation will be treated as owning the trust asset (or pro rata portion thereof) for purposes of determining its U.S. assets under this section.

(5) *Property that is not a U.S. asset*—(i) *Property that does not give rise to ECEP.* Property described in paragraphs (d)(1) through (4) of this section shall not be treated as a U.S. asset of a foreign corporation if, on the determination date, income from the use of the property, or gain or loss from the disposition of the property, would be described in paragraph (f)(2) of this section (relating to certain income that does not produce ECEP).

(ii) *Assets acquired to increase U.S. net equity artificially.* U.S. assets shall not include assets acquired or used by a foreign corporation if one of the principal purposes of such acquisition or use is to increase artificially the U.S. assets of a foreign corporation on the determination date. Whether assets are acquired or used for such purpose will depend upon all the facts and circumstances of each case. Factors to be considered in determining whether one of the principal purposes in acquiring or using an asset is to increase artificially the U.S. assets of a foreign corporation include the length of time during which the asset was used in a U.S. trade or business, whether the asset was acquired from, or disposed of to, a related person, and whether the aggregate value of the U.S. assets of the foreign corporation increased temporarily on the determination date. For purposes of this paragraph (d)(5)(ii), to be one of the principal purposes, a purpose must be important, but it is not necessary that it be the primary purpose.

(iii) *Interbranch transactions.* A transaction of any type between separate offices or branches of the same taxpayer does not create a U.S. asset.

(6) *E&P basis of a U.S. asset*—(i) *General rule.* The E&P basis of a U.S. asset for purposes of this section is its adjusted basis for purposes of computing the foreign corporation's earnings and profits. In determining the E&P basis of a U.S. asset, the adjusted basis of the asset (for purposes of computing taxable income) must be increased or decreased to take into account inclusions of income or gain, and deductions or similar charges, that affect the basis of the asset where such items are taken into account in a different manner for purposes of computing earnings and profits than for purposes of computing taxable income. For example, if section 312(k) requires that depreciation with respect to a U.S. asset be determined using the straight line method for purposes of computing earnings and profits, but depreciation with respect to the asset is determined using a different method for purposes of computing taxable income, the E&P basis of the property for purposes of this section must be computed using the straight line method of depreciation.

(ii) *Installment obligations*—(A) *Sales in taxable year beginning on or after January 1, 1987.* For purposes of this section, the E&P basis of an installment obligation described in paragraph (d)(2)(iii) of this section that arises in connection with an installment sale occurring in a taxable year beginning on or after January 1, 1987, shall equal the sum of the total amount of gain from the sale if the obligation were satisfied in full and the adjusted basis of the property sold as of the date of sale, reduced by payments received with respect to the obligation that are not interest or original issue discount. See paragraph (j)(2)(ii) of this section, however, for a special E&P basis rule for an installment obligation arising in connection with a sale of a U.S. asset by a foreign corporation described in section 312(k)(4), where such sale occurs in a taxable year beginning in 1987.

(B) *Sales in taxable year prior to January 1, 1987.* For purposes of this section, the E&P basis of an installment obligation described in paragraph (d)(2)(iii) of this section that arises in connection with an installment sale occurring in a taxable year beginning before January 1, 1987, shall equal zero.

(iii) *Computation of E&P basis in a partnership.* For purposes of this section, a foreign corporation's E&P basis in a partnership interest shall be the foreign corporation's adjusted basis in such interest (as determined under paragraph (d)(3)(vi) of this section), further adjusted to take into account any differences between the foreign corporation's distributive share of items of partnership income, gain, loss, and deduction for purposes of computing the taxable income of the foreign corporation and the foreign corporation's distributive share of items of partnership income, gain, loss, and deduction for purposes of computing the earnings and profits of the foreign corporation.

Reg. § 1.884-1(d)(4)

(iv) *Computation of E&P basis of a loss property.* The E&P basis of a loss property (as defined in paragraph (d)(2)(ix) of this section) shall equal the E&P basis, immediately before the loss, of the U.S. asset with respect to which the loss was sustained, reduced (but not below zero) by—

    (A) The amount of any deduction claimed under section 165 by the foreign corporation with respect to the loss for earnings and profits purposes; and

    (B) Any compensation received with respect to the loss.

(v) *Computation of E&P basis of financial instruments.* [Reserved]

(vi) *Example.* The application of paragraph (d)(6)(ii) of this section is illustrated by the following example.

Example. Sale in taxable year beginning on or after January 1, 1987. Foreign corporation A, a calendar year taxpayer, sells a U.S. asset on the installment method in 1993. Under the terms of the sale, A is to receive $100, payable in ten annual installments of $10 beginning in 1994, plus an arm's-length rate of interest on the unpaid balance of the sales price. A's adjusted basis in the property sold is $70. The obligation received in connection with the installment sale is treated as a U.S. asset with an E&P basis of $100 ($30 (the amount of gain from the sale if the obligation were satisfied in full) + $70 (the adjusted basis of the property sold)). If A receives a payment of $10 (not including interest) in 1994 with respect to the obligation, the obligation is treated as a U.S. asset with an E&P basis of $90 ($100 − $10) as of the close of 1994.

(e) *U.S. liabilities.* The term "U.S. liabilities" means the amount of liabilities determined under paragraph (e)(1) of this section decreased by the amount of liabilities determined under paragraph (e)(3) of this section, and increased by the amount of liabilities determined under paragraph (e)(2) of this section.

(1) *Liabilities based on § 1.882-5.* The amount of liabilities determined under this paragraph (e)(1) is the amount of U.S.-connected liabilities of a foreign corporation under § 1.882-5 if the U.S.-connected liabilities were computed using the assets and liabilities of the foreign corporation as of the determination date (rather than the average of such assets and liabilities for the taxable year) and without regard to paragraph (e)(3) of this section.

(2) *Additional liabilities—Insurance reserves.* (i) The amount of liabilities determined under this paragraph (e)(2)(i) is the amount (as of the determination date) of the total insurance liabilities on United States business (within the meaning of section 842 (b)(2)(B)) of a foreign corporation described in section 842(a) (relating to foreign corporations carrying on an insurance business in the United States) to the extent that such liabilities are not otherwise treated as U.S. liabilities by reason of paragraph (e)(1) of this section.

(ii) *Liabilities described in § 1.882-5(a)(1)(ii).* The amount of liabilities determined under this paragraph (e)(2)(ii) is the amount (as of the determination date) of liabilities described in § 1.882-5(a)(1)(ii) (relating to liabilities giving rise to interest expense that is directly allocated to income from a U.S. asset).

(3) *Election to reduce liabilities*—(i) *General rule.* The amount of liabilities determined under this paragraph (e)(3) is the amount by which a foreign corporation elects to reduce its liabilities under paragraph (e)(1) of this section.

(ii) *Limitation.* For any taxable year, a foreign corporation may elect to reduce the amount of its liabilities determined under paragraph (e)(1) of this section by an amount that does not exceed the excess, if any, of the amount of liabilities in paragraph (e)(1) of this section over the amount, as of the determination date, of U.S. booked liabilities (determined under § 1.882-5(d)(2)) and liabilities described in paragraph (e)(2) of this section.

(iii) *Effect of election on interest deduction and branch-level interest tax.* A foreign corporation that elects to reduce its liabilities under this paragraph (e)(3) must, for purposes of computing the amount of its interest apportioned to ECI under § 1.882-5, reduce its U.S.-connected liabilities for the taxable year of the election by the amount of the reduction in liabilities under this paragraph (e)(3). The reduction of its U.S.-connected liabilities will also require a corresponding decrease in the amount of its interest apportioned to ECI under § 1.882-5 for purposes of § 1.884-4(a) and for all other Code sections for which the amount of interest apportioned under § 1.882-5 is relevant.

(iv) *Method of election.* A foreign corporation that elects the benefits of this paragraph (e)(3) for a taxable year shall state on its return for the taxable year (or on a statement attached to the return) that it has elected to reduce its liabilities for the taxable year under this paragraph (e)(3) and that it has reduced the amount of its U.S.-connected liabilities as provided in paragraph (e)(3)(iii) of this section, and shall indicate the amount of such reductions on the return or attachment. An election under this paragraph (e)(3) must be made before the due date (including extensions) for the foreign corporation's income tax return for the taxable year.

(v) *Effect of election on complete termination.* If a foreign corporation completely terminates its U.S. trade or business (within the meaning of § 1.884-2T (a)(2)), notwithstanding § 1.884-2T(a), the foreign corporation will be subject to tax on a dividend equivalent amount that equals the lesser of—

(A) The foreign corporation's accumulated ECEP that is attributable to an election to reduce liabilities; or

(B) The amount by which the corporation elected to reduce liabilities at the end of the taxable year preceding the year of complete termination.

For purposes of the preceding sentence, accumulated ECEP is attributable to an election to reduce liabilities to the extent that the ECEP was accumulated because of such an election rather than because of an increase in U.S. assets. For example, if a foreign corporation did not have positive ECEP in any year for which an election was made, it would not be required to include an amount as a dividend equivalent amount under this paragraph (e)(3)(v) because any accumulated ECEP that it may have is not attributable to an election to reduce liabilities.

(4) *Artificial decrease in U.S. liabilities.* If a foreign corporation repays or otherwise decreases its U.S. liabilities and one of the principal purposes of such decrease is to decrease artificially its U.S. liabilities on the determination date, then such decrease shall not be taken into account for purposes of computing the foreign corporation's U.S. net equity. Whether the U.S. liabilities of a foreign corporation are artificially decreased will depend on all the facts and circumstances of each case. Factors to be considered in determining whether one of the principal purposes for the repayment or decrease of the liabilities is to decrease artificially the U.S. liabilities of a foreign corporation shall include whether the aggregate liabilities are temporarily decreased on or before the determination date by, for example, the repayment of liabilities, or U.S. liabilities are temporarily decreased on or before the determination date by the acquisition with contributed funds of passive-type assets that are not U.S. assets. For purposes of this paragraph (e)(4), to be one of the principal purposes, a purpose must be important, but it is not necessary that it be the primary purpose.

(5) *Examples.* The application of this paragraph (e) is illustrated by the following examples.

Example 1. General rule for computation of U.S. liabilities. As of the close of 1997, foreign corporation A, a calendar year taxpayer computes its U.S.-connected liabilities under § 1.882-5(c) using its actual ratio of liabilities to assets. For purposes of computing its U.S. connected liabilities under § 1.882-5(c), A must determine the average total value of its assets that are U.S. assets. Assume that the average value of such assets is $100, while the amount of such assets as of the close of 1997 is $125. For purposes of § 1.882-5(c)(2), A must determine the ratio of the average of its worldwide liabilities for the year to the average total value of worldwide assets for the taxable year. Assume that A's average liabilities-to-assets ratio under § 1.882-5(c)(2) is 55 percent, while its liabilities-to-assets ratio at the close of 1997 is only 50 percent. Thus, assuming no further adjustments under paragraph (e)(3) of this section, A's U.S.-connected liabilities for purposes of § 1.882-5 are $55 ($100 x 55%). However, A's U.S. liabilities are $62.50 for purposes of this section, the value of its assets determined under § 1.882-5(b)(2) as of the close of December ($125) multiplied by the liabilities-to-assets ratio (50%) as of such date.

Example 2. Election made to reduce liabilities. (i) As of the close of 1997, foreign corporation A, a real estate company, owns U.S. assets with an E&P basis of $1000. A has $800 of liabilities under paragraph (e)(1) of this section and $300 of liabilities properly reflected on the books of its U.S. trade or business under § 1.882-5(d)(2). A has accumulated ECEP of $500 and in 1998, A has $60 of ECEP that it intends to retain for future expansion of its U.S. trade or business. A elects under paragraph (e) (3) of this section to reduce its liabilities by $60 from $800 to $740. As a result of the election, assuming A's U.S. assets and U.S. liabilities would otherwise have remained constant, A's U.S. net equity as of the close of 1998 will increase by the amount of the decrease in liabilities ($60) from $200 to $260 and its ECEP will be reduced to zero. Under paragraph (e)(3)(iii) of this section, A's interest expense for the taxable year is reduced by the amount of interest attributable to $60 of liabilities and A's excess interest is reduced by the same amount. A's taxable income and ECEP are increased by the amount of the reduction in interest expense attributable to the liabilities, and A may make an election under paragraph (e)(3) of this section to further reduce its liabilities, thus increasing its U.S. net equity and reducing the amount of additional ECEP created by the election.

(ii) In 1999, assuming A again has $60 of ECEP, A may again make the election under paragraph (e)(3) to reduce its liabilities. However,

Reg. § 1.884-1(e)(4)

assuming A's U.S. assets and liabilities under paragraph (e)(1) of this section remain constant, A will need to make an election to reduce its liabilities by $120 to reduce to zero its ECEP in 1999 and to continue to retain for expansion (without the payment of the branch profits tax) the $60 of ECEP earned in 1998. Without an election to reduce liabilities, A's dividend equivalent amount for 1999 would be $120 ($60 of ECEP plus the $60 reduction in U.S. net equity from $260 to $200). If A makes the election to reduce liabilities by $120 (from $800 to $680), A's U.S. net equity will increase by $60 (from $260 at the end of the previous year to $320), the amount necessary to reduce its ECEP to $0. However, the reduction of liabilities will itself create additional ECEP subject to section 884 because of the reduction in interest expense attributable to the $120 of liabilities. A can make the election to reduce liabilities by $120 without exceeding the limitation on the election provided in paragraph (e)(3)(ii) of this section because $120 does not exceed the excess of $800 (the amount of A's liabilities under paragraph (e)(1) of this section) over $300 (the amount of liabilities on A's books).

(iii) If A terminates its U.S. trade or business in 1999 in accordance with the rules in § 1.884-2T(a), A would not be subject to the branch profits tax on the $60 of ECEP earned in that year. Under paragraph (e)(3)(v) of this section, however, it would be subject to the branch profits tax on the portion of the $60 of ECEP that it earned in 1998 that became accumulated ECEP because of an election to reduce liabilities.

(f) *Effectively connected earnings and profits*— (1) *In general.* Except as provided in paragraph (f)(2) of this section and as modified by § 1.884-2T (relating to the incorporation or complete termination of a U.S. trade or business or the reorganization or liquidation of a foreign corporation or its domestic subsidiary), the term "effectively connected earnings and profits" ("ECEP") means the earnings and profits (or deficits therein) determined under section 312 and this paragraph (f) that are attributable to ECI (within the meaning of paragraph (d)(1)(iii) of this section). Because the term "ECI" includes income treated as effectively connected, income that is ECI under section 842(b) (relating to minimum net investment income of an insurance business) or 864(c)(7) (relating to gain from property formerly held for use in a U.S. trade or business) gives rise to ECEP. ECEP also includes earnings and profits attributable to ECI of a foreign corporation earned through a partnership, and through a trust or estate. For purposes of section 884, gain on the sale of a U.S. real property interest by a foreign corporation that has made an election to be treated as a domestic corporation under section 897(i) will also give rise to ECEP. ECEP is not reduced by distributions made by the foreign corporation during any taxable year or by the amount of branch profits tax or tax on excess interest (as defined in § 1.884-4(a)(2)) paid by the foreign corporation. Earnings and profits are treated as attributable to ECI even if the earnings and profits are taken into account under section 312 in an earlier or later taxable year than the taxable year in which the ECI is taken into account.

(2) *Income that does not produce ECEP.* The term "ECEP" does not include any earnings and profits attributable to—

(i) Income excluded from gross income under section 883(a)(1) or 883(a)(2) (relating to certain income derived from the operation of ships or aircraft);

(ii) Income that is ECI by reason of section 921(d) or 926(b) (relating to certain income of a FSC and certain dividends paid by a FSC to a foreign corporation or nonresident alien) that is not otherwise ECI;

(iii) Gain on the disposition of a U.S. real property interest described in section 897(c)(1)(A)(ii) (relating to certain interests in a domestic corporation);

(iv) Income that is ECI by reason of section 953(c)(3)(C) (relating to certain income of a captive insurance company that a corporation elects to treat as ECI) that is not otherwise ECI;

(v) Income that is exempt from tax under section 892 (relating to certain income of foreign governments); and

(vi) Income that is ECI by reason of section 882(e) (relating to certain interest income of banks organized under the laws of a possession of the United States) that is not otherwise ECI.

(3) *Allocation of deductions attributable to income that does not produce ECEP.* In determining the amount of a foreign corporation's ECEP for the taxable year, deductions and other adjustments shall be allocated and apportioned under the principles of § 1.861-8 between ECI that gives rise to ECEP and income described in paragraph (f)(2) of this section (relating to income that is ECI but does not give rise to ECEP).

(4) *Examples.* The principles of paragraph (f) of this section are illustrated by the following examples.

Example 1. Tax-exempt income. Foreign corporation A owns a tax-exempt municipal bond that is a U.S. asset as of the close of its 1989 taxable year. The municipal bond gives rise in 1989 to ECI (even though the income is excluded

Reg. § 1.884-1(f)(3)

from gross income under section 103(a) and is not gross income of a foreign corporation by reason of section 882(b)), and therefore gives rise to ECEP in 1989.

Example 2. Income exempt under a treaty. Foreign corporation A derives ECI that constitutes business profits that are not attributable to a permanent establishment maintained by A in the United States. The ECI is exempt from taxation under section 882(a) by reason of an income tax treaty and section 894(a). The income nevertheless gives rise to ECEP under this paragraph (f). However, a dividend equivalent amount attributable to such ECEP may be exempt from the branch profits tax by reason of paragraph (g) of this section (relating to the application of the branch profits tax to corporations that are residents of countries with which the United States has an income tax treaty).

(g) *Corporations resident in countries with which the United States has an income tax treaty*—(1) *General rule.* Except as provided in paragraph (g)(2) of this section, a foreign corporation that is a resident of a country with which the United States has an income tax treaty in effect for a taxable year in which it has a dividend equivalent amount and that meets the requirements, if any, of the limitation on benefits provisions of such treaty with respect to the dividend equivalent amount shall not be subject to the branch profits tax on such amount (or will qualify for a reduction in the amount of tax with respect to such amount) only if—

(i) The foreign corporation is a qualified resident of such country for the taxable year, within the meaning of § 1.884-5(a); or

(ii) The limitation on benefits provision, or an amendment to that provision, entered into force after December 31, 1986.

If, after application of § 1.884-5(e)(4)(iv), a foreign corporation is a qualified resident under § 1.884-5(e) (relating to the active trade or business test) only with respect to one of its trades or businesses in the United States, i.e., the trade or business that is an integral part of its business conducted in its country of residence, and not with respect to another, the rules of this paragraph shall apply only to that portion of its dividend equivalent amount attributable to the trade or business for which the foreign corporation is a qualified resident.

(2) *Special rules for foreign corporations that are qualified residents on the basis of their ownership*—(i) *General rule.* A foreign corporation that, in any taxable year, is a qualified resident of a country with which the United States has an income tax treaty in effect solely by reason of meeting the requirements of § 1.884-5(b) and (c) (relating, respectively, to stock ownership and base erosion) shall be exempt from the branch profits tax or subject to a reduced rate of branch profits tax under paragraph (g)(1) of this section with respect to the portion of its dividend equivalent amount for the taxable year attributable to accumulated ECEP only if the foreign corporation is a qualified resident of such country within the meaning of § 1.884-5(a) for the taxable years includible, in whole or in part, in a consecutive 36-month period that includes the taxable year of the dividend equivalent amount. A foreign corporation that fails the 36-month test described in the preceding sentence shall be exempt from the branch profits tax or subject to the branch profits tax at a reduced rate under paragraph (g)(1) of this section with respect to accumulated ECEP (determined on a last-in-first-out basis) accumulated only during prior years in which the foreign corporation was a qualified resident of such country within the meaning of § 1.884-5(a).

(ii) *Rules of application.* A foreign corporation that has not satisfied the 36-month test as of the close of the taxable year of the dividend equivalent amount but satisfies the test with respect to such dividend equivalent amount by meeting the 36-month test by the close of the second taxable year succeeding the taxable year of the dividend equivalent amount shall be subject to the branch profits tax for the year of the dividend equivalent amount without regard to paragraph (g)(1) of this section on the portion of the dividend equivalent amount attributable to accumulated ECEP derived in a taxable year in which the foreign corporation was not a qualified resident within the meaning of § 1.884-5(a). Upon meeting the 36-month test, the foreign corporation shall be entitled to claim by amended return a refund of the tax paid with respect to the dividend equivalent amount in excess of the branch profits tax calculated by taking into account paragraph (g)(2)(i) of this section, provided the foreign corporation establishes in the amended return for the taxable year that it has met the requirements of such paragraph. For purposes of section 6611 (dealing with interest on overpayments), any overpayment of branch profits tax by reason of this paragraph (g)(2)(ii) shall be deemed not to have been made before the filing date for the taxable year in which the foreign corporation establishes that it has met the 36-month test.

(iii) *Example.* The application of this paragraph (g)(2) is illustrated by the following example.

Example. (i) Foreign corporation A, a calendar year taxpayer, is a resident of the United

Kingdom. A has a dividend equivalent amount for its taxable year 1991 of $300, of which $100 is attributable to 1991 ECEP and $200 to accumulated ECEP. A is a qualified resident for its taxable year 1991 because for that year it meets the requirements of § 1.884-5(b) and (c), relating, respectively, to stock ownership and base erosion. For 1991 A does not meet the requirements of § 1.884-5(d), (e), or (f) for qualified residence. A is not a qualified resident of the United Kingdom for any taxable year prior to 1990 but is a qualified resident for its taxable years 1990 and 1992.

(ii) Because A is a qualified resident for the 3-year period (1990, 1991, and 1992) that includes the taxable year of the dividend equivalent amount (1991), A satisfies the 36-month test of this paragraph (g)(2) and no branch profits tax is imposed on the total $300 dividend equivalent amount. However, since A was not a qualified resident for any taxable year prior to 1990 and therefore cannot establish that it has satisfied the 36-month test until the taxable year following the year of the dividend equivalent amount, A must pay the branch profits tax for its taxable year 1991 with respect to the portion of the dividend equivalent amount attributable to accumulated ECEP relating to years prior to 1990 without regard to paragraph (g)(1) of this section. A may file for a refund of the branch profits tax paid with respect to its 1991 taxable year at any time after it establishes that it is a qualified resident for its 1992 taxable year.

(3) *Exemptions for foreign corporations resident in certain countries with income tax treaties in effect on January 1, 1987.* The branch profits tax shall not be imposed on the portion of the dividend equivalent amount with respect to which a foreign corporation satisfies the requirements of paragraphs (g)(1) and (2) of this section for a country listed below, so long as the income tax treaty between the United States and that country, as in effect on January 1, 1987, remains in effect, except to the extent the treaty is modified on or after January 1, 1987, to expressly provide for the imposition of the branch profits tax:

Aruba	Greece	Netherlands
Austria	Hungary	Netherlands
Belgium	Iceland	Antilles
People's	Ireland	Norway
Republic	Italy	Pakistan
of China	Jamaica	Philippines
Cyprus	Japan	Sweden
Denmark	Korea	Switzerland
Egypt	Luxembourg	United
Finland	Malta	Kingdom
Germany	Morocco	

(4) *Modifications with respect to other income tax treaties*—(i) *Limitation on rate of tax*—(A) *General rule.* If, under paragraphs (g)(1) and (2) of this section, a corporation qualifies for a reduction in the amount of the branch profits tax and paragraph (g)(3) of this section does not apply, the rate of tax shall be the rate of tax on branch profits specified in the treaty between the United States and the corporation's country of residence or, if no rate of tax on branch profits is specified, the rate of tax that would apply under such treaty to dividends paid to the foreign corporation by a wholly-owned domestic corporation.

(B) *Certain treaties in effect on January 1, 1987.* The branch profits tax shall generally be imposed at the following rates on the portion of the dividend equivalent amount with respect to which a foreign corporation satisfies the requirements of paragraphs (g)(1) and (2) of this section for a country listed below, for as long as the relevant provisions of those income tax treaties remain in effect and are not modified or superseded by subsequent agreement:

Australia (15%)	New Zealand (5%)	Trinidad &
Barbados (5%)	Poland (5%)	Tobago (10%)
Canada (10%)	Romania (10%)	U.S.S.R. (30%)
France (5%)	South Africa (30%)	

However, for special rates imposed on corporations resident in France and Trinidad & Tobago that have certain amounts of dividend and interest income, see the dividend articles of the income tax treaties with those countries.

(ii) *Limitations other than rate of tax.* If, under paragraphs (g)(1) and (2) of this section, a foreign corporation qualifies for a reduction in the amount of branch profits tax and paragraph (g)(3) of this section does not apply, then—

(A) The foreign corporation shall be entitled to the benefit of any limitations on imposition of a tax on branch profits (in addition to any limitations on the rate of tax) contained in the treaty; and

Reg. § 1.884-1(g)(4)

(B) No branch profits tax shall be imposed with respect to a dividend equivalent amount out of ECEP or accumulated ECEP of the foreign corporation unless the ECEP or accumulated ECEP is attributable to a permanent establishment in the United States or, if not otherwise prohibited under the treaty, to gain from the disposition of a U.S. real property interest described in section 897(c)(1)(A)(i), except to the extent the treaty specifically permits the imposition of the branch profits tax on such earnings and profits.

No article in such treaty shall be construed to provide any limitations on imposition of the branch profits tax other than as provided in this paragraph (g)(4).

(iii) *Computation of the dividend equivalent amount if a foreign corporation has both ECEP attributable to a permanent establishment and not attributable to a permanent establishment.* To determine the dividend equivalent amount of a foreign corporation out of ECEP that is attributable to a permanent establishment, the foreign corporation may only take into account its U.S. assets, U.S. liabilities, U.S. net equity and ECEP attributable to its permanent establishment. Thus, a foreign corporation may not reduce the amount of its ECEP attributable to its permanent establishment by reinvesting all or a portion of that amount in U.S. assets not attributable to the permanent establishment.

(iv) *Limitations under the Canadian treaty.* The limitations on the imposition of the branch profits tax under the Canadian treaty include, but are not limited to, those described in paragraphs (g)(4)(iv)(A) and (B).

(A) *Effect of deficits in earnings and profits.* In the case of a foreign corporation that is a qualified resident of Canada, the dividend equivalent amount for any taxable year shall not exceed the foreign corporation's accumulated ECEP as of the beginning of the taxable year plus the corporation's ECEP for the taxable year. Thus, for example, if a foreign corporation that is a qualified resident of Canada has a deficit in accumulated ECEP of $200 as of the beginning of the taxable year and ECEP of $100 for the taxable year, it will have no dividend equivalent amount for the taxable year because it would have a cumulative deficit in ECEP of $100 as of the close of the taxable year. For purposes of this paragraph (g)(4)(iii)(A), any net deficit in accumulated earnings and profits attributable to taxable years beginning before January 1, 1987, shall be includible in determining accumulated ECEP.

(B) *One-time exemption of Canadian $500,000—(1) General rule.* In the case of a foreign corporation that is a qualified resident of Canada, the branch profits tax shall be imposed only with respect to that portion of the dividend equivalent amount for the taxable year that, when translated into Canadian dollars and added to the dividend equivalent amounts for preceding taxable years translated into Canadian dollars, exceeds Canadian $500,000. The value of the dividend equivalent amount in Canadian currency shall be determined by translating the ECEP for each taxable year that is includible in the dividend equivalent amount (as determined in U.S. dollars under the currency translation method used in determining the foreign corporation's taxable income for U.S. tax purposes) by the weighted average exchange rate for the taxable year (determined under the rules of section 989(b)(3)) during which the earnings and profits were derived.

(2) *Reduction in amount of exemption in the case of related corporations.* The amount of a foreign corporation's exemption under this paragraph (g)(4)(iii)(B) shall be reduced by the amount of any exemption that reduced the dividend equivalent amount of an associated foreign corporation with respect to the same or a similar business. For purposes of this paragraph (g)(4)(iii)(B), a foreign corporation is an associated foreign corporation if it is related to the foreign corporation for purposes of section 267(b) or it and the foreign corporation are stapled entities (within the meaning of section 269B(c)(2)) or are effectively stapled entities. A business is the same as or similar to another business if it involves the sale, lease, or manufacture of the same or a similar type of property or the provision of the same or a similar type of services. A U.S. real property interest described in section 897(c)(1)(A)(i) shall be treated as a business and all such U.S. real property interests shall be treated as businesses that are the same or similar.

(3) *Coordination with second-tier withholding tax.* The value of the dividend equivalent amount that is exempt from the branch profits tax by reason of paragraph (g)(4)(iii)(B)(*1*) of this section shall not be subject to tax under section 871(a) or 881, or to withholding under section 1441 or 1442, when distributed by the foreign corporation.

(5) *Benefits under treaties other than income tax treaties.* A treaty that is not an income tax treaty does not exempt a foreign corporation from the branch profits tax or reduce the amount of the tax.

(h) *Stapled entities.* Any foreign corporation that is treated as a domestic corporation by rea-

Reg. § 1.884-1(g)(5)

son of section 269B (relating to stapled entities) shall continue to be treated as a foreign corporation for purposes of section 884 and the regulations thereunder, notwithstanding section 269B or the regulations thereunder. Dividends paid by such foreign corporation shall be treated as paid by a domestic corporation and shall be subject to the tax imposed by section 871(a) or 881(a), and to withholding under section 1441 or 1442, as applicable, to the extent paid out of earnings and profits that are not subject to tax under section 884(a). Dividends paid by such foreign corporation out of earnings and profits subject to tax under section 884(a) shall be exempt from the tax imposed by sections 871(a) and 881(a) and shall not be subject to withholding under section 1441 or 1442. Whether dividends are paid out of earnings and profits that are subject to tax under section 884(a) shall be determined under section 884(e)(3)(A) and the regulations thereunder. The limitation on the application of treaty benefits in section 884(e)(3)(B) (relating to qualified residents) shall apply to a foreign corporation described in this paragraph (h).

(i) *Effective date*—(1) *General rule.* This section is effective for taxable years beginning on or after [*the date that is 30 days after these regulations are published in the Federal Register*]. With respect to a taxable year beginning before [*the date that is 30 days after these regulations are published in the Federal Register*] and after December 31, 1986, a foreign corporation may elect to apply this section in lieu of § 1.884-1T of the temporary regulations (as contained in the CFR edition revised as of April 1, 1992), but only if the foreign corporation also makes an election under § 1.884-4(e) to apply § 1.884-4 in lieu of § 1.884-4T (as contained in the CFR edition revised as of April 1, 1992) for that taxable year, and the statute of limitations for assessment of a deficiency has not expired for that taxable year. Once an election has been made, an election under this section shall apply to all subsequent taxable years. However, paragraph (f)(2)(vi) of this section (relating to certain interest income of Possessions banks) shall not apply for taxable years beginning before January 1, 1990.

(2) *Election to reduce liabilities.* A foreign corporation may make an election to reduce its liabilities under paragraph (e)(3) of this section with respect to a taxable year for which an election under paragraph (i)(1) of this section is in effect by filing an amended return for the taxable year and recomputing its interest deduction and any other item affected by the election on an amended Form 1120F to take into account the reduction in liabilities for such year.

(3) *Separate election for installment obligations.* A foreign corporation may make a separate election to apply paragraphs (d)(2)(iii) and (d)(6)(ii) of this section (relating to installment obligations treated as U.S. assets) to any prior taxable year without making an election under paragraph (i)(1) of this section, provided the statute of limitations for assessment of a deficiency has not expired for that taxable year and each succeeding taxable year. Once an election under this paragraph (i)(3) has been made, it shall apply to all subsequent taxable years.

(4) *Special rules for certain U.S. assets and liabilities.* Paragraphs (c)(2)(i) and (ii), (d)(3), (d)(4), (d)(5)(iii), (d)(6)(iii), (d)(6)(vi), (e)(2), and (e)(3)(ii), of this section are effective for taxable years beginning on or after June 6, 1996.

(j) *Transition rules*—(1) *General rule.* Except as provided in paragraph (j)(2) of this section, in order to compute its dividend equivalent amount in the first taxable year to which this section applies (whether or not such year begins before [*the date that is 30 days after these regulations are published in the Federal Register*]), a foreign corporation must recompute its U.S. net equity as of close of the preceding taxable year using the rules of this section and use such recomputed amount, rather than the amount computed under § 1.884-1T (as contained in the CFR edition revised as of April 1, 1992), to determine the amount of any increase or decrease in the U.S. net equity as of the close of that taxable year.

(2) *Installment obligations*—(i) *Interest election.* In recomputing its U.S. net equity as of the close of the preceding taxable year, a foreign corporation that holds an installment obligation treated as a U.S. asset under § 1.884-1T(d)(7) (as contained in the CFR edition revised as of April 1, 1992) as of such date may apply the rules of paragraph (d)(2)(iii) of this section without regard to the rule in that paragraph that requires interest or original issue discount on the obligation to be treated as ECI in order for such obligation to be treated as a U.S. asset.

(ii) *1987 sales by certain foreign corporations.* The E&P basis of an installment obligation arising in connection with a sale of property by a foreign corporation described in section 312(k)(4), where such sale occurs in a taxable year beginning in 1987, shall equal the E&P basis of the property sold as of the determination date reduced by payments received with respect to the obligation that do not represent gain for earnings and profits purposes, interest or original issue discount. [Reg. § 1.884-1.]

☐ [T.D. 8432, 9-10-92. Amended by T.D. 8657, 3-5-96.]

[Reg. § 1.884-2]

§ 1.884-2. **Special rules for termination or incorporation of a U.S. trade or business or liquidation or reorganization of a foreign corporation or its domestic subsidiary.**—(a) through (a)(2)(i) [Reserved]. For further information, see § 1.884-2T(a) through (a)(2)(i).

(a)(2)(ii) *Waiver of period of limitations.* The waiver referred to in § 1.884-2T(a)(2)(i)(D) shall be executed on Form 8848, or substitute form, and shall extend the period for assessment of the branch profits tax for the year of complete termination to a date not earlier than the close of the sixth taxable year following that taxable year. This form shall include such information as is required by the form and accompanying instructions. The waiver must be signed by the person authorized to sign the income tax returns for the foreign corporation (including an agent authorized to do so under a general or specific power of attorney). The waiver must be filed on or before the date (including extensions) prescribed for filing the foreign corporation's income tax return for the year of complete termination. With respect to a complete termination occurring in a taxable year ending prior to June 6, 1996, a foreign corporation may also satisfy the requirements of this paragraph (a)(2)(ii) by applying § 1.884-2T(a)(2)(ii) of the temporary regulations (as contained in the CFR edition revised as of April 1, 1995). A properly executed Form 8848, substitute form, or other form of waiver authorized by this paragraph (a)(2)(ii) shall be deemed to be consented to and signed by a Service Center Director or the Assistant Commissioner (International) for purposes of § 301.6501(c)-1(d) of this chapter.

(a)(3) through (a)(4) [Reserved]. For further information, see § 1.884-2T(a)(3) through (a)(4).

(a)(5) *Special rule if a foreign corporation terminates an interest in a trust.* A foreign corporation whose beneficial interest in a trust terminates (by disposition or otherwise) in any taxable year shall be subject to the branch profits tax on ECEP attributable to amounts (including distributions of accumulated income or gain) treated as ECI to such beneficiary in such taxable year notwithstanding any other provision of § 1.884-2T(a).

(b) through (c)(2)(ii) [Reserved]. For further information, see § 1.884-2T(b) through (c)(2)(ii).

(c)(2)(iii) *Waiver of period of limitations and transferee agreement.* In the case of a transferee that is a domestic corporation, the provisions of § 1.884-2T(c)(2)(i) shall not apply unless, as part of the section 381(a) transaction, the transferee executes a Form 2045 (Transferee Agreement) and a waiver of period of limitations as described in this paragraph (c)(2)(iii), and files both documents with its timely filed (including extensions) income tax return for the taxable year in which the section 381(a) transaction occurs. The waiver shall be executed on Form 8848, or substitute form, and shall extend the period for assessment of any additional branch profits tax for the taxable year in which the section 381(a) transaction occurs to a date not earlier than the close of the sixth taxable year following the taxable year in which such transaction occurs. This form shall include such information as is required by the form and accompanying instructions. The waiver must be signed by the person authorized to sign Form 2045. With respect to a complete termination occurring in a taxable year ending prior to June 6, 1996, a foreign corporation may also satisfy the requirements of this paragraph (c)(2)(iii) by applying § 1.884-2T(c)(2)(iii) of the temporary regulations (as contained in the CFR edition revised as of April 1, 1995). A properly executed Form 8848, substitute form, or other form of waiver authorized by this paragraph (c)(2)(iii) shall be deemed to be consented to and signed by a Service Center Director or the Assistant Commissioner (International) for purposes of § 301.6501(c)-1(d) of this chapter.

(c)(3) through (f) [Reserved]. For further information, see § 1.884-2T(c)(3) through (f).

(g) *Effective dates.* Paragraphs (a)(2)(ii) and (c)(2)(iii) of this section are effective for taxable years beginning after December 31, 1986. Paragraph (a)(5) of this section is effective for taxable years beginning on or after June 6, 1996. [Reg. § 1.884-2.]

☐ [*T.D.* 8657, 3-5-96.]

[Reg. § 1.884-2T]

§ 1.884-2T. **Special rules for termination or incorporation of a U.S. trade or business or liquidation or reorganization of a foreign corporation or its domestic subsidiary (Temporary).**—(a) *Complete termination of a U.S. trade or business*—(1) *General rule.* A foreign corporation shall not be subject to the branch profits tax for the taxable year in which it completely terminates all of its U.S. trade or business within the meaning of paragraph (a)(2) of this section. A foreign corporation's non-previously taxed accumulated effectively connected earnings and profits as of the close of the taxable year of complete termination shall be extinguished for purposes of section 884 and the regulations thereunder, but not for other purposes (for example, sections 312, 316 and 381).

(2) *Operating rules*—(i) *Definition of complete termination.* A foreign corporation shall have completely terminated all of its U.S. trade or business for any taxable year ("the year of complete termination") only if—

(A) As of the close of that taxable year, the foreign corporation either has no U.S. assets, or its shareholders have adopted an irrevocable resolution in that taxable year to completely liquidate and dissolve the corporation and, before the close of the immediately succeeding taxable year (also a "year of complete termination" for purposes of applying this paragraph (a)(2)), all of its U.S. assets are either distributed, used to pay off liabilities, or cease to be U.S. assets;

(B) Neither the foreign corporation nor a related corporation uses, directly or indirectly, any of the U.S. assets or the terminated U.S. trade or business, or property attributable thereto or to effectively connected earnings and profits earned by the foreign corporation in the year of complete termination, in the conduct of a trade or business in the United States at any time during a period of three years from the close of the year of complete termination;

(C) The foreign corporation has no income that is, or is treated as, effectively connected with the conduct of a trade or business in the United States (other than solely by reason of section 864(c)(6) or (c)(7)) during the period of three years from the close of the year of complete termination; and

(D) The foreign corporation attaches to its income tax return for each year of complete termination a waiver of the period of limitations, as described in paragraph (a)(2)(ii) of this section.

If a foreign corporation fails to completely terminate all of its U.S. trade or business because of the failure to meet any of the requirements of this paragraph (a)(2), then its branch profits tax liability for the taxable year and all subsequent taxable years shall be determined under the provisions of § 1.884-1, without regard to any provisions in this paragraph (a), taking into account any reduction in U.S. net equity that results from a U.S. trade or business of the foreign corporation ceasing to have U.S. assets. Any additional branch profits tax liability that may result, together with interest thereon (charged at the underpayment rates determined under section 6621(a)(2) with respect to the period between the date that was prescribed for filing the foreign corporation's income tax return for the taxable year with respect to which the branch profits tax liability arises and the date on which the additional tax for that year is paid), and applicable penalties, if any, shall be the liability of the foreign corporation (or of any person who is a transferee of the foreign corporation within the meaning of section 6901).

(ii) *Waiver of period of limitations.* [Reserved] See § 1.884-2(a)(2)(ii) for rules relating to this paragraph.

(iii) *Property subject to reinvestment prohibition rule.* For purposes of paragraph (a)(2)(i)(B) of this section—

(A) The term "U.S. assets of the terminated U.S. trade or business" shall mean all the money and other property that qualified as U.S. assets of the foreign corporation as of the close of the taxable year immediately preceding the year of complete termination; and

(B) Property attributable to U.S. assets or to effectively connected earnings and profits earned by the foreign corporation in the year of complete termination shall mean money or other property into which any part or all of such assets or effectively connected earnings and profits are converted at any time before the expiration of the three-year period specified in paragraph (a)(2)(i)(B) of this section by way of sale, exchange, or other disposition, as well as any money or other property attributable to the sale by a shareholder of the foreign corporation of its interest in the foreign corporation (or a successor corporation) at any time after a date which is 12 months before the close of the year of complete termination (24 months in the case of a foreign corporation that makes an election under paragraph (b) of this section).

(iv) *Related corporation.* For purposes of paragraph (a)(2)(i)(B) of this section, a corporation shall be related to a foreign corporation if either corporation is a 10-percent shareholder of the other corporation or, where the foreign corporation completely liquidates, if either corporation would have been a 10-percent shareholder of the other corporation had the foreign corporation remained in existence. For this purpose, the term "10-percent shareholder" means any person described in section 871(h)(3)(B) as well as any person who owns 10 percent or more of the total value of the stock of the corporation, and stock ownership shall be determined on the basis of the attribution rules described in section 871(h)(3)(C).

(v) *Direct or indirect use of U.S. assets.* The use of any part or all of the property referred to in paragraph (a)(2)(i)(B) of this section shall include the loan thereof to a related corporation or the use thereof as security (as a pledge, mortgage, or otherwise) for any indebtedness of a related corporation.

(3) *Complete termination in the case of a section 338 election.* A foreign corporation whose

Reg. § 1.884-2T

stock is acquired by another corporation that makes (or is deemed to make) an election under section 338 with respect to the stock of the foreign corporation shall be treated as having completely liquidated as of the close of the acquisition date (as defined in section 338(h)(2)) and to have completely terminated all of its U.S. trade or business with respect to the taxable year ending on such acquisition date provided the foreign corporation that exists prior to the section 338 transactions complies with the requirements of paragraph (a)(2)(i)(B) and (D) of this section. For purposes of the preceding sentence, any of the money or other property paid as consideration for the acquisition of the stock in the foreign corporation (and for any debt claim against the foreign corporation) shall be treated as property attributable to the U.S. assets of the terminated U.S. trade or business and to the effectively connected earnings and profits of the foreign corporation earned in the year of complete termination.

(4) *Complete termination in the case of a foreign corporation with income under section 864(c)(6) or 864(c)(7).* No branch profits tax shall be imposed on effectively connected earnings and profits attributable to income that is treated as effectively connected with the conduct of a trade or business in the United States solely by reason of section 864(c)(6) or 864(c)(7) if—

(i) No income of the foreign corporation for the taxable year is, or is treated as, effectively connected with the conduct of a trade or business in the United States, without regard to section 864(c)(6) or 864(c)(7);

(ii) The foreign corporation has no U.S. assets as of the close of the taxable year, and

(iii) Such effectively connected earnings and profits would not have been subject to branch profits tax pursuant to the complete termination provisions of paragraph (a)(1) of this section if income or gain subject to section 864(c)(6) had not been deferred or if property subject to section 864(c)(7) had been sold immediately prior to the date the property ceased to have been used in the conduct of a trade or business in the United States.

(5) *Special rule if a foreign corporation terminates an interest in a trust.* [Reserved] See § 1.884-2(a)(5) for rules relating to this paragraph.

(6) *Coordination with second-level withholding tax.* Effectively connected earnings and profits and non-previously taxed accumulated effectively connected earnings and profits of a foreign corporation that are exempt from branch profits tax by reason of the provisions of paragraph (a)(1) of this section shall not be subject to tax under section 871(a), 881(a), 1441 or 1442 when paid as a dividend by such foreign corporation (or a successor-in-interest).

(b) *Election to remain engaged in a U.S. trade or business*—(1) *General rule.* A foreign corporation that would be considered to have completely terminated all of its U.S. trade or business for the taxable year under the provisions of paragraph (a)(2)(i) of this section, but for the provisions of paragraph (a)(2)(i)(B) of this section that prohibit reinvestment within a three-year period, may make an election under this paragraph (b) for the taxable year in which it completely terminates all its U.S. trade or business (as determined without regard to paragraph (a)(2)(i)(B) of this section) and, if it so chooses, for the following taxable year (but not for any succeeding taxable year). The election under this paragraph (b) is an election by the foreign corporation to designate an amount of marketable securities as U.S. assets for purposes of § 1.884-1. The marketable securities identified pursuant to the election under paragraph (b)(3) of this section shall be treated as being U.S. assets in an amount equal, in the aggregate, to the lesser of the adjusted basis of the U.S. assets that ceased to be U.S. assets during the taxable year in which the election is made (determined on the date or dates the U.S. assets ceased to be U.S. assets) or the adjusted basis of the marketable securities as of the end of the taxable year. The securities must be held from the date that they are identified until the end of the taxable year for which the election is made, or if disposed of during the taxable year, must be replaced on the date of disposition with other marketable securities that are acquired on or before that date and that have a fair market value as of the date of substitution not less than their adjusted basis.

(2) *Marketable security.* For purposes of this paragraph (b), the term "marketable security" means a security (including stock) that is part of an issue any portion of which is regularly traded on an established securities market (within the meaning of § 1.884-5(d)(2) and (4)) and a deposit described in section 871(i)(3)(A) or (B).

(3) *Identification requirements.* In order to qualify for this election—

(i) The marketable securities must be identified on the books and records of the U.S. trade or business within 30 days of the date an equivalent amount of U.S. assets ceases to be U.S. assets; and

(ii) On the date a marketable security is identified, its adjusted basis must not exceed its fair market value.

(4) *Treatment of income from deemed U.S. assets.* The income or gain from the marketable securities (or replacement securities) subject to an

election under this paragraph (b) that arises in a taxable year for which an election is made shall be treated as ECI (other than for purposes of section 864(c)(7)), and losses from the disposition of such marketable securities shall be allocated entirely to income that is ECI. In addition, all such securities shall be treated as if they had been sold for their fair market value on the earlier of the last business day of a taxable year for which an election is in effect or the day immediately prior to the date of substitution by the foreign corporation of a U.S. asset for the marketable security, and any gain (but not loss) and accrued interest on the securities shall also be treated as ECI. The adjusted basis of such property shall be increased by the amount of any gain recognized by reason of this paragraph (b).

(5) *Method of election.* A foreign corporation may make an election under this paragraph (b) by attaching to its income tax return for the taxable year a statement—

(i) Identifying the marketable securities treated as U.S. assets under this paragraph (b);

(ii) Setting forth the E&P bases of such securities; and

(iii) Agreeing to treat any income, gain or loss as provided in paragraph (b)(4) of this section.

Such statement must be filed on or before the due date (including extensions) of the foreign corporation's income tax return for the taxable year. A foreign corporation shall not be permitted to make an election under this paragraph (b) more than once.

(6) *Effective date.* This paragraph (b) is effective for taxable years beginning on or after October 13, 1992. However, if a foreign corporation has made a valid election under § 1.884-1 (i) to apply that section with respect to a taxable year beginning before October 13, 1992, and after December 31, 1986, this paragraph (b) shall be effective beginning with such taxable year.

(c) *Liquidation, reorganization, etc., of a foreign corporation.* The following rules apply to the transfer by a foreign corporation engaged (or deemed engaged) in the conduct of a U.S. trade or business (the "transferor") of its U.S. assets to another corporation (the "transferee") in a complete liquidation or reorganization described in section 381(a) (a "section 381(a) transaction") if the transferor is engaged (or deemed engaged) in the conduct of a U.S. trade or business immediately prior to the section 381(a) transaction. For purposes of this paragraph (c), a section 381(a) transaction is considered to occur in the taxable year that ends on the date of distribution or transfer (as defined in § 1.381(b)-1(b)) pursuant to the section 381(a) transaction.

(1) *Inapplicability of paragraph (a)(1) of this section to section 381(a) transactions.* Paragraph (a)(1) of this section (relating to the complete termination of a U.S. trade or business of a foreign corporation) does not apply to exempt the transferor from branch profits tax liability for the taxable year in which the section 381(a) transaction occurs or in any succeeding taxable year.

(2) *Transferor's dividend equivalent amount for the taxable year in which a section 381(a) transaction occurs.* The dividend equivalent amount for the taxable year, including a short taxable year, in which a section 381(a) transaction occurs shall be determined under the provisions of § 1.884-1, as modified under the provisions of this paragraph (c)(2).

(i) *U.S. net equity.* The transferor's U.S. net equity as of the close of the taxable year shall be determined without regard to any transfer in that taxable year of U.S. assets to or from the transferee pursuant to a section 381(a) transaction, and without regard to any U.S. liabilities assumed or acquired by the transferee from the transferor in that taxable year pursuant to a section 381(a) transaction. The transferor's adjusted basis (for earnings and profits purposes) in U.S. assets transferred to the transferee pursuant to a section 381(a) transaction shall be the adjusted basis of those assets (for earnings and profits purposes) immediately prior to the section 381(a) transaction, adjusted as provided under section 362(b), treating the transferor, for that purpose, as though it were the transferee and treating the gain taken into account for earnings and profits purposes as gain recognized.

(ii) *Effectively connected earnings and profits.* The transferor's effectively connected earnings and profits for the taxable year in which the section 381(a) transaction occurs and its nonpreviously taxed accumulated effectively connected earnings and profits shall be determined without regard to the carryover to the transferee of the transferor's earnings and profits under section 381(a) and (c)(2) of paragraph (c)(4) of this section. Effectively connected earnings and profits for the taxable year in which a section 381(a) transaction occurs shall be adjusted by the amount of any gain recognized to the transferor in that year pursuant to the section 381(a) transaction (to the extent taken into account for earnings and profits purposes).

(iii) *Waiver of period of limitations and transferee agreement.* [Reserved] See § 1.884-2(c)(2)(iii) for rules relating to this paragraph.

Reg. § 1.884-2T(c)(2)

(3) *Transferor's dividend equivalent amount for any taxable year succeeding the taxable year in which the section 381(a) transaction occurs.* Any decrease in U.S. net equity in any taxable year succeeding the taxable year in which the section 381(a) transaction occurs shall increase the transferor's dividend equivalent amount for those years without regard to the limitation in § 1.884-1(b)(3)(ii), to the extent such decrease in U.S. net equity does not exceed the balance of effectively connected earnings and profits and non-previously taxed accumulated effectively connected earnings and profits carried over to the transferee pursuant to section 381(a) and (c)(2), as determined under paragraph (c)(4) of this section.

(4) *Earnings and profits of the transferor carried over to the transferee pursuant to the section 381(a) transaction*—(i) *Amount.* The amount of effectively connected earnings and profits and non-previously taxed accumulated effectively connected earnings and profits of the transferor that carry over to the transferee under section 381(a) and (c)(2) shall be the effectively connected earnings and profits and the non-previously taxed accumulated effectively connected earnings and profits of the transferor immediately before the close of the taxable year in which the section 381(a) transaction occurs. For this purpose, the provisions in § 1.381(c)(2)-1 shall generally apply with proper adjustments to reflect the fact that effectively connected earnings and profits and non-previously taxed accumulated effectively connected earnings and profits are not affected by distributions to shareholders but, rather, by dividend equivalent amounts. Therefore, the amounts of effectively connected earnings and profits and non-previously taxed accumulated effectively connected earnings and profits that carry over to the transferee pursuant to those provisions are reduced by the transferor's dividend equivalent amount for the taxable year in which the section 381(a) transaction occurs. Such amounts are also reduced to the extent of any dividend equivalent amount determined for any succeeding taxable year solely as a result of the provisions of paragraph (c)(3) of this section. For purposes of this paragraph (c)(4)(i), if the transferor accumulates non-previously taxed effectively connected earnings and profits, or incurs a deficit in effectively connected earnings and profits, attributable to a period that is after the close of the taxable year in which the section 381(a) transaction occurs and before the liquidation of the transferor, then such effectively connected earnings and profits, or deficits therein, shall be deemed to have been accumulated or incurred on or before the close of the taxable year in which the section 381(a) transaction occurs.

(ii) *Retention of character.* All of the transferor's effectively connected earnings and profits and non-previously taxed accumulated effectively connected earnings and profits that carry over to the transferee shall constitute non-previously taxed accumulated effectively connected earnings and profits of the transferee. In the case of a domestic transferee, such non-previously taxed accumulated effectively connected earnings and profits shall also constitute accumulated earnings and profits of the transferee for purposes of section 316(a)(2).

(iii) *Treatment of distributions by a domestic transferee out of non-previously taxed accumulated effectively connected earnings and profits.* In the event the transferee is a domestic corporation, distributions out of the transferee's non-previously taxed accumulated effectively connected earnings and profits that are received by a foreign distributee shall qualify for benefits under an applicable income tax treaty only (A) if the distributee qualifies for the benefits under such treaty and (B) to the extent that the transferor foreign corporation would have qualified under the principles of § 1.884-1(g)(1) and (2)(i) for an exemption or reduction in rate with respect to the branch profits tax if the non-previously taxed accumulated effectively connected earnings and profits had been reflected in a dividend equivalent amount for the taxable year in which the section 381(a) transaction occurs. (The tax rate on dividends specified in the treaty between the distributee's country of residence and the United States shall apply to any dividends received by a distributee who qualifies for a treaty benefit under the preceding sentence.) In addition, distributions out of such non-previously taxed accumulated effectively connected earnings and profits shall retain their character in the hands of any domestic distributee up a chain of corporate shareholders for purposes of applying this paragraph (c)(4)(iii) to distributions made by any such person to a foreign distributee. If a domestic transferee has non-previously taxed accumulated effectively connected earnings and profits carried over from the transferor as well as accumulated earnings and profits, then each category of earnings and profits shall be accounted for in two separate pools, and any distribution of earnings and profits shall be treated as a distribution out of each pool in proportion to the respective amount of undistributed earnings and profits in each pool. Section 871(i) (relating, in part, to dividends paid by a domestic corporation meeting the 80-percent foreign business requirements of section 861(c)(1)) shall not apply to any dividends

Reg. § 1.884-2T(c)(3)

paid by a domestic transferee out of its non-previously taxed accumulated effectively connected earnings and profits.

(5) *Determination of U.S. net equity of a transferee that is a foreign corporation.* In the event the transferee is a foreign corporation, then for purposes of determining the transferee's increase or decrease in U.S. net equity under § 1.884-1 for its taxable year during which the section 381(a) transaction occurs, its U.S. net equity as of the close of its immediately preceding taxable year shall be increased by the amount of U.S. net equity acquired by the transferee from the transferor pursuant to the section 381(a) transaction, taking into account the adjustments to the basis (for earnings and profits purposes) of U.S. assets under the principles of section 362(b).

(6) *Special rules in the case of the disposition of stock or securities in a domestic transferee or in the transferor*—(i) *General rule.* This paragraph (c)(6)(i) shall apply where the transferee is a domestic corporation, subdivision (A), (B), or (C) of this paragraph applies and subdivision (D) of this paragraph applies.

(A) Shareholders of the transferor sell, exchange or otherwise dispose of stock in the transferor at any time during a 12-month period before the date of distribution or transfer (as defined in § 1.381(b)-1(b)) and the aggregate amount of such stock sold, exchanged or otherwise disposed of exceeds 25 percent of the value of the stock of the transferor, determined on a date that is 12 months before the date of distribution or transfer.

(B) Shareholders of the transferee (or of the transferee's parent in the case of a reorganization described in the parenthetical clause in section 368(a)(1)(C)) who in the aggregate owned more than 25 percent of the value of the stock of the transferor at any time within the 12-month period preceding the close of the year in which the section 381(a) transaction occurs sell, exchange or otherwise dispose of their stock or securities in the transferee at any time during a period of three years from the close of the taxable year in which the section 381(a) transaction occurs.

(C) In the case of a reorganization described in the parenthetical clause in section 368(a)(1)(C), the transferee's parent sells, exchanges or otherwise disposes of its stock or securities in the transferee at any time during a period of three years from the close of the taxable year in which the section 381(a) transaction occurs.

(D) A corporation related to any such shareholder or the shareholder itself if it is a corporation (subsequent to an event described in subdivision (A) or (B) of this paragraph (c)(6)(i)), or the transferee's parent (subsequent to an event described in subdivision (C) of this paragraph (c)(6)(i)), uses, directly or indirectly, the proceeds or property received in such sale, exchange or disposition, or property attributable thereto, in the conduct of a trade or business in the United States at any time during a period of three years from the date of sale in the case of a disposition of stock in the transferor, or from the close of the taxable year in which the section 381(a) transaction occurs in the case of a disposition of the stock or securities in the transferee (or the transferee's parent in the case of a reorganization described in the parenthetical clause in section 368(a)(1)(C)). Where this paragraph (c)(6)(i) applies, the transferor's branch profits tax liability for the taxable year in which the section 381(a) transaction occurs shall be determined under § 1.884-1, taking into account all the adjustments in U.S. net equity that result from the transfer of U.S. assets and liabilities to the transferee pursuant to the section 381(a) transaction, without regard to any provisions in this paragraph (c). If an event described in paragraph (c)(6)(i)(A), (B), or (C) of this section occurs after the close of the taxable year in which the section 381(a) transaction occurs, and if additional branch profits tax is required to be paid by reason of the application of this paragraph (c)(6)(i), then interest must be paid on that amount at the underpayment rates determined under section 6621(a)(2), with respect to the period between the date that was prescribed for filing the transferor's income tax return for the year in which the section 381(a) transaction occurs and the date on which the additional tax for that year is paid. Any such additional tax liability together with interest thereon shall be the liability of the transferee within the meaning of section 6901 pursuant to section 6901 and the regulations thereunder.

(ii) *Operating rule.* For purposes of paragraph (c)(6)(i) of this section paragraph (a)(2)(iii)(B), (iv) and (v) of this section shall apply for purposes of making the determinations under paragraph (c)(6)(i)(D) of this section.

(d) *Incorporation under section 351*—(1) *In general.* The following rules apply to the transfer by a foreign corporation engaged (or deemed engaged) in the conduct of a U.S. trade or business (the "transferor") of part or all of its U.S. assets to a U.S. corporation (the "transferee") in exchange for stock or securities in the transferee in a transaction that qualifies under section 351(a) (a "section 351 transaction"), provided that immediately after the transaction, the transferor is in control (as defined in section 368(c)) of the transferee, without regard to other transferors.

Reg. § 1.884-2T(d)(1)

(2) *Inapplicability of paragraph (a)(1) of this section to section 351 transactions.* Paragraph (a)(1) of this section does not apply to exempt the transferor from branch profits tax liability for the taxable year in which a section 351 transaction described in paragraph (d)(1) of this section occurs and shall not apply for any subsequent taxable year of the transferor in which it, or a successor-in-interest, owns stock or securities of a transferee as of the close of the transferor's taxable year.

(3) *Transferor's dividend equivalent amount for the taxable year in which a section 351 transaction occurs.* The dividend equivalent amount of the transferor for the taxable year in which a section 351 transaction described in paragraph (d)(1) of this section occurs shall be determined under the provisions of § 1.884-1, as modified by the provisions of this paragraph (d)(3) provided that the transferee elects under paragraph (d)(4) of this section to be allocated a proportionate amount of the transferor's effectively connected earnings and profits and non-previously taxed accumulated effectively connected earnings and profits and the foreign corporation files a statement as provided in paragraph (d)(5)(i) of this section and complies with the agreement included in such statement with respect to a subsequent disposition of the transferee's stock.

(i) *U.S. net equity.* The transferor's U.S. net equity as of the close of the taxable year shall be determined without regard to any transfer in that taxable year of U.S. assets to or from the transferee pursuant to a section 351 transaction, and without regard to any U.S. liabilities assumed or acquired by the transferee from the transferor in that taxable year pursuant to a section 351 transaction. The transferor's adjusted basis for earnings and profits purposes in U.S. assets transferred to the transferee pursuant to a section 351 transaction shall be the adjusted basis of those assets for earnings and profits purposes immediately prior to the section 351 transaction, increased by the amount of any gain recognized by the transferor on the transfer of such assets in the section 351 transaction to the extent taken into account for earnings and profits purposes.

(ii) *Effectively connected earnings and profits.* Subject to the limitation in paragraph (d)(3)(iii) of this section, the calculation of the transferor's dividend equivalent amount shall take into account the transferor's effectively connected earnings and profits for the taxable year in which a section 351 transaction occurs (including any amount of gain recognized to the transferor pursuant to the section 351 transaction to the extent the gain is taken into account for earnings and profits purposes) and, for purposes of applying the limitation of § 1.884-1(b)(3)(ii), its non-previously taxed accumulated effectively connected earnings and profits, determined without regard to the allocation to the transferee of the transferor's effectively connected earnings and profits and non-previously taxed accumulated effectively connected earnings and profits pursuant to the election under paragraph (d)(4)(i) of this section.

(iii) *Limitation on dividend equivalent amount.* The dividend equivalent amount determined under this paragraph (d)(3) shall not exceed the sum of the transferor's effectively connected earnings and profits and non-previously taxed accumulated effectively connected earnings and profits determined after taking into account the allocation to the transferee of the transferor's earnings pursuant to an election under paragraph (d)(4)(i) of this section.

(4) *Election to increase earnings and profits*—(i) *General rule.* The election referred to in paragraph (d)(3) of this section is an election by the transferee to increase its earnings and profits by the amount determined under paragraph (d)(4)(ii) of this section. An election under this paragraph (d)(4)(i) shall be effective only if the transferee attaches a statement to its timely filed (including extensions) income tax return for the taxable year in which the section 351 transaction occurs, in which—

(A) It agrees to be subject to the rules of paragraph (c)(4)(ii) and (iii) of this section with respect to the transferor's effectively connected earnings and profits and non-previously accumulated effectively connected earnings and profits allocated to the transferee pursuant to the election under this paragraph (d)(4)(i) in the same manner as if such earnings and profits had been carried over to the transferee pursuant to section 381(a) and (c)(2), and

(B) It identifies the amount of effectively connected earnings and profits and non-previously taxed accumulated effectively connected earnings and profits that are allocated from the transferor.

An election with respect to a taxable year ending on or before December 1, 1988, may be made by filing an amended Form 1120F on or before January 3, 1989, to which the statement described in this paragraph (d)(4)(i) shall be attached.

(ii) *Amount of the transferor's effectively connected earnings and profits and non-previously taxed accumulated effectively connected earnings and profits allocated to the transferee.* The amount referred to in paragraph (d)(4)(i) of this section is equal to the same proportion of the

Reg. § 1.884-2T(d)(2)

transferor's effectively connected earnings and profits and non-previously taxed accumulated effectively connected earnings and profits (determined immediately prior to the section 351 transaction and without regard to this paragraph (d)(4) or any dividend equivalent amount for the taxable year) that the adjusted bases for purposes of computing earnings and profits in all the U.S. assets transferred to the transferee by the transferor pursuant to the section 351 transaction bear to the adjusted bases for purposes of computing earnings and profits in all the U.S. assets of the transferor, determined immediately prior to the section 351 transaction.

(iii) *Effect of election on transferor.* For purposes of computing the transferor's dividend equivalent amount for the taxable year succeeding the taxable year in which a section 351 transaction occurs, the transferor's effectively connected earnings and profits and non-previously taxed accumulated effectively connected earnings and profits as of the close of the taxable year in which the section 351 transaction occurs shall be reduced by the amount of its effectively connected earnings and profits and non-previously taxed accumulated effectively connected earnings and profits allocated to the transferee pursuant to the election under paragraph (d)(4)(i) of this section (and by its dividend equivalent amount for the taxable year in which the section 351 transaction occurs).

(5) *Dispositions of stock or securities of the transferee by the transferor*—(i) *General rule.* The statement referred to in paragraph (d)(3) of this section is a statement executed by the transferor stating the transferor's agreement that, upon the disposition of part or all of the stock or securities it owns in the transferee (or a successor-in-interest), it shall treat as a dividend equivalent amount for the taxable year in which the disposition occurs an amount equal to the lesser of (A) the amount realized upon such disposition or (B) the total amount of effectively connected earnings and profits and non-previously taxed accumulated effectively connected earnings and profits that was allocated from the transferor to that transferee pursuant to an election under paragraph (d)(4)(i) of this section, which amount shall be reduced to the extent previously taken into account by the transferor as dividends or dividend equivalent amounts for tax or branch profits tax purposes. The extent and manner in which such dividend equivalent amount may be subject to the branch profits tax in the taxable year of disposition shall be determined under the provisions of section 884 and the regulations thereunder, including the provisions of paragraph (a) of this section (relating to complete terminations), as limited under paragraph (d)(2) of this section. Except as otherwise provided in paragraph (d)(5)(ii) of this section, the term "disposition" means any transfer that would constitute a disposition by the transferor for any purpose of the Internal Revenue Code and the regulations thereunder. This paragraph (d)(5)(i) shall apply regardless of whether the stock or securities of the transferee are U.S. assets in the hands of the transferor at the time of sale, exchange or disposition.

(ii) *Exception for certain tax-free dispositions.* For purposes of paragraph (d)(5)(i) of this section, a disposition does not include a transfer of stock or securities of the transferee by the transferor in a transaction that qualifies as a transfer pursuant to a complete liquidation described in section 332(b) or a transfer pursuant to a reorganization described in section 368(a)(1)(F). Any other transfer that qualifies for non-recognition of gain or loss shall be treated as a disposition for purposes of paragraph (d)(5)(i) of this section, unless the Commissioner has, by published guidance or by prior ruling issued to the taxpayer upon its request, determined such transfer not to be a disposition for purposes of paragraph (d)(5)(i) of this section.

(iii) *Distributions governed by section 355.* In the case of a distribution or exchange of stock or securities of a transferee to which section 355 applies (or so much of section 356 as relates to section 355) and that is not in pursuance of a plan meeting the requirements of a reorganization as defined in section 368(a)(1)(D), § 1.312-10(b) (relating to the allocation of earnings and profits in certain corporate separations) shall not apply to reduce the transferor's effectively connected earnings and profits or non-previously taxed accumulated effectively connected earnings and profits.

(iv) *Filing of statement.* The statement referred to in paragraph (d)(5)(i) of this section shall be attached to a timely filed (including extensions) income tax return of the transferor for the taxable year in which the section 351 transaction occurs. An election with respect to a taxable year ending on or before December 1, 1988, may be made by filing an amended Form 1120F on or before January 3, 1989, to which the statement described in this paragraph (d)(5)(iv) shall be attached.

(6) *Example.* The provisions of this paragraph (d) are illustrated by the following example.

Example. Foreign corporation X has a calendar taxable year. X's only assets are U.S. assets and X computes its interest deduction using the actual ratio of liabilities to assets under § 1.882-5(b)(2)(ii). X's U.S. net equity as of the

Reg. § 1.884-2T(d)(6)

close of its 1988 taxable year is $2,000, resulting from the following amounts of U.S. assets and liabilities:

U.S. assets	
U.S. building A	$1,000
U.S. building B	$2,500
Other U.S. assets	$ 800
Total	$4,300

U.S. liabilities	
Mortgage A	$ 800
Mortgage B	$1,500
	$2,300

Assume that X's adjusted basis in its assets is equal to X's adjusted basis in its assets for earnings and profits purposes. On September 30, 1989, X transfers building A, which has a fair market value of $1,800, to a newly created U.S. corporation Y under section 351 in exchange for 100% of the stock of Y with a fair market value of $800, other property with a fair market value of $200, and the assumption of Mortgage A. Assume that under sections 11 and 351(b), tax of $30 is imposed with respect to the $200 of other property received by X. X's non-previously taxed accumulated effectively connected earnings and profits as of the close of its 1988 taxable year are $200 and its effectively connected earnings and profits for its 1989 taxable year are $330, including $170 of gain recognized to X on the transfer as adjusted for earnings and profits purposes (i.e., $200 of gain recognized minus $30 of tax paid with respect to the gain). Y takes a $1,200 basis in the building transferred from X, equal to the basis in the hands of X ($1,000) increased by the amount of gain recognized to X in the section 351 transaction ($200). Y makes an election in the manner described in paragraph (d)(4)(i) of this section to increase its earnings and profits by the amount described in paragraph (d)(4)(ii) of this section and X files a statement as provided in paragraph (d)(5)(i) of this section. The branch profits tax consequences to X and Y in the taxable year in which the section 351 transaction occurs and in subsequent taxable years are as follows:

(i) *X's dividend equivalent amount for 1989.* The determination of X's dividend equivalent amount for 1989 is a three-step process: determining X's U.S. net equity as of the close of its 1989 taxable year under paragraph (d)(3)(i) of this section; determining the amount of X's effectively connected earnings and profits and non-previously taxed accumulated effectively connected earnings and profits for its 1989 taxable year under paragraph (d)(3)(ii) of this section; and applying the limitation in paragraph (d)(3)(iii) of this section.

Step one: Pursuant to paragraph (d)(3)(i) of this section, X's U.S. net equity as of the close of its 1989 taxable year is calculated without regard to the section 351 transaction except that X's basis in its U.S. assets is increased by the $170 amount of gain it has recognized for earnings and profits in connection with the section 351 transaction. Thus, X's U.S. net equity as of the close of its 1989 taxable year is $1,870, consisting of the following U.S. assets and liabilities, taking into account the fact that X's other U.S. assets have decreased to $500:

U.S. assets	
Building A	$1,170
Building B	$2,500
Other U.S. assets	$ 500
Total	$4,170

U.S. liabilities	
Mortgage A	$ 800
Mortgage B	$1,500
	$2,300

Thus, X's U.S. net equity as of the close of its 1989 taxable year has decreased by $130 relative to its U.S. net equity as of the close of its 1988 taxable year.

Step two: Pursuant to paragraph (d)(3)(ii) of this section, X's effectively connected earnings and profits and non-previously taxed accumulated effectively connected earnings and profits for the taxable year are determined without taking into account the allocation to Y of X's effectively connected earnings and profits and non-previously taxed accumulated effectively connected earnings and profits pursuant to the election under paragraph (d)(4)(i) of this section. Thus, X's effectively connected earnings and profits for its 1989 taxable year are $330 and X's non-previously taxed accumulated effectively connected earnings and profits are $200. Thus, but for the limitation in paragraph (d)(3)(iii) of this section, X's dividend equivalent amount for the taxable year would be $460, equal to X's effectively connected earnings and profits for the taxable year ($330), increased by the decrease in X's U.S. net equity ($130).

Step three: Pursuant to paragraph (d)(3)(iii) of this section, X's dividend equivalent amount for its 1989 taxable year may not exceed the sum of the transferor's effectively connected earnings and profits and non-previously taxed accumulated effectively connected earnings and profits, deter-

Reg. § 1.884-2T(d)(6)

mined as of the close of its 1989 taxable year, after taking into account the allocation of the transferor's earnings and profits pursuant to the election under paragraph (d)(4)(i) of this section. Based upon subdivision (ii) of this example, X's dividend equivalent amount for 1989 cannot exceed $423, which is equal to the total amount of X's effectively connected earnings and profits and non-previously taxed accumulated effectively connected earnings and profits, determined as of the close of its 1989 taxable year without regard to the allocation of earnings and profits to Y pursuant to Y's election under paragraph (d)(4)(i) of this section ($530), reduced by the amount of X's effectively connected earnings and profits and non-previously taxed accumulated effectively connected earnings and profits allocated to Y pursuant to Y's election under paragraph (d)(4)(i) of this section ($107). Thus, X's dividend equivalent amount for its 1989 taxable year is limited to $423.

(ii) *Amount of X's effectively connected earnings and profits and non-previously taxed accumulated effectively connected earnings and profits transferred to Y.* Pursuant to Y's election under paragraph (d)(4)(i) of this section, Y increases its earnings and profits by the amount prescribed in paragraph (d)(4)(ii) of this section. This amount is equal to the sum of X's effectively connected earnings and profits and non-previously taxed accumulated effectively connected earnings and profits determined immediately before the section 351 transaction, without regard to X's dividend equivalent amount for the year, allocated in the same proportion that X's basis in the U.S. assets transferred to Y bears to the bases of all of X's U.S. assets, which bases are determined immediately prior to the section 351(a) transaction. The amount of X's effectively connected earnings and profits immediately before the section 351 transaction is assumed to be $260. The total amount of effectively connected earnings and profits ($260) and non-previously taxed accumulated effectively connected earnings and profits ($200) determined immediately before the section 351 transaction is, therefore, $460. The portion of $460 that is allocated to Y pursuant to Y's election under paragraph (d)(4)(i) of this section is $107, calculated as $460 multiplied by a fraction, the numerator of which is the basis of the U.S. assets transferred to Y pursuant to the section 351 transaction ($1,000), and the denominator of which is the bases of X's U.S. assets determined immediately before the section 351 transaction ($4,300). Pursuant to paragraph (d)(4)(i) of this section, the amount of $107 of X's effectively connected earnings and profits and non-previously taxed accumulated effectively connected earnings and profits allocated to Y pursuant to paragraph (d)(4)(i) of this section constitutes non-previously taxed accumulated effectively connected earnings and profits of Y.

(iii) *X's non-previously taxed accumulated effectively connected earnings and profits for 1990.* Pursuant to paragraph (d)(4)(iii) of this section, X's non-previously taxed accumulated effectively connected earnings and profits as of the close of its 1989 taxable year for purposes of computing its dividend equivalent amount for its taxable year 1990 are zero, *i.e.,* $530 of effectively connected earnings and profits and non-previously taxed accumulated effectively connected earnings and profits reduced by $107 of effectively connected earnings and profits and non-previously taxed accumulated effectively connected earnings and profits allocated to Y, and further reduced by X's $423 dividend equivalent amount for its 1989 taxable year.

(iv) *X's U.S. net equity for purposes of determining the dividend equivalent amount for succeeding taxable years.* For 1990, X must determine its U.S. net equity as of December 31, 1989, in order to determine whether there has been an increase or decrease in its U.S. net equity as of December 31, 1990. For this purpose, X's U.S. net equity as of December 31, 1989 is determined under the provisions of § 1.884-1 without regard to the special rules in paragraph (d)(3)(i) of this section. Thus, X's U.S. net equity as of December 31, 1989 is $1,500, consisting of the following U.S. assets and liabilities:

U.S. assets	
Building B	$2,500
Other U.S. assets	500
	$3,000

U.S. liabilities	
Mortgage B	$1,500
	$1,500

(e) *Certain transactions with respect to a domestic subsidiary.* In the case of a section 381(a) transaction in which a domestic subsidiary of a foreign corporation transfers assets to that foreign corporation or to another foreign corporation with respect to which the first foreign corporation owns stock (directly or indirectly) meeting the requirements of section 1504(a)(2), the transferee's non-previously taxed accumulated effectively connected earnings and profits for the taxable year in which the section 381(a) transaction occurs shall be increased by all of the domestic subsidiary's current earnings and profits and earnings and profits accumulated after December 31, 1986,

Reg. § 1.884-2T(e)

that carry over to the transferee under sections 381(a) and (c)(1) (including non-previously taxed accumulated effectively connected earnings and profits, if any, transferred to the domestic subsidiary under paragraphs (c)(4) and (d)(4) of this section and treated as earnings and profits under paragraphs (c)(4)(ii) and (d)(4)(ii) of this section). For purposes of determining the transferee's dividend equivalent amount for the taxable year in which the section 381(a) transaction occurs, the transferee's U.S. net equity as of the close of its taxable year immediately preceding the taxable year during which the section 381(a) transaction occurs shall be increased by the greater of (1) the amount by which the transferee's U.S. net equity computed immediately prior to the transfer would have increased due to the transfer of the subsidiary's assets and liabilities if U.S. net equity were computed immediately prior to the transfer and immediately after the transfer (taking into account in the earnings and profits basis of the assets transferred any gain recognized on the transfer to the extent reflected in earnings and profits), or (2) the total amount of U.S. net equity transferred (directly or indirectly) by the foreign parent to the domestic subsidiary in one or more prior section 351 or 381(a) transactions.

(f) *Effective date.* This section is effective for taxable years beginning after December 31, 1986. [Temporary Reg. § 1.884-2T.]

☐ [T.D. 8223, 8-29-88. Amended by T.D. 8432, 9-10-92 and T.D. 8657, 3-5-96.]

[Reg. § 1.884-3T]

§ 1.884-3T. **Coordination of branch profits tax with second-tier withholding (Temporary).**—[Reserved.]

[Reg. § 1.884-4]

§ 1.884-4. **Branch-level interest tax.**—(a) *General rule*—(1) *Tax on branch interest.* In the case of a foreign corporation that, during the taxable year, is engaged in trade or business in the United States or has gross income that is ECI (as defined in § 1.884-1(d)(1)(iii)), any interest paid by such trade or business (hereinafter "branch interest," as defined in paragraph (b) of this section) shall, for purposes of subtitle A (Income Taxes), be treated as if it were paid by a domestic corporation (other than a corporation described in section 861(c)(1), relating to a domestic corporation that meets the 80 percent foreign business requirement). Thus, for example, whether such interest is treated as income from sources within the United States by the person who receives the interest shall be determined in the same manner as if such interest were paid by a domestic corporation (other than a corporation described in section 861(c)(1)). Such interest shall be subject to tax under section 871(a) or 881, and to withholding under section 1441 or 1442, in the same manner as interest paid by a domestic corporation (other than a corporation described in section 861(c)(1)) if received by a foreign person and not effectively connected with the conduct by the foreign person of a trade or business in the United States, unless the interest, if paid by a domestic corporation, would be exempt under section 871(h) or 881(c) (relating to exemption for certain portfolio interest received by a foreign person), section 871(i) or 881(d) (relating, in part, to exemption for certain bank deposit interest received by a foreign person), or another provision of the Code. Such interest shall also be treated as interest paid by a domestic corporation (other than a corporation described in section 861(c)(1)) for purposes of sections 864(c), 871(b) and 882(a) (relating to income that is effectively connected with the conduct of a trade or business within the United States) and section 904 (relating to the limitation on the foreign tax credit). For purposes of this section, a foreign corporation also shall be treated as engaged in trade or business in the United States if, at any time during the taxable year, it owns an asset taken into account under § 1.882-5(a)(1)(ii) or (b)(1) for purposes of determining the amount of the foreign corporation's interest expense allocated or apportioned to ECI. See paragraph (b)(8) of this section for the effect of income tax treaties on branch interest.

(2) *Tax on excess interest*—(i) *Definition of excess interest.* For purposes of this section, the term "excess interest" means—

(A) The amount of interest allocated or apportioned to ECI of the foreign corporation under § 1.882-5 for the taxable year, after application of § 1.884-1(e)(3); minus

(B) The foreign corporation's branch interest (as defined in paragraph (b) of this section) for the taxable year, but not including interest accruing in a taxable year beginning before January 1, 1987; minus

(C) The amount of interest determined under paragraph (c)(2) of this section (relating to interest paid by a partnership).

(ii) *Imposition of tax.* A foreign corporation shall be liable for tax on excess interest under section 881(a) in the same manner as if such excess interest were interest paid to the foreign corporation by a wholly-owned domestic corporation (other than a corporation described in section 861(c)(1)) on the last day of the foreign corporation's taxable year. Excess interest shall be exempt from tax under section 881(a) only as provided in paragraph (a)(2)(iii) of this section (relating to treatment of certain excess interest of banks as interest on deposits) or paragraph (c)(3) of this section (relating to income tax treaties).

(iii) *Treatment of a portion of the excess interest of banks as interest on deposits.* A portion of the excess interest of a foreign corporation that is a bank (as defined in section 585(a)(2)(B) without regard to the second sentence thereof) provided that a substantial part of its business in the United States, as well as all other countries in which it operates, consists of receiving deposits and making loans and discounts, shall be treated as interest on deposits (as described in section 871(i)(3)), and shall be exempt from the tax imposed by section 881(a) as provided in such section. The portion of the excess interest of the foreign corporation that is treated as interest on deposits shall equal the product of the foreign corporation's excess interest and the greater of—

(A) The ratio of the amount of interest bearing deposits, within the meaning of section 871(i)(3)(A), of the foreign corporation as of the close of the taxable year to the amount of all interest bearing liabilities of the foreign corporation on such date; or

(B) 85 percent.

(iv) *Reporting and payment of tax on excess interest.* The amount of tax due under section 884(f) and this section with respect to excess interest of a foreign corporation shall be reported on the foreign corporation's income tax return for the taxable year in which the excess interest is treated as paid to the foreign corporation under section 884(f)(1)(B) and paragraph (a)(2) of this section, and shall not be subject to withholding under section 1441 or 1442. The tax shall be due and payable as provided in section 6151 and such other sections of Subtitle F of the Internal Revenue Code as apply, and estimated tax payments shall be due with respect to a foreign corporation's liability for the tax on excess interest as provided in section 6655.

(3) *Original issue discount.* For purposes of this section, the term "interest" includes original issue discount, as defined in section 1273(a)(1).

(4) *Examples.* The application of this paragraph (a) is illustrated by the following examples.

Example 1. Taxation of branch interest and excess interest. Foreign corporation A, a calendar year taxpayer that is not a corporation described in paragraph (a)(2)(iii) of this section (relating to banks), has $120 of interest allocated or apportioned to ECI under § 1.882-5 for 1997. A's branch interest (as defined in paragraph (b) of this section) for 1997 is as follows: $55 of portfolio interest (as defined in section 871(h)(2)) to B, a nonresident alien; $25 of interest to foreign corporation C, which owns 15 percent of the combined voting power of A's stock, with respect to bonds issued by A; and $20 to D, a domestic corporation. B and C are not engaged in the conduct of a trade or business in the United States. A, B and C are residents of countries with which the United States does not have an income tax treaty. The interest payments made to B and D are not subject to tax under section 871(a) or 881 and are not subject to withholding under section 1441 or 1442. The payment to C, which does not qualify as portfolio interest because C owns at least 10 percent of the combined voting power of A's stock, is subject to withholding of $7.50 ($25 × 30%). In addition, because A's interest allocated or apportioned to ECI under § 1.882-5 ($120) exceeds its branch interest ($100), A has excess interest of $20, which is subject to a tax of $6 ($20 × 30%) under section 881. The tax on A's excess interest must be reported on A's income tax return for 1997.

Example 2. Taxation of excess interest of a bank. Foreign corporation A, a calendar year taxpayer, is a corporation described in paragraph (a)(2)(iii) of this section (relating to banks) and is a resident of a country with which the United States does not have an income tax treaty. A has excess interest of $100 for 1997. At the close of 1997, A has $10,000 of interest-bearing liabilities (including liabilities that give rise to branch interest), of which $8,700 are interest-bearing deposits. For purposes of computing the tax on A's excess interest, $87 of the excess interest ($100 excess interest × ($8,700 interest-bearing deposits/ $10,000 interest-bearing liabilities)) is treated as interest on deposits. Thus, $87 of A's excess interest is exempt from tax under section 881(a) and the remaining $13 of excess interest is subject to a tax of $3.90 ($13 × 30%) under section 881(a).

(b) *Branch interest*—(1) *Definition of branch interest.* For purposes of this section, the term "branch interest" means interest that is—

(i) Paid by a foreign corporation with respect to a liability that is—

(A) A U.S. booked liability within the meaning of § 1.882-5(d)(2) (other than a U.S. booked liability of a partner within the meaning of § 1.882-5(d)(2)(vii)); or

(B) Described in § 1.884-1(e)(2) (relating to insurance liabilities on U.S. business and liabilities giving rise to interest expense that is directly allocated to income from a U.S. asset); or

(ii) In the case of a foreign corporation other than a corporation described in paragraph (a)(2)(iii) of this section, a liability specifically identified (as provided in paragraph (b)(3)(i) of this section) as a liability of a U.S. trade or

Reg. § 1.884-4(b)(1)

business of the foreign corporation on or before the earlier of the date on which the first payment of interest is made with respect to the liability or the due date (including extensions) of the foreign corporation's income tax return for the taxable year, provided that—

(A) The amount of such interest does not exceed 85 percent of the amount of interest of the foreign corporation that would be excess interest before taking into account interest treated as branch interest by reason of this paragraph (b)(1)(ii);

(B) The requirements of paragraph (b)(3)(ii) of this section (relating to notification of recipient of interest) are satisfied; and

(C) The liability is not described in paragraph (b)(3)(iii) of this section (relating to liabilities incurred in the ordinary course of a foreign business or secured by foreign assets) or paragraph (b)(1)(i) of this section.

(2) [Reserved]

(3) *Requirements relating to specifically identified liabilities*—(i) *Method of identification.* A liability described in paragraph (b)(1)(ii) of this section is identified as a liability of a U.S. trade or business only if the liability is shown on the records of the U.S. trade or business, or is identified as a liability of the U.S. trade or business on other records of the foreign corporation or on a schedule established for the purpose of identifying the liabilities of the U.S. trade or business. Each such liability must be identified with sufficient specificity so that the amount of branch interest attributable to the liability, and the name and address of the recipient, can be readily identified from such records or schedule. However, with respect to liabilities that give rise to portfolio interest (as defined in sections 871(h) and 881(c)) or that are payable 183 days or less from the date of original issue, and form part of a larger debt issue, such liabilities may be identified by reference to the issue and maturity date, principal amount and interest payable with respect to the entire debt issue. Records or schedules described in this paragraph that identify liabilities that give rise to branch interest must be maintained in the United States by the foreign corporation or an agent of the foreign corporation for the entire period commencing with the due date (including extensions) of the income tax return for the taxable year to which the records or schedules relate and ending with the expiration of the period of limitations for assessment of tax for such taxable year. A foreign corporation that is subject to this section may identify a liability under paragraph (b)(1)(ii) of this section whether or not it is actually engaged in the conduct of a trade or business in the United States.

(ii) *Notification to recipient.* Interest with respect to a liability described in paragraph (b)(1)(ii) of this section shall not be treated as branch interest unless the foreign corporation paying the interest either—

(A) Makes a return, pursuant to section 6049, with respect to the interest payment; or

(B) Sends a notice to the person who receives such interest in a confirmation of the transaction, a statement of account, or a separate notice, within two months of the end of the calendar year in which the interest was paid, stating that the interest paid with respect to the liability is from sources within the United States.

(iii) *Liabilities that do not give rise to branch interest under paragraph (b)(1)(ii) of this section.* A liability is described in this paragraph (b)(3)(iii) (and interest with respect to the liability may not be treated as branch interest of a foreign corporation by reason of paragraph (b)(1)(ii) of this section) if—

(A) The liability is directly incurred in the ordinary course of the profit-making activities of a trade or business of the foreign corporation conducted outside the United States, as, for example, an account or note payable arising from the purchase of inventory or receipt of services by such trade or business; or

(B) The liability is secured (during more than half the days during the portion of the taxable year in which the interest accrues) predominantly by property that is not a U.S. asset (as defined in § 1.884-1(d)) unless such liability is secured by substantially all the property of the foreign corporation.

(4) [Reserved]

(5) *Increase in branch interest where U.S. assets constitute 80 percent or more of a foreign corporation's assets*—(i) *General rule.* If a foreign corporation would have excess interest before application of this paragraph (b)(5) and the amount of the foreign corporation's U.S. assets as of the close of the taxable year equals or exceeds 80 percent of all money and the aggregate E&P basis of all property of the foreign corporation on such date, then all interest paid and accrued by the foreign corporation during the taxable year that was not treated as branch interest before application of this paragraph (b)(5) and that is not paid with respect to a liability described in paragraph (b)(3)(iii) of this section (relating to liabilities incurred in the ordinary course of a foreign business or secured by non-U.S. assets) shall be treated as branch interest. However, if applica-

Reg. § 1.884-4(b)(2)

tion of the preceding sentence would cause the amount of the foreign corporation's branch interest to exceed the amount permitted by paragraph (b)(6)(i) of this section (relating to branch interest in excess of a foreign corporation's interest allocated or apportioned to ECI under § 1.882-5) the amount of branch interest arising by reason of this paragraph shall be reduced as provided in paragraphs (b)(6)(ii) and (iii) of this section, as applicable.

(ii) *Example.* The application of this paragraph (b)(5) is illustrated by the following example.

Example. Application of 80 percent test. Foreign corporation A, a calendar year taxpayer, has $90 of interest allocated or apportioned to ECI under § 1.882-5 for 1993. Before application of this paragraph (b)(5), A has $40 of branch interest in 1993. A pays $60 of other interest during 1993, none of which is attributable to a liability described in paragraph (b)(3)(iii) of this section (relating to liabilities incurred in the ordinary course of a foreign business and liabilities predominantly secured by foreign assets). As of the close of 1993, A has an amount of U.S. assets that exceeds 80 percent of the money and E&P bases of all A's property. Before application of this paragraph (b)(5), A would have $50 of excess interest (*i.e.*, the $90 interest allocated or apportioned to its ECI under § 1.882-5 less $40 of branch interest). Under this paragraph (b)(5), the $60 of additional interest paid by A is also treated as branch interest. However, to the extent that treating the $60 of additional interest as branch interest would create an amount of branch interest that would exceed the amount of branch interest permitted under paragraph (b)(6) of this section (relating to branch interest that exceeds a foreign corporation's interest allocated or apportioned to ECI under § 1.882-5) the amount of the additional branch interest is reduced under paragraph (b)(6)(iii) of this section, which generally allows a foreign corporation to specify certain liabilities that do not give rise to branch interest or paragraph (b)(6)(ii) of this section, which generally specifies liabilities that do not give rise to branch interest beginning with the most-recently incurred liability.

(6) *Special rule where branch interest exceeds interest allocated or apportioned to ECI of a foreign corporation*—(i) *General rule.* If the amount of branch interest that is both paid and accrued by a foreign corporation during the taxable year (including interest that the foreign corporation elects under paragraph (c)(1) of this section to treat as paid during the taxable year) exceeds the amount of interest allocated or apportioned to ECI of a foreign corporation under § 1.882-5 for the taxable year, then the amount of the foreign corporation's branch interest shall be reduced by the amount of such excess as provided in paragraphs (b)(6)(ii) and (iii) of this section, as applicable. The rules of paragraphs (b)(6)(ii) and (iii) of this section shall also apply where the amount of branch interest with respect to liabilities identified under paragraph (b)(1)(ii) of this section exceeds the maximum amount that may be treated as branch interest under that paragraph. This paragraph (b)(6) shall apply whether or not a reduction in the amount of branch interest occurs as a result of adjustments made during the examination of the foreign corporation's income tax return, such as a reduction in the amount of interest allocated or apportioned to ECI of the foreign corporation under § 1.882-5.

(ii) *Reduction of branch interest beginning with most-recently incurred liability.* Except as provided in paragraph (b)(6)(iii) of this section (relating to an election to specify liabilities that do not give rise to branch interest), the amount of the excess in paragraph (b)(6)(i) of this section shall first reduce branch interest attributable to liabilities described in paragraph (b)(1)(ii) of this section (relating to liabilities identified as giving rise to branch interest) and then, if such excess has not been reduced to zero, branch interest attributable to the group of liabilities described in paragraph (b)(1)(i) of this section. The reduction of branch interest attributable to each group of liabilities (*i.e.*, liabilities described in paragraph (b)(1)(ii) of this section and liabilities described in paragraph (b)(1)(i) of this section) shall be made beginning with interest attributable to the latest-incurred liability and continuing, in reverse chronological order, with branch interest attributable to the next-latest incurred liability. The branch interest attributable to a liability must be reduced to zero before a reduction is made with respect to branch interest attributable to the next-latest incurred liability. Where only a portion of the branch interest attributable to a liability is reduced by reason of this paragraph (b)(6)(ii), the reduction shall be made beginning with the last interest payment made with respect to the liability during the taxable year and continuing, in reverse chronological order, with the next-latest payment until the amount of branch interest has been reduced by the amount specified in paragraph (b)(6)(i) of this section. The amount of interest that is not treated as branch interest by reason of this paragraph (b)(6)(ii) shall not be treated as paid by a domestic corporation and thus shall not be subject to tax under section 871(a) or 881(a).

Reg. § 1.884-4(b)(6)

(iii) *Election to specify liabilities that do not give rise to branch interest.* For purposes of reducing the amount of branch interest under paragraph (b)(6)(i) of this section, a foreign corporation may, instead of using the method described in paragraph (b)(6)(ii) of this section, elect for any taxable year to specify which liabilities will not be treated as giving rise to branch interest or will be treated as giving rise only in part to branch interest. Branch interest paid during the taxable year with respect to a liability specified under this paragraph (b)(6)(iii) must be reduced to zero before a reduction is made with respect to branch interest attributable to the next-specified liability. If all interest payments with respect to a specified liability, when added to all interest payments with respect to other liabilities specified under this paragraph (b)(6)(iii), would exceed the amount of the reduction under paragraph (b)(6)(i) of this section, then only a portion of the branch interest attributable to that specified liability shall be reduced under this paragraph (b)(6)(iii), and the reduction shall be made beginning with the last interest payment made with respect to the liability during the taxable year and continuing, in reverse chronological order, with the next-latest payment until the amount of branch interest has been reduced by the amount of the reduction under paragraph (b)(6)(i) of this section. A foreign corporation that elects to have this paragraph (b)(6)(iii) apply shall note on its books and records maintained in the United States that the liability is not to be treated as giving rise to branch interest, or is to be treated as giving rise to branch interest only in part. Such notation must be made after the close of the taxable year in which the foreign corporation pays the interest and prior to the due date (with extensions) of the foreign corporation's income tax return for the taxable year. However, if the excess interest in paragraph (b)(6)(i) of this section occurs as a result of adjustments made during the examination of the foreign corporation's income tax return, the election and notation may be made at the time of examination. The amount of interest that is not treated as branch interest by reason of this paragraph (b)(6)(iii) shall not be treated as paid by a domestic corporation and thus shall not be subject to tax under section 871(a) or 881(a).

(iv) *Examples.* The application of this paragraph (b)(6) is illustrated by the following examples.

Example 1. Branch interest exceeds interest apportioned to ECI with no election in effect. Foreign corporation A, a calendar year, accrual method taxpayer, has interest expense apportioned to ECI under § 1.882-5 of $230 for 1997. A's branch interest for 1997 is as follows:

(i) $130 paid to B, a domestic corporation, with respect to a note issued on March 10, 1997, and secured by real property located in the United States;

(ii) $60 paid to C, an individual resident of country X who is entitled to a 10 percent rate of withholding on interest payments under the income tax treaty between the United States and X, with respect to a note issued on October 15, 1996, which gives rise to interest subject to tax under section 871(a);

(iii) $80 paid to D, an individual resident of country Y who is entitled to a 15 percent rate of withholding on interest payments under the income tax treaty between the United States and Y, with respect to a note issued on February 15, 1997, which gives rise to interest subject to tax under section 871(a); and

(iv) $70 of portfolio interest (as defined in section 871(h)(2)) paid to E, a nonresident alien, with respect to a bond issued on March 1, 1997.

A's branch interest accrues during 1997 for purposes of calculating the amount of A's interest apportioned to ECI under § 1.882-5. A has identified under paragraph (b)(1)(ii) of this section the liabilities described in paragraphs (ii), (iii) and (iv) of this example. A has not made an election under paragraph (b)(6)(iii) of this section to specify liabilities that do not give rise to branch interest. The amount of A's branch interest in 1997 is limited under paragraph (b)(6)(i) of this section to $230, the amount of the interest apportioned to A's ECI for 1997. The amount of A's branch interest must thus be reduced by $110 ($340 − $230) under paragraph (b)(6)(ii) of this section. The reduction is first made with respect to interest attributable to liabilities described in paragraph (b)(1)(ii) of this section (*i.e.*, liabilities identified as giving rise to branch interest) and, within the group of liabilities described in paragraph (b)(1)(ii) of this section, is first made with respect to the latest-incurred liability. Thus, the $70 of interest paid to E with respect to the bond issued on March 1, 1997, and $40 of the $80 of interest paid to D with respect to the note issued on February 15, 1997, are not treated as branch interest. The interest paid to D is no longer subject to tax under section 871(a), and D may claim a refund of amounts withheld with respect to the interest payments. There is no change in the tax consequences to E because the interest received by E was portfolio interest and was not subject to tax when it was treated as branch interest.

Example 2. Effect of election to specify liabilities. Assume the same facts as in *Example 1* except that A makes an election under paragraph (b)(6)(iii) of this section to specify which liabili-

Reg. § 1.884-4(b)(6)

ties are not to be treated as giving rise to branch interest. A specifies the liability to D, who would be taxable at a rate of 15 percent on interest paid with respect to the liability, as a liability that does not give rise to branch interest, and D is therefore not subject to tax under section 871(a) and is entitled to a refund of amounts withheld with respect to the interest payments. A also specifies the liability to C as a liability that gives rise to branch interest only in part. As a result, $30 of the $60 of interest paid to C is not treated as branch interest, and C is entitled to a refund with respect to the $30 of interest that is not treated as branch interest.

(7) *Effect of election under paragraph (c)(1) of this section to treat interest as if paid in year of accrual.* If a foreign corporation accrues an interest expense in a taxable year earlier than the taxable year of payment and elects under paragraph (c)(1) of this section to compute its excess interest as if the interest expense were branch interest paid in the year of accrual, the interest expense shall be treated as branch interest that is paid at the close of such year (and not in the actual year of payment) for all purposes of this section. Such interest shall thus be subject to tax under section 871(a) or 881(a) and withholding under section 1441 or section 1442, as if paid on the last day of the taxable year of accrual. Interest that is treated under paragraph (c)(1) of this section as paid in a later year for purposes of computing excess interest shall be treated as paid only in the actual year of payment for all purposes of this section other than paragraphs (a)(2) and (c)(1) of this section (relating to excess interest).

(8) *Effect of treaties*—(i) *Payor's treaty.* In the case of a foreign corporation's branch interest, relief shall be available under an article of an income tax treaty between the United States and the foreign corporation's country of residence relating to interest paid by the foreign corporation only if, for the taxable year in which the branch interest is paid (or if the branch interest is treated as paid in an earlier taxable year under paragraph (b)(7) of this section, for the earlier taxable year)—

(A) The foreign corporation meets the requirements of the limitation on benefits provision, if any, in the treaty, and either—

(*1*) The corporation is a qualified resident (as defined in § 1.884-5(a)) of that foreign country in such year; or

(*2*) The corporation meets the requirements of paragraph (b)(8)(iii) of this section in such year; or

(B) The limitation on benefits provision, or an amendment to that provision, entered into force after December 31, 1986.

(ii) *Recipient's treaty.* A foreign person (other than a foreign corporation) that derives branch interest is entitled to claim benefits under provisions of an income tax treaty between the United States and its country of residence relating to interest derived by the foreign person. A foreign corporation may claim such benefits if it meets, with respect to the branch interest, the requirements of the limitation on benefits provision, if any, in the treaty and—

(A) The foreign corporation meets the requirements of paragraphs (b)(8)(i)(A) or (B) of this section; and

(B) In the case of interest paid in a taxable year beginning after December 31, 1988, with respect to an obligation with a maturity not exceeding one year, each foreign corporation that beneficially owned the obligation prior to maturity was a qualified resident (for the period specified in paragraph (b)(8)(i) of this section) of a foreign country with which the United States has an income tax treaty or met the requirements of the limitation on benefits provision in a treaty with respect to the interest payment and such provision entered into force after December 31, 1986.

(iii) *Presumption that a foreign corporation continues to be a qualified resident.* For purposes of this paragraph (b)(8), a foreign corporation that was a qualified resident for the prior taxable year because it fulfills the requirements of § 1.884-5 shall be considered a qualified resident with respect to branch interest that is paid or received during the current taxable year if—

(A) In the case of a foreign corporation that met the stock ownership and base erosion tests in § 1.884-5(b) and (c) for the preceding taxable year, the foreign corporation does not know, or have reason to know, that either 50 percent of its stock (by value) is not beneficially owned (or treated as beneficially owned by reason of § 1.884-5(b)(2)) by qualifying shareholders at any time during the portion of the taxable year that ends with the date on which the interest is paid, or that the base erosion test is not met during the portion of the taxable year that ends with the date on which the interest is paid;

(B) In the case of a foreign corporation that met the requirements of § 1.884-5(d) (relating to publicly-traded corporations) for the preceding taxable year, the foreign corporation is listed on an established securities exchange in the United States or its country of residence at all

Reg. § 1.884-4(b)(8)

times during the portion of the taxable year that ends with the date on which the interest is paid and does not fail the requirements of § 1.884-5(d)(4)(iii) (relating to certain closely-held corporations) at any time during such period; or

(C) In the case of a foreign corporation that met the requirements of § 1.884-5(e) (relating to the active trade or business test) for the preceding taxable year, the foreign corporation continues to operate (other than in a nominal degree), at all times during the portion of the taxable year that ends with the date on which the interest is paid, the same business in the U.S. and its country of residence that caused it to meet such requirements for the preceding taxable year.

(iv) *Treaties other than income tax treaties.* A treaty that is not an income tax treaty does not provide any benefits with respect to branch interest.

(v) *Effect of income tax treaties on interest paid by a partnership.* If a foreign corporation is a partner (directly or indirectly) in a partnership that is engaged in a trade or business in the United States and owns an interest of 10 percent or more (as determined under the attribution rules of section 318) in the capital, profits, or losses of the partnership at any time during the partner's taxable year, the relief that may be claimed under an income tax treaty with respect to the foreign corporation's distributive share of interest paid or treated as paid by the partnership shall not exceed the relief that would be available under paragraphs (b)(8)(i) and (ii) of this section if such interest were branch interest of the foreign corporation. See paragraph (c)(2) of this section for the effect on a foreign corporation's excess interest of interest paid by a partnership of which the foreign corporation is a partner.

(vi) *Examples.* The following examples illustrate the application of this paragraph (b)(8).

Example 1. Payor's treaty. The income tax treaty between the United States and country X provides that the United States may not impose a tax on interest paid by a corporation that is a resident of that country (and that is not a domestic corporation) if the recipient of the interest is a nonresident alien or a foreign corporation. Corp A is a qualified resident of country X and meets the limitation on benefits provision in the treaty. A's branch interest is not subject to tax under section 871(a) or 881(a) regardless of whether the recipient is entitled to benefits under an income tax treaty.

Example 2. Recipient's treaty and interest received from a partnership. A, a foreign corporation, and B, a nonresident alien, are partners in a partnership that owns and operates U.S. real estate and each has a distributive share of partnership interest deductions equal to 50 percent of the interest deductions of the partnership. There is no income tax treaty between the United States and the countries of residence of A and B. The partnership pays $1,000 of interest to a bank that is a resident of a foreign country, Y, and that qualifies under an income tax treaty in effect with the United States for a 5 percent rate of tax on U.S. source interest paid to a resident of country Y. However, the bank is not a qualified resident of country Y and the limitation on benefits provision of the treaty has not been amended since December 31, 1986. The partnership is required to withhold at a rate of 30 percent on $500 of the interest paid to the bank (*i.e.*, A's 50 percent distributive share of interest paid by the partnership) because the bank cannot, under paragraph (b)(8)(iv) of this section, claim greater treaty benefits by lending money to the partnership than it could claim if it lent money to A directly and the $500 were branch interest of A.

(c) *Rules relating to excess interest*—(1) *Election to compute excess interest by treating branch interest that is paid and accrued in different years as if paid in year of accrual*—(i) *General rule.* If branch interest is paid in one or more taxable years before or after the year in which the interest accrues, a foreign corporation may elect to compute its excess interest as if such branch interest were paid on the last day of the taxable year in which it accrues, and not in the taxable year in which it is actually paid. The interest expense will thus reduce the amount of the foreign corporation's excess interest in the year of accrual rather than in the year of actual payment. Except as provided in paragraph (c)(1)(ii) of this section, if an election is made for a taxable year, this paragraph (c)(1)(i) shall apply to all branch interest that is paid or accrued during that year. See paragraph (b)(7) of this section for the effect of an election under this paragraph (c)(1) on branch interest that accrues in a taxable year after the year of payment.

(ii) *Election not to apply in certain cases.* An election under this paragraph (c)(1) shall not apply to an interest expense that accrued in a taxable year beginning before January 1, 1987, and shall not apply to an interest expense that was paid in a taxable year beginning before such date unless the interest was income from sources within the United States. An election under this paragraph (c)(1) shall not apply to branch interest that accrues during the taxable year and is paid in an earlier taxable year if the branch interest reduced excess interest in such earlier year. However, a foreign corporation may amend its income tax return for such earlier taxable year

Reg. § 1.884-4(c)(1)

so that the branch interest does not reduce excess interest in such year.

(iii) *Requirements for election.* A foreign corporation that elects to apply this paragraph (c)(1) shall attach to its income tax return (or to an amended income tax return) a statement that it elects to have the provisions of this paragraph (c)(1) apply, or shall provide written notice to the Commissioner during an examination that it elects to apply this paragraph (c)(1). The election shall be effective for the taxable year to which the return relates and for all subsequent taxable years unless the Commissioner consents to revocation of the election.

(iv) *Examples.* The following examples illustrate the application of this paragraph (c)(1).

Example 1. Interest accrued before paid. Foreign corporation A, a calendar year, accrual method taxpayer, has $100 of interest allocated or apportioned to ECI under § 1.882-5 for 1997. A has $60 of branch interest in 1997 before application of this paragraph (c)(1). A has an interest expense of $20 that properly accrues for tax purposes in 1997 but is not paid until 1998. When the interest is paid in 1998 it will meet the requirements for branch interest under paragraph (b)(1) of this section. A makes a timely election under this paragraph (c)(1) to treat the accrued interest as if it were paid in 1997. A will be treated as having branch interest of $80 for 1997 and excess interest of $20 in 1997. The $20 of interest treated as branch interest of A in 1997 will not again be treated as branch interest in 1998.

Example 2. Interest paid before accrued. Foreign corporation A, a calendar year, accrual method taxpayer, has $60 of branch interest in 1997. The interest expense does not accrue until 1998 and the amount of interest allocated or apportioned to A's ECI under § 1.882-5 is zero for 1997 and $60 for 1998. A makes an election under this paragraph (c)(1) with respect to 1997. As a result of the election, A's $60 of branch interest in 1997 reduces the amount of A's excess interest for 1998 rather than in 1997.

(2) *Interest paid by a partnership*—(i) *General rule.* Except as otherwise provided in paragraphs (c)(2)(i) and (ii) of this section, if a foreign corporation is a partner in a partnership that is engaged in trade or business in the United States, the amount of the foreign corporation's distributive share of interest paid or accrued by the partnership shall reduce (but not below zero) the amount of the foreign corporation's excess interest for the year to the extent such interest is taken into account by the foreign corporation in that year for purposes of calculating the interest allocated or apportioned to the ECI of the foreign corporation under § 1.882-5. A foreign corporation's excess interest shall not be reduced by its distributive share of partnership interest that is attributable to a liability described in paragraph (b)(3)(iii) of this section (relating to interest on liabilities incurred in the ordinary course of a foreign business or secured predominantly by assets that are not U.S. assets) or would be described in paragraph (b)(3)(iii) of this section if entered on the partner's books. See paragraph (b)(8)(v) of this section for the effect of income tax treaties on interest paid by a partnership.

(ii) *Special rule for interest that is paid and accrued in different years.* Paragraph (c)(2)(i) of this section shall not apply to any portion of a foreign corporation's distributive share of partnership interest that is paid and accrued in different taxable years unless the foreign corporation has an election in effect under paragraph (c)(1) of this section that is effective with respect to such interest and any tax due under section 871(a) or 881(a) with respect to such interest has been deducted and withheld at source in the earlier of the taxable year of payment or accrual.

(3) *Effect of treaties*—(i) *General rule.* The rate of tax imposed on the excess interest of a foreign corporation that is a resident of a country with which the United States has an income tax treaty shall not exceed the rate provided under such treaty that would apply with respect to interest paid by a domestic corporation to that foreign corporation if the foreign corporation meets, with respect to the excess interest, the requirements of the limitation on benefits provision, if any, in the treaty and either—

(A) The corporation is a qualified resident (as defined in § 1.884-5(a)) of that foreign country for the taxable year in which the excess interest is subject to tax; or

(B) The limitation on benefits provision, or an amendment to that provision, entered into force after December 31, 1986.

(ii) *Provisions relating to interest paid by a foreign corporation.* Any provision in an income tax treaty that exempts or reduces the rate of tax on interest paid by a foreign corporation does not prevent imposition of the tax on excess interest or reduce the rate of such tax.

(4) *Example.* The application of paragraphs (c)(2) and (3) of this section is illustrated by the following example.

Example. Interest paid by a partnership. Foreign corporation A, a calendar year taxpayer, is not a resident of a foreign country with which the United States has an income tax treaty. A is engaged in the conduct of a trade or business both

Reg. § 1.884-4(c)(4)

in the United States and in foreign countries, and owns a 50 percent interest in X, a calendar year partnership engaged in the conduct of a trade or business in the United States. For 1997, all of X's liabilities are of a type described in paragraph (b)(1) of this section (relating to liabilities on U.S. books) and none are described in paragraph (b)(3)(iii) of this section (relating to liabilities that may not give rise to branch interest). A's distributive share of interest paid by X in 1997 is $20. For 1997, A has $150 of interest allocated or apportioned to its ECI under § 1.882-5, $120 of which is attributable to branch interest. Thus, the amount of A's excess interest for 1997, before application of paragraph (c)(2)(i) of this section, is $30. Under paragraph (c)(2)(i) of this section, A's $30 of excess interest is reduced by $20, representing A's share of interest paid by X. Thus, the amount of A's excess interest for 1997 is reduced to $10. A is subject to a tax of 30 percent on its $10 of excess interest.

(d) *Stapled entities.* A foreign corporation that is treated as a domestic corporation by reason of section 269B (relating to stapled entities) shall continue to be treated as a foreign corporation for purposes of section 884(f) and this section, notwithstanding section 269B and the regulations thereunder. Interest paid by such foreign corporation shall be treated as paid by a domestic corporation and shall be subject to the tax imposed by section 871(a) or 881(a), and to withholding under sections 1441 and 1442, as applicable, to the extent such interest is not subject to tax by reason of section 884(f) and this section.

(e) *Effective dates*—(1) *General rule.* Except as provided in paragraph (e)(2) of this section, this section is effective for taxable years beginning October 13, 1992, and for payments of interest described in section 884(f)(1)(A) made (or treated as made under paragraph (b)(7) of this section) during taxable years of the payor beginning after such date. With respect to taxable years beginning before October 13, 1992 and after December 31, 1986, a foreign corporation may elect to apply this section in lieu of § 1.884-4T of the temporary regulations (as contained in the CFR edition revised as of April 1, 1992) as they applied to the foreign corporation after issuance of Notice 89-80, 1989-2 C.B. 394, but only if the foreign corporation has made an election under § 1.884-1(i) to apply § 1.884-1 in lieu of § 1.884-1T (as contained in the CFR edition revised as of April 1, 1992) for that year, and the statute of limitations for assessment of a deficiency has not expired for that taxable year. Once an election has been made, an election under this section shall apply to all subsequent taxable years.

(2) *Special rule.* Paragraphs (a)(1), (a)(2)(i)(A), (a)(2)(iii), (b)(1), (b)(3), (b)(5)(i), (b)(6)(i), (b)(6)(ii), and (c)(2)(i) of this section are effective for taxable years beginning on or after June 6, 1996.

(f) *Transition rules*—(1) *Election under paragraph (c)(1) of this section.* If a foreign corporation has made an election described in § 1.884-4T(b)(7) (as contained in the CFR edition revised as of April 1, 1992) with respect to interest that has accrued and been paid in different taxable years, such election shall be effective for purposes of paragraph (c)(1) of this section as if the corporation had made the election under paragraph (c)(1) of this section of these regulations.

(2) *Waiver of notification requirement for non-banks under Notice 89-80.* If a foreign corporation that is not a bank has made an election under Notice 89-80 to apply the rules in Part 2 of Section I of the Notice in lieu of the rules in § 1.884-4T(b) (as contained in the CFR edition revised as of April 1, 1992) to determine the amount of its interest paid and excess interest in taxable years beginning prior to 1990, the requirement that the foreign corporation satisfy the notification requirements described in paragraph (b)(3)(ii) of this section is waived with respect to interest paid in taxable years ending on or before the date the Notice was issued.

(3) *Waiver of legending requirement for certain debt issued prior to January 3, 1989.* For purposes of sections 871(h), 881(c), and this section, branch interest of a foreign corporation that would be treated as portfolio interest under section 871(h) or 881(c) but for the fact that it fails to meet the requirements of section 163 (f)(2)(B)(ii)(II) (relating to the legend requirement), shall nevertheless be treated as portfolio interest provided the interest arises with respect to a liability incurred by the foreign corporation before January 3, 1989, and interest with respect to the liability was treated as branch interest in a taxable year beginning before January 1, 1990. [Reg. § 1.884-4.]

☐ [*T.D.* 8432, 9-10-92. Amended by *T.D.* 8657, 3-5-96.]

[Reg. § 1.884-5]

§ 1.884-5. **Qualified resident.**—(a) *Definition of qualified resident.* A foreign corporation is a qualified resident of a foreign country with which the United States has an income tax treaty in effect if, for the taxable year, the foreign corporation is a resident of that country (within the meaning of such treaty) and either—

(1) Meets the requirements of paragraphs (b) and (c) of this section (relating to stock ownership and base erosion);

(2) Meets the requirements of paragraph (d) of this section (relating to publicly-traded corporations);

(3) Meets the requirements of paragraph (e) of this section (relating to the conduct of an active trade or business); or

(4) Obtains a ruling as provided in paragraph (f) of this section that it shall be treated as a qualified resident of its country of residence.

(b) *Stock ownership requirement*—(1) *General rule*—(i) *Ownership by qualifying shareholders.* A foreign corporation satisfies the stock ownership requirement of this paragraph (b) for the taxable year if more than 50 percent of its stock (by value) is beneficially owned (or is treated as beneficially owned by reason of paragraph (b)(2) of this section) during at least half of the number of days in the foreign corporation's taxable year by one or more qualifying shareholders. A person shall be treated as a qualifying shareholder only if such person meets the requirements of paragraph (b)(3) of this section and is either—

(A) An individual who is either a resident of the foreign country of which the foreign corporation is a resident or a citizen or resident of the United States;

(B) The government of the country of which the foreign corporation is a resident (or a political subdivision or local authority of such country), or the United States, a State, the District of Columbia, or a political subdivision or local authority of a State;

(C) A corporation that is a resident of the foreign country of which the foreign corporation is a resident and whose stock is primarily and regularly traded on an established securities market (within the meaning of paragraph (d) of this section) in that country or the United States or a domestic corporation whose stock is primarily and regularly traded on an established securities market (within the meaning of paragraph (d) of this section) in the United States;

(D) A not-for-profit organization described in paragraph (b)(1)(iv) of this section that is not a pension fund as defined in paragraph (b)(8)(i)(A) of this section and that is organized under the laws of the foreign country of which the foreign corporation is a resident or the United States; or

(E) A beneficiary of certain pension funds (as defined in paragraph (b)(8)(i)(A) of this section) administered in or by the country in which the foreign corporation is a resident to the extent provided in paragraph (b)(8) of this section.

Beneficial owners of an association taxable as a corporation shall be treated as shareholders of such association for purposes of this paragraph (b)(1). If stock of a foreign corporation is owned by a corporation that is treated as a qualifying shareholder under paragraph (b)(1)(i)(C) of this section, such stock shall not also be treated as owned, directly or indirectly, by any qualifying shareholders of such corporation for purposes of this paragraph (b). Notwithstanding the above, a foreign corporation will not be treated as a qualified resident unless it obtains the documentation described in paragraph (b)(3) of this section to show that the requirements of this paragraph (b)(1)(i) have been met and maintains the documentation as provided in paragraph (b)(9) of this section. See also paragraph (b)(1)(iii) of this section, which treats certain publicly-traded classes of stock as owned by qualifying shareholders.

(ii) *Special rules relating to qualifying shareholders.* For purposes of applying paragraph (b)(1)(i) of this section—

(A) Stock owned on any day shall be taken into account only if the beneficial owner is a qualifying shareholder on that day or, in the case of a corporation or not-for-profit organization that is a qualifying shareholder under paragraph (b)(1)(i)(C) or (D) of this section, for a one-year period that includes such day; and

(B) An individual, corporation or not-for-profit organization is a resident of a foreign country if it is a resident of that country for purposes of the income tax treaty between the United States and that country.

(iii) *Publicly-traded class of stock treated as owned by qualifying shareholders.* A class of stock of a foreign corporation shall be treated as owned by qualifying shareholders if—

(A) The class of stock is listed on an established securities market in the United States or in the country of residence of the foreign corporation seeking qualified resident status; and

(B) The class of stock is primarily and regularly traded on such market (within the meaning of paragraphs (d)(3) and (4) of this section, applied as if the class of stock were the sole class of stock relied on to meet the requirements of paragraph (d)(4)(i)(A)).

For purposes of this paragraph (b), stock in such class shall not also be treated as owned by any qualifying shareholders who own such stock, either directly or indirectly.

(iv) *Special rule for not-for-profit organizations.* A not-for-profit organization is described in

Reg. § 1.884-5(b)(1)

paragraph (b)(1)(iv) of this section if it meets the following requirements—

(A) It is a corporation, association taxable as a corporation, trust, fund, foundation, league or other entity operated exclusively for religious, charitable, educational, or recreational purposes, and it is not organized for profit;

(B) It is generally exempt from tax in its country of organization by virtue of its not-for-profit status; and

(C) Either—

(*1*) More than 50 percent of its annual support is expended on behalf of persons described in paragraphs (b)(1)(i)(A) through (E) of this section or on qualified residents of the country in which the organization is organized; or

(*2*) More than 50 percent of its annual support is derived from persons described in paragraphs (b)(1)(i)(A) through (E) of this section or from persons who are qualified residents of the country in which the organization is organized.

For purposes of meeting the requirements of paragraph (b)(1)(iv)(C) of this section, a not-for-profit organization may rely on the addresses of record of its individual beneficiaries and supporters to determine if such persons are resident in the country in which the not-for-profit organization is organized, provided that the addresses of record are not nonresidential addresses such as a post office box or in care of a financial intermediary, and the officers, directors or administrators of the organization do not know or have reason to know that the individual beneficiaries or supporters do not reside at that address.

(2) *Rules for determining constructive ownership*—(i) *General rules for attribution.* For purposes of this section, stock owned by a corporation, partnership, trust, estate, or mutual insurance company or similar entity shall be treated as owned proportionately by its shareholders, partners, beneficiaries, grantors or other interest holders as provided in paragraph (b)(2)(ii) through (v) of this section. The proportionate interest rules of this paragraph (b)(2) shall apply successively upward through a chain of ownership, and a person's proportionate interest shall be computed for the relevant days or period that is taken into account in determining whether a foreign corporation is a qualified resident. Except as otherwise provided, stock treated as owned by a person by reason of this paragraph (b)(2) shall, for purposes of applying this paragraph (b)(2), be treated as actually owned by such person.

(ii) *Partnerships.* A partner shall be treated as having an interest in stock of a foreign corporation owned by a partnership in proportion to the least of—

(A) The partner's percentage distributive share of the partnership's dividend income from the stock;

(B) The partner's percentage distributive share of gain from disposition of the stock by the partnership;

(C) The partner's percentage distributive share of the stock (or proceeds from the disposition of the stock) upon liquidation of the partnership.

For purposes of this paragraph (b)(2)(ii), however, all qualifying shareholders that are partners of a partnership shall be treated as one partner. Thus, the percentage distributive shares of dividend income, gain and liquidation rights of all qualifying shareholders that are partners in a partnership are aggregated prior to determining the least of the three percentages.

(iii) *Trusts and estates*—(A) *Beneficiaries.* In general, a person shall be treated as having an interest in stock of a foreign corporation owned by a trust or estate in proportion to the person's actuarial interest in the trust or estate, as provided in section 318(a)(2)(B)(i), except that an income beneficiary's actuarial interest in the trust will be determined as if the trust's only asset were the stock. The interest of a remainder beneficiary in stock will be equal to 100 percent minus the sum of the percentages of any interest in the stock held by income beneficiaries. The ownership of an interest in stock owned by a trust shall not be attributed to any beneficiary whose interest cannot be determined under the preceding sentence, and any such interest, to the extent not attributed by reason of this paragraph (b)(2)(iii)(A), shall not be considered owned by a beneficiary unless all potential beneficiaries with respect to the stock are qualifying shareholders. In addition, a beneficiary's actuarial interest will be treated as zero to the extent that a grantor is treated as owning the stock under paragraph (b)(2)(iii)(B) of this section. A substantially separate and independent share of a trust, within the meaning of section 663(c), shall be treated as a separate trust for purposes of this paragraph (b)(2)(iii)(A), provided that payment of income, accumulated income or corpus of a share of one beneficiary (or group of beneficiaries) cannot affect the proportionate share of income, accumulated income or corpus of another beneficiary (or group of beneficiaries).

(B) *Grantor trusts.* A person is treated as the owner of stock of a foreign corporation owned by a trust to the extent that the stock is included in the portion of the trust that is treated

Reg. § 1.884-5(b)(2)

as owned by the person under sections 671 to 679 (relating to grantors and others treated as substantial owners).

(iv) *Corporations that issue stock.* A shareholder of a corporation that issues stock shall be treated as owning stock of a foreign corporation that is owned by such corporation on any day in a proportion that equals the value of the stock owned by such shareholder to the value of all stock of such corporation. If there is an agreement, express or implied, that a shareholder of a corporation will not receive distributions from the earnings of stock owned by the corporation, the shareholder will not be treated as owning that stock owned by the corporation.

(v) *Mutual insurance companies and similar entities.* Stock held by a mutual insurance company, mutual savings bank, or similar entity (including an association taxable as a corporation that does not issue stock interests) shall be considered owned proportionately by the policy holders, depositors, or other owners in the same proportion that such persons share in the surplus of such entity upon liquidation or dissolution.

(vi) *Pension funds.* See paragraphs (b)(8)(ii) and (iii) of this section for the attribution of stock owned by a pension fund (as defined in paragraph (b)(8)(i)(A)) to beneficiaries of the fund.

(vii) *Examples.* The rules of paragraph (b)(2)(ii) of this section are illustrated by the following examples.

Example 1. Stock held solely by qualifying shareholders through a partnership. A and B, residents of country X, are qualifying shareholders, within the meaning of paragraphs (b)(1)(i)(A) through (E) of this section, and the sole partners of partnership P. P's only asset is the stock of foreign corporation Z, a country X corporation seeking qualified resident status under this section. A's distributive share of P's income and gain on the disposition of P's assets is 80 percent, but A's distributive share of P's assets (or the proceeds therefrom) on P's liquidation is 20 percent. B's distributive share of P's income and gain is 20 percent and S is entitled to 80 percent of the assets (or proceeds therefrom) on P's liquidation. Under the attribution rules of paragraph (b)(2)(ii) of this section, A and B will be treated as a single partner owning in the aggregate 100 percent of the stock of Z owned by P.

Example 2. Stock held by both qualifying and nonqualifying shareholders through a partnership. Assume the same facts as in *Example 1* except that C, an individual who is not a qualifying shareholder, is also a partner in P and that C's distributive share of P's income is 60 percent. The distributive shares of A and B are the same as in *Example 1* except that A's distributive share of income is 20 percent. Under the attribution rules of paragraph (b)(2)(ii) of this section, A and B will be treated as a single partner owning in the aggregate 40 percent of the stock of Z owned by P (*i.e.*, the least of A and B's aggregate distributive shares of dividend income (40 percent), gain (100 percent), and liquidation rights (100 percent) with respect to the Z stock).

Example 3. Stock held through tiered partnerships. Assume the same facts as in *Example 1,* except that P does not own the stock of Z directly, but rather is a partner in partnership PI, which owns the stock of Z. Assume that P's distributive share of the dividend income, gain and liquidation rights with respect to the Z stock held by PI is 40 percent. Assume that of the remaining partners of PI only D is a qualifying shareholder. D's distributive share of P1's dividend income and gain is 15 percent; D's distributive share of P1's assets on liquidation is 25 percent. Under the attribution rules of paragraph (b)(2)(ii) of this section, A and B, treated as a single partner, will own 40 percent of the Z stock owned by P1 (100 percent × 40 percent) and D will be treated as owning 15 percent of the Z stock owned by P1 (the least of D's dividend income (15 percent), gain (15 percent), and liquidation rights (25 percent) with respect to the Z stock). Thus, 55 percent of the Z stock owned by P1 is treated as owned by qualifying shareholders under paragraph (b)(2)(ii) of this section.

(3) *Required documentation*—(i) *Ownership statements, certificates of residency and intermediary ownership statements.* Except as provided in paragraphs (b)(3)(ii), (iii) and (iv) and paragraph (b)(8) of this section, a person shall only be treated as a qualifying shareholder of a foreign corporation if—

(A) For the relevant period, the person completes an ownership statement described in paragraph (b)(4) of this section and, in the case of an individual who is not a U.S. citizen or resident, also obtains a certificate of residency described in paragraph (b)(5) of this section;

(B) In the case of a person owning stock in the foreign corporation indirectly through one or more intermediaries (including mere legal owners or recordholders acting as nominees), each intermediary completes an intermediary ownership statement described in paragraph (b)(6) of this section; and

(C) Such ownership statements and certificates of residency are received by the foreign corporation on or before the earlier of the date it files its income tax return for the taxable year to

Reg. § 1.884-5(b)(3)

which the statements relate or the due date (including extensions) for filing such return or, in the case of a foreign corporation claiming treaty benefits under § 1.884-4(b)(8)(i) or (ii) (relating to branch interest) on or before the date on which such interest is paid.

(ii) *Substitution of intermediary verification statement for ownership statements and certificates of residency.* If a qualifying shareholder owns stock through an intermediary that is either a domestic corporation, a resident of the United States, or a resident (for treaty purposes) of a country with which the United States has an income tax treaty in effect, the intermediary may provide an intermediary verification statement (as described in paragraph (b)(7) of this section) in place of any relevant ownership statements and certificates of residency from qualifying shareholders, and in place of intermediary ownership statements (or, where applicable, intermediary verification statements) from all intermediaries standing in the chain of ownership between the qualifying shareholders and the intermediary issuing the intermediary verification statement. An intermediary verification statement generally certifies that the verifying intermediary holds the documentation described in the preceding sentence and agrees to make it available to the District Director on request. Such intermediary verification statements, along with an intermediary ownership statement from the verifying intermediary, must be received by the foreign corporation on or before the earlier of the date it files its income tax return for the taxable year to which the statements relate or the due date (including extensions) for filing such return. An indirect owner of a foreign corporation is thus treated as a qualifying shareholder of a foreign corporation if the foreign corporation receives, on or before the time specified above, an intermediary verification statement and an intermediary ownership statement from the verifying intermediary and an intermediary ownership statement from all intermediaries standing in the chain of the verifying intermediary's ownership of its interest in the foreign corporation.

(iii) *Special rule for registered shareholders of widely-held corporations.* An ownership statement and a certificate of residency shall not be required in the case of an individual who is a shareholder of record of a corporation that has at least 250 shareholders if—

(A) The individual owns less than one percent of the stock (by value) (applying the attribution rules of section 318) of the corporation at all times during the taxable year;

(B) The individual's address of record is in the corporation's country of residence and is not a nonresidential address such as a post office box or in care of a financial intermediary or stock transfer agent; and

(C) The officers and directors of the corporation do not know or have reason to know that the individual does not reside at that address.

The rule in this paragraph (b)(3)(iii) may also be applied with respect to individual owners of mutual insurance companies, mutual savings banks or similar entities, provided that the same conditions set forth in this paragraph (b)(3)(iii) are met with respect to such individuals.

(iv) *Special rule for pension funds.* See paragraphs (b)(8)(ii) through (v) of this section for special documentation rules applicable to pension funds (as defined in paragraph (b)(8)(i)(A) of this section).

(v) *Reasonable cause exception.* If a foreign corporation does not obtain the documentation described in this paragraph (b)(3) or (b)(8) of this section in a timely manner but is able to show prior to notification of an examination of the return for the taxable year that the failure was due to reasonable cause and not willful neglect, the foreign corporation may perfect the documentation after the deadlines specified in this paragraph (b)(3) or (b)(8) of this section. It may make such a showing by providing a written statement to the District Director having jurisdiction over the taxpayer's return or the Office of the Assistant Commissioner (International), as applicable, setting forth the reasons for the failure to obtain the documentation in a timely manner and describing the documentation that was received after the deadline had passed. Whether a failure to obtain the documentation in a timely manner was due to reasonable cause shall be determined by the District Director or the Office of the Assistant Commissioner (International), as applicable, under all the facts and circumstances.

(4) *Ownership statements from qualifying shareholders*—(i) *Ownership statements from individuals.* An ownership statement from an individual is a written statement signed by the individual under penalties of perjury stating—

(A) The name, permanent address, and country of residence of the individual and, if the individual was not a resident of the country for the entire taxable year of the foreign corporation seeking qualified resident status, the period during which it was a resident of the foreign corporation's country of residence;

(B) If the individual is a direct beneficial owner of stock in the foreign corporation, the

Reg. § 1.884-5(b)(4)

name of the corporation, the number of shares in each class of stock of the corporation that are so owned, and the period of time during the taxable year of the foreign corporation during which the individual owned the stock (or, in the case of an association taxable as a corporation, the amount and nature of the owner's interest in such association);

(C) If the individual directly owns an interest in a corporation, partnership, trust, estate or other intermediary that owns (directly or indirectly) stock in the foreign corporation, the name of the intermediary, the number and class of shares or amount and nature of the interest of the individual in such intermediary (that is relevant for purposes of attributing ownership in paragraph (b)(2) of this section), and the period of time during the taxable year of the foreign corporation during which the individual held such interest; and

(D) To the extent known by the individual, a description of the chain of ownership through which the individual owns stock in the foreign corporation, including the name and address of each intermediary standing between the intermediary described in paragraph (b)(4)(i)(C) of this section and the foreign corporation.

(ii) *Ownership statements from governments.* An ownership statement from a government that is a qualifying shareholder is a written statement signed by either—

(A) An official of the governmental authority, agency or office that has supervisory authority with respect to the government's ownership interest who is authorized to sign such a statement on behalf of the authority, agency or office; or

(B) The competent authority of the foreign country (as defined in the income tax treaty between the United States and the foreign country).

Such statement shall provide the title of the official signing the statement and the name and address of the government agency, and shall provide the information described in paragraphs (b)(4)(i)(B) through (D) of this section (substituting "government" for "individual") with respect to the government's direct or indirect ownership of stock in the foreign corporation seeking qualified resident status.

(iii) *Ownership statements from publicly-traded corporations.* An ownership statement from a corporation that is a qualifying shareholder under paragraph (b)(1)(i)(C) of this section is a written statement signed by a person authorized to sign a tax return on behalf of the corporation under penalties of perjury stating—

(A) The name, permanent address, and principal place of business of the corporation (if different from its permanent address);

(B) The information described in paragraphs (b)(4)(i)(B) through (D) of this section (substituting "corporation" for "individual"); and

(C) That the corporation's stock is primarily and regularly traded on an established securities exchange (within the meaning of paragraph (d) of this section) in the United States or its country of residence.

(iv) *Ownership statements from not-for-profit organizations.* An ownership statement from a not-for-profit organization (other than a pension fund as defined in paragraph (b)(8)(i)(A) of this section) is a written statement signed by a person authorized to sign a tax return on behalf of the organization under penalties of perjury stating—

(A) The name, permanent address, and principal location of the activities of the organization (if different from its permanent address);

(B) The information described in paragraphs (b)(4)(i)(B) through (D) of this section (substituting "not-for-profit organization" for "individual") with respect to the not-for-profit organization's direct or indirect ownership of stock in the foreign corporation seeking qualified resident status; and

(C) That the not-for-profit organization satisfies the requirements of paragraph (b)(1)(iv) of this section.

(v) *Ownership through a nominee.* For purposes of this paragraph (b)(4) and paragraph (b)(6) of this section, a person who owns either stock in a foreign corporation seeking qualified resident status or an interest in an intermediary described in paragraph (b)(4)(i)(C) of this section through a nominee shall be treated as owning such stock or interest directly and must, therefore, provide the information described in paragraphs (b)(4)(i) through (iv) of this section, as applicable. Such person must also provide the name and address of the nominee.

(5) *Certificate of residency.* A certificate of residency must be signed by the relevant authorities (as described below) of the country of residence of the individual shareholder and must state that the individual is a resident of that country for purposes of its income tax laws or, if the authorities do not customarily make such a determination, that the individual has filed a tax return claiming resident status and subjecting the individual's income to tax on a resident basis for the taxable year or period that ends with or within the taxable year for which the corporation

Reg. § 1.884-5(b)(5)

is seeking qualified resident status. In the case of an individual who is not legally required to file a tax return in his or her country of residence or in any other country, a certificate of residency of a parent or guardian residing at such individual's address shall be considered sufficient to meet that individual's obligation under this paragraph (b)(5). The relevant authorities shall be the competent authority of the foreign country of which the foreign corporation is a resident, as defined in the income tax treaty between the foreign country and the United States, or such other governmental office of the foreign country (or political subdivision thereof) that customarily provides statements of residence. Notwithstanding the foregoing, the Commissioner may consult with the competent authority of a country regarding the procedures set forth in this paragraph (b)(5) and if necessary agree on additional or alternative procedures under which these certificates may be issued.

(6) *Intermediary ownership statement.* An intermediary ownership statement is a written statement signed under penalties of perjury by the intermediary (if the intermediary is an individual) or a person that would be authorized to sign a tax return on behalf of the intermediary (if the intermediary is not an individual) containing the following information:

(i) The name, address, country of residence, and principal place of business (in the case of a corporation or partnership) of the intermediary and, if the intermediary is a trust or estate, the name and permanent address of all trustees or executors (or equivalent under foreign law);

(ii) The information described in paragraphs (b)(4)(i)(B) through (D) (substituting "intermediary making the ownership statement" for "individual") with respect to the intermediary's direct or indirect ownership in the stock in the foreign corporation seeking qualified resident status;

(iii) If the intermediary is a nominee for a qualifying shareholder or another intermediary, the name and permanent address of the qualifying shareholder, or the name and principal place of business of such other intermediary;

(iv) If the intermediary is not a nominee for a qualifying shareholder or another intermediary, the proportionate interest in the intermediary of each direct shareholder, partner, beneficiary, grantor, or other interest holder (or if the direct holder is a nominee, of its beneficial shareholder, partner, beneficiary, grantor, or other interest holder) from which the intermediary received an ownership statement and the period of time during the taxable year for which the interest in the intermediary was owned by such shareholder, partner, beneficiary, grantor or other interest holder. For purposes of this paragraph (b)(6)(iv), the proportionate interest of a person in an intermediary is the percentage interest (by value) held by such person, determined using the principles for attributing ownership in paragraph (b)(2) of this section. If an intermediary is not required to receive an ownership statement from its individual registered shareholders or other interest holders by reason of paragraph (b)(3)(iii) of this section, then it must provide a list of the names and addresses of such registered shareholders or other interest holders and the aggregate proportionate interest in the intermediary of such registered shareholders or other interest holders.

(7) *Intermediary verification statement.* An intermediary verification statement that may be substituted for certain documentation under paragraph (b)(3)(ii) of this section is a written statement signed under penalties of perjury by the intermediary (if the intermediary is an individual) or by a person that would be authorized to sign a tax return on behalf of the intermediary (if the verifying intermediary is not an individual) containing the following information—

(i) The name, principal place of business, and country of residence of the verifying intermediary;

(ii) A statement that the verifying intermediary has obtained either—

(A) An ownership statement and, if applicable, a certificate of residency from a qualifying shareholder with respect to the foreign corporation seeking qualified resident status, and an intermediary ownership statement from each intermediary standing in the chain of ownership between the verifying intermediary and the qualifying shareholder; or

(B) An intermediary verification statement substituting for the documentation described in paragraph (b)(7)(ii)(A) and an intermediary ownership statement from such intermediary and each intermediary standing in the chain of ownership between such intermediary and the verifying intermediary;

(iii) The proportionate interest (as computed using the documentation described in paragraph (b)(7)(ii) of this section) in the intermediary owned directly or indirectly by qualifying shareholders;

(iv) An agreement to make available to the Commissioner at such time and place as the Commissioner may request the underlying documentation described in paragraph (b)(7)(ii) of this section; and

Reg. § 1.884-5(b)(6)

(v) A specific and valid waiver of any right to bank secrecy or other secrecy under the laws of the country in which the verifying intermediary is located, with respect to any qualifying shareholder ownership statements, certificates of residency, intermediary ownership statements or intermediary verification statements that the verifying intermediary has obtained pursuant to paragraph (b)(7)(ii) of this section.

A foreign corporation may combine, in a single statement, the information in an intermediary ownership statement and the information in an intermediary verification statement.

(8) *Special rules for pension funds*—(i) *Definitions*—(A) *Pension fund.* For purposes of this section, the term "pension fund" shall mean a trust, fund, foundation, or other entity that is established exclusively for the benefit of employees or former employees of one or more employers, the principal purpose of which is to provide retirement, disability, and death benefits to beneficiaries of such entity and persons designated by such beneficiaries in consideration for prior services rendered.

(B) *Beneficiary.* For purposes of this section, the term "beneficiary" of a pension fund shall mean any person who has made contributions to the pension fund, or on whose behalf contributions have been made, and who is currently receiving retirement, disability, or death benefits from the pension fund or can reasonably be expected to receive such benefits in the future, whether or not the person's right to receive benefits from the fund has vested.

(ii) *Government pension funds.* An individual who is a beneficiary of a pension fund that would be a controlled entity of a foreign sovereign within the principles of § 1.892-2T(c)(1) of the regulations (relating to pension funds established for the benefit of employees or former employees of a foreign government) shall be treated as a qualifying shareholder of a foreign corporation in which the pension fund owns a direct or indirect interest without having to meet the documentation requirements under paragraph (b)(3)(i)(A) of this section, if the foreign corporation is resident in the country of the foreign sovereign and the trustees, directors, or other administrators of the pension fund provide, with the pension fund's intermediary ownership statement described in paragraph (b)(6) of this section, a written statement that the fund is a controlled entity described in this paragraph (b)(8)(ii). See paragraph (b)(4)(ii) of this section regarding an ownership statement from a pension fund that is an integral part of a foreign government.

(iii) *Non-government pension funds.* For purposes of this section, an individual who is a beneficiary of a pension fund not described in paragraph (b)(8)(ii) of this section shall be treated as a qualifying shareholder of a foreign corporation owned directly or indirectly by such pension fund without having to meet the documentation requirements under paragraph (b)(3)(i)(A) of this section, if—

(A) The pension fund is administered in the foreign corporation's country of residence and is subject to supervision or regulation by a governmental authority (or other authority delegated to perform such supervision or regulation by a governmental authority) in such country;

(B) The pension fund is generally exempt from income taxation in its country of administration;

(C) The pension fund has 100 or more beneficiaries;

(D) The beneficiary's address, as it appears on the records of the fund, is in the foreign corporation's country of residence or the United States and is not a nonresidential address, such as a post office box or in care of a financial intermediary, and none of the trustees, directors or other administrators of the pension fund know, or have reason to know, that the beneficiary is not an individual resident of such foreign country or the United States;

(E) In the case of a pension fund that has fewer than 500 beneficiaries, the beneficiary's employer provides (if the beneficiary is currently contributing to the fund) to the trustees, directors or other administrators a written statement that the beneficiary is currently employed in the country in which the fund is administered or is usually employed in such country but is temporarily employed by the company outside of the country; and

(F) The trustees, directors or other administrators of the pension fund provide, with the pension fund's intermediary ownership statement described in paragraph (b)(6) of this section, a written statement signed under penalties of perjury declaring that the pension fund meets the requirements in paragraphs (b)(8)(iii)(A), (B) and (C) of this section and giving the number of beneficiaries who meet the requirements of paragraph (b)(8)(iii) (D) of this section, and, if applicable, paragraph (b)(8)(iii)(E) of this section.

(iv) *Computation of beneficial interests in nongovernment pension funds.* The number of shares in a foreign corporation that are held indirectly by beneficiaries of a pension fund who are qualifying shareholders may be computed based on the ratio of the number of such beneficiaries to

Reg. § 1.884-5(b)(8)

all beneficiaries of the pension fund (rather than on the basis of the rules in paragraph (b)(2) of this section) if—

(A) The pension fund meets the requirements of paragraphs (b)(8)(iii) (A), (B) and (C) of this section;

(B) The trustees, directors or other administrators of the pension fund have no knowledge, and no reason to know, that the ratio of the pension fund's beneficiaries who are residents of either the country in which the pension fund is administered or of the United States to all beneficiaries of the pension fund would differ significantly from the ratio of the sum of the actuarial interests of such residents in the pension fund to the actuarial interests of all beneficiaries in the pension fund (or, if the beneficiaries' actuarial interest in the stock held directly or indirectly by the pension fund differs from the beneficiaries's actuarial interest in the pension fund, the ratio of actuarial interests computed by reference to the beneficiaries' actuarial interest in the stock);

(C) Either—

(*1*) Any overfunding of the pension fund would be payable, pursuant to the governing instrument or the laws of the foreign country in which the pension fund is administered, only to, or for the benefit of, one or more corporations that are qualified residents of the country in which the pension fund is administered, individual beneficiaries of the pension fund or their designated beneficiaries, or social or charitable causes (the reduction of the obligation of the sponsoring company or companies to make future contributions to the pension fund by reason of overfunding shall not itself result in such overfunding being deemed to be payable to or for the benefit of such company or companies); or

(*2*) The foreign country in which the pension fund is administered has laws that are designed to prevent overfunding of a pension fund and the funding of the pension fund is within the guidelines of such laws; or

(*3*) The pension fund is maintained to provide benefits to employees in a particular industry, profession, or group of industries or professions and employees of at least 10 companies (other than companies that are owned or controlled, directly or indirectly, by the same interests) contribute to the pension fund or receive benefits from the pension fund; and

(D) The trustees, directors or other administrators provide, with the pension fund's intermediary ownership statement described in paragraph (b)(6) of this section, a written statement signed under penalties of perjury certifying that the requirements in paragraphs (b)(8)(iv)(A), (B), and either (C)(*1*), (C)(*2*) or (C)(*3*) of this section have been met.

The statement described in paragraph (b)(8)(iv)(D) of this section may be combined, in a single statement, with the information required in paragraph (b)(8)(iii)(F) of this section.

(v) *Time for making determinations.* The determinations required to be made under this paragraph (b)(8) shall be made using information shown on the records of the pension fund for a date on or after the beginning of the foreign corporation's taxable year to which the determination is relevant.

(9) *Availability of documents for inspection*—(i) *Retention of documents by the foreign corporation.* The documentation described in paragraphs (b)(3) and (b)(8) of this section must be retained by the foreign corporation until expiration of the period of limitations for the taxable year to which the documentation relates and must be made available for inspection by the District Director at such time and place as the District Director may request.

(ii) *Retention of documents by an intermediary issuing an intermediary verification statement.* The documentation upon which an intermediary relies to issue an intermediary verification statement under paragraph (b)(7) of this section must be retained by the intermediary for a period of six years from the date of issuance of the intermediary verification statement and must be made available for inspection by the District Director at such time and place as the District Director may request.

(10) *Examples.* The application of this paragraph (b) is illustrated by the following examples.

Example 1. Foreign corporation A is a resident of country L, which has an income tax treaty in effect with the United States. Foreign corporation A has one class of stock issued and outstanding consisting of 1,000 shares, which are beneficially owned by the following alien individuals, directly or by application of paragraph (b)(2) of this section:

Individual	Shares owned, directly or indirectly by application of paragraph (b) (2) of this section	Percentage
T —resident of the U.S.	200	20%
U —resident of country L	400	40%
V —resident of country M	100	10%

Reg. § 1.884-5(b)(9)

W—resident of country L	210	21%
X—resident of country N	90	9%
Total	1,000	100%

(i) T owns his 200 shares directly and is a beneficial owner.

(ii) U and V own, respectively, an 80 percent and a 20 percent actuarial interest in foreign trust FT, (which interest does not differ from their respective interests in the stock owned by FT), which beneficially owns 100 percent of the stock of a foreign corporation B with bearer shares, which beneficially owns 500 shares of foreign corporation A. Foreign corporation B is incorporated in a country that does not have an income tax treaty with the United States. The foreign trust has deposited the bearer shares it owns in B with a bank in a foreign country that has an income tax treaty with the United States.

(iii) W beneficially owns all the shares of foreign corporation C, which are registered in the name of individual Z, a nominee, who resides in country L; foreign corporation C beneficially owns a 70 percent interest in foreign corporation D, which beneficially owns 300 shares of A. D's shares are bearer shares that C (not a resident of a country with which the United States has an income tax treaty) has deposited with a bank in a foreign country that has an income tax treaty with the United States.

(iv) X beneficially owns a 30 percent interest in foreign corporation D.

(v) A is a qualified resident of country L if it obtains the applicable documentation described in paragraph (b)(3) of this section either with respect to ownership by individuals U and W or with respect to ownership by individuals T and U, since either combination of qualifying shareholders of foreign corporation A will exceed 50 percent.

Example 2. Assume the same facts as in *Example 1* and assume that foreign corporation A chooses to obtain documentation with respect to individuals T and U.

(i) A must obtain, pursuant to paragraph (b)(3)(i) of this section, an ownership statement (as described in paragraph (b)(4)(i) of this section) signed by T. T is not required to furnish a certificate of residency because T is a U.S. resident.

(ii) U must provide foreign trust FT with an ownership statement and certificate of residency, as described in paragraphs (b)(4) and (b)(5) of this section. The trustees of FT must provide the depository bank holding foreign corporation B's bearer shares with an intermediary ownership statement concerning its beneficial ownership of B's shares and must attach to it the documentation provided by U. The depository bank must provide B with an intermediary ownership statement regarding its holding of B shares on behalf of FT and has the choice of attaching—

(A) The documentation from U and the intermediary ownership statement from FT; or

(B) An intermediary verification statement described in paragraph (b)(7) of this section, in which case foreign corporation B would not be provided with U's individual documentation or FT's intermediary ownership statement, both of which are retained by the depository bank.

(iii) In either case, B must then provide foreign corporation A with an intermediary ownership statement regarding its direct beneficial ownership of shares in A and, as the case may be, either—

(A) U's documentation and the intermediary ownership statements by FT and the depository bank; or

(B) The depository bank's intermediary ownership and verification statements.

(iv) Thus, with respect to U, A must obtain under paragraph (b)(3)(i) of this section the individual documentation regarding U and an intermediary ownership statement from each intermediary standing in the chain of U's indirect beneficial ownership of shares in A, *i.e.,* from FT, the depository bank and B. In the alternative, A must obtain under paragraph (b)(3)(ii) of this section an intermediary verification statement issued by the depository bank and an intermediary ownership statement from the bank and from B, which, in this example, are the only intermediaries standing in the chain of ownership of the verifying intermediary (*i.e.,* the depository bank).

Example 3. Assume the same facts as in *Example 1.* In addition, assume that foreign corporation A chooses to obtain documentation with respect to individuals U and W. With respect to U, A must obtain the same documentation that is described in *Example 2.* With respect to W, A must obtain, under paragraph (b)(3)(i) of this section, individual documentation regarding W and an intermediary ownership statement from each intermediary standing in the chain of W's indirect beneficial ownership of shares in A, *i.e.,* from individual Z, foreign corporation C, the depository bank in the foreign treaty country, and foreign corporation D. In the alternative, A must obtain, under paragraph (b)(3)(ii) of this section, either—

Reg. § 1.884-5(b)(10)

(i) An intermediary verification statement by the depository bank in the foreign treaty country and an intermediary ownership statement from the bank and from D; or

(ii) An intermediary verification statement from Z and an intermediary ownership statement from Z and from each intermediary standing in the chain of ownership of shares in foreign corporation A, *i.e.*, from C, the depository bank in the foreign treaty country and D. C may not issue an intermediary verification statement because it is not a resident of a country with which the United States has an income tax treaty.

(c) *Base erosion.* A foreign corporation satisfies the requirement relating to base erosion for a taxable year if it establishes that less than 50 percent of its income for the taxable year is used (directly or indirectly) to make deductible payments in the current taxable year to persons who are not residents (or, in the case of foreign corporations, qualified residents) of the foreign country of which the foreign corporation is a resident and who are not citizens or residents (or, in the case of domestic corporations, qualified residents) of the United States. Whether a domestic corporation is a qualified resident of the United States shall be determined under the principles of this section. For purposes of this paragraph (c), the term "deductible payments" includes payments that would be ordinarily deductible under U.S. income tax principles without regard to other provisions of the Code that may require the capitalization of the expense, or disallow or defer the deduction. Such payments include, for example, interest, rents, royalties and reinsurance premiums. For purposes of this paragraph (c), the income of a foreign corporation means the corporation's gross income for the taxable year (or, if the foreign corporation has no gross income for the taxable year, the average of its gross income for the three previous taxable years) under U.S. tax principles, but not excluding items of income otherwise excluded from gross income under U.S. tax principles.

(d) *Publicly-traded corporations*—(1) *General rule.* A foreign corporation that is a resident of a foreign country shall be treated as a qualified resident of that country for any taxable year in which—

(i) Its stock is primarily and regularly traded (as defined in paragraphs (d)(3) and (4) of this section) on one or more established securities markets (as defined in paragraph (d)(2) of this section) in that country, or in the United States, or both; or

(ii) At least 90 percent of the total combined voting power of all classes of stock of such foreign corporation entitled to vote and at least 90 percent of the total value of the stock of such foreign corporation is owned, directly or by application of paragraph (b)(2) of this section, by a foreign corporation that is a resident of the same foreign country or a domestic corporation and the stock of such parent corporation is primarily and regularly traded on an established securities market in that foreign country or in the United States, or both.

(2) *Established securities market*—(i) *General rule.* For purposes of section 884, the term "established securities market" means, for any taxable year—

(A) A foreign securities exchange that is officially recognized, sanctioned, or supervised by a governmental authority of the country in which the market is located, is the principal exchange in that country, and has an annual value of shares traded on the exchange exceeding $1 billion during each of the three calendar years immediately preceding the beginning of the taxable year;

(B) A national securities exchange that is registered under section 6 of the Securities Act of 1934 (15 U.S.C. 78f); and

(C) A domestic over-the-counter market (as defined in paragraph (d)(2)(iv) of this section).

(ii) *Exchanges with multiple tiers.* If a principal exchange in a foreign country has more than one tier or market level on which stock may be separately listed or traded, each such tier shall be treated as a separate exchange.

(iii) *Computation of dollar value of stock traded.* For purposes of paragraph (d)(2)(i)(A) of this section, the value in U.S. dollars of shares traded during a calendar year shall be determined on the basis of the dollar value of such shares traded as reported by the International Federation of Stock Exchanges, located in Paris, or, if not so reported, then by converting into U.S. dollars the aggregate value in local currency of the shares traded using an exchange rate equal to the average of the spot rates on the last day of each month of the calendar year.

(iv) *Definition of over-the-counter market.* An over-the-counter market is any market reflected by the existence of an interdealer quotation system. An interdealer quotation system is any system of general circulation to brokers and dealers that regularly disseminates quotations of stocks and securities by identified brokers or dealers, other than by quotation sheets that are prepared and distributed by a broker or dealer in the regular course of business and that contain only quotations of such broker or dealer.

Reg. § 1.884-5(c)

(v) *Discretion to determine that an exchange qualifies as an established securities market.* The Commissioner may, in his sole discretion, determine in a published document that a securities exchange that does not meet the requirements of paragraph (d)(2)(i)(A) of this section qualifies as an established securities market. Such a determination will be made only if it is established that—

(A) The exchange, in substance, has the attributes of an established securities market (including adequate trading volume, and comparable listing and financial disclosure requirements);

(B) The rules of the exchange ensure active trading of listed stocks; and

(C) The exchange is a member of the International Federation of Stock Exchanges.

(vi) *Discretion to determine that an exchange does not qualify as an established securities market.* The Commissioner may, in his sole discretion, determine in a published document that a securities exchange that meets the requirements of paragraph (d)(2)(i) of this section does not qualify as an established securities market. Such determination shall be made if, in the view of the Commissioner—

(A) The exchange does not have adequate listing, financial disclosure, or trading requirements (or does not adequately enforce such requirements); or

(B) There is not clear and convincing evidence that the exchange ensures the active trading of listed stocks.

(3) *Primarily traded.* For purposes of this section, stock of a corporation is "primarily traded" on one or more established securities markets in the corporation's country of residence or in the United States in any taxable year if, with respect to each class described in paragraph (d)(4)(i)(A) of this section (relating to classes of stock relied on to meet the regularly traded test)—

(i) The number of shares in each such class that are traded during the taxable year on all established securities markets in the corporation's country of residence or in the United States during the taxable year exceeds

(ii) The number of shares in each such class that are traded during that year on established securities markets in any other single foreign country.

(4) *Regularly traded*—(i) *General rule.* For purposes of this section, stock of a corporation is "regularly traded" on one or more established securities markets in the foreign corporation's country of residence or in the United States for the taxable year if—

(A) One or more classes of stock of the corporation that, in the aggregate, represent 80 percent or more of the total combined voting power of all classes of stock of such corporation entitled to vote and of the total value of the stock of such corporation are listed on such market or markets during the taxable year;

(B) With respect to each class relied on to meet the 80 percent requirement of paragraph (d)(4)(i)(A) of this section—

(*1*) Trades in each such class are effected, other than in *de minimis* quantities, on such market or markets on at least 60 days during the taxable year (or 1/6 of the number of days in a short taxable year); and

(*2*) The aggregate number of shares in each such class that is traded on such market or markets during the taxable year is at least 10 percent of the average number of shares outstanding in that class during the taxable year (or, in the case of a short taxable year, a percentage that equals at least 10 percent of the number of days in the short taxable year divided by 365).

If stock of a foreign corporation fails the 80 percent requirement of paragraph (d)(4)(i)(A) of this section, but a class of such stock meets the trading requirements of paragraph (d)(4)(i)(B) of this section, such class of stock may be taken into account under paragraph (b)(1)(iii) of this section as owned by qualifying shareholders for purposes of meeting the ownership test of paragraph (b)(1) of this section.

(ii) *Classes of stock traded on a domestic established securities market treated as meeting trading requirements.* A class of stock that is traded during the taxable year on an established securities market located in the United States shall be treated as meeting the trading requirements of paragraph (d)(4)(i)(B) of this section if the stock is regularly quoted by brokers or dealers making a market in the stock. A broker or dealer makes a market in a stock only if the broker or dealer holds himself out to buy or sell the stock at the quoted price.

(iii) *Closely-held classes of stock not treated as meeting trading requirement*—(A) *General rule.* A class of stock shall not be treated as meeting the trading requirements of paragraph (d)(4)(i)(B) of this section (or the requirements of paragraph (d)(4)(ii) of this section) for a taxable year if, at any time during the taxable year, one or more persons who are not qualifying shareholders (as defined in paragraph (b)(1) of this section) and who each beneficially own 5 percent or more of the value of the outstanding shares of the class

Reg. § 1.884-5(d)(4)

of stock own, in the aggregate, 50 percent or more of the outstanding shares of the class of stock for more than 30 days during the taxable year. For purposes of the preceding sentence, shares shall not be treated as owned by a qualifying shareholder unless such shareholder provides to the foreign corporation, by the time prescribed in paragraph (b)(3) of this section, the documentation described in paragraph (b)(3) of this section necessary to establish that it is a qualifying shareholder. For purposes of this paragraph (d)(4)(iii)(A), shares of stock owned by a pension fund, as defined in paragraph (b)(8)(i)(A) of this section, shall be treated as beneficially owned by the beneficiaries of such fund, as defined in paragraph (b)(8)(i)(B) of this section.

(B) *Treatment of related persons.* Persons related within the meaning of section 267(b) shall be treated as one person for purposes of this paragraph (d)(4)(iii). In determining whether two or more corporations are members of the same controlled group under section 267(b)(3), a person is considered to own stock owned directly by such person, stock owned with the application of section 1563(e)(1), and stock owned with the application of section 267(c). Further, in determining whether a corporation is related to a partnership under section 267(b)(10), a person is considered to own the partnership interest owned directly by such person and the partnership interest owned with the application of section 267(e)(3).

(iv) *Anti-abuse rule.* Trades between persons described in section 267(b)(as modified in paragraph (d)(4)(iii)(B) of this section) and trades conducted in order to meet the requirements of paragraph (d)(4)(i)(B) of this section shall be disregarded. A class of stock shall not be treated as meeting the trading requirements of paragraph (d)(4)(i)(B) of this section if there is a pattern of trades conducted to meet the requirements of that paragraph. For example, trades between two persons that occur several times during the taxable year may be treated as an arrangement or a pattern of trades conducted to meet the trading requirements of paragraph (d)(4)(i)(B) of this section.

(5) *Burden of proof for publicly-traded corporations.* A foreign corporation that relies on this paragraph (d) to establish that it is a qualified resident of a country with which the United States has an income tax treaty shall have the burden of proving all the facts necessary for the corporation to be treated as a qualified resident, except that with respect to paragraphs (d)(4)(iii) and (iv) of this section, a foreign corporation, with either registered or bearer shares, will meet the burden of proof if it has no reason to know and no actual knowledge of facts that would cause the corporation's stock not to be treated as regularly traded under such paragraphs. A foreign corporation that has shareholders of record must also maintain a list of such shareholders and, on request, make available to the District Director such list and any other relevant information known to the foreign corporation.

(e) *Active trade or business*—(1) *General rule.* A foreign corporation that is a resident of a foreign country shall be treated as a qualified resident of that country with respect to any U.S. trade or business if, during the taxable year—

(i) It is engaged in the active conduct of a trade or business (as defined in paragraph (e)(2) of this section) in its country of residence;

(ii) It has a substantial presence (within the meaning of paragraph (e)(3) of this section) in its country of residence; and

(iii) Either—

(A) Such U.S. trade or business is an integral part (as defined in paragraph (e)(4) of this section) of an active trade or business conducted by the foreign corporation in its country of residence; or

(B) In the case of interest received by the foreign corporation for which a treaty exemption or rate reduction is claimed pursuant to § 1.884-4(b)(8)(ii), the interest is derived in connection with, or is incidental to, a trade or business described in paragraph (e)(1)(i) of this section.

A foreign corporation may determine whether it is a qualified resident under this paragraph (e) by applying the rules of this paragraph (e) to the entire affiliated group (as defined in section 1504(a) without regard to section 1504(b)(2) or (3)) of which the foreign corporation is a member rather than to the foreign corporation separately. If a foreign corporation chooses to apply the rules of this paragraph (e) to its entire affiliated group as provided in the preceding sentence, then it must apply such rules consistently to all of its U.S. trades or businesses conducted during the taxable year.

(2) *Active conduct of a trade or business.* A foreign corporation is engaged in the active conduct of a trade or business only if either—

(i) It is engaged in the active conduct of a trade or business within the meaning of section 367(a)(3) and the regulations thereunder; or

(ii) It qualifies as a banking or financing institution under the laws of the foreign country of which it is a resident, it is licensed to do business with residents of its country of residence, and it is engaged in the active conduct of a

Reg. § 1.884-5(d)(5)

banking, financing, or similar business within the meaning of § 1.864-4(c)(5)(i) in its country of residence.

A foreign corporation that is an insurance company within the meaning of § 1.801-3(a) or (b) is engaged in the active conduct of a trade or business only if it is predominantly engaged in the active conduct of an insurance business within the meaning of section 952(c)(1)(B)(v) and the regulations thereunder.

(3) *Substantial presence test*—(i) *General rule.* Except as provided in paragraph (e)(3)(ii) of this section, a foreign corporation that is engaged in the active conduct of a trade or business in its country of residence has a substantial presence in that country if, for the taxable year, the average of the following three ratios exceeds 25 percent and each ratio is at least equal to 20 percent—

(A) The ratio of the value of the assets of the foreign corporation used or held for use in the active conduct of a trade or business in its country of residence at the close of the taxable year to the value of all assets of the foreign corporation at the close of the taxable year;

(B) The ratio of gross income from the active conduct of the foreign corporation's trade or business in its country of residence that is derived from sources within such country for the taxable year to the worldwide gross income of the foreign corporation for the taxable year; and

(C) The ratio of the payroll expenses in the foreign corporation's country of residence for the taxable year to the foreign corporation's worldwide payroll expenses for the taxable year.

(ii) *Special rules*—(A) *Asset ratio.* For purposes of paragraph (e)(3)(i)(A) of this section, the value of an asset shall be determined using the method used by the taxpayer in keeping its books for purposes of financial reporting in its country of residence. An asset shall be treated as used or held for use in a foreign corporation's trade or business if it meets the requirements of § 1.367(a)-2T(b)(5). Stock held by a foreign corporation shall not be treated as an asset of the foreign corporation for purposes of paragraph (e)(3)(i)(A) of this section if the foreign corporation owns 10 percent or more of the total combined voting power of all classes of stock of such corporation entitled to vote. The rules of § 1.954-2T(b)(3) (other than § 1.954-2T(b)(3)(x)) shall apply to determine the location of assets used or held for use in a trade or business. Loans originated or acquired in the course of the normal customer loan activities of a banking, financing or similar institution, and securities and derivative financial instruments held by dealers, traders and insurance companies for use in a trade or business shall be treated as located in the country in which an office or other fixed place of business is primarily responsible for the acquisition of the asset and the realization of income, gain or loss with respect to the asset.

(B) *Gross income ratio*—(*1*) *General rule.* For purposes of paragraph (e)(3)(i)(B) of this section, the term "gross income" means the gross income of a foreign corporation for purposes of financial reporting in its country of residence. Gross income shall not include, however, dividends, interest, rents, or royalties unless such corporation derives such dividends, interest, rents, or royalties in the active conduct of its trade or business. Gross income shall also not include gain from the disposition of stock if the foreign corporation owns 10 percent or more of the total combined voting power of all classes of stock of such corporation entitled to vote. Except as provided in this paragraph (e)(3)(ii)(B), the principles of sections 861 through 865 shall apply to determine the amount of gross income of a foreign corporation derived within its country of residence.

(*2*) *Banks, dealers and traders.* Dividend income and gain from the sale of securities, or from entering into or disposing of derivative financial instruments by dealers and traders in such securities or derivative financial instruments shall be treated as derived within the country where the assets are located under paragraph (e)(3)(ii)(A) of this section. Other income, including interest and fees, earned in the active conduct of a banking, financing or similar business shall be treated as derived within the country where the payor of such interest or other income resides. For purposes of the preceding sentence, if a branch or similar establishment outside the country in which the payor resides makes a payment of interest or other income, such amounts shall be treated as derived within the country in which the branch or similar establishment is located.

(*3*) *Insurance companies.* The gross income of a foreign insurance company shall include only gross premiums received by the company.

(*4*) *Other corporations.* Gross income from the performance of services, including transportation services, shall be treated as derived within the country of residence of the person for whom the services are performed. Gross income from the sale of property by a foreign corporation shall be treated as derived within the country in which the purchaser resides.

(*5*) *Anti-abuse rule.* The Commissioner may disregard the source of income from a transaction determined under this paragraph (e)(3)(ii)(B) if it is determined that one of the

Reg. § 1.884-5(e)(3)

principal purposes of the transaction was to increase the source of income derived within the country of residence of the foreign corporation for purposes of this section.

(C) *Payroll ratio.* For purposes of paragraph (e)(3)(i)(C) of this section, the payroll expenses of a foreign corporation shall include expenses for "leased employees" (within the meaning of section 414(n)(2) but without regard to subdivision (B) of that section) and commission expenses paid to employees and agents for services performed for or on behalf of the corporation. Payroll expense for an employee, agent or a "leased employee" shall be treated as incurred where the employee, agent or "leased employee" performs services on behalf of the corporation.

(iii) *Exception to gross income test for foreign corporations engaged in certain trades or businesses.* In determining whether a foreign corporation engaged primarily in selling tangible property or in manufacturing, producing, growing, or extracting tangible property has a substantial presence in its country of residence for purposes of paragraph (e)(3)(i) of this section, the foreign corporation may apply the ratio provided in this paragraph (e)(3)(iii) instead of the ratio described in paragraph (e)(3)(i)(B) of this section (relating to the ratio of gross income derived from its country of residence). This ratio shall be the ratio of the direct material costs of the foreign corporation with respect to tangible property manufactured, produced, grown, or extracted in the foreign corporation's country of residence to the total direct material costs of the foreign corporation.

(4) *Integral part of an active trade or business in a foreign corporation's country of residence*—(i) *In general.* A U.S. trade or business of a foreign corporation is an integral part of an active trade or business conducted by a foreign corporation in its country of residence if the active trade or business conducted by the foreign corporation in both its country of residence and in the United States comprise, in principal part, complementary and mutually interdependent steps in the United States and its country of residence in the production and sale or lease of goods or in the provision of services. Subject to the presumption and de minimis rule in paragraphs (e)(4)(iii) and (iv) of this section, if a U.S. trade or business of a foreign corporation sells goods that are not, in principal part, manufactured, produced, grown, or extracted by the foreign corporation in its country of residence, such business shall not be treated as an integral part of an active trade or business conducted in the foreign corporation's country of residence unless the foreign corporation takes physical possession of the goods in a warehouse or other storage facility that is located in its country of residence and in which goods of such type are normally stored prior to sale to customers in such country.

(ii) *Presumption for banks.* A U.S. trade or business of a foreign corporation that is described in § 1.884-4(a)(2)(iii) shall be presumed to be an integral part of an active banking business conducted by the foreign corporation in its country of residence provided that a substantial part of the business of the foreign corporation in both its country of residence and the United States consists of receiving deposits and making loans and discounts. This paragraph shall be effective for taxable years beginning on or after June 6, 1996.

(iii) *Presumption if business principally conducted in country of residence.* A U.S. trade or business of a foreign corporation shall be treated as an integral part of an active trade or business of a foreign corporation in its country of residence with respect to the sale or lease of property (or the performance of services) if at least 50 percent of the foreign corporation's worldwide gross income from the sale or lease of property of the type sold in the United States (or from the performance of services of the type performed in the United States) is derived from the sale or lease of such property for consumption, use, or disposition in the foreign corporation's country of residence (or from the performance of such services in the foreign corporation's country of residence). In determining whether property or services are of the same type, a foreign corporation shall follow recognized industry or trade usage or the three-digit major groups (or any narrower classification) of the Standard Industrial Classification as prepared by the Statistical Policy Division of the Office of Management and Budget, Executive Office of the President. The determination of whether income is of the same kind must be made in a consistent manner from year to year.

(iv) *De minimis rule.* If a foreign corporation is engaged in more than one U.S. trade or business and if at least 80 percent of the sum of the ECEP from the current year and the preceding two years is attributable to one or more trades or businesses that meet the integral part test of this paragraph (e)(4), all of the U.S. trades or businesses of the foreign corporation shall be treated as an integral part of an active trade or business conducted by the foreign corporation. If a foreign corporation has more than one U.S. trade or business and does not meet the requirements of the preceding sentence but otherwise meets the requirements of this paragraph (e)(4) with regard to one or more trade or business, see

Reg. § 1.884-5(e)(4)

§ 1.884-1(g)(1) to determine the extent to which treaty benefits apply to such corporation.

(f) *Qualified resident ruling*—(1) *Basis for ruling.* In his or her sole discretion, the Commissioner may rule that a foreign corporation is a qualified resident of its country of residence if the Commissioner determines that individuals who are not residents of the foreign country of which the foreign corporation is a resident do not use the treaty between that country and the United States in a manner inconsistent with the purposes of section 884. The purposes of section 884 include, but are not limited to, the prevention of treaty shopping by an individual with respect to any article of an income tax treaty between the country of residence of the foreign corporation and the United States.

(2) *Factors.* In order to make this determination, the Commissioner may take into account the following factors, including, but not limited to:

(i) The business reasons for establishing and maintaining the foreign corporation in its country of residence;

(ii) The date of incorporation of the foreign corporation in relation to the date that an income tax treaty between the United States and the foreign corporation's country of residence entered into force;

(iii) The continuity of the historical business and ownership of the foreign corporation;

(iv) The extent to which the foreign corporation meets the requirements of one or more of the tests described in paragraphs (b) through (e) of this section;

(v) The extent to which the U.S. trade or business is dependent on capital, assets, or personnel of the foreign trade or business;

(vi) The extent to which the foreign corporation receives special tax benefits in its country of residence;

(vii) Whether the foreign corporation is a member of an affiliated group (as defined in section 1504(a) without regard to section 1504(b)(2) or (3)), that has no members resident outside the country of residence of the foreign corporation; and

(viii) The extent to which the foreign corporation would be entitled to comparable treaty benefits with respect to all articles of an income tax treaty that would apply to that corporation if it had been incorporated in the country or countries of residence of the majority of its shareholders. For purposes of the preceding sentence, shareholders taken into account shall generally be limited to persons described in paragraph (b)(1)(i) of this section but for the fact that they are not residents of the foreign corporation's country of residence.

(3) *Procedural requirements.* A request for a ruling under this paragraph (f) must be submitted on or before the due date (including extensions) of the foreign corporation's income tax return for the taxable year for which the ruling is requested. A foreign corporation receiving a ruling will be treated as a qualified resident of its country of residence for the taxable year for which the ruling is requested and for the succeeding two taxable years. If there is a material change in any fact that formed the basis of the ruling, such as the ownership or the nature of the trade or business of the foreign corporation, the foreign corporation must notify the Secretary within 90 days of such change and submit a new private letter ruling request. The Commissioner will then rule whether the change affects the foreign corporation's status as a qualified resident, and such ruling will be valid for the taxable year in which the material change occurred and the two succeeding taxable years, subject to the requirement in the preceding sentence to notify the Commissioner of a material change.

(g) *Effective dates.* Except as provided in paragraph (e)(4)(ii) of this section, this section is effective for taxable years beginning on or after October 13, 1992.

(h) *Transition rule.* If a foreign corporation elects to apply this section in lieu of § 1.884-5T (as contained in the CFR edition revised as of April 1, 1992) as provided in paragraph (g) of this section, and the application of paragraph (b) of this section results in additional documentation requirements in order for the foreign corporation to be treated as a qualified resident, the foreign corporation must obtain the documentation required under that paragraph on or before March 11, 1993. [Reg. § 1.884-5.]

☐ [*T.D.* 8432, 9-10-92. *Amended by T.D.* 8657, 3-5-96.]

[Reg. § 1.892-1T]

§ 1.892-1T. **Purpose and scope of regulations (Temporary).**—(a) *In general.* These regulations provide guidance with respect to the taxation of income derived by foreign governments and international organizations from sources within the United States. Under section 892, certain specific types of income received by foreign governments are excluded from gross income and are exempt, unless derived from the conduct of a commercial activity or received from or by a controlled commercial entity. This section sets forth the effective date of the regulations. Section 1.892-2T defines a foreign government. In particular it describes the extent to which either an integral part of a foreign sovereign or an entity which is not an integral part of a foreign sovereign will be treated as a foreign government for purposes of section 892. Section 1.892-3T describes the types of income that generally qualify for exemption and certain limitations on the exemption. Section 1.892-4T provides rules concerning the characterization of activities as commercial activities. Section 1.892-5T defines a controlled commercial entity. Section 1.892-6T sets forth the extent to which income of international organizations from sources within the United States is excluded from gross income and is exempt from taxation. Section 1.892-7T sets forth the relationship of section 892 to other Internal Revenue Code sections.

(b) *Effective date.* The regulations set forth in §§ 1.892-1T through 1.892-7T apply to income received by a foreign government on or after July 1, 1986. No amount of income shall be required to be deducted and withheld, by reason of the amendment of section 892 by section 1247 of the Tax Reform Act of 1986 (Pub.L. 99-514, 100 Stat. 2085, 2583) from any payment made before October 22, 1986. [Temporary Reg. § 1.892-1T.]

☐ [T.D. 8211, 6-24-88.]

[Reg. § 1.892-2T]

§ 1.892-2T. **Foreign government defined (Temporary).**—(a) *Foreign government*—(1) *Definition.* The term "foreign government" means only the integral parts or controlled entities of a foreign sovereign.

(2) *Integral part.* An "integral part" of a foreign sovereign is any person, body of persons, organization, agency, bureau, fund, instrumentality, or other body, however designated, that constitutes a governing authority of a foreign country. The net earnings of the governing authority must be credited to its own account or to other accounts of the foreign sovereign, with no portion inuring to the benefit of any private person. An integral part does not include any individual who is a sovereign, official, or administrator acting in a private or personal capacity. Consideration of all the facts and circumstances will determine whether an individual is acting in a private or personal capacity.

(3) *Controlled entity.* The term "controlled entity" means an entity that is separate in form from a foreign sovereign or otherwise constitutes a separate juridical entity if it satisfies the following requirements:

(i) It is wholly owned and controlled by a foreign sovereign directly or indirectly through one or more controlled entities;

(ii) It is organized under the laws of the foreign sovereign by which owned;

(iii) Its net earnings are credited to its own account or to other accounts of the foreign sovereign, with no portion of its income inuring to the benefit of any private person; and

(iv) Its assets vest in the foreign sovereign upon dissolution.

A controlled entity does not include partnerships or any other entity owned and controlled by more than one foreign sovereign. Thus, a foreign financial organization organized and wholly owned and controlled by several foreign sovereigns to foster economic, financial, and technical cooperation between various foreign nations is not a controlled entity for purposes of this section.

(b) *Inurement to the benefit of private persons.* For purposes of this section, income will be presumed not to inure to the benefit of private persons if such persons (within the meaning of section 7701(a)(1)) are the intended beneficiaries of a governmental program which is carried on by the foreign sovereign and the activities of which constitute governmental functions (within the meaning of § 1.892-4T (c)(4)). Income will be considered to inure to the benefit of private persons if such income benefits:

(1) Private persons through the use of a governmental entity as a conduit for personal investment; or

(2) Private persons who divert such income from its intended use by the exertion of influence or control through means explicitly or implicitly approved of by the foreign sovereign.

(c) *Pension trusts*—(1) *In general.* A controlled entity includes a separately organized pension trust if it meets the following requirements:

(i) The trust is established exclusively for the benefit of (A) employees or former employees of a foreign government or (B) employees or former employees of a foreign government and nongovernmental employees or former employees that perform or performed governmental or social services;

(ii) The funds that comprise the trust are managed by trustees who are employees of, or persons appointed by, the foreign government;

(iii) The trust forming a part of the pension plan provides for retirement, disability, or death benefits in consideration for prior services rendered; and

(iv) Income of the trust satisfies the obligations of the foreign government to participants under the plan, rather than inuring to the benefit of a private person.

Income of a pension trust is subject to the rules of § 1.892-5T(b)(3) regarding the application of the rules for controlled commercial entities to pension trusts. Income of a superannuation or similar pension fund of an integral part or controlled entity (which is not a separate pension trust as defined in this paragraph (c)(1)) is subject to the rules that generally apply to a foreign sovereign. Such a pension fund may also benefit non-governmental employees or former employees that perform or performed governmental or social services.

(2) *Illustrations.* The following examples illustrate the application of paragraph (c)(1).

Example (1). The Ministry of Welfare (MW), an integral part of foreign sovereign FC, instituted a retirement plan for FC's employees and former employees. Retirement benefits under the plan are based on a percentage of the final year's salary paid to an individual, times the number of years of government service. Pursuant to the plan, contributions are made by MW to a pension trust managed by persons appointed by MW to the extent actuarially necessary to fund accrued pension liabilities. The pension trust in turn invests such contributions partially in United States Treasury obligations. The income of the trust is credited to the trust's account and subsequently used to satisfy the pension plan's obligations to retired employees. Under these circumstances, the income of the trust is not deemed to inure to the benefit of private persons. Accordingly, the trust is considered a controlled entity of FC.

Example (2). The facts are the same as in *Example* (1), except that the retirement plan also benefits employees performing governmental or social services for the following non-government institutions: (i) a university in a local jurisdiction; (ii) a harbor commission; and (iii) a library system. The retirement benefits under the plan are based on the total amounts credited to an individual's account over the term of his or her employment. MW makes annual contributions to each covered employee's account equal to a percentage of annual compensation. In addition, the income derived from investment of the annual contributions is credited annually to individual accounts. The annual contributions do not exceed an amount that is determined to be actuarially necessary to provide the employee with reasonable retirement benefits. Notwithstanding that retirement benefits vary depending upon the investment experience of the trust, no portion of the income of the trust is deemed to inure to the benefit of private persons. Accordingly, the trust is considered a controlled entity of FC.

Example (3). The facts are the same as in *Example* (1), except that employees are allowed to make unlimited contributions to the trust, and such contributions are credited to the employee's account as well as interest accrued on such contributions. Retirement benefits will reflect the amounts credited to the individual accounts in addition to the usual annuity computation based on the final year's salary and years of service. A pension plan established under these rules is in part acting as an investment conduit. As a result, the income of the trust is deemed to inure to the benefit of private persons. Accordingly, the trust is not considered a controlled entity of FC.

Example (4). (a) The facts are the same as in *Example* (2), except that MW establishes a pension fund rather than a separate pension trust. A pension fund is merely assets of an integral part or controlled entity allocated to a separate account and held and invested for purposes of providing retirement benefits. Under these circumstances, the income of the pension fund is not deemed to inure to the benefit of private persons. Accordingly, income earned from the United States Treasury obligations by the pension fund is considered to be received by a foreign government and is exempt from taxation under section 892.

(b) The facts are the same as in *Example* (4)(a), except that MW is a controlled entity of foreign sovereign FC. The result is the same as in *Example* (4)(a). However, should MW engage in commercial activities (whether within or outside the United States), the income from the Treasury obligations earned by the pension fund will not be exempt from taxation under section 892 since MW will be considered a controlled commercial entity within the meaning of § 1.892-5T(a).

(d) *Political subdivision and transnational entity.* The rules that apply to a foreign sovereign apply to political subdivisions of a foreign country and to transnational entities. A transnational entity is an organization created by more than one foreign sovereign that has broad powers over external and domestic affairs of all participating foreign countries stretching beyond economic subjects to those concerning legal relations and transcending state or political boundaries. [Temporary Reg. § 1.892-2T.]

☐ [*T.D.* 8211, 6-24-88.]

[Reg. § 1.892-3T]

§ 1.892-3T. Income of foreign governments (Temporary).—(a) *Types of income exempt*—(1) *In general.* Subject to the exceptions contained in §§ 1.892-4T and 1.892-5T for income derived from the conduct of a commercial activity or received from or by a controlled commercial entity, the following types of income derived by a

Reg. § 1.892-3T(a)(1)

foreign government (as defined in § 1.892-2T) are not included in gross income and are exempt:

(i) Income from investments in the United States in stocks, bonds, or other securities;

(ii) Income from investments in the United States in financial instruments held in the execution of governmental financial or monetary policy; and

(iii) Interest on deposits in banks in the United States of moneys belonging to such foreign government.

Income derived from sources other than described in this paragraph (such as income earned from a U.S. real property interest described in section 897(c)(1)(A)(i)) is not exempt from taxation under section 892. Furthermore, any gain derived from the disposition of a U.S. real property interest defined in section 897(c)(1)(A)(i) shall in no event qualify for exemption under section 892.

(2) *Income from investments.* For purposes of paragraph (a) of this section, income from investments in stocks, bonds or other securities includes gain from their disposition and income earned from engaging in section 1058 securities lending transactions. Gain on the disposition of an interest in a partnership or a trust is not exempt from taxation under section 892.

(3) *Securities.* For purposes of paragraph (a) of this section, the term "other securities" includes any note or other evidence of indebtedness. Thus, an annuity contract, a mortgage, a banker's acceptance or a loan are securities for purposes of this section. However, the term "other securities" does not include partnership interests (with the exception of publicly traded partnerships within the meaning of section 7704) or trust interests. The term also does not include commodity forward or futures contracts and commodity options unless they constitute securities for purposes of section 864(b)(2)(A).

(4) *Financial instrument.* For purposes of paragraph (a) of this section, the term "financial instrument" includes any forward, futures, options contract, swap agreement or similar instrument in a functional or nonfunctional currency (see section 985(b) for the definition of functional currency) or in precious metals when held by a foreign government or central bank of issue (as defined in § 1.895-1(b)). Nonfunctional currency or gold shall be considered a "financial instrument" also when physically held by a central bank of issue.

(5) *Execution of financial or monetary policy—* (i) *Rule.* A financial instrument shall be deemed held in the execution of governmental financial or monetary policy if the primary purpose for holding the instrument is to implement or effectuate such policy.

(ii) *Illustration.* The following example illustrates the application of this paragraph (a)(5).

Example. In order to ensure sufficient currency reserves, the monetary authority of foreign country FC issues short-term government obligations. The amount received from the obligations is invested in U.S. financial instruments. Since the primary purpose for obtaining the U.S. financial instruments is to implement FC's monetary policy, the income received from the financial instruments is exempt from taxation under section 892.

(b) *Illustrations.* The principles of paragraph (a) of this section may be illustrated by the following examples.

Example (1). X, a foreign corporation not engaged in commercial activity anywhere in the world, is a controlled entity of a foreign sovereign within the meaning of § 1.892-2T(a)(3). X is not a central bank of issue as defined in § 1.895-1(b). In 1987, X received the following items of income from investments in the United States: (i) dividends from a portfolio of publicly traded stocks in U.S. corporations in which X owns less than 50 percent of the stock; (ii) dividends from BTB Corporation, an automobile manufacturer, in which X owns 50 percent of the stock; (iii) interest from bonds issued by noncontrolled entities and from interest bearing bank deposits in noncontrolled entities; (iv) rents from a net lease on real property; (v) gains from silver futures contracts; (vi) gains from wheat futures contracts; (vii) gains from spot sales of nonfunctional foreign currency in X's possession; (viii) gains from the disposition of a publicly traded partnership interest, and (ix) gains from the disposition of the stock of Z Corporation, a United States real property holding company as defined in section 897, of which X owns 12 percent of the stock. Only income derived from sources described in paragraph (a)(1) of this section is treated as income of a foreign government eligible for exemption from taxation. Accordingly, only income received by X from items (i), (iii), (v) provided that the silver futures contracts are held in the execution of governmental financial or monetary policy, and (ix) is exempt from taxation under section 892.

Example (2). The facts are the same as in *Example (1),* except that X is also a central bank of issue within the meaning of section 895. Since physical possession of nonfunctional foreign currency when held by a central bank of issue is considered a financial instrument, the item (vii) gains from spot sales of nonfunctional foreign currency are exempt from taxation under paragraph (a)(1) of this section, if physical possession of the currency was an essential part of X's reserve policy in the execution of its governmental financial or monetary policy.

Example (3). State Concert Bureau, an integral part of a foreign sovereign within the meaning of § 1.892-2T(a)(2), entered into an agreement with a U.S. corporation engaged in the business of promoting international cultural programs. Under the agreement the State Concert Bureau agreed to send a ballet troupe on tour for 5 weeks in the United States. The Bureau received approximately $60,000 from the performances. Regardless of whether the performances themselves constitute commercial activities under § 1.892-4T, the income received by the Bureau is not exempt from taxation under section 892 since the income is from sources other than described in paragraph (a)(1) of this section. [Temporary Reg. § 1.892-3T.]

☐ [*T.D.* 8211, 6-24-88.]

[Reg. § 1.892-4T]

§ 1.892-4T. Commercial activities (Temporary).—(a) *Purpose.* The exemption generally applicable to a foreign government (as defined in § 1.892-2T) for income described in § 1.892-3T does not apply to income derived from the conduct of a commercial activity or income received by a controlled commercial entity or received (directly or indirectly) from a controlled commercial entity. This section provides rules for determining whether income is derived from the conduct of a commercial activity. These rules also apply in determining under § 1.892-5T whether an entity is a controlled commercial entity.

(b) *In general.* Except as provided in paragraph (c) of this section, all activities (whether conducted within or outside the United States) which are ordinarily conducted by the taxpayer or by other persons with a view towards the current or future production of income or gain are commercial activities. An activity may be considered a commercial activity even if such activity does not constitute the conduct of a trade or business in the United States under section 864(b).

(c) *Activities that are not commercial*—(1) *Investments*—(i) *In general.* Subject to the provisions of paragraphs (ii) and (iii) of this paragraph (c)(1), the following are not commercial activities: investments in stock, bonds, and other securities; loans; investments in financial instruments held in the execution of governmental financial or monetary policy; the holding of net leases on real property or land which is not producing income (other than on its sale or from an investment in net leases on real property); and the holding of bank deposits in banks. Transferring securities under a loan agreement which meets the requirements of section 1058 is an investment for purposes of this paragraph (c)(1)(i). An activity will not cease to be an investment solely because of the volume of transactions of that activity or because of other unrelated activities.

(ii) *Trading.* Effecting transactions in stocks, securities, or commodities for a foreign government's own account does not constitute a commercial activity regardless of whether such activities constitute a trade or business for purposes of section 162 or a U.S. trade or business for purposes of section 864. Such transactions are not commercial activities regardless of whether they are effected by the foreign government through its employees or through a broker, commission agent, custodian, or other independent agent and regardless of whether or not any such employee or agent has discretionary authority to make decisions in effecting the transactions. An activity undertaken as a dealer, however as defined in § 1.864-2(c)(2)(iv)(a) will not be an investment for purposes of this paragraph (c)(1)(i). For purposes of this paragraph (c)(1)(ii), the term "commodities" means commodities of a kind customarily dealt in on an organized commodity exchange but only if the transaction is of a kind customarily consummated at such place.

(iii) *Banking, financing, etc.* Investments (including loans) made by a banking, financing, or similar business constitute commercial activities, even if the income derived from such investments is not considered to be income effectively connected to the active conduct of a banking, financing, or similar business in the U.S. by reason of the application of § 1.864-4(c)(5).

(2) *Cultural events.* Performances and exhibitions within or outside the United States of amateur athletic events and events devoted to the promotion of the arts by cultural organizations are not commercial activities.

(3) *Non-profit activities.* Activities that are not customarily attributable to or carried on by private enterprise for profit are not commercial activities. The fact that in some instances Federal, State, or local governments of the United States also are engaged in the same or similar activity does not mean necessarily that it is a non-profit activity. For example, even though the United States Government may be engaged in the activity of operating a railroad, operating a railroad is not a non-profit activity.

(4) *Governmental functions.* Governmental functions are not commercial activities. The term "governmental functions" shall be determined under U.S. standards. In general, activities performed for the general public with respect to the

common welfare or which relate to the administration of some phase of government will be considered governmental functions. For example, the operation of libraries, toll bridges, or local transportation services and activities substantially equivalent to the Federal Aviation Authority, Interstate Commerce Commission, or United States Postal Service will all be considered governmental functions for purposes of this section.

(5) *Purchasing.* The mere purchasing of goods for the use of a foreign government is not a commercial activity. [Temporary Reg. § 1.892-4T.]

☐ [T.D. 8211, 6-24-88.]

[Reg. § 1.892-5T]

§ 1.892-5T. **Controlled commercial entity (Temporary).**—(a) *In general.* The exemption generally applicable to a foreign government (as defined in § 1.892-2T) for income described in § 1.892-3T does not apply to income received by a controlled commercial entity or received (directly or indirectly) from a controlled commercial entity. The term "controlled commercial entity" means any entity engaged in commercial activities as defined in § 1.892-4T (whether conducted within or outside the United States) if the government—

(1) holds (directly or indirectly) any interest in such entity which (by value or voting power) is 50 percent or more of the total of such interests in such entity, or

(2) holds (directly or indirectly) a sufficient interest (by value or voting power) or any other interest in such entity which provides the foreign government with effective practical control of such entity.

For purposes of this paragraph, the term "entity" encompasses corporations and trusts (including pension trusts described in § 1.892-2T(c)) and estates.

(b) *Entities treated as engaged in commercial activity*—(1) *U.S. real property holding corporations.* A United States real property holding corporation, as defined in section 897(c)(2) or a foreign corporation that would be a United States real property holding corporation if it was a United States corporation, shall be treated as engaged in commercial activity and, therefore, is a controlled commercial entity if the requirements of paragraph (a)(1) or (a)(2) of this section are satisfied.

(2) *Central banks.* Notwithstanding paragraph (a) of this section, a central bank of issue (as defined in § 1.895-1(b)) shall be treated as a controlled commercial entity only if it engages in commercial activities within the United States.

(3) *Pension trusts.* A pension trust, described in § 1.892-2T(c), which engages in commercial activities within or outside the United States, shall be treated as a controlled commercial entity. Income derived by such a pension trust is not income of a foreign government for purposes of the exemption from taxation provided in section 892. A pension trust described in § 1.892-2T(c) shall not be treated as a controlled commercial entity if such trust solely earns income which would not be unrelated business taxable income (as defined in section 512(a)(1)) if the trust were a qualified trust described in section 401(a). However, only income derived by a pension trust that is described in § 1.892-3T and which is not from commercial activities as defined in § 1.892-4T is exempt from taxation under section 892.

(c) *Control*—(1) *Attribution*—(i) *Rule.* In determining for purposes of paragraph (a) of this section the interest held by a foreign government, any interest in an entity (whether or not engaged in commercial activity) owned directly or indirectly by an integral part or controlled entity of a foreign sovereign shall be treated as actually owned by such foreign sovereign.

(ii) *Illustration.* The following example illustrates the application of paragraph (c)(1)(i) above.

Example. FX, a controlled entity of foreign sovereign FC, owns 20 percent of the stock of Corp 1. Neither FX nor Corp 1 is engaged in commercial activity anywhere in the world. Corp 1 owns 60 percent of the stock of Corp 2, which is engaged in commercial activity. The remaining 40 percent of Corp 2's stock is owned by Bureau, an integral part of foreign sovereign FC. For purposes of determining whether Corp 2 is a controlled commercial entity of FC, Bureau will be treated as actually owning the 12 percent of Corp 2's stock indirectly owned by FX. Therefore, since Bureau directly and indirectly owns 52 percent of the stock of Corp 2, Corp 2 is a controlled commercial entity of FC within the meaning of paragraph (a) of this section. Accordingly, dividends or other income received, directly or indirectly, from Corp 2 by either Bureau or FX will not be exempt from taxation under section 892. Furthermore, dividends from Corp 1 to the extent attributable to dividends from Corp 2 will not be exempt from taxation. Thus, a distribution from Corp 1 to FX shall be exempt only to the extent such distribution exceeds Corp 1's earnings and profits attributable to the Corp 2 dividend amount received by Corp 1.

(2) *Effective practical control.* An entity engaged in commercial activity may be treated as a controlled commercial entity if a foreign govern-

ment holds sufficient interests in such entity to give it "effective practical control" over the entity. Effective practical control may be achieved through a minority interest which is sufficiently large to achieve effective control, or through creditor, contractual or regulatory relationships which, together with ownership interests held by the foreign government, achieve effective control. For example, an entity engaged in commercial activity may be treated as a controlled commercial entity if a foreign government, in addition to holding a small minority interest (by value or voting power), is also a substantial creditor of the entity or controls a strategic natural resource which such entity uses in the conduct of its trade or business, giving the foreign government effective practical control over the entity.

(d) *Related controlled entities*—(1) *Brother/sister entities.* Commercial activities of a controlled entity are not attributed to such entity's other brother/sister related entities. Thus, investment income described in § 1.892-2T that is derived by a controlled entity that is not itself engaged in commercial activity within or outside the United States is exempt from taxation notwithstanding the fact that such entity's brother/sister related entity is a controlled commercial entity.

(2) *Parent/subsidiary entities*—(i) *Subsidiary to parent attribution.* Commercial activities of a subsidiary controlled entity are not attributed to its parent. Thus, investment income described in § 1.892-3T that is derived by a parent controlled entity that is not itself engaged in commercial activity within or outside the United States is exempt from taxation notwithstanding the fact that its subsidiary is a controlled commercial entity. Dividends or other payments of income received by the parent controlled entity from the subsidiary are not exempt under section 892, because it constitutes income received from a controlled commercial entity. Furthermore, dividends paid by the parent are not exempt to the extent attributable to the dividends received by the parent from the subsidiary. Thus, a distribution by the parent shall be exempt only to the extent such distribution exceeds earnings and profits attributable to the dividend received from its subsidiary.

(ii) *Parent to subsidiary attribution.* Commercial activities of a parent controlled entity are attributed to its subsidiary. Thus, investment income described in § 1.892-3T that is derived by a subsidiary controlled entity (not engaged in commercial activity within or outside the United States) is not exempt from taxation under section 892 if its parent is a controlled commercial entity.

(3) *Partnerships.* Except for partners of publicly traded partnerships, commercial activities of a partnership are attributable to its general and limited partners for purposes of section 892. For example, where a controlled entity is a general partner in a partnership engaged in commercial activities, the controlled entity's distributive share of partnership income (including income described in § 1.892-3T) will not be exempt from taxation under section 892.

(4) *Illustrations.* The principles of this section may be illustrated by the following examples.

Example (1). (a) The Ministry of Industry and Development is an integral part of a foreign sovereign under § 1.892-2T(a)(2). The Ministry is engaged in commercial activity within the United States. In addition, the Ministry receives income from various publicly traded stocks and bonds, soybean futures contracts and net leases on U.S. real property. Since the Ministry is an integral part, and not a controlled entity, of a foreign sovereign, it is not a controlled commercial entity within the meaning of paragraph (a) of this section. Therefore, income described in § 1.892-3T is ineligible for exemption under section 892 only to the extent derived from the conduct of commercial activities. Accordingly, the Ministry's income from the stocks and bonds is exempt from U.S. tax.

(b) The facts are the same as in *Example* (1)(a), except that the Ministry also owns 75 percent of the stock of R, a U.S. holding company that owns all the stock of S, a U.S. operating company engaged in commercial activity. Ministry's dividend income from R is income received indirectly from a controlled commercial entity. The Ministry's income from the stocks and bonds, with the exception of dividend income from R, is exempt from U.S. tax.

(c) The facts are the same as in *Example* (1)(a), except that the Ministry is a controlled entity of a foreign sovereign. Since the Ministry is a controlled entity and is engaged in commercial activity, it is a controlled commercial entity within the meaning of paragraph (a) of this section, and none of its income is eligible for exemption.

Example (2). (a) Z, a controlled entity of a foreign sovereign, has established a pension trust as part of a pension plan for the benefit of its employees and former employees. The pension trust (T), which meets the requirements of § 1.892-2T(c), has investments in the U.S. in various stocks, bonds, annuity contracts, and a shopping center which is leased and managed by an independent real estate management firm. T also makes securities loans in transactions that qualify

Reg. § 1.892-5T(d)(4)

under section 1058. T's investment in the shopping center is not considered an unrelated trade or business within the meaning of section 513(b). Accordingly, T will not be treated as engaged in commercial activity. Since T is not a controlled commercial entity, its investment income described in § 1.892-3T, with the exception of income received from the operations of the shopping center, is exempt from taxation under section 892.

(b) The facts are the same as *Example* (2)(a), except that T has an interest in a limited partnership which owns the shopping center. The shopping center is leased and managed by the partnership rather than by an independent management firm. Managing a shopping center, directly or indirectly through a partnership of which a trust is a member, would be considered an unrelated trade or business within the meaning of section 513(b) giving rise to unrelated business taxable income. Since the commercial activities of a partnership are attributable to its partners, T will be treated as engaged in commercial activity and thus will be considered a controlled commercial entity. Accordingly, none of T's income will be exempt from taxation under section 892.

(c) The facts are the same as *Example* (2)(a), except that Z is a controlled commercial entity. The result is the same as in *Example* (2)(a).

Example (3). (a) The Department of Interior, an integral part of foreign sovereign FC, wholly owns corporations G and H. G, in turn, wholly owns S. G, H and S are each controlled entities. G, which is not engaged in commercial activity anywhere in the world, receives interest income from deposits in banks in the United States. Both H and S do not have any investments in the U.S. but are both engaged in commercial activities. However, only S is engaged in commercial activities within the United States. Because neither the commercial activities of H nor the commercial activities of S are attributable to the Department of Interior or G, G's interest income is exempt from taxation under section 892.

(b) The facts are the same as *Example* (3)(a), except that G rather than S is engaged in commercial activities and S rather than G receives the interest income from the United States. Since the commercial activities of G are attributable to S, S's interest income is not exempt from taxation.

Example (4). (a) K, a controlled entity of a foreign sovereign, is a general partner in the Daj partnership. The Daj partnership has investments in the U.S. in various stocks and bonds and also owns and manages an office building in New York. K will be deemed to be engaged in commercial activity by being a general partner in Daj even if K does not actually make management decisions with regard to the partnership's commercial activity, the operation of the office building. Accordingly, K's distributive share of partnership income (including income derived from stocks and bonds) will not be exempt from taxation under section 892.

(b) The facts are the same as in *Example* (4)(a), except that the Daj partnership has hired a real estate management firm to lease offices and manage the building. Notwithstanding the fact that an independent contractor is performing the activities, the partnership shall still be deemed to be engaged in commercial activity. Accordingly, K's distributive share of partnership income (including income derived from stocks and bonds) will not be exempt from taxation under section 892.

(c) The facts are the same as in *Example* (4)(a), except that K is a partner whose partnership interest is considered a publicly traded partnership interest within the meaning of section 7704. Under paragraph (d)(3) of this section, the partnership's commercial activity will not be attributed to K. Since K will not be deemed to be engaged in commercial activity, K's distributive share of partnership income derived from stocks and bonds will be exempt from taxation under section 892. [Temporary Reg. § 1.892-5T.]

□ [T.D. 8211, 6-24-88.]

[Reg. § 1.892-6T]

§ 1.892-6T. **Income of international organizations (Temporary).**—(a) *Exempt from tax.* Subject to the provisions of section 1 of the International Organizations Immunities Act (22 U.S.C. 288) (the provisions of which are set forth in paragraph (b)(3) of § 1.893-1), the income of an international organization (as defined in section 7701(a)(18)) received from investments in the United States in stocks, bonds, or other domestic securities, owned by such international organization, or from interest on deposits in banks in the United States of moneys belonging to such international organization, or from any other source within the United States, is exempt from Federal income tax.

(b) *Income received prior to Presidential designation.* An organization designated by the President through appropriate Executive order as entitled to enjoy the privileges, exemptions, and immunities provided in the International Organizations Immunities Act may enjoy the benefits of the exemption with respect to income of the prescribed character received by such organization prior to the date of the issuance of such Executive order, if (i) the Executive order does not provide otherwise and (ii) the organization is a public

Reg. § 1.892-6T(a)

international organization in which the United States participates, pursuant to a treaty or under the authority of an act of Congress authorizing such participation or making an appropriation for such participation, at the time such income is received. [Temporary Reg. § 1.892-6T.]

☐ [T.D. 8211, 6-24-88.]

[Reg. § 1.892-7T]

§ 1.892-7T. Relationship to other Internal Revenue Code sections (Temporary).—(a) *Section 893.* The term "foreign government" referred to in section 893 (relating to the exemption for compensation of employees of foreign governments) has the same meaning as given such term in § 1.892-2T.

(b) *Section 895.* A foreign central bank of issue (as defined in § 1.895-1(b)) that fails to qualify for the exemption from tax provided by this section (for example, it is not wholly owned by a foreign sovereign) may nevertheless be exempt from tax on the items of income described in section 895.

(c) *Section 883(b).* Nothing in section 892 or these regulations shall limit the exemption provided under section 883(b) relating generally to the exemption of earnings derived by foreign participants from the ownership or operation of communications satellite systems.

(d) *Section 884.* Earnings and profits attributable to income of a controlled entity of a foreign sovereign which is exempt from taxation under section 892 shall not be subject to the tax imposed by section 884(a).

(e) *Sections 1441 and 1442.* No withholding is required under sections 1441 and 1442 in the case of income exempt from taxation under section 892. [Temporary Reg. § 1.892-7T.]

☐ [T.D. 8211, 6-24-88.]

[Reg. § 1.893-1]

§ 1.893-1. Compensation of employees of foreign governments or international organizations.—(a) *Employees of foreign governments.*—(1) *Exempt from tax.* Except to the extent that the exemption is limited by the execution and filing of the waiver provided for in section 247(b) of the Immigration and Nationality Act (8 U.S.C. 1257(b)), all employees of a foreign government (including consular or other officers, or nondiplomatic representatives) who are not citizens of the United States, or are citizens of the Republic of the Philippines (whether or not citizens of the United States), are exempt from Federal income tax with respect to wages, fees, or salaries received by them as compensation for official services rendered to such foreign government, provided (i) the services are of a character similar to those performed by employees of the Government of the United States in that foreign country and (ii) the foreign government whose employees are claiming exemption grants an equivalent exemption to employees of the Government of the United States performing similar services in that foreign country.

(2) *Certificate by Secretary of State.* Section 893(b) provides that the Secretary of State shall certify to the Secretary of the Treasury the names of the foreign countries which grant an equivalent exemption to the employees of the Government of the United States performing services in such foreign countries, and the character of the services performed by employees of the Government of the United States in foreign countries.

(3) *Items not exempt.* The income received by employees of foreign governments from sources other than their salaries, fees, or wages, referred to in subparagraph (1) of this paragraph, is subject to Federal income tax.

(4) *Immigration and Nationality Act.* Section 247(b) of the Immigration and Nationality Act provides as follows:

Sec. 247. Adjustment of status of certain resident aliens. * * *

(b) The adjustment of status required by subsection (a) [of section 247 of the Immigration and Nationality Act] shall not be applicable in the case of any alien who requests that he be permitted to retain his status as an immigrant and who, in such form as the Attorney General may require, executes and files with the Attorney General a written waiver of all rights, privileges, exemptions, and immunities under any law or any executive order which would otherwise accrue to him because of the acquisition of an occupational status entitling him to a nonimmigrant status under paragraph (15)(A), (15)(E), or (15)(G) of section 101(a).

(5) *Effect of waiver.* An employee of a foreign government who executes and files with the Attorney General the waiver provided for in section 247(b) of the Immigration and Nationality Act thereby waives the exemption conferred by section 893 of the Code. As a consequence, that exemption does not apply to income received by that alien after the date of filing of the waiver.

(6) *Citizens of the United States.* The compensation of citizens of the United States (other than those who are also citizens of the Republic of the Philippines) who are officers or employees of a foreign government is not exempt from income tax pursuant to this paragraph. But see section 911 and the regulations thereunder.

(b) *Employees of international organizations.*— (1) *Exempt from tax.* Except to the extent that the exemption is limited by the execution and filing of the waiver provided for in section 247(b) of the Immigration and Nationality Act and subject to the provisions of sections 1, 8, and 9 of the International Organizations Immunities Act (22 U.S.C. 288, 288e, 288f), wages, fees, or salary of any officer or employee of an international organization (as defined in section 7701(a)(18)) received as compensation for official services to that international organization is exempt from Federal income tax, if that officer or employee (i) is not a citizen of the United States or (ii) is a citizen of the Republic of the Philippines (whether or not a citizen of the United States).

(2) *Income earned prior to executive action.* An individual of the prescribed class who receives wages, fees, or salary as compensation for official services to an organization designated by the President through appropriate Executive order as entitled to enjoy the privileges, exemptions, and immunities provided in the International Organizations Immunities Act and who has been duly notified to, and accepted by, the Secretary of State as an officer or employee of that organization, or who has been designated by the Secretary of State, prior to formal notification and acceptance, as a prospective officer or employee of that organization, may enjoy the benefits of the exemption with respect to compensation of the prescribed character earned by that individual, either prior to the date of the issuance of the Executive order, or prior to the date of the acceptance or designation by the Secretary of State, for official services to that organization, if (i) the Executive order does not provide otherwise, (ii) the organization is a public international organization in which the United States participates, pursuant to a treaty or under the authority of an act of Congress authorizing such participation or making an appropriation for such participation, at the time the compensation is earned, and (iii) the individual is an officer or employee of that organization at that time.

(3) *International Organizations Immunities Act.* Sections 1, 8, and 9 of the International Organizations Immunities Act (22 U.S.C. 288, 288e, 288f) provide in part as follows:

Section 1. For the purposes of this title [International Organizations Immunities Act], the term "international organization" means a public international organization in which the United States participates pursuant to any treaty or under the authority of any Act of Congress authorizing such participation or making an appropriation for such participation, and which shall have been designated by the President through appropriate Executive order as being entitled to enjoy the privileges, exemptions, and immunities herein provided. The President shall be authorized, in the light of the functions performed by any such international organization, by appropriate Executive order to withhold or withdraw from any such organization or its officers or employees any of the privileges, exemptions, and immunities provided for in this title (including the amendments made by this title) or to condition or limit the enjoyment by any such organization or its officers or employees of any such privilege, exemption, or immunity. The President shall be authorized, if in his judgment such action should be justified by reason of the abuse by an international organization or its officers and employees of the privileges, exemptions, and immunities herein provided or for any other reason, at any time to revoke the designation of any international organization under this section, whereupon the international organization in question shall cease to be classed as an international organization for the purposes of this title.

* * *

Sec. 8. (a) No person shall be entitled to the benefits of this title [International Organizations Immunities Act] unless he (1) shall have been duly notified to and accepted by the Secretary of State as a * * * officer, or employee; or (2) shall have been designated by the Secretary of State, prior to formal notification and acceptance, as a prospective * * * officer, or employee; * * *

(b) Should the Secretary of State determine that the continued presence in the United States of any person entitled to the benefits of this title is not desirable, he shall so inform the * * * international organization concerned * * * and after such person shall have had a reasonable length of time, to be determined by the Secretary of State, to depart from the United States, he shall cease to be entitled to such benefits.

(c) No person shall, by reason of the provisions of this title, be considered as receiving diplomatic status or as receiving any of the privileges incident thereto other than such as are specifically set forth herein.

Sec. 9. The privileges, exemptions, and immunities of international organizations and of their officers and employees * * * provided for in this title [International Organizations Immunities Act], shall be granted notwithstanding the fact that the similar privileges, exemptions, and immunities granted to a foreign government, its officers, or employees, may be conditioned upon the existence of reciprocity by that foreign government: *Provided,* That nothing contained in

Reg. § 1.893-1(b)(1)

this title shall be construed as precluding the Secretary of State from withdrawing the privileges, exemptions, and immunities herein provided from persons who are nationals of any foreign country on the ground that such country is failing to accord corresponding privileges, exemptions, and immunities to citizens of the United States.

(4) *Effect of waiver.* An officer or employee of an international organization who executes and files with the Attorney General the waiver provided for in section 247(b) of the Immigration and Nationality Act (8 U.S.C. 1257(b)) thereby waives the exemption conferred by section 893 of the Code. As a consequence, that exemption does not apply to income received by that individual after the date of filing of the waiver.

(5) *Citizens of the United States.* The compensation of citizens of the United States (other than those who are also citizens of the Republic of the Philippines) who are officers or employees of an international organization is not exempt from income tax pursuant to this paragraph. But see section 911 and the regulations thereunder.

(c) *Tax conventions, consular conventions, and international agreements.*—(1) *Exemption dependent upon internal revenue laws.* A tax convention or consular convention between the United States and a foreign country, which provides that the United States may include in the tax base of its residents all income taxable under the internal revenue laws, and which makes no specific exception for the income of the employees of that foreign government, does not provide any exemption (with respect to residents of the United States) beyond that which is provided by the internal revenue laws. Accordingly, the effect of the execution and filing of a waiver under section 247(b) of the Immigration and Nationality Act by an employee of a foreign government which is a party to such a convention is to subject the employee to tax to the same extent as provided in paragraph (a)(5) of this section with respect to the waiver of exemption under section 893.

(2) *Exemption not dependent upon internal revenue laws.* If a tax convention, consular convention, or international agreement provides that compensation paid by the foreign government or international organization to its employees is exempt from Federal income tax, and the application of this exemption is not dependent upon the provisions of the internal revenue laws, the exemption so conferred is not affected by the execution and filing of a waiver under section 247(b) of the Immigration and Nationality Act. For examples of exemptions which are not affected by the Immigration and Nationality Act, see article X of the income tax convention between the United States and the United Kingdom (60 Stat. 1383); article IX, section 9(b), of the Articles of Agreement of the International Monetary Fund (60 Stat. 1414); and article VII, section 9(b), of the Articles of Agreement of the International Bank for Reconstruction and Development (60 Stat. 1458). [Reg. § 1.893-1.]

☐ [T.D. 6258, 10-23-57.]

[Reg. § 1.894-1]

§ 1.894-1. **Income affected by treaty.**—(a) *Income exempt under treaty.* Income of any kind is not included in gross income and is exempt from tax under subtitle A (relating to income taxes), to the extent required by any income tax convention to which the United States is a party. However, unless otherwise provided by an income tax convention, the exclusion from gross income under section 894(a) and this paragraph does not apply in determining the accumulated taxable income of a foreign corporation under section 535 and the regulations thereunder or the undistributed personal holding company income of a foreign corporation under section 545 and the regulations thereunder. Moreover, the distributable net income of a foreign trust is determined without regard to section 894 and this paragraph, to the extent provided by section 643(a)(6)(B). Further, the compensating tax adjustment required by section 819(a)(3) in the case of a foreign life insurance company is to be determined without regard to section 894 and this paragraph, to the extent required by section 819(a)(3)(A). See § 1.871-12 for the manner of determining the tax liability of a nonresident alien individual or foreign corporation whose gross income includes income on which the tax is reduced under a tax convention.

(b) *Taxpayer treated as having no permanent establishment in the United States*—(1) *In general.* A nonresident alien individual or a foreign corporation, that is engaged in trade or business in the United States through a permanent establishment located therein at any time during a taxable year beginning after December 31, 1966, shall be deemed not to have a permanent establishment in the United States at any time during that year for purposes of applying any exemption from, or reduction in the rate of, any tax under subtitle A of the Code which is provided by any income tax convention with respect to income which is not effectively connected for that year with the conduct of a trade or business in the United States by the taxpayer. This paragraph applies to all treaties or conventions entered into by the United States, whether entered into before, on, or after November 13, 1966, the date of enactment of the Foreign Investors Tax Act of 1966 (80

Reg. § 1.894-1(b)(1)

Stat. 1539). This paragraph is not considered to be contrary to any obligation of the United States under an income tax convention to which it is a party. The benefit granted under section 894(b) and this paragraph applies only to those items of income derived from sources within the United States which are subject to the tax imposed by section 871(a) or 881(a), and section 1441, 1442, or 1451, on the noneffectively connected income received from sources within the United States by a nonresident alien individual or a foreign corporation. The benefit does not apply to any income from real property in respect of which an election is in effect for the taxable year under § 1.871-10 or in determining under section 877(b) the tax of a nonresident alien individual who has lost United States citizenship at any time after March 8, 1965. The benefit granted by section 894(b) and this paragraph is not elective.

(2) *Illustrations.* The application of this paragraph may be illustrated by the following examples:

Example (1). M, a corporation organized in foreign country X, uses the calendar year as the taxable year. The United States and country X are parties to an income tax convention which provides in part that dividends received from sources within the United States by a corporation of country X not having a permanent establishment in the United States are subject to tax under chapter 1 of the Code at a rate not to exceed 15 percent. During 1967, M is engaged in business in the United States through a permanent establishment located therein and receives $100,000 in dividends from domestic corporation B, which under section 861(a)(2)(A) constitute income from sources within the United States. Under section 864(c)(2) and § 1.864-4(c), the dividends received from B are not effectively connected for 1967 with the conduct of a trade or business in the United States by M. Although M has a permanent establishment in the United States during 1967, it is deemed, under section 894(b) and this paragraph, not to have a permanent establishment in the United States during that year with respect to the dividends. Accordingly, in accordance with paragraph (c)(3) of § 1.871-12 the tax on the dividends is $15,000, that is, 15 percent of $100,000, determined without the allowance of any deductions.

Example (2). T, a corporation organized in foreign country X, uses the calendar year as the taxable year. The United States and country X are parties to an income tax convention which provides in part that an enterprise of country X is not subject to tax under chapter 1 of the Code in respect of its industrial or commercial profits unless it is engaged in trade or business in the United States during the taxable year through a permanent establishment located therein and that, if it is so engaged, the tax may be imposed upon the entire income of that enterprise from sources within the United States. The convention also provides that the tax imposed by chapter 1 of the Code on dividends received from sources within the United States by a corporation of X which is not engaged in trade or business in the United States through a permanent establishment located therein shall not exceed 15 percent of the dividend. During 1967, T is engaged in a business (business A) in the United States which is carried on through a permanent establishment in the United States; in addition, T is engaged in a business (business B) in the United States which is not carried on through a permanent establishment. During 1967, T receives from sources within the United States $60,000 in service fees through the operation of business A and $10,000 in dividends through the operation of business B, both of which amounts are, under section 864(c)(2)(B), and § 1.864-4(c)(3), effectively connected for that year with the conduct of a trade or business in the United States by that corporation. The service fees are considered to be industrial or commercial profits under the tax convention with country X. Since T has no income for 1967 which is not effectively connected for that year with the conduct of a trade or business in the United States by that corporation, section 894(b), this paragraph, and § 1.871-12 do not apply. Accordingly, for 1967 T's entire income of $70,000 from sources within the United States is subject to tax, after allowance of deductions, in accordance with section 882(a)(1) and paragraph (b)(2) of § 1.882-1.

Example (3). S, a corporation organized in foreign country W, uses the calendar year as the taxable year. The United States and country W are parties to an income tax convention which provides in part that a corporation of country W is not subject to tax under chapter 1 of the Code in respect of its industrial or commercial profits unless it is engaged in trade or business in the United States during the taxable year through a permanent establishment located therein and that, if it is so engaged, the tax may be imposed upon the entire income of that corporation from sources within the United States. The convention also provides that the tax imposed by chapter 1 of the Code on dividends received from sources within the United States by a corporation of country W which is not engaged in trade or business in the United States through a permanent establishment located therein shall not exceed 15 percent of the dividend. During 1967, S is engaged in business in the United States through a permanent establishment located therein and derives

Reg. § 1.894-1(b)(2)

from sources within the United States $100,000 in service fees which, under section 864(c)(2)(B) and § 1.864-4(c)(3), are effectively connected for that year with the conduct of a trade or business in the United States by S and which are considered to be industrial or commercial profits under the tax convention with country W. During 1967, S also derives from sources within the United States, through another business it carries on in foreign country X, $10,000 in sales income which, under section 864(c)(3) and § 1.864-4(b), is effectively connected for that year with the conduct of a trade or business in the United States by S and $5,000 in dividends which, under section 864(c)(2)(A) and § 1.864-4(c)(2), are not effectively connected for that year with the conduct of a trade or business in the United States by S. The sales income is considered to be industrial or commercial profits under the tax convention with country W. Although S is engaged in a trade or business in the United States during 1967 through a permanent establishment located therein, it is deemed, under section 894(b) and this paragraph, not to have a permanent establishment therein with respect to the $5,000 in dividends. Accordingly, in accordance with paragraph (c) of § 1.871-12, for 1967 S is subject to a tax of $750 on the dividends ($5,000 × .15) and a tax, determined under section 882(a) and § 1.882-1, on its $110,000 industrial or commercial profits.

Example (4). (a) N, a corporation organized in foreign country Z, uses the calendar year as the taxable year. The United States and country Z are parties to an income tax convention which provides in part that the tax imposed by chapter 1 of the Code on dividends received from sources within the United States by a corporation of country Z shall not exceed 15 percent of the amount distributed if the recipient does not have a permanent establishment in the United States or, where the recipient does have a permanent establishment in the United States, if the shares giving rise to the dividends are not effectively connected with the permanent establishment. The tax convention also provides that if a corporation of country Z is engaged in industrial or commercial activity in the United States through a permanent establishment in the United States, income tax may be imposed by the United States on so much of the industrial or commercial profits of such corporation as are attributable to the permanent establishment in the United States.

(b) During 1967, N is engaged in a business (business A) in the United States which is not carried on through a permanent establishment in the United States. In addition, N has a permanent establishment in the United States through which it carries on another business (business B) in the United States. During 1967, N holds shares of stock in domestic corporation D which are not effectively connected with N's permanent establishment in the United States. During 1967, N receives $100,000 in dividends from D which, pursuant to section 864(c)(2)(A) and § 1.864-4(c)(2), are effectively connected for that year with the conduct of business A. Under section 861(a)(2)(A) these dividends are treated as income from sources within the United States. In addition, during 1967, N receives from sources within the United States $150,000 in sales income which, pursuant to section 864(c)(3) and § 1.864-4(b), is effectively connected with the conduct of a trade or business in the United States and which is considered to be industrial or commercial profits under the tax convention with country Z. Of these total profits, $70,000 is from business A and $80,000 is from business B. Only the $80,000 of industrial or commercial profits is attributable to N's permanent establishment in the United States.

(c) Since N has no income for 1967 which is not effectively connected for that year with the conduct of a trade or business in the United States by that corporation, section 894(b) and this paragraph do not apply. However, N is entitled to the reduced rate of tax under the tax convention with country Z with respect to the dividends because the shares of stock are not effectively connected with N's permanent establishment in the United States. Accordingly, assuming that there are no deductions connected with N's industrial or commercial profits, the tax for 1967, determined as provided in paragraph (c) of § 1.871-12, is $46,900 as follows:

Tax on nontreaty income:	
$80,000 × .48	$38,400
Less $25,000 × .26	6,500
	31,900
Tax on treaty income:	
$100,000 (gross dividends) × .15	15,000
Total tax	$46,900

Example (5). M, a corporation organized in foreign country Z, uses the calendar year as the taxable year. The United States and country Z are parties to an income tax convention which provides in part that a corporation of country Z is not subject to tax under chapter 1 of the Code in respect of its commercial and industrial profits except such profits as are allocable to its permanent establishment in the United States. The regulations in this chapter under the tax convention with country Z provide that a corporation of country Z having a permanent establishment in the United States is subject to U.S. tax upon its industrial and commercial profits from sources

Reg. § 1.894-1(b)(2)

within the United States and that its industrial and commercial profits from such sources are deemed to be allocable to the permanent establishment in the United States. During 1967, M is engaged in a business (business A) in the United States, which is carried on through a permanent establishment in the United States; in addition, M is engaged in a business (business B) in foreign country X and none of such business is carried on in the United States. During 1967, M receives from sources within the United States $40,000 in sales income through the operation of business A and $10,000 in sales income through the operation of business B, both of which amounts are, under section 864(c)(3) and § 1.864-4(b), effectively connected for that year with the conduct of a trade or business in the United States by that corporation. The sales income is considered to be industrial and commercial profits under the tax convention with country Z. Since M has no income for 1967 which is not effectively connected for that year with the conduct of a trade or business in the United States by that corporation, section 894(b) and this paragraph do not apply. Accordingly, for 1967 M's entire income of $50,000 from sources within the United States is subject to tax, after allowance of deductions, in accordance with section 882(a)(1) and paragraph (b)(2) of § 1.882-1.

(c) *Substitute interest and dividend payments.* The provisions of an income tax convention dealing with interest or dividends paid to or derived by a foreign person include substitute interest or dividend payments that have the same character as interest or dividends under § 1.864-5(b)(2)(ii), 1.871-7(b)(2) or 1.881-2(b)(2). The provisions of this paragraph (c) shall apply for purposes of securities lending transactions or sale-repurchase transactions as defined in § 1.861-2(a)(7) and § 1.861-3(a)(6).

(d) *Special rule for items of income received by entities*—(1) *In general.* The tax imposed by sections 871(a), 881(a), 1443, 1461, and 4948(a) on an item of income received by an entity, wherever organized, that is fiscally transparent under the laws of the United States and/or any other jurisdiction with respect to an item of income shall be eligible for reduction under the terms of an income tax treaty to which the United States is a party only if the item of income is derived by a resident of the applicable treaty jurisdiction. For this purpose, an item of income may be derived by either the entity receiving the item of income or by the interest holders in the entity or, in certain circumstances, both. An item of income paid to an entity shall be considered to be derived by the entity only if the entity is not fiscally transparent under the laws of the entity's jurisdiction, as defined in paragraph (d)(3)(ii) of this section, with respect to the item of income. An item of income paid to an entity shall be considered to be derived by the interest holder in the entity only if the interest holder is not fiscally transparent in its jurisdiction with respect to the item of income and if the entity is considered to be fiscally transparent under the laws of the interest holder's jurisdiction with respect to the item of income, as defined in paragraph (d)(3)(iii) of this section. Notwithstanding the preceding two sentences, an item of income paid directly to a type of entity specifically identified in a treaty as a resident of a treaty jurisdiction shall be treated as derived by a resident of that treaty jurisdiction.

(2) *Application to domestic reverse hybrid entities*—(i) *In general.* An income tax treaty may not apply to reduce the amount of federal income tax on U.S. source payments received by a domestic reverse hybrid entity. Further, notwithstanding paragraph (d)(1) of this section, the foreign interest holders of a domestic reverse hybrid entity are not entitled to the benefits of a reduction of U.S. income tax under an income tax treaty on items of income received from U.S. sources by such entity. A domestic reverse hybrid entity is a domestic entity that is treated as not fiscally transparent for U.S. tax purposes and as fiscally transparent under the laws of the interest holder's jurisdiction, with respect to the item of income received by the domestic entity.

(ii) *Payments by domestic reverse hybrid entities.* [Reserved].

(3) *Definitions*—(i) *Entity.* For purposes of this paragraph (d), the term *entity* shall mean any person that is treated by the United States or the applicable treaty jurisdiction as other than an individual. The term *entity* includes disregarded entities, including single member disregarded entities with individual owners.

(ii) *Fiscally transparent under the law of the entity's jurisdiction*—(A) *General rule.* For purposes of this paragraph (d), an entity is fiscally transparent under the laws of the entity's jurisdiction with respect to an item of income to the extent that the laws of that jurisdiction require the interest holder in the entity, wherever resident, to separately take into account on a current basis the interest holder's respective share of the item of income paid to the entity, whether or not distributed to the interest holder, and the character and source of the item in the hands of the interest holder are determined as if such item were realized directly from the source from which realized by the entity. However, the entity will be fiscally transparent with respect to the item of income even if the item of income is not separately taken into account by the interest holder,

Reg. § 1.894-1(c)

provided the item of income, if separately taken into account by the interest holder, would not result in an income tax liability for that interest holder different from that which would result if the interest holder did not take the item into account separately, and provided the interest holder is required to take into account on a current basis the interest holder's share of all such nonseparately stated items of income paid to the entity, whether or not distributed to the interest holder. In determining whether an entity is fiscally transparent with respect to an item of income in the entity's jurisdiction, it is irrelevant that, under the laws of the entity's jurisdiction, the entity is permitted to exclude such item from gross income or that the entity is required to include such item in gross income but is entitled to a deduction for distributions to its interest holders.

(B) *Special definitions*. For purposes of this paragraph (d)(3)(ii), an entity's jurisdiction is the jurisdiction where the entity is organized or incorporated or may otherwise be considered a resident under the laws of that jurisdiction. An interest holder will be treated as taking into account that person's share of income paid to an entity on a current basis even if such amount is taken into account by the interest holder in a taxable year other than the taxable year of the entity if the difference is due solely to differing taxable years.

(iii) *Fiscally transparent under the law of an interest holder's jurisdiction*—(A) *General rule*. For purposes of this paragraph (d), an entity is treated as fiscally transparent under the law of an interest holder's jurisdiction with respect to an item of income to the extent that the laws of the interest holder's jurisdiction require the interest holder resident in that jurisdiction to separately take into account on a current basis the interest holder's respective share of the item of income paid to the entity, whether or not distributed to the interest holder, and the character and source of the item in the hands of the interest holder are determined as if such item were realized directly from the source from which realized by the entity. However, an entity will be fiscally transparent with respect to the item of income even if the item of income is not separately taken into account by the interest holder, provided the item of income, if separately taken into account by the interest holder, would not result in an income tax liability for that interest holder different from that which would result if the interest holder did not take the item into account separately, and provided the interest holder is required to take into account on a current basis the interest holder's share of all such nonseparately stated items of income paid to the entity, whether or not distributed to the interest holder. An entity will not be treated as fiscally transparent with respect to an item of income under the laws of the interest holder's jurisdiction, however, if, under the laws of the interest holder's jurisdiction, the interest holder in the entity is required to include in gross income a share of all or a part of the entity's income on a current basis year under any type of anti-deferral or comparable mechanism. In determining whether an entity is fiscally transparent with respect to an item of income under the laws of an interest holder's jurisdiction, it is irrelevant how the entity is treated under the laws of the entity's jurisdiction.

(B) *Special definitions*. For purposes of this paragraph (d)(3)(iii), an interest holder's jurisdiction is the jurisdiction where the interest holder is organized or incorporated or may otherwise be considered a resident under the laws of that jurisdiction. An interest holder will be treated as taking into account that person's share of income paid to an entity on a current basis even if such amount is taken into account by such person in a taxable year other than the taxable year of the entity if the difference is due solely to differing taxable years.

(iv) *Applicable treaty jurisdiction*. The term *applicable treaty jurisdiction* means the jurisdiction whose income tax treaty with the United States is invoked for purposes of reducing the rate of tax imposed under sections 871(a), 881(a), 1461, and 4948(a).

(v) *Resident*. The term *resident* shall have the meaning assigned to such term in the applicable income tax treaty.

(4) *Application to all income tax treaties*. Unless otherwise explicitly agreed upon in the text of an income tax treaty, the rules contained in this paragraph (d) shall apply in respect of all income tax treaties to which the United States is a party. Notwithstanding the foregoing sentence, the competent authorities may agree on a mutual basis to depart from the rules contained in this paragraph (d) in appropriate circumstances. However, a reduced rate under a tax treaty for an item of U.S. source income paid will not be available irrespective of the provisions in this paragraph (d) to the extent that the applicable treaty jurisdiction would not grant a reduced rate under the tax treaty to a U.S. resident in similar circumstances, as evidenced by a mutual agreement between the relevant competent authorities or by a public notice of the treaty jurisdiction. The Internal Revenue Service shall announce the terms of any such mutual agreement or public notice of the treaty jurisdiction. Any denial of tax treaty benefits as a consequence of such a mutual agreement

Reg. § 1.894-1(d)(4)

or notice shall affect only payment of U.S. source items of income made after announcement of the terms of the agreement or of the notice.

(5) *Examples.* This paragraph (d) is illustrated by the following examples:

Example 1. Treatment of entity treated as partnership by U.S. and country of organization. (i) *Facts.* Entity A is a business organization formed under the laws of Country X that has an income tax treaty in effect with the United States. A is treated as a partnership for U.S. federal income tax purposes. A is also treated as a partnership under the laws of Country X, and therefore Country X requires the interest holders in A to separately take into account on a current basis their respective shares of the items of income paid to A, whether or not distributed to the interest holders, and the character and source of the items in the hands of the interest holders are determined as if such items were realized directly from the source from which realized by A. A receives royalty income from U.S. sources that is not effectively connected with the conduct of a trade or business in the United States.

(ii) *Analysis.* A is fiscally transparent in its jurisdiction within the meaning of paragraph (d)(3)(ii) of this section with respect to the U.S. source royalty income in Country X and, thus, A does not derive such income for purposes of the U.S.-X income tax treaty.

Example 2. Treatment of interest holders in entity treated as partnership by U.S. and country of organization. (i) *Facts.* The facts are the same as under *Example 1.* A's partners are M, a corporation organized under the laws of Country Y that has an income tax treaty in effect with the United States, and T, a corporation organized under the laws of Country Z that has an income tax treaty in effect with the United States. M and T are not fiscally transparent under the laws of their respective countries of incorporation. Country Y requires M to separately take into account on a current basis M's respective share of the items of income paid to A, whether or not distributed to M, and the character and source of the items of income in M's hands are determined as if such items were realized directly from the source from which realized by A. Country Z treats A as a corporation and does not require T to take its share of A's income into account on a current basis whether or not distributed.

(ii) *Analysis.* M is treated as deriving its share of the U.S. source royalty income for purposes of the U.S.-Y income tax treaty because A is fiscally transparent under paragraph (d)(3)(iii) with respect to that income under the laws of Country Y. Under Country Z law, however, because T is not required to take into account its share of the U.S. source royalty income received by A on a current basis whether or not distributed, A is not treated as fiscally transparent. Accordingly, T is not treated as deriving its share of the U.S. source royalty income for purposes of the U.S.-Z income tax treaty.

Example 3. Dual benefits to entity and interest holder. (i) *Facts.* The facts are the same as under *Example 2,* except that A is taxable as a corporation under the laws of Country X. Article 12 of the U.S.-X income tax treaty provides for a source country reduced rate of taxation on royalties of 5-percent. Article 12 of the U.S.-Y income tax treaty provides that royalty income may only be taxed by the beneficial owner's country of residence.

(ii) *Analysis.* A is treated as deriving the U.S. source royalty income for purposes of the U.S.-X income tax treaty because it is not fiscally transparent with respect to the item of income within the meaning of paragraph (d)(3)(ii) of this section in Country X, its country of organization. M is also treated as deriving its share of the U.S. source royalty income for purposes of the U.S.-Y income tax treaty because A is fiscally transparent under paragraph (d)(3)(iii) of this section with respect to that income under the laws of Country Y. T is not treated as deriving the U.S. source royalty income for purposes of the U.S.-Z income tax treaty because under Country Z law A is not fiscally transparent. Assuming all other requirements for eligibility for treaty benefits have been satisfied, A is entitled to the 5-percent treaty reduced rate on royalties under the U.S.-X income tax treaty with respect to the entire royalty payment. Assuming all other requirements for treaty benefits have been satisfied, M is also entitled to a zero rate under the U.S.-Y income tax treaty with respect to its share of the royalty income.

Example 4. Treatment of grantor trust. (i) *Facts.* Entity A is a trust organized under the laws of Country X, which does not have an income tax treaty in effect with the United States. M, the grantor and owner of A for U.S. income tax purposes, is a resident of Country Y, which has an income tax treaty in effect with the United States. M is also treated as the grantor and owner of the trust under the laws of Country Y. Thus, Country Y requires M to take into account all items of A's income in the taxable year, whether or not distributed to M, and determines the character of each item in M's hands as if such item was realized directly from the source from which realized by A. Country X does not treat M as the owner of A and does not require M to account for A's income on a current basis whether or not

Reg. § 1.894-1(d)(5)

distributed to M. A receives interest income from U.S. sources that is neither portfolio interest nor effectively connected with the conduct of a trade or business in the United States.

(ii) *Analysis.* A is not fiscally transparent under the laws of Country X within the meaning of paragraph (d)(3)(ii) of this section with respect to the U.S. source interest income, but A may not claim treaty benefits because there is no U.S.-X income tax treaty. M, however, does derive the income for purposes of the U.S.-Y income tax treaty because under the laws of Country Y, A is fiscally transparent.

Example 5. Treatment of complex trust. (i) *Facts.* The facts are the same as in *Example 4* except that M is treated as the owner of the trust only under U.S. tax law, after application of section 672(f), but not under the law of Country Y. Although the trust document governing A does not require that A distribute any of its income on a current basis, some distributions are made currently to M. There is no requirement under Country Y law that M take into account A's income on a current basis whether or not distributed to him in that year. Under the laws of Country Y, with respect to current distributions, the character of the item of income in the hands of the interest holder is determined as if such item were realized directly from the source from which realized by A. Accordingly, upon a current distribution of interest income to M, the interest income retains its source as U.S. source income.

(ii) *Analysis.* M does not derive the U.S. source interest income because A is not fiscally transparent under paragraph (d)(3)(ii) of this section with respect to the U.S. source interest income under the laws of Country Y. Although the character of the interest in the hands of M is determined as if realized directly from the source from which realized by A, under the laws of Country Y, M is not required to take into account his share of A's interest income on a current basis whether or not distributed. Accordingly, neither A nor M is entitled to claim treaty benefits, since A is a resident of a non-treaty jurisdiction and M does not derive the U.S. source interest income for purposes of the U.S.-Y income tax treaty.

Example 6. Treatment of interest holders required to include passive income under anti-deferral regime. (i) *Facts.* The facts are the same as under *Example 2.* However, Country Z does require T, who is treated as owning 60-percent of the stock of A, to take into account its respective share of the royalty income of A under an anti-deferral regime applicable to certain passive income of controlled foreign corporations.

(ii) *Analysis.* T is still not eligible to claim treaty benefits with respect to the royalty income. T is not treated as deriving the U.S. source royalty income for purposes of the U.S.-Z income tax treaty under paragraph (d)(3)(iii) of this section because T is only required to take into account its pro rata share of the U.S. source royalty income by reason of Country Z's anti-deferral regime.

Example 7. Treatment of contractual arrangements operating as collective investment vehicles. (i) *Facts.* A is a contractual arrangement without legal personality for all purposes under the laws of Country X providing for joint ownership of securities. Country X has an income tax treaty in effect with the United States. A is a collective investment fund which is of a type known as a Common Fund under Country X law. Because of the absence of legal personality in Country X of the arrangement, A is not liable to tax as a person at the entity level in Country X and is thus not a resident within the meaning of the Residence Article of the U.S.-X income tax treaty. A is treated as a partnership for U.S. income tax purposes and receives U.S. source dividend income. Under the laws of Country X, however, investors in A only take into account their respective share of A's income upon distribution from the Common Fund. Some of A's interest holders are residents of Country X and some of Country Y. Country Y has no income tax treaty in effect with the United States.

(ii) *Analysis.* A is not fiscally transparent under paragraph (d)(3)(ii) of this section with respect to the U.S. source dividend income because the interest holders in A are not required to take into account their respective shares of such income in the taxable year whether or not distributed. Because A is an arrangement without a legal personality that is not considered a person in Country X and thus not a resident of Country X under the Residence Article of the U.S.-X income tax treaty, however, A does not derive the income as a resident of Country X for purposes of the U.S.-X income tax treaty. Further, because A is not fiscally transparent under paragraph (d)(3)(iii) of this section with respect to the U.S. source dividend income, A's interest holders that are residents of Country X do not derive the income as residents of Country X for purposes of the U.S.-X income tax treaty.

Example 8. Treatment of person specifically listed as resident in applicable treaty. (i) *Facts.* The facts are the same as in *Example 7* except that A (the Common Fund) is organized in Country Z and the Residence Article of the U.S.-Z income tax treaty provides that "the term 'resident of a Contracting State' includes, in the case of Country Z, Common Funds...."

(ii) *Analysis.* A is treated, for purposes of the U.S.-Z income tax treaty as deriving the dividend income as a resident of Country Z under paragraph (d)(1) of this section because the item of income is paid directly to A, A is a Common Fund under the laws of Country Z, and Common Funds are specifically identified as residents of Country Z in the U.S.-Z treaty. There is no need to determine whether A meets the definition of fiscally transparent under paragraph (d)(3)(ii) of this section.

Example 9. Treatment of investment company when entity receives distribution deductions, and all distributions sourced by residence of entity. (i) *Facts.* Entity A is a business organization formed under the laws of Country X, which has an income tax treaty in effect with the United States. A is treated as a partnership for U.S. income tax purposes. Under the laws of Country X, A is an investment company taxable at the entity level and a resident of Country X. It is also entitled to a distribution deduction for amounts distributed to its interest holders on a current basis. A distributes all its net income on a current basis to its interest holders and, thus, in fact, has no income tax liability to Country X. A receives U.S. source dividend income. Under Country X law, all amounts distributed to interest holders of this type of business entity are treated as dividends from sources within Country X and Country X imposes a withholding tax on all payments by A to foreign persons. Under Country X laws, the interest holders in A do not have to separately take into account their respective shares of A's income on a current basis if such income is not, in fact, distributed.

(ii) *Analysis.* A is not fiscally transparent under paragraph (d)(3)(ii) of this section with respect to the U.S. source dividends because the interest holders in A do not have to take into account their respective share of the U.S. source dividends on a current basis whether or not distributed. A is also not fiscally transparent under paragraph (d)(3)(ii) of this section because there is a change in source of the income received by A when A distributes the income to its interest holders and, thus, the character and source of the income in the hands of A's interest holder are not determined as if such income were realized directly from the source from which realized by A. Accordingly, A is treated as deriving the U.S. source dividends for purposes of the U.S.-Country X treaty.

Example 10. Item by item determination of fiscal transparency. (i) *Facts.* Entity A is a business organization formed under the laws of Country X, which has an income tax treaty in effect with the United States. A is treated as a partnership for U.S. income tax purposes. Under the laws of Country X, A is an investment company taxable at the entity level and a resident of Country X. It is also entitled to a distribution deduction for amounts distributed to its interest holders on a current basis. A receives both U.S. source dividend income and interest income from U.S. sources that is neither portfolio interest nor effectively connected with the conduct of a trade or business in the United States. Country X law sources all distributions attributable to dividend income based on the residence of the investment company. In contrast, Country X law sources all distributions attributable to interest income based on the residence of the payor of the interest. No withholding applies with respect to distributions attributable to U.S. source interest and the character of the distributions attributable to the interest income remains the same in the hands of A's interest holders as if such items were realized directly from the source from which realized by A. However, under Country X law the interest holders in A do not have to take into account their respective share of the interest income received by A on a current basis whether or not distributed.

(ii) *Analysis.* An item by item analysis is required under paragraph (d) of this section. The analysis is the same as *Example 9* with respect to the dividend income. A is also not fiscally transparent under paragraph (d)(3)(ii) of this section with respect to the interest income because, although the character of the distributions attributable to the interest income in the hands of A's interest holders is determined as if realized directly from the source from which realized by A, under Country X law the interest holders in A do not have to take into account their respective share of the interest income received by A on a current basis whether or not distributed. Accordingly, A derives the U.S. source interest income for purpose of the U.S.-X treaty.

Example 11. Treatment of charitable organizations. (i) *Facts.* Entity A is a corporation organized under the laws of Country X that has an income tax treaty in effect with the United States. Entity A is established and operated exclusively for religious, charitable, scientific, artistic, cultural, or educational purposes. Entity A receives U.S. source dividend income from U.S. sources. A provision of Country X law generally exempts Entity A's income from Country X tax due to the fact that Entity A is established and operated exclusively for religious, charitable, scientific, artistic, cultural, or educational purposes.

Reg. § 1.894-1(d)(5)

But for such provision, Entity A's income would be taxed by Country X.

(ii) *Analysis.* Entity A is not fiscally transparent under paragraph (d)(3)(ii) of this section with respect to the U.S. source dividend income because, under Country X law, the dividend income is treated as an item of income of A and no other persons are required to take into account their respective share of the item of income on a current basis, whether or not distributed. Accordingly, Entity A is treated as deriving the U.S. source dividend income.

Example 12. Treatment of pension trusts. (i) *Facts.* Entity A is a trust established and operated in Country X exclusively to provide pension or other similar benefits to employees pursuant to a plan. Entity A receives U.S. source dividend income. A provision of Country X law generally exempts Entity A's income from Country X tax due to the fact that Entity A is established and operated exclusively to provide pension or other similar benefits to employees pursuant to a plan. Under the laws of Country X, the beneficiaries of the trust are not required to take into account their respective share of A's income on a current basis, whether or not distributed and the character and source of the income in the hands of A's interest holders are not determined as if realized directly from the source from which realized by A.

(ii) *Analysis.* A is not fiscally transparent under paragraph (d)(3)(ii) of this section with respect to the U.S. source dividend income because under the laws of Country X, the beneficiaries of A are not required to take into account their respective share of A's income on a current basis, whether or not distributed. A is also not fiscally transparent under paragraph (d)(3)(ii) of this section with respect to the U.S. source dividend income because under the laws of Country X, the character and source of the income in the hands of A's interest holders are not determined as if realized directly from the source from which realized by A. Accordingly, A derives the U.S. source dividend income for purposes of the U.S.-X income tax treaty.

(6) *Effective date.* This paragraph (d) applies to items of income paid on or after June 30, 2000.

(e) *Effective dates.* Paragraphs (a) and (b) of this section apply for taxable years beginning after December 31, 1966. For corresponding rules applicable to taxable years beginning before January 1, 1967, (see 26 CFR part 1 revised April 1, 1971). Paragraph (c) of this section is applicable to payments made after November 13, 1997. See paragraph (d)(6) of this section for applicability dates for paragraph (d) of this section. [Reg. § 1.894-1.]

☐ [*T.D.* 6258, 10-23-57. *Amended by T.D.* 7293, 11-27-73; *T.D.* 8735, 10-6-97 *and T.D.* 8889, 6-30-2000 (*corrected* 12-7-2000).]

[Reg. § 1.895-1]

§ 1.895-1. Income derived by a foreign central bank of issue, or by Bank for International Settlements, from obligations of the United States or from bank deposits.—(a) *In general.* Income derived by a foreign central bank of issue from obligations of the United States or of any agency or instrumentality thereof, or from interest on deposits with persons carrying on the banking business, is excluded from the gross income of such bank and is exempt from income tax if the bank is the owner of the obligations or deposits and does not hold the obligations or deposits for, or use them in connection with, the conduct of a commercial banking function or other commercial activity by such bank. For purposes of this section and paragraph (i) of § 1.1441-4, obligations of the United States or of any agency or instrumentality thereof include beneficial interests, participations, and other instruments issued under section 302(c) of the Federal National Mortgage Association Charter Act (12 U.S.C. 1717). See 24 CFR Part 1600 et seq.

(b) *Foreign central bank of issue.* (1) A foreign central bank of issue is a bank which is by law or government sanction the principal authority, other than the government itself, issuing instruments intended to circulate as currency. Such a bank is generally the custodian of the banking reserves of the country under whose law it is organized. See also paragraph (b)(5) of § 1.861-2.

(2) The exclusion granted by section 895 applies to an instrumentality that is separate from a foreign government, whether or not owned in whole or in part by a foreign government. For example, foreign banks organized along the lines of, and performing functions similar to, the Federal Reserve System qualify as foreign central banks of issue for purposes of this section.

(3) The Bank for International Settlements shall be treated as though it were a foreign central bank of issue for purposes of obtaining the exclusion granted by section 895.

(c) *Ownership of United States obligations or bank deposits.* The exclusion does not apply if the obligations or bank deposits from which the income is derived are not owned by the foreign central bank of issue. Obligations held, or deposits made, by a foreign central bank of issue as agent, custodian, trustee, or in any other fiduciary ca-

Reg. § 1.895-1(c)

pacity, shall be considered as not owned by such bank for purposes of this section.

(d) *Commercial banking function or other commercial activity.* The exclusion applies only to obligations of the United States or of any agency or instrumentality thereof, or to bank deposits, held for, or used in connection with, the conduct of a central banking function and not to obligations or deposits held for, or used in connection with, the conduct of commercial banking functions or other commercial activities by the foreign central bank.

(e) *Other exclusions.* See section 861(a)(1)(A) and (E) and § 1.861-2(b)(1) and (4), for special rules relating to interest paid or credited before January 1, 1977, on deposits and on similar amounts and for rules on interest derived from bankers' acceptances. For exemption from withholding under § 1.1441-1 on income derived by a foreign central bank of issue, or by the Bank for International Settlements, from obligations of the United States or of any agency or instrumentality thereof, or from bank deposits, see § 1.441-4(i).

(f) *Effective date.* This section shall apply with respect to taxable years beginning after December 31, 1966. For corresponding rules applicable to taxable years beginning before January 1, 1967, see 26 CFR 1.85-1 (Rev. as of Jan. 1, 1972). [Reg. § 1.895-1.]

☐ [T.D. 6636, 2-25-63. Amended by T.D. 7378, 9-29-75.]

[Reg. § 1.897-1]

§ 1.897-1. Taxation of foreign investment in United States real property interests, definition of terms.—(a) *In general*—(1) *Purpose and scope of regulations.* These regulations provide guidance with respect to the taxation of foreign investment in U.S. real property interests and related matters. This section defines various terms for purposes of sections 897, 1445, and 6039C and the regulations thereunder. Section 1.897-2 provides rules regarding the definition of, and consequences of, U.S. real property holding corporation status. Section 1.897-3 sets forth rules pursuant to which certain foreign corporations may elect under section 897(i) to be treated as domestic corporations for purposes of sections 897 and 6039C. Finally, § 1.897-4 provides rules concerning the similar election under section 897(k) for certain foreign corporations in the process of liquidation.

(2) *Effective date.* The regulations set forth in §§ 1.897-1 through 1.897-4 are effective for transactions occurring after June 18, 1980. However, with respect to all transactions occurring after June 18, 1980, and before January 30, 1985, taxpayers may at their option choose to apply the Temporary Regulations under section 897 (in their entirety). The Temporary Regulations are located at 26 CFR §§ 6a. 897-1 through 6a. 897-4 (Revised as of April 1, 1983), and were originally published in the *Federal Register* for September 21, 1982 (47 FR 41532) and amended by T.D. 7890, published in the *Federal Register* on April 28, 1983 (48 FR 19163).

(b) *Real property*—(1) *In general.* The term "real property" includes the following three categories of property: Land and unsevered natural products of the land, improvements, and personal property associated with the use of real property. The three categories of real property are defined in subparagraphs (2), (3), and (4) of this paragraph (b). Local law definitions will not be controlling for purposes of determining the meaning of the term "real property" as it is used in sections 897, 1445, and 6039C and the regulations thereunder.

(2) *Land and unsevered natural products of the land.* The term "real property" includes land, growing crops and timber, and mines, wells, and other natural deposits. Crops and timber cease to be real property at the time that they are severed from the land. Ores, minerals, and other natural deposits cease to be real property when they are extracted from the ground. The storage of severed or extracted crops, timber, or minerals in or upon real property will not cause such property to be recharacterized as real property.

(3) *Improvements*—(i) *In general.* The term "real property" includes improvements on land. An improvement is a building, any other inherently permanent structure, or the structural components of either, as defined in subdivisions (ii) through (iv) of this paragraph (b)(3).

(ii) *Building.* The term "building" generally means any structure or edifice enclosing a space within its walls, and usually covered by a roof, the purpose of which is, for example, to provide shelter or housing or to provide working, office, parking, display, or sales space. The term includes, for example, structures such as apartment houses, factory and office buildings, warehouses, barns, garages, railway or bus stations, and stores. Any structure that is classified as a building for purposes of section 48(a)(1)(B) and § 1.48-1 shall be treated as such for purposes of this section.

(iii) *Inherently permanent structure*—(A) *In general.* The term "inherently permanent structure" means any property not otherwise described in this paragraph (b)(3) that is affixed to real property and that will ordinarily remain affixed for an indefinite period of time. Property that is not classified as a building for purposes of section 48(a)(1)(B) and § 1.48-1 may nevertheless constitute an inherently permanent structure. For purposes of this section, affixation to real property may be accomplished by weight alone.

(B) *Use of precedents under section 48.* Any property not otherwise described in this paragraph (b)(3) that constitutes "other tangible property" under the principles of section 48(a)(1)(B) and § 1.48-1(c) and (d) shall be treated for purposes of this section as an inherently permanent structure. Thus, for example, the term includes swimming pools, paved parking areas and other pavements, special foundations for heavy equipment, wharves and docks, bridges, fences, inherently permanent advertising displays, inherently permanent outdoor lighting facilities, railroad tracks and signals, telephone poles, permanently installed telephone and television cables, broadcasting towers, oil derricks, oil and gas pipelines, oil and gas storage tanks, grain storage bins, and silos. However, property that is determined to be either property in the nature of machinery under § 1.48-1(c) or property which is essentially an item of machinery or equipment under § 1.48-1(e)(1)(i) shall not be treated as an inherently permanent structure.

(C) *Absence of precedents under section 48.* Where precedents developed under the principles of section 48 fail to provide adequate guidance with respect to the classification of particular property, the determination of whether such property constitutes an inherently permanent structure shall be made in view of all the facts and circumstances. In particular, the following factors must be taken into account:

(*1*) The manner in which the property is affixed to real property;

(*2*) Whether the property was designed to be easily removable or to remain in place indefinitely;

(*3*) Whether the property has been moved since its initial installation;

(*4*) Any circumstances that suggest the expected period of affixation (e.g., a lease that requires removal of the property upon its expiration);

(*5*) The amount of damage that removal of the property would cause to the property itself or to the real property to which it is affixed; and

(*6*) The extent of the effort that would be required to remove the property, in terms of time and expense.

(iv) *Structural components of buildings and other inherently permanent structures.* Structural components of buildings and other inherently permanent structures, as defined in § 1.48-1(e)(2), themselves constitute improvements. Structural components include walls, partitions, floors, ceilings, windows, doors, wiring, plumbing, central heating and central air conditioning systems, lighting fixtures, pipes, ducts, elevators, escalators, sprinkler systems, fire escapes, and other components relating to the operation or maintenance of a building. However, the term "structural components" does not include machinery the sole justification for the installation of which is the fact that such machinery is required to meet temperature or humidity requirements which are essential for the operation of other machinery or the processing of materials or foodstuffs. Machinery may meet the "sole justification" test provided by the preceding sentence even though it incidentally provides for the comfort of employees or serves to an insubstantial degree areas where such temperature or humidity requirements are not essential.

(4) *Personal property associated with the use of the real property*—(i) *In general.* The term "real property" includes movable walls, furnishings, and other personal property associated with the use of the real property. Personal property is associated with the use of real property only if it is described in one of the categories set forth in subdivisions (A) through (D) of this paragraph (b)(4)(i). "Personal property" for purposes of this section means any property that constitutes "tangible personal property" under the principles of § 1.48-1(c), without regard to whether such property qualifies as section 38 property. Such property will be associated with the use of the real property only where both the personal property and the United States real property interest with which it is associated are held by the same person or by related persons within the meaning of § 1.897-1(i). For purposes of this paragraph (b)(4)(i), property is used "predominantly" in a named activity if it is devoted to that activity during at least half of the time in which it is in use during a calendar year.

(A) *Property used in mining, farming, and forestry.* Personal property is associated with the use of real property if it is predominantly used to exploit unsevered natural products in or upon the land. Such property includes mining equipment used to extract ores, minerals, and other natural deposits from the ground. It also includes any property used to cultivate the soil and harvest its products, such as farm machinery, draft animals, and equipment used in the growing and cutting of timber. However, personal property used to process or transport minerals, crops, or

Reg. § 1.897-1(b)(4)

timber after they are severed from the land is not associated personal property.

(B) *Property used in the improvement of real property.* Personal property is associated with the use of real property if it is predominantly used to construct or otherwise carry out improvements to real property. Such property includes equipment used to alter the natural contours of the land, equipment used to clear and prepare raw land for construction, and equipment used to carry out the construction of improvements.

(C) *Property used in the operation of a lodging facility.* Personal property is associated with the use of real property if it is predominantly used in connection with the operation of a lodging facility. Property that is used in connection with the operation of a lodging facility includes property used in the living quarters of such facility, such as beds and other furniture, refrigerators, ranges and other equipment, as well as property used in the common areas of such facility, such as lobby furniture and laundry equipment. Such property constitutes personal property associated with the use of real property in the hands of the owner or operator of the facility, not of the tenant or guest. A lodging facility is an apartment house or apartment, hotel, motel, dormitory, residence, or any other facility (or part of a facility) predominantly used to provide, at a charge, living and/or sleeping accommodations, whether on a daily, weekly, monthly, annual, or other basis. The term "lodging facility" does not include a personal residence occupied solely by its owner, or a facility used primarily as a means of transportation (such as an aircraft, vessel, or a railroad car) or used primarily to provide medical or convalescent services, even though sleeping accommodations are provided. Nor does the term include temporary living quarters provided by an employer due to the unavailability of lodgings within a reasonable distance of a worksite (such as a mine or construction project). The term "lodging facility" does not include any portion of a facility that constitutes a nonlodging commercial facility and that is available to persons not using the lodging facility on the same basis that it is available to tenants of the lodging facility. Examples of nonlodging commercial facilities include restaurants, drug stores, and grocery stores located in a lodging facility.

(D) *Property used in the rental of furnished office and other work space.* Personal property is associated with the use of real property if it is predominantly used by a lessor to provide furnished office or other work space to lessees. Property that is so used includes office furniture and equipment included in the rental of furnished space. Such property constitutes personal property associated with the use of real property in the hands of the lessor, not of the lessee.

(ii) *Dispositions of associated personal property*—(A) *In general.* Personal property that has become associated with the use of a real property interest shall itself be treated as real property interest upon its disposition, unless either:

(*1*) The personal property is disposed of more than one year before the disposition of any present right to use or occupy the real property with which it was associated (and subject to the provisions of subdivision (B) of this paragraph (b)(4)(ii));

(*2*) The personal property is disposed of more than one year after the disposition of all present rights to use or occupy the real property with which it was associated (and subject to the provisions of subdivision (C) of this paragraph (b)(4)(ii)); or

(*3*) The personal property and the real property with which it was associated are separately sold to persons that are related neither to the transferor nor to one another (and subject to the provisions of subdivision (D) of this paragraph (b)(4)(ii)).

(B) *Personalty disposed of one year before realty.* A transferor of personal property associated with the use of real property need not treat such property as a real property interest upon disposition if on the date of disposition the transferor does not expect or intend to dispose of the real property until more than one year later. However, if the real property is in fact disposed of within the following year, the transferor must treat the personal property as having been a real property interest as of the date on which the personalty was disposed of. If the transferor had not previously filed an income tax return, a return must be filed and tax paid, together with any interest due thereon, by the later of the date on which a tax return or payment is actually due (with extensions), or the 60th day following the date of disposition. If the transferor had previously filed an income tax return, an amended return must be filed and tax paid, together with any interest due thereon, by the later of the dates specified above. Such a transferor may be liable to penalties for failure to file, for late payment of tax, or for understatement of liability, but only if the transferor knew or had reason to anticipate that the real property would be disposed of within one year of the disposition of the associated personal property.

(C) *Personalty disposed of one year after realty.* A disposition of real property shall be

Reg. § 1.897-1(b)(4)

disregarded for purposes of subdivision (A) (*2*) of this paragraph (b)(4)(ii) if any right to use or occupy the real property is reacquired within the one-year period referred to in that subdivision. However, the disposition shall not be disregarded if such reacquisition is made in foreclosure of a mortgage or other security interest, in the exercise of a contractual remedy, or in the enforcement of a judgment. If, however, the reacquisition of the property is made pursuant to a plan the principal purpose of which is the avoidance of the provisions of section 897, 1445, or 6039C and the regulations thereunder, then the initial disposition shall be disregarded for purposes of subdivision (A)(*2*) of this paragraph (b)(4)(ii).

(D) *Separate dispositions of personality and realty.* A transferor of personal property associated with the use of real property need not treat such property as a real property interest upon disposition if within 90 days before or after such disposition the transferor separately disposes of the real property interest to persons that are related neither to the transferor nor to the purchaser of the personal property. A transferor may rely upon this rule unless the transferor knows or has reason to know that the purchasers of the real property and the personal property—

(*1*) Are related persons; or

(*2*) Intend to reassociate the personal property with the use of the real property within one year of the date of disposition of the personal property.

(E) *Status of property in hands of transferee.* Personal property that has been associated with the use of real property and that is sold to an unrelated party will be treated as real property in the hands of the transferee only if the personal property becomes associated with the use of real property held or acquired by the transferee, in the manner described in paragraph (b)(4)(i) of this section.

(iii) *Determination dates.* The determination of whether personal property is personal property associated with the use of real property as defined in this paragraph (b)(4) is to be made on the date the personal property is disposed of and on each applicable determination date. See § 1.897-2(c).

(c) *United States real property interest*—(1) *In general.* The term "United States real property interest" means any interest, other than an interest solely as a creditor, in either:

(i) Real property located in the United States or the Virgin Islands, or

(ii) A domestic corporation unless it is established that the corporation was not a U.S. real property holding corporation within the period described in section 897(c)(1)(A)(ii).

In addition, for the limited purpose of determining whether any corporation is a U.S. real property holding corporation, the term "United States real property interest" means an interest, other than an interest solely as a creditor, in a foreign corporation unless it is established that the foreign corporation is not a U.S. real property holding corporation within the period prescribed in section 897(c)(1)(A)(ii). See § 1.897-2 for rules regarding the manner of establishing that a corporation is not a United States real property holding corporation.

(2) *Exceptions and special rules*—(i) *Domestically-controlled REIT.* An interest in a domestically-controlled real estate investment trust (REIT) is not a U.S. real property interest. A domestically-controlled REIT is one in which less than 50 percent of the fair market value of the outstanding stock was directly or indirectly held by foreign persons during the five-year period ending on the applicable determination date (or the period since June 18, 1980, if shorter). For purposes of this determination the actual owners of stock, as determined under § 1.857-8, must be taken into account.

(ii) *Corporation that has disposed of all U.S. real property interests.* The term "United States real property interest" does not include an interest in a corporation which has disposed of all its U.S. real property interests in transactions in which the full amount of gain, if any, was recognized, as provided in section 897(c)(1)(B). See § 1.897-2(f) for rules regarding the requirements of section 897(c)(1)(B).

(iii) *Publicly-traded corporations.* If, at any time during the calendar year, any class of stock of a domestic corporation is regularly traded on an established securities market, an interest in such corporation shall be treated as a U.S. real property interest only in the case of:

(A) A regularly traded interest owned by a person who beneficially owned more than 5 percent of the total fair market value of that class of interests at any time during the five-year period ending either on the date of disposition of such interest or other applicable determination date (or the period since June 18, 1980, if shorter), or

(B) [Reserved]

(iv) *Publicly traded partnerships and trusts.* If any class of interests in a partnership or trust is, within the meaning of § 1.897-1(m) and (n), regularly traded on an established securities market, then for purposes of sections 897(g) and 1445 and § 1.897-2(d) and (e) an interest in the

Reg. § 1.897-1(c)(2)

entity shall not be treated as an interest in a partnership or trust. Instead, such an interest shall be subject to the rules applicable to interests in publicly traded corporations pursuant to paragraph (c)(2)(iii) of this section. Such interests can be real property interests in the hands of a person that holds a greater than 5 percent interest. Therefore, solely for purposes of determining whether greater than 5 percent interests in such an entity constitutes U.S. real property interests the disposition of which is subject to tax, the entity is required to determine pursuant to the provisions of § 1.897-2 whether the assets it holds would cause it to be classified as a U.S. real property holding corporation if it were a corporation. The treatment of dispositions of U.S. real property interests by publicly traded partnerships and trusts is not affected by the rules of this paragraph (c)(2)(iv); by reason of the operation of section 897(a), foreign partners or beneficiaries are subject to tax upon their distributive share of any gain recognized upon such dispositions by the partnership or trust. The rules of this paragraph (c)(2)(iv) are illustrated by the following example.

Example. PTP is a partnership one class of interests in which is regularly traded on an established securities market. A is a nonresident alien individual who owns 1 percent of a class of limited partnership interests in PTP. B is a nonresident alien individual who owns 10 percent of the same class of limited partnership interests in PTP. On July 1, 1986, A and B sell their interests in PTP. Pursuant to the rules of this paragraph (c)(2)(iv), neither disposition is treated as the disposition of a partnership interest subject to the provisions of section 897(g). Instead, A and B are treated as having disposed of interests in a publicly traded corporation. Therefore, pursuant to the rule of paragraph (c)(2)(iii) of this section, A's disposition of a 1 percent interest has no consequences under section 897. However, B's disposition of a 10 percent interest will constitute the disposition of a U.S. real property interest subject to tax by reason of the operation of section 897 unless it is established pursuant to the rules of § 1.897-2 that the interest is not a U.S. real property interest.

(d) *Interest other than an interest solely as a creditor*—(1) *In general.* This paragraph defines an interest other than an interest solely as a creditor, with respect to real property, and with respect to corporations, partnerships, trusts, and estates. An interest solely as a creditor either in real property or in a domestic corporation does not constitute a United States real property interest. Similarly, where one corporation holds an interest solely as a creditor in a second corporation or in a partnership, trust, or estate, that interest will be disregarded for purposes of determining whether the first corporation is a U.S. real property holding corporation (except to the extent that such interest constitutes an asset used or held for use in a trade or business, in accordance with the rules of § 1.897-1(f)). In addition, the disposition of an interest solely as a creditor in a partnership, trust, or estate is not subject to sections 897, 1445, and 6039C. Whether an interest is considered debt under any provisions of the Code is not determinative of whether it constitutes an interest solely as a creditor for purpose of sections 897, 1445, and 6039C and the regulations thereunder.

(2) *Interests in real property other than solely as creditor*—(i) *In general.* An interest in real property other than an interest solely as a creditor includes a fee ownership, co-ownership, or leasehold interest in real property, a time sharing interest in real property, and a life estate, remainder, or reversionary interest in such property. The term also includes any direct or indirect right to share in the appreciation in the value, or in the gross or net proceeds or profits generated by, the real property. A loan to an individual or entity under the terms of which a holder of the indebtedness has any direct or indirect right to share in the appreciation in value of, or the gross or net proceeds or profits generated by, an interest in real property of the debtor or of a related person is, in its entirety, an interest in real property other than solely as a creditor. An interest in production payments described in section 636 does not generally constitute an interest in real property other than solely as a creditor. However, a right to production payments shall constitute an interest in real property other than solely as a creditor if it conveys a right to share in the appreciation in value of the mineral property. A production payment that is limited to a quantum of mineral (including a percentage of recoverable reserves produced) or a period of time will be considered to convey a right to share in the appreciation in value of the mineral property. The rules of this paragraph (d)(2)(i) are illustrated by the following example.

Example. A, a U.S. citizen, purchases a condominium unit located in the United States for $500,000. A makes a $100,000 down payment and borrows $400,000 from B, a foreign person, to pay the balance of the purchase price. Under the terms of the loan, A is to pay B 13 percent annual interest each year for 10 years and 35 percent of the appreciation in the fair market value of the condominium at the end of the 10-year period. Because B has a right to share in the appreciation in value of the condominium, B has an interest other than solely as a creditor in the condominium. B's entire interest in the obligation from A,

Reg. § 1.897-1(d)(1)

therefore, is a United States real property interest.

(ii) *Special rules*—(A) *Installment obligations.* A right to installment or other deferred payments from the disposition of an interest in real property will constitute an interest solely as a creditor if the transferor elects not to have the installment method of section 453(a) apply, any gain or loss is recognized in the year of disposition, and all tax due is timely paid. See section 1445 and regulations thereunder for further guidance concerning the availability of installment sale treatment under section 453. If an agreement for the payment of tax with respect to an installment sale is entered into with the Internal Revenue Service pursuant to section 1445, that agreement may specify whether or not the installment obligation will constitute an interest solely as a creditor. If an installment obligation constitutes an interest other than solely as a creditor then the receipt of each payment shall be treated as the disposition of an interest in real property that is subject to section 897(a) to the extent of any gain required to be taken into account pursuant to section 453. If the original holder of an installment obligation that constitutes an interest other than solely as a creditor subsequently disposes of the obligation to an unrelated party and recognizes gain or loss pursuant to section 453B, the obligation will constitute an interest in real property solely as a creditor in the hands of the subsequent holder. However, if the obligation is disposed of to a related person and the full amount of gain realized upon the disposition of the real property has not been recognized upon such disposition of the installment obligation, then the obligation shall continue to be an interest in real property other than solely as a creditor in the hands of the subsequent holder subject to the rules of this paragraph (d)(2)(ii)(A).

In addition, if the obligation is disposed of to any person for a principal purpose of avoiding the provisions of section 897, 1445, or 6039C, then the obligation shall continue to be an interest in real property other than solely as a creditor in the hands of the subsequent holder subject to the rules of this paragraph (d)(2)(ii)(A). However, rights to payments arising from dispositions that took place before June 19, 1980, shall in no event constitute interests in real property other than solely as a creditor, even if such payments are received after June 18, 1980. In addition, rights to payments arising from dispositions to unrelated parties that took place before January 1, 1985, and that were not subject to U.S. tax pursuant to the provisions of a U.S. income tax treaty, shall not constitute interests in real property other than solely as a creditor, even if such payments are received after December 31, 1984.

(B) *Options.* An option, a contract, or a right of first refusal to acquire any interest in real property (other than an interest solely as a creditor) will itself constitute an interest in real property other than solely as a creditor.

(C) *Security interests.* A right to repossess or foreclose on real property under a mortgage, security agreement, financing statement, or other collateral instrument securing a debt will not be considered a reversionary interest in, or a right to share in the appreciation in value of or gross or net proceeds or profits generated by, an interest in real property. Thus, no such right of repossession or foreclosure will of itself cause an interest in real property which is otherwise an interest solely as a creditor to become an interest other than solely as a creditor. In addition, a person acting as mortgagee in possession shall not be considered to hold an interest in real property other than solely as a creditor, if the mortgagee's interest in the property otherwise constitutes an interest solely as a creditor.

(D) *Indexed interest rates.* An interest will not constitute a right to share in the appreciation in the value of, or gross or net proceeds or profits generated by, real property solely because it bears a rate of interest that is tied to an index of any kind that is intended to reflect general inflation or deflation of prices and interest rates (e.g., the Consumer Price Index). However, where an interest in real property bears a rate of interest that is tied to an index the principal purpose of which is to reflect changes in real property values, the real property interest will be considered an indirect right to share in the appreciation in value of, or gross or net proceeds or profits generated by, real property. Such an indirect right constitutes an interest in real property other than solely as a creditor.

(E) *Commissions.* A right to payment of a commission, brokerage fee, or similar charge for professional services rendered in connection with the arrangement or financing of a purchase, sale, or lease of real property does not constitute a right to share in the appreciation in value of, or gross or net proceeds or profits of, real property solely because it is based upon a percentage of the purchase price or rent. Thus, a right to a commission earned by a real estate agent based on a percentage of the sales price does not constitute an interest in real property other than solely as a creditor. However, a right to a commission, brokerage fee, or similar charge will constitute an interest other than solely as a creditor if the total amount of the payment is contingent upon appre-

Reg. § 1.897-1(d)(2)

ciation, proceeds, or profits of the real property occurring or arising after the date of the transaction with respect to which the professional services were rendered. For example, a commission earned in connection with the purchase of a real property interest that is contingent upon the amount of gain ultimately realized by the purchaser will constitute an interest in real property other than solely as a creditor.

(F) *Trustees' fees, etc.* A right to payment of reasonable compensation for services rendered as a trustee, as an administrator of an estate, or in a similar capacity does not constitute a right to share in the appreciation in the value of, or gross or net proceeds or profits of, real property solely because the assets of the trust or estate include U.S. real property interests.

(3) *Interest in an entity other than solely as a creditor*—(i) *In general.* For purposes of sections 897, 1445, and 6039C, an interest in an entity other than an interest solely as a creditor is—

(A) Stock of a corporation;

(B) An interest in a partnership as a partner within the meaning of section 761(b) and the regulations thereunder;

(C) An interest in a trust or estate as a beneficiary within the meaning of section 643(c) and the regulations thereunder or an ownership interest in any portion of a trust as provided in section 671 through 679 and the regulations thereunder;

(D) An interest which is, in whole or in part, a direct or indirect right to share in the appreciation in value of an interest in an entity described in subdivision (A), (B), or (C) of this paragraph (d)(3)(i) or a direct or indirect right to share in the appreciation in value of assets of, or gross or net proceeds or profits derived by, the entity; or

(E) A right (whether or not presently exercisable) directly or indirectly to acquire, by purchase, conversion, exchange, or in any other manner, an interest described in subdivision (A), (B), (C), or (D) of this paragraph (d)(3)(i).

(ii) *Special rules*—(A) *Installment obligations.* A right to installment or other deferred payments from the disposition of an interest in an entity will constitute an interest solely as a creditor if the transferor elects not to have the installment method of section 453(a) apply, any gain or loss is recognized in the year of disposition, and tax due is timely paid. See section 1445 and regulations thereunder for further guidance concerning the availability of installment sale treatment under section 453. If an agreement for the payment of tax with respect to an installment sale is entered into with the Internal Revenue Service pursuant to section 1445, that agreement may specify whether or not the installment obligation will constitute an interest solely as a creditor. If an installment obligation constitutes an interest other than solely as a creditor then the receipt of each payment shall be treated as the disposition of such an interest and shall be subject to section 897(a) to the extent that: (*1*) It constitutes the disposition of a U.S. real property interest and (*2*) Gain or loss is required to be taken into account pursuant to section 453. Such treatment shall apply to payments arising from dispositions of interests in a corporation any class of the stock of which is regularly traded on an established securities market, but only in the case of a disposition of any portion of an interest described in paragraph (c)(2)(iii)(A) or (B) of this section. If the original holder of an installment obligation that constitutes an interest other than solely as a creditor subsequently disposes of the obligation to an unrelated party and recognizes gain or loss pursuant to section 453B, the obligation will constitute an interest in the entity solely as a creditor in the hands of the subsequent holder. However, if the obligation is disposed of to a related person and the full amount of gain realized upon the disposition of the interest in the entity has not been recognized upon such disposition of the installment obligation, then the obligation shall continue to be an interest in the entity other than solely as a creditor in the hands of the subsequent holder subject to the rules of this paragraph (d)(3)(ii)(A). In addition, if the obligation is disposed of to any person for a principal purpose of avoiding the provisions of section 897, 1445, or 6039C, then the obligation shall continue to be an interest in the entity other than solely as a creditor in the hands of the subsequent holder subject to the rules of this paragraph (d)(3)(ii)(A). However, rights to payments arising from dispositions that took place before June 19, 1980, shall in no event constitute interests in an entity other than solely as a creditor, even if such payments are received after June 18, 1980. In addition, such treatment shall not apply to payments arising from dispositions to unrelated parties that took place before January 1, 1985, and that were not subject to U.S. tax pursuant to the provisions of a U.S. income tax treaty, regardless of when such payments are received.

(B) *Contingent interests.* The interests described in subdivision (D) of paragraph (d)(3)(i) of this section include any right to a payment from an entity the amount of which is contingent on the appreciation in value of an interest described in subdivision (A), (B), or (C) or paragraph (d)(3)(i) of this section or which is

Reg. § 1.897-1(d)(3)

contingent on the appreciation in value of assets of, or the general gross or net proceeds or profits derived by, such entity. The right to such a payment is itself an interest in the entity other than solely as a creditor, regardless of whether the holder of such right actually holds an interest in the entity described in subdivision (A), (B), or (C) of paragraph (d)(3)(i) of this section. For example, a stock appreciation right constitutes an interest in a corporation other than solely as a creditor even if the holder of such right actually holds no stock in the corporation. However, the interests described in subdivision (D) of paragraph (d)(3)(i) of this section do not include any right to a payment that is (*1*) exclusively contingent upon and exclusively paid out of revenues from sales of personal property (whether tangible or intangible) or from services, or (*2*) exclusively contingent upon the resolution of a claim asserted against the entity by a person related neither to the entity nor to the holder of the interest.

(C) *Security interests.* A right to repossess or foreclose on an interest in an entity under a mortgage, security agreement, financing statement, or other collateral instrument securing a debt will not of itself cause an interest in an entity which is otherwise an interest solely as a creditor to become an interest other than solely as a creditor.

(D) *Royalties.* The interests described in subdivision (D) of paragraph (d)(3)(i) of this section do not include rights to payments representing royalties, license fees, or similar charges for the use of patents, inventions, formulas, copyrights, literary, musical or artistic compositions, trademarks, trade names, franchises, licenses, or similar intangible property.

(E) *Commissions.* The interests described in subdivision (D) of paragraph (d)(3)(i) of this section do not include a right to a commission, brokerage fee or similar charge for professional services rendered in connection with the purchase or sale of an interest in an entity. However, a right to such a payment will constitute an interest other than solely as a creditor if the total amount of the payment is contingent upon appreciation in value of assets of, or proceeds or profits derived by, the entity after the date of the transaction with respect to which the payment was earned.

(F) *Trustee's fees.* The interests described in subdivision (D) of paragraph (d)(3)(i) of this section do not include a right to payment representing reasonable compensation for services rendered as a trustee, as an administrator of an estate, or in a similar capacity.

(4) *Aggregation of interests.* If a person holds both interests solely as a creditor and interests other than solely as a creditor in real property or in an entity, those interests will generally be treated as separate and distinct interests. However, such interests shall be aggregated and treated as interests other than solely as a creditor in their entirety if the interest solely as a creditor has been separated from, or acquired separately from, the interest other than solely as a creditor, for a principal purpose of avoiding the provisions of section 897, 1445, or 6039C by causing one or more of such interests to be an interest solely as a creditor. The existence of such a purpose will be determined with reference to all the facts and circumstances. Where an interest solely as a creditor has arm's-length interest and repayment terms it shall in no event be aggregated with and treated as an interest other than solely as a creditor. For purposes of this paragraph (d)(4), an interest rate that does not exceed 120 percent of the applicable Federal rate (as defined in section 1274(d)) shall be presumed to be an arm's-length interest rate. For purposes of applying the rules of this paragraph (d)(4), a person shall be treated as holding any interests held by a related person within the meaning of § 1.897-1(i).

(5) *"Interest" means "interest other than solely as a creditor."* Unless otherwise stated, the term "interest" as used with regard to real property or with regard to an entity hereafter in the regulations under sections 897, 1445, and 6039C, means an interest in such real property or entity other than an interest solely as a creditor.

(e) *Proportionate share of assets held by an entity*—(1) *In general.* A person that holds an interest in an entity is for certain purposes treated as holding a proportionate or pro rata share of the assets held by the entity. Such proportionate share must be calculated, in accordance with the rules of this paragraph, for the following purposes.

(i) In determining whether a corporation is a U.S. real property holding corporation—

(A) A person holding an interest in a partnership, trust, or estate is treated as holding a proportionate share of the assets held by the partnership, trust, or estate (see § 1.897-2(e)(2)), and

(B) A corporation that holds a controlling interest in a second corporation is treated as holding a proportionate share of the assets held by the second corporation (see § 1.897-2(e)(3)).

(ii) In determining reporting obligations that may be imposed under section 6039C, the holder of an interest in a partnership, trust, or estate is treated as owning a proportionate share

Reg. § 1.897-1(e)(1)

of the U.S. real property interests held by the partnership, trust, or estate.

(2) *Proportionate share of assets held by a corporation or partnership*—(i) *In general.* A person's proportionate or pro rata share of assets held by a corporation or partnership is determined by multiplying—

    (A) The person's percentage ownership interest in the entity, by

    (B) The fair market value of the assets held by the entity (or the book value of such assets, in the case of a determination pursuant to § 1.897-2(b)(2)).

   (ii) *Percentage ownership interest.* A person's percentage ownership interest in a corporation or partnership is the percentage equal to the ratio of (A) the sum of the liquidation values of all interests in the entity held by the person to (B) the sum of the liquidation values of all outstanding interests in the entity. The liquidation value of an interest in an entity is the amount of cash and the fair market value of any property that would be distributed with respect to such interest upon the liquidation of the entity after satisfaction of liabilities to persons having interests in the entity solely as creditors. With respect to an entity that has interests outstanding that grant a presently-exercisable option to acquire or right to convert into or otherwise acquire an interest in the entity other than solely as a creditor, the liquidation value of all interests in such entity shall be calculated as though such option or right had been exercised, giving effect both to the payment of any consideration required to exercise the option or right and to the issuance of the additional interest.

The fair market value of the assets of the entity, the amount of cash held by the entity, and the amount of liabilities to persons having interests solely as creditors is determined for this purpose on the date with respect to which the percentage ownership interest is determined.

   (iii) *Examples.* The rules of this paragraph (e)(2) are illustrated by the following examples.

   Example (1). Corporation K's only assets are stock and securities with a fair market value as of the applicable determination date of $20,000,000. K's assets are subject to liabilities of $10,000,000. Among K's liabilities are a $1,000,000 loan from L, under the terms of which L is entitled, upon payment of the loan principal, to a profit share equal to 10 percent of the excess of the fair market value of K's assets over $18,000,000, but only if all other corporate liabilities have been paid. K has two classes of stock, common and preferred. PS1 and PS2 each own 100 of the 200 outstanding shares of preferred stock. CS1 and CS2 each own 500 of the 1,000 outstanding shares of common stock. Each preferred shareholder is entitled to $10,000 per share of preferred stock upon liquidation, subject to payment of all corporate liabilities and to any amount owed to L, but before any common shareholder is paid. The liquidation value of L's interest in K, which constitutes an interest other than an interest solely as a creditor, is $1,200,000 ($1,000,000 principal of the loan to K plus $200,000 (10 percent of the excess of $20,000,000 over $18,000,000). The liquidation value of each of PS1's and PS2's blocks of preferred stock is $1,000,000 ($10,000 times 100 shares each). The liquidation value of each of CS1's and CS2's blocks of common stock is $3,900,000 [$20,000,000 (the total fair market value of K's assets) − $9,000,000 (liabilities to creditors other than L) − $1,200,000 (L's liquidation value) − $2,000,000 (PS1's and PS2's liquidation value)) times 50 percent (the percentage of common stock owned by each)]. The sum of the liquidation values of all of the outstanding interests in K (i.e., interests other than solely as a creditor) is $11,000,000 [$1,200,000 (L's liquidation value) + $2,000,000 (PS1's and PS2's liquidation values) + $7,800,000 (CS1's and CS2's liquidation values)]. Each of CS1's and CS2's percentage ownership interests in K is 35.5 percent ($3,900,000 divided by $11,000,000). Each of PS1's and PS2's percentage ownership interests in K is 9 percent ($1,000,000 divided by $11,000,000). L's percentage ownership interest in K is 11 percent ($1,200,000 divided by $11,000,000).

   Example (2). A, a U.S. person, and B, a foreign person are partners in a partnership the only asset of which is a parcel of undeveloped land located in the United States that was purchased by the partnership in 1980 for $300,000. The partnership has no liabilities, and its capital is $300,000. A's and B's interests in the capital of the partnership are 25 percent and 75 percent, respectively, and A and B each has a 50 percent profit interest in the partnership. The partnership agreement provides that upon liquidation any unrealized gain will be distributed in accordance with the partners' profit interests. In 1984 the partnership has no items of income or deduction, and the fair market value of its parcel of undeveloped land is $500,000. In 1984 the percentage ownership interest of A in the partnership is 35 percent [the ratio of $100,000 (the liquidation value of A's profit interest in 1984) plus $75,000 (the liquidation value of A's 25 percent interest in the partnership's $300,000 capital) to $500,000 (the sum of the liquidation values of all outstanding interests in the partnership)]. The percentage ownership interest of B in the partnership in 1984 is 65 percent [the ratio of $325,000 (B's $100,000 profit interest plus his $225,000 capital interest) to $500,000].

(3) *Proportionate share of assets held by trusts and estates*—(i) *In general.* A person's proportionate or pro rata share of assets held by a trust or estate is determined by multiplying—

(A) The person's percentage ownership interest in the trust or estate, by

(B) The fair market value of the assets held by the trust or estate (or the book value of such assets, in the case of a determination pursuant to § 1.897-2(b)(2)).

(ii) *Percentage ownership interest*—(A) *General rule.* A person's percentage ownership interest in a trust or an estate—is the percentage equal to the ratio of: (*1*) The sum of the actuarial values of such person's interests in the cash and other assets held by the trust or estate after satisfaction of the liabilities of the trust or estate to persons holding interests in the trust or estate solely as creditors, to (*2*) the entire amount of such cash and other assets after satisfaction of liabilities to persons holding interests in the trust or estate solely as creditors. For purposes of calculating this ratio, the fair market value of the trust's or estate's assets, the amount of cash held by the trust or estate, and the amount of the liabilities to persons having interests solely as creditors is determined on the date with respect to which the percentage ownership interest is determined. With respect to a trust or estate that has interests outstanding that grant a presently-exercisable option to acquire or right to convert into or otherwise acquire an interest in the trust or estate other than solely as a creditor, the liquidation value of all interests in such entity shall be calculated as though such option or right had been exercised, giving effect both to the payment of any consideration required to exercise the option or right and to the issuance of the additional interest. With respect to a trust or estate that has interests outstanding that entitle any person to a distribution of U.S. real property interests upon liquidation that is disproportionate to such person's interest in the total assets of the trust or estate, such disproportionate right shall be disregarded in the calculation of the interest-holders' proportionate share of the U.S. real property interests held by the entity. For purposes of determining his own percentage ownership interest in a trust, a grantor or other person will be treated as owning any portion of the trust's cash and other assets which such person is treated as owning under sections 671 through 679.

(B) *Discretionary trusts and estates.* In determining percentage ownership interest in a trust or an estate, the sum of the definitely ascertainable actuarial values of interests in the cash and the other assets of the trust or estate held by persons in existence on the date with respect to which such determination is made must equal the amount in paragraph (e)(3)(ii)(A)(*2*) of this section. If the amount in paragraph (e)(3)(ii)(A)(*2*) of this section exceeds the sum of the definitely ascertainable actuarial values of the interests held by persons in existence on the determination date, the excess will be considered to be owned in total by each beneficiary who is in existence on such date, whose interest in the excess is not definitely ascertainable and who is potentially entitled to such excess. However, such excess shall not be considered to be owned in total by each beneficiary if the discretionary terms of the trust or estate were included for a principal purpose of avoiding the provisions of section 897, 1445, or 6039C by causing assets other than U.S. real property interests to be attributed in total to each beneficiary. The rules of this paragraph (e)(3) are illustrated by the following example.

Example. A, a U.S. person, established a trust on December 31, 1984, and contributed real property with a fair market value of $10,000 to the trust. The terms of that trust provided that the trustee, a bank that is unrelated to A, at its discretion may retain trust income or may distribute it to X, a foreign person, or to the head of state of any country other than the United States. The remainder upon the death of X is to go in equal shares to such of Y and Z, both foreign persons, as survive X. On December 31, 1984, the total value of the trust's assets is $10,000. On the same date, the actuarial values of the remainder interests of Y and Z in the corpus of the trust are definitely ascertainable. They are $1,000 and $500, respectively. Neither the income interest of X nor of the head of state of any country other than the United States has a definitely ascertainable actuarial value on December 31, 1984. The interests of Y and Z in the income portion of the trust similarly have no definitely ascertainable actuarial values on such date since the income may be distributed rather than retained by the trust. Since the sum of the actuarial values of definitely ascertainable interests of persons in existence ($1,500) is less than $10,000, the difference ($8,500) is treated as owned by each beneficiary who is in existence on December 31, 1984, and who is potentially entitled to such excess. Therefore, X, Y, Z, and the head of state of any country other than the United States are each considered as owning the entire $8,500 income interest in the trust. On December 31, 1984, the total actuarial value of X's interest is $8,500, and his percentage ownership interest is 85 percent.

Reg. § 1.897-1(e)(3)

The total actuarial value of Y's interest in the trust is $9,500 ($1,000 plus $8,500), and his percentage ownership interest is 95 percent. The total actuarial value of Z's interest is $9,000 ($500 plus $8,500), and his percentage ownership interest is 90 percent. The actuarial value of the interest of the head of state of each country other than the United States is $8,500, and his percentage ownership interest is 85 percent.

(4) *Dates with respect to which percentage ownership interests are determined.* The dates with respect to which percentage ownership interests are determined are the applicable determination dates outlined in § 1.897-2 or in regulations under section 6039C.

(f) *Asset used or held for use in a trade or business*—(1) *In general.* The term "asset used or held for use in a trade or business" means—

(i) Property, other than a U.S. real property interest, that is—

(A) Stock in trade of an entity or other property of a kind which would properly be included in the inventory of the entity if on hand at the close of the taxable year, or property held by the entity primarily for sale to customers in the ordinary course of its trade or business, or

(B) Depreciable property used or held for use in the trade or business, as described in section 1231(b)(1) but without regard to the holding period limitations of section 1231(b), or

(C) Livestock, including poultry, used or held for use in a trade or business for draft, breeding, dairy, or sporting purposes, and

(ii) Goodwill and going concern value, patents, inventions, formulas, copyrights, literary, musical, or artistic compositions, trademarks, trade names, franchises, licenses, customer lists, and similar intangible property, but only to the extent that such property is used or held for use in the entity's trade or business and subject to the valuation rules of § 1.897-1(o)(4), and

(iii) Cash, stock, securities, receivables of all kinds, options or contracts to acquire any of the foregoing, and options or contracts to acquire commodities, but only to the extent that such assets are used or held for use in the corporation's trade or business and do not constitute U.S. real property interests.

(2) *Used or held for use in a trade or business.* An asset is used or held for use in an entity's trade or business if it is, under the principles of § 1.864-4(c)(2)—

(i) Held for the principal purpose of promoting the present conduct of the trade or business,

(ii) Acquired and held in the ordinary course of the trade or business, as, for example, in the case of an account or note receivable arising from that trade or business (including the performance of services), or

(iii) Otherwise held in a direct relationship to the trade or business.

In determining whether an asset is held in a direct relationship to the trade or business, consideration shall be given to whether the asset is needed in that trade or business. An asset shall be considered to be needed in a trade or business only if the asset is held to meet the present needs of that trade or business and not its anticipated future needs. An asset shall be considered as needed in the trade or business if, for example, the asset is held to meet the operating expenses of that trade or business. Conversely, an asset shall be considered as not needed in the trade or business if, for example, the asset is held for the purpose of providing for future diversification into a new trade or business, future expansion of trade or business activities, future plant replacement, or future business contingencies. An asset that is held to meet reserve or capitalization requirements imposed by applicable law shall be presumed to be held in a direct relationship to the trade or business.

(3) *Special rules concerning liquid assets*—(i) *Safe harbor amount.* Assets described in paragraph (f)(1)(iii) of this section shall be presumed to be used or held for use in a trade or business, in an amount up to 5 percent of the fair market value of other assets used or held for use in the trade or business. However, the rule of this paragraph (f)(3)(i) shall not apply with respect to any assets described in paragraph (f)(1)(iii) of this section that are held or acquired for the principal purpose of avoiding the provisions of section 897 or 1445.

(ii) *Investment companies.* Assets described in paragraph (f)(1)(iii) of this section shall be presumed to be used or held for use in an entity's trade or business if the principal business of the entity is trading or investing in such assets for its own account. An entity's principal business shall be presumed to be trading or investing in assets, described in paragraph (f)(1)(iii) of this section if the fair market value of such assets held by the entity equals or exceeds 90 percent of the sum of the fair market values of the entity's U.S. real property interests, interests in real property located outside the United States, assets otherwise used or held for use in a trade or business, and assets described in paragraph (f)(1)(iii) of this section.

Reg. § 1.897-1(e)(4)

(4) *Examples.* The application of this paragraph (f) may be illustrated by the following examples:

Example (1). M, a domestic corporation engaged in industrial manufacturing, is required to hold a large current cash balance for the purposes of purchasing materials and meeting its payroll. The amount of the cash balance so required varies because of the fluctuating seasonal nature of the corporation's business. In months when large cash balances are not required, the corporation invests the surplus amount in U.S. Treasury bills. Since both the cash and the Treasury bills are held to meet the present needs of the business, they are held in a direct relationship to that business, and, therefore, constitute assets used or held for use in the trade or business.

Example (2). R, a domestic corporation engaged in the manufacture of goods, engages a stock brokerage firm to manage securities which were purchased with funds from R's general surplus reserves. The funds invested in these securities are intended to provide for the future expansion of R into a new trade or business. Thus, the funds are not necessary for the present needs of the business; they are accordingly not held in a direct relationship to the business and do not constitute assets used or held for use in the trade or business.

Example (3). B, a federally chartered and regulated bank, is required by law to hold substantial reserves of cash, stock, and securities. Pursuant to the rule of paragraph (f)(2) of this section, such assets are presumed to be held in a direct relationship to B's business, and thus constitute assets used or held for use in the trade or business. In addition, B holds substantial loan receivables which are acquired and held in the ordinary course of its banking business. Pursuant to the rule of paragraph (f)(1)(iii) of this section, such receivables constitute assets used or held for use in the trade or business.

(g) *Disposition:* For purposes of sections 897, 1445, and 6039C, the term "disposition" means any transfer that would constitute a disposition by the transferor for any purpose of the Internal Revenue Code and regulations thereunder. The severance of crops or timber and the extraction of minerals do not alone constitute the disposition of a U.S. real property interest.

(h) *Gain or loss,* the amount of gain or loss arising from the disposition of the U.S. real property interest shall be determined as provided in section 1001(a) and (b). Such gain or loss shall be subject to the provisions of section 897(a) and (b), unless a nonrecognition provision is applicable pursuant to section 897(d) or (e) and regulations thereunder. Amounts otherwise treated for Federal income tax purposes as principal and interest payments on debt obligations of all kinds (including obligations that are interests other than solely as a creditor) do not give rise to gain or loss that is subject to section 897(a). However, principal payments on installment obligations described in §§ 1.897-1(d)(2)(ii)(A) and 1.897-1(d)(3)(ii)(A) do give rise to gain or loss that is subject to section 897(a), to the extent such gain or loss is required to be recognized pursuant to section 453. The rules of paragraphs (g) and (h) are illustrated by the following examples.

Example (1). Foreign individual C has an undivided fee interest in a parcel of real property located in the United States. The fair market value of C's interest is $70,000, and C's basis in such interest is $50,000. The only liability to which the real property is subject is the liability of $65,000 secured by a mortgage in the same amount. C transfers his fee interest in the property subject to the mortgage by gift to D. C realizes $15,000 of gain upon such transfer. As a transfer by gift constitutes a disposition for purposes of the Code, and as gain is realized upon that transfer, the gift is a disposition for purposes of sections 897, 1445, and 6039C and is subject to section 897(a) to the extent of the gain realized. However, section 897(a) would not be applicable to the transfer if the mortgage on the U.S. real property were equal to or less than C's $50,000 basis, since the transfer then would not give rise to the realization of gain or loss under the Internal Revenue Code.

Example (2). Foreign corporation Y makes a loan of $1 million to domestic individual Z, secured by a mortgage on residential real property purchased with the loan proceeds. The loan agreement provides that Y is entitled to receive fixed monthly payments from Z, constituting repayment of principal plus interest at a fixed rate. In addition, the agreement provides that Y is entitled to receive a percentage of the appreciation in value of the real property as of the time that the loan is retired. The obligation in its entirety is considered debt for Federal income tax purposes. However, because of Y's right to share in the appreciation in value of the real property, the debt obligation gives Y an interest in the real property other than solely as a creditor. Nevertheless, as principal and interest payments do not constitute gain under section 1001 and paragraph (h) of this section, and both the monthly and final payments received by Y are considered to consist solely of principal and interest for Federal income tax purposes, section 897(a) shall not apply to Y's receipt of such payments. However, Y's sale of the

Reg. § 1.897-1(h)

debt obligation to foreign corporation A would give rise to gain that is subject to section 897(a).

(i) *Related person.* For purposes of sections 897, 1445, and 6039C, persons are considered to be related if they are partners or partnerships described in section 707(b)(1) of the Code or if they are related within the meaning of section 267(b) and (c) of the Code (except that section 267(f) shall apply without regard to section 1563(b)(2)).

(j) *Domestic corporation.* The term "domestic corporation" has the same meaning as set forth in section 7701(a)(3) and (4) and § 301.7701-5. For purposes of sections 897 and 6039C, it also includes a foreign corporation with respect to which an election under section 897(i) and § 1.897-3 or section 897(k) and § 1.897-4 to be treated as domestic corporation is in effect.

(k) *Foreign person.* [Reserved]

(l) *Foreign corporation.* The term "foreign corporation" has the meaning ascribed to such term in section 7701(a)(3) and (5) and § 301.7701-5. For purposes of sections 897 and 6039C, however, the term does not include a foreign corporation with respect to which there is in effect an election under section 897(i) and § 1.897-3 or section 897(k) and § 1.897-4 to be treated as a domestic corporation.

(m) *Established securities market.* For purposes of sections 897, 1445, and 6039C, the term "established securities market" means—

(1) A national securities exchange which is registered under section 6 of the Securities Exchange Act of 1934 (15 U.S.C. 78f);

(2) A foreign national securities exchange which is officially recognized, sanctioned, or supervised by governmental authority, and

(3) Any over-the-counter market.

An over-the-counter market is any market reflected by the existence of an interdealer quotation system. An interdealer quotation system is any system of general circulation to brokers and dealers which regularly disseminates quotations of stocks and securities by identified brokers or dealers, other than by quotation sheets which are prepared and distributed by a broker or dealer in the regular course of business and which contain only quotations of such broker or dealer.

(n) *Regularly traded.* [Reserved]

(o) *Fair market value*—(1) *In general.* For purposes of sections 897, 1445, and 6039C only, the term "fair market value" means the value of the property determined in accordance with the rules, contained in this paragraph (o). The definition of fair market value provided herein is not to be used in the calculation of gain or loss from the disposition of a U.S. real property interest pursuant to section 1001. An independent professional appraisal of the value of property must be submitted only if such an appraisal is specifically requested in connection with the negotiation of a security agreement pursuant to section 1445.

(2) *Method of calculating fair market value*—(i) *In general.* The fair market value of property is its gross value (as defined in paragraph (o)(2)(ii) of this section) reduced by the outstanding balance of any debts secured by the property which are described in paragraph (o)(2)(iii) of this section. See § 1.897-2(b) for the alternative use of book values in certain limited circumstances.

(ii) *Gross value.* Gross value is the price at which the property would change hands between an unrelated willing buyer and willing seller, neither being under any compulsion to buy or sell and both having reasonable knowledge of all relevant facts. Generally, with respect to trade or business assets, going concern value should be used as it will provide the most accurate reflection of such a price. However, taxpayers may use other methods of valuation if they can establish that such method will provide a more accurate determination of gross value and if they consistently apply such method to all assets to be valued. See subdivisions (3) and (4) of this paragraph (o) for special rules with respect to the valuation of leases and of intangible assets.

(iii) *Debts secured by the property.* The gross value of property shall be reduced by the outstanding balance of debts that are:

(A) Secured by a mortgage or other security interest in the property that is valid and enforceable under the law of the jurisdiction in which the property is located, and

(B) Either (*1*) incurred to acquire the property (including long-term financing obtained in replacement of construction loans or other short-term debt within one year of the acquisition or completion of the property), or (*2*) otherwise incurred in direct connection with the property, such as property tax liens upon real property or debts incurred to maintain or improve property.

In addition, if any debt described in this paragraph (o)(2)(iii) is refinanced for a valid business purpose (such as obtaining a more favorable rate of interest), the principal amount of the replacement debt does not exceed the outstanding balance of the original debt, and the replacement debt is secured by the property, then the gross value of the property shall be reduced by the replacement debt. Obligations to related persons shall not be taken into account for purposes of this paragraph (o)(2)(iii) unless such obligations constitute interests, solely as a creditor pursuant to

Reg. § 1.897-1(i)

the provisions of paragraph (d)(4) of this section and unless the related person has made similar loans to unrelated persons on similar terms and conditions.

(iv) *Anti-abuse rule.* The gross value of real property located outside the United States and of assets used or held for use in a trade or business shall be reduced by the outstanding balance of any debt that was entered into for the principal purpose of avoiding the provisions of section 897, 1445, or 6039C by enabling the corporation to acquire such assets. The existence of such a purpose shall be determined with reference to all the facts and circumstances. Debts that a particular corporation routinely enters into the ordinary course of its acquisition of assets used or held for use in its trade or business will not be considered to be entered into for the principal purpose of avoiding the provisions of section 897, 1445, or 6039C.

(3) *Fair market value of leases and options.* For purposes of sections 897, 1445, and 6039C, the fair market value of a leasehold interest in real property is the price at which the lease could be assigned or the property sublet, neither party to such transaction being under any compulsion to enter into the transaction and both having reasonable knowledge of all relevant facts. Thus, the value of a leasehold interest will generally consist of the present value, over the period of the lease remaining, of the difference between the rental provided for in the lease and the current rental value of the real property. A leasehold interest bearing restrictions on its assignment or sublease has a fair market value of zero, but only if those restrictions in practical effect preclude (rather than merely condition) the lessee's ability to transfer, at a gain, the benefits of a favorable lease. The normal commercial practice of lessors may be used to determine whether restrictions in a lease have the practical effect of precluding transfer at a gain. The fair market value of an option to purchase any property is, similarly, the price at which the option could be sold, consisting generally of the difference between the option price and the fair market value of the property, taking proper account of any restrictions upon the transfer of the option.

(4) *Fair market value of intangible assets.* For purposes of determining whether a corporation is a U.S. real property holding corporation, the fair market value of intangible assets described in § 1.897-1(f)(1)(ii) may be determined in accordance with the following rules.

(i) *Purchase price.* Intangible assets described in § 1.897-1(f)(1)(ii) that were acquired by purchase from a person not related to the purchaser within the meaning of § 1.897-1(i) may be valued at their purchase price. However, such purchase price must be adjusted to reflect any amortization required by generally accepted accounting principles applied in the United States. Intangible assets acquired by purchase shall include any amounts allocated to goodwill or going concern value pursuant to section 338(b)(3) and regulations thereunder. Intangible assets acquired by purchase shall not include assets that were acquired indirectly through an acquisition of stock to which section 338 does not apply. Such assets must be valued pursuant to a method described in subdivision (ii) or (iii) of this paragraph (o)(4).

(ii) *Book value.* Intangible assets described in § 1.897-1(f)(1)(ii) (other than goodwill and going concern value) may be valued at the amount at which such assets are carried on the financial accounting records of the holder of such assets, provided that such amount is determined in accordance with generally accepted accounting principles applied in the United States. However, this method may not be used with respect to assets acquired by purchase from a related person within the meaning of § 1.897-1(i).

(iii) *Other methods.* Intangible assets described in § 1.897-1(f)(1)(ii) may be valued pursuant to any other reasonable method at an amount reflecting the price at which the asset would change hands between an unrelated willing buyer and willing seller, neither being under any compulsion to buy or to sell and both having reasonable knowledge of all relevant facts. However, a corporation that uses a method of valuation other than the purchase price or book value methods may be required to comply with the special notification requirements of § 1.897-2(h)(1)(iii)(A).

(p) *Identifying number.* The "identifying number" of an individual is the individual's United States social security number. The "identifying number" of any other person is its United States employer identification number. [Reg. § 1.897-1.]

☐ [*T.D.* 7999, 12-26-84. *Amended by T.D.* 8113, 12-18-86; *T.D.* 8198, 5-4-88 *and T.D.* 8657, 3-5-96.]

[Reg. § 1.897-2]

§ 1.897-2. **United States real property holding corporations.**—(a) *Purpose and scope.* This section provides rules regarding the definition and consequences of U.S. real property holding corporation status. U.S. real property holding corporation status is important for determining whether gain from the disposition by a foreign person of an interest in a domestic corporation is taxable. Such status is also important for purposes of the withholding and reporting requirements of sections 1445 and 6039C. For example, a person that buys stock of a U.S. real property holding corporation from a foreign person is required to withhold under section 1445. In addition, for purposes of determining whether another corporation is a U.S. real property holding corporation, an interest in a foreign corporation is a U.S. real property interest unless it is established that the foreign corporation is not a U.S. real property holding corporation. The general definition of a U.S. real property holding corporation is provided in paragraph (b) of this section. Paragraph (c) provides rules regarding the dates on which U.S. real property holding corporation status must be determined. The assets that must be included in making the determination of a corporation's status are set forth in paragraph (d), while paragraph (e) provides special rules regarding the treatment of interests held by a corporation in partnerships, trusts, estates, and other corporations. Rules regarding the termination of U.S. real property holding corporation status are set forth in paragraph (f). Paragraph (g) explains the manner in which an interest-holder can establish that a corporation is not a U.S. real property holding corporation, and paragraph (h) provides rules regarding certain notification requirements applicable to corporations.

(b) *U.S. real property holding corporation*—(1) *In general.* A corporation is a U.S. real property holding corporation if the fair market value of the U.S. real property interests held by the corporation on any applicable determination date equals or exceeds 50 percent of the sum of the fair market values of its—

(i) U.S. real property interests;

(ii) Interests in real property located outside the United States; and

(iii) Assets other than those described in subdivision (i) or (ii) of this paragraph (b)(1) that are used or held for use in its trade or business.

See paragraphs (d) and (e) of this section for rules regarding the directly and indirectly held assets that must be included in the determination of whether a corporation is a U.S. real property holding corporation. The term "interest in real property located outside the United States" means an interest other than solely as a creditor (as defined in § 1.897-1(d)) in real property (as defined in § 1.897-1(b)) that is located outside the United States or the Virgin Islands. If a corporation qualifies as a U.S. real property holding corporation on any applicable determination date after June 18, 1980, any interest in it shall be treated as a U.S. real property interest for a period of five years from that date, unless the provisions of paragraph (f)(2) of this section are applicable.

(2) *Alternative test*—(i) *In general.* The fair market value of a corporation's U.S. real property interests shall be presumed to be less than 50 percent of the fair market value of the aggregate of its assets described in paragraphs (d) and (e) of this section if on an applicable determination date the total book value of the U.S. real property interests held by the corporation is 25 percent or less of the book value of the aggregate of the corporation's assets described in paragraphs (d) and (e) of this section.

(ii) *Definition of book value.* For purposes of this section and § 1.897-1(e) the term "book value" shall be defined as follows. In the case of assets that are held directly by the corporation, the term means the value at which an item is carried on the financial accounting records of the corporation, if such value is determined in accordance with generally accepted accounting principles applied in the United States. In the case of assets of which a corporation is treated as holding a pro rata share pursuant to paragraphs (e)(2) and (3) of this section and § 1.897-1(e), the term "book value" means the corporation's share of the value at which the asset is carried on the financial accounting records of the entity that directly holds the asset, if such value is determined in accordance with generally accepted accounting principles applied in the United States. For purposes of this paragraph (b)(2)(ii), an entity need not keep all of its books in accordance with U.S. accounting principles, so long as the value of the relevant assets is determined in accordance therewith.

(iii) *Denial of presumption.* If the Internal Revenue Service determines, on the basis of information as to the fair market values of a corporation's assets, that the presumption allowed by this paragraph (b)(2) may not accurately reflect the status of the corporation, the Service will notify the corporation that it may not rely upon the presumption. The Service will provide a written notice to the corporation that sets forth the general grounds for the Service's conclusion that the presumption may be inaccurate. By the 90th day following the date on which the corporation receives the Service's notification, the corporation must determine whether on its most recent determination date it was a U.S. real property holding corporation pursuant to the general rule set forth in paragraph (b)(1) of this section and must notify the Service of its determination. If the corporation determines that it was not a U.S. real property holding corporation pursuant to the general rule, then the corporation may upon future

Reg. § 1.897-2(b)(1)

determination dates rely upon the presumption allowed by this paragraph (b)(2), unless on the basis of additional information the Service again requests that the determination be made pursuant to the general rule. If the corporation determines that it was a U.S. real property holding corporation on its most recent determination date, then by the 180th day following the date on which the corporation received the Service's notification the corporation (if a domestic corporation) must notify each holder of an interest in it that contrary to any prior representations it was a U.S. real property holding corporation as of its most recent determination date.

(iv) *Applicability of penalties.* A corporation that had previously relied upon the presumption allowed by this paragraph (b)(2) but that is determined to be a U.S. real property holding corporation shall not be subject to penalties for any incorrect notice previously given pursuant to the requirements of paragraph (h) of this section, if:

(A) The corporation in fact carried out the necessary calculations enabling it to rely upon the presumption allowed by this paragraph (b)(2); and

(B) The corporation complies with the provisions of paragraph (b)(2)(iii) of this section.

However, a corporation shall remain subject to any applicable penalties if at the time of its reliance on the presumption allowed by this paragraph (b)(2) the corporation knew that the book values of relevant assets was substantially higher or lower than the fair market value of those assets and therefore had reason to believe that under the general test of paragraph (b)(1) of this section the corporation would probably be a U.S. real property holding corporation. Information with respect to the fair market value of its assets is known by a corporation if such information is included on any books and records of the corporation or its agent, is known by its directors or officers, or is known by employees who in the course of their employment have reason to know such information. A corporation relying upon the presumption allowed by this paragraph (b)(2) has no affirmative duty to determine the fair market value of assets if such values are not otherwise known to it in accordance with the preceding sentence. The rules of this paragraph (b)(2)(iv) may be illustrated by the following examples.

Example 1. DC is a domestic corporation engaged in light manufacturing that knows that it has foreign shareholders. On its December 31, 1985 determination date DC held assets used in its trade or business, consisting largely of recently-purchased equipment, with a book value of $500,000. DC's only real property interest was a factory that it had occupied for over 50 years, which had a book value of $200,000. The factory was located in a deteriorated downtown area, and DC had no knowledge of any facts indicating that the fair market value of the property was substantially higher than its book value. Therefore, DC was entitled to rely upon the presumption allowed by § 1.897-2(b)(2) and any incorrect statement pursuant to § 1.897-2(h) that arose out of such reliance would not give rise to penalties.

Example 2. The facts are the same as in Example 1, except as follows. By the time of DC's December 31, 1989 determination date, the downtown area in which DC's factory was located had become the subject of an extensive urban renewal program. On December 1, 1989, the president of DC was offered $750,000 for the factory by a developer who planned to convert the property into condominiums. Because DC thus had knowledge of the fair market value of its assets which made it clear that the corporation would probably be a U.S. real property holding corporation under the general rule of § 1.897-2(b)(1), DC was not entitled to rely upon the presumption allowed by § 1.897-2(b)(2) after December 1, 1989, and any false statements arising out of such reliance thereafter would give rise to penalties.

(v) *Effect on interestholders and related persons.* For the effect on interestholders and related persons of reliance on a statement issued by a corporation that made a determination as to whether it was a U.S. real property holding corporation under the provisions of § 1.897-2(b), see § 1.897-2(g)(1)(ii)(A) and 1.897-2(g)(2)(ii).

(c) *Determination dates for applying U.S. real property holding corporation test* —(1) *In general.* Whether a corporation is a U.S. real property holding corporation is to be determined as of the following dates:

(i) The last day of the corporation's taxable year;

(ii) The date on which the corporation acquires any U.S. real property interest;

(iii) The date on which the corporation disposes of an interest in real property located outside the United States or disposes of other assets used or held for use in a trade or business during the calendar year, subject to the provisions of paragraph (c)(2)(i) of this section; and

(iv) In the case of a corporation that is treated pursuant to paragraph (d)(4) or (5) of this section as owning a portion of the assets held by an entity in which the corporation directly or indirectly holds an interest, the date on which that entity either (A) acquires a U.S. real property interest, (B) disposes of an interest in real

Reg. § 1.897-2(c)(1)

property located outside the United States or (C) disposes of other assets used or held for use in a trade or business during the calendar year, subject to the provisions of paragraph (c)(2)(ii) of this section. A determination that is triggered by a transaction described in subdivision (ii), (iii), or (iv) of this paragraph (c)(1) must take such transaction into account. However, the first determination of a corporation's status need not be made until the 120th day after the later of the date of incorporation or of the date on which the corporation first acquires a shareholder. In addition, no determination of a corporation's status need be made during the 12-month period beginning on the date on which a corporation adopts a plan of complete liquidation, provided that all the assets of the corporation (other than assets retained to meet claims) are distributed within such period.

(2) *Transactions not requiring a determination*—(i) *Transactions by corporation.* Notwithstanding the provisions of paragraph (c)(1) of this section, a determination of U.S. real property holding corporation status need not be made on the date of:

(A) A corporation's disposition of inventory or livestock (as described in § 1.897-1(f)(1)(i)(A) and (C));

(B) The satisfaction of accounts receivable arising from the disposition of inventory or livestock or from the performance of services;

(C) The disbursement of cash to meet the regular operating needs of the business (e.g., to acquire inventory or to pay wages and salaries);

(D) A corporation's disposition of assets used or held for use in a trade or business (other than inventory or livestock) not in excess of a limitation amount determined in accordance with the rules of subdivision (iii) of this paragraph (c)(2); or

(E) A corporation's acquisition of U.S. real property interests not in excess of a limitation amount determined in accordance with the rules of subdivision (iii) of this paragraph (c)(2).

(ii) *Transactions by entity other than corporation.* Notwithstanding the provisions of paragraph (c)(1)(iv) or (c)(2)(v) of this section, in the case of a corporation that is treated as owning a portion of the assets held by an entity in which the corporation directly or indirectly holds an interest, a determination of U.S. real property holding corporation status need not be made on the date of:

(A) The entity's disposition of inventory or livestock (as described in § 1.897-1(f)(1)(i)(A) and (C));

(B) The satisfaction of accounts receivable arising from the entity's disposition of inventory or livestock or from the performance of personal services;

(C) The entity's disbursement of cash to meet the regular operating needs of its business (e.g. to acquire inventory or to pay wages and salaries);

(D) The entity's disposition of assets used or held for use in a trade or business (other than inventory or livestock) not in excess of a limitation amount determined in accordance with the rules of subdivision (iii) of this paragraph (c)(2); or

(E) The entity's acquisition of U.S. real property interests not in excess of a limitation amount determined in accordance with the rules of subdivision (iii) of this paragraph (c)(2).

(iii) *Calculation of limitation amount.* The amount of assets used or held for use in a trade or business that may be disposed of, and the amount of U.S. real property interests that may be acquired, by a corporation or other entity without triggering a determination date shall be calculated in accordance with the following rules.

(A) If, in accordance with the provisions of paragraphs (d) and (e) of this section, a corporation on its most recent determination date was considered to hold U.S. real property interests having a fair market value that was less than 25 percent of the aggregate fair market value of all the assets it was considered to hold, then the applicable limitation amount shall be 10 percent of the fair market value of all trade or business assets or all U.S. real property interests (as applicable) held directly by the corporation or by another entity described in paragraph (c)(1)(iv) of this section on that determination date.

(B) If, in accordance with the provisions of paragraphs (d) and (e) of this section, a corporation on its most recent determination date was considered to hold U.S. real property interests having a fair market value that was equal to or greater than 25 and less than 35 percent of the aggregate fair market value of all the assets it was considered to hold, then the applicable limitation amount shall be 5 percent of the fair market value of all trade or business assets or all U.S. real property interests (as applicable) held directly by the corporation or by another entity described in paragraph (c)(1)(iv) of this section on that determination date.

(C) If, in accordance with the provisions of paragraphs (d) and (e) of this section, a corporation on its most recent determination date was considered to hold U.S. real property interests having a fair market value that was equal to or

Reg. § 1.897-2(c)(2)

greater than 35 percent of the aggregate fair market value of all the assets it was considered to hold, then the applicable limitation amount shall be 2 percent of the fair market value of all trade or business assets or all U.S. real property interests (as applicable) held directly by the corporation or by another entity described in paragraph (c)(1)(iv) of this section on that determination date.

(D) If a corporation is not a U.S. real property holding corporation under the alternative test of paragraph (b)(2) of this section (relating to the book value of the corporation's assets), then the applicable limitation shall be 10 percent of the book value of all trade or business assets or all U.S. real property interests (as applicable) held directly by the corporation or by another entity described in paragraph (c)(1)(iv) of this section on the most recent determination date.

Dispositions or acquisitions by the corporation or other entity of assets having a value less than the applicable limitation amount must be cumulated by the corporation or entity making such dispositions or acquisitions, and a determination must be made on the date of a transaction that causes the total of either type to exceed the applicable limitation. Once a determination is triggered by a transaction that causes the applicable limitation to be exceeded, the computation of the amount of trade or business assets disposed of or real property interests acquired after that date shall begin again at zero.

The rules of this paragraph (c)(2) may be illustrated by the following examples.

Example (1). DC is a domestic corporation, no class of stock of which is regularly traded on an established securities market, that knows that it has several foreign shareholders. As of December 31, 1984, DC holds U.S. real property interests with a fair market value of $500,000, no real property interests located outside the U.S., and other assets used in its trade or business with a fair market value of $1,600,000. Thus, the fair market value of DC's U.S. real property interests ($500,000) is less than 25% ($525,000) of the total ($2,100,000) of DC's U.S. real property interests ($500,000), interests in real property located outside the United States (zero), and assets used or held for use in a trade or business ($1,600,000). DC is not a U.S. real property holding corporation, and under the rule of paragraph (c)(2)(i) of this section it may dispose of trade or business assets with a fair market value equal to 10 percent ($160,000) of the total fair market value ($1,600,000) of such assets held by it on its most recent determination date (December 31, 1984), without triggering a determination of its U.S. real property holding corporation status. Therefore, when DC disposes of $60,000 worth of trade or business assets (other than inventory or livestock) on March 1, 1985, and again on April 1, 1985, no determination of its status is required on either date. However, when DC disposes of a further $60,000 worth of such trade or business assets on May 1, its total disposition of such assets ($180,000) exceeds its applicable limitation amount, and DC is therefore required to determine its U.S. real property holding corporation status. On May 1, 1985, the fair market value of DC's U.S. real property interests ($500,000) is greater than 25 percent or ($480,000) and less than 35 percent ($672,000) of the total ($1,920,000) of DC's U.S. real property interests ($500,000), interests in real property located outside the United States (zero), and assets used or held for use in a trade or business ($1,420,000). DC is still not a U.S. real property holding corporation, but must now compute its applicable limitation amount as of the May 1 determination date. Under the rule of paragraph (c)(2)(iii)(B) of this section, DC could now dispose of trade or business assets other than inventory or livestock with a total fair market value equal to 5 percent of the fair market value of all trade or business assets held by DC on the May 1 determination date. Therefore, disposition of such trade or business assets with a fair market value of more than $71,000 (5 percent of $1,420,000) will trigger a further determination date for DC.

Example (2). DC is a domestic corporation, no class of stock of which is regularly traded on an established securities market, that knows that it has several foreign shareholders. As of December 31, 1986, DC's only assets are a U.S. real property interest with a fair market value of $300,000 other assets used or held for use in its trade or business with a fair market value of $600,000, and a 50 percent partnership interest in domestic partnership DP. DC's interest in DP constitutes a percentage ownership interest in the partnership of 50 percent, and pursuant to the rules of paragraph (e)(2) of this section DC is treated as owning a portion of the assets of DP determined by multiplying that percentage by the fair market value of DP's assets. As of December 31, 1986, DP's only assets are U.S. real property interests with a fair market value of $120,000 and other assets used in its trade or business with a fair market value of $380,000. As of its December 31, 1986, determination date, the fair market value ($360,000) of the U.S. real property interests DC holds ($300,000) and is treated as holding ($60,000 [The fair market value of DP's U.S. real property interest ($120,000) multiplied by DC's percentage ownership interest in DP (50 per-

Reg. § 1.897-2(c)(2)

cent)]), is equal to 31 percent of the sum of the fair market values ($1,150,000) of the U.S. real property interests DC holds and is treated as holding ($360,000) DC's interest in real property located outside the United States (zero), and assets used or held for use in a trade or business that DC holds or is treated as holding ($790,000 [$600,000 (held directly) plus $190,000 (DC's 50 percent share of assets used or held for use in a trade or business by DP)]). Thus, under the rules of paragraph (c)(2)(i) and (iii)(B) of this section DC may dispose of assets used or held for use in its trade or business with a fair market value equal to 5 percent ($30,000) of the total fair market value ($600,000) of such assets held directly by it on its most recent determination date (December 31, 1986), without triggering a determination of its U.S. real property holding corporation status. In addition, under the rules of paragraph (c)(2)(ii) and (iii)(A) of this section, a determination date for DC would not be triggered by DP's disposition of trade or business assets (other than inventory or livestock) with a fair market value equal to 5 percent ($19,000) of the total fair market value ($380,000) of such assets held by it as of DC's most recent determination date (December 31, 1986). However, any disposition of such assets by DP exceeding that limitation would trigger a determination of DC's U.S. real property holding corporation status. In addition, under the rule of paragraph (c)(1)(iv) of this section, any disposition of a U.S. real property interest by DP would trigger a determination date for DC, while under the rule of paragraph (c)(2)(ii) of this section no disposition of inventory or livestock by DP would trigger a determination for DC.

(3) *Alternative monthly determination dates*—(i) *In general.* Notwithstanding the provisions of paragraph (c)(1) and (2) of this section, a corporation may choose to determine its U.S. real property holding corporation status in accordance with the rules of this paragraph (c)(3). In the case of a corporation that has determined that it is not a U.S. real property holding corporation pursuant to the alternative test of paragraph (b)(2) of this section (relating to the book value of the corporation's assets), the rules of this paragraph (c)(3) may be applied by using book values rather than fair market values in all relevant calculations.

(ii) *Monthly determinations.* A corporation that determines its U.S. real property holding corporation status in accordance with the rules of this paragraph (c)(3) must make a determination at the end of each calendar month.

(iii) *Transactional determinations.* A corporation that determines its U.S. real property holding corporation status in accordance with the rules of this paragraph (c)(3) must make a determination as of the date on which, pursuant to a single transaction (consisting of one or more transfers):

(A) U.S. real property interests are acquired, and/or

(B) Interests in real property located outside the U.S. and/or assets used or held for use in a trade or business are disposed of,

if the total fair market value of the assets acquired and/or disposed of exceeds 5 percent of the sum of the fair market values of the U.S. real property interests, interests in real property located outside the U.S., and assets used or held for use in a trade or business held by the corporation.

(iv) *Exceptions.* Notwithstanding any other provision of this paragraph (c)(3), the first determination of a corporation's status need not be made until the 120th day after the later of the date of incorporation or the date on which the corporation first acquires a shareholder. In addition, no determination of a corporation's status need be made during the 12-month period beginning on the date on which a corporation adopts a plan of complete liquidation, if all the assets of the corporation (other than assets retained to meet claims) are distributed within such period.

(4) *Valuation date methods*—(i) *In general.* For purposes of determining whether a corporation is a U.S. real property holding corporation on any applicable determination date, the fair market value of the assets held by the corporation (in accordance with § 1.897-2(d)) as of that determination date must be used.

(ii) *Alternative valuation date method for determination dates other than the last day of the taxable year.* For purposes of paragraph (c)(4)(i) of this section, if an applicable determination date under paragraph (c)(1), (2), or (3) of this section is other than the last day of the taxable year, property may be valued as of the later of the last day of the previous taxable year or the date such property was acquired. For purposes of the determination date that falls on the last day of the taxable year, fair market value as of that date must always be used.

(iii) *Consistent methods.* The valuation date method selected under this paragraph (c)(4) for the first determination date in a taxable year must be used for all subsequent determination dates for such year. In addition, the valuation date method selected must be used for all property with respect to which the determination is made. The use of one method for one taxable year does not preclude the use of the other method for any other taxable year.

Reg. § 1.897-2(c)(3)

Nonresident Aliens and Foreign Corporations

See p. 20,601 for regulations not amended to reflect law changes

(5) *Illustrations.* The rules of this paragraph (c) are illustrated by the following examples:

Example (1). Nonresident alien individual C purchased 100 shares of stock of domestic corporation K on July 26, 1985. Although K has additional shares of common stock outstanding, its stock has never been traded on an established securities market. At all times during calendar year 1985, K's only assets were a parcel of U.S. real estate (parcel A) and a parcel of country Z real estate (parcel B). On December 31, 1985, the fair market value of parcel A was $1,000,000 and the fair market value of parcel B was $2,000,000. For purposes of determining whether K was a U.S. real property holding corporation during 1985, the only applicable determination date was December 31, 1985, because K did not make any acquisitions or dispositions described in paragraph (c)(1) of this section during the year. The test of paragraph (b) of this section is applied using the fair market value of the property held on that date. K was not a U.S. real property holding corporation during 1985 because as of December 31, 1985, the fair market value ($1,000,000) of the U.S. real property interests held by K did not equal or exceed 50 percent ($1,500,000) of the sum ($3,000,000) of the fair market value of K's U.S. real property interest ($1,000,000), the interests in real property located outside the United States ($2,000,000), plus other assets used or held for use by K in a trade or business (zero).

Example (2). The facts are the same as in example (1), except that on April 7, 1986, K purchased another parcel of U.S. real estate for $2,000,000. K's purchase of real property on April 7 triggered a determination on that date. As provided in paragraph (c)(3)(ii) of this section, K chooses to use the value of parcels A and B as of the previous December 31, while newly acquired parcel C must be valued as of its acquisition on April 7, 1986. On that date, K qualifies as a U.S. real property holding corporation, since the fair market value of its U.S. real property interests ($3,000,000) exceeds 50 percent ($2,500,000) of the sum ($5,000,000) of the fair market value of K's U.S. real property interests ($3,000,000), its interests in real property located outside the U.S. ($2,000,000), and its other assets used or held for use in a trade or business (zero).

(d) *Assets held by a corporation.* The assets that must be included in the determination of whether a corporation is a U.S. real property holding corporation are the following:

(1) U.S. real property interests that are held directly by the corporation (including directly-held interests in foreign corporations that are treated as U.S. real property interests pursuant to the rules of paragraph (e)(1) of this section);

(2) Interests in real property located outside the United States that are held directly by the corporation;

(3) Assets used or held for use in a trade or business that are held directly by the corporation;

(4) A proportionate share of assets held through a partnership, trust, or estate pursuant to the rules of paragraph (e)(2) of this section; and

(5) A proportionate share of assets held through a domestic or foreign corporation in which a corporation holds a controlling interest, pursuant to the rules of paragraph (e)(3) of this section.

(e) *Special rules regarding assets held by a corporation*—(1) *Interests in foreign corporations.* For purposes only of determining whether any corporation is a U.S. real property holding corporation, an interest in a foreign corporation shall be treated as a U.S. real property interest unless it is established that the interest was not a U.S. real property interest under the rules of this section on the applicable determination date. The rules of paragraph (g)(2) of this section must be complied with to establish that the interest is not a U.S. real property interest. However, regardless of whether an interest in a foreign corporation is treated as a U.S. real property interest for this purpose, gain or loss from the disposition of an interest in such corporation will not be treated as effectively connected with the conduct of a U.S. trade or business by reason of section 897(a). The rules of this paragraph (e)(1) are illustrated by the following examples. In each example, fair market value is determined as of the applicable determination dates under paragraph (c)(4)(i) of this section.

Example (1). Nonresident alien individual F holds all of the stock of domestic corporation DC. DC's only assets are 40 percent of the stock of foreign corporation FC, with a fair market value of $500,000, and a parcel of country W real estate, with a fair market value of $400,000. Foreign corporation FP, unrelated to DC, holds the other 60 percent of the stock of FC. FC's only asset is a parcel of U.S. real estate with a fair market value of $1,250,000. FC is a U.S. real property holding corporation because the fair market value of its U.S. real property interests ($1,250,000) exceeds 50 percent ($625,000) of the sum of the fair market values of its U.S. real property interests ($1,250,000), its interests in real property located outside the United States (zero), plus its other assets used or held for use in a trade or business (zero). Consequently DC's interest in FC is treated as a U.S. real property

Reg. § 1.897-2(e)(1)

interest under the rules of this paragraph (e)(1). DC is a U.S. real property holding corporation because the fair market value ($500,000) of its U.S. real property interest (the stock of FC) exceeds 50 percent ($450,000) of the sum ($900,000) of the fair market value of its U.S. real property interests ($500,000), its interests in real property located outside the United States ($400,000), plus its other assets used or held for use in a trade or business (zero). If F disposes of her stock within 5 years of the current determination date, her gain or loss on the disposition of her stock in DC will be treated as effectively connected with a U.S. trade or business under section 897(a). However, FP's gain on the disposition of its FC stock would not be subject to the provisions of section 897(a) because the stock of FC is a U.S. real property interest only for purposes of determining whether DC is a U.S. real property holding corporation.

Example (2). Nonresident alien individual B holds all of the stock of domestic corporation US. US's only assets are 40 percent of the stock of foreign corporation FC1. Nonresident alien individual N, unrelated to US, holds the other 60 percent of FC1's stock. FC1's only assets are 40 percent of the stock of foreign corporation FC2. The remaining 60 percent of the stock of FC2 is owned by nonresident alien individual X, who is unrelated to FC1. FC2's only asset is a parcel of U.S. real estate with fair market value of $1,000,000. FC2, therefore, is a U.S. real property holding corporation, and the stock of FC2 held by FC1 is a U.S. real property interest for purposes of determining whether FC1 is a U.S. real property holding corporation (but not for purposes of treating FC1's gain from the disposition of FC2 stock as effectively connected with a U.S. trade or business under section 897(a)). As all of FC1's assets are U.S. real property interests, the stock of FC1 held by US is a U.S. real property interest for purposes of determining whether US is a U.S. real property holding corporation (but not for purposes of subjecting N's gain on the disposition of FC1 stock to the provisions of section 897(a)). As US is a domestic corporation and as all of its assets are U.S. real property interests, US is a U.S. real property holding corporation, and the stock of US held by B is a U.S. real property interest for purposes of section 897(a). Therefore, B's gain or loss upon the disposition of the stock of US within 5 years of the most recent determination date is subject to the provisions of section 897(a).

(2) *Proportionate ownership of assets held by partnerships, trusts, and estates.* For purposes of determining whether a corporation is a U.S. real property holding corporation, a holder of an interest in a partnership, a trust, or an estate (whether domestic or foreign) shall be treated pursuant to section 897(c)(4)(B) as holding a proportionate share of the assets held by the entity. However, a holder of an interest shall not be treated as holding a proportionate share of assets that in the hands of the entity are subject to the rule of § 1.897-1(f)(3)(ii) (concerning the trade or business assets of investment companies). Such proportionate share is to be determined in accordance with the rules of § 1.897-1(e) on each applicable determination date. The interest in the entity shall itself be disregarded when a proportionate share of the entity's assets is attributed to the interest-holder pursuant to the rule of this paragraph (e)(2). Any asset treated as held by a holder of an interest by reason of this paragraph (e)(2) which is used or held for use in a trade or business by the partnership, trust, or estate shall be treated as so used or held for use by the holder of the interest. The proportionate ownership rule of this paragraph (e)(2) applies successively upward through a chain of ownership. The proportionate ownership rule of this paragraph (e)(2) is illustrated by the following examples. In each example fair market value is determined as of the applicable determination date under paragraph (c)(4)(i) of this section.

Example (1). Nonresident alien individual F holds all of the stock of domestic corporation DC. DC is a partner in foreign partnership FP, and DC's percentage ownership interest in FP is 50 percent. DC's other assets are a parcel of country F real estate with a fair market value of $500,000 and other assets which it uses in its business with a fair market value of $100,000. FP's assets are a parcel of country Z real estate with a fair market value of $300,000 and a parcel of U.S. real estate with a fair market value of $2,000,000. For purposes of determining whether DC is a U.S. real property holding corporation, DC is treated as holding its pro rata share of the assets held by FP. DC's pro rata share of the U.S. real estate held by FP is $1,000,000, determined by multiplying the fair market value ($2,000,000) of the U.S. real property interests held by FP by DC's percentage ownership interest in FP (50 percent). DC's pro rata share of the country Z real estate held by FP is $150,000, determined in the same manner. DC is a U.S. real property holding corporation because the fair market value ($1,000,000) of its U.S. real property interests (the U.S. real estate it is treated as holding proportionately) exceeds 50 percent ($875,000) of the sum ($1,750,000) of the fair market value of its U.S. real property interests ($1,000,000), its interests in real property located outside the United States [($650,000) (its country F real estate and its pro rata share of the country Z real estate)], plus its other assets which are used or held for use in a trade or business

Reg. § 1.897-2(e)(2)

($100,000). Because DC is a domestic U.S. real property holding corporation, the stock of DC is a U.S. real property interest and F's gain or loss on the disposition of his DC stock within 5 years of the current determination date will be treated as effectively connected with a U.S. trade or business under section 897(a).

Example (2). Nonresident alien individual B holds all of the stock of domestic corporation US. US is a beneficiary of foreign trust FT. US's percentage ownership interest in FT is 90 percent. US has no other assets. FT is a partner in domestic partnership DP. FT's percentage ownership interest in DP is 30 percent. FT has no other assets. DP's only asset is a parcel of U.S. real estate with a fair market value of $1,000,000. FT is treated as holding U.S. real estate with a fair market value of $300,000 (30 percent of the U.S. real estate held by DP with a fair market value of $1,000,000). For purposes of determining whether US is a U.S. real property holding corporation, the proportionate ownership rule is applied successively upward through the chain of ownership. Thus, US is treated as holding 90 percent of FT's $300,000 pro rata share of the U.S. real estate held by DP. US is a U.S. real property holding corporation because the fair market value ($270,000) of its U.S. real property interests (its pro rata share of the U.S. real estate held by DP) exceeds 50 percent ($135,000) of the sum of the fair market values of its U.S. real property interests ($270,000), its interests in real property located outside the United States (zero), plus its other assets used or held for use in a trade or business (zero). Because US is a domestic U.S. real property holding corporation, the stock of US is a U.S. real property interest, and B's gain or loss from the disposition of US stock within 5 years of the current determination date will be treated as effectively connected with a U.S. trade or business under section 897(a).

(3) *Controlling interests in corporations.* For purposes only of determining whether a corporation is a U.S. real property holding corporation, if the corporation (the "first corporation") holds a controlling interest in a second corporation—

(i) The first corporation is treated as holding a proportionate share of each asset (i.e., U.S. real property interests, interests in real property located outside the United States, and assets used or held for use in a trade or business) held by the second corporation, determined in accordance with the rules of § 1.897-1(e);

(ii) Any asset so treated as held proportionately by the first corporation which is used or held for use by the second corporation in a trade or business shall be treated as so used or held for use by the first corporation; and

(iii) Interests in the second corporation held by the first corporation are not themselves taken into account as U.S. real property interests (regardless of whether the second corporation is a U.S. real property holding corporation) or as trade or business assets.

However, the first corporation shall not be treated as holding a proportionate share of assets that in the hands of the second corporation are subject to the rule of § 1.897-1(f)(3)(ii) (concerning the trade or business assets of investment companies). A determination of what portion of the assets of the second corporation are considered to be held by the first corporation shall be made as of the applicable dates for determining whether the first corporation is a U.S. real property holding corporation. A "controlling interest" means 50 percent or more of the fair market value of all classes of stock of the corporation, determined as of the applicable determination date. In determining whether a corporation holds a controlling interest in another corporation, section 318(a) shall apply (except that sections 318(a)(2)(C) and (3)(C) are applied by substituting the phrase "5 percent" for "50 percent"). However, a corporation that does not directly hold any interest in a second corporation shall not be treated as holding a controlling interest in the second corporation by reason of the application of section 318(a)(3)(C). The rules of this paragraph (e)(3) apply successively upward through a chain of ownership. For example, if the second corporation owns a controlling interest in a third corporation, the rules of this paragraph shall be applied first to determine the portion of the assets of the third corporation that is considered to be held by the second corporation and then to determine the portion of the assets held and considered to be held by the second corporation that is considered to be held by the first corporation. The controlling interest rules of this paragraph (e)(3) apply, regardless of whether a corporation is domestic or foreign, whenever it is necessary to determine whether a corporation is a U.S. real property holding corporation. The rules of this paragraph (e)(3) are illustrated by the following examples. In each example fair market value is determined as of the applicable determination date under paragraph (c)(4)(i) of this section and no corporation holds constructively any interest not specified in the example.

Example (1). Nonresident alien individual N owns all of the stock of domestic corporation DC. DC's only assets are 60 percent of the fair market value of all classes of stock of foreign

Reg. § 1.897-2(e)(3)

corporation FS and 60 percent of the fair market value of all classes of stock of domestic corporation DS. The percentage ownership interest of DC in each of FS and DS is 60 percent. The balance of the stock in FS and DS is held by nonresident alien individual B, who is unrelated to DC. FS's only asset is a parcel of country F real estate with a fair market value of $1,000,000. DS's only asset is a parcel of U.S. real estate with a fair market value of $2,000,000. The value of DC stock in FS and DS is not taken into account for purposes of determining whether DC is a U.S. real property holding corporation. Rather, because DC holds a controlling interest (60 percent) in each of FS and DS, DC is treated as holding a portion of each asset held by FS and DS. DC's portion of the country F real estate held by FS is $600,000, determined by multiplying the fair market value ($1,000,000) of the country F real estate by DC's percentage ownership interest (60 percent). Similarly, DC's portion of the U.S. real estate held by DS is $1,200,000 (60 percent of $2,000,000). DC is a U.S. real property holding corporation, because the fair market value ($1,200,000) of its U.S. real property interests (its portion of the U.S. real estate) exceeds 50 percent ($900,000) of the sum ($1,800,000) of the fair market values of its U.S. real property interests ($1,200,000), its interests in real property located outside the United States (the $600,000 portion of country F real estate), plus its other assets used or held for use in a trade or business (zero). Because DC is a domestic U.S. real property holding corporation, the stock of DC is a U.S. real property interest, and N's gain or loss on the disposition of DC stock within 5 years of the current determination date would be treated as effectively connected with a U.S. trade or business under section 897(a).

Example (2). (i) Nonresident alien individual F owns all of the stock of domestic corporation US1. US1's only asset is 85 percent of the fair market value of all classes of stock of domestic corporation US2. US2's only assets are 60 percent of the fair market value of all classes of stock of domestic corporation US3, with a fair market value of $800,000, and a parcel of country D real estate with a fair market value of $800,000. US3's only asset is a parcel of U.S. real estate with a fair market value of $2,000,000. The percentage ownership interest of F in US1 is 100 percent. Although US1 owns 85 percent of the stock of US2, US1's percentage ownership interest in US2 is 75 percent, because US2 has other interests other than solely as a creditor outstanding. US2's percentage ownership interest in US3 is 60 percent.

(ii) US2 holds a controlling interest in US3, since it holds more than 50 percent of the fair market value of all classes of stock of US3. Consequently, the value of US2's stock in US3 is not taken into account in determining whether US2 is a U.S. real property holding corporation, even though US3 is a U.S. real property holding corporation. Instead, US2 is treated as holding a portion of the U.S. real estate held by US3. US2's portion of the U.S. real estate is $1,200,000, determined by multiplying US2's percentage ownership interest (60 percent) by the fair market value ($2,000,000) of the U.S. real estate. US1 holds a controlling interest in US2 (75 percent). By reapplying the rules of paragraph (e)(3) of this section successively upward through the chain of ownership, US1's stock in US2 is not taken into account, and US1 is treated as holding a portion of the country D real estate held by US2 and the U.S. real estate which US2 is treated as holding proportionately. US1's portion of the country D real estate is $800,000, determined by multiplying US1's percentage ownership interest (75 percent) by the fair market value ($800,000) of the country D real estate. US1's portion of the U.S. real estate which US2 is treated as owning is $900,000, determined by multiplying US1's percentage ownership interest (75 percent) by the fair market value ($1,200,000) of US2's portion of U.S. real estate held by US3. US1 is a U.S. real property holding corporation, because the fair market value ($900,000) of its U.S. real property interests (its portion of US2's portion of U.S. real estate) is more than 50 percent ($750,000) of the sum ($1,500,000) of fair market values of its U.S. real property interests ($900,000), its interests in real property located outside the United States ($800,000), plus its other assets used or held for use in a trade or business (zero). Because US1 is a U.S. real property holding corporation and is a domestic corporation, the stock of US1 is a U.S. real property interest, and F's gain or loss on the disposition of US1 stock within 5 years of the current determination date will be treated as effectively connected with a U.S. trade or business under section 897(a).

Example (3). Nonresident alien individual B holds all of the stock of domestic corporation DC. DC's only assets are 40 percent of the fair market value of all classes of stock of foreign corporation FC and a parcel of country R real estate with a fair market value of $100,000. FC's only asset is one parcel of U.S. real estate with a fair market value of $1,000,000. The fair market value of the FC stock held by DC is $200,000. FC is a U.S. real property holding corporation. Since DC does not hold a controlling interest in FC, the controlling interest rules of paragraph (e)(3) of this section do not apply to treat DC as holding a portion of the U.S. real estate held by FC. However, because FC is a U.S. real property holding

Reg. § 1.897-2(e)(3)

corporation, the stock of FC is a U.S. real property interest for purposes of determining whether DC is a U.S. real property holding corporation. DC is a U.S. real property holding corporation because the fair market value ($200,000) of its U.S. real property interest (the stock of FC) exceeds 50 percent ($150,000) of the sum ($300,000) of the fair market values of its U.S. real property interest ($200,000), its interests in real property located outside the United States ($100,000), plus its other assets used or held for use in a trade or business (zero). Because DC is a U.S. real property holding corporation and is a domestic corporation, its stock is a U.S. real property interest, and B's gain or loss on the disposition of DC stock within 5 years of the current determination date would be subject to the provisions of section 897(a).

Example (4). Nonresident alien individual C owns all of the stock of domestic corporation DC1. DC1's only assets are 25 percent of the fair market value of all classes of stock of domestic corporation DC2, and a parcel of U.S. real estate with a fair market value of $100,000. The stock of DC2 is not an asset used or held for use in DC1's trade or business. DC2's only assets are a building located in the U.S. with a fair market value of $100,000 and manufacturing equipment and inventory with a fair market value of $200,000. DC2 is not a U.S. real property holding corporation. Since DC1 does not hold a controlling interest in DC2, the rules of this paragraph (e)(3) do not apply to treat DC1 as holding a portion of the assets held by DC2. In addition, since DC2 is not a U.S. real property holding corporation, its stock does not constitute a U.S. real property interest. Therefore, for purposes of determining whether DC1 is a U.S. real property holding corporation, its interest in DC2 is not taken into account. Since DC1's only other asset is a parcel of U.S. real estate, DC1 is a U.S. real property holding corporation, and C's gain or loss on the disposition of DC1 stock within 5 years of the current determination date would be subject to the provisions of section 897(a).

(4) *Co-application of rules of this paragraph (e).* The rules of this paragraph (e) apply in conjunction with one another for purposes of determining whether a corporation is a U.S. real property holding corporation. The rule of this paragraph (e)(4) is illustrated by the following example. In the example fair market value is determined as of the applicable determination date in accordance with paragraph (c)(4)(i) of this section.

Example. Nonresident alien individual B holds 100 percent of the stock of domestic corporation US. US's only asset is 10 percent of the stock of foreign corporation FC1. FC1's only asset is 100 percent of the stock of foreign corporation FC2. FC2's only asset is a 50 percent interest in domestic partnership DP. FC2's percentage ownership interest in DP is 50 percent. DP's only asset is a parcel of U.S. real estate with a fair market value of $10,000,000. In determining whether US is a U.S. real property holding corporation, the rules of this paragraph (e) apply in conjunction with one another. Consequently, under paragraph (e)(2) of this section FC2 is treated as holding U.S. real estate with a fair market value of $5,000,000 (50 percent of $10,000,000, its pro rata share of real estate held by DP). Under paragraph (e)(3) of this section, FC1 is treated as holding 100 percent of the assets of FC2 (U.S. real estate with a fair market value of $5,000,000). FC1, therefore, is a U.S. real property holding corporation. Under paragraph (e)(1) of this section, the stock of FC1 is treated as U.S. real property interest. US is a U.S. real property holding corporation because 100 percent of its assets (the stock of FC1) are U.S. real property interests. As US is a U.S. real property holding corporation and is a domestic corporation, the stock of US is a U.S. real property interest, and B's gain or loss from the disposition of stock of US within 5 years of the current determination date will be subject to the provisions of section 897(a).

(f) *Termination of U.S. real property holding corporation status*—(1) *In general.* A U.S. real property holding corporation may voluntarily determine its status as of the date of any acquisition or disposition of assets. If the fair market value of its U.S. real property interests on such date no longer equals or exceeds 50 percent of the fair market value of all assets described in paragraphs (d) and (e) of this section, such corporation shall cease to be U.S. real property holding corporation as of such date, and on the day that is five years after such date interests in such corporation shall cease to be treated as U.S. real property interests (unless subsequent transactions within the five-year period have caused the fair market value of the corporation's U.S. real property interests to equal or exceed 50 percent of the fair market value of assets described in paragraphs (d) and (e) of this section). A corporation that determines that interests in it have ceased to be U.S. real property interests pursuant to the rules of this paragraph (f) may so inform the Internal Revenue Service, as provided in paragraph (h) of this section.

(2) *Early termination.* Interests in a U.S. real property holding corporation shall immediately cease to be U.S. real property interests as of the

first date on which the following conditions are met—

(i) The corporation does not hold any U.S. real property interests, and

(ii) All of the U.S. real property interests directly or indirectly held by such corporation at any time during the previous five years (but disregarding any disposed of before June 19, 1980) either (A) were directly or indirectly disposed of in transactions in which the full amount of the gain (if any) was recognized or (B) ceased to be U.S. real property interests by reason of the application of this paragraph (f) to one or more other corporations.

For purposes of this paragraph (f)(2), a corporation that disposes of all U.S. real property interests other than a lease that has a fair market value of zero will be considered to have disposed of all of its U.S. real property interests, provided that the leased property is used in the conduct by the corporation of a trade or business in the United States. Such a lease may include an option to renew, but only if such option is for a renewal at fair market rental rates prevailing at the time of renewal.

(g) *Establishing that a corporation is not a U.S. real property holding corporation*—(1) *Foreign persons disposing of interests*—(i) *In general.* A foreign person disposing of an interest in a domestic corporation (other than an interest solely as a creditor) must establish that the interest was not a U.S. real property interest as of the date of disposition, either by:

(A) Obtaining a statement from the corporation pursuant to the provisions of subdivision (ii) of this paragraph (g)(1), or

(B) Obtaining a determination by the Director, Foreign Operations District ("Director") pursuant to the provisions of subdivision (iii) of this paragraph (g)(1).

If the foreign person does not establish by either method that the interest disposed of was not a U.S. real property interest then the interest shall be presumed to have been a U.S. real property interest the disposition of which is subject to section 897(a). See paragraph (g)(3) of this section for certain exceptions to this rule. It should be noted that the rules of this section relate solely to interests in a corporation that are interests other than solely as a creditor. Therefore, a statement by a corporation or a determination by the Director (under paragraphs (g) and (h) of this section) that an interest is not a U.S. real property interest depends solely upon whether or not the corporation was a U.S. real property holding corporation during the period described in section 897(c)(1)(A)(ii) (subject to certain special rules).

The determination of whether an interest is one solely as a creditor is made under the rules of § 1.897-1(d).

(ii) *Statement from corporation*—(A) *In general.* A foreign person disposing of an interest in a domestic corporation may establish that the interest was not a U.S. real property interest as of the date of the disposition by requesting and obtaining from the corporation a statement that the interest was not a U.S. real property interest as of that date. However, a corporation's statement shall not be valid for purposes of this rule, and thus may not be relied upon for purposes of establishing that an interest was not a U.S. real property interest, unless the corporation complies with the notice requirements of paragraph (h)(2) or (h)(4) of this section.

A foreign person that requests and obtains such a statement is not required to forward the statement to the Internal Revenue Service and is not required to take any further action to establish that the interest disposed of was not a U.S. real property interest. To qualify under this rule, the foreign person must obtain the corporation's statement no later than the date, including any extensions, on which a tax return would otherwise be due with respect to a disposition. A foreign person that relies in good faith upon a statement from the corporation is not thereby excused from filing a return and paying any taxes and interest due thereon if the corporation's statement is later found to have been incorrect. However, such reliance shall be taken into account in determining whether the foreign person shall be subject to any penalty for the previous failure to file. However, a foreign person that knew or had reason to know that a corporation's statement was incorrect is not entitled to rely upon such statement and shall remain liable for all applicable penalties.

(B) *Coordination with section 1445.* Pursuant to section 1445 and regulations thereunder, withholding of tax is not required with respect to a foreign person's disposition of an interest in a domestic corporation, if the transferee is furnished with a statement by the corporation under paragraph (h) of this section that the interest is not a U.S. real property interest. A foreign person that obtains a corporation's statement for that purpose prior to the date of disposition may also rely upon the statement for purposes of this paragraph (g)(1)(ii), unless the corporation informs the foreign person (pursuant to paragraph (h)(1)(iv)(C) of this section) that it became a U.S. real property holding corporation after the date of the notice but prior to the actual date of disposition.

Reg. § 1.897-2(g)(1)

(iii) *Determination by Director*—(A) *In general.* A foreign person disposing of an interest in a domestic corporation may establish that the interest was not a U.S. real property interest as of the date of disposition by requesting and obtaining a determination to that effect from the Director. Such a determination may be requested pursuant to the provisions of subdivision (B) or (C) of this paragraph (g)(1)(iii). A request for a determination should be addressed to: Director, Foreign Operations District; 1325 K St. N.W.; Washington, D.C. 20225. A foreign transferor who has requested a determination by the Director pursuant to the rules of this paragraph (g)(1)(iii) is not thereby excused from filing a return and paying any tax due by the date, including any extensions, on which such return and payment would otherwise be due with respect to a disposition. If the Director subsequently determines and notifies the foreign transferor that the interest was not a U.S. real property interest, the foreign transferor shall be entitled to a refund of any taxes, penalties, and interest paid by reason of the application of section 897(a) pursuant to the rules of paragraph (g)(1)(i) of this section, together with any interest otherwise due on such refund, if a claim for refund is made within the applicable time limits.

(B) *Determination based on Director's information.* A foreign person may request that the Director make a determination based on information contained in the Director's records, if:

(1) The foreign person made a request to the corporation for information as to the status of its interest no later than the 90th day before the date, including any extensions, on which a tax return would otherwise be due with respect to a disposition, and

(2) The corporation failed to respond to such request by the 30th day following the date the request was delivered to the corporation.

If the Director is unable to make a determination based on information available to him, he shall inform the foreign person that the interest must be treated as a U.S. real property interest unless the person subsequently obtains either the necessary statement from the corporation or a determination pursuant to subdivision (C) of this paragraph (g)(1)(iii).

(C) *Determination based on information supplied by foreign person.* A foreign person may request that the Director make a determination based on information supplied by the foreign person. Such information may be drawn, for example, from annual reports, financial statements, or records of the corporation, and must establish to the satisfaction of the Director that the foreign person's interest was not a U.S. real property interest as of the date of disposition.

(D) *Determination by Director on his own motion.* Notwithstanding any other provision of this section, a foreign person shall not treat the disposition of an interest in a domestic corporation as a disposition of a U.S. real property interest if such person is notified that the Director has upon his own motion determined that the interest was not a U.S. real property interest as of the date of disposition.

(2) *Corporations determining U.S. real property holding corporation status*—(i) *In general.* A corporation that must determine whether it is a U.S. real property holding corporation, and that holds an interest in another corporation (other than a controlling interest as defined in paragraph (e)(3) of this section), must determine whether or not that interest was a U.S. real property interest as of its own determination date, by either:

(A) Obtaining a statement from the second corporation pursuant to the provisions of subdivision (ii) of this paragraph (g)(2);

(B) Obtaining a determination by the Director pursuant to the provisions of subdivision (iii) of this paragraph (g)(2); or

(C) Making an independent determination pursuant to the provisions of subdivision (iv) of this paragraph (g)(2).

A corporation that is unable to determine by any of the above methods whether its interest in a second corporation is a U.S. real property interest must presume that such interest is a U.S. real property interest.

(ii) *Statement from corporation.* A corporation may determine whether or not an interest in a second corporation was a U.S. real property interest as of its own determination date by obtaining from the second corporation a statement that the interest was not a U.S. real property interest as of that date. However, the second corporation's statement shall not be valid for purposes of this rule, and thus may not be relied upon for purposes of establishing that an interest was not a U.S. real property interest, unless such corporation complies with the notice requirements of paragraph (h)(2) or (h)(4) of this section.

A corporation that requests and obtains such a statement is not required to forward the statement to the Internal Revenue Service and is not required to take any further action to establish that the interest in the second corporation was not a U.S. real property interest. If the second corporation's statement is later found to have been incorrect, the first corporation shall not be subject

Reg. § 1.897-2(g)(2)

to penalties arising out of past failures to comply with the requirements of section 897 or 1445, if such failures were attributable to reliance upon the second corporation's statement. By the 90th day following receipt of a notification from the Service or from the second corporation that a prior statement was incorrect, the first corporation must redetermine its status (as of its most recent determination date) and if appropriate notify the Internal Revenue Service that it is a U.S. real property holding corporation in accordance with paragraph (h)(1)(ii)(C) of this section. However, a corporation that knew or had reason to know that a second corporation's statement was incorrect is not entitled to rely upon such statement and shall remain liable for all applicable taxes, penalties, and interest arising out of the second corporation's status as a U.S. real property holding corporation.

(iii) *Determination by Director*—(A) *In general.* A corporation may determine whether or not an interest in a second corporation was a U.S. real property interest as of its own determination date by requesting and obtaining a determination to that effect from the Director. Such a determination may be requested pursuant to the provisions of subdivision (B) or (C) of this paragraph (g)(2)(iii). A request for a determination must be addressed to: Director, Foreign Operations District; 1325 K St. N.W.; Washington, D.C. 20225. A corporation that has requested a determination by the Director pursuant to the provisions of this paragraph is not thereby excused from taking any action required by section 897 or 1445 by the date on which such action would otherwise be due. However, the Director may grant a reasonable extension of time for the satisfaction of any requirement if the Director is satisfied that the corporation has not sought a determination pursuant to this paragraph (g)(2)(iii) for a principal purpose of delay.

(B) *Determination based on Director's information.* A corporation may request that the Director make a determination based on information contained in the Director's records, if:

(1) The corporation made a request to the second corporation for information as to the status of its interest no later than the fifth day following the first corporation's determination date, and

(2) The second corporation failed to respond to such request by the 30th day following the date the request was delivered to the second corporation.

Pending his resolution of such a request, the Director will generally grant an extension with respect to the change-of-status notification that may otherwise be required pursuant to paragraph (h)(1)(ii) of this section. If the Director is unable to make a determination based on information available to him, he shall inform the corporation that the interest must be treated as a U.S. real property interest unless the corporation subsequently obtains either the necessary statement from the second corporation or a determination pursuant to paragraph (g)(2)(iii)(C) or (g)(2)(iv) of this section.

(C) *Determination based on information supplied by corporation.* A corporation may request that the Director make a determination based on information supplied by the corporation. Such information may be drawn, for example, from annual reports, financial statements, or records of the second corporation, and must establish to the satisfaction of the Director that the interest in the second corporation was not a U.S. real property interest as of the first corporation's determination date.

(D) *Determination by Director on his own motion.* Notwithstanding any other provision of this section, a corporation shall not treat an interest in a second corporation as a U.S. real property interest if the corporation is notified that the Director has upon his own motion determined that the interest in the second corporation is not a U.S. real property interest.

(iv) *Independent determination by corporation.* A corporation may independently determine whether or not an interest in a second corporation was a U.S. real property interest as of the first corporation's own determination date. Such determination must be based upon the best evidence available, drawn from annual reports, financial statements, records of the second corporation, or from any other source, that demonstrates to a reasonable certainty that the interest in the second corporation was not a U.S. real property interest. A corporation that makes an independent determination pursuant to this paragraph (g)(2)(iv) shall be subject to the special notification rule of paragraph (h)(1)(iii)(D) of this section. If the Director subsequently determines that the corporation's independent determination was incorrect, the corporation shall be subject to penalties for any past failure to comply with the requirements of section 897 or 1445 only if the corporation's determination was unreasonable in view of facts that the corporation knew or had reason to know.

(3) *Requirements not applicable.* If at any time during the calendar year any class of stock of a corporation is regularly traded on an established securities market, the requirements of this paragraph (g) shall not apply with respect to any

Reg. § 1.897-2(g)(3)

holder of an interest in such corporation other than a person who holds an interest described in § 1.897-1(c)(2)(iii)(A) or (B). For example, a corporation determining whether it is a U.S. real property holding corporation need not ascertain from a regularly traded corporation in which it neither holds, nor has held during the period described in section 897(c)(1)(A)(ii), more than a 5 percent interest whether that regularly traded corporation is itself a U.S. real property holding corporation. In addition, the requirements of this paragraph (g) do not apply to any holder of an interest in a domestically-controlled REIT, as defined in section 897(h)(4)(B).

(h) *Notice requirements applicable to corporations*—(1) *Statement to foreign interest-holder*—(i) *In general.* A domestic corporation must, within a reasonable period after receipt of a request from a foreign person holding an interest in it, inform that person whether the interest constitutes a U.S. real property interest. No particular form is required for this statement, which need only indicate the corporation's determination. The statement must be dated and signed by a responsible corporate officer who must verify under penalties of perjury that the statement is correct to his knowledge and belief.

(ii) *Required determination.* For purposes of the statement required by paragraph (h)(1)(i) of this section, an interest in a corporation is a U.S. real property interest if the corporation was a U.S. real property holding corporation on any determination date during the 5-year period ending on the date specified in the interest-holder's request, or on the date such request was received if no date is specified (or during such shorter period ending on the date that is applicable pursuant to section 897(c)(1)(A)(ii)). However, an interest in a corporation is not a U.S. real property interest if such interest is excluded under section 897(c)(1)(B).

(2) *Notice to the Internal Revenue Service.* If a foreign interest holder requests that a domestic corporation provide a statement described in paragraph (h)(1) of this section, then such corporation must provide a notice to the Internal Revenue Service in accordance with this paragraph (h)(2). No particular form is required for such notice, but the following must be provided:

(i) A statement that the notice is provided pursuant to the requirements of § 1.897-2(h)(2);

(ii) The name, address, and identifying number of the corporation providing the notice;

(iii) The name, address, and identifying number (if any) of the foreign interest holder that requested the statement (this information may be omitted from the notice if fully set forth in the statement to the foreign interest holder attached to the notice);

(iv) Whether the interest in question is a U.S. real property interest;

(v) A statement signed by a responsible corporate officer verifying under penalties of perjury that the notice (including any attachments thereto) is correct to his knowledge and belief. A copy of any statement provided to the foreign interest holder must be attached to the notice. The notice must be mailed to the Assistant Commissioner (International), Director, Office of Compliance, OP:I:C:E:666, 950 L'Enfant Plaza South, SW, COMSAT Building, Washington, D.C. 20024 on or before the 30th day after the statement referred to in § 1.897-2(h)(1) is mailed to the interest holder that requested it. Failure to mail such notice within the time period set forth in the preceding sentence will cause the statement provided pursuant to § 1.897-2(h)(1) to become an invalid statement.

(3) *Requirements not applicable.* The requirements of this paragraph (h) do not apply to domestically-controlled REITS, as defined in section 897(h)(4)(B). These requirements also do not apply to a corporation any class of stock in which is regularly traded on an established securities market at any time during the calendar year. However, such a corporation may voluntarily choose to comply with the requirements of paragraph (h)(4) of this section.

(4) *Voluntary notice to Internal Revenue Service*—(i) *In general.* A domestic corporation which determines that it is not a U.S. real property holding corporation—

(A) on each of the applicable determination dates in a taxable year, or

(B) pursuant to section 897(c)(1)(B),

may attach to its income tax return for that year a statement informing the Internal Revenue Service of its determination. A corporation that has provided a voluntary notice described in this § 1.897-2(h)(4)(i) for the immediately preceding taxable year and that does not have an event described in § 1.897-2(c)(1)(ii), (iii) or (iv) prior to receiving a request from a foreign person under § 1.897-2(h)(1), is exempt from the notice requirement of § 1.897-2(h)(2).

(ii) *Early termination of real property holding corporation status.* A corporation that determines during the course of its taxable year that interests in it have ceased to be U.S. real property interests pursuant to the rules of section 897(c)(1)(B) may, on the day of its determination or thereafter, provide a statement to the Assistant Commissioner (International); Director, Office of

Reg. § 1.897-2(h)(4)

Compliance, OP:I:C:E:666; 950 L'Enfant Plaza South, S.W.; COMSAT Building; Washington, D.C. 20024, informing the Service of its determination. No particular form is required but the statement must set forth the corporation's name, address, identification number, a brief statement regarding its determination and the date such determination was made. Such statement will enable foreign interest-holders to dispose of their interests without being subject to section 897(a), as provided in paragraph (g) of this section.

(5) *Supplemental statements*—(i) *By corporations with substantial intangible assets.* A corporation that is subject to the requirements of paragraph (h)(2) of this section (or that voluntarily complies with the requirements of paragraph (h)(4) of this section) must submit a supplemental statement to the Internal Revenue Service if—

(A) Such corporation values any of the intangible assets described in § 1.897-1(f)(1)(ii) (other than goodwill or going concern value) by a method other than the purchase price or book value methods described in § 1.897-1(o)(4); and

(B) The fair market value of such intangible assets equals or exceeds 25 percent of the total of the fair market values of the assets the corporation is considered to hold in accordance with the provisions of paragraphs (d) and (e) of this section.

The supplemental statement must inform the Internal Revenue Service that the corporation meets the criteria of subdivisions (A) and (B) of this paragraph (h)(5)(i), and must summarize the methods and calculations upon which the corporation's determination of the fair market value of its intangible assets is based. In addition, the supplemental statement must list any intangible assets that were purchased from any person that have been valued by the corporation at an amount other than their purchase price, and must provide a justification for such a departure from the purchase price. The supplemental statement must be attached to or incorporated in the statement provided under paragraph (h)(2) or (h)(4) of this section.

(ii) *Corporation not valuing goodwill or going concern value at purchase price.* A corporation that is subject to the requirements of paragraph (h)(2) of this section (or that voluntarily complies with the requirements of paragraph (h)(4) of this section) must submit a supplemental statement to the Internal Revenue Service if such corporation values goodwill or going concern value pursuant to § 1.897-1(o)(4)(iii). The supplemental statement must set forth that it is made pursuant to this paragraph (h)(5)(ii), and must summarize the methods and calculations upon which the corporation's determination of the fair market value of such intangible assets is based. In addition, the supplemental statement must list any such assets that were purchased from any person that have been valued by the corporation at an amount other than their purchase price, and must provide a justification for such a departure from the purchase price. The supplemental statement must be attached to or incorporated in the statement provided under paragraph (h)(2) or (h)(4) of this section.

(iii) *Corporation using alternative U.S. real property holding corporation test.* A corporation that is subject to the requirements of paragraph (h)(2) of this section (or that voluntarily complies with the requirements of paragraph (h)(4) of this section) must submit a supplemental statement to the Internal Revenue Service if—

(A) Such corporation utilizes the rule of paragraph (b)(2) of this section (regarding the book values of assets held by the corporation) to presume that it is not a U.S. real property holding corporation; and

(B) Such corporation is engaged in or is planning to engage in a trade or business of mining, farming, or forestry, or of buying and selling or developing real property, or of leasing real property to tenants.

The supplemental statement must inform the Internal Revenue Service that the corporation meets the criteria of subdivisions (A) and (B) of this paragraph (h)(5)(iii), and must be attached to or incorporated in the statement provided under paragraph (h)(2) or (h)(4) of this section.

(iv) *Corporation determining real property holding corporation status of second corporation.* A corporation that is subject to the requirements of paragraph (h)(2) of this section (or that voluntarily complies with the requirements of paragraph (h)(4) of this section) must submit a supplemental statement to the Internal Revenue Service if such corporation independently determines whether or not an interest in a second corporation is a U.S. real property interest, pursuant to paragraph (g)(2)(iv) of this section. The supplemental statement must set forth that it is made pursuant to this paragraph (h)(5)(iv) and must briefly summarize the facts upon which the corporation's determination is based and the sources of the information relied upon by the corporation. The supplemental statement must be attached to or incorporated in the statement provided under paragraph (h)(2) or (h)(4) of this section.

(i) *Transition Rules*—(1) *General waiver of penalties for failure to file.* If a foreign person disposed of an interest in a domestic corporation

Reg. § 1.897-2(h)(5)

between June 18, 1980 and January 23, 1987, and such person establishes under the rules of paragraph (g) of this section at any time that the interest disposed of was not a U.S. real property interest, then such person shall not be subject to tax under section 897 and shall not be subject to penalties (or interest) for failure to file an income tax return with respect to such disposition.

(2) *Foreign persons that met the requirements of prior regulations.* A foreign person that disposed of an interest in a domestic corporation between June 18, 1980 and January 23, 1987, shall be deemed to have satisfied the requirements of paragraph (g) of this section with respect to such disposition if such person established under prior temporary or prior final regulations issued under section 897 that the interest disposed of was not a U.S. real property interest. [Reg. § 1.897-2.]

☐ [T.D. 7999, 12-26-84. Amended by T.D. 8113, 12-18-86.]

[Reg. § 1.897-3]

§ 1.897-3. **Election by foreign corporation to be treated as a domestic corporation under section 897(i).**—(a) *Purpose and scope.* This section provides rules pursuant to which a foreign corporation may elect under section 897(i) to be treated as a domestic corporation for purposes of sections 897, 1445, and 6039C and the regulations thereunder. A foreign corporation with respect to which an election under section 897(i) is in effect is subject to all rules under sections 897 and 1445 that apply to domestic corporations. Thus, for example, if a foreign corporation that has made an election under section 897(i) is a U.S. real property holding corporation, interests in it are U.S. real property interests that are subject to withholding under section 1445, and any gain or loss from the disposition of such interests by a foreign person will be treated as effectively connected with a U.S. trade or business under section 897(a). Similarly, if a foreign corporation makes an election under section 897(i), its distribution of a U.S. real property interest pursuant to section 301 will be subject to the carryover basis rule of section 897(f). However, an interest in an electing corporation is not a U.S. real property interest if following the election the interest is described in section 897(c)(1)(B) or § 1.897-1(c)(2) (subject to the exceptions of subdivisions (i) and (ii) of that section). In addition, section 897(d) will not apply to any distribution of a U.S. real property interest by such corporation or to any sale or exchange of such interest pursuant to a plan of complete liquidation under section 337. A foreign corporation that makes an election under section 897(i) shall not be treated as a domestic corporation for purposes of any other provision of the Code or regulations, except to the extent that it is required to consent to such treatment as a condition to making the election. For further information concerning the effect of an election under section 897(i) upon the withholding requirements of section 1445, see § 1.1445-7. An election under section 897(i) is the exclusive remedy of any foreign person claiming discriminatory treatment under any treaty with respect to the application of sections 897, 1445, and 6039C to a foreign corporation. Therefore, if a corporation does not make an effective election, relief under a nondiscrimination article of any treaty shall not be otherwise available with respect to the application of sections 897, 1445, and 6039C to such corporation.

(b) *General conditions.* A foreign corporation may make an election under section 897(i) only if it meets all three of the following conditions.

(1) *Holding a U.S. real property interest.* The foreign corporation must hold a U.S. real property interest at the time of the election. This condition is satisfied when a U.S. real property interest is acquired simultaneously with the effective date of an election. For example, this condition is satisfied when real property is acquired in an exchange described in section 351 that is carried out simultaneously with the effective date of the election. This condition is also satisfied by a corporation that indirectly holds a U.S. real property interest through a partnership, trust, or estate.

(2) *Entitlement to nondiscriminatory treatment.* The foreign corporation must be entitled to nondiscriminatory treatment with respect to its U.S. real property interest under any treaty to which the United States is a party. Where the corporation indirectly holds a U.S. real property interest through a partnership, trust, or estate, the corporation itself must be entitled to nondiscriminatory treatment with respect to such property interest.

(3) *Submission of election in proper form.* The foreign corporation must comply with the requirements of paragraph (c) of this section respecting the manner and form in which an election must be submitted.

(c) *Manner and form of election.* An election under section 897(i) is made by filing the documents described in subparagraphs (1) through (5) of this paragraph (c) with the Director of the Foreign Operations District, 1325 K St., N.W., Washington, D.C. 20225. The required items may be incorporated in a single document.

(1) *General statement.* The foreign corporation must supply a general statement indicating that an election under section 897(i) is being made. The general statement must be signed by a

Reg. § 1.897-3(c)(1)

responsible corporate officer, who must verify under penalty of perjury that the statement and all other documents submitted pursuant to the requirements of this paragraph (c) are true and correct to his knowledge and belief. No particular form is required for the statement, which must set forth—

(i) The name, address, identifying number (if any), and place and date of incorporation of the foreign corporation;

(ii) The treaty and article under which the foreign corporation is seeking nondiscriminatory treatment;

(iii) A description of the U.S. real property interests held by the corporation, either directly or through a partnership, trust, or estate, including the dates such interests were acquired, the corporation's adjusted bases in such interests, and their fair market values as of the date of the election (or book values if the corporation is not a U.S. real property holding corporation under the alternative test of § 1.897-2(b)(2)); and

(iv) A list of all dispositions of any interests in the foreign corporation after December 31, 1979, and before June 19, 1980, between related persons (as defined in section 453(f)(1)), giving the type and the amount of any interest transferred, the name and address of the related person to whom the interest was transferred, the transferor's basis in the interest transferred, and the amount of any nontaxed gain as defined in section 1125(d) of Pub. L. 96-499.

(2) *Waiver of treaty benefits.* The foreign corporation must submit a binding waiver of the benefits of any U.S. treaty with respect to any gain or loss from the disposition of a U.S. real property interest during the period in which the election is in effect.

(3) *Consent to be taxed.* The foreign corporation must submit a binding agreement to treat as though it were a domestic corporation any gain or loss, that is recognized upon—

(i) The disposition of any U.S. real property interest during the period in which the election is in effect, and

(ii) The disposition of any property that it acquired in exchange for a U.S. real property interest in a nonrecognition transaction (as defined under section 897(e)) during the period in which the election is in effect.

(4) *Interest-holders' consent to election*—(i) *In general.* The foreign corporation must submit both a signed consent to the making of the election and a waiver of U.S. treaty benefits with respect to any gain or loss from the disposition of an interest in the corporation from each person who holds an interest in the corporation on the date the election is made. In the case of a corporation any class of stock of which is regularly traded on an established securities market at any time during the calendar year, the signed consent and waiver need only be provided by a person who holds an interest described in § 1.897-1(c)(2)(iii)(A) or (B) (determined after application of the constructive ownership rules of section 897(c)(6)(C)). The foreign corporation must also include with the signed consents and waivers a list that identifies and describes the interest in the corporation held by each interest holder, including the type and amount of such interest and its fair market value as of the date of the election.

(ii) *Corporation's retention of interest-holders' consents.* A corporation need not file the consents and waivers of its interest-holders as required by paragraph (c)(4)(i) of this section, if it instead complies with the requirements of subdivisions (A) through (D) of this paragraph (c)(4)(ii).

(A) The corporation must place a legend on each outstanding certificate for shares of its stock that reads substantially as follows: "[Name of corporation] has made an election under section 897(i) of the United States Internal Revenue Code to be treated as a U.S. corporation for certain tax purposes, and any purchaser of this interest may therefore be required to withhold tax at the time of the purchase." The corporation must certify that the foregoing requirement has been met and that it will place an equivalent legend on every stock certificate that is issued while the election under section 897(i) is in effect and the corporation retains the consents and waivers of its interest-holders under the rules of this paragraph (c)(4)(ii). However, with respect to any registered certificate issued prior to January 30, 1985, in lieu of placing a legend on the certificate the corporation may certify that it will provide the purchaser of the interest with a copy of the legend at the time the certificate is surrendered for issuance of a new certificate.

(B) The corporation must include with its election a statement that the corporation has received both a signed consent to the making of the election and a waiver of U.S. treaty benefits with respect to any gain or loss from the disposition of an interest in the corporation from each person who holds an interest in the corporation on the date the election is made. In the case of a corporation any class of stock of which is regularly traded on an established securities market at any time during the calendar year, the signed consent and waiver need only be provided by a person who

Reg. § 1.897-3(c)(2)

holds or has held an interest described in § 1.897-1(c)(2)(iii)(A) or (B) (determined after application of the constructive ownership rules of section 897(c)(6)(C)).

(C) The corporation must include with its election a list that describes the interests in the corporation held by each interest-holder. The list need not identify the interest-holders by name, but must set forth the type, amount, and fair market value of the interests held by each.

(D) The corporation must include with its election an agreement that the corporation will retain all signed consents and waivers for a period of three years from the date of the election and supply such documents to the Director within 30 days of his request for production thereof. The Director's review of the signed consents and waivers pursuant to this provision shall not constitute an examination for purposes of section 7605(b).

(5) *Statement regarding prior dispositions.* The foreign corporation must state that no interest in the corporation was disposed of during the shortest of (A) the period from June 19, 1980, through the date of the election, (B) the period from the date on which the corporation first holds a U.S. real property interest through the date of the election, or (C) the five-year period ending on the date of the election. If the corporation cannot state that no such dispositions have been made, it may make the section 897(i) election only if it states that it has complied with the requirements of paragraph (d)(2) of this section.

(d) *Time and duration of election*—(1) *In general.* A foreign corporation that meets the conditions of paragraph (b) of this section may make an election under section 897(i) at any time before the first disposition of an interest in the corporation which would be subject to section 897(a) if the election had been made before that disposition, except as otherwise provided in paragraph (d)(2) of this section. The period to which the election applies begins on the date on which the election is made, or such earlier date as is specified in the election, but not earlier than June 19, 1980. Unless revoked, an election applies for the duration of the time for which the corporation remains in existence. An election is made on the date that the statements described in paragraph (c) of this section are delivered to the Foreign Operations District. If the election is delivered by United States mail, the provisions of section 7502 and the regulations thereunder shall apply in determining the date of delivery.

(2) *Election after disposition of stock.* An election under section 897(i) may be made after any disposition of an interest in the corporation which would have been subject to section 897(a) if the election had been made before that disposition, but only if the requirements of either subdivision (i) or (ii) of this paragraph (d)(2) are met with respect to all dispositions of interests during the period described in paragraph (c)(5) of this section.

(i) There is a payment of an amount equal to any taxes which would have been imposed by reason of the application of section 897 upon all persons who had disposed of interests in the corporation during the period described in paragraph (c)(5) of this section had the corporation made the election prior to such dispositions. Such payment must be made by the later of the date the election is made, or the date on which payment of such taxes would otherwise have been due, and must include any interest that would have accrued had tax actually been due with respect to the disposition. As an election made prior to any disposition of interests in the corporation would have been conditioned on a waiver of treaty benefits by the interest-holders, payment of an amount equal to tax and any interest with respect to such prior disposition is required as a condition to making a subsequent election under this subdivision (i) irrespective of the application of any treaty provision. For this purpose, it is not necessary that the payment be made by the person who would have owed the tax if the election under this section had been made prior to the disposition, and that person is under no obligation to supply any information to the present holders of interests in the electing corporation. The payment shall be made to the Director, ——————————, Foreign Operations District. Where the payment is made by a present holder of an interest, the basis of the person's interest in the corporation shall be increased to the extent of the amount paid.

(ii) Each person that acquired an interest in the electing corporation took a basis in the interest that was equal to the basis of the interest in the hands of the person from which the interest was acquired, increased by the sum of any gain recognized by the transferor of the interest and any tax paid under chapter 1 by the person that acquired the interest, if such interest was acquired after June 18, 1980.

(3) *Adequate proof of basis.* For purposes of meeting the conditions of paragraph (d)(2)(i) or (ii) of this section, a corporation must establish the bases of and amount of gain realized by all persons who disposed of interests in the corporation during the period described in paragraph (c)(5) of this section. See paragraph (g)(3) of this section for an exception to this rule.

(4) *Acknowledgment of receipt.* Within 60 days after its receipt of an election under section

Reg. § 1.897-3(d)(4)

897(i), the Internal Revenue Service will acknowledge receipt of the election. Such acknowledgment either will indicate that the information submitted with the election is complete or will specify any documents that remain to be submitted pursuant to the requirements of paragraph (c) of this section respecting the manner and form in which an election must be made.

(e) *Anti-abuse rule*—(1) *In general.* A corporation that is otherwise eligible to make an election under section 897(i) may do so only by complying with the requirements of subdivision (2) of this paragraph, if during the period described in paragraph (c)(5) of this section—

(i) Prior to receipt of a U.S. real property interest by the corporation seeking to make the election, stock in such corporation (or in any corporation controlled by such corporation) was acquired in a transaction in which the person acquiring such stock obtained an increase in basis in the stock over the adjusted basis of the stock in the hands of the person from whom it was acquired;

(ii) The full amount of gain realized by the person from whom the stock was acquired was not subject to U.S. tax; and

(iii) The corporation seeking to make the election received the U.S. real property interest in a transaction or series of transactions to which section 897(d)(1)(B) or (e)(1) applies to allow for nonrecognition of gain.

(2) *Recognition of gain.* A corporation described in subparagraph (1) of this paragraph (e) may make an election under section 897(i) only if it pays an amount equal to the tax on the full amount of gain realized by the transferors of the stock of such corporation (or of any corporation controlled by it) in the transaction described in paragraph (e)(1)(i) of this section. However, such amount must be paid only if the stock of the corporation seeking to make the election (or the stock of a corporation controlled by it) would have constituted a U.S. real property interest had it (or a corporation controlled by it) made the election before that acquisition. Such amount must be paid by the later of the date of the election or the date on which such tax would otherwise be due, and must include any interest that would have accrued had tax actually been due with respect to the disposition.

(3) *Definition of control.* For purposes of this paragraph, a corporation controls a second corporation if it holds 80 percent or more of the total combined voting power of all classes of stock entitled to vote, and 80 percent or more of the total number of shares of all other classes of stock of the second corporation. In a chain of corporations where each succeeding corporation is controlled within the meaning of this subparagraph (3) by the corporation immediately above it in the chain, each corporation in the chain shall be considered to be controlled by all corporations that preceded it in the chain.

(4) *Examples.* The rules of this paragraph (e) are illustrated by the following examples.

Example 1. Nonresident alien individual X owns 100 percent of the stock of foreign corporation L which was organized in 1981. L's only asset is a parcel of U.S. real property which it has held since 1981. The fair market value of the U.S. real property held by L on January 1, 1984, is $1,000,000. L's basis in the property is $200,000. X's basis in the L stock is $500,000. On June 1, 1984, M corporation, a foreign corporation owned by foreign persons who are unrelated to X, purchases the stock of L from X for $1,000,000 with title passing outside of the United States. Since the stock of L is not a U.S. real property interest, X's gain from the disposition of the L stock ($500,000) is not treated as effectively connected with a U.S. trade or business under section 897(a). In addition, since X was neither engaged in a U.S. trade or business nor present in the U.S. at any time during 1984, such gain is not subject to U.S. tax under section 871. On January 1, 1987, M liquidates L under a plan of liquidation adopted on that same date. Under section 332 of the Code M recognizes no gain on receipt of the parcel of U.S. real property distributed by L in liquidation. Under section 334 (b)(1) M takes $200,000 as its basis in the U.S. real property received from L. Under section 897(d)(1)(B) no gain would be recognized to L under section 897(d)(1)(A) on the liquidating distribution. As a consequence, no gain is recognized to L under section 336 of the Code. After its receipt of the U.S. real property from L, M seeks to make an election to be treated as a domestic corporation. Thus, M acquired the L stock in a transaction in which it obtained a basis in such stock in excess of the adjusted basis of X in the stock, U.S. tax was not paid on the full amount of the gain realized by X, and M has received the property in a distribution in which section 897(d)(1)(B) applied to provide for nonrecognition of gain to L. Therefore, M may make the election only if it pays an amount equal to the tax on the full amount of X's gain, pursuant to the rule of subparagraph (e)(2) of this section.

Example 2. Nonresident alien individual X owns 100 percent of the stock of foreign corporation A which owns 100 percent of the stock of foreign corporation B. X's basis in the A stock is $500,000. A's basis in the B stock is $500,000. B

Reg. § 1.897-3(e)(1)

Nonresident Aliens and Foreign Corporations

See p. 20,601 for regulations not amended to reflect law changes

owns U.S. real property with a fair market value of $1,000,000. B's basis in the U.S. real property is $500,000. On January 1, 1985, X sells the stock of A to Y, an unrelated individual, for $1,000,000 with title passing outside of the United States. In addition, X was neither engaged in a U.S. trade or business nor present in the U.S. at any time during 1985. Since the A stock is not a U.S. real property interest, X's gain on such disposition is not treated as effectively connected with a U.S. trade or business under section 897(a) and is therefore not subject to U.S. tax under section 871. On July 1, 1987, a plan of liquidation is adopted, and B is liquidated into A. Under sections 332, 334(b)(1), 336, and 897(d)(1)(B), there is no tax to A on receipt of U.S. real property from B and no tax to B on the distribution of the U.S. real property interest to A. After receipt of the property A seeks to make an election under section 897(i). Under the rules of paragraph (e) of this section, A may make the election only if it pays an amount equal to the tax on the full amount of X's gain. (Assuming that A is a U.S. real property holding corporation, the same result would be required by the rule of paragraph (d)(2) of this section.)

(f) *Revocation of election*—(1) *In general.* An election under section 897(i) may be revoked only with the consent of the Commissioner. A request for revocation shall be in writing and shall be addressed to the Director, Foreign Operations District, 1325 K St. NW., Washington, D.C. 20225. The request shall include the name, address, and identifying number of the corporation seeking to revoke the election, and a description of all U.S. real property interests held by the corporation on the date of the request for revocation, including the dates such interests were acquired, the corporation's adjusted bases in such interests, and their fair market values as of the date of the request (or book value if the corporation is not a U.S. real property holding corporation under the alternative test of § 1.897-2(b)(2)). The request shall be signed by a responsible officer of the corporation under penalty of perjury and shall contain a statement either that the corporation has made no distributions described in subparagraph (2) of this paragraph (f) or that the conditions of that subparagraph have been satisfied. A revocation will be effective as of the date the request is delivered to the Foreign Operations District (unless the Commissioner provides otherwise in his consent to the revocation. If the request is delivered by United States mail, the provisions of section 7502 and the regulations thereunder shall apply in determining the date of delivery. The Commissioner will generally consent to a revocation, provided either that there have been no distributions described in subparagraph (2) of this paragraph (f), or that the conditions of that subparagraph have been satisfied. Within 90 days after its receipt of a request to revoke an election under section 897(i), the Internal Revenue Service will acknowledge receipt of the request. Such acknowledgement either will indicate that the information submitted with the request is complete or will specify any information that remains to be submitted pursuant to the requirements of this paragraph (f).

(2) *Revocation after distribution.* If there have been any distributions of U.S. real property interests by the corporation during the period to which an election made under section 897(i) applies, the Commissioner shall consent to the revocation of such election only if one of the following conditions is met.

(i) The full amount of gain realized by the corporation upon the distribution was subject to U.S. income tax.

(ii) There is a payment of an amount equal to the taxes that would have been imposed upon the corporation by reason of the application of section 897 if the election had not been in effect on the date of the distribution. Such payment must be made by the later of the date of the request for revocation or the date on which payment of such tax would otherwise have been due, and must include any interest that would have accrued had tax actually been due with respect to the distribution. If under the terms of any treaty to which the United States is a party such distribution would not have been subject to U.S. income tax notwithstanding the provisions of section 897, then this condition may be satisfied by providing a statement with the request for revocation setting forth the treaty and article which would have exempted the distribution from U.S. tax had the election under section 897(i) not been in effect on the date thereof.

(iii) At the time of the receipt of the distributed property, the distributee would be subject to taxation under chapter 1 of the Code on a subsequent disposition of the distributed property, and the basis of the distributed property in the hands of the distributee is no greater than the adjusted basis of such property before the distribution, increased by the amount of gain (if any) recognized by the distributing corporation. For purposes of this paragraph (f)(2)(i)(C), a distributee shall be considered to be subject to taxation upon a subsequent disposition of distributed property only if such distributee waives the benefits of any U.S. treaty that would otherwise render such disposition not taxable by the United States. Such

Reg. § 1.897-3(f)(2)

waiver must be attached to the corporation's request for revocation.

(g) *Transitional rules*—(1) *In general.* An election under section 897(i) that was made at any time after June 18, 1980, must be amended to comply with the requirements of paragraphs (b), (c), and (d) of this section. Such amendment must be delivered in writing to the Director of the Foreign Operations District by [the date which is 3 months after the date of publication of this document in the *Federal Register*]. If the amendment is delivered by United States mail, the provisions of section 7502 and the regulations thereunder shall apply in determining the date of delivery. An election that is properly amended pursuant to the requirements of this section shall be effective as of the date of the original election.

(2) *Corporations previously entitled to make election.* A foreign corporation that would have been entitled under the rules of this section to make a section 897(i) election at any time between June 19, 1980, and January 30, 1985, may retroactively make such an election pursuant to the requirements of this section. Such election must be delivered to the Director, Foreign Operations District, by March 1, 1985.

(3) *Interests in corporation disposed of prior to publication.* Where interests in a corporation were disposed of before January 3, 1984, the requirement of paragraph (d)(2) of this section may be met, notwithstanding the requirement of paragraph (d)(3), by paying a tax that is based upon a reasonable estimate of the gain upon the prior dispositions. Such estimate must be based on all facts and circumstances known to, and ascertainable through the exercise of reasonable diligence by, the corporation seeking to make the election. [Reg. § 1.897-3.]

☐ [T.D. 7999, 12-26-84. Amended by T.D. 8115, 12-16-86.]

[Reg. § 1.897-4AT]

§ 1.897-4AT. Table of contents (Temporary).

§ 1.897-5T. *Corporate distributions (Temporary).*

(a) Purpose and scope.

(b) Distributions by domestic corporations.

(1) Limitation of basis upon dividend distribution of U.S. real property interest.

(2) Distributions by U.S. real property holding corporation under generally applicable rules.

(3) Section 332 liquidations of U.S. real property holding corporations.

(i) General rules.

(ii) Distribution to a foreign corporation under section 332 after June 18, 1980, and before the repeal of the General Utilities doctrine.

(iii) Distribution to a foreign corporation under section 332 and former section 334(b)(2) after June 18, 1980.

(iv) Distribution to a foreign corporation under section 332(a) after July 31, 1986 and after the repeal of the General Utilities doctrine.

(A) Liquidation of domestic corporation.

(B) Liquidation of certain foreign corporations making a section 897(i) election.

(v) Transfer of foreign corporation stock followed by a section 332 liquidation treated as a reorganization.

(4) Section 897(i) companies.

(5) Examples.

(6) Section 333 elections.

(i) General rule.

(ii) Example.

(c) Distributions of U.S. real property interests by foreign corporations.

(1) Recognition of gain required.

(2) Recognition of gain not required.

(i) Statutory exception.

(ii) Section 332 liquidations.

(A) In general.

(B) Recognition of gain required in certain section 332 liquidations.

(iii) Examples.

(3) Limitation of gain recognized under paragraph (c)(1) of this section for certain section 355 distributions.

(i) In general.

(ii) Example.

(4) Distribution by a foreign corporation in certain reorganizations.

(i) In general.

(ii) Statutory exception.

(iii) Regulatory limitation on gain recognized.

(iv) Examples.

(5) Sales of U.S. real property interests by foreign corporations under section 337.

(6) Section 897(l) credit.

(7) Other applicable rules.

(d) Rules of general application.

(1) Interests subject to taxation upon later dispositions.

(i) In general.

(ii) Effects of income tax treaties.

(A) Effect of treaty exemption from tax.

(B) Effect of treaty reduction of tax.

(C) Waiver of treaty benefits to preserve nonrecognition.

(iii) Procedural requirements.

(2) Treaty exception to imposition of tax.

(3) Withholding.

(4) Effect on earnings and profits.

(e) Effective date.

§ 1.897-6T. Nonrecognition exchanges applicable to corporations, their shareholders, and other taxpayers, and certain transfers of property in corporate reorganizations (Temporary).

(a) Nonrecognition exchanges.

(1) In general.

(2) Definition of nonrecognition provision.

(3) Consequence of nonapplication of nonrecognition provisions.

(4) Section 355 distributions treated as exchanges.

(5) Section 1034 rollover of gain.

(i) Purchase of foreign principal residence.

(ii) Purchase of U.S. principal residence.

(6) Determination of basis.

(7) Examples.

(8) Treatment of nonqualifying property.

(i) In general.

(ii) Treatment of mixed exchanges.

(A) Allocation of nonqualifying property.

(B) Recognition of gain.

(C) Treatment of other amounts.

(iii) Example.

(9) Treaty exception to imposition of tax.

(b) Certain foreign to foreign exchanges.

(1) Exceptions to the general rule.

(2) Applicability of exception.

(3) No exceptions.

(4) Examples.

(5) Contribution of property.

(c) Denial of nonrecognition with respect to certain tax avoidance transfers.

(1) In general.

(2) Certain transfers to domestic corporations.

(i) General rule.

(ii) Example.

(3) Basis adjustment for certain related person transactions.

(4) Rearrangement of ownership to gain treaty benefit.

(d) Effective date.

§ 1.897-7T. Treatment of certain partnership interests as entirely U.S. real property interests under section 897(g) (Temporary).

(a) Rule.

(b) Effective date.

§ 1.897-8T. Status as a U.S. real property holding corporation as a condition for electing section 897(i) pursuant to § 1.897-3 (Temporary).

(a) Purpose and scope.

(b) General conditions.

(c) Effective date.

§ 1.897-9T. Treatment of certain interests in publicly traded corporations, definition of foreign person, and foreign governments and international organizations (Temporary).

(a) Purpose and scope.

(b)

(c) Foreign person.

(d) Regularly traded.

(e) Foreign governments and international organizations.

(f) Effective date.

[Temporary Reg. § 1.897-4AT.]

☐ [T.D. 8198, 5-4-88.]

[Reg. § 1.897-5T]

§ 1.897-5T. Corporate distributions (Temporary).—(a) *Purpose and scope.* This section provides rules concerning the recognition of gain or loss and adjustments to basis required with respect to certain corporate distributions that are subject to section 897. Paragraph (b) of this section provides rules concerning such distributions by domestic corporations, including distributions under section 301, distributions in redemption of stock, and distributions in liquidation. Paragraph (c) sets forth rules concerning distributions by foreign corporations, including distributions under sections 301 and 355, distributions in redemption of stock, and distributions in liquidation. Finally, various rules generally applicable to distributions subject to this section, as well as to transfers subject to § 1.897-6T, are set forth in paragraph (d). The rules contained in this section are also subject to the tax avoidance rules of § 1.897-6T(c).

(b) *Distributions by domestic corporations*—(1) *Limitation of basis upon dividend distribution of U.S. real property interest.* Under section 897(f), if any domestic corporation (distributing corporation) distributes a U.S. real property interest to a shareholder that is a foreign person (distributee) in a distribution to which section 301 applies, then the basis of the distributed U.S. real property interest in the hands of the foreign distributee shall be determined in accordance with the

Reg. § 1.897-5T(b)(1)

provisions of section 301(d), and shall not exceed—

(i) The adjusted basis of the property before the distribution in the hands of the distributing corporation, increased by

(ii) The sum of—

(A) Any gain recognized by the distributing corporation on the distribution, and

(B) Any U.S. tax paid by or on behalf of the distributee with respect to the distribution.

(2) *Distributions by U.S. real property holding corporations which are taxable exchanges of stock under generally applicable rules.* If a domestic corporation, stock in which is treated as a U.S. real property interest, distributes property with respect to such stock to a foreign shareholder, the distributee shall be treated as having disposed of a U.S. real property interest, and shall recognize gain or loss on the stock of such domestic corporation to the extent that, with respect to the distributees—

(i) Part or all of the distribution is treated pursuant to section 301(c)(3)(A) as a sale or exchange of stock;

(ii) Part or all of the distribution is treated pursuant to section 302(a) as made in part or full payment in exchange for stock; or

(iii) Part or all of the distribution is treated pursuant to section 331(a) as made in full payment in exchange for stock.

Stock in a domestic corporation shall not be considered a U.S. real property interest pursuant to the provisions of § 1.897-2(f)(2) if the corporation does not hold any U.S. real property interests and has disposed of all of its U.S. real property interests owned within the previous five years in transactions in which the full amount of gain was recognized under the rules of § 1.897-2(f)(2). If gain is recognized at the corporate level on either a distribution of a U.S. real property interest or a sale of a U.S. real property interest in a liquidation, such distribution or sale shall be considered a disposition for purposes of § 1.897-2(f)(2). With regard to the consequences of a distribution from a U.S. real property holding corporation under section 355(a), see § 1.897-6T(a)(1) and (4).

(3) *Section 332 liquidations of U.S. real property holding corporations*—(i) *General rules.* Exchanges that are subject to section 897(e) are normally covered by § 1.897-6T(a)(1), (2) and (3). This paragraph (b)(3) provides rules concerning the application of section 897(e) and the general principles of § 1.897-6T(a)(1), (2) and (3) to section 332 liquidations of U.S. real property holding corporations.

(ii) *Distribution to a foreign corporation under section 332 after June 18, 1980, and before the repeal of the General Utilities doctrine.* Except for distributions under paragraph (b)(3)(iii) of this section (relating to section 332 and former section 334(b)(2)), the rules of this paragraph (b)(3)(ii) shall apply to section 332 distributions after June 18, 1980, and before January 1, 1990, pursuant to section 336(a) as in effect prior to the effective dates of the amendments made by section 631 of the Tax Reform Act of 1986. A foreign corporation that meets the stock ownership requirements of section 332(b) with respect to stock in a domestic corporation that is a U.S. real property interest shall not, after December 31, 1984, be subject to taxation by reason of section 367(a). The foreign corporation shall recognize gain pursuant to section 897(e)(1) on such stock upon the receipt of property in a section 332(a) liquidation from such domestic corporation, but only to the extent that the property received constitutes property other than a U.S. real property interest. The gain on the stock in the domestic corporation to be recognized by the foreign corporation pursuant to section 897(e)(1) shall be determined by multiplying the gain realized on the distribution by a fraction. The numerator of the fraction shall be the fair market value of the property other than U.S. real property interests received by the foreign corporation on the distribution, and the denominator shall be the fair market value of all property received by the foreign corporation on the distribution. The bases of the distributed U.S. real property interests in the hands of the foreign corporation shall be the same as the bases in the hands of the domestic corporation. The bases of the property other than U.S. real property interests in the hands of the foreign corporation shall be the same as the bases in the hands of the domestic corporation, plus any gain recognized by the foreign corporation on the distribution allocated among such assets in proportion to the potential gain inherent in each such asset at the time of distribution. However, the basis of each asset is limited to its fair market value. Property, other than a U.S. real property interest that is distributed by the domestic corporation, shall not be considered to be distributed by the domestic corporation pursuant to a section 332 liquidation (that is, the foreign corporation shall not be considered to be a corporation for purposes of section 332) if the requirements of section 367(a) are not satisfied. See, for example, sections 1245(b)(3) and 1250(d)(3) regarding the consequences to the distributing domestic corporation if the requirements of section 367(a) are not satisfied.

(iii) *Distribution to a foreign corporation under section 332 and former section 334(b)(2) after June 18, 1980.* The rules of this paragraph (b)(2)(iii) shall apply to section 332 distributions after June 18, 1980 where the basis of the distrib-

Reg. § 1.897-5T(b)(2)

uted property in the hands of the foreign corporation is determined under section 334(b)(2) as in effect prior to the Tax Equity and Fiscal Responsibility Act of 1982. A foreign corporation that meets the stock ownership requirements of section 332(b) with respect to stock in a domestic corporation that is a U.S. real property interest shall recognize gain on the receipt of property in a section 332(a) liquidation where section 334(b)(2) applies to the extent that the fair market value of the distributed assets that are not U.S. real property interests exceeds the basis of such assets determined under section 334(b)(2) (for example, if the liquidation does not occur immediately upon the purchase of stock in the domestic corporation). The gain recognized shall not exceed the excess of the fair market value of the stock of the domestic corporation in the hands of the foreign corporation at the time of the distribution over the shareholder's adjusted basis in such stock. The basis of the distributed U.S. real property interests in the hands of the foreign corporation shall be determined under section 334(b)(2), by reference to the adjusted basis of the stock with respect to which the distribution was made. The basis of such property other than U.S. real property interests shall be tentatively determined under section 334(b)(2), and then increased by any gain recognized by the foreign corporation on the distribution allocated among such assets in proportion to the potential gain inherent in each such asset at the time of distribution (computed using the tentative basis as determined under section 334(b)(2)). The basis of each asset is limited, however, to its fair market value.

(iv) *Distribution to a foreign corporation under section 332 after July 31, 1986 and after the repeal of the General Utilities doctrine.* The rules of this subdivision (iv) shall apply to section 332 distributions after July 31, 1986, pursuant to section 337(a) as in effect after the effective dates of the amendments of section 631 of the Tax Reform Act of 1986.

(A) *Liquidation of domestic corporation.* A foreign corporation that meets the stock ownership requirements of section 332(b) with respect to stock in a domestic corporation that is a U.S. real property interest (except a foreign corporation that has made an effective election under section 897(i) and the stock of which is treated as a U.S. real property interest) shall not recognize any gain under sections 367(a) or 897(e)(1) on the receipt of property in a section 332(a) liquidation. The domestic corporation shall not recognize gain under section 367(e)(2) on the distribution of U.S. real property interests (other than stock in a former U.S. real property holding corporation which is treated as a U.S. real property interest) to the foreign corporation. The domestic corporation shall recognize gain under section 367(e)(2) on the distribution of stock in a former U.S. real property holding corporation which is treated as a U.S. real property interest. With respect to the recognition of gain or loss by the domestic corporation under section 367(e)(2) on the distribution of property other than U.S. real property interests, see the regulations under section 367(e)(2). The basis of the distributed U.S. real property interests (other than stock in a former U.S. real property holding corporation) in the hands of the foreign corporation shall be the same as it was in the hands of the domestic corporation. The basis of any property (other than U.S. real property interests) and stock in a former U.S. real property holding corporation that is a U.S. real property interest in the hands of the foreign corporation shall be the same as it was in the hands of the domestic corporation increased by any gain recognized by the distributing corporation on the distribution that was subject to U.S. taxation.

(B) *Liquidation of certain foreign corporations making a section 897(i) election.* A foreign corporation that meets the stock ownership requirements of section 332(b) with respect to stock in another foreign corporation, that has made an effective election under section 897(i) and the stock of which is treated as a U.S. real property interest, shall recognize gain pursuant to section 897(e)(1) on such stock upon the receipt from the distributing foreign corporation of property that is not a U.S. real property interest, and that is not used by the distributee foreign corporation in the conduct of a trade or business within the United States (if the distributee foreign corporation is not a resident of a country with which the United States maintains an income tax treaty) or in a permanent establishment within the United States (if the distributee foreign corporation is a resident of a country with which the United States maintains an income tax treaty). The gain on the stock in the foreign corporation (making an effective election under section 897(i)) to be recognized by the distributee foreign corporation pursuant to section 897(e)(1) shall be determined by multiplying the gain realized on the distribution by a fraction. The numerator of the fraction shall be the fair market value of the property received by the distributee foreign corporation upon which it must recognize gain, and the denominator of the fraction shall be the fair market value of all property received by the distributee foreign corporation on the distribution. The distributing foreign corporation shall not recognize gain under section 367(e)(2) on the distribution of U.S. real property interests to the distributee foreign corporation. With respect to the recognition of gain or loss under section 367(e)(2) on the distribution of property other than U.S. real property interests,

Reg. § 1.897-5T(b)(3)

see the regulations under section 367(e)(2). The basis of the distributed U.S. real property interests in the hands of the distributee foreign corporation shall be the same as it was in the hands of the distributing foreign corporation. The basis of the property upon which the distributee foreign corporation recognized gain in the hands of the distributee foreign corporation shall be the same as the basis in the hands of the distributing foreign corporation, plus any gain recognized by the distributee foreign corporation on the receipt of such property allocated among such property in proportion to the potential gain inherent in each such property at the time of the distribution. In regard to the basis of any other property received by the distributee foreign corporation in the liquidation, see the regulations under section 367(e)(2). However, the basis of each asset is limited to its fair market value.

(v) *Transfer of foreign corporation stock followed by a section 332 liquidation treated as a reorganization.* If a nonresident alien or foreign corporation transfers the stock of a foreign corporation that owns a U.S. real property interest to a domestic corporation in exchange for stock of the domestic corporation (or its domestic or foreign parent corporation) in a reorganization under section 368(a)(1)(B) or in an exchange under section 351(a), and if the foreign corporation then distributes the U.S. real property interest to the domestic corporation in a liquidation described in section 332(a) within five years of the transfer of the stock of the foreign corporation to the domestic corporation, then the transfer of the foreign corporation stock and the liquidation shall be treated as a reorganization described in section 368(a)(1)(C) or (D). The rules of § 1.897-6T(a)(1) shall apply to the transfer of the U.S. real property interest to the domestic corporation in exchange for domestic corporation stock, and the rules of § 1.897-5T(c)(4) shall apply to the distribution of domestic corporation stock by the foreign corporation. However, the rules of this paragraph (b)(3)(v) shall not apply if the transfer of the foreign corporation stock and the liquidation under section 332(a) are separate and independent transactions justified by substantial and verifiable business purposes.

(4) *Section 897 (i) companies.* Except as otherwise provided herein for purposes of this section and § 1.897-6T, a foreign corporation that has made a valid election under section 897(i) shall be treated as a domestic corporation and not as a foreign corporation in determining the application of section 897. For rules concerning the making of a section 897(i) election, see §§ 1.897-3 and 1.897-8T. In regard to section 367(e)(2) and foreign corporations that have made an effective election under section 897(i), see paragraph (b)(3)(iv) of this section.

(5) *Examples.* The following examples illustrate the rules of this paragraph (b). In each example there is no applicable income tax treaty to which the United States is a party.

Example (1). (i) A is a nonresident alien who owns 100 percent of the stock of DC, a U.S. real property holding corporation. DC's only asset is Parcel P, a U.S. real property interest, with a fair market value of $500,000 and an adjusted basis of $300,000. DC completely liquidates in 1987 and distributes Parcel P to A in exchange for the DC stock held by A.

(ii) Under section 336(a), DC must recognize gain to the extent of the excess of the fair market value ($500,000) over the adjusted basis ($300,000), or $200,000.

(iii) A does not recognize any gain under section 897(a) because the DC stock in the hands of A is no longer a U.S. real property interest under paragraph (b)(2) of this section and paragraph 2(f) of § 1.897-2. A does recognize gain (if any) under section 331(a); however, the gain is not subject to taxation under section 871(a). A's adjusted basis in Parcel P is $500,000.

(iv) If DC did not recognize all of the gain on the disposition under a transitional rule to section 631 of the Tax Reform Act of 1986, then paragraph (b)(2) of this section and paragraph 2(f) of § 1.897-2 would not apply to A. A would recognize gain (if any) under paragraph (b)(2) because the distribution is treated as in full payment in exchange for the DC stock under section 897(a).

Example (2). (i) FC, a Country F corporation, owns 100 percent of the stock of DC, a U.S. real property holding corporation. FC's basis in the stock of DC is $400,000, and the fair market value of the DC stock is $800,000. DC owns a U.S. real property interest with an adjusted basis of $350,000 and a fair market value of $600,000. DC also owns other assets that are not U.S. real property interests that have an adjusted basis of $125,000 and a fair market value of $200,000. DC completely liquidates in 1985 and distributes all of its property to FC in exchange for the DC stock held by FC.

(ii) Under paragraph (b)(3)(ii) of this section, FC recognizes $100,000 of gain under section 897(a) on the disposition of the DC stock. This is determined by multiplying FC's gain realized ($400,000) by a fraction. The numerator of the fraction is the fair market value of the property other than U.S. real property interests ($200,000), and the denominator of the fraction is the fair market value of all property received ($800,000). FC takes a carryover adjusted basis in the U.S. real property interest ($350,000). FC's adjusted

Reg. § 1.897-5T(b)(4)

basis in the assets that are not U.S. real property interests ($200,000) is the basis of those assets in the hands of DC ($125,000) plus the gain recognized by FC on the distribution ($100,000) not to exceed the fair market value ($200,000).

Example (3). (i) FC, a Country F corporation, owns 100 percent of the stock of DC, a U.S. real property holding corporation. FC's basis in the stock of DC is $300,000, and the fair market value of the DC stock is $500,000. DC owns Parcel P, a U.S. real property interest, with an adjusted basis of $250,000 and a fair market value of $400,000. DC also owns all of the stock of DX, a former U.S. real property holding corporation whose stock is a U.S. real property interest, with an adjusted basis of $50,000 and a fair market value of $100,000. DC completely liquidates in 1987 and distributes all of its property to FC in exchange for the DC stock held by FC.

(ii) Under paragraph (b)(3)(iv)(A) of this section, DC recognizes $50,000 of gain on the distribution to FC of the DX stock. DC does not recognize any gain for purposes of section 367(e)(2) on the distribution to FC of Parcel P.

(iii) Under paragraph (b)(3)(iv)(A) of this section, FC's disposition of its DC stock is not treated as a disposition of a U.S. real property interest. Under section 334(b)(1), FC takes a carryover adjusted basis of $250,000 in Parcel P. FC takes an increased basis of $100,000 in the DX stock which is equal to DC's basis ($50,000) increased by the gain recognized by DC ($50,000).

(iv) The result would be the same if FC had made an effective election under section 897(i).

(6) *Section 333 elections*—(i) *General rule.* A foreign shareholder that elects section 333 as in effect prior to its repeal by the Tax Reform Act of 1986 upon the distribution of property in a liquidation by a domestic corporation whose stock is treated as a U.S. real property interest shall recognize gain on such stock to the extent that—

(A) The property received by the foreign shareholder constitutes property other than U.S. real property interests subject to U.S. taxation upon its disposition as specified by paragraph (a)(1) of this section, or

(B) The basis of a U.S. real property interest subject to U.S. taxation upon its disposition in the hands of the recipient foreign shareholder exceeds the basis of the U.S. real property interest in the hands of the liquidating domestic corporation.

In determining the amount of gain recognized by the foreign shareholder, the foreign shareholder shall be considered to have exchanged the domestic corporation stock for all the property distributed on a proportionate fair market value basis. The gain recognized on a respective portion of domestic corporation stock shall not exceed the gain realized on that portion. Property other than U.S. real property interests subject to U.S. taxation upon disposition shall have a fair market value basis in the hands of the foreign shareholder. The basis of U.S. real property interests subject to U.S. taxation upon disposition shall be the basis of the proportionate part of the domestic corporation stock cancelled or redeemed in the liquidation, increased in the amount of gain recognized (other than gain recognized under this section) by the shareholder in respect to that proportionate part of the domestic corporation stock.

(ii) *Example.* The rules of paragraph (b)(6)(i) of this section may be illustrated by the following example.

Example. (i) A is a citizen and resident of Country F with which the U.S. does not have an income tax treaty. A owns all of the stock of DC, a U.S. real property holding corporation. The DC stock has a fair market value of $1,000,000. A acquired the DC stock in two purchases. The basis of one lot of the DC stock is $150,000, and the basis of the other lot is $650,000.

(ii) DC owns Parcel P, a U.S. real property interest, with a fair market value of $750,000 and an adjusted basis of $400,000. DC's only other property is equipment with a fair market value of $250,000 and an adjusted basis of $100,000. DC does not have any earnings and profits.

(iii) DC completely liquidates in 1985 in accordance with section 333 by distributing Parcel P and the equipment to A. A elects section 333 treatment.

(iv) A is considered as having exchanged 75 percent (fair market value of Parcel P/fair market value of all property distributed) of the DC stock for Parcel P. A realized gain of $150,000 on that portion of the DC stock ($750,000 − $600,000). All of the gain of $150,000 is recognized under section 897(a) because A's basis in Parcel P under section 334(c) ($600,000) would exceed DC's basis in Parcel P ($400,000) by at least the amount of realized gain. A takes a basis of $750,000 in Parcel P.

(v) A is considered as having exchanged 25 percent (fair market value of equipment/fair market value of all property distributed) of the DC stock for the equipment. A realized gain of $50,000 on that portion of the DC stock ($250,000 − $200,000). All of the gain of $50,000 is recognized under section 897(a). A takes a basis of $250,000 in the equipment.

(c) *Distributions of U.S. real property interests by foreign corporations*—(1) *Recognition of gain required.* If a foreign corporation makes a distribution (including a distribution in liquidation or

Reg. § 1.897-5T(c)(1)

redemption) of a U.S. real property interest to a shareholder (whether foreign or domestic), then, except as provided in paragraph (c)(2), (3) or (4) of this section, the distributing corporation shall recognize gain (but not loss) on the distribution under section 897(d)(1). The gain recognized shall be equal to the excess of the fair market value of the U.S. real property interest (as of the time of the distribution) over its adjusted basis. Except as otherwise provided, the distributee's basis in the distributed U.S. real property interest shall be determined under the otherwise applicable sections of the Code. The distributee (whether domestic or foreign) of a foreign corporation in a liquidation under section 332 shall take the foreign corporation's basis in the distributed U.S. real property interest increased by any gain recognized (and subject to U.S. income taxation) by the foreign corporation on the distribution of such U.S. real property interest.

(2) *Recognition of gain not required*—(i) *Statutory exception rule.* Under section 897(d)(2)(A), gain shall not be recognized by a distributing foreign corporation if—

(A) At the time of the receipt of the distributed U.S. real property interest, the distributee would be subject to U.S. income taxation on a subsequent disposition of the U.S. real property interest, determined in accordance with the rules of paragraph (d)(1) of this section;

(B) The basis of the distributed U.S. real property interest in the hands of the distributee is no greater than the adjusted basis of such property before the distribution, increased by the amount of gain (if any) recognized by the distributing corporation upon the distribution and added to the adjusted basis under the otherwise applicable provisions; and

(C) The distributing corporation complies with the filing requirements of paragraph (d)(1)(iii) of this section.

(ii) *Section 332 liquidations*—(A) *In general.* A distributing foreign corporation that meets the requirements of paragraph (c)(2)(i) in a section 332(a) liquidation shall not recognize gain on the distribution of U.S. real property interests to a foreign corporation meeting the stock ownership requirements of section 332(b) if the distributing corporation complies with the procedural requirements of paragraph (d)(1)(iii). Whether a foreign corporation recognizes gain on the distribution of U.S. real property interests to a U.S. corporation meeting the stock ownership requirements of section 332(b) depends upon whether the U.S. corporation satisfies the subject to tax requirement provided in paragraph (d)(1)(i) (in addition to the procedural requirements of paragraph (d)(1)(iii)). With respect to section 332 distributions by a foreign corporation occurring after July 31, 1986, section 367(e)(2) shall not affect the application of section 337(a) (as in effect after the Tax Reform Act of 1986) and paragraph (c)(2)(i) of this section to the distribution of a U.S. real property interest.

(B) *Recognition of gain required in certain section 332 liquidations.* Notwithstanding the other rules of this paragraph (c), a foreign corporation shall, pursuant to the authority conferred by section 897(e)(2), recognize gain on its distribution after May 5, 1988 of a U.S. real property interest to a domestic corporation meeting the stock ownership requirements of section 332(b) if—

(*1*) the foreign corporation has not made an election under section 897(i), and any gain on the stock in the foreign corporation would be subject to U.S. taxation if an election were made on the date of the liquidation; and

(*2*) The distribution of the U.S. real property interest by the foreign corporation to the domestic corporation pursuant to section 332(a) occurs less than five years after the date of the last gain from the disposition of stock of the foreign corporation that would be subject to payment of tax under section 1.897-3(d)(2)(i) if an election under section 897(i) were made by the foreign corporation on the date of its liquidation.

With regard to the treatment of certain foreign corporations as domestic corporations under section 897(i), however, see §§ 1.897-3 and 1.897-8T.

(iii) *Examples.* The rules of this paragraph (c)(2) may be illustrated by the following examples.

Example (1). (i) DC, a domestic corporation, owns 100 percent of the stock of FC, a Country F corporation. FC's only asset is Parcel P, a U.S. real property interest, with a fair market value of $500x and an adjusted basis of $100x. In September 1987, FC liquidates under section 332(a) and transfers Parcel P to DC. The transitional rules contained in section 633 of the Tax Reform Act of 1986 concerning the repeal of the *General Utilities* doctrine would not be applicable to a subsequent distribution or disposition of assets by DC.

(ii) Assume that FC complies with the filing requirements of paragraph (d)(1)(iii). DC will be subject to U.S. income taxation on a subsequent disposition of Parcel P under the rules of paragraph (d)(1). The basis of Parcel P in the hands of DC will be $100x under section 334(b)(1), and thus no greater than the basis of Parcel P in the hands of FC. FC does not recognize any gain under the rules of paragraph (c)(1) of this section on the distribution because the exception of paragraph (d)(2)(i) applies.

Reg. § 1.897-5T(c)(2)

Example (2). If in *Example (1)* the distribution by FC to DC occurred in September 1985, and DC sold or exchanged Parcel P under sections 336(a) or 337(a) as in effect prior to the Tax Reform Act of 1986, then FC must recognize gain of $400x on the distribution of Parcel P. The gain must be recognized because Parcel P in the hands of DC is not considered subject to U.S. income taxation on a subsequent disposition under the rules of paragraph (d)(1) of this section.

(3) *Limitation of gain recognized under paragraph (c)(1) of this section for certain section 355 distributions*—(i) *In general.* Under paragraph (c)(1) of this section, a foreign corporation that distributes stock in a domestic corporation that constitutes a U.S. real property interest in a distribution to which section 355 applies shall recognize gain on the distribution to the extent that the fair market value of the distributed stock exceeds its adjusted basis in the hands of the distributing foreign corporation. The gain recognized shall be limited under this paragraph (c)(3), however, to the amount by which the aggregate basis of the distributed stock in the hands of the distributees exceeds the aggregate adjusted basis of the distributed stock in the hands of the distributing corporation. The distributees' basis in the distributed U.S. real property interest shall be determined under the otherwise applicable provisions of section 358. (Thus, the distributees' basis in the distributed U.S. real property interest shall be determined without any increase for any gain recognized by the foreign corporation).

(ii) *Example.* The rules of paragraph (c)(3)(i) of this section may be illustrated by the following example.

Example. (i) C is a citizen and resident of Country F. C owns all of the stock of FC, a Country F corporation. The fair market value of the FC stock is 1000x, and C has a basis of 600x in the FC stock. Country F does not have an income tax treaty with the United States.

(ii) In a transaction qualifying as a distribution of stock of a controlled corporation under section 355(a), FC distributes to C all of the stock of DC, a U.S. real property holding corporation. C does not surrender any of the FC stock. The DC stock has a fair market value of 600x, and FC has an adjusted basis of 200x in the DC stock. After the distribution, the FC stock has a fair market value of 400x.

(iii) Under paragraph (c)(3)(i) of this section, FC must recognize gain on the distribution of the DC stock to C equal to the difference between the fair market value of the DC stock (600x) and FC's adjusted basis in the DC stock (200x). This results in a potential gain of 400x. Under section 358, C takes a 360x adjusted basis in the DC stock. Provided that FC complies with the filing requirements of paragraph (d)(1)(iii) of this section, the gain recognized by FC is limited under paragraph (c)(3)(i) to 160x because (A) this is the amount by which the basis of the DC stock in the hands of C (360x) exceeds the adjusted basis of the DC stock in the hands of FC (200x), and (B) at the time of receipt of the DC stock, C would be subject to U.S. taxation on a subsequent disposition of the stock.

(iv) C's adjusted basis in the DC stock is not increased by the 160x recognized by FC.

(4) *Distribution by a foreign corporation in certain reorganizations*—(i) *In general.* Under paragraph (c)(1) of this section, a foreign corporation that transfers property to another corporation in an exchange under section 361(a) for stock of a domestic corporation which is a United States real property holding corporation immediately after the transfer in a reorganization under section 368(a)(1)(C), (D) or (F) shall recognize gain under section 897(d)(1) on the distribution (whether actual or deemed) of the stock of the domestic corporation received by the foreign corporation to its shareholders (whether domestic or foreign). See § 1.897-6T(a) of the regulations for the consequences to the foreign corporation of the exchange of its property for the domestic corporation stock.

(ii) *Statutory exception.* Pursuant to the exception provided in section 897(d)(2)(A), no gain shall be recognized by the foreign corporation on its distribution of the domestic corporation stock if—

(A) At the time of the distribution, the distributee (*i.e.*, the exchanging shareholder in the section 354 exchange) would be subject to U.S. taxation on a subsequent disposition of the stock of the domestic corporation, determined in accordance with the rules of paragraph (d)(1) of this section;

(B) The distributee's adjusted basis in the stock of the foreign corporation immediately before the distribution was no greater than the foreign corporation's basis in the stock of the domestic corporation determined under section 358; and

(C) The distributing corporation complies with the filing requirements of paragraph (d)(1)(iii) of this section.

(iii) *Regulatory limitation on gain recognized.* If the requirements of subdivisions (A) and (C) of paragraph (c)(4)(ii) are met, the amount of any gain recognized by the foreign corporation shall not exceed the excess of the distributee's adjusted basis in the stock of the foreign corporation immediately before the distribution over the foreign corporation's basis in the stock of the

Reg. § 1.897-5T(c)(4)

domestic corporation immediately before the distribution as determined under section 358.

(iv) *Examples.* The rules of paragraph (c)(4) of this section may be illustrated by the following examples.

Example (1). (i) A, a nonresident alien, organized FC, a Country W corporation, in September 1980 to invest in U.S. real estate. In 1986, FC's only asset is Parcel P, a U.S. real property interest with a fair market value of $600,000 and an adjusted basis to FC of $200,000. Parcel P is subject to a mortgage with an outstanding balance of $100,000. The fair market value of the FC stock is $500,000, and A's adjusted basis in the stock is $100,000. FC does not have liabilities in excess of the adjusted basis in Parcel P. The United States does not have a treaty with Country W that entitles FC to nondiscriminatory treatment as described in section 1.897-3(b)(2) of the regulations.

(ii) Pursuant to a plan of reorganization under section 368(a)(1)(D), FC transfers Parcel P to DC, a newly formed domestic corporation, in exchange for DC stock. FC distributes the DC stock to A in exchange for A's FC stock.

(iii) FC's exchange of Parcel P for the DC stock is a disposition of a U.S. real property interest. Under § 1.897-6T(a)(1), there is an exchange of a U.S. real property interest (Parcel P) for another U.S. real property interest (DC stock) so that no gain is recognized on the exchange under section 897(e). DC takes FC's basis of $200,000 in Parcel P under section 362(b). Under section 358(a)(1), FC takes a $100,000 basis in the DC stock because FC's substituted basis of $200,000 in the DC stock is reduced by the $100,000 of liabilities to which Parcel P is subject.

(iv) Under section 897(d)(1) and paragraph (c)(4)(i) of this section, FC generally must recognize gain on the distribution of the DC stock received in exchange for FC's assets equal to the difference between the fair market value of the DC stock ($500,000) and FC's adjusted basis in the DC stock prior to the distribution ($100,000). This results in a potential gain of $400,000. Under section 358(a)(1), A takes a basis in the DC stock equal to the its basis in the FC stock of $100,000. Provided that FC complies with the filing requirements of paragraph (d)(1)(iii) of this section, no gain is recognized by FC on the distribution of the DC stock under the statutory exception to the general rule of section 897(d)(1) provided in section 897(d)(2)(A) and paragraph (c)(4)(ii) of this section because (*1*) A's basis in the DC stock ($100,000) does not exceed FC's adjusted basis in the DC stock ($100,000) immediately prior to the distribution and (*2*) A, at the time of receipt of the DC stock, would be subject to U.S. taxation on a subsequent disposition of the stock.

(v) The FC stock in the hands of A is not a U.S. real property interest because FC is a foreign corporation that has not elected to be treated as a domestic corporation under section 897(i). Accordingly, the exchange of the FC stock by A for DC stock is not a disposition of a U.S. real property interest under section 897(a).

Example (2). The facts are the same as in *Example* (1), except that A purchased the FC stock in September 1983 for $100,000 from S, a nonresident alien, and that S had a basis of $40,000 in the FC stock at the time of the sale to A. The results are the same as in Example 1.

Example (3). (i) The facts are the same as in *Example* 1, except that A's adjusted basis in the FC stock prior to the reorganization is $300,000. Following the distribution, A takes its basis of $300,000 in the FC stock as its basis in the DC stock pursuant to section 358(a)(1).

(ii) FC does not qualify under the statutory exception of paragraph (c)(4)(ii) to the general recognition rule of section 897(d)(1) and paragraph (c)(4)(i) of this section because A's basis in the DC stock ($300,000) exceeds FC's adjusted basis in the DC stock ($100,000) immediately prior to the distribution. However, provided that FC complies with the filing requirements of paragraph (d)(1)(iii) of this section, the gain recognized by FC is limited to $200,000 under the regulatory limitation of gain provided by paragraph (c)(4)(iii). This is the excess of A's basis in the FC stock immediately before the distribution ($300,000) over A's adjusted basis in the DC stock immediately before the distribution ($100,000).

(iii) A takes a basis of $300,000 in the DC stock under section 358(a)(1). A's basis in the DC stock is not increased by the gain recognized by FC. DC takes a basis of $200,000 in Parcel P under section 362(b).

Example (4). (i) The facts are the same as in *Example* (3), except that the United States has an income tax treaty with Country W entitling FC to nondiscriminatory treatment under section 1.897-3(b) (2) of the regulations. A valid election under section 897(i) is made to treat FC as a U.S. corporation.

(ii) FC is treated as a domestic corporation for purposes of section 897 and is not required to recognize gain under section 897(d)(1) and paragraph (c)(4)(i) of this section on the distribution of the DC stock as described in *Example* 3. (If a valid section 897(i) election were not made, the result would be same as in *Example* (3).)

(iii) The FC stock in the hands of A is a U.S. real property interest because an election

Reg. § 1.897-5T(c)(4)

was made under section 897(i) to treat FC as a U.S. corporation. The exchange of the FC stock for DC stock by A is a disposition of a U.S. real property interest. Under section 897(e)(1) and paragraph (a) of § 1.897-6T, A does not recognize gain on the exchange because there is an exchange of a U.S. real property interest (the FC stock) for another U.S. real property interest (the DC stock). Under section 358(a)(1), A takes as its basis in the DC stock A's basis in the FC stock ($300,000).

(5) *Sales of U.S. real property interests by foreign corporations under section 337.* Section 337 as in effect prior to the Tax Reform Act of 1986 shall not apply to any sale or exchange (including a deemed section 337 sale pursuant to an election under section 338(a) to treat a stock purchase as an asset acquisition) of a U.S. real property interest by a foreign corporation.

(6) *Section 897(l) credit.* If a foreign corporation adopts a plan of complete liquidation and if, solely by reason of section 897(d) and this section, section 337(a)(as in effect before the Tax Reform Act of 1986) does not apply to sales or exchanges of, or section 336 (as in effect before the Tax Reform Act of 1986) does not apply to distributions of, United States real property interests by the liquidating corporation, then—

(i) The amount realized by the shareholder on the distribution shall be increased by its proportionate share of the amount by which the tax imposed by chapter 1 of the Code, as modified by the provisions of any applicable U.S. income tax treaty, on the liquidating corporation would have been reduced if section 897(d) and this section had not been applicable, and

(ii) For purposes of the Code, the shareholder shall be deemed to have paid, on the last day prescribed by law for the payment of the tax imposed by subtitle A of the Code on the shareholder for the taxable year, an amount of tax equal to the amount of increase in the amount realized described in subdivision (i) of this paragraph (c).

The special rule provided by this paragraph (c)(5) applies only to shareholders who are United States citizens or residents, and who have held stock in the liquidating corporation continuously since June 18, 1980. This special rule also only applies for the first taxable year of any such shareholder in which the shareholder receives a distribution in complete liquidation from the foreign corporation.

(7) *Other applicable rules.* For rules concerning exemption of gain pursuant to a U.S. income tax treaty, withholding of tax from distributions, and other applicable rules, see paragraph (d) of this section. For the treatment of liquidations described in section 334(b)(2)(A) of certain foreign corporations acquired before November 6, 1980, see § 1.897-4.

(d) *Rules of general application*—(1) *Interests subject to taxation upon later disposition*—(i) *In general.* Pursuant to the otherwise applicable rules of this section and § 1.897-6T, nonrecognition of gain or loss may apply with respect to certain distributions or exchanges of U.S. real property interests if any gain from a subsequent disposition of the interests that are distributed or received by the transferor in the exchange would be included in the gross income of the distributee or transferor and be subject to U.S. taxation. Gain is considered subject to U.S. taxation if the gain is included on the income tax return of a U.S. tax paying entity even if there is no U.S. tax liability (for example, because of net operating losses or an investment tax credit). Gain is not considered subject to U.S. taxation if the gain is derived by a tax exempt entity. A real estate investment trust is considered to be a pass-through entity for purposes of the rule of taxability of this paragraph (d)(1)(i). Thus, for example, a tax exempt entity holding an interest in a real estate investment trust is not subject to tax. A domestic corporation (including a foreign corporation that makes an effective section 897(i) election after receipt of the U.S. real property interest) shall not be considered subject to U.S. taxation on a subsequent disposition of a U.S. real property interest if it received the U.S. real property interest prior to the effective date of the repeal of sections 336(a) or 337(a) as in effect prior to the Tax Reform Act of 1986, unless the U.S. real property interest has not been sold or exchanged by the domestic corporation prior to such effective date in a transaction to which either section 336(a) or section 337(a)(as in effect prior to such effective date) applied. In addition, an interest shall be considered to be subject to U.S. taxation upon its subsequent disposition only if the requirements set forth in subdivision (iii) of this paragraph (d)(1) are met.

(ii) *Effects of income tax treaties*—(A) *Effect of treaty exemption from tax.* Except as otherwise provided in subdivision (C) of this paragraph (d)(1)(ii), a U.S. real property interest shall not be considered to be subject to U.S. taxation upon a subsequent disposition if, at the time of its distribution or exchange, the recipient is entitled pursuant to the provisions of a U.S. income tax treaty to an exemption from U.S. taxation upon a disposition of the interest.

(B) *Effect of treaty reduction of tax.* If, at the time of a distribution or exchange, a distributee of a U.S. real property interest in a distribution or a transferor who receives a U.S. real property interest in an exchange would be entitled pursuant to the provisions of a U.S. income tax treaty to reduced U.S. taxation upon the

Reg. § 1.897-5T(d)(1)

disposition of the interest, then a portion of the interest received shall be treated as an interest subject to U.S. taxation upon its disposition, and, therefore, that portion shall be entitled to nonrecognition treatment under the rules of this section or § 1.897-6T. The portion of the interest that is treated as subject to U.S. taxation is determined by multiplying the fair market value of the interest by a fraction. The numerator of the fraction is the amount of tax that would be due pursuant to the provisions of the applicable U.S. income tax treaty upon the recipient's disposition of the interest, determined as of the date of the distribution or transfer. The denominator of the fraction is the amount of tax that would be due upon such disposition but for the provisions of the treaty. However, nonrecognition treatment may be preserved in accordance with the provisions of subdivision (C) of this paragraph (d)(1)(ii). With regard to the provisions of this paragraph, see Article XIII (9) of the United States-Canada Income Tax Convention.

(C) *Waiver of treaty benefits to preserve nonrecognition.* Notwithstanding the provisions of subdivisions (A) and (B) of this paragraph (d)(1)(ii), an interest shall be considered to be subject to U.S. taxation upon its subsequent disposition if, in accordance with paragraph (d)(1)(iii)(F) of this section, the recipient waives the benefits of a U.S. income tax treaty that would otherwise entitle the recipient to an exemption from (or reduction of) U.S. tax upon a disposition of the interest.

(iii) *Procedural requirements.* If a U.S. real property interest is distributed or transferred after December 31, 1987, the transferor or distributor (that is a nonresident alien individual or a foreign corporation) shall file an income tax return for the taxable year of the distribution or transfer. Also, if a U.S. real property interest is distributed or transferred in a transaction before January 1, 1988, with respect to which nonrecognition treatment would not have been available under the express provisions of section 897(d) or (e) of the Code but is available under the provisions of this section or § 1.897-6T, then the person that would otherwise be subject to tax by reason of the operation of section 897 must file an income tax return for the taxable year of the distribution or transfer. This requirement is satisfied by filing a tax return or an amended tax return for the year of the distribution or transfer by May 5, 1989, or by the date that the filing of the return is otherwise required. The person filing the return must attach thereto a document setting forth the following:

(A) A statement that the distribution or transfer is one to which section 897 applies;

(B) A description of the U.S. real property interest distributed or transferred, including its location, its adjusted basis in the hands of the distributor or transferor immediately before the distribution or transfer, and the date of the distribution or transfer;

(C) A description of the U.S. real property interest received in an exchange;

(D) A declaration signed by an officer of the corporation that the distributing foreign corporation has substantiated the adjusted basis of the shareholder in its stock if the distributing corporation has nonrecognition or recognition limitation under paragraph (c)(3) or (4) of this section;

(E) The amount of any gain recognized and tax withheld by any person with respect to the distribution or transfer;

(F) Identification by name and address of the distributee or transferee, including the distributee's or transferee's taxpayer identification number (if any);

(G) The treaty and article (if any) under which the distributee or transferor would be exempt from U.S. taxation on a sale of the distributed U.S. real property interest or the U.S. real property interest received in the transfer; and

(H) A declaration, signed by the distributee or transferor or its authorized legal representative, that the distributee or transferor shall treat any subsequent sale, exchange, or other disposition of the U.S. real property interest as a disposition that is subject to U.S. taxation, notwithstanding the provisions of any U.S. income tax treaty or intervening change in circumstance.

A person who has provided or filed a notice described in § 1.1445-2(d)(2)(iii) or § 1.1445-5(b)(2)(ii) in connection with a transaction may satisfy the requirement of this paragraph (d)(1)(iii) by attaching to his return a copy of that notice together with any information or declaration required by this subdivision not contained in that notice.

(2) *Treaty exception to imposition of tax.* If gain that would be currently recognized pursuant to the provisions of this section or § 1.897-6T is subject to an exemption from (or reduction of) U.S. tax pursuant to a U.S. income tax treaty, then gain shall be recognized only as provided by that treaty, for dispositions occurring before January 1, 1985. For dispositions occurring after December 31, 1984, all gain shall be recognized as provided in section 897 and the regulations thereunder, except as provided by Articles XIII (9) and XXX (5) of the United States-Canada Income Tax Convention or other income tax treaty entered into force after June 6, 1988. With regard to Article XXX (5) of the Income Tax Treaty with

Reg. § 1.897-5T(d)(2)

Canada, see, Rev. Rul. 85-76, 1985-1 C.B. 409. With regard to basis adjustments for certain related person transactions, see, § 1.897-6T (c)(3).

(3) *Withholding.* Under sections 1441 and 1442, as modified by the provisions of any applicable U.S. income tax treaty, a corporation must withhold tax from a dividend distribution to which section 301 applies to a shareholder that is a foreign person, if the dividend is considered to be from sources inside the United States. For a description of dividends that are considered to be from sources inside the United States, see section 861(a)(2). Under section 1445, withholding is required with respect to certain dispositions and distributions of U.S. real property interests.

(4) *Effect on earnings and profits.* With respect to adjustments to earnings and profits for gain recognized to a distributing corporation on a distribution, see section 312 and the regulations thereunder.

(e) *Effective date.* Except as otherwise specifically provided in the text of these regulations, this section shall be effective for transfers, exchanges, distributions and other dispositions occurring after June 18, 1980. [Temporary Reg.§ 1.897-5T.]

☐ [*T.D.* 8198, 5-4-88.]

[Reg. § 1.897-6T]

§ 1.897-6T. **Nonrecognition exchanges applicable to corporations, their shareholders, and other taxpayers, and certain transfers of property in corporate reorganizations (Temporary).**—(a) *Nonrecognition exchanges*—(1) *In general.* Except as otherwise provided in this section and in § 1.897-5T, for purposes of section 897(e) any nonrecognition provision shall apply to a transfer by a foreign person of a U.S. real property interest on which gain is realized only to the extent that the transferred U.S. real property interest is exchanged for a U.S. real property interest which, immediately following the exchange, would be subject to U.S. taxation upon its disposition, and the transferor complies with the filing requirements of paragraph (d)(1)(iii) of § 1.897-5T. No loss shall be recognized pursuant to section 897(e) or the rules of this section unless such loss is otherwise permitted to be recognized. In the case of an exchange of a U.S. real property interest for stock in a domestic corporation (that is otherwise treated as a U.S. real property interest), such stock shall not be considered a U.S. real property interest unless the domestic corporation is a U.S. real property holding corporation immediately after the exchange. Whether an interest would be subject to U.S. taxation in the hands of the transferor upon its disposition shall be determined in accordance with the rules of § 1.897-5T (d)(1).

(2) *Definition of "nonrecognition" provision.* A "nonrecognition provision" is any provision of the Code which provides that gain or loss shall not be recognized if the requirements of that provision are met. Nonrecognition provisions relevant to this section include, but are not limited to, sections 332, 351, 354, 355, 361, 721, 731, 1031, 1033, 1034 and 1036. For purposes of section 897(e), sections 121 and 453 are not nonrecognition provisions.

(3) *Consequence of nonapplication of nonrecognition provisions.* If a nonrecognition provision does not apply to a transaction, then the U.S. real property interest transferred shall be considered exchanged pursuant to a transaction that is subject to U.S. taxation by reason of the operation of section 897. See, however, § 1.897-5T (d)(2) with respect to the treaty exceptions to the imposition of tax. If a U.S. real property interest is exchanged for an interest the disposition of which is only partially subject to taxation under chapter 1 of the Code (as modified by the provisions of any applicable U.S. income tax treaty), then any nonrecognition provision shall apply only to the extent that the interest received in the exchange would be subject to taxation under chapter 1 of the Code, as modified. For example, the exchange of a U.S. real property interest for an interest in a partnership will receive nonrecognition treatment pursuant to section 721 only to the extent that a disposition of the partnership interest will be subject to U.S. taxation by reason of the operation of section 897(g).

(4) *Section 355 distributions treated as exchanges.* If a domestic corporation, stock in which is treated as a U.S. real property interest, distributes stock in a foreign corporation or stock in a domestic corporation that is not a U.S. real property holding corporation to a foreign person under section 355(a), then the foreign person shall be considered as having exchanged a proportionate part of the stock in the domestic corporation that is treated as a U.S. real property interest for stock that is not treated as a U.S. real property interest.

(5) *Section 1034 rollover of gain*—(i) *Purchase of foreign principal residence.* A nonresident alien individual shall not be entitled to nonrecognition under section 1034 on the sale of a principal residence when the new principal residence acquired is not a U.S. real property interest.

(ii) *Purchase of U.S. principal residence.* A nonresident alien individual who sells his principal residence that is a U.S. real property interest and, within a period beginning two years before the date of such sale and ending on the date (with extensions) of filing his income tax return for the taxable year of the sale of the principal residence, purchases and uses another U.S. real property

Reg. § 1.897-6T

interest as a principal residence, shall, to the extent provided by section 1034, not recognize gain on the sale of the principal residence. If the individual has not purchased another U.S. real property interest as a principal residence at the time of the filing of the return for the year of sale, the individual must file a timely income tax return for the year of sale without claiming the benefit of section 1034. If the individual subsequently purchases another U.S. property interest as a principal residence that otherwise qualifies under section 1034 after the due date of the income tax return for the year of the sale of the principal residence and before a date that is two years after the sale of the principal residence, the individual may then apply section 1034 by filing an amended income tax return for the year of the sale of the principal residence and claim a refund. A nonresident alien may not claim the benefits of section 1034 unless such individual files a complete and timely income tax return with the appropriate forms for the year of the sale of the principal residence. The rules of this paragraph (a)(5)(ii) shall first apply to the sale of principal residences after June 6, 1988. A nonresident alien individual who sells his principal residence that is a U.S. real property interest on or before June 6, 1988, shall, to the extent provided by section 1034, not recognize gain on the sale of the principal residence if the new principal residence is a U.S. real property interest.

(6) *Determination of basis.* If a nonrecognition provision applies to the transfer of a U.S. real property interest pursuant to the provisions of this section, then the basis of the property received in the exchange shall be determined in accordance with the rules generally applicable with respect to such nonrecognition provision. Similarly, the basis of the exchanged property in the hands of the transferee shall be determined in accordance with the rules that generally apply to such transfer.

(7) *Examples.* The rules of paragraph (a)(1) through (6) of this section may be illustrated by the following examples. In each instance, the filing requirements of paragraph (d)(1)(iii) of § 1.897-5T have been satisfied.

Example (1). (i) A is a citizen and resident of Country F with which the U.S. does not have an income tax treaty. A owns Parcel P, a U.S. real property interest, with a fair market value of $500,000 and an adjusted basis of $300,000. A transfers Parcel P to DC, a newly formed U.S. real property holding corporation wholly owned by A, in exchange for DC stock.

(ii) Under paragraph (a)(1) of this section, A has exchanged a U.S. real property interest (Parcel P) for another U.S. real property interest (DC stock) which is subject to U.S. taxation upon its disposition. The nonrecognition provisions of section 351(a) apply to A's transfer of Parcel P.

(iii) Under paragraph (a)(6) of this section, the basis of the DC stock received by A is determined in accordance with the rules generally applicable to the transfer. A takes a $300,000 adjusted basis in the DC stock under the rules of section 358(a)(1).

Example (2). (i) A is a citizen and resident of Country F who is stationed in Washington, DC as a full-time employee of an international organization. A sells his principal residence in Washington, and in the same taxable year A purchases another principal residence in Washington. The cost of the new residence exceeds the adjusted sales price of the old residence.

(ii) Under section 7701(b), A is a nonresident alien for U.S. tax purposes, and is subject to taxation under section 897(a). Under paragraphs (a)(1) and (5)(ii) of this section, A is considered to have exchanged a U.S. real property interest (the old principal residence) for another U.S. real property interest (the new principal residence) which is subject to U.S. taxation upon its disposition. The nonrecognition and basis provisions of section 1034(a) apply to A.

Example (3). If in *Example* (2) A had instead purchased a new principal residence in Country F, there would be an exchange of a U.S. real property interest for property that is not a U.S. real property interest. Under paragraph (a)(5)(i) of this section, A would recognize gain under section 897(a) on the disposition of the old principal residence.

Example (4). (i) B is a citizen and resident of Country F with which the U.S. does not have an income tax treaty. B owns stock in DC1, a U.S. real property holding corporation. In a reorganization qualifying for nonrecognition under section 368(a)(1)(B), B exchanges the DC1 stock under section 354(a) for stock in DC2, a U.S. real property holding corporation.

(ii) A does not recognize any gain under paragraph (a)(1) of this section on the exchange of the DC1 stock for DC2 stock because there is an exchange of a U.S. real property interest (the DC1 stock) for another U.S. real property interest (the DC2 stock) which is subject to U.S. taxation upon its disposition.

Example (5). (i) C is a citizen and resident of Country F with which the U.S. does not have an income tax treaty. C owns all of the stock of DC, a U.S. real property holding corporation. The fair market value of the DC stock is 500x, and C has a basis of 100x in the DC stock.

(ii) In a transaction qualifying as a distribution of stock of a controlled corporation under section 355(a), DC distributes to C all of the stock

Reg. § 1.897-6T

of FC, a foreign corporation that has not made a section 897(i) election. C does not surrender any of the DC stock. The FC stock has a fair market value of 200x. After the distribution, the DC stock has a fair market value of 300x.

(iii) Under the rules of paragraph (a)(4) of this section, C is considered to have exchanged DC stock with a fair market value of 200x and an adjusted basis of 40x for FC stock with a fair market value of 200x. Because the FC stock is not a U.S. real property interest, C must recognize gain of 160x under section 897(a) on the distribution. C takes a basis of 200x in the FC stock. C's basis in the DC stock is reduced to 60x pursuant to section 358(c).

Example (6). (i) A is an individual citizen and resident of Country F. F has an income tax treaty with the United States that exempts gain from the sale of stock, but not real property, by a resident of F from U.S. taxation. In 1981, A transferred Parcel P, an appreciated U.S. real property interest, to DC, a U.S. real property holding corporation, in exchange for DC stock. A owned all of the stock of DC.

(ii) Under the rules of paragraph (a)(1) of this section, A must recognize gain on the transfer of Parcel P. Even though there is an exchange of a U.S. real property interest for another U.S. real property interest, there is gain recognition because the U.S. real property interest received (the DC stock) would not have been subject to U.S. taxation upon a disposition immediately following the exchange. A may not convert a U.S. real property interest that was subject to taxation under section 897 into a U.S. real property interest that could be sold without taxation under section 897 due to a treaty exemption.

Example (7). (i) A, a nonresident alien, organized FC1, a Country W corporation in September 1980 to invest in U.S. real property. FC1's only asset is Parcel P, a U.S. real property interest with a fair market value of $500,000 and an adjusted basis of $200,000. The FC1 stock has a fair market value of $500,000 and A's basis in the FC1 stock is $100,000. The United States does not have a treaty with Country W.

(ii) A, organized FC2, a Country W corporation in July 1987. FC2 organized DC in August 1987. Pursuant to a plan of reorganization under section 368(a)(1)(C), FC1 transfers Parcel P to DC in exchange for FC2 voting stock. As a result of the transfer, DC is a U.S. real property holding corporation wholly owned by FC2. The FC2 stock used by DC in the acquisition had been transferred by FC2 to DC as part of the plan of reorganization. FC1 distributes the FC2 stock to A in exchange for A's FC1 stock.

(iii) FC1's exchange of Parcel P for the FC2 stock under section 361(a) is a disposition of a U.S. real property interest. FC1 must recognize gain of $300,000 under section 897(e) and paragraph (a)(1) of this section on the exchange because the FC2 stock received in exchange for Parcel P is not a U.S. real property interest.

(iv) Under section 362(b), DC takes a basis of $500,000 in Parcel P. FC2 takes a basis of $500,000 in the DC stock. A takes a basis of $100,000 in the FC2 stock under section 358(a)(1). Section 897(d) and paragraph (c)(1) of § 1.897-5T do not apply to FC1's distribution of the FC2 stock because the FC2 stock is not a U.S. real property interest.

Example (8). The facts are the same as in Example 7, except that the United States has a treaty with Country W that entitles FC1 and FC2 to nondiscriminatory treatment as described in § 1.897-3(b)(2). FC1, but not FC2, makes a valid section 897(i) election prior to the transaction.

(ii) FC1's transfer of Parcel P to DC in exchange for FC2 stock is not subject to section 897(e) and paragraph (a)(1) of this section because FC1 made an election under section 897(i). DC takes a basis of $200,000 in Parcel P under section 362(b).

(iii) FC1's distribution of the FC2 stock to A in exchange for the FC1 stock is not subject to the section 897(d) and paragraph (c)(1) of § 1.897-5T because FC1 made an election under section 897(i).

(iv) A must recognize gain on the exchange under section 354(a) of the FC1 stock for the FC2 stock. A exchanged a U.S. real property interest (the FC1 stock) for an interest which is not a U.S. real property interest (the FC2 stock). A recognizes gain of $400,000. Under section 1012, A takes a $500,000 basis in the FC2 stock.

Example (9). (i) The facts are the same as in Example 7 except that the United States has a treaty with Country W that entitles FC1 and FC2 to nondiscriminatory treatment as described in § 1.897-3(b)(2). FC2, but not FC1, makes a valid section 897(i) election prior to the transaction.

(ii) FC1's exchange of Parcel P for the FC2 stock under section 361(a) is a disposition of a U.S. real property interest. FC1 does not recognize any gain under section 897(e) and paragraph (a)(1) of this section because there is an exchange of a U.S. real property interest (Parcel P) for another U.S. real property interest (the FC2 stock). DC takes a basis of $200,000 in Parcel P under section 362(b). FC2 takes a basis of $200,000 in the DC stock.

(iii) FC1's distribution of the FC2 stock to A in exchange for the FC1 stock is subject to section 897(d) and paragraph (c)(1) of § 1.897-5T. Be-

Reg. § 1.897-6T

cause A takes a basis of $100,000 in the FC2 stock under section 358(a) (which is less than the $200,000 basis of the FC2 stock in the hands of FC1), and A would be subject to U.S. taxation under section 897(a) on a subsequent disposition of the FC2 stock, FC1 does not recognize any gain under paragraph (c)(1) of § 1.897-5T due to the statutory exception of paragraph (c)(2)(i) of that section, provided that FC1 complies with the filing requirements of paragraph (d)(1)(C) of § 1.897-5T.

(iv) Since the FC1 stock was not a U.S. real property interest, its disposition by A in the section 354(a) exchange for FC2 stock is not subject to section 897(e) and paragraph (a)(1) of this section.

Example (10). The facts are the same as in Example 7, except that the United States has a treaty with Country W that entitles FC1 and FC2 to nondiscriminatory treatment as described in § 1.897-3(b)(2). FC1 and FC2 made valid section 897(i) elections prior to the transactions.

(ii) FC1's transfer of Parcel P to DC in exchange for FC2 stock is not subject to section 897(e) and paragraph (a)(1) of this section because FC1 made an election under section 897(i). DC takes a basis of $200,000 in Parcel P under section 362(a). FC2 takes a basis of $200,000 in the DC stock.

(iii) FC1's distribution of the FC2 stock to A in exchange for the FC1 stock is not subject to section 897(d) and paragraph (c)(1) of § 1.897-5T because FC1 made an election under section 897(i).

(iv) A does not recognize any gain on the exchange of the FC1 stock for the FC2 stock under section 354(a). Under paragraph (a)(1) of this section, there is an exchange of a U.S. real property interest (FC1 stock) for another U.S. real property interest (FC2 stock). A takes a basis of $100,000 in the FC2 stock under section 358(a).

(8) *Treatment of nonqualifying property*—(i) *In general.* If, under paragraph (a)(1) of this section, a nonrecognition provision would apply to an exchange but for the fact that nonqualifying property (cash or property other than U.S. real property interests) is received in addition to property (U.S. real property interests) that is permitted to be received under paragraph (a)(1) of this section, then the transferor shall recognize gain under this section equal to the lesser of—

(A) The sum of the cash received plus the fair market value of the nonqualifying property received, or

(B) The gain realized with respect to the U.S. real property interest transferred.

However, no loss shall be recognized pursuant to this paragraph (a)(8) unless such loss is otherwise permitted to be recognized.

(ii) *Treatment of mixed exchanges.* In a mixed exchange where both a U.S. real property interest and other property (including cash) is transferred in exchange both for property the receipt of which would qualify for nonrecognition treatment pursuant to paragraph (a)(1) of this section and for other property (including cash) which would not so qualify, the transferor will recognize gain in accordance with the rules set forth in subdivisions (A) through (C) of this paragraph (a)(8)(ii).

(A) *Allocation of nonqualifying property.* The amount of nonqualifying property (including cash) considered to be received in exchange for U.S. real property interests shall be determined by multiplying the fair market value of the nonqualifying property received by a fraction ("real property fraction"). The numerator of the fraction is the fair market value of the U.S. real property interest transferred in the exchange. The denominator of the fraction is the fair market value of all property transferred in the exchange.

(B) *Recognition of gain.* The amount of gain that must be recognized, and that shall be subject to U.S. taxation by reason of the operation of section 897, shall be equal to the lesser of:

(*1*) The amount determined under subdivision (A) of this paragraph (a)(8)(ii), or

(*2*) The gain or loss realized with respect to the U.S. real property interest exchanged.

(C) *Treatment of other amounts.* The treatment of other amounts received in a mixed exchange shall be determined as follows:

(*1*) The amount of nonqualifying property (including cash) considered to be received in exchange for property (including cash) other than U.S. real property interests shall be treated in the manner provided in the relevant nonrecognition provision. Such amounts shall be determined by subtracting the amount determined under subdivision (A) of this paragraph (a)(8)(ii) from the total amount of nonqualifying property received in the exchange.

(*2*) The amount of qualifying property considered to be received in exchange for U.S. real property interests shall be treated in the manner provided in paragraph (a)(1) of this section. Such amount shall be determined by multiplying the total fair market value of qualifying property received in the exchange by the real property fraction described in subdivision (A) of this paragraph (a)(8)(ii).

Reg. § 1.897-6T

(3) The amount of qualifying property considered to be received in exchange for property other than U.S. real property interests shall be treated in the manner provided in the relevant nonrecognition provision. Such amount shall be determined by subtracting the amount determined under subdivision (2) of this paragraph (a)(8)(ii)(C) from the total fair market value of qualifying property received in the exchange.

(iii) *Example.* The rules of paragraph (a)(8)(ii) of this section may be illustrated by the following example.

Example. (i) A is an individual citizen and resident of country F. Country F does not have an income tax treaty with the United States. A is the sole proprietor of a business located in the United States, the assets of which consist of a U.S. real property interest with a fair market value of $1,000,000 and an adjusted basis of $700 000, and equipment used in the business with a fair market value of $500,000 and an adjusted basis of $250,000. A decides to incorporate the business, and on January 1, 1987, A transfers his assets to domestic corporation DC in exchange for 100 percent of the stock of DC, with a fair market value of $900,000. In addition, A receives a long term note (constituting a security) from DC for $600,000, bearing arm's length interest and repayment terms. DC has no assets other than those received in the exchange with A. Pursuant to section 897(c)(2) and § 1.897-2, DC is a U.S. real property holding corporation. Therefore, the stock of DC is a U.S. real property interest. Assume that the note from DC constitutes an interest in the corporation solely as a creditor as provided by § 1.897-1(d)(4) of the regulation. A complies with the filing requirements of paragraph (d)(1)(iii) of § 1.897-5T.

(ii) Because the note from DC would not be subject to U.S. taxation upon its disposition, it is nonqualifying property for purposes of determining whether A is entitled to receive nonrecognition treatment pursuant to section 351 with respect to his exchange of the U.S. real property interest. Thus, A must recognize gain in the manner provided in paragraph (a)(8)(ii) of this section. Pursuant to paragraph (a)(8)(ii)(A), the amount of nonqualifying property received in exchange for the real property interests is determined by multiplying the fair market value of such property ($600,000) by the real property fraction. The numerator of the fraction is $1,000,000, the fair market value of the real property transferred by A. The denominator is $1,500,000, the fair market value of all property transferred by A. Thus, A is considered to have received $400,000 of the note in exchange for the real property ($600,000 × $1,000,000/$1,500,000). Pursuant to paragraph (a)(8)(ii)(B), A must recognize the lesser of the amount initially determined or the gain realized with respect to the U.S. real property interest. Therefore, A must recognize the $300,000 gain realized with respect to the real property.

(iii) Pursuant to paragraph (a)(8)(ii)(C) of this section, A is considered to have received $200,000 of the note in exchange for equipment ($600,000 [total value of note received] minus $400,000 [portion of note received in exchange for real property]), $600,000 of the stock in exchange for real property ($900,000 [total value of stock received] times $1,000,000/1,500,000 [proportion of property exchanged consisting of real property]), and $300,000 of the stock in exchange for equipment ($900,000 [total value of stock received] minus $600,000 [portion of stock received in exchange for real property]). All three amounts are entitled to nonrecognition treatment pursuant to section 351.

(iv) Pursuant to paragraph (a)(2) of this section, A's basis in the stock and note received and DC's basis in the U.S. real property interest and equipment will be determined in accordance with the generally applicable rules. The $400,000 portion of the note received in exchange for the real property interest is other property. Pursuant to section 358(a)(2), A takes a fair market value ($400,000) basis for that portion of the note. Pursuant to section 358(a)(1), A's basis in the property received without the recognition of gain (the DC stock and the other portion of the note) will be equal to the basis of the property transferred ($950,000 [$700,000 basis of U.S. real property interest plus $250,000 basis of equipment]), decreased by the fair market value of the other property received ($400,000 portion of the note), and increased by the amount of gain recognized to A on the transaction ($300,000). Thus, A's basis in the stock and the nonrecognition portion of the note is $850,000 ($950,000 − $400,000 + $300,000). Under § 1.358-2(b)(2) of the regulations, the $850,000 is allocated between the stock and the nonrecognition portion of the note in proportion to their fair market values. A takes a basis of $697,000 in the DC stock ($850,000 × 900,000/1,100,000). A takes a basis of $153,000 in the nonrecognition portion of the note ($850,000 × 200,000/1,100,000). A's basis in the note is $553,000 ($400,000 + $153,000). DC's basis in the property received from A will be determined under section 362(a). DC takes a basis of $1,000,000 in the real property interest (A's basis of $700,000 increased by the $300,000 of gain recognized by A on it). DC takes a basis of $250,000 in the equipment (A's basis of $250,000).

Reg. § 1.897-6T

(9) *Treaty exception to imposition of tax.* If gain that would be currently recognized pursuant to the provisions of this section is subject to an exemption from, or reduction of, U.S. tax pursuant to a U.S. income tax treaty, then gain shall be recognized only as provided by that treaty for dispositions occurring before January 1, 1985. For dispositions occurring after December 31, 1984, all gain shall be recognized as provided in section 897 and the regulations thereunder, except as provided by Articles XII (9) and XXX (5) of the United States-Canada Income Tax Convention or other income tax treaty entered into after June 6, 1988. In regard to Article XXX (5) the Income Tax Treaty with Canada, see, Rev. Rul. 85-76, 1985-1 C.B. 409.

(b) *Certain foreign to foreign exchanges*—(1) *Exceptions to the general rule.* Notwithstanding the provisions of paragraph (a)(1) of this section and pursuant to authority conferred by section 897(e)(2), a foreign person shall not recognize gain, in the instances described in paragraph (b)(2) of this section, on the transfer of a U.S. real property interest to a foreign corporation in exchange for stock in a foreign corporation, but only if the transferee's subsequent disposition of the transferred U.S. real property interest would be subject to U.S. taxation, as determined in accordance with the provisions of § 1.897-5T (d)(1), if the filing requirements of paragraph (d)(1)(iii) of § 1.897-5T have been satisfied, if one of the five conditions set forth in paragraph (b)(2) exists, and if one of the following three forms of exchange takes place.

(i) The exchange is made by a foreign corporation pursuant to section 361(a) in a reorganization described in section 368(a)(1)(D) or (F) and there is an exchange of the transferor corporation stock for the transferee corporation stock under section 354(a); or

(ii) The exchange is made by a foreign corporation pursuant to section 361(a) in a reorganization described in section 368(a)(1)(C); there is an exchange of the transferor corporation stock for the transferee corporation stock (or stock of the transferee corporation's parent in the case of a parenthetical C reorganization) under section 354(a); and the transferor corporation's shareholders own more than fifty percent of the voting stock of the transferee corporation (or stock of the transferee corporation's parent in the case of a parenthetical C reorganization) immediately after the reorganization; or

(iii) The U.S. real property interest exchanged is stock in a U.S. real property holding corporation; the exchange qualifies under section 351(a) or section 354(a) in a reorganization described in section 368(a)(1)(B); and immediately after the exchange, all of the outstanding stock of the transferee corporation (or stock of the transferee corporation's parent in the case of a parenthetical B reorganization) is owned in the same proportions by the same nonresident alien individuals and foreign corporations that, immediately before the exchange, owned the stock of the U.S. real property holding corporation.

If, however, a nonresident alien individual or foreign corporation which received stock in an exchange described in subdivision (iii) of this paragraph (b)(1) (or the transferee corporation's parent) disposes of any of such foreign stock within three years from the date of its receipt, then that individual or corporation shall recognize that portion of the gain realized with respect to the stock in the U.S. real property holding corporation for which foreign stock disposed of was received.

(2) *Applicability of exception.* The exception to the provisions of paragraph (a)(1) provided by paragraph (b)(1) shall apply only if one of the following five conditions exists.

(i) Each of the interests exchanged or received in a transferor corporation or transferee corporation would not be a U.S. real property interest as defined in § 1.897-1(c)(1) if such corporations were domestic corporations; or

(ii) The transferee corporation (and the transferee corporation's parent in the case of a parenthetical B or C reorganization) is incorporated in a foreign country that maintains an income tax treaty with the United States that contains an information exchange provision; the transfer occurs after May 5, 1988; and the transferee corporation (and the transferee corporation's parent in the case of a parenthetical B or C reorganization) submit a binding waiver of all benefits of the respective income tax treaty (including the opportunity to make an election under section 897(i)), which must be attached to each of the transferor and transferee corporation's income tax returns for the year of the transfer; or

(iii) The transferee foreign corporation (and the transferee corporation's parent in the case of a parenthetical B or C reorganization) is a qualified resident as defined in section 884(e) and any regulations thereunder of the foreign country in which it is incorporated; or

(iv) The transferee foreign corporation (and the transferee corporation's parent in the case of a parenthetical B or C reorganization) is incorporated in the same foreign country as the transferor foreign corporation; and there is an income tax treaty in force between that foreign country and the United States at the time of the transfer that contains an exchange of information provision; or

Reg. § 1.897-6T(b)(1)

(v) The transferee foreign corporation is incorporated in the same foreign country as the transferor foreign corporation; and the transfer is incident to a mere change in identity, form, or place of organization of one corporation under section 368(a)(1)(F).

For purposes of any election by a transferee foreign corporation (or the transferee corporation's parent in the case of a parenthetical C reorganization) to be treated as a domestic corporation under section 897(i) and § 1.897-3 where the exchange was described in subdivisions (i) or (ii) of paragraph (b)(1) of this section, any prior dispositions of the transferor foreign corporation stock will be subject to the requirements of § 1.897-3(d)(2) upon an election under section 897(i) by the transferee foreign corporation (or the transferee corporation's parent in the case of a parenthetical C reorganization).

(3) *No exceptions.* No exception to recognition of gain under paragraph (a)(1) of this section is provided for the transfer of a U.S. real property interest by a foreign person to a foreign corporation in exchange for stock in a foreign corporation other than as provided in this paragraph (b). Thus, no exception is provided where—

(i) Such exchange is made pursuant to section 351 and the U.S. real property interest transferred is not stock in a U.S. real property holding corporation; or

(ii) Such exchange is made pursuant to section 361(a) in a reorganization described in section 368 (a)(1) that does not qualify for nonrecognition of gain under this paragraph (b). With regard to the treatment of certain foreign corporations as domestic corporations under section 897(i), see §§ 1.897-3 and 1.897-8T.

(4) *Examples.* The rules of paragraph (b)(1) and (2) of this section may be illustrated by the following examples. In each instance, the filing requirements of paragraph (d)(1)(iii) of § 1.897-5T have been satisfied.

Example (1). (i) FC is a Country F corporation that has not made a section 897(i) election. FC owns Parcel P, a U.S. real property interest, with a fair market value of $450x and an adjusted basis of 100x.

(ii) FC transfers Parcel P to FS, its wholly owned Country F subsidiary, in exchange for FS stock under section 351(a). FS has not made a section 897 (i) election. Under the rules of paragraph (a)(1) of this section, FC must recognize gain of 350x under section 897(a) because the FS stock received in the exchange is not a U.S. real property interest. No exception to the recognition rule of paragraph (a)(1) is provided under this paragraph (b) for a transfer under section 351(a) of a U.S. real property interest (that is not stock in a U.S. real property holding corporation) by a foreign corporation to another foreign corporation in exchange for stock of the transferee corporation.

Example (2). (i) FC is a Country F corporation that has not made a section 897(i) election. FC owns several U.S. real property interests that have appreciated in value since FC purchased the interests. FP, a Country F corporation, owns all of the outstanding stock of FC. Country F maintains an income tax treaty with the United States.

(ii) For valid business purposes, FC transferred substantially all of its assets including all of its U.S. real property interests to FS in 1989 under section 361(a) in a reorganization in exchange for FS stock. FS is a newly formed Country F corporation that is owned by FC. The transfer qualifies as a reorganization under section 368(a)(1)(D). FC immediately distributes the FS stock to FP in exchange for the FC stock and FC dissolves. FP has no gain or loss on the exchange of the FC stock for the FS stock under section 354(a).

(iii) Under the rules of paragraph (b)(1)(i) of this section, FC does not recognize any gain on the transfer of the U.S. real property interests to FS under section 361(a) in the reorganization under section 368(a)(1)(D) because FS would be subject to U.S. taxation on a subsequent disposition of the interests, as required by paragraph (b)(1) of this section; there is an exchange of stock under section 354(a), as required by paragraph (b)(1)(i); and FC and FS are incorporated in Country F which maintains an income tax treaty with the United States, as required by paragraph (b)(2)(iv).

(5) *Contributions of property.* A foreign person that contributes a U.S. real property interest to a foreign corporation as paid in surplus or as a contribution to capital (including a contribution provided in section 304(a)) shall be treated, for purposes of section 897(j) and this section, as exchanging the U.S. real property interest for stock in the foreign corporation.

(c) *Denial of nonrecognition with respect to certain tax avoidance transfers*—(1) *In general.* The provisions of § 1.897-5T and paragraphs (a) and (b) of this section are subject to the rules of this paragraph (c).

(2) *Certain transfers to domestic corporations*— (i) *General rule.* If a foreign person transfers property, that is not a U.S. real property interest, to a domestic corporation in a nonrecognition exchange, where—

(A) The adjusted basis of such property transferred exceeded its fair market value on the date of the transfer to the domestic corporation;

(B) The property transferred will not immediately be used in, or held by the domestic corporation for use in, the conduct of a trade or business as defined in § 1.897-1(f); and

(C) Within two years of the transfer to the domestic corporation, the property transferred is sold at a loss;

then, it will be presumed, absent clear and convincing evidence to the contrary, that the purpose for transferring the loss property was the avoidance of taxation on the disposition of U.S. real property interests by the domestic corporation. Any loss recognized by the domestic corporation on the sale or exchange of such property shall not be used by the domestic corporation, either by direct offset or as part of a net operating loss or capital loss carryback or carryover, to offset any gain recognized from the sale or exchange of a U.S. real property interest by the domestic corporation.

(ii) *Example.* The rules of paragraph (e)(2)(i) of this section may be illustrated by the following example.

Example. A is an individual citizen and resident of country F, which does not have an income tax treaty with the U.S. On January 1, 1987, A transfers a U.S. real property interest with a basis of $100,000 and a fair market value of $600,000 to domestic corporation DC in exchange for all of the stock of DC. On October 20, 1987, A transfers stock of a publicly traded domestic corporation with a basis in his hands of $900,000 and a fair market value of $500,000, in exchange for additional stock of DC. The stock of the publicly traded domestic corporation does not constitute an asset used or held for use in DC's trade or business. If DC sells the stock of the publicly traded domestic corporation before October 20, 1989 and recognizes a loss, the loss may not be used to offset any gain recognized on the sale of the U.S. real property interests by DC.

(3) *Basis adjustment for certain related person transactions.* In the case of any disposition after December 31, 1979, of a U.S. real property interest to a related person (within the meaning of section 453(f)(1)), the basis of the interest in the hands of the person acquiring such interest shall be reduced by the amount of any gain which is not subject to taxation under section 871(b)(1) or 882(a)(1) because the disposition occurred before June 19, 1980 or because of any treaty obligation of the United States. If a foreign corporation makes an election under section 897 (i), and the stock of such corporation was transferred between related persons after December 31, 1979 and before June 19, 1980, then such stock shall be treated as a U.S. real property interest solely for purposes of this paragraph (c)(3).

(4) *Rearrangement of ownership to gain treaty benefit.* A foreign person who directly or indirectly owns a U.S. real property interest may not directly or indirectly rearrange the incidents of ownership of the U.S. real property interest through the use of nonrecognition provisions in order to gain the benefit of a treaty exemption from taxation. Such nonrecognition will not apply to the foreign transferor. The transferor will recognize gain but not loss on the transfer under section 897(a).

(d) *Effective date.* Except as specifically provided otherwise in the text of the regulations, paragraphs (a) through (c) shall be effective for transfers, exchanges and other dispositions occurring after June 18, 1980. Paragraph (a)(5)(ii) of this section shall be effective for exchanges and elections occurring after June 6, 1988. [Temporary Reg. § 1.897-6T.]

☐ [T.D. 8198, 5-4-88.]

[Reg. § 1.897-7T]

§ 1.897-7T. Treatment of certain partnership interests as entirely U.S. real property interests under sections 897(g) and 1445(e) (Temporary).—(a) *Rule.* Pursuant to section 897(g), an interest in a partnership in which, directly or indirectly, fifty percent or more of the value of the gross assets consist of U.S. real property interests, and ninety percent or more of the value of the gross assets consist of U.S. real property interests plus any cash or cash equivalents shall, for purposes of section 1445, be treated as entirely a U.S. real property interest. For purposes of section 897(g), such interest shall be treated as a U.S. real property interest only to the extent that the gain on the disposition is attributable to U.S. real property interests (and not cash, cash equivalents or other property). Consequently, a disposition of any portion of such partnership interest shall be subject to partial taxation under section 897(a) and full withholding under section 1445(a). For purposes of this paragraph, cash equivalent means any asset readily convertible into cash (whether or not denominated in U.S. dollars) including, but not limited to, bank accounts, certificates of deposit, money market accounts, commercial paper, U.S. and foreign treasury obligations and bonds, corporate obligations and bonds, precious metals or commodities, and publicly traded instruments.

(b) *Effective date.* Section 1.897-7T shall be effective for transfers, exchanges, distributions and other dispositions occurring after June 6, 1988. [Temporary Reg. § 1.897-7T.]

☐ [T.D. 8198, 5-4-88.]

Nonresident Aliens and Foreign Corporations 48,495

See p. 20,601 for regulations not amended to reflect law changes

[Reg. § 1.897-8T]

§ 1.897-8T. **Status as a U.S. real property holding corporation as a condition for electing section 897(i) pursuant to § 1.897-3 (Temporary).**—(a) *Purpose and scope.* This section provides a temporary regulation that, if and when adopted as a final regulation, will be added to paragraph (b) of § 1.897-3. Paragraph (b) of this section would then appear as paragraph (b)(4) of § 1.897-3.

(b) *General conditions.* The foreign corporation upon making an election under section 897(i) (including any retroactive election) must qualify as a U.S. real property holding corporation as defined in paragraph (b) (1) of § 1.897-2.

(c) *Effective date.* Section 1.897-8T shall be effective as of June 6, 1988, with respect to foreign corporations making an election under section 897(i) after May 5, 1988. [Temporary Reg. § 1.897-8T.]

☐ [T.D. 8198, 5-4-88.]

[Reg. § 1.897-9T]

§ 1.897-9T. **Treatment of certain interest in publicly traded corporations, definition of foreign person, and foreign governments and international organizations (Temporary).**—(a) *Purpose and scope.* This section provides a temporary regulation that, if and when adopted as a final regulation, will be added as new paragraphs (c)(2)(iii)(B), (k), (n) and (q) of § 1.897-1. Paragraph (b) of this section would then appear as paragraph (c)(2)(iii)(B) of § 1.897-1. Paragraph (c) of this section would then appear as paragraph (k) of § 1.897-1. Paragraph (d) of this section would then appear as paragraph (n) of § 1.897-1. Paragraph (e) of this section would then appear as paragraph (q) of § 1.897-1.

(b) Any other interest in the corporation (other than an interest solely as a creditor) if on the date such interest was acquired by its present holder it had a fair market value greater than the fair market value on that date of 5 percent of the regularly traded class of the corporation's stock with the lowest fair market value. However, if a non-regularly traded class of interests in the corporation is convertible into a regularly traded class of interests in the corporation, an interest in such non-regularly traded class shall be treated as a U.S. real property interest if on the date it was acquired by its present holder it had a fair market value greater than the fair market value on that date of 5 percent of the regularly traded class of the corporation's stock into which it is convertible. If a person holds interests in a corporation of a class that is not regularly traded, and subsequently acquires additional interests of the same class, then all such interests must be aggregated and valued as of the date of the subsequent acquisition. If the subsequent acquisition causes that person's interests to exceed the applicable limitation, then all such interests shall be treated as U.S. real property interests, regardless of when acquired. In addition, if a person holds interests in a corporation of separate classes that are not regularly traded, and if such interests were separately acquired for a principal purpose of avoiding the applicable 5 percent limitation of this paragraph, then such interests shall be aggregated for purposes of applying that limitation. This rule shall not apply to interests of separate classes acquired in transactions more than three years apart. For purposes of paragraph (c)(2)(iii) of § 1.897-1, section 318(a) shall apply (except that section 318(a)(2)(C) and (3)(C) shall each be applied by substituting "5 percent" for "50 percent").

(c) *Foreign person.* The term "foreign person" means a nonresident alien individual (including an individual subject to the provisions of section 877), a foreign corporation as defined in paragraph (1) of this section, a foreign partnership, a foreign trust or a foreign estate, as such persons are defined respectively by § 1.871-2 and by 7701 and the regulations thereunder. A resident alien individual, including a nonresident alien with respect to whom there is in effect an election under section 6013(g) or (h) to be treated as United States resident, is not a foreign person. With respect to the status of foreign governments and international organizations, see paragraph (e) of this section.

(d) *Regularly traded*—(1) *General rule*—(i) *Trading requirements.* A class of interests that is traded on one or more established securities markets is considered to be regularly traded on such market or markets for any calendar quarter during which—

(A) Trades in such class are effected, other than in *de minimis* quantities, on at least 15 days during the calendar quarter;

(B) The aggregate number of the interests in such class traded is at least 7.5 percent or more of the average number of interests in such class outstanding during the calendar quarter; and

(C) The requirements of paragraph (d)(3) of this section are met.

(ii) *Exceptions*—(A) In the case of the class of interests which is held by 2,500 or more record shareholders, the requirements of paragraph (d)(1)(i)(B) of this section shall be applied by substituting "2.5 percent" for "7.5 percent".

(B) If at any time during the calendar quarter 100 or fewer persons own 50 percent or more of the outstanding shares of a class of inter-

Reg. § 1.897-9T(d)(1)

ests, such class shall not be considered to be regularly traded for purposes of sections 897, 1445 and 6039C. Related persons shall be treated as one person for purposes of this paragraph (d)(1)(ii)(B).

(iii) *Anti-abuse rule.* Trades between related persons shall be disregarded. In addition, a class of interests shall not be treated as regularly traded if there is an arrangement or a pattern of trades designed to meet the requirements of this paragraph (d)(1). For example, trades between two persons that occur several times during the calendar quarter may be treated as an arrangement or a pattern of trades designed to meet the requirements of this paragraph (d)(1).

(2) *Interests traded on domestic established securities markets.* For purposes of sections 897, 1445 and 6039C, a class of interests that is traded on an established securities market located in the United States is considered to be regularly traded for any calendar quarter during which it is regularly quoted by brokers or dealers making a market in such interests. A broker or dealer makes a market in a class of interests only if the broker or dealer holds himself out to buy or sell interests in such class at the quoted price. Stock of a corporation that is described in section 851(a)(1) and units of a unit investment trust registered under the Investment Company Act of 1940 (15 U.S.C. sections 80a-1 to 80a-2) shall be treated as regularly traded within the meaning of this paragraph.

(3) *Reporting requirement for interests traded on foreign securities markets.* A class of interests in a domestic corporation that is traded on one or more established securities markets located outside the United States shall not be considered to be regularly traded on such market or markets unless such class is traded in registered form, and—

(i) The corporation registers such class of interests pursuant to section 12 of the Securities Exchange Act of 1934, 15 U.S.C. sec. 78, or

(ii) The corporation attaches to its federal income tax return a statement providing the following:

(A) A caption which states "The following information concerning certain shareholders of this corporation is provided in accordance with the requirements of § 1.897-9T."

(B) The name under which the corporation is incorporated, the state in which such corporation is incorporated, the principal place of business of the corporation, and its employer identification number, if any;

(C) The identity of each person who, at any time during the corporation's taxable year, was the beneficial owner of more than 5 percent of any class of interests of the corporation to which this paragraph (d)(3) applies;

(D) The title, and the total number of shares issued, of any class of interests so owned; and

(E) With respect to each beneficial owner of more than 5 percent of any class of interests of the corporation, the number of shares owned, the percentage of the class represented thereby, and the nature of the beneficial ownership of each class of shares so owned.

Interests in a domestic corporation which has filed a report pursuant to this paragraph (d)(3)(ii) shall be considered to be regularly traded on an established securities market only for the taxable year of the corporation with respect to which such a report is filed.

(4) *Coordination with section 1445.* For purposes of section 1445, a class of interests in a corporation shall be presumed to be regularly traded during a calendar quarter if such interests were regularly traded within the meaning of this paragraph during the previous calendar quarter.

(e) *Foreign governments and international organizations.* A foreign government shall be treated as a foreign person with respect to U.S. real property interests, and shall be subject to sections 897, 1445, and 6039C on the disposition of a U.S. real property interest except to the extent specifically otherwise provided in the regulations issued under section 892. An international organization (as defined in section 7701(a)(18)) is not a foreign person with respect to U.S. real property interests, and is not subject to sections 897, 1445, and 6039C on the disposition of a U.S. real property interest. Buildings or parts of buildings and the land ancillary thereto (including the residence of the head of the diplomatic mission) used by the foreign government for a diplomatic mission shall not be a U.S. real property interest in the hands of the respective foreign government.

(f) *Effective date.* Section 1.897-9T with the exception of paragraph (e) shall be effective for transfers, exchanges, distributions and other dispositions occurring on or after June 6, 1988. Paragraph (e) of this section shall be effective for transfers, exchanges, distributions and other dispositions occurring on or after July 1, 1986. [Temporary Reg. § 1.897-9T.]

☐ [T.D. 8198, 5-4-88.]

[The next page is 48,801.]

Reg. § 1.897-9T(d)(2)

Income from Sources Without the United States
[Reg. § 1.901-1]

§ 1.901-1. Allowance of credit for taxes.—(a) *In general.* Citizens of the United States, domestic corporations, and certain aliens resident in the United States or Puerto Rico may choose to claim a credit, as provided in section 901, against the tax imposed by chapter 1 of the Code for taxes paid or accrued to foreign countries and possessions of the United States, subject to the conditions prescribed in the following subparagraphs:

(1) *Citizen of the United States.* A citizen of the United States, whether resident or nonresident, may claim a credit for (i) the amount of any income, war profits, and excess profits taxes paid or accrued (or deemed paid or accrued under section 905(b)) during the taxable year to any foreign country or to any possession of the United States; and (ii) his share of any such taxes of a partnership of which he is a member, or of an estate or trust of which he is a beneficiary.

(2) *Domestic corporation.* A domestic corporation may claim a credit for (i) the amount of any income, war profits, and excess profits taxes paid or accrued during the taxable year to any foreign country or to any possession of the United States; and (ii) the taxes deemed to have been paid or accrued under section 902, 905(b), or 960.

(3) *Alien resident of the United States or Puerto Rico.* An alien resident of the United States, or an alien individual who is a bona fide resident of Puerto Rico during the entire taxable year, may claim a credit for—

(i) The amount of any income, war profits, and excess profits taxes paid or accrued during the taxable year to any possession of the United States;

(ii) The amount of any such taxes paid or accrued (or deemed paid or accrued under section 905(b)) during the taxable year to any foreign country, if the foreign country of which such alien resident is a citizen or subject, in imposing such taxes, allows a similar credit to citizens of the United States residing in such country; and

(iii) His share of any such taxes of a partnership of which he is a member, or of an estate or trust of which he is a beneficiary, paid or accrued (or deemed paid or accrued under section 905(b)) during the taxable year,

(a) To any foreign country, if the foreign country of which such alien resident is a citizen or subject, in imposing such taxes, allows a similar credit to citizens of the United States residing in such country, or

(b) To any possession of the United States, as the case may be.

(4) *Limitation.* Section 907(a) limits the credit against the tax imposed by chapter 1 of the Code for certain foreign taxes paid or accrued with respect to foreign oil or gas extraction income. See § 1.907(a)-1.

(b) *Foreign countries which satisfy the similar credit requirement*—(1) *Taxes of foreign country of which alien resident is citizen or subject.* A foreign country of which an alien resident is a citizen or subject allows a similar credit, within the meaning of section 901(b)(3), to a United States citizen residing in such country either—

(i) If such country allows him a credit against its income taxes for the amount of income taxes paid or accrued to the United States; or

(ii) If, in imposing such taxes, such country exempts from taxation the income received by him from sources within the United States (as determined under part I (section 861 and following), subchapter N, chapter 1 of the Code).

(2) *Taxes of foreign country other than one of which alien resident is citizen or subject.* An alien resident of the United States may claim a credit for income taxes paid or accrued by him to a foreign country other than the one of which he is a citizen or subject if the country of which he is a citizen or subject either—

(i) Allows a credit to a United States citizen residing therein for income taxes paid or accrued by him to such other foreign country; or

(ii) In imposing its income taxes, exempts from taxation the income of a United States citizen residing therein from sources within such other foreign country.

(c) *Deduction denied if credit claimed.* If a taxpayer chooses with respect to any taxable year to claim a credit for taxes to any extent, such choice will be considered to apply to income, war profits, and excess profits taxes paid or accrued in such taxable year to all foreign countries and possessions of the United States, and no portion of any such taxes shall be allowed as a deduction from gross income in such taxable year or any succeeding taxable year. See section 275(a)(4).

(d) *Period during which election can be made or changed.* The taxpayer may, for a particular taxable year, claim the benefits of section 901 (or claim a deduction in lieu of a foreign tax credit) at any time before the expiration of the period prescribed by section 6511(d)(3)(A) (or section 6511(c) if the period is extended by agreement).

(e) *Joint return.* In the case of a husband and wife making a joint return, credit for taxes paid or accrued to any foreign country or to any possession of the United States shall be computed upon the basis of the total taxes so paid by or accrued against the spouses.

(f) *Taxes against which credit not allowed.* The credit for taxes shall be allowed only against the tax imposed by chapter 1 of the Code, but it shall not be allowed against the following taxes imposed under that chapter:

(1) The minimum tax for tax preferences imposed by section 56;

(2) The 10 percent tax on premature distributions to owner-employees imposed by section 72(m)(5)(B);

(3) The tax on lump sum distributions imposed by section 402(e);

(4) The additional tax on income from certain retirement accounts imposed by section 408(f);

(5) The tax on accumulated earnings imposed by section 531;

(6) The personal holding company tax imposed by section 541;

(7) The additional tax relating to war loss recoveries imposed by section 1333; and

(8) The additional tax relating to recoveries of foreign expropriation losses imposed by section 1351.

(g) *Taxpayers to whom credit not allowed.* Among those to whom the credit for taxes is not allowed are the following:

(1) A foreign corporation (see section 882(c)(4));

(2) A China Trade Act corporation (see section 942);

(3) A citizen or domestic corporation entitled to the benefits of the exemption provided by section 931 for income from possessions of the United States (see section 931(g));

(4) A nonresident alien, other than an alien individual who is a bona fide resident of Puerto Rico during the entire taxable year (see sections 874(c) and 901(b)(3));

(5) A citizen of a possession of the United States (except Puerto Rico) who is not otherwise a citizen of the United States and who is not a resident of the United States and persons who are inhabitants of the Virgin Islands (see section 932).

(h) *Taxpayers denied credit in a particular taxable year.* Taxpayers who are denied the credit for taxes for particular taxable years are the following:

(1) An individual who elects to pay the optional tax imposed by section 3, or one who elects under section 144 to take the standard deduction (see section 36);

(2) A taxpayer who elects to deduct taxes paid or accrued to any foreign country or possession of the United States (see sections 164 and 275);

(3) A regulated investment company which has exercised the election under section 853.

(i) *Dividends from a DISC treated as foreign.* For purposes of sections 901 through 906 and the regulations thereunder, any amount treated as a dividend from a corporation which is a DISC or former DISC (as defined in section 992(a)(1) or (3) as the case may be) will be treated as a dividend from a foreign corporation to the extent such dividend is treated under section 861(a)(2)(D) as income from sources without the United States. [Reg. § 1.901-1.]

☐ [*T.D.* 6275, 12-2-57. *Amended by T.D.* 6466, 5-12-60, *T.D.* 6780, 12-21-64, *T.D.* 6798, 12-30-64, *T.D.* 6795, 1-28-65, *T.D.* 7283, 8-2-73, *T.D.* 7564, 9-11-78, *T.D.* 7636, 8-9-79, *T.D.* 7961, 6-20-84, *and T.D.* 8160, 9-8-87.]

[Reg. § 1.901-2]

§ 1.901-2. **Income, war profits, or excess profits tax paid or accrued.**—(a) *Definition of income, war profits, or excess profits tax*—(1) *In general.* Section 901 allows a credit for the amount of income, war profits or excess profits tax (referred to as "income tax" for purposes of this section and §§ 1.901-2A and 1.903-1) paid to any foreign country. Whether a foreign levy is an income tax is determined independently for each separate foreign levy. A foreign levy is an income tax if and only if—

(i) It is a tax; and

(ii) The predominant character of that tax is that of an income tax in the U.S. sense.

Except to the extent otherwise provided in paragraphs (a)(3)(ii) and (c) of this section, a tax either is or is not an income tax, in its entirety, for all persons subject to the tax. Paragraphs (a), (b) and (c) of this section define an income tax for purposes of section 901. Paragraph (d) of this section contains rules describing what constitutes a separate foreign levy. Paragraph (e) of this section contains rules for determining the amount of tax paid by a person. Paragraph (f) of this section contains rules for determining by whom foreign tax is paid. Paragraph (g) of this section contains definitions of the terms "paid by," "foreign country," and "foreign levy." Paragraph (h) of this section states the effective date of this section.

(2) *Tax*—(i) *In general.* A foreign levy is a tax if it requires a compulsory payment pursuant to the authority of a foreign country to levy taxes. A penalty, fine, interest, or similar obligation is

not a tax, nor is a customs duty a tax. Whether a foreign levy requires a compulsory payment pursuant to a foreign country's authority to levy taxes is determined by principles of U.S. law and not by principles of law of the foreign country. Therefore, the assertion by a foreign country that a levy is pursuant to the foreign country's authority to levy taxes is not determinative that, under U.S. principles, it is pursuant thereto. Notwithstanding any assertion of a foreign country to the contrary, a foreign levy is not pursuant to a foreign country's authority to levy taxes, and thus is not a tax, to the extent a person subject to the levy receives (or will receive), directly or indirectly, a specific economic benefit (as defined in paragraph (a)(2)(ii)(B) of this section) from the foreign country in exchange for payment pursuant to the levy. Rather, to that extent, such levy requires a compulsory payment in exchange for such specific economic benefit. If, applying U.S. principles, a foreign levy requires a compulsory payment pursuant to the authority of a foreign country to levy taxes and also requires a compulsory payment in exchange for a specific economic benefit, the levy is considered to have two distinct elements: a tax and a requirement of compulsory payment in exchange for such specific economic benefit. In such a situation, these two distinct elements of the foreign levy (and the amount paid pursuant to each such element) must be separated. No credit is allowable for a payment pursuant to a foreign levy by a dual capacity taxpayer (as defined in paragraph (a)(2)(ii)(A) of this section) unless the person claiming such credit establishes the amount that is paid pursuant to the distinct element of the foreign levy that is a tax. See paragraph (a)(2)(ii) of this section and § 1.901-2A.

(ii) *Dual capacity taxpayers*—(A) *In general.* For purposes of this section and §§ 1.901-2A and 1.903-1, a person who is subject to a levy of a foreign state or of a possession of the United States or of a political subdivision of such a state or possession and who also, directly or indirectly (within the meaning of paragraph (a)(2)(ii)(E) of this section) receives (or will receive) a specific economic benefit from the state or possession or from a political subdivision of such state or possession or from an agency or instrumentality of any of the foregoing is referred to as a "dual capacity taxpayer." Dual capacity taxpayers are subject to the special rules of § 1.901-2A.

(B) *Specific economic benefit.* For purposes of this section and §§ 1.901-2A and 1.903-1, the term "specific economic benefit" means an economic benefit that is not made available on substantially the same terms to substantially all persons who are subject to the income tax that is generally imposed by the foreign country, or, if there is no such generally imposed income tax, an economic benefit that is not made available on substantially the same terms to the population of the country in general. Thus, a concession to extract government-owned petroleum is a specific economic benefit, but the right to travel or to ship freight on a government-owned airline is not, because the latter, but not the former, is made generally available on substantially the same terms. An economic benefit includes property; a service; a fee or other payment; a right to use, acquire or extract resources, patents or other property that a foreign country owns or controls (within the meaning of paragraph (a)(2)(ii)(D) of this section); or a reduction or discharge of a contractual obligation. It does not include the right or privilege merely to engage in business generally or to engage in business in a particular form.

(C) *Pension, unemployment, and disability fund payments.* A foreign levy imposed on individuals to finance retirement, old-age, death, survivor, unemployment, illness, or disability benefits, or for some substantially similar purpose, is not a requirement of compulsory payment in exchange for a specific economic benefit, as long as the amounts required to be paid by the individuals subject to the levy are not computed on a basis reflecting the respective ages, life expectancies or similar characteristics of such individuals.

(D) *Control of property.* A foreign country controls property that it does not own if the country exhibits substantial indicia of ownership with respect to the property, for example, by both regulating the quantity of property that may be extracted and establishing the minimum price at which it may be disposed of.

(E) *Indirect receipt of a benefit.* A person is considered to receive a specific economic benefit indirectly if another person receives a specific economic benefit and that other person—

(1) Owns or controls, directly or indirectly, the first person or is owned or controlled, directly or indirectly, by the first person or by the same persons that own or control, directly or indirectly, the first person; or

(2) Engages in a transaction with the first person under terms and conditions such that the first person receives, directly or indirectly, all or part of the value of the specific economic benefit.

(3) *Predominant character.* The predominant character of a foreign tax is that of an income tax in the U.S. sense—

(i) If, within the meaning of paragraph (b)(1) of this section, the foreign tax is likely to

Reg. § 1.901-2(a)(3)

reach net gain the normal circumstances in which it applies,

(ii) But only to the extent that liability for the tax is not dependent, within the meaning of paragraph (c) of this section, by its terms or otherwise, on the availability of a credit for the tax against income tax liability to another country.

(b) *Net gain*—(1) *In general.* A foreign tax is likely to reach net gain in the normal circumstances in which it applies if and only if the tax, judged on the basis of its predominant character, satisfies each of the realization, gross receipts, and net income requirements set forth in paragraphs (b)(2), (b)(3) and (b)(4), respectively, of this section.

(2) *Realization*—(i) *In general.* A foreign tax satisfies the realization requirement if, judged on the basis of its predominant character, it is imposed—

(A) Upon or subsequent to the occurrence of events ("realization events") that would result in the realization of income under the income tax provisions of the Internal Revenue Code;

(B) Upon the occurrence of an event prior to a realization event (a "prerealization event") provided the consequence of such event is the recapture (in whole or part) of a tax deduction, tax credit or other tax allowance previously accorded to the taxpayer; or

(C) Upon the occurrence of a prerealization event, other than one described in paragraph (b)(2)(i)(B) of this section, but only if the foreign country does not, upon the occurrence of a later event (other than a distribution or a deemed distribution of the income), impose tax ("second tax") with respect to the income on which tax is imposed by reason of such prerealization event (or, if it does impose a second tax, a credit or other comparable relief is available against the liability for such a second tax for tax paid on the occurrence of the prerealization event) and—

(1) The imposition of the tax upon such prerealization event is based on the difference in the values of property at the beginning and end of a period; or

(2) The prerealization event is the physical transfer, processing, or export of readily marketable property (as defined in paragraph (b)(2)(iii) of this section).

A foreign tax that, judged on the basis of its predominant character, is imposed upon the occurrence of events described in this paragraph (b)(2)(i) satisfies the realization requirement even if it is also imposed in some situations upon the occurrence of events not described in this paragraph (b)(2)(i). For example, a foreign tax that, judged on the basis of its predominant character, is imposed upon the occurrence of events described in this paragraph (b)(2)(i) satisfies the realization requirement even though the base of that tax also includes imputed rental income from a personal residence used by the owner and receipt of stock dividends of a type described in section 305(a) of the Internal Revenue Code. As provided in paragraph (a)(1) of this section, a tax either is or is not an income tax, in its entirety, for all persons subject to the tax; therefore, a foreign tax described in the immediately preceding sentence satisfies the realization requirement even though some persons subject to the tax will on some occasions not be subject to the tax except with respect to such imputed rental income and such stock dividends. However, a foreign tax based only or predominantly on such imputed rental income or only or predominantly on receipt of such stock dividends does not satisfy the realization requirement.

(ii) *Certain deemed distributions.* A foreign tax that does not satisfy the realization requirement under paragraph (b)(2)(i) of this section is nevertheless considered to meet the realization requirement if it is imposed with respect to a deemed distribution (*e.g.*, by a corporation to a shareholder) of amounts that meet the realization requirement in the hands of the person that, under foreign law, is deemed to distribute such amount, but only if the foreign country does not, upon the occurrence of a later event (*e.g.*, an actual distribution), impose tax ("second tax") with respect to the income on which tax was imposed by reason of such deemed distribution (or, if it does impose a second tax, a credit or other comparable relief is available against the liability for such a second tax for tax paid with respect to the deemed distribution).

(iii) *Readily marketable property.* Property is readily marketable if—

(A) It is stock in trade or other property of a kind that properly would be included in inventory if on hand at the close of the taxable year or if it is held primarily for sale to customers in the ordinary course of business, and

(B) It can be sold on the open market without further processing or it is exported from the foreign country.

(iv) *Examples.* The provisions of paragraph (b)(2) of this section may be illustrated by the following examples:

Example (1). Residents of country X are subject to a tax of 10 percent on the aggregate net appreciation in fair market value during the calendar year of all shares of stock held by them at

Reg. § 1.901-2(b)(1)

the end of the year. In addition, all such residents are subject to a country X tax that qualifies as an income tax within the meaning of paragraph (a)(1) of this section. Included in the base of the income tax are gains and losses realized on the sale of stock, and the basis of stock for purposes of determining such gain or loss is its cost. The operation of the stock appreciation tax and the income tax as applied to sales of stock is exemplified as follows: A, a resident of country X, purchases stock in June, 1983 for 100u (units of country X currency) and sells it in May, 1985 for 160u. On December 31, 1983, the stock is worth 120u and on December 31, 1984, it is worth 155u. Pursuant to the stock appreciation tax, A pays 2u for 1983 (10 percent of (120u − 100u)), 3.5u for 1984 (10 percent of (155u − 120u)), and nothing in 1985 because no stock was held at the end of that year. For purposes of the income tax, A must include 60u (160u − 100u) in his income for 1985, the year of sale. Pursuant to paragraph (b)(2)(i)(C) of this section, the stock appreciation tax does not satisfy the realization requirement because country X imposes a second tax upon the occurrence of a later event (i.e., the sale of stock) with respect to the income that was taxed by the stock appreciation tax and no credit or comparable relief is available against such second tax for the stock appreciation tax paid.

Example (2). The facts are the same as in example (1) except that if stock was held on December 31 last preceding the date of its sale, the basis of such stock for purposes of computing gain or loss under the income tax is the value of the stock on such December 31. Thus, in 1985, A includes only 5u (160u − 155u) as income from the sale for purposes of the income tax. Because the income tax imposed upon the occurrence of a later event (the sale) does not impose a tax with respect to the income that was taxed by the stock appreciation tax, the stock appreciation tax satisfies the realization requirement. The result would be the same if, instead of a basis adjustment to reflect taxation pursuant to the stock appreciation tax, the country X income tax allowed a credit (or other comparable relief) to take account of the stock appreciation tax. If a credit mechanism is used, see also paragraph (e)(4)(i) of this section.

Example (3). Country X imposes a tax on the realized net income of corporations that do business in country X. Country X also imposes a branch profits tax on corporations organized under the law of a country other than country X that do business in country X. The branch profits tax is imposed when realized net income is remitted or deemed to be remitted by branches in country X to home offices outside of country X. The branch profits tax is imposed subsequent to the occurrence of events that would result in realization of income (i.e., by corporations subject to such tax) under the income tax provisions of the Internal Revenue Code; thus, in accordance with paragraph (b)(2)(i)(A) of this section, the branch profits tax satisfies the realization requirement.

Example (4). Country X imposes a tax on the realized net income of corporations that do business in country X (the "country X corporate tax"). Country X also imposes a separate tax on shareholders of such corporations (the "country X shareholder tax"). The country X shareholder tax is imposed on the sum of the actual distributions received during the taxable year by such a shareholder from the corporation's realized net income for that year (i.e., income from past years is not taxed in a later year when it is actually distributed) plus the distributions deemed to be received by such a shareholder. Deemed distributions are defined as (A) a shareholder's pro rata share of the corporation's realized net income for the taxable year, less (B) such shareholder's pro rata share of the corporation's country X corporate tax for that year, less (C) actual distributions made by such corporation to such shareholder from such net income. A shareholder's receipt of actual distributions is a realization event within the meaning of paragraph (b)(2)(i)(A) of this section. The deemed distributions are not realization events, but they are described in paragraph (b)(2)(ii) of this section. Accordingly, the country X shareholder tax satisfies the realization requirement.

(3) *Gross receipts*—(i) *In general.* A foreign tax satisfies the gross receipts requirement if, judged on the basis of its predominant character, it is imposed on the basis of—

(A) Gross receipts; or

(B) Gross receipts computed under a method that is likely to produce an amount that is not greater than fair market value.

A foreign tax that, judged on the basis of its predominant character, is imposed on the basis of amounts described in this paragraph (b)(3)(i) satisfies the gross receipts requirement even if it is also imposed on the basis of some amounts not described in this paragraph (b)(3)(i).

(ii) *Examples.* The provisions of paragraph (b)(3)(i) of this section may be illustrated by the following examples:

Example (1). Country X imposes a "headquarters company tax" on country X corporations that serve as regional headquarters for affiliated nonresident corporations, and this tax is a separate tax within the meaning of paragraph (d) of this section. A headquarters company for purposes of this tax is a corporation that performs

Reg. § 1.901-2(b)(3)

administrative, management or coordination functions solely for nonresident affiliated entities. Due to the difficulty of determining on a case-by-case basis the arm's length gross receipts that headquarters companies would charge affiliates for such services, gross receipts of a headquarters company are deemed, for purposes of this tax, to equal 110 percent of the business expenses incurred by the headquarters company. It is established that this formula is likely to produce an amount that is not greater than the fair market value of arm's length gross receipts from such transactions with affiliates. Pursuant to paragraph (b)(3)(i)(B) of this section, the headquarters company tax satisfies the gross receipts requirement.

Example (2). The facts are the same as in Example (1), with the added fact that in the case of a particular taxpayer, A, the formula actually produces an amount that is substantially greater than the fair market value of arm's length gross receipts from transactions with affiliates. As provided in paragraph (a)(1) of this section, the headquarters company tax either is or is not an income tax, in its entirety, for all persons subject to the tax. Accordingly, the result is the same as in example (1) for all persons subject to the headquarters company tax, including A.

Example (3). Country X imposes a separate tax (within the meaning of paragraph (d) of this section) on income from the extraction of petroleum. Under that tax, gross receipts from extraction income are deemed to equal 105 percent of the fair market value of petroleum extracted. This computation is designed to produce an amount that is greater than the fair market value of actual gross receipts; therefore, the tax on extraction income is not likely to produce an amount that is not greater than fair market value. Accordingly, the tax on extraction income does not satisfy the gross receipts requirement. However, if the tax satisfies the criteria of § 1.903-1(a), it is a tax in lieu of an income tax.

(4) *Net income*—(i) *In general.* A foreign tax satisfies the net income requirement if, judged on the basis of its predominant character, the base of the tax is computed by reducing gross receipts (including gross receipts as computed under paragraph (b)(3)(i)(B) of this section) to permit—

(A) Recovery of the significant costs and expenses (including significant capital expenditures) attributable, under reasonable principles, to such gross receipts; or

(B) Recovery of such significant costs and expenses computed under a method that is likely to produce an amount that approximates, or is greater than, recovery of such significant costs and expenses.

A foreign tax law permits recovery of significant costs and expenses even if such costs and expenses are recovered at a different time than they would be if the Internal Revenue Code applied, unless the time of recovery is such that under the circumstances there is effectively a denial of such recovery. For example, unless the time of recovery is such that under the circumstances there is effectively a denial of such recovery, the net income requirement is satisfied where items deductible under the Internal Revenue Code are capitalized under the foreign tax system and recovered either on a recurring basis over time or upon the occurrence of some future event or where the recovery of items capitalized under the Internal Revenue Code occurs less rapidly under the foreign tax system. A foreign tax law that does not permit recovery of one or more significant costs or expenses, but that provides allowances that effectively compensate for nonrecovery of such significant costs or expenses, is considered to permit recovery of such costs or expenses. Principles used in the foreign tax law to attribute costs and expenses to gross receipts may be reasonable even if they differ from principles that apply under the Internal Revenue Code (*e.g.*, principles that apply under section 265, 465, or 861(b) of the Internal Revenue Code). A foreign tax whose base, judged on the basis of its predominant character, is computed by reducing gross receipts by items described in paragraph (b)(4)(i)(A) or (B) of this section satisfies the net income requirement even if gross receipts are not reduced by some such items. A foreign tax whose base is gross receipts or gross income does not satisfy the net income requirement except in the rare situation where that tax is almost certain to reach some net gain in the normal circumstances in which it applies because costs and expenses will almost never be so high as to offset gross receipts or gross income, respectively, and the rate of the tax is such that after the tax is paid persons subject to the tax are almost certain to have net gain. Thus, a tax on the gross receipts or gross income of businesses can satisfy the net income requirement only if businesses subject to the tax are almost certain never to incur a loss (after payment of the tax). In determining whether a foreign tax satisfies the net income requirement, it is immaterial whether gross receipts are reduced, in the base of the tax, by another tax, provided that other tax satisfies the realization, gross receipts and net income requirements.

(ii) *Consolidation of profits and losses.* In determining whether a foreign tax satisfies the net income requirement, one of the factors to be

Reg. § 1.901-2(b)(4)

taken into account is whether, in computing the base of the tax, a loss incurred in one activity (*e.g.,* a contract area in the case of oil and gas exploration) in a trade or business is allowed to offset profit earned by the same person in another activity (*e.g.,* a separate contract area) in the same trade or business. If such an offset is allowed, it is immaterial whether the offset may be made in the taxable period in which the loss is incurred or only in a different taxable period, unless the period is such that under the circumstances there is effectively a denial of the ability to offset the loss against profit. In determining whether a foreign tax satisfies the net income requirement, it is immaterial that no such offset is allowed if a loss incurred in one such activity may be applied to offset profit earned in that activity in a different taxable period, unless the period is such that under the circumstances there is effectively a denial of the ability to offset such loss against profit. In determining whether a foreign tax satisfies the net income requirement, it is immaterial whether a person's profits and losses from one trade or business (*e.g.,* oil and gas extraction) are allowed to offset its profits and losses from another trade or business (*e.g.,* oil and gas refining and processing), or whether a person's business profits and losses and its passive investment profits and losses are allowed to offset each other in computing the base of the foreign tax. Moreover, it is immaterial whether foreign law permits or prohibits consolidation of profits and losses of related persons, unless foreign law requires separate entities to be used to carry on separate activities in the same trade or business. If foreign law requires that separate entities carry on such separate activities, the determination whether the net income requirement is satisfied is made by applying the same considerations as if such separate activities were carried on by a single entity.

(iii) *Carryovers.* In determining whether a foreign tax satisfies the net income requirement, it is immaterial, except as otherwise provided in paragraph (b)(4)(ii) of this section, whether losses incurred during one taxable period may be carried over to offset profits incurred in different taxable periods.

(iv) *Examples.* The provisions of this paragraph (b)(4) may be illustrated by the following examples:

Example (1). Country X imposes an income tax on corporations engaged in business in country X; however, that income tax is not applicable to banks. Country X also imposes a tax (the "bank tax") of 1 percent on the gross amount of interest income derived by banks from branches in country X; no deductions are allowed. Banks doing business in country X incur very substantial costs and expenses (*e.g.,* interest expense) attributable to their interest income. The bank tax neither provides for recovery of significant costs and expenses nor provides any allowance that significantly compensates for the lack of such recovery. Since such banks are not almost certain never to incur a loss on their interest income from branches in country X, the bank tax does not satisfy the net income requirement. However, if the tax on corporations is generally imposed, the bank tax satisfies the criteria of § 1.903-1(a) and therefore is a tax in lieu of an income tax.

Example (2). Country X law imposes an income tax on persons engaged in business in country X. The base of that tax is realized net income attributable under reasonable principles to such business. Under the tax law of country X, a bank is not considered to be engaged in business in country X unless it has a branch in country X and interest income earned by a bank from a loan to a resident of country X is not considered attributable to business conducted by the bank in country X unless a branch of the bank in country X performs certain significant enumerated activities, such as negotiating the loan. Country X also imposes a tax (the "bank tax") of 1 percent on the gross amount of interest income earned by banks from loans to residents of country X if such banks do not engage in business in country X or if such interest income is not considered attributable to business conducted in country X. For the same reasons as are set forth in example (1), the bank tax does not satisfy the net income requirement. However, if the tax on persons engaged in business in country X is generally imposed, the bank tax satisfies the criteria of § 1.903-1(a) and therefore is a tax in lieu of an income tax.

Example (3). A foreign tax is imposed at the rate of 40 percent on the amount of gross wages realized by an employee; no deductions are allowed. Thus, the tax law neither provides for recovery of costs and expenses nor provides any allowance that effectively compensates for the lack of such recovery. Because costs and expenses of employees attributable to wage income are almost always insignificant compared to the gross wages realized, such costs and expenses will almost always not be so high as to offset the gross wages and the rate of the tax is such that, under the circumstances, after the tax is paid, employees subject to the tax are almost certain to have net gain. Accordingly, the tax satisfies the net income requirement.

Example (4). Country X imposes a tax at the rate of 48 percent of the "taxable income" of

Reg. § 1.901-2(b)(4)

nonresidents of country X who furnish specified types of services to customers who are residents of country X. "Taxable income" for purposes of the tax is defined as gross receipts received from residents of country X (regardless of whether the services to which the receipts relate are performed within or outside country X) less deductions that permit recovery of the significant costs and expenses (including significant capital expenditures) attributable under reasonable principles to such gross receipts. The country X tax satisfies the net income requirement.

Example (5). Each of country X and province Y (a political subdivision of country X) imposes a tax on corporations, called the "country X income tax" and the "province Y income tax," respectively. Each tax has an identical base, which is computed by reducing a corporation's gross receipts by deductions that, based on the predominant character of the tax, permit recovery of the significant costs and expenses (including significant capital expenditures) attributable under reasonable principles to such gross receipts. The country X income tax does not allow a deduction for the province Y income tax for which a taxpayer is liable, nor does the province Y income tax allow a deduction for the country X income tax for which a taxpayer is liable. As provided in paragraph (d)(1) of this section, each of the country X income tax and the province Y income tax is a separate levy. Both of these levies satisfy the net income requirement; the fact that neither levy's base allows a deduction for the other levy is immaterial in reaching that determination.

(c) *Soak-up taxes*—(1) *In general.* Pursuant to paragraph (a)(3)(ii) of this section, the predominant character of a foreign tax that satisfies the requirement of paragraph (a)(3)(i) of this section is that of an income tax in the U.S. sense only to the extent that liability for the foreign tax is not dependent (by its terms or otherwise) on the availability of a credit for the tax against income tax liability to another country. Liability for foreign tax is dependent on the availability of a credit for the foreign tax against income tax liability to another country only if and to the extent that the foreign tax would not be imposed on the taxpayer but for the availability of such a credit. See also § 1.903-1(b)(2).

(2) *Examples.* The provisions of paragraph (c)(1) of this section may be illustrated by the following examples:

Example (1). Country X imposes a tax on the receipt of royalties from sources in country X by nonresidents of country X. The tax is 15 percent of the gross amount of such royalties unless the recipient is a resident of the United States or of country A, B, C or D, in which case the tax is 20 percent of the gross amount of such royalties. Like the United States, each of countries A, B, C and D allows its residents a credit against the income tax otherwise payable to it for income taxes paid to other countries. Because the 20 percent rate applies only to residents of countries which allow a credit for taxes paid to other countries and the 15 percent rate applies to residents of countries which do not allow such a credit, one-fourth of the country X tax would not be imposed on residents of the United States but for the availability of such a credit. Accordingly, one-fourth of the country X tax imposed on residents of the United States who receive royalties from sources in country X is dependent on the availability of a credit for the country X tax against income tax liability to another country.

Example (2). Country X imposes a tax on the realized net income derived by all nonresidents from carrying on a trade or business in country X. Although country X law does not prohibit other nonresidents from carrying on business in country X, United States persons are the only nonresidents of country X that carry on business in country X in 1984. The country X tax would be imposed in its entirety on a nonresident of country X irrespective of the availability of a credit for country X tax against income tax liability to another country. Accordingly, no portion of that tax is dependent on the availability of such a credit.

Example (3). Country X imposes tax on the realized net income of all corporations incorporated in country X. Country X allows a tax holiday to qualifying corporations incorporated in country X that are owned by nonresidents of country X, pursuant to which no country X tax is imposed on the net income of a qualifying corporation for the first ten years of its operations in country X. A corporation qualifies for the tax holiday if it meets certain minimum investment criteria and if the development office of country X certifies that in its opinion the operations of the corporation will be consistent with specified development goals of country X. The development office will not so certify to any corporation owned by persons resident in countries that allow a credit (such as that available under section 902 of the Internal Revenue Code) for country X tax paid by a corporation incorporated in country X. In practice, tax holidays are granted to a large number of corporations, but country X tax is imposed on a significant number of other corporations incorporated in country X (*e.g.,* those owned by country X persons and those which have had operations for more than 10 years) in addition to corporations denied a tax holiday because their

Reg. § 1.901-2(c)(1)

shareholders qualify for a credit for the country X tax against income tax liability to another country. In the case of corporations denied a tax holiday because they have U.S. shareholders, no portion of the country X tax during the period of the denied 10-year tax holiday is dependent on the availability of a credit for the country X tax against income tax liability to another country.

Example (4). The facts are the same as in example (3), except that corporations owned by persons resident in countries that will allow a credit for country X tax at the time when dividends are distributed by the corporations are granted a provisional tax holiday. Under the provisional tax holiday, instead of relieving such a corporation from country X tax for 10 years, liability for such tax is deferred until the corporation distributes dividends. The result is the same as in example (3).

(d) *Separate levies.* (1) *In general.* For purposes of sections 901 and 903, whether a single levy or separate levies are imposed by a foreign country depends on U.S. principles and not on whether foreign law imposes the levy or levies in a single or separate statutes. A levy imposed by one taxing authority (*e.g.,* the national government of a foreign country) is always separate for purposes of sections 901 and 903 from a levy imposed by another taxing authority (*e.g.,* a political subdivision of that foreign country). Levies are not separate merely because different rates apply to different taxpayers. For example, a foreign levy identical to the tax imposed on U.S. citizens and resident alien individuals by section 1 of the Internal Revenue Code is a single levy notwithstanding the levy has graduated rates and applies different rate schedules to unmarried individuals, married individuals who file separate returns and married individuals who file joint returns. In general, levies are not separate merely because some provisions determining the base of the levy apply, by their terms or in practice, to some, but not all, persons subject to the levy. For example, a foreign levy identical to the tax imposed by section 11 of the Internal Revenue Code is a single levy even though some provisions apply by their terms to some but not all corporations subject to the section 11 tax (*e.g.,* section 465 is by its terms applicable to corporations described in sections 465(a)(1)(B) and 465(a)(1)(C), but not to other corporations), and even though some provisions apply in practice to some but not all corporations subject to the section 11 tax (*e.g.,* section 611 does not, in practice, apply to any corporation that does not have a qualifying interest in the type of property described in section 611(a)). However, where the base of a levy is different in kind, and not merely in degree, for different classes of persons subject to the levy, the levy is considered for purposes of sections 901 and 903 to impose separate levies for such classes of persons. For example, regardless of whether they are contained in a single or separate foreign statutes, a foreign levy identical to the tax imposed by section 871(b) of the Internal Revenue Code is a separate levy from a foreign levy identical to the tax imposed by section 1 of the Internal Revenue Code as it applies to persons other than those described in section 871(b), and foreign levies identical to the taxes imposed by sections 11, 541, 881, 882, 1491 and 3111 of the Internal Revenue Code are each separate levies, because the base of each of those levies differs in kind, and not merely in degree, from the base of each of the others. Accordingly, each such levy must be analyzed separately to determine whether it is an income tax within the meaning of paragraph (a)(1) of this section and whether it is a tax in lieu of an income tax within the meaning of paragraph (a) of § 1.903-1. Where foreign law imposes a levy that is the sum of two or more separately computed amounts, and each such amount is computed by reference to a separate base, separate levies are considered, for purposes of sections 901 and 903, to be imposed. A separate base may consist, for example, of a particular type of income or of an amount unrelated to income, *e.g.,* wages paid. Amounts are not separately computed if they are computed separately merely for purposes of a preliminary computation and are then combined as a single base. In the case of levies that apply to dual capacity taxpayers, see also § 1.901-2A(a).

(2) *Contractual modifications.* Notwithstanding paragraph (d)(1) of this section, if foreign law imposing a levy is modified for one or more persons subject to the levy by a contract entered into by such person or persons and the foreign country, then foreign law is considered for purposes of sections 901 and 903 to impose a separate levy for all persons to whom such contractual modification of the levy applies, as contrasted to the levy as applied to all persons to whom such contractual modification does not apply. In applying the provisions of paragraph (c) of this section to a tax as modified by such a contract, the provisions of § 1.903-1(b)(2) shall apply.

(3) *Examples.* The provisions of paragraph (d)(1) of this section may be illustrated by the following examples:

Example (1). A foreign statute imposes a levy on corporations equal to the sum of 15% of the corporation's realized net income plus 3% of its net worth. As the levy is the sum of two separately computed amounts, each of which is computed by reference to a separate base, each of the portion of the levy based on income and the portion of the levy based on net worth is considered, for purposes of sections 901 and 903, to be a separate levy.

Example (2). A foreign statute imposes a levy on nonresident alien individuals analogous to the taxes imposed by section 871 of the Internal Revenue Code. For the same reasons as set forth in example (1), each of the portion of the foreign levy analogous to the tax imposed by section 871(a) and the portion of the foreign levy analogous to the tax imposed by sections 871(b) and 1, is considered, for purposes of sections 901 and 903, to be a separate levy.

Example (3). A single foreign statute or separate foreign statutes impose a foreign levy that is the sum of the products of specified rates applied to specified bases, as follows:

base	rate
net income from mining	45%
net income from manufacturing	50%
net income from technical services	50%
net income from other services	45%
net income from investments	15%
all other net income	50%

In computing each such base, deductible expenditures are allocated to the type of income they generate. If allocated deductible expenditures exceed the gross amount of a specified type of income, the excess may not be applied against income of a different specified type. Accordingly, the levy is the sum of several separately computed amounts, each of which is computed by reference to a separate base. Each of the levies on mining net income, manufacturing net income, technical services net income, other services net income, investment net income and other net income is, therefore, considered, for purposes of sections 901 and 903, to be a separate levy.

Example (4). The facts are the same as in example (3), except that excess deductible expenditures allocated to one type of income are applied against other types of income to which the same rate applies. The levies on mining net income and other services net income together are considered, for purposes of sections 901 and 903, to be a single levy since, despite a separate preliminary computation of the bases, by reason of the permitted application of excess allocated deductible expenditures, the bases are not separately computed. For the same reason, the levies on manufacturing net income, technical services net income and other net income together are considered, for purposes of sections 901 and 903, to be a single levy. The levy on investment net income is considered, for purposes of sections 901 and 903, to be a separate levy. These results are not dependent on whether the application of excess allocated deductible expenditures to a different type of income, as described above, is permitted in the same taxable period in which the expenditures are taken into account for purposes of the preliminary computation, or only in a different (*e.g.,* later) taxable period.

Example (5). The facts are the same as in example (3), except that excess deductible expenditures allocated to any type of income other than investment income are applied against the other types of income (including investment income) according to a specified set of priorities of application. Excess deductible expenditures allocated to investment income are not applied against any other type of income. For the reason expressed in example (4), all of the levies are together considered, for purposes of sections 901 and 903, to be a single levy.

(e) *Amount of income tax that is creditable*—(1) *In general.* Credit is allowed under section 901 for the amount of income tax (within the meaning of paragraph (a)(1) of this section) that is paid to a foreign country by the taxpayer. The amount of income tax paid by the taxpayer is determined separately for each taxpayer.

(2) *Refunds and credits*—(i) *In general.* An amount is not tax paid to a foreign country to the extent that it is reasonably certain that the amount will be refunded, credited, rebated, abated, or forgiven. It is not reasonably certain that an amount will be refunded, credited, rebated, abated, or forgiven if the amount is not greater than a reasonable approximation of final tax liability to the foreign country.

(ii) *Examples.* The provisions of paragraph (e)(2)(i) of this section may be illustrated by the following examples:

Example (1). The internal law of country X imposes a 25 percent tax on the gross amount of interest from sources in country X that is received by a nonresident of country X. Country X law imposes the tax on the nonresident recipient and requires any resident of country X that pays such interest to a nonresident to withhold and pay over to country X 25 percent of such interest, which is applied to offset the recipient's liability for the 25 percent tax. A tax treaty between the United States and country X overrides internal law of country X and provides that country X may not tax interest received by a resident of the United States from a resident of country X at a rate in excess of 10 percent of the gross amount of such interest. A resident of the United States may claim the benefit of the treaty only by applying for a refund of the excess withheld amount (15

Reg. § 1.901-2(e)(1)

percent of the gross amount of interest income) after the end of the taxable year. *A*, a resident of the United States, receives a gross amount of 100u (units of country X currency) of interest income from a resident of country X from sources in country X in the taxable year 1984, from which 25u of country X tax is withheld. *A* files a timely claim for refund of the 15u excess withheld amount. 15u of the amount withheld (25u − 10u) is reasonably certain to be refunded; therefore, 15u is not considered an amount of tax paid to country X.

Example (2). *A*'s initial income tax liability under country X law is 100u (units of country X currency). However, under country X law *A*'s initial income tax liability is reduced in order to compute its final tax liability by an investment credit of 15u and a credit for charitable contributions of 5u. The amount of income tax paid by *A* is 80u.

Example (3). *A* computes his income tax liability in country X for the taxable year 1984 as 100u (units of country X currency), files a tax return on that basis, and pays 100u of tax. The day after *A* files that return, *A* files a claim for refund of 90u. The difference between the 100u of liability reflected in *A*'s original return and the 10u of liability reflected in *A*'s refund claim depends on whether a particular expenditure made by *A* is nondeductible or deductible, respectively. Based on an analysis of the country X tax law, *A*'s country X tax advisors have advised *A* that it is not clear whether or not that expenditure is deductible. In view of the uncertainty as to the proper treatment of the item in question under country X tax law, no portion of the 100u paid by *A* is reasonably certain to be refunded. If *A* receives a refund, *A* must treat the refund as required by section 905(c) of the Internal Revenue Code.

Example (4). A levy of country X, which qualifies as an income tax within the meaning of paragraph (a)(1) of this section, provides that each person who makes payment to country X pursuant to the levy will receive a bond to be issued by country X with an amount payable at maturity equal to 10 percent of the amount paid pursuant to the levy. *A* pays 38,000u (units of country X currency) to country X and is entitled to receive a bond with an amount payable at maturity of 3800u. It is reasonably certain that a refund in the form of property (the bond) will be made. The amount of that refund is equal to the fair market value of the bond. Therefore, only the portion of the 38,000u payment in excess of the fair market value of the bond is an amount of tax paid.

(3) *Subsidies*—(i) *General rule*. An amount of foreign income tax is not an amount of income tax paid or accrued by a taxpayer to a foreign country to the extent that—

(A) The amount is used, directly or indirectly, by the foreign country imposing the tax to provide a subsidy by any means (including, but not limited to, a rebate, a refund, a credit, a deduction, a payment, a discharge of an obligation, or any other method) to the taxpayer, to a related person (within the meaning of section 482), to any party to the transaction, or to any party to a related transaction; and

(B) The subsidy is determined, directly or indirectly, by reference to the amount of the tax or by reference to the base used to compute the amount of the tax.

(ii) *Subsidy*. The term "subsidy" includes any benefit conferred, directly or indirectly, by a foreign country to one of the parties enumerated in paragraph (e)(3)(i)(A) of this section. Substance and not form shall govern in determining whether a subsidy exists. The fact that the U.S. taxpayer may derive no demonstrable benefit from the subsidy is irrelevant in determining whether a subsidy exists.

(iii) *Official exchange rate*. A subsidy described in paragraph (e)(3)(i)(B) of this section does not include the actual use of an official foreign government exchange rate converting foreign currency into dollars where a free exchange rate also exists if—

(A) The economic benefit represented by the use of the official exchange rate is not targeted to or tied to transactions that give rise to a claim for a foreign tax credit;

(B) The economic benefit of the official exchange rate applies to a broad range of international transactions, in all cases based on the total payment to be made without regard to whether the payment is a return of principal, gross income, or net income, and without regard to whether it is subject to tax; and

(C) Any reduction in the overall cost of the transaction is merely coincidental to the broad structure and operation of the official exchange rate.

In regard to foreign taxes paid or accrued in taxable years beginning before January 1, 1987, to which the Mexican Exchange Control Decree, effective as of December 20, 1982, applies, see Rev. Rul. 84-143, 1984-2 C.B. 127.

(iv) *Examples*. The provisions of this paragraph (e)(3) may be illustrated by the following examples:

Reg. § 1.901-2(e)(3)

Example 1. (i) Country X imposes a 30 percent tax on nonresident lenders with respect to interest which the nonresident lenders receive from borrowers who are residents of Country X, and it is established that this tax is a tax in lieu of an income tax within the meaning of § 1.903-1(a). Country X provides the nonresident lenders with receipts upon their payment of the 30 percent tax. Country X remits to resident borrowers an incentive payment for engaging in foreign loans, which payment is an amount equal to 20 percent of the interest paid to nonresident lenders.

(ii) Because the incentive payment is based on the interest paid, it is determined by reference to the base used to compute the tax that is imposed on the nonresident lender. The incentive payment is considered a subsidy under this paragraph (e)(3) since it is provided to a party (the borrower) to the transaction and is based on the amount of tax that is imposed on the lender with respect to the transaction. Therefore, two-thirds (20 percent/30 percent) of the amount withheld by the resident borrower from interest payments to the nonresident lender is not an amount of income tax paid or accrued for purposes of section 901(b).

Example 2. (i) A U.S. bank lends money to a development bank in Country X. The development bank relends the money to companies resident in Country X. A withholding tax is imposed by Country X on the U.S. bank with respect to the interest that the development bank pays to the U.S. bank, and appropriate receipts are provided. On the date that the tax is withheld, fifty percent of the tax is credited by Country X to an account of the development bank. Country X requires the development bank to transfer the amount credited to the borrowing companies.

(ii) The amount successively credited to the account of the development bank and then to the account of the borrowing companies is determined by reference to the amount of the tax and the tax base. Since the amount credited to the borrowing companies is a subsidy provided to a party (the borrowing companies) to a related transaction and is based on the amount of tax and the tax base, it is not an amount paid or accrued as an income tax for purposes of section 901(b).

Example 3. (i) A U.S. bank lends dollars to a Country X borrower. Country X imposes a withholding tax on the lender with respect to the interest. The tax is to be paid in Country X currency, although the interest is payable in dollars. Country X has a dual exchange rate system, comprised of a controlled official exchange rate and a free exchange rate. Priority transactions such as exports of merchandise, imports of merchandise, and payments of principal and interest on foreign currency loans payable abroad to foreign lenders are governed by the official exchange rate which yields more dollars per unit of Country X currency than the free exchange rate. The Country X borrower remits the net amount of dollar interest due to the U.S. bank (interest due less withholding tax), pays the tax withheld in Country X currency to the Country X government, and provides to the U.S. bank a receipt for payment of the Country X taxes.

(ii) The use of the official exchange rate by the U.S. bank to determine foreign taxes with respect to interest is not a subsidy described in paragraph (e)(3)(i)(B) of this section. The official exchange rate is not targeted to or tied to transactions that give rise to a claim for a foreign tax credit. The use of the official exchange rate applies to the interest paid and to the principal paid. Any benefit derived by the U.S. bank through the use of the official exchange rate is merely coincidental to the broad structure and operation of the official exchange rate.

Example 4. (i) B, a U.S. corporation, is engaged in the production of oil and gas in Country X pursuant to a production sharing agreement between B, Country X, and the state petroleum authority of Country X. The agreement is approved and enacted into law by the Legislature of Country X. Both B and the petroleum authority are subject to the Country X income tax. Each entity files an annual income tax return and pays, to the tax authority of Country X, the amount of income tax due on its annual income. B is a dual capacity taxpayer as defined in § 1.901-2(a)(2)(ii)(A). Country X has agreed to return to the petroleum authority one-half of the income taxes paid by B by allowing it a credit in calculating its own tax liability to Country X.

(ii) The petroleum authority is a party to a transaction with B and the amount returned by Country X to the petroleum authority is determined by reference to the amount of the tax imposed on B. Therefore, the amount returned is a subsidy as described in this paragraph (e)(3) and one-half the tax imposed on B is not an amount of income tax paid or accrued.

Example 5. Assume the same facts as in *Example 4*, except that the state petroleum authority of Country X does not receive amounts from Country X related to tax paid by B. Instead, the authority of Country X receives a general appropriation from Country X which is not calculated with reference to the amount of tax paid by B. The general appropriation is therefore not a subsidy described in this paragraph (e)(3).

Reg. § 1.901-2(e)(3)

(v) *Effective Date.* This paragraph (e)(3) shall apply to foreign taxes paid or accrued in taxable years beginning after December 31, 1986.

(4) *Multiple levies*—(i) *In general.* If, under foreign law, a taxpayer's tentative liability for one levy (the "first levy") is or can be reduced by the amount of the taxpayer's liability for a different levy (the "second levy"), then the amount considered paid by the taxpayer to the foreign country pursuant to the second levy is an amount equal to its entire liability for that levy, and the remainder of the amount paid is considered paid pursuant to the first levy. This rule applies regardless of whether it is or is not likely that liability for one such levy will always exceed liability for the other such levy. For an example of the application of this rule, see example (5) of § 1.903-1(b)(3). If, under foreign law, the amount of a taxpayer's liability is the greater or lesser of amounts computed pursuant to two levies, then the entire amount paid to the foreign country by the taxpayer is considered paid pursuant to the levy that imposes such greater or lesser amount, respectively, and no amount is considered paid pursuant to such other levy.

(ii) *Integrated tax systems.* [Reserved]

(5) *Noncompulsory amounts*—(i) *In general.* An amount paid is not a compulsory payment, and thus is not an amount of tax paid, to the extent that the amount paid exceeds the amount of liability under foreign law for tax. An amount paid does not exceed the amount of such liability if the amount paid is determined by the taxpayer in a manner that is consistent with a reasonable interpretation and application of the substantive and procedural provisions of foreign law (including applicable tax treaties) in such a way as to reduce, over time, the taxpayer's reasonably expected liability under foreign law for tax, and if the taxpayer exhausts all effective and practical remedies, including invocation of competent authority procedures available under applicable tax treaties, to reduce, over time, the taxpayer's liability for foreign tax (including liability pursuant to a foreign tax audit adjustment). Where foreign tax law includes options or elections whereby a taxpayer's tax liability may be shifted, in whole or part, to a different year or years, the taxpayer's use or failure to use such options or elections does not result in a payment in excess of the taxpayer's liability for foreign tax. An interpretation or application of foreign law is not reasonable if there is actual notice or constructive notice (*e.g.*, a published court decision) to the taxpayer that the interpretation or application is likely to be erroneous. In interpreting foreign tax law, a taxpayer may generally rely on advice obtained in good faith from competent foreign tax advisors to whom the taxpayer has disclosed the relevant facts. A remedy is effective and practical only if the cost thereof (including the risk of offsetting or additional tax liability) is reasonable in light of the amount at issue and the likelihood of success. A settlement by a taxpayer of two or more issues will be evaluated on an overall basis, not on an issue-by-issue basis, in determining whether an amount is a compulsory amount. A taxpayer is not required to alter its form of doing business, its business conduct, or the form of any business transaction in order to reduce its liability under foreign law for tax.

(ii) *Examples.* The provisions of paragraph (e)(5)(i) of this section may be illustrated by the following examples:

Example (1). A, a corporation organized and doing business solely in the United States, owns all of the stock of B, a corporation organized in country X. In 1984 A buys merchandise from unrelated persons for $1,000,000, shortly thereafter resells that merchandise to B for $600,000, and B later in 1984 resells the merchandise to unrelated persons for $1,200,000. Under the country X income tax, which is an income tax within the meaning of paragraph (a)(1) of this section, all corporations organized in country X are subject to a tax equal to 3% of their net income. In computing its 1984 country X income tax liability B reports $600,000 ($1,200,000 − $600,000) of profit from the purchase and resale of the merchandise referred to above. The country X income tax law requires that transactions between related persons be reported at arm's length prices, and a reasonable interpretation of this requirement, as it has been applied in country X, would consider B's arm's length purchase price of the merchandise purchased from A to be $1,050,000. When it computes its country X tax liability B is aware that $600,000 is not an arm's length price (by country X standards). B's knowing use of a non-arm's length price (by country X standards) of $600,000, instead of a price of $1,050,000 (an arm's length price under country X's law), is not consistent with a reasonable interpretation and application of the law of country X, determined in such a way as to reduce over time B's reasonably expected liability for country X income tax. Accordingly, $13,500 (3% of $450,000 ($1,050,000 − $600,000)), the amount of country X income tax paid by B to country X that is attributable to the purchase of the merchandise from B's parent at less than an arm's length price, is in excess of the amount of B's liability for country X tax, and thus is not an amount of tax.

Reg. § 1.901-2(e)(5)

Example (2). A, a corporation organized and doing business solely in the United States, owns all of the stock of B, a corporation organized in country X. Country X has in force an income tax treaty with the United States. The treaty provides that the profits of related persons shall be determined as if the persons were not related. A and B deal extensively with each other. A and B, with respect to a series of transactions involving both of them, treat A as having $300,000 of income and B as having $700,000 of income for purposes of A's United States income tax and B's country X income tax, respectively. B has no actual or constructive notice that its treatment of these transactions under country X law is likely to be erroneous. Subsequently, the Internal Revenue Service reallocates $200,000 of this income from B to A under the authority of section 482 and the treaty. This reallocation constitutes actual notice to A and constructive notice to B that B's interpretation and application of country X's law and the tax treaty is likely to be erroneous. B does not exhaust all effective and practical remedies to obtain a refund of the amount of country X income tax paid by B to country X that is attributable to the reallocated $200,000 of income. This amount is in excess of the amount of B's liability for country X tax and thus is not an amount of tax.

Example (3). The facts are the same as in example (2), except that B files a claim for refund (an administrative proceeding) of country X tax and A or B invokes the competent authority procedures of the treaty, the cost of which is reasonable in view of the amount at issue and the likelihood of success. Nevertheless, B does not obtain any refund of country X tax. The cost of pursuing any judicial remedy in country X would be unreasonable in light of the amount at issue and the likelihood of B's success, and B does not pursue any such remedy. The entire amount paid by B to country X is a compulsory payment and thus is an amount of tax paid by B.

Example (4). The facts are the same as in example (2), except that, when the Internal Revenue Service makes the reallocation, the country X statute of limitations on refunds has expired; and neither the internal law of country X nor the treaty authorizes the country X tax authorities to pay a refund that is barred by the statute of limitations. B does not file a claim for refund, and neither A nor B invokes the competent authority procedures of the treaty. Because the country X tax authorities would be barred by the statute of limitations from paying a refund, B has no effective and practicable remedies. The entire amount paid by B to country X is a compulsory payment and thus is an amount of tax paid by B.

Example (5). A is a U.S. person doing business in country X. In computing its income tax liability to country X, A is permitted, at its election, to recover the cost of machinery used in its business either by deducting that cost in the year of acquisition or by depreciating that cost on the straight line method over a period of 2, 4, 6 or 10 years. A elects to depreciate machinery over 10 years. This election merely shifts A's tax liability to different years (compared to the timing of A's tax liability under a different depreciation period); it does not result in a payment in excess of the amount of A's liability for country X income tax in any year since the amount of country X tax paid by A is consistent with a reasonable interpretation of country X law in such a way as to reduce over time A's reasonably expected liability for country X tax. Because the standard of paragraph (e)(5)(i) of this section refers to A's reasonably expected liability, not its actual liability, events actually occurring in subsequent years (*e.g.*, whether A has sufficient profit in such years so that such depreciation deductions actually reduce A's country X tax liability or whether the country X tax rates change) are immaterial.

Example (6). The internal law of country X imposes a 25 percent tax on the gross amount of interest from sources in country X that is received by a nonresident of country X. Country X law imposes the tax on the nonresident recipient and requires any resident of country X that pays such interest to a nonresident to withhold and pay over to country X 25 percent of such interest, which is applied to offset the recipient's liability for the 25 percent tax. A tax treaty between the United States and country X overrides internal law of country X and provides that country X may not tax interest received by a resident of the United States from a resident of country X at a rate in excess of 10 percent of the gross amount of such interest. A resident of the United States may claim the benefit of the treaty only by applying for a refund of the excess withheld amount (15 percent of the gross amount of interest income) after the end of the taxable year. A, a resident of the United States, receives a gross amount of 100u (units of country X currency) of interest income from a resident of country X from sources in country X in the taxable year 1984, from which 25u of country X tax is withheld. A does not file a timely claim for refund. 15u of the amount withheld (25u − 10u) is not a compulsory payment and hence is not an amount of tax.

(f) *Taxpayer*—(1) *In general.* The person by whom tax is considered paid for purposes of sections 901 and 903 is the person on whom foreign law imposes legal liability for such tax, even if another person (*e.g.*, a withholding agent) remits

Reg. § 1.901-2(f)(1)

such tax. For purposes of this section, § 1.901-2A and § 1.903-1, the person on whom foreign law imposes such liability is referred to as the "taxpayer." A foreign tax of a type described in paragraph (a)(2)(ii)(C) of this section is considered to be imposed on the recipients of wages if such tax is deducted from such wages under provisions that are comparable to section 3102(a) and (b) of the Internal Revenue Code.

(2) *Party undertaking tax obligation as part of transaction*—(i) *In general.* Tax is considered paid by the taxpayer even if another party to a direct or indirect transaction with the taxpayer agrees, as a part of the transaction, to assume the taxpayer's foreign tax liability. The rules of the foregoing sentence apply notwithstanding anything to the contrary in paragraph (e)(3) of this section. See § 1.901-2A for additional rules regarding dual capacity taxpayers.

(ii) *Examples.* The provisions of paragraphs f(1) and (f)(2)(i) of this section may be illustrated by the following examples:

Example (1). Under a loan agreement between A, a resident of country X, and B, a United States person, A agrees to pay B a certain amount of interest net of any tax that country X may impose on B with respect to its interest income. Country X imposes a 10 percent tax on the gross amount of interest income received by nonresidents of country X from sources in country X, and it is established that this tax is a tax in lieu of an income tax within the meaning of § 1.903-1(a). Under the law of country X this tax is imposed on the nonresident recipient, and any resident of country X that pays such interest to a nonresident is required to withhold and pay over to country X 10 percent of the amount of such interest, which is applied to offset the recipient's liability for the tax. Because legal liability for the tax is imposed on the recipient of such interest income, B is the taxpayer with respect to the country X tax imposed on B's interest income from B's loan to A. Accordingly, B's interest income for federal income tax purposes includes the amount of country X tax that is imposed on B with respect to such interest income and that is paid on B's behalf by A pursuant to the loan agreement, and, under paragraph (f)(2)(i) of this section, such tax is considered for purposes of section 903 to be paid by B.

Example (2). The facts are the same as in example (1), except that in collecting and receiving the interest B is acting as a nominee for, or agent of, C, who is a United States person. Because C (not B) is the beneficial owner of the interest, legal liability for the tax is imposed in C, not B (C's nominee or agent). Thus, C is the taxpayer with respect to the country X tax imposed on C's interest income from C's loan to A. Accordingly, C's interest income for federal income tax purposes includes the amount of country X tax that is imposed on C with respect to such interest income and that is paid on C's behalf by A pursuant to the loan agreement. Under paragraph (f)(2)(i) of this section, such tax is considered for purposes of section 903 to be paid by C. No such tax is considered paid by B.

Example (3). Country X imposes a tax called the "country X income tax." A, a United States person engaged in construction activities in country X, is subject to that tax. Country X has contracted with A for A to construct a naval base. A is a dual capacity taxpayer (as defined in paragraph (a)(2)(ii)(A) of this section) and, in accordance with paragraphs (a)(1) and (c)(1) of § 1.901-2A, A has established that the country X income tax as applied to dual capacity persons and the country X income tax as applied to persons other than dual capacity persons together constitute a single levy. A has also established that that levy is an income tax within the meaning of paragraph (a)(1) of this section. Pursuant to the terms of the contract, country X has agreed to assume any country X tax liability that A may incur with respect to A's income from the contract. For federal income tax purposes, A's income from the contract includes the amount of tax liability that is imposed by country X on A with respect to its income from the contract and that is assumed by country X; and for purposes of section 901 the amount of such tax liability assumed by country X is considered to be paid by A. By reason of paragraph (f)(2)(i) of this section, country X is not considered to provide a subsidy, within the meaning of paragraph (e)(3) of this section, to A.

(3) *Taxes paid on combined income.* If foreign income tax is imposed on the combined income of two or more related persons (for example, a husband and wife or a corporation and one or more of its subsidiaries) and they are jointly and severally liable for the income tax under foreign law, foreign law is considered to impose legal liability on each such person for the amount of the foreign income tax that is attributable to its portion of the base of the tax, regardless of which person actually pays the tax.

(g) *Definitions.* For purposes of this section and §§ 1.901-2A and 1.903-1, the following definitions apply:

(1) The term "paid" means "paid or accrued"; the term "payment" means "payment or accrual"; and the term "paid by" means "paid or accrued by or on behalf of."

Reg. § 1.901-2(g)(1)

(2) The term "foreign country" means any foreign state, any possession of the United States, and any political subdivision of any foreign state or of any possession of the United States. The term "possession of the United States" includes Puerto Rico, the Virgin Islands, Guam, the Northern Mariana Islands and American Samoa.

(3) The term "foreign levy" means a levy imposed by a foreign country.

(h) *Effective date*—(1) *In general.* This section, § 1.901-2A, and § 1.903-1 apply to taxable years beginning after November 14, 1983. In addition, a person may elect to apply the provisions of this section, § 1.901-2A, and § 1.903-1 to earlier years. See paragraph (h)(2) of this section.

(2) *Election to apply regulations to earlier years*—(i) *Scope of election.* An election to apply the provisions of this section, § 1.901-2A, and § 1.903-1 to taxable years beginning on or before November 14, 1983 is made with respect to one or more foreign states and possessions of the United States with respect to a taxable year of the person making the election beginning on or before November 14, 1983. Such election requires all of the provisions of this section, § 1.901-2A and § 1.903-1 to be applied to such taxable year and to all subsequent taxable years of the person making the election ("elected years"). If an election applies to a foreign state or to a possession of the United States ("election country"), it applies to all taxes of the election country and to all taxes of all political subdivisions of the election country. An election does not apply to foreign taxes carried forward to any elected year from any taxable year to which the election does not apply. Such election does apply to foreign taxes carried back or forward from any elected year to any taxable year.

(ii) *Effect of election.* An election to apply the regulations to earlier years has no effect on the limitations on assessment and collection or on the limitations on credit or refund (see Chapter 66 of the Internal Revenue Code).

(iii) *Manner of making election.* An election to apply the regulations to one or more earlier taxable years is made by attaching a statement to a return, amended return, or claim for refund for the earliest taxable year to which the election relates. Such statement shall state that the election is made and, unless the election is to apply to all foreign countries, the statement shall designate the election countries. In the absence of such a designation of the election countries, all foreign countries shall be election countries.

(iv) *Time for making election.* An election to apply the regulations to earlier taxable years must be made by October 12, 1984, except that if a person who has deducted (instead of credited) foreign taxes in its United States income tax return for such an earlier taxable year validly makes an election to credit (instead of deduct) such taxes in a timely filed amended return for such earlier taxable year and such amended return is filed after such date, an election to apply the regulations to such earlier taxable year must be made in such amended return.

(v) *Revocation of election.* An election to apply the regulations to earlier taxable years may not be revoked.

(vi) *Affiliated groups.* A member of an affiliated group that files a consolidated United States income tax return may apply the regulations to earlier years only if an election to so apply them has been made by the common parent of such affiliated group on behalf of all members of the group. [Reg. § 1.901-2.]

☐ [*T.D. 7918, 10-6-83. Amended by T.D. 8372, 10-30-91.*]

[Reg. § 1.901-2A]

§ 1.901-2A. **Dual capacity taxpayers.**—(a) *Application of separate levy rules as applied to dual capacity taxpayers*—(1) *In general.* If the application of a foreign levy (as defined in § 1.901-2(g)(3)) is different, either by the terms of the levy or in practice, for dual capacity taxpayers (as defined in § 1.901-2(a)(2)(ii)(A)) from its application to other persons, then, unless the only such difference is that a lower rate (but the same base) applies to dual capacity taxpayers, such difference is considered to be related to the fact that dual capacity taxpayers receive, directly or indirectly, a specific economic benefit (as defined in § 1.901-2(a)(2)(ii)(B)) from the foreign country and thus to be a difference in kind, and not merely of degree. In such a case, notwithstanding any contrary provision of § 1.901-2(d), the levy as applicable to such dual capacity taxpayers is a separate levy (within the meaning of § 1.901-2(d)) from the levy as applicable to such other persons, regardless of whether such difference is in the base of the levy, in the rate of the levy, or both. In such a case, each of the levy as applied to dual capacity taxpayers and the levy as applied to other persons must be analyzed separately to determine whether it is an income tax within the meaning of § 1.901-2(a)(1) and whether it is a tax in lieu of an income tax within the meaning of § 1.903-1(a). However, if the application of the levy is neither different by its terms nor different in practice for dual capacity taxpayers from its application to other persons, or if the only difference is that a lower rate (but the same base) applies to dual capacity taxpayers, then, in accordance with § 1.901-2(d), such foreign levy as applicable to dual capacity taxpayers and such levy

Reg. § 1.901-2A(a)(1)

Income from Sources Without the United States 48,817
See p. 20,601 for regulations not amended to reflect law changes

as applicable to other persons together constitute a single levy. In such a case, no amount paid (as defined in § 1.901-2(g)(1)) pursuant to such levy by any such dual capacity taxpayer is considered to be paid in exchange for a specific economic benefit, and such levy, as applicable in the aggregate to such dual capacity taxpayers and to such other persons, is analyzed to determine whether it is an income tax within the meaning of § 1.901-2(a)(1) or a tax in lieu of an income tax within the meaning of § 1.903-1(a). Application of a foreign levy to dual capacity taxpayers will be considered to be different in practice from application of that levy to other persons, even if no such difference is apparent from the terms of the levy, unless it is established that application of that levy to dual capacity taxpayers does not differ in practice from its application to other persons.

(2) *Examples.* The provisions of paragraph (a)(1) of this section may be illustrated by the following examples:

Example (1). Under a levy of country X called the country X income tax, every corporation that does business in country X is required to pay to country X 40% of its income from its business in country X. Income for purposes of the country X income tax is computed by subtracting specified deductions from the corporation's gross income derived from its business in country X. The specified deductions include the corporation's expenses attributable to such gross income and allowances for recovery of the cost of capital expenditures attributable to such gross income, except that under the terms of the country X income tax a corporation engaged in the exploitation of minerals K, L or M in country X is not permitted to recover, currently or in the future, expenditures it incurs in exploring for those minerals. In practice, the only corporations that engage in exploitation of the specified minerals in country X are dual capacity taxpayers. Thus, the application of the country X income tax to dual capacity taxpayers is different from its application to other corporations. The country X income tax as applied to corporations that engage in the exploitation of minerals K, L or M (dual capacity taxpayers) is, therefore, a separate levy from the country X income tax as applied to other corporations. Accordingly, each of (i) the country X income tax as applied to such dual capacity taxpayers and (ii) the country X income tax as applied to such other persons, must be analyzed separately to determine whether it is an income tax within the meaning of § 1.901-2(a)(1) and whether it is a tax in lieu of an income tax within the meaning of § 1.903-1(a).

Example (2). The facts are the same as in example (1), except that it is demonstrated that corporations that engage in exploitation of the specified minerals in country X and that are subject to the levy include both dual capacity taxpayers and other persons. The country X income tax as applied to all corporations is, therefore, a single levy. Accordingly, no amount paid pursuant to the country X income tax by a dual capacity taxpayer is considered to be paid in exchange for a specific economic benefit; and, if the country X income tax is an income tax within the meaning of § 1.901-2(a)(1) or a tax in lieu of an income tax within the meaning of § 1.903-1(a), it will be so considered in its entirety for all corporations subject to it.

Example (3). Under a levy of country Y called the country Y income tax, each corporation incorporated in country Y is required to pay to country Y a percentage of its worldwide income. The applicable percentage is greater for such corporations that earn more than a specified amount of income than for such corporations that earn less than that amount. Income for purposes of the levy is computed by deducting from gross income specified types of expenses and specified allowances for capital expenditures. The expenses for which deductions are permitted differ depending on the type of business in which the corporation subject to the levy is engaged, *e.g.*, a deduction for interest paid to a related party is not allowed for corporations engaged in enumerated types of activities. In addition, carryover of losses from one taxable period to another is permitted for corporations engaged in specified types of activities, but not for corporations engaged in other activities. By its terms, the foreign levy makes no distinction between dual capacity taxpayers and other persons. It is established that in practice the higher rate of the country Y income tax applies to both dual capacity taxpayers and other persons and that in practice the differences in the base of the country Y income tax (*e.g.*, the lack of a deduction for interest paid to related parties for some corporations subject to the levy and the lack of a carryover provision for some corporations subject to the levy) apply to both dual capacity taxpayers and other persons. The country Y income tax as applied to all corporations incorporated in country Y is therefore a single levy. Accordingly, no amount paid pursuant to the country Y income tax by a dual capacity taxpayer is considered to be paid in exchange for a specific economic benefit; and if the country Y income tax is an income tax within the meaning of § 1.901-2(a)(1) or a tax in lieu of an income tax within the meaning of § 1.903-1(a), it will be so considered in its entirety for all persons subject to it.

Reg. § 1.901-2A(a)(2)

Example (4). The facts are the same as in example (3), except that it is not established that in practice the higher rate does not apply only to dual capacity taxpayers. By reason of such higher rate, application of the country Y income tax to dual capacity taxpayers is different in practice from application of the country Y income tax to other persons subject to it. The country Y income tax as applied to dual capacity taxpayers is therefore a separate levy from the country Y income tax as applied to other corporations incorporated in country Y. Accordingly, each of (i) the country Y income tax as applied to dual capacity taxpayers and (ii) the country Y income tax as applied to other corporations incorporated in country Y, must be analyzed separately to determine whether it is an income tax within the meaning of § 1.901-2(a)(1) and whether it is a tax in lieu of an income tax within the meaning of § 1.903-1(a).

Example (5). Under a levy of country X called the country X tax, all persons who do not engage in business in country X and who receive interest income from residents of country X are required to pay to country X 25 percent of the gross amount of such interest income. It is established that the country X tax applies by its terms and in practice to certain banks that are dual capacity taxpayers and to persons who are not dual capacity taxpayers and that application to such dual capacity taxpayers does not differ by its terms or in practice from application to such other persons. The country X tax as applied to all such persons (both the dual capacity taxpayers and the other persons) is, therefore, a single levy. Accordingly, no amount paid pursuant to the country X tax by such a dual capacity taxpayer is considered to be paid in exchange for a specific economic benefit; and, if the country X tax is a tax in lieu of an income tax within the meaning of § 1.903-1(a), it will be so considered in its entirety for all persons subject to it.

Example (6). Under a levy of country X called the country X tax, every corporation incorporated outside of country X ("foreign corporation") that maintains a branch in country X is required annually to pay to country X 52 percent of its net income attributable to that branch. It is established that the application of the country X tax is neither different by its terms nor different in practice for certain banks that are dual capacity taxpayers from its application to persons (which may, but do not necessarily, include other banks) that are not dual capacity taxpayers. The country X tax as applied to all foreign corporations with branches in country X (*i.e.*, both those banks that are dual capacity taxpayers and the foreign corporations that are not dual capacity taxpayers) is, therefore, a single levy. Accordingly, no amount paid pursuant to the country X tax by a bank that is a dual capacity taxpayer is considered to be paid in exchange for a specific economic benefit; and, if the country X tax is an income tax within the meaning of § 1.901-2(a)(1) or a tax in lieu of an income tax within the meaning of § 1.903-1(a), it will be so considered in its entirety for all persons subject to it.

Example (7). Under a levy of country H called the country H tax, all corporations that are organized outside country H and that do not engage in business in country H are required to pay to country H a percentage of the gross amount of interest income derived from residents of country H. The percentage is 30 percent, except that it is 15 percent for a specified category of corporations. All corporations in that category are dual capacity taxpayers. It is established that the country H tax applies by its terms and in practice to dual capacity taxpayers and to persons that are not dual capacity taxpayers and that the only difference in application between such dual capacity taxpayers and such other persons is that a lower rate (but the same base) applies to such dual capacity taxpayers. The country H tax as applied to all such persons (both the dual capacity taxpayers and the other persons) is, therefore, a single levy. Accordingly, no amount paid pursuant to the country H tax by such a dual capacity taxpayer is considered to be paid in exchange for a specific economic benefit, and if the country H tax is a tax in lieu of an income tax within the meaning of § 1.903-1(a), it will be so considered in its entirety for all persons subject to it.

(b) *Burden of proof for dual capacity taxpayers*—(1) *In general.* For credit to be allowable under section 901 or 903, the person claiming credit must establish that the foreign levy with respect to which credit is claimed is an income tax within the meaning of § 1.901-2(a)(1) or a tax in lieu of an income tax within the meaning of § 1.903-1(a), respectively. Thus, such person must establish, among other things, that such levy is a tax. See § 1.901-2(a)(2)(i) and § 1.903-1(a). Where a person claims credit under section 901 or 903 for an amount paid by a dual capacity taxpayer pursaunt to a foreign levy, § 1.901-2(a)(2)(i) and § 1.903-1(a), respectively, require such person to establish the amount, if any, that is paid pursuant to the distinct element of the levy that is a tax. If, pursuant to paragraph (a)(1) of this section and § 1.901-2(d), such levy as applicable to dual capacity taxpayers and such levy as applicable to other persons together constitute a single levy, then no amount paid pursuant to that levy by any such dual capacity taxpayer is considered to be paid in exchange for a specific economic benefit. Accordingly, such levy has only one distinct ele-

Reg. § 1.901-2A(b)(1)

ment, and the levy either is or is not, in its entirety, a tax. If, however, such levy as applicable to dual capacity taxpayers is a separate levy from such levy as applicable to other persons, then a person claiming credit under section 901 or 903 for an amount paid by a dual capacity taxpayer pursuant to such separate levy may establish the amount, if any, that is paid pursuant to the distinct element of the levy that is a tax only by the facts and circumstances method or the safe harbor method described in paragraph (c) of this section. If such person fails to so establish such amount, no portion of the amount that is paid pursuant to the separate levy by the dual capacity taxpayer to such foreign country shall be treated as an amount of tax. Any amount that, either by reason of application of the methods of paragraph (c) of this section or by reason of the immediately preceding sentence, is not treated as an amount of tax shall (i) be considered to have been paid in exchange for a specific economic benefit; (ii) be characterized (e.g., as royalty, purchase price, cost of sales, reduction of the proceeds of a sale, or reduction of interest income) according to the nature of the transaction and of the specific economic benefit received; and (iii) be treated according to such characterization for all purposes of Chapter 1 of the Internal Revenue Code, except that any determination that an amount is not tax for purposes of section 901 or 903 by reason of application of the safe harbor method shall not be taken into account in determining whether or not such an amount is to be characterized and treated as tax for purposes of computing an allowance for percentage depletion under sections 611 and 613.

(2) *Effect of certain treaties.* If, irrespective of whether such credit would be allowable under section 901 or 903 in the absence of a treaty, the United States has in force a treaty with a foreign country that treats a foreign levy as an income tax for purposes of allowing credit for United States tax and if the person claiming credit is entitled to the benefit of such treaty, then, unless such person claims credit not under the treaty but under section 901 or 903, and except to the extent the treaty provides otherwise and subject to all terms, conditions and limitations provided in the treaty, no portion of an amount paid with respect to such levy by a dual capacity taxpayer shall be considered to be paid in exchange for a specific economic benefit. If, however, such person claims credit not under such treaty but rather under section 901 or 903 (e.g., so as not to be subject to a limitation contained in such treaty), the provisions of this section apply to such levy.

(c) *Satisfaction of burden of proof*—(1) *In general.* This paragraph (c) sets out the methods by which a person who claims credit under section 901 or 903 for an amount paid by a dual capacity taxpayer pursuant to a foreign levy that satisfies all of the criteria of section 901 or 903 other than the determination of the distinct element of the levy that is a tax and of the amount that is paid pursuant to that distinct element (a "qualifying levy") may establish such distinct element and amount. Such person must establish the amount paid pursuant to a qualifying levy that is paid pursuant to the distinct element of the levy that is a tax (which amount therefore is an amount of income tax within the meaning of § 1.901-2(a)(1) or an amount of tax in lieu of income tax within the meaning of § 1.903-1(a) (a "qualifying amount")) only by the facts and circumstances method set forth in paragraph (c)(2) of this section or the safe harbor method set forth in paragraph (c)(3) of this section. A levy is not a qualifying levy, and neither the facts and circumstances method nor the safe harbor method applies to an amount paid by a dual capacity taxpayer pursuant to a foreign levy, if it has been established pursuant to § 1.901-2(d) and paragraph (a)(1) of this section that levy as applied to that dual capacity taxpayer and that levy as applied to persons other than dual capacity taxpayers together constitute a single levy, or if it has been established in accordance with the first sentence of paragraph (b)(2) of this section that credit is allowable by reason of a treaty for an amount paid with respect to such levy.

(2) *Facts and circumstances method*—(i) *In general.* If the person claiming credit establishes, based on all of the relevant facts and circumstances, the amount, if any, paid by the dual capacity taxpayer pursuant to the qualifying levy that is not paid in exchange for a specific economic benefit, such amount is the qualifying amount with respect to such qualifying levy. In determining the qualifying amount with respect to a qualifying levy under the facts and circumstances method, neither the methodology nor the results that would have obtained if a person had elected to apply the safe harbor method to such qualifying levy is a relevant fact or circumstance. Accordingly, neither such methodology nor such results shall be taken into account in applying the facts and circumstances method.

(ii) *Examples.* The application of the facts and circumstances method is illustrated by the following examples:

Example (1). Country A, which does not have a generally imposed income tax, imposes a levy, called the country A income tax, on corporations that carry on the banking business through a branch in country A. All such corporations lend

Reg. § 1.901-2A(c)(2)

money to the government of country A, and the consideration (interest) paid by the government of country A for the loans is not made available by the government on substantially the same terms to the population of country A in general. Thus, the country A income tax is imposed only on dual capacity taxpayers. L, a corporation that carries on the banking business through a branch in country A and that is a dual capacity taxpayer, establishes that all of the criteria of section 901 are satisfied by the country A income tax, except for the determination of the distinct element of the levy that is a tax and of L's qualifying amount with respect thereto. The country A income tax is, therefore, a qualifying levy. L establishes that, although all persons subject to the country A income tax are dual capacity taxpayers, the country A income tax applies in the same manner to income from such persons' transactions with the government of country A as it does to income from their transactions with private persons; that there are significant transactions (either in volume or in amount) with private persons; and that the portion of such persons' income that is derived from transactions with the government of country A on the one hand or private persons on the other varies greatly among persons subject to the country A income tax. By making this showing, L has demonstrated that no portion of the amount paid by it to country A pursuant to the levy is paid in exchange for a specific economic benefit (the interest income). Accordingly, L has demonstrated under the facts and circumstances method that the entire amount it has paid pursuant to the country A income tax is a qualifying amount.

Example (2). A, a domestic corporation that is a dual capacity taxpayer subject to a qualifying levy of country X, pays 1000u (units of country X currency) to country X in 1986 pursuant to the qualifying levy. A does not elect to apply the safe harbor method to country X, but if it had so elected, 800u would have been A's qualifying amount with respect to the levy. Based on all of the relevant facts and circumstances (which do not include either the methodology of the safe harbor method or the qualifying amount that would have obtained under that method), A establishes that 628u of such 1000u is not paid in exchange for a specific economic benefit. A has demonstrated under the facts and circumstances method that 628u is a qualifying amount. Pursuant to paragraph (b)(1) of this section, 372u (1000u − 628u) is considered to have been paid by A in exchange for a specific economic benefit. That amount is characterized and treated as provided in paragraph (b)(1) of this section.

Example (3). The facts are the same as in example (2), except that under the safe harbor method 580u would have been A's qualifying amount with respect to the levy. That amount is not a relevant fact or circumstance and the result is the same as in example (2).

(3) *Safe harbor method.* Under the safe harbor method, the person claiming credit makes an election as provided in paragraph (d) of this section and, pursuant to such election, applies the safe harbor formula described in paragraph (e) of this section to the qualifying levy or levies to which the election applies.

(d) *Election to use the safe harbor method* —(1) *Scope of election.* An election to use the safe harbor method is made with respect to one or more foreign states and possessions of the United States with respect to a taxable year of the person making the election (the "electing person"). Such election applies to such taxable year and to all subsequent taxable years of the electing person ("election years"), unless the election is revoked in accordance with paragraph (d)(4) of this section. If an election applies to a foreign state or possession of the United States ("elected country"), it applies to all qualifying levies of the elected country and to all qualifying levies of all political subdivisions of the elected country with respect to which the electing person claims credit for amounts paid (or deemed to be paid) by any dual capacity taxpayer. A member of an affiliated group that files a consolidated United States income tax return may use the safe harbor method for a foreign state or U.S. possession only if an election to use the safe harbor method for that state or possession has been made by the common parent of such affiliated group on behalf of all members of the group. Similarly, a member of an affiliated group that does not file a consolidated United States income tax return may elect to use the safe harbor method for a foreign state or U.S. possession only if an election to use the safe harbor method for that state or possession is made by each member of the affiliated group which claims credit for taxes paid to such state or possession or to any political subdivision thereof. An election to use the safe harbor method for an elected country does not apply to foreign taxes carried back or forward to any election year from any taxable year to which the election does not apply. Such election does apply to foreign taxes carried back or forward from any election year to any taxable year. A person who elects to use the safe harbor method for one or more foreign countries may, in a later taxable year, also elect to use that method for other foreign countries.

(2) *Effect of election.* An election to use the safe harbor method described in paragraph (c)(3) of this section requires the electing person to

apply the safe harbor formula of paragraph (e) of this section to all qualifying levies of all elected countries and their political subdivisions, and constitutes a specific waiver by such person of the right to use the facts and circumstances method described in paragraph (c)(2) of this section with respect to any levy of any elected country or any political subdivision thereof.

(3) *Time and manner of making election*—(i) *In general.* To elect to use the safe harbor method, an electing person must attach a statement to its United States income tax return for the taxable year for which the election is made and must file such return by the due date (including extensions) for the filing thereof. Such statement shall state that the electing person elects to use the safe harbor method for the foreign states and the possessions of the United States designated in the statement and their political subdivisions, and that the electing person waives the right, for any election year, to use the facts and circumstances method for any levy of the designated states, possessions and political subdivisions. Notwithstanding the foregoing, a person may, with the consent of the Commissioner, elect to use the safe harbor method for a taxable year for one or more foreign states or possessions of the United States, at a date later than that specified in the first sentence of this paragraph (d)(3)(i), *e.g.*, upon audit of such person's United States income tax return for such taxable year. The Commissioner will normally consent to such a later election if such person demonstrates that it failed to make a timely election for such a foreign state or possession for such taxable year because such person reasonably believed either that it was not a dual capacity taxpayer with respect to such state or possession or that no levy that it paid to such state or possession or any political subdivision thereof was a qualifying levy (for example, because it reasonably, but incorrectly, believed that the levy it paid was not a separate levy from that applicable to persons other than dual capacity taxpayers). The Commissioner will not, however, consent to such a later election with respect to any state or possession for a taxable year if such person (or any other member of an affiliated group of which such person is a member) applied the facts and circumstances method to any levy of such state or possession or any political subdivision thereof for such taxable year.

(ii) *Certain retroactive elections.* Notwithstanding the requirements of paragraph (d)(3)(i) of this section relating to the time and manner of making an election, an election may be made for a taxable year beginning on or before November 14, 1983, provided the electing person elects in accordance with § 1.901-2(h) to apply all of the provisions of this section, § 1.901-2 and § 1.903-1 to such taxable year and provided all of the requirements set forth in this paragraph (d)(3)(ii) are satisfied. Such an election shall be made by timely (including extensions) filing a federal income tax return or an amended federal income tax return for such taxable year; by attaching to such return a statement containing the statements and information set forth in paragraph (d)(3)(i) of this section; and by filing amended income tax returns for all subsequent election years for which income tax returns have previously been filed in which credit is claimed under section 901 or 903 and applying the safe harbor method in such amended returns. All amended returns referred to in the immediately preceding sentence must be filed on or before October 12, 1984 and at a time when neither assessment of a deficiency for any of such election years nor the filing of a claim for any refund claimed in any such amended return is barred.

(iii) *Election to credit taxes made in amended return.* If a person has filed a United States income tax return for a taxable year to which this § 1.901-2A applies (including application by reason of the election provided in § 1.901-2(h)(2)) in which such person has deducted (instead of credited) qualifying foreign taxes and such person validly makes an election to credit (instead of deduct) such taxes in a timely filed amended return for such taxable year, an election to use the safe harbor method may be made in such amended return provided all of the requirements of paragraph (d)(3)(ii) of this section are satisfied other than the requirement that such amended return and the other amended returns referred to in that paragraph be filed on or before October 12, 1984.

(4) *Revocation of election.* An election to use the safe harbor method described in paragraph (c)(3) of this section may not be revoked without the consent of the Commissioner. An application for consent to revoke such election with respect to one or more elected countries shall be made to the Commissioner of Internal Revenue, Washington, D.C. 20224. Such application shall be made not later than the 30th day before the due date (including extensions) for the filing of the income tax return for the first taxable year for which the revocation is sought to be effective, except in the case of an event described in (i), (ii), (iii) or (iv) below, in which case an application for revocation with retroactive effect may be made within a reasonable time after such event. The Commissioner may make his consent to any revocation conditioned upon adjustments being made in one or more taxable years so as to prevent the revocation from resulting in a distortion of the amount

of any item relating to tax liability in any taxable year. The Commissioner will normally consent to a revocation (including, in the case of (i), (ii), (iii) or (iv) below, one with retroactive effect), if—

(i) An amendment to the Internal Revenue Code or the regulations thereunder is made which applies to the taxable year for which the revocation is to be effective and the amendment substantially affects the taxation of income from sources outside the United States under subchapter N of Chapter 1 of the Internal Revenue Code; or

(ii) After a safe harbor election is made with respect to a foreign state, a tax treaty between the United States and that state enters into force; that treaty covers a foreign tax to which the safe harbor election applies; and that treaty applies to the taxable year for which the revocation is to be effective; or

(iii) After a safe harbor election is made with respect to a foreign state or possession of the United States, a material change is made in the tax law of that state or possession or of a political subdivision of that state or possession; and the changed law applies to the taxable year for which the revocation is to be effective and has a material effect on the taxpayer; or

(iv) With respect to a foreign country to which a safe harbor election applies, the Internal Revenue Service issues a letter ruling to the electing person and that letter ruling (A) relates to the availability or application of the safe harbor method to one or more levies of such foreign country; (B) does not relate to the facts and circumstances method described in paragraph (c)(2) of this section; and (C) fails to include a ruling requested by the electing person or includes a ruling contrary to one requested by such person (in either case, other than one relating to the facts and circumstances method) and such failure or inclusion has a material adverse effect on the amount of such electing person's credit for taxes paid to such foreign country for the taxable year for which the revocation is to be effective; or

(v) A corporation ("new member") becomes a member of an affiliated group; the new member and one or more pre-existing members of such group are dual capacity taxpayers with respect to the same foreign country; and, with respect to such country, either the new member or the pre-existing members (but not both) have made a safe harbor election; and the Commissioner in his discretion determines that obtaining the benefit of the right to revoke the safe harbor election with respect to such foreign country was not the principal purpose of the affiliation between such new member and such group; or

(vi) The election has been in effect with respect to at least three taxable years prior to the taxable year for which the revocation is to be effective.

The Commissioner may, in his discretion, consent to a revocation even if none of the foregoing subdivisions (i) through (vi) is applicable. If an election has been revoked with respect to an elected country, a subsequent election to apply the safe harbor method with respect to such elected country may be made only with the consent of the Commissioner and upon such terms and conditions as the Commissioner in his discretion may require.

(e) *Safe harbor formula*—(1) *In general*. The safe harbor formula applies to determine the distinct element of a qualifying levy that is a tax and the amount paid by a dual capacity taxpayer pursuant to such qualifying levy that is the qualifying amount with respect to such levy. Under the safe harbor formula the amount paid in a taxable year pursuant to a qualifying levy that is the qualifying amount with respect to such levy is an amount equal to:

$$(A-B-C) \times D/(1-D)$$

where (except as otherwise provided in paragraph (e)(5) of this section):

A = the amount of gross receipts as determined under paragraph (e)(2) of this section

B = the amount of costs and expenses as determined under paragraph (e)(2) of this section

C = the total amount paid in the taxable year by the dual capacity taxpayer pursuant to the qualifying levy (the "actual payment amount")

D = the tax rate as determined under paragraph (e)(3) of this section

In no case, however, shall the qualifying amount exceed the actual payment amount; and the qualifying amount is zero if the safe harbor formula yields a qualifying amount less than zero. The safe harbor formula is intended to yield a qualifying amount that is approximately equal to the amount of generally imposed income tax within the meaning of paragraphs (a) and (b)(1) of § 1.903-1 ("general tax") of the foreign country that would have been required to be paid in the taxable year by the dual capacity taxpayer if it had not been a dual capacity taxpayer and if the base of the general tax had allowed a deduction in such year for the amount ("specific economic benefit amount") by which the actual payment amount exceeds the qualifying amount. See, however, paragraph (e)(5) of this section if an elected country has no general tax. The specific economic

Reg. § 1.901-2A(e)(1)

benefit amount is considered to be the portion of the actual payment amount that is paid pursuant to the distinct portion of the qualifying levy that imposes an obligation in exchange for a specific economic benefit. The specific economic benefit amount is therefore considered to be an amount paid by the dual capacity taxpayer in exchange for such specific economic benefit, which amount must be treated for purposes of Chapter 1 of the Internal Revenue Code as provided in paragraph (b)(1) of this section.

(2) *Determination of gross receipts and costs and expenses.* For purposes of the safe harbor formula, gross receipts and costs and expenses are, except as otherwise provided in this paragraph (e), the gross receipts and the deductions for costs and expenses, respectively, as determined under the foreign law applicable in computing the actual payment amount of the qualifying levy to which the safe harbor formula applies. However, except as otherwise provided in this paragraph (e), if provisions of the qualifying levy increase or decrease the liability imposed on dual capacity taxpayers compared to the general tax liability of persons other than dual capacity taxpayers by reason of the determination or treatment of gross receipts or of costs or expenses, the provisions generally applicable in computing such other persons' tax base under the general tax shall apply to determine gross receipts and costs and expenses for purposes of computing the qualifying amount. If provisions of the qualifying levy relating to gross receipts meet the requirements of § 1.901-2(b)(3)(i), such provisions shall apply to determine gross receipts for purposes of computing the qualifying amount. If neither the general tax nor the qualifying levy permits recovery of one or more costs or expenses, and by reason of the failure to permit such recovery the qualifying levy does not satisfy the net income requirement of § 1.901-2(b)(4) (even though the general tax does satisfy that requirement), then such cost or expense shall be considered a cost or expense for purposes of computing the qualifying amount. If the qualifying levy does not permit recovery of one or more significant costs or expenses, but provides allowances that effectively compensate for nonrecovery of such significant costs or expenses, then, for purposes of computing the qualifying amount, costs and expenses shall not include the costs and expenses under the general tax whose nonrecovery under the qualifying levy is compensated for by such allowances but shall instead include such allowances. In determining costs and expenses for purposes of computing the qualifying amount with respect to a qualifying levy, the actual payment amount with respect to such levy shall not be considered a cost or expense. For purposes of this paragraph, the following differences in gross receipts and costs and expenses between the qualifying levy and the general tax shall not be considered to increase the liability imposed on dual capacity taxpayers compared to the general tax liability of persons other than dual capacity taxpayers, but only if the general tax would be an income tax within the meaning of § 1.901-2(a)(1) if such different treatment under the qualifying levy had also applied under the general tax:

(i) Differences in the time of realization or recognition of one or more items of income or in the time when recovery of one or more costs and expenses is allowed (unless the period of recovery of such costs and expenses pursuant to the qualifying levy is such that it effectively is a denial of recovery of such costs and expenses, as described in § 1.901-2(b)(4)(i)); and

(ii) Differences in consolidation or carryover provisions of the types described in paragraphs (b)(4)(ii) and (b)(4)(iii) of § 1.901-2.

(3) *Determination of tax rate.* The tax rate for purposes of the safe harbor formula is the tax rate (expressed as a decimal) that is applicable in computing tax liability under the general tax. If the rate of the general tax varies according to the amount of the base of that tax, the rate to be applied in computing the qualifying amount is the rate that applies under the general tax to a person whose base is, using the terminology of paragraph (e)(1) of this section, "A" minus "B" minus the specific economic benefit amount paid by the dual capacity taxpayer pursuant to the qualifying levy, provided such rate applies in practice to persons other than dual capacity taxpayers, or, if such rate does not so apply in practice, the next lowest rate of the general tax that does so apply in practice.

(4) *Determination of applicable provisions of general tax*—(i) *In general.* If the general tax is a series of income taxes (*e.g.,* on different types of income), or if the application of the general tax differs by its terms for different classes of persons subject to the general tax (*e.g.,* for persons in different industries), then, except as otherwise provided in this paragraph (e), the qualifying amount shall be computed by reference to the income tax contained in such series of income taxes, or in the case of such different applications the application of the general tax, that by its terms and in practice imposes the highest tax burden on persons other than dual capacity taxpayers. Notwithstanding the preceding sentence, the general tax amount shall be computed by reference to the application of the general tax to entities of the same type (as determined under the

general tax) as the dual capacity taxpayer and to persons of the same resident or nonresident status (as determined under the general tax) as the dual capacity taxpayer; and, if the general tax treats business income differently from non-business (e.g., investment) income (as determined under the general tax), the dual capacity taxpayer's business and non-business income shall be treated as the general tax treats such income. If, for example, the dual capacity taxpayer would, under the general tax, be treated as a resident (e.g., because the general tax treats an entity that is organized in the foreign country or managed or controlled there as a resident) and as a corporation (i.e., because the rules of the general tax treat an entity like the dual capacity taxpayer as a corporation), and if some of the dual capacity taxpayer's income would, under the general tax, be treated as business income and some as non-business income, the dual capacity taxpayer and its income shall be so treated in computing the qualifying amount.

(ii) *Establishing that provisions apply in practice.* For purposes of the safe harbor formula a provision (including tax rate) shall be considered a provision of the general tax only if it is reasonably likely that that provision applies by its terms and in practice to persons other than dual capacity taxpayers. In general, it will be assumed that a provision (including tax rate) that by its terms applies to persons other than dual capacity taxpayers is reasonably likely to apply in practice to such other persons, unless the person claiming credit knows or has reason to know otherwise. However, in cases of doubt, the person claiming credit may be required to demonstrate that such provision is reasonably likely so to apply in practice.

(5) *No general tax.* If a foreign country does not impose a general tax (and thus a levy, in order to be a qualifying levy must satisfy all of the criteria of section 901 (because section 903 cannot apply, other than the determination of the distinct element of the levy that is a tax and of the amount that is paid pursuant to that distinct element), paragraphs (e)(2), (3) and (4) of this section to not apply to a qualifying levy of such country, and the terms of the safe harbor formula set forth in paragraph (e)(1) of this section are defined with respect to such levy as follows:

A = the amount of gross receipts as determined under the qualifying levy;

B = the amount of deductions for costs and expenses as determined under the qualifying levy;

C = the actual payment amount; and

D = the lower of the rate of the qualifying levy, or the rate of tax specified in section 11(b)(5) (or predecessor or successor section, as the case may be) of the Internal Revenue Code as applicable to the taxable year in which the actual payment amount is paid.

(6) *Certain taxes in lieu of an income tax.* To the extent a tax in lieu of an income tax (within the meaning of § 1.903-1(a)) that applies in practice to persons other than dual capacity taxpayers would actually have been required to be paid in the taxable year by a dual capacity taxpayer if it had not been a dual capacity taxpayer (e.g., in substitution for the general tax with respect to a type of income, such as interest income, dividend income, royalty income, insurance income), such tax in lieu of an income tax shall be treated as if it were an application of the general tax for purposes of applying the safe harbor formula of this paragraph (e) to such dual capacity taxpayer, and such formula shall be applied to yield a qualifying amount that is approximately equal to the general tax (so defined) that would have been required to be paid in the taxable year by such dual capacity taxpayer if the base of such general tax had allowed a deduction in such year for the specific economic benefit amount.

(7) *Multiple levies.* If, in any election year of an electing person, with respect to any elected country and all of its political subdivisions,

(i) Amounts are paid by a dual capacity taxpayer pursuant to more than one qualifying levy or pursuant to one or more levies that are qualifying levies and one or more levies that are not qualifying levies by reason of the last sentence of paragraph (c)(1) of this section but with respect to which credit is allowable, or

(ii) More than one general tax (including a tax treated as if it were an application of the general tax under paragraph (e)(6)) would have been required to be paid by a dual capacity taxpayer (or taxpayers) if it (or they) had not been a dual capacity taxpayer (or taxpayers), or

(iii) Credit is claimed with respect to amounts paid by more than one dual capacity taxpayer,

the provisions of this paragraph (e) shall be applied such that the aggregate qualifying amount with respect to such qualifying levy or levies plus the aggregate amount paid with respect to levies referred to in (e)(7)(i) that are not qualifying levies shall be the aggregate amount that would have been required to be paid in the taxable year by such dual capacity taxpayer (or taxpayers) pursuant to such general tax or taxes if it (or they) had not been a dual capacity taxpayer (or taxpayers) and if the base of such general tax or

Reg. § 1.901-2A(e)(5)

Income from Sources Without the United States 48,825
See p. 20,601 for regulations not amended to reflect law changes

taxes had allowed a deduction in such year for the aggregate specific economic benefit amount (except that, if paragraph (e)(5) applies to any levy of such elected country or any political subdivision thereof, the aggregate qualifying amount for qualifying levies of such elected country and all of its political subdivisions plus the aggregate amount paid with respect to levies referred to in paragraph (e)(7)(i) that are not qualifying levies shall not exceed the greater of the aggregate amount paid with respect to levies referred to in paragraph (e)(7)(i) that are not qualifying levies and the amount determined in accordance with paragraph (e)(5) where "D" is the rate of tax specified in section 11(b)(5) (or predecessor or successor section, as the case may be) of the Internal Revenue Code as applicable to the taxable year in which the actual payment amount is paid). However, in no event shall such aggregate amount exceed the aggregate actual payment amount plus the aggregate amount paid with respect to levies referred to in (e)(7)(i) that are not qualifying levies, nor be less than the aggregate amount paid with respect to levies referred to in (e)(7)(i) that are not qualifying levies. In applying (e)(7)(ii) a person who is not subject to a levy but who is considered to receive a specific economic benefit by reason of § 1.901-2(a)(2)(ii)(E) shall be treated as a dual capacity taxpayer. See example (12) in paragraph (e)(8) of this section.

(8) *Examples.* The provisions of this paragraph (e) may be illustrated by the following examples:

Example (1). Under a levy of country X called the country X income tax, every corporation that does business in country X is required to pay to country X 40% of its income from its business in country X. Income for purposes of the country X income tax is computed by subtracting specified deductions from the corporation's gross income derived from its business in country X. The specified deductions include the corporation's expenses attributable to such gross income and allowances for recovery of the cost of capital expenditures attributable to such gross income, except that under the terms of the country X income tax a corporation engaged in the exploitation of minerals K, L or M in country X is not permitted to recover, currently or in the future, expenditures it incurs in exploring for those minerals. Under the terms of the country X income tax interest is not deductible to the extent it exceeds an arm's length amount (*e.g.,* if the loan to which the interest relates is not in accordance with normal commercial practice or to the extent the interest rate exceeds an arm's length rate). In practice, the only corporations that engage in exploitation of the specified minerals in country X are dual capacity taxpayers. Because no other persons subject to the levy engage in exploitation of minerals K, L or M in country X, the application of the country X income tax to dual capacity taxpayers is different from its application to other corporations. The country X income tax as applied to corporations that engage in the exploitation of minerals K, L or M (dual capacity taxpayers) is, therefore, a separate levy from the country X income tax as applied to other corporations.

A is a U.S. corporation that is engaged in country X in exploitation of mineral K. Natural deposits of mineral K in country X are owned by country X, and *A* has been allowed to extract mineral K in consideration of payment of a bonus and of royalties to an instrumentality of country X. Therefore, *A* is a dual capacity taxpayer. In 1984, *A* does business in country X within the meaning of the levy. *A* has validly elected the safe harbor method for country X for 1984. In 1984, as determined in accordance with the country X income tax as applied to *A*, *A* has gross receipts of 120u (units of country X currency), deducts 20u of costs and expenses, and pays 40u (40% of (120u − 20u)) to country X pursuant to the levy. *A* also incurs in 1984 10u of nondeductible expenditures for exploration for mineral K and 2u of nondeductible interest costs attributable to an advance of funds from a related party to finance an undertaking relating to the exploration for mineral K for which normal commercial financing was unavailable because of the substantial risk inherent in the undertaking. *A* establishes that the country X income tax as applied to persons other than dual capacity taxpayers is an income tax within the meaning of § 1.901-2(a)(1), that it is the generally imposed income tax of country X and hence the general tax, and that all of the criteria of section 903 are satisfied with respect to the country X income tax as applied to dual capacity taxpayers, except for the determination of the distinct element of the levy that is a tax and of *A* 's qualifying amount with respect thereto. (No conclusion is reached whether the country X income tax as applied to dual capacity taxpayers is an income tax within the meaning of § 1.901-2(a)(1). Such a determination would require, among other things, that the country X income tax as so applied, judged on the basis of its predominant character, meets the net income requirement of § 1.901-2(b)(4) notwithstanding its failure to permit recovery of exploration expenses.) *A* has therefore demonstrated that the country X income tax as applied to dual capacity taxpayers is a qualifying levy.

In applying the safe harbor formula, in accordance with paragraph (e)(2), the amount of

Reg. § 1.901-2A(e)(8)

A's costs and expenses includes the 10u of nondeductible exploration expenses. The failure to permit recovery of interest in excess of arm's length amounts, a provision of both the general tax and the qualifying levy, does not cause the qualifying levy to fail to satisfy the net income requirement of § 1.901-2(b)(4); therefore, the amount of A's cost and expenses does not include the 2u of nondeductible interest costs. Thus, under the safe harbor method, A's qualifying amount with respect to the levy is 33.33u ((120u − 30u − 40u) × .40/(1 − .40)). A's specific economic benefit amount is 6.67u (A's actual payment amount (40u) less A's qualifying amount (33.33u)). Under paragraph (a) of this section, this 6.67u is considered to be consideration paid by A for the right to extract mineral K. Pursuant to paragraph (b) of this section, this amount is characterized according to the nature of A's transactions with country X and its instrumentality and of the specific economic benefit received (the right to extract mineral K), as an additional royalty or other business expense paid or accrued by A and is so treated for all purposes of Chapter 1 of the Internal Revenue Code, except that if an allowance for percentage depletion is allowable to A under sections 611 and 613 with respect to A's interest in mineral K, the determination whether this 6.67u is tax or royalty for purposes of computing the amount of such allowance shall be made under sections 611 and 613 without regard to the determination that under the safe harbor formula such 6.67u is not tax for purposes of section 901 or 903.

Example (2). Under a levy of country Y called the country Y income tax, each corporation incorporated in country Y is required to pay to country Y a percentage of its worldwide income. The applicable percentage is 40 percent of the first 1,000u (units of country Y currency) of income and 50 percent of income in excess of 1,000u. Income for purposes of the levy is computed by deducting from gross income specified types of expenses and specified allowances for capital expenditures. The expenses for which deductions are permitted differ depending on the type of business in which the corporation subject to the levy is engaged, *e.g.*, a deduction for interest paid to a related party is not allowed for corporations engaged in enumerated types of activities. In addition, carryover of losses from one taxable period to another is permitted for corporations engaged in specified types of activities, but not for corporations engaged in other activities. By its terms, the foreign levy makes no distinction between dual capacity taxpayers and other persons. In practice the differences in the base of the country Y income tax (*e.g.*, the lack of a deduction for interest paid to related parties for some corporations subject to the levy and the lack of a carryover provision for some corporations subject to the levy) apply to both dual capacity taxpayers and other persons, but the 50 percent rate applies only to dual capacity taxpayers. By reason of such higher rate, application of the country Y income tax to dual capacity taxpayers is different in practice from application of the country Y income tax to other persons subject to it. The country Y income tax as applied to dual capacity taxpayers is therefore a separate levy from the country Y income tax as applied to other corporations incorporated in country Y.

B is a corporation incorporated in country Y that is engaged in construction activities in country Y. B has a contract with the government of country Y to build a hospital in country Y for a fee that is not made available on substantially the same terms to substantially all persons who are subject to the general tax of country X. Accordingly, B is a dual capacity taxpayer. B has validly elected the safe harbor method for country Y for 1985. In 1985, as determined in accordance with the country Y income tax as applied to B, B has gross receipts of 10,000u, deducts 6,000u of costs and expenses, and pays 1900u ((1,000u × 40%) + (3,000u × 50%)) to Country Y pursuant to the levy.

It is assumed that B has established that the country Y income tax as applied to persons other than dual capacity taxpayers is an income tax within the meaning of § 1.901-2(a)(1) and is the general tax. It is further assumed that B has demonstrated that all of the criteria of section 901 are satisfied with respect to the country Y income tax as applied to dual capacity taxpayers, except for the determination of the distinct element of such levy that is a tax and of B's qualifying amount with respect to that levy, and therefore that the country Y income tax as applied to dual capacity taxpayers is a qualifying levy.

In applying the safe harbor formula, in accordance with paragraph (e)(3), the 50 percent rate is not used because it does not apply in practice to persons other than dual capacity taxpayers. The next lowest rate of the general tax that does apply in practice to such persons, 40 percent, is used. Accordingly, under the safe harbor formula, B's qualifying amount with respect to the levy is 1400u ((10,000u − 6000u − 1900u) × .40/(1 − .40)). B's specific economic benefit amount is 500u (B's actual payment amount (1900u) less B's qualifying amount (1400u)). Pursuant to paragraph (b) of this section, B's specific economic benefit amount is characterized according to the nature of B's transactions with country

Y and of the specific economic benefit received, as a reduction of B's proceeds of its contract with country Y; and this amount is so treated for all purposes of Chapter 1 of the Code, including the computation of B's accumulated profits for purposes of section 902.

Example (3). The facts are the same as in example (2), with the following additional facts: The contract between B and country Y is a cost plus contract. One of the costs of the contract which country Y is required to pay or for which it is required to reimburse B is any tax of country Y on B's income or receipts from the contract. Instead of reimbursing B therefor, country Y agrees with B to assume any such tax liability. Under country Y tax law, B is not considered to have additional income or receipts by reason of country Y's assumption of B's country Y tax liability. In 1985, B's gross receipts of 10,000u include 3000u from the contract, and its costs and expenses of 6000u include 2000u attributable to the contract. B's other gross receipts and expenses do not relate to any transaction in which B receives a specific economic benefit. In accordance with the contract, country Y, and not B, is required to bear the amount of B's country Y income tax liability on B's 1000u (3000u − 2000u) income from the contract. In accordance with the contract B computes its country Y income tax without taking this 1000u into account and therefore pays 1400u ((1000u × 40%) + (2000u × 50%)) to country Y pursuant to the levy.

In accordance with § 1.901-2(f)(2)(i), the country Y income tax which country Y is, under the contract, required to bear is considered to be paid by country Y on behalf of B. B's proceeds of its contract, for all purposes of Chapter 1 of the Code (including the computation of B's accumulated profits for purposes of section 902), therefore, are increased by the additional 500u (1900u computed as in example (2) less 1400u as computed above) of B's liability under the country Y income tax that is assumed by country Y and such 500u is considered to be paid pursuant to the levy by country Y on behalf of B. In applying the safe harbor formula, therefore, the computation is exactly as in example (2) and the results are the same as in example (2).

Example (4). Country L issues a decree (the "April 11 decree"), in which it states it is exercising its tax authority to impose a tax on all corporations on their "net income" from country L. "Net income" is defined as actual gross receipts less all expenses attributable thereto, except that in the case of income from extraction of petroleum, gross receipts are defined as 105% of actual gross receipts, and no deduction is allowed for interest incurred on loans whose proceeds are used for exploration for petroleum. Under the April 11 decree, wages paid by corporations subject to the decree are deductible in the year of payment, except that corporations engaged in the extraction of petroleum may deduct such wages only by amortization over a 5-year period and, to the extent such wages are paid to officers, they may be deducted only by amortization over a period of 50 years. The April 11 decree permits related corporations subject to the decree to file consolidated returns in which net income and net losses of related corporations offset each other in computing net income for purposes of the April 11 decree, except that corporations engaged in petroleum exploration or extraction activities are not eligible for inclusion in such a consolidated return. The law of country L does not require separate entities to carry on separate activities in connection with exploring for or extracting petroleum. Net losses of a taxable year may be carried over for 10 years to offset income, except that no more than 25% of net income (before deducting the loss carryover) in any such future year may be offset by a carryover of net loss, and, in the case of any corporation engaged in exploration or extraction of petroleum, losses incurred prior to such a corporation's having net income from production may be carried forward for only 8 years and no more than 15% of net income in any such future year may be offset by such a net loss. The rate to be paid under the April 11 decree is 50% of net income (as defined in the levy), except that if net income exceeds 10,000u (units of country L currency), the rate is 75% of the corporation's net income (including the first 10,000u thereof). In practice, no corporations other than corporations engaged in extraction of petroleum have net income in excess of 10,000u. All petroleum resources of country L are owned by the government of country L, whose petroleum ministry licenses corporations to explore for and extract petroleum in consideration for payment of royalties as petroleum is produced.

J is a U.S. corporation that is engaged in country L in the exploration and extraction of petroleum and therefore is a dual capacity taxpayer. J has validly elected the safe harbor method for country L for the year of 1983, the year that J commenced activities in country L, and has not revoked such election. For the years 1983 through 1986, J's gross receipts, deductions and net income before application of the carryover provisions, determined in accordance with the April 11 decree, are as follows:

Reg. § 1.901-2A(e)(8)

48,828 Income from Sources Without the United States
See p. 20,601 for regulations not amended to reflect law changes

Year A.	gross receipts (105% of actual gross receipts) B.	deductions other than wages C.	wages paid other than to officers (amortizable at 20%) D.	wages paid to officers (amortizable at 2%) E.	nondeductible exploration interest expense F.	net income (loss) (B-C-amortization of cumulative D-amortization of cumulative E) G.
1983	0	13,000u	100u	50u	1,000u	(13,021u)
1984	0	17,000u	100u	50u	2,800u	(17,042u)
1985	42,000u	15,000u	100u	50u	2,800u	26,937u
1986	105,000u	20,000u	100u	50u	2,800u	84,916u

After application of the carryover provisions, J's net income and actual payment amounts pursuant to the April 11 levy are as follows:

Year H.	Net income (loss) I.	Actual payment amount (I × 75%) J.
1983	(13,021u)	0
1984	(17,042u)	0
1985	22,896u	17,172u
1986	72,179u	54,134u

Pursuant to paragraph (a)(1) of this section, the April 11 decree as applied to corporations engaged in the exploration or extraction of petroleum in country L is a separate levy from the April 11 decree as applied to all other corporations. J establishes that the April 11 decree, as applied to such other corporations, is an income tax within the meaning of § 1.901-2(a)(1) and that the decree as so applied is the general tax.

The April 11 decree as applied to corporations engaged in the exploration or extraction of petroleum in country L does not meet the gross receipts requirement of § 1.901-2(b)(3); therefore, irrespective of whether it meets the other requirements of § 1.901-2(b)(1), it is not an income tax within the meaning of § 1.901-2(a)(1). However, the April 11 decree as applied to such corporations is a qualifying levy because J has demonstrated that all of the criteria of section 903 are satisfied with respect to the April 11 decree as applied to such corporations, except for the determination of the distinct element of such levy that imposes a tax and of J's qualifying amount with respect thereto.

In applying the safe harbor formula, in accordance with paragraph (e)(2), gross receipts are computed by reference to the general levy, and thus are 100%, not 105%, of actual gross receipts. Similarly, costs and expenses include exploration interest expense. In accordance with paragraph (e)(2)(i) of this section the difference between the general tax and the qualifying levy in the timing of the deduction for wages, other than wages of officers, is not considered to increase the liability of dual capacity taxpayers because the general tax would not have failed to be an income tax within the meaning of § 1.901-2(a)(1) if it had provided for 5-year amortization of such wages instead of for current deduction. See § 1.901-2(b)(4)(i). However, amortization of wages paid to officers over a 50-year period is such a deferred recovery of such wages that it effectively is a denial of the deduction of the excess of such wages paid in any year over the amortization of such cumulative wages permitted in such year. See § 1.901-2(b)(4)(i). The different treatment of wages paid to officers under the general tax and the qualifying levy is thus not merely a difference in timing within the meaning of paragraph (e)(2)(i) of this section. Accordingly, the difference between the amount of wages paid by J to officers in any year and J's deduction (in computing the actual payment amount) for amortization of such cumulative wages allowed in such year is, pursuant to paragraph (e)(2) of this section, treated as a cost and expense in computing J's qualifying amount for such year with respect to the April 11 decree. The differences in the consolidation and carryover provisions between the general tax and the qualifying levy are of the types described in paragraph (e)(2)(ii) of this section and, pursuant to paragraphs (b)(4)(ii) and (b)(4)(iii) of § 1.901-2, the general tax would not fail to be an income tax within the meaning of § 1.901-2(a)(i) even if it contained the consolidation and carryover provisions of the qualifying levy. Thus, such differences are not considered to increase the liability of dual capacity taxpayers pursuant to the qualifying levy as compared to

Reg. § 1.901-2A(e)(8)

Income from Sources Without the United States

See p. 20,601 for regulations not amended to reflect law changes

the general tax liability of persons other than dual capacity taxpayers.

Accordingly, in applying the safe harbor formula to the qualifying levy for 1985 and 1986, gross receipts and costs and expenses are computed as follows:

Gross receipts
1985: 42,000u × (100/105) = 40,000u
1986: 105,000u × (100/105) = 100,000u

Costs and expenses

Item	1985	1986
1. Deductions other than wages (column C in the preceding chart)	15,000u	20,000u
2. Amortization of cumulative wages paid in 1983 and thereafter other than to officers	60u	80u
3. Deduction of wages to officers paid in current year, instead of amortization allowed in current year of such cumulative wages paid in 1983 and thereafter	50u	50u
4. Deduction of exploration interest expense	2,800u	2,800u
5. Costs and expenses before carryover of net loss (sum of lines 1 through 4)	17,910u	22,930u

6. Recalculation of loss carryover by recalculating 1983 and 1984 net income (loss) to reflect current deduction of wages to officers and exploration interest expense:
1983 adjusted net loss carryover:
(13,021u) + (49u) + (1000u) = (14,070u)
1984 adjusted net loss carryover:
(17,042u) + (48u) + (2800u) = (19,890u)
7. Recalculation of limitation on use of net loss carryover deduction:

Item	1985	1986
gross receipts	40,000u	100,000u
less costs and expenses	(17,910u)	(22,930u)
	22,090u	77,070u
times 15% limitation	3,314u	11,561u

8. Costs and expenses including net loss carryover deduction (line 5 plus line 7) 21,224u 34,491u

In years after 1986, costs and expenses for purposes of determining the qualifying amount would reflect net loss carryforward deductions based on the recomputed losses carried forward from 1983 and 1984 (14,070u and 19,890u, respectively) less the amounts thereof that were utilized in determining costs and expenses for 1985 and 1986 (3,314u and 11,561u, respectively). The 1983 and 1984 loss carryforwards would be considered utilized in accordance with the order of priority in which such losses are utilized under the terms of the qualifying levy.

In applying the safe harbor formula, the tax rate to be used, in accordance with paragraph (e)(3) of this section, is .50.

Accordingly, under the safe harbor method, J's qualifying amounts with respect to the April 11 decree for 1985 and 1986 are computed as follows:

1985: (40,000u
− 21,224u   × .50/(1−.50) = 1604u
− 17,172u)

1986: (100,000u
− 34,491u   × .50/(1−.50) = 11,375u
− 54,134u)

Under the safe harbor method J's qualifying amounts with respect to the April 11 decree for 1985 and 1986 are thus 1604u and 11,375u, respectively; and its specific economic benefit amounts are 15,568u (17,172u − 1604u) and 42,759u (54,134u − 11,375u), respectively. Pursuant to paragraph (b) of this section, J's specific economic benefit amounts are characterized according to the nature of J's transactions with country L and of the specific economic benefit received by J as additional royalties paid to country L with respect to the petroleum extracted by J in country L in 1985 and 1986, and these amounts are so treated for all purposes of Chapter 1 of the Code.

Reg. § 1.901-2A(e)(8)

Example (5). Country E, which has no generally imposed income tax, imposes a levy called the country E income tax only on corporations carrying on the banking business through a branch in Country E and on corporations engaged in the extraction of petroleum in country E. All of the petroleum resources of country E are owned by the government of country E, whose petroleum ministry licenses corporations to explore for and extract petroleum in consideration of payment of royalties as petroleum is extracted. The base of the country E income tax is a corporation's actual gross receipts from sources in country E less all expenses attributable, on reasonable principles, to such gross receipts; the rate of tax is 29%.

A is a U.S. corporation that carries on the banking business through a branch in country E. *B* is a U.S. corporation (unrelated to *A*) that is engaged in the extraction of petroleum in country E. In 1984 *A* receives interest on loans it has made to 160 borrowers in country E, seven of which are agencies and instrumentalities of the government of country E. The economic benefits received by *A* and *B* (*i.e.*, the interest received by *A* from the government and *B*'s license to extract petroleum owned by the government) are not made available on substantially the same terms to the population of country E in general.

A and *B* are dual capacity taxpayers. Each of them has validly elected the safe harbor method for country E for 1984. *A* demonstrates that the country E income tax as applied to it (a dual capacity taxpayer) is not different by its terms or in practice from the country E income tax as applied to persons (in this case other banks) that are not dual capacity taxpayers. *A* has therefore established pursuant to paragraph (a)(1) of this section and § 1.901-2(d) that the country E income tax as applied to it and the country E income tax as applied to persons other than dual capacity taxpayers are together a single levy. *A* establishes that such levy is an income tax within the meaning of § 1.901-2(a)(1). In accordance with paragraph (a)(1) of this section, no portion of the amount paid by *A* pursuant to such levy is considered to be paid in exchange for a specific economic benefit. Thus, the entire amount paid by *A* pursuant to this levy is an amount of income tax paid.

B does not demonstrate that the country E income tax as applied to corporations engaged in the extraction of petroleum in country E (dual capacity taxpayers) is not different by its terms or in practice from the country E income tax as applied to persons other than dual capacity taxpayers (*i.e.*, banks that are not dual capacity taxpayers). Accordingly, pursuant to paragraph (a)(1) of this section and § 1.901-2(d), the country E income tax as applied to corporations engaged in the extraction of petroleum in country E is a separate levy from the country E income tax as applied to other persons.

B demonstrates that all of the criteria of section 901 are satisfied with respect to the country E income tax as applied to corporations engaged in the exploration of petroleum in country E, except for the determination of the distinct element of such levy that imposes a tax and of *B*'s qualifying amount with respect to the levy. Pursuant to paragraph (e)(5) of this section, in applying the safe harbor formula to *B*, "A" is the amount of *B*'s gross receipts as determined under the country E income tax as applied to *B*; "B" is the amount of *B*'s costs and expenses as determined thereunder; "C" is *B*'s actual payment amount; and "D" is .29, the lower of the rate (29 percent) of the qualifying levy (the country E income tax as applied to corporations engaged in the extraction of petroleum in country E) or the rate (46 percent) of tax specified for 1984 in section 11(b)(5) of the Internal Revenue Code. Thus, *B*'s qualifying amount is equal to its actual payment amount.

Example (6). The facts are the same as in example (5), except that the rate of the country E income tax is 55 percent. For the reasons stated in example (5), the results with respect to *A* are the same as in example (5). In applying the safe harbor formula to *B*, "A," "B," and "C" are the same as in example (5), but "D" is .46, as that rate is less than .55. Thus, *B*'s qualifying amount is less than *B*'s actual payment amount, and the difference is *B*'s specific economic benefit amount.

Example (7). Country E imposes a tax (called the country E income tax) on the realized net income derived by corporations from sources in country E, except that, with respect to interest income received from sources in country E and certain insurance income, nonresident corporations are instead subject to other levies. With respect to such interest income a levy (called the country E interest tax) requires nonresident corporations to pay to country E 20 percent of such gross interest income unless the nonresident corporation falls within a specified category of corporations ("special corporations"), all of which are dual capacity taxpayers, in which case the rate is instead 25 percent. With respect to such insurance income nonresident corporations are subject to a levy (called the country E insurance tax), which is not an income tax within the meaning of § 1.901-2(a)(1).

The country E interest tax applies at the 20 percent rate by its terms and in practice to persons other than dual capacity taxpayers. The

Reg. § 1.901-2A(e)(8)

country E interest tax as applied at the 25 percent rate to special corporations applies only to dual capacity taxpayers; therefore, the country E interest tax as applied to special corporations is a separate levy from the country E interest tax as applied at the 20 percent rate.

A is a U.S. corporation which is a special corporation subject to the 25 percent rate of the country E interest tax. A does not have insurance income that is subject to the country E insurance tax. A, a dual capacity taxpayer, has validly elected the safe harbor formula for 1984. In 1984 A receives 100u (units of country E currency) of gross interest income subject to the country E interest tax and pays 25u to country E.

A establishes that the country E income tax is the generally imposed income tax of country E; that all of the criteria of section 903 are satisfied with respect to the country E interest tax as applied to special corporations except for the determination of the distinct element of the levy that is a tax and of A's qualifying amount with respect thereto. A has therefore demonstrated that the country E interest tax as applied to special corporations is a qualifying levy. A establishes that the country E interest tax at the 20 percent rate is a tax in lieu of an income tax within the meaning of § 1.903-1(a). Pursuant to paragraph (e)(6) of this section the country E interest tax at the 20 percent rate is treated as if it were an application of the general tax for purposes of the safe harbor formula of this paragraph (e), since that tax would actually have been required to have been paid by A with respect to its interest income had A not been a dual capacity taxpayer (special corporation) instead subject to the qualifying levy (the country E interest tax at the 25 percent rate).

Even if the country E insurance tax is a tax in lieu of an income tax within the meaning of § 1.903-1(a), that tax is not treated as if it were an application of the general tax for purposes of applying the safe harbor formula to A since A had no insurance income in 1984 and hence such tax would not actually have been required to be paid by A had A not been a dual capacity taxpayer.

Example (8). Under a levy of country S called the country S income tax, each corporation operating in country S is required to pay country S 50 percent of its income from operations in country S. Income for purposes of the country S income tax is computed by subtracting all attributable costs and expenses from a corporation's gross receipts derived from its business in country S. Among corporations on which the country S income tax is imposed are corporations engaged in the exploitation of mineral K in country S. Natural deposits of mineral K in country S are owned by country S, and all corporations engaged in the exploitation thereof do so under concession agreements with an instrumentality of country S. Such corporations, in addition to the 50 percent country S income tax, are also subject to a levy called a surtax, which is equal to 60 percent of posted price net income less the amount of the country S income tax. The surtax is not deductible in computing the country S income tax of corporations engaged in the exploitation of mineral K in country S.

A is a U.S. corporation engaged in country S in the exploitation of mineral K, and A has been allowed to extract mineral K under a concession agreement with an instrumentality of country S. Therefore, A is a dual capacity taxpayer. In accordance with a term of the concession agreement, certain of A's income (net of expenses attributable thereto) is exempted from the income tax and surtax.

The results for A in 1984 are as follows:

	Income Tax	Surtax
Gross Receipts		
Realized—Taxable	120u	—
Realized—Exempt	15u	—
Posted Price—Taxable	—	145u
Costs		
Attributable to Taxable Receipts	20u	20u
Attributable to Exempt Receipts	5u	—
Taxable Income	100u	125u
Tentative Surtax (60%)	—	75u
Petroleum Levy at 50%	50u	50u
Surtax	—	25u

Because of the difference (nondeductibility of the surtax) in the country S income tax as applied to dual capacity taxpayers from its application to other persons, the country S income tax as applied to dual capacity taxpayers and the country S income tax as applied to persons other than dual capacity taxpayers are separate levies. Moreover, because A's concession agreement provides for a modification (exemption of certain income) of the country S income tax and surtax as they otherwise apply to other persons engaged in the exploitation of mineral K in country S, those levies (contractual levies) as applied to A are separate levies from those levies as applied to other persons engaged in the exploitation of mineral K in country S.

A establishes that the country S income tax as applied to persons other than dual capacity taxpayers is an income tax within the meaning of § 1.901-2(a)(1) and is the general tax. A demonstrates that all the criteria of section 903 are satisfied with respect to the country S income tax as applied to A and with respect to the surtax as

Reg. § 1.901-2A(e)(8)

applied to A, except for the determination of the distinct elements of such levies that are taxes and of A's qualifying amounts with respect to such levies. Therefore, both the country S income tax as applied to A and the surtax as applied to A are qualifying levies.

In applying the safe harbor formula, in accordance with paragraph (e)(2), the amount of A's gross receipts includes the exempt realized income, and the amount of A's costs and expenses includes the costs attributable to such exempt income. In accordance with paragraph (e)(7)(i), the amount of the qualifying levy for purposes of the formula is the sum of A's liability for the country S income tax and A's liability for the surtax. Accordingly, under the safe harbor formula, A's qualifying amount with respect to the country S income tax and the surtax is 35u ((135u − 25u − 75u) × .50/(1 − .50)). A's specific economic benefit amount is 40u (A's actual payment amount (75u) less A's qualifying amount (35u)).

Example (9). Country T imposes a levy on corporations, called the country T income tax. The country T income tax is imposed at a rate of 50 percent on gross receipts less all costs and expenses, and affiliated corporations are allowed to consolidate their results in applying the country T income tax. Corporations engaged in the exploitation of mineral L in country T are subject to a levy that is identical to the country T income tax except that no consolidation among affiliated corporations is allowed. The levy allows unlimited loss carryforwards.

C and D are affiliated U.S. corporations engaged in country T in the exploitation of mineral L. Natural deposits of mineral L in country T are owned by country T, and C and D have been allowed to extract mineral L in consideration of certain payments to an instrumentality of country T. Therefore, C and D are dual capacity taxpayers.

The results for C and D in 1984 and 1985 are as follows:

	1984 C	1984 D	1985 C	1985 D
Gross Receipts	120u	0	120u	120u
Costs	20u	50u	20u	20u
Loss Carryforward	....	...	....	50u
Net Income (Loss)	100u	(50u)	100u	50u
Income Tax	50u	...	50u	25u

C and D establish that the country T income tax as applied to persons other than dual capacity taxpayers is an income tax within the meaning of § 1.901-2(a)(1) and is the general tax. C and D demonstrate that all of the criteria of section 901 are satisfied with respect to the country T income tax as applied to dual capacity taxpayers, except for the determination of the distinct element of such levy that is a tax and of C and D's qualifying amounts with respect to that levy. Therefore, the country T income tax as applied to dual capacity taxpayers is a qualifying levy.

In applying the safe harbor formula, in accordance with paragraphs (e)(2)(ii) and (e)(7)(iii), the gross receipts, costs and expenses, and actual payment amounts of C and D are aggregated, except that in D's loss year (1984) its gross receipts and costs and expenses are disregarded. The results of any loss year are disregarded since the country T income tax as applied to dual capacity taxpayers does not allow consolidation, and, pursuant to paragraph (e)(2)(ii), differences in consolidation provisions between such levy and the country T income tax as applied to persons that are not dual capacity taxpayers are not considered. Accordingly, in 1984 the qualifying amount with respect to the country T income tax is 50u ((120u − 20u − 50u) × .50/(1 − .50)), all of which is considered paid by C. In 1985 the qualifying amount is 75u ((120u + 120u − 20u − 20u − 50u (loss carryforward) − 50u − 25u) × .50/(1 − .50)), of which 50u is considered to be paid by C and 25u by D.

Example (10). Country W imposes a levy called the country W income tax on corporations doing business in country W. The country W income tax is imposed at a 50 percent rate on gross receipts less all costs and expenses. Corporations engaged in the exploitation of mineral M in country W are subject to a levy that is identical in all respects to the country W income tax except that it is imposed at a rate of 80 percent (the "80 percent levy").

A is a U.S. corporation engaged in country W in exploitation of mineral M and is subject to the 80 percent levy. Natural deposits of mineral M in country W are owned by country W, and A has been allowed to extract mineral M in consideration of certain payments to an instrumentality of country W. Therefore, A is a dual capacity taxpayer. B, a U.S. corporation affiliated with A, also is engaged in business in country W, but has no transactions with country W. B is subject to the country W income tax. B is a dual capacity taxpayer within the meaning of § 1.901-2(a)(2)(ii)(A) by virtue of its affiliation with A.

The results for A and B in 1984 are as follows:

	A	B
Gross Receipts	120u	100u
Costs	20u	40u
Net Income	100u	60u
Tax Rate	.80	.50
Tax	80u	30u

Reg. § 1.901-2A(e)(8)

Income from Sources Without the United States

See p. 20,601 for regulations not amended to reflect law changes

A and B establish that the country W income tax as applied to persons other than dual capacity taxpayers is an income tax within the meaning of § 1.901-2(a)(1) and is the general tax. It is assumed that B has demonstrated that the country W income tax as applied to B does not differ by its terms or in practice from the country W income tax as applied to persons other than dual capacity taxpayers and hence that the country W income tax as applied to B, a dual capacity taxpayer, and the country W income tax as applied to such other persons is a single levy. Thus, with respect to B, the country W income tax is not a qualifying levy by reason of the last sentence of paragraph (c)(1) of this section. A demonstrates that all the criteria of section 901 are satisfied with respect to the 80 percent levy, except for the determination of the distinct element of such levy that is a tax and of A's qualifying amount with respect thereto. Accordingly, the 80 percent levy as applied to A is a qualifying levy.

In applying the safe harbor formula in accordance with paragraphs (e)(7)(i) and (e)(7)(iii) in the instant case, it is not necessary to incorporate B's results in the safe harbor formula because B's taxation in country W is identical to the taxation of persons other than dual capacity taxpayers and because neither A's and B's results nor their taxation in country W interact in any way to change A's taxation. All of the amount paid by B, 30u, is an amount of income tax paid by B within the meaning of § 1.901-2(a)(1). Accordingly, under the safe harbor formula, the qualifying amount for A with respect to the 80 percent levy is 20u ((120u − 20u − 80u) × .50/1(1 − .50)). The remaining 60u paid by A (80u − 20u) is A's specific economic benefit amount.

Example (11). The facts are the same as in example (10), except that it is assumed that B has not demonstrated that the country W income tax as applied to B does not differ by its terms or in practice from the country W income tax as applied to persons other than dual capacity taxpayers. In addition, A and B demonstrate that all the criteria of section 901 are satisfied with respect to each of the country W income tax and the 80 percent levy as applied to dual capacity taxpayers, except for the determination of the distinct elements of such levies that are taxes and of A and B's qualifying amounts with respect to such levies. Therefore, the country W income tax and 80 percent levy as applied to dual capacity taxpayers are qualifying levies.

In applying the safe harbor formula in accordance with paragraphs (e)(7)(i) and (e)(7)(iii), the results of A and B are aggregated. Accordingly, under the safe harbor formula, the aggregate qualifying amount for A and B with respect to the country W income tax and 80 percent levy is 50u ([(120u + 100u) − (20u + 40u) − (80u + 30u)] × .50/(1 − .50)).

Example (12). Country Y imposes a levy on corporations operating in country Y, called the country Y income tax. Income for purposes of the country Y income tax is computed by subtracting all costs and expenses from a corporation's gross receipts derived from its business in country Y. The rate of the country Y income tax is 50 percent. Country Y also imposes a 20 percent tax (the "withholding tax") on the gross amount of certain income, including dividends, received by persons who are not residents of country Y from persons who are residents of country Y and from corporations that operate there. Corporations engaged in the exploitation of mineral K in country Y are subject to a levy (the "75 percent levy") that is identical in all respects to the country Y income tax except that it is imposed at a rate of 75 percent. Dividends received from such corporations are not subject to the withholding tax.

C, a wholly-owned country Y subsidiary of D, a U.S. corporation, is engaged in country Y in the exploitation of mineral K. Natural deposits of mineral K in country Y are owned by country Y, and C has been allowed to extract mineral K in consideration of certain payments to an instrumentality of country Y. Therefore, C is a dual capacity taxpayer. D has elected the safe harbor method for country Y for 1984. In 1984, C's gross receipts are 120u (units of country Y currency), its costs and expenses are 20u, and its liability under the 75 percent levy is 75u. C distributes the amount that remains, 25u, as a dividend to D.

D establishes that the country Y income tax as applied to persons other than dual capacity taxpayers is an income tax within the meaning of § 1.901-2(a)(1) and the general tax, and that all the criteria of section 901 are satisfied with respect to the 75 percent levy, except for the determination of the distinct element of such levy that is tax and of C's qualifying amount with respect thereto. Accordingly, the 75 percent levy is a qualifying levy.

Pursuant to paragraph (e)(7), D (which is not subject to a levy of country Y but is considered to receive a specific economic benefit by reason of § 1.901-2(a)(2)(ii)(E)) is treated as a dual capacity taxpayer in applying paragraph (e)(7)(ii). D demonstrates that the withholding tax is a tax in lieu of an income tax within the meaning of § 1.903-1, which tax applies in practice to persons other than dual capacity taxpayers, and that such tax actually would have

Reg. § 1.901-2A(e)(8)

applied to D had D not been a dual capacity taxpayer (i.e., had C not been a dual capacity taxpayer, in which case D also would not have been one). Accordingly, the withholding tax is treated for purposes of the safe harbor formula as if it were an application of the general tax.

In applying the safe harbor formula to this situation in accordance with paragraph (e)(7)(ii), the rates of the country Y income tax and the withholding tax are aggregated into a single effective general tax rate. In this case, that rate is .60 $(.50 + [(1 - .50) \times .20])$. Accordingly, under the safe harbor forumla, C's qualifying amount with respect to the 75 percent levy is 37.5u [(120u − 20u − 75u) × .60/(1 − .60)], the aggregate amount that C and D would have paid if C had been subject to the country Y income tax and had distributed to D as a dividend subject to the withholding tax the entire amount that remained for the year after payment of the country Y income tax. Because C is in fact the only taxpayer, the entire qualifying amount is paid by C.

Example (13). The facts are the same as in example (12), except that dividends received from corporations engaged in the exploitation of mineral K in country Y are subject to the withholding tax. Thus, C's liability under the 75 percent levy is 75u, and D's liability under the withholding tax on the 25u distribution is 5u.

D, which is a dual capacity taxpayer, demonstrates that the withholding tax as applied to D does not differ by its terms or in practice from the withholding tax as applied to persons other than dual capacity taxpayers and hence that the withholding tax as applied to D and that levy as applied to such other persons is a single levy. D demonstrates that all of the criteria of section 903 are satisfied with respect to the withholding tax. The withholding tax is not a qualifying levy by reason of the last sentence of paragraph (c)(1) of this section.

Paragraphs (e)(7)(i), (e)(7)(ii) and (e)(7)(iii) all apply in this situation. As in example (10), it is not necessary to incorporate the withholding tax into the safe harbor formula. All of the amount paid by D, 5u, is an amount of tax paid by D in lieu of an income tax. In applying the safe harbor formula to C, therefore, with respect to the 75 percent levy, "A" is 120, "B" is "20", "C" is 75 and "D" is .50. Accordingly, C's qualifying amount with respect to the 75 percent levy is 25u; the remaining 50u that it paid is its specific economic benefit amount.

Example (14). The facts are the same as in example (12), except that dividends received from corporations engaged in the exploitation of mineral K in country Y are subject to a 10 percent withholding tax (the "10 percent withholding tax"). Thus, C's liability under the 75 percent levy is 75u, and D's liability under the 10 percent withholding tax on the 25u distribution is 2.5u.

The only difference between the withholding tax and the 10 percent withholding tax applicable only to dual capacity taxpayers (including D) is that a lower rate (but the same base) applies to dual capacity taxpayers. Although the withholding tax and the 10 percent withholding tax are together a single levy, this difference makes it necessary, when dealing with multiple levies, to incorporate the withholding tax and D's payment pursuant to the 10 percent withholding tax in the safe harbor formula. Accordingly, as in example (12), the safe harbor formula is applied by aggregation.

The aggregate effective rate of the general taxes for purposes of the safe harbor formula is .60 $(.50 + [(1 - .50) \times .20])$. Pursuant to paragraph (e)(7), the aggregate actual payment amount of the qualifying levies for purposes of the formula is the sum of C and D's liability for the 75 percent levy and the 10 percent withholding tax. Accordingly, under the safe harbor formula, the aggregate qualifying amount with respect to the 75 percent levy on C and the 10 percent withholding tax on D is 33.75u ((120u − 20u − [75u + 2.5u]) × .60(1 − .60)), which is the aggregate amount of tax that C and D would have paid if C had been subject to the country Y income tax and had paid out its entire amount remaining after payment of that tax to D as a dividend subject to the withholding tax.

Example (15). The facts are the same as in example (5), except that the rate of the country E income tax is 45 percent and a political subdivision of country E also imposes a levy, called the "local tax," on all corporations subject to the country E income tax. The base of the local tax is the same as the base of the country E income tax; the rate is 10 percent.

The reasoning of example (5) with regard to the country E income tax as applied to A and B, respectively, applies equally with regard to the local tax as applied to A and B, respectively. Accordingly, the entire amount paid by A pursuant to each of the country E income tax and the local tax is an amount of income tax paid, and both the country E income tax as applied to B and the local tax as applied to B are qualifying levies.

Pursuant to paragraph (e)(7), in applying the safe harbor formula to B, "A" is the amount of B's gross receipts as determined under the (identical) country E income tax and local tax as applied to B; "B" is the amount of B's costs and expenses thereunder; and "C" is the sum of B's actual payment amounts with respect to the two levies. Pursuant to paragraph (e)(7), in applying the safe harbor formula to B, B's aggregate qualifying amount with respect to the two levies is limited to the amount determined in accordance with paragraph (e)(5) where "D" is the rate of tax specified in section 11(b)(5) of the Internal Revenue Code. Accordingly, "D" is .46, which is the lower of the aggregate rate (55 percent) of the qualifying levies or the section 11(b)(5) rate (46 percent). B's aggregate qualifying amount is, therefore, identical to B's qualifying amount in example (6), which is less than its aggregate actual payment amount, and the difference is B's specific economic benefit amount.

(f) *Effective date.* The effective date of this section is as provided in § 1.901-2(h). [Reg. § 1.901-2A.]

☐ [*T.D. 7918, 10-6-83.*]

[Reg. § 1.901-3]

§ 1.901-3. Reduction in amount of foreign taxes on foreign mineral income allowed as a credit.—(a) *Determination of amount of reduction*—(1) *In general.* For purposes of determining the amount of taxes which are allowed as a credit under section 901(a) for taxable years beginning after December 31, 1969, the amount of any income, war profits, and excess profits taxes paid or accrued, or deemed to be paid under section 902, during the taxable year to any foreign country or possession of the United States with respect to foreign mineral income (as defined in paragraph (b) of this section) from sources within such country or possession shall be reduced by the amount, if any, by which—

(i) The smaller of—

(*a*) The amount of such foreign income, war profits, and excess profits taxes, or

(*b*) The amount of the tax which would be computed under chapter 1 of the Code for such year with respect to such foreign mineral income if the deduction for depletion were determined under section 611 without regard to the deduction for percentage depletion under section 613, exceeds

(ii) The amount of the tax computed under chapter 1 of the Code for such year with respect to such foreign mineral income.

The reduction required by this subparagraph must be made on a country-by-country basis whether the taxpayer uses for the taxable year the per-country limitation under section 904(a)(1), or the overall limitation under section 904(a)(2), on the amount of taxes allowed as credit under section 901(a).

(2) *Determination of amount of tax on foreign mineral income*—(i) *Foreign tax.* For purposes of subparagraph (1)(i)(*a*) of this paragraph, the amount of the income, war profits, and excess profits taxes paid or accrued during the taxable year to a foreign country or possession of the United States with respect to foreign mineral income from sources within such country or possession is an amount which is the greater of—

(*a*) The amount by which the total amount of the income, war profits, and excess profits taxes paid or accrued during the taxable year to such country or possession exceeds the amount of such taxes that would be paid or accrued for such year to such country or possession without taking into account such foreign mineral income, or

(*b*) The amount of the income, war profits, and excess profits taxes that would be paid or accrued to such country or possession if such foreign mineral income were the taxpayer's only income for the taxable year,

except that in no case shall the amount so determined exceed the total of all income, war profits, and excess profits taxes paid or accrued during the taxable year to such country or possession. For such purposes taxes which are paid or accrued also include taxes which are deemed paid under section 902. In the case of a dividend described in paragraph (b)(2)(i)(*a*) of this section which is from sources within a foreign country or possession of the United States and is attributable in whole or in part to foreign mineral income, the amount of the income, war profits, and excess profits taxes deemed paid under section 902 during the taxable year to such country or possession with respect to foreign mineral income from sources within such country or possession is an amount which bears the same ratio to the amount of the income, war profits, and excess profits taxes deemed paid under section 902 during such year to such country or possession with respect to such dividend as the portion of the dividend which is attributable to foreign mineral income bears to the total dividend. For purposes of (*a*) and (*b*) of this subdivision, foreign mineral income is to be reduced by any credits, expenses, losses, and other deductions which are properly allocable to such income under the law of the foreign country or possession of the United States from which such income is derived.

(ii) *U.S. tax.* For purposes of subparagraph (1)(ii) of this paragraph, the amount of the tax computed under chapter 1 of the Code for the taxable year with respect to foreign mineral income from sources within a foreign country or possession of the United States is the greater of—

Reg. § 1.901-3(a)(2)

Income from Sources Without the United States

(a) The amount by which the tax under chapter 1 of the Code on the taxpayer's taxable income for the taxable year exceeds a tax determined under such chapter on the taxable income for such year determined without regard to such foreign mineral income, or

(b) The amount of tax that would be determined under chapter 1 of the Code if such foreign mineral income were the taxpayer's only income for the taxable year.

For purposes of this subdivision the tax is to be determined without regard to any credits against the tax and without taking into account any tax against which a credit is not allowed under section 901(a). For purposes of (b) of this subdivision, the foreign mineral income is to be reduced only by expenses, losses, and other deductions properly allocable under chapter 1 of the Code to such income and is to be computed without any deduction for personal exemptions under section 151 or 642(b).

(iii) *U.S. income tax computed without deduction allowed by section 613.* For purposes of subparagraph (1)(i)(b) of this paragraph, the amount of the tax which would be computed under chapter 1 of the Code (without regard to section 613) for the taxable year with respect to foreign mineral income from sources within a foreign country or possession of the United States is the amount of the tax on such income that would be computed under such chapter by using as the allowance for depletion cost depletion computed upon the adjusted depletion basis of the property. For purposes of this subdivision the tax is to be determined without regard to any credits against the tax and without taking into account any tax against which credit is not allowed under section 901(a). If the greater tax with respect to the foreign mineral income under subdivision (ii) of this subparagraph is the tax determined under (a) of such subdivision, the tax determined for purposes of subparagraph (1)(i)(b) of this paragraph is to be determined by applying the principles of (a) (rather than of (b)) of subdivision (ii) of this subparagraph. On the other hand, if the greater tax with respect to the foreign mineral income under subdivision (ii) of this subparagraph is the tax determined under (b) of such subdivision, the tax determined for purposes of subparagraph (1)(i)(b) of this paragraph is to be determined by applying the principles of (b) (rather than of (a)) of subdivision (ii) of this subparagraph.

(3) *Special rules.* (i) The reduction required by this paragraph in the amount of taxes paid, accrued, or deemed to be paid to a foreign country or possession of the United States applies only where the taxpayer is allowed a deduction for percentage depletion under section 613 with respect to any part of his foreign mineral income for the taxable year from sources within such country or possession, whether or not such deduction is allowed with respect to the entire mineral income from sources within such country or possession for such year.

(ii) For purposes of this section, the term "foreign country" or "possession of the United States" includes the adjacent continental shelf areas to the extent, and in the manner, provided by section 638(2) and the regulations thereunder.

(iii) The provisions of this section are to be applied before making any reduction required by section 1503(b) in the amount of income, war profits, and excess profits taxes paid or accrued to foreign countries or possessions of the United States by a Western Hemisphere trade corporation.

(iv) If a taxpayer chooses with respect to any taxable year to claim a credit under section 901 and has any foreign mineral income from sources within a foreign country or possession of the United States for such year with respect to which the deduction under section 613 is allowed, he must attach to his return for such year a schedule showing the computations required by subdivisions (i), (ii), and (iii) of subparagraph (2) of this paragraph.

(v) A taxpayer who has elected to use the overall limitation under section 904(a)(2) on the amount of the foreign tax credit for any taxable year beginning before January 1, 1970, may, for his first taxable year beginning after December 31, 1969, revoke his election without first securing the consent of the Commissioner. See paragraph (d) of § 1.904-1.

(b) *Foreign mineral income defined*—(1) *In general.* The term "foreign mineral income" means income (determined under chapter 1 of the Code) from sources within a foreign country or possession of the United States derived from—

(i) The extraction of minerals from mines, wells, or other natural deposits,

(ii) The processing of minerals into their primary products, or

(iii) The transportation, distribution, or sale of minerals or of the primary products derived from minerals.

Any income of the taxpayer derived from an activity described in either subdivision (i), (ii), or (iii) of this subparagraph is foreign mineral income, since it is not necessary that the taxpayer extract, process, and transport, distribute, or sell minerals or their primary products for the income derived from any such activity to be foreign mineral income. Thus, for example, an integrated oil company must treat as foreign mineral income

Reg. § 1.901-3(a)(3)

from sources within a foreign country or possession of the United States all income from such sources derived from the production of oil, the refining of crude oil into gasoline, the distribution of gasoline to marketing outlets, and the retail sale of gasoline. Similarly, income from such sources from the refining, distribution, or marketing of fuel oil by the taxpayer is foreign mineral income, whether or not the crude oil was extracted by the taxpaper. In further illustration, income from sources within a foreign country or possession of the United States derived from the processing of minerals into their primary products by the taxpayer is foreign mineral income, whether or not the minerals were extracted, or the primary products were sold, by the taxpayer. Section 901(e) and this section apply whether or not the extraction, processing, transportation, distribution, or selling of the minerals or primary products is done by the taxpayer. Thus, for example, an individual who derives royalty income from the extraction of oil from an oil well in a foreign country has foreign mineral income for purposes of this paragraph. Income from the manufacture, distribution, and marketing of petrochemicals is not foreign mineral income. Foreign mineral income is not limited to gross income from the property within the meaning of section 613(c) and § 1.613-3.

(2) *Income included in foreign mineral income*—(i) *In general.* Foreign mineral income from sources within a foreign country or possession of the United States includes, but is not limited to—

(a) Dividends from such sources, as determined under § 1.902-1(h)(1), received from a foreign corporation in respect of which taxes are deemed paid by the taxpayer under section 902, to the extent such dividends are attributable to foreign mineral income described in subparagraph (1) of this paragraph. The portion of such a dividend which is attributable to such income is that amount which bears the same ratio to the total dividend received as the earnings and profits out of which such dividend is paid that are attributable to foreign mineral income bear to the total earnings and profits out of which such dividend is paid. For such purposes, the foreign mineral income of a foreign corporation is its foreign mineral income described in this paragraph (including any dividends described in this (a) which are received from another foreign corporation), whether or not such income is derived from sources within the foreign country or possession of the United States in which, or under the laws of which, the former corporation is created or organized. A foreign corporation is considered to have no foreign mineral income for any taxable year beginning before January 1, 1970.

(b) Any section 78 dividend to which a dividend described in (a) of this subdivision gives rise, but only to the extent such section 78 dividend is deemed paid under paragraph (a)(2)(i) of this section with respect to foreign mineral income from sources within such country or possession and to the extent it is treated under § 1.902-1(h)(1) as income from sources within such country or possession.

(c) Any amounts includible in income of the taxpayer under section 702(a) as his distributive share of the income of a partnership consisting of income described in subparagraph (1) of this paragraph.

(d) Any amounts includible in income of the taxpayer by virtue of section 652(a), 662(a), 671, 682(a), or 691(a), to the extent such amounts consist of income described in subparagraph (1) of this paragraph.

(ii) *Illustration.* The provisions of this subparagraph may be illustrated by the following example:

Example. (a) Throughout 1974, M, a domestic corporation, owns all the one class of stock of N, a foreign corporation which is not a less developed country corporation within the meaning of section 902(d). Both corporations use the calendar year as the taxable year. N is incorporated in foreign country Y. During 1974, N has income from sources within foreign country X, all of which is foreign mineral income. During 1974, N also has income from sources within country Y, none of which is foreign mineral income. N is taxed in each foreign country only on income derived from sources within that country. Neither country X nor country Y allows a credit against its tax for foreign income taxes. N pays a dividend of $40,000 to M for 1974. For purposes of section 902, the dividend is paid from earnings and profits for 1974.

(b) N's earnings and profits and taxes for 1974 are determined as follows:

Foreign mineral income from country X		$100,000
Less:		
Intangible drilling and development costs	$21,000	
Cost depletion	3,000	24,000
Taxable income from country X		76,000
Income tax rate of country X		× 50%
Tax paid to country X...............		38,000

Reg. § 1.901-3(b)(2)

48,838   Income from Sources Without the United States
See p. 20,601 for regulations not amended to reflect law changes

Income from country Y	100,000
Less deductions	25,000
Taxable income from country Y	75,000
Income tax rate of country Y	× 60%
Tax paid to country Y	45,000
Total taxable income	151,000
Less total foreign income taxes	83,000
Total earnings and profits	68,000
Taxable income from foreign mineral income	76,000
Less: Tax paid on foreign mineral income	38,000
Earnings and profits from foreign mineral income	38,000

(c) For 1974, M has foreign mineral income from country Y of $49,636.68, determined in the following manner and by applying this section, § 1.78-1, and § 1.902-1(h)(1):

Portion of dividend from country Y attributable to foreign mineral income (subdivision (i)(a) of this subparagraph) ($40,000 × $38,000/$68,000)	$22,352.94
Foreign income tax deemed paid by M to country Y under section 902(a)(1) ($83,000 × $40,000/$68,000)	48,823.53
Foreign income tax deemed paid by M to country Y with respect to foreign mineral income from country Y (par. (a)(2)(i) of this section) ($48,823.53 × $22,352.94/$40,000)	27,283.74
Foreign mineral income from country Y:	
Dividend attributable to foreign mineral income from country Y	22,352.94
Sec. 78 dividend deemed paid with respect to foreign mineral income (subdivision (i)(b) of this subparagraph)	27,283.74
Total foreign mineral income	49,636.68

(c) *Limitations on foreign tax credit* —(1) *In general.* The reduction under section 901(e) and paragraph (a)(1) of this section in the amount of foreign taxes allowed as a credit under section 901(a) is to be made whether the per-country limitation under section 904(a)(1) or the overall limitation under section 904(a)(2) is used for the taxable year, but the reduction in the amount of foreign taxes allowed as a credit under section 901(a) must be made on a country-by-country basis before applying the limitation under section 904(a) to the reduced amount of taxes. If for the taxable year the separate limitation under section 904(f) applies to any foreign mineral income, that limitation must also be applied after making the reduction under section 901(e) and paragraph (a)(1) of this section.

(2) *Carrybacks and carryovers of excess tax paid* —(i) *In general.* Any amount by which (a) any income, war profits, and excess profits taxes paid or accrued, or deemed to be paid under section 902, during the taxable year to any foreign country or possession of the United States with respect to foreign mineral income from sources within such country or possession exceed (b) the reduced amount of such taxes as determined under paragraph (a)(1) of this section may not be deemed paid or accrued under section 904(d) in any other taxable year. See § 1.904-2(b)(2)(iii). However, to the extent such reduced amount of taxes exceeds the applicable limitation under section 904(a) for the taxable year it shall be deemed paid or accrued under section 904(d) in another taxable year as a carryback or carryover of an unused foreign tax. The amount so deemed paid or accrued in another taxable year is not, however, deemed paid or accrued with respect to foreign mineral income in such other taxable year. See § 1.904-2(c)(3).

(ii) *Carryovers to taxable years beginning after December 31, 1969.* Where, under the provisions of section 904(d), taxes paid or accrued, or deemed to be paid under section 902, to any foreign country or possession of the United States in any taxable year beginning before January 1, 1970, are deemed paid or accrued in one or more taxable years beginning after December 31, 1969, the amount of such taxes so deemed paid or accrued shall not be deemed paid or accrued with respect to foreign mineral income and shall not be reduced under section 901(e) and paragraph (a)(1) of this section.

(iii) *Carrybacks to taxable years beginning before January 1, 1970.* Where income, war profits, and excess profits taxes are paid or accrued, or deemed to be paid under section 902, to any foreign country or possession of the United States in any taxable year beginning after December 31, 1969, with respect to foreign mineral income from sources within such country or possession, they must first be reduced under section 901(e) and paragraph (a)(1) of this section before they may be deemed paid or accrued under section 904(d) in one or more taxable years beginning before January 1, 1970.

(d) *Illustrations.* The application of this section may be illustrated by the following examples, in which the surtax exemption provided by section 11(d) and the tax surcharge provided by section

Reg. § 1.901-3(c)(1)

Income from Sources Without the United States

51(a) are disregarded for purposes of simplification:

Example (1). (a) M, a domestic corporation using the calendar year as the taxable year, is an operator drilling for oil in foreign country W. For 1971, M's gross income under chapter 1 of the Code is $100,000, all of which is foreign mineral income from a property in country W and is subject to the allowance for depletion. During 1971, M incurs intangible drilling and development costs of $15,000, which are currently deductible for purposes of the tax of both countries. Cost depletion amounts to $2,000 for purposes of the tax of both countries, and only cost depletion is allowed as a deduction under the law of country W. It is assumed that no other deductions are allowable under the law of either country. Based upon the facts assumed, the income tax paid to country W on such foreign mineral income is $41,500, and the U.S. tax on such income before allowance of the foreign tax credit is $30,240, determined as follows:

	U.S. Tax	W Tax
Foreign mineral income	$100,000	$100,000
Less:		
Intangible drilling and development costs	15,000	15,000
Cost depletion	....	2,000
Percentage depletion (22% of $100,000, but not to exceed 50% of $85,000)	22,000	....
Taxable income	63,000	83,000
Income tax rate	48%	50%
Tax	$ 30,240	$ 41,500

(b) Without taking this section into account, M would be allowed a foreign tax credit for 1971 of $30,240 ($30,240 × $63,000/$63,000), and foreign income tax in the amount of $11,260 ($41,500 less $30,240) would first be carried back to 1969 under section 904(d).

(c) Pursuant to paragraph (a)(1) of this section, however, the foreign income tax allowable as a credit against the U.S. tax is reduced to $31,900, determined as follows:

Foreign income tax paid on foreign mineral income	$41,500
Less reduction under sec. 901(e): Smaller of $41,500 (tax paid to country W on foreign mineral income) or $39,840 (U.S. tax on foreign mineral income of $83,000 ($83,000 × 48%), determined by deducting cost depletion of $2,000 in lieu of percentage depletion of $22,000) $39,840	
Less: U.S. tax on foreign mineral income (before credit) 30,240	9,600
Foreign income tax allowable as a credit	31,900

(d) After taking this section into account, M is allowed a foreign tax credit for 1971 of $30,240 ($30,240 × $63,000/$63,000). The amount of foreign income tax which may be first carried back to 1969 under section 904(d) is reduced from $11,260 to $1,660 ($31,900 less $30,240).

Example (2). (a) M, a domestic corporation using the calendar year as the taxable year, is an operator drilling for oil in foreign country X. For 1972, M has gross income under chapter 1 of the Code of $100,000, all of which is foreign mineral income from a property in country X and is subject to the allowance for depletion. During 1972, M incurs intangible drilling and development costs of $50,000 which are currently deductible for purposes of the U.S. tax but which must be amortized for purposes of the tax of country X. Percentage depletion of $22,000 is allowed as a deduction by both countries. For purposes of the U.S. tax, cost depletion for 1972 amounts to $15,000. It is assumed that no other deductions are allowable under the law of either country. Based upon these facts, the income tax paid to country X on such foreign mineral income is $27,200, and the U.S. tax on such income before allowance of the foreign tax credit is $13,440, determined as follows:

	U.S. Tax	X Tax
Foreign mineral income	$100,000	$100,000
Less:		
Intangible drilling and development costs	50,000	10,000
Percentage depletion	22,000	22,000
Taxable income	28,000	68,000
Income tax rate	48%	40%
Tax	$ 13,440	$ 27,200

Reg. § 1.901-3(d)

48,840   **Income from Sources Without the United States**
See p. 20,601 for regulations not amended to reflect law changes

(b) Without taking this section into account, M would be allowed a foreign tax credit for 1972 of $13,440 ($13,440 × $28,000/$28,000), and foreign income tax in the amount of $13,760 ($27,200 less $13,440) would first be carried back to 1970 under section 904(d).

(c) Pursuant to paragraph (a)(1) of this section, however, the foreign income tax allowable as a credit against the U.S. tax is reduced to $23,840, determined as follows:

Foreign income tax paid on foreign mineral income		$ 27,200
Less reduction under section 901(e):		
Smaller of $27,200 (tax paid to country X on foreign mineral income) or $16,800 (U.S. tax on foreign mineral income of $35,000 ($35,000 × 48%), determined by deducting cost depletion of $15,000 in lieu of percentage depletion of $22,000)	$ 16,800	
Less: U.S. tax on foreign mineral income (before credit)	13,440	3,360
Foreign income tax allowable as a credit		23,840

(d) After taking this section into account, M is allowed a foreign tax credit of $13,440 ($13,440 × $28,000/$28,000). The amount of foreign income tax which may be first carried back to 1970 under section 904(d) is reduced from $13,760 to $10,400 ($23,840 less $13,440).

Example (3). (a) N, a domestic corporation using the calendar year as the taxable year, is an operator drilling for oil in foreign country Y. For 1972, N's gross income under chapter 1 of the Code is $100,000, all of which is foreign mineral income from a property in country Y and is subject to the allowance for depletion. During 1972, N incurs intangible drilling and development costs of $15,000, which are currently deductible for purposes of the U.S. tax but are not deductible under the law of country Y. Depreciation of $40,000 is allowed as a deduction for purposes of the U.S. tax; and of $20,000, for purposes of the Y tax. Cost depletion amounts to $10,000 for purposes of the tax of both countries, and only cost depletion is allowed as a deduction under the law of country Y. It is assumed that no other deductions are allowable under the law of either country. Based upon the facts assumed, the income tax paid to country Y on such foreign mineral income is $14,000, and the U.S. tax on such income before allowance of the foreign tax credit is $11,040, determined as follows:

	U.S. Tax	Y Tax
Foreign mineral income	$100,000	$100,000
Less:		
Intangible drilling and development costs	15,000	....
Depreciation	40,000	20,000
Cost depletion	....	10,000
Percentage depletion (22% of $100,000, but not to exceed 50% of $45,000)	22,000	....
Taxable income	23,000	70,000
Income tax rate	48%	20%
Tax	$ 11,040	$ 14,000

(b) Without taking this section into account, N would be allowed a foreign tax credit for 1972 of $11,040 ($11,040 × $23,000/$23,000), and foreign income tax in the amount of $2,960 ($14,000 less $11,040) would first be carried back to 1970 under section 904(d).

(c) Pursuant to paragraph (a)(1) of this section, however, the foreign income tax allowable as a credit against the U.S. tax is reduced to $11,040, determined as follows:

Foreign income tax paid on foreign mineral income		$ 14,000
Less reduction under section 901(e):		
Smaller of $14,000 (tax paid to country Y on foreign mineral income) or $16,800 (U.S. tax on foreign mineral income of $35,000 ($35,000 × 48%), determined by deducting cost depletion of $10,000 in lieu of percentage depletion of $22,000)	$ 14,000	
Less: U.S. tax on foreign mineral income (before credit)	11,040	2,960
Foreign income tax allowable as a credit		$ 11,040

Reg. § 1.901-3(d)

Income from Sources Without the United States

See p. 20,601 for regulations not amended to reflect law changes

(d) After taking this section into account, N is allowed a foreign tax credit for 1972 of $11,040 ($11,040 × $23,000/$23,000), but no foreign income tax is carried back to 1970 under section 904(d) since the allowable credit of $11,040 does not exceed the limitation of $11,040.

Example (4). (a) D, a domestic corporation using the calendar year as the taxable year, is an operator drilling for oil in foreign country Z. For 1971, D's gross income under chapter 1 of the Code is $100,000, all of which is foreign mineral income from a property in country Z and is subject to the allowance for depletion. During 1971, D incurs intangible drilling and development costs of $85,000, which are currently deductible for purposes of the U.S. tax but are not deductible under the law of country Z. Cost depletion in the amount of $10,000 is allowed as a deduction for purposes of both the U.S. tax and the tax of country Z. Percentage depletion is not allowed as a deduction under the law of country Z and is not taken as a deduction for purposes of the U.S. tax. It is assumed that no other deductions are allowable under the law of either country. Based upon the facts assumed, the income tax paid to country Z on such foreign mineral income is $27,000, and the U.S. tax on such income before allowance of the foreign tax credit is $2,400, determined as follows:

	U.S. Tax	Z Tax
Foreign mineral income	$100,000	$100,000
Less:		
Intangible drilling and development costs	85,000	....
Cost depletion	10,000	10,000
Taxable income	5,000	90,000
Income tax rate	48%	30%
Tax	$ 2,400	$ 27,000

(b) Section 901(e) and this section do not apply to reduce the amount of the foreign income tax paid to country Z with respect to the foreign mineral income since for 1971 D is not allowed the deduction for percentage depletion with respect to any foreign mineral income from sources within country Z. Accordingly, D is allowed a foreign tax credit of $2,400 ($2,400 × $5,000/$5,000), and foreign income tax in the amount of $24,600 ($27,000 less $2,400) is first carried back to 1969 under section 904(d).

Example (5). (a) R, a domestic corporation using the calendar year as the taxable year, is an operator drilling for oil in the United States and in foreign country Z. For 1971, R's gross income under chapter 1 of the Code is $250,000, of which $100,000 is foreign mineral income from a property in foreign country Z and $150,000 is from a property in the United States, all being subject to the allowance for depletion. During 1971, R incurs intangible drilling and development costs of $125,000 in the United States and of $25,000 in country Z, all of which are currently deductible for purposes of the U.S. tax. Of these costs of $25,000 incurred in country Z, only $2,500 is currently deductible under the law of country Z. Cost depletion in the case of the U.S. property amounts to $60,000; and in the case of the property in country Z, to $5,000, which is allowed as a deduction under the laws of such country. Percentage depletion is not allowed as a deduction under the law of country Z. In computing the U.S. tax for 1971, R is required to use cost depletion with respect to the mineral income from the U.S. property and percentage depletion with respect to the foreign mineral income from the property in country Z. It is assumed that no other deductions are allowed under the law of either country. Based upon the facts assumed, the income tax paid to country Z on the foreign mineral income from sources therein is $37,000, and the U.S. tax on the entire mineral income before allowance of the foreign tax credit is $8,640, determined as follows:

	U.S. Tax	Z Tax
Gross income (including foreign mineral income)	$250,000	$100,000
Less:		
Intangible drilling and development costs	150,000	2,500
Cost depletion	60,000	5,000
Percentage depletion on foreign mineral income (22% of $100,000, but not to exceed 50% of [$100,000 − $25,000])	22,000	....
Taxable income	18,000	92,500
Income tax rate	48%	40%
Tax	$ 8,640	$ 37,000

(b) Without taking this section into account, R would be allowed a foreign tax credit for 1971 of $8,640 ($8,640 × $18,000/$18,000), and foreign income tax in the amount of $28,360 ($37,000 less $8,640) would first be carried back to 1969 under section 904(d).

Reg. § 1.901-3(d)

48,842 Income from Sources Without the United States
See p. 20,601 for regulations not amended to reflect law changes

(c) Under paragraph (a)(2)(ii) of this section, the amount of the U.S. tax for 1971 with respect to foreign mineral income from country Z is $25,440, which is the greater of the amounts of tax determined under subparagraphs (1) and (2):

(1) U.S. tax on total taxable income in excess of U.S. tax on taxable income excluding foreign mineral income from country Z (determined under paragraph (a)(2)(ii)(a) of this section):

U.S. tax on total taxable income		$8,640
Less U.S. tax on taxable income other than foreign mineral income from country Z:		
Income from U.S. property	$150,000	
Intangible drilling and development costs	125,000	
Cost depletion	60,000	
Taxable income	0	
Income tax rate	48%	
U.S. tax	$ 0	0
Excess tax		8,640

(2) U.S. tax on foreign mineral income from country Z (determined under paragraph (a)(2)(ii)(b) of this section):

Foreign mineral income	$100,000
Intangible drilling and development costs	25,000
Percentage depletion (22% of $100,000, but not to exceed 50% of $75,000)	22,000
Taxable income	53,000
Income tax rate	48%
U.S. tax	$ 25,440

(d) Under paragraph (a)(2)(iii) of this section, the amount of the U.S. tax which would be computed for 1971 (without regard to section 613) with respect to foreign mineral income from sources within country Z is $33,600, computed by applying the principles of paragraph (a)(2)(ii)(b) of this section:

Foreign mineral income	$100,000
Intangible drilling and developments costs	25,000
Cost depletion	5,000
Taxable income	70,000
Income tax rate	48%
U.S. tax	$ 33,600

(e) Pursuant to paragraph (a)(1) of this section, the foreign income tax allowable as a credit against the U.S. tax for 1971 is reduced to $28,840, determined as follows:

Foreign income tax paid on foreign mineral income		$37,000
Less reduction under sec. 901(e):		
Smaller of $37,000 (tax paid to country Z on foreign mineral income) or $33,600 (U.S. tax on foreign mineral income of $70,000, as determined under par. (d) of this example	$33,600	
Less: U.S. tax on foreign mineral income of $53,000, as determined under par. (c) of this example	25,440	8,160
Foreign income tax allowable as a credit		28,840

(f) After taking this section into account, R is allowed a foreign tax credit for 1971 of $8,640 ($8,640 × $18,000/$18,000). The amount of foreign income tax which may be first carried back to 1969 under section 904(d) is reduced from $28,360 to $20,200 ($28,840 less $8,640).

Example (6). (a) B, a single individual using the calendar year as the taxable year, is an operator drilling for oil in foreign countries X and Y. For 1972, B's gross income under chapter 1 of the Code is $250,000, of which $150,000 is foreign mineral income from a property in country X and $100,000 is foreign mineral income from a property in country Y, all being subject to the allowance for depletion. The assumption is made that B's earned taxable income for 1972 is insufficient to cause section 1348 to apply. During 1972, B incurs intangible drilling and development costs of $16,000 in country X and of $9,000 in country Y, which are currently deductible for purposes of both the U.S. tax and the tax of countries X and

Reg. § 1.901-3(d)

Income from Sources Without the United States 48,843
See p. 20,601 for regulations not amended to reflect law changes

Y, respectively. For purposes of both the U.S. tax and the tax of countries X and Y, respectively, cost depletion in the case of the X property amounts to $8,000, and in the case of the Y property, to $7,000; and only cost depletion is allowed as a deduction under the law of countries X and Y. For 1972, B uses the overall limitation under section 904(a)(2) on the foreign tax credit. Percentage depletion is not allowed as a deduction under the law of countries X and Y. It is assumed that the only other allowable deductions amount to $2,250. None of these deductions is attributable to the income from the properties in countries X and Y, and none is deductible under the laws of country X or country Y. Based upon the facts assumed, the income tax paid to countries X and Y on the foreign mineral income from each such country is $71,820 and $25,200, respectively, and the U.S. tax on B's total taxable income before allowance of the foreign tax credit is $99,990, determined as follows:

	U.S. Tax	X Tax	Y Tax
Total income (including foreign mineral income from countries X and Y)	$250,000	$150,000	$100,000
Intangible drilling and development costs	25,000	16,000	9,000
Cost depletion	....	8,000	7,000
Percentage depletion (22% of $150,000, but not to exceed 50% of $134,000; plus 22% of $100,000, but not to exceed 50% of $91,000)	55,000	....	....
Adjusted gross income	170,000	....	....
Other deductions	2,250	....	....
Personal exemption	750	....	....
Taxable income	$167,000	$126,000	$ 84,000
Income tax rate	....	57%	30%
Foreign tax	....	$71,820	$25,200
U.S. tax ($53,090 plus 70% of $67,000)	$99,990	....	....

(b) Without taking this section into account, B would be allowed a foreign tax credit for 1972 of $97,020 ($71,820 + $25,200), but not to exceed the overall limitation under section 904(a)(2) of $99,990 ($99,990 × $167,750/$167,750). There would be no foreign income tax carried back to 1970 under section 904(d) since the allowable credit of $97,020 does not exceed the limitation of $99,990.

(c) Under paragraph (a)(2)(ii) of this section, the amount of the U.S. tax for 1972 with respect to foreign mineral income from sources within country X is $69,760, which is the greater of the amounts of tax determined under subparagraphs (1) and (2):

(1) U.S. tax on total taxable income in excess of U.S. tax on taxable income excluding foreign mineral income from country X (determined under paragraph (a)(2)(ii)(a) of this section):

U.S. tax on total taxable income	$99,990
Less U.S. tax on taxable income other than foreign mineral income from country X:	
Foreign mineral income from country Y	$100,000
Intangible drilling and development costs	9,000
Percentage depletion (22% of $100,000, but not to exceed 50% of $91,000)	22,000

Adjusted gross income	69,000
Other deductions	2,250
Personal exemption	750
Taxable income	66,000
U.S. tax ($26,390 plus 64% of $6,000)	$30,230
Excess tax	69,760

(2) U.S. tax on foreign mineral income from country X (determined under paragraph (a)(2)(ii)(b) of this section):

Foreign mineral income from country X	$150,000
Intangible drilling and development costs	16,000
Percentage depletion (22% of $150,000, but not to exceed 50% of $134,000)	33,000
Adjusted gross income	101,000
Other deductions	....
Taxable income	101,000
U.S. tax ($53,090 plus 70% of excess over $100,000)	53,790

(d) Under paragraph (a)(2)(iii) of this section, and by applying the principles of paragraph (a)(2)(ii)(a) of this section, the amount of the U.S. tax which would be computed for 1972 (without regard to section 613) with respect to foreign mineral income from sources within country X is $87,920, which is the excess of the U.S. tax ($127,990) determined under subparagraph (1) over the U.S. tax ($40,070) determined under subparagraph (2):

(1) U.S. tax on total taxable income determined without regard to section 613:

Reg. § 1.901-3(d)

48,844 Income from Sources Without the United States

See p. 20,601 for regulations not amended to reflect law changes

Total income	$250,000
Intangible drilling and development costs	25,000
Cost depletion	15,000
Adjusted gross income	210,000
Other deductions	2,250
Personal exemption	750
Taxable income	207,000
U.S. tax ($53,090 plus 70% of $107,000)	127,990

(2) U.S. tax on total taxable income other than foreign mineral income from country X, determined without regard to section 613:

Foreign mineral income from country Y	$100,000
Intangible drilling and development costs	9,000
Cost depletion	7,000
Adjusted gross income	84,000
Other deductions	2,250
Personal exemption	750
Taxable income	81,000
U.S. tax ($39,390 plus 68% of $1,000)	40,070

(e) Under paragraph (a)(2)(i) of this section, the amount of income tax paid to country X for 1972 with respect to foreign mineral income from sources within such country is $71,820. This is the amount determined under both (a) and (b) of paragraph (a)(2)(i) of this section, since, in this case, there is no income from sources within country X other than foreign mineral income, and there are no deductions allowed under the law of country X which are not allocable to such foreign mineral income.

(f) Pursuant to paragraph (a)(1) of this section, the foreign income tax with respect to foreign mineral income from sources within country X which is allowable as a credit against the U.S. tax for 1972 is reduced to $69,760, determined as follows:

Foreign income tax paid to country X on foreign mineral income		$71,820
Less reduction under sec. 901(e):		
Smaller of $71,820 (tax paid to country X on foreign mineral income) or $87,920 (U.S. tax on foreign mineral income from sources within country X, as determined under par. (d) of this example)	$71,820	
Less: U.S. tax on foreign mineral income from sources within country X, determined under par. (c) of this example	69,760	2,060

Foreign income tax of country X allowable as a credit	69,760

(g) Under paragraph (a)(2)(ii) of this section, the amount of the U.S. tax for 1972 with respect to foreign mineral income from sources within country Y is $48,280, which is the greater of the amounts of tax determined under subparagraphs (1) and (2):

(1) U.S. tax on total taxable income in excess of U.S. tax on taxable income excluding foreign mineral income from country Y (determined under paragraph (a)(2)(ii)(a) of this section):

U.S. tax on total taxable income		$99,990
Less U.S. tax on taxable income other than foreign mineral income from country Y:		
Foreign mineral income from country X	$150,000	
Intangible drilling and development costs	16,000	
Percentage depletion (22% of $150,000, but not to exceed 50% of $134,000)	33,000	
Adjusted gross income	101,000	
Other deductions	2,250	
Personal exemption	750	
Taxable income	98,000	
U.S. tax ($46,190 plus 69% of $8,000)		51,710
Excess tax		48,280

(2) U.S. tax on foreign mineral income from country Y (determined under paragraph (a)(2)(ii)(b) of this section):

Foreign mineral income from country Y		$100,000
Intangible drilling and development costs		9,000
Percentage depletion (22% of $100,000, but not to exceed 50% of $91,000)		$22,000
Adjusted gross income		69,000
Other deductions		
Taxable income		69,000
U.S. tax ($26,390 plus 64% of $9,000)		32,150

(h) Under paragraph (a)(2)(iii) of this section, and by applying the principles of paragraph (a)(2)(ii)(a) of this section, the amount of the U.S. tax which would be computed for 1972 (without regard to section 613) with respect to foreign mineral income from sources within country Y is $58,800, which is the excess of the U.S. tax ($127,990) determined under paragraph (d)(1) of this example over the U.S. tax ($69,190) on total taxable income other than foreign mineral income

Reg. § 1.901-3(d)

Income from Sources Without the United States

See p. 20,601 for regulations not amended to reflect law changes

from country Y, determined without regard to section 613, as follows:

Foreign mineral income from country X	$150,000
Intangible drilling and development costs	16,000
Cost depletion	8,000
Adjusted gross income	126,000
Other deductions	2,250
Personal exemption	750
Taxable income	123,000
U.S. tax ($53,090 plus 70% of $23,000)	69,190

(i) Under paragraph (a)(2)(i) of this section, the amount of income tax paid to country Y for 1972 with respect to foreign mineral income from sources within such country is $25,200. This is the amount determined under both (a) and (b) of paragraph (a)(2)(i) of this section, since, in this case, there is no income from sources within country Y other than foreign mineral income, and there are no deductions allowed under the law of country Y which are not allocable to such foreign mineral income.

(j) Pursuant to paragraph (a)(1) of this section, the foreign income tax with respect to foreign mineral income from sources within country Y which is allowable as a credit against the U.S. tax for 1972 is not reduced from $25,200, as follows:

Foreign income tax paid to country Y on foreign mineral income		$25,200
Less reduction under sec. 901(e):		
Smaller of $25,200 (tax paid to country Y on foreign mineral income) or $58,800 (U.S. tax on foreign mineral income from sources within country Y, as determined under par. (h) of this example)	$25,200	
Less: U.S. tax on foreign mineral income from sources within country Y, as determined under par. (g) of this example	48,280	......
Foreign income tax of country Y allowable as a credit		25,200

(k) After taking this section into account, B is allowed a foreign tax credit for 1972 of $94,960 ($69,760 + $25,200), but not to exceed the overall limitation under section 904(a)(2) of $99,990 ($99,990 × $167,750/$167,750). There would be no foreign income tax carried back to 1970 under section 904(d) since the allowable credit of $94,960 does not exceed the limitation of $99,990.

Example (7). (a) P, a domestic corporation using the calendar year as the taxable year, is an operator mining for iron ore in foreign country X. For 1971, P's gross income under chapter 1 of the Code is $100,000, all of which is foreign mineral income from a property in country X and is subject to the allowance for depletion. For 1971, cost depletion amounts to $5,000 for purposes of the tax of both countries, and only cost depletion is allowed as a deduction under the law of country X. It is assumed that deductions (other than for depletion) attributable to the mineral property in country X amount to $8,000, and these deductions are allowable under the law of both countries. Based upon the facts assumed, the income tax paid to country X on such foreign mineral income is $39,150, and the U.S. tax on such income before allowance of the foreign tax credit is $37,440 determined as follows:

	U.S. Tax	X Tax
Foreign mineral income	$100,000	$100,000
Less:		
Percentage depletion (14% of $100,000, but not to exceed 50% of $92,000)	14,000	......
Cost depletion	......	5,000
Other deductions	8,000	8,000
Taxable income	78,000	87,000
Income tax rate	48%	45%
Tax	$37,440	$39,150

(b) Without taking this section into account, P would be allowed a foreign tax credit for 1971 of $37,440 ($37,440 × $78,000/$78,000), and foreign income tax in the amount of $1,710 ($39,150 less $37,440) would first be carried back to 1969 under section 904(d).

(c) Pursuant to paragraph (a)(1) of this section, however, the foreign income tax allowable as a credit against the U.S. tax is reduced to $37,440, determined as follows:

Foreign income tax paid on foreign mineral income	$39,150
Less reduction under sec. 901(e):	
Smaller of $39,150 (tax paid to country X on foreign mineral income) or $41,760 (U.S. tax on foreign mineral income of $87,000 ($87,000 × 48%), determined by deducting cost depletion of $5,000 in lieu of percentage depletion of $14,000)	$39,150

Reg. § 1.901-3(d)

48,846 Income from Sources Without the United States
See p. 20,601 for regulations not amended to reflect law changes

Less: U.S. tax on foreign mineral income (before credit).........	37,440	1,710
Foreign income tax allowable as a credit		37,440

(d) After taking this section into account, P is allowed a foreign tax credit for 1971 of $37,440 ($37,440 × $78,000/$78,000), but no foreign income tax is carried back to 1969 under section 904(d) since the allowable credit of $37,440 does not exceed the limitation of $37,440.

Example (8). (a) The facts are the same as in example (7), except that P is assumed to have received dividends for 1971 of $25,000 from R, a foreign corporation incorporated in country X which is not a less developed country corporation within the meaning of section 902(d). Income tax of $2,500 ($25,000 × 10%) on such dividends is withheld at the source in country X. It is assumed that P is deemed under section 902(a)(1) and § 1.902-1(h) to have paid income tax of $22,500 to country X in respect of such dividends and that under paragraphs (a)(2)(i) and (b)(2)(i) of this section such dividends are deemed to be attributable to foreign mineral income from sources in country X and that such tax is deemed to be paid with respect to such foreign mineral income. Based upon the facts assumed, the U.S. tax on the foreign mineral income from sources in country X is $60,240 before allowance of the foreign tax credit, determined as follows:

Foreign mineral income from country X:		
Income from mining property	$100,000	
Dividends from R	25,000	
Sec. 78 dividend .	22,500	$147,500
Less:		
Percentage depletion (14% of $100,000, but not to exceed 50% of $92,000)		$ 14,000
Other deductions		8,000
Taxable income		125,500
Income tax rate		48%
U.S. tax		$ 60,240

(b) Without taking this section into account, P would be allowed a foreign tax credit for 1971 of $60,240 ($60,240 × $125,500/$125,500), and foreign income tax in the amount of $3,910 ([39,150 + $22,500 + $2,500] less $60,240) would first be carried back to 1969 under section 904(d).

(c) Pursuant to paragraph (a)(1) of this section, however, the foreign income tax allowable as a credit against the U.S. tax is reduced from $64,150 to $60,240, determined as follows:

Foreign income tax paid, and deemed to be paid, to country X on foreign mineral income ($39,150 + $22,500 + $2,500).........................		$64,150
Less reduction under section 901(e): Smaller of $64,150 (tax paid and deemed paid to country X on foreign mineral income) or $64,560 (U.S. tax on foreign mineral income of $134,500 ($134,500 × 48%), determined by deducting cost depletion of $5,000 in lieu of percentage depletion of $14,000)	$64,150	
Less: U.S. tax on foreign mineral income (before credit)	60,240	$3,910
Foreign income tax allowable as a credit		60,240

(d) After taking this section into account, P is allowed a foreign tax credit for 1971 of $60,240 ($60,240 × $125,500/$125,500), but no foreign income tax is carried back to 1969 under section 904(d) since the allowable credit of $60,240 does not exceed the limitation of $60,240.

[Reg. § 1.901-3.]

☐ [*T.D. 7294, 11-29-73. Amended by T.D. 7481, 4-15-77.*]

[Reg. § 1.902-0]

§ 1.902-0. Outline of regulations provisions for section 902.—This section lists the provisions under section 902.

§ 1.902-1. Credit for domestic corporate shareholder of a foreign corporation for foreign income taxes paid by the foreign corporation.

(a) Definitions and special effective date.

(1) Domestic shareholder.

(2) First-tier corporation.

(3) Second-tier corporation.

(4) Third-tier corporation.

(5) Example.

(6) Upper—and lower-tier corporations.

(7) Foreign income taxes.

(8) Post-1986 foreign income taxes.

(i) In general.

(ii) Distributions out of earnings and profits accumulated by a lower-tier corporation in its taxable years beginning before January 1, 1987, and included in the gross income of an upper-tier

Reg. § 1.902-0

Income from Sources Without the United States

See p. 20,601 for regulations not amended to reflect law changes

corporation in its taxable year beginning after December 31, 1986.

(iii) Foreign income taxes paid or accrued with respect to high withholding tax interest.

(9) Post-1986 undistributed earnings.

(i) In general.

(ii) Distributions out of earnings and profits accumulated by a lower-tier corporation in its taxable years beginning before January 1, 1987, and included in the gross income of an upper-tier corporation in its taxable year beginning after December 31, 1986.

(iii) Reduction for foreign income taxes paid or accrued.

(iv) Special allocations.

(10) Pre-1987 accumulated profits.

(i) Definition.

(ii) Computation of pre-1987 accumulated profits.

(iii) Foreign income taxes attributable to pre-1987 accumulated profits.

(11) Dividend.

(12) Dividend received.

(13) Special effective date.

(i) Rule.

(ii) Example.

(b) Computation of foreign income taxes deemed paid by a domestic shareholder, first-tier corporation, and second-tier corporation.

(1) General rule.

(2) Allocation rule for dividends attributable to post-1986 undistributed earnings and pre-1987 accumulated profits.

(i) Portion of dividend out of post-1986 undistributed earnings.

(ii) Portion of dividend out of pre-1987 accumulated profits.

(3) Dividends paid out of pre-1987 accumulated profits.

(4) Deficits in accumulated earnings and profits.

(5) Examples.

(c) Special rules.

(1) Separate computations required for dividends from each first-tier and lower-tier corporation.

(i) Rule.

(ii) Example.

(2) Section 78 gross-up.

(i) Foreign income taxes deemed paid by a domestic shareholder.

(ii) Foreign income taxes deemed paid by an upper-tier corporation.

(iii) Example.

(3) Creditable foreign income taxes.

(4) Foreign mineral income.

(5) Foreign taxes paid or accrued in connection with the purchase or sale of certain oil and gas.

(6) Foreign oil and gas extraction income.

(7) United States shareholders of controlled foreign corporations.

(8) Credit for foreign taxes deemed paid in a section 304 transaction.

(9) Effect of section 482 adjustments on post-1986 foreign income taxes and post-1986 undistributed earnings.

(d) Dividends from controlled foreign corporations.

(1) General rule.

(2) Look-through.

(i) Dividends.

(ii) Coordination with section 960.

(3) Dividends distributed out of earnings accumulated before a controlled foreign corporation became a controlled foreign corporation.

(i) General rule.

(ii) Dividend distributions out of earnings and profits for a year during which a shareholder that is currently a more-than-90-percent United States shareholder of a controlled foreign corporation was not a United States shareholder of the controlled foreign corporation.

(e) Information to be furnished.

(f) Examples.

(g) Effective date.

§ 1.902-2. Treatment of deficits in post-1986 undistributed earnings and pre-1987 accumulated profits of a first-, second-, or third-tier corporation for purposes of computing an amount of foreign taxes deemed paid § 1.902-1.

(a) Carryback of deficits in post-1986 undistributed earnings of a first-, second-, or third-tier corporation to pre-effective date taxable years.

(1) Rule.

(2) Examples.

(b) Carryforward of deficits in pre-1987 accumulated profits of a first-, second-, or third-tier corporation to post-1986 undistributed earnings for purposes of section 902.

(1) General rule.

(2) Effect of pre-effective date deficit.

(3) Examples.

48,847

Reg. § 1.902-0

§ 1.902-3. Credit for domestic corporate shareholder of a foreign corporation for foreign income taxes paid with respect to accumulated profits of taxable years of the foreign corporation beginning before January 1, 1987.

(a) Definitions.

(1) Domestic shareholder.

(2) First-tier corporation.

(3) Second-tier corporation.

(4) Third-tier corporation.

(5) Foreign income taxes.

(6) Dividend.

(7) Dividend received.

(b) Domestic shareholder owning stock in a first-tier corporation.

(1) In general.

(2) Amount of foreign taxes deemed paid by a domestic shareholder.

(c) First-tier corporation owning stock in a second-tier corporation.

(1) In general.

(2) Amount of foreign taxes deemed paid by a first-tier corporation.

(d) Second-tier corporation owning stock in a third-tier corporation.

(1) In general.

(2) Amount of foreign taxes deemed paid by a second-tier corporation.

(e) Determination of accumulated profits of a foreign corporation.

(f) Taxes paid on or with respect to accumulated profits of a foreign corporation.

(g) Determination of earnings and profits of a foreign corporation.

(1) Taxable year to which section 963 does not apply.

(2) Taxable year to which section 963 applies.

(3) Time and manner of making choice.

(4) Determination by district director.

(h) Source of income from first-tier corporation and country to which tax is deemed paid.

(1) Source of income.

(2) Country to which taxes deemed paid.

(i) United Kingdom income taxes paid with respect to royalties.

(j) Information to be furnished.

(k) Illustrations.

(l) Effective date.

§ 1.902-4. Rules for distributions attributable to accumulated profits for taxable years in which a first-tier corporation was a less developed country corporation.

(a) In general.

(b) Combined distributions.

(c) Distributions of a first-tier corporation attributable to certain distributions from second- or third-tier corporations.

(d) Illustrations. [Reg. § 1.902-0.]

☐ [T.D. 8708, 1-6-97.]

[Reg. § 1.902-1]

§ 1.902-1. Credit for domestic corporate shareholder of a foreign corporation for foreign income taxes paid by the foreign corporation.—(a) *Definitions and special effective date.* For purposes of section 902, this section, and § 1.902-2, the definitions provided in paragraphs (a)(1) through (12) of this section and the special effective date of paragraph (a)(13) of this section apply.

(1) *Domestic shareholder.* In the case of dividends received by a domestic corporation from a foreign corporation after December 31, 1986, the term domestic shareholder means a domestic corporation, other than an S corporation as defined in section 1361(a), that owns at least 10 percent of the voting stock of the foreign corporation at the time the domestic corporation receives a dividend from that foreign corporation.

(2) *First-tier corporation.* In the case of dividends received by a domestic shareholder from a foreign corporation in a taxable year beginning after December 31, 1986, the term first-tier corporation means a foreign corporation, at least 10 percent of the voting stock of which is owned by a domestic shareholder at the time the domestic shareholder receives a dividend from that foreign corporation. The term first-tier corporation also includes a DISC or former DISC, but only with respect to dividends from the DISC or former DISC that are treated under sections 861(a)(2)(D) and 862(a)(2) as income from sources without the United States.

(3) *Second-tier corporation.* In the case of dividends paid to a first-tier corporation by a foreign corporation in a taxable year beginning after December 31, 1986, the foreign corporation is a second-tier corporation if, at the time a first-tier corporation receives a dividend from that foreign corporation, the first-tier corporation owns at least 10 percent of the foreign corporation's voting stock and the product of the following equals at least 5 percent—

(i) The percentage of voting stock owned by the domestic shareholder in the first-tier corporation; multiplied by

Reg. § 1.902-1(a)(1)

(ii) The percentage of voting stock owned by the first-tier corporation in the second-tier corporation.

(4) *Third-tier corporation.* In the case of dividends paid to a second-tier corporation by a foreign corporation in a taxable year beginning after December 31, 1986, a foreign corporation is a third-tier corporation if, at the time a second-tier corporation receives a dividend from that foreign corporation, the second-tier corporation owns at least 10 percent of the foreign corporation's voting stock and the product of the following equals at least 5 percent—

(i) The percentage of voting stock owned by the domestic shareholder in the first-tier corporation; multiplied by

(ii) The percentage of voting stock owned by the first-tier corporation in the second-tier corporation; multiplied by

(iii) The percentage of voting stock owned by the second-tier corporation in the third-tier corporation.

(5) *Example.* The following example illustrates the ownership requirements of paragraphs (a)(1) through (4) of this section:

Example. (i) Domestic corporation M owns 30 percent of the voting stock of foreign corporation A on January 1, 1991, and for all periods thereafter. Corporation A owns 40 percent of the voting stock of foreign corporation B on January 1, 1991, and continues to own that stock until June 1, 1991, when Corporation A sells its stock in Corporation B. Both Corporation A and Corporation B use the calendar year as the taxable year. Corporation B pays a dividend out of its post-1986 undistributed earnings to Corporation A, which Corporation A receives on February 16, 1991. Corporation A pays a dividend out of its post-1986 undistributed earnings to Corporation M, which Corporation M receives on January 20, 1992. Corporation M uses a fiscal year ending on June 30 as the taxable year.

(ii) On February 16, 1991, when Corporation B pays a dividend to Corporation A, Corporation M satisfies the 10-percent stock ownership requirement of paragraphs (a)(1) and (2) of this section with respect to Corporation A. Therefore, Corporation A is a first-tier corporation within the meaning of paragraph (a)(2) of this section and Corporation M is a domestic shareholder of Corporation A within the meaning of paragraph (a)(1) of this section. Also on February 16, 1991, Corporation B is a second-tier corporation within the meaning of paragraph (a)(3) of this section because Corporation A owns at least 10 percent of its voting stock, and the percentage of voting stock owned by Corporation M in Corporation A on February 16, 1991 (30 percent) multiplied by the percentage of voting stock owned by Corporation A in Corporation B on February 16, 1991 (40 percent) equals 12 percent. Corporation A shall be deemed to have paid foreign income taxes of Corporation B with respect to the dividend received from Corporation B on February 16, 1991.

(iii) On January 20, 1992, Corporation M satisfies the 10-percent stock ownership requirement of paragraphs (a)(1) and (2) of this section with respect to Corporation A. Therefore, Corporation A is a first-tier corporation within the meaning of paragraph (a)(2) of this section and Corporation M is a domestic shareholder within the meaning of paragraph (a)(1) of this section. Accordingly, for its taxable year ending on June 30, 1992, Corporation M is deemed to have paid a portion of the post-1986 foreign income taxes paid, accrued, or deemed to be paid, by Corporation A. Those taxes will include taxes paid by Corporation B that were deemed paid by Corporation A with respect to the dividend paid by Corporation B to Corporation A on February 16, 1991, even though Corporation B is no longer a second-tier corporation with respect to Corporations A and M on January 20, 1992, and has not been a second-tier corporation with respect to Corporations A and M at any time during the taxable years of Corporations A and M that include January 20, 1992.

(6) *Upper—and lower-tier corporations.* In the case of a third-tier corporation, the term upper-tier corporation means a first—or second-tier corporation. In the case of a second-tier corporation, the term upper-tier corporation means a first-tier corporation. In the case of a first-tier corporation, the term lower-tier corporation means a second—or third-tier corporation. In the case of a second-tier corporation, the term lower-tier corporation means a third-tier corporation.

(7) *Foreign income taxes.* The term foreign income taxes means income, war profits, and excess profits taxes as defined in § 1.901-2(a), and taxes included in the term income, war profits, and excess profits taxes by reason of section 903, that are imposed by a foreign country or a possession of the United States, including any such taxes deemed paid by a foreign corporation under this section. Foreign income, war profits, and excess profits taxes shall not include amounts excluded from the definition of those taxes pursuant to section 901 and the regulations under that section. See also paragraphs (c)(4) and (5) of this section (concerning foreign taxes paid with respect to foreign mineral income and in connection with the purchase or sale of oil and gas).

Reg. § 1.902-1(a)(7)

(8) *Post-1986 foreign income taxes*—(i) *In general*. Except as provided in paragraphs (a)(10) and (13) of this section, the term post-1986 foreign income taxes of a foreign corporation means the sum of the foreign income taxes paid, accrued, or deemed paid in the taxable year of the foreign corporation in which it distributes a dividend plus the foreign income taxes paid, accrued, or deemed paid in the foreign corporation's prior taxable years beginning after December 31, 1986, to the extent the foreign taxes were not paid or deemed paid by the foreign corporation on or with respect to earnings that in prior taxable years were distributed to, or otherwise included (e.g., under sections 304, 367(b), 551, 951(a), 1248 or 1293) in the income of, a foreign or domestic shareholder. Except as provided in paragraph (b)(4) of this section, foreign taxes paid or deemed paid by the foreign corporation on or with respect to earnings that weredistributed or otherwise removed from post-1986 undistributed earnings in prior post-1986 taxable years shall be removed from post-1986 foreign income taxes regardless of whether the shareholder is eligible to compute an amount of foreign taxes deemed paid under section 902, and regardless of whether the shareholder in fact chose to credit foreign income taxes under section 901 for the year of the distribution or inclusion. Thus, if an amount is distributed or deemed distributed by a foreign corporation to a United States person that is not a domestic shareholder within the meaning of paragraph (a)(1) of this section (e.g., an individual or a corporation that owns less than 10% of the foreign corporation's voting stock), or to a foreign person that does not meet the definition of a first-or second-tier corporation under paragraph (a)(2) or (3) of this section, then although no foreign income taxes shall be deemed paid under section 902, foreign income taxes attributable to the distribution or deemed distribution that would have been deemed paid had the shareholder met the ownership requirements of paragraphs (a) (1) through (4) of this section shall be removed from post-1986 foreign income taxes. Further, if a domestic shareholder chooses to deduct foreign taxes paid or accrued for the taxable year of the distribution or inclusion, it shall nonetheless be deemed to have paid a proportionate share of the foreign corporation's post-1986 foreign income taxes under section 902(a), and the foreign taxes deemed paid must be removed from post-1986 foreign income taxes. In the case of a foreign corporation the foreign income taxes of which are determined based on an accounting period of less than one year, the term year means that accounting period. See sections 441(b)(3) and 443.

(ii) *Distributions out of earnings and profits accumulated by a lower-tier corporation in its taxable years beginning before January 1, 1987, and included in the gross income of an upper-tier corporation in its taxable year beginning after December 31, 1986*. Post-1986 foreign income taxes shall include foreign income taxes that are deemed paid by an upper-tier corporation with respect to distributions from a lower-tier corporation out of non-previously taxed pre-1987 accumulated profits, as defined in paragraph (a)(10) of this section, that are received by an upper-tier corporation in any taxable year of the upper-tier corporation beginning after December 31, 1986, provided the upper-tier corporation's earnings and profits in that year are included in its post-1986 undistributed earnings under paragraph (a)(9) of this section. Foreign income taxes deemed paid with respect to a distribution of pre-1987 accumulated profits shall be translated from the functional currency of the lower-tier corporation into dollars at the spot exchange rate in effect on the date of the distribution. To determine the character of the earnings and profits and associated taxes for foreign tax credit limitation purposes, see section 904 and § 1.904-7(a).

(iii) *Foreign income taxes paid or accrued with respect to high withholding tax interest*. Post-1986 foreign income taxes shall not include foreign income taxes paid or accrued by a noncontrolled section 902 corporation (as defined in section 904(d)(2)(E)(i)) with respect to high withholding tax interest (as defined in section 904(d)(2)(B)) to the extent the foreign tax rate imposed on such interest exceeds 5 percent. See section 904(d)(2)(E)(ii) and § 1.904-4(g)(2)(iii). The reduction in foreign income taxes paid or accrued by the amount of tax in excess of 5 percent imposed on high withholding tax interest income must be computed in functional currency before foreign income taxes are translated into U.S. dollars and included in post-1986 foreign income taxes.

(9) *Post-1986 undistributed earnings*—(i) *In general*. Except as provided in paragraphs (a)(10) and (13) of this section, the term post-1986 undistributed earnings means the amount of the earnings and profits of a foreign corporation (computed in accordance with sections 964(a) and 986) accumulated in taxable years of the foreign corporation beginning after December 31, 1986, determined as of the close of the taxable year of the foreign corporation in which it distributes a dividend. Post-1986 undistributed earnings shall not be reduced by reason of any earnings distributed or otherwise included in income, for example under section 304, 367(b), 551, 951(a), 1248 or 1293, during the taxable year. Post-1986 undis-

Reg. § 1.902-1(a)(8)

tributed earnings shall be reduced to account for distributions or deemed distributions that reduced earnings and profits and inclusions that resulted in previously-taxed amounts described in section 959(c)(1) and (2) or section 1293(c) in prior taxable years beginning after December 31, 1986. Thus, post-1986 undistributed earnings shall not be reduced to the extent of the ratable share of a controlled foreign corporation's subpart F income, as defined in section 952, attributable to a shareholder that is not a United States shareholder within the meaning of section 951(b) or section 953(c)(1)(A), because that amount has not been included in a shareholder's gross income. Post-1986 undistributed earnings shall be reduced as provided herein regardless of whether any shareholder is deemed to have paid any foreign taxes, and regardless of whether any domestic shareholder chose to claim a foreign tax credit under section 901(a) for the year of the distribution. For rules on carrybacks and carryforwards of deficits and their effect on post-1986 undistributed earnings, see § 1.902-2. In the case of a foreign corporation the foreign income taxes of which are computed based on an accounting period of less than one year, the term year means that accounting period. See sections 441(b)(3) and 443.

(ii) *Distributions out of earnings and profits accumulated by a lower-tier corporation in its taxable years beginning before January 1, 1987, and included in the gross income of an upper-tier corporation in its taxable year beginning after December 31, 1986.* Distributions by a lower-tier corporation out of non-previously taxed pre-1987 accumulated profits, as defined in paragraph (a) (10) of this section, that are received by an upper-tier corporation in any taxable year of the upper-tier corporation beginning after December 31, 1986, shall be treated as post-1986 undistributed earnings of the upper-tier corporation, provided the upper-tier corporation's earnings and profits for that year are included in its post-1986 undistributed earnings under paragraph (a)(9)(i) of this section. To determine the character of the earnings and profits and associated taxes for foreign tax credit limitation purposes, see section 904 and § 1.904-7(a).

(iii) *Reduction for foreign income taxes paid or accrued.* In computing post-1986 undistributed earnings, earnings and profits shall be reduced by foreign income taxes paid or accrued regardless of whether the taxes are creditable. Thus, earnings and profits shall be reduced by foreign income taxes paid with respect to high withholding tax interest even though a portion of the taxes is not creditable pursuant to section 904(d)(2)(E)(ii) and is not included in post-1986 foreign income taxes under paragraph (a)(8)(iii) of this section. Earnings and profits of an upper-tier corporation, however, shall not be reduced by foreign income taxes paid by a lower-tier corporation and deemed to have been paid by the upper-tier corporation.

(iv) *Special allocations.* The term post-1986 undistributed earnings means the total amount of the earnings of the corporation determined at the corporate level. Special allocations of earnings and taxes to particular shareholders, whether required or permitted by foreign law or a shareholder agreement, shall be disregarded. If, however, the Commissioner establishes that there is an agreement to pay dividends only out of earnings in the separate categories for passive or high withholding tax interest income, then only taxes imposed on passive or high withholding tax interest earnings shall be treated as related to the dividend. See § 1.904-6(a)(2).

(10) *Pre-1987 accumulated profits*—(i) *Definition.* The term pre-1987 accumulated profits means the amount of the earnings and profits of a foreign corporation computed in accordance with section 902 and attributable to its taxable years beginning before January 1, 1987. If the special effective date of paragraph (a)(13) of this section applies, pre-1987 accumulated profits also includes any earnings and profits (computed in accordance with sections 964(a) and 986) attributable to the foreign corporation's taxable years beginning after December 31, 1986, but before the first day of the first taxable year of the foreign corporation in which the ownership requirements of section 902(c)(3)(B) and paragraphs (a)(1) through (4) of this section are met with respect to that corporation.

(ii) *Computation of pre-1987 accumulated profits.* Pre-1987 accumulated profits must be computed under United States principles governing the computation of earnings and profits. Pre-1987 accumulated profits are determined at the corporate level. Special allocations of accumulated profits and taxes to particular shareholders with respect to distributions of pre-1987 accumulated profits in taxable years beginning after December 31, 1986, whether required or permitted by foreign law or a shareholder agreement, shall be disregarded. Pre-1987 accumulated profits of a particular year shall be reduced by amounts distributed from those accumulated profits or otherwise included in income from those accumulated profits, for example under sections 304, 367(b), 551, 951(a), 1248 or 1293. If a deficit in post-1986 undistributed earnings is carried back to offset pre-1987 accumulated profits, pre-1987 accumulated profits of a particular taxable year shall be

Reg. § 1.902-1(a)(10)

reduced by the amount of the deficit carried back to that year. See § 1.902-2. The amount of a distribution out of pre-1987 accumulated profits, and the amount of foreign income taxes deemed paid under section 902, shall be determined and translated into United States dollars by applying the law as in effect prior to the effective date of the Tax Reform Act of 1986. See §§ 1.902-3, 1.902-4 and 1.964-1.

(iii) *Foreign income taxes attributable to pre-1987 accumulated profits.* The term pre-1987 foreign income taxes means any foreign income taxes paid, accrued, or deemed paid by a foreign corporation on or with respect to its pre-1987 accumulated profits. Pre-1987 foreign income taxes of a particular year shall be reduced by the amount of taxes paid or deemed paid by the foreign corporation on or with respect to amounts distributed or otherwise included in income from pre-1987 accumulated profits of that year. Thus, pre-1987 foreign income taxes shall be reduced by the amount of taxes deemed paid by a domestic shareholder (regardless of whether the shareholder chose to credit foreign income taxes under section 901 for the year of the distribution or inclusion) or a first-tier or second-tier corporation, and by the amount of taxes that would have been deemed paid had any other shareholder been eligible to compute an amount of foreign taxes deemed paid under section 902. Foreign income taxes deemed paid with respect to a distribution of pre-1987 accumulated profits shall be translated from the functional currency of the distributing corporation into United States dollars at the spot exchange rate in effect on the date of the distribution.

(11) *Dividend.* For purposes of section 902, the definition of the term dividend in section 316 and the regulations under that section applies. Thus, for example, distributions and deemed distributions under sections 302, 304, 305(b) and 367(b) that are treated as dividends within the meaning of section 301(c)(1) also are dividends for purposes of section 902. In addition, the term dividend includes deemed dividends under sections 551 and 1248, but not deemed inclusions under sections 951(a) and 1293. For rules concerning excess distributions from section 1291 funds that are treated as dividends solely for foreign tax credit purposes, (see Regulation Project INTL-656-87 published in 1992-1 C.B. 1124; see § 601.601(d)(2)(ii)(*b*) of this chapter).

(12) *Dividend received.* A dividend shall be considered received for purposes of section 902 when the cash or other property is unqualifiedly made subject to the demands of the distributee. See § 1.301-1(b). A dividend also is considered received for purposes of section 902 when it is deemed received under section 304, 367(b), 551, or 1248.

(13) *Special effective date*—(i) *Rule.* If the first day on which the ownership requirements of section 902(c)(3)(B) and paragraphs (a)(1) through (4) of this section are met with respect to a foreign corporation, without regard to whether a dividend is distributed, is in a taxable year of the foreign corporation beginning after December 31, 1986, then—

(A) The post-1986 undistributed earnings and post-1986 foreign income taxes of the foreign corporation shall be determined by taking into account only taxable years beginning on and after the first day of the first taxable year of the foreign corporation in which the ownership requirements are met, including subsequent taxable years in which the ownership requirements of section 902(c)(3)(B) and paragraphs (a)(1) through (4) of this section are not met; and

(B) Earnings and profits accumulated prior to the first day of the first taxable year of the foreign corporation in which the ownership requirements of section 902(c)(3)(13) and paragraphs (a) (1) through (4) of this section are met shall be considered pre-1987 accumulated profits.

(ii) *Example.* The following example illustrates the special effective date rules of this paragraph (a)(13):

Example. As of December 31, 1991, and since its incorporation, foreign corporation A has owned 100 percent of the stock of foreign corporation B. Corporation B is not a controlled foreign corporation. Corporation B uses the calendar year as its taxable year, and its functional currency is the u. Assume 1u equals $1 at all relevant times. On April 1, 1992, Corporation B pays a 200u dividend to Corporation A and the ownership requirements of section 902(c)(3)(B) and paragraphs (a) (1) through (4) of this section are not met at that time. On July 1, 1992, domestic corporation M purchases 10 percent of the Corporation B stock from Corporation A and, for the first time, Corporation B meets the ownership requirements of section 902(c)(3)(B) and paragraph (a) (2) of this section. Corporation M uses the calendar year as its taxable year. Corporation B does not distribute any dividends to Corporation M during 1992. For its taxable year ending December 31, 1992, Corporation B has 500u of earnings and profits (after foreign taxes but before taking into account the 200u distribution to Corporation A) and pays 100u of foreign income taxes that is equal to $100. Pursuant to paragraph (a)(13)(i) of this section, Corporation

Reg. § 1.902-1(a)(11)

Income from Sources Without the United States 48,853
See p. 20,601 for regulations not amended to reflect law changes

B's post-1986 undistributed earnings and post-1986 foreign income taxes will include earnings and profits and foreign income taxes attributable to Corporation B's entire 1992 taxable year and all taxable years thereafter. Thus, the April 1, 1992, dividend to Corporation A will reduce post-1986 undistributed earnings to 300u (500u − 200u) under paragraph (a)(9)(i) of this section. The foreign income taxes attributable to the amount distributed as a dividend to Corporation A will not be creditable because Corporation A is not a domestic shareholder. Post-1986 foreign income taxes, however, will be reduced by the amount of foreign taxes attributable to the dividend. Thus, as of the beginning of 1993, Corporation B has $60 ($100 − [$100 x 40% (200u/500u)]) of post-1986 foreign income taxes. See paragraphs (a)(8)(i) and (b)(1) of this section.

(b) *Computation of foreign income taxes deemed paid by a domestic shareholder, first-tier corporation, and second-tier corporation*—(1) *General rule.* If a foreign corporation pays a dividend in any taxable year out of post-1986 undistributed earnings to a shareholder that is a domestic shareholder or an upper-tier corporation at the time it receives the dividend, the recipient shall be deemed to have paid the same proportion of any post-1986 foreign income taxes paid, accrued or deemed paid by the distributing corporation on or with respect to post-1986 undistributed earnings which the amount of the dividend out of post-1986 undistributed earnings (determined without regard to the gross-up under section 78) bears to the amount of the distributing corporation's post-1986 undistributed earnings. An upper-tier corporation shall not be entitled to compute an amount of foreign taxes deemed paid on a dividend from a lower-tier corporation, however, unless the ownership requirements of paragraphs (a)(1) through (4) of this section are met at each tier at the time the upper-tier corporation receives the dividend. Foreign income taxes deemed paid by a domestic shareholder or an upper-tier corporation must be computed under the following formula:

$$\begin{array}{l}\text{Foreign income taxes}\\ \text{deemed paid by do-}\\ \text{mestic shareholder}\\ \text{(or upper-tier}\\ \text{corporation)}\end{array} = \begin{array}{l}\text{Post-1986 foreign in-}\\ \text{come taxes of first-}\\ \text{tier corporation (or}\\ \text{lower-tier}\\ \text{corporation)}\end{array} \times \frac{\text{Dividend paid to domestic shareholder (or upper-tier corporation) by first-tier corporation (or lower-tier corporation)}}{\text{Post-1986 undistributed earnings of first-tier corporation (or lower-tier corporation)}}$$

(2) *Allocation rule for dividends attributable to post-1986 undistributed earnings and pre-1987 accumulated profits*—(i) *Portion of dividend out of post-1986 undistributed earnings.* Dividends will be deemed to be paid first out of post-1986 undistributed earnings to the extent thereof. If dividends exceed post-1986 undistributed earnings and dividends are paid to more than one shareholder, then the dividend to each shareholder shall be deemed to be paid pro rata out of post-1986 undistributed earnings, computed as follows:

$$\begin{array}{l}\text{Portion of Dividend to a}\\ \text{Shareholder Attributable to}\\ \text{Post-1986 Undistributed}\\ \text{Earnings}\end{array} = \begin{array}{l}\text{Post-1986 Undistributed}\\ \text{Earnings}\end{array} \times \frac{\text{Dividend to Shareholder}}{\text{Total Dividends Paid To all Shareholders}}$$

(ii) *Portion of dividend out of pre-1987 accumulated profits.* After the portion of the dividend attributable to post-1986 undistributed earnings is determined under paragraph (b)(2)(i) of this section, the remainder of the dividend received by a shareholder is attributable to pre-1987 accumulated profits to the extent thereof. That part of the dividend attributable to pre-1987 accumulated profits will be treated as paid first from the most recently accumulated earnings and profits. See § 1.902-3. If dividends paid out of pre-1987 accumulated profits are attributable to more than one pre-1987 taxable year and are paid to more than one shareholder, then the dividend to each shareholder attributable to earnings and profits accumulated in a particular pre-1987 taxable year shall be deemed to be paid pro rata out of accumulated profits of that taxable year, computed as follows:

$$\begin{array}{l}\text{Portion of Dividend to a}\\ \text{Shareholder Attributable to}\\ \text{Accumulated Profits of a}\\ \text{Particular Pre-1987 Taxa-}\\ \text{ble Year}\end{array} = \begin{array}{l}\text{Dividend Paid Out of}\\ \text{Pre-1987 Accumulated}\\ \text{Profits with Respect to the}\\ \text{Particular Pre-1987 Taxa-}\\ \text{ble Year}\end{array} \times \frac{\text{Dividend to Shareholder}}{\text{Total Dividends Paid to all Shareholders}}$$

(3) *Dividends paid out of pre-1987 accumulated profits.* If dividends are paid by a first-tier corporation or a lower-tier corporation out of pre-1987 accumulated profits, the domestic shareholder or upper-tier corporation that receives the dividends shall be deemed to have paid foreign income taxes to the extent provided under section 902 and the regulations thereunder as in effect

Reg. § 1.902-1(b)(3)

prior to the effective date of the Tax Reform Act of 1986. See paragraphs (a)(10) and (13) of this section and §§ 1.902-3 and 1.902-4.

(4) *Deficits in accumulated earnings and profits.* No foreign income taxes shall be deemed paid with respect to a distribution from a foreign corporation out of current earnings and profits that is treated as a dividend under section 316(a)(2), and post-1986 foreign income taxes shall not be reduced, if as of the end of the taxable year in which the dividend is paid or accrued, the corporation has zero or a deficit in post-1986 undistributed earnings and the sum of current plus accumulated earnings and profits is zero or less than zero. The dividend shall reduce post-1986 undistributed earnings and accumulated earnings and profits.

(5) *Examples.* The following examples illustrate the rules of this paragraph (b):

Example 1. Domestic corporation M owns 100 percent of foreign corporation A. Both Corporation M and Corporation A use the calendar year as the taxable year, and Corporation A uses the u as its functional currency. Assume that 1u equals $1 at all relevant times. All of Corporation A's pre-1987 accumulated profits and post-1986 undistributed earnings are non-subpart F general limitation earnings and profits under section 904(d)(1)(I). As of December 31, 1992, Corporation A has 100u of post-1986 undistributed earnings and $40 of post-1986 foreign income taxes. For its 1986 taxable year, Corporation A has accumulated profits of 200u (net of foreign taxes) and paid 60u of foreign income taxes on those earnings. In 1992, Corporation A distributes 150u to Corporation M. Corporation A has 100u of post-1986 undistributed earnings and the dividend, therefore, is treated as paid out of post-1986 undistributed earnings to the extent of 100u. The first 100u distribution is from post-1986 undistributed earnings, and, because the distribution exhausts those earnings, Corporation M is deemed to have paid the entire amount of post-1986 foreign income taxes of Corporation A ($40). The remaining 50u dividend is treated as a dividend out of 1986 accumulated profits under paragraph (b) (2) of this section. Corporation M is deemed to have paid $15 (60u x 50u/200u, translated at the appropriate exchange rates) of Corporation A's foreign income taxes for 1986. As of January 1, 1993, Corporation A's post-1986 undistributed earnings and post-1986 foreign income taxes are 0. Corporation A has 150u of accumulated profits and 45u of foreign income taxes remaining in 1986.

Example 2. Domestic corporation M (incorporated on January 1, 1987) owns 100 percent of foreign corporation A (incorporated on January 1, 1987). Both Corporation M and Corporation A use the calendar year as the taxable year, and Corporation A uses the u as its functional currency. Assume that 1u equals $1 at all relevant times. Corporation A has no pre-1987 accumulated profits. All of Corporation A's post-1986 undistributed earnings are non-subpart F general limitation earnings and profits under section 904(d)(1)(I). On January 1, 1992, Corporation A has a deficit in accumulated earnings and profits and a deficit in post-1986 undistributed earnings of (200u). No foreign taxes have been paid with respect to post-1986 undistributed earnings. During 1992, Corporation A earns 100u (net of foreign taxes), pays $40 of foreign taxes on those earnings and distributes 50u to Corporation M. As of the end of 1992, Corporation A has a deficit of (100u) ((200u) post-1986 undistributed earnings + 100u current earnings and profits) in post-1986 undistributed earnings. Corporation A, however, has current earnings and profits of 100u. Therefore, the 50u distribution is treated as a dividend in its entirety under section 316(a)(2). Under paragraph (b)(4) of this section, Corporation M is not deemed to have paid any of the foreign taxes paid by Corporation A because post-1986 undistributed earnings and the sum of current plus accumulated earnings and profits are (100u). The dividend reduces both post-1986 undistributed earnings and accumulated earnings and profits. Therefore, as of January 1, 1993, Corporation A's post-1986 undistributed earnings are (150u) and its accumulated earnings and profits are (150u). Corporation A's post-1986 foreign income taxes at the start of 1993 are $40.

(c) *Special rules.*—(1) *Separate computations required for dividends from each first-tier and lower-tier corporation*—(i) *Rule.* If in a taxable year dividends are received by a domestic shareholder or an upper-tier corporation from two or more first-tier corporations or two or more lower-tier corporations, the foreign income taxes deemed paid by the domestic shareholder or the upper-tier corporation under sections 902(a) and (b) and paragraph (b) of this section shall be computed separately with respect to the dividends received from each first-tier corporation or lower-tier corporation. If a domestic shareholder receives dividend distributions from one or more first-tier corporations and in the same taxable year the first-tier corporation receives dividends from one or more lower-tier corporations, then the amount of foreign income taxes deemed paid shall be computed by starting with the lowest-tier corporation and working upward.

(ii) *Example.* The following example illustrates the application of this paragraph (c)(1):

Reg. § 1.902-1(b)(4)

Example. P, a domestic corporation, owns 40 percent of the voting stock of foreign corporation S. S owns 30 percent of the voting stock of foreign corporation T, and 30 percent of the voting stock of foreign corporation U. Neither S, T, nor U is a controlled foreign corporation. P, S, T and U all use the calendar year as their taxable year. In 1993, T and U both pay dividends to S and S pays a dividend to P. To compute foreign taxes deemed paid, paragraph (c)(1) of this section requires P to start with the lowest tier corporations and to compute foreign taxes deemed paid separately for dividends from each first-tier and lower-tier corporation. Thus, S first will compute foreign taxes deemed paid separately on its dividends from T and U. The deemed paid taxes will be added to S's post-1986 foreign income taxes, and the dividends will be added to S's post-1986 undistributed earnings. Next, P will compute foreign taxes deemed paid with respect to the dividend from S. This computation will take into account the taxes paid by T and U and deemed paid by S.

(2) *Section 78 gross-up*—(i) *Foreign income taxes deemed paid by a domestic shareholder.* Except as provided in section 960(b) and the regulations under that section (relating to amounts excluded from gross income under section 959(b)), any foreign income taxes deemed paid by a domestic shareholder in any taxable year under section 902(a) and paragraph (b) of this section shall be included in the gross income of the domestic shareholder for the year as a dividend under section 78. Amounts included in gross income under section 78 shall, for purposes of section 904, be deemed to be derived from sources within the United States to the extent the earnings and profits on which the taxes were paid are treated under section 904(g) as United States source earnings and profits. Section 1.904-5(m)(6). Amounts included in gross income under section 78 shall be treated for purposes of section 904 as income in a separate category to the extent that the foreign income taxes were allocated and apportioned to income in that separate category. See section 904(d)(3)(G) and § 1.904-6(b)(3).

(ii) *Foreign income taxes deemed paid by an upper-tier corporation.* Foreign income taxes deemed paid by an upper-tier corporation on a distribution from a lower-tier corporation are not included in the earnings and profits of the upper-tier corporation. For purposes of section 904, foreign income taxes shall be allocated and apportioned to income in a separate category to the extent those taxes were allocated to the earnings and profits of the lower-tier corporation in that separate category. See section 904(d)(3)(G) and § 1.904-6(b)(3). To the extent that section 904(g) treats the earnings of the lower-tier corporation on which those foreign income taxes were paid as United States source earnings and profits, the foreign income taxes deemed paid by the upper-tier corporation on the distribution from the lower-tier corporation shall be treated as attributable to United States source earnings and profits. See section 904(g) and § 1.904-5(m)(6).

(iii) *Example.* The following example illustrates the rules of this paragraph (c)(2):

Example. P, a domestic corporation, owns 100 percent of the voting stock of controlled foreign corporation S. Corporations P and S use the calendar year as their taxable year, and S uses the u as its functional currency. Assume that 1u equals $1 at all relevant times. As of January 1, 1992, S has -0- post-1986 undistributed earnings and -0- post-1986 foreign income taxes. In 1992, S earns 150u of non-subpart F general limitation income net of foreign taxes and pays 60u of foreign income taxes. As of the end of 1992, but before dividend payments, S has 150u of post-1986 undistributed earnings and $60 of post-1986 foreign income taxes. Assume that 50u of S's earnings for 1992 are from United States sources. S pays P a dividend of 75u which P receives in 1992. Under § 1.904-5(m)(4), one-third of the dividend, or 25u (75u x 50u/150u), is United States source income to P. P computes foreign taxes deemed paid on the dividend under paragraph (b)(1) of this section of $30 ($60 x 50%[75u/150u]) and includes that amount in gross income under section 78 as a dividend. Because 25u of the 75u dividend is United States source income to P, $10 ($30 x 33.33%[25u/75u]) of the section 78 dividend will be treated as United States source income to P under this paragraph (c)(2).

(3) *Creditable foreign income taxes.* The amount of creditable foreign income taxes under section 901 shall include, subject to the limitations and conditions of sections 902 and 904, foreign income taxes actually paid and deemed paid by a domestic shareholder that receives a dividend from a first-tier corporation. Foreign income taxes deemed paid by a domestic shareholder under paragraph (b) of this section shall be deemed paid by the domestic shareholder only for purposes of computing the foreign tax credit allowed under section 901.

(4) *Foreign mineral income.* Certain foreign income, war profits and excess profits taxes paid or accrued with respect to foreign mineral income will not be considered foreign income taxes for purposes of section 902. See section 901(e) and § 1.901-3.

Reg. § 1.902-1(c)(4)

48,856 Income from Sources Without the United States

See p. 20,601 for regulations not amended to reflect law changes

(5) *Foreign taxes paid or accrued in connection with the purchase or sale of certain oil and gas.* Certain income, war profits, or excess profits taxes paid or accrued to a foreign country in connection with the purchase and sale of oil or gas extracted in that country will not be considered foreign income taxes for purposes of section 902. See section 901(f).

(6) *Foreign oil and gas extraction income.* For rules relating to reduction of the amount of foreign income taxes deemed paid with respect to foreign oil and gas extraction income, see section 907(a) and the regulations under that section.

(7) *United States shareholders of controlled foreign corporations.* See paragraph (d) of this section and sections 960 and 962 and the regulations under those sections for special rules relating to the application of section 902 in computing foreign income taxes deemed paid by United States shareholders of controlled foreign corporations.

(8) *Credit for foreign taxes deemed paid in a section 304 transaction.* [Reserved].

(9) *Effect of section 482 adjustments on post-1986 foreign income taxes and post-1986 undistributed earnings.* [Reserved].

(d) *Dividends from controlled foreign corporations*— (1) *General rule.* Except as provided in paragraph (d) (3) of this section, if a dividend is received by a domestic shareholder that is a United States shareholder (as defined in section 951(b) or section 953(c) a (A)) from a first-tier corporation that is a controlled foreign corporation (as defined in section 957(a) or section 953(c)(1)(B)), or by an upper-tier corporation from a lower-tier corporation if the corporations are related look-through entities within the meaning of § 1.904-5(i), the following rule applies. If a dividend is paid out of post-1986 undistributed earnings or pre-1987 accumulated profits of the upper- or lower-tier controlled foreign corporation attributable to more than one separate category under section 904(d), the amount of foreign income taxes deemed paid by the domestic shareholder or the upper-tier corporation under section 902 and paragraph (b) of this section shall be computed separately with respect to the post-1986 undistributed earnings or pre1987 accumulated profits in each separate category out of which the dividend is paid. See § 1.904-5(c)(4) and paragraph (d)(2) of this section. The separately computed deemed paid taxes shall be added to other taxes paid by the U.S. shareholder or upper-tier corporation with respect to income in the appropriate separate category.

(2) *Look-through*—(i) *Dividends.* Except as otherwise provided in paragraph (d)(3) of this section, any dividend distribution out of post-1986 undistributed earnings of a look-through entity to a related look-through entity shall be deemed to be paid pro rata out of each separate category of income. See § § 1.904-5(c)(4) and 1.904-7. The portion of the foreign income taxes attributable to a particular separate category that shall be deemed paid by the domestic shareholder or upper-tier corporation must be computed under the following formula:

$$\text{Foreign taxes deemed paid by domestic shareholder or upper-tier corporation with respect to a separate category under section 904(d)} = \text{Post-1986 foreign income taxes of first-tier or lower-tier corporation allocated and apportioned to a separate category under § 1.904-6} \times \frac{\text{Dividend amount attributable to a separate category}}{\text{Post-1986 undistributed earnings of first-tier or lower-tier corporation attributable to the separate category}}$$

(ii) *Coordination with section 960.* For rules coordinating the computation of foreign taxes deemed paid with respect to amounts included in gross income under section 951(a) and dividends distributed by a controlled foreign corporation, see section 960 and the regulations under that section.

(3) *Dividends distributed out of earnings accumulated before a controlled foreign corporation became a controlled foreign corporation*—(i) *General rule.* Any dividend distributed by a controlled foreign corporation out of earnings accumulated before the controlled foreign corporation became a controlled foreign corporation shall be treated as a dividend from a noncontrolled section 902 corporation regardless of whether the earnings were accumulated in a taxable year beginning before January 1, 1987, or after December 31, 1986.

(ii) *Dividend distributions out of earnings and profits for a year during which a shareholder that is currently a more-than-90-percent United States shareholder of a controlled foreign corporation was not a United States shareholder of the controlled foreign corporation.* [Reserved]. For rules regarding dividend distributions before August 6, 1997, to certain more-than-90-percent United States shareholders of a controlled foreign corporation, see § 1.904-4(g)(3)(ii).

(e) *Information to be furnished.* If the credit for foreign income taxes claimed under section 901 includes foreign income taxes deemed paid under

Reg. § 1.902-1(c)(5)

section 902 and paragraph (b) of this section, the domestic shareholder must furnish the same information with respect to the foreign income taxes deemed paid as it is required to furnish with respect to the foreign income taxes it directly paid or accrued and for which the credit is claimed. See § 1.905-2. For other information required to be furnished by the domestic shareholder for the annual accounting period of certain foreign corporations ending with or within the shareholder's taxable year, and for reduction in the amount of foreign income taxes paid, accrued, or deemed paid for failure to furnish the required information, see section 6038 and the regulations under that section.

(f) *Examples.* The following examples illustrate the application of this section:

Example 1. Since 1987, domestic corporation M has owned 10 percent of the one class of stock of foreign corporation A. The remaining 90 percent of Corporation A's stock is owned by Z, a foreign corporation. Corporation A is not a controlled foreign corporation. Corporation A uses the u as its functional currency, and 1u equals $1 at all relevant times. Both Corporation A and Corporation M use the calendar year as the taxable year. In 1992, Corporation A pays a 30u dividend out of post-1986 undistributed earnings, 3u to Corporation M and 27u to Corporation Z. Corporation M is deemed, under paragraph (b) of this section, to have paid a portion of the post-1986 foreign income taxes paid by Corporation A and includes the amount of foreign taxes deemed paid in gross income under section 78 as a dividend. Both the foreign taxes deemed paid and the dividend would be subject to a separate limitation for dividends from Corporation A, a noncontrolled section 902 corporation. Under paragraph (a)(9)(i) of this section, Corporation A must reduce its post-1986 undistributed earnings as of January 1, 1993, by the total amount of dividends paid to Corporation M and Corporation Z in 1992. Under paragraph (a)(8)(i) of this section, Corporation A must reduce its post-1986 foreign income taxes as of January 1, 1993, by the amount of foreign income taxes that were deemed paid by Corporation M and by the amount of foreign income taxes that would have been deemed paid by Corporation Z had Corporation Z been eligible to compute an amount of foreign income taxes deemed paid with respect to the dividend received from Corporation A. Foreign income taxes deemed paid by Corporation M and Corporation A's opening balances in post-1986 undistributed earnings and post-1986 foreign income taxes for 1993 are computed as follows:

1.	Assumed post-1986 undistributed earnings of Corporation A at start of 1992	25u
2.	Assumed post-1986 foreign income taxes of Corporation A at start of 1992	$25
3.	Assumed pre-tax earnings and profits of Corporation A for 1992	50u
4.	Assumed foreign income taxes paid or accrued by Corporation A in 1992	15u
5.	Post-1986 undistributed earnings in Corporation A for 1992 (pre-dividend) (Line 1 plus Line 3 minus Line 4)	60u
6.	Post-1986 foreign income taxes in Corporation A for 1992 (pre-dividend) (Line 2 plus Line 4 translated at the appropriate exchange rates)	$40
7.	Dividends paid out of post-1986 undistributed earnings of Corporation A to Corporation M in 1992	3u
8.	Percentage of Corporation A's post-1986 undistributed earnings paid to Corporation M (Line 7 divided by Line 5)	5%
9.	Foreign income taxes of Corporation A deemed paid by Corporation M under section 902(a) (Line 6 multiplied by Line 8)	$2
10.	Total dividends paid out of post-1986 undistributed earnings of Corporation A to all shareholders in 1992	30u
11.	Percentage of Corporation A's post-1986 undistributed earnings paid to all shareholders in 1992 (Line 10 divided by Line 5)	50%
12.	Post-1986 foreign income taxes paid with respect to post-1986 undistributed earnings distributed to all shareholders in 1992 (Line 6 multiplied by Line 11)	$20
13.	Corporation A's post-1986 undistributed earnings at the start of 1993 (Line 5 minus Line 10)	30u
14.	Corporation A's post-1986 foreign income taxes at the start of 1993 (Line 6 minus Line 12)	$20

Example 2. (i) The facts are the same as in *Example 1,* except that Corporation M has also owned 10 percent of the one class of stock of foreign corporation B since 1987. Corporation B

Reg. § 1.902-1(f)

48,858 Income from Sources Without the United States

See p. 20,601 for regulations not amended to reflect law changes

uses the calendar year as the taxable year. The remaining 90 percent of Corporation B's stock is owned by Corporation Z. Corporation B is not a controlled foreign corporation. Corporation B uses the u as its functional currency, and 1u equals $1 at all relevant times. In 1992, Corporation B has earnings and profits and pays foreign income taxes, a portion of which are attributable to high withholding tax interest, as defined in section 904(d)(2)(B)(i). Corporation B must reduce its pool of post-1986 foreign income taxes by the amount of tax imposed on high withholding tax interest in excess of 5 percent because that amount is not treated as a tax for purposes of section 902. See section 904(d)(2)(E)(ii) and paragraph (a)(8)(iii) of this section. Corporation B pays 50u in dividends in 1992, 5u to Corporation M and 45u to Corporation Z. Corporation M must compute its section 902(a) deemed paid taxes separately for the dividends it receives in 1992 from Corporation A (as computed in *Example 1*) and from Corporation B. Foreign income taxes of Corporation B deemed paid by Corporation M, and Corporation B's opening balances in post-1986 undistributed earnings and post-1986 foreign income taxes for 1993 are computed as follows:

1. Assumed post-1986 undistributed earnings of Corporation B at start of 1992 ..... (100u)
2. Assumed post-1986 foreign income taxes of Corporation B at start of 1992 ..... $0
3. Assumed pre-tax earnings and profits of Corporation B for 1992 (including 50u of high withholding tax interest on which 5u of tax is withheld) 302.50u
4. Assumed foreign income taxes paid or accrued by Corporation B in 1992 ..... 102.50u
5. Post-1986 undistributed earnings in Corporation B for 1992 (pre-dividend) (Line 1 plus Line 3 minus Line 4) 100u
6. Amount of foreign income tax of Corporation B imposed on high withholding tax interest in excess of 5% (5u withholding tax − [5% × 50u high withholding tax interest]) 2.50u
7. Post-1986 foreign income taxes in Corporation B for 1992 (pre-dividend) (Line 2 plus [Line 4 minus Line 6 translated at the appropriate exchange rate]) $100
8. Dividends paid out of post-1986 undistributed earnings to Corporation M in 1992 . ..... 5u
9. Percentage of Corporation B's post-1986 undistributed earnings paid to Corporation M (Line 8 divided by Line 5) 5%
10. Foreign income taxes of Corporation B deemed paid by Corporation M under section 902(a) (Line 7 multiplied by Line 9) $5
11. Total dividends paid out of post-1986 undistributed earnings of Corporation B to all shareholders in 1992 ..... 50u
12. Percentage of Corporation B's post-1986 undistributed earnings paid to all shareholders in 1992 (Line 11 divided by Line 5) 50%
13. Post-1986 foreign income taxes of Corporation B paid on or with respect to post-1986 undistributed earnings distributed to all shareholders in 1992 (Line 7 multiplied by Line 12) $50
14. Corporation B's post-1986 undistributed earnings at start of 1993 (Line 5 minus Line 11) 50u
15. Corporation B's post-1986 foreign income taxes at start of 1993 (Line 7 minus Line 13) $50

(ii) For 1992, as computed in *Example 1*, Corporation M is deemed to have paid $2 of the post-1986 foreign income taxes paid by Corporation A and includes $2 in gross income as a dividend under section 78. Both the income inclusion and the credit are subject to a separate limitation for dividends from Corporation A, a noncontrolled section 902 corporation. Corporation M also is deemed to have paid $5 of the post-1986 foreign income taxes paid by Corporation B and includes $5 in gross income as a deemed dividend under section 78. Both the income inclusion and the foreign taxes deemed paid are subject to a separate limitation for dividends from Corporation B, a noncontrolled section 902 corporation.

Example 3. (i) Since 1987, domestic corporation M has owned 50 percent of the one class of stock of foreign corporation A. The remaining 50 percent of Corporation A is owned by foreign corporation Z. For the same time period, Corporation A has owned 40 percent of the one class of stock of foreign corporation B, and Corporation B has owned 30 percent of the one class of stock of foreign corporation C. The remaining 60 percent

Reg. § 1.902-1(f)

Income from Sources Without the United States 48,859
See p. 20,601 for regulations not amended to reflect law changes

of Corporation B is owned by foreign corporation Y, and the remaining 70 percent of Corporation C is owned by foreign corporation X. Corporations A, B, and C are not controlled foreign corporations. Corporations A, B, and C use the u as their functional currency, and 1u equals $1 at all relevant times. Corporation B uses a fiscal year ending June 30 as its taxable year; all other corporations use the calendar year as the taxable year. On February 1, 1992, Corporation C pays a 500u dividend-out of post-1986 undistributed earnings, 150u to Corporation B and 350u to Corporation X. On February 15, 1992, Corporation B pays a 300u dividend out of post-1986 undistributed earnings computed as of the close of Corporation B's fiscal year ended June 30, 1992, 120u to Corporation A and 180u to Corporation Y. On August 15, 1992, Corporation A pays a 200u dividend out of post-1986 undistributed earnings, 100u to Corporation M and 100u to Corporation Z. In computing foreign taxes deemed paid by Corporations B and A, section 78 does not apply and Corporations B and A thus do not have to include the foreign taxes deemed paid in earnings and profits. See paragraph (c)(2)(ii) of this section. Foreign income taxes deemed paid by Corporations B, A and M, and the foreign corporations' opening balances in post-1986 undistributed earnings and post-1986 foreign income taxes for Corporation B's fiscal year beginning July 1, 1992, and Corporation C's and Corporation A's 1993 calendar years are computed as follows:

A. Corporation C (third-tier corporation):

1. Assumed post-1986 undistributed earnings in Corporation C at start of 1992 ...... 1300u
2. Assumed post-1986 foreign income taxes in Corporation C at start of 1992 .... $500
3. Assumed pre-tax earnings and profits of Corporation C for 1992 .... 500u
4. Assumed foreign income taxes paid or accrued in 1992 .... 300u
5. Post-1986 undistributed earnings in Corporation C for 1992 (pre-dividend) (Line 1 plus Line 3 minus Line 4) 1500u
6. Post-1986 foreign income taxes in Corporation C for 1992 (pre-dividend) (Line 2 plus Line 4 translated at the appropriate exchange rates).................. $800
7. Dividends paid out of post-1986 undistributed earnings of Corporation C to Corporation B in 1992 .... 150u
8. Percentage of Corporation C's post-1986 undistributed earnings paid to Corporation B (Line 7 divided by Line 5) 10%
9. Foreign income taxes of Corporation C deemed paid by Corporation B under section 902(b)(2) (Line 6 multiplied by Line 8) $80
10. Total dividends paid out of post-1986 undistributed earnings of Corporation C to all shareholders in 1992 .... 500u
11. Percentage of Corporation C's post-1986 undistributed earnings paid to all shareholders in 1992 (Line 10 divided by Line 5)......................... 33.33%
12. Post-1986 foreign income taxes paid with respect to post-1986 undistributed earnings distributed to all shareholders in 1992 (Line 6 multiplied by Line 11) .. $266.66
13. Post-1986 undistributed earnings in Corporation C at start of 1993 (Line 5 minus Line 10)... 1000u
14. Post-1986 foreign income taxes in Corporation C at start of 1993 (Line 6 minus Line 12)... $533.34

B. Corporation B (second-tier corporation):

1. Assumed post-1986 undistributed earnings in Corporation B as of July 1, 1991.... 0
2. Assumed post-1986 foreign income taxes in Corporation B as of July 1, 1991...... 0
3. Assumed pre-tax earnings and profits of Corporation B for fiscal year ended June 30, 1992, (including 150u dividend from Corporation B)..................... 1000u
4. Assumed foreign income taxes paid or accrued by Corporation B in fiscal year ended June 30, 1992.. 200u
5. Foreign income taxes of Corporation C deemed paid by Corporation B in its fiscal year ended June 30, 1992 (Part A, Line 9 of paragraph (i) of this *Example 3*).... $80
6. Post-1986 undistributed earnings in Corporation B for fiscal year ended June 30, 1992 (pre-dividend) (Line 1 plus Line 3 minus Line 4) 800u

Reg. § 1.902-1(f)

48,860 Income from Sources Without the United States
See p. 20,601 for regulations not amended to reflect law changes

7.	Post-1986 foreign income taxes in Corporation B for fiscal year ended June 30, 1992 (pre-dividend) (Line 2 plus Line 4 translated at the appropriate exchange rates plus Line 5)	$280
8.	Dividends paid out of post-1986 undistributed earnings of Corporation B to Corporation A on February 15, 1992	120u
9.	Percentage of Corporation B's post-1986 undistributed earnings for fiscal year ended June 30, 1992, paid to Corporation A (Line 8 divided by Line 6)	15%
10.	Foreign income taxes paid and deemed paid by Corporation B as of June 30, 1992, deemed paid by Corporation A under section 902(b)(1) (Line 7 multiplied by Line 9)	$42
11.	Total dividends paid out of post-1986 undistributed earnings of Corporation B for fiscal year ended June 30, 1992	300u
12.	Percentage of Corporation B's post-1986 undistributed earnings for fiscal year ended June 30, 1992, paid to all shareholders (Line 11 divided by Line 6)	37.5%
13.	Post-1986 foreign income taxes paid and deemed paid with respect to post-1986 undistributed earnings distributed to all shareholders during Corporation B's fiscal year ended June 30, 1992 (Line 7 multiplied by Line 12)	$105
14.	Post-1986 undistributed earnings in Corporation B as of July 1, 1992 (Line 6 minus Line 11)	500u
15.	Post-1986 foreign income taxes in Corporation B as of July 1, 1992 (Line 7 minus Line 13)	$175

C. Corporation A (first-tier corporation):

1.	Assumed post-1986 undistributed earnings in Corporation A at start of 1992	250u
2.	Assumed post-1986 foreign income taxes in Corporation A at start of 1992	$100
3.	Assumed pre-tax earnings and profits of Corporation A for 1992 (including 120u dividend from Corporation B)	250u
4.	Assumed foreign income taxes paid or accrued by Corporation A in 1992	100u
5.	Foreign income taxes paid or deemed paid by Corporation B as of June 30, 1992, that are deemed paid by Corporation A in 1992 (Part B, Line 10 of paragraph (i) of this *Example 3*)	$42
6.	Post-1986 undistributed earnings in Corporation A for 1992 (pre-dividend) (Line 1 plus Line 3 minus Line 4)	400u
7.	Post-1986 foreign income taxes in Corporation A for 1992 (pre-dividend) (Line 2 plus Line 4 translated at the appropriate exchange rates plus Line 5)	$242
8.	Dividends paid out of post-1986 undistributed earnings of Corporation A to Corporation M on August 15, 1992	100u
9.	Percentage of Corporation A's post-1986 undistributed earnings paid to Corporation M in 1992 (Line 8 divided by Line 6)	25%
10.	Foreign income taxes paid and deemed paid by Corporation A in 1992 that are deemed paid by Corporation M under section 902(a) (Line 7 multiplied by Line 9)	$60.50
11.	Total dividends paid out of post-1986 undistributed earnings of Corporation A to all shareholders in 1992	200u
12.	Percentage of Corporation A's post-1986 undistributed earnings paid to all shareholders in 1992 (Line 11 divided by Line 6)	50%
13.	Post-1986 foreign income taxes paid and deemed paid by Corporation A with respect to post-1986 undistributed earnings distributed to all shareholders in 1992 (Line 7 multiplied by Line 12)	$121
14.	Post-1986 undistributed earnings in Corporation A at start of 1993 (Line 6 minus Line 11)	200u
15.	Post-1986 foreign income taxes in Corporation A at start of 1993 (Line 7 minus Line 13)	$121

Reg. § 1.902-1(f)

(ii) Corporation M is deemed, under section 902(a) and paragraph (b) of this section, to have paid $60.50 of post-1986 foreign income taxes paid, or deemed paid, by Corporation A on or with respect to its post-1986 undistributed earnings (Part C, Line 10) and Corporation M includes that amount in gross income as a dividend under section 78. Both the income inclusion and the credit are subject to a separate limitation for dividends from Corporation A, a noncontrolled section 902 corporation.

Example 4. (i) Since 1987, domestic corporation M has owned 100 percent of the voting stock of controlled foreign corporation A, and Corporation A has owned 100 percent of the voting stock of controlled foreign corporation B. Corporations M, A and B use the calendar year as the taxable year. Corporations A and B are organized in the same foreign country and use the u as their functional currency. 1u equals $1 at all relevant times. Assume that all of the earnings of Corporations A and B are general limitation earnings and profits within the meaning of section 904(d)(2)(I), and that neither Corporation A nor Corporation B has any previously taxed income accounts. In 1992, Corporation B pays a dividend of 150u to Corporation A out of post-1986 undistributed earnings, and Corporation A computes an amount of foreign taxes deemed paid under section 902(b)(1). The dividend is not subpart F income to Corporation A because section 954(c)(3)(B)(i) (the same country dividend exception) applies. Pursuant to paragraph (c)(2)(ii) of this section, Corporation A is not required to include the deemed paid taxes in earnings and profits. Corporation A has no pre-1987 accumulated profits and a deficit in post-1986 undistributed earnings for 1992. In 1992, Corporation A pays a dividend of 100u to Corporation M out of its earnings and profits for 1992 (current earnings and profits). Under paragraph (b)(4) of this section, Corporation M is not deemed to have paid any of the foreign income taxes paid or deemed paid by Corporation A because Corporation A has a deficit in post-1986 undistributed earnings as of December 31, 1992, and the sum of its current plus accumulated profits is less than zero. Note that if instead of paying a dividend to Corporation A in 1992, Corporation B had made an additional investment of $150 in United States property under section 956, that amount would have been included in gross income by Corporation M under section 951(a)(1)(B) and Corporation M would have been deemed to have paid $50 of foreign income taxes paid by Corporation B. See sections 951(a)(1)(B) and 960. Foreign income taxes of Corporation B deemed paid by Corporation A and the opening balances in post-1986 undistributed earnings and post-1986 foreign income taxes for Corporation A and Corporation B for 1993 are computed as follows:

A. Corporation B (second-tier corporation):

1. Assumed post-1986 undistributed earnings in Corporation B at start of 1992 .... 200u
2. Assumed post-1986 foreign income taxes in Corporation B at start of 1992 .... $50
3. Assumed pre-tax earnings and profits of Corporation B for 1992 .... 150u
4. Assumed foreign income taxes paid or accrued in 1992 .... 50u
5. Post-1986 undistributed earnings in Corporation B for 1992 (pre-dividend) (Line 1 plus Line 3 minus Line 4) 300u
6. Post-1986 foreign income taxes in Corporation B for 1992 (pre-dividend) (Line 2 plus Line 4 translated at the appropriate exchange rates) $100
7. Dividends paid out of post-1986 undistributed earnings of Corporation B to Corporation A in 1992 .... 150u
8. Percentage of Corporation B's post-1986 undistributed earnings paid to Corporation A (Line 7 divided by Line 5) 50%
9. Foreign income taxes of Corporation B deemed paid by Corporation A under section 902(b)(1) (Line 6 multiplied by Line 8) $50
10. Post-1986 undistributed earnings in Corporation B at start of 1993 (Line 5 minus Line 7) 150u
11. Post-1986 foreign income taxes in Corporation B at start of 1993 (Line 6 minus Line 9) $50

B. Corporation A (first-tier corporation):

1. Assumed post-1986 undistributed earnings in Corporation A at start of 1992 .... (200u)
2. Assumed post-1986 foreign income taxes in Corporation A at start of 1992 0

Reg. § 1.902-1(f)

48,862   Income from Sources Without the United States
See p. 20,601 for regulations not amended to reflect law changes

3. Assumed pre-tax earnings and profits of Corporation A for 1992 (including 150u dividend from Corporation B) 200u
4. Assumed foreign income taxes paid or accrued by Corporation A in 1992 .... 40u
5. Foreign income taxes paid by Corporation B in 1992 that are deemed paid by Corporation A (Part A, Line 9 of paragraph (i) of this *Example 4*) $50
6. Post-1986 undistributed earnings in Corporation A for 1992 (pre-dividend) (Line 1 plus Line 3 minus Line 4) .... (40u)
7. Post-1986 foreign income taxes in Corporation A for 1992 (pre-dividend) (Line 2 plus Line 4 translated at the appropriate exchange rates plus Line 5) $90
8. Dividends paid out of current earnings and profits of Corporation A for 1992 ...... 100u
9. Percentage of post-1986 undistributed earnings of Corporation A paid to Corporation M in 1992 (Line 8 divided by the greater of Line 6 or zero) 0
10. Foreign income taxes paid and deemed paid by Corporation A in 1992 that are deemed paid by Corporation M under section 902(a) (Line 7 multiplied by Line 9) .. 0
11. Post-1986 undistributed earnings in Corporation A at start of 1993 (line 6 minus line 8) .... (140u)
12. Post-1986 foreign income taxes in Corporation A at start of 1993 (Line 7 minus Line 10) $90

(ii) For 1993, Corporation A has 500u of earnings and profits on which it pays 160u of foreign income taxes. Corporation A receives no dividends from Corporation B, and pays a 100u dividend to Corporation M. The 100u dividend to Corporation M carries with it some of the foreign income taxes paid and deemed paid by Corporation A in 1992, which were not deemed paid by Corporation M in 1992 because Corporation A had no post-1986 undistributed earnings. Thus, for 1993, Corporation M is deemed to have paid $125 of post-1986 foreign income taxes paid and deemed paid by Corporation A and includes that amount in gross income as a dividend under section 78, determined as follows:

1. Post-1986 undistributed earnings in Corporation A at start of 1993 .... (140u)
2. Post-1986 foreign income taxes in Corporation A at start of 1993 .... $90
3. Pre-tax earnings and profits of Corporation A for 1993 .... 500u
4. Foreign income taxes paid or accrued by Corporation A in 1993 .... 160u
5. Post-1986 undistributed earnings in Corporation A for 1993 (pre-dividend) (Line 1 plus Line 3 minus Line 4) 200u
6. Post-1986 foreign income taxes in Corporation A for 1993 (pre-dividend) (Line 2 plus Line 4 translated at the appropriate exchange rates) $250
7. Dividends paid out of post-1986 undistributed earnings of Corporation A to Corporation M in 1993 .... 100u
8. Percentage of post-1986 undistributed earnings of Corporation A paid to Corporation M in 1993 (Line 7 divided by Line 5) 50%
9. Foreign income taxes paid and deemed paid by Corporation A that are deemed paid by Corporation M in 1993 (Line 6 multiplied by Line 8) $125
10. Post-1986 undistributed earnings in Corporation A at start of 1994 (Line 5 minus Line 7) 100u
11. Post-1986 foreign income taxes in Corporation A at start of 1994 (Line 6 minus Line 9) $125

Example 5. (i) Since 1987, domestic corporation M has owned 100 percent of the voting stock of controlled foreign corporation A. Corporation M also conducts operations through a foreign branch. Both Corporation A and Corporation M use the calendar year as the taxable year. Corporation A uses the u as its functional currency and 1u equals $1 at all relevant times. Corporation A has no subpart F income, as defined in section 952, and no increase in earnings invested in United States property under section 956 for 1992. Corporation A also has no previously taxed income accounts. Corporation A has general limitation income and high withholding tax interest income that, by operation of section 954(b)(4), does not constitute foreign base company income under section 954(a). Because Corporation A is a controlled foreign corporation, it is not required to reduce post-1986 foreign income taxes by foreign taxes paid or accrued with respect to high withholding

Reg. § 1.902-1(f)

Income from Sources Without the United States

See p. 20,601 for regulations not amended to reflect law changes

tax interest in excess of 5 percent. See § 1.902-1(a)(8)(iii). Corporation A pays a 60u dividend to Corporation M in 1992. For 1992, Corporation M is deemed, under paragraph (b) of this section, to have paid $24 of the post-1986 foreign income taxes paid by Corporation A and includes that amount in gross income under section 78 as a dividend, determined as follows:

1. Assumed post-1986 undistributed earnings in Corporation A at start of 1992 attributable to:

    (a) Section 904(d)(1)(B) high withholding tax interest........................... 20u
    (b) Section 904(d)(1)(I) general limitation income 55u

2. Assumed post-1986 foreign income taxes in Corporation A at start of 1992 attributable to:

    (a) Section 904(d)(1)(B) high withholding tax interest........................... $5
    (b) Section 904(d)(1)(I) general limitation income $20

3. Assumed pre-tax earnings and profits of Corporation A for 1992 attributable to:

    (a) Section 904(d)(1)(B) high withholding tax interest........................... 20u
    (b) Section 904(d)(1)(I) general limitation income 20u

4. Assumed foreign income taxes paid or accrued in 1992 on or with respect to:

    (a) Section 904(d)(1)(B) high withholding tax interest........................... 10u
    (b) Section 904(d)(1)(I) general limitation income 5u

5. Post-1986 undistributed earnings in Corporation A for 1992 (pre-dividend) attributable to:

    (a) Section 904(d)(1)(B) high withholding tax interest (Line 1(a) + Line 3(a) minus Line 4(a)) 30u
    (b) Section 904(d)(1)(I) general limitation income (Line 1(b) + Line 3(b) minus Line 4(b)) 70u
    (c) Total 100u

6. Post-1986 foreign income taxes in Corporation A for 1992 (pre-dividend) attributable to:

    (a) Section 904(d)(1)(B) high withholding tax interest (Line 2(a) + Line 4(a) translated at the appropriate exchange rates) $15
    (b) Section 904(d)(1)(I) general limitation income (Line 2(b) + Line 4(b) translated at the appropriate exchange rates) $25

7. Dividends paid to Corporation M in 1992..................................... 60u

8. Dividends paid to Corporation M in 1992 attributable to section 904(d) separate categories pursuant to § 1.904-5(d):

    (a) Dividends paid to Corporation M in 1992 attributable to section 904(d)(1)(B) high withholding tax interest (Line 7 multiplied by Line 5(a) divided by Line 5(c)) 18u
    (b) Dividends paid to Corporation M in 1992 attributable to section 904(d)(1)(I) general limitation income (Line 7 multiplied by Line 5(b) divided by Line 5(c)) 42u

9. Percentage of Corporation A's post-1986 undistributed earnings for 1992 paid to Corporation M attributable to:

    (a) Section 904(d)(1)(B) high withholding tax interest (Line 8(a) divided by Line 5(a)) 60%
    (b) Section 904(d)(1)(I) general limitation income (Line 8(b) divided by Line 5(b))... 60%

10. Foreign income taxes of Corporation A deemed paid by Corporation M under section 902(a) attributable to:

    (a) Foreign income taxes of Corporation A deemed paid by Corporation M under section 902(a) with respect to section 904(d)(1)(B) high withholding tax interest (Line 6(a) multiplied by Line 9(a)) $9
    (b) Foreign income taxes of Corporation A deemed paid by Corporation M under section 902(a) with respect to section 904(d)(1)(I) general limitation income (Line 6(b) multiplied by Line 9(b) $15

Reg. § 1.902-1(f)

48,864 Income from Sources Without the United States

See p. 20,601 for regulations not amended to reflect law changes

11. Post-1986 undistributed earnings in Corporation A at start of 1993 attributable to:
   (a) Section 904(d)(1)(B) high withholding tax interest (Line 5(a) minus Line 8(a)) .. 12u
   (b) Section 904(d)(1)(I) general limitation income (Line 5(b) minus Line 8(b)) 28u

12. Post-1986 foreign income taxes in Corporation A at start of 1989 allocable to:
   (a) Section 904(d)(1)(B) high withholding tax interest (Line 6(a) minus Line 10(a)) $6
   (b) Section 904(d)(1)(I) general limitation income (Line 6(b) minus Line 10(b)) $10

(ii) For purposes of computing Corporation M's foreign tax credit limitation, the post-1986 foreign income taxes of Corporation A deemed paid by Corporation M with respect to income in separate categories will be added to the foreign income taxes paid or accrued by Corporation M associated with income derived from Corporation M's branch operation in the same separate categories. The dividend (and the section 78 inclusion with respect to the dividend) will be treated as income in separate categories and added to Corporation M's other income, if any, attributable to the same separate categories. See section 904(d) and § 1.904-6.

(g) *Effective date.* This section applies to any distribution made in and after a foreign corporation's first taxable year beginning on or after January 1, 1987. [Reg. § 1.902-1.]

☐ [T.D. 8708, 1-6-97. Amended by T.D. 8916, 12-29-2000.]

[Reg. § 1.902-2]

§ 1.902-2. Treatment of deficits in post-1986 undistributed earnings and pre-1987 accumulated profits of a first-, second-, or third-tier corporation for purposes of computing an amount of foreign taxes deemed paid under § 1.902-1.—(a) *Carryback of deficits in post-1986 undistributed earnings of a first-, second-, or third-tier corporation to pre-effective date taxable years.*—(1) *Rule.* For purposes of computing foreign income taxes deemed paid under § 1.902-1(b) with respect to dividends paid by a first-, second-, or third-tier corporation, when there is a deficit in the post-1986 undistributed earnings of that corporation and the corporation makes a distribution to shareholders that is a dividend or would be a dividend if there were current or accumulated earnings and profits, then the post-1986 deficit shall be carried back to the most recent pre-effective date taxable year of the first-, second-, or third-tier corporation with positive accumulated profits computed under section 902. See § 1.902-3(e). For purposes of this § 1.902-2, a pre-effective date taxable year is a taxable year beginning before January 1, 1987, or a taxable year beginning after December 31, 1986, if the special effective date of § 1.902-1(a)(13) applies. The deficit shall reduce the section 902 accumulated profits in the most recent pre-effective date year to the extent thereof, and any remaining deficit shall be carried back to the next preceding year or years until the deficit is completely allocated. The amount carried back shall reduce the deficit in post-1986 undistributed earnings. Any foreign income taxes paid in a post-effective date year will not be carried back to pre-effective date taxable years or removed from post-1986 foreign income taxes. See section 960 and the regulations under that section for rules governing the carryback of deficits and the computation of foreign income taxes deemed paid with respect to deemed income inclusions from controlled foreign corporations.

(2) *Examples.* The following examples illustrate the rules of this paragraph (a):

Example 1. (i) From 1985 through 1990, domestic corporation M owns 10 percent of the one class of stock of foreign corporation A. The remaining 90 percent of Corporation A's stock is owned by Z, a foreign corporation. Corporation A is not a controlled foreign corporation and uses the u as its functional currency. 1u equals $1 at all relevant times. Both Corporation A and Corporation M use the calendar year as the taxable year. Corporation A has pre-1987 accumulated profits and post-1986 undistributed earnings or deficits in post-1986 undistributed earnings, pays pre-1987 and post-1986 foreign income taxes, and pays dividends as summarized below:

Taxable year	1985	1986	1987	1988	1989	1990
Current E & P (Deficits) of Corp. A	150u	150u	(100u)	100u	–0–	–0–
Current Plus Accumulated E & P of Corp. A .	150u	300u	200u	250u	250u	200u
Post-'86 Undistributed Earnings of Corp. A ..			(100u)	100u	100u	50u
Post-'86 Undistributed Earnings of Corp. A Reduced By Current Year Dividend Distributions (increased by deficit carryback)			–0–	100u	50u	50u
Foreign Income Taxes of Corp. A (Annual) ..	120u	120u	$10	$50	–0–	–0–

Reg. § 1.902-2

Income from Sources Without the United States

See p. 20,601 for regulations not amended to reflect law changes

Post-'86 Foreign Income Taxes of Corp. A . . .			$10	$60	$60	$30
12/31 Distributions to Corp. M	–0–	–0–	5u	–0–	5u	–0–
12/31 Distributions to Corp. Z	–0–	–0–	45u	–0–	45u	–0–

(ii) On December 31, 1987, Corporation A distributes a 5u dividend to Corporation M and a 45u dividend to Corporation Z. At that time Corporation A has a deficit of (100u) in post-1986 undistributed earnings and $10 of post-1986 foreign income taxes. The (100u) deficit (but not the post-1986 foreign income taxes) is carried back to offset the accumulated profits of 1986 and removed from post-1986 undistributed earnings. The accumulated profits for 1986 are reduced to 50u (150u − 100u). The dividend is paid out of the reduced 1986 accumulated profits. Foreign taxes deemed paid by Corporation M with respect to the 5u dividend are 12u (120u x (5u/50u)). See § 1.902-1(b)(3). Corporation M must include 12u in gross income (translated under the rule applicable to foreign income taxes paid on earnings accumulated in pre-effective date years) under section 78 as a dividend. Both the income inclusion and the foreign taxes deemed paid are subject to a separate limitation for dividends from Corporation A, a noncontrolled section 902 corporation. No accumulated profits remain in Corporation A with respect to 1986 after the carryback of the 1987 deficit and the December 31, 1987, dividend distributions to Corporations M and Z.

(iii) On December 31, 1989, Corporation A distributes a 5u dividend to Corporation M and a 45u dividend to Corporation Z. At that time Corporation A has 100u of post-1986 undistributed earnings and $60 of post-1986 foreign income taxes. Therefore, the dividend is considered paid out of Corporation A's post-1986 undistributed earnings. Foreign taxes deemed paid by Corporation M with respect to the 5u dividend are $3 ($60 x 5% [5u/100u]). Corporation M must include $3 in gross income under section 78 as a dividend. Both the income inclusion and the foreign taxes deemed paid are subject to a separate limitation for dividends from noncontrolled section 902 corporation A. Corporation A's post-1986 undistributed earnings as of January 1, 1990, are 50u (100u − 50u). Corporation A's post-1986 foreign income taxes must be reduced by the amount of foreign taxes that would have been deemed paid if both Corporations M and Z were eligible to compute an amount of deemed paid taxes. Section 1.902-1(a)(8)(i). The amount of foreign income taxes that would have been deemed paid if both Corporations M and Z were eligible to compute an amount of deemed paid taxes on the 50u dividend distributed by Corporation A is $30 ($60 x 50% [50u/100u]). Thus, post-1986 foreign income taxes as of January 1, 1990, are $30 ($60 − $30).

Example 2. The facts are the same as in *Example 1*, except that Corporation A has a deficit in its post-1986 undistributed earnings of (150u) on December 31, 1987. The deficit is carried back to 1986 and reduces accumulated profits for that year to -0-. Thus, the foreign income taxes paid with respect to the 1986 accumulated profits will never be deemed paid. The 1987 dividend is deemed to be out of Corporation A's 1985 accumulated profits. Foreign taxes deemed paid by Corporation M under section 902 with respect to the 5u dividend paid on December 31, 1987, are 4u (120u x 5u/150u). See § 1.902-1(b)(3). As a result of the December 31, 1987, dividend distributions, 100u (150u − 50u) of accumulated profits and 80u (120u reduced by 40u[120u x 50u/150u] of foreign taxes that would have been deemed paid had all of Corporation A's shareholders been eligible to compute an amount of foreign taxes deemed paid with respect to the dividend paid out of 1985 accumulated profits) remain in Corporation A with respect to 1985.

Example 3. (i) From 1986 through 1991, domestic corporation M owns 10 percent of the one class of stock of foreign corporation A. The remaining 90 percent of Corporation A's stock is owned by Corporation Z, a foreign corporation. Corporation A is not a controlled foreign corporation and uses the u as its functional currency. 1u equals $1 at all relevant times. Both Corporation A and Corporation M use the calendar year as the taxable year. Corporation A has pre-1987 accumulated profits and post-1986 undistributed earnings or deficits in post-1986 undistributed earnings, pays pre-1987 and post-1986 foreign income taxes, and pays dividends as summarized below:

Taxable year	1986	1987	1988	1989	1990	1991
Current E & P (Deficits) of Corp. A	100u	(50u)	150u	75u	25u	–0–
Current Plus Accumulated E & P of Corp. A	100u	50u	200u	175u	200u	80u
Post-'86 Undistributed Earnings of Corp. A		(50u)	100u	75u	100u	–0–
Post-'86 Undistributed Earnings of Corp. A Reduced By Current Year Dividend Distributions (increased by deficit carryback) . .		(50u)	–0–	75u	–0–	–0–

Reg. § 1.902-2

48,866 Income from Sources Without the United States
See p. 20,601 for regulations not amended to reflect law changes

Foreign Income Taxes (Annual) of Corp. A	80u	–0–	$120	$20	$20	–0–
Post-'86 Foreign Income Taxes of Corp. A		–0–	$120	$20	$40	–0–
12/31 Distributions to Corp. M	–0–	–0–	10u	–0–	12u	–0–
12/31 Distributions to Corp. Z	–0–	–0–	90u	–0–	108u	–0–

(ii) On December 31, 1988, Corporation A distributes a 10u dividend to Corporation M and a 90u dividend to Corporation Z. At that time Corporation A has 100u in its post-1986 undistributed earnings and $120 in its post-1986 foreign income taxes. Corporation M is deemed, under § 1.902-1(b)(1), to have paid $12 ($120 x 10% [10u/100u]) of the post-1986 foreign income taxes paid by Corporation A and includes that amount in gross income under section 78 as a dividend. Both the income inclusion and the foreign taxes deemed paid are subject to a separate limitation for dividends from noncontrolled section 902 corporation A. Corporation A's post-1986 undistributed earnings as of January 1, 1989, are -0- (100u – 100u). Its post-1986 foreign taxes as of January 1, 1989, also are -0-, $120 reduced by $120 of foreign income taxes paid that would have been deemed paid if both Corporations M and Z were eligible to compute an amount of foreign taxes deemed paid on the dividend from Corporation A ($120 x 100% [100u/100u]).

(iii) On December 31, 1990, Corporation A distributes a 12u dividend to Corporation M and a 108u dividend to Corporation Z. At that time Corporation A has 100u in its post-1986 undistributed earnings and $40 in its post-1986 foreign income taxes. The dividend is paid out of post-1986 undistributed earnings to the extent thereof (100u), and the remainder of 20u is paid out of 1986 accumulated profits. Under § 1.902-1(b)(2), the 12u dividend to Corporation M is deemed to be paid out of post-1986 undistributed earnings to the extent of 10u (100u x 12u/120u) and the remaining 2u is deemed to be paid out of Corporation A's 1986 accumulated profits. Similarly, the 108u dividend to Corporation Z is deemed to be paid out of post-1986 undistributed earnings to the extent of 90u (100u x 108u/120u) and the remaining 18u is deemed to be paid out of Corporation A's 1986 accumulated profits. Foreign income taxes deemed paid by Corporation M under section 902 with respect to the portion of the dividend paid out of post-1986 undistributed earnings are $4 ($40 x 10% [10u/100u]), and foreign taxes deemed paid by Corporation M with respect to the portion of the dividend deemed paid out of 1986 accumulated profits are 1.6u (80u x 2u/100u). Corporation M must include $4 plus 1.6u translated under the rule applicable to foreign income taxes paid on earnings accumulated in taxable years prior to the effective date of the Tax Reform Act of 1986 in gross income as a dividend under section 78. The income inclusion and the foreign income taxes deemed paid are subject to a separate limitation for dividends from noncontrolled section 902 Corporation A. As of January 1, 1991, Corporation A's post-1986 undistributed earnings are -0- (100u – 100u). 80u (100u – 20u) of accumulated profits remain with respect to 1986. Post-1986 foreign income taxes as of January 1, 1991, are -0-, $40 reduced by $40 of foreign income taxes paid that would have been deemed paid if both Corporations M and Z were eligible to compute an amount of deemed paid taxes on the 100u dividend distributed by Corporation A out of post-1986 undistributed earnings ($40 x 100% [100u/100u]). Corporation A has 64u of foreign income taxes remaining with respect to 1986, 80u reduced by 16u [80u x 20u/100u] of foreign income taxes that would have been deemed paid if Corporations M and Z both were eligible to compute an amount of deemed paid taxes on the 20u dividend distributed by Corporation A out of 1986 accumulated profits.

(b) *Carryforward of deficits in pre-1987 accumulated profits of a first-, second-, or third-tier corporation to post-1986 undistributed earnings for purposes of section 902*—(1) *General rule.* For purposes of computing foreign income taxes deemed paid under § 1.902-1(b) with respect to dividends paid by a first-, second-, or third-tier corporation out of post-1986 undistributed earnings, the amount of a deficit in accumulated profits of the foreign corporation determined under section 902 as of the end of its last pre-effective date taxable year is carried forward and reduces post-1986 undistributed earnings on the first day of the foreign corporation's first taxable year beginning after December 31, 1986, or on the first day of the first taxable year in which the ownership requirements of section 902(c)(3)(B) and § 1.902-1(a)(1) through (4) are met if the special effective date of § 1.902-1(a)(13) applies. Any foreign income taxes paid with respect to a pre-effective date year shall not be carried forward and included in post-1986 foreign income taxes. Post-1986 undistributed earnings may not be reduced by the amount of a pre-1987 deficit in earnings and profits computed under section 964(a). See section 960 and the regulations under that section for rules governing the carryforward of deficits and the computation of foreign income taxes deemed paid with respect to deemed income inclusions from controlled foreign corporations.

Reg. § 1.902-2(b)

Income from Sources Without the United States

For translation rules governing carryforwards of deficits in pre-1987 accumulated profits to post-1986 taxable years of a foreign corporation with a dollar functional currency, see § 1.985-6(d)(2).

(2) *Effect of pre-effective date deficit.* If a foreign corporation has a deficit in accumulated profits as of the end of its last pre-effective date taxable year, then the foreign corporation cannot pay a dividend out of pre-effective date years unless there is an adjustment made (for example, a refund of foreign taxes paid) that restores section 902 accumulated profits to a pre-effective date taxable year or years. Moreover, if a foreign corporation has a deficit in section 902 accumulated profits as of the end of its last pre-effective date taxable year, then no deficit in post-1986 undistributed earnings will be carried back under paragraph (a) of this section. For rules concerning carrybacks of eligible deficits from post-1986 undistributed earnings to reduce pre-1987 earnings and profits computed under section 964(a), see section 960 and the regulations under that section.

(3) *Examples.* The following examples illustrate the rules of this paragraph (b):

Example 1. (i) From 1984 through 1988, domestic corporation M owns 10 percent of the one class of stock of foreign corporation A. The remaining 90 percent of Corporation A's stock is owned by Corporation Z, a foreign corporation. Corporation A is not a controlled foreign corporation and uses the u as its functional currency. 1u equals $1 at all relevant times. Both Corporation A and Corporation M use the calendar year as the taxable year. Corporation A has pre-1987 accumulated profits or deficits in accumulated profits and post-1986 undistributed earnings, pays pre-1987 and post-1986 foreign income taxes, and pays dividends as summarized below:

Taxable year	1984	1985	1986	1987	1988
Current E & P (Deficits) of Corp. A	25u	(100u)	(25u)	200u	100u
Current Plus Accumulated E & P (Deficits) of Corp. A	25u	(75u)	(100u)	100u	50u
Post-'86 Undistributed Earnings of Corp. A				100u	50u
Post-'86 Undistributed Earnings of Corp. A Reduced By Current Year Dividend Distributions (reduced by deficit carryforward)				(50u)	50u
Foreign Income Taxes (Annual) of Corp. A	20u	5u	–0–	$100	$50
Post-'86 Foreign Income Taxes of Corp. A				$100	$50
12/31 Distributions to Corp. M	–0–	–0–	–0–	15u	–0–
12/31 Distributions to Corp. Z	–0–	–0–	–0–	135u	–0–

(ii) On December 31, 1987, Corporation A distributes a 150u dividend, 15u to Corporation M and 135u to Corporation Z. Corporation A has 200u of current earnings and profits for 1987, but its post-1986 undistributed earnings are only 100u as a result of the reduction for pre-1987 accumulated deficits required under paragraph (b)(1) of this section. Corporation A has $100 of post-1986 foreign income taxes. Only 100u of the 150u distribution is a dividend out of post-1986 undistributed earnings. Foreign income taxes deemed paid by Corporation M in 1987 with respect to the 10u dividend attributable to post-1986 undistributed earnings, computed under § 1.902-1(b), are $10 ($100 x 10% [10u/100u]). Corporation M includes this amount in gross income under section 78 as a dividend. Both the income inclusion and the foreign taxes deemed paid are subject to a separate limitation for dividends from noncontrolled section 902 corporation A. After the distribution, Corporation A has (50u) of post-1986 undistributed earnings (100u − 150u) and -0- post-1986 foreign income taxes, $100 reduced by $100 of foreign income taxes paid that would have been deemed paid if both Corporations M and Z were eligible to compute an amount of deemed paid taxes on the 100u dividend distributed by Corporation A out of post-1986 undistributed earnings ($100 x 100% [100u/100u]).

(iii) The remaining 50u of the 150u distribution cannot be deemed paid out of accumulated profits of a pre-1987 year because Corporation A has an accumulated deficit as of the end of 1986 that eliminated all pre-1987 accumulated profits. See paragraph (b)(2) of this section. The 50u is a dividend out of current earnings and profits under section 316(a)(2); but Corporation M is not deemed to have paid any additional foreign income taxes paid by Corporation A with respect to that 50u dividend out of current earnings and profits. See § 1.902-1(b)(4).

Example 2. (i) From 1986 through 1991, domestic corporation M owns 10 percent of the one class of stock of foreign corporation A. The re-

Reg. § 1.902-2(b)(3)

48,868 Income from Sources Without the United States

See p. 20,601 for regulations not amended to reflect law changes

maining 90 percent of Corporation A's stock is owned by Corporation Z, a foreign corporation. Corporation A is not a controlled foreign corporation and uses the u as its functional currency. 1u equals $1 at all relevant times. Both Corporation A and Corporation M use the calendar year as the taxable year. Corporation A has pre-1987 accumulated profits or deficits in accumulated profits and post-1986 undistributed earnings, pays post-1986 foreign income taxes, and pays dividends as summarized below:

Taxable year	1986	1987	1988	1989	1990
Current E & P (Deficits) of Corp. A	(100u)	150u	(150u)	100u	250u
Current Plus Accumulated E & P (Deficits) of Corp. A	(100u)	50u	(200u)	(100u)	50u
Post-'86 Undistributed Earnings of Corp. A		50u	(200u)	(100u)	50u
Post-'86 Undistributed Earnings of Corp. A Reduced By Current Year Dividend Distributions (reduced by deficit carryforward)		(50u)	(200u)	(200u)	–0–
Foreign Income Taxes (Annual) of Corp. A	–0–	$120	–0–	$50	$100
Post-'86 Foreign Income Taxes of Corp. A		$120	–0–	$50	$150
12/31 Distributions to Corp. M	–0–	10u	–0–	10u	5u
12/31 Distributions to Corp. Z	–0–	90u	–0–	90u	45u

(ii) On December 31, 1987, Corporation A distributes a 10u dividend to Corporation M and a 90u dividend to Corporation Z. At the time of the distribution, Corporation A has 50u of post-1986 undistributed earnings and 150u of current earnings and profits. Thus, 50u of the dividend distribution (5u to Corporation M and 45u to Corporation Z) is a dividend out of post-1986 undistributed earnings. The remaining 50u is a dividend out of current earnings and profits under section 316(a)(2), but Corporation M is not deemed to have paid any additional foreign income taxes paid by Corporation A with respect to that 50u dividend out of current earnings and profits. See § 1.902-1(b)(4). Note that even if there were no current earnings and profits in Corporation A, the remaining 50u of the 100u distribution cannot be deemed paid out of accumulated profits of a pre-1987 year because Corporation A has an accumulated deficit as of the end of 1986 that eliminated all pre-1987 accumulated profits. See paragraph (b)(2) of this section. Corporation A has $120 of post-1986 foreign income taxes. Foreign taxes deemed paid by Corporation M under section 902 with respect to the 5u dividend out of post-1986 undistributed earnings are $12 ($120 x 10% [5u/50u]). Corporation M includes this amount in gross income as a dividend under section 78. Both the foreign taxes deemed paid and the deemed dividend are subject to a separate limitation for dividends from noncontrolled section 902 corporation A. As of January 1, 1988, Corporation A has (50u) in its post-1986 undistributed earnings (50u-100u) and -0- in its post-1986 foreign income taxes, $120 reduced by $120 of foreign taxes that would have been deemed paid if both Corporations M and Z were eligible to compute an amount of deemed paid taxes on the dividend distributed by Corporation A out of post-1986 undistributed earnings ($120 x 100% [50u/50u]).

(iii) On December 31, 1989, Corporation A distributes a 10u dividend to Corporation M and a 90u dividend to Corporation Z. Although the distribution is considered a dividend in its entirety out of 1989 earnings and profits pursuant to section 316(a)(2), post-1986 undistributed earnings are (100u). Accordingly, for purposes of section 902, Corporation M is deemed to have paid no post-1986 foreign income taxes. See § 1.902-1(b)(4). Corporation A's post-1986 undistributed earnings as of January 1, 1990, are (200u) ((100u)-100u). Corporation A's post-1986 foreign income taxes are not reduced because no taxes were deemed paid.

(iv) On December 31, 1990, Corporation A distributes a 5u dividend to Corporation M and a 45u dividend to Corporation Z. At that time Corporation A has 50u of post-1986 undistributed earnings, and $150 of post-1986 foreign income taxes. Foreign taxes deemed paid by Corporation M under section 902 with respect to the 5u dividend are $15 ($150 x 10% [5u/50u]). Post-1986 undistributed earnings as of January 1, 1991, are -0- (50u − 50u). Post-1986 foreign income taxes as of January 1, 1991, also are -0-, $150 reduced by $150 ($150 x 100% [50u/50u]) of foreign income taxes that would have been deemed paid if both Corporations M and Z were eligible to compute an amount of deemed paid taxes on the 50u dividend.

[Reg. § 1.902-2.]

☐ [T.D. 8708, 1-6-97.]

Reg. § 1.902-2(b)(3)

[Reg. § 1.902-3]

§ 1.902-3. Credit for domestic corporate shareholder of a foreign corporation for foreign income taxes paid with respect to accumulated profits of taxable years of the foreign corporation beginning before January 1, 1987.—(a) *Definitions.* For purposes of section 902 and §§ 1.902-3 and 1.902-4:

(1) *Domestic shareholder.* In the case of dividends received by a domestic corporation after December 31, 1964, from a foreign corporation, the term "domestic shareholder" means a domestic corporation which owns at least 10 percent of the voting stock of the foreign corporation at the time it receives a dividend from such foreign corporation.

(2) *First-tier corporation.* In the case of dividends received by a domestic shareholder after December 31, 1964, from a foreign corporation, the term "first-tier corporation" means a foreign corporation at least 10 percent of the voting stock of which is owned by a domestic shareholder at the time it receives a dividend from such foreign corporation. The term "first-tier corporation" also means a DISC or former DISC, but only with respect to dividends from the DISC or former DISC to the extent they are treated under sections 861(a)(2)(D) and 862(a)(2) as income from sources without the United States.

(3) *Second-tier corporation.* (i) In the case of dividends paid to a first-tier corporation by a foreign corporation after January 12, 1971 (*i.e.*, the date of enactment of Pub. L. 91-684, 84 Stat. 2068), but only for purposes of applying this section for a taxable year of a domestic shareholder ending after that date, the foreign corporation is a "second-tier corporation" if at least 10 percent of its voting stock is owned by the first-tier corporation at the time the first-tier corporation receives the dividend.

(ii) In the case of dividends paid to a first-tier corporation by a foreign corporation after January 12, 1971, but only for purposes of applying this section for a taxable year of a domestic shareholder ending before January 13, 1971, or in the case of any dividend paid to a first-tier corporation by a foreign corporation before January 13, 1971, the foreign corporation is a "second-tier corporation" if at least 50 percent of its voting stock is owned by the first-tier corporation at the time the first-tier corporation receives the dividend.

(4) *Third-tier corporation.* In the case of dividends paid to a second-tier corporation (as defined in paragraph (a)(3)(i) or (ii) of this section) by a foreign corporation after January 12, 1971, but only for purposes of applying this section for a taxable year of a domestic shareholder ending after that date, the foreign corporation is a "third-tier corporation" if at least 10 percent of its voting stock is owned by the second-tier corporation at the time the second-tier corporation receives the dividend.

(5) *Foreign income taxes.* The term "foreign income taxes" means income, war profits, and excess profits taxes, and taxes included in the term "income, war profits, and excess profits taxes" by reason of section 903, imposed by a foreign country or a possession of the United States.

(6) *Dividend.* For the definition of the term "dividend" for purposes of applying section 902 and this section, see section 316 and the regulations thereunder.

(7) *Dividend received.* A dividend shall be considered received for purposes of section 902 and this section when the cash or other property is unqualifiedly made subject to the demands of the distributee. See § 1.301-1(b).

(b) *Domestic shareholder owning stock in a first-tier corporation*—(1) *In general.* (i) If a domestic shareholder receives dividends in any taxable year from its first-tier corporation, the credit for foreign income taxes allowed by section 901 includes, subject to the conditions and limitations of this section, the foreign income taxes deemed, in accordance with paragraph (b)(2) of this section, to be paid by such domestic shareholder for such year.

(ii) If dividends are received by a domestic shareholder from more than one first-tier corporation, the taxes deemed to be paid by such shareholder under section 902(a) and this paragraph (b) shall be computed separately with respect to the dividends received from each of such first-tier corporations.

(iii) Any taxes deemed paid by a domestic shareholder for the taxable year pursuant to section 902(a) and paragraph (b)(2) of this section shall, except as provided in § 1.960-3(b), be included in the gross income of such shareholder for such year as a dividend pursuant to section 78 and § 1.78-1. For the source of such a section 78 dividend, see paragraph (h)(1) of this section.

(iv) Any taxes deemed, under paragraph (b)(2) of this section, to be paid by the domestic shareholder shall be deemed to be paid by such shareholder only for purposes of the foreign tax credit allowed under section 901. See section 904 for other limitations on the amount of the credit.

(v) For rules relating to reduction of the amount of foreign income taxes deemed paid or accrued with respect to foreign mineral income, see section 901(e) and § 1.901-3.

(vi) For the nonrecognition as a foreign income tax for purposes of this section of certain income, profits, or excess profits taxes paid or accrued to a foreign country in connection with the purchase and sale of oil or gas extracted in such country, see section 901(f) and the regulations thereunder.

(vii) For rules relating to reduction of the amount of foreign income taxes deemed paid with respect to foreign oil and gas extraction income, see section 907(a) and the regulations thereunder.

(viii) See the regulations under sections 960, 962, and 963 for special rules relating to the application of section 902 in computing the foreign tax credit of United States shareholders of controlled foreign corporations.

(2) *Amount of foreign taxes deemed paid by a domestic shareholder.* To the extent dividends are paid by a first-tier corporation to its domestic shareholder out of accumulated profits, as defined in paragraph (e) of this section, for any taxable year, the domestic shareholder shall be deemed to have paid the same proportion of any foreign income taxes paid, accrued or deemed, in accordance with paragraph (c)(2) of this section, to be paid by such first-tier corporation on or with respect to such accumulated profits for such year which the amount of such dividends (determined without regard to the gross-up under section 78) bears to the amount by which such accumulated profits exceed the amount of such taxes (other than those deemed, under paragraph (c)(2) of this section, to be paid). For determining the amount of foreign income taxes paid or accrued by such first-tier corporation on or with respect to the accumulated profits for the taxable year of such first-tier corporation, see paragraph (f) of this section.

(c) *First-tier corporation owning stock in a second-tier corporation*—(1) *In general.* For purposes of applying section 902(a) and paragraph (b)(2) of this section, if a first-tier corporation receives dividends in any taxable year from its second-tier corporation, the foreign income taxes deemed to be paid by the first-tier corporation on or with respect to its own accumulated profits for such year shall be the amount determined in accordance with paragraph (c)(2) of this section. This paragraph (c) shall not apply unless the product of—

(i) The percentage of voting stock owned by the domestic shareholder in the first-tier corporation at the time that the domestic shareholder receives dividends from the first-tier corporation in respect of which foreign income taxes are deemed to be paid by the domestic shareholder under paragraph (b)(1) of this section, and

(ii) The percentage of voting stock owned by the first-tier corporation in the second-tier corporation equals at least 5 percent. The percentage under paragraph (c)(1)(ii) of this section of voting stock owned by the first-tier corporation in the second-tier corporation is determined as of the time that the dividend distributed by the second-tier corporation is received by the first-tier corporation and thus included in accumulated profits of the first-tier corporation out of which dividends referred to in paragraph (c)(1)(i) of this section are distributed by the first-tier corporation to the domestic shareholder.

Example. On February 10, 1976, foreign corporation B pays a dividend out of its accumulated profits for 1975 to foreign corporation A. On February 16, 1976, the date on which it receives the dividend, A Corporation owns 40 percent of the voting stock of B Corporation. Both corporations use the calendar year as the taxable year. On June 1, 1976, A Corporation sells its stock in B Corporation. On January 17, 1977, A Corporation pays a dividend out of its accumulated profits for 1976 to domestic corporation M. M Corporation owns 30 percent of the voting stock of A Corporation on January 20, 1977, the date on which it receives the dividend. M Corporation uses a fiscal year ending on April 30 as the taxable year. On February 16, 1976, A Corporation satisfies the 10-percent stock ownership requirement referred to in paragraph (a)(3) of this section with respect to B Corporation, and on January 20, 1977, M Corporation satisfies the 10-percent stock ownership requirement referred to in paragraph (a)(2) of this section with respect to A Corporation. The 5-percent requirement of this paragraph (c)(1) is also satisfied since 30 percent (the percentage of voting stock owned by M Corporation in A Corporation on January 20, 1977), when multiplied by 40 percent (the percentage of voting stock owned by A Corporation in B Corporation on February 16, 1976), equals 12 percent. Accordingly, for its taxable year ending on April 30, 1977, M Corporation is entitled to a credit for a portion of the foreign income taxes paid, accrued, or deemed to be paid, by A Corporation for 1976; and for 1976 A Corporation is deemed to have paid a portion of the foreign income taxes paid or accrued by B Corporation for 1975.

(2) *Amount of foreign taxes deemed paid by a first-tier corporation.* A first-tier corporation which receives dividends in any taxable year from its second-tier corporation shall be deemed to have paid for such year the same proportion of any foreign income taxes paid, accrued, or deemed, in

Reg. § 1.902-3(b)(2)

accordance with paragraph (d)(2) of this section, to be paid by its second-tier corporation on or with respect to the accumulated profits, as defined in paragraph (e) of this section, for the taxable year of the second-tier corporation from which such dividends are paid which the amount of such dividends bears to the amount by which such accumulated profits of the second-tier corporation exceed the taxes so paid or accrued. For determining the amount of the foreign income taxes paid or accrued by such second-tier corporation on or with respect to the accumulated profits for the taxable year of such second-tier corporation, see paragraph (f) of this section.

(d) *Second-tier corporation owning stock in a third-tier corporation*—(1) *In general.* For purposes of applying section 902(b)(1) and paragraph (c)(2) of this section, if a second-tier corporation receives dividends in any taxable year from its third-tier corporation, the foreign income taxes deemed to be paid by the second-tier corporation on or with respect to its own accumulated profits for such year shall be the amount determined in accordance with paragraph (d)(2) of this section. This paragraph (d) shall not apply unless the product of—

(i) The percentage of voting stock arrived at in applying the 5-percent requirement of paragraph (c)(1) of this section with respect to dividends received by the first-tier corporation from the second-tier corporation, and

(ii) The percentage of voting stock owned by the second-tier corporation in the third-tier corporation

equal at least 5 percent. The percentage under paragraph (d)(1)(ii) of this section of voting stock owned by the second-tier corporation in the third-tier corporation is determined as of the time that the dividend distributed by the third-tier corporation is received by the second-tier corporation and thus included in accumulated profits of the second-tier corporation out of which dividends referred to in paragraph (d)(1)(i) of this section are distributed by the second-tier corporation to the first-tier corporation.

Example. On February 27, 1975, foreign corporation C pays a dividend out of its accumulated profits for 1974 to foreign corporation B. On March 3, 1975, the date on which it receives the dividend, B Corporation owns 50 percent of the voting stock of C Corporation. On February 10, 1976, B Corporation pays a dividend out of its accumulated profits for 1975 to foreign corporation A. On February 16, 1976, the date on which it receives the dividend, A Corporation owns 40 percent of the voting stock of B Corporation. All three corporations use the calendar year as the taxable year. On January 17, 1977, A Corporation pays a dividend out of its accumulated profits for 1976 to domestic corporation M. M Corporation owns 30 percent of the voting stock of A Corporation on January 20, 1977, the date on which it receives the dividend. M Corporation uses a fiscal year ending on April 30 as the taxable year. On February 16, 1976, A Corporation satisfies the 10-percent stock ownership requirement referred to in paragraph (a)(3) of this section with respect to B Corporation, and on January 20, 1977, M Corporation satisfies the 10-percent stock ownership requirement referred to in paragraph (a)(2) of this section with respect to A Corporation. The 5-percent requirement of paragraph (c)(1) of this section is also satisfied since 30 percent (the percentage of voting stock owned by M Corporation in A Corporation on January 20, 1977), when multiplied by 40 percent (the percentage of voting stock owned by A Corporation in B Corporation on February 16, 1976), equals 12 percent. On March 3, 1975, B Corporation satisfies the 10-percent stock ownership requirement referred to in paragraph (a)(4) of this section with respect to C Corporation. The 5-percent requirement of this paragraph (d)(1) is also satisfied since 12 percent (the percentage of voting stock arrived at in applying the 5-percent requirement of paragraph (c)(1) of this section with respect to the dividends received by A Corporation from B Corporation on February 16, 1976), when multiplied by 50 percent (the percentage of voting stock owned by B Corporation in C Corporation on March 3, 1975), equals 6 percent. Accordingly, for its taxable year ending on April 30, 1977, M Corporation is entitled to a credit for a portion of the foreign income taxes paid, accrued, or deemed to be paid, by A Corporation for 1976; for 1976 A Corporation is deemed to have paid a portion of the foreign income taxes paid, accrued, or deemed to be paid, by B Corporation for 1975; and for 1975 B Corporation is deemed to have paid a portion of the foreign income taxes paid or accrued by C Corporation for 1974.

(2) *Amount of foreign taxes deemed paid by a second-tier corporation.* For purposes of applying paragraph (c)(2) of this section to a first-tier corporation, a second-tier corporation which receives dividends in its taxable year from its third-tier corporation shall be deemed to have paid for such year the same proportion of any foreign income taxes paid or accrued by its third-tier corporation on or with respect to the accumulated profits, as defined in paragraph (e) of this section, for the taxable year of the third-tier corporation from which such dividends are paid which the amount of such dividends bears to the amount by which such accumulated profits of the third-tier

Reg. § 1.902-3(d)(2)

corporation exceed the taxes so paid or accrued. For determining the amount of the foreign income taxes paid or accrued by such third-tier corporation on or with respect to the accumulated profits for the taxable year of such third-tier corporation, see paragraph (f) of this section.

(e) *Determination of accumulated profits of a foreign corporation.* The accumulated profits for any taxable year of a first-tier corporation and the accumulated profits for any taxable year of a second-tier or third-tier corporation, which are taken into account in applying paragraph (c)(2) or (d)(2) of this section with respect to such first-tier corporation, shall be the sum of—

(1) The earnings and profits of such corporation for such year, and

(2) The foreign income taxes imposed on or with respect to the gains, profits, and income to which such earnings and profits are attributable.

(f) *Taxes paid on or with respect to accumulated profits of a foreign corporation.* For purposes of this section, the amount of foreign income taxes paid or accrued on or with respect to the accumulated profits of a foreign corporation for any taxable year shall be the entire amount of the foreign income taxes paid or accrued for such year on or with respect to such gains, profits, and income. For purposes of this paragraph (f), the gains, profits, and income of a foreign corporation for any taxable year shall be determined after reduction by any income, war profits, or excess profits taxes imposed on or with respect to such gains, profits, and income by the United States.

(g) *Determination of earnings and profits of a foreign corporation*—(1) *Taxable year to which section 963 does not apply.* For purposes of this section, the earnings and profits of a foreign corporation for any taxable year beginning after December 31, 1962, other than a taxable year to which paragraph (g)(2) of this section applies, may, if the domestic shareholder chooses, be determined under the rules provided by § 1.964-1 exclusive of paragraphs (d) and (e) of such section. The translation of amounts so determined into United States dollars or other foreign currency shall be made at the proper exchange rate for the date of distribution with respect to which the determination is made.

(2) *Taxable year to which section 963 applies.* For any taxable year of a foreign corporation with respect to which there applies under § 1.963-1(c)(1) an election by a corporate United States shareholder to exclude from its gross income for the taxable year the subpart F income of a controlled foreign corporation, the earnings and profits of such foreign corporation for such year with respect to such shareholder must be determined, for purposes of this section, under the rules provided by § 1.964-1, even though the amount of the minimum distribution required under § 1.963-2(a) to be received by such shareholder from such earnings and profits of such foreign corporation, or from the consolidated earnings and profits of the chain or group which includes such foreign corporation, is zero. Effective for taxable years of foreign corporations beginning after December 31, 1975, section 963 is repealed by section 602(a)(1) of the Tax Reduction Act of 1975 (89 Stat. 58); accordingly, this paragraph (g)(2) is inapplicable with respect to computing earnings and profits for such taxable years.

(3) *Time and manner of making choice.* The controlling United States shareholders (as defined in § 1.964-1(c)(5)) of a foreign corporation shall make the choice referred to in paragraph (g)(1) of this section (including the elections permitted by § 1.964-1(b) and (c)) by filing a written statement to such effect with the Director of the Internal Revenue Service Center, 11601 Roosevelt Boulevard, Philadelphia, Pennsylvania 19155, within 180 days after the close of the first taxable year of the foreign corporation during which such shareholders receive a distribution of earnings and profits with respect to which the benefits of this section are claimed or on or before November 15, 1965, whichever is later. For purposes of this paragraph (g)(3), the 180-day period shall commence on the date of receipt of any distribution which is considered paid from the accumulated profits of a preceding year or years under paragraph (g)(4) of this section. See § 1.964-1(c)(3)(ii) and (iii) for procedures requiring notification of the Director of the Internal Revenue Service Center and noncontrolling shareholders of action taken.

(4) *Determination by district director.* The district director in whose district is filed the income tax return of the domestic shareholder claiming a credit under section 901 for foreign income taxes deemed, under section 902 and this section, to be paid by such shareholder shall have the power to determine, with respect to a foreign corporation, from the accumulated profits of what taxable year or years the dividends were paid. In making such determination the district director shall, unless it is otherwise established to his satisfaction, treat any dividends which are paid in the first 60 days of any taxable year of such a corporation as having been paid from the accumulated profits of the preceding taxable year or years of such corporation and shall, in other respects, treat any dividends as having been paid from the most recently accumulated profits. For purposes of this paragraph (g)(4), in the case of a foreign corporation the foreign income taxes of which are deter-

Reg. § 1.902-3(e)(1)

Income from Sources Without the United States

mined on the basis of an accounting period of less than 1 year, the term "year" shall mean such accounting period. See sections 441(b)(3) and 443.

(h) *Source of income from first-tier corporation and country to which tax is deemed paid* —(1) *Source of income.* For purposes of section 904(a)(1) (relating to the per-country limitation), in the case of a dividend received by a domestic shareholder from a first-tier corporation there shall be deemed to be derived from sources within the foreign country or possession of the United States under the laws of which the first-tier corporation is created or organized the sum of the amounts which under paragraph (a)(3)(ii) of § 1.861-3 are treated, with respect to such dividend, as income from sources without the United States.

(2) *Country to which taxes deemed paid.* For purposes of section 904, all foreign income taxes paid, or deemed under paragraph (c) of this section to be paid, by a first-tier corporation shall be deemed to be paid to the foreign country or possession of the United States under the laws of which such first-tier corporation is created or organized.

(i) *United Kingdom income taxes paid with respect to royalties.* A taxpayer shall not be deemed under section 902 and this section to have paid any taxes with respect to which a credit is allowable to such taxpayer or any other taxpayer by virtue of section 905(b).

(j) *Information to be furnished.* If the credit for foreign income taxes claimed under section 901 includes taxes deemed, under paragraph (b)(2) or (3) of this section, to be paid, the domestic shareholder must furnish the same information with respect to such taxes as it is required to furnish with respect to the taxes actually paid or accrued by it and for which credit is claimed. See § 1.905-2. For other information required to be furnished by the domestic shareholder for the annual accounting period of certain foreign corporations ending with or within such shareholder's taxable year, and for reduction in the amount of foreign income taxes paid or deemed to be paid for failure to furnish such information, see section 6038 and the regulations thereunder.

(k) *Illustrations.* The application of this section may be illustrated by the following examples:

Example (1). Throughout 1978, domestic corporation M owns all the one class of stock of foreign corporation A. Both corporations use the calendar year as the taxable year. Corporation A has accumulated profits, pays foreign income taxes, and pays dividends for 1978 as summarized below. For 1978, M Corporation is deemed, under paragraph (b)(2) of this section, to have paid $20 of the foreign income taxes paid by A Corporation for 1978 and includes such amount in gross income under section 78 as a dividend, determined as follows:

Gains, profits, and income of A Corp.	$100
Foreign income taxes imposed on or with respect to gains, profits, and income	40
Accumulated profits	100
Foreign income taxes paid on or with respect to accumulated profits (total foreign income taxes)	40
Accumulated profits in excess of foreign income taxes	60
Dividends paid to M Corp.	30
Foreign income taxes of A Corp. deemed paid by M Corp. under sec. 902(a) ($40 × $30/$60)	20

Example (2). The facts are the same as in example (1), except that M Corporation also owns all of the one class of stock of foreign corporation B which also uses the calendar year as the taxable year. Corporation B has accumulated profits, pays foreign income taxes, and pays dividends for 1978 as summarized below. For 1978, M Corporation is deemed under paragraph (b)(2) of this section, to have paid $20 of the foreign income taxes paid by A Corporation for 1978 and to have paid $50 of the foreign income taxes paid by B Corporation for 1978, and includes $70 in gross income as a dividend under section 78, determined as follows:

B Corporation

Gains, profits and income	$200
Foreign income taxes imposed on or with respect to gains, profits, and income	100
Accumulated profits	200
Foreign income taxes paid by B Corp. on or with respect to accumulated profits	100
Accumulated profits in excess of foreign income taxes	100
Dividends paid to M Corp.	50
Foreign income taxes of B Corporation deemed paid by M Corporation under section 902(a) ($100 × $50/100)	50

M Corporation

Foreign income taxes deemed paid under sec. 902(a):	
Taxes of A Corp. (from example (1))	$20
Taxes of B Corp. (as determined above)	50
Total	70
Foreign income taxes included in gross income under sec. 78 as a dividend:	
Taxes of A Corp. (from example (1))	20
Taxes of B Corp.	50
Total	70

Example (3). For 1978, domestic corporation M owns all the one class of stock of foreign corporation A, which in turn owns all the one class stock of foreign corporation B. All corporations use the calendar year as the taxable year. For 1978, M

Reg. § 1.902-3(k)

48,874 Income from Sources Without the United States
See p. 20,601 for regulations not amended to reflect law changes

Corporation is deemed under paragraph (b)(2) of this section to have paid $50 of the foreign income taxes paid, or deemed under paragraph (c)(2) of this section to be paid, by A Corporation for such year and includes such amount in gross income as a dividend under section 78, determined as follows upon the basis of the facts assumed:

B Corp. (second-tier corporation):	
Gains, profits, and income	$300
Foreign income taxes imposed on or with respect to gains, profits, and income	120
Accumulated profits	300
Foreign income taxes paid by B Corp. on or with respect to its accumulated profits (total foreign income taxes)	120
Accumulated profits in excess of foreign income taxes	180
Dividends paid on Dec. 31, 1978 to A Corp.	90
Foreign income taxes of B Corp. deemed paid by A Corp. for 1978 under sec. 902(b)(1) ($120 × $90/$180)	60
A Corp. (first-tier corporation):	
Gains, profits, and income:	
Business operations	200
Dividends from B Corp	90
Total	290
Foreign income taxes imposed on or with respect to gains, profits, and income	40
Accumulated profits	290
Foreign income taxes paid by A Corp. on or with respect to its accumulated profits (total foreign income taxes)	40
Accumulated profits in excess of foreign income taxes	250
Foreign income taxes paid, and deemed to be paid, by A Corp. for 1978 on or with respect to its accumulated profits for such year ($60 + $40)	100
Dividends paid on Dec. 31, 1978, to M Corp.	125
M Corp. (domestic shareholder):	
Foreign income taxes of A Corp. deemed paid by M Corp. for 1978 under sec. 902(a) ($100 × $125/$250)	50
Foreign income taxes included in gross income of M Corp. under sec. 78 as a dividend received from A Corp.	$50

Example (4). Throughout 1978, domestic corporation M owns 50 percent of the voting stock of foreign corporation A. A Corporation has owned 40 percent of the voting stock of foreign corporation B since 1970; B Corporation has owned 30 percent of the voting stock of foreign corporation C since 1972. B Corporation uses a fiscal year ending on June 30 as its taxable year; all other corporations use the calendar year as the taxable year. On February 1, 1977, B Corporation receives a dividend from C Corporation out of C Corporation's accumulated profits for 1976. On February 15, 1977, A Corporation receives a dividend from B Corporation out of B Corporation's accumulated profits for its fiscal year ending in 1977. On February 15, 1978, M Corporation receives a dividend from A Corporation out of A Corporation's accumulated profits for 1977. For 1978, M Corporation is deemed under paragraph (b)(2) of this section to have paid $81.67 of the foreign income taxes paid, or deemed under paragraph (c)(2) of this section to be paid, by A Corporation on or with respect to its accumulated profits for 1977, and M Corporation includes that amount in gross income as a dividend under section 78, determined as follows upon the basis of the facts assumed:

C Corp. (third-tier corporation):	
Gains, profits, and income for 1976	$2,000.00
Foreign income taxes imposed on or with respect to such gains, profits, and income	800.00
Accumulated profits	2,000.00
Foreign income taxes paid by C Corp. on or with respect to its accumulated profits (total foreign income taxes)	800.00
Accumulated profits in excess of foreign income taxes	1,200.00
Dividends paid on Feb. 1, 1977 to B Corp.	150.00
Foreign income taxes of C Corp. for 1976 deemed paid by B Corp. for its fiscal year ending in 1977 ($800 × $150/$1,200)	100.00
B Corp. (second-tier corporation):	
Gains, profits, and income for fiscal year ending in 1977:	
Business operations	850.00
Dividends from C Corp.	150.00
Total	1,000.00
Foreign income taxes imposed on or with respect to gains, profits, and income	200.00
Accumulated profits	1,000.00
Foreign income taxes paid by B Corp. on or with respect to its accumulated profits (total foreign income taxes)	200.00
Accumulated profits in excess of foreign income taxes	800.00
Foreign income taxes paid, and deemed to be paid, by B Corp. for its fiscal year on or with respect to its accumulated profits for such year ($100 + $200)	300.00
Dividends paid on Feb. 15, 1977 to A Corp.	120.00
Foreign income taxes of B Corp. for its fiscal year deemed paid by A Corp. for 1977 ($300 × $120/$800)	45.00
A Corp. (first-tier corporation):	
Gains, profits, and income for 1977:	
Business operations	380.00
Dividends from B Corp.	120.00
Total	500.00
Foreign income taxes imposed on or with respect to gains, profits, and income	200.00
Accumulated profits	500.00

Reg. § 1.902-3(k)

Income from Sources Without the United States

Foreign income taxes paid by A Corp. on or with respect to its accumulated profits (total foreign income taxes)	200.00
Accumulated profits in excess of foreign taxes	300.00
Foreign income taxes paid, and deemed to be paid, by A Corp. for 1977 on or with respect to its accumulated profits for such year ($45 + $200)	245.00
Dividends paid on Feb. 15, 1978 to M Corp.	100.00
M Corp. (domestic shareholder):	
Foreign income taxes of A Corp. for 1974 deemed paid by M Corp. for 1978 under sec. 902(a) ($245 × $100/$30)	81.67
Foreign income taxes included in gross income of M Corp. under sec. 78 as a dividend received from A Corp.	81.67

(l) *Effective date.* Except as provided in § 1.902-4, this section applies to any distribution received from a first-tier corporation by its domestic shareholder after December 31, 1964, and before the beginning of the foreign corporation's first taxable year beginning after December 31, 1986. If, however, the first day on which the ownership requirements of section 902(c)(3)(B) and § 1.902-1(a)(1) through (4) are met with respect to the foreign corporation is in a taxable year of the foreign corporation beginning after December 31, 1986, then this section shall apply to all taxable years beginning after December 31, 1964, and before the year in which the ownership requirements are first met. See § 1.902-1(a)(13)(i). For corresponding rules applicable to distributions received by the domestic shareholder prior to January 1, 1965, see § 1.902-5 as contained in the 26 CFR part 1 edition revised April 1, 1976. [Reg. § 1.902-3.]

☐ [T.D. 7481, 4-15-77. *Amended by T.D.* 7490, 6-10-77; *T.D.* 7649, 10-17-79 *and T.D.* 8708, 1-6-97.]

[Reg. § 1.902-4]

§ 1.902-4. Rules for distributions attributable to accumulated profits for taxable years in which a first-tier corporation was a less developed country corporation.—(a) *In general.* If a domestic shareholder receives a distribution from a first-tier corporation before January 1, 1978, in a taxable year of the domestic shareholder beginning after December 31, 1964, which is attributable to accumulated profits of the first-tier corporation for a taxable year beginning before January 1, 1976, in which the first-tier corporation was a less developed country corporation (as defined in 26 CFR § 1.902-2 rev. as of April 1, 1978), then the amount of the credit deemed paid by the domestic shareholder with respect to such distribution shall be calculated under the rules relating to less developed country corporations contained in (26 CFR § 1.902-1 rev. as of April 1, 1978).

(b) *Combined distributions.* If a domestic shareholder receives a distribution before January 1, 1978, from a first-tier corporation, a portion of which is described in paragraph (a) of this section, and a portion of which is attributable to accumulated profits of the first-tier corporation for a year in which the first-tier corporation was not a less developed country corporation, then the amount of taxes deemed paid by the domestic shareholder shall be computed separately on each portion of the dividend. The taxes deemed paid on that portion of the dividend described in paragraph (a) shall be computed as specified in paragraph (a). The taxes deemed paid on that portion of the dividend described in this paragraph (b), shall be computed as specified in § 1.902-3.

(c) *Distributions of a first-tier corporation attributable to certain distributions from second- or third-tier corporations.* Paragraph (a) shall apply to a distribution received by a domestic shareholder before January 1, 1978, from a first-tier corporation out of accumulated profits for a taxable year beginning after December 31, 1975, if:

(1) The distribution is attributable to a distribution received by the first-tier corporation from a second- or third-tier corporation in a taxable year beginning after December 31, 1975.

(2) The distribution from the second- or third-tier corporation is made out of accumulated profits of the second- or third-tier corporation for a taxable year beginning before January 1, 1976, and

(3) The first-tier corporation would have qualified as a less developed country corporation under section 902(d) (as in effect on December 31, 1975), in the taxable year in which it received the distribution.

(d) *Illustrations.* The application of this section may be illustrated by the following examples:

Example (1). M, a domestic corporation owns all of the one class of stock of foreign corporation A. Both corporations use the calendar year as the taxable year. A Corporation pays a dividend to M Corporation on January 1, 1977, partly out of its accumulated profits for calendar year 1976 and partly out of its accumulated profits for calendar year 1975. For 1975 A Corporation qualified as a less developed country corporation under the former section 902(d) (as in effect on December 31, 1975). M Corporation is deemed under paragraphs (a) and (b) of this section to have paid $63 of foreign income taxes paid by A Corporation on or with respect to its accumulated profits for 1976 and 1975 and M Corporation includes $36 of that amount in gross income as a dividend under

Reg. § 1.902-4(d)

section 78, determined as follows upon the basis of the facts assumed:

1976

Gains, profits, and income of A Corp. for 1976	$120.00
Foreign income taxes imposed on or with respect to such gains, profits, and income	36.00
Accumulated profits	120.00
Foreign income taxes paid by A Corp. on or with respect to its accumulated profits (total foreign income taxes)	36.00
Accumulated profits in excess of foreign income taxes	84.00
Dividend to M Corp. out of 1976 accumulated profits	84.00
Foreign income taxes of A for 1976 deemed paid by M Corp. ($84/$84 × $36)	36.00
Foreign income taxes included in gross income of M Corp. under sec. 78 as a dividend from A Corp.	36.00

1975

Gains, profits, and income of A Corp. for 1975	$257.14
Foreign income taxes imposed on or with respect to such gains, profits, and income	77.14
Accumulated profits (under sec. 902(c)(1)(B) as in effect prior to amendment by the Tax Reform Act of 1976)	180.00
Foreign income taxes paid by A Corp. on or with respect to its accumulated profits ($77.14 × $180/$257.14)	54.00
Dividends paid to M Corp. out of accumulated profits of A Corp. for 1975	90.00
Foreign income taxes of A Corp. for 1975 deemed paid by M Corp. (under sec. 902(a)(2) as in effect prior to amendment by the Tax Reform Act of 1976) ($54 × $90/$180)	27.00
Foreign income taxes included in gross income of M Corp. under sec. 78 as a dividend from A Corp.	0

Example (2). The facts are the same as in example (1), except that the distribution from A Corporation to M Corporation on January 1, 1977, was from accumulated profits of A Corporation for 1976. A Corporation's accumulated profits for 1976 were made up of income from its trade or business, and a dividend paid by B, a second-tier corporation in 1976. The dividend from B Corporation to A Corporation was from accumulated profits of B Corporation for 1975. A Corporation would have qualified as a less developed country corporation for 1976 under the former section 902(d) (as in effect on December 31, 1975), M Corporation is deemed under paragraphs (b) and (c) of this section to have paid $543 of the foreign taxes paid or deemed paid by A Corporation on or with respect to its accumulated profits for 1976, and M Corporation includes $360 of that amount in gross income as a dividend under section 78, determined as follows upon the basis of the facts assumed:

Total gains, profits, and income of A Corp. for 1976	$1,500
Gains and profits from business operations	1,200
Gains and profits from dividend A Corp. received in 1976 from B Corp. out of accumulated profits of B Corp. for 1975	300
Foreign taxes imposed on or with respect to such profits and income	450
Foreign taxes paid by A Corp. attributable to gains and profits from A Corp.'s business operations	360
Foreign taxes paid by A Corp. attributable to dividend from B Corp. in 1976	90
Dividends from A Corp. to M Corp. on Jan. 1, 1977	1,050
Portion of dividend attributable to gains and profits of A Corp. from business operations ($1,200/$1,500 × $1,050)	840
Portion of dividends attributable to gains on profits of A Corp. from dividend from B Corp. ($300/$1,500 × $1,050)	210

(a) *Amount of foreign taxes of A Corp. deemed paid by M Corp. on A Corp.'s gains and profits for 1976 from business operations.*

Reg. § 1.902-4(d)

Income from Sources Without the United States

Gains, profits, and income of A Corp. from business operations	$1,200
Foreign income taxes imposed on or with respect to gains, profits, and income	360
Accumulated profits	1,200
Foreign income taxes paid A Corp. on or with respect to its accumulated profits (total foreign income taxes)	360
Accumulated profits in excess of foreign income taxes	840
Dividend to M Corp	840
Foreign taxes of A Corp. deemed paid by M Corp. ($360 × $840/$840)	360
Foreign taxes included in gross income of M Corp. under sec. 78 as a dividend	360

(b) *Amount of foreign taxes of A Corp. deemed paid by M Corp. on portion of the dividend attributable to B Corp.'s accumulated profits for 1975.*

B Corp. (second-tier corporation):	
Gains, profits, and income for calendar year 1975	$1,000
Foreign income taxes imposed on or with respect to gains, profits, and income	400
Accumulated profits (under sec. 902(c)(1)(B) as in effect prior to amendment by the Tax Reform Act of 1976)	600
Foreign income taxes paid by B Corp. on or with respect to its accumulated profits ($400 × $600/$1,000)	240
Dividend to A Corp. in 1976	300
Foreign taxes of B Corp. for 1975 deemed paid by A Corp. (under sec. 902(b)(1)(B) as in effect prior to amendment by the Tax Reform Act of 1976) ($240 × $300/$600)	120
A Corp. (first-tier corporation):	
Gains, profits, and income for 1976 attributable to dividend from B Corp.'s accumulated profits for 1975	300
Foreign income taxes imposed on or with respect to such gains, profits, and income	90
Accumulated profits (under sec. 902(c)(1)(B) as in effect prior to amendment by the Tax Reform Act of 1976)	210
Foreign taxes paid by A Corp. on or with respect to such accumulated profits ($90 × $210/$300)	63
Foreign income taxes paid and deemed to be paid by A Corp. for 1976 on or with respect to such accumulated profits ($120 + $63)	183
Dividend paid to M Corp. attributable to dividend from B Corp. out of accumulated profits for 1975	210
Foreign taxes of A Corp. deemed paid by M Corp. (under sec. 902(a)(2) as in effect prior to amendment by the Tax Reform Act of 1976) ($183 × $210/$210)	183
Amount included in gross income of M Corp. under sec. 78	0

[Reg. § 1.902-4.]

☐ [T.D. 6805, 3-8-65. Amended by T.D. 7283, 8-2-73; T.D. 7481, 4-15-77; T.D. 7649, 10-17-79 and T.D. 8708, 1-6-97.]

[Reg. § 1.903-1]

§ 1.903-1. Taxes in lieu of income taxes.—(a) *In general.* Section 903 provides that the term "income, war profits, and excess profits taxes" shall include a tax paid in lieu of a tax on income, war profits, or excess profits ("income tax") otherwise generally imposed by any foreign country. For purposes of this section and §§ 1.901-2 and 1.901-2A, such a tax is referred to as a "tax in lieu of an income tax"; and the terms "paid" and "foreign country" are defined in § 1.901-2(g). A foreign levy (within the meaning of § 1.901-2(g)(3)) is a tax in lieu of an income tax if and only if—

(1) It is a tax within the meaning of § 1.901-2(a)(2); and

(2) It meets the substitution requirement as set forth in paragraph (b) of this section.

The foreign country's purpose in imposing the foreign tax (*e.g.*, whether it imposes the foreign tax because of administrative difficulty in determining the base of the income tax otherwise generally imposed) is immaterial. It is also immaterial whether the base of the foreign tax bears any relation to realized net income. The base of the tax may, for example, be gross income, gross receipts or sales, or the number of units produced or exported. Determinations of the amount of a tax in lieu of an income tax that is paid by a person and determinations of the person by whom such tax is paid are made under § 1.901-2(e) and (f), respectively, substituting the phrase "tax in lieu of an income tax" for the phrase "income tax" wherever the latter appears in those sections. Section 1.901-2A contains additional rules applicable to dual capacity taxpayers (as defined in § 1.901-2(a)(2)(ii)(A)). The rules of this section are applied independently to each separate levy (within the meaning of §§ 1.901-2(d) and 1.901-2A(a)) imposed by the foreign country. Except as otherwise provided in paragraph (b)(2) of this section, a foreign tax either is or is not a tax in lieu of an income tax in its entirety for all persons subject to the tax.

(b) *Substitution*—(1) *In general.* A foreign tax satisfies the substitution requirement if the tax in fact operates as a tax imposed in substitution for, and not in addition to, an income tax or a series of income taxes otherwise generally imposed. However, not all income derived by persons subject to the foreign tax need be exempt from the income tax. If, for example, a taxpayer is subject to a generally imposed income tax except that, pursuant to an agreement with the foreign country, the taxpayer's income from insurance is subject to a gross receipts tax and not to the income tax, then the gross receipts tax meets the substitution requirement notwithstanding the fact that the taxpayer's income from other activities, such as the operation of a hotel, is subject to the generally imposed income tax. A comparison between the tax burden of this insurance gross receipts tax and the tax burden that would have obtained under the generally imposed income tax is irrelevant to this determination.

(2) *Soak-up taxes.* A foreign tax satisfies the substitution requirement only to the extent that liability for the foreign tax is not dependent (by its terms or otherwise) on the availability of a credit for the foreign tax against income tax liability to another country. If, without regard to this paragraph (b)(2), a foreign tax satisfies the requirement of paragraph (b)(1) of this section (including for this purpose any foreign tax that both satisfies such requirement and also is an income tax within the meaning of § 1.901-2(a)(1)), liability for the foreign tax is dependent on the availability of a credit for the foreign tax against income tax liability to another country only to the extent of the lesser of—

(i) The amount of foreign tax that would not be imposed on the taxpayer but for the availability of such a credit to the taxpayer (within the meaning of § 1.901-2(c)), or

(ii) The amount, if any, by which the foreign tax paid by the taxpayer exceeds the amount of foreign income tax that would have been paid by the taxpayer if it had instead been subject to the generally imposed income tax of the foreign country.

(3) *Examples.* The provisions of this paragraph (b) may be illustrated by the following examples:

Example (1). Country X has a tax on realized net income that is generally imposed except that nonresidents are not subject to that tax. Nonresidents are subject to a gross income tax on income from country X that is not attributable to a trade or business carried on in country X. The gross income tax imposed on nonresidents satisfies the substitution requirement set forth in this paragraph (b). See also examples (1) and (2) of § 1.901-2(b)(4)(iv).

Example (2). The facts are the same as in example (1), with the additional fact that payors located in country X are required by country X law to withhold the gross income tax from payments they make to nonresidents, and to remit such withheld tax to the government of country X. The result is the same as in example (1).

Example (3). The facts are the same as in example (2), with the additional fact that the gross income tax on nonresidents applies to payments for technical services performed by them outside of country X. The result is the same as in example (2).

Example (4). Country X has a tax that is generally imposed on the realized net income of nonresident corporations that is attributable to a trade or business carried on in country X. The tax applies to all nonresident corporations that engage in business in country X except for such corporations that engage in contracting activities, each of which is instead subject to two different taxes. The taxes applicable to nonresident corporations that engage in contracting activities satisfy the substitution requirement set forth in this paragraph (b).

Example (5). Country X imposes both an excise tax and an income tax. The excise tax, which is payable independently of the income tax, is allowed as a credit against the income tax. For 1984 A has a tentative income tax liability of 100u (units of country X currency) but is allowed a credit for 30u of excise tax that it has paid. Pursuant to paragraph (e)(4)(i) of § 1.901-2, the amount of excise tax A has paid to country X is 30u and the amount of income tax A has paid to country X is 70u. The excise tax paid by A does not satisfy the substitution requirement set forth in this paragraph (b) because the excise tax is imposed on A in addition to, and not in substitution for, the generally imposed income tax.

Example (6). Pursuant to a contract with country X, A, a domestic corporation engaged in manufacturing activities in country X, must pay tax to country X equal to the greater of (i) 5u (units of country X currency) per item produced, or (ii) the maximum amount creditable by A against its U.S. income tax liability for that year with respect to income from its country X operations. Also pursuant to the contract, A is exempted from country X's otherwise generally imposed income tax. A produces 16 items in 1984 and the maximum amount creditable by A against its U.S. income tax liability for 1984 is 125u. If A had been subject to country X's otherwise generally imposed income tax it would have paid a tax of 150u. Pursuant to paragraph (b)(2) of this section, the amount of tax paid by A that is

Reg. § 1.903-1(b)(2)

dependent on the availability of a credit against income tax of another country is 0 (lesser of (i) 45u, the amount that would not be imposed but for the availability of a credit (125u − 80u), or (ii) 0, the amount by which the contractual tax (125u) exceeds the generally imposed income tax (150u)).

Example (7). The facts are the same as in example (6) except that, of the 150u *A* would have paid if it had been subject to the otherwise generally imposed income tax, 60u is dependent on the availability of a credit against income tax of another country. The amount of tax actually paid by *A* (*i.e.*, 125u) that is dependent on the availability of a credit against income tax of another country is 35u (lesser of (i) 45u, computed as in example (6), or (ii) 35u, the amount by which the contractual tax (125u) exceeds the amount *A* would have paid as income tax if it had been subject to the otherwise generally imposed income tax (90u, *i.e.*, 150u − 60u)).

(c) *Effective date.* The effective date of this section is as provided in § 1.901-2(h). [Reg. § 1.903-1.]

☐ [T.D. 7918, 10-6-83.]

[Reg. § 1.904-0]

§ 1.904-0. **Outline of regulation provisions for section 904.**—This section lists the regulations under section 904 of the Internal Revenue Code of 1986.

§ 1.904-1. *Limitation on credit for foreign taxes.*

(a) Per-country limitation.

(1) General.

(2) Illustration of principles.

(b) Overall limitation.

(1) General.

(2) Illustration of principles.

(c) Special computation of taxable income.

(d) Election of overall limitation.

(1) In general.

(i) Manner of making election.

(ii) Revocation for first taxable year beginning after December 31, 1969.

(2) Method of making the initial election.

(3) Method of revoking an election and making a new election.

(e) Joint return.

(1) General.

(2) Electing the overall limitation.

§ 1.904-2. *Carryback and carryover of unused foreign tax.*

(a) Credit for foreign tax carryback or carryover.

(b) Years to which carried.

(1) General.

(2) Definitions.

(3) Taxable years beginning before January 1, 1958.

(c) Tax deemed paid or accrued.

(1) Unused foreign tax for per-country limitation year.

(2) Unused foreign tax for overall limitation year.

(3) Unused foreign tax with respect to foreign mineral income.

(d) Determination of excess limitation for certain years.

(e) Periods of less than 12 months.

(f) Statement with tax return.

(g) Illustration of carrybacks and carryovers.

§ 1.904-3. *Carryback and carryover of unused foreign tax by husband and wife.*

(a) In general.

(b) Joint unused foreign tax and joint excess limitation.

(c) Continuous use of joint return.

(d) From separate to joint return.

(e) Amounts carried from or through a joint return year to or through a separate return year.

(f) Allocation of unused foreign tax and excess limitation.

(1) Limitation.

(i) Per-country limitation.

(ii) Overall limitation.

(2) Unused foreign tax.

(i) Per-country limitation.

(ii) Overall limitation.

(3) Excess limitation.

(i) Per-country limitation taxpayer.

(ii) Overall limitation.

(4) Excess limitation to be applied.

(5) Reduction of excess limitation.

(6) Spouses using different limitations.

(g) Illustrations.

§ 1.904-4. *Separate application of section 904 with respect to certain categories of income.*

(a) In general.

(b) Passive income.

(1) In general.

(i) Rule.

(ii) Example.

(2) Active rents or royalties.

(i) In general.

48,880 Income from Sources Without the United States

See p. 20,601 for regulations not amended to reflect law changes

    (ii) Exception for certain rents and royalties.
    (iii) Unrelated person.
    (iv) Example.
  (c) High-taxed income.
    (1) In general
    (2) Grouping of items of income in order to determine whether passive income is high-taxed income.
      (i) Effective dates.
        (A) In general.
        (B) Application to prior periods.
      (ii) Grouping rules.
        (A) Initial allocation and apportionment of deductions and taxes.
        (B) Reallocation of loss groups.
    (3) Amounts received or accrued by United States persons.
    (4) Income of controlled foreign corporations and foreign QBUs.
    (5) Special rules.
      (i) Certain rents and royalties.
      (ii) Treatment of partnership income.
      (iii) Currency gain or loss.
      (iv) Certain passive dividends.
      (v) Coordination with section 954(b)(4).
    (6) Application of this paragraph to additional taxes paid or deemed paid in the year of receipt of previously taxed income.
      (i) Determination made in year of inclusion.
      (ii) Exception.
      (iii) Allocation of foreign taxes imposed on distributions of previously taxed income.
      (iv) Increase in taxes paid by successors.
        (A) General rule.
        (B) Exception for U.S. shareholders not entitled to look-through.
    (7) Application of this paragraph to certain reductions of tax on distributions of income.
      (i) In general.
      (ii) Allocation of reductions of foreign tax.
      (iii) Interaction with section 954(b)(4).
    (8) Examples.
  (d) High withholding tax interest.
  (e) Financial services income.
    (1) In general.
    (2) Active financing income.
      (i) Income included.
    (3) Financial services entities.

      (i) In general.
      (ii) Special rule for affiliated groups.
      (iii) Treatment of partnerships and other pass-through entities.
        (A) Rule.
        (B) Examples.
      (iv) Examples.
    (4) Definition of incidental income.
      (i) In general.
        (A) Rule.
        (B) Examples.
      (ii) Income that is not incidental income.
    (5) Exceptions.
  (f) Shipping income.
  (g) Non-controlled section 902 corporations.
    (1) Definition.
    (2) Treatment of dividends for each separate non-controlled section 902 corporation.
      (i) In general.
      (ii) Special rule for dividends received by a controlled foreign corporation.
      (iii) Special rule for high withholding tax interest.
      (iv) Treatment of inclusions under section 1293.
      (v) Examples.
    (3) Special rule for dividends paid by a controlled foreign corporation.
      (i) Distributions out of earnings and profits accumulated when the distributing corporation was not a controlled foreign corporation.
        (A) General rule.
        (B) Ordering rule.
        (C) Effect of intervening noncontrolled status.
        (D) Examples.
      (ii) Pre-August 6, 1997, dividend distributions out of earnings and profits accumulated before a more-than-90-percent United States shareholder became a United States shareholder.
        (A) General rule.
        (B) Exception for intra-group acquisitions.
        (C) Ordering rule.
        (D) Distributions after August 5, 1997.
        (E) Examples.
      (iii) Treatment of earnings and profits for transition year.
      (iv) Definitions.
      (v) Effective date.

Reg. § 1.904-0

Income from Sources Without the United States

(h) Export financing interest.
  (1) Definitions.
    (i) Export financing.
    (ii) Fair market value.
    (iii) Related person.
  (2) Treatment of export financing interest.
  (3) Exceptions.
    (i) Export financing interest that is high withholding tax interest.
    (ii) Export financing interest that is also related person factoring income.
    (iii) Export financing interest that is related person factoring income and is received or accrued by a financial services entity.
    (iv) Export financing interest that is related person factoring income and high withholding tax interest.
  (4) Examples.
  (5) Income eligible for section 864(d)(7) exception (same country exception) from related person factoring treatment.
    (i) Income other than interest.
    (ii) Interest income.
    (iii) Examples.
(i) Interaction of section 907(c) and income described in this section.
(j) Special rule for certain currency gains and losses.
(k) Special rule for alternative minimum tax foreign tax credit.
(l) Priority rules.
  (1) In general.
  (2) Examples.

§ 1.904-5. Look-through rules as applied to controlled foreign corporations and other entities.
(a) Definitions.
(b) In general.
(c) Rules for specific types of inclusions and payments.
  (1) Subpart F inclusions.
    (i) Rule.
    (ii) Examples.
  (2) Interest.
    (i) In general.
    (ii) Allocating and apportioning expenses including interest paid to a related person.
    (iii) Definitions.
      (A) Value of assets and reduction in value of assets and gross income.
      (B) Related person debt allocated to passive assets.
      (iv) Examples.
  (3) Rents and royalties.
  (4) Dividends.
    (i) Look-through rule.
    (ii) Special rule for dividends attributable to certain loans.
    (iii) Examples.
(d) Effect of exclusions from Subpart F income.
  (1) De minimis amount of Subpart F income.
  (2) Exception for certain income subject to high foreign tax.
  (3) Examples.
(e) Treatment of Subpart F income in excess of 70 percent of gross income.
  (1) Rule.
  (2) Example.
(f) Modifications of look-through rules for certain income.
  (1) High withholding tax interest.
  (2) Dividends from a non-controlled section 902 corporation.
    (i) Rule.
    (ii) Example.
  (3) Distributions from a FSC.
  (4) Example.
(g) Application of the look-through rules to certain domestic corporations.
(h) Application of the look-through rules to partnerships and other pass-through entities.
  (1) General rule.
  (2) Exception for certain partnership interests.
    (i) Rule.
    (ii) Exceptions.
  (3) Income from the sale of a partnership interest.
  (4) Value of a partnership interest.
(i) Application of look-through rules to related entities.
  (1) In general.
  (2) Exception for distributive shares of partnership income.
  (3) Special rule for dividends.
  (4) Examples.
(j) Look-through rules applied to passive foreign investment company inclusions.
(k) Ordering rules.
  (1) In general.
  (2) Specific rules.
(l) Examples.

Reg. § 1.904-0

48,882   Income from Sources Without the United States

See p. 20,601 for regulations not amended to reflect law changes

(m) Application of section 904(g).

(1) In general.

(2) Treatment of interest payments.

(3) Examples.

(4) Treatment of dividend payments.

  (i) Rule.

  (ii) Determination of earnings and profits from United States sources.

  (iii) Example.

(5) Treatment of Subpart F inclusions.

  (i) Rule.

  (ii) Example.

(6) Treatment of section 78 amount.

(7) Coordination with treaties.

  (i) Rule.

  (ii) Example.

(n) Order of application of sections 904(d) and (g).

(o) Effective date.

§ 1.904-6. Allocation and apportionment of taxes.

(a) Allocation and apportionment of taxes to a separate category or categories of income.

(1) Allocation of taxes to a separate category or categories of income.

  (i) Taxes related to a separate category of income.

  (ii) Apportionment of taxes related to more than one separate category.

  (iii) Apportionment of taxes for purposes of applying the high tax income test.

  (iv) Special rule for base and timing differences.

(2) Treatment of certain dividends from noncontrolled section 902 corporations.

(b) Application of paragraph (a) to sections 902 and 960.

(1) Determination of foreign taxes deemed paid.

(2) Distributions received from foreign corporations that are excluded from gross income under section 959(b).

(3) Application of section 78.

(4) Increase in limitation.

(c) Examples.

§ 1.904-7. Transition rules.

(a) Characterization of distributions and section 951(a)(1)(A)(ii) and (iii) and (B) inclusions of earnings of a controlled foreign corporation accumulated in taxable years beginning before January 1, 1987, during taxable years of both the payor controlled foreign corporation and the recipient which begin after December 31, 1986.

(1) Distributions and section 951(a)(1)(A)(ii) and (iii) and (B) inclusions.

(2) Limitation on establishing the character of earnings and profits.

(b) Application of look-through rules to distributions (including deemed distributions) and payments by an entity to a recipient when one's taxable year begins before January 1, 1987 and the other's taxable year begins after December 31, 1986.

(1) In general.

(2) Payor of interest, rents, or royalties is subject to the Act and recipient is not subject to the Act.

(3) Recipient of interest, rents, or royalties is subject to the Act and payor is not subject to the Act.

(4) Recipient of dividends and subpart F inclusions is subject to the Act and payor is not subject to the Act.

(5) Examples.

(c) Installment sales.

(d) Special effective date for high withholding tax interest earned by persons with respect to qualified loans described in section 1201(e)(2) of the Act.

(e) Treatment of certain recapture income.

§ 1.904(b)-1. Treatment of capital gains for corporations.

(a) In general.

(1) Inclusion in foreign source taxable income.

(2) Inclusion in entire taxable income.

(3) Treatment of capital losses.

(b) Definitions.

(1) Capital gain net income.

(2) Foreign source capital gain net income.

(3) Net capital gain.

(4) Foreign source net capital gain.

(5) Rate differential portion.

(6) Net capital loss.

(7) Allocation and apportionment.

(8) Computation of net section 1231 gain.

(c) Illustrations.

§ 1.904(b)-2. Treatment of capital gains for other taxpayers.

(a) In general.

(1) Inclusion in foreign source taxable income.

(2) Inclusion in entire taxable income.

Reg. § 1.904-0

Income from Sources Without the United States 48,883
See p. 20,601 for regulations not amended to reflect law changes

(3) Treatment of capital losses.

(b) Definition of net capital loss.

(c) Illustrations.

§ 1.904(b)-3. Sale of personal property.

(a) General rule.

(b) Special rules.

(c) Exception.

(d) Application of source rules.

(e) Gain from liquidation of certain foreign corporations.

(f) Residence defined.

(g) Tax rate applicable to gain.

(h) Country in which gross income derived.

§ 1.904(b)-4. Effective date.

§ 1.904(f)-1. Overall foreign loss and the overall foreign loss account.

(a) Overview of regulations.

(b) Overall foreign loss accounts.

(c) Determination of a taxpayer's overall foreign loss.

   (1) Overall foreign loss defined.

   (2) Separate limitation defined.

   (3) Method of allocation and apportionment of deductions.

(d) Additions to the overall foreign loss account.

   (1) General rule.

   (2) Overall foreign net capital loss.

   (3) Overall foreign losses of another taxpayer.

   (4) Additions to overall foreign loss account created by loss carryovers.

   (5) Adjustments.

      (i) Adjustment due to reduction in foreign source income under section 904(b).

      (ii) Adjustment to account for rate differential between ordinary income rate and capital gain rate.

(e) Reductions of overall foreign loss accounts.

   (1) Pre-recapture reduction for amounts allocated to other taxpayers.

   (2) Reduction for amounts recaptured.

(f) Illustrations.

§ 1.904(f)-2. Recapture of overall foreign losses.

(a) In general.

(b) Determination of taxable income from sources without the United States for purposes of recapture.

   (1) In general.

(c) Section 904(f)(1) recapture.

   (1) In general.

   (2) Election to recapture more of the overall foreign loss than is required under paragraph (c)(1).

   (3) Special rule for recapture of losses incurred prior to section 936 election.

   (4) Recapture of pre-1983 overall foreign losses determined on a combined basis.

   (5) Illustrations.

(d) Recapture of overall foreign losses from dispositions under section 904(f)(3).

   (1) In general.

   (2) Treatment of net capital gain.

   (3) Dispositions where gain is recognized irrespective of section 904(f)(3).

   (4) Dispositions in which gain would not otherwise be recognized.

      (i) Recognition of gain to the extent of the overall foreign loss account.

      (ii) Basis adjustment.

      (iii) Recapture of overall foreign loss to the extent of amount recognized.

      (iv) Priorities among dispositions in which gain is deemed to be recognized.

   (5) Definitions.

      (i) Disposition.

      (ii) Property used in a trade or business.

      (iii) Property used predominantly outside the United States.

      (iv) Property which is a material factor in the realization of income.

   (6) Carryover of overall foreign loss accounts in a corporate acquisition to which section 381(a) applies.

   (7) Illustrations.

§ 1.904(f)-3. Allocation of net operating losses and net capital losses.

(a) Allocation of net operating loss carrybacks and carryovers that include overall foreign losses.

(b) Allocation of net capital loss carrybacks and carryovers that include overall foreign losses.

(c) Transitional rule.

(d) Illustrations.

§ 1.904(f)-4. Recapture of foreign losses out of accumulation distributions from a foreign trust.

(a) In general.

(b) Effect of recapture on foreign tax credit limitation under section 667(d).

(c) Recapture if taxpayer deducts foreign taxes deemed distributed.

(d) Illustrations.

§ 1.904(f)-5. Special rules for recapture of overall foreign losses of a domestic trust.

Reg. § 1.904-0

48,884 Income from Sources Without the United States

See p. 20,601 for regulations not amended to reflect law changes

(a) In general.

(b) Recapture of trust's overall foreign loss.

(1) Trust accumulates income.

(2) Trust distributes income.

(3) Trust accumulates and distributes income.

(c) Amounts allocated to beneficiaries.

(d) Section 904(f)(3) dispositions to which § 1.904(f)-2(d)(4)(i) is applicable.

(e) Illustrations.

§ 1.904(f)-6. *Transitional rule for recapture of FORI and general limitation overall foreign losses incurred in taxable year beginning before January 1, 1983, from foreign source taxable income subject to the general limitation in taxable years beginning after December 31, 1982.*

(a) General rule.

(b) Recapture of pre-1983 FORI and general limitation overall foreign losses from post-1982 income.

(1) Recapture from income subject to the same limitation.

(2) Recapture from income subject to the other limitation.

(c) Coordination of recapture of pre-1983 and post-1982 overall foreign losses.

(d) Illustrations.

§ 1.904(f)-12. *Transition rules.*

(a) Recapture in years beginning after December 31, 1986, of overall foreign losses incurred in taxable years beginning before January 1, 1987.

(1) In general.

(2) Rule for general limitation losses.

(i) In general.

(ii) Exception.

(3) Priority of recapture of overall foreign losses incurred in pre-effective date taxable years.

(4) Examples.

(b) Treatment of overall foreign losses that are part of net operating losses incurred in pre-effective date taxable years which are carried forward to post-effective date taxable years.

(1) Rule.

(2) Example.

(c) Treatment of overall foreign losses that are part of net operating losses incurred in post-effective date taxable years which are carried back to pre-effective date taxable years.

(1) Allocation to analogous income category.

(2) Allocation to U.S. source income.

(3) Allocation to other separate limitation categories.

(4) Examples.

(d) Recapture of FORI and general limitation overall foreign losses incurred in taxable years beginning before January 1, 1983.

(e) Recapture of pre-1983 overall foreign losses determined on a combined basis.

(f) Transition rules for taxable years beginning before December 31, 1990.

§ 1.904(i)-1. *Limitation on use of deconsolidation to avoid foreign tax credit limitations.*

(a) General rule.

(1) Determination of taxable income.

(2) Allocation.

(b) Definitions and special rules.

(1) Affiliate.

(i) Generally.

(ii) Rules for consolidated groups.

(iii) Exception for newly acquired affiliates.

(2) Includible corporation.

(c) Taxable years.

(d) Consistent treatment of foreign taxes paid.

(e) Effective date.

[Reg. § 1.904-0.]

☐ [*T.D.* 8214, 7-15-88. *Amended by T.D.* 8412, 5-13-92; T.D. 8627, 11-6-95; T.D. 8805, 1-8-99 *and T.D.* 8916, 12-29-2000.]

[Reg. § 1.904-1]

§ 1.904-1. **Limitation on credit for foreign taxes.**—(a) *Per-country limitation*—(1) *General.* In the case of any taxpayer who does not elect the overall limitation under section 904(a)(2), the amount allowable as a credit for income or profits taxes paid or accrued to a foreign country or a possession of the United States is subject to the per-country limitation prescribed in section 904(a)(1). Such limitation provides that the credit for such taxes paid or accrued (including those deemed to have been paid or accrued other than by reason of section 904(d)) to each foreign country or possession of the United States shall not exceed that proportion of the tax against which credit is taken which the taxpayer's taxable income from sources within such country or possession (but not in excess of the taxpayer's entire taxable income) bears to his entire taxable income for the same taxable year. For special rules regarding the application of the per-country limitation when the taxpayer has derived section 904(f) interest or section 904(f) dividends, see § 1.904-4 or § 1.904-5.

(2) *Illustration of principles.* The operation of the per-country limitation under section 904(a)(1) on the credit for foreign taxes paid or accrued may be illustrated by the following examples:

Reg. § 1.904-1(a)(1)

Income from Sources Without the United States 48,885
See p. 20,601 for regulations not amended to reflect law changes

Example (1). The credit for foreign taxes allowable for 1954 in the case of X, an unmarried citizen of the United States who in 1954 received the income shown below and had three exemptions under section 151, is $14,904, computed as follows:

Taxable income (computed without deductions for personal exemptions) from sources within the United States	$50,000
Taxable income (computed without deductions for personal exemptions) from sources within Great Britain	25,000
Total taxable income	75,000
United States income tax (based on taxable income computed with the deductions for personal exemptions)	44,712
British income and profits taxes	18,000

Per-country limitation $\left(\dfrac{25,000}{75,000} \text{ of } \$44,712 \quad 14,904 \right)$

Credit for British income and profits taxes (total British income and profits taxes, reduced in accordance with the per-country limitation) 14,904

Example (2). Assume the same facts as in example (1), except that the sources of X's income and taxes paid are as shown below. The credit for foreign taxes allowable to X is $13,442.40, computed as follows:

Taxable income (computed without deductions for personal exemptions) from sources within the United States	$ 50,000
Taxable income (computed without deductions for personal exemptions) from sources within Great Britain	15,000
Taxable income (computed without deductions for personal exemptions) from sources within Canada	10,000
Total taxable income	75,000
United States income tax (based on taxable income computed with the deductions for personal exemptions)	44,712
British income and profits taxes	10,800

Per-country limitation on British income and profits taxes

$\left(\dfrac{15,000}{75,000} \text{ of } \$44,712 \right)$ 8,942.40

Credit for British income and profits taxes as limited by per-country limitation	8,942.40
Canadian income and profits taxes	4,500.00

Per-country limitation on Canadian income and profits

taxes $\left(\dfrac{10,000}{75,000} \text{ of } \$44,712 \right)$ 5,961.60

Credit for Canadian income and profits taxes (total Canadian income and profits taxes, since such amount does not exceed the per-country limitation)	4,500.00
Total amount of credit allowable (sum of credits—$8,942.40 plus $4,500)	13,442.40

Example (3). A domestic corporation realized taxable income in 1954 in the amount of $100,000, consisting of $50,000 from United States sources and dividends of $50,000 from a Brazilian corporation, more than 10 percent of whose voting stock it owned. The Brazilian corporation paid income and profits taxes to Brazil on its income and in addition paid a dividend tax for the account of its shareholders on income distributed to them, the latter tax being withheld and paid at the source. The domestic corporation's credit for foreign taxes is $23,250, computed as follows:

Taxable income from sources within the United States	$ 50,000
Taxable income from sources within Brazil	50,000
Total taxable income	100,000
United States income tax	46,500
Dividend tax paid at source to Brazil	19,000

Reg. § 1.904-1(a)(2)

48,886   Income from Sources Without the United States
See p. 20,601 for regulations not amended to reflect law changes

Income and profits taxes deemed under section 902 to have been paid to Brazil, computed as follows:

Dividends received from Brazilian corporation during 1954	$ 50,000
Income of Brazilian corporation during 1954	200,000
Income and profits taxes paid to Brazil on $200,000	30,000
Accumulated profits ($200,000 minus $30,000)	170,000
Brazilian taxes applicable to accumulated profits distributed:	
$\dfrac{50,000}{170,000}$ of $\dfrac{170,000}{200,000}$ of $30,000$	$ 7,500
Total income and profits taxes paid and deemed to have been paid to Brazil	26,500
Per-country limitation $\left(\dfrac{50,000}{100,000}\text{ of }\$46,500\right)$	23,250
Credit for Brazilian income and profits taxes as limited by per-country limitation	23,250

(b) *Overall limitation*—(1) *General.* In the case of any taxpayer who elects the overall limitation provided by section 904(a)(2), the total credit for taxes paid or accrued (including those deemed to have been paid or accrued other than by reason of section 904(d)) shall not exceed that proportion of the tax against which such credit is taken which the taxpayer's taxable income from sources without the United States (but not in excess of the taxpayer's entire taxable income) bears to his entire taxable income for the same taxable year. For special rules regarding the application of the overall limitation when the taxpayer has derived section 904(f) interest or section 904(f) dividends, see § 1.904-4 or § 1.904-5.

(2) *Illustration of principles.* The operation of the overall limitation under section 904(a)(2) may be illustrated by the following example:

Example. Corporation X, a domestic corporation, for its taxable year beginning January 1, 1961, elects the overall limitation provided by section 904(a)(2). For taxable year 1961 corporation X has taxable income of $275,000 of which $200,000 is from sources without the United States. The United States income tax is $137,500. During the taxable year corporation X pays or accrues to foreign countries $105,000 in income and profits taxes, consisting of $45,000 paid or accrued to foreign country Y and $60,000 to foreign country Z. The credit for such foreign taxes is limited to $100,000, i.e.,

$$\dfrac{200,000}{275,000} \times \$137,500.$$

The limitation would be the same whether or not some portion of the $200,000 of taxable income from sources without the United States is from sources on the high seas or in a foreign country (other than Y and Z) which imposed no taxes allowable as a credit.

(c) *Special computation of taxable income.* For purposes of computing the limitations under paragraphs (a) and (b) of this section, the taxable income in the case of an individual, estate, or trust shall be computed without any deduction for personal exemptions under section 151 or 642(b).

(d) *Election of overall limitation*—(1) *In general*—(i) *Manner of making election.* The initial election under section 904(b) of the overall limitation provided by section 904(a)(2) may be made by the taxpayer for any taxable year beginning after December 31, 1960, without securing the consent of the Commissioner. The taxpayer may, for the first taxable year for which the election is to be made, make such election at any time before the expiration of the period referred to in paragraph (d) of § 1.901-1 for choosing the benefits of section 901 for such taxable year. Having made the initial election, the taxpayer may, within the time prescribed for making such election for such taxable year, revoke such election without the consent of the Commissioner. If such revocation is timely and properly made, the taxpayer may make his initial election of the overall limitation for a later taxable year without the consent of the Commissioner. If, however, the taxpayer makes the initial election for a taxable year and the period prescribed for making such election for such taxable year expires, the taxpayer must continue the election of the overall limitation for all subsequent taxable years (whether or not foreign taxes were paid or accrued for any such year and notwithstanding that a deduction for foreign taxes under section 164 was claimed for any such year)

Reg. § 1.904-1(b)(1)

until revoked with the consent of the Commissioner. See section 904(b)(1). If the election for any taxable year is revoked with the consent of the Commissioner, the taxpayer may not make a new election for such taxable year or for any subsequent taxable year without the consent of the Commissioner. If the election of the overall limitation is revoked for a taxable year, the per-country limitation shall apply to such taxable year and to all taxable years thereafter unless a new election of the overall limitation is made, either with or without the consent of the Commissioner in accordance with this section.

(ii) *Revocation for first taxable year beginning after December 31, 1969.* Notwithstanding subdivision (i) of this subparagraph, if the taxpayer has made an initial election under section 904(b) of the overall limitation for a taxable year beginning before January 1, 1970, and the period prescribed for making such election for such taxable year has expired, or if he has made a new election for such a taxable year with the consent of the Commissioner, he may revoke such election effective with respect to his first taxable year beginning after December 31, 1969, without the consent of the Commissioner. Such revocation may be made within the time prescribed for making an initial election for such first taxable year beginning after December 31, 1969. If such revocation is timely and properly made, the taxpayer may make a new election of the overall limitation for a later taxable year without the consent of the Commissioner. Such new election for a later taxable year may be made at any time before the expiration of the period referred to in paragraph (d) of § 1.901-1 for choosing the benefits of section 901 for such taxable year. The revocation of an election, or the making of a new election, pursuant to this subdivision shall be made in the same manner provided in subparagraph (2) of this paragraph for revoking or making an initial election. This subdivision applies even though the taxpayer is not required under section 901(e) and § 1.901-3 to reduce the amount of any foreign taxes paid, accrued, or deemed to be paid with respect to foreign mineral income for any taxable year beginning after December 31, 1969.

(2) *Method of making the initial election.* The initial election of the overall limitation under section 904(b) shall be made on Form 1116 in the case of an individual or on Form 1118 in the case of a corporation. The form shall be attached to the appropriate income tax return for the taxable year to which such election applies. Such election may be made, however, only for a taxable year for which the taxpayer chooses to claim a credit under section 901. If the taxpayer revokes the initial election without the consent of the Commissioner, he must file amended Form 1116 or 1118 and amended income tax returns or claims for refund, where applicable, for the taxable years to which the revocation applies. For rules relating to the filing of such forms, see paragraph (a) of § 1.905-2.

(3) *Method of revoking an election and making a new election.* A request to revoke an election of the overall limitation under section 904(b) when such revocation requires the consent of the Commissioner, or to make a new election when such election requires the consent of the Commissioner, shall be in writing and shall be addressed to the Commissioner of Internal Revenue, Washington, D.C. 20224. The request shall include the name and address of the taxpayer and shall be signed by the taxpayer or his duly authorized representative. It must specify the taxable year for which the revocation or new election is to be effective and shall be mailed within 75 days after the close of the first taxable year for which it is desired to make the change. It must be accompanied by a statement specifying the nature of the taxpayer's business, the countries in which the business is carried on, or expected to be carried on, within the taxable year of the requested change, and grounds considered as justifying the requested revocation or new election. The Commissioner may require such other information as may be necessary in order to determine whether the proposed change will be permitted. Generally, a request for consent to revoke an election or make a new election will be granted if the basic nature of the taxpayer's business changes or if there are changes in conditions in a foreign country which substantially affect the taxpayer's business. For example, a taxpayer who enters substantial operations in a new foreign country or who loses existing investment due to nationalization, expropriation, or war would be granted consent to revoke an election or make a new election.

(e) *Joint return*—(1) *General.* In the case of a husband and wife making a joint return, the applicable limitation prescribed by section 904(a) on the credit for taxes paid or accrued to foreign countries and possessions of the United States shall be applied with respect to the aggregate taxable income from sources within each such country or possession, or from sources without the United States, as the case may be, and the aggregate taxable income from all sources, of the spouses.

Reg. § 1.904-1(e)(1)

(2) *Electing the overall limitation.* If a husband and wife make a joint return for the current taxable year, but made a separate return for the preceding taxable year and the overall limitation applied for such preceding taxable year to one spouse or to both spouses (whether or not then married), then, unless revoked with the consent of the Commissioner, the overall limitation shall apply for the current taxable year and for subsequent taxable years of both spouses, whether or not they remain married, whether or not joint returns are filed for such subsequent taxable years, and whether or not one of such spouses could have elected the overall limitation for the current taxable year only with the consent of the Commissioner if he had filed a separate return for such year. [Reg. § 1.904-1.]

☐ [T.D. 6275, 12-2-57. Amended by T.D. 6789, 12-30-64, T.D. 7292, 11-30-73, T.D. 7294, 11-29-73 and T.D. 7490, 6-10-77.]

[Reg. § 1.904-2]

§ 1.904-2. **Carryback and carryover of unused foreign tax.**—(a) *Credit for foreign tax carryback or carryover.* A taxpayer who chooses to claim a credit under section 901 for a taxable year is allowed a credit under that section not only for taxes otherwise allowable as a credit but also for taxes deemed paid or accrued in that year as a result of a carryback or carryover of an unused foreign tax under section 904(d). However, the taxes so deemed paid or accrued shall not be allowed as a deduction under section 164(a). The following paragraphs of this section provide rules for the computation of carryovers and carrybacks under section 904(d). For special rules regarding the application of section 904(d) and this section in the case of taxes paid or accrued with respect to section 904(f) interest see section 904(f) and § 1.904-4. For special rules regarding the application of section 904(d) and this section in the case of taxes paid, accrued, or deemed to be paid with respect to section 904(f) dividends see section 904(f) and § 1.904-5. For special rules regarding these computations in the case of taxes paid, accrued, or deemed to be paid with respect to foreign oil and gas extraction income or foreign oil related income, see section 907(b), (e), and (f) and the regulations thereunder.

(b) *Years to which carried*—(1) *General.* If the taxpayer chooses the benefits of section 901 for a taxable year beginning after December 31, 1957, any unused foreign tax (as defined in subparagraph (2) of this paragraph) for such year shall, under section 904(d), be carried to the second preceding taxable year, the first preceding taxable year, and the first, second, third, fourth, and fifth succeeding taxable years, in that order and to the extent not absorbed as taxes deemed paid or accrued, under paragraph (c) of this section, in a prior taxable year. The entire unused foreign tax for any taxable year shall first be carried to the earliest of the taxable years to which, under the preceding sentence, such unused foreign tax may be carried. Any portion of such unused foreign tax not deemed paid or accrued under paragraph (c) of this section in such earliest taxable year shall then be carried to the next earliest taxable year to which such unused foreign tax may be carried, and any portion not absorbed in that year shall then be carried to the next earliest year, and so on.

(2) *Definitions.* (i) When used with reference to a taxable year for which the per-country limitation provided in section 904(a)(1) applies, the term "unused foreign tax" means, with respect to a particular foreign country or possession of the United States, the excess of (a) the income, war profits, and excess profits taxes paid or accrued (or deemed paid or accrued other than by reason of section 904(d)) in such year to such foreign country or possession, over (b) the applicable per-country limitation under section 904(a)(1) for such year.

(ii) When used with reference to a taxable year for which the overall limitation provided in section 904(a)(2) applies, the term "unused foreign tax" means the excess of (a) the income, war profits, and excess profits taxes paid or accrued (or deemed paid or accrued other than by reason of section 904(d)) in such year to all foreign countries and possessions of the United States, over (b) the overall limitation under section 904(a)(2) for such year.

(iii) The term "unused foreign tax" does not include any amount by which the income, war profits, and excess profits taxes paid or accrued, or deemed to be paid, to any foreign country or possession of the United States with respect to foreign mineral income are reduced under section 901(e)(1) and § 1.901-3(b)(1).

(3) *Taxable years beginning before January 1, 1958.* For purposes of this paragraph, the terms "second preceding taxable year" and "first preceding taxable year" do not include any taxable year beginning before January 1, 1958.

(c) *Tax deemed paid or accrued*—(1) *Unused foreign tax for per-country limitation year.* (i) The amount of an unused foreign tax with respect to a particular foreign country or possession of the United States, for a taxable year for which the per-country limitation under section 904(a)(1) applies, which shall be deemed paid or accrued in any taxable year to which such unused foreign tax may be carried under paragraph (b) of this section shall, except as provided in subdivision (iii) of this subparagraph, be equal to the smaller of—

   (a) The portion of such unused foreign tax which, under paragraph (b) of this section, is carried to such taxable year, or

   (b) Any excess limitation for such taxable year with respect to such unused foreign tax (as determined under subdivision (ii) of this subparagraph).

   (ii) The excess limitation for any taxable year (hereinafter called the "excess limitation year") with respect to an unused foreign tax in respect of a particular foreign country or possession of the United States for another taxable year (hereinafter called the "year of origin") shall be the amount, if any, by which the limitation for the excess limitation year with respect to that foreign country or possession (computed under section 904(a)(1)) exceeds the sum of—

   (a) The income, war profits, and excess profits taxes actually paid or accrued to such foreign country or possession in the excess limitation year,

   (b) The income, war profits, and excess profits taxes deemed paid or accrued in such year to such foreign country or possession other than by reason of section 904(d), and

   (c) The portion of the unused foreign tax, with respect to such foreign country or possession for any taxable year earlier than the year of origin, which is absorbed as taxes deemed paid or accrued in the excess limitation year under subdivision (i) of this subparagraph.

   (iii) An unused foreign tax for a taxable year for which the per-country limitation provided in section 904(a)(1) applies shall not be deemed paid or accrued in a taxable year for which the overall limitation provided in section 904(a)(2) applies, notwithstanding that under paragraph (b) of this section such overall limitation year is counted as one of the years to which such unused foreign tax may be carried.

   (iv) Any portion of an unused foreign tax with respect to a particular foreign country or possession of the United States which is deemed paid or accrued under section 904(d) in the year to which it is carried shall be deemed paid or accrued to the same foreign country or possession to which such foreign tax was paid or accrued (or deemed paid or accrued other than by reason of section 904(d)) for the year in which it originated.

   (v) For determination of excess limitation for a year for which the taxpayer does not choose to claim a credit under section 901, see paragraph (d) of this section.

(2) *Unused foreign tax for overall limitation year.* (i) The amount of an unused foreign tax with respect to all foreign countries and possessions of the United States, for a taxable year for which the overall limitation provided in section 904(a)(2) applies, which shall be deemed paid or accrued in any taxable year to which such unused foreign tax may be carried under paragraph (b) of this section shall, except as provided in subdivision (iii) of this subparagraph, be equal to the smaller of—

   (a) The portion of such unused foreign tax which, under paragraph (b) of this section, is carried to such taxable year, or

   (b) Any excess limitation for such taxable year with respect to such unused foreign tax (as determined under subdivision (ii) of this subparagraph).

   (ii) The excess limitation for any taxable year (hereinafter called the "excess limitation year") with respect to an unused foreign tax in respect of all foreign countries and possessions of the United States for another taxable year (hereinafter called the "year of origin") shall be the amount, if any, by which the limitation for the excess limitation year with respect to all foreign countries and possessions of the United States (computed under section 904(a)(2)) exceeds the sum of—

   (a) The income, war profits, and excess profits taxes actually paid or accrued to all foreign countries and possessions in the excess limitation year,

   (b) The income, war profits, and excess profits taxes deemed paid or accrued in such year to all foreign countries and possessions other than by reason of section 904(d), and

   (c) The portion of the unused foreign tax, with respect to all foreign countries and possessions for any taxable year earlier than the year of origin, which is absorbed as taxes deemed paid or accrued in the excess limitation year under subdivision (i) of this subparagraph.

   (iii) An unused foreign tax for a taxable year for which the overall limitation provided in section 904(a)(2) applies shall not be deemed paid or accrued in a taxable year for which the per-country limitation provided in section 904(a)(1) applies, notwithstanding that under paragraph (b) of this section such per-country limitation year is counted as one of the years to which such unused foreign tax may be carried.

   (iv) For determination of excess limitation for a year for which the taxpayer does not choose to claim a credit under section 901, see paragraph (d) of this section.

Reg. § 1.904-2(c)(2)

48,890 Income from Sources Without the United States

See p. 20,601 for regulations not amended to reflect law changes

(3) *Unused foreign tax with respect to foreign mineral income.* If any portion of an unused foreign tax for any taxable year beginning after December 31, 1969, consists of tax paid or accrued, or deemed to be paid, with respect to foreign mineral income, as defined in § 1.901-3(c), such portion shall not be deemed paid or accrued with respect to foreign mineral income in the taxable year to which it is carried under section 904(d).

(d) *Determination of excess limitation for certain years.* An excess limitation for a taxable year may exist, and may absorb all or some portion of an unused foreign tax, even though the taxpayer does not choose to claim a credit under section 901 for such year. In such case, the amount of the excess limitation, if any, for such year (hereinafter called the "deduction year") shall be determined in the same manner as though the taxpayer had chosen to claim a credit under section 901 for that year. For purposes of the preceding sentence—

(1) If the taxpayer has not chosen the benefits of section 901 for any taxable year before the deduction year, the per-country limitation under section 904(a)(1) shall be considered to be applicable for such year, and

(2) If the taxpayer has chosen the benefits of section 901 for any taxable year before the deduction year, the limitation (per-country or overall) applicable for the last taxable year (preceding such deduction year) for which a credit was claimed under section 901 shall be considered to be applicable for such deduction year.

(e) *Periods of less than 12 months.* A fractional part of a year which is a taxable year under sections 441(b) and 7701(a)(23) is a preceding or a succeeding taxable year for the purpose of determining under section 904(d) the years to which the unused foreign tax may be carried, and any unused foreign tax or excess limitation for such fractional part of a year is the unused foreign tax or excess limitation for a taxable year.

(f) *Statement with tax return.* Every taxpayer claiming the benefit of a carryback or carryover of the unused foreign tax to any taxable year for which he chooses to claim a credit under section 901 shall file with his return (or with his claim for refund, if appropriate) for that year as an attachment to his Form 1116 or 1118, as the case may be, a statement setting forth the unused foreign tax deemed paid or accrued under this section and all material and pertinent facts relative thereto, including a detailed schedule showing the computation of the unused foreign tax so carried back or over.

(g) *Illustration of carrybacks and carryovers.* The application of this section may be illustrated by the following examples:

Example (1). (i) A, a calendar year taxpayer using the cash receipts and disbursements method of accounting, chooses to claim a credit under section 901 for each of the taxable years set forth below. Based upon the taxes actually paid to country X, and the section 904(a)(1) limitation applicable in respect of country X, in each of the taxable years, the unused foreign tax deemed paid under section 904(d) in each of the appropriate taxable years is as follows:

Taxable years	1958	1959	1960	1961	1962	1963	1964	1965	1966
Per-country limitation	$175	$150	$100	$100	$100	$300	$400	$200	$600
Taxes actually paid to country X in taxable year	75	60	830	170	150	100	200	140	400
Unused foreign tax to be carried back or over from year of origin	X	X	730	70	50	X	X	X	X
Excess limitation with respect to unused foreign tax for 1960	(100)	(90)	X	X	X	(200)	(200)	(60)	X
1961	X	X	X	X	X	X	X	X	(200)
1962	X	X	X	X	X	X	X	X	(130)
Unused foreign tax absorbed as taxes deemed paid under the carryback and carryover provisions as carried from—									
1960	$100	$90	X	X	X	$200	$200	$60	X
1961	X	X	X	X	X	X	X	X	$70
1962	X	X	X	X	X	X	X	X	50

(ii) The excess limitation for 1958, 1959, 1963, 1964 and 1965, respectively, which is available to absorb the unused foreign tax for 1960 is the amount by which the per-country limitation for each of those years exceeds the taxes actually paid to country X in each such year. The unused

Reg. § 1.904-2(c)(3)

Income from Sources Without the United States

foreign tax for 1961 and 1962 are not taken into account, since neither of those years is a year earlier than 1960, the year of origin in respect of which the excess limitation is being determined. Thus, for example, the excess limitation for 1963 is $200, unreduced by the unused foreign tax for 1961 and 1962. There is no excess limitation for 1966 with respect to the unused foreign tax for 1960, since the unused foreign tax may be carried forward only 5 taxable years. The unused foreign tax ($730) for 1960 is thus absorbed as taxes deemed paid to the extent of the excess limitation for each of the taxable years 1958, 1959, 1963, 1964, and 1965, respectively, and in that order, leaving unused foreign tax in the amount of $80 which cannot be absorbed because it cannot be carried beyond 1965.

(iii) The amount of unused foreign tax for 1961 which is deemed paid in 1966 is $70, the smaller of *(a)* that portion of the unused foreign tax carried to 1966 ($70), or *(b)* the excess limitation for 1966 with respect to such unused foreign tax ($200). The unused foreign tax for 1962 ($50) is not taken into account for such purposes, since that year is not a year earlier than 1961, the year of origin in respect of which the excess limitation for 1966 is being determined.

(iv) The excess limitation for 1966 with respect to the unused foreign tax for 1962 is $130, the amount by which the limitation applicable under section 904(a)(1) for 1966 ($600) exceeds the sum of the taxes actually paid ($400) to country X in that year and the unused foreign tax ($70) for 1961 which is absorbed in 1966 as taxes deemed paid and which is carried from a taxable year earlier than 1962, the year of origin in respect of which the excess limitation for 1966 which is available to absorb the unused foreign unused foreign tax for 1960, a year earlier than 1962, is not taken into account in computing the excess limitation for 1966, since the unused foreign tax for 1960 may not be carried beyond 1965. The unused foreign tax ($50) for 1962 is thus absorbed in full in 1966 as taxes deemed paid, since the unused foreign tax does not exceed the excess limitation ($130) for that year.

Example (2). Assume the same facts as those in example (1) except that the taxpayer does not choose to have the benefits of section 901 for 1961. In that case there is no unused foreign tax for that year to carry back or over to be absorbed in other taxable years as taxes deemed paid. Moreover, the excess limitation is being determined. The unabsorbed part ($80) of the tax for 1962 is $200, instead of $130, that is, the amount by which the limitation applicable under section 904(a)(1) for 1966 ($600) exceeds the taxes actually paid ($400) to country X in that year. The amount of the unused foreign tax absorbed in each taxable year as taxes deemed paid is the same as in example (1) except for 1966. In that year only the unused foreign tax ($50) for 1962 is absorbed as taxes deemed paid.

Example (3). Assume the same facts as those in example (1) except that the taxpayer does not choose the benefits of section 901 for 1959. Since the excess limitation for a taxable year for which the taxpayer does not claim a credit under section 901 is determined in the same manner as though the taxpayer had chosen such credit, the excess limitation for 1959 is determined to be $90 just as in example (1). Moreover, even though such excess limitation absorbs a carryback of $90 from the unused tax for 1960, none of such $90 so deemed paid in 1959 is allowed as a deduction under section 164 or as a credit under section 901 for 1959 or for any other taxable year.

Example (4). (i) B, a calendar year taxpayer using the cash receipts and disbursements method of accounting, chooses the benefits of section 901 for each of the taxable years 1957, 1958, and 1959. Based upon the taxes actually paid to country Y and the per-country limitation applicable with respect to country Y, in each of the taxable years, the unused foreign tax deemed paid under section 904(d) for taxable year 1959 is as follows:

Taxable years	1957	1958
Per-country limitation on credit for taxes paid to Y	$300	$200
Taxes actually paid to Y in taxable year	200	300
Unused foreign tax to be carried back or over from year of origin	X	100
Excess limitation applicable to unused credit	X	X
Unused foreign tax absorbed as taxes deemed paid	X	X

(ii) Since a taxable year beginning before January 1, 1958, cannot constitute a preceding taxable year in which the unused foreign tax for 1958 may be absorbed as taxes deemed paid, the entire unused foreign tax ($100) is absorbed as taxes deemed paid in 1959.

Example (5). (i) C, a calendar year taxpayer using an accrual method of accounting, accrues foreign taxes for the first time in 1961. C chooses the benefits of section 901 for each of the taxable years set forth below and for 1962 elects the overall limitation provided by section 904(a)(2)

Reg. § 1.904-2(g)

48,892 Income from Sources Without the United States

See p. 20,601 for regulations not amended to reflect law changes

which, with the Commissioner's consent, is revoked for 1966. Based upon the taxes actually accrued with respect to foreign countries X and Y for each of the taxable years, the unused foreign tax deemed accrued under section 904(d) in the appropriate taxable years is as follows:

Taxable year	Per country 1961	Overall 1962	Overall 1963	Overall 1964	Overall 1965	Per country 1966
Limitation:						
Country X	$175	X	X	X	X	$290
Country Y	125	X	X	X	X	95
Overall	X	$250	$800	$300	$400	X
Taxes actually accrued:						
Country X	$325	X	X	X	X	$200
Country Y	85	X	X	X	X	100
Aggregate	X	$350	$380	$425	$450	X
Unused foreign tax to be carried back or over from year of origin:						
Country X	150	X	X	X	X	X
Country Y	X	X	X	X	X	$5
Aggregate	X	100	X	125	50	X
Excess limitation:						
Country X	X	X	X	X	X	90
Country Y	40	X	X	X	X	X
Overall	X	X	420	X	X	X
Unused foreign tax absorbed as taxes deemed accrued under section 904(d) and carried from—						
1961 (Country X)	X	X	X	X	X	(90)
1962 (Overall)	X	X	(100)	X	X	X
1964 (Overall)	X	X	(125)	X	X	X
1965 (Overall)	X	X	(50)	X	X	X

(ii) Since the per-country limitation is applicable for 1961 and 1966 only, any unused foreign tax with respect to such years may not be deemed accrued in 1962, 1963, 1964, or 1965, years for which the overall limitation applies. However, the excess limitation for 1966 with respect to country X ($90) is available to absorb a part of the unused foreign tax for 1961 with respect to country X. The difference with respect to country X between the unused foreign tax for 1961 ($150) and the amount absorbed as taxes deemed accrued ($90) in 1966, or $60, may not be carried beyond 1966 since the unused foreign tax may be carried forward only 5 taxable years. There is no excess limitation with respect to country Y for 1961 in respect of the unused foreign tax of country Y for 1966, since the unused foreign tax may be carried back only 2 taxable years.

(iii) Since the overall limitation is applicable for 1962, 1963, 1964, and 1965, any unused foreign tax with respect to such years may not be absorbed as taxes deemed accrued in 1961 or 1966, years for which the per-country limitation applies. However, the excess limitation for 1963 ($420) computed on the basis of the overall limitation is available to absorb the unused foreign tax for 1962 ($100), the unused foreign tax for 1964 ($125), and the unused foreign tax for 1965 ($50), leaving an excess limitation above such absorption of $145 ($420 − $275). [Reg. § 1.904-2.]

☐ [T.D. 6789, 12-30-64. Amended by T.D. 7292, 11-30-73, T.D. 7294, 11-29-73, T.D. 7490, 6-10-77 and T.D. 7961, 6-27-84.]

[Reg. § 1.904-3]

§ 1.904-3. Carryback and carryover of unused foreign tax by husband and wife.—(a) *In general.* This section provides rules, in addition to those prescribed in § 1.904-2, for the carryback and carryover of the unused foreign tax paid or accrued to a foreign country or possession by a husband and wife making a joint return for one or more of the taxable years involved in the computation of the carryback or carryover.

(b) *Joint unused foreign tax and joint excess limitation.* In the case of a husband and wife the joint unused foreign tax or the joint excess limitation for a taxable year for which a joint return is made shall be computed on the basis of the combined income, deductions, taxes, and credit of both spouses as if the combined income, deductions, taxes, and credit were those of one individual.

(c) *Continuous use of joint return.* If a husband and wife make a joint return for the current taxable year, and also make joint returns for each

Reg. § 1.904-3(a)

of the other taxable years involved in the computation of the carryback or carryover of the unused foreign tax to the current taxable year, the joint carryback or the joint carryover to the current taxable year shall be computed on the basis of the joint unused foreign tax and the joint excess limitations.

(d) *From separate to joint return.* If a husband and wife make a joint return for the current taxable year, but make separate returns for all of the other taxable years involved in the computation of the carryback or carryover of the unused foreign tax to the current taxable year, the separate carrybacks or separate carryovers shall be a joint carryback or a joint carryover to the current taxable year. If for such current year the per-country limitation applies, then only the unused foreign tax for a taxable year of a spouse for which the per-country limitation applied to such spouse may constitute a carryover or carryback to the current taxable year. If for such current taxable year the overall limitation applies, then only the unused foreign tax for a taxable year of a spouse for which the overall limitation applied to such spouse may constitute a carryover or carryback to the current taxable year.

(e) *Amounts carried from or through a joint return year to or through a separate return year.* It is necessary to allocate to each spouse his share of an unused foreign tax or excess limitation for any taxable year for which the spouses filed a joint return if—

(1) The husband and wife file separate returns for the current taxable year and an unused foreign tax is carried thereto from a taxable year for which they filed a joint return;

(2) The husband and wife file separate returns for the current taxable year and an unused foreign tax is carried to such taxable year from a year for which they filed separate returns but is first carried through a year for which they filed a joint return; or

(3) The husband and wife file a joint return for the current taxable year and an unused foreign tax is carried from a taxable year for which they filed joint returns but is first carried through a year for which they filed separate returns.

In such cases, the separate carryback or carryover of each spouse to the current taxable year shall be computed in the manner described in § 1.904-2 but with the modifications set forth in paragraph (f) of this section. Where applicable, appropriate adjustments shall be made to take into account the fact that, for any taxable year involved in the computation of the carryback or the carryover, either spouse has interest income described in section 904(f)(2) with respect to which the provisions of section 904(f) and § 1.904-4 apply, dividends described in section 904(f)(1)(B) with respect to which the provisions of section 904(f) and § 1.904-5 apply, or foreign oil related income described in section 907(c) with respect to which the separate limitation on section 907(b) applies.

(f) *Allocation of unused foreign tax and excess limitation*—(1) *Limitation*—(i) *Per-country limitation.* The per-country limitation of a particular spouse with respect to a foreign country or United States possession for a taxable year for which a joint return is made shall be the portion of the limitation on the joint return which bears the same ratio to such limitation as such spouse's taxable income (with gross income and deductions taken into account to the same extent as taken into account on the joint return) from sources within such country or possession (but not in excess of the joint taxable income from sources within such country or possession) bears to the joint taxable income from such sources.

(ii) *Overall limitation.* The overall limitation of a particular spouse for a taxable year for which a joint return is made shall be the portion of the limitation on the joint return which bears the same ratio to such limitation as such spouse's taxable income (with gross income and deductions taken into account to the same extent as taken into account on the joint return) from sources without the United States (but not in excess of the joint taxable income from such sources) bears to the joint taxable income from such sources.

(2) *Unused foreign tax*—(i) *Per-country limitation.* The unused foreign tax of a particular spouse with respect to a foreign country or United States possession for a taxable year for which a joint return is made shall be the excess of his tax paid or accrued to such country or possession over his limitation determined under subparagraph (1)(i) of this paragraph.

(ii) *Overall limitation.* The unused foreign tax of a particular spouse for a taxable year to which the overall limitation applies and for which a joint return is made shall be the excess of his tax paid or accrued to foreign countries and United States possessions over his limitation determined under subparagraph (1)(ii) of this paragraph.

(3) *Excess limitation*—(i) *Per-country limitation taxpayer.* A spouse's excess limitation with respect to a foreign country or possession for a taxable year for which a joint return is made shall be the excess of his limitation determined under subparagraph (1)(i) of this paragraph over his taxes paid or accrued to such country or possession for such taxable year.

(ii) *Overall limitation.* A spouse's excess limitation for a taxable year to which the overall

Reg. § 1.904-3(f)(3)

Income from Sources Without the United States

See p. 20,601 for regulations not amended to reflect law changes

limitation applies and for which a joint return is made shall be the excess of his limitation determined under subparagraph (1)(ii) of this paragraph over his taxes paid or accrued to foreign countries and United States possessions for such taxable year.

(4) *Excess limitation to be applied.* The excess limitation of the particular spouse for any taxable year which is applied against the unused foreign tax of that spouse for another taxable year in order to determine the amount of the unused foreign tax which shall be carried back or over to a third taxable year shall be, in a case in which the excess limitation is determined on a joint return, the sum of the following amounts:

(i) Such spouse's excess limitation determined under subparagraph (3) of this paragraph reduced as provided in subparagraph (5)(i) of this paragraph, and

(ii) The excess limitation of the other spouse determined under subparagraph (3) of this paragraph for that taxable year reduced as provided in subparagraph (5)(i) and (ii) of this paragraph.

(5) *Reduction of excess limitation.*—(i) The part of the excess limitation which is attributable to each spouse for the taxable year, as determined under subparagraph (3) of this paragraph, shall be reduced by absorbing as taxes deemed paid or accrued under section 904(d) in that year the unabsorbed separate unused foreign tax of such spouse, and the unabsorbed unused foreign tax determined under subparagraph (2) of this paragraph of such spouse, for taxable years which begin before the beginning of the year of origin of the unused foreign tax of the particular spouse against which the excess limitation so determined is being applied.

(ii) In addition, the part of the excess limitation which is attributable to the other spouse for the taxable year, as determined under subparagraph (3) of this paragraph, shall be reduced by absorbing as taxes deemed paid or accrued under section 904(d) in that year the unabsorbed unused foreign tax, if any, of such other spouse for the taxable year which begins on the same date as the beginning of the year of origin of the unused foreign tax of the particular spouse against which the excess limitation so determined is being applied.

(6) *Spouses using different limitations.* If an unused foreign tax is carried through a taxable year for which spouses made a joint return and the credit under section 901 for such taxable year is not claimed, and in the prior taxable year separate returns are made in which the per-country limitation applies to one spouse and the overall limitation applies to the other spouse, the amount treated as absorbed in the taxable year for which a joint return is made—

(i) With respect to the spouse for which the per-country limitation applies shall be determined on the basis of the excess limitation which would be allocated to such spouse under subparagraph (3)(i) of this paragraph had the per-country limitation applied for such year to both spouses;

(ii) With respect to the other spouse for which the overall limitation applies shall be determined on the basis of the excess limitation which would be allocated to such spouse under subparagraph (3)(ii) of this paragraph had the overall limitation applied for such year to both spouses.

This subparagraph shall be applied without regard to subparagraph (4)(ii) of this paragraph.

(g) *Illustrations.* This section may be illustrated by the following examples:

Example (1). (a) H and W, calendar year taxpayers, file joint returns for 1961 and 1963, and separate returns for 1962, 1964, and 1965; and for each of those taxable years they choose to claim a credit under section 901. For the taxable years involved, they had unused foreign tax, excess limitations, and carrybacks and carryovers of unused foreign tax as set forth below. The overall limitation applies to both spouses for all taxable years involved in this example. Neither H nor W had an unused foreign tax or excess limitation for any year before 1961 or after 1965. For purposes of this example, any reference to an excess limitation means such a limitation as determined under paragraph (c)(2)(ii) of § 1.904-2 but without regard to any taxes deemed paid or accrued under section 904(d):

Taxable year	1961	1962	1963	1964	1965
Return	Joint	Separate	Joint	Separate	Separate
H's unused foreign tax to be carried over or back, or excess limitation (enclosed in parentheses)..........	$500	$250	$(650)	$400	$(500)
W's unused foreign tax to be carried over or back, or excess limitation (enclosed in parentheses)..........	300	(200)	(300)	150	(100)
Total......................	800	x	(950)	x	x

Reg. § 1.904-3(f)(4)

Income from Sources Without the United States

See p. 20,601 for regulations not amended to reflect law changes

Taxable year Return	1961 Joint	1962 Separate	1963 Joint	1964 Separate	1965 Separate
Carryovers absorbed:					
W's, from 1961		$200W[1]	$100W		
H's, from 1961			500H[2]		
H's, from 1962			150H		
			100W		
W's, from 1964					$ 50W
H's, from 1964					400H
Carrybacks absorbed:					
W's, from 1964			0	100W	
H's, from 1964				0	

[1] W—absorbed by W's excess limitation.
[2] H—absorbed by H's excess limitation.

(b) Two hundred dollars of the $300 constituting W's part of the joint unused foreign tax for 1961 is absorbed by her separate excess limitation of $200 for 1962, and the remaining $100 of such part is absorbed by her part ($300) of the joint excess limitation for 1963. The excess limitation of $300 for 1963 is not required first to be reduced by any amount, since neither H nor W has any unused foreign tax for taxable years beginning before 1961.

(c) H's part ($500) of the joint unused foreign tax for 1961 is absorbed by his part ($650) of the joint excess limitation for 1963. The excess limitation of $650 for 1963 is not required first to be reduced by any amount, since neither H nor W has any unused foreign tax for taxable years beginning before 1961.

(d) H's unused foreign tax of $250 for 1962 is first absorbed (to the extent of $150) by H's part of the joint excess limitation for 1963, which must first be reduced from $650 to $150 by the absorption as taxes deemed paid or accrued in 1963 of H's unused foreign tax of $500 for 1961, which is a taxable year beginning before 1962. The remaining part ($100) of H's unused foreign tax for 1962 is then absorbed by W's part of the joint excess limitation for 1963, which must first be reduced from $300 to $200 by the absorption as taxes deemed paid or accrued in 1963 of the unabsorbed part ($100) of W's unused foreign tax for 1961, which is a taxable year beginning before 1962.

(e) W's unused foreign tax of $150 for 1964 is first absorbed (to the extent of $100) by W's part of the joint excess limitation for 1963, which must first be reduced from $300 to $100 by the absorption as taxes deemed paid or accrued in 1963 of the unabsorbed part ($100) of W's unused foreign tax for 1961 and the unabsorbed part ($100) of H's unused foreign tax for 1962, which are taxable years beginning before 1964. No part of W's unused foreign tax for 1964 is absorbed by H's part of the joint excess limitation for 1963, since H's part of that excess must first be reduced from $650 to $0 by the absorption as taxes deemed paid or accrued in 1963 of H's unused foreign tax of $500 for 1961 and of the unabsorbed part ($150) of H's unused foreign tax for 1962, which are taxable years beginning before 1964. The unabsorbed part ($50) of W's unused foreign tax for 1964 is then absorbed by W's excess limitation of $100 for 1965. No part of W's unused foreign tax for 1964 is absorbed by W's excess limitation for 1962, since that excess limitation must first be reduced from $200 to $0 by W's unused foreign tax for 1961, which is a taxable year beginning before 1964.

(f) No part of H's unused foreign tax of $400 for 1964 is absorbed by H's part of the joint excess limitation for 1963, since H's part of that excess must first be reduced from $650 to $0 by the absorption as taxes deemed paid or accrued in 1963 of H's unused foreign tax of $500 for 1961 and of a part ($150) of H's unused foreign tax for 1962, which are taxable years beginning before 1964. Moreover, no part of H's unused foreign tax of $400 for 1964 is absorbed by W's part of the joint excess limitation for 1963, since W's part of that excess must first be reduced from $300 to $0 by the absorption as taxes deemed paid or accrued in 1963 of the unabsorbed part ($100) of W's unused foreign tax for 1961 and of the unabsorbed part ($100) of H's unused foreign tax for 1962, which are taxable years beginning before 1964, and also by the absorption of a part ($100) of W's unused foreign tax of $150 for 1964, which is a taxable year beginning on the same date as the beginning of H's taxable year 1964. The unabsorbed part ($400) of H's unused foreign tax for 1964 is then absorbed by H's excess limitation of $500 for 1965.

Example (2). (a) Assume the same facts as those in example (1) except that for 1964 W's unused foreign tax is $20, instead of $150. The carrybacks and carryovers absorbed are the same as in example (1) except as indicated in paragraphs (b) and (c) of this example.

Reg. § 1.904-3(g)

(b) No part of W's unused foreign tax of $20 for 1964 is absorbed by W's excess limitation for 1962, since that excess must first be reduced from $200 to $0 by W's unused foreign tax for 1961, which is a taxable year beginning before 1964. W's unused foreign tax of $20 for 1964 is absorbed by W's part of the joint excess limitation for 1963, which must first be reduced from $300 to $100 by the absorption as taxes deemed paid or accrued in 1963 of the unabsorbed part ($100) of W's unused foreign tax for 1961 and the unabsorbed part ($100) of H's unused foreign tax for 1962, which are taxable years beginning before 1964.

(c) For the reason given in paragraph (f) of example (1), no part of H's unused foreign tax of $400 for 1964 is absorbed by H's part of the joint excess limitation for 1963. H's unused foreign tax of $400 for 1964 is first absorbed (to the extent of $80) by W's part of the joint excess limitation for 1963, which must first be reduced from $300 to $80 by the absorption as taxes deemed paid or accrued in 1963 of the unabsorbed part ($100) of W's unused foreign tax for 1961 and of the unabsorbed part ($100) of H's unused foreign tax for 1962, which are taxable years beginning before 1964, and also by the absorption of W's unused foreign tax of $20 for 1964, which is a taxable year beginning on the same date as the beginning of H's taxable year 1964. The unabsorbed part ($320) of H's unused foreign tax for 1964 is then absorbed by H's excess limitation of $500 for 1965.

Example (3). The facts are the same as in example (1) except that the per-country limitation applies to both spouses for all taxable years involved in the example and that excess limitations and the unused foreign taxes relate to a single foreign country. The carryovers and carrybacks are the same as in example (1). [Reg. § 1.904-3.]

☐ [T.D. 6789, 12-30-64. Amended by T.D. 7292, 11-30-73; T.D. 7490, 6-10-77 and T.D. 7961, 6-27-84.]

[Reg. § 1.904-4]

§ 1.904-4. Separate application of section 904 with respect to certain categories of income.—(a) *In general.* A taxpayer is required to compute a separate foreign tax credit limitation for income received or accrued in a taxable year that is described in section 904(d)(1)(A) (passive income), (B) (high withholding tax interest), (C) (financial services income), (D) (shipping income), (E) (dividends from each noncontrolled section 902 corporation), (F) (dividends from a DISC or former DISC), (G) (foreign trade income), (H) (distributions from a FSC or former FSC), or (I) (general limitation income).

(b) *Passive income*—(1) *In general*—(i) *Rule.* The term "passive income" means any—

(A) Income received or accrued by any person that is of a kind that would be foreign personal holding company income (as defined in section 954(c)) if the taxpayer were a controlled foreign corporation, including any amount of gain on the sale or exchange of stock in excess of the amount treated as a dividend under section 1248; or

(B) Amount includible in gross income under section 551 or section 1293.

Passive income does not include any income that is also described in section 904(d)(1)(B) through (H), any export financing interest (as defined in section 904(d)(2)(G) and paragraph (h) of this section), any high taxed income (as defined in section 904(d)(2)(F) and paragraph (c) of this section), or, for taxable years beginning before January 1, 1993, any foreign oil and gas extraction income (as defined in section 907(c)). In addition, passive income does not include any income that would otherwise be passive but is characterized as income in another separate category under the look-through rules. In determining whether any income is of a kind that would be foreign personal holding company income, the rules of section 864(d)(5)(A)(i) and (6) (treating related person factoring income of a controlled foreign corporation as foreign personal holding company income that is not eligible for the export financing income exception to the separate limitation for passive income) shall apply only in the case of income of a controlled foreign corporation (as defined in section 957). Thus, income earned directly by a United States person that is related person factoring income may be eligible for the exception for export financing interest.

(ii) *Example.* The following example illustrates the application of paragraph (b)(1)(i) of this section:

P is a domestic corporation with a branch in foreign country X. P does not have any financial services income. For 1988, P has a net foreign currency gain that would not constitute foreign personal holding company income if P were a controlled foreign corporation because the gain is directly related to the business needs of P. The currency gain is, therefore, general limitation income to P because it is not income of a kind that would be foreign personal holding company income.

(2) *Active rents or royalties*—(i) *In general.* Passive income does not include any rents or royalties that are derived in the active conduct of a trade or business and received from a person who is an unrelated person. Except as provided in

paragraph (b)(2)(ii) of this section, the principles of section 954(c)(2)(A) and the regulations under that section shall apply in determining whether rents or royalties are derived in the active conduct of a trade or business. For this purpose, the term "taxpayer" shall be substituted for the term "controlled foreign corporation" if the recipient of the rents or royalties is not a controlled foreign corporation.

(ii) *Exception for certain rents and royalties.* Rents or royalties are considered derived in the active conduct of a trade or business by a United States person or by a controlled foreign corporation (or other entity to which the look-through rules apply) for purposes of section 904 (but not for purposes of section 954) if the requirements of section 954(c)(2)(A) are satisfied by one or more corporations that are members of an affiliated group of corporations (within the meaning of section 1504(a) without regard to section 1504(b)(3)) of which the recipient is a member.

(iii) *Unrelated person.* For purposes of this paragraph (b)(2), a person is considered to be an unrelated person if the person is not a related person within the meaning of section 954(d)(3), without regard to whether the relationship described in section 954(d)(3) is between a controlled foreign corporation and another person or between two persons neither one of which is a controlled foreign corporation.

(iv) *Example.* The following example illustrates the application of paragraph (b)(2)(ii) of this section.

Example. Controlled foreign corporation S is a wholly-owned subsidiary of P, a domestic corporation. S is regularly engaged in the restaurant franchise business. P licenses trademarks, tradenames, certain know-how, related services, and certain restaurant designs for which S pays P an arm's length royalty. P is regularly engaged in the development and licensing of such property. The royalties received by P for the use of its property are allocable under the look-through rules of §1.904-5 to the royalties S receives from the franchisees. All of the franchisees are unrelated to S or P and operate in S's country of incorporation. S does not satisfy, but P does satisfy, the active trade or business requirements of section 954(c)(2)(A) and the regulations under that section. The royalty income earned by S with regard to its franchisees is foreign personal holding company income that is general limitation income, and the royalties paid to P are general limitation income to P.

(c) *High-taxed income*—(1) *In general.* Income received or accrued by a United States person that would otherwise be passive income shall not be treated as passive income if the income is determined to be high-taxed income. Income shall be considered to be high-taxed income if, after allocating expenses, losses and other deductions of the United States person to that income under paragraph (c)(2)(ii) of this section, the sum of the foreign income taxes paid or accrued by the United States person with respect to such income and the foreign taxes deemed paid or accrued by the United States person with respect to such income under section 902 or section 960 exceeds the highest rate of tax specified in section 1 or 11, whichever applies (and with reference to section 15 if applicable), multiplied by the amount of such income (including the amount treated as a dividend under section 78). If, after application of this paragraph (c), income that would otherwise be passive income is determined to be high-taxed income, such income shall be treated as general limitation income, and any taxes imposed on that income shall be considered related to general limitation income under §1.904-6. If, after application of this paragraph (c), passive income is zero or less than zero, any taxes imposed on the passive income shall be considered related to general limitation income. For additional rules regarding losses related to passive income, see paragraph (c)(2) of this section. Income and taxes shall be translated at the appropriate rates, as determined under sections 986, 987 and 989 and the regulations under those sections, before application of this paragraph (c). For purposes of allocating taxes to groups of income, United States source passive income is treated as any other passive income. In making the determination whether income is high-taxed, however, only foreign source income, as determined under United States tax principles, is relevant. See paragraph (c)(8) *Examples* 10 through 13 of this section for examples illustrating the application of this paragraph (c)(1) and paragraph (c)(2) of this section. This paragraph (c)(1) is applicable for taxable years beginning after March 12, 1999.

(2) *Grouping of items of income in order to determine whether passive income is high-taxed income*—(i) *Effective dates*—(A) *In general.* For purposes of determining whether passive income is high-taxed income, the grouping rules of paragraphs (c)(3)(i) and (ii), (c)(4), and (c)(5) of this section apply to taxable years beginning after December 31, 1987. Except as provided in paragraph (c)(2)(i)(B) of this section, the rules of paragraph (c)(3)(iii) apply to taxable years beginning after December 31, 1987, and ending before December 31, 1998, and the rules of paragraph (c)(3)(iv) apply to taxable years ending on or after December 31, 1998. See Notice 87-6 (1987-1 C.B.417) for the grouping rules applicable to taxa-

Reg. § 1.904-4(c)(2)

ble years beginning after December 31, 1986 and before January 1, 1988. Paragraph (c)(2)(ii) of this section is applicable for taxable years beginning after March 12, 1999.

(B) *Application to prior periods.* A taxpayer may apply the rules of paragraph (c)(3)(iv) to any taxable year beginning after December 31, 1991, and all subsequent years, provided that—

(*1*) The taxpayer's tax liability as shown on an original or amended tax return is consistent with the rules of this section for each such year for which the statute of limitations does not preclude the filing of an amended return on June 30, 1999; and

(*2*) The taxpayer makes appropriate adjustments to eliminate any double benefit arising from the application of this section to years that are not open for assessment.

(ii) *Grouping rules*—(A) *Initial allocation and apportionment of deductions and taxes.* For purposes of determining whether passive income is high-taxed, expenses, losses and other deductions shall be allocated and apportioned initially to each of the groups of passive income (described in paragraphs (c)(3), (4), and (5) of this section) under the rules of §§ 1.861-8 through 1.861-14T and 1.865-1 and 1.865-2. Taxpayers that allocate and apportion interest expense on an asset basis may nevertheless apportion passive interest expense among the groups of passive income on a gross income basis. Foreign taxes are allocated to groups under the rules of § 1.904-6(a)(iii). If a loss on a disposition of property gives rise to foreign tax (i.e., the transaction giving rise to the loss is treated under foreign law as having given rise to a gain), the foreign tax shall be allocated to the group of passive income to which gain on the sale would have been assigned under paragraph (c)(3) or (4) of this section. A determination of whether passive income is high-taxed shall be made only after application of paragraph (c)(2)(ii)(B) of this section (if applicable).

(B) *Reallocation of loss groups.* If, after allocation and apportionment of expenses, losses and other deductions under paragraph (c)(2)(ii)(A) of this section, the sum of the allocable deductions exceeds the gross income in one or more groups, the excess deductions shall proportionately reduce income in the other groups (but not below zero).

(3) *Amounts received or accrued by United States persons.* Except as provided in paragraph (c)(5) of this section, all passive income received by a United States person shall be subject to the rules of this paragraph (c)(3). However, subpart F inclusions that are passive income and income that is earned by a United States person through a foreign qualified business unit (foreign QBU) that is passive income shall be subject to the rules of this paragraph only to the extent provided in paragraph (c)(4)(ii) of this section. For purposes of this section, a foreign QBU is a QBU (as defined in section 989(a)) other than a controlled foreign corporation, that has its principal place of business outside the United States. These rules shall apply whether the income is received from a controlled foreign corporation of which the United States person is a United States shareholder or from any other person. For purposes of determining whether passive income is high-taxed income, the following rules apply:

(i) All passive income received during the taxable year that is subject to a withholding tax of fifteen percent or greater shall be treated as one item of income.

(ii) All passive income received during the taxable year that is subject to a withholding tax of less than fifteen percent (but greater than zero) shall be treated as one item of income.

(iii) For taxable years ending before December 31, 1998 (except as provided in paragraph (c)(2)(i)(B) of this section), all passive income received during the taxable year that is subject to no withholding tax shall be treated as one item of income.

(iv) For taxable years ending on or after December 31, 1998, all passive income received during the taxable year that is subject to no withholding tax or other foreign tax shall be treated as one item of income, and all passive income received during the taxable year that is subject to no withholding tax but is subject to a foreign tax other than a withholding tax shall be treated as one item of income.

(4) *Income of controlled foreign corporations and foreign QBUs.* Except as provided in paragraph (c)(5) of this section, all amounts included in gross income of a United States shareholder under section 951(a)(1) for a particular year that (after application of the look-through rules of section 904(d)(3) and § 1.904-5) are attributable to passive income received or accrued by a controlled foreign corporation and all amounts of passive income received or accrued by a United States person through a foreign QBU shall be subject to the rules of this paragraph (c)(4). This paragraph (c)(4) shall be applied separately to inclusions with respect to each controlled foreign corporation of which the taxpayer is a United States shareholder. This paragraph (c)(4) also shall be applied separately to income attributable to each QBU of a controlled foreign corporation or any other look-through entity as defined in § 1.904-5(i), except that if the entity subject to the look-through rules

Reg. § 1.904-4(c)(3)

is a United States person, then this paragraph (c)(4) shall be applied separately only to each foreign QBU of that United States person.

(i) *Income from sources within the QBU's country of operation.* Passive income from sources within the QBU's country of operation shall be treated as one item of income.

(ii) *Income from sources without the QBU's country of operation.* Passive income from sources without the QBU's country of operation shall be grouped on the basis of the tax imposed on that income as provided in paragraphs (c)(3)(i) through (iv) of this section.

(iii) *Determination of the source of income.* For purposes of this paragraph (c)(4), income will be determined to be from sources within or without the QBU's country of operation under the laws of the foreign country of the payor of the income.

(5) *Special rules*—(i) *Certain rents and royalties.* All items of rent or royalty income to which an item of rent or royalty expense is directly allocable shall be treated as a single item of income and shall not be grouped with other amounts.

(ii) *Treatment of partnership income.* A partner's distributive share of income from a foreign or United States partnership that is not subject to the look-through rules and that is treated as passive income under § 1.904-5(h)(2)(i) (generally providing that a less than 10 percent partner's distributive share of partnership income is passive income) shall be treated as a single item of income and shall not be grouped with other amounts. A distributive share of income from a foreign partnership that is treated as passive income under the look-through rules shall be grouped according to the rules in paragraph (c)(4) of this section. A distributive share of income from a United States partnership that is treated as passive income under the look-through rules shall be grouped according to the rules in paragraph (c)(3) of this section, except that the portion, if any, of the distributive share of income attributable to income earned by a United States partnership through a foreign QBU shall be grouped under the rules of paragraph (c)(4) of this section.

(iii) *Currency gain or loss*—(A) *Section 986(c).* Any currency gain or loss with respect to a distribution received by a United States shareholder (other than a foreign QBU of that shareholder) of previously taxed earnings and profits that is recognized under section 986(c) and that is treated as an item of passive income shall be subject to the rules provided in paragraph (c)(3)(iii) of this section. If that item, however, is received or accrued by a foreign QBU of the United States shareholder, it shall be treated as an item of passive income from sources within the QBU's country of operation for purposes of paragraph (c)(4)(i) of this section. This paragraph (c)(5)(iii)(A) shall be applied separately for each foreign QBU of a United States shareholder.

(B) *Section 987(3).* Any currency gain or loss with respect to remittances or transfers of property between QBUs of a United States shareholder that is recognized under section 987(3)(B) and that is treated as an item of passive income shall be subject to the rules provided in paragraph (c)(3)(iii) of this section. If that item, however, is received or accrued by a foreign QBU of the United States shareholder, it shall be treated as an item of passive income from sources within the QBU's country of operation for purposes of paragraph (c)(4)(i) of this section. This paragraph (c)(5)(iii)(B) shall be applied separately for each foreign QBU of a United States shareholder.

(C) *Example.* The following example illustrates the provisions of this paragraph (c)(5)(iii).

Example. P, a domestic corporation, owns all of the stock of S, a controlled foreign corporation that uses x as its functional currency. In 1993, S earns 100x of passive foreign personal holding company income. When included in P's income under subpart F, the exchange rate is 1x equals $1. Therefore, P's subpart F inclusion is $100. At the end of 1993, S has previously taxed earnings and profits of 100x and P's basis in those earnings is $100. In 1994, S has no earnings and distributes 100x to P. The value of the earnings when distributed is $150. Assume that under section 986(c), P must recognize $50 of passive income attributable to the appreciation of the previously taxed income. Country X does not recognize any gain or loss on the distribution. Therefore, the section 986(c) gain is not subject to any foreign withholding tax or other foreign tax. Thus, under paragraph (c)(3)(iii) of this section, the section 986(c) gain shall be grouped with other items of P's income that are subject to no withholding tax or other foreign tax.

(iv) *Certain passive dividends.* A dividend from a controlled foreign corporation that is treated as passive income under the look-through rules shall be grouped according to the rules of paragraph (c)(4) of this section.

(v) *Coordination with section 954(b)(4).* For rules relating to passive income of a controlled foreign corporation that is exempt from subpart F treatment because the income is subject to high foreign tax, see section 904(d)(3)(E), § 1.904-4(c)(7)(iii), and § 1.904-5(d)(2).

Reg. § 1.904-4(c)(5)

(6) *Application of this paragraph to additional taxes paid or deemed paid in the year of receipt of previously taxed income*—(i) *Determination made in year of inclusion.* The determination of whether an amount included in gross income under section 951(a) is high-taxed income shall be made in the taxable year the income is included in the gross income of the United States shareholder under section 951(a) (hereinafter the "taxable year of inclusion"). Any increase in foreign taxes paid or accrued, or deemed paid or accrued, when the taxpayer receives an amount that is excluded from gross income under section 959(a) and that is attributable to a controlled foreign corporation's earnings and profits relating to the amount previously included in gross income will not be considered in determining whether the amount included in income in the taxable year of inclusion is high-taxed income.

(ii) *Exception.* Paragraph (c)(6)(i) of this section shall not apply to an increase in tax in a case in which the taxpayer is required to adjust its foreign taxes in the year of inclusion under section 905(c).

(iii) *Allocation of foreign taxes imposed on distributions of previously taxed income.* If an item of income is considered high-taxed income in the year of inclusion and paragraph (c)(6)(i) of this section applies, then any increase in foreign income taxes imposed with respect to that item shall be considered to be related to general limitation income. If an item of income is not considered to be high-taxed income in the taxable year of inclusion and paragraph (c)(6)(i) of this section applies, the following rules shall apply. The taxpayer shall treat an increase in taxes paid or accrued, or deemed paid or accrued, on any distribution of the earnings and profits attributable to the amount included in gross income in the taxable year of inclusion as taxes related to passive income to the extent of the excess of the product of (A) the highest rate of tax in section 11 (determined with regard to section 15 and determined as of the year of inclusion) and (B) the amount of the inclusion (after allocation of parent expenses) over (C) the taxes paid or accrued, or deemed paid or accrued, in the year of inclusion. The taxpayer shall treat any taxes paid or accrued, or deemed paid or accrued, on the distribution in excess of this amount as taxes related to general limitation income. If these additional taxes are not creditable in the year of distribution the carryover rules of section 904(c) apply. For purposes of this paragraph, the foreign tax on a subpart F inclusion shall be considered increased on distribution of the earnings and profits associated with that inclusion if the total of taxes paid and deemed paid on the inclusion and the distribution (taking into account any reductions in tax and any withholding taxes) is greater than the total taxes deemed paid in the year of inclusion. Any foreign currency loss associated with the earnings and profits that are distributed with respect to the inclusion is not to be considered as giving rise to an increase in tax.

(iv) *Increase in taxes paid by successors*—(A) *General rule.* Except as provided in paragraph (c)(6)(iv)(B) of this section, if passive earnings and profits previously included in income of a United States shareholder are distributed to a person that was not a United States shareholder of the distributing corporation in the year the earnings were included, any increase in foreign taxes paid or accrued, or deemed paid or accrued, on that distribution shall be treated as taxes related to general limitation income, regardless of whether the previously-taxed income was considered high-taxed income under section 904(d)(2)(F) in the year of inclusion.

(B) *Exception for U.S. shareholders not entitled to look-through.* In the case of a United States shareholder that, by reason of paragraph (g)(3)(ii) of this section (relating to distributions prior to August 6, 1997, to new shareholders acquiring more than 90 percent of a controlled foreign corporation), is not entitled to look-through treatment with respect to pre-acquisition earnings and profits of the distributing corporation, the increase in foreign taxes described in paragraph (c)(6)(iv)(A) of this section shall be treated as taxes related to the noncontrolled section 902 corporation income of the distributing corporation.

(C) *Effective date.* This paragraph (c)(6)(iv) applies to taxable years beginning after December 31, 1986. However, for taxable years beginning before January 1, 2001, taxpayers may rely on § 1.904-4(c)(6)(iv) of regulations project INTL-1-92, published at 1992-1 C.B. 1209. See § 601.601(d)(2) of this chapter.

(7) *Application of this paragraph to certain reductions of tax on distributions of income*—(i) *In general.* If the effective rate of tax imposed by a foreign country on income of a foreign corporation that is included in a taxpayer's gross income is reduced under foreign law on distribution of such income, the rules of this paragraph (c) apply at the time that the income is included in the taxpayer's gross income without regard to the possibility of subsequent reduction of foreign tax on the distribution. If the inclusion is considered to be high-taxed income, then the taxpayer shall treat the inclusion as general limitation income. When the foreign corporation distributes the earnings and profits to which the inclusion was attributable and the foreign tax on the inclusion is

reduced, then the taxpayer shall redetermine whether the inclusion should be considered to be high-taxed income provided that a redetermination of United States tax liability is required under section 905(c). If, taking into account the reduction in foreign tax, the inclusion would not have been considered high-taxed income, then the taxpayer, in redetermining its United States tax liability for the year or years affected, shall treat the inclusion and the associated taxes (as reduced on the distribution) as passive income and taxes. See section 905(c) and the regulations thereunder regarding the method of adjustment. For this purpose, the foreign tax on a subpart F inclusion shall be considered reduced on distribution of the earnings and profits associated with the inclusion if the total of taxes paid and deemed paid on the inclusion and the distribution (taking into account any reductions in tax and any withholding taxes) is less than the total taxes deemed paid in the year of inclusion. Any foreign currency gain associated with the earnings and profits that are distributed with respect to the inclusion is not to be considered a reduction of tax.

(ii) *Allocation of reductions of foreign tax.* For purposes of paragraph (c)(7)(i) of this section, reductions in foreign tax shall be allocated among the separate categories under the same principles as those of § 1.904-6 for allocating taxes among the separate categories. Thus, for purposes of determining to which year's taxes the reduction in taxes relates, foreign law shall apply. If, however, foreign law does not attribute a reduction in taxes to a particular year or years, then the reduction in taxes shall be attributable, on an annual last infirst out (LIFO) basis, to foreign taxes potentially subject to reduction that are associated with previously taxed income, then on a LIFO basis to foreign taxes associated with income that under paragraph (c)(7)(iii) of this section remains as passive income but that was excluded from subpart F income under section 954(b)(4), and finally on a LIFO basis to foreign taxes associated with other earnings and profits. Furthermore, in applying the ordering rules of section 959(c), distributions shall be considered made on a LIFO basis first out of earnings described in section 959(c)(1) and (2), then on a LIFO basis out of earnings and profits associated with income that remains passive income under paragraph (c)(7)(iii) of this section but that was excluded from subpart F under section 954(b)(4), and finally on a LIFO basis out of other earnings and profits. For purposes of this paragraph (c)(7)(ii), foreign law is not considered to attribute a reduction in tax to a particular year or years if foreign law attributes the tax reduction to a pool or group containing income from more than one taxable year and such pool or group is defined based on a characteristic of the income (for example, the rate of tax paid with respect to the income) rather than on the taxable year in which the income is derived.

(iii) *Interaction with section 954(b)(4).* If the effective rate of tax imposed by a foreign country on income of a foreign corporation is reduced under foreign law on distribution of that income, the rules of section 954(b)(4) shall be applied without regard to the possibility of subsequent reduction of foreign tax. If a taxpayer excludes passive income from a controlled foreign corporation's foreign personal holding company income under these circumstances, then, notwithstanding the general rule of § 1.904-5(d)(2), the income shall be considered to be passive income until distribution of that income. At that time, the rules of this paragraph shall apply to determine whether the income is high-taxed income and, therefore, general limitation income. For purposes of determining whether a reduction in tax is attributable to taxes on income excluded under section 954(b)(4), the rules of paragraph (c)(7)(ii) of this section apply. The rules of paragraph (c)(7)(ii) of this section shall apply for purposes of ordering distributions to determine whether such distributions are out of earnings and profits associated with such excluded income. For an example illustrating the operation of this paragraph (c)(7)(iii), see paragraph (c)(8) *Example (7)* of this section.

(8) *Examples.* The following examples illustrate the application of this paragraph (c).

Example (1). Controlled foreign corporation S is a wholly-owned subsidiary of domestic corporation P. S is a single qualified business unit (QBU) operating in foreign country X. In 1988, S earns $130 of gross passive royalty income from country X sources, and incurs $30 of expenses that do not include any payments to P. S's $100 of net passive royalty income is subject to $30 of foreign tax, and is included under section 951 in P's gross income for the taxable year. P allocates $50 of expenses to the $100 (consisting of the $70 section 951 inclusion and $30 section 78 amount), resulting in a net inclusion of $50. After application of the high-tax kick-out rules of paragraph (c)(1) of this section, the $50 inclusion is treated as general limitation income, and the $30 of taxes deemed paid are treated as taxes imposed on general limitation income, because the foreign taxes paid and deemed paid on the income exceed the highest United States tax rate multiplied by the $50 inclusion ($30>$17 (.34 × $50)).

Example (2). The facts are the same as in *Example (1)* except that instead of earning $130 of gross passive royalty income, S earns $65 of

Reg. § 1.904-4(c)(8)

gross passive royalty income from country X sources and $65 of gross passive interest income from country Y sources. S incurs $15 of expenses and $5 of foreign tax with regard to the royalty income and incurs $15 of expenses and $10 of foreign tax with regard to the interest income. P allocates $50 of expenses pro rata to the $50 inclusion ($45 section 951 inclusion and $5 section 78 amount) attributable to the royalty income earned by S and the $50 inclusion ($40 section 951 inclusion and $10 section 78 amount) attributable to the interest income earned by S. Under paragraph (c)(4) of this section, the high-tax test is applied separately to the section 951 inclusion attributable to the income from X sources and the section 951 inclusion attributable to the income from Y sources. Therefore, after allocation of P's $50 of expenses, the resulting $25 inclusion attributable to the royalty income from X sources is still treated as passive income because the foreign taxes paid and deemed paid on the income do not exceed the highest United States tax rate multiplied by the $25 inclusion ($5<$8.50 (.34 × $25)). The $25 inclusion attributable to the interest income from Y sources is treated as general limitation income because the foreign taxes paid and deemed paid exceed the highest United States tax rate multiplied by the $25 inclusion ($10>$8.50 (.34 × $25)).

Example (3). Controlled foreign corporation S is a wholly-owned subsidiary of domestic corporation P. S is incorporated and operating in country Y and has a branch in country Z. S has two QBUs (QBU Y and QBU Z). In 1988, S earns $65 of gross passive royalty income in country Y through QBU Y and $65 of gross passive royalty income in country Z through QBU Z. S allocates $15 of expenses to the gross passive royalty income earned by each QBU, resulting in net income of $50 in each QBU. Country Y imposes $5 of foreign tax on the royalty income earned in Y, and country Z imposes $10 of tax on royalty income earned in Z. All of S's income constitutes subpart F foreign personal holding company income that is passive income and is included in P's gross income for the taxable year. P allocates $50 of expenses pro rata to the $100 subpart F inclusion attributable to the QBUs (consisting of the $45 section 951 inclusion derived through QBU Y, the $5 section 78 amount attributable to QBU Y, the $40 section 951 inclusion derived through QBU Z, and the $10 section 78 amount attributable to QBU Z), resulting in a net inclusion of $50. Pursuant to paragraph (c)(4) of this section, the high-tax kickout rules must be applied separately to the subpart F inclusion attributable to the income earned by QBU Y and the income earned by QBU Z. After application of the high-tax kickout rules, the $25 inclusion attributable to Y will still be treated as passive income because the foreign taxes paid and deemed paid on the income do not exceed the highest United States tax rate multiplied by the $25 inclusion ($5<$8.50 (.34 × $25)). The $25 inclusion attributable to Z will be treated as general limitation income because the foreign taxes paid and deemed paid on the income exceed the highest United States tax rate multiplied by the $25 inclusion ($10>$8.50 (.34 × $25)).

Example (4). Domestic corporation M operates in branch form in foreign countries X and Y. The branches are qualified business units (QBUs), within the meaning of section 989(a). In 1988, QBU X earns passive royalty income, interest income and rental income. All of the QBU X passive income is from Country Z sources. The royalty income is not subject to a withholding tax, and is not taxed by Country X, and the interest and the rental income are subject to a 5 percent and 10 percent withholding tax, respectively. QBU Y earns interest income in Country Y that is not subject to foreign tax. For purposes of determining whether M's foreign source passive income is high-taxed income, the rental income and the interest income earned in QBU X are treated as one item of income pursuant to paragraphs (c)(4)(ii) and (3)(ii) of this section. The interest income earned in QBU Y and the royalty income earned in QBU X are each treated as a separate item of income under paragraphs (c)(4)(i) (with respect to QBU Y's interest income) and (c)(4)(ii) and (3)(iii) (with respect to QBU X's royalty income) of this section.

Example (5). S, a controlled foreign corporation incorporated in foreign country R, is a wholly-owned subsidiary of P, a domestic corporation. For 1988, P is required under section 951(a) to include in gross income $80 (not including the section 78 amount) attributable to the earnings and profits of S for such year, all of which is foreign personal holding company income that is passive rent or royalty income. S does not make any distributions in 1988 or 1989. Foreign income taxes paid by S for 1988 that are deemed paid by P for such year under section 960(a) with respect to the section 951(a) inclusion equal $20. Twenty dollars ($20) of P's expenses are properly allocated to the section 951(a) inclusion. The foreign income tax paid with respect to the section 951(a) inclusion does not exceed the highest United States tax rate multiplied by the amount of income after allocation of parent expenses ($20<$27.20 (.34 × $80)). Thus, P's section 951(a) inclusion for 1988 is included in P's passive income and the $20 of taxes attributable to that inclusion are treated as taxes related to passive

Income from Sources Without the United States

income. In 1990, S distributes $80 to P, and under section 959 that distribution is treated as attributable to the earnings and profits with respect to the amount included in income by P in 1988 and is excluded from P's gross income. Foreign country R imposes a withholding tax of $15 on the distribution in 1990. Under paragraph (c)(6)(i) of this section, the withholding tax in 1990 does not affect the characterization of the 1988 inclusion as passive income nor does it affect the characterization of the $20 of taxes paid in 1988 as taxes paid with respect to passive income. No further parent expenses are allocable to the receipt of that distribution. In 1990, the foreign taxes paid ($15) exceed the product of the highest United States tax rate and the amount of the inclusion reduced by taxes deemed paid in the year of inclusion ($15 > ((.34 \times $80) - $20)$). Thus, under paragraph (c)(6)(iii) of this section, $7.20 ((.34 \times $80) - $20)$ of the $15 withholding tax paid in 1990 is treated as taxes related to passive income and the remaining $7.80 ($15 - $7.20) of the withholding tax is treated as related to general limitation income.

Example (6). S, a controlled foreign corporation, is a wholly-owned subsidiary of P, a domestic corporation. P and S are calendar year taxpayers. In 1987, S's only earnings consist of $200 of passive income that is foreign personal holding company income that is earned in foreign country X. Under country X's tax system, the corporate tax on particular earnings is reduced on distribution of those earnings and no withholding tax is imposed. In 1987, S pays $100 of foreign tax. P does not elect to exclude this income from subpart F under section 954(b)(4) and includes $200 in gross income ($100 of net foreign personal holding company income and $100 of the section 78 amount). At the time of the inclusion, the income is considered to be high-taxed income under paragraphs (c)(1) and (c)(6)(i) of this section and is general limitation income to P. S does not distribute any of its earnings in 1987. In 1988, S has no earnings. On December 31, 1988, S distributes the $100 of earnings from 1987. At that time, S receives a $50 refund from X attributable to the reduction of the country X corporate tax imposed on those earnings. Under paragraph (c)(7)(i) of this section, P must redetermine whether the 1987 inclusion should be considered to be high-taxed income. By taking into account the reduction in foreign tax, the inclusion would not have been considered high-taxed income. Therefore, P must redetermine its foreign tax credit for 1987 and treat the inclusion and the taxes associated with the inclusion as passive income and taxes. P must follow the appropriate section 905(c) procedures.

Example (7). The facts are the same as in Example (6) except that P elects to apply section 954(b)(4) to S's passive income that is subpart F income. Although the income is not considered to be subpart F income, it remains passive income until distribution. In 1988, S distributes $150 to P. The distribution is a dividend to P because S has $150 of accumulated earnings and profits (the $100 of earnings in 1987 and the $50 refund in 1988). P has no expenses allocable to the dividend from S. In 1988, the income is subject to the high-tax kick-out rules under paragraph (c)(7)(iii) of this section. The income is passive income to P because the foreign taxes paid and deemed paid by P with respect to the income do not exceed the highest United States tax rate on that income.

Example (8). The facts are the same as in Example (6) except that the distribution in 1988 is subject to a withholding tax of $25. Under paragraph (c)(7)(i) of this section, P must redetermine whether the 1987 inclusion should be considered to be high-taxed income because there is a net $25 reduction of foreign tax. By taking into account both the reduction in foreign corporate tax and the withholding tax, the inclusion would continue to be considered high-taxed income. P must follow the appropriate section 905(c) procedures. P must redetermine its foreign tax credit for 1987, but the inclusion and the $75 taxes ($50 of deemed paid tax and $25 withholding tax) will continue to be treated as general limitation income and taxes.

Example (9). (i) S, a controlled foreign corporation operating in country G, is a wholly-owned subsidiary of P, a domestic corporation. P and S are calendar year taxpayers. Country G imposes a tax of 50 percent on S's earnings. Under country G's system, the foreign corporate tax on particular earnings is reduced on distribution of those earnings to 30 percent and no withholding tax is imposed. Under country G's law, distributions are treated as made out of a pool of undistributed earnings subject to the 50% tax rate. For 1987, S's only earnings consist of passive income that is foreign personal holding company income that is earned in foreign country G. S has taxable income of $110 for United States purposes and $100 for country G purposes. Country G, therefore, imposes a tax of $50 on the 1987 earnings of S. P does not elect to exclude this income from subpart F under section 954(b)(4) and includes $110 in gross income ($60 of net foreign personal holding company income and $50 of the section 78 amount). At the time of the inclusion, the income is considered to be high-taxed income under paragraph (c) of this section and is general limitation income to P. S does not distribute any of its taxable income in 1987.

Reg. § 1.904-4(c)(8)

(ii) In 1988, S earns general limitation income that is not subpart F income. S again has $110 in taxable income for United States purposes and $100 in taxable income for country G purposes, and S pays $50 of tax to foreign country G. In 1989, S has no taxable income or earnings. On December 31, 1989, S distributes $60 of earnings and receives a refund of foreign tax of $24. Country G treats the distribution of earnings as out of the 50% tax rate pool of earnings accumulated in 1987 and 1988. However, under paragraph (c)(7)(ii) of this section, the distribution, and, therefore, the reduction of tax is treated as first attributable to the $60 of passive earnings attributable to income previously taxed in 1987. However, because, under foreign law, only 40 percent (the reduction in tax rates from 50 percent to 30 percent is a 40 percent reduction in tax) of the $50 of foreign taxes on the passive earnings can be refunded, $20 of the $24 foreign tax refund reduces foreign taxes on passive earnings. The other $4 of the tax refund reduces the general limitation taxes from $50 to $46 (even though for United States purposes the $60 distribution is entirely out of passive earnings).

(iii) Under paragraph (c)(7) of this section, P must redetermine whether the 1987 inclusion should be considered to be high-taxed income. By taking into account the reduction in foreign tax, the inclusion would not have been considered high-taxed income ($30 < .34 × $110). Therefore, P must redetermine its foreign tax credit for 1987 and treat the inclusion and the taxes associated with the inclusion as passive income and taxes. P must follow the appropriate section 905(c) procedures.

Example (10). P, a domestic corporation, earns $100 of passive royalty income from sources within the United States. Under the laws of Country X, however, that royalty is considered to be from sources within Country X and Country X imposes a 10 percent withholding tax on the payment of the royalty. P also earns $100 of passive foreign source dividend income subject to a 10 percent withholding tax to which $15 of expenses are allocated. In determining whether P's passive income is high-taxed, the $10 withholding tax on P's royalty income is allocated to passive income, and within the passive category to the group of income described in paragraph (c)(3)(ii) of this section (passive income subject to a withholding tax of less than 15 percent (but greater than zero)). For purposes of determining whether the income is high-taxed, however, only the foreign source dividend income is taken into account. The foreign source dividend income will still be treated as passive income because the foreign taxes paid on the passive income in the group ($20) do not exceed the highest United States tax rate multiplied by the $85 of net foreign source income in the group ($20 is less than $28.90 ($100 − $15) × .34).

Example 11. In 2001, P, a U.S. citizen with a tax home in Country X, earns the following items of gross income: $400 of foreign source, passive limitation interest income not subject to foreign withholding tax but subject to Country X income tax of $100, $200 of foreign source, passive limitation royalty income subject to a 5 percent foreign withholding tax (foreign tax paid is $10), $1,300 of foreign source, passive limitation rental income subject to a 25 percent foreign withholding tax (foreign tax paid is $325), $500 of foreign source, general limitation income that gives rise to a $250 foreign tax, and $2,000 of U.S. source capital gain that is not subject to any foreign tax. P has a $900 deduction allocable to its passive rental income. P's only other deduction is a $700 capital loss on the sale of stock that is allocated to foreign source passive limitation income under § 1.865-2(a)(3)(i). The $700 capital loss is initially allocated to the group of passive income subject to no withholding tax but subject to foreign tax other than withholding tax. The $300 amount by which the capital loss exceeds the income in the group must be reapportioned to the other groups under paragraph (c)(2)(ii)(B) of this section. The royalty income is thus reduced by $100 to $100 ($200 − ($300 x (200/600))) and the rental income is thus reduced by $200 to $200 ($400 − ($300 x (400/600))). The $100 royalty income is not high-taxed and remains passive income because the foreign taxes do not exceed the highest United States rate of tax on that income. Under the high-tax kick-out, the $200 of rental income and the $325 of associated foreign tax are assigned to the general limitation category.

Example 12. The facts are the same as in *Example 11* except the amount of the capital loss that is allocated under § 1.865-2(a)(3)(i) and paragraph (c)(2) of this section to the group of foreign source passive income subject to no withholding tax but subject to foreign tax other than withholding tax is $1,200. Under paragraph (c)(2)(ii)(B) of this section, the excess deductions of $800 must be reapportioned to the $200 of net royalty income subject to a 5 percent withholding tax and the $400 of net rental income subject to a 15 percent or greater withholding tax. The income in each of these groups is reduced to zero, and the foreign taxes imposed on the rental and royalty income are considered related to general limitation income. The remaining loss of $200 constitutes a separate limitation loss with respect to passive income.

Reg. § 1.904-4(c)(8)

Income from Sources Without the United States

Example 13. In 2001, P, a domestic corporation, earns a $100 dividend that is foreign source passive limitation income subject to a 30-percent withholding tax. A foreign tax credit for the withholding tax on the dividend is disallowed under section 901(k). A deduction for the tax is allowed, however, under sections 164 and 901(k)(7). In determining whether P's passive income is high-taxed, the $100 dividend and the $30 deduction are allocated to the first group of income described in paragraph (c)(3)(iv) of this section (passive income subject to no withholding tax or other foreign tax).

(d) *High withholding tax interest.* The term "high withholding tax interest" means any interest if such interest is subject to a withholding tax of a foreign country or a possession of the United States and the rate of tax applicable to such interest is at least 5 percent. For purposes of the preceding sentence, a withholding tax is any tax imposed by a foreign country or possession of the United States that is determined on a gross basis. A withholding tax shall not be considered to be determined on a gross basis if the tax is not the final tax payable on the interest income, but is merely a prepayment or credit against a final foreign tax liability determined on a net basis on the interest alone or on interest and other income. High withholding tax interest does not include any interest described as export financing interest (as defined in section 904(d)(2)(G) and paragraph (h) of this section).

(e) *Financial services income*—(1) *In general.* The term "financial services income" means income derived by a financial services entity, as defined in paragraph (e)(3) of this section, that is:

(i) Income derived in the active conduct of a banking, insurance, financing, or similar business (active financing income as defined in paragraph (e)(2) of this section), except income described in paragraph (e)(2)(i)(W) of this section (high withholding tax interest);

(ii) Passive income as defined in section 904(d)(2)(A) and paragraph (b) of this section as determined before the application of the exception for high-taxed income;

(iii) Export financing interest as defined in section 904(d)(2)(G) and paragraph (h) of this section that, but for section 904(d)(2)(B)(ii), would also meet the definition of high withholding tax interest; or

(iv) Incidental income as defined in paragraph (e)(4) of this section.

(2) *Active financing income*—(i) *Income included.* For purposes of paragraph (e)(1) and (e)(3) of this section, income is active financing income only if it is described in any of the following subdivisions.

(A) Income that is of a kind that would be insurance income as defined in section 953(a) (including related party insurance income as defined in section 953(c)(2)) and determined without regard to those provisions of section 953(a)(1)(A) that limit insurance income to income from countries other than the country in which the corporation was created or organized.

(B) Income from the investment by an insurance company of its unearned premiums or reserves ordinary and necessary to the proper conduct of the insurance business, income from providing services as an insurance underwriter, income from insurance brokerage or agency services, and income from loss adjuster and surveyor services.

(C) Income from investing funds in circumstances in which the taxpayer holds itself out as providing a financial service by the acceptance or the investment of such funds, including income from investing deposits of money and income earned investing funds received for the purchase of traveller's checks or face amount certificates.

(D) Income from making personal, mortgage, industrial, or other loans.

(E) Income from purchasing, selling, discounting, or negotiating on a regular basis, notes, drafts, checks, bills of exchange, acceptances, or other evidences of indebtedness.

(F) Income from issuing letters of credit and negotiating drafts drawn thereunder.

(G) Income from providing trust services.

(H) Income from arranging foreign exchange transactions, or engaging in foreign exchange transactions.

(I) Income from purchasing stock, debt obligations, or other securities from an issuer or holder with a view to the public distribution thereof or offering or selling stock, debt obligations, or other securities for an issuer or holder in connection with the public distribution thereof, or participating in any such undertaking.

(J) Income earned by broker-dealers in the ordinary course of business (such as commissions) from the purchase or sale of stock, debt obligations, commodities futures, or other securities or financial instruments and dividend and interest income earned by broker dealers on stock, debt obligations, or other financial instruments that are held for sale.

(K) Service fee income from investment and correspondent banking.

Reg. § 1.904-4(e)(2)

48,906   Income from Sources Without the United States
See p. 20,601 for regulations not amended to reflect law changes

(L) Income from interest rate and currency swaps.

(M) Income from providing fiduciary services.

(N) Income from services with respect to the management of funds.

(O) Bank-to-bank participation income.

(P) Income from providing charge and credit card services or for factoring receivables obtained in the course of providing such services.

(Q) Income from financing purchases from third parties.

(R) Income from gains on the disposition of tangible or intangible personal property or real property that was used in the active financing business (as defined in paragraph (e)(3)(i) of this section) but only to the extent that the property was held to generate or generated active financing income prior to its disposition.

(S) Income from hedging gain with respect to other active financing income.

(T) Income from providing traveller's check services.

(U) Income from servicing mortgages.

(V) Income from a finance lease. For this purpose, a finance lease is any lease that is a direct financing lease or a leveraged lease for accounting purposes and is also a lease for tax purposes.

(W) High withholding tax interest that would otherwise be described as active financing income.

(X) Income from providing investment advisory services, custodial services, agency paying services, collection agency services, and stock transfer agency services.

(Y) Any similar item of income that is disclosed in the manner provided in the instructions to the Form 1118 or 1116 or that is designated as a similar item of income in guidance published by the Internal Revenue Service.

(3) *Financial services entities*—(i) *In general.* The term "financial services entity" means an individual or entity that is predominantly engaged in the active conduct of a banking, insurance, financing, or similar business (active financing business) for any taxable year. Except as provided in paragraph (e)(3)(ii) of this section, a determination of whether an entity is a financial services entity shall be done on an entity-by-entity basis. An individual or entity is predominantly engaged in the active financing business for any year if for that year at least 80 percent of its gross income is income described in paragraph (e)(2)(i) of this section. For this purpose, gross income includes all income realized by an individual or entity, whether includible or excludible from gross income under other operative provisions of the Code, but excludes gain from the disposition of stock of a corporation that prior to the disposition of its stock is related to the transferor within the meaning of section 267(b). For this purpose, income received from a related person that is a financial services entity shall be excluded if such income is characterized under the look-through rules of section 904(d)(3) and § 1.904-5. In addition, income received from a related person that is not a financial services entity but that is characterized as financial services income under the look-through rules shall be excluded. See paragraph (e)(3)(iv) *Example (5)* of this section. Any income received from a related person that is characterized under the look-through rules and that is not otherwise excluded by this paragraph will retain its character either as active financing income or other income in the hands of the recipient for purposes of determining if the recipient is a financial services entity and if the income is financial services income to the recipient. For purposes of this paragraph, related person is defined in § 1.904-5(i)(1).

(ii) *Special rule for affiliated groups.* In the case of any corporation that is not a financial services entity under paragraph (e)(3)(i) of this section, but is a member of an affiliated group, such corporation will be deemed to be a financial services entity if the affiliated group as a whole meets the requirements of paragraph (e)(3)(i) of this section. For purposes of this paragraph (e)(3)(ii), affiliated group means an affiliated group as defined in section 1504(a), determined without regard to section 1504(b)(3). In counting the income of the group for purposes of determining whether the group meets the requirements of paragraph (e)(3)(i) of this section, the following rules apply. Only the income of group members that are United States corporations or foreign corporations that are controlled foreign corporations in which United States members of the affiliated group own, directly or indirectly, at least 80 percent of the total voting power and value of the stock shall be included. For purposes of this paragraph (e)(3)(ii), indirect ownership shall be determined under section 318 and the regulations under that section. The income of the group will not include any income from transactions with other members of the group. Passive income will not be considered to be active financing income merely because that income is earned by a member of the group that is a financial services entity without regard to the rule of this paragraph (e)(3)(ii). This paragraph (e)(3)(ii) applies to taxable years beginning after December 31, 2000.

Reg. § 1.904-4(e)(3)

(iii) *Treatment of partnerships and other pass-through entities.* For purposes of determining whether a partner (including a partnership that is a partner in a second partnership) is a financial services entity, all of the partner's income shall be taken into account, except that income that is excluded under paragraph (e)(3)(i) of this section shall not be taken into account. Thus, if a partnership is determined to be a financial services entity none of the income of the partner received from the partnership that is characterized under the look-through rules shall be included for purpose of determining if the partner is a financial services entity. If a partnership is determined not to be a financial services entity, then income of the partner from the partnership that is characterized under the look-through rules will be taken into account (unless such income is financial services income) and such income will retain its character either as active financing income or as other income in the hands of the partner for purposes of determining if the partner is a financial service entity and if the income is financial services income to the partner. If a partnership is a financial services entity and the partner's income from the partnership is characterized as financial services income under the look-through rules, then, for purposes of determining a partner's foreign tax credit limitation, the income from the partnership shall be considered to be financial services income to the partner regardless of whether the partner is itself a financial services entity. The rules of this paragraph (e)(3)(iii) will apply for purposes of determining whether an owner of an interest in any other pass-through entity the character of the income of which is preserved when such income is included in the income of the owner of the interest is a financial services entity.

(iv) *Examples.* The principles of paragraph (e)(3) of this section are illustrated by the following examples.

Example (1). P is a domestic corporation that owns 100 percent of the stock of S, a controlled foreign corporation incorporated in Country X. For the 1990 taxable year, 60 percent of S's income is active financing income that consists of income that will be considered general limitation or passive income if S is not a financial services entity. The other 40 percent of S's income is passive non-active financing income. S is not a financial services entity and its active financing income thus retains its character as general limitation and passive income. S makes an interest payment to P in 1990 that is characterized under the look-through rules. Although the interest is not financial services income to S under the look-through rules, it retains its character as active financing income when paid to P and P must take that income into account in determining whether it is a financial services entity under paragraph (e)(3)(i) of this section. If P is determined to be a financial services entity, both the portion of the interest payment characterized as active financing income (whether general limitation or passive income in S's hands) and the portion characterized as passive non-active financing income received from S will be recharacterized as financial services income.

Example 2. Foreign corporation A, which is not a controlled foreign corporation, owns 100 percent of the stock of domestic corporation B, which owns 100 percent of the stock of domestic corporation C. A also owns 100 percent of the stock of foreign corporation D. D owns 100 percent of the stock of domestic corporation E, which owns 100 percent of the stock of controlled foreign corporation F. All of the corporations are members of an affiliated group within the meaning of section 1504(a) (determined without regard to section 1504(b)(3)). Pursuant to paragraph (e)(3)(ii) of this section, however, only the income of B, C, E, and F is counted in determining whether the group meets the requirements of paragraph (e)(3)(i) of this section. For the 2001 taxable year, B's income consists of $95 of active financing income and $5 of passive non-active financing income. C has $40 of active financing income and $20 of passive non-active financing income. E has $70 of active financing income and $15 of passive non-active financing income. F has $10 of passive income. B and E qualify as financial services entities under the entity test of paragraph (e)(3)(i) of this section. Therefore, B and E are financial services entities without regard to whether the group as a whole is a financial services entity and all of the income of B and E shall be treated as financial services income. C and F do not qualify as financial services entities under the entity test of paragraph (e)(3)(i) of this section. However, under the affiliated group test of paragraph (e)(3)(ii) of this section, C and F are financial services entities because at least 80 percent of the group's total income consists of active financing income ($205 of active financing income is 80.4 percent of $255 total income). B's and E's passive income is not treated as active financing income for purposes of the affiliated group test of paragraph (e)(3)(ii) of this section even though it is treated as financial services income without regard to whether the group satisfies the affiliated group test. Once C and F are determined to be financial services entities under the affiliated group test, however, all of the passive income of the group is treated as financial services income. Thus, 100 percent of the income of B, C, E, and F for 2001 is financial services income.

Reg. § 1.904-4(e)(3)

Example (3). PS is a domestic partnership operating in branch form in foreign country X. PS has two equal general partners, A and B. A and B are domestic corporations that each operate in branch form in foreign countries Y and Z. All of A's income, except that derived through PS, is manufacturing income. All of B's income, except that derived through PS, is active financing income. A and B's only income from PS are distributive shares of PS's income. PS is a financial services entity and all of its income is financial services income. The income from PS is excluded in determining if A or B are financial services entities. Thus, A is not a financial services entity because none of A's income is active financing income and B is a financial services entity because all of B's income is active financing income. However, both A and B's distributive shares of PS's taxable income consist of financial services income even though A is not a financial services entity.

Example (4). PS is a domestic partnership operating in foreign country X. A and B are domestic corporations that are equal general partners in PS and, therefore, the look-through rules apply for purposes of characterizing A's and B's distributive shares of PS's income. Fifty (50) percent of PS's gross income is active financing income that is not high withholding tax interest. The active financing income includes income that also meets the definition of passive income and income that meets the definition of general limitation income. The other 50 percent of PS's income is from manufacturing. PS is, therefore, not a financial services entity. A's and B's distributive shares of partnership taxable income consist of general limitation manufacturing income and active financing income. Under paragraph (c)(3)(i) of this section, the active financing income shall be financial services income to A or B if either A or B is determined to be a financial services entity. If A or B is not a financial services entity, the distributive shares of income from PS will not be financial services income to A or B and will consist of passive and general limitation income. All of the income from PS is included in determining if A or B are financial services entities.

Example (5). P is a United States corporation that is not a financial services entity. P owns 100 percent of the stock of S, a controlled foreign corporation that is not a financial services entity. S owns 100 percent of the stock of T, a controlled foreign corporation that is a financial services entity. In 1991, T pays a dividend to S. The dividend from T is characterized under the look-through rules of section 904(d)(3). Pursuant to paragraph (e)(3)(i) of this section, the dividend from T is excluded in determining whether S is a financial services entity. S is determined not to be a financial services entity but the dividend retains its character as financial services income in S's hands. Any subpart F inclusion or dividend to P out of earnings and profits attributable to the dividend from T will be excluded in determining whether P is a financial services entity but the inclusion or dividend will retain its character as financial services income.

(4) *Definition of incidental income*—(i) *In general*—(A) *Rule.* Incidental income is income that is integrally related to active financing income of a financial services entity. Such income includes, for example, income from precious metals trading and commodity trading that is integrally related to futures income. If securities, shares of stock, or other types of property are acquired by a financial services entity as an ordinary and necessary incident to the conduct of a active financing business, the income from such property will be considered to be financial services income but only so long as the retention of such property remains an ordinary or necessary incident to the conduct of such business. Thus property, including stock, acquired as the result of, or in order to prevent, a loss in an active financing business upon a loan held by the taxpayer in the ordinary course of such business will be considered ordinary and necessary to the conduct of such business, but income from such property will be considered financial services income only so long as the holding of such property remains an ordinary and necessary incident to the conduct of such business. If an entity holds such property for five years or less then the property is considered held incident to the financial services business. If an entity holds such property for more than five years, a presumption will be established that the entity is not holding such property incident to its financial services business. An entity will be able to rebut the presumption by demonstrating that under the facts and circumstances it is not holding the property as an investment. However, the fact that an entity holds the property for more than five years and is not able to rebut the presumption that it is not holding the property incident to its financial services business will not affect the characterization of any income received from the property during the first five years as financial services income.

(B) *Examples.* The following examples illustrate the application of paragraph (e)(4)(i) of this section.

Example (1). X is a financial services entity within the meaning of paragraph (e)(3)(i) of this section. In 1987, X made a loan in the ordinary course of its business to an unrelated foreign corporation, Y. As security for that loan, Y pledged certain operating assets. Those assets generate income of a type that would be subject to the general limitation. In January 1989, Y defaulted on the loan and forfeited the collateral. During the period X held the assets, X earned operating income generated by those assets. This income was applied in partial satisfaction of Y's obligation. In 1993, X sold the forfeited assets. The sales proceeds were in excess of the remainder of Y's obligation. The operating income received in the period from 1989 to 1993 and the income on the sale of the assets in 1993 are financial services income of X.

Example (2). The facts are the same as in *Example (1)*, except that instead of pledging its operating assets as collateral for the loan, Y pledged the stock of its operating subsidiary Z. In 1993, X sold the stock of Z in complete satisfaction of Y's obligation. X's income from the sale of Z stock in satisfaction of Y's obligation is financial services income.

Example (3). P, a domestic corporation, is a financial services entity within the meaning of paragraph (e)(3)(i) of this section. P holds a United States dollar denominated debt (the "obligation") of the Central Bank of foreign country X. The obligation evidences a loan of $100 made by P to the Central Bank. In 1988, pursuant to a program of country X, P delivers the obligation to the Central Bank which credits 70 units of country X currency to M, a country X corporation. M issues all of its only class of capital stock to P. M invests the 70 units of country X currency in the construction and operation of a new hotel in X. In 1994, M distributes 10 units of country X currency to P as a dividend. P is not able to rebut the presumption that it is not holding the stock of M incident to its financial services business. The dividend to P is, therefore, not financial services income.

(ii) *Income that is not incidental income.* Income that is attributable to non-financial activity is not incidental income within the meaning of paragraph (e)(4)(i) and (ii) of this section solely because such income represents a relatively small proportion of the taxpayer's total income or that the taxpayer engages in non-financial activity on a sporadic basis. Thus, for example, income from data processing services provided to related or unrelated parties or income from the sale of goods or non-financial services (for example travel services) is not financial services income, even if the recipient is a financial services entity.

(5) *Exceptions.* Financial services income does not include income that is:

(i) Export financing interest as defined in section 904(d)(2)(G) and paragraph (h) of this section unless that income would be high withholding tax interest as defined in section 904(d)(2)(B) but for paragraph (d)(2)(B)(ii) of that section;

(ii) High withholding tax interest as defined in section 904(d)(2)(B) unless that income also meets the definition of export financing interest; and

(iii) Dividends from noncontrolled section 902 corporations as defined in section 904(d)(2)(E) and paragraph (g) of this section.

(f) *Shipping income.* The term "shipping income" means any income received or accrued by any person that is of a kind that would be foreign base company shipping income (as defined in section 954(f) and the regulations thereunder). Shipping income does not include any dividends received or accrued from a noncontrolled section 902 corporation, any income that is financial services income, or any income described in section 904(d)(1)(G) (foreign trade income within the meaning of section 923(b)).

(g) *Noncontrolled section 902 corporation*—(1) *Definition.* Except as otherwise provided, the term "noncontrolled section 902 corporation" means any foreign corporation with respect to which the taxpayer meets the stock ownership requirements of section 902(a) or, for purposes of applying the look-through rules described in section 904(d)(3) and § 1.904-5, the taxpayer meets the requirements of section 902(b). Except as provided in section 902 and the regulations under that section and paragraph (g)(3) of this section, a controlled foreign corporation shall not be treated as a noncontrolled section 902 corporation with respect to any distributions out of its earnings and profits for periods during which it was a controlled foreign corporation. In the case of a partnership owning a foreign corporation, the determination of whether a taxpayer meets the ownership requirements of section 902(a) or (b) will be made with respect to the partner's indirect ownership, and not the partnership's direct ownership, in the foreign corporation.

(2) *Treatment of dividends from each separate noncontrolled section 902 corporation*—(i) *In general.* Except as otherwise provided, a separate foreign tax credit limitation applies to dividends received or accrued by a corporation from each noncontrolled section 902 corporation. Any dividend distribution made by a noncontrolled section 902 corporation out of earnings and profits attributable to periods in which the shareholder did not meet the stock ownership requirements of section 902(a) or section 902(b) shall be treated as distri-

Reg. § 1.904-4(g)(2)

butions made by a noncontrolled section 902 corporation.

(ii) *Special rule for dividends received by a controlled foreign corporation.* If—

(A) Stock in a foreign corporation that is not a controlled foreign corporation is owned by a controlled foreign corporation, see paragraph (g)(4) *Example (1),*

(B) There are two or more shareholders of that controlled foreign corporation, and

(C) The ownership requirements of section 902(b) with respect to the foreign corporation are met by at least one of the United States shareholders of the controlled foreign corporation,

then any dividends received by the controlled foreign corporation from the foreign corporation shall be treated in their entirety to the controlled foreign corporation as dividends from a noncontrolled section 902 corporation, notwithstanding that all the United States shareholders of the controlled foreign corporation do not meet the requirements of section 902(b). Any income received or accrued by a United States shareholder of a controlled foreign corporation described in the preceding sentence that is attributable to a dividend paid by a foreign corporation shall be considered to be passive income if the shareholder's interest in that foreign corporation does not satisfy the requirements of section 902(b).

(iii) *Special rules for high withholding tax interest.* If a taxpayer receives or accrues a dividend distribution from a noncontrolled section 902 corporation out of earnings and profits attributable to high withholding tax interest earned or accrued by the noncontrolled section 902 corporation, any gross basis foreign tax (as defined in paragraph (d) of this section) imposed on such interest, to the extent that the taxes are imposed at a rate in excess of 5 percent, shall not be treated as foreign taxes for purposes of determining the amount of foreign taxes deemed paid or accrued by the taxpayer under section 902. The preceding sentence shall have no effect upon the determination of the amount of earnings and profits of a noncontrolled section 902 corporation.

(iv) *Treatment of inclusions under section 1293.* If a foreign corporation is a noncontrolled section 902 corporation with respect to a taxpayer, and inclusion in the taxpayer's gross income under section 1293 with respect to that corporation shall be treated as a dividend from a noncontrolled section 902 corporation and thus shall be subject to a separate limitation.

(v) *Examples.* The following examples illustrate the application of this paragraph (g).

Example (1). A and B are domestic corporations. A owns 90 percent of the stock of C, a foreign corporation and B owns the remaining 10 percent of the C stock. C is a controlled foreign corporation. A and B are United States shareholders. C owns 20 percent of the stock of D, a foreign corporation, not a controlled corporation, that is incorporated in a different country than C. D is a noncontrolled section 902 corporation with respect to C and A, but not with respect to B. In 1987, C has foreign personal holding company income of $1000, $100 of which is attributable to a dividend from D. The remainder of the foreign personal holding company income is passive income. Assume that gross income and net income are equal and that C pays no foreign taxes on its foreign personal holding company income. In 1987, A and B have section 951(a)(1)(A) inclusions of $900 and $100, respectively, attributable to the foreign personal holding company income. Under paragraph (g)(2)(ii) of this section, the $900 included by A consists of $810 passive income and $90 of income attributable to a dividend from a noncontrolled section 902 corporation. The $100 included by B in gross income is characterized as passive income in its entirety although $10 of the $100 is attributable to the dividend from D, and, as to C, that dividend is characterized as a dividend from a noncontrolled section 902 corporation. As to B, the $10 is characterized as passive income because B does not meet the ownership requirements of section 902(b) with regard to D.

Example (2). In 1987, A, a domestic corporation, owned 9 percent of the stock of B, a foreign corporation. In 1988, A acquired an additional 20 percent of the stock of B. Thus, in 1988, B is a noncontrolled section 902 corporation with regard to A. In 1989, A acquired an additional 25 percent of the stock of B. A acquired no additional stock in 1990. In 1989 and 1990, A owned 54 percent of the stock of B. For 1989 and 1990, B is a controlled foreign corporation in which A is a United States shareholder. B has no subpart F income in 1989 or 1990. In 1990, B pays a dividend of $3,000 to A. One thousand dollars ($1,000) of the dividend is attributable to earnings and profits from 1987, $1,000 is attributable to earnings and profits from 1988, and $1,000 is attributable to earnings and profits from 1989. Under paragraph (g)(1) of this section, the $1,000 attributable to the earnings and profits from 1989 is subject to the look through rules of section 904(d)(3) and § 1.904-5(c)(4) and is characterized in A's hands according to those rules. Under section 904(d)(2)(E)(i) and paragraph (g)(3) of this section, the $2,000 attributable to the 1987 and 1988 earnings and profits is treated as income

Reg. § 1.904-4(g)(2)

Income from Sources Without the United States

See p. 20,601 for regulations not amended to reflect law changes

subject to a separate limitation for dividends from a noncontrolled section 902 corporation (B corporation).

Example (3). M owns 40 percent of the voting stock of foreign corporation N. N is a noncontrolled section 902 corporation. In 1987, N earns $2,000 of gross interest income and incurs $1,700 of interest expense. N incurs no other expenses and earns no other income. One-thousand dollars ($1,000) of the interest income is subject to a 10 percent withholding tax and is, therefore, high withholding tax interest. N's earnings and profits are $200 ($2,000 gross interest income less $1,700 interest expense less $100 withholding tax). N pays the full $200 out as a dividend. M receives $80 (40 percent of the $200). Under paragraph (g)(2)(iii) of this section, $50 ($100 − 5% × $1,000) of the $100 withholding tax is not treated as a foreign tax for purposes of determining the amount of foreign taxes deemed paid by M under section 902. M's deemed paid credit with respect to the $80 dividend it receives is, therefore, reduced from $40 ($100 × $80/$200) to $20 ($50 × $80/$200).

(3) *Special rule for dividends paid by a controlled foreign corporation*—(i) *Distributions out of earnings and profits accumulated when the distributing corporation was not a controlled foreign corporation*—(A) *General rule.* Distributions from a controlled foreign corporation shall be treated as dividends from a noncontrolled section 902 corporation, and therefore not subject to the look-through rules of § 1.904-5, to the extent that the distribution is out of earnings and profits accumulated during periods when the distributing corporation was not a controlled foreign corporation.

(B) *Ordering rule.* The determination of the earnings to which a distribution from a controlled foreign corporation is attributable shall be made on a last-in first-out (LIFO) basis. Thus, a distribution shall be deemed made first from post-1986 undistributed earnings attributable to the period after the distributing corporation became a controlled foreign corporation (look-through pools), next from the non-look-through pool of post-1986 undistributed earnings, if any, and finally on a LIFO basis from pre-1987 accumulated profits.

(C) *Effect of intervening noncontrolled status.* [Reserved]

(D) *Examples.* The following examples illustrate the application of paragraph (g)(3)(i):

Example 1. S is a foreign corporation formed in 1980. Until 1992, S had no United States shareholders. In 1992, P, a domestic corporation, acquires 10 percent of the stock of S. Thus, for 1992 and subsequent years, S is a noncontrolled section 902 corporation. Because the 10-percent ownership requirement of section 902(a) was not satisfied until 1992, earnings accumulated by S before 1992 will be treated as pre-1987 accumulated profits for purposes of section 902, and the amount of foreign taxes deemed paid with respect to any distribution out of such pre-1987 accumulated profits will be computed on a year-by-year basis under the rules of section 902(c)(6)(A) and § 1.902-1(b)(3). In 2000, P acquires an additional 45% of the stock of S. Thus, for 2000 and subsequent years, S is a controlled foreign corporation. In 2000, S has no earnings and profits and pays a dividend out of prior years' earnings and profits. Pursuant to paragraph (g)(3)(i) of this section, because S was not a controlled foreign corporation before 2000, the dividend to P will be treated as a dividend from a noncontrolled section 902 corporation. The dividend is treated as paid first out of S's non-look-through pool of post-1986 undistributed earnings to the extent thereof, and then out of S's pre-1987 accumulated profits on a LIFO basis. The entire dividend will be subject to a single separate limitation for dividends from a noncontrolled section 902 corporation.

Examples 2 through 4. [Reserved]

(ii) *Pre-August 6, 1997, dividend distributions out of earnings and profits accumulated before a more-than-90-percent United States shareholder became a United States shareholder*—(A) *General rule.* Look-through principles do not apply to distributions made before August 6, 1997, to a more-than-90-percent United States shareholder in the distributing corporation, to the extent the distributions are made from earnings and profits accumulated before the taxpayer became a United States shareholder of the distributing corporation (pre-acquisition earnings). Therefore, in the case of a distribution made before August 6, 1997, a dividend shall be treated as a dividend from a noncontrolled section 902 corporation, and the look-through rules of section 904(d)(3) and § 1.904-5 shall not apply, if—

(*1*) The distribution is received by a United States shareholder, or by an upper-tier controlled foreign corporation of a United States shareholder, at a time when such United States shareholder is a more-than-90-percent United States shareholder of the distributing corporation; and

(*2*) The more-than-90-percent United States shareholder was not a United States shareholder at the time the distributed earnings and profits were accumulated by the distributing corporation.

Reg. § 1.904-4(g)(3)

(B) *Exception for certain intra-group acquisitions.* Notwithstanding paragraph (g)(3)(ii)(A) of this section, a dividend recipient shall be entitled to look-through treatment on a distribution out of pre-acquisition earnings if—

(*1*) The dividend recipient is a United States shareholder of the distributing corporation;

(*2*) The immediately preceding owner or owners were entitled to look-through treatment on distributions from the distributing corporation (determined after the application of paragraphs (g)(3)(i) and (g)(3)(ii)(A) of this section); and

(*3*) Both at the time of such distribution and at the time that the dividend recipient acquired its interest from such immediately preceding owner or owners, such recipient and such preceding owner or owners are members of the same affiliated group (within the meaning of section 1504(a), determined without regard to section 1504(b)(3)).

(C) *Ordering rule.* If, under paragraph (g)(3)(ii) of this section (or under paragraphs (g)(3)(i)(A) and (g)(3)(ii) of this section), a shareholder is not entitled to look-through treatment, the determination of whether a distribution from its controlled foreign corporation is attributable to pre-acquisition earnings shall be made on a last-in first-out (LIFO) basis. Thus, a distribution shall be deemed made first from the post-1986 undistributed earnings attributable to the period after the shareholder became a United States shareholder in the distributing corporation, and then from pre-acquisition earnings, in the order described in paragraph (g)(3)(i)(B) of this section.

(D) *Distributions after August 5, 1997.* Look-through principles shall apply to distributions made after August 5, 1997, to a distribution from a controlled foreign corporation to a more-than-90-percent United States shareholder out of pre-acquisition earnings that were accumulated in years during which the corporation was a controlled foreign corporation. Post-1986 undistributed earnings attributable to the period after the shareholder became a United States shareholder in the distributing corporation and other post-1986 undistributed earnings accumulated while the distributing corporation was a controlled foreign corporation shall be combined into a single set of post-1986 undistributed earnings pools for each separate category described in § 1.904-5(a)(1) as of August 6, 1997.

(E) *Examples.* The following examples illustrate the application of this paragraph (g)(3)(ii):

Example 1. (i) P, a domestic corporation, owns 100 percent of the stock of U, a controlled foreign corporation. In 1992, P sells 100 percent of the stock of U to T, an unrelated domestic corporation. In 1992, U has no earnings and pays a dividend to T out of earnings and profits attributable to prior years. T is not related to P and P's ownership of U will not be attributed to T. Because the dividend to T in 1992 is out of post-1986 undistributed earnings that are pre-acquisition earnings, the dividend will be treated as a dividend from a noncontrolled section 902 corporation. In 1993, U pays a dividend to T out of current earnings and profits. T is entitled to look-through treatment on the dividend.

(ii) In September 1997, U pays a dividend to T out of both post-acquisition earnings and pre-acquisition earnings accumulated while U was a controlled foreign corporation. Under paragraph (g)(3)(ii)(D) of this section, T is entitled to look-through treatment on the full amount of the dividend.

Example 2. (i) Domestic corporation P has owned 95 percent of the stock of S, a controlled foreign corporation, from the time of S's organization in 1990. Domestic corporation R owns the remaining 5 percent of the stock of S. On December 1, 1996, T, an unrelated domestic corporation, acquires P's 95 percent interest in S. On December 31, 1996, S pays a dividend out of current and prior years' earnings and profits. T is a more-than-90-percent United States shareholder of S at the time it receives the dividend, but was not a United States shareholder at the time the distributed earnings were accumulated. Under this paragraph (g)(3)(ii), the portion of the dividend to T attributable to pre-acquisition earnings will be treated as a dividend from a noncontrolled section 902 corporation. Under paragraph (g)(3)(iii) of this section, T will be entitled to look-through treatment on the portion of the dividend attributable to 1996 earnings and profits. Under paragraph (g)(3)(ii)(C) of this section, the dividend received by T will be treated as coming first from S's post-1986 undistributed earnings attributable to 1996, and then from pre-acquisition earnings.

(ii) On December 31, 1997, S pays a second dividend out of current and prior years' earnings and profits. Under paragraph (g)(3)(ii)(D) of this section, T will be entitled to look-through treatment on the full amount of the dividend because all of S's earnings and profits were accumulated in years during which S was a controlled foreign corporation. The dividends to R will be treated as passive income because R owns less than 10 percent of the stock of S and, therefore, is not entitled to look-through treatment.

Example 3. The facts are the same as in *Example 2* except that R, rather than T, acquires from P an 86 percent interest in S in 1996. Although R was a shareholder of S before the acquisition, it was not a United States shareholder because it did not own 10 percent of the voting stock of S. Thus, because R owns more than 90 percent of the stock of S, and received a distribution of earnings before August 7, 1997, that were accumulated before it became a United States shareholder of S, this paragraph (g)(3)(ii) applies and R is not entitled to look-through treatment on the 1996 dividend. R is entitled to look-through treatment on the 1997 dividend.

Example 4. Since its organization in 1980, S, a controlled foreign corporation, has been owned 60 percent by domestic corporation P and 40 percent by domestic corporation R. On November 15, 1996, domestic corporation T acquires R's 40 percent interest in the stock of S. S has no income in 1996 and pays a dividend on December 15, 1996, out of prior years' earnings and profits. This paragraph (g)(3)(ii) does not apply because T acquired less than 90 percent of the stock of S. Thus, T is entitled to look-through treatment on dividends distributed out of pre-acquisition earnings, because such earnings are attributable to periods in which S was a controlled foreign corporation.

(iii) *Treatment of earnings and profits accumulated in a transition year.* Earnings and profits accumulated in the taxable year in which a corporation became a controlled foreign corporation or in which a more-than-90-percent United States shareholder became a United States shareholder shall be considered earnings and profits accumulated after the corporation became a controlled foreign corporation or the shareholder became a United States shareholder, respectively.

(iv) *Definitions.* The following definitions apply for purposes of this paragraph (g)(3):

(A) *More-than-90-percent United States shareholder.* The term *more-than-90-percent United States shareholder* means, with respect to any controlled foreign corporation, a United States shareholder that owns more than 90 percent of the total combined voting power of all classes of stock entitled to vote of the controlled foreign corporation. In determining ownership for purposes of this definition, the indirect stock ownership rules of sections 958 and 318 and the regulations under those sections shall apply.

(B) *Non-look-through pool.* Except as otherwise provided, the term *non-look-through pool* means post-1986 undistributed earnings accumulated during periods in which the distributing corporation was a noncontrolled section 902 corporation that was not a controlled foreign corporation.

(C) *Post-1986 undistributed earnings.* The term *post-1986 undistributed earnings* has the meaning set forth in § 1.902-1(a)(9).

(D) *Pre-1987 accumulated profits.* The term *pre-1987 accumulated profits* has the meaning set forth in § 1.902-1(a)(10).

(E) *Upper tier controlled foreign corporation.* The term *upper tier controlled foreign corporation* of a United States shareholder means a controlled foreign corporation in which the taxpayer is a United States shareholder and which is an upper-tier corporation as defined in § 1.902-1(a)(6) with respect to the distributing corporation.

(v) *Effective date.* The provisions of this paragraph (g)(3) apply to taxable years beginning after December 31, 1986. However, for taxable years beginning before January 1, 2001, taxpayers may rely on § 1.904-4(g)(3)(ii), (iii) and (iv) of regulations project INTL-1-92, published at 1992-1 C.B. 1209. See § 601.601(d)(2) of this chapter.

(h) *Export financing interest*—(1) *Definitions*—(i) *Export financing interest.* The term "export financing interest" means any interest derived from financing the sale (or other disposition) for use or consumption outside the United States of any property that is manufactured, produced, grown, or extracted in the United States by the taxpayer or a related person, and not more than 50 percent of the fair market value of which is attributable to products imported into the United States. For purposes of this paragraph, the term "United States" includes the fifty States, the District of Columbia, and the Commonwealth of Puerto Rico.

(ii) *Fair market value.* For purposes of this paragraph, the fair market value of any property imported into the United States shall be its appraised value, as determined by the Secretary under section 402 of the Tariff Act of 1930 (19 U.S.C. 1401a) in connection with its importation. For purposes of determining the foreign content of an item of property imported into the United States, see section 927 and the regulations thereunder.

(iii) *Related person.* For purposes of this paragraph, the term "related person" has the meaning given it by section 954(d)(3) except that such section shall be applied by substituting "the person with respect to whom the determination is being made" for "controlled foreign corporation" each place it applies.

(2) *Treatment of export financing interest.* Except as provided in paragraph (h)(3) of this section, if a taxpayer (including a financial services entity) receives or accrues export financing

interest from an unrelated person, then that interest shall be treated as general limitation income.

(3) *Exceptions*—(i) *Export financing interest that is high withholding tax interest.* If a financial services entity receives or accrues export financing interest that would also be high withholding tax interest but for section 904(d)(2)(B)(ii), that income shall be treated as financial services income.

(ii) *Export financing interest that is also related person factoring income.* Export financing interest shall be treated as passive income if that income is also related person factoring income. For this purpose, related person factoring income is—

(A) Income received or accrued by a controlled foreign corporation that is income described in section 864(d)(6) (income of a controlled foreign corporation from a loan for the purpose of financing the purchase of inventory property of a related person); or

(B) Income received or accrued by any person that is income described in section 864(d)(1) (income from a trade receivable acquired from a related person).

(iii) *Export financing interest that is related person factoring income and is received or accrued by a financial services entity.* If a financial services entity receives or accrues export financing interest that is also related person factoring income, then the income shall be treated as financial services income. See section 864(d)(5)(A)(i).

(iv) *Export financing interest that is related person factoring income and high withholding tax interest.* If any taxpayer (including a financial services entity) receives or accrues export financing interest that is also related person factoring income and high withholding tax interest, then that income shall be treated as high withholding tax interest. See section 864(d)(5)(A)(i).

(4) *Examples.* The following examples illustrate the operation of paragraph (h)(3) of this section:

Example (1). Controlled foreign corporation S is a wholly-owned subsidiary of domestic corporation P. S is not a financial services entity and has accumulated cash reserves. P has uncollected trade and service receivables of foreign obligors. P sells the receivables at a discount ("factors") to S. The income derived by S on the receivables is related person factoring income. The income is also export financing interest. Because the income is related person factoring income, the income is passive income to S.

Example (2). The facts are the same as in Example (1) except that S is a financial services entity and derives the income in an active financing business. The income derived by S on the receivables is related person factoring income and is also export financing interest. Therefore, pursuant to paragraph (h)(3)(iii) of this section, the income is financial services income to S.

Example (3). Domestic corporation S is a wholly-owned subsidiary of domestic corporation P. S is not a financial services entity and has accumulated cash reserves. P has uncollected trade and service receivables of foreign obligors. P factors the receivables to S. The income derived by S on the receivables is related person factoring income. The income is also export financing interest. The income will be passive income to S.

Example (4). The facts are the same as in Example (3) except that instead of factoring P's receivables, S finances the sales of P's goods by making loans to the purchasers of P's goods. The interest derived by S on these loans is export financing interest and is not related person factoring income. The income will be general limitation income to S.

(5) *Income eligible for section 864(d)(7) exception (same country exception) from related person factoring treatment*—(i) *Income other than interest.* If any foreign person that is not a financial services entity receives or accrues income that is described in section 864(d)(7) (income on a trade or service receivable acquired from a related person in the same foreign country as the recipient) and such income would also meet the definition of export financing interest if section 864(d)(1) applied to such income (income on a trade or service receivable acquired from a related person treated as interest), then the income shall be considered to be export financing interest and shall be treated as general limitation income. If a financial services entity receives or accrues that income, the income shall not be considered to be export financing interest and, therefore, shall be treated as financial services income.

(ii) *Interest income.* If export financing interest is received or accrued by any foreign person and that income would otherwise be treated as related person factoring income under section 864(d)(6) if section 864(d)(7) did not apply, section 904(d)(2)(A)(iii)(II) shall apply, and the interest shall be treated as general limitation income unless the interest is received or accrued by a financial services entity. If that interest is received or accrued by a financial services entity, section 904(d)(2)(C)(iii)(III) shall apply and the interest shall be treated as general limitation income. If that interest also would be high withhold-

Reg. § 1.904-4(h)(3)

ing tax interest but for section 904(d)(2)(B)(ii), then the interest shall be treated as financial services income.

(iii) *Examples.* The following examples illustrate the operation of this paragraph (h)(5):

Example (1). Controlled foreign corporation S is a wholly-owned subsidiary of domestic corporation P. Controlled foreign corporation T is a wholly-owned subsidiary of controlled foreign corporation S. S and T are incorporated in Country M. In 1987, P sells tractors to T, which T sells to X, an unrelated foreign corporation organized in country M. The tractors are to be used in country M. T uses a substantial part of its assets in its trade or business located in Country M. T has uncollected trade receivables from X that it factors to S. S derived more than 20 percent of its gross income for 1987 other than from an active financing business and the income derived by S from the receivables is not derived in an active financing business. Thus, pursuant to paragraph (e)(3)(i) of this section, S is not a financial services entity. The income is not related person factoring income because it is described in section 864(d)(7) (income eligible for the same country exception). If section 864(d)(1) applied, the income S derived from the receivables would meet the definition of export financing interest. The income, therefore, is considered to be export financing interest and is general limitation income to S.

Example (2). The facts are the same as in Example (1) except that S is a financial services entity and derives the income on the receivables from the conduct of an active financing business. The income S derives from the receivables is not related person factoring income because it is described in section 864(d)(7). If the income would be high withholding tax interest but for section 904(d)(2)(B)(ii), then the income will not be considered to be export financing interest and will be financial services income to S. Otherwise, the income will [be] considered to be export financing interest and will be general limitation income to S.

Example (3). Controlled foreign corporation S is a wholly-owned subsidiary of domestic corporation, P. Controlled foreign corporation T is a wholly-owned subsidiary of controlled foreign corporation S. S and T are incorporated in country M. S is not a financial services entity. In 1987, P sells tractors to T, which T sells to X, a foreign partnership that is organized in country M and is related to S and T. S makes a loan to X to finance the tractor sales. The interest earned by S from financing the sales is described in section 864(d)(7) and is export financing interest. Therefore, the income shall be general limitation income to S.

Example (4). The facts are the same as in Example (3) except that S is a financial services entity and derives the interest on the loan to X in an active financing business. The interest S earns is export financing interest that is not described in section 864(d)(1) because it is described in section 864(d)(7). Because the interest is described in section 864(d)(7) and is export financing interest, section 904(d)(2)(C)(iii)(III) shall apply and the income shall be general limitation income to S, unless it would also be high withholding tax interest but for section 904(d)(2)(B)(ii), in which case it will be financial services income to S.

(i) *Interaction of section 907(c) and income described in this section.* If a person receives or accrues income that is income described in section 907(c) (relating to oil and gas income), the rules of section 907(c) and the regulations thereunder, as well as the rules of this section, shall apply to the income. Thus, for example, if a taxpayer receives or accrues a dividend distribution from two separate noncontrolled section 902 corporations out of earnings and profits attributable to income received or accrued by the noncontrolled section 902 corporations that is income described in section 907(c), the rules provided in section 907 shall apply separately to the dividends received from each noncontrolled section 902 corporation. The reduction in amount allowed as foreign tax provided by section 907(a) shall therefore be calculated separately for dividends received or accrued by the taxpayer from each separate noncontrolled section 902 corporation.

(j) *Special rule for DASTM gain or loss.* Any DASTM gain or loss computed under § 1.985-3(d) must be allocated among the categories of income under the rules of § 1.985-3(e)(2)(iv) or (e)(3). The rules of § 1.985-3(e) apply before the rules of section 904(d)(2)(A)(iii)(III) (the exception from passive income for high-taxed income).

(k) *Special rule for alternative minimum tax foreign tax credit.* For purposes of computing the alternative minimum tax foreign tax credit under section 59(a), items included in alternative minimum taxable income by reason of section 56(g) (adjustments based on adjusted current earnings) shall be characterized as income described in a separate category under section 904(d) and this section based on the character of the underlying items of income.

(l) *Priority rules*—(1) *In general.* In the case of income that meets the definitions of more than one category of separate limitation income, the following priority rules apply:

Reg. § 1.904-4(l)(1)

(i) Income that meets the definitions of passive income and of any other separate limitation income described in section 904(d)(1)(B) through (H) will be subject to the other separate limitation;

(ii) Income that meets the definitions of financial services income and of either shipping income or passive income will be subject to the separate limitation for financial services income;

(iii) Income that meets the definitions of financial services income and of any separate limitation income other than shipping or passive income will be subject to the other separate limitation;

(iv) Income that meets the definitions of dividends from a noncontrolled section 902 corporation and of any other separate limitation income will be subject to the separate limitation for dividends from a noncontrolled section 902 corporation unless that income is foreign oil and gas extraction income defined in section 907(c), in which case it will be treated as general limitation income pursuant to § 1.907(a)-1(f);

(v) Income that meets the definitions of high withholding tax interest and of any other separate limitation income will be high withholding tax interest; and

(vi) Income that meets the definitions of shipping income and of foreign trade income will be subject to the separate limitation for foreign trade income.

(2) *Examples.* The provisions of this paragraph (1) are illustrated by the following examples:

Example (1). Controlled foreign corporation S is a wholly-owned subsidiary of domestic corporation P. S owns 20 percent of the voting stock of T, a foreign corporation that is not a controlled foreign corporation. In 1987, T pays S a dividend that qualifies as foreign base company shipping income to S under § 1.954-6(f)(1). The dividend from T is also a dividend from a noncontrolled section 902 corporation. Therefore, pursuant to section 904(d)(2)(D) and paragraph (l)(1)(iv) of this section, the dividend from T is treated as a dividend from a noncontrolled section 902 corporation.

Example (2). In 1987, domestic corporation P received a dividend from R, a foreign corporation that is not a controlled foreign corporation. P owns 30 percent of the voting stock of R. P is a financial services entity and the dividend from R qualifies as financial services income under paragraph (e)(4)(i)(A) of this section. The dividend from R is also a dividend from a noncontrolled section 902 corporation. Therefore, pursuant to section 904(d)(2)(C)(iii)(II) and paragraphs (l)(i)(iii) and (iv) of this section, the dividend from R is treated as a dividend from a noncontrolled section 902 corporation.

Example (3). P, a domestic corporation, owns 10 percent of foreign corporation S. S is a noncontrolled section 902 corporation. In 1990, S earns foreign oil and gas extraction income which is general limitation income. S pays a dividend to P out of its earnings and profits for 1990. The dividend from S is a dividend from a noncontrolled section 902 corporation that is also foreign oil and gas extraction income. Pursuant to section 907(c)(3)(A), § 1.907(a)-1(f) and paragraph (l)(1)(iv) of this section, P will include the dividend in income as general limitation income. [Reg. § 1.904-4.]

☐ [T.D. 8214, 7-15-88. Amended by T.D. 8412, 5-13-92; T.D. 8556, 7-22-94; T.D. 8805, 1-8-99 (corrected 6-16-99); T.D. 8916, 12-29-2000 (corrected 3-22-2001) and T.D. 8973, 12-27-2001.]

[Reg. § 1.904-5]

§ 1.904-5. **Look-through rules as applied to controlled foreign corporations and other entities.**—(a) *Definitions.* For purposes of section 904(d)(3) and the regulations under section 904 the following definitions apply:

(1) The term "separate category" means, as the context requires, any category of income described in section 904(d)(1)(A), (B), (C), (D), (E), (F), (G), (H), or (I) and in § 1.904-4(b), (d), (e), (f), and (g), or any category of earnings and profits to which income described in such provisions is attributable.

(2) The term "controlled foreign corporation" has the meaning given such term by section 957 (taking into account the special rule for certain captive insurance companies contained in section 953 (c)).

(3) The term "United States shareholder" has the meaning given such term by section 951(b) (taking into account the special rule for certain captive insurance companies contained in section 953(c)), except that for purposes of this section, a United States shareholder shall include any member of the controlled group of the United States shareholder. For this purpose the controlled group is any member of the affiliated group within the meaning of section 1504(a)(1) except that "more than 50 percent" shall be substituted for "at least 80 percent" wherever it appears in section 1504(a)(2). For taxable years beginning before January 1, 2001, the preceding sentence shall be applied by substituting "50 percent" for "more than 50 percent".

Income from Sources Without the United States

(b) *In general.* Except as otherwise provided in section 904(d)(2)(E) and (3) and this section, dividends, interest, rents, and royalties received or accrued by a taxpayer from a controlled foreign corporation in which the taxpayer is a United States shareholder shall be treated as general limitation income.

(c) *Rules for specific types of inclusions and payments*—(1) *Subpart F inclusions*—(i) *Rule.* Any amount included in gross income under section 951(a)(1)(A) shall be treated as income in a separate category to the extent the amount so included is attributable to income received or accrued by the controlled foreign corporation that is described as income in such category. For purposes of this § 1.904-5, income shall be characterized under the rules of § 1.904-4 prior to the application of the rules of paragraph (c) of this section. For rules concerning inclusions under section 951(a)(1)(B), see paragraph (c)(4)(i) of this section.

(ii) *Examples.* The following examples illustrate the application of this paragraph (c)(1):

Example (1). Controlled foreign corporation S is a wholly-owned subsidiary of P, a domestic corporation. S earns $200 of net income, $85 of which is foreign base company shipping income, $15 of which is foreign personal holding company income, and $100 of which is non-subpart F general limitation income. No foreign tax is imposed on the income. One hundred dollars ($100) of S's income is subpart F income taxed currently to P under section 951(a)(1)(A). Because $85 of the subpart F inclusion is attributable to shipping income of S, $85 of the subpart F inclusion is shipping income to P. Because $15 of the subpart F inclusion is attributable to passive income of S, $15 of the subpart F inclusion is passive income to P.

Example (2). Controlled foreign corporation S is a wholly-owned subsidiary of domestic corporation P. S is a financial services entity. P manufactures cars and is not a financial services entity. In 1987, S earns $200 of interest income unrelated to its banking business and $900 of interest income related to its banking business. Assume that S pays no foreign taxes and has no expenses. All of S's income is included in P's gross income as foreign personal holding company income. Because S is a financial services entity, income that would otherwise be passive income is considered to be financial services income. P, therefore, treats the entire subpart F inclusion as financial services income.

Example (3). Controlled foreign corporation S is a wholly-owned subsidiary of domestic corporation P. P is a financial services entity. S manufactures cars and is not a financial services entity. In 1987, S earns $200 of passive income that is subpart F income and $900 of general limitation non-subpart F income. Assume that S pays no foreign taxes on its passive earnings and has no expenses. P includes the $200 of subpart F income in gross income. Because P is a financial services entity, the inclusion will be financial services income to P.

Example (4). Controlled foreign corporation S is a wholly-owned subsidiary of domestic corporation P. Neither P nor S is a financial services entity. Controlled foreign corporation T is a wholly-owned subsidiary of controlled foreign corporation S. T is a financial services entity. In 1991, T pays a dividend to S. For purposes of determining whether S is a financial services entity under § 1.904-4(e)(3)(i), the dividend from T is ignored. For purposes of characterizing the dividend in S's hands under the look-through rules of paragraph (c)(4) of this section, however, the dividend retains its character as financial services income. Similarly, any subpart F inclusion or dividend to P out of the earnings and profits attributable to the dividend from S is excluded in determining whether P is a financial services entity under § 1.904-4(e)(3)(i), but retains its character in P's hands as financial services income under paragraph (c)(4) of this section.

Example (5). Controlled foreign corporation S is a wholly-owned subsidiary of domestic corporation P. S owns 40 percent of foreign corporation A, 45 percent of foreign corporation B, 30 percent of foreign corporation C and 20 percent of foreign corporation D. A, B, C, and D are noncontrolled section 902 corporations. In 1987, S's only income is a $100 dividend from each foreign corporation. Assume that S pays no foreign taxes and has no expenses. All $400 of the income is foreign personal holding company income and is included in P's gross income. P must include $100 in its separate limitation for dividends from A, $100 in its separate limitation for dividends from B, $100 in its separate limitation for dividends from C, and $100 in its separate limitation for dividends from D.

(2) *Interest*—(i) *In general.* For purposes of this paragraph, related person interest is any interest paid or accrued by a controlled foreign corporation to any United States shareholder in that corporation (or to any other related person) to which the look-through rules of section 904(d)(3) and this section apply. Unrelated person interest is all interest other than related person interest. Related person interest shall be treated as income in a separate category to the extent it is allocable to income of the controlled

Reg. § 1.904-5(c)(2)

foreign corporation in that category. If related person interest is received or accrued from a controlled foreign corporation by two or more persons, the amount of interest received or accrued by each person that is allocable to any separate category of income shall be determined by multiplying the amount of related person interest allocable to that separate category of income by a fraction. The numerator of the fraction is the amount of related person interest received or accrued by that person and the denominator is the total amount of related person interest paid or accrued by the controlled foreign corporation.

(ii) *Allocating and apportioning expenses including interest paid to a related person.* Related person interest and other expenses of a controlled foreign corporation shall be allocated and apportioned in the following manner:

(A) Gross income in each separate category shall be determined;

(B) Any expenses that are definitely related to less than all of gross income as a class, including unrelated person interest that is directly allocated to income from a specific property, shall be allocated and apportioned under the principles of §§ 1.861-8 or 1.861-10T, as applicable, to income in each separate category;

(C) Related person interest shall be allocated to and shall reduce (but not below zero) the amount of passive foreign personal holding company income as determined after the application of paragraph (c)(2)(ii)(B) of this section;

(D) To the extent that related person interest exceeds passive foreign personal holding company income as determined after the application of paragraphs (c)(2)(ii)(B) and (C) of this section, the related person interest shall be apportioned under the rules of this paragraph to separate categories other than passive income.

(*1*) If under § 1.861-9T, the modified gross income method of apportioning interest expense is elected, related person interest shall be apportioned as follows:

$$\left(\text{Related person interest} - \text{Related person interest allocated under paragraph (c)(2)(ii)(C) of this section}\right) \times \frac{\text{Gross income in a separate category (other than passive)}}{\text{Total gross income (other than passive)}}$$

(*2*) If under § 1.861-9T, the asset method of apportioning interest expense is elected, related person interest shall be apportioned according to the following formula:

$$\left(\text{Related person interest} - \text{Related person interest allocated under paragraph (c)(2)(ii)(C) of this section}\right) \times \frac{\text{Value of assets in a separate category (other than passive)}}{\text{Value of total assets (other than passive)}}$$

(E) Any other expenses (including unrelated person interest that is not directly allocated to income from a specific property) that are not definitely related expenses or that are definitely related to all of gross income as a class shall be apportioned under the rules of this paragraph to reduce income in each separate category.

(*1*) If under § 1.861-9T, the modified gross income method of apportioning interest expense is elected, the interest expense shall be apportioned as follows:

Expense apportionable to a separate category =

$$\text{Expense} \times \frac{\begin{array}{c}\text{Gross income in a separate category}\\ \text{(minus related person interest}\\ \text{allocated under paragraph (c)(2)(ii)(C)}\\ \text{of this section if the category is passive)}\end{array}}{\begin{array}{c}\text{Total gross income minus related person}\\ \text{interest allocated to passive income}\\ \text{under paragraph (c)(2)(ii)(C) of this section}\end{array}}$$

(*2*) If under § 1.861-9T, the asset method of apportioning interest expense is elected, then the expense shall be apportioned as follows:

Expense apportionable to a separate category =

$$\text{Expense} \times \frac{\begin{array}{c}\text{Value of assets in a separate}\\ \text{category (minus related person debt}\\ \text{allocated to passive assets}\\ \text{if the category is passive)}\end{array}}{\begin{array}{c}\text{Value of total assets minus related}\\ \text{person debt allocated to passive assets}\end{array}}$$

Reg. § 1.904-5(c)(2)

Income from Sources Without the United States

See p. 20,601 for regulations not amended to reflect law changes

(3) Expenses other than interest shall be apportioned in a similar manner depending on the apportionment method used. See § 1.861-8T(c)(1)(i)-(vi).

(iii) *Definitions*—(A) *Value of assets and reduction in value of assets and gross income.* For purposes of paragraph (c)(2)(ii)(D) and (E) of this section, the value of total assets is the value of assets in all categories (determined under the principles of § 1.861-9T(g)). See § 1.861-10T(d)(2) to determine the reduction in value of assets and gross income for purposes of apportioning additional third person interest expense that is not directly allocated when some interest expense has been directly allocated. For purposes of this paragraph and paragraph (c)(2)(ii)(E) of this section, any reduction in the value of assets for indebtedness that relates to interest allocated under paragraph (c)(2)(ii)(C) of this section is made before determining the average of asset values. For rules relating to the averaging of reduced asset values see § 1.861-9T(g)(2).

(B) *Related person debt allocated to passive assets.* For purposes of paragraph (c)(2)(ii)(E) of this section, related person debt allocated to passive assets is determined as follows:

$$\text{Related person debt allocated to the passive category} = \text{Total related person debt} \times \frac{\text{Related person interest allocable to passive income under paragraph (c)(2)(ii)(C)}}{\text{All related person interest}}$$

For this purpose, the term "total related person debt" means the sum of the principal amounts of obligations of a controlled foreign corporation owed to any United States shareholder of such corporation or to any related entity (within the meaning of paragraph (g) of this section) determined at the end of the taxable year.

(iv) *Examples.* The following examples illustrate the operation of this paragraph (c)(2).

Example (1). (i) Controlled foreign corporation S is a wholly-owned subsidiary of P, a domestic corporation. In 1987, S earns $200 of foreign personal holding company income that is passive income. S also earns $100 of foreign base company sales income that is general limitation income. S has $2000 of passive assets and $2000 of general limitation assets. In 1987, S makes a $150 interest payment to P with respect to a $1500 loan from P. S also pays $100 of interest to an unrelated person on a $1000 loan from that person. S has no other expenses. S uses the asset method to apportion interest expense.

(ii) Under paragraph (c)(2)(ii)(C) of this section, the $150 related person interest payment is allocable to S's passive foreign personal holding company income. Therefore, the $150 interest payment is passive income to P. Because the entire related person interest payment is allocated to passive income under paragraph (c)(2)(ii)(C) of this section, none of the related person interest payment is apportioned to general limitation income under paragraph (c)(2)(ii)(D) of this section. Under paragraph (c)(2)(iii)(B) of this section, the entire amount of the related person debt is allocable to passive assets ($1500 = $1500 × $150/$150). Under paragraph (c)(2)(ii)(E) of this section, $20 of interest expense paid to an unrelated person is apportioned to passive income ($20 = $100 × ($2000 − $1500)/($4000 − $1500)). Eighty dollars ($80) of the interest expense paid to an unrelated person is apportioned to general limitation income ($80 = $100 × $2000 /($4000 − $1500)).

Example (2). The facts are the same as in *Example* (1), except that S uses the gross income method to apportion interest expense. Under paragraph (c)(2)(ii)(E) of this section, the unrelated person interest expense would be apportioned on a gross income method. Therefore, $33 of interest expense paid to unrelated persons would be apportioned to passive income ($33 = $100 × ($200 − $150)/($300 − $150)) and $67 of interest expense paid to unrelated persons would be apportioned to general limitation income ($67 = $100 × $100/($300 − $150)).

Example (3). (i) The facts are the same as in *Example* (1), except that S has an additional $50 of third person interest expense that is directly allocated to income from a specific property that produces only passive income. The principal amount of indebtedness to which the interest relates is $500. S also has $50 of additional non-interest expenses that are not definitely related expenses and that are apportioned on an asset basis.

(ii) Under paragraph (c)(2)(ii)(B) of this section, the $50 of directly allocated third person interest is first allocated to reduce the passive income of S. Under paragraph (c)(2)(ii)(C) of this section, the $150 of related person interest is allocated to the remaining $150 of passive income. Under paragraph (c)(2)(iii)(B) of this sec-

Reg. § 1.904-5(c)(2)

tion, all of the related person debt is allocated to passive assets. ($1500 = $1500 × $150/$150).

(iii) Under paragraph (c)(2)(ii)(E) of this section, the non-interest expenses that are not definitely related are apportioned on the basis of the asset values reduced by the allocated related person debt. Therefore, $10 of these expenses are apportioned to the passive category ($50 × ($2000 − $1500)/($4000 − $1500)) and $40 are apportioned to the general limitation category ($50 × $2000/($4000 − $1500)).

(iv) In order to apportion third person interest between the categories of assets, the value of assets in a separate category must also be reduced under the principles of § 1.861-8 by the indebtedness relating to the specifically allocated interest. Therefore, under paragraph (c)(2)(iii)(B) of this section, the value of assets in the passive category for purposes of apportioning the additional third person interest = 0 ($2000 minus $500 (the principal amount of the debt, the interest payment on which is directly allocated to specific interest producing properties) minus $1500 (the related person debt allocated to passive assets)). Under paragraph (c)(2)(ii)(E) of this section, all $100 of the non-definitely related third person interest is apportioned to the general limitation category ($100 = $100 × $2000/($4000 − $500 − $1500)).

Example (4). (i) Controlled foreign corporation S is a wholly-owned subsidiary of P, a domestic corporation. In 1987, S earns $100 of foreign personal holding company income that is passive income. S also earns $100 of foreign base company sales income that is general limitation income. S has $1000 of general limitation assets and $1000 of passive assets. In 1987, S makes a $150 interest payment to P on a $1500 loan from P and has $20 of general and administrative expenses (G & A) that under the principles of §§ 1.861-8 through 1.861-14T is treated as directly allocable to all of P's gross income. S also makes a $25 interest payment to an unrelated person on a $250 loan from the unrelated person. S has no other expenses. S uses the asset method to apportion interest expense. S uses the gross income method to apportion G & A.

(ii) Under paragraph (c)(2)(ii)(C) of this section, $100 of the interest payment to P is allocable to S's passive foreign personal holding company income. Under paragraph (c)(2)(ii)(D) of this section, the additional $50 of related person interest expense is apportioned to general limitation income ($50 = $50 × $1000/$1000). Under paragraph (c)(2)(iii)(B) of this section, related person debt allocated to passive assets equals $1000 ($1000 = $1500 × $100/$150).

(iii) Under paragraph (c)(2)(ii)(E) of this section, none of the $25 of interest expense paid to an unrelated person is apportioned to passive income ($0 = $25 × ($1000 − $1000)/($2000 − $1000)). Twenty-five dollars ($25) of the interest expense paid to an unrelated person is apportioned to general limitation income ($25 = $25 × $1000/($2000 − $1000)). Under paragraph (c)(2)(ii)(E) of this section, none of the G & A is apportioned to S's passive foreign personal holding company income ($0 = $20 × ($100 − $100)/($200 − $100)). All $20 of the G & A is apportioned to S's general limitation income ($20 = $20 × $100/($200 − $100)).

Example (5). The facts are the same as in *Example (4),* except that S uses the gross income method to apportion interest expense. As in *Example (4),* $100 of the interest payment to P is allocated to passive income under paragraph (c)(2)(ii)(C) of this section. Under paragraph (c)(2)(ii)(D) of this section, the additional $50 of related person interest expense is apportioned to general limitation income ($150 − 100 × $100/$100). Under paragraph (c)(2)(ii)(E) of this section, none of the unrelated person interest expense and none of the G & A is apportioned to passive income, because after the application of paragraph (c)(2)(ii)(C) of this section, no passive income remains in the passive income category.

Example (6). Controlled foreign corporation T is a wholly-owned subsidiary of S, a controlled foreign corporation. S is a wholly-owned subsidiary of P, a domestic corporation. S is not a financial services entity. S and T are incorporated in the same country. In 1987, P sells tractors to T, which T sells to X, a foreign corporation that is related to both S and T and is organized in the same country as S and T. S makes a loan to X to finance the tractor sales. Assume that the interest earned by S from financing the sales is export financing interest that is neither related person factoring income nor foreign personal holding company income. The export financing interest earned by S is, therefore, general limitation income. S earns no other income. S makes a $100 interest payment to P. The $100 of interest paid is allocable under the look-through rules of paragraph (c)(2)(ii) of this section to the general limitation income earned by S and is therefore general limitation income to P.

(3) *Rents and royalties.* Any rents or royalties received or accrued from a controlled foreign corporation in which the taxpayer is a United States shareholder shall be treated as income in a separate category to the extent they are allocable to income of the controlled foreign corporation in

Reg. § 1.904-5(c)(3)

that category under the principles of §§ 1.861-8 through 1.861-14T.

(4) *Dividends*—(i) *Look-through rule.* Any dividend paid or accrued out of the earnings and profits of any controlled foreign corporation, shall be treated as income in a separate category in proportion to the ratio of the portion of earnings and profits attributable to income in such category to the total amount of earnings and profits of the controlled foreign corporation. For purposes of this paragraph, the term "dividend" includes any amount included in gross income under section 951(a)(1)(B) as a pro rata share of a controlled foreign corporation's increase in earnings invested in United States property.

(ii) *Special rule for dividends attributable to certain loans.* If a dividend is distributed to a taxpayer by a controlled foreign corporation, that controlled foreign corporation is the recipient of loan proceeds from a related look-through entity (within the meaning of § 1.904-5 (i) of this section), and the purpose of such loan is to alter the characterization of the dividend for purposes of this section, then, to the extent of the principal amount of the loan, the dividend shall be characterized with respect to the earnings and profits of the related person lender rather than with respect to the earnings and profits of the dividend payor. A loan will not be considered made for the purpose of altering the characterization of a dividend if the loan would have been made or maintained on substantially the same terms irrespective of the dividend. The determination of whether a loan would have been made or maintained on substantially the same terms irrespective of the dividend will be made taking into account all the facts and circumstances of the relationship between the lender and the borrower. Thus, for example, a loan by a related party lender to a controlled foreign corporation that arises from the sale of inventory in the ordinary course of business will not be considered a loan made for the purpose of altering the character of any dividend paid by the borrower.

(iii) *Examples.* The following examples illustrate the application of this paragraph (c)(4).

Example (1). Controlled foreign corporation S is a wholly-owned subsidiary of P, a domestic corporation. In 1987, S has earnings and profits of $1,000, $600 of which is attributable to general limitation income and $400 of which is attributable to dividends received by S from its wholly-owned subsidiary, T. T is a controlled foreign corporation and is incorporated and operates in the same country as S. All of T's income is financial services income. Neither S's general limitation income nor the dividend from T is subpart F income. In December 1987, S pays a dividend to P of $200, all of which is attributable to earnings and profits earned in 1987. Six-tenths of the dividend ($120) is treated as general limitation income because six-tenths of S's earnings and profits are attributable to general limitation income. Four-tenths of the dividend ($80) is treated as financial services income because four-tenths of S's earnings and profits are attributable to dividends from T, and all of T's earnings are financial services income.

Example (2). A, a United States person, has been the sole shareholder in controlled foreign corporation X since its organization on January 1, 1963. Both X and A are calendar year taxpayers. X's earnings and profits for 1963 through the end of 1987 totaled $3,000. A sells his stock in X at the end of 1987 and realizes a gain of $4,000. Of the total $4,000 gain, $3,000 (A's share of the post-1962 earnings and profits) is includible in A's gross income as a dividend and is subject to the look-through rules including the transition rule of § 1.904-7(a) with respect to the portion of the distribution out of pre- 87 earnings and profits. The remaining $1,000 of the gain is includible as gain from the sale or exchange of the X stock and is passive income to A.

(d) *Effect of exclusions from subpart F income*—(1) *De minimis amount of subpart F income.* If the sum of a controlled foreign corporation's gross foreign base company income (determined under section 954(a) without regard to section 954(b)(5)) and gross insurance income (determined under section 953(a)) for the taxable year is less than the lesser of 5 percent of gross income of $1,000,000, then all of that income (other than income that would be financial services income without regard to this paragraph (d)(1)) shall be treated as general limitation income. In addition, if the test in the preceding sentence is satisfied, for purposes of paragraphs (c)(2)(ii)(D) and (E) of this section (apportionment of interest expense to passive income using the asset method), any passive limitation assets shall be treated as general limitation assets. The determination in the first sentence shall be made prior to the application of the exception for certain income subject to a high rate of foreign tax described in paragraph (d)(2) of this section.

(2) *Exception for certain income subject to high foreign tax.* Except as provided in § 1.904-4(c)(7)(iii) (relating to reductions in tax upon distribution), for purposes of the dividend look-through rule of paragraph (c)(4)(i) of this section, an item of net income that would otherwise be passive income (after application of the priority rules of § 1.904-4(l)) and that is received

Reg. § 1.904-5(d)(2)

or accrued by a controlled foreign corporation shall be treated as general limitation income, and the earnings and profits attributable to such income shall be treated as general limitation earnings and profits, if the taxpayer establishes to the satisfaction of the Secretary that such income was subject to an effective rate of income tax imposed by a foreign country greater than 90 percent of the maximum rate of tax specified in section 11 (with reference to section 15, if applicable). The preceding sentence has no effect on amounts (other than dividends) paid or accrued by a controlled foreign corporation to a United States shareholder of such controlled foreign corporation to the extent those amounts are allocable to passive income of the controlled foreign corporation.

(3) *Examples.* The following examples illustrate the application of this paragraph.

Example (1). Controlled foreign corporation S is a wholly-owned subsidiary of P, a domestic corporation. In 1987, S earns $100 of gross income, $4 of which is interest that is subpart F foreign personal holding company income and $96 of which is gross manufacturing income that is not subpart F income. S has no other earnings for 1987. S has no expenses and pays no foreign taxes. S pays P a $100 dividend. Under the de minimis rule of section 954(b)(3), none of S's income is treated as foreign base company income. All of S's income, therefore, is treated as general limitation income. The entire $100 dividend is general limitation income to P.

Example (2). (i) Controlled foreign corporation S is a wholly-owned subsidiary of P, a domestic corporation. In 1987, S earns $50 of shipping income of a type that is foreign base company shipping income. S also earns $50 of dividends from T, a foreign corporation in which S owns 45 percent of the voting stock, and receives $50 of dividends from U, a foreign corporation in which S owns 5% of the voting stock. Foreign persons hold the remaining voting stock of both T and U. S, T, and U are all incorporated in different foreign countries. The dividends S receives from T and U are of a type that normally would be subpart F foreign personal holding company income that is passive income. Under § 1.904-4(l)(1)(iv), however, the dividends from T are dividends from a noncontrolled section 902 corporation rather than passive income. S has no expenses. The earnings and profits of S are equal to the net income after taxes of S. The dividends and the shipping income are taxed abroad by S's country of incorporation at an effective rate of 40 percent. P establishes to the satisfaction of the Secretary that the effective rate of tax on both the dividends and the shipping income exceeds 90 percent of the maximum United States tax rate. Thus, under section 954(b)(4), neither the shipping income nor the dividends are taxed currently to P under subpart F. S's earnings attributable to shipping income and dividends from a noncontrolled section 902 corporation retain their character as such. Under paragraph (d)(2) of this section, S's earnings attributable to the dividends from U are treated as earnings attributable to general limitation income. See §§ 1.905-3T and 1.905-4T, however, for rules concerning adjustments to the pools of earnings and profits and foreign taxes and redeterminations of United States tax liability when foreign taxes are refunded in a later year.

(ii) In 1988, S has no earnings and pays a $150 dividend (including gross-up) to P. The dividend is paid out of S's post-1986 pool of earnings and profits. One-third of the dividend ($50) is attributable to S's shipping earnings, one-third ($50) is attributable to the dividend from T, and one-third ($50) is attributable to the dividend from U. Pursuant to section 904(d)(3)(E) and paragraph (c)(4) of this section, one-third of the dividend is shipping income, one-third is a dividend from a noncontrolled section 902 corporation, T, and one-third is general limitation income to P.

(e) *Treatment of subpart F income in excess of 70 percent of gross income*—(1) *Rule.* If the sum of a controlled foreign corporation's gross foreign base company income (determined without regard to section 954(b)(5)) and gross insurance income for the taxable year exceeds 70 percent of the gross income, then all of the controlled foreign corporation's gross income shall be treated as foreign base company income or gross insurance income (whichever is appropriate) and, thus, included in a United States shareholder's gross income. However, the inclusion in gross income of an amount that would not otherwise be subpart F income does not affect its character for purposes of determining whether the income is within a separate category. The determination of whether the controlled foreign corporation's gross foreign base company income and gross insurance income exceeds 70 percent of gross income is made before the exception for certain income subject to a high rate of foreign tax.

(2) *Example.* The following example illustrates the application of this paragraph.

Example. Controlled foreign corporation S is a wholly-owned subsidiary of P, a domestic corporation. S earns $100, $75 of which is foreign personal holding company income and $25 of which is non-subpart F services income. S is not a financial services entity. S's gross and net income are equal. Under the 70 percent full inclusion rule of section

Reg. § 1.904-5(d)(3)

954(b)(3)(B), the entire $100 is foreign base company income currently taxable to P under section 951. Because $75 of the $100 section 951 inclusion is attributable to S's passive income, $75 of the inclusion is passive income to P. The remaining $25 of the inclusion is treated as general limitation income to P because $25 is attributable to S's general limitation income.

(f) *Modification of look-through rules for certain income*—(1) *High withholding tax interest.* If a taxpayer receives or accrues interest from a controlled foreign corporation that is a financial services entity, and the interest would be described as high withholding tax interest if section 904(d)(3) and paragraph (c)(2) of this section (the look-through rules for interest) did not apply, then the interest shall be treated as high withholding tax interest to the extent that the interest is allocable under section 904(d)(3) and paragraph (c)(2)(i) of this section to financial services income of the controlled foreign corporation. See section 904(d)(3)(H). The amount treated as high-withholding tax interest under this paragraph (f)(1) shall not exceed the interest, or equivalent income, of the payor that would be taken into account in determining the financial services income of the payor if the look-through rules applied.

(2) *Dividends from a noncontrolled section 902 corporation*—(i) *Rule.* If a United States shareholder that is a corporation receives or accrues income from a controlled foreign corporation that is attributable to dividends from a noncontrolled section 902 corporation, such income shall be subject to a separate limitation for such dividends except as provided in § 1.904-4(g)(2)(ii) (relating to dividends from a foreign corporation with respect to which the United States shareholder does not meet the stock ownership requirements of section 902).

(ii) *Example.* The following example illustrates the provisions of this paragraph (f)(2).

Example. P, a domestic corporation, owns 40 percent of S, a controlled foreign corporation. U, an unrelated domestic corporation, owns the remaining 60 percent of S. S owns 10 percent of T, a noncontrolled section 902 corporation. In 1990, T pays S a dividend, which S includes in its gross income as a dividend from a noncontrolled section 902 corporation. S has no other income during 1990. P and U must include S's dividend income from T in their gross income under subpart F. Pursuant to § 1.904-4(g)(2)(ii)(C), the subpart F inclusion to U is characterized as a dividend from a noncontrolled section 902 corporation because U meets the 5 percent ownership requirement of section 902(b) (60% × 10% = 6%). The subpart F inclusion to P is characterized as passive income because P does not meet the 5 percent ownership requirement of section 902(b) (40% × 10% = 4%).

(3) *Distributions from a FSC.* Income received or accrued by a taxpayer that, under the rules of paragraph (c)(4) of this section (look-through rules for dividends), would be treated as foreign trade income or as passive income that is interest and carrying charges (as defined in section 927(d)(1)), and that is also a distribution from a FSC (or a former FSC), shall be treated as a distribution from a FSC (or a former FSC).

(4) *Example.* The following example illustrates the operation of paragraph (f)(1) of this section.

Example. Controlled foreign corporation S is a wholly-owned subsidiary of P, a domestic corporation. S is a financial services entity. In 1988, S earns $80 of interest that meets the definition of financial services income and $20 of high withholding tax interest. S makes a $100 interest payment to P. The interest payment to P is subject to a withholding tax of 15 percent. Twenty dollars ($20) of the interest payment to P is considered to be high withholding tax interest because, under section 904(d)(3), it is allocable to the high withholding tax interest earned by S. The remaining eighty dollars ($80) of the interest payment is also treated as high withholding tax interest to P because, under paragraph (f)(1) of this section, interest that is subject to a high withholding tax but would not be considered to be high withholding tax interest under the look-through rules of paragraph (c)(2) of this section, shall be treated as high withholding tax interest to the extent that the interest would have been treated as financial services interest income under the look-through rules of paragraph (c)(2)(i) of this section.

(g) *Application of look-through rules to certain domestic corporations.* The principles of section 904(d)(3) and this section shall apply to any foreign source interest, rents and royalties paid by a United States corporation to a related corporation. For this purpose, a United States corporation and another corporation are considered to be related if one owns, directly or indirectly, stock possessing more than 50 percent of the total voting power of all classes of stock of the other corporation or more than 50 percent of the total value of the other corporation. In addition, a United States corporation and another corporation shall be considered to be related if the same United States shareholders own, directly or indirectly, stock possessing more than 50 percent of the total voting power of all classes of stock or more than 50 percent of the total value of each corporation. For purposes of this paragraph, the

Reg. § 1.904-5(g)

constructive stock ownership rules of section 318 and the regulations under that section apply. For taxable years beginning before January 1, 2001, this paragraph (g) shall be applied by substituting "50 percent or more" for "more than 50 percent" each place it appears.

(h) *Application of look-through rules to partnerships and other pass-through entities*—(1) *General rule.* Except as provided in paragraph (h)(2) of this section, a partner's distributive share of partnership income shall be characterized as income in a separate category to the extent that the distributive share is a share of income earned or accrued by the partnership in such category. Payments to a partner described in section 707 (*e.g.*, payments to a partner not acting in capacity as a partner) shall be characterized as income in a separate category to the extent that the payment is attributable under the principles of § 1.861-8 and this section to income earned or accrued by the partnership in such category, if the payments are interest, rents, or royalties that would be characterized under the look-through rules of this section if the partnership were foreign corporation, and the partner who receives the payment owns 10 percent or more of the value of the partnership. A payment by a partnership to a member of the controlled group (as defined in paragraph (a)(3) of this section) of the partner shall be characterized under the look-through rules of this section if the payment would be a section 707 payment entitled to look-through treatment if it were made to the partner.

(2) *Exception for certain partnership interests*—(i) *Rule.* Except as otherwise provided, if any limited partner or corporate general partner owns less than 10 percent of the value in a partnership, the partner's distributive share of partnership income from the partnership shall be passive income to the partner, and the partner's distributive share of partnership deductions from the partnership shall be allocated and apportioned under the principles of § 1.861-8 only to the partner's passive income from that partnership.

(ii) *Exceptions.* To the extent a partner's distributive share of income from a partnership is a share of high withholding tax interest received or accrued by the partnership, that partner's distributive share of partnership income will be high withholding tax interest regardless of the partner's level of ownership in the partnership. If a partnership interest described in paragraph (h)(2)(i) of this section is held in the ordinary course of a partner's active trade or business, the rules of paragraph (h)(1) of this section shall apply for purposes of characterizing the partner's distributive share of the partnership income. A partnership interest will be considered to be held in the ordinary course of a partner's active trade or business if the partner (or a member of the partner's affiliated group of corporations (within the meaning of section 1504(a) and without regard to section 1504(b)(3))) engages (other than through a less than 10 percent interest in a partnership) in the same or related trade or business as the partnership.

(3) *Income from the sale of a partnership interest.* To the extent a partner recognizes gain on the sale of a partnership interest, that income shall be treated as passive income to the partner, unless the income is considered to be high-taxed under section 904(d)(2)(A)(iii)(III) and § 1.904-4(c).

(4) *Value of a partnership interest.* For purposes of paragraphs (i), (h)(1), and (h)(2) of this section, a partner will be considered as owning 10 percent of the value of a partnership for a particular year if the partner has 10 percent of the capital and profits interest of the partnership. Similarly, a partnership (first partnership) is considered as owning 50 percent of the value of another partnership (second partnership) if the first partnership owns fifty percent of the capital and profits interests of another partnership. For this purpose, value will be determined at the end of the partnership's taxable year. Similarly, a partnership (first partnership) is considered as owning more than 50 percent of the value of another partnership (second partnership) if the first partnership owns more than 50 percent of the capital and profits interests of the second partnership. For this purpose, value will be determined at the end of the partnership's taxable year. For taxable years beginning before January 1, 2001, the second preceding sentence shall be applied by substituting "50 percent" for "more than 50 percent".

(i) *Application of look-through rules to related entities*—(1) *In general.* Except as provided in paragraphs (i)(2) and (3) of this section, the principles of this section shall apply to distributions and payments that are subject to the look-through rules of section 904(d)(3) and this section from a controlled foreign corporation or other entity otherwise entitled to look-through treatment (a "look-through entity") under this section to a related look-through entity. Two look-through entities shall be considered to be related to each other if one owns, directly or indirectly, stock possessing more than 50 percent of the total voting power of all classes of voting stock of the other entity or more than 50 percent of the total value of such entity. In addition, two look-through entities are

Income from Sources Without the United States

related if the same United States shareholders own, directly or indirectly, stock possessing more than 50 percent of the total voting power of all voting classes of stock (in the case of a corporation) or more than 50 percent of the total value of each look-through entity. In the case of a corporation, value shall be determined by taking into account all classes of stock. In the case of a partnership, value shall be determined under the rules in paragraph (h)(4) of this section. For purposes of this section, indirect ownership shall be determined under section 318 and the regulations thereunder. For taxable years beginning before January 1, 2001, the third sentence of this paragraph (i)(1) shall be applied by substituting "50 percent or more" for "more than 50 percent" each place it appears.

(2) *Exception for distributive shares of partnership income.* In the case of tiered partnership arrangements, a distributive share of partnership income will be characterized under the look-through rules of section 904(d)(3) and this section if the partner meets the requirements of paragraph (h)(1) of this section with respect to the partnership (first partnership), whether or not the income is received through another partnership or partnerships (second partnership) and whether or not the first partnership and the second partnership are considered to be related under the rules of paragraph (i)(1) of this section.

(3) *Special rule for dividends.* Solely for purposes of dividend payments between controlled foreign corporations in taxable years beginning after December 31, 2000, two controlled foreign corporations shall be considered related look-through entities if the same United States shareholder owns, directly or indirectly, at least 10 percent of the total voting power of all classes of stock of each foreign corporation. Taxpayers may choose to apply this paragraph (i)(3) in taxable years beginning after December 31, 1991, provided that appropriate adjustments are made to eliminate any double benefit arising from the application of this paragraph (i)(3) to taxable years that are not open for assessment.

(4) *Examples.* The following examples illustrate the provisions of this paragraph (i):

Example 1. P, a domestic corporation, owns all of the stock of S, a controlled foreign corporation. S owns 40 percent of the stock of T, a Country X corporation that is a controlled foreign corporation. The remaining 60 percent of the stock of T is owned by V, a domestic corporation. The percentages of value and voting power of T owned by S and V correspond to their percentages of stock ownership. T owns 40 percent (by vote and value) of the stock of U, a Country Z corporation that is a controlled foreign corporation. The remaining 60 percent of U is owned by unrelated U.S. persons. U earns exclusively general limitation non-subpart F income. In 2001, U makes an interest payment of $100 to T. Look-through principles do not apply because T and U are not related look-through entities under paragraph (i)(1) of this section (because T does not own more than 50 percent of the voting power or value of U). The interest is passive income to T, and is subpart F income to P and V. Under paragraph (c)(1) of this section, look-through principles determine P and V's characterization of the subpart F inclusion from T. P and V therefore must characterize the inclusion as passive income.

Example 2. The facts are the same as in Example 1 except that instead of a $100 interest payment, U pays a $50 dividend to T in 2001. P and V each own, directly or indirectly, more than 10 percent of the voting power of all classes of stock of both T and U. Pursuant to paragraph (i)(3) of this section, for purposes of applying this section to the dividend from U to T, U and T are treated as related look-through entities. Therefore, look-through principles apply to characterize the dividend income as general limitation income to T. The dividend is subpart F income of T that is taxable to P and V. The subpart F inclusions of P and V are also subject to look-through principles, under paragraph (c)(1) of this section, and are characterized as general limitation income to P and V because the income is general limitation income of T.

Example 3. The facts are the same as in Example 1, except that U pays both a $100 interest payment and a $50 dividend to T, and T owns 80 percent (by vote and value) of U. Under paragraph (i)(1) of this section, T and U are related look-through entities, because T owns more than 50 percent (by vote and value) of U. Therefore, look-through principles apply to both the interest and dividend income paid or accrued by U to T, and T treats both types of income as general limitation income. Under paragraph (c)(1) of this section, P and V apply look-through principles to the resulting subpart F inclusions, which therefore are also general limitation income to P and V.

(j) *Look-through rules applied to passive foreign investment company inclusions.* If a passive foreign investment company is a controlled foreign corporation and the taxpayer is a United States shareholder in that passive foreign investment company, any amount included in gross income under section 1293 shall be treated as income in a separate category to the extent the amount so included is attributable to income received or accrued by that controlled foreign corpo-

Reg. § 1.904-5(j)

ration that is described as income in the separate category. For purposes of this paragraph (j), the priority rules of § 1.904-4(l) shall apply prior to the application of the rules of this paragraph.

(k) *Ordering rules*—(1) *In general.* Income received or accrued by a related person to which the look-through rules apply is characterized before amounts included from, or paid or distributed by that person and received or accrued by a related person. For purposes of determining the character of income received or accrued by a person from a related person if the payor or another related person also receives or accrues income from the recipient and the look-through rules apply to the income in all cases, the rules of paragraph (k)(2) of this section apply.

(2) *Specific rules.* For purposes of characterizing income under this paragraph, the following types of income are characterized in the order stated:

(i) Rents and royalties;

(ii) Interest;

(iii) Subpart F inclusions and distributive shares of partnership income;

(iv) Dividend distributions.

If an entity is both a recipient and a payor of income described in any one of the categories described in (i) through (iv) of this paragraph, the income received will be characterized before the income that is paid. In addition, the amount of interest paid or accrued, directly or indirectly, by a person to a related person shall be offset against and eliminate any interest received or accrued, directly or indirectly, by a person from that related person before application of the ordering rules of this paragraph. In a case in which a person pays or accrues interest to a related person, and also receives or accrues interest indirectly from the related person, the smallest interest payment is eliminated and the amount of all other interest payments are reduced by the amount of the smallest interest payment.

(l) *Examples.* The following examples illustrate the application of paragraphs (g), (h), (i), and (k) of this section.

Example (1). S and T, controlled foreign corporations, are wholly-owned subsidiaries of P, a domestic corporation. S and T are incorporated in two different foreign countries and T is a financial services entity. In 1987, S earns $100 of income that is general limitation foreign base company sales income. After expenses, including a $50 interest payment to T, S's income is subject to foreign tax at an effective rate of 40 percent. P elects to exclude S's $50 of net income from subpart F under section 954(b)(4). T earns $350 of income that consists of $300 of subpart F financial services income and $50 of interest received from S. The $50 of interest is foreign personal holding company income in T's hands because section 954(c)(3)(A)(i) (same country exception for interest payments) does not apply. The $50 of interest is also general limitation income to T because S and T are related look-through entities within the meaning of paragraph (i)(1) of this section and, therefore, the look-through rules of paragraph (c)(2)(i) of this section apply to characterize the interest payment. Thus, with respect to T, P includes in its gross income $50 of general limitation foreign personal holding company income and $300 of financial services income.

Example (2). The facts are the same as in Example (1) except that instead of earning $100 of general limitation foreign base company sales income, S earns $100 of foreign personal holding company income that is passive income. Although the interest payment to T would otherwise be passive income, T is a financial services entity and, under § 1.904-4(e)(1), the income is treated as financial services income in T's hands. Thus, P's entire $350 section 951 inclusion consists of financial services income.

Example (3). P, a domestic corporation, wholly-owns S, a domestic corporation that is a 80/20 corporation. In 1987, S's earnings consist of $100 of foreign source shipping income and $100 of foreign source high withholding tax interest. S makes a $100 foreign source interest payment to P. The interest payment to P is subject to the look-through rules of paragraph (c)(2)(i) of this section, and is characterized as shipping income and high withholding tax interest to the extent that it is allocable to such income in S's hands.

Example (4). PS is a domestic partnership that is the sole shareholder of controlled foreign corporation S. PS has two general partners, A and B. A and B each have a greater than 10 percent interest in PS. PS also has two limited partners, C and D. C has a 50 percent interest in the partnership and D has a 9 percent interest. A, B, C and D are all United States persons. In 1987, S has $100 of general limitation non-subpart F income on which it pays no foreign tax. S pays a $100 dividend to PS. The dividend is the only income of PS. Under the look-through rule of paragraph (c)(4) of this section, the dividend to PS is general limitation income. Under paragraph (h)(1) of this section, A's, B's, and C's distributive shares of PS's income are general limitation income. Under paragraph (h)(2) of this section, because D is a limited partner with a less than 10 percent interest in PS, D's distributive share of PS's income is passive income.

Reg. § 1.904-5(k)(1)

Example (5). P has a 25 percent interest in partnership PS that he sells to X for $110. P's basis in his partnership interest is $35. P recognizes $75 of gain on the sale of its partnership interest and is subject to no foreign tax. Under paragraph (h)(3) of this section, the gain is treated as passive income.

Example (6). P, a domestic corporation, owns 100 percent of the stock of S, a controlled foreign corporation, and S owns 100 percent of the stock of T, a controlled foreign corporation. S has $100 of passive foreign personal holding company income from unrelated persons and $100 of general limitation income. S also has $50 of interest income from T. S pays T $100 of interest. Under paragraph (k)(2) of this section, the $100 interest payment from S to T is reduced for limitation purposes to the extent of the $50 interest payment from T to S before application of the rules in paragraph (c)(2)(ii) of this section. Therefore, the interest payment from T to S is disregarded. S is treated as if it paid $50 of interest to T, all of which is allocable to S's passive foreign personal holding company income. Therefore the $50 interest payment from S to T is passive income.

Example (7). P, a domestic corporation, owns 100 percent of the stock of S, a controlled foreign corporation. S owns 100 percent of the stock of T, a controlled foreign corporation and 100 percent of the stock of U, a controlled foreign corporation. In 1988, T pays S $5 of interest, S pays U $10 of interest and U pays T $20 of interest. Under paragraph (k)(2) of this section, the interest payments from S to U must be offset by the amount of interest that S is considered as receiving indirectly from U and the interest payment from U to T is offset by the amount of the interest payment that U is considered as receiving indirectly from T. The $10 payment by S to U is reduced by $5, the amount of the interest payment from T to S that is treated as being paid indirectly by U to S. Similarly, the $20 interest payment from U to T is reduced by $5, the amount of the interest payment from S to U that is treated as being paid indirectly by T to U. Therefore, under paragraph (k)(2) of this section, T is treated as having made no interest payment to S, S is treated as having paid $5 of interest to U, and U is treated as having paid $15 to T.

Example (8). (i) P, a domestic corporation, owns 100 percent of the stock of S, a controlled foreign corporation, and S owns 100 percent of the stock of T, a controlled foreign corporation. In 1987, S earns $100 of passive foreign personal holding company income and $100 of general limitation non-subpart F sales income from unrelated persons and $100 of general limitation non-sub-part F interest income from a related person, W. S pays $150 of interest to T. T earns $200 of general limitation sales income from unrelated persons and the $150 interest payment from S. T pays S $100 of interest.

(ii) Under paragraph (k)(2) of this section, the $100 interest payment from T to S reduces the $150 interest payment from S to T. S is treated as though it paid $50 of interest to T. T is treated as though it made no interest payment to S.

(iii) Under paragraph (k)(2)(ii) of this section, the remaining $50 interest payment from S to T is then characterized. The interest payment is first allocable under the rules of paragraph (c)(2)(ii)(C) of this section to S's passive income. Therefore, the $50 interest payment to T is passive income. The interest income is foreign personal holding company income in T's hands. T, therefore, has $50 of subpart F passive income and $200 of non-subpart F general limitation income.

(iv) Under paragraph (k)(2)(iii) of this section, subpart F inclusions are characterized next. P has a subpart F inclusion with respect to S of $50 that is attributable to passive income of S and is treated as passive income to P. P has a subpart F inclusion with respect to T of $50 that is attributable to passive income of T and is treated as passive income to P.

Example (9). (i) P, a domestic corporation, owns 100 percent of the stock of S, a controlled foreign corporation, and S owns 100 percent of the stock of T, a controlled foreign corporation. P also owns 100 percent of the stock of U, a controlled foreign corporation. In 1987, S earns $100 of passive foreign personal holding company income and $200 of non-subpart F general limitation income from unrelated persons. S also receives $150 of dividend income from T. S pays $100 of interest to T and $100 of interest to U. U earns $300 of non-subpart F general limitation income and the $100 of interest received from S. U pays a $100 royalty to T. T earns the $100 interest payment received from S and the $100 royalty received from U.

(ii) Under paragraph (k)(2)(i) of this section, the royalty paid by U to T is characterized first. Assume that the royalty is directly allocable to U's general limitation income. Also assume that the royalty is not subpart F income to T. With respect to T, the royalty is general limitation income.

(iii) Under paragraph (k)(2)(ii) of this section, the interest payments from S to T and U are characterized next. This characterization is done without regard to any dividend income received by S because, under paragraph (k)(2) of this section, dividends are characterized after interest payments from a related person. The interest payments are first allocable to S's passive income under paragraph (c)(2)(ii)(C) of this section. Therefore, $50 of the interest payment to T is passive and $50 of the interest payment to U is passive. The remaining $50 paid to T is general limitation income and the remaining $50 paid to U is general limitation income. All of the interest payments to T and U are subpart F foreign personal holding company income to both recipients.

(iv) Under paragraph (k)(2)(iii) of this section, P has a $100 subpart F inclusion with respect to T that is characterized next. Fifty dollars ($50) of the subpart F inclusion is passive income to P because it is attributable to the passive income portion of the interest income received by T from S, and $50 of the inclusion is treated as general limitation income to P because it is attributable to the general limitation portion of the interest income received by T from S. Under paragraph (k)(2)(iii) of this section, P also has a $100 subpart F inclusion with respect to U. Fifty dollars ($50) of the subpart F inclusion is passive income to P because it is attributable to the passive portion of the interest income received by U from S, and $50 of the inclusion is general limitation income to P because it is attributable to the general limitation portion of the interest income received by U from S.

(v) Under paragraph (k)(2)(iv) of this section, the $150 distribution from T to S is characterized next. One hundred dollars ($100) of the distribution is out of earnings and profits attributable to previously taxed income. Therefore, only $50 is a dividend that is subject to the look-through rules of paragraph (d) of this section. The $50 dividend is attributable to T's general limitation income and is general limitation income to S in its entirety.

Example (10). (i) P, a domestic corporation, owns 100 percent of the stock of S, a controlled foreign corporation, and S owns 100 percent of the stock of T, a controlled foreign corporation. P also owns 100 percent of the stock of U, a controlled foreign corporation. S, T and U are all incorporated in the same foreign country. In 1987, S earns $100 of passive foreign personal holding income and $200 of general limitation non-subpart F income from unrelated persons. S pays $100 of interest to T and $100 of interest to U. U earns $300 of general limitation non-subpart F income and the $100 of interest received from S. T's only income is the $100 interest payment received from S.

(ii) Under paragraph (k)(2)(ii) of this section, the interest payments from S to T and U are characterized first. The interest payments are first allocated under the rule of paragraph (c)(2)(ii)(C) of this section to S's passive income. Therefore, under that provision and paragraph (c)(2)(i) of this section, $50 of the interest payment to T is passive income to T and $50 of the interest payment to U is passive income to U. The remaining $50 paid to T is general limitation income and the remaining $50 paid to U is general limitation income.

(iii) Under paragraph (k)(2)(iii) of this section, any subpart F inclusion of P is determined and characterized next. Under paragraph (c)(1)(i) of this section, paragraphs (c)(2)(i) and (c)(2)(ii) apply not only for purposes of determining the separate category of income of S to which the interest payments from S to T and U are allocable but also for purposes of determining the subpart F income of T and U. Although the interest payments from S to T and U are "same country" interest payments that would otherwise be excludible from T's and U's subpart F income under section 954(c)(3)(A)(i), section 954(c)(3)(B) provides that the exception for same country payments between related persons shall not apply to the extent such payments have reduced the subpart F income of the payor. In this case, $50 of the $100 interest payment from S to T reduced S's subpart F income and $50 of the $100 interest payment from S to U reduced the remaining $50 of S's subpart F income. Therefore, T has $50 of subpart F income that is passive income and U has $50 of subpart F income that is passive income. P includes $100 of subpart F income in gross income that is passive income to P.

(iv) The remaining $50 of interest paid by S to T and the remaining $50 of interest paid by S to U is not subpart F income to T or U because it did not reduce S's subpart F income and is therefore eligible for the same country exception.

Example (11). P, a domestic corporation, owns 100 percent of the stock of S, a controlled foreign corporation, and S owns 100 percent of the stock of T, a controlled foreign corporation. P also owns 100 percent of the stock of U, a controlled foreign corporation. In 1991, T earns $100 of general limitation income that is not subpart F income and distributes the entire amount to S as a dividend. S earns $100 of passive foreign personal holding company income and the $100 dividend from T. S pays $100 of interest to U. U earns $200 of general limitation income that is foreign base company income and $100 of interest income from S. This transaction does not involve circular payments and, therefore, the ordering rules of paragraph (k)(2) of this section do not apply. Instead, pursuant to paragraph (k)(1) of this section, income received is characterized first. T's earnings and, thus, the dividend from T to S are characterized first. S includes the $100 dividend from T in gross income as general limitation income because all of T's earnings are general limitation income. S thus has $100 of passive foreign personal holding company income and $100 of general limitation income. The interest payment to U is then characterized as $100 passive income under paragraph (c)(2)(ii)(C) of this section (allocation of related person interest to passive foreign personal holding company income). For 1991, U thus has $200 of general limitation income that is subpart F income, and $100 of passive foreign personal holding company income. For 1991, P includes in its gross income $200 of general limitation subpart F income from U, $100 of passive subpart F income from U (relating to the interest payment from S to U), and $100 of general limitation subpart F income from S (relating to the dividend from T to S).

(m) *Application of section 904(g)*—(1) *In general.* For purposes of determining the portion of an interest payment that is allocable to income earned or accrued by a controlled foreign corporation from sources within the United States under section 904(g)(3), the rules in paragraph (m)(2) of this section apply. For purposes of determining the portion of a dividend paid or accrued (or amount treated as a dividend, including amounts described in section 951(a)(1)(B)) by a controlled foreign corporation that is treated as from sources within the United States under section 904(g)(4), the rules in paragraph (m)(4) of this section apply. For purposes of determining the portion of an amount included in gross income under section 951(a)(1)(A) that is attributable to income of the controlled foreign corporation from sources within the United States under section 904(g)(2), the rules in paragraph (m)(5) of this section apply. In order to determine whether section 904(g) applies, section 904(g)(5) (exception if controlled foreign corporation has a de minimis amount of United States source income) shall be applied to the total amount of earnings and profits of a controlled foreign corporation for a taxable year without regard to the characterization of those earnings under section 904(d).

(2) *Treatment of interest payments.* If interest is received or accrued by a United States shareholder or a person related to a United States shareholder (within the meaning of paragraph (c)(2)(ii) of this section) from a controlled foreign corporation, the interest shall be considered to be allocable to income of the controlled foreign corporation from sources within the United States for purposes of section 904(d) to the extent that the interest is allocable under paragraph (c)(2)(ii)(C) of this section to passive income that is from sources within the United States. If related person interest is less than or equal to passive income, the related person interest will be allocable to United States source passive income based on the ratio of United States source passive income to total passive income. To the extent that related person interest exceeds passive income, and, therefore, is allocated under paragraph (c)(2)(ii)(D) of this section to income in a separate category other than passive, the following formulas apply in determining the portion of the interest payment that is from sources within the United States. If the taxpayer uses the gross income method to allocate interest, the portion of the interest payment from sources within the United States is determined as follows:

$$\text{The amount of the interest payment allocated to the separate category under paragraph (c)(2)(ii)(D) of this section} \times \frac{\text{Gross income from United States sources in that category}}{\text{Gross income from all sources in that category}}$$

If the taxpayer uses the asset method to allocate interest, then the portion of the interest payment from sources within the United States is determined as follows:

$$\text{The amount of the interest payment allocated to the separate category under paragraph (c)(2)(ii)(D) of this section} \times \frac{\text{Value of domestic assets in that catetory}}{\text{Value of total assets in that category}}$$

For purposes of this paragraph, the value of assets in a separate category is the value of assets as determined under the principles of § 1.861-9T(g). See § 1.861-10T(d)(2) for purposes of determining the value of assets and gross income in a separate category as reduced for indebtedness the interest on which is directly allocated.

(3) *Examples.* The following examples illustrate the application of this paragraph.

Example (1). Controlled foreign corporation S is a wholly-owned subsidiary of P, a domestic corporation. In 1988, S pays P $300 of interest. S has no other expenses. In 1988, S has $3000 of assets that generate $650 of foreign source general

Reg. § 1.904-5(m)(3)

limitation sales income and a $1000 loan to an unrelated foreign person that generates $20 of foreign source passive interest income. S also has a $4000 loan to an unrelated United States person that generates $70 of United States source passive income and $4000 of inventory that generates $100 of United States source general limitation income. S uses the asset method to allocate interest expense. The following chart summarizes S's assets and income:

Assets

	Foreign	U.S.	Totals
Passive	1000	4000	5000
General	3000	4000	7000
Total	4000	8000	12000

Income

	Foreign	U.S.	Totals
Passive	20	70	90
General	650	100	750
Total	670	170	840

Under paragraph (c)(2)(ii)(C) of this section, $90 of the related person interest payment is allocable to S's passive income. Under paragraph (m)(2) of this section, $70 is from sources within the United States and $20 is from foreign sources. Under paragraph (c)(2)(ii)(D) of this section, the remaining $210 of the related person interest payment is allocated to general limitation income. Under paragraph (m)(2) of this section, $120 of the remaining $210 is treated as income from sources within the United States ($120 = $210 × $4000/$7000) and $90 is treated as income from foreign sources ($90 = $210 × $3000/$7000).

Example (2). The facts are the same as in Example (1) except that S uses the gross income method to allocate interest expense. The first $90 of related person interest expense is allocated to passive income in the same manner as in Example (1). Under paragraph (c)(2)(ii)(D) of this section, the remaining $210 of the related person interest expense is allocated to general limitation income. Under paragraph (m)(2) of this section, $28 of the remaining $210 is treated as income from United States sources ($28 = $210 × $100/$750) and $182 is treated as income from foreign sources ($182 = $210 × $650/$750).

Example (3). Controlled foreign corporation S is a wholly-owned subsidiary of P, a domestic corporation. In 1988, S pays $300 of interest to P. S has no other expenses. S uses the asset method to allocate interest expense. In 1988, S has $4000 of assets that generate $650 of foreign source general limitation manufacturing income and a $1000 loan to an unrelated foreign person that generates $100 of foreign source passive interest income. S has $500 of shipping assets that generate $200 of foreign source shipping income and $500 of shipping assets that generate $200 of United States source shipping income. S also has a $1000 loan to an unrelated United States person that generates $100 of United States source passive income. S's passive income is not also described as shipping income. The following chart summarizes S's assets and income:

Assets

	Foreign	U.S.	Totals
Passive	1000	1000	2000
Shipping	500	500	1000
General	4000	0	4000
Total	5500	1500	7000

Income

	Foreign	U.S.	Totals
Passive	100	100	200
Shipping	200	200	400
General	650	0	650
Total	950	300	1250

Under paragraph (c)(2)(ii)(C) of this section, $200 of the related person interest payment is allocable to S's passive income. Under paragraph (m)(2) of this section, $100 of this amount is from foreign sources and $100 is from sources within the United States.

Under paragraph (c)(2)(ii)(D) of this section, $80 of the remaining $100 of the related person interest payment is allocated to general limitation income ($80 = $100 × $4000/$5000) and $20 is allocated to shipping income ($20 = $100 × $1000/$5000).

Under paragraph (m)(2) of this section, none of $80 of the interest payment allocated to general limitation income is treated as income from United States sources ($0 = $80 × $0/$4000). Therefore, the entire $80 is treated as income from foreign sources.

Under paragraph (m)(2) of this section, $10 of the $20 of the interest payment allocated to the shipping income is treated as income from United States sources ($10 = $20 × $500/$1000) and $10 of the $20 is treated as income from foreign sources ($10 = $20 × $500/$1000).

Example (4). The facts are the same as in Example (3) except that S uses the gross income method to allocate interest expense. The interest allocated to passive income under paragraph (c)(2)(ii)(C) of this section is the same, $200, $100 from United States sources and $100 from foreign sources.

Under paragraph (c)(2)(ii)(D) of this section, the remaining $100 of related person interest is allocated between the shipping and general limitation categories based on the gross income in

Reg. § 1.904-5(m)(3)

Income from Sources Without the United States

those categories. Therefore, $38 of the remaining $100 interest payment is allocated to shipping income ($38 = $100 × $400/($1250 − $200)) and $62 is treated as allocated to general limitation income ($62 = $100 × $650/($1250 − $200)).

Under paragraph (m)(2) of this section, $19 of the $38 allocable to shipping income is treated as income from United States sources ($19 = $38 × $200/$400) and $19 is treated as income from foreign sources ($19 = $38 × $200/$400).

Under paragraph (m)(2) of this section, all of the $62 allocated to general limitation income is treated as income from foreign sources ($62 = $62 × $650/$650).

(4) *Treatment of dividend payments*—(i) *Rule.* Any dividend or distribution treated as a dividend under this section (including an amount included in gross income under section 951(a)(1)(B)) that is received or accrued by a United States shareholder from a controlled foreign corporation shall be treated as income in a separate category derived from sources within the United States in proportion to the ratio of the portion of the earnings and profits of the controlled foreign corporation in the corresponding separate category from United States sources to the total amount of earnings and profits of the controlled foreign corporation in that separate category.

(ii) *Determination of earnings and profits from United States sources.* In order to determine the portions of earnings and profits from United States sources and from foreign sources within each separate category, related person interest shall be allocated to the United States source portion of income in a separate category by applying the rules of paragraph (m)(2) of this section. Other expenses shall be allocated by applying the rules of paragraph (c)(2)(ii) of this section separately to the United States source income and the foreign source income in each category. For example, unrelated person interest expense that is allocated among categories of income based upon the relative amounts of assets in a category must be allocated between United States and foreign source income within each category by applying the rules of paragraph (c)(2)(ii)(E) of this section separately to United States source and foreign source assets in the separate category.

(iii) *Example.* The following example illustrates the application of this paragraph.

Example. Controlled foreign corporation, S, is a wholly owned subsidiary of P, a domestic corporation. S is a financial services entity. In 1987, S has $100 of non-subpart F general limitation earnings and profits and $100 of non-subpart F financial services income. None of the general limitation earnings and profits are from sources within the United States, and $50 of the financial services earnings and profits are from United States sources. In 1988, S earns $300 of non-subpart F general limitation earnings and profits and $500 of non-subpart F financial services earnings and profits. One hundred dollars ($100) of the general limitation earnings and profits are from sources within the United States. None of the financial services earnings and profits are from United States sources. In 1988, S pays P a $500 dividend. Under paragraph (c)(4) of this section, $200 of the dividend is attributable to general limitation earnings and profits ($200 = $500 × $400/$1000). Under this paragraph (m)(3), the portion of the dividend that is attributable to general limitation earnings and profits from sources within the United States is $50 ($200 × $100/$400). Under paragraph (c)(4) of this section, $300 of the dividend is attributable to financial services earnings and profits ($300 = $500 × $600/$1000). Under this paragraph (m)(3), the portion of the dividend that is attributable to financial services earnings and profits from sources within the United States is $25 ($300 × $50/$600).

(5) *Treatment of subpart F inclusions*—(i) *Rule.* Any amount included in the gross income of a United States shareholder of a controlled foreign corporation under section 951(a)(1)(A) shall be treated as income subject to a separate limitation that is derived from sources within the United States to the extent such amount is attributable to income of the controlled foreign corporation in the corresponding category of income from sources within the United States. In order to determine a controlled foreign corporation's taxable income and earnings and profits from sources within the United States in each separate category, the principles of paragraph (m)(4)(ii) of this section shall apply.

(ii) *Example.* The following example illustrates the application of this paragraph (m)(5).

Example. Controlled foreign corporation S is a wholly-owned subsidiary of domestic corporation, P. In 1987, S earns $100 of subpart F foreign personal holding company income that is passive income. Of this amount, $40 is derived from sources within the United States. S also earns $50 of subpart F general limitation income. None of this income is from sources within the United States. Assume that S pays no foreign taxes and has no expenses. P is required to include $150 in gross income under section 951(a). Of this amount, $60 will be foreign source passive income to P and $40 will be United States source passive

Reg. § 1.904-5(m)(5)

income to P. Fifty dollars ($50) will be foreign source general limitation income to P.

(6) *Treatment of section 78 amount.* For purposes of treating taxes deemed paid by a taxpayer under section 902(a) and section 960(a)(1) as a dividend under section 78, taxes that are paid or accrued with respect to United States source income in a separate category shall be treated as United States source income in that separate category.

(7) *Coordination with treaties*—(i) *Rule.* If any amount of income derived from a United States-owned foreign corporation, as defined in section 904(g)(6), would be treated as derived from sources within the United States under section 904(g) and this paragraph (m) and, pursuant to an income tax convention with the United States, the taxpayer chooses to avail itself of benefits of the convention that treat that amount as arising from sources outside the United States under a rule explicitly treating the income as foreign source, then that amount will be treated as foreign source income. However, sections 904(a), (b), (c), (d) and (f), 902, 907, and 960 shall be applied separately to amounts described in the preceding sentence with respect to each treaty under which the taxpayer has claimed benefits and, within each treaty, to each separate category of income.

(ii) *Example.* The following example illustrates the application of this paragraph (m)(7).

Example. Controlled foreign corporation S is incorporated in Country A and is a wholly-owned subsidiary of P, a domestic corporation. In 1990, S earns $80 of foreign base company sales income in Country A which is general limitation income and $40 of U.S. source interest income. S incurs $20 of expenses attributable to its sales business. S pays P $40 of interest that is allocated to U.S. source passive income under paragraphs (c)(2)(ii)(C) and (m)(2) of this section. Assume that earnings and profits equal net income. All of S's net income of $60 is includible in P's gross income under subpart F (section 951 (a)(1)). For 1990, P also has $100 of passive income derived from investments in Country B. Pursuant to section 904(g)(3) and paragraph (m)(2) of this section, the $40 interest payment from S is United States source income to P because it is attributable to United States source interest income of S. The United States-Country A income tax treaty, however, treats all interest payments by residents of Country A as Country A sourced and P elects to apply the treaty. Pursuant to section 904(g)(10) and this paragraph (m)(7), the entire interest payment will be treated as foreign source income to P. P thus has $60 of foreign source general limitation income, $40 of foreign source passive income from S, and $100 of other foreign source passive income. In determining P's foreign tax credit limitation on passive income, the passive income from Country A shall be treated separately from any other passive income.

(n) *Order of application of sections 904(d), and (g).* In order to apply the rules of this section, section 904(d)(1) shall first be applied to the controlled foreign corporation to determine the amount of income and earnings and profits derived by the controlled foreign corporation in each separate category. The income and earnings and profits in each separate category that is from United States sources shall then be determined. Sections 904(d)(3), 904(g), and this section shall then be applied for purposes of characterizing and sourcing income received, accrued, or included by a United States shareholder in the controlled foreign corporation that is attributable or allocable to income or earnings and profits of the controlled foreign corporation.

(o) *Effective date.* Section 904(d)(3) and this section apply to distributions and section 951 inclusions of earnings and profits of a controlled foreign corporation (or other entity to which this section applies) derived during the first taxable year of the controlled foreign corporation (or other entity) beginning after December 31, 1986, and thereafter, and to payments made by a controlled foreign corporation (or other entity) during such taxable years, without regard to whether the corresponding taxable year of the recipient of the distribution or payment or of one or more of the United States shareholders of the controlled foreign corporation begins after December 31, 1986. [Reg. § 1.904-5.]

☐ [*T.D. 8214, 7-15-88. Amended by T.D. 8412, 5-13-92; T.D. 8767, 3-23-98; T.D. 8827, 7-12-99 (corrected 10-29-99) and T.D. 8916, 12-29-2000.*]

[Reg. § 1.904-6]

§ 1.904-6. **Allocation and apportionment of taxes.**—(a) *Allocation and appointment of taxes to a separate category or categories of income*— (1) *In general*—(i) *Taxes related to a separate category of income.* The amount of foreign taxes paid or accrued with respect to a separate category of income (including United States source income) shall include only those taxes that are related to income in that separate category. Taxes are related to income if the income is included in the base upon which the tax is imposed. If, for example, foreign law exempts certain types of income from foreign taxes, or certain types of income are exempt from foreign tax under an income tax convention, then no taxes are considered to be related to such income for purposes of this paragraph. As another example, if foreign law provides for a specific rate of tax with respect to certain types of income (*e.g.,* capital gains), or certain expenses, deductions, or credits are allowed under foreign law only with respect to a particular type of income, then such provisions shall be taken into account in determining the amount of foreign tax imposed on such income. A withholding tax (unless it is a withholding tax that is not the final tax payable on the income as described in § 1.904-4 (d)) is related to the income from which it is withheld. A tax that is imposed on a base that includes more than one separate category of income is considered to be imposed on income in all such categories, and, thus, the taxes are related to all such categories included within the foreign country or possession's taxable income base.

(ii) *Apportionment of taxes related to more than one separate category.* If a tax is related to more than one separate category, then, in order to determine the amount of the tax paid or accrued with respect to each separate category, the tax shall be apportioned on an annual basis among the separate categories on the basis of the following formula:

$$\begin{array}{c}\text{Foreign tax}\\\text{related to more}\\\text{than one}\\\text{separate category}\end{array} \times \frac{\begin{array}{c}\text{Net income subject to}\\\text{that foreign tax}\\\text{included in a separate category}\end{array}}{\begin{array}{c}\text{Net income subject to}\\\text{that foreign tax}\end{array}}$$

For purposes of apportioning foreign taxes among the separate categories, gross income is determined under the law of the foreign country or a possession of the United States to which the foreign income taxes have been paid or accrued. Gross income, as determined under foreign law, in the passive category shall first be reduced by any related person interest expense that is allocated to the income under the principles of section 954(b)(5) and § 1.904-5(c)(2)(ii)(C) (adjusted gross passive income). Gross income in all separate categories (including adjusted gross passive income) is next reduced by deducting any expenses, losses, or other amounts that are deductible under foreign law that are specifically allocable to the gross amount of such income under the laws of that foreign country or possession. If expenses are not specifically allocated under foreign law then the expenses will be apportioned under the principles of foreign law but only after taking into account the reduction of passive income by the application of section 954(b)(5). Thus, for example, if foreign law provides that expenses will be apportioned on a gross income basis, the gross income amounts will be those amounts determined under foreign law except that, in the case of passive income, the amount will be adjusted gross passive income. If foreign law does not provide for the direct allocation or apportionment of expenses, losses, or other deductions to a particular category of income, then the principles of §§ 1.861-8 through 1.861-14T and section 954(b)(5) shall apply in allocating and apportioning such expenses, losses, or other deductions to gross income as determined under foreign law after reduction of passive income by the amount of related person interest allocated to passive income under section 954(b)(5) and § 1.904-5(c)(2)(ii)(C). For example, the principles of §§ 1.861-8 through 1.861-14T apply to require definitely related expenses to be directly allocated to particular categories of gross income and provide the methods of apportioning expenses that are definitely related to more than one category of gross income or that are not definitely related to any particular category of gross income. For this purpose, the apportionment of expenses required to be made under §§ 1.861-8 through 1.861-14T need not be made on other than a separate company basis. The rules in this paragraph apply only for purposes of the apportionment of taxes among separate categories of income and do not affect the computation of a taxpayer's foreign tax credit limitation with respect to a specific category of income.

(iii) *Apportionment of taxes for purposes of applying the high-tax income test.* If taxes have been allocated and apportioned to passive income under the rules of paragraph (a)(1)(i) or (ii) of this section, the taxes must further be apportioned to the groups of income described in § 1.904-4(c)(3), (4) and (5) for purposes of determining if the group is high-taxed income. Taxes will be related to income in a particular group under the same rules as those in paragraph (a)(1)(i) and (ii) of this section except that those rules shall be applied by substituting the term "group" for the term "category."

(iv) *Special rule for base and timing differences.* If, under the law of a foreign country or possession of the United States, a tax is imposed on an item of income that does not constitute income under United States tax principles, that tax shall be treated as imposed with respect to general limitation income. If, under the law of a foreign country or possession of the United States,

Reg. § 1.904-6(a)(1)

a tax is imposed on an item that would be income under United States tax principles in another year, that tax will be allocated to the appropriate separate category or categories as if the income were recognized under United States tax principles in the year in which the tax was imposed.

(2) *Treatment of certain dividends from noncontrolled section 902 corporations.* If a taxpayer receives or accrues a dividend from a noncontrolled section 902 corporation, and if the Commissioner establishes that there is an agreement, express or implied, that such dividend is paid out of the passive earnings or high withholding tax interest income of the foreign corporation, then only the foreign taxes imposed on passive income or high withholding tax interest income of the noncontrolled section 902 corporation will be considered to be taxes related to the dividend. For an illustration of this rule, see paragraph (c) *Example (7)* of this section.

(b) *Application of paragraph (a) to sections 902 and 960*—(1) *Determination of foreign taxes deemed paid.* If, for the taxable year, there is included in the gross income of a domestic corporation under section 951 an amount attributable to the earnings and profits of a controlled foreign corporation for any taxable year and the amount included consists of income in more than one separate category of the controlled foreign corporation, then the domestic corporation shall be deemed to have paid only a portion of the taxes paid or accrued, or deemed paid or accrued, by the controlled foreign corporation that are allocated to each separate category to which the inclusion is attributable. The portion of the taxes allocated to a particular separate category that shall be deemed paid by the United States shareholder shall be equal to the taxes allocated to that separate category multiplied by the amount of the inclusion with respect to that category (as determined under § 1.904-5(c)(1)) and divided by the earnings and profits of the controlled foreign corporation with respect to that separate category (in accordance with § 1.904-5(c)(2)(ii)). The rules of this paragraph (b)(1) also apply for purposes of computing the foreign taxes deemed paid by United States shareholders of controlled foreign corporations under section 902.

(2) *Distributions received from foreign corporations that are excluded from gross income under section 959 (b).* The principles of this paragraph shall be applied to—

(i) Any portion of a distribution received from a first-tier corporation by a domestic corporation or individual that is excluded from the domestic corporation's or individual's income under section 959(a) and § 1.959-1; and

(ii) Any portion of a distribution received from an immediately lower-tier corporation by a second- or first-tier corporation that is excluded from such foreign corporation's gross income under section 959(b) and § 1.959-2, if such distribution is treated as a dividend pursuant to § 1.960-2(a).

(3) *Application of section 78.* For purposes of treating taxes deemed paid by a taxpayer under section 902(a) and section 960(a)(1) as a dividend under section 78, taxes that were allocated to income in a separate category shall be treated as income in that same separate category.

(4) *Increase in limitation.* The amount of the increase in the foreign tax credit limitation allowed by section 960(b) and § 1.960-4 shall be determined with regard to the applicable category of income under section 904(d).

(c) *Examples.* The following examples illustrate the application of this section.

Example (1). M, a domestic corporation, conducts business in foreign country X. M earns $400 of shipping income, $200 of general limitation income and $200 of passive income as determined under foreign law. Under foreign law, none of M's expenses are directly allocated or apportioned to a particular category of income. Under the principles of §§ 1.861-8 through 1.861-14T, M allocates $75 of directly allocable expenses to shipping income, $10 of directly allocable expenses to general limitation income, and no such expenses to passive income. M also apportions expenses that are not directly allocable to a specific class of gross income—$40 to shipping income, $20 to general limitation income, and $20 to passive income. Therefore, for purposes of paragraph (a) of this section, M has $285 of net shipping income, $170 of net general limitation income, and $180 of net passive income. Country X imposes tax of $100 on a base that includes M's shipping income and general limitation income. Country X exempts passive income from tax. The tax paid by M is related to M's shipping and general limitation income. The $100 tax is apportioned between those limitations. Thus, M is considered to have paid $63 of X tax on its shipping income ($100 × $285/$455) and $37 of tax on its general limitation income ($100 × $170/$455). None of the X tax is allocated to M's passive income.

Example (2). The facts are the same as in example (1) except that X does not exempt all passive income from tax but only exempts interest income. M's passive income consists of $100 of gross dividend income, to which $10 of expenses that are not directly allocable are apportioned, and $100 of interest income, to which $10 of expenses that are not directly allocable are appor-

Reg. § 1.904-6(a)(2)

tioned. The $90 of net dividend income is subject to X tax, and $90 of net interest income is exempt from X tax. M pays $130 of tax to X. The $130 of tax is related to M's general, shipping, and passive income. The tax is apportioned among those limitations as follows: $68 to shipping income ($130 × $285/$545) $41 to general limitation income ($130 × $170/$545), and $21 to passive income ($130 × $90/$545).

Example (3). P, a domestic corporation, owns 100 percent of S, a controlled foreign corporation organized in country X. S owns 100 percent of T, a controlled foreign corporation that is also organized in country X. Country X grants group relief to S and T. In 1987, S earns $100 of income and T incurs an $80 loss. Under country X's group relief provisions, only $20 of S's income is subject to country X tax. Country X imposes a 30 percent tax on this income ($6). P includes $100 of S's income in gross income under section 951. Six dollars ($6) of foreign tax is related to that income for purposes of section 960.

Example (4). P, a domestic corporation, owns 100 percent of S, a controlled foreign corporation organized in country X and 100 percent of T, a controlled foreign corporation organized in country Y. T has $200 of gross manufacturing general limitation income and $50 of passive income. T also pays S $100 for shipping T's goods, a price that may be justified under section 482. T has no other expenses and S has no other income or expense. T's income and earnings and profits are the same. Foreign country X does not tax S on its shipping income. Foreign country Y taxes all of T's income at a rate of 20 percent. Under the law of foreign country Y, T is only allowed a $50 deduction for the payment to S. Therefore, for foreign law purposes, T has $150 of manufacturing income and earnings and profits and $50 of passive income and earnings and profits upon which it pays $40 of tax. Under the principles of foreign law, $30 of that tax is imposed on the general limitation manufacturing income and $10 of the tax is imposed on passive income. Therefore, the foreign effective rate on the general limitation income is 30 percent and the foreign effective rate on the passive income is 20 percent. T has $100 of general limitation income and $50 of passive income and pays $30 of general limitation taxes and $10 of passive taxes. S has $100 of shipping income and pays no foreign tax.

Example (5). R, a domestic corporation, owns 50 percent of T a foreign corporation that is not a controlled foreign corporation and that is organized in foreign country X. R licenses certain property to T. T then relicenses this property to a third person. In 1987, T paid R a royalty of $100 all of which is treated as passive income to R because it was not an active royalty as defined in § 1.904-4(b)(2). R has $10 of expenses associated with the royalty income and no foreign tax was imposed on the royalty so the high-tax kickout does not apply. In 1988, the Commissioner determined that the correct arm's length royalty was $150 and under the authority of section 482 reallocated an additional $50 of income to R for 1987. Under a closing agreement with the Commissioner, R elected the benefits of Rev. Proc. 65-17 in relation to the income reallocated from R and established an account receivable from T. In 1988, T paid R an additional $50 to reflect the section 482 adjustment and the account receivable that was established because of the adjustment. Foreign country X treats the $50 payment in 1988 as a dividend by T and imposes a $10 withholding tax on the payment. Under paragraph (a)(1) of this section, the $10 of withholding tax is treated as fully allocable to the $50 payment because under foreign law the tax is imposed only on that income. For U.S. purposes, the income is not characterized as a dividend but as a repayment of a bona fide debt and, therefore, the $50 of income is not required to be recognized by R in 1988. The $10 of tax is treated as a tax paid in 1988 on the $50 of passive income included by R in 1987 pursuant to the section 482 adjustment rather than as a tax associated with a dividend from a noncontrolled section 902 corporation. The $10 tax is a tax imposed on passive income under paragraph (a)(1)(iv) of this section.

Example (6). P, a domestic corporation owns all of the stock of S, a controlled foreign corporation that is incorporated in country X. In 1989, S has $100 of passive income, $200 of dividends from a non-controlled section 902 corporation and $200 of general limitation income. S also has $100 of related person interest expense and $100 of other expenses that under foreign law are directly allocable to the general limitation income of S. S has no other expenses. Country X imposes a tax of 25% on all of the net income of S and S, therefore, pays $75 in foreign tax. Under paragraph (a)(1)(ii) of this section, the passive income of S is first reduced by the amount of related person interest for purposes of determining the net amount for purposes of allocating the $75 of tax. Under paragraph (a)(1)(ii) of this section, the general limitation income of S is reduced by the $100 of other expenses. Therefore, $50 of the foreign tax is allocated to the dividends from a noncontrolled section 902 corporation ($50 = $75 × $200/$300), $25 is allocated to the general limitation income of S ($25 = $75 × $100/$300), and no taxes are allocated to S's passive income.

Reg. § 1.904-6(c)

48,936 Income from Sources Without the United States
See p. 20,601 for regulations not amended to reflect law changes

Example (7). R, a domestic corporation owns preferred stock in T, a foreign corporation that is not a controlled foreign corporation, incorporated in foreign country X. R's stock represents 15 percent of the value of T. Dividends on the preferred stock are paid only out of certain designated passive investments of T. Foreign country X does not tax the passive income of T. Under paragraph (a)(2) of this section, no taxes will be considered to be related to any dividend paid by T to R.

Example (8). Domestic corporation P owns all of the stock of controlled foreign corporation S, which owns all of the stock of controlled foreign corporation T. All such corporations use the calendar year as the taxable year. Assume that earnings and profits are equal to net income and that the income amounts are identical under United States and foreign law principles. In 1987, T earns (before foreign taxes) $187.50 of net passive income and $62.50 of net general limitation income and pays $50 of foreign taxes. S earns no income in 1987 and pays no foreign taxes. For 1987, P is required under section 951 to include in gross income $175 attributable to the earnings and profits of T for that year. One hundred and fifty dollars ($150) of the subpart F inclusion is attributable to passive income earned by T, and $25 of the subpart F inclusion is attributable to general limitation income earned by T. In 1988, T earns no income and pays no foreign taxes. T pays a $200 dividend to S, consisting of $175 from its earnings and profits attributable to amounts required to be included in P's gross income with respect to T and $25 from its other earnings and profits. Assume that no withholding tax is imposed with respect to the distribution from T to S. In 1988, S earns $100 of net general limitation income and receives a $200 dividend from T. S pays $30 in foreign taxes. For 1988, P is required under section 951 to include in gross income $22.50 attributable to the earnings and profits of S for such year. The entire subpart F inclusion is attributable to general limitation income earned by S. In 1988, S pays P a dividend of $247.50, consisting of $157.50 from its earnings and profits attributable to the amount required under section 951 to be included in P's gross income with respect to T, $22.50 from its earnings and profits attributable to the amount required under section 951 to be included in P's gross income with respect to S, and $67.50 from its other earnings and profits. Assume that the de minimis rule of section 954(b)(3)(A) and the full inclusion rule of section 954(b)(3)(B) do not apply to the gross amounts of income earned by S and T. The foreign income taxes deemed paid by P for 1987 and 1988 under section 960(a)(1) and section 902(a) are determined as follows on the basis of the following facts and computations.

1. T corporation (second-tier corporation):
   - (a) Pre-tax earnings and profits:
     - Passive income (p.i.) 187.50
     - Plus:
   - (b) General limitation income (g.l.i.) 62.50
   - (c) Total 250
     - Less:
   - (d) Foreign income taxes paid on or with respect to T's earnings and profits (20%) . 50
   - (e) Earnings and profits 200
2. Allocation of taxes:
   - (a) Foreign income taxes paid by T that are allocable to p.i. earned by T:
     - Line 1(d) taxes 50
     - Multiplied by: foreign law net p.i. 187.50
     - Divided by: foreign law total net income 250
     - Result 37.50
   - (b) Foreign income taxes paid by T that are allocable to g.l.i. earned by T:
     - Line 1(d) taxes 50
     - Multiplied by: foreign law net g.l.i. 62.50
     - Divided by: foreign law total net income 250
     - Result 12.50

Reg. § 1.904-6(c)

Income from Sources Without the United States

See p. 20,601 for regulations not amended to reflect law changes

3. T's earnings and profits:
   (a) Earnings and profits attributable to T's p.i.:

Line (1)(a) e & p	187.50
Less: line 2(a) taxes	37.50
Result	150

   (b) Earnings and profits attributable to T's g.l.i.:

Line (1)(b) e & p	62.50
Less: line 2(b) taxes	12.50
Result	50

4. Subpart F inclusion attributable to T:
   (a) Amount required to be included in P's gross income for 1987 under section 951 with respect to T that is attribuable to T's p.i. 150
   (b) Amount required to be included in P's gross income for 1987 under section 951 with respect to T that is attributable to T's g.l.i. 25

5. Foreign income taxes deemed paid by P under section 960(a)(1) with respect to T:
   (a) Taxes deemed paid that are attributable to T's subpart F inclusion that are attributable to T's p.i.:

Line 2(a) taxes	37.50
Multiplied by: line 4(a) sec. 951 incl.	150
Divided by: line 3(a) e & p	150
Result	37.50

   (b) Taxes deemed paid that are attributable to T's subpart F inclusion that are attributable to T's g.l.i.:

Line 2(b) taxes	12.50
Multiplied by: line 4(b) sec. 951 incl.	25
Divided by: line 3(b) e & p	50
Result	6.25

6. Dividends paid to S:
   (a) Dividends attributable to T's previously taxed p.i. 150
       Plus:
   (b) Dividends attributable to T's previously taxed g.l.i. 25
       Plus:
   (c) Dividends from T's non-previously taxed earnings and profits attributable to p.i. 0
       Plus:
   (d) Dividends from T's non-previously taxed earnings and profits attributable to g.l.i. 25
   (e) Total dividends paid to S 200

7. Taxes deemed paid by S:
   (a) Taxes of T deemed paid by S for 1987 under section 902(b)(1) with regard to T's p.i.:

Line 2(a) taxes	37.50
Multiplied by: line 6(c) dividend	0
Divided by: line 3(a) e & p	150
Result	0

   (b) Taxes of T deemed paid by S for 1987 under section 902(b)(1) with regard to T's g.l.i.:

Line 2(b) taxes	12.50
Multiplied by: line 6(d) dividend	25
Divided by: line 3(b) e & p	50
Result	6.25

Reg. § 1.904-6(c)

48,938   **Income from Sources Without the United States**
See p. 20,601 for regulations not amended to reflect law changes

S corporation (first-tier corporation):

8. Pre-tax earnings and profits:
   - (a) Dividends from T attributable to T's non-previously taxed p.i. 0
   Plus:
   - (b) Dividends from T attributable to T's non-previously taxed g.l.i. 25
   Plus:
   - (c) Dividends from T attributable to T's previously taxed p.i. 150
   Plus:
   - (d) Dividends from T attributable to T's previously taxed g.l.i. 25
   Plus:
   - (e) Passive income other than dividend from T 0
   Plus:
   - (f) General limitation income other than dividend from T 100
   - (g) Total pre-tax earnings and profits 300
   - (h) Foreign income taxes paid on or with respect to S's earnings and profits (10%) . 30
   - (i) Earnings and profits   270

9. Allocation of taxes:
   - (a) Foreign income taxes paid by S that are allocable to non-previously taxed p.i. earned by S:
     - Line 8(h) taxes 30
     - Multiplied by: foreign law line 8(a) & 8(e) p.i. amounts 0
     - Divided by: foreign law total net income 300
     - Result 0
   - (b) Foreign income taxes paid by S that are allocable to S's previously taxed p.i. received from T:
     - Line 8(h) taxes 30
     - Multiplied by: foreign law line 8(c) p.i. amount 150
     - Divided by: foreign law total net income 300
     - Result 15
   - (c) Foreign income taxes paid by S that are allocable to non-previously taxed g.l.i. earned by S:
     - Line 8(h) taxes 30
     - Multiplied by: foreign law line 8(b) & line 8(f) g.l.i. amounts 125
     - Divided by: foreign law total net income 300
     - Result 12.50
   - (d) Foreign income taxes paid by S that are allocable to S's previously taxed g.l.i. received from T:
     - Line 8(h) taxes 30
     - Multiplied by: foreign law line 8(d) amount 25
     - Divided by: foreign law total net income 300
     - Result 2.50

10. (a) Non-previously taxed earnings and profits of S:
    - Lines 8(a), 8(b), 8(e), & 8(f) e & p 125
    - Less: lines 9(a) & 9(c) taxes 12.50
    - Result 112.50
    - (b) Portion of result in 10(a) attributable to S's p.i. 0
    - (c) Portion of result in 10(a) attributable to S's g.l.i. 112.50

11. (a) Previously taxed earnings and profits of S:
    - Lines 8(c) and 8(d) e & p 175
    - Less: lines 9(b) & 9(d) taxes 17.50
    - Result 157.50
    - (b) Portion of result in 11(a) attributable to T's p.i.:
      - Line 8(c) 150
      - Less: line 9(b) taxes 15
      - Result 135

Reg. § 1.904-6(c)

Income from Sources Without the United States 48,939
See p. 20,601 for regulations not amended to reflect law changes

	(c)	Portion of result in 11(a) attributable to T's g.l.i.:		
		Line 8(d)	25	
		Less: line 9(d) taxes	2.50	
		Result		22.50
12.		Subpart F inclusion attributable to S:		
	(a)	Amount required to be included in P's gross income for 1988 under section 951 with respect to S that is attributable to S's p.i.		0
	(b)	Amount required to be included in P's gross income for 1988 under section 951 with respect to S that is attributable to S's g.l.i.		22.50
13.		Foreign income taxes deemed paid by P under section 960(a)(1) with respect to S:		
	(a)	Taxes deemed paid that are attributable to S's subpart F inclusion that are attributable to S's p.i.:		
		Line 9(a) taxes	0	
		Multiplied by: line 12(a) sec. 951 incl.	0	
		Divided by: line 10(b) e & p	0	
		Result		0
	(b)	Taxes deemed paid that are attributable to S's subpart F inclusion that are attributable to S's g.l.i.:		
		Line 9(c) taxes	12.50	
		Multiplied by: line 12(b) sec. 951 incl	22.50	
		Divided by: line 10(c) e & p	112.50	
		Result		2.50
	(c)	Foreign income taxes deemed paid by S deemed paid by P that are allocable to S's p.i.:		
		Line 7(a) taxes deemed paid by S	0	
		Multiplied by: line 12(a) sec. 951 incl	0	
		Divided by: line 10(b) e & p	0	
		Result		0
	(d)	Foreign income taxes deemed paid by S deemed paid by P that are allowable to S's g.l.i.:		
		Line 7(b) taxes deemed paid by S	6.25	
		Multiplied by: line 12(b) sec. 951 incl	22.50	
		Divided by: line 10(c) e & p	112.50	
		Result		1.25
14.		Dividends paid to P:		
	(a)	Dividends from S attributable to S's previously taxed p.i. ...	0	
		Plus:		
	(b)	Dividends from S attributable to S's previously taxed g.l.i. ...	22.50	
		Plus:		
	(c)	Dividends to which section 902(a) applies:		
		(i) Consisting of S's earnings and profits attributable to T's previously taxed p.i.	135	
		Plus:		
		(ii) Consisting of S's earnings and profits attributable to T's previously taxed g.l.i.	22.50	
		Plus:		
		(iii) Consisting of S's other p.i. earnings and profits	0	
		Plus:		
		(iv) Consisting of S's other g.l.i. earnings and profits	67.50	
		(v) Total section 902 dividend		225
	(d)	Total dividends paid to P		247.50

Reg. § 1.904-6(c)

48,940 **Income from Sources Without the United States**
See p. 20,601 for regulations not amended to reflect law changes

15. Foreign income taxes deemed paid by P under section 902 and section 960(a)(3) with respect to S:

  (a) Taxes paid by S deemed paid by P under section 902(a) with regard to S's p.i.:

Line 9(a) taxes	0
Multiplied by: line 14(c)(iii) div	0
Divided by: line 10(b) e & p	0
Result	0

  (b) Taxes paid by S deemed paid by P under section 902(a) with regard to S's g.l.i.:

Line 9(c) taxes	12.50
Multiplied by: line 14(c)(iv) div	67.50
Divided by: line 10(c) e & p	112.50
Result	7.50

  (c) Taxes deemed paid by S deemed paid by P under section 902(a) with regard to S's p.i.:

Line 7(a) deemed paid taxes	0
Multiplied by: line 14(c)(iii) div	0
Divided by: line 10(b) e & p	0
Result	0

  (d) Taxes deemed paid by S deemed paid by P under section 902(a) with regard to S's g.l.i.:

Line 7(b) deemed paid taxes	6.25
Multiplied by: line 14(c)(iv) div	67.50
Divided by: line 10(c) e & p	112.50
Result	3.75

  (e) Foreign income taxes paid by S under section 960(a)(3) deemed paid by P with regard to S's previously taxed p.i.:

Line 9(b) taxes	15
Multiplied by: line 14(c)(i) div	135
Divided by: line 11(b) e & p	135
Result	15

  (f) Foreign income taxes paid by S under section 960(a)(3) deemed paid by P with regard to S's previously taxed g.l.i.:

Line 9(d) taxes	2.50
Multiplied by: line 14(c)(ii) div	22.50
Divided by: line 11(c) e & p	22.50
Result	2.50

SUMMARY

Total taxes deemed paid by P under section 960(a)(1) with respect to—

Passive income of S and T included under section 951 in income of P:

Line 5(a)	37.50
Plus:	
Line 13(a)	0
Plus:	
Line 13(c)	0
Result	37.50

General limitation income of S and T included under section 951 in income of P:

Line 5(b)	6.25
Plus:	
Line 13(b)	2.50
Plus:	
Line 13(d)	1.25
Result	10
Total deemed paid taxes under section 960(a)(1)	47.50
Total taxes deemed paid by P under section 902 and section 960(a)(3) attributable to passive income of S and T (line 15(e))	15

Reg. § 1.904-6(c)

Income from Sources Without the United States   **48,941**
See p. 20,601 for regulations not amended to reflect law changes

Total taxes deemed paid by P under section 902 and section 960(a)(3) attributable to general limitation income of S and T:

Line 15(b)	7.50
Plus:	
Line 15(d)	3.75
Plus:	
Line 15(f)	2.50
Result	13.75

[Reg. § 1.904-6.]

☐ [T.D. 8214, 7-15-88. Amended by T.D. 8412, 5-13-92.]

[Reg. § 1.904-7]

§ 1.904-7. **Transition rules.**—(a) *Characterization of distributions and section 951(a)(1)(A)(ii) and (iii) and (B) inclusions of earnings of a controlled foreign corporation accumulated in taxable years beginning before January 1, 1987, during taxable years of both the payor controlled foreign corporation and the recipient which begin after December 31, 1986*—(1) *Distributions and section 951(a)(1)(A)(ii) and (iii) and (B) inclusions.* Earnings accumulated in taxable years beginning before January 1, 1987, by a foreign corporation that was a controlled foreign corporation when such earnings were accumulated are characterized in that foreign corporation's hands under section 904(d)(1)(A) (separate limitation interest income) or section 904(d)(1)(E) (general limitation income) (prior to their amendment by the Tax Reform Act of 1986 (the Act)) after application of the de minimis rule of former section 904(d)(3)(C) (prior to its amendment by the Act). When, in a taxable year after the effective date of the Act, earnings and profits attributable to such income are distributed to, or included in the gross income of, a United States shareholder under section 951(a)(1)(A)(ii) or (iii) or (B) (hereinafter in this section "inclusions"), the ordering rules of section 904(d)(3)(D) and § 1.904-5(c)(4) shall be applied in determining initially the character of the income of the distributee or United States shareholder. Thus, a proportionate amount of a distribution described in this paragraph initially will be characterized as separate limitation interest income in the hands of the distributee based on the ratio of the separate limitation interest earnings and profits out of which the dividend was paid to the total earnings and profits out of which the dividend was paid. The distribution or inclusions must then be recharacterized in the hands of the distributee or United States shareholder on the basis of the following principles:

(i) Distributions and inclusions that are initially characterized as separate limitation interest income shall be treated as passive income;

(ii) Distributions and inclusions that initially are characterized as old general limitation income shall be treated as general limitation income, unless the taxpayer establishes to the satisfaction of the Commissioner that the distribution or inclusion is attributable to:

(A) Earnings and profits accumulated with respect to shipping income, as defined in section 904(d)(2)(D) and § 1.904-4(f); or

(B) In the case of a financial services entity, earnings and profits accumulated with respect to financial services income, as defined in section 904(d)(2)(C)(ii) and § 1.904-4(e)(1); or

(C) Earnings and profits accumulated with respect to high withholding tax interest, as defined in section 904(d)(2)(B) and § 1.904-4(d).

(2) *Limitation on establishing the character of earnings and profits.* In order for a taxpayer to establish that distributions or inclusions that are attributable to general limitation earnings and profits of a particular taxable year beginning before January 1, 1987, are attributable to shipping, financial services or high withholding tax interest earnings and profits, the taxpayer must establish the amounts of foreign taxes paid or accrued with respect to income attributable to those earnings and profits that are to be treated as taxes paid or accrued with respect to shipping, financial services or high withholding tax interest income, as the case may be, under section 904(d)(2)(I). Conversely, in order for a taxpayer to establish the amounts of general limitation taxes paid or accrued in a taxable year beginning before January 1, 1987, that are to be treated as taxes paid or accrued with respect to shipping, financial services or high withholding tax interest income, as the case may be, the taxpayer must establish the amount of any distributions or inclusions that are attributable to shipping, financial services or high withholding tax interest earnings and profits. For purposes of establishing the amounts of general limitation taxes that are to be treated as taxes paid or accrued with respect to shipping, financial services or high withholding tax interest income, the principles of § 1.904-6 shall be applied.

(b) *Application of look-through rules to distributions (including deemed distributions) and pay-*

Reg. § 1.904-7(b)

ments by an entity to a recipient when one's taxable year begins before January 1, 1987 and the other's taxable year begins after December 31, 1986—(1) *In general.* This paragraph provides rules relating to the application of section 904(d)(3) to payments made by a controlled foreign corporation or other entity to which the look-through rules apply during its taxable year beginning after December 31, 1986, but received in a taxable year of the recipient beginning before January 1, 1987. The paragraph also provides rules relating to distributions (including deemed distributions) or payments made by a controlled foreign corporation to which section 904(d)(3) (as in effect before the Act) applies during its taxable year beginning before January 1, 1987, and received in a taxable year of the recipient beginning after December 31, 1986.

(2) *Payor of interest, rents, or royalties is subject to the Act and recipient is not subject to the Act.* If interest, rents, or royalties are paid or accrued on or after the start of the payor's first taxable year beginning on or after January 1, 1987, but prior to the start of the recipient's first taxable year beginning on or after January 1, 1987, such interest, rents, or royalties shall initially be characterized in accordance with section 904(d)(3) and § 1.904-5. To the extent that interest payments in the hands of the recipient are initially characterized as passive income under these rules, they will be treated as separate limitation interest in the hands of the recipient. To the extent that rents or royalties in the hands of the recipient are initially characterized as passive income under these rules, they will be recharacterized as general limitation income in the hands of the recipient.

(3) *Recipient of interest, rents, or royalties is subject to the Act and payor is not subject to the Act.* If interest, rents, or royalties are paid or accrued before the start of the payor's first taxable year beginning on or after January 1, 1987, but on or after the start of the recipient's first taxable year beginning after January 1, 1987, the income in the recipient's hands shall be initially characterized in accordance with former section 904(d)(3) (prior to its amendment by the Act). To the extent interest income is characterized as separate limitation interest income under these rules, that income shall be recharacterized as passive income in the hands of the recipient. Rents or royalties will be characterized as general limitation income.

(4) *Recipient of dividends and subpart F inclusions is subject to the Act and payor is not subject to the Act.* If dividends are paid or accrued or section 951(a)(1) inclusions occur before the start of the first taxable year of a controlled foreign corporation beginning on or after January 1, 1987, but on or after the start of the first taxable year of the distributee or United States shareholder beginning on or after January 1, 1987, the dividends or section 951(a)(1) inclusions in the hands of the distributee or United States shareholder shall be initially characterized in accordance with former section 904(d)(3) (including the ordering rules of section 904(d)(3)(A). Therefore, under former section 904(d)(3)(A), dividends are considered to be paid or derived first from earnings attributable to separate limitation interest income. To the extent the dividend or section 951(a)(1) inclusion is initially characterized under these rules as separate limitation interest income in the hands of the distributee or United States shareholder, the dividend or section 951(a)(1) inclusion shall be recharacterized as passive income in the hands of the distributee or United States shareholder. The portion, if any, of the dividend or section 951(a)(1) inclusion that is not characterized as passive income shall be characterized according to the rules in paragraph (a) of this section. Therefore, a taxpayer may establish that income that would otherwise be characterized as general limitation income is shipping or financial services income. Rules comparable to the rules contained in section 904(d)(2)(I) shall be applied for purposes of characterizing foreign taxes deemed paid with respect to distributions and section 951(a)(1) inclusions covered by this paragraph (b)(4).

(5) *Examples.* The following examples illustrate the application of this paragraph (b).

Example (1). P is a domestic corporation that is a fiscal year taxpayer (July 1-June 30). S, a controlled foreign corporation, is a wholly-owned subsidiary of P and has a calendar taxable year. On June 1, 1987, S makes a $100 interest payment to P. Because the payment is made after January 1, 1987 (the first day of S's first taxable year beginning after December 31, 1986), the look-through rules of section 904(d)(3) apply to characterize the payment made by S. To the extent, however, that the interest payment to P is allocable to passive income earned by S, the payment will be included in P's separate limitation for interest as provided in former section 904(d)(1)(A).

Example (2). P is a domestic corporation that is a calendar year taxpayer. S, a controlled foreign corporation, is a wholly-owned subsidiary of P and has a July 1-June 30 taxable year. On June 1, 1987, S makes a $100 interest payment to P. Because the payment is made prior to July 1, 1987 (the first day of S's first taxable year beginning after December 31, 1986), the look-through rules of section 904(d)(3) do not apply. Assume that, under former section 904(d)(3), the interest payment would be characterized as separate limitation interest income. For purposes of determining P's foreign tax credit limitation, the interest payment will be passive income as provided in section 904(d)(1)(A).

Example (3). The facts are the same as in *Example (2)* except that on June 1, 1987, S makes a $100 dividend distribution to P. Because the dividend is paid prior to July 1, 1987 (the first day of S's first taxable year beginning after December 31, 1986), the look-through rules of section 904(d)(3) do not apply. Assume that, under former section 904(d)(3), S's earnings and profits for the taxable year ending June 30, 1987 consist of $200 of earnings attributable to general limitation income and $75 of earnings attributable to separate limitation interest income. The portion of the dividend that is attributable to S's separate limitation interest and is treated as separate limitation interest income under former section 904(d)(3) is $75. The remaining $25 of the dividend is treated as general limitation income under former section 904(d)(3). For purposes of determining P's foreign tax credit limitation, $75 of the dividend will be recharacterized as passive income. The remaining $25 of the dividend will be characterized as general limitation income, unless P can establish that the general limitation portion is attributable to shipping or financial services income.

(c) *Installment sales.* If income is received or accrued by any person on or after the effective date of the Act (as applied to such person) that is attributable to a disposition of property by such person with regard to which section 453 or section 453A applies (installment sale treatment), and the disposition occurred prior to the effective date of the Act, that income shall be characterized according to the rules of §§ 1.904-4 through 1.904-7.

(d) *Special effective date for high withholding tax interest earned by persons with respect to qualified loans described in section 1201(e)(2) of the Act.* For purposes of characterizing interest received or accrued by any person, the definition of high withholding tax interest in § 1.904-4(d) shall apply to taxable years beginning after December 31, 1986 except as provided in section 1201(e)(2) of the Act.

(e) *Treatment of certain recapture income.* Except as otherwise provided, if income is subject to recapture under section 585(c), the income shall be general limitation income. If the income is recaptured by a taxpayer that is a financial services entity, the entity may treat the income as financial services income if the taxpayer establishes to the satisfaction of the Secretary that the deduction to which the recapture amount is attributable is allocable to financial services income. If the taxpayer establishes to the satisfaction of the Secretary that the deduction to which the recapture amount is attributable is allocable to high-withholding tax interest income, the taxpayer may treat the income as high-withholding tax interest. [Reg. § 1.904-7.]

☐ [*T.D.* 8214, 7-15-88. *Amended by T.D.* 8412, 5-13-92.]

[Reg. § 1.904(b)-1]

§ 1.904(b)-1. **Treatment of capital gains for corporations.**—(a) *In general.* For purposes of computing the foreign tax credit limitation of corporations, the following rules apply:

(1) *Inclusion in foreign source taxable income.* The taxable income of a corporation from sources without the United States includes gain from the sale or exchange of capital assets only in an amount equal to—

(i) Foreign source capital gain net income (as defined in paragraph (b)(2)), reduced by

(ii) The rate differential portion (as defined in paragraph (b)(5) of this section) of foreign source net capital gain (as defined in paragraph (b)(4) of this section).

(2) *Inclusion in entire taxable income.* The entire taxable income of a corporation includes gain from the sale or exchange of capital assets only in an amount equal to—

(i) Capital gain net income (as defined in paragraph (b)(1) of this section), reduced by

(ii) The rate differential portion of net capital gain (as defined in paragraph (b)(3) of this section).

(3) *Treatment of capital losses.* The taxable income of a corporation from sources without the United States shall be reduced by an amount equal to—

(i) Any net capital loss (as defined in paragraph (b)(6) of this section) allocable or apportionable to sources without the United States to the extent taken into account in determining capital gain net income for the taxable year, less

(ii) An amount equal to the differential portion of the excess of net capital gain from sources within the United States over net capital gain (from all sources).

(b) *Definitions.* For purposes of section 904(b) and §§ 1.904(b)-1 through (b)-3, the following definitions shall apply:

Reg. § 1.904(b)-1(b)

48,944 Income from Sources Without the United States
See p. 20,601 for regulations not amended to reflect law changes

(1) *Capital gain net income.* The term "capital gain net income" means the excess of the gains from the sales or exchanges of capital assets over the losses from such sales or exchanges. Such term shall include net section 1231 gain, but shall not include gains from the sale or exchange of capital assets to the extent that such gains are not treated as capital gains. In determining capital gain net income, gains and losses which are not from the sale or exchange of capital assets but which are treated as capital gains and losses under the Internal Revenue Code are included.

(2) *Foreign source capital gain net income.* The term "foreign source capital gain net income" means the lesser of—

(i) Capital gain net income from sources without the United States, or

(ii) Capital gain net income (from all sources).

(3) *Net capital gain.* The term "net capital gain" means the excess of the net long-term capital gain (including net section 1231 gain) for the taxable year over the net short-term capital loss for such year, but shall not include gains from the sale or exchange of capital assets to the extent that such gains are not treated as capital gains. In determining net capital gain, gains and losses which are not from the sale or exchange of capital assets but which are treated as capital gains and losses under the Internal Revenue Code are included.

(4) *Foreign source net capital gain.* The term "foreign source net capital gain" means the lesser of—

(i) Net capital gain from sources without the United States, or

(ii) Net capital gain (from all sources).

(5) *Rate differential portion.* The term "rate differential portion" of foreign source net capital gain, or the excess of net capital gain, from sources within the United States over net capital gain, as the case may be, is the same proportion of such amount as the excess of the highest rate of tax specified in section 11(b) over the alternative rate of tax under section 1201(a) bears to the highest rate of tax specified in section 11(b).

(6) *Net capital loss.* Except as provided in § 1.904(b)-2(b), the term "net capital loss" means the excess of the losses from sales and exchanges of capital assets over the sum allowed under section 1211. For purposes of paragraph (a) of this section, the term "net capital loss" includes any amounts which are short-term capital losses under section 1212(a). Net capital losses do not include losses from the sales or exchanges of capital assets which are not treated as capital losses under the Internal Revenue Code. In determining net capital loss, gains and losses which are not from the sale or exchange of capital assets but which are treated as capital gains and losses under the Internal Revenue Code are included.

(7) *Allocation and apportionment.* For purposes of this section and §§ 1.904(b)-2 and (b)-3, the rules under § 1.861-8(e)(7) with respect to the allocation and apportionment of losses are to be applied with respect to losses on the sale, exchange or other disposition of property.

(8) *Computation of net section 1231 gain.* For purposes of this section and § 1.904(b)-2, the netting of section 1231 gains and losses is determined by aggregating the gains and loss from sources both within and without the United States. The gain or loss determined by this aggregation determines the character of the section 1231 gains (and losses allocable or apportionable thereto) from sources without the United States and from all sources for purposes of computing the foreign tax credit limitation fraction.

(c) *Illustrations.* The principles of paragraph (a) of this section may be illustrated by the following examples:

Example (1). Corporation A had the following business taxable income, capital gains and capital losses for 1979:

	Foreign source	United States source	All sources
Business income	$1200	$2000	$3200
Long-term capital gain	300	200	500
Long-term capital loss	0	400	400
Short-term capital gain	100	400	500
Short-term capital loss	200	300	500

In Thousands

For purposes of computing the foreign tax credit limitations, the foreign source taxable income and the entire taxable income of A are computed as follows:

Step (1) First compute the net long-term capital gain and net short-term capital gain and the net long-term capital loss and net short-term capital loss allocable or apportionable to such sources, from sources without the United States and from all sources, as follows:

Reg. § 1.904(b)-1(b)(1)

Income from Sources Without the United States

See p. 20,601 for regulations not amended to reflect law changes

	In Thousands	
	Sources without the U.S.	All sources
Net long-term capital gain	$300	$100
Net long-term capital loss	0	0
Net short-term capital gain	0	0
Net short-term capital loss	100	0

Step (2) Next compute capital gain net income and net capital gain from sources without the United States and from all sources as follows:

	In Thousands	
	Sources without the U.S.	All sources
Capital gain net income	(a) $200	(b) $100
Net capital gain	(c) $200	(d) $100

Step (3) Next calculate foreign source capital gain net income and foreign source net capital gain, which is the lesser of (a) or (b) and the lesser of (c) or (d) respectively. Foreign source capital gain net income is $100,000, and foreign source net capital gain is $100,000.

Step (4) Compute taxable income from sources without the United States, using 18/46 as the rate differential portion, as follows:

Foreign business income + Foreign source capital gain net income − 18/46 (foreign source net capital gain)
$1,200,000 + $100,000 − 18/46 ($100,000) = $1,260,870
($39,130)

Step (5) Compute the entire taxable income as follows:

Business income + Capital gain net income − 18/46 (net capital gain)
$3,200,000 + $100,000 − 18/46 ($100,000) = $3,260,870
($39,130)

Example (2). Corporation B had the following business taxable income, capital gains, and capital losses for 1979:

	In Thousands		
	Foreign source	United States source	All sources
Business income	$1200	$2000	$3200
Long-term capital gain	300	200	500
Long-term capital loss	500	100	600
Short-term capital gain	600	200	800
Short-term capital loss	100	200	300

For purposes of computing the foreign tax credit limitation, the foreign source taxable income and the entire taxable income of B are computed as follows:

Step (1) First compute the net long-term capital gain and net short-term capital gain and the net long-term capital loss and net short-term capital loss allocable or apportionable to such sources, from sources without the United States and from all sources, as follows:

	In Thousands	
	Sources without the U.S.	All sources
Net long-term capital gain	$ 0	$ 0
Net long-term capital loss	200	100
Net short-term capital gain	500	500
Net short-term capital loss	0	0

Reg. § 1.904(b)-1(c)

48,946 Income from Sources Without the United States
See p. 20,601 for regulations not amended to reflect law changes

Step (2) Next compute capital gain net income and net capital gain from sources without the United States and from all sources as follows:

	In Thousands Sources without the U.S.	All sources
Capital gain net income	(a) $300	(b) $400
Net capital gain	(c) 0	(d) 0

Step (3) Next calculate foreign source capital gain net income and foreign source net capital gain which is the lesser of (a) or (b) and the lesser of (c) or (d), respectively. Foreign source capital gain net income is $300,000 and foreign source net capital gain is zero.

Step (4) Compute taxable income from sources without the United States, using 18/46 as the rate differential portion, as follows:

Foreign business income $1,200,000 + Foreign source capital gain net income $300,000 − 18/46 (foreign source net capital gain) − 18/46 (0) = $1,500,000

Step (5) Compute the entire taxable income as follows:

Business income $3,200,000 + Capital gain net income $400,000 − 18/46 (net capital gain) − 18/46 (0) = $3,600,000

Example (3). Corporation C had the following business taxable income, capital gains, and capital losses for 1979:

	Foreign source	In Thousands United States source	All sources
Business income	$1200	$2000	$3200
Long-term capital gain	200	500	700
Long-term capital loss	600	100	700
Short-term capital gain	300	400	700
Short-term capital loss	500	100	600

For purposes of computing the foreign tax credit limitation, the foreign source taxable income and the entire taxable income of C are computed as follows:

Step (1) First compute the net long-term capital gain and net short-term capital gain and the net long-term capital loss and net short-term capital loss allocable or apportionable to such sources, from sources without the United States and from all sources, as follows:

	In Thousands Sources without the U.S.	All sources
Net long-term capital gain	0	0
Net long-term capital loss	$400	0
Net short-term capital gain	0	$100
Net short-term capital loss	200	0

Step (2) Next compute capital gain net income and net capital gain from sources without the United States and from all sources:

	In Thousands Sources without the U.S.	All sources
Capital gain net income	(a) 0	(b) $100
Net capital gain	(c) 0	(d) 0

Step (3) Next calculate foreign source capital gain net income and foreign source net capital gain which is the lesser of (a) or (b) and the lesser of (c) or (d) respectively. Foreign source capital gain net

Reg. § 1.904(b)-1(c)

Income from Sources Without the United States

See p. 20,601 for regulations not amended to reflect law changes

income is zero and foreign source net capital gain is zero.

Step (4) Under paragraph (a)(3)(i) of this section, the taxable income from sources without the United States is reduced by the amount by which the net capital loss allocable or apportionable to sources without the United States reduces capital gains (long and short-term) from sources within the United States when computing capital gain net income. This is determined by first computing the net capital loss allocable or apportionable to sources without the United States ($600,000) and the capital gain net income from sources within the United States ($700,000). In this case, $600,000 of net capital loss allocable or apportionable to sources without the United States reduces $600,000 of net long and short-term capital gains from sources within the United States in computing capital gain net income.

Step (5) Under paragraph (a)(3)(ii) of this section, the adjustment under paragraph (a)(3)(i) of this section is reduced by an amount equal to the rate differential portion of net capital gain from sources within the United States over net capital gain (from all sources). In this case, net capital gain from sources within the United States is $400,000 and net capital gain is zero, so an amount equal to 18/46 multiplied by $400,000 is added to the numerator of the foreign tax credit limitation fraction in computing taxable income from sources without the United States.

Step (6) Computation of foreign tax credit limitation fraction.

(i) Taxable income from sources without the United States is as follows:

Foreign business income + Foreign source capital gain net income − 18/46 (foreign source − net capital gain)

(paragraph (a)(3)(i) adjustment − paragraph (a)(3)(ii) adjustment)

$1,200,000 + 0 − 0 − $600,000 + 18/46 ($400,000) = $756,522
($156,522)

(ii) The entire taxable income is as follows:

Business income + Capital gain net income − 18/46 (net capital gain)
$3,200,000 + $100,000 − 0 = $3,300,000

Note that no adjustment under paragraph (a)(3) is made with respect to the denominator.

Example (4). Corporation D had the following business taxable income, capital gains, and capital losses in 1979:

	In Thousands		
	Foreign source	United States source	All sources
Business income	$2000	$2500	$4500
Long-term capital gain	100	200	300
Long-term capital loss	100	100	200
Short-term capital gain	300	400	700
Short-term capital loss	800	0	800

For purposes of computing the foreign tax credit limitation, the foreign source taxable income and the entire taxable income are computed as follows:

Step (1) First compute the net long-term capital gain and net short-term capital gain and the net long-term capital loss and net short-term capital loss allocable or apportionable to such sources, from sources without the United States and from all sources, as follows:

	In Thousands	
	Sources without the U.S.	All sources
Net long-term capital gain	0	$100
Net long-term capital loss	0	0
Net short-term capital gain	0	0
Net short-term capital loss	$500	100

Step (2) Next compute capital gain net income and net capital gain from sources without the United States and from all sources:

Reg. § 1.904(b)-1(c)

48,948 Income from Sources Without the United States

See p. 20,601 for regulations not amended to reflect law changes

	In Thousands Sources without the U.S.	All sources
Capital gain net income	(a) 0	(b) 0
Net capital gain	(c) 0	(d) 0

Step (3) Next compute foreign source capital gain net income and foreign source net capital gain, which is the lesser of (a) or (b) and the lesser of (c) or (d), respectively. Foreign source capital gain net income is zero and foreign source net capital gain is zero.

Step (4) Under paragraph (a)(3)(i) of this section, the taxable income from sources without the United States is reduced by the amount by which the net capital loss allocable or apportionable to sources without the United States reduces capital gains (long- and short-term) from sources within the United States when computing capital gain net income. This is determined by first computing the net capital loss allocable or apportionable to sources without the United States ($500,000), and the capital gain net income from sources within the United States ($500,000). In this case, $500,000 of net capital loss allocable or apportionable to sources without the United States reduces $500,000 of net long- and short-term gains from sources within the United States in computing capital gain net income.

Step (5) Under paragraph (a)(3)(ii) of this section, the adjustment under paragraph (a)(3)(i) of this section is reduced by an amount equal to the rate differential portion of net capital gain from sources within the United States over net capital gain (from all sources). In this case, net capital gain from sources within the United States is $100,000 and the net capital gain is zero, so an amount equal to 18/46 multiplied by $100,000 is added to the numerator of the foreign tax credit limitation fraction in computing taxable income from sources without the United States.

Step (6) Computation of foreign tax credit limitation fraction.

(i) Taxable income from sources without the United States is as follows:

$$\begin{pmatrix} \text{Foreign} \\ \text{business} \\ \text{income} \end{pmatrix} + \begin{pmatrix} \text{Foreign source} \\ \text{capital gain} \\ \text{net income} \end{pmatrix} - \begin{pmatrix} 18/46 \text{ (foreign source} \\ - \text{ net capital gain)} \end{pmatrix}$$

$$\begin{pmatrix} \text{paragraph} \\ (a)(3)(i) \\ \text{adjustment} \end{pmatrix} - \text{paragraph (a)(3)(ii) adjustment}$$

$$\$2{,}000{,}000 + 0 - 0 - \$500{,}000 + 18/46 \ (\$100{,}000) = \$1{,}539{,}130$$
$$(\$\ 39{,}130)$$

(ii) The entire taxable income is determined as follows:

$$\begin{pmatrix} \text{Business} \\ \text{income} \\ \$4{,}500{,}000 \end{pmatrix} + \begin{pmatrix} \text{Capital gain} \\ \text{net income} \\ 0 - 0 \end{pmatrix} - 18/46 \ (\text{net capital gain})$$
$$= \$4{,}500{,}000$$

Note that no adjustment under paragraph (a)(3) of this section is made with respect to the denominator. [Reg. § 1.904(b)-1.]

☐ [T.D. 7914, 9-28-83.]

[Reg. § 1.904(b)-2]

§ 1.904(b)-2. Treatment of capital gains for other taxpayers.—(a) *In general.* For purposes of computing the foreign tax credit limitation of persons other than corporations, the following rules apply:

(1) *Inclusion in foreign source taxable income.* The taxable income from sources without the United States shall include gain from the sale or exchange of capital assets only to the extent of foreign source capital gain net income (as defined in paragraph (b)(2) of § 1.904(b)-1, reduced by an amount determined by multiplying foreign source net capital gain (as defined in paragraph (b)(4) of § 1.904(b)-1) by the percentage specified under section 1202(a).

(2) *Inclusion in entire taxable income.* The entire taxable income of a taxpayer other than a corporation shall include gains from the sale or exchange of capital assets only to the extent of capital gain net income (as defined in paragraph (b)(1) of § 1.904(b)-1), reduced by an amount determined by multiplying net capital gain (as defined in paragraph (b)(3) of § 1.904(b)-1) by the percentage specified under section 1202(a).

(3) *Treatment of capital losses.* The taxable income from sources without the United States shall be reduced by:

(i) Any net capital loss (as defined in paragraph (b) of this section) allocable or apportionable to sources without the United States to the extent taken into account in determining capital gain net income, less

Reg. § 1.904(b)-2(a)(1)

Income from Sources Without the United States

See p. 20,601 for regulations not amended to reflect law changes

(ii) An amount equal to the excess of net capital gain from sources within the United States over net capital gain, multiplied by the percentage specified under section 1202(a).

(b) *Definition of net capital loss.* For purposes of paragraph (a), the term "net capital loss" means the excess of the losses from the sale or exchange of capital assets treated as capital losses under the Internal Revenue Code and any carryforward as determined under section 1212 over the amount allowed under section 1211(b). In determining net capital loss, gains and losses which are not from the sale or exchange of capital assets but which are treated as capital gains and losses under the Internal Revenue Code are included.

(c) *Illustrations.* The principles of paragraph (a) are illustrated by the following examples:

Example (1). X, an individual, has $1,500,000 of foreign source taxable income and $2,500,000 of U.S. source taxable income (exclusive of capital gains and losses) for 1979 and the following capital gains and losses:

	Foreign source	In Thousands United States source	All sources
Long-term capital gain	$300	$500	$800
Long-term capital loss	100	500	600
Short-term capital gain	100	400	500
Short-term capital loss	100	200	300

For purposes of computing the foreign tax credit limitation, the foreign source taxable income and the entire taxable income of X are computed as follows:

Step (1) First, compute the net long-term capital gain and net short-term capital gain and the net long-term capital loss and net short-term capital loss allocable or apportionable to such sources, from sources without the United States and from all sources, as follows:

	In Thousands Sources without the U.S.	All sources
Net long-term capital gain	$200	$200
Net long-term capital loss	0	0
Net short-term capital gain	0	200
Net short-term capital loss	0	0

Step (2) Next compute capital gain net income and net capital gain from sources without the United States and from all sources as follows:

	In Thousands Sources without the U.S.	All sources
Capital gain net income	(a) $200	(b) $400
Net capital gain	(c) 200	(d) 200

Step (3) Next calculate foreign source capital gain net income and foreign source net capital gain, which is the lesser of (a) or (b) and the lesser of (c) or (d), respectively. Foreign source capital gain net income is $200,000 and foreign source net capital gain is $200,000.

Step (4) Compute taxable income from sources without the United States, using 0.60 as the percentage specified in section 1202(a), as follows:

Foreign taxable income exclusive of capital gains and losses)	+	Foreign source capital gain net income	−	0.60 (foreign source net capital gain)
$1,500,000	+	$200,000	−	0.60 ($200,000) = $1,580,000

Step (5) Compute the entire taxable income as follows:

Taxable income (exclusive of capital gains and losses)	+	Capital gain net income	−	0.60 (net capital gain)
$4,000,000	+	$400,000	−	0.06 ($200,000) ($120,000) = $4,280,000

Example (2). Y, an individual, has $2,000,000 of foreign source taxable income and $3,000,000 of U.S. source taxable income (exclusive of capital

Reg. § 1.904(b)-2(c)

48,950 Income from Sources Without the United States
See p. 20,601 for regulations not amended to reflect law changes

gains and losses) for 1979 and the following capital gains and losses:

	In Thousands		
	Foreign source	United States source	All sources
Long-term capital gain	$200	$800	$1000
Long-term capital loss	700	100	800
Short-term capital gain	100	300	400
Short-term capital loss	300	200	500

For purposes of computing the foreign tax credit limitation, the foreign source taxable income and the entire taxable income of Y are computed as follows:

Step (1) First, compute the net long-term capital gain and net short-term capital gain and the net long-term capital loss and net short-term capital loss allocable or apportionable to such sources, from sources without the United States and from all sources, as follows:

	In Thousands	
	Sources without the U.S.	All sources
Net long-term capital gain	$ 0	$200
Net long-term capital loss	500	0
Net short-term capital gain	0	0
Net short-term capital loss	200	100

Step (2) Next compute the capital gain net income and net capital gain from sources without the United States and from all sources as follows:

	In Thousands	
	Sources without the U.S.	All sources
Capital gain net income	(a) 0	(b) $100
Net capital gain	(c) 0	(d) 100

Step (3) Next calculate foreign source capital gain net income and foreign source net capital gain, which is the lesser of (a) or (b) and the lesser of (c) of (d), respectively. Foreign source capital gain net income is zero and foreign source net capital gain is also zero.

Step (4) Under paragraph (a)(3)(i) of this section, the taxable income from sources without the United States is reduced by the amount by which the net capital loss allocable or apportionable to sources without the United States reduces capital gains (long- and short-term) from sources within the United States when computing capital gain net income. This is determined by first computing the net capital loss allocable or apportionable to sources without the United States ($700,000) and the capital gain net income from sources within the United States ($800,000). In this case, $700,000 of net capital loss allocable or apportionable to sources without the United States reduces $700,000 of long- and short-term capital gain in computing capital gain net income.

Step (5) Under paragraph (a)(3)(ii) of this section, the adjustment under paragraph (a)(3)(i) of this section is reduced by an amount equal to the difference between net capital gain from sources within the United States and net capital gain (from all sources), multiplied by the percentage specified under section 1212(a). In this case, the net capital gain from sources within the United States is $700,000, the net capital gain is $100,000 and the percentage specified under section 1202(a) is 0.60.

Step (6) Computation of foreign tax credit limitation fraction.

(i) Taxable income from sources without the United States is as follows:

Foreign income (exclusive of capital gains and losses) + Foreign source capital gain net income − 0.60 (foreign source net capital gain)

$$- \begin{pmatrix} \text{paragraph (a)(3)(i)} \\ \text{adjustment} \end{pmatrix} - \begin{pmatrix} \text{paragraph (a)(3)(ii)} \\ \text{adjustment} \end{pmatrix}$$

$2,000,000 + 0 − 0 − $700,000 + 0.60 ($600,000) = $1,660,000
[or] ($360,000)

(ii) The entire taxable income is as follows:

Taxable income (exclusive of capital gains and losses) + Capital gains net income − 0.60 (net capital gain)
$5,000,000 + $100,000 − $60,000 = $5,040,000

Reg. § 1.904(b)-2(c)

Income from Sources Without the United States

Note that no adjustment under paragraph (a)(3) of this section is made with respect to the denominator. [Reg. § 1.904(b)-2.]

☐ [T.D. 7914, 9-28-83.]

[Reg. § 1.904(b)-3]

§ 1.904(b)-3. Sale of personal property.—(a) *General rule.* For purposes of section 904 and the regulations thereunder, there shall be included as gain from sources within the United States any gain from sources without the United States arising from the sale or exchange of a capital asset which is personal property (as defined in § 1.1245-3(b)). For purposes of this paragraph, gain from the sale or exchange of a capital asset shall include net section 1231 gain, but shall not include gain from the sale or exchange of a capital asset which is not treated as capital gain. However, gains and losses which are not from the sale or exchange of capital assets but which are treated as capital gains and losses under the Internal Revenue Code are included. The special source rules provided under this section shall be applied on an item by item basis with respect to the sale of personal property within any taxable year, except that if substantially all the assets of a trade or business (within the meaning of section 368(a)(1)(C)) are sold within any one country within any taxable year, the gains and losses from such sales or such assets shall be netted before applying the source rules under this section.

(b) *Special rules.* Paragraph (a) of this section shall not apply in each of the following cases:

(1) In the case of an individual, if the property is sold or exchanged within the country or possession of the individual's residence.

(2) In the case of a corporation, if the property is stock in a second corporation, and is sold in a country or possession in which the second corporation derived more than 50 percent of its gross income for the 3-year period ending with the close of such second corporation's taxable year immediately preceding the year during which the sale or exchange occurred (or for such part of such period as the corporation has been in existence, but in no event less than a 12-month period). For purposes of this paragraph (b)(2) of this section, the gross income of any foreign corporation shall be computed in the same manner as if the foreign corporation were a domestic corporation. Thus, the gross income of a foreign corporation for this purpose includes income from all sources, which is not specifically excluded from gross income under any other provisions of the Code.

(3) In the case of any taxpayer, if the property is personal property (other than stock in a corporation) which is sold or exchanged in a country or possession in which the property is used in a trade or business of the taxpayer, or in which the taxpayer derived more than 50 percent of its gross income for the 3-year period ending with the close of its taxable year immediately preceding the year during which the sale or exchange occurred (or, in case of a taxpayer other than an individual, for such part of such period as the taxpayer has been in existence, but in no event less than a 12-month period). In the case of property sold or exchanged by a partnership, trust, or estate, the determination required by the preceding sentence shall be made at the level of the partnership, trust (other than a grantor trust), or estate. For purposes of this paragraph (b)(3) of this section, the gross income of any foreign corporation (or other entity) shall be computed in the same manner as if the foreign corporation were a domestic corporation (or a domestic entity).

(c) *Exception.* Paragraph (a) of this section shall not apply to a sale of personal property if the gain (determined under chapter 1 of the Internal Revenue Code and computed on an item by item basis as provided under paragraph (a) of this section) from the sale or exchange of the personal property is subject to an income, war profits, or excess profits tax (including a tax withheld with respect to nonresident aliens or foreign corporations) with respect to a foreign country or a possession of the United States in which the sale or exchange occurs, and the rate of tax imposed by such country or possession applicable to such gain is 10 percent or more. For purposes of this paragraph, the tax must be 10 percent or more of the total amount of gain (whether ordinary or capital) arising from the sale or exchange of the item of personal property.

(d) *Application of source rules.* In determining the foreign country or possession where property is sold or exchanged for purposes of paragraphs (b) and (c) of this section, and the foreign country or possession where gross income is derived for purposes of paragraphs (b)(2), (b)(3) and (e) of this section, the source of any gain or income shall be determined by applying the principles under sections 861, 862, and 863 and the regulations thereunder.

(e) *Gain from liquidation of certain foreign corporations.* Paragraph (a) shall not apply with respect to a distribution in liquidation of a foreign corporation to which Part II of subchapter C applies, if such corporation derived less than 50 percent of its gross income from sources within the United States for the 3-year period ending with the close of such corporation's taxable year immediately preceding the year during which the distribution occurred (or for such part of such

Reg. § 1.904(b)-3(e)

period as the corporation has been in existence, but in no event less than a 12-month period). For purposes of this paragraph (e) of this section, the gross income of the foreign corporation shall be computed in the same manner as if the foreign corporation were a domestic corporation.

(f) *Residence defined.* For purposes of paragraph (b)(1) of this section, the country of an individual's residence is to be determined by applying the rules under §§ 301.7701(b)-1 through 301.7701(b)-9 of this chapter.

(g) *Tax rate applicable to gain.* For purposes of paragraph (c) of this section, the tax rate applicable to the gain on the sale or exchange of personal property (as determined under Chapter 1 of the Internal Revenue Code of 1954) shall be determined by applying the tax laws of the foreign country or possession (and any applicable reduction under a tax treaty) to such gain and by treating the gain from such transaction as if such gain were the only income derived by the taxpayer during the taxable year (and the only deductions allowed are deductions directly attributable to such gain).

(h) *Country in which gross income derived.* Notwithstanding paragraph (d) of this section, for purposes of this section, dividends received by a shareholder who is not a U.S. person from a foreign corporation shall be deemed to be derived from sources within the foreign country under the laws of which the foreign corporation is created or organized. [Reg. § 1.904(b)-3.]

☐ [T.D. 7914, 9-28-83. Amended by T.D. 8411, 4-24-92.]

[Reg. § 1.904(b)-4]

§ 1.904(b)-4. **Effective date.**—Sections 1.904(b)-1 and 1.904(b)-2 shall apply to taxable years beginning after December 31, 1975 and § 1.904(b)-3 shall apply to sales and exchanges made after November 12, 1975. [Reg. § 1.904(b)-4.]

☐ [T.D. 7914, 9-28-83.]

[Reg. § 1.904(f)-1]

§ 1.904(f)-1. **Overall foreign loss and the overall foreign loss account.**—(a) *Overview of regulations.* In general, section 904(f) and these regulations apply to any taxpayer that sustains an overall foreign loss (as defined in paragraph (c)(1) of this section) in a taxable year beginning after December 31, 1975. For taxable years ending after December 31, 1984, and beginning before January 1, 1987, there can be five types of overall foreign losses: a loss under each of the five separate limitations contained in former section 904(d)(1)(A) (passive interest limitation), (d)(1)(B) (DISC dividend limitation), (d)(1)(C) (foreign trade income limitation), (d)(1)(D) (foreign sales corporation (FSC) distributions limitation), and (d)(1)(E) (general limitation). For taxable years beginning after December 31, 1982, and ending before January 1, 1985, there can be three types of overall foreign losses under former section 904(d)(1)(A) (passive interest limitation), former section 904(d)(1)(B) (DISC dividend limitation) and former section 904(d)(1)(C) (general limitation). For taxpayers subject to section 907, the post-1982 general limitation overall foreign loss account may be further subdivided, as provided in § 1.904(f)-6. For taxable years beginning after December 31, 1975, and before January 1, 1983, taxpayers should have computed overall foreign losses separately under the passive interest limitation, the DISC dividend limitation, the general limitation, and the section 907(b) (FORI) limitation. However, for taxable years beginning after December 31, 1975, and before January 1, 1983, taxpayers may have computed only two types of overall foreign losses: a foreign oil related loss under the FORI limitation and an overall foreign loss computed on a combined basis for the passive interest limitation, the DISC dividend limitation, and the general limitation. A taxpayer that computed overall foreign losses for these years on a combined basis will not be required to amend its return to recompute such losses on a separate basis. If a taxpayer computed its overall foreign losses for these years separately under the passive interest limitation, the DISC dividend limitation, and the general limitation, on returns previously filed, a taxpayer may not amend those returns to compute such overall foreign losses on a combined basis. Section 1.904(f)-1 provides rules for determining a taxpayer's overall foreign losses, for establishing overall foreign loss accounts, and for making additions to and reductions of such accounts for purposes of section 904(f). Section 1.904(f)-2 provides rules for recapturing the balance in any overall foreign loss account under the general recapture rule of section 904(f)(1) and under the special recapture rule of section 904(f)(3) when the taxpayer disposes of property used predominantly outside the United States in a trade or business. Section 1.904(f)-3 provides rules for allocating overall foreign losses that are part of net operating losses or net capital losses to foreign source income in years to which such losses are carried. In addition, § 1.904(f)-3 provides transition rules for the treatment of net operating losses incurred in taxable years beginning after December 31, 1982, and carried back to taxable years beginning before January 1, 1983, and of net operating losses incurred in taxable years beginning before January 1, 1983, and carried forward to taxable years beginning after December 31, 1982. Section 1.904(f)-4 provides rules for recapture out of an accumulation distribution of a foreign trust. Section 1.904(f)-5 provides rules for recapture of overall foreign losses of domestic trusts. Section 1.904(f)-6 provides a transition rule for recapturing a taxpayer's pre-1983 overall foreign losses under the general limitation and the FORI limitation out of taxable income subject to the general limitation in taxable years beginning after December 31, 1982. Section § 1.1502-9 provides rules concerning the application of these regulations to corporations filing consolidated returns.

(b) *Overall foreign loss accounts.* Any taxpayer that sustains an overall foreign loss under paragraph (c) of this section must establish an account for such loss. Separate types of overall foreign losses must be kept in separate accounts. For taxable years beginning prior to January 1, 1983, taxpayers that computed losses on a combined basis in accordance with § 1.904(f)-1(c)(1) will keep one overall foreign loss account for such overall foreign loss. The balance in each overall foreign loss account represents the amount of such overall foreign loss subject to recapture by the taxpayer in a given year. From year to year, amounts may be added to or subtracted from the balances in such accounts as provided in paragraphs (d) and (e) of this section. The taxpayer must report the balances (if any) in its overall foreign loss accounts annually on a Form 1116 or 1118. Such forms must be filed for each taxable year ending after September 24, 1987. The balance in each account does not have to be attributed to the year or years in which the loss was incurred.

(c) *Determination of a taxpayer's overall foreign loss*—(1) *Overall foreign loss defined.* For taxable years beginning after December 31, 1982, and before January 1, 1987, a taxpayer sustains an overall foreign loss in any taxable year in which its gross income from sources without the United States subject to a separate limitation (as defined in paragraph (c)(2) of this section) is exceeded by the sum of the deductions properly allocated and apportioned thereto. Such losses are to be determined separately in accordance with the principles of the separate limitations. Accordingly, income and deductions subject to a separate limitation are not to be netted with income and deductions subject to another separate limitation for purposes of determining the amount of an overall foreign loss. A taxpayer may, for example, have an overall foreign loss under the general limitation in the same taxable year in which it has taxable income under the DISC dividend limitation. The same principles of calculating overall foreign losses on a separate limitation basis apply for taxable years beginning before January 1, 1983, except that a taxpayer shall determine its overall foreign losses on a combined basis, except for income subject to the FORI limitation, if the taxpayer filed its pre-1983 returns on such basis. Thus, for taxable years beginning prior to January 1, 1983, a taxpayer can net income and losses among the passive interest limitation, the DISC dividend limitation, and the general limitation if the taxpayer calculated its overall foreign losses that way at the time. Taxpayers that computed overall foreign losses separately under each of the separate limitations on their returns filed for taxable years beginning prior to January 1, 1983, may not amend such returns to compute their overall foreign losses for pre-1983 years on a combined basis.

(2) *Separate limitation defined.* For purposes of paragraph (c)(1) of this section and these regulations, the term separate limitation means any of the separate limitations under former section 904(d)(1)(A) (passive interest limitation), (B) (DISC dividend limitation), (C) (foreign trade income limitation), (D) (FSC distributions limitation), and (E) (general limitation) and the separate limitation under section 907(b) (FORI limitation) (for taxable years ending after December 31, 1975, and beginning before January 1, 1983).

(3) *Method of allocation and apportionment of deductions.* In determining its overall foreign loss, a taxpayer shall allocate and apportion expenses, losses, and other deductions to the appropriate category of gross income in accordance with section 862(b) and § 1.861-8 of the regulations. However, the following deductions shall not be taken into account:

(i) The amount of any net operating loss deduction for such year under section 172(a); and

(ii) To the extent such losses are not compensated for by insurance or otherwise, the amount of any—

(A) Expropriation losses for such year (as defined in section 172(h)), or

(B) Losses for such year which arise from fire, storm, shipwreck, or other casualty, or from theft.

(d) *Additions to the overall foreign loss account*—(1) *General rule.* A taxpayer's overall foreign loss as determined under paragraph (c) of this section shall be added to the applicable overall foreign loss account at the end of its taxable year to the extent that the overall foreign loss has reduced United States source income during the taxable year or during a year to which the loss has been carried back. For rules with respect to carry-

Reg. § 1.904(f)-1(d)(1)

overs see paragraph (d)(4) of this section and § 1.904(f)-3.

(2) *Overall foreign net capital loss.* An overall foreign net capital loss shall be added to the applicable overall foreign loss account at the end of the taxable year to the extent that the foreign source capital loss has reduced United States source capital gain net income during the taxable year or during a year to which the loss has been carried back, subject to the adjustments in paragraph (d)(5) of this section. For rules with respect to carryovers, see paragraph (d)(4) of this section and § 1.904(f)-3. As provided under § 1211(b), to the extent that a foreign source net capital loss has reduced United States source capital loss has reduced United States source income other than United States source capital gain net income, this additional amount would be added to the taxpayer's overall foreign loss account as if the United states source income had been offset by a foreign net operating loss that is not a capital loss.

(3) *Overall foreign losses of another taxpayer.* If any portion of any overall foreign loss of another taxpayer is allocated to the taxpayer in accordance with § 1.904(f)-5 (relating to overall foreign losses of domestic trusts) or § 1.1502-9 (relating to consolidated overall foreign losses), the taxpayer shall add such amount to its applicable overall foreign loss account.

(4) *Additions to overall foreign loss account created by loss carryovers.* Subject to the adjustments under § 1.904(f)-1(d)(5), the taxpayer shall add to each overall foreign loss account—

(i) All net operating loss carryovers to the current taxable year attributable to the same limitation to the extent that overall foreign losses included in the net operating loss carryovers reduced United States source income for the taxable year, and

(ii) All capital loss carryovers to the current taxable year attributable to the same limitation to the extent that foreign source capital loss carryovers reduced United States source capital gain net income for the taxable year.

(5) *Adjustments.* The amount of overall foreign loss determined in paragraph (d)(1) of this section and the amount of overall foreign net capital loss determined in paragraph (d)(2) of this section which shall be added to a taxpayer's overall foreign loss account shall be adjusted as follows prior to being added to an account.

(i) *Adjustment due to reduction in foreign source income under section 904(b).* A taxpayer's overall foreign loss acount shall not include any net capital loss from sources without the United States to the extent that the application of section 904(b) would result in a reduction of foreign source taxable income (but not below zero) for purposes of the numerator of the foreign tax credit limitation fraction.

(ii) *Adjustment to account for rate differential between ordinary income rate and capital gain rate.* Subject to the provisions of paragraph (d)(5)(i) of this section, if an overall foreign loss for a taxable year includes an overall foreign net capital loss, such amount shall be reduced as follows, in accordance with the provisions of section 904(b), before being added to the overall foreign loss account:

(A) In the case of a corporate taxpayer, to the extent that the United States source capital gain net income reduced by the foreign source net capital loss consists of the United States source net capital gain, by an amount equal to the rate differential portion (as defined in section 904(b)(3)(D) of the Code and the regulations thereunder) of the United States source net capital gain; or

(B) In the case of a taxpayer other than a corporate taxpayer, for taxable years beginning prior to January 1, 1979, an amount equal to the taxpayer's United States source net capital gain that is offset by such foreign source net capital loss reduced by 50 percent of such gain, and for taxable years beginning after December 31, 1978, and before January 1, 1987, reduced by an amount equal to 60 percent of such gain.

(e) *Reductions of overall foreign loss accounts.* The taxpayer shall subtract the following amounts from its overall foreign loss accounts at the end of its taxable year in the following order, if applicable:

(1) *Pre-recapture reduction for amounts allocated to other taxpayers.* An overall foreign loss account is reduced by the amount of any foreign loss which is allocated to another taxpayer in accordance with § 1.904(f)-5 (relating to overall foreign losses of domestic trusts) or § 1.1502-9 (relating to consolidated overall foreign losses).

(2) *Reduction for amounts recaptured.* An overall foreign loss account is reduced by the amount of any foreign source income that is subject to the same limitation as the loss that resulted in the account and that is recaptured in accordance with §§ 1.904(f)-2(c) (relating to recapture under section 904(f)(1)); 1.904(f)-2(d) (relating to recapture when the taxpayer disposes of certain properties under section 904(f)(3)); and 1.904(f)-4 (relating to recapture when the taxpayer receives an accumulation distribution from a foreign trust under section 904(f)(4)).

(f) *Illustrations.* The rules of this section are illustrated by the following examples.

Example (1). X Corporation is a domestic corporation with foreign branch operations in country C. X's taxable income and losses for its taxable year 1983 are as follows:

U.S. source taxable income	$1,000
Foreign source taxable income (loss) subject to general limitation	($500)
Foreign source taxable income subject to the passive interest limitation	$200

X has a general limitation overall foreign loss of $500 for 1983 in accordance with paragraph (c)(1) of this section. Since the general limitation overall foreign loss is not considered to of set income under the separate limitation for passive interest income, it therefore offsets $500 of United States source taxable income. This amount is added to X's general limitation overall foreign loss account at the end of 1983 in accordance with paragraphs (c)(1) and (d)(1) of this section.

Example (2). Y Corporation is a domestic corporation with foreign branch operations in Country C. Y's taxable income and losses for its taxable year 1982 are as follows:

U.S. source taxable income	$1,000
Foreign source taxable income (loss) subject to general limitation	($500)
Foreign source taxable income subject to the passive interest limitation	$250

For its pre-1983 taxable years, Y filed its returns determining its overall foreign losses on a combined basis. In accordance with paragraphs (a) and (c)(1) of this section, Y may net the foreign source income and loss before offsetting the United States source income. Y therefore has a section 904(d)(1)(A-C) overall foreign loss account of $250 at the end of 1982.

Example (3). X Corporation is a domestic corporation with foreign branch operations in Country C. For its taxable year 1985, X has taxable income (loss) determined as follows:

U.S. source taxable income	$200
Foreign source taxable income (loss) subject to general limitation	($1,000)
Foreign source taxable income (loss) subject to the passive limitation	$1,800

X has a general limitation overall foreign loss of $1,000 in accordance with paragraph (c)(1) of this section. The overall foreign loss offsets $200 of United States source taxable income in 1985 and therefore, X has a $200 general limitation overall foreign loss account at the end of 1985. The remaining $800 general limitation loss is offset by the passive interest limitation income in 1985 so that X has no net operating loss carryover that is attributable to the general limitation loss and no additional amount attributable to that loss will be added to the overall foreign loss account in 1985 or in any other year.

Example (4). In 1986, V Corporation has $1,000 of general limitation foreign source taxable income and $500 of general limitation foreign source net capital loss which has reduced $500 of United States source capital gain net income ("short term gain") (none of which is net capital gain). Under section 904(b), the numerator of V's foreign tax credit limitation fraction for income subject to the general limitation is reduced by $500 (see § 1.904(b)-1(a)(3)). Under paragraph (d)(5)(i) of this section, none of that $500 goes into its general limitation overall foreign loss account.

Example (5). Z Corporation is a domestic corporation with foreign branch operations. For the taxable year 1984, Z's taxable income and (losses) are as follows:

U.S. source taxable ordinary income	$1,000
U.S. source net capital gain	$ 460
Foreign source taxable ordinary income subject to the general limitation	$ 200
Foreign source net capital loss subject to the general limitation	($ 800)

Z had no capital gain net income in any prior taxable year. Under paragraph (d)(2) and (5) of this section, the amount to be added to Z's general limitation overall foreign loss account is the excess of the amount which has reduced United States source capital gain net income for the taxable year ($460), adjusted for the rate differential because it has reduced United States source net capital gain ($460 × 28/46 = $280), over the amount which has reduced the numerator of Z's foreign tax credit limitation fraction under section 904(b)(2), which is $200. (The $200 amount is foreign source net capital loss that has reduced United States source net capital gain in the denominator of the fraction, but not exceeding the amount of foreign source income in the numerator before the section 904(b)(2) adjustment.) Thus, Z must add $80 (the excess of the $280 over $200) to its general limitation overall foreign loss account in 1984. [Reg. § 1.904(f)-1.]

☐ [*T.D.* 8153, 8-21-87.]

[Reg. § 1.904(f)-2]

§ 1.904(f)-2. **Recapture of overall foreign losses.**—(a) *In general.* A taxpayer shall be required to recapture an overall foreign loss as provided in this section. Recapture is accomplished by treating as United States source income a portion of the taxpayer's foreign source taxable income of the same limitation as the foreign source loss that resulted in an overall foreign loss account. As a result, if the taxpayer elects the benefits of section 901 or section 936, the tax-

Reg. § 1.904(f)-2(a)

payer's foreign tax credit limitation with respect to such income is decreased. As provided in § 1.904(f)-1(e)(2), the balance in a taxpayer's overall foreign loss account is reduced by the amount of loss recaptured. Recapture continues until such time as the amount of foreign source taxable income recharacterized as United States source income equals the amount in the overall foreign loss account. As provided in § 1.904(f)-1(e)(2), the balance in an overall foreign loss account is reduced at the end of each taxable year by the amount of the loss recaptured during that taxable year. Regardless of whether recapture occurs in a year in which a taxpayer elects the benefits of section 901 or in a year in which a taxpayer deducts its foreign taxes under section 164, the overall foreign loss account is recaptured only to the extent of foreign source taxable income remaining after applying the appropriate section 904(b) adjustments, if any, as provided in paragraph (b) of this section.

(b) *Determination of taxable income from sources without the United States for purposes of recapture*—(1) *In general.* For purposes of determining the amount of an overall foreign loss subject to recapture, the taxpayer's taxable income from sources without the United States shall be computed with respect to each of the separate limitations described in § 1.904(f)-1(c)(2) in accordance with the rules set forth in § 1.904(f)-1(c)(1) and (3). This computation is made without taking into account foreign source taxable income (and deductions properly allocated and apportioned thereto) subject to other separate limitations. Before applying the recapture rules to foreign source taxable income, the following provisions shall be applied to such income in the following order:

(i) Former section 904(f)(3)(C) (prior to its removal by the Tax Reform Act of 1986) and the regulations thereunder shall be applied to treat certain foreign source gain as United States source gain; and

(ii) Section 904(b)(2) and the regulations thereunder shall be applied to make adjustments in the foreign tax credit limitation fraction for certain capital gains and losses.

(c) *Section 904(f)(1) recapture*—(1) *In general.* In a year in which a taxpayer elects the benefits of sections 901 or 936, the amount of any foreign source taxable income subject to recapture in a taxable year in which paragraph (a) of this section is applicable is the lesser of the balance in the applicable overall foreign loss account (after reduction of such account in accordance with § 1.904(f)-1(e)) or fifty percent of the taxpayer's foreign source taxable income of the same limitation as the loss that resulted in the overall foreign loss account (as determined under paragraph (b) of this section). If, in any year, in accordance with sections 164(a) and section 275(a)(4)(A), a taxpayer deducts rather than credits its foreign taxes, recapture is applied to the extent of the lesser of (i) the balance in the applicable overall foreign loss account or (ii) foreign source taxable income of the same limitation type that resulted in the overall foreign loss minus foreign taxes imposed on such income.

(2) *Election to recapture more of the overall foreign loss than is required under paragraph (c)(1).* In a year in which a taxpayer elects the benefits of sections 901 or 936, a taxpayer may make an annual revocable election to recapture a greater portion of the balance in an overall foreign loss account than is required to be recaptured under paragraph (c)(1) of this section. A taxpayer may make such an election or amend a prior election by attaching a statement to its annual Form 1116 or 1118. If an amendment is made to a prior year's election, an amended tax return should be filed. The statement attached to the Form 1116 or 1118 must indicate the percentage and dollar amount of the taxpayer's foreign source taxable income that is being recharacterized as United States source income and the percentage and dollar amount of the balance (both before and after recapture) in the overall foreign loss account that is being recaptured. Except for the special recapture rules for section 936 corporations and for recapture of pre-1983 overall foreign losses determined on a combined basis, the taxpayer that elects to credit its foreign taxes may not elect to recapture an amount in excess of the taxpayer's foreign source taxable income subject to the same limitation as the loss that resulted in the overall foreign loss account.

(3) *Special rule for recapture of losses incurred prior to section 936 election.* If a corporation elects the application of section 936 and at the time of the election has a balance in any overall foreign loss account, such losses will be recaptured from the possessions source income of the electing section 936 corporation that qualifies for the section 936 credit, including qualified possession source investment income as defined in section 936(d)(2), even though the overall foreign loss to be recaptured may not be attributable to a loss in an income category of a type that would meet the definition of qualified possession source investment income. For purposes of recapturing an overall foreign loss incurred by a consolidated group including a corporation that subsequently elects to use section 936, the electing section 936 corporation's possession source income that qualifies for the section 936 credit, including qualified

Reg. § 1.904(f)-2(b)

Income from Sources Without the United States

See p. 20,601 for regulations not amended to reflect law changes

possession source investment income, shall be used to recapture the section 936 corporation's share of previously incurred overall foreign loss accounts. Rules for determining the section 936 corporation's share of the consolidated group's overall foreign loss accounts are provided in § 1.1502-9(c).

(4) *Recapture of pre-1983 overall foreign losses determined on a combined basis.* If a taxpayer computed its overall foreign losses on a combined basis in accordance with § 1.904(f)-1(c)(1) for taxable years beginning before January 1, 1983, any losses recaptured in taxable years beginning after December 31, 1982, shall be recaptured from income subject to the general limitation, subject to the rules in § 1.904(f)-6(a) and (b). Ordering rules for recapture of these losses are provided in § 1.904(f)-6(c).

(5) *Illustrations.* The rules of this paragraph (c) are illustrated by the following examples, all of which assume a United States corporate tax rate of 50 percent unless otherwise stated.

Example (1). X Corporation is a domestic corporation that does business in the United States and abroad. On December 31, 1983, the balance in X's general limitation overall foreign loss account is $600, all of which is attributable to a loss incurred in 1983. For 1984, X has United States source taxable income of $500 and foreign source taxable income subject to the general limitation of $500. For 1984, X pays $200 in foreign taxes and elects section 901. Under paragraph (c)(1) of this section, X is required to recapture $250 (the lesser of $600 or 50 percent of $500) of its overall foreign loss. As a consequence, X's foreign tax credit limitation under the general limitation is $250/$1,000 × $500, or $125, instead of $500/$1,000 × $500, or $250. The balance in X's general limitation overall foreign loss account is reduced by $250 in accordance with § 1.904(f)-1(e)(2).

Example (2). The facts are the same as in example (1) except that X makes an election to recapture its overall foreign loss to the extent of 80 percent of its foreign source taxable income subject to the general limitation (or $400) in accordance with paragraph (c)(2) of this section. As a result of recapture, X's 1984 foreign tax credit limitation for income subject to the general limitation is $100/$1,000 × $500, or $50, instead of $500/$1,000 × $500, or $250. X's general limitation overall foreign loss account is reduced by $400 in accordance with § 1.904(f)-1(e)(2).

Example (3). The facts are the same as in example (1) except that X does not elect the benefits of section 901 in 1984 and instead deducts its foreign taxes paid. In 1984, X recaptures $300 of its overall foreign loss, the difference between X's foreign source taxable income of $500 and $200 of foreign taxes paid. The balance in X's general limitation overall foreign loss account is reduced by $300 in accordance with § 1.904(f)-1(e)(2).

Example (4). The facts are the same as in example (1) except that in 1984, X also has $1,000 of foreign source DISC dividend income subject to the separate limitation for DISC dividends which carries a foreign tax of $50. Under paragraph (c)(1) of this section the amount of X's general limitation overall foreign loss subject to recapture is $250 (the lesser of the balance in the overall foreign loss account or 50 percent of the foreign source taxable income subject to the general limitation). There is no recapture with respect to the DISC dividend income. X's separate limitation for DISC dividend income is $1,000/$2,000 × $1,000, or $500. Its general limitation is $250/$2,000 × $1,000, or $125, instead of $500/$2,000 × $1,000, or $250. The balance in X's general limitation overall foreign loss account is reduced by $250 in accordance with § 1.904(f)-1(e)(2).

Example (5). On December 31, 1980, V, a domestic corporation that does business in the United States and abroad, has a balance in its section 904(d)(1)(A-C) overall foreign loss account of $600. V also has a balance in its FORI limitation overall foreign loss account of $900. For 1981, V has foreign source taxable income subject to the general limitation of $500 and $500 of United States source income. V also has foreign source taxable income subject to the FORI limitation of $800. V is required to recapture $250 of its section 904(d)(1)(A-C) overall foreign loss account (the lesser of $600 or 50% of $500) and its general limitation foreign tax credit limitation is $250/$1,800 × $900, or $125 instead of $500/$1,800 × $900, or $250. V is also required to recapture $400 of its FORI limitation overall foreign loss account (the lesser of $900 or 50% of $800). V's foreign tax credit limitation for FORI is $400/$1,800 × $900, or $200, instead of $800/$1,800 × $900, or $400. The balance in V's FORI limitation overall foreign loss account is reduced to $500 and the balance in V's section 904(d)(1)(A-C) account is reduced to $350, in accordance with § 1.904(f)-1(e)(2).

Example (6). This example assumes a United States corporate tax rate of 46 percent (under section 11(b)) and an alternative rate of tax under section 1201(a) of 28 percent. W is a domestic corporation that does business in the United States and abroad. On December 31, 1984, W has $350 in its general limitation overall foreign loss

Reg. § 1.904(f)-2(c)(5)

account. For 1985, W has $500 of United States source taxable income, and has foreign source income subject to the general limitation as follows:

Foreign source taxable income other than net capital gain	$720
Foreign source net capital gain	$460

Under paragraph (b)(2) of this section, foreign source taxable income for purposes of recapture includes foreign source capital gain net income, reduced, under section 904(b)(2), by the rate differential portion of foreign source net capital gain, which adjusts for the reduced tax rate for net capital gain under section 1201(a):

Foreign source capital gain net income ..	$460
Rate differential portion of foreign source net capital gain (18/46 of $460)	− 180
Foreign source capital gain included in foreign source taxable income	$280

The total foreign source taxable income of W for purposes of recapture in 1985 is $1,000 ($720 + $280). Under paragraph (c)(1) of this section, W is required to recapture $350 (the lesser of $350 or 50 percent of $1,000), and W's general limitation overall foreign loss account is reduced to zero. W's foreign tax credit limitation for income subject to the general limitation is $650/$1,500 × $690 ((.46) (500 + 720) + (.28) (460)), or $299, instead of $1,000/$1,500 × $690, or $460.

(d) *Recapture of overall foreign losses from dispositions under section 904(f)(3)*—(1) *In general.* If a taxpayer disposes of property used or held for use predominantly without the United States in a trade or business during a taxable year and that property generates foreign source taxable income subject to a separate limitation to which paragraph (a) of this section is applicable, (i) gain will be recognized on the disposition of such property, (ii) such gain will be treated as foreign source income subject to the same limitation as the income the property generated, and (iii) the applicable overall foreign loss account shall be recaptured as provided in paragraphs (d)(2), (d)(3), and (d)(4) of this section. See paragraph (d)(5) of this section for definitions.

(2) *Treatment of net capital gain.* If the gain from a disposition of property to which this paragraph (d) applies is treated as net capital gain, all references to such gain in paragraphs (d)(3) and (d)(4) of this section shall mean such gain as adjusted under paragraph (b) of this section. The amount by which the overall foreign loss account shall be reduced shall be determined from such adjusted gain.

(3) *Dispositions where gain is recognized irrespective of section 904(f)(3).* If a taxpayer recognizes foreign source gain subject to a separate limitation on the disposition of property described in paragraph (d)(1) of this section, and there is a balance in a taxpayer's overall foreign loss account that is attributable to a loss under such limitation after applying paragraph (c) of this section, an additional portion of such balance shall be recaptured in accordance with paragraphs (a) and (b) of this section. The amount recaptured shall be the lesser of such balance or 100 percent of the foreign source gain recognized on the disposition that was not previously recharacterized.

(4) *Dispositions in which gain would not otherwise be recognized*—(i) *Recognition of gain to the extent of the overall foreign loss account.* If a taxpayer makes a disposition of property described in paragraph (d)(1) of this section in which any amount of gain otherwise would not be recognized in the year of the disposition, and such property was used or held for use to generate foreign source taxable income subject to a separate limitation under which the taxpayer had a balance in its overall foreign loss account (including a balance that arose in the year of the disposition), the taxpayer shall recognize foreign source taxable income in an amount equal to the lesser of:

(A) The sum of the balance in the applicable overall foreign loss account (but only after such balance has been increased by amounts added to the account for the year of the disposition or has been reduced by amounts recaptured for the year of the disposition under paragraph (c) and paragraph (d)(3) of this section) plus the amount of any overall foreign loss that would be part of a net operating loss for the year of the disposition if gain from the disposition were not recognized under section 904(f)(3), plus the amount of any overall foreign loss that is part of a net operating loss carryover from a prior year, or

(B) The excess of the fair market value of such property over the taxpayer's adjusted basis in such property.

The excess of the fair market value of such property over its adjusted basis shall be determined on an asset by asset basis. Losses from the disposition of an asset shall not be recognized. Any foreign source taxable income deemed received and recognized under this paragraph (d)(4)(i) will have the same character as if the property had been sold or exchanged in a taxable transaction and will constitute gain for all purposes.

(ii) *Basis adjustment.* The basis of the property received in an exchange to which this

Reg. § 1.904(f)-2(d)(1)

paragraph (d)(4) applies shall be increased by the amount of gain deemed recognized, in accordance with applicable sections of subchapters C (relating to corporate distributions and adjustments), K (relating to partners and partnerships), O (relating to gain or loss on the disposition of property), and P (relating to capital gains and losses). If the property to which this paragraph (d)(4) applies was transferred by gift, the basis of such property in the hands of the donor immediately preceding such gift shall be increased by the amount of the gain deemed recognized.

(iii) *Recapture of overall foreign loss to the extent of amount recognized.* The provisions of paragraphs (a) and (b) of this section shall be applied to the extent of 100 percent of the foreign source taxable income which is recognized under paragraph (d)(4)(i) of this section. However, amounts of foreign source gain that would not be recognized except by application of section 904(f)(3) and paragraph (d)(4)(i) of this section, and which are treated as United States source gain by application of section 904(b)(3)(C) (prior to its removal by the Tax Reform Act of 1986) and paragraph (b)(1) of this section, shall reduce the overall foreign loss account (subject to the adjustments described in paragraph (d)(2) of this section) if such gain is net capital gain, notwithstanding the fact that such amounts would otherwise not be recaptured under the ordering rules in paragraph (b) of this section.

(iv) *Priorities among dispositions in which gain is deemed to be recognized.* If, in a single taxable year, a taxpayer makes more than one disposition to which this paragraph (d)(4) is applicable, the rules of this paragraph (d)(4) shall be applied to each disposition in succession starting with the disposition which occurred earliest, until the balance in the applicable overall foreign loss account is reduced to zero. If the taxpayer simultaneously makes more than one disposition to which this paragraph (d)(4) is applicable, the rules of paragraph (d)(4) shall be applied so that the balance in the applicable overall foreign loss account to be recaptured will be allocated pro rata among the assets in proportion to the excess of the fair market value of each asset over the adjusted basis of each asset.

(5) *Definitions*—(i) *Disposition.* A disposition to which this paragraph (d) applies includes a sale; exchange; distribution; gift; transfer upon the foreclosure of a security interest (but not a mere transfer of title to a creditor upon creation of a security interest or to a debtor upon termination of a security interest); involuntary conversion; contribution to a partnership, trust, or corporation; transfer at death; or any other transfer of property whether or not gain or loss is recognized under other provisions of the Code. However, a disposition to which this paragraph (d) applies does not include:

(A) A distribution or transfer of property to a domestic corporation described in section 381(a) (provided that paragraph (d)(6) of this section applies);

(B) A disposition of property which is not a material factor in the realization of income by the taxpayer (as defined in paragraph (d)(5)(iv) of this section);

(C) A transaction in which gross income is not realized; or

(D) The entering into of a unitization or pooling agreement (as defined in § 1.614-8(b)(6) of the regulations) containing a valid election under section 761(a)(2), and in which the source of the entire gain from any disposition of the interest created by the agreement would be determined to be foreign source under section 862(a)(5) if the disposition occurred presently.

(ii) *Property used in a trade or business.* Property is used in a trade or business if it is held for the principal purpose of promoting the present or future conduct of the trade or business. This generally includes property acquired and held in the ordinary course of a trade or business or otherwise held in a direct relationship to a trade or business. In determining whether an asset is held in a direct relationship to a trade or business, principal consideration shall be given to whether the asset is used in the trade or business. Property will be treated as held in a direct relationship to a trade or business if the property was acquired with funds generated by that trade or business or if income generated from the asset is available for use in that trade or business. Property used in a trade or business may be tangible or intangible, real or personal property. It includes property, such as equipment, which is subject to an allowance for depreciation under section 167 or cost recovery under section 168. Property may be considered used in a trade or business even if it is a capital asset in the hands of the taxpayer. However, stock of another corporation shall not be considered property used in a trade or business if a substantial investment motive exists for acquiring and holding the stock. On the other hand, stock acquired or held to assure a source of supply for a trade or business shall be considered property used in that trade or business. Inventory is generally not considered property used in a trade or business. However, when disposed of in a manner not in the ordinary course of a trade or business, inventory will be considered property used in the trade or business. A partnership interest

Reg. § 1.904(f)-2(d)(5)

will be treated as property used in a trade or business if the underlying assets of the partnership would be property used in a trade or business. For purposes of section 904(f)(3) and §§ 1.904(f)-2(d)(1) and (5), a disposition of a partnership interest to which this section applies will be treated as a disposition of a proportionate share of each of the assets of the partnership. For purposes of allocating the purchase price of the interest and the seller's basis in the interest to those assets, the principles of § 1.751-1(a) will apply.

(iii) *Property used predominantly outside the United States.* Property will be considered used predominantly outside the United States if for a 3-year period ending on the date of the disposition (or, if shorter, the period during which the property has been used in the trade or business) such property was located outside the United States more than 50 percent of the time. An aircraft, railroad rolling stock, vessel, motor vehicle, container, or other property used for transportation purposes is deemed to be used predominantly outside the United States if, during the 3-year (or shorter) period, either such propery is located outside the United States more than 50 percent of the time or more than 50 percent of the miles traversed in the use of such property are traversed outside the United States.

(iv) *Property which is a material factor in the realization of income.* For purposes of this section, property used in a trade or business will be considered a material factor in the realization of income unless the taxpayer establishes that it is not (or, if the taxpayer did not realize income from the trade or business in the taxable year, would not be expected to be) necessary to the realization of income by the taxpayer.

(6) *Carryover of overall foreign loss accounts in a corporate acquisition to which section 381(a) applies.* In the case of a distribution or transfer described in section 381(a), an overall foreign loss account of the distributing or transferor corporation shall be treated as an overall foreign loss account of the acquiring or transferee corporation as of the close of the date of the distribution or transfer. If the transferee corporation had an overall foreign loss account under the same separate limitation prior to the distribution or transfer, the balance in the transferor's account must be added to the transferee's account. If not, the transferee must adopt the transferor's overall foreign loss account. An overall foreign loss of the transferor will be treated as incurred by the transferee in the year prior to the year of the transfer.

(7) *Illustrations.* The rules of this paragraph (d) are illustrated by the following examples which assume that the United States corporate tax rate is 50 percent (unless otherwise stated). For purposes of these examples, none of the foreign source gains are treated as net capital gains (unless so stated).

Example (1). X Corporation has a balance in its general limitation overall foreign loss account of $600 at the close of its taxable year ending December 31, 1984. In 1985, X sells assets used predominantly outside the United States in a trade or business and recognizes $1,000 of gain on the sale under section 1001. This gain is subject to the general limitation. This sale is a disposition within the meaning of paragraph (d)(5)(i) of this section, and to which this paragraph (d) applies. X has no other foreign source taxable income in 1985 and has $1,000 of United States source taxable income. Under paragraph (c), X is required to recapture $500 (the lesser of the balance in X's general limitation overall foreign loss account ($600) or 50 percent of $1,000) of its overall foreign loss account. The balance in X's general limitation overall foreign loss account is reduced to $100 in accordance with § 1.904(f)-1(e)(2). In addition, under paragraph (d)(3) of this section, X is required to recapture $100 (the lesser of the remaining balance in its general limitation overall foreign loss account ($100) or 100 percent of its foreign source taxable income recognized on such disposition that has not been previously recharacterized ($500)). The total amount recaptured is $600. X's foreign tax credit limitation for income subject to the general limitation in 1985 is $200 ($400/$2,000 × $1,000) instead of $500 ($1,000/$2,000 × $1,000). The balance in X's general limitation overall foreign loss account is reduced to zero in accordance with § 1.904(f)-1(e)(2).

Example (2). On December 31, 1984, Y Corporation has a balance in its general limitation overall foreign loss account of $1,500. In 1985, Y has $500 of United States source taxable income and $200 of foreign source taxable income subject to the general limitation. Y's foreign source taxable income is from the sale of property used predominantly outside of the United States in a trade or business. This sale is a disposition to which this paragraph (d) is applicable. In 1985, Y also transferred property used predominantly outside of the United States in a trade or business to another corporation. Under section 351, no gain was recognized on this transfer. Such property had been used to generate foreign source taxable income subject to the general limitation. The excess of the fair market value of the property transferred over Y's adjusted basis in such property was $2,000. In accordance with paragraph (c) of this section, Y is required to recapture $100

Reg. § 1.904(f)-2(d)(6)

(the lesser of $1,500, the amount in Y's general limitation overall foreign loss account, or 50 percent of $200, the amount of general limitation foreign source taxable income for the current year) of its general limitation overall foreign loss. Y is then required to recapture an additional $100 of its general limitation overall foreign loss account under paragraph (d)(3) of this section out of the remaining gain recognized on the sale of assets, because 100 percent of such gain is subject to recapture. The balance in Y's general limitation overall foreign loss account is reduced to $1,300 in accordance with § 1.904(f)-1(e)(2). Y corporation is then required to recognize $1,300 of foreign source taxable income on its section 351 transfer under paragraph (d)(4) of this section. The remaining $700 of potential gain associated with the section 351 transfer is not recognized. Under paragraph (d)(4), 100 percent of the $1,300 is recharacterized as United States source taxable income, and Y's general limitation overall foreign loss account is reduced to zero. Y's entire taxable income for 1985 is:

U.S. source taxable income	$ 500
Foreign source taxable income subject to the general limitation that is recharacterized as U.S. source income by paragraphs (c) and (d)(3) of this section	$ 200
Gain recognized under section 904(f)(3) and paragraph (d)(4) of this section, and recharacterized as U.S. source income	$1,300
Total	$2,000

Y's foreign tax credit limitation for 1985 for income subject to the general limitation is $0 ($0/$2,000 × $1,000) instead of $100 ($200/$700 × $350).

Example (3). W Corporation is a calendar year domestic corporation with foreign branch operations in country C. As of December 31, 1984, W has no overall foreign loss accounts and has no net operating loss carryovers. W's entire taxable income in 1985 is:

U.S. source taxable income	$ 800
Foreign source taxable income (loss) subject to the general limitation	($1,000)

W cannot carry back its 1985 NOL to any earlier year. As of December 31, 1985, W therefore has $800 in its general limitation overall foreign loss account. In 1986, W earns $400 United States source taxable income and has an additional $1,000 loss from the operations of the foreign branch. Income in the loss category would be subject to the general limitation. Also in 1986, W disposes of property used predominantly outside the United States in a trade or business. Such property generated income subject to the general limitation. The excess of the property's fair market value over its adjusted basis is $3,000. The disposition is of a type described in § 1.904(f)-2(d)(4)(i). W has no other income in 1986. Under § 1.904(f)-2(d)(4)(i), W is required to recognize foreign source taxable income on the disposition in an amount equal to the lesser of $2,000 ($800 (the balance in the general limitation overall foreign loss account as of 1985) + $400 (the increase in the general limitation overall foreign loss account attributable to the disposition year) + $600 (the general limitation overall foreign loss that is part of the NOL from 1986) + $200 (the general limitation overall foreign loss that is part of the NOL from 1985)) or $3,000. The $2,000 foreign source income required to be recognized under section 904(f)(3) is reduced to $1,200 by the remaining $600 loss in 1986 and the $200 net operating loss carried forward from 1985. This $1,200 of income is subject to the general limitation. In computing the foreign tax credit limitation for general limitation income, the $1,200 of foreign source income is treated as United States source income and, therefore, W's foreign tax credit limitation for income subject to the general limitation is zero. W's overall foreign loss account is reduced to zero.

Example (4). Z Corporation has a balance in its FORI overall foreign loss account of $1,500 at the end of its taxable year 1980. In 1981, Z has $1,600 of foreign oil related income subject to the separate limitation for FORI income and no United States source income. In addition, in 1981, Z makes two dispositions of property used predominantly outside the United States in a trade or business on which no gain was recognized. Such property generated foreign oil related income. The excess of the fair market value of the property transferred in the first disposition over Z's adjusted basis in such property is $575. The excess of the fair market value of the property transferred in the second disposition over Z's adjusted basis in such property is $1,000. Under paragraph (c) of this section, Z is required to recapture $800 (the lesser of 50 percent of its foreign oil related income of $1,600 or the balance ($1,500) in its FORI overall foreign loss account) of its foreign oil related loss. In accordance with paragraphs (d)(4)(i) and (iv) of this section, Z is required to recognize foreign oil related income in the amount of $575 on the first disposition and, since the foreign oil related loss account is now reduced by $1,375 (the $800 and $575 amounts previously recaptured), Z is required to recognize foreign oil related income in the amount of $125 on the second disposition. In accordance with paragraph (d)(4)(iii) of this section, the entire

Reg. § 1.904(f)-2(d)(7)

amount recognized is treated as United States source income and the balance in the FORI overall foreign loss account is reduced to zero under § 1.904(f)-1(e)(2). Z's foreign tax credit limitation for FORI is $400 ($800/$2,300 × $1,150) instead of $800 ($1,600/$1,600 × $800).

Example (5). The facts are the same as in example (4), except that the gain from the two dispositions of property is treated as net capital gain and the United States corporate tax rate is assumed to be 46 percent. As in example (4), Z is required to recapture $800 of its foreign oil related loss from its 1981 ordinary foreign oil related income. In accordance with paragraph (d)(4)(i) and (iv) of this section, Z is first required to recognize foreign oil related income (which is net capital gain) on the first disposition in the amount of $575. Under paragraphs (b) and (d)(2) of this section, this net capital gain is adjusted by subtracting the rate differential portion of such gain from the total amount of such gain to determine the amount by which the foreign oil related loss account is reduced, which is $350 ($575 − ($575 × 18/46)). The balance remaining in Z's foreign oil related loss account after this step is $350. Therefore, this process will be repeated, in accordance with paragraph (d)(4)(iv) of this section, to recapture that remaining balance out of the gain deemed recognized on the second disposition, resulting in reduction of the foreign oil related loss account to zero and net capital gain required to be recognized from the second disposition in the amount of $575, which must also be adjusted by subtracting the rate differential portion to determine the amount by which the foreign oil related loss account is reduced (which is $350). The $575 of net capital gain from each disposition is recharacterized as United States source net capital gain. Z's section 907(b) foreign tax credit limitation is the same as in example (4), and Z has $1,150 ($575 + $575) of United States source net capital gain. [Reg. § 1.904(f)-2.]

☐ [T.D. 8153, 8-21-87.]

[Reg. § 1.904(f)-3]

§ 1.904(f)-3. Allocation of net operating losses and net capital losses.—(a) *Allocation of net operating loss carrybacks and carryovers that include overall foreign losses.* If a taxpayer sustains an overall foreign loss that is part of a net operating loss for the year, then, in carrying such net operating loss back to an earlier year or forward to a later year in accordance with section 172 (or § 1.1502-21(b) (or §§ 1.1502-21A(b) and 1.1502-79A(a), as appropriate)), the portion, if any, of the net operating loss attributable to a United States source loss shall be allocated first to United States source income and the portion of the net operating loss attributable to an overall foreign loss shall be allocated first to foreign source taxable income subject to the same separate limitation in the carryback or carryover year. To the extent that the overall foreign loss component of the net operating loss exceeds foreign source taxable income subject to the same separate limitation in the year to which it is carried, it shall be allocated next to the taxpayer's United States source income for such year and then to foreign source taxable income subject to another separate limitation. See paragraph § 1.904(f)-1(d) of this section for additions to the applicable overall foreign loss account to the extent that United States source taxable income is reduced in the taxable year to which the loss is carried.

(b) *Allocation of net capital loss carrybacks and carryovers that include overall foreign losses.* If a taxpayer sustains an overall foreign loss that is part of net capital loss for the year, then in carrying the net capital loss back to an earlier year or forward to a later year in accordance with section 1212 (or § 1.1502-22(b) (or §§ 1.1502-22A and 1.1502-79A(b), as appropriate)), the portion of the net capital loss that is attributable to a foreign source capital loss shall be allocated first to foreign source capital gain net income subject to the same separate limitation in the carryback or carryover year. To the extent that such foreign source capital loss exceeds foreign source capital gain net income subject to the same separate limitation in the year to which it is carried, it shall be allocated first to United States source capital gain net income in such year and then to foreign source capital gain net income subject to another separate limitation. An overall foreign source net capital loss carried over to a later year in accordance with this paragraph (b) shall be taken into consideration in determining the taxpayer's overall foreign loss in the year to which it is carried and shall be added to the applicable overall foreign loss account for such year in accordance with paragraph (c) of this section. An overall foreign source net capital loss carried back to an earlier year in accordance with this paragraph (b) shall be added to the applicable overall foreign loss account in the year in which the loss occurred.

(c) *Transitional rule.* When a taxpayer incurs a net operating loss in a post-1982 taxable year that is carried back to a pre-1983 taxable year and creates an overall foreign loss in the pre-1983 year, for purposes of this section, § 1.904(f)-1(c)(1), and § 1.904(f)-2(b), that loss will be treated as if it arose in the post-1982 year; thus the loss will first offset United States source income before it offsets foreign source income subject to another limitation. When a taxpayer incurs a net operating loss in a pre-1983 taxable year that is carried forward to a post-1982 taxable year and creates an overall foreign loss in the carryover year, for purposes of this section, § 1.904(f)-1(c)(1), and § 1.904(f)-2(b), that loss is treated as if it arose in the post-1982 taxable year; thus the loss will first offset United States source income before it offsets foreign source income subject to another limitation.

(d) *Illustrations.* The following examples illustrate the application of this section.

Example (1). X Corporation is a domestic corporation with foreign branch operations in Country C. For its taxable year 1985, X has a net operating loss of ($1250), determined as follows:

U.S. source taxable income (loss) . ($ 250)
Foreign source taxable income
   (loss) subject to the general
   limitation .... ($1,000)

The only prior year to which the net operating loss can be carried under section 172 is 1983. For its taxable year 1983, X had the following taxable income:

U.S. source taxable income $1,900
Foreign source taxable income
   subject to the general limitation
   .... $ 400

X has a general limitation overall foreign loss for 1985 of $1,000. X's overall foreign loss is part of a net operating loss of $1,250 for 1985. In accordance with § 1.904(f)-3(a), the foreign loss carried back to 1983 is first allocated to X's foreign source taxable income subject to the limitation under which the loss arose, the general limitation. This amount is not added to X's overall foreign loss account under paragraph (c)(1)(i). The remaining $600 of 1985 foreign source loss is allocated to and thus reduces 1983 United States source income, and this amount is added to X's general limitation overall foreign loss account in 1985.

Example (2). The facts are the same as in example (1), except that in 1983, X's United States source taxable income was zero. No amount is added to X's overall foreign loss account at the end of 1985. X's income and deductions for 1986 are as follows:

U.S. source taxable income $1,250
Foreign source taxable income
   subject to the general limitation
   .... $ 300

X has a net operating loss carryover to 1986 of $850 ($1,250 − $400). The $850 net operating loss carryover is comprised of $600 of foreign losses ($1,000 of 1985 loss, minus $400 offset by foreign source income in the carryback year) and $250 of United States source loss. The $600 foreign source component of the net operating loss is first allocated to X's foreign source taxable income subject to the general limitation in 1986, in accordance with § 1.904(f)-3(a), prior to reducing United States source income. The $250 United States source component of the net operating loss component is also allocated first to United States income in the carryover year before reducing any foreign source income. Thus, $300 of the remaining $600 of foreign source net operating loss carryover is first applied to eliminate foreign source income in the carryover year, leaving $300 of foreign source net operating loss. The $250 United States source component of the net operating loss reduces United States source taxable income to $1,000 in 1986. This $1,000 of United States source income is then further reduced by the remaining $300 of foreign source net operating loss. Therefore, in 1986, X has $700 of United States source income and $300 is added to X's general limitation overall foreign loss account in accordance with § 1.904(f)-1(d)(4) of this section.

Example (3). Z is a domestic corporation that does business in the United States and abroad. For taxable years prior to 1983, Z computed its overall foreign losses on a separate limitation basis. In 1980, Z had $100 of United States source income and ($100) of foreign source loss subject to the general limitation. On December 31, 1980, the balance in Z's general limitation overall foreign loss account was $100. In 1981, Z had $50 of United States source income and $100 of general limitation foreign source income. In 1982, Z also had $50 United States source income and $100 foreign source general limitation income. Therefore, in both 1981 and 1982, Z recaptured $50 and at the end of 1982, Z's general limitation overall foreign loss account was reduced to zero. In 1983, Z had no income. In 1984, Z had a ($150) United States source loss and a ($150) general limitation foreign source loss. The 1984 net operating loss is carried back first to 1981 and then to 1982. Because of the overall foreign loss recapture that occurred in those years, Z is considered to have $100 of United States source income and $50 of foreign source income in each year. Thus, in 1981, ($50) of the ($150) foreign source component of the carryback eliminated the $50 foreign source income in that year and ($100) of the ($150) domestic source component of the carryback eliminated the United States source income in that year. In 1982, ($50) of the remaining domestic source component of the net operating loss reduced the United States source income to $50. The remaining ($100) of the foreign source component of the loss first reduced the foreign source income to zero and then reduced the remaining United States source income to zero, thus creating a $50 overall foreign loss. Therefore, at the end of 1984, Z has $50 in its general limitation overall foreign loss account.

Reg. § 1.904(f)-3(d)

Example (4). In 1985, V Corporation has a general limitation loss of <$1,000> and no other income or loss in that year. The 1985 loss is carried back to 1982. For taxable years prior to 1983, V computed its overall foreign losses on a combined basis for income subject to the passive interest limitation, the DISC dividend limitation, and the general limitation. In 1982, V had $400 of passive interest limitation income and $200 of general limitation income and $1,000 of United States source taxable income. Under paragraph (d) of this section, the $1,000 NOL attributable to the 1985 loss is first offset by the general limitation income in 1982 and then the United States source passive interest limitation income in that year. V therefore adds $800 to its general limitation overall foreign loss account in 1985.

Example (5). In 1982, W Corporation has a general limitation loss of <$500> and $200 of passive interest limitation income. For taxable years prior to 1983, W computed its overall foreign losses on a combined basis. W has no other taxable income or loss. W cannot carry back the $300 NOL and so it carries it forward to 1983, a year in which it has $600 passive interest limitation income and $500 of United States source income and no general limitation income. Under paragraph (d) of this section, the NOL is not offset by the foreign source income in 1984 but first is applied against United States source income. Thus, $300 is added to W's general limitation overall foreign loss account in 1984. [Reg. § 1.904(f)-3.]

☐ [T.D. 8153, 8-21-87. Amended by T.D. 8677, 6-26-96 and T.D. 8823, 6-25-99.]

[Reg. § 1.904(f)-4]

§ 1.904(f)-4. Recapture of foreign losses out of accumulation distributions from a foreign trust.—(a) *In general.* If a taxpayer receives a distribution of foreign source taxable income subject to a separate limitation in which the taxpayer had a balance in an overall foreign loss account and that income is treated under section 666 as having been distributed by a foreign trust in a preceding taxable year, a portion of the balance in the taxpayer's applicable overall foreign loss account shall be subject to recapture under this section. The amount subject to recapture shall be the lesser of the balance in the taxpayer's overall foreign loss account (after applying §§ 1.904(f)-1, 1.904(f)-2, 1.904(f)-3, and 1.904(f)-6 to the taxpayer's other income or loss in the current taxable year) or the entire amount of foreign source taxable income deemed distributed in a preceding year or years under section 666.

(b) *Effect of recapture on foreign tax credit limitation under section 667(d).* If paragraph (a) of this section is applicable, then in applying the separate limitation (in accordance with section 667(d)(1)(A) and (C)) to determine the amount of foreign taxes deemed distributed under section 666(b) and (c) that can be credited against the increase in tax in a computation year, a portion of the foreign source taxable income deemed distributed in such computation year shall be treated as United States source income. Such portion shall be determined by multiplying the amount of foreign source taxable income deemed distributed in the computation year by a fraction. The numerator of this fraction is the balance in the taxpayer's overall foreign loss account (after application of §§ 1.904(f)-1, 1.904(f)-2, 1.904(f)-3, and 1.904(f)-6), and the denominator of the fraction is the entire amount of foreign source taxable income deemed distributed under section 666. However, the numerator of this fraction shall not exceed the denominator of the fraction.

(c) *Recapture if taxpayer deducts foreign taxes deemed distributed.* If paragraph (a) of this section is applicable and if, in accordance with section 667(d)(1)(B), the beneficiary deducted rather than credited its taxes in the computation year, the beneficiary shall reduce its overall foreign loss account (but not below zero) by an amount equal to the lesser of the balance in the applicable overall foreign loss account or the amount of the actual distribution deemed distributed in the computation year (without regard to the foreign taxes deemed distributed).

(d) *Illustrations.* The provisions of this section are illustrated by the following examples:

Example (1). X Corporation is a domestic corporation that has a balance of $10,000 in its general limitation overall foreign loss account on December 31, 1980. For its taxable year beginning January 1, 1981, X's only income is an accumulation distribution from a foreign trust of $20,000 of general limitation foreign source taxable income. Under section 666, the amount distributed and the foreign taxes paid on such amount ($4,000) are deemed distributed in two prior taxable years. In determining the partial tax on such distribution under section 667(b), the amount added to each computation year is $12,000 (the sum of the actual distribution plus the taxes deemed distributed ($24,000) divided by the number of accumulation years (2)). Of that amount, $5,000 ($10,000/$24,000 × $12,000) is treated as United States source taxable income in accordance with paragraph (b) of this section. Assuming the United States tax rate is 50 percent, X's separate foreign tax credit limitation against the increase in tax in each computation year is $3,500 ($7,000/$12,000 × $6,000) instead of $6,000 ($12,000/$12,000 × $6,000). X's overall foreign loss account is reduced to zero in accordance with paragraph (a) of this section.

Example (2). Assume the same facts as in Example (1), except that X deducted rather than credited its foreign taxes in the computation years. In 1979, the amount added to X's income is $12,000 under section 667(b), $2,000 of which is deductible under section 667(d)(1)(B). X must reduce its overall foreign loss account by $10,000, the amount of the actual distribution that is deemed distributed in 1979 (without regard to the $2,000 foreign taxes also deemed distributed). The entire overall foreign loss account is therefore reduced to $0 in 1979. [Reg. § 1.904(f)-4.]

☐ [T.D. 8153, 8-21-87.]

[Reg. § 1.904(f)-5]

§ 1.904(f)-5. **Special rules for recapture of overall foreign losses of a domestic trust.**—(a) *In general.* Except as provided in this section, the rules contained in §§ 1.904(f)-1, 1.904(f)-2, 1.904(f)-3, 1.904(f)-4, and 1.904(f)-6 apply to domestic trusts.

(b) *Recapture of trust's overall foreign loss.* In taxable years in which a trust has foreign source taxable income subject to a separate limitation in which the trust has a balance in its overall foreign loss account, the balance in the trust's overall foreign loss account shall be recaptured as follows:

(1) *Trust accumulates income.* If the trust accumulates all of its foreign source taxable income subject to the same limitation as the loss that created the balance in the overall foreign loss account, its overall foreign loss shall be recaptured out of such income in accordance with §§ 1.904(f)-1, 1.904(f)-2, 1.904(f)-3, 1.904(f)-4, and 1.904(f)-6.

(2) *Trust distributes income.* If the trust distributes all of its foreign source taxable income subject to the same limitation as the loss that created the overall foreign loss account, the amount of the overall foreign loss that would be subject to recapture by the trust under paragraph (b)(1) of this section shall be allocated to the beneficiaries in proportion to the amount of such income which is distributed to each beneficiary in that year.

(3) *Trust accumulates and distributes income.* If the trust accumulates part of its foreign source taxable income subject to the same limitation as the loss that created the overall foreign loss account and distributes part of such income, the portion of the overall foreign loss that would be subject to recapture by the trust under paragraph (b)(1) of this section if the distributed income were accumulated shall be allocated to the beneficiaries receiving income distributions. The amount of overall foreign loss to be allocated to such beneficiaries shall be the same portion of the total amount of such overall foreign loss that would be recaptured as the amount of such income which is distributed to each beneficiary bears to the total amount of such income of the trust for such year. That portion of the overall foreign loss subject to recapture in such year that is not allocated to the beneficiaries in accordance with this paragraph (b)(3) shall be recaptured by the trust in accordance with paragraph (b)(1).

(c) *Amounts allocated to beneficiaries.* Amounts of a trust's overall foreign loss allocated to any beneficiary in accordance with paragraph (b)(2) or (3) of this section shall be added to the beneficiary's applicable overall foreign loss account and treated as an overall foreign loss of the beneficiary incurred in the taxable year preceding the year of such allocation. Such amounts shall be recaptured in accordance with §§ 1.904(f)-1, 1.904(f)-2, 1.904(f)-3, 1.904(f)-4, and 1.904(f)-6 out of foreign source taxable income distributed by the trust which is subject to the same separate limitation.

(d) *Section 904(f)(3) dispositions to which § 1.904(f)-2(d)(4)(i) is applicable.* Foreign source taxable income recognized by a trust under § 1.904(f)-2(d)(4) on a disposition of property used in a trade or business outside the United States shall be deemed to be accumulated by the trust. All such income shall be used to recapture the trust's overall foreign loss in accordance with § 1.904(f)-2(d)(4).

(e) *Illustrations.* The provisions of this section are illustrated by the following examples:

Example (1). T, a domestic trust, has a balance of $2,000 in a general limitation overall foreign loss account on December 31, 1983. For its taxable year ending on December 31, 1984, T has foreign source taxable income subject to the general limitation of $1,600, all of which it accumulates. Under paragraph (b)(1) of this section, T is required to recapture $800 in 1984 (the lesser of the overall foreign loss or 50 percent of the foreign source taxable income). This amount is treated as United States source income for purposes of taxing T in 1984 and upon subsequent distribution to T's beneficiaries. At the end of its 1984 taxable year, T has a balance of $1,200 in its overall foreign loss account.

Example (2). The facts are the same as in example (1). In 1985, T has general limitation foreign source taxable income of $1,000, which it distributes to its beneficiaries as follows: $500 to A, $250 to B, and $250 to C. Under paragraph (b)(1) of this section, T would have been required to recapture $500 of its overall foreign loss if it had accumulated all of such income. Therefore, under paragraph (b)(2) of this section, T must allocate $500 of its overall foreign loss to A, B, and C as follows: $250 to A ($500 × $500/$1,000), $125 to B ($500 × $250/$1,000), and $125 to C ($500 × $250/$1,000). Under paragraph (c) of this section and § 1.904(f)-1(d)(4), A, B, and C must add the amounts of general limitation overall foreign loss allocated to them from T to their overall foreign loss accounts and treat such amounts as overall foreign losses incurred in 1984. A, B, and C must then apply the rules of §§ 1.904(f)-1, 1.904(f)-2, 1.904(f)-3, 1.904(f)-4, and 1.904(f)-6 to recapture their overall foreign losses. T's overall foreign loss account is reduced in accordance with § 1.904(f)-1(e)(1) by the $500 that is allocated to A, B, and C. At the end of 1985, T's general limitation overall foreign loss account has a balance of $700.

Example (3). The facts are the same as in example (2), including an overall foreign loss account at the end of 1984 of $1,200, except that in 1985 T's general limitation foreign source taxable income is $1,500 instead of $1,000, and T accumulates the additional $500. Under paragraph (b)(1) of this section, T would be required to recapture $750 of its overall foreign loss if it accumulated all of the $1,500. Under paragraph (b)(3) of this section, T must allocate $500 of its overall foreign loss to A, B, and C as follows: $250 to A ($750 × $500/$1,500) and $125 each to B and C ($750 × $250/$1,500). T must also recapture $250 of its overall foreign loss, which is the amount subject to recapture in 1985 that is not allocated to the beneficiaries ($750 − $500 = $250). Under § 1.904(f)-1(e)(1), T reduces its general limitation overall foreign loss account by $500. Under § 1.904(f)-1(e)(2), T reduces its general limitation overall foreign loss account by $250. At the end of 1985 there is a balance in the general limitation overall foreign loss account of $450 (($1,200 − $500) − $250). [Reg. § 1.904(f)-5.]

☐ [T.D. 8153, 8-21-87.]

[Reg. § 1.904(f)-6]

§ 1.904(f)-6. Transitional rule for recapture of FORI and general limitation overall foreign losses incurred in taxable years beginning before January 1, 1983, from foreign source taxable income subject to the general limitation in taxable years beginning after December 31, 1982.—(a) *General Rule.* For taxable years beginning after December 31, 1982, foreign source taxable income subject to the general limitation includes foreign oil related income (as defined in section 907(c)(2) prior to its amendment by section 211 of the Tax Equity and Fiscal Responsibility Act of 1982). However, for purposes of recapturing general limitation overall foreign losses incurred in taxable years beginning before January 1, 1983 (pre-1983) out of foreign source taxable income subject to the general limitation in taxable years beginning after December 31, 1982 (post-1982), the taxpayer shall make separate determinations of foreign oil related income and other general limitation income (as if the FORI limitation under "old section 907(b)" (prior to its amendment by section 211 of the Tax Equity and Fiscal Responsibility Act of 1982) were still in effect), and shall apply the rules set forth in this section. The taxpayer shall maintain separate accounts for its pre-1983 FORI limitation overall foreign losses, its pre-1983 general limitation overall foreign losses (or its pre-1983 section 904(d)(1) (A-C) overall foreign losses if such losses were computed on a combined basis), and its post-1982 general limitation overall foreign losses. The taxpayer shall continue to maintain such separate accounts, make such separate determinations, and apply the rules of this section separately to each account until the earlier of—

(1) Such time as the taxpayer's entire pre-1983 FORI limitation overall foreign loss account and pre-1983 general limitation overall foreign loss account (or, if the taxpayer determined pre-1983 overall foreign losses on a combined basis, the section 904(d)(1) (A-C) account) have been recaptured, or

(2) The end of the taxpayer's 8th post-1982 taxable year, at which time the taxpayer shall add any remaining balance in its pre-1983 FORI limitation account and pre-1983 general limitation overall foreign loss account (or the section 904(d)(1) (A-C) account) to its post-1982 general limitation overall foreign loss account.

(b) *Recapture of pre-1983 FORI and general limitation overall foreign losses from post-1982 income.* A taxpayer having a balance in its pre-1983 FORI limitation overall foreign loss account or its pre-1983 general limitation overall foreign loss account (or its pre-1983 section 904(d)(1)(A-C) account) in a post-1982 taxable year shall recapture such overall foreign loss as follows:

(1) *Recapture from income subject to the same limitation.* The taxpayer shall first apply the rules of §§ 1.904(f)-1 through 1.904(f)-5 to the taxpayer's separately determined foreign oil related income to recapture the pre-1983 FORI limitation overall foreign loss account, and shall apply such rules to the taxpayer's separately determined general limitation income (exclusive of foreign oil related income) to recapture the

Reg. § 1.904(f)-6(b)(1)

Income from Sources Without the United States

pre-1983 general limitation overall foreign loss account (or the section 904(d)(1)(A-C) overall foreign loss account). Rules for determining the recapture of the pre-1983 section 904(d)(1)(A-C) losses are contained in section 1.904(f)-2(c)(4).

(2) *Recapture from income subject to the other limitation.* The taxpayer shall next apply the rules of §§ 1.904(f)-1 through -5 to the taxpayer's separately determined foreign oil related income to recapture the pre-1983 general limitation overall foreign loss account (or the section 904(d)(1)(A-C) overall foreign loss account) and shall apply such rules to the taxpayer's separately determined general limitation income to recapture foreign oil related losses to the extent that—

(i) The amount recaptured from such separately determined income under paragraph (b)(1) of this section is less than 50 percent (or such larger percentage as the taxpayer elects) of such separately determined income, and

(ii) The amount recaptured from such separately determined income under this paragraph (b)(2) does not exceed an amount equal to 12½ percent of the balance in the taxpayer's pre-1983 FORI limitation overall foreign loss account or the pre-1983 general limitation overall foreign loss account (or the section 904(d)(1)(A-C) overall foreign loss account) at the beginning of the taxpayer's first post-1982 taxable year, multiplied by the number of post-1982 taxable years (including the year to which this rule is being applied) which have elapsed, less the amount (if any) recaptured in prior post-1982 taxable years under this paragraph (b)(2) from such separately determined income.

The taxpayer may elect to recapture a pre-1983 overall foreign loss from post-1982 income subject to the general limitation at a faster rate than is required by this paragraph (b)(2). This election shall be made in the same manner as an election to recapture more than 50 percent of the income subject to recapture under section 904(f)(1), as provided in § 1.904(f)-2(c)(2).

(c) *Coordination of recapture of pre-1983 and post-1982 overall foreign losses.* A taxpayer incurring a general limitation overall foreign loss in any post-1982 taxable year in which the taxpayer has a balance in a pre-1983 FORI limitation or its pre-1983 general limitation overall foreign loss account (or the section 904(d)(1)(A-C) overall foreign loss account) shall establish a separate overall foreign loss account for such loss. The taxpayer shall recapture its overall foreign losses in succeeding taxable years by first applying the rules of this section to recapture its pre-1983 overall foreign losses, and then applying the rules of §§ 1.904(f)-1 through 1.904(f)-5 to recapture its post-1982 general limitation overall foreign loss. A post-1982 general limitation overall foreign loss is required to be recaptured only to the extent that the amount of foreign source taxable income recharacterized under paragraph (b) of this section is less than 50 percent of the taxpayer's total general limitation foreign source taxable income (including foreign oil related income) for such taxable year (except as required by section 904(f)(3)). However, a taxpayer may elect to recapture at a faster rate.

(d) *Illustrations.* The provisions of this section are illustrated by the following examples:

Example (1). X Corporation is a domestic corporation which has the calendar year as its taxable year. On December 31, 1982, X has a balance of $1,000 in its section 904(d)(1) (A-C) overall foreign loss account. X does not have a balance in a FORI limitation overall foreign loss account. For 1983, X has income of $1,200, which was subject to the general limitation and includes foreign oil related income of $1,000 and other general limitation income of $200. In 1983, X is required to recapture $225 of its pre-1983 section 904(d)(1) (A-C) overall foreign loss account computed as follows:

Amount recaptured under paragraph (b)(1) of this section............................	$100
The amount recaptured from general limitation income exclusive of foreign oil related income is the lesser of $1,000 (the pre-1983 loss reflected in the section 904(d)(1) (A-C) overall foreign loss account) or 50 percent of $200 (the separately determined general limitation income (exclusive of foreign oil related income)).	
Amount recaptured under paragraph (b)(2) of this section.............	$125
The amount recaptured from foreign oil related income is the lesser of $900 (the remaining pre-1983 section 904(d)(1) (A-C) overall foreign loss account after recapture under paragraph (b)(1) of this section) or 50 percent of $1,000 (the separately determined foreign oil related income), but as limited by paragraph (b)(2)(ii) of this section to (12½ percent of $1,000 × 1) − $0, which is $125.	
Total amount recaptured in 1983..........	$225

Example (2). The facts are the same as in example (1), except that X has general limitation

Reg. § 1.904(f)-6(d)

income of $50 for 1984 and $600 for 1985, all of which is foreign oil related income. X is required to recapture $25 in 1984 and $225 in 1985 of its pre-1983 section 904(d)(1) (A-C) overall foreign loss account computed as follows:

Amount recaptured under paragraph
(b)(2) of this section in 1984 .... $ 25
The amount recaptured from foreign oil related income is the lesser of $775 (the remaining pre-1983 section 904(d)(1) (A-C) overall foreign loss account) or 50 percent of $50 (the separately determined foreign oil related income). This amount is within the limitation of paragraph (b)(2)(ii) of this section (12½ percent of $1,000 × 2) − $125, which is $125.

Amount recaptured under paragraph
(b)(2) of this section in 1985 .... $225
The amount recaptured from foreign oil related income is the lesser of $750 (the remaining pre-1983 section 904(d)(1) (C-C) overall foreign loss account) or 50 percent of $600 (the separately determined foreign oil related income), but as limited by paragraph (b)(2)(ii) of this section to (12½ percent of $1,000 × 3) − ($125 + $25), which is $225. ($125 is the amount recaptured in 1983 under paragraph (b)(2) of this section, and $25 is the amount recaptured in 1984 under paragraph (b)(2) of this section.)

Example (3). Y Corporation is a domestic corporation which has the calendar year as its taxable year. On December 31, 1982, Y has a balance of $400 in its section 904(d)(1) (A-C) overall foreign loss account. Y does not have a balance in a FORI overall foreign loss account. For 1983, Y has a general limitation overall foreign loss of $200. For 1984, Y has general limitation income of $1,200, all of which is foreign oil related income. In 1984, Y is required to recapture a total of $300 computed as follows:

Amount of pre-1983 overall foreign
loss recaptured under paragraph
(b)(2) of this section $100
The amount of the pre-1983 section 904(d)(1) (A-C) overall loss account attributable to a general limitation loss recaptured from foreign oil related income is the lesser of $400 (the loss) or 50 percent of $1,200 (the separately determined foreign oil related income), but as limited by paragraph (b)(2)(ii) of this section to (12½ percent of $400 × 2) − $0, which is $100.

Amount of post-1982 overall foreign
loss recaptured under paragraph
(c) of this section $200
The amount of post-1982 general limitation overall foreign loss recaptured is the amount computed under § 1.904(f)-2(c)(1), which is the lesser of $200 (the post-1982 loss) or 50 percent of $1,200 (the income), but only to the extent that the amount of pre-1983 loss recaptured under paragraph (b) of this section is less than 50 percent of such income ((50 percent of $1,200) − $100 recaptured under paragraph (b) = $500).

Total amount recaptured in 1984 .... $300

At the end of 1984, Y has a balance in its pre-1983 section 904 (d)(1)(A-C) overall foreign loss account of $300, and has reduced its post-1982 general limitation overall foreign loss account to zero.

Example (4). Z is a domestic corporation which has the calendar year as its taxable year. On December 31, 1982, Z has a balance of $400 in its section 904(d)(1)(A-C) overall foreign loss account, and a balance of $1,000 in its FORI limitation overall foreign loss account. For 1983, Z has general limitation income of $2,000, which includes foreign oil related income of $1,000 and other general limitation income of $1,000. Keeping these amounts separate for purposes of this section, Z is required to recapture a total of $1,000 in 1983, computed as follows:

Amount recaptured under paragraph
(b)(1) of this section .... $ 900
The amount of pre-1983 section 904 (d)(1)(A-C) overall foreign loss account recaptured from general limitation income exclusive of foreign oil related income, in accordance with § 1.904(f)-2(c)(1), is the lesser of $400 (the section 904(d)(1)(A-C) overall foreign loss) or 50 percent of $1,000, the general limitation income exclusive of foreign oil related income), which is $400.

The amount of pre-1983 FORI overall foreign loss recaptured from foreign oil related income, in accordance with § 1.904(f)-2(c)(1), is the lesser of $1,000 (the FORI overall foreign loss) or 50 percent of $1,000 (the foreign oil related income), which is $500.

Amount recaptured under paragraph
(b)(2) of this section $100

Reg. § 1.904(f)-6(d)

The amount of pre-1983 FORI 907(b) overall foreign loss recaptured from section general limitation income exclusive of foreign oil related income is the lesser of $500 (the remaining balance in that loss account) or 50 percent of $1,000 (the general limitation income exclusive of foreign oil related income), but only to the extent that the amount recaptured from such income under paragraph (b)(1) of this section is less than 50 percent of such income, or $100 ((50 percent of $1,000) − $400 recapture due to section 904(d)(1)(A-C) overall foreign loss account), and only up to the amount permitted by paragraph (b)(2)(ii) of this section, which is (12½ percent of $1,000 × 1) − $0, or $125.

Total amount recaptured in 1983........... $1,000

At the end of 1983, Z has reduced its pre-1983 section 904(d)(1)(A-C) overall foreign loss account to zero, and has a balance in its pre-1983 FORI overall foreign loss account of $400.

[Reg. § 1.904(f)-6.]

☐ [T.D. 8153, 8-21-87.]

[Reg. § 1.904(f)-12]

§ 1.904(f)-12. Transition rules.

(a) *Recapture in years beginning after December 31, 1986, of overall foreign losses incurred in taxable years beginning before January 1, 1987*— (1) *In general.* If a taxpayer has a balance in an overall foreign loss account at the end of its last taxable year beginning before January 1, 1987 (pre-effective date years), the amount of that balance shall be recaptured in subsequent years by recharacterizing income received in the income category described in section 904(d) as in effect for taxable years beginning after December 31, 1986 (post-effective date years), that is analogous to the income category for which the overall foreign loss account was established, as follows:

(i) Interest income as defined in section 904(d)(1)(A) as in effect for pre-effective date taxable years is analogous to passive income as defined in section 904(d)(1)(A) as in effect for post-effective date years;

(ii) Dividends from a DISC or former DISC as defined in section 904(d)(1)(B) as in effect for pre-effective date taxable years is analogous to dividends from a DISC or former DISC as defined in section 904(d)(1)(F) as in effect for post-effective date taxable years;

(iii) Taxable income attributable to foreign trade income as defined in section 904(d)(1)(C) as in effect for pre-effective date taxable years is analogous to taxable income attributable to foreign trade income as defined in section 904(d)(1)(G) as in effect for post-effective date years;

(iv) Distributions from a FSC (or former FSC) as defined in section 904(d)(1)(D) as in effect for pre-effective date taxable years is analogous to distributions from a FSC (or former FSC) as defined in section 904(d)(1)(H) as in effect for post-effective date taxable years;

(v) For general limitation income as described in section 904(d)(1)(E) as in effect for pre-effective date taxable years, see the special rule in paragraph (a)(2) of this section.

(2) *Rule for general limitation losses*—(i) *In general.* Overall foreign losses incurred in the general limitation category of section 904(d)(1)(E), as in effect for pre-effective date taxable years, that are recaptured in post-effective date taxable years shall be recaptured from the taxpayer's general limitation income, financial services income, shipping income, and dividends from each noncontrolled section 902 corporation. If the sum of the taxpayer's general limitation income, financial services income, shipping income and dividends from each noncontrolled section 902 corporation for a taxable year subject to recapture exceeds the overall foreign loss to be recaptured, then the amount of each type of separate limitation income that will be treated as U.S. source income shall be determined as follows:

$$\text{Overall foreign loss subject to recapture} \times \frac{\text{Amount of income in each separate category from which the loss may be recaptured}}{\text{Sum of income in all separate categories from which the loss may be recaptured}}$$

This recapture shall be made after the allocation of separate limitation losses pursuant to section 904(f)(5)(B) and before the recharacterization of post-effective date separate limitation income pursuant to section 904(f)(5)(C).

(ii) *Exception.* If a taxpayer can demonstrate to the satisfaction of the district director that an overall foreign loss in the general limitation category of section 904(d)(1)(E), as in effect for pre-effective date taxable years, is attributa-

Reg. § 1.904(f)-12(a)(2)

ble, in sums certain, to losses in one or more separate categories of section 904(d)(1) (including for this purpose the passive income category and the high withholding tax interest category), as in effect for post-effective date taxable years, then the taxpayer may recapture the loss (in the amounts demonstrated) from those separate categories only.

(3) *Priority of recapture of overall foreign losses incurred in pre-effective date taxable years.* An overall foreign loss incurred by a taxpayer in pre-effective date taxable years shall be recaptured to the extent thereof before the taxpayer recaptures an overall foreign loss incurred in a post-effective date taxable year.

(4) *Examples:* The following examples illustrate the application of this paragraph (a).

Example (1). X corporation is a domestic corporation which operates a branch in Country Y. For its taxable year ending December 31, 1988, X has $800 of financial services income, $100 of general limitation income and $100 of shipping income. X has a balance of $100 in its general limitation overall foreign loss account which resulted from an overall foreign loss incurred during its 1986 taxable year. X is unable to demonstrate to which of the income categories set forth in section 904(d)(1) as in effect for post-effective date taxable years the loss is attributable. In addition, X has a balance of $100 in its shipping overall foreign loss account attributable to a shipping loss incurred during its 1987 taxable year. X has no other overall foreign loss accounts. Pursuant to section 904(f)(1), the full amount in each of X corporation's overall foreign loss accounts is subject to recapture since $200 (the sum of those amounts) is less than 50% of X's foreign source taxable income for its 1988 taxable year, or $500. X's overall foreign loss incurred during its 1986 taxable year is recaptured before the overall foreign loss incurred during its 1987 taxable year, as follows: $80 ($100 × 800/1000) of X's financial services income, $10 ($100 × 100/1000) of X's general limitation income, and $10 ($100 × 100/1000) of X's shipping income will be treated as U.S. source income. The remaining $90 of X corporation's 1988 shipping income will be treated as U.S. source income for the purpose of recapturing X's $100 overall foreign loss attributable to the shipping loss incurred in 1987. $10 remains in X's shipping overall foreign loss account for recapture in subsequent taxable years.

Example (2). The facts are the same as in *Example* (1) except that X has $800 of financial services income, $100 of general limitation income, a $100 dividend from a noncontrolled section 902 corporation and a ($100) shipping loss for its taxable year ending December 31, 1988. Separate limitation losses are allocated pursuant to the rules of section 904(f)(5) before the recapture of overall foreign losses. Therefore, the ($100) shipping loss incurred by X will be allocated to its separate limitation income as follows: $80 ($100 × 800/1000) will be allocated to X's financial services income, $10 ($100 × 100/1000) will be allocated to its general limitation income and $10 ($100 × 100/1000) will be allocated to X's dividend from the noncontrolled section 902 corporation. Accordingly, after allocation of the 1988 shipping loss, X has $720 of financial services income, $90 of general limitation income, and a $90 dividend from the noncontrolled section 902 corporation. Pursuant to section 904(f)(1), the full amount in each of X corporation's overall foreign loss accounts is subject to recapture since $200 (the sum of those amounts) is less than 50% of X's net foreign source taxable income for its 1988 taxable year, or $450. X's overall foreign loss incurred during its 1986 taxable year is recaptured as follows: $80 ($100 × 720/900) of X's financial services income, $10 ($100 × 90/900) of its general limitation income and $10 ($100 × 90/900) of its dividend from the noncontrolled section 902 corporation will be treated as U.S. source income. Accordingly, after application of section 904(f), X has $100 of U.S. source income, $640 of financial services income, $80 of general limitation income and a $80 dividend from the noncontrolled section 902 corporation for its 1988 taxable year. X must establish a separate limitation loss account for each portion of the 1988 shipping loss that was allocated to its financial services income, general limitation income and dividends from the noncontrolled section 902 corporation. X's overall foreign loss account for the 1986 general limitation loss is reduced to zero. X still has a $100 balance in its overall foreign loss account that resulted from the 1987 shipping loss.

Example (3). Y is a domestic corporation which has a branch operation in Country Z. For its 1988 taxable year, Y has $5 of shipping income, $15 of general limitation income and $100 of financial services income. Y has a balance of $100 in its general limitation overall foreign loss account attributable to its 1986 taxable year. Y has no other overall foreign loss accounts. Pursuant to section 904(f)(1), $60 of the overall foreign loss is subject to recapture since 50% of Y's foreign source income for 1988 is less than the balance in its overall foreign loss account. Y can demonstrate that the entire $100 overall foreign loss was attributable to a shipping limitation loss incurred in 1986. Accordingly, only Y's $5 of shipping limitation income received in 1988 will be treated as U.S. source income. Because Y can

Reg. § 1.904(f)-12(a)(3)

demonstrate that the 1986 loss was entirely attributable to a shipping loss, none of Y's general limitation income or financial services income received in 1988 will be treated as U.S. source income.

Example (4). The facts are the same as in Example (3) except that Y can only demonstrate that $50 of the 1986 overall foreign loss account was attributable to a shipping loss incurred in 1986. Accordingly, Y's $5 of shipping limitation income received in 1988 will be treated as U.S. source income. The remaining $50 of the 1986 overall foreign loss that Y cannot trace to a particular separate limitation will be recaptured and treated as U.S. source income as follows: $43 ($50 × 100/115) of Y's financial services income will be treated as U.S. source income and $7 ($50 × 15/115) of Y's general limitation income will be treated as U.S. source income. Y has $45 remaining in its overall foreign loss account to be recaptured from shipping income in a future year.

(b) *Treatment of overall foreign losses that are part of net operating losses incurred in pre-effective date taxable years which are carried forward to post-effective date taxable years*—(1) *Rule.* An overall foreign loss that is part of a net operating loss incurred in a pre-effective date taxable year which is carried forward, pursuant to section 172, to a post-effective date taxable year will be carried forward under the rules of section 904(f)(5) and the regulations under that section. *See also* Notice 89-3, 1989-1 C.B. 623. For this purpose the loss must be allocated to income in the category analogous to the income category set forth in section 904(d) as in effect for pre-effective date taxable years in which the loss occurred. The analogous category shall be determined under the rules of paragraph (a) of this section.

(2) *Example.* The following example illustrates the rule of paragraph (b)(1) of this section.

Example. Z is a domestic corporation which has a branch operation in Country D. For its taxable year ending December 31, 1988, Z has $100 of passive income and $200 of general limitation income. Z also has a $60 net operating loss which was carried forward pursuant to section 172 from its 1986 taxable year. The net operating loss resulted from an overall foreign loss attributable to the general limitation income category. Z can demonstrate that the loss is a shipping loss. Therefore, the net operating loss will be treated as a shipping loss for Z's 1988 taxable year. Pursuant to section 904(f)(5), the shipping loss will be allocated as follows: $20 ($60 × 100/300) will be allocated to Z's passive income and $40 ($60 × 200/300) will be allocated to Z's general limitation income. Accordingly, after application of section 904(f), Z has $80 of passive income and $160 of general limitation income for its 1988 taxable year. Although no addition to Z's overall foreign loss account for shipping income will result from the NOL carry forward, shipping income earned by Z in subsequent taxable years will be subject to recharacterization as passive income and general limitation income pursuant to the rules set forth in section 904(f)(5).

(c) *Treatment of overall foreign losses that are part of net operating losses incurred in post-effective date taxable years which are carried back to pre-effective date taxable years*—(1) *Allocation to analogous income category.* An overall foreign loss that is part of a net operating loss incurred by the taxpayer in a post-effective date taxable year which is carried back, pursuant to section 172, to a pre-effective date taxable year shall be allocated first to income in the pre-effective date income category analogous to the income category set forth in section 904(d) as in effect for post-effective date taxable years in which the loss occurred. Except for the general limitation income category, the pre-effective date income category that is analogous to a post-effective date income category shall be determined under paragraphs (a)(1)(i) through (iv) of this section. The general limitation income category for pre-effective date years shall be treated as the income category that is analogous to the post-effective date categories for general limitation income, financial services income, shipping income, dividends from each noncontrolled section 902 corporation and high withholding tax interest income. If the net operating loss resulted from separate limitation losses in more than one post-effective date income category and more than one loss is carried back to pre-effective date general limitation income, then the losses shall be allocated to the pre-effective date general limitation income based on the following formula:

$$\text{Pre-effective date general limitation income} \times \frac{\text{Loss in each post-effective date separate limitation category that is analogous to pre-effective date general limitation income}}{\text{Losses in all post-effective categories that are analogous to pre-effective date general limitation income.}}$$

(2) *Allocation to U.S. source income.* If an overall foreign loss is carried back to a pre-effective date taxable year and the loss exceeds the foreign source income in the analogous category for the carry back year, the remaining loss shall be allocated against U.S. source income as set forth in § 1.904(f)-3. The amount of the loss that

offsets U.S. source income must be added to the taxpayer's overall foreign loss account. An addition to an overall foreign loss account resulting from the carry back of a net operating loss incurred by a taxpayer in a post-effective date taxable year shall be treated as having been incurred by the taxpayer in the year in which the loss arose and shall be subject to recapture pursuant to section 904(f) as in effect for post-effective date taxable years.

(3) *Allocation to other separate limitation categories.* To the extent that an overall foreign loss that is carried back as part of a net operating loss exceeds the separate limitation income to which it is allocated and the U.S. source income of the taxpayer for the taxable year to which the loss is carried, the loss shall be allocated pro rata to other separate limitation income of the taxpayer for the taxable year. However, there shall be no recharacterization of separate limitation income pursuant to section 904(f)(5) as a result of the allocation of such a net operating loss to other separate limitation income of the taxpayer.

(4) *Examples.* The following examples illustrate the rules of paragraph (c) of this section.

Example (1). X is a domestic corporation which has a branch operation in Country A. For its taxable year ending December 31, 1987, X has a $60 net operating loss which is carried back pursuant to section 172 to its taxable year ending December 31, 1985. The net operating loss resulted from a shipping loss; X had no U.S. source income in 1987. X had $20 of general limitation income, $40 of DISC limitation income and $10 of U.S. source income for its 1985 taxable year. The $60 NOL is allocated first to X's 1985 general limitation income to the extent thereof ($20) since the general limitation income category of section 904(d) as in effect for pre-effective date taxable years is the income category that is analogous to shipping income for post-effective date taxable years. Therefore, X has no general limitation income for its 1985 taxable year. Next, pursuant to section 904(f) as in effect for pre-effective date taxable years, the remaining $40 of the NOL is allocated first to X's $10 of U.S. source income and then to $30 of X's DISC limitation income for its 1985 taxable year. Accordingly, X has no U.S. source income and $10 of DISC limitation income for its 1985 taxable year after allocation of the NOL. X has a $10 balance in its shipping overall foreign loss account which is subject to recapture pursuant to section 904(f) as in effect for post-effective date taxable years. X will not be required to recharacterize, pursuant to section 904(f)(5), subsequent shipping income as DISC limitation income.

Example (2). Y is a domestic corporation which has a branch operation in Country B. For its taxable year ending December 31, 1987, X has a $200 net operating loss which is carried back pursuant to section 172 to its taxable year ending December 31, 1986. The net operating loss resulted from a ($100) general limitation loss and a ($100) shipping loss. Y had $100 of general limitation income and $200 of U.S. source income for its taxable year ending December 31, 1986. The separate limitation losses for 1987 are allocated pro rata to Y's 1986 general limitation income as follows: $50 of the ($100) general limitation loss ($100 × 100/200) and $50 of the ($100) shipping loss ($100 × 100/200) is allocated to Y's $100 of 1986 general limitation income. The remaining $50 of Y's general limitation loss and the remaining $50 of Y's shipping loss are allocated to Y's 1986 U.S. source income. Accordingly, Y has no foreign source income and $100 of U.S. source income for its 1986 taxable year. Y has a $50 balance in its general limitation overall foreign loss account and a $50 balance in its shipping overall foreign loss account, both of which will be subject to recapture pursuant to section 904(f) as in effect for post-effective date taxable years.

(d) *Recapture of FORI and general limitation overall foreign losses incurred in taxable years beginning before January 1, 1983.* For taxable years beginning after December 31, 1986, and before January 1, 1991, the rules set forth in § 1.904(f)-6 shall apply for purposes of recapturing general limitation and foreign oil related income (FORI) overall foreign losses incurred in taxable years beginning before January 1, 1983 (pre-1983). For taxable years beginning after December 31, 1990, the rules set forth in this section shall apply for purposes of recapturing pre-1983 general limitation and FORI overall foreign losses.

(e) *Recapture of pre-1983 overall foreign losses determined on a combined basis.* The rules set forth in paragraph (a)(2) of this section shall apply for purposes of recapturing overall foreign losses incurred in taxable years beginning before January 1, 1983, that were computed on a combined basis in accordance with § 1.904(f)-1(c)(1).

(f) *Transition rules for taxable years beginning before December 31, 1990.* For transition rules for taxable years beginning before January 1, 1990, see 26 CFR § 1.904(f)-13T as it appeared in the Code of Federal Regulations revised as of April 1, 1990. [Reg. § 1.904(f)-12.]

☐ [*T.D.* 8306, 8-1-90.]

Reg. § 1.904(f)-12(c)(3)

[Reg. § 1.904(i)-1]

§ 1.904(i)-1. Limitation on use of deconsolidation to avoid foreign tax credit limitations.—(a) *General rule.* If two or more includible corporations are affiliates, within the meaning of paragraph (b)(1) of this section, at any time during their taxable years, then, solely for purposes of applying the foreign tax credit provisions of section 59(a), sections 901 through 908, and section 960, the rules of this section will apply.

(1) *Determination of taxable income*—(i) Each affiliate must compute its net taxable income or loss in each separate category (as defined in § 1.904-5(a)(1), and treating U.S. source income or loss as a separate category) without regard to sections 904(f) and 907(c)(4). Only affiliates that are members of the same consolidated group use the consolidated return regulations (other than those under sections 904(f) and 907(c)(4)) in computing such net taxable income or loss. To the extent otherwise applicable, other provisions of the Internal Revenue Code and regulations must be used in the determination of an affiliate's net taxable income or loss in a separate category.

(ii) The net taxable income amounts in each separate category determined under paragraph (a)(1)(i) of this section are combined for all affiliates to determine one amount for the group of affiliates in each separate category. However, a net loss of an affiliate (first affiliate) in a separate category determined under paragraph (a)(1)(i) of this section will be combined under this paragraph (a) with net income or loss amounts of other affiliates in the same category only if, and to the extent that, the net loss offsets taxable income, whether U.S. or foreign source, of the first affiliate. The consolidated return regulations that apply the principles of sections 904(f) and 907(c)(4) to consolidated groups will then be applied to the combined amounts in each separate category as if all affiliates were members of a single consolidated group.

(2) *Allocation.* Any net taxable income in a separate category calculated under paragraph (a)(1)(ii) of this section for purposes of the foreign tax credit provisions must then be allocated among the affiliates under any consistently applied reasonable method, taking into account all of the facts and circumstances. A method is consistently applied if used by all affiliates from year to year. Once chosen, an allocation method may be changed only with the consent of the Commissioner. This allocation will only affect the source and foreign tax credit separate limitation character of the income for purposes of the foreign tax credit separate limitation of each affiliate, and will not otherwise affect an affiliate's total net income or loss. This section applies whether the federal income tax consequences of its application favor, or are adverse to, the taxpayer.

(b) *Definitions and special rules*—For purposes of this section only, the following terms will have the meanings specified.

(1) *Affiliate*—(i) *Generally.* Affiliates are includible corporations—

(A) That are members of the same affiliated group, as defined in section 1504(a); or

(B) That would be members of the same affiliated group, as defined in section 1504(a) if—

(*1*) Any non-includible corporation meeting the ownership test of section 1504(a)(2) with respect to any such includible corporation was itself an includible corporation; or

(*2*) The constructive ownership rules of section 1563(e) were applied for purposes of section 1504(a).

(ii) *Rules for consolidated groups.* Affiliates that are members of the same consolidated group are treated as a single affiliate for purposes of this section. The provisions of paragraph (a) of this section shall not apply if the only affiliates under this definition are already members of the same consolidated group without operation of this section.

(iii) *Exception for newly acquired affiliates*—(A) With respect to acquisitions after December 7, 1995, an includible corporation acquired from unrelated third parties (First Corporation) will not be considered an affiliate of another includible corporation (Second Corporation) during the taxable year of the First Corporation beginning before the date on which the First Corporation originally becomes an affiliate with respect to the Second Corporation.

(B) With respect to acquisitions on or before December 7, 1995, an includible corporation acquired from unrelated third parties will not be considered an affiliate of another includible corporation during its taxable year beginning before the date on which the first includible corporation first becomes an affiliate with respect to that other includible corporation.

(C) This exception does not apply where the acquisition of an includible corporation is used to avoid the application of this section.

(2) *Includible corporation.* The term *includible corporation* has the same meaning it has in section 1504(b).

(c) *Taxable years.* If all of the affiliates use the same U.S. taxable year, then that taxable year must be used for purposes of applying this section. If, however, the affiliates use more than one U.S.

taxable year, then an appropriate taxable year must be used for applying this section. The determination whether a taxable year is appropriate must take into account all of the relevant facts and circumstances, including the U.S. taxable years used by the affiliates for general U.S. income tax purposes. The taxable year chosen by the affiliates for purposes of applying this section must be used consistently from year to year. The taxable year may be changed only with the prior consent of the Commissioner. Those affiliates that do not use the year determined under this paragraph (c) as their U.S. taxable year for general U.S. income tax purposes must, for purposes of this section, use their U.S. taxable year or years ending within the taxable year determined under this paragraph (c). If, however, the stock of an affiliate is disposed of so that it ceases to be an affiliate, then the taxable year of that affiliate will be considered to end on the disposition date for purposes of this section.

(d) *Consistent treatment of foreign taxes paid.* All affiliates must consistently either elect under section 901(a) to claim a credit for foreign income taxes paid or accrued, or deemed paid or accrued, or deduct foreign taxes paid or accrued under section 164. See also § 1.1502-4(a); § 1.905-1(a).

(e) *Effective date.* Except as provided in paragraph (b)(1)(iii) of this section (relating to newly acquired affiliates), this section is effective for taxable years of affiliates beginning after December 31, 1993. [Reg. § 1.904(i)-1.]

☐ [*T.D.* 8627, 11-6-95.]

[Reg. § 1.905-1]

§ 1.905-1. **When credit for taxes may be taken.**—(a) *In general.* The credit for taxes provided in subpart A (section 901 and following), part III, subchapter N, chapter 1 of the Code, may ordinarily be taken either in the return for the year in which the taxes accrued or in which the taxes were paid, dependent upon whether the accounts of the taxpayer are kept and his returns filed using an accrual method or using the cash receipts and disbursements method. Section 905(a) allows the taxpayer, at his option and irrespective of the method of accounting employed in keeping his books, to take such credit for taxes as may be allowable in the return for the year in which the taxes accrued. An election thus made under section 905(a) (or under the corresponding provisions of prior internal revenue laws) must be followed in returns for all subsequent years, and no portion of any such taxes accrued in a year in which a credit is claimed will be allowed as a deduction from gross income in any year. See also § 1.905-4.

(b) *Foreign income subject to exchange controls.* If, however, under the provisions of the regulations under section 461, an amount otherwise constituting gross income for the taxable year from sources without the United States is, owing to monetary, exchange, or other restrictions imposed by a foreign country, not includible in gross income of the taxpayer for such year, the credit for income taxes imposed by such foreign country with respect to such amount shall be taken proportionately in any subsequent taxable year in which such amount or portion thereof is includible in gross income. [Reg. § 1.905-1.]

☐ [*T.D.* 6275, 12-2-57.]

[Reg. § 1.905-2]

§ 1.905-2. **Conditions of allowance of credit.**—(a) *Forms and information.* (1) Whenever the taxpayer chooses, in accordance with paragraph (d) of § 1.901-1, to claim the benefits of the foreign tax credit, the claim for credit shall be accompanied by Form 1116 in the case of an individual or by Form 1118 in the case of a corporation.

(2) The form must be carefully filled in with all the information called for and with the calculations of credits indicated. Except where it is established to the satisfaction of the district director that it is impossible for the taxpayer to furnish such evidence, the taxpayer must provide upon request the receipt for each such tax payment if credit is sought for taxes already paid or the return on which each such accrued tax was based if credit is sought for taxes accrued. The receipt or return must be either the original, a duplicate original, or a duly certified or authenticated copy. The preceding two sentences are applicable for returns whose original due date falls on or after January 1, 1988. If the receipt or the return is in a foreign language, a certified translation thereof must be furnished by the taxpayer. Any additional information necessary for the determination under part I (section 861 and following), subchapter N, chapter 1 of the Code, of the amount of income derived from sources without the United States and from each foreign country shall, upon the request of the district director, be furnished by the taxpayer. If the taxpayer upon request fails without justification to furnish any such additional information which is significant, including any significant information which he is requested to furnish pursuant to § 1.861-8(f)(5) as proposed in the Federal Register for November 8, 1976, the District Director may disallow the claim of the taxpayer to the benefits of the foreign tax credit.

(b) *Secondary evidence.* Where it has been established to the satisfaction of the district director

Reg. § 1.905-1(a)

that it is impossible to furnish a receipt for such foreign tax payment, the foreign tax return, or direct evidence of the amount of tax withheld at the source, the district director, may, in his discretion, accept secondary evidence thereof as follows:

(1) *Receipt for payment.* In the absence of a receipt for payment of foreign taxes there shall be submitted a photostatic copy of the check, draft, or other medium of payment showing the amount and date thereof, with certification identifying it with the tax claimed to have been paid, together with evidence establishing that the tax was paid for taxpayer's account as his own tax on his own income. If credit is claimed on an accrual method, it must be shown that the tax accrued in the taxable year.

(2) *Foreign tax return.* If the foreign tax return is not available, the foreign tax has not been paid, and credit is claimed on an accrual method, there shall be submitted—

(i) A certified statement of the amount claimed to have accrued,

(ii) Excerpts from the taxpayer's accounts showing amounts of foreign income and tax thereon accrued on its books,

(iii) A computation of the foreign tax based on income from the foreign country carried on the books and at current rates of tax to be established by data such as excerpts from the foreign law, assessment notices, or other documentary evidence thereof,

(iv) A bond, if deemed necessary by the district director, filed in the manner provided in cases where the foreign return is available, and

(v) In case a bond is not required, a specific agreement wherein the taxpayer shall recognize its liability to report the correct amount of tax when ascertained, as required by the provisions of section 905(c).

If at any time the foreign tax receipts or foreign tax returns become available to the taxpayer, they shall be promptly submitted to the district director.

(3) *Tax withheld at source.* In the case of taxes withheld at the source from dividends, interest, royalties, compensation, or other form of income, where evidence of withholding and of the amount withheld cannot be secured from those who have made the payments, the district director may, in his discretion, accept secondary evidence of such withholding and of the amount of the tax so withheld, having due regard to the taxpayer's books of account and to the rates of taxation prevailing in the particular foreign country during the period involved.

(c) In the case of a credit sought for a tax accrued but not paid, the district director may, as a condition precedent to the allowance of a credit, require a bond from the taxpayer, in addition to Form 1116 or 1118. If such a bond is required, Form 1117 shall be used by an individual or by a corporation. It shall be in such sum as the Commissioner may prescribe, and shall be conditioned for the payment by the taxpayer of any amount of tax found due upon any redetermination of the tax made necessary by such credit proving incorrect, with such further conditions as the district director may require. This bond shall be executed by the taxpayer, or the agent or representative of the taxpayer, as principal, and by sureties satisfactory to and approved by the Commissioner. See also 6 U.S.C. 15. [Reg. § 1.905-2.]

☐ [*T.D.* 6275, 12-2-57. *Amended by T.D.* 6789, 12-30-64; *T.D.* 7292, 11-30-74; *T.D.* 7456, 1-3-77; *T.D.* 8210, 6-22-88; *T.D.* 8412, 5-13-92 *and T.D.* 8759, 1-26-98.]

[Reg. § 1.905-3T]

§ 1.905-3T. **Adjustments to the pools of foreign taxes and earnings and profits when the allowable foreign tax credit changes (Temporary).**—(a) *Foreign tax redeterminations subject to sections 985 through 989 of the Internal Revenue Code.* This section applies to a foreign tax redetermination that occurs in a taxpayer's taxable year beginning after December 31, 1986 with respect to—

(1) Tax that is paid or accrued by or on behalf of a taxpayer (including taxes paid or accrued prior to January 1, 1987), or

(2) Tax that is deemed paid or accrued by a taxpayer under section 902 or section 960 with respect to earnings and profits of a foreign corporation accumulated in taxable years of the foreign corporation beginning after December 31, 1986.

(b) *Currency translation rules*—(1) *Accrual of foreign tax.* Accrued and unpaid foreign tax liabilities denominated in foreign currency, as determined under foreign law, shall be translated into dollars at the exchange rate as of the last day of the taxable year of the taxpayer.

(2) *Payments of foreign tax.* Foreign tax liabilities denominated in foreign currency shall be translated into dollars at the rate of exchange for the date of the payment of the foreign tax. Tax withheld in foreign currency shall be translated into dollars at the rate for the date on which the tax is withheld. Estimated tax paid in foreign currency shall be translated into dollars at the rate for the date on which the estimated tax payment is made.

(3) *Refunds of foreign tax.* A refund of foreign tax shall be translated into dollars using the exchange rate for the date of the payment of the foreign taxes. If a refund of foreign tax relates to foreign taxes paid on more than one date, then the refund shall be deemed to be derived from, and shall reduce, the last payment of foreign taxes first, to the extent thereof. See § 1.905-3T(d)(3) relating to the method of adjustment of a foreign corporation's pools of earnings and profits and foreign taxes.

(4) *Allocation of refunds of foreign tax.* Refunds of foreign tax shall be allocated to the same separate category as foreign taxes to which the refunded taxes relate. Refunds are related to foreign taxes of a separate category if the foreign tax that was refunded was imposed with respect to that separate category. See section 904(d) and § 1.904-6 concerning the allocation of taxes to separate categories of income. Earnings and profits of a foreign corporation in the separate category to which the refund relates shall be increased to reflect the foreign tax refund.

(5) *Basis of foreign currency refunded.* A recipient of a refund of foreign tax shall determine its basis in the currency refunded under the following rules.

(i) If the functional currency of the qualified business unit (as defined in section 989 and the regulations thereunder, hereinafter "QBU") that paid the tax and received the refund is the United States dollar or the person receiving the refund is not a QBU, then the recipient's basis in the foreign currency refunded shall be the dollar value of the refund determined, under paragraph (b)(2) of this section, on the date the foreign tax was paid.

(ii) If the functional currency of the QBU receiving the refund is not the United States dollar and is different from the currency in which the foreign tax was paid, then the recipient's basis in the foreign currency refunded shall be equal to the functional currency value of the non-functional refunded translated into functional currency at the exchange rate between the functional currency and the non-functional currency, determined under paragraph (b)(2) of this section, on the date the foreign tax was paid.

(iii) If the functional currency of the QBU receiving the refund is the currency in which the refund was made, then the recipient's basis in the currency received shall be the amount of the functional currency received.

For purposes of determining exchange gain or loss on the initial payment of foreign tax in a non-functional currency, see section 988. For purposes of determining subsequent exchange gain or loss on the disposition of non-functional currency the basis of which is determined under this rule, see section 988.

(c) *Foreign tax redetermination.* For purposes of this section, the term "foreign tax redetermination" means a change in the foreign tax liability that may affect a United States taxpayer's foreign tax credit. A foreign tax redetermination includes—

(1) A refund of foreign taxes;

(2) A difference between the dollar value of the accrued foreign tax and the dollar value of the foreign tax actually paid attributable to differences in the units of foreign currency paid and the units of foreign currency accrued; or

(3) A difference between the dollar value of the accrued foreign tax and the dollar value of the foreign tax actually paid attributable to fluctuations in the value of the foreign currency relative to the dollar between the date of accrual and the date of payment.

(d) *Redetermination of United States tax liability*—(1) *Foreign taxes paid directly by a United States person.* If a foreign tax redetermination occurs with respect to foreign tax paid or accrued by or on behalf of a United States taxpayer, then a redetermination of United States tax liability is required for the taxable year for which the foreign tax was claimed as a credit. See § 1.905-4T(b) which requires notification to the Internal Revenue Service of a foreign tax redetermination in situations in which a redetermination of United States liability is required. However, a redetermination of United States tax liability is not required (and a taxpayer need not notify the Service) if the foreign tax redetermination is described in paragraph (c)(3) (that is, it is caused solely by a foreign currency fluctuation), and the amount of the foreign tax redetermination with respect to the foreign country is less than the lesser of ten thousand dollars or two percent of the total dollar amount of the foreign tax initially accrued with respect to that foreign country for the taxable year. In such case, an appropriate adjustment shall be made to the taxpayer's United States tax liability in the taxable year during which the foreign tax redetermination occurs.

Reg. § 1.905-3T(b)(3)

→ *Caution: Temporary Reg. § 1.905-3T(d)(2)(ii)(A) and so much of (C) as refers to (A) has been suspended by Notice 90-26.*←

(2) *Foreign taxes deemed paid under sections 902 or 960*—(i) *Redetermination of United States tax liability not required.* Subject to the special rule of paragraph (d)(4), a redetermination of United States tax liability is not required to account for the effect of a redetermination of foreign tax paid or accrued by a foreign corporation on the foreign taxes deemed paid by a United States corporation under sections 902 or section 960. Instead, adjustments shall be made, and notification of such adjustments shall be filed, as required by paragraphs (d)(2) and (3) of this section.

(ii) *Adjustments to pools.* In the case of a foreign tax redetermination that affects the amount of foreign taxes deemed paid by a United States corporation for a taxable year—

(A) If the foreign tax redetermination occurs more than 90 days before the due date (determined with extensions) of the United States taxpayer's United States income tax return for such taxable year and before the taxpayer actually files that return, then that United States taxpayer shall adjust the foreign tax credit to be claimed on that return for such taxable year to account for the effect of the foreign tax redetermination (including the impact of the foreign tax redetermination on the earnings and profits of the foreign corporation);

(B) If a foreign tax redetermination occurs after the filing of the United States tax return for such taxable year, then appropriate upward or downward adjustments shall be made at the time of the foreign tax redetermination to the pool of foreign taxes and the pool of earnings and profits of the foreign corporation as provided in paragraph (d)(3) to reflect the effect of the foreign tax redetermination in calculating foreign taxes deemed paid with respect to distributions and inclusions (and the amount of such distributions and inclusions) that are includible in taxable years subsequent to the taxable year for which such tax return is filed; and

(C) If the foreign tax redetermination occurs within 90 days of the due date (determined with extensions) of the United States tax return and before the taxpayer actually files its tax return, then the taxpayer may elect either to adjust the foreign tax credit to be claimed on that return in the manner described in subparagraph (A) of this paragraph (d)(2)(ii) or adjust the pools of foreign taxes and earnings and profits to reflect the effect of the foreign tax redetermination in the manner described in paragraph (d)(2)(ii)(B), provided that consistent elections are made by the taxpayer and all other members of the affiliated group, as defined in section 1504(a), of which the taxpayer is a member, with respect to all foreign tax redeterminations occurring on or before any date within the 90 day period.

(iii) *Reporting requirements.* If an adjustment to the appropriate pool of foreign taxes and earnings and profits is required under paragraphs (d)(2)(ii)(B) or (C), the United States corporation shall attach a notice of such adjustment to its return for the year with or within which ends the foreign corporation's taxable year during which the foreign tax redetermination occurs. The United States corporation shall provide: its name and identifying number; the foreign corporation's name, address, and identifying number (if any); the amount of any refunds of foreign taxes and the exchange rate as of the time of the original payment of the refunded foreign taxes; the amounts of unrefunded foreign taxes when paid and when accrued in foreign currency, the exchange rates for the accrual and payment dates of unrefunded foreign taxes, and the dollar amounts of unrefunded foreign taxes paid and accrued; the current balances of the pools of earnings and profits and foreign taxes before and after the foreign tax redetermination; and such other information as the Service may require. If a taxpayer may be required to redetermine its United States tax liability under paragraph (d)(4)(ii) of § 1.905-3T (relating to foreign tax adjustments of two percent or more), the notice shall specifically identify foreign tax adjustments described in such paragraph and shall include a complete factual description justifying the overaccrual of foreign tax. If the United States corporation fails to attach the required notice, to provide the necessary information, or to make the required adjustments, then it must provide notification of the foreign tax redetermination under § 1.905-4T. The Service may, in its discretion, make a redetermination of United States tax liability, and subject the taxpayer to the interest provisions of section 6601 and the penalty provisions of section 6689 and the regulations thereunder.

(iv) *Examples.* The following examples illustrate the application of paragraph (d)(2)(ii) and (iii) of this section. In each case, the exceptions of paragraph (d)(4) do not apply.

Example (1). Controlled foreign corporation S is a wholly-owned subsidiary of domestic corporation, P. P is a fiscal year taxpayer whose taxable year ends on June 30. P does not request an extension for filing its United States tax return for the taxable year ending June 30, 1988 and files its return on its September 15, 1988 due

Reg. § 1.905-3T(d)(2)

data. S is a calendar year taxpayer. In 1987, S earned 100u of Subpart F income and accrued foreign taxes with respect to that income of 20u. At the time of accrual, the exchange rate was $1:4u. S paid the 20u of accrued tax with respect to its income on June 15, 1988, when the exchange rate was $1:2u. P includes the 100u in gross income under section 951(a) and claims a credit under section 960. P must use the amount of taxes actually paid by S (20u = $10) in determining foreign taxes deemed paid by P. Pursuant to paragraph (d)(2)(ii)(A), P is required to compute foreign taxes deemed paid taking into account the foreign tax redetermination that occurred on June 15, which was more than 90 days before the due date of P's tax return (September 15, 1988) and before P actually filed its return.

Example (2). The facts are the same as in Example (1), except that S paid its tax liability on October 16, 1988. P filed its United States income tax return for 1987 on September 15, 1987, before the foreign tax redetermination. P properly computed its section 960 credit on its 1987 return with respect to its 100u Subpart F inclusion on the basis of the amount of accrued foreign tax. Subject to the special rule of paragraph (d)(3)(iv), P is required, pursuant to the provisions of paragraph (d)(2)(ii)(B), to make the appropriate adjustments to the relevant pool of foreign taxes and pool of earnings and profits for purposes of calculating foreign taxes deemed paid in subsequent taxable years.

Example (3). Controlled foreign corporation S is a wholly-owned subsidiary of domestic corporation, P. P is a fiscal year (June 30) taxpayer, and S is a calendar year taxpayer. In 1987, S earned 100u of general limitation manufacturing income that was not Subpart F income. S accrued 40u in foreign tax with respect to that income as of the end of its taxable year when the exchange rate was $1:4u. During 1987 and 1988, P received no distributions (and had no section 951(a)(1) inclusions) from S. S paid its taxes on March 15, 1988 when the exchange rate was $1:2u (40u = $20). S received a refund of foreign tax of 20u on July 1, 1988. No section 905(c) adjustment is required on these facts. As of the end of 1988, S's pool of general limitation accumulated earnings and profits equals 80u (100u − 20u), and its pool of foreign taxes imposed on general limitation income equals $10 (40u − 20u = 20u, translated as of the date of payment ($1:2u), equals $10).

(3) *Adjustments to the pools of earnings and profits and foreign taxes*—(i) *In general.* If a foreign corporation is required to adjust its earnings and profits and foreign taxes under § 1.905-3T(d)(2)(ii)(B) or (C), then that adjustment shall be made in accordance with the provisions of this section.

(ii) *Refunds of foreign taxes.* A foreign corporation shall reduce its pool of foreign taxes in the appropriate separate category by the United States dollar amount of a foreign tax refund translated as provided in paragraph (b)(3). A foreign corporation shall increase its pool of earnings and profits in the appropriate separate category by the functional currency amount of the foreign tax refund. The allocation of the refund to the appropriate separate categories shall be made in accordance with §§ 1.905-3T(b)(4) and 1.904-6. If a foreign corporation receives a refund of foreign tax in a currency other than its functional currency, that refund shall be translated into its functional currency, for purposes of computing the increase to its pool of earnings and profits, at the exchange rate as of the date of the payment of the foreign tax.

(iii) *Additional assessments of foreign tax.* A foreign corporation shall increase its pool of foreign taxes in the appropriate separate category by the United States dollar amount of the additional foreign tax paid or accrued translated as provided in paragraphs (b)(1) and (2). A foreign corporation shall decrease its earnings and profits in the appropriate separate category by the functional currency amount of the additional foreign tax paid or accrued. The allocation of the additional amount of foreign tax among separate categories shall be made in accordance with § 1.904-6.

(iv) *Refunds of foreign taxes of lower tier foreign corporations that cause deficits in foreign tax pools.* If a lower tier foreign corporation receives a refund of foreign tax after making a distribution to an upper tier foreign corporation and the refund would have the effect of reducing below zero the lower tier corporation's pool of foreign taxes in any separate category, then both the lower tier and upper tier corporations shall adjust the appropriate pool of foreign taxes to reflect that refund. The upper tier foreign corporation shall adjust its pool of foreign taxes by the difference between the United States dollar amount of foreign tax deemed paid by the upper tier foreign corporation prior to the refund and the United States dollar amount of foreign tax recomputed as if the refund occurred prior to the distribution. The upper tier foreign corporation shall not make any adjustment to its earnings and profits because foreign taxes deemed paid by the upper tier corporation are not included in the upper tier corporation's earnings and profits. The lower tier foreign corporation shall adjust its pool of foreign taxes by the difference between the United States dollar amount of the refund and the

Reg. § 1.905-3T(d)(3)

Income from Sources Without the United States 48,979

See p. 20,601 for regulations not amended to reflect law changes

United States dollar amount of the adjustment to the upper tier foreign corporation's pool of foreign taxes. The earnings and profits of the lower tier foreign corporation shall be adjusted to reflect the full amount of the refund. The provisions of this paragraph (d)(3)(iv) do not apply to distributions or inclusions to a United States person. See § 1.905-3T(d)(4)(iv) for rules relating to actual or deemed distributions made to a United States person.

(v) *Examples.* The following examples illustrate the application of this paragraph (d)(3).

Example (1). Controlled foreign corporation (CFC) is a wholly-owned subsidiary of its domestic parent, P. Both CFC and P are calendar year taxpayers. CFC has a functional currency, the u, other than the dollar and maintains its pool of earnings and profits in that currency. At the end of year 1, CFC paid 100u in taxes with respect to non-Subpart F income when the exchange rate was $1:1u. In year 2, on a date that is after P filed its United States tax return, CFC receives a refund of 50u of its year 1 taxes. CFC made no distributions to P in year 1. In accordance with paragraph (d)(3)(ii) and subject to paragraph (d)(4), CFC shall reduce its pool of foreign taxes by $50 and increase its pool of earnings and profits by 50u.

Example (2). Controlled foreign corporation (CFC) is a wholly-owned subsidiary of its domestic parent, P. Both CFC and P are calendar year taxpayers. In year 1 CFC earned 400u of general limitation manufacturing income and 200u of shipping income. On date 1, CFC paid 200u of foreign tax, 100u with respect to general limitation manufacturing income, and 100u with respect to shipping income. On date 1, the exchange rate is $1:1u. On date 2, a date that is after the filing of P's United States tax return, CFC receives a refund of 75u, 25u of which is related to the manufacturing income and 50u of which is related to the shipping income. Subject to paragraph (d)(4), CFC shall reduce its pools of foreign taxes related to general limitation income and shipping income by $25 and $50, respectively (because the refund is translated at the rate of exchange prevailing on the date of payment of the foreign tax), and increase the respective pools of earnings and profits by 25u and 50u (because the earnings and profits are increased by the functional currency amount of the refund received). If the refund to CFC was not specifically related to any separate category of income, CFC, pursuant to § 1.904-6, is required to allocate that refund in accordance with the provisions of that section.

Example (3). CFC1 is a foreign corporation that is wholly-owned by P, a domestic corporation. CFC2 is a foreign corporation that is wholly-owned by CFC1. Unless stated otherwise, the exchange rate is always $1:1u. In year 1, CFC2 has earnings and profits of 100u (net of foreign taxes) and paid 100u in foreign taxes with respect to those earnings. CFC2 has no income and pays no foreign taxes in years 2 and 3. CFC1 has no earnings and profits other than those resulting from distributions from CFC2 and pays no foreign taxes.

Situation (i). In year 2, CFC2 receives a refund of foreign taxes of 25u. In year 3, CFC2 makes a distribution to CFC1 of 50u. CFC1 is deemed to have paid $30 of foreign taxes with respect to that distribution (50u/125u × $75). At the end of year 3, the following reflects the pools of earnings and profits and foreign taxes of CFC1 and CFC2.

CFC2	Earnings and Profits(u)			Foreign Taxes		
Y1	100			$100		
Y2	100 + 25	=	125	$100 − <$25>	=	$75
Y3	125 − <50>	=	75	$ 75 − <$30>	=	$45

CFC1	Earnings and Profits(u)	Foreign Taxes
Y3	50	30

Situation (ii). The facts are the same as situation (i), except that CFC2 makes a distribution of 50u in year 2 and receives a refund of 75u in year 3. In year 2 the amount of foreign taxes deemed paid by CFC1 would be $50 (50u/100u × $100). Both CFC1 and CFC2 must adjust their pools of foreign taxes in year 3 because the year 3 refund would have the effect of reducing below zero CFC2's pool of foreign taxes. CFC1 reduces its pool of foreign taxes by $42.86 determined as follows: $50 (foreign taxes deemed paid on the distribution from CFC2) - $7.14 (the foreign taxes that would have been deemed paid had the refund occurred prior to the distribution (50u/175u × $25)). CFC2 reduces its pool of foreign taxes by $32.14 (the difference between the dollar value of 75u refund determined as of the date of payment of the foreign tax and the $42.86 adjustment to CFC1's pool of foreign taxes). At the and of year 3, the following reflects the pools of foreign taxes and earnings and profits for CFC1 and CFC2.

Reg. § 1.905-3T(d)(3)

Income from Sources Without the United States

See p. 20,601 for regulations not amended to reflect law changes

CFC2	Earnings and Profits (u)			Foreign Taxes		
Y1	100			$100		
Y2	100 −	<50>	= 50	$100 −	<$50>	= $50
Y3	50 +	75	= 125	$ 50 −	<$32.14>	= $17.86

CFC1	Earnings and Profits (u)	Foreign Taxes		
Y2	50	$50		
Y3	50	$ 50 −	<$42.86>	= $ 7.14

(4) *Exceptions.* The provisions of paragraph (d)(2) of this section shall not apply and a redetermination of United States tax liability is required to account for the effect of a redetermination of foreign tax on foreign taxes deemed paid by a United States corporation under section 902 or section 960 to the extent provided in this paragraph (d)(4).

(i) *Hyperinflationary currencies.* A redetermination of United States tax liability is required if the foreign tax liability is in a hyperinflationary currency. The term "hyperinflationary currency" means the currency of a country in which there is cumulative inflation during the base period of at least 100% as determined by reference to the consumer price index of the country listed in the monthly issues of International Financial Statistics, or a successor publication, of the International Monetary Fund. "Base period" means, with respect to any taxable year, the thirty-six calendar months immediately preceding the last day of such taxable year (see § 1.985-2T(b)(2)).

(ii) *Foreign tax adjustment of two percent or more.* If the foreign tax liability of a United States taxpayer is in a currency other than a hyperinflationary currency and the amount of foreign tax accrued for the taxable year to a foreign country, as measured in units of foreign currency, exceeds the amount of foreign tax paid to that foreign country for the taxable year (as measured in units of foreign currency) by at least two percent, then the Service, in its discretion, may require a redetermination of United States tax liability.

(iii) *Example.* The provisions of paragraph (d)(4)(ii) are illustrated by the following example.

Example. Controlled foreign corporation is a wholly-owned subsidiary of its domestic parent, P. Both CFC and P are calendar year taxpayers. In year 1, CFC has general limitation income of 200u and, by year-end, had accrued foreign taxes with respect to that income of 100u when the exchange rate is $1:1u. In year 1, CFC makes a distribution to P of 50u, half of its earnings and profits of 100u. P is deemed to have paid $50 of foreign tax with respect to that distribution (50u/100u × $100). In year 2, after P has filed its United States tax return, CFC pays its actual foreign tax liability of 98.50 when the exchange rate is $1:1u. Subject to paragraph (d)(4), CFC must reduce its pool of foreign taxes by $1.50 and increase the corresponding pool of earnings and profits by 1.50u. (The refund is translated into dollars at the rate of exchange prevailing on the date of payment of the foreign tax, and the adjustment to earnings and profits is in "u"s.) In year 2, CFC earns 200u of general limitation income and accrues 120u of tax when the exchange rate is $1:1u. In year 2, CFC distributes 100u to P. P is deemed to have paid $128 of foreign tax (($48.50 + $120) × 100u/(51.50u + 80u)). In year 3, after P filed its year 2 United States tax return, CFC pays its actual year 2 tax liability of 100u when the exchange rate is $1:1u. The Service may require P to recompute its year 2 United States tax liability to account for the effect of the overaccrual of foreign tax pursuant to § 1.905-3T(d)(4)(ii).

(iv) *Deficit in foreign tax pool.* A redetermination of United States tax liability is required if a foreign tax redetermination occurs with respect to foreign taxes deemed paid with respect to a Subpart F inclusion or an actual distribution which has the effect of reducing below zero the distributing foreign corporation's pool of foreign taxes in any separate category. Whether a foreign corporation's pool of foreign taxes is reduced below zero shall be determined at the close of the taxable year of the foreign corporation in which the foreign tax redetermination occurred. In no case shall taxes paid or accrued with respect to one separate category be applied to offset a negative balance in any other separate category.

(v) *Example.* The provisions of paragraph (d)(4)(iv) are illustrated by the following example.

Example. Controlled foreign corporation (CFC) is a wholly-owned subsidiary of P, a domestic corporation. Both P and CFC are calendar year taxpayers. In year 1, CFC has 200u of general limitation income with respect to which 100 of taxes are paid when the exchange rate was $1:1u. In year 1, CFC distributes half (50u) of its earnings and profits (100u). Under section 902, P is deemed to have paid $50 of the foreign taxes paid by CFC with respect to that distribution (50u/100u × $100). In year 2, CFC receives a refund of all of its year 1 taxes (100u). In year 2, CFC earns an additional 290u of income—200u of shipping income with respect to which 100u of taxes are paid, and 90u of general limitation in-

Reg. § 1.905-3T(d)(4)

Income from Sources Without the United States

See p. 20,601 for regulations not amended to reflect law changes

come with respect to which 45u of taxes are paid when the exchange rate was $1:1u. P is required to redetermine its year 1 United States tax liability to account for the foreign tax redetermination occurring in year 2 because, if an adjustment to CFC's pool of general limitation taxes were made, the pool would be <$5>. CFC is not permitted to carry a deficit in any pool of foreign taxes; therefore, P must redetermine its United States liability for year 1.

(e) *Foreign tax imposed on foreign refund.* If the redetermination of foreign tax for a taxable year or years is occasioned by the refund to the taxpayer of taxes paid to a foreign country or possession of the United States and the foreign country or possession imposed tax on the refund, then the amount of the refund shall be considered to be reduced by the amount of any tax described in section 901 imposed by the foreign country or possession of the United States with respect to such refund. In such case, no other credit under section 901, and no deduction under section 164, shall be allowed for any taxable year with respect to such tax imposed on such refund.

(f) *Reduction of corporate level tax on distribution of earnings and profits.* If a United States shareholder of a controlled foreign corporation receives a distribution out of previously taxed earnings and profits and a foreign country has imposed tax on the income of the controlled foreign corporation, which tax is reduced on distribution of the earnings and profits of the corporation, then the United States shareholder shall redetermine its United States tax liability for the year or years affected. [Temporary Reg. § 1.905-3T.]

☐ [T.D. 8210, 6-22-88.]

[Reg. § 1.905-4T]

§ 1.905-4T. Notification and redetermination of United States tax liability (Temporary).—(a) *Application of this section.* The rules of this section shall apply if, as a result of a foreign tax redetermination as defined in § 1.905-3T(c), a redetermination of United States tax liability is required under § 1.905-3T.

(b) *Notification*—(1) *General rules.* Any United States taxpayer for which a redetermination of United States tax liability is required shall notify the Secretary in the manner described in this paragraph (b), and the Service will redetermine the United States tax liability of the United States taxpayer. Notification shall be made by filing Form 1120X or 1040X, and Form 1118 or 1116, in the manner described in the instructions to Form 1118 with the Service Center where the taxpayer filed the tax return claiming the foreign tax credit to which the notice relates. Notification shall be filed within the time prescribed by and shall contain the information required by this paragraph (b). The amount of tax, if any, due upon a redetermination shall be paid by the taxpayer after notice and demand has been made by the Service. Subchapter B of chapter 63 of the Code (relating to deficiency procedures) shall not apply with respect to the assessment of the amount due upon such redetermination. In accordance with section 905(c) and section 6501(c)(5), the amount of additional tax due shall be assessed and collected without regard to the provisions of section 6401(a) (relating to limitations on assessment and collection). The amount of tax, if any, shown by a redetermination to have bean overpaid shall be credited or refunded to the taxpayer in accordance with the provisions of § 301.6511(d)-3.

(2) *Time for filing.* If a redetermination of United States tax liability is necessitated by a foreign tax redetermination that reduced the amount of foreign taxes paid or deemed paid, then the United States taxpayer shall file the notification with respect to such foreign tax redetermination within 180 days after the date that the foreign tax redetermination occurs. If a redetermination of United States liability is necessitated by a foreign tax redetermination that increased the amount of foreign taxes paid or deemed paid, then the United States taxpayer claiming foreign tax credits for accrued foreign taxes must notify the Service within the period provided by section 6511(d)(3)(A). Filing of the appropriate notification within the prescribed time shall constitute a claim for refund of United States tax.

(3) *Notification contents*—(i) *In general.* The taxpayer shall provide the Service with information sufficient to redetermine the tax including, but not limited to, the following: the United States taxpayer's name, address, and identifying number; the taxable year or years of the taxpayer that are affected by the redetermination of United States tax liability; information required in paragraph (b)(ii) and (iii) below with respect to foreign tax redeterminations affecting the redetermination of United States tax liability, including information in a form that will enable the Service to verify and compare the original computations with respect to a claimed foreign tax credit, the revised computations resulting from the foreign tax redeterminations, and the net changes resulting therefrom.

(ii) *Direct foreign tax credit.* In the case of foreign taxes paid by or on behalf of the taxpayer, if—

(A) The taxpayer receives a refund of foreign tax, the taxpayer's information shall in-

Reg. § 1.905-4T(b)(3)

clude: the amount of foreign taxes paid in foreign currency; the date or dates the foreign taxes were paid; the rate of exchange on each date the foreign taxes were paid; the amount of the foreign taxes refunded in foreign currency;

(B) The foreign taxes when paid differ from the accrued amounts claimed as credits by the taxpayer because of fluctuation in the value of the foreign currency in which the foreign taxes were paid, the taxpayer's information shall include the following: the date on which foreign taxes were accrued and the dates on which the foreign taxes were paid; the rates of exchange for each such date; and the amount of foreign taxes accrued or paid in foreign currency on each such date;

(C) The foreign taxes when paid differ from accrued amounts claimed as credits by the taxpayer because the taxpayer is assessed additional or less foreign tax. The taxpayer's information shall include the following: the original amounts and information described in subdivision (B) of this paragraph (b)(3)(ii); the amount of additional or reduced foreign tax in foreign currency; and the revised amounts and information described in subdivision (B) of this paragraph (b)(3)(ii).

(iii) *Foreign taxes deemed paid.* In the case of foreign taxes paid or accrued by a foreign corporation that are deemed paid or accrued under section 902 or section 960 and with respect to which the taxpayer is required to redetermine its United States tax liability, the United States taxpayer's information shall include the following: the foreign corporation's name and identifying number (if any); the dates and amounts of any dividend distributions or other inclusions made out of earnings and profits for the affected year or years; and the amount of earnings and profits from which such dividends were paid for the affected year or years; and information described in paragraph (b)(3)(ii) as applied to the foreign corporation. In the case of a failure to attach the required notification or to make the required adjustments described in § 1.905-3T(d)(2)(iii), the taxpayer's information shall also include a complete factual description justifying that failure.

(c) *Interest and penalty*—(1) *General rules.* If a foreign tax redetermination results in a redetermination of United States tax liability, then interest shall be computed on the deficiency or overpayment in accordance with sections 6601 and 6611 and the regulations thereunder. No interest shall be assessed or collected on any deficiency resulting from a refund of foreign tax for any period before the receipt of the refund, except to the extent interest was paid by the foreign country or possession of the United States on the refund for the period. In no case, however, shall interest assessed and collected pursuant to the preceding sentence for any period before receipt of the refund exceed the amount that otherwise would have been assessed and collected under section 6601 and the regulations thereunder for that period. Interest shall be assessed from the time the taxpayer (or the foreign corporation of which the taxpayer is a shareholder) receives a refund until the taxpayer pays the additional tax due the United States.

(2) *No interest on adjustments to pools of foreign taxes.* A deficiency or overpayment of United States tax liability does not result from a redetermination of foreign tax unless a redetermination of United States liability is required. Consequently, no interest will be paid by or to a United States corporation as a result of adjustments by a foreign corporation to its pools of foreign taxes and earnings and profits under paragraph (d)(2) of § 1.905-3T.

(3) *Imposition of penalty.* Failure to comply with the provisions of this section shall subject the taxpayer to the penalty provisions of section 6689 and the regulations thereunder.

(d) *Effective date.* The provisions of this section apply to foreign tax redeterminations described in § 1.905-3T(a). Notwithstanding paragraph (b)(2) of this section (relating to time for filing the required notice), the taxpayer shall have 180 days after the publication of an Announcement in the Internal Revenue Bulletin notifying taxpayers of the availability of the Forms and instructions to comply with the provisions of this section. In no case, however, shall this paragraph (d) operate to extend the statute of limitations provided by section 6511(d)(3)(A). [Temporary Reg. § 1.905-4T.]

☐ [T.D. 8210, 6-22-88.]

[Reg. § 1.905-5T]

§ 1.905-5T. **Foreign tax redeterminations and currency translation rules for foreign tax redeterminations occurring in taxable years beginning prior to January 1, 1987 (Temporary).**—(a) *In general.* This section sets forth rules governing the application of section 905(c) to foreign tax redeterminations occurring prior to January 1, 1987. However, the rules of this section also apply to foreign tax redeterminations occurring after December 31, 1986 with respect to foreign tax deemed paid under section 902 or section 960 with respect to earnings and profits accumulated in taxable years of a foreign corporation beginning prior to January 1, 1987.

Income from Sources Without the United States

See p. 20,601 for regulations not amended to reflect law changes

(b) *Currency translation rules*—(1) *Foreign taxes paid by the taxpayer and certain foreign taxes deemed paid.* Foreign taxes paid in foreign currency that are paid by or on behalf of a taxpayer or deemed paid under section 960 (or under section 902 in a deemed distribution under section 1248) shall be translated into dollars at the rate of exchange for the date of the payment of the foreign tax. Refunds of such taxes shall be translated into dollars at the rate of exchange for the date of the refund.

(2) *Foreign taxes deemed paid on an actual distribution.* Foreign taxes deemed paid by a taxpayer under section 902 with respect to an actual distribution and refunds of such taxes shall be translated into dollars at the rate of exchange for the date of the distribution of the earnings to which the taxes relate.

(c) *Foreign tax redetermination.* The term "foreign tax redetermination" means a foreign tax redetermination as defined in § 1.905-3T(c).

(d) *Redetermination of United States tax liability*—(1) *In general.* A redetermination of United States tax liability is required with respect to any foreign tax redetermination subject to this section and shall be subject to the requirements of § 1.905-4T(b). The content of the notification required by this paragraph (d) shall be the same as provided in § 1.905-4T(b)(3), except as modified by paragraphs (d)(2), (3), and (4) of this section.

(2) *Refunds.* In the case of any refund of foreign tax, the rate of exchange on the date of the refund shall be included in the information required by § 1.905-4T(b)(3)(ii)(A).

(3) *Foreign taxes deemed paid under section 902.* In the case of foreign taxes paid or accrued by a foreign corporation that are deemed paid or accrued under section 902 with respect to an actual distribution and with respect to which there was a redetermination of foreign tax, the United States taxpayer's information shall include, in lieu of the information required by paragraph (b)(3)(iii), the following: the foreign corporation's name and identifying number (if any); the date on which the foreign taxes were accrued and the dates on which the foreign taxes were paid; the amounts of the foreign taxes accrued or paid in foreign currency on each such date; the dates on which any foreign taxes were refunded and the amounts thereof; the dates and amounts of any dividend distributions made out of earnings and profits for the affected year or years; the rate of exchange on the date of any such distribution; and the amount of earnings and profits from which such dividends were paid for the affected year or years.

(4) *Foreign taxes deemed paid under section 960.* In the case of foreign taxes paid under section 960 (or under section 902 in the case of an amount treated as a dividend under section 1248), the rate of exchange determined under § 1.964-1 for translating accrued foreign taxes shall be included in the information required by § 1.905-4T(b)(3)(iii) in lieu of the exchange rate for the date of the accrual.

(e) *Exception for de minimis currency fluctuations.* A United States taxpayer need not notify the Service of a foreign tax redetermination that results solely from a currency fluctuation if the amount of such redetermination with respect to the foreign country is less than the lesser of ten thousand dollars or two percent of the total dollar amount of the foreign tax, prior to the adjustment, initially accrued with respect to that foreign country for the taxable year.

(f) *Special effective date.* If a foreign tax redetermination within the meaning of this section occurs after December 31, 1979, and before July 25, 1988, and the taxpayer has not notified the Service before that date of the redetermination as required under § 1.905-3 as it appeared in the CFR dated April 1, 1988, then the taxpayer shall have 180 days after the publication of an Announcement in the Internal Revenue Bulletin notifying taxpayers of the availability of the Forms and instructions to comply with the provisions of this section. Failure to comply with the provisions of this section shall subject the taxpayer to the penalty provisions of section 6689 and the regulations thereunder. In no case, however, shall this paragraph operate to extend the statute of limitations provided by section 6511(d)(3)(A). [Temporary Reg. § 1.905-5T.]

☐ [T.D. 8210, 6-22-88.]

[Reg. § 1.907-0]

§ 1.907-0. **Outline of regulation provisions for section 907.**—This section lists the paragraphs contained in §§ 1.907(a)-0 through 1.907(f)-1.

§ 1.907(a)-0. Introduction (for taxable years beginning after December 31, 1982).

(a) Effective dates.

(b) Key terms.

(c) FOGEI tax limitation.

(d) Reduction of creditable FORI taxes.

(e) FOGEI and FORI.

(f) Posted prices.

(g) Transitional rules.

(h) Section 907(f) carrybacks and carryovers.

(i) Statutes covered.

48,984 Income from Sources Without the United States

See p. 20,601 for regulations not amended to reflect law changes

§ 1.907(a)-1. Reduction in taxes paid on FOGEI (for taxable years beginning after December 31, 1982).
  (a) Amount of reduction.
  (b) Foreign taxes paid or accrued.
    (1) Foreign taxes.
    (2) Foreign taxes paid or accrued.
  (c) Limitation level.
    (1) In general.
    (2) Limitation percentage for corporations.
    (3) Limitation percentage for individuals.
    (4) Losses.
    (5) Priority.
  (d) Illustrations.
  (e) Effect on other provisions.
    (1) Deduction denied.
    (2) Reduction inapplicable.
    (3) Section 78 dividend.
  (f) Section 904 limitation.

§ 1.907(b)-1. Reduction of creditable FORI taxes (for taxable years beginning after December 31, 1982).

§ 1.907(c)-1. Definitions relating to FOGEI and FORI (for taxable years beginning after December 31, 1982).
  (a) Scope.
  (b) FOGEI.
    (1) General rule.
    (2) Amount.
    (3) Other circumstances.
    (4) Income directly related to extraction.
    (5) Income not included.
    (6) Fair market value.
    (7) Economic interest.
  (c) Carryover of foreign oil extraction losses.
    (1) In general.
    (2) Reduction.
    (3) Foreign oil extraction loss defined.
    (4) Affiliated groups.
    (5) FOGEI taxes.
    (6) Examples.
  (d) FORI.
    (1) In general.
    (2) Transportation.
    (3) Distribution or sale.
    (4) Processing.
    (5) Primary product from oil.
    (6) Primary product from gas.
    (7) Directly related income.

  (e) Assets used in a trade or business.
    (1) In general.
    (2) Section 907(c) activities.
    (3) Stock.
    (4) Losses on sale of stock.
    (5) Character of gain or loss.
    (6) Allocation of amount realized.
    (7) Interest.
  (f) Terms and items common to FORI and FOGEI.
    (1) Minerals.
    (2) Taxable income.
    (3) Interest on working capital.
    (4) Exchange gain or loss.
    (5) Allocation.
    (6) Facts and circumstances.
  (g) Directly related income.
    (1) In general.
    (2) Directly related services.
    (3) Leases and licenses.
    (4) Related person.
    (5) Gross income.
  (h) Coordination with other provisions.
    (1) Certain adjustments.
    (2) Section 901(f).

§ 1.907(c)-2. Section 907(c)(3) items (for taxable years beginning after December 31, 1982).
  (a) Scope.
  (b) Dividend.
    (1) Section 1248.
    (2) Section 78 dividend.
  (c) Taxes deemed paid.
    (1) Voting stock test.
    (2) Dividends and interest.
    (3) Amounts included under section 951(a).
  (d) Amount attributable to certain items.
    (1) Certain dividends.
    (2) Interest received from certain foreign corporations.
    (3) Dividends from domestic corporation.
    (4) Amounts with respect to which taxes are deemed paid under section 960(a).
    (5) Section 78 dividend.
    (6) Special rule.
    (7) Deficits.
    (8) Illustrations.
  (e) Dividends, interest, and other amounts from sources within a possession.
  (f) Income from partnerships, trusts, etc.

Reg. § 1.907-0

Income from Sources Without the United States

§ 1.907(c)-3. FOGEI and FORI taxes (for taxable years beginning after December 31, 1982).

(a) Tax characterization, allocation and apportionment.

(1) Scope.

(2) Three classes of income.

(3) More than one class in a foreign tax base.

(4) Allocation of tax within a base.

(5) Modified gross income.

(6) Allocation of tax credits.

(7) Withholding taxes.

(b) Dividends.

(1) In general.

(2) Section 78 dividend.

(c) Includable amounts under section 951(a).

(d) Partnerships.

(e) Illustrations.

§ 1.907(d)-1. Disregard of posted prices for purposes of chapter 1 of the Code (for taxable years beginning after December 31, 1982).

(a) In general.

(1) Scope.

(2) Initial computation requirement.

(3) Burden of proof.

(4) Related parties.

(b) Adjustments.

(c) Definitions.

(1) Foreign government.

(2) Minerals.

(3) Posted price.

(4) Other pricing arrangement.

(5) Fair market value.

§ 1.907(f)-1. Carryback and carryover of credits disallowed by section 907(a) (for amounts carried between taxable years that each begin after December 31, 1982).

(a) In general.

(b) Unused FOGEI.

(1) In general.

(2) Year of origin.

(c) Tax deemed paid or accrued.

(d) Excess extraction limitation.

(e) Excess general section 904 limitation.

(f) Section 907(f) priority.

(g) Cross-reference.

(h) Example.

[Reg. § 1.907-0.]

☐ [T.D. 8240, 1-19-89. Amended by T.D. 8338, 3-14-91 and T.D. 8655, 1-5-96.]

[Reg. § 1.907(a)-0]

§ 1.907(a)-0. Introduction (for taxable years beginning after December 31, 1982).—(a) *Effective dates.* The provisions of §§ 1.907(a)-0 through § 1.907(f)-1 apply to taxable years beginning after December 31, 1982. For provisions that apply to taxable years beginning before January 1, 1983, see §§ 1.907(a)-0A through 1.907(f)-1A.

(b) *Key terms.* For purposes of the regulations under section 907 —

(1) "FOGEI" means foreign oil and gas extraction income.

(2) "FORI" means foreign oil related income.

(3) "FOGEI taxes" mean foreign oil and gas extraction taxes as defined in section 907(c)(5).

(4) "FORI taxes" mean foreign taxes on foreign oil related income. See § 1.907(c)-3.

(c) *FOGEI tax limitation.* Section 907(a) limits the foreign tax credit for taxes paid or accrued on FOGEI. See § 1.907(a)-1.

(d) *Reduction of creditable FORI taxes.* Section 907(b) recharacterizes FORI taxes as non-creditable deductible expenses to the extent that the foreign law imposing the FORI taxes is structured, or in fact operates, so that the amount of tax imposed with respect to FORI will be materially greater, over a reasonable period of time, than the amount generally imposed on income that is neither FOGEI nor FORI. See § 1.907(b)-1.

(e) *FOGEI and FORI.* FOGEI includes the taxable income from the extraction of minerals from oil or gas wells by a taxpayer (or another person) and from the sale or exchange of assets used in the extraction business. FORI includes taxable income from the activities of processing oil and gas into their primary products, transporting or distributing oil and gas and their primary products, and from the disposition of assets used in these activities. For this purpose, a disposition includes only a sale or exchange. FOGEI and FORI may also include taxable income from the performance of related services or from the lease of related property and certain dividends, interest, or amounts described in section 951(a). See §§ 1.907(c)-1 through 1.907(c)-3.

(f) *Posted prices.* Certain sales prices are disregarded when computing FOGEI for purposes of chapter 1 of the Code. See § 1.907(d)-1.

(g) *Transitional rules.* Section 907(e) provides rules for the carryover of unused FOGEI taxes from taxable years beginning before January 1, 1983, and carryback of FOGEI taxes arising in taxable years beginning after December 31, 1982. See § 1.907(e)-1.

Reg. § 1.907(a)-0(g)

(h) *Section 907(f) carrybacks and carryovers.* FOGEI taxes disallowed under section 907(a) may be carried back or forward to other taxable years. These FOGEI taxes may be absorbed in another taxable year to the extent of the lesser of the separate excess extraction limitation or the excess limitation in the general limitation category (section 904 (d)(1)(I)) for the carryback or carryover year. See § 1.907(f)-1.

(i) *Statutes covered.* The regulations under section 907 are issued as a result of the enactment of section 601 of the Tax Reduction Act of 1975, of section 1035 of the Tax Reform Act of 1976, of section 301(b)(14) of the Revenue Act of 1978, of section 211 of the Tax Equity and Fiscal Responsibility Act of 1982 and of section 1012(g)(6)(A)-(B) of the Technical and Miscellaneous Revenue Act of 1988. [Reg. § 1.907(a)-0.]

☐ [T.D. 8338, 3-14-91.]

[Reg. § 1.907(a)-1]

§ 1.907(a)-1. **Reduction in taxes paid on FOGEI (for taxable years beginning after December 31, 1982).**—(a) *Amount of reduction.* FOGEI taxes are reduced by the amount by which they exceed a limitation level (as defined in paragraph (c) of this section).

(b) *Foreign taxes paid or accrued.* For purposes of the regulations under section 907—

(1) *Foreign taxes.* The term "foreign taxes" means income, war profits, or excess profits taxes of foreign countries or possessions of the United States otherwise creditable under section 901 (including those creditable by reason of section 903).

(2) *Foreign taxes paid or accrued.* The terms "foreign taxes paid or accrued," "FOGEI taxes paid or accrued," and "FORI taxes paid or accrued" include foreign taxes deemed paid under sections 902 and 960. Unless otherwise expressly provided, these terms do not include foreign taxes deemed paid by reason of sections 904(c) and 907(f).

(c) *Limitation level*—(1) *In general.* The limitation level is FOGEI for the taxable year multiplied by the limitation percentage for that year.

(2) *Limitation percentage for corporations.* A corporation's limitation percentage is the highest rate of tax specified in section 11(b) for the particular year.

(3) *Limitation percentage for individuals.* Section 907(a)(2)(B) provides that the limitation percentage for individual taxpayers is the effective rate of tax for those taxpayers. The effective rate of tax is computed by dividing the entire tax, before the credit under section 901(a) is taken, by the taxpayer's entire taxable income.

(4) *Losses.* (i) For purposes of determining whether income is FOGEI, a taxpayer's FOGEI will be recharacterized as foreign source non-FOGEI to the extent that FOGEI losses for preceding taxable years beginning after December 31, 1982, exceed the amount of FOGEI already recharacterized. See § 1.907(c)-1(c). However, taxes that were paid or accrued on the recharacterized FOGEI will remain FOGEI taxes.

(ii) Taxes paid or accrued by a person to a foreign country may be FOGEI taxes even though that person has under U.S. law a net operating loss from sources within that country.

(iii) For purposes of determining whether income is FOGEI, a taxpayer's income will be treated as income from sources outside the United States even though all or a portion of that income may be resourced as income from sources within the United States under section 904(f)(1) and (4).

(5) *Priority.* (i) Section 907(a) applies before section 908, relating to reduction of credit for participation in or cooperation with an international boycott.

(ii) Section 901(f) (relating to certain payments with respect to oil and gas not considered as taxes) applies before section 907.

(d) *Illustrations.* Paragraphs (a) through (c) of this section are illustrated by the following examples.

Example 1. M, a U.S. corporation, uses the accrual method of accounting and the calendar year as its taxable year. For 1984, M has $20,000 of FOGEI, derived from operations in foreign countries X and Y, and has accrued $11,500 of foreign taxes with respect to FOGEI. The highest tax rate specified in section 11(b) for M's 1984 taxable year is 46 percent. Pursuant to section 907(a), M's FOGEI taxes limitation level for 1984 is $9,200 (46% × $20,000). The foreign taxes in excess of this limitation level ($2,300) may be carried back or forward. See section 907(f) and § 1.907(f)-1 and section 907(e) and § 1.907(e)-1.

Example 2. The facts are the same as in *Example 1* except that M is a partnership owned equally by U.S. citizens A and B who each file as unmarried individuals and do not itemize deductions. Pursuant to section 905(a), A and B have elected to credit foreign taxes in the year accrued. The total amount of foreign taxes accrued by A and B with respect to their distributive shares of M's FOGEI is $11,500 ($5,750 accrued by A and $5,750 accrued by B). A and B have no other FOGEI. A's only taxable income for 1984 is his 50% distributive share ($10,000) of M's FOGEI and A has a preliminary U.S. tax liability of $1,079. B has $112,130 of taxable income for 1984 (including his 50% distributive share ($10,000) of

M's FOGEI) and has a preliminary U.S. tax liability of $44,000. Pursuant to section 907(a), A's FOGEI taxes limitation level for 1984 is $1,079 (($1,079/$10,000) × $10,000)) and B's FOGEI taxes limitation level for 1984 is $3,924 (($44,000/$112,130) × $10,000)).

(e) *Effect on other provisions*—(1) *Deduction denied.* If a credit is claimed under section 901, no deduction under section 164(a)(3) is allowed for the amount of the FOGEI taxes that exceed a taxpayer's limitation level for the taxable year. See section 275(a)(4)(A). Thus, FOGEI taxes disallowed under section 907(a) are not added to the cost or inventory amount of oil or gas.

(2) *Reduction inapplicable.* The reduction under section 907(a) does not apply to a taxpayer that deducts foreign taxes and does not claim the benefits of section 901 for a taxable year.

(3) *Section 78 dividend.* The reduction under section 907(a) has no effect on the amount of foreign taxes that are treated as dividends under section 78.

(f) *Section 904 limitation.* FOGEI taxes as reduced under section 907(a) are creditable only to the extent permitted by the general limitation of section 904(d)(1)(I). [Reg. § 1.907(a)-1.]

☐ [T.D. 8338, 3-14-91.]

[Reg. § 1.907(b)-1]

§ 1.907(b)-1. Reduction of creditable FORI taxes (for taxable years beginning after December 31, 1982).—If the foreign law imposing a FORI tax (as defined in § 1.907(c)-3) is either structured in a manner, or operates in a manner, so that the amount of tax imposed on FORI is generally materially greater than the tax imposed by the foreign law on income that is neither FORI nor FOGEI ("described manner"), section 907(b) provides a special rule which limits the amount of FORI taxes paid or accrued by a person to a foreign country which will be considered income, war profits, or excess profits taxes. Section 907(b) will apply to a person regardless of whether that person is a dual capacity taxpayer as defined in § 1.901-2(a)(2)(ii)(A). (In general, a dual capacity taxpayer is a person who pays an amount to a foreign country part of which is attributable to an income tax and the remainder of which is a payment for a specific economic benefit derived from that country.) Foreign law imposing a tax on FORI will be considered either to be structured in or to operate in the described manner only if, under the facts and circumstances, there has been a shifting of tax by the foreign country from a tax on FOGEI to a tax on FORI. [Reg. § 1.907(b)-1.]

☐ [T.D. 8338, 3-14-91.]

[Reg. § 1.907(c)-1]

§ 1.907(c)-1. Definitions relating to FOGEI and FORI (for taxable years beginning after December 31, 1982).—(a) *Scope.* This section explains the meaning to be given certain terms and items in section 907(c)(1), (2), and (4). See also §§ 1.907(a)-0(b) and 1.907(c)-2 for further definitions.

(b) FOGEI—(1) *General rule.* Under section 907(c)(1), FOGEI means taxable income (or loss) derived from sources outside the United States and its possessions from the extraction (by the taxpayer or any other person) of minerals from oil or gas wells located outside the United States and its possessions or from the sale or exchange of assets used by the taxpayer in the trade or business of extracting those minerals. Extraction of minerals from oil or gas wells will result in gross income from extraction in every case in which that person has an economic interest in the minerals in place. For other circumstances in which gross income from extraction may arise, see paragraph (b)(3) of this section. For determination of the amount of gross income from extraction, see paragraph (b)(2) of this section. For definition of the phrase "assets used by the taxpayer in the trade or business" and for rules relating to that type of FOGEI, see paragraph (e)(1) of this section. The term "minerals" is defined in paragraph (f)(1) of this section. For determination of taxable income, see paragraph (f)(2) of this section. FOGEI includes, in addition, items listed in section 907(c)(3) (relating to dividends, interest, partnership distributions, etc.) and explained in § 1.907(c)-2. For the reduction of what would otherwise be FOGEI by losses incurred in a prior year, see section 907(c)(4) and paragraph (c) of this section.

(2) *Amount.* The gross income from extraction is determined by reference to the fair market value of the minerals in the immediate vicinity of the well. Fair market value is determined under paragraph (b)(6) of this section.

(3) *Other circumstances.* Gross income from extraction or the sale or exchange of assets described in section 907(c)(1)(B) includes income from any arrangement, or a combination of arrangements or transactions, to the extent the income is in substance attributable to the extraction of minerals or such a sale or exchange. For instance, a person may have gross income from such a sale or exchange if the person purchased minerals from a foreign government at a discount and the discount reflects an arm's-length amount in consideration for the government's nationalization of assets that person owned and used in the extraction of minerals.

(4) *Income directly related to extraction.* Gross income from extraction includes directly related income under paragraph (g) of this section.

(5) *Income not included.* FOGEI as otherwise determined under this paragraph (b), nevertheless, does not include income to the extent attributable to marketing, distributing, processing or transporting minerals or primary products. Income from the purchase and sale of minerals is not ordinarily FOGEI. If the foreign taxes paid or accrued in connection with income from a purchase and sale are not creditable by reason of section 901(f), that income is not FOGEI. A taxpayer to whom section 901(f) applies is not a producer.

(6) *Fair market value.* For purposes of this paragraph (b), the fair market value of oil or gas in the immediate vicinity of the well depends on all of the facts and circumstances as they exist relative to a party in any particular case. The facts and circumstances that may be taken into account include, but are not limited to, the following—

(i) The facts and circumstances pertaining to an independent market value (if any) in the immediate vicinity of the well,

(ii) The facts and circumstances pertaining to the relationships between the taxpayer and the foreign government. If an independent fair market value in the immediate vicinity of the well cannot be determined but fair market value at the port, or a similar point, in the foreign country can be determined (port price), an analysis of the arrangements between the taxpayer and the foreign government that retains a share of production could be evidence of the appropriate, arm's-length difference between the port price and the field price, and

(iii) The other facts and circumstances pertaining to any difference in the producing country between the field and port prices.

(7) *Economic interest.* For purposes of this paragraph (b), the term "economic interest" means an economic interest as defined in § 1.611-1(b)(1), whether or not a deduction for depletion is allowable under section 611.

(c) *Carryover of foreign oil extraction losses—*(1) *In general.* Pursuant to section 907(c)(4), the determination of FOGEI for a particular taxable year takes into account a foreign oil extraction loss incurred in prior taxable years beginning after December 31, 1982. There is no time limitation on this carryover of foreign oil extraction losses. Section 907(c)(4) does not provide for any carryback of these losses. Section 907(c)(4) operates solely for purposes of determining FOGEI and thus operates independently of section 904(f).

(2) *Reduction.* That portion of the income of the taxpayer for the taxable year which but for this paragraph (c) would be treated as FOGEI is reduced (but not below zero) by the excess of—

(i) The aggregate amount of foreign oil extraction losses for preceding taxable years beginning after December 31, 1982, over

(ii) The aggregate amount of reductions under this paragraph (c) for preceding taxable years beginning after December 31, 1982.

(3) *Foreign oil extraction loss defined—*(i) *In general.* For purposes of this paragraph (c), the term "foreign oil extraction loss" means the amount by which the gross income for the taxable year that is taken into account in determining FOGEI for that year is exceeded by the sum of the deductions properly allocated and apportioned to that gross income (as determined under paragraph (f)(2) of this section). A person can have a foreign oil extraction loss for a taxable year even if the person has not chosen the benefits of section 901 for that year.

(ii) *Items not taken into account.* For purposes of paragraph (c)(3)(i) of this section, the following items are not taken into account—

(A) The net operating loss deduction allowable for the taxable year under section 172(a),

(B) Any foreign expropriation loss (as defined in section 172(h)) for the taxable year, and

(C) Any loss for the taxable year which arises from fire, storm, shipwreck, or other casualty, or from theft.

A loss mentioned in paragraph (c)(3)(ii)(B) or (C) of this section is taken into account, however, to the extent compensation (for instance by insurance) for the loss is included in gross income.

(4) *Affiliated groups.* The foreign oil extraction loss of an affiliated group of corporations (within the meaning of section 1504(a)) that files a consolidated return is determined on a group basis. If the group does not have a foreign oil extraction loss, the foreign oil extraction loss of a member of that group will not reduce on a separate basis that member's FOGEI for a later taxable year. For special rules affecting the foreign oil extraction loss in the case of certain related domestic corporations that are not members of the same affiliated group, see section 904(i).

(5) *FOGEI taxes.* If FOGEI is reduced pursuant to this paragraph (c) (and thereby recharacterized as non-FOGEI income), any foreign taxes imposed on the FOGEI that is

Reg. § 1.907(c)-1(b)(4)

recharacterized as other income retain their character as FOGEI taxes. See section 907(c)(5).

(6) *Examples.* The provisions of this paragraph (c) may be illustrated by the following examples.

Example 1—(i) *Facts.* X, a U.S. corporation using the accrual method of accounting and the calendar year as its taxable year, is engaged in extraction activities in three foreign countries. X has only the following combined foreign tax items for the three countries (prior to the application of this paragraph (c)) for 1983, 1984, and 1985:

	1983	1984	1985
FOGEI	$(700)	$100	$450
FOGEI taxes	10	60	200
Net operating loss deduction	(200)	0	0
Foreign oil extraction loss allowable after adjustment for paragraph (c)(3)(ii) amounts	(500)	0	0
General limitation taxes other than FOGEI taxes	30	90	230

(ii) *1983.* Because X's FOGEI for 1983 is a loss of $(700), X's section 907(a) limitation for 1983 is $0 (.46 × $0). Thus, none of the FOGEI taxes paid or accrued in 1983 ($10) can be credited in 1983. They can, however, be carried back to 1981 or 1982 pursuant to the provisions of section 907(e)(2) and § 1.907(e)-1 and carried forward pursuant to the provisions of section 907(f) and § 1.907(f)-1.

(iii) *1984.* X's FOGEI for 1984, prior to the application of this paragraph (c), is $100. X has a foreign oil extraction loss for 1983 of $(500). This loss must be applied against X's preliminary FOGEI of $100 for 1984. Thus, X's FOGEI for 1984 is $0 and X has $(400) ($500-$100) of foreign oil extraction loss from 1983 to be carried to 1985. Since X's FOGEI for 1984 is $0, its section 907(a) limitation is $0 (.46 × $0). Therefore, none of the FOGEI taxes paid or accrued in 1984 ($60) can be credited in 1984. They can, however, be carried back pursuant to the provisions of section 907(e)(2) and § 1.907(e)-1 and carried forward pursuant to the provisions of section 907(f) and § 1.907(f)-1.

(iv) *1985.* X's FOGEI for 1985, prior to the application of this paragraph (c), is $450. X's remaining foreign oil extraction loss carryover from 1983 is $(400) and this must be applied against X's preliminary FOGEI of $450 for 1985. Thus, X's FOGEI for 1984 is $50 ($450 − $400). X's section 907(a) limitation is $23 (.46 × $50). Therefore, $23 of the FOGEI taxes paid or accrued in 1985, together with the other $230 of general limitation taxes, can be credited in 1985, subject to the general limitation of section 904(d)(1)(E) (as in effect prior to 1987). The excess of FOGEI taxes, $177 ($200 − $23), can be carried back pursuant to the provisions of section 907(e)(2) and § 1.907(e)-1 and carried forward pursuant to the provisions of section 907(f) and § 1.907(f)-1.

Example 2—(i) *Facts.* The facts are the same as in *Example 1* except that X's paragraph (c)(3)(ii) items for 1983 allocable to FOGEI are $(800) instead of $(200). FOGEI remains a loss of $(700). Thus, X does not have a foreign oil extraction loss for 1983 because it has $100 of FOGEI when its paragraph (c)(3)(ii) items are not taken into account ($(700) + $800).

(ii) *1983.* The results are the same as in *Example 1*.

(iii) *1984.* Although X had a FOGEI loss of $(700) in 1983, there is not a loss that can be carried forward after adjustment for paragraph (c)(3)(ii) items. Thus, X's FOGEI for 1984 is not reduced by the 1983 loss. X's section 907(a) limitation for 1984 is $46 (.46 × $100). Therefore, $46 of the FOGEI taxes paid or accrued in 1984, together with the other $90 of general limitation taxes, can be credited in 1984, subject to the general limitation of section 904(d)(1)(E) (as in effect prior to 1987). The excess of $14 ($60 − $46) can be carried back to 1982 pursuant to the provisions of section 907(e)(2) and § 1.907(e)-1 and carried forward pursuant to the provisions of section 907(f) and § 1.907(f)-1.

(iv) *1985.* Since there is no foreign oil extraction loss for either 1983 or 1984 to be applied in 1985, X's FOGEI for 1985 is $450. Thus, its section 907(a) limitation for 1985 is $207 (.46 × $450) and all of its FOGEI taxes paid or accrued in 1985 ($200), together with the other $230 of general limitation taxes, can be credited in 1985, subject to the general limitation of section 904(d)(1)(E)(as in effect prior to 1987). FOGEI taxes in the amount of $10 from 1983 and $14 from 1984 may be carried forward to 1985 if they have not been used in carryback years. However, because the excess section 907(a) limitation for 1985 is only $7, that is the maximum potential FOGEI taxes from 1983 or 1984 that may be used in 1985.

Example 3—(i) *Facts.* Y, a U.S. corporation using the accrual method of accounting and the calendar year as its taxable year, is engaged in extraction activities in three foreign countries. Y's only foreign taxable income is income subject to the general limitation of section 904(d)(1)(E) (as in effect prior to 1987). Y has no paragraph (c)(3)(ii) items. Y has the following foreign tax items for 1983 and 1984:

Reg. § 1.907(c)-1(c)(6)

Income from Sources Without the United States

See p. 20,601 for regulations not amended to reflect law changes

	1983	1984
FOGEI	$ (400)	$ 300
Other foreign taxable income	250	200
U.S. taxable income	1,000	1,100
Worldwide taxable income	850	1,600
FOGEI taxes	10	180
Other general limitation taxes	50	40
Foreign oil extraction loss	(400)	0

(ii) *1983*—(A) *Section 907(a) limitation.* Because Y's FOGEI for 1983 is a loss of $(400), Y's section 907(a) limitation for 1983 is $0. Thus, none of the FOGEI taxes paid or accrued in 1983 ($10) can be credited in 1983. They can, however, be carried back to 1981 or 1982 pursuant to the provisions of section 907(e)(2) and § 1.907(e)-1 and carried forward pursuant to the provisions of section 907(f) and § 1.907(f)-1.

(B) *Section 904(d) fraction.* Y has a foreign loss of $(150) ($(400) + $250) for 1983. Thus, its fraction for purposes of determining its general limitation of section 904(d)(1)(E) is $0/$850.

(iii) *1984*—(A) *Section 907(a) limitation.* Y's foreign oil extraction loss for 1983 is $(400). Applying this loss to its preliminary FOGEI for 1984 ($300) eliminates all of Y's FOGEI for 1984. Because Y's FOGEI for 1984 is $0, its section 907(a) limitation is also $0. Thus, none of the FOGEI taxes paid or accrued in 1984 ($180) can be credited in 1984. They can, however, be carried back to 1982 pursuant to the provisions of section 907(e)(2) and § 1.907(e)-1 and carried forward pursuant to the provisions of section 907(f) and § 1.907(f)-1. Y has a remaining foreign oil extraction loss of $(100) from 1983 to be carried to 1985.

(B) *Section 904(d) fraction.* Y's preliminary foreign taxable income for purposes of determining its general limitation of section 904(d)(1)(E) is $500 ($300 + $200). However, Y has an overall foreign loss from 1983 of $(150) ($(400) + $250) and thus, pursuant to section 904(f), Y must recharacterize $150 (lesser of $150 or 50% of $500) of its 1984 foreign taxable income as U.S. taxable income. Thus, Y's fraction for purposes of determining its general limitation of section 904(d)(1)(E) for 1984 is $350/$1,600.

Example 4—(i) *Facts.* Assume the same facts as in *Example 3* except that Y has the following foreign tax items:

	1983	1984	1985
FOGEI		$(100)	$ 225
Other foreign source taxable income subject to the general limitation of section 904(d)(1)(E)	$ (50)		
U.S. source taxable income	50		
Worldwide taxable income		(100)	225
FOGEI taxes		10	125
Foreign oil extraction loss		(100)	

(ii) *1983.* For 1983, Y has a section 904(d)(1)(E) overall foreign loss account of $50; see section 904(f) and § 1.904(f)-1(b).

(iii) *1984.* Because Y's FOGEI for 1984 is a loss of $(100), Y's section 907(a) limitation for 1984 is $0. Thus, none of the FOGEI taxes paid or accrued in 1984 ($10) can be credited in 1984. They can, however, be carried back under the provisions of section 907(e)(2) and § 1.907(e)-1 and carried forward under the provisions of section 907(f) and § 1.907(f)-1.

(iv) *1985.* Y's FOGEI loss of $(100) for 1984 is carried forward to 1985 and offsets FOGEI income in that amount in 1985. The entire section 904(d)(1)(E) overall foreign loss account of $50 is recaptured in 1985; therefore, Y has $75 of foreign source income and $50 of U.S. source income. However, Y has $125 of FOGEI since, for purposes of section 907(a), the $50 resourced by section 904(f) will be treated as income from sources outside the United States; see § 1.907(a)-1(c)(4)(iii). Accordingly, Y's section 907(a) limitation is $57.50 (.46 × $125). Y's section 904(d)(1)(E) limitation is, however, only $34.50 (.46 × $75). Thus, Y may claim a foreign tax credit of $34.50 in 1985. Y may carry back or carry forward $23 ($57.50 − $34.50) and that amount is not subject to the section 907(a) limitation in the carry to year. In addition, $67.50 ($125 − $57.50) may be carried back pursuant to the provisions of section 907(e)(2) and § 1.907(e)-1 and carried forward pursuant to the provisions of section 907(f) and § 1.907(f)-1. This amount is subject to the section 907(a) limitation in the carry to year.

(d) *FORI*—(1) *In general.* Section 907(c)(2) defines FORI to include taxable income from the processing of oil and gas into their primary products, from the transportation or distribution and sale of oil and gas and their primary products, from the disposition of assets used in these activities and from the performance of any other related service. FORI may also include, under section 907(c)(3), certain dividends, interest, or amounts described in section 951(a). This paragraph (d) defines certain terms and items applicable to FORI.

(2) *Transportation.* Gross income from transportation of minerals or primary products ("gross transportation income") is gross income arising from carrying minerals or primary products between two places (including time or voyage charter hires) by any means of transportation, such as a vessel, pipeline, truck, railroad, or aircraft. Ex-

Reg. § 1.907(c)-1(d)(1)

cept for directly related income under paragraphs (d)(7) and (g) of this section, gross transportation income does not include gross income received by a lessor from a bareboat charter hire of a means of transportation, certain other rental income, or income from the performance of certain services.

(3) *Distribution or sale.* The term "distribution or sale" means the sale or exchange of minerals or primary products to processors, users who purchase, store, or use in bulk quantities, other persons for further distribution, retailers, or consumers. Gross income from distribution or sale includes interest income attributable to the distribution of minerals or primary products on credit.

(4) *Processing.* The term "processing" means the destructive distillation, or a process similar in effect to destructive distillation, of crude oil and the processing of natural gas into their primary products including processes used to remove pollutants from crude oil or natural gas.

(5) *Primary product from oil.* The term "primary product" (in the case of oil) means all products derived from the processing of crude oil, including volatile products, light oils (such as motor fuel and kerosene), distillates (such as naphtha), lubricating oils, greases and waxes, and residues (such as fuel oil).

(6) *Primary product from gas.* The term "primary product" (in the case of gas) means all gas and associated hydrocarbon components from gas wells or oil wells, whether recovered at the lease or upon further processing, including natural gas, condensates, liquefiable petroleum gases (such as ethane, propane, and butane), and liquid products (such as natural gasoline).

(7) *Directly related income.* FORI also includes directly related income under paragraph (g) of this section.

(e) *Assets used in a trade or business*—(1) *In general.* The term "assets used by the taxpayer in the trade or business" in section 907(c)(1)(B) and (2)(D) means property primarily used in one or more of the trades or businesses that are section 907(c) activities. For purposes of this paragraph (e), assets used in a trade or business are assets described in section 1231(b) (applied without regard to any holding period or the character of the asset as being subject to the allowance for depreciation under section 167).

(2) *Section 907(c) activities.* Section 907(c) activities are those described in section 907(c)(1)(A) (for FOGEI) or (c)(2)(A) through (C) (for FORI). If an asset is used primarily in one or more section 907(c) activities, then the entire gain (or loss) will be considered attributable to those activities. For example, if a person uses a service station primarily to distribute primary products from oil, then all of the gain (or loss) on the sale of the station is FORI even though the person uses the station to distribute products that are not primary products (such as tires or batteries). If an asset is not primarily used in one or more section 907(c) activities, then the entire gain or loss will not be FOGEI or FORI.

(3) *Stock.* Stock of any corporation (whether foreign or domestic) will not be treated as an asset used by a person in section 907(c) activities.

(4) *Losses on sale of stock.* If, under § 1.861-8(e)(7), a loss on the sale, exchange, or disposition of stock is considered a deduction which is definitely related and allocable to FOGEI or FORI, then notwithstanding § 1.861-8(e)(7) and paragraph (f)(2) of this section, this loss shall be allocated and apportioned to the same class of income that would have been produced if there were capital gain from the sale, exchange or disposition.

(5) *Character of gain or loss.* Except in the case of stock, gain or loss from the sale, exchange or disposition of assets used in the trade or business may be FORI or FOGEI to the extent taken into account in computing taxable income for the taxable year, whether or not the gain or loss is ordinary income or ordinary loss.

(6) *Allocation of amount realized.* The amount realized from the sale, exchange or disposition of several assets in one transaction is allocated among them in proportion to their respective fair market values. This allocation is made under the principles set forth in § 1.1245-1(a)(5) (relating to allocation between section 1245 property and non-section 1245 property).

(7) *Interest.* Gross income from the sale, exchange or disposition of an asset used in a section 907(c) activity includes interest income from such a sale, exchange or disposition.

(f) *Terms and items common to FORI and FOGEI*—(1) *Minerals.* The term "minerals" means hydrocarbon minerals extracted from oil and gas wells, including crude oil or natural gas (as defined in section 613A (e)). The term includes incidental impurities from these wells, such as sulphur, nitrogen, or helium. The term does not include hydrocarbon minerals derived from shale oil or tar sands.

(2) *Taxable income.* Deductions to be taken into account in computing taxable income or net operating loss attributable to FOGEI or FORI are determined under the principles of § 1.861-8. For an exception with regard to losses, see paragraph (e)(4) of this section.

Reg. § 1.907(c)-1(f)(2)

(3) *Interest on working capital.* FORI and FOGEI may include interest on bank deposits or on any other temporary investment which is not in excess of funds reasonably necessary to meet the working capital requirements and the specifically anticipated business needs of the person that is engaged in the conduct of the activities described in section 907(c)(1) or (2).

(4) *Exchange gain or loss.* Exchange gain (and loss) may be FORI and FOGEI. For taxable years beginning after 1986, exchange gain or loss from a section 988 transaction may be FORI or FOGEI only if directly related to the business needs (under the principles of section 954(c)(1)(D)) attributable to the conduct of the section 907(c) activity.

(5) *Allocation.* Interest income and exchange gain (or loss) described, respectively, in paragraph (f)(3) and (4) of this section are allocated among FORI, FOGEI, and any other class of income relevant for purposes of the foreign tax credit limitations under any reasonable method which is consistently applied from year-to-year.

(6) *Facts and circumstances.* Income not described elsewhere in this section may be FOGEI or FORI if, under the facts and circumstances in the particular case, the income is in substance directly attributable to the activities described in section 907(c)(1) or (2). For example, assume that a producer in the North Sea suffers a casualty caused by an explosion, fire, and resulting destruction of a drilling platform. Insurance proceeds received for the platform's destruction in excess of the producer's basis is extraction income if the excess constitutes income from sources outside the United States. In addition, income from an insurance policy for business interruption may be extraction income to the extent the payments under the policy are geared directly to the loss of income from production and are treated as income from sources outside the United States. Also, if an oil company's oil concession or assets used in extraction activities described in section 907(c)(1)(A) and located outside the United States are nationalized or expropriated by a foreign government, or instrumentality thereof, income derived from that nationalization or expropriation (including interest on the income paid pursuant to the nationalization or expropriation) is FOGEI. Likewise, if a company's assets used in the activities described in section 907(c)(2)(A) through (C) and located outside the United States are nationalized or expropriated by a foreign government, or instrumentality thereof, income (including interest on the income paid pursuant to the nationalization or expropriation) derived from the nationalization or expropriation will be FORI. Nationalization or expropriation is deemed to be a sale or exchange for purposes of section 907(c)(1)(B) and a disposition for purposes of section 907(c)(2)(D). In further example, assume that an oil company has an exclusive right to buy all the oil in country X from Y, an instrumentality of the foreign sovereign which owns all of the oil in X. The oil company does not have an economic interest in any oil in country X. Y has a temporary cash-flow problem and demands that the oil company make advance deposits for the purchase of oil not yet delivered. In return, Y grants the oil company a discount on the price of the oil when delivered. Income represented by the discount on the later disposition of the oil is FORI described in section 907(c)(2)(C). The result would be the same if Y credited the oil company with interest on the advance deposits, which had to be used to purchase oil (the interest income would be FORI).

(g) *Directly related income*—(1) *In general.* Section 907(c)(2)(E) and this paragraph (g) include in FORI, and this paragraph (g) includes in FOGEI, income from the performance of directly related services (as defined in paragraph (g)(2) of this section). This paragraph (g) also includes in FORI and FOGEI income from the lease or license of related property (as defined in paragraph (g)(3) of this section). Section 907(c)(2)(E) with regard to FORI and this paragraph (g) with regard to both FORI and FOGEI do not apply to a person if—

(i) Neither that person nor a related person (as defined in paragraph (g)(4) of this section) has FOGEI described in paragraph (b) of this section (other than paragraph (b)(4) of this section relating to directly related income) or FORI described in paragraph (d) of this section (other than paragraph (d)(7) of this section relating to directly related income), or

(ii) Less than 50 percent of that person's gross income from sources outside the United States which is related exclusively to the performance of services and from the lease or license of property described in paragraph (g)(2) and (3) of this section, respectively, is attributable to services performed for (or on behalf of), leases to, or licenses with, related persons, but

(iii) Paragraph (g)(1)(ii) of this section will not apply to a person if 50 percent or more of that person's total gross income from sources outside the United States is FOGEI and FORI (as both are described in paragraph (g)(1)(i) of this section).

A person described in paragraph (g)(1)(i) or (ii) of this section will, however, have directly related services income which is FOGEI if the income is

Reg. § 1.907(c)-1(f)(3)

Income from Sources Without the United States

See p. 20,601 for regulations not amended to reflect law changes

so classified by reason of the income based on output test set forth in paragraph (g)(2)(i)(B) of this section.

(2) *Directly related services*—(i) *FOGEI.* (A) Income from directly related services will be FOGEI, as that term is defined in paragraph (b)(1) and (3) of this section, if those services are directly related to the active conduct of extraction (including exploration) of minerals from oil and gas wells. Paragraph (b)(1) of this section provides that, in order to have extraction income, a person must have an economic interest in the minerals in place. However, paragraph (b)(3) of this section recognizes that income arising from "other circumstances" is extraction income if that income is in substance attributable to the extraction of minerals.

(B) An example of "other circumstances" under paragraph (b)(3) of this section is the "income based on output test." This income based on output test provides that, if the amount of compensation paid or credited to a person for services is dependent on the amount of minerals discovered or extracted, the income of the person from the performance of the services will be directly related services income which is FOGEI. This test will apply whether or not the person performing the services has, or had, an economic interest in the minerals discovered or extracted.

(ii) *FORI.* With regard to the determination of directly related services income which is FORI, directly related services are those services directly related to the active conduct of the operations described in section 907(c)(2)(A) through (C). Those services include, for example, services performed in relation to the distribution of minerals or primary products or in connection with the operation of a refinery, or the types of services described in § 1.954-6(d) (other than § 1.954-6(d)(4)) which relate to foreign base company shipping income.

(iii) *Recipient of the services.* Directly related services described in paragraph (g)(2)(i) and (ii) of this section may be performed for any person without regard to whether that person is a related person.

(iv) *Excluded services*—(A) *FOGEI.* Directly related services which produce FOGEI do not include insurance, accounting or managerial services.

(B) *FORI.* Directly related services which produce FORI do not, generally, include insurance, accounting or managerial services. These services will, however, produce FORI if they are performed by the person performing the operations described in section 907(c)(2)(A) through (C). For these purposes, insurance income which is FORI means taxable income as defined in section 832(a).

(3) *Leases and licenses.* A lease or license of related property is the lease or license of assets used (or held for use) by the lessor, licensor, or another person (including the lessee or a sublessee) in the active conduct of the activities described in section 907(c)(1)(A) or (c)(2)(A) through (C). The leases or licenses described in this paragraph (g)(3) include, for example, a lease of a means of transportation under a bareboat charter hire, of drilling equipment used in extraction operations, or the license of a patent, know-how, or similar intangible property used in extracting, transporting, distributing or processing minerals or primary products. This paragraph (g)(3) applies without regard to whether the parties are related persons.

(4) *Related person.* A person will be treated as a related person for purposes of this paragraph (g) if that person would be so treated within the meaning of section 954(d)(3) (as applied by substituting the word "corporation" for the word "controlled foreign corporation") or that person is a partnership or partner described in section 707(b)(1).

(5) *Gross income.* A foreign corporation shall be treated as a domestic corporation for the purpose of applying the gross-income rules in paragraph (g)(1)(ii) and (iii) of this section.

(h) *Coordination with other provisions*—(1) *Certain adjustments.* The character of income as FOGEI or FORI is determined before making any adjustment under section 482 or section 907(d). For example, assume that X and Y are related parties, Y's only income is from the sale of oil that Y purchased from X, and FOGEI from X is diverted to Y through an arrangement described in paragraph (b)(3) of this section. Accordingly, Y has FOGEI. If under section 482 the Commissioner reallocates the FOGEI from Y to X, then Y's remaining income represents only a profit from distributing the oil, and thus is FORI. If the foreign taxes paid by Y on this income are otherwise creditable under section 901, the foreign taxes that are not refunded to Y retain their characterization as FOGEI taxes.

(2) *Section 901(f).* Section 901(f) (relating to certain payments with respect to oil and gas not considered as taxes) applies before section 907. Taxes disallowed by section 901(f) are added to the cost or inventory amount of oil or gas. [Reg. § 1.907(c)-1.]

☐ [T.D. 8338, 3-14-91.]

Reg. § 1.907(c)-1(h)(2)

[Reg. § 1.907(c)-2]

§ 1.907(c)-2. Section 907(c)(3) items (for taxable years beginning after December 31, 1982).—(a) *Scope.* This section provides rules relating to certain items listed in section 907(c)(3). The rules of this section are expressed in terms of FORI but apply for determining FOGEI by substituting "FOGEI" for "FORI" whenever appropriate. FOGEI does not include interest described in section 907(c)(3)(A). Dividends paid prior to January 1, 1987, and described in section 907(c)(3)(B), as in effect prior to amendment by the Technical and Miscellaneous Revenue Act of 1988, are included in FORI and not FOGEI.

(b) *Dividend*—(1) *Section 1248 dividend.* A section 1248 dividend is a dividend described in section 907(c)(3)(A). Except as otherwise provided in this paragraph (b)(1), gain (or loss) from the disposition of stock in any corporation is not FOGEI or FORI. See § 1.907(c)-1(e)(3) and (4).

(2) *Section 78 dividend.* A section 78 dividend is FORI to the extent it arises from a dividend described in section 907(c)(3)(A), or an amount described in section 907(c)(3)(C).

(c) *Taxes deemed paid*—(1) *Voting stock test.* Items described in section 907(c)(3)(A) or (C) are FORI only if a deemed-paid-tax test is met under the criteria of section 902 or 960. The purpose of this test is to require minimum direct or indirect ownership by a domestic corporation in the voting stock of a foreign corporation as a prerequisite for the item to qualify as FORI in the hands of the domestic corporation. The test is whether a domestic corporation would be deemed to pay any taxes of a foreign corporation when a dividend or an amount described in section 907(c)(3)(A) or (C), respectively, is included in the domestic corporation's gross income. In the case of interest described in section 907(c)(3)(A), the test is whether any taxes would be deemed paid if there were a hypothetical dividend.

(2) *Dividends and interest.* For purposes of section 907(c)(3)(A), a domestic corporation is deemed under section 902 to pay taxes in respect of dividends and interest received from a foreign corporation whether or not the foreign corporation:

    (i) Actually pays or is deemed to pay taxes, or

    (ii) In the case of interest, actually pays dividends.

This paragraph (c)(2) also applies to dividends received by a foreign corporation from a second-tier or third-tier foreign corporation (as defined in § 1.902-1(a)(3)(i) and (4), respectively). In the case of interest received by a foreign corporation from another foreign corporation, this paragraph (c)(2) applies if the taxes of both foreign corporations would be deemed paid under section 902(a) or (b) for purposes of applying section 902(a) to the same taxpayer which is a domestic corporation. In the case of interest received by any corporation (whether foreign or domestic), all members of an affiliated group filing a consolidated return will be treated as the same taxpayer under section 907(c)(3)(A) if the foreign taxes of the payor and (if the recipient is a foreign corporation) the foreign taxes of the recipient would be deemed paid under section 902 by at least one member. The term "member" is defined in § 1.1502-1(b). Thus, for example, assume that P owns all of the stock of D1 and D2 and P, D1, and D2 are members of an affiliated group filing a consolidated return. Assume further that D1 owns all of the stock of F1 and D2 owns all of the stock of F2, where F1 and F2 are foreign corporations. Interest paid by F1 to P, D2, or F2 may be FORI.

(3) *Amounts included under section 951(a).* For purposes of section 907(c)(3)(C), a domestic corporation is deemed under section 960 to pay taxes in respect of a foreign corporation, whether or not the foreign corporation actually pays taxes on the amounts included in gross income under section 951(a).

(d) *Amount attributable to certain items*—(1) *Certain dividends*—(i) *General rule.* The portion of a dividend described in section 907(c)(3)(A) that is FORI equals—

Amount of dividend × a/b

a = FORI accumulated profits in excess of FORI taxes paid or accrued, and

b = Total accumulated profits in excess of total foreign taxes paid or accrued.

This paragraph (d)(1)(i) applies even though the FORI accumulated profits arose in a taxable year of a foreign corporation beginning before January 1, 1983. Determination of the FORI amount of dividends under this paragraph (d)(1)(i) must be made separately for FORI accumulated profits and total accumulated profits that arose in taxable years beginning before January 1, 1987, and for FORI accumulated profits and total accumulated profits that arose in taxable years beginning after December 31, 1986. Dividends are deemed to be paid first out of FORI and total accumulated profits that arose in taxable years beginning after December 31, 1986. With regard to FORI accumulated profits and total accumulated profits that arose in taxable years beginning after December 31, 1986, the portion of a dividend that is FORI equals—

Reg. § 1.907(c)-2(a)

Income from Sources Without the United States

See p. 20,601 for regulations not amended to reflect law changes

Amount of dividend × a/b

a = Post-1986 undistributed FORI earnings determined under the principles of section 902(c)(1), and

b = Post-1986 undistributed earnings determined under the principles of section 902(c)(1).

(ii) *Cross-references.* See § 1.902-1(g) for the determination of a foreign corporation's earnings and profits and of those out of which a dividend is paid. See § 1.1248-2 or 1.1248-3 for the determination of the earnings and profits attributable to the sale or exchange of stock in certain foreign corporations.

(2) *Interest received from certain foreign corporations.* Interest described in section 907(c)(3)(A) is FORI to the extent the corresponding interest expense of the paying corporation is properly allocable and apportionable to the gross income of the paying corporation that would be FORI were that corporation a domestic corporation. This allocation and apportionment is made in a manner consistent with the rules of section 954(b)(5) and § 1.861-8(e)(2).

(3) *Dividends from domestic corporation.* The amount of a dividend from a corporation described in section 907(c)(3)(B), as in effect prior to amendment by the Technical and Miscellaneous Revenue Act of 1988, paid in a taxable year of that corporation beginning before December 31, 1986, that is FORI is determined under the principles of paragraph (d)(1)(i) of this section with respect to its current earnings and profits under section 316(a)(2) or its accumulated earnings and profits under section 316(a)(1), as the case may be.

(4) *Amounts with respect to which taxes are deemed paid under section 960(a)*—(i) *Portion attributable to FORI.* The portion of an amount described in section 907(c)(3)(C) that is FORI equals:

A × B/C

A = Amount described in section 907(c)(3)(C)
B = FORI earnings and profits
C = Total earnings and profits

For taxable years ending after January 23, 1989, the facts and circumstances will be used to determine what part of the amount of the section 907(c)(3)(C) amount is directly attributable to FOGEI, FORI and other income.

(ii) *Earnings and profits.* Total earnings and profits are those of the foreign corporation for a taxable year under section 964 and the regulations under that section.

(5) *Section 78 dividend.* The portion of a section 78 dividend that will be considered FORI will equal the amount of taxes deemed paid under either section 902(a) or section 960(a)(1) with respect to the dividend to the extent the taxes deemed paid are FORI taxes under § 1.907(c)-3(b) or (c). See § 1.907(c)-3(a)(1).

(6) *Special rule.* (i) No item in the formula described in paragraph (d)(1)(i) of this section includes amounts excluded from the gross income of a United States shareholder under section 959(a)(1).

(ii) With respect to a foreign corporation, earnings and profits in the formula described in paragraph (d)(4)(i) of this section do not include amounts excluded under section 959(b) from its gross income.

(7) *Deficits*—(i) *Allocation of deficits within a separate category.* In a taxable year in which a foreign corporation described in section 907(c)(3)(A) pays a dividend or has income that is subject to inclusion under section 951, if the foreign corporation has positive post-1986 undistributed earnings in a separate category but within that separate category there is a deficit in post-1986 undistributed earnings attributable to earnings other than FOGEI and FORI, that deficit shall be allocated ratably between the FOGEI and FORI post-1986 undistributed earnings within that separate category. Any deficit in post-1986 undistributed earnings attributable to either FOGEI or FORI shall be allocated first to FOGEI or FORI post-1986 undistributed earnings (as the case may be) to the extent thereof. Post-1986 undistributed FORI earnings are the post-1986 undistributed earnings (as defined in section 902 and the regulations under that section) attributable to FORI as defined in section 907(c)(2) and (3). Post-1986 undistributed FOGEI earnings are the post-1986 undistributed earnings (as defined in section 902 and the regulations under that section) attributable to FOGEI as defined in section 907(c)(1) and (3).

Example. Foreign corporation X for years 1987 and 1988 had the following undistributed earnings (none of which is income that is subject to inclusion under section 951) and foreign taxes:

	Earnings	Taxes
FOGEI	$800	$400
FORI	(750)	—
Other	700	250
Total	$750	$650

On December 31, 1988, X paid a dividend of all of its post-1986 undistributed earnings to its sole shareholder Y. Under paragraph (d)(5) and (7)(i) of this section and § 1.907(c)-2(d)(5), $450 of Y's dividend is attributable to FOGEI ($50 from undistributed earnings plus a $400 section 78 dividend) and $950 is attributable to other

Reg. § 1.907(c)-2(d)(7)

earnings ($700 from undistributed earnings plus a $250 section 78 dividend).

(ii) *Deficits allocated among separate categories.* If a deficit in a separate category ("first separate category") is allocated to another separate category ("second separate category") under sections 902 and 960 pursuant to Notice 88-71, 1988-2 CB 374 and the regulations under those sections, the following rules shall apply. Any deficit in post-1986 undistributed earnings attributable to either FOGEI (or FORI) from the first separate category shall be allocated to post-1986 undistributed earnings in the second separate category to the extent thereof in the following order:

(A) FOGEI (or FORI),

(B) FORI (or FOGEI), and

(C) Other income.

Any deficit in post-1986 undistributed earnings attributable to other income from the first separate category shall be allocated first to other post-1986 undistributed earnings and then ratably to FOGEI and FORI post-1986 undistributed earnings in the second separate category.

(iii) *Pre-1987 deficits.* The amount of a dividend paid by a foreign corporation described in section 907(c)(3)(A) out of positive pre-1987 earnings that is attributable to FOGEI and FORI shall be determined in a manner similar to that used in paragraph (d)(7)(i) and (ii) of this section except that the determinations shall be made on an annual basis.

(8) *Illustrations.* The application of this paragraph (d) is illustrated by the following examples.

Example 1. X, a domestic corporation, owns all of the stock of Y, a foreign corporation organized in country S. Y owns all of the stock of Z, a foreign corporation also organized in country S. Each corporation uses the calendar year as its taxable year. In 1983, Z has $150 of FOGEI earnings and profits and $250 of earnings and profits other than FOGEI or FORI. Assume that Z paid no taxes to S and X must include $100 in its gross income under section 951(a) with respect to Z. Under paragraph (d)(4)(i) of this section, $37.50 of the amount described in section 951(a) is FOGEI ($100 × $150/$400). The remaining $62.50 of the section 951(a) amount represents other income.

Example 2. Assume the same facts as in Example 1 except that the taxable year in question is 1988. In addition, under the facts and circumstances, it is determined that of the $100 section 951(a) amount included in X's gross income, $30 is directly attributable to Z's FOGEI activity, $60 is directly attributable to Z's FORI activity and $10 is directly attributable to Z's other activity. Accordingly, under paragraph (d)(4)(i), $30 will be FOGEI and $60 will be FORI to X.

Example 3. (i) Assume the same facts as in Example 1. Assume further that, in 1983, Z distributes its entire earnings and profits ($400) to Y, which consists of a dividend of $300 and a section 959(a)(1) distribution of $100. Y has no other earnings and profits during 1983. Assume that the dividend and distribution are not foreign personal holding company income under section 954(c). Y pays no taxes to S. In 1983, Y distributes its entire earnings and profits to X.

(ii) Under paragraphs (c)(2) and (d)(1)(i) of this section, Y has FOGEI of $112.50, *i.e.*, the amount of the dividend received by Y ($300) multiplied by the fraction described in paragraph (d)(1)(i). The numerator of the fraction is Z's FOGEI accumulated profits in excess of the FOGEI taxes paid ($112.50) and the denominator is Z's total accumulated profits in excess of total foreign taxes paid ($400) minus the amount excluded from Y's gross income under section 959(a)(1) ($100). The rule of paragraph (d)(6)(ii) of this section does not apply since X does not include any amount in its gross income under section 951(a) with respect to Y. If Y paid taxes to S, this paragraph (d) would apply to characterize those taxes as FOGEI taxes or other taxes. See § 1.907(c)-3(a)(8) and *Example 2* (iii) under § 1.907(c)-3(e).

(iii) The distribution from Y to X is a dividend to the extent of $300, *i.e.*, the amount of the distribution ($400) minus the amount excluded from X's gross income under section 959(a)(1) ($100). Under paragraph (d)(1)(i) and (6)(i) of this section, $112.50 of the dividend is FOGEI, *i.e.*, the amount of the dividend ($300) multiplied by a fraction. The numerator of the fraction is $112.50, *i.e.*, the FOGEI accumulated profits of Y in excess of FOGEI taxes paid ($150) minus the FOGEI accumulated profits of Y in excess of FOGEI taxes paid excluded from X's gross income under section 959(a)(1) ($37.50). The denominator of the fraction is $300, *i.e.*, the total accumulated profits of Y in excess of taxes paid ($400) minus the amount excluded from X's gross income under section 959(a)(1) ($100).

Example 4. Assume the same facts as in Example 1 with the following modifications: In 1983, Z's only earnings and profits are FORI earnings and profits which are included in X's gross income under section 951(a). Z distributes its entire earnings and profits to Y. In 1983, Y has total earnings and profits of $100 without regard to the dividend from Z, $60 of which are

Reg. § 1.907(c)-2(d)(8)

Income from Sources Without the United States

See p. 20,601 for regulations not amended to reflect law changes

FORI earnings and profits. Y also has $40 which is included in X's gross income under section 951(a). Under paragraph (d)(6)(ii) of this section, the dividend from Z is disregarded for purposes of applying paragraph (d)(4)(i) of this section to the $40 included in X's gross income under section 951(a) with respect to Y. Accordingly, $24 of the amount described in section 951(a) is FORI ($40 × $60/$100). Had these circumstances existed in 1988, and if the $40 included in X's gross income under section 951(a) was directly attributable to FORI activity, all of that income would be FORI to X.

(e) *Dividends, interest, and other amounts from sources within a possession.* FORI includes the items listed in section 907(c)(3)(A) and (C) to the extent attributable to FORI of a corporation that is created or organized in or under the laws of a possession of the United States.

(f) *Income from partnerships, trusts, etc.* FORI and FOGEI include a person's distributive share (determined under the principles of section 704) of the income of any partnership and amounts included in income under subchapter J of chapter 1 of the Code (relating to the taxation of trusts, estates, and beneficiaries) to the extent the income and amounts are attributable to FORI and FOGEI. For taxable years beginning after 1986, the principles of § 1.904-5(h) and (i) shall be applied to determine whether (and to what extent) a person's distributive share is FORI and FOGEI. Thus, for example, a less-than-10 percent corporate partner's share of income of the partnership would generally be treated as passive income to the partner, and not as FORI or FOGEI, unless an exception under § 1.904-5(h) and (i) applies. [Reg. § 1.907(c)-2.].

☐ [*T.D.* 8338, 3-14-91.]

[Reg. § 1.907(c)-3]

§ 1.907(c)-3. FOGEI and FORI taxes (for taxable years beginning after December 31, 1982).—(a) *Tax characterization, allocation and apportionment*—(1) *Scope.* Paragraph (a)(2) through (6) of this section provides rules for the characterization, allocation, and apportionment of the income taxes (other than withholding taxes) paid or accrued to a foreign country among FOGEI, FORI, and other income relevant for purposes of sections 907 and 904. Some of the rules in this section are expressed in terms of FOGEI taxes but they apply to FORI taxes by substituting "FORI taxes" for "FOGEI taxes" whenever appropriate. For the treatment of withholding taxes, see paragraph (a)(8) of this section. FOGEI taxes are determined without any reduction under section 907(a). In addition, determination of FOGEI taxes will not be affected by recharacterization of FOGEI by section 907(c)(4). See § 1.907(c)-1(c)(5). Foreign taxes will not be characterized as creditable FORI taxes if section 907(b) and § 1.907(b)-1 apply.

(2) *Three classes of income.* There are three classes of income: FOGEI, FORI, and other income.

(3) *More than one class in a foreign tax base.* If more than one class of income is taxed under one tax base under the law of a foreign country, the amount of pre-credit foreign tax for each base must be determined. This amount is the foreign taxes paid or accrued to that country for the base as increased by the tax credits (if any) which reduced those taxes and were allowed in the country for that tax. More than one class of income is taxed under the same base, if, under a foreign country's law, deductions from one class of income may reduce the income of any other class and the classes are subject to foreign tax at the same rates.

(4) *Allocation of tax within a base.* If more than one class of income is taxed under the same base under a foreign country's law, the pre-credit foreign tax for the base is apportioned to each class of income in proportion to the income of each class. Tax credits are then allocated (under paragraph (a)(6) of this section) to the apportioned pre-credit tax. Income of a class is the excess of modified gross income for a class over the deductions allowed under foreign law for, and which are attributable to, that class.

(5) *Modified gross income.* Modified gross income is not necessarily the same as gross income as defined for purposes of chapter 1 of the Internal Revenue Code. Modified gross income is determined with reference to the foreign tax base for gross income (or its equivalent). However, the characterization of the base as a particular class of income is governed by general principles of U.S. tax law. Thus, for example—

(i) Gross income from extraction is the fair market value of oil or gas in the immediate vicinity of the well (as determined under § 1.907(c)-1(b)(6) (without any deductions)).

(ii) Whether cost of goods sold (or any other deduction) is a deduction from modified gross income and the amount of such a deduction is determined under foreign law.

(iii) Modified gross income includes items that are part of the foreign tax base even though they are not gross income under U.S. law so long as the foreign taxes paid on the base constitute creditable taxes under section 901 (including taxes described in section 903). For example, if a foreign country imposes a tax (creditable under section 901) on a tax base that includes in small

Reg. § 1.907(c)-3(a)(5)

part a percentage of the value of a company's oil reserves in place, modified gross income from extraction includes such a percentage of value solely for purposes of making the tax allocation in paragraph (a)(4) of this section.

(iv) Modified gross income from extraction is increased for purposes of this paragraph (a)(5) by the entire excess of the posted price over fair market value if the foreign country uses a posted price system or other pricing arrangement described in section 907(d) in imposing its income tax.

(v) Modified gross income from FORI is that income attributable to the activities in section 907(c)(2)(A) through (C) and (E).

(vi) Modified gross income for any class may not include gross income that is not subject to taxation by the foreign country.

(6) *Allocation of tax credits.* The foreign taxes paid or accrued on a particular class of income equals the pre-credit tax on the class reduced (but not below zero) by the credits allowed under foreign law against the foreign tax on the particular class. Any tax credit attributable to a class that is not allocated to that class is allocated to the other class in the base or, if there are three classes in the base, is apportioned ratably among the taxes paid or accrued on the other two classes (as reduced in accordance with the preceding sentence).

(7) *Withholding taxes.* Paragraph (a)(2) through (6) of this section does not apply to withholding taxes imposed by a foreign country. FOGEI taxes may include withholding taxes imposed with respect to a distribution from a corporation. The portion of the total withholding taxes on a distribution that constitutes FOGEI taxes is determined by the portion of the distribution that is FOGEI. In addition, FOGEI taxes may include taxes imposed on a distribution described in section 959(a)(1) or on amounts described in section 959(b). The portion of the total withholding taxes imposed on a distribution described in section 959(a)(1) or on amounts described in section 959(b) is determined by reference to the portion of the amount included in gross income under section 951(a) that was FOGEI.

(b) *Dividends*—(1) *In general*—(i) FOGEI taxes deemed paid with respect to a dividend equal the total taxes deemed paid with respect to the dividend multiplied by the fraction:

FOGEI taxes paid or accrued by the payor/
Total foreign taxes paid or accrued by the payor.

(ii) With regard to dividends received in taxable years beginning after December 31, 1986, FOGEI taxes deemed paid with respect to a dividend equal the total taxes deemed paid with respect to the portion of the dividend within a separate category multiplied by the fraction:

Post-1986 FOGEI taxes as determined under the principles of section 902(c)(2) that are allocable to that separate category
-----
Post-1986 foreign income taxes as determined under the principles of section 902(c)(2) that are allocable to that separate category.

(iii) This paragraph (b) applies to a dividend described in section 907(c)(3)(A) (including a section 1248 dividend) with reference to the particular taxable year or years of those accumulated profits out of which a dividend is paid. Determination of FOGEI taxes under this paragraph (b) must be made separately—

(A) For FOGEI taxes paid on FOGEI accumulated profits and total taxes paid on accumulated profits that arose in taxable years beginning before January 1, 1987, to which paragraph (b)(1)(i) of this section applies, and

(B) For FOGEI taxes paid on FOGEI accumulated profits and total taxes paid on accumulated profits that arose in taxable years beginning after December 31, 1986, to which paragraph (b)(1)(ii) of this section applies.

For purposes of these determinations, dividends are deemed to be paid first out of FOGEI and total accumulated profits that arose in taxable years beginning after December 31, 1986. See § 1.907(c)-2(d)(1)(i). See section 960(a)(3) and § 1.960-2 relating to distributions that are treated as dividends for purposes of section 902.

(2) *Section 78 dividend.* There are no FOGEI taxes with respect to section 78 dividends.

(c) *Includable amounts under section 951(a).*—(1) FOGEI taxes deemed paid with respect to an amount includable in gross income under section 951(a) equal the total taxes deemed paid with respect to that amount multiplied by the fraction:

FOGEI taxes paid or accrued by the foreign corporation

Total foreign taxes paid or accrued by the foreign corporation.

(2) With regard to an amount includable in gross income under section 951(a) in taxable years beginning after December 31, 1986, FOGEI taxes deemed paid with respect to that amount equal the total taxes deemed paid with respect to that amount within a separate category multiplied by the fraction:

Reg. § 1.907(c)-3(a)(6)

Income from Sources Without the United States 48,999
See p. 20,601 for regulations not amended to reflect law changes

Post-1986 FOGEI taxes as determined under the principles of section 902(c)(2) that are allocable to that separate category

---

Post-1986 foreign income taxes as determined under the principles of section 902(c)(2) that are allocable to that separate category.

Taxes in the fraction in this paragraph (c)(2) of this section include only those foreign taxes that may be deemed paid under section 960(a) by reason of such inclusion. See §§ 1.960-1(c)(3) and 1.960-2(c).

(d) *Partnerships*. A partner's distributive share of the partnership's FOGEI taxes is determined under the principles of section 704.

(e) *Illustrations*. The application of this section may be illustrated by the following examples.

Example 1. X, a domestic corporation, owns all of the stock of Y, a foreign corporation organized in country S. Y owns all of the stock of Z, a foreign corporation organized in country T. Each corporation used the calendar year as its taxable year. In 1983, X includes in its gross income an amount described in section 951(a) with respect to Z. Assume that the taxes deemed paid under section 902(a) by X by reason of such an inclusion is $70. Assume further that Z paid total taxes of $120, $80 of which is FOGEI tax. Under paragraph (c) of this section, the FOGEI tax deemed paid is $46.67 (*i.e.*, $70 × $80/$120). This $46.67 is also FOGEI under § 1.907(c)-2(d)(5) because it must be included in X's gross income under section 78.

Example 2. (i) Assume the same facts as in *Example 1*. Assume further that in 1983, Z distributes its entire earnings and profits to Y. Y has no earnings and profits during 1983 other than this dividend. Y paid a tax of $50 to S. Assume that Y is deemed under section 902(b)(1) to pay $50 of the tax paid by Z which was not deemed paid by X under section 960(a)(1) in 1983. In 1983, Y distributes its entire earnings and profits to X. Assume that X is deemed under section 902(a) to pay $100 of the taxes actually paid, and deemed paid, by Y.

(ii) Paragraph (b)(1) of this section applies to characterize the $50 tax of Z that Y is deemed to pay under section 902(b)(1). Y is deemed to pay $33.33 of FOGEI tax, *i.e.*, the amount of the tax deemed paid by Y ($50) multiplied by a fraction. The numerator of the fraction is the amount of Z's FOGEI tax ($80) and the denominator is the total taxes paid by Z ($120).

(iii) Under paragraph (a)(8) of this section, a portion of the $50 tax actually paid by Y on the earnings and profits received from Z is FOGEI tax. The amount of tax actually paid by Y that is FOGEI tax depends on the amount of the distribution from Z that is FOGEI (see § 1.907(c)-2(d)(1)(i) and *Example 2* (ii) under § 1.907(c)-2(d)(8)). This result does not depend upon whether a portion of the distribution from Z is described in section 959(b) and it follows even though a portion of Y's earnings and profits will be excluded from X's gross income under section 959(a)(1) when distributed by Y. Assume that $12.50 of the $50 tax actually paid by Y is FOGEI tax.

(iv) Under paragraph (b)(1) of this section, X is deemed to pay $45.83 of FOGEI tax by reason of the distribution from Y. This amount is determined by multiplying the total taxes deemed paid by X by reason of such distribution ($100) by a fraction. The numerator of the fraction is the FOGEI tax paid, and deemed paid, by Y ($45.83, *i.e.*, $33.33 under paragraph (2)(ii) of this example plus $12.50 under paragraph (2)(iii) of this example). The denominator of the fraction is the total taxes paid, and deemed paid, by Y ($100). This $45.83 is FOGEI under § 1.907(c)-2(d)(5) because it is included in X's gross income as a section 78 dividend.

Example 3. (i) X, a domestic corporation, has a concession with foreign country Y that gives it the exclusive right to extract and export the crude oil and natural gas owned by Y. The concession agreement and location of the oil and gas wells mandate that X construct a system of pipelines to transport the minerals that are extracted to a port where they are loaded onto tankers for export. X owns the transportation facilities. Y has an income tax system under which income from mineral operations is subject to a 50 percent tax rate. The taxation by Y of the mineral operations is a separate tax base under paragraph (a)(3) of this section. Under this system, Y imposes the tax at the port prior to export and it establishes a posted price of $12 per barrel. Y also collects royalties of $1.44 per barrel (*i.e.*, 12 percent of this posted price) which is deductible in computing the petroleum tax. Y also allows X deductible lifting costs of $.20 per barrel and deductible transporting costs of $.80 per barrel. Y does not allow any credits against the mineral tax. Assume that X does not have any income in Y other than the mineral income. (In 1983, X extracts, transports, and exports 10,000,000 barrels of crude oil, but for convenience, all computations are in terms of one barrel). X pays foreign taxes of $4.78 per barrel, computed as follows:

Sales		$12.00
Royalties	$1.44	
Lifting	.20	
Transporting	.80	
	2.44	(2.44)

Reg. § 1.907(c)-3(e)

Income from Sources Without the United States

See p. 20,601 for regulations not amended to reflect law changes

Income base	9.56
Tax rate (percent)	.50
Tax	4.78

Assume that these taxes are creditable taxes under section 901, that the fair market value of the oil at the port is $10 per barrel, and that under § 1.907(c)-1(b)(6) fair market value in the immediate vicinity of the oil wells is $9 per barrel. Thus, at the port, the excess of posted price ($12) over fair market value ($10) is $2.

(ii) The $4.78 foreign tax paid to Y is allocated to FOGEI and FORI in accordance with the rules in paragraph (a)(2) through (5) of this section.

(iii) Under paragraph (a)(3) of this section, FOGEI and FORI are subject to foreign taxation under one tax base. This foreign tax is allocated between FOGEI tax and FORI tax in accordance with paragraph (a)(4) and (5) of this section.

(iv) The modified gross income for FOGEI is $11, *i.e.*, fair market value in the immediate vicinity of the well ($9) plus the excess at the port of posted price over fair market value ($2). The modified gross income for FORI is $1, *i.e.*, value added to the oil beyond the wellhead which is part of Y's tax base ($10 − $9).

(v) The royalty deductions are all directly attributable to FOGEI.

(vi) Under paragraph (a)(4) of this section, the income of each class is determined as follows:

	FOGEI	FORI
Modified gross income	$11.00	$1.00
Deductions:		
Royalties	1.44	0
Lifting	.20	0
Transporting	0	.80
Total	1.64	.80
Net Income	9.36	.20

(vii) Under paragraph (a)(4) of this section, the total tax paid to Y is allocated to FOGEI and FORI in proportion to the income in each class. The calculation is as follows:

FOGEI tax = $4.78 × $9.36/$9.56 = $4.68
FORI tax = $4.78 × $0.20/$9.56 = $0.10

Thus, for the 10,000,000 barrels, the FOGEI tax is $46,800,000 and the FORI tax is $1,000,000.

(viii) The allocation under paragraph (a)(4) of this section, rather than the direct application of stated foreign tax rates to foreign-law taxable income in each class of income (which would produce the same results in the facts of this example), is necessary when a foreign country taxes more than one class of income under a progressive rate structure. See *Example 4* in this paragraph (e).

Example 4. Assume the same facts as in *Example 3* except that Y's tax is imposed at 40 percent for the first $20,000,000 of income and at 60 percent for all other income. The foreign taxes are allocated under paragraph (a)(4) of this section between FOGEI and FORI in the same manner as in paragraphs (vi) and (vii) of *Example 3*, as follows:

(1) Taxable income	$95,600,000
(2) Tax:	
(a) 40% of $20,000,000	$ 8,000,000
(b) 60% of $75,600,000	45,360,000
(c) Total tax	53,360,000
(3) FOGEI tax (line 2(c) × $9.36/$9.56)	52,243,680
(4) FORI tax (line 2(c) × $0.20/$9.56)	1,116,320

Example 5. Assume the same facts as in *Example 3*. Assume further that X refines the crude oil into primary products prior to export and Y imposes its tax on the basis of crude oil equivalences of $12 per barrel, rather than the value of the primary products, to establish port prices. Assume that this arrangement is a pricing arrangement described in section 907(d). Thus, Y does not tax the refinery income. The results are the same as in *Example 3* even if $12 per barrel is equal to, more than, or less than, the value of the primary products at the port. See paragraph (a)(5)(vi) of this section. [Reg. § 1.907(c)-3.]

☐ [T.D. 8338, 3-14-91.]

[Reg. § 1.907(d)-1]

§ 1.907(d)-1. **Disregard of posted prices for purposes of chapter 1 of the Code (for taxable years beginning after December 31, 1982).**—(a) *In general*—(1) *Scope.* Section 907(d) applies if a person has FOGEI from the—

(i) Acquisition (other than from a foreign government) or

(ii) Disposition of minerals at a posted price that differs from the fair market value at the time of the transaction. Also, if a seller (other than a foreign government) derives FOGEI upon a disposition described in the preceding sentence, section 907(d) applies to the acquisition by the purchaser whether or not the purchaser has FOGEI. Thus, section 907(d) may apply in determining a person's FORI.

(2) *Initial computation requirement.* If section 907(d) applies to any person, income on the transaction as initially reflected on the person's return shall be computed as if the transaction were effected at fair market value. This requirement applies the first time a person has taxable income derived from either the transaction or an item (such as a dividend described in section 907(c)(3)(A)) determined with reference to that income.

(3) *Burden of proof.* The taxpayer must be able to demonstrate the transaction as it actually occurred and the basis for reporting the transaction under the principles of paragraph (a)(2) of this section.

(4) *Related parties.* Section 907(d) (as a rule of characterization) applies whether or not the parties to the transaction are related. Thus, the excess of the posted price over the fair market value may never be taken into account in determining a person's FOGEI under section 907(a) but may be taken into account in determining a person's FORI.

(b) *Adjustments.* If a taxpayer does not comply with the initial requirement of paragraph (a)(2) of this section, adjustments under section 907(d) may be made only by the Commissioner in the same manner that section 482 is administered. Correlative and similar adjustments consistent with the substantive and procedural principles of section 482 and § 1.482-1(d) apply. However, section 907(d) is not a limitation on section 482. If a taxpayer disposing of minerals at a posted price does comply with the initial computation requirement of this section, adjustments and correlative and similar adjustments consistent with the substantive and procedural aspects of section 482 and § 1.482-1(d) shall apply, whether made on the return by the taxpayer or on a later audit. This paragraph (b) does not apply to an actual sale or exchange of minerals made between persons with respect to whom adjustments under section 482 would never apply (but see paragraph (a)(4) of this section).

(c) *Definitions.* For purposes of this section—

(1) *Foreign government.* The term "foreign government" means only the integral parts or controlled entities of a foreign sovereign and political subdivisions of a foreign country.

(2) *Minerals.* The term "minerals" has the same meaning as in § 1.907(c)-1(f)(1).

(3) *Posted price.* The term "posted price" means the price set by, or at the direction of, a foreign government to calculate income for purposes of its tax or at which minerals must be sold.

(4) *Other pricing arrangement.* The term "other pricing arrangement" in section 907(d) means a pricing arrangement having the effect of a posted price.

(5) *Fair market value.* The term "fair market value," whether or not at the port prior to export, is determined in the same way that the wellhead price is determined under § 1.907(c)-1(b)(6). [Reg. § 1.907(d)-1.]

□ [T.D. 8338, 3-14-91.]

[Reg. § 1.907(f)-1]

§ 1.907(f)-1. **Carryback and carryover of credits disallowed by section 907(a) (for amounts carried between taxable years that each begin after December 31, 1982).**—(a) *In general.* If a taxpayer chooses the benefits of section 901, any unused FOGEI tax paid or accrued in a taxable year beginning after December 31, 1982, may be carried to the taxable years specified in section 907(f) under the carryback and carryover principles of this section and § 1.904-2(b). See section 907(e) and § 1.907(e)-1 for transitional rules that apply to unused FOGEI taxes carried back or forward between a taxable year beginning before January 1, 1983, and a taxable year beginning after December 31, 1982.

(b) *Unused FOGEI tax*—(1) *In general.* The "unused FOGEI tax" for purposes of this section is the excess of the FOGEI taxes for a taxable year (year of origin) over that year's limitation level (as defined in § 1.907(a)-1(b)).

(2) *Year of origin.* The term "year of origin" in the regulations under section 904 corresponds to the term "unused credit year" under section 907(f).

(c) *Tax deemed paid or accrued.* The unused FOGEI tax from a year of origin that may be deemed paid or accrued under section 907(f) in any preceding or succeeding taxable year ("excess limitation year") may not exceed the lesser of—

(1) The excess extraction limitation for the excess limitation year, or

(2) The excess general section 904 limitation for the excess limitation year.

(d) *Excess extraction limitation.* Under section 907(f)(2)(A), the "excess extraction limitation" for an excess limitation year is the amount by which that year's section 907(a) extraction limitation exceeds the sum of—

(1) The FOGEI taxes paid or accrued, and

(2) The FOGEI taxes deemed paid or accrued in that year by reason of a section 907(f) carryback or carryover from preceding years of origin.

Reg. § 1.907(f)-1(d)(2)

(e) *Excess general section 904 limitation.* Under section 907(f)(2)(B), the "excess general section 904 limitation" for an excess limitation year is the amount by which that year's section 904 general limitation exceeds the sum of—

(1) The general limitation taxes paid or accrued (or deemed to have been paid under section 902 or 960) to all foreign countries and possessions of the United States during the taxable year,

(2) The general limitation taxes deemed paid or accrued in such taxable year under section 904(c) and which are attributable to taxable years preceding the unused credit year, plus

(3) The FOGEI taxes deemed paid or accrued in that year by reason of a section 907(f) carryover (or carryback) from preceding years of origin.

(f) *Section 907(f) priority.* If a taxable year is a year of origin under both section 907(f) and section 904(c), section 907(f) applies first. See section 907(f)(3)(A).

(g) *Cross-reference.* In computing the carryback and carryover of disallowed credits under section 907(f), the principles of § 1.904-2(d), (e), and (f) apply.

(h) *Example.* The following example illustrates the application of section 907(f).

Example. X, a U.S. corporation organized on January 1, 1983, uses the accrual method of accounting and the calendar year as its taxable year. X's only income is income which is not subject to a separate tax limitation under section 904(d). X's preliminary U.S. tax liability indicates an effective rate of 46% for taxable years 1983-1985. X has the following foreign tax items for 1983-1985:

	1983	1984	1985
1. FOGEI	$15,000	$20,000	$10,000
2. FOGEI taxes	7,500	9,200	4,200
3. Other foreign taxable income	8,000	5,000	10,000
4. Other foreign taxes	3,200	2,000	3,000
5. (a) Section 907(a) limitation (.46 × Line 1)	6,900	9,200	4,600
(b) General section 904 limitation (.46 × (line 1 plus line 3))	10,580	11,500	9,200
6. (a) Unused FOGEI taxes (excess of line 2 over line 5(a))	600	0	0
(b) Unused general limitation taxes (excess of line 4 plus lesser of line 2 or line 5(a) over line 5(b))	0	0	0
7. (a) FOGEI taxes from years preceding 1983 deemed accrued under section 907(f)	0	0	0
(b) Section 904 general limitation taxes from years preceding 1983 deemed accrued under section 904(c)	0	0	0
8. (a) Excess section 907(a) limitation (excess of line 5(a) over sum of line 2 and line 7(a))	0	0	400
(b) Excess section 904 general limitation (excess of line 5(b) over sum of line 4, lesser of line 2 and line 5(a), and line 7(b))	480	300	2,000
9. Limit on FOGEI taxes that will be deemed accrued under section 907(f) (lesser of line 8(a) and line 8(b))	0	0	400

X has unused 1983 FOGEI taxes of $600. Since the excess section 907(a) limitation for 1984 is zero, the unused FOGEI taxes are carried to 1985. Of the $600 carryover, $400 is deemed accrued in 1985 and the balance of $200 is carried to following years (but not to a year after 1988). After the carryover from 1983 to 1985, the excess section 904 general limitation for 1985 (line 8(b)) is reduced by $400 to $1,600 to reflect the amount of 1983 FOGEI taxes deemed accrued in 1985 under section 907(f). [Reg. § 1.907(f)-1.]

☐ [T.D. 8338, 3-14-91.]

[Reg. § 1.911-1]

§ 1.911-1. **Partial exclusion for earned income from sources within a foreign country and foreign housing costs.**—(a) *In general.* Section 911 provides that a qualified individual may elect to exclude the individual's foreign earned income and the housing cost amount from the individual's gross income for the taxable year. Foreign earned income is excludable to the extent of the applicable limitation for the taxable year. The housing cost amount for the taxable year is excludable to the extent attributable to employer provided amounts. If a portion of the housing cost amount for the taxable year is attributable to non-employer provided amounts, such amount may be deductible by the qualified individual subject to a limitation. The amounts excluded under section 911(a) and the amount deducted under section 911(c)(3)(A) for the taxable year shall not exceed the individual's foreign earned income for such taxable year. Foreign earned income must be earned during a period for which the individual qualifies to make an election under section 911(d)(1). A housing cost amount that would be deductible except for the application of this limitation may be carried over to the next taxable year and is deductible to the extent of the limita-

Reg. § 1.911-1(a)

Income from Sources Without the United States

tion for that year. Except as otherwise provided, §§ 1.911-1 through 1.911-7 apply to taxable years beginning after December 31, 1981. These sections do not apply to any item of income, expense, deduction, or credit arising before January 1, 1982, even if such item is attributable to services performed after December 31, 1981.

(b) *Scope.* Section 1.911-2 provides rules for determining whether an individual qualifies to make an election under section 911. Section 1.911-3 provides rules for determining the amount of foreign earned income that is excludable under section 911(a)(1). Section 1.911-4 provides rules for determining the housing cost amount and the portions excludable under section 911(a)(2) or deductible under section 911(c)(3). Section 1.911-5 provides special rules applicable to married couples. Section 1.911-6 provides for the disallowance of deductions, exclusions, and credits attributable to amounts excluded under section 911. Section 1.911-7 provides procedural rules for making or revoking an election under section 911. Section 1.911-8 provides a reference to rules applicable to taxable years beginning before January 1, 1982. [Reg. § 1.911-1.]

☐ [T.D. 8006, 1-17-85. Amended by T.D. 8240, 1-19-89.]

[Reg. § 1.911-2]

§ 1.911-2. **Qualified individuals.**—(a) *In general.* An individual is a qualified individual if:

(1) The individual's tax home is in a foreign country or countries throughout—

(i) The period of bona fide residence described in paragraph (a)(2)(i) of this section, or

(ii) The 330 full days of presence described in paragraph (a)(2)(ii) of this section; and

(2) The individual is either—

(i) A citizen of the United States who establishes to the satisfaction of the Commissioner or his delegate that the individual has been a bona fide resident of a foreign country or countries for an uninterrupted period which includes an entire taxable year, or

(ii) A citizen or resident of the United States who has been physically present in a foreign country or countries for at least 330 full days during any period of twelve consecutive months.

(b) *Tax home.* For purposes of paragraph (a)(1) of this section, the term "tax home" has the same meaning which it has for purposes of section 162 (a)(2) (relating to travel expenses away from home). Thus, under section 911, an individual's tax home is considered to be located at his regular or principal (if more than one regular) place of business or, if the individual has no regular or principal place of business because of the nature of the business, then at his regular place of abode in a real and substantial sense. An individual shall not, however, be considered to have a tax home in a foreign country for any period for which the individual's abode is in the United States. Temporary presence of the individual in the United States does not necessarily mean that the individual's abode is in the United States during that time. Maintenance of a dwelling in the United States by an individual, whether or not that dwelling is used by the individual's spouse and dependents, does not necessarily mean that the individual's abode is in the United States.

(c) *Determination of bona fide residence.* For purposes of paragraph (a)(2)(i) of this section, whether an individual is a bona fide resident of a foreign country shall be determined by applying, to the extent practical, the principles of section 871 and the regulations thereunder, relating to the determination of the residence of aliens. Bona fide residence in a foreign country or countries for an uninterrupted period may be established, even if temporary visits are made during the period to the United States or elsewhere on vacation or business. An individual with earned income from sources within a foreign country is not a bona fide resident of that country if:

(1) The individual claims to be a nonresident of that foreign country in a statement submitted to the authorities of that country, and

(2) The earned income of the individual is not subject, by reason of nonresidency in the foreign country, to the income tax of that country.

If an individual has submitted a statement of nonresidence to the authorities of a foreign country the accuracy of which has not been resolved as of any date when a determination of the individual's bona fide residence is being made, then the individual will not be considered a bona fide resident of the foreign country as of that date.

(d) *Determination of physical presence.* For purposes of paragraph (a)(2)(ii) of this section, the following rules apply.

(1) *Twelve-month test.* A period of twelve consecutive months may begin with any day but must end on the day before the corresponding day in the twelfth succeeding month. The twelve month period may begin before or after arrival in a foreign country and may end before or after departure.

(2) *330-day test.* The 330 full days need not be consecutive but may be interrupted by periods during which the individual is not present in a foreign country. In computing the minimum 330 full days of presence in a foreign country or countries, all separate periods of such presence during

the period of twelve consecutive months are aggregated. A full day is a continuous period of twenty-four hours beginning with midnight and ending with the following midnight. An individual who has been present in a foreign country and then travels over areas not within any foreign country for less than twenty-four hours shall not be deemed outside a foreign country during the period of travel. If an individual who is in transit between two points outside the United States is physically present in the United States for less than twenty-four hours, such individual shall not be treated as present in the United States during such transit but shall be treated as travelling over areas not within any foreign country. For purposes of this paragraph (d)(2), the term "transit between two points outside the United States" has the same meaning that it has when used in section 7701(b)(6)(C).

(3) *Illustrations of the physical presence requirement.* The physical presence requirement of paragraph (a)(2)(ii) of this section is illustrated by the following examples:

Example (1). B, a U.S. citizen, arrives in Venezuela from New York at 12 noon on April 24, 1982. B remains in Venezuela until 2 p.m. on March 21, 1983, at which time B departs for the United States. Among other possible twelve month periods, B is present in a foreign country an aggregate of 330 full days during each of the following twelve month periods: March 21, 1982 through March 20, 1983; and April 25, 1982 through April 24, 1983.

Example (2). C, a U.S. citizen, travels extensively from the time C leaves the United States on March 5, 1982, until the time C departs the United Kingdom on January 1, 1984, to return to the United States permanently. The schedule of C's travel and the number of full days at each location are listed below:

Country	Time and date of arrival	Time and date of departure	Full days in foreign country
United States		10 p.m. (by air) Mar. 5, 1982	
United Kingdom	9 a.m. Mar. 6, 1982	10 p.m. (by ship) June 25, 1982	110
United States	11 a.m. June 30, 1982	1 p.m. (by ship) July 19, 1982	0
France	3 p.m. July 24, 1982	11 a.m. (by air) Aug. 22, 1983	393
United States	4 p.m. Aug. 22, 1983	9 a.m. (by air) Sept. 4, 1983	0
United Kingdom	9 a.m. Sept. 5, 1983	9 a.m. (by air) Jan. 1, 1984	117
United States	1 p.m. Jan. 1, 1984		

Among other possible twelve month periods, C is present in a foreign country or countries an aggregate of 330 full days during the following twelve month periods: March 2, 1982 through March 1, 1983; and January 21, 1983 through January 20, 1984. The computation of days with respect to each twelve month period may be illustrated as follows:

First twelve month period (March 2, 1982 through March 1, 1983):

	Full days in foreign country
Mar. 2, 1982 through Mar. 6, 1982	0
Mar. 7, 1982 through June 24, 1982	110
June 25, 1982 through July 24, 1982	0
July 25, 1982 through Mar. 1, 1983	220
Total full days	330

Second twelve month period (January 21, 1983 through January 20, 1984):

	Full days in foreign country
Jan. 21, 1983 through Aug. 21, 1983	213
Aug. 22, 1983 through Sept. 5, 1983	0
Sept. 6, 1983 through Dec. 31, 1983	117
Jan. 1, 1984 through Jan. 20, 1984	0
Total full days	330

(e) *Special rules.* For purposes only of establishing that an individual is a qualified individual under paragraph (a) of this section, residence or presence in a foreign country while there employed by the U.S. government or any agency or instrumentality of the U.S. government counts towards satisfaction of the requirements of § 1.911-2(a). (But see section 911(b)(1)(B)(ii) and § 1.911-3(c)(3) for the rule excluding amounts paid by the U.S. government to an employee from the definition of foreign earned income.) Time spent in a foreign country prior to January 1, 1982, counts toward satisfaction of the bona fide residence and physical presence requirements, even though no exclusion or deduction may be allowed under section 911 for income attributable to services performed during that time. For purposes of paragraph (a)(2)(ii) of this section, the term "resident of the United States" includes an individual for whom a valid election is in effect under section 6013(g) or (h) for the taxable year or years during which the physical presence requirement is satisfied.

(f) *Waiver of period of stay in foreign country due to war or civil unrest.* Notwithstanding the requirements of paragraph (a) of this section, an individual whose tax home is in a foreign country, and who is a bona fide resident of, or present in, a foreign country for any period, who leaves the foreign country after August 31, 1978, before meeting the requirements of paragraph (a) of this section, may, as provided in this paragraph, qualify to make an election under section 911(a) and § 1.911-7(a). If the Secretary determines, after consultation with the Secretary of State or his delegate, that war, civil unrest, or similar adverse conditions existed in a foreign country, then the Secretary shall publish the name of the foreign country and the dates between which such conditions were deemed to exist. In order to qualify to make an election under this paragraph, the individual must establish to the satisfaction of the Secretary that the individual left a foreign country, the name of which has been published by the Secretary, during the period when adverse conditions existed and that the individual could reasonably have expected to meet the requirements of paragraph (a) of this section but for the adverse conditions. The individual shall attach to his return for the taxable year a statement that the individual expected to meet the requirements of paragraph (a) of this section but for the conditions in the foreign country which precluded the normal conduct of business by the individual. Such individual shall be treated as a qualified individual, but only for the actual period of residence or presence. Thus, in determining the number of the individual's qualifying days, only days within the period of actual residence or presence shall be counted.

(g) *United States.* The term "United States" when used in a geographical sense includes any territory under the sovereignty of the United States. It includes the states, the District of Columbia, the possessions and territories of the United States, the territorial waters of the United States, the air space over the United States, and the seabed and subsoil of those submarine areas which are adjacent to the territorial waters of the United States and over which the United States has exclusive rights, in accordance with international law, with respect to the exploration and exploitation of natural resources.

(h) *Foreign country.* The term "foreign country" when used in a geographical sense includes any territory under the sovereignty of a government other than that of the United States. It includes the territorial waters of the foreign country (determined in accordance with the laws of the United States), the air space over the foreign country, and the seabed and subsoil of those submarine areas which are adjacent to the territorial waters of the foreign country and over which the foreign country has exclusive rights, in accordance with international law, with respect to the exploration and exploitation of natural resources. [Reg. § 1.911-2.]

☐ [*T.D.* 8006, 1-17-85.]

[Reg. § 1.911-3]

§ 1.911-3. Determination of amount of foreign earned income to be excluded.—(a) *Definition of foreign earned income.* For purposes of section 911 and the regulations thereunder, the term "foreign earned income" means earned income (as defined in paragraph (b) of this section) from sources within a foreign country (as defined in § 1.911-2(h)) that is earned during a period for which the individual qualifies under § 1.911-2(a) to make an election. Earned income is from sources within a foreign country if it is attributable to services performed by an individual in a foreign country or countries. The place of receipt of earned income is immaterial in determining whether earned income is attributable to services performed in a foreign country or countries.

(b) *Definition of earned income*—(1) *In general.* The term "earned income" means wages, salaries, professional fees, and other amounts received as compensation for personal services actually rendered including the fair market value of all remuneration paid in any medium other than cash. Earned income does not include any portion of an amount paid by a corporation which represents a distribution of earnings and profits rather than a reasonable allowance as compensation for personal services actually rendered to the corporation.

(2) *Earned income from business in which capital is material.* In the case of an individual engaged in a trade or business (other than in corporate form) in which both personal services and capital are material income producing factors, a reasonable allowance as compensation for the personal services actually rendered by the individual shall be considered earned income, but the total amount which shall be treated as the earned income of the individual from such trade or business shall in no case exceed thirty percent of the individual's share of the net profits of such trade or business.

(3) *Professional fees.* Earned income includes all fees received by an individual engaged in a professional occupation (such as doctor or lawyer) in the performance of professional activities. Professional fees constitute earned income even though the individual employs assistants to perform part or all of the services, provided the patients or clients are those of the individual and look to the individual as the person responsible for the services rendered.

(c) *Amounts not included in foreign earned income.* Foreign earned income does not include an amount:

Reg. § 1.911-3(c)

(1) Excluded from gross income under section 119;

(2) Received as a pension or annuity (including social security benefits);

(3) Paid to an employee by an employer which is the U.S. government or any U.S. government agency or instrumentality;

(4) Included in the individual's gross income by reason of section 402(b) (relating to the taxability of a beneficiary of a nonexempt trust) or section 403(c) (relating to the taxability of a beneficiary under a nonqualified annuity or under annuities purchased by exempt organizations);

(5) Included in gross income by reason of § 1.911-6(b)(4)(ii); or

(6) Received after the close of the first taxable year following the taxable year in which the services giving rise to the amounts were performed. For treatment of amounts received after December 31, 1962, which are attributable to services performed on or before December 31, 1962, and with respect to which there existed on March 12, 1962, a right (whether forfeitable or nonforfeitable) to receive such amounts, see § 1.72-8.

(ii) *Annual rate for the taxable year.* The annual rate for the taxable year is the rate set forth in section 911(b)(2)(A).

(3) *Number of qualifying days.* For purposes of section 911 and the regulations thereunder, the number of qualifying days is the number of days in the taxable year within the period during which the individual met the tax home requirement and either the bona fide residence requirement or the physical presence requirement of § 1.911-2(a). Although the period of bona fide residence must include an entire taxable year, the entire uninterrupted period of residence may include fractional parts of a taxable year. For instance, if an individual who was a calendar year taxpayer established a tax home and a residence in a foreign country as of November 1, 1982, and maintained the tax home and the residence through March 31, 1984, then the uninterrupted period of bona fide residence includes fractional parts of the years 1982 and 1984, and all of 1983. The number of qualifying days in 1982 is sixty-one. The number of qualifying days in 1983 is 365. The number of qualifying days in 1984 is ninety-one. The period during which the physical presence requirement of § 1.911-2(a)(2)(ii) is met is any twelve consecutive month period during which the individual is physically present in one or more foreign countries for 330 days and the individual's tax home is

(d) *Determination of the amount of foreign earned income that may be excluded under section 911(a)(1)* —(1) *In general.* Foreign earned income described in this section may be excluded under section 911(a)(1) and this paragraph only to the extent of the limitation specified in paragraph (d)(2) of this section. Income is considered to be earned in the taxable year in which the services giving rise to the income are performed. The determination of the amount of excluded earned income in this manner does not affect the time for reporting any amounts included in gross income.

(2) *Limitation*—(i) *In general.* The term "section 911(a)(1) limitation" means the amount of foreign earned income for a taxable year which may be excluded under section 911(a)(1). The section 911(a)(1) limitation shall be equal to the lesser of the qualified individual's foreign earned income for the taxable year in excess of amounts that the individual elected to exclude from gross income under section 911(a)(2) or the product of the annual rate for the taxable year (as specified in paragraph (d)(2)(ii) of this section) multiplied by the following fraction:

$$\frac{\text{The number of qualifying days in the taxable year}}{\text{The number of days in the taxable year}}$$

in a foreign country during each day of such physical presence. Such period may include days when the individual is not physically present in a foreign country, and days when the individual does not maintain a tax home in a foreign country. Such period may include fractional parts of a taxable year. Thus, if an individual's period of physical presence is the twelve-month period beginning June 1, 1982, and ending May 31, 1983, the number of qualifying days in 1982 is 214 and the number of qualifying days in 1983 is 151.

(e) *Attribution rules*—(1) *In general.* Foreign earned income is considered to be earned in the taxable year in which the individual performed the services giving rise to the income. If income is earned in one taxable year and received in another taxable year, then, for purposes of determining the amount of foreign earned income that the individual may exclude under section 911(a), the individual must attribute the income to the taxable year in which the services giving rise to the income were performed. Thus, any reimbursement would be attributable to the taxable year in which the services giving rise to the obligation to pay the reimbursement were performed, not the taxable year in which the reimbursement was received. For example, tax equalization payments are normally received in the year after the year in which the services giving rise to the obligation to pay the

Reg. § 1.911-3(c)(1)

tax equalization payment were performed. Therefore, such payments will almost always have to be attributed to the prior year. Foreign earned income attributable to services performed in a preceding taxable year shall be excludable from gross income in the year of receipt only to the extent such amount could have been excluded under paragraph (d)(1) in the preceding taxable year, had such amount been received in the preceding taxable year. The taxable year to which income is attributable will be determined on the basis of all the facts and circumstances.

(2) *Priority of use of the section 911(a)(1) limitation.* Foreign earned income received in the year in which it is earned shall be applied to the section 911(a)(1) limitation for that year before applying income earned in that year that is received in any other year. Foreign earned income that is earned in one year and received in another year shall be applied to the section 911(a)(1) limitation for the year in which it was earned, on a year by year basis, in any order that the individual chooses. (But see section 911(b)(1)(B)(iv)). An individual may not amend his return to change the treatment of income with respect to the section 911(a)(1) exclusion after the period provided by section 6511(a). The special period of limitation provided by section 6511(d)(3) does not apply for this purpose. For example, C, a qualified individual, receives an advance bonus of $10,000 in 1982, salary of $70,000 in 1983, and a performance bonus of $10,000 in 1984, all of which are foreign earned income for 1983. C has a section 911(a)(1) limitation for 1983 of $80,000, and has no housing cost amount exclusion. On his income tax return for 1983, C elects to exclude foreign earned income of $70,000 received in 1983. C may also exclude his $10,000 advance bonus received in 1982 (by filing an amended return for 1982), or he may exclude the $10,000 performance bonus received in 1984 on his 1984 income tax return. However, C may not exclude part of the 1982 bonus and part of the 1984 bonus.

(3) *Exception for year-end payroll period.* Notwithstanding paragraph (e)(1) of this section, salary or wage payments of a cash basis taxpayer shall be attributed entirely to the year of receipt under the following circumstances:

(i) The period for which the payment is made is a normal payroll period of the employer which regularly applies to the employee;

(ii) The payroll period includes the last day of the employee's taxable year;

(iii) The payroll period does not exceed 16 days; and

(iv) The payment is part of a normal payroll of the employer that is distributed at the same time, in relation to the payroll period, that such payroll would normally be distributed, and is distributed before the end of the next succeeding payroll period.

(4) *Attribution of bonuses and substantially nonvested property to periods in which services were performed* —(i) *In general.* Bonuses and substantially nonvested property are attributable to all of the services giving rise to the income on the basis of all the facts and circumstances. If an individual receives a bonus or substantially nonvested property (as defined in § 1.83-3(b)) and it is determined to be attributable to services performed in more than one taxable year, then, for purposes of determining the amount eligible for exclusion from gross income in the year the bonus is received or the property vests, a portion of such amount shall be treated as attributable to services performed in each taxable year (or portion thereof) during the period when services giving rise to the bonus or the substantially nonvested property were performed. Such portion shall be determined by dividing the amount of the bonus or the excess of the fair market value of the vested property over the amount paid, if any, for the vested property, by the number of months in the period when services giving rise to such amount were performed, and multiplying the quotient by the number of months in such period in the taxable year. For purposes of this section, the term "month" means a calendar month. A fraction of a calendar month shall be deemed a month if it includes fifteen or more days.

(ii) *Examples.* The following examples illustrate the application of this paragraph (e)(4).

Example (1). A, an employee of M Corporation during all of 1983 and 1984, worked in the United States from January 1 through April 30, 1983, and received $12,000 of salary for that period. A worked in country F from May 1, 1983 through the end of 1984, and is a qualified individual under § 1.911-2(a) for that period. For the period from May 1 through December 31, 1983, A received $32,000 of salary. M pays a bonus on December 20, 1983 to each of M's employees in an amount equal to 10 percent of the employee's regular wages or salary for the 1983 calendar year. The amount of A's bonus is $4,400 for 1983. The portion of A's bonus that is attributable to services performed in country F and is foreign earned income for 1983 is $3,200, or $32,000 × 10 percent. The remaining $1,200 of A's bonus is attributable to services performed in the United States, and is not foreign earned income.

Example (2). The facts are the same as in example (1), except that M determines bonuses separately for each country based on the produc-

Reg. § 1.911-3(e)(4)

tivity of the employees in that country. M pays a bonus to employees in country F, in the amount of 15 percent of each employee's wages or salary earned in country F. A's country F bonus is $4,800 for 1983 ($32,000 × 15 percent), and is foreign earned income for 1983. If A also receives a bonus (or if A's bonus is increased) for working in the United States during 1983, that amount is not foreign earned income.

Example (3). X corporation offers its employees a bonus of $40,000 if the employee accepts employment in a foreign country and remains in a foreign country for a period of at least four years. A, an employee of X, is a calendar year and cash basis taxpayer. A accepts employment with X in foreign country F. A begins work in F on July 1, 1983 and continues to work in F for X until June 30, 1987. In 1987 X pays A a $40,000 bonus. The bonus is attributable to services A performed from July 1, 1983 through June 30, 1987. The amount of the bonus attributable to 1987 is $5,000 (($40,000 ÷ 48) × 6). The amount of the bonus attributable to 1986 is $10,000 (($40,000 ÷ 48) × 12). A may exclude the $10,000 attributable to 1986 only to the extent that amount could have been excluded under section 911(a)(1) had A received it in 1986. The remaining $25,000 is attributable to services performed in taxable years before 1986. Such amounts may not be excluded under section 911 because they are received after the close of the taxable year following the taxable year in which the services giving rise to the income were performed.

(iii) *Special rule for elections under section 83(b).* If an individual receives substantially nonvested property and makes an election under section 83(b) and § 1.83-2(a) to include in his gross income the amount determined under section 83(b)(1)(A) and (B) and § 1.83-2(a) for the taxable year in which the property is transferred (as defined in § 1.83-3(a)), then, for the purpose of determining the amount eligible for exclusion in the year of receipt, the individual may elect either of the following options:

(A) Substantially nonvested property may be treated as attributable entirely to services performed in the taxable year in which an election to include it in income is made. If so treated, then the amount otherwise included in gross income as determined under § 1.83-2(a) will be excludable under section 911(a) for such year subject to the limitation provided in § 1.911-3(d)(2) for such year.

(B) A portion of the substantially nonvested property may be treated as attributable to services performed or to be performed in each taxable year during which the substantial risk of forfeiture (as defined in section 83(c) and § 1.83-3(c)) exists. The portion treated as attributable to services performed or to be performed in each taxable year is determined by dividing the amount of the substantially nonvested property included in gross income as determined under § 1.83-2(a) by the number of months during the period when a substantial risk of forfeiture exists. The quotient is multiplied by the total number of months in the taxable year during which a substantial risk of forfeiture exists. The amount determined to be attributable to services performed in the year the election is made shall be excluded from gross income for such year as provided in paragraph (d)(2) of this section. Amounts treated as attributable to services performed in subsequent taxable years shall be excludable in the year of receipt only to the extent such amounts could be excluded under paragraph (d)(2) of this section in such subsequent year. An individual may obtain such additional exclusion by filing an amended return for the taxable year in which the property was transferred. The individual may only amend his or her return within the period provided by section 6511(a) and the regulations thereunder.

(5) *Moving expense reimbursements*—(i) *Source of reimbursements.* For the purpose of determining whether a moving expense reimbursement is attributable to services performed within a foreign country or within the United States, in the absence of evidence to the contrary, the reimbursement shall be attributable to future services to be performed at the new principal place of work. Thus, a reimbursement received by an employee from his employer for the expenses of a move to a foreign country will generally be attributable to services performed in the foreign country. A reimbursement received by an employee from his employer for the expenses of a move from a foreign country to the United States will generally be attributable to services performed in the United States. For purposes of this paragraph (e)(5), evidence to the contrary includes, but is not limited to, an agreement, between the employer and the employee, or a statement of company policy, which is reduced to writing before the move to the foreign country and which is entered into or established to induce the employee or employees to move to a foreign country. The writing must state that the employer will reimburse the employee for moving expenses incurred in returning to the United States regardless of whether the employee continues to work for the employer after the employee returns to the United States. The writing may contain conditions upon which the right to reimbursement is

Reg. § 1.911-3(e)(5)

determined as long as the conditions set forth standards that are definitely ascertainable and the conditions can only be fulfilled prior to, or through completion of, the employee's return move to the United States that is the subject of the writing. In no case will an oral agreement or statement of company policy concerning moving expenses be considered evidence to the contrary. For the purpose of determining whether a storage expense reimbursement is attributable to services performed within a foreign country, in the case of storage expenses incurred after December 31, 1983, the reimbursement shall be attributable to services performed during the period of time for which the storage expenses are incurred.

(ii) *Attribution of foreign source reimbursements to taxable years in which services are performed*—(A) *In general.* If a reimbursement for moving expenses is determined to be from foreign sources under paragraph (e)(5)(i) of this section, then for the purpose of determining the amount eligible for exclusion in accordance with paragraphs (d)(2) and (e)(2) of this section, the reimbursement shall be considered attributable to services performed in the year of the move as long as the individual is a qualified individual for a period that includes 120 days in the year of the move. The period that is used in determining the number of qualifying days for purposes of the individual's section 911(a)(1) limitation (under paragraph (d)(2) of this section) must also be used in determining whether the individual is a qualified individual for a period that includes 120 days in the year of the move. If the individual is not a qualified individual for such period, then the individual shall treat a portion of the reimbursement as attributable to services performed in the year of the move, and a portion as attributable to services performed in the succeeding taxable year, if the move is from the United States to a foreign country, or to the prior taxable year, if the move is from a foreign country to the United States. The portion of the reimbursement treated as attributable to services performed in the year of the move shall be determined by multiplying the total reimbursement by the following fraction:

$$\frac{\text{The number of qualifying days (as defined in paragraph (d)(3) of this section) in the year of the move}}{\text{The number of days in the taxable year of the move.}}$$

The remaining portion of the reimbursement shall be treated as attributable to services performed in the year succeeding or preceding the year of the move. Amounts treated as attributable to services performed in a year succeeding or preceding the year of the move shall be excludable in the year of receipt only to the extent such amounts could be excluded under paragraph (d)(2) of this section in such succeeding or preceding year.

(B) *Moves beginning before January 1, 1984.* Notwithstanding paragraph (e)(5)(ii)(A) of this section, this paragraph (e)(5)(ii)(B) shall apply for moves begun before January 1, 1984. If a reimbursement for moving expenses is determined to be from foreign sources under paragraph (e)(5)(i) of this section, then for the purpose of determining the amount eligible for exclusion in accordance with paragraphs (d)(2) and (e)(2) of this section, the reimbursement shall be considered attributable to services performed in the year of the move. However, if the individual does not qualify under section 911(d)(1) and § 1.911-2(a) for the entire taxable year of the move, then the individual shall treat a portion of the reimbursement as attributable to services performed in the succeeding taxable year, if the move is from the United States to a foreign country, or to the prior taxable year, if the move is from a foreign country to the United States. The portion of the reimbursement treated as attributable to services performed in the year succeeding or preceding the move shall be determined by multiplying the total reimbursement by the following fraction:

$$\frac{\text{The number of qualifying days (as defined in paragraph (d)(3) of this section) in the year of the move}}{\text{The number of days in the taxable year of the move.}}$$

and subtracting the product from the total reimbursement. Amounts treated as attributable to services performed in a year succeeding or preceding the year of the move shall be excludable in the year of receipt only to the extent such amounts could be excluded under paragraph (d)(2) of this section in such succeeding or preceding year.

(f) *Examples.* The following examples illustrate the application of this section.

Example (1). A is a U.S. citizen and calendar year taxpayer. A's tax home was in foreign country F and A was physically present in F for 330 days during the period from July 4, 1982 through July 3, 1983. The number of A's qualifying days in 1982 as determined under paragraph (d)(2) of this section is 181. In 1982 A receives $40,000 attributable to services performed in foreign country F in 1982. Under paragraph (d)(2) of this section A's section 911(a)(1) limitation is $37,192,

Reg. § 1.911-3(f)

that is the lesser of $40,000 (foreign earned income) or

$$75{,}000 \text{ (annual rate)} \times \frac{181 \text{ (qualifying days)}}{365 \text{ (days in taxable year)}}.$$

Example (2). The facts are the same as in example (1) except that in 1982 A receives $30,000 attributable to services performed in foreign country F. A excludes this amount from gross income under paragraph (d) of this section. In addition, in 1983 A receives $10,000 attributable to services performed in F in 1982 and $35,000 attributable to services performed in F in 1983. On his return for 1983, A must report $45,000 of income. A's section 911(a)(1) limitation for 1983 is the lesser of $35,000 (foreign earned income) or $40,329, the annual rate for the taxable year multiplied by a fraction the numerator of which is A's qualifying days in the taxable year and the denominator of which is the number of days in the taxable year ($80,000 × 184/365). On his tax return for 1983 A may exclude $35,000 attributable to services performed in 1983. A may only exclude $7,192 of the $10,000 received in 1983 attributable to services performed in 1982 because such amount is only excludable in 1983 to the extent such amount could have been excluded in 1982 subject to the section 911(a)(1) limitation for 1982 which is $37,192 ($75,000 × 181/365). No portion of amounts attributable to services performed in 1982 may be used in calculating A's section 911(a)(1) limitation for 1983. Thus, even though A could have excluded an additional $6,329 in 1983 if A had had more foreign earned income attributable to 1983, A may not exclude the $2,808 of remaining foreign earned income attributable to 1982.

Example (3). C is a U.S. citizen and calendar year taxpayer. C establishes a bona fide residence and a tax home in foreign country J on March 1, 1982, and maintains a tax home and a residence in J until December 31, 1986. In March of 1982 C's employer, Y corporation, transfers stock in Y to C. The stock is subject to forfeiture if C returns to the U.S. before January 1, 1985. C elects under section 83(b) to include $15,000, the amount determined with respect to such stock under section 83(b)(1), in gross income in 1982. C's other foreign earned income in 1982 is $58,000. C elects under paragraph (e)(4)(iii)(B) of this section to treat the stock as if earned over the period of the substantial risk of forfeiture. The number of months in the period of the substantial risk of forfeiture is thirty-four. The number of months in the taxable year 1982 within the period of foreign employment is ten. For purposes of determining C's section 911(a)(1) limitation, $4,412 (($15,000/34) × 10) of the amount included in gross income under section 83(b) is treated as attributable to services performed in 1982, $5,294 is treated as attributable to services to be performed in 1983, and $5,294 is treated as attributable to services to be performed in 1984. In 1982, C excludes $62,412 under section 911(a)(1). That is the lesser of foreign earned income for 1982 ($56,000 + $4,412) or the annual rate for the taxable year multiplied by a fraction the numerator of which is C's qualifying days in the taxable year and the denominator of which is the number of days in the taxable year ($75,000 × 306/365). C continues to perform services in foreign country J throughout 1983 and 1984. C would be able to exclude the remaining $5,294 attributable to services performed in 1983 and $5,294 attributable to services performed in 1984 if those amounts would be excludable if they had been received in 1983 or 1984 respectively. If C is entitled to exclude the additional amounts, C must claim the exclusion by filing an amended return for 1982.

Example (4). D is a U.S. citizen and calendar year taxpayer. In September, 1984 D moves to foreign country K. D is physically present in K, and D's tax home is in K, from September 15, 1984 through December 31, 1985. D receives $6,000 in April, 1985 from his employer, as a reimbursement for expenses of moving to K, pursuant to a written agreement that such moving expenses would be reimbursed to D upon successful completion of 6 months employment in K. Under paragraph (e)(5)(i) of this section, the reimbursement is attributable to services performed in K. Under the physical presence test of § 1.911-2(a)(2)(ii), among other periods D is a qualified individual for the period of August 10, 1984 through August 9, 1985, which includes 144 days in 1984. Under paragraph (e)(5)(ii)(A) of this section, for the purpose of determining the amount eligible for exclusion, the reimbursement is considered attributable to services performed in 1984 (the year of the move) because D is a qualified individual under § 1.911-2(a) for a period that includes 120 days in 1984. The reimbursement may be excluded under paragraphs (d)(2) and (c)(2) of this section, to the extent that D's foreign earned income for 1984 that was earned and received in 1984 was less than the annual rate for the taxable year multiplied by the number of D's qualifying days in the taxable year over the number of days in D's taxable year ($80,000 × 144/366), or $31,475.

Reg. § 1.911-3(f)

Income from Sources Without the United States

Example (5). The facts are the same as in example (4) except that D is not a qualified individual under the physical presence test, but is a qualified individual under the bona fide residence test for the period of September 15, 1984 through December 31, 1985. Under paragraph (e)(5)(ii)(A) of this section, for the purpose of determining the amount eligible for exclusion, the reimbursement is considered attributable to services performed in 1984 and 1985 because D is not a qualified individual for a period that includes 120 days in 1984 (the year of the move). The portion of the reimbursement treated as attributable to services performed in 1984 is $6,000 × 108/366, or $1,770, and may be excluded, subject to D's 1984 section 911(a)(1) limitation. The balance of the reimbursement, $4,230, is treated as attributable to services performed in 1985, and may be excluded to the extent provided in paragraphs (d)(2) and (e)(2) of this section.

Example (6). The facts are the same as in Example (4), with the following additions. Before D moved to K, D and his employer signed a written agreement that D would perform services for the employer for at least one year, primarily in country K, and, if D did not voluntarily cease to work for the employer primarily in country K before one year had elapsed, the employer would reimburse D for one-half of D's expenses, up to a maximum of $4,000, of moving back to the United States. The agreement also stated that, if D did not voluntarily leave the employment in K before two years had elapsed, the employer would reimburse D for all of D's reasonable expenses of moving back to the United States. The agreement further stated that D's right to reimbursement would not be conditioned upon the performance of services after D ceased to work in K. D worked in country K for all of 1985. On January 1, 1986, D left K and moved to the United States. In February, 1986 the employer paid D $3,500 as reimbursement for one-half of D's expenses of moving to the United States. Although D did not fulfill the condition in the agreement to receive full reimbursement, all of the conditions in the agreement set forth definitely ascertainable standards and no condition could be fulfilled after D moved back to the United States. The agreement fulfills the requirements of paragraph (e)(5)(i) of this section, and therefore is evidence that the reimbursement should not be attributable to future services to be performed at D's new principal place of work. Under the facts and circumstances, the reimbursement is attributable to services performed in K. Under paragraph (e)(5)(ii)(A) of this section, the entire reimbursement is attributable to services performed in 1985. The amount attributable in 1985 may be excluded to the extent provided in paragraphs (d)(2) and (e)(2) of this section. [Reg. § 1.911-3.]

☐ [T.D. 8006, 1-17-85.]

[Reg. § 1.911-4]

§ 1.911-4. **Determination of housing cost amount eligible for exclusion or deduction.**—(a) *Definition of housing cost amount.* The term "housing cost amount" means an amount equal to the reasonable expenses paid or incurred (as defined in section 7701(a)(25)) during the taxable year by or on behalf of the individual attributable to housing in a foreign country for the individual and any spouse or dependents who reside with the individual (or live in a second foreign household described in paragraph (b)(5) of this section) less the base housing amount as defined in paragraph (c) of this section. The housing cost amount must be reduced by the amount of any military or section 912 allowance or similar allowance excludable from gross income that is intended to compensate the individual or the individual's spouse in whole or in part for the expenses of housing during the same period for which the individual claims a housing cost amount exclusion or deduction.

(b) *Housing expenses.*—(1) *Included expenses.* For purposes of paragraph (a) of this section, housing expenses include rent, the fair rental value of housing provided in kind by the employer, utilities (other than telephone charges), real and personal property insurance, occupancy taxes not described in paragraph (b)(2)(v) of this section, nonrefundable fees paid for securing a leasehold, rental of furniture and accessories, household repairs, and residential parking.

(2) *Excluded expenses.* Housing expenses do not include:

(i) The cost of house purchase, improvements, and other costs that are capital expenditures;

(ii) The cost of purchased furniture or accessories or domestic labor (maids, gardeners, etc.);

(iii) Amortized payments of principal with respect to an evidence of indebtedness secured by a mortgage on the taxpayers housing;

(iv) Depreciation of housing owned by the taxpayer, or amortization or depreciation of capital improvements made to housing leased by the taxpayer;

(v) Interest and taxes deductible under section 163 or 164 or other amounts deductible under section 216(a) (relating to deduction of interest and taxes by cooperative housing corporation tenant);

Reg. § 1.911-4(b)(2)

(vi) The expenses of more than one foreign household except as provided in paragraph (b)(5) of this section;

(vii) Expenses excluded from gross income under section 119;

(viii) Expenses claimed as deductible moving expenses under section 217; or

(ix) The cost of a pay television subscription.

(3) *Limitation.* Housing expenses are taken into account for purposes of this section only to the extent attributable to housing for portions of the taxable year within the period during which the individual satisfies the requirements of § 1.911-2(a). Housing expenses are not taken into account for the period during which the value of the individual's housing is excluded from gross income under section 119, unless the individual maintains a second foreign household described in paragraph (b)(5) of this section. If an individual maintains two foreign households, only expenses incurred with respect to the abode which bears the closest relationship, not necessarily geographic, with respect to the individual's tax home shall be taken into account, unless one of the households is a second foreign household.

(4) *Reasonableness.* An amount paid for housing shall not be treated as reasonable, for purposes of paragraph (a) of this section, to the extent that the expense is lavish or extravagant under the circumstances.

(5) *Expenses of a second foreign household*—(i) *In general.* The term "second foreign household" means a separate abode maintained by an individual outside of the U.S. for his or her spouse or dependents (who, if minors, are in the individual's legal custody or the joint custody of the individual and the individual's spouse) at a place other than the tax home of the individual because of adverse living conditions at the individual's tax home. If an individual maintains a second foreign household the expenses of the second foreign household may be included in the individual's housing expenses under paragraph (b)(1) of this section. Under no circumstances shall an individual be considered to maintain more than one second foreign household at the same time.

(ii) *Adverse living conditions.* Solely for purposes of paragraph (b)(5)(i) of this section, adverse living conditions are living conditions which are dangerous, unhealthful, or otherwise adverse. Adverse living conditions include a state of warfare or civil insurrection in the general area of the individual's tax home. Adverse living conditions exist if the individual resides on the business premises of the employer for the convenience of the employer and, because of the nature of the business (for example, a construction site or drilling rig), it is not feasible for the employer to provide housing for the individual's spouse or dependents. The criteria used by the Department of State in granting a separate maintenance allowance are relevant, but not determinative, for purposes of determining whether a separate household is provided because of adverse living conditions.

(c) *Base housing amount*—(1) *In general.* The base housing amount is equal to the product of 16 percent of the annual salary of an employee of the United States who is compensated at a rate equal to the annual salary rate paid for step 1 of grade GS-14, multiplied by the following fraction:

$$\frac{\text{The number of qualifying days}}{\text{The number of days in the taxable year}}$$

For purposes of the above fraction, the number of qualifying days is determined in accordance with § 1.911-3(d)(3).

(2) *Annual salary of step 1 of grade GS-14.* The annual salary rate for a step 1 of grade GS-14 is determined on January first of the calendar year in which the individual's taxable year begins.

(d) *Housing costs amount exclusion.*—(1) *Limitation.* A qualified individual who has elected to exclude his or her housing cost amount may only exclude the lesser of the full amount of either the individual's housing cost amount attributable to employer provided amounts or the individual's foreign earned income for the taxable year. A qualified individual who elects to exclude his or her housing cost amount may not claim less than the full amount of the housing cost exclusion determined under this paragraph.

(2) *Employer provided amounts.* For purposes of this section, the term "employer provided amounts" means any amounts paid or incurred on behalf of the individual by the individual's employer which are foreign earned income included in the individual's gross income for the taxable year (without regard to section 911). Employer provided amounts include, but are not limited to, the following amounts: any salary paid by the employer to the employee; any reimbursement paid by the employer to the employee for housing expenses, educational expenses for the individual's dependents, or as part of a tax equalization plan; the fair market value of compensation provided in kind (including lodging, unless excluded under section 119, relating to meals and lodging furnished for the convenience of the employer); and any amount paid by the employer to any third party on behalf of the employee. An individual will only have earnings that are not employer

Reg. § 1.911-4(b)(3)

Income from Sources Without the United States

provided amounts if the individual has earnings from self-employment.

(3) *Housing cost amount attributable to employer provided amounts.* For the purpose of determining what portion of the housing cost amount is excludable and what portion is deductible the following rules apply. If the individual has no income from self-employment, then the entire housing cost amount is attributable to employer provided amounts and is, therefore, excludable to the extent of the limitation provided in paragraph (d)(1) of this section. If the individual only has income from self-employment, then the entire housing cost amount is attributable to non-employer provided amounts and is, therefore, deductible to the extent of the limitation provided in paragraph (e) of this section. In all other instances, the housing cost amount attributable to employer provided amounts shall be determined by multiplying the housing cost amount by the following fraction: employer provided amounts over foreign earned income for the taxable year. The housing cost amount attributable to non-employer provided amounts shall be determined by subtracting the portion of the housing cost amount attributable to employer provided amounts from the total housing cost amount.

(e) *Housing cost amount deduction*—(1) *In general.* If a portion of the individual's housing cost amount is determined under paragraph (d)(3) of this section to be attributable to non-employer provided amounts, the individual may deduct that amount from gross income for the taxable year but only to the extent of the individual's foreign earned income (as defined in § 1.911-3) for the taxable year in excess of foreign earned income excluded and the housing cost amount excluded from gross income for the taxable year under § 1.911-3 and this section.

(2) *Carryover.* If any portion of the individual's housing cost amount deduction is disallowed for the taxable year under paragraph (e)(1) of this section, such portion shall be carried over and treated as a deduction from gross income for the succeeding taxable year (but only for the succeeding taxable year) to the extent of the excess, if any, of:

(i) The amount of foreign earned income for the succeeding taxable year less the foreign earned income and the housing cost amount excluded from gross income under § 1.911-3 and this section for the succeeding taxable year over,

(ii) The portion, if any, of the housing cost amount that is deductible under paragraph (e)(1) of this section for the succeeding taxable year.

(f) *Examples.* The following examples illustrate the application of this section. In all examples the annual rate for a step 1 of GS-14 as of January first of the calendar year in which the individual's taxable year begins is $39,689.

Example (1). B, a U.S. citizen, is a calendar year taxpayer who was a bona fide resident of and whose tax home was located in foreign country G for the entire taxable year 1982. B receives an $80,000 salary from B's employer for services performed in G. B incurs no business expenses. B receives housing provided by B's employer with a fair rental value of $15,000. The value of the housing furnished by B's employer is not excluded from gross income under section 119. B pays $10,000 for housing expenses. B's gross income and foreign earned income for 1982 is $95,000. B elects the foreign earned income exclusion of section 911(a)(1) and the housing cost amount exclusion of section 911(a)(2). B must first compute his housing cost amount exclusion. B's housing cost amount is $18,650 determined by reducing B's housing expenses, $25,000 ($15,000 fair rental value of housing and $10,000 of other expenses), by the base housing amount of $6,350 (($39,689 × .16) × 365/365). Because B has no income from self-employment, the entire amount is attributable to employer provided amounts and, therefore, is excludable. B's section 911(a)(1) limitation is over $75,000. That is the lesser of $75,000 × 365/365 or $95,000 − 18,650. B's total exclusion for 1982 under section 911(a)(1) and (2) is $93,650.

Example (2). The facts are the same as in example (1) except that B's salary for 1982 is $70,000. B's foreign earned income for 1982 is $85,000. B's housing cost amount is $18,650, all of which is attributable to employer provided amounts. B's housing cost amount is excludable to the extent of the lesser of B's housing cost amount attributable to employer provided amounts, $18,650, or the foreign earned income for the taxable year, $85,000. Thus, B excludes $18,650 under section 911(a)(2). B's section 911(a)(1) limitation for 1982 is $66,350 (the lesser of $75,000 × 365/365 or $85,000 − 18,650). B's total exclusion for 1982 under section 911(a)(1) and (2) is $85,000.

Example (3). The facts are the same as in example (2) except that in 1983, B receives $5,000 attributable to services performed in 1982. B may exclude the entire $5,000 in 1983 because such amount would have been excludable under § 1.911-3(d)(1) had it been received in 1982.

Example (4). C is a U.S. citizen, self-employed, and a calendar year and cash basis taxpayer. C arrived in foreign country H on October 3, 1982, and departed from H on March 8, 1984. C's tax home was located in H throughout that period. C

Reg. § 1.911-4(f)

was physically present for 330 full days during the twelve consecutive month period August 30, 1982 through August 29, 1983. The number of C's qualifying days in 1982 is 124. During 1982 C had $35,000 of foreign earned income, none of which was attributable to employer provided amounts, and $8,000 of reasonable housing expenses. C's housing cost amount is $5,843 ($8,000 − ((39,689 × .16) × 124/365)). C elects to exclude her foreign earned income under § 1.911-3(d)(1). C's section 911(a)(1) limitation for 1982 is $25,479 (the lesser of C's foreign earned income for the taxable year ($35,000) or the annual rate for the taxable year multiplied by the number of C's qualifying days over the number of days in the taxable year ($75,000 × 124/365 = $25,479)). C may not claim the housing cost amount exclusion under section 911(a)(2) because no portion of the housing cost amount is attributable to employer provided amounts. C may deduct the lesser of her housing cost amount ($5,843) or her foreign earned income in excess of amounts excluded under section 911(a) ($35,000 − 25,479 = $9,521). Thus, C's housing cost amount deduction is $5,843.

Example (5). The facts are the same as in example (4) except that C had $30,000 of foreign earned income for 1982, none of which was attributable to employer provided amounts. C elects to exclude $25,479 under § 1.911-3(d)(1). C may only deduct $4,521 of her housing cost amount under paragraph (e)(1) of this section because her foreign earned income in excess of amounts excluded under section 911(a) is $4,521 ($30,000 − 25,479). The $1322 of unused housing cost amount deduction may be carried over to the subsequent taxable year.

Example (6). The facts are the same as in example (4) except that C had $15,000 of foreign earned income for 1982, none of which was attributable to employer provided amounts. C elects to exclude the entire $15,000 under § 1.911-3(d)(1). C is not entitled to a housing cost amount deduction for 1982 since she has no foreign earned income in excess of amounts excluded under section 911(a). C may carryover her entire housing cost amount deduction to 1983.

Example (7). The facts are the same as in example (6). In addition, during taxable year 1983 C had $115,000 of foreign earned income, none of which was attributable to employer provided amounts, and $40,000 of reasonable housing expenses. C elects to exclude her foreign earned income under § 1.911-3(d)(1). C's section 911(a)(1) limitation is the lesser of $115,000 or $80,000 ($80,000 × 365/365). C's housing cost amount for 1983 is $33,650 (40,000 − (($39,689 ×

.16) × 365/365). Since no portion of that amount is attributable to employer provided amounts, C may not claim a housing cost amount exclusion. C may deduct the lesser of her housing cost amount ($33,650) or her foreign earned income in excess of amounts excluded under section 911(a) ($115,000 − 80,000 = 35,000). Thus, C may deduct her $33,650 housing cost amount in 1983. In addition, C may deduct $1,350 of the housing cost amount deduction carried over from taxable year 1982 (($115,000 − 80,000) − 33,650 = $1,350). The remaining $4,493 ($5,843 − 1,350) of the housing cost amount deduction carried over from taxable year 1982 may not be deducted in 1983 or carried over to 1984.

Example (8). D is a U.S. citizen and a calendar year and cash basis taxpayer. D is a bona fide resident of and maintains his tax home in foreign country J for all of taxable year 1984. In 1984, D earns $80,000 of foreign earned income, $60,000 of which is an employer provided amount and $20,000 of which is a non-employer provided amount. D's total housing cost amount for 1984 is $25,000. D elects to exclude, under section 911(a)(2), the portion of his housing cost amount that is attributable to employer provided amounts. D's excludable housing cost amount is $18,750; that is the total housing cost amount ($25,000) multiplied by employer provided amounts for the taxable year ($60,000) over foreign earned income for the taxable year ($80,000). D also elects to exclude his foreign earned income under § 1.911-3(d)(1). D's section 911(a)(1) limitation for 1984 is $61,250 (the lesser of $80,000 − $18,750 or $80,000 × 366/366). D's total exclusion for 1984 under section 911(a)(1) and (2) is $80,000. D cannot claim a housing cost amount deduction in 1984 because D has no foreign earned income in excess of his foreign earned income and housing cost amount excluded from gross income for the taxable year under § 1.911-3 and this section. D may carry over his housing cost amount deduction of $6,250, the total housing cost amount less the portion attributable to employer provided amounts ($25,000 − 18,750), to taxable year 1985. [Reg. § 1.911-4.]

☐ [T.D. 8006, 1-17-85.]

[Reg. § 1.911-5]

§ 1.911-5. Special rules for married couples.—(a) *Married couples with two qualified individuals.*—(1) *In general.* In the case in which a husband and wife both are qualified individuals under § 1.911-2(a), each individual may make one or more elections under § 1.911-7 and exclude from gross income foreign earned income and exclude or deduct housing cost amounts subject to

Reg. § 1.911-5(a)(1)

the rules of paragraph (a)(2) and (3) of this section.

(2) *Computation of excluded foreign earned income.* The amount of excludable foreign earned income is determined separately for each spouse under the rules of § 1.911-3 on the basis of the income attributable to the services of that spouse. If the spouses file separate returns each may exclude the amount of his or her foreign earned income attributable to his or her services subject to the limitations of § 1.911-3(d)(2). If the spouses file a joint return, the sum of these foreign earned income amounts so determined for each spouse may be excluded. For example, H and W both qualify under § 1.911-2(a)(2)(i) for the entire 1983 taxable year. During 1983 W earns $100,000 of foreign earned income and H earns $45,000 of foreign earned income. H and W file a joint return for 1983. On their joint return H and W may exclude from gross income a total of $125,000. That amount is determined by adding W's section 911(a)(1) limitation, $80,000 (the lesser of $80,000 × 365/365 or $100,000), and H's section 911(a)(1) limitation, $45,000 (the lesser of $80,000 × 365/365 or $45,000).

(3) *Computation of housing cost amount* — (i) *Spouses residing together.* If the spouses reside together, and file a joint return, they may compute their housing cost amount either jointly or separately. If the spouses reside together and file separate returns, they must compute their housing cost amounts separately. If the spouses compute their housing cost amounts separately, they may allocate the housing expenses to either of them or between them for the purpose of calculating separate housing cost amounts, but each spouse claiming a housing cost amount exclusion or deduction must use his or her full base housing amount in such computation. If the spouses compute their housing cost amount jointly, then only one of the spouses may claim the housing cost amount exclusion or deduction. Either spouse may claim the housing cost amount exclusion or deduction; however, if the spouses have different periods of residence or presence and the spouse with the shorter period of residence or presence claims the exclusion or deduction, then only the expenses incurred in that shorter period may be claimed as housing expenses. The spouse claiming the exclusion or deduction may aggregate the couple's housing expenses, and subtract his or her base housing amount. For example, H and W reside together and file a joint return. H was a bona fide resident of and maintained his tax home in foreign country M from August 17, 1982 through December 31, 1983. W was a bona fide resident of and maintained her tax home in foreign country M from September 15, 1982 through December 31, 1983. During 1982, H and W earn and receive, respectively, $25,000 and $10,000 of foreign earned income. H paid $10,000 for qualified housing expenses in 1982, $7,500 of that was for qualified housing expenses incurred from September 15, 1982 through December 31, 1982. W paid $3,000 for qualified housing expenses in 1982 all of which were incurred during her period of residence. H and W may choose to compute their housing cost amount jointly. If they do so and H claims the housing cost amount exclusion his exclusion would be $10,617. H's housing expenses would be $13,000 ($10,000 + $3,000) and his base housing amount would be $2,383 (($39,689 × .16) × 137/365 = $2,383). If instead W claims the housing cost amount exclusion her exclusion would be $8,621. W's housing expenses would be $10,500 ($7,500 + 3,000) and her base housing amount would be $1,879 (($39,689 × .16) × 108/365 = $1,879). If H and W file jointly and both claim a housing cost amount exclusion, then H's and W's housing cost amounts would be, respectively, $7,617 ($10,000 − 2,383) and $1,121 ($3,000 − 1,879).

(ii) *Spouses residing apart.* If the spouses reside apart, both spouses may exclude or deduct their housing cost amount if the spouses have different tax homes that are not within reasonable commuting distance (as defined in § 1.119-(d)(4)) of each other and neither spouse's residence is within a reasonable commuting distance of the other spouse's tax home. If the spouses' tax homes, or one spouse's residence and the other spouse's tax home, are within a reasonable commuting distance of each other, only one spouse may exclude or deduct his or her housing cost amount. Regardless of whether the spouses file joint or separate returns, the amount of the housing cost amount exclusion or deduction must be determined separately for each spouse under the rules of § 1.911-4. If both spouses claim a housing cost amount exclusion or deduction directly as qualified individuals, neither may claim any such exclusion or deduction under section 911(c)(2)(B)(ii), relating to a second foreign household maintained for the other spouse. If one spouse fails to claim a housing cost amount exclusion or deduction which that spouse could claim directly, the other spouse may claim such exclusion or deduction under section 911(c)(2)(B)(ii), relating to a second foreign household maintained for the first spouse, provided that all the requirements of that section are met. Spouses may not claim more than one second foreign household and the expenses of such household may only be claimed by one spouse. For example, if both H and W are qualified individuals and H's tax home is in London and W's tax home is in Paris, then both H

Reg. § 1.911-5(a)(3)

and W may exclude or deduct their housing cost amounts; however, H and W must compute these amounts separately regardless of whether they file joint or separate returns. If instead of living in Paris, W lives in an area where there are adverse living conditions and W maintains H's home in London, then W may add those housing expenses to her housing expenses and compute one base housing amount. In that case H may not claim a housing cost amount exclusion or deduction.

(iii) *Housing cost amount attributable to employer provided amounts.* Each spouse claiming a housing cost amount exclusion or deduction shall compute the portion of the housing cost amount that is attributable to employer provided amounts separately, based on his or her separate foreign earned income, in accordance with § 1.911-4(d)(3).

(b) *Married couples with community income.* The amount of excludable foreign earned income of a husband and wife with community income is determined separately for each spouse in accordance with paragraph (a) of this section on the basis of income attributable to that spouse's services without regard to community property laws. See sections 879 and 6013(g) and (h) for special rules regarding treatment of community income of a nonresident alien individual married to a U.S. citizen or resident. [Reg. § 1.911-5.]

☐ [T.D. 8006, 1-17-85.]

[Reg. § 1.911-6]

§ 1.911-6. Disallowance of deductions, exclusions, and credits.—(a) *In general.* No deduction or exclusion from gross income under Subtitle A of the Code or credit against the tax imposed by chapter 1 of the Code shall be allowed to the extent the deduction, exclusion, or credit is properly allocable to or chargeable against amounts excluded from gross income under section 911(a). For purposes of the preceding sentence, deductions, exclusions, and credits which are definitely related (as provided in § 1.861-8), in whole or in part, to earned income shall be allocated and apportioned to foreign earned income and U.S. source earned income in accordance with the rules contained in § 1.861-8. Deductions, exclusions, and credits which are definitely related to all gross income under § 1.861-8, including deductions for interest described in § 1.861-8(e)(2)(ii), are definitely related, in whole or in part, to earned income. In the case of interest expense allocable, in whole or in part, to foreign earned income under § 1.861-8(e)(2)(ii), the expense shall normally be apportioned under option one of the optional gross income methods of apportionment (§ 1.861-8(e)(2)(vi)(A)), but without regard to conditions *(1)* and *(2)* of subdivision (vi)(A) (the fifty percent conditions). Such interest expense shall not normally be apportioned under the asset method of § 1.861-8(e)(2)(v). This is because, where section 911 is the operative section, the expense normally relates more closely to gross income generated from activities than to the amount of capital utilized or invested in activities or property. Deductions that are allocated and apportioned to foreign earned income must then be allocated and apportioned to foreign earned income that is excluded under section 911(a). If an individual has foreign earned income from both self-employment and other employment, the amount excluded under section 911(a)(1) shall be deemed to include a pro rata amount of the self-employment income and the income from other employment; thus, a pro rata portion of deductible expenses attributable to self-employment income must be disallowed. For purposes of section 911(d)(6) and this section only, deductions, exclusions, or credits which are not definitely related to any class of gross income shall not be allocable or chargeable to excluded amounts and are, therefore, deductible to the extent allowed by chapter 1 of the Code. Examples of deductions that are not definitely related to a class of gross income are personal and family medical expenses, qualified retirement contributions (but see section 219(b)(1)), real estate taxes and mortgage interest on a personal residence, charitable contributions, alimony payments, and deductions for personal exemptions. In addition, for purposes of this section, amounts excludable or deductible under section 911 or 119 shall not be allocable or chargeable to other amounts excluded under section 911(a). Thus, an individual's housing cost amount which is excludable or deductible under § 1.911-4(d) for a taxable year is not apportioned in part to the individual's foreign earned income which is excluded for such year under § 1.911-3(d). Therefore, the entire amount of such exclusion or deduction is allowed to the extent provided in § 1.911-4. This section does not affect the time for claiming any deduction, exclusion, or credit that is not allocated or apportioned to excluded amounts.

(b) *Moving expenses*—(1) *In general.* No deduction shall be allowed for moving expenses under section 217 to the extent the deduction is properly allocable to or chargeable against amounts of foreign earned income excluded from gross income under section 911(a). If an individual's new principal place of work is in a foreign country, deductible moving expenses will be allocable to foreign earned income. If an individual treats a reimbursement from his employer for the expenses of a move from a foreign country to the United States as attributable to services performed in a foreign country under § 1.911-3(e)(5)(i), then deductible moving expenses attributable to that move will be allocable to foreign earned income. If the individual is a qualified individual who elects to exclude foreign earned income under section 911(a), then some or all of such moving expenses must be disallowed as a deduction.

(2) *Attribution of moving expense deduction to taxable years in which services are performed.* If a moving expense deduction is properly allocable to foreign earned income, the deduction shall be considered attributable to services performed in the year of the move as long as the individual is a qualified individual under § 1.911-2(a) for a period that includes 120 days in the year of the move. If the individual is not a qualified individual for such period, then the individual shall treat the deduction as attributable to services performed in both the year of the move and the succeeding taxable year, if the move is from the United States to the foreign country, or the prior taxable year, if the move is from a foreign country to the United States. Notwithstanding the preceding two sentences, storage expenses incurred after December 31, 1983 shall be treated as attributable to services performed in the year in which the expenses are incurred.

(3) *Formula for disallowance of moving expense deduction.* The portion of the moving expense deduction that is disallowed shall be determined by multiplying the moving expense deduction by a fraction the numerator of which is all amounts excluded under section 911(a) for the year or years to which the deduction is attributable (under paragraph (b)(2) of this section) and the denominator of which is foreign earned income (as defined in § 1.911-3(a)) for that year or years.

(4) *Effect of disallowance based on attribution of deduction to subsequent year's income.* An individual may claim a moving expense deduction in the taxable year in which the amount of the expense is paid or incurred even if attributable, in part, to the succeeding year. However, at such time as the individual excludes income under section 911(a) for the year or years to which the deduction is attributable, the individual shall either—

(i) file an amended return for the year in which the deduction was claimed that does not claim the portion of the deduction that is disallowed because it is chargeable against excluded income, or

(ii) include in income for the year following the year in which the deduction was claimed an amount equal to the amount of the deduction that is disallowed.

Any amount included in income under paragraph (b)(4)(ii) of this section is not foreign earned income.

(5) *Moves beginning before January 1, 1984.* Notwithstanding paragraph (b)(1) through (3) of this section, the rules of this paragraph (b)(5) shall apply for moves beginning before January 1, 1984.

(i) *Individual qualifies for the entire taxable year of the move.* If the individual is a qualified individual for the entire taxable year of the move, then the amount of moving expenses disallowed shall be determined by multiplying the moving expense deduction otherwise allowable by a fraction the numerator of which is the foreign earned income excluded under section 911(a) for the taxable year of the move and the denominator of which is the foreign earned income for the same taxable year.

(ii) *Individual qualifies for less than the entire taxable year of the move.* If the individual is a qualified individual for less than the entire taxable year of the move, then, for the purpose of determining the portion of the otherwise allowable moving expense deduction that is disallowed, the individual must attribute a portion of the otherwise allowable moving expense deduction either to the succeeding taxable year, if the move is from the United States to a foreign country, or to the prior taxable year, if the move is from a foreign country to the United States. The portion of the moving expense deduction treated as attributable to services performed in the year of the move shall be determined by multiplying the otherwise allowable moving expense deduction by the following fraction:

$$\frac{\text{The number of qualifying days (as defined in § 1.911-3(d)(3)) in the year of the move}}{\text{The number of days in the taxable year of the move.}}$$

The portion of the moving expense deduction treated as attributable to the year succeeding or preceding the move shall be determined by subtracting the portion of the moving expense deduction that is attributable to the year of the move from the total moving expense deduction. The allocation of a portion of the moving expense deduction to a succeeding or preceding taxable year does not affect the time for claiming the allowable moving expense deduction. The portion of the moving expense deduction that is disallowed shall be determined by multiplying the moving expense deduction attributable to the year of the move or the succeeding or preceding year, as the case may be, by a fraction the numerator of which is amounts excluded under section 911(a) for that year and the denominator of which is foreign earned income for that year.

(c) *Foreign taxes*—(1) *Amount disallowed.* No deduction or credit is allowed for foreign income, war profits, or excess profits taxes paid or accrued with respect to amounts excluded from gross income under section 911. To determine the amount of disallowed foreign taxes, multiply the foreign tax imposed on foreign earned income (as defined in § 1.911-3(a)) received or accrued during the taxable year by a fraction, the numerator of which is amounts excluded under section 911(a) in such taxable year less deductible expenses properly allocated to such amounts (see paragraphs (a) and (b) of this section), and the denominator of which is foreign earned income (as defined in § 1.911-3(a)) received or accrued during the taxable year less deductible expenses properly allocated or apportioned thereto. For the purpose of determining the extent to which foreign taxes are disallowed, the housing cost amount deduction is treated as definitely related to foreign earned income that is not excluded. If the foreign tax is imposed on foreign earned income and some other income (for example, earned income from sources within the United States or an amount not subject to tax in the United States), and the taxes on the other amount cannot be segregated, then the denominator equals the total of the amounts subject to tax less deductible expenses allocable to all such amounts.

(2) *Definitions and special rules*—(i) *Taxable year.* For purposes of paragraph (c)(1) of this section, the term "taxable year" means the individual's taxable year for U.S. tax purposes. Such term includes the portion of any foreign taxable year within the individual's U.S. taxable year and excludes the portion of any foreign taxable year not within the individual's U.S. taxable year.

(ii) *Apportionment of foreign taxes.* For purposes of this paragraph (c), foreign taxes imposed on foreign earned income shall be deemed to accrue, on a pro rata basis, to income as the income is received or accrued. The taxes so accrued shall be apportioned to the taxable year during which the income is received or accrued. This rule applies for all individuals, regardless of their method of accounting.

(iii) *Effect of disallowance.* The disallowance of foreign taxes under this paragraph (c) shall not affect the time for claiming any deduction or credit for foreign taxes paid. Rather, the disallowance shall only affect the amount of taxes considered paid or accrued to any foreign country.

(iv) *Interest on foreign taxes.* Any interest expense incurred on a liability for foreign taxes is allocated and apportioned not under this paragraph (c) but under paragraph (a) of this section to foreign earned income and then to excluded foreign earned income and to that extent disallowed as a deduction under paragraph (a). In that regard, see also § 1.861-8(e)(2) for the specific rules for allocation and apportionment of interest expense.

(d) *Examples.* The following examples illustrate the application of this section.

Example (1). In 1982 A, an architect, operates his business as a sole proprietorship in which capital is not a material income producing factor. A receives $1,000,000 in gross receipts, all of which is foreign source earned income, and incurs $500,000 of otherwise deductible business expenses definitely related to the foreign earned income. A elects to exclude $75,000 under section 911(a)(1). The expenses must be apportioned to excluded earned income as follows: $500,000 × $75,000/1,000,000. Thus, $37,500 of the business expenses are not deductible.

Example (2). The facts are the same as in example (1), except that $100,000 of A's gross receipts is U.S. source earned income and $68,000 of A's business expenses are attributable to the U.S. source earned income. Thus, A has $900,000 of foreign earned income and $432,000 of deductions allocated to foreign earned income. The expenses apportioned to excluded earned income are $432,000 × $75,000/$900,000, or $36,000, which are not deductible.

Example (3). B is a U.S. citizen, calendar year and cash basis taxpayer. B moves to foreign country N and maintains a tax home and is physically present there from July 1, 1984 through May 26, 1985. Among other possible periods, B is a qualified individual for 219 days in the year of the move. B pays $6,000 of otherwise deductible moving expenses in 1984. For 1984, B's foreign earned income is $60,000 and B excludes $47,869 ($80,000 × 219/366) under section 911(a). Under paragraph (b)(2) of this section, B's moving expenses are attributable to services performed in 1984. Under paragraph (b)(3) of this section, $6,000 × $47,869/$60,000, or $4,789, of B's moving expense deduction is disallowed. B may deduct $1,211 of moving expenses on his 1984 return.

Example (4). The facts are the same as in example (3) except that B maintains a tax home and is physically present in foreign country N from October 9, 1984 through September 3, 1985. Among other possible periods, B is a qualified individual for no more than 119 days in 1984 and 281 days in 1985. B's foreign earned income for

Reg. § 1.911-6(c)(1)

Income from Sources Without the United States

1984 is $60,000. B's foreign earned income for 1985 is $150,000. Because B is a qualified individual for less than 120 days in the year of the move, under paragraph (b)(2) of this section, B's moving expenses are attributable to services performed in 1984 and 1985. At the close of 1984, B may either seek an extension of time to file under § 1.911-7(c) or may file an income tax return without claiming the exclusions or deduction under section 911. B does not seek an extension and files without excluding foreign earned income; thus B may deduct his moving expenses in full. B later amends his 1984 return and excludes foreign earned income for that year. B excludes foreign earned income for 1985. B must determine the portion of the moving expense deduction that is disallowed. The portion of the moving expense deduction that is disallowed is determined by multiplying the otherwise allowable moving expense deduction by a fraction. The numerator of the fraction is the sum of amounts excluded under section 911(a) for 1984 and 1985, that is, $26,082, or $80,000 × 119/365, plus $61,589, or $80,000 × 281/365, which totals $87,671. The denominator of the fraction is the sum of foreign earned income for 1984 and 1985, that is, $60,000 plus $150,000, or $210,000. B's allowable moving expense deduction is $3,495, or $6,000—($6,000 × $87,671/$210,000). If B does not file an amended 1984 return (and does not exclude foreign earned income for 1984), but excludes foreign earned income under section 911(a) for 1985, a portion of his moving expense deduction is disallowed, based on the same formula. The amount disallowed is $6,000 × $61,589/$210,000, or $1,760. This amount may be recaptured either by filing an amended return for 1984 or by including it in income for 1985 (in which case it is not foreign earned income).

Example (5). C is a U.S. citizen, a self-employed individual, and a cash basis and calendar year taxpayer. For the entire 1982 taxable year C maintained his tax home and his bona fide residence in foreign country P. During 1982 C earned and received $120,000 of foreign earned income, none of which was attributable to employer provided amounts. C paid $40,000 of business expenses. C elected to exclude foreign earned income under section 911(a)(1) and claimed a housing cost amount deduction of $15,000. C received $10,000 of foreign source interest income which was included with C's earned income in a single tax base and taxed at graduated rates. For 1982, C paid $30,000 in income tax to foreign country P. The amount of C's business expenses that is properly apportioned to excluded amounts (and therefore, not deductible) equals $25,000, which is determined by multiplying the otherwise allowable deductions by C's excluded amounts over C's foreign earned income ($40,000 × $75,000/$120,000). The amount of country P tax that is properly apportioned to excluded amounts (and therefore, not deductible or creditable) equals $20,000, which is determined by multiplying the tax of $30,000 by the following fraction:

$$\frac{\$50,000\ (\$75,000\ \text{excluded amounts less}\ \$25,000\ \text{of deductible expenses allocable thereto})}{\$75,000\ ((\$120,000\ \text{foreign earned income less}\ \$40,000\ \text{of deductible expenses allocable thereto})\ \text{less}\ \$15,000\ (\text{housing cost amount deduction allocable thereto})\ \text{plus}\ \$10,000\ \text{other taxable income}).}$$

Example (6). D is a U.S. citizen and an accrual basis and calendar year taxpayer for U.S. tax purposes. For the entire period from January 1, 1982 through December 31, 1983, D maintains his tax home and his bona fide residence in foreign country R. For purposes of R's income tax, D is a cash basis taxpayer and uses a fiscal year that begins on April 1 and ends on the following March 31. During his entire period of residence in R, D receives foreign earned income of $10,000 each month, all of which is attributable to employer provided amounts. For his foreign taxable year ending March 31, 1982, D pays $10,000 of income tax to R. For his foreign taxable year ending March 31, 1983, D pays $54,000 of income tax to R. Under paragraph (c)(2)(ii) of this section, all of the $10,000 of tax paid for his foreign taxable year ending March 31, 1982 is imposed on foreign earned income received in 1982, as is $40,500 or 9/12 × $54,000, of tax paid for his foreign taxable year ending March 31, 1983. (D received $10,000 per month for the last 3 months of his foreign taxable year ending March 31, 1982, all of which are within his U.S. taxable year ending December 31, 1982 under paragraph (c)(2)(i) of this section, and $10,000 per month for each month of his foreign taxable year ending March 31, 1983, of which the first 9 months are within his U.S. taxable year ending December 31, 1982. Under paragraph (c)(2)(ii) of this section, foreign taxes are deemed to accrue on a pro rata basis to income as it is received or accrued. Thus, all of the $10,000 of foreign taxes imposed on the income received during D's foreign taxable year ending March 31, 1982 accrue to D's 1982 foreign earned income, as do 9/12 (or $90,000/$120,000) of foreign taxes imposed on income received during D's foreign taxable year ending March 31, 1983, for purposes of determining the amount of D's foreign taxes that is disallowed.) For 1982, D has no deductible expenses, and elects to exclude his housing cost amount of $21,000 under section 911(a)(2) and foreign earned income of $75,000 under section 911(a)(1). The amount of D's foreign taxes disal-

Reg. § 1.911-6(d)

lowed for deduction or credit purposes for 1982 is $8,000 (that is, $10,000 × $96,000/$120,000) of the taxes for his foreign taxable year ending March 31, 1982, plus $32,400 (that is, $40,500 × $96,000/$120,000) of the taxes for his foreign taxable year ending March 31, 1983, or $40,400. From 1982, D has $2,000 ($10,000 − $8,000) of deductible or creditable taxes accrued on March 31, 1982, and $8,100 ($40,500 − $32,400) of deductible or creditable taxes accrued on March 31, 1983, after the disallowance based on his 1982 excluded income.

Example (7). E is a United States citizen, calendar year and cash basis taxpayer. E is physically present in and establishes his tax home in foreign country S on May 1, 1981. For purposes of country S, E's taxable year begins on April 1 and ends the following March 31. E receives foreign earned income of $15,000 each month beginning May 1, 1981. At the end of his foreign taxable year ending on March 31, 1982, E pays $70,000 of income tax to S on $165,000 of foreign earned income. Under section 911, as in effect for taxable years beginning before January 1, 1982, E may not exclude any income that is earned or received during 1981. None of E's taxes paid in 1982 that are attributable to income earned or received in 1981 are subject to disallowance because, under paragraph (c)(2)(ii) of this section, the only taxes disallowed are those deemed to accrue on income earned and received after December 31, 1981, and excluded from gross income. The amount of E's taxes paid in 1982 that are attributable to 1981 is $50,909, or $70,000 × $120,000/$165,000. E elects to exclude foreign earned income for 1982. The amount of E's taxes paid to S in 1982 that accrue to 1982 foreign earned income, and are therefore subject to disallowance based on excluded income, is $19,091, or $70,000 × $45,000/$165,000. [Reg. § 1.911-6.]

☐ [T.D. 8006, 1-17-85.]

[Reg. § 1.911-7]

§ 1.911-7. **Procedural rules.**—(a) *Elections of a qualified individual*—(1) *In general.* In order to receive either exclusion provided by section 911(a), a qualified individual must elect, separately with respect to each exclusion, to exclude foreign earned income under section 911(a)(1) and the housing cost amount under section 911(a)(2). Any such elections may be made on Form 2555 or on a comparable form. Each election must be filed either with the income tax return, or with an amended return, for the first taxable year of the individual for which the election is to be effective. An election once made remains in effect for that year and all subsequent years unless revoked under paragraph (b) of this section. Each election shall contain information sufficient to determine whether the individual is a qualified individual as provided in § 1.911-2. The statement shall include the following information:

(i) The individual's name, address, and social security number;

(ii) The name of the individual's employer;

(iii) Whether the individual claimed exclusions under section 911 for earlier years after 1981 and within the five preceding taxable years;

(iv) Whether the individual has revoked a previously made election and the taxable year for which such revocation was effective;

(v) The exclusion or exclusions the individual is electing;

(vi) The foreign country or countries in which the individual's tax home is located and the date when such tax home was established;

(vii) The status (either bona fide residence or physical presence) under which the individual claims the exclusion;

(viii) The individual's qualifying period of residence or presence;

(ix) The individual's foreign earned income for the taxable year including the fair market value of all noncash remuneration; and,

(x) If the individual elects to exclude the housing cost amount, the individual's housing expenses.

(2) *Requirement of a return*—(i) *In general.* In order to make a valid election under this paragraph (a), the election must be made:

(A) With an income tax return that is timely filed (including any extensions of time to file),

(B) With a later return filed within the period prescribed in section 6511(a) amending the foregoing timely filed income tax return,

(C) With an original income tax return that is filed within one year after the due date of the return (determined without regard to any extension of time to file); this one year period does not constitute an extension of time for any purpose—it is merely a period during which a valid election may be made on a late return, or

(D) With an income tax return filed after the period described in paragraphs (a)(2)(i)(A), (B), or (C) of this section provided—

(*1*) The taxpayer owes no federal income tax after taking into account the exclusion and files Form 1040 with Form 2555 or a comparable form attached either before or after the Internal Revenue Service discovers that the taxpayer failed to elect the exclusion; or

Reg. § 1.911-7(a)(1)

(2) The taxpayer owes federal income tax after taking into account the exclusion and files Form 1040 with Form 2555 or a comparable form attached before the Internal Revenue Service discovers that the taxpayer failed to elect the exclusion.

(3) A taxpayer filing an income tax return pursuant to paragraph (a)(2)(i)(D)(*1*) or (*2*) of this section must type or legibly print the following statement at the top of the first page of the Form 1040: "Filed Pursuant to Section 1.911-7(a)(2)(i)(D)."

(ii) *Election for 1982 and 1983 taxable years.* Solely for purposes of paragraph (a)(2)(i)(A) of this section, an income tax return for any taxable year beginning before January 1, 1984 shall be considered timely filed if it is filed on or before July 23, 1985.

(3) *Housing cost amount deduction.* An individual does not have to make an election in order to claim the housing cost amount deduction. However, such individual must provide the Commissioner with information sufficient to determine the individual's correct amount of tax. Such information shall include the following: the individual's name, address, and social security number; the name of the individual's employer; the foreign country in which the individual's tax home was established; the status under which the individual claims the deduction; the individual's qualifying period of residence or presence; the individual's foreign earned income for the taxable year; and the individual's housing expenses.

(4) *Effect of immaterial error or omission.* An inadvertent error or omission of information required to be provided to make an election under this paragraph (a) shall not render the election invalid if the error or omission is not material in determining whether the individual is a qualified individual or whether the individual intends to make the election.

(b) *Revocation of election*—(1) *In general.* An individual may revoke any election made under paragraph (a) of this section for any taxable year. A revocation must be made separately with respect to each election. The individual may revoke an election for any taxable year, including the first taxable year for which an election was effective, by filing a statement that the individual is revoking one or more of the previously made elections. The statement must be filed with the income tax return, or with an amended return, for the first taxable year of individual for which the revocation is to be effective. A revocation once made is effective for that year and all subsequent years. If an election is revoked for any taxable year, including the first taxable year for which the election was effective, the individual may not, without the consent of the Commissioner, again make the same election until the sixth taxable year following the taxable year for which the revocation was first effective. For example, a qualified individual makes an election to exclude foreign earned income under section 911(a)(1) and files it with his 1982 income tax return. The individual files 1983 and 1984 income tax returns on which he excludes his foreign earned income. Then, within 3 years after filing his 1982 income tax return, the individual files an amended 1982 income tax return with a statement revoking his election to exclude foreign earned income under section 911(a)(1). The revocation of the election is effective for taxable years 1982, 1983, and 1984. The individual may not elect to exclude income under section 911(a)(1) for any taxable year before 1988, unless he obtains consent to reelect under paragraph (b)(2) of this section.

(2) *Reelection before sixth taxable year after revocation.* If an individual revoked an election under paragraph (b)(1) of this section and within five taxable years the individual wishes to reelect the same exclusion, then the individual may apply for consent to the reelection. The application for consent shall be made by requesting a ruling from the Associate Chief Counsel (Technical), National Office, Internal Revenue Service, 1111 Constitution Avenue NW., Washington, D.C. 20224. In determining whether to consent to a reelection the Associate Chief Counsel or his delegate shall consider any facts and circumstances that may be relevant to the determination. Relevant facts and circumstances may include the following: a period of United States residence, a move from one foreign country to another foreign country with differing tax rates, a substantial change in the tax laws of the foreign country of residence or physical presence, and a change of employer.

(c) *Returns and extensions*—(1) *In general.* Any return filed before completion of the period necessary to qualify an individual for any exclusion or deduction provided by section 911 shall be filed without regard to any exclusion or deduction provided by that section. A claim for a credit or refund of any overpayment of tax may be filed, however, if the taxpayer subsequently qualifies for any exclusion or deduction under section 911. See section 6012(c) and § 1.6012-1(a)(3), relating to returns to be filed and information to be furnished by individuals who qualify for any exclusion or deduction under section 911.

(2) *Extensions.* An individual desiring an extension of time (in addition to the automatic extension of time granted by § 1.6081-2) for filing a return until after the completion of the qualifying

period described in paragraph (c)(1) of this section for claiming any exclusion or deduction under section 911 may apply for an extension. An individual whose moving expense deduction is attributable to services performed in two years may apply for an extension of time for filing a return until after the end of the second year. The individual may make such application on Form 2350 or a comparable form. The application must be filed with the Director, Internal Revenue Service Center, Philadelphia, Pennsylvania 19255. The application must set forth the facts relied on to justify the extension of time requested and must include a statement as to the earliest date the individual expects to become entitled to any exclusion or deduction by reason of completion of the qualifying period.

(d) *Declaration of estimated tax.* In estimating gross income for the purpose of determining whether a declaration of estimated tax must be made for any taxable year, an individual is not required to take into account income which the individual reasonably believes will be excluded from gross income under the provisions of section 911. In computing estimated tax, however, the individual must take into account, among other things, the denial of the foreign tax credit for foreign taxes allocable to the excluded income (see § 1.911-6(c)). [Reg. § 1.911-7.]

☐ [T.D. 8006, 1-17-85. Amended by T.D. 8480, 6-29-93.]

[Reg. § 1.911-8]

§ 1.911-8. Former deduction for certain expenses of living abroad.—For rules relating to the deduction for certain expenses of living abroad applicable to taxable years beginning before January 1, 1982, see 26 CFR §§ 1.913-1 through 1.913-13 as they appeared in the Code of Federal Regulations revised as of April 1, 1982. [Reg. § 1.911-8.]

☐ [T.D. 8006, 1-17-85.]

[Reg. § 1.912-1]

§ 1.912-1. Exclusion of certain cost-of-living allowances.—(a) Amounts received by Government civilian personnel stationed outside the continental United States as cost-of-living allowances in accordance with regulations approved by the President are, by the provisions of section 912(1), excluded from gross income. Such allowances shall be considered as retaining their characteristics under section 912(1) notwithstanding any combination thereof with any other allowance. For example, the cost-of-living portion of a "living and quarters allowance" would be excluded from gross income whether or not any other portion of such allowance is excluded from gross income.

(b) For purposes of section 912(1), the term "continental United States" includes only the 48 States existing on February 25, 1944 (the date of the enactment of the Revenue Act of 1943 (58 Stat. 21)) and the District of Columbia [Reg. § 1.912-1.]

☐ [T.D. 6249, 8-21-57. Amended by T.D. 6365, 2-13-59.]

[Reg. § 1.912-2]

§ 1.912-2. Exclusion of certain allowances of Foreign Service personnel.—Gross income does not include amounts received by personnel of the Foreign Service of the United States as allowances or otherwise under the provisions of chapter 9 of title I of the Foreign Service Act of 1980 or the provisions of section 28 of the State Department Basic Authorities Act (formerly section 914 of title IX of the Foreign Service Act of 1946). [Reg. § 1.912-2.]

☐ [T.D. 6249, 8-21-57. Amended by T.D. 8256, 7-5-89.]

[Reg. § 1.921-1T]

§ 1.921-1T. Temporary regulations providing transition rules for DISCs and FSCs (Temporary).—(a) *Termination of a DISC*—(1) *At end of 1984.*

Question 1: What is the effect of the termination on December 31, 1984 of a DISC's taxable year?

Answer 1: Without regard to the annual accounting period of the DISC, the last taxable year of each DISC beginning during 1984 shall be deemed to close on December 31, 1984. The corporation's DISC election also shall be deemed revoked at the close of business on December 31, 1984. (A DISC that does not elect to be an interest charge DISC as of January 1, 1985, in addition to a corporation described in section 992(a)(3), shall be referred to as a "former DISC".) A corporation which wishes to be treated as a FSC, a small FSC, or an interest charge DISC must make an election as provided under paragraph (b) (Q & A #1) of this section.

(2) *Deemed distributions for short taxable years.*

Question 2: If the termination of the DISC's taxable year on December 31, 1984, results in a short taxable year, how are the deemed distributions under section 995(b)(1)(E) determined?

Answer 2: The deemed distributions are determined on the basis of the DISC's taxable income for its short taxable year ending on December 31, 1984. In computing the incremental distribution under section 995(b)(1)(E), the export gross receipts for the short taxable year must be annualized.

(3) Qualification as a DISC for 1984.

Question 3: Must the DISC satisfy all the tests set forth in section 992(a)(1) for the DISC's taxable year ending December 31, 1984?

Answer 3: All of the tests under section 992(a)(1), except the qualified assets test under section 992(a)(1)(B), must be satisfied.

(4) Commissions for 1984.

Question 4: Must commissions be paid by a related supplier to a DISC with respect to the DISC's taxable year ending December 31, 1984?

Answer 4: No.

Question 4A: Must commissions which were earned prior to January 1, 1985, be paid by a related supplier if the last date payment is required (as set forth in § 1.994-1(e)(3)) is after December 31, 1984?

Answer 4A: No.

(5) Producer's loans for 1984.

Question 5: Must the producer's loan rules under section 993(d) be satisfied with respect to the DISC's taxable year ending December 31, 1984?

Answer 5: Yes.

(6) Accumulated DISC income.

Question 6: Under what circumstances is any remaining accumulated DISC income treated as previously taxed income (and not taxed)?

Answer 6: The accumulated DISC income of a DISC (but not a DISC described in section 992(a)(3)) as of December 31, 1984, is treated as previously taxed income when actually distributed after December 31, 1984. Any amounts distributed by the former DISC (including a DISC which has elected to be an interest charge DISC) after December 31, 1984, shall be treated as made first out of current earnings and profits and then out of previously taxed income to the extent thereof. For purposes of the preceding sentence, amounts distributed before July 1, 1985 shall be treated as made first out of previously taxed income to the extent thereof. If property other than money is distributed and if such property was a qualified export asset within the meaning of section 993(b) on December 31, 1984, then for purposes of section 311, no gain or loss will be recognized on the distribution and the distributee will have the same basis in the property as the distributor.

Question 7: May a DISC that was previously disqualified, but has requalified as of December 31, 1984, treat any accumulated DISC income as previously taxed income?

Answer 7: If a DISC was previously disqualified, but has requalified as of December 31, 1984, any accumulated DISC income previously required to be taken into income upon prior disqualification shall not be treated as previously taxed income. All accumulated DISC income derived since requalification, however, will be treated as previously taxed income.

(7) Distribution of previously taxed income.

Question 8: What effect will the distribution of previously taxed income have on earnings and profits of corporate shareholders of the former DISC?

Answer 8: The earnings and profits of the corporate shareholders of the former DISC will be increased by the amount of money and the adjusted basis of any property which is distributed out of previously taxed income.

Question 9: Will the distribution of the former DISC's accumulated DISC income as previously taxed income after December 31, 1984, result in a reduction in the shareholder's basis of the stock of the former DISC and consequent taxation of the excess of the distribution over such basis as capital gain under section 996(d)?

Answer 9: No. This distribution will be treated both as amounts representing deemed distributions under section 995(b)(1) and as previously taxed income. Thus, no capital gain will arise.

(8) Qualifying distributions.

Question 10: How is a qualifying distribution to satisfy the qualified export receipts tests under section 992(c)(1)(A) which is made with respect to the DISC's taxable year ending on December 31, 1984, treated?

Answer 10: The distribution will not be treated as previously taxed income but will be taxed to the shareholder of the former DISC, as provided under section 992(c) and 996(a)(2) and the regulations thereunder, in the shareholder's taxable year in which the distribution is made.

(9) Deficiency distributions.

Question 11: With respect to an audit adjustment made after December 31, 1984, may a deficiency distribution be made, and if so, in what manner may it be made?

Answer 11: A deficiency distribution may be made notwithstanding the fact that after December 31, 1984 the former DISC is a taxable corporation under subchapter C, has elected to be treated as an interest charge DISC, or has been liquidated, reorganized or is otherwise no longer in existence. However, such deficiency distribution shall be treated as made out of accumulated DISC income which is not previously taxed income be-

Reg. § 1.921-1T(a)(9)

cause it will be treated as distributed prior to December 31, 1984 to the DISC's shareholders.

Question 11A: Must a former DISC remain in existence in order for a former DISC shareholder to take advantage of the spread provided in section 995(b)(2) with respect to DISC disqualification?

Answer 11A: No. With respect to distributions deemed to be received by a former DISC shareholder under section 995(b)(2) for taxable years beginning after December 31, 1984, if the former DISC shareholder elects, the rules of section 995(b)(2)(B) shall apply even though the former DISC does not continue in existence. If the former DISC is no longer in existence, the former DISC's shareholders will be deemed to have received the distribution on the last day of their taxable years over the applicable period of time determined under section 995(b)(2) as if the former DISC had remained in existence.

(10) Deemed distribution for 1984.

Question 12: How is the deemed distribution to a shareholder for the DISC's taxable year ending December 31, 1984, taken into account?

Answer 12 (i) If the taxable year of the DISC ending on December 31, 1984, (A) is the first taxable year of the DISC which begins in 1984, (B) begins after the date in 1984 on which the taxable year of the DISC's shareholder begins, and (C) if the DISC's shareholder makes an election under section 805(b)(3) of the Tax Reform Act of 1984, the deemed distribution under section 995(b) with respect to income derived by the DISC for such taxable year of the DISC shall be treated as received by the shareholder in 10 equal installments (unless the shareholder elects to be treated as receiving the deemed distribution in income over a smaller number of equal installments). The first installment shall be treated as received by the shareholder on the last day of the shareholder's second taxable year beginning in 1984 (if any), or if the shareholder had only one taxable year which began in 1984, on the last day of the shareholder's first taxable year beginning in 1985. One installment shall be treated as received by the shareholder on the last day of each succeeding taxable year of the shareholder until the entire amount of the DISC's 1984 deemed distribution has been included in the shareholder's taxable income. To make the election under section 805(b)(3) of the Tax Reform Act of 1984, the DISC shareholder must attach a statement to its timely filed tax return (including extensions) for its taxable year which includes December 31, 1984, indicating the total amount of the shareholder's pro rata share of the DISC's deemed distribution for 1984 (determined under section 995(b) of the Code without regard to the election under section 805(b)(3) of the Tax Reform Act of 1984), and the number of equal installments, if less than 10, over which the shareholder wishes to spread its pro rata share of the deemed distribution for 1984. If the election under section 805(b)(3) of the Tax Reform Act of 1984 is made, it may not be changed or revoked. In determining estimated tax payments, the portion of the deemed distribution includible in the shareholder's taxable income for any taxable year under this subdivision (i) shall be treated as received by the shareholder on the last day of such taxable year.

(ii) Except as provided in subdivision (i), the deemed distribution under section 995(b) with respect to income derived by the DISC for its taxable year ending on December 31, 1984, shall be included in the shareholder's taxable income for its taxable year which includes December 31, 1984. Thus, if the taxable year of the DISC and the DISC's shareholder both begin on January 1, 1984, and end on December 31, 1984 (or, if the taxable year of the DISC beginning in 1984 begins before the taxable year of the DISC's shareholder), the deemed distribution with respect to the DISC's taxable year ending on December 31, 1984, will be included in the DISC shareholder's taxable year ending on (or including) December 31, 1984, and the election described in subdivision (i) may not be made.

(iii) The provisions of this Question and Answer-12 apply without regard to any existence of the DISC after December 31, 1984, as an interest charge DISC.

Question 12A: If under section 805(b)(3) of the Tax Reform Act of 1984 the shareholders of the DISC are permitted to make an election to treat the DISC's 1984 deemed distribution as received over a ten year period, must the DISC distribute that amount to its shareholders ratably over the 10-year period?

Answer 12A: No. Under section 805(b)(3) of the Tax Reform Act of 1984, if the DISC's deemed distribution for its taxable year which ended on December 31, 1984, is a qualified distribution, the shareholders of the DISC are permitted to make an election to treat the distribution as received over a 10-year period. The 10-year treatment applies even though the amount of the deemed distribution is distributed to the DISC's shareholders prior to the period in which the distribution is taken into income by the shareholders. In addition, under section 996(e) of the Code, the shareholder's basis in the stock of the DISC will be considered as increased, as of the date of liquidation, by the shareholder's pro rata share of the

Income From Sources Without the United States

See p. 20,601 for regulations not amended to reflect law changes

amount of the undistributed qualified distribution even though that amount is treated as received by the shareholder in later years. Further, the actual distribution in liquidation of the former DISC after 1984 will increase the earnings and profits of a corporate distributee, and the amount actually distributed shall be treated under the rules of section 996.

(11) Conformity of accounting period.

Question 13: May a DISC be established or change its annual accounting period for taxable years beginning after March 21, 1984, and before January 1, 1985?

Answer 13: A DISC that is established or that changes its annual accounting period after March 21, 1984, must conform its annual accounting period to that of its principal shareholder (the shareholder with the highest percentage of voting power as defined in section 441(h)).

(12) DISC gains and distributions from U.S. sources.

Question 14: What is the effective date of the amendment to section 996(g), made by section 801(d)(10) of the Tax Reform Act of 1984, which treats certain DISC gains and distributions as derived from sources within the United States?

Answer 14: Under section 805(a)(3) of the Act, the amendment to section 996(g) shall apply to all gains referred to in section 995(c) and all distributions out of accumulated DISC income including deemed distributions made on or after June 22, 1984.

(b) *Establishing and electing status as a FSC, small FSC or interest charge DISC*—*(1) Ninety-day period.*

Question 1: How does a corporation elect to be treated as a FSC, a small FSC, or an interest charge DISC?

Answer 1: A corporation electing FSC or small FSC status must file Form 8279. A corporation electing interest charge DISC status must file Form 4876A. A corporation electing to be treated as a FSC, small FSC, or interest charge DISC for its first taxable year shall make its election within 90 days after the beginning of that year. A corporation electing to be treated as a FSC, small FSC, or interest charge DISC for any taxable year other than its first taxable year shall make its election during the 90-day period immediately preceding the first day of that taxable year. The election to be a FSC, small FSC, or interest charge DISC may be made by the corporation, however, during the first 90 days of a taxable year, even if that taxable year is not the corporation's first taxable year, if that taxable year begins before July 1, 1985. Likewise, the election to be a FSC (or a small FSC) may be made during the first 90 days of any taxable year of a corporation if the corporation had in a prior taxable year elected small FSC (or FSC) status and the corporation revokes the small FSC (or FSC) election within the 90 day period. A corporation which was a DISC for its taxable year ending December 31, 1984, which wishes to be treated as an interest charge DISC beginning with its first taxable year beginning after December 31, 1984, may make the election to be treated as an interest charge DISC by filing Form 4876A on or before July 1, 1987. Also, if a corporation which has elected FSC, small FSC or interest charge DISC status, or a shareholder of that corporation, is acquired in a qualified stock purchase under section 338(d)(3), and if an election under section 338(a) is effective with regard to that corporation, the corporation may re-elect FSC, small FSC or interest charge DISC status, (whichever is applicable,) not later than the date of the election under section 338(a), see section 338(g)(i) and § 1.338-2(d). This re-election is necessary because the original elections are deemed terminated if an election is made under section 338(a). The rules contained in § 1.992-2(a)(1), (b)(1) and (b)(3) shall apply to the manner of making the election and the manner and form of shareholder consent.

(2) FSC incorporated in a possession.

Question 2: Where does a FSC which is incorporated in a U.S. possession file its election?

Answer 2: The election is filed with the Internal Revenue Service Center, Philadelphia, Pennsylvania 19255.

(3) Information returns.

Question 3: Must Form 5471 be filed with respect to the organization of a FSC pursuant to section 6046 or to provide information with respect to a FSC pursuant to section 6038?

Answer 3: A Form 5471 required under section 6046 need not be filed with respect to the organization of a FSC. The requirements of section 6046 shall be satisfied by the filing of a Form 8279 dealing with the election to be treated as a FSC or small FSC. However, a Form 5471 will be required with respect to a reorganization of a FSC (or small FSC) or an acquisition of stock of a FSC (or small FSC), as required under section 6046 and the regulations thereunder. Provided that a Form 1120 FSC is filed, a Form 5471 need not be filed to satisfy the requirements of section 6038.

(4) Conformity of accounting period.

Question 4: Since a FSC, small FSC, and interest charge DISC must use the same annual accounting period as the principal shareholder, must such corporation delay the beginning of its first

Reg. § 1.921-1T(b)(4)

taxable year beyond January 1, 1985 if the principal shareholder (the shareholder with the highest percentage of voting power as defined in section 441(h)) is not a calendar year taxpayer?

Answer 4: No. Where the principal shareholder is not a calendar year taxpayer, a corporation may elect to be treated as a FSC, small FSC, or interest charge DISC for a taxable year beginning January 1, 1985. However, such corporation must close its first taxable year and adopt the annual accounting period of its principal shareholder as of the first day of the principal shareholder's first taxable year beginning in 1985. A FSC, small FSC, or interest charge DISC need not obtain the consent of the Commissioner under section 442 to conform its annual accounting period to the annual accounting period of its principal shareholder.

(5) Dollar limitations for short taxable years.

Question 5: If a small FSC or an interest charge DISC has a short taxable year, how are the dollar limitations on foreign trading export gross receipts and qualified export gross receipts, respectively, determined for small FSCs and interest charge DISCs?

Answer 5: The dollar limitations are to be prorated on a daily basis. Thus, for example, if for its 1985 taxable year a small FSC has a short taxable year of 73 days, then in determining exempt foreign trade income, any foreign trading gross receipts that exceed $1 million (73/365 × $5 million) will not be taken into account.

(6) Change of accounting period.

Question 6: If the principal shareholder of a FSC, a small FSC, or an interest charge DISC (hereinafter referred to as a "FSC") changes its annual accounting period or is replaced by a new principal shareholder during a taxable year, is it necessary for the FSC to change its annual accounting period?

Answer 6: If the principal shareholder changes its annual accounting period, the FSC must also change its annual accounting period to conform to that of its principal shareholder. If the voting power of the principal shareholder is reduced by an amount equal to at least 10 percent of the total shares entitled to vote and such shareholder is no longer the principal shareholder, the FSC must conform its accounting period to that of its new principal shareholder. However, in determining whether a shareholder is a principal shareholder, the voting power of the shareholders is determined as of the beginning of the FSC's taxable year. Thus, for example, assume that for 1985 a FSC adopts a calendar year period as its annual accounting period to conform to that of its principal shareholder. Assume further that in March 1985 there is a 10 percent change in voting power and a different shareholder whose annual accounting period begins on July 1 becomes the new principal shareholder. The FSC will not be required to adopt the annual accounting period of its new principal shareholder until July 1, 1986. The FSC will have a short taxable year for the period January 1 to June 30, 1986.

(7) Transition transfers.

Question 7: Under what circumstances may a DISC or former DISC transfer its assets to a FSC or small FSC without incurring any tax liability on the transfer?

Answer 7: A DISC or former DISC will recognize no income, gain, or loss on a transfer of its qualified assets (as defined in section 993(b)) to a FSC or small FSC if all of the following conditions are met:

(1) The assets transferred were held by the DISC on August 4, 1983, and were transferred by the DISC or former DISC to the FSC or small FSC in a transfer completed before January 1, 1986; and

(2) The assets are transferred in a transaction which would qualify for nonrecognition under subchapter C of Chapter 1 of the Code, or would so qualify but for section 367 of the Code.

In such case, section 367 shall not apply to the transfer. In addition, other provisions of subchapter C will apply to the transfer, such as section 358 (basis to shareholders), section 362 (basis to corporations), and section 381 (carryovers in corporate acquisitions). In determining whether a transfer by a DISC to a FSC or small FSC qualifies for nonrecognition under subchapter C, a liquidation of the assets of the DISC into a parent corporation followed by a transfer by the parent of those assets to the FSC or small FSC will be treated as a transaction described in section 368(a)(1)(D).

Notwithstanding the foregoing answer, a taxpayer which transfers a right to use its corporate name to a FSC in a transaction described in sections 332, 351, 354, 356 and 361 shall not be treated as having sold that right under section 367(d) or as having transferred that right to an entity that is not a corporation under section 367(a) provided that the corporate name is used only by the FSC and is not licensed or otherwise made available to others by the FSC.

(8) Completed contract method.

Question 8: Under what conditions is a taxpayer using the completed contract method of accounting as defined in § 1.451-3(d) exempted from satisfying the foreign management and for-

Reg. § 1.921-1T(b)(5)

Income From Sources Without the United States

eign economic process requirements of subsections (c) and (d) of section 924?

Answer 8: If the taxpayer has entered into a binding contract before March 16, 1984, or has on March 15, 1984, and at all times thereafter a firm plan, evidenced in writing, to enter the contract and enters into a binding contract by December 31, 1984, then the taxpayer will be treated as having satisfied the foreign management tests of section 924(c) for periods before December 31, 1984, and the foreign economic process tests of section 924(d) with respect to costs incurred before December 31, 1984, with respect to the transaction. The FSC rules will apply to the income from the long-term contract if an election is made and the general FSC requirements under section 922 are satisfied. However, such taxpayer need not satisfy the activities test under section 925(c) for activities which occur before January 1, 1985 in order to use the transfer pricing rules under section 925.

(9) Long-term contract—before March 15, 1984.

Question 9: Under what conditions is a taxpayer who enters into a binding long-term contract (i.e., a contract which is not completed in the taxable year in which it is entered into) before March 15, 1984, but does not use the completed contract method of accounting exempted from satisfying the foreign management and economic process requirements of subsections (c) and (d) of section 924?

Answer 9: If a taxpayer enters into a binding contract before March 15, 1984, the taxpayer will be treated as having satisfied the foreign management tests of section 924(c) for periods before December 31, 1984, and the foreign economic process tests of section 924(d) with respect to costs incurred before December 31, 1984, but only with respect to income attributable to such contracts that is recognized before December 31, 1986. The FSC rules will apply to the income from the long-term contract if an election is made and the general FSC requirements under section 922 are satisfied. However, such taxpayer need not satisfy the activities test under section 925(c) for activities which occur before January 1, 1985, in order to use the transfer pricing rules under section 925.

(10) Long-term contract—after March 15, 1984.

Question 10: Under what conditions is a taxpayer who has a long-term contract (i.e., a contract which is not completed in the taxable year in which it is entered into) but does not use the completed contract method of accounting exempted from satisfying the foreign management and economic process requirements of subsections (c) and (d) of section 924 if such taxpayer enters into a binding contract after March 15, 1984 and before January 1, 1985?

Answer 10: If a taxpayer enters into a contract after March 15, 1984, and before January 1, 1985, the taxpayer will be treated as having satisfied the foreign management tests of section 924(c) for periods before December 31, 1984, and the foreign economic process tests of section 924(d) with respect to costs incurred before December 31, 1984, but only with respect to income attributable to such contract that is recognized before December 31, 1985.

The FSC rules will apply to the income from the long-term contract if an election is made and the general requirements under section 922 are satisfied. However, such taxpayer need not satisfy the activities test under section 925(c) for activities which occur before January 1, 1985 in order to use the transfer pricing rules under section 925.

(11) Incomplete transactions.

Question 11: In computing its foreign trade income, how should a FSC treat transfers of export property from a related supplier to a DISC which is subsequently resold by a FSC after the DISC's termination?

Answer 11: In applying the gross receipts and combined taxable income methods under section 925(a)(1) and (a)(2), the transaction is treated as if the transfer of export property were made by the related supplier to the FSC except that the foreign management and economic processes tests under section 924 and the activities test under section 925(c) shall be deemed to be satisfied for purposes of the transaction.

(12) Pre-effective date costs and activities.

Question 12: Are costs incurred and activities performed prior to January 1, 1985 taken into account for purposes of satisfying the foreign management and foreign economic processes requirements of subsections (c) and (d) of section 924 and the activities test under section 925(c)?

Answer 12: For purposes of determining the costs incurred and the activities performed to be taken into account with respect to contracts entered into after December 31, 1984, only those costs incurred and activities performed after December 31, 1984 are taken into consideration. Costs incurred and activities performed by a related supplier prior to January 1, 1985 (or prior to the effective date of a corporation's election to be treated as a FSC if other than January 1, 1985) with respect to transactions occurring after January 1, 1985 (or after the effective date of a corporation's election to be treated as a FSC) need not

Reg. § 1.921-1T(b)(12)

be taken into account for purposes of computing the FSC's profit under section 925 but are treated for section 925(c) purposes as if they were performed on behalf of the FSC.

(13) FSC and interest charge DISC.

Question 13: Can a FSC and an interest charge DISC be members of the same controlled group?

Answer 13: A FSC and an interest charge DISC cannot be members of the same controlled group. If any controlled group of corporations of which an interest charge DISC is a member establishes a FSC, then any interest charge DISC which is a member of such group shall be treated as having terminated its status as an interest charge DISC.

(c) *Export Trade Corporations—(1) Previously taxed income.*

Question 1: Under what circumstances are earnings of an export trade corporation that have not been included in income under section 951 treated as previously taxed income previously included in the income of a U.S. shareholder for purposes of section 959 (and not taxed)?

Answer 1: A corporation which qualifies as an export trade corporation (ETC) with respect to its last taxable year beginning before January 1, 1985, and elects to discontinue operations as an ETC for all taxable years beginning after December 31, 1984, shall not be required to take into income earnings attributable to previously excluded export trade income, as defined in § 1.970-1(b), derived with respect to taxable years beginning before January 1, 1985. However, any amounts distributed by the former ETC (*i.e.* a corporation which was an ETC for its last taxable year beginning before January 1, 1985) shall be treated as being made out of current earnings and profits and then out of previously taxed income. For purposes of determining the shareholder's basis in the ETC stock, distributions of previously excluded export trade income shall be treated as if made out of previously taxed income which has already been included in gross income under section 951(a)(1)(B). Thus, no basis adjustment under section 961 is necessary. In addition, upon the sale or exchange of the stock of such corporation in a transaction described in section 1248(a), the earnings and profits of the corporation attributable to such previously untaxed income shall not be subject to section 1248(a).

(2) Qualification as an ETC for last year.

Question 2: Must an ETC satisfy all of the tests set forth in section 971(a)(1) for the ETC's last taxable year beginning before January 1, 1985?

Answer 2: All of the tests in section 971(a)(1) must be satisfied, except that for purposes of the working capital requirements set forth in section 971(c)(1), the working capital of the ETC at the close of its last taxable year beginning before January 1, 1985 shall be deemed reasonable.

(3) Continuation of ETC status.

Question 3: May a corporation which chooses to remain an ETC after December 31, 1984 continue to do so?

Answer 3: Yes. However, previously untaxed income of such ETC shall not be treated as previously taxed income in accordance with Q&A #1 of this section.

(4) Discontinuation of ETC status.

Question 4: How does an ETC make an election to discontinue its operations as an ETC?

Answer 4: The United States shareholders (as defined in section 951(b)) must file a statement of election on behalf of the ETC indicating the intent of the ETC to discontinue operations as an ETC for taxable years beginning after December 31, 1984. In addition, the statement of election must include the name, address, taxpayer identification number and stock interest of each United States shareholder. The statement must also indicate that the corporation on behalf of which the shareholders are making the election qualified as an ETC for its last taxable year beginning before January 1, 1985, and also the amount of earnings attributable to previously excluded export trade income. The statement must be jointly signed by each United States shareholder with each shareholder stating under penalties of perjury that he or she holds the stock interest specified for such shareholder in the statement of election. A copy of the statement of election must be attached to Form 5471 (information return with respect to a foreign corporation) filed with respect to the ETC's last taxable year beginning before January 1, 1985.

(5) Transition transfers.

Question 5: Under what circumstances may an electing ETC transfer its assets to a FSC without incurring any tax liability on the transfer?

Answer 5: An electing ETC will recognize no income, gain, or loss on a transfer of its assets to a FSC but only if all of the following conditions are met:

(1) The assets transferred were held by the ETC on August 4, 1983, and were transferred by the ETC to the FSC in a transfer completed before January 1, 1986; and

(2) The assets are transferred in a transaction which would qualify for nonrecognition under subchapter C of Chapter 1 of the Code, or would so qualify but for section 367 of the Code.

In such case, section 367 shall not apply to the transfer. In addition, other provisions of sub-

Reg. § 1.921-1T(b)(13)

Income From Sources Without the United States

See p. 20,601 for regulations not amended to reflect law changes

chapter C will apply to the transfer such as section 358 (basis to shareholders), section 362 (basis to corporations) and section 381 (carryovers in corporate acquisitions). In determining whether a transfer by an ETC to a FSC qualifies for nonrecognition under subchapter C, a liquidation of the assets of the ETC into a parent corporation followed by a transfer by the parent of those assets to the FSC will be treated as a transaction described in section 368(a)(1)(D). [Temporary Reg. § 1.921-1T.]

☐ [T.D. 7983, 10-5-84. Amended by T.D. 7992, 12-7-84; T.D. 8126, 3-2-87; T.D. 8515, 1-12-94; T.D. 8858, 1-5-2000 and T.D. 8940, 2-12-2001.]

[Reg. § 1.921-2]

§ 1.921-2. Foreign Sales Corporation—General Rules.—(a) *Definition of a FSC and the Effect of a FSC Election.*

Q-1. What is the definition of a Foreign Sales Corporation (hereinafter referred to as a "FSC" (All references to FSCs include small FSCs unless indicated otherwise))?

A-1. As defined in section 922(a), an FSC must satisfy the following eight requirements.

(i) The FSC must be a corporation organized or created under the laws of a foreign country that meets the requirements of section 927(e)(3) (a "qualifying foreign country") or a U.S. possession other than Puerto Rico (an "eligible possession"). See Q&As 3, 4, and 5 of § 1.922-1.

(ii) A FSC may not have more than 25 shareholders at any time during the taxable year. See Q&A 6 of § 1.922-1.

(iii) A FSC may not have any preferred stock outstanding during the taxable year. See Q&As 7 and 8 of § 1.922-1.

(iv) A FSC must maintain an office outside of the United States in a qualifying foreign country or an eligible possession and maintain a set of permanent books of account (including invoices or summaries of invoices) at such office. See Q&As 9, 10, 11, 12, 13, 14, and 15 of § 1.922-1.

(v) A FSC must maintain within the United States the records required under section 6001. See Q&A 16 of § 1.922-1.

(vi) The FSC must have a board of directors which includes at least one individual who is not a resident of the United States at all times during the taxable year. See Q&As 17, 18, 19, 20, and 21 of § 1.922-1.

(vii) A FSC may not be a member, at any time during the taxable year, of any controlled group of corporations of which an interest charge DISC is a member. See Q&A 2 of this section and Q&A 13, of § 1.921-1T(b)(13).

(viii) A FSC must have made an election under section 927(f)(1) which is in effect for the taxable year. See Q&A 1 of § 1.921-1T(b)(1) and § 1.927(f)-1. In addition, under section 441(h), the taxable year of a FSC must conform to the taxable year of its principal shareholder. See Q&A 4 of § 1.921-1T(b)(4).

Q-2. Does the reference to a DISC under section 922(a)(1)(F) which provides that a FSC cannot be a member, at any time during the taxable year, of any controlled group of corporations of which a DISC is a member refer solely to an interest charge DISC?

A-2. Yes.

(b) *Small FSC.*

Q-3. What is a small FSC?

A-3. A small FSC is a Foreign Sales Corporation which meets the requirements of section 922(a)(1) enumerated in Q&A 1 of this section as well as the requirements of section 922(b). Section 922(b) requires that a small FSC make a separate election to be treated as a small FSC. See Q&A 1 of § 1.921-1T(b) and § 1.927(f)-1. In addition, section 922(b) requires that the small FSC not be a member, at any time during the taxable year, of a controlled group of corporations which includes a FSC unless such FSC is a small FSC.

Q-4. What is the effect of an election as a small FSC?

A-4. Under section 924(b)(2), a small FSC need not meet the foreign management and economic processes tests of section 924(b)(1) in order to have foreign trading gross receipts. However, in determining the exempt foreign trade income of a small FSC, any foreign trading gross receipts for the taxable year in excess of $5 million are not taken into account. If the foreign trading gross receipts of a small FSC for the taxable year exceed the $5 million limitation, the FSC may select the gross receipts to which the limitation is allocated. In order to use the administrative pricing rules under section 925(a), a small FSC must satisfy the activities test under section 925(c). In addition, under section 441(h), the taxable year of a small FSC must conform to the taxable year of its principal shareholder (defined in Q&A 4 of § 1.921-1T(b)(4) as the shareholder with the highest percentage of its voting power).

Q-5. What is the effect on a small FSC (or FSC) ("target") if it is acquired, directly or indirectly, by a corporation if that acquiring corporation ("acquiring"), or a member of the acquiring corporation's controlled group, is a FSC (or small FSC)?

A-5. Unless the corporations in the controlled group elect to terminate the FSC (or small FSC)

Reg. § 1.921-2(b)

election of the acquiring corporation, the target's small FSC's (or FSC's) taxable year and election will terminate as of the day preceding the date the target small FSC and acquiring FSC became members of the same controlled group. The target small FSC will receive FSC benefits for the period prior to termination, but the $5 million small FSC limitation will be reduced to the amount which bears the same ratio to the $5 million as the number of days in the short year created by the termination bears to 365. The due date of the income tax return for the short taxable year created by this provision will be the date prescribed by section 6072(b), including extensions, starting with the last day of the short taxable year. If the short taxable year created by this provision ends prior to March 3, 1987, the filing date of the tax return for the short taxable year will be automatically extended until the earlier of May 18, 1987, or the date under section 6072(b) assuming a short taxable year had not been created by these regulations.

(c) *Comparison of FSC to DISC.*

Q-6. How does a FSC differ from a DISC?

A-6. A DISC is a domestic corporation which is not itself taxable while a FSC must be created or organized under the laws of a jurisdiction which is outside of the United States (including certain U.S. possessions) and may be taxable on its income except for its exempt foreign trade income. The DISC provisions enable a shareholder to obtain a partial deferral of tax on income from export sales and certain services, if 95 percent of its receipts and assets are export related. The FSC provisions contain no assets test, but a portion of income for export sales and certain services is exempt from U.S. taxes if the FSC satisfies certain foreign presence, foreign management, and foreign economic processes tests.

(d) *Organization of a FSC.*

Q-7. Under the laws of what countries may a FSC be organized?

A-7. A FSC may not be created or organized under the laws of the United States, a state, or other political subdivision. However, a FSC may be created or organized under the laws of a possession of the United States, including Guam, American Samoa, the Commonwealth of the Northern Mariana Islands and the Virgin Islands of the United States, but not Puerto Rico. These eligible possessions are located outside the U.S. customs territory. In addition, a FSC may incorporate under the laws of a foreign country that is a party to (i) an exchange of information agreement that meets the standards of the Caribbean Basin Economic Recovery Act of 1983 (Code section 274(h)(6)(C)), or (ii) a bilateral income tax treaty with the United States if the Secretary certifies that the exchange of information program under the treaty carries out the purpose of the exchange of information requirements of the FSC legislation as set forth in section 927(e)(3), if the company is covered under the exchange of information program under subdivision (i) or (ii). The Secretary may terminate the certification. Any termination by the Secretary will be effective six months after the date of the publication of the notice of such termination in the Federal Register.

(e) *Foreign Trade Income.*

Q-8. How is foreign trade income defined?

A-8. Foreign trade income, defined in section 923(b), is gross income of a FSC attributable to foreign trading gross receipts. It includes both the profits earned by the FSC itself from exports and commissions earned by the FSC from products and services exported by others.

(f) *Investment Income and Carrying Charges.*

Q-9. What do the terms "investment income" and "carrying charges" mean?

A-9. (i) Investment income means:

(A) Dividends,

(B) Interest,

(C) Royalties,

(D) Annuities,

(E) Rents (other than rents from the lease or rental of export property for use by the lessee outside of the United States);

(F) Gains from the sale of stock or securities,

(G) Gains from futures transactions in any commodity on, or subject to the rules of, a board of trade or commodity exchange (other than gains which arise out of a bona fide hedging transaction reasonably necessary to conduct the business of the FSC in the manner in which such business is customarily conducted by others),

(H) Amounts includible in computing the taxable income of the corporation under part I of subchapter J, and

(I) Gains from the sale or other disposition of any interest in an estate or trust.

(ii) Carrying charges means:

(A) Charges that are imposed by a FSC or a related supplier and that are identified as carrying charges, ("stated carrying charges") and

(B)(*1*) Charges that are considered to be included in the price of the property or services sold by a FSC or a related supplier, as provided under Q&As 1 and 2 of § 1.927(d)-1, and (*2*) any other unstated interest.

Reg. § 1.921-2(c)

Income From Sources Without the United States

Q-10. How are investment income and carrying charges treated?

A-10. Investment income and carrying charges are not foreign trading gross receipts. Investment income and carrying charges are includible in the taxable income of a FSC, except in the case of a commission FSC where carrying charges are treated as income of the related supplier, and are treated as income effectively connected with a trade or business conducted through a permanent establishment within the United States. The source of investment income and carrying charges is determined under sections 861, 862, and 863 of the Code.

(g) *Small Businesses.*

Q-11. What options are available to small businesses engaged in exporting?

A-11. A small business may elect to be treated as either a small FSC or an interest charge DISC. See Q&As 3 & 4 of § 1.921-2 relating to a small FSC. Rules with respect to interest charge DISCs are the subject of another regulations project. [Reg. § 1.921-2.]

☐ [T.D. 8127, 3-2-87.]

[Reg. § 1.921-3T]

§ 1.921-3T. Temporary Regulations; Foreign sales corporation general rules (Temporary).—(a) *Exclusion*—(1) *Classifications of income.* The extent to which income of a FSC (any further reference to a FSC in this section shall include a small FSC unless indicated otherwise) is subject to the corporate income tax of section 11, or, in the alternative, section 1201(a), is dependent upon the allocation of the FSC's income to the following five categories:

(i) Exempt foreign trade income determined under section 923 and § 1.923-1T;

(ii) Non-exempt foreign trade income determined with regard to the administrative pricing rules of section 925(a)(1) or (2);

(iii) Non-exempt foreign trade income determined without regard to the administrative pricing rules of section 925(a)(1) or (2) (section 923(a)(2) non-exempt income as defined in section 927(d)(6));

(iv) Investment income and carrying charges; and

(v) Other non-foreign trade income.

(2) *Source and characterization of FSC income*—(i) *Exempt foreign trade income.* The exempt foreign trade income of a FSC determined under section 923 and § 1.923-1T is treated as foreign source income which is not effectively connected with a United States trade or business. See § 1.923-1T(a) for the definition of foreign trade income and § 1.923-1T(b) for the definition of exempt foreign trade income.

(ii) *Non-exempt foreign trade income determined with regard to the administrative pricing rules.* The FSC's non-exempt foreign trade income with respect to a transaction or group of transactions will be treated as United States source income which is effectively connected with the FSC's trade or business which is conducted through its permanent establishment within the United States if either of the administrative pricing rules of section 925(a)(1) or (2) is used to determine the FSC's foreign trade income from a transaction or group of transactions. See § 1.923-1T(b) for the definition of non-exempt foreign trade income.

(iii) *Non-exempt foreign trade income determined without regard to the administrative pricing rules.* The source and taxation of the FSC's non-exempt foreign trade income not classified in paragraph (a)(2)(ii) of this section will be determined under the appropriate sections of the Internal Revenue Code and the regulations under those sections. This type of income (section 923(a)(2) non-exempt income) includes both income that is not effectively connected with the conduct of a trade or business in the United States and income that is effectively connected.

(iv) *Investment income and carrying charges.* All of the FSC's investment income and carrying charges will be treated as income which is effectively connected with the FSC's trade or business which is conducted through its permanent establishment within the United States. The source of that income will be determined under the appropriate sections of the Internal Revenue Code and the regulations under those sections. See § 1.921-2(f) (Q&A9) for definition of investment income and carrying charges.

(v) *Non-foreign trade income (other than investment income and carrying charges).* The source and taxation of the FSC's non-foreign trade income (other than investment income and carrying charges) will be determined under the appropriate sections of the Internal Revenue Code and the regulations under those sections.

(b) *Allocation and apportionment of deductions.* Expenses, losses and deductions incurred by the FSC shall be allocated and apportioned under the rules set forth in § 1.861-8 to the FSC's foreign trade income and to the FSC's non-foreign trade income. Any deductions incurred by the FSC on a transaction, or group of transactions, which are allocated and apportioned to the FSC's foreign trade income from that transaction, or group of transactions, shall be allocated on a proportionate

Reg. § 1.921-3T(b)

basis between exempt foreign trade income and non-exempt foreign trade income.

(c) *Net operating losses and capital losses*—

(1) *General rule.* (i) If a FSC for any taxable year incurs a deficit in earnings and profits attributable to foreign trade income determined without regard to the administrative pricing rules of section 925(a) (1) or (2), that deficit shall be applied to reduce current earnings and profits, if any, attributable to—

(A) First, exempt foreign trade income determined with regard to the administrative pricing rules,

(B) Second, non-exempt foreign trade income determined with regard to the administrative pricing rules,

(C) Third, investment income and carrying charges, and

(D) Fourth, other non-foreign trade income.

(ii) If a FSC for any taxable year incurs a deficit in earnings and profits attributable to non-foreign trade income (other than investment income, carrying charges and net capital losses), that deficit shall be applied to reduce current earnings and profits, if any, attributable to—

(A) First, investment income and carrying charges,

(B) Second, exempt foreign trade income determined with regard to the administrative pricing rules,

(C) Third, exempt foreign trade income determined without regard to the administrative pricing rules,

(D) Fourth, non-exempt foreign trade income determined with regard to the administrative pricing rules, and

(E) Fifth, section 923(a)(2) non-exempt income.

(iii) If a FSC for any taxable year incurs a deficit in earnings and profits attributable to investment income and carrying charges, that deficit shall be applied to reduce current earnings and profits, if any, attributable to—

(A) First, non-foreign trade income other than capital gains,

(B) Second, exempt foreign trade income determined with regard to the administrative pricing rules,

(C) Third, exempt foreign trade income determined without regard to the administrative pricing rules,

(D) Fourth, non-exempt foreign trade income determined with regard to the administrative pricing rules, and

(E) Fifth, section 923(a)(2) non-exempt income.

(iv) Net capital losses will be available for carryback or carryover pursuant to paragraph (c)(2) of this section.

(v) Because the no-loss rules provide that a related supplier may always compensate the FSC for its expenses either as part of the commission payment or as part of the transfer price if the administrative pricing rules are used (see § 1.925(a)-1T(e)(1)(i)), a FSC will not have a deficit in its earnings and profits relating to foreign trade income determined with regard to the administrative pricing rules. To determine the amount of any division of earnings and profits for the purpose of determining under § 1.926(a)-1T(a) and (b) the treatment and order of distributions, the portion of a deficit in earnings and profits chargeable under this paragraph to such division prior to such distribution shall be determined in a manner consistent with the rules in § 1.316-2(b) for determining the amount of earnings and profits available on the date of any distribution.

(2) *Carryback or carryover of net operating losses and capital losses to other taxable years of a FSC (or former FSC).* (i) The amount of the deduction for the taxable year under section 172 for a net operating loss carryback or carryover, or under section 1212 for a capital loss carryback or carryover, shall be determined in the same manner as if the FSC were a foreign corporation which had not elected to be treated as a FSC. Thus, the amount of the deduction will be the same whether or not the corporation was a FSC in the year of the loss or in the year to which the loss is carried.

(ii) Any carryback or carryover of a FSC's (or former FSC's) net operating loss which is attributable to transactions which give rise to foreign trade income shall be charged—

(A) First, to earnings and profits attributable to exempt foreign trade income which is determined without regard to the administrative pricing rules,

(B) Second, to earnings and profits attributable to section 923(a)(2) non-exempt income,

(C) Third, to earnings and profits attributable to exempt foreign trade income determined with regard to the administrative pricing rules,

(D) Fourth, to earnings and profits attributable to non-exempt foreign trade income determined with regard to the administrative pricing rules,

Reg. § 1.921-3T(c)(1)

(E) Fifth, to earnings and profits attributable to investment income and carrying charges (other than capital gain income), and

(F) Sixth, to earnings and profits attributable to non-foreign trade income (other than investment income, carrying charges and capital gain income).

(iii) Any carryback or carryover of a FSC's (or former FSC's) net operating loss which is attributable to non-foreign trade income (other than capital gain income) shall be charged—

(A) First, to earnings and profits attributable to non-foreign trade income (other than investment income, carrying charges and capital gain income),

(B) Second, to earnings and profits attributable to investment income and carrying charges,

(C) Third, to earnings and profits attributable to exempt foreign trade income determined with regard to the administrative pricing rules,

(D) Fourth, to earnings and profits attributable to non-exempt foreign trade income determined with regard to the administrative pricing rules,

(E) Fifth, to earnings and profits attributable to exempt foreign trade income which is determined without regard to the administrative pricing rules, and

(F) Sixth, to earnings and profits attributable to section 923(a)(2) non-exempt income.

(iv) Any carryback or carryover of a net operating loss to a year in which the corporation was (or is) a FSC from a taxable year in which the corporation was not a FSC shall be applied in a manner consistent with subdivision (iii) of this paragraph.

(d) *Credits against tax*—(1) *General rule.* Notwithstanding any other provision of chapter 1, subtitle A, a FSC is allowed under section 921(c) as credits against tax only the following credits:

(i) The foreign tax credit, section 27(a);

(ii) The credit for tax withheld at source on foreign corporations, section 33; and

(iii) The certain uses of gasoline and special fuels credit, section 34.

(2) *Foreign tax credit.* (i) The direct foreign tax credit of section 901(b)(4) as determined under section 906 for income, war profits, and excess profits taxes (or taxes in lieu thereof) paid or accrued to any foreign country or possession of the United States is allowed a FSC only to the extent that those taxes are attributable to the FSC's foreign source non-foreign trade income which is effectively connected with its conduct of a trade or business within the United States. See section 906(b)(5).

(ii) The foreign tax credit for domestic corporate shareholders in foreign corporations (the deemed paid credit) provided under section 901(a) as determined under section 902 is allowed for income, war profits, and excess profits taxes deemed paid or accrued by a FSC (or former FSC) only to the extent those taxes are deemed paid or accrued with respect to the FSC's (or former FSC's) section 923(a)(2) non-exempt income and its non-foreign trade income.

(iii) The foreign tax credit allowed by sections 901 and 903 for tax withheld at source is allowed only to the extent the dividends paid to the FSC's (or former FSC's) shareholder are attributable to the FSC's (or former FSC's) section 923(a)(2) non-exempt income and its non-foreign trade income.

(3) *Foreign tax credit limitation.* (i) For purposes of computation of the direct foreign tax credit of section 901(b)(4) as determined under section 906, the separate limitation of section 904(d)(1)(C) for the FSC's taxable income attributable to its foreign trade income will apply. The direct foreign tax credit is not allowed to a FSC with regard to taxes it paid which are attributable to its foreign trade income. Since the foreign tax credit is not allowed for that type of income, the effect of the separate limitation is to remove the FSC's foreign trade income from the numerator of the fraction used to compute the FSC's overall foreign tax credit limitation.

(ii) A separate limitation under section 904(d)(1)(D) is provided for distributions from a FSC (or former FSC) that arise through operation of the deemed paid credit of section 902 and are attributable to foreign trade income earned during the period when the distributing corporation was a FSC. This limitation is computed by multiplying the FSC's shareholder's tentative United States tax by a fraction the numerator of which is the foreign source dividend (determined with regard to section 78) attributable to the foreign trade income less dividends received deductions and other expenses allocated and apportioned under § 1.861-8 allowed to the shareholder and the denominator of which is the shareholder's worldwide income. The effect of this separate limitation is to remove dividends attributable to the FSC's foreign trade income from the numerator of the fraction used to compute the overall foreign tax credit limitation of the FSC's shareholder.

(iii) The separate limitation under section 904(d)(1)(D) also applies to the foreign tax credit allowed to a FSC shareholder by sections 901 and 903 for tax withheld at source on dividends paid

Reg. § 1.921-3T(d)(3)

by the FSC. The numerator of this fraction is the part of the dividend attributable to the FSC's foreign trade income and the denominator is the shareholder's worldwide income. The effect of this separate limitation is to remove dividends attributable to foreign trade income of a FSC (or former FSC) from the numerator of the fraction used to compute the overall foreign tax credit limitation of the FSC's shareholder.

(e) *Deduction for foreign income, war profits and excess profits taxes.* Under section 275(a)(4)(B), income, war profits and excess profits taxes imposed by a foreign country or possession of the United States may not be deducted by a FSC to the extent those taxes are paid or accrued with respect to its foreign trade income.

(f) *Payment of estimated tax.* Every FSC which is subject to tax under section 11 or 1201(a) and section 882 must make payment of its estimated tax in accordance with section 6154 and the regulations under that section. In determining the amount of the estimated tax, the FSC must treat the tax imposed by section 881 as though it were a tax imposed by section 11. See section 6154(g).

(g) *Accumulated earnings, personal holding company and foreign personal holding company.* The provisions covering the accumulated earnings tax (sections 531-537), personal holding companies (sections 541-547) and foreign personal holding companies (sections 551-558) apply to FSCs to the extent they would apply to foreign corporations that are not FSCs.

(h) *Subpart F income and increase of earnings invested in U.S. property.* For the mandatory inclusion in the gross income of the U.S. shareholders of the subpart F income and of the increase in earnings invested in U.S. property of a FSC, see sections 951 through 964 and the regulations under those sections. However, the foreign trade income (other than section 923(a)(2) nonexempt income) and, generally, the investment income and carrying charges of a FSC and any deductions which are allocated and apportioned to those classes of income, are not taken into account under sections 951 through 964. See sections 951(e) and 952(b).

(i) *Certain accumulations of earnings and profits.* For the inclusion in the gross income of U.S. persons as a dividend on the gain recognized on certain sales or exchanges of stock in a FSC, to the extent of certain earnings and profits attributable to the stock which were accumulated while the FSC was a controlled foreign corporation, see section 1248 and the regulations under that section. However, section 1248 and the regulations under that section do not apply to a FSC's earnings and profits attributable to foreign trade income, see section 1248(d)(6).

(j) *Limitations on certain multiple tax benefits.* The provisions of section 1561, Limitations on Certain Multiple Tax Benefits in the Case of Certain Controlled Corporations, and section 1563, Definitions and Special Rules, and the regulations under those sections apply to a FSC and its controlled group. [Temporary Reg. § 1.921-3T.]

☐ [*T.D.* 8126, 3-2-87.]

[Reg. § 1.922-1]

§ 1.922-1. **Requirements that a corporation must satisfy to be a FSC or a small FSC.**—(a) *FSC requirements.*

Q-1. What are the requirements that a corporation must satisfy to be a FSC?

A-1. A corporation must satisfy all of the requirements of section 922(a).

(b) *Small FSC requirements.*

Q-2. What are the requirements that a corporation must satisfy to be a small FSC?

A-2. A corporation must satisfy all of the requirements of sections 922(a)(1) and (b).

(c) *Definition of corporation.*

Q-3. What type of entity is considered a corporation for purposes of qualifying as a FSC or a small FSC under section 922?

A-3. A foreign entity that is classified as a corporation under section 7701(a)(3) (other than an insurance company) is considered a corporation for purposes of this requirement.

(d) *Eligible possessions.*

Q-4. For purposes of meeting the place of incorporation requirement of section 922(a)(1)(A), what is a possession of the United States?

A-4. For purposes of section 922(a)(1)(A), the possessions of the United States are Guam, American Samoa, the Commonwealth of the Northern Mariana Islands, and the Virgin Islands of the United States ("eligible possessions"). Puerto Rico, although a possession for certain tax purposes, does not qualify as a jurisdiction in which a FSC or small FSC may be incorporated.

(e) *Qualifying countries.*

Q-5. For purposes of meeting the place of incorporation requirement of section 922(a)(1)(A), what is a foreign country and which foreign countries meet the requirements of section 927(e)(3)?

A-5. (i) A foreign country is a jurisdiction outside the 50 states, the District of Columbia, the Commonwealth of Puerto Rico, and the possessions of the United States. (ii) A list of the foreign countries that meet the requirements of section 927(e)(3) ("qualifying countries") will be

Reg. § 1.922-1(a)

published from time to time in the Federal Register and the Internal Revenue Bulletin. A corporation is considered to be created or organized under the laws of a foreign country that meets the requirements of section 927(e)(3) only if the foreign country is a party to (A) an exchange of information agreement under the Caribbean Basin Economic Recovery Act (Code section 274(h)(6)(C)), or (B) a bilateral income tax treaty with the United States if the Secretary certifies that the exchange of information program under the treaty carries out the purposes of the exchange of information requirements of the FSC legislation as set forth in Code section 927(e)(3) and if the corporation is covered under exchange of information program under subdivision (A) or (B).

(f) *Number of shareholders.*

Q-6. Who is counted as a shareholder of a corporation for purposes of determining whether a corporation meets the limitation on the number of shareholders to no more than 25 under section 922(a)(1)(B)?

A-6. Solely for purposes of the limitation on the number of shareholders, the following rules apply:

(i) In general, an individual who owns an interest in stock of the corporation is counted as a shareholder. In the case of joint owners, each joint owner is counted as a shareholder. A member of a corporation's board of directors who holds qualifying shares that are required to be owned by a resident of the country of incorporation is not counted as a shareholder.

(ii) A corporation that owns an interest in stock of the corporation is counted as a single shareholder.

(iii) An estate that owns an interest in stock of the corporation is counted as a single shareholder. If the limitation on number of shareholders is not satisfied by reason of the closing of an estate, the FSC will continue to qualify for the taxable year of the FSC in which the estate is closed.

(iv) A trust is not counted as a shareholder. In the case of a trust all of which is treated as owned by one or more persons under sections 671-679, those persons are counted as shareholders. In the case of all other trusts, a beneficiary is counted as a shareholder.

(v) A partnership is not counted as a shareholder. A general or limited partner is counted as a shareholder if it is a corporation, an individual, or an estate, under the rules contained in subdivisions (i) through (iii). A general or limited partner is not counted as a shareholder if it is a partnership or a trust; the rules contained in subdivision

(iv) and this subdivision (v) apply to the determination of who is counted as a shareholder.

(g) *Class of stock.*

Q-7. What is preferred stock for purposes of determining whether a corporation satisfies the requirement under section 922(a)(1)(C) that no preferred stock be outstanding?

A-7. Preferred stock is stock that is limited and preferred as to dividends or distributions in liquidation.

Q-8. Can a corporation have outstanding more than one class of common stock?

A-8. Yes. However, the rights of a class of stock will be disregarded if the right has the effect of avoidance of federal income tax. For instance, dividend rights may not be used to direct dividends from exempt foreign trade income to shareholders that have taxable income and to direct other dividends to shareholders that have net operating loss carryovers.

(h) *Office.*

Q-9. What is an office for purposes of determining whether a corporation satisfies the requirement of section 922(a)(1)(D)(i)?

A-9. An office is a place for the transaction of the business of the corporation. To be an office a place must meet all of the following requirements:

(i) *It must have a fixed location.*

A transient location is not a fixed location.

(ii) *It must be a building or a portion of a building consisting of at least one room.*

A room is a partitioned part of the inside of a building. The building or portion thereof used as the corporation's office must be large enough to accommodate the equipment required in subdivision (iii) of this answer 9 and the activity required in subdivision (iv) of this answer 9. However, an office is not limited to a room with communication equipment or an adjacent room. Non-contiguous space within the same building will also constitute an office if it is equipped for the retention of the documentation required to be stored by the FSC and if access to the necessary communication equipment is available for use by the FSC.

(iii) *It must be equipped for the performance of the corporation's business.*

An office must be equipped for the communication and retention of information and must be supplied with communication services.

(iv) *It must be regularly used for some business activity of the corporation.* A corporation's business activities must include the maintenance of the documentation described in Q&A 12 of this section. These documents need not be prepared at the office. Any person, whether or not related to

Reg. § 1.922-1(h)

the corporation, may perform the business activities of the corporation at the office if the activity is performed pursuant to a contract, oral or written, for the performance of the activity on behalf of the corporation.

(v) *It must be operated, and owned or leased, by the corporation or by a person, whether or not related to the corporation, under contract to the corporation.*

(vi) *It must be maintained by the corporation or by a person, whether or not related, to the corporation, under contract to the corporation at all times during the taxable year.* In the case of a corporation newly organized as a FSC, thirty days may elapse between the time the corporation is organized as a FSC (*i.e.*, the first day for which the FSC election is effective) and the time an office is maintained by the corporation or a person under contract with the corporation. A place that meets the requirements in subdivision (i) through (vi) of this answer 9 can also be used for activities that are unrelated to the business activity of the corporation.

Q-10. Can a corporation locate an office in any foreign country if it has at least one office in a U.S. possession or in a foreign country that meets the requirements of section 927(e)(3) as provided Q&A 5 of this section?

A-10. Yes.

Q-11. Must a corporation locate the office that is required under section 922(a)(1)(D)(i) in the country or possession of its incorporation?

A-11. No.

(i) *Documentation.*

Q-12. What documentation must be maintained at the corporation's office for purposes of section 922(a)(1)(D)(ii)?

A-12. At least the following documentation must be maintained at the corporation's office under section 922(a)(1)(D)(ii):

(i) The quarterly income statements, a final year-end income statement and a year-end balance sheet of the FSC; and

(ii) All final invoices (or a summary of them) or statements of account with respect to (A) sales by the FSC, and (B) sales by a related person if the FSC realizes income with respect to such sales. A final invoice is an invoice upon which payment is made by the customer. A final invoice must contain, at a minimum, the customer's name or identifying number and, with respect to the transaction or transactions, the date, product or product code or service or service code, quantity, price, and amount due. In the alternative, a document will be acceptable as a final invoice even though it does not include all of the above listed information if the FSC establishes that the document is considered to be a final invoice under normal commercial practices. An invoice forwarded to the customer after payment has been tendered or received pursuant to a letter of credit, as a receipt for payment, satisfies this definition. A single final invoice may cover more than one transaction with a customer.

(iii) A summary of final invoices may be in any reasonable form provided that the summary contains all substantive information from the invoices. All substantive information includes the customer's name or identifying number, the invoice number, date, product or product code, and amount owed. In the alternative, all substantive information includes a summary of the information that is included on documents considered to be final invoices under normal commercial practice. A statement of account is any summary statement forwarded to a customer to inform of, or confirm, the status of transactions occurring within an accounting period during a taxable year that is not less than one month. A statement of account must contain, at a minimum, the customer's name or identifying number, date of the statement of account and the balance due (even if the balance due is zero) as of the last day of the accounting period covered by the statement of account. In the alternative, a document will be accepted as a statement of account even though it does not include all of the above listed information if the FSC establishes that the document is considered a statement of account under normal commercial practice. For these purposes, a document will be considered to be a statement of account under normal commercial practice if it is sent to domestic as well as to export customers in order to inform the customers of the status of transactions during an accounting period. With regard to quarterly income statements, a reasonable estimate of the FSC's income and expense items will be acceptable. If the FSC is a commission FSC, 1.83% of the related supplier's gross receipts will be considered a reasonable estimate of the FSC's income. The documents required by this Q&A 12 need not be prepared by the FSC. In addition they need not be prepared at the FSC's office.

(iv) The FSC will satisfy the requirement that the documents be maintained at its office even if not all final invoices (or summaries) or statements of account or items to be included on statements of account are maintained at its office as long as it makes a good faith effort to do so and provided that any failure to maintain the required documents is cured within a reasonable time of discovery of the failure.

Reg. § 1.922-1(i)

Q-13. If the required documents are not prepared at the FSC's office, by what date must the documents be maintained at its office?

A-13. With regard to the applicable quarters or years prior to March 3, 1987, the quarterly income statements, final invoices (or summaries), or statements of account and the year-end balance sheet must be maintained at the FSC's office no later than the due date, including extensions, of the FSC tax return for the applicable taxable year in which the period ends. With regard to the applicable quarters or years ending after March 3, 1987, the quarterly income statements for the first three quarters of the FSC year must be maintained at the FSC's office no later than 90 days after the end of the quarter. The quarterly income statement for the fourth quarter of the FSC year, the final year-end income statement, the year-end balance sheet, and the final invoices (or summaries) or statements of account must be maintained at the FSC's office no later than the due date, including extensions, of the FSC tax return for the applicable taxable year.

Q-14. In what form must the documentation required under section 922(a)(1)(D)(ii) be maintained?

A-14. The documentation required to be maintained by the office may be originals or duplicates and may be in any form that qualifies as a record under Rev. Rul. 71-20, 1971-1 C.B. 392. Therefore, documentation may be maintained in the form of punch cards, magnetic tapes, disks, and other machine-sensible media used for recording, consolidating, and summarizing accounting transactions and records within a taxpayer's automatic data processing system. The corporation need not maintain at its office equipment capable of reading the machine-sensible media. That equipment, however, must be situated in a location that is readily accessible to the corporation. The equipment need not be owned by the corporation.

Q-15. How long must the documentation required under section 922(a)(1)(D)(ii) be maintained?

A-15. The documentation required under section 922(a)(1)(D)(ii) for a taxable year must be maintained at the FSC's office described in section 922(a)(1)(D)(i) until the period of limitations for assessment of tax for the taxable year has expired under section 6501.

Q-16. Under what circumstances will a corporation be considered to satisfy the requirement of section 922(a)(1)(D)(iii) that it maintain the records it is required to keep under section 6001 at a location within the United States?

A-16. A corporation will be considered to satisfy this requirement if the records required under section 6001 are kept by any person at any location in the United States provided that the records are retained in accordance with section 6001 and the regulations thereunder.

(j) *Board of directors.*

Q-17. What is a corporation's "board of directors" for purposes of the requirement under section 922(a)(1)(E) that, at all times during the taxable year, the corporation must have a board of directors which includes at least one individual who is not a resident of the United States?

A-17. The "board of directors" is the body that manages and directs the corporation according to the law of the qualifying country or eligible possession under the laws of which the corporation was created or organized.

Q-18. Can the member of the board of directors who is a nonresident of the United States be a citizen of the United States?

A-18. Yes. For purposes of meeting the requirement under section 922(a)(1)(E), the member of the board who cannot be a United States resident can be a United States citizen. The principles of section 7701(b) shall be used to determine whether a United States citizen is a United States resident.

Q-19. If the only member of the board of directors who is not a resident of the United States dies, or resigns, is removed from the board or becomes a resident of the United States will the corporation be considered to fail the requirement under section 922(a)(1)(E)?

A-19. If the corporation appoints a new member who is a nonresident of the United States to the board within 30 days after the death, resignation or removal of the former nonresident member, the corporation will be considered to satisfy the requirement under section 922(a)(1)(E).

Also, the corporation will be considered to satisfy the requirement under section 922(a)(1)(E) if the corporation appoints a new member who is a nonresident of the United States to the board within 30 days after the corporation has knowledge, or reason to know, that the board's former nonresident member was in fact a resident of the United States.

Q-20. Is a nonresident alien individual who elects to be treated as a resident of the United States for a taxable year under section 6013(g) considered a nonresident of the United States for purposes of the requirement under section 922(a)(1)(E)?

A-20. Yes.

Q-21. Will the requirement that a FSC's board of directors have a nonresident member at all times during the taxable year be satisfied if the

Reg. § 1.922-1(j)

nonresident member is elected or appointed to the board of directors no later than 30 days after the first day for which the FSC election is effective?

A-21. Yes.

[Reg. § 1.922-1.]

☐ [T.D. 8127, 3-2-87.]

[Reg. § 1.923-1T]

§ 1.923-1T. Temporary Regulations; Exempt foreign trade income.—(a) *Foreign trade income.* Foreign trade income of a FSC is the FSC's gross income attributable to its foreign trading gross receipts. (Any further reference to a FSC in this section shall include a small FSC unless indicated otherwise.) If the FSC is the principal on the sale of export property which it purchased from a related supplier, the FSC's gross income is determined by subtracting from its foreign trading gross receipts the transfer price determined under the transfer pricing methods of section 925(a). If the FSC is the commission agent on the sale of export property by its related supplier, the FSC's gross income is the commission paid or payable by the related supplier to the FSC with respect to the transactions that would have generated foreign trading gross receipts had the FSC been the principal on the transaction. See § 1.925(a)-1T(f) *Examples (1)* and *(6)* for illustrations of the computation of a FSC's foreign trade income, exempt foreign trade income and taxable income.

(b) *Exempt foreign trade income*—(1) *Determination.* (i) If a FSC uses either of the two administrative pricing rules, provided for by section 925(a)(1) and (2), to determine its income from a transaction, or group of transactions, to which section 925 applies (see § 1.925(a)-1T(b)(2)(ii) and (iii)), 15/23 of the foreign trade income that it earns from the transaction, or group of transactions, will be exempt foreign trade income. If a FSC has a non-corporate shareholder (shareholders), 16/23 of its foreign trade income attributable to the noncorporate shareholder's (shareholders') proportionate interest in the FSC will be exempt foreign trade income. See section 291(a)(4).

(ii) If a FSC does not use the administrative pricing rules to determine its income from a transaction, or group of transactions, which gives rise to foreign trade income, 30 percent of its foreign trade income will be exempt foreign trade income. If a FSC has a non-corporate shareholder (shareholders), 32 percent of its foreign trade income attributable to the non-corporate shareholder's (shareholders') proportionate interest in the FSC will be exempt foreign trade income. See section 291(a)(4).

(iii) Exempt foreign trade income so determined under subdivisions (1)(i) and (ii) of this paragraph is treated as foreign source income which is not effectively connected with the conduct of a trade or business within the United States. See section 921(a).

(2) *Special rule for foreign trade income allocable to a qualified cooperative.* (i) Pursuant to section 923(a)(4), if a qualified cooperative is a shareholder of a FSC, the FSC's non-exempt foreign trade income determined by use of either of the administrative pricing methods of section 925(a)(1) or (2) which is allocable to the marketing of agricultural or horticultural products, or the providing of related services, for any taxable year will be treated as exempt foreign trade income to the extent that it is distributed to the qualified cooperative shareholder. A qualified cooperative is defined as any organization to which chapter 1, subchapter T, part 1 of the Code applies. See section 1381(a).

(ii) This special rule of section 923(a)(4) shall apply only if the distribution is made before the due date under section 6072(b), including extensions, for filing the FSC's income tax return for that year. Any distribution which satisfies this requirement will be treated as made on the last day of the FSC's taxable year. In addition, this special rule shall apply only if the income of the cooperative is based on arm's length transactions between the cooperative and its members or patrons.

(iii) Income attributable to the marketing of agricultural or horticultural products, or the providing of related services, shall be allocated to the FSC shareholders on a per share basis. See § 1.926(a)-1T(b) for ordering rules for distributions from a FSC.

(3) *Special rule for military property.* (i) Under section 923(a)(5), the exempt foreign trade income of a FSC relating to the disposition of, or services relating to, military property shall be equal to 50 percent of the amount which, but for section 923(a)(5), would be treated as exempt foreign trade income under section 923(a)(2) or (3). The foreign trade income no longer treated as exempt because of this special rule of section 923(a)(5) will remain income of the FSC and will be treated as non-exempt foreign trade income.

(ii) The term "military property" is defined in section 995(b)(3)(B) and includes any property which is an arm, ammunition, or implement of war designated in the munitions list published pursuant to section 38 of the International Security Assistance and Arms Export Control Act of 1976 (22 U.S.C. 2778) (which repealed and

Reg. § 1.923-1T(a)

replaced the Military Security Act of 1954). [Temporary Reg. § 1.923-1T.]

☐ [T.D. 8126, 3-2-87.]

[Reg. § 1.924(a)-1T]

§ 1.924(a)-1T. Temporary Regulations; Definition of foreign trading gross receipts (Temporary).—(a) *In general.* The term "foreign trading gross receipts" means any of the five amounts described in paragraphs (b) through (f) of this section, except to the extent that any of the five amounts is an excluded receipt within the meaning of paragraph (g) of this section. These amounts will not be foreign trading gross receipts if the FSC is not managed outside the United States, pursuant to section 924(c), or if the economic processes with regard to a transaction, or group of transactions, that are required of a FSC by section 924(d) do not take place outside the United States. The requirement that these activities take place outside the United States does not apply to a small FSC. The activities required by section 924(c) and (d) may be performed either by the FSC or by any person (whether or not related to the FSC) acting under contract with the FSC for the performance of the required activities. Sections 1.924(c)-1 and 1.924(d)-1 provide rules to determine whether these requirements have been met. For purposes of this section—

(1) *FSC.* All references to a FSC in this section mean a FSC, except when the context indicates that such term means a corporation in the process of meeting the conditions necessary for that corporation to become a FSC. All references to a FSC in this section shall include a small FSC unless indicated otherwise.

(2) *Sale and lease.* The term "sale" includes an exchange or other disposition and the term "lease" includes a rental or a sublease. The term "license" includes a sublicense. All rules under this section applicable to leases of export property apply in the same manner to licenses of export property. See § 1.927(a)-1T(f)(3) for a description of intangible property which cannot be export property.

(3) *Gross receipts.* The term "gross receipts" is defined by section 927(b) and § 1.927(b)-1T.

(4) *Export property.* The term "export property" is defined by section 927(a) and § 1.927(a)-1T.

(5) *Controlled group.* The term "controlled group" is defined by paragraph (h) of this section.

(6) *Related supplier and related party.* The terms related supplier and related party are defined by § 1.927(d)-2T.

(b) *Sales of export property.* Foreign trading gross receipts of a FSC include gross receipts from the sale of export property by the FSC, or by any principal for whom the FSC acts as a commission agent (whether or not the principal is a related supplier), pursuant to the terms of a contract entered into with a purchaser by the FSC or by the principal at any time or by any other person and assigned to the FSC or the principal at any time prior to the shipment of the property to the purchaser. Any agreement, oral or written, which constitutes a contract at law, satisfies the contractual requirements of this paragraph. Gross receipts from the sale of export property, whenever received, do not constitute foreign trading gross receipts unless the seller (or the corporation acting as commission agent for the seller) is a FSC at the time of the shipment of the property to the purchaser. For example, if a corporation which sells export property under the installment method is not a FSC for the taxable year in which the property is shipped to the purchaser, gross receipts from the sale do not constitute foreign trading gross receipts for any taxable year of the corporation.

(c) *Leases of export property*—(1) *In general.* Foreign trading gross receipts of a FSC include gross receipts from the lease of export property provided that—

(i) The property is held by the FSC (or by a principal for whom the FSC acts as commission agent with respect to the lease) either as an owner or lessee at the beginning of the term of the lease, and

(ii) The FSC qualified (or was treated) as a FSC for its taxable year in which the term of the lease began.

(2) *Prepayment of lease receipts.* If the gross receipts from a lease of export property are prepaid, then—

(i) All the prepaid gross receipts are foreign trading gross receipts of a FSC if it is reasonably expected at the time of the prepayment that, throughout the term of the lease, the lease will meet the requirements of this paragraph and the property will be export property; or

(ii) If it is reasonably expected at the time of the prepayment that the prepaid receipts would not be foreign trading gross receipts throughout the term of the lease if those receipts were not received as a prepayment, then only those prepaid receipts, for the taxable years of the FSC for which they would be foreign trading gross receipts, are foreign trading gross receipts. Thus, for example, if a lessee makes a prepayment of the first and last years' rent, and it is reasonably expected that the leased property will be export property for the first half of the lease period but not the second half of such period, the amount of

Reg. § 1.924(a)-1T(c)(2)

the prepayment which represents the first year's rent will be considered foreign trading gross receipts if it would otherwise qualify, whereas the amount of the prepayment which represents the last year's rent will not be considered foreign trading gross receipts.

(d) *Related and subsidiary services*—(1) *In general.* Foreign trading gross receipts of a FSC include gross receipts from services furnished by the FSC which are related and subsidiary to any sale or lease (as described in paragraph (b) or (c) of this section) of export property by the FSC or with respect to which the FSC acts as a commission agent, provided that the FSC derives foreign trading gross receipts from the sale or lease. The services may be performed within or without the United States.

(2) *Services furnished by the FSC.* Services are considered to be furnished by a FSC for purposes of this paragraph if the services are provided by—

(i) The person who sold or leased the export property to which the services are related and subsidiary, provided that the FSC acts as a commission agent with respect to the sale or lease of the property and with respect to the services,

(ii) The FSC as principal, or any other person pursuant to a contract with the FSC, provided the FSC acted as principal or commission agent with respect to the sale or lease of the property, or

(iii) A member of the same controlled group as the FSC if the sale or lease of the export property is made by another member of the controlled group provided, however, that the FSC acts as principal or commission agent with respect to the sale or lease and as commission agent with respect to the services.

(3) *Related services.* Services which may be related to a sale or lease of export property include but are not limited to warranty service, maintenance service, repair service, and installation service. Transportation (including insurance related to such transportation) will be related to a sale or lease of export property, if the cost of the transportation is included in the sale price or rental of the property or, if the cost is separately stated, is paid by the FSC (or its principal) which sold or leased the property to the person furnishing the transportation service. Financing or the obtaining of financing for a sale or lease is not a related service for purposes of this paragraph. A service is related to a sale or lease of export property if—

(i) The service is of the type customarily and usually furnished with the type of transaction in the trade or business in which the sale or lease arose, and

(ii) The contract to furnish the service—

(A) Is expressly provided for in or is provided for by implied warranty under the contract of sale or lease,

(B) Is entered into on or before the date which is 2 years after the date on which the contract under which the sale or lease was entered into, provided that the person described in paragraph (d)(2) of this section which is to furnish the service delivers to the purchaser or lessor a written offer or option to furnish the services on or before the date on which the first shipment of goods with respect to which the service is to be performed is delivered, or

(C) Is a renewal of the services contract described in subdivision (ii)(A) and (B) of this paragraph.

(4) *Subsidiary services*—(i) *In general.* Services related to a sale or lease of export property are subsidiary to the sale or lease only if it is reasonably expected at the time of the sale or lease that the gross receipts from all related services furnished by the FSC (as defined in this paragraph (d)(2)) will not exceed 50 percent of the sum of the gross receipts from the sale or lease and the gross receipts from related services furnished by the FSC (as described in this paragraph (d)(2)). In the case of a sale, reasonable expectations at the time of the sale are based on the gross receipts from all related services which may reasonably be performed at any time before the end of the 10-year period following the date of the sale. In the case of a lease, reasonable expectations at the time of the lease are based on the gross receipts from all related services which may reasonably be performed at any time before the end of the term of the lease (determined without regard to renewal options).

(ii) *Allocation of gross receipts from services.* In determining whether the services related to a sale or lease of export property are subsidiary to the sale or lease, the gross receipts to be treated as derived from the furnishing of services may not be less than the amount of gross receipts reasonably allocated to the services as determined under the facts and circumstances of each case without regard to whether—

(A) The services are furnished under a separate contract or under the same contract pursuant to which the sale or lease occurs, or

(B) The cost of the services is specified in the contract of sale or lease.

(iii) *Transactions involving more than one item of export property.* If more than one item of

Reg. § 1.924(a)-1T(d)(1)

export property is sold or leased in a single transaction pursuant to one contract, the total gross receipts from the transaction and the total gross receipts from all services related to the transaction are each taken into account in determining whether the services are subsidiary to the transaction. However, the provisions of this subdivision apply only if the items could be included in the same product line, as determined under § 1.925(a)-1T(c)(8).

(iv) *Renewed service contracts.* If under the terms of a contract for related services, the contract is renewable within 10 years after a sale of export property, or during the term of a lease of export property, related services to be performed under the renewed contract are subsidiary to the sale or lease if it is reasonably expected at the time of the renewal that the gross receipts from all related services which have been and which are to be furnished by the FSC (as described in paragraph (d)(2) of this section) will not exceed 50 percent of the sum of the gross receipts from the sale or lease and the gross receipts from related services furnished by the FSC (as so described). Reasonable expectations are determined as provided in subdivision (i) of this paragraph.

(v) *Parts used in services.* If a services contract described in paragraph (d)(3) of this section provides for the furnishing of parts in connection with the furnishing of related services, gross receipts from the furnishing of the parts are not taken into account in determining whether under this paragraph (d)(4) the services are subsidiary. See paragraph (b) or (c) of this section to determine whether the gross receipts from the furnishing of parts constitute foreign trading gross receipts. See § 1.927(a)-1T(c)(2) and (e)(3) for rules regarding the treatment of the parts with respect to the manufacture of export property and the foreign content of the property, respectively.

(5) *Relation to leases.* If the gross receipts for services which are related and subsidiary to a lease of property have been prepaid at any time for all the services which are to be performed before the end of the term of the lease, then the rules in paragraph (c)(2) of this section (relating to prepayment of lease receipts) will determine whether prepaid services under this paragraph (d)(5) are foreign trading gross receipts. Thus, for example, if it is reasonably expected that leased property will be export property for the first year of the term of the lease but will not be export property for the second year of the term, prepaid gross receipts for related and subsidiary services to be furnished in the first year may be foreign trading gross receipts. However, any prepaid gross receipts for the services to be furnished in the second year cannot be foreign trading gross receipts.

(6) *Relation with export property determination.* The determination as to whether gross receipts from the sale or lease of export property constitute foreign trading gross receipts does not depend upon whether services connected with the sale or lease are related and subsidiary to the sale or lease. Thus, for example, assume that a FSC receives gross receipts of $1,000 from the sale of export property and gross receipts of $1,100 from installation and maintenance services which are to be furnished by the FSC within 10 years after the sale and which are related to the sale. The $1,100 which the FSC receives for the services would not be foreign trading gross receipts since the gross receipts from the services exceed 50 percent of the sum of the gross receipts from the sale and the gross receipts from the related services furnished by the FSC. The $1,000 which the FSC receives from the sale of export property would, however, be foreign trading gross receipts if the sale met the requirements of paragraph (b) of this section.

(e) *Engineering and architectural services*—(1) *In general.* Foreign trading gross receipts of a FSC include gross receipts from engineering services (as described in paragraph (e)(5) of this section) or architectural services (as described in paragraph (e)(6) of this section) furnished by such FSC (as described in paragraph (e)(7) of this section) for a construction project (as defined in paragraph (e)(8) of this section) located, or proposed for location, outside the United States. Such services may be performed within or without the United States.

(2) *Services included.* Engineering and architectural services include feasibility studies for a proposed construction project whether or not such project is ultimately initiated.

(3) *Excluded services.* Engineering and architectural services do not include—

(i) Services connected with the exploration for oil or gas, or

(ii) Technical assistance or know-how. For purposes of this paragraph, the term "technical assistance or know-how" includes activities or programs designed to enable business, commerce, industrial establishments, and governmental organizations to acquire or use scientific, architectural, or engineering information.

(4) *Other services.* Receipts from the performance of construction activities other than engineering and architectural services constitute foreign trading gross receipts to the extent that the activities are related and subsidiary services (within the meaning of paragraph (d) of this sec-

Reg. § 1.924(a)-1T(e)(4)

tion) with respect to a sale or lease of export property.

(5) *Engineering services.* For purposes of this paragraph, engineering services in connection with any construction project (within the meaning of paragraph (e)(8) of this section) include any professional services requiring engineering education, training, and experience and the application of special knowledge of the mathematical, physical, or engineering sciences to those professional services as consultation, investigation, evaluation, planning, design, or responsible supervision of construction for the purpose of assuring compliance with plans, specifications, and design.

(6) *Architectural services.* For purposes of this paragraph, architectural services include the offering or furnishing of any professional services such as consultation, planning, aesthetic and structural design, drawings and specifications, or responsible supervision of construction (for the purpose of assuring compliance with plans, specifications, and design) or erection, in connection with any construction project (within the meaning of paragraph (e)(8) of this section).

(7) *Definition of "furnished by the FSC".* For purposes of this paragraph, the term "furnished by the FSC" means architectural and engineering services furnished:

(i) By the FSC,

(ii) By another person (whether or not that person is a United States person) pursuant to a contract entered into with the FSC at any time prior to the furnishing of the services, provided that the FSC acts as principal, or

(iii) By another person (whether or not that person is a United States person) pursuant to a contract for the furnishing of the services entered into by, or assigned to, the person at any time, provided that the FSC acts as a commission agent for the furnishing of the services.

(8) *Definition of "construction project".* For purposes of this paragraph, the term "construction project" includes the erection, expansion, or repair (but not including minor remodeling or minor repairs) of new or existing buildings or other physical facilities including, for example, roads, dams, canals, bridges, tunnels, railroad tracks, and pipelines. The term also includes site grading and improvement and installation of equipment necessary for the construction. Gross receipts from the sale or lease of construction equipment are not foreign trading gross receipts unless the equipment is export property.

(f) *Managerial services*—(1) *In general.* Foreign trading gross receipts of a first FSC for its taxable year include gross receipts from the furnishing of managerial services provided for an unrelated FSC or unrelated interest charge DISC to aid the unrelated FSC or unrelated interest charge DISC in deriving foreign trading gross receipts or qualified export receipts, as the case may be, provided that at least 50 percent of the first FSC's gross receipts for such year consists of foreign trading gross receipts derived from the sale or lease of export property and the furnishing of related and subsidiary services. For purposes of this paragraph, managerial services are considered furnished by a FSC if the services are provided—

(i) By the first FSC,

(ii) By another person (whether or not a United States person) pursuant to a contract entered into by that person with the first FSC at any time prior to the furnishing of the services, provided that the first FSC acts as principal with respect to the furnishing of the services, or

(iii) By another person (whether or not a United States person) pursuant to a contract for the furnishing of services entered into at any time prior to the furnishing of the services provided that the first FSC acts as commission agent with respect to those services.

(2) *Definition of "managerial services".* The term "managerial services" as used in this paragraph means activities relating to the operation of an unrelated FSC or an unrelated interest charge DISC which derives foreign trading gross receipts or qualified export receipts as the case may be from the sale or lease of export property and from the furnishing of services related and subsidiary to those sales or leases. The term includes staffing and operational services necessary to operate the unrelated FSC or unrelated interest charge DISC, but does not include legal, accounting, scientific, or technical services. Examples of managerial services are: conducting export market studies, making shipping arrangements, and contacting potential foreign purchasers.

(3) *Status of recipient of managerial services.* Foreign trading gross receipts of a first FSC include receipts from the furnishing of managerial services during any taxable year of a recipient of such services if the recipient qualifies as a FSC or interest charge DISC for the taxable year. For purposes of this paragraph, a recipient is deemed to qualify as a FSC or interest charge DISC for its taxable year if the first FSC obtains from the recipient a copy of the recipient's election to be treated as a FSC or interest charge DISC together with the recipient's sworn statement that an election has been timely filed with the Internal Revenue Service Center. The recipient may mark out the names of its shareholders on a copy of its

Reg. § 1.924(a)-1T(e)(5)

election to be treated as a FSC or interest charge DISC before submitting it to the first FSC. The copy of the election and the sworn statement of the recipient must be received by the first FSC within six months after the first FSC furnishes managerial services for the recipient. The copy of the election and the sworn statement of the recipient need not be obtained by the first FSC for subsequent taxable years of the recipient. A recipient of managerial services is not treated as a FSC or interest charge DISC with respect to the services performed during a taxable year for which the recipient does not qualify as a FSC or interest charge DISC if the first FSC performing such services does not believe or if a reasonable person would not believe (taking into account the furnishing FSC's managerial relationship with such recipient FSC or interest charge DISC) at the beginning of such taxable year that the recipient will qualify as a FSC or an interest charge DISC for such taxable year.

(g) *Excluded receipts*—(1) *In general.* Notwithstanding the provisions of paragraphs (b) through (f) of this section, foreign trading gross receipts of a FSC do not include any of the six amounts described in paragraph (g)(2) through (7) of this section.

(2) *Sales and leases of property for ultimate use in the United States.* Property which is sold or leased for ultimate use in the United States does not constitute export property. See § 1.927(a)-1T(d)(4) relating to determination of where the ultimate use of the property occurs. Thus, foreign trading gross receipts of a FSC described in paragraph (b) or (c) of this section do not include gross receipts of the FSC from the sale or lease of this property.

(3) *Sales or leases of export property and furnishing of services accomplished by subsidy.* Foreign trading gross receipts of a FSC do not include gross receipts described in paragraphs (b) through (f) of this section if the sale or lease of export property or the furnishing of services is accomplished by a subsidy granted by the United States or any instrumentality thereof, see section 924(f)(1)(B). Subsidies covered by section 924 (f)(1)(B) are listed in subdivisions (i) through (vi) of this paragraph.

(i) The development loan program, or grants under the technical cooperation and development grants program of the Agency for International Development, or grants under the military assistance program administered by the Department of Defense, pursuant to the Foreign Assistance Act of 1961, as amended (22 U.S.C. 2151) unless the FSC shows to the satisfaction of the Commissioner that, under the conditions existing at the time of the sale (or at the time of the lease or at the time the services were rendered), the purchaser (or lessor or recipient of the services) had a reasonable opportunity to purchase (or lease or contract for services) on competitive terms and from a seller (or lessor or performer of services) who was not a U.S. person, goods (or services) which were substantially identical to such property (or services) and which were not manufactured, produced, grown, or extracted in the United States (or performed by a U.S. person);

(ii) The Public Law 480 program authorized under Title I of the Agricultural Trade Development and Assistance Act of 1954, as amended (7 U.S.C. 1691, 1701-1714);

(iii) The Export Payment program of the Commodity Credit Corporation authorized by section 5(d) and (f) of the Commodity Credit Corporation Charter Act, as amended (15 U.S.C. 714c(d) and (f));

(iv) The section 32 export payment programs authorized by section 32 of the Act of August 24, 1935, as amended (7 U.S.C. 612c);

(v) The Export Sales program of Commodity Credit Corporation authorized by sections 5(d) and (f) of the Commodity Credit Corporation Charter Act, as amended (15 U.S.C. 714c(d) and (f)), other than the GSM-4 program provided under 7 CFR 1488, and section 407 of the Agricultural Act of 1949, as amended (7 U.S.C. 1427), for the purpose of disposing of surplus agricultural commodities and exporting or causing to be exported agricultural commodities; and

(vi) The Foreign Military Sales direct credit program (22 U.S.C. 2763) or the Foreign Military Sales loan guaranty program (22 U.S.C. 2764) if—

(A) The borrowing country is released from its contractual liability to repay the United States government with respect to those credits or guaranteed loans;

(B) The repayment period exceeds twelve years; or

(C) The interest rate charged is less than the market rate of interest as defined in 22 U.S.C. 2763(c)(2)(B);

unless the FSC shows to the satisfaction of the Commissioner that, under the conditions existing at the time of the sale, the purchaser had a reasonable opportunity to purchase, on competitive terms from a seller who was not a U.S. person, goods which were substantially identical to this property and which were not manufactured, produced, grown, or extracted in the United States. Information regarding whether an export is financed, in whole or in part, with funds derived

Reg. § 1.924(a)-1T(g)(3)

from the programs identified in this subdivision may be obtained from the Comptroller, Defense Security Assistance Agency, Department of Defense, Washington, D.C. 20301.

(4) *Sales or leases of export property and furnishing of architectural or engineering services for use by the United States*—(i) *In general.* Foreign trading gross receipts of a FSC do not include gross receipts described in paragraph (b), (c), or (e) of this section if a sale or lease of export property, or the furnishing of architectural or engineering services, is for use by the United States or an instrumentality thereof in any case in which any law or regulation requires in any manner the purchase or lease of property manufactured, produced, grown, or extracted in the United States or requires the use of architectural or engineering services performed by a United States person. See section 924(f)(1)(A)(ii). For example, a sale by a FSC of export property to the Department of Defense for use outside the United States would not produce foreign trading gross receipts for the FSC if the Department of Defense purchased the property from appropriated funds subject to either any provision of the Department of Defense Federal Acquisition Regulations Supplement (48 CFR Chapter 2) or any appropriations act for the Department of Defense for the applicable year if the regulations or appropriations act requires that the items purchased must have been grown, reprocessed, reused, or produced in the United States. The Department of Defense's regulations do not require that items purchased by the Department for resale in post or base exchanges and commissary stores located on United States military installations in foreign countries be items grown, reprocessed, reused or produced in the United States. Therefore, receipts arising from the sale by a FSC to those post or base exchanges and commissary stores will not be excluded from the definition of foreign trading gross receipts by this paragraph (g)(4).

(ii) *Direct or indirect sales or leases.* Any sale or lease of export property is for use by the United States or an instrumentality thereof if such property is sold or leased by a FSC (or by a principal for whom the FSC acts as commission agent) to—

(A) A person who is a related person with respect to the FSC or such principal and who sells or leases the property for use by the United States or an instrumentality thereof, or

(B) A person who is not a related person with respect to the FSC or such principal if, at the time of the sale or lease, there is an agreement or understanding that the property will be sold or leased for use by the United States or an instrumentality thereof (or if a reasonable person would have known at the time of the sale or lease that the property would be sold or leased for use by the United States or an instrumentality thereof) within 3 years after the sale or lease.

(iii) *Excluded programs.* The provisions of subdivision (4)(i) and (ii) of this paragraph do not apply in the case of a purchase by the United States or an instrumentality thereof if the purchase is pursuant to—

(A) The Foreign Military Sales Act, as amended (22 U.S.C. § 2751 et seq.), or a program under which the United States government purchases property for resale, on commercial terms, to a foreign government or agency or instrumentality thereof, or

(B) A program (whether bilateral or multilateral) under which sales to the United States government are open to international competitive bidding.

(5) *Services.* Foreign trading gross receipts of a FSC do not include gross receipts described in paragraph (d) of this section (concerning related and subsidiary services) if the services from which such gross receipts are derived are related and subsidiary to the sale or lease of property which results in excluded receipts under this paragraph.

(6) *Receipts within controlled group.* (i) For purposes of the transfer pricing methods of section 925(a), gross receipts of a corporation do not constitute foreign trading gross receipts for any taxable year of the corporation if at the time of the sale, lease, or other transaction resulting in the gross receipts, the corporation and the person from whom the gross receipts, are directly or indirectly derived (whether or not such corporation and such person are the same person) are members of the same controlled group, and either

(A) The corporation and the person each qualifies as a FSC (or if related FSCs are commission agents of each party to the transaction) for its taxable year in which its receipts arise, or

(B) With regard to sale transactions, a sale of export property to a FSC (or to a related person if the FSC is the commission agent of the related person) by a non-FSC within the same controlled group follows any sale of the export property to a FSC (or to a related person if the FSC is the commission agent of the related person) within the same controlled group if foreign trading gross receipts resulted from the sale. Thus for example, assume that R, S, X, and Y are members of the same controlled group and that X and Y are FSCs. If R sells property to S and pays X a commission relating to that sale and if S sells the same property to an unrelated foreign party and pays Y a commission relating to that sale, the

Reg. § 1.924(a)-1T(g)(4)

receipts received by X from the sale of such property by R to S will be considered to be derived from Y, a FSC which is a member of the same controlled group as X, and thus will not result in foreign trading gross receipts to X. The receipts received by Y from the sale to an unrelated foreign party may, however, result in foreign trading gross receipts to Y. For another example, if R and S both assign the commissions to X, receipts derived from the sale from R to S will be considered to be derived from X acting as commission agent for S and will not result in foreign trading gross receipts to X. Receipts derived by X from the sale of property by S to an unrelated foreign party may, however, constitute foreign trading gross receipts.

(ii) Section 1.927(a)-1T(f)(2) provides rules regarding property not constituting export property in certain cases where such property is leased to any corporation which is a member of the same controlled group as the lessor.

(7) *Factoring of receivables by a related supplier.* If an account receivable arising with respect to export property is transferred to any person for an amount reflecting a discount from the selling price of the export property, then the gross receipts from the sale which are treated as foreign trading gross receipts for purposes of computing a FSC's profit under the administrative pricing methods of section 925(a)(1) and (2) shall be reduced by the amount of the discount. See § 1.925(a)-1T(f) *Example (11)* for illustration of how this special rule affects computation of combined taxable income of a FSC and its related supplier.

(h) *Definition of "controlled group".* For purposes of sections 921 through 927 and the regulations under those sections, the term "controlled group" has the same meaning as is assigned to the term "controlled group of corporations" by section 1563(a), except that (1) the phrase "more than 50 percent" is substituted for the phrase "at least 80 percent" each place the latter phrase appears in section 1563(a), and (2) section 1563(b) shall not apply. Thus, for example, a foreign corporation subject to tax under section 882 may be a member of a controlled group. Furthermore, two or more corporations (including a foreign corporation) are members of a controlled group at any time such corporations meet the requirements of section 1563(a) (as modified by this paragraph).

(i) *FSC's entitlement to income*—(1) *Application of administrative pricing rules of section 925(a).* A corporation which meets the requirements of section 922(a) (or section 922(b) if the corporation elects small FSC status) and § 1.921-2(a) (Q&A1) to be treated as a FSC (or small FSC) for a taxable year is entitled to income, and the administrative pricing rules of section 925(a)(1) or (2) apply, in the case of any transaction described in § 1.925(a)-1T(b)(iii) between the FSC and its related supplier (as defined in § 1.927(d)-2T(a)) as long as the FSC, or someone under contract to it, satisfies the requirements of section 925(c). The requirements of section 925(c) must be met by a commission FSC as well as by a buy-sell FSC. See § 1.925(a)-1T(a)(3)(i) and (b)(2)(ii).

(2) *Other transactions.* In the case of a transaction to which the provisions of paragraph (i)(1) of this section do not apply but from which a FSC derives gross receipts, the income to which the FSC is entitled as a result of the transaction is determined pursuant to the terms of the contract for the transaction and, if applicable, section 482 and the regulations under that section. For applicability of the section 482 transfer pricing method, see § 1.925(a)-1T(a)(3)(ii) and (b)(2)(i).

(j) *Small FSC limitation*—(1) *In general.* Under section 924(b)(2)(B), in determining exempt foreign trade income of a small FSC, the foreign trading gross receipts of the small FSC for the taxable year which exceed $5 million are not taken into account. The foreign trading gross receipts of the small FSC not taken into account for purposes of computing the small FSC's exempt foreign trade income shall be taken into account in computing the small FSC's non-exempt foreign trade income. If the foreign trading gross receipts of the small FSC exceed the $5 million limitation, the small FSC may select the gross receipts to which the limitation is allocated. See section 922(b) and § 1.921-2(b) (Q&A3) for a definition of a small FSC.

(2) *Members of a controlled group limited to one $5 million amount*—(i) *General rule.* All small FSCs which are members of a controlled group on a December 31, shall, for their taxable years which include that December 31, be limited to one $5 million amount. The $5 million amount shall be allocated equally among the member small FSCs of the controlled group for their taxable years including that December 31, unless all of the member small FSCs consent to an apportionment plan providing for an unequal allocation of the $5 million amount. The apportionment plan shall provide for the apportionment of a fixed dollar amount to one or more of the corporations, and the sum of the amounts so apportioned shall not exceed the $5 million amount. If the taxable year including the December 31 of any member small FSC is a short period (as defined in section 443), the portion of the $5 million amount allocated to that member small FSC for that short

Reg. § 1.924(a)-1T(j)(2)

period under the preceding sentence shall be reduced to the amount which bears the same ratio to the amount so allocated as the number of days in such short period bears to 365. The consent of each member small FSC to the apportionment plan for the taxable year shall be signified by a statement which satisfies the requirements of and is filed in the manner specified in § 1.1561-3(b). An apportionment plan may be amended in the manner prescribed in § 1.1561-3(c), except that an original or an amended plan may not be adopted with respect to a particular December 31 if at the time the original or amended plan is sought to be adopted, less than 12 full months remain in the statutory period (including extensions) for the assessment of a deficiency against any shareholder of a member small FSC the tax liability of which would change by the adoption of the original or amended plan. If less than 12 full months of the period remain with respect to any such shareholder, the director of the service center with which the shareholder files its income tax return will, upon request, enter into an agreement extending the statutory period for the limited purpose of assessing any deficiency against that shareholder attributable to the adoption of the original or amended apportionment plan.

(ii) *Membership determined under section 1563(b).* For purposes of this paragraph (j)(2), the determination of whether a small FSC is a member of a controlled group of corporations with respect to any taxable year shall be made in the manner prescribed in section 1563(b) and the regulations under that section.

(iii) *Certain short taxable years*—(A) *General rule.* If a small FSC has a short period (as defined in section 443) which does not include a December 31, and that small FSC is a member of a controlled group of corporations which includes one or more other small FSC's with respect to the short period, then the amount described in section 924(b)(2)(B) with respect to the short period of that small FSC shall be determined by—

(*1*) Dividing $5 million by the number of small FSCs which are members of that group on the last day of the short period, and

(*2*) Multiplying the result by a fraction, the numerator of which is the number of days in the short period and the denominator of which is 365.

For purposes of the preceding sentence, section 1563(b) shall be applied as if the last day of the short period were substituted for December 31. Except as provided in subdivision (2)(iii)(B) of this paragraph, the small FSC having a short period not including a December 31 may not enter into an apportionment plan with respect to the short period.

(B) *Exception.* If the short period not including a December 31 of two or more small FSCs begins on the same date and ends on the same date and those small FSCs are members of the same controlled group, those small FSCs may enter into an apportionment plan for such short period in the manner provided in subdivision (2)(i) of this paragraph with respect to the combined amount allowed to each of those small FSCs under subdivision (2)(iii)(A) of this paragraph. [Temporary Reg. § 1.924(a)-1T.]

☐ [*T.D.* 8126, 3-2-87.]

[Reg. § 1.924(c)-1]

§ 1.924(c)-1. **Requirement that a FSC be managed outside the United States.**—(a) *In general.* Section 924(b)(1)(A) provides that a FSC shall be treated as having foreign trading gross receipts for the taxable year only if the management of the FSC during the year takes place outside the United States, as provided in section 924(c). Section 924(c) and this section set forth the management activities that must take place outside the United States in order to satisfy the requirement of section 924(b)(1)(A). Paragraph (b) of this section provides rules for determining whether the requirements of section 924(c)(1) have been met. Section 924(c)(1) requires that all meetings of the board of directors of the FSC during the taxable year and all meetings of the shareholders of the FSC during the taxable year take place outside the United States. Paragraph (c) of this section provides rules for maintaining the FSC's principal bank account outside the United States as provided in section 924(c)(2). Paragraph (d) of this section provides rules for disbursements required by section 924(c)(3) to be made from bank accounts of the FSC maintained outside the United States.

(b) *Meetings of board of directors and meetings of shareholders must be outside the United States.* All meetings of the board of directors of the FSC and all meetings of the shareholders of the FSC that take place during a taxable year must take place outside the United States to meet the requirements of section 924(c)(1). Only meetings that are formally convened as meetings of the board of directors or as shareholder meetings will be taken into account in determining whether those requirements have been met. In addition, all such meetings must comply with the local laws of the foreign country or possession of the United States in which the FSC was created or organized. The local laws determine whether a meeting must be held, when and where it must be held (if it is held at all), who must be present, quorum require-

Reg. § 1.924(c)-1(a)

ments, use of proxies, and so on. Where the local law permits action by the board of directors or shareholders to be taken by written consent without a meeting, use of such procedure will not constitute a meeting for purposes of section 924(c)(1). Section 924(c)(1) and this section impose no other requirements except the requirement that meetings that are actually held take place outside the United States. If the participants in a meeting are not all physically present in the same location, the location of the meeting is determined by the location of the persons exercising a majority of the voting power (including proxies) participating in the meeting. For example, a FSC has five directors, and is organized in country A. Country A's law requires that a majority of the directors of a corporation must participate in a meeting to constitute a quorum (and, thus, a meeting), but there is no requirement that the meeting be held in country A or that the directors must be physically present to participate. One director is in country A, another director is in country B, and a third director is in the United States. These three directors convene a meeting by telephone that constitutes a meeting under the law of country A. The meeting occurs outside the United States because the persons exercising a majority of the voting power participating in the meeting are located outside the United States.

(c) *Maintenance of the principal bank account outside the United States*—(1) *In general.* For purposes of section 924 (c), the bank account that shall be regarded as the principal bank account of a FSC is the bank account from which the disbursements described in paragraph (d) of this section are made. A FSC may have more than one principal bank account. The bank account that is regarded as the principal bank account must be maintained in a foreign country which meets the requirements of section 927(e)(3), or in any possession of the United States (as defined in section 927(d)(5)), and it must be so maintained at all times during the taxable year. For taxable years beginning on or after February 19, 1987, a principal bank account or accounts must be designated on the annual return of the FSC by providing the bank name(s) and account number(s).

(2) *Maintenance of the account in a bank.* The bank account that is regarded as the principal bank account must be maintained in an institution that is engaged in the conduct of a banking, financing, or similar business, as defined in § 1.954-2(d)(2)(ii) (without regard to whether it is a controlled foreign corporation). The institution may be a U.S. bank, provided that the account is maintained in a branch outside the United States.

(3) *Maintenance of an account outside the United States.* Maintenance of the principal bank account outside the United States means that the account regarded as the principal bank account must be an account maintained on the books of the banking institution at an office outside the United States, but does not require that access to the account may be made only outside the United States. Instructions providing for deposits into or disbursements from the account may originate in the United States without affecting the status of maintenance of the account outside the United States.

(4) *Maintenance of the account at all times during the taxable year.* The term "at all times during the taxable year" generally means for each day of the taxable year. In the case of a newly created or organized corporation, thirty days may elapse between the effective date of the corporation's election to be treated as a FSC and the date a bank account is opened without causing the FSC to fail the requirement that it maintain its principal bank account outside the United States at all times during the taxable year. For example, if a corporation is created or organized prior to January 1, 1985 and makes an election to be treated as a FSC within the first 90 days of 1985, the election is effective as of January 1, 1985. Thus, the FSC must open a bank account within 30 days of January 1, or as of January 31, 1985, to satisfy this requirement. Also, a FSC shall be treated as satisfying this requirement if the account that is regarded as its principal bank account is terminated during the taxable year, provided that (i) such termination is the result of circumstances beyond the FSC's control, and (ii) the FSC establishes a new principal bank account within thirty days after such termination. A FSC may close its principal bank account and replace it with another account that qualifies under this paragraph (c) as a principal bank account at any time provided that no lapse of time occurs between the closing of the principal bank account and the opening of the replacement account.

(5) *Other accounts.* The FSC may maintain other bank accounts in addition to its principal bank account. Such other accounts may be located anywhere, without limitation. The mere existence of such other accounts will not cause the FSC to fail to satisfy the requirements of section 924(c).

(d) *Disbursement of dividends, legal and accounting fees, and salaries of officers and directors out of the principal bank account of the FSC*—(1) *In general.* All dividends, legal fees, accounting fees, salaries of officers of the FSC, and salaries or fees paid to members of the board of directors of the FSC that are disbursed during the taxable

Reg. § 1.924(c)-1(d)

year must be disbursed out of bank account(s) of the FSC maintained outside the United States. Such an account is treated as the principal bank account of the FSC for purposes of section 924(c). Dividends, however, may be netted against amounts owed to the FSC (*e.g.*, commissions) by a related supplier through book entries. If the FSC regularly disburses its legal or accounting fees, salaries of officers, and salaries or fees of directors out of its principal bank account, the occasional, inadvertent payment by mistake of fact or law of such amounts out of another bank account will not be considered a disbursement by the FSC if, upon determination that such payment was made from another account, reimbursement to such other account is made from the principal bank account of the FSC within a reasonable period from the date of the determination. Disbursement out of the principal bank account of the FSC may be made by transferring funds from the principal bank account to a U.S. account of the FSC provided that (i) the payment of the dividends, salaries or fees to the recipients is made within 12 months of the transfer, (ii) the purpose of the expenditures is designated, and (iii) the payment of the dividends, salaries or fees is actually made out of the same U.S. account that received the disbursement from the principal bank account.

(2) *Reimbursement.* Legal or accounting fees, salaries of officers, and salaries or fees of directors that are paid by a related person wholly or partially on behalf of a FSC must be reimbursed by the FSC. The amounts paid by the related person are not considered disbursed by the FSC until the related person is reimbursed by the FSC. The related person must be reimbursed no later than the last date prescribed for filing the FSC's tax return (including extensions) for the taxable year to which the reimbursement relates. Any reimbursement for amounts paid on behalf of the FSC must be disbursed out of the FSC's principal bank account (and not netted against any obligation owed by the related person to the FSC), as set forth in paragraph (c) of this section. To determine the amounts paid on behalf of the FSC, the FSC may rely upon a written statement or invoice furnished to it by the related person which shows the following:

(i) the actual fees charged for performing the legal or accounting services for the FSC or, if such fees cannot be ascertained by the related person, a good faith estimate thereof, and the actual salaries or fees paid for services as officers and directors of the FSC, and

(ii) the person who performed or provided the services.

(3) *Good faith exception.* If, after the FSC has filed its tax return, a determination is made by the Commissioner that all or a part of the legal or accounting fees, salaries of officers, and salaries or fees of directors of the FSC were paid by a related person without receiving reimbursement, the FSC may, nonetheless, satisfy the requirements of section 924(c)(3) if the fees and salaries were paid by the related person in good faith, and the FSC reimburses the related person for the fees and salaries paid within 90 days after the determination. The reimbursement shall be treated as made as of the end of the taxable year of the FSC for which the reimbursement is made.

(4) *Dividends*—(i) *Definition.* For purposes of section 924(c) and this section only, the term "dividends" refers solely to cash dividends (including a dividend paid in a foreign functional currency) actually paid pursuant to a declaration or authorization by the FSC. Accordingly, a "dividend" will not include a constructive dividend that is deemed to be paid (regardless of the source of such constructive dividend) or a distribution of property that is a dividend under section 316 other than a distribution of U.S. dollars or a foreign functional currency.

(ii) *Offset accounting entries.* Payment of dividends by the FSC to its related supplier may be in the form of an accounting entry offsetting an amount payable to the related supplier for the dividend against an existing debt owed to the FSC. The offset accounting entries must be clearly identified in the books of account of both the related supplier and the FSC.

(5) *Legal and accounting fees.* For purposes of this section, legal and accounting fees do not include salaries paid to legal and accounting employees of the FSC (or a related person). Legal and accounting fees are limited to fees paid to independent persons performing legal or accounting services for or with respect to the FSC.

(6) *Salaries of officers and directors.* For purposes of this section, salaries of officers and salaries or fees of directors are only those salaries or fees paid for services as officers or directors of the FSC. Salaries do not include reimbursed travel and entertainment expenses. If an individual officer, director, or employee of a related person is also an officer or director of a FSC and receives additional compensation for services performed for the FSC, the portion of the compensation paid to the individual which is for services performed for the FSC is required to be disbursed out of the FSC's principal bank account. For purposes of this section, the term "compensation" is defined as set forth in paragraphs (d)(1) and (2) of § 1.415-2. [Reg. § 1.924(c)-1.]

☐ [*T.D.* 8125, 2-3-87.]

Reg. § 1.924(c)-1(d)(2)

Income From Sources Without the United States

See p. 20,601 for regulations not amended to reflect law changes

[Reg. § 1.924(d)-1]

§ 1.924(d)-1. Requirement that economic processes take place outside the United States.—(a) *In general.* Section 924(b)(1)(B) provides that a FSC has foreign trading gross receipts from any transaction only if economic processes with respect to such transaction take place outside the United States as provided in section 924(d). Section 924(d) and this section set forth the rules for determining whether a sufficient amount of the economic processes of a transaction take place outside the United States. Generally, a transaction will qualify if the FSC satisfies two different requirements: participation outside the United States in the sales portion of the transaction, and satisfaction of either the 50-percent or the 85-percent foreign direct cost test. The activities comprising these economic processes may be performed by the FSC or by any other person acting under contract with the FSC. (All references to "FSC" in §§ 1.924(d)-1 and 1.924(e)-1 shall mean the FSC or, if applicable, the person performing the relevant activity under contract on behalf of the FSC). The FSC may act upon standing instructions from another person in the performance of any activity, whether a sales activity under paragraph (c) of this section or an activity relating to the disposition of export property under paragraph (d) of this section and § 1.924(e)-1. The identity of the FSC as a separate entity is not required to be disclosed in the performance of any of the activities comprising the economic processes. Except as otherwise provided, the location of any activity is determined by the place where the activity is initiated by the FSC, and not by the location of any person transmitting instructions to the FSC.

(b) *Activities performed by another person*—(1) *In general.* Any person, whether domestic or foreign, and whether related or unrelated to the FSC, may perform any activity required to satisfy this section, provided that the activity is performed pursuant to a contract for the performance of that activity on behalf of the FSC. Such a contract may be any oral or written agreement which constitutes a contract at law. The person performing the activity is not required to enter into a contract directly with the FSC and, thus, may be a direct or indirect subcontractor of a person under contract with the FSC. For example, assume that a buy-sell FSC enters into an agreement with its related supplier in which the related supplier agrees to perform on behalf of the FSC all sales activities with respect to the FSC's transactions with its foreign customers. Through its existing agreements with a domestic unrelated person, the related supplier subcontracts the performance of these activities to the domestic unrelated person, who, in turn, subcontracts the performance of the sales activities to foreign sales agents. The sales activities performed by the foreign sales agents are considered to be performed on behalf of the FSC for purposes of meeting the requirements of section 924(d)(1)(A).

(2) *Proof of compliance.* If the FSC does not perform the activity itself, it must maintain records adequate to establish, with respect to each transaction or group of transactions, that the activity was performed and that the performance of such activity took place outside the United States. If the person who performed the activity on behalf of the FSC is an independent contractor, the FSC may rely upon a written declaration from that person stating that the activities were performed by that person on behalf of the FSC, and were performed outside the United States. An invoice or a receipt for payment will be considered to be such a written declaration if it specifies that the activities were performed outside the United States or specifies a particular place outside the United States where the activities were performed. If the person performing the activities on behalf of the FSC is a related person, the FSC must maintain records adequate to establish that the activities were actually performed and where the activities were performed. Such records may be stored with the related person provided that the FSC makes such records available to the Commissioner upon request.

(c) *Participation outside the United States in the sales portion of the transaction*—(1) *In general.* The requirement of section 924(d)(1)(A) is met with respect to the gross receipts of a FSC derived from any transaction if the FSC has participated outside the United States in the solicitation, the negotiation, or the making of the contract relating to such transaction (hereinafter described as "sales activities"), as provided in this paragraph (c). A sale need not occur in order that the solicitation or negotiation tests be satisfied. Once the FSC has participated outside the United States in an activity that constitutes the solicitation, negotiation, or the making of the contract with respect to a transaction, any prior or subsequent activity by the FSC with respect to such transaction that would otherwise constitute the sales activity will be disregarded for purposes of determining whether the FSC has met the requirements of section 924(d)(1)(A). For example, if a FSC sells a product to a foreign customer by first meeting with the customer in New York to discuss the product and then by mailing to it from outside the Untied States a brochure describing the product, the prior meeting is disregarded and

Reg. § 1.924(d)-1(c)(1)

only the mailing is considered in determining whether there was solicitation outside the United States by the FSC with respect to the transaction which has occurred.

(2) *Solicitation (other than advertising).* For purposes of this paragraph (c), "solicitation" refers to any communication (by any method, including, but not limited to, telephone, telegraph, mail, or in person) by the FSC, at any time during the 12 month period (measured from the date the communication is mailed or transmitted) immediately preceding the execution of a contract relating to the transaction to a specific, targeted customer or potential customer, that specifically addresses the customer's attention to the product or service which is the subject of the transaction. For purposes of paragraph (c)(2) of this section, communication by mail means depositing the communication in a mailbox. Except as provided in § 1.924(e)-1(a)(1) with respect to second mailings, activities that would otherwise constitute advertising (such as sending sales literature to a customer or potential customer) will be considered solicitation if the activities are directed at a specific, targeted customer or potential customer, and the costs of the activity are not taken into account as advertising under the foreign direct cost tests. Activities that would otherwise constitute sales promotion (such as a promotional meeting in person with a customer) will be considered to be solicitation if the activities are directed at a specific, targeted customer or potential customer, and the costs of the activity are not taken into account as sales promotion under the foreign direct cost tests. Except as provided in § 1.924(e)-1(a)(1) with respect to second mailings, the same or similar activities cannot be considered both solicitation and advertising, or both solicitation and sales promotion, with respect to the same customer. Solicitation, however, may take place at the same time as, and in conjunction with, another sales activity. Additionally, it may take place with respect to any person, whether domestic or foreign, and whether or not related to the FSC.

(3) *Negotiation.* For purposes of this paragraph (c), "negotiation" refers to any communication by the FSC to a customer or potential customer aimed at an agreement on one or more of the terms of a transaction, including, but not limited to, price, credit terms, quantity, or time or manner of delivery. For purposes of this paragraph (c)(3), communication by mail has the same meaning as provided in paragraph (c)(2) of this section. Negotiation does not include the mere receipt of a communication from a customer (such as an order) that includes terms of a sale. Negotiation may take place at the same time as, and in conjunction with, another sales activity. Additionally, it may take place with respect to any person, whether domestic or foreign, and whether or not related to the FSC.

(4) *Making of a contract.* For purposes of this paragraph (c), "making of a contract" refers to performance by the FSC of any of the elements necessary to complete a sale, such as making an offer or accepting an offer. A requirements contract is considered an open offer to be accepted from time to time when the customer submits an order for a specified quantity. Thus, the acceptance of such an order will be considered the making of a contract. The written confirmation by the FSC to the customer of the acceptance of the open order will also be considered the making of a contract. Acceptance of an unsolicited bid or order is considered the "making of a contract" even if no solicitation or negotiation occurred with respect to the transaction. The written confirmation by the FSC to the customer of an oral or written agreement which confirms variable contract terms, such as price, credit terms, quantity, or time or manner of delivery, or specifies (directly or by cross-reference) additional contract terms will be considered the making of a contract. A written confirmation is any confirmation expressed in writing, including a telegram, telex, or other similar written communication. The making of a contract may take place at the same time as, and in conjunction with, another sales activity. Additionally, it may take place with respect to any person, whether domestic or foreign, and whether or not related to the FSC.

(5) *Grouping transactions.* Generally, the sales activities under this paragraph (c) are to be applied on a transaction-by-transaction basis. By annual election of the FSC, however, any of the sales activities may be applied on the basis of a group as set forth in this paragraph (c)(5). Any groupings used must be supported by adequate documentation of performance of activities relating to the groupings used. An election by the FSC to group transactions must be made on its annual income tax return. The FSC, however, may amend its tax return to group in a manner different from that elected on its original return before the expiration of the statute of limitations.

(i) *Standards of groups.* A determination by a FSC as to a grouping will be accepted by a district director if such determination conforms to any of the following standards:

(A) *Product or product line groupings.* A product or product line grouping may be based upon either a recognized trade or industry usage, or upon a two digit major group (or on any inferior classification or combination of inferior classi-

Reg. § 1.924(d)-1(c)(2)

fications within a major group) of the Standard Industrial Classification as prepared by the Statistical Policy Division of the Office of Management and Budget, Executive Office of the President. For taxable years beginning on or before February 19, 1987, any sales activity that is performed outside the United States with respect to any transaction covered by the product or product line grouping during the FSC's taxable year shall apply to all transactions covered by the product or product line. However, for taxable years beginning after February 19, 1987, the requirement of section 924(d)(1)(A) is met with respect to all transactions covered by the product or product line grouping only if the sales activities are performed outside the United States with respect to customers with sales representing either: (i) 20-percent or more of the foreign trading gross receipts of the product or product line grouping during the current year or (ii) 50 percent or more of the foreign trading gross receipts of the product or product line grouping for the prior year irrespective of whether any sales occurred within the current year to the prior year customers. If during the prior taxable year, the controlled group of which the FSC is a member had a DISC or interest charge DISC, the FSC may use the 50 percent rule with respect to the preceding DISC or interest charge DISC year, substituting qualified export receipts for foreign trading gross receipts. A corporation which has not been treated in the prior year as a FSC, interest charge DISC, or DISC does not have to meet either the 20 percent test or the 50 percent test for the first year in which it is treated as a FSC.

(B) *Customer groupings.* A customer grouping includes all transactions of the FSC with a particular customer during the FSC's taxable year. Thus, any sales activity that is performed outside the United States with respect to any transaction with the customer during the taxable year shall apply to all transactions within the customer grouping.

(C) *Contract groupings.* A contract grouping includes all transactions of the FSC under a particular contract for a taxable year. Thus, any sales activity that is performed outside the United States with respect to any transaction under the contract will apply to all transactions under the contract for such taxable year. For long-term contracts between unrelated parties, the sales activities tests need be satisfied only once for the life of the contract. With respect to requirements contracts and long-term contracts between related parties, the sales activities test must be satisfied annually.

(D) *Product or product line groupings within customer or contract groupings.* Groupings may be based upon product or product line groupings within customer or contract groupings. If, however, the primary grouping is a customer or contract grouping, the 20 percent test set forth in subdivision (A) of this paragraph relating to product or product line grouping will not be applicable.

(ii) *Transactions included in a grouping.* A choice by a FSC to group transactions shall generally apply to all transactions within the scope of that grouping. The choice of a grouping, however, applies only to transactions covered by the grouping and, for transactions not encompassed by the grouping, the determinations may be made on a transaction-by-transaction basis or other grouping basis. For example, a FSC may choose a product grouping with respect to one product and use the transaction-by-transaction method for another product within the same taxable year. In addition, if a FSC applies sales activity rules on the basis of other types of groupings, such as all sales to a particular customer, transactions included in those other groupings shall be excluded from product groupings.

(iii) *Different groupings allowed for different purposes.* A choice by the FSC to group transactions may be made separately for each of the sales activities under section 924(d)(1)(A). Groupings used for purposes of section 924(d)(1)(A) will have no relationship to groupings used for other purposes, such as satisfying the foreign direct cost tests. This paragraph (c)(5) does not apply for purposes of section 925.

(6) *Examples.* The provisions of this paragraph (c) may be illustrated by the following examples:

Example (1). In November, a calendar year FSC mailed from its foreign office its catalog to a potential foreign customer. The catalog displayed numerous products along with a brief description and the price of each. In February of the following year, the FSC sold to the customer a product displayed in the catalog. Since the FSC communicated with the customer during the 12-month period prior to the sale, although during the previous taxable year, the FSC participated outside the United States in the solicitation relating to the transaction.

Example (2). A FSC with a taxable year ending April 30, 1986, solicits customer X during that taxable year with respect to Product A. In the previous taxable year, the FSC sold product A to customers V, W, X, Y, Z, none of whom were customers in the taxable year ending April 30, 1986. The sales proceeds from sales to customer X

Reg. § 1.924(d)-1(c)(6)

represented 50 percent of the foreign trading gross receipts for the previous FSC year. The FSC meets the 50 percent test for product or product line grouping for the taxable year ending April 30, 1986. If the facts were changed so that there was not a FSC, DISC or interest charge DISC in the same controlled group in the previous taxable year, the single solicitation directed to any customer would qualify all transactions within the product group as meeting the solicitation requirement for that taxable year. For subsequent taxable years, the 50 percent test or the 20 percent test would be applicable.

Example (3). A FSC earns commissions on the sale of export property by its domestic related supplier to United States wholesalers for final sale to foreign customers. The related supplier receives an order from one of its United States wholesalers. The related supplier telephones the United States wholesaler to inform it of the new price and the probability of another price increase soon. The United States wholesaler orally agrees to the new price and the related supplier instructs the FSC to telex the wholesaler from its foreign office a confirmation that the product will be sold at the current new price. The written confirmation by the FSC of an oral agreement on a variable contract term constitutes the making of a contract. Thus, the requirements of section 924(d)(1)(A) are met with respect to the transaction relating to the product.

(d) *Satisfaction of either the 50-percent or the 85-percent foreign direct cost test*—(1) *In general.* Section 924(d)(1)(B) requires, in order for the gross receipts of a transaction to qualify as foreign trading gross receipts, that the foreign direct costs incurred by the FSC attributable to the transaction equal or exceed 50 percent of the total direct costs incurred by the FSC attributable to the transaction. The direct costs are those costs attributable to activities described in the five categories of section 924(e). Section 924(d)(2) provides that, instead of satisfying the 50-percent foreign direct cost test of section 924(d)(1)(B), the FSC may incur foreign direct costs attributable to activities described in each of two of those categories that equal or exceed 85 percent of the total direct costs incurred by the FSC attributable to the activity described in each of the two categories. If no direct costs are incurred by the FSC in a particular category, that category shall not be taken into account for purposes of determining satisfaction of either the 50-percent or the 85-percent foreign direct cost test. If any amount of direct costs is incurred in a particular category, that category shall be taken into account for purposes of the foreign direct costs tests.

(2) *Direct costs*—(i) *Definition of direct costs.* For purposes of section 924(d), direct costs are those costs which are incident to and necessary for the performance of any activity described in section 924(e). Direct costs include the cost of materials which are consumed in the performance of the activity, and the cost of labor which can be identified or associated directly with the performance of the activity (but only to the extent of wages, salaries, fees for professional services, and other amounts paid for personal services actually rendered, such as bonuses or compensation paid for services on the basis of a percentage of profits). Direct costs also include the allowable depreciation deduction for equipment or facilities (or the rental cost for use thereof) that can be specifically identified or associated with the activity, as well as the contract price of an activity performed on behalf of the FSC by a contractor. If costs of services or the use of facilities are only incidentally related to the performance of an activity described in section 924(e), only the incremental cost is considered to be identified directly with the activity. For example, supervisory, administrative, and general overhead expenses, such as telephone service, normally are not identified directly with particular activities described in section 924(e). The cost of a long distance telephone call made to arrange for delivery of export property, however, is identified directly with the activities described in section 924(e)(2). Direct costs for purposes of section 924(d) do not necessarily include all of the expenses taken into account for purposes of determining the taxable income of the FSC or the combined taxable income of the FSC and its related supplier.

(ii) *Allocation of direct costs.* For purposes of this section only, if costs are identified with more than one activity (whether or not all of the activities are described in section 924(e)), the portion of the costs attributable to each activity shall be determined by allocating the costs among the activities in any manner that is consistently applied and, if applicable, that reasonably reflects relative costs that would be incurred by performing each activity independently. If costs of an activity are attributable to more than one transaction or grouping of transactions, the portion of the costs attributable to each transaction or grouping shall be determined by allocating the costs among the transactions or groupings in any manner that is consistently applied and, if applicable, that reasonably reflects relative costs that would be incurred by performing the activity independently with respect to each transaction or grouping.

(3) *Total direct costs.* The term "total direct costs" means all of the direct costs of any transac-

Reg. § 1.924(d)-1(d)(1)

tion attributable to activities described in any paragraph of section 924(e). For purposes of the 50-percent foreign direct cost test of section 924(d)(1)(B), total direct costs are determined based on the direct costs of all activities described in all of the paragraphs of section 924(e). For purposes of the 85-percent foreign direct cost test of section 924(d)(2), however, the total direct costs are determined separately for each paragraph of section 924(e). If more than one activity is included within a paragraph of section 924(e), direct costs must be incurred with respect to at least one activity listed in the paragraph. If costs are incurred with respect to more than one activity, all direct costs must be considered for purposes of satisfying the direct costs test.

(4) *Foreign direct costs.* The term "foreign direct costs" means the portion of the total direct costs of any transaction which is attributable to activities performed outside the United States. For purposes of the 50-percent foreign direct cost test, foreign direct costs are determined based on the direct costs of all activities described in all of the paragraphs of section 924(e). For purposes of the 85-percent foreign direct cost test, however, foreign direct costs are determined separately for each paragraph of section 924(e).

(5) *Fifty percent foreign direct cost test.* To satisfy the requirement of section 924(d)(1)(B), the foreign direct costs incurred by the FSC attributable to the transaction must equal or exceed 50 percent of the total direct costs attributable to the transaction. This test looks to the cost of the activities described in section 924(e) on an aggregate basis; therefore, it is not necessary that the foreign direct costs of each activity, or of each paragraph of section 924(e), equal or exceed 50 percent of the total direct costs of that activity or paragraph.

(6) *Eighty-five percent foreign direct cost test*—(i) *General rule.* To satisfy the requirement of section 924(d)(2), the foreign direct costs of a transaction incurred by the FSC attributable to activities described in each of at least two paragraphs of section 924(e) must equal or exceed 85 percent of the total direct costs attributable to activities described in that paragraph. This test looks to costs of the activities on a paragraph-by-paragraph basis (but not on an activity-by-activity basis). As an example, the foreign direct costs of advertising and sales promotion are aggregated with each other for this purpose, but they are not aggregated with the foreign direct costs of transportation.

(ii) *Satisfaction of the 85-percent test.* If, after the FSC files its tax return indicating that it has satisfied the 85-percent foreign direct cost test with respect to each of at least two paragraphs of subsection 924(e) and a determination is made by the Commissioner that the foreign direct costs attributable to one or both of the two paragraphs of section 924(e) specified on the return did not equal or exceed 85 percent of the total direct costs attributable to such activities, the FSC may, nonetheless, satisfy the 85-percent foreign direct cost test if the foreign direct costs attributable to any two paragraphs of section 924(e) equal or exceed 85 percent of the total direct costs attributable to those other paragraphs.

(e) *Grouping transactions.* Generally, the foreign direct cost tests under paragraph (d) of this section are to be applied on a transaction-by-transaction basis. By annual election of the FSC, however, the foreign direct cost tests may be applied on a customer, contract or product or product line grouping basis. Any groupings used must be supported by adequate documentation of performance of activities and costs of activities relating to the groupings used. An election by the FSC to group transactions must be made on its annual income tax return. The FSC may, however, amend its tax return before the expiration of the statute of limitations under section 6501 of the Code to group in a manner different from that elected on its original return.

(1) *Standards for groupings.* A determination by a FSC as to a grouping will be accepted by the district director if such determination conforms to any of the following standards:

(i) *Product or product line groupings.* A product or product line grouping may be based either on a recognized trade or industry usage, or on a two digit major grouping (or on any inferior classification or combination of inferior classifications within a major grouping) of the Standard Industrial Classification as prepared by the Statistical Policy Division of the Office of Management and Budget, Executive Office of the President.

(ii) *Customer groupings.* A customer grouping includes all transactions of the FSC with a particular customer during the FSC's taxable year.

(iii) *Contract groupings.* A contract grouping includes all transactions of the FSC under a particular contract, including a requirements contract. The tests will be applied to all transactions within a contract grouping during each taxable year of the FSC; however, by election of the FSC, all transactions under a contract that occur in the first or the last year of the contract may be included with, respectively, the next succeeding or the immediately preceding taxable year in applying these tests. For example, if with respect to

Reg. § 1.924(d)-1(e)(1)

transactions during the first calendar year of a 5-year contract, a calendar year FSC incurs direct costs attributable to the transactions of $100X for advertising, all of which are foreign direct costs, and $10X for processing of customer orders and for arranging for delivery, $9X (or 90 percent of the total direct costs) of which are foreign direct costs, the FSC has satisfied the 85-percent foreign direct cost test with respect to those transactions for the taxable year. If with respect to transactions during the second year of the contract, the FSC only incurs $18X of direct costs for processing of customer orders and arranging for delivery, $15X (83.3 percent of the total direct costs) of which are foreign direct costs, the FSC may include the transactions from the first year of the contract to meet the 85-percent foreign direct cost test in the second taxable year. Thus, with respect to the transactions in the second year, the FSC satisfies the foreign direct costs test for advertising (because the entire $100X of direct costs are foreign direct costs) and for processing of customer orders and arranging for delivery (because of the $28X of direct costs, $24X or 85.7 percent of the total direct costs are foreign direct costs). If, however, with respect to transactions in the third year, the FSC satisfies the foreign direct costs test, those transactions cannot be included with the transactions in the fourth year. The FSC may aggregate the direct costs in the fourth and fifth years in the same manner as for the first and second years as described above in order to satisfy the 85 percent foreign direct costs test.

(iv) *Product or product line groupings within customer or contract groupings.* Groupings may be based on product or product line groupings within customer or contract groupings.

(2) *Transactions included in a grouping.* An election by the FSC to group transactions shall generally apply to all transactions within the scope of that grouping. The election of a grouping, however, applies only to transactions covered by the grouping and, as to transactions not encompassed by the grouping, the determinations may be made on a transaction-by-transaction basis or other grouping basis. For example, the FSC may elect a product grouping with respect to one product and elect the transaction-by-transaction method for another product within the same taxable year. In addition, if a FSC is permitted to apply either the 50-percent or the 85-percent foreign direct cost test on the basis of other types of groupings, such as all transactions with respect to a particular customer, transactions included in those other groupings shall be excluded from product groupings.

(3) *Different groupings allowed for different purposes.* An election by the FSC to group transactions may be made separately for each of the activities relating to disposition of export property under section 924(d)(1)(B) or section 924(d)(2). Groupings used for purposes of section 924 will have no bearing on groupings for other purposes. This paragraph (e) does not apply for purposes of section 925.

(f) *Exception for foreign military property*—(1) *General rule.* The requirements of this section do not apply to any activities performed in connection with foreign military sales except those activities described in section 924(e). The FSC is deemed to have satisfied the requirements of section 924(d)(1)(A).

(2) *Example.* The principles of paragraph (f)(1) of this section may be illustrated by the following example:

Example. A FSC earns commissions on foreign military sales by its related supplier. All solicitation, negotiation, and contract making activities occur in the United States solely between the related supplier and the United States government. The property is delivered, title passes, and payment is made in the United States in accordance with standard United States government practices. The FSC incurs direct costs in the amount of $155X to process the government's orders and arrange for delivery of the goods, all of which are foreign direct costs. In addition, it incurs foreign direct costs in the amount of $250X for assembling and transmitting its final invoice to the government from outside the U.S. and foreign direct costs of $200X associated with receiving payment from the related supplier in accordance with the rules of § 1.924(e)-1(d)(2)(iii). No other activities occur with respect to the foreign military sales. The FSC has satisfied the 85-percent foreign direct cost test and thus has foreign trading gross receipts with respect to the foreign military sales. The fact that the FSC did not participate outside the United States in any of the sales activities has no bearing on the qualification of the receipts since the FSC is deemed to have met the requirements of § 924(d)(1)(A). [Reg. § 1.924(d)-1.]

☐ [T.D. 8125, 2-13-87.]

[Reg. § 1.924(e)-1]

§ 1.924(e)-1. **Activities relating to the disposition of export property.**—(a) *Advertising and sales promotion.* For purposes of section 924(e), advertising and sales promotion are defined as follows.

(1) *Advertising*—(i) *Advertising defined*—(A) *General rule.* Advertising means the an-

Reg. § 1.924(e)-1(a)(1)

nouncement or description of property or services described in section 924(a), in some medium of mass communication (such as radio, television, newspaper, trade journals, mass mailings, or billboards), in order to induce multiple customers or potential customers to buy or rent the property or services from the FSC or related supplier. Advertising is not required to be directed to the general public, but may be focused toward any group of export customers or potential export customers. Advertising except for the advertising described in § 1.924(e)-1(a)(1)(i)(B) must describe one or more specific products or product lines (or services) and identify the product as a product offered by the FSC or related supplier. Advertising intended solely to build a favorable image of a company or group of companies is not included in this definition of advertising. Additionally, advertising primarily directed at customers or potential customers in the United States is not included in this definition of advertising, nor is advertising related to property or services not described in section 924(a).

(B) *Special rules for sales to distributors.* If the customer is a distributor (whether domestic or foreign, related or unrelated to the FSC), an expense that is incurred by the distributor and charged to the FSC or related supplier as a reduction in the purchase price or as a separate charge for an announcement or description described in paragraph (a)(1)(A) of this section to induce the distributor's customers, potential customers, or the ultimate users to buy or rent the property or services is advertising for these purposes (i) if the FSC incurs 20 percent or more of the total advertising costs of the distributor or (ii) if the FSC pays the total charge of an advertisement either directly or indirectly. For these purposes, a distributor is anyone other than an end user or a final consumer. A FSC may incur direct advertising costs to a foreign end consumer even though the FSC sells to a U.S. distributor.

(ii) *Direct costs of advertising.* Direct costs of advertising include costs of transmitting, displaying, or distributing the advertising to customers or potential customers and the costs of printing in the case of sales literature, but do not include fees paid to an independent advertising agency to develop the announcement or description, translation costs, or costs of preparing the announcement or description for potential use as advertising. Direct costs of sending sales literature to customers or potential customers may be taken into account as advertising costs as long as the activity is not taken into account for purposes of the sales activity requirements of § 1.924(d)-1(c).

(iii) *Location of advertising.*

(A) *General rule.* The location of advertising activity is the place to which the advertising is transmitted, displayed, distributed, mailed, or otherwise conveyed to the customers or potential customers (or in the case of advertising described in paragraph (a)(i)(B) of this section, the distributor's customers, or the ultimate users). For example, a television advertisement that is broadcast to a foreign country constitutes advertising activity outside the United States even though the broadcast signal originates in the United States. Therefore, the cost of that advertising activity is a foreign cost. The FSC may rely upon the distribution statistics of the publisher of print media or the broadcaster of broadcast media through which the advertising is distributed. If the distribution statistics show that 85 percent or more of the readership, radio listeners, or viewership are outside the United States, all direct costs of advertising are considered foreign direct costs of advertising.

(B) *Foreign editions of journals, magazines, etc.* Costs related to advertising in foreign English editions of U.S. publications as well as advertising in any publication in a foreign language are foreign direct costs.

(C) *United States editions.* Costs related to advertising in United States publications are not treated as direct costs even if the publication also has a foreign edition in English.

(iv) *Second mailings.* In general, direct costs of sending sales literature to customers may be treated as solicitation or advertising, but not both. A distinction may be made, however, between a first and second mailing so that one may be treated as advertising and the other may be treated as solicitation. To qualify under this second mailing rule, the two mailings must be generically different items such as a price list and a description of the product itself. An amended price list would not be distinguishable from an original price list and would, therefore, not constitute a second mailing.

(v) *Examples.* The principles of paragraph (a)(1) of this section may be illustrated by the following examples:

Example (1). The related supplier, under contract with a buy-sell FSC to advertise export product D on the FSC's behalf to its foreign unrelated customers, engaged a French advertising agency to develop an advertising campaign to induce French customers to buy the product. As a part of the advertising campaign, the agency places a one-page advertisement in a relevant French trade journal. The advertisement consti-

Reg. § 1.924(e)-1(a)(1)

tutes advertising within the meaning of paragraph (a)(1) of this section.

Example (2). A United States weekly magazine publishes, in addition to its United States edition, a Canadian edition in English and a Mexican edition in Spanish. A FSC incurs costs of $200 X for a one-page display in each of the three editions for a total advertising cost of $600 X. The $200 X cost relating to the advertising in the United States edition is not a direct cost because it relates to United States sales. The total costs of $400 X relating to advertising in the English language Canadian edition and the Spanish language Mexican edition are foreign direct costs.

Example (3). A FSC earns commissions on the sale of export product E by its domestic related supplier to United States distributors for resale to Canadian retail customers. The related supplier, under contract with the FSC to advertise product E, pays an amount equal to 1-percent of its annual gross receipts with respect to product E under a cooperative advertising arrangement with the distributor. The amount, which represents 20 percent of the total advertising costs for product E, is reimbursed by the FSC. The 20-percent amount represents a significant portion of the total advertising costs and thus constitutes advertising within the meaning of paragraph (a)(1)(i) of this section.

Example (4). A FSC mails two items to each customer on its customer list within one taxable year. The first mailing consists of a price list which merely lists the various products by name and provides a price next to each product name. The second mailing consists of a brochure which fully describes and illustrates each product. The two mailings are generically different. Therefore, one mailing may be counted as advertising while the other mailing may be counted as solicitation.

(2) *Sales promotion*—(i) *Sales promotion defined.* Sales promotion means an appeal made in person to an export customer or potential export customer for the sale or rental of property or services described in section 924(a), made in the context of a trade show or customer meeting. A customer meeting means a periodic meeting (*e.g.,* quarterly, semi-annual, or annual) in which 10 or more customers or potential customers are reasonably expected to attend. However, for taxable years beginning before February 19, 1987, a customer meeting may, at the option of the taxpayer, mean any meeting with a customer or potential customer regardless of the frequency of the meetings or the number of customers or potential customers in attendance. A meeting, show or event in the United States that is primarily aimed at the export of goods or services described in section 924(a) constitutes sales promotion. Sales promotion does not include an appeal made in the context of any meeting, show or event primarily aimed at U. S. customers or an appeal for the sale or rental of property or services not described in section 924(a). Whether any meeting, show or event is primarily aimed at U.S. customers or at the export of goods or services described in section 924(a) shall be determined by all of the facts and circumstances including the announced objective of the meeting, show or event; the attendees; the location of the meeting, show or event; and the product or special feature of the product.

(ii) *Direct costs of sales promotion.* Direct costs of sales promotion include costs such as rental of space at trade shows, payments to organizers or other persons hired for the event, rental of display equipment and decorations for the event, and costs of maintaining a showroom. Direct costs of sales promotion also include costs for travel, meals, and lodging for direct sales people attending the event if these costs are paid by the FSC or related supplier. In the case of a customer meeting, direct costs of sales promotion include the costs of materials printed specifically for the meeting and the costs of travel, lodging, and food for both the direct sales people and customers or potential customers attending the meeting. Direct costs of sales promotion do not include the cost of salaries and commissions of direct sales people or the cost of discount coupons, samples of the product, or printed advertising materials that are used for general advertising as well as sales promotion.

(iii) *Location of sales promotion.* The location of sales promotion activity is the place where the trade show or customer meeting is held.

(iv) *Examples.* The principles of paragraph (a)(2)(i) of this section may be illustrated by the following examples:

Example (1). The related supplier sells various export products described in section 924(a) to its foreign customers. As a commission agent for the related supplier with respect to such sales, the FSC performs sales promotion. It contracts with the related supplier to serve as its agent for such purposes. To stimulate the sale of its export products, the related supplier conducts semi-annual meetings with the purchasing agents of its customers at its Kansas City headquarters. Ten or more purchasing agents are reasonably expected to attend each meeting. At such meetings, the purchasing agents see the related supplier's manufacturing facilities, visit with its executives, attend technical updates, and see new export products. These semi-annual customer meetings

Reg. § 1.924(e)-1(a)(2)

constitute sales promotion within the meaning of paragraph (a)(2)(i) of this section. Direct costs incurred with respect to the customer meetings are U.S. direct costs because the sales promotion activities occur within the United States.

Example (2). Assume the same facts as in Example (1), except that the related supplier exhibits products that only operate on 220 volts at a trade show in the United States. According to the trade show sponsors, the purpose of the show is to increase sales abroad of United States-manufactured products. Since the products exhibited are designed for operation in foreign countries and the purpose of the trade show is to boost sales in those countries, the trade show held in the United States is primarily aimed at the export products described in section 924(a) and not at United States customers. Thus, the trade show constitutes sales promotion within the meaning of paragraph (a)(2)(i) of this section and the direct costs incurred in connection with the trade show are treated as United States direct costs.

(b) *Processing of customer orders and arranging for delivery of the export property*. For purposes of section 924(e), the processing of customer orders and the arranging for delivery of the export property are defined in paragraph (b)(1) and paragraph (b)(2), respectively, of this section. For taxable years beginning after February 19, 1987, if the FSC performs the activities of processing of customer orders and arranging for delivery of the export property and elects to group its transactions, it is considered to have performed the activities with respect to all transactions in the grouping elected by the FSC under § 1.924(d)-1(e) during the taxable year if it performs the activities of processing of customer orders and arranging for delivery of the export property with respect to customers generating 20 percent or more of foreign trading gross receipts within the elected grouping.

(1) *Processing of customer orders*—(i) *Processing of customer orders defined*. The processing of customer orders means notification by the FSC to the related supplier of the order and of the requirements for delivery. The related supplier may have independent knowledge of the order and requirements for delivery. If the FSC does not have a related supplier, the processing of customer orders means communication with the customer by any method such as telephone, telegram, or mail to acknowledge receipt of the order and requirements for delivery. Once the related supplier has been notified by the FSC, or the customer has received an acknowledgement from the FSC, of the order and requirements for delivery, subsequent or prior communications with respect to an order (such as changes in quantity or prospective delivery date) are not included in the definition of processing of customer orders.

(ii) *Direct costs of processing customer orders*. Direct costs of processing of customer orders include salaries of clerical personnel and costs of telephone, telegram, mail, or other communication media (including the costs of operating transmission equipment).

(iii) *Location of processing of customer orders*. The location of this activity is the place where the communication is initiated by the FSC.

(iv) *Examples*. The principles of paragraph (b)(1) of this section may be illustrated by the following examples:

Example (1). A domestic related supplier, using a FSC as its commission agent on the sale of export property to foreign customers, receives an order from one of its foreign customers. Information concerning the receipt of such order and its requirements for delivery are transmitted to the FSC. The FSC from its office outside the United States notifies the related supplier of the order and the requirements for delivery by telex. This notification by the FSC to the related supplier constitutes the processing of the customer's order within the meaning of paragraph (b)(1)(i) of this section. In addition, its direct costs of processing the customer's order are foreign direct costs because the communication is initiated by the FSC from outside the United States.

Example (2). A domestic unrelated supplier manufactures a product which it sells to a buy-sell FSC located in Germany for resale to the FSC's German customers. Upon receiving an order from one of its customers, the FSC telephones the customer from its German office to acknowledge receipt of the order and the requirements for delivery. The acknowledgement constitutes the processing of the customer's order within the meaning of paragraph (b)(1)(i) of this section and the direct costs attributable thereto are foreign direct costs.

(2) *Arranging for delivery*—(i) *Arranging for delivery defined*. The arranging for delivery of export property means the taking of necessary steps to have the export property delivered to the customer in accordance with the requirements of the order. Arranging for delivery does not include preparation of shipping documents (*e.g.*, bill of lading) or the property for shipment (*i.e.*, packaging or crating), or shipment of property (*i.e.*, transportation). Arranging for delivery does include communications with a carrier or freight forwarder to provide transportation (as defined in § 1.924(e)-1(c)(1), but without regard to when the commission relationship for purposes of transpor-

Reg. § 1.924(e)-1(b)(2)

tation begins) for the export property from the FSC or related supplier to the place where the customer takes possession of the property. Arranging for delivery also includes communications with the customer to notify the customer of the time and place of delivery. The carrier or freight forwarder and the customer may already have knowledge of the information communicated. If the FSC has communicated with the carrier or freight forwarder, where applicable, and the customer to notify it of the time and place of delivery, prior or subsequent communications to either about delivery are not included in the definition of arranging for delivery.

(ii) *Direct costs of arranging for delivery.* The direct costs of arranging for delivery include salaries of clerical personnel and costs of telephone, telegraph, mail, and other communications media, but do not include any actual shipping costs.

(iii) *Location of arranging for delivery.* The location of arranging for delivery activity is the place where the activity is initiated by the FSC.

(iv) *Examples.* The principles of paragraph (b)(2)(i) of this section may be illustrated by the following examples:

Example (1). A FSC earns commissions on the sale of export property by its domestic related supplier to foreign customers. The shipment term of all of the related supplier's sales is F.O.B. (Free on Board) its manufacturing plant in Gary, Indiana. Thus, there is no transportation as defined in § 1.924(e)-1(c)(1) with respect to its sales. From its shipping department at the plant, the related supplier telephones carriers to arrange for delivery. It also notifies the FSC by mail of the time and place of delivery of the customer's orders. The FSC from its office outside the United States transmits the received information to the customers. Because there is no transportation to be arranged, this communication alone by the FSC to the customers to notify them of the time and place of delivery constitutes arranging for delivery within the meaning of paragraph (b)(2)(i) of this section.

Example (2). Assume the same facts as in *Example (1),* except that the shipment term of all of the related supplier's sales is C.I.F. (Cost, Insurance, Freight) and that the commission relationship for transportation begins after the export property leaves the United States customs territory. The related supplier telephones a trucking firm and an overseas carrier from its plant in Gary, Indiana to ascertain information on transporting its property by truck to the docks, and by overseas carrier from the docks to the place where the customer takes possession. Upon receiving the necessary information, the related supplier electronically transmits to the FSC the shipping information and the time and place of delivery to the customer. In addition, it instructs the FSC to communicate the necessary shipping information to the carriers to ensure shipment and to notify the customer of the time and place of delivery. The FSC does both from its office located outside of the United States. The communications by the FSC to the carriers and the customer constitute arranging for delivery within the meaning of paragraph (b)(2)(i) of this section.

(c) *Transportation*—(1) *Transportation defined.* For purposes of section 924(e), transportation means moving or shipping the export property during the period when the FSC owns or is responsible for the property, or, if the FSC is acting as a commission agent, during the period when the related supplier owns or is responsible for the property but after the commission relationship for purposes of transportation begins (even if the relationship begins after the property leaves the U.S. customs territory). The FSC or related supplier is treated as responsible for the property when it either has title, bears the risk of loss, or insures the property during shipment. Since a commission FSC will not generally have title or bear the risk of loss, it will, nevertheless, satisfy the transportation test if the related supplier has either title, bears the risk of loss, or insures the property during shipment. Examples of methods of shipping which would qualify as transportation include F.O.B. (Free on Board) destination, C.I.F. (Cost, Insurance, Freight), Ex Ship, and Ex Quay, but do not include C. & F. (Cost and Freight) or F.O.B. shipping point.

(2) *Direct costs of transportation.* The direct costs of transportation include the expenses of shipping, such as fees paid to carriers and freight forwarders, costs of freight insurance, and documentation fees. With respect to fungible commodities, direct costs include only those costs incurred after the goods have been identified to a contract. Transportation costs do not include any of the costs of arranging for delivery. The FSC is considered to engage in transportation activity whenever it pays the costs of shipping the export property and the property is shipped during the period when the FSC owns or is responsible for the property as provided in paragraph (c)(1) of this section. If the customer pays the shipping costs directly, the FSC is not considered to engage in transportation activity. If, however, the FSC pays the shipping costs, the ultimate transfer of those costs to the customer will not disqualify the FSC from engaging in transportation for purposes of section 924(e) regardless of whether the costs are

Income From Sources Without the United States 49,059
See p. 20,601 for regulations not amended to reflect law changes

included in the sale price of the export property or separately stated.

(3) *Location of transportation.* The location of transportation activity is the area over which the property is transported. Thus, the portion of total direct costs of transportation treated as foreign direct costs is the portion attributable to transportation outside the United States, determined on the basis of the ratio of mileage outside the U.S. customs territory to total mileage. For purposes of determining mileage outside U.S. customs territory, goods are treated as leaving U.S. customs territory when they have been tendered to an international carrier for shipment to a foreign location, as long as they are not removed from the custody of the carrier before they reach a point outside U.S. customs territory. The same rule for determining mileage outside the U.S. customs territory will apply to freight forwarders if (i) the forwarder has the risk of loss or is an insurer of the goods, and (ii) the property is shipped on a single bill of lading issued to the FSC or its agent as the shipper.

(4) *Examples.* The principles of paragraph (c) of this section may be illustrated by the following examples:

Example (1). A buy-sell FSC sells export property to a customer located in Canada. The contract between the FSC and the customer requires that the property be shipped F.O.B. its Canadian destination. Under this shipment term, the FSC holds title and bears the risk of loss until the property is tendered at its Canadian destination. Thus, it is responsible for the property during shipment. The FSC instructs its related supplier to ship the property from its manufacturing facilities in St. Louis. The related supplier negotiates two contracts, one for domestic transportation and the second for foreign transportation. A domestic trucking firm transports the property to the Canadian border where a Canadian trucking company is used to transport the property to its Canadian destination. The documentation fees and the fees for the two trucking firms are paid by the FSC. Because the FSC paid the costs of shipping and the property was shipped during the period when the FSC was responsible for the property, the FSC has engaged in transportation activity, the direct costs of which are the fees paid by the FSC. If 70 percent of the mileage from St. Louis to the Canadian destination is associated with the transportation from the Canadian border to the Canadian destination, 70 percent of the FSC's direct transportation costs are foreign direct costs. If, instead of using two trucking firms, the FSC had tendered the goods to a freight forwarder for shipment to a foreign location and the freight forwarder assumed the risk of loss for the goods and issued a single bill of lading, all of the fees paid by the FSC to the freight forwarder would be foreign direct costs.

Example (2). A related supplier sells export property to its foreign customer in Liverpool, England. The contract between the related supplier and the customer requires that the property be shipped C.I.F. Liverpool. The related supplier engages the FSC as its commission agent with respect to its sales to the customer, requiring the FSC to provide transportation to the customer. The FSC contracts with the related supplier to provide the transportation on behalf of the FSC. The commission agreement between the related supplier and the FSC provides that the FSC's responsibilities with respect to transportation of the export property begins after the property leaves the U.S. customs territory. The related supplier hires a domestic trucking firm to transport the shipment to a New York City port where it is loaded on a cargo ship destined for Liverpool at a total cost of $3,000X, $2,750X of which is allocable to mileage from the U.S. customs territory to Liverpool, England. Because the related supplier insures the property during shipment under C.I.F., the property is shipped during the period when the related supplier is treated as responsible for the property. Thus, the FSC, as the related supplier's commission agent, has satisfied the transportation test. In addition, because the FSC's responsibilities with respect to transportation begins when the property leaves U.S. customs territory, the FSC's payment of $2750X is a foreign direct cost of transportation. The remaining $250X is not a direct cost of transportation to the FSC because the amount was expended before the commission relationship between the FSC and related supplier began.

Example (3). A FSC earns commissions on sales by the related supplier of export property, all of which falls within a single two-digit SIC group. The related supplier is under contract to the FSC to perform on the FSC's behalf all of the section 924(e) activities attributable to the sales. Of all of the sales made during the year, the FSC has no transportation costs with respect to the sales to customer R because the shipment term is F.O.B. the related supplier's Chicago plant. With respect to the sales to customer S, the FSC ships the property F.O.B. its destination and pays 100 percent of the transportation costs, all of which are foreign direct costs because the commission relationship for transportation begins outside the U.S. customs territory. For purposes of determining whether the FSC has satisfied the 85-percent foreign direct cost test for transportation, the FSC

Reg. § 1.924(e)-1(c)(4)

49,060   Income From Sources Without the United States
See p. 20,601 for regulations not amended to reflect law changes

groups the sales by product. Because the transportation costs for sales to customer S are 100-percent foreign direct costs and because there are no transportation costs on sales to customer R, the FSC is considered to have met the 85-percent foreign direct cost test for transportation for all the sales in the single two-digit SIC group.

(d) *Determination and transmittal of a final invoice or statement of account and receipt of payment.* For purposes of section 924(e), the determination and transmittal of a final invoice or statement of account and the receipt of payment are defined as follows.

(1) *Determination and transmittal of a final invoice or statement of account*—(i) *Definitions*—(A) *In general.* The determination and transmittal of a final invoice or statement of account means the assembly of either a final invoice or statement of account and the forwarding of that document to the customer. A FSC may elect to send either final invoices or statements of account and disregard any costs of the alternative not elected. For taxable years beginning after February 19, 1987, a special grouping rule is provided. If the FSC assembles and forwards either a statement of account or a final invoice from outside the United States to customers with sales representing 50 percent of the current year foreign trading gross receipts within a product or product line grouping or to customers with sales representing 50 percent of the prior year foreign trading gross receipts within a product or product line grouping utilized for the current year, all other U.S. costs will be disregarded and the FSC will be deemed to have no U.S. costs with respect to the determination and transmittal of a final invoice or statement of account. If, during the prior taxable year, the controlled group of which the FSC is a member had a DISC or interest charge DISC, the FSC may apply the 50 percent rule by taking into account the customers and sales of the DISC or interest charge DISC for the preceding taxable year. If no foreign trading gross receipts (or qualified export receipts for DISC purposes) were received in the prior year either by the FSC or by a DISC or interest charge DISC within the controlled group of which the FSC is a member, the FSC must apply the 50 percent rule taking into account customers and foreign trading gross receipts for the current year. In the event that the 50 percent rule is not satisfied, all costs associated with assembly and forwarding of the selected documents (invoices or statements of account) must be included in the costs attributable to activities described in section 924(e)(4).

(B) *Final invoice defined.* A final invoice is an invoice upon which payment is made by the customer. A final invoice must contain the customer's name or identifying number and, with respect to the transaction or transactions, the date, product or service, quantity, price, and amount due. In the alternative, a document will be acceptable as a final invoice even though it does not include all of the above listed information if the FSC establishes that the document is considered to be a final invoice under normal commercial practices. An invoice forwarded to the customer after payment has been tendered or received pursuant to a letter of credit as a receipt for payment satisfies this definition.

(C) *Statement of account defined.* A statement of account is any summary statement forwarded to a customer to inform of, or confirm, the status of transactions occurring within an accounting period during a taxable year that is not less than one month. A statement of account must contain, at a minimum, the customer's name or identifying number, date of the statement of account as of the last day of the accounting period covered by the statement of account and the balance due (even if the balance due is zero). A single final invoice or statement of account can cover more than one transaction with one customer. In the alternative, a document will be accepted as a statement of account even though it does not include all of the above listed information if the FSC establishes that the document is considered a statement of account under normal commercial practice. For these purposes, a document will be considered to be a statement of account under normal commercial practices if it is sent to domestic as well as to export customers in order to inform the customers of the status of transactions during an accounting period. Additional information may be sent separately, such as summary statements forwarded to a related party for purposes of reconciling intercompany accounts for financial reporting requirements. If the information is sent separately, the direct costs associated with the assembly and forwarding of that information are not considered for purposes of section 924(d).

(D) *Assembly and forwarding defined.* Assembly means folding the documents (where applicable), filling envelopes, and addressing envelopes (if window envelopes are not used). Forwarding means mailing or delivery.

(ii) *Direct costs of determination and transmittal of final invoice or statement of account.* Direct costs of this activity include costs of office supplies, office equipment, clerical salaries and costs of mailing or other delivery services, if the costs can be identified or associated directly with the assembly and transmittal of a final in-

Reg. § 1.924(e)-1(d)(1)

voice or statement of account. Costs of establishing a price, or of communicating prices or other billing information between the FSC and a related supplier are not direct costs of this activity. In addition, the costs of preparing and mailing the final invoices or statements of account to the FSC and the costs of accumulating and formatting data for invoicing or statements of account on computer discs, tapes, or some other storage media along with the costs of transmitting or transporting this data to the FSC are not direct costs of this activity.

(iii) *Location of determination and transmittal of a final invoice or statement of account.* For taxable years beginning before February 19, 1987, the location of this activity is the place where the final invoice or statement of account is assembled for forwarding to the customer or the place from which it is forwarded to the customer. Thus, the forwarding of the final invoice or statement of account from outside the United States is sufficient to source this activity outside the United States. For all other taxable years, the location of this activity is the place where the final invoice or statement of account is both assembled and forwarded to the customer.

(iv) *Examples.* The principles of paragraph (d)(1) of this section may be illustrated by the following examples, all of which apply to taxable years beginning on or after February 19, 1987.

Example (1). A related supplier sells export property to its foreign customers. The related supplier engages the FSC as its commission agent with respect to the sales, requiring the FSC to determine and transmit final invoices or statements of account to the customers with respect to the sales. Annually, the FSC assembles and forwards statements of account to customers representing 40 percent of current year export sales and 35 percent of prior year sales. The statements are sent from its office outside of the United States. The remaining statements of account are sent from the Albany, New York office of the related supplier. The statements are recognized in its industry as a statement of account. Although the statement does not contain all of the information described in § 1.924(e)-1(d)(1)(i), it is sent to both domestic and foreign customers of the related supplier to inform the customer of the status of its transactions with the related supplier. The document qualifies as a statement of account under § 1.924(e)-1(d)(1)(i); however, the 50 percent test set forth in § 1.924(e)-1(d)(1)(i)(A) is not satisfied. Therefore, the FSC must take into account all domestic direct costs attributable to assembly and forwarding of statements of account from its domestic office in determining whether the FSC has satisfied the direct cost test with respect to section 924 (e)(4) and paragraph § 924(e)-1(d).

Example (2). Employees of a FSC, in the FSC's foreign office, fold and place in envelopes the sheet or sheets that constitute the final invoices provided by the related supplier. In addition, the employees address, affix postage to, and mail the envelopes. These activities constitute the determination and transmittal of the final invoices within the meaning of paragraph (d)(1)(i) of this section and, because the final invoices are assembled and forwarded to the customers from outside the United States, all the direct costs of the activities are foreign direct costs.

Example (3). The related supplier sends to the FSC's foreign office a computer tape to be used to prepare a statement of account. A management company, working under contract with the FSC, transcribes the data to a piece of paper which is a statement of account for purposes of § 1.924(d)(1)(i), folds the document, and fills, affixes postage to, and mails the envelopes. Only the costs performed by the management company under contract with the FSC that constitute the assembly and forwarding of a statement of account under § 1.924(e)-1(d)(1)(i)(D) are direct costs. Therefore, the costs attributable to transcribing the data to a piece of paper are not direct costs for purposes of section 924(e)(4).

(2) *Receipt of payment*—(i) *Receipt of payment defined.* Receipt of payment means the crediting of the FSC's bank account by an amount which is not less than 1.83 percent of the gross receipts ("gross receipts amount") associated with the transaction. The FSC's bank account is not credited unless the FSC has the authority to withdraw the amount deposited. Where sales proceeds are factored or where payments from related foreign subsidiaries are netted against amounts owed to these foreign subsidiaries in an intercompany account, crediting of the FSC's bank account with no less than the gross receipts amount of the factoring proceeds or the proceeds, net of offsets, respectively, qualifies as receipt of payment. In addition, where a FSC is precluded from receiving a portion of the proceeds of the export transaction, the FSC may satisfy receipt of payment by receiving no less than the gross receipts amount of the remaining portion of the proceeds in its bank account. In the case of advance or progress payments, each payment constitutes a payment for receipt of payment purposes.

(ii) *Direct costs of receipt of payment.* Direct costs of receiving payment include the expenses of maintaining a bank account of the FSC in which payment is deposited, any fees or

Reg. § 1.924(e)-1(d)(2)

service charges incurred for converting the payment into U.S. currency, and any transfer fees incurred with respect to the transfer of funds into and out of the FSC's bank account in accordance with the 35 calendar day rule in paragraph (d)(2)(iii) of this section. The transfer fees and the fees or service charges incurred for currency conversion are considered to be foreign direct costs of receiving payment; however, exchange losses are not costs of receiving payment.

(iii) *Location of receipt of payment.* The location of this activity is the office of the banking institution at which the account is maintained. If payment is made by the purchaser directly to the FSC or the related supplier in the United States, and the FSC or related supplier transfers the gross receipts amount associated with the transaction to a bank account of the FSC outside the United States after receipt of payment (*i.e.,* cash, check, wire transfer, etc.), but no later than 35 calendar days after receipt of good funds (*i.e.,* the clearance of the check) the FSC is considered to have received payment outside the United States. Therefore, all transfer fees and the costs of the foreign bank account are treated as foreign direct costs. The United States bank costs are disregarded. If, however, the related supplier does not transfer the gross receipts amount within 35 calendar days, United States bank costs are not disregarded and are domestic direct costs. In either case, the transfer costs, currency conversion charges, and foreign bank costs remain foreign direct costs. The preceding rules apply both to commission FSC's and buy-sell FSCs.

(iv) *Examples.* The principles of paragraph (d)(2) of this section may be illustrated by the following examples:

Example (1). A FSC earns commissions on sales of export property by its related supplier. The related supplier manufactures and sells its export property to its foreign subsidiaries for resale in their respective countries. From time to time, the foreign subsidiaries will return products to the related supplier for credit and, from time to time, the foreign subsidiaries purchase products in their respective countries and sell such products to the related supplier. These transactions result in various amounts being owed to the foreign subsidiaries. Each month the various inter-company obligations are reviewed. The result of such review of inter-company indebtedness is a netting out of the various intercompany liabilities on the books, to the extent possible, and a flow of funds for the net obligation. Due to the nature of these transactions, the amounts owed by the foreign subsidiaries exceed the amounts which the related supplier owes to the foreign subsidiaries. The gross receipts amount (*i.e.,* 1.83 percent of this net amount) is credited to the FSC's bank account. This constitutes receipt of payment for purposes of paragraph (d)(2)(i) of this section.

Example (2). In a leveraged lease transaction, a FSC-lessor obtains purchase financing from a lending institution. The lending institution retains a security interest in the proceeds and requires that a portion of each rental payment be paid by the lessee directly to the lending institution. Since the FSC is precluded from receiving a portion of the proceeds of the export transaction, the FSC may satisfy the receipt of payment requirement by receiving the gross receipts amount with respect to the remaining proceeds.

Example (3). A buy-sell FSC sells its export property to a foreign customer and is paid by means of a "draw-down" letter of credit. Over a substantial period of time prior to delivery of the export property, amounts are advanced to the FSC under the letter of credit. At delivery, the remaining amount available is paid. Each payment made to the FSC constitutes a payment for receipt of payment purposes and thus the gross receipts amount related to each payment must be credited to the FSC's bank account.

Example (4). A FSC earns commissions on sales of export property by its related supplier. The related supplier regularly collects payments from its foreign customers in a San Francisco bank account and, after the San Francisco bank has collected on the checks, transfers, within 35 calendar days, the gross receipts amounts from its New York bank account to the FSC's bank account located outside the United States. The FSC incurred transfer fees of $160X in addition to a fee of $35X for the maintenance of the FSC's bank account outside the United States during the 35 calendar day period. The maintenance fee relating to the United States bank account for the 35 calendar day period is $45X. The receipt of payment test is met because the gross receipts amounts are transferred after payment but within 35 calendar days to the FSC's bank account located outside the United States. The transfer fees of $160X and the maintenance fee of $35X relating to the FSC's foreign bank account are foreign direct costs. The $45X maintenance fee related to the United States bank account is not a direct cost. If the gross receipts amounts had not been transferred to the FSC's foreign bank account within 35 calendar days, the $45X maintenance fee related to the United States bank account would be considered a United States direct cost. The transfer fee of $160X and the maintenance fee of $35X relating to the FSC's foreign bank account, however, would, nonetheless, be considered as foreign direct costs. The same funds received in San Francisco need not be transferred to the FSC's foreign bank account because money is fungible. For the same reason, the gross receipts amounts need not be transferred from the same bank account in which the payments are received.

(e) *Assumption of credit risk*—(1) *Assumption of credit risk defined.* For purposes of section 924(e), the assumption of credit risk means bearing the economic risk of nonpayment with respect to a transaction. If the FSC is acting as a commission agent for the related supplier, this risk is borne by the FSC if the commission contract transfers the costs of the economic risk of nonpayment with respect to the transaction from the related supplier to the FSC. The FSC may elect on its annual return to bear the economic risk of nonpayment with respect to its transactions during a taxable year by either—

(i) assuming the risk of a bad debt in accordance with the rules of paragraph (e)(4)(i) of this section,

(ii) obtaining insurance to cover nonpayment,

(iii) investigating credit of a customer or a potential customer,

(iv) factoring trade receivables, or

(v) selling by means of letters of credit or banker's acceptances.

Only the alternative elected to be performed by the FSC during a taxable year is relevant for purposes of section 924(d). For example, if a buy-sell FSC elects to bear the economic risk of nonpayment with respect to its transaction during a taxable year by assuming the risk of a bad debt in accordance with the rules of paragraph (e)(4)(i) of this section, and also factors the transaction's trade receivables, only the direct costs of assuming the risk of a bad debt are relevant for purposes of section 924(d). For purposes of this paragraph, a potential customer is an unrelated person who is engaged in the purchase or sale of export property on whom an investigation is performed, but with whom no export sales contract is executed.

(2) *Direct costs of assumption of credit risk.* (i) With respect to assuming the risk of a bad debt, the direct costs of the assumption of credit risk in the case of a buy-sell FSC include debts that become uncollectible and charges taken into account in determining additions to bad debt reserves of the FSC. In the case of a commission FSC, the direct costs of the assumption of credit risk include the assumption of the debts and charges of the related supplier attributable to export sales that are allowed as deductions under section 166.

(ii) With respect to insurance, the direct costs of the assumption of credit risk are the costs of obtaining insurance against the risk of nonpayment. Qualifying insurance must be obtained from an unrelated insurer and must cover the risk of nonpayment due to default and bankruptcy by the purchaser. Insurance obtained from a related insurer, or insurance that covers default and bankruptcy due to risks of war or political unrest without covering ordinary default or bankruptcy is not sufficient.

(iii) With respect to investigating credit, the direct costs of assumption of credit risk are the external costs of investigating credit for customers or potential customers, including costs of membership in a credit agency or association for that purpose (but not the costs of approving credit by an internal credit agency).

(iv) With respect to factoring trade receivables, the direct costs of assumption of credit risk are the costs of factoring trade receivables of related and unrelated customers (*e.g.,* the amount of the discount and the fees relating to factoring).

(v) With respect to letters of credit or banker's acceptances, the direct costs of assumption of credit risk are the costs of letters of credit or banker's acceptances and the documentary collection costs.

(3) *Location of assumption of credit risk.* The location of the activity of assumption of credit risk is the location of the customer or obligor whose payment is at risk, except that the location of investigating credit is the location of the credit agency or association performing the investigation. A foreign branch of a United States corporation and a foreign office of the United States government are not foreign obligors for purposes of this test. A foreign branch of a United States credit investigation agency or association, however, is treated as located outside the United States.

(4) *Special rules*—(i) *Assuming the risk of a bad debt.* (A) *In general.* If a FSC chooses to bear the economic risk of nonpayment by assuming the risk of a bad debt with respect to a transaction or grouping of transactions and an actual bad debt loss on a foreign trading gross receipt is not incurred in any three consecutive years, the FSC will be deemed to have performed this activity during the first two years of the three year period. For the third year, the FSC will not be deemed to have performed this activity and must satisfy the 85 percent foreign direct costs test by satisfying any two paragraphs included within section 924(e) other than assumption of credit risk activ-

Reg. § 1.924(e)-1(e)(4)

ity under section 924(e)(5). An actual bad debt loss will only satisfy the activity test with respect to a single three consecutive year period.

(B) *Example.* The principles of this paragraph may be illustrated by the following example:

Example. In year 1, a related supplier of a commission FSC incurs a bad debt with respect to foreign trading gross receipts owed by a foreign obligor. This expense is the only bad debt incurred with respect to foreign trading gross receipts in year 1. Therefore, the direct costs for the bearing of the economic risk of nonpayment for year 1 are all foreign direct costs and the 85-percent test is satisfied. In year 2, the FSC incurs a bad debt with respect to a U.S. broker/consolidator. The direct costs for year 2 are U.S. direct costs and, therefore, the 85-percent test is not satisfied. No bad debt is incurred in year 3. Because a bad debt with respect to a foreign obligor is incurred in year 1, the FSC is deemed to have satisfied the economic risk of nonpayment for each of years 1, 2 and 3.

(ii) *Grouping with respect to other risk activities.* For taxable years beginning after February 19, 1987, if a FSC elects to bear the economic risk of nonpayment by performing one of the activities described in paragraph (e) of this section and elects to group transactions, it is considered to have performed the elected activity with respect to all transactions within the group during the taxable year if it performs the activity in accordance with the following rules. If a FSC elects to factor trade receivables, at least 20 percent of the face amount of a group's receivables must be factored. If a FSC elects to sell by means of letters of credit or banker's acceptances, a fee must be incurred with respect to 20 percent of the foreign trading gross receipts attributable to sales within the group. If the FSC elects to obtain insurance to cover nonpayment, 20 percent of the face amount of receivables attributable to sales included in the § 1.924(d)-1(e) grouping elected by the FSC must be insured. If a FSC elects to investigate credit of customers or potential customers, 20 percent of new or potential customers for which a credit investigation is performed must be investigated. [Reg. § 1.924(e)-1.]

☐ [T.D. 8125, 2-13-87.]

[Reg. § 1.925(a)-1]

§ 1.925(a)-1. Transfer pricing rules for FSCs.—(a) through (c)(7) [Reserved] For further guidance, see § 1.925(a)-1T(a) through (c)(7).

(c)(8) *Grouping transactions*—(i) The determinations under this section are to be made on a transaction-by-transaction basis. However, at the annual choice made by the related supplier if the administrative pricing methods are used, some or all of these determinations may be made on the basis of groups consisting of products or product lines. The election to group transactions shall be evidenced on Schedule P of the FSC's U.S. income tax return for the taxable year. No untimely or amended returns filed later than one year after the due date of the FSC's timely filed (including extensions) U.S. income tax return will be allowed to elect to group, to change a grouping basis, or to change from a grouping basis to a transaction-by-transaction basis (collectively "grouping redeterminations"). The rule of the previous sentence is applicable to taxable years beginning after December 31, 1999. For any taxable year beginning before January 1, 2000, a grouping redetermination may be made no later than the due date of the FSC's timely filed (including extensions) U.S. income tax return for the FSC's first taxable year beginning on or after January 1, 2000. Notwithstanding the time limits for filing grouping redeterminations otherwise specified in the previous three sentences, a grouping redetermination may be made at any time during the one-year period commencing upon notification of the related supplier by the Internal Revenue Service of an examination, provided that both the FSC and the related supplier agree to extend their respective statutes of limitations for assessment by one year. In addition, any grouping redeterminations made under this paragraph must meet the requirements under § 1.925(a)-1T(e)(4) with respect to redeterminations other than grouping. The language "or grouping of transactions" is removed from the fourth sentence of § 1.925(a)-1T(e)(4), applicable to taxable years beginning after December 31, 1997. See also § 1.925(b)-1T(b)(3)(i).

(c)(8)(ii) through (f) [Reserved] For further guidance, see § 1.925(a)-1T(c)(8)(ii) through (f).

(g) *Effective date.* The provisions of this section apply on or after March 2, 2001. [Reg. § 1.925(a)-1.]

☐ [T.D. 8944, 3-2-2001.]

[Reg. § 1.925(a)-1T]

§ 1.925(a)-1T. **Temporary Regulations; Transfer pricing rules for FSCs.**—(a) *Scope*— (1) *Transfer pricing rules.* In the case of a transaction described in paragraph (b) of this section, section 925 permits a related party to a FSC to determine the allowable transfer price charged the FSC (or commission paid to the FSC) by its choice of the three transfer pricing methods described in paragraph (c)(2), (3), and (4) of this section: The "1.83 percent" gross receipts method and the "23 percent" combined taxable income method (the administrative pricing rules) of section 925(a)(1) and (2), respectively, and the section 482 method of section 925(a)(3). (Any further reference to a FSC in this section shall include a small FSC unless indicated otherwise.) Subject to the special no-loss rule of § 1.925(a)-1T (e)(1)(iii), any, or all, of the transfer pricing methods may be used in the same taxable year of the FSC for separate transactions (or separate groups of transactions). If either of the administrative pricing methods (the gross receipts method or combined taxable income method) is applied to a transaction, the Commissioner may not make distributions, apportionments, or allocations as provided by section 42 and the regulations under that section. The transfer price charged the FSC (or the commission paid to the FSC) on a transaction with a person that is not a related party to the FSC may be determined in any manner agreed to by the FSC and that person. However, the Commissioner will use special scrutiny to determine whether a person selling export property to a FSC (or paying a commission to a FSC) is a related party to the FSC with respect to a transaction if the FSC earns a profit on the transaction in excess of the profit it would have earned had the administrative pricing rules applied to the transaction.

(2) *Special rules.* For rules as to certain "incomplete transactions" and for computing full costing combined taxable income, see paragraph (c)(5) and (6) of this section. For a special rule as to cooperatives and computation of their combined taxable incomes, see paragraph (c)(7) of this section. Grouping of transactions for purposes of applying the administrative pricing method chosen is provided for by paragraph (c)(8) of this section. The rules in paragraph (c) of this section are directly applicable only in the case of sales or exchanges of export property to a FSC for resale, and are applicable by analogy to leases, commissions, and services as provided in paragraph (d) of this section. For a rule providing for the recovery of the FSC's costs in an overall loss situation, see paragraph (e)(1)(i) of this section. Paragraph (e)(2) of this section provides for the applicability of section 482 to resales by the FSC to related persons or to sales between related persons prior to the sale to the FSC. Paragraph (e)(3) of this section provides for the creation of receivables if the transfer price, rental payment, commission or payment for services rendered is not paid by the due date of the FSC's income tax return for the taxable year under section 6072(b), including extensions provided for by section 6081. Provisions for the subsequent determination and further adjustment to the relevant amounts are set forth in paragraph (e)(4) and (5) of this section. Paragraph (f) of this section has several examples illustrating the provisions of this section. Section 1.925(b)-1T prescribes the marginal costing rules authorized by section 925(b)(2). Section 1.927(d)-2T provides definitions of related supplier and related party.

(3) *Performance of substantial economic functions*—(i) *Administrative pricing methods.* The application of the administrative pricing methods of section 925(a)(1) and (2) does not depend on the extent to which the FSC performs substantial economic functions beyond those required by section 925(c). See paragraph (b)(2)(ii) of this section and § 1.924(a)-1T (i)(1).

(ii) *Section 482 method.* In order to apply the section 482 method of section 925(a)(3), the arm's length standards of section 482 and the regulations under that section must be satisfied. In applying the standards of section 482, all of the rules of section 482 will apply. Thus, if the FSC would not be recognized as a separate entity, it would also not be recognized on application of the section 482 method. Similarly, if a FSC performs no substantial economic function with respect to a transaction, no income will be allocable to the FSC under the section 482 method. See § 1.924(a)-1T(i)(2). If a related supplier performs services under contract with a FSC, the FSC will not be deemed to have performed substantial economic functions for purposes of the section 482 method unless it compensates the related supplier under the provisions of § 1.482-2(b)(1) through (7). See § 1.925(a)-1T(c)(6)(ii) for the applicability of the regulations under section 482 in determination of the FSC's profit under the administrative pricing methods.

(b) *Transactions to which section 925 applies*—(1) *In general.* The transfer pricing methods of section 925 (the administrative pricing methods and the section 482 method) will apply, generally, only if a transaction, or group of transactions, gives rise to foreign trading gross receipts (within the meaning of section 924(a) and § 1.924(a)-1T) to the FSC (or small FSC, as defined in section 922(b) and § 1.921-2(b) (Q&A3)). However, the transfer pricing methods will apply as well if the FSC is acting as commission agent for a related supplier with regard to a transaction, or group of transactions, on which the related supplier is the principal if the transaction, or group of transactions, would have resulted in foreign trading gross receipts had the FSC been the principal.

(2) *Application of the transfer pricing rules*—(i) *Section 482 method.* The section 482 transfer pricing method may be applied to any transaction between a related supplier and a FSC if the requirements of paragraph (a)(3)(ii) of this section have been met.

Reg. § 1.925(a)-1T(b)(2)

(ii) *Administrative pricing methods.* The administrative pricing methods may be applied in situations in which the FSC is either the principal or commission agent on the transaction, or group of transactions, only if the requirements of section 925(c) are met. Section 925(c) requires that the FSC performs all the activities described in subsections (d)(1)(A) and (e) of section 924 that are attributable to a particular transaction, or group of transactions. The FSC need not perform any activities with respect to a particular transaction merely to comply with section 925(c) if that activity would not have been performed but for the requirements of that subsection. The FSC need not perform all of the activities outside the United States. None of the activities need be performed outside the United States by a small FSC. Rather than the FSC itself performing the activities required by section 925(c), another person under contract, written or oral, directly or indirectly, with the FSC may perform the activities (see § 1.924(d)-1(b)). If a related supplier is performing the required activities on behalf of the FSC with regard to a transaction, or group of transactions, the requirements of section 925(c) will be met if the FSC pays the related supplier an amount equal to the direct and indirect expenses related to the required activities. See paragraph (c)(6)(ii) of this section for the amount of compensation due the related supplier. The payment made to the related supplier must be reflected on the FSC's books and must be taken into account in computing the FSC's and related supplier's combined taxable income. If it is determined that the related supplier was not compensated for all the expenses related to the required activities or if the entire payment is not reflected on the FSC's books or in computing combined taxable income, the administrative pricing methods may be used but proper adjustments will be made to the FSC's and related supplier's books or income. At the election of the FSC and related supplier, the requirements of section 925(c) will be deemed to have been met if the related supplier is paid by the FSC an amount equal to all of the costs under paragraph (c)(6)(iii)(D) of this section (limited by paragraph (c)(6)(ii) of this section) related to the export sale, other than expenses relating to activities performed directly by the FSC or by a person other than the related supplier, and if that payment is reflected on the FSC's books and in computing the FSC's and related supplier's combined taxable income on the transaction, or group of transactions. If it is determined that the related supplier was not compensated for all its expenses or if the entire payment is not reflected on the FSC's books or in computing combined taxable income, the administrative pricing methods may be used but proper adjustments will be made to the FSC's and related supplier's books or income. All activities that are performed in connection with foreign military sales are considered to be performed by the FSC, or under contract with the FSC, if they are performed by the United States government even though the United States government has not contracted for the performance of those activities. All actual costs incurred by the FSC and related supplier in connection with the performance of those activities must be taken into account, however, in determining the combined taxable income of the FSC and related supplier.

(iii) *Allowable transactions for purposes of the administrative pricing methods.* If the required performance of activities has been met, the administrative pricing methods may be applied to a transaction between a related supplier and a FSC only in the following circumstances:

(A) The related supplier sells export property (as defined in section 927(a) and § 1.927(a)-1T) to the FSC for resale or the FSC acts as a commission agent for the related supplier on sales by the related supplier of export property to third parties, whether or not related parties. For purposes of this section, references to sales include references to exchanges or other dispositions.

(B) The related supplier leases export property to the FSC for sublease for a comparable period with comparable terms of payment, or the FSC acts as commission agent for the related supplier on leases of export property by the related supplier, to third parties whether or not related parties.

(C) Services are furnished by a FSC as principal or by a related supplier if a FSC is a commission agent for the related supplier which are related and subsidiary to any sale or lease by the FSC, acting as principal or commission agent, of export property under subdivision (iii)(A) or (B) of this paragraph.

(D) Engineering or architectural services for construction projects located (or proposed for location) outside of the United States are furnished by the FSC if the FSC is acting as principal, or by the related supplier if the FSC is a commission agent for the related supplier, with respect to the furnishing of the services to a third party whether or not a related party.

(E) The FSC acting as principal, or the related supplier where the FSC is a commission agent, furnishes managerial services in furtherance of the production of foreign trading gross receipts of an unrelated FSC or the production of qualified export receipts of an unrelated interest charge DISC. This subdivision (iii)(E) shall not

Reg. § 1.925(a)-1T(b)(2)

Income from Sources Without the United States

apply for any taxable year unless at least 50 percent of the gross receipts for such taxable year of the FSC or of the related supplier, whichever party furnishes the managerial services, is derived from activities described in subdivision (iii)(A), (B) or (C) of this paragraph.

(c) *Transfer price for sales of export property*—(1) *In general.* Under this paragraph, rules are prescribed for computing the allowable price for a transfer from a related supplier to a FSC in the case of a sale, described in paragraph (b)(2)(iii)(A) of this section, of export property.

(2) *The "1.83 percent" gross receipts method*—Under the gross receipts method of pricing, described in section 925(a)(1), the transfer price for a sale by the related supplier to the FSC is the price as a result of which the profit derived by the FSC from the sale will not exceed 1.83 percent of the foreign trading gross receipts of the FSC derived from the sale of the export property. Pursuant to section 925(d), the amount of profit derived by the FSC under this method may not exceed twice the amount of profit determined under, at the related supplier's election, either the combined taxable income method of § 1.925(a)-1T(c)(3) or the marginal costing rules of § 1.925(b)-1T. For FSC taxable years beginning after December 31, 1986, if the related supplier elects to determine twice the profit determined under the combined taxable income method using the marginal costing rules, because of the no-loss rule of § 1.925 (a)-1T(e)(1)(i), the profit that may be earned by the FSC is limited to 100% of the full costing combined taxable income as determined under § 1.925(a)-1T(c)(3) and (6). Interest or carrying charges with respect to the sale are not foreign trading gross receipts.

(3) *The "23 percent" combined taxable income method.* Under the combined taxable income method of pricing, described in section 925(a)(2), the transfer price for a sale by the related supplier to the FSC is the price as a result of which the profit derived by the FSC from the sale will not exceed 23 percent of the full costing combined taxable income (as defined in paragraph (c)(6) of this section) of the FSC and the related supplier attributable to the foreign trading gross receipts from such sale.

(4) *Section 482 method.* If the methods of paragraphs (c)(2) and (3) of this section are inapplicable to a sale or if the related supplier does not choose to use them, the transfer price for a sale by the related supplier to the FSC is to be determined on the basis of the sales price actually charged but subject to the rules provided by section 482 and the regulations for that section and by § 1.925(a)-1T(a)(3)(ii).

(5) *Incomplete transactions*—(i) For purposes of the gross receipts and combined taxable income methods, if export property which the FSC purchased from the related supplier is not resold by the FSC before the close of either the FSC's taxable year or the taxable year of the related supplier during which the export property was purchased by the FSC from the related supplier, then—

(A) The transfer price of the export property sold by the FSC during that year shall be computed separately from the transfer price of the export property not sold by the FSC during that year.

(B) With respect to the export property not sold by the FSC during that year, the transfer price paid by the FSC for that year shall be the related supplier's cost of goods sold (see paragraph (c)(6)(iii)(C) of this section) with respect to the property.

(C) For the subsequent taxable year during which the export property is resold by the FSC, an additional amount shall be paid by the FSC (to be treated as income for the later year in which it is received or accrued by the related supplier) equal to the excess of the amount which would have been the transfer price under this section had the transfer to the FSC by the related supplier and the resale by the FSC taken place during the taxable year of the FSC during which it resold the property over the amount already paid under subdivision (B) of this paragraph.

(D) The time and manner of payment of transfer prices required by subdivision (i)(B) and (C) of this paragraph shall be determined under paragraph (e)(3), (4) and (5) of this section.

(ii) For purposes of this paragraph, a FSC may determine the year in which it received property from a related supplier and the year in which it resells property in accordance with the method of identifying goods in its inventory properly used under section 471 or section 472 (relating repectively to the general rule for inventories and to the rule for LIFO inventories). Transportation expense of the related supplier in connection with a transaction to which this paragraph applies shall be treated as an item of cost of goods sold with respect to the property if the related supplier includes the cost of intracompany transportation between its branches, divisions, plants, or other units in its cost of goods sold (see paragraph (c)(6)(iii)(C) of this section).

(6) *Full costing combined taxable income*—(i) *In general.* For purposes of section 925 and this section, if a FSC is the principal on the sale of export property, the full costing combined taxable income of the FSC and its related supplier from

Reg. § 1.925(a)-1T(c)(6)

the sale is the excess of the foreign trading gross receipts of the FSC from the sale over the total costs of the FSC and related supplier including the related supplier's cost of goods sold and its and the FSC's noninventoriable costs (see § 1.471-11(c)(2)(ii)) which relate to the foreign trading gross receipts. Interest or carrying charges with respect to the sale are not foreign trading gross receipts.

(ii) *Section 482 applicability.* Combined taxable income under this paragraph shall be determined after taking into account under paragraph (e)(2) of this section all adjustments required by section 482 with respect to transactions to which the section is applicable. If a related supplier performs services under contract with a FSC, the FSC shall compensate the related supplier with an arm's length amount under the provisions of § 1.482-2(b)(1) through (6). Section 1.482-2(b)(7), which provides that an arm's length charge shall not be deemed equal to costs or deductions with respect to services which are an integral part of the business activity of either the member rendering the services (*i.e.*, the related supplier) or the member receiving the benefit of the services (*i.e.*, the FSC), shall not apply if the administrative pricing methods of section 925(a)(1) and (2) are used to compute the FSC's profit and if the related supplier is the person rendering the services. Section 1.482-2(b)(7) shall apply, however, if a related person other than the related supplier is the person rendering the services or if the section 482 method of section 925(a)(3) is used to compute the FSC's profit. See § 1.925(a)-1T(a)(3)(ii). For a special rule for computation of combined taxable income where the related supplier is a qualified cooperative shareholder of the FSC, see paragraph (c)(7) of this section.

(iii) *Rules for determination of gross receipts and total costs.* In determining the gross receipts of the FSC and the total costs of the FSC and related supplier which relate to such gross receipts, the rules set forth in subdivision (iii)(A) through (E) of this paragraph shall apply.

(A) Subject to the provisions of subdivision (iii)(B) through (E) of this paragraph, the methods of accounting used by the FSC and related supplier to compute their taxable incomes will be accepted for purposes of determining the amounts of items of income and expense (including depreciation) and the taxable year for which those items are taken into account.

(B) A FSC may, generally, choose any method of accounting permissible under section 446(c) and the regulations under that section. However, if a FSC is a member of a controlled group (as defined in section 927(d)(4) and § 1.924(a)-1T(h)), the FSC may not choose a method of accounting which, when applied to transactions between the FSC and other members of the controlled group, will result in a material distortion of the income of the FSC or of any other member of the controlled group. Changes in the method of accounting of a FSC are subject to the requirements of section 446(e) and the regulations under that section.

(C) Cost of goods sold shall be determined in accordance with the provisions of § 1.61-3. See sections 471 and 472 and the regulations thereunder with respect to inventories. With respect to property to which an election under section 631 applies (relating to cutting of timber considered as a sale or exchange), cost of goods sold shall be determined by applying § 1.631-1(d)(3) and (e) (relating to fair market value as of the beginning of the taxable year of the standing timber cut during the year considered as its cost).

(D) Costs (other than cost of goods sold) which shall be treated as relating to gross receipts from sales of export property are the expenses, losses, and deductions definitely related, and therefore allocated and apportioned thereto, and a ratable part of any other expenses, losses, or deductions which are not definitely related to any class of gross income, determined in a manner consistent with the rules set forth in § 1.861-8. The deduction for depletion allowed by section 611 relates to gross receipts from sales of export property and shall be taken into account in computing the combined taxable income of the FSC and its related supplier.

(7) *Cooperatives and combined taxable income method.* If a qualified cooperative, as defined in section 1381(a), sells export property to a FSC of which it is a shareholder, the combined taxable income of the FSC and the cooperative shall be computed without taking into account deductions allowed under section 1382(b) and (c) for patronage dividends, per-unit retain allocations and nonpatronage distributions. The FSC and cooperative must take into account, however, when computing combined taxable income, the cooperative's cost of goods sold, or cost of purchases.

(8) *Grouping transactions*—(i) [Reserved] For further guidance, see § 1.925(a)-1(c)(8)(i).

(ii) A determination by the related supplier as to a product or a product line will be accepted by a district director if such determination conforms to either of the following standards: Recognized trade or industry usage, or the two-digit major groups (or any inferior classifications

Reg. § 1.925(a)-1T(c)(7)

or combinations thereof, within a major group) of the Standard Industrial Classification as prepared by the Statistical Policy Division of the Office of Management and Budget, Executive Office of the President. A product shall be included in only one product line for purposes of this section if a product otherwise falls within more than one product line classification.

(iii) A choice by the related supplier to group transactions for a taxable year on a product or product line basis shall apply to all transactions with respect to that product or product line consummated during the taxable year. However, the choice of a product or product line grouping applies only to transactions covered by the grouping and, as to transactions not encompassed by the grouping, the determinations are to be made on a transaction-by-transaction basis. For example, the related supplier may choose a product grouping with respect to one product and use the transaction-by-transaction method for another product within the same taxable year. Sale transactions may not be grouped, however, with lease transactions.

(iv) For purposes of this section, transactions involving military property, as defined in section 923(a)(5) and § 1.923-1T(b)(3)(ii), may be grouped only with other military property included within the same product or product line grouping determined under the standards of subdivision (8)(ii) of this paragraph. Non-military property included within a product or product line grouping which includes military property may be grouped, at the election of the related supplier, under the general grouping rules of subdivisions (i) through (iii) of this paragraph.

(v) A special grouping rule applies to agricultural and horticultural products sold to the FSC by a qualified cooperative if the FSC satisfies the requirements of section 923(a)(4). Section 923(a)(4) increases the amount of the FSC's exempt foreign trade income with regard to sales of these products; see § 1.923-1T(b)(2). This special grouping rule provides that if the related supplier elects to group those products that no other export property may be included within that group. Export property which would have been grouped under the general grouping rules of subdivisions (i) through (iii) of this paragraph with the export property covered by this special grouping rule may be grouped, however, at the election of the related supplier, under the general grouping rules.

(vi) For rules as to grouping certain related and subsidiary services, see paragraph (d)(3)(ii) of this section.

(vii) If there is more than one FSC (or more than one small FSC) within a controlled group of corporations, the same grouping transactions, if any, must be used by all FSCs (or small FSCs) within the controlled group. If the same grouping of transactions is required by this subdivision, and if grouping is elected, the same transfer pricing method must be used to determine each FSC's (or small FSC's) taxable income with respect to that grouping.

(viii) The product or product line groups that are established for purposes of determining combined taxable income may be different from the groups that are established with regard to economic processes (see § 1.924(d)-1(e)).

(d) *Rules under section 925(a)(1) and (2) for transactions other than sales by a FSC.* The following rules are prescribed for purposes of applying the gross receipts method or combined taxable income method to transactions other than sales by a FSC.

(1) *Leases.* In the case of a lease of export property by a related supplier to a FSC for sublease by the FSC, the amount of rent the FSC must pay to the related supplier shall be computed in a manner consistent with the rules in paragraph (c) of this section for computing the transfer price in the case of sales and resales of export property under the gross receipts method or combined taxable income method. Transactions may not be so grouped on a product or product line basis under the rules of paragraph (c)(8) of this section as to combine in any one group of transactions both lease transactions and sale transactions.

(2) *Commissions.* If any transaction to which section 925 applies is handled on a commission basis for a related supplier by a FSC and if commissions paid to the FSC give rise to gross receipts to the related supplier which would have been foreign trading gross receipts under section 924(a) had the FSC made the sale directly then—

(i) The administrative pricing methods of section 925(a)(1) and (2) may be used to determine the FSC's commission income only if the requirements of section 925(c) (relating to activities that must be performed in order to use the administrative pricing methods) are met; see § 1.925(a)-1T(b)(2)(ii).

(ii) The amount of the income that may be earned by the FSC in any year is the amount, computed in a manner consistent with paragraph (c) of this section, which the FSC would have been permitted to earn under the gross receipts method, the combined taxable income method, or the section 482 method if the related supplier had sold (or leased) the property or service to the FSC and the FSC had in turn sold (or subleased) to a third party, whether or not a related party.

Reg. § 1.925(a)-1T(d)(2)

(iii) The combined taxable income of a FSC and the related supplier from the transaction is the excess of the related supplier's gross receipts from the transaction which would have been foreign trading gross receipts had the sale been made by the FSC directly over the related supplier's and the FSC's total costs, excluding the commission paid or payable to the FSC, but including the related supplier's cost of goods sold and its and the FSC's noninventoriable costs (see § 1.471-11(c)(2)(ii)) which relate to the gross receipts from the transaction. The related supplier's gross receipts for purposes of the administrative pricing methods shall be reduced by carrying charges, if any, as computed under § 1.927(d)-1(a) (Q & A2). These carrying charges shall remain income of the related supplier.

(iv) The maximum commission the FSC may charge the related supplier is the amount of income determined under subdivisions (ii) and (iii) of this paragraph plus the FSC's total costs for the transaction as determined under paragraph (c)(6) of this section.

(3) *Receipts from services*—(i) *Related and subsidiary services attributable to the year of the export transaction.* The gross receipts for related and subsidiary services described in paragraph (b)(2)(iii)(C) of this section shall be treated as part of the receipts from the export transaction to which such services are related and subsidiary, but only if, under the arrangement between the FSC and its related supplier and the accounting method otherwise employed by the FSC, the income from such services is includible for the same taxable year as income from such export transaction.

(ii) *Other services.* Income from the performance of related and subsidiary services will be treated as a separate type of income if subdivision (i) of this paragraph does not apply. Income from the performance of engineering and architectural services and certain managerial services, as defined in paragraph (b)(2)(iii)(D) and (E), respectively, of this section, will in all situations be treated as separate types of income. If this subdivision (ii) applies, the amount of taxable income which the FSC may derive for any taxable year shall be determined under the arrangement between the FSC and its related supplier and shall be computed in a manner consistent with the rules in paragraph (c) of this section for computing the transfer price in the case of sales for resale of export property under the transfer pricing rules of section 925. Related and subsidiary services to which the above subdivision (i) of this paragraph does not apply may be grouped, under the rules for grouping of transactions in paragraph (c)(8) of this section, with the products or product lines to which they are related and subsidiary, so long as the grouping of services chosen is consistent with the grouping of products or product lines chosen for the taxable year in which either the products or product lines were sold or in which payment for the services is received or accrued. Grouping of transactions shall not be allowed with respect to the determination of taxable income which the FSC may derive from services described in paragraph (b)(2)(iii)(D) or (E) of this section whether performed by the FSC or by the related supplier. Those determinations shall be made only on a transaction-by-transaction basis.

(e) *Special rules for applying paragraphs (c) and (d) of this section*—(1) *Limitation on FSC income ("no loss" rules).* (i) If there is a combined loss on a transaction or group of transactions, a FSC may not earn a profit under either the combined taxable income method or the gross receipts method. Also, for FSC taxable years beginning after December 31, 1986, in applying the gross receipts method, the FSC's profit may not exceed 100% of full costing combined taxable income determined under the full costing method of § 1.925(a)-1T(c)(3) and (6). This rule prevents pricing at a loss to the related supplier. The related supplier may in all situations set a transfer price or rental payment or pay a commission in an amount that will allow the FSC to recover an amount not in excess of its costs, if any, even if to do so would create, or increase, a loss in the related supplier.

(ii) For purposes of determining whether a combined loss exists, the basis for grouping transactions chosen by the related supplier under paragraph (c)(8) of this section for the taxable year shall apply.

(iii) If a FSC recognizes income while the related supplier recognizes a loss on a sale transaction under the section 482 method, neither the combined taxable income method nor the gross receipts method may be used by the FSC and related supplier (or by a FSC in the same controlled group and the related supplier) for any other sale transaction, or group of sale transactions, during a year which fall within the same three digit Standard Industrial Classification as the subject sale transaction. The reason for this rule is to prevent the segregation of transactions for the purposes of allowing the related supplier to recognize a loss on the subject transactions, while allowing the FSC to earn a profit under the administrative pricing methods on other transactions within the same three digit Standard Industrial Classification.

Reg. § 1.925(a)-1T(d)(3)

(2) *Relationship to section 482.* In applying the administrative pricing methods, it may be necessary to first take into account the price of a transfer (or other transaction) between the related supplier (or FSC) and a related party which is subject to the arm's length standard of section 482. Thus, for example, if a related supplier sells to a FSC export property which the related supplier purchased from related parties, the costs taken into account in computing the combined taxable income of the FSC and the related supplier are determined after any necessary adjustment under section 482 of the price paid by the related supplier to the related parties. In applying section 482 to a transfer by a FSC to a related party, the parties are treated as if they were a single entity carrying on all the functions performed by the FSC and the related supplier with respect to the transaction. The FSC shall be allowed to receive under the section 482 standard the amount the related supplier would have received had there been no FSC.

(3) *Creation of receivables.* (i) If the amount of the transfer price or rental payment actually charged by a related supplier to a FSC or the sales commission actually charged by a FSC to a related supplier has not been paid, an account receivable and payable will be deemed created as of the due date under section 6072(b), including extensions provided for under section 6081, of the FSC's tax return for the taxable year of the FSC during which a transaction to which section 925 is applicable occurs. The receivable and payable will be in an amount equal to the difference between the amount of the transfer price or rental payment or commission determined under section 925 and this section and the amount (if any) actually paid or received. For example, a calendar year FSC's related supplier paid the FSC on July 1, 1985, a commission of $50 on the sale of export property. On September 15, 1986, the extended due date of the FSC's income tax return for taxable year 1985, the related supplier determined that the commission should have been $60. The additional $10 of commission had not been paid. Accordingly, an interest-bearing payable to the FSC from the related supplier in the amount of $10 was created as of September 15, 1986. A $10 interest bearing receivable was also created on the FSC's books.

(ii) An indebtedness arising under the above subdivision (i) shall bear interest at an arm's length rate, computed in the manner provided by § 1.482-2(a)(2), from the due date under section 6072(b), including extensions provided for under section 6081, of the FSC's tax return for the taxable year of the FSC in which the transaction occurred which gave rise to the indebtedness to the date of payment of the indebtedness. The interest so computed shall be accrued and included in the taxable income of the person to whom the indebtedness is owed for each taxable year during which the indebtedness is unpaid if that person is an accrual basis taxpayer or when the interest is paid if a cash basis taxpayer. Because the transactions covered by this subdivision are between the related supplier and FSC, the carrying charges provisions of § 1.927(d)-1(a) do not apply.

(iii) Payment of dividends, transfer prices, rents, commissions, service fees, receivables, or payables may be in the form of money, property, sales discount, or an accounting entry offsetting the amount due the related supplier, or FSC, whichever applies, against an existing debt of the other party to the transaction. This provision does not eliminate the requirement that actual cash payments be made by the related supplier to a commission FSC if the receipt of payment test of section 924(e)(4) is used to meet the foreign economic process requirements of section 924(d). The offset accounting entries must be clearly identified in both the related supplier's and FSC's books of account.

(4) *Subsequent determination of transfer price, rental income or commission.* The FSC and its related supplier would ordinarily determine under section 925 and this section the transfer price or rental payment payable by the FSC or the commission payable to the FSC for a transaction before the FSC files its return for the taxable year of the transaction. After the FSC has filed its return, a redetermination of those amounts by the Commissioner may only be made if specifically permitted by a Code provision or regulations under the Code. Such a redetermination would include a redetermination by reason of an adjustment under section 482 and the regulations under that section or section 861 and § 1.861-8 which affects the amounts which entered into the determination. In addition, a redetermination may be made by the FSC and related supplier if their taxable years are still open under the statute of limitations for making claims for refund under section 6511 if they determine that a different transfer pricing method may be more beneficial. Also, the FSC and related supplier may redetermine the amount of foreign trading gross receipts and the amount of the costs and expenses that are used to determine the FSC's and related supplier's profits under the transfer pricing methods. Any redetermination shall affect both the FSC and the related supplier. The FSC and the related supplier may not redetermine that the FSC was operating as a commission FSC rather than a buy-sell FSC, and vice versa.

Reg. § 1.925(a)-1T(e)(4)

(5) *Procedure for adjustments to redeterminations.* (i) If a redetermination under paragraph (e)(4) of this section is made of the transfer price, rental payment or commission for a transaction, or group of transactions, the person who was underpaid under this redetermination shall establish (or be deemed to have established), at the date of the redetermination, an account receivable from the person with whom it engaged in the transaction equal to the difference between the amounts as redetermined and the amounts (if any) previously paid and received, plus the amount (if any) of the account receivable determined under paragraph (e)(3) of this section that remains unpaid. A corresponding account payable will be established by the person who underpaid the amount due.

(ii) An account receivable established in accordance with the above subdivision (5)(i) of this paragraph shall bear interest at an arm's length rate, computed in the manner provided by § 1.482-2(a)(2), from the day after the date the account receivable is deemed established to the date of payment. The interest so computed shall be accrued and included in the taxable income for each taxable year during which the account receivable is outstanding of an accrual basis taxpayer or when paid if a cash basis taxpayer.

(iii) In lieu of establishing an account receivable in accordance with the above subdivision (5)(i) of this paragraph for all or part of an amount due a related supplier, the related supplier and FSC are permitted to treat all or part of any current or prior distribution which was made by the FSC as an additional payment of transfer price or rental payment or repayment of commission (and not as a distribution) made as of the date the distribution was made. Any additional amount arising on the redetermination due the related supplier after this treatment shall be represented by an account receivable established under the above subdivision (5)(i) of this paragraph. To the extent that a distribution is so treated under this subdivision (5)(iii), it shall cease to qualify as a distribution for any Federal income tax purpose. If all or part of any distribution made to a shareholder other than the related supplier is recharacterized under this subdivision (5)(iii), the related supplier shall establish an account receivable from that shareholder for the amount so recharacterized. The Commissioner may prescribe by Revenue Procedure conditions and procedures that must be met in order to obtain the relief provided by this subdivision (5)(iii).

(iv) The procedure for adjustments to transfer price provided by this paragraph does not apply to incomplete transactions described in paragraph (c)(5) of this section. Such procedure will, however, be applied to any such transaction with respect to the taxable year in which the transaction is completed.

(f) *Examples.* The provisions of this section may be illustrated by the following examples:

Example (1). In 1985, F, a FSC, purchases export property from R, a domestic manufacturer of export property A. R is F's related supplier. The sale from R to F is made under a written agreement which provides that the transfer price between R and F shall be that price which allocates to F the maximum amount permitted to be received under the transfer pricing rules of section 925. F resells property A in 1985 to an unrelated purchaser for $1,000. The terms of the sales contract between F and the unrelated purchaser provide that payment of the $1,000 sales price will be made within 90 days after sale. The purchaser pays the entire sales price within 60 days. F incurs indirect and direct expenses in the amount of $260 attributable to the sale which relate to the activities and functions referred to in section 924(c), (d) and (e). In addition, F incurs additional expenses attributable to the sale in the amount of $35. R's cost of goods sold attributable to the export property is $550. R incurred direct selling expenses in connection with the sale of $50. R's deductible general and administrative expenses allocable to all gross income are $200. Apportionment of those supportive expenses on the basis of gross income does not result in a material distortion of income and is a reasonable method of apportionment. R's direct selling expenses and its general and administrative expenses were not required to be incurred by F. R's gross income from sources other than the transaction is $17,550 resulting in total gross income of R and F (excluding the transfer price paid by F) of $18,000 ($450 plus $17,550). For purposes of this example, it is assumed that if R sold the export property to F for $690, the price could be justified as satisfying the standards of section 482. Under these facts, F may earn, under the combined taxable income method, the more favorable of the three transfer pricing rules, a profit of $23 on the sale. (Unless otherwise indicated, all examples in this section assume that the marginal costing method of § 1.925(b)-1T does not result in a higher profit than the profit under the full costing combined taxable income method of paragraph (c)(3) and (6) of this section.) F's profit and the transfer price to F from the transaction, using the administrative pricing methods, and F's profit if the transfer price is determined under section 482, would be as follows:

Combined taxable income:

Reg. § 1.925(a)-1T(e)(5)

Income from Sources Without the United States 49,073

See p. 20,601 for regulations not amended to reflect law changes

F's foreign trading gross receipts	$1,000.00
R's cost of goods sold	(550.00)
Combined gross income	450.00
Less:	
R's direct selling expenses	50.00
F's expenses	295.00
Apportionment of R's general and administrative expenses:	
R's total G/A expenses.. $ 200.00	
Combined gross income . 450.00	
R's and F's total gross income (foreign and domestic) 18,000.00	
Apportionment of G/A expenses: $200 × $450/$18,000	5.00
Total	(350.00)
Combined taxable income	$ 100.00

The section 482 method—Transfer price to F and F's profit:

Transfer price to F	$ 690.00
F's profit:	
F's foreign trading gross receipts	$1,000.00
Less:	
F's cost of goods sold	690.00
F's expenses	295.00
Total	(985.00)
F's profit	$ 15.00

The gross receipts method—F's profit and transfer price to F:

F's profit—lesser of 1.83% of F's foreign trading gross receipts ($18.30) or two times F's profit under the combined taxable income method ($46.00) (See below) (Unless otherwise indicated, all examples in this section assume that the marginal costing method of § 1.925(b)-1T does not result in a higher profit than the profit under the full costing combined taxable income method)	$ 18.30
Transfer price to F:	
F's foreign trading gross receipts	$1,000.00
Less:	
F's expenses	295.00
F's profit	18.30
Total	(313.30)
Transfer price	$ 686.70

The combined taxable income method—F's profit and transfer price to F:

F's profit—23% of combined taxable income ($100)	$ 23.00
Transfer price to F:	
F's foreign trading gross receipts	$1,000.00
Less:	
F's expenses	295.00
F's profit	23.00
Total	(318.00)
Transfer price	$ 682.00

With a profit of $23 under the most favorable of the transfer pricing methods, F's exempt foreign trade income under section 923 would be $207.39, computed as follows:

F's foreign trading gross receipts	$1,000.00
F's costs of purchases (transfer price)	(682.00)
F's foreign trade income	$ 318.00
F's exempt foreign trade income $318 × 15/23	207.39

F's taxable income would be $8.00, computed as follows:

F's foreign trade income	$ 318.00
F's exempt foreign trade income	(207.39)
F's non-exempt foreign trade income	110.61
Less:	
F's expenses allocable to non-exempt foreign trade income $295 × $110.61/$318	(102.61)
F's taxable income	$ 8.00

Of F's total expenses, $192.39 ($295 × $207.39/$318) are allocated to F's exempt foreign trade income and are disallowed for purposes of computing F's taxable income.

Example (2). Assume the same facts as in Example (1) except that the purchaser pays the entire sales price 96 days after delivery, well beyond the 60 day period in which payment must be made to avoid recharacterization of part of the contract price as carrying charges. Therefore, the contract price of $1,000 includes $10 of carrying charges, assuming a discount rate of 10%. See § 1.927(d)-1(a) (Q & A2) for computation method for determining amount of carrying charges. Under these facts, F may earn, under the combined taxable income method, the most favorable of the three transfer pricing rules, a profit of $20.73 on the sale. F's profit and the transfer price to F under the transfer pricing rules, assuming that a carrying charge is incurred, would be as follows:

Reg. § 1.925(a)-1T(f)

49,074 Income from Sources Without the United States
See p. 20,601 for regulations not amended to reflect law changes

Combined taxable income:

F's foreign trading gross receipts	$ 990.00
R's cost of goods sold	(550.00)
Combined gross income	440.00
Less:	
R's direct selling expenses	50.00
R's apportioned G/A expenses: $200 × $440/$18,000	4.89
F's expenses	295.00
Total	$ (349.89)
Combined taxable income	$ 90.11

The combined taxable income method—F's profit and transfer price to F:

F's profit—23% of combined taxable income ($90.11)	$ 20.73
Transfer price to F:	
F's foreign trading gross receipts	$ 990.00
Less:	
F's expenses	295.00
F's profit	20.73
Total	(315.73)
Transfer price	$ 674.27

The gross receipts method—F's profit and transfer price to F

F's profit—lesser of 1.83% of F's foreign trading gross receipts ($18.12) or two times F's profit under the combined taxable income method ($41.46)	$ 18.12
Transfer price to F:	
F's foreign trading gross receipts	$ 990.00
Less:	
F's expenses	295.00
F's profit	18.12
Total	(313.12)
Transfer price	$ 676.88

The section 482 method—Transfer price to F and F's profit:

Transfer price to F	$ 690.00
F's profit:	
F's foreign trading gross receipts	$ 990.00
Less:	
F's cost of goods sold	690.00
F's expenses	295.00
Total	(985.00)
F's profit	$ 5.00

Example (3). R and F are calendar year taxpayers. R, a domestic manufacturing company, owns all the stock of F, a FSC for the taxable year. During 1985, R produces and sells a product line of export property to F for $157, a price which can be justified as satisfying the arm's length price standard of section 482. The sale from R to F is made under a written agreement which provides that the transfer price between R and F shall be that price which allocates to F the maximum amount permitted to be received under the transfer pricing rules of section 925. F resells the export property for $200. R's cost of goods sold attributable to the export property is $115 so that the combined gross income from the sale of the export property is $85 (*i.e.,* $200 minus $115). R incurs $18 in direct selling expenses in connection with the sale of the property. R's deductible general and administrative expenses allocable to all gross income are $120. R's direct selling and its general and administrative expenses were not required to be incurred by F. R's gross income from sources other than the transaction is $5,015 resulting in the total gross income of R and F (excluding the transfer price paid by F) of $5,100 (*i.e.,* $85 plus $5,015). F incurs $50 in direct and indirect expenses attributable to resale of the export property. Of those expenses, $45 relate to activities and functions referred to in section 924(c), (d) and (e). The maximum profit which F may earn with respect to the product line is $3.66, computed as follows:

Combined taxable income:

F's foreign trading gross receipts	$ 200.00
R's cost of goods sold	(115.00)
Combined gross income	85.00
Less:	
R's direct selling expenses	18.00
R's apportioned G/A expenses:	
F's expenses	50.00
Total	(70.00)
Combined taxable income	$ 15.00

The combined taxable income method—F's profit:

F's profit—23% of combined taxable income ($15)	$ 3.45

The gross receipts method—F's profit:

F's profit—lesser of 1.83% of F's foreign trading gross receipts ($3.66) or two times F's profit under the combined taxable income method ($6.90)	$ 3.66

Reg. § 1.925(a)-1T(f)

Income from Sources Without the United States 49,075
See p. 20,601 for regulations not amended to reflect law changes

The section 482 method—F's profit:

F's foreign trading gross receipts	$ 200.00
Less:	
F's cost of goods sold	157.00
F's expenses	50.00
Total	(207.00)
F's profit (loss)	$ (7.00)

Since the gross receipts method results in a greater profit to F ($3.66) than does either the combined taxable income method ($3.45) or the section 482 method (a loss of $7), and does not exceed twice the profit under the combined taxable income method, F may earn a maximum profit of $3.66. Accordingly, the transfer price from R to F may be readjusted as long as the transfer price is not readjusted below $146.34, computed as follows:

Transfer price to F:

F's foreign trading gross receipts	$ 200.00
Less:	
F's expenses	50.00
F's profit	3.66
Total	(53.66)
Transfer price	$ 146.34

Example (4). R and F are fiscal year May 31 year-end taxpayers. R, a domestic manufacturing company, owns all the stock of F, a FSC for the taxable year. During August of 1987, R produces and sells 100 units of export property A to F under a written agreement which provides that the transfer price between R and F shall be that price which allocates to F the maximum profit permitted to be received under the transfer pricing rules of section 925. Thereafter, the 100 units are resold for export by F for $950. R's cost of goods sold attributable to the 100 units is $650. R incurs costs, both direct and indirect, in the amount of $270 with regard to activities and functions referred to in section 924(c), (d) and (e) which it was under contract with F to perform for F. R's direct selling expenses are $40. Those expenses were not required to be incurred by F. For purposes of this example, assume that R has no general and administrative expenses other than those relating to the section 924(c), (d) and (e) activities and functions. F incurs expenses in the amount of $290 attributable to the resale which relate to the activities and functions referred to in section 924(c), (d) and (e). Of that amount, $270 was paid to R under contract to perform the activities in section 924. The remaining $20 was paid to independent contractors. R chooses not to apply the section 482 transfer pricing method to determine F's profit on the transaction. F may not earn any income under either the gross receipts (see the special no-loss rule of paragraph (e)(1)(i) of this section) or the combined taxable income administrative pricing methods with respect to resale of the 100 units because there is a combined loss of $(30) on the transaction, computed as follows:

Combined taxable income:

F's foreign trading gross receipts	$ 950.00
R's cost of goods sold	(650.00)
Combined gross income	300.00
Less:	
R's direct selling expenses	40.00
F's expenses	290.00
Total	(330.00)
Combined taxable income (loss)	$ (30.00)

Under paragraph (e)(1)(i) of this section, F is permitted to recover its expenses attributable to the sale ($290) even though such recovery results in a loss or increased loss to the related supplier. Accordingly, the transfer price from R to F may be readjusted as long as the transfer price is not readjusted below $660, computed as follows:

Transfer price to F:

F's foreign trading gross receipts	$ 950.00
Less:	
F's expenses	(290.00)
Transfer price	$ 660.00

Example (5). Assume the same facts as in *Example (4)* except that F performs the section 924(c), (d) and (e) activities and functions and that R chooses to apply the section 482 transfer pricing method. Under the standards of section 482, a transfer price from R to F of $650 is an arm's length price. Accordingly, the transfer price to F and F's profit on the subsequent resale of product A ($10) are as follows:

The section 482 method—Transfer price to F and F's profit:

Transfer price to F	$ 650.00

F's profit:	
F's foreign trading gross receipts	$ 950.00
F's cost of purchases	(650.00)
F's gross income	300.00
Less:	
F's expenses	(290.00)
F's profit	$ 10.00

This sale of product A results in a loss to R of $40 (transfer price of $650 less R's cost of goods sold of $650 and direct selling expenses of $40). Since R chose to use the section 482 transfer pricing method on this loss transaction, under the special

Reg. § 1.925(a)-1T(f)

49,076 Income from Sources Without the United States

See p. 20,601 for regulations not amended to reflect law changes

no loss rule of paragraph (e)(1)(iii) of this section, the administrative pricing methods of section 925(a)(1) and (2) may not be used for any other sale transactions, or group of sale transactions, during the same year of other products which fall within the same three digit Standard Industrial Classification as product A. F's profit, if any, on these sales must be computed under the section 482 transfer pricing method.

Example (6). R and F are calendar year taxpayers. R, a domestic manufacturing company, owns all the stock of F, a FSC for the taxable year. During 1985, R manufactures 100 units of export property A. R enters into a written agreement with F whereby F is granted a sales franchise with respect to export property A and F will receive commissions with respect to these exports equal to the maximum amount permitted to be received under the administrative pricing rules of section 925(a)(1) and (2). Thereafter, the 100 units are sold for export by R for $1,000. The total sales price of $1,000 was paid by the purchaser to R within 60 days of the sales transaction. The entire $1,000 would have been foreign trading gross receipts had F been the principal on the sale. R's cost of goods sold attributable to the 100 units is $650. R's direct selling expenses so attributable are $50. R's deductible general and administrative expenses, other than those attributable to the section 924(c), (d) and (e) activities and functions, allocable to all gross income are $200. Apportionment of those supportive expenses on the basis of gross income does not result in a material distortion of income and is a reasonable method of apportionment. R's direct selling expenses and the portion of the general and administrative expenses not relating to the activities and functions referred to in section 924(c), (d) and (e) were not required to be incurred by F. R's gross income from sources other than the transaction is $17,650 resulting in total gross income of $18,000 ($350 plus $17,650). R and a related person perform on F's behalf the activities and functions referred to in section 924(c), (d) and (e). In performing these activities, R and the related person incurred expenses, both direct and indirect, of $200 and $45, respectively. F pays $200 to R under contract and $50 to the related person. The maximum profit which F may earn under the franchise pursuant to the administrative pricing rules is $18.30, computed as follows:

Combined taxable income:
R's gross receipts from the sale $1,000.00
R's cost of goods sold .... (650.00)

    Combined gross income 350.00

Less:
    R's direct selling expenses 50.00
    F's expenses 250.00

Apportionment of R's general and administrative expenses:
R's total G/A expenses .... $ 200.00
Combined gross income 350.00
R's and F's total gross income (foreign and domestic) 18,000.00
Apportionment of G/A expenses:
$200 × $350/$18,000 .... 3.89

    Total................... (303.89)
Combined taxable income .... $ 46.11

As reflected in the above computation, F included on its books $200 of expenses related to the section 924 activities and performed by R on behalf of F. R incurred $253.89 of expenses. These expenses were reflected on its books. Under paragraph (b)(2)(ii) of this section, R and F may elect to include all of the expenses related to the export sales on F's books. This will satisfy the requirements of section 925(c) without requiring an allocation of the expenses between R and F. Under this election, as reflected in the following computation, combined taxable income will still be $46.11 but, as reflected in a later part of this example, the commission due F will be increased by $253.89:

Combined taxable income:

R's gross receipts from the sale $1,000.00
R's cost of goods sold .... (650.00)

    Combined gross income 350.00

Less:
    F's expenses .... (303.89)
Combined taxable income .... $ 46.11

The combined taxable income method—F's profit:

F's profit—23% of combined taxable income ($46.11) .... $ 10.61

The gross receipts method—F's profit:

F's profit—lesser of 1.83% of R's gross receipts ($18.30) or two times F's profit under the combined taxable income method ($21.22).................... $ 18.30

If the election provided for in paragraph (b)(2)(ii) of this section is not made, F may receive a commission from R in the amount of $268.30, computed as follows:

F's expenses .... $ 250.00
F's profit........................... 18.30

F's commission .... $ 268.30

Reg. § 1.925(a)-1T(f)

Income from Sources Without the United States

This $268.30 is F's foreign trade income. F's exempt foreign trade income is $174.98 ($268.30 × 15/23). F's taxable income is $6.37, computed as follows:

F's foreign trade income		$ 268.30
F's exempt foreign trade income		(174.98)
F's non-exempt foreign trade income		93.32
Less:		
F's expenses allocable to non-exempt foreign trade income $250 × $93.32/$268.30		(86.95)
F's taxable income	$	6.37

Of F's total expenses, $163.05 ($250 × $174.98/$268.30) are allocated to F's exempt foreign trade income and are disallowed for purposes of computing F's taxable income.

If R and F make the election provided for in paragraph (b)(2)(ii) of this section, F may receive a commission from R in the amount of $322.19, computed as follows:

F's expenses	$	303.89
F's profit		18.30
F's commission	$	322.19

With this election, this $322.19 is F's foreign trade income. F's exempt foreign trade income is $210.12 ($322.19 × 15/23). F's taxable income is still $6.37, computed as follows:

F's foreign trade income	$	322.19
F's exempt foreign trade income		(210.12)
F's non-exempt foreign trade income		112.07
Less:		
F's expenses allocable to non-exempt foreign trade income $303.89 × $112.07/$322.19		(105.70)
F's taxable income	$	6.37

Of F's total expenses, $198.19 ($303.89 × $210.12/$322.19) are allocated to F's exempt foreign trade income and are disallowed for purposes of computing F's taxable income.

Example (7). Assume the same facts as in Example (6) except that R's direct selling expenses are $60. The profit which F may earn under the franchise pursuant to the administrative pricing rules is $16.62, computed as follows:

Combined taxable income:

R's gross receipts from the sale	$1,000.00
R's cost of goods sold	(650.00)
Combined gross income	350.00
Less:	
R's direct selling expenses	60.00
R's apportioned G/A expenses	3.89
F's expenses	250.00
	(313.89)
Combined taxable income	$ 36.11

The combined taxable income method—F's profit:

F's profit—23% of combined taxable income ($36.11)	$ 8.31

The gross receipts method—F's profit:

F's profit—lesser of 1.83% of R's gross receipts ($18.30) or two times F's profit under the combined taxable income method ($16.62)	$ 16.62

F may receive a commission from R in the amount of $266.62, computed as follows:

F's expenses	$ 250.00
F's profit	16.62
F's commission	$ 266.62

If the election provided for in paragraph (b)(2)(ii) of this section is made by R and F, the profit which F may earn under the franchise pursuant to the administrative pricing rules will remain at $16.62 but will be computed as follows:

Combined taxable income:

R's gross receipts from the sale	$1,000.00
R's cost of goods sold	(650.00)
Combined gross income	350.00
Less: F's expenses	(313.89)
Combined taxable income	$ 36.11

The combined taxable income method—F's profit:

F's profit—23% of combined taxable income ($36.11)	$ 8.31

Reg. § 1.925(a)-1T(f)

49,078 Income from Sources Without the United States
See p. 20,601 for regulations not amended to reflect law changes

The gross receipts method—F's profit:

F's profit—lesser of 1.83% of R's gross receipts ($18.30) or two times F's profit under the combined taxable income method ($16.62).....................	$ 16.62

F may receive a commission from R in the amount of $330.51, computed as follows:

F's expenses	$ 313.89
F's profit.........................	16.62
F's commission	$ 330.51

As illustrated by *Example (6)*, F's exempt taxable income and taxable income will be the same regardless of which method is used to compute F's commission.

Example (8). Assume the same facts as in *Example (6)* except that F's expenses are $300. With this assumption, there is a combined loss of $(3.89) on the transaction under the full costing combined taxable income method, computed as follows:

Combined taxable income:

R's gross receipts from the sale		$1,000.00
R's cost of goods sold		(650.00)
Combined gross income		350.00
Less:		
R's direct selling expenses	50.00	
R's apportioned G/A expenses	3.89	
F's expenses	300.00	
		(353.89)
Combined taxable income (loss)	$	(3.89)

Since there is a combined loss, F will not have a profit under the full costing combined taxable income method. However, for purposes of this example, it is assumed that under the marginal costing rules of § 1.925(b)-1T the maximum combined taxable income is $75 and the overall profit percentage limitation is $30. Accordingly, F's profit would be $6.90 (23% of $30) under the marginal costing rules. F's profit under the gross receipts method will be $13.80 (1.83% of $1,000 limited by section 925(d) to two times the profit determined under marginal costing). The commission F may receive from R is $313.80. Had all of the expenses been reflected on F's books pursuant to the election of paragraph (b)(2)(ii) of this section, F's commission would have been $367.69.

Example (9). Assume the same facts as in *Example (6)* except that F's expenses are $300 and the transaction occurred in 1987. F will not earn a profit under the sales franchise pursuant to the administrative pricing rules. This is shown by the following computation:

Combined taxable income:

R's gross receipts from the sale		$1,000.00
R's cost of goods sold		(650.00)
Combined gross income		350.00
Less:		
R's direct selling expenses	50.00	
R's apportioned G/A expenses	3.89	
F's expenses	300.00	
		(353.89)
Combined taxable income (loss)	$	(3.89)

F will not have a profit under the full costing combined taxable income method since there is a combined loss of $(3.89). Also, F will not have a profit under the gross receipts method due to section 925(d) and the special no loss rule of paragraph (e)(1)(i) of this section. In addition, F will not have a profit under the marginal costing rules because the profit may not exceed full costing combined taxable income, see § 1.925(b)-1T(b)(4). Although F may not earn a profit, it is entitled to recoup its expenses. Therefore, the commission F may receive from R is $300.00. R will bear the entire loss. Had all of the expenses been reflected on F's books pursuant to the election of paragraph (b)(2)(ii) of this section, F's commission would have been $353.89.

Example (10). Assume the same facts as in *Example (6)* except that R receives total payment of the sale price of $1,000 on the 96th day after delivery, well beyond the 60 day period in which payment must be made to avoid recharacterization of part of the contract price as carrying charges. Therefore, the contract price of $1,000 includes $10 of carrying charges, assuming a discount rate of 10%. See § 1.927(d)-1(a) (Q & A2) for computation method for determining amount of carrying charges. This $10 of carrying charges is R's income. The profit which F may earn under the franchise pursuant to the administrative pricing rules is $16.66, computed as follows (the election of paragraph (b)(2)(ii) of this section is not made by R and F):

Combined taxable income:

R's gross receipts from the sale		$ 990.00
R's cost of goods sold		(650.00)
Combined gross income		340.00
Less:		
R's direct selling expenses		50.00
R's apportioned G/A expenses:		
$200 × $340/$18,000		3.78
F's expenses		250.00
Total		(303.78)
Combined taxable income	$	36.22

Reg. § 1.925(a)-1T(f)

Income from Sources Without the United States 49,079

See p. 20,601 for regulations not amended to reflect law changes

The combined taxable income method—F's profit:

F's profit—23% of combined taxable income ($36.22) .... $ 8.33

The gross receipts method—F's profit:

F's profit—lesser of 1.83% of R's gross receipts ($18.12) or two times F's profit under the combined taxable income method ($16.66)..................... $ 16.66

F may receive a commission from R in the amount of $266.66, computed as follows:

F's expenses .... $ 250.00
F's profit......................... 16.66
    F's commission .... $ 266.66

Example (11). Assume the same facts as in Example (6). In addition, assume that R also manufactures products K, L, M, N and P all of which are export property as defined in section 927(a). Product K is military property as defined in section 923(a)(5) and § 1.923-1T(b)(3)(ii). Assume further that products A, L and P are included within product line X and that products K, L, M and N are included within product line W. R has entered into a written agreement with F under which F is granted a sales franchise with respect to exporting the products. Under this agreement, F will receive commissions with respect to those exports equal to the maximum amount permitted to be received under the administrative pricing rules. The table set forth below details F's foreign trading gross receipts, R's cost of goods sold and R's and F's expenses allocable and apportioned under § 1.861-8 to the sale of products A, L, M, N and P. For purposes of this example, it is assumed that R does not incur any general and administrative expenses. Because of the special grouping rule of paragraph (c)(8)(ii) of this section, product L may be included for purposes of the administrative pricing rules in only one product line, at the option of R. Also for these purposes, product K, which is military property, may not be grouped with products L, M and N. See paragraph (c)(8)(iv) of this section. Under these facts, F will have profits under the franchise agreement from the sale of products A, L, M, N and P and may receive commissions from R relating to the sale of those products, assuming the election of paragraph (b)(2)(ii) of this section is not made, in the following amounts:

	Profit	F's Expenses	Commissions
Product Line X (products A and P) ...	$36.34	$490.00	$526.34
Product Line W (products L, M and N).......	$40.48	$421.00	$461.48

On the sale of product K, R received gross receipts of $150. R's cost of goods sold was $130. R's and F's expenses allocable to product K totaled $10 ($7 of R's expenses and $3 of F's). Under the gross receipts method, F earned a profit of $2.75 (1.83% of $150) and $2.30 under the combined taxable income method. F may receive a commission, assuming the election of paragraph (b)(2)(ii) of this section is made by R and F, from R in the amount of $12.75, computed as follows:

F's expenses .... $ 10.00
F's profit......................... 2.75
    F's commission .... $ 12.75

Reg. § 1.925(a)-1T(f)

49,080 Income from Sources Without the United States

See p. 20,601 for regulations not amended to reflect law changes

	Product A	Product L	Product M	Product N	Product P	Total
Product Line X						
Combined Taxable Income						
R's GR from sale	$ 1,000	......	......	......	$ 1,000	$ 2,000
R's cost of goods sold	(650)	......	......	......	(650)	(1,300)
Combined gross income	350	......	......	......	350	700
Less:						
R's expenses	50	......	......	......	81	131
F's expenses	250	......	......	......	240	490
Total	(300)	......	......	......	(321)	(621)
Combined taxable income (loss)	$ 50	......	......	......	$ 29	$ 79
23% of CTI	$ 11.50	......	......	......	$ 6.67	$ 18.17
1.83% of GR from sale	$ 18.30	......	......	......	$ 13.34	$ 36.34
Product Line W						
Combined Taxable Income						
R's GR from sale	......	$ 1,000	$ 625	$ 1,800	......	$ 3,425
R's cost of goods sold	......	(650)	(445)	(1,600)	......	(2,695)
Combined gross income	......	350	180	200	......	730
Less:						
R's expenses	......	81	70	70	......	221
F's expenses	......	230	60	131	......	421
Total	......	(311)	(130)	(201)	......	(642)
Combined taxable income (loss)	......	$ 39	$ 50	$ (1)	......	$ 88
23% of CTI	......	$ 8.97	$ 11.50	$ -0-	......	$ 20.24
1.83% of GR From sale	......	$ 17.94	$ 11.44	$ -0-	......	$ 40.48

Example (12). R and F are calendar year taxpayers. R owns all the stock of F, a FSC for the taxable year. During 1985, R purchases 100 units of export property A from B, an unrelated domestic manufacturing company for $850. R's direct selling expenses so attributable are $20. R enters into a written agreement with F whereby F is granted a sales franchise with respect to export product A and F will receive commissions with respect to these exports equal to the maximum amount permitted to be received under the administrative pricing rules of section 925. Thereafter, the 100 units are sold for export by R for $1,050. R factors the trade receivable to unrelated person X for $1,000. Under § 1.924(a)-1T(g)(7), total gross receipts for purposes of computing R's and F's combined taxable income is $1,000 (total receipts ($1,050) less the discount ($50)). This $1,000 would have been foreign trading gross receipts had F been the principal on the sale. For purposes of this example, it is assumed that R did not incur any general and administrative expenses. F incurs expenses in the amount of $110, all of which were performed by R under contract to F. The profit which F may earn under the franchise pursuant to the administrative pricing rules is $9.20 computed as follows:

Combined taxable income:

R's gross receipts from the sale	$1,000.00
R's cost of goods sold	(850.00)
	150.00
Less:	
R's direct selling expenses	20.00
F's expenses	110.00
Total	130.00
Combined taxable income	$ 20.00

Reg. § 1.925(a)-1T(f)

Income from Sources Without the United States 49,081
See p. 20,601 for regulations not amended to reflect law changes

The combined taxable income method—F's profit:

F's profit—23% of combined taxable income ($20)	$ 4.60

The gross receipts method—F's profit:

F's profit—lesser of 1.83% of R's gross receipts ($18.30) or two times F's profit under the combined taxable income method ($9.20)	$ 9.20

F may receive a commission from R in the amount of $119.20, computed as follows (the election of § 1.925(a)-1T(b)(2)(ii) has not been made):

F's expenses	$ 110.00
F's profit.....................	9.20
F's commission	$ 119.20

Example (13). R and F are calendar year taxpayers. R, a domestic manufacturing company, owns all the stock of F, a FSC for the taxable year. During March 1985, R manufactures office equipment, export property within the definition of section 927(a)(1), which it leases on April 1, 1985, to F for a term of 1 year at a monthly rental of $1,000, a rent which satisfies the standard of arm's length rental under section 482. F subleases the product on April 1, 1985, for a term of 1 year at a monthly rental of $1,200. R's cost for the product leased is $40,000. R's other deductible expenses attributable to the product are $200, all of which are incurred in 1985. Those expenses were not incurred under contract to F. F's expenses attributable to sublease of the export property are $1,150, all of which are incurred in 1985 directly by F. R depreciates the property on a straight line basis, using a half-year convention, assuming a 10 year recovery period (see section 168(f)(2)(C), § 1.48-1(g)). The profit which F may earn with respect to the transaction is $1,483.50 for 1985 and $600 for 1986, computed as follows:

COMPUTATION FOR 1985

Combined taxable income:

F's sublease rental receipts for year ($1,200 × 9 months)	$10,800.00
Less:	
R's depreciation (($40,000 × 1/10) × 9/12)	3,000.00
R's expenses	200.00
F's expense	1,150.00
Total	(4,350.00)

Combined taxable income	$ 6,450.00

The combined taxable income method—F's profit:

F's profit—23% of combined taxable income ($6,450).....................	$ 1,483.50

The gross receipts method—F's profit:

F's profit—lesser of 1.83% of F's foreign trading gross receipts ($197.64) or two times F's profit under the combined taxable income method ($2,967)	$ 197.64

The section 482 method—F's profit:

F's sublease rental receipts for year ...	$10,800.00
Less:	
F's lease rental payments for year	9,000.00
F's expenses	1,150.00
Total.....................	(10,150.00)
F's profit.......................	$ 650.00

Since the combined taxable income method results in greater profit to F ($1,483.50) than does either the gross receipts method ($197.64) or the section 482 method ($650), F may earn a profit of $1,483.50 for 1985. Accordingly, the monthly rental payable by F to R for 1985 may be readjusted as long as the monthly rental payable is not readjusted below $907.39, computed as follows:

Monthly rental payable by F to R for 1985:

F's sublease rental receipts for year ...	$10,800.00
Less:	
F's expenses	1,150.00
F's profit.......................	1,483.50
Total.....................	(2,633.50)
Rental payable for 1985	$ 8,166.50
Rental payable each month ($8,166.50 / 9 months)........................	$ 907.39

COMPUTATION FOR 1986

Combined taxable income:

F's sublease rental receipts for year ($1,200 × 3 months)	$3,600.00
Less:	
R's depreciation (($40,000 × 1/10) × 3/12)	(1,000.00)
Combined taxable income	$2,600.00

The combined taxable income method—F's profit:

Reg. § 1.925(a)-1T(f)

F's profit—23% of combined taxable income ($2,600) .... $ 598.00

The gross receipts method—F's profit:

F's profit—lesser of 1.83% of F's foreign trading gross receipts ($3,600) or two times F's profit under the combined taxable income method ($1,196) .... $ 65.88

The section 482 method—F's profit:

F's sublease rental receipts for year	$3,600.00
Less: F's lease rental payments for year	(3,000.00)
F's profit	$ 600.00

Since the section 482 method results in a greater profit to F ($600) than does either the combined taxable income method ($598) or the gross receipts method ($65.88), F may earn a profit of $600 for 1986. Accordingly, the monthly rental payable by F to R for 1986 may be readjusted as long as the monthly rental payable is not readjusted below $1,000, computed as follows:

Monthly rental payable by F to R for 1986:

F's sublease rental receipts for year	$3,600.00
Less: F's profit	(600.00)
Rental payable for 1986	$3,000.00
Rental payable for each month ($3,000 / 3 months)	$1,000.00

(g) *Effective date.* The provisions of this section and § 1.925(b)-1T apply with respect to taxable years ending after December 31, 1984, except that a corporation may not be a FSC for any taxable year beginning before January 1, 1985.

[Temporary Reg. § 1.925(a)-1T.]

☐ [T.D. 8126, 3-2-87. Amended by T.D. 8764, 3-2-98 and T.D. 8944, 3-2-2001.]

[Reg. § 1.925(b)-1T]

§ 1.925(b)-1T. Temporary regulations; Marginal costing rules.—(a) *In general.* This section prescribes the marginal costing rules authorized by section 925(b)(2). If under paragraph (c)(1) of this section a FSC is treated for its taxable year as seeking to establish or maintain a foreign market for sales of an item, product, or product line of export property (as defined in § 1.927(a)-1T) from which foreign trading gross receipts (as defined in § 1.924(a)-1T) are derived, the marginal costing rules prescribed in paragraph (b) of this section may be applied at the related supplier's election to compute combined taxable income of the FSC and related supplier derived from those sales. (Any further reference to a FSC in this section shall include a small FSC unless indicated otherwise.) The combined taxable income determined under these marginal costing rules may be used to determine whether the "twice the amount determined under the combined taxable income method" limitation for the 1.83% of gross receipts test of section 925(d) has been met. For FSC taxable years beginning after December 31, 1986, if the marginal costing rules are used to determine the section 925(d) limitation, the FSC may not earn more than 100% of full costing combined taxable income determined under the full costing combined taxable income method of § 1.925(a)-1T(c)(3) and (6). The marginal costing rules may be applied even if the related supplier does not manufacture, produce, grow, or extract the export property sold. The marginal costing rules do not apply to sales of export property which in the hands of a purchaser related under section 954(d)(3) to the seller give rise to foreign base company sales income as described in section 954(d) unless, for the purchaser's year in which it resells the export property, section 954(b)(3)(A) is applicable or that income is under the exceptions in section 954(b)(4). In addition, the marginal costing rules do not apply to leases of property or to the performances of any services even if they are related and subsidiary services (as defined in § 1.924(a)-1T(d) and § 1.925(a)-1T(b)(2)(iii)(C)).

(b) *Marginal costing rules*—(1) *In general.* Marginal costing is a method under which only direct production costs of producing a particular item, product, or product line are taken into account for purposes of computing the combined taxable income of the FSC and its related supplier under section 925(a)(2). The costs to be taken into account are the related supplier's direct material and labor costs (as defined in § 1.471-11(b)(2)(i)). Costs which are incurred by the FSC and which are not taken into account in computing combined taxable income are deductible by the FSC only to the extent of the FSC's non-foreign trade income. If the related supplier is not the manufacturer or producer of the export property that is sold, the related supplier's purchase price shall be taken into account.

(2) *Overall profit percentage limitation.* Under marginal costing, the combined taxable income of the FSC and its related supplier may not exceed the overall profit percentage (determined under paragraph (c)(2) of this section) multiplied by the FSC's foreign trading gross receipts if the FSC is the principal on the sale (or the related supplier's gross receipts if the FSC is a commission agent) from the sale of export property.

Reg. § 1.925(b)-1T(a)

(3) *Grouping of transactions*—(i) In general, for purposes of this section, an item, product, or product line is the item or group consisting of the product or product line pursuant to § 1.925(a)-1T(c)(8) used by the taxpayer for purposes of applying the full costing combined taxable income method of § 1.925(a)-1T(c)(3) and (6).

(ii) However, for purposes of determining the overall profit percentage under paragraph (c)(2) of this section, any product or product line grouping permissible under § 1.925(a)-1T(c)(8) may be used at the annual choice of the FSC even though it may not be the same item or grouping referred to in subdivision (i) of this paragraph as long as the grouping chosen for determining the overall profit percentage is at least as broad as the grouping referred to in the above subdivision (i) of this paragraph. A product may be included for this purpose, however, in only one product group even though under the grouping rules it would otherwise fall in more than one group. Thus, the marginal costing rules will not apply with respect to any regrouping if the regrouping does not include any product (or products) that was included in the group for purposes of the full costing method.

(4) *Application of limitation on FSC income ("no loss" rules).* The marginal costing rules of this section will not apply if there is a combined loss of the related supplier and the FSC determined in accordance with paragraph (b)(1) of this section. In addition, for FSC taxable years beginning after December 31, 1986, the profit determined under the marginal costing method may be allowed to the FSC only to the extent it does not exceed the FSC's and the related supplier's full costing combined taxable income determined under the full costing combined taxable income method of § 1.925(a)-lT(c)(3) and (6). This rule prevents pricing at a loss to the related supplier. If either of these "no loss" rules apply, the related supplier may nonetheless charge a transfer price or pay a commission in an amount that will allow the FSC to recover an amount not in excess of its full costs, if any, even if to do so would create or increase a loss in the related supplier. The effect of these no-loss rules and of the overall profit percentage limitation of paragraph (c)(2) of this section is that the FSC's profit under these marginal costing rules is limited to the lesser of the following:

(i) 23% of maximum combined taxable income determined under the marginal costing rules,

(ii) 23% of the overall profit percentage limitation, or

(iii) for FSC taxable years beginning after December 31, 1986, 100% of the full costing combined taxable income determined under the full costing combined taxable income method of § 1.925(a)-1T(c)(3) and (6).

(c) *Definitions*—(1) *Establishing or maintaining a foreign market.* A FSC shall be treated for its taxable year as seeking to establish or maintain a foreign market with respect to sales of an item, product, or product line of export property from which foreign trading gross receipts are derived if the combined taxable income computed under paragraph (b) of this section is greater than the full costing combined taxable income computed under the full costing combined taxable income method of § 1.925(a)-1T(c)(3) and (6).

(2) *Overall profit percentage*—(i) For purposes of this section, the overall profit percentage for a taxable year of the FSC for a product or product line is the percentage which—

(A) The combined taxable income of the FSC and its related supplier from the sale of export property plus all other taxable income of its related supplier from all sales (domestic and foreign) of such product or product line during the FSC's taxable year, computed under the full costing method, is of

(B) The total gross receipts (determined under § 1.927(b)-1T) of the FSC and related supplier from all sales of the product or product line.

(ii) At the annual option of the related supplier, the overall profit percentage for the FSC's taxable year for all products and product lines may be determined by aggregating the amounts described in subdivision (i)(A) and (B) of this paragraph of the FSC, and all domestic members of the controlled group (as defined in section 927(d)(4) and § 1.924(a)-1T(h)) of which the FSC is a member, for the FSC's taxable year and for taxable years of the members ending with or within the FSC's taxable year.

(iii) For purposes of determining the amounts in subdivisions (i) and (ii) of this paragraph, a sale of property between a FSC and its related supplier or between domestic members of the controlled group shall be taken into account only during the FSC's taxable year (or taxable year of the member ending within the FSC's taxable year) during which the property is ultimately sold to a person which is not related to the FSC or if related, is a foreign person that is not a FSC.

(3) *Full costing method.* For purposes of section 925 and this section, the term "full costing combined taxable income method" is the method for determining full costing combined taxable income set forth in § 1.925(a)-1T(c)(3) and (6).

Reg. § 1.925(b)-1T(c)(3)

49,084 Income from Sources Without the United States

See p. 20,601 for regulations not amended to reflect law changes

(d) *Examples.* The provisions of this section may be illustrated by the following examples:

Example (1). R and F are calendar year taxpayers. R, a domestic manufacturing company, owns all the stock of F, a FSC for the taxable year. During 1985, R produces and sells 100 units of export property A to F under a written agreement which provides that the transfer price between R and F shall be that price which allocates to F the maximum profit permitted to be received under the administrative pricing rules of section 925(a)(1) and (2). Thereafter, the 100 units are resold for export by F for $950. R's cost of goods sold attributable to the 100 units is $650 consisting in part of $400 of direct materials and $200 of direct labor. R incurs selling expenses directly attributable to the sale in the amount of $100. Those expenses were not required to be incurred by F. For purposes of this example, it is assumed that R does not have general and administrative expenses that are not definitely allocable to any item of gross income. F's expenses attributable to the resale of the 100 units are $120. For purposes of this example, R and F have gross receipts of $4,000 from all domestic and foreign sales, R's total cost of goods sold and total expenses relating to its foreign and domestic sales are $2,730 and $450, respectively. Under full costing, the combined taxable income will be $80, computed as follows:

Combined taxable income—full costing:

F's foreign trading gross receipts	$ 950.00
R's cost of goods sold	(650.00)
Combined gross income	300.00
Less:	
R's direct selling expenses	100.00
F's expenses	120.00
Total	(220.00)
Combined taxable income (loss)	$ 80.00

F's profit under the full costing combined taxable income method is $18.40, i.e., 23% of full costing combined taxable income ($80). F's profit under the gross receipts method will be $17.39, i.e., 1.83% of F's foreign trading gross receipts ($950). However, under the marginal costing rules, F would have a profit attributable to the export sale in the amount of $38.24, i.e., 23% of combined taxable income as determined under the marginal costing rules (23% of $166.25). As shown by the computation below, the combined taxable income under marginal costing is limited to the overall profit percentage limitation ($166.25) since that amount is less than the maximum combined taxable income amount ($350):

Maximum combined taxable income (determined under paragraph (b)(1) of this section):

F's foreign trading gross receipts	$ 950.00
Less:	
R's direct materials	400.00
R's direct labor	200.00
Total	(600.00)
Maximum combined total income	$ 350.00

Overall profit percentage limitation calculation (determined under paragraph (c)(2) of this section):

Gross receipts of R and F from all domestic and foreign sales	$4,000.00
R's cost of goods sold	(2,730.00)
Combined gross income	1,270.00
Less:	
R's expenses	450.00
F's expenses	120.00
Total	(570.00)
Total taxable income from all sales computed on a full costing method	$ 700.00

Overall profit percentage (total taxable income ($700) divided by total gross receipts ($4,000)) ... 17.5%

Overall profit percentage limitation (overall profit percentage times F's foreign trading gross receipts (17.5% times $950.00)) ... $ 166.25

The transfer price from R to F may be set at $791.76, computed as follows:

Transfer price to F:

F's foreign trading gross receipts	$ 950.00
Less:	
F's expenses	120.00
F's profit	38.24
Total	(158.24)
Transfer price	$ 791.76

Example (2). Assume the same facts as in Example (1), except that F's expenses are $170. Under full costing, the combined taxable income will be $30, computed as follows:

Combined taxable income—full costing:

F's foreign trading gross receipts	$ 950.00
R's cost of goods sold	(650.00)
Combined gross income	300.00
Less:	
R's expenses	100.00
F's expenses	170.00

Reg. § 1.925(b)-1T(d)

Income from Sources Without the United States 49,085
See p. 20,601 for regulations not amended to reflect law changes

Total......................	(270.00)
Combined taxable income (loss)	$ 30.00

F's profit under the full costing combined taxable income method is $6.90, i.e., 23% of combined taxable income, $30. Under the marginal costing rules, F may earn a profit attributable to the export sale in the amount of $35.51, i.e., 23% of combined taxable income as determined under the marginal costing rules (23% of $154.38). Had the transaction occurred in 1987, F would have had a profit attributable to the export sale under these marginal costing rules of only $30, i.e., 23% of combined taxable income as determined under the marginal costing rules (23% of $154.38) limited, for FSC taxable years beginning after December 31, 1986, to combined taxable income determined under full costing ($30), see paragraph (b)(4) of this section. F's profit under the gross receipts method will be $17.39, i.e., 1.83% of F's foreign trading gross receipts ($950). The computations are as follows:

Maximum combined taxable income (determined under paragraph (b)(1) of this section):

F's foreign trading gross receipts	$ 950.00
Less:	
R's direct materials	400.00
R's direct labor.....................	200.00
Total.....................	(600.00)
Maximum combined taxable income ...	$ 350.00

Overall profit percentage limitation calculation (determined under paragraph (c)(2) of this section):

Gross receipts of R and F from all domestic and foreign sales	$4,000.00
R's cost of goods sold	(2,730.00)
Combined gross income	1,270.00
Less:	
R's expenses	450.00
F's expenses	170.00
Total.....................	(620.00)
Total taxable income from all sales computed on a full costing method	$ 650.00

Overall profit percentage (total taxable income ($650) divided by total gross receipts ($4,000)) .... | 16.25%

Overall profit percentage limitation
Overall profit percentage times F's foreign trading gross receipts (16.25% times $950.00) .... | $ 154.38

The transfer price from R to F may be set at $744.49, computed as follows:

Transfer price to F:

F's foreign trading gross receipts	$ 950.00
Less:	
F's expenses	170.00
F's profit...........................	35.51
Total.....................	(205.51)
Transfer price.....................	$ 744.49

Example (3). Assume the same facts as in *Example (1)* except that the transaction occurs in 1987 and that F incurs expenses in the amount of $250. Since a $50 combined loss, as computed below, is incurred, F will not have any profit under either the full costing combined taxable income method, the gross receipts method or the marginal costing rules:

Combined taxable income—full costing:

F's foreign trading gross receipts	$ 950.00
R's cost of goods sold	(650.00)
Combined gross income	300.00
Less:	
R's expenses	100.00
F's expenses	250.00
Total.....................	(350.00)
Combined taxable income (loss)	$ (50.00)

The transfer price to R may be set at $700 so that F may recover its expenses.

Example (4). R and F are calendar year taxpayers. R, a domestic manufacturing company, owns all the stock of F, a FSC for the taxable year. During 1985, R manufactures export property A. R enters into a written agreement with F whereby F will receive a commission with respect to sales of export property A by R which result in gross receipts to R which would have been foreign trading gross receipts had F and not R been the principal on the sale. F will receive commissions with respect to such export sales equal to the maximum amount permitted to be received under the transfer pricing rules of section 925. The maximum commission may be earned by F under these marginal costing rules. In this example, R received $950 from the sale of export property A. R's cost of goods sold for that property was $620. R incurred direct selling expenses of $20. Also, it is assumed that R incurred total general and administrative expenses, in addition to those incurred relating to its contract to perform on behalf of F the functions and activities of section 924(c), (d) and (e), of $50. R incurred direct and indirect expenses of $130 in performing those functions and activities on behalf of F. During 1985, R had gross receipts from all domestic and

Reg. § 1.925(b)-1T(d)

49,086   Income from Sources Without the United States
See p. 20,601 for regulations not amended to reflect law changes

foreign sales of $3,500, total cost of goods sold and total expenses relating to the domestic and foreign sales of $1,600 and $259, respectively. The election provided for in § 1.925(a)-1T(b)(2)(ii) was not made by R and F.

Combined taxable income—full costing:

R's gross receipts from the sale of the export property	$ 950.00
R's cost of goods sold	(620.00)
Combined gross income	330.00
Less:	
R's direct selling expenses	20.00
F's expenses	130.00
Apportionment of R's general and administrative expenses:	
R's total G/A expenses ...... $ 50	
Combined gross income 330	
R's total gross income 1,900	
Apportionment of G/A expenses $50 × $330/$1,900	8.68
Total	(158.68)
Combined taxable income (loss)	$ 171.32

Maximum combined taxable income (determined under paragraph (b)(1) of this section):

R's gross receipts from the sale of the export property	$ 950.00
Less:	
R's direct materials	450.00
R's direct labor	100.00
Total	(550.00)
Maximum combined taxable income	$ 400.00

Overall profit percentage limitation calculation (determined under paragraph (c)(2) of this section):

Gross receipts of R from all domestic and foreign sales	$3,500.00
R's cost of goods sold	(1,600.00)
Combined gross income	1,900.00
Less:	
R's total expenses	259.00
F's total expenses	130.00
Total	(450.00)
Total taxable income from all sales computed on a full costing method	$1,511.00
Overall profit percentage (total taxable income ($1,511) divided by total gross receipts ($3,500))	43.17%
Overall profit percentage limitation Overall profit percentage times R's gross receipts from the sale of export property (i.e., 43.17% times $950.00)	$ 410.12

Since the overall profit percentage limitation ($410.12) is greater than the maximum combined taxable income ($400), combined taxable income under marginal costing and for purposes of computing F's commission is limited to $400. Under these marginal costing rules, F will have a profit attributable to the sale of $92, *i.e.*, 23% of combined taxable income as determined under the marginal costing rules (23% of $400). Accordingly, the commission F receives from R is $222, *i.e.*, F's expenses ($130) plus F's profit ($92).

Example (5). Assume the same facts as in *Example (4)*, except that R's gross receipts from the sale of export property (which would have been foreign trading gross receipts had F been the principal on the sale) are $1,050 and gross receipts from all sales, domestic and foreign, remain at $3,500. For purposes of applying the combined taxable income method, R and F may compute their combined taxable income attributable to the product line of export property under the marginal costing rules as follows:

Combined taxable income—full costing:

R's gross receipts from the sale of the export property	$1,050.00
R's cost of goods sold	(620.00)
Combined gross income	430.00
Less:	
R's direct selling expenses	20.00
F's expenses	130.00
Apportionment of R's G/A expenses $50 × $430/$1,900	11.32
Total	(161.32)
Combined taxable income (loss)	$ 268.68

Maximum combined taxable income (determined under paragraph (b)(1) of this section):

R's gross receipts from the sale of export property	$1,050.00
Less:	
R's direct materials	450.00
R's direct labor	100.00
Total	(550.00)
Maximum combined taxable income	$ 500.00
Overall profit percentage (see example (4))	43.17%
Overall profit percentage limitation (determined under paragraph (c)(2) of this section) (R's gross receipts from sale ($1,050.00) times the overall profit percentage (43.17%))	$ 453.29

Since maximum combined taxable income ($500) is greater than the overall profit percentage limitation ($453.29), combined taxable income under marginal costing and for purposes of computing

Reg. § 1.925(b)-1T(d)

Income from Sources Without the United States

F's commission is limited to $453.29. Under these marginal costing rules, F will have a profit attributable to the sales of $104.26, i.e., 23% of combined taxable income (23% of $453.29). Accordingly, the commission F receives from R is $234.26, i.e., F's expenses ($130) plus F's profit ($104.26).

Example (6). Assume the same facts as in *Example (5)*, except that F has expenses of $140 and R's cost of goods sold for the export sale was $900. R does not incur any direct selling expenses. Since cost of goods sold has increased by $280, R's total gross income has been reduced from $1,900 to $1,620. For purposes of applying the combined taxable income method, R and F may compute their combined taxable income under the marginal costing rules as follows:

Combined taxable income—full costing:

R's gross receipts from the sale of the export property	$1,050.00
R's cost of goods sold	(900.00)
Combined gross income	150.00
Less:	
F's expenses	140.00
Apportionment of R's G/A expenses $50 × $150/$1,620	4.63
Total	(144.63)
Combined taxable income (loss)	$ 5.37

Maximum combined taxable income (determined under paragraph (b)(1) of this section):

R's gross receipts from the sale of the export property	$1,050.00
Less:	
R's direct materials	630.00
R's direct labor	200.00
Total	(830.00)
Maximum combined taxable income	$ 220.00

Overall profit percentage limitation calculation (determined under paragraph (c)(2) of this section):

Gross receipts of R and F from all domestic and foreign sales	$3,500.00
R's cost of goods sold	(1,880.00)
Combined gross income	1,620.00
Less:	
R's total expenses	259.00
F's total expenses	140.00
Total	(399.00)
Total taxable income from all sales computed on a full costing method	$1,221.00

Overall profit percentage (total taxable income ($1,1221) divided by total gross receipts ($3,500))	34.89%
Overall profit percentage limitation Overall profit percentage times R's gross receipts from the sale of export property (i.e., 34.89% times $1,050)	$ 366.35

Since the overall profit percentage limitation ($366.35) is greater than the maximum combined taxable income ($220), combined taxable income under marginal costing and for purposes of computing F's commission is limited to $220. Under these marginal costing rules, F will have a profit attributable to the sale of $50.60, i.e., 23% of combined taxable income as determined under the marginal costing rules (23% of $220). If the transaction occurred in 1987, F's profit would be limited, however, by paragraph (b)(4) of this section to the full costing combined taxable income of $5.37. [Temporary Reg. § 1.925(b)-1T.]

☐ [T.D. 8126, 3-2-87. Amended by T.D. 8764, 3-2-98 and T.D. 8944, 3-2-2001.]

[Reg. § 1.926(a)-1]

§ 1.926(a)-1. Distributions to shareholders.—(a) *Treatment of distributions.* [Reserved] For guidance, see § 1.926(a)-1T(a).

(b) *Order of distribution*—(1) *In general*—(i) Distributions by a FSC received by a shareholder in a taxable year of the shareholder beginning before January 1, 1990. Any actual distribution to a shareholder by a FSC (all references to a FSC in this section shall include a small FSC and a former FSC) that is received by the shareholder in a taxable year of the shareholder beginning before January 1, 1990, and made out of earnings and profits shall be treated as made in the following order, to the extent thereof—

    (A) Out of earnings and profits attributable to exempt foreign trade income determined solely because of operation of section 923(a)(4),

    (B) Out of earnings and profits attributable to other exempt foreign trade income,

    (C) Out of earnings and profits attributable to non-exempt foreign trade income determined under either of the administrative pricing methods of section 925(a)(1) or (2),

    (D) Out of earnings and profits attributable to section 923(a)(2) non-exempt income, and

    (E) Out of other earnings and profits.

  (ii) *Distributions by a FSC received by a shareholder in a taxable year of the shareholder beginning after December 31, 1989.* Any actual distribution to a shareholder by a FSC that is received by the shareholder in a taxable year beginning after December 31, 1989, and that is

Reg. § 1.926(a)-1(b)(1)

49,088 Income from Sources Without the United States

See p. 20,601 for regulations not amended to reflect law changes

made out of earnings and profits shall be treated as made in the following order, to the extent thereof—

(A) Out of earnings and profits attributable to exempt foreign trade income determined solely because of the operation of section 923(a)(4),

(B) Out of earnings and profits attributable to foreign trade income (other than exempt foreign trade income determined solely because of the operation of section 923(a)(4)) allocable to the marketing of agricultural or horticultural products (or the providing of related services) by a qualified cooperative which is a shareholder of the FSC,

(C) Out of earnings and profits attributable to non-exempt foreign trade income and other exempt foreign trade income determined under either of the administrative pricing methods of section 925(a)(1) or (2). Distributions out of this classification will be made on a pro rata basis so that 15/23 (16/23 with regard to distributions to a non-corporate shareholder) of each distribution will be out of earnings and profits attributable to exempt foreign trade income and the remainder will be out of earnings and profits attributable to non-exempt foreign trade income. To the extent the distributions are out of earnings and profits attributable to the disposition of, or services related to, military property, 75/23 (8/23 with regard to distributions to a non-corporate shareholder) of each distribution will be out of earnings and profits attributable to exempt foreign trade income and the remainder will be out of earnings and profits attributable to non-exempt foreign trade income,

(D) Out of earnings and profits attributable to other exempt foreign trade income determined under the transfer pricing method of section 925(a)(3),

(E) Out of earnings and profits attributable to section 923(a)(2) non-exempt income,

(F) Out of earnings and profits attributable to effectively connected income, as defined in section 245(c)(4)(B), and

(G) Out of other earnings and profits.

(2) *Determination of earnings and profits.* [Reserved] For guidance, see § 1.926(a)-1T(b)(1).

(c) *Definition of "former FSC".* [Reserved] For guidance, see § 1.926(a)-1T(c).

(d) *Personal holding company income.* [Reserved] For guidance, see § 1.926(a)-1T(d).

Reg. § 1.926(a)-1T(a)

(e) *Sale of stock if section 1248 applies.* [Reserved] For guidance, see § 1.926(a)-1T(e). [Reg. § 1.926(a)-1.]

☐ [*T.D.* 8340, 3-14-91.]

[Reg. § 1.926(a)-1T]

§ 1.926(a)-1T. Temporary Regulations; Distributions to shareholders.—(a) *Treatment of distributions.* Any distribution by a FSC (or former FSC) to its shareholder with respect to its stock will be includible in the shareholder's gross income in accordance with the provisions of section 301. (Any further reference to a FSC in this section shall include a small FSC unless indicated otherwise.) See section 245(c) for treatment of distributions to domestic corporate shareholders of the FSC. If earnings and profits of a FSC (or former FSC) attributable to foreign trade income are distributed to a shareholder which is a foreign person (or a nonresident alien individual), that distribution shall be treated as United States source income which is effectively connected with the conduct of a trade or business conducted through a permanent establishment of such shareholder within the United States. For this purpose, distributions to a foreign partnership, foreign trust, foreign estate or other foreign entities that would be treated as pass-through entities under U.S. law shall be treated as made directly to the partners or beneficiaries in proportion to their respective interest in the entity.

(b) *Order of distribution*—(1) *In general.* For guidance, see § 1.926(a)-1(b)(1).

(2) *Determination of earnings and profits.* For purposes of this section, the earnings and profits of a FSC (or former FSC) shall be the earnings and profits computed in accordance with the rules, where applicable, prescribed in § 1.964-1 (relating to determination of the earnings and profits of a foreign corporation) other than subsections (d) and (e) of that section.

(c) *Definition of "former FSC".* Under section 926(c), the term "former FSC" refers to a corporation which is not a FSC for a taxable year but which was a FSC for a prior taxable year. However, a corporation is not a former FSC for a taxable year unless such corporation has, at the beginning of such taxable year, earnings and profits attributable to foreign trade income. A corporation which is a former FSC for a taxable year is a former FSC for all purposes of the Code.

(d) *Personal holding company income*—(1) *Treatment of dividends.* Any amount includible in a shareholder's gross income as a dividend with respect to the stock of a FSC (or former FSC) under paragraph (a) of this section shall be treated as a dividend for all purposes of the Code, except that that part of the dividend attributable to foreign trade income, other than an amount attributable to section 923(a)(2) non-exempt income, shall not be considered in applying the personal holding company and foreign personal holding company provisions (sections 541 through 547 and 551 through 558, respectively).

(2) *Look through option.* With regard to distributions from a FSC (or former FSC) which are not treated as personal holding company income under paragraph (d)(1) of this section, the shareholder may, however, treat any amount of that distribution as an item of income described under section 543 (or section 553) (for example, rents) if it establishes to the satisfaction of the Commissioner that such amount is attributable to earnings and profits of the FSC derived from such item of income. For example, distributions from a FSC relating to section 923(a)(2) non-exempt income will be treated as dividends for purposes of the personal holding company provisions of sections 541 through 547 unless the look through option is elected. Under this option, if earnings and profits out of which those distributions are made are attributable to the lease of export property, the FSC shareholder may treat the distribution for purposes of the personal holding company provisions as rents rather than as dividends. This may be beneficial to the shareholder because rents are not considered under section 543(a)(2) as personal holding company income, if in general, rents constitute 50% or more of the shareholder's adjusted ordinary gross income.

(e) *Sale of stock if section 1248 applies.* For purposes of section 1248, the earnings and profits of a FSC (or former FSC) shall not include earnings and profits attributable to foreign trade income. [Temporary Reg. § 1.926(a)-1T.]

☐ [T.D. 8126, 3-2-87. Amended by T.D. 8340, 3-14-91.]

[Reg. § 1.927(a)-1T]

§ 1.927(a)-1T. Temporary Regulations; Definition of export property.—(a) *General rule.* Under section 927(a), except as otherwise provided with respect to excluded property in paragraphs (f), (g) and (h) of this section and with respect to certain short supply property in paragraph (i) of this section, export property is property in the hands of any person (whether or not a FSC) (any further reference to a FSC in this section shall include a small FSC unless indicated otherwise)—

(1) *U.S. manufactured, produced, grown or extracted.* Manufactured, produced, grown, or extracted in the United States by any person or persons other than a FSC (see paragraph (c) of this section),

(2) *Foreign use, consumption or disposition.* Held primarily for sale, lease or rental in the ordinary course of a trade or business by a FSC to a FSC or to any other person for direct use, consumption, or disposition outside the United States (see paragraph (d) of this section),

(3) *Foreign content.* Not more than 50 percent of the fair market value of which is attributable to articles imported into the United States (see paragraph (e) of this section), and

(4) *Non-related FSC purchaser or user.* Which is not sold, leased or rented by a FSC, or with a FSC as commission agent, to another FSC which is a member of the same controlled group (as defined in section 927(d)(4) and § 1.924 (a)-1T(h)) as the FSC.

(b) *Services.* For purposes of this section, services (including the written communication of services in any form) are not export property. Whether an item is property or services shall be determined on the basis of the facts and circumstances attending the development and disposition of the item. Thus, for example, the preparation of a map of a particular construction site would constitute services and not export property, but standard maps prepared for sale to customers generally would not constitute services and would be export property if the requirements of this section were otherwise met.

(c) *Manufacture, production, growth, or extraction of property*—(1) *By a person other than a FSC.* Export property may be manufactured, produced, grown, or extracted in the United States by any person, provided that that person does not qualify as a FSC. Property held by a FSC which was manufactured, produced, grown or extracted by it at a time when it did not qualify as a FSC is not export property of the FSC. Property which sustains further manufacture, production or processing outside the United States prior to sale or lease by a person but after manufacture, production, processing or extraction in the United States will be considered as manufactured, produced, grown or extracted in the United States by that person only if the property is reimported into the United States for further manufacturing, production or processing prior to final export sale. In order to be considered export property, the property manufactured, produced, grown or extracted in the United States must satisfy all of the provisions of section 927(a) and this section.

(2) *Manufactured, produced or processed.* For purposes of this section, property which is sold or leased by a person is considered to be

manufactured, produced or processed by that person or by another person pursuant to a contract with that person if the property is manufactured or produced, as defined in § 1.954-3(a)(4). For purposes of this section, however, in determining if the 20% conversion test of § 1.954-3(a)(4)(iii) has been met, conversion costs include assembly and packaging costs but do not include the value of parts provided pursuant to a services contract as described in § 1.924(a)-1T(d)(3). In addition, for purposes of this section, the 20% conversion test is extended and applied to the export property's adjusted basis rather than to its cost of goods sold if it is leased or held for lease.

(d) *Foreign use, consumption or disposition*—(1) *In general.* (i) Under paragraph (a)(2) of this section, export property must be held primarily for the purpose of sale, lease or rental in the ordinary course of a trade or business, by a FSC to a FSC or to any other person, and the sale or lease must be for direct use, consumption, or disposition outside the United States. Thus, property cannot qualify as export property unless it is sold or leased for direct use, consumption, or disposition outside the United States. Property is sold or leased for direct use, consumption, or disposition outside the United States if the sale or lease satisfies the destination test described in subdivision (2) of this paragraph, the proof of compliance requirements described in subdivision (3) of this paragraph, and the use outside the United States test described in subdivision (4) of this paragraph.

(ii) *Factors not taken into account.* In determining whether property which is sold or leased to a FSC is sold or leased for direct use, consumption, or disposition outside the United States, the fact that the acquiring FSC holds the property in inventory or for lease prior to the time it sells or leases it for direct use, consumption, or disposition outside the United States will not affect the characterization of the property as export property. Fungible export property must be physically segregated from non-export property at all times after purchase by or rental by a FSC or after the start of the commission relationship between the FSC and related supplier with regard to the export property. Non-fungible export property need not be physically segregated from non-export property.

(2) *Destination test.* (i) For purposes of paragraph (d)(1) of this section, the destination test of this paragraph is satisfied with respect to property sold or leased by a seller or lessor only if it is delivered by the seller or lessor (or an agent of the seller or lessor) regardless of the F.O.B. point or the place at which title passes or risk of loss shifts from the seller or lessor—

(A) Within the United States to a carrier or freight forwarder for ultimate delivery outside the United States to a purchaser or lessee (or to a subsequent purchaser or sublessee),

(B) Within the United States to a purchaser or lessee, if the property is ultimately delivered outside the United States (including delivery to a carrier or freight forwarder for delivery outside the United States) by the purchaser or lessee (or a subsequent purchaser or sublessee) within 1 year after the sale or lease,

(C) Within or outside the United States to a purchaser or lessee which, at the time of the sale or lease, is a FSC or an interest charge DISC and is not a member of the same controlled group as the seller or lessor,

(D) From the United States to the purchaser or lessee (or a subsequent purchaser or sublessee) at a point outside the United States by means of the seller's or lessor's own ship, aircraft, or other delivery vehicle, owned, leased, or chartered by the seller or lessor,

(E) Outside the United States to a purchaser or lessee from a warehouse, storage facility, or assembly site located outside the United States, if the property was previously shipped by the seller or lessor from the United States, or

(F) Outside the United States to a purchaser or lessee if the property was previously shipped by the seller or lessor from the United States and if the property is located outside the United States pursuant to a prior lease by the seller or lessor, and either (*1*) the prior lease terminated at the expiration of its term (or by the action of the prior lessee acting alone), (*2*) the sale occurred or the term of the subsequent lease began after the time at which the term of the prior lease would have expired, or (*3*) the lessee under the subsequent lease is not a related person with respect to the lessor and the prior lease was terminated by the action of the lessor (acting alone or together with the lessee).

(ii) For purposes of this paragraph (d)(2) (other than paragraph (d)(2)(i)(C) and (F)(3)), any relationship between the seller or lessor and any purchaser, subsequent purchaser, lessee, or sublessee is immaterial.

(iii) In no event is the destination test of this paragraph (d)(2) satisfied with respect to property which is subject to any use (other than a resale or sublease), manufacture, assembly, or other processing (other than packaging) by any person between the time of the sale or lease by such seller or lessor and the delivery or ultimate delivery outside the United States described in this paragraph (d)(2).

Reg. § 1.927(a)-1T(d)(1)

(iv) If property is located outside the United States at the time it is purchased by a person or leased by a person as lessee, such property may be export property in the hands of such purchaser or lessee only if it is imported into the United States prior to its further sale or lease (including a sublease) outside the United States. Paragraphs (a)(3) and (e) of this section (relating to the 50 percent foreign content test) are applicable in determining whether such property is export property. Thus, for example, if such property is not subjected to manufacturing or production (as defined in paragraph (c) of this section) within the United States after such importation, it does not qualify as export property.

(3) *Proof of compliance with destination test*—(i) *Delivery outside the United States.* For purposes of paragraph (d)(2) of this section (other than subdivision (i)(C) thereof), a seller or lessor shall establish ultimate delivery, use, or consumption of property outside the United States by providing—

(A) A facsimile or carbon copy of the export bill of lading issued by the carrier who delivers the property,

(B) A certificate of an agent or representative of the carrier disclosing delivery of the property outside the United States,

(C) A facsimile or carbon copy of the certificate of lading for the property executed by a customs officer of the country to which the property is delivered,

(D) If that country has no customs administration, a written statement by the person to whom delivery outside the United States was made,

(E) A facsimile or carbon copy of the Shipper's Export Declaration, a monthly shipper's summary declaration filed with the Bureau of Customs, or a magnetic tape filed in lieu of the Shipper's Export Declaration, covering the property, or

(F) Any other proof (including evidence as to the nature of the property or the nature of the transaction) which establishes to the satisfaction of the Commissioner that the property was ultimately delivered, or directly sold, or directly consumed outside the United States within 1 year after the sale or lease.

(ii) The requirements of subdivision (i)(A), (B), (C), or (E) of this paragraph will be considered satisfied even though the name of the ultimate consignee and the price paid for the goods is marked out provided that, in the case of a Shipper's Export Declaration or other document listed in subdivision (i)(E) of this paragraph or a document such as an export bill of lading, such document still indicates the country in which delivery to the ultimate consignee is to be made and, in the case of a certificate of an agent or representative of the carrier, that the document indicates that the property was delivered outside the United States.

(iii) A seller or lessor shall also establish the meeting of the requirement of paragraph (d)(2)(i) of this section (other than subdivision (i)(C) thereof), that the property was delivered outside the United States without further use, manufacture, assembly, or other processing within the United States.

(iv) For purposes of paragraph (d)(2)(i)(C) of this section, a purchaser or lessee of property is deemed to qualify as a FSC or an interest charge DISC for its taxable year if the seller or lessor obtains from the purchaser or lessee a copy of the purchaser's or lessee's election to be treated as a FSC or interest charge DISC together with the purchaser's or lessee's sworn statement that the election has been timely filed with the Internal Revenue Service Center. The copy of the election and the sworn statement of the purchaser or lessee must be received by the seller or lessor within 6 months after the sale or lease. A purchaser or lessee is not treated as a FSC or interest charge DISC with respect to a sale or lease during a taxable year for which the purchaser or lessee does not qualify as a FSC or interest charge DISC if the seller or lessor does not believe or if a reasonable person would not believe at the time the sale or lease is made that the purchaser or lessee will qualify as a FSC or interest charge DISC for the taxable year.

(v) If a seller or lessor fails to provide proof of compliance with the destination test as required by this paragraph (d)(3), the property sold or leased is not export property.

(4) *Sales and leases of property for ultimate use in the United States*—(i) *In general.* For purposes of paragraph (d)(1) of this section, the use test in this paragraph (d)(4) is satisfied with respect to property which—

(A) Under subdivision (4)(ii) through (iv) of this paragraph is not sold for ultimate use in the United States, or

(B) Under subdivision (4)(v) of this paragraph is leased for ultimate use outside the United States.

(ii) *Sales of property for ultimate use in the United States.* For purposes of subdivision (4)(i) of this paragraph, a purchaser of property (including components, as defined in subdivision (4)(vii) of this paragraph) is deemed to use the

Reg. § 1.927(a)-1T(d)(4)

property ultimately in the United States if any of the following conditions exist:

(A) The purchaser is a related party with respect to the seller and the purchaser ultimately uses the property, or a second product into which the property is incorporated as a component, in the United States.

(B) At the time of the sale, there is an agreement or understanding that the property, or a second product into which the property is incorporated as a component, will be ultimately used by the purchaser in the United States.

(C) At the time of the sale, a reasonable person would have believed that the property or the second product would be ultimately used by the purchaser in the United States unless, in the case of a sale of components, the fair market value of the components at the time of delivery to the purchaser constitutes less than 20 percent of the fair market value of the second product into which the components are incorporated (determined at the time of completion of the production, manufacture, or assembly of the second product).

For purposes of subdivision (4)(ii)(B) of this paragraph, there is an agreement or understanding that property will ultimately be used in the United States if, for example, a component is sold abroad under an express agreement with the foreign purchaser that the component is to be incorporated into a product to be sold back to the United States. As a further example, there would also be such an agreement or understanding if the foreign purchaser indicated at the time of the sale or previously that the component is to be incorporated into a product which is designed principally for the United States market. However, such an agreement or understanding does not result from the mere fact that a second product, into which components exported from the United States have been incorporated and which is sold on the world market, is sold in substantial quantities in the United States.

(iii) *Use in the United States.* For purposes of subdivision (4)(ii) of this paragraph, property (including components incorporated into a second product) is or would be ultimately used in the United States by the purchaser if, at any time within 3 years after the purchase of such property or components, either the property is or the components (or the second product into which the components are incorporated) are resold by the purchaser for use by a subsequent purchaser within the United States or the purchaser or subsequent purchaser fails, for any period of 365 consecutive days, to use the property or second product predominantly outside the United States (as defined in subdivision (4)(vi) of this paragraph).

(iv) *Sales to retailers.* For purposes of subdivision (4)(ii)(C) of this paragraph, property sold to any person whose principal business consists of selling from inventory to retail customers at retail outlets outside the United States will be considered to be used predominantly outside the United States.

(v) *Leases of property for ultimate use outside the United States.* For purposes of subdivision (4)(i) of this paragraph, a lessee of property is deemed to use property ultimately outside the United States during a taxable year of the lessor if the property is used predominantly outside the United States (as defined in subdivision (4)(vi) of this paragraph) by the lessee during the portion of the lessor's taxable year which is included within the term of the lease. A determination as to whether the ultimate use of leased property satisfies the requirements of this subdivision is made for each taxable year of the lessor. Thus, leased property may be used predominantly outside the United States for a taxable year of the lessor (and, thus, constitute export property if the remaining requirements of this section are met) even if the property is not used predominantly outside the United States in earlier taxable years or later taxable years of the lessor.

(vi) *Predominant use outside the United States.* For purposes of this paragraph (d)(4), property is used predominantly outside the United States for any period if, during that period, the property is located outside the United States more than 50 percent of the time. An aircraft, railroad rolling stock, vessel, motor vehicle, container, or other property used for transportation purposes is deemed to be used predominantly outside the United States for any period if, during that period, either the property is located outside the United States more than 50 percent of the time or more than 50 percent of the miles traversed in the use of the property are traversed outside the United States. However, property is deemed to be within the United States at all times during which it is engaged in transport between any two points within the United States, except where the transport constitutes uninterrupted international air transportation within the meaning of section 4262(c)(3) and the regulations under that section (relating to tax on air transportation of persons). An orbiting satellite is deemed to be located outside the United States. For purposes of applying section 4262(c)(3) to this subdivision, the term "United States" includes the Commonwealth of Puerto Rico.

Reg. § 1.927(a)-1T(d)(4)

(vii) *Component.* For purposes of this paragraph (d)(4), a component is property which is (or is reasonably expected to be) incorporated into a second product by the purchaser of such component by means of production, manufacture, or assembly.

(e) *Foreign content of property*—(1) *The 50 percent test.* Under paragraph (a)(3) of this section, no more than 50 percent of the fair market value of export property may be attributable to the fair market value of articles which were imported into the United States. For purposes of this paragraph (e), articles imported into the United States are referred to as "foreign content." The fair market value of the foreign content of export property is computed in accordance with paragraph (e)(4) of this section. The fair market value of export property which is sold to a person who is not a related person with respect to the seller is the sale price for such property (not including interest, finance or carrying charges, or similar charges.)

(2) *Application of 50 percent test.* The 50 percent test is applied on an item-by-item basis. If, however, a person sells or leases a large volume of substantially identical export property in a taxable year and if all of that property contains substantially identical foreign content in substantially the same proportion, the person may determine the portion of foreign content contained in that property on an aggregate basis.

(3) *Parts and services.* If, at the time property is sold or leased the seller or lessor agrees to furnish parts pursuant to a services contract (as provided in § 1.924(a)-1T(d)(3)) and the price for the parts is not separately stated, the 50 percent test is applied on an aggregate basis to the property and parts. If the price for the parts is separately stated, the 50 percent test is applied separately to the property and to the parts.

(4) *Computation of foreign content*—(i) *Valuation.* For purposes of applying the 50 percent test, it is necessary to determine the fair market value of all articles which constitutes foreign content of the property being tested to determine if it is export property. The fair market value of the imported articles is determined as of the time the articles are imported into the United States.

(A) *General rule.* Except as provided in paragraph (e)(4)(i)(B), the fair market value of the imported articles which constitutes foreign content is their appraised value, as determined under section 403 of the Tariff Act of 1930 (19 U.S.C. 1401a) in connection with their importation. The appraised value of the articles is the full dutiable value of the articles, determined, however, without regard to any special provision in the United States tariff laws which would result in a lower dutiable value.

(B) *Special election.* If all or a portion of the imported article was originally manufactured, produced, grown, or extracted in the United States, the taxpayer may elect to determine the fair market value of the imported articles which constitutes foreign content under the provisions of this paragraph (e)(4)(i)(B) if the property is subjected to manufacturing or production (as defined in paragraph (c) of this section) within the United States after importation. A taxpayer making the election under this paragraph may determine the fair market value of the imported articles which constitutes foreign content to be the fair market value of the imported articles reduced by the fair market value at the time of the initial export of the portion of the property that was manufactured, produced, grown, or extracted in the United States. The taxpayer must establish the fair market value of the imported articles and of the portion of the property manufactured, produced, grown, or extracted in the United States at the time of the initial export in accordance with subdivision (4)(ii)(B) of this paragraph.

(ii) *Evidence of fair market value*—(A) *General rule.* For purposes of subdivision (4)(i)(A) of this paragraph, the fair market value of the imported articles is their appraised value, which may be evidenced by the customs invoice issued on the importation of such articles into the United States. If the holder of the articles is not the importer (or a related person with respect to the importer), the appraised value of the articles may be evidenced by a certificate based upon information contained in the customs invoice and furnished to the holder by the person from whom the articles (or property incorporating the articles) were purchased. If a customs invoice or certificate described in the preceding sentences is not available to a person purchasing property, the person shall establish that no more than 50 percent of the fair market value of such property is attributable to the fair market value of articles which were imported into the United States.

(B) *Special election.* For purposes of the special election set forth in subdivision (4)(i)(B) of this property, if the initial export is made to a controlled person within the meaning of section 482, the fair market value of the imported articles and of the portion of the articles that are manufactured, produced, grown, or extracted within the United States shall be established by the taxpayer in accordance with the rules under section 482 and the regulations under that section. If the initial export is not made to a controlled person,

Reg. § 1.927(a)-1T(e)(4)

the fair market value must be established by the taxpayer under the facts and circumstances.

(iii) *Interchangeable component articles.* (A) If identical or similar component articles can be incorporated interchangeably into property and a person acquires component articles that are imported into the United States and other component articles that are not imported into the United States, the determination whether imported component articles were incorporated in the property that is exported from the United States shall be made on a substitution basis as in the case of the rules relating to drawback accounts under the customs laws. See section 313(b) of the Tariff Act of 1930, as amended (19 U.S.C. 1313(b)).

(B) The provisions of subdivision (4)(iii)(A) of this paragraph may be illustrated by the following example:

Example. Assume that a manufacturer produces a total of 20,000 electronic devices. The manufacturer exports 5,000 of the devices and subsequently sells 11,000 of the devices to a FSC which exports the 11,000 devices. The major single component article in each device is a tube which represents 60 percent of the fair market value of the device at the time the device is sold by the manufacturer. The manufacturer imports 8,000 of the tubes and produces the remaining 12,000 tubes. For purposes of this subdivision, in accordance with the substitution principle used in the customs drawback laws, the 5,000 devices exported by the manufacturer are each treated as containing an imported tube because the devices were exported prior to the sale to the FSC. The remaining 3,000 imported tubes are treated as being contained in the first 3,000 devices purchased and exported by the FSC. Thus, since the 50 percent test is not met with respect to the first 3,000 devices purchased and exported by the FSC, those devices are not export property. The remaining 8,000 devices purchased and exported by the FSC are treated as containing tubes produced in the United States, and those devices are export property (if they otherwise meet the requirements of this section).

(f) *Excluded property*—(1) *In general.* Notwithstanding any other provision of this section, the following property is not export property—

(i) Property described in subdivision (2) of this paragraph (relating to property leased to a member of controlled group),

(ii) Property described in subdivision (3) of this paragraph (relating to certain types of intangible property),

(iii) Products described in paragraph (g) of this section (relating to oil and gas products), and

(iv) Products described in paragraph (h) of this section (relating to certain export controlled products).

(2) *Property leased to member of controlled group*—(i) *In general.* Property leased to a person (whether or not a FSC) which is a member of the same controlled group as the lessor constitutes export property for any period of time only if during the period—

(A) The property is held for sublease, or is subleased, by the person to a third person for the ultimate use of the third person;

(B) The third person is not a member of the same controlled group; and

(C) The property is used predominantly outside the United States by the third person.

(ii) *Predominant use.* The provisions of paragraph (d)(4)(vi) of this section apply in determining under subdivision (2)(i)(C) of this paragraph whether the property is used predominantly outside the United States by the third person.

(iii) *Leasing rule.* For purposes of this paragraph (f)(2), leased property is deemed to be ultimately used by a member of the same controlled group as the lessor if such property is leased to a person which is not a member of the controlled group but which subleases the property to a person which is a member of the controlled group. Thus, for example, if X, a FSC for the taxable year, leases a movie film to Y, a foreign corporation which is not a member of the same controlled group as X, and Y then subleases the film to persons which are members of the controlled group for showing to the general public, the film is not export property. On the other hand, if X, a FSC for the taxable year, leases a movie film to Z, a foreign corporation which is a member of the same controlled group as X, and Z then subleases the film to Y, another foreign corporation, which is not a member of the same controlled group for showing to the general public, the film is not disqualified from being export property.

(iv) *Certain copyrights.* With respect to a copyright which is not excluded by subdivision (3) of this paragraph from being export property, the ultimate use of the property is the sale or exhibition of the property to the general public. Thus, if A, a FSC for the taxable year, leases recording tapes to B, a foreign corporation which is a member of the same controlled group as A, and if B makes records from the recording tape and sells the records to C, another foreign corporation, which is not a member of the same controlled group, for sale by C to the general public, the recording tape is not disqualified under this paragraph from being export property, notwithstand-

Reg. § 1.927(a)-1T(f)(1)

ing the leasing of the recording tape by A to a member of the same controlled group, since the ultimate use of the tape is the sale of the records (*i.e.*, property produced from the recording tape).

(3) *Intangible property.* Export property does not include any patent, invention, model, design, formula, or process, whether or not patented, or any copyright (other than films, tapes, records, or similar reproductions, for commercial or home use), goodwill, trademark, tradebrand, franchise, or other like property. Although a copyright such as copyright on a book or computer software does not constitute export property, a copyrighted article (such as a book or standardized, mass marketed computer software) if not accompanied by a right to reproduce for extenal use is export property if the requirements of this section are otherwise satisfied. Computer software referred to in the preceding sentence may be on any medium, including, but not limited to, magnetic tape, punched cards, disks, semi-conductor chips and circuit boards. A license of a master recording tape for reproduction outside the United States is not disqualified under this paragraph from being export property.

(g) *Oil and Gas*—(1) *In general.* Under section 927(a)(2)(C), export property does not include oil or gas (or any primary product thereof).

(2) *Primary product from oil or gas.* A primary product from oil or gas is not export property. For purposes of this paragraph—

(i) *Primary product from oil.* The term "primary product from oil" means crude oil and all products derived from the destructive distillation of crude oil, including—

(A) Volatile products,

(B) Light oils such as motor fuel and kerosene,

(C) Distillates such as naphtha,

(D) Lubricating oils,

(E) Greases and waxes, and

(F) Residues such as fuel oil.

For purposes of this paragraph, a product or commodity derived from shale oil which would be a primary product from oil if derived from crude oil is considered a primary product from oil.

(ii) *Primary product from gas.* The term "primary product from gas" means all gas and associated hydrocarbon components from gas wells or oil wells, whether recovered at the lease or upon further processing, including—

(A) Natural gas,

(B) Condensates,

(C) Liquefied petroleum gases such as ethane, propane, and butane, and

(D) Liquid products such as natural gasoline.

(iii) *Primary products and changing technology.* The primary products from oil or gas described in subdivision (2)(i) and (ii) of this paragraph and the processes described in those subdivisions are not intended to represent either the only primary products from oil or gas, or the only processes from which primary products may be derived under existing and future technologies. For example, petroleum coke, although not derived from the destructive distillation of crude oil, is a primary product from oil derived from an existing technology.

(iv) *Non-primary products.* For purposes of this paragraph, petrochemicals, medicinal products, insecticides and alcohols are not considered primary products from oil or gas.

(h) *Export controlled products*—(1) *In general.* Section 927(a)(2)(D) provides that an export controlled product is not export property. A product or commodity may be an export controlled product at one time but not an export controlled product at another time. For purposes of this paragraph, a product or commodity is an "export controlled product" at a particular time if at that time the export of such product or commodity is prohibited or curtailed under section 7(a) of the Export Administration Act of 1979, to effectuate the policy relating to the protection of the domestic economy set forth in paragraph (2)(C) of section 3 of the Export Administration Act of 1979. That policy is to use export controls to the extent necessary to protect the domestic economy from the excessive drain of scarce materials and to reduce the serious inflationary impact of foreign demand.

(2) *Products considered export controlled products*—(i) *In general.* For purposes of this paragraph, an export controlled product is a product or commodity, which is subject to short supply export controls under 15 CFR Part 377. A product or commodity is considered an export controlled product for the duration of each control period which applies to such product or commodity. A control period of a product or commodity begins on and includes the initial control date (as defined in subdivision (2)(ii) of this paragraph) and ends on and includes the final control date (as defined in subdivision (2)(iii) of this paragraph).

(ii) *Initial control date.* The initial control date of a product or commodity which is subject to short supply export controls is the effective date stated in the regulations to 15 CFR Part 377 which subjects the product or commodity to short supply export controls. If there is no effective date stated in these regulations, the initial control

Reg. § 1.927(a)-1T(h)(2)

date of the product or commodity will be thirty days after the effective date of the regulations which subject the product or commodity to short supply export controls.

(iii) *Final control date.* The final control date of a product or commodity is the effective date stated in the regulations to 15 CFR Part 377 which removes the product or commodity from short supply export controls. If there is no effective date stated in those regulations, the final control date of the product or commodity is the date which is thirty days after the effective date of the regulations which remove the product or commodity from short supply export control.

(iv) *Expiration of Export Administration Act.* An initial control date and final control date cannot occur after the expiration date of the Export Administration Act under the authority of which the short supply export controls were issued.

(3) *Effective dates*—(i) *Products controlled on January 1, 1985.* If a product or commodity was subject to short supply export controls on January 1, 1985, this paragraph shall apply to all sales, exchanges, other dispositions, or leases of the product or commodity made after January 1, 1985, by the FSC or by the FSC's related supplier if the FSC is the commission agent on the transaction.

(ii) *Products first controlled after January 1, 1985.* If a product or commodity becomes subject to short supply export controls after January 1, 1985, this paragraph applies to sales, exchanges, other dispositions, or leases of such product or commodity made on or after the initial control date of such product or commodity, and to owning such product or commodity on or after such date.

(iii) *Date of sales, exchange, lease, or other disposition.* For purposes of this paragraph (h)(3), the date of sale, exchange, or other disposition of a product or commodity is the date as of which title to such product or commodity passes. The date of a lease is the date as of which the lessee takes possession of a product or commodity. The accounting method of a person is not determinative of the date of sale, exchange, other disposition, or lease.

(i) *Property in short supply.* If the President determines that the supply of any property which is otherwise export property as defined in this section is insufficient to meet the requirements of the domestic economy, he may by Executive Order designate such property as in short supply. Any property so designated will be treated under section 927 (a)(3) as property which is not export property during the period beginning with the date specified in such Executive Order and ending with the date specified in an Executive Order setting forth the President's determination that such property is no longer in short supply. [Temporary Reg. § 1.927(a)-1T.]

☐ [*T.D.* 8126, 3-2-87.]

[Reg. § 1.927(b)-1T]

§ 1.927(b)-1T. **Temporary Regulations; Definition of gross receipts.**—(a) *General rule.* Under section 927(b), for purposes of section 921 through 927, the gross receipts of a person for a taxable year are—

(1) *Business income.* The total amounts received or accrued by the person from the sale or lease of property held primarily for sale or lease in the ordinary course of a trade or business, and

(2) *Other income.* Gross income recognized from whatever source derived, such as, for example, from—

(i) The furnishing of services (whether or not related to the sale or lease of property described in subdivision (1) of this paragraph),

(ii) Dividends and interest (including tax exempt interest),

(iii) The sale at a gain of any property not described in subdivision (1) of this paragraph, and

(iv) Commission transactions to the extent described in paragraph (e) of this section.

(b) *Non-gross receipts items.* For purposes of paragraph (a) of this section, gross receipts do not include amounts received or accrued by a person from—

(1) *Loan transactions.* The proceeds of a loan or of the repayment of a loan, or

(2) *Non-taxable transactions.* A receipt of property in a transaction to which section 118 (relating to contribution to capital) or section 1032 (relating to exchange of stock for property) applies.

(c) *Non-reduction of total amounts.* For purposes of paragraph (a) of this section, the total amounts received or accrued by a person are not reduced by costs of goods sold, expenses, losses, a deduction for dividends received, or any other deductible amounts. The total amounts received or accrued by a person are reduced by returns and allowances.

(d) *Method of accounting.* For purposes of paragraph (a) of this section, the total amounts received or accrued by a person shall be determined under the method of accounting used in computing its taxable income. If, for example, a FSC receives advance or installment payments for the sale or lease of property described in paragraph (a)(1) of this section, for the furnishing of services,

Reg. § 1.927(b)-1T(a)(1)

or which represent recognized gain from the sale of property not described in paragraph (a)(1) of this section, any amount of such advance payments is considered to be gross receipts of the FSC for the taxable year for which such amount is included in the gross income of the FSC.

(e) *Commission transactions*—(1) *In general*—(i) *With a related supplier.* In the case of transactions which give rise to a commission from the FSC's related supplier on the sale or lease of property or the furnishing of services by a principal, the FSC's gross income from all such transactions is the commission paid or payable to the FSC by the related supplier. The FSC's gross receipts for purposes of computing its profit under the administrative pricing methods of section 925 (a)(1) and (2) shall be the gross receipts (other than gross receipts which would not be foreign trading gross receipts had they been received by the FSC) derived by the related supplier from the sale or lease of the property or from the furnishing of services, with respect to which the commissions are derived. Also, in determining whether the 50% test in section 924(a) has been met, the relevant gross receipts are the gross receipts of the related supplier.

(ii) *With an unrelated principal.* In the case of transactions which give rise to a commission from an unrelated principal to a FSC on the sale or lease of property or the furnishing of services by a principal, the amount recognized by the FSC as gross income from all such transactions shall be the commission received from the principal.

(2) *Selective commission arrangements*—(i) *In general.* A commission arrangement between the FSC and its related supplier may provide that the FSC will not be the related supplier's commission agent with respect to sales or leases of export property, or the furnishing of services, which do not result in foreign trading gross receipts. In addition, the commission agreement may provide that the FSC will not be the related supplier's commission agent on transactions which would result in a loss to the related supplier under the transfer pricing rules of section 925(a). In a buy-sell FSC situation, selective commission arrangements are not applicable. Determination of which transactions fall within the selective commission arrangement may be made up to the due date under section 6072(b), including extensions provided for under section 6081, of the FSC's income tax return for the taxable year of the FSC during which a transaction occurs.

(ii) *Example.* The treatment of a selective commission arrangement may be illustrated by the following example:

Example. A calendar year commission FSC ("F") entered into a selective commission arrangement with related supplier RS which provided that F will not be RS's commission agent on transactions which would result in a loss to RS under the transfer pricing rules of section 925(a). During 1987, RS sold three different articles of export property A, B and C, all of which fall within the same three digit Standard Industrial Classification. In July of 1988, while preparing the FSC's 1987 income tax return, RS determined that the sale of export property A resulted in a loss to RS under the section 482 method of section 925(a)(3) and that applying that method to the sales of export property B and C resulted in only a small amount of income to both RS and F. In addition, RS determined that grouping export property B and C, while excluding export property A from the grouping, resulted in the highest profit to F under the combined taxable income administrative pricing method of section 925(a)(2). Using the same grouping, the gross receipts method of section 925(a)(1) would result in a lower profit to F. Under the special no-loss rule of § 1.925(a)-1T(e)(1)(iii), RS would be prohibited from using the combined taxable income administrative pricing method to determine F's profit for the grouping of export property B and C if it used the section 482 method on the sale of export property A. This results because there was a loss to RS on the sale of export property A. Under the selective commission arrangement, RS could exercise its option and exclude the sale of export property A. Since F is no longer deemed to have been operating as RS's commission agent on that sale, the combined taxable income method may be used to compute F's profit on the grouping of the sales of export property B and C.

(f) *Example.* The definition of gross receipts under this section may be illustrated by the following example:

Example. During 1985, M, a related supplier of N, is engaged in the manufacture of machines in the United States. N, a calendar year FSC, is engaged in the sale and lease of such machines in foreign countries. N furnishes services which are related and subsidiary to its sale and lease of those machines. N also acts as a commission agent in foreign countries for Z, an unrelated supplier, with respect to Z's sale of products. N receives dividends on stock owned by it, interest on loans, and proceeds from sales of business assets located outside the United States resulting in recognized gains and losses. N's gross receipts for 1985 are $3,550, computed on the basis of the additional facts assumed in the table below:

Reg. § 1.927(b)-1T(f)

N's sales receipts for machines manufactured by M (without reduction for cost of goods sold and selling expenses)	$1,500
N's lease receipts for machines manufactured by M (without reduction for depreciation and leasing expenses)	500
N's gross income from related and subsidiary services for machines manufactured by M (without reduction for service expenses)	400
N's sales receipts for products manufactured by Z (without reduction for Z's cost of goods sold, commissions on sales and commission sales expenses)	550
Dividends received by N	150
Interest received by N	200
Proceeds received by N representing recognized gain (but not losses) from sales of business assets located outside the United States	250
N's gross receipts	$3,550

[Temporary Reg. § 1.927(b)-1T.]

☐ [T.D. 8126, 3-2-87.]

[Reg. § 1.927(d)-1]

§ 1.927(d)-1. Other definitions.—(a) *Carrying Charges.*

Q-1. Under what circumstances is the sales price of property or services sold by a FSC or a related supplier considered to include carrying charges as defined in subdivision (ii)(B)(*1*) of Q&A 9 of § 1.921-2T?

A-1. (i) The proceeds received from a sale of export property by a FSC or a related supplier (or the amount paid for services rendered or from rental of export property) may include carrying charges if any part of the sale proceeds (or service or rental payment) is paid after the end of the normal payment period. If the export property is sold or leased by, or if the services are rendered by, the FSC, the entire carrying charges amount as determined in Q&A-2 of this section will be the income of the FSC. If, however, the FSC is the commission agent of a related supplier on these transactions, the carrying charges amount so determined is income of the related supplier. The commission payable to the FSC will be computed by reducing the related supplier's gross receipts from the transaction by the amount of the carrying charges. No carrying charges will be assessed on the commissions paid by the related supplier to the FSC. The carrying charges provisions, likewise, do not apply to any other transaction that does not give rise to foreign trading gross receipts.

(ii) The normal payment period for a sale transaction is 60 days from the earlier of date of sale or date of exchange of property under the contract. For this purpose, the date of sale will be the date the sale is recorded on the seller's books of account under its normal accounting method. The date the transaction was recorded on the seller's books of account shall be disregarded if recording is delayed in order to delay the start of the normal payment period. In these circumstances, the earlier of the date of the contract or date of exchange of property will be deemed the date of sale. For related and subsidiary services that are not separately stated from the sale or lease transaction, the earlier of the date of the sale or date the export property is delivered to the purchaser is the applicable date. For related and subsidiary services which are separately stated from the sale or lease transaction and for other services, such as engineering and architectural services, the normal payment period is 60 days from the earlier of the date payment is due for the services or the date services under the contract are completed. The date of completion of a services contract is the date of final approval of the services by the recipient. With regard to transactions involving the lease or rental of export property, the normal payment period will begin on the date the rental payment is due under the lease. The date the normal payment period begins under this subdivision (ii) will be the same whether or not the transaction is with a related person.

(iii) The carrying charges are computed for the period beginning with the first day after the end of the normal payment period and ending with the date of payment. A FSC may elect at any time prior to the close of the statute of limitations of section 6501(a) for the FSC taxable year to treat the final date of payment stated in the contract as the date of payment if—

(A) the contracts for all transactions completed during the taxable year require that payment be received within the normal payment period,

(B) no more than 20% of transactions for which final payment is received in the taxable year involve payment after the end of the normal payment period.

For FSC taxable years beginning after March 3, 1987, the 20% test will apply only to the dollar value of the transactions and not to the number of transactions. For prior taxable years, the 20% test will apply to either the dollar value of the transactions or to the number of transactions. The special grouping rules applicable to determination of the FSC's profit under the administrative pricing rules of section 925 may be applied to this elective

Income from Sources Without the United States

provision. Accordingly, transactions may be grouped into product or product-line groupings to determine whether 20% or less of the dollar value (or number of transactions, if applicable) of the grouped transactions involve payment after the end of the normal payment period.

Q-2. How are carrying charges as defined in subdivision (ii)(B)(*1*) of Q&A 9 of § 1.921-2T computed?

A-2. If carrying charges as defined in subdivision (ii)(B)(*1*) of Q&A 9 of § 1.921-2T are considered to be included in the sales price of property services, income or rental payment the amount of the carrying charges is equal to the amount in subdivision (i) of this answer if the contract provides for stated interest or the amount in subdivisions (ii) or (iii) of this answer, whichever is applicable, if the contract does not so provide.

(i) If a contract provides for stated interest beginning on the day after the end of the normal payment period, carrying charges will accrue only if the stated interest rate is less than the short-term, monthly Federal rate as of the day after the end of normal payment period and then only to the extent the stated interest is less than the short-term, monthly Federal rate. The short-term, monthly Federal rate is that rate as determined for purposes of section 1274(d) and which is published in the Internal Revenue Bulletin. Carrying charges will not accrue, however, unless payments are made after the end of the normal payment period.

(ii) If a contract for a transaction does not provide for stated interest, and if the taxpayer does not elect the method described in subdivision (iii) below, the amount of carrying charges is equal to the excess of—

(A) The amount of the sales price of property, services income or rental payment that is unpaid on the day after the end of the normal payment period, over

(B) The present value, as of the day after the end of the normal payment period, of all payments that are required to be made under the contract and that are unpaid on the day after the end of the normal payment period.

The amount of the sales price of property, services income or rental payment is the amount under the contract whether it be the sales price, amount paid for services or the rental amount determined as of the actual payment date unless a FSC makes the election provided under subdivision (iii) of Q&A 1. If a FSC makes the election provided under subdivision (iii) of Q&A 1, the amount of the sales price is the sales price, services income or rental payment under the contract determined as of the final payment date stated in the contract.

All payments that are required to be made under the contract include the stated sales price, services income or rental payment as well as stated amounts of interest and carrying charges. The discount rate for the present value computation is simple interest at the short-term monthly Federal rate published in the Internal Revenue Bulletin, determined as of the day after the end of the normal payment period.

The present value of a payment is calculated as follows:

$$P = S \frac{1}{(1 + (i \times t))}$$

P = present value of a payment that is required and unpaid after the end of the normal payment period

S = amount of a payment that is required and unpaid after the end of the normal payment period

i = the short-term monthly Federal rate

t = the number of days after the end of the normal payment period and before date of payment divided by 365.

If a sale is made, or if services are completed, or if rent is due under a lease in a taxable year and the required date of payment is in a later taxable year, carrying charges for the first taxable year are computed for the number of days after the end of the normal payment period and before the end of the taxable year. For the following taxable year, carrying charges are computed for the number of days after the beginning of the taxable year and before the date of payment.

(iii) At the election of the taxpayer, the amount of carrying charges may be determined under the method described in this subdivision (iii). If the taxpayer elects this method, it must be used for all applicable transactions within the taxable year of the FSC. If this optional method is used, the computation of carrying charges must be made separately for transactions involving related persons and for those transactions involving unrelated persons. In addition, the computation of carrying charges must be made separately for each of the five types of income of the FSC (or of the related supplier if the related supplier is the principal on the transaction) listed in paragraphs (1) through (5) of section 924(a). These groupings are separate and distinct from the groupings that are established for purposes of determining the FSC's profit on the export transactions. The optional method allowed in this subdivision provides that the amount of carrying charges for a taxable year of a FSC (or related supplier if the related

Reg. § 1.927(d)-1(a)

49,100 Income from Sources Without the United States

See p. 20,601 for regulations not amended to reflect law changes

supplier is the principal on the export transaction) is computed using the average of receivables of unrelated persons (or of related persons) and the average time those receivables are outstanding. Receivables are included in this computation only if they are from transactions on which foreign trading gross receipts, as defined in section 924(a), are received by the FSC (or which are received by a related supplier of a FSC and which would have been foreign trading gross receipts had they been received by the FSC). Carrying charges are calculated under this method as follows:

CC = (AR)(I/365)(X)(Y)
CC = Carrying charges
AR = Average monthly receivables balance for the taxable year
I = The average short-term, monthly Federal rate for the year
X = The number of times receivables turn over in the year
Y = The number of days the average receivables are outstanding over 60 days.

This optional method is illustrated in *Example (5)* in subdivision (v) of this answer.

(iv) The computation of carrying charges under this answer 2 applies only to the determination of carrying charges under subdivision (ii)(B)(*1*) of Q&A 9 of § 1.921-2 and does not apply to the determination of any other unstated interest or for any other purpose.

(v) The following examples illustrate the computation of carrying charges under this section:

Example (1). On January 1, 1985, a FSC sells export property for $10,000. The export property is delivered to the purchaser on January 10, 1985. The terms of the contract require payment within 90 days after sale. The normal payment period is 60 days. The FSC does not make an election under subdivision (iii) of Q&A 1. The contract does not require the payment of any interest or carrying charges. The purchaser pays the entire sales price on March 1, 1985. The sales price is not considered to include any carrying charges because the purchaser paid the entire sales price within the normal payment period.

Example (2). The facts are the same as in example (1) except that the purchaser pays the entire sales price on April 6, 1985, 96 days after the earlier of the date of sale or date of delivery (*i.e.*, January 1, 1985). Therefore, the sales price is considered to include carrying charges computed as follows:

Step 1: Determine the short-term monthly Federal rate as of the earlier of date of sale or date of delivery. For purposes of this example, the rate is 10%.

Step 2: Determine the fraction of the year represented by the number of days after 60 days and before date of payment. In this example, the number of days beyond 60 is 96 − 60 = 36, which is divided by 365

$$\frac{36 \text{ days}}{365 \text{ days}} = .099 \text{ fraction of the year}$$

Step 3: Using the short-term monthly Federal rate and the fraction of the year, compute the present value of the payment.

$$P = S \frac{1}{(1 + (i \times t))}$$

$$P = \$10,000 \frac{1}{(1 + (.10 \times .099))}$$

P = $10,000 (.99)
P = $9,900

Step 4: Using the present value of all payments, compute the carrying charges.

Carrying Charges = Sales Price Less Present Value.

$10,000 Sales Price
−9,900 Present Value
$100 Carrying charges

Example (3). On October 15, 1985, F, a FSC, leases export property to X for one month with a total rental due of $20,000. Under the terms of the lease, A agreed to pay F $10,000 on October 15, 1985, and the remaining $10,000 on January 15, 1986. The contract does not require the payment of any interest or carrying charges. The second $10,000 payment is made on January 3, 1986. This payment does not include any carrying charges because X paid the $10,000 before the start of the normal payment period.

Example (4). On October 15, 1985, F, a FSC, leases export property to X, for one month with a total amount due under the lease of $10,000, payable on October 15, 1985. X delays payment until January 19, 1986, which was 96 days after the start of the normal payment period. The 60 day normal payment period terminated on December 14, 1985. Therefore, the lease payment is considered to include carrying charges of $100 computed in the same manner as in *Example (2)*. Of this $100, $17/36$, or $47.22, is carrying charges for 1985 (*i.e.*, 17 days in December), and $19/36$, or $52.78, is carrying charges for 1986.

Example (5). During 1986, F, a FSC, sold on account export properties A and B to related and unrelated persons.

Reg. § 1.927(d)-1(a)

Income from Sources Without the United States

See p. 20,601 for regulations not amended to reflect law changes

(A) *Unrelated persons.* During 1986, the sales on account to unrelated persons totaled $6,000. On the last day of each of the months of 1986, F had total receivables from unrelated persons from sales of export properties A and B, as follows:

January 31	$ 1,400
February 28	1,400
March 31	1,000
April 30	1,000
May 31	1,200
June 30	1,300
July 31	1,000
August 31	1,300
September 30	1,500
October 31	1,100
November 30	1,200
December 31	1,000
	$14,400

Carrying charges for 1986 with unrelated persons under the optional method of subdivision (iii) of this answer will be $19.23, computed as follows:

Step 1: Determine the average short-term, monthly Federal rate for the year. For purposes of this example, the rate is assumed to be 9%.

Step 2: Determine the average receivables for the year. This average is calculated by totaling the end of the month receivables balance of each month of the year and dividing by twelve. In this example, the average monthly receivables balance is $1,200, calculated as follows:

$$\$1,200 = \$14,400/12$$

Step 3: Determine the number of times the receivables turn over during the year. This is calculated by dividing the sales on account for the year by the average monthly receivables balance for the year. For purposes of this example, receivables turned over 5 times for 1986, computed as follows:

$$5 = \frac{\$6,000}{\$1,200}$$

Step 4: Determine the number of days the average receivables are outstanding in excess of 60 days. In this example, there are 13 receivable days in excess of 60 days, computed as follows:

$$13 \text{ days} = (365/5) - 60 \text{ days}$$

Step 5: The amount of carrying charges, $19.23, is calculated by using the following equation:

CC = (AR) (I/365) (X) (Y)
CC = Carrying charges
AR = Average monthly receivables balance for the taxable year (step 2)

I = The average short-term monthly Federal rate for the year (step 1)
X = The number of times receivables turn over in the year (step 3)
Y = The number of days the average receivables are outstanding over 60 days (step 4).
CC = $19.23 = ($1,200) (.09/365) (5) (13)

(B) *Related persons.* Carrying charges, if any, on the sales on account to related persons must be computed separately using this optional method.

Q-3. Is a discount from the sales price of property or services for prompt payment considered to be stated carrying charges as defined in subdivision (ii)(A) of Q&A 9 of § 1.921-2?

A-3. No.

Q-4. Is the receipt of an arm's length factoring payment from an unrelated person considered a payment of the sales proceeds for purposes of determining whether payment is made within the normal payment period and the possible imposition of carrying charges?

A-4. Yes.

[Reg. § 1.927(d)-1.]

☐ [T.D. 8127, 3-2-87.]

[Reg. § 1.927(d)-2T]

§ 1.927(d)-2T. Temporary Regulations; Definitions and special rules relating to Foreign Sales Corporation.—(a) *Definition of related supplier.* For purposes of section 921 through 927 and the regulations under those sections, the term "related supplier" means a related party which directly supplies to a FSC any property or services which the FSC disposes of in a transaction producing foreign trading gross receipts, or a related party which uses the FSC as a commission agent in the disposition of any property or services producing foreign trading gross receipts. A FSC may have different related suppliers with respect to different transactions. If, for example, X owns all the stock of Y, a corporation, and of F, a FSC, and X sells a product to Y which is resold to F, only Y is the related supplier of F. If, however, X sells directly to F and Y also sells directly to F, then, as to the transactions involving direct sales to F, each of X and Y is a related supplier of F.

(b) *Definition of related party.* The term "related party" means a person which is owned or controlled directly or indirectly by the same interests as the FSC within the meaning of section 482 and § 1.482-1(a). [Temporary Reg. § 1.927(d)-2T.]

☐ [T.D. 8126, 3-2-87.]

Reg. § 1.927(d)-2T(b)

Income from Sources Without the United States

See p. 20,601 for regulations not amended to reflect law changes

[Reg. § 1.927(e)-1]

§ 1.927(e)-1. **Special sourcing rule.**—(a) *Source rules for related persons*—(1) *In general.* The income of a person described in section 482 from a sale of export property giving rise to foreign trading gross receipts of a FSC that is treated as from sources outside the United States shall not exceed the amount that would be treated as foreign source income earned by such person if the pricing rule under section 994 that corresponds to the rule used under section 925 with respect to such transaction applied to such transaction. This special sourcing rule also applies if the FSC is acting as a commission agent for the related supplier with respect to the transaction described in the first sentence of this paragraph (a)(1) that gives rise to foreign trading gross receipts and the transfer pricing rules of section 925 are used to determine the commission payable to the FSC. No limitation results under this section with respect to a transaction to which the section 482 pricing rule under section 925(a)(3) applies.

(2) *Grouping of transactions.* If, for purposes of determining the FSC's profits under the administrative pricing rules of sections 925(a)(1) and (2), grouping of transactions under § 1.925(a)-1T(c)(8) was elected, the same grouping shall be used for making the determinations under the special sourcing rule in this section.

(3) *Corresponding DISC pricing rules*—(i) *In general.* For purposes of this section—

(A) The DISC gross receipts pricing rule of section 994(a)(1) corresponds to the gross receipts pricing rule of section 925(a)(1);

(B) The DISC combined taxable income pricing rule of section 994(a)(2) corresponds to the combined taxable income pricing rule of section 925(a)(2); and

(C) The DISC section 482 pricing rule of section 994(a)(3) corresponds to the section 482 pricing rule of section 925(a)(3).

(ii) *Special rules.* For purposes of this section—

(A) The DISC pricing rules of section 994(a)(1) and (2) shall be determined without regard to export promotion expenses;

(B) Qualified export receipts under section 994(a)(1) and (2) shall be deemed to be an amount equal to the foreign trading gross receipts arising from the transaction; and

(C) Combined taxable income for purposes of section 994(a)(2) shall be deemed to be an amount equal to the combined taxable income for purposes of section 925(a)(2) arising from the transaction.

(b) *Examples.* The provisions of this section may be illustrated by the following examples:

Example 1. (i) R and F are calendar year taxpayers. R, a domestic manufacturing company, owns all the stock of F, which is a FSC acting as a commission agent for R. For the taxable year, R and F used the combined taxable income pricing rule of section 925(a)(2). For the taxable year, the combined taxable income of R and F is $100 from the sale of export property, as defined in section 927(a), manufactured by R using production assets located in the United States. Title to the export property passed outside of the United States.

(ii) Under section 925(a)(2), 23 percent of the $100 combined taxable income of R and F ($23) is allocated to F and the remaining $77 is allocated to R. Absent the special sourcing rule, under section 863(b) the $77 income allocated to R would be sourced $38.50 U.S. source and $38.50 foreign source. Under the special sourcing rule, the amount of foreign source income earned by a related supplier of a FSC shall not exceed the amount that would result if the corresponding DISC pricing rule applied. The DISC combined taxable income pricing rule of section 994(a)(2) corresponds to the combined taxable income pricing rule of section 925(a)(2). Under section 994(a)(2), $50 of the combined taxable income ($100 x .50) would be allocated to the DISC and the remaining $50 would be allocated to the related supplier. Under section 863(b), the $50 income allocated to the DISC's related supplier would be sourced $25 U.S. source and $25 foreign source. Accordingly, under the special sourcing rule, the foreign source income of R shall not exceed $25.

Example 2. (i) Assume the same facts as in Example 1 except that R and F used the gross receipts pricing rule of section 925(a)(1). In addition, for the taxable year foreign trading gross receipts derived from the sale of the export property are $2,000.

(ii) Under section 925(a)(1), 1.83 percent of the $2,000 foreign trading gross receipts ($36.60) is allocated to F and the $63.40 remaining combined taxable income ($100 - $36.60) is allocated to R. Absent the special sourcing rule, under section 863(b) the $63.40 income allocated to R would be sourced $31.70 U.S. source and $31.70 foreign source. Under the special sourcing rule, the amount of foreign source income earned by a related supplier of a FSC shall not exceed the amount that would result if the corresponding DISC pricing rule applied. The DISC gross receipts pricing rule of section 994(a)(1) corresponds to the gross receipts pricing rule of section

Reg. § 1.927(e)-1(a)(1)

925(a)(1). Under section 994(a)(1), $80 ($2,000 x .04) would be allocated to the DISC and the $20 remaining combined taxable income would be allocated to the related supplier. Under section 863(b), the $20 income allocated to the DISC's related supplier would be sourced $10 U.S. source and $10 foreign source. Accordingly, under the special sourcing rule, the foreign source income of R shall not exceed $10.

(c) *Effective date.* The rules of this section are applicable to taxable years beginning after December 31, 1997. [Reg. § 1.927(e)-1.]

☐ [T.D. 8782, 9-17-98.]

[Reg. § 1.927(e)-2T]

§ 1.927(e)-2T. Temporary Regulations; Effect of boycott participation on FSC and small FSC benefits.—(a) *International Boycott Factor.* If the FSC (or small FSC) or any member of the FSC's (or small FSC's) controlled group participates in or cooperates with an international boycott within the meaning of section 999, the FSC's (or small FSC's) exempt foreign trade income as determined under section 923(a) shall be reduced by an amount equal to the product of the FSC's (or small FSC's) exempt foreign trade income multiplied by the international boycott factor determined under section 999. The amount of the reduction will be considered as non-exempt foreign trade income.

(b) *Specifically Attributable Taxes and Income Method.* If the taxpayer clearly demonstrates that the income earned for the taxable year is attributable to specific operations, then in lieu of applying the international boycott factor for such taxable year, the amount of the exempt foreign trade income as determined under section 923(a) that will be reduced by this section shall be the amount specifically attributable to the operations in which there was participation in or cooperation with an international boycott under section 999(b)(1). The amount of the reduction will be considered as non-exempt foreign trade income. [Temporary Reg. § 1.927(e)-2T.]

☐ [T.D. 8126, 3-2-87.]

[Reg. § 1.927(f)-1]

§ 1.927(f)-1. Election and termination of status as a Foreign Sales Corporation.—(a) *Election of status as a FSC or a small FSC.*

Q-1. What is the effect of an election by a corporation to be treated as a FSC or small FSC?

A-1. A valid election to be treated as a FSC or a small FSC applies to the taxable year of the corporation for which made and remains in effect for all succeeding taxable years in which the corporation qualifies to be a FSC unless revoked by the corporation or unless the corporation fails for five consecutive years to qualify as a FSC (in case of a FSC election) or as a small FSC (in case of a small FSC election).

Q-2. Can a corporation established prior to January 1, 1985 be treated as a FSC or a small FSC prior to making a FSC or a small FSC election?

A-2. A corporation cannot be treated as a FSC or a small FSC until it has made a FSC or a small FSC election. An election made within the first 90 days of 1985 relates back to January 1, 1985 unless the taxpayer indicates otherwise.

Q-3. If a shareholder who has not consented to a FSC or small FSC election transfers some or all of its shares before or during the first taxable year for which the election is made, may the holder of the transferred shares consent to the election?

A-3. A holder of the transferred shares may consent to a FSC or small FSC election under the circumstances described in § 1.992-2(c)(1). The rules contained in § 1.992-2(c) shall apply to the consent by a holder of transferred shares.

Q-4. If a shareholder who has consented to a FSC or a small FSC election transfers some or all of its shares before the first taxable year for which the election is made, must the holder of the transferred shares consent to the election?

A-4. Yes. Consent must be made by any recipient of such shares on or before the 90th day after the first day of such first taxable year. If such recipient fails to file his consent on or before such 90th day, an extension of time for filing such consent may be granted in the manner, and subject to the conditions, described in paragraph (b)(3) of § 1.992-2.

Q-5. May an election of a corporation to be a FSC or a small FSC be effective as of a time other than the start of the corporation's taxable year?

A-5. No.

Q-6. If a fiscal year foreign corporation was in existence on December 31, 1984, must it wait until the first day of its taxable year beginning after January 1, 1985, to elect FSC status?

A-6. No. If a fiscal year foreign corporation was in existence on December 31, 1984, its taxable year will be deemed to have terminated on that date if the foreign corporation elects FSC status to be effective January 1, 1985. An income tax return will be required for any short years created by the deemed closing of the taxable year unless the corporation is relieved from the necessity of making a return by section 6012 and the regulations under that section. If the corporation's taxable year is deemed closed by operation of this regulation, the filing date of tax returns for the short taxable year ended on December 31, 1984, will be automatically extended until May 18, 1987.

Q-7. What is the effect of an election to be treated as a FSC or as a small FSC if the corporation or any other member of the controlled group has in effect an election to be treated as an interest charge DISC?

A-7. The interest charge DISC election shall be treated as revoked for all purposes under the Code as of the date the FSC election is effective. An affirmative revocation of the DISC election is unnecessary. The FSC election shall take effect. As long as the FSC election remains in effect, neither the corporation nor any other member of the controlled group is permitted to elect to be treated as an interest charge DISC for any taxable year including any part of a taxable year during which the corporation's FSC election continues to be effective.

Q-8. What is the effect of an election to be treated as a small FSC if the corporation or any other member of the controlled group has in effect an election to be treated as a FSC?

A-8. As long as a FSC election remains in effect, neither the corporation nor any other member of the controlled group is permitted to elect to be treated as a small FSC for any taxable year including any part of a taxable year during which a FSC election continues to be effective. Any FSC within the controlled group must affirmatively revoke its FSC election for a taxable year including any part of a taxable year for which small FSC status is elected.

Q-9. What is the effect of an election to be treated as a FSC if the corporation or any other member of the controlled group has in effect an election to be treated as a small FSC?

A-9. As long as a small FSC election remains in effect, neither the corporation nor any other member of the controlled group is permitted to elect to be treated as a FSC for any taxable year including any part of the taxable year during which a small FSC election continues to be effective. Any small FSC within the controlled group must affirmatively revoke its small FSC election for a taxable year including any part of a taxable year for which FSC status is elected. An election to be treated as a small FSC is permitted if the corporation or any other member of the controlled group has in effect an election to be treated as a small FSC.

For a special rule providing for conversion of a small FSC to a FSC within one taxable year, see § 1.921-1T(b)(1) (Q&A 1).

(b) *Termination of election of status as a FSC or a small FSC.*

Q-10. How is the status of a corporation as a FSC or a small FSC terminated?

A-10. The status of a corporation as a FSC or a small FSC is terminated through revocation or by its continued failure to be a FSC.

Q-11. For what taxable year may a corporation revoke its election to be treated as a FSC or a small FSC?

A-11. A corporation may revoke its election to be treated as a FSC or as a small FSC for any taxable year of the corporation after the first taxable year for which the election is effective.

Q-12. When must a corporation revoke a FSC or a small FSC election if revocation is to be effective for the taxable year in which revocation takes place?

A-12. If a corporation files a statement revoking its election to be treated as a FSC or as a small FSC during the first 90 days of a taxable year (other than the first taxable year for which such election is effective), such revocation will be effective for such taxable year and all taxable years thereafter. If the corporation files a statement revoking its election to be treated as a FSC or a small FSC after the first 90 days of a taxable year, the revocation will be effective for all taxable years following such taxable year.

Q-13. Can a FSC change its status to a small FSC, or can a small FSC change its status to a FSC as of a date other than the first day of a taxable year?

A-13. No. Since a revocation of an election to be a FSC or a small FSC is effective only for entire taxable year, a corporation's change between FSC and small FSC status is effective as of the first day of a taxable year.

Q-14. How may a corporation revoke an election by a corporation to be treated as a FSC or a small FSC?

A-14. A corporation may revoke its election by filing a statement that the corporation revokes its election under section 922(a) to be treated as a FSC or under section 922(b) to be treated as a small FSC. Such statement shall indicate the corporation's name, address, employer identification number, and the first taxable year of the corporation for which the revocation is to be effective. The statement shall be signed by any person authorized to sign a corporate return under section 6062. Such revocation shall be filed with the Service Center with which the corporation filed its return.

Q-15. What is the effect if a corporation that has elected to be treated as a FSC or a small FSC fails to qualify as a FSC because it does not meet the requirements of section 922 for a taxable year?

Reg. § 1.927(f)-1(b)

Income from Sources Without the United States

See p. 20,601 for regulations not amended to reflect law changes

A-15. If a corporation that has elected to be treated as a FSC or a small FSC does not qualify as a FSC or a small FSC for a taxable year, the corporation will not be treated as a FSC or a small FSC for the taxable year. However, the failure of a corporation to qualify to be treated as a FSC or a small FSC for a taxable year does not terminate the election of the corporation to be treated as FSC or a small FSC unless the corporation does not qualify under section 922 for each of 5 consecutive taxable years, as provided in Q&A 16 of this section.

Q-16. Under what circumstances is the FSC or small FSC election terminated for continued failure to be a FSC?

A-16. If a corporation that has elected to be treated as a FSC or a small FSC does not qualify under section 922 to be treated as a FSC or a small FSC for each of 5 consecutive taxable years, such election terminates and will not be effective for any taxable year after such fifth taxable year. Such termination will be effective automatically without notice to such corporation or to the Internal Revenue Service. [Reg. § 1.927(f)-1.]

☐ [T.D. 8127, 3-2-87.]

[Reg. § 1.931-1]

§ 1.931-1. **Citizens of the United States and domestic corporations deriving income from sources within a possession of the United States.**—(a) *Definitions.*—(1) As used in section 931 and this section, the term "possession of the United States" includes American Samoa, Guam, Johnston Island, Midway Islands, the Panama Canal Zone, Puerto Rico, and Wake Island. However, the term does not include (i) the Virgin Islands and (ii), when used with respect to citizens of the United States, the term does not include Puerto Rico or, in the case of taxable years beginning after December 31, 1972, Guam.

(2) As used in section 931 and this section, the term "United States" includes only the States, the Territories of Alaska and Hawaii, and the District of Columbia.

(b) *General rule*—(1) *Qualifications.* In the case of a citizen of the United States or a domestic corporation satisfying the following conditions, gross income means only gross income from sources within the United States—

(i) If 80 percent or more of the gross income of such citizen or domestic corporation (computed without the benefit of section 931) for the 3-year period immediately preceding the close of the taxable year (or for such part of such period immediately preceding the close of such taxable year as may be applicable) was derived from sources within a possession of the United States, and

(ii) If 50 percent or more of the gross income of such citizen or domestic corporation (computed without the benefit of section 931) for such period or such part thereof was derived from the active conduct of a trade or business within a possession of the United States. In the case of a citizen, the trade or business may be conducted on his own account or as an employee or agent of another. The salary or other compensation paid by the United States to the members of its civil, military, or naval personnel for services rendered within a possession of the United States represents income derived from the active conduct of a trade or business within a possession of the United States. The salary or other compensation paid for services performed by a citizen of the United States as an employee of the United States or any agency thereof shall, for the purposes of section 931 and this section, be deemed to be derived from sources within the United States. Dividends received by a citizen from a corporation whose income was derived from the active conduct of a business within a possession of the United States, does not represent income derived from the active conduct of a trade or business within the possession of the United States even though such citizen was actively engaged in the management of such corporation. For a determination of income from sources within the United States, see part I (section 861 and following), subchapter N, chapter 1 of the Code, and section 931(i), and the regulations thereunder.

(2) *Relationship of sections 931 and 911.* A citizen of the United States who cannot meet the 80-percent and the 50-percent requirements of section 931 but who receives earned income from sources within a possession of the United States, is not deprived of the benefits of the provisions of section 911 (relating to the exemption of earned income from sources outside the United States), provided he meets the requirements thereof. In such a case none of the provisions of section 931 is applicable in determining the citizen's tax liability. For what constitutes earned income, see section 911(b).

(3) *Meaning of "gross income" on joint return.* In the case of a husband and wife making a joint return, the term "gross income," as used in this section, means the combined gross income of the spouses.

(4) *Returns.* A citizen entitled to the benefits of section 931 is required to file with his individual return Form 1040 the schedule on Form 1040E. If a citizen entitled to the benefits of section 931 has no income from sources within the

Reg. § 1.931-1(b)(4)

United States and does not receive within the United States any income derived from sources without the United States he is not required to file a return or the schedule on Form 1040E.

(5) *Illustration of the operation of section 931.* This section may be illustrated by the following example:

Example. On July 1, 1954, A, who is a citizen of the United States, went to a possession of the United States and established a business there which he actively conducted during the remainder of that year. His gross income from the business during such period was $20,000. In addition, he made a profit of $12,000 from the sale during the latter part of 1954 of some real estate located in such possession and not connected with his trade or business. In the first six months of 1954 he also derived $8,000 gross income from rental property located in the United States. He derived a like amount of gross income from such property during the last six months of 1954. On these facts, A may exclude the $32,000 derived from sources within the possession of the United States, since he qualified under section 931 with respect to that amount. The period of July 1, 1954, through December 31, 1954, constitutes the applicable part of the 3-year period immediately preceding the close of the taxable year (the calendar year 1954), and for that period, 80 percent of A's gross income was derived from sources within a possession of the United States ($32,000, or 80 percent of $40,000) and 50 percent or more of A's gross income was derived from the active conduct of a trade or business within a possession of the United States ($20,000, or 50 percent of $40,000). A is required to report on his return for 1954 only the gross income derived by him from sources within the United States ($16,000 from the rental property located in the United States).

(c) *Amounts received in United States.* Notwithstanding the provisions of section 931(a), there shall be included in the gross income of citizens and domestic corporations therein specified all amounts, whether derived from sources within or without the United States, which are received by such citizens or corporations within the United States. From the amounts so included in gross income there shall be deducted only the expenses properly apportioned or allocated thereto. For instance, if in the example set forth in paragraph (b)(5) of this section the taxpayer during the latter part of 1954 returned to the United States for a few weeks and while there received the proceeds resulting from the sale of the real estate located in the possession, the profits derived from such transaction should be reported in gross income. Such receipt in the United States, however, would not deprive the taxpayer of the benefits of section 931 with respect to other items of gross income excluded by that section.

(d) *Deductions*—(1) *Individuals.* In the case of a citizen entitled to the benefits of section 931, the deductions allowed in computing taxable income, except the standard deduction and a deduction for one personal exemption (see sections 142(b)(2) and 931(e), respectively), are allowed only if and to the extent that they are connected with income from sources within the United States. The provisions of section 873 and the regulations thereunder, relating to the allowance to nonresident alien individuals, who at any time within the taxable year were engaged in trade or business within the United States, of the deductions provided in section 165(c)(2) and (3) for losses not connected with the trade or business, are applicable in the case of citizens entitled to the benefits of section 931. The provisions of section 873(c) and the regulations thereunder pertaining to the allowance to such nonresident alien individuals of deductions for contributions provided in section 170 are also applied in the case of such citizens.

(2) *Corporations.* Corporations entitled to the benefits of section 931 are allowed the same deductions from their gross income arising from sources within the United States as are allowed to domestic corporations to the extent that such deductions are connected with such gross income, except that the so-called charitable contribution deduction provided by section 170 to corporations is allowed whether or not connected with income from sources within the United States. The proper apportionment and allocation of the deductions with respect to sources within and without the United States shall be determined as provided in part I (section 861 and following), subchapter N, chapter 1 of the Code, and the regulations thereunder.

(e) *Deduction for personal exemption.* A citizen of the United States entitled to the benefits of section 931 is allowed a deduction for only one exemption under section 151.

(f) *Allowance of deductions and credits.* Unless a citizen of the United States or a domestic corporation entitled to the benefits of section 931 shall file or cause to be filed with the district director a true and accurate return of total income from all sources within the United States, in the manner prescribed in subtitle F of the Code, the tax shall be collected on the basis of the gross income (not the taxable income) from sources within the United States. If such citizen or corporation fails to file a necessary income tax return, the Commissioner will cause a return to be made, including

Reg. § 1.931-1(b)(5)

therein all income from sources within the United States and allowing no deductions or credits (except credit for tax withheld at source).

(g) *Foreign tax credit.* Persons entitled to the benefits of section 931 are not allowed the credits provided for in section 901 (relating to credits for taxes of foreign countries and possessions).

(h) *Internees.* If a citizen of the United States—

(1) Was interned by the enemy while serving as an employee within a possession of the United States; and

(2) Was confined in any place not within a possession of the United States, then

(i) Such place of confinement shall be considered as within a possession of the United States for the purposes of section 931; and

(ii) Section 931(b) shall not apply to any compensation received within the United States by such citizen attributable to the period of time during which such citizen was interned by the enemy.

(i) *Employees of the United States.* For the purposes of section 931, amounts paid for services performed by a citizen of the United States as an employee of the United States or any agency thereof shall be deemed to be derived from sources within the United States.

(j) *Nonapplication to a DISC or shareholder thereof.* Section 931 does not apply to a corporation for a taxable year (1) for which it qualifies (or is treated) as a DISC or (2) during which it owns directly or indirectly at any time stock in a corporation which, at such time, is (or is treated as) a DISC or former DISC. (See section 992(a)(1) and (3), respectively, for the definitions of the terms "DISC" and "former DISC".) For example, assume X Corporation and Y Corporation have the same taxable years. On the first day of its taxable year, X owns and sells all of the stock in Y. Y on such day owns and sells all of the stock in Z Corporation, and Z qualifies as a DISC as of such day. Section 931 will not apply to X and Y for their taxable years. Section 931 will likewise not apply to Z for the taxable year for which it qualifies as a DISC. [Reg. § 1.931-1.]

☐ [T.D. 6249, 8-21-57. Amended by T.D. 7283, 8-2-73 and T.D. 7385, 10-28-75.]

[Reg. § 1.932-1]

§ 1.932-1. **Status of citizens of United States possessions.**—(a) *General rule*—(1) *Definition and treatment.* A citizen of a possession of the United States (except Puerto Rico and, for taxable years beginning after December 31, 1972, Guam), who is not otherwise a citizen or resident of the United States, including only the States and the District of Columbia, is treated for the purpose of the taxes imposed by subtitle A of the Code (relating to income taxes) as if he were a nonresident alien individual. However, for purposes of the tax imposed on self-employment income by chapter 2 of the Code, the term "possession of the United States" as used in section 932 and the preceding sentence does not include American Samoa, Guam, or the Virgin Islands. See section 1402(a)(9). See subpart A (section 871 and following), part II, subchapter N, chapter 1 of the Code, and the regulations thereunder, for rules relating to imposition of tax on nonresident alien individuals. For Federal income tax purposes, a citizen of a possession of the United States who is not otherwise a citizen of the United States is a citizen of a possession of the United States who has not become a citizen of the United States by naturalization in a State, Territory, or the District of Columbia. The fixed or determinable annual or periodical income from sources within the United States of a citizen of a possession of the United States who is treated as if he were a nonresident alien individual is subject to withholding. See section 1441.

(2) *Classification of citizens of United States possessions.* For the purpose of this section citizens of the possessions of the United States who are not otherwise citizens of the United States are divided into two classes: (i) Citizens of possessions of the United States who at any time within the taxable year are not engaged in trade or business within the United States, and (ii) citizens of possessions of the United States who at any time within the taxable year are engaged in trade or business within the United States. The provisions of subpart A (section 871 and following) and the regulations thereunder, applicable to nonresident alien individuals not engaged in trade or business within the United States are applicable to the citizens of possessions falling within the first class, while the provisions of such sections applicable to nonresident alien individuals who at any time within the taxable year are engaged in trade or business within the United States are applicable to citizens of possessions falling within the second class.

(b) *Nonapplication to citizen of Puerto Rico or Guam.* The provisions of section 932(a) and paragraph (a) of this section do not apply in the case of a citizen of Puerto Rico or, for taxable years beginning after December 31, 1972, a citizen of Guam. Thus, for example, any such citizen who is not a resident of the United States will not be treated by the United States as a nonresident alien individual for purposes of section 2(b)(3)(A) or (d), relating to definitions and special rules;

Reg. § 1.932-1(b)

section 4(d)(1), relating to taxpayers not eligible to use the optional tax tables; section 37(h), relating to denial of retirement income credit; section 116(d), relating to taxpayers ineligible for dividend exclusion; section 142(b)(1), relating to taxpayers ineligible for standard deduction; section 152(b)(3), relating to definition of "dependent"; section 402(a)(4), relating to distributions by the United States to nonresident aliens; section 545(d), relating to certain foreign corporations; section 565(e), relating to certain consent dividends; section 861(a)(1), relating to interest from sources within the United States; sections 871 to 877, relating to nonresident alien individuals; section 1303(b), relating to individuals not eligible for income averaging; section 1371(a)(3), relating to definition of small business corporation; section 1402(b), relating to definition of "self-employment income"; section 1441, relating to withholding of tax on nonresident aliens; section 3401(a), relating to definition of wages; section 6013(a)(1), relating to inability to make a joint return; section 6015(b) and (i), relating to declaration of estimated income tax by nonresident alien individuals; section 6017, relating to self-employment tax returns; section 6042(b)(2), relating to returns regarding payments of dividends; section 6049(b)(2), relating to returns regarding payments of interest; section 6072(c), relating to time for filing returns of nonresident alien individuals; section 6091(b), relating to place for filing returns of nonresident aliens; and section 6096(a), relating to designation of tax payments to Presidential Election Campaign Fund. For other rules applicable to citizens of Puerto Rico, see §§ 1.1-1(b) and 1.933-1. For other rules applicable to citizens of Guam, see §§ 1.1-1(b) and 1.935-1 of this chapter (Income Tax Regulations) and § 301.7654-1 of this chapter (Regulations on Procedure and Administration). [Reg. § 1.932-1.]

☐ [T.D. 6249, 8-21-57. Amended by T.D. 6462, 5-5-60, T.D. 7332, 12-20-74 and T.D. 7385, 10-28-75.]

[Reg. § 1.933-1]

§ 1.933-1. Exclusion of certain income from sources within Puerto Rico.—(a) *General rule.* An individual (whether a United States citizen or an alien), who is a bona fide resident of Puerto Rico during the entire taxable year, shall exclude from his gross income the income derived from sources within Puerto Rico, except amounts received for services performed as an employee of the United States or any agency thereof. Whether the individual is a bona fide resident of Puerto Rico shall be determined in general by applying to the facts and circumstances in each case the principles of §§ 1.871-2, 1.871-3, 1.871-4, and 1.871-5, relating to what constitutes residence or nonresidence, as the case may be, in the United States in the case of an alien individual. Once bona fide residence in Puerto Rico has been established, temporary absence therefrom in the United States or elsewhere on vacation or business trips will not necessarily deprive an individual of his status as a bona fide resident of Puerto Rico. An individual taking up residence in Puerto Rico during the course of the taxable year is not entitled for such year to the exclusion provided in section 933.

(b) *Taxable year of change of residence from Puerto Rico.* A citizen of the United States who changes his residence from Puerto Rico after having been a bona fide resident thereof for a period of at least two years immediately preceding the date of such change in residence shall exclude from his gross income the income derived from sources within Puerto Rico which is attributable to that part of such period of Puerto Rican residence which preceded the date of such change in residence, except amounts received for services performed as an employee of the United States or any agency thereof.

(c) *Deductions.* In any case in which any amount otherwise constituting gross income is excluded from gross income under the provisions of section 933, there shall not be allowed as a deduction from gross income any items of expenses or losses or other deductions (except the deduction under section 151, relating to personal exemptions) properly allocable to, or chargeable against, the amounts so excluded from gross income. [Reg. § 1.933-1.]

☐ [T.D. 6249, 8-21-57.]

[Reg. § 1.934-1]

§ 1.934-1. Limitation on reduction in income tax liability incurred to the Virgin Islands.—(a) *General rule.* Section 934(a) provides that tax liability incurred to the Virgin Islands shall not be reduced or remitted in any way, directly or indirectly, whether by grant, subsidy, or other similar payment, by any law enacted in the Virgin Islands, except to the extent provided in section 934(b) or (c). For purposes of the preceding sentence, the term "tax liability" means the liability incurred to the Virgin Islands pursuant to subtitle A of the Code, as made applicable in the Virgin Islands by the Act of July 12, 1921 (48 U.S.C. 1397), or pursuant to section 28(a) of the Revised Organic Act of the Virgin Islands (48 U.S.C. 1642).

(b) *Exception for certain domestic and Virgin Islands corporations*—(1) *General rule.* Section 934(b) provides an exception to the application of

Reg. § 1.933-1(a)

Income from Sources Without the United States

section 934(a). Under this exception, section 934(a) does not apply with respect to tax liability incurred to the Virgin Islands by a domestic or Virgin Islands corporation for any taxable year (or for such part of such year as may be applicable) to the extent that such tax liability is attributable to income derived from sources without the United States, if such corporation satisfies the conditions provided in section 934(b)(1) and (2), and if the information required by section 934(d) is supplied. These conditions are enumerated in the remainder of this paragraph, and the information requirement is set forth in paragraph (d) of this section.

(2) *Conditions to be satisfied for exception.* A domestic or Virgin Islands corporation satisfies the conditions of section 934(b)(1) and (2) if—

(i) Eighty percent or more of the gross income of such corporation for the 3-year period immediately preceding the close of the taxable year (or for such part of such period immediately preceding the close of such taxable year as may be applicable) was derived from sources within the Virgin Islands; and

(ii) Fifty percent or more of the gross income of such corporation for such period (or such part thereof) was derived from the active conduct of a trade or business within the Virgin Islands.

(3) *Computation rule.* Except as provided in subparagraph (5) of this paragraph, tax liability incurred to the Virgin Islands by a domestic or Virgin Islands corporation for the taxable year (or such part of such year as may be applicable) attributable to income derived from sources without the United States shall be computed as follows:

(i) Add to the income tax liability incurred to the Virgin Islands any credit against the tax allowed under section 901(a);

(ii) Multiply by taxable income from sources without the United States for the applicable period;

(iii) Divide by total taxable income for the period;

(iv) Subtract any credit against the tax allowed under section 901(a).

Tax liability incurred to the Virgin Islands attributable to income derived from sources without the United States, as cattributable to income derived from sources without the United States, as computed in this subparagraph, however, shall not exceed the total amount of income tax liability actually incurred.

(4) *Examples.* The rule of the preceding subparagraph may be illustrated by the following examples:

Example (1). Corporation X, which satisfies the requirements of section 934(b), incurs an income tax liability to the Virgin Islands for taxable year 1963 of $290 as follows:

Taxable income from sources within the U.S.	$ 200
Taxable income from sources without the U.S.	800
Total taxable income	$ 1,000
Credit allowed under section 901(a)	10
Tax liability incurred to the Virgin Islands	290

The income tax liability incurred to the Virgin Islands attributable to income derived from sources without the United States is $230, computed as follows:

(i) Tax liability incurred to the Virgin Islands	$ 290	
Plus credit allowed under section 901(a)	10	
		$ 300
(ii) Multiply by taxable income from sources without the U.S.	800	
		240,000
(iii) Divide by total taxable income	1,000	
		240
(iv) Subtract credit allowed under section 901(a)	10	
		230

Example (2). Corporation Y, which satisfies the requirements of section 934(b), incurs an income tax liability to the Virgin Islands for taxable year 1963 of $140, as follows:

Reg. § 1.934-1(b)(4)

49,110 Income from Sources Without the United States

See p. 20,601 for regulations not amended to reflect law changes

Taxable income from sources within the U.S.	($300 net loss)	
Taxable income from sources without the U.S.	800	
Total taxable income		$ 500
Credit allowed under section 901(a)		10
Tax liability incurred to the Virgin Islands		140

The income tax liability incurred to the Virgin Islands attributable to income derived from sources without the United States is $140, computed as follows:

(i) Tax liability incurred to the Virgin Islands	$ 140	
Plus credit allowed under section 901(a)	10	
		$ 150
(ii) Multiply by taxable income from sources without the U.S.	800	
		120,000
(iii) Divide by total taxable income	500	
		240
(iv) Subtract credit allowed under section 901(a)	10	
		230

Since the $230 derived from the computation is in excess of the actual tax liability incurred, the income tax liability incurred to the Virgin Islands attributable to income derived from sources without the United States is limited to $140, the actual liability incurred.

(5) *Special computation rule for certain domestic corporations.* For purposes of section 934(b) and this paragraph, tax liability incurred to the Virgin Islands by a domestic corporation which is required to file an income tax return with the United States for the taxable year (or such part of such year as may be applicable) attributable to income derived from sources without the United States shall be the actual income tax liability incurred to the Virgin Islands for such year.

(6) *Source of income.* For purposes of section 934(b) and this paragraph, the income of a Virgin Islands corporation, and the sources from which the income of such corporation is derived, shall be determined as if such corporation were a domestic corporation. However, all amounts received by a corporation within the United States, whether derived from sources within or without the United States, shall be considered as being derived from sources within the United States. In determining the sources from which the income of a domestic or Virgin Islands corporation is derived, the principles of part 1 (section 861 and following), subchapter N, chapter 1 of the Code, and the regulations thereunder shall apply.

(c) *Exception for certain residents of the Virgin Islands*—(1) *General rule.* Section 934(c) provides another exception to the application of section 934(a). Under this exception, section 934(a) does not apply with respect to the tax liability incurred by an individual citizen of the United States to the Virgin Islands for any taxable year to the extent that such tax liability is attributable to income derived from sources within the Virgin Islands, if such individual is a bona fide resident of the Virgin Islands during the entire taxable year and if he supplies the information required under section 934(d).

(2) *Definition—bona fide resident and United States citizen.* In determining whether a United States citizen is a bona fide resident of the Virgin Islands, the principles of §§ 1.871-2, 1.871-3, 1.871-4, and 1.871-5, relating to the determination of residence and nonresidence in the United States, shall apply. Once a bona fide residence in the Virgin Islands is established by an individual, temporary absence therefrom will not necessarily deprive such individual of his status as a bona fide resident of the Virgin Islands. For purposes of section 934(c), a citizen of the United States includes any individual who is a citizen of the United States by reason of being a citizen of any possession of the United States.

(3) *Computation rule.* For purposes of section 934(c) and this paragraph, tax liability incurred to the Virgin Islands for the taxable year attributable to income derived from sources within the Virgin Islands shall be computed as follows:

(i) Add to the income tax liability incurred to the Virgin Islands any credit against the tax allowed under section 901(a);

(ii) Multiply by taxable income from sources within the Virgin Islands;

(iii) Divide by total taxable income.

Reg. § 1.934-1(b)(5)

Income from Sources Without the United States

Tax liability incurred to the Virgin Islands attributable to income derived from sources within the Virgin Islands, as computed in this subparagraph, however, shall not exceed the total amount of income tax liability actually incurred.

(4) *Examples.* The rule of the preceding subparagraph may be illustrated by the following examples:

Example (1). A, an individual who satisfies the requirements of section 934(c), incurs an income tax liability to the Virgin Islands for taxable year 1963 of $380, as follows:

Taxable income from sources within the Virgin Islands	$1,200
Taxable income from sources without the Virgin Islands	800
Taxable income	$2,000
Credit allowed under section 901(a)	20
Tax liability incurred to the Virgin Islands	380

The income tax liability incurred to the Virgin Islands attributable to income derived from sources within the Virgin Islands is $240, computed as follows:

(i) Tax liability incurred to the Virgin Islands	$ 380
plus credit allowed under section 901(a)	20
	$400
(ii) Multiply by taxable income from sources within the Virgin Islands	1,200
	480,000
(iii) Divide by total taxable income	2,000
	240

Example (2). B, an individual who satisfies the requirements of section 934(c), incurs an income tax liability to the Virgin Islands for taxable year 1963 of $100, as follows:

Taxable income from sources within the Virgin Islands	$800
Taxable income from sources without the Virgin Islands	($200 net loss)
Total taxable income	$600
Credit allowed under section 901(a)	20
Tax liability incurred to the Virgin Islands	100

The income tax liability incurred to the Virgin Islands attributable to income derived from sources within the Virgin Islands is $100, computed as follows:

(i) Tax liability incurred to the Virgin Islands	$100
Plus credit allowed under section 901(a)	20
	$ 120
(ii) Multiply by taxable income from sources within the Virgin Islands	800
	96,000
(iii) Divide by total taxable income	600
	160

Since the $160 derived from the computation is in excess of the actual tax liability incurred, the income tax liability incurred to the Virgin Islands attributable to income derived from sources within the Virgin Islands is limited to $100, the actual liability incurred.

(5) *Source of income.* For purposes of section 934(c) and this paragraph, in determining taxable income from sources within and without the Virgin Islands the principles of part 1 (section 861 and following), subchapter N, chapter 1 of the Code, and the regulations thereunder shall apply, except that—

(i) Any deductions for personal exemptions allowable under section 151 shall be deducted in computing taxable income from sources within the

Reg. § 1.934-1(c)(5)

Virgin Islands but shall not be deducted in computing taxable income from sources without the Virgin Islands;

(ii) Amounts received for services performed as an employee of the United States or any agency thereof shall not be considered as income derived from sources within the Virgin Islands; and

(iii) Gain or loss from the sale or exchange of any security (as defined in section 165(g)(2)) shall not be treated as derived from sources within the Virgin Islands.

(6) *Definition—"taxable income" on a joint return.* In the case of a husband and wife making a joint return, the term "taxable income", as used in this paragraph, means the combined taxable income of both spouses.

(d) *Information required.* Section 934(d) provides that the exceptions in section 934(b) and (c) shall apply only in the case of persons who supply such information as the Secretary or his delegate may by regulations prescribe for purposes of determining the applicability of such exceptions. The following portions of this paragraph, together with paragraphs (e) and (f) of this section, prescribe the information which must be filed. Any person seeking to come within an exception must provide the following information:

(1) The name and address of such person;

(2) If such person is one of two or more organizations, trades, or businesses (whether or not incorporated, whether or not organized in the United States, and whether or not affiliated) owned or controlled directly or indirectly by the same interests within the meaning of section 482 and the regulations thereunder—

(i) The name and address of each such organization, trade, or business;

(ii) The relationship which each such organization, trade, or business bears to the other organizations, trades, or businesses in such group; and

(iii) The nature of the activity or activities conducted by each such organization, trade, or business.

(3) Any person seeking to come within an exception must make available for inspection by the Director of International Operations such records, and underlying contracts and documents, as are necessary to determine the applicability of section 934(b) or (c).

(e) *Information required—corporations.* Corporations seeking to come within the exception provided in section 934(b) shall, in addition to the information required by paragraph (d) of this section, submit the following information with respect to each taxable year:

(1) The date and place of incorporation;

(2) The name and address of any shareholder of record owning at any time during the taxable year 5 percent or more of the voting stock of any class or 5 percent or more of the value of any class of outstanding stock, and the nature and amount of the stock owned; and

(3) For the 3-year period immediately preceding the close of the corporation's taxable year (or for such part of such period immediately preceding the close of such taxable year as may be applicable)—

(i) The total amount of its gross income;

(ii) The amount of such gross income derived from the active conduct of a trade or business within the Virgin Islands;

(iii) The amount of such gross income from sources within (a) the Virgin Islands, (b) the United States (including therein and specifically itemizing all amounts received within the United States), and (c) all other countries as a group;

(iv) The ratio which gross income derived from sources within the Virgin Islands bears to total gross income;

(v) The ratio which gross income derived from the active conduct of a trade or business within the Virgin Islands bears to total gross income.

(f) *Information required—individuals.* Individuals seeking to come within the exception provided in section 934(c) shall, in addition to the information required by paragraph (d) of this section, submit the following information with respect to each taxable year:

(1) The date on which such individual became a bona fide resident of the Virgin Islands;

(2) If such individual maintains a place of abode for himself or his family in the United States or elsewhere outside the Virgin Islands, the location of such place of abode and the purpose for which such place is maintained;

(3) The beginning and the ending dates of each period of absence from the Virgin Islands during such taxable year;

(4) The amount of gross income for such taxable year from sources within the Virgin Islands, excluding—

(i) The amount of gain or loss from the sale or exchange of any security, as defined in Section 165(g)(2);

(ii) The amount of gross income received for services performed as an employee of the United States or any agency thereof;

Reg. § 1.934-1(c)(6)

(5) Any amounts excluded from gross income from sources within the Virgin Islands under subparagraphs (4)(i) and (ii) of this paragraph.

(g) *Time and place for filing statement.* The statement, in duplicate, providing the information required under section 934(d) and paragraphs (d), (e), and (f) of this section shall be attached to the income tax return filed with the Government of the Virgin Islands for the taxable year with respect to which an exception is claimed under section 934(b) or (c). If an exception is claimed with respect to any taxable year for which the time prescribed by law for filing the return expires prior to 30 days from the publication of these regulations, the required statement must be filed in duplicate on or before 90 days from the publication of these regulations. The return and statement must be available for examination by the Director of International Operations.

(h) *Effective date.* The provisions of this section shall apply to taxable years beginning after December 31, 1959. [Reg. § 1.934-1.]

☐ [T.D. 6629, 12-27-62.]

[Reg. § 1.935-1]

§ 1.935-1. Coordination of U.S. and Guam individual income taxes.—(a) *Application of section*—(1) *Scope.* Section 935 and this section set forth the special rules relating to the filing of income tax returns, income tax liabilities, and estimated income tax of individuals described in subparagraph (2) of this paragraph. For additional rules relating to the collection of income tax at source on the wages of certain individuals, the furnishing of certain information with the returns of certain individuals, and the covering over to the treasury of Guam of net collections of income taxes imposed on certain individuals, see section 7654 and § 301.7654-1 of this chapter (Regulations on Procedure and Administration).

(2) *Individuals covered.* This section shall apply for a taxable year to any individual who—

(i) Is a resident of Guam, whether or not he is a citizen of the United States,

(ii) Is a citizen of Guam but not otherwise a citizen of the United States,

(iii) Has income derived from Guam for the taxable year and is a citizen or a resident of the United States, or

(iv) Files a joint return for the taxable year with any individual described in subdivision (i), (ii), or (iii) of this subparagraph.

(3) *Determination of residence and citizenship.* For purposes of this section, determinations of residence and citizenship for a taxable year shall be made (except as provided to the contrary in paragraph (d)(1) and (2) of this section) as of the close of the taxable year. A citizen of the United States is any individual who is a citizen within the meaning of paragraph (c) of § 1.1-1, except that the term does not include an individual who is a citizen of Guam but not otherwise a citizen of the United States. An individual who is a citizen of Guam but not otherwise a citizen of the United States is any individual who has become a citizen of the United States by birth or naturalization in Guam. Whether an individual is a resident of Guam or a resident of the United States shall generally be determined by applying to the facts and circumstances in each case the principles of §§ 1.871-2 through 1.871-5 relating to what constitutes residence or nonresidence, as the case may be, in the United States in the case of an alien individual. However, for special rules for determining the residence for tax purposes of individuals under military or naval orders, see section 514 of the Soldiers' and Sailors' Civil Relief Act of 1940, 50 App. U.S.C. 574. The residence of an individual, and, therefore, the jurisdiction with which he is required to file an income tax return under paragraph (b) of this section, may change from year to year.

(b) *Filing requirement*—(1) *Tax Jurisdiction.* An individual described in paragraph (a)(2) of this section shall file his return of income tax for the taxable year—

(i) With the United States if he is a resident of the United States, whether or not he is a citizen of the United States,

(ii) With Guam if he is a resident of Guam, whether or not he is a citizen of Guam, or

(iii) If neither subdivision (i) nor (ii) of this subparagraph applies,

(A) With Guam if he is a citizen of Guam but not otherwise a citizen of the United States, as defined in paragraph (a)(3) of this section, or

(B) With the United States if he is a citizen of the United States, as defined in paragraph (a)(3) of this section.

Thus, for example, if a U.S. citizen employed by the United States in Guam becomes a resident of Guam for the taxable year, he must file his return of income tax for such year with Guam. The tax shown on the return shall be paid to the jurisdiction with which such return is required to be filed and shall be determined by taking into account any credit under section 31 for tax withheld by Guam or the United States on wages, any credit under section 6402(b) for an overpayment of income tax to Guam or the United States, and any payments under section 6315 of estimated income

Reg. § 1.935-1(b)(1)

49,114 Income from Sources Without the United States
See p. 20,601 for regulations not amended to reflect law changes

tax paid to Guam or the United States. See paragraph (a)(3) of this section for the rule that determinations of residence and citizenship are to be made as of the close of the taxable year.

(2) *Joint returns.* In the case of married persons, if one or both spouses is an individual described in paragraph (a)(2) of this section and they file a joint return of income tax, the spouses shall file their joint return with, and pay the tax due on such return to, the jurisdiction where the spouse who has the greater adjusted gross income for the taxable year would be required under subparagraph (1) of this paragraph to file his return if separate returns were filed. For this purpose, adjusted gross income of each spouse is determined under section 62 and the regulations thereunder but without regard to community property laws; and, if one of the spouses dies, the taxable year of the surviving spouse shall be treated as ending on the date of such death.

(3) *Place for filing returns*—(i) *U.S. returns.* A return required under this paragraph to be filed with the United States shall be filed in accordance with § 1.6091-2, except that such return of a citizen or resident of the United States who is described in § 301.7654-1(a)(2) of this chapter (Regulations on Procedure and Administration) shall be filed with the Internal Revenue Service Center, 11601 Roosevelt Boulevard, Philadelphia, Pennsylvania 19155.

(ii) *Guam returns.* A return required under this paragraph to be filed with Guam shall be filed with the Commissioner of Revenue and Taxation, Agana, Guam 96910.

(4) *Tax accounting standards.* A taxpayer who has filed his return with one of the jurisdictions named in subparagraph (1) of this paragraph for a prior taxable year and is required to file his return for a later taxable year with the other such jurisdiction may not, for such later taxable year, change his accounting period, method of accounting, or any election to which he is bound with respect to his reporting of taxable income to the first jurisdiction unless he obtains the consent of the second jurisdiction to make such change. However, such change will not be effective for returns filed thereafter with the first jurisdiction unless before such later date of filing he also obtains consent of the first jurisdiction to make such change. Any request for consent to make a change pursuant to this subparagraph must be made to the office where the return is required to be filed under subparagraph (3) of this paragraph and in sufficient time to permit a copy of the consent to be attached to the return for the taxable year.

(c) *Extent of liability for income tax*—(1) *Extension of territory*—(i) *General rule.* With respect to an individual who, for a taxable year, is described in paragraph (a)(2) of this section—

(A) For purposes of so much of the Internal Revenue Code of 1954 as relates to the normal taxes and surtaxes imposed by chapter 1 thereof, the United States shall be treated, in a geographical and governmental sense, as including Guam, and

(B) For purposes of the Guam Territorial income tax (48 U.S.C. 1421 i), Guam shall be treated, in a geographical and governmental sense, as including the United States except that this subdivision shall not apply for purposes of this section, section 7651, and section 7654.

(ii) *Application of general rule.* (A) The significance of the application of the rule of subdivision (i) of this subparagraph will depend upon the facts and circumstances of the particular case. The rule will not be applied where its application would be manifestly inapplicable or incompatible with the intent thereof. Thus, the rule will not be applied for purposes of section 3401, relating to definition of wages. Also, the rule will not be applied in determining the sources of dividends and interest from a domestic corporation. For example, if less than 20 percent of a domestic corporation's gross income is from U.S. sources for the period described in section 861(a)(1)(B) and (2)(A), but more than 20 percent of its gross income is from U.S. and Guam sources taken together for such period, the dividends and interest derived from it will be treated as derived from sources without the United States. In addition, for purposes of section 1372(e)(4), relating to whether an election of a small business corporation has been terminated because it derived more than 80 percent of its gross receipts from sources outside the United States, gross receipts from sources within Guam will be treated as gross receipts from sources outside the United States. On the other hand, some of the conclusions which may be reached as a result of the application of subdivision (i) of this subparagraph to a U.S. taxpayer (that is, an individual described in paragraph (b)(1)(i) or (iii)(B) of this section) are as follows. A U.S. taxpayer may not claim a foreign tax credit based upon his income from sources within Guam. Income tax paid to Guam may be taken into account under section 31, 6315, and 6402(b) as payments to the United States. For purposes of section 116(a), relating to the partial exclusion of dividends received by individuals, dividends paid to a U.S. taxpayer by a corporation created or organized in Guam or under tha law of Guam will be treated as dividends paid by a domestic corpo-

Reg. § 1.935-1(b)(2)

ration. Taxes paid to Guam and otherwise satisfying the requirements of section 164(a) will be allowed as a deduction under that section, but income taxes paid to Guam will be disallowed as a deduction under section 275(a).

(B) If a U.S. taxpayer has a net operating loss carryback or carryover under section 172, a foreign tax credit carryback or carryover under section 904, an investment credit carryback or carryover under section 46, a capital loss carryover under section 1212, or a charitable contributions carryover under section 170, the United States will take such carryback or carryover into account for a taxable year for which the taxpayer's return is required to be filed with the United States, and make a refund to the extent required under section 6402, even though the return of the taxpayer for the taxable year (whether beginning on, before, or after December 31, 1972) giving rise to the carryback or carryover was required to be filed with Guam.

(C) For purposes of income averaging of a U.S. taxpayer under sections 1301 through 1305, the taxpayer will not be denied status as an "eligible individual" merely because he was during the base period defined in section 1302(c)(2) treated under section 932 as a nonresident alien individual because he was a citizen of Guam but not otherwise a citizen of the United States. See section 1303(b). Furthermore, in determining the base period of such a U.S. taxpayer under section 1302(c)(2), taxable years for which a return was required to be filed with Guam shall be taken into account.

(D) In applying the Guam Territorial income tax the converse of the preceding rules under this subdivision will apply. Thus, for example, income tax paid to the United States may be taken into account under sections 31, 6315, and 6402(b) as payments to Guam. Moreover, a citizen of the United States (as defined in paragraph (a)(3) of this section) not a resident of Guam will not be treated as a nonresident alien individual for purposes of the Guam Territorial income tax. Thus, for example, a citizen of the United States (as so defined), or a resident of the United States, will not be treated as a nonresident alien individual for purposes of section 1371(a)(3) of the Guamanian Territorial income tax.

(2) *Liability to other jurisdiction*—(i) *Filing with Guam.* If for a taxable year an individual is required under paragraph (b)(1) of this section to file a return with Guam, he is relieved of liability to file an income tax return with, and to pay an income tax to, the United States for the taxable year.

(ii) *Filing with the United States.* If for a taxable year an individual is required under paragraph (b)(1) of this section to file a return with the United States, he is relieved of liability to file an income tax return with, and to pay an income tax to, Guam for the taxable year.

(d) *Special rules for estimated income tax*—(1) *Declaration of estimated income tax.* If, under all the facts and circumstances existing at the date an individual is required to file a declaration of estimated income tax, there is reason to believe that he will, for the taxable year, be an individual described in paragraph (a)(2) of this section, he must file his declaration of estimated income tax (and all amendments thereof) with the jurisdiction with which he would be required to file a return under paragraph (b)(1) of this section if his taxable year had closed on the date he is first required to file a declaration of estimated income tax for the taxable year. Except as provided in paragraph (6) of this section (relating to underpayments of estimated income tax), payments of estimated income tax shall be made to the jurisdiction with which he is required to file the declaration even though for the taxable year he is required under paragraph (b)(1) of this section to file his return with the other jurisdiction. In determining the amount of such estimated income tax, income tax paid to Guam may be taken into account under sections 31 and 6402(b) as payments to the United States, and vice versa. For rules relating to the determination of, and time for filing, declarations of estimated tax, see sections 6015 and 6073; for rules relating to the time for paying installments of the tax, see section 6153.

(2) *Joint declaration of estimated income tax.* In the case of married persons, if, under all the facts and circumstances existing at the date a spouse is required to file a declaration of estimated income tax, there is reason to believe that he will, for the taxable year, be an individual described in paragraph (a)(2) of this section and the spouses file a joint declaration of estimated income tax, the spouses must file their joint declaration of estimated income tax (and all amendments thereof) with the jurisdiction where the spouse who has the greater estimated adjusted gross income for the taxable year would be required under subparagraph (1) of this paragraph to file his declaration of estimated income tax if separate declarations were filed. For this purpose, estimated adjusted gross income of each spouse for the taxable year is determined without regard to community property laws. Except as provided in paragraph (6) of this section, payments of estimated income tax shall be made to the juris-

Reg. § 1.935-1(d)(2)

diction with which the spouses are required to file the joint declaration.

(3) *Early filing of declarations.* If the individual or spouses have in fact filed a declaration or joint declaration of estimated income tax earlier than the time he or they are first required to file the declaration and such declaration was not filed where it is required to be filed under paragraph (d)(1) or (2) of this section, as the case may be, of this paragraph, only subsequent amendments of the declaration are required to be filed pursuant to such paragraph (d)(1) or (2) of this section with the other jurisdiction and only subsequent installments of the estimated income tax are required to be paid to the other jurisdiction.

(4) *Place for filing declarations.* A declaration of estimated income tax required under subparagraph (1) of this paragraph to be filed with Guam, shall be filed as prescribed in paragraph (b)(3)(ii) of this section. A declaration of estimated income tax required under subparagraph (1) of this paragraph to be filed with the United States shall be filed at the place prescribed by § 1.6073-1(c).

(5) *Liability to other jurisdiction*—(i) *Filing with Guam.* If, for a taxable year, an individual is required under this paragraph to file a declaration of estimated income tax with Guam, he is relieved of liability to file a declaration of estimated income tax (and any amendments thereof) with, and to make payments of estimated income tax to, the United States for the taxable year.

(ii) *Filing with the United States.* If, for a taxable year, an individual is required under this paragraph to file a declaration of estimated income tax with the United States, he is relieved of liability to file a declaration of estimated income tax (and any amendments thereof) with, and to make payments of estimated income to, Guam for the taxable year.

(6) *Underpayments.* The liability of an individual described in paragraph (a)(2) of this section for underpayments of estimated income tax for a taxable year, as determined under section 6654 and the regulations thereunder, shall be to the jurisdiction with which he is required under paragraph (b) of this section to file his return for the taxable year.

(e) *Illustration.* The application of this section may be illustrated by the following examples:

Example (1). B, an individual, files returns on a calendar year basis. B is a resident of the United States at the time he is required to file his declaration of estimated income tax for 1974. If, under the facts and circumstances, B does not reasonably expect at the time he files his declaration of estimated income tax that he will be a resident of Guam at the close of 1974, he will not be subject to this section at the time of such filing. However, B subsequently receives Guam source income which necessitates an amendment of his declaration, and some time later in 1974 he becomes a resident of Guam for the remainder of the year. B is required under paragraph (d)(1) of this section to file his amended declaration with the United States and to make payments of the estimated tax to the United States. However, B is required to file his income tax return for 1974 with Guam and to make any underpayments of estimated tax to Guam, pursuant to paragraphs (b)(1) and (d)(6) of this section.

Example (2). C, an individual, files returns on a calendar year basis. On March 1, 1974, C is a resident of the United States, files his declaration of estimated income tax for 1974 with the United States, and pays his first installment of estimated tax to the United States. Prior to the date C would otherwise be required to file his declaration of estimated income tax for 1974 (April 15, 1974), C becomes a resident of Guam for the remainder of the year. C is required under paragraph (d)(1) of this section to make only his remaining payments of installments of estimated tax to Guam. C is also required to file his income tax return for 1974 with Guam and to make any underpayments of estimated tax to Guam, pursuant to paragraphs (b)(1) and (d)(6) of this section.

Example (3). D, an individual, files returns on a calendar year basis. On August 1, 1974, D ceases to be a resident of the United States for the year and becomes a resident of Guam for the remainder of the year. D is first required to file a declaration of estimated income tax for 1974 on September 15, 1974, because of his receipt of an extraordinary item of income after June 15, 1974. D is required under paragraph (d)(1) of this section to file his declaration with Guam and to make payments of the estimated tax to Guam. D is also required to file his income tax return for 1974 with Guam and to make any underpayments of estimated tax to Guam, pursuant to paragraphs (b)(1) and (d)(6) of this section.

(f) *Effective date.* This section shall apply for taxable years beginning after December 31, 1972. [Reg. § 1.935-1.]

☐ [*T.D.* 7385, 10-28-75.]

[Reg. § 1.936-1]

§ 1.936-1. Elections.—(a) *Making an election.* A domestic corporation shall make an election under section 936(e), for any taxable year beginning after December 31, 1975, by filing Form 5712 on or before the later of—

(1) The date on which such corporation is required, pursuant to sections 6072(b) and 6081, to file its Federal income tax return for the first taxable year for which the election is made; or

(2) April 8, 1980.

Form 5712 shall be filed with the Internal Revenue Service Center, 11601 Roosevelt Boulevard, Philadelphia, Pennsylvania 19155 (Philadelphia Center).

(b) *Revoking an election.* Any corporation to which an election under section 936(e) applies on February 8, 1980 is hereby granted the consent of the Secretary to revoke that election for the first taxable year to which the election applied. (The corporation may make a new election under § 1.936-1(a) for any subsequent taxable year.) The corporation shall make this revocation by sending to the Philadelphia Center a written statement of revocation on or before February 8, 1980. [Reg. § 1.936-1.]

☐ [T.D. 7673, 2-7-80.]

[Reg. § 7.936-1]

§ 7.936-1. Qualified possession source investment income (Temporary).—For purposes of this section, interest earned after September 30, 1976 (less applicable deductions), by a domestic corporation, engaged in the active conduct of a trade or business in Puerto Rico, which elects the application of section 936 with respect to deposits with certain Puerto Rican financial institutions will be treated as qualified possession source investment income within the meaning of section 936(d)(2) if (1) the interest qualifies for exemption from Puerto Rican income tax under regulations issued by the Secretary of the Treasury of Puerto Rico, as in effect on September 28, 1976, under the authority of section 2(j) of the Puerto Rico Industrial Incentive Act of 1963, as amended, (2) the interest is from sources within Puerto Rico (within the meaning of section 936(d)(2)(A)), and (3) the funds with respect to which the interest is earned are derived from the active conduct of a trade or business in Puerto Rico or from investment of funds so derived. [Temporary Reg. § 7.936-1.]

☐ [T.D. 7452, 12-27-76.]

[Reg. § 1.936-4]

§ 1.936-4. Intangible property income in the absence of an election out.—The rules in this section apply for purposes of section 936(h) and also for purposes of section 934(e), where applicable.

QUESTION 1: If a possessions corporation and its affiliates do not make an election under either the cost sharing or 50/50 profit split option, what rules will govern the treatment of income attributable to intangible property owned or leased by the possessions corporation?

ANSWER 1: Intangible property income will be allocated to the possessions corporation's U.S. shareholders with the proration of income based on shareholdings. If a shareholder of the possessions corporation is a foreign person or a tax-exempt person, the possessions corporation will be taxable on that shareholder's pro rata amount of the intangible property income. If any class of the stock of a possessions corporation is regularly traded on an established securities market, then the intangible property income will be taxable to the possessions corporation rather than the corporation's U.S. shareholders. For these purposes, a United States shareholder includes any shareholder who is a United States person as described under section 7701(a)(30). The term "intangible property income" means the gross income of a possessions corporation attributable to any intangible property other than intangible property which has been licensed to such corporation since prior to 1948 and which was in use by such corporation on September 3, 1982.

QUESTION 2: What is the source of the intangible property income described in question 1?

ANSWER 2: The intangible property income is U.S. source, whether taxed to U.S. shareholders or taxed to the possessions corporation. Such intangible property income, if treated as income of the possessions corporation, does not enter into the calculation of the 80-percent possessions source test or the 65-percent active trade or business test of section 936(a)(2)(A) and (B).

QUESTION 3: How will the amount of income attributable to intangible property be measured?

ANSWER 3: Income attributable to intangible property includes the amount received by a possessions corporation from the sale, exchange, or other disposition of any product or from the rendering of a service which is in excess of the reasonable costs it incurs in manufacturing the product or rendering the service (other than costs incurred in connection with intangibles) plus a reasonable profit margin. A reasonable profit margin shall be computed with respect to direct and indirect costs other than (i) costs incurred in connection with intangibles, (ii) interest expense, and (iii) the cost of materials which are subject to processing or which are components in a product manufactured by the possessions corporation. Notwithstanding the above, certain taxpayers who have been permitted by the Internal Revenue Service in taxable years beginning before January 1, 1983, to use the cost-plus method of pricing without reflecting a return from intangibles, but including the cost of materials in the cost base, will not be precluded from doing so. (Sec. 3.02(3), Rev. Proc. 63-10, 1963-1 C.B. 490.) Thus, the Internal Revenue Service may continue in appropriate cases to permit such taxpayers to continue to report their income as they have been under existing procedures described in the previous sentence if it is appropriate under all the facts and circumstances and does not distort the income of the taxpayer.

QUESTION 4: If there is no intangible property related to a product produced in whole or in part by a possessions corporation, what method may the possessions corporation use to compute its income?

ANSWER 4: The taxpayer may compute its income using the appropriate method as provided under sectio 482 and the regulations thereunder. The taxpayer may also elect the cost sharing or profit split method. [Reg. § 1.936-4.]

☐ [T.D. 8090, 6-9-86.]

[Reg. § 1.936-5]

§ 1.936-5. Intangible property income when an election out is made: Product, business presence, and contract manufacturing.—The rules in this section apply for purposes of section 936(h) and also for purposes of section 934(e), where applicable.

(a) *Definition of product.*

QUESTION 1: What does the term "product" mean?

ANSWER 1: The term "product" means an item of property which is the result of a production process. The term "product" includes component products, integrated products, and end-product forms. A component product is a product which is subject to further processing before sale to an unrelated party. A component product may be produced from other items of property, and if it is so produced, may be treated as including or not including (at the choice of the possessions corporation) one or more of such other items of property for all purposes of section 936(h)(5). An integrated product is a product which is not subject to any further processing before sale to an unrelated party and which includes all component products from which it is produced. An end-product form is a product which—

(1) Is not subject to any further processing before sale to an unrelated party;

(2) Is produced from a component product or products; and

(3) Is treated as not including certain component products for all purposes of section 936(h)(5).

A possessions corporation may treat a component product, integrated product, or end-product form as its possession product even though the final stage or stages of production occur outside the possession. Further processing includes transformation, incorporation, assembly, or packaging.

QUESTION 2: If a possessions corporation produces both a component product and an integrated product (which by definition includes the end-product form), may the possessions corporation use the options under section 936(h)(5) to compute its income with respect to either the component product, the integrated product or the end-product form?

ANSWER 2: Yes. The possessions corporation may choose to treat the component product, the integrated product, or the end-product form as the product for purposes of determining whether the possessions corporation satisfies the significant business presence test. The possessions corporation must treat the same item of property as its product (the possession product) for all purposes of section 936(h)(5) for that taxable year, including the significant business presence test under section 936(h)(5)(B)(ii), the possessions sales calculation under section 936(h)(5)(C)(i)(I), the determination of income under section 936(h)(5)(C)(i)(II), and the combined taxable income computations under section 936(h)(5)(C)(ii). Although the possessions corporation must treat the same item of property as its product for all purposes of section 936(h)(5) in a particular taxable year, its choice of the component product, integrated product or end-product form may be different from year to year. The possessions corporation must specify the possession product on a statement attached to its return (Schedule P of Form 5735). The possessions corporation may specify its choice by either listing the components that are included in the possession product or the components that are excluded from the possession product. The possessions corporation must file a separate Schedule P with respect to each possession product. The possessions corporation must attach to each Schedule P detailed computations indicating how the significant business presence test is satisfied with respect to the possession product identified in that Schedule P.

QUESTION 3: A possessions corporation produces a product that is sometimes sold to unrelated parties without further processing and is sometimes sold to unrelated parties after further processing. May the possessions corporation choose to treat the same item of property as the possession product even though in some cases it is an integrated product and in some cases it is a component product?

Reg. § 1.936-5(a)

Income from Sources Without the United States

ANSWER 3: Yes. Except as provided in questions and answers 4 and 5, the possessions corporation must designate a single possession product even though it is sometimes a component product and sometimes an integrated product.

QUESTION 4: A possessions corporation produces a product that is sometimes sold without further processing by any member of the affiliated group to unrelated parties or to related parties for their own consumption and is sometimes sold after further processing by any member of the affiliated group to unrelated parties or to related parties for their own consumption. May the possessions corporation designate two products as possession products?

ANSWER 4: The possessions corporation may designate two or more possession products. The possessions corporation must use a consistent definition of the possession product for all items of property that are sold to unrelated parties or consumed by related parties at the same stage in the production process. The significant business presence test shall apply separately to each product designated by the possessions corporation. The possessions corporation shall compute its income separately with respect to each product.

QUESTION 5: A possessions corporation produces a product in one taxable year and does not sell all of the units that it produced. In the next taxable year the possessions corporation produces a product which includes the product produced in the prior year. The possessions corporation could not have satisfied the significant business presence test with respect to the units produced the first taxable year if the larger possession product had been designated. May the possessions corporation designate two possession products in the second year?

ANSWER 5: Yes. The possessions corporation may designate two possession products. However, once a product has been designated for a particular year all sales of units produced in that year must be defined in the same manner. In addition, the taxpayer must maintain a significant business presence in a possession with respect to that product. Sales shall be deemed made first out of the current year's production. If all of the current year's production is sold and some inventory is liquidated, then the taxpayer's method of inventory accounting shall be applied to determine what year's layer of inventory is liquidated.

Example (1). A possessions corporation, S, manufactures a bulk pharmaceutical in a possession. S transfers the bulk pharmaceutical to its U.S. parent, P, for encapsulation and sale by P to customers. S satisfies the significant business presence test with respect to the bulk pharmaceutical (the component product) and the combination of the bulk pharmaceutical and the capsule (the integrated product). S may use the cost sharing or profit split method to compute its income with respect to either the component product or the integrated product.

Example (2). The facts are the same as in example (1) except that S does not satisfy the significant business presence test with respect to the integrated product. S may use the cost sharing or profit split method to compute its income only with respect to the component product. However, if in a later taxable year S satisfies the significant business presence test with respect to the integrated product, then S may use the cost sharing or profit split method to compute its income with respect to that integrated product for that later taxable year.

Example (3). P, a domestic corporation, produces in bulk form in the United States the active ingredient for a pharmaceutical product. P transfers the bulk form to S, a wholly owned possessions corporation. S uses the bulk form to produce in Puerto Rico the finished dosage form drug. S transfers the drug in finished dosage form to P, which sells the drug to unrelated customers in the U.S. The direct labor costs incurred in Puerto Rico by S during its taxable year in formulating, filling and finishing the dosage form are at least 65 percent of the total direct labor costs incurred by the affiliated group in producing the bulk and finished forms during that period. S manufactures (within the meaning of section 954(d)(1)(A)) the finished dosage form. S has elected out under section 936(h)(5) under the profit split option for the drug product area (SIC 283). P and S may treat the bulk and finished dosage forms as parts of an integrated product. Since S satisfies the significant business presence requirement with respect to the integrated product, it is entitled to 50 percent of the combined taxable income on the integrated product.

Example (4). A possessions corporation, S, produces the keyboard of an electric typewriter and incorporates the keyboard with components acquired from a related corporation into finished typewriters. S does not satisfy the significant business presence test with respect to the typewriters (the integrated product). Therefore, S may use the cost sharing or profit split method to compute its income only with respect to a component product or end-product form. For taxable year 1983, S specifies on a statement attached to its return (Schedule P of Form 5735) that the possession product is the end-product form. The statement identifies the components—for example, the keyboard structure and frame—which are included in

Reg. § 1.936-5(a)

the possession product. S's definition of the possession product will apply to all units of the electric typewriters which S produces in whole or in part in the possession and which are sold in 1983. Thus, all units of a given component incorporated into such typewriters will be treated in the same way. For example, all keyboards and all frames will be included in the possession product, and all electric drive mechanisms and rollers will be excluded from the possession product.

Example (5). Possessions corporation A produces printed circuit boards in a possession. The printed circuit boards are sold to unrelated parties. A also uses the boards to produce personal computers in the possession. A may designate two possession products: printed circuit boards and personal computers. The significant business presence test applies separately with respect to each of these products. Thus, for those printed circuit boards that are sold to unrelated parties, only the costs of the possessions corporation and the other members of the affiliated group that are incurred with respect to units of the printed circuit boards which are produced in whole or in part in the possessions and sold to third parties shall be taken into account. Conversely, with respect to personal computers, only the costs incurred with respect to the personal computers shall be taken into account. This would include the costs with respect to printed circuit boards that are incorporated into personal computers but not the costs incurred with respect to printed circuit boards that are sold without further processing to unrelated parties.

Example (6). Possessions corporation S produces integrated circuits in a possession. P, an affiliate of S, produces circuit boards in the United States. P transfers the circuit boards to S. S assembles the integrated circuits and the circuit boards. S sells some of the loaded circuit boards to third parties. S retains some of the loaded circuit boards and incorporates them into central processing units. The central processing units are then sold to third parties. S may designate two possession products. S must use a consistent definition of the possession product for all units that are sold at the same stage in the production process. Thus, with respect to those units sold after assembly of the integrated circuits and the printed circuit boards, if S cannot satisfy the significant business presence test with respect to all the loaded circuit boards (the integrated product), then S must designate a lesser product, either the integrated circuit (the component product) or the loaded circuit board less the printed circuit board (the end-product form) as its possession product. With respect to the central processing units sold the same rule would apply. Thus, if S cannot satisfy the significant business presence test with respect to the entire central processing unit for all of the central processing units sold, S must designate some lesser product as its possession product.

Example (7). S is a possessions corporation. In 1985, S produced 100 units of product X. Those units were finished into product Y in 1985 by affiliates of S. Product X is a component of product Y. In 1985, S satisfies the direct labor test with respect to product X but not with respect to product Y. S designates the component product X as its possession product. In 1986 S produces 100 units of product X and finishes those units into product Y. S would have satisfied the significant business presence test with respect to product X if S had designated product X as its possession product in 1986. In addition, in 1986 S satisfies the significant business presence test with respect to the integrated product Y. In 1986, S sells 150 units of Y. One hundred of those units would be deemed to be produced in 1986. With respect to those units S may designate the integrated product Y as its possession product. Under S's method of inventory accounting the remaining 50 units were determined to have been produced in 1985. With respect to those units S must define its possession product as it did for the taxable year in which those units were produced. Thus, S's possession product would be the component product X.

QUESTION 6: May an affiliated group establish groupings of possession products and treat the groupings as single products?

ANSWER 6: An affiliated group may establish reasonable groupings of possession products based on similarities in the production processes of the possession products. Possession products that are grouped shall be treated as a single product. The determination of whether the production processes involved in producing the products that are to be grouped are similar is based on the production processes of the components that are included in the possession product. The affiliated group may establish new groupings each year. Any grouping which materially distorts a taxpayer's income or the application of the significant business presence test may be disallowed by the Commissioner. The mere fact that a grouping results in an increased allocation of income to the possessions corporation does not, of itself, create a material distortion of income. If the Commissioner determines that the taxpayer's grouping is improper with respect to one or more products in a group, then those products shall be excluded from the group. The effect of excluding a product or products from the group is that the taxpayer must demonstrate that the group without the excluded products (and each excluded product

Reg. § 1.936-5(a)

itself) satisfies the significant business presence test. If the group without the excluded products, or any of the excluded products themselves, fails to satisfy the significant business presence test, then the possessions corporation's income from those products shall be determined under section 936(h)(1) through (4) and the regulations thereunder.

Example (1). The following are examples of possession products the processes of production of which are sufficiently similar that they may be grouped and treated as a single product:

(A) Beverage bases or concentrates for different soft drinks or soft drink syrups, regardless of whether some include sweeteners and some do not;

(B) Different styles of clothing;

(C) Different styles of shoes;

(D) Equipment which relies on gravity to deliver solutions to patients intravenously;

(E) Equipment which relies on machines to deliver solutions to patients intravenously;

(F) Video game cartridges, even though the concept and design of each game title is, in part, protected against infringement by separate copyrights;

(G) All integrated circuits;

(H) All printed circuit boards; and

(I) Hardware and software if the software is one of several alternative types of software offered by the manufacturer and sold only with the hardware, and a purchaser of the hardware would ordinarily purchase one or more of the manufacturer-provided alternative types of software. In all other cases, hardware and software may not be grouped and treated as a single product.

Groupings (D) and (E) do not include any solutions which are delivered through the equipment described therein.

Example (2). A possessions corporation produces in Puerto Rico non-programmable, interactive cathode ray tube computer terminals that vary in price. These terminals all interact with a computer or controller to perform their functions of data entry, graphics word processing, and program development. The terminals can be purchased with options that include a built-in printer, different language keyboards, specialized cathode ray tubes, and different power supply features. All terminals are produced in one integrated process requiring the same skills and operations. The differences in the production of the terminals include differences in the number of printed circuit boards incorporated in each terminal, the use of unique keyboards, and the installation and testing of the built-in printer. Some difference in direct labor time to manufacture the terminals occurs, primarily due to the differing number and complexity of printed circuit boards incorporated into each terminal. Different model numbers are assigned to various computer terminals. A grouping by the taxpayer of all of the terminals as one product will be respected by the Service, unless the Service establishes that substantial distortion results. This grouping is proper because the processes of producing each of the terminals are similar.

Example (3). A possessions corporation, S, produces several models of serial matrix impact printers and teleprinters. These products have differing performance standards based on such factors as speed (in characters per second), numbers of columns, and cost. The production process for all types of printers involves production of three basic elements: electronic circuitry, the printing head, and the mechanical parts. The process of producing all the printers is similar. Thus, all printers could be grouped and treated as a single product. S purchases electronic circuitry and mechanical parts from a U.S affiliate. S performs manufacturing functions relative to the printing head and assembles and tests the finished printers. S does not satisfy the significant business presence test with respect to the integrated products. S therefore specifies on a statement attached to its return (Schedule P of Form 5735) that the possession product for both the serial matrix printers and the teleprinters is the end-product form. The statement identifies the components which are included in each possession product. S may group and treat as a single product the serial matrix printers and the teleprinters if both end-product forms include and exclude similar components. Thus, if the end-product form for both the serial matrix printers and the teleprinters includes the mechanical parts and excludes the electronic circuitry, then S may group and treat as a single product the two end-product forms. If, however, the end-product forms for the two items of property contain components that are not similar and as a result of this definition of the end-product forms the production processes involved in producing the two end-product forms are not similar, then S may not group the end-product forms.

QUESTION 7: Is the affiliated group permitted to include in a group an item of property that is not produced in whole or in part in a possession?

ANSWER 7: No.

Example (1). Possessions corporation S produces 70 units of product A in a possession. P, an affiliate of S, produces 30 units of product A entirely in the United States. All of the units are sold to unrelated parties. The affiliated group is

Reg. § 1.936-5(a)

not permitted to group the 30 units of product A produced in the United States with the 70 units produced in the possession because those units are not produced in whole or in part in a possession.

Example (2). The facts are the same as in example (1) except that the 30 units of product A are transferred to possessions corporation S. S incorporates the 100 units of product A into product B. This incorporation takes place in the possession. S may group and treat as a single product all of the units of product B even though some of those units contain units of product A that were produced in the possession and some that were produced in the United States.

QUESTION 8: What factors should be disregarded in determining whether a particular grouping of similar items of property is reasonable?

ANSWER 8: In general, differences in the following factors will be disregarded in determining whether a particular grouping of items of property is reasonable:

(1) Differences in testing requirements (*e.g.,* some products sold for military use may require more extensive or different testing than products sold for commercial use);

(2) Differences in the product specifications that are designed to accommodate the product to its area of use or for conditions under which used (*e.g.,* electrical products designed for ultimate use in the United States differ from electrical products designed for ultimate use in Europe);

(3) Differences in packaging or labeling (*e.g.,* differences in the number of units of the items shipped in one package); and

(4) Minor differences in the operations of the items of property.

QUESTION 9: What rules apply for purposes of determining whether pharmaceutical products are properly grouped and treated as a single product?

ANSWER 9: The rules contained in questions and answers 6 through 8 of this section shall apply. Thus, an affiliated group may establish reasonable groupings based on similarities in the production processes of two or more possession products. In establishing a group the affiliated group may only compare the production processes involved in producing the possession products. The fact that two pharmaceutical products contain different active or inert ingredients is not relevant to the determination of whether the pharmaceutical products may be grouped. For example, if the possession products are bulk chemicals and the production processes involved in producing the bulk chemicals are similar, those bulk chemicals may be grouped and treated as a single product even though they contain different active or inert ingredients. The affiliated group may also group and treat as a single product the finished dosage form drug as long as the production processes involved in producing the finished dosage forms are similar. For these purposes, the production processes involved in producing the following classes of items shall be considered to be sufficiently similar that possession products delivered in a form described in one of the categories may be grouped with other possession products delivered in a form described in the same category.

The categories are:

(1) Capsules, tablets, and pills;

(2) Liquids, ointments, and creams; or

(3) Injectable and intravenous preparations.

No distinctions should be based on packaging, list numbers, or size of dosage. The affiliated group may group and treat as a single product the integrated product (combination of the bulk and the delivery form) only if all the production processes involved in producing the integrated products are similar. The rules of this question and answer are illustrated by the following examples.

Example (1). Possessions corporation S produces two chemical active ingredients X and Y. Both chemical ingredients are produced through the process of fermentation. The affiliated group is permitted to group and treat as a single product the two chemical ingredients.

Example (2). The facts are the same as in example (1) and possessions corporation S finishes chemical ingredient X into tablets and chemical ingredient Y into capsules. The affiliated group is permitted to group and treat as a single product the combination of the bulk pharmaceutical and the finishing because the production processes involved in producing the integrated products are similar.

Example (3). Possessions corporation S produces in a possession a bulk chemical, X, by fermentation. A United States affiliate, P, produces in the United States a bulk chemical, Y, by fermentation. Both bulk chemicals are finished by S in the possession. The finished dosage form of X is in pill form. The finished dosage form of Y is in injectable form. If S's possession product is the integrated product or the end-product form then S may not group X and Y because the production processes involved in producing the finished dosage forms of X and Y are not similar. If S's possession product is the component then S may not group X and Y because the bulk chemical Y is not produced in whole or in part in a possession.

QUESTION 10: Will the fact that a manufacturer of a drug must submit a New Drug Application ("NDA") or a supplemental NDA to the Food and Drug Administration have any effect on the definition or grouping of a product?

ANSWER 10: No.

QUESTION 11: A possessions corporation which produced a product or rendered a type of service in a possession on or before September 3, 1982, is not required to meet the significant business presence test in a possession with respect to such product or type of service for its taxable years beginning before January 1, 1986 (the interim period). During such interim period, how will the term "product" be defined for purposes of allocating income under the cost sharing or profit split methods?

ANSWER 11: During the interim period the product will be determined based on the activities performed by the possessions corporation within a possession on September 3, 1982. During the interim period the possessions corporation may compute its income under the cost sharing or profit split method only with respect to the product that is produced or manufactured within the meaning of section 954(d)(1)(A) within the possession. If the product is manufactured from a component or components produced by an affiliated corporation or a contract manufacturer, then the product will not be treated as including such component or components for purposes of the computation of income under the cost sharing or profit split methods. Thus, the possessions corporation is not entitled to any return on the intangibles associated with the component or components. Notwithstanding the preceding sentences, for taxable years beginning before January 1, 1986, a possessions corporation may compute its income under the cost sharing or profit split method with respect to a product which includes a component or components produced by an affiliated corporation or contract manufacturer if the possessions corporation satisfies with respect to such product the significant business presence test described in section 936(h)(5)(B)(ii) and the regulations thereunder.

Example (1). A possessions corporation, S, was manufacturing (within the meaning of section 954(d)(1)(A)) integrated circuits in a possession on September 3, 1982. S transferred those integrated circuits to related corporation P. P incorporated the integrated circuits into central processing units (CPUs in the United States) and sold the CPUs to unrelated parties. S continued to manufacture integrated circuits in the possession through January 1, 1986. For taxable years beginning before January 1, 1986, S may compute its income under the cost sharing or profit split method with respect to the integrated circuits regardless of whether S satisfies the significant business presence test. However, unless S satisfies the significant business presence test with respect to the central processing units, S may not compute its income under the cost sharing or profit split methods with respect to the CPUs, and thus, S is not entitled to any return on manufacturing intangibles associated with CPUs to the extent that they are not related to the integrated circuits produced by S, nor (except as provided in the profit split method) to any return on marketing intangibles.

Example (2). A possessions corporation, S, was engaged on September 3, 1982, in the manufacture (within the meaning of section 954(d)(1)(A)) of a bulk pharmaceutical in Puerto Rico from raw materials. S sold the bulk pharmaceutical to its U.S. parent, P, for encapsulation and sale by P to customers as the product X. Because S was not engaged in the encapsulation of X, S is not considered to have manufactured the integrated product, X, in Puerto Rico. During the interim period, S may compute its income under the cost sharing or profit split methods with respect to the integrated product, X, only if S satisfies the significant business presence test with respect to X. S may compute its income under the cost sharing or profit split methods with respect to the component product (the bulk pharmaceutical).

Example (3). P is a domestic corporation that is not a possessions corporation. P manufactures a bulk pharmaceutical in the United States. P transfers the bulk pharmaceutical to its wholly owned subsidiary, S, a possessions corporation. On September 3, 1982, S was engaged in the encapsulation of the bulk pharmaceutical in Puerto Rico in a manner which satisfies the test of section 954(d)(1)(A). For taxable years beginning before January 1, 1986, S may compute its income under the cost sharing or profit split methods with respect to the end-product form (the encapsulated drug) regardless of whether S meets the significant business presence test. However, unless S satisfies the significant business presence test with respect to the integrated product, S may not compute its income under the cost sharing or profit split methods with respect to the integrated product, and thus, S is not entitled to any return on the intangibles associated with the bulk pharmaceutical.

QUESTION 12: On September 3, 1982, a possessions corporation, S, was engaged in the manufacture (within the meaning of section

Reg. § 1.936-5(a)

954(d)(1)(A)) of X in a possession. During the interim period, after September 3, 1982, but before January 1, 1986, S produced Y, which differs from X in terms of minor design features. S did not produce Y in a possession on September 3, 1982. Will S be considered to have commenced production of a new product after September 3, 1982, for purposes of the application of the significant business presence test for the interim period?

ANSWER 12: No. X and Y will be considered to be a single product, and therefore S will not be required to satisfy the business presence test separately with respect to Y during the interim period. In all cases in which the items of property produced on or before September 3, 1982 and the items of property produced after that date could have been grouped together under the guidelines provided in § 1.936-5(a) questions and answers 6 through 10, the possessions corporation will not be considered to manufacture a new product after September 3, 1982.

QUESTION 13: May the term "product" be defined differently for export sales than for domestic sales?

ANSWER 13: Yes. For rules concerning the application of the separate election for export sales see § 1.936-7(b).

(b) *Requirement of significant business presence*—(1) *General rules.*

QUESTION 1: In general, a possessions corporation may compute its income under the cost sharing or profit split methods with respect to a product only if the possessions corporation has a significant business presence in a possession with respect to that product. When will a possessions corporation be considered to have a significant business presence in a possession?

ANSWER 1: For purposes of the cost sharing method, the significant business presence test is met if the possessions corporation satisfies either a value added test or a direct labor test. For purposes of the profit split method, the significant business presence test is met if the possessions corporation satisfies either a value added test or a direct labor test and also manufactures the product in the possession within the meaning of section 954(d)(1)(A).

QUESTION 2: How may a possessions corporation satisfy the direct labor test with respect to a product?

ANSWER 2: The possessions corporation will satisfy the direct labor test with respect to a product if the direct labor costs incurred by the possessions corporation as compensation for services performed in a possession are greater than or equal to 65 percent of the direct labor costs of the affiliated group for units of the possession product produced during the taxable year in whole or in part by the possessions corporation.

QUESTION 3: How may a possessions corporation satisfy the value added test?

ANSWER 3: In order to satisfy the value added test, the production costs of the possessions corporation incurred in the possession with respect to units of the possession product produced in whole or in part by the possessions corporation in the possession and sold or otherwise disposed of during the taxable year by the affiliated group to unrelated parties must be greater than or equal to twenty-five percent of the difference between gross receipts from such sales or other dispositions and the direct material costs of the affiliated group for materials purchased for such units from unrelated parties.

QUESTION 4: Must the significant business presence test be met with respect to all units of the product produced during the taxable year by the affiliated group?

ANSWER 4: No. The significant business presence test must be met with respect to only those units of the product produced during the taxable year in whole or in part by the possessions corporation in a possession.

QUESTION 5: For purposes of determining whether a possessions corporation satisfies the significant business presence test, how shall the possessions corporation treat the cost of components transferred to the possessions corporation by a member of the affiliated group?

ANSWER 5: The treatment of the cost of components transferred from an affiliate depends on whether the possession product is treated as including the components for purposes of section 936(h). If it is, then for purposes of the value added test, the production costs associated with the component shall be treated as production costs of the affiliated group that are not incurred by the possessions corporation. Those production costs, other than the cost of materials, shall not be treated as a cost of materials. For purposes of the direct labor test and the alternative significant business presence test, the direct labor costs associated with such components shall be treated as direct labor costs of the affiliated group that are not incurred by the possessions corporation. If the possession product is treated as not including such component for purposes of section 936(h), then, solely for purposes of determining whether the possessions corporation satisfies the value added test, the cost of the component shall not be treated as either a cost of materials or as a production cost. For purposes of the direct labor test and the alternative significant business presence

Reg. § 1.936-5(b)(1)

test, the direct labor costs associated with such component shall not be treated as direct labor costs of the affiliated group. If the possession product is treated as not including such component, then the possessions corporation shall not be entitled to any return on the intangibles associated with the manufacturing or marketing of the component.

QUESTION 6: May two or more related possessions corporations aggregate their production or direct labor costs for purposes of determining whether they satisfy the significant business presence test with respect to a single product?

ANSWER 6: No.

QUESTION 7: A possessions corporation, S, purchases raw materials and components from a unrelated corporation which conducts business outside of a possession. The unrelated corporation is not a contract manufacturer. What is the treatment of such raw materials and components for purposes of the significant business presence test?

ANSWER 7: Where corporation S purchases raw materials or components from an unrelated corporation which is not a contract manufacturer, the raw materials and components are treated as materials, and the costs related thereto are treated as a cost of materials.

(2) *Direct labor costs.*

QUESTION 1: How is the term "direct labor costs" to be defined?

ANSWER 1: The term "direct labor costs" has the same meaning which it has for purposes of § 1.471-11(b)(2)(i). Thus, direct labor costs include the cost of labor which can be identified or associated with particular units or groups of units of a specific product. The elements of direct labor include such items as basic compensation, overtime pay, vacation and holiday pay, sick leave pay (other than payments pursuant to a wage continuation plan under section 105(d)), shift differential, payroll taxes, and payments to a supplemental unemployment benefit plan paid or incurred on behalf of employees engaged in direct labor.

QUESTION 2: May a taxpayer treat a cost as a direct labor cost if it is not included in inventoriable costs under section 471 and the regulations thereunder?

ANSWER 2: No. A cost may be treated as a direct labor cost only if it is included in inventoriable costs. However, a cost may be considered a direct labor cost even though the activity to which it relates would not constitute manufacturing under section 954(d)(1)(A) as long as the cost is included in inventoriable costs.

QUESTION 3: May the members of the affiliated group include as direct labor costs the labor element in indirect production costs?

ANSWER 3: No. The labor element of indirect production costs may not be considered as part of direct labor costs.

QUESTION 4: Do direct labor costs include the costs which can be identified or associated with particular units or groups of units of a specific product if those costs could also be described as quality control and inspection?

ANSWER 4: Yes. Direct labor costs include costs which can be identified or associated with particular units or groups of units of a specific product. Thus, if quality control and inspection is an integral part of the production process, then the labor associated with that quality control and inspection shall be considered direct labor. For example, integrated circuits are soldered to printed circuit boards by passing the boards over liquid solder. Employees inspect each of the boards and repair any imperfectly soldered joints discovered on that inspection. The labor associated with this process is direct labor. However, if a person performs random inspections on limited numbers of products, then that labor associated with those inspections shall be considered quality control and therefore indirect labor.

QUESTION 5: Do direct labor costs of the possessions corporation include only the costs which were actually incurred or do they take into account, in addition, any labor savings which result because the activities were performed in a possession rather than in the United States?

ANSWER 5: Direct labor costs include only the costs which were actually incurred.

QUESTION 6: For purposes of determining whether a possessions corporation satisfies the significant business presence test for a taxable year with respect to a product, how shall the possessions corporation compute its direct labor costs of units of the product?

ANSWER 6: The direct labor tests shall be applied separately to products produced in whole or in part by the possessions corporation in the possession during each taxable year. Sales shall be deemed to be made first out of the current year's production. If sales are made only out of the current year's production, then the direct labor costs of producing those units that are sold shall be the pro rata portion of the total direct labor costs of producing all the units that are produced in whole or in part in the possession by the possessions corporation during the current year. If all of the current year's production is sold and some inventory is liquidated, then the direct labor test shall be applied separately to the current year's

Reg. § 1.936-5(b)(2)

production and the liquidated inventory. The direct labor costs of producing the liquidated inventory shall be the pro rata portion of the total direct labor costs that were incurred in producing all the units that were produced in whole or in part by the possessions corporation in the possessions in the layer of liquidated inventory determined under the member's method of inventory accounting.

Example. S is a cash basis calendar year taxpayer that has made an election under section 936(a). In 1985 S produced 100 units of product X. Fifty percent of the direct labor costs of the affiliated group were incurred by S and were compensation for services performed in the possession. Thus, S did not satisfy the significant business presence test with respect to product X in taxable year 1985. During 1986 S produced 100 units of product X. One hundred percent of the direct labor costs of the affiliated group were incurred by S and were compensation for services performed in the possession. In 1986 S sells 150 units of product X. One hundred of those units are deemed to be from the units produced in 1986. With respect to those units S satisfies the significant business presence test. Under S's method of inventory accounting the remaining 50 units were determined to be produced in 1985. With respect to those units S does not satisfy the significant business presence test because only 50% of the direct labor costs incurred in producing those units were incurred by S and were compensation for services performed in the possession.

QUESTION 7: What is the result if in a particular taxable year the possessions corporation satisfies the significant business presence test with respect to units of the product produced in one year and fails the significant business with respect to units produced in another year?

ANSWER 7: For those units of the product with respect to which the possessions corporation satisfies the significant business presence test, the possessions corporation may compute its income under the provisions of section 936(h)(5). For those units of the product with respect to which the possessions corporations fails the significant business presence test, the possessions corporation must compute its income under section 936(h)(1) through (4).

QUESTION 8: Do direct labor costs include costs incurred in a prior taxable year with respect to units of the possession product that are finished in a later taxable year?

ANSWER 8: Yes.

(3) *Direct material costs.*

QUESTION 1: How is the term "direct material costs" to be defined?

ANSWER 1: Direct material costs include the cost of those materials which become an integral part of the specific product and those materials which are consumed in the ordinary course of manufacturing and can be identified or associated with particular units or groups of units of that product. See § 1.471-3 for the elements of direct material costs.

QUESTION 2: May a taxpayer treat a cost as a direct material cost if it is not included in inventoriable costs under section 471 and the regulations thereunder?

ANSWER 2: A taxpayer may not treat such costs as direct material costs.

(4) *Production costs.*

QUESTION 1: How is the term "production costs" defined?

ANSWER 1: The term "production costs" has the same meaning which it has for purposes of § 1.471-11(b) except that the term does not include direct material costs and interest. Thus, production costs include direct labor costs and fixed and variable indirect production costs (other than interest).

QUESTION 2: With respect to indirect production costs described in § 1.471-11(c)(2)(ii) and (iii), may a possessions corporation include these costs in production costs for purposes of section 936, if they are not included in inventoriable costs under section 471 and the regulations thereunder?

ANSWER 2: No. A possessions corporation may include these costs only if they are included for purposes of section 471 and the regulations thereunder. If a possessions corporation and the other members of the affiliated group include and exclude different indirect production costs in their inventoriable costs, then, for purposes of the significant business presence test, the possessions corporation shall compute its production costs and the production costs of the other members of the affiliated group by subtracting from the production costs of each member all indirect costs included by that member that are not included in production costs by all other members of the affiliated group.

QUESTION 3: Does a change in a taxpayer's method of accounting for purposes of section 471 affect the taxpayer's computation of production costs for purposes of section 936?

ANSWER 3: Yes. If a taxpayer changes its method of accounting for purposes of section 471, then the same change shall apply for purposes of section 936.

QUESTION 4: For purposes of determining whether a possessions corporation satisfies the significant business presence test for a taxable year

Reg. § 1.936-5(b)(3)

with respect to a product, how shall the possessions corporation compute its costs of producing units of the product sold or otherwise disposed to unrelated parties during the taxable year?

ANSWER 4: All members of the affiliated group may elect to use their current year production costs regardless of whether the members use the FIFO or LIFO method of inventory accounting. If some or all of the current year's production of a product is sold, then the production costs of producing those units sold shall be the pro rata portion of the total production costs of producing all the units produced in the current year. If all of the current year's production of a product is sold and some inventory is liquidated, then the production costs of producing the liquidated inventory shall be the pro rata portion of the production costs incurred in producing the layer of liquidated inventory as determined under the member's method of inventory accounting.

QUESTION 5: How should the members of the affiliated group determine the portion of their production costs that is allocable to units of the product sold or otherwise disposed of during the taxable year?

ANSWER 5: The members of the affiliated group may use either standard production costs (so long as variances are not material), average production costs, or FIFO production costs to determine the production costs that will be considered to be attributable to units of the product sold or otherwise disposed of during the taxable year. However, all members of the affiliated group must use the same method.

QUESTION 6: When is the quality control and inspection of a product considered to be part of the production activity for that product?

ANSWER 6: Quality control and inspection of a manufactured product before its sale or other disposition by the manufacturer, or before its incorporation into other products, is considered to be part of the indirect production activity for that initial product. Subsequent testing of a product to ensure that the product is compatible with other products is not a part of the production activity for the initial product. When a component is incorporated into an end-product form and the end-product form is then tested, the latter testing will be considered to be a part of the indirect production activity for the end-product form and will not be considered to be a part of the production activity for the component.

QUESTION 7: For purposes of the significant business presence test and the allocation of income to a possessions corporation, what is the treatment of the cost of installation of a product?

ANSWER 7: For purposes of the significant business presence test and the allocation of income to a possessions corporation, product installation costs need not be taken into account as costs incurred in the manufacture of that product, if the taxpayer keeps such permanent books of account or records as are sufficient to establish the fair market price of the uninstalled product. In such a case, the cost of installation materials, the cost of the labor for installation, and a reasonable profit for installation will not be included in the costs and income associated with the possession product. If the taxpayer does not keep such permanent books of account or records, then the cost of installation materials and the cost of labor for installation shall be treated as costs associated with the possession product and income will be allocated to the possessions corporation and its affiliates under the rules provided in these regulations.

QUESTION 8: For purposes of the significant business presence test and the allocation of income to a product or service, what is the treatment of the cost of servicing and maintaining a possession product that is sold to an unrelated party?

ANSWER 8: The cost of servicing and maintaining a possession product after it is sold is not associated with the production of that product.

QUESTION 9: For purposes of the significant business presence test and the allocation of income to a possessions corporation, what is the treatment of the cost of samples?

ANSWER 9: The cost of producing samples will be treated as a marketing expense and not as inventoriable costs for these purposes. However, for taxable years beginning prior to January 1, 1986, the cost of producing samples may be treated as either a marketing expense or as inventoriable costs.

(5) *Gross receipts.*

QUESTION 1: How shall the affiliated group determine gross receipts from sales or other dispositions by the affiliated group to unrelated parties of the possession product?

ANSWER 1: Gross receipts shall be determined in the same manner as possession sales under the rules contained in § 1.936-6(a)(2).

(6) *Manufacturing within the meaning of section 954(d)(1)(A).*

QUESTION 1: What is the test for determining, within the meaning of section 954(d)(1)(A), whether a product is manufactured or produced by a possessions corporation in a possession?

ANSWER 1: A product is considered to have been manufactured or produced by a possessions

Reg. § 1.936-5(b)(6)

corporation in a possession within the meaning of section 954(d)(1)(A) and § 1.954-3(a)(4) if—

(i) The property has been substantially transformed by the possessions corporation in the possession;

(ii) The operations conducted by the possessions corporation in the possession in connection with the property are substantial in nature and are generally considered to constitute the manufacture or production of property; or

(iii) The conversion costs sustained by the possessions corporation in the possession, including direct labor, factory burden, testing of components before incorporation into an end product and testing of the manufactured product before sales account for 20 percent or more of the total cost of goods sold of the possessions corporation.

In no event, however, will packaging, repackaging, labeling, or minor assembly operations constitute manufacture or production of property. See particularly examples (2) and (3) of § 1.954-3(a)(4)(iii).

QUESTION 2: Does the requirement that a possession product be produced or manufactured in a possession within the meaning of section 954(d)(1)(A) apply to taxable years beginning before January 1, 1986?

ANSWER 2: A possessions corporation must satisfy this requirement for taxable years beginning before January 1, 1986, in the following cases:

(i) If the possessions corporation makes a separate election under section 936(h)(5)(F)(iv)(II) with respect to export sales;

(ii) If the possessions corporation is electing as its possession product a product that is subject to the interim period rules of § 1.936-5(a) question and answer (10); or

(iii) If the possessions corporation is electing as its possession product a product that is not subject to the interim period rules of § 1.936-5(a) question and answer (10) and the possessions corporation computes its income under the profit split method with respect to that product.

For rules concerning products first produced in a possession after September 3, 1982, see § 1.936-5(b)(7) question and answer (2).

(7) *Start-up operations.*

QUESTION 1: With respect to products not produced (and types of services not rendered) in the possession on or before September 3, 1982, when must a possessions corporation first satisfy the 25 percent value added test or the 65 percent direct labor test?

ANSWER 1: A transitional period is established such that a possessions corporation engaged in start-up operations with respect to a product or service need not satisfy the 25 percent value added test or the 65 percent labor test until the third taxable year following the taxable year in which such product is first sold by the possessions corporation or such service is first rendered by the possessions corporation. During the transitional period, the applicable percentages for these tests will be as follows:

	Any year after 1982		
	1	2	3
Value added test	10	15	20
Labor test	35	45	55

QUESTION 2: Does the requirement that a possession product be produced or manufactured in a possession within the meaning of section 954(d)(1)(A) apply to a product if the possessions corporation is engaged in start-up operations with respect to that product?

ANSWER 2: The possessions corporation must produce or manufacture the possessions product within the meaning of section 954(d)(1)(A) if the possessions corporation computes its income with respect to that product under the profit split method.

QUESTION 3: When will a possessions corporation be considered to be engaged in start-up operations?

ANSWER 3: A possessions corporation is engaged in start-up operations if it begins operations in a possession with respect to a product or type of service after September 3, 1982. Subject to the further provisions of this answer, a possessions corporation will be considered to begin operations with respect to a product if, under the rules of § 1.936-5(a) questions and answers (6) through (10), such product could not be grouped with any other item of property manufactured in whole or in part in the possessions by any member of the affiliated group in any preceding taxable year. Any improvement or other change in a possession product which does not substantially change the production process would not be deemed to create a new product. A change in the division of manufacturing activity between the possessions corporation and its affiliates with respect to an item of property will not give rise to a new product. If a possessions corporation was producing a possession product that was either a component product or an end-product form and the possessions corporation expands its operations in the same possession so that it is now producing a product that includes the earlier possession product, the possessions corporation will not be entitled to use the

Reg. § 1.936-5(b)(7)

start-up significant business presence test unless the production costs incurred by the possessions corporation in the possession in producing a unit of its new possession product are at least double the production costs incurred by the possessions corporation in the possession in producing a unit of the earlier possession product. If any member of an affiliated group actually groups two or more items of property then, solely for the purposes of determining whether any item of property in that group is a new product, that grouping shall be respected. However, the fact that an affiliated group does not actually group two or more items of property shall be disregarded in determining whether any item of property is a new product. Notwithstanding the above, if a possessions corporation is producing a possession product in one possession and such corporation or a member of its affiliated group begins operations in a different possession, regardless of whether the items of property could be grouped, the affiliated group may treat the units of the item of property produced at the new site of operations in the different possession as a new product.

(8) *Alternative significant business presence test.*

QUESTION 1: Will the Secretary adopt a significant business presence test other than those set forth in section 936(h)(5)(B)(ii)?

ANSWER 1: Yes. The following significant business presence test is adopted both for the transitional period and thereafter. A possessions corporation will have a significant business presence in a possession for a taxable year with respect to a product or type of service if—

(i) No less than 50 percent of the direct labor costs of the affiliated group for units of the product produced, in whole or in part, during the taxable year by the possessions corporation or for the type of service rendered by the possessions corporation during the taxable year are incurred by the possessions corporation as compensation for services performed in the possession; and

(ii) The direct labor costs of the possessions corporation for units of the product produced or the type of service rendered plus the base period construction costs are no less than 70 percent of the sum of such base period construction costs and the direct labor costs of the affiliated group for such units of the product produced or the type of service rendered.

Notwithstanding satisfaction of the above test, for purposes of determining whether a possessions corporation may compute its income under the profit split method, a possessions corporation will not be treated as having a significant business presence in a possession with respect to a product unless the possessions corporation manufactures the product in the possession within the meaning of section 954(d)(1)(A).

QUESTION 2: How is the term "base period construction costs" defined?

ANSWER 2: The term "base period construction costs" means the average construction costs incurred by or on behalf of the possessions corporation for services in the possession during the taxable year and the preceding four taxable years for section 1250 property (as defined in section 1250(c) and the regulations thereunder) that is used for the production of the product or the rendering of the service in the possession, and which represents the original use of the section 1250 property. For purposes of the preceding sentence, if the possessions corporation was not in existence during one or more of the four preceding taxable years, its construction costs for that year or years shall be deemed to be zero. Construction costs include architects' and engineers' fees, labor costs, and overhead and profit (if the construction is performed by a person that is not a member of the affiliated group).

(c) *Definition and treatment of contract manufacturing.*

QUESTION 1: For purposes of determining whether a possessions corporation satisfies the significant business presence test with respect to a product, the costs incurred by the possessions corporation or by any of its affiliates in connection with contract manufacturing which is related to that product and is performed outside the possession shall be treated as direct labor costs of the affiliated group and shall not be treated as production costs of the possessions corporation or as material costs. How is the term "contract manufacturing" to be defined?

ANSWER 1: The term "contract manufacturing" includes any arrangement between a possessions corporation (or another member of the affiliated group) and an unrelated person if the unrelated person:

(1) Performs work on inventory owned by a member of the affiliated group for a fee without the passage of title;

(2) Performs production activities (including manufacturing, assembling, finishing, or packaging) under the direct supervision and control of a member of the affiliated group; or

(3) Does not undertake any significant risk in manufacturing its product (*e.g.*, it is paid by the hour).

QUESTION 2: Does an arrangement between a member of the affiliated group and an unrelated party constitute contract manufacturing if the

Reg. § 1.936-5(c)

unrelated party uses an intangible owned or licensed by a member of the affiliated group?

ANSWER 2: Such an arrangement will be treated as contract manufacturing if the unrelated party makes use of a patent owned or licensed by a member of the affiliated group in producing the product which becomes part of the possession product of the possessions corporation. In addition, such use of manufacturing intangibles other than patents may be treated as contract manufacturing if it is established that the arrangement has the effect of materially distorting the application of the significant business presence test. However, the preceding sentence shall not apply if the possessions corporation establishes that the arrangement was entered into for a substantial business purpose (e.g., to obtain the benefit of special expertise of the manufacturer or economies of scale). These rules shall not apply to such contract manufacturing performed in taxable years beginning before January 1, 1986, nor shall the rules apply to binding contracts for the performance of such contract manufacturing entered into before June 13, 1986.

QUESTION 3: For purposes of the significant business presence test, how shall a possessions corporation treat the cost of contract manufacturing performed within a possession?

ANSWER 3: If the possessions corporation uses the value added test, it will be permitted to treat the cost of the contract manufacturing performed in a possession, not including material costs, as a production cost of the possessions corporation. If it uses the direct labor test or the alternative significant business presence test set forth in § 1.936-5(b)(8), it is permitted to treat the direct labor costs of the contract manufacturer associated with such contract manufacturing as a cost of direct labor of the possessions corporation. The allowable amount of the direct labor cost shall be determined in accordance with question and answer 4 below.

QUESTION 4: How are the amounts paid by a possessions corporation to a contract manufacturer for services rendered in a possession to be treated by the possessions corporation in computing the direct labor cost of the product to which such contract manufacturing relates?

ANSWER 4: If the possessions corporation can establish the contract manufacturer's direct labor cost which was incurred in the possession, such cost will be treated as incurred by the possessions corporation as compensation for services performed in the possession. If the possessions corporation cannot establish such cost, then 50 percent of the amount paid to such contract manufacturer may be treated as incurred by the possessions corporation as compensation for services performed in the possession: provided, that not more than 50 percent of the fair market value of the product manufactured by the contract manufacturer is attributable to articles shipped into the possession, and the possessions corporation receives a statement from the contract manufacturer that this test has been satisfied. If this fair market value test is not satisfied, then the cost of contract manufacturing performed within a possession shall not be treated as a production cost or a direct labor cost of either the possessions corporation or the affiliated group.

QUESTION 5: For purposes of the significant business presence test, what is the treatment of costs which are incurred by a member of the affiliated group (including the possessions corporation) for contract manufacturing performed outside of the possession with respect to an item of property which is a component of the possession product?

ANSWER 5: If the possession product is treated as including such component, the cost of the contract manufacturing shall be treated as a direct labor cost of members of the affiliated group other than the possessions corporation for purposes of the direct labor test and the alternative significant business presence test, and shall not be treated as a production cost of the possessions corporation or as a cost of materials for purposes of the value added test. If the possession product is treated as not including such component, the cost of the contract manufacturing shall not be treated as a direct labor cost of any member of the affiliated group for purposes of the direct labor test and the alternative significant business presence test, and shall not be treated as a production cost of the possessions corporation or as a cost of materials for purposes of the value added test. [Reg. § 1.936-5.]

☐ [T.D. 8090, 6-9-86.]

[Reg. § 1.936-6]

§ 1.936-6. Intangible property income when an election out is made: cost sharing and profit split options; covered intangibles. The rules in this section apply for purposes of section 936(h) and also for purposes of section 934(e), where applicable.

(a) *Cost sharing option*—(1) *Product area research.*

QUESTION 1: Cost sharing payments are based on research undertaken by the affiliated group in the "product area" which includes the possession product. The term "product area" is defined by reference to the three-digit classification under the Standard Industrial Classification

Reg. § 1.936-6(a)(1)

(SIC) code. Which governmental agency has jurisdiction to decide the proper SIC category for any specific product?

Answer 1: Solely for the purpose of determining the tax consequences of operating in a possession, the Secretary or his delegate has exclusive jurisdiction to decide the proper SIC category under which a product is classified. For this purpose, the product area under which a product is classified will be determined according to the 1972 edition of the SIC code. From time to time and in appropriate cases, the Secretary may prescribe regulations or issue rulings determining the proper SIC category under which a particular product is to be classified, and may prescribe regulations for aggregating two or more three-digit classifications of the SIC code and for classifying product areas according to a system other than under the SIC code.

Question 2: How is the term "affiliated group" defined for purposes of the cost sharing option?

Answer 2: For purposes of the cost sharing option, the term "affiliated group" means the possessions corporation and all other organizations, trades or businesses (whether or not incorporated, whether or not organized in the United States, and whether or not affiliated) owned or controlled directly or indirectly by the same interests, within the meaning of section 482.

Question 3: Are research and development expenditures that are included in product area research limited to research and development expenditures that are deductible under section 174 or that are incurred by U.S. affiliates?

Answer 3: No, product area research is not limited to product area research expenditures deductible under section 174 or to expenses incurred by U.S. affiliates. Product area research also includes deductions permitted under section 168 with respect to research property which are not deductible under section 174; qualified research expenses within the meaning of section 30(b); payments (such as royalties) for the use of, or right to use, a patent, invention, formula, process, design, pattern or know-how; and a proper allowance for amounts incurred in the acquisition of manufacturing intangible property. In the case of an acquisition of depreciable or amortizable manufacturing intangible property, the annual amount of product area research shall be equal to the allowable depreciation or amortization on the intangible property for the taxable year. In the case of an acquisition of nondepreciable or nonamortizable manufacturing intangible property, the amount expended for the acquisition shall be deemed to be amortized over a five year period and included in product area research in the year of the deemed amortization. Any contingent payment made with respect to the acquisition of nonamortizable manufacturing intangible property shall be treated as amounts incurred in the acquisition of nonamortizable manufacturing intangible property when paid or accrued.

Question 4: Does royalty income from a person outside the affiliated group with respect to the manufacturing intangibles within a product area reduce the product area research pool within the same product area?

Answer 4: Yes.

Question 5: Does income received from a person outside the affiliated group from the sale of a manufacturing intangible reduce the product area research pool within the same product area?

Answer 5: In determining product area research, the income from the sale attributable to noncontingent payments will reduce product area research ratably over the remaining useful life of the property in the case of an amortizable intangible and ratably over a 5-year period in the case of a nonamortizable intangible. Any income attributable to contingent amounts received with respect to the sale of manufacturing intangible property shall be treated as amounts received from the sale of the manufacturing intangible property in the year in which such contingent amounts are received or accrued.

Question 6: If a member of an affiliated group incurs research and development expenses pursuant to a contract with an unrelated person who is entitled to exclusive ownership of all the technology resulting from the expenditures, is the amount of product area research reduced by the amount of such expenditures?

Answer 6: To the extent that the product area research expenditures can be allocated solely to the technology produced for the unrelated person, such expenditures will not be included in product area research expenditures provided, however, that the unrelated person has exclusive ownership of all the technology resulting from these expenditures, and further that no member of the affiliated group has a right to use any of the technology.

Question 7: What is the treatment of product area research expenditures attributable to a component where the component and the integrated product fall within different product areas?

Answer 7: For purposes of the computation of product area research expenditures in the product area by the affiliated group, the product area in which the component falls is aggregated with the product area in which the integrated product falls. However, if the component product and inte-

Reg. § 1.936-6(a)(1)

grated product are in separate SIC codes and if the component product is not included in the definition of the possession product, then the product area research expenditures are not aggregated. The same rule applies where the taxpayer elects a component product which encompasses another component product and the two component products fall into separate SIC codes. In such case, the product area in which the first component falls is aggregated with the product area in which the second component falls.

(2) Possession sales and total sales.

Question 1: The cost sharing payment is the same proportion of the total cost of product area research which the amount of "possession sales" of the affiliated group bears to the "total sales" of the affiliated group within the product area. How are "possession sales" defined for purposes of the cost sharing fraction?

Answer 1: The term "possession sales" means the aggregate sales or other dispositions of the possession product, to persons who are not members of the affiliated group, less returns and allowances and less indirect taxes imposed on the production of the product, for the taxable year. Except as otherwise indicated in § 1.936-6(a)(2), the sales price to be used is the sales price received by the affiliated group from persons who are not members of the affiliated group.

Question 2: For purposes of the numerator of the cost sharing fraction, how are possession sales computed where the possession product is a component product or an end-product form?

Answer 2: (i) The sales price of the component product or end-product form is determined as follows. With respect to a component product, an independent sales price from comparable uncontrolled transactions must be used if such price can be determined in accordance with § 1.482-2(e)(2). If an independent sales price of the component product from comparable uncontrolled transactions cannot be determined, then the sales price of the component product shall be deemed to be equal to the transfer price, determined under the appropriate section 482 method, which the possessions corporation uses under the cost sharing method in computing the income it derives from the active conduct of a trade or business in the possession with respect to the component product. The possessions corporation in lieu of using the transfer price determined under the preceding sentence may treat the sales price for the component product as equal to the same proportion of the third party sales price of the integrated product which the production costs attributable to the component product bear to the total production cost for the integrated product. Production cost will be the sum of direct and indirect production costs as defined in § 1.936-5(b)(4). If the possessions corporation determines the sales price of the component product using the production cost ratio, the transfer price used by the possessions corporation in computing its income from the component product under the cost sharing method may not be greater than such sales price. (ii) With respect to an end-product form, the sales price of the end-product form is equal to the difference between the third party sales price of the integrated product and the independent sales price of the excluded component(s) from comparable uncontrolled transactions, if such price can be determined under § 1.482-2(e)(2). If an independent sales price of the excluded component(s) from uncontrolled transactions cannot be determined, then the sales price of the end-product form shall be deemed to be equal to the transfer price, determined under the appropriate section 482 method, which the possessions corporation uses under the cost sharing method in computing the income it derives from the active conduct of a trade or business in the possession with respect to such end-product form. The possessions corporation in lieu of using the transfer price determined under the preceding sentence may use the production cost ratio method described above to determine the sales price of the end-product form (*i.e.,* the same proportion which the production costs attributable to the end-product form bear to the total production costs for the integrated product). If the possessions corporation determines the sales price of the end-product form using the production cost ratio, the transfer price used by the possessions corporation in computing its income from the end-product form under the cost sharing method may not be greater than such sales price. For similar rules applicable to the profit split option see § 1.936-6(b)(1), question and answer 12.

Question 3: For purposes of determining possessions sales in the numerator of the cost sharing fraction, will the replacement part price of the product be treated as a price from comparable uncontrolled transactions?

Answer 3: Prices for replacement parts are generally higher than prices for equipment sold as part of an original system. Thus, prices for replacement parts cannot generally be used directly as prices for comparable uncontrolled transactions. However, replacement part prices may be used for estimating comparable uncontrolled prices where the price differential can be reasonably determined and taken into account under § 1.482-2(e)(2).

Reg. § 1.936-6(a)(2)

Question 4: For purposes of determining possession sales in the cost sharing fraction, what is the treatment of components that are purchased by one possessions corporation from an affiliated possessions corporation and which are incorporated into a possession product where the transferor possessions corporation treats the transferred component as a possession product?

Answer 4: When one possessions corporation purchases components from a second possessions corporation which is an affiliated corporation, the purchase price of the components paid to the second possessions corporation shall be subtracted from the sales proceeds of the product produced in the possession by the first possessions corporation, and only the remainder is included in the numerator of the cost sharing formula for the first corporation. For example, assume that N corporation manufactures a component for sale to O corporation for $100 (a price which reflects prices in comparable uncontrolled transactions). Both N and O are affiliated possessions corporations. N has designated that component product as its possession product. O then incorporates that product into a second product which is sold to customers for $300. N and O must make separate cost sharing payments. The cost sharing payment of N corporation is determined by including $100 as possession sales, and the payment of O is determined by subtracting that $100 purchase price from the $300 received from customers. Thus, the possessions sales amount of O is $200. This rule is intended to prevent the double counting of the sales of a component produced by one possessions corporation and incorporated into another product by an affiliated possessions corporation.

Question 5: Are pre-TEFRA sales included in the cost sharing fraction?

Answer 5: No. Pre-TEFRA sales are sales of products produced by the possessions corporation and transferred to an affiliate prior to a possessions corporation's first taxable year beginning after December 31, 1982. Pre-TEFRA sales are not included in either the numerator or denominator of the cost sharing fraction. If the U.S. affiliate uses the FIFO method of costing inventory, the pre-TEFRA inventory will be treated as the first inventory sold by the U.S. affiliate during the first year in which section 936(h) applies. If the U.S. affiliate uses the LIFO method of costing inventory (either dollar-value or specific goods LIFO), pre-TEFRA inventory will be treated as inventory sold by the U.S. affiliate in the year in which the U.S. affiliate's LIFO layer containing pre-TEFRA LIFO inventory is liquidated.

Question 6: How are "possession sales" determined under the cost sharing formula if members of the affiliated group (other than the possessions corporation) include purchases of the possession product, X, in a dollar-value LIFO inventory pool (as provided under § 1.472-8)?

Answer 6: Possession sales may be determined by applying the revenue identification method provided under paragraph (b)(1) Question and Answer 18 of this section.

Question 7: Do possession sales include excise taxes paid by the possessions corporation when the product is sold for ultimate use or consumption in the possession?

Answer 7: No. The amount of excise taxes is excluded from both the numerator and denominator of the cost sharing fraction.

Question 8: How are "total sales" defined for purposes of the cost sharing fraction?

Answer 8: The term "total sales" means aggregate sales or other dispositions of products in the same product area as the possession product, less returns and allowances and less indirect taxes imposed on the production of the product, for the taxable year to persons who are not members of the affiliated group. The sales price to be used is the sales price received by the affiliated group from persons who are not members of the affiliated group.

Question 9: In computing the cost sharing payment, how are "total sales" computed if the dollar-value LIFO inventory pool includes some products which are not included in the product area (determined under the 3-digit SIC code) on which the denominator of the cost sharing fraction is based?

Answer 9: In such case, the amount of the total sales within the product area to persons who are not members of the affiliated group by persons who are members of the affiliated group is determined by multiplying the total sales of the products within the dollar-value LIFO inventory pool by a fraction. The numerator of the fraction includes the dollar-value of purchases by members of the affiliated group (including the possessions corporation) of products within the product area made during the year, plus any added production costs (as defined in § 1.471-11(b), (c), and (d) but not including the cost of materials) incurred by the affiliates during the same period. The denominator of the fraction includes the dollar-value of purchases by members of the affiliated group (including the possessions corporation) of products within the dollar-value LIFO inventory pool made during the same period (including any production costs, as described above, incurred by the affiliate during the same period). For these purposes, purchases of a possession product are determined

Reg. § 1.936-6(a)(2)

on the basis of the possessions corporation's cost for its inventory purposes.

Question 10: May a possessions corporation compute its income under the cost sharing method with respect to a possession product which the possessions corporation sells to a member of its affiliated group and which that member then leases to an unrelated person or uses in its own trade or business?

Answer 10: Yes, provided that an independent sales price for the possession product from comparable uncontrolled transactions can be determined in accordance with § 1.482-2(e)(2), and, provided further, that such member complies with the requirements of § 1.936-6(a)(2), question and answer 14. If, however, there is a comparable uncontrolled price for an integrated product and the possession product is a component product or end-product form thereof, the possessions corporation may, if such member complies with the requirements of § 1.936-6(a)(2), question and answer 14, compute its income under the cost sharing method with respect to such possession product. In that case, the cost sharing payment shall be computed under the following question and answer.

Question 11: How are possession sales snd total sales to be determined for purposes of computing the cost sharing payment with respect to a possession product which the possessions corporation sells to a member of its affiliated group where that member then leases the possession product to unrelated persons or uses it in its own trade or business?

Answer 11: If the possessions corporation is entitled to compute its income from such sales of the possession product under the cost sharing method, both possession sales and total sales shall be determined as if the possession product had been sold by the affiliate to an unrelated person at the time the possession product was first leased or otherwise placed in service by the affiliate. The sales price on such deemed sale shall be equal to the independent sales price from comparable uncontrolled transactions determined in accordance with § 1.482-2(e)(2), if any. If the possession product is a component product or an end-product form for which there is no such independent sales price but there is a comparable uncontrolled price for the integrated product which includes the possession product, the deemed sales price of the possession product shall be computed under the rules of § 1.936-6(a)(2) question and answer 2. The full amount of income received under the lease shall be treated as income of (and taxed to) the affiliate and not the possessions corporation.

Question 12: When may a possessions corporation take into account in computing total sales under the cost sharing method products in the same product area as the possession product (other than the possession product itself) where such products are leased by members of the affiliated group to unrelated persons or used by any such member in its own trade or business?

Answer 12: For purposes of computing total sales under the cost sharing method, the possessions corporation may take into account products in the same product area as the possession product itself where such products are leased by members of the affiliated group to unrelated persons or used in the trade or business of any such member, but only if an independent sales price for such products from comparable uncontrolled transactions may be determined under § 1.482-2(e)(2). In such cases, the units of such products which are leased or otherwise used internally by members of the affiliated group may be treated as sold to unrelated persons for such independent sales price for purposes of computing total sales.

Question 13: Assuming that a possessions corporation is entitled to compute its income under the cost sharing method with respect to sales of a possession product to affiliates in cases where those affiliates lease units of the possession product to unrelated persons or use them internally, is the possessions corporation's income from the possession product any different than if the affiliates had sold the product to unrelated parties?

Answer 13: No.

Question 14: If a possessions corporation sells units of a possession product to a member of its affiliated group and that affiliate then leases those units to an unrelated person or uses the units in its own trade or business, what requirements must the affiliate meet in order for the possessions corporation to be entitled to the benefits of the cost sharing method with respect to such units?

Answer 14: (i) For taxable years of the possessions corporation beginning on or before June 13, 1986, the affiliate need not meet any special requirements in order for the possessions corporation be entitled to the benefits of the cost sharing method with respect to such units. Thus, the affiliate's basis in such units shall be equal to the transfer price used for computing the possessions corporation's gross income with respect to such units under section 936(h)(5)(C)(i)(II), and the income derived by the affiliate from such lease or internal use shall be reported by the affiliate when and to the extent actually derived. The affiliate shall not be deemed to have sold such units to an unrelated party at the time they were

Reg. § 1.936-6(a)(2)

first leased or otherwise placed in service for any purpose other than the computation of possession sales and total sales. A similar rule applies to other products in the same product area as the possession product which are sold by any member in its own trade or business and which the possessions corporation takes into account in computing total sales under the cost sharing method.

(ii) For taxable years of the possessions corporations beginning after June 13, 1986, a possessions corporation will not be entitled to the benefits of the cost sharing method with respect to units of the possession product which the possessions corporation sells to an affiliate where the affiliate then leases such units to an unrelated person or uses them in its own trade or business, unless the affiliate agrees to be treated for all tax purposes as having sold such units to an unrelated party at the time they were first leased or otherwise placed in service by such affiliate. The affiliate must demonstrate such agreement by reporting its income from such units as if: (A) it had sold such units to an unrelated person at such time at a price equal to the price used to compute possessions sales under § 1.936-6(a)(2), question and answer 11; (B) it had immediately repurchased such units for the same price; and (C) its basis in such units for all subsequent purposes was equal to its cost basis from such deemed repurchase. For treatment of other products in the same product area as the possession product see § 1.936-6(a)(2), question and answer 12.

(iii) The principles contained in questions and answers 11, 12, 13, and 14 are illustrated by the following example:

Example. Possessions corporation S and its affiliate A are calendar year taxpayers. In 1985, S manufactures 100 units of possession product X. S sells 50 units of X to unrelated persons in arm's length transactions for $10 per unit. In applying the cost sharing method to determine the portion of its gross income from such sales which qualifies for the possessions tax credit, S determines that $8 of the $10 sales price may be taken into account. S sells the remaining 50 units of X to A, and A then leases such units to unrelated persons. In 1985, A also manufactures 100 units of product Y, the only other product in the same product area as X manufactured or sold by any member of the affiliated group. A manufactured the 100 units of Y at a cost of $15 per unit, sold 50 units of Y to unrelated persons in arm's length transactions for $20 per unit, and leased the remaining 50 units of Y to unrelated persons.

S may compute its income under the cost sharing method with respect to the 50 units of X it sold to A because S can determine an independent sales price of X from comparable uncontrolled transactions under § 1.482-2(e)(2). For purposes of computing both possessions sales and total sales, the 50 units of X sold to A will be deemed to have been sold by A to an unrelated person for $10 per unit. The income of S qualifying for the possessions tax credit from the sale of those 50 units of X to A, and A's basis in those units, will both be determined using the $8 transfer price determined under section 936(h)(5)(C)(i)(II). For purposes of computing total sales in the denominator of the cost sharing fraction, S may also take into account the 50 units of Y leased by A to unrelated persons, as if A had sold those units for $20 per unit. A's basis in those units of Y will continue to be its actual cost basis of $15 per unit.

If all of the above transactions had occurred in 1987, S would be entitled to compute its income under the cost sharing method with respect to the 50 units of X it sold to A only if A agreed to be treated for all tax purposes as if it had sold such units for $10 per unit, realized income on such deemed sale of $2 per unit, repurchased such units immediately for $10 per unit, and then leased such units, which would then have a $10 per unit basis in A's hands. For purposes of computing total sales, S would be entitled to take into account the 50 units of X leased by A to unrelated persons as if A had sold such units for $20 per unit.

(3) *Credits against cost sharing payments.*

Question 1: Is the cost of product area research paid or accrued by the possessions corporation in a taxable year creditable against the cost sharing payment?

Answer 1: Yes, if the cost of the product area research is paid or accrued solely by the possessions corporation. Thus, payments by the possessions corporation under cost sharing arrangements with, or royalties paid to, unrelated persons are so creditable. Amounts (such as royalties) paid directly or indirectly to, or on behalf of, related persons and amounts paid under any cost sharing agreements with related persons are not creditable against the cost sharing payment.

Question 2: Do royalties or other payments made by an affiliate of the possessions corporation to another member of the affiliated group reduce the cost sharing payment if such royalties or other payments are based, in part, on activity of the possessions corporation?

Answer 2: No. Payments made between affiliated corporations do not reduce the cost sharing payment. Thus, for example, if a possessions corporation sells a component to a foreign affiliate for incorporation by the foreign affiliate into an integrated product sold to unrelated persons, and

Reg. § 1.936-6(a)(3)

the foreign affiliate pays a royalty to the U.S. parent of the possessions corporation based on the total value of the integrated product, the cost sharing payment of the possessions corporation is not reduced.

(4) *Computation of cost sharing payment.*

Question 1: S is a possessions corporation engaged in the manufacture and sale of four products (A, B, C, and D) all of which are classified under the same three-digit SIC code. S sells its production to a U.S. affiliate, P, which resells it to unrelated parties in the United States. P's third party sales of each of these products produced in whole or in part by S (computed as provided under paragraph (a)(2) of § 1.936-6) are $1 million or a total of $4 million for A, B, C, and D. P's other sales of products in the same SIC code are $3,000,000; and the defined worldwide product area research of the affiliated group is $350,000. How should S compute the cost sharing amount for products A, B, C, and D?

Answer 1: The cost sharing amount is computed separately for each product on Schedule P of Form 5735. S should use the following formula for each of the products A, B, C, and D:

$$\frac{\text{Sales to unrelated persons of possession product}}{\text{Total sales of products in SIC code}} \times \text{Worldwide product area research}$$

$$\frac{\$1,000,000}{\$7,000,000} \times \$350,000 = \$50,000$$

Question 2: The facts are the same as in question 1 except that S manufactures product D under a license from an unrelated person. S pays the unrelated party an annual license fee of $20,000. Thus, the worldwide product area research expense of the affiliated group is $370,000. How should the cost sharing payment be adjusted?

Answer 2: The cost sharing fee should be reduced by the $20,000 license fee made as a direct annual payment to a third party on account of product D. The cost sharing payment with respect to product D in this example will be adjusted as follows:

$$\frac{\text{Sales to unrelated persons of possession product}}{\text{Total sales of products in SIC code}} \times \text{Worldwide product area research} - \text{Amount paid by the possessions corporation to an unrelated party}$$

$$\frac{(\$1,000,000)}{\$7,000,000} \times \$370,000 - \$20,000 = \$32,857$$

Question 3: The facts are the same as in question 1 except that S also manufactures and exports product E to a foreign affiliate, which resells it to unrelated persons for $1 million. S makes a separate election for its export sales. How should S compute the cost sharing amount for product E?

Answer 3: The numerator of the cost sharing fraction is the aggregate sales or other dispositions by members of the affiliated group of the units of product E produced in whole or in part in the possession to persons who are not members of the affiliated group. The cost sharing amount for product E would be computed as follows:

$$\frac{\text{Export sales of E}}{\text{Total sales of products in SIC code (In this example, U.S. Sales of A, B, C, and D + export sales of E)}} \times \text{Worldwide product area research}$$

or

$$\frac{\$1,000,000}{(\$7,000,000 + \$1,000,000)} \times \$350,000 = \$43,750$$

Question 4: The facts are the same as in question 1, except that S also receives $10,000 in royalty income from unrelated persons for the licensing of certain manufacturing intangible property rights. What is the amount of the product area research that must be allocated in determining the cost sharing amount?

Answer 4: If the affiliated group receives royalty income from unrelated persons with respect to manufacturing intangibles in the same product area, then the product area research to be considered shall be first reduced by such royalty income. In this case, the amount of product area research to be used in determining S's cost sharing pay-

Reg. § 1.936-6(a)(4)

ment should be reduced by the $10,000 royalty payment received to $340,000.

Question 5: May a possessions corporation redetermine the amount of its required cost sharing payment after filing its tax return?

Answer 5: If after filing its tax return, a possessions corporation files an amended return, or if an adjustment is made on audit, either of which affects the amount of the cost sharing payment required, then a redetermination of the cost sharing payment must be made. See, however, section 936(h)(5)(C)(i)(III)(*a*) with respect to the increase in the cost sharing payment due to interest imposed under section 6601(a).

(5) *Effect of election under the cost sharing method.*

Question 1: What is the effect of the cost sharing method?

Answer 1: The cost sharing payment reduces the amount of deductions (and the amount of reductions in earnings and profits) otherwise allowable to the U.S. affiliates (other than tax-exempt affiliates) within the affiliated group as determined under section 936(h)(5)(C)(i)(I)(*b*) which have incurred research expenditures (as defined in § 1.936-6(a)(1), question and answer (3) in the same product area for which the cost sharing option is elected, during the taxable year in which the cost sharing payment accrues. If there are no such U.S. affiliates, the reductions with respect to deductions and earnings and profits, as the case may be, are made with respect to foreign affiliates within the same affiliated group which have incurred product area research expenditures in such product area attributable to a U.S. trade or business. If there are no affiliates which have incurred research expenditures in such product area, the reductions are then made with respect to any other U.S. affiliate and, if there is no such U.S. affiliate, then to any other foreign affiliate. The allocations of these reductions in each case shall be made in proportion to the gross income of the affiliates. In the case of foreign affiliates, the allocation shall be made in proportion to gross income attributable to the U.S. trade or business or worldwide gross income, as the case may be. With respect to each group above, the reduction of deductions shall be applied first to deductions under section 174, then to deductions under section 162, and finally to any other deductions on a pro rata basis.

Question 2: For purposes of estimated tax payments, when is the cost sharing amount deemed to accrue?

Answer 2: The cost sharing amount is deemed to accrue to the appropriate affiliate on the last day of the taxable year of each such affiliate in which or with which the taxable year of the possessions corporation ends.

Question 3: If the cost sharing method is elected and the year of accrual of the cost sharing payment to the appropriate affiliate (described in question and answer 1 of this paragraph (a)(5)) differs from the year of actual payment by the possessions corporation, in what year are the deductions of the recipients reduced?

Answer 3: In the year the cost sharing payment has accrued.

Question 4: What is the treatment of income from intangibles under the cost sharing method?

Answer 4: Under the cost sharing method, a possessions corporation is treated as the owner, for purposes of obtaining a return thereon, of manufacturing intangibles related to a possession product. The term "manufacturing intangible" means any patent, invention, formula, process, design, pattern, or know-how. The possessions corporation will not be treated as the owner, for purposes of obtaining a return thereon, of any manufacturing intangibles related to a component product produced by an affiliated corporation and transferred to the possessions corporation for incorporation into the possession product, except in the case that the possession product is treated as including such component product for all purposes of section 936(h)(5). Further, the possessions corporation will not be treated as the owner, for purposes of obtaining a return thereon, of any marketing intangibles except "covered intangibles." (See § 1.936-6(c).)

Question 5: If the cost sharing option is elected, is it necessary for the possessions corporation to be the legal owner of the manufacturing intangibles related to the possession product in order for the possessions corporation to receive a full return with respect to such intangibles?

Answer 5: No. There is no requirement that manufacturing intangibles be owned by the possessions corporation.

Question 6: How is income attributable to marketing intangibles treated under the cost sharing method?

Answer 6: Except in the case of "covered intangibles" (see § 1.936-6(c)), the possessions corporation is not treated as the owner of any marketing intangibles, and income attributable to marketing intangibles of the possessions corporation will be allocated to the possessions corporation's U.S. shareholders with the proration of income based on shareholdings. If a shareholder of the possessions corporation is a foreign person or is otherwise tax exempt, the possessions corporation is taxable on that shareholder's pro rata

Reg. § 1.936-6(a)(5)

amount of the intangible property income. If the possessions corporation is a corporation any class of the stock of which is regularly traded on an established securities market, then the income attributable to marketing intangibles will be taxable to the possessions corporation rather than the corporation's U.S. shareholders.

Question 7: What is the source of the intangible property income described in question and answer 6?

Answer 7: The intangible property income is U.S. source whether taxed to the U.S. shareholder or taxed to the possessions corporation and section 863(b) does not apply for this purpose. However, such intangible property income, if treated as income of the possessions corporation, does not enter into the calculation of the 80-percent possession source test or the 65-percent active trade or business test.

Question 7a: What is the source of the taxpayer's gross income derived from a sale in the United States of a possession product purchased by the taxpayer (or an affiliate) from a corporation that has an election in effect under section 936, if the income from such sale is taken into account to determine benefits under cost sharing for the section 936 corporation? Is the result different if the taxpayer (or an affiliate) derives gross income from a sale in the United States of an integrated product incorporating a possession product purchased by the taxpayer (or an affiliate) from the section 936 corporation, if the taxpayer (or an affiliate) processes the possession product or an excluded component in the United States?

Answer 7a: Under either scenario, the income is U.S. source, without regard to whether the possession product is a component, end-product, or integrated product. Section 863 does not apply in determining the source of the taxpayer's income. This Q&A 7a is applicable for taxable years beginning on or after November 13, 1998.

Question 8: May marketing intangible income, if any, be allocated to the possessions corporation with respect to custom-made products?

Answer 8: No. If the cost sharing option is elected, then income attributable to marketing intangibles (other than "covered intangibles" described in § 1.936-6(c)) will be taxed as discussed in questions and answers 6 and 7 of paragraph (a)(5) of this section. It is immaterial whether the product is custom-made.

Question 9: In order to sell a pharmaceutical product in the United States, a New Drug Application ("NDA") for the product must be approved by the U.S. Food and Drug Administration. Is an NDA considered a manufacturing or marketing intangible for purposes of the allocation of income under the cost sharing method?

Answer 9: A manufacturing intangible.

Question 10: Can a copyright be, in whole or in part, a manufacturing intangible for purposes of the allocation of income under the cost sharing method?

Answer 10: In general, a copyright is a marketing intangible. See section 936(h)(3)(B)(ii). However, copyrights may be treated either as manufacturing intangibles or nonmanufacturing intangibles (or as partly each) depending upon the function or the use of the copyright. If the copyright is used in manufacturing, it will be treated as a manufacturing intangible; but if it is used in marketing, even if it is also classified as know-how, it will be treated as a marketing intangible.

Question 11: If the cost sharing option is elected and a patent is related to the product produced by the possessions corporation, does the return to the possessions corporation with respect to the manufacturing intangible include the make, use, and sell elements of the patent?

Answer 11: Yes. A patent confers an exclusive right for 17 years to sell a product covered by the patent. During this period, the return to the possessions corporation includes the make, use and sell elements of the patent.

Question 12: For purposes of the cost sharing option, may a safe haven rule be applied to determine the amount of marketing intangible income?

Answer 12: No. The amount of marketing intangible income is determined on the basis of all relevant facts and circumstances. The section 482 regulations will continue to apply except to the extent modified by the election. Rev. Proc. 63-10 and Rev. Proc. 68-22 do not apply for this purpose.

Question 13: If a product covered by the cost sharing election is sold by a possessions corporation to an affiliated corporation for resale to an unrelated party, may the resale price method under section 482 be used to determine the intercompany price of the possessions corporation?

Answer 13: In general, the resale price method may be used if (a) no comparable uncontrolled price for the product exists, and (b) the affiliated corporation does not add a substantial amount of value to the product by manufacturing or by the provision of services which are reflected in the sales price of the product to the customer. The possessions corporation will not be denied use of the resale price method for purposes of such intercompany pricing merely because the reseller adds more than an insubstantial amount to the

Reg. § 1.936-6(a)(5)

value of the product by the use of intangible property.

Question 14: If a possessions corporation makes the cost sharing election and uses the cost-plus method under section 482 to determine the arm's-length price of a possession product, will the cost base include the cost of materials which are subject to processing or which are components in the possession product?

Answer 14: A taxpayer may include the cost of materials in the cost base if it is appropriate under the regulations under § 1.482-2(e)(4).

Question 15: If the possessions corporation computes its income with respect to a product under the cost sharing method, and the price of the product is determined under the cost-plus method under section 482, does the cost base used in computing cost-plus under section 482 include the amount of the cost sharing payment?

ANSWER 15: The amount of the cost sharing payment is included in the cost base. However, no profit with respect to the cost sharing payment will be allowed.

QUESTION 16: If a member of the affiliated group transfers to a possessions corporation a component which is incorporated into a possession product, how will the transfer price for the component be determined?

ANSWER 16: The transfer price for the component will be determined under section 482, and as follows. If the possession product is treated as not including such component for purposes of section 936(h)(5), the transfer price paid for the component will include a return on all intangibles related to the component product. If the possession product is treated as including such component for purposes of section 936(h)(5), then the transfer price paid for the component by the possessions corporation will not include a return on any manufacturing intangible related to the component product, and the possessions corporation will obtain the return on the manufacturing intangibles associated with the component.

QUESTION 17: If the possessions corporation computes its income with respect to a product under the cost sharing method, with respect to which units of the product shall the possessions corporation be treated as owning intangible property as a result of having made the cost sharing election?

ANSWER 17: The possessions corporation shall not be treated as owning intangible property, as a result of having made the cost sharing election, with respect to any units of a possession product which were not taken into account by the possessions corporation in applying the significant business presence test for the current taxable year or for any prior taxable year in which the possessions corporation also had a significant business presence in the possession with respect to such product.

(b) *Profit split option*—(1) *Computation of combined taxable income.*

QUESTION 1: In determining combined taxable income from sales of a possession product, how are the allocations and apportionments of expenses, losses, and other deductions to be determined?

ANSWER 1: (i) Expenses, losses, and other deductions are to be allocated and apportioned on a "fully-loaded" basis under § 1.861-8 to the combined gross income of the possessions corporation and other members of the affiliated group (other than foreign affiliates). For purposes of the profit split option, the term "affiliated group" is defined the same as under § 1.936-6(a)(1) question and answer 2. The amount of research, development, and experimental expenses allocated and apportioned to combined gross income is to be determined under § 1.861-8(e)(3). The amount of research, development and experimental expenses and related deductions (such as royalties paid or accrued with respect to manufacturing intangibles by the possessions corporation or other domestic members of the affiliated group to unrelated persons or to foreign affiliates) allocated and apportioned to combined gross income shall in no event be less than the amount of the cost sharing payment that would have been required under the rules set forth in section 936(h)(5)(C)(i)(II) and paragraph (a) of this section if the cost sharing option had been elected. Other expenses which are subject to § 1.861-8(e) are to be allocated and apportioned in accordance with that section. For example, interest expense (including payments made with respect to bonds issued by the Puerto Rican Industrial, Medical and Environmental Control Facilities Authority (AFICA)) is to be allocated and apportioned under § 1.861-8(e)(2). With the exception of marketing and distribution expenses discussed below, the other remaining expenses which are definitely related to a class of gross income shall be allocated to that class of gross income and shall be apportioned on the basis of any reasonable method, as described in § 1.861-8(b)(3) and (c)(1). Examples of such methods may include, but are not limited to, those specified in § 1.861-8(c)(1)(i) through (vi).

(ii) The class of gross income to which marketing and distribution expenses relate and shall be allocated is generally to be defined by the same "product area" as is determined for the relevant research, development, and experimental ex-

Reg. § 1.936-6(b)(1)

penses (*i.e.*, the appropriate 3-digit SIC code), but shall include only gross income generated or reasonably expected to be generated from the geographic area or areas to which the expenses relate. It shall be presumed that marketing and distribution expenses relate to all product sales within the same product area. If, however, it can be established that any of these expenses are separately identifiable expenses, such as advertising, and relate, directly or indirectly, solely to a specific product or a specific group of products, such expenses shall be allocated to the class of gross income defined by the specific product or group of products. Thus, advertising and other separately identifiable marketing expenses which relate specifically and exclusively to a particular product must be allocated entirely to the gross income from that product, even though the taxpayer or other members of an affiliated group which includes the taxpayer produce and market other products in the same 3-digit SIC code classification. The mere display of a company logo or mention of a company name solely in the context of identifying the manufacturer shall not prevent an advertisement from relating specifically and exclusively to a particular product or group of products.

(iii) If marketing and distribution expenses are allocated to a class of gross income which consists both of income from sales of possession products (the statutory grouping) and other income such as from sales by U.S. affiliates of products not produced in the possession (the residual grouping), then these marketing and distribution expenses shall be apportioned on a "fully-loaded" basis which reflects, to a reasonably close extent, the factual relationship between these deductions and the statutory and residual groupings of gross income. Apportionment methods based upon comparisons of amounts incurred before ultimate sale of a product (including apportionment on a comparison of costs of goods sold, other expenses incurred, or other comparisons set forth in § 1.861-8(c)(1)(v), such as time spent) are not on a "fully-loaded" basis and do not reflect this required factual relationship. These deductions shall be apportioned on a basis of comparison of the amount of gross sales or receipts or another method if it is established that such method similarly reflects the required factual relationship. Thus, for example, a comparison of units sold may be used only where the units are of the same or similar value and are, thus, in fact comparable.

(iv) The rules for allocation and apportionment of marketing and distribution expenses may be illustrated by the following examples:

Example (1). Assume that possessions corporation A manufactures prescription pharmaceutical product #1 for resale by P, its U.S. parent corporation, in the United States. Additionally, assume that P manufactures prescription pharmaceutical products #2 and #3 in the United States for sale there. Further, assume that all three products are within the same product area, and that marketing and distribution expenses are internally divided by P among the three products on the basis of time spent by sales persons of P on marketing of the three products, as follows:

PRODUCT #1 —	50X
PRODUCT #2 —	80X
PRODUCT #3 —	110X
TOTAL	240X

These expenses of 240X are allocated to gross income generated by all three products and shall be apportioned on the basis of gross sales or receipts of product #1 as compared to products #2 and #3 or another method which similarly reflects the factual relationship between these expenses and gross income derived from product #1 and products #2 and #3. Thus, if a sales method were used and sales of product #1 accounted for one-third of sales receipts from the three products, 80X (240 ÷ 3) of marketing and distribution expenses would be apportioned to the combined gross income from product #1.

Example (2). Corporation B produces and sells Brand W whiskey, in the United States. B's subsidiary, S, which is a possessions corporation, produces soft drink extract in Puerto Rico which it sells to independent bottlers to produce Brand S soft drinks for sale in the United States. Corporation B's advertisements and other promotional materials for Brand W whiskey make no reference to Brand S soft drinks (or any other Corporation B products), and Brand S soft drink advertisements and other promotional materials make no reference to Brand W whiskey (or any other Corporation B products). For purposes of section 936(h), the advertising and other promotional expenses for Brand W whiskey must be allocated entirely to the gross income from sales of Brand W whiskey and the advertising and other promotional expenses for Brand S soft drink must be allocated entirely to the gross income from the sales of soft drink extract, notwithstanding the fact that whiskey and soft drink extract are both included in SIC code 208. A similar result would apply, for example, to separately identifiable advertising and other marketing expenses which relate specifically and exclusively to one or the other of the following pairs of products: chewing gum and granulated sugar (SIC code 206); canned tuna fish and freeze-dried coffee (SIC code 209); children's

Income from Sources Without the United States

underwear and ladies' brassieres (SIC code 234); aspirin tablets and prescription antibiotic tablets (SIC code 283); floor wax and perfume (SIC code 284); adhesives and inks (SIC code 289); semiconductors and cathode-ray tubes (SIC code 367); batteries and extension cords (SIC code 369); bandages and dental supplies (SIC code 384); stainless steel flatware and jewelry parts (SIC code 391); children's toys and sporting goods (SIC code 394); hair curlers and zippers (SIC code 396); and paint brushes and linoleum tiles (SIC code 399).

Example (3). Assume the same facts as in Example (1) and that possessions corporation A also manufactures aspirin, a non-prescription product, for resale by its U.S. parent corporation, P. Further, assume that the advertising and separately identifiable marketing expenses which relate specifically and exclusively to aspirin sales total $100 and that these expenses are allocable solely to gross income derived from aspirin sales. The sales method continues to be used to apportion the marketing and distribution expenses related, directly or indirectly, to products #1, #2, and #3, and the apportionment of such expenses to product #1 for purposes of determining combined taxable income from product #1 will remain as stated in Example (1). None of the advertising and other separately identifiable marketing expenses which relate specifically and exclusively to aspirin will be taken into account in allocating and apportioning the marketing and distribution expenses relating to the gross income attributable to products #1, #2, and #3. Gross income attributable to aspirin will be considered as a separate class of gross income, and all the advertising and separately identifiable marketing expenses which relate specifically and exclusively to aspirin sales of $100 will be allocated to the class of gross income derived from aspirin sales. Similarly, none of the marketing and distribution expenses, directly or indirectly, related solely to the group of products #1, #2, and #3 will be taken into account in determining the combined taxable income from aspirin sales. The remaining marketing and distribution expenses which do not, directly or indirectly, relate solely to any specific product or group of products (*e.g.,* the salaries of a Vice-President of Marketing who has responsibility for marketing all products and his staff) shall be allocated and apportioned on the basis of the gross receipts from the sales of all of the products (or a similar method) in determining combined taxable income of any product.

Question 2: How may the allocation and apportionment of expenses to combined gross income be verified?

Answer 2: Substantiation of the allocation and apportionment of expenses will be required upon audit of the possessions corporation and affiliates. Detailed substantiation may be necessary, particularly where the entities are engaged in multiple lines of business involving distinct product areas. Sources of substantiation may include certified financial reports. Form 10-K's, annual reports, internal production reports, product line assembly work papers, and other relevant materials. In this regard, see § 1.861-8(f)(5).

Question 3: Does section 936(h) overide the moratorium provided by section 223 of the Economic Recovery Tax Act of 1981 and any subsequent similar moratorium?

Answer 3: Yes. Thus, the allocation and apportionment of product area research described in question and answer 1 must be made without regard to the moratorium.

Question 4: Is the cost of samples treated as a marketing expense?

Answer 4: Yes. The cost of producing samples will be treated as a marketing expense and not as inventoriable costs for purposes of determining combined taxable income (and compliance with the significant business presence test). However, for taxable years beginning prior to January 1, 1986, the cost of producing samples may be treated as either a marketing expense or as inventoriable costs.

Question 5: If a possessions corporation uses the profit split method to determine its taxable income from sales of a product, how does it determine its gross income for purposes of the 80-percent possession source test and the 65-percent active trade or business test of section 936(a)(2)?

Answer 5: One-half of the deductions of the affiliated group (other than foreign affiliates) which are used in determining the combined taxable income from sales of the product are added to the portion of the combined taxable income allocated to the possessions corporation in order to determine the possessions corporation's gross income from sales of such product.

Question 6: How will income from intangibles related to a possession product be treated under the profit split method?

Answer 6: Combined taxable income of the possessions corporation and affiliates from the sale of the possession product will include income attributable to all intangibles, including both manufacturing and marketing intangibles, associated with the product.

Question 7: Can a possessions corporation apply the profit split option to a possession product if no

Reg. § 1.936-6(b)(1)

U.S. affiliates derive income from the sale of the possession product?

Answer 7: Yes.

Question 8: With respect to the factual situation discussed in question and answer 7 how is combined taxable income computed?

Answer 8: The profit split option is applied to the taxable income of the possessions corporation from sales of the possession product to foreign affiliates and unrelated persons. Fifty percent of that income is allocated to the possessions corporation, and the remainder is allocated to the appropriate affiliates as described in question and answer 13 of this paragraph (b)(1).

Question 9: May a possessions corporation compute its income under the profit split method with respect to units of a possession product which it sells to a U.S. affiliate if the U.S. affiliate leases such units to unrelated persons or to foreign affiliates or uses such units in its own trade or business?

Answer 9: Yes, provided that an independent sales price for the possession product from comparable uncontrolled transactions can be determined in accordance with § 1.482-2(e)(2). If, however, there is a comparable uncontrolled price for an integrated product and the possession product is a component product or end-product form thereof, the possessions corporation may compute its income under the profit split method with respect to such units. In either case, the possessions corporation shall compute combined taxable income with respect to such units under the following question and answer.

Question 10: If the possessions corporation is entitled to use the profit split method in the situation described in Q. 9 (leasing units of the possession product or use of such units in the taxpayer's own trade or business), how should it compute combined taxable income with respect to such units?

Answer 10: (i) Combined taxable income shall be computed as if the U.S. affiliate had sold the units to an unrelated person (or to a foreign affiliate) at the time the units were first leased or otherwise placed in service by the U.S. affiliate. The sales price on such deemed sale shall be equal to the independent sales price from comparable uncontrolled transactions determined in accordance with § 1.482-2(e)(2), if any.

(ii) If the possession product is a component product or an end-product form, the combined taxable income with respect to the possession product shall be determined under Q&A. 12 of this paragraph (b)(1).

(iii) For purposes of determining the basis of a component product or an end-product form, the deemed sales price of such product must be determined. The deemed sales price of the component product shall be determined by multiplying the deemed sales price of the integrated product that includes the component product by a ratio, the numerator of which is the production costs of the component product and the denominator of which is the production costs of the integrated product that includes the component product. The deemed sales price of an end-product form shall be determined by multiplying the deemed sales price of the integrated product that includes the end-product form by a ratio, the numerator of which is the production costs of the end-product form and the denominator of which is the production costs of the integrated product that includes the end-product form. For the definition of production costs, see Q&A. 12 of this paragraph (b)(1).

(iv)(A) If combined taxable income is determined under paragraph (v) of A. 12 of this paragraph (b)(1), in the case of a component product, the deemed sales price shall be determined by using the actual sales price of that product when sold as an integrated product (as adjusted under the rules of the fourth sentence of § 1.482-3(b)(2)(ii)(A)).

(B) If combined taxable income is determined under paragraph (v) of A. 12 of this paragraph (b)(1), in the case of an end-product form, the deemed sales price shall be determined by subtracting from the deemed sales price of the integrated product that includes the end-product form (e.g., the leased property) the actual sales price of the excluded component when sold as an integrated product to an unrelated person (as adjusted under the rules of the fourth sentence of § 1.482-3(b)(2)(ii)(A)).

(v) The full amount of income received under the lease shall be treated as income of (and be taxed to) the U.S. affiliate and not the possessions corporation.

Question 11: In the situation described in question 9, how does the U.S. affiliate determine its basis in such units for purposes of computing depreciation and similar items?

Answer 11: The U.S. affiliate shall be treated, for purposes of computing its basis in such units, as if it had repurchased such units immediately following the deemed sale and at the deemed sales price as provided in Q&A.10 of this paragraph (b)(1).

The principles of questions and answers 10 and 11 are illustrated by the following example.

Example: Possessions corporation S manufactures 100 units of possession product X. S sells 50

Reg. § 1.936-6(b)(1)

Income from Sources Without the United States

See p. 20,601 for regulations not amended to reflect law changes

units of X to an unrelated person in an arm's length transaction for $10 per unit. S sells the remaining 50 units to its U.S. affiliate, A, which leases such units to unrelated persons. The combined taxable income for the 100 units of X is computed below on the basis of the given production, sales, and cost data:

Sales

1. Total sales by S to unrelated persons (50 × $10) .... $ 500
2. Total deemed sales by A to unrelated persons (50 × $10).................. 500
3. Total gross receipts (line 1 plus line 2) .. 1,000

Total Costs

4. Material Costs 200
5. Production costs..................... 300
6. Research expenses 0
7. Other expenses 100
8. Total (add lines 4 through 7).......... 600

Combined taxable income attributable to the 100 units of X:

9. Combined taxable income (line 3 minus line 8) 400
10. Share of combined taxable income apportioned to S (50% of line 9) 200
11. Share of combined taxable income apportioned to A (line 9 minus line 10) . 200

A's basis in 50 units of X leased by it to unrelated persons:

12. 50 units times $10 deemed repurchase price 500

Subsequent leasing income is entirely taxed to A.

Question 12: If the possession product is a component product or an end-product form, how is the combined taxable income for such product to be determined?

Answer 12: (i) Except as provided in paragraph (v) of this *A. 12*, combined taxable income for a component product or an end-product form is computed under the production cost ratio (PCR) method.

(ii) Under the PCR method, the combined taxable income for a component product will be the same proportion of the combined taxable income for the integrated product that includes the component product that the production costs attributable to the component product bear to the total production costs (including costs incurred by the U.S. affiliates) for the integrated product that includes the component product. Production costs will be the sum of the direct and indirect production costs as defined under § 1.936-5(b)(4) except that the costs will not include any costs of materials. If the possession product is a component product that is transformed into an integrated product in whole or in part by a contract manufacturer outside of the possession, within the meaning of § 1.936-5(c), the denominator of the PCR shall be computed by including the same amount paid to the contract manufacturer, less the costs of materials of the contract manufacturer, as is taken into account for purposes of the significant business presence test under § 1.936-5(c) Q&A. 5.

(iii) Under the PCR method the combined taxable income for an end-product form will be the same proportion of the combined taxable income for the integrated product that includes the end-product form that the production costs attributable to the end-product form bear to the total production costs (including costs incurred by the U.S. affiliates) for the integrated product that includes the end-product form. Production costs will be the sum of the direct and indirect production costs as defined under § 1.936-5(b)(4) except that the costs will not include any costs of materials. If the possession product is an endproduct form and an excluded component is contract manufactured outside of the possession, within the meaning of § 1.936-5(c), the denominator shall be computed by including the same amount paid to the contract manufacturer, less cost of materials of the contract manufacturer, as is also taken into account for purposes of the significant business presence test under § 1.936-5(c) Q&A. 5.

(iv) This paragraph (iv) of *A. 12* illustrates the computation of combined taxable income for a component product or end-product form under the PCR method. S, a possessions corporation, is engaged in the manufacture of microprocessors. S obtains a component from a U.S. affiliate, O. S sells its production to another U.S. affiliate, P, which incorporates the microprocessors into central processing units (CPUs). P transfers the CPUs to a U.S. affiliate, Q, which incorporates the CPUs into computers for sale to unrelated persons. S chooses to define the possession product as the CPUs. The combined taxable income for the sale of the possession product on the basis of the given production, sales, and cost data is computed as follows:

Production costs (excluding costs of materials):

1. O's costs for the component......... 100
2. S's costs for the microprocessors 500
3. P's costs for the CPUs (the possession product)....................... 200
4. Q's costs for the computers 400
5. Total production costs for the computer (Add lines 1 through 4) 1,200
6. Combined production costs for the CPU (the possession product) (Add lines 1 through 3) 800
7. Ratio of production costs for the CPUs (the possession product) to the production costs for the computer 0.667

Reg. § 1.936-6(b)(1)

49,144 Income from Sources Without the United States

See p. 20,601 for regulations not amended to reflect law changes

Determination of combined taxable income for computers:
Sales:
8. Total possession sales of computers to unrelated customers and foreign affiliates 7,500

Total costs of O, S, P, and Q incurred in production of a computer:
9. Production costs (enter from line 5) .. 1,200
10. Material costs 100
11. Total costs (line 9 plus line 10) 1,300
12. Combined gross income from sale of computers (line 8 minus line 11)... 6,200

Expenses of the affiliated group (other than foreign affiliates) allocable and apportionable to the computers or any component thereof under the rules of §§ 1.861-8 through 1.861-14T and 1.936-6(b)(1), Q& A. 1:
13. Expenses (other than research expenses) 980

Research expenses of the affiliated group allocable and apportionable to the computers:
14. Total sales in the 3-digit SIC Code ... 12,500
15. Possession sales of the computers (enter from line 8) 7,500
16. Cost sharing fraction (divide line 15 by line 14) 0.6
17. Research expenses incurred by the affiliated group in 3-digit SIC Code multiplied by 120 percent 700
18. Cost sharing amount (multiply line 16 by line 17) 420
19. Research of the affiliated group (other than foreign affiliates) allocable and apportionable under §§ 1.861-17 and 1.861-14T(e)(2) to the computers 300
20. Enter the greater of line 18 or line 19 . 420

Computation of combined taxable income of the computer and the CPU:
21. Combined taxable income attributable to the computer (line 12 minus line 13 and line 20) 4,800
22. Combined taxable income attributable to CPUs (multiply line 21 by line 7) (production cost ratio) 3,200
23. Share of combined taxable income apportioned to S (50 percent of line 22) 1,600

Share of combined taxable income apportioned to U.S. affiliate(s) of S:
24. Adjustments for research expenses (line 18 minus line 19 multiplied by line 7) 80
25. Adjusted combined taxable income (line 22 plus line 24) 3,280
26. Share of combined taxable S (line 25 minus line 23) 1,680

(v)(A) If a possession product is sold by a taxpayer or its affiliate to unrelated persons in covered sales both as an integrated product and as a component product and the conditions of paragraph (v)(C) of this A. 12 are satisfied, the taxpayer may elect to determine the combined taxable income derived from covered sales of the component product under this paragraph (v). In that case, the combined taxable income derived from covered sales of the component product shall be determined by using the same per unit combined taxable income as is derived from covered sales of the product as an integrated product, but subject to the limitation of paragraph (v)(D) of this A. 12.

(B) In the case of a possession product that is an end-product form, if all of the excluded components are also separately sold by the taxpayer or its affiliate to unrelated persons in uncontrolled transactions and the conditions of paragraph (v)(C) of this A. 12 are satisfied, the taxpayer may elect to determine the combined taxable income of such end-product form under this paragraph (v). In that case, the combined taxable income derived from covered sales of the end-product form shall be determined by reducing the per unit combined taxable income from the integrated product that includes the end-product form by the per unit combined taxable income for excluded components determined under the rules of this paragraph (v), but subject to the limitation of paragraph (v)(D) of this A. 12. For this purpose, combined taxable income of the excluded components must be determined under section 936 as if the excluded components were possession products.

(C) In the case of component products, this paragraph (v) applies only if the sales price of the possession product sold in covered sales as an integrated product (i.e., in uncontrolled transactions) would be the most direct and reliable measure of an arm's length price within the meaning of the fourth sentence of § 1.482-3(b)(2)(ii)(A) for the component product. For purposes of applying the fourth sentence of § 1.482-3(b)(2)(ii)(A), the sale of the integrated product that includes the component product is treated as being immediately preceded by a sale of the component (i.e. without further processing) in a controlled transaction. In the case of end-product forms, this paragraph (v) applies only if the sales price of excluded components separately sold in uncontrolled transactions would be the most direct and reliable measure of an arm's length price within the meaning of the fourth sentence of § 1.482-3(b)(2)(ii)(A) for all excluded components of an integrated product that includes an end-product form. For purposes of applying the fourth sentence of § 1.482-3(b)(2)(ii)(A), the sale of the integrated product that includes excluded components is treated as being immediately preceded by

Reg. § 1.936-6(b)(1)

a sale of the excluded components (i.e. without further processing) in a controlled transaction. Under the fourth sentence of § 1.482-3(b)(2)(ii)(A), the uncontrolled transactions referred to in this paragraph (v)(C) must have no differences with the controlled transactions that would affect price, or have only minor differences that have a definite and reasonably ascertainable effect on price and for which appropriate adjustments are made (resulting in appropriate adjustments to the computation of combined taxable income). If such adjustments cannot be made, or if there are more than minor differences between the controlled and uncontrolled transactions, the method provided by this paragraph (v)(C) cannot be used. Thus, for example, these uncontrolled transactions must involve substantially identical property in the same or a substantially identical geographic market, and must be substantially identical to the controlled transaction in terms of their volumes, contractual terms, and market level. See § 1.482-3(b)(2)(ii)(B).

(D) In no case can the per unit combined taxable income as determined under paragraph (v)(A) or (B) of this *A. 12* be greater than the per unit combined taxable income of the integrated product that includes the component product or end-product form.

(E) The provisions of this paragraph (v) are illustrated by the following example. Taxpayer manufactures product A in a U.S. possession. Some portion of product A is sold to unrelated persons as an integrated product and the remainder is sold to related persons for transformation into product AB. The combined taxable income of integrated product A is $400 per unit and the combined taxable income of product AB is $300 per unit. The production cost ratio with respect to product A when sold as a component of product AB, is 2/3. Unless the taxpayer elects and satisfies the conditions of this paragraph (v), the combined taxable income with respect to A will be $200 per unit (combined taxable income for AB of $300 x the production cost ratio of 2/3). If, however, the comparability standards of paragraph (v)(C) of this *A. 12* are met, the taxpayer may elect to determine combined taxable income of product A when sold as a component of product AB using the same per unit combined taxable income as product A when sold as an integrated product. However, the per unit combined taxable income from sales of product A as a component product may not exceed the per unit combined taxable income on the sale of product AB. Therefore, the combined taxable income of component product A may not exceed $300 per unit.

(vi) Taxpayers that have not elected the percentage limitation under section 936(a)(1) for the first taxable year beginning after December 31, 1993, may do so if the taxpayer has elected the profit split method and computation of combined taxable income is affected by *Q&A.12* of this paragraph (b)(1).

(vii) The rules of *Q&A. 12* of this paragraph (b)(1) apply for taxable years ending after June 9, 1996. If, however, the election under paragraph (v) of *A. 12* of § 1.936-6(b)(1) is made, this election must be made for the taxpayer's first taxable year beginning after December 31, 1993, and if not made effective for that year, the election cannot be made for any later taxable year. A successor corporation that makes the same or substantially similar products as its predecessor corporation cannot make an election under paragraph (v) of A.12 of § 1.936-6(b)(1) unless the election was made by its predecessor corporation for its first taxable year beginning after December 31, 1993.

Question 13: If the profit split option is elected, how is the portion of combined taxable income not allocated to the possessions corporation to be treated?

Answer 13: (i) The income shall be allocated to affiliates in the following order, but no allocations will be made to affiliates described in a later category if there are any affiliates in a prior category—

(A) First, to U.S. affiliates (other than tax exempt affiliates) within the group (as determined under section 482) that derive income with respect to the product produced in whole or in part in the possession;

(B) Second, to U.S. affiliates (other than tax exempt affiliates) that derive income from the active conduct of a trade or business in the same product area as the possession product;

(C) Third, to other U.S. affiliates (other than tax-exempt affiliates);

(D) Fourth, to foreign affiliates that derive income from the active conduct of a U.S. trade or business in the same product area as the possession product (or, if the foreign members are resident in a country with which the U.S. has an income tax convention, then to those foreign members that have a permanent establishment in the United States that derives income in the same product area as the possession product); and

(E) Fifth, to all other affiliates.

(ii) The allocations made under paragraph (i)(A) of this *A. 13* shall be made on the basis of the relative gross income derived by each such affiliate with respect to the product produced in

Reg. § 1.936-6(b)(1)

whole or in part in the possession. For this purpose, gross income must be determined consistently for each affiliate and consistently from year to year.

(iii) The allocations made under paragraphs (i)(B) and (i)(D) of this *A. 13* shall be made on the basis of the relative gross income derived by each such affiliate from the active conduct of the trade or business in the same product area.

(iv) The allocations made under paragraphs (i)(C) and (i)(E) of this *A. 13* shall be made on the basis of the relative total gross income of each such affiliate before allocating income under this section.

(v) Income allocated to affiliates shall be treated as U.S. source and section 863(b) does not apply for this purpose.

(vi) For purposes of determining an affiliate's estimated tax liability for income thus allocated for taxable years beginning prior to January 1, 1995, the income shall be deemed to be received on the last day of the taxable year of each such affiliate in which or with which the taxable year of the possessions corporation ends. For taxable years beginning after December 31, 1994, quarterly estimated tax payments will be required as provided under section 711 of the Uruguay Round Agreements, Public Law 103-465 (1994), page 230, and any administrative guidance issued by the Internal Revenue Service thereunder.

Question 14: What is the source of the portion of combined taxable income allocated to the possessions corporation?

Answer 14: Income allocated to the possessions corporation shall be treated as possession source income and as derived from the active conduct of a trade or business within the possession.

Question 15: How is the profit split option to be applied to properly account for costs incurred in a year with respect to products which are sold by the possessions corporation to a U.S. affiliate during such year, but are not resold by the U.S. affiliate to persons who are not members of the affiliated group or to foreign affiliates until a later year?

Answer 15: The rules under § 1.994-1(c)(5) are to be applied. Incomplete transactions will not be taken into consideration in computing combined taxable income. Thus, for example, if in 1983, A, a possessions corporation, sells units of a product with a cost to A of $5000 to B corporation, its U.S. affiliate, which uses the dollar-value LIFO method of costing inventory, and B sells units with a cost of $4000 (representing A's cost) to C corporation, a foreign affiliate, only $4000 of such costs shall be taken into consideration in computing the combined taxable income of the possessions corporation and U.S. affiliates for 1983. If a specific goods LIFO inventory method is used by B, the determination of whether A's goods remain in B's inventory shall be based on whether B's specific goods LIFO grouping has experienced an increment or decrement for the year on the specific LIFO cost of such units, rather than on an average unit cost of such units. If the FIFO method of costing inventory is used by B, transfers may be based on the cost of the specific units transferred or on the average unit production cost of the units transferred, but in each case a FIFO flow assumption shall be used to identify the units transferred. For a determination of which goods are sold by taxpayers using the LIFO method, see question and answer 19.

Question 16: If a possessions corporation purchases materials from an affiliate and computes combined taxable income for a possession product which includes such materials, how are those materials to be treated in the possessions corporation's inventory?

Answer 16: The cost of those materials is considered to be equal to the affiliate's cost using the affiliate's method of costing inventory.

Question 17: If the possessions corporation uses the FIFO method of costing inventory and the U.S. affiliate uses the LIFO method of costing inventory, or *vice versa*, what method of costing inventory should be used in computing combined taxable income?

Answer 17: The transferor corporation's method of costing inventory determines the cost of inventory for purposes of combined taxable income while the transferee corporation's method of costing inventory determines the flow. Assume, for example, that X corporation, a possessions corporation, using the FIFO method of costing inventory purchases materials from Y corporation, a U.S. affiliate, also using the FIFO method. X corporation produces a product which it transfers to Z corporation, another U.S. affiliate using the LIFO method. Assume also that the final product satisfies the significant business presence test. Under these facts, the cost of the materials purchased by X from Y is Y's FIFO cost. The costs of the inventory transferred by X to Z are determined under X's FIFO method of accounting as is the flow of the inventory from X to Z. The costs added by Z are determined under Z's LIFO method of inventory, as is the flow of the inventory from Z to unrelated persons or foreign affiliates.

Question 18: How are the costs of a possession product and the revenues derived from the sale of a possession product determined if the U.S. affili-

Reg. § 1.936-6(b)(1)

Income from Sources Without the United States

See p. 20,601 for regulations not amended to reflect law changes

ate includes purchases of the possession product in a dollar-value LIFO inventory pool (as provided under § 1.472-8)?

Answer 18: The following method will be accepted in determining the revenues derived from the sale of a possession product and the costs of a possession product if the U.S. affiliate includes purchases of the possession product in a dollar-value LIFO inventory pool. The rules apply solely for the cost sharing and profit options under section 936 (h).

(i) *Revenue Identification:* The identification of revenues derived from sales of a possession product must generally be made on a specific identification basis. The particular method employed by a taxpayer for valuing its inventory will have no impact on the determination of what units are sold or how much revenue is derived from such sales. Thus, if a U.S. affiliate sells both item A (a possession product) and item B (a non-possession product), the actual sales revenues received by the U.S. affiliate from item A sales would constitute possession product revenue for purposes of the profit split option and possession sales for purposes of the cost sharing option regardless of whether the U.S. affiliate values its inventories on the FIFO or the LIFO method. In instances where sales of item A (*i.e.,* the possession product) cannot be determined by use of specific identification (for example, in cases where items A and B are identical except that one is produced in the possession (item A) and the other (item B) is produced outside of the possession and it is not possible to segregate these items in the hands of the U.S. affiliate), it will be necessary to identify the portion of the combined sales of items A and B (which together can be identified on a specific identification basis) which is attributed to item A sales and the portion which is attributed to item B sales. The determination of the portion of aggregated sales attributable to item A and item B is independent of the LIFO method used to determine the cost of such sales and may be made under the following approach. A taxpayer may, for purposes of this section of the regulations, use the relative purchases (in units) of items A and B by the U.S. affiliate during the taxable year (or other appropriate measuring period such as the period during the taxable year used to determine current-year costs, *i.e.,* earliest acquisitions period, latest acquisitions period, etc.) in determining the ratio to apply against the combined items A and B sales revenue. If the sales exceed current purchases, the taxpayer can use a FIFO unit approach which identifies actual unit sales on a first-in, first-out basis. Revenue determination where specific identification is not possible is illustrated by the following example:

Example. At the end of year 1, there are 600 units of combined items A and B which are to be allocated between A and B on the basis of annual purchases of A and B units during year 1. During year 1, 1,000 units of item A, a possession product, and 2,000 units of item B, a non-possession product, were purchased. Thus, the 600 units in year 1 ending inventory are allocated 200 (*i.e.* 1/3) to item A units and 400 (*i.e.* 2/3) to item B units based on the relative purchases of A (1,000) and B (2,000) in year 1. These units appear as beginning inventory in year 2.

In year 2, 1,500 units of item A are purchased and 1,500 units of item B are purchased. However, 3,300 units of items A and B in the aggregate are sold for $600,000. The relative proportion of the $600,000 attributable to item A and to item B sales would be determined as follows:

Year 2 Sales	Item A	Item B
Unit sales from opening inventory	200	400
Unit sales from current-year purchases	1,350	1,350
Total unit sales	1,550	1,750 = 3,300
Percentage	47%	53%
Revenues from item A sales	$281,818	$600,000 × 1550/3300
Revenues from item B sales	$318,182	$600,000 × 1750/3300

Year 2 Closing Inventory

	Units
Item A	150
Item B	150

Thus, revenues from item A sales for purposes of computing possession sales for the cost sharing option and revenues for the profit split option are $281,818.

(ii) *Cost Identification:* The determination of the cost of possession product sales by the U.S. affiliate must be based on the LIFO inventory method of the U.S. affiliate. The LIFO cost of

Reg. § 1.936-6(b)(1)

Income from Sources Without the United States

See p. 20,601 for regulations not amended to reflect law changes

possession product sales will, for purposes of this section of the regulations, be determined by maintaining a separate LIFO cost for possession products in a taxpayer's opening and closing LIFO inventory and using this cost to calculate an independent cost of possession product sales. This separate LIFO cost for possession products in the LIFO pool of a taxpayer is to be determined as follows:

(A) Determine the base-year cost of possession products in ending inventory in a LIFO pool.

(B) Determine the percentage of the base-year cost of possession products in the pool as compared to the total base-year cost of all items in the pool.

(C) Multiply the percentage determined in step (B) above by the ending LIFO inventory value of the pool to determine the deemed LIFO cost attributable to possession products in the pool.

(D) Subtract the LIFO cost of possession products in ending inventory in the pool (as calculated in step (C) above) from the sum of: (1) possession product purchases for the year, plus (2) the portion of the opening LIFO inventory value of the pool attributed to possession products (i.e., the result obtained in step (C) above for the prior year). The number determined by this calculation is the LIFO cost of possession product sales from the taxpayer's LIFO pool.

Example: Assume that item A is a possession product and item B is a non-posession product and also assume the inventory and purchases with respect to the LIFO pool as provided below:

Year 1—Ending Inventory

	Number of Units	Base-Year Cost/Unit	Base-Year Cost	%
Item A	100	$2.00	$200	20%
Item B	200	4.00	800	80%

Year 1—LIFO Value

	Base-Year Cost	Index	LIFO Cost
Increment layer 2	$ 300	3.0	$ 900
Increment layer 1	400	2.0	800
Base layer	300	1.0	300
Pool total	$1,000		$2,000

Year 1—LIFO Value Per Item

	Base-Year Cost	LIFO Value
Total pool	$1,000	$2,000
Item A	200	400
Item B	800	1,600

Year 2—Purchases

	Total Purchases
Item A	$6,000
Item B	4,000

Year 2—Ending Inventory

	Number of Units	Base-Year Cost/Unit	Base-Year Cost	%
Item A	200	$2.00	$400	50%

Year 2—LIFO Value

	Base-Year Cost	Index	LIFO Cost
Increment layer 2	$ 100	3.0	$ 300
Increment layer 1	400	2.0	800
Base layer	300	1.0	300
Pool total	$ 800		$1,400

The year 2 LIFO cost of possession product A sales will be calculated as follows:

(1) Base-year cost of item in year 2 ending inventory = $400

(2) Percentage of item A base-year cost to total base-year cost ($400 ÷ $800) = 50%

(3) LIFO value of item A ($1,400 × 50%) = $700

(4) LIFO cost of item A sales is determined by adding to the beginning inventory in year 2 the purchases of item A in year 2 and subtracting from this amount the ending inventory in year 2 ($400 + $6000 − $700 = $5700). The beginning inventory in year 2 is determined by multiplying the LIFO cost of the year 1 ending inventory by a percentage of item A base year cost to the total

Reg. § 1.936-6(b)(1)

Income from Sources Without the United States

See p. 20,601 for regulations not amended to reflect law changes

base-year cost in year 1. The ending inventory in year 2 is determined under (3) above.

Question 19: If a possession product is purchased from a possessions corporation by a U.S. affiliate using the dollar-value LIFO method of costing its inventory and is included in a LIFO pool of the U.S. affiliate which includes products purchased from the possessions corporation in pre-TEFRA years, how should the LIFO index computation of the U.S. affiliate be made in the first year in which section 936(h) applies and in subsequent taxable years?

Answer 19: The U.S. affiliate should treat the first taxable year for which section 936(h) applies as a new base year in accordance with procedures provided by regulations under section 472. Thus, the opening inventory for the first year, for which section 936(h) applies (valuing possession products purchased from the possessions corporation on the basis of the cost of such possession products), would equal the new base year cost of the inventory of such pool of the U.S. affiliate. Increments and decrements at new base year cost would be valued for LIFO purposes pursuant to the procedures provided by regulations under section 472.

Question 20: If the possessions corporation computes its income with respect to a product under the profit split method, with respect to which units of the product shall the profit split method apply?

Answer 20: The profit split method shall apply to units of the possession product produced in whole or in part by the possessions corporation in the possession and sold during the taxable year by members of the affiliated group (other than foreign affiliates) to unrelated parties or to foreign affiliates. In no event shall the profit split method apply to units of the product which were not taken into account by the possessions corporation in applying the significant business presence test for the current taxable year or for any prior taxable year in which the possessions corporation also had a significant business presence in the possession with respect to such product.

(2) *Pre-TEFRA Inventory.*

Question 1: How is pre-TEFRA inventory to be determined if the profit split option is elected and the FIFO method of costing inventory is used by the U.S. affiliate?

Answer 1: Pre-TEFRA inventory is inventory which was produced by the possessions corporation and transferred to a U.S. affiliate prior to the possessions corporation's first taxable year beginning after December 31, 1982. Pre-TEFRA inventory will not be included for purposes of the profit split option. If the U.S. affiliate uses the FIFO method of costing inventory, the pre-TEFRA inventory will be treated as the first inventory sold by the U.S. affiliate during the first year in which section 936(h) applies and will not be included in the computation of combined taxable income for purposes of the profit split option. The treatment of pre-TEFRA inventory when FIFO costing is used by both the U.S. affiliate and the possessions corporation is illustrated by the following example in which FIFO unit costing is used:

Example: Assume the following:

	X Possessions corporation		Y U.S. affiliate	
	Number of units	Cost per unit	Number of units	Cost per unit
Beginning inventory	500	$150	200	$225
Units produced during 1983	1,000	200	....	....
Ending inventory	400	200	300	....

In 1983, the beginning inventory of X, a possessions corporation, is 500 units with a unit cost of $150 and the beginning inventory of Y, the U.S. affiliate, is 200 units with a unit cost of $225, which represents the section 482 price paid by Y. Y's beginning inventory in 1983 represents purchases made in 1982 of products produced by X in that year. Y sells all the units it purchases from X to Z, a foreign affiliate. In 1983, X produces 1000 units at a unit cost of $200 and sells 1100 units to Y (the difference between 1500 units, representing X's 1983 beginning inventory (500) and the units produced by X in 1983 (1000), and X's ending inventory of 400 units). Of the 1100 units sold by X to Y in 1983, only 800 units (and not 1000 units) which were sold by Y to Z are taken into consideration in computing combined taxable income for 1983. Since FIFO costing by the possessions corporation is used, the cost is $150 per unit for the first 500 units and $200 per unit for the remaining 300 units. The 200 units sold by X to Y in 1982 are pre-TEFRA inventory and are not included in the computation of combined taxable income for 1983. They are also treated as the first units sold by Y to Z in 1983. This inventory has a unit cost of $225, which reflects the section 482 transfer price from X to Y in 1982. Y's 1983 ending inventory of 300 units will not be taken into consideration in computing the combined taxable income of X and Y for 1983

Reg. § 1.936-6(b)(2)

because the units have not been sold to a foreign affiliate or to persons who are not members of the affiliated group. In a subsequent year when the units are sold to Z, the cost to X and selling price to Z of these units will enter into the computation of combined taxable income for that year.

(c) *Covered Intangibles.*

Question 1: What are "covered intangibles" under section 936(h)(5)(C)(i)(II)?

Answer 1: The term "covered intangibles" means (1) intangible property developed in a possession solely by the possessions corporation and owned by it, (2) manufacturing intangible property (described in section 936(h)(3)(B)(i)) which is acquired by the possessions corporation from unrelated persons, and (3) any other intangible property (described in section 936(h)(3)(B)(ii) through (v), to the extent not described in section 936(h)(3)(B)(i)) which relates to sales of products or services to unrelated persons for ultimate consumption or use in the possession in which the possessions corporation conducts its business. The possessions corporation is treated as the owner of covered intangibles for purposes of obtaining a return thereon.

Question 2: Do covered intangibles include manufacturing intangible property which is acquired by an affiliate and subsequently transferred to the possessions corporation?

Answer 2: No. In order for a manufacturing intangible to be treated as a covered intangible, the intangible property must be acquired directly by the possessions corporation from an unrelated person unless the manufacturing intangible was acquired by an affiliate from an unrelated person and was transferred to the possessions corporation by the affiliate prior to September 3, 1982.

Question 3: If a possessions corporation licenses a manufacturing intangible from an unrelated party, will the licensed intangible be treated as a covered intangible?

Answer 3: No.

Question 4: How is ultimate consumption or use determined for purposes of the definition of covered intangibles?

Answer 4: A product will be treated as having its ultimate use or consumption in a possession if it is sold by the possessions corporation to a related or unrelated person in a possession and is not resold or used or consumed outside of the possession within one year after the date of the sale.

Question 5: Are sales of products that relate to covered intangibles excluded from the cost sharing fraction?

Answer 5: If no manufacturing intangibles other than covered intangibles are associated with the possession product, then sales of such product will be excluded from the cost sharing fraction. If both covered and non-covered manufacturing intangibles are associated with the possession product, then sales of such product will be included in the cost sharing fraction.

Question 6: If the cost sharing option is elected, is it necessary for the possessions corporation to be the legal owner of covered intangibles described in section 936(h)(5)(C)(i)(II)(c) related to the product in order for the possessions corporation to receive a full return with respect to such intangibles?

Answer 6: No. For purposes of section 936(h), it is immaterial whether such covered intangibles are owned by the possessions corporation or by another member of the affiliated group. Moreover, if the legal owner of such covered intangibles which are subject to section 936(h)(5) is an affiliate of the possessions corporation, such person will not be required to charge an arm's-length royalty under section 482 to the possessions corporation. [Reg. § 1.936-6.]

☐ [T.D. 8090, 6-9-86. Amended by T.D. 8669, 5-9-96 and T.D. 8786, 10-13-98.]

[Reg. § 1.936-7]

§ 1.936-7. Manner of making election under section 936(h)(5); special election for export sales; revocation of election under section 936(a).—The rules in this section apply for purposes of section 936(h) and also for purposes of section 934(e), where applicable.

(a) *Manner of making election.*

Question 1: How does a possessions corporation make an election to use the cost sharing method or profit split method?

Answer 1: A possessions corporation makes an election to use the cost sharing or profit split method by filing Form 5712-A and attaching it to its tax return. Form 5712-A must be filed on or before the due date (including extensions) of the tax return of the possessions corporation for its first taxable year beginning after December 31, 1982. The electing corporation must set forth on the form the name and the taxpayer identification number or address of all members of the affiliated group (including foreign affiliates not required to file a U.S. tax return). All members of the affiliated group must consent to the election. An authorized officer of the electing corporation must sign the statement of election and must declare that he has received a signed statement of consent from an authorized officer, director, or other appropriate official of each member of the affiliated group. The election is not valid unless all affiliates consent. However, a failure to obtain an affiliate's written consent will not invalidate the election out if the possessions corporation made a good faith effort to obtain all the necessary consents or the failure to obtain the missing consent was inadvertent. Subsequently created or acquired affiliates are bound by the election. If an election out is revoked under section 936(h)(5)(F)(iii), a new election out with respect to that product area cannot be made without the consent of the Commissioner. The possessions corporation shall file an amended Form 5712-A with its timely filed income tax return to reflect any changes in the names or number of the members of the affiliated group for any taxable year after the first taxable year to which the election out applies. By consenting to the election out, all affiliates agree to provide information necessary to compute the cost sharing payment under the cost sharing method or combined taxable income under the profit split method, and failure to provide such information shall be treated as a request to revoke the election out under section 936(h)(5)(F)(iii).

Question 2: May the "election out" under section 936(h)(5) be made on a product-by-product basis, or must it be made on a wider basis?

Answer 2: An electing corporation is required to treat products in the same product area in the same manner.

Similarly, all possessions corporations in the same affiliated group that produce any products or render any services in the same product area must make the same election for all products that fall within the same product area. However, § 1.936-7(b) provides that the electing corporation may make a different election for export sales than for domestic sales. The electing corporation or corporations may also make different elections for products that fall within different product areas.

Question 3: May the possessions corporation elect to define product area more narrowly than the 3-digit SIC code?

Answer 3: No. Certain alternatives, such as the 4-digit SIC code, would not be permitted under the statute. However, other methods for defining product area may be considered by the Commissioner in the future.

Question 4: May a possessions corporation make an election out under the cost sharing method with respect to a product area if the affiliated group incurs no research, development or experimental costs in that product area?

Answer 4: Yes. In that case the cost sharing payment will be zero.

Question 5: If the significant business presence test is not satisfied for a product or type of service within the product area covered by the election out under section 936(h)(5) what rules will apply with respect to that product?

Answer 5: With respect to the product which does not satisfy the significant business presence test, the provisions of section 936(h)(1) through (h)(4) will apply to the allocation of income. However, if a cost sharing or a profit split election has been made with respect to the product area, the cost sharing payment or the research and development floor under section 936(h)(5)(C)(ii)(II) will not be reduced.

Question 6: Is a taxpayer permitted to make a change of election with respect to the cost sharing and profit split methods?

Answer 6: In general, once the election is properly made, it is binding for the first year in which it applies and all subsequent years (including upon any later created or acquired affiliates), and revocation is only permitted with the consent of the Commissioner of Internal Revenue. However, a taxpayer will be permitted to change its election once from the cost sharing method to the profit split method or *vice versa,* or from the method permitted under section 936(h)(1) through (h)(4) to cost sharing or profit split or *vice versa,* without the consent of the Commissioner if the change is made on the taxpayer's return for its first taxable year ending after June 13, 1986. Such change will aply to such taxable year and all subsequent taxable years, and, at the taxpayer's option, may also apply to all prior taxable years for which section 936(h) was in effect. A change of election will be treated as an election subject to the procedures set forth above and to section 481 of the Internal Revenue Code.

Question 7: If the Commissioner determines that a possessions corporation does not meet the 80-percent possession source test or the 65-percent active trade or business test (the "qualification tests") for any taxable year beginning after 1982, under what circumstances is the possessions corporation permitted to make a distribution of property after the close of its taxable year to meet the qualification tests?

Answer 7: A possessions corporation may make a pro rata distribution of property to its shareholders after the close of the taxable year if the Commissioner determines that the possessions corporation does not satisfy the qualification tests (a) by reason of the exclusion from gross income of intangible income under section 936(h)(1)(B) or section 936(h)(5)(C)(i)(II) or (b) by reason of the allocation to the shareholders of the possessions corporation of income under section

Reg. § 1.936-7(a)

49,152 Income from Sources Without the United States

See p. 20,601 for regulations not amended to reflect law changes

936(h)(5)(C)(ii)(III); provided, however, that the determination of the Commissioner does not contain a finding that the failure of such corporation to satisfy the qualification tests was due, in whole or in part, to fraud with intent to evade tax or willful neglect on the part of the possessions corporation. The possessions corporation must designate the distribution at the time the distribution is made as a distribution to meet qualification requirements, and it will be subject to the provisions of section 936(h)(4). Such distributions will not qualify for the dividends received deduction.

Question 8: If a possessions corporation owns stock in a subsidiary possessions corporation, any intangible property income allocated to the parent possessions corporation under section 936(h) will be treated as U.S. source income and taxable to the parent possessions corporation. Is the intangible property income taken into consideration in determining whether the parent possessions corporation meets the income tests of section 936(a)(2)?

Answer 8: While taxable to the parent possessions corporation, the intangible property income does not enter into the calculation of the 80-percent possession source test or the 65-percent active trade or business test of section 936(a)(2)(A) and (B). This would also be the case if the subsidiary possessions corporation made a qualifying distribution under section 936(h)(4).

(b) *Separate election for export sales.*

Question 1: What methods of computing income can a possessions corporation use under the separate election for export sales?

Answer 1: The only two methods which are available under the separate election for export sales are the cost sharing method and the profit split method.

Question 2: What is the definition of export sales for purposes of the separate election for export sales?

Answer 2: The determination of export sales is based upon the destination of the product, i.e., where it is to be used or consumed. If the product is sold to a U.S. affiliate, it will be treated as an export sale only if resold or otherwise transferred abroad to a foreign person (including a foreign affiliate or foreign branch of a U.S. affiliate) within one year from the date of sale to the U.S. affiliate for ultimate use or consumption outside the United States as provided under § 1.954-3(a)(3)(ii).

Question 3: Assume that a possessions corporation sells a product to both foreign affiliates and foreign branches of U.S. affiliates. In addition, it sells the product to its U.S. parent for resale in the U.S. The possessions corporation makes a profit split election for domestic sales and a cost sharing election for export sales. Will the sales to foreign branches of U.S. affiliates be treated as exports subject to the cost sharing method or as domestic sales subject to the profit split method?

Answer 3: The sales to a foreign branch of a U.S. corporation are exports if for ultimate use or consumption outside of the United States as provided under § 1.954-3(a)(3)(ii).

Question 4: Under what circumstances may a possessions corporation make the separate election under section 936(h)(5)(F)(iv)(II) for computing its income from products exported to a foreign person when the income derived by such foreign person on the resale of such products is included in foreign base company income under section 954(a)?

Answer 4: If the income derived by a foreign person on the resale of products manufactured, in whole or in part, by a possessions corporation is included in foreign base company income under section 954(a), then the possessions corporation may make the separate export election under section 936(h)(5)(F)(iv)(II) for computing its income from such products only if such foreign person has been formed or is availed of for substantial business reasons that are unrelated to an affiliated corporation's U.S. tax liability. For purposes of the preceding sentence, a foreign person will be considered to be formed or availed of for such substantial business reasons if the foreign person in the normal course of business purchases substantial quantities of products from both the possessions corporation and its affiliates for resale, and, in addition provides support services for affiliated companies such as centralized testing, marketing of products, management of local currency exposures, or other similar services. However, a foreign person that purchases and resells products only from a possessions corporation is presumed to be formed or availed of for other than such substantial business reasons, even if the foreign person provides additional services.

Question 5: When will the "manufacturing" test set forth in subsection (d)(1)(A) of section 954 be applicable to the export sales of a product of a possessions corporation which makes a separate election for export sales?

Answer 5: An electing corporation will be required to meet the "manufacturing" test set forth in subsection (d)(1)(A) of section 954 with respect to export sales of its product in each taxable year in which the separate election for export sales is in effect.

(c) *Revocation of election under section 936(a).*

Question 1: When may an election under section 936(a) be revoked?

Reg. § 1.936-7(b)

Answer 1: An election under section 936(a) may be revoked during the first ten years of section 936 status only with the consent of the Commissioner, and without the Commissioner's consent after that time. The Commissioner hereby consents to all requests for revocation that are made with respect to the taxpayer's first taxable year beginning after December 31, 1982 provided that the section 936(a) election was in effect for the corporation's last taxable year beginning before January 1, 1983, if the taxpayer agrees not to re-elect section 936(a) prior to its first taxable year beginning after December 31, 1988. A taxpayer that wishes to revoke a section 936(a) election under the terms of the blanket revocation must attach a "Statement of Revocation—Section 936" to the taxpayer's timely filed return (including extensions) and must state that in revoking the election the taxpayer agrees not to re-elect section 936(a) prior to its first taxable year beginning after December 31, 1983. Other requests to revoke not covered by the Commissioner's blanket consent should be addressed to the District Director having jurisdiction over the taxpayer's tax return. [Reg. § 1.936-7.]

☐ [T.D. 8090, 6-9-86.]

[Reg. § 1.936-8T]

§ 1.936-8T. **Qualified possession source investment income (Temporary).** [Reserved]

[Reg. § 1.936-9T]

§ 1.936-9T. **Source of qualified possession source investment income (Temporary).** [Reserved]

[Reg. § 1.936-10]

§ 1.936-10. **Qualified investments.**—(a) *In general.* [Reserved]

(b) *Qualified Investments in Puerto Rico.* [Reserved]

(c) *Qualified investment in certain Caribbean Basin countries*—(1) *General rule.* An investment of qualified funds described in this section shall be treated as a qualified investment of funds for use in Puerto Rico if the funds are used for a qualified investment in a qualified Caribbean Basin country. A qualified investment in a qualified Caribbean Basin country is a loan of qualified funds by a qualified financial institution (described in paragraph (c)(3) of this section) directly to a qualified recipient (described in paragraph (c)(9) of this section) or indirectly through a single financial intermediary for investment in active business assets (as defined in paragraph (c)(4) of this section) in a qualified Caribbean Basin country (described in paragraph (c)(10)(ii) of this section) or for investment in development projects (as defined in paragraph (c)(5) of this section) in a qualified Caribbean Basin country, provided—

(i) The investment is authorized, prior to disbursement of the funds, by the Commissioner of Financial Institutions of Puerto Rico (or his delegate) pursuant to regulations issued by such Commissioner; and

(ii) The agreement, certification, and due diligence requirements under paragraphs (c)(11), (12), and (13) of this section are met.

A loan by a qualified financial institution shall not be disqualified merely because the loan transaction is processed by the central bank of issue of the country into which the loan is made pursuant to, and solely for purposes of complying with, the exchange control laws or regulations of such country. Further, a loan by a qualified financial institution shall not be disqualified merely because the loan is acquired by another person, provided such other person is also a qualified financial institution.

(2) *Termination of qualification*—(i) *In general.* An investment that, at any time after having met the requirements for a qualified investment in a qualified Caribbean Basin country under the terms of this paragraph (c), fails to meet any of the conditions enumerated in this paragraph (c) shall no longer be considered a qualified investment in a qualified Caribbean Basin country from the time of such failure, unless the investment satisfies the requirements for a timely cure described in paragraph (c)(2)(ii) of this section. Such a failure includes, but is not limited to, the occurrence of any of the following events:

(A) Active business assets cease to qualify as such;

(B) Proceeds from the investment are diverted for the financing of assets, projects, or operations that are not active business assets or development projects or are not the assets or the project of the qualified recipient;

(C) The holder of the qualified recipient's obligation is not a qualified financial institution;

(D) The qualified recipient's qualified business activity ceases to qualify as such; or

(E) The qualified Caribbean Basin country ceases to be a country described in paragraph (c)(10)(ii) of this section.

(ii) *Timely cure*—(A) *In general.* A timely cure shall be considered to have been made if the event or events that cause disqualification of the investment are corrected within a reasonable period of time. For purposes of this section, a reasonable period of time shall not exceed 60 days after

Reg. § 1.936-10(c)(2)

such event or events come to the attention of the qualified recipient or the qualified financial institution or should have come to their attention by the exercise of reasonable diligence.

(B) *Due diligence requirements.* A timely cure of a failure to comply with the due diligence requirements of paragraphs (c)(11), (12), and (13) of this section shall be considered to be made if the failure to comply is due to reasonable cause and, upon request of the Commissioner of Financial Institutions of Puerto Rico (or his delegate) or of the Assistant Commissioner (International) (or his authorized representative), the qualified financial institution (and its trustee or agent, if any), the financial intermediary, or the qualified recipient establishes to the satisfaction of the Commissioner of Financial Institutions of Puerto Rico (or his delegate) or of the Assistant Commissioner (International) (or his authorized representative) that it has exercised due diligence in ensuring that the funds were properly disbursed to a qualified recipient and applied by or on behalf of such qualified recipient to uses that qualify the investment as an investment in qualified business assets or a development project under the provisions of this paragraph (c).

(iii) *Assumption of qualified recipient's obligation.* An investment shall not cease to qualify merely because the qualified recipient's obligation to the qualified financial institution (or to a financial intermediary, if any) is assumed by another person, provided such other person assumes the qualified recipient's agreement and certification requirements under paragraph (c)(11)(i) of this section and is either—

(A) A qualified recipient on the date of assumption, in which case such person shall be treated for purposes of this section as the original qualified recipient and shall be subject to all the requirements of this section for continued qualification of the loan as a qualified investment in a qualified Caribbean Basin country; or

(B) An international organization, the principal purpose of which is to foster economic development in developing countries and which is described in section 1 of the International Organizations Immunities Act (22 U.S.C. § 288), if the assumption of the obligation is pursuant to a bona fide guarantee agreement.

(3) *Qualified financial institution*—(i) *General rule.* For purposes of section 936(d)(4)(A) and this section, a qualified financial institution includes only—

(A) A banking, financing, or similar business defined in § 1.864-4(c)(5)(i) that is an eligible institution described in paragraph (c)(3)(ii) of this section, but not including branches of such institution outside of Puerto Rico;

(B) A single-purpose entity described in paragraph (c)(3)(iii) of this section;

(C) The Government Development Bank for Puerto Rico;

(D) The Puerto Rico Economic Development Bank; and

(E) Such other entity as may be determined by the Commissioner by Revenue Procedure or other guidance published in the Internal Revenue Bulletin.

(ii) *Eligible institution.* An eligible institution means an institution—

(A) That is an entity organized under the laws of the Commonwealth of Puerto Rico or is the Puerto Rican branch of an entity organized under the laws of another jurisdiction, if such entity is engaged in a banking, financing, or similar business defined in § 1.864-4(c)(5)(i), and

(B) That is licensed as an eligible institution under Regulation No. 3582 (or any successor regulation) issued by the Commissioner of Financial Institutions of Puerto Rico (hereinafter "Puerto Rican Regulation No. 3582").

(iii) *Single-purpose entity.* A single-purpose entity is an entity that meets all of the following conditions:

(A) The entity is organized under the laws of the Commonwealth of Puerto Rico and is a corporation, a partnership or a trust, which conducts substantially all of its activities in Puerto Rico.

(B) The sole purpose of the entity is to use qualified funds from possessions corporations to make one or more qualified investments in a qualified Caribbean Basin country and the entity actually uses such funds only for such purpose.

(C) In the case of an entity that is a trust, one of the trustees is a qualified financial institution described in paragraph (c)(3)(i) of this section.

(D) The entity is licensed as an eligible institution under Puerto Rican Regulation No. 3582 (or any successor regulation).

(E) Any temporary investment by the entity for its own account of funds received from a possessions corporation, and the income from the investment thereof, and any temporary investment by the entity for its own account of principal and interest paid by a borrower to the entity, and the income from the investment thereof, are limited to investments in eligible activities, as described in section 6.2.4 of Puerto Rican Regulation No. 3582, as in effect on September 22, 1989.

Reg. § 1.936-10(c)(3)

(4) *Investments in active business assets*—(i) *In general.* For purposes of section 936(d)(4)(A)(i)(I) and this section and subject to the provisions of paragraph (c)(8) of this section, a loan qualifies as an investment in active business assets if—

(A) The amounts disbursed to a qualified recipient under the loan or bond issue are promptly applied (as defined in paragraphs (c)(6) and (7) of this section) by (or on behalf of) the qualified recipient solely for capital expenditures for the construction, rehabilitation (including demolition associated therewith), improvement, or upgrading of qualified assets described in paragraphs (c)(4)(ii)(A), (B), (E), and (F) of this section, for the acquisition of qualified assets described in paragraphs (c)(4)(ii)(B), (C), (E), and (F) of this section, for the expenditures described in paragraph (c)(4)(ii)(D), (E), and (F) of this section, and, if applicable, for the financing of incidental expenditures described in paragraph (c)(4)(iii) of this section;

(B) The qualified recipient owns the assets for United States income tax purposes and uses them in a qualified business activity (as defined in paragraph (c)(4)(iv)); and

(C) The requirements of paragraph (c)(6) of this section (regarding temporary investments and time periods within which the funds must be invested) and of paragraph (c)(7) of this section (regarding the refinancing of existing funding and the time periods within which funding for investments must be secured) are satisfied.

(ii) *Definition of qualified assets.* For purposes of this paragraph (c), qualified assets mean—

(A) Real property;

(B) Tangible personal property (such as furniture, machinery, or equipment) that is not property described in section 1221(1) and that is either new property or property which at no time during the period specified in paragraph (c)(4)(v) of this section was used in a business activity in the qualified Caribbean Basin country in which the property is to be used;

(C) Rights to intangible property that is a patent, invention, formula, process, design, pattern, know-how, or similar item, or rights under a franchise agreement, provided that such rights—

(*1*) Were not at any time during the period specified in paragraph (c)(4)(v) of this section used in a business activity in the qualified Caribbean Basin country in which the rights are to be used,

(*2*) Are not rights the use of which gives rise, or would give rise if used, to United States source income, and

(*3*) Are not rights acquired by the qualified recipient from a person related (within the meaning of section 267(b), using "10 percent" instead of "50 percent" in the places where it appears) to the qualified recipient;

(D) Exploration and development expenditures incurred by a qualified recipient for the purpose of ascertaining the existence, location, extent or quality of any deposit of ore, oil, gas, or other mineral in a qualified Caribbean Basin country, as well as for purposes of developing such deposit (within the meaning of section 616 of the Code and the regulations thereunder);

(E) Living plants and animals (other than crops, plants, and animals that are acquired primarily to hold as inventory by the qualified recipient for resale in the ordinary course of trade or business) acquired in connection with a farming business (as defined in § 1.263-1T(c)(4)(i)), expenditures of a preparatory nature to prepare the land or area for farming (such as planting trees, drilling wells, clearing brush, leveling land, laying pipes, building roads, constructing tanks and reservoirs), expenditures for soil and water conservation of a type described in section 175(c)(1), and expenditures of a development nature incurred in connection with, and during, the preproductive period of property produced in a farming business (as defined in § 1.263-1T(c)(4)(ii));

(F) Other assets or expenditures that are not described in paragraphs (c)(4)(ii)(A) through (E) of this section and that the Commissioner may, by Revenue Procedure or other guidance published in the Internal Revenue Bulletin or by ruling issued to a qualified financial institution or qualified recipient upon its request, determine to be qualified assets.

(iii) *Incidental expenditures.* An amount in addition to the loan proceeds borrowed to make an investment in active business assets shall be considered an investment in active business assets if such amount is applied to finance expenditures that are incidental to making the investment in active business assets, provided such amount is disbursed at or about the same time the proceeds for making the investment in active business assets are disbursed. For purposes of this section, expenditures incidental to an investment in active business assets include only the following items:

(A) A reasonable amount of costs (other than the cost of credit enhancement or bond insurance premiums) associated with arranging the financing of an investment in active business as-

Reg. § 1.936-10(c)(4)

sets, not to exceed 3.5 percent of the proceeds of the loan or bond issue.

(B) A reasonable amount of installation costs and other reasonable costs associated with placing an active business asset in service in the qualified business activity.

(C) An amount not in excess of 10 percent of the total amount of investment in qualified assets to finance the acquisition of inventory, and other working capital requirements, but if an investment is in connection with a manufacturing or farming business, the percentage limitation shall be 50 percent rather than 10 percent provided the excess over the 10 percent limitation is used to finance inventory property. For purposes of this paragraph (c), whether a business is a manufacturing business shall be determined under principles similar to those described in section 954(d)(1)(A) and the regulations thereunder; whether a business is a farming business shall be determined under § 1.263-1T(c)(4)(i).

(D) An amount not in excess of 5 percent of the sum of the investment in active business assets and the costs described in paragraphs (c)(4)(iii)(A), (B), and (C) of this section for the refinancing of an existing debt of the qualified recipient if such refinancing is incidental to an investment in active business assets. For this purpose, the replacement of an existing loan arrangement shall not be considered the refinancing of an existing indebtedness to the extent that the funds under such loan arrangement have not yet been disbursed to the qualified recipient

(iv) *Qualified business activity.* A qualified business activity is a lawful industrial or commercial activity that is conducted as an active trade or business (under principles similar to those described in § 1.367(a)-2T(b)(2) and (3)) in a qualified Caribbean Basin country. A trade or business for purposes of this paragraph (c)(4)(iv) is any business activity meeting the principles of section 367 of the Code and described in Divisions A through I (excluding group 43 in Division E (relating to the United States Postal Service) and groups 84 (relating to museums, art galleries, and botanical and zoological gardens), 86 (relating to membership organizations), and 88 (relating to private households) in Division I) of the 1987 Standard Industrial Classification Manual issued by the Executive Office of the President, Office of Management and Budget, or in the comparable provisions of any successor Standard Industrial Classification Manual that is adopted by the Commissioner of Internal Revenue in a notice, regulation, or other document published in the Internal Revenue Cumulative Bulletin.

(v) *Period of use.* The period referred to in paragraphs (c)(4)(ii)(B) and (C) of this section shall be a five year period preceding the date of acquisition with the loan proceeds, if the date of acquisition is on or before May 13, 1991. If the date of acquisition is after May 13, 1991, then the period specified in this paragraph (c)(4)(v) shall be three years preceding the date of acquisition with the loan proceeds.

(5) *Investments in development projects*—(i) *In general.* Subject to the provisions of paragraph (c)(8) of this section, this paragraph (c)(5)(i) describes the requirements in order for a loan by a qualified financial institution to qualify as an investment in a development project for purposes of section 936(d)(4)(A)(i)(II) and for this section.

(A) The amounts disbursed under the loan or bond issue must be promptly applied (as defined in paragraphs (c)(6) and (7) of this section) by (or on behalf of) the qualified recipient solely for one or more investments described in paragraph (c)(4)(i)(A) of this section and in any land, buildings, or other property functionally related and subordinate to a facility described in paragraph (c)(5)(ii) of this section (determined under principles similar to those described in § 1.103-8(a)(3)), for use (under principles similar to those described in § 1.367(a)2T(b)(5)) in connection with one or more activities described in paragraph (c)(5)(i)(B) of this section.

(B) The activities referred to in paragraph (c)(5)(i)(A) of this section are—

(*1*) A development project described in paragraph (c)(5)(ii) of this section in a qualified Caribbean Basin country; or

(*2*) The performance in a qualified Caribbean Basin country of a non-commercial governmental function described in paragraph (c)(5)(iv) of this section;

(C) The qualified recipient must own the assets for United States income tax purposes;

(D) The requirements of paragraph (c)(6) of this section (regarding temporary investments and time periods within which the funds must be invested) and of paragraph (c)(7) of this section (regarding the refinancing of existing funding and time periods within which funding for investments must be secured) must be satisfied.

(*1*) [Reserved]

(ii) *Development project.* For purposes of this paragraph (c), a development project is one or more facilities in a qualified Caribbean Basin country that support economic development in that country and that satisfy the public use requirement of paragraph (c)(5)(iii) of this section.

Reg. § 1.936-10(c)(5)

Examples of facilities that may meet the public use requirement include, but are not limited to—

(A) Transportation systems and equipment, including sea, surface, and air, such as roads, railways, air terminals, runways, harbor facilities, and ships and aircraft;

(B) Communications facilities;

(C) Training and education facilities related to qualified business activities;

(D) Industrial parks, including necessary support facilities such as roads; transmission lines for water, gas, electricity, and sewage; docks; plant sites preparations; power generation; sewage disposal; and water treatment;

(E) Sports facilities;

(F) Convention or trade show facilities;

(G) Sewage, solid waste, water, and electric facilities;

(H) Housing projects pursuant to a government program designed to provide affordable housing to low or moderate income families, based upon local standards; and

(I) Hydroelectric generating facilities.

(iii) *Public use requirement.* To satisfy the public use requirement in paragraph (c)(5)(ii) of this section, a facility must serve or be available on a regular basis for general public use, as contrasted with similar types of facilities which are constructed for the exclusive use of a limited number of persons as determined under principles similar to those described in § 1.103-8(a)(2).

(iv) *Non-commercial governmental functions.* For purposes of paragraph (c)(5)(i)(B) of this section, the term "non-commercial governmental functions" refers to activities that, under U.S. standards, are not customarily attributable to or carried on by private enterprises for profit and are performed for the general public with respect to the common welfare or which relate to the administration of some phase of government. For example, the operation of libraries, toll bridges, or local transportation services, and activities substantially equivalent to those carried out by the Federal Aviation Authority, Interstate Commerce Commission, or United States Postal Service, are considered non-commercial governmental functions. For purposes of this section, non-commercial government functions shall not include military activities.

(v) [Reserved]

(6) *Prompt application of borrowed proceeds.* This paragraph (c)(6) provides rules for determining whether amounts disbursed to a qualified recipient by a qualified financial institution (or a financial intermediary) shall be considered to have been promptly applied for the purpose of paragraphs (c)(4)(i)(A) and (c)(5)(i)(A) of this section.

(i) *In general.* Except as otherwise provided in paragraphs (c)(6)(ii) and (c)(7)(iii)(B) of this section, amounts disbursed to a qualified recipient by a qualified financial institution (or a financial intermediary) shall be considered to have been promptly applied for the purpose of paragraphs (c)(4)(i)(A) and (c)(5)(i)(A) of this section if the amounts are fully expended for any of the purposes described in paragraphs (c)(4)(i)(A) or (c)(5)(i)(A) of this section no later than six months from the date of such disbursement and any temporary investment of such funds by the qualified recipient during such period complies with the rules of paragraph (c)(6)(iii)(A) of this section. Where the amounts disbursed are bond proceeds described in paragraph (c)(6)(iv)(A) of this section, the six-month period shall begin on the date of issuance of the bonds. In the event the qualified financial institution (or financial intermediary) invests any part of the bond proceeds before disbursement of those proceeds to the qualified recipient, all earnings from any such investment shall be paid to the qualified recipient or applied for its benefit.

(ii) *Special rules for long term projects financed out of bond proceeds.* In the case of a long term project described in paragraph (c)(6)(iv)(B) of this section that is financed out of bond proceeds, the six-month period described in paragraph (c)(6)(i) of this section shall be extended with respect to the amount of bond proceeds used to fund the project for such reasonable period of time as shall be necessary until completion of the project or until beginning of production (in the case of a farming business), but, in any event, not to exceed three years from the date of issuance of the bonds, and only if—

(A) The project that is financed out of bond proceeds was identified as of the date of issue;

(B) A construction and expenditure plan certified by an independent expert (such as an engineer, an architect, or a farming expert) is filed with, and approved by, the Commissioner of Financial Institutions of Puerto Rico (or his delegate) prior to the date of issue, which makes a reasonable estimate, as of the date of filing of the plan, of the amounts and uses of the bond proceeds and the time of completion or production, and includes a schedule of progress payments until such time;

(C) The terms of the construction and expenditure plan are disclosed in the public offering memorandum, private placement memoran-

Reg. § 1.936-10(c)(6)

dum, or similar document prepared for information or disclosure purposes in relation to the issuance of bonds; and

(D) Any temporary investment of the bond proceeds complies with the rules of paragraph (c)(6)(iii)(A) and (B) of this section.

(iii) *Temporary investments*—(A) *During six-month period.* During the six-month period described in paragraph (c)(6)(i) of this section, during the first six months of the period described in paragraph (c)(6)(ii) of this section, and during the 30-day period described in paragraph (c)(7)(iii)(A) of this section, loan proceeds disbursed to a qualified recipient, bond proceeds, and income from the investment thereof, may be held in unrestricted yield investments, provided such yield reflects normal market yield for such type of investments and provided the income from such investments, if any, is or would be sourced either in Puerto Rico or in a country in which the investment in active business assets or development project is to be made.

(B) *During other periods.* During any other period, any temporary investment of bond proceeds, and of income from such investments, shall be limited to investments in eligible activities. For purposes of this paragraph (c)(6)(iii)(B), the term "eligible activities" shall mean those investments described in section 6.2.4 of Puerto Rican Regulation No. 3582, as in effect on September 22, 1989.

(iv) *Definitions*—(A) *Bond proceeds.* For purposes of this paragraph (c), bond proceeds shall mean the proceeds from the issuance of obligations by way of a public offering or a private placement by a qualified financial institution for investment in active business assets or a development project that has been identified at the time of issue and is described in a public offering memorandum, private placement memorandum, or similar document prepared for information or disclosure purposes in relation to the issuance of the bonds.

(B) *Long term project.* For purposes of this section, the term long term project means—

(*1*) A project, whether or not under a contract, for the construction, rehabilitation, improvement, upgrading, or production of qualified assets, or for expenditures, described in paragraph (c)(4)(ii) of this section (other than paragraph (c)(4)(ii)(C) of this section), which is reasonably expected to require more than 12 months to complete; or

(*2*) The production of property in a farming business referred to in paragraph (c)(4)(ii)(E) of this section, which is reasonably expected to require a preproductive period in excess of 12 months.

(7) *Financing of previously incurred costs.* Loan or bond proceeds which are disbursed after a qualified recipient has paid or incurred part or all of the costs of acquiring active business assets or investing in a development project shall be considered to have been applied for such purposes only as provided in this paragraph (c)(7).

(i) *Replacement of temporary non-section 936 financing of a qualified investment.* This paragraph (c)(7)(i) prescribes the maximum time limits within which temporary non-section 936 financing of qualified investments may be replaced with section 936 funds without being considered a prohibited refinancing transaction. This paragraph (c)(7)(i) applies to the refinancing of costs incurred with respect to investments that, at the time the costs were first incurred, were either qualified investments in a qualified Caribbean Basin country or were investments by a qualified recipient in active business assets or a development project in a qualified Caribbean Basin country. This paragraph (c)(7)(i) applies also to the refinancing of costs incurred with respect to any other investment. However, in the latter case, the amount of costs that may be refinanced with section 936 funds is limited to the amount of costs that are incurred with respect to the investment after the investment becomes a qualified investment in a qualified Caribbean Basin country. For purposes of this paragraph (c)(7)(i), the time when costs are incurred shall be determined under principles similar to those applicable under section 461(h) dealing with the economic performance test for the accrual of deductible liabilities. This paragraph (c)(7)(i) applies only to the situations described in this paragraph (c)(7)(i).

(A) In the case of an investment in active business assets or a development project, a loan shall be a qualified investment for purposes of this paragraph (c) if the loan proceeds are disbursed, or the obligations are issued, no later than six months after the date on which the qualified recipient takes possession of the asset or the facility or, if earlier, places the asset or the facility in service. However, in the case of a small project described in paragraph (c)(8)(v) of this section, the six-month period shall be one year.

(B) In the case of an investment in active business assets or a development project that is part of a long term project described in paragraph (c)(6)(iv)(B) of this section, a loan shall also be a qualified investment for purposes of this paragraph (c) if the loan proceeds are disbursed, or the obligations are issued, no later than six months after completion of the project or, in the

Reg. § 1.936-10(c)(7)

case of a farming business, after the beginning of production, and in any event, no later than three years after the date on which the first payment is made toward the eligible costs of the project. The amount of the qualified investment may not exceed the sum of—

(1) The eligible costs relating to investments described in paragraph (c)(4)(i)(A) in the case of an investment in active business assets, or the eligible costs relating to investments described in paragraph (c)(5)(i) of this section in the case of a development project, but only to the extent of the costs that are incurred after the date described in paragraph (c)(7)(i)(D) of this section, and

(2) The portion of unpaid interest that would be required to be capitalized under U.S. tax rules and that accrued on prior temporary non-section 936 financing from the date described in paragraph (c)(7)(i)(D) of this section through the date the section 936 loan proceeds are disbursed or the section 936 obligations are issued.

(C) In order to qualify for the special rules of this paragraph (c)(7)(i), a plan must be filed with the Commissioner of Financial Institutions of Puerto Rico (or his delegate) stating the qualified recipient's intention to refinance the costs of the long term project with section 936 funds.

(D) The date referred to in paragraph (c)(7)(i)(B)(1) and (2) of this section is a date that is the later of—

(1) the date the plan described in paragraph (c)(7)(i)(C) is filed, or

(2) the date the investment becomes a qualified investment by a qualified recipient in active business assets or a development project in a qualified Caribbean Basin country.

(ii) *Refinancing of section 936 financing.* A section 936 loan or bond issue used to finance a qualified investment described in paragraph (c)(1) of this section may be refinanced with section 936 funds through a new loan or bond issue to the extent of the remaining principal balance on such existing qualified financing, increased by the amount of unpaid interest accrued through the date the new loan proceeds are disbursed or the new obligations are issued and that would be required to be capitalized under U.S. tax rules.

(iii) *Prompt application of borrowed proceeds*—(A) *In general.* In the case of a loan or bond issue described in paragraphs (c)(7)(i) or (ii) of this section, the rules of paragraph (c)(6) of this section shall apply but the six-month period described in paragraph (c)(6)(i) of this section shall be limited to 30 days from the date of disbursement of loan proceeds to the qualified recipient or from the date of issuance in the case of a bond issue.

(B) *Special rules for long term projects financed out of bond proceeds.* In the case of a long term project described in paragraph (c)(6)(iv)(B) of this section that is financed out of bond proceeds, the 30-day period described in paragraph (c)(7)(iii)(A) of this section shall be extended with respect to the amount of bond proceeds used for the permanent financing of the long term project for such reasonable period of time as shall be necessary until completion of the project or beginning of production (in the case of a farming business), but, in any event, not to exceed three years from the date of issuance of the bonds. For purposes of this paragraph (c)(7)(iii)(B), the period of time shall be considered reasonable only if—

(1) A construction and expenditure plan certified by an independent expert (such as an engineer, an architect, or a farming expert) is filed with, and approved by, the Commissioner of Financial Institutions of Puerto Rico (or his delegate) prior to the date of issue, which makes a reasonable estimate, as of the date of issue, of the amounts and uses of the bond proceeds and the time of completion or production, and includes a schedule of progress payments until such time; and

(2) The terms of the construction and expenditure plan are disclosed in the public offering memorandum, private placement memorandum, or similar document prepared for information or disclosure purposes in relation to the bond issue.

(8) *Miscellaneous operating rules*—(i) *Sale and leaseback.* An asset that is acquired and leased back to the person from whom acquired does not constitute an investment in an active business asset or an investment in a development project.

(ii) *Use of asset in qualified business activity.* For purposes of paragraph (c)(4)(i)(B), an asset shall be considered used or held for use in a qualified business activity if it is used or held for use in such activity under principles similar to those described in § 1.367(a)2T-(b)(5), or a successor provision.

(iii) *Definition of capital expenditures.* For purposes of this paragraph (c), capital expenditures mean those expenditures described in section 263(a) of the Code (without regard to paragraphs (A) through (G) of section 263(a)(1)), and those costs required to be capitalized under section 263A with respect to property described in

Reg. § 1.936-10(c)(8)

section 263A(b)(1), relating to self-constructed assets.

(iv) *Loans through certain financial intermediaries.* A loan by a qualified financial institution shall not be disqualified from being an investment in active business assets or in a development project merely because the proceeds are first lent to a financial intermediary (as defined in paragraph (c)(8)(iv)(H) of this section) which, in turn, on-lends the proceeds directly to a qualified recipient, provided the requirements of this paragraph (c)(8)(iv) are satisfied.

(A) The loan to the qualified recipient must satisfy the requirements of paragraph (c)(4)(i) of this section in the case of an investment in active business assets, or of paragraph (c)(5)(i) of this section in the case of an investment in a development project.

(B) The qualified recipient and the active business assets or development project in which the proceeds are to be invested must be identified prior to disbursement of any part of the proceeds by the qualified financial institution to the financial intermediary.

(C) The effective interest rate charged by the qualified financial institution to the financial intermediary must not exceed the average interest rate paid by the qualified financial institution with respect to its eligible funds, increased by such number of basis points as is required to provide reasonable compensation to the qualified financial institution for services performed and risks assumed with respect to the loan to the financial intermediary that are not ordinarily required to be performed or assumed with respect to a deposit, loan, repurchase agreement or other transfer of eligible funds with another qualified financial institution. The average interest rate shall be the average rate, determined on a daily basis, paid by the qualified financial institution on its eligible funds over the most recent quarter preceding the date on which the rate on the loan to the financial intermediary is committed.

(D) The effective interest rate charged by the financial intermediary to the qualified recipient must not exceed the effective interest rate charged to the financial intermediary by the qualified financial institution, increased by such number of basis points as is required to provide reasonable compensation to the financial intermediary for services performed and risks assumed with respect to the loan to the qualified recipient.

(E) The financial intermediary must borrow from the qualified financial institution under substantially the same terms as it lends to the qualified recipient. In particular, both loans must have disbursement terms, repayment schedules and maturity dates for interest and principal amounts such that the financial intermediary does not retain for more than 48 hours any of the funds disbursed by the qualified financial institution nor any of the funds paid by the qualified recipient in repayment of principal or interest on the loan.

(F) The financial institution and the financial intermediary must agree to comply with the due diligence requirements described in paragraphs (c)(11), (12), and (13) of this section;

(G) The time periods and temporary investments rules in paragraphs (c)(6) and (7) of this section must be complied with; and

(H) For purposes of this paragraph (c), the financial intermediary must be—

(*1*) An active trade or business which a person maintains in a qualified Caribbean Basin country and which consists of a banking, financing or similar business as defined in § 1.864-4(c)(5)(i) (other than a central bank of issue); or

(*2*) A public international organization, the principal purpose of which is to foster economic development in developing countries and which is described in section 1 of the International Organizations Immunities Act (22 U.S.C. § 288).

For purposes of paragraphs (c)(8)(iv)(C) and (D) of this section, the determination of whether compensation is reasonable shall be made in relation to normal commercial practices for comparable transactions carrying a similar degree of commercial, currency and political risk. Reasonable credit enhancement fees and other reasonable fees and amounts charged to the financial intermediary or the qualified recipient with respect to the loan transaction in addition to interest shall be added to the interest cost in determining the effective interest rate.

(v) *Small project.* For purposes of this paragraph (c), a small project shall be a project (including the acquisition of an asset) for which the total amount of section 936 funds used for its financing does not exceed $1,000,000 in the aggregate, or such other amount as the Commissioner may publish, from time to time, in the Internal Revenue Bulletin.

(9) *Qualified recipient.* For purposes of this section, a qualified recipient is any person described in paragraphs (c)(9)(i) or (ii) of this section. The term "person" means a person described in section 7701(a)(1) or a government (within the meaning of § 1.892-2T(a)(1)) of a qualified Caribbean Basin country.

Reg. § 1.936-10(c)(9)

(i) In the case of an investment described in paragraph (c)(4) of this section (relating to investments in active business assets), a qualified recipient is a person that carries on a qualified business activity in a qualified Caribbean Basin country, and complies with the agreement and certification requirements described in paragraph (c)(11)(i) of this section at all times during the period in which the investment remains outstanding.

(ii) In the case of an investment described in paragraph (c)(5) of this section (relating to investments in development projects), a qualified recipient is the borrower (including a person empowered by the borrower to authorize expenditures for the investment in the development project) that has authority to comply, and complies, with the agreement and certification requirements described in paragraph (c)(11)(i) of this section at all times during the period in which the investment remains outstanding.

(10) *Investments in a qualified Caribbean Basin country*—(i) *Rules for determining the place of an investment.* The rules of this paragraph (c)(10)(i) shall apply to determine the extent to which an investment in an active business asset or a development project will be considered made in a qualified Caribbean Basin country.

(A) An investment in real property is considered made in the qualified Caribbean Basin country in which the real property is located.

(B) Except as otherwise provided in this paragraph (c)(10)(i)(B), an investment in tangible personal property is considered made in a qualified Caribbean Basin country so long as the tangible personal property is predominantly used in that country. Whether property is used predominantly in a qualified Caribbean Basin country shall be determined under principles similar to those described in § 1.48-1(g)(1), (g)(2)(ii), (g)(2)(iv), (g)(2)(vi), (g)(2)(viii), and (g)(2)(x) (relating to investment tax credits for property used outside the United States) as in effect on December 31, 1985. A vessel, container, or aircraft shall be considered for use predominantly in a qualified Caribbean Basin country in any year if it is used for transport to and from such country with some degree of frequency during that year and at least 30 percent of the income from the use of such vessel, container or aircraft for that year is sourced in such country under principles similar to those described in section 863(c)(1) and (2) (relating to source rules for certain transportation income). Cables and pipelines which are permanently installed as part of a communication or transportation system between a qualified Caribbean Basin country and another country or among several countries which include a qualified Caribbean Basin country shall be considered used in a qualified Caribbean Basin country to the extent of 50 percent of the portion of the facility that directly links the qualified country to another country or to a hub, unless it is established by notice or other guidance published in the Internal Revenue Bulletin or by ruling issued to a qualified institution or qualified recipient upon request that it is appropriate to attribute a greater portion of the cost of the facility to the qualified Caribbean Basin country.

(C) An investment in rights to intangible property is considered made in a qualified Caribbean Basin country to the extent such rights are used in that country. Where rights to intangible property are used shall be determined under principles similar to those described in § 1.954-2T(b)(3)(vii) or a successor provision.

(ii) *Qualified Caribbean Basin country.* For purposes of this section, the term "qualified Caribbean Basin country" means any beneficiary country (within the meaning of section 212(a)(1)(A) of the Caribbean Basin Economic Recovery Act, P.L. 98-67 (Aug. 5, 1983), 97 Stat. 384, 19 USC § 2702(a)(1)(A)), which meets the requirements of section 274(h)(6)(A)(i) and (ii) and the U.S. Virgin Islands, and includes the territorial waters and continental shelf thereof.

(11) *Agreements and certifications by qualified recipients and financial intermediaries*—(i) *In general.* In order for an investment to be considered a qualified investment under section 936(d)(4) and paragraph (c)(1) of this section, a qualified recipient must certify to the qualified financial institution (or to the financial intermediary, if the loan is made through a financial intermediary) on the date of closing of the loan agreement and on each anniversary date thereof, that it is a qualified recipient described in paragraph (c)(9) of this section. In addition, the qualified recipient must agree in the loan agreement with the qualified financial institution (or with the financial intermediary, if the loan is made through a financial intermediary)—

(A) To use the funds at all times during the period the loan is outstanding solely for the purposes and in the manner described in paragraph (c)(4) of this section (regarding investment in active business assets) or in paragraph (c)(5) of this section (regarding investment in development projects);

(B) To comply with the requirements of paragraph (c)(6) of this section (regarding temporary investments and time periods within which the funds must be invested) and paragraph (c)(7) of this section (regarding the refinancing of ex-

Reg. § 1.936-10(c)(11)

isting funding and the time periods within which funding for investments must be secured);

(C) To notify the Assistant Commissioner (International), the qualified financial institution (or the financial intermediary, if the loan is made through a financial intermediary), and the Commissioner of Financial Institutions of Puerto Rico (or his delegate) pursuant to paragraph (c)(14) of this section if it no longer is a qualified recipient or if, for any other reason, the investment has ceased to qualify as a qualified investment described in paragraph (c)(1) of this section, promptly upon the occurrence of such disqualifying event; and

(D) To permit examination by the office of the Assistant Commissioner (International) (or by the office of any District Director authorized by the Assistant Commissioner (International)) and the Commissioner of Financial Institutions of Puerto Rico (or his delegate) of all necessary books and records that are sufficient to verify that the funds were used for investments in active business assets or development projects in conformity with the terms of the loan agreement.

(ii) *Certification by a financial intermediary.* In the case of a loan by a qualified financial institution to a financial intermediary, the financial intermediary must certify to the qualified financial institution (using the procedures described in paragraph (c)(11)(i) of this section) that it is a financial intermediary described in paragraph (c)(8)(iv)(H) of this section, and must furnish to the qualified financial institution a copy of the qualified recipient's certification described in paragraph (c)(11)(i) of this section and of its loan agreement with the qualified recipient. In addition, the financial intermediary must agree in the loan agreement with the qualified financial institution:

(A) To comply with the requirements of paragraph (c)(8)(iv) of this section; and

(B) To permit examination by the office of the Assistant Commissioner (International) (or by the office of any District Director authorized by the Assistant Commissioner (International)) and the Commissioner of Financial Institutions of Puerto Rico (or his delegate) of all its necessary books and records that are sufficient to verify that the funds were used in conformity with the terms of the loan agreements.

(12) *Certification requirements.* In order for an investment to be considered a qualified investment under section 936(d)(4), section 936(d)(4)(C)(i) requires that both the person in whose trade or business such investment is made and the financial institution certify to the Secretary of the Treasury and the Commissioner of Financial Institutions of Puerto Rico that the proceeds of the loan will be promptly used to acquire active business assets or to make other authorized expenditures. This certification requirement is satisfied as to the qualified financial institution, the financial intermediary (if any), and the qualified recipient if the qualified financial institution submits a certificate to both the Assistant Commissioner (International) and to the Commissioner of Financial Institutions of Puerto Rico (or his delegate) pursuant to paragraph (c)(14) of this section upon authorization of the investment by the Commissioner of Financial Institutions and, in any event, prior to the first disbursement of the loan proceeds to the qualified recipient or to the financial intermediary (if any), in which the qualified financial institution—

(i) Represents that, as of the date of the certification, the qualified recipient and the financial intermediary (if any) have complied with the requirements described in paragraph (c)(11) of this section;

(ii) Describes the important terms of the loan to the financial intermediary (if any) and to the qualified recipient, including the amount of the loan, the nature of the investment, the basis for its qualification as an investment in active business assets or a development project under this section, the identity of the financial intermediary (if any) and of the qualified recipient, the qualified Caribbean Basin country involved, and the nature of the collateral or other security used, including any guarantee;

(iii) Agrees to permit examination by the Assistant Commissioner (International) (or by the office of any District Director authorized by the Assistant Commissioner (International)) and the Commissioner of Financial Institutions of Puerto Rico (or his delegate) of all its necessary books and records that are sufficient to verify that the funds were used for investments in active business assets or development projects in conformity with the terms of the loan agreement or agreements with the financial intermediary (if any) and with the qualified recipient; and

(iv) In the case of a single-purpose entity that is a qualified financial institution, discloses the name and address of the entity's trustee or agent, if any, that assists the qualified financial institution in the performance of its due diligence requirement under paragraph (c) of this section, and represents that the trustee or agent has agreed with the qualified financial institution to permit examination by the Assistant Commissioner (International) (or by the office of any District Director authorized by the Assistant Commissioner (International)) and the Commissioner of Financial Institutions of Puerto Rico (or his delegate) of all necessary books and records of such trustee or agent that are sufficient to verify that the funds were used for investments in active business assets or development projects in conformity with the terms of the loan agreement or agreements with the financial intermediary (if any) and with the qualified recipient.

(13) *Continuing due diligence requirements.* In order to maintain the qualification for an investment under paragraph (c)(1) of this section, the continuing due diligence requirements described in this paragraph (c)(13) must be satisfied.

(i) *Requirements of qualified recipient.* A qualified recipient must—

(A) Submit annually to the qualified financial institution or to the financial intermediary from which its qualified funds were obtained a copy of its most recent annual financial statement accompanied by an opinion of an independent accountant familiar with the financials of the qualified recipient disclosing the amount of the loan, the current outstanding balance of the loan, describing the assets financed with such loan and the qualified business activity in which such assets are used or the development project for which the loan is used, and stating that there are no reasons to doubt that the loan proceeds have been properly used and continue to be properly used, and

(B) Act in a manner consistent with its representations and agreements described in paragraph (c)(11) of this section.

(ii) *Requirements of qualified financial institutions.* Except as otherwise provided in paragraph (c)(13)(iii) of this section, a qualified financial institution described in paragraph (c)(3) of this section must maintain in its records and have available for inspection the documentation described in paragraph (c)(13)(ii)(A) or (B) of this section. In addition, the qualified financial institution is required to notify the Assistant Commissioner (International) and the Commissioner of Financial Institutions of Puerto Rico (or his delegate) pursuant to paragraph (c)(14) of this section upon becoming aware that a loan has ceased to be an investment in active business assets or a development project under this section. For purposes of this paragraph (c)(13)(ii), multiple loans for investment in a single qualified business activity or development project will be aggregated in determining what due diligence requirements apply.

(A) In the case of a small project described in paragraph (c)(8)(v) of this section, the following documents must be maintained and available for inspection:

(*1*) The loan application or other similar document;

(*2*) The financial statements of the qualified recipient filed as part of the loan application;

(*3*) The statement required by section 6.4.3(a)(iii) of Puerto Rican Regulation No. 3582 or any successor thereof, signed by the qualified recipient (or its duly authorized representative), acknowledging the receipt of the loan proceeds, describing the assets financed with such loan and the business activity in which such assets are to be used or the development project for which the funds will be utilized, the collateral to be provided for the transaction including any guarantee, and the basis for its qualification as a qualified recipient;

(*4*) The loan documents; and

(*5*) In the case of a qualified financial institution that is a single-purpose entity, a copy of the agreement with the entity's trustee or agent, if any, described in paragraph (c)(12)(iv) of this section.

(B) In the case of a disbursement concerning a project that is not a small project described in paragraph (c)(8)(v) of this section, the following documents must be maintained and available for inspection, in addition to the documents required by paragraph (c)(13)(ii)(A) of this section:

(*1*) A memorandum of credit prepared by an officer of the qualified financial institution (or, in the case of a single purpose entity, an agent of the entity or a trustee for the entity, if any) and signed by the officer of the qualified financial institution, containing the details of the investigation and review that the qualified financial institution, or its trustee or agent, if any, conducted in order to evaluate whether the investment is qualified under paragraph (c)(1) of this section and the opinion of the officer of the qualified financial institution, or the opinion of an officer of the agent of, or of the trustee for, the qualified financial institution, if any, that there is no reasonable ground for belief that the qualified funds will be diverted to a use that is not permitted under the provisions of this section; in making this investigation and review, factors that must be utilized are ones similar to those listed in Puerto Rico Regulation No. 3582, section 6.4.2;

(*2*) The annual financial statement of the qualified recipient; and

(*3*) The written report of an officer of the qualified financial institution, or of an officer of an agent of, or of the trustee for, the qualified financial institution, if any, documenting discus-

Reg. § 1.936-10(c)(13)

sions, both before and after the disbursement of the loan proceeds, with each recipient's accounting, financial and executive personnel with respect to the proposed and actual use of the loan proceeds and his analysis of the annual financial statements of the qualified recipient including an analysis of the statement of sources and uses of funds. After the loan disbursement, such discussions and review shall occur annually during the term of the loan. Such report shall include the conclusion that in such officer's opinion there is no reasonable ground for belief that the qualified recipient is improperly utilizing the funds.

(iii) *Requirements in the case of a financial intermediary.* Where a qualified financial institution lends funds to a financial intermediary which are on-lent to a qualified recipient—

(A) The obligation to maintain the documentation described in paragraph (c)(13)(ii)(A) or (B) of this section shall apply only to the financial intermediary and not to the qualified financial institution and the provisions of paragraph (c)(13)(ii)(A) or (B) of this section shall be read so as to impose on the financial intermediary any obligation imposed on the qualified financial institution.

(B) The financial intermediary shall forward annually to the qualified financial institution a copy of the documentation it is required to maintain in its records pursuant to the provisions of this paragraph (c)(13)(iii) and shall notify the Assistant Commissioner (International), the Commissioner of Financial Institutions of Puerto Rico (or his delegate), and the qualified financial institution pursuant to paragraph (c)(14) of this section upon becoming aware that a loan has ceased to be an investment in active business assets or a development project under this section. The qualified financial institution must maintain in its records and have available for inspection the documentation furnished by the financial intermediary pursuant to this paragraph (c)(13)(iii)(B).

(C) The qualified financial institution shall cause one of its officers (or one of the officers of its agent or trustee, if any) to prepare a written report documenting his analysis of the documentation furnished by the financial intermediary pursuant to paragraph (c)(13)(iii)(B) of this section, his discussions, both before and after the disbursement of the loan proceeds, with the financial intermediary's accounting, financial and executive personnel with respect to the proposed and actual use of the loan proceeds, and his analysis of the annual financial statements of the qualified recipient including an analysis of the statement of sources and uses of funds. After the loan disbursement, such discussions and review shall occur annually during the term of the loan. Such report shall include the conclusion that in such officer's opinion there is no reasonable ground for belief that the qualified recipient is improperly utilizing the funds.

(14) *Procedures for notices and certifications.* Notices and certifications to the Assistant Commissioner (International) required under paragraphs (c)(11), (12) and (13) of this section shall be addressed to the attention of the Assistant Commissioner (International), Office of Taxpayer Service and Compliance, IN:C, 950 L'Enfant Plaza South, S.W., Washington, DC 20024. Notices and certifications to the Commissioner of Financial Institutions of Puerto Rico required under paragraphs (c)(11), (12), and (13) of this section shall be addressed as follows: Commissioner of Financial Institutions, GPO Box 70324, San Juan, Puerto Rico 00936.

(15) *Effective date.* This paragraph (c) is effective May 13, 1991. It is applicable to investments by a possessions corporation in a financial institution that are used by a financial institution for investments in accordance with a specific authorization granted by the Commissioner of Financial Institutions of Puerto Rico (or his delegate) after September 22, 1989. However, the taxpayer may choose to apply § 1.936-10T for periods before June 12, 1991. [Reg. § 1.936-10.]

☐ [*T.D.* 8350, 5-10-91.]

[Reg. § 1.936-11]

§ 1.936-11. **New lines of business prohibited.**—(a) *In general.* A possessions corporation that is an existing credit claimant, as defined in section 936(j)(9)(A) and this section, that adds a substantial new line of business during a taxable year, or that has a new line of business that becomes substantial during the taxable year, loses its status as an existing credit claimant for that year and all years subsequent.

(b) *New line of business*—(1) *In general.* A new line of business is any business activity of the possessions corporation that is not closely related to a pre-existing business of the possessions corporation. The term *closely related* is defined in paragraph (b)(2) of this section. The term *pre-existing business* is defined in paragraph (b)(3) of this section.

(2) *Closely related.* To determine whether a new activity is closely related to a pre-existing business of the possessions corporation all the facts and circumstances must be considered, including those set forth in paragraphs (b)(2)(i)(A) through (G) of this section.

(i) *Factors.* The following factors will help to establish that a new activity is closely related to a pre-existing business activity of the possessions corporation—

(A) The new activity provides products or services very similar to the products or services provided by the pre-existing business;

(B) The new activity markets products and services to the same class of customers;

(C) The new activity is of a type that is normally conducted in the same business location;

(D) The new activity requires the use of similar operating assets;

(E) The new activity's economic success depends on the success of the pre-existing business;

(F) The new activity is of a type that would normally be treated as a unit with the pre-existing business in the business' accounting records; and

(G) The new activity and the pre-existing business are regulated or licensed by the same or similar governmental authority.

(ii) *Safe harbors.* An activity is not a new line of business if—

(A) If the activity is within the same six-digit North American Industry Classification System (NAICS) code (or four-digit Standard Industrial Classification (SIC) code). The similarity of the NAICS or SIC codes may not be relied upon to determine whether the activity is closely related to a preexisting business where the code indicates a miscellaneous category;

(B) If the new activity is within the same five-digit NAICS code (or three-digit SIC code) and the facts relating to the new activity also satisfy at least three of the factors listed in paragraphs (b)(2)(i)(A) through (G) of this section; or

(C) If the pre-existing business is making a component product or end-product form, as defined in § 1.936-5(a)(1), Q & A1, and the new business activity is making an integrated product, or an end-product form with fewer excluded components, that is not within the same six-digit NAICS code (or four-digit SIC code) as the pre-existing business solely because the component product and the integrated product (or two end-product forms) have different end-uses.

(3) *Pre-existing business*—(i) *In general.* Except as provided in paragraph (b)(3)(ii) of this section, a business activity is a pre-existing business of the existing credit claimant if—

(A) The existing credit claimant was actively engaged in the activity within the possession on or before October 13, 1995; and

(B) The existing credit claimant had elected the benefits of the Puerto Rico and possession tax credit pursuant to an election which was in effect for the taxable year that included October 13, 1995.

(ii) *Acquisition of an existing credit claimant*—(A) If all the assets of one or more trades or businesses of a corporation of an existing credit claimant are acquired by an affiliated or non-affiliated existing credit claimant which carries on the business activity of the predecessor existing credit claimant, the acquired business activity will be treated as a pre-existing business of the acquiring corporation. A non-affiliated acquiring corporation will not be bound by any section 936(h) election made by the predecessor existing credit claimant with respect to that business activity.

(B) Where all of the assets of one or more trades or businesses of a corporation of an existing credit claimant are acquired by a corporation that is not an existing credit claimant, the acquiring corporation may make a section 936(e) election for the taxable year in which the assets are acquired with the following effects—

(*1*) The acquiring corporation will be treated as an existing credit claimant for the year of acquisition;

(*2*) The activity will be considered a pre-existing business of the acquiring corporation;

(*3*) The acquiring corporation will be deemed to satisfy the rules of section 936(a)(2) for the year of acquisition; and

(*4*) After making an election under section 936(e), a nonaffiliated acquiring corporation will not be bound by elections under sections 936(a)(4) and (h) made by the predecessor existing credit claimant.

(C) For purposes of this section the assets of a trade or business are determined at the time of acquisition provided that the transferee actively conducts the trade or business acquired.

(D) A mere change in the stock ownership of a possessions corporation will not affect its status as an existing credit claimant for purposes of this section.

(4) *Leasing of assets*—(i) The leasing of assets (and employees to operate leased assets) will not, for purposes of this section, be considered a new line of business of the existing credit claimant if—

(A) the existing credit claimant used the leased assets in an active trade or business for at least five years;

(B) the existing credit claimant does not through its own officers or staff of employees

Reg. § 1.936-11(b)(4)

perform management or operational functions (but not including operational functions performed through leased employees) with respect to the leased assets; and

(C) the existing credit claimant does not perform marketing functions with respect to the leasing of the assets.

(ii) Any income from the leasing of assets not considered a new line of business pursuant to paragraph (b)(4)(i) of this section will not be income from the active conduct of a trade or business (and, therefore, the existing credit claimant may not receive a possession tax credit with respect to such income).

(5) *Timing rule.* The tests for a new line of business in this paragraph (whether the new activity is closely related to a pre-existing business) are applied only at the end of the taxable year during which the new activity is added.

(c) *Substantial*—(1) *In general.* A new line of business is considered to be substantial as of the earlier of—

(i) The taxable year in which the possessions corporation derives more than 15 percent of its gross income from that new line of business (gross income test); or

(ii) The taxable year in which the possessions corporation directly uses in that new line of business more than 15 percent of its assets (assets test).

(2) *Gross income test.* The denominator in the gross income test is the amount that is the gross income of the possessions corporation for the current taxable year, while the numerator is the amount that is the gross income of the new line of business for the current taxable year. The gross income test is applied at the end of each taxable year. For purposes of this test, if a new line of business is added late in the taxable year, the income is not to be annualized in that year. In the case of a new line of business acquired through the purchase of assets, the gross income of such new line of business for the taxable year of the acquiring corporation that includes the date of acquisition is determined from the date of acquisition through the end of the taxable year. In the case of a consolidated group election made pursuant to section 936(i)(5), the test applies on a company by company basis and not on a consolidated basis.

(3) *Assets test*—(i) *Computation.* The denominator is the adjusted tax basis of the total assets of the possessions corporation for the current taxable year. The numerator is the adjusted tax basis of the total assets utilized in the new line of business for the current taxable year. The assets test is computed annually using all assets including cash and receivables.

(ii) *Exception.* A new line of business of a possessions corporation will not be treated as substantial as a result of meeting the assets test if an event that is not reasonably anticipated causes assets used in the new line of business of the possessions corporation to exceed 15 percent of the adjusted tax basis of the possessions corporation's total assets. For example, an event that is not reasonably anticipated would include the destruction of plant and equipment of the preexisting business due to a hurricane or other natural disaster, or other similar circumstances beyond the control of the possessions corporation. The expiration of a patent is not such an event and will not permit use of this exception.

(d) *Examples.* The following examples illustrate the rules described in paragraphs (a), (b), and (c) of this section. In the following examples, X Corp. is an existing credit claimant unless otherwise indicated:

Example 1. X Corp. is a pharmaceutical corporation which manufactured bulk chemicals (a component product). In March 1997, X Corp. began to also manufacture pills (e.g., finished dosages or an integrated product). The new activity provides products very similar to the products provided by the preexisting business. The new activity is of a type that is normally conducted in the same business location as the preexisting business. The activity's economic success depends on the success of the pre-existing business. The manufacture of bulk chemicals is in NAICS code 325411, Medicinal and Botanical Manufacturing, while the manufacture of the pills is in NAICS code 325412, Pharmaceutical Preparation Manufacturing. Although the products have a different end-use, may be marketed to a different class of customers, and may not use similar operating assets, they are within the same five-digit NAICS code and the activity also satisfies paragraphs (b)(2)(i)(A), (C), and (E) of this section. The manufacture of the pills by X Corp. will be considered closely related to the manufacture of the bulk chemicals. Therefore, X Corp. will not be considered to have added a new line of business for purposes of paragraph (b) of this section because it falls within the safe harbor rule of (b)(2)(ii)(B).

Example 2. X Corp. currently manufactures printed circuit boards in a possession. As a result of a technological breakthrough, X Corp. could produce the printed circuit boards more efficiently if it modified its existing production methods. Because demand for its products was high, X Corp. expanded when it modified its production methods. After these modifications to the facilities

Reg. § 1.936-11(b)(5)

Income from Sources Without the United States

and production methods, the products produced through the new technology were in the same six-digit NAICS code as products produced previously by X Corp. See paragraph (b)(2)(ii)(A) of this section. Therefore, X Corp. will not be considered to have added a new line of business for purposes of paragraph (b) of this section because it falls within the safe harbor rule of (b)(2)(ii)(A).

Example 3. X Corp. has manufactured Device A in Puerto Rico for a number of years and began to manufacture Device B in Puerto Rico in 1997. Device A and Device B are both used to conduct electrical current to the heart and are both sold to cardiologists. There is no significant change in the type of activity conducted in Puerto Rico after the transfer of the manufacturing of Device B to Puerto Rico. Similar manufacturing equipment, manufacturing processes and skills are used in the manufacture of both devices. Both are regulated and licensed by the Food and Drug Administration. The economic success of Device B is dependent upon the success of Device A only to the extent that the liability and manufacturing prowess with respect to one reflects favorably on the other. Depending upon the heart abnormality, the cardiologist may choose to use Device A, Device B or both on a patient. The manufacture of Device B is treated as a unit with the manufacture of Device A in X Corp.'s accounting records. The manufacture of Device A is in the six-digit NAICS code 339112, Surgical and Medical Instrument Manufacturing. The manufacture of Device B is in the six-digit NAICS code 334510, Electromedical and electrotherapeutic Apparatus Manufacturing. (The manufacture of Device A is in the four-digit SIC code 3845, Electromedical and Electrotherapeutic Apparatus. The manufacture of Device B is in the four-digit SIC code 3841, Surgical and Medical Instruments and Apparatus.) The safe harbor of paragraph (b)(2)(ii)(B) of this section applies because the two activities are within the same three-digit SIC code and Corp. X satisfies paragraphs (b)(2)(i)(A), (B), (C), (D), (F), and (G) of this section.

Example 4. X Corp. has been manufacturing house slippers in Puerto Rico since 1990. Y Corp. is a U.S. corporation that is not affiliated with X Corp. and is not an existing credit claimant. Y Corp. has been manufacturing snack food in the United States. In 1997, X Corp. purchased the assets of Y Corp. and began to manufacture snack food in Puerto Rico. House slipper manufacturing is in the six-digit NAICS code 316212 (Four-digit SIC code 3142, House Slippers). The manufacture of snack foods falls under the six-digit NAICS code 311919, Other Snack Food Manufacturing (four-digit SIC code 2052, Cookies and Crackers (pretzels)). Because these activities are not within the same five or six digit NAICS code (or the same three or four-digit SIC code), and because snack food is not an integrated product that contains house slippers, the safe harbor of paragraph (b)(2)(ii) of this section cannot apply. Considering all the facts and circumstances, including the seven factors of paragraph (b)(2)(i) of this section, the snack food manufacturing activity is not closely related to the manufacture of house slippers, and is a new line of business, within the meaning of paragraph (b) of this section.

Example 5. X Corp., a calendar year taxpayer, is an existing credit claimant that has elected the profit-split method for computing taxable income. P Corp. was not an existing credit claimant and manufactured a product in a different five-digit NAICS code than the product manufactured by X Corp. In 1997, X Corp. acquired the stock of P Corp. and liquidated P Corp. in a tax-free liquidation under section 332, but continued the business activity of P Corp. as a new business segment. Assume that this new business segment is a new line of business within the meaning of paragraph (c) of this section. In 1997, X Corp. has gross income from the active conduct of a trade or business in a possession computed under section 936(a)(2) of $500 million and the adjusted tax basis of its assets is $200 million. The new business segment had gross income of $60 million, or 12 percent of the X Corp. gross income, and the adjusted basis of the new segment's assets was $20 million, or 10 percent of the X Corp. total assets. In 1997, X Corp. does not derive more than 15 percent of its gross income, or directly use more that 15 percent of its total assets, from the new business segment. Thus, the new line of business acquired from P Corp. is not a *substantial* new line of business within the meaning of paragraph (c) of this section, and the new activity will not cause X Corp. to lose its status as an existing credit claimant during 1997. In 1998, however, the gross income of X Corp. grew to $750 million while the gross income of the new line of business grew to $150 million, or 20% of the X Corp. 1998 gross income. Thus, in 1998, the new line of business is substantial within the meaning of paragraph (c) of this section, and X Corp. loses its status as an existing credit claimant for 1998 and all years subsequent.

(e) *Loss of status as existing credit claimant.* An existing credit claimant that adds a substantial new line of business in a taxable year, or that has a new line of business that becomes substantial in a taxable year, loses its status as an existing credit claimant for that year and all years subsequent.

Reg. § 1.936-11(e)

Income from Sources Without the United States

See p. 20,601 for regulations not amended to reflect law changes

(f) *Effective date*—(1) *General rule.* This section applies to taxable years of a possessions corporation beginning on or after January 25, 2000.

(2) *Election for retroactive application.* Taxpayers may elect to apply retroactively all the provisions of this section for any open taxable year beginning after December 31, 1995. Such election will be effective for the year of the election and all subsequent taxable years. This section will not apply to activities of pre-existing businesses for taxable years beginning before January 1, 1996. [Reg. § 1.936-11.]

☐ [T.D. 8868, 1-21-2000.]

[Reg. § 1.951-1]

§ 1.951-1. **Amounts included in gross income of United States shareholders.**—(a) *In general.* If a foreign corporation is a controlled foreign corporation (within the meaning of section 957) for an uninterrupted period of 30 days or more (determined under paragraph (f) of this section) during any taxable year of such corporation beginning after December 31, 1962, every person—

(1) Who is a United States shareholder (as defined in section 951(b) and paragraph (g) of this section) of such corporation at any time during such taxable year, and

(2) Who owns (within the meaning of section 958(a)) stock in such corporation on the last day, in such year, on which such corporation is a controlled foreign corporation

shall include in his gross income for his taxable year in which or with which such taxable year of the corporation ends, the sum of—

(i) Except as provided in section 963, such shareholder's pro rata share (determined under paragraph (b) of this section) of the corporation's subpart F income (as defined in section 952) for such taxable year of the corporation,

(ii) Such shareholder's pro rata share (determined under paragraph (c)(1) of this section) of the corporation's previously excluded subpart F income withdrawn from investment in less developed countries for such taxable year of the corporation,

(iii) Such shareholder's pro rata share (determined under paragraph (c)(2) of this section) of the corporation's previously excluded subpart F income withdrawn from investment in foreign base company shipping operations for such taxable year of the corporation, and

(iv) Such shareholder's pro rata share (determined under paragraph (d) of this section) of the corporation's increase in earnings invested in United States property for such taxable year of the corporation (but only to the extent such pro rata share is not excluded from such shareholder's gross income for his taxable year under section 959(a)(2)).

For purposes of determining whether a United States shareholder which is a domestic corporation is a personal holding company under section 542 and § 1.542-1, the character of the amount includible in gross income of such domestic corporation under this paragraph shall be determined as if such amount were realized directly by such corporation from the source from which it is realized by the controlled foreign corporation. See paragraph (a) of § 1.957-2 for special limitation on the amount of subpart F income in the case of a controlled foreign corporation described in section 957(b). See section 970(a) and § 1.970-1 which provides for the reduction of subpart F income of export trade corporations.

(b) *Limitation on a United States shareholder's pro rata share of subpart F income*—(1) *In general.* For purposes of paragraph (a)(2)(i) of this section, a United States shareholder's pro rata share (determined in accordance with the rules of paragraph (e) of this section) of the foreign corporation's subpart F income for the taxable year of such corporation is—

(i) The amount which would have been distributed with respect to the stock which such shareholder owns (within the meaning of section 958(a)) in such corporation if on the last day, in such corporation's taxable year, on which such corporation is a controlled foreign corporation it had distributed pro rata to its shareholders an amount which bears the same ratio to its subpart F income for such taxable year as the part of such year during which such corporation is a controlled foreign corporation bears to the entire taxable year, reduced by—

(ii) The amount of distributions received by any other person during such taxable year as a dividend with respect to such stock, but only to the extent that such distributions do not exceed the dividend which would have been received by such other person if the distributions by such corporation to all its shareholders had been the amount which bears the same ratio to the subpart F income of such corporation for the taxable year as the part of such year during which such shareholder did not own (within the meaning of section 958(a)) such stock bears to the entire taxable year.

(2) *Illustrations.* The application of this paragraph may be illustrated by the following examples:

Example (1). A, a United States shareholder, owns 100 percent of the only class of stock of M, a

Income from Sources Without the United States

See p. 20,601 for regulations not amended to reflect law changes

controlled foreign corporation throughout 1963. Both A and M Corporation use the calendar year as a taxable year. For 1963, M Corporation derives $100 of subpart F income, has $100 of earnings and profits, and makes no distributions. A must include $100 in his gross income for 1963 under section 951(a)(1)(A)(i).

Example (2). The facts are the same as in example (1), except that instead of holding 100 percent of the stock of M Corporation for the entire year, A sells 60 percent of such stock to B, a nonresident alien, on May 26, 1963. Thus, M Corporation is a controlled foreign corporation for the period January 1, 1963, through May 26, 1963. A must include $40 ($100 × 146/365) in his gross income for 1963 under section 951(a)(1)(A)(i).

Example (3). The facts are the same as in example (1), except that instead of holding 100 percent of the stock of M Corporation for the entire year, A holds 60 percent of such stock on December 31, 1963, having acquired such interest on May 26, 1963, from B, a nonresident alien, who owned such interest from January 1, 1963. Before A's acquisition of such stock, M Corporation had distributed a dividend of $15 to B in 1963 with respect to such stock. A must include $21 in his gross income for 1963 under section 951(a)(1)(A)(i), such amount being determined as follows:

Corporation M's subpart F income for 1963	$100
Less: Reduction under sec. 951(a)(2)(A) for period (1-1-63 through 5-26-63) during which M Corporation is not a controlled foreign corporation ($100 × 146/365)	40
Subpart F income for 1963 as limited by sec. 951(a)(2)(A)	60
A's pro rata share of subpart F income as determined under sec. 951(a)(2)(A) (60 percent of $60)	36
Less: Reduction under sec. 951(a)(2)(B) for dividends received by B during 1963 with respect to the stock acquired by A in M Corporation:	
(i) Dividend received by B	$15
(ii) B's pro rata share of the amount which bears the same ratio to M Corporation's subpart F income for 1963 ($100) as the period during which A did not own (within the meaning of section 958(a)) his stock (146 days) bears to the entire taxable year (365 days) (60 percent of ($100 × 146/365))	$24
(iii) Amount of reduction (lesser of (i) or (ii))	$ 15
A's pro rata share of subpart F income as determined under sec. 951(a)(2)	21

Example (4). A, a United States shareholder, owns 100 percent of the only class of stock of P, a controlled foreign corporation throughout 1963, and P owns 100 percent of the only class of stock of R, a controlled foreign corporation throughout 1963. A and Corporations P and R each use the calendar year as a taxable year. For 1963, R Corporation derives $100 of subpart F income, has $100 of earnings and profits, and distributes a dividend of $20 to P Corporation. Corporation P has no income for 1963 other than the dividend received from R Corporation. A must include $100 in his gross income for 1963 under section 951(a)(1)(A)(i) as subpart F income of R Corporation for such year. Such subpart F income is not reduced under sec. 951(a)(2)(B) for the dividend of $20 paid to P Corporation because there was no part of the year 1963 during which A did not own (within the meaning of section 958(a)) the stock of R Corporation. By reason of the application of section 959(b), the $20 distribution from R Corporation to P Corporation is not again includible in the gross income of A under section 951(a).

Example (5). The facts are the same as in example (4), except that instead of holding the stock of R Corporation for the entire year, P Corporation acquires 60 percent of the only class of stock of R Corporation on March 14, 1963, from C, a nonresident alien, after R Corporation distributes in 1963 a dividend of $35 to C with respect to the stock so acquired by P Corporation. The stock interest so acquired by P Corporation was owned by C from January 1, 1963, until acquired by P Corporation. A must include $36 in his gross income for 1963 under section 951(a)(1)(A)(i), such amount being determined as follows:

Corporation R's subpart F income for 1963	$100
Less: Reduction under sec. 951(a)(2)(A) for period (1-1-63 through 3-14-63) during which R Corporation is not a controlled foreign corporation ($100 × 73/365)	20
Subpart F income for 1963 as limited by sec. 951(a)(2)(A)	80
A's pro rata share of subpart F income as determined under sec. 951(a)(2)(A) (60 percent of $80)	48

Reg. § 1.951-1(b)(2)

49,170 Income from Sources Without the United States
See p. 20,601 for regulations not amended to reflect law changes

Less: Reduction under sec. 951(a)(2)(B) for dividends received by C during 1963 with respect to the stock indirectly acquired by A in R Corporation:

(i) Dividend received by C $35

(ii) C's pro rata share of the amount which bears the same ratio to R Corporation's subpart F income for 1963 ($100) as the period during which A did not in indirectly own (within the meaning of section 958(a)(2)) his stock (73 days) bears to the entire taxable year (365 days) (60 percent of ($100 × 73/365)) $12

(iii) Amount of reduction (lesser of (i) or (ii)) .... $ 12

A's pro rata share of subpart F income as determined under sec. 951(a)(2) 36

(c) *Limitation on a United States shareholder's pro rata share of previously excluded subpart F income withdrawn from investments*—(1) *Investments in less developed countries.* For purposes of paragraph (a)(2)(ii) of this section, a United States shareholder's pro rata share (determined in accordance with the rules of paragraph (e) of this section) of the foreign corporation's previously excluded subpart F income withdrawn from investment in less developed countries for the taxable year of such corporation shall not exceed an amount which bears the same ratio to such shareholder's pro rata share of such income withdrawn (as determined under section 955(a)(3), as in effect before the enactment of the Tax Reduction Act of 1975, and paragraph (c) of § 1.955-1) for such taxable year as the part of such year during which such corporation is a controlled foreign corporation bears to the entire taxable year. See paragraph (c)(2) of § 1.955-1 for a special rule applicable to exclusions and withdrawals occurring before the date on which the United States shareholder acquires his stock.

(2) *Investments in foreign base company shipping operations.* For purposes of paragraph (a)(2)(iii) of this section, a United States shareholder's pro rata share (determined in accordance with the rules of paragraph (e) of this section) of the foreign corporation's previously excluded subpart F income withdrawn from investment in foreign base company shipping operations for the taxable year of such corporation shall not exceed an amount which bears the same ratio to such shareholder's pro rata share of such income withdrawn (as determined under section 955(a)(3) and paragraph (c) of § 1.955A-1) for such taxable year as the part of such year during which such corporation is a controlled foreign corporation bears to the entire taxable year. See paragraph (c)(2) of § 1.955A-1 for a special rule applicable to exclusions and withdrawals occurring before the date on which the United States shareholder acquires his stock.

(d) *Limitation on a United States shareholder's pro rata share of increase in investment in United States property.* For purposes of paragraph (a)(2)(iv) of this section, a United States shareholder's pro rata share (determined in accordance with the rules of paragraph (e) of this section) of the foreign corporation's increase in earnings invested in United States property for the taxable year of such corporation shall not exceed an amount which bears the same ratio to such shareholder's pro rata share of such increase (as determined under section 956(a)(2) and paragraph (c) of § 1.956-1) for such taxable year as the part of such year during which such corporation is a controlled foreign corporation bears to the entire taxable year. The amount determined under the preceding sentence, however, shall be taken into account under paragraph (a)(2)(iv) of this section only to the extent such amount is not excluded from such shareholder's gross income for his taxable year under section 959(a)(2) and the regulations thereunder.

(e) *"Pro rata share" defined*—(1) *In general.* For purposes of paragraphs (b), (c), and (d) of this section, a United States shareholder's pro rata share of a controlled foreign corporation's subpart F income, previously excluded subpart F income withdrawn from investment in less developed countries, previously excluded subpart F income withdrawn from investment in foreign base company shipping operations, or increase in earnings invested in United States property, respectively, for any taxable year is his pro rata share determined under paragraph (a) of § 1.952-1, paragraph (c) of § 1.955-1, paragraph (c) of § 1.955A-1, or paragraph (c) of § 1.956-1, respectively.

(2) *More than one class of stock.* If a controlled foreign corporation for a taxable year has more than one class of stock outstanding, the amount of such corporation's subpart F income, withdrawal, or increase in investment, for the taxable year which shall be taken into account with respect to any one class of such stock for purposes of subparagraph (1) of this paragraph shall be that amount which bears the same ratio to the total of such subpart F income, withdrawal, or increase in investment for such year as the earnings and profits which would be distributed with respect to such class of stock if all earnings and profits of such corporation for such year were distributed on the last day of such corporation's taxable year on which such corporation is a con-

Reg. § 1.951-1(c)(2)

trolled foreign corporation bear to the total earnings and profits of such corporation for such taxable year. For purposes of the preceding sentence, if an arrearage in dividends for prior taxable years exists with respect to a class of preferred stock of such corporation, the earnings and profits for the taxable year shall be attributed to such arrearage only to the extent such arrearage exceeds the earnings and profits of such corporation remaining from prior taxable years beginning after December 31, 1962.

(3) *Discretionary power to allocate earnings to different classes of stock.* If the allocation of a foreign corporation's earnings and profits for the taxable year between two or more classes of stock depends upon the exercise of discretion by that body of persons which exercises with respect to such corporation the powers ordinarily exercised by the board of directors of a domestic corporation, the allocation of earnings and profits to such classes shall be made for purposes of this paragraph as if such classes constituted one class of stock in which each share has the same rights to dividends as any other share, unless a different method of allocation of earnings and profits is established as proper by the United States shareholder.

(4) *Illustrations.* The application of this paragraph may be illustrated by the following examples:

Example (1). Throughout its taxable year 1964, controlled foreign corporation A has outstanding 40 shares of common stock and 60 shares of 6-percent, nonparticipating, nonvoting, preferred stock with a par value of $100 per share. D, a United States citizen who uses the calendar year as a taxable year, owns 30 shares of the common, and 15 shares of the preferred, stock during 1964; Corporation A for 1964 has earnings and profits of $1,000, and income of $500 with respect to which amounts are required to be included in gross income of United States shareholders under section 951(a). In such case, if the total $1,000 of earnings and profits were distributed on December 31, 1964, $360 (0.06 × $100 × 60) would be distributed with respect to A Corporation's preferred stock and $640 ($1,000 minus $360) would be distributed with respect to its common stock. Accordingly, of the $500 with respect to which amounts are required to be included in gross income of United States shareholders under section 951(a), $180 ($360/$1,000 × $500) is allocated to the outstanding preferred stock and $320 ($640/$1,000 × $500) is allocated to the outstanding common stock. D's pro rata share of such amounts for 1964 is $285 [($180 × 15/60) + ($320 × 30/40)].

Example (2). The facts are the same as in example (1), except that the preferred stock is cumulative and there is an arrearage in dividends with respect to such stock of $900; on December 31, 1963, Corporation A has accumulated earnings and profits for 1963 of $700; therefore, for purposes of this paragraph, Corporation A's earnings and profits for 1964 attributable to such arrearage may not exceed $200 ($900 minus $700). In such case, for purposes of this paragraph, if the $1,000 earnings and profits for 1964 were distributed on December 31, 1964, $560 [(0.06 × $100 × 60) + $200] would be distributed with respect to A Corporation's preferred stock and $440 ($1,000 minus $560) would be distributed with respect to its common stock. Accordingly, of the $500 with respect to which amounts are required to be included in gross income of United States shareholders under section 951(a), $280 ($560/$1,000 × $500) is allocated to the outstanding preferred stock and $220 ($440/$1,000 × $500) is allocated to the outstanding common stock. D's pro rata share of such amounts for 1964 is $235 [($280 × 15/60) + ($220 × 30/40)].

(f) *Determination of holding period.* For purposes of sections 951 through 964, the holding period of an asset (including stock of a controlled foreign corporation) shall be determined by excluding the day on which such asset is acquired and including the day on which such asset is disposed of. The application of this paragraph may be illustrated by the following example:

Example. On June 30, 1963, United States person E acquires 70 of the 100 shares of the only class of stock of foreign corporation A from nonresident alien B, who until such time owns all such 100 shares. E sells 10 shares of stock of such corporation on November 30, 1963, and 60 shares on December 31, 1963, to nonresident alien F. Corporation A is a controlled foreign corporation for the period beginning with July 1, 1963, and extending through December 31, 1963. As to the 10 shares of stock sold on November 30, 1963, E is treated as not owning such shares at any time after November 30, 1963, nor before July 1, 1963. As to the remaining 60 shares of stock, E is treated as not owning them before July 1, 1963, or after December 31, 1963.

(g) *United States shareholder defined*—(1) *In general.* For purposes of sections 951 through 964, the term "United States shareholder" means, with respect to a foreign corporation, a United States person (as defined in section 957(d)) who owns within the meaning of section 958(a), or is considered as owning by applying the rules of ownership of section 958(b), 10 percent or more of the total

Reg. § 1.951-1(g)(1)

combined voting power of all classes of stock entitled to vote of such foreign corporation.

(2) *Percentage of total combined voting power owned by United States person*—(i) *Meaning of combined voting power.* In determining for purposes of subparagraph (1) of this paragraph whether a United States person owns the requisite percentage of voting power of all classes of stock entitled to vote, consideration will be given to all the facts and circumstances in each case. In any case where—

(*a*) A foreign corporation has more than one class of stock outstanding, and

(*b*) One or more United States persons own (within the meaning of section 958) shares of any one class of stock which possesses the power to elect, appoint, or replace a person, or persons, who with respect to such corporation, exercise the powers ordinarily exercised by a member of the board of directors of a domestic corporation,

the percentage of the total combined voting power with respect to such corporation owned by any such United States person shall be his proportionate share of the percentage of the persons exercising the powers ordinarily exercised by members of the board of directors of a domestic corporation (described in (*b*) of this subdivision) which such class of stock (as a class) possesses the power to elect, appoint, or replace. In all cases, however, a United States person will be deemed to own 10 percent or more of the total combined voting power with respect to a foreign corporation if such person owns (within the meaning of section 958) 20 percent or more of the total number of shares of a class of stock of such corporation possessing one or more powers enumerated in paragraph (b)(1) of § 1.957-1. Whether a foreign corporation is a controlled foreign corporation for purposes of sections 951 through 964 shall be determined by applying the rules of section 957 and §§ 1.957-1 through 1.957-4.

(ii) *Illustration.* The application of this paragraph may be illustrated by the following examples:

Example (1). Foreign corporation S has two classes of capital stock outstanding, consisting of 60 shares of class A stock and 40 shares of class B stock. Each class of the outstanding stock is entitled to participate on a share for share basis in any dividend distributions by S Corporation. The owners of a majority of the class A stock are entitled to elect 7 of the 10 corporate directors, and the owners of a majority of the class B stock are entitled to elect the other 3 of the 10 directors. Thus, the class A stock (as a class) possesses 70 percent of the total combined voting power of all classes of stock entitled to vote of S Corporation, and the class B stock (as a class) possesses 30 percent of such voting power. D, a United States person, owns 31 shares of the class A stock and thus owns 36.167 percent (31/60 × 70 percent) of the total combined voting power of all classes of stock entitled to vote of S Corporation. By reason of the ownership of such voting power, D is a United States shareholder of S Corporation under section 951(b). For purposes of section 957, S Corporation is a controlled foreign corporation by reason of D's ownership of a majority of the class A stock, as illustrated in example (2) of paragraph (c) of § 1.957-1. E, a United States person, owns eight shares of the class A stock and thus owns 9.333 percent (8/60 × 70 percent) of the total combined voting power of all classes of stock entitled to vote of S Corporation. Since E owns only 9.333 percent of such voting power and less than 20 percent of the number of shares of the class A stock, he is not a United States shareholder of S Corporation under section 951(b). F, a United States person, owns 14 shares of the class B stock and thus owns 10.5 percent (14/40 × 30 percent) of the total combined voting power of all classes of stock entitled to vote of S Corporation. By reason of the ownership of such voting power, F is a United States shareholder of S Corporation under section 951(b).

Example (2). Foreign corporation R has three classes of stock outstanding, consisting of 10 shares of class A stock, 20 shares of class B stock, and 300 shares of class C stock. Each class of the outstanding stock is entitled to participate on a share for share basis in any distribution by R Corporation. The owners of a majority of the class A stock are entitled to elect 6 of the 10 corporate directors, and the owners of a majority of the class B stock are entitled to elect the other 4 of the 10 directors. The class C stock is not entitled to vote. D, E, and F, United States persons, each own 2 shares of the class A stock and 100 shares of the class C stock. As owners of a majority of the class A stock, D, E, and F elect 6 members of the board of directors. D, E, and F are United States shareholders of R Corporation under section 951(b) since each owns 20 percent of the total number of shares of the class A stock which possesses the power to elect a majority of the board of directors of R Corporation. For purposes of section 957, R Corporation is a controlled foreign corporation by reason of the ownership by D, E, and F of a majority of the class A stock, as illustrated in example (2) of paragraph (c) of § 1.957-1. [Reg. § 1.951-1.]

☐ [*T.D.* 6795, 1-28-65. *Amended by T.D.* 7893, 5-11-83.]

Reg. § 1.951-1(g)(2)

Income from Sources Without the United States

[Reg. § 1.951-2]

§ 1.951-2. Coordination of subpart F with election of a foreign investment company to distribute income.—A United States shareholder who for his taxable year is a qualified shareholder (within the meaning of section 1247(c)) of a foreign investment company with respect to which an election under section 1247(a) and the regulations thereunder is in effect for the taxable year of such company which ends with or within such taxable year of such shareholder shall not be required to include any amount in his gross income for his taxable year under paragraph (a) of § 1.951-1 with respect to such company for that taxable year of such company. [Reg. § 1.951-2.]

☐ [T.D. 6795, 1-28-65.]

[Reg. § 1.951-3]

§ 1.951-3. Coordination of subpart F with foreign personal holding company provisions.—A United States shareholder (as defined in section 951(b)) who is required under section 551(b) to include in his gross income for his taxable year his share of the undistributed foreign personal holding company income for the taxable year of a foreign personal holding company (as defined in section 552) which for that taxable year is a controlled foreign corporation (as defined in section 957) shall not be required to include in his gross income for his taxable year under section 951(a) and paragraph (a) of § 1.951-1 any amount attributable to the earnings and profits of such corporation for that taxable year of such corporation. If a foreign corporation is both a foreign personal holding company and a controlled foreign corporation for the same period which is only a part of its taxable year, then, for purposes of applying the immediately preceding sentence, such corporation shall be deemed to be, for such part of such year, a foreign personal holding company and not a controlled foreign corporation and the earnings and profits of such corporation for the taxable year shall be deemed to be that amount which bears the same ratio to its earnings and profits for the taxable year as such part of the taxable year bears to the entire taxable year. The application of this section may be illustrated by the following examples:

Example (1). A, a United States shareholder, owns 100 percent of the only class of stock of controlled foreign corporation M which, in turn, owns 100 percent of the only class of stock of controlled foreign corporation N. A and Corporations M and N use the calendar year as a taxable year. During 1963, N Corporation derives $40,000 of gross income all of which is foreign personal holding company income within the meaning of section 553; thus, N Corporation is a foreign personal holding company for such year within the meaning of section 552(a). For 1963, N Corporation has undistributed foreign personal holding company income (as defined in section 556(a)) of $30,000, derives $25,000 of subpart F income, and has earnings and profits of $32,000. During 1963, M Corporation derives $100,000 of gross income (including as a dividend under section 555(c)(2) the $30,000 of N Corporation's undistributed foreign personal holding company income), 65 percent of which is foreign personal holding company income within the meaning of section 553. Therefore, M Corporation is a foreign personal holding company for such year. For 1963, M Corporation has undistributed foreign personal holding company income (as defined in section 556(a)) of $90,000, determined by taking into account under section 552(c)(1) N Corporation's $30,000 of undistributed foreign personal holding company income for such year; in addition, M Corporation derives $50,000 of subpart F income and has earnings and profits of $92,000. Neither M Corporation nor N Corporation makes any actual distributions during 1963. A is required under section 551(b) to include in his gross income for 1963 as a dividend the $90,000 of M Corporation's undistributed foreign personal holding company income for such year. For 1963, A is not required to include in his gross income under section 951(a) any of the $50,000 subpart F income of M Corporation or of the $25,000 subpart F income of N Corporation.

Example (2). The facts are the same as in example (1), except that only 45 percent of M Corporation's gross income (determined by including under section 555(c)(2) the $30,000 of N Corporation's undistributed foreign personal holding company income) is foreign personal holding company income within the meaning of section 553; accordingly, M Corporation is not a foreign personal holding company for 1963. Since for such year M Corporation is not a foreign personal holding company, the undistributed foreign personal holding company income ($30,000) of N Corporation is not required under section 555(b) to be included in the gross income of M Corporation for 1963; as a result, such income is not required under section 551(b) to be included in the gross income of A for such year even though N Corporation is a foreign personal holding company for that year. For 1963, A is required to include $75,000 in his gross income under section 951(a)(1)(A)(i) and paragraph (a) of § 1.951-1, consisting of the $50,000 subpart F income of M Corporation and the $25,000 subpart F income of N Corporation.

Example (3). The facts are the same as in example (1), except that in 1963 N Corporation actually distributes $30,000 to M Corporation and M Corporation, in turn, actually distributes $90,000 to A. Under section 556 the undistributed foreign personal holding company income of both M Corporation and N Corporation is thus reduced to zero; accordingly, no amount is included in the gross income of A under section 551(b) by reason of his interest in corporations M and N. A must include $75,000 in his gross income for 1963 under section 951(a)(1)(A)(i) and paragraph (a) of § 1.951-1, consisting of the $50,000 subpart F income of M Corporation and the $25,000 subpart F income of N Corporation. Of the $90,000 distribution received by A from M Corporation, $75,000 is excludable from his gross income under section 959(a)(1) as previously taxed earnings and profits; the remaining $15,000 is includible in his gross income for 1963 as a dividend.

Example (4). (a) A, a United States shareholder, owns 100 percent of the only class of stock of controlled foreign corporation P, organized on January 1, 1963. Both A and P Corporation use the calendar year as a taxable year. During 1963, 1964, and 1965, P Corporation is not a foreign personal holding company as defined in section 552(a); in each of such years, P Corporation derives dividend income of $10,000 which constitutes foreign personal holding company income (within the meaning of § 1.954-2) but under 26 CFR § 1.954-1(b)(1) (Rev. as of Apr. 1, 1975) excludes such amounts from foreign base company income as dividends received from, and reinvested in, qualified investments in less developed countries. Corporation P's earnings and profits accumulated for 1963, 1964, and 1965 and determined under paragraph (b)(2) of § 1.955-1 are $40,000. For 1966, P Corporation is a foreign personal holding company, has predistribution earnings and profits of $10,000, derives $10,000 of income which is both foreign personal holding company income within the meaning of section 553 and subpart F income within the meaning of section 952, distributes $8,000 to A, and has undistributed foreign personal holding company income of $2,000 within the meaning of section 556. In addition, for 1966 P Corporation has a withdrawal (determined under section 955(a), as in effect before the enactment of the Tax Reduction Act of 1975, but without regard to its earnings and profits for such year) of $25,000 of previously excluded subpart F income from investment in less developed countries. A is required under section 551(b) to include in his gross income for 1966 as a dividend the $2,000 undistributed foreign personal holding company income. The $8,000 distribution is includible in A's gross income for 1966 under sections 61(a)(7) and 301 as a distribution to which section 316(a)(2) applies. Corporation P's $25,000 withdrawal of previously excluded subpart F income from investment in less developed countries is includible in A's gross income for 1966 under section 951(a)(1)(A)(ii) and paragraph (a)(2) of § 1.951-1.

(b) If P Corporation's earnings and profits accumulated for 1963, 1964, and 1965 were $15,000, instead of $40,000, the result would be the same as in paragraph (a) of this example, except that a withdrawal of only $15,000 of previously excluded subpart F income from investment in less developed countries would be includible in A's gross income for 1966 under section 951(a)(1)(A)(ii) and paragraph (a)(2) of § 1.951-1.

(c) The principles of this example also apply to withdrawals (determined under section 955(a), as in effect before the enactment of the Tax Reduction Act of 1975) of previously excluded subpart F income from investment in less developed countries effected after the effective date of such Act, and to withdrawals (determined under section 955(a), as amended by such Act) of previously excluded subpart F income from investment in foreign base company shipping operations.

Example (5). (a) The facts are the same as in paragraph (a) of example (4), except that, instead of having a $25,000 decrease in qualified investments in less developed countries for 1966, P Corporation invests $20,000 in tangible property (not described in section 956(b)(2)) located in the United States and such investment constitutes an increase (determined under section 956(a) but without regard to the earnings and profits of P Corporation for 1966) in earnings invested in United States property. Corporation P's earnings and profits accumulated for 1963, 1964, and 1965 and determined under paragraph (b)(1) of § 1.956-1 are $22,000. The result is the same as in paragraph (a) of example (4), except that instead of including the $25,000 withdrawal, A must include $20,000 in his gross income for 1966 under section 951(a)(1)(B) and paragraph (a)(2)(iv) of § 1.951-1 as an investment of earnings in United States property.

(b) If P Corporation's earnings and profits accumulated for 1963, 1964, and 1965 were $9,000 instead of $22,000, the result would be the same as in paragraph (a) of this example, except that only $9,000 would be includible in A's gross income for 1966 under section 951(a)(1)(B) and paragraph (a)(2)(iv) of § 1.951-1 as investment of earnings in United States property. [Reg. § 1.951-3.]

☐ [T.D. 6795, 1-28-65. Amended by T.D. 7893, 5-11-83.]

Income from Sources Without the United States

See p. 20,601 for regulations not amended to reflect law changes

[Reg. § 1.952-1]

§ 1.952-1. Subpart F income defined.—(a) *In general.* For purposes of sections 951 through 964, a controlled foreign corporation's subpart F income for any taxable year shall, except as provided in paragraph (b) of this section and subject to the limitations of paragraphs (c) and (d) of this section, consist of the sum of—

(1) The income derived by such corporation for such year from the insurance of United States risks (determined in accordance with the provisions of section 953 and §§ 1.953-1 through 1.953-6),

(2) The income derived by such corporation for such year which constitutes foreign base company income (determined in accordance with the provisions of section 954 and §§ 1.954-1 through 1.954-8),

(3)(i) An amount equal to the product of—

(A) The income of such corporation other than income which—

(*1*) Is attributable to earnings and profits of the foreign corporation included in the gross income of a United States person under section 951 (other than by reason of this paragraph) (determined in accordance with the provisions of section 951 and § 1.951-1), or

(*2*) Is described in section 952(b), multiplied by

(B) The international boycott factor determined in accordance with the provisions of section 999(c)(1), or

(ii) In lieu of the amount determined under paragraph (a)(3)(i) of this section, the amount described under section 999(c)(2) of such international boycott income, and

(4) The sum of the amount of any illegal bribes, kickbacks, or other payments paid after November 3, 1976, by or on behalf of the corporation during the taxable year of the corporation directly or indirectly to an official, employee, or agent in fact of a government. An amount is paid by a controlled foreign corporation where it is paid by an officer, director, employee, shareholder or agent of such corporation for the benefit of such corporation. For purposes of this section, the principles of section 162(c) and the regulations thereunder shall apply. In the case of payments made after September 3, 1982, a payment is illegal if the payment would be unlawful under the Foreign Corrupt Practices Act of 1977 if the payor were a United States person. The fair market value of an illegal payment made in the form of property or services shall be considered the amount of such illegal payment.

Pursuant to section 951(a)(1)(A)(i) and § 1.951-1, a United States shareholder of such controlled foreign corporation must include his pro rata share of such subpart F income in his gross income for his taxable year in which or with which such taxable year of the foreign corporation ends. See section 952(a). However, see paragraph (a) of § 1.957-2 for special rule limiting the subpart F income to the income derived from the insurance of United States risks in the case of certain controlled foreign corporations described in section 957(b).

(b) *Exclusion of U.S. income*—(1) *Taxable years beginning before January 1, 1967.* For rules applicable to taxable years beginning before January 1, 1967, see 26 CFR § 1.952-1(b)(1) (Rev. as of April 1, 1975).

(2) *Taxable years beginning after December 31, 1966.* Notwithstanding paragraph (a) of this section, a controlled foreign corporation's subpart F income for any taxable year beginning after December 31, 1966, shall not include any item of income from sources within the United States which is effectively connected for that year with the conduct by such corporation of a trade or business in the United States unless, pursuant to a treaty to which the United States is a party, such item of income either is exempt from the income tax imposed by chapter 1 (relating to normal taxes and surtaxes) of the Code or is subject to such tax at a reduced rate. Thus, for example, dividends received from sources within the United States by a foreign corporation engaged in business in the United States during the taxable year, which are not effectively connected for that year with the conduct of a trade or business in the United States by that corporation, shall not be excluded from subpart F income under section 952(b) and this subparagraph even though such dividends are subject to the tax of 30 percent imposed by section 881(a). Also, for example, if, by reason of an income tax convention to which the United States is a party, an amount of interest from sources within the United States which is effectively connected for the taxable year with the conduct of a business in the United States by a foreign corporation is subject to tax under chapter 1 at a flat rate of 15 percent, as provided in § 1.871-12, such interest is not excluded from subpart F income under section 952(b) and this subparagraph. The deductions attributable to items of income which are excluded from subpart F income under this subparagraph shall not be taken into account for purposes of section 952.

(3) *Rule applicable under section 956(b)(2).* For purposes only of paragraph (b)(1)(viii) of § 1.956-2, an item of income derived by a con-

trolled foreign corporation from sources within the United States with respect to which for the taxable year a tax is imposed in accordance with section 882(a) shall be considered described in section 952(b) whether or not such item of income would have constituted subpart F income for such year.

(c) *Limitation on a controlled foreign corporation's subpart F income*—(1) *In general.* A United States shareholder's pro rata share (determined in accordance with the rules of paragraph (e) of § 1.951-1) of a controlled foreign corporation's subpart F income for any taxable year shall not exceed his pro rata share of the earnings and profits (as defined in section 964(a) and § 1.964-1) of such corporation for such taxable year, computed as of the close of such taxable year without diminution by reason of any distributions made during such taxable year, minus the sum of—

(i) The amount, if any, by which such shareholder's pro rata share of—

(*a*) The sum of such corporation's deficits in earnings and profits for prior taxable years beginning after December 31, 1962, plus

(*b*) The sum of such corporation's deficits in earnings and profits for taxable years beginning after December 31, 1959, and before January 1, 1963 (reduced by the sum of the earnings and profits (as so defined) of such corporation for any of such taxable years) exceeds

(*c*) The sum of such corporation's earnings and profits for prior taxable years beginning after December 31, 1962, which, with respect to such shareholder, are allocated to other earnings and profits under section 959(c)(3) and § 1.959-3; and

(ii) Such shareholder's pro rata share of any deficits in earnings and profits of other foreign corporations for a taxable year beginning after December 31, 1962, which are attributable to stock of such other foreign corporations owned by such shareholder within the meaning of section 958(a) and which, in accordance with section 952(d) and paragraph (d) of this section, are taken into account as a reduction in the controlled foreign corporation's earnings and profits for such taxable year.

For purposes of applying this subparagraph, the reduction (if any) provided by subdivision (i) of this subparagraph in a United States shareholder's pro rata share of the earnings and profits of a controlled foreign corporation shall be taken into account before the reduction provided by subdivision (ii) of this subparagraph. See section 952(c).

(2) *Special rules.* For purposes only of determining the limitation under subparagraph (1) of this paragraph on a United States shareholder's pro rata share of a controlled foreign corporation's subpart F income for any taxable year—

(i) *Status of foreign corporation.* The earnings and profits, or deficit in earnings and profits, of a foreign corporation for any taxable year shall be taken into account whether or not such foreign corporation is a controlled foreign corporation at the time such earnings and profits are derived or such deficit in earnings and profits is incurred.

(ii) *Deficits in earnings and profits taken into account only once.* A controlled foreign corporation's deficit in earnings and profits for any taxable year preceding the taxable year shall be taken into account for the taxable year only to the extent such deficit has not been taken into account under this paragraph, paragraph (d) of this section, or paragraph (d)(2)(ii) of § 1.963-2 (applied as if section 963 had not been repealed by the Tax Reduction Act of 1975) in computing a minimum distribution, for any taxable year preceding the taxable year, to reduce earnings and profits of such preceding year of such controlled foreign corporation or of any other controlled foreign corporation. To the extent a controlled foreign corporation's (the "first corporation") excess foreign base company shipping deductions for any taxable year (determined under § 1.955A-3(c)(2)(i)) reduce the foreign base company shipping income of another member of a related group (as defined in § 1.955A-2(b)), such deductions shall not be taken into account in determining the earnings and profits or deficit in earnings and profits of such first corporation for such taxable year for purposes of this paragraph (c) and paragraph (d) of this section. The rule of the preceding sentence shall not apply to the extent the excess foreign base company shipping deductions of the first corporation reduce the foreign base company shipping income of another member of a related group below zero.

(iii) *Determination of pro rata share.* A United States shareholder's pro rata share of a controlled foreign corporation's earnings and profits, or deficit in earnings and profits, for any taxable year shall be determined in accordance with the principles of paragraph (e) of § 1.951-1 and paragraph (d)(2)(ii) of § 1.963-2.

(3) *Illustrations.* The application of this paragraph may be illustrated by the following examples:

Example (1). (a) A is a United States shareholder who owns 100 percent of the only class of stock of M Corporation, a controlled foreign corporation organized on January 1, 1963. Both A and

Reg. § 1.952-1(c)(1)

M Corporation use the calendar year as a taxable year.

(b) During 1963, M Corporation derives $20,000 of subpart F income and has earnings and profits of $30,000. Corporation M makes no distributions to A during such year. The limitation under section 952(c) on M Corporation's subpart F income for 1963 is $30,000; and $20,000 is includible in A's gross income for such year under section 951(a)(1)(A)(i).

(c) On January 1, 1964, M Corporation acquires 100 percent of the only class of stock of N Corporation, a controlled foreign corporation which uses the calendar year as a taxable year. During 1964, N Corporation derives $6,000 of subpart F income, has $7,000 of earnings and profits, and distributes $5,000 to M Corporation. The limitation under section 952(c) on N Corporation's subpart F income for 1964 is $7,000; and $6,000 of subpart F income is includible in A's gross income for such year under section 951(a)(1)(A)(i).

(d) During 1964, M Corporation derives $8,000 of rents which constitute subpart F income, makes a $10,000 distribution to A, and has earnings and profits of $12,000 (including the $5,000 dividend received from N Corporation). The limitation under section 952(c) on M Corporation's subpart F income for 1964 is $7,000, determined as follows:

Corporation M's earnings and profits for 1964 (determined under section 964(a) and § 1.964-1 as of the close of such year without diminution for any distributions made during such year)	$12,000
Less: Corporation M's earnings and profits for 1964 described in section 959(b)	5,000
Limitation on M Corporation's subpart F income for 1964	$ 7,000

Thus, for 1964 with respect to A's interest in M Corporation, $7,000 of subpart F income is includible in his gross income under section 951(a)(1)(A)(i). The $10,000 dividend received from M Corporation is excludable from A's gross income for 1964 under section 959(a)(1) and paragraph (b) of § 1.959-1.

Example (2). A is a United States shareholder who owns 100 percent of the only class of stock of R Corporation which was organized on January 1, 1961. R Corporation is a controlled foreign corporation for the entire period after December 31, 1962, here involved. Both A and R Corporation use the calendar year as a taxable year. During 1963, R Corporation derives $25,000 of subpart F income and has $50,000 of earnings and profits. Corporation R has $15,000 of earnings and profits for 1961, and a deficit in earnings and profits of $45,000 for 1962. Thus, R Corporation has as of December 31, 1963, a net deficit in earnings and profits of $30,000 for the years 1961 and 1962. Corporation R makes no distributions to A during 1963. The limitation under section 952(c) on R Corporation's subpart F income for 1963 is $20,000 ($50,000 minus $30,000), and $20,000 of subpart F income is includible in A's gross income for 1963 under section 951(a)(1)(A)(i). During 1964, R Corporation derives $18,000 of subpart F income and has $30,000 of earnings and profits. Corporation R makes no distributions to A during 1964. The entire $18,000 of subpart F income is includible in A's gross income for 1964 under section 951(a)(1)(A)(i).

(d) *Treatment of deficits in earnings and profits attributable to stock of other foreign corporations indirectly owned by a United States shareholder*—(1) *In general.* For purposes of paragraph (c)(1)(ii) of this section, if—

(i) A United States shareholder owns (within the meaning of section 958(a)) stock in two or more foreign corporations in a chain of foreign corporations (as defined in subparagraph (2)(ii) of this paragraph), and

(ii) Any of the corporations in such chain has a deficit in earnings and profits for taxable year beginning after December 31, 1962,

then, with respect to such shareholder and only for purposes of determining the limitation on subpart F income under paragraph (c) of this section, the earnings and profits for the taxable year of each such foreign corporation which is a controlled foreign corporation shall, in accordance with the rules of subparagraph (2) of this paragraph, be reduced to take into account any deficit in earnings and profits referred to in subdivision (ii) of this subparagraph. See section 952(d).

(2) *Special rules.* For purposes of this paragraph—

(i) *Applicable rules.* The special rules set forth in paragraph (c)(2) of this section shall apply.

(ii) *"Chain" defined.* A chain of foreign corporations shall, with respect to a United States shareholder, include—

(a) Any foreign corporation in which such shareholder owns (within the meaning of section 958(a)(1)(A)) stock, but only to the extent of the stock so owned, and

(b) All foreign corporations in which such shareholder owns (within the meaning of section 958(a)(2)) stock, but only to the extent of

Reg. § 1.952-1(d)(2)

the stock so owned by reason of his ownership of the stock referred to in (*a*) of this subdivision.

(iii) *Allocation of deficit.* If one or more foreign corporations (whether or not a controlled foreign corporation) includible in a chain of foreign corporations has a deficit in earnings and profits (determined under section 964(a) and § 1.964-1) for the taxable year, the amount of deficit taken into account under section 952(d) with respect to a United States shareholder in such chain as a reduction in earnings and profits for the taxable year of a controlled foreign corporation includible in such chain shall be an amount which bears the same ratio to such shareholder's pro rata share of the total deficits in earnings and profits for the taxable year of all includible foreign corporations as his pro rata share of the earnings and profits (determined under paragraph (c) of this section but without regard to the provisions of subparagraph (1)(ii) of such paragraph) for the taxable year of such includible controlled foreign corporation bears to his pro rata share of the total earnings and profits (as so determined under paragraph (c) of this section) for the taxable year of all includible controlled foreign corporations. The amount of deficit taken into account under this subdivision with respect to any controlled foreign corporation includible in a chain of foreign corporations shall not exceed the United States shareholder's pro rata share of the controlled foreign corporation's earnings and profits for the taxable year.

(iv) *Taxable year.* The taxable year from which a deficit is allocated under this paragraph, and the taxable year to which such deficit is allocated to reduce earnings and profits, shall be the taxable year of the foreign corporation ending with or within the taxable year of the United States shareholder described in subparagraph (1)(i) of this paragraph.

(3) *Illustration.* The application of this paragraph may be illustrated by the following examples:

Example (1). (a) Domestic corporation M owns 100 percent, 20 percent, and 100 percent, respectively, of the only class of stock of foreign corporations A, B, and F, respectively. Corporation A owns 80 percent of the only class of stock of each of foreign corporations B and C, respectively. Corporation F owns 20 percent of such stock of C Corporation. Corporation B owns 75 percent of the only class of stock of foreign corporation D, and 50 percent of the only class of stock of each of foreign corporations G and H, respectively. C Corporation owns 75 percent of the only class of stock of foreign corporation E. All the corporations use the calendar year as a taxable year, and all of the foreign corporations, except corporations G and H, are controlled foreign corporations throughout the period here involved.

(b) The subpart F income, and the earnings and profits (determined under paragraph (c) of this section but without regard to subparagraph (1)(ii) of such paragraph) or deficit in earnings and profits (determined under section 964(a) and § 1.964-1), of each of the foreign corporations for 1963 are as follows, the deficits being set forth in parentheses:

	Subpart F income	Earnings and profits (deficits)
A Corporation	$ 6,000	$18,000
B Corporation	......	(7,500)
C Corporation	......	(2,500)
D Corporation	4,000	5,000
E Corporation	12,000	15,000
F Corporation	8,000	20,250
G Corporation	......	(10,000)
H Corporation	......	7,000

(c) The chains of foreign corporations (within the meaning of subparagraph (2)(ii) of this paragraph) for 1963 are the "A" chain, consisting of corporations A, B, C, D, E, G, and H, but only to the extent of M Corporation's stock interest in such corporations under section 958(a) by reason of its ownership of stock in A Corporation; the "B" chain, consisting of corporations B, D, G, and H, but only to the extent of M Corporation's stock interest in such corporations under section 958(a) by reason of its ownership of stock in B Corporation; and the "F" chain, consisting of corporations F, C, and E, but only to the extent of M Corporation's stock interest in such corporations under section 958(a) by reason of its ownership of stock in F Corporation.

(d) Corporation M's stock interest under section 958(a) in each of the chains of foreign corporations is as follows for 1963:

	A %	B %	C %	D %	E %	F %	G %	H %
A chain:								
Direct interest	100							
(100% × 80%)		80						
(100% × 80%)			80					
(80% × 75%)				60				
(80% × 75%)					60			
(80% × 50%)							40	
(80% × 50%)								40

Reg. § 1.952-1(d)(3)

Income from Sources Without the United States

See p. 20,601 for regulations not amended to reflect law changes

B chain:
Direct interest	20						
(20% × 75%)		15					
(20% × 50%)					10		
(20% × 50%)							10

F chain:
Direct interest				100			
(100% × 20%)	20						
(20% × 75%)		15					
Total interests	100	100	100	75	75	100	50	50

(e) Corporation M's pro rata share of the earnings and profits (determined under paragraph (c) of this section but without regard to subparagraph (1)(ii) of such paragraph), or of the deficit, of each controlled foreign corporation or each foreign corporation, respectively, includible in the respective chains for 1963 is as follows:

	Earnings and profits	Deficit
A chain:		
A Corporation (100%)	$18,000	....
B Corporation (80%)	....	($ 6,000)
C Corporation (80%)	....	(2,000)
D Corporation (60%)	3,000	....
E Corporation (60%)	9,000	....
G Corporation (40%)	....	(4,000)
H Corporation (40%)	....	....
Total	$30,000	($12,000)
B chain:		
B Corporation (20%)	....	($ 1,500)
D Corporation (15%)	$ 750	....
G Corporation (10%)	....	(1,000)
H Corporation (10%)	....	....
Total	$ 750	($ 2,500)
F chain:		
F Corporation (100%)	$20,250	....
C Corporation (20%)	....	($ 500)
E Corporation (15%)	2,250	....
Total	$22,500	($ 500)

* The earnings and profits of H Corporation are not included in the total earnings and profits for the chain because H Corporation is not a controlled foreign corporation.

(f) The amount by which M Corporation's pro rata share of the earnings and profits for 1963 of the controlled foreign corporations in each respective chain shall be reduced under section 952(d) by M Corporation's pro rata share of the deficits of corporations B, C, and G for 1963 is determined as follows:

	Amount of reduction
A chain:	
A Corporation ($12,000 × $18,000/$30,000)	$ 7,200
D Corporation ($12,000 × $3,000/$30,000)	1,200
E Corporation ($12,000 × $9,000/$30,000)	3,600
Total	$12,000
B chain:	
D Corporation ($2,500 × $750/$750)	$2,500
Limitation: M Corporation's pro rata share of D Corporation's earnings and profits	750
Allocation of used deficit ($750) to M Corporation's pro rata share of the deficits of corporations B and G:	
B Corporation	
($750 × ($1,500/$2,500))	$ 450

Reg. § 1.952-1(d)(3)

49,180 Income from Sources Without the United States
See p. 20,601 for regulations not amended to reflect law changes

G Corporation ($750 × ($1,000/$2,500))	300	
Total..	$ 750	$ 750
F chain:		
F Corporation ($500 × $20,250/$22,500).................................		$ 450
E Corporation ($500 × $2,250/$22,500)		50
Total		$ 500

(g) Corporation M's pro rata share of the earnings and profits (determined after reduction for deficits under section 952(d)) for 1963 of each controlled foreign corporation in the respective chains, determined on a chain-by-chain basis, is determined as follows:

	Earnings and profits before reduction	Reduction (sec. 952(d))	Reduced earnings and profits
A chain:			
A Corporation	$18,000	$7,200	$10,800
D Corporation	3,000	1,200	1,800
E Corporation	9,000	3,600	5,400
B chain:			
D Corporation	750	750	....
F chain:			
F Corporation	20,250	450	19,800
E Corporation	2,250	50	2,200

(h) Corporation M's pro rata share of each controlled foreign corporation's subpart F income, limited as provided by section 952(c) and paragraph (c) of this section, for 1963 which is includible in its gross income for such year under section 951(a)(1)(A)(i) and §1.951-1 is determined as follows:

	Subpart F income (before limitation)	Earnings and profits (sec. 952(c))	Amount includible in income
A Corporation (100%)	$6,000	$10,800	$ 6,000
D Corporation (75%)	3,000	1,800	1,800
E Corporation (75%)	9,000	7,600	7,600
F Corporation (100%)	8,000	19,800	8,000
Total includible under section 951(a)(1)(A)(i)			$23,400

Example (2). The facts are the same as in example (1) except that, in addition, for 1964, foreign corporations C, D, and E have no subpart F income and no earnings and profits and foreign corporations G and H have no earnings and profits. For 1964, B Corporation has subpart F income of $1,000 and earnings and profits (determined in accordance with section 964(a) and §1.964-1) of $1,500; A Corporation has subpart F income of $800 and earnings and profits of $1,000; and F Corporation has subpart F income of $500 and earnings and profits of $1,000. Such earnings and profits are determined without regard to distributions for 1964. Corporation B has an unused deficit in earnings and profits of $1,050 for 1963 ($1,500 minus $450) applicable to M Corporation's interest in such corporation (paragraph (f) of example (1)), and, under paragraph (c)(1)(i)(a) of this section, with respect to M Corporation, such deficit reduces B Corporation's earnings and profits for 1964 to $450. Inasmuch as G Corporation is not a controlled foreign corporation for 1964, such corporation's unused deficit in earnings and profits of $700 for 1963 ($1,000 minus $300) applicable to M Corporation's interest in such corporation (paragraph (f) of example (1)) may be used under paragraph (c)(1)(i)(a) of this section to reduce M Corporation's interest in G Corporation's earnings and profits in a later year or years for which G Corporation is a controlled foreign corporation. Corporation M's pro rata share of each controlled foreign corporation's subpart F income, limited as provided by section 952(c) and paragraph (c) of this section, for 1964 which is includible in its gross income for such year under section 951(a)(1)(A)(i) and §1.951-1 is determined as follows:

	Subpart F income (before limitation)	Earnings and profits (sec. 952(c))	Amount includible in income
A Corporation	$ 800	$1,000	$800
B Corporation.........................	1,000	450	450
F Corporation.........................	500	1,000	500

Reg. § 1.952-1(d)(3)

Example (3). The facts are the same as in example (2), except that for 1964 B Corporation has subpart F income of $550 and earnings and profits (determined in accordance with section 964(a) and § 1.964-1) of $550; such earnings and profits are determined without regard to distributions for 1964. Under paragraph (c)(1)(i)(a) of this section, B Corporation's unused deficit of $1,050 for 1963 reduces its earnings and profits for 1964 with respect to M Corporation to zero. The remaining $500 of the unused deficit for 1963 applicable to M Corporation's interest in B Corporation may be used under paragraph (c)(1)(i)(a) of this section in later years to reduce M Corporation's interest in B Corporation's earnings and profits.

(e) *Application of current earnings and profits limitation*—(1) *In general.* If the subpart F income (as defined in section 952(a)) of a controlled foreign corporation exceeds the foreign corporation's earnings and profits for the taxable year, the subpart F income includible in the income of the corporation's United States shareholders is reduced under section 952(c)(1)(A) in accordance with the following rules. The excess of subpart F income over current year earnings and profits shall—

(i) First, proportionately reduce subpart F income in each separate category of the controlled foreign corporation, as defined in § 1.904-5(a)(1), in which current earnings and profits are zero or less than zero;

(ii) Second, proportionately reduce subpart F income in each separate category in which subpart F income exceeds current earnings and profits; and

(iii) Third, proportionately reduce subpart F income in other separate categories.

(2) *Allocation to a category of subpart F income.* An excess amount that is allocated under paragraph (e)(1) of this section to a separate category must be further allocated to a category of subpart F income if the separate category contains more than one category of subpart F income described in section 952(a) or, in the case of foreign base company income, described in § 1.954-1(c)(1)(iii)(A)(*1*) or (*2*). In such case, the excess amount that is allocated to the separate category must be allocated to the various categories of subpart F income within that separate category on a proportionate basis.

(3) *Recapture of subpart F income reduced by operation of earnings and profits limitation.* Any amount in a category of subpart F income described in section 952(a) or, in the case of foreign base company income, described in § 1.954-1(c)(1)(iii)(A)(*1*) or (*2*) that is reduced by operation of the current year earnings and profits limitation of section 952(c)(1)(A) and this paragraph (e) shall be subject to recapture in a subsequent year under the rules of section 952(c)(2) and paragraph (f) of this section.

(4) *Coordination with sections 953 and 954.* The rules of this paragraph (e) shall be applied after the application of sections 953 and 954 and the regulations under those sections, except as provided in § 1.954-1(d)(4)(ii).

(5) *Earnings and deficits retain separate limitation character.* The income reduction rules of paragraph (e)(1) of this section shall apply only for purposes of determining the amount of an inclusion under section 951(a)(1)(A) from each separate category as defined in § 1.904-5(a)(1) and the separate categories in which recapture accounts are established under section 952(c)(2) and paragraph (f) of this section. For rules applicable in computing post-1986 undistributed earnings, see generally section 902 and the regulations under that section. For rules relating to the allocation of deficits for purposes of computing foreign taxes deemed paid under section 960 with respect to an inclusion under section 951(a)(1)(A), see § 1.960-1(i).

(f) *Recapture of subpart F income in subsequent taxable year*—(1) *In general.* If a controlled foreign corporation's subpart F income for a taxable year is reduced under the current year earnings and profits limitation of section 952(c)(1)(A) and paragraph (e) of this section, recapture accounts will be established and subject to recharacterization in any subsequent taxable year to the extent the recapture accounts were not previously recharacterized or distributed, as provided in paragraphs (f)(2) and (3) of this section.

(2) *Rules of recapture*—(i) *Recapture account.* If a category of subpart F income described in section 952(a) or, in the case of foreign base company income, described in § 1.954-1(c)(1)(iii)(A)(*1*) or (*2*) is reduced under the current year earnings and profits limitation of section 952(c)(1)(A) and paragraph (e) of this section for a taxable year, the amount of such reduction shall constitute a recapture account.

(ii) *Recapture.* Each recapture account of the controlled foreign corporation will be recharacterized, on a proportionate basis, as subpart F income in the same separate category (as defined in § 1.904-5(a)(1)) as the recapture account to the extent that current year earnings and profits exceed subpart F income in a taxable year. The United States shareholder must include his pro rata share (determined under the rules of

§ 1.951-1(e)) of each recharacterized amount in income as subpart F income in such separate category for the taxable year.

(iii) *Reduction of recapture account and corresponding earnings.* Each recapture account, and post-1986 undistributed earnings in the separate category containing the recapture account, will be reduced in any taxable year by the amount which is recharacterized under paragraph (f)(2)(ii) of this section. In addition, each recapture account, and post-1986 undistributed earnings in the separate category containing the recapture account, will be reduced in the amount of any distribution out of that account (as determined under the ordering rules of section 959(c) and paragraph (f)(3)(ii) of this section).

(3) *Distribution ordering rules*—(i) *Coordination of recapture and distribution rules.* If a controlled foreign corporation distributes an amount out of earnings and profits described in section 959(c)(3) in a year in which current year earnings and profits exceed subpart F income and there is an amount in a recapture account for such year, the recapture rules will apply first.

(ii) *Distributions reduce recapture accounts first.* Any distribution made by a controlled foreign corporation out of earnings and profits described in section 959(c)(3) shall be treated as made first on a proportionate basis out of the recapture accounts in each separate category to the extent thereof (even if the amount in the recapture account exceeds post-1986 undistributed earnings in the separate category containing the recapture account). Any remaining distribution shall be treated as made on a proportionate basis out of the remaining earnings and profits of the controlled foreign corporation in each separate category. See section 904(d)(3)(D).

(4) *Examples.* The application of paragraphs (e) and (f) of this section may be illustrated by the following examples:

Example 1. (i) A, a U.S. person, is the sole shareholder of CFC, a controlled foreign corporation formed on January 1, 1998, whose functional currency is the u. In 1998, CFC earns 100u of foreign base company sales income that is general limitation income described in section 904(d)(1)(I) and incurs a (200u) loss attributable to activities that would have produced general limitation income that is not subpart F income. In 1998 CFC also earns 100u of foreign personal holding company income that is passive income described in section 904(d)(1)(A), and 100u of foreign personal holding company income that is dividend income subject to a separate limitation described in section 904(d)(1)(E) for dividends from a noncontrolled section 902 corporation.

CFC's subpart F income for 1998, 300u, exceeds CFC's current earnings and profits, 100u, by 200u. Under section 952(c)(1)(A) and paragraph (e) of this section, subpart F income is limited to CFC's current earnings and profits of 100u, all of which is included in A's gross income under section 951(a)(1)(A). The 200u of CFC's 1998 subpart F income that is not included in A's income in 1998 by reason of section 952(c)(1)(A) is subject to recapture under section 952(c)(2) and paragraph (f) of this section.

(ii) For purposes of determining the amount and type of income included in A's gross income and the amount and type of income in CFC's recapture account, the rules of paragraphs (e)(1) and (2) of this section apply. Under paragraph (e)(1)(i) of this section, the amount by which CFC's subpart F income exceeds its earnings and profits for 1998, 200u, first reduces from 100u to 0 CFC's subpart F income in the general limitation category, which has a current year deficit of (100u) in earnings and profits. Next, under paragraph (e)(1)(iii) of this section, the remaining 100u by which CFC's 1998 subpart F income exceeds earnings and profits is applied proportionately to reduce CFC's subpart F income in the separate categories for passive income (100u) and dividends from the noncontrolled section 902 corporation (100u). Thus, A includes 50u of passive limitation/foreign personal holding company income and 50u of dividends from the noncontrolled section 902 corporation/foreign personal holding company income in gross income in 1998. CFC has 100u in its general limitation/foreign base company sales income recapture account attributable to the 100u of foreign base company sales income that is not included in A's income by reason of the earnings and profits limitation of section 952(c)(1)(A). CFC also has 50u in its passive limitation recapture account, all of which is attributable to foreign personal holding company income, and 50u in its recapture account for dividends from the noncontrolled section 902 corporation, all of which is attributable to foreign personal holding company income.

(iii) For purposes of computing post-1986 undistributed earnings, the rules of sections 902 and 960, including the rules of § 1.960-1(i), apply. Under § 1.960-1(i), the general limitation deficit of (100u) is allocated proportionately to reduce passive limitation earnings of 100u and noncontrolled section 902 dividend earnings of 100u. Thus, passive limitation earnings are reduced by 50u to 50u (100u passive limitation earnings/200u total earnings in positive separate categories x (100u) general limitation deficit = 50u reduction), and the noncontrolled section 902 corporation earnings are reduced by 50u to 50u

(100u noncontrolled section 902 corporation earnings/200u total earnings in positive separate categories x (100u) general limitation deficit = 50u reduction). All of CFC's post-1986 foreign income taxes with respect to passive limitation income and dividends from the noncontrolled section 902 corporation are deemed paid by A under section 960 with respect to the subpart F inclusions (50u inclusion/50u earnings in each separate category). After the inclusion and deemed-paid taxes are computed, at the close of 1998 CFC has a (100u) deficit in general limitation earnings (100u subpart F earnings + (200u) nonsubpart F loss), 50u of passive limitation earnings (100u of earnings attributable to foreign personal holding company income − 50u inclusion) with a corresponding passive limitation/foreign personal holding company income recapture account of 50u, and 50u of earnings subject to a separate limitation for dividends from the noncontrolled section 902 corporation (100u earnings − 50u inclusion) with a corresponding noncontrolled section 902 corporation/foreign personal holding company income recapture account of 50u.

Example 2. (i) The facts are the same as in *Example 1* with the addition of the following facts. In 1999, CFC earns 100u of foreign base company sales income that is general limitation income and 100u of foreign personal holding company income that is passive limitation income. In addition, CFC incurs (10u) of expenses that are allocable to its separate limitation for dividends from the noncontrolled section 902 corporation. Thus, CFC's subpart F income for 1999, 200u, exceeds CFC's current earnings and profits, 190u, by 10u. Under section 952(c)(1)(A) and paragraph (e) of this section, subpart F income is limited to CFC's current earnings and profits of 190u, all of which is included in A's gross income under section 951(a)(1)(A).

(ii) For purposes of determining the amount and type of income included in A's gross income and the amount and type of income in CFC's recapture accounts, the rules of paragraphs (e)(1) and (2) of this section apply. While CFC's general limitation post-1986 undistributed earnings for 1999 are 0 ((100u) opening balance + 100u subpart F income), CFC's general limitation subpart F income (100u) does not exceed its general limitation current earnings and profits (100u) for 1999. Accordingly, under paragraph (e)(1)(iii) of this section, the amount by which CFC's subpart F income exceeds its earnings and profits for 1999, 10u, is applied proportionately to reduce CFC's subpart F income in the separate categories for general limitation income, 100u, and passive income, 100u. Thus, A includes 95u of general limitation foreign base company sales income and 95u of passive limitation foreign personal holding company income in gross income in 1999. At the close of 1999 CFC has 105u in its general limitation/foreign base company sales income recapture account (100u from 1998 + 5u from 1999), 55u in its passive limitation/foreign personal holding company income recapture account (50u from 1998 + 5u from 1999), and 50u in its dividends from the noncontrolled section 902 corporation/ foreign personal holding company income recapture account (all from 1998).

(iii) For purposes of computing post-1986 undistributed earnings in each separate category, the rules of sections 902 and 960, including the rules of § 1.960-1(i), apply. Thus, post-1986 undistributed earnings (or an accumulated deficit) in each separate category are increased (or reduced) by current earnings and profits or current deficits in each separate category. The accumulated deficit in CFC's general limitation earnings and profits (100u) is reduced to 0 by the addition of 100u of 1999 earnings and profits. CFC's passive limitation earnings of 50u are increased by 100u to 150u, and CFC's noncontrolled section 902 corporation earnings of 50u are decreased by (10u) to 40u. After the addition of current year earnings and profits and deficits to the separate categories there are no deficits remaining in any separate category. Thus, the allocation rules of § 1.960-1(i)(4) do not apply in 1999. Accordingly, in determining the post-1986 foreign income taxes deemed paid by A, post-1986 undistributed earnings in each separate category are unaffected by earnings in the other categories. Foreign taxes deemed paid under section 960 for 1999 would be determined as follows for each separate category: with respect to the inclusion of 95u of foreign base company sales income out of general limitation earnings, the section 960 fraction is 95u inclusion/0 total earnings; with respect to the inclusion of 95u of passive limitation income the section 960 fraction is 95u inclusion/150u passive earnings. Thus, no general limitation taxes would be associated with the inclusion of the general limitation earnings because there are no accumulated earnings in the general limitation category. After the deemed-paid taxes are computed, at the close of 1999 CFC has a (95u) deficit in general limitation earnings and profits ((100u) opening balance + 100u current earnings − 95u inclusion), 55u of passive limitation earnings and profits (50u opening balance + 100u current foreign personal holding company income − 95u inclusion), and 40u of earnings and profits subject to the separate limitation for dividends from the noncontrolled section 902 corporation (50u opening balance + (10u) expense).

Reg. § 1.952-1(f)(4)

Example 3. (i) A, a U.S. person, is the sole shareholder of *CFC*, a controlled foreign corporation whose functional currency is the u. At the beginning of 1998, CFC has post-1986 undistributed earnings of 275u, all of which are general limitation earnings described in section 904(d)(1)(I). CFC has no previously-taxed earnings and profits described in section 959(c)(1) or (c)(2). In 1998, CFC has a (200u) loss in the shipping category described in section 904(d)(1)(D), 100u of foreign personal holding company income that is passive income described in section 904(d)(1)(A), and 125u of general limitation manufacturing earnings that are not subpart F income. CFC's subpart F income for 1998, 100u, exceeds CFC's current earnings and profits, 25u, by 75u. Under section 952(c)(1)(A) and paragraph (e) of this section, subpart F income is limited to CFC's current earnings and profits of 25u, all of which is included in A's gross income under section 951(a)(1)(A). The 75u of CFC's 1998 subpart F income that is not included in A's income in 1998 by reason of section 952(c)(1)(A) is subject to recapture under section 952(c)(2) and paragraph (f) of this section.

(ii) For purposes of determining the amount and type of income included in A's gross income and the amount and type of income in CFC's recapture account, the rules of paragraphs (e)(1) and (2) of this section apply. Under paragraph (e)(1) of this section, the amount of CFC's subpart F income in excess of earnings and profits for 1998, 75u, reduces the 100u of passive limitation foreign personal holding company income. Thus, A includes 25u of passive limitation foreign personal holding company income in gross income, and CFC has 75u in its passive limitation/foreign personal holding company income recapture account.

(iii) For purposes of computing post-1986 undistributed earnings in each separate category the rules of sections 902 and 960, including the rules of § 1.960-1(i), apply. Under § 1.960-1(i), the shipping limitation deficit of (200u) is allocated proportionately to reduce general limitation earnings of 400u and passive limitation earnings of 100u. Thus, general limitation earnings are reduced by 160u to 240u (400u general limitation earnings/500u total earnings in positive separate categories x (200u) shipping deficit = 160u reduction), and passive limitation earnings are reduced by 40u to 60u (100u passive earnings/500u total earnings in positive separate categories x (200u) shipping deficit = 40u reduction). Five-twelfths of CFC's post-1986 foreign income taxes with respect to passive limitation earnings are deemed paid by A under section 960 with respect to the subpart F inclusion (25u inclusion/60u passive earnings). After the inclusion and deemed-paid taxes are computed, at the close of 1998 CFC has 400u of general limitation earnings (275u opening balance + 125u current earnings), 75u of passive limitation earnings (100u of foreign personal holding company income − 25u inclusion), and a (200u) deficit in shipping limitation earnings.

Example 4. (i) The facts are the same as in *Example 3* with the addition of the following facts. In 1999, CFC earns 50u of general limitation earnings that are not subpart F income and 75u of passive limitation income that is foreign personal holding company income. Thus, CFC has 125u of current earnings and profits. CFC distributes 200u to A. Under paragraph (f)(3)(i) of this section, the recapture rules are applied first. Thus, the amount by which 1999 current earnings and profits exceed subpart F income, 50u, is recharacterized as passive limitation foreign personal holding company income. CFC's total subpart F income for 1999 is 125u of passive limitation foreign personal holding company income (75u current earnings plus 50u recapture account), and the passive limitation/foreign personal holding company income recapture account is reduced from 75u to 25u.

(ii) CFC has 150u of previously-taxed earnings and profits described in section 959(c)(2) (25u attributable to 1998 and 125u attributable to 1999), all of which is passive limitation earnings and profits. Under section 959(c), 150u of the 200u distribution is deemed to be made from earnings and profits described in section 959(c)(2). The remaining 50u is deemed to be made from earnings and profits described in section 959(c)(3). Under paragraph (f)(3)(ii) of this section, the dividend distribution is deemed to be made first out of the passive limitation recapture account to the extent thereof (25u). Under paragraph (f)(2)(iii) of this section, the passive limitation recapture account is reduced from 25u to 0. The remaining distribution of 25u is treated as made out of CFC's general limitation earnings and profits.

(iii) For purposes of computing post-1986 undistributed earnings, the rules of section 902 and 960, including the rules of § 1.960-1(i), apply. Thus, the shipping limitation accumulated deficit of (200u) reduces general limitation earnings and profits of 450u and passive limitation earnings and profits of 150u on a proportionate basis. Thus, 100% of CFC's post-1986 foreign income taxes with respect to passive limitation earnings are deemed paid by A under section 960 with respect to the 1999 subpart F inclusion of 125u (100u inclusion (numerator limited to denominator)/100u passive earnings). No post-1986 foreign

Income from Sources Without the United States

income taxes remain to be deemed paid under section 902 in connection with the 25u distribution from the passive limitation/foreign personal holding company income recapture account. One-twelfth of CFC's post-1986 foreign income taxes with respect to general limitation earnings are deemed paid by A under section 902 with respect to the distribution of 25u general limitation earnings and profits described in section 959(c)(3) (25u inclusion/300u general limitation earnings). After the deemed-paid taxes are computed, at the close of 1999 CFC has 425u of general limitation earnings and profits (400u opening balance + 50u current earnings − 25u distribution), 0 of passive limitation earnings (75u recapture account + 75u current foreign personal holding company income − 125u inclusion − 25u distribution), and a (200u) deficit in shipping limitation earnings.

(5) *Effective date.* Paragraph (e) of this section and this paragraph (f) apply to taxable years of a controlled foreign corporation beginning after March 3, 1997. [Reg. § 1.952-1.]

☐ [T.D. 6795, 1-28-65. *Amended by* T.D. 6892, 8-22-66; T.D. 7293, 11-27-73; T.D. 7545, 5-5-78; T.D. 7862, 12-16-82; T.D. 7893, 5-11-83; T.D. 7894, 5-11-83; T.D. 8331, 1-24-91 *and* T.D. 8704, 12-31-96.]

[Reg. § 1.952-2]

§ 1.952-2. Determination of gross income and taxable income of a foreign corporation.—(a) *Determination of gross income*—(1) *In general.* Except as provided in subparagraph (2) of this paragraph, the gross income of a foreign corporation for any taxable year shall, subject to the special rules of paragraph (c) of this section, be determined by treating such foreign corporation as a domestic corporation taxable under section 11 and by applying the principles of section 61 and the regulations thereunder.

(2) *Insurance gross income*—(i) *Life insurance gross income.* The gross income for any taxable year of a controlled foreign corporation which is engaged in the business of reinsuring or issuing insurance or annuity contracts and which, if it were a domestic corporation engaged only in such business, would be taxable as a life insurance company to which part I (sections 801 through 820) of subchapter L of chapter 1 of the Code applies, shall, subject to the special rules of paragraph (c) of this section, be the sum of—

(*a*) The gross investment income, as defined under section 804(b), except that interest which is excluded from gross income under section 103 shall not be taken into account;

(*b*) The sum of the items taken into account under section 809(c), except that advance premiums shall not be taken into account; and

(*c*) The amount by which the net long-term capital gain exceeds the net short-term capital loss.

(ii) *Mutual and other insurance gross income.* The gross income for any taxable year of a controlled foreign corporation which is engaged in the business of reinsuring or issuing insurance or annuity contracts and which, if it were a domestic corporation engaged only in such business, would be taxable as a mutual insurance company to which part II (sections 821 through 826) of subchapter L of chapter 1 of the Code applies or as a mutual marine insurance or other insurance company to which part III (sections 831 and 832) of subchapter L of chapter 1 of the Code applies, shall, subject to the special rules of paragraph (c) of this section, be—

(*a*) The sum of—

(*1*) The gross income, as defined in section 832(b)(1);

(*2*) The amount of losses incurred, as defined in section 832(b)(5); and

(*3*) The amount of expenses incurred, as defined in section 832(b)(6); reduced by

(*b*) The amount of interest which under section 103 is excluded from gross income.

(b) *Determination of taxable income*—(1) *In general.* Except as provided in subparagraph (2) of this paragraph, the taxable income of a foreign corporation for any taxable year shall, subject to the special rules of paragraph (c) of this section, be determined by treating such foreign corporation as a domestic corporation taxable under section 11 and by applying the principles of section 63.

(2) *Insurance taxable income.* The taxable income for any taxable year of a controlled foreign corporation which is engaged in the business of reinsuring or issuing insurance or annuity contracts and which, if it were a domestic corporation engaged only in such business, would be taxable as an insurance company to which subchapter L of chapter 1 of the Code applies shall, subject to the special rules of paragraph (c) of this section, be determined by treating such corporation as a domestic corporation taxable under subchapter L of chapter 1 of the Code and by applying the principles of §§ 1.953-4 and 1.953-5 for determining taxable income.

(c) *Special rules for purposes of this section*—(1) *Nonapplication of certain provisions.* Except where otherwise distinctly expressed, the provisions of subchapters F, G, H, L, M, N, S, and T of

49,186 Income from Sources Without the United States

See p. 20,601 for regulations not amended to reflect law changes

chapter 1 of the Internal Revenue Code shall not apply and, for taxable years of a controlled foreign corporation beginning after March 3, 1997, the provisions of section 103 of the Internal Revenue Code shall not apply.

(2) *Application of principles of § 1.964-1.* The determinations with respect to a foreign corporation shall be made as follows:

(i) *Books of account.* The books of account to be used shall be those regularly maintained by the corporation for the purpose of accounting to its shareholders.

(ii) *Accounting principles.* Except as provided in subparagraphs (3) and (4) of this paragraph, the accounting principles to be employed are those described in paragraph (b) of § 1.964-1. Thus, in applying accounting principles generally accepted in the United States for purposes of reflecting in the financial statements of a domestic corporation the operations of foreign affiliates, no adjustment need be made unless such adjustment will have a material effect, within the meaning of paragraph (a) of § 1.964-1.

(iii) *Translation into United States dollars*—(a) *In general.* Except as provided in (b) of this subdivision, the amounts determined in accordance with subdivision (ii) of this subparagraph shall be translated into United States dollars in accordance with the principles of paragraph (d) of § 1.964-1.

(b) *Special rule.* In any case in which the value of the foreign currency in relation to the United States dollar fluctuates more than 10 percent during any translation period (within the meaning of paragraph (d)(6) of § 1.964-1), the subpart F income and non-subpart F income shall be separately translated as if each constituted all the income of the controlled foreign corporation for the translation period.

(iv) *Tax accounting methods.* The tax accounting methods to be employed as those established or adopted by or on behalf of the foreign corporation under paragraph (c) of § 1.964-1. Thus, such accounting methods must be consistent with the manner of treating inventories, depreciation, and elections referred to in subdivisions (ii), (iii), and (iv) of paragraph (c)(1) of § 1.964-1 and used for purposes of such paragraph; however, if, in accordance with paragraph (c)(6) of § 1.964-1, a foreign corporation receives foreign base company income before any elections are made or before an accounting method is adopted by or on behalf of such corporation under paragraph (c)(3) of § 1.964-1, the determinations of whether an exclusion set forth in section 954(b) applies shall be made as if no elections had been made and no accounting method had been adopted.

(v) *Exchange gain or loss.* (a) Exchange gain or loss, determined in accordance with the principles of § 1.964-1(e), shall be taken into account for purposes of determining gross income and taxable income.

(b) Exchange gain or loss shall be treated as foreign base company shipping income (or as a deduction allocable thereto) to the extent that it is attributable to foreign base company shipping operations. The extent to which exchange gain or loss is attributable to foreign base company shipping operations may be determined under any reasonable method which is consistently applied from year to year. For example, the extent to which the exchange gain or loss is attributable to foreign base company shipping operations may be determined on the basis of the ratio which the foreign base company shipping income of the corporation for the taxable year bears to its total gross income for the taxable year, such ratio to be determined without regard to this subdivision (v).

(c) The remainder of the exchange gain or loss shall be allocated between subpart F income and non-subpart F income under any reasonable method which is consistently applied from year to year. For example, such remainder may be allocated to subpart F income in the same ratio that the gross subpart F income (exclusive of foreign base company shipping income) of the corporation for the taxable year bears to its total gross income (exclusive of foreign base company shipping income) for the taxable year, such ratio to be determined without regard to this subdivision (v).

(3) *Necessity for recognition of gain or loss.* Gross income of a foreign corporation (including an insurance company) includes gain or loss only if such gain or loss would be recognized under the provisions of the Internal Revenue Code if the foreign corporation were a domestic corporation taxable under section 11 (subject to the modifications of subparagraph (1) of this paragraph). See section 1002. However, a foreign corporation shall not be treated as a domestic corporation for purposes of determining whether section 367 applies.

(4) *Gross income and gross receipts.* The term "gross income" may not have the same meaning as the term "gross receipts". For example, in a manufacturing, merchandising, or mining business, gross income means the total sales less the cost of goods sold, plus any income from investments and from incidental or outside operations or sources.

Reg. § 1.952-2(c)(2)

(5) *Treatment of capital loss and net operating loss.* In determining taxable income of a foreign corporation for any taxable year—

(i) *Capital loss carryback and carryover.* The capital loss carryback and carryover provided by section 1212(a) shall not be allowed.

(ii) *Net operating loss deduction.* The net operating loss deduction under section 172(a) or the operations loss deduction under section 812 shall not be allowed.

(6) *Corporations which have insurance income.* For purposes of paragraphs (a)(2) and (b)(2) of this section, in determining whether a controlled foreign corporation which is engaged in the business of reinsuring or issuing insurance or annuity contracts and which, if it were a domestic corporation engaged only in such business, would be taxable as an insurance company to which subchapter L of chapter 1 of the Code applies, it is immaterial that—

(i) The corporation would be exempt from taxation as an organization described in section 501(a),

(ii) The corporation would not be taxable as an insurance company to which subchapter L of the Code applies, or

(iii) The corporation would be subject to the alternative tax for small mutual insurance companies provided by section 821(c). [Reg. § 1.952-2.]

☐ [*T.D.* 6795, 1-28-65. *Amended by T.D.* 7893, 5-11-83; *T.D.* 7894, 5-11-83 *and T.D.* 8704, 12-31-96.]

[Reg. § 1.953-1]

§ 1.953-1. **Income from insurance of United States risks.**—(a) *In general.* The subpart F income of a controlled foreign corporation for any taxable year includes its income derived from the insurance of United States risks for such taxable year. See section 952(a)(1). A controlled foreign corporation shall have income derived from the insurance of United States risks for such purpose if it has taxable income, as determined under § 1.953-4 or § 1.953-5, which is attributable to the reinsuring or the issuing of any insurance or annuity contract in connection with United States risks, as defined in § 1.953-2 or § 1.953-3, and if it satisfies the 5-percent minimum premium requirement prescribed in paragraph (b) of this section. It is immaterial for purposes of this section whether the person insured or the beneficiary of any insurance, annuity, or reinsurance contract is, as to such corporation, a related person or a United States shareholder. For definition of the term "controlled foreign corporation" for purposes of taking into account income derived from the insurance of United States risks under section 953, see section 957(a) and (b) and §§ 1.957-1 and 1.957-2.

(b) *5-percent minimum premium requirement.* A controlled foreign corporation shall not have income derived from the insurance of United States risks for purposes of this section unless the premiums received by such corporation during the taxable year which are attributable to the reinsuring and the issuing of insurance and annuity contracts in connection with the United States risks exceed 5 percent of the total premiums which are received by such corporation during such taxable year and which are attributable to the reinsuring and the issuing of insurance and annuity contracts in connection with all risks.

(c) *General definitions.* For purposes of §§ 1.953-1 to 1.953-6, inclusive—

(1) *Reinsurance, etc.* The terms "reinsurance", "insurance", and "annuity contract" have the same meaning which they have for purposes of applying section 809(c)(1) or section 832(b)(4), as the case may be.

(2) *Premiums.* The term "premiums" means the items taken into account for the taxable year under section 809(c)(1), or the amount computed for the taxable year under section 832(b)(4) without the application of subparagraph (B) thereof, as the case may be; except that, for purposes of determining the amount of premiums received in applying paragraph (b) of this section or paragraph (a) of § 1.953-3, advance premiums and deposits shall not be taken into account.

(3) *Insurance company.* The term "insurance company" has the same meaning which it has for purposes of applying section 801(a), determined by applying the principles of paragraph (a) of § 1.801-3.

(4) *Related person.* The term "related person", when used with respect to a controlled foreign corporation, shall have the meaning assigned to it by paragraph (e) of § 1.954-1.

(5) *Policy period.* With respect to any insurance or annuity contract under which a corporation is potentially liable at any time during its taxable year, the term "policy period" means with respect to such year each period of coverage under the contract if such period begins or ends with or within the taxable year, except that, if such period of coverage is more than one year, such term means such of the following periods as are applicable, each one of which is a policy period with respect to the taxable year:

(i) The one-year period which begins with the effective date of the contract and begins or ends with or within the taxable year,

Reg. § 1.953-1(c)(5)

(ii) The one-year period which begins with an anniversary of the contract and begins or ends with or within the taxable year, and

(iii) The period of less than one year if such period begins with an anniversary of the contract, ends with the date on which coverage under the contract terminates, and begins or ends with or within the taxable year.

For such purposes, the effective date of the contract is the date on which coverage under the contract begins, and the anniversary of the contract is the annual return of the effective date. The period of coverage under a contract is the period beginning with the effective date of the contract and ending with the date on which the coverage under the contract expires; except that, if the risk under the contract has been transferred by assumption reinsurance, the period of coverage shall end with the effective date of such transfer or, if the contract is cancelled, with the effective date of cancellation. For this purpose, the term "assumption reinsurance" shall have the meaning provided by paragraph (a)(7)(ii) of § 1.809-5. The application of this subparagraph may be illustrated by the following examples:

Example (1). Controlled foreign corporation A issues to domestic corporation M an insurance contract which provides coverage for the 2½ year period beginning on July 1, 1963. Corporation A uses the calendar year as the taxable year. For 1963, the policy period under such contract as to A Corporation is July 1, 1963, to June 30, 1964. For 1964, the policy periods under such contract as to A Corporation are July 1, 1963, to June 30, 1964, and July 1, 1964, to June 30, 1965. For 1965, the policy periods under such contract as to A Corporation are July 1, 1964, to June 30, 1965, and July 1, 1965, to December 31, 1965.

Example (2). The facts are the same as in example (1) except that M Corporation cancels the contract on August 31, 1963. For 1963, the policy period under such contract as to A Corporation is July 1, 1963, to August 31, 1963.

Example (3). The facts are the same as in example (1) except that on January 15, 1965, A Corporation cedes insurance under the contract to controlled foreign corporation B, which also uses the calendar year as the taxable year. For 1964, the policy periods under such contract as to A Corporation are July 1, 1963, to June 30, 1964, and July 1, 1964, to June 30, 1965. For 1965, the policy periods under such contract as to both A Corporation and B Corporation are July 1, 1964, to June 30, 1965, and July 1, 1965, to December 31, 1965.

Example (4). Controlled foreign corporation C, which uses the calendar year as the taxable year, issues to domestic corporation N an insurance contract which covers the marine risks in connection with shipping a machine to Europe. The contract does not specify the dates during which the machine is covered, but provides coverage from the time the machine is delivered alongside a named vessel in Hoboken, New Jersey, until the machine is delivered alongside such vessel in Liverpool, England. Such deliveries in New Jersey and England take place on February 1, and February 28, 1963, respectively. For 1963, the policy period under such contract as to C Corporation is February 1, to February 28, 1963.

(6) *Foreign country.* The term "foreign country" includes, where not otherwise expressly provided, a possession of the United States. [Reg. § 1.953-1.]

☐ [*T.D.* 6781, 12-22-64.]

[Reg. § 1.953-2]

§ 1.953-2. **Actual United States risks.**—(a) *In general.* For purposes of paragraph (a) of § 1.953-1, the term "United States risks" means risks described in section 953(a)(1)(A)—

(1) In connection with property in the United States (as defined in paragraph (b) of this section),

(2) In connection with liability arising out of activity in the United States (as defined in paragraph (c) of this section), or

(3) In connection with the lives or health of residents of the United States (as defined in paragraph (d) of this section).

For purposes of section 953(a), the term "United States" is used in a geographical sense and includes only the States and the District of Columbia. Therefore, the reinsuring or the issuing of insurance or annuity contracts by a controlled foreign corporation in connection with property located in a foreign country or a possession of the United States, in connection with activity in a foreign country or a possession, or in connection with the lives or health of citizens of the United States who are not residents of the United States will not give rise to income to which paragraph (a) of § 1.953-1 applies, unless the income derived by the controlled foreign corporation from such contracts constitutes income derived in connection with risks which are deemed to be United States risks, as defined in § 1.953-3.

(b) *Property in the United States.* The term "property in the United States" means property, as defined in subparagraph (1) of this paragraph, which is in the United States, within the meaning of subparagraph (2) of this paragraph.

Reg. § 1.953-2(a)(1)

(1) *Property defined.* The term "property" means any interest of an insured in tangible (including real and personal) or intangible property. Such interests include, but are not limited to, those of an owner, landlord, tenant, mortgagor, mortgagee, trustee, beneficiary, or partner. Thus, for example, if insurance is issued against loss from fire and theft with respect to an insured's home and its contents, such risks are risks in connection with property, whether the insured is the owner or lessee and whether the contents include furniture or cash and securities. Furthermore, if insurance is issued against all risks of damage or loss with respect to the automobile of an insured, such risks are risks in connection with property, whether the risks insured against may be caused by the insured, another person, or natural forces.

(2) *United States location*—(i) *In general.* Property will be considered property in the United States when it is exclusively located in the United States. Conversely, property will be considered property not in the United States when it is exclusively located outside the United States. In addition, property which is ordinarily located in, but temporarily located outside, the United States will be considered property in the United States both when it is ordinarily located in, and when it is temporarily located outside, the United States if the premium which is attributable to the reinsuring or issuing of any insurance contract in connection with such property cannot be allocated to, or apportioned between, risks incurred when such property is actually located in the United States and risks incurred when it is actually located outside the United States. If such premium can be so allocated or apportioned on a reasonable basis, however, such property will be considered property not in the United States when it is actually located outside the United States. However, property will not be considered property in the United States if it is neither property which is exclusively located in the United States nor property which is ordinarily located in, but temporarily located outside, the United States. The rules prescribed in subdivision (ii) of this subparagraph shall apply in determining whether a premium can be allocated or apportioned on a reasonable basis to or between risks incurred when property is actually located in the United States and risks incurred when such property is actually located outside the United States. The rules prescribed in subdivisions (iii) through (x) of this subparagraph shall apply in determining whether property is, or will be considered, exclusively located in or outside the United States and whether property is, or will be considered, ordinarily located in the United States; such rules also limit the rule of premium allocation and apportionment prescribed in this subdivision and subdivision (ii) of this subparagraph. The determinations required by this subparagraph shall be made with respect to the location of property during the policy period applicable to the taxable year of the insuring or reinsuring corporation, or, if more than one policy period exists with respect to such taxable year, such determinations shall be made separately with respect to the location of property during each such policy period.

(ii) *Premium allocation or apportionment.* Whether a premium can be allocated or apportioned on a reasonable basis to or between risks incurred when property is actually located in the United States and risks incurred when such property is actually located outside the United States shall depend on the intention of the parties to the insurance contract, as determined from its provisions and the facts and circumstances preceding its execution. Contract provisions on the basis of which the premium reasonably may be so allocated or apportioned include, but are not limited to, provisions which separately describe each risk covered, the period of coverage of each risk, the special warranties for each risk, the premium for each risk (or the basis for determining such premium), and the conditions of paying the premium for each risk. For purposes of this subdivision, it shall be unnecessary formally to make a separate policy with respect to each risk covered or with respect to each clause attached to the policy, provided that the intention of the parties to the contract is reasonably clear. For example, if in the ordinary course of carrying on an insurance business an insurance policy is issued which covers fire, theft, and water damage risks incurred when property is actually located in the United States and marine risks incurred when such property is actually located outside the United States and which, pursuant to accepted insurance principles, properly describes the premium rates as percentages of the amount of coverage as ".825% plus .3% fire, etc. risk plus .12% water risks = 1.245%", a reasonable basis exists to allocate a $124.50 premium paid for $10,000 of such coverage to $82.50 for foreign risks and $42.00 ($30.00 + $12.00) to United States risks.

(iii) *Property in general*—(a) *Ordinary and temporary location.* Except as otherwise provided in subdivisions (iv) and through (x) of this subparagraph, the determination of whether property is ordinarily located in the United States will depend on all the facts and circumstances in each case. Property is ordinarily located in the United States if its location in the United States is regular, usual, or often occurring. However, in all cases property will be considered ordinarily located in

Reg. § 1.953-2(b)(2)

the United States if it is actually located in the United States for an aggregate of more than 50 percent of the days in the applicable policy period whereas property will, under no circumstances, be considered ordinarily located in the United States if it is actually located in the United States for an aggregate of not more than 30 percent of the days in the applicable policy period. Property which is ordinarily located in the United States is temporarily located outside the United States when it is actually located outside the United States. For purposes of determining the number and percent of the days in an applicable policy period, the term "day" means, not any 24-consecutive-hour period, but a continuous period of twenty-four hours commencing from midnight and ending with the following midnight; in determining the location of property for such purposes, an amount of time which is at least one-half of such a day, but less than the entire day, shall be considered a day, and an amount of time which is less than one-half of such a day shall not be considered a day.

(b) *Illustrations.* The application of this subdivision may be illustrated by the following examples:

Example (1). Controlled foreign corporation A issues to domestic corporation M a comprehensive blanket or floater insurance policy which, for one year, covers inventory samples which M Corporation regularly ships from the United States in order to encourage sales. Such shipments are made on the condition that they be returned to the United States within 5 days after they are received. During the one-year policy period, such samples are sent from, and returned to, the United States 50 times, and during such one-year period are acually located in the United States for an aggregate of 120 days. Since the location of the samples in the United States during such one-year period is often recurring, they are property ordinarily located in, but temporarily located outside, the United States. Therefore, they will be considered property in the United States even though for such one-year period their location in the United States is not regular or usual and is not for an aggregate of more than 50 percent of the days in the policy period. However, if, by considering such factors as the terms and premium schedule of the insurance contract as well as the number, value, and duration of the location in and outside the United States, of such samples, the premium which is attributable to the issuing of such contract can be allocated to, or apportioned between, risks occurring when such samples are actually located in the United States and risks occurring when they are actually located outside the United States, such samples will be considered property not in the United States when they are actually located outside the United States.

Example (2). A machine, located for several years in a foreign branch of a United States manufacturer, is permanently transferred to the home office of such manufacturer, where it arrives on January 1, 1963, and remains for the remainder of 1963. Under a separate insurance contract issued by a controlled foreign corporation, which uses the calendar year as the taxable year, such machine is insured against damage for the three-year period commencing on May 1, 1962. Because of the change in location of the machine, the premiums are increased as of January 1, 1963. Since the machine is in the United States from January 1, 1963, to April 30, 1963, its location in the United States is regular and usual during the policy period of May 1, 1962, to April 30, 1963. Accordingly, the machine is ordinarily located in the United States for such policy period. However, since the premium which is attributable to the issuing of such contract is allocable to risks occurring when the machine is actually located in, and when it is actually located outside, the United States, such machine will be considered property not in the United States from May 1, 1962, through December 31, 1962.

(iv) *Commercial motor vehicles, ships, aircraft, railroad rolling stock, and containers.* Any motor vehicle, ship, aircraft, railroad rolling stock, or any container transported thereby, which is used exclusively in the commercial transportation of persons or property to or from the United States (including such transportation from one place to another in the United States) and is ordinarily located in the United States will be considered property in the United States both when such property is ordinarily located in, and when such property is temporarily located outside, the United States. Whether such property is used in the transportation of persons or property to or from the United States and is ordinarily located in the United States are issues to be determined from all the facts and circumstances in each case. However, in all cases such transportation property will be considered ordinarily located in the United States if either more than 50 percent of the miles traversed during the applicable policy period in the use of such property are traversed within the United States or such property is located in the United States more than 50 percent of the time during such period. Further, such transportation property will not at any time be considered property in the United States if either not more than 30 percent of the miles traversed during the applicable policy period in the use of such property are traversed within the United States or such property is located in the

United States for not more than 30 percent of the time during such period. Nevertheless, if not more than 30 percent of the miles traversed during the applicable policy period in the use of such transportation property are traversed within the United States, such property will be considered ordinarily located in the United States if it is located in the United States more than 50 percent of the time during such period. Moreover, if such transportation property is located in the United States for not more than 30 percent of the time during the applicable policy period, such property will be considered ordinarily located in the United States if more than 50 percent of the miles traversed during such period in the use of such property are traversed within the United States. If such transportation property is considered property in the United States because more than 50 percent of the miles traversed during the applicable policy period in the use of such property are traversed within the United States, the apportionment of premium provided in subdivison (i) of this subparagraph shall be made on a mileage basis. If, however, such property is considered property in the United States because such property is located in the United States more than 50 percent of the time during the applicable policy period, the apportionment of premium provided in subdivision (i) of this subparagraph shall be made on a time basis.

(v) *Noncommercial motor vehicles, ships, aircraft, and railroad rolling stock.* Except as provided in subdivision (iv) of this subparagraph, any motor vehicle, ship or boat, aircraft, or railroad rolling stock which at any time is actually located in the United States and which either (*a*) is registered with the United States, a State (including any political subdivision thereof), or any agency thereof or (*b*), if not so registered, is owned by a citizen, resident, or corporation of the United States will be considered property which is ordinarily located in the United States. Unless the premium which is attributable to the reinsuring or issuing of any insurance contract in connection with such property considered ordinarily located in the United States is specifically allocated under the contract to risks incurred when such property is actually located in the United States and to risks incurred when it is actually located outside the United States, such property will be considered property in the United States both when it is ordinarily located in, and when it is temporarily located outside, the United States; under no circumstances will such property be considered outside the United States on the basis of any apportionment of such premium.

(vi) *Property exported or imported by railroad or motor vehicle.* Any property which is exported from, or imported to, the United States by railroad or motor vehicle will be considered property ordinarily located in the United States which, when such property is not actually located in the United States, is temporarily located outside the United States. For example, if an insurance contract reinsured or issued in connection with property exported from the United States by motor vehicle covers risks commencing when such property is loaded on the motor vehicle at the United States warehouse and terminating when such property is unloaded at the foreign warehouse, and if the premium payable with respect to risks incurred when the property is in the United States and risks incurred when the property is in the foreign country is not separately stated, such property will be considered property in the United States only until such property is actually located outside the United States, provided that the premium can be properly apportioned (for example) on the basis of time or mileage, between risks incurred when the property is actually located in the United States and risks incurred when it is actually located outside the United States. If in such case the premium is not so apportionable, such property will be considered property in the United States both when such property is ordinarily located in, and when it is temporarily located outside, the United States.

(vii) *Property exported by ship or aircraft.* If an insurance contract which is reinsured or issued in connection with property which is exported from the United States by ship or aircraft covers risks all of which terminate when such property is placed aboard a ship or aircraft at the United States port of exit for shipment from the United States, such property will be considered property in the United States. If such insurance contract covers risks all of which commence when such property is placed aboard a ship or aircraft at the United States port of exit for shipment from the United States, such property will be considered property not in the United States. If such insurance contract covers risks commencing before, and terminating after, such property is placed aboard a ship or aircraft at the United States port of exit for shipment from the United States, such property will be considered property ordinarily located in the United States which, after such property is placed aboard such ship or aircraft at the United States port of exit, is temporarily located outside the United States. The application of this subdivision may be illustrated by the following example:

Example. A controlled foreign corporation issues an insurance contract in connection with property exported from the United States by ship. The contract covers risks commencing after such

Reg. § 1.953-2(b)(2)

property is removed from the United States warehouse and terminating when such property is unloaded at the foreign port of entry. Assuming that the premium payable with respect to the risks incurred before and the risks incurred after the property is placed aboard the ship at the United States port of exit for shipment from the United States or with respect to the steps in handling such property during such coverage, such as transporting the property to the United States port of exit, unloading the property there, placing the property aboard the ship, holding the property aboard the ship in port, the actual voyage, and unloading the property at the foreign port of entry, is separately stated in, or is determinable from, such contract, the property will be considered property in the United States only until such property is placed aboard the ship at the United States port of exit for shipment from the United States. Assuming, however, that the premiums payable with respect to such steps, or with respect to the risks incurred before and the risks incurred after the property is placed aboard the ship at the United States port of exit, are not allocable or apportionable under the contract, such property will be considered property in the United States both before and after such property is placed aboard the ship at the United States port of exit.

(viii) *Property imported by ship or aircraft.* If an insurance contract which is reinsured or issued in connection with property which is imported to the United States by ship or aircraft covers risks all of which terminate when such property is unloaded at the United States port of entry, such property will be considered property not in the United States. If such insurance contract covers risks all of which commence after such property is unloaded at the United States port of entry, such property will be considered property in the United States. If such insurance contract covers risks commencing before, and terminating after, such property is unloaded at the United States port of entry, such property will be considered property ordinarily located in the United States which, before such property is unloaded at the United States port of entry, is temporarily located outside the United States. For an illustration pertaining to the allocation or apportionment of the premium, see the example in subdivision (vii) of this subparagraph.

(ix) *Shipments originating and terminating in the United States.* Any property which is shipped from one place in the United States to another place in the United States, on or over a foreign country, the high seas, or the coastal waters of the United States will be considered property actually located at all times in the United States. For example, property which is shipped from New York City to Los Angeles via the Panama Canal or from San Francisco to Hawaii or Alaska will be considered property actually located at all times in the United States.

(x) *Shipments originating and terminating in a foreign country.* Any property which is shipped by any means, or a combination of means, of transportation from one foreign country to another foreign country, or from a contiguous foreign country to the same contiguous foreign country, on or over the United States will be considered property exclusively located outside the United States. Notwithstanding the foregoing, any property which is shipped by any means, or a combination of means, of transportation from one contiguous foreign country to another contiguous foreign country on or over the United States will be considered property ordinarily located in the United States which, when such property is not actually located in the United States, is temporarily located outside the United States.

(c) *Liability from United States activity.* The term "liability arising out of activity in the United States" means a loss, as described in subparagraph (1) of this paragraph, or a liability, as described in subparagraph (2) of this paragraph, which could arise from activity performed in the United States, as defined in subparagraph (3) of this paragraph.

(1) *Loss described.* The term "loss" includes all loss of an insured which could arise from the occurrence of the event insured against except that such term does not include any loss in connection with property described in paragraph (b) of this section. For example, such term includes, in the case of a promoter of outdoor sporting events, the loss which could arise from the cancellation of such an event because of inclement weather.

(2) *Liability described.* The term "liability" includes all liability of an insured in tort, contract, property, or otherwise. It includes, for example, the liability of a principal for the acts of his agent, of a husband for the acts of his spouse, and of a parent for the acts of his child. The term not only includes the direct liability which may be incurred, for example, by a tortfeasor to the person harmed, but also the indirect liability which may be incurred, for example, by a manufacturer to the purchaser at retail for a breach of warranty.

(3) *Activity in the United States*—(i) *In general.* A loss or liability will be considered a loss or liability which could arise from activity performed in the United States if the loss or liability would result, if at all, from an activity exclusively carried on in the United States. Conversely, a loss

Reg. § 1.953-2(c)(1)

or liability will be considered a loss or liability which could not arise from activity performed in the United States if the loss or liability would result, if at all, from an activity exclusively carried on outside the United States. In addition, a loss or liability will be considered a loss or liability which could arise from activity performed in the United States if the loss or liability would result, if at all, from an activity ordinarily carried on in, but partly carried on outside, the United States. If the premium which is attributable to the reinsuring or issuing of any insurance contract in connection with an activity ordinarily carried on in, but partly carried on outside, the United States can, on a reasonable basis, be allocated to, or apportioned between, the risks incurred with respect to the activity carried on in, and the risks incurred with respect to the activity carried on outside, the United States, such loss or liability will be considered a loss or liability which could not arise from activity performed in the United States to the extent the loss or liability would result, if at all, from that activity carried on outside the United States. However, a loss or liability will not be considered a loss or liability which could arise from an activity performed in the United States if such loss or liability would result, if at all, from an activity which is neither exclusively carried on in the United States nor ordinarily carried on in, but partly carried on outside, the United States. The principles of paragraph (b)(2)(ii) of this section for allocating or apportioning a premium on a reasonable basis to or between risks incurred when property is actually located in the United States and risks incurred when such property is actually located outside the United States shall apply for allocating or apportioning a premium on a reasonable basis to or between the risks incurred with respect to the activity carried on in, and the risks incurred with respect to the activity carried on outside, the United States. The rules prescribed in subdivisions (ii) through (vi) of this subparagraph shall apply in determining whether an activity is, or will be considered, exclusively carried on in or outside the United States and whether an activity is, or will be considered, ordinarily carried on in the United States and in determining what is the activity which is performed by the insured from which a loss or liability results or could result; such rules also limit the rule of premium allocation and apportionment prescribed in this subdivision. The determinations required by this subparagraph shall be made with respect to the location of an activity of the insured performed during the policy period applicable to the taxable year of the insuring or reinsuring corporation, or, if more than one policy period exists with respect to such taxable year, such determinations shall be made separately with respect to the location of the activity during each such policy period.

(ii) *Substantial activity carried on in the United States.* The term "activity" is used in its broadest sense and includes the performance of an act unlawfully undertaken, the wrongful performance of an act lawfully undertaken, and the wrongful failure to perform an act lawfully required to be undertaken. With respect to a loss described in subparagraph (1) of this paragraph, the term "activity" includes the occurrence of the event insured against. The determination of whether an activity ordinarily is carried on in, but is partly carried on outside, the United States will depend on all the facts and circumstances in each case. An activity ordinarily is carried on in the United States if a substantial amount of such activity is carried on in the United States. Factors which will be taken into account in determining whether a substantial amount of activity is carried on in the United States are those which are connected with the activity and include, but are not limited to, the location of the insured's assets, the place where personal services are performed, and the place where sales occur, but only if such assets, services, and sales are connected with the activity. In all cases an activity will be considered substantially carried on in the United States if more than 50 percent of the insured's total assets, personal services, and sales, if any, connected with such activity are located, performed, or occur in the United States. On the other hand, an activity will, under no circumstances, be considered substantially carried on in the United States if not more than 30 percent of the insured's total assets, personal services, and sales, if any, connected with such activity are located, performed, or occur in the United States. For this purpose the mean of the value of the total assets at the beginning and end of the policy period shall be used, determined by taking assets into account at their actual value (not reduced by liabilities), which, in the absence of affirmative evidence to the contrary, shall be deemed to be (*a*) face value in the case of bills receivable, accounts receivable, notes receivable, and open accounts held by an insured using the cash receipts and disbursements method of accounting and (*b*) adjusted basis in the case of all other assets. Personal services shall be measured by the amount of compensation paid or accrued for such services, and sales shall be measured by the volume of gross sales. An activity is carried on partly outside the United States if it is carried on, whether substantially or insubstantially, outside the United States.

(iii) *Manufacturing, producing, constructing, or assembling activity.* If a person who manu-

Reg. § 1.953-2(c)(3)

factures, produces, constructs, or assembles property is liable with regard to the consumption or use of such property, such liability will be considered to result from the activity performed of manufacturing, producing, constructing, or assembling such property. If such person manufactures, produces, constructs, or assembles more than one type of product, the liability with regard to the consumption or use of one of such products will be considered to result from the activity performed of manufacturing, producing, constructing, or assembling that particular product. For example, the liability of a building contractor, which constructs apartment buildings only in the United States, for the improper construction of, or the failure to construct, an apartment building, will be considered to result from an activity exclusively carried on in the United States and will be considered a liability which could arise from activity performed in the United States. In further illustration, the liability (which is covered by a single policy of insurance) of a domestic corporation, which assembles refrigerators exclusively in the United States and manufactures automobiles both in a foreign country and in the United States through substantial activity carried on in each of such countries, for the negligent manufacturing of a part for one of the automobiles by the foreign branch, will be considered to result from an activity ordinarily carried on in, but partly carried on outside, the United States and will be considered a liability which could arise from activity performed in the United States.

(iv) *Selling activity.* If a person is liable with regard to selling activity performed, such liability will be considered, except as provided in subdivisions (iii), (v), and (vi) of this subparagraph, to result from such selling activity. A person will be considered to be engaged in selling activity if such person engages in an activity resulting in the sale of property. Thus, it is immaterial that, under the Code, such activity would not constitute engaging in or carrying on a trade or business in the country in which such activity is carried on, the property in the goods does not pass in such country, or delivery of the property is not made in such country. For example, if a foreign wholesale distributor, which manages its entire business operations in a foreign country and sells its inventory exclusively in the United States—its only contact in the United States being the promotion of such sales to United States retail outlets by advertising in trade publications and distributing sales catalogues—is liable for a breach of warranty with regard to the sale of property to a United States retail outlet, such liability will be considered to result from an activity exclusively carried on in the United States and will be considered a liability which could arise from activity performed in the United States.

(v) *Liability from service or driving activity*—(a) *In general.* If a person is liable with regard to any service activity performed, or is liable with regard to driving activity performed in connection with a motor vehicle, ship or boat, aircraft, or railroad rolling stock, whether or not exclusively used in the commercial transportation of persons or property, such liability will be considered to result from such service or driving activity. For example, if an oil company which drills for oil exclusively in a foreign country is liable with regard to the negligent handling by its employees of explosives in the course of such drilling there, such liability will be considered to result from an activity exclusively carried on outside the United States and will be considered a liability which could not arise from activity performed in the United States. In further illustration, if a corporation which services machinery exclusively in a foreign country under servicing contracts is liable with regard to the negligent repairing of a machine under such a contract, such liability will be considered to result from an activity exclusively carried on outside the United States and will be considered a liability which could not arise from activity performed in the United States.

(b) *Location of activities in connection with transportation property.* For purposes of (a) of this subdivision, service or driving activity performed in connection with a motor vehicle, ship or boat, aircraft, or railroad rolling stock, whether or not exclusively used in the commercial transportation of persons or property, will be considered activity performed in the United States if the activity is carried on at a time when such property is or will be considered, in accordance with subdivision (iv) or (v) of paragraph (b)(2) of this section, actually in the United States or ordinarily located in the United States. However, if the premium which is attributable to the reinsuring or issuing of any insurance contract in connection with such service or driving activity which is carried on at a time when such property is, or will be considered, ordinarily located in the United States can be allocated to, or apportioned between, the risks incurred when such property is actually located in the United States and risks incurred when it is actually located outside the United States, such liability will be considered a liability which could arise from activity performed in the United States only when such property is actually located in the United States. Any allocation or apportionment of premium under the preceding sentence shall be made in accordance with the rules of allocation and apportionment

Reg. § 1.953-2(c)(3)

provided in subdivision (iv) or (v) of paragraph (b)(2) of this section. For example, if a person is liable with regard to the performance of services outside the United States in the operation of a motor vehicle which is used exclusively in the commercial transportation of persons to and from the United States and which, because more than 50 percent of the miles traversed during the applicable policy period in the use of such property are traversed within the United States, is considered ordinarily located in the United States, such liability will be considered to be a liability which could not arise from activity performed in the United States only to the extent that the premium which is attributable to the reinsuring or issuing of any insurance contract in connection with such service activity is apportioned on a mileage basis between the risks incurred when such motor vehicle is actually located in the United States and when such vehicle is actually located outside the United States. See paragraph (b)(2)(iv) of this section. In further illustration, if a person is liable with regard to his negligent driving of a motor vehicle which is not used exclusively in the commercial transportation of persons or property, which is registered with any State, and which is driven both in the United States and a foreign country, such liability will be considered a liability which could arise from activity performed in the United States, unless the premium which is attributable to the reinsuring or issuing of an insurance contract in connection with such driving performed in such motor vehicle ordinarily located in the United States is specifically allocated under the contract to risks incurred with respect to driving performed in, and to risks incurred with respect to driving performed outside, the United States. See paragraph (b)(2)(v) of this section.

(c) *Illustration.* The application of this subdivision may be further illustrated by the following example:

Example. Controlled foreign corporation A is a wholly owned subsidiary of domestic corporation M. Both corporations are insurance companies and use the calendar year as the taxable year. Corporation M is exclusively engaged in issuing to owners of commercial rental property which is located in the United States insurance contracts which cover any harm which may be caused in 1963 by the tortious conduct of the owners' employees in managing and maintaining such property. The owners insured under such contracts include both residents and nonresidents of the United States. In 1963, M Corporation cedes to A Corporation one-half of the insurance contracts issued by M Corporation in that year, including the contracts issued to nonresidents. Income of A Corporation derived in 1963 from reinsuring the risks of M Corporation is income from the insurance of United States risks since all the insurance contracts reinsured by it are in connection with a liability which could arise from service activity performed in the United States.

(vi) *Liability from delivery of property.* If the person who is obligated to deliver property is liable with regard to such delivery, such liability will be considered to result from the activity performed of delivering such property. For example, if a corporation which exports all of its inventory from the United States to foreign countries or possessions of the United States is liable with regard to its failure to make delivery outside the United States of inventory it has sold, such liability will be considered to result from an activity exclusively carried on outside the United States and will be considered a liability which could not arise from activity performed in the United States. In further illustration, if a corporation which exports all of its inventory from a foreign country to the United States is liable with regard to its improper delivery in the United States of inventory it has sold, such liability will be considered to result from an activity exclusively carried on in the United States and will be considered a liability which could arise from activity performed in the United States.

(d) *Lives or health of United States residents.* Risks in connection with the lives or health of residents of the United States include those risks which are the subject of insurance contracts referred to in section 801(a), relating to the definition of a life insurance company. If the insured is a resident of the United States at the time the insurance contract is approved, the risk is in connection with the life or health of a resident of the United States for the period of coverage under the contract. However, if during such period of coverage the insured notifies the insurer, or circumstances known to the insurer indicate, that the insured is no longer a resident of the United States, the risk shall cease to be a risk in connection with the life or health of a resident of the United States for the policy period in which the insured gives such notice or such circumstances are known to the insurer, and for each subsequent policy period. Conversely, if the insured is a resident of a particular foreign country at the time the insurance contract is approved, the risk is in connection with the life or health of a resident of such foreign country for the period of coverage under the contract. However, if during such period of coverage the insured notifies the insurer, or circumstances known to the insurer indicate, that the insured is no longer a resident of such foreign country, the risk shall cease to be a risk in connec-

Reg. § 1.953-2(d)

tion with the life or health of a resident of such particular foreign country for the policy period in which the insured gives such notice or such circumstances are known to the insurer, and for each subsequent policy period. In determining the country of residence of an insured, the principles of §§ 301.7701(b)-1 through 301.7701(b)-9 of this chapter, relating to the determination of residence and nonresidence in the United States and of foreign residence, shall apply. Citizens of the United States are not residents of the United States merely because of their citizenship. The application of this paragraph may be illustrated by the following example:

Example. Controlled foreign corporation A is a wholly owned subsidiary of domestic corporation M. Corporation A uses the calendar year as the taxable year and is engaged in the life insurance business in foreign country X. In 1963, A Corporation issues ordinary life insurance contracts on the lives of residents of the United States, including one issued on February 1, 1963, to R, a citizen of foreign country Y and a resident of the United States on such date. All activity in connection with the issuing of such contracts is transacted by mail. On May 1, 1963, R abandons his United States residence and establishes residence in foreign country Z. There are no circumstances known to A Corporation that R has changed his residence until R, on March 1, 1964, actually notifies A Corporation of that change. Income of A Corporation for the policy period of February 1, 1963, to January 31, 1964, from issuing such insurance contracts is income derived from the insurance of United States risks. However, income of A Corporation derived for the policy period of February 1, 1964, to January 31, 1965, from R's insurance contract is not income derived from the insurance of United States risks. [Reg. § 1.953-2.]

☐ [T.D. 6781, 12-22-64. Amended by T.D. 7736, 11-14-80 and T.D. 8411, 4-24-92.]

[Reg. § 1.953-3]

§ 1.953-3. Risks deemed to be United States risks.—(a) *Artificial arrangements.* For purposes of paragraph (a) of § 1.953-1, the term "United States risks" also includes under section 953(a)(1)(B) risks which are deemed to be United States risks. They are risks (other than United States risks described in section 953(a)(1)(A) and § 1.953-2) which a controlled foreign corporation reinsures under an insurance or annuity contract, or with respect to which a controlled foreign corporation issues any insurance or annuity contract, in accordance with any arrangement whereby another corporation which is not a controlled foreign corporation receives an amount of premiums (for reinsuring or issuing any insurance or annuity contract in connection with the United States risks described in section 953(a)(1)(A) and § 1.953-2) which is substantially equal to the amount of premiums which the controlled foreign corporation receives under its contracts. Arrangements to which this rule applies include those entered into by the controlled foreign corporation, by its United States shareholders, or by a related person.

(b) *Evidence of arrangements.* The determination of the existence of an arrangement referred to in paragraph (a) of this section shall depend on all the facts and circumstances in each case. In making this determination, it will be recognized that arrangements of this type generally are orally entered into outside the United States and that direct evidence of such an arrangement is not ordinarily available. Therefore, in determining the existence of such an arrangement, consideration will be given to whether or not there is substantial similarity between the type, location, profit margin expected, and loss experience of the risks which the corporation which is not a controlled foreign corporation insures or reinsures and the risks which the controlled foreign corporation insures or reinsures. Further, consideration will be given to the existence of prior similar arrangements between, and the identity of the directors or shareholders of, the corporation which is not a controlled foreign corporation, its shareholders, or related persons and the controlled foreign corporation, its shareholders, or related persons. However, the absence of such prior arrangements or identity of directors or shareholders will not of itself establish the nonexistence of an arrangement referred to in paragraph (a) of this section. In determining whether the amounts received by the controlled foreign corporation and the corporation which is not a controlled foreign corporation are substantially equal, the period in which the controlled foreign corporation receives premiums need not be the same as, or identical in length with, that of the corporation which is not a controlled foreign corporation nor limited to a taxable year of the controlled foreign corporation.

(c) *Illustrations.* The application of this section may be illustrated by the following examples:

Example (1). Controlled foreign corporation A is a wholly owned subsidiary of domestic corporation M. Foreign corporation B is a wholly owned subsidiary of foreign corporation R. All corporations use the calendar year as the taxable year. Corporations M and R, which are not related persons, agree that from July 1, 1963, through December 31, 1963, B Corporation will reinsure all risks of M Corporation which are United States risks described in section 953(a)(1)(A), and that from January 1, 1964, through June 30, 1964, A Corporation will reinsure all risks of R Corporation which are not United States risks described in section 953(a)(1)(A). The amount of premiums received by A Corporation and B Corporation, respectively, as a result of the agreement are substantially equal. The income of A Corporation derived in 1964 from reinsuring the risks of R Corporation is income derived from the insurance of United States risks described in section 953(a)(1)(B).

Example (2). Assume the same facts as in example (1), except that M and R Corporations also agree, as part of their arrangement, that from July 1, 1964, through December 31, 1964, B Corporation will reinsure all risks of M Corporation which are United States risks described in section 953 (a)(1)(A), and that from January 1, 1965, through June 30, 1965, A Corporation will reinsure all risks of R Corporation which are not United States risks described in section 953(a)(1)(A). The amount of premiums derived by B Corporation from July 1, 1963, through December 31, 1963, under the agreement is not substantially equal to the amount of premiums derived by A Corporation from January 1, 1964, through June 30, 1964, and the amount of premiums derived by B Corporation from July 1, 1964, through December 31, 1964, is not substantially equal to the amount of premiums derived by A Corporation from January 1, 1965, through June 30, 1965. However, the aggregate amount of premiums received by B Corporation under the arrangement is substantially equal to the aggregate amount of premiums received by A Corporation. The income of A Corporation derived in 1964 and 1965 from reinsuring the risks of R Corporation is income derived from the insurance of United States risks described in section 953(a)(1)(B).

Example (3). Assume the same facts as in example (1), except that foreign corporation C is also a wholly owned subsidiary of R Corporation. Assume that C Corporation uses the calendar year as its taxable year. Assume further that M Corporation and R Corporation agree that from July 1, 1963, through December 31, 1963, B Corporation and C Corporation together will reinsure the United States risks described in section 953(a)(1)(A) of M Corporation. The amount of premiums received by B Corporation in respect of such United States risks is equal to one-third of the amount received by A Corporation in respect of the risks which are not United States risks described in section 953(a)(1)(A), and the amount of premiums received by C Corporation in respect of such United States risks is equal to two-thirds of the amount so received by A Corporation. The income of A Corporation derived in 1964 from reinsuring the risks of R Corporation is income derived from the insurance of United States risks described in section 953(a)(1)(B).

Example (4). Assume the same facts as in example (3), except that controlled foreign corporation D is also a wholly owned subsidiary of M Corporation and uses the calendar year as its taxable year. Assume further that M Corporation and R Corporation agree that in 1964 R Corporation will pay premiums of $300,000 to A Corporation and $700,000 to D Corporation to reinsure all risks of R Corporation which are not United States risks described in section 953(a)(1)(A), and that in 1963 M Corporation will pay premiums of $400,000 to B Corporation and $600,000 to C Corporation to reinsure all risks of M Corporation which are United States risks described in section 953(a)(1)(A). The income of A Corporation and D Corporation derived in 1964 from reinsuring the risks of R Corporation is income derived from the insurance of United States risks described in section 953(a)(1)(B).

Example (5). Controlled foreign corporation A is a wholly owned subsidiary of domestic insurance corporation M. Controlled foreign corporation B is a wholly owned subsidiary of domestic insurance corporation N. All corporations use the calendar year as the taxable year. As a result of an arrangement between M Corporation and N Corporation, in 1963 A Corporation reinsures all the United States risks described in section 953(a)(1)(A) of N Corporation, and B Corporation reinsures all the United States risks described in section 953(a)(1)(A) of M Corporation. The premiums and other consideration received by A Corporation and B Corporation in respect of such reinsurance are not substantially equal. The income of A Corporation and B Corporation in 1963 from reinsuring the risks of N Corporation and M Corporation, respectively, is income derived from the insurance of United States risks described in section 953(a)(1)(A) and is not income derived from the insurance of United States risks described in section 953(a)(1)(B).

Example (6). Assume the same facts as in example (5), except that B Corporation is not a controlled foreign corporation. The income of A Corporation in 1963 from reinsuring the risks of N Corporation is income derived from the insurance of United States risks described in section 953(a)(1)(A) and is not income derived from the insurance of United States risks described in section 953(a)(1)(B). [Reg. § 1.953-3.]

☐ [T.D. 6781, 12-22-64.]

Reg. § 1.953-3(c)

[Reg. § 1.953-4]

§ 1.953-4. Taxable income to which section 953 applies.—(a) *Taxable income defined*—(1) *Life insurance taxable income.* For a controlled foreign corporation which is engaged in the business of reinsuring or issuing insurance or annuity contracts and which, if it were a domestic corporation engaged only in such business, would be taxable as a life insurance company to which part I (sections 801 through 820) of subchapter L of the Code applies, the term "taxable income" means for purposes of paragraph (a) of § 1.953-1 the gain from operations, as defined in section 809(b) and as modified by this section, derived from, and attributable to, the insurance of United States risks. For purposes of determining such taxable income, the provisions of section 802(b) (relating to the definition of life insurance company taxable income) shall not apply. Determinations for purposes of this subparagraph shall be made without regard to section 501(a).

(2) *Mutual and other insurance taxable income.* For a controlled foreign corporation which is engaged in the business of reinsuring or issuing insurance or annuity contracts and which, if it were a domestic corporation engaged only in such business, would be taxable as a mutual insurance company to which part II (sections 821 through 826) of subchapter L of the Code applies or as a mutual marine insurance or other insurance company to which part III (sections 831 and 832) of subchapter L of the Code applies, the term "taxable income" means for purposes of paragraph (a) of § 1.953-1 taxable income as defined in section 832(a) and as modified by this section, derived from, and attributable to, the insurance of United States risks. Determinations for purposes of this subparagraph shall be made without regard to section 501(a).

(3) *Corporations not qualifying as insurance companies.* For special rules applicable under this section in the case of a controlled foreign corporation which, if it were a domestic corporation, would not qualify as an insurance company, see § 1.953-5.

(b) *Certain provisions inapplicable.* In determining taxable income under this section, the following provisions of subchapter L of the Code shall not apply:

(1) Section 809(d)(4), relating to the operations loss deduction;

(2) Section 809(d)(5), relating to certain nonparticipating contracts;

(3) Section 809(d)(6), relating to certain accident and health insurance and group life insurance;

(4) Section 809(d)(10), relating to small business deduction;

(5) Section 817(b), relating to gain on property held on December 31, 1958, and certain substituted property acquired after 1958; and

(6) Section 832(c)(5), relating to capital losses.

(c) *Computation of reserves required by law*—(1) *Law applicable in determining reserves.* The reserves which will be taken into account as reserves required by law under section 801(b)(2), both in determining for any taxable year whether a controlled foreign corporation is a controlled foreign corporation described in paragraph (a)(1) or paragraph (2) of this section and in determining taxable income of such corporation for the taxable year under paragraph (a) of this section, shall be the following reserves:

(i) *Reserves required by the law of a State.* The reserves which are required by the law of the State or States to which the insurance business of the controlled foreign corporation is subject, but only with respect to its United States business, if any, which is taxable under section 819(a).

(ii) *Reserves deemed to be required.* To the extent of such controlled foreign corporation's insurance business not taxable under section 819(a)—

(a) Except as provided in subdivision (b) of this subdivision (ii), the reserves which would result if such reserves were determined by applying the minimum standards of the law of New York as if such controlled foreign corporation were an insurance company transacting all of its insurance business (other than its United States business which is taxable under section 819(a)) for such taxable year in such State, and

(b) With respect to all risks covered by insurance ceded to such controlled foreign corporation by an insurance company to which apply the provisions of subchapter L of the Code (determined without regard to section 501(a)) and in respect of which an election is made by or on behalf of such controlled foreign corporation to determine its reserves in accordance with this subdivision (b), the amount of reserves against such risks which would result if all of such reserves were determined by applying the law of the State, to which the risks in the hands of such insurance company are subject, as if such controlled foreign corporation were an insurance company engaged in reinsuring such risks in such State.

(2) *Rules of application.* For purposes of subparagraph (1) of this paragraph, the following rules shall apply:

Income from Sources Without the United States

(i) *Life insurance reserves computed on preliminary term basis.* For purposes of determining under paragraph (a) of this section the taxable income of a controlled foreign corporation, an election may be made by or on behalf of such corporation that the amount of reserves which are taken into account as life insurance reserves with respect to contracts for which reserves are computed on a preliminary term basis shall be determined as provided in section 818(c). This election shall apply, subject to section 818(c), to all life insurance reserves of the controlled foreign corporation, whether or not reserves applicable to the United States business taxable under section 819(a). However, reserves determined as provided in section 818(c) shall not be taken into account in determining whether a controlled foreign corporation is a controlled foreign corporation described in paragraph (a)(1) or paragraph (2) of this section.

(ii) *Actual reserves required.* (*a*) A controlled foreign corporation will be considered to have a reserve only to the extent the reserve has been actually held during the taxable year for which such reserve is claimed.

(*b*) For determining when reserves are required by the law of a State, see paragraph (b) of § 1.801-5 of this Chapter.

(iii) *Total reserves to be taken into account.* The total reserves of a controlled foreign corporation shall be taken into account in determining whether such corporation is a controlled foreign corporation described in paragraph (a)(1) or paragraph (2) of this section. Therefore, in making such determination, the reserves which, under subparagraph (1)(i) of this paragraph, are required by the law of any State shall be taken into account together with the reserves which, under subparagraph (1)(ii) of this paragraph, are deemed to be required. Moreover, reserves applicable to the reinsuring or the issuing of insurance or annuity contracts of both United States risks and foreign risks shall be taken into account. Finally, except as provided in subdivision (i) of this subparagraph, the reserves which are taken into account in determining whether a controlled foreign corporation is a controlled foreign corporation described in paragraph (a)(1) or paragraph (2) of this section shall be the same reserves which are taken into account in determining under paragraph (a) of this section the taxable income of such corporation.

(iv) *Method of comparing reserves when subject to more than one State.* If the insurance business of a controlled foreign corporation is subject to the law of more than one State, the amount of reserves taken into account under subparagraph (1)(i) of this paragraph shall be the amount of the highest aggregate reserve required by any State, determined as provided in paragraph (a) of § 1.801-5 of this Chapter.

(d) *Domestic corporation tax attributes.* In determining taxable income of a controlled foreign corporation under this section there shall be allowed, except as provided in section 953(b), this section, and § 1.953-5, the exclusions and deductions from gross income which would be allowed if such corporation were a domestic insurance company engaged in the business of only reinsuring or issuing the insurance or annuity contracts which have been reinsured or issued by such corporation. For this purpose, the provisions of sections 819, 821(e), 822(e), 831(b), and 832(d), relating to foreign insurance companies, shall not apply; however, for the exclusion from the taxable income determined under section 953 of amounts derived from sources within the United States, see section 952(b) and paragraph (b) of § 1.952-1. Furthermore, taxable income shall be determined under this section without regard to section 882(b) and (c), relating to gross income and deductions of a foreign corporation, and without regard to whether the controlled foreign corporation is carrying on an insurance business in the United States. For other rules relating to the determination of gross income and taxable income of a foreign corporation for purposes of subpart F, see § 1.952-2.

(e) *Limitation on certain amounts in respect of United States risks.* In determining taxable income under this section the following accounts shall not, in accordance with section 953(b)(4), be taken into account except to the extent they are attributable to the reinsuring or issuing of any insurance or annuity contract in connection with United States risks described in § 1.953-2 or § 1.953-3:

(1) The amount of premiums determined under section 809(c)(1);

(2) The net decrease in reserves determined under section 809(c)(2);

(3) The net increase in reserves determined under section 809(d)(2); and

(4) The premiums earned on insurance contracts during the taxable year, as determined under section 832(b)(4).

For the allocation and apportionment of such amounts to income from the insurance of United States risks, see paragraphs (f) and (g) of this section.

(f) *Items allocated or apportioned*—(1) *Rules of allocation or apportionment.* In determining taxable income under this section, first determine

Reg. § 1.953-4(f)(1)

49,200 Income from Sources Without the United States
See p. 20,601 for regulations not amended to reflect law changes

all items of income, expenses, losses, and other deductions which directly relate to the premiums received for the reinsuring or the issuing of any insurance or annuity contract in connection with United States risks, as defined in §§ 1.953-2 and 1.953-3, and allocate such items to the insurance of United States risks. For example, the deductions allowed by section 809(d)(1), relating to death benefits, section 809(d)(3), relating to dividends to policyholders, and section 809(d)(7), relating to the assumption by another person of liabilities under insurance contracts, shall be allocated to the insurance of United States risks to the extent they relate directly to the premiums received for reinsuring or issuing insurance or annuity contracts in connection with United States risks. Next, determine all items of income, expenses, losses, and other deductions which directly relate to the premiums received for the reinsuring or the issuing of any insurance or annuity contract in connection with foreign risks and allocate such items to the reinsuring of foreign risks. Finally, determine all items of income, expenses, losses, and other deductions which relate to the premiums received for the reinsuring or the issuing of any insurance or annuity contract in connection with both United States risks and foreign risks, and, except as provided in paragraph (g) of this section, apportion such items between the insurance of United States risks and the insurance of foreign risks in the manner prescribed in subparagraph (2) or (3) of this paragraph, as the case may be. As used in this section, the term "foreign risks" means risks which are not United States risks as defined in § 1.953-2 or § 1.953-3.

(2) *Method of apportionment in determination of life insurance taxable income*—(i) *Investment yield and net long-term capital gain.* Unless they can be allocated to the insurance of United States risks, as provided in subparagraph (1) of this paragraph, in determining a controlled foreign corporation's taxable income for any taxable year under paragraph (a)(1) of this section—

(a) The investment yield under section 804(c),

(b) The amount (if any) under section 809(b)(1)(B) by which the net long-term capital gain exceeds the net short-term capital loss, and

(c) Those deductions allowed under section 809(d)(8), (9), and (12) which relate to gross investment income

shall be apportioned to the reinsuring and issuing of insurance and annuity contracts in connection with United States risks in an amount which bears the same ratio to each of such amounts of investment yield, excess gain, and deductions as the sum of the mean of each of the items described in section 810(c) at the beginning and end of the taxable year attributable to reinsuring and issuing any insurance and annuity contracts in connection with United States risks bears to the sum of the mean of each of the items described in section 810(c) at the beginning and end of the taxable year attributable to reinsuring and issuing all insurance and annuity contracts. Thus, for example, if the ratio which the sum of the mean of each of the items described in section 810(c) at the beginning and end of the taxable year attributable to reinsuring and issuing insurance and annuity contracts in connection with United States risks bears to the sum of the mean of each of the items described in section 810(c) at the beginning and end of the taxable year attributable to reinsuring and issuing all insurance and annuity contracts in one to three, then, unless an allocation to the insurance of United States risks can be made as provided in subparagraph (1) of this paragraph, one-third of each of such amounts of investment yield, excess gain, and deductions shall be apportioned to the reinsuring and issuing of insurance and annuity contracts in connection with United States risks, and two-thirds of each of such amounts shall be apportioned to the reinsuring and issuing of insurance and annuity contracts in connection with foreign risks.

(ii) *Other income and deductions*—(a) *Amount taken into account.* In determining a controlled foreign corporation's taxable income for any taxable year under paragraph (a)(1) of this section, all items of income taken into acccount under section 809 (c)(3), relating to other amounts of gross income, and the other deductions allowed under section 809(d)(12) to the extent that such other deductions do not relate to gross investment income shall be apportioned to the reinsuring and issuing of insurance and annuity contracts in connection with United States risks in an amount which bears the same ratio to each of such items of income or of such other deductions as the numerator determined under (b) of this subdivision bears to the denominator determined under (c) of this subdivision.

(b) *Numerator.* The numerator used for purposes of the apportionment under (a) of this subdivision shall be an amount which equals the amount determined under (c) of this subdivision, but only to the extent that the amount so determined is taken into account under paragraph (e) of this section in determining taxable income for the taxable year.

(c) *Denominator.* The denominator used for purposes of the apportionment under (a) of this subdivision shall be an amount which equals—

Reg. § 1.953-4(f)(2)

Income from Sources Without the United States

See p. 20,601 for regulations not amended to reflect law changes

(1) The amount of premiums determined under section 809(c)(1) for the taxable year, plus

(2) The net decrease in reserves determined under section 809(c)(2) for such year, minus

(3) The net increase in reserves determined under section 809(d)(2) for such year.

(iii) *Reserves used in apportionment formula.* The rules for determining which reserves are taken into account in determining the taxable income of a controlled foreign corporation under paragraph (a) of this section shall also apply under subdivision (ii)(*b*) and (*c*) of this subparagraph in determining the net decrease in reserves under section 809(c)(2) or the net increase in reserves under section 809(d)(2). See paragraph (c) of this section.

(3) *Method of apportionment in determination of mutual and other insurance income*—(i) *In general.* In determining a controlled foreign corporation's taxable income for any taxable year under paragraph (a)(2) of this section, any item which is required to be apportioned under subparagraph (1) of this paragraph shall be apportioned to the reinsuring and issuing of insurance and annuity contracts in connection with United States risks in an amount which bears the same ratio to the total amount of such item as the amount of premiums earned on insurance contracts during the taxable year which is required to be taken into account by such corporation under paragraph (e)(4) of this section in determining such taxable income bears to the total amount of all its premiums earned (as determined under section 832(b)(4)) on insurance contracts during the taxable year.

(ii) *Reserves used in apportionment formula.* The principles of subparagraph (2)(iii) of this paragraph shall apply in determining the reserves included in premiums earned on insurance contracts during the taxable year for purposes of subdivision (i) of this subparagraph.

(g) *Separate accounting.* The methods of apportionment prescribed in subparagraphs (2) and (3) of paragraph (f) of this section for determining taxable income under this section shall not apply if the district director determines that the controlled foreign corporation, in good faith and unaffected by considerations of tax liability, regularly employs in its books of account a detailed segregation of receipts, expenditures, assets, liabilities, and net worth which clearly reflects the income derived from the reinsuring or issuing of insurance or annuity contracts in connection with United States risks. The district director, in making such determination, shall give effect to any foreign law, satisfactory evidence of which is presented by the United States shareholder to the district director, which requires a reasonable segregation of those items of income, expense, losses, and other deductions which relate to determining such taxable income.

(h) *Illustration.* The application of paragraphs (e) and (f) of this section may be illustrated by the following example:

Example. Controlled foreign corporation A, incorporated under, and engaged in an insurance business subject to, the laws of foreign country X, is a wholly owned subsidiary of domestic corporation M. Both corporations use the calendar year as the taxable year. Corporation M is a life insurance company as defined in section 801(a); A Corporation would, if it were a domestic corporation, be taxable under part I of subchapter L of the Code. In 1963, A Corporation derives income from the insurance of United States risks as a result of reinsuring the life insurance policies issued by M Corporation on lives of residents of the United States. In 1963, A Corporation also issues policies of life insurance on individuals who are not residents of the United States, but its premiums from the reinsuring of United States risks exceed the 5-percent minimum premium requirement prescribed in paragraph (b) of § 1.953-1. Based upon the facts set forth in paragraph (a) of this example, A Corporation for 1963 has taxable income under this section of $40,200, which is attributable to the reinsuring of life insurance contracts in connection with United States risks, determined in the manner provided in paragraphs (b), (c), and (d) of this example.

(a) A summary of the entire operations of A Corporation for 1963, determined under this section as though such corporation were a domestic life insurance company but without applying paragraph (f) of this section, is as follows:

Reg. § 1.953-4(h)

Income from Sources Without the United States

See p. 20,601 for regulations not amended to reflect law changes

Item	Attributable to all insurance	Attributable to reinsuring U.S. risks	Attributable to insuring foreign risks
Investment Income:			
(1) Investment yield under sec. 804(c)	$ 90,000	unallocable	unallocable
(2) Sum of the mean of each of the items described in sec. 810(c) at beginning and end of 1963	2,500,000	$1,000,000	$1,500,000
(3) Required interest under sec. 809(a)(2)	60,000	25,000	35,000
(4) Deductions allowed under sec. 809(d)(8), (9), and (12) which relate to gross investment income	10,000	unallocable	unallocable
Underwriting Income:			
(5) Premiums under sec. 809(c)(1)	$ 600,000	$200,000	$400,000
(6) Net decrease in reserves under sec. 809(c)(2)	10,000	none	10,000
(7) Net increase in reserves under sec. 809(d)(2)	40,000	40,000	none
(8) Deductions allowed under sec. 809(d) (other than deduction allowed under sec. 809(d)(2) and other than those deductions allowed under sec. 809(d)(8), (9), and (12) which relate to gross investment income):			
(i) allocable	330,000	110,000	220,000
(ii) unallocable	60,000	unallocable	unallocable

(b) The unallocable investment yield ($90,000) under paragraph (a)(1) of this example and the unallocable deductions ($10,000) under paragraph (a)(4) relating to gross investment income are apportioned to the reinsuring of United States risks under paragraph (f)(1)(i) of this section in the amounts of $36,000, and $4,000, respectively, determined as follows:

(1) Sum of the mean of each of the items described in sec. 810(c) at beginning and end of 1963, attributable to reinsuring U.S. risks (paragraph (a)(2)) $1,000,000
(2) Sum of the mean of each of the items described in sec. 810(c) at beginning and end of 1963, attributable to all insurance (paragraph (a)(2)) $2,500,000
(3) Ratio of amount under subparagraph (1) to amount under subparagraph (2) ($1,000,000/$2,500,000) 40%
(4) Amount of investment yield attributable to reinsuring of U.S. risks (40% of $90,000) .... $ 36,000
(5) Amount of such deductions attributable to reinsuring of U.S. risks (40% of $10,000) .... $ 4,000

(c) The unallocable deductions ($60,000) under paragraph (a)(8)(ii) of this example which do not relate to gross investment income are apportioned to the reinsuring of United States risks under paragraph (f)(2)(ii) of this section in the amount of $16,800, determined as follows:

(1) The numerator determined under paragraph (f)(2)(ii)(b) of this section is $160,000, determined as follows:

(i) Premiums under sec. 809(c)(1) attributable to reinsuring U.S. risks (paragraph (a)(5)) $200,000
(ii) Plus: Net decrease in reserves under sec. 809(c)(2) attributable to reinsuring U.S. risks (paragraph (a)(6)) .... none $200,000
(iii) Less: Net increase in reserves under sec. 809(d)(2) attributable to reinsuring U.S. risks (paragraph (a)(7)) .... $ 40,000
$160,000

(2) The denominator determined under paragraph (f)(2)(ii)(c) of this section is $570,000, determined as follows:

(i) Premiums under sec. 809(c)(1) attributable to all insurance (paragraph (a)(5)) $600,000
(ii) Plus: Net decrease in reserves under sec. 809(c)(2) attributable to all insurance (paragraph (a)(6)) 10,000 $610,000
(iii) Less: Net increase in reserves under sec. 809(d)(2) attributable to all insurance (paragraph (a)(7)) 40,000
$570,000

Reg. § 1.953-4(h)

Income from Sources Without the United States

See p. 20,601 for regulations not amended to reflect law changes

(3) Ratio which the numerator determined under subparagraph (1) bears to the denominator determined under subparagraph (2) ($160,000/$570,000) 28%

(4) Amount of deductions attributable to reinsuring of U.S. risks (28% of $60,000) $16,800

(d) The taxable income of A Corporation for 1963 which constitutes its income derived from the insurance of United States risks for purposes of paragraph (a) of § 1.953-1 is $40,200, determined as follows:

Item:	Attributable to all insurance		Attributable to reinsuring U.S. risks		Attributable to insuring foreign risks	
(1) Investment yield under sec. 804(c) (paragraph (a)(1), unallocable but as apportioned under paragraph (b)(4))	$90,000		$36,000		$54,000	
(2) Less: Required interest under sec. 809(a)(2) (paragraph (a)(3))	60,000		25,000		35,000	
(3) Life insurance company's share of investment yield under sec. 809(b)(1)(A) .		$30,000		$11,000		$19,000
Plus sum of:						
(4) Premiums under sec. 809(c)(1) (paragraph (a)(5))	600,000		200,000		400,000	
(5) Net decrease in reserves under sec. 809(c)(2) (paragraph (a)(6))	10,000	610,000	none	200,000	10,000	410,000
Sum determined under sec. 809(b)(1)		640,000		211,000		429,000
Less sum of:						
(6) Net increase in reserves under sec. 809(d)(2) (paragraph (a)(7))	$40,000		$40,000		none	
(7) Deductions allowed under sec. 809(d)(8), (9), and (12) which relate to gross investment income (paragraph (a)(4)), unallocable but as apportioned under paragraph (b)(5)	10,000		4,000		$6,000	
(8) Deductions allowed under sec. 809(d) (other than deduction allowed under sec. 809(d)(2) and other than those deductions allowed under sec. 809(d)(8), (9), and (12) which relate to gross investment income) (paragraph (a)(8)):						
(i) allocable	330,000		110,000		220,000	
(ii) unallocable, but as apportioned under paragraph (c)(4) ...	60,000	$440,000	16,800	$170,800	43,200	$269,200
Gain from operations		200,000		40,200		159,800

[Reg. § 1.953-4.]

☐ [T.D. 6781, 12-22-64.]

[Reg. § 1.953-5]

§ 1.953-5. Corporations not qualifying as insurance companies.—(a) *In general.* A controlled foreign corporation is not excluded from the application of paragraph (a) of § 1.953-1 because such corporation, if it were a domestic corporation, would not be taxable as an insurance company to which subchapter L of the Code applies. Thus, if a controlled foreign corporation

Reg. § 1.953-5(a)

reinsures or issues insurance or annuity contracts in connection with United States risks, as defined in § 1.953-2 or § 1.953-3, and satisfies the 5-percent minimum premium requirement prescribed in paragraph (b) of § 1.953-1, such corporation may derive income from the insurance of United States risks even though the primary and predominant business activity of such corporation during the taxable year is not the issuing of insurance or annuity contracts or the reinsuring of risks underwritten by insurance companies.

(b) *Income from insurance of United States risks by noninsurance company.* For purposes of paragraph (a) of § 1.953-1, the taxable income derived from the reinsuring or the issuing of any insurance or annuity contract in connection with United States risks by a controlled foreign corporation which, if it were a domestic corporation, would not be taxable as an insurance company to which subchapter L of the Code applies shall be determined under § 1.953-4, subject to, and to the extent not inconsistent with, the special rules prescribed in paragraph (c) or (d) of this section, whichever applies.

(c) *Special rules in determining taxable income*—(1) *In general.* The rules prescribed in this paragraph apply in order to exclude from the determination under § 1.953-4 of the taxable income described in paragraph (b) of this section those items of the controlled foreign corporation's gross income and deductions which are not attributable to the reinsuring and issuing of insurance and annuity contracts.

(2) *Life insurance taxable income*—(i) *Amount of investment yield taken into account.* For purposes of determining the taxable income of a controlled foreign corporation which would not be taxable as an insurance company to which subchapter L of the Code applies if it were a domestic corporation but would be taxable as an insurance company to which part I of such subchapter applies if it were a domestic insurance company engaged in the business of only reinsuring or issuing the insurance or annuity contracts which have been reinsured or issued by such corporation, the investment yield under section 804(c), the amount (if any) by which the net long-term capital gain exceeds the net short-term capital loss, and all items of income taken into account under section 809(c)(3) shall be taken into account, subject to the provisions of paragraphs (e) and (f) of § 1.953-4, in an amount which bears the same ratio to each of such amounts of investment yield, excess gain, and income items, as the case may be, as the numerator determined under subdivision (ii) of this subparagraph bears to the denominator determined under subdivision (iii) of this subparagraph.

(ii) *Numerator.* The numerator used for purposes of the apportionment under subdivision (i) of this subparagraph shall be the sum of—

(*a*) The mean of each of the items described in section 810(c) at the beginning and end of the taxable year, determined in accordance with the rules prescribed in paragraph (c) of § 1.953-4 for purposes of determining taxable income of a controlled foreign corporation under paragraph (a) of § 1.953-4,

(*b*) The mean of other liabilities at the beginning and end of the taxable year which are attributable to the reinsuring and issuing of insurance and annuity contracts, and

(*c*) The mean of the earnings and profits accumulated by the controlled foreign corporation at the beginning and end of the taxable year (determined without diminution by reason of any distributions made during the taxable year) which are attributable to the reinsuring and issuing of insurance and annuity contracts.

(iii) *Denominator.* The denominator used for purposes of the apportionment under subdivision (i) of this subparagraph shall be the mean of the value of the total assets held by the controlled foreign corporation at the beginning and end of the taxable year, determined by taking assets into account at their actual value (not reduced by liabilities), which, in the absence of affirmative evidence to the contrary, shall be deemed to be (*a*) face value in the case of bills receivable, accounts receivable, notes receivable, and open accounts held by a controlled foreign corporation using the cash receipts and disbursements method of accounting and (*b*) adjusted basis in the case of all other assets.

(3) *Mutual and other insurance taxable income*—(i) *Amount of insurance income taken into account.* For purposes of determining the taxable income of a controlled foreign corporation which, if it were a domestic corporation, would not be taxable as an insurance company to which subchapter L of the Code applies but which if it were a domestic insurance company engaged in the business of only reinsuring or issuing the insurance or annuity contracts which have been reinsured or issued by such corporation, would be taxable as a mutual insurance company to which part II of subchapter L of the Code applies, or would be taxable as a mutual marine insurance or other insurance company to which part III of subchapter L of the Code applies, the sum of the items of gross income referred to in section 832(b)(1) (except the gross amount earned during the taxable year from underwriting income de-

Reg. § 1.953-5(b)

scribed in section 832(b)(1)(A)) reduced by the deductions allowable under section 832(c) which are related to such items of gross income shall be taken into account, subject to the provisions of paragraphs (e) and (f) of § 1.953-4, in an amount which bears the same proportion to the sum of such items of gross income reduced by such deductions as the numerator determined under subdivision (ii) of this subparagraph bears to the denominator determined under subdivision (iii) of this subparagraph.

(ii) *Numerator.* The numerator used for purposes of the apportionment under subdivision (i) of this subparagraph shall be the sum of—

(*a*) The mean of the controlled foreign corporation's unearned premiums at the beginning and end of the taxable year, determined under section 832(b)(4)(B) and in accordance with the rules prescribed in paragraph (c) of § 1.953-4 for purposes of determining taxable income of a controlled foreign corporation under paragraph (a) of § 1.953-4,

(*b*) The mean of such corporation's unpaid losses at the beginning and end of the taxable year, determined under section 832(b)(5)(B),

(*c*) The mean of the items described in section 810(c)(4) at the beginning and end of the taxable year, to the extent allowable to such corporation under section 832(c)(11),

(*d*) The mean of other liabilities at the beginning and end of the taxable year which are attributable to the reinsuring and issuing of insurance and annuity contracts, and

(*e*) The mean of the earnings and profits accumulated by such corporation at the beginning and end of the taxable year (determined without diminution by reason of any distributions made during the taxable year) which are attributable to the reinsuring and issuing of insurance and annuity contracts.

(iii) *Denominator.* The denominator used for purposes of the apportionment under subdivision (i) of this subparagraph shall be the mean of the value of the total assets held by the controlled foreign corporation at the beginning and end of the taxable year, determined in the manner prescribed in subparagraph (2) (iii) of this paragraph.

(d) *Separate accounting.* The special rules prescribed in paragraph (c) of this section shall not apply if the district director determines that the controlled foreign corporation, in good faith and unaffected by considerations of tax liability, regularly employs in its books of account a detailed segregation of receipts, expenditures, assets, liabilities, and net worth which clearly reflects the income derived from the reinsuring or issuing of insurance or annuity contracts. The district director, in making such determination, shall give effect to any foreign law, satisfactory evidence of which is presented by the United States shareholder to the district director, which requires a reasonable segregation of the insurance assets of the controlled foreign corporation. [Reg. § 1.953-5.]

☐ [*T.D.* 6781, 12-22-64.]

[Reg. § 1.953-6]

§ 1.953-6. **Relationship of sections 953 and 954.**—(a) *Priority of application.* For purposes of determining the subpart F income of a controlled foreign corporation under section 952 for any taxable year, the provisions of section 954, relating to foreign base company income, shall be applied, after first applying section 953, only with respect to income which is not income derived from the insurance of United States risks under section 953. For example, the provisions of section 954 may be applied with respect to the income of a controlled foreign corporation which is not income derived from the insurance of United States risks under section 953 because such corporation does not satisfy the 5-percent minimum premium requirement prescribed in paragraph (b) of § 1.953-1, even though such corporation has taxable income, as determined under § 1.953-4, which is attributable to the reinsuring or the issuing of any insurance or annuity contracts in connection with United States risks. In addition, the provisions of section 954 may apply with respect to the income of a controlled foreign corporation to the extent such income is not allocated or apportioned under § 1.953-4 to the insurance of United States risks.

(b) *Decrease in income not material.* It is not material that the income of a controlled foreign corporation is decreased as a result of the application of paragraph (a) of this section. Thus, in applying § 1.953-4 to the income of a controlled foreign corporation described in paragraph (c)(2) of § 1.953-5 which would, but for paragraph (a) of this section, be subject to the provisions of section 954, there shall be allowed, in determining the taxable income derived from the insurance of United States risks under § 1.953-4, a deduction under section 809(a)(1) for the share of each and every item of investment yield set aside for policyholders; it is not material that in determining foreign base company income such deduction would not be allowed under section 954(b)(5). Further, income of a controlled foreign corporation which is required to be taken into account under section 953 in determining income derived from the insurance of United States risks and would, but for the provisions of paragraph (a) of this section, constitute foreign base company income under section 954 shall not be taken into account under section 954(b)(3)(B) in determining whether foreign base company income exceeds 70 percent of gross income for the taxable year.

(c) *Increase in income not material.* It is not material that the income of a controlled foreign corporation is increased as a result of the application of paragraph (a) of this section. Thus, in applying § 1.953-4 to income of a controlled foreign corporation which would, but for paragraph (a) of this section, be subject to the provisions of section 954, it is not material that the dividends, interest, and gains from the sale or exchange of stock or securities derived from certain investments which would not be included in foreign personal holding company income under section 954(c)(3)(B) are included under section 953 in income derived from the insurance of United States risks. Further, income of a controlled foreign corporation which is required to be taken into account under section 953 in determining income derived from the insurance of United States risks and would, but for paragraph (a) of this section, constitute foreign base company income shall not be excluded under section 954(b)(3)(A) for the taxable year. [Reg. § 1.953-6.]

☐ [*T.D.* 6781, 12-22-64.]

[Reg. § 1.954-0]

§ 1.954-0. Introduction.—(a) *Effective dates*—(1) *Final regulations*—(i) *In general.* Except as otherwise specifically provided, the provisions of §§ 1.954-1 and 1.954-2 apply to taxable years of a controlled foreign corporation beginning after November 6, 1995. If any of the rules described in §§ 1.954-1 and 1.954-2 are inconsistent with provisions of other regulations under subpart F, these final regulations are intended to apply instead of such other regulations.

(ii) *Election to apply final regulations retroactively*—(A) *Scope of election.* An election may be made to apply the final regulations retroactively with respect to any taxable year of the controlled foreign corporation beginning on or after January 1, 1987. If such an election is made, these final regulations must be applied in their entirety for such taxable year and all subsequent taxable years. All references to section 11 in the final regulations shall be deemed to include section 15, where applicable.

(B) *Manner of making election.* An election under this paragraph (a)(1)(ii) is binding on all United States shareholders of the controlled foreign corporation and must be made—

(*1*) By the controlling United States shareholders, as defined in § 1.964-1(c)(5), by attaching a statement to such effect with their original or amended income tax returns for the taxable year of such United States shareholders in which or with which the taxable year of the CFC ends, and including any additional information required by applicable administrative pronouncements, or

(*2*) In such other manner as may be prescribed in applicable administrative pronouncements.

(C) *Time for making election.* An election may be made under this paragraph (a)(1)(ii) with respect to a taxable year of the controlled foreign corporation beginning on or after January 1, 1987 only if the time for filing a return or claim for refund has not expired for the taxable year of any United States shareholder of the controlled foreign corporation in which or with which such taxable year of the controlled foreign corporation ends.

(D) *Revocation of election.* An election made under this paragraph (a)(1)(ii) may not be revoked.

(2) *Temporary regulations.* The provisions of §§ 4.954-1 and 4.954-2 of this chapter apply to taxable years of a controlled foreign corporation beginning after December 31, 1986 and on or before November 6, 1995. However, the provisions of § 4.954-2(b)(6) of this chapter continue to apply. For transactions entered into on or before October 9, 1995, taxpayers may rely on Notice 89-90, 1989-2 C.B. 407, in applying the temporary regulations.

(3) *§§ 1.954A-1 and 1.954A-2.* The provisions of §§ 1.954A-1 and 1.954A-2 (as contained in 26 CFR part 1 edition revised April 1, 1995) apply to taxable years of a controlled foreign corporation beginning before January 1, 1987. All references therein to sections of the Code are to the Internal Revenue Code of 1954 prior to the amendments made by the Tax Reform Act of 1986.

(b) *Outline of §§ 1.954-0, 1.954-1 and 1.954-2.*
§ 1.954-0. Introduction.
(a) Effective dates.
(1) Final regulations.
(i) In general.
(ii) Election to apply final regulations retroactively.
(A) Scope of election.
(B) Manner of making election.
(C) Time for making election.
(D) Revocation of election.
(2) Temporary regulations.
(3) §§ 1.954A-1 and 1.954A-2.
(b) Outline of §§ 1.954-0, 1.954-1, and 1.954-2.
§ 1.954-1. Foreign base company income.
(a) In general.
(1) Purpose and scope.
(2) Gross foreign base company income.

Income from Sources Without the United States

See p. 20,601 for regulations not amended to reflect law changes

(3) Adjusted gross foreign base company income.

(4) Net foreign base company income.

(5) Adjusted net foreign base company income.

(6) Insurance income.

(7) Additional items of adjusted net foreign base company income or adjusted net insurance income by reason of section 952(c).

(b) Computation of adjusted gross foreign base company income and adjusted gross insurance income.

(1) De minimis and full inclusion tests.

    (i) De minimis test.

        (A) In general.

        (B) Currency translation.

        (C) Coordination with sections 864(d) and 881(c).

    (ii) Seventy percent full inclusion test.

(2) Character of gross income included in adjusted gross foreign base company income.

(3) Coordination with section 952(c).

(4) Anti-abuse rule.

    (i) In general.

    (ii) Presumption.

    (iii) Related persons.

    (iv) Example.

(c) Computation of net foreign base company income.

(1) General rule.

    (i) Deductions against gross foreign base company income.

    (ii) Losses reduce subpart F income by operation of earnings and profits limitation.

    (iii) Items of income.

        (A) Income other than passive foreign personal holding company income.

        (B) Passive foreign personal holding company income.

(2) Computation of net foreign base company income derived from same country insurance income.

(d) Computation of adjusted net foreign base company income or adjusted net insurance income.

(1) Application of high tax exception.

(2) Effective rate at which taxes are imposed.

(3) Taxes paid or accrued with respect to an item of income.

    (i) Income other than passive foreign personal holding company income.

    (ii) Passive foreign personal holding company income.

(4) Special rules.

    (i) Consistency rule.

    (ii) Coordination with earnings and profits limitation.

    (iii) Example.

(5) Procedure.

(6) Coordination of full inclusion and high tax exception rules.

(7) Examples.

(e) Character of income.

(1) Substance of the transaction.

(2) Separable character.

(3) Predominant character.

(4) Coordination of categories of gross foreign base company income or gross insurance income.

    (i) In general.

    (ii) Income excluded from other categories of gross foreign base company income.

(f) Definition of related person.

(1) Persons related to controlled foreign corporation.

    (i) Individuals.

    (ii) Other persons.

(2) Control.

    (i) Corporations.

    (ii) Partnerships.

    (iii) Trusts and estates.

    (iv) Direct or indirect ownership.

§ 1.954-2. Foreign personal holding company income.

(a) Computation of foreign personal holding company income.

(1) Categories of foreign personal holding company income.

(2) Coordination of overlapping categories under foreign personal holding company provisions.

    (i) In general.

    (ii) Priority of categories.

(3) Changes in the use or purpose for which property is held.

    (i) In general.

    (ii) Special rules.

        (A) Anti-abuse rule.

        (B) Hedging transactions.

    (iii) Example.

(4) Definitions and special rules.

    (i) Interest.

Reg. § 1.954-0(b)

49,208 Income from Sources Without the United States

See p. 20,601 for regulations not amended to reflect law changes

(ii) Bona fide hedging transaction.
   (A) Definition.
   (B) Identification.
   (C) Effect of identification and non-identification.
      (*1*) Transactions identified.
      (*2*) Inadvertent identification.
      (*3*) Transactions not identified.
      (*4*) Inadvertent error.
      (*5*) Anti-abuse rule.
(iii) Inventory and similar property.
   (A) Definition.
   (B) Hedging transactions.
(iv) Regular dealer.
(v) Dealer property.
   (A) Definition.
   (B) Securities dealers.
   (C) Hedging transactions.
(vi) Examples.
(vii) Debt instrument.

(b) Dividends, interest, rents, royalties and annuities.
 (1) In general.
 (2) Exclusion of certain export financing interest.
   (i) In general.
   (ii) Exceptions.
   (iii) Conduct of a banking business.
   (iv) Examples.
 (3) Treatment of tax-exempt interest. [RESERVED]
 (4) Exclusion of dividends or interest from related persons.
   (i) In general.
      (A) Corporate payor.
      (B) Payment by a partnership.
   (ii) Exceptions.
      (A) Dividends.
      (B) Interest paid out of adjusted foreign base company income or insurance income.
         (*1*) In general.
         (*2*) Rule for corporations that are both recipients and payors of interest.
      (C) Coordination with sections 864(d) and 881(c).
   (iii) Trade or business requirement.
   (iv) Substantial assets test.
   (v) Valuation of assets.
   (vi) Location of tangible property.
      (A) In general.
      (B) Exception.
   (vii) Location of intangible property.
      (A) In general.
      (B) Exception for property located in part in the payor's country of incorporation.
   (viii) Location of inventory and dealer property.
      (A) In general.
      (B) Inventory and dealer property located in part in the payor's country of incorporation.
   (ix) Location of debt instruments.
   (x) Treatment of certain stock interests.
   (xi) Treatment of banks and insurance companies. [Reserved]
 (5) Exclusion of rents and royalties derived from related persons.
   (i) In general.
      (A) Corporate payor.
      (B) Payment by a partnership.
   (ii) Exceptions.
      (A) Rents or royalties paid out of adjusted foreign base company income or insurance income.
      (B) Property used in part in the controlled foreign corporation's country of incorporation.
 (6) Exclusion of rents and royalties derived in the active conduct of a trade or business.

(c) Excluded rents.
 (1) Active conduct of a trade or business.
 (2) Special rules.
   (i) Adding substantial value.
   (ii) Substantiality of foreign organization.
   (iii) Active leasing expenses.
   (iv) Adjusted leasing profit.
 (3) Examples.

(d) Excluded royalties.
 (1) Active conduct of a trade or business.
 (2) Special rules.
   (i) Adding substantial value.
   (ii) Substantiality of foreign organization.
   (iii) Active licensing expenses.
   (iv) Adjusted licensing profit.
 (3) Examples.

(e) Certain property transactions.
 (1) In general.
   (i) Inclusions.
   (ii) Exceptions.

Reg. § 1.954-0(b)

Income from Sources Without the United States

(iii) Treatment of losses.

(iv) Dual character property.

(2) Property that gives rise to certain income.

(i) In general.

(ii) Gain or loss from the disposition of a debt instrument.

(3) Property that does not give rise to income.

(f) Commodities transactions.

(1) In general.

(i) Inclusion in foreign personal holding company income.

(ii) Exception.

(iii) Treatment of losses.

(2) Definitions.

(i) Commodity.

(ii) Commodities transaction.

(iii) Qualified active sale.

(A) In general.

(B) Active conduct of a commodities business.

(C) Substantially all.

(D) Activities of employees of a related entity.

(E) Financial activities.

(iv) Qualified hedging transaction.

(A) In general.

(B) Exception.

(g) Foreign currency gain or loss.

(1) Scope and purpose.

(2) In general.

(i) Inclusion.

(ii) Exclusion for business needs.

(A) General rule.

(B) Business needs.

(C) Regular dealers.

(D) Example.

(iii) Special rule for foreign currency gain or loss from an interest-bearing liability.

(3) Election to characterize foreign currency gain or loss that arises from a specific category of subpart F income as gain or loss in that category.

(i) In general.

(ii) Time and manner of election.

(iii) Revocation of election.

(iv) Example.

(4) Election to treat all foreign currency gains or losses as foreign personal holding company income.

(i) In general.

(ii) Time and manner of election.

(iii) Revocation of election.

(5) Gains and losses not subject to this paragraph.

(i) Capital gains and losses.

(ii) Income not subject to section 988.

(iii) Qualified business units using the dollar approximate separate transactions method.

(iv) Gain or loss allocated under § 1.861-9. [Reserved]

(h) Income equivalent to interest.

(1) In general.

(i) Inclusion in foreign personal holding company income.

(ii) Exceptions.

(A) Liability hedging transactions.

(B) Interest.

(2) Definition of income equivalent to interest.

(i) In general.

(ii) Income from the sale of property.

(3) Notional principal contracts.

(i) In general.

(ii) Regular dealers.

(4) Income equivalent to interest from factoring.

(i) General rule.

(ii) Exceptions.

(iii) Factored receivable.

(iv) Examples.

(5) Receivables arising from performance of services.

(6) Examples.

[Reg. § 1.954-0.]

□[*T.D. 8618, 9-6-95. Amended by T.D. 8767, 3-23-98.*]

[Reg. 4.954-0]

§ 4.954-0. Introduction.—(a) *Effective date*— (1) The provisions of §§ 4.954-1 and 4.954-2 apply to taxable years of a controlled foreign corporation beginning after December 31, 1986. Consequently, any gain or loss (including foreign currency gain or loss as defined in section 988(b)) recognized during such taxable years of a controlled foreign corporation is subject to these provisions. For further guidance, see § 1.954-0(a) of this chapter.

(2) The provisions of §§ 1.954A-1 and 1.954A-2 apply to taxable years of a controlled foreign corporation beginning before January 1,

49,210 Income from Sources Without the United States

See p. 20,601 for regulations not amended to reflect law changes

1987. All references therein to sections of the Code are to the Internal Revenue Code of 1954 prior to the amendments made by the Tax Reform Act of 1986.

(b) *Outline of regulation provisions for sections 954(b)(3), 954(b)(4), 954(b)(5) and 954(c) for taxable years of a controlled foreign corporation beginning after December 31, 1986.*

§ 4.954-0. Introduction.

(a) Effective dates.

(b) Outline.

§ 4.954-1. Foreign base company income.

(a) In general.

(1) Purpose and scope.

(2) Definition of gross foreign base company income.

(3) Definition of adjusted gross foreign base company income.

(4) Definition of net foreign base company income.

(5) Definition of adjusted net foreign base company income.

(6) Insurance income definitions.

(7) Additional items of adjusted net foreign base company income or adjusted net insurance income by reason of section 952(c).

(8) Illustration.

(b) Computation of adjusted gross foreign base company income and adjusted gross insurance income.

(1) De minimis rule and full inclusion rule.

(i) In general.

(ii) Five percent de minimis test.

(iii) Seventy percent full inclusion test.

(2) Character of items of adjusted gross foreign base company income.

(3) Coordination with section 952(c).

(4) Anti-abuse rule.

(i) In general.

(ii) Presumption.

(iii) Definition of related person.

(iv) Illustration.

(5) Illustration.

(c) Computation of net foreign base company income.

(d) Computation of adjusted net foreign base company income or adjusted net insurance income.

(1) Application of high tax exception.

(2) Effective rate at which taxes are imposed.

(3) Taxes paid or accrued with respect to an item of income.

(i) Income other than foreign personal holding company income.

(ii) Foreign personal holding company income.

(4) Definition of an item of income.

(i) Income other than foreign personal holding company income.

(ii) Foreign personal holding company income.

(A) In general.

(B) Consistency rule.

(5) Procedure.

(6) Illustrations.

(e) Character of an item of income.

(1) Substance of the transaction.

(2) Separable character.

(3) Predominant character.

(4) Coordination of categories of gross foreign base company income or gross insurance income.

§ 4.954-2. Foreign personal holding company income.

(a) Computation of foreign personal holding company income.

(1) In general.

(2) Coordination of overlapping definitions.

(3) Changes in use or purpose with which property is held.

(i) In general.

(ii) Illustrations.

(4) Definitions.

(i) Interest.

(ii) Inventory and similar property.

(iii) Regular dealer.

(iv) Dealer property.

(v) Debt instrument.

(b) Dividends, etc.

(1) In general.

(2) Exclusion of certain export financing.

(i) In general.

(ii) Conduct of a banking business.

(iii) Illustration.

(3) Exclusion of dividends and interest from related persons.

(i) Excluded dividends and interest.

(ii) Interest paid out of adjusted foreign base company income or insurance income.

(iii) Dividends paid out of prior years' earnings.

Reg. § 4.954-0(b)

Income from Sources Without the United States

See p. 20,601 for regulations not amended to reflect law changes

(iv) Fifty percent substantial assets test.
(v) Value of assets.
(vi) Location of tangible property used in a trade or business.
    (A) In general.
    (B) Exception.
(vii) Location of intangible property used in a trade or business.
    (A) In general.
    (B) Property located in part in the payor's country of incorporation and in part in other countries.
(viii) Location of property held for sale to customers.
    (A) In general.
    (B) Inventory located in part in the payor's country of incorporation and in part in other countries.
(ix) Location of debt instruments.
(x) Treatment of certain stock interests.
(xi) Determination of period during which property is used in a trade or business.
(xii) Treatment of banks and insurance companies. [Reserved]
(4) Exclusion of rents and royalties derived from related persons.
    (i) In general.
    (ii) Rents or royalties paid out of adjusted foreign base company income or insurance income.
(5) Exclusion of rents and royalties derived in the active conduct of a trade or business.
(6) Treatment of tax exempt interest.
(c) Excluded rents.
(1) Trade or business cases.
(2) Special rules.
    (i) Adding substantial value.
    (ii) Substantiality of foreign organization.
    (iii) Definition of active leasing expense.
    (iv) Adjusted leasing profits.
(3) Illustrations.
(d) Excluded royalties.
(1) Trade or business cases.
(2) Special rules.
    (i) Adding substantial value.
    (ii) Substantiality of foreign organization.
    (iii) Definition of active licensing expense.
    (iv) Definition of adjusted licensing profit.
(3) Illustrations.
(e) Certain property transactions.

(1) In general.
    (i) Inclusion of FPHC income.
    (ii) Dual character property.
(2) Property that gives rise to certain income.
    (i) In general.
    (ii) Exception.
(3) Property that does not give rise to income.
(4) Classification of gain or loss from the disposition of a debt instrument or on a deferred payment sale.
    (i) Gain.
    (ii) Loss.
(5) Classification of options and other rights to acquire or transfer property.
(6) Classification of certain interests in pass-through entities. [Reserved]
(f) Commodities transactions.
(1) In general.
(2) Definitions.
    (i) Commodity.
    (ii) Commodities transaction.
(3) Definition of the term "qualified active sales".
    (i) In general.
    (ii) Sale of commodities.
    (iii) Active conduct of a commodities business.
    (iv) Definition of the term "substantially all."
(4) Definition of the term "qualified hedging transaction".
(g) Foreign currency gain.
(1) In general.
(2) Exceptions.
    (i) Qualified business units using the dollar approximate separate transactions method.
    (ii) Tracing to exclude foreign currency gain or loss from qualified business and hedging transactions.
    (iii) Election out of tracing.
(3) Definition of the term "qualified business transaction".
    (i) In general.
    (ii) Specific section 988 transactions attributable to the sale of goods or services.
        (A) Acquisition of debt instruments.
        (B) Becoming the obligor under debt instruments.
        (C) Accrual of any item of gross income.

Reg. § 4.954-0(b)

(D) Accrual of any item of expense.

(E) Entering into forward contracts, futures contracts, options, and similar instruments.

(F) Disposition of nonfunctional currency.

(4) Definition of the term "qualified hedging transaction".

(i) In general.

(ii) Change in purpose of hedging transaction.

(5) Election out of tracing.

(i) In general.

(ii) Exception.

(iii) Procedure.

(A) In general.

(B) Time and manner.

(C) Termination.

(h) Income equivalent to interest.

(1) In general.

(2) Illustrations.

(3) Income equivalent to interest from factoring.

(i) General rule.

(ii) Exceptions.

(iii) Factored receivable.

(iv) Illustrations.

(4) Determination of sales income.

(5) Receivables arising from performance of services.

[Reg. § 4.954-0.]

☐[T.D. 8216, 7-20-88. Redesignated and amended by T.D. 8618, 9-6-95.]

[Reg. § 1.954-1]

§ 1.954-1. Foreign base company income.—(a) *In general*—(1) *Purpose and scope.* Section 954 and §§ 1.954-1 and 1.954-2 provide rules for computing the foreign base company income of a controlled foreign corporation. Foreign base company income is included in the subpart F income of a controlled foreign corporation under the rules of section 952. Subpart F income is included in the gross income of a United States shareholder of a controlled foreign corporation under the rules of section 951 and thus is subject to current taxation under section 1, 11 or 55 of the Internal Revenue Code. The determination of whether a foreign corporation is a controlled foreign corporation, the subpart F income of which is included currently in the gross income of its United States shareholders, is made under the rules of section 957.

(2) *Gross foreign base company income.* The gross foreign base company income of a controlled foreign corporation consists of the following categories of gross income (determined after the application of section 952(b))—

(i) Foreign personal holding company income, as defined in section 954(c);

(ii) Foreign base company sales income, as defined in section 954(d);

(iii) Foreign base company services income, as defined in section 954(e);

(iv) Foreign base company shipping income, as defined in section 954(f); and

(v) Foreign base company oil related income, as defined in section 954(g).

(3) *Adjusted gross foreign base company income.* The term *adjusted gross foreign base company income* means the gross foreign base company income of a controlled foreign corporation as adjusted by the de minimis and full inclusion rules of paragraph (b) of this section.

(4) *Net foreign base company income.* The term *net foreign base company income* means the adjusted gross foreign base company income of a controlled foreign corporation reduced so as to take account of deductions (including taxes) properly allocable or apportionable to such income under the rules of section 954(b)(5) and paragraph (c) of this section.

(5) *Adjusted net foreign base company income.* The term *adjusted net foreign base company income* means the net foreign base company income of a controlled foreign corporation reduced, first, by any items of net foreign base company income excluded from subpart F income pursuant to section 952(c) and, second, by any items excluded from subpart F income pursuant to the high tax exception of section 954(b). See paragraph (d)(4)(ii) of this section. The term *foreign base company income* as used in the Internal Revenue Code and elsewhere in the Income Tax Regulations means adjusted net foreign base company income, unless otherwise provided.

(6) *Insurance income.* The term *gross insurance income* includes all gross income taken into account in determining insurance income under section 953. The term *adjusted gross insurance income* means gross insurance income as adjusted by the de minimis and full inclusion rules of paragraph (b) of this section. The term *net insurance income* means adjusted gross insurance income reduced under section 953 so as to take into account deductions (including taxes) properly allocable or apportionable to such income. The term *adjusted net insurance income* means net insurance income reduced by any items of net insurance income that are excluded from subpart F income pursuant to section 952(b) or pursuant to

Reg. § 1.954-1(a)(1)

the high tax exception of section 954(b). The term *insurance income* as used in subpart F of the Internal Revenue Code and in the regulations under that subpart means adjusted net insurance income, unless otherwise provided.

(7) *Additional items of adjusted net foreign base company income or adjusted net insurance income by reason of section 952(c).* Earnings and profits of the controlled foreign corporation that are recharacterized as foreign base company income or insurance income under section 952(c) are items of adjusted net foreign base company income or adjusted net insurance income, respectively. Amounts subject to recharacterization under section 952(c) are determined after adjusted net foreign base company income and adjusted net insurance income are otherwise determined under subpart F and are not again subject to any exceptions or special rules that would affect the amount of subpart F income. Thus, for example, items of gross foreign base company income or gross insurance income that are excluded from adjusted gross foreign base company income or adjusted gross insurance income because the de minimis test is met are subject to recharacterization under section 952(c). Further, the de minimis and full inclusion tests of paragraph (b) of this section, and the high tax exception of paragraph (d) of this section, for example, do not apply to such amounts.

(b) *Computation of adjusted gross foreign base company income and adjusted gross insurance income*—(1) *De minimis and full inclusion tests*—(i) *De minimis test*—(A) *In general.* Except as provided in paragraph (b)(1)(i)(C) of this section, adjusted gross foreign base company income and adjusted gross insurance income are equal to zero if the sum of the gross foreign base company income and the gross insurance income of a controlled foreign corporation is less than the lesser of—

(*1*) 5 percent of gross income; or

(*2*) $1,000,000.

(B) *Currency translation.* Controlled foreign corporations having a functional currency other than the United States dollar shall translate the $1,000,000 threshold using the exchange rate provided under section 989(b)(3) for amounts included in income under section 951(a).

(C) *Coordination with sections 864(d) and 881(c).* Adjusted gross foreign base company income or adjusted gross insurance income of a controlled foreign corporation always includes income from trade or service receivables described in section 864(d)(1) or (6), and portfolio interest described in section 881(c), even if the de minimis test of this paragraph (b)(1)(i) is otherwise satisfied.

(ii) *Seventy percent full inclusion test.* Except as provided in section 953, adjusted gross foreign base company income consists of all gross income of the controlled foreign corporation other than gross insurance income and amounts described in section 952(b), and adjusted gross insurance income consists of all gross insurance income other than amounts described in section 952(b), if the sum of the gross foreign base company income and the gross insurance income for the taxable year exceeds 70 percent of gross income. See paragraph (d)(6) of this section, under which certain items of full inclusion foreign base company income may nevertheless be excluded from subpart F income.

(2) *Character of gross income included in adjusted gross foreign base company income.* The gross income included in the adjusted gross foreign base company income of a controlled foreign corporation generally retains its character as foreign personal holding company income, foreign base company sales income, foreign base company services income, foreign base company shipping income, or foreign base company oil related income. However, gross income included in adjusted gross foreign base company income because the full inclusion test of paragraph (b)(1)(ii) of this section is met is termed *full inclusion foreign base company income,* and constitutes a separate category of adjusted gross foreign base company income for purposes of allocating and apportioning deductions under paragraph (c) of this section.

(3) *Coordination with section 952(c).* Income that is included in subpart F income because the full inclusion test of paragraph (b)(1)(ii) of this section is met does not reduce amounts that, under section 952(c), are subject to recharacterization.

(4) *Anti-abuse rule*—(i) *In general.* For purposes of applying the de minimis test of paragraph (b)(1)(i) of this section, the income of two or more controlled foreign corporations shall be aggregated and treated as the income of a single corporation if a principal purpose for separately organizing, acquiring, or maintaining such multiple corporations is to prevent income from being treated as foreign base company income or insurance income under the de minimis test. A purpose may be a principal purpose even though it is outweighed by other purposes (taken together or separately).

(ii) *Presumption.* Two or more controlled foreign corporations are presumed to have been organized, acquired or maintained to prevent income from being treated as foreign base company

Reg. § 1.954-1(b)(4)

49,214 Income from Sources Without the United States
See p. 20,601 for regulations not amended to reflect law changes

income or insurance income under the de minimis test of paragraph (b)(1)(i) of this section if the corporations are related persons, as defined in paragraph (b)(4)(iii) of this section, and the corporations are described in paragraph (b)(4)(ii)(A), (B), or (C) of this section. This presumption may be rebutted by proof to the contrary.

(A) The activities carried on by the controlled foreign corporations, or the assets used in those activities, are substantially the same activities that were previously carried on, or assets that were previously held, by a single controlled foreign corporation. Further, the United States shareholders of the controlled foreign corporations or related persons (as determined under paragraph (b)(4)(iii) of this section) are substantially the same as the United States shareholders of the one controlled foreign corporation in a prior taxable year. A presumption made in connection with the requirements of this paragraph (b)(4)(ii)(A) may be rebutted by proof that the activities carried on by each controlled foreign corporation would constitute a separate branch under the principles of § 1.367(a)-6T(g)(2) if carried on directly by a United States person.

(B) The controlled foreign corporations carry on a business, financial operation, or venture as partners directly or indirectly in a partnership (as defined in section 7701(a)(2) and § 301.7701-3 of this chapter) that is a related person (as defined in paragraph (b)(4)(iii) of this section) with respect to each such controlled foreign corporation.

(C) The activities carried on by the controlled foreign corporations would constitute a single branch operation under § 1.367(a)-6T(g)(2) if carried on directly by a United States person.

(iii) *Related persons.* For purposes of this paragraph (b), two or more persons are related persons if they are in a relationship described in section 267(b). In determining for purposes of this paragraph (b) whether two or more corporations are members of the same controlled group under section 267(b)(3), a person is considered to own stock owned directly by such person, stock owned with the application of section 1563(e)(1), and stock owned with the application of section 267(c). In determining for purposes of this paragraph (b) whether a corporation is related to a partnership under section 267(b)(10), a person is considered to own the partnership interest owned directly by such person and the partnership interest owned with the application of section 267(e)(3).

(iv) *Example.* The following example illustrates the application of this paragraph (b)(4).

Example. (i)(1) *USP* is the sole United States shareholder of three controlled foreign corporations: *CFC1, CFC2* and *CFC3.* The three controlled foreign corporations all have the same taxable year. The three controlled foreign corporations are partners in *FP,* a foreign entity classified as a partnership under section 7701(a)(2) and § 301.7701-3 of the regulations. For their current taxable years, each of the controlled foreign corporations derives all of its income other than foreign base company income from activities conducted through *FP,* and its foreign base company income from activities conducted both jointly through *FP* and separately without *FP.* Based on the facts in the table below, the foreign base company income derived by each controlled foreign corporation for its current taxable year, including income derived from *FP,* is less than five percent of the gross income of each controlled foreign corporation and is less than $1,000,000:

	CFC1	CFC2	CFC3
Gross income	$ 4,000,000	$ 8,000,000	$ 12,000,000
Five percent of gross income	200,000	400,000	600,000
Foreign base company income	199,000	398,000	597,000

(2) Thus, without the application of the anti-abuse rule of this paragraph (b)(4), each controlled foreign corporation would be treated as having no foreign base company income after the application of the de minimis test of section 954(b)(3)(A) and paragraph (b)(1)(i) of this section.

(ii) However, under these facts, the requirements of paragraph (b)(4)(i) of this section are met unless the presumption of paragraph (b)(4)(ii) of this section is successfully rebutted. The sum of the foreign base company income of the controlled foreign corporations is $1,194,000. Thus, the amount of gross foreign base company income of each controlled foreign corporation will not be reduced by reason of the de minimis rule of section 954(b)(3)(A) and this paragraph (b).

(c) *Computation of net foreign base company income*—(1) *General rule.* The net foreign base company income of a controlled foreign corporation (as defined in paragraph (a)(4) of this section) is computed under the rules of this paragraph (c)(1). The principles of § 1.904-5(k) shall apply where payments are made between controlled foreign corporations that are related persons (within the meaning of section 954(d)(3)). Consistent with these principles, only payments

Reg. § 1.954-1(c)(1)

Income from Sources Without the United States

described in § 1.954-2(b)(4)(ii)(B)(*2*) may be offset as provided in § 1.904-5(k)(2).

(i) *Deductions against gross foreign base company income.* The net foreign base company income of a controlled foreign corporation is computed first by taking into account deductions in the following manner:

(A) First, the gross amount of each item of income described in paragraph (c)(1)(iii) of this section is determined.

(B) Second, any expenses definitely related to less than all gross income as a class shall be allocated and apportioned under the principles of sections 861, 864 and 904(d) to the gross income described in paragraph (c)(1)(i)(A) of this section.

(C) Third, foreign personal holding company income that is passive within the meaning of section 904 (determined before the application of the high-taxed income rule of § 1.904-4(c)) is reduced by related person interest expense allocable to passive income under § 1.904-5(c)(2); such interest must be further allocated and apportioned to items described in paragraph (c)(1)(iii)(B) of this section.

(D) Fourth, the amount of each item of income described in paragraph (c)(1)(iii) of this section is reduced by other expenses allocable and apportionable to such income under the principles of sections 861, 864 and 904(d).

(ii) *Losses reduce subpart F income by operation of earnings and profits limitation.* Except as otherwise provided in § 1.954-2(g)(4), if after applying the rules of paragraph (c)(1)(i) of this section, the amount remaining in any category of foreign base company income or foreign personal holding company income is less than zero, the loss in that category may not reduce any other category of foreign base company income or foreign personal holding company income except by operation of the earnings and profits limitation of section 952(c)(1).

(iii) *Items of income*—(A) *Income other than passive foreign personal holding company income.* A single item of income (other than foreign personal holding company income that is passive) is the aggregate amount from all transactions that falls within a single separate category (as defined in § 1.904-5(a)(1)), and either—

(*1*) Falls within a single category of foreign personal holding company income as—

(*i*) Dividends, interest, rents, royalties and annuities;

(*ii*) Gain from certain property transactions;

(*iii*) Gain from commodities transactions;

(*iv*) Foreign currency gain; or

(*v*) Income equivalent to interest; or

(*2*) Falls within a single category of foreign base company income, other than foreign personal holding company income, as—

(*i*) Foreign base company sales income;

(*ii*) Foreign base company services income;

(*iii*) Foreign base company shipping income;

(*iv*) Foreign base company oil related income; or

(*v*) Full inclusion foreign base company income.

(B) *Passive foreign personal holding company income.* A single item of foreign personal holding company income that is passive is an amount of income that falls within a single group of passive income under the grouping rules of § 1.904-4(c)(3), (4) and (5) and a single category of foreign personal holding company income described in paragraphs (c)(1)(iii)(A)(*1*)(*i*) through (*v*).

(2) *Computation of net foreign base company income derived from same country insurance income.* Deductions relating to foreign base company income attributable to the issuing (or reinsuring) of any insurance or annuity contract in connection with risks located in the country under the laws of which the controlled foreign corporation is created or organized shall be allocated and apportioned in accordance with the rules set forth in section 953.

(d) *Computation of adjusted net foreign base company income or adjusted net insurance income*—(1) *Application of high tax exception.* Adjusted net foreign base company income (or adjusted net insurance income) equals the net foreign base company income (or net insurance income) of a controlled foreign corporation, reduced by any net item of such income that qualifies for the high tax exception provided by section 954(b)(4) and this paragraph (d). Any item of income that is foreign base company oil related income, as defined in section 954(g), or portfolio interest, as described in section 881(c), does not qualify for the high tax exception. See paragraph (c)(1)(iii) of this section for the definition of the term *item of income.* For rules concerning the treatment for foreign tax credit purposes of amounts excluded from subpart F under section

Reg. § 1.954-1(d)

954(b)(4), see § 1.904-4(c). A net item of income qualifies for the high tax exception only if—

(i) An election is made under section 954(b)(4) and paragraph (d)(5) of this section to exclude the income from the computation of subpart F income; and

(ii) It is established that the net item of income was subject to foreign income taxes imposed by a foreign country or countries at an effective rate that is greater than 90 percent of the maximum rate of tax specified in section 11 for the taxable year of the controlled foreign corporation.

(2) *Effective rate at which taxes are imposed.* The effective rate with respect to a net item of income shall be determined separately for each controlled foreign corporation in a chain of corporations through which a distribution is made. The effective rate at which taxes are imposed on a net item of income is—

(i) The United States dollar amount of foreign income taxes paid or accrued (or deemed paid or accrued) with respect to the net item of income, determined under paragraph (d)(3) of this section; divided by

(ii) The United States dollar amount of the net item of foreign base company income or insurance income, described in paragraph (c)(1)(iii) of this section, increased by the amount of foreign income taxes referred to in paragraph (d)(2)(i) of this section.

(3) *Taxes paid or accrued with respect to an item of income*—(i) *Income other than passive foreign personal holding company income.* The amount of foreign income taxes paid or accrued with respect to a net item of income (other than an item of foreign personal holding company income that is passive) for purposes of section 954(b)(4) and this paragraph (d) is the United States dollar amount of foreign income taxes that would be deemed paid under section 960 with respect to that item if that item were included in the gross income of a United States shareholder under section 951(a)(1)(A) (determined, in the case of a United States shareholder that is an individual, as if an election under section 962 has been made, whether or not such election is actually made). For this purpose, in accordance with the regulations under section 960, the amounts that would be deemed paid under section 960 shall be determined separately with respect to each controlled foreign corporation and without regard to the limitation applicable under section 904(a). The amount of foreign income taxes paid or accrued with respect to a net item of income, determined in the manner provided in this paragraph (d), will not be affected by a subsequent reduction in foreign income taxes attributable to a distribution to shareholders of all or part of such income.

(ii) *Passive foreign personal holding company income.* The amount of income taxes paid or accrued with respect to a net item of foreign personal holding company income that is passive for purposes of section 954(b)(4) and this paragraph (d) is the United States dollar amount of foreign income taxes that would be deemed paid under section 960 and that would be taken into account for purposes applying the provisions of § 1.904-4(c) with respect to that net item of income.

(4) *Special rules*—(i) *Consistency rule.* An election to exclude income from the computation of subpart F income for a taxable year must be made consistently with respect to all items of passive foreign personal holding company income eligible to be excluded for the taxable year. Thus, high-taxed passive foreign personal holding company income of a controlled foreign corporation must either be excluded in its entirety, or remain subject to subpart F in its entirety.

(ii) *Coordination with earnings and profits limitation.* If the amount of income included in subpart F income for the taxable year is reduced by the earnings and profits limitation of section 952(c)(1), the amount of income that is a net item of income, within the meaning of paragraph (c)(1)(iii) of this section, is determined after the application of the rules of section 952(c)(1).

(iii) *Example.* The following example illustrates the provisions of paragraph (d)(4)(ii) of this section. All of the taxes referred to in the following example are foreign income taxes. For simplicity, this example assumes that the amount of taxes that are taken into account as a deduction under section 954(b)(5) and the amount of the gross-up required under sections 960 and 78 are equal. Therefore, this example does not separately illustrate the deduction for taxes and gross-up.

Example. During its 1995 taxable year, CFC, a controlled foreign corporation, earns royalty income, net of taxes, of $100 that is foreign personal holding company income. CFC has no expenses associated with this royalty income. CFC pays $50 of foreign income taxes with respect to the royalty income. For 1995, CFC has current earnings and profits of $50. CFC's subpart F income, as determined prior to the application of this paragraph (d), exceeds its current earnings and profits. Thus, under paragraph (d)(4)(ii) of this section, the amount of CFC's only net item of income, the royalty income, will be limited to $50. The remaining $50 will be subject to recharacterization in a subsequent taxable year under section

Reg. § 1.954-1(d)(2)

952(c)(2). Because the amount of foreign income taxes paid with respect to this net item of income is $50, the effective rate of tax on the item, for purposes of this paragraph (d), is 50 percent ($50 of taxes/$50 net item + $50 of taxes). Accordingly, an election under paragraph (d)(5) of this section may be made to exclude the item of income from the computation of subpart F income.

(5) *Procedure.* An election made under the procedure provided by this paragraph (d)(5) is binding on all United States shareholders of the controlled foreign corporation and must be made—

(i) By the controlling United States shareholders, as defined in § 1.964-1(c)(5), by attaching a statement to such effect with their original or amended income tax returns, and including any additional information required by applicable administrative pronouncements; or

(ii) In such other manner as may be prescribed in applicable administrative pronouncements.

(6) *Coordination of full inclusion and high tax exception rules.* Notwithstanding paragraph (b)(1)(ii) of this section, full inclusion foreign base company income will be excluded from subpart F income if more than 90 percent of the adjusted gross foreign base company income and adjusted gross insurance company income of a controlled foreign corporation (determined without regard to the full inclusion test of paragraph (b)(1) of this section) is attributable to net amounts excluded from subpart F income pursuant to an election to have the high tax exception described in section 954(b)(4) and this paragraph (d) apply.

(7) *Examples.* (i) The following examples illustrate the rules of this paragraph (d). All of the taxes referred to in the following examples are foreign income taxes. For simplicity, these examples assume that the amount of taxes that are taken into account as a deduction under section 954(b)(5) and the amount of the gross-up required under sections 960 and 78 are equal. Therefore, these examples do not separately illustrate the deduction for taxes and gross-up. Except as otherwise stated, these examples assume there are no earnings, deficits, or foreign income taxes in the post-1986 pools of earnings and profits or foreign income taxes.

Example 1. (i) *Items of income.* During its 1995 taxable year, controlled foreign corporation CFC earns from outside its country of operation portfolio dividend income of $100 and interest income, net of taxes, of $100 (consisting of a gross payment of $150 reduced by a third-country withholding tax of $50). For purposes of illustration, assume that CFC incurs no expenses. None of the income is taxed in CFC's country of operation. The dividend income was not subject to third-country withholding taxes. Pursuant to the operation of section 904, the interest income is high withholding tax interest and the dividend income is passive income. Accordingly, pursuant to paragraph (c)(1)(iii) of this section, CFC has two net items of income—

(1) $100 of foreign personal holding company (FPHC)/passive income (the dividends); and

(2) $100 of FPHC/high withholding tax income (the interest).

(ii) *Effective rates of tax.* No foreign tax would be deemed paid under section 960 with respect to the net item of income described in paragraph (i)(1) of this *Example 1.* Therefore, the effective rate of foreign tax is 0, and the item may not be excluded from subpart F income under the rules of this paragraph (d). Foreign tax of $50 would be deemed paid under section 960 with respect to the net item of income described in paragraph (i)(2) of this *Example 1.* Therefore, the effective rate of foreign tax is 33 percent ($50 of creditable taxes paid, divided by $150, consisting of the net item of foreign base company income ($100) plus creditable taxes paid thereon ($50)). The highest rate of tax specified in section 11 for the 1995 taxable year is 35 percent. Accordingly, the net item of income described in paragraph (i)(2) of this *Example 1* may be excluded from subpart F income if an election under paragraph (d)(5) of this section is made, since it is subject to foreign tax at an effective rate that is greater than 31.5 percent (90 percent of 35 percent). However, for purposes of section 904(d), it remains high withholding tax interest.

Example 2. (i) The facts are the same as in *Example 1*, except that CFC's country of operation imposes a tax of $50 with respect to CFC's dividend income (and thus CFC earns portfolio dividend income, net of taxes, of only $50). The interest income is still high withholding tax interest. The dividend income is still passive income (without regard to the possible applicability of the high tax exception of section 904(d)(2)). Accordingly, CFC has two items of income for purposes of this paragraph (d)—

(1) $50 of FPHC/passive income (net of the $50 foreign tax); and

(2) $100 of FPHC/high withholding tax interest income.

(ii) Each item is taxed at an effective rate greater than 31.5 percent. The net item of income described in paragraph (i)(1) of this *Example 2*: foreign tax ($50) divided by sum ($100) of net item of income ($50) plus creditable tax thereon

Reg. § 1.954-1(d)(7)

($50) equals 50 percent. The net item of income described in paragraph (i)(2) of this *Example 2*: Foreign tax ($50) divided by sum ($150) of income item ($100) plus creditable tax thereon ($50) equals 33 percent. Accordingly, an election may be made under paragraph (d)(5) of this section to exclude either or both of the net items of income described in paragraphs (i)(1) and (2) of this *Example 2* from subpart F income. If no election is made the items would be included in the subpart F income of *CFC*.

Example 3. (i) The facts are the same as in *Example 1*, except that the $100 of portfolio dividend income is subject to a third-country withholding tax of $50, and the $150 of interest income is from sources within *CFC*'s country of operation, is subject to a $10 income tax therein, and is not subject to a withholding tax. Although the interest income and the dividend income are both passive income, under paragraph (c)(1)(iii)(B) of this section they constitute separate items of income pursuant to the application of the grouping rules of § 1.904-4(c). Accordingly, *CFC* has two net items of income for purposes of this paragraph (d)—

(1) $50 (net of $50 tax) of FPHC/non-country of operation/greater than 15 percent withholding tax income; and

(2) $140 (net of $10 tax) of FPHC/country of operation income.

(ii) The item described in paragraph (i)(1) of this *Example 3* is taxed at an effective rate greater than 31.5 percent, but Item 2 is not. The net item of income described in paragraph (i)(1) of this *Example 3*: foreign tax ($50) divided by sum ($100) of net item of income ($50) plus creditable tax thereon ($50) equals 50 percent. The net item of income described in paragraph (i)(2) of this *Example 3*: foreign tax ($10) divided by sum ($150) of net item of income ($140) plus creditable tax thereon ($10) equals 6.67 percent. Therefore, an election may be made under paragraph (d)(5) of this section to exclude the net item of income described in paragraph (i)(1) of this *Example 3* but not the net item of income described in paragraph (i)(2) of this *Example 3* from subpart F income.

Example 4. The facts are the same as in *Example 3*, except that the $150 of interest income is subject to an income tax of $50 in *CFC*'s country of operation. Accordingly, *CFC*'s items of income are the same as in *Example 3*, but both items are taxed at an effective rate greater than 31.5 percent. The net item of income described in paragraph (i)(1) of *Example 3*: Foreign tax ($50) divided by sum ($100) of net item of income ($50) plus creditable tax thereon ($50) equals 50 per- cent. The net item of income described in paragraph (i)(2) of *Example 3*: foreign tax ($50) divided by sum ($150) of net item of income ($100) plus creditable tax thereon ($50) equals 33 percent. Pursuant to the consistency rule of paragraph (d)(4)(i) of this section, an election made by *CFC*'s controlling United States shareholders must exclude from subpart F income both items of FPHC income under the high tax exception of section 954(b)(4) and this paragraph (d). The election may not be made only with respect to one item.

Example 5. The facts are the same as in *Example 1*, except that *CFC* earns $5 of portfolio dividend income and $150 of interest income. In addition, *CFC* earns $45 for performing consulting services within its country of operation for unrelated persons. *CFC*'s gross foreign base company income for 1995 of $155 ($150 of gross interest income and $5 of portfolio dividend income) is greater than 70 percent of its gross income of $200. Therefore, under the full inclusion test of paragraph (b)(1)(ii) of this section, *CFC*'s adjusted gross foreign base company income is $200, and under paragraph (b)(2) of this section, the $45 of consulting income is full inclusion foreign base company income. If *CFC* elects, under paragraph (d)(5) of this section, to exclude the interest income from subpart F income pursuant to the high tax exception, the $45 of full inclusion foreign base company income will be excluded from subpart F income under paragraph (d)(6) of this section because the $150 of gross interest income excluded under the high tax exception is more than 90 percent of *CFC*'s adjusted gross foreign base company income of $155.

(ii) The following examples generally illustrate the application of paragraph (c) of this section and this paragraph (d). *Example 1* illustrates the order of computations. *Example 2* illustrates the computations required by sections 952 and 954 and this § 1.954-1 if the full inclusion test of paragraph (b)(1)(ii) of this section is met and the income is not excluded from subpart F income under section 952(b). Computations in these examples involving the operation of section 952(c) are included for purposes of illustration only and do not provide substantive rules concerning the operation of that section. For simplicity, these examples assume that the amount of taxes that are taken into account as a deduction under section 954(b)(5) and the amount of the gross-up required under sections 960 and 78 are equal. Therefore, these examples do not separately illustrate the deduction for taxes and gross-up.

Example 1. (i) *Gross income.* *CFC*, a controlled foreign corporation, has gross income of

Reg. § 1.954-1(d)(7)

$1000 for the current taxable year. Of that $1000 of income, $100 is interest income that is included in the definition of foreign personal holding company income under section 954(c)(1)(A) and § 1.954-2(b)(1)(ii), is not income from a trade or service receivable described in section 864(d)(1) or (6), or portfolio interest described in section 881(c), and is not excluded from foreign personal holding company income under any provision of section 952(b) or section 954(c). Another $50 is foreign base company sales income under section 954(d). The remaining $850 of gross income is not included in the definition of foreign base company income or insurance income under sections 954(c), (d), (e), (f) or (g) or 953, and is foreign source general limitation income described in section 904(d)(1)(I).

(ii) *Expenses.* For the current taxable year, CFC has expenses of $500. This amount includes $8 of interest paid to a related person that is allocable to foreign personal holding company income under section 904, and $2 of other expense that is directly related to foreign personal holding company income. Another $20 of expense is directly related to foreign base company sales. The remaining $470 of expenses is allocable to general limitation income that is not foreign base company income or insurance income.

(iii) *Earnings and losses.* CFC has earnings and profits for the current taxable year of $500. In the prior taxable year, CFC had losses with respect to income other than gross foreign base company income or gross insurance income. By reason of the limitation provided under section 952(c)(1)(A), those losses reduced the subpart F income (consisting entirely of foreign source general limitation income) of CFC by $600 for the prior taxable year.

(iv) *Taxes.* Foreign income tax of $30 is considered imposed on the interest income under the rules of section 954(b)(4), this paragraph (d), and § 1.904-6. Foreign income tax of $14 is considered imposed on the foreign base company sales income under the rules of section 954(b)(4), paragraph (d) of this section, and § 1.904-6. Foreign income tax of $177 is considered imposed on the remaining foreign source general limitation income under the rules of section 954(b)(4), this paragraph (d), and § 1.904-6. For the taxable year of CFC, the maximum United States rate of taxation under section 11 is 35 percent.

(v) *Conclusion.* Based on these facts, if CFC elects to exclude all items of income subject to a high foreign tax under section 954(b)(4) and this paragraph (d), it will have $500 of subpart F income as defined in section 952(a) (consisting entirely of foreign source general limitation income) determined as follows:

Step 1—Determine gross income:

(1) Gross income $1000

Step 2—Determine gross foreign base company income and gross insurance income:

(2) Interest income included in gross foreign personal holding company income under section 954(c) 100

(3) Gross foreign base company sales income under section 954(d) 50

(4) Total gross foreign base company income and gross insurance income as defined in sections 954(c), (d), (e), (f) and (g) and 953 (line (2) plus line (3)) 150

Step 3—Compute adjusted gross foreign base company income and adjusted gross insurance income:

(5) Five percent of gross income (.05 × line (1)) 50

(6) Seventy percent of gross income (.70 × line (1))700

(7) Adjusted gross foreign base company income and adjusted gross insurance income after the application of the de minimis test of paragraph (b) (line (4), or zero if line (4) is less than the lesser of line (5) or $1,000,000) (if the amount on this line 7 is zero, proceed to Step 8) 150

(8) Adjusted gross foreign base company income and adjusted gross insurance income after the application of the full inclusion test of paragraph (b) (line (4), or line (1) if line (4) is greater than line (6)) 150

Step 4—Compute net foreign base company income:

(9) Expenses directly related to adjusted gross foreign base company sales income 20

(10) Expenses (other than related person interest expense) directly related to adjusted gross foreign personal holding company income . 2

(11) Related person interest expense allocable to adjusted gross foreign personal holding company income under section 904 8

(12) Net foreign personal holding company income after allocating deductions under section 954(b)(5) and paragraph (c) of this section (line (2) reduced by lines (10) and (11)) 90

(13) Net foreign base company sales income after allocating deductions under section 954(b)(5) and paragraph (c) of this section (line (3) reduced by line (9)) 30

(14) Total net foreign base company income after allocating deductions under section

Reg. § 1.954-1(d)(7)

49,220 Income from Sources Without the United States
See p. 20,601 for regulations not amended to reflect law changes

954(b)(5) and paragraph (c) of this section (line (12) plus line (13)) 120

Step 5—Compute net insurance income:

(15) Net insurance income under section 953.. 0

Step 6—Compute adjusted net foreign base company income:

(16) Foreign income tax imposed on net foreign personal holding company income (as determined under section 954(b)(4) and this paragraph (d)) 30

(17) Foreign income tax imposed on net foreign base company sales income (as determined under section 954(b)(4) and this paragraph (d)) 14

(18) Ninety percent of the maximum United States corporate tax rate 31.5%

(19) Effective rate of foreign income tax imposed on net foreign personal holding company income ($90 of interest) under section 954(b)(4) and this paragraph (d) (line (16) divided by line (12)) 33%

(20) Effective rate of foreign income tax imposed on $30 of net foreign base company sales income under section 954(b)(4) and this paragraph (d) (line (17) divided by line (13)) 47%

(21) Net foreign personal holding company income subject to a high foreign tax under section 954(b)(4) and this paragraph (d) (zero, or line (12) if line (19) is greater than line (18)) .. 90

(22) Net foreign base company sales income subject to a high foreign tax under section 954(b)(4) and this paragraph (d) (zero, or line (13) if line (20) is greater than line (18)) 30

(23) Adjusted net foreign base company income after applying section 954(b)(4) and this paragraph (d) (line (14), reduced by the sum of line (21) and line (22)) 0

Step 7—Compute adjusted net insurance income:

(24) Adjusted net insurance income .. 0

Step 8—Additions to or reduction of adjusted net foreign base company income by reason of section 952(c):

(25) Earnings and profits for the current year 500

(26) Amount subject to being recharacterized as subpart F income under section 952(c)(2) (excess of line (25) over the sum of lines (23) and (24)); if there is a deficit, then the limitation of section 952(c)(1) may apply for the current year 500

(27) Amount of reduction in subpart F income for prior taxable years by reason of the limitation of section 952(c)(1) 600

(28) Subpart F income as defined in section 952(a), assuming section 952(a)(3), (4), and (5) do not apply (the sum of line (23), line (24), and the lesser of line (26) or line (27) .. 500

(29) Amount of prior year's deficit to be recharacterized as subpart F income in later years under section 952(c) (excess of line (27) over line (26)) 100

Example 2. (i) *Gross income.* CFC, a controlled foreign corporation, has gross income of $1000 for the current taxable year. Of that $1000 of income, $720 is interest income that is included in the definition of foreign personal holding company income under section 954(c)(1)(A) and § 1.954-2(b)(1)(ii), is not income from trade or service receivables described in section 864(d)(1) or (6), or portfolio interest described in section 881(c), and is not excluded from foreign personal holding company income under any provision of section 954(c) and § 1.954-2 or section 952(b). The remaining $280 is services income that is not included in the definition of foreign base company income or insurance income under sections 954(c), (d), (e), (f), or (g) or 953, and is foreign source general limitation income for purposes of section 904(d)(1)(I).

(ii) *Expenses.* For the current taxable year, CFC has expenses of $650. This amount includes $350 of interest paid to related persons that is allocable to foreign personal holding company income under section 904, and $50 of other expense that is directly related to foreign personal holding company income. The remaining $250 of expenses is allocable to services income other than foreign base company income or insurance income.

(iii) *Earnings and losses.* CFC has earnings and profits for the current taxable year of $350. In the prior taxable year, CFC had losses with respect to income other than foreign base company income or insurance income. By reason of the limitation provided under section 952(c)(1)(A), those losses reduced the subpart F income of CFC (consisting entirely of foreign source general limitation income) by $600 for the prior taxable year.

(iv) *Taxes.* Foreign income tax of $120 is considered imposed on the $720 of interest income under the rules of section 954(b)(4), paragraph (d) of this section, and § 1.904-6. Foreign income tax of $2 is considered imposed on the services income under the rules of section 954(b)(4), paragraph (d) of this section, and § 1.904-6. For the taxable year of CFC, the maximum United States rate of taxation under section 11 is 34 percent.

Reg. § 1.954-1(d)(7)

Income from Sources Without the United States

(v) *Conclusion.* Based on these facts, if CFC elects to exclude all items of income subject to a high foreign tax under section 954(b)(4) and this paragraph (d), it will have $350 of subpart F income as defined in section 952(a), determined as follows.

Step 1—Determine gross income:

(1) Gross income $1000

Step 2—Determine gross foreign base company income and gross insurance income:

(2) Gross foreign base company income and gross insurance income as defined in sections 954(c), (d), (e), (f) and (g) and 953 (interest income) 720

Step 3—Compute adjusted gross foreign base company income and adjusted gross insurance income:

(3) Seventy percent of gross income (.70 × line (1)) 700

(4) Adjusted gross foreign base company income and adjusted gross insurance income after the application of the full inclusion rule of this paragraph (b)(1) (line (2), or line (1) if line (2) is greater than line (3)) 1000

(5) Full inclusion foreign base company income under paragraph (b)(1)(ii) (line (4) minus line (2)) 280

Step 4—Compute net foreign base company income:

(6) Expenses (other than related person interest expense) directly related to adjusted gross foreign personal holding company income 50

(7) Related person interest expense allocable to adjusted gross foreign personal holding company income under section 904 350

(8) Deductions allocable to full inclusion foreign base company income under section 954(b)(5) and paragraph (c) of this section . . . 250

(9) Net foreign personal holding company income after allocating deductions under section 954(b)(5) and paragraph (c) of this section (line (2) reduced by line (6) and line (7)) 320

(10) Full inclusion foreign base company income after allocating deductions under section 954(b)(5) and paragraph (c) of this section (line (5) reduced by line (8)) 30

(11) Total net foreign base company income after allocating deductions under section 954(b)(5) and paragraph (c) of this section (line (9) plus line (10)) 350

Step 5—Compute net insurance income:

(12) Net insurance income under section 953 0

Step 6—Compute adjusted net foreign base company income:

(13) Foreign income tax imposed on net foreign personal holding company income (interest) 120

(14) Foreign income tax imposed on net full inclusion foreign base company income 2

(15) Ninety percent of the maximum United States corporate tax rate 31.5%

(16) Effective rate of foreign income tax imposed on $320 of net foreign personal holding company income under section 954(b)(4) and this paragraph (d) (line (13) divided by line (9)) . 38%

(17) Effective rate of foreign income tax imposed on $30 of net full inclusion foreign base company income under section 954(b)(4) and this paragraph (d) (line (14) divided by line (10)) . 7%

(18) Net foreign personal holding company income subject to a high foreign tax under section 954(b)(4) and this paragraph (d) (zero, or line (9) if line (16) is greater than line (15)) . . 320

(19) Net full inclusion foreign base company income subject to a high foreign tax under section 954(b)(4) and this paragraph (d) (zero, or line (10) if line (17) is greater than line (15)) . . . 0

(20) Adjusted net foreign base company income after applying section 954(b)(4) and this paragraph (d) (line (11) reduced by the sum of line (18) and line (19)) 30

Step 7—Compute adjusted net insurance income:

(21) Adjusted net insurance income . . 0

Step 8—Reduction of adjusted net foreign base company income or adjusted net insurance income by reason of paragraph (d)(6) of this section:

(22) Adjusted gross foreign base company income and adjusted gross insurance income (determined without regard to the full inclusion test of paragraph (b)(1) of this section) (line (4) reduced by line (5)) 720

(23) Ninety percent of adjusted gross foreign base company income and adjusted gross insurance income (determined without regard to the full inclusion test of paragraph (b)(1)(ii) of this section) (90% of the amount on line (22)) 648

(24) Net foreign base company income and net insurance income excluded from subpart F income under section 954(b)(4), increased by the amount of expenses that reduced this income under section 954(b)(5) and paragraph (c) of this section (line (18) increased by the sum of line (6) and line (7)) 720

Reg. § 1.954-1(d)(7)

49,222 Income from Sources Without the United States
See p. 20,601 for regulations not amended to reflect law changes

(25) Adjusted net full inclusion foreign base company income excluded from subpart F income under paragraph (d)(6) of this section (zero, or line (10) reduced by line (19) if line (24) is greater than line (23)) 30

(26) Adjusted net foreign base company income after application of paragraph (d)(6) of this section (line (20) reduced by line (25)) 0

Step 9—Additions to or reduction of subpart F income by reason of section 952(c):

(27) Earnings and profits for the current year 350

(28) Amount subject to being recharacterized as subpart F income under section 952(c)(2) (excess of line (27) over the sum of line (21) and line (26)); if there is a deficit, then the limitation of 952(c)(1) may apply for the current year 350

(29) Amount of reduction in subpart F income for prior taxable years by reason of the limitation of section 952(c)(1) 600

(30) Subpart F income as defined in section 952(a), assuming section 952(a)(3), (4), and (5) do not apply (the sum of line (21) and line (26) plus the lesser of line (28) or line (29)) ... 350

(31) Amount of prior years' deficit remaining to be recharacterized as subpart F income in later years under section 952(c) (excess of line (29) over line (28)).................... 250

(e) *Character of income*—(1) *Substance of the transaction.* For purposes of section 954, income shall be characterized in accordance with the substance of the transaction, and not in accordance with the designation applied by the parties to the transaction. For example, an amount that is designated as rent by the taxpayer but actually constitutes income from the sale of property, royalties, or income from services shall not be characterized as rent but shall be characterized as income from the sale of property, royalties or income from services, as the case may be. Local law shall not be controlling in characterizing income.

(2) *Separable character.* To the extent the definitional provisions of section 953 or 954 describe the income or gain derived from a transaction, or any portion or portions thereof, that income or gain, or portion or portions thereof, is so characterized for purposes of subpart F. Thus, a single transaction may give rise to income in more than one category of foreign base company income described in paragraph (a)(2) of this section. For example, if a controlled foreign corporation, in its business of purchasing personal property and selling it to related persons outside its country of incorporation, also performs services outside its country of incorporation with respect to the property it sells, the sales income will be treated as foreign base company sales income and the services income will be treated as foreign base company services income for purposes of these rules.

(3) *Predominant character.* The portion of income or gain derived from a transaction that is included in the computation of foreign personal holding company income is always separately determinable and thus must always be segregated from other income and separately classified under paragraph (e)(2) of this section. However, the portion of income or gain derived from a transaction that would meet a particular definitional provision under section 954 or 953 (other than the definition of foreign personal holding company income) in unusual circumstances may not be separately determinable. If such portion is not separately determinable, it must be classified in accordance with the predominant character of the transaction. For example, if a controlled foreign corporation engineers, fabricates, and installs a fixed offshore drilling platform as part of an integrated transaction, and the portion of income that relates to services is not accounted for separately from the portion that relates to sales, and is otherwise not separately determinable, then the classification of income from the transaction shall be made in accordance with the predominant character of the arrangement.

(4) *Coordination of categories of gross foreign base company income or gross insurance income*—(i) *In general.* The computations of gross foreign base company income and gross insurance income are limited by the following rules:

(A) If income is foreign base company shipping income, pursuant to section 954(f), it shall not be considered insurance income or income in any other category of foreign base company income.

(B) If income is foreign base company oil related income, pursuant to section 954(g), it shall not be considered insurance income or income in any other category of foreign base company income, except as provided in paragraph (e)(4)(i)(A) of this section.

(C) If income is insurance income, pursuant to section 953, it shall not be considered income in any category of foreign base company income except as provided in paragraph (e)(4)(i)(A) or (B) of this section.

(D) If income is foreign personal holding company income, pursuant to section 954(c), it shall not be considered income in any other category of foreign base company income, other than as provided in paragraph (e)(4)(i)(A), (B) or (C) of this section.

Reg. § 1.954-1(e)(1)

Income from Sources Without the United States

(ii) *Income excluded from other categories of gross foreign base company income.* Income shall not be excluded from a category of gross foreign base company income or gross insurance income under this paragraph (e)(4) by reason of being included in another category of gross foreign base company income or gross insurance income, if the income is excluded from that other category by a more specific provision of section 953 or 954. For example, income derived from a commodity transaction that is excluded from foreign personal holding company income under § 1.954-2(f) as income from a qualified active sale may be included in gross foreign base company income if it also meets the definition of foreign base company sales income. See § 1.954-2(a)(2) for the coordination of overlapping categories within the definition of foreign personal holding company income.

(f) *Definition of related person*—(1) *Persons related to controlled foreign corporation.* Unless otherwise provided, for purposes of section 954 and § § 1.954-1 through 1.954-8 inclusive, the following persons are considered under section 954(d)(3) to be related persons with respect to a controlled foreign corporation:

(i) *Individuals.* An individual, whether or not a citizen or resident of the United States, who controls the controlled foreign corporation.

(ii) *Other persons.* A foreign or domestic corporation, partnership, trust or estate that controls or is controlled by the controlled foreign corporation, or is controlled by the same person or persons that control the controlled foreign corporation.

(2) *Control*—(i) *Corporations.* With respect to a corporation, control means the ownership, directly or indirectly, of stock possessing more than 50 percent of the total voting power of all classes of stock entitled to vote or of the total value of the stock of the corporation.

(ii) *Partnerships.* With respect to a partnership, control means the ownership, directly or indirectly, of more than 50 percent (by value) of the capital or profits interest in the partnership.

(iii) *Trusts and estates.* With respect to a trust or estate, control means the ownership, directly, or indirectly, of more than 50 percent (by value) of the beneficial interest in the trust or estate.

(iv) *Direct or indirect ownership.* For purposes of this paragraph (f), to determine direct or indirect ownership, the principles of section 958 shall be applied without regard to whether a corporation, partnership, trust or estate is foreign or domestic or whether or not an individual is a citizen or resident of the United States. [Reg. § 1.954-1.]

☐ [T.D. 8618, 9-6-95. Amended by T.D. 8704, 12-31-96; T.D. 8767, 3-23-98 and T.D. 8827, 7-12-99.]

[Reg § 4.954-1]

§ 4.954-1. Foreign base company income; taxable years beginning after December 31, 1986.—(a) *In general*—(1) *Purpose and scope.* Section 954(b) through (g) and § § 1.954-1T and 1.954-2T provide rules for computing the foreign base company income of a controlled foreign corporation. Foreign base company income is included in the subpart F income of a controlled foreign corporation under the rules of section 952 and the regulations thereunder. Subpart F income is included in the gross income of a United States shareholder of a controlled foreign corporation under the rules of section 951 and the regulations thereunder, and thus is subject to current taxation under section 1 or 11 of the Code. The determination of whether a foreign corporation is a controlled foreign corporation, the subpart F income of which is included currently in the gross income of its United States shareholders, is made under the rules of section 957 and the regulations thereunder.

(2) *Gross foreign base company income.* For taxable years of a controlled foreign corporation beginning after December 31, 1986, the gross foreign base company income of a controlled foreign corporation consists of the following categories of gross income:

(i) Its foreign personal holding company income, as defined in section 954(c) and § 1.954-2T,

(ii) Its foreign base company sales income, as defined in section 954(d) and the regulations thereunder,

(iii) Its foreign base company services income, as defined in section 954(e) and the regulations thereunder,

(iv) Its foreign base company shipping income, as defined in section 954(f) and the regulations thereunder, and

(v) Its foreign base company oil related income, as defined in section 954(g) and the regulations thereunder.

(3) *Adjusted gross foreign base company income.* The term "adjusted gross foreign base company income" means the gross foreign base company income of a controlled foreign corporation as adjusted by the de minimis and full inclusion rules of paragraph (b) of this section.

(4) *Net foreign base company income.* The term "net foreign base company income" means the adjusted gross foreign base company income of a controlled foreign corporation reduced so as to

Reg. § 4.954-1(a)(4)

take account of deductions properly allocable to such income under the rules of section 954(b)(5) and paragraph (c) of this section. In computing net foreign base company income, foreign personal holding company income is reduced (but not below zero) by related person interest expense before allocating and apportioning other expenses in accordance with the rules of paragraph (c) of this section and § 1.904(d)-5(c)(2).

(5) *Adjusted net foreign base company income.* The term "adjusted net foreign base company income" means the net foreign base company income of a controlled foreign corporation reduced by any items of net foreign base company income for which the high tax exception of paragraph (d) is elected. The term "foreign base company income" as used in the Code and elsewhere in the regulations generally means adjusted net foreign base company income.

(6) *Insurance income definitions.* The term "gross insurance income" includes any item of gross income taken into account in determining insurance income under section 953 and the regulations thereunder. The term "adjusted gross insurance income" means gross insurance income as adjusted by the de minimis and full inclusion rules of paragraph (b). The term "net insurance income" means adjusted gross insurance income reduced under section 953 and the regulations thereunder so as to take into account deductions properly allocable or apportionable to such income. The term "adjusted net insurance income" means net insurance income reduced by any items of net insurance income for which the high tax exception of paragraph (d) is elected.

(7) *Additional items of adjusted net foreign base company income or adjusted net insurance income by reason of section 952(c).* Earnings and profits of the controlled foreign corporation that are recharacterized as foreign base company income or insurance income under section 952(c) are items of adjusted net foreign base company income or adjusted net insurance income. Thus, they are not included in the gross foreign base company income or gross insurance income of the controlled foreign corporation in computing adjusted gross foreign base company income or adjusted gross insurance income (for purposes of applying the de minimis and full inclusion tests of paragraph (b) of this section).

(8) *Illustration.* The order of computation is illustrated by the following example. Computations in this paragraph (a)(8) and in paragraph (b)(5) of this section involving the operation of section 952(c) are included for purposes of illustration only and do not provide substantive rules concerning the operation of that section.

Example. (i) *Gross income.* CFC, a controlled foreign corporation, has gross income of $1000 for the current taxable year. Of that $1000 of income, $100 is interest income that is included in the definition of foreign personal holding company income under section 954(c)(1)(A) and § 1.954-2T(b)(1)(ii), is not income from a trade or service receivable described in section 864(d)(1) or (6), and is not excluded from foreign personal holding company income under any provision of section 954(c) and § 1.954-2T. Another $50 is foreign base company sales income under section 954(d) and the regulations thereunder. The remaining $850 of gross income is not included in the definition of foreign base company income or insurance income under sections 954(c), (d), (e), (f), (g), or 953 and the regulations thereunder, and is foreign source general limitation income described in section 904(d)(1)(I) and the regulations thereunder.

(ii) *Expenses.* CFC has expenses for the current taxable year of $500. Of that $500, $8 is from interest paid to a related person and is allocable to foreign personal holding company income along with $2 of other expense. Another $20 of expense is allocable to foreign base company sales. The remaining $470 of expense is allocable to income other than foreign base company income or insurance income.

(iii) *Earnings and deficits.* CFC has earnings and profits for the current taxable year of $500. In the prior taxable year, CFC had losses with respect to income other than gross foreign base company income or gross insurance income. By reason of the limitation provided under section 952(c)(1)(A) and the regulations thereunder, those losses reduced the subpart F income (consisting entirely of foreign source general limitation income) of CFC by $600 for the prior taxable year.

(iv) *Taxes.* Foreign tax of $30 is considered imposed on the interest income under the rules of section 954(b)(4) and paragraph (d) of this section. Foreign tax of $14 is considered imposed on the foreign base company sales income under the rules of section 954(b)(4) and paragraph (d) of this section. Foreign tax of $177 is considered imposed on the remaining foreign source general limitation income under the rules of section 954(b)(4) and paragraph (d) of this section. For the taxable year of the foreign corporation, the maximum U.S. rate of taxation under section 11 is 34 percent.

(v) *Conclusion.* Based on these facts, if CFC elects to exclude all items of income subject to a high foreign tax under section 954(b)(4) and paragraph (d), it will have $500 of subpart F income as defined in section 952(a) (consisting entirely of

Reg. § 4.954-1(a)(5)

Income from Sources Without the United States 49,225
See p. 20,601 for regulations not amended to reflect law changes

foreign source general limitation income) determined as follows. The following steps do not illustrate the computation of the subpart F income of a controlled foreign corporation that has income from a trade or service receivable treated as interest under section 864(d)(1) or interest described in section 864(d)(6).

Step 1—Determine gross income:

    (1) Gross income $1000

Step 2—Determine gross foreign base company income and gross insurance income:

    (2) Interest income included in foreign personal holding company income under section 954(c) 100

    (3) Foreign base company sales income under section 954(d) 50

    (4) Total gross foreign base company income gross insurance income as defined in sections 954(c), (d), (e), (f) and (g) and 953 and the regulations thereunder (line (3) plus line (4)) . 150

Step 3—Determine adjusted gross foreign base company income and adjusted gross insurance income:

    (5) Five percent of gross income (.05 × line (1)) 50

    (6) Seventy percent of gross income (.70 × line (1)) 700

    (7) Adjusted gross foreign base company income and adjusted gross insurance income after the application of the de minimis test of paragraph (b) (line (4), or zero if line (4) is less than the lesser of line (5) or $1,000,000) 150

    (8) Adjusted gross foreign base company income and adjusted gross insurance income after the application of the full inclusion test of paragraph (b) (line (4), or line (1) if line (4) is greater than line (6)) 150

Step 4—Compute net foreign base company income:

    (9) Related person interest expense and other expense allocable and apportionable to foreign personal holding company income 10

    (10) Deductions allocable and apportionable to foreign base company sales income . 20

    (11) Foreign personal holding company income after allocating deductions under section 954(b)(5) and paragraph (c) of this section (the lesser of line (2) or line (7), reduced (but not below zero) by line (9)) 90

    (12) Foreign base company sales income after allocating deductions under section 954(b)(5) and paragraph (c) of this section (the lesser of line (3) or line (7), reduced (but not below zero) by line (10)) 30

    (13) Total net foreign base company income after allocating deductions under section 954(b)(5) and paragraph (c) (line (11) plus line (12)) 120

Step 5—Compute net insurance income:

    (14) Net insurance income under section 953 and the regulations thereunder 0

Step 6—Compute adjusted net foreign base company income:

    (15) Foreign tax imposed on foreign personal holding company income (as determined under paragraph (d)) 30

    (16) Foreign tax imposed on foreign base company sales income (as determined under paragraph (d)) 14

    (17) Ninety percent of the maximum U.S. corporate tax rate 30.6

    (18) Effective rate of foreign tax imposed on foreign personal holding company income (interest) under section 954(b)(4) and paragraph (d) (line (15) divided by line (11)) . . 33

    (19) Effective rate of foreign tax imposed on $40 of foreign base company sales income under section 954(b)(4) and paragraph (d) (line (16) divided by line (12)) 47

    (20) Foreign personal holding company income subject to a high foreign tax under section 954(b)(4) and paragraph (d) (zero, or line (11) if line (18) is greater than line (17)) 90

    (21) Foreign base company sales income subject to a high foreign tax under section 954(b)(4) and paragraph (d) (zero, or line (12) if line (19) is greater than line (17)) 30

    (22) Adjusted net foreign base company income after applying section 954(b)(4) and paragraph (d) (line (13), reduced by the sum of line (20) and line (21)) 0

Step 7—Compute adjusted net insurance income:

    (23) Adjusted net insurance income . . 0

Step 8—Additions to or reduction of adjusted net foreign base company income by reason of section 952(c):

    (24) Earnings and profits for the current year 500

    (25) The excess in earnings and profits over subpart F income subject to being recharacterized as adjusted net foreign base company income under section 952(c)(2) (excess of line (24) over the sum of lines (22) and (23); if there is a deficit, then the limitation of section 952(c)(1) may apply for the current year) . . . 500

    (26) Amount of reduction in subpart F income for prior taxable years by reason of the

Reg. § 4.954-1(a)(8)

limitation of section 952(c)(1) and the regulations thereunder............................ 600

(27) Subpart F income as defined in section 952(a), assuming section 952(a)(3), (4), or (5) does not apply (the sum of line (22), line (23), and the lesser of line (25) or line (26)) 500

(b) *Computation of adjusted gross foreign base company income and adjusted gross insurance income*—(1) *De minimis rule, etc.*—(i) *In general.* If the de minimis rule of paragraph (b)(1)(ii) of this section applies, then adjusted gross foreign base company income and adjusted gross insurance income are each equal to zero. If the full inclusion rule of paragraph (b)(1)(iii) applies, then adjusted gross foreign base company income consists of all items of gross income of the controlled foreign corporation other than gross insurance income, and adjusted gross insurance income consists of all items of gross insurance income. Otherwise, the adjusted gross foreign base company income of a controlled foreign corporation consists of the gross foreign base company income of the controlled foreign corporation, and the adjusted gross insurance income of a controlled foreign corporation consists of the gross insurance income of the controlled foreign corporation.

(ii) *Five percent de minimis test*—(A) *In general.* The de minimis rule of this paragraph (b)(1)(ii) applies if the sum of the gross foreign base company income and the gross insurance income of a controlled foreign corporation is less than the lesser of—

(*1*) 5 percent of gross income, or

(*2*) $1,000,000.

Controlled foreign corporations having a functional currency other than the U.S. dollar shall translate the $1,000,000 threshold using the exchange rate provided under section 989(b)(3) and the regulations thereunder for amounts included in income under section 951(a).

(B) *Coordination with section 864(d).* Gross foreign base company income or gross insurance income of a controlled foreign corporation always includes items of income from trade or service receivables described in section 864(d)(1) or (6), even if the de minimis rule of this paragraph (b)(1)(ii) is otherwise applicable. In that case, adjusted gross foreign base company income consists only of the items of income from trade or service receivables described in section 864(d)(1) or (6) that are included in gross foreign base company income, and adjusted gross insurance income consists only of the items of income from trade or service receivables described in section 864(d)(1) or (6) that are included in gross insurance income.

(iii) *Seventy percent full inclusion test.* The full inclusion rule of this paragraph (b)(1)(iii) applies if the sum of the foreign base company income and the gross insurance income for the taxable year exceeds 70 percent of gross income.

(2) *Character of items of gross income included in adjusted gross foreign base company income.* The items of gross income included in the adjusted gross foreign base company income of a controlled foreign corporation retain their character as foreign personal holding company income, foreign base company sales income, foreign base company services income, foreign base company shipping income, or foreign base company oil related income. Items of gross income included in adjusted gross income because the full inclusion test of paragraph (b)(1)(iii) is met are termed "full inclusion foreign base company income," and constitute a separate category of adjusted gross foreign base company income for purposes of allocating and apportioning deductions under paragraph (c).

(3) *Coordination with section 952(c).* Items of gross foreign base company income or gross insurance income that are excluded from adjusted foreign base company income or adjusted gross insurance income because the de minimis test of paragraph (b)(1)(ii) is met are potentially subject to recharacterization as adjusted net foreign base company income or adjusted net insurance income (or other categories of income included in the computation of subpart F income under section 952 and the regulations thereunder) for the taxable year under the rules of section 952(c). Items of full inclusion foreign base company income that are included in adjusted gross foreign base company income because the full inclusion test of paragraph (b)(1)(iii) is met, and are included in subpart F income under section 952 and the regulations thereunder, do not reduce amounts that, under section 952(c), are subject to recharacterization in later years on account of deficits in prior years.

(4) *Anti-abuse rule*—(i) *In general.* For purposes of applying the de minimis and full inclusion tests of paragraph (b)(1) of this section, the income of two or more controlled foreign corporations shall be aggregated and treated as the income of a single corporation if one principal purpose for separately organizing, acquiring, or maintaining such multiple corporations is to avoid the application of the de minimis or full inclusion requirements of paragraph (b)(1) of this section. For purposes of this paragraph (b), a principal purpose need not be the purpose of first importance.

Reg. § 4.954-1(b)(2)

(ii) *Presumption.* Two or more controlled foreign corporations are presumed to have been organized, acquired or maintained to avoid the effect of the de minimis and full inclusion requirements of paragraph (b)(1) of this section if the corporations are related persons as defined in subdivision (iii) of this paragraph (b)(4) and the corporations are described in subdivision (A), (B), or (C). This presumption may be rebutted by proof to the contrary.

(A) The activities now carried on by the controlled foreign corporations, or the assets used in those activities, are substantially the same activities that were carried on, or assets that were previously held by a single controlled foreign corporation, and the United States shareholders of the controlled foreign corporations or related persons (as determined under subdivision (iii) of this paragraph (b)(4)) are substantially the same as the United States shareholders of the one controlled foreign corporation in that prior taxable year. A presumption made in connection with the requirements of this subdivision (A) of paragraph (b)(4)(ii) may be rebutted by proof that the activities carried on by each controlled foreign corporation would constitute a separate branch under the principles of § 1.367(a)-6T(g) if carried on directly by a United States person.

(B) The controlled foreign corporations carry on a business, financial operation, or venture as partners directly or indirectly in a partnership (as defined in section 7701(a)(2) and § 301.7701-3) that is a related person (as defined in subdivision (iii) of this paragraph (b)(4)) with respect to each such controlled foreign corporation.

(C) The activities carried on by the controlled foreign corporations would constitute a single branch operation under § 1.367(a)-6T(g)(2) if carried on directly by a United States person.

(iii) *Related persons.* For purposes of this paragraph (b), two or more persons are related persons if they are in a relationship described in section 267(b). In determining for purposes of this paragraph (b) whether two or more corporations are members of the same controlled group under section 267(b)(3), a person is considered to own stock owned directly by such person, stock owned with the application of section 1563(e)(1), and stock owned with the application of section 267(c). In determining for purposes of this paragraph (b) whether a corporation is related to a partnership under section 267(b)(10), a person is considered to own the partnership interest owned directly by such person and the partnership interest owned with the application of section 267(e)(3).

(iv) *Illustration.* The following example illustrates the application of this paragraph (b)(4).

Example. USP is the sole United States shareholder of three controlled foreign corporations: CFC1, CFC2 and CFC3. The three controlled foreign corporations all have the same taxable year. The three controlled foreign corporations are partners in FP, a foreign entity classified as a partnership under section 7701(a)(2) and § 301.7701-3 of the regulations. For their current taxable years, each of the controlled foreign corporations derives all of its income other than foreign base company income from activities conducted through FP, and its foreign base company income from activities conducted both jointly through FP and separately without FP. Based on the facts in the table below, for their current taxable years, the foreign base company income derived by each controlled foreign corporation, including income derived from FP, is less than five percent of the gross income of each controlled foreign corporation and is less than $1,000,000:

	CFC1	CFC2	CFC3
Gross income	$4,000,000	$8,000,000	$12,000,000
Five percent of gross income	200,000	400,000	600,000
Foreign base company income	199,000	398,000	597,000

Thus, without the application of the anti-abuse rule of this subparagraph (5), each controlled foreign corporation would be treated as having no foreign base company income after the application of the de minimis rule of section 954(b)(3)(A) and § 1.954-1T(b)(1).

However, under these facts the requirements of subdivision (i) of this paragraph (b)(4) are presumed to be met. The sum of the foreign base company income of the controlled foreign corporations is $1,194,000. Thus, the amount of adjusted gross foreign base company income will not be less than the amount of gross foreign base company income by reason of the de minimis rule of section 954(b)(3)(A) and this paragraph (b).

(5) *Illustration.* The following example illustrates computations required by sections 952 and 954 and this § 1.954-1T if the full inclusion test of paragraph (b)(1)(iii) is met (see paragraph (a)(8) for an example illustrating computations required if the de minimis test of paragraph (b)(1)(ii) is met):

Example. (i) *Gross income.* CFC, a controlled foreign corporation, has gross income of $1000 for the current taxable year. Of that $1000 of income, $720 is interest income that is included in the

Reg. § 4.954-1(b)(5)

49,228   Income from Sources Without the United States

See p. 20,601 for regulations not amended to reflect law changes

definition of foreign personal holding company income under section 954(c)(1)(A) and § 1.954-2T(b)(ii), is not income from trade or service receivables described in section 864(d)(1) or (6), and is not excluded from foreign personal holding company income under any provision of section 954(c) and § 1.954-2T. The remaining $280 is services income that is not included in the definition of foreign base company income or insurance income under sections 954(c), (d), (e), (f), (g) or 953 and the regulations thereunder, and is foreign source general limitation income for purposes of section 904(d)(1)(I).

(ii) *Expenses.* CFC has expenses for the current taxable year of $650. Of that $650, $350 is from interest paid to related persons that is allocable to foreign personal holding company income along with $50 of other expense. The remaining $250 of expense is allocable to services income other than foreign base company income or insurance income.

(iii) *Earnings and deficits.* CFC has earnings and profits for the current taxable year of $350. In the prior taxable year, CFC had losses with respect to income other than foreign base company income or insurance income. By reason of the limitation provided under section 952(c)(1)(A) and the regulations thereunder, those losses reduced the subpart F income of CFC (consisting entirely of foreign source general limitation income) by $600 for the prior taxable year.

(iv) *Taxes.* A foreign tax of $120 is considered imposed on the $720 of interest income under the rules of section 954(b)(4) and paragraph (d) of this section, and a foreign tax of $2 is considered imposed on the services income under the rules of section 954(b)(4) and paragraph (d) of this section. For the taxable year of the foreign corporation, the maximum U.S. rate of taxation under section 11 is 34 percent.

(v) *Conclusion.* Based on these facts, if CFC elects to exclude all items of income subject to a high foreign tax under section 954(b)(4) and paragraph (d), it will have $350 of subpart F income as defined in section 952(a) determined as follows:

Step 1—Determine gross income:

(1) Gross income $1,000

Step 2—Compute gross foreign base company income and gross insurance income:

(2) Gross foreign base company income and insurance income as defined in sections 954(c), (d), (e), (f), (g) and 953 and the regulations thereunder (interest income).......... 720

Step 3—Compute adjusted gross foreign base company income:

(3) Seventy percent of gross income (.70 × line (1)) 700

(4) Adjusted gross foreign base company income or insurance income after the application of the full inclusion rule of this paragraph (b)(1) (line (2), or line (1) if line (2) is greater than line (3)) 1,000

(5) Full inclusion foreign base company income under paragraph (a)(2)(vi)(line (4) minus line (2)) 280

Step 4—Compute net foreign base company income:

(6) Related person interest expense and other deductions allocable and apportionable to foreign personal holding company income under section 954(b)(5) and paragraph (c) 400

(7) Deductions allocable and apportionable to full inclusion foreign base company income under section 954(b)(5) and paragraph (c) ... 250

(8) Foreign personal holding company income after allocating deductions under section 954(b)(5) and paragraph (c) of this section (line (2) reduced (but not below zero) by line (6)) .. 320

(9) Full inclusion foreign base company income after allocating deductions under section 954(b)(5) and paragraph (c) of this section (line (5) reduced (but not below zero) by line (7)) ... 30

(10) Total gross foreign base company income after allocating deductions under section 954(b)(5) and paragraph (c)(line (8) plus line (9)) 350

Step 5—Compute net insurance income:

(11) Net insurance income under section 953 and the regulations thereunder 0

Step 6—Compute adjusted net foreign base company income:

(12) Foreign tax imposed on foreign personal holding company income (interest) 120

(13) Foreign tax imposed on full inclusion foreign base company income 2

(14) Ninety percent of the maximum U.S. corporate tax rate 30.6

(15) Effective rate of foreign tax imposed on $320 of foreign personal holding company income under section 954(b)(4) and paragraph (d) (line (12) divided by line (8)) ... 38

(16) Effective rate of foreign tax imposed on $30 of full inclusion foreign base company income under section 954(b)(4) and paragraph (d)(line (13) divided by line (9)) 7

(17) Foreign personal holding company income subject to a high foreign tax under section 954(b)(4) and paragraph (d)(zero, or line (8) if line (15) is greater than line (14)) 320

Reg. § 4.954-1(b)(5)

(18) Full inclusion foreign base company income subject to a high foreign tax under section 954(b)(4) and paragraph (d)(zero, or line (9) if line (16) is greater than line (14)) 0

(19) Adjusted net foreign base company income after applying section 954(b)(4) and paragraph (d)(line (10), reduced by the sum of line (17) and line (18)) 30

Step 7—Compute adjusted net insurance income:

(20) Adjusted net insurance income . . 0

Step 8—Additions to or reduction of adjusted net foreign base company income by reason of section 952(c):

(21) Earnings and profits for the current year 350

(22) The excess in earnings and profits over subpart F income, which is subject to being recharacterized as adjusted net foreign base company income under section 952(c)(2) (excess of line (21) over the sum of line (19) and line (20)); if there is a deficit, then the limitation of 952(c)(1) may apply for the current year 320

(23) Amount of reduction in subpart F income for prior taxable years by reason of the limitation of section 952(c)(1) and the regulations thereunder. 600

(24) Subpart F income as defined in section 952(a), assuming section 952(a)(3), (4), or (5) does not apply (the sum of line (19) and line (20) plus the lesser of line (22) or line (23)) . . . 350

(25) Amount of prior years' deficit remaining to be recharacterized as subpart F income in later years under section 952(c) (excess of line (23) over line (22)) 280

(c) *Computation of net foreign base company income*—The net foreign base company income of a controlled foreign corporation is computed by reducing (but not below zero) the amount of gross income in each of the categories of adjusted gross foreign base company income described in paragraph (b)(2) of this section, so as to take into account deductions allocable and apportionable to such income. For purposes of section 954 and this section, expenses must be allocated and apportioned consistent with the allocation and apportionment of expenses for purposes of section 904(d). For purposes of this § 1.954-1T, an item of net foreign base company income must be categorized according to the category of adjusted gross foreign base company income from which it is derived. Thus, an item of net foreign base company income must be categorized as a net item of—

(1) Foreign personal holding company income,

(2) Foreign base company sales income,

(3) Foreign base company services income,

(4) Foreign base company shipping income,

(5) Foreign base company oil related income, or

(6) Full inclusion foreign base company income.

(d) *Computation of adjusted net foreign base company income or adjusted net insurance income*—(1) *Application of high tax exception.* Adjusted net foreign base company income (or adjusted net insurance income) equals the net foreign base company income (or net insurance income) of a controlled foreign corporation, reduced by any item of such income (other than foreign base company oil related income as defined in section 954(g)) subject to the high tax exception provided by section 954(b)(4) and this paragraph (d). An item of income is subject to the high tax exception only if—

(i) It is established that the income was subject to creditable income taxes imposed by a foreign country or countries at an effective rate that is greater than 90 percent of the maximum rate of tax specified in section 11 or 15 for the taxable year of the controlled foreign corporation; and

(ii) An election is made under section 954(b)(4) and paragraph (d)(5) of this section to exclude the income from the computation of subpart F income.

See paragraph (d)(4) of this section for the definition of the term "item of income." For rules concerning the treatment for foreign tax credit purposes of amounts excluded from subpart F under section 954(b)(4), see § 1.904-4(c)(1).

(2) *Effective rate at which taxes are imposed.* For purposes of this paragraph (d), the effective rate at which taxes are imposed on an item of income is—

(i) The amount of income taxes paid or accrued (or deemed paid or accrued) with respect to the item of income, determined under paragraph (d)(3), divided by

(ii) The item of net foreign base company income or net insurance income, determined under paragraph (d)(4) (including the appropriate amount of income taxes referred to in subdivision (i) of this paragraph (d)(2), immediately above).

(3) *Taxes paid or accrued with respect to an item of income*—(i) *Income other than passive foreign personal holding company income.* The amount of income taxes paid or accrued with respect to an item of income (other than an item of foreign personal holding company income that

Reg. § 4.954-1(d)(3)

is passive income) for purposes of section 954(b)(4) and this paragraph (d) is the amount of foreign income taxes that would be deemed paid under section 960 with respect to that item if that item were included in the gross income of a U.S. shareholder under section 951(a)(1)(A). For this purpose, the amounts that would be deemed paid under section 960 shall be determined separately with respect to each controlled foreign corporation and without regard to the limitation applicable under § 904(a).

(ii) *Passive foreign personal holding company income.* The amount of income taxes paid or accrued with respect to an item of foreign personal holding company income that is passive income for purposes of section 954(b)(4) and this paragraph (d) is the amount of foreign income taxes paid or accrued or deemed paid by the foreign corporation that would be taken into account for purposes of applying the provisions of § 1.904-4(c) with respect to that item of income.

(4) *Item of income*—(i) *Income other than passive foreign personal holding company income.* The high tax exception applies (when elected) to all income that constitutes a single item under this paragraph (d)(4). A single item of net foreign base company income or net insurance income is an amount of net foreign base company income (other than foreign personal holding company income that is passive income) or net insurance income that:

(A) Falls within a single category of net foreign base company income, as defined in paragraph (c) of this section, or net insurance income, and

(B) Also falls within a single separate limitation category for purposes of sections 904(d) and 960 and the regulations thereunder.

(ii) *Passive foreign personal holding company income*—(A) *In general.* For purposes of this paragraph (d) a single item of net foreign personal holding company income that is passive income is an amount of such income that falls within a single group of passive income under the grouping rules of § 1.904-4(c)(3), (4) and (5).

(B) *Consistency rule.* An election to exclude income from subpart F must be consistently made with respect to all items of passive foreign personal holding company income eligible to be excluded. Thus, high-taxed passive foreign personal holding company income of a controlled foreign corporation must be excluded in its entirety, or remain subject to subpart F.

(5) *Procedure.* The election provided by this paragraph (d) must be made—

(i) By controlling United States shareholders, as defined in § 1.964-1(c)(5), by attaching a statement to such effect with their original or amended income tax returns, and including any additional information required by subsequent administrative pronouncements, or

(ii) In such other manner as may be prescribed in subsequent administrative pronouncements.

An election made under the procedure provided by this paragraph (d)(5) is binding on all United States shareholders of the controlled foreign corporation.

(6) *Illustrations.* The rules of this paragraph (d) are illustrated by the following examples.

Example (1). (i) *Items of income.* During its 1987 taxable year, controlled foreign corporation CFC receives from outside its country of operation portfolio dividend income of $100 and interest income of $100 (consisting of a gross payment of $150 reduced by a third-country withholding tax of $50). For purposes of illustration, assume that the CFC incurs no expenses. None of the income is taxed in CFC's country of operation. The dividend income was not subject to third-country withholding taxes. The interest income was subject to withholding taxes equal to $50, and is therefore high withholding tax interest for purposes of section 960 (pursuant to the operation of section 904). The dividend income is passive income for purposes of section 960. Accordingly, pursuant to paragraph (d)(4) of this section, CFC has two items of income: (1) $100 of FPHC/passive income (the dividends) and (2) $100 of FPHC/high withholding tax income (the interest). The election under paragraph (d)(5) of this section to exclude high-taxed income from the operation of subpart F is potentially applicable to each such item in its entirety.

(ii) *Effective rates of tax.* No foreign tax would be deemed paid under section 960 with respect to item (1). Therefore, the effective rate of foreign tax is 0, and the item may not be excluded from subpart F under the rules of this paragraph (d). Foreign tax of $50 would be deemed paid under section 960 with respect to item (2). Therefore, the effective rate of foreign tax is 33 percent ($50 of creditable taxes paid, divided by $150, consisting of the item of net foreign base company income ($100) plus creditable taxes paid thereon ($50)). The highest rate of tax specified in section 11 for the 1987 taxable year is 34 percent. Accordingly, item (2) may be excluded from subpart F pursuant to an election under paragraph (d)(5) of this section, since it is subject to foreign tax at an effective rate that is greater than 30.6 percent (90

Reg. § 4.954-1(d)(4)

Income from Sources Without the United States

percent of 34 percent). However, it remains high withholding tax interest when included.

Example (2). The facts are the same as in Example (1), except that CFC's country of operation imposes a tax of $50 with respect to CFC's dividend income. The interest income is still high withholding tax interest. The dividend income is still passive income (without regard to the possible applicability of the high tax exception of section 904(d)(2)). Accordingly, CFC has two items of income for purposes of this paragraph (d): (1) $100 of FPHC/high withholding tax interest income, and (2) $50 of FPHC/passive income (net of the $50 foreign tax). Both items are taxed at an effective rate greater than 31.6 percent. Item 1: foreign tax ($50) divided by sum ($150) of income item ($100) plus creditable tax thereon ($50) equals 33 percent. Item 2: foreign tax ($50) divided by sum ($100) of income item ($50) plus creditable tax thereon ($50) equals 50 percent. Accordingly, an election may be made under paragraph (d)(5) of this section to exclude either, both, or neither of items 1 and 2 from subpart F.

Example (3). The facts are the same as in Example (1), except that the $100 of portfolio dividend income is subject to a third-country withholding tax of $50, and the $150 of interest income is from sources within CFC's country of operation, is subject to a $10 income tax therein, and is not subject to a withholding tax. Although the interest income and the dividend income are both passive income, under paragraph (d)(4)(ii)(A) of this section they constitute separate items of income pursuant to the application of the grouping rules of § 1.904-4(c). Accordingly, CFC has two items of income for purposes of this paragraph (d): (1) $50 (net of tax) of FPHC/non-country of operation/greater than 15 percent withholding tax income; and (2) $140 (net of $10 tax) of FPHC/country of operation income. Item 1 is taxed at an effective rate greater than 30.6 percent, but Item 2 is not. Item 1: foreign tax ($50) divided by sum ($100) of income item ($50) plus creditable tax thereon ($50) equals 50 percent. Item 2: foreign tax ($10) divided by sum ($150) of income item ($140) plus creditable tax thereon ($10) equals 6.67 percent. Therefore, an election may be made under paragraph (d)(5) of this section to exclude Item 1 but not Item 2 from subpart F.

Example (4). The facts are the same as in Example (3), except that the $150 of interest income is subject to an income tax of $50 in CFC's country of operation. Accordingly, CFC has two items of income, as in Example (4), but both items are taxed at an effective rate greater than 30.6 percent. Item 1: foreign tax ($50) divided by sum ($100) of income item ($50) plus creditable tax thereon ($50) equals 50 percent. Item 2: foreign tax ($50) divided by sum ($150) of income item ($100) plus creditable tax thereon ($50) equals 33 percent. Pursuant to the consistency rule of paragraph (d)(4)(ii)(B) of this section, CFC's shareholders must consistently elect or not elect to exclude from subpart F all items of FPHC income that are eligible to be excluded. Therefore, an election may be made to exclude both Item 1 and Item 2 from subpart F, or neither may be excluded.

(e) *Character of an item of income*—(1) *Substance of the transaction.* For purposes of section 954 and the regulations thereunder, items of income shall be characterized in accordance with the substance of the transaction, and not in accordance with the designation applied by the parties to the transaction. For example, an amount received as "rent" which actually constitutes income from the sale of property, royalties, or income from services shall not be characterized as "rent" but shall be characterized as income from the sale of property, royalties or income from services, respectively. Local law shall not be controlling in characterizing an item of income.

(2) *Separable character.* To the extent one of the definitional provisions of section 953 or 954 describes a portion of the income or gain derived from a transaction, that portion of income or gain is so characterized. Thus, a single transaction may give rise to income in more than one category of foreign base company income described in paragraph (a)(2). For example, if a controlled foreign corporation, in its business of purchasing and selling personal property, receives interest (including imputed interest and market discount) on an account receivable arising from a sale, a portion of the income derived from the transaction by the controlled foreign corporation will be interest, and another portion will be gain (or loss) from the sale of personal property. If the sale is denominated in a currency other than a functional currency as defined in section 985 and the regulations thereunder, the controlled foreign corporation may have additional income in the form of foreign currency gain as defined in section 988.

(3) *Predominant character.* The portion of income derived from a transaction that meets the definition of foreign personal holding company income is always separately determinable, and thus must always be segregated from other income and separately classified under subparagraph (2) of this paragraph (e). However, the portion of income derived from a transaction that would meet a particular definitional provision under section 954 or 953 and the regulations

Reg. § 4.954-1(e)(3)

thereunder (other than the definition of foreign personal holding company income) in unusual circumstances may be indeterminable. If such portion is indeterminable, it must be classified in accordance with the predominant character of the transaction. For example, if a controlled foreign corporation engineers, fabricates, and installs a fixed offshore drilling platform as part of an integrated transaction, and the portion of income that relates to services is not accounted for separately from the portion that relates to sales, and is otherwise indeterminable, then the classification of income from the transaction shall be made in accordance with the predominant character of the particular integrated arrangement.

(4) *Coordination of categories of gross foreign base company income or gross insurance income.* The definitions of gross foreign base company income and gross insurance income are limited by the following rules (to be applied in numerical order):

(i) If an item of income is included in subpart F income under section 952(a)(1) and the regulations thereunder as insurance income, it is by definition excluded from any other category of subpart F income.

(ii) If an item of income is included in the foreign base company oil related income of a controlled foreign corporation, it is by definition excluded from any other category of foreign base company income, other than as provided in subdivision (i) of this paragraph (e)(4).

(iii) If an item of income is included in the foreign base company shipping income of a controlled foreign corporation, it is by definition excluded from any other category of foreign base company income, other than as provided in subdivisions (i) and (ii) of this paragraph (e)(4).

(iv) If an item of income is included in foreign personal holding company income of a controlled foreign corporation, it is by definition not included in any other category of foreign base company income, other than as provided in subdivisions (i), (ii), and (iii) of this paragraph (e)(4).

An item of income shall not be excluded from the definition of a category of gross foreign base company income or gross insurance income under this paragraph (e)(4) by reason of being included in the general definition of another category of gross foreign base company income or gross insurance income, if the item of income is excluded from that other category by a more specific provision of section 953 or 954 and the regulations thereunder. For example, income derived from a commodity transaction that is excluded from foreign personal holding company income under § 1.954-2T(f) as income from qualified active sales may be included in gross foreign base company income if it also meets the definition of foreign base company sales income. See § 1.954-2T(a)(2) for the coordination of overlapping categories within the definition of foreign personal holding company income. [Reg. § 4.954-1.]

☐[*T.D.* 8216, 7-20-88. *Redesignated by T.D.* 8618, 9-6-95.]

[§ 1.954-2]

§ 1.954-2. **Foreign personal holding company income.**—(a) *Computation of foreign personal holding company income*—(1) *Categories of foreign personal holding company income.* For purposes of subpart F and the regulations under that subpart, foreign personal holding company income consists of the following categories of income—

(i) Dividends, interest, rents, royalties, and annuities as described in paragraph (b) of this section;

(ii) Gain from certain property transactions as described in paragraph (e) of this section;

(iii) Gain from commodities transactions as described in paragraph (f) of this section;

(iv) Foreign currency gain as described in paragraph (g) of this section; and

(v) Income equivalent to interest as described in paragraph (h) of this section.

(2) *Coordination of overlapping categories under foreign personal holding company provisions*—(i) *In general.* If any portion of income, gain or loss from a transaction is described in more than one category of foreign personal holding company income (as described in paragraph (a)(2)(ii) of this section), that portion of income, gain or loss is treated solely as income, gain or loss from the category of foreign personal holding company income with the highest priority.

(ii) *Priority of categories.* The categories of foreign personal holding company income, listed from highest priority (paragraph (a)(2)(ii)(A) of this section) to lowest priority (paragraph (a)(2)(ii)(E) of this section), are—

(A) Dividends, interest, rents, royalties, and annuities, as described in paragraph (b) of this section;

(B) Income equivalent to interest, as described in paragraph (h) of this section without regard to the exceptions in paragraph (h)(1)(ii)(A) of this section;

(C) Foreign currency gain or loss, as described in paragraph (g) of this section without regard to the exclusion in paragraph (g)(2)(ii) of this section;

(D) Gain or loss from commodities transactions, as described in paragraph (f) of this section without regard to the exclusion in paragraph (f)(1)(ii) of this section; and

(E) Gain or loss from certain property transactions, as described in paragraph (e) of this section without regard to the exceptions in paragraph (e)(1)(ii) of this section.

(3) *Changes in the use or purpose for which property is held*—(i) *In general.* Under paragraphs (e), (f), (g) and (h) of this section, transactions in certain property give rise to gain or loss included in the computation of foreign personal holding company income if the controlled foreign corporation holds that property for a particular use or purpose. The use or purpose for which property is held is that use or purpose for which it was held for more than one-half of the period during which the controlled foreign corporation held the property prior to the disposition.

(ii) *Special rules*—(A) *Anti-abuse rule.* If a principal purpose of a change in use or purpose of property was to avoid including gain or loss in the computation of foreign personal holding company income, all the gain or loss from the disposition of the property is treated as foreign personal holding company income. A purpose may be a principal purpose even though it is outweighed by other purposes (taken together or separately).

(B) *Hedging transactions.* The provisions of paragraph (a)(3)(i) of this section shall not apply to bona fide hedging transactions, as defined in paragraph (a)(4)(ii) of this section. A transaction will be treated as a bona fide hedging transaction only so long as it satisfies the requirements of paragraph (a)(4)(ii) of this section.

(iii) *Example.* The following example illustrates the application of this paragraph (a)(3).

Example. At the beginning of taxable year 1, *CFC*, a controlled foreign corporation, purchases a building for investment. During taxable years 1 and 2, *CFC* derives rents from the building that are included in the computation of foreign personal holding company income under paragraph (b)(1)(iii) of this section. At the beginning of taxable year 3, *CFC* changes the use of the building by terminating all leases and using it in an active trade or business. At the beginning of taxable year 4, *CFC* sells the building at a gain. The building was not used in an active trade or business of *CFC* for more than one-half of the period during which it was held by *CFC*. Therefore, the building is considered to be property that gives rise to rents, as described in paragraph (e)(2) of this section, and gain from the sale is included in the computation of *CFC*'s foreign personal holding company income under paragraph (e) of this section.

(4) *Definitions and special rules.* The following definitions and special rules apply for purposes of computing foreign personal holding company income under this section.

(i) *Interest.* The term *interest* includes all amounts that are treated as interest income (including interest on a tax-exempt obligation) by reason of the Internal Revenue Code or Income Tax Regulations or any other provision of law. For example, interest includes stated interest, acquisition discount, original issue discount, de minimis original issue discount, market discount, de minimis market discount, and unstated interest, as adjusted by any amortizable bond premium or acquisition premium.

(ii) *Bona fide hedging transaction*—(A) *Definition.* The term *bona fide hedging transaction* means a transaction that meets the requirements of § 1.1221-2(a) through (c) and that is identified in accordance with the requirements of paragraph (a)(4)(ii)(B) of this section, except that in applying § 1.1221-2(b)(1), the risk being hedged may be with respect to ordinary property, section 1231 property, or a section 988 transaction. A transaction that hedges the liabilities, inventory or other assets of a related person (as defined in section 954(d)(3)), that is entered into to assume or reduce risks of a related person, or that is entered into by a person other than a person acting in its capacity as a regular dealer (as defined in paragraph (a)(4)(iv) of this section) to reduce risks assumed from a related person, will not be treated as a bona fide hedging transaction. For an illustration of how this rule applies with respect to foreign currency transactions, see paragraph (g)(2)(ii)(D) of this section.

(B) *Identification.* The identification requirements of this section shall be satisfied if the taxpayer meets the identification and recordkeeping requirements of § 1.1221-2(e). However, for bona fide hedging transactions entered into prior to March 7, 1996, the identification and record-keeping requirements of § 1.1221-2 shall not apply. Rather, for bona fide hedging transactions entered into on or after July 22, 1988 and prior to March 7, 1996, the identification and recordkeeping requirements shall be satisfied if such transactions are identified by the close of the fifth day after the day on which they are entered into. For bona fide hedging transactions entered into prior to July 22, 1988, the identification and record-keeping requirements shall be satisfied if such transactions are identified reasonably contemporaneously with the date they are entered into, but no later than within the normal period prescribed

Reg. § 1.954-2(a)(4)

under the method of accounting of the controlled foreign corporation used for financial reporting purposes.

(C) *Effect of identification and non-identification*—(*1*) *Transactions identified.* If a taxpayer identifies a transaction as a bona fide hedging transaction for purposes of this section, the identification is binding with respect to any loss arising from such transaction whether or not all of the requirements of paragraph (a)(4)(ii)(A) of this section are satisfied. Accordingly, such loss will be allocated against income that is not subpart F income (or, in the case of an election under paragraph (g)(3) of this section, against the category of subpart F income to which it relates) and apportioned among the categories of income described in section 904(d)(1). If the transaction is not in fact a bona fide hedging transaction described in paragraph (a)(4)(ii)(A) of this section, however, then any gain realized with respect to such transaction shall not be considered as gain from a bona fide hedging transaction. Accordingly, such gain shall be treated as gain from the appropriate category of foreign personal holding company income. Thus, the taxpayer's identification of the transaction as a hedging transaction does not itself operate to exclude gain from the appropriate category of foreign personal holding company income.

(*2*) *Inadvertent identification.* Notwithstanding paragraph (a)(4)(ii)(C)(*1*) of this section, if the taxpayer identifies a transaction as a bona fide hedging transaction for purposes of this section, the characterization of the loss is determined as if the transaction had not been identified as a bona fide hedging transaction if—

(*i*) The transaction is not a bona fide hedging transaction (as defined in paragraph (a)(4)(ii)(A) of this section);

(*ii*) The identification of the transaction as a bona fide hedging transaction was due to inadvertent error; and

(*iii*) All of the taxpayer's transactions in all open years are being treated on either original or, if necessary, amended returns in a manner consistent with the principles of this section.

(*3*) *Transactions not identified.* Except as provided in paragraphs (a)(4)(ii)(C)(*4*) and (*5*) of this section, the absence of an identification that satisfies the requirements of paragraph (a)(4)(ii)(B) of this section is binding and establishes that a transaction is not a bona fide hedging transaction. Thus, subject to the exceptions, the characterization of gain or loss is determined without reference to whether the transaction is a bona fide hedging transaction.

(*4*) *Inadvertent error.* If a taxpayer does not make an identification that satisfies the requirements of paragraph (a)(4)(ii)(B) of this section, the taxpayer may treat gain or loss from the transaction as gain or loss from a bona fide hedging transaction if—

(*i*) The transaction is a bona fide hedging transaction (as defined in paragraph (a)(4)(ii)(A) of this section);

(*ii*) The failure to identify the transaction was due to inadvertent error; and

(*iii*) All of the taxpayer's bona fide hedging transactions in all open years are being treated on either original or, if necessary, amended returns as bona fide hedging transactions in accordance with the rules of this section.

(*5*) *Anti-abuse rule.* If a taxpayer does not make an identification that satisfies all the requirements of paragraph (a)(4)(ii)(B) of this section but the taxpayer has no reasonable grounds for treating the transaction as other than a bona fide hedging transaction, then loss from the transaction shall be treated as realized with respect to a bona fide hedging transaction. Thus, a taxpayer may not elect to exclude loss from its proper characterization as a bona fide hedging transaction. The reasonableness of the taxpayer's failure to identify a transaction is determined by taking into consideration not only the requirements of paragraph (a)(4)(ii)(A) of this section but also the taxpayer's treatment of the transaction for financial accounting or other purposes and the taxpayer's identification of similar transactions as hedging transactions.

(iii) *Inventory and similar property*—(A) *Definition.* The term *inventory and similar property* (or *inventory or similar property*) means property that is stock in trade of the controlled foreign corporation or other property of a kind that would properly be included in the inventory of the controlled foreign corporation if on hand at the close of the taxable year (if the controlled foreign corporation were a domestic corporation), or property held by the controlled foreign corporation primarily for sale to customers in the ordinary course of its trade or business.

(B) *Hedging transactions.* A bona fide hedging transaction with respect to inventory or similar property (other than a transaction described in section 988(c)(1) without regard to section 988(c)(1)(D)(i)) shall be treated as a transaction in inventory or similar property.

(iv) *Regular dealer.* The term *regular dealer* means a controlled foreign corporation that—

Reg. § 1.954-2(a)(4)

Income from Sources Without the United States

(A) Regularly and actively offers to, and in fact does, purchase property from and sell property to customers who are not related persons (as defined in section 954(d)(3)) with respect to the controlled foreign corporation in the ordinary course of a trade or business; or

(B) Regularly and actively offers to, and in fact does, enter into, assume, offset, assign or otherwise terminate positions in property with customers who are not related persons (as defined in section 954(d)(3)) with respect to the controlled foreign corporation in the ordinary course of a trade or business.

(v) *Dealer property*—(A) *Definition.* Property held by a controlled foreign corporation is *dealer property* if—

(*1*) The controlled foreign corporation is a regular dealer in property of such kind (determined under paragraph (a)(4)(iv) of this section); and

(*2*) The property is held by the controlled foreign corporation in its capacity as a dealer in property of such kind without regard to whether the property arises from a transaction with a related person (as defined in section 954(d)(3)) with respect to the controlled foreign corporation. The property is not held by the controlled foreign corporation in its capacity as a dealer if the property is held for investment or speculation on its own behalf or on behalf of a related person (as defined in section 954(d)(3)).

(B) *Securities dealers.* If a controlled foreign corporation is a licensed securities dealer, only the securities that it has identified as held for investment in accordance with the provisions of section 475(b) or section 1236 will be considered to be property held for investment or speculation under this section. A licensed securities dealer is a controlled foreign corporation that is both a securities dealer, as defined in section 475, and a regular dealer, as defined in paragraph (a)(4)(iv) of this section, and that is either—

(*1*) registered as a securities dealer under section 15(a) of the Securities Exchange Act of 1934 or as a Government securities dealer under section 15C(a) of such Act; or

(*2*) licensed or authorized in the country in which it is chartered, incorporated, or organized to purchase and sell securities from or to customers who are residents of that country. The conduct of such securities activities must be subject to bona fide regulation, including appropriate reporting, monitoring, and prudential (including capital adequacy) requirements, by a securities regulatory authority in that country that regularly enforces compliance with such requirements and prudential standards.

(C) *Hedging transactions.* A bona fide hedging transaction with respect to dealer property shall be treated as a transaction in dealer property.

(vi) *Examples.* The following examples illustrate the application of paragraphs (a)(4)(ii), (iv) and (v) of this section.

Example 1. (i) *CFC1* and *CFC2* are related controlled foreign corporations (within the meaning of section 954(d)(3)) located in Countries F and G, respectively. *CFC1* and *CFC2* regularly purchase securities from and sell securities to customers who are not related persons with respect to *CFC1* or *CFC2* (within the meaning of section 954(d)(3)) in the ordinary course of their businesses and regularly and actively hold themselves out as being willing to, and in fact do, enter into either side of options, forward contracts, or other financial instruments. *CFC1* uses securities that are traded in securities markets in Country G to hedge positions that it enters into with customers located in Country F. *CFC1* is not a member of a securities exchange in Country G, so it purchases such securities from *CFC2* and unrelated persons that are registered as securities dealers in Country G and that are members of Country G securities exchanges. Such hedging transactions qualify as bona fide hedging transactions under paragraph (a)(4)(ii) of this section.

(ii) Transactions that *CFC1* and *CFC2* enter into with each other do not affect the determination of whether they are regular dealers. Because *CFC1* and *CFC2* regularly purchase securities from and sell securities to customers who are not related persons within the meaning of section 954(d)(3) in the ordinary course of their businesses and regularly and actively hold themselves out as being willing to, and in fact do, enter into either side of options, forward contracts, or other financial instruments, however, they qualify as regular dealers in such property within the meaning of paragraph (a)(4)(iv) of this section. Moreover, because *CFC1* purchases securities from *CFC2* as bona fide hedging transactions with respect to dealer property, the securities are dealer property under paragraph (a)(4)(v)(C) of this section. Similarly, because *CFC2* sells securities to *CFC1* in the ordinary course of its business as a dealer, the securities are dealer property under paragraph (a)(4)(v)(A) of this section.

Example 2. (i) *CFC* is a controlled foreign corporation located in Country B. *CFC* serves as the currency coordination center for the controlled group, aggregating currency risks incurred by the group and entering into hedging transactions that transfer those risks outside of the group. *CFC* regularly and actively holds itself out as being

Reg. § 1.954-2(a)(4)

willing to, and in fact does, enter into either side of options, forward contracts, or other financial instruments with other members of the same controlled group. CFC hedges risks arising from such transactions by entering into transactions with persons who are not related persons (within the meaning of section 954(d)(3)) with respect to CFC. However, CFC does not regularly and actively hold itself out as being willing to, and does not, enter into either side of transactions with unrelated persons.

(ii) CFC is not a regular dealer in property under paragraph (a)(4)(iv) of this section and its options, forwards, and other financial instruments are not dealer property within the meaning of paragraph (a)(4)(v) of this section.

(vii) *Debt instrument.* The term *debt instrument* includes bonds, debentures, notes, certificates, accounts receivable, and other evidences of indebtedness.

(b) *Dividends, interest, rents, royalties, and annuities*—(1) *In general.* Foreign personal holding company income includes—

(i) Dividends, except certain dividends from related persons as described in paragraph (b)(4) of this section and distributions of previously taxed income under section 959(b);

(ii) Interest, except export financing interest as defined in paragraph (b)(2) of this section and certain interest received from related persons as described in paragraph (b)(4) of this section;

(iii) Rents and royalties, except certain rents and royalties received from related persons as described in paragraph (b)(5) of this section and rents and royalties derived in the active conduct of a trade or business as defined in paragraph (b)(6) of this section; and

(iv) Annuities.

(2) *Exclusion of certain export financing interest*—(i) *In general.* Foreign personal holding company income does not include interest that is export financing interest. The term *export financing interest* means interest that is derived in the conduct of a banking business and is export financing interest as defined in section 904(d)(2)(G). Solely for purposes of determining whether interest is export financing interest, property is treated as manufactured, produced, grown, or extracted in the United States if it is so treated under § 1.927(a)-1T(c).

(ii) *Exceptions.* Export financing interest does not include income from related party factoring that is treated as interest under section 864(d)(1) or (6) after the application of section 864(d)(7).

(iii) *Conduct of a banking business.* For purposes of this section, export financing interest is considered derived in the conduct of a banking business if, in connection with the financing from which the interest is derived, the corporation, through its own officers or staff of employees, engages in all the activities in which banks customarily engage in issuing and servicing a loan.

(iv) *Examples.* The following examples illustrate the application of this paragraph (b)(2).

Example 1. (i) *DS*, a domestic corporation, manufactures property in the United States. In addition to selling inventory (property described in section 1221(1)), *DS* occasionally sells depreciable equipment it manufactures for use in its trade or business, which is property described in section 1221(2). Less than 50 percent of the fair market value, determined in accordance with section 904(d)(2)(G), of each item of inventory or equipment sold by *DS* is attributable to products imported into the United States. *CFC*, a controlled foreign corporation with respect to which *DS* is a related person (within the meaning of section 954(d)(3)), provides loans described in section 864(d)(6) to unrelated persons for the purchase of property from *DS*. This property is purchased exclusively for use or consumption outside the United States and outside *CFC*'s country of incorporation.

(ii) If, in issuing and servicing loans made with respect to purchases from *DS* of depreciable equipment used in its trade or business, which is property described in section 1221(2) in the hands of *DS*, *CFC* engages in all the activities in which banks customarily engage in issuing and servicing loans, the interest accrued from these loans would be export financing interest meeting the requirements of this paragraph (b)(2) and, thus, not included in foreign personal holding company income. However, interest from the loans made with respect to purchases from *DS* of property that is inventory in the hands of *DS* cannot be export financing interest because it is treated as income from a trade or service receivable under section 864(d)(6) and the exception under section 864(d)(7) does not apply. Thus the interest from loans made with respect to this inventory is included in foreign personal holding company income under paragraph (b)(1)(ii) of this section.

Example 2. (i) *DS*, a domestic corporation manufactures property in the United States. *DS* wholly owns two controlled foreign corporations organized in Country A, *CFC1* and *CFC2*. *CFC1* has a substantial part of its assets used in its trade or business in Country A. *CFC1* purchases the property that *DS* manufactures and sells it without further manufacture for use or consump-

Reg. § 1.954-2(b)(1)

tion within Country A. This property is inventory property, as described in section 1221(1), in the hands of *CFC1*. Less than 50 percent of the fair market value, determined in accordance with section 904(d)(2)(G), of each item of inventory sold by *CFC1* is attributable to products imported into the United States. *CFC2* provides loans described in section 864(d)(6) to unrelated persons in Country A for the purchase of the property from *CFC1*.

(ii) If, in issuing and servicing loans made with respect to purchases from *CFC1* of the inventory property, *CFC2* engages in all the activities in which banks customarily engage in issuing and servicing loans, the interest accrued from these loans would be export financing interest meeting the requirements of paragraph (b)(2) of this section. It is not treated as income from a trade or service receivable under section 864(d)(6) because the exception under section 864(d)(7) applies. Thus the interest is excluded from foreign personal holding company income.

Example 3. The facts are the same as in *Example 2* except that the property sold by *CFC1* is manufactured by *CFC1* in Country A from component parts that were manufactured by *DS* in the United States. The interest accrued from the loans by *CFC2* is not export financing interest as defined in section 904(d)(2)(G) because the property is not manufactured in the United States under § 1.927(a)-1T(c). No portion of the interest is export financing interest as defined in this paragraph (b)(2). The full amount of the interest is, therefore, included in foreign personal holding company income under paragraph (b)(1)(ii) of this section.

(3) *Treatment of tax exempt interest.* For taxable years of a controlled foreign corporation beginning after March 3, 1997, foreign personal holding company income includes all interest income, including interest that is described in section 103 (see § 1.952-2(c)(1)).

(4) *Exclusion of dividends or interest from related persons*—(i) *In general*—(A) *Corporate payor.* Foreign personal holding company income received by a controlled foreign corporation does not include dividends or interest if the payor—

(*1*) Is a corporation that is a related person with respect to the controlled foreign corporation, as defined in section 954(d)(3);

(*2*) Is created or organized under the laws of the same foreign country (the *country of incorporation*) as is the controlled foreign corporation; and

(*3*) Uses a substantial part of its assets in a trade or business in its country of incorporation, as determined under this paragraph (b)(4).

(B) *Payment by a partnership.* For purposes of this paragraph (b)(4), if a partnership with one or more corporate partners makes a payment of interest, a corporate partner will be treated as the payor of the interest—

(*1*) If the interest payment gives rise to a partnership item of deduction under the Internal Revenue Code or Income Tax Regulations, to the extent that the item of deduction is allocable to the corporate partner under section 704(b); or

(*2*) If the interest payment does not give rise to a partnership item of deduction under the Internal Revenue Code or Income Tax Regulations, to the extent that a partnership item reasonably related to the payment would be allocated to that partner under an existing allocation under the partnership agreement (made pursuant to section 704(b)).

(ii) *Exceptions*—(A) *Dividends.* Dividends are excluded from foreign personal holding company income under this paragraph (b)(4) only to the extent that they are paid out of earnings and profits that are earned or accumulated during a period in which—

(*1*) The stock on which dividends are paid with respect to which the exclusion is claimed was owned by the recipient controlled foreign corporation directly, or indirectly through a chain of one or more subsidiaries each of which meets the requirements of paragraph (b)(4)(i)(A) of this section; and

(*2*) Each of the requirements of paragraph (b)(4)(i)(A) of this section is satisfied or, to the extent earned or accumulated during a taxable year of the related foreign corporation ending on or before December 31, 1962, during a period in which the payor was a related corporation as to the controlled foreign corporation and the other requirements of paragraph (b)(4)(i)(A) of this section were substantially satisfied.

(*3*) This paragraph (b)(4)(ii)(A) is illustrated by the following example:

Example. A, a domestic corporation, owns all of the stock of B, a corporation created and organized under the laws of Country Y, and C, a corporation created and organized under the laws of Country X. The taxable year of each of the corporations is the calendar year. In Year 1, B earns $100 of income from the sale of products in Country Y that it manufactured in Country Y. C had no earnings and profits in Year 1. On January 1 of Year 2, A contributes all of the stock of B and C to Newco, a Country Y corporation, in exchange for all of the stock of Newco. Neither B nor C earns any income in Year 2, but at the end of Year 2 B distributes the $100 accumulated earn-

Reg. § 1.954-2(b)(4)

ings and profits to Newco. Newco's income from the distribution, $100, is foreign personal holding company income because the earnings and profits distributed by B were not earned or accumulated during a period in which the stock of B was owned by Newco and in which each of the requirements of paragraph (b)(4)(i)(A) of this section was satisfied.

(B) *Interest paid out of adjusted foreign base company income or insurance income*—(*1*) *In general.* Interest may not be excluded from the foreign personal holding company income of the recipient under this paragraph (b)(4) to the extent that the deduction for the interest is allocated under § 1.954-1(a)(4) and (c) to the payor's adjusted gross foreign base company income (as defined in § 1.954-1(a)(3)), adjusted gross insurance income (as defined in § 1.954-1(a)(6)), or any other category of income included in the computation of subpart F income under section 952(a).

(*2*) *Rule for corporations that are both recipients and payors of interest.* If a controlled foreign corporation is both a recipient and payor of interest, the interest that is received will be characterized before the interest that is paid. In addition, the amount of interest paid or accrued, directly or indirectly, by the controlled foreign corporation to a related person (as defined in section 954(d)(3)) shall be offset against and eliminate any interest received or accrued, directly or indirectly, by the controlled foreign corporation from that related person. In a case in which the controlled foreign corporation pays or accrues interest to a related person, as defined in section 954(d)(3), and also receives or accrues interest indirectly from the related person, the smallest interest payment is eliminated and the amounts of all other interest payments are reduced by the amount of the smallest interest payment.

(C) *Coordination with sections 864(d) and 881(c).* Income of a controlled foreign corporation that is treated as interest under section 864(d)(1) or (6), or that is portfolio interest, as defined by section 881(c), is not excluded from foreign personal holding company income under section 954(c)(3)(A)(i) and this paragraph (b)(4).

(iii) *Trade or business requirement.* Except as otherwise provided under this paragraph (b)(4), the principles of section 367(a) apply for purposes of determining whether the payor has a trade or business in its country of incorporation and whether its assets are used in that trade or business. Property purchased or produced for use in a trade or business is not considered used in a trade or business before it is placed in service or after it is retired from service as determined in accordance with the principles of sections 167 and 168.

(iv) *Substantial assets test.* A substantial part of the assets of the payor will be considered to be used in a trade or business located in the payor's country of incorporation for a taxable year only if the average value of the payor's assets for such year that are used in the trade or business and are located in such country equals more than 50 percent of the average value of all the assets of the payor (including assets not used in a trade or business). The average value of assets for the taxable year is determined by averaging the values of assets at the close of each quarter of the taxable year. The value of assets is determined under paragraph (b)(4)(v) of this section, and the location of assets used in a trade or business of the payor is determined under paragraphs (b)(4)(vi) through (xi) of this section.

(v) *Valuation of assets.* For purposes of determining whether a substantial part of the assets of the payor are used in a trade or business in its country of incorporation, the value of assets shall be their fair market value (not reduced by liabilities), which, in the absence of affirmative evidence to the contrary, shall be deemed to be their adjusted basis.

(vi) *Location of tangible property*—(A) *In general.* Tangible property (other than inventory and similar property as defined in paragraph (a)(4)(iii) of this section, and dealer property as defined in paragraph (a)(4)(v) of this section) used in a trade or business is considered located in the country in which it is physically located.

(B) *Exception.* An item of tangible personal property that is used in the trade or business of a payor in the payor's country of incorporation is considered located within the payor's country of incorporation while it is temporarily located elsewhere for inspection or repair if the property is not placed in service in a country other than the payor's country of incorporation and is not to be so placed in service following the inspection or repair.

(vii) *Location of intangible property*—(A) *In general.* Intangible property (other than inventory and similar property as defined in paragraph (a)(4)(iii) of this section, dealer property as defined in paragraph (a)(4)(v) of this section, and debt instruments) is considered located entirely in the payor's country of incorporation for a quarter of the taxable year only if the payor conducts all of its activities in connection with the use or exploitation of the property in that country during that entire quarter. For this purpose, the country in which the activities connected to the use or exploitation of the property are conducted

Reg. § 1.954-2(b)(4)

is the country in which the expenses associated with these activities are incurred. Expenses incurred in connection with the use or exploitation of an item of intangible property are included in the computation provided by this paragraph (b)(4) if they would be deductible under section 162 or includible in inventory costs or the cost of goods sold if the payor were a domestic corporation. If the payor conducts such activities through an agent or independent contractor, then the expenses incurred by the payor with respect to the agent or independent contractor shall be deemed to be incurred by the payor in the country in which the expenses of the agent or independent contractor were incurred by the agent or independent contractor.

(B) *Exception for property located in part in the payor's country of incorporation.* If the payor conducts its activities in connection with the use or exploitation of an item of intangible property, including goodwill (other than inventory and similar property, dealer property and debt instruments) during a quarter of the taxable year both in its country of incorporation and elsewhere, then the value of the intangible considered located in the payor's country of incorporation during that quarter is a percentage of the value of the item as of the close of the quarter. That percentage equals the ratio that the expenses incurred by the payor (described in paragraph (b)(4)(vii)(A) of this section) during the entire quarter by reason of activities that are connected with the use or exploitation of the item of intangible property and are conducted in the payor's country of incorporation bear to all expenses incurred by the payor during the entire quarter by reason of all such activities worldwide.

(viii) *Location of inventory and dealer property*—(A) *In general.* Inventory and similar property, as defined in paragraph (a)(4)(iii) of this section, and dealer property, as defined in paragraph (a)(4)(v) of this section, are considered located entirely in the payor's country of incorporation for a quarter of the taxable year only if the payor conducts all of its activities in connection with the production and sale, or purchase and resale, of such property in its country of incorporation during that entire quarter. If the payor conducts such activities through an agent or independent contractor, then the location of such activities is the place in which they are conducted by the agent or independent contractor.

(B) *Inventory and dealer property located in part in the payor's country of incorporation.* If the payor conducts its activities in connection with the production and sale, or purchase and resale, of inventory or similar property or dealer property during a quarter of the taxable year both in its country of incorporation and elsewhere, then the value of the inventory or similar property or dealer property considered located in the payor's country of incorporation during each quarter is a percentage of the value of the inventory or similar property or dealer property as of the close of the quarter. That percentage equals the ratio that the costs and expenses incurred by the payor during the entire quarter by reason of activities connected with the production and sale, or purchase and resale, of inventory or similar property or dealer property that are conducted in the payor's country of incorporation bear to all costs or expenses incurred by the payor during the entire quarter by reason of all such activities worldwide. A cost incurred in connection with the production and sale or purchase and resale of inventory or similar property or dealer property is included in this computation if it—

(*1*) Would be included in inventory costs or otherwise capitalized with respect to inventory or similar property or dealer property under section 61, 263A, 471, or 472 if the payor were a domestic corporation; or

(*2*) Would be deductible under section 162 if the payor were a domestic corporation and is definitely related to gross income derived from such property (but not to all classes of gross income derived by the payor) under the principles of § 1.861-8.

(ix) *Location of debt instruments.* For purposes of this paragraph (b)(4), debt instruments, other than debt instruments that are inventory or similar property (as defined in paragraph (a)(4)(iii) of this section) or dealer property (as defined in paragraph (a)(4)(v) of this section) are considered to be used in a trade or business only if they arise from the sale of inventory or similar property or dealer property by the payor or from the rendition of services by the payor in the ordinary course of a trade or business of the payor, and only until such time as interest is required to be charged under section 482. Debt instruments that arise from the sale of inventory or similar property or dealer property during a quarter are treated as having the same location, proportionately, as the inventory or similar property or dealer property held during that quarter. Debt instruments arising from the rendition of services in the ordinary course of a trade or business are considered located on a proportionate basis in the countries in which the services to which they relate are performed.

(x) *Treatment of certain stock interests.* Stock in a controlled foreign corporation (lower-tier corporation) that is incorporated in the same

Reg. § 1.954-2(b)(4)

country as the payor and that is more than 50-percent owned, directly or indirectly, by the payor within the meaning of section 958(a) shall be considered located in the payor's country of incorporation and, solely for purposes of section 954(c)(3), used in a trade or business of the payor in proportion to the value of the assets of the lower-tier corporation that are used in a trade or business in the country of incorporation. The location of assets used in a trade or business of the lower-tier corporation shall be determined under the rules of this paragraph (b)(4).

(xi) *Treatment of banks and insurance companies.* [Reserved]

(5) *Exclusion of rents and royalties derived from related persons*—(i) *In general*—(A) *Corporate payor.* Foreign personal holding company income received by a controlled foreign corporation does not include rents or royalties if—

(*1*) The payor is a corporation that is a related person with respect to the controlled foreign corporation, as defined in section 954(d)(3); and

(*2*) The rents or royalties are for the use of, or the privilege of using, property within the country under the laws of which the controlled foreign corporation receiving the payments is created or organized (the country of incorporation).

(B) *Payment by a partnership.* For purposes of this paragraph (b)(5), if a partnership with one or more corporate partners makes a payment of rents or royalties, a corporate partner will be treated as the payor of the rents or royalties—

(*1*) If the rent or royalty payment gives rise to a partnership item of deduction under the Internal Revenue Code or Income Tax Regulations, to the extent the item of deduction is allocable to the corporate partner under section 704(b); or

(*2*) If the rent or royalty payment does not give rise to a partnership item of deduction under the Internal Revenue Code or Income Tax Regulations, to the extent that a partnership item reasonably related to the payment would be allocated to that partner under an existing allocation under the partnership agreement (made pursuant to section 704(b)).

(ii) *Exceptions*—(A) *Rents or royalties paid out of adjusted foreign base company income or insurance income.* Rents or royalties may not be excluded from the foreign personal holding company income of the recipient under this paragraph (b)(5) to the extent that deductions for the payments are allocated under section 954(b)(5) and § 1.954-1(a)(4) and (c) to the payor's adjusted gross foreign base company income (as defined in § 1.954-1(a)(3)), adjusted gross insurance income (as defined in § 1.954-1(a)(6)), or any other category of income included in the computation of subpart F income under section 952(a).

(B) *Property used in part in the controlled foreign corporation's country of incorporation.* If the payor uses the property both in the controlled foreign corporation's country of incorporation and elsewhere, the part of the rent or royalty attributable (determined under the principles of section 482) to the use of, or the privilege of using, the property outside such country of incorporation is included in the computation of foreign personal holding company income under this paragraph (b).

(6) *Exclusion of rents and royalties derived in the active conduct of a trade or business.* Foreign personal holding company income shall not include rents or royalties that are derived in the active conduct of a trade or business and received from a person that is not a related person (as defined in section 954(d)(3)) with respect to the controlled foreign corporation. For purposes of this section, rents or royalties are derived in the active conduct of a trade or business only if the provisions of paragraph (c) or (d) of this section are satisfied.

(c) *Excluded rents*—(1) *Active conduct of a trade or business.* Rents will be considered for purposes of paragraph (b)(6) of this section to be derived in the active conduct of a trade or business if such rents are derived by the controlled foreign corporation (the lessor) from leasing any of the following—

(i) Property that the lessor has manufactured or produced, or has acquired and added substantial value to, but only if the lessor is regularly engaged in the manufacture or production of, or in the acquisition and addition of substantial value to, property of such kind;

(ii) Real property with respect to which the lessor, through its own officers or staff of employees, regularly performs active and substantial management and operational functions while the property is leased;

(iii) Personal property ordinarily used by the lessor in the active conduct of a trade or business, leased temporarily during a period when the property would, but for such leasing, be idle; or

(iv) Property that is leased as a result of the performance of marketing functions by such lessor if the lessor, through its own officers or staff of employees located in a foreign country, maintains and operates an organization in such country that is regularly engaged in the business of

Reg. § 1.954-2(b)(5)

marketing, or of marketing and servicing, the leased property and that is substantial in relation to the amount of rents derived from the leasing of such property.

(2) *Special rules*—(i) *Adding substantial value.* For purposes of paragraph (c)(1)(i) of this section, the performance of marketing functions will not be considered to add substantial value to property.

(ii) *Substantiality of foreign organization.* For purposes of paragraph (c)(1)(iv) of this section, whether an organization in a foreign country is substantial in relation to the amount of rents is determined based on all of the facts and circumstances. However, such an organization will be considered substantial in relation to the amount of rents if active leasing expenses, as defined in paragraph (c)(2)(iii) of this section, equal or exceed 25 percent of the adjusted leasing profit, as defined in paragraph (c)(2)(iv) of this section.

(iii) *Active leasing expenses.* The term *active leasing expenses* means the deductions incurred by an organization of the lessor in a foreign country that are properly allocable to rental income and that would be allowable under section 162 to the lessor if it were a domestic corporation, other than—

(A) Deductions for compensation for personal services rendered by shareholders of, or related persons (as defined in section 954(d)(3)) with respect to, the lessor;

(B) Deductions for rents paid or accrued;

(C) Deductions that, although generally allowable under section 162, would be specifically allowable to the lessor (if the lessor were a domestic corporation) under any section of the Internal Revenue Code other than section 162; and

(D) Deductions for payments made to agents or independent contractors with respect to the leased property other than payments for insurance, utilities and other expenses for like services, or for capitalized repairs.

(iv) *Adjusted leasing profit.* The term *adjusted leasing profit* means the gross income of the lessor from rents, reduced by the sum of—

(A) The rents paid or incurred by the lessor with respect to such rental income;

(B) The amounts that would be allowable to such lessor (if the lessor were a domestic corporation) as deductions under sections 167 or 168 with respect to such rental income; and

(C) The amounts paid by the lessor to agents or independent contractors with respect to such rental income other than payments for insurance, utilities and other expenses for like services, or for capitalized repairs.

(3) *Examples.* The application of this paragraph (c) is illustrated by the following examples.

Example 1. Controlled foreign corporation *A* is regularly engaged in the production of office machines which it sells or leases to others and services. Under paragraph (c)(1)(i) of this section, the rental income of Corporation *A* from these leases is derived in the active conduct of a trade or business for purposes of section 954(c)(2)(A).

Example 2. Controlled foreign corporation *D* purchases motor vehicles which it leases to others. In the conduct of its short-term leasing of such vehicles in foreign country X, Corporation *D* owns a large number of motor vehicles in country X which it services and repairs, leases motor vehicles to customers on an hourly, daily, or weekly basis, maintains offices and service facilities in country X from which to lease and service such vehicles, and maintains therein a sizable staff of its own administrative, sales, and service personnel. Corporation *D* also leases in country X on a long-term basis, generally for a term of one year, motor vehicles that it owns. Under the terms of the long-term leases, Corporation *D* is required to repair and service, during the term of the lease, the leased motor vehicles without cost to the lessee. By the maintenance in country X of office, sales, and service facilities and its complete staff of administrative, sales, and service personnel, Corporation *D* maintains and operates an organization therein that is regularly engaged in the business of marketing and servicing the motor vehicles that are leased. The deductions incurred by such organization satisfy the 25-percent test of paragraph (c)(2)(ii) of this section; thus, such organization is substantial in relation to the rents Corporation *D* receives from leasing the motor vehicles. Therefore, under paragraph (c)(1)(iv) of this section, such rents are derived in the active conduct of a trade or business for purposes of section 954(c)(2)(A).

Example 3. Controlled foreign corporation *E* owns a complex of apartment buildings that it has acquired by purchase. Corporation *E* engages a real estate management firm to lease the apartments, manage the buildings and pay over the net rents to Corporation *E*. The rental income of Corporation *E* from such leases is not derived in the active conduct of a trade or business for purposes of section 954(c)(2)(A).

Example 4. Controlled foreign corporation *F* acquired by purchase a twenty-story office building in a foreign country, three floors of which it occupies and the rest of which it leases. Corporation *F* acts as rental agent for the leasing of

Reg. § 1.954-2(c)(3)

offices in the building and employs a substantial staff to perform other management and maintenance functions. Under paragraph (c)(1)(ii) of this section, the rents received by Corporation F from such leasing operations are derived in the active conduct of a trade or business for purposes of section 954(c)(2)(A).

Example 5. Controlled foreign corporation G owns equipment that it ordinarily uses to perform contracts in foreign countries to drill oil wells. For occasional brief and irregular periods it is unable to obtain contracts requiring immediate performance sufficient to employ all such equipment. During such a period it sometimes leases such idle equipment temporarily. After the expiration of such temporary leasing of the property, Corporation G continues the use of such equipment in the performance of its own drilling contracts. Under paragraph (c)(1)(iii) of this section, rents Corporation G receives from such leasing of idle equipment are derived in the active conduct of a trade or business for purposes of section 954(c)(2)(A).

(d) *Excluded royalties*—(1) *Active conduct of a trade or business.* Royalties will be considered for purposes of paragraph (b)(6) of this section to be derived in the active conduct of a trade or business if such royalties are derived by the controlled foreign corporation (the licensor) from licensing—

(i) Property that the licensor has developed, created, or produced, or has acquired and added substantial value to, but only so long as the licensor is regularly engaged in the development, creation or production of, or in the acquisition of and addition of substantial value to, property of such kind; or

(ii) Property that is licensed as a result of the performance of marketing functions by such licensor if the licensor, through its own officers or staff of employees located in a foreign country, maintains and operates an organization in such country that is regularly engaged in the business of marketing, or of marketing and servicing, the licensed property and that is substantial in relation to the amount of royalties derived from the licensing of such property.

(2) *Special rules*—(i) *Adding substantial value.* For purposes of paragraph (d)(1)(i) of this section, the performance of marketing functions will not be considered to add substantial value to property.

(ii) *Substantiality of foreign organization.* For purposes of paragraph (d)(1)(ii) of this section, whether an organization in a foreign country is substantial in relation to the amount of royalties is determined based on all of the facts and circumstances. However, such an organization will be considered substantial in relation to the amount of royalties if active licensing expenses, as defined in paragraph (d)(2)(iii) of this section, equal or exceed 25 percent of the adjusted licensing profit, as defined in paragraph (d)(2)(iv) of this section.

(iii) *Active licensing expenses.* The term *active licensing expenses* means the deductions incurred by an organization of the licensor in a foreign country that are properly allocable to royalty income and that would be allowable under section 162 to the licensor if it were a domestic corporation, other than—

(A) Deductions for compensation for personal services rendered by shareholders of, or related persons (as defined in section 954(d)(3)) with respect to, the licensor;

(B) Deductions for royalties paid or incurred;

(C) Deductions that, although generally allowable under section 162, would be specifically allowable to the licensor (if the controlled foreign corporation were a domestic corporation) under any section of the Internal Revenue Code other than section 162; and

(D) Deductions for payments made to agents or independent contractors with respect to the licensed property.

(iv) *Adjusted licensing profit.* The term *adjusted licensing profit* means the gross income of the licensor from royalties, reduced by the sum of—

(A) The royalties paid or incurred by the licensor with respect to such royalty income;

(B) The amounts that would be allowable to such licensor as deductions under section 167 or 197 (if the licensor were a domestic corporation) with respect to such royalty income; and

(C) The amounts paid by the licensor to agents or independent contractors with respect to such royalty income.

(3) *Examples.* The application of this paragraph (d) is illustrated by the following examples.

Example 1. Controlled foreign corporation A, through its own staff of employees, owns and operates a research facility in foreign country X. At the research facility, employees of Corporation A who are scientists, engineers, and technicians regularly perform experiments, tests, and other technical activities, that ultimately result in the issuance of patents that it sells or licenses. Under paragraph (d)(1)(i) of this section, royalties received by Corporation A for the privilege of using patented rights that it develops as a result of such research activity are derived in the active conduct of a trade or business for purposes of section 954(c)(2)(A), but only so long as the licensor is

Reg. § 1.954-2(d)(1)

regularly engaged in the development, creation or production of, or in the acquisition of and addition of substantial value to, property of such kind.

Example 2. Assume that Corporation *A* in *Example 1,* in addition to receiving royalties for the use of patents that it develops, receives royalties for the use of patents that it acquires by purchase and licenses to others without adding any value thereto. Corporation *A* generally consummates royalty agreements on such purchased patents as the result of inquiries received by it from prospective licensees when the fact becomes known in the business community, as a result of the filing of a patent, advertisements in trade journals, announcements, and contacts by employees of Corporation *A,* that Corporation *A* has acquired rights under a patent and is interested in licensing its rights. Corporation *A* does not, however, maintain and operate an organization in a foreign country that is regularly engaged in the business of marketing the purchased patents. The royalties received by Corporation *A* for the use of the purchased patents are not derived in the active conduct of a trade or business for purposes of section 954(c)(2)(A).

Example 3. Controlled foreign corporation *B* receives royalties for the use of patents that it acquires by purchase. The primary business of Corporation *B,* operated on a regular basis, consists of licensing patents that it has purchased raw from inventors and, through the efforts of a substantial staff of employees consisting of scientists, engineers, and technicians, made susceptible to commercial application. For example, Corporation *B,* after purchasing patent rights covering a chemical process, designs specialized production equipment required for the commercial adaptation of the process and, by so doing, substantially increases the value of the patent. Under paragraph (d)(1)(i) of this section, royalties received by Corporation *B* from the use of such patent are derived in the active conduct of a trade or business for purposes of section 954(c)(2)(A).

Example 4. Controlled foreign corporation *C* receives royalties for the use of a patent that it developed through its own staff of employees at its facility in country X. Corporation *C* has developed no other patents. It does not regularly employ a staff of scientists, engineers or technicians to create new products to be patented. Further, it does not purchase and license patents developed by others to which it has added substantial value. The royalties received by Corporation *C* are not derived from the active conduct of a trade or business for purposes of section 954(c)(2)(A).

Example 5. Controlled foreign corporation *D* finances independent persons in the development of patented items in return for an ownership interest in such items from which it derives a percentage of royalty income, if any, subsequently derived from the use by others of the protected right. Corporation *D* also attempts to increase its royalty income from such patents by contacting prospective licensees and rendering to licensees advice that is intended to promote the use of the patented property. Corporation *D* does not, however, maintain and operate an organization in a foreign country that is regularly engaged in the business of marketing the patents. Royalties received by Corporation *D* for the use of such patents are not derived in the active conduct of a trade or business for purposes of section 954(c)(2)(A).

(e) *Certain property transactions*—(1) *In general*—(i) *Inclusions.* Gain from certain property transactions described in section 954(c)(1)(B) includes the excess of gains over losses from the sale or exchange of—

(A) Property that gives rise to dividends, interest, rents, royalties or annuities, as described in paragraph (e)(2) of this section;

(B) Property that is an interest in a partnership, trust or REMIC; and

(C) Property that does not give rise to income, as described in paragraph (e)(3) of this section.

(ii) *Exceptions.* Gain or loss from certain property transactions described in section 954(c)(1)(B) and paragraph (e)(1)(i) of this section does not include gain or loss from the sale or exchange of—

(A) Inventory or similar property, as defined in paragraph (a)(4)(iii) of this section;

(B) Dealer property, as defined in paragraph (a)(4)(v) of this section; or

(C) Property that gives rise to rents or royalties described in paragraph (b)(6) of this section that are derived in the active conduct of a trade or business from persons that are not related persons (as defined in section 954(d)(3)) with respect to the controlled foreign corporation.

(iii) *Treatment of losses.* Section 1.954-1(c)(1)(ii) provides for the treatment of losses in excess of gains from the sale or exchange of property described in paragraph (e)(1)(i) of this section.

(iv) *Dual character property.* Property may, in part, constitute property that gives rise to certain income as described in paragraph (e)(2) of this section or, in part, constitute property that does not give rise to any income as described in paragraph (e)(3) of this section. However, property that is described in paragraph (e)(1)(i)(B) of

Reg. § 1.954-2(e)(1)

this section cannot be dual character property. Dual character property must be treated as two separate properties for purposes of paragraph (e)(2) or (3) of this section. Accordingly, the sale or exchange of such dual character property will give rise to gain or loss that in part must be included in the computation of foreign personal holding company income under paragraph (e)(2) or (3) of this section, and in part is excluded from such computation. Gain or loss from the disposition of dual character property must be bifurcated under this paragraph (e)(1)(iv) pursuant to the method that most reasonably reflects the relative uses of the property. Reasonable methods may include comparisons in terms of gross income generated or the physical division of the property. In the case of real property, the physical division of the property will in most cases be the most reasonable method available. For example, if a controlled foreign corporation owns an office building, uses 60 percent of the building in its trade or business, and rents out the other 40 percent, then 40 percent of the gain recognized on the disposition of the property would reasonably be treated as gain that is included in the computation of foreign personal holding company income under this paragraph (e)(1). This paragraph (e)(1)(iv) addresses the contemporaneous use of property for dual purposes. For rules concerning changes in the use of property affecting its classification for purposes of this paragraph (e), see paragraph (a)(3) of this section.

(2) *Property that gives rise to certain income*—(i) *In general.* Property the sale or exchange of which gives rise to foreign personal holding company income under this paragraph (e)(2) includes property that gives rise to dividends, interest, rents, royalties or annuities described in paragraph (b) of this section, including—

(A) Property that gives rise to export financing interest described in paragraph (b)(2) of this section; and

(B) Property that gives rise to income from related persons described in paragraph (b)(4) or (5) of this section.

(ii) *Gain or loss from the disposition of a debt instrument.* Gain or loss from the sale, exchange or retirement of a debt instrument is included in the computation of foreign personal holding company income under this paragraph (e) unless—

(A) In the case of gain—

(*1*) It is interest (as defined in paragraph (a)(4)(i) of this section); or

(*2*) It is income equivalent to interest(as described in paragraph (h) of this section); and

(B) In the case of loss—

(*1*) It is directly allocated to, or treated as an adjustment to, interest income (as described in paragraph (a)(4)(i) of this section) or income equivalent to interest (as defined in paragraph (h) of this section) under any provision of the Internal Revenue Code or Income Tax Regulations; or

(*2*) It is required to be apportioned in the same manner as interest expense under section 864(e) or any other provision of the Internal Revenue Code or Income Tax Regulations.

(3) *Property that does not give rise to income.* Except as otherwise provided in this paragraph (e)(3), for purposes of this section, the term *property that does not give rise to income* includes all rights and interests in property (whether or not a capital asset) including, for example, forwards, futures and options. Property that does not give rise to income shall not include—

(i) Property that gives rise to dividends, interest, rents, royalties or annuities described in paragraph (e)(2) of this section;

(ii) Tangible property (other than real property) used or held for use in the controlled foreign corporation's trade or business that is of a character that would be subject to the allowance for depreciation under section 167 or 168 and the regulations under those sections (including tangible property described in § 1.167(a)-2);

(iii) Real property that does not give rise to rental or similar income, to the extent used or held for use in the controlled foreign corporation's trade or business;

(iv) Intangible property (as defined in section 936(h)(3)(B)), goodwill or going concern value, to the extent used or held for use in the controlled foreign corporation's trade or business;

(v) Notional principal contracts (but see paragraphs (f)(2), (g)(2) and (h)(3) of this section for rules that include income from certain notional principal contracts in gains from commodities transactions, foreign currency gains and income equivalent to interest, respectively); or

(vi) Other property that is excepted from the general rule of this paragraph (e)(3) by the Commissioner in published guidance. See § 601.601(d)(2) of this chapter.

(f) *Commodities transactions*—(1) *In general*—(i) *Inclusion in foreign personal holding company income.* Foreign personal holding company income includes the excess of gains over losses from commodities transactions.

Reg. § 1.954-2(e)(2)

(ii) *Exception.* Gains and losses from qualified active sales and qualified hedging transactions are excluded from the computation of foreign personal holding company income under this paragraph (f).

(iii) *Treatment of losses.* Section 1.954-1(c)(1)(ii) provides for the treatment of losses in excess of gains from commodities transactions.

(2) *Definitions*—(i) *Commodity.* For purposes of this section, the term *commodity* includes tangible personal property of a kind that is actively traded or with respect to which contractual interests are actively traded.

(ii) *Commodities transaction.* The term *commodities transaction* means the purchase or sale of a commodity for immediate (spot) delivery or deferred (forward) delivery, or the right to purchase, sell, receive, or transfer a commodity, or any other right or obligation with respect to a commodity accomplished through a cash or off-exchange market, an interbank market, an organized exchange or board of trade, or an over-the-counter market, or in a transaction effected between private parties outside of any market. Commodities transactions include, but are not limited to—

(A) A futures or forward contract in a commodity;

(B) A leverage contract in a commodity purchased from a leverage transaction merchant;

(C) An exchange of futures for physical transaction;

(D) A transaction, including a notional principal contract, in which the income or loss to the parties is measured by reference to the price of a commodity, a pool of commodities, or an index of commodities;

(E) The purchase or sale of an option or other right to acquire or transfer a commodity, a futures contract in a commodity, or an index of commodities; and

(F) The delivery of one commodity in exchange for the delivery of another commodity, the same commodity at another time, cash, or nonfunctional currency.

(iii) *Qualified active sale*—(A) *In general.* The term *qualified active sale* means the sale of commodities in the active conduct of a commodities business as a producer, processor, merchant or handler of commodities if substantially all of the controlled foreign corporation's business is as an active producer, processor, merchant or handler of commodities. The sale of commodities held by a controlled foreign corporation other than in its capacity as an active producer, processor, merchant or handler of commodities is not a qualified active sale. For example, the sale by a controlled foreign corporation of commodities that were held for investment or speculation would not be a qualified active sale.

(B) *Active conduct of a commodities business.* For purposes of this paragraph, a controlled foreign corporation is engaged in the active conduct of a commodities business as a producer, processor, merchant or handler of commodities only with respect to commodities sales for which each of the following conditions is satisfied—

(*1*) It holds the commodities directly, and not through an agent or independent contractor, as inventory or similar property (as defined in paragraph (a)(4)(iii) of this section) or as dealer property (as defined in paragraph (a)(4)(v) of this section); and

(*2*) With respect to such commodities, it incurs substantial expenses in the ordinary course of a commodities business from engaging in one or more of the following activities directly, and not through an independent contractor—

(*i*) Substantial activities in the production of the commodities, including planting, tending or harvesting crops, raising or slaughtering livestock, or extracting minerals;

(*ii*) Substantial processing activities prior to the sale of the commodities, including the blending and drying of agricultural commodities, or the concentrating, refining, mixing, crushing, aerating or milling of commodities; or

(*iii*) Significant activities as described in paragraph (f)(2)(iii)(B)(*3*) of this section.

(*3*) For purposes of paragraph (f)(2)(iii)(B)(*2*)(*iii*) of this section, the significant activities must relate to—

(*i*) The physical movement, handling and storage of the commodities, including preparation of contracts and invoices, arranging freight, insurance and credit, arranging for receipt, transfer or negotiation of shipping documents, arranging storage or warehousing, and dealing with quality claims;

(*ii*) Owning and operating facilities for storage or warehousing; or

(*iii*) Owning or chartering vessels or vehicles for the transportation of the commodities.

(C) *Substantially all.* Substantially all of the controlled foreign corporation's business is as an active producer, processor, merchant or handler of commodities if the sum of its gross receipts from all of its qualified active sales (as defined in this paragraph (f)(2)(iii) without regard to the substantially all requirement) of commodities and

Reg. § 1.954-2(f)(2)

its gross receipts from all of its qualified hedging transactions (as defined in paragraph (f)(2)(iv) of this section, applied without regard to the substantially all requirement of this paragraph (f)(2)(iii)(C)) equals or exceeds 85 percent of its total gross receipts for the taxable year (computed as though the corporation were a domestic corporation). In computing gross receipts, the District Director may disregard any sale or hedging transaction that has as a principal purpose manipulation of the 85 percent gross receipts test. A purpose may be a principal purpose even though it is outweighed by other purposes (taken together or separately).

(D) *Activities of employees of a related entity.* For purposes of this paragraph (f), activities of employees of an entity related to the controlled foreign corporation, who are made available to and supervised on a day-to-day basis by, and whose salaries are paid by (or reimbursed to the related entity by), the controlled foreign corporation, are treated as activities engaged in directly by the controlled foreign corporation.

(E) *Financial activities.* For purposes of this paragraph (f), a corporation is not engaged in a commodities business as a producer, processor, merchant or handler of commodities if its business is primarily financial. For example, the business of a controlled foreign corporation is primarily financial if its principal business is making a market in notional principal contracts based on a commodities index.

(iv) *Qualified hedging transaction*—(A) *In general.* The term *qualified hedging transaction* means a bona fide hedging transaction, as defined in paragraph (a)(4)(ii) of this section, with respect to qualified active sales (other than transactions described in section 988(c)(1) without regard to section 988(c)(1)(D)(i)).

(B) *Exception.* The term *qualified hedging transaction* does not include transactions that are not reasonably necessary to the conduct of business of the controlled foreign corporation as a producer, processor, merchant or handler of a commodity in the manner in which such business is customarily and usually conducted by others.

(g) *Foreign currency gain or loss*—(1) *Scope and purpose.* This paragraph (g) provides rules for the treatment of foreign currency gains and losses. Paragraph (g)(2) of this section provides the general rule. Paragraph (g)(3) of this section provides an election to include foreign currency gains or losses that would otherwise be treated as foreign personal holding company income under this paragraph (g) in the computation of another category of subpart F income. Paragraph (g)(4) of this section provides an alternative election to treat any net foreign currency gain or loss as foreign personal holding company income. Paragraph (g)(5) of this section provides rules for certain gains and losses not subject to this paragraph (g).

(2) *In general*—(i) *Inclusion.* Except as otherwise provided in this paragraph (g), foreign personal holding company income includes the excess of foreign currency gains over foreign currency losses attributable to any section 988 transactions (foreign currency gain or loss). Section 1.954-1(c)(1)(ii) provides rules for the treatment of foreign currency losses in excess of foreign currency gains. However, if an election is made under paragraph (g)(4) of this section, the excess of foreign currency losses over foreign currency gains to which the election would apply may be apportioned to, and offset, other categories of foreign personal holding company income.

(ii) *Exclusion for business needs*—(A) *General rule.* Foreign currency gain or loss directly related to the business needs of the controlled foreign corporation is excluded from foreign personal holding company income.

(B) *Business needs.* Foreign currency gain or loss is directly related to the business needs of a controlled foreign corporation if—

(*1*) The foreign currency gain or loss—

(*i*) Arises from a transaction (other than a hedging transaction) entered into, or property used or held for use, in the normal course of the controlled foreign corporation's trade or business, other than the trade or business of trading foreign currency;

(*ii*) Arises from a transaction or property that does not itself (and could not reasonably be expected to) give rise to subpart F income other than foreign currency gain or loss;

(*iii*) Does not arise from a transaction described in section 988(c)(1)(B)(iii); and

(*iv*) Is clearly determinable from the records of the controlled foreign corporation as being derived from such transaction or property; or

(*2*) The foreign currency gain or loss arises from a bona fide hedging transaction, as defined in paragraph (a)(4)(ii) of this section, with respect to a transaction or property that satisfies the requirements of paragraphs (g)(2)(ii)(B)(*1*)(*i*) through (*iii*) of this section, provided that any gain or loss arising from such transaction or property that is attributable to changes in exchange rates is clearly determinable from the records of the CFC as being derived from such transaction or property. For purposes of this paragraph (g)(2)(ii)(B)(*2*), a hedging transaction

Reg. § 1.954-2(g)(1)

will satisfy the aggregate hedging rules of § 1.1221-2(c)(7) only if all (or all but a de minimis amount) of the aggregate risk being hedged arises in connection with transactions or property that satisfy the requirements of paragraphs (g)(2)(ii)(B)(*1*)(*i*) through (*iii*) of this section, provided that any gain or loss arising from such transactions or property that is attributable to changes in exchange rates is clearly determinable from the records of the CFC as being derived from such transactions or property.

(C) *Regular dealers.* Transactions in dealer property (as defined in paragraph (a)(4)(v) of this section) described in section 988(c)(1)(B) or (C) that are entered into by a controlled foreign corporation that is a regular dealer (as defined in paragraph (a)(4)(iv) of this section) in such property in its capacity as a dealer will be treated as directly related to the business needs of the controlled foreign corporation under paragraph (g)(2)(ii)(A) of this section.

(D) *Example.* The following example illustrates the provisions of this paragraph (g)(2).

Example. (i) *CFC1* and *CFC2* are controlled foreign corporations located in Country B, and are members of the same controlled group. *CFC1* is engaged in the active conduct of a trade or business that does not produce any subpart F income. *CFC2* serves as the currency coordination center for the controlled group, aggregating currency risks incurred by the group and entering into hedging transactions that transfer those risks outside of the group. Pursuant to this arrangement, and to hedge the currency risk on a noninterest bearing receivable incurred by *CFC1* in the normal course of its business, on Day 1 *CFC1* enters into a forward contract to sell Japanese Yen to *CFC2* in 30 days. Also on Day 1, *CFC2* enters into a forward contract to sell Yen to unrelated Bank X on Day 30. *CFC2* is not a regular dealer in Yen spot and forward contracts, and the Yen is not the functional currency for either *CFC1* or *CFC2*.

(ii) Because the forward contract entered into by *CFC1* to sell Yen hedges a transaction entered into in the normal course of *CFC1*'s business that does not give rise to subpart F income, it qualifies as a bona fide hedging transaction as defined in paragraph (a)(4)(ii) of this section. Therefore, *CFC1*'s foreign exchange gain or loss from that forward contract will not be treated as foreign personal holding company income or loss under this paragraph (g).

(iii) Because the forward contract to purchase Yen was entered into by *CFC2* in order to assume currency risks incurred by *CFC1* it does not qualify as a bona fide hedging transaction, as defined in paragraph (a)(4)(ii) of this section. Thus, foreign exchange gain or loss recognized by *CFC2* from that forward contract will be foreign personal holding company income. Because *CFC2* entered into the forward contract to sell Yen in order to hedge currency risks of *CFC1*, that forward contract also does not qualify as a bona fide hedging transaction. Thus, *CFC2*'s foreign currency gain or loss arising from that forward contract will be foreign personal holding company income.

(iii) *Special rule for foreign currency gain or loss from an interest-bearing liability.* Except as provided in paragraph (g)(5)(iv) of this section, foreign currency gain or loss arising from an interest-bearing liability is characterized as subpart F income and non-subpart F income in the same manner that interest expense associated with the liability would be allocated and apportioned between subpart F income and non-subpart F income under § § 1.861-9T and 1.861-12T.

(3) *Election to characterize foreign currency gain or loss that arises from a specific category of subpart F income as gain or loss in that category*—(i) *In general.* For taxable years of a controlled foreign corporation beginning on or after November 6, 1995, elect, under this paragraph (g)(3), to exclude foreign currency gain or loss otherwise includible in the computation of foreign personal holding company income under this paragraph (g) from the computation of foreign personal holding company income under this paragraph (g) and include such foreign currency gain or loss in the category (or categories) of subpart F income (described in section 952(a), or, in the case of foreign base company income, described in § 1.954-1(c)(1)(iii)(A)(*1*) or (*2*)) to which such gain or loss relates. If an election is made under this paragraph (g)(3) with respect to a category (or categories) of subpart F income described in section 952(a), or, in the case of foreign base company income, described in § 1.954-1(c)(1)(iii)(A)(*1*) or (*2*), the election shall apply to all foreign currency gain or loss that arises from—

(A) A transaction (other than a hedging transaction) entered into, or property used or held for use, in the normal course of the controlled foreign corporation's trade or business that gives rise to income in that category (or categories) and that is clearly determinable from the records of the controlled foreign corporation as being derived from such transaction or property; and

(B) A bona fide hedging transaction, as defined in paragraph (a)(4)(ii) of this section, with respect to a transaction or property described in paragraph (g)(3)(i)(A) of this section.

Reg. § 1.954-2(g)(3)

For purposes of this paragraph (g)(3)(i)(B), a hedging transaction will satisfy the aggregate hedging rules of § 1.1221-2(c)(7) only if all (or all but a de minimis amount) of the aggregate risk being hedged arises in connection with transactions or property that generate the same category of subpart F income described in section 952(a), or, in the case of foreign base company income, described in § 1.954-1(c)(1)(iii)(A)(*1*) or (*2*).

(ii) *Time and manner of election.* The controlling United States shareholders, as defined in § 1.964-1(c)(5), make the election on behalf of the controlled foreign corporation by filing a statement with their original income tax returns for the taxable year of such United States shareholders ending with or within the taxable year of the controlled foreign corporation for which the election is made, clearly indicating that such election has been made. If the controlling United States shareholders elect to apply these regulations retroactively, under § 1.954-0(a)(1)(ii), the election under this paragraph (g)(3) may be made by the amended return filed pursuant to the election under § 1.954-0(a)(1)(ii). The controlling United States shareholders filing the election statement described in this paragraph (g)(3)(ii) must provide copies of the election statement to all other United States shareholders of the electing controlled foreign corporation. Failure to provide copies of such statement will not cause an election under this paragraph (g)(3) to be voidable by the controlled foreign corporation or the controlling United States shareholders. However, the District Director has discretion to void the election if it is determined that there was no reasonable cause for the failure to provide copies of such statement. The statement shall include the following information—

(A) The name, address, taxpayer identification number, and taxable year of each United States shareholder;

(B) The name, address, and taxable year of the controlled foreign corporation for which the election is effective; and

(C) Any additional information required by the Commissioner by administrative pronouncement.

(iii) *Revocation of election.* This election is effective for the taxable year of the controlled foreign corporation for which it is made and all subsequent taxable years of such corporation unless revoked by or with the consent of the Commissioner.

(iv) *Example.* The following example illustrates the provisions of this paragraph (g)(3).

Example. (i) *CFC*, a controlled foreign corporation, is a sales company that earns foreign base company sales income under section 954(d). *CFC* makes an election under this paragraph (g)(3) to treat foreign currency gains or losses that arise from a specific category (or categories) of subpart F income (as described in section 952(a), or, in the case of foreign base company income, as described in § 1.954-1(c)(1)(iii)(A)(*1*) or (*2*)) as that type of income. *CFC* aggregates the currency risk on all of its transactions that generate foreign base company sales income and hedges this net currency exposure.

(ii) Assuming no more than a de minimis amount of risk in the pool of risks being hedged arises from transactions or property that generate income other than foreign base company sales income, pursuant to its election under (g)(3), *CFC*'s net foreign currency gain from the pool and the hedging transactions will be treated as foreign base company sales income under section 954(d), rather than as foreign personal holding company income under section 954(c)(1)(D). If the pool of risks and the hedging transactions generate a net foreign base company sales loss, however, *CFC* must apply the rules of § 1.954-1(c)(1)(ii).

(4) *Election to treat all foreign currency gains or losses as foreign personal holding company income*—(i) *In general.* If the controlling United States shareholders make an election under this paragraph (g)(4), the controlled foreign corporation shall include in its computation of foreign personal holding company income the excess of foreign currency gains over losses or the excess of foreign currency losses over gains attributable to any section 988 transaction (except those described in paragraph (g)(5) of this section) and any section 1256 contract that would be a section 988 transaction but for section 988(c)(1)(D). Separate elections for section 1256 contracts and section 988 transactions are not permitted. An election under this paragraph (g)(4) supersedes an election under paragraph (g)(3) of this section.

(ii) *Time and manner of election.* The controlling United States shareholders, as defined in § 1.964-1(c)(5), make the election on behalf of the controlled foreign corporation in the same time and manner as provided in paragraph (g)(3)(ii) of this section.

(iii) *Revocation of election.* This election is effective for the taxable year of the controlled foreign corporation for which it is made and all subsequent taxable years of such corporation unless revoked by or with the consent of the Commissioner.

(5) *Gains and losses not subject to this paragraph*—(i) *Capital gains and losses.* Gain or loss that is treated as capital gain or loss under section

Reg. § 1.954-2(g)(4)

Income from Sources Without the United States

988(a)(1)(B) is not foreign currency gain or loss for purposes of this paragraph (g). Such gain or loss is treated as gain or loss from the sale or exchange of property that is included in the computation of foreign personal holding company income under paragraph (e)(1) of this section. Paragraph (a)(2) of this section provides other rules concerning income described in more than one category of foreign personal holding company income.

(ii) *Income not subject to section 988.* Gain or loss that is not treated as foreign currency gain or loss by reason of section 988(a)(2) or (d) is not foreign currency gain or loss for purposes of this paragraph (g). However, such gain or loss may be included in the computation of other categories of foreign personal holding company income in accordance with its characterization under section 988(a)(2) or (d) (for example, foreign currency gain that is treated as interest income under section 988(a)(2) will be included in the computation of foreign personal holding company income under paragraph (b)(ii) of this section).

(iii) *Qualified business units using the dollar approximate separate transactions method.* This paragraph (g) does not apply to any DASTM gain or loss computed under § 1.985-3(d). Such gain or loss is allocated under the rules of § 1.985-3(e)(2)(iv) or (e)(3). However, the provisions of this paragraph (g) do apply to section 988 transactions denominated in a currency other than the United States dollar or the currency that would be the qualified business unit's functional currency were it not hyperinflationary.

(iv) *Gain or loss allocated under § 1.861-9.* [Reserved]

(h) *Income equivalent to interest*—(1) *In general*—(i) *Inclusion in foreign personal holding company income.* Except as provided in this paragraph (h), foreign personal holding company income includes income equivalent to interest as defined in paragraph (h)(2) of this section.

(ii) *Exceptions*—(A) *Liability hedging transactions.* Income, gain, deduction or loss that is allocated and apportioned in the same manner as interest expense under the provisions of § 1.861-9T is not income equivalent to interest for purposes of this paragraph (h).

(B) *Interest.* Amounts treated as interest under section 954(c)(1)(A) and paragraph (b) of this section are not income equivalent to interest for purposes of this paragraph (h).

(2) *Definition of income equivalent to interest*—(i) *In general.* The term *income equivalent to interest* includes income that is derived from—

(A) A transaction or series of related transactions in which the payments, net payments, cash flows or return predominantly reflect the time value of money;

(B) Transactions in which the payments (or a predominant portion thereof) are, in substance, for the use or forbearance of money;

(C) Notional principal contracts, to the extent provided in paragraph (h)(3) of this section;

(D) Factoring, to the extent provided in paragraph (h)(4) of this section;

(E) Conversion transactions, but only to the extent that gain realized with respect to such a transaction is treated as ordinary income under section 1258;

(F) The performance of services, to the extent provided in paragraph (h)(5) of this section;

(G) The commitment by a lender to provide financing, if any portion of such financing is actually provided;

(H) Transfers of debt securities subject to section 1058; and

(I) Other transactions, as provided by the Commissioner in published guidance. See § 601.601(d)(2) of this chapter.

(ii) *Income from the sale of property.* Income from the sale of property will not be treated as income equivalent to interest by reason of paragraph (h)(2)(i)(A) or (B) of this section. Income derived by a controlled foreign corporation will be treated as arising from the sale of property only if the corporation in substance carries out sales activities. Accordingly, an arrangement that is designed to lend the form of a sales transaction to a transaction that in substance constitutes an advance of funds will be disregarded. For example, if a controlled foreign corporation acquires property on 30-day payment terms from one person and sells that property to another person on 90-day payment terms and at prearranged prices and terms such that the foreign corporation bears no substantial economic risk with respect to the purchase and sale other than the risk of nonpayment, the foreign corporation has not in substance derived income from the sale of property.

(3) *Notional principal contracts*—(i) *In general.* Income equivalent to interest includes income from notional principal contracts denominated in the functional currency of the taxpayer (or a qualified business unit of the taxpayer, as defined in section 989(a)), the value of which is determined solely by reference to interest rates or interest rate indices, to the extent that

Reg. § 1.954-2(h)(3)

the income from such transactions accrues on or after August 14, 1989.

(ii) *Regular dealers.* Income equivalent to interest does not include income earned by a regular dealer (as defined in paragraph (a)(4)(iv) of this section) from notional principal contracts that are dealer property (as defined in paragraph (a)(4)(v) of this section).

(4) *Income equivalent to interest from factoring*—(i) *General rule.* Income equivalent to interest includes factoring income. Except as provided in paragraph (h)(4)(ii) of this section, the term *factoring income* includes any income (including any discount income or service fee, but excluding any stated interest) derived from the acquisition and collection or disposition of a factored receivable. The amount of income equivalent to interest realized with respect to a factored receivable is the difference (if a positive number) between the amount paid for the receivable by the foreign corporation and the amount that it collects on the receivable (or realizes upon its sale of the receivable). The rules of this paragraph (h)(4) apply only with respect to the tax treatment of factoring income derived from the acquisition and collection or disposition of a factored receivable and shall not affect the characterization of an expense or loss of either the person whose goods or services gave rise to a factored receivable or the obligor under a receivable.

(ii) *Exceptions.* Factoring income shall not include—

(A) Income treated as interest under section 864(d)(1) or (6) (relating to income derived from trade or service receivables of related persons), even if such income is treated as not described in section 864(d)(1) by reason of the same-country exception of section 864(d)(7);

(B) Income derived from a factored receivable if payment for the acquisition of the receivable is made on or after the date on which stated interest begins to accrue, but only if the rate of stated interest equals or exceeds 120 percent of the Federal short-term rate (as defined under section 1274) (or the analogous rate for a currency other than the dollar) as of the date on which the receivable is acquired by the foreign corporation; or

(C) Income derived from a factored receivable if payment for the acquisition of the receivable by the foreign corporation is made only on or after the anticipated date of payment of all principal by the obligor (or the anticipated weighted average date of payment of a pool of purchased receivables).

(iii) *Factored receivable.* For purposes of this paragraph (h)(4), the term *factored receivable* includes any account receivable or other evidence of indebtedness, whether or not issued at a discount and whether or not bearing stated interest, arising out of the disposition of property or the performance of services by any person, if such account receivable or evidence of indebtedness is acquired by a person other than the person who disposed of the property or provided the services that gave rise to the account receivable or evidence of indebtedness. For purposes of this paragraph (h)(4), it is immaterial whether the person providing the property or services agrees to transfer the receivable at the time of sale (as by accepting a third-party charge or credit card) or at a later time.

(iv) *Examples.* The following examples illustrate the application of this paragraph (h)(4).

Example 1. DP, a domestic corporation, owns all of the outstanding stock of FS, a controlled foreign corporation. FS acquires accounts receivable arising from the sale of property by unrelated corporation X. The receivables have a face amount of $100, and after 30 days bear stated interest equal to at least 120 percent of the applicable Federal short-term rate (determined as of the date the receivables are acquired by FS). FS purchases the receivables from X for $95 on Day 1 and collects $100 plus stated interest from the obligor under the receivables on Day 40. Income (other than stated interest) derived by FS from the factored receivables is factoring income within the meaning of paragraph (h)(4)(i) of this section and, therefore, is income equivalent to interest.

Example 2. The facts are the same as in *Example 1*, except that, rather than collecting $100 plus stated interest from the obligor under the factored receivables on Day 40, FS sells the receivables to controlled foreign corporation Y on Day 15 for $97. Both the income derived by FS on the factored receivables and the income derived by Y (other than stated interest) on the receivables are factoring income within the meaning of paragraph (h)(4)(i) of this section, and therefore, constitute income equivalent to interest.

Example 3. The facts are the same as in *Example 1*, except that FS purchases the receivables from X for $98 on Day 30. Income derived by FS from the factored receivables is excluded from factoring income under paragraph (h)(4)(ii)(B) of this section and, therefore, does not give rise to income equivalent to interest.

Example 4. The facts are the same as in *Example 3*, except that it is anticipated that all principal will be paid by the obligor of the receivables by Day 30. Income derived by FS from this maturity factoring of the receivables is excluded

Reg. § 1.954-2(h)(4)

Income from Sources Without the United States

from factoring income under paragraph (h)(4)(ii)(C) of this section and, therefore, does not give rise to income equivalent to interest.

Example 5. The facts are the same as in Example 4, except that FS sells the factored receivables to Y for $99 on day 45, at which time stated interest is accruing on the unpaid balance of $100. Because interest was accruing at the time Y acquired the receivables at a rate equal to at least 120 percent of the applicable Federal short-term rate, income derived by Y from the factored receivables is excluded from factoring income under paragraph (h)(4)(ii)(B) of this section and, therefore, does not give rise to income equivalent to interest.

Example 6. DP, a domestic corporation engaged in an integrated credit card business, owns all of the outstanding stock of FS, a controlled foreign corporation. On Day 1, individual A uses a credit card issued by DP to purchase shoes priced at $100 from X, a foreign corporation unrelated to DP, FS, or A. On Day 7, X transfers the receivable (which does not bear stated interest) arising from A's purchase to FS in exchange for $95. FS collects $100 from A on Day 45. Income derived by FS on the factored receivable is factoring income within the meaning of paragraph (h)(4)(i) of this section and, therefore, is income equivalent to interest.

(5) *Receivables arising from performance of services.* If payment for services performed by a controlled foreign corporation is not made until more than 120 days after the date on which such services are performed, then the income derived by the controlled foreign corporation constitutes income equivalent to interest to the extent that interest income would be imputed under the principles of section 483 or the original issue discount provisions (sections 1271 through 1275), if—

(i) Such provisions applied to contracts for the performance of services;

(ii) The time period referred to in sections 483(c)(1) and 1274(c)(1)(B) were 120 days rather than six months; and (iii) The time period referred to in section 483(c)(1)(A) were 120 days rather than one year.

(6) *Examples.* The following examples illustrate the application of this paragraph (h).

Example 1. CFC, a controlled foreign corporation, promises that Corporation A may borrow up to $500 in principal for one year beginning at any time during the next three months at an interest rate of 10 percent. In exchange, Corporation A pays CFC a commitment fee of $2. Pursuant to this agreement, CFC lends $80 to Corporation A. As a result, the entire $2 fee is included in the computation of CFC'S foreign personal holding company income under paragraph (h)(2)(i)(G) of this section.

Example 2. (i) At the beginning of its current taxable year, CFC, a controlled foreign corporation, purchases at face value a one-year debt instrument issued by Corporation A having a $100 principal amount and bearing a floating rate of interest set at the LIBOR plus one percentage point. Contemporaneously, CFC borrows $100 from Corporation B for one year at a fixed interest rate of 10 percent, using the debt instrument as security.

(ii) During its current taxable year, CFC accrues $11 of interest from Corporation A on the bond. Because interest is excluded from the definition of income equivalent to interest under paragraph (h)(1)(ii)(B) of this section, the $11 is not income equivalent to interest.

(iii) During its current taxable year, CFC incurs $10 of interest expense with respect to the borrowing from Corporation B. That expense is allocated and apportioned to, and reduces, subpart F income to the extent provided in section 954(b)(5) and §§ 1.861-9T through 1.861-12T and 1.954-1(c).

Example 3. (i) On January 1, 1994, CFC, a controlled foreign corporation with the United States dollar as its functional currency, purchases at face value a 10-year debt instrument issued by Corporation A having a $100 principal amount and bearing a floating rate of interest set at the (LIBOR) plus one percentage point payable on December 31st of each year. CFC subsequently determines that it would prefer receiving a fixed rate of return. Accordingly, on January 1, 1995, CFC enters into a 9-year interest rate swap agreement with Corporation B whereby Corporation B promises to pay CFC on December 31st of each year an amount equal to 10 percent on a notional principal amount of $100. In exchange, CFC promises to pay Corporation B an amount equal to LIBOR plus one percentage point on the notional principal amount.

(ii) On December 31, 1995, CFC receives $9 of interest income from Corporation A with respect to the debt instrument. On the same day, CFC receives a total of $10 from Corporation B and pays $9 to Corporation B with respect to the interest rate swap.

(iii) The $9 of interest income is foreign personal holding income under section 954(c)(1). Pursuant to § 1.446-3(d), CFC recognizes $1 of swap income for its 1995 taxable year that is also foreign personal holding company income because it is income equivalent to interest under paragraph (h)(2)(i)(C) of this section.

Reg. § 1.954-2(h)(6)

Income from Sources Without the United States

Example 4. (i) *CFC*, a controlled foreign corporation, purchases commodity X on the spot market for $100 and, contemporaneously, enter into a 3 month forward contract to sell commodity X for $104, a price set by the forward market.

(ii) Assuming that substantially all of *CFC*'s expected return is attributable to the time value of the net investment, as described in section 1258(c)(1), the transaction is a conversion transaction under section 1258(c). Accordingly, any gain treated as ordinary income under section 1258(a) will be foreign personal holding company income because it is income equivalent to interest under paragraph (h)(2)(i)(E) of this section. [Reg. § 1.954-2.]

☐ [*T.D.* 8618, 9-6-95. Amended by *T.D.* 8704, 12-31-96.]

[Reg. § 4.954-2.]

§ 4.954-2. **Foreign personal holding company income; taxable years beginning after December 31, 1986.**—(a) *Computation of foreign personal holding company income*—(1) *In general.* Foreign personal holding company income consists of the following categories of income:

(i) Dividends, interest, rents, royalties, and annuities as defined in paragraph (b) of this section;

(ii) Gain from certain property transactions as defined in paragraph (e) of this section;

(iii) Gain from commodities transactions as defined in paragraph (f) of this section;

(iv) Foreign currency gain as defined in paragraph (g) of this section; and

(v) Income equivalent to interest as defined in paragraph (h) of this section.

Paragraph (a)(3) provides rules for determining the use or purpose for which property is held, if a change in use or purpose would affect the computation of foreign personal holding company income under paragraphs (e), (f), and (g). Paragraphs (c) and (d) provide rules for determining certain rents and royalties that are excluded from foreign personal holding company income under paragraph (b).

(2) *Coordination of overlapping definitions.* If a particular portion of income from a transaction in substance falls within more than one of the definitional rules of section 954(c) and this section, its character is determined under the rules of subdivision (i) through (iii) of this paragraph (a)(2). The character of loss from a transaction must be similarly determined under the rules of this paragraph (a)(2).

(i) If a portion of the income from a transaction falls within the definition of income equivalent to interest under paragraph (h) of this section and the definition of gain from certain property transactions under paragraph (e) of this section, gain from a commodities transaction under paragraph (f) of this section (whether or not derived from a qualified hedging transaction or qualified active sales), or foreign currency gain under paragraph (g) of this section (whether or not derived from a qualified business transaction or a qualified hedging transaction), that portion of income is treated as income equivalent to interest for purposes of section 954(c) and this section.

(ii) If a portion of the income from a transaction falls within the definition of foreign currency gain under paragraph (g) of this section (whether or not derived from a qualified business transaction or a qualified hedging transaction) and the definition of gain from certain property transactions under paragraph (e) of this section, or gain from a commodities transaction under paragraph (f) of this section (whether or not derived from a qualified hedging transaction or qualified active sales), that portion of income is treated as foreign currency gain for purposes of section 954(c) and this section.

(iii) If a portion of the income from a transaction falls within the definition of gain from a commodities transaction under paragraph (f) of this section (whether or not derived from a qualified hedging transaction or qualified active sales) and the definition of gain from certain property transactions under paragraph (e) of this section, that portion of income is treated as gain from a commodities transaction for purposes of section 954(c) and this section.

(3) *Changes in the use or purpose with which property is held*—(i) *In general.* Under paragraphs (e), (f), and (g) of this section, transactions in certain property give rise to gain or loss included in the computation of foreign personal holding company income if the controlled foreign corporation holds that property for a particular use or purpose. For purposes of this section, in determining the purpose or use for which property is held, the period shortly before disposition is the most significant period. However, if a controlled foreign corporation held property with a purpose that would have caused its disposition to give rise to gain or loss included in the computation of foreign personal holding company income under this section, and prior to disposition the controlled foreign corporation changed the purpose or use for which it held the property to one that would cause its disposition to give rise to gain or loss excluded from the computation of foreign personal holding company income, then the later purpose or use shall be ignored unless it was continuously present

Reg. § 4.954-2(a)(1)

for a predominant portion of the period during which the controlled foreign corporation held the property. Under paragraph (g)(4)(iii) of this section, a currency hedging transaction may be treated as two or more separate hedging transactions, such that each portion is separately considered in applying this paragraph (a)(3).

(ii) *Illustrations.* The following examples illustrate the application of this paragraph (a)(3).

Example (1). At the beginning of taxable year 1, CFC, a controlled foreign corporation, purchases a building for investment. During taxable years 1 and 2, CFC derives rents from this building that are included in the computation of foreign personal holding company income under paragraph (b)(1)(iii) of this section. At the beginning of taxable year 3, CFC changes the use of the building by terminating all leases and using it in an active trade or business. At the beginning of taxable year 4, CFC sells the building at a gain. For purposes of paragraph (e) of this section (gains from the sale or exchange of certain property) the building is considered to be property that gives rise to rents, as described in paragraph (e)(2). Because there was a change of use at the beginning of year 3 that would cause the disposition of the building to give rise to gain or loss excluded from the computation of foreign personal holding company income, the characterization of the gain derived at the beginning of year 4 is determined according to the property's use during the predominant portion of the period from purchase to date of sale. Therefore, gain from the sale of that building is included in the computation of foreign personal holding company income under paragraph (e) of this section.

Example (2). For taxable years 1, 2, and 3, CFC, a controlled foreign corporation, is engaged in the active conduct of a commodity business as a handler of gold, as defined in paragraph (f)(3)(iii), and substantially all of its business is as an active handler of gold, as defined in paragraph (f)(3)(iv). At the beginning of taxable year 1, CFC purchases 1000 ounces of gold for investment. At the beginning of taxable year 3, CFC begins holding that gold in physical form for sale to customers. During taxable year 3, CFC sells the entire 1000 ounces of gold in transactions described in paragraph (f)(3)(ii) at a gain. For purposes of paragraph (f), CFC is considered to hold the gold for investment, and not in its capacity as an active handler of gold. Thus, under paragraph (f)(3)(i), the gold is not considered to be sold in the active trade or business of the CFC as a handler of gold, and gain from the sale is included in the computation of foreign personal holding company income under paragraph (f) of this section.

Example (3). CFC, a controlled foreign corporation, is a regular dealer in unimproved land. The functional currency (as defined in section 985 and the regulations thereunder) of CFC is country X currency. On day 1 of its current taxable year, CFC enters into an agreement with A to pay $100 for certain real property to be held by CFC for investment. On day 10, under its method of accounting, CFC accrues the value of $100 in country X currency, but payment will not be made until the first day of the next taxable year (day 366). On day 190, CFC determines to hold the property for sale to customers in a transaction that would be a qualified business transaction under paragraph (g)(3) of this section. For purposes of this section, the land is considered to be held for investment, and the foreign currency gain attributable to that transaction is included in the computation of foreign personal holding company income under paragraph (g) of this section.

Example (4). CFC, a controlled foreign corporation, is a regular dealer in widgets. The functional currency (as defined in section 985 and the regulations thereunder) of CFC is country X currency. On day 1 of its current taxable year, CFC sells widgets held in inventory to A for delivery on day 60. The sales price is denominated in U.S. dollars, and payment is to be made by A on the same day the widgets are to be delivered to A. The remaining facts and circumstances are such that this sale would meet the definition of a qualified business transaction under paragraph (g)(4), the foreign currency gain from which would be excluded from the computation of foreign personal holding company income under paragraph (g). On day 1, CFC sells U.S. dollars forward for delivery in 60 days in a transaction that would be a qualified hedging transaction under paragraph (g)(5). On day 25 the sale of widgets to A is cancelled in a transaction that does not result in CFC realizing any foreign currency gain or loss with respect to the sale of widgets. However, CFC holds the dollar forward contract to maturity. Because the forward contract does not hedge a qualified business transaction during the period shortly before its maturity, it is not to be considered a qualified hedging transaction under paragraph (g), and any foreign currency gain or loss recognized therefrom is included in the computation of foreign personal holding company income under paragraph (g). However, if CFC identifies the portion of the foreign currency gain or loss derived from the forward contract that is attributable to days 1 through 25, and the portion that is attributable to

Reg. § 4.954-2(a)(3)

days 25 through 60, the forward contract may be considered two separate transactions in accordance with the rules provided by paragraph (g)(4)(ii) of this section. Thus, the forward sale may be separately considered a qualified hedging transaction for day 1 through day 25, and the foreign currency gain or loss attributable to day 1 through day 25 may be excluded from the computation of foreign personal holding company income under paragraph (g) of this section.

Example (5). CFC, a controlled foreign corporation, has country X currency as its functional currency under section 985 and the regulations thereunder. On day 1 of the current taxable year, CFC, speculating on exchange rates, sells dollars forward for delivery in 120 days. On day 65, CFC sells widgets held in inventory at a price denominated in dollars to be paid on day 120 in a transaction that is a qualified business transaction. CFC had not made any other dollar sales between day 1 and day 65 and does not anticipate making any other dollar sales during the taxable year. On day 65, CFC accrues the value of $100 in country X currency. On day 120, CFC receives $100 payment for the widgets and recognizes foreign currency loss pursuant to that transaction. On day 120 CFC also delivers dollars in connection with the forward sale, and recognizes foreign currency gain pursuant to the delivery. Under this paragraph (a)(3) the currency transaction is considered to have been entered into for speculation, and any currency gain recognized by CFC on the forward sale of dollars must be included in the computation of foreign personal holding company income under paragraph (g). However, if CFC identifies the portion of the forward sale, and the foreign currency gain or therefrom, that is attributable to day 1 through day 64, and the portion that is attributable to day 65 through day 120, the forward sale may be considered two separate transactions in accordance with the rules provided by paragraph (g)(4)(ii) of this section. Thus, the transaction for day 65 through day 120 may be considered a separate transaction that is a qualified hedging transaction, and the foreign currency gain attributable to day 65 through day 120 may be excluded from the computation of foreign personal holding company income under this paragraph (g) if all the other requirements for treatment as a qualified hedging transaction under paragraph (g) are met.

(4) *Definitions.* The following definitions apply for purposes of computing foreign personal holding company income under this section.

(i) *Interest.* The term "interest" includes amounts that are treated as ordinary income, original issue discount or interest income (including original issue discount and interest on a tax-exempt obligation) by reason of sections 482, 483, 864(d), 1273, 1274, 1276, 1281, 1286, 1288, 7872 and the regulations thereunder, or as interest or original issue discount income by reason of any other provision of law. For special rules concerning interest exempt from U.S. tax pursuant to section 103, see paragraph (b)(6) of this section.

(ii) *Inventory and similar property.* The term "inventory and similar property" (or "inventory or similar property") means property that is stock in trade of the controlled foreign corporation or other property of a kind which would properly be included in the inventory of the controlled corporation if on hand at the close of the taxable year (were the controlled foreign corporation a domestic corporation), or property held by the controlled foreign corporation primarily for sale to customers in the ordinary course of its trade or business. Rights to property held in bona fide hedging transactions that reduce the risk of price changes in the cost of "inventory and similar property" are included in the definition of that term if they are an integral part of the system by which a controlled foreign corporation purchases such property, and they are so identified by the close of the fifth day after the day on which the hedging transaction is entered into.

(iii) *Regular dealer.* The term "regular dealer" means a merchant with an established place of business that—

(A) Regularly and actively engages as a merchant in purchasing property and selling it to customers in the ordinary course of business with a view to the gains and profits that may be derived therefrom, or

(B) Makes a market in derivative financial products of property (such as forward contracts to buy or sell property, option contracts to buy or sell property, interest rate and currency swap contracts or other notional principal contracts) by regularly and actively offering to enter into positions in such products to the public in the ordinary course of business.

Purchasing and selling property through a regulated exchange or established off-exchange market (for example, engaging in futures transactions) is not actively engaging as a merchant for purposes of this section.

(iv) *Dealer property.* Property held by a controlled foreign corporation is "dealer property" if—

(A) The controlled foreign corporation is a regular dealer in property of such kind, and

Reg. § 4.954-2(a)(4)

(B) The property is held by the controlled foreign corporation in its capacity as a dealer.

Property which is held by the controlled foreign corporation for investment or speculation is not such property.

(v) *Debt instrument.* The term "debt instrument" includes bonds, debentures, notes, certificates, accounts receivable, and other evidences of indebtedness.

(b) *Dividends, etc.*—(1) *In general.* Foreign personal holding company includes:

(i) Dividends, except certain dividends from related persons as described in paragraph (b)(3) of this section and distributions of previously taxed income under section 959(b) and the regulations thereunder;

(ii) Interest, except export financing interest as defined in paragraph (b)(2) of this section and certain interest received from related persons as described in paragraph (b)(3) of this section;

(iii) Rents and royalties, except certain rents and royalties received from related persons as described in (b)(4) of this section and rents and royalties derived in the active conduct of a trade or business as defined in paragraph (b)(5); and

(iv) Annuities.

(2) *Exclusion of certain export financing*—(i) *In general.* Pursuant to section 954(c)(2)(B), foreign personal holding company income computed under section 954(c)(1)(A) and this paragraph (b) does not include interest that is export financing interest. For purposes of section 954(c)(2)(B) and this section, the term "export financing interest" means interest that is derived in the conduct of a banking business and is export financing interest as defined in section 904(d)(2)(G) and the regulations thereunder. Pursuant to section 864(d)(5)(A)(iii), it does not include income from related party factoring that is treated as interest under section 864(d)(1) or interest described in section 864(d)(6).

(ii) *Conduct of a banking business.* For purposes of this section, export financing interest as defined in section 904(d)(2)(G) and the regulations thereunder is considered derived in the conduct of a banking business if, in connection with the financing from which the interest is derived, the corporation, through its own officers or staff of employees, engages in all the activities in which banks customarily engage in issuing and servicing a loan.

(iii) *Illustration.* The following example illustrates the application of this provision:

Example. DS, a domestic corporation, manufactures property in the United States. In addition to selling inventory (property described in section 1221(1)), DS occasionally sells depreciable equipment it manufactures for use in its trade or business, which is property described in section 1221(2). Less than 50 percent of the fair market value, determined in accordance with section 904(d)(2)(G) and the regulations thereunder, of each item of inventory or equipment sold by DS is attributable to products imported into the United States. CFC, a controlled foreign corporation related (as defined in section 954(d)) to DS, provides loans for the purchase of property from DS, if the property is purchased exclusively for use or consumption outside the United States.

If, in issuing and servicing loans made with respect to purchases from DS of depreciable equipment used in its trade or business, which is property described in section 1221(2) in the hands of DS, CFC engages in all the activities in which banks customarily engage in issuing and servicing loans, the interest accrued from these loans would be export financing interest meeting the requirements of paragraph (b)(2) of this section, which would not be included in foreign personal holding company income under section 954(c) and paragraph (b)(1)(ii) of this section. However, interest from the loans made with respect to purchases from DS of property which is inventory in the hands of DS cannot be export financing interest because it is treated as income from a trade or service receivable under section 864(d)(6) and the regulations thereunder, and thus is included in foreign personal holding company income under paragraph (b)(1)(ii) of this section. See § 1.864-8T(d) for rules concerning certain income from trade and service receivables qualifying under the same country exception of section 864(d)(7).

(3) *Exclusion of dividends and interest from related persons*—(i) *Excluded dividends and interest.* Foreign personal holding company income does not include dividends and interest if—

(A) The payor is a corporation that is a related person as defined in section 954(d)(3),

(B) The payor is created or organized ("incorporated") under the laws of the same foreign country as the controlled foreign corporation, and

(C) A substantial part of the payor's assets are used in a trade or business in the payor's country of incorporation as determined under subdivision (iv) of this paragraph (b)(3).

Except as otherwise provided under this paragraph (b)(3), the principles of section 367(a) and regulations thereunder shall apply in determining whether the payor has a trade or business in its

Reg. § 4.954-2(b)(3)

country of incorporation, and whether its assets are used in that trade or business.

(ii) *Interest paid out of adjusted foreign base company income or insurance income.* Interest may not be excluded from the foreign personal holding company income of the recipient under this paragraph (b)(3) to the extent that the deduction for the interest is allocated under § 1.954-1T(c) to the payor's adjusted gross foreign base company income (as defined in § 1.954-1T(a)(3)), adjusted gross insurance income (as defined in § 1.954-1T(a)(6)), or other categories of income included in the computation of subpart F income under section 952(a), for purposes of computing the payor's net foreign base company income (as defined in § 1.954-1T(a)(4)), net insurance income (as defined in § 1.954-1T(a)(6)), or income described in sections 952(a)(3), (4), and (5).

(iii) *Dividends paid out of prior years' earnings.* Dividends are excluded from foreign personal holding company income under this paragraph (b)(3) only to the extent they are paid out of earnings and profits which were earned or accumulated during a period in which the requirements of subdivision (i) of this paragraph (b)(3) were satisfied or, to the extent earned or accumulated during a taxable year of the related foreign corporation ending on or before December 31, 1962, during a period in which the payor was a related corporation as to the controlled foreign corporation and the other requirements of subdivision (i) of this paragraph (b)(3) are substantially satisfied.

(iv) *Fifty percent substantial assets test.* A substantial part of the assets of the payor will be considered used in a trade or business located in its country of incorporation only if, for each quarter during such taxable year, the average value (as of the beginning and end of the quarter) of its assets which are used in the trade or business and are located in such country constitutes over 50 percent of the average value (as of the beginning and end of the quarter) of all the assets of the payor (including assets not used in a trade or business). For such purposes the value of assets shall be determined under subdivision (v) of this paragraph (b)(3), and the location of assets used in a trade or business of the payor shall be determined under subdivisions (vi) through (xi) of this paragraph (b)(3).

(v) *Value of assets.* For purposes of determining whether a substantial part of the assets of the payor are used in a trade or business in its country of incorporation, the value of assets shall be their actual value (not reduced by liabilities), which, in the absence of affirmative evidence to the contrary, shall be deemed to be their adjusted basis.

(vi) *Location of tangible property used in a trade or business*—(A) *In general.* Tangible property (other than inventory and similar property) used in a trade or business is considered located in the country in which it is physically located.

(B) *Exception.* If tangible personal property used in a trade or business is intended for use in the payor's country of incorporation, but is temporarily located elsewhere, it will be considered located within payor's country of incorporation if the reason for its location elsewhere is for inspection or repair, and it is not currently in service in a country other than the payor's country of incorporation and is not to be placed in service in a country other than the payor's country of incorporation following the inspection or repair.

(vii) *Location of intangible property used in a trade or business*—(A) *In general.* The location of intangible property (other than inventory or similar property and debt instruments) used in a trade or business is determined based on the site of the activities conducted by the payor during the current year in connection with using or exploiting that property. An item of intangible property is located in the payor's country of incorporation during each quarter of the current taxable year if the activities connected with its use or exploitation are conducted during the entire current taxable year by the payor in its country of incorporation. For this purpose, the determination of the country in which services are performed shall be made under the principles of section 954(e) and § 1.954-4(c).

(B) *Property located in part in the payor's country of incorporation and in part in other countries.* If the activities connected with the use or exploitation of an item of intangible property are conducted during the current taxable year by the payor in the payor's country of incorporation and in other countries, then a percentage of the intangible (measured by the average value of the item as of the beginning and end of the quarter) is considered located in the payor's country of incorporation during each quarter. That percentage equals the ratio that the expenses of the payor incurred during the entire taxable year by reason of such activities that are conducted in the payor's country of incorporation bear to the expenses of the payor incurred during the entire taxable year by reason of all such activities worldwide. Expenses incurred in connection with the use or exploitation of an item of intangible property are included in the computation provided by

Reg. § 4.954-2(b)(3)

this paragraph (b)(3) if they are deductible under section 162 or includible in inventory costs or the costs of goods sold (were the payor a domestic corporation).

(viii) *Location of property held for sale to customers*—(A) *In general.* Inventory or similar property is considered located in the payor's country of incorporation during each quarter of the taxable year if the activities of the payor in connection with the production and sale, or purchase and resale, of such property are conducted in the payor's country of incorporation during the entire taxable year. If the payor conducts such activities through an independent contractor, then the location of such activities shall be the place in which they are conducted by the independent contractor.

(B) *Inventory located in part in the payor's country of incorporation and in part in other countries.* If the activities connected with the production and sale, or purchase and resale, of inventory or similar property are conducted by the payor in the payor's country of incorporation and other countries, then a percentage of the inventory or similar property (measured by the average value of the item as of the beginning and end of the quarter) is considered located in the payor's country of incorporation each quarter. That percentage equals the ratio that the costs of the payor incurred during the entire taxable year by reason of such activities that are conducted in the payor's country of incorporation bear to all such costs incurred by reason of such activities worldwide. A cost incurred in connection with the production and sale or purchase and resale of inventory or similar property is included in this computation if it—

(*1*) Must be included in inventory costs or otherwise capitalized with respect to inventory or similar property under section 61, 263A, 471, or 472 and the regulations thereunder (whichever would be applicable were the payor a domestic corporation), or

(*2*) Would be deductible under section 162 (were the payor a domestic corporation) and is definitely related to gross income derived from such property (but not to all classes of gross income derived by the payor) under the principles of § 1.861-8.

(ix) *Location of debt instruments.* For purposes of this paragraph (b)(3), debt instruments are considered to be used in a trade or business only if they arise from the sale of inventory or similar property by the payor or from the rendition of services by the payor in the ordinary course of a trade or business of the payor, but only until such time as interest is required to be charged under section 482 and the regulations thereunder. Debt instruments that arise from the sale of inventory or similar property are treated as having the same location, proportionately, as inventory or similar property that is held during the same calendar quarter. Debt instruments arising from the rendition of services in the ordinary course of a trade or business are considered located on a proportionate basis in the countries in which the services to which they relate are performed.

(x) *Treatment of certain stock interests.* For the purpose of determining the value of assets used in a trade or business in the country of incorporation, stock directly or indirectly owned by the payor within the meaning of section 958(a) in a controlled foreign corporation ("lower-tier corporation"), which is incorporated in the same country as the payor, shall be considered located in the country of incorporation and used in a trade or business of the payor in proportion to the value of the assets of the lower-tier corporation that are used in a trade or business in the country of incorporation. The location of assets used in a trade or business of the lower-tier corporation shall be determined under the rules of this paragraph (b)(3).

(xi) *Determination of period during which property is used in a trade or business.* Property purchased or produced for use in a trade or business shall not be considered used in a trade or business until it is placed in service, and shall cease to be considered used in a trade or business when it is retired from service. The dates during which depreciable property is determined to be in use must be consistent with the determination of depreciation under sections 167 and 168 and the regulations thereunder.

(xii) *Treatment of banks and insurance companies.* [Reserved.]

(4) *Exclusion of rents and royalties derived from related persons*—(i) *In general.* Foreign personal holding company income does not include rents or royalties if—

(A) The payor is a corporation that is a related person as defined in section 954(d)(3), and

(B) The rents or royalties are for the use of, or the privilege of using, property within the country under the laws of which the recipient of the payments is created or organized.

If the property is used both within and without the country under the laws of which the controlled foreign corporation is created or organized, the part of the rent or royalty attributable to the use of, or the privilege of using, the property outside such country of incorporation is, unless otherwise

Reg. § 4.954-2(b)(4)

provided, foreign personal holding company income under this paragraph (b).

(ii) *Rents or royalties paid out of adjusted foreign base company income or insurance income.* Rents or royalties may not be excluded from the foreign personal holding company income of the recipient under this paragraph (b)(4) to the extent that deductions for the payments are allocated under section 954(b)(5) and § 1.954-1T(a)(4) to the payor's adjusted gross foreign base company income (as defined in § 1.954-1T(a)(3)), adjusted gross insurance income (as defined in § 1.954-1T(a)(6)), or other categories of income included in the computation of subpart F income under section 952(a), for purposes of computing the payor's net foreign base company income (as defined in § 1.954-1T(a)(4)), net insurance income (as defined in § 1.954-1T(a)(6)), or income described in section 952(a)(3), (4), or (5).

(5) *Exclusion of rents and royalties derived in the active conduct of a trade or business.* Foreign personal holding company income shall not include rents or royalties which are derived in the active conduct of a trade or business and which are received from a person other than a related person within the meaning of section 954(d)(3). Whether or not rents or royalties are derived in the active conduct of a trade or business is to be determined from the facts and circumstances of each case; but see paragraph (c) or (d) of this section for specific cases in which rents or royalties will be considered for purposes of this paragraph to be derived in the active conduct of a trade or business. The frequency with which a foreign corporation enters into transactions from which rents or royalties are derived will not of itself establish the fact that such rents or royalties are derived in the active conduct of a trade or business.

(6) *Treatment of tax exempt interest.* Foreign personal holding company income includes all interest income, including interest that is exempt from U.S. tax pursuant to section 103 ("tax-exempt interest"). However, the net foreign base company income of a controlled foreign corporation that is attributable to such tax-exempt interest shall be treated as tax-exempt interest in the hands of the U.S. shareholders of the foreign corporation. Accordingly, any net foreign base company income that is included in the subpart F income of a U.S. shareholder and that is attributable to such tax-exempt interest shall remain exempt from the regular income tax, but potentially subject to the alternative minimum tax, in the hands of the U.S. shareholder.

(c) *Excluded rents*—(1) *Trade or business cases.* Rents will be considered for purposes of paragraph (b)(5) of this section to be derived in the active conduct of a trade or business if such rents are derived by the controlled foreign corporation ("lessor") from leasing—

(i) Property which the lessor has manufactured or produced, or has acquired and added substantial value to, but only if the lessor is regularly engaged in the manufacture or production of, or in the acquisition and addition of substantial value to, property of such kind,

(ii) Real property with respect to which the lessor, through its own officers or staff of employees, regularly performs active and substantial management and operational functions while the property is leased,

(iii) Personal property ordinarily used by the lessor in the active conduct of a trade or business, leased during a temporary period when the property would, but for such leasing, be idle, or

(iv) Property which is leased as a result of the performance of marketing functions by such lessor if the lessor, through its own officers or staff of employees located in a foreign country, maintains and operates an organization in such country which is regularly engaged in the business of marketing, or of marketing and servicing, the leased property and which is substantial in relation to the amount of rents derived from the leasing of such property.

(2) *Special rules*—(i) *Adding substantial value.* For purposes of paragraph (c)(1)(i) of this section, the performance of marketing functions will not be considered to add substantial value to property.

(ii) *Substantiality of foreign organization.* An organization in a foreign country will be considered substantial in relation to the amount of rents, for purposes of paragraph (c)(1)(iv) of this section, if active leasing expenses, as defined in paragraph (c)(2)(iii), equal or exceed 25 percent of the adjusted leasing profit, as defined in paragraph (c)(2)(iv).

(iii) *Active leasing expenses.* The term "active leasing expenses" means the deductions incurred by an organization of the lessor in a foreign country which are properly allocable to rental income and which would be allowable under section 162 to the lessor (were the lessor a domestic corporation) other than—

(A) Deductions for compensation for personal services rendered by shareholders of, or related persons with respect to, the lessor,

Reg. § 4.954-2(b)(5)

(B) Deductions for rents paid or accrued,

(C) Deductions which, although generally allowable under section 162, would be specifically allowable to the lessor (were the lessor a domestic corporation) under sections other than section 162 (such as sections 167 and 168), and

(D) Deductions for payments made to independent contractors with respect to the leased property.

(iv) *Adjusted leasing profit.* The term "adjusted leasing profit" means the gross income of the lessor from rents, reduced by the sum of—

(A) The rents paid or incurred by the controlled foreign corporation with respect to such gross rental income,

(B) The amounts which would be allowable to such lessor (were the lessor a domestic corporation) as deductions under section 167 or 168 with respect to such rental income, and

(C) The amounts paid to independent contractors with respect to such rental ilcome.

(3) *Illustrations.* The application of this paragraph (c) is illustrated by the following examples.

Example (1). Controlled foreign corporation A is regularly engaged in the production of office machines which it sells or leases to others and services. Under paragraph (c)(1)(i) of this section, the rental income of A Corporation from the leases is derived in the active conduct of a trade or business for purposes of section 954(c)(2)(A).

Example (2). Controlled foreign corporation D purchases motor vehicles which it leases to others. In the conduct of its short-term leasing of such vehicles in foreign country X, Corporation D owns a large number of motor vehicles in country X which it services and repairs, leases motor vehicles to customers on an hourly, daily, or weekly basis, maintains offices and service facilities in country X from which to lease and service such vehicles, and maintains therein a sizable staff of its own administrative, sales, and service personnel. Corporation D also leases in country X on a long-term basis, generally for a term of one year, motor vehicles which it owns. Under the terms of the long-term leases, Corporation D is required to repair and service, during the term of the lease, the leased motor vehicles without cost to the lessee. By the maintenance in country X of office, sales, and service facilities and its complete staff of administrative, sales, and service personnel, Corporation D maintains and operates an organization therein which is regularly engaged in the business of marketing and servicing the motor vehicles which are leased. The deductions incurred by such organization satisfy the 25-percent test of paragraph (c)(2)(ii) of this section; thus, such organization is substantial in relation to the rents Corporation D receives from leasing the motor vehicles. Therefore, under paragraph (c)(1)(iv) of this section, such rents are derived in the active conduct of a trade or business for purposes of section 954(c)(2)(A).

Example (4). Controlled foreign corporation E owns a complex of apartment buildings which it has acquired by purchase. Corporation E engages a real estate management firm to lease the apartments, manage the buildings and pay over the net rents to the owner. The rental income of E Corporation from such leases is not derived in the active conduct of a trade or business for purposes of section 954(c)(2)(A).

Example (5). Controlled foreign corporation F acquired by purchase a twenty-story office building in a foreign country, three floors of which it occupies and the rest of which it leases. Corporation F acts as rental agent for the leasing of offices in the building and employs a substantial staff to perform other management and maintenance functions. Under paragraph (c)(1)(ii) of this section, the rents received by Corporation F from such leasing operations are derived in the active conduct of a trade or business for purposes of section 954(c)(2)(A).

Example (6). Controlled foreign corporation G owns equipment which it ordinarily uses to perform contracts in foreign countries to drill oil wells. For occasional brief and irregular periods it is unable to obtain contracts requiring immediate performance sufficient to employ all such equipment. During such a period it sometimes leases such idle equipment temporarily. After the expiration of such temporary leasing of the property, Corporation G continues the use of such equipment in the performance of its own drilling contracts. Under paragraph (c)(1)(iii) of this section, rents G receives from such leasing of idle equipment are derived in the active conduct of a trade or business for purposes of section 954(c)(2)(A).

(d) *Excluded royalties*—(1) *Trade or business cases.* Royalties will be considered for purposes of paragraph (b)(5) of this section to be derived in the active conduct of a trade or business if such royalties are derived by the controlled foreign corporation ("licensor") from licensing—(i) Property which the licensor has developed, created, or produced, or has acquired and added substantial value to, but only so long as the licensor is regularly engaged in the development, creation, or production of, or in the acquisition of and addition of substantial value to, property of such kind, or

Reg. § 4.954-2(d)(1)

(ii) Property which is licensed as a result of the performance of marketing functions by such licensor and the licensor, through its own staff of employees located in a foreign country, maintains and operates an organization in such country which is regularly engaged in the business of marketing, or of marketing and servicing, the licensed property and which is substantial in relation to the amount of royalties derived from the licensing of such property.

(2) *Special rules*—(i) *Adding substantial value.* For purposes of paragraph (d)(1)(i), the performance of marketing functions will not be considered to add substantial value to property.

(ii) *Substantiality of foreign organization.* An organization in a foreign country will be considered substantial in relation to the amount of royalties, for purposes of paragraph (d)(1)(ii) of this section, if the active licensing expenses, as defined in paragraph (d)(2)(iii) of this section, equal or exceed 25 percent of the adjusted licensing profit, as defined in paragraph (d)(2)(iv).

(iii) *Active licensing expenses.* The term "active licensing expenses" means the deductions incurred by an organization of the licensor which are properly allocable to royalty income and which would be allowable under section 162 to the licensor (were the licensor a domestic corporation) other than—

(A) Deductions for compensation for personal services rendered by shareholders of, or related persons with respect to, the licensor,

(B) Deductions for royalties paid or incurred,

(C) Deductions which, although generally allowable under section 162, would be specifically allowable to the licensor (were the controlled foreign corporation a domestic corporation) under sections other than section 162 (such as section 167), and

(D) Deductions for payments made to independent contractors with respect to the licensed property.

(iv) *Adjusted licensing profit.* The term "adjusted licensing profit" means the gross income of the licensor from royalties, reduced by the sum of—

(A) The royalties paid or incurred by the controlled foreign corporation with respect to such gross royalty income,

(B) The amounts which would be allowable to such licensor as deductions under section 167 (were the licensor a domestic corporation) with respect to such royalty income, and

(C) The amounts paid to independent contractors with respect to such royalty income.

(3) *Illustrations.* The application of this paragraph (d) is illustrated by the following examples.

Example (1). Controlled foreign corporation A, through its own staff of employees, owns and operates a research facility in foreign country X. At the research facility employees of Corporation A who are full time scientists, engineers, and technicians regularly perform experiments, tests, and other technical activities, which ultimately result in the issuance of patents that it sells or licenses. Under paragraph (d)(1)(i) of this section, royalties received by Corporation A for the privilege of using patented rights which it develops as a result of such research activity are derived in the active conduct of a trade or business for purposes of section 954(c)(2)(A).

Example (2). Assume that Corporation A in Example (1), in addition to receiving royalties for the use of patents which it develops, receives royalties for the use of patents which it acquires by purchase and licenses to others without adding any value thereto. Corporation A generally consummates royalty agreements on such purchased patents as the result of inquiries received by it from prospective licensees when the fact becomes known in the business community, as a result of the filing of a patent, advertisements in trade journals, announcements, and contacts by employees of Corporation A, that Corporation A has acquired rights under a patent and is interested in licensing its rights. Corporation A does not, however, maintain and operate an organization in a foreign country which is regularly engaged in the business of marketing the purchased patents. The royalties received by Corporation A for the use of the purchased patents are not derived in the active conduct of a trade or business for purposes of section 954(c)(2)(A).

Example (3). Controlled foreign corporation B receives royalties for the use of patents which it acquires by purchase. The primary business of Corporation B, operated on a regular basis, consists of licensing patents which it has purchased "raw" from inventors and, through the efforts of a substantial staff of employees consisting of scientists, engineers, and technicians, made susceptible to commercial application. For example, Corporation B, after purchasing patent rights covering a chemical process, designs specialized production equipment required for the commercial adaptation of the process and, by so doing, substantially increases the value of the patent. Under paragraph (d)(1)(i) of this section, royalties received by Corporation B from the use of such patent are derived in the active conduct of a trade or business for purposes of section 954(c)(2)(A).

Reg. § 4.954-2(d)(2)

Example (4). Controlled foreign corporation *D* finances independent persons in the development of patented items in return for an ownership interest in such items from which it derives a percentage of royalty income, if any, subsequently derived from the use by others of the protected right. Corporation *D* also attempts to increase its royalty income from such patents by contacting prospective licensees and rendering to licensees advice which is intended to promote the use of the patented property. Corporation *D* does not, however, maintain and operate an organization in a foreign country which is regularly engaged in the business of marketing the patents. Royalties received by Corporation *D* for the use of such patents are not derived in the active conduct of a trade or business for purposes of section 954(c)(2)(A).

(e) *Certain property transactions*—(1) *In general*—(i) *Inclusion in FPHC income.* Foreign personal holding company income includes the excess of gains over losses from the sale or exchange of—

(A) Property which gives rise to dividends, interest, rents, royalties or annuities as described in paragraph (e)(2) of this section, and

(B) Property which does not give rise to income, as described in paragraph (e)(3) of this section.

If losses from the sale or exchange of such property exceed gains, the net loss is not within the definition of foreign personal holding company income under this paragraph (e), and may not be allocated to, or otherwise reduce, other foreign personal holding company income under section 954(b)(5) and § 1.954-1T(c). Gain or loss from a transaction that is treated as capital gain or loss under section 988(a)(1)(B) is not foreign currency gain or loss as defined in paragraph (g), but is gain or loss from the sale or exchange of property which is included in the computation of foreign personal holding company income under this paragraph (e)(1). Paragraphs (e)(4) and (5) of this section provide specific rules for determining whether gain or loss from dispositions of debt instruments and dispositions of options or similar property must be included in the computation of foreign personal holding company income under this paragraph (e)(1). A loss that is deferred or that otherwise may not be taken into account under any provision of the Code may not be taken into account for purposes of determining foreign personal holding company income under any provision of this paragraph (e).

(ii) *Dual character property.* Property may only in part constitute property that gives rise to certain income as described in paragraph (e)(2) of this section or property that does not give rise to any income as described in paragraph (e)(3) of this section. In such cases, the property must be treated as two separate properties for purposes of this paragraph (e). Accordingly, the sale or exchange of such dual character property will give rise to gain or loss that in part must be included in the computation of foreign personal holding company income under this paragraph (e), and in part is excluded from such computation. Gain or loss from the disposition of dual character property must be bifurcated for purposes of this paragraph (e)(1)(i) pursuant to the method that most reasonably reflects the relative uses of the property. Reasonable methods may include comparisons in terms of gross income generated or the physical division of the property. In the case of real property, the physical division of the property will in most cases be the most reasonable method available. For example, if a controlled foreign corporation owns an office building, uses 60 percent of the building in its business, and rents out the other 40 percent, then 40 percent of the gain recognized on the disposition of the property would reasonably be treated as gain which is included in the computation of foreign personal holding company income under this paragraph (e)(1). This paragraph (e)(1)(ii) addresses the contemporaneous use of property for dual purposes; for rules concerning changes in the use of property affecting its classification for purposes of this paragraph (e), see paragraph (a)(3) of this section.

(2) *Property that gives rise to certain income*—(i) *In general.* Property the sale or exchange of which gives rise to foreign personal holding company income under this paragraph (e)(2) includes property that gives rise to dividends, interest, rents, royalties and annuities described in paragraph (b) of this section, except for rents and royalties derived from unrelated persons in the active conduct of a trade or business under paragraph (b)(5) of this section. The property described by this paragraph (e)(2) includes property which gives rise to export financing interest described in paragraph (b)(2) of this section and property which gives rise to income from related persons described in paragraphs (b)(3) and (b)(4).

(ii) *Exception.* Property described in this paragraph (e)(2) does not include—

(A) Dealer property (as defined in paragraph (a)(4)(iv) of this section), and

(B) Inventory and similar property (as defined in paragraph (a)(4)(ii) of this section) other than securities.

(3) *Property that does not give rise to income.* The term "property that does not give rise to income" for purposes of this section includes all

Reg. § 4.954-2(e)(3)

rights and interests in property (whether or not a capital asset) except—

(i) Property that gives rise to dividends, interest, rents, royalties and annuities described in paragraph (e)(2) of this section and property that gives rise to rents and royalties derived in the active conduct of a trade or business under paragraph (b)(5) of this section;

(ii) Dealer property (as defined in paragraph (a)(4)(iv) of this section);

(iii) Inventory and similar property (as defined in paragraph (a)(4)(ii)) other than securities;

(iv) Property (other than real property) used in the controlled foreign corporation's trade or business that is of a character which would be subject to the allowance for depreciation under section 167 or 168 and the regulations thereunder (including tangible property described in § 1.167(a)-2 and intangibles described in § 1.167(a)-3);

(v) Real property that does not give rise to rental or similar income, to the extent used in the controlled foreign corporation's trade or business; and

(vi) Intangible property as defined in section 936(h)(3)(B) and goodwill that is not subject to the allowance for depreciation under section 167 and the regulations thereunder to the extent used in the controlled foreign corporation's trade or business and disposed of in connection with the sale of a trade or business of the controlled foreign corporation.

(4) *Classification of gain or loss from the disposition of a debt instrument or on a deferred payment sale*—(i) *Gain.* Gain from the sale, exchange, or retirement of a debt instrument is included in the computation of foreign personal holding company income under this paragraph (e) unless—

(A) It is treated as interest income (as defined in paragraph (a)(4)(i)); or

(B) It is treated as income equivalent to interest under paragraph (h) of this section.

(ii) *Loss.* Loss from the sale, exchange, or retirement of a debt instrument is included in the computation of foreign personal holding company income under this paragraph (e) unless—

(A) It is directly allocated to interest income (as defined in paragraph (a)(4)(i) of this section) or income equivalent to interest (as defined in paragraph (h) of this section) under any provision of the Code or regulations thereunder;

(B) It is required to be apportioned in the same manner as interest expense under section 864(e) or any other provision of the Code or regulations thereunder; or

(C) The debt instrument was taken in consideration for the sale or exchange of property (or the provision of services) by the controlled foreign corporation and gain or loss from that sale or exchange (or income from the provision of services) is not includible in foreign base company income under this section.

(5) *Classification of options and other rights to acquire or transfer property.* Subject to the exceptions provided in paragraphs (e)(3)(ii) and (iii) (relating to certain dealer property and inventory property), rights to acquire or transfer property, including property that gives rise to income, are classified as property that does not give rise to income under paragraph (e)(3). These rights include options, warrants, futures contracts, options on a futures contract, forward contracts, and options on an index relating to stocks, securities or interest rates.

(6) *Classification of certain interests in pass through entities.* [Reserved.]

(f) *Commodities transactions*—(1) *In general.* Except as otherwise provided in this paragraph (f), foreign personal holding company income includes the excess of gains over losses from commodities transactions. If losses from commodities transactions exceed gains, the net loss is not within the definition of foreign personal holding company income under this paragraph (f), and may not be allocated to, or otherwise reduce, foreign personal holding company income under section 954(b)(5) and § 1.954-1T(a)(4). The terms "commodity" and "commodities transactions" are defined in paragraph (f)(2) of this section. Gains and losses from qualified active sales and qualified hedging transactions are excluded from the computation of foreign personal holding company income under this paragraph (f). The term "qualified active sales" is defined in paragraph (f)(3). The term "qualified hedging transaction" is defined in paragraph (f)(4). An election is provided under paragraph (g)(5) of this section to include all gains and losses from section 1256 foreign currency transactions, which would otherwise be commodities transactions, in the computation of foreign personal holding company income under paragraph (g) instead of this paragraph (f). A loss that is deferred or that otherwise may not be taken into account under any provision of the Code may not be taken into account for purposes of determining foreign personal holding company income under any provision of this paragraph (f).

(2) *Definitions*—(i) *Commodity.* For purposes of this section, the term "commodity" means:

Reg. § 4.954-2(e)(4)

(A) Tangible personal property of a kind which is actively traded or with respect to which contractual interests are actively traded, and

(B) Nonfunctional currency (as defined under section 988 and the regulations thereunder).

(ii) *Commodities transaction.* A commodities transaction means the purchase or sale of a commodity for immediate (spot) delivery, or deferred (forward) delivery, or the right to purchase, sell, receive, or transfer a commodity, or any other right or obligation with respect to a commodity, accomplished through a cash or off-exchange market, an interbank market, an organized exchange or board of trade, an over-the- counter market, or in a transaction effected between private parties outside of any market. Commodities transactions include, but are not limited to:

(A) A futures or forward contract in a commodity,

(B) A leverage contract in a commodity purchased from leverage transaction merchants,

(C) An exchange of futures for physical transaction,

(D) A transaction in which the income or loss to the parties is measured by reference to the price of a commodity, a pool of commodities, or an index of commodities,

(E) The purchase or sale of an option or other right to acquire or transfer a commodity, a futures contract in a commodity, or an index of commodities, and

(F) The delivery of one commodity in exchange for the delivery of another commodity, the same commodity at another time, cash, or nonfunctional currency.

(3) *Definition of the term "qualified active sales"*—(i) *In general.* The term "qualified active sales" means the sale of commodities in the active conduct of a commodity business as a producer, processor, merchant, or handler of commodities if substantially all of the controlled foreign corporation's business is as an active producer, processor, merchant, or handler of commodities of like kind. The sale of commodities held by a controlled foreign corporation other than in its capacity as an active producer, processor, merchant or handler of commodities of like kind is not a qualified active sale.

(ii) *Sale of commodities.* The term "sale of commodities" means any transaction in which the controlled foreign corporation intends to deliver to a purchaser a commodity held by the controlled foreign corporation in physical form.

(iii) *Active conduct of a commodities business.* For purposes of this paragraph, a controlled foreign corporation is engaged in the active conduct of a commodities business as a producer, processor, merchant, or handler of commodities only if—

(A) It holds commodities as inventory or similar property (as defined in paragraph (a)(4)(ii)); and

(B) It incurs substantial expenses in the ordinary course of a commodities business from engaging in one of the following activities directly, and not through an independent contractor:

(*1*) Substantial activities in the production of commodities, including planting, tending or harvesting crops, raising or slaughtering livestock, or extracting minerals.

(*2*) Substantial processing activities prior to the sale of commodities including concentrating, refining, mixing, crushing, aerating, or milling; or

(*3*) Significant activities relating to the physical movement, handling and storage of commodities including preparation of contracts and invoices; arranging freight, insurance and credit; arranging for receipt, transfer or negotiation of shipping documents; arranging storage or warehousing, and dealing with quality claims; owning and operating facilities for storage or warehousing or owning or chartering vessels or vehicles for the transportation of commodities.

For purposes of this paragraph (f), a corporation is not engaged in a commodities business as a producer, processor, merchant, or handler of commodities if its business is primarily financial. In general, the business of a controlled foreign corporation is financial if it primarily engages in commodities transactions for investment or speculation, or if it primarily provides products or services to customers for investment or speculation.

(iv) *Substantially all.* Substantially all of the controlled foreign corporation's business is as an active producer, processor, merchant, or handler of commodities if the activities described in paragraph (f)(3)(iii) give rise to 85 percent of the taxable income of the controlled foreign corporation (computed as though the corporation were a domestic corporation). For this purpose, gains or losses from qualified hedging transactions, as defined in paragraph (f)(4), are considered derived from the qualified active sales to which they relate or are expected to relate.

(4) *Definition of the term "qualified hedging transaction."* The term "qualified hedging transaction" means a bona fide hedging transaction that:

Reg. § 4.954-2(f)(4)

(i) Is reasonably necessary to the conduct of business as a producer, processor, merchant or handler of a commodity in the manner in which such business is customarily and usually conducted by others;

(ii) Is entered into primarily to reduce the risk of price change (but not the risk of currency fluctuations) with respect to commodities sold or to be sold in qualified active sales described in paragraph (f)(3); and

(iii) Is clearly identified on the controlled foreign corporation's records before the close of the fifth day after the day during which the hedging transaction is entered into and at a time when there is a reasonable risk of loss; however, if the controlled foreign corporation does not at such time specifically and properly identify the qualified active sales (or category of such sales) to which a hedging transaction relates, the district director in his sole discretion may determine which hedging transactions (if any) are related to qualified active sales.

(g) *Foreign currency gain*—(1) *In general.* Except as provided in paragraph (g)(2), foreign personal holding company income includes the excess of foreign currency gains over losses (as defined in section 988(b)) attributable to any section 988 transactions. If foreign currency losses exceed gains, the net loss is not within the definition of foreign personal holding company income under this paragraph (g), and may not be allocated to, or otherwise reduce, foreign personal holding company income under section 954(b)(5) and § 1.954-1T(a)(4). To the extent the gain or loss from a transaction is treated as interest income or expense under sections 988(a)(2) or 988(d) and the regulations thereunder, it is not included in the computation of foreign personal holding company income under this paragraph (g). (For other rules concerning income described in more than one category of foreign personal holding company income, see § 1.954-2(a)(2).) A loss that is deferred or that otherwise may not be taken into account under any provision of the Code may not be taken into account for purposes of determining foreign personal holding company income under any provision of this paragraph (g).

(2) *Exceptions*—(i) *Qualified business units using the dollar approximate separate transactions method.* Any DASTM gain or loss computed under § 1.985-3(d) must be allocated under the rules of § 1.985-3(e)(2)(iv) or (e)(3).

(ii) *Tracing to exclude foreign currency gain or loss from qualified business and hedging transactions.* A foreign currency gain or loss is excluded from the computation of foreign personal holding company income under this paragraph (g) if it is clearly identified on the records of the controlled foreign corporation as being derived from a qualified business transaction or a qualified hedging transaction. The term "qualified business transaction" is defined in paragraph (g)(3) of this section. The term "qualified hedging transaction" is defined in paragraph (g)(4) of this section. However, currency gain or loss of a qualified business unit included in the computation of currency gain or loss under subdivision (i) of this paragraph (g)(2) may not be excluded from foreign personal holding company income under the tracing rule of this paragraph (g)(2)(ii). Furthermore, the tracing rule of this paragraph (g)(2)(ii) will not apply if a controlled foreign corporation makes the election provided by paragraph (g)(2)(iii).

(iii) *Election out of tracing.* A controlled foreign corporation may elect a method of accounting under which all foreign currency gains or losses attributable to section 988 transactions are included in foreign personal holding company income. The scope and requirements for this election are provided in paragraph (g)(5) of this section. This election does not apply to foreign currency gains or losses of a qualified business unit included in the computation of gain or loss under paragraph (g)(2)(i).

(3) *Definition of the term "qualified business transaction"*—(i) *In general.* The term "qualified business transaction" means a transaction (other than a "qualified hedging transaction" as described in paragraph (g)(4) of this section) that:

(A) Does not have investment or speculation as a significant purpose;

(B) Is not attributable to property or an activity of the kind that gives rise to subpart F income (other than foreign currency gain under this paragraph (g)), or could reasonably be expected to give rise to subpart F income (including upon disposition); for example, the transaction may not be attributable to stock or debt of another corporation (including related corporations organized and operating in the same country), or property likely to give rise to foreign base company sales or services income; and

(C) Is attributable to business transactions described in subdivision (ii) of this paragraph (g)(3).

A qualified business transaction includes the disposition of a debt instrument that constitutes inventory property under paragraph (a)(4)(ii) or dealer property under paragraph (a)(4)(iv) of this section. The provisions of this paragraph (g)(3) do not apply to the foreign currency gain or loss of a qualified business unit (as determined under § 1.985-3T(d)(2)) included in the computation of

Reg. § 4.954-2(g)(1)

gain or loss under paragraph (g)(2)(i). The provisions of this paragraph (g)(3) do, however, apply to other currency transactions of a qualified business unit that elects (or is deemed to elect) the U.S. dollar as its functional currency under section 985(b)(3) and § 1.985-2T. Qualified business transactions and the amount of foreign currency gain or loss derived therefrom must be clearly identified on its records by the controlled foreign corporation. If the controlled foreign corporation is unable to specifically identify the qualified business transactions and the foreign currency gain or loss derived therefrom, the district director in his sole discretion may determine which transactions of the corporation giving rise to the foreign currency gains or losses are attributable to qualified business transactions.

(ii) *Specific business transactions.* A transaction of a controlled foreign corporation must meet the requirements of any of subdivisions (A) through (F) of this paragraph (g)(3)(ii) to be a qualified business transaction under this paragraph (g)(3).

(A) *Acquisition of debt instruments.* If the transaction is the acquisition of a debt instrument described in section 988(c)(1)(B)(i) and the regulations thereunder, the debt must be derived from—

(*1*) The sale of inventory and similar property to customers by the controlled foreign corporation in the ordinary course of regular business operations, or

(*2*) The rendition of services by the corporation in the ordinary course of regular business operations.

For purposes of this paragraph (g)(3)(ii)(A), a debt instrument will not be considered derived in the ordinary course of regular business operations unless the instrument matures, and is reasonably expected to be satisfied, within the period for which interest need not be charged under section 482 and the regulations thereunder.

(B) *Becoming the obligor under debt instruments.* If the transaction is becoming the obligor under a debt instrument described in section 988(c)(1)(B)(i) and the regulations thereunder, the debt must be incurred for:

(*1*) Payment of expenses that are includible by the controlled foreign corporation in the cost of goods sold under § 1.61-3 for property held primarily for sale to customers in the ordinary course of regular business operations, are inventoriable costs under section 471 and the regulations thereunder, or are allocable or apportionable under the rules of § 1.861-8 to gross income derived from inventory and similar property,

(*2*) Payment of expenses that are allocable or apportionable under the rules of § 1.861-8 to gross income derived from services provided by the controlled foreign corporation in the ordinary course of regular business operations,

(*3*) Acquisition of an asset that does not give rise to subpart F income during the current taxable year (other than by application of section 952(c)) and is not reasonably expected to give rise to subpart F income in subsequent taxable years, or

(*4*) Acquisition of dealer property as defined in paragraph (a)(4)(iv) of this section.

The identification requirements of subdivision (i) of this paragraph (g)(3) will not be met with respect to a borrowing if the controlled foreign corporation fails to clearly identify the debt and the expenses (or categories of expenses) to which it relates before the close of the fifth day after the day on which the expenses are incurred.

(C) *Accrual of any item of gross income.* If the transaction is the accrual (or otherwise taking into account) of any item of gross income or receipts as described in section 988(c)(1)(B)(ii) and the regulations thereunder, the item of gross income or receipts must be derived from:

(*1*) The sale of inventory and similar property in the ordinary course of regular business operations, or

(*2*) The provision of services by the controlled foreign corporation to customers in the ordinary course of regular business operations.

(D) *Accrual of any item of expense.* If the transaction is the accrual (or otherwise taking into account) of any item of expense as described in section 988(c)(1)(B)(ii) and the regulations thereunder, the item of expense must be:

(*1*) An expense that is includible by the controlled foreign corporation in the cost of goods sold under § 1.61-3 for property held primarily for sale to customers in the ordinary course of regular business operations, is an inventoriable cost under section 471 and the regulations thereunder, or is allocable or apportionable under the rules of § 1.861-8 to gross income derived from inventory and similar property, or

(*2*) An expense that is allocable or apportionable under the rules of § 1.861-8 to gross income derived from services provided by the controlled foreign corporation in the ordinary course of regular business operations.

(E) *Entering into forward contracts, futures contracts, options and similar instruments.* If the transaction is entering into any forward contract, futures contract, option or similar financial instrument and if such contract or instrument

Reg. § 4.954-2(g)(3)

is not marked to market at the close of the taxable year under section 1256, as described in section 988(c)(1)(B)(iii) and the regulations thereunder, then the contract or instrument must be property held as dealer property as defined in paragraph (a)(4)(ii) of this section.

(F) *Disposition of nonfunctional currency.* If the transaction is the disposition of nonfunctional currency, as described in section 988(c)(1)(C) and the regulations thereunder, then the transaction must be for a purpose described in paragraph (g)(3)(ii)(B), for the payment of taxes not attributable to subpart F income, or must be the disposition of property held as dealer property as defined in paragraph (a)(4)(iv) of this section.

(G) *Transactions in business assets.* The acquisition or disposition of an asset that is used or held for use in the active conduct of a trade or business.

(4) *Definition of the term "qualified hedging transaction"*—(i) *In general.* The term "qualified hedging transaction" means a bona fide hedging transaction meeting all the requirements of subdivisions (A) through (D) of this paragraph (g)(4)(i):

(A) The transaction must be reasonably necessary to the conduct of regular business operations in the manner in which such business operations are customarily and usually conducted by others.

(B) The transaction must be entered into primarily to reduce the risk of currency fluctuations with respect to property or services sold or to be sold or expenses incurred or to be incurred in transactions that are qualified business transactions under paragraph (g)(3).

(C) The hedging transaction and the property or expense (or category of property or expense) to which it relates must be clearly identified on the records of the controlled foreign corporation before the close of the fifth day after the day during which the hedging transaction is entered into and at a time during which there is a reasonable risk of currency loss.

(D) The amount of foreign currency gain or loss that is attributable to a specific hedging transaction must be clearly identifiable on the records of the controlled foreign corporation or its controlling shareholder (as defined in § 1.964-1(c)(5)).

The provisions of this paragraph (g)(4) do not apply to transactions of a qualified business unit included in the computation of gain or loss under paragraph (g)(2)(i). The provisions of this paragraph (g)(4) do apply, however, to other currency transactions of a qualified business unit that elects (or is deemed to elect) the U.S. dollar as its functional currency under section 985(b)(3) and § 1.985-3T. If the controlled foreign corporation does not specifically identify the qualified business transactions (or category of qualified business transactions) to which a hedging transaction relates or is unable to specifically identify the amount of foreign currency gain or loss derived from the hedging transactions, the district director in his sole discretion may make the identifications required of the controlled foreign corporation and determine which hedging transactions (if any) are related to qualified business transactions, and the amount of foreign currency gain or loss attributable to the qualified hedging transactions.

(ii) *Change in purpose of hedging transaction.* If a hedging transaction is entered into for one purpose, and the purpose for that transaction subsequently changes, the transaction may be treated as two separate hedging transactions for purposes of this paragraph (g)(4). In such a case, the portion of the transaction that relates to a qualified business transaction is considered a qualified hedging transaction if it separately meets all the other requirements of this paragraph (g)(4) for treatment as a qualified hedging transaction. For purposes of paragraph (g)(4)(i)(C), the foreign corporation must identify on its records the portion of the transaction that relates to a qualified business transaction by the close of the fifth day after the day on which the hedge becomes so related (*i.e.,* either the day on which the hedge is first entered into or on the day on which it first relates to a qualified business transaction due to a change in its purpose). The foreign corporation must identify on its records the portion of the transaction that does not relate to a qualified business transaction by the close of the fifth day after the day on which the purpose for the hedging transaction changes.

(5) *Election out of tracing*—(i) *In general.* A controlled foreign corporation may elect to account for currency gains and losses under section 988 and gains and losses from section 1256 currency contracts by including in the computation of foreign personal holding company income under this paragraph (g) all foreign currency gains or losses attributable to section 988 transactions, and all gains or losses from section 1256 foreign currency contracts. Separate elections for section 1256 foreign currency contracts and section 988 transactions are not permitted. If a controlled foreign corporation makes the election described in this paragraph (g)(5)(i), the election is effective for all related persons as defined in section 954(d)(3) and the regulations thereunder.

Reg. § 4.954-2(g)(4)

Income from Sources Without the United States

See p. 20,601 for regulations not amended to reflect law changes

(ii) *Exception.* The election provided by this paragraph (g)(5) does not apply to foreign currency gain or loss of a qualified business unit determined under § 1.985-3T(d)(2). It does, however, apply to other foreign currency gains or losses of a qualified business unit that elects (or is deemed to elect) the U.S. dollar as its functional currency.

(iii) *Procedure*—(A) *In general.* The election provided by this paragraph (g)(5) shall be made in the manner prescribed in this paragraph and in subsequent administrative pronouncements.

(B) *Time and manner.* The controlled foreign corporation may make the election by filing a statement with its original or amended information return for the taxable year for which the election is made. The controlling United States shareholders, as defined in § 1.964-1(c)(5), may make the election on behalf of the controlled foreign corporation and related corporations by filing a statement to such effect with their original or amended income tax returns for the taxable year during which the taxable year of the controlled foreign corporation for which the election is made ends. The election is effective for the taxable year of the controlled foreign corporation for which the election is made, for the taxable years of all related controlled foreign corporations ending within such taxable year, and for all subsequent years of such corporations. The statement shall include the following information:

(*1*) The name, address, taxpayer identification number, and taxable year of each United States shareholder;

(*2*) The name, address, and taxable year of each controlled foreign corporation for which the election is effective; and

(*3*) Any additional information to be required by the Secretary by administrative pronouncement.

Each United States shareholder or controlled foreign corporation filing the election must provide copies of the election to all controlled foreign corporations for which the election is effective, and all United States shareholders of such corporations. However, failure to provide such copies will not void (or cause to be voidable) an election under this paragraph (g)(5).

(C) *Termination.* The election provided by this paragraph (g)(5) may be terminated only with the consent of the Commissioner: Attn.: CC:INTL.

(h) *Income equivalent to interest*—(1) *In general.* Foreign personal holding company income includes income that is equivalent to interest.

Income equivalent to interest includes, but is not limited to, income derived from the following categories of transactions:

(i) An investment, or series of integrated transactions which include an investment, in which the payments, net payments, cash flows, or return predominantly reflect the time value of money, and

(ii) Transactions in which the payments or a predominant portion thereof are in substance for the use or forbearance of money, but are not generally treated as interest.

However, amounts treated as interest under section 954(c)(1)(A) and paragraph (b) of this section are not income equivalent to interest under this paragraph (h). Income from the sale of property will not be treated as income equivalent to interest for purposes of this paragraph (h), subject to the rule of paragraph (h)(4) of this section, unless the sale is part of an integrated transaction that gives rise to interest or income equivalent to interest. See sections 482, 483 and 1274 for the extent to which such income may be characterized as interest income subject to paragraph (b) of this section. Income equivalent to interest for purposes of this paragraph (h) includes all income attributable to a transfer of securities subject to section 1058. Income equivalent to interest also includes a portion of certain deferred payments received for the performance of services, in accordance with the provisions of paragraph (h)(5) of this section. Income equivalent to interest does not include income attributable to notional principal contracts such as interest rate swaps, currency swaps, interest rate floor agreements, or similar contracts except to the extent that such contracts are part of an integrated transaction that gives rise to income equivalent to interest. Income derived from notional contracts by a person acting in its capacity as a regular dealer in such contracts will be presumed not to be integrated with an investment.

(2) *Illustrations.* The following examples illustrate the application of this paragraph (h):

Example (1). CFC, a controlled foreign corporation, promises that *A*, an unrelated person, may borrow up to $500 in principal for one year beginning at any time during the next three months at an interest rate of 10 percent. In exchange, *A* pays *CFC* a commitment fee of $2.00. Pursuant to this loan commitment, *CFC* lends $80 to *A*. As a result, the entire $2.00 fee is included in the computation of foreign personal holding company income under this paragraph (h)(1)(ii).

Example (2). (i) At the beginning of its current taxable year, *CFC*, a controlled foreign corporation, purchases at face value a one-year debt

Reg. § 4.954-2(h)(2)

instrument issued by A having a $100 principal amount and bearing a floating rate of interest set at the London Interbank Offered Rate ("LIBOR") plus one percentage point. Contemporaneously, CFC borrows $100 from B for one year at a fixed interest rate of 10 percent, using the debt instrument as security.

(ii) During its current taxable year, CFC accrues $11 of interest from A on the bond. That interest is foreign personal holding company income under section 954(c)(1) and § 1.954-2T(b), and thus is not income equivalent to interest. During its current taxable year, CFC incurs $10 of interest expense with respect to the borrowing from B. That expense is allocated and apportioned to, and reduces, foreign base company income or insurance income to the extent provided in sections 954(b)(5), 863(e), and 864(e) and the regulations thereunder.

Example (3). (i) At the beginning of its 1988 taxable year, CFC, a controlled foreign corporation, purchases at face value a one-year debt instrument issued by A having a $100 principal amount and bearing a floating rate of interest set at the London Interbank Offered Rate ("LIBOR") plus one percentage point payable on the last day of CFC's current taxable year. CFC subsequently determines that it would prefer receiving interest at a fixed rate, and, on January 1, 1989, enters into an agreement with B, an unrelated person, whereby B promises to pay CFC on the last day of CFC's 1989 taxable year an amount equal to 10 percent on a notional principal amount of $100. In exchange, CFC promises to pay B on the last day of CFC's 1989 taxable year an amount equal to LIBOR plus one percentage point on the notional principal amount.

(ii) CFC receives a total of $10 from B, and pays $9 to B. CFC also receives $9 from A. The $9 paid to B is directly allocated to, or is otherwise an adjustment to, the $10 received from B. The transactions are considered an integrated transaction giving rise to $9 of interest income (paid by A) and, under paragraph (h)(1)(i), $1 of income equivalent to interest (paid by B).

Example (4). The facts are the same as in Example (3), except that CFC does not hold any debt obligations. Since the transaction with B is not integrated with an investment giving rise to interest or income equivalent to interest, the net $1 of income realized by CFC does not constitute income equivalent to interest.

Example (5). (i) CFC, a controlled foreign corporation, enters into an agreement with A whereby CFC purchases commodity X from A at a price of $100, and A contemporaneously repurchases commodity X from CFC for payment and delivery in 3 months at a price of $104 set by the forward market.

(ii) The transaction is in substance a loan from CFC to A secured by commodity X. Thus, CFC accrues $4 of gross income which is included in foreign personal holding company income as interest under section 954(c)(1)(A) and paragraph (b) of this section.

Example (6). (i) CFC purchases commodity Y on the spot market for $100 and contemporaneously, sells commodity Y forward for delivery and payment in 3 months at a price of $104 set by the forward market.

(ii) The $100 paid on the spot purchase of commodity Y offsets any market risk on the forward sale so that the $4 of income to be derived predominantly reflects time value of money. Thus, under paragraph (h)(1)(i), the spot purchase of commodity Y and the offsetting forward sale will be treated as an integrated transaction giving rise to $4 of income equivalent to interest.

(3) *Income equivalent to interest from factoring*—(i) *General rule.* Income equivalent to interest includes factoring income. Except as provided in paragraph (h)(3)(ii) of this section, the term "factoring income" includes any income (including any discount income or service fee, but excluding any stated interest) derived from the acquisition and collection or disposition of a factored receivable. The rules of this paragraph (h)(3) apply only with respect to the tax treatment of factoring income derived from the acquisition and collection or disposition of a factored receivable and shall not affect the characterization of an expense or loss of either the person whose goods or services gave rise to a factored receivable or the obligor under a receivable. The amount of income equivalent to interest realized with respect to a factored receivable is the difference (if a positive number) between the amount paid for the receivable by the foreign corporation and the amount that it collects on the receivable (or realizes upon its sale of the receivable).

(ii) *Exceptions.* Factoring income shall not include—

(A) Income treated as interest under section 864(d)(1) or (6) and the regulations thereunder (relating to income derived from trade or service receivables of related persons), even if such income is not treated as described in section 864(d)(1) by reason of the same-country exception of section 864(d)(7);

(B) Income derived from a factored receivable if payment for the acquisition of the receivable is made on or after the date on which stated interest begins to accrue, but only if the

Income from Sources Without the United States

rate of stated interest equals or exceeds 120 percent of the Federal short term rate (as defined under section 1274) (or the equivalent rate for a currency other than the dollar) as of the date on which the receivable is acquired by the foreign corporation; or

(C) Income derived from a factored receivable if payment for the acquisition of the receivable by the foreign corporation is made only on or after the anticipated date of payment of all principal by the obligor (or the anticipated weighted average date of payment of a pool of purchased receivables).

(iii) *Factored receivable.* For purposes of this paragraph (h)(3), the term "factored receivable" includes any account receivable or other evidence of indebtedness, whether or not issued at a discount and whether or not bearing stated interest, arising out of the disposition of property or the performance of services by any person, if such account receivable or evidence of indebtedness is acquired by a person other than the person who disposed of the property or provided the services that gave rise to the account receivable or evidence of indebtedness. For purposes of this paragraph (h)(3), it is immaterial whether the person providing the property or services agrees to transfer the receivable at the time of sale (as by accepting a third-party charge or credit card) or at a later time.

(iv) *Illustrations.* The following examples illustrate the application of this paragraph (h)(3).

Example (1). DP, a domestic corporation, owns all of the outstanding stock of FS, a controlled foreign corporation. FS acquires accounts receivable arising from the sale of property by unrelated corporation X. The receivables have a face amount of $100, and after 30 days bear stated interest equal to at least 120 percent of the applicable short term Federal rate (determined as of the date the receivable is acquired). FS purchases the receivables from X for $95 on Day 1 and collects $100 from the obligor under the receivable on Day 40. Income (other than stated interest) derived by FS from the factored receivables is factoring income within the meaning of paragraph (h)(3)(i) of this section and, therefore, is income equivalent to interest.

Example (2). The facts are the same as in example (1), except that FS does not pay X for the receivables until Day 30. Income derived by FS from the factored receivables is not factoring income by reason of paragraph (h)(3)(ii)(B) of this section.

Example (3). The facts are the same as in Example (2), except that it is anticipated that all principal will be paid by the obligor of the receivables by Day 30. Income derived by FS from this "maturity factoring" of the receivables is not factoring income by reason of paragraph (h)(3)(ii)(C) of this section, and therefore does not give rise to income equivalent to interest.

Example (4). The facts are the same as in example (1), except that, rather than collecting $100 from the obligor under the factored receivable on Day 40, FS sells the receivable to controlled foreign corporation Y on Day 15 for $97. Both the income derived by FS on the factored receivable and the income derived by Y (other than stated interest) on the receivable are factoring income within the meaning of paragraph (h)(3)(i) of this section, and, therefore, constitute income equivalent to interest.

Example (5). The facts are the same as in example (4), except that FS sells the factored receivable to Y for $99 on day 45, at which time interest is accruing on the unpaid balance of $100. FS has $4 of net factoring income that is income equivalent to interest. Because interest was accruing at the time Y acquired the receivable at a rate equal to at least 120 percent of the applicable short term Federal rate, income derived by Y from the factored receivable is not factoring income by reason of paragraph (h)(3)(ii)(B).

Example (6). DP, a domestic corporation engaged in an integrated credit card business, owns all of the outstanding stock of FS, a controlled foreign corporation. On Day 1 individual A uses a credit card issued by DP to purchase shoes priced at $100 from X, a foreign corporation unrelated to DP, FS, or A. By prearrangement with DP, on Day 7, X transfers the receivable arising from A's purchase to FS in exchange for $95. FS collects $100 from A on Day 45. Income derived by FS on the factored receivable is factoring income within the meaning of paragraph (h)(3)(i) of this section and, therefore, is income equivalent to interest.

(4) *Determination of sales income.* Income equivalent to interest for purposes of this paragraph (h) does not include income from the sale of property unless the sale is part of an integrated transaction that gives rise to interest or income equivalent to interest. Income derived by a controlled foreign corporation will be treated as arising from the sale of property only if the corporation in substance carries out sales activities. Accordingly, an arrangement that is designed to lend the form of a sales transaction to a transaction that in substance constitutes an advance of funds will be disregarded. For example, if a controlled foreign corporation acquires property on 30-day payment terms from one person and sells that property to another person on 90 day pay-

Reg. § 4.954-2(h)(4)

ment terms and at prearranged prices and terms such that the foreign corporation bears no substantial economic risk with respect to the purchase and sale other than the risk of nonpayment, the foreign corporation has not in substance derived income from the sale of property.

(5) *Receivables arising from performance of services.* If payment for services performed by a controlled foreign corporation is not made until more than 120 days after the date on which such services are performed, then the income derived by the foreign corporation constitutes income equivalent to interest to the extent that interest income would be imputed under the principles of section 483 or the original issue discount provisions (section 1271 et seq.), if—

    (A) Such provisions applied to contracts for the performance of services,

    (B) The time period referred to in sections 483(c)(1) and 1274(c)(1)(B) were 120 days rather than six months, and

    (C) The time period referred to in section 483(c)(1)(A) were 120 days rather than one year. [Reg. § 4.954-2.]

☐ [T.D. 8216, 7-20-88. Amended by T.D. 8556, 7-22-94. Redesignated by T.D. 8618, 9-6-95.]

[Reg. § 1.954-3]

§ 1.954-3. Foreign base company sales income.—(a) *Income included* —(1) *In general*—(i) *General rules.* Foreign base company sales income of a controlled foreign corporation shall, except as provided in subparagraphs (2), (3), and (4) of this paragraph, consist of gross income (whether in the form of profits, commissions, fees, or otherwise) derived in connection with (a) the purchase of personal property from a related person and its sale to any person, (b) the sale of personal property to any person on behalf of a related person, (c) the purchase of personal property from any person and its sale to a related person, or (d) the purchase of personal property from any person on behalf of a related person. See section 954(d)(1). This section shall apply to the purchase and/or sale of personal property, whether or not such property was purchased and/or sold in the ordinary course of trade or business, except that income derived in connection with the sale of tangible personal property will not be considered to be foreign base company sales income if such property is sold to an unrelated person, as defined in paragraph (e)(2) of § 1.954-1, after substantial use has been made of the property by the controlled foreign corporation in its trade or business. This section shall not apply to the excess of gains over losses from sales or exchanges of securities or from future transactions, to the extent such excess gains are includible in foreign personal holding company income of the controlled foreign corporation under § 1.954-2 or foreign base company shipping income under § 1.954-6; nor shall it apply to the sale of the controlled foreign corporation's property (other than its stock in trade or other property of a kind which would properly be included in its inventory if on hand at the close of the taxable year, or property held primarily for sale to customers in the ordinary course of its trade or business) if substantially all the property of such corporation is sold pursuant to the discontinuation of the trade or business previously carried on by such corporation. The term "any person" as used in this subparagraph includes a related person, as defined in paragraph (e)(1) of § 1.954-1.

(ii) *Special rule*—(a) *In general.* The term "personal property" as used in section 954(d) and this section shall not include agricultural commodities which are not grown in the United States (within the meaning of section 7701(a)(9)) in commercially marketable quantities. All of the agricultural commodities listed in Table I shall be considered grown in the United States in commercially marketable quantities. Bananas, black pepper, cocoa, coconut, coffee, crude rubber, and tea shall not be considered grown in the United States in commercially marketable quantities. All other agricultural commodities shall not be considered grown in the United States in commercially marketable quantities when, in consideration of all of the facts and circumstances of the individual case, such commodities are shown to be produced in the United States in insufficient quantity and quality to be marketed commercially. The term "agricultural commodities" includes, but is not limited to, livestock, poultry, fish produced in fish farms, fruit, furbearing animals as well as the products of truck farms, ranches, nurseries, ranges, and orchards. A fish farm is an area where fish are grown or raised (artificially protected and cared for), as opposed to merely caught or harvested. However, the term "agricultural commodities" shall not include timber (either standing or felled), or any commodity at least 50 percent of the fair market value of which is attributable to manufacturing or processing, determined in a manner consistent with the regulations under section 993(c) (relating to the definition of export property). For purposes of applying such regulations, the term "processing" shall be deemed not to include handling, packing, packaging, grading, storing, transporting, slaughtering, and harvesting. Subdivision (ii) shall apply in the computation of foreign base company sales income for taxable years of controlled foreign corporations beginning after December 31, 1975, and to taxa-

Income from Sources Without the United States 49,271
See p. 20,601 for regulations not amended to reflect law changes

ble years of United States shareholders (within the meaning of section 951 (b)) within which or with which such taxable years of such foreign corporations end.

(b) *Table.*

Table I—Agricultural Commodities Grown in the United States in Commercially Marketable Quantities

Livestock and Products

Beeswax	Horses
Cattle and calves	Milk
Chickens	Mink
Chicken eggs	Mohair
Ducks	Rabbits
Geese	Sheep and lambs
Goats	Turkeys
Hogs	Wool
Honey	

Crops

Alfalfa	Eggplant	Peanuts
Almonds	Escarole	Pears
Apples	Figs	Peas
Apricots	Filberts	Peppers
Artichokes	Flaxseed	Plums and prunes
Asparagus	Garlic	Potatoes
Avocadoes	Grapes	Potted plants
Barley	Grapefruit	Raspberries
Beans	Grass seed	Rice
Beets	Hay	Rhubarb
Blackberries	Honeydew melons	Rye
Blueberries	Hops	Sorghum grain
Brussel sprouts	Lemons	Soybeans
Broccoli	Lettuce	Spinach
Bulbs	Limes	Strawberries
Cabbage	Macadamia nuts	Sugar beets
Cantaloupes	Maple syrup and sugar	Sugarcane
Carrots	Mint	Sweet potatoes
Cauliflower	Mushrooms	Tangelos
Celery	Nectarines	Tangerines
Cherries	Oats	Tobacco
Corn	Olives	Tomatoes
Cotton	Onions	Walnuts
Cranberries	Oranges	Watermelons
Cucumbers	Papayas	Wheat
Cut flowers	Pecans	
Dates	Peaches	

(iii) *Examples.* The application of this subparagraph may be illustrated by the following examples:

Example (1). Controlled foreign corporation A, incorporated under the laws of foreign country X, is a wholly owned subsidiary of domestic corporation M. Corporation A purchases from M Corporation, a related person, articles manufactured in the United States and sells the articles in the form in which purchased to P, not a related person, for delivery and use in foreign country Y. Gross income of A Corporation derived from the purchase and sale of the personal property is foreign base company sales income.

Example (2). Corporation A in example (1) also purchases from P, not a related person, articles manufactured in country Y and sells the articles in the form in which purchased to foreign corporation B, a related person, for use in foreign country Z. Gross income of A Corporation derived from the purchase and sale of the personal property is foreign base company sales income.

Example (3). Controlled foreign corporation C, incorporated under the laws of foreign country X, is a wholly owned subsidiary of domestic corporation N. By contract, N Corporation agrees to pay C Corporation, a related person, a commission equal to 6 percent of the gross selling price of all personal property shipped by N Corporation as the result of orders solicited by C Corporation in foreign countries Y and Z. In fulfillment of such orders, N Corporation ships products manufactured by it in the United States. Corporation C does not assume title to the property sold. Gross commissions received by C Corporation from N Corporation in connection with the sale of such property for use in countries Y and Z constitute foreign base company sales income.

Example (4). Controlled foreign corporation D, incorporated under the laws of foreign country Y, is a wholly owned subsidiary of domestic corporation R. In 1964, D Corporation acquires a United States manufactured lathe from R Corporation. In 1972, after having made a substantial use of the lathe in its manufacturing business, D Corporation sells the lathe to an unrelated person for use in foreign country Z. Gross income from the sale of the lathe is not foreign base company sales income since it is sold to an unrelated person after substantial use has been made of it by D Corporation in its business.

Example (5). Controlled foreign corporation E, incorporated under the laws of foreign country Y, is a wholly owned subsidiary of domestic corporation P. Corporation E purchases from P Corporation articles manufactured by P Corporation outside of country Y and sells the articles to F Corporation, an unrelated person, for use in foreign country Z. Corporation E finances the purchase of the articles by F Corporation by agreeing to accept payment over an extended period of time and receives not only the purchase price but also interest and service fees. All gross income of E Corporation derived in connection with the purchase and sale of the personal property, including interest and service fees derived from financing the sale to F Corporation, constitutes foreign base company sales income.

Reg. § 1.954-3(a)(1)

Income from Sources Without the United States

(2) *Property manufactured, produced, constructed, grown, or extracted within the country in which the controlled foreign corporation is created or organized.* Foreign base company sales income does not include income derived in connection with the purchase and sale of personal property (or purchase or sale of personal property on behalf of a related person) in a transaction described in subparagraph (1) of this paragraph if the property is manufactured, produced, constructed, grown, or extracted in the country under the laws of which the controlled foreign corporation which purchases and sells the property (or acts on behalf of a related person) is created or organized. See section 954(d)(1)(A). The principles set forth in subparagraph (4) of this paragraph with respect to the manufacture, production, or construction of personal property shall apply under this subparagraph in determining what constitutes manufacture, production, or construction of property. The application of this subparagraph may be illustrated by the following examples:

Example (1). Controlled foreign corporation A, incorporated under the laws of foreign country X, is a wholly owned subsidiary of domestic corporation M. Corporation A purchases coffee beans grown in country X from foreign corporation P, a related person, and sells the beans to M Corporation, a related person, for use in the United States. Income from the purchase and sale of the coffee beans by A Corporation is not foreign base company sales income since the beans were grown in country X.

Example (2). Controlled foreign corporation B, incorporated under the laws of foreign country X, is a wholly owned subsidiary of controlled foreign corporation C, also incorporated under the laws of country X. Corporation B purchases and imports into country X rough diamonds mined in foreign country Y; in country X it cuts, polishes, and shapes the diamonds in a process which constitutes manufacturing within the meaning of subparagraph (4) of this paragraph. Corporation B sells the finished diamonds to C Corporation, a related person, which in turn sells them for use in foreign country Z. Since for purposes of this subparagraph the finished diamonds are manufactured in country X, gross income derived by C Corporation from their sale is not foreign base company sales income.

(3) *Property sold for use, consumption, or disposition within the country in which the controlled foreign corporation is created or organized* —(i) *In general.* Foreign base company sales income does not include income derived in connection with the purchase and sale of personal property (or purchase or sale of personal property on behalf of a related person) in a transaction described in subparagraph (1) of this paragraph, (a) if the property is sold for use, consumption, or disposition in the country under the laws of which the controlled foreign corporation which purchases and sells the property (or sells on behalf of a related person) is created or organized or (b), where the property is purchased by the controlled foreign corporation on behalf of a related person, if such property is purchased for use, consumption, or disposition in the country under the laws of which such controlled foreign corporation is created or organized. See section 954(d)(1)(B).

(ii) *Rules for determining country of use, consumption, or disposition.* As a general rule, personal property which is sold to an unrelated person will be presumed for purposes of this subparagraph to have been sold for use, consumption, or disposition in the country of destination of the property sold; for such purpose, the occurrence in a country of a temporary interruption in shipment of goods shall not constitute such country the country of destination. However, if at the time of a sale or personal property to an unrelated person the controlled foreign corporation knew, or should have known from the facts and circumstances surrounding the transaction, that the property probably would not be used, consumed, or disposed of in the country of destination, the controlled foreign corporation must determine the country of ultimate use, consumption, or disposition of the property or the property will be presumed to have been used, consumed, or disposed of outside the country under the laws of which the controlled foreign corporation is created or organized. A controlled foreign corporation which sells personal property to a related person is presumed to sell such property for use, consumption, or disposition outside the country under the laws of which the controlled foreign corporation is created or organized unless such corporation establishes the use made of the property by the related person; once it has established that the related person has disposed of the property, the rules in the two preceding sentences relating to sales by a controlled foreign corporation to an unrelated person will apply at the first stage in the chain of distribution at which a sale is made by a related person to an unrelated person. Notwithstanding the preceding provisions of this subdivision, a controlled foreign corporation which sells personal property to any person all of whose business except for an insubstantial part consists of selling from inventory to retail customers at retail outlets all within one country may assume at the time of such sale to such person that such property will be used, consumed, or disposed of within such country.

Reg. § 1.954-3(a)(2)

(iii) *Fungible goods.* For purposes of this subparagraph, a controlled foreign corporation which sells to a purchaser personal property which because of its fungible nature cannot reasonably be specifically traced to other purchasers and to the countries of ultimate use, consumption, or disposition shall, unless such corporation establishes a different disposition as being proper, treat such property as being sold, for ultimate use, consumption, or disposition in those countries, and to those other purchasers, in the same proportions in which property from the fungible mass of the first purchaser is sold in the regular course of business by such first purchaser. No apportionment need be made, however, on the basis of sporadic sales by the first purchaser. This subdivision shall apply only in a case where the controlled foreign corporation knew, or should have known from the facts and circumstances surrounding the transaction, the manner in which the first purchaser disposes of goods from the fungible mass.

(iv) *Illustrations.* The application of this subparagraph may be illustrated by the following examples:

Example (1). Controlled foreign corporation A, incorporated under the laws of foreign country X, and controlled foreign corporation B, incorporated under the laws of foreign country Y, are related persons. Corporation A purchases from B Corporation electric transformers produced by B Corporation in country Y and sells the transformers to D Corporation, an unrelated person, for installation in a factory building being constructed in country X. Since the personal property purchased and sold by A Corporation is to be used within the country in which A Corporation is incorporated, income of A Corporation derived from the purchase and sale of the electric transformers is not foreign base company sales income.

Example (2). Controlled foreign corporation C, incorporated under the laws of foreign country X, is a wholly owned subsidiary of domestic corporation N. Corporation C purchases from N Corporation sewing machines manufactured in the United States by N Corporation and sells the sewing machines to retail department stores, unrelated persons, located in foreign country X. The entire activities of the department stores to which C Corporation sells the machines consist of selling goods from inventory to retail customers at retail outlets in country X. Under these circumstances, at the time of sale C Corporation may assume the sewing machines will be used, consumed, or disposed of in country X, and no attempt need be made by C Corporation to determine where the sewing machines will ultimately be used by the customers of the retail department stores. Gross income of C Corporation derived from the sales to the department stores located in country X is not foreign base company sales income.

Example (3). Controlled foreign corporation D, incorporated under the laws of foreign country Y, and controlled foreign corporation E, incorporated under the laws of foreign country X, are related persons. Corporation D purchases from E Corporation sulphur extracted by E Corporation from deposits located in country X. Corporation D sells the sulphur to F Corporation, an unrelated person, for delivery to F Corporation's storage facilities located in country Y. At the time of the sale of the sulphur from D Corporation to F Corporation, D Corporation knows that F Corporation is actively engaged in the business of selling a large amount of sulphur in country Y but also that F Corporation sells, in the normal course of its business, 25 percent of its sulphur for ultimate consumption in foreign country Z. However, D Corporation has no knowledge at the time of sale whether any portion of the particular shipment it sells to F Corporation will be resold by F Corporation for ultimate use, consumption, or disposition outside country Y. Moreover, delivery of the sulphur to F Corporation's storage facilities constitutes more than a temporary interruption in the shipment of the sulphur. Under such circumstances, D Corporation may, but is not required to, trace the ultimate disposition by F Corporation of the personal property sold to F Corporation; however, if D Corporation does not trace the ultimate disposition and if it does not establish a different disposition as being proper, 25 percent of the sulphur sold by D Corporation to F Corporation will be treated as being sold for consumption in country Z and 25 percent of the gross income from the sale of sulphur by D Corporation to F Corporation will be treated as foreign base company sales income.

Example (4). Controlled foreign corporation G, incorporated under the laws of foreign country X, is a wholly owned subsidiary of domestic corporation P. Corporation G purchases from P Corporation toys manufactured in the United States by P Corporation and sells the toys to R, an unrelated person, for delivery to a duty-free port in country X. Instructions for the assembly and operation of the toys are printed in a language which is not commonly used in country X. From the facts and circumstances surrounding the sales to R, G Corporation knows, or should know, that the toys will probably not be used, consumed, or disposed of within country X. Therefore, unless G Corporation determines the use to be made of the toys by R, such property will be presumed to have been sold by R for use, consumption, or disposi-

Reg. § 1.954-3(a)(3)

tion outside of country X, and the entire gross income of G Corporation derived from the sales will be considered foreign base company sales income.

(4) *Property manufactured or produced by the controlled foreign corporation*—(i) *In general.* Foreign base company sales income does not include income of a controlled foreign corporation derived in connection with the sale of personal property manufactured, produced, or constructed by such corporation in whole or in part from personal property which it has purchased. A foreign corporation will be considered, for purposes of this subparagraph, to have manufactured, produced, or constructed personal property which it sells if the property sold is in effect not the property which it purchased. In the case of the manufacture, production, or construction of personal property, the property sold will be considered, for purposes of this subparagraph, as not being the property which is purchased if the provisions of subdivision (ii) or (iii) of this subparagraph are satisfied. For rules of apportionment in determining foreign base company sales income derived from the sale of personal property purchased and used as a component part of property which is not manufactured, produced, or constructed, see subparagraph (5) of this paragraph.

(ii) *Substantial transformation of property.* If purchased personal property is substantially transformed prior to sale, the property sold will be treated as having been manufactured, produced, or constructed by the selling corporation. The application of this subdivision may be illustrated by the following examples:

Example (1). Controlled foreign corporation A, incorporated under the laws of foreign country X, operates a paper factory in foreign country Y. Corporation A purchases from a related person wood pulp grown in country Y. Corporation A, by a series of processes, converts the wood pulp to paper which it sells for use in foreign country Z. The transformation of wood pulp to paper constitutes the manufacture or production of property for purposes of this subparagraph.

Example (2). Controlled foreign corporation B, incorporated under the laws of foreign country X, purchases steel rods from a related person who produces the steel in foreign country Y. Corporation B operates a machining plant in country X in which it utilizes the purchased steel rods to make screws and bolts. The transformation of steel rods to screws and bolts constitutes the manufacture or production of property for purposes of this subparagraph.

Example (3). Controlled foreign corporation C, incorporated under the laws of foreign country X, purchases tuna fish from unrelated persons who own fishing boats which catch such fish on the high seas. Corporation C receives such fish in country X in the condition in which taken from the fishing boats and in such country processes, cans, and sells the fish to related person D, incorporated under the laws of foreign country Y, for consumption in foreign country Z. The transformation of such fish into canned fish constitutes the manufacture or production of property for purposes of this subparagraph.

(iii) *Manufacture of a product when purchased components constitute part of the property sold.* If purchased property is used as a component part of personal property which is sold, the sale of the property will be treated as the sale of a manufactured product, rather than the sale of component parts, if the operations conducted by the selling corporation in connection with the property purchased and sold are substantial in nature and are generally considered to constitute the manufacture, production, or construction of property. Without limiting this substantive test, which is dependent on the facts and circumstances of each case, the operations of the selling corporation in connection with the use of the purchased property as a component part of the personal property which is sold will be considered to constitute the manufacture of a product if in connection with such property conversion costs (direct labor and factory burden) of such corporation account for 20 percent or more of the total cost of goods sold. In no event, however, will packaging, repackaging, labeling, or minor assembly operations constitute the manufacture, production, or construction of property for purposes of section 954(d)(1). The application of this subdivision may be illustrated by the following examples:

Example (1). Controlled foreign corporation A, incorporated under the laws of foreign country X, sells industrial engines for use, consumption, and disposition outside country X. Corporation A, in connection with the assembly of such engines, performs machining and assembly operations. In addition, A Corporation purchases, from related and unrelated persons, components manufactured in foreign country Y. On a per unit basis, A Corporation's selling price and costs of such engines are as follows:

Selling price $400
Cost of goods sold:
  Material—
    Acquired from related
      persons $100
    Acquired from others .   40

      Total material $140

Reg. § 1.954-3(a)(4)

Income from Sources Without the United States

See p. 20,601 for regulations not amended to reflect law changes

Conversion costs (direct labor and factory burden)	70
Total cost of goods sold	$210
Gross profit	$190
Administrative and selling expenses	50
Taxable income	$140

The conversion costs incurred by A Corporation are more than 20 percent of total costs of goods sold ($70/$210 or 33 percent). Although the product sold, an engine, is not sufficiently distinguishable from the components to constitute a substantial transformation of the purchased parts within the meaning of subdivision (ii) of this subparagraph, A Corporation will be considered under this subdivision to have manufactured the product it sells.

Example (2). Controlled foreign corporation B, incorporated under the laws of foreign country X, operates an automobile assembly plant. In connection with such activity, B Corporation purchases from related persons assembled engines, transmissions, and certain other components, all of which are manufactured outside of country X; purchases additional components from unrelated persons; conducts stamping, machining, and subassembly operations; and has a substantial investment in tools, jigs, welding equipment, and other machinery and equipment used in the assembly of an automobile. On a per unit basis, B Corporation's selling price and costs of such automobiles are as follows:

Selling price		$2,500
Cost of goods sold:		
Material—		
Acquired from related persons	$1,200	
Acquired from others	275	
Total material	$1,475	
Conversion costs (direct labor and factory burden)	325	
Total cost of goods sold		$1,800
Gross profit		700
Administrative and selling expenses		300
Taxable income		$ 400

The product sold, an automobile, is not sufficiently distinguishable from the components purchased (the engine, transmission, etc.) to constitute a substantial transformation of purchased parts within the meaning of subdivision (ii) of this subparagraph. Although conversion costs of B Corporation are less than 20 percent of total cost of goods sold ($325/$1,800 or 18 percent), the operations conducted by B Corporation in connection with the property purchased and sold are substantial in nature and are generally considered to constitute the manufacture of a product. Corporation B will be considered under this subdivision to have manufactured the product it sells.

Example (3). Controlled foreign corporation C, incorporated under the laws of foreign country X, purchases from related persons radio parts manufactured in foreign country Y. Corporation C designs radio kits, packages component parts required for assembly of such kits, and sells the parts in a knocked-down condition to unrelated persons for use outside country X. These packaging operations of C Corporation do not constitute the manufacture, production, or construction of personal property for purposes of section 954(d)(1).

(5) *Rules for apportionment of income derived from the sale of purchased components used in property not manufactured, produced, or constructed.* The foreign base company sales income derived by a controlled foreign corporation for the taxable year from sales of personal property purchased and used as a component part of property which is not manufactured, produced, or constructed by such corporation within the meaning of subparagraph (4) of this paragraph shall, unless the records of the controlled foreign corporation show that a different apportionment of income is proper or unless all the income from such sales is treated as foreign base company sales income, be determined by first making for such year the following separate classifications and subclassifications with respect to the property which is sold and then by apportioning the income for such year from such sales in accordance with the rules of this subparagraph:

(i) A classification of the cost of components used in the property which is sold into two classes consisting of the cost of components manufactured, produced, constructed, grown, or extracted—

(a) Within the country under the laws of which the controlled foreign corporation is created or organized, and

(b) Outside such country;

(ii) A subclassification of the class described in subdivision (i)(b) of this subparagraph into—

(a) The cost of such components purchased from unrelated persons, and

(b) The cost of such components purchased from related persons;

(iii) A classification of the income derived from such sales into two classes consisting of in-

Reg. § 1.954-3(a)(5)

Income from Sources Without the United States

See p. 20,601 for regulations not amended to reflect law changes

come derived from sales for use, consumption, or disposition—

    (a) Within the country under the laws of which the controlled foreign corporation is created or organized, and

    (b) Outside such country; and

  (iv) A subclassification of the class described in subdivision (iii)(b) of this subparagraph into income from—

    (a) Sales to unrelated persons, and

    (b) Sales to related persons. The foreign base company sales income for the taxable year from purchases of the property from related persons and sales to unrelated persons shall be the amount which bears to the amount described in subdivision (iv)(a) of this subparagraph the same ratio that the amount described in subdivision (ii)(b) of this subparagraph bears to the total cost of components used in the product which is sold. The foreign base company sales income for the taxable year from purchases of the property from related persons and sales to related persons is the amount which bears to the amount described in subdivision (iv)(b) of this subparagraph the same ratio that the amount described in subdivision (ii)(b) of this subparagraph bears to the total cost of components used in the product which is sold. The foreign base company sales income for the taxble year from purchases of the property from unrelated persons and sales to related persons is the amount which bears to the amount described in subdivision (iv)(b) of this subparagraph the same ratio that the amount described in subdivision (ii)(a) of this subparagraph bears to the total cost of components used in the product which is sold. The application of this subparagraph may be illustrated by the following examples:

    Example (1). Controlled foreign corporation C, which is incorporated under the laws of foreign country X, uses the calendar year as the taxable year. For 1964, C Corporation purchases radio parts of which some are manufactured in foreign country Y; and others, in country X. Some of the parts manufactured in country Y are purchased from related persons. Corporation C uses the purchased parts in radio kits which it designs and sells for assembly by its customers, unrelated persons, some of whom use the kits outside country X. Unless the records of C Corporation show that a different apportionment of income is proper, the foreign base company sales income for 1964 is determined in the following manner upon the basis of the following factual classifications for such year:

Cost of components purchased from all persons:		
Manufactured within country X		$ 20
Manufactured outside country X		40
Total cost		60
Cost of components manufactured outside country X:		
Purchased from unrelated persons		10
Purchased from related persons		30
Total cost		40
Gross income from sales:		
Gross receipts from sales		$120
Cost of goods sold:		
Components	$60	
Direct labor and factory burden	10	70
Gross income		50
Gross income from sales:		
For use within country X		$ 26
For use outside country X		24
Gross income		50
Foreign base company sales income from purchases from related persons and sales to unrelated persons ($24×$30/$60)		12

    Example (2). The facts are the same as in example (1) except that none of the purchases are from related persons and some of the sales for use outside country X are to related persons. Unless the records of C Corporation show that a different apportionment of income is proper, the foreign base company sales income for 1964 is determined in the following manner upon the basis of the following additional factual classification for such year:

Gross income from sales for use outside country X—		
To unrelated persons	$	8
To related persons		16
Total gross income		24
Foreign base company sales income from purchases from unrelated persons and sales to related persons ($16 × $40/$60)		$10.67

    Example (3). The facts are the same as in example (1) except that some of the sales for use outside country X are to related persons as in example (2). Unless the records of C Corporation show that a different apportionment of income is proper, the foreign base company sales income for 1964 is determined in the following manner:

Foreign base company sales income from purchases from related persons and sales to unrelated persons ($8 × $30/$60)		$ 4.00

Reg. § 1.954-3(a)(5)

Foreign base company sales income from purchases from related persons and sales to related persons ($16 × $30/$60)	8.00
Foreign base company sales income from purchases from unrelated persons and sales to related persons ($16 × $10/$60)	2.67
Total foreign base company sales income	$14.67

(b) *Branches of controlled foreign corporation treated as separate corporations*—(1) *General rules for determining when to apply separate treatment* —(i) *Sales or purchase branch* —(a) *In general.* If a controlled foreign corporation carries on purchasing or selling activities by or through a branch or similar establishment located outside the country under the laws of which such corporation is created or organized and the use of the branch or similar establishment for such activities has substantially the same tax effect as if the branch or similar establishment were a wholly owned subsidiary corporation of such controlled foreign corporation, the branch or similar establishment and the remainder of the controlled foreign corporation will be treated as separate corporations for purposes of determining foreign base company sales income of such corporation. See section 954(d)(2).

(*b*) *Allocation of income and comparison of effective rates of tax.* The determination as to whether such use of the branch or similar establishment has the same tax effect as if it were a wholly owned subsidiary corporation of the controlled foreign corporation shall be made by allocating to such branch or similar establishment only that income derived by the branch or establishment which, when the special rules of subparagraph (2)(i) of this paragraph are applied, is described in paragraph (a) of this section (but determined without applying subparagraphs (2), (3), and (4) of such paragraph). The use of the branch or similar establishment for such activities will be considered to have substantially the same tax effect as if it were a wholly owned subsidiary corporation of the controlled foreign corporation if the income allocated to the branch or similar establishment under the immediately preceding sentence is, by statute, treaty obligation, or otherwise, taxed in the year when earned at an effective rate of tax that is less than 90 percent of, and at least 5 percentage points less than, the effective rate of tax which would apply to such income under the laws of the country in which the controlled foreign corporation is created or organized, if, under the laws of such country, the entire income of the controlled foreign corporation were considered derived by the corporation from sources within such country from doing business through a permanent establishment therein, received in such country, and allocable to such permanent establishment, and the corporation were managed and controlled in such country.

(*c*) *Use of more than one branch.* If a controlled foreign corporation carries on purchasing or selling activities by or through more than one branch or similar establishment located outside the country under the laws of which such corporation is created or organized, or by or through one or more such branches or similar establishments in a case where subdivision (ii) of this subparagraph also applies, then (*b*) of this subdivision shall be applied separately to the income derived by each such branch or similar establishment (by treating such purchasing or selling branch or similar establishment as if it were the only branch or similar establishment of the controlled foreign corporation and as if any such other branches or similar establishments were separate corporations) in determining whether the use of such branch or similar establishment has substantially the same tax effect as if such branch or similar establishment were a wholly owned subsidiary corporation of the controlled foreign corporation.

(ii) *Manufacturing branch* —(a) *In general.* If a controlled foreign corporation carries on manufacturing, producing, constructing, growing, or extracting activities by or through a branch or similar establishment located outside the country under the laws of which such corporation is created or organized and the use of the branch or similar establishment for such activities with respect to personal property purchased or sold by or through the remainder of the controlled foreign corporation has substantially the same tax effect as if the branch or similar establishment were a wholly owned subsidiary corporation of such controlled foreign corporation, the branch or similar establishment and the remainder of the controlled foreign corporation will be treated as separate corporations for purposes of determining foreign base company sales income of such corporation. See section 954(d)(2).

(*b*) *Allocation of income and comparison of effective rates of tax.* The determination as to whether such use of the branch or similar establishment has substantially the same tax effect as if the branch or similar establishment were a wholly owned subsidiary corporation of the controlled foreign corporation shall be made by allocating to the remainder of such controlled foreign corporation only that income derived by the remainder of such corporation, which, when the special rules of subparagraph (2)(i) of this para-

Reg. § 1.954-3(b)(1)

graph are applied, is described in paragraph (a) of this section (but determined without applying subparagraphs (2), (3), and (4) of such paragraph). The use of the branch or similar establishment for such activities will be considered to have substantially the same tax effect as if it were a wholly owned subsidiary corporation of the controlled foreign corporation if income allocated to the remainder of the controlled foreign corporation under the immediately preceding sentence is, by statute, treaty obligation, or otherwise, taxed in the year when earned at an effective rate of tax that is less than 90 percent of, and at least 5 percentage points less than, the effective rate of tax which would apply to such income under the laws of the country in which the branch or similar establishment is located, if, under the laws of such country, the entire income of the controlled foreign corporation were considered derived by such corporation from sources within such country from doing business through a permanent establishment therein, received in such country, and allocable to such permanent establishment, and the corporation were created or organized under the laws of, and managed and controlled in, such country.

(c) *Use of one or more sales or purchase branches in addition to a manufacturing branch.* If, with respect to personal property manufactured, produced, constructed, grown, or extracted by or through a branch or similar establishment located outside the country under the laws of which the controlled foreign corporation is created or organized, purchasing or selling activities are carried on by or through more than one branch or similar establishment, or by or through one or more branches or similar establishments located outside such country, of such corporation, then (b) of this subdivision shall be applied separately to the income derived by each such purchasing or selling branch or similar establishment (by treating such purchasing or selling branch or similar establishment as though it alone were the remainder of the controlled foreign corporation) for purposes of determining whether the use of such manufacturing, producing, constructing, growing, or extracting branch or similar establishment has substantially the same tax effect as if such branch or similar establishment were a wholly owned subsidiary corporation of the controlled foreign corporation.

(2) *Special rules*—(i) *Determination of treatment as a wholly owned subsidiary corporation.* For purposes of determining under this paragraph whether the use of a branch or similar establishment which is treated as a separate corporation has substantially the same tax effect as if the branch or similar establishment were a wholly owned subsidiary corporation of a controlled foreign corporation—

(a) *Treatment as separate corporations.* The branch or similar establishment will be treated as a wholly owned subsidiary corporation of the controlled foreign corporation, and such branch or similar establishment will be deemed to be incorporated in the country in which it is located.

(b) *Activities treated as performed on behalf of remainder of corporation.* With respect to purchasing or selling activities performed by or through the branch or similar establishment, such purchasing or selling activities shall—

(1) With respect to personal property manufactured, produced, constructed, grown, or extracted by the controlled foreign corporation, or

(2) With respect to personal property (other than property described in (1) of this subdivision (b)) purchased or sold, or purchased and sold, by the controlled foreign corporation.

be treated as performed on behalf of the controlled foreign corporation.

(c) *Activities treated as performed on behalf of branch.* With respect to manufacturing, producing, constructing, growing, or extracting activities performed by or through the branch or similar establishment, purchasing or selling activities performed by or through the remainder of the controlled foreign corporation with respect to the personal property manufactured, produced, constructed, grown, or extracted by or through the branch or similar establishment shall be treated as performed on behalf of the branch or similar establishment.

(d) *Determination of hypothetical tax.* To the extent applicable, the principles of paragraph (b)(4)(ii) of § 1.954-1 shall be used in determining, under subdivision (i) of subparagraph (1) of this paragraph, the effective rate of tax which would apply to the income of the branch or similar establishment under the laws of the country in which the controlled foreign corporation is created or organized, or in determining, under subdivision (ii) of such subparagraph, the effective rate of tax which would apply to the income of the branch or similar establishment under the laws of the country in which the manufacturing, producing, constructing, growing, or extracting branch or similar establishment is located.

(e) *Tax laws to be taken into account.* Tax determinations shall be made by taking into account only the income, war profits, excess profits, or similar tax laws (or the absence of such laws) of the countries involved.

Reg. § 1.954-3(b)(2)

(ii) *Determination of foreign base company sales income.* Once it has been determined under subparagraph (1) of this paragraph that a branch or similar establishment and the remainder of the controlled foreign corporation are to be treated as separate corporations, the determination of whether such branch or similar establishment, or the remainder of the controlled foreign corporation, as the case may be, has foreign base company sales income shall be made by applying the following rules:

(*a*) *Treatment as separate corporations.* The branch or similar establishment will be treated as a wholly owned subsidiary corporation of the controlled foreign corporation, and such branch or similar establishment will be deemed to be incorporated in the country in which it is located.

(*b*) *Activities treated as performed on behalf of remainder of corporation.* With respect to purchasing or selling activities performed by or through the branch or similar establishment, such purchasing or selling activities shall—

(*1*) With respect to personal property manufactured, produced, constructed, grown, or extracted by the controlled foreign corporation, or

(*2*) With respect to personal property (other than property described in (*1*) of this subdivision (*b*)) purchased or sold, or purchased and sold, by the controlled foreign corporation,

be treated as performed on behalf of the controlled foreign corporation.

(*c*) *Activities treated as performed on behalf of branch.* With respect to manufacturing, producing, constructing, growing, or extracting activities performed by or through the branch or similar establishment, purchasing or selling activities performed by or through the remainder of the controlled foreign corporation with respect to the personal property manufactured, produced, constructed, grown, or extracted by or through the branch or similar establishment shall be treated as performed on behalf of the branch or similar establishment.

(*d*) *Items not to be twice included in income.* Income which is classified as foreign base company sales income as a result of the application of subdivision (i) of subparagraph (1) of this paragraph shall not be again classified as foreign base company sales income as a result of the application of subdivision (ii) of such subparagraph.

(*e*) *Comparison with ordinary treatment.* Income derived by the branch or similar establishment, or by the remainder of the controlled foreign corporation, shall not be considered foreign base company sales income if the income would not be so considered if it were derived by a separate controlled foreign corporation under like circumstances.

(*f*) *Priority of application.* If income derived by the branch or similar establishment, or by the remainder of the controlled foreign corporation, from a transaction would be classified as foreign base company sales income of such controlled foreign corporation under section 954(d)(1) and paragraph (a) of this section, the income shall, notwithstanding this paragraph, be treated as foreign base company sales income under paragraph (a) of this section and the branch or similar establishment shall not be treated as a separate corporation with respect to such income.

(3) *Inclusion of amounts in gross income of United States shareholders.* A branch or similar establishment of a controlled foreign corporation and the remainder of such corporation shall be treated as separate corporations under this paragraph solely for purposes of determining the foreign base company sales income of each such corporation and for purposes of including an amount in subpart F income of the controlled foreign corporation under section 952(a). See section 954(b)(3) and paragraph (d)(4) of § 1.954-1 for rules relating to the treatment of a branch or similar establishment of a controlled foreign corporation and the remainder of such corporation as separate corporations for purposes of independently determining if the foreign base company income of each such corporation is less than 10 percent, or more than 70 percent, of its gross income. For all other purposes, however, a branch or similar establishment of a controlled foreign corporation and the remainder of such corporation shall not be treated as separate corporations. For example, if the controlled foreign corporation has a deficit in earnings and profits to which section 952(c) applies, the limitation of such section on the amount includible in the subpart F income of such corporation will apply. Moreover, income, war profits, or excess profits taxes paid by a branch or similar establishment to a foreign country will be treated as having been paid by the controlled foreign corporation for purposes of section 960 (relating to special rules for foreign tax credit) and the regulations thereunder. Also, income of a branch or similar establishment, treated as a separate corporation under this paragraph, will not be treated as dividend income of the controlled foreign corporation of which it is a branch or similar establishment.

(4) *Illustrations.* The application of this paragraph may be illustrated by the following examples:

Example (1). Controlled foreign corporation A, incorporated under the laws of foreign country X, is engaged in the manufacturing business in such country. Corporation A negotiates sales of its products for use outside of country X through a sales office, branch B, maintained in foreign country Y. These activities constitute the only activities of A Corporation. Country X levies an income tax at an effective rate of 50 percent on the income of A Corporation derived by the manufacturing plant in country X but does not tax the sales of income of A Corporation derived by branch B in country Y. Country Y levies an income tax at an effective rate of 10 percent on the sales income derived by branch B but does not tax the income of A Corporation derived by the manufacturing plant in country X. If the sales income derived by branch B were, under the laws of country X, derived from sources within country X by A Corporation, such income would be taxed by such country at an effective rate of 50 percent. In determining foreign base company sales income of A Corporation, branch B is treated as a separate wholly owned subsidiary corporation of A Corporation, the 10 percent rate of tax on branch B's income being less than 90 percent of, and at least 5 percentage points less than, the 50 percent rate. Income derived by branch B, treated as a separate corporation, from the sale by or through it for use, consumption, or disposition outside country Y of the personal property produced in country X is treated as income from the sale of personal property on behalf of A Corporation, a related person, and constitutes foreign base company sales income. The remainder of A Corporation, treated as a separate corporation, derives no foreign base company sales income since it produces the product which is sold.

Example (2). Controlled foreign corporation C is incorporated under the laws of foreign country X. Corporation C maintains branch B in foreign country Y. Branch B manufactures articles in country Y which are sold through the sales offices of C Corporation located in country X. These activities constitute the only activities of C Corporation. Country Y levies an income tax at an effective rate of 30 percent on the manufacturing profit of C Corporation derived by branch B but does not tax the sales income of C Corporation derived by the sales offices in country X. Country X does not impose an income, war profits, excess profits, or similar tax, and no tax is paid to any foreign country with respect to income of C Corporation which is not derived by branch B. If C Corporation were incorporated under the laws of country Y, the sales income of the sales offices in country X would be taxed by country Y at an effective rate of 30 percent. In determining foreign base company sales income of C Corporation, branch B is treated as a separate wholly owned subsidiary corporation of C Corporation, the zero rate of tax on the income derived by the remainder of C Corporation being less than 90 percent of, and at least 5 percentage points less than, the 30 percent rate. Branch B, treated as a separate corporation, derives no foreign base company sales income since it produces the product which is sold. Income derived by the remainder of C Corporation, treated as a separate corporation, from the sale by or through it for use, consumption, or disposition outside country X of the personal property produced in country Y is treated as income from the sale of personal property on behalf of branch B, a related person, and constitutes foreign base company sales income.

Example (3). Controlled foreign corporation E, incorporated under the laws of foreign country X, is a wholly owned subsidiary of controlled foreign corporation D, also incorporated under the laws of country X. Corporation E maintains branch B in foreign country Y. Both corporations use the calendar year as the taxable year. In 1964, E Corporation's sole activity, carried on through branch B, consists of the purchase of articles manufactured in country X by D Corporation, a related person, and the sale of the articles through branch B for use outside country X. The income of E Corporation derived by branch B from such transactions is taxed to E Corporation by country X only at the time E Corporation distributes such income to D Corporation and is then taxed on the basis of what the tax (a 40 percent effective rate) would have been if the income had been derived in 1964 by E Corporation from sources within country X from doing business through a permanent establishment therein. Country Y levies an income tax at an effective rate of 50 percent on income derived from sources within such country, but the income of branch B for 1964 is effectively taxed by country Y at a 5 percent rate since, under the laws of such country, only 10 percent of branch B's income is derived from sources within such country. Corporation E makes no distributions to D Corporation in 1964. In determining foreign base company sales income of E Corporation for 1964, branch B is treated as a separate wholly owned subsidiary corporation of E Corporation, the 5 percent rate of tax on branch B's income being less than 90 percent of, and at least 5 percentage points less than, the 40 percent rate. Income derived by branch B, treated as a separate corporation, from the sale by or through it for use, consumption, or disposition outside country Y of the personal property produced in country X is treated as income from the sale of personal prop-

Reg. § 1.954-3(b)(4)

erty on behalf of E Corporation, a related person, and constitutes foreign base company sales income.

Example (4). Controlled foreign corporation F, incorporated under the laws of foreign country X, is a wholly owned subsidiary of domestic corporation M. Corporation F, through its branch B in foreign country Y, purchases from controlled foreign corporation G, a wholly owned subsidiary of M Corporation incorporated under the laws of foreign country Z, personal property which G Corporation manufactures in country Z. Corporation F sells such property for use in foreign country W. Since the income of F Corporation from such purchases and sales is classified as foreign base company sales income under section 954(d)(1) and paragraph (a) of this section, branch B will not be treated as a separate corporation with respect to such income even if the tax differential between countries X and Y would otherwise justify such treatment.

Example (5). Controlled foreign corporation A, incorporated under the laws of foreign country X, is engaged in manufacturing articles through its home office, located in country X, and selling such articles through branch B, located in foreign country Y, and through branch C, located in foreign country Z, for use outside country X. These activities constitute the only activities of A Corporation for its taxable year 1963. Each such country levies an income tax on only the income derived from sources within such country, and all income derived in 1963 by the home office, branch B, and branch C, respectively, is derived from sources within countries X, Y, and Z, respectively. The income and income taxes of A Corporation for 1963 are as follows:

	X Country	Y Country	Z Country
Income of:			
Home office	$200,000	....	....
Branch B ...	....	$100,000	....
Branch C ..	....	....	$100,000
Income tax ...	100,000	20,000	20,000
Effective rate of tax	50%	20%	20%

By applying subparagraph (1)(i) of this paragraph and by treating branch B as though it were the only branch of A Corporation, branch B is treated as a separate wholly owned subsidiary corporation of A Corporation in determining foreign base company sales income of A Corporation for 1963, the 20 percent rate of tax on the income of such branch being less than 90 percent of, and at least 5 percentage points less than, the 50 percent rate of tax which would apply to the income of branch B under the laws of country X if, under the laws of such country, all the income of A Corporation for 1963 derived through the home office and branch B were derived from sources within country X. Moreover, by applying subparagraph (1)(i) of this paragraph and by treating branch C as though it were the only branch of A Corporation, branch C is treated as a separate wholly owned subsidiary corporation of A Corporation, the 20 percent rate of tax on the income of such branch being less than 90 percent of, and at least 5 percentage points less than, the 50 percent rate of tax which would apply to the income of branch C under the laws of country X if, under the laws of such country, all the income of A Corporation for 1963 derived through the home office and branch C were derived from sources within country X. The income derived by branch B and branch C, respectively, each treated as a separate corporation, from the sale by or through each of them for use, consumption, or disposition outside country Y and country Z, respectively, is treated as income from the sale of personal property on behalf of A Corporation, a related person, and constitutes foreign base company sales income for 1963. The home office of A Corporation, treated as a separate corporation, derives no foreign base company sales income for 1963 since it produces the articles which are sold.

Example (6). Controlled foreign corporation A, incorporated under the laws of foreign country X, is engaged in manufacturing articles through branch B, located in foreign country Y, and selling such articles through branch C, located in foreign country Z, and through its home office, located in country X, for use outside country X. These activities constitute the only activities of A Corporation for its taxable year 1963. Each such country levies an income tax on only the income derived from sources within such country, and all income derived in 1963 by the home office, branch B, and branch C, respectively, is derived from sources within countries X, Y, and Z, respectively. The income and income taxes of A Corporation for 1963 are as follows:

	X Country	Y Country	Z Country
Income of:			
Home office .	$100,000	....	....
Branch B ...	....	$200,000	....
Branch C ..	....	....	$100,000
Income tax ...	20,000	100,000	20,000
Effective rate of tax	20%	50%	20%

In determining foreign base company sales income of A Corporation for 1963 neither branch B nor branch C is treated, by applying subparagraph (1)(i) of this paragraph, as a separate wholly owned subsidiary corporation of A Corporation since branch B derives no income from the

Reg. § 1.954-3(b)(4)

purchase or sale of personal property and since, in the case of branch C treated as though it were the only branch of A Corporation, the 20 percent rate of tax on the income of branch C is not less than 90 percent of, and not as much as 5 percentage points less than, the 20 percent rate of tax which would apply to the income of branch C under the laws of country X if, under the laws of such country, all the income of A Corporation for 1963 derived through the home office and branch C were derived from sources within country X. However, by applying subparagraph (1)(ii) of this paragraph and by treating the home office in country X as though it alone were the remainder of A Corporation, branch B is treated as a separate wholly owned subsidiary corporation of A Corporation, the 20 percent rate of tax on the income of the home office being less than 90 percent of, and at least 5 percentage points less than, the 50 percent rate of tax which would apply to the income of the home office under the laws of country Y if, under the laws of such country, all the income of A Corporation for 1963 derived through the home office and branch B were derived from sources within country Y. Moreover, by applying subparagraph (1)(ii) of this paragraph and by treating branch C as though it alone were the remainder of A Corporation, branch B and branch C are treated as separate wholly owned subsidiary corporations of A Corporation, the 20 percent rate of tax on the income of branch C being less than 90 percent of, and at least 5 percentage points less than, the 50 percent rate of tax which would apply to the income of branch C under the laws of country Y if, under the laws of such country, all the income of A Corporation for 1963 derived through branch B and branch C were derived from sources within country Y. The income derived by the home office and branch C, respectively, each treated as a separate corporation, from the sale by or through each of them for use, consumption, or disposition outside country X and country Z, respectively, is treated as income from the sale of personal property on behalf of branch B, a related person, and constitutes foreign base company sales income for 1963. Branch B, treated as a separate corporation, derives no foreign base company sales income since it produces the articles which are sold.

Example (7). Controlled foreign corporation A, incorporated under the laws of foreign country X, is engaged in manufacturing articles through branch B, located in foreign country Y, and selling such articles through the home office, located in country X, and through branch C, located in foreign country Z, for use outside country X. These activities constitute the only activities of A Corporation for its taxable year 1963. Each such country levies an income tax on only the income derived from sources within such country, and all income derived in 1963 by the home office, branch B, and branch C, respectively, is derived from sources within countries X, Y, and Z, respectively. The income and income taxes of A Corporation for 1963 are as follows:

Income of:

	X Country	Y Country	Z Country
Home office	$100,000	....	....
Branch B	....	$200,000	....
Branch C	....	....	$100,000
Income tax	40,000	100,000	20,000
Effective rate of tax	40%	50%	20%

By applying subparagraph (1)(i) of this paragraph and by treating branch C as though it were the only branch of A Corporation, branch C is treated as a separate wholly owned subsidiary corporation of A Corporation in determining foreign base company sales income of A Corporation for 1963, the 20 percent rate of tax on the income of branch C being less than 90 percent of, and at least 5 percentage points less than, the 40 percent rate of tax which would apply to the income of branch C under the laws of country X if, under the laws of such country, all the income of A Corporation for 1963 derived through the home office and branch C were derived from sources within country X. In addition, by applying subparagraph (1)(ii) of this paragraph and by treating the home office in country X as though it alone were the remainder of A Corporation, branch B is treated as a separate wholly owned subsidiary corporation of A Corporation, the 40 percent rate of tax on the income of the home office being less than 90 percent of, and at least 5 percentage points less than, the 50 percent rate of tax which would apply to the income of the home office under the laws of country Y if, under the laws of such country, all the income of A Corporation for 1963 derived through the home office and branch B were derived from sources within country Y. Moreover, by applying subparagraph (1)(ii) of this paragraph and by treating branch C as though it alone were the remainder of A Corporation, branch B and branch C would again be treated as separate wholly owned subsidiary corporations of A Corporation, the 20 percent rate of tax on the income of branch C being less than 90 percent of, and at least 5 percentage points less than, the 50 percent rate of tax which would apply to the income of branch C under the laws of country Y if, under the laws of such country, all the income of A Corporation for 1963 derived through branch B and branch C were derived from sources within country Y; however, for purposes of determining foreign base company sales

Reg. § 1.954-3(b)(4)

income of A Corporation for 1963, only the classification under subparagraph (1)(i) of this paragraph shall, by reason of the application of subparagraph (2)(ii)(*d*) of this paragraph, be applied with respect to the income derived by branch C. The income derived by the home office and branch C, respectively, each treated as a separate corporation, from the sale by or through each of them for use, consumption, or disposition outside country X and country Z, respectively, is treated as income from the sale of personal property on behalf of branch B, a related person, and constitutes foreign base company sales income for 1963. Branch B, treated as a separate corporation, derives no foreign base company sales income since it produces the articles which are sold.

(c) *Shipping income for taxable years beginning after December 31, 1975.* For taxable years beginning after December 31, 1975, foreign base company shipping income (as determined under § 1.954-6) of a controlled foreign corporation shall not also be considered foreign base company sales income of that controlled foreign corporation. [Reg. § 1.954-3]

☐ [*T.D.* 6734, 5-14-64. *Amended by T.D.* 7497, 7-6-77, T.D. 7555, 7-25-78, T.D. 7893, 5-11-83 and T.D. 7894, 5-11-83.]

[Reg. § 1.954-4]

§ 1.954-4. **Foreign base company services income.**—(a) *Items included.* Except as provided in paragraph (d) of this section, foreign base company services income means income of a controlled foreign corporation, whether in the form of compensation, commissions, fees, or otherwise, derived in connection with the performance of technical, managerial, engineering, architectural, scientific, skilled, industrial, commercial, or like services which—

(1) Are performed for, or on behalf of, a related person, as defined in paragraph (e)(1) of § 1.954-1, and

(2) Are performed outside the country under the laws of which the controlled foreign corporation is created or organized.

(b) *Services performed for, or on behalf of, a related person*—(1) *Specific cases.* For purposes of paragraph (a)(1) of this section, "services which are performed for, or on behalf of, a related person" include (but are not limited to) services performed by a controlled foreign corporation in a case where—

(i) The controlled foreign corporation is paid or reimbursed by, is released from an obligation to, or otherwise receives substantial financial benefit from, a related person for performing such services;

(ii) The controlled foreign corporation performs services (whether or not with respect to property sold by a related person) which a related person is, or has been, obligated to perform;

(iii) The controlled foreign corporation performs services with respect to property sold by a related person and the performance of such services constitutes a condition or a material term of such sale; or

(iv) Substantial assistance contributing to the performance of such services has been furnished by a related person or persons.

(2) *Special rules*—(i) *Guaranty of performance.* Subparagraph (1)(ii) of this paragraph shall not apply with respect to services performed by a controlled foreign corporation pursuant to a contract the performance of which is guaranteed by a related person, if (*a*) the related person's sole obligation with respect to the contract is to guarantee performance of such services, (*b*) the controlled foreign corporation is fully obligated to perform the services under the contract, and (*c*) the related person (or any other person related to the controlled foreign corporation) does not in fact (*1*) pay for performance of, or perform, any of such services the performance of which is so guaranteed or (*2*) pay for performance of, or perform, any significant services related to such services. If the related person (or any other person related to the controlled foreign corporation) does in fact pay for performance of, or perform, any of such services or any significant services related to such services, subparagraph (1)(ii) of this paragraph shall apply with respect to the services performed by the controlled foreign corporation pursuant to the contract the performance of which is guaranteed by the related person, even though such payment or performance is not considered to be substantial assistance for purposes of subparagraph (1)(iv) of this paragraph. For purposes of this subdivision, a related person shall be considered to guarantee performance of the services by the controlled foreign corporation whether it guarantees performance of such services by a separate contract of guaranty or enters into a service contract solely for purposes of guaranteeing performance of such services and immediately thereafter assigns the entire contract to the controlled foreign corporation for execution.

(ii) *Application of substantial assistance test.* For purposes of subparagraph (1)(iv) of this paragraph—

(*a*) Assistance furnished by a related person or persons to the controlled foreign corporation shall include, but shall not be limited to, direction, supervision, services, know-how, finan-

Reg. § 1.954-4(b)(2)

cial assistance (other than contributions to capital), and equipment, material, or supplies.

(*b*) Assistance furnished by a related person or persons to a controlled foreign corporation in the form of direction, supervision, services, or know-how shall not be considered substantial unless either (*1*) the assistance so furnished provides the controlled foreign corporation with skills which are a principal element in producing the income from the performance of such services by such corporation or (*2*) the cost to the controlled foreign corporation of the assistance so furnished equals 50 percent or more of the total cost to the controlled foreign corporation of performing the services performed by such corporation. The term "cost," as used in this subdivision (*b*), shall be determined after taking into account adjustments, if any, made under section 482.

(*c*) Financial assistance (other than contributions to capital), equipment, material, or supplies furnished by a related person to a controlled foreign corporation shall be considered assistance only in that amount by which the consideration actually paid by the controlled foreign corporation for the purchase or use of such item is less than the arm's length charge for such purchase or use. The total of such amounts so considered to be assistance in the case of financial assistance, equipment, material, and supplies furnished by all related persons shall be compared with the profits derived by the controlled foreign corporation from the performance of the services to determine whether the financial assistance, equipment, material, and supplies furnished by a related person or persons are by themselves substantial assistance contributing to the performance of such services. For purposes of this subdivision (*c*), determinations shall be made after taking into account adjustments, if any, made under section 482 and the term "consideration actually paid" shall include any amount which is deemed paid by the controlled foreign corporation pursuant to such an adjustment.

(*d*) Even though assistance furnished by a related person or persons to a controlled foreign corporation in the form of direction, supervision, services, or know-how is not considered to be substantial under (*b*) of this subdivision and assistance furnished by a related person or persons in the form of financial assistance (other than contributions to capital), equipment, material, or supplies is not considered to be substantial under (*c*) of this subdivision, such assistance may nevertheless constitute substantial assistance when taken together or in combination with other assistance furnished by a related person or persons which in itself is not considered to be substantial.

(*e*) Assistance furnished by a related person or persons to a controlled foreign corporation in the form of direction, supervision, services, or know-how shall not be taken into account under (*b*) or (*d*) of this subdivision unless the assistance so furnished assists the controlled foreign corporation directly in the performance of the services performed by such corporation.

(3) *Illustrations.* The application of this paragraph may be illustrated by the following examples:

Example (1). Controlled foreign corporation A is paid by related corporation M for the installation and maintenance of industrial machines which M Corporation manufactures and sells to B Corporation. Such installation and maintenance services by A Corporation are performed for, or on behalf of, M Corporation for purposes of section 954(e).

Example (2). Controlled foreign corporation B enters into a contract with an unrelated person to drill an oil well in a foreign country. Domestic corporation M owns all the outstanding stock of B Corporation. Corporation B employs a relatively small clerical and administrative staff and owns the necessary well-drilling equipment. Most of the technical and supervisory personnel who oversee the drilling of the oil well by B Corporation are regular employees of M Corporation who are temporarily employed by B Corporation. In addition, B Corporation hires on the open market unskilled and semiskilled laborers to work on the drilling project. The services performed by B Corporation under the well-drilling contract are performed for, or on behalf of, a related person for purposes of section 954(e) because the services of the technical and supervisory personnel which are provided by M Corporation are of substantial assistance in the performance of such contract in that they assist B Corporation directly in the execution of the contract and provide B Corporation with skills which are a principal element in producing the income from the performance of such contract.

Example (3). Controlled foreign corporation F enters into a contract with an unrelated person to construct a dam in a foreign country. Domestic corporation M owns all the outstanding stock of F Corporation. Corporation F leases or buys from M Corporation, on an arm's length basis, the equipment and material necessary for the construction of the dam. The technical and supervisory personnel who design and oversee the construction of the dam are regular full-time employees of F Corporation who are not on loan from any related person. The principal clerical work, and the financial accounting, required in connection with the construction of the dam by F Corporation are

Reg. § 1.954-4(b)(3)

performed, on a remunerated basis, by full-time employees of M Corporation. All other assistance F Corporation requires in completing the construction of the dam is paid for by that corporation and furnished by unrelated persons. The services performed by F Corporation under the contract for the construction of the dam are not performed for, or on behalf of, a related person for purposes of section 954(e) because the clerical and accounting services furnished by M Corporation do not assist F Corporation directly in the performance of the contract.

Example (4). Controlled foreign corporation D, a wholly owned subsidiary of domestic corporation M, procures and enters a contract with an unrelated person to construct a superhighway in a foreign country, but such person enters the contract only on the condition that M Corporation agrees to perform, or to pay for the performance by some person other than D Corporation of, the services called for by the contract if D Corporation should fail to complete their performance. Corporation D is capable of performing such contract. No related person as to D Corporation pays for, or performs, any services called for by the contract, or pays for, or performs, any significant services related to such services. The construction of the superhighway by D Corporation is not considered for purposes of section 954(e) to be the performance of services for, or on behalf of, M Corporation.

Example (5). Domestic corporation M is obligated under a contract with an unrelated person to construct a superhighway in a foreign country. At a later date M Corporation assigns the entire contract to its wholly owned subsidiary, controlled foreign corporation C, and the unrelated person releases M Corporation from any obligation under the contract. The construction of such highway by C Corporation is considered for purposes of section 954(e) to be the performance of services for, or on behalf of, M Corporation.

Example (6). Domestic corporation M enters a contract with an unrelated person to construct a superhighway in a foreign country. Corporation M immediately assigns the entire contract to its wholly owned subsidiary, controlled foreign corporation C. The unrelated person does not release M Corporation of its obligation under the contract, the sole purpose of these arrangements being to have M Corporation guarantee performance of the contract by C Corporation. Corporation C is capable of performing the construction contract. Neither M Corporation nor any other person related to C Corporation pays for, or performs, any services called for by the construction contract or at any time pays for, or performs, any significant services related to the services performed under such contract. The construction of the superhighway by C Corporation is not considered for purposes of section 954(e) to be the performance of services for, or on behalf of, M Corporation.

Example (7). The facts are the same as in example (6) except that M Corporation, preparatory to entering the construction contract, prepares plans and specifications which enable the submission of bids for the contract. Since M Corporation has performed significant services related to the services the performance of which it has guaranteed, the construction of such highway by C Corporation is considered for purposes of section 954(e) to be the performance of services for, or on behalf of, M Corporation.

Example (8). Domestic corporation M manufactures an industrial machine which requires specialized installation. Corporation M sells the machines for a basic price if the contract of sale contains no provision for installation. If, however, the customer agrees to employ controlled foreign corporation E, a wholly owned subsidiary of M Corporation, to install the machine and to pay E Corporation a specified installation charge, M Corporation sells the machine at a price which is less than the basic price. The installation services performed by E Corporation for customers of M Corporation purchasing the machine at the reduced price are considered for purposes of section 954(e) to be performed for, or on behalf of, M Corporation.

Example (9). Domestic corporation M manufactures and sells industrial machines with a warranty as to their performance conditional upon their installation and maintenance by a factory-authorized service agency. Controlled foreign corporation F, a wholly owned subsidiary of M Corporation, is the only authorized service agency. Any installation or maintenance services performed by F Corporation on such machines are considered for purposes of section 954(e) to be performed for, or on behalf of, M Corporation.

Example (10). Domestic corporation M manufactures electric office machines which it sells at a basic price without any provision for, or understanding as to, adjustment or maintenance of the machines. The machines require constant adjustment and maintenance services which M Corporation, certain wholly owned subsidiaries of M Corporation, and certain unrelated persons throughout the world are qualified to perform. From among the numerous persons qualified and available to perform adjustment and maintenance services with respect to such office machines, foreign corporation B, a customer of M Corporation, employs controlled foreign corporation G, a wholly

Reg. § 1.954-4(b)(3)

owned subsidiary of M Corporation, to adjust and maintain the office machines which B Corporation purchases from M Corporation. The adjustment and maintenance services performed by G Corporation for B Corporation are not considered for purposes of section 954(e) to be performed for, or on behalf of, M Corporation.

(c) *Place where services are performed.* The place where services will be considered to have been performed for purposes of paragraph (a)(2) of this section will depend on the facts and circumstances of each case. As a general rule, services will be considered performed where the persons performing services for the controlled foreign corporation which derives income in connection with the performance of technical, managerial, architectural, engineering, scientific, skilled, industrial, commercial, or like services are physically located when they perform their duties in the execution of the service activity resulting in such income. Therefore, in many cases, total gross income of a controlled foreign corporation derived in connection with each service contract or arrangement performed for or on behalf of a related person must be apportioned, between income which is not foreign base company services income and that which is foreign base company services income, on a basis of employee-time spent within the foreign country under the laws of which the controlled foreign corporation is created or organized and employee-time spent without the foreign country under the laws of which such corporation is created or organized. In allocating time spent within and without the foreign country under the laws of which the controlled foreign corporation is created or organized, relative weight must also be given to the value of the various functions performed by persons in fulfillment of the service contract or arrangement. For example, clerical work will ordinarily be assigned little value, while services performed by technical, highly skilled, and managerial personnel will be assigned greater values in relation to the type of function performed by each individual.

(d) *Items excluded.* Foreign base company services income does not include—

(1) Income derived in connection with the performance of services by a controlled foreign corporation if—

(i) The services directly relate to the sale or exchange of personal property by the controlled foreign corporation,

(ii) The property sold or exchanged was manufactured, produced, grown, or extracted by such controlled foreign corporation, and

(iii) The services were performed before the sale or exchange of such property by the controlled foreign corporation;

(2) Income derived in connection with the performance of services by a controlled foreign corporation if the services directly relate to an offer or effort to sell or exchange personal property which was, or would have been, manufactured, produced, grown, or extracted by such controlled foreign corporation whether or not a sale or exchange of such property was in fact consummated; or

(3) For taxable years beginning after December 31, 1975, foreign base company shipping income (as determined under § 1.954-6). [Reg. § 1.954-4.]

☐ [*T.D.* 6734, 5-14-64. *Amended by T.D.* 6981, 11-12-68 *and T.D.* 7894, 5-11-83.]

[Reg. § 1.954-5]

§ 1.954-5. **Increase in qualified investments in less developed countries; taxable years of controlled foreign corporations beginning before January 1, 1976.**—For rules applicable to taxable years of controlled foreign corporations beginning before January 1, 1976, see section 954(b)(1) (as in effect before the enactment of the Tax Reduction Act of 1975) and 26 CFR § 1.954-5 (Rev. as of April 1, 1975). [Reg. § 1.954-5.]

☐ [*T.D.* 6734, 5-14-64. *Amended by T.D.* 7893, 5-11-83.]

[Reg. § 1.954-6]

§ 1.954-6. **Foreign base company shipping income.**—(a) *Scope*—(1) *In general.*—This section prescribes rules for determining foreign base company shipping income under the provisions of section 954(f), as amended by the Tax Reduction Act of 1975.

(2) *Effective date.*—(i) The rules prescribed in this section apply to taxable years of foreign corporations beginning after December 31, 1975, and to taxable years of United States shareholders (as defined in section 951(b)) within which or with which such taxable years of such foreign corporations end.

(ii) Except as described in paragraph (b)(1)(viii) of this section, foreign base company shipping income does not include amounts earned by a foreign corporation in a taxable year of such corporation beginning before January 1, 1976. See example (1) of paragraph (g)(2) of this section for an illustration of the effect of this subparagraph on partnership income. See example (3) of paragraph (f)(4)(ii) of this section for an illustration of the effect of this subparagraph on certain dividend income. See paragraph (f)(5)(iii) of this section for the effect of this subparagraph on certain interest and gains.

(b) *Definitions*—(1) *Foreign base company shipping income.*—The term "foreign base company shipping income" means—

(i) Gross income derived from, or in connection with, the use (or hiring or leasing for use) of any aircraft or vessel in foreign commerce (see paragraph (c) of this section),

(ii) Gross income derived from, or in connection with, the performance of services directly related to the use of any aircraft or vessesl in foreign commerce (see paragraph (d) of this section),

(iii) Gross income incidental to income described in subdivisions (i) and (ii) of this subparagraph, as provided in paragraph (e) of this section,

(iv) Gross income derived from the sale, exchange, or other disposition of any aircraft or vessel used or held for use (by the seller or by a person related to the seller) in foreign commerce,

(v) In the case of a controlled foreign corporation, dividends, interest, and gains described in paragraph (f) of this section,

(vi) Income described in paragraph (g) of this section (relating to partnerships, trusts, etc.),

(vii) Exchange gain, to the extent allocable to foreign base company shipping income (see § 1.952-2(c)(2)(v)(*b*)), and

(viii) In the case of a controlled foreign corporation and at its option, dividends, interest, and gains attributable to income derived from aircraft and vessels (as defined in 26 CFR § 1.954-1(b)(2) (Rev. as of April 1, 1975)) by a less developed country shipping company (described in § 1.955-5(b)) in taxable years beginning after December 31, 1962, and before January 1, 1976. The portion of a dividend, interest, or gain attributable to such income shall be determined by the same method as that for determining the portion of a dividend, interest, or gain attributable to foreign base company shipping income under paragraphs (f)(4), (5), and (6) of this section, but without regard to paragraphs (f)(6)(ii) and (iv)(B).

(2) *Foreign base company shipping operations.*—For purposes of sections 951 through 964, the term "foreign base company shipping operations" means the trade or business from which gross income described in subparagraph (1)(i) and (ii) of this paragraph is derived.

(3) *Foreign commerce.*—For purposes of section 951 through 964—

(i) An aircraft or vessel is used in foreign commerce to the extent it is used in transportation of property or passengers—

(A) Between a port (or airport) in the United States or possession of the United States and a port (or airport) in a foreign country, or

(B) Between a port (or airport) in a foreign country and another in the same country or between a port (or airport) in a foreign country and one in another foreign country.

Thus, for example, a trawler, a factory ship, and an oil drilling ship are not considered to be used in foreign commerce. On the other hand, a cruise ship which visits one or more foreign ports is considered to be so used. Notwithstanding subdivision (i)(B) of this paragraph (b)(3), foreign base company income does not include income derived from, or in connection with, the use of an aircraft or vessel in transportation of property or passengers between a port (or airport) in a foreign country and another port (or airport) in the same country if both the foreign corporation is created or organized and the aircraft or vessel is registered in that country.

(ii) The term "vessel" includes all water craft and other artificial contrivances of whatever description and at whatever stage of construction, whether on the stocks or launched, which are used or are capable of being used or are intended to be used as a means of transportation on water. This definition does not apply for purposes of section 956(b)(2)(G) and § 1.956-2(b)(1)(ix).

(iii) The term "port" means any place (whether on or off shore) where aircraft or vessels are accustomed to load or unload goods or to take on or let off passengers.

(iv) Any vessel (such as a lighter or beacon lightship) which serves other vessels used in foreign commerce (within the meaning of subdivision (i) of this subparagraph) shall, to the extent so used, also be considered to be used in foreign commerce.

(v) For the meaning of the term "foreign country", see section 638(2).

(4) *Use in foreign commerce.* For purposes of sections 951 through 964, the use of an aircraft or vessel in foreign commerce includes the hiring or leasing (or subleasing) of an aircraft or vessel to another for use in foreign commerce. Thus, for example, an aircraft or vessel is "used in foreign commerce" within the meaning of section 955(b)(1)(A) if such aircraft or vessel is chartered (whether pursuant to a bareboat charter, time charter, or otherwise) to another for use in foreign commerce.

Reg. § 1.954-6(b)(4)

49,288 Income from Sources Without the United States
See p. 20,601 for regulations not amended to reflect law changes

(5) *Related person.* With respect to a controlled foreign corporation, the term "related person" means a related person as defined in § 1.954-1(e)(1), and the term "unrelated person" means an unrelated person as defined in § 1.954-1(e)(2).

(c) *Aircraft or vessel income*—(1) *In general.* The term "income derived from, or in connection with, the use (or hiring or leasing for use) of any aircraft or vessel in foreign commerce" as used in paragraph (b)(1)(i) of this section means—

(i) Income derived from transporting passengers or property by aircraft or vessel in foreign commerce and

(ii) Income derived from hiring or leasing an aircraft or vessel to another for use in foreign commerce.

(2) *Illustrations.* The application of this paragaraph may be illustrated by the following examples:

Example (1). Foreign corporation C owns a foreign flag vessel which it charters under a long-term charter to foreign corporation D. The vessel is used by D as a tramp which has no fixed or regular schedule. The vessel carries bulk and packaged cargoes, as well as occasional passengers, under charter parties, contracts of affreightment, or other contracts of carriage. The carriage of cargoes and passengers is between a port in the United States and a port in a foreign country or between a port in one foreign country and another port in the same or a different foreign country. The charter hire paid to C by D constitutes income derived from the use of the vessel in foreign commerce, but is not foreign base company income to the extent the charter hire is allocable to income derived from the use of the vessel between ports in the same foreign country in which both C is incorporated and the vessel is registered. The charter hire and freight and passenger revenue (including demurrage and dead freight) derived by D also constitute income derived from the use of the vessel in foreign commerce, but is not foreign base company income to the extent the charter hire and freight and passenger revenue are allocable to the use of the vessel between ports in the same foreign country in which both D is incorporated and the vessel is registered.

Example (2). (a) Foreign corporation E owns a foreign flag tanker which it charters under a long-term bareboat charter to foreign corporation F for use in foreign commerce. F produces oil in a foreign country and ships the oil to other foreign countries and to the United States. The vessel, when not engaged in carrying F's oil, is used to carry bulk cargoes for unrelated persons in foreign commerce as opportunity offers. The charter hire received by E constitutes income derived from the use of the vessel in foreign commerce. The income derived by F from carrying bulk cargoes for unrelated persons also constitutes income derived from the use of the vessel in foreign commerce.

(b) F is forced to lay up the vessel as a result of adverse market developments. Pursuant to the terms of the charter, F continues to pay charter hire to E during the period of lay-up. The charter hire received by E during the period of lay-up constitutes income derived from the use of the vessel in foreign commerce.

Example (3). (a) A shipment of cheese is loaded into a container owned by controlled foreign corporation S at the consignor's place of business in Hamar, Norway. The cheese is transported to Milan, Italy, by the following routings:

(1) Overland by road from Hamar, Norway, to Gothenburg, Sweden, by unrelated motor carriers via Oslo, Norway,

(2) By sea from Gothenburg to Rotterdam, Netherlands, by feeder vessel under foreign flag, time chartered to S by unrelated owner,

(3) By sea from Rotterdam to Algeciras, Spain, by feeder vessel under foreign flag, time chartered to S by unrelated owner,

(4) By sea from Algeciras to Genoa, Italy, by line-haul vessel under U.S. flag, chartered by S from related company, and

(5) Overland from Genoa to Milan, Italy, by unrelated motor carrier.

(b) The consignor pays S total charges of $1,710, and S pays $676 to unrelated third parties, which amounts may be broken down as follows:

Description of charges	Amount billed to customer and collected by S	Revenue collected by S on behalf of an unrelated party	Costs paid to unrelated 3d party and absorbed by S
Ocean freight	$1,420		
Trucking charge of empty equipment to shipper's facility	50	$ 50	

Reg. § 1.954-6(b)(5)

Trucking charges Hamar to Oslo	60	60	
Trucking charges Oslo to Gothenburg			$315
Trucking charges Genoa to Milan	180	180	
Brokerage Commission in Europe			71
Total	1,710	290	386

(c) Of the $1,710 amount billed to the consignor and collected by S, $290 is collected by S on behalf of unrelated third parties. This $290 amount is not includible in S's gross income, and is therefore not includible in S's foreign base company shipping income. The remaining $1,420 amount (i.e., $1,710 − $290) is includible in S's foreign base company shipping income. The $386 amount paid by S to unrelated third parties and absorbed by S is deductible from foreign base company shipping income under § 1.954-1(c).

(d) *Services directly related*—(1) *In general.* The term "income derived from, or in connection with, the performance of services directly related to the use of an aircraft or vessel in foreign commerce", as used in paragraph (b)(1)(ii) of this section, means—

(i) Income derived from, or in connection with, the performance of services described in subparagraph (2) or (3) of this paragraph, and

(ii) Income treated as foreign base company shipping income under subparagraph (4) of this paragraph.

(2) *Intragroup services.* The services described in this subparagraph are services performed for a person who is the owner, lessor, lessee or operator of an aircraft or vessel used in foreign commerce, by such person or by a person related to such person, and which fall into one or more of the following categories:

(i) Terminal services, such as dockage, wharfage, storage, lights, water, refrigeration, and similar services;

(ii) Stevedoring and other cargo handling services;

(iii) Container related services (including the rental of containers and related equipment) performed either in connection with the local drayage or inland haulage of cargo or in the course of transportation in foreign commerce;

(iv) Services performed by tugs, lighters, barges, scows, launches, floating cranes, and other similar equipment;

(v) Maintenance and repairs;

(vi) Training of pilots and crews;

(vii) Licensing of patents, know-how, and similar intangible property developed and used in the course of foreign base company shipping operations;

(viii) Services performed by a booking, operating, or managing agent; and

(ix) Any service performed in the course of the actual transportation of passengers or property.

(3) *Services for passenger, consignor, or consignee.* The services described in this subparagraph are services provided by the operator (or person related to the operator) of an aircraft or vessel in foreign commerce for the passenger, consignor, or consignee, such as—

(i) Services described in one or more of the categories set out in subparagraph (2)(i) through (iv) and (ix) of this paragraph.

(ii) The rental of staterooms, berths, or living accommodations and the furnishing of meals.

(iii) Barber shop and other services to passengers aboard vessels,

(iv) Excess baggage, and

(v) Demurrage, dispatch, and dead freight.

(4) *The 70-percent test.* At the option of the foreign corporation all the gross income for a taxable year derived by a foreign corporation from any facility used in connection with the performance of services described in one or more of the categories set out in subparagraph (2)(i) through (ix) of this paragraph is foreign base company shipping income if more than 70 percent of such gross income for either—

(i) Such taxable year, or

(ii) Such taxable year and the two preceding taxable years,

is foreign base company shipping income (determined without regard to this subparagraph). Thus, for example, if 80 percent of the gross income derived by a controlled foreign corporation at a stevedoring facility is treated as foreign base company shipping income under subparagraph (2) of this paragraph, then the remaining 20 percent is treated as foreign base company shipping income under this subparagraph.

(5) *Rules for applying subparagraph (4).* (i) Solely for purposes of applying subparagraph (4) of this paragraph, foreign base company shipping income and gross income shall be deemed to in-

Reg. § 1.954-6(d)(5)

Income from Sources Without the United States

See p. 20,601 for regulations not amended to reflect law changes

clude an arm's length charge (see paragraph (h)(5) of this section) for services performed by the foreign corporation for itself.

(ii) In determining whether services performed by a foreign corporation are performed at a single facility or at two or more different facilities, all of the facts and circumstances involved will be taken into account. Ordinarily, all services performed by a foreign corporation within a single port area will be considered performed at a single facility.

(iii) The application of this subparagraph and subparagraph (4) of this paragraph may be illustrated by the following example in which it is assumed that the foreign corporation has chosen to apply the 70-percent test of subparagraph (4):

Example. (a) Controlled foreign corporation X uses the calendar year as the taxable year. For 1976, X is divided into two operating divisions, A and B. Division A operates a number of vessels in foreign commerce. Division B operates a terminal facility at which it performs services described in subparagraph (2)(i) of this paragraph for vessels some of which are operated by division A, some of which are operated by persons related to X, and some of which are operated by persons unrelated to X. For 1976, X includes under subparagraph (5) as foreign base company shipping income and gross income, for purposes of subparagraph (4), and arm's length charge for services performed for itself. For 1976, the gross income derived by division B is reconstructed for purposes of subparagraph (4) of this paragraph as follows, based on the facts shown in the following table:

(1) Gross income derived from persons unrelated to X	$ 20
(2) Gross income derived from persons related to X	10
(3) Actual gross income (line (1) plus line (2))	30
(4) Hypothetical gross income derived from division A (determined by the application of subdivision (i) of this subparagraph)	70
(5) Total reconstructed gross income (line (3) plus line (4))	100

(b) Since 80 percent of the reconstructed gross income derived by division B would be treated as foreign base company shipping income under subparagraph (2) of this paragraph, the entire $30 amount of the gross income actually derived by division B is treated as foreign base company shipping income under subparagraph (4) of this paragraph.

(6) *Arm's length charge.* For purposes of this section, the arm's length charge for services performed by a foreign corporation for itself shall be determined by applying the principles of section 482 and the regulations thereunder as if the party for whom the services are performed and the party by whom the services are performed were not the same person, but were controlled taxpayers within the meaning of § 1.482-1(a)(4).

(7) *Illustrations.* The application of this paragraph may be illustrated by the following examples:

Example (1). Controlled foreign corporation A acts as a managing agent for foreign corporation B, a related person which contracts to construct and charter a foreign flag vessel for use in foreign commerce. As managing agent for B, A performs a broad range of services relating to the use of the vessel, including arranging for, and supervising of, construction and chartering of the vessel, and handling of operating services after construction is completed. The income derived by A from its management and operating services constitutes income derived in connection with the performance of services directly related to the use of the vessel in foreign commerce.

Example (2). Controlled foreign corporation C uses the calendar year as the taxable year. During 1976, C is engaged in the trade or business of acting as a steamship agent solely for unrelated persons. C's activities as steamship agent range from "husbanding" (i.e., arranging for fuel, supplies and port services, and attending to crew and customs matters) to the solicitation and booking of cargo at a number of foreign ports. None of C's other gross income for 1976 is foreign base company shipping income. Under these circumstances, C's gross income derived from its steamship agency does not constitute foreign base company shipping income.

(e) *Incidental income*—(1) *In general.* Foreign base company shipping income includes all incidental income derived by a foreign corporation in the course of its active conduct of foreign base company shipping operations.

(2) *Examples.* Examples of incidental income derived in the course of the active conduct of foreign base company shipping operations include—

(i) Gain from the sale, exchange or other disposition of assets which are related shipping assets within the meaning of § 1.955A-2(b),

(ii) Income derived from temporary investments described in § 1.955A-2(b)(2)(i) and (iii),

(iii) Interest on accounts receivable and evidences of indebtedness described in § 1.955A-2(b)(2)(ii),

Reg. § 1.954-6(d)(6)

(iv) Income derived from granting concessions to others aboard aircraft or vessels used in foreign commerce,

(v) Income derived from stock and currency futures described in § 1.955A-2(b)(2)(vii) and (viii),

(vi) Income derived by the lessor of an aircraft or vessel used in foreign commerce from additional rentals for the use of related equipment (such as a complement of containers), and

(vii) Interest derived by the seller from a purchase money mortgage loan in respect of the sale of an aircraft or vessel described in § 1.955A-2(a)(1)(i).

(f) *Certain dividends, interest, and gain*—(1) *In general.* (i) The foreign base company shipping income of a controlled foreign corporation (referred to in subdivision (ii)(A) of this paragraph (f)(1) as "first corporation") includes—

(A) Dividends and interest received from foreign corporations listed in subdivision (ii) of this paragraph (f)(1) and

(B) Gain recognized from the sale, exchange, or other disposition of stock or obligations of foreign corporations listed in subdivision (ii) of this paragraph (f)(1),

but only to the extent that such dividends, interest, and gains are attributable to foreign base company shipping income of the foreign corporations listed in subdivision (ii) of this paragraph (f)(1).

(ii) The foreign corporations referred to in subdivision (i) of this paragraph (f)(1) are—

(A) Foreign corporations with respect to which the first corporation (see subdivision (i) of this paragraph (f)(1)) would be deemed under section 902(b) to pay taxes,

(B) Controlled foreign corporations which are related persons (within the meaning of section 954(d)(3)), and

(C) Less developed country shipping companies described in § 1.955-5(b).

(2) *Corporation deemed to pay taxes.* (i) For purposes of this paragraph, a controlled foreign corporation would be deemed under section 902(b) to pay taxes in respect of any other foreign corporation if such controlled foreign corporation would be deemed, for purposes of applying section 902(a) to any United States shareholder of such controlled foreign corporation, to pay taxes in respect of dividends which were received from such other foreign corporation (whether or not such other foreign corporation actually pays any taxes or dividends).

Solely for purposes of this subdivision, each United States shareholder (within the meaning of section 951(b)) shall be deemed to be a domestic corporation.

(ii) The application of subdivision (i) of this subparagraph may be illustrated by the following examples:

Example (1). Domestic corporation M owns 100 percent of the one class of stock of controlled foreign corporation X, which in turn owns 40 percent of the one class of stock of foreign corporation Y. Y is not a controlled foreign corporation. For purposes of subdivision (i) of this subparagraph, X is deemed to pay taxes in respect of Y.

Example (2). The facts are the same as in example (1), except that United States shareholder A, an individual, owns 80 percent of the stock of corporation X, and United States shareholders B and C, parent and child, own the other 20 percent in equal shares. For purposes of applying this paragraph to all three United States shareholders (A, B, and C), X is deemed to pay taxes in respect of Y.

(3) *Obligation defined.* For purposes of this section, the term "obligation" means any bond, note, debenture, certificate, or other evidence of indebtedness, and a debt recorded in the books of account of both the creditor and the debtor. In the absence of legal, governmental, or business reasons to the contrary, the indebtedness must bear interest or be issued at a discount.

(4) *Dividends.* (i) For purposes of this paragraph and § 1.954-1(b)(2), the portion of a dividend which is attributable to foreign base company shipping income is that amount which bears the same ratio to the total dividend received as the earnings and profits out of which such dividend is paid that are attributable to foreign base company shipping income bears to the total earnings and profits out of which such dividend is paid. For purposes of this subdivision, the source of the earnings and profits out of which a distribution is made shall be determined under section 316(a), except that the source of the earnings and profits out of which a distribution is made by a controlled foreign corporation with respect to stock owned (within the meaning of section 958(a)) by a United States shareholder of such controlled foreign corporation shall be determined under § 1.959-3.

(ii) The application of this subparagraph may be illustrated by the following examples:

Example (1). Domestic corporation M owns 100 percent of the one class of stock of controlled foreign corporation X, which in turn owns 40 percent of the one class of stock of foreign

Reg. § 1.954-6(f)(4)

corporation Y. Y, which is not (and has not been) either a controlled foreign corporation or a less developed country shipping company, makes a distribution of $100 to X. Under section 316(a), such distribution is made out of Y's earnings and profits for 1978. Sixty percent of Y's earnings and profits for 1978 are attributable to foreign base company shipping income. As a result, $60 of the $100 distribution constitutes foreign base company shipping income to X under subdivision (i) of this subparagraph.

Example (2). The facts are the same as in example (1), except that under section 316(a) $20 of the $100 dividend is paid out of Y's earnings and profits for 1979, and the other $80 is paid out of Y's earnings and profits for 1978. Thirty percent of Y's earnings and profits for 1979 are attributable to foreign base company shipping income. Since 60 percent of Y's earnings and profits for 1978 are also attributable to foreign base company shipping income, $54, i.e. (.60 × $80) + (.30 × $20), of the $100 distribution constitutes foreign base company shipping income to X under subdivision (i) of this subparagraph.

Example (3). The facts are the same as in example (1) except that under section 316(a) the $100 dividend is made out of Y's earnings and profits for 1972. Since under paragraph (a)(2)(ii) of this section foreign base company shipping income does not include amounts earned by a foreign corporation (not a less developed country shipping company) in a taxable year beginning before January 1, 1976, no amount of such $100 distribution constitutes foreign base company shipping income to X under subdivision (i) of this subparagraph.

Example (4). Domestic corporation N owns 100 percent of the one class of stock of controlled foreign corporation S, which in turn owns 100 percent of the one class of stock of controlled foreign corporation T. T makes a distribution of $100 to S, of which $80 is allocable under § 1.959-3 to earnings and profits for 1977 which are described in § 1.959-3(b)(2), and $20 is allocable to earnings and profits for 1978 which are described in § 1.959-3(b)(3). The $80 amount is excluded from S's gross income under section 959(b) and therefore is not included in S's foreign base company shipping income. One hundred percent of T's earnings and profits for 1978 described in § 1.959-3(b)(3) were attributable to reinvested foreign base company shipping income. As a result, the entire $20 amount is included in S's foreign base company shipping income under this paragraph. See § 1.954-1(b)(2) for the rule that such $20 amount may be excluded from the foreign base company income of S.

(5) *Interest and gain.* (i) Except as provided in subdivisions (ii) and (iii) of this subparagraph, the portion of any interest paid by a foreign corporation, or gain recognized from the sale, exchange, or other disposition of stock or obligations of a foreign corporation, which is attributable to the foreign base company shipping income of such foreign corporation is that amount which bears the same ratio to such interest or gain as the foreign base company shipping income of such corporation for the period described in subparagraph (6) of this paragraph bears to its gross income for such period.

(ii) Interest which is paid by a controlled foreign corporation is attributable to such corporation's foreign base company shipping income to the same extent that such interest is allocable (under the principles of § 1.954-1(c) to its foreign base company shipping income.

(iii) If interest is paid by a foreign corporation, or if stock or obligations of a foreign corporation are sold, exchanged, or otherwise disposed of, during a taxable year of such foreign corporation beginning before January 1, 1976, then no portion of such interest or gain is attributable to foreign base company shipping income.

(iv) Solely for purposes of subdivision (i) of this subparagraph, if a controlled foreign corporation (the "first corporation") owns more than 10 percent of the stock of another controlled foreign corporation (the "second corporation"), then

(A) The gross income of the first corporation for any taxable year shall be—

(1) Increased by its pro rata share of the gross income of the second corporation for the taxable year which ends with or within such taxable year of the first corporation, and

(2) Decreased by the amount of any dividends received from the second corporation; and

(B) The foreign base company shipping income of the first corporation for any taxable year shall be—

(1) Increased by its pro rata share of the foreign base company shipping income of the second corporation for the taxable year which ends with or within such taxable year of the first corporation, and

(2) Decreased by the amount of any dividends received from the second corporation which constitute foreign base company income.

(v) Solely for purposes of applying subdivision (i) of this subparagraph, the district director shall make such other adjustments to the gross income and the foreign base company shipping income of any foreign corporation as are necessary

Reg. § 1.954-6(f)(5)

to properly determine the extent to which any interest or gain is attributable to foreign base company shipping income, including proper adjustments to reflect any transaction during the test period described in subparagraph (6) of this paragraph to which section 332, 351, 354, 355, 356, or 361 applies.

(6) *Test period.* (i) Except as provided in subdivisions (ii) and (iii) of this subparagraph, the period described in this subparagraph with respect to any foreign corporation is the 3-year period ending with the close of such corporation's taxable year preceding the year during which interest was paid or stock or obligations were sold, exchanged, or otherwise disposed of, or such part of such period as such corporation was in existence.

(ii) The period described in this paragraph shall not include any part of a taxable year beginning before January 1, 1976.

(iii) If interest is paid by a foreign corporation, or if stock or obligations of a foreign corporation are sold, exchanged, or otherwise disposed of during its first taxable year, then the period described in this paragraph shall be such first taxable year.

(iv) For purposes of subdivision (iii) of this subparagraph, the first taxable year of a foreign corporation is the later of—

(A) The first taxable year of its existence, or

(B) Its first taxable year beginning after December 31, 1975.

(g) *Income from partnerships, trusts, etc.*—(1) *In general.* The foreign base company shipping income of any foreign corporation includes—

(i) Its distributive share of the gross income of any partnership, and

(ii) Any amounts includible in its gross income under section 652(a), 662(a), 671, or 691(a),

to the extent that such items would have been includible in its foreign base company shipping income had they been realized by it directly.

(2) *Illustrations.*—The application of subparagraph (1) of this paragraph may be illustrated by the following examples:

Example (1). Controlled foreign corporations X and Y are equal partners in partnership P. The taxable years end on December 31 for X, June 30 for Y, and March 31 for P. In the fiscal year ending March 31, 1976, P's sole business activity is the use of a vessel in foreign commerce. P derives gross income of $200 from the use of the vessel, and incurs expenses, taxes, and other deductions of $160. Assume X's distributive share of such $200 of P's gross income is $100, all of which is includible in X's gross income. If X had realized its distributive share of $100 directly, then the amount which would have been includible in X's foreign base company shipping income under this paragraph is the portion allocable to the months of January, February, and March of 1976. Such amount, $25 (i.e., $1/2 \times \$200 \times 3$ months/12 months), is included in X's foreign base company shipping income for its taxable year ending December 31, 1976. Similarly, X is entitled under this paragraph to a deduction from foreign base company shipping income of $20 (i.e., $1/2 \times \$160 \times 3$ months/12 months). Since foreign base company shipping income does not include amounts earned by a foreign corporation (not a less developed country shipping corporation) in a taxable year beginning before January 1, 1976, Y has no foreign base company shipping income (under this paragraph or otherwise) for its taxable year beginning on July 1, 1975.

Example (2). The facts are the same as in example (1), except that P incurs expenses, taxes, and deductions of $240 in its taxable year ending on March 31, 1976. Accordingly, $25 is includible in X's foreign base company shipping income, and the amount deductible therefrom under this paragraph is $30 (i.e., $1/2 \times \$240 \times 3$ months/12 months).

(3) *Other income.* Except as expressly provided in subparagraph (1) of this paragraph, foreign base company shipping income does not include any amount includible in the gross income of a controlled foreign corporation under part I of subchapter J (section 641 and following, relating to estates, trusts, and beneficiaries), and gains from the sale or other disposition of any interest in an estate or trust.

(h) *Additional rules*—(1) *Gross income.* For purposes of this section and § 1.955A-2, the gross income of a foreign corporation (whether or not a controlled foreign corporation) shall be determined in accordance with the provisions of section 952 and § 1.952-2. Thus, for example, section 883 (relating to exclusions from gross income of foreign corporations) is inapplicable under § 1.952-2(a)(1) and (c)(1). In addition, the gross income of a controlled foreign corporation shall be determined, with respect to a United States shareholder of such controlled foreign corporation, by excluding distributions received by such corporation which are excluded from gross income under section 959(b) with respect to such shareholder.

(2) *Earnings and profits.* For purposes of this section, the earnings and profits of a foreign corporation (whether or not a controlled foreign corporation) shall be determined in accordance with

Reg. § 1.954-6(h)(2)

the provisions of section 964 and the regulations thereunder.

(3) *No double counting.* No item of gross income shall be counted as foreign base company shipping income under more than one provision of this section. For example, if $200 of gross income derived from the use of a lighter is treated as foreign base company shipping income under both paragraph (b)(1)(i) and paragraph (b)(1)(ii) of this section, then such $200 is counted only once as foreign base company shipping income. A taxpayer may choose under which provision to include an item of income.

(4) *Losses.* (i) Generally, if a controlled foreign corporation has losses which are properly allocable to foreign base company shipping income, the extent to which such losses are deductible from such income shall be determined by treating such foreign corporation as a domestic corporation and applying the principles of section 63. See §§ 1.954-1(c) and 1.952-2(b). Thus, for example, losses from sales or exchanges of capital assets are allowable only to the extent of gains from such sales or exchanges.

(ii) If gain from the sale, exchange, or other disposition of any stock or obligation would be treated (to any extent) as foreign base company shipping income, then loss from such sale, exchange, or other disposition is properly allocable to foreign base company shipping income (to the same extent).

(iii) In determining the extent to which any loss on the disposition of a qualified investment in foreign base company shipping operations is deductible from foreign base company shipping income, it is immaterial that such loss is taken into account under § 1.955A-1(b)(1)(ii) as a reduction in the amount of the decrease in (withdrawal from) qualified investments in foreign base company shipping operations.

(5) *Hypothetical charges.* Under paragraph (d)(5)(i) of this section and § 1.955A-2(a)(4)(ii)(A), gross income may be deemed to include hypothetical arm's length charges for services performed by a controlled foreign corporation for itself. Under paragraph (d)(2) of this section, certain of these hypothetical charges may be treated as foreign base company shipping income. Such hypothetical charges are deemed to be income solely for purposes of applying the "extent of use" tests prescribed by paragraph (d)(4) of this section and § 1.955A-2(a)(4). Charges for services performed by a controlled foreign corporation for itself shall in no event be included in income for any other purpose. [Reg. § 1.954-6.]

☐ [*T.D.* 7894, 5-11-83.]

[Reg. § 1.954-7]

§ 1.954-7. **Increase in qualified investments in foreign base company shipping operations.**—(a) *Determination of investments at close of taxable year*—(1) *In general.* Under section 954(g), the increase in qualified investments in foreign base company shipping operations, for purposes of section 954(b)(2) and paragraph (b)(1) of § 1.954-1, of any controlled foreign corporation for any taxable year is, except as provided in paragraph (b) of this section, the amount by which—

(i) The controlled foreign corporation's qualified investments in foreign base company shipping operations at the close of the taxable year, exceed

(ii) Its qualified investments in foreign base company shipping operations at the close of the preceding taxable year.

(2) *Preceding taxable year.* For purposes of this section, a taxable year which begins before January 1, 1976, may be a preceding taxable year.

(3) *Cross-reference.* See section 955(b) and § 1.955A-2 for the definition of the term "qualified investments in foreign base company shipping operations."

(b) *Election to determine investments at close of following taxable year*—(1) *General rule.* In lieu of determining an increase in qualified investments in foreign base company shipping operations for a taxable year in the manner provided in paragraph (a) of this section, a United States shareholder of a controlled foreign corporation may make an election under section 955(b)(3) to determine the increase for the corporation's taxable year by ascertaining the amount by which—

(i) Such corporation's qualified investments in foreign base company shipping operations at the close of the taxable year immediately following such taxable year, exceed

(ii) Its qualified investments in foreign base company shipping operations at the close of the taxable year immediately preceding such following taxable year.

(2) *Election with respect to first taxable year.* Notwithstanding subparagraph (1) of this paragraph, if an election is made without consent by a United States shareholder under § 1.955A-4(b)(1) with respect to a controlled foreign corporation, the increase in such controlled foreign corporation's qualified investments in foreign base company shipping operations for the first taxable year to which such election applies shall be the amount by which—

Reg. § 1.954-7(a)(1)

Income from Sources Without the United States

See p. 20,601 for regulations not amended to reflect law changes

(i) Such corporation's qualified investments in foreign base company shipping operations at the close of the taxable year immediately following such first taxable year, exceed

(ii) Its qualified investments in foreign base company shipping operations at the close of the taxable year immediately preceding such first taxable year.

(3) *Manner of making election.* For the manner of making an election under section 955(b)(3), and for rules pertaining to the revocation of such an election, see § 1.955A-4.

(4) *Coordination with prior law.* If a United States shareholder makes an election without consent under § 1.955A-4(b)(1) with respect to a controlled foreign corporation, then such corporation's increase in qualified investments in foreign base company shipping operations for the first taxable year to which such election applies shall be determined by disregarding any change which occurs during such taxable year in the amount of such corporation's investments in stock or obligations of a less developed country shipping company described in § 1.955-5(b) if both of the following conditions exist:

(i) Such taxable year is the first taxable year of such corporation which begins after December 31, 1975, and

(ii) Such United States shareholder has elected to determine the change in such corporation's qualified investments in less developed countries for its last taxable year beginning before January 1, 1976, under § 1.954-5(b) or § 1.955-3.

(5) *Illustrations.* The application of this paragraph may be illustrated by the following examples:

Example (1). (a) Controlled foreign corporation X is a wholly owned subsidiary of domestic corporation M. X uses the calendar year as the taxable year. The amounts of X's qualified investments in foreign base company shipping operations at the close of 1975 through 1979 are as follows:

Qualified investments at Dec. 31, 1975	$16,000
Qualified investments at Dec. 31, 1976	17,000
Qualified investments at Dec. 31, 1977	23,000
Qualified investments at Dec. 31, 1978	28,000
Qualified investments at Dec. 31, 1979	30,000

(b) Assume that M properly files without consent a timely election under § 1.955A-4(b)(1) to determine X's increase for 1976 in qualified investments in foreign base company shipping operations pursuant to this paragraph, and that the election remains in force through 1978. Then X's increases for 1976 through 1978 in qualified investments in foreign base company shipping operations are as follows:

Increase for 1976 ($23,000 minus $16,000)	$7,000
Increase for 1977 ($28,000 minus $23,000)	5,000
Increase for 1978 ($30,000 minus $28,000)	2,000

Example (2). Assume the same facts as in example (1), except that M never files an election under § 1.955A-4(b)(1). X's increases for 1976 through 1978 in qualified investments in foreign base company shipping operations are as follows:

Increase for 1976 ($17,000 minus $16,000)	$1,000
Increase for 1977 ($23,000 minus $17,000)	6,000
Increase for 1978 ($28,000 minus $23,000)	5,000

Example (3). The facts are the same as in example (1), except that X's qualified investments in foreign base company shipping operations include an investment in less developed country shipping companies described in § 1.955-5(b) of $500 on December 31, 1975, and $750 on December 31, 1976. Assume further that M has made an election under section 955(b)(3) (as in effect before the enactment of the Tax Reduction Act of 1975) with respect to X's taxable year 1975. Then X's increase in qualified investments in foreign base company shipping operations for 1976 is $6,750 (i.e., $7,000 − $250).

(c) *Illustration.* The application of this section may be illustrated by the following example:

Example. (a) Controlled foreign corporation X uses the calendar year as the taxable year. On December 31, 1975, X's qualified investments in foreign base company shipping operations (determined as provided in § 1.955A-2(g)) consist of the following amounts:

Cash	$ 6,000
Readily marketable securities	1,000
Stock of related controlled foreign corporations	4,000
Traffic and other receivables	14,000
Marine insurance claims receivables	1,000
Foreign income tax refunds receivable	1,000
Prepaid shipping expenses and shipping inventories ashore	1,000
Vessel construction funds	0
Vessels	123,000
Vessel plans and construction in progress	3,000
Containers and chassis	0
Terminal property and equipment	2,000

Reg. § 1.954-7(c)

49,296 Income from Sources Without the United States
See p. 20,601 for regulations not amended to reflect law changes

Shipping office (land and building)..	1,000
Vessel spare parts ashore	1,000
Performance deposits	2,000
Deferred charges	2,000
Stock of less developed country shipping company described in § 1.955-5(b)	10,000
	$172,000

(b) On December 31, 1976, X's qualified investments in foreign base company shipping operations (determined as provided in § 1.955A-2(g)) consist of the following amounts:

Cash	$ 5,000
Readily marketable securities	2,000
Stock of related controlled foreign corporations	4,000
Traffic and other receivables	16,000
Foreign income tax refunds receivable	3,000
Prepaid shipping expenses and shipping inventories ashore	2,000
Vessel construction funds	1,000
Vessels	117,000
Vessel plans and construction in progress	12,000
Containers and chassis	4,000
Terminal property and equipment	2,000
Shipping office (land and building)..	1,000
Vessel spare parts ashore	1,000
Performance deposits	2,000
Deferred charges	2,000
Stock of less developed country shipping company described in § 1.955-5(b)	0
	$174,000

(c) For 1976, X's increase in qualified investments in foreign base company shipping operations is $2,000, which amount is determined as follows:

Qualified investments at Dec. 31, 1976	$174,000
Qualified investments at Dec. 31, 1975	172,000
Increase for 1976	$ 2,000

[Reg. § 1.954-7.]

☐ [T.D. 7894, 5-11-83.]

[Reg. § 1.954-8]

§ 1.954-8. Foreign base company oil related income.—(a) *Foreign base company oil related income*—(1) *In general.* Under section 954(g), the foreign base company oil related income of a controlled foreign corporation (except as provided under paragraph (b) of this section) consists of the items of foreign oil related income ("FORI") described in section 907(c)(2) and (3), other than such income derived from a source within a foreign country in connection with—

(i) Oil or gas which was extracted from an oil or gas well located in that foreign country ("extraction exception"), or

(ii) Oil, gas, or a primary product of oil or gas which is sold by the controlled foreign corporation or a related person for use or consumption within that country or is loaded in that country on a vessel or aircraft as fuel for the vessel or aircraft ("use or consumption exception").

A taxpayer claiming the use or consumption exception must establish its applicability on the basis of facts and circumstances. For special rules for applying the extraction exception, see paragraph (c) of this section.

(2) *Source of income.* The source of foreign base company oil related income is determined generally under the principles of §§ 1.861-1 to 1.863-5. See § 1.863-6. Thus, income from the performance of a service generally is sourced in the country where the service is performed. See § 1.861-4. Underwriting income from insuring a foreign oil related activity is sourced at the location of the risk. See section 861(a)(7) and § 1.953-2.

(3) *Primary product.* The term "primary product" of oil or gas has the meaning given this term by § 1.907(c)-1(d)(5) and (6).

(4) *Vessel.* For the definition of the term "vessel", see § 1.954-6(b)(3)(ii).

(5) *Foreign country.* For purposes of this section, the term "foreign country" has the same meaning as in section 638 (relating to continental shelf areas). Thus, for example, oil or gas extracted from a sea area will be deemed to be extracted in the country which has exclusive rights of exploitation of natural resources with respect to that area if the other conditions of section 638 are met.

(6) *Country of use or consumption.* For rules for determining the country of use or consumption, see § 1.954-3(a)(3)(ii).

(7) *Insurance income.* For purposes of this section, income derived from or attributable to insurance of section 907(c)(2) activities means taxable income as defined in section 832(a) and as modified by the principles of § 1.953-4 (other than as the section is applied to life insurance).

(8) *Fuel product.* For purposes of this section, the term "fuel product" means oil, gas or a primary product of oil or gas.

(9) *Effective date.* The provisions of section 954(g) and this section are applicable to taxable years of foreign corporations beginning on or after January 1, 1983, and to taxable years of United States shareholders in which or with which those taxable years of foreign corporations end.

Reg. § 1.954-8(a)(1)

Income from Sources Without the United States 49,297
See p. 20,601 for regulations not amended to reflect law changes

(b) *Exemption for small oil producers*—(1) *In general.* Foreign base company oil related income does not include any income of a foreign corporation which is not a large oil producer.

(2) *Large oil producer.* A corporation is a large oil producer (within the meaning of section 954(g)(2)) if the average daily production (extraction) of foreign crude oil and natural gas by the related group which includes the corporation and related persons (within the meaning of section 954(d)(3)) for the taxable year or immediately preceding taxable year is 1,000 or more barrels. The average daily production of foreign crude oil or natural gas for any taxable year (and the conversion of cubic feet of natural gas into barrels) is determined under rules similar to the rules of section 613A, except that only crude oil or natural gas from a well located outside the United States is taken into account.

(c) *Special rules for applying the extraction exception of paragraph (a)(1)(i) of this section*— (1) *Refining income described in section 907(c)(2)(A).* With regard to a controlled foreign corporation's refining income from the processing of minerals extracted (by the taxpayer or by any other person) from oil or gas wells into their primary products, as described in section 907(c)(2)(A), a pro rata method will be applied for purposes of determining the part of the refining income that qualifies for the extraction exception of paragraph (a)(1)(i) of this section. The pro rata method will be based on the proportion that the barrels of the fuel product extracted in the country of processing bears to the total barrels of the fuel product processed in that country and will apply regardless of the country of sale of the primary product.

(2) *Marketing income described in section 907(c)(2)(C).* With regard to a controlled foreign corporation's marketing income from the distribution or sale of minerals extracted from oil or gas wells or of primary products, as described in section 907(c)(2)(C), a pro rata method will be applied for purposes of determining the part of the marketing income that qualifies for the extraction exception of paragraph (a)(1)(i) of this section. When applying the pro rata method to the sale of a fuel product other than a primary product, the pro rata method will be based on the proportion that the barrels of the fuel product extracted in the country of sale bears to the total barrels of the fuel product sold in that country. When applying the pro rata method to the sale of primary products, the method will be based on the proportion that the barrels of the fuel product extracted in the country of sale bears to the total barrels of the fuel product processed. For purposes of applying the pro rata method, data of the controlled foreign corporation's related group (as defined in section 954(g)(2)(C)) will be taken into account. The pro rata method will not apply, however, if the mineral or primary product is purchased by the controlled foreign corporation from a person not within the controlled foreign corporation's related group. In that situation, the marketing income will be presumed to qualify for the extraction exception if the country of the source of the marketing income is a net exporter of crude oil or gas, whichever is relevant. If the country of the source of the marketing income is not a net exporter of crude oil or gas, whichever is relevant, the marketing income will be presumed not to qualify for the extraction exception. The controlled foreign corporation may, however, rebut this latter presumption by demonstrating on the basis of all the facts and circumstances that its marketing income does qualify for the extraction exception. If a primary product that is acquired from a person within the controlled foreign corporation's related group is commingled with like products acquired from persons not within that related group, the pro rata method based on the proportion that the barrels of the fuel product extracted in the country of sale bears to the total barrels of the fuel product processed will be applied to that portion of the total products sold that was purchased from persons within the related group, to the extent that that person did not sell product purchased from an unrelated person, and either the presumption or facts and circumstances will determine the characterization of the remainder.

(3) *Transportation income described in section 907(c)(2)(B).* With regard to a controlled foreign corporation's income from the transportation of minerals from oil and gas wells or of primary products, as described in section 907(c)(2)(B), the rules set forth in paragraph (c)(2) of this section will apply for purposes of determining the part of the transportation income that qualifies for the extraction exception of paragraph (a)(1)(i) of this section.

(4) *Illustrations.* The following examples illustrate the application of this paragraph.

Example 1. Controlled foreign corporation M has a refinery in foreign country A that refines 250x barrels of oil during its taxable year beginning in 1984. It is determined that 125x barrels of its 250x barrels were extracted in country A. M sold 150x barrels of its 250x barrels in country A for consumption in country A which resulted in $225x of income from refining and $225x of marketing income, as described in section 907(c)(2)(C). M also sold within foreign country B, for consumption in country B, 100x barrels of its 250x barrels which resulted in an additional $150x of income from refining for M and $170x of marketing income for M. The 100x barrels sold by M within country B, a contiguous country, were

Reg. § 1.954-8(c)(4)

49,298 Income from Sources Without the United States
See p. 20,601 for regulations not amended to reflect law changes

transported from M's refinery in country A to country B by a pipeline which is owned by M, and M recognized a total of $10x of income from the transportation of the 100x barrels. Of this $10x, $8x was recognized in country A and $2x was recognized in country B. Under the source of income rules of paragraph (a)(2) of this section, income from refining is considered derived from the country in which the refining occurs and not from the country where the sale of the refined product occurs.

(i) *M's refining income.* M has $75x of foreign base company oil related income with respect to its refining of the 250x barrels, determined as follows:

(A) Total amount of income from refining attributable to oil refined in country A by M	$375x
(B) Amount of income from refining with respect to oil sold for consumption ($225x) in country A (use or consumption exception under paragraph (a)(1)(ii) of this section)	(225x)
(C) Pro rata amount of income from refining attributable to sales in country B considered extracted from country A ($150x times 125x barrels/250x barrels) (extraction exception under paragraph (a)(1)(i) of this section)	(75x)
(D) Foreign base company oil related income	$ 75x

(ii) *M's marketing income.* M does not have foreign base company oil related income with respect to its sale of the 100x barrels in country B and 150x barrels in country A because the $170x and $225x, respectively, of marketing income was derived from the country in which the oil was sold for consumption (an exception under paragraph (a)(1)(ii) of this section).

(iii) *M's transportation income.* M does not have foreign base company oil related income with respect to its $2x of pipeline transportation income recognized in country B because the income was derived from the country in which the 100x barrels were sold for consumption, an exception under paragraph (a)(1)(ii) of this section. With regard to the $8x of pipeline transportation income recognized in country A, however, M has $4x of foreign base company oil related income since of the total barrels refined in country A (250x) only one-half were extracted in that country. Therefore, only one-half of the transportation income qualifies for the extraction exception of paragraph (a)(1)(i) of this section.

(iv) *M's extraction income.* M does not have foreign base company oil related income for its extraction activity because extraction income is excluded in all events. See section 954(g)(1)(A).

Example 2. Assume the same facts as in *Example 1* except that M sold all of the 250x barrels of refined oil in country A. In addition, assume that country A is a net exporter of crude oil. As in *Example 1,* M sold 150x barrels for consumption in country A with the same resulting income. M sold in country A the remaining 100x barrels to unrelated controlled foreign corporation N which resulted in an additional $150x of income from refining for M and $170x of marketing income for M. N immediately resold in country A for export those 100x barrels. N did not commingle the 100x barrels with any other refined oil. N earned $10x of marketing income on that sale.

(i) *M's refining income.* M has $75x foreign base company oil related income with respect to its refining of the 250x barrels determined as follows:

(A) Total amount of income from refining attributable to oil refined in country A by M	$375x
(B) Amount of income from refining with respect to oil sold for consumption ($225x) in country A (use or consumption exception under paragraph (a)(1)(ii) of this section)	(225x)
(C) Pro rata amount of income from refining attributable to sales in country A (for consumption outside of country A) considered extracted from country A ($150x times 125x barrels/250x barrels) (extraction exception under paragraph (a)(1)(i) of this section)	(75x)
(D) Foreign base company oil related income	$ 75x

(ii) *M's marketing income.* M does not have foreign base company oil related income with respect to its marketing income from the sale of the 150x barrels in country A because the $225x of marketing income was derived from the country in which the oil was sold for consumption (an exception under paragraph (a)(1)(ii) of this section). M has $85x of foreign base company oil related income with respect to its marketing income from sale to N of the 100x barrels, determined as follows:

(A) Total amount of marketing income from the sale	$170x
(B) Pro rata amount of marketing income attributable to oil product considered extracted in country A ($170x times 125x barrels/250x barrels) (extraction exception under paragraph (a)(1)(i) of this section)	(85x)
(C) Foreign base company oil related income	$ 85x

Reg. § 1.954-8(c)(4)

(iii) *N's marketing income.* N is not related to M. Therefore, since N sold the 100x barrels in country A, a net exporter of crude oil, and since N did not commingle the 100x barrels with other refined products, it is presumed that all of the 100x barrels were extracted in country A. Accordingly, all of N's $10x of marketing income is excepted under paragraph (a)(1)(i) of this section.

Example 3. Assume the same facts as in Example 2 except that N is related to M. Characterization of M's income remains the same as in Example 2. N will have, however, $5x of foreign base company oil related income with regard to its marketing income, determined as follows:

(i) Total amount of marketing income from the sale	$ 10x
(ii) Pro rata amount of marketing income considered extracted from country A ($10x times 125x barrels/250x barrels) (extraction exception under paragraph (a)(1)(i) of this section)	5x
(iii) Foreign base company oil related income	$ 5x

Example 4. Assume that controlled foreign corporation M has a refinery in foreign country A that refines 200x barrels of oil during its taxable year beginning in 1984. It is determined that 100x barrels of that oil were extracted in country A and that the other 100x barrels were extracted in country B. Neither country A nor country B is a net exporter of crude oil. In addition, M purchased from an unrelated country A refiner 100x barrels of already refined oil. M does not know where this oil was extracted. These 100x barrels of purchased refined oil were commingled with the 200x barrels of refined oil from M's refinery. M sold 225x barrels of refined oil in country A for consumption in country A which resulted in $250x of income from refining and $225x of marketing income. M sold within foreign country B for consumption outside of country B 75x barrels of refined oil which resulted in $100x of income from refining and $75x of marketing income. The refined product was transported between country A and country B by an unrelated person.

(i) *M's refining income.* With regard to the sales in country A, M has $50x of foreign base company oil related income with respect to its refining of the 100x barrels, determined as follows:

(A) Total amount of income from refining attributable to oil refined in country A by M	$350x
(B) Amount of income from refining with respect to oil sold for consumption in country A ($250x) (use or consumption exception under paragraph (a)(1)(ii) of this section)	(250x)
(C) Pro rata amount of income from refining attributable to sales in country B considered extracted from country A ($100x times 100x barrels/200x barrels) (extraction exception under paragraph (a)(1)(i) of this section)	(50x)
(D) Foreign base company oil related income	$ 50x

(ii) *M's marketing income.* Since the barrels from M's refinery and those that M purchased were commingled, a portion, as follows, of the marketing income is deemed to derive from both purchased and refined products. Since M refined 200x barrels and purchased 100x barrels, its marketing income of $225x from the sale of the 225x barrels in country A for consumption in country A will be deemed to consist of $150x (200x/300x × $225x) from the sale of products refined by M and $75x (100x/300x × $225x) from the sale of purchased products. Likewise, its marketing income of $75x from the sale of the 75x barrels in country B for consumption outside of country B will be deemed to consist of $50x (200x/300x × $75x) from the sale of products refined by M and $25x (100x/300x × $75x) from the sale of purchased products.

(A) *Purchased products.* M is considered as having $75x of marketing income from the sale of purchased products in country A for consumption in country A. None of this marketing income is foreign base company oil related income since the marketing income is earned in country A, the country of consumption. See paragraph (a)(1)(ii) of this section. All of the $25x of M's marketing income from the sale of purchased products in country B will be foreign base company oil related income. The exception at paragraph (a)(1)(ii) of this section does not apply since the refined oil is not sold for use or consumption in country B. Likewise, the extraction exception under paragraph (a)(1)(i) of this section does not apply. The purchased product cannot be presumed to be extracted in country B since country B is not a net exporter of crude oil. In addition, M cannot show, on a facts and circumstances basis, that purchased products were refined from crude oil extracted in country B.

(B) *Products refined by M.* With regard to M's marketing income attributable to the sale of products refined by M, M does not have any foreign base company oil related income with regard to its $150x of marketing income in country A since that income was derived from the country in which the oil was sold for consumption (the use or consumption exception under paragraph (a)(1)(ii) of this section). M has $25x of foreign base company oil related income with regard to its

$50x of marketing income in country B determined as follows:

(1) Total amount of income from marketing attributable to oil refined by M and sold in country B .... $ 50x
(2) Pro rata amount of income from marketing attributable to sales in country B considered extracted from country B ($50x times 100x barrels/200x barrels) (extraction exception under paragraph (a)(1)(i) of this section) .... (25x)
(3) Foreign base company oil related income .... $ 25x

[Reg. § 1.954-8.]

☐ [T.D. 8331, 1-24-91.]

[Reg. § 1.955-0]

§ 1.955-0. Effective dates.—(a) *Section 955 as in effect before the enactment of the Tax Reduction Act of 1975*—(1) *In general.* In general, §§ 1.955-1 through 1.955-6 are applicable with respect to withdrawals of previously excluded subpart F income from qualified investment in less developed countries for taxable years of foreign corporations beginning after December 31, 1962, and to taxable years of United States shareholders (as defined in section 951(b)) within which or with which such taxable years of such foreign corporations end. However, such sections are effective with respect to withdrawals of amounts invested in less developed country shipping companies described in section 955(c)(2) (as in effect before the enactment of the Tax Reduction Act of 1975) only for taxable years of foreign corporations beginning before January 1, 1976, and for taxable years of United States shareholders (as defined in section 951(b)) within which or with which such taxable years of such foreign corporations end. For rules applicable to withdrawals of amounts invested in less developed country shipping companies described in section 955(c)(2) (as in effect before such enactment), in taxable years of foreign corporations beginning after December 31, 1975, see section 955(b)(5) (as amended by such Act) and §§ 1.955A-1 through 1.955A-4.

(2) *References.* Except as otherwise provided therein, all references contained in §§ 1.955-1 through 1.955-6 to section 954 or 955 or to the regulations under section 954 are to those sections and regulations as in effect before the enactment of the Tax Reduction Act of 1975. For regulations under section 954 (as in effect before such enactment), see 26 CFR §§ 1.954-1 through 1.954-5 (Rev. as of April 1, 1975). For taxable years of foreign corporations beginning after December 31, 1975, and for taxable years of United States shareholders (as described in section 951(b)) within which or with which such taxable years of such foreign corporations end, the definitions of less developed countries and less developed country corporations contained in section 902(d) (as amended by such Act) and § 1.902-2 apply for purposes of determining the credit for corporate stockholders in foreign corporations under section 902.

(b) *Section 955 as amended by the Tax Reduction Act of 1975.* Except as otherwise provided therein, §§ 1.955A-1 through 1.955A-4 are applicable to taxable years of foreign corporations beginning after December 31, 1975, and to taxable years of United States shareholders (as defined in section 951(b)) within which or with which such taxable years of such foreign corporations end. [Reg. § 1.955-0.]

☐ [T.D. 7893, 5-11-83.]

[Reg. § 1.955-1]

§ 1.955-1. **Shareholder's pro rata share of amount of previously excluded subpart F income withdrawn from investment in less developed countries.**—(a) *In general.* Pursuant to section 951(a)(1)(A)(ii) and the regulations thereunder, a United States shareholder of a controlled foreign corporation must include in its gross income its pro rata share (as determined in accordance with paragraph (c) of this section) of the amount of such controlled foreign corporation's previously excluded subpart F income which is withdrawn for any taxable year from investment in less developed countries. Section 955 provides rules for determining the amount of a controlled foreign corporation's previously excluded subpart F income for any taxable year of the corporation beginning after December 31, 1962 that is withdrawn from investment in less developed countries for any taxable year of the corporation beginning before January 1, 1976. Except for investments in less developed country shipping companies, section 955 also provides rules for determining the amount of a controlled foreign corporation's previously excluded subpart F income for any taxable year of the corporation beginning after December 31, 1962 which is withdrawn from investment in less developed countries in taxable years of the corporation beginning after December 31, 1975. To determine the amount of a controlled foreign corporation's previously excluded subpart F income withdrawn from investment in less developed country shipping companies described in section 955(c)(2) in taxable years of a controlled foreign corporation beginning after December 31, 1975, see section 955(b)(5) (as in effect after amendment by the Tax Reduction Act of 1975) and §§ 1.955A-1 through 1.955A-4. For effective dates, see § 1.955-0.

(b) *Amount withdrawn by controlled foreign corporation*—(1) *In general.* For purposes of sections 951 through 964, the amount of a controlled foreign corporation's previously excluded subpart F income which is withdrawn for any taxable year from investment in less developed countries is an amount equal to the decrease for such year in such corporation's qualified investments in less developed countries. Such decrease is, except as provided in § 1.955-3—

(i) An amount equal to the excess of the amount of its qualified investments in less developed countries at the close of the preceding taxable year over the amount of its qualified investments in less developed countries at the close of the taxable year, minus

(ii) The amount (if any) by which recognized losses on sales or exchanges by such corporation during the taxable year of qualified investments in less developed countries exceed its recognized gains on sales or exchanges during such year of qualified investments in less developed countries, but only to the extent that the net amount so determined does not exceed the limitation determined under subparagraph (2) of this paragraph. See § 1.955-2 for determining the amount of qualified investments in less developed countries.

(2) *Limitations applicable in determining decreases*—(i) *General.* The limitation referred to in subparagraph (1) of this paragraph for any taxable year of a controlled foreign corporation shall be the lesser of the following two limitations:

(*a*) The sum of the controlled foreign corporation's earnings and profits (or deficit in earnings and profits) for the taxable year, computed as of the close of the taxable year without diminution by reason of any distributions made during the taxable year, plus the sum of its earnings and profits (or deficits in earnings and profits) accumulated for prior taxable years beginning after December 31, 1962 (including prior taxable years beginning after December 31, 1975), or

(*b*) The sum of the amounts excluded under section 954(b)(1) and paragraph (b)(1) of § 1.954-1 from the foreign base company income of such corporation for all prior taxable years, minus the sum of the amounts (determined under this paragraph) of its previously excluded subpart F income withdrawn from investment in less developed countries for all prior taxable years.

(ii) *Treatment of earnings and profits.* For purposes of determining earnings and profits of a controlled foreign corporation under subdivision (i)(*a*) of this subparagraph, such earnings and profits shall be considered not to include any amounts which are attributable to—

(*a*)(*1*) Amounts which, for the current taxable year, are included in the gross income of a United States shareholder of such controlled foreign corporation under section 951(a)(1)(A)(i) or (iii), or

(*2*) Amounts which, for any prior taxable year, have been included in the gross income of a United States shareholder of such controlled foreign corporation under section 951(a) and have not been distributed; or

(*b*)(*1*) Amounts which, for the current taxable year, are included in the gross income of a United States shareholder of such controlled foreign corporation under section 551(b) or would be so included under such section but for the fact that such amounts were distributed to such shareholder during the taxable year, or

(*2*) Amounts which, for any prior taxable year, have been included in the gross income of a United States shareholder of such controlled foreign corporation under section 551(b) and have not been distributed.

The rules of this subdivision apply only in determining the limitation on a controlled foreign corporation's decrease in qualified investments in less developed countries. See section 959 and the regulations thereunder for limitations on the exclusion from gross income of previously taxed earnings and profits.

(3) *Taxable years beginning after December 31, 1975.* (i) In the case of a taxable year of a controlled foreign corporation beginning after December 31, 1975, § 1.955-2(b)(5) must be applied in determining the amount of its qualified investments in less developed countries on both of the determination dates applicable to such taxable year.

(ii) The application of this subparagraph may be illustrated by the following examples:

Example (1). (a) Controlled foreign corporation M uses the calendar year as the taxable year. Throughout 1974 through 1976, M owns 100 percent of the only class of stock of foreign corporation N, a less developed country shipping company described in § 1.955-5(b), and M owns no other stock or obligations. The amount taken into account under § 1.955-2(d) with respect to the stock of N is $10,000 at the close of 1974, 1975,

Reg. § 1.955-1(b)(3)

49,302 Income from Sources Without the United States

See p. 20,601 for regulations not amended to reflect law changes

and 1976. The amount of M's previously excluded subpart F income which is withdrawn for 1975 (a year to which § 1.955-2(b)(5) does not apply) from investment in less developed countries is zero, determined as follows:

(1) Qualified investments in less developed countries at the close of 1974	$10,000
(2) Less: qualified investments in less developed countries at the close of 1975	10,000
(3) Balance	0

(Further computations similar to those set out in lines (iv) through (ix) of example (1) of paragraph (d) of this section are unnecessary because the balance in line (3) of this example is zero.)

(b) As a result of § 1.955-2(b)(5)(ii), the amount of M's previously excluded subpart F income which is withdrawn for 1976 from investment in less developed countries is zero, determined as follows:

(1) Qualified investments in less developed countries at the close of 1975	$ 0
(2) Less: qualified investments in less developed countries at the close of 1976	0
(3) Balance	0

Example (2). The facts are the same as in example (1), except that foreign corporation N is a less developed country corporation described in § 1.955-5(a). The amount of M's previously excluded subpart F income withdrawn for 1976 from investment in less developed countries is zero, determined as follows:

(1) Qualified investments in less developed countries at the close of 1975	$10,000
(2) Less: qualified investments in less developed countries at the close of 1976	10,000
(3) Balance	0

(c) *Shareholder's pro rata share of amount withdrawn by controlled foreign corporation*—(1) *In general.* A United States shareholder's pro rata share of a controlled foreign corporation's previously excluded subpart F income withdrawn for any taxable year from investment in less developed countries is his pro rata share of the amount withdrawn for such year by such corporation, as determined under paragraph (b) of this section. See section 955(a)(3).

(2) *Special rule.* A United States shareholder's pro rata share of the net amount determined under paragraph (b)(2)(i)(*b*) of this section with respect to any stock of the controlled foreign corporation owned by such shareholder shall be determined without taking into account any amount attributable to a period prior to the date on which such shareholder acquired such stock. See section 1248 and the regulations thereunder for rules governing treatment of gain from sales or exchanges of stock in certain foreign corporations.

(d) *Illustrations.* The application of this section may be illustrated by the following examples:

Example (1). A, a United States shareholder, owns 60 percent of the only class of stock of M Corporation, a controlled foreign corporation throughout the entire period here involved. Both A and M Corporation use the calendar year as a taxable year. Corporation M's qualified investments in less developed countries at the close of 1964 amount to $125,000; and, at the close of 1965, to $75,000. During 1965, M Corporation realizes recognized gains of $5,000 and recognized losses of $15,000, on sales of qualified investments in less developed countries. Corporation M's earnings and profits for 1965 and its accumulated earnings and profits for 1963 and 1964 amount to $45,000, as determined under paragraph (b)(2) of this section. The amount excluded under section 954(b)(1) for 1963 from its foreign base company income is $75,000, and the amount of its previously excluded subpart F income withdrawn for 1964 from investment in less developed countries is $25,000. The amount of M Corporation's previously excluded subpart F income withdrawn for 1965 from investment in less developed countries is $40,000, and A's pro rata share of such amount is $24,000, determined as follows:

(i) Qualified investments in less developed countries at the close of 1964	$125,000
(ii) Less: Qualified investments in less developed countries at the close of 1965	75,000
(iii) Balance	50,000
(iv) Less: Excess of recognized losses over recognized gains on sales during 1965 of qualified investments in less developed countries ($15,000 less $5,000)	10,000
(v) Tentative decrease in qualified investments in less developed countries for 1965	40,000
(vi) Earnings and profits for 1963, 1964, and 1965	45,000
(vii) Excess of amount excluded under sec. 954(b)(1) from foreign base company income for 1963 ($75,000) over amount of previously excluded subpart F income withdrawn for 1964 from investment in less developed countries ($25,000)	50,000

Reg. § 1.955-1(c)(1)

(viii) M Corporation's amount of previously excluded subpart F income withdrawn for 1965 from investment in less developed countries (item (v), but not to exceed the lesser of item (vi) or item (vii)) 40,000

(ix) A's pro rata share of M Corporation's amount of previously excluded subpart F income withdrawn for 1965 from investment in less developed countries (60 percent of $40,000) 24,000

Example (2). The facts are the same as in example (1), except that M Corporation's earnings and profits (determined under paragraph (b)(2) of this section) for 1963, 1964, and 1965 (item (vi)) are $30,000 instead of $45,000. Corporation M's amount of previously excluded subpart F income withdrawn for 1965 from investment in less developed countries is $30,000. A's pro rata share of such amount is $18,000 (60 percent of $30,000).

Example (3). The facts are the same as in example (1), except that the excess of the amount excluded under section 954(b)(1) for 1963 from M Corporation's foreign base company income over the amount of its previously excluded subpart F income withdrawn for 1964 from investment in less developed countries (item (vii)) is $20,000 instead of $50,000. Corporation M's amount of previously excluded subpart F income withdrawn for 1965 from investment in less developed countries is $20,000. A's pro rata share of such amount is $12,000 (60 percent of $20,000). [Reg. § 1.955-1.]

☐ [*T.D.* 6683, 10-17-63. *Amended by T.D.* 6795, 1-28-65 *and T.D.* 7894, 5-11-83.]

[Reg. § 1.955-2]

§ 1.955-2. Amount of a controlled foreign corporation's qualified investments in less developed countries.—(a) *Included property.* For purposes of sections 951 through 964, a controlled foreign corporation's "qualified investments in less developed countries" are items of property (other than property excluded under paragraph (b)(1) of this section) owned directly by such corporation on the applicable determination date for purposes of section 954(f) or section 955(a)(2) and consisting of one or more of the following:

(1) Stock of a less developed country corporation if the controlled foreign corporation owns (within the meaning of paragraph (b)(2) of this section) on the applicable determination date 10 percent or more of the total combined voting power of all classes of stock of such less developed country corporation;

(2) An obligation (as defined in paragraph (b)(3) of this section) of a less developed country corporation which, at the time of acquisition (as defined in paragraph (b)(4) of this section) of such obligation by the controlled foreign corporation, has a maturity of one year or more, but only if the controlled foreign corporation owns (within the meaning of paragraph (b)(2) of this section) on the applicable determination date 10 percent or more of the total combined voting power of all classes of stock of such less developed country corporation; and

(3) An obligation (as defined in paragraph (b)(3) of this section) of a less developed country, including obligations issued or guaranteed by the government of such country or of a political subdivision thereof and obligations of any agency or instrumentality of such country, in which such country is financially committed. The application of this subparagraph may be illustrated by the following example:

Example. A, a political subdivision of foreign country X, constructs and operates a toll bridge. Country X is a less developed country throughout the period here involved. A issues bonds under an indenture which provides for amortization of the principal and interest of such bonds only out of the net revenues derived from operation of the bridge. The bonds of A are obligations in which X Country is financially committed and, in the hands of a controlled foreign corporation, are qualified investments in less developed countries.

(b) *Special rules*—(1) *Excluded property.* For purposes of paragraph (a) of this section, property which is disposed of within 6 months after the date of its acquisition shall be excluded from a controlled foreign corporation's qualified investments in less developed countries. However, the fact that property acquired by a controlled foreign corporation has not been held on an applicable determination date for more than 6 months after the date of its acquisition shall not prevent such property from being included in the controlled foreign corporation's qualified investments in less developed countries on such date. Proper adjustments shall be made subsequently, however, to exclude any item of property so included, if the property is in fact disposed of within 6 months after the date of its acquisition. See section 955(b)(4).

(2) *Determination of stock ownership.* In determining for purposes of paragraph (a)(1) and (2) of this section whether a controlled foreign corporation owns 10 percent or more of the total combined voting power of all classes of stock of a less developed country corporation, only stock owned directly by such controlled foreign corpora-

Reg. § 1.955-2(b)(2)

tion shall be taken into account and the provisions of section 958 and the regulations thereunder shall not apply. See section 958(a)(1).

(3) *Obligation defined.* For purposes of paragraph (a)(2) and (3) of this section, the term "obligation" means any bond, note, debenture, certificate, or other evidence of indebtedness. In the absence of legal, governmental, or business reasons to the contrary, the indebtedness must bear interest or be issued at a discount.

(4) *Date of acquisition.* For purposes of paragraphs (a)(2) and (b)(5)(i) of this section, stock or an obligation shall be considered acquired by a foreign corporation as of the date such corporation acquires an adjusted basis in the stock or obligation. For this purpose, in a case in which a foreign corporation acquires stock or an obligation in a transaction (other than a reorganization of the type described in section 368(a)(1)(E) or (F)) in which no gain or loss would be recognized had the transaction been between two domestic corporations, such corporation will be considered to have acquired an adjusted basis in such stock or obligation as of the date such transaction occurs.

(5) *Taxable years beginning after December 31, 1975.* For taxable years beginning after December 31, 1975, qualified investments in less developed countries do not include—

(i) Any property acquired after the latest determination date applicable to a taxable year beginning before December 31, 1975.

(ii) Stock or obligations of a less developed country shipping company described in § 1.955-5(b), and

(iii) Stock or obligations which were not treated as qualified investments in less developed countries on the later of the two determination dates applicable to the preceding taxable year.

See § 1.955-1(b)(3) for rules relating to the application of this subparagraph. See § 1.955A-2(h) for rules relating to the treatment of investments in stock or obligations described in subdivision (ii) of this subparagraph as qualified investments in foreign base company shipping operations.

(6) *Determination dates.* For purposes of subparagraph (5) of this paragraph and § 1.955-1(b)(3), the determination dates applicable to a taxable year of a controlled foreign corporation are—

(i) Except as provided in subdivision (ii) of this subparagraph, the close of such taxable year and the close of the preceding taxable year, and

(ii) With respect to a United States shareholder who has made an election under section 955(b)(3) to determine such corporation's increase in qualified investments in less developed countries at the close of the following taxable year, the close of such taxable year and the close of the taxable year immediately following such taxable year.

(c) *Termination of designation as a less developed country.* For purposes of sections 951 through 964, property which would constitute a qualified investment in a less developed country but for the fact that a foreign country or United States possession has, after the acquisition of such property by the controlled foreign corporation, ceased to be a less developed country shall be treated as a qualified investment in a less developed country. The application of this paragraph may be illustrated by the following example:

Example. On December 31, 1969, in accordance with the provisions of § 1.955-4, the designation of foreign country X as an economically less developed country is terminated. Corporation M, a controlled foreign corporation, has $50,000 of qualified investments in country X acquired before December 31, 1969. After 1969 such investments are treated as qualified investments in a less developed country notwithstanding the termination of the status of X Country as an economically less developed country. However, if such qualified investments of M Corporation are reduced to $40,000, each United States shareholder of M Corporation is required, subject to the provisions of § 1.955-1, to include his pro rata share of the $10,000 decrease in his gross income under section 951(a)(1)(A)(ii) and the regulations thereunder.

(d) *Amount attributable to property*—(1) *General rule.* For purposes of this section, the amount taken into account with respect to any property which constitutes a qualified investment in a less developed country shall be its adjusted basis as of the applicable determination date, reduced by any liability (other than a liability described in subparagraph (2) of this paragraph) to which such property is subject on such date. To be taken into account under this subparagraph, a liability must constitute a specific charge against the property involved. Thus, a liability evidenced by an open account or a liability secured only by the general credit of the controlled foreign corporation will not be taken into account. On the other hand, if a liability constitutes a specific charge against several items of property and cannot definitely be allocated to any single item of property, the liability shall be apportioned against each of such items of property in that ratio which the adjusted basis of such item on the applicable determination date bears to the adjusted basis of all such items at such time. A liability in excess of the adjusted basis of the property which is subject to such

Reg. § 1.955-2(b)(3)

liability shall not be taken into account for the purpose of reducing the adjusted basis of other property which is not subject to such liability.

(2) *Excluded charges.* For purposes of subparagraph (1) of this paragraph, a specific charge created with respect to any item of property principally for the purpose of artificially increasing or decreasing the amount of a controlled foreign corporation's qualified investments in less developed countries will not be recognized; whether a specific charge is created principally for such purpose will depend upon all the facts and circumstances of each case. One of the factors that will be considered in making such a determination with respect to a loan is whether the loan is from a related person, as defined in section 954(d)(3) and paragraph (e) of § 1.954-1.

(3) *Statement required.* If for purposes of this section a United States shareholder of a controlled foreign corporation reduces the adjusted basis of property which constitutes a qualified investment in a less developed country on the ground that such property is subject to a liability, he shall attach to his return a statement setting forth the adjusted basis of the property before the reduction and the amount and nature of the reduction.

(4) *Taxable years beginning after December 31, 1975.* For taxable years beginning after December 31, 1975, the amount taken into account under subparagraph (1) of this paragraph with respect to any property which constitutes a qualified investment in less developed countries shall not exceed the amount taken into account with respect to such property at the close of the preceding taxable year. [Reg. § 1.955-2.]

☐ [T.D. 6683, 10-17-63. Amended by T.D. 7894, 5-11-83.]

[Reg. § 1.955-3]

§ 1.955-3. **Election as to date of determining qualified investments in less developed countries.**—(a) *Nature of election.* In lieu of determining the increase for a taxable year of a foreign corporation beginning before January 1, 1976, under the provisions of section 954(f) and paragraph (a) of § 1.954-5, or the decrease under the provisions of section 955(a)(2) and paragraph (b) of § 1.955-1, in a controlled foreign corporation's qualified investments in less developed countries for a taxable year in the manner provided in such provisions, a United States shareholder of such controlled foreign corporation may elect, under the provisions of section 955(b)(3) and this section, to determine such increase in accordance with the provisions of paragraph (b) of § 1.954-5 and to determine such decrease by ascertaining the amount by which—

(1) Such controlled foreign corporation's qualified investments in less developed countries at the close of such taxable year exceed its qualified investments in less developed countries at the close of the taxable year immediately following such taxable year, and reducing such excess by

(2) The amount determined under paragraph (b)(1)(ii) of § 1.955-1 for such taxable year,

subject to the limitation provided in paragraph (b)(2) of § 1.955-1 for such taxable year. An election under this section may be made with respect to each taxable year. An election under this section may be made with respect to each controlled foreign corporation with respect to which a person is a United States shareholder within the meaning of section 951(b), but the election may not be exercised separately with respect to the increases and the decreases of such controlled foreign corporation. If an election is made under this section to determine the increase of a controlled foreign corporation in accordance with the provisions of paragraph (b) of § 1.954-5, subsequent decreases of such controlled foreign corporation shall be determined in accordance with this paragraph and not in accordance with paragraph (b) of § 1.955-1.

(b) *Time and manner of making election*—(1) *Without consent.* An election under this section with respect to a controlled foreign corporation shall be made without the consent of the Commissioner by a United States shareholder's filing a statement to such effect with his return for his taxable year in which or with which ends the first taxable year of such controlled foreign corporation in which—

(i) Such shareholder owns, within the meaning of section 958(a), or is considered as owning by applying the rules of ownership of section 958(b), 10 percent or more of the total combined voting power of all classes of stock entitled to vote of such controlled foreign corporation, and

(ii) Such controlled foreign corporation realizes foreign base company income from which amounts are excluded under section 954(b)(1) and paragraph (b)(1) of § 1.954-1.

The statement shall contain the name and address of the controlled foreign corporation and identification of such first taxable year of such corporation. For taxable years of a foreign corporation beginning after December 31, 1975, no election under this section with respect to a controlled foreign corporation may be made without the consent of the Commissioner.

Reg. § 1.955-3(b)(1)

(2) *With consent.* An election under this section with respect to a controlled foreign corporation may be made by a United States shareholder at any time with the consent of the Commissioner. Consent will not be granted if the first taxable year of the controlled foreign corporation with respect to which the shareholder desires to compute an amount described in section 954(b)(1) in accordance with the election provided in this section begins after December 31, 1975. Consent will not be granted unless the United States shareholder and the Commissioner agree to the terms, conditions, and adjustments under which the election will be effected. The application for consent to elect shall be made by the United States shareholder's mailing a letter for such purpose to the Commissioner of Internal Revenue, Washington, D.C. 20224. The application shall be mailed before the close of the first taxable year of the controlled foreign corporation with respect to which the shareholder desires to compute an amount described in section 954(b)(1) in accordance with the election provided in this section. The application shall include the following information:

(i) The name, address, and taxable year of the United States shareholder;

(ii) The name and address of the controlled foreign corporation;

(iii) The first taxable year of the controlled foreign corporation for which income is to be computed under the election;

(iv) The amount of the controlled foreign corporation's qualified investments in less developed countries at the close of its preceding taxable year; and

(v) The sum of the amounts excluded under section 954(b)(1) and paragraph (b)(1) of § 1.954-1 from the foreign base company income of the controlled foreign corporation for all prior taxable years during which such shareholder was a United States shareholder of such corporation and the sum of the amounts of its previously excluded subpart F income withdrawn from investment in less developed countries for all prior taxable years during which such shareholder was a United States shareholder of such corporation.

(c) *Effect of election*—(1) *General.* Except as provided in subparagraphs (3) and (4) of this paragraph, an election under this section with respect to a controlled foreign corporation shall be binding on the United States shareholder and shall apply to all qualified investments in less developed countries acquired, or disposed of, by such controlled foreign corporation during the taxable year following its taxable year for which income is first computed under the election and during all succeeding taxable years of such corporation.

(2) *Returns.* Any return of a United States shareholder required to be filed before the completion of a period with respect to which determinations are to be made as to a controlled foreign corporation's qualified investments in less developed countries for purposes of computing such shareholder's taxable income shall be filed on the basis of an estimate of the amount of the controlled foreign corporation's qualified investments in less developed countries at the close of the period. If the actual amount of such investments is not the same as the amount of the estimate, the United States shareholder shall immediately notify the Commissioner. The Commissioner will thereupon redetermine the amount of tax of such United States shareholder for the year or years with respect to which the incorrect amount was taken into account. The amount of tax, if any, due upon such redetermination shall be paid by the United States shareholder upon notice and demand by the district director. The amount of tax, if any, shown by such redetermination to have been overpaid shall be credited or refunded to the United States shareholder in accordance with the provisions of sections 6402 and 6511 and the regulations thereunder.

(3) *Revocation.* Upon application by the United States shareholder, the election made under this section may, subject to the approval of the Commissioner, be revoked. Approval will not be granted unless the United States shareholder and the Commissioner agree to the terms, conditions, and adjustments under which the revocation will be effected. Unless such agreement provides otherwise, the change in the controlled foreign corporation's qualified investments in less developed countries for its first taxable year for which income is computed without regard to the election previously made will be considered to be zero for purposes of effectuating the revocation. The application for consent to revocation shall be made by the United States shareholder's mailing a letter for such purpose to the Commissioner of Internal Revenue, Washington, D.C. 20224. The application shall be mailed before the close of the first taxable year of the controlled foreign corporation with respect to which the shareholder desires to compute the amounts described in section 954(b)(1) or 955(a) without regard to the election provided in this section. The application may also be filed in a taxable year beginning after December 31, 1975. The application shall include the following information:

(i) The name, address, and taxpayer identification number of the United States shareholder;

(ii) The name and address of the controlled foreign corporation;

(iii) The taxable year of the controlled foreign corporation for which such amounts are to be so computed;

(iv) The amount of the controlled foreign corporation's qualified investments in less developed countries at the close of its preceding taxable year;

(v) The sum of the amounts excluded under section 954(b)(1) and paragraph (b)(1) of § 1.954-1 from the foreign base company income of the controlled foreign corporation for all prior taxable years during which such shareholder was a United States shareholder of such corporation and the sum of the amounts of its previously excluded subpart F income withdrawn from investment in less developed countries for all prior taxable years during which such shareholder was a United States shareholder of such corporation; and

(vi) The reasons for the request for consent to revocation.

(4) *Transfer of stock.* If during any taxable year of a controlled foreign corporation—

(i) A United States shareholder who has made an election under this section with respect to such controlled foreign corporation sells, exchanges, or otherwise disposes of all or part of his stock in such controlled foreign corporation, and

(ii) The foreign corporation is a controlled foreign corporation immediately after the sale, exchange, or other disposition,

then, with respect to the stock so sold, exchanged, or disposed of, the controlled foreign corporation's acquisitions and dispositions of qualified investments in less developed countries for such taxable year shall be considered to be zero. If the United States shareholder's successor in interest is entitled to and does make an election under paragraph (b)(1) of this section to determine the controlled foreign corporation's increase in qualified investments in less developed countries for the taxable year in which he acquires such stock, such increase with respect to the stock so acquired shall be determined in accordance with the provisions of paragraph (b)(1) of § 1.954-5. If the controlled foreign corporation realizes no foreign base company income from which amounts are excluded under section 954(b)(1) and paragraph (b)(1) of § 1.954-1 for the taxable year in which the United States shareholder's successor in interest acquires such stock and such successor in interest makes an election under paragraph (b)(1) of this section with respect to a subsequent taxable year of such controlled foreign corporation, the increase in the controlled foreign corporation's qualified investments in less developed countries for such subsequent taxable year shall be determined in accordance with the provisions of paragraph (b)(2) of § 1.954-5.

(d) *Illustrations.* The application of this section may be illustrated by the following examples:

Example (1). Foreign corporation A is a wholly owned subsidiary of domestic corporation M. Both corporations use the calendar year as a taxable year. In a statement filed with its return for 1963, M Corporation makes an election under section 955(b)(3) and the election remains in force for the taxable year 1964. At December 31, 1964, A Corporation's qualified investments in less developed countries amount to $100,000; and, at December 31, 1965, to $80,000. For purposes of paragraph (a)(1) of this section, A Corporation's decrease in qualified investments in less developed countries for the taxable year 1964 is $20,000 and is determined by ascertaining the amount by which A Corporation's qualified investments in less developed countries at December 31, 1964 ($100,000) exceed its qualified investments in less developed countries at December 31, 1965 ($80,000).

Example (2). The facts are the same as in example (1) except that A Corporation experiences no changes in qualified investments in less developed countries during its taxable years 1966 and 1967. If M Corporation's election were to remain in force, A Corporation's acquisitions and dispositions of qualified investments in less developed countries during A Corporation's taxable year 1968 would be taken into account in determining whether A Corporation has experienced an increase or a decrease in qualified investments in less developed countries for its taxable year 1967. However, M Corporation duly files before the close of A Corporation's taxable year 1967 an application for consent to revocation of M Corporation's election under section 955(b)(3), and, pursuant to an agreement between the Commissioner and M Corporation, consent is granted by the Commissioner. Assuming such agreement does not provide otherwise, A Corporation's change in qualified investments in less developed countries for its taxable year 1967 is zero because the effect of the revocation of the election is to treat acquisitions and dispositions of qualified investments in less developed countries actually occurring in 1968 as having occurred in such year rather than in 1967.

Example (3). The facts are the same as in example (2) except that A Corporation's qualified

Reg. § 1.955-3(d)

investments in less developed countries at December 31, 1968, amount to $70,000. For purposes of paragraph (b)(1)(i) of § 1.955-1, the decrease in A Corporation's qualified investments in less developed countries for the taxable year 1968 is $10,000 and is determined by ascertaining the amount by which A Corporation's qualified investments in less developed countries at December 31, 1967 ($80,000) exceed its qualified investments in less developed countries at December 31, 1968 ($70,000).

Example (4). The facts are the same as in example (1) except that on September 30, 1965, M Corporation sells 40 percent of the only class of stock of A Corporation to N Corporation, a domestic corporation. Corporation N uses the calendar year as a taxable year. Corporation A remains a controlled foreign corporation immediately after such sale of its stock. Corporation A's qualified investments in less developed countries at December 31, 1966, amount to $90,000. The changes in A Corporation's qualified investments in less developed countries occurring in its taxable year 1965 are considered to be zero with respect to the 40-percent stock interest acquired by N Corporation. The entire $20,000 reduction in A Corporation's qualified investments in less developed countries which occurs during the taxable year 1965 is taken into account by M Corporation for purposes of paragraph (a)(1) of this section in determining its tax liability for the taxable year 1964. Corporation A's increase in qualified investments in less developed countries for the taxable year 1965 with respect to the 60-percent stock interest retained by M Corporation is $6,000 and is determined by ascertaining M Corporation's pro rata share (60 percent) of the amount by which A Corporation's qualified investments in less developed countries at December 31, 1966 ($90,000) exceed its qualified investments in less developed countries at December 31, 1965 ($80,000). Corporation N does not make an election under section 955(b)(3) in its return for its taxable year 1966. Corporation A's increase in qualified investments in less developed countries for the taxable year 1966 with respect to the 40-percent stock interest acquired by N Corporation is $4,000. [Reg. § 1.955-3.]

☐ [T.D. 6683, 10-17-63. Amended by T.D. 7893, 5-11-83 and T.D. 7894, 5-11-83.]

[Reg. § 1.955-4]

§ 1.955-4. Definition of less developed country.—(a) *Designation by Executive order.* For purposes of sections 951 through 964, the term "less developed country" means any foreign country (other than an area within the Sino-Soviet bloc) or any possession of the United States with respect to which, on the first day of the foreign corporation's taxable year, there is in effect an Executive order by the President of the United States designating such country or possession as an economically less developed country for purposes of such sections. Each territory, department, province, or possession of any foreign country other than a country within the Sino-Soviet bloc may be treated as a separate foreign country for purposes of such designation if the territory, department, province, or possession is overseas from the country of which it is a territory, department, province, or possession. Thus, for example, an overseas possession of a foreign country may be designated by Executive order as an economically less developed country even though the foreign country itself has not been designated as an economically less developed country; or the foreign country may be so designated even though the overseas possessions of such country have not been designated as economically less developed countries. The term "possession of the United States", for purposes of section 955(c)(3) and this section, shall be construed to have the same meaning as that contained in paragraph (b)(2) of § 1.957-3.

(b) *Countries not eligible for designation.* Section 955(c)(3) provides that no designation by Executive order may be made under section 955(c)(3) and paragraph (a) of this section with respect to—

Australia
Austria
Belgium
Canada
Denmark
France
Germany (Federal Republic)
Hong Kong
Italy
Japan
Liechtenstein
Luxembourg
Monaco
Netherlands
New Zealand
Norway
Union of South Africa
San Marino
Sweden
Switzerland
United Kingdom

(c) *Termination of designation.* Section 955(c)(3) provides that, after the President has designated any foreign country or possession of the United States as an economically less developed country for purposes of sections 951 through 964, he may not terminate such designation (ei-

Reg. § 1.955-4(a)

ther by issuing an Executive order for the purpose of terminating such designation or by issuing an Executive order which has the effect of terminating such designation) unless, at least 30 days prior to such termination, he has notified the Senate and the House of Representatives of his intention to terminate such designation. If such 30-day notice is given, no action by the Congress of the United States is necessary to effectuate the termination. The requirement for giving 30-day notice to the Senate and House of Representatives applies also to the termination of a designation with respect to an overseas territory, department, province, or possession of a foreign country. See paragraph (c) of § 1.955-2 for the effect of a termination of a Presidential designation upon property which would be a qualified investment in a less developed country but for the fact of such termination. [Reg. § 1.955-4.]

☐ [T.D. 6683, 10-17-63.]

[Reg. § 1.955-5]

§ 1.955-5. Definition of less developed country corporation.—(a) *Less developed country corporation*—(1) *In general.* For purposes of sections 951 through 964, the term "less developed country corporation" means a foreign corporation described in paragraph (b) of this section and also any foreign corporation—

(i) Which is engaged in the active conduct of one or more trades or businesses during the entire taxable year;

(ii) Which derives 80 percent or more of its gross income, if any, for such taxable year from sources within less developed countries, as determined under the provisions of § 1.955-6; and

(iii) Which has 80 percent or more in value (within the meaning of paragraph (d) of this section) of its assets on each day of such taxable year consisting of one or more of the following items of property:

(*a*) Property (other than property described in (*b*) through (*h*) of this subdivision) which is used, or held for use, in such trades or businesses and is located in one or more less developed countries;

(*b*) Money;

(*c*) Deposits with persons carrying on the banking business;

(*d*) Stock of any other less developed country corporation;

(*e*) Obligations (within the meaning of paragraph (b)(3) of § 1.955-2) of another less developed country corporation which at the time of their acquisition (within the meaning of paragraph (b)(4) of § 1.955-2) by the foreign corporation have a maturity of one year or more;

(*f*) Obligations (within the meaning of paragraph (b)(3) of § 1.955-2) of any less developed country;

(*g*) Investments which are required to be made or held because of restrictions imposed by the government of any less developed country; and

(*h*) Property described in section 956(b)(2).

For purposes of this subparagraph, if a foreign corporation is a partner in a foreign partnership, as defined in section 7701(a)(2) and (5) and the regulations thereunder, such corporation will be considered to be engaged in the active conduct of a trade or business to the extent and in the manner in which the partnership is so engaged and to own directly its proportionate share of each of the assets of the partnership. For purposes of subdivision (i) of this subparagraph, a newly-organized foreign corporation will be considered engaged in the active conduct of a trade or business from the date of its organization if such corporation commences business operations as soon as practicable after such organization. In the absence of affirmative evidence showing that the 80-percent requirement of subdivision (iii) of this subparagraph has not been satisfied on each day of the taxable year, such requirement will be considered satisfied if it is established to the satisfaction of the district director that such requirement has been satisfied on the last day of each quarter of the taxable year of the foreign corporation. For purposes of subdivision (iii) of this subparagraph, property (other than stock in trade or other property of a kind which would properly be included in inventory of the foreign corporation if on hand at the close of the taxable year, or property held primarily for sale to customers in the ordinary course of the trade or business of the foreign corporation) purchased for use in a trade or business and temporarily located outside less developed countries will be considered located in less developed countries if, but only if, such property is shipped to and received in less developed countries promptly after such purchase.

(2) *Special rules.* For purposes of subparagraph (1)(iii)(*a*) of this paragraph—

(i) *Treatment of receivables.* Bills receivable, accounts receivable, notes receivable and open accounts shall be considered to be used in the trade or business and located in less developed countries if, but only if—

(*a*) Such obligations arise out of the rental of property located in less developed countries, the performance of services within less de-

Reg. § 1.955-5(a)(2)

veloped countries, or the sale of property manufactured, produced, grown, or extracted in less developed countries, but only to the extent that the aggregate amount of such obligations at any time during the taxable year does not exceed an amount which is ordinary and necessary to carry on the business of both parties to the transactions if such transactions are between unrelated persons or, if such transactions are between related persons, an amount which would be ordinary and necessary to carry on the business of both parties to the transactions if such transactions were between unrelated persons;

(b) In the case of bills receivable, accounts receivable, notes receivable, and open accounts arising out of transactions other than those referred to in (a) of this subdivision—

(1) If the obligor is an individual, such individual is a resident of one or more less developed countries and of no other country which is not a less developed country;

(2) If the obligor is a corporation which as to the foreign corporation is a related person as defined in section 954(d)(3) and paragraph (e) of § 1.954-1, such obligor meets, with respect to the period ending with the close of its annual accounting period in which occurs the date on which the obligation is incurred, the 80-percent gross income requirement of paragraph (b)(1)(ii) of § 1.955-6; or

(3) If the obligor is a corporation which as to the foreign corporation is not a related person as defined in section 954(d)(3) and paragraph (e) of § 1.954-1, it is reasonable, on the basis of ascertainable facts, for the obligee to believe that the obligor meets, with respect to such period, the 80-percent gross income requirement of paragraph (b)(1)(ii) of § 1.955-6.

(ii) *Location of interests in real estate.* Interests in real estate such as leaseholds of land or improvements thereon, mortgages on real property (including interests in mortgages on leaseholds of land or improvements thereon), and mineral, oil, or gas interests shall be considered located in less developed countries if, but only if, the underlying real estate is located in less developed countries.

(iii) *Location of certain other intangibles.* Intangible property (other than any such property described in subdivision (i) or (ii) of this subparagraph) used in the trade or business of the foreign corporation shall be considered to be located in less developed countries in the same ratio that the amount of the foreign corporation's tangible property and property described in subdivision (i) or (ii) of this subparagraph used in its trades or businessses and located or deemed located in less developed countries bears to the total amount of its tangible property and property described in subdivision (i) or (ii) of this subparagraph used in its trades or businesses.

(3) *Illustration.* The provisions of subparagraph (1) of this paragraph may be illustrated by the following example:

Example. Foreign corporation A is formed on November 1, 1963, to engage in the business of manufacturing and selling radios in Brazil, a less developed country as of November 1, 1963. Corporation A uses the calendar year as a taxable year. Shortly after it is formed, A Corporation acquires a plant site and begins construction of a plant which is completed on August 1, 1964. Corporation A commences business operations as soon as practicable and continues such operations through December 31, 1964, and thereafter, after completion of the plant and continues such operations through December 31, 1964, and thereafter. Corporation A will be considered for purposes of subparagraph (1)(i) of this paragraph to be engaged in the active conduct of a trade or business for its entire taxable years ending on December 31, 1963, and 1964. The plant site and the plant (while under construction and after completion) will be considered to be property held during such taxable years for use in A Corporation's trade or business.

(b) *Shipping companies.* For purposes of sections 951 through 964, the term "less developed country corporation" also means any foreign corporation—

(1) Which has 80 percent or more of its gross income, if any, for the taxable year consisting of one or more of—

(i) Gross income derived—

(a) From, or in connection with, the using (or hiring or leasing for use) in foreign commerce of aircraft or vessels registered under the laws of a less developed country,

(b) From, or in connection with, the performance of services directly related to the use in foreign commerce of aircraft or vessels registered under the laws of a less developed country, or

(c) From the sale or exchange of aircraft or vessels registered under the laws of a less developed country and used in foreign commerce by such foreign corporation;

(ii) Dividends and interest received from other foreign corporations which are less developed country corporations within the meaning of this paragraph and 10 percent or more of the total combined voting power of all classes of stock of which is owned at the time such dividends and interest are received or accrued by such foreign corporation; and

(iii) Gain from the sale or exchange of stock or obligations of other foreign corporations which are less developed country corporations within the meaning of this paragraph and 10 percent or more of the total combined voting power of all classes of stock of which is owned by such foreign corporation immediately before such sale or exchange; and

(2) Which has 80 percent or more in value (within the meaning of paragraph (d) of this section) of its assets on each day of the taxable year consisting of—

(i) Assets used, or held for use, for the production of income described in subparagraph (1) of this paragraph, or in connection with the production of such income, whether or not such income is received during the taxable year, and

(ii) Property described in section 956(b)(2).

In the absence of affirmative evidence showing that the 80-percent requirement of this subparagraph has not been satisfied on each day of the taxable year, such requirement will be considered satisfied if it is established to the satisfaction of the district director that such requirement has been satisfied on the last day of each quarter of the taxable year of the foreign corporation. The provisions of this subparagraph may be illustrated by the following example:

Example. Foreign corporation A is formed on November 1, 1963, for the purpose of constructing and operating a vessel and, on that date, enters a charter agreement which provides that such vessel will be registered under the laws of Liberia, a less developed country as of November 1, 1963, and operated between South American and European ports. Corporation A uses the calendar year as a taxable year. Construction of the vessel is completed on September 1, 1965, and the vessel is registered under the laws of Liberia and operated between South American and European ports through December 31, 1965, and thereafter. The charter and the vessel (while under construction and after completion), or any interest of A Corporation in such assets, will be considered assets which are held by A Corporation during its taxable years ending on December 31, 1963, 1964, and 1965, for use in the production of income described in subparagraph (1) of this paragraph.

(c) *Determination of stock ownership.* In determining for purposes of paragraph (b)(1)(ii) and (iii) of this section whether a foreign corporation owns 10 percent or more of the total combined voting power of all classes of stock of a less developed country corporation, only stock owned directly by such foreign corporation shall be taken into account and the provisions of section 958 and the regulations thereunder shall not apply. See section 958(a)(1).

(d) *Determination of value.* For purposes of paragraphs (a)(1)(iii) and (b)(2) of this section—

(1) *General.* Except as provided in subparagraph (2) of this paragraph, the value at which property shall be taken into account is its actual value (not reduced by liabilities) which, in the absence of affirmative evidence to the contrary, shall be deemed to be its adjusted basis.

(2) *Treatment of certain receivables.* The value at which receivables described in paragraph (a)(2)(i) of this section and held by a foreign corporation using the cash receipts and disbursements method of accounting shall be taken into account is their actual value (not reduced by liabilities) which, in the absence of affirmative evidence to the contrary, shall be deemed to be their face value. [Reg. § 1.955-5.]

☐ [*T.D.* 6683, 10-17-63.]

[Reg. § 1.955-6]

§ 1.955-6. Gross income from sources within less developed countries.—(a) *General.* For purposes of paragraph (a)(1)(ii) of § 1.955-5, the determination whether a foreign corporation has derived 80 percent or more of its gross income from sources within less developed countries for any taxable year shall be made by the application of the provisions of sections 861 through 864, and §§ 1.861-1 through 1.863-5, in application of which the name of a less developed country shall be substituted for "the United States", except that if income is derived by the foreign corporation from—

(1) Interest (other than interest to which subparagraph (3) of this paragraph applies), the rules set forth in paragraph (b) of this section shall apply;

(2) Dividends, the rules set forth in paragraph (c) of this section shall apply; or

(3) Income (including interest) derived in connection with the sale of tangible personal property, the rules set forth in paragraph (d) of this section shall apply.

The source of income described in subparagraphs (1), (2), or (3) of this paragraph shall be determined solely under the rules of this section and without regard to the rules of sections 861 through 864, and the regulations thereunder.

(b) *Interest*—(1) *In general.* Except as provided in subparagraph (2) of this paragraph and paragraph (d) of this section, gross income derived

Reg. § 1.955-6(b)(1)

by the foreign corporation from interest on any indebtedness—

(i) Of an individual shall be treated as income from sources within a less developed country if, but only if, such individual is a resident of one or more less developed countries and of no other country which is not a less developed country.

(ii) Of a corporation shall be treated as income from sources within less developed countries if, but only if, 80 percent or more of the gross income of the payer corporation for the 3-year period ending with the close of its annual accounting period in which such interest is paid, or for such part of such 3-year period as such corporation has been in existence, or for such part of such 3-year period as occurs on and after the beginning of such corporation's first annual accounting period beginning after December 31, 1962, whichever period is shortest, was derived from sources within less developed countries as determined in accordance with the principles of this section; or

(iii) Of a less developed country, including obligations issued or guaranteed by the government of such country or of a political subdivision thereof and obligations of any agency or instrumentality of such country, in which such country is financially committed shall be treated as income from sources within such country.

(2) *Special rule.* Gross income derived by the foreign corporation from interest on obligations of the United States shall be treated as income from sources within less developed countries without regard to the provisions of subparagraph (1) of this paragraph.

(3) *Payers other than related persons.* For purposes of subparagraph (1)(ii) of this paragraph, a payer corporation which as to the recipient corporation is not a related person as defined in section 954(d)(3) and paragraph (e) of § 1.954-1 shall be deemed to have satisfied the 80-percent gross income requirement if, on the basis of ascertainable facts, it is reasonable for the recipient corporation to believe that such requirement is satisfied.

(c) *Dividends*—(1) *In general.* Gross income derived by the foreign corporation from dividends, as defined in section 316 and the regulations thereunder, shall be treated as income from sources within less developed countries if, but only if, 80 percent or more of the gross income of the payer corporation for the 3-year period ending with the close of its annual accounting period in which such dividends are distributed, or for such part of such 3-year period as such corporation has been in existence, or for such part of such 3-year period as occurs on and after the beginning of such corporation's first annual accounting period beginning after December 31, 1962, whichever period is shortest, was derived from sources within less developed countries as determined in accordance with the principles of this section.

(2) *Payers other than related persons.* See paragraph (b)(3) of this section for rule governing satisfaction of the 80-percent gross income requirement by payers other than related persons.

(d) *Sale of tangible personal property*—(1) *In general.* Income (whether in the form of profits, commissions, fees, interest, or otherwise) derived by the foreign corporation in connection with the sale of tangible personal property shall be treated as income from sources within less developed countries if, but only if—

(i) Such property is produced (within the meaning of subparagraph (2) of this paragraph) within less developed countries; or

(ii) Such property is sold for use, consumption, or disposition within less developed countries even though produced outside less developed countries and the selling corporation is engaged within less developed countries, in connection with sales of such property, in continuous operational activities which are substantial in relation to such sales, as evidenced, for example, by the maintenance within less developed countries of a substantial sales or service organization or substantial facilities for the storage, handling, transportation, assembly, packaging, or servicing of such property.

(2) *Production defined.* For purposes of this paragraph, the term "produced" means manufactured, grown, extracted, or constructed and includes a substantial transformation of property purchased for resale or the manufacture of a product when purchased components constitute part of the property which is sold. See paragraph (a)(4)(ii) and (iii) of § 1.954-3 for a statement and illustration of the principles set forth in the preceding sentence. [Reg. § 1.955-6.]

☐ [T.D. 6683, 10-17-63.]

[Reg. § 1.955A-1]

§ 1.955A-1. Shareholder's pro rata share of amount of previously excluded subpart F income withdrawn from investment in foreign base company shipping operations.—(a) *In general.* Section 955 provides rules for determining the amount of a controlled foreign corporation's previously excluded subpart F income which is withdrawn for any taxable year beginning after December 31, 1975, from investment in foreign base company shipping operations. Pursuant to section 951(a)(1)(A)(iii) and the regulations thereunder, a United States shareholder of such

Income from Sources Without the United States 49,313

See p. 20,601 for regulations not amended to reflect law changes

controlled foreign corporation must include in his gross income his pro rata share of such amount as determined in accordance with paragraph (c) of this section.

(b) *Amount withdrawn by controlled foreign corporation.*—(1) *In general.* For purposes of sections 951 through 964, the amount of a controlled foreign corporation's previously excluded subpart F income which is withdrawn for any taxable year from investment in foreign base company shipping operations is an amount equal to the decrease for such year in such corporation's qualified investments in foreign base company shipping operations. Such decrease is, except as provided in § 1.955A-4—

(i) An amount equal to the excess of the amount of its qualified investments in foreign base company shipping operations at the close of the preceding taxable year over the amount of its qualified investments in foreign base company shipping operations at the close of the taxable year, minus

(ii) The amount (if any) by which recognized losses on sales or exchanges by such corporation during the taxable year of qualified investments in foreign base company shipping operations exceed its recognized gains on sales or exchanges during such year of qualified investments in foreign base company shipping operations,

but only to the extent that the net amount so determined does not exceed the limitation determined under subparagraph (2) of this paragraph. See § 1.955A-2 for determining the amount of qualified investments in foreign base company shipping operations.

(2) *Limitation applicable in determining decreases*—(i) *In general.* The limitation referred to in subparagraph (1) of this paragraph for any taxable year of a controlled foreign corporation shall be the lesser of the following two limitations:

(A) The sum of (*1*) the controlled foreign corporation's earnings and profits (or deficit in earnings and profits) for the taxable year, computed as of the close of the taxable year without diminution by reason of any distribution made during the taxable year, (*2*) the sum of its earnings and profits (or deficits in earnings and profits) accumulated for prior taxable years beginning after December 31, 1975, and (*3*) the amount described in subparagraph (3) of this paragraph; or

(B) The sum of the amounts excluded under section 954(b)(2) (see subparagraph (4) of this paragraph) from the foreign base company income of such corporation for all prior taxable years beginning after December 31, 1975, minus the sum of the amounts (determined under this paragraph) of its previously excluded subpart F income withdrawn from investment in foreign base company shipping operations for all such prior taxable years.

(C) For purposes of the immediately preceding subparagraph (B), the amount excluded under section 954(b)(2) for a taxable year of a controlled foreign corporation (the "first corporation") includes (*1*) an amount excluded under section 954(b)(2) by another corporation which is a member of a related group (as defined in § 1.955A-3(b)(1)) attributable to the first corporation's excess investment (see § 1.955A-3(c)(4)) for a taxable year beginning after December 31, 1983, (*2*) an amount excluded by a corporation under § 1.954-1(b)(4)(ii)(*b*) by reason of the application of the carryover rule there set forth, and (*3*) an amount equal to the first corporation's pro rata share of a group excess deduction (see § 1.955A-3(c)(2)) of a related group for a taxable year beginning after December 31, 1983 (but not in excess of that portion of such pro rata share which would reduce the first corporation's foreign base company shipping income to zero). Such amounts will not be treated as excluded under section 954(b)(2) by any other corporation.

(ii) *Certain exclusions from earnings and profits.* For purposes of determining the earnings and profits of a controlled foreign corporation under subdivision (i)(A)(*1*) and (*2*) of this subparagraph, such earnings and profits shall be considered not to include any amounts which are attributable to—

(A)(*1*) Amounts which, for the current taxable year, are included in the gross income of a United States shareholder of such controlled foreign corporation under section 951(a)(1)(A)(i), or

(*2*) Amounts which, for any prior taxable year, have been included in the gross income of a United States shareholder of such controlled foreign corporation under section 951(a) and have not been distributed; or

(B)(*1*) Amounts which, for the current taxable year, are included in the gross income of a United States shareholder of such controlled foreign corporation under section 551(b) or would be so included under such section but for the fact that such amounts were distributed to such shareholder during the taxable year, or

(*2*) Amounts which, for any prior taxable year, have been included in the gross income of a United States shareholder of such controlled foreign corporation under section 551(b) and have not been distributed.

The rules of this subdivision apply only in determining the limitation on a controlled foreign cor-

Reg. § 1.955A-1(b)(2)

49,314 Income from Sources Without the United States

See p. 20,601 for regulations not amended to reflect law changes

poration's decrease in qualified investments in foreign base company shipping operations. See section 959 and the regulations thereunder for rules relating to the exclusion from gross income of previously taxed earnings and profits.

(3) *Carryover of amounts relating to investments in less developed country shipping companies*—(i) *In general.* The amount described in this subparagraph for any taxable year of a controlled foreign corporation beginning after December 31, 1975, is the lesser of—

(A) The excess of the amount described in subdivision (ii) of this subparagraph, over the amount described in subdivision (iii) of this subparagraph, or

(B) The limitation determined under subdivision (iv) of this subparagraph.

(ii) *Previously excluded subpart F income invested in less developed country shipping companies.* The amount described in this subdivision for all taxable years of a controlled foreign corporation beginning after December 31, 1975, is the lesser of—

(A) The amount of such corporation's qualified investments (determined under § 1.955-2 other than paragraph (b)(5) thereof) in less developed country shipping companies described in § 1.955-5(b) at the close of the last taxable year of such corporation beginning before January 1, 1976, or

(B) The limitation determined under § 1.955-1(b)(2)(i)(*b*) (relating to previously excluded subpart F income) for the first taxable year of such corporation beginning after January 1, 1976.

(iii) *Amounts previously carried over.* The amount described in this subdivision for any taxable year of a controlled foreign corporation shall be the sum of the excess determined for each prior taxable year beginning after December 31, 1976, of—

(A) The amount (determined under this paragraph) of such corporation's previously excluded subpart F income withdrawn from investment in foreign base company shipping operations, over

(B) The sum of the earnings and profits determined under subparagraph (2)(i)(A)(*1*) and (*2*) of this paragraph.

(iv) *Extent attributable to accumulated earnings and profits.* The limitation determined under this subdivision for any taxable year of a controlled foreign corporation is the sum of such controlled foreign corporation's earnings and profits (or deficits in earnings and profits) accumulated for taxable years beginning after December 31, 1962, and before January 1, 1976. For purposes of the preceding sentence, earnings and profits shall be determined by excluding the amounts described in subparagraph (2)(ii) (A) and (B) of this paragraph.

(v) *Illustration.* The application of this subparagraph may be illustrated by the following example:

Example. (a) Throughout the period here involved A is a United States shareholder of controlled foreign corporation M. M is not a foreign personal holding company, and M uses the calendar year as the taxable year.

(b) The amount described in this subparagraph for M's taxable year 1978 with respect to A is determined as follows, based on the facts shown in the following table:

(1) Investment in less developed country shipping companies on December 31, 1975 (subdivision (ii)(A) amount)	$10,000
(2) § 1.955-1(b)(2)(i)(*b*) limitation for 1976 (previously excluded subpart F income not withdrawn from investment in less developed countries) (subdivision (ii)(B) amount)	50,000
(3) Subdivision (ii) amount (lesser of lines (1) and (2))	10,000
(4) Subdivision (iii) amount: Excess for 1977 of M's previously excluded subpart F income withdrawn from investment in foreign base country shipping operations, $3,000, over the sum of the amounts determined under subparagraphs (2)(i)(A) (*1*) and (*2*) of this paragraph, $1,000	2,000
(5) Excess of line (3) over line (4)	8,000
(6) Sum of M's earnings and profits accumulated for 1962 through 1975, determined on December 31, 1978	26,000
(7) Amount described in this subparagraph for 1978 (lesser of line (5) and line (6))	8,000

(c) For 1978, M's earnings and profits (reduced as provided in § 1.955-1(b)(2)(ii)(*a*) (*1*)) are $19,000, and the amount of M's previously excluded subpart F income withdrawn from investment in less developed countries determined under § 1.955-1(b)) is $42,000. Consequently,

Reg. § 1.955A-1(b)(3)

Income from Sources Without the United States

$23,000 of M's earnings and profits accumulated for 1962 through 1975 are attributable to such $42,000 amount, and will therefore be excluded under subparagraph (2)(ii)(A) (*2*) of this paragraph from M's earnings and profits accumulated for 1962 through 1975, determined as of December 31, 1979. No other portion of M's earnings and profits accumulated for 1962 through 1975 is distributed or included in the gross income of a United States shareholder in 1978.

(d) The amount described in this subparagraph for M's taxable year 1979 with respect to A is determined as follows, based on the additional facts shown in the following table:

(1) Subdivision (ii) amount (line (3) from paragraph (b) of this example)	$10,000
(2) Subdivision (iii) amount: (i) Excess for 1977 from line (4) of paragraph (b) of this example	2,000
(ii) Plus: excess for 1978 of M's previously excluded subpart F income withdrawn from investment in foreign base country shipping operations, $6,000, over the sum of the amounts determined under subparagraphs (2)(i)(A) (*1*) and (*2*) of this paragraph, $25,000.............	0
(iii) Subdivision (iii) amount	2,000
(3) Excess of line (1) over line (2)(iii) ..	8,000
(4) Sum of M's earnings and profits accumulated for 1962 through 1975, determined on December 31, 1979 ($26,000 minus $23,000)	3,000
(5) Amount described in this subparagraph for 1979 (lesser of line (3) and line (4))	3,000

(4) *Amount excluded.* For purposes of subparagraph (2)(i)(B) of this paragraph, the amount excluded under section 954(b)(2) from the foreign base company income of a controlled foreign corporation for any taxable year beginning after December 31, 1975, is the excess of—

(i) The amount which would have been equal to the subpart F income of such corporation for such taxable year if such corporation had had no increase in qualified investments in foreign base company shipping operations for such taxable year, over

(ii) The subpart F income of such corporation for such taxable year.

(c) *Shareholder's pro rata share of amount withdrawn by controlled foreign corporation*—(1) *In general.* A United States shareholder's pro rata share of a controlled foreign corporation's previously excluded subpart F income withdrawn for any taxable year from investment in foreign base company shipping operations is his pro rata share of the amount withdrawn for such year by such corporation, as determined under paragraph (b) of this section. See section 955(a)(3). Such pro rata share shall be determined in accordance with the principles of § 1.951-1(e).

(2) *Special rule.* A United States shareholder's pro rata share of the net amount determined under paragraph (b)(2)(i)(B) of this section with respect to any stock of the controlled foreign corporation owned by such shareholder shall be determined without taking into account any amount attributable to a period prior to the date on which such shareholder acquired such stock. See section 1248 and the regulations thereunder for rules governing treatment of gain from sales or exchanges of stock in certain foreign corporations.

(d) *Illustrations.* The application of this section may be illustrated by the following examples:

Example (1). A, a United States shareholder, owns 60 percent of the only class of stock of M Corporation, a controlled foreign corporation throughout the entire period here involved. Both A and M use the calendar year as a taxable year. The amount of M's previously excluded subpart F income withdrawn for 1978 from investment in foreign base company shipping operations is $40,000, and A's pro rata share of such amount is $24,000, determined as follows based on the facts shown in the following table:

(a) Qualified investments in foreign base company shipping operations at the close of 1977	$125,000
(b) Less: qualified investments in foreign base company shipping operations at the close of 1978	75,000
(c) Balance	50,000
(d) Less: excess of recognized losses ($15,000) over recognized gains ($5,000) on sales during 1978 of qualified investments in foreign base company shipping operations	10,000
(e) Tentative decrease in qualified investments in foreign base company shipping operations for 1978......................	40,000
(f) Earnings and profits for 1976, 1977, and 1978	45,000
(g) Plus: amount determined under paragraph (b)(3) of this section ..	0
(h) Earnings and profits limitation....	45,000

Reg. § 1.955A-1(d)

49,316   Income from Sources Without the United States

See p. 20,601 for regulations not amended to reflect law changes

(i) Excess of amount excluded under section 954(b)(2) from foreign base company income for 1976 ($75,000) over amount of previously excluded subpart F income withdrawn for 1977 from investment in foreign base company shipping operations ($25,000) ... 50,000

(j) M's amount of previously excluded subpart F income withdrawn for 1978 from investment in foreign base company shipping operations (item (e), but not to exceed the lesser of item (h) or item (i)) 40,000

(k) A's pro rata share of M Corporation's amount of previously excluded subpart F income withdrawn for 1978 from investment in foreign base company shipping operations (60 percent of $40,000) .... $ 24,000

Example (2). The facts are the same as in example (1), except that M's earnings and profits (determined under paragraph (b)(2) of this section) for 1976, 1977, and 1978 (item (f)) are $30,000 instead of $45,000. M's amount of previously excluded subpart F income withdrawn for 1978 from investment in foreign base company shipping operations is $30,000. A's pro rata share of such amount is $18,000 (60 percent of $30,000).

Example (3). The facts are the same as in example (1), except that the excess of the amount excluded under section 954(b)(2) for 1976 from M Corporation's foreign base company income over the amount of its previously excluded subpart F income withdrawn for 1977 from investment in foreign base company shipping operations (item (i)) is $20,000 instead of $50,000. M's amount of previously excluded subpart F income withdrawn for 1978 from investment in foreign base company shipping operations is $20,000. A's pro rata share of such amount is $12,000 (60 percent of $20,000). [Reg. § 1.955A-1.]

☐ [*T.D.* 7894, 5-11-83.]

[Reg. § 1.955A-2]

§ 1.955A-2. Amount of a controlled foreign corporation's qualified investments in foreign base company shipping operations.—(a) *Qualified investments*—(1) *In general.* Under section 955(b), for purposes of sections 951 through 964, a controlled foreign corporation's "qualified investments in foreign base company shipping operations" are investments in—

(i) Any aircraft or vessel, to the extent that such aircraft or vessel is used (or hired or leased for use) in foreign commerce.

(ii) Related shipping assets (within the meaning of paragraph (b) of this section),

(iii) Stock or obligations of a related controlled foreign corporation, to the extent provided in paragraph (c) of this section,

(iv) A partnership, to the extent provided in paragraph (d) of this section, and

(v) Stock or obligations of a less developed country shipping company described in § 1.955-5(b), as provided in paragraph (h) of this section.

(2) *Coordination of provisions.* No amount shall be counted as a qualified investment in foreign base company shipping operations under more than one provision of this section. Thus, for example, if a $10,000 investment in stock of a controlled foreign corporation is treated as a qualified investment in foreign base company shipping operations under both subparagraph (1) (iii) and (v) of this paragraph, then such $10,000 is counted only once as a qualified investment in foreign base company shipping operations.

(3) *Definitions.* If the meaning of any term is defined or explained in § 1.954-6, then such term shall have the same meaning when used in this section.

(4) *Extent of use.* (i) For purposes of subparagraph (1)(i) of this paragraph and paragraph (b)(1) of this section, the extent to which an asset of a controlled foreign corporation is used during a taxable year in foreign base company shipping operations shall be determined on the basis of the proportion for such year which the foreign base company shipping income derived from the use of such asset bears to the total gross income derived from the use of such asset.

(ii) For purposes of determining under subdivision (i) of this subparagraph the amounts of foreign base company shipping income and gross income of a controlled foreign corporation—

(A) Such amounts shall be deemed to include an arm's length charge (see § 1.954-6(h)(5)) for services performed by such corporation for itself,

(B) Such amounts shall be deemed to include an arm's length charge for the use of an asset (such as a vessel under construction or laid up for repairs) which is held for use in foreign base company shipping operations, but is not actually so used,

(C) Foreign base company shipping income shall be deemed to include amounts earned in taxable years beginning before January 1, 1976, and

(D) The district director shall make such other adjustments to such amounts as are necessary to properly determine the extent to

Reg. § 1.955A-2(a)(1)

which any asset is used in foreign base company shipping operations.

(b) *Related shipping assets*—(1) *In general.* For purposes of this section, the term "related shipping asset" means any asset which is used (or held for use) for or in connection with the production of income described in § 1.954-6(b)(1) (i) or (ii), but only to the extent that such asset is so used (or is so held for use).

(2) *Examples.* Examples of assets of a controlled foreign corporation which are used (or held for use) for or in connection with the production of income described in subparagraph (1) of this paragraph include—

(i) Money, bank deposits, and other temporary investments which are reasonably necessary to meet the working capital requirements of such corporation in its conduct of foreign base company shipping operations,

(ii) Accounts receivable and evidences of indebtedness which arise from the conduct of foreign base company shipping operations by such corporation or by a related person,

(iii) Amounts (other than amounts described in subdivision (i) of this subparagraph) deposited in bank accounts or invested in readily marketable securities pursuant to a specific, definite, and feasible plan to purchase any tangible asset for use in foreign base company shipping operations,

(iv) Amounts paid into escrow to secure the payment of (A) charter hire for an aircraft, vessel, or other asset used in foreign base company shipping operations or (B) a debt which constitutes a specific charge against such an asset,

(v) Capitalized expenditures (such as progress payments) made under a contract to purchase any asset for use in foreign base company shipping operations,

(vi) Prepaid expenses and deferred charges incurred in the course of foreign base company shipping operations,

(vii) Stock acquired and retained to insure a source of supplies or services used in the conduct of foreign base company shipping operations, and

(viii) Currency futures acquired and retained as a hedge against international currency fluctuations in connection with foreign base company shipping operations.

(3) *Limitations*—(i) *Vessels generally.* Notwithstanding any other provision of this paragraph, the term "related shipping assets" does not include any money or other intangible assets of a controlled foreign corporation, to the extent that such assets are permitted to accumulate in excess of the reasonably anticipated needs of the business.

(ii) *Safe harbor.* If a controlled foreign corporation accumulates money or other intangible assets pursuant to a plan to purchase one or more vessels for use in foreign commerce, and if—

(A) The amount so accumulated, plus

(B) The sum of the amounts accumulated by other controlled foreign corporations which are related persons (within the meaning of section 954(d)(3)) pursuant to similar plans,

does not exceed 110 percent of a reasonable down payment on each vessel so planned to be purchased within a reasonable period, then such plan will be considered to be feasible. For purposes of the preceding sentence, a reasonable down payment shall not exceed 28 percent of the total cost of acquisition. The determination dates applicable to the taxable year of a controlled foreign corporation are those set forth in paragraph (c)(2)(ii) of this section. In the case of accumulation of assets which do not come within the safe harbor limitation of this subdivision (ii), in determining whether such assets have accumulated beyond the reasonably anticipated needs of the business, factors to be taken into account include, but are not limited to, the availability of financing to purchase a vessel and the availability of a vessel suitable for the purposes to which the vessel is to be put.

(iii) *Other assets.* In determining whether a plan to purchase any asset other than a vessel for use in foreign base company shipping operations is feasible, principles similar to those states in subdivision (ii) of this subparagraph shall be applied.

(4) *Cross-reference.* See § 1.954-7(c) for additional illustrations bearing on the application of this paragraph.

(c) *Stock and obligations*—(1) *In general.* Investments by a controlled foreign corporation (the "first corporation") in stock or obligations of a second controlled foreign corporation which is a related person (within the meaning of section 954(d)(3)) are considered to be qualified investments in foreign base company shipping operations to the extent that the assets of such second operation are used (or held for use) in foreign base company shipping operations. See subparagraph (2) of this paragraph. However, an investment in an obligation of the second corporation will not be considered a qualified investment in foreign base company shipping operations if the obligation represents a liability which constitutes a specific charge (nonrecourse or otherwise) against an asset of the second corporation which is not either—

Reg. § 1.955A-2(c)(1)

(i) An aircraft or vessel used (or held for use) to some extent in foreign commerce, or

(ii) An asset described in paragraph (a)(1)(ii) through (v) of this section.

(2) *Extent of use.* On any determination date applicable to a taxable year of the first corporation, the extent to which the assets of the second corporation are used in foreign base company shipping operations shall be determined on the basis of the proportion which the amount of such second corporation's qualified investments in foreign base company shipping operations bears to its net worth, such proportion to be determined at the close of the second corporation's last taxable year which ends on or before such determination date. For purposes of the preceding sentence—

(i) A controlled foreign corporation's net worth is the total adjusted basis of the corporate assets reduced by the total outstanding principal amount of the corporate liabilities, and

(ii) The determination dates applicable to a taxable year of a controlled foreign corporation are—

(A) Except as provided in (B) of this subdivision, the close of such taxable year and the close of the preceding taxable year, and

(B) With respect to a United States shareholder who has made an election under section 955(b)(3) to determine such corporation's increase in qualified investments in foreign base company shipping operations at the close of the following taxable year, the close of such taxable year and the close of the taxable year immediately following such taxable year.

(3) *Illustrations.* The application of this paragraph may be illustrated by the following examples:

Example (1). On December 31, 1976, controlled foreign corporation X owns 100 percent of the single class of stock of controlled foreign corporation Y. X and Y both use the calendar year as the taxable year. On December 31, 1976, Y's assets consist of a vessel used in foreign commerce, related shipping assets, and other assets unrelated to its foreign base company shipping operations. On such date Y has qualified investments in foreign based company shipping operations (determined under paragraph (g) of this section) of $60,000, and a net worth of $100,000. If X's investment in the stock of Y is $50,000, then $30,000 of such amount, i.e.,

$$\frac{\$60,000}{\$100,000} \times \$50,000$$

is a qualified investment in foreign base company shipping operations.

Example (2). The facts are the same as in example (1), except that on December 31, 1976, Y's assets consist entirely of a vessel used in foreign commerce and related shipping assets, Y has qualified investments in foreign base company shipping operations (determined under paragraph (g) of this section) of $16,000 and (therefore) a net worth of $16,000. If X's investment in the stock of Y is $50,000, then the entire $50,000, i.e.,

$$\frac{\$16,000}{\$16,000} \times \$50,000$$

is a qualified investment in foreign base company shipping operations.

Example (3). On December 31, 1980, controlled foreign corporation J owns two notes of controlled foreign corporation K, which is a related person (within the meaning of section 954(d)(3)). Both J and K use the calendar year as the taxable year. J's adjusted basis in each of the two notes is $100,000. The first note is secured only by the general credit of K. The second note is secured by (and, therefore, constitutes a specific charge on) a hotel owned by K in a foreign country. On December 31, 1980, K has qualified investments in foreign base company shipping operations with an adjusted basis of $500,000 (before applying the rules of paragraph (g) of this section). The adjusted basis of all of K's corporate assets is $1,100,000. K's only liabilities are the two notes. The amount of K's qualified investments in foreign base company shipping operations (determined under paragraph (g) of this section) is $450,000. K's net worth is $900,000. The amount of J's qualified investment in foreign base company shipping operations in respect of the first note is $50,000, i.e.,

$$\frac{\$450,000}{\$900,000} \times \$100,000.$$

The amount of J's qualified investment in respect of the second note is zero (see the last sentence of paragraph (c)(1) of this section).

(d) *Partnerships*—(1) *In general.* A controlled foreign corporation's investment in a partnership at the close of any taxable year of such corporation shall be considered a qualified investment in foreign base company shipping operations to the extent of the proportion which such corporation's foreign base company shipping income for such taxable would bear to its gross income for such taxable year if—

(i) Such corporation had realized no income other than its distributive share of the partnership gross income, and

Reg. § 1.955A-2(c)(2)

(ii) Such corporation's income was adjusted in accordance with the rules stated in paragraph (a)(4)(ii)(B) and (D) of this section.

(2) *Transitional rule.* For purposes of subparagraph (1)(i) of this paragraph, the controlled foreign corporation's distributive share of the partnership gross income shall not include any amount attributable to income earned by the partnership before the first day of such corporation's first taxable year beginning after December 31, 1975.

(3) *Cross-reference.* See paragraph (g)(4) of this section for rules relating to the determination of the amount of a controlled foreign corporation's investment in a partnership.

(e) *Trusts*—(1) *In general.* An investment in a trust is not a qualified investment in foreign base company shipping operations.

(2) *Grantor trusts.* Notwithstanding subparagraph (1) of this paragraph, if a controlled foreign corporation is treated as the owner of any portion of a trust under Subpart E of Part I of Subchapter J (relating to grantors and others treated as substantial owners), then for purposes of this section such controlled foreign corporation is deemed to be the actual owner of such portion of the assets of the trust. Accordingly, its investments in such assets (as determined under paragraph (g)(5) of this section) may be treated as a qualified investment in foreign base company shipping operations.

(3) *Definitions.* For purposes of this section the term "trust" means a trust as defined in § 301.7701-4.

(f) *Excluded property.* For purposes of paragraph (a) of this section, property acquired principally for the purpose of artificially increasing the amount of a controlled foreign corporation's qualified investments in foreign base company shipping operations will not be recognized; whether an item of property is acquired principally for such purpose will depend upon all the facts and circumstances of each case. One of the factors that will be considered in making such a determination with respect to an item of property is whether the item is disposed of within 6 months after the date of its acquisition.

(g) *Amount attributable to property*—(1) *General rule.* For purposes of this section, the amount taken into account under section 955(b)(4) with respect to any property which constitutes a qualified investment in foreign base company shipping operations shall be its adjusted basis as of the applicable determination date, reduced by the outstanding principal amount of any liability (other than a liability described in subparagraph (2) of this paragraph) to which such property is subject on such date, including a liability secured only by the general credit of the controlled foreign corporation. Liabilities shall be taken into account in the following order:

(i) The adjusted basis of each and every item of corporate property shall be reduced by any specific charge (nonrecourse or otherwise) to which such item is subject. For this purpose, if a liability constitutes a specific charge against several items of property and cannot definitely be allocated to any single item of property, the specific charge shall be apportioned against each of such items of property in that ratio which the adjusted basis of such item on the applicable determination date bears to the adjusted basis of all such items on such date. The excess against property over the adjusted basis of such property shall be taken into account as a liability secured only by the general credit of the corporation.

(ii) A liability which is evidenced by an open account or which is secured only by the general credit of the controlled foreign corporation shall be apportioned against each and every item of corporate property in that ratio which the adjusted basis of such item on the applicable determination date (reduced as provided in subdivision (i) of this subparagraph) bears to the adjusted basis of all the corporate property on such date (reduced as provided in subdivision (i) of this subparagraph); provided that no liability shall be apportioned under this subdivision against any stock or obligations described in paragraph (h)(1) of this section.

(2) *Excluded charges.* For purposes of subparagraph (1) of this paragraph, a liability created principally for the purpose of artificially increasing or decreasing the amount of a controlled foreign corporation's qualified investments in foreign base company shipping operations will not be recognized. Whether a liability is created principally for such purpose will depend upon all the facts and circumstances of each case. One of the factors that will be considered in making such a determination with respect to a loan is whether the loan was both created after November 20, 1974, and is from a related person, as defined in section 954(d)(3) and paragraph (e) of § 1.954-1. Another such factor is whether the liability was created after March 29, 1975, in a taxable year beginning before January 1, 1976. For purposes of this paragraph (g)(2), payments on liabilities which are represented by an open account are credited against the account transactions arising earliest in time.

(3) *Statement required.* If for purposes of this section the adjusted basis of property which constitutes a qualified investment in foreign base

company shipping operations by a controlled foreign corporation is reduced on the ground that such property is subject to a liability, each United States shareholder shall attach to his return a statement setting forth the adjusted basis of the property before the reduction and the amount and nature of the reduction.

(4) *Partnership interest.* If a controlled foreign corporation is a partner in a partnership, its investment in the partnership taken into account under section 955(b)(4) shall be its adjusted basis in the partnership determined under section 722 or 742, adjusted as provided in section 705, and reduced as provided in subparagraph (1) of this paragraph. (However, if the partnership is not engaged solely in the conduct of foreign base company shipping operations, such amount shall be taken into account only to the extent provided in paragraph (d)(1) of this section.)

(5) *Grantor trust.* If a controlled foreign corporation is deemed to own a portion of the assets of a trust under paragraph (e)(2) of this section, then the amount taken into account under section 955(b)(4) with respect to such assets shall be determined as provided in subparagraph (1) of this paragraph by the application of the following rules:

(i) Such controlled foreign corporation's adjusted basis in such assets shall be deemed to be a proportionate share of the trust's adjusted basis in such assets, and

(ii) A proportionate share of the liabilities of the trust shall be deemed to be liabilities of such controlled foreign corporation and to constitute specific charges against such assets.

(6) *Translation into United States dollars.* The amounts determined in accordance with this paragraph shall be translated into United States dollars in accordance with the principles of § 1.964-1(e)(4).

(h) *Investments in shipping companies under prior law*—(1) *In general.* If an amount invested in stock or obligations of a less developed country shipping company described in § 1.955-5(b) is treated as a qualified investment in less developed countries under § 1.955-2 (applied without regard to paragraph (b)(5)(ii) thereof) on the applicable determination date for purposes of section 954(g) of section 955(a)(2) with respect to a taxable year beginning after December 31, 1975, then such amount shall be treated as a qualified investment in foreign base company shipping operations on such determination date. See section 955(b)(5).

(2) *Effect on prior law.* See § 1.955-2(b)(5)(ii) for the rule that investments which are treated as qualified investments in foreign base company shipping operations under subparagraph (1) of this paragraph shall not be treated as qualified investments in less developed countries for purposes of section 951(a)(1)(A)(ii).

(3) *Illustration.* The application of this paragraph may be illustrated by the following example:

Example. (a) Throughout the period here involved, controlled foreign corporation X owns 100 percent of the single class of stock of controlled foreign corporation Y. X and Y each use the calendar years as the taxable year. At the close of 1975, X's $50,000 investment in the stock of Y is treated as a qualified investment in less developed countries under § 1.955-2 (applied without regard to § 1.955-2(b)(5)(ii)), and Y is a less developed country shipping company described in § 1.955-5(b).

(b) On December 31, 1976, Y is still a less developed country shipping company and X's $50,000 investment in the stock of Y is still treated as a qualified investment in less developed countries under § 1.955-2 (applied without regard to § 1.955-2(b)(5)(ii)). Under subparagraph (1) of this paragraph, X's entire $50,000 investment in the stock of Y is treated as a qualified investment in foreign base company shipping operations.

(c) For 1977, Y's gross income is $10,000 and Y's foreign base company shipping income is $7,500. Since Y fails to meet the 80-percent income test of § 1.955-5(b)(1), Y is no longer a less developed country shipping company described in § 1.955-5(b), and X's investment in the stock of Y is no longer treated as a qualified investment in less developed countries under § 1.955-2 (applied without regard to § 1.955-2(b)(5)(ii)). However, assume that on December 31, 1977, Y's net worth (as defined in paragraph (c)(2)(i) of this section) is $100,000, that Y's qualified investments in foreign base company shipping operations (determined under this section) on December 31, 1977, are $75,000, and that X's investment in the stock of Y (as determined under paragraph (g) of this section) continues to be $50,000. Then $37,500, i.e.,

$$\frac{\$\ 75,000}{\$100,000} \times \$50,000$$

of X's $50,000 investment in the stock of Y is treated as a qualified investment in foreign company shipping operations under paragraph (c) of this section.

(d) For 1978, all of Y's gross income is foreign base company shipping income. Although Y is again a less developed country shipping company described in § 1.955-5(b), X's investment in the stock of Y is no longer treated as a qualified investment in less developed countries under § 1.955-2(b)(5)(iii). Thus, X's investment in the stock of Y is not treated as a qualified investment in foreign base company shipping operations under subparagraph (1) of this paragraph. However, X's investment in the stock of Y may be so treated under another provision of this section, as was the case in item (c) of this example. [Reg. § 1.955A-2.]

☐ [T.D. 7894, 5-11-83. Amended by T.D. 7959, 5-29-84.]

[Reg. § 1.955A-3]

§ 1.955A-3. Election as to qualified investments by related persons.—(a) *In general.* If a United States shareholder elects the benefits of section 955(b)(2) with respect to a related group (as defined in paragraph (b)(1) of this section) of controlled foreign corporations, then an investment in foreign base company shipping operation made by one member of such group will be treated as having been made by another member to the extent provided in paragraph (c)(4) of this section, and each member will be subject to the other provisions of paragraph (c) of this section. An election once made shall apply for the taxable year for which it is made and for all subsequent years unless the election is revoked or a new election is made to add one or more controlled foreign corporations to election coverage. For the manner of making an election under section 955(b)(2), and for rules relating to the revocation of such an election, see paragraph (d) of this section. For rules relating to the coordination of sections 955(b)(2) and 955(b)(3), see paragraph (e) of this section.

(b) *Related group*—(1) *Related group defined.* The term "related group" means two or more controlled foreign corporations, but only if all of the following requirements are met:

(i) All such corporations use the same taxable year,

(ii) The same United States shareholder controls each such corporation within the meaning of section 954(d)(3) at the end of such taxable year, and

(iii) Such United States shareholder elects to treat such corporations as a related group.

(iv) If any of the corporations is on a 52-53 week taxable year and if all the taxable years of the corporations end within the same 7-day period, the rule of paragraph (b)(1)(i) of this section shall be deemed satisfied.

(v) An election under paragraph (b)(1)(iii) of this section will not be valid in the case of an election by a U.S. shareholder (the "first U.S. shareholder") if—

(A) The first U.S. shareholder controls a second U.S. shareholder,

(B) The second U.S. shareholder controls one or more controlled foreign corporations, and

(C) Any of the controlled foreign corporations are the subject of the election by the first U.S. shareholder,

unless the second U.S. shareholder consents to the election by the first U.S. shareholder.

(2) *Group taxable years defined.* The "group taxable year" is the common taxable year of a related group.

(3) *Limitation.* If a United States shareholder elects to treat two or more corporations as a related group for a group taxable year (the "first group taxable year"), then such United States shareholder (and any other United States shareholder which is controlled by such shareholder) may not also elect to treat two or more other corporations as a related group for a group taxable year any day of which falls within the first group taxable year.

(4) *Illustrations.* The application of this paragraph may be illustrated by the following examples:

Example (1). Domestic corporation M owns 100 percent of the only class of stock of controlled foreign corporations A, B, C, D, and E. A, B, and C use the calendar year as the taxable year. D and E use the fiscal year ending on June 30 as the taxable year. M may elect to treat A, B, and C as a related group. However, M may not elect to treat C, D, and E as a related group.

Example (2). The facts are the same as in example (1). In addition, M elects to treat A, B, and C as a related group for the group taxable year which ends on December 31, 1976. M may not also elect to treat D and E as a related group for the group taxable year ending on June 30, 1977.

Example (3). United States shareholder A owns 60 percent of the only class of stock of controlled foreign corporation X and 40 percent of the only class of stock of controlled foreign corporation Y. United States shareholder B owns the other 40 percent of the stock of X and the other 60 percent of the stock of Y. Neither A nor B (nor both together) may elect to treat X and Y as a related group.

(c) *Effect of election.* If a United States shareholder elects to treat two or more controlled foreign corporations as a related group for any group taxable year then, for purposes of determining the foreign base company income (see § 1.954-1) and

Reg. § 1.955A-3(c)

the increase or decrease in qualified investments in foreign base company shipping operations (see §§ 1.954-7, 1.955A-1, and 1.955A-4) of each member of such group for such year, the following rules shall apply:

(1) *Intragroup dividends.* The gross income of each member of the related group shall be deemed not to include dividends received from any other member of such group, to the extent that such dividends are attributable (within the meaning of § 1.954-6(f)(4)) to foreign base company shipping income. In determining net foreign base company shipping income, deductions allocable to intragroup dividends attributable to foreign base company shipping income shall not be allowed.

(2) *Group excess deduction.* (i) The deduction allocable under § 1.954-1(c) to the foreign base company shipping income of each member of the related group shall be deemed to include such member's pro rata share of the group excess deduction.

(ii) The group excess deduction for the group taxable year is the sum of the excesses for each member of the related group (having an excess) of—

(A) The member's deductions (determined without regard to this subparagraph) allocable to foreign base company shipping income for such year, over

(B) The member's foreign base company shipping income for such year.

(iii) A member's pro rata share of the group excess deduction is the amount which bears the same ratio to such group excess deduction as—

(A) The excess of such member's foreign base company shipping income over the deductions (so determined) allocable thereto, bears to

(B) The sum of such excesses for each member of the related group having an excess.

(iv) For purposes of this subparagraph, "foreign base company shipping income" means foreign base company shipping income (as defined in § 1.954-6), reduced by excluding therefrom all amounts which are—

(A) Excluded from subpart F income under section 952(b) (relating to exclusion of United States income) or

(B) Excluded from foreign base company income under section 954(b)(4) (relating to exception for foreign corporation not availed of to reduce taxes).

(v) The application of this subparagraph may be illustrated by the following example:

Example. Controlled foreign corporations X, Y, and Z are a related group for calendar year 1976. The excess group deduction for 1976 is $9, X's pro rata share of the group excess deduction is $6, and Y's pro rata share is $3, determined as follows on the basis of the facts shown in the following table:

	X	Y	Z	Group
(1) Gross shipping income	$100	$90	$80	...
(2) Shipping deductions	60	70	89	...
(3) Net shipping income	40	20	(9)	...
(4) Group excess deduction				$9
(5) X's pro rata share of group excess deduction ($9 × $40/$60)	6			
(6) Y's pro rata share of group excess deduction ($9 × $20/$60)		3		

(3) *Intragroup investments.* On both of the determination dates applicable to the group taxable year for purposes of section 954(g) or section 955(a)(2), the qualified investments in foreign base company shipping tions of each member of the related group shall be deemed not to include stock of any other member of the related group. In addition, neither the gains nor the losses on dispositions of such stock during the group taxable year shall be taken into account under § 1.955A-1(b)(1)(ii) in determining the decrease in qualified investments in foreign company shipping operations of any member of such related group.

(4) *Gross excess investment.* (i) On the later (and only the later) of the two determination dates applicable to the group taxable year for purposes of section 954(g) or section 955(a)(2), the qualified investments in foreign base company shipping operations of each member of the related group shall be deemed to include such member's pro rata share of the group excess investment.

(ii) The group excess investment for the group taxable year is the sum of the excess for each member of the related group (having an excess) of—

(A) The member's increase in qualified investments in foreign base company shipping operations (determined under § 1.954-7 after the application of subparagraph (3) of this paragraph) for such year, over

(B) The member's foreign base company shipping income for such year.

(iii) A member's pro rata share of the group excess investment is the amount which

Reg. § 1.955A-3(c)(1)

bears the same ratio to such group excess investment as—

(A) Such member's shortfall in qualified investments bears to

(B) The sum of the shortfalls in qualified investments of each member of such related group having a shortfall.

(iv) If a member has an increase in qualified investments in foreign base company shipping operations (determined as provided in § 1.954-7 after the application of subparagraph (3) of this paragraph) for the group taxable year, then such member's "shortfall in qualified investments" is the excess of—

(A) Such member's foreign base company shipping income for such year, over

(B) Such increase.

(v) If a member has a decrease in qualified investments in foreign base company shipping operations (determined under § 1.955A-1(b)(1) or § 1.955A-4(a), whichever is applicable, after the application of subparagraph (3) of this paragraph) for the group taxable year, then such member's "shortfall in qualified investments" is the sum of—

(A) Such member's foreign base company shipping income for such year and

(B) Such decrease.

(vi) For purposes of this subparagraph, "foreign base company shipping income" means foreign base company shipping income (as defined in subparagraph (2)(iv) of this paragraph), reduced by the deductions allocable thereto under § 1.954-1(c) (including the additional deductions described in subparagraph (2) of this paragraph).

(vii) The application of paragraphs (c)(1), (3), and (4) of this section may be illustrated by the following example:

Example. (a) Controlled foreign corporations R, S, and T are a related group for calendar year 1977. R and S do not own the stock of any member of the related group.

(b) On December 31, 1977, T has qualified investments in foreign base company shipping operations (determined without regard to paragraphs (c)(3) and (4)) of $105, of which $15 consists of stock of S. After application of paragraph (c)(3) (but before application of paragraph (c)(4)), on December 31, 1977, T has qualified investments in foreign base company shipping operations of $90, determined as follows:

(1) Qualified investments (determined without regard to paragraph (c)(3)) on December 31, 1977 .... $105
(2) Less: Qualified investments in stock of another member of a related group (as required by paragraph (c)(3)) 15
(3) Balance 90

(c) During 1977, T's foreign base company shipping income is $180, determined without regard to paragraph (c)(1). Included in the $180 is $5 in dividends in respect of T's stock in S. During 1977, T has shipping deductions of $91. Of T's shipping deductions, $1 is allocable to the dividends from S. After application of paragraph (c)(1), T's net shipping income during 1977 is $85, determined as follows:

(1) Foreign base company shipping income $180
(2) Less: intragroup dividends (as required by paragraph (c)(1)) 5
(3) Balance 175
(4) Shipping deductions $91
(5) Less: deductions allocable to intragroup dividends (as required by paragraph (c)(1)) 1
(6) Balance 90
(7) Net shipping income (line (3) minus line (6)) 85

(d) During 1977 (without regard to paragraph (c)(4)), R's increase in qualified investments in foreign base company shipping operations is $120; S's decrease is $55; and T's increase is $35, determined on the basis of the facts shown in the following table. In all cases, the listed amounts of qualified investments on December 31, 1976, reflect any adjustments required by paragraph (c)(3) for 1976, but not any adjustment required by paragraph (c)(4) for 1976 (see §§ 1.955A-3(c)(3) and (4)(i)).

	R	S	T
(1) Qualified investments on December 31, 1977 (in the case of T, taken from line (3) of part (b) of this example)	$220	$150	$90
(2) Qualified investments on December 31, 1976	100	205	55
(3) Increase (decrease) (line (1) minus (2))	120	(55)	35

Reg. § 1.955A-3(c)(4)

49,324 Income from Sources Without the United States

See p. 20,601 for regulations not amended to reflect law changes

(e) In 1977, R's net shipping income is $100; S's is $95; and T's is $85, determined as follows:

	R	S	T
(1) Gross foreign base company shipping income (in the case of T, taken from line (3) of part (c) of this example)	$200	$180	$175
(2) Shipping deductions (in the case of T, taken from line (6) of part (c) of this example)	$100	$ 85	$ 90
(3) Net shipping income (line (1) minus line (2))	$100	$ 95	$ 85

(f) By application of paragraph (c)(4) for 1977, S's pro rata share of the group excess investment is $15, and T's pro rata share is $5, determined as follows:

	R	S	T	Group
(1) Net shipping income (taken from line (3) of part (e) of this example)	$100	$ 95	$85	....
(2) Increase (decrease) in qualified investments (taken from line (3) of part (d) of this example)	120	(55)	35	....
(3) Excess investment	20	....	....	$ 20
(4) Shortfall	....	150	50	200
(5) S's pro rata share of group excess investment ($20 × $150/$200)	....	15	...	....
(6) T's pro rata share of group excess investment ($20 × $50/$200)	....	....	5	....

(g) After application of paragraph (c)(4), for purposes of determining their increase or decrease in qualified investments in foreign base company shipping operations for 1977, on December 31, 1977, the amount of R's qualified investments is $200; the amount of S's is $165; and the amount of T's is $95, determined as follows:

(1) Qualified investments on December 31, 1977 (taken from line (1) of part (d) of this example)	$220
(2) Plus: pro rata share of group excess investment (as required by paragraph (c)(4)) (taken from lines (5) and (6) of part (f) of this example)	....
(3) Minus: Excess investment treated as investments of related group members (taken from line (3) of part (f) of this example)	20
(4) Total qualified investments	200

(h) After application of paragraph (c)(1), (3), and (4), during 1977, R's increase in qualified investments in foreign base company shipping operations is $100; S's decrease is $40; and T's increase is $40, determined as set forth in the table below. In all cases, the listed amounts of qualified investments on December 31, 1976, reflect any similar adjustments required by paragraph (c)(3) for 1976, but not any adjustment required by paragraph (c)(4) for 1976 (see §§ 1.955A-3(c)(3) and (4)(i)).

	R	S	T
(1) Qualified investments on December 31, 1977 (taken from line (4) of part (g) of this example)	$200	$165	$95
(2) Qualified investments on December 31, 1976 (see line (2) of part (d) of this example)	$100	$205	$55
(3) Increase (decrease) (line (1) minus line (2))	$100	$(40)	$40

(5) *Collateral effect.* (i) An election under this section by a United States shareholder to treat two or more controlled foreign corporations as a related group for a group taxable year shall have no effect on—

(A) Any other United States shareholder (including a minority shareholder of a member of such related group),

(B) Any other controlled foreign corporation, and

(C) The foreign personal holding company income, foreign base company sales income, and foreign base company services income, and the deductions allocable under § 1.954-1(c) thereto, of any member of such related group.

(ii) See § 1.952-1(c)(2)(ii) for the effect of an election under this section on the computation of earnings and profits and deficits in earnings and profits under section 952(c) and (d).

(iii) The application of this subparagraph may be illustrated by the following example:

Example. United States shareholder A owns 80 percent of the only class of stock of controlled foreign corporations X and Y. United States shareholder B owns the other 20 percent of the stock of X and Y. X and Y both use the calendar year as the taxable year. A elects to treat

Reg. § 1.955A-3(c)(5)

X and Y as a related group for 1977. For purposes of determining the amounts includible in B's gross income under section 951(a) in respect of X and Y, the election made by A shall be disregarded and all of B's computations shall be made without regard to this section, as illustrated in § 1.952-3(d).

(d) *Procedure.*—(1) *Time and manner of making election.* A United States shareholder shall make an election under this section to treat two or more controlled foreign corporations as a related group for a group taxable year and subsequent years by filing a statement to such effect with the return for the taxable year within which or with which such group taxable year ends. The statement shall include the following information:

(i) The name, address, taxpayer identification number, and taxable year of the United States shareholder;

(ii) The name, address, and taxable year of each controlled foreign corporation which is a member of the related group and is to be subject to the election; and

(iii) A schedule showing the calculations by which the amounts described in this section have been determined for the taxable year for which the election is first effective. With respect to each subsequent taxable year to which the election applies, a new schedule showing calculations of such amounts for that taxable year must be filed with the return for that taxable year. A consent to an election required by paragraph (b)(1)(v) of this section shall include the same information required for the election statement.

(2) *Revocation.* (i) Except as provided in subdivision (ii) of this subparagraph, an election under this section by a United States shareholder shall be binding for the group taxable year for which it is made and for subsequent years.

(ii) Upon application by the United States shareholder (and any other United States shareholder controlled by such shareholder which consented under paragraph (b)(1)(v) of this section to the election), an election made under this section may, subject to the approval of the Commissioner, be revoked. An application to revoke the election, as of a specified group taxable year, with respect to one or more (but not all) controlled foreign corporations, subject to an election shall be deemed to be an application to revoke the election. Approval will not be granted unless a material and substantial change in circumstances occurs which could not have been anticipated when the election was made. The application for consent to revocation shall be made by mailing a letter for such purpose to Commissioner of Internal Revenue, Attention: T:C:C, Washington, D.C. 20224, containing a statement of the facts which justify such consent. If a member of a related group subject to an election ceases to meet the requirements of paragraph (b) of this section for membership in the group by reason of any action taken by it or any member of the group or the electing United States shareholder, then the election will be deemed to be revoked as of the beginning of the taxable year in which such action occurred. If such action is taken principally for the purpose of revoking the election without applying for and obtaining the approval of the Commissioner to the revocation, then no further election covering any member of that related group may be made by any United States shareholder for the remainder of the taxable year in which the action occurred and the five succeeding taxable years.

(e) *Coordination with section 955(b)(3).* If a United States shareholder elects under this section to treat two or more controlled foreign corporations as a related group for any taxable year, and if such United States shareholder is required under § 1.955A-4(c)(2) for purposes of filing any return to estimate the qualified investments in foreign base company shipping operations of any member of such group, then such United States shareholder shall, for purposes of filing such return, determine the amount includible in his gross income in respect of each member of such related group on the basis of such estimate. If the actual amount of such investments is not the same as the amount of the estimate, the United States shareholder shall immediately notify the Commissioner. The Commissioner will thereupon redetermine the amount of tax of such United States shareholder for the year or years with respect to which the incorrect amount was taken into account. The amount of tax, if any, due upon such redetermination shall be paid by the United States shareholder upon notice and demand by the district director. The amount of tax, if any, shown by such redetermination to have been overpaid shall be credited or refunded to the United States shareholder in accordance with the provisions of sections 6402 and 6511 and the regulations thereunder. If a United States shareholder elects under this section and if the United States shareholder has made an election under section 955(b)(3) as to at least one member of the related group, then the qualified investment amounts necessary for the calculations of paragraphs (c)(3) and (4) of this section shall be obtained, for each member of the related group, as of the determination dates applicable to each of the members.

(f) *Illustrations.* The application of this section may be illustrated by the following examples:

Reg. § 1.955A-3(f)

Income from Sources Without the United States
See p. 20,601 for regulations not amended to reflect law changes

Example (1). (a) Controlled foreign corporations X and Y are wholly owned subsidiaries of domestic corporation M. X and Y use the calendar year as the taxable year. For 1977, X and Y are not export trade corporations (as defined in section 971(a)), nor have they any income derived from the insurance of United States risks (within the meaning of section 953(a)). M does not elect to treat X and Y as a related group for 1977.

(b) For 1977, X and Y each have gross income (determined as provided in § 1.954-6(h)(1)) of $1,000. X's foreign base company income is $20 and Y's foreign base company shipping income is $0, determined as follows, based on the facts shown in the following table:

	X	Y
(1) Foreign base company shipping income	$1,000	$1,000
(2) Less: amounts excluded from subpart F income under section 952(b) (relating to U.S. income) and amounts excluded from foreign base company income under section 954(b)(4) (relating to corporation not availed of to reduce taxes)	0	0
(3) Balance	1,000	1,000
(4) Less: deductions allocable under § 1.954-1(c) to balance	800	1,040
(5) Remaining balance	200	0
(6) Less: increase in qualified investments in foreign base company shipping operations	180	.....
(7) Foreign base company income	20	.....

(c) For 1977, Y has a withdrawal of previously excluded subpart F income from investment in foreign base company shipping operations of $20, determined as follows, on the basis of the facts shown in the following table:

(1) Qualified investments in foreign base company shipping operations at Dec. 31, 1976	$1,210
(2) Less: qualified investments in foreign base company shipping operations at Dec. 31, 1977	1,170
(3) Balance	40
(4) Less: excess of recognized losses over recognized gains on sales during 1977 of qualified investments in foreign base company shipping operations	20
(5) Tentative decrease in qualified investments in foreign base company shipping operations for 1977	20
(6) Limitation described in § 1.955A-1(b)(2)	160
(7) Y's amount of previously excluded subpart F income withdrawn from investment in foreign base company shipping operations (lesser of lines (5) and (6))	20

Example (2). (a) The facts are the same as in example (1), except that M does elect to treat X and Y as a related group for 1977.

(b) The group excess deduction, which is solely attributable to Y's net shipping loss, is $40 (i.e., $1,040 − $1,000). Since X is the only member of the related group with net shipping income, X's pro rata share of the group excess deduction is the entire $40 amount.

(c) X's foreign base company income for 1977 is zero, determined as follows:

(1) Preliminary net foreign base company shipping income (line (b)(5) of example (1))	$ 200
(2) Less: X's pro rata share of group excess deduction	$ 40
(3) Remaining balance	160
(4) Less: increase in qualified investments in foreign base company shipping operations	180
(5) Foreign base company income	0

(d) The group excess investment, which is solely attributable to X's excess investment, is $20 (i.e., $180 minus $160). Since Y is the only member of the related group with a shortfall in qualified investments, Y's share of the group excess investment is the entire $20 amount.

(e) During 1976 and 1977, Y owns no stock of X. Y's withdrawal of previously excluded subpart F income from investment in foreign base company shipping operations for 1977 is zero, determined as follows:

Reg. § 1.955A-3(f)

Income from Sources Without the United States

(1) Qualified investments at Dec. 31, 1976	$1,210
(2) (i) Qualified investments at Dec. 31, 1977 (determined without regard to paragraph (c)(4) of this section)	1,170
(ii) Y's pro rata share of group excess investment	20
(iii) Total qualified investments at Dec. 31, 1977 (line (i) plus line (ii))	1,190
(3) Balance (line (1) minus line (2)(iii)) . .	20
(4) Less: excess of recognized losses over recognized gains on sales during 1977 of qualified investments in foreign base company shipping operations . . .	20
(5) Decrease in qualified investments for 1977	0

[Reg. § 1.955A-3.]

☐ [T.D. 7894, 5-11-83. Amended by T.D. 7959, 5-29-84.]

[Reg. § 1.955A-4]

§ 1.955A-4. Election as to date of determining qualified investment in foreign base company shipping operations.—(a) *Nature of election.* In lieu of determining the increase under the provisions of section 954(g) and § 1.954-7(a) or the decrease under the provisions of section 955(a)(2) and § 1.955A-1(b) in a controlled foreign corporation's qualified investments in foreign base company shipping operations for a taxable year in the manner provided in such provisions, a United States shareholder of such controlled foreign corporation may elect, under the provisions of section 955(b)(3) and this section, to determine such increase in accordance with the provisions of § 1.954-7(b) and to determine such decrease by ascertaining the amount by which—

(1) Such controlled foreign corporation's qualified investments in foreign base company shipping operations at the close of such taxable year exceed its qualified investments in foreign base company shipping operations at the close of the taxable year immediately following such taxable year, and reducing such excess by

(2) The amount determined under § 1.955A-1(b)(1)(ii) for such taxable year,

subject to the limitation provided in § 1.955A-1(b)(2) for such taxable year. An election under this section may be made with respect to each controlled foreign corporation with respect to which a person is a United States shareholder within the meaning of section 951(b), but the election may not be exercised separately with respect to the increases and the decreases of such controlled foreign corporation. If an election is made under this section to determine the increase of a controlled foreign corporation in accordance with the provisions of § 1.954-7(b), subsequent decreases of such controlled foreign corporation shall be determined in accordance with this paragraph and not in accordance with § 1.955A-1(b).

(b) *Time and manner of making election*—(1) *Without consent.* An election under this section with respect to a controlled foreign corporation shall be made without the consent of the Commissioner by a United States shareholder's filing a statement to such effect with his return for his taxable year in which or with which ends the first taxable year of such controlled foreign corporation in which—

(i) Such shareholder is a United States shareholder, and

(ii) Such controlled foreign corporation realizes foreign base company shipping income, as defined in § 1.954-6.

The statement shall contain the name and address of the controlled foreign corporation and identification of such first taxable year of such corporation.

(2) *With consent.* An election under this section with respect to a controlled foreign corporation may be made by a United States shareholder at any time with the consent of the Commissioner. Consent will not be granted unless the United States shareholder and the Commissioner agree to the terms, conditions, and adjustments under which the election will be effected. The application for consent to elect shall be made by the United States shareholder's mailing a letter for such purpose to the Commissioner of Internal Revenue, Washington, D.C. 20224. The application shall be mailed before the close of the first taxable year of the controlled foreign corporation with respect to which the shareholder desires to compute an amount described in section 954(b)(2) in accordance with the election provided in this section. The application shall include the following information:

(i) The name, address, and taxpayer identification number, and taxable year of the United States shareholder;

(ii) The name and address of the controlled foreign corporation;

(iii) The first taxable year of the controlled foreign corporation for which income is to be computed under the election;

(iv) The amount of the controlled foreign corporation's qualified investments in foreign base company shipping operations at the close of its preceding taxable year; and

(v) The sum of the amounts excluded under section 954(b)(2) and § 1.954-1(b)(1) from the foreign base company income of the controlled foreign corporation for all prior taxable years during which such shareholder was a United States shareholder of such corporation and the sum of the amounts of its previously excluded subpart F income withdrawn from investment in foreign base company shipping operations for all prior taxable years during which such shareholder was a United States shareholder of such corporation.

(c) *Effect of election*—(1) *General.* Except as provided in subparagraphs (3) and (4) of this paragraph, an election under this section with respect to a controlled foreign corporation shall be binding on the United States shareholder and shall apply to all qualified investments in foreign base company shipping operations acquired, or disposed of, by such controlled foreign corporation during the taxable year following its taxable year for which income is first computed under the election and during all succeeding taxable years of such corporation.

(2) *Returns.* Any return of a United States shareholder required to be filed before the completion of a period with respect to which determinations are to be made as to a controlled foreign corporation's qualified investments in foreign base company shipping operations for purposes of computing such shareholder's taxable income shall be filed on the basis of an estimate of the amount of the controlled foreign corporation's qualified investments in foreign base company shipping operations at the close of the period. If the actual amount of such investments is not the same as the amount of the estimate, the United States shareholder shall immediately notify the Commissioner. The Commissioner will thereupon redetermine the amount of tax of such United States shareholder for the year or years with respect to which the incorrect amount was taken into account. The amount of tax, if any, due upon such redetermination shall be paid by the United States shareholder upon notice and demand by the district director. The amount of tax, if any, shown by such redetermination to have been overpaid shall be credited or refunded to the United States shareholder in accordance with the provisions of sections 6402 and 6511 and the regulations thereunder.

(3) *Revocation.* Upon application by the United States shareholder, the election made under this section may, subject to the approval of the Commissioner, be revoked. Approval will not be granted unless the United States shareholder and the Commissioner agree to the terms, conditions, and adjustments under which the revocation will be effected. Unless such agreement provides otherwise, the change in the controlled foreign corporation's qualified investments in foreign base company shipping operations for its first taxable year for which income is computed without regard to the election previously made will be considered to be zero for purposes of effectuating the revocation. The application for consent to revocation shall be made by the United States shareholder's mailing a letter for such purpose to the Commissioner of Internal Revenue, Washington, D.C. 20224. The application shall be mailed before the close of the first taxable year of the controlled foreign corporation with respect to which the shareholder desires to compute the amounts described in section 954(b)(2) or 955(a) without regard to the election provided in this section. The application shall include the following information:

(i) The name, address, and taxpayer identification number of the United States shareholder;

(ii) The name and address of the controlled foreign corporation;

(iii) The taxable year of the controlled foreign corporation for which such amounts are to be so computed;

(iv) The amount of the controlled foreign corporation's qualified investments in foreign base company shipping operations at the close of its preceding taxable year;

(v) The sum of the amounts excluded under section 954(b)(2) and § 1.954-1(b)(1) from the foreign base company income of the controlled foreign corporation for all prior taxable years during which such shareholder was a United States shareholder of such corporation and the sum of the amounts of its previously excluded subpart F income withdrawn from investment in foreign base company shipping operations for all prior taxable years during which such shareholder was a United States shareholder of such corporation; and

(vi) The reasons for the request for consent to revocation.

(4) *Transfer of stock.* If during any taxable year of a controlled foreign corporation—

(i) A United States shareholder who has made an election under this section with respect to such controlled foreign corporation sells, exchanges, or otherwise disposes of all or part of his stock in such controlled foreign corporation, and

(ii) The foreign corporation is a controlled foreign corporation immediately after the sale, exchange, or other disposition,

then, with respect to the stock so sold, exchanged, or disposed of, the change in the controlled foreign corporation's qualified investments in foreign

Reg. § 1.955A-4(c)(1)

base company shipping operations for such taxable year shall be considered to be zero. If the United States shareholder's successor in interest is entitled to and does make an election under paragraph (b)(1) of this section to determine the controlled foreign corporation's increase in qualified investments in foreign base company shipping operations for the taxable year in which he acquires such stock, such increase with respect to the stock so acquired shall be determined in accordance with the provisions of § 1.954-7(b)(1). If the controlled foreign corporation realizes no foreign base company income from which amounts are excluded under section 954(b)(2) and § 1.954-1(b)(1) for the taxable year in which the United States shareholder's successor in interest acquires such stock and such successor in interest makes an election under paragraph (b)(1) of this section with respect to a subsequent taxable year of such controlled foreign corporation, the increase in the controlled foreign corporation's qualified investments in foreign base company shipping operations for such subsequent taxable year shall be determined in accordance with the provisions of § 1.954-7(b)(2).

(d) *Illustrations.* The application of this section may be illustrated by the following examples:

Example (1). Foreign Corporation A is a wholly owned subsidiary of domestic Corporation M. Both corporations use the calendar year as a taxable year. In a statement filed with its return for 1977, M makes an election under section 955(b)(3) and the election remains in force for the taxable year 1978. At December 31, 1978, A's qualified investments in foreign base company shipping operations amount to $100,000; and, at December 31, 1979, to $80,000. For purposes of paragraph (a)(1) of this section, A Corporation's decrease in qualified investments in foreign base company shipping operations for the taxable year 1978 is $20,000 and is determined by ascertaining the amount by which A Corporation's qualified investments in foreign base company shipping operations at December 31, 1978 ($100,000) exceed its qualified investments in foreign base company shipping operations at December 31, 1979 ($80,000).

Example (2). The facts are the same as in example (1) except that A experiences no changes in qualified investments in foreign base company shipping operations during its taxable years 1980 and 1981. If M's election were to remain in force, A's acquisitions and dispositions of qualified investments in foreign base company shipping operations during A's taxable year 1982 would be taken into account in determining whether A has experienced an increase or a decrease in qualified investments in foreign base company shipping operations for its taxable year 1981. However, M duly files before the close of A's taxable year 1981 an application for consent to revocation of M Corporation's election under section 955(b)(3), and, pursuant to an agreement between the Commissioner and M, consent is granted by the Commissioner. Assuming such agreement does not provide otherwise, A's change in qualified investments in foreign base company shipping operations for its taxable year 1981 is zero because the effect of the revocation of the election is to treat acquisitions and dispositions of qualified investments in foreign base company shipping operations actually occurring in 1982 as having occurred in such year rather than in 1981.

Example (3). The facts are the same as in example (2) except that A's qualified investments in foreign base company shipping operations at December 31, 1982, amount to $70,000. For purposes of paragraph (b)(1)(i) of § 1.955A-1, the decrease in A's qualified investments in foreign base company shipping operations for the taxable year 1982 is $10,000 and is determined by ascertaining the amount by which A's qualified investments in foreign base company shipping operations at December 31, 1981 ($80,000) exceed its qualified investments in foreign base company shipping operations at December 31, 1982 ($70,000).

Example (4). The facts are the same as in Example (1). Assume further that on September 30, 1979, M sells 40 percent of the only class of stock of A to N Corporation, a domestic corporation. N uses the calendar year as a taxable year. A remains a controlled foreign corporation immediately after such sale of its stock. A's qualified investment in foreign base company shipping operations at December 31, 1980, amount to $90,000. The changes in A Corporation's qualified investments in foreign base company shipping operations occurring in its taxable year 1979 are considered to be zero with respect to the 40-percent stock interest acquired by N Corporation. The entire $20,000 reduction in A Corporation's qualified investments in foreign base company shipping operations which occurs during the taxable year 1979 is taken into account by M for purposes of paragraph (c)(1) of this section in determining its tax liability for the taxable year 1978. A's increase in qualified investments in foreign base company shipping operations for the taxable year 1979 with respect to the 60-percent stock interest retained by M is $6,000 and is determined by ascertaining M's pro rata share (60 percent) of the amount by which A's qualified investments in foreign base company shipping operations at December 31, 1980 ($90,000) exceed

Reg. § 1.955A-4(d)

its qualified investments in foreign base company shipping operations at December 31, 1979 ($80,000). N does not make an election under section 955(b)(3) in its return for its taxable year 1980. Corporation A's increase in qualified investments in foreign base company shipping operations for the taxable year 1980 with respect to the 40-percent stock interest acquired by N is $4,000. [Reg. § 1.955A-4.]

☐ [T.D. 7894, 5-11-83.]

[Reg. § 1.956-1]

§ 1.956-1. Shareholder's pro rata share of a controlled foreign corporation's increase in earnings invested in United States property.— (a) *In general.* Section 956(a)(1) and paragraph (b) of this section provide rules for determining the amount of a controlled foreign corporation's earnings invested in United States property at the close of any taxable year. Such amount is the aggregate amount invested in United States property to the extent such amount would have constituted a dividend if it had been distributed on such date. Subject to the provisions of section 951(a)(4) and the regulations thereunder, a United States shareholder of a controlled foreign corporation is required to include in his gross income his pro rata share, as determined in accordance with paragraph (c) of this section, of the controlled foreign corporation's increase for any taxable year in earnings invested in United States property but only to the extent such share is not excludable from his gross income under the provisions of section 959(a)(2) and the regulations thereunder.

(b) *Amount of a controlled foreign corporation's investment of earnings in United States property*—(1) *Dividend limitation.* The amount of a controlled foreign corporation's earnings invested at the close of its taxable year in United States property is the aggregate amount of such property held, directly or indirectly, by such corporation at the close of its taxable year to the extent such amount would have constituted a dividend under section 316 and §§ 1.316-1 and 1.316-2 (determined after the application of section 955(a)) if it had been distributed on such closing day. For purposes of this subparagraph, the determination of whether an amount would have constituted a dividend if distributed shall be made without regard to the provisions of section 959(d) and the regulations thereunder.

(2) *Aggregate amount of United States property.* For purposes of determining an increase in earnings invested in United States property for any taxable year beginning after December 31, 1975, the aggregate amount of United States property held by a controlled foreign corporation at the close of—

(i) Any taxable year beginning after December 31, 1975, and

(ii) The last taxable year beginning before January 1, 1976

does not include stock or obligations of a domestic corporation described in section 956(b)(2)(F) or movable property described in section 956(b)(2)(G).

(3) *Treatment of earnings and profits.* For purposes of making the determination under subparagraph (1) of this paragraph as to whether an amount of investment would have constituted a dividend if distributed at the close of any taxable year of a controlled foreign corporation, earnings and profits of the controlled foreign corporation shall be considered not to include any amounts which are attributable to—

(i) Amounts which have been included in the gross income of a United States shareholder of such controlled foreign corporation under section 951(a)(1)(B) (or which would have been so included but for section 959(a)(2)) and have not been distributed, or

(ii)(*a*) Amounts which are included in the gross income of a United States shareholder of such controlled foreign corporation under section 551(b) or would be so included under such section but for the fact that such amounts were distributed to such shareholder during the taxable year, or

(*b*) Amounts which, for any prior taxable year, have been included in the gross income of a United States shareholder of such controlled foreign corporation under section 551(b) and have not been distributed.

The rules of this subparagraph apply only in determining the limitation on a controlled foreign corporation's increase in earnings invested in United States property. See section 959 and the regulations thereunder for limitations on the exclusion from gross income of previously taxed earnings and profits.

(4) [Reserved.]

(c) *Shareholder's pro rata share of increase*—(1) *General rule.* A United States shareholder's pro rata share of a controlled foreign corporation's increase for any taxable year in earnings invested in United States property is the amount determined by subtracting the shareholder's pro rata share of—

(i) The controlled foreign corporation's earnings invested in United States property at the close of its preceding taxable year, as determined under paragraph (b) of this section, reduced by amounts paid by such corporation during such preceding taxable year to which section 959(c)(1)

Income from Sources Without the United States

See p. 20,601 for regulations not amended to reflect law changes

and the regulations thereunder apply, from his pro rata share of

(ii) The controlled foreign corporation's earnings invested in United States property at the close of its current taxable year, as determined under paragraph (b) of this section.

(2) *Illustration.* The application of this paragraph may be illustrated by the following examples:

Example (1). A is a United States shareholder and direct owner of 60 percent of the only class of stock of R Corporation, a controlled foreign corporation during the entire period here involved. Both A and R Corporation use the calendar year as a taxable year. Corporation R's aggregate investment in United States property on December 31, 1964, which would constitute a dividend (as determined under paragraph (b) of this section) if distributed on such date is $150,000. During the taxable year 1964, R Corporation distributed $50,000 to which section 959(c)(1) applies. Corporation R's aggregate investment in United States property on December 31, 1965, is $250,000; and R Corporation's current and accumulated earnings and profits on such date (determined as provided in paragraph (b) of this section) are $225,000. A's pro rata share of R Corporation's increase for 1965 in earnings invested in United States property is $75,000, determined as follows:

(i) Aggregate investment in United States property on Dec. 31, 1965	$250,000
(ii) Current and accumulated earnings and profits on December 31, 1965	225,000
(iii) Amount of earnings invested in United States property on December 31, 1965, which would constitute a dividend if distributed on such date (lesser of item (i) or item (ii))	225,000
(iv) Aggregate investment in United States property on December 31, 1964, which would constitute a dividend if distributed on such date ....$150,000 Less: Amounts distributed during 1964 to which sec. 959(c)(1) applies ....$ 50,000	$100,000
(v) R Corporation's increase for 1965 in earnings invested in United States property (item (iii) minus item (iv))	$125,000
(vi) A's pro rata share of R Corporation's increase for 1965 in earnings invested in United States property (item (v) times 60 percent)	75,000

Example (2). The facts are the same as in example (1), except that R Corporation's current and accumulated earnings and profits on December 31, 1965, are $100,000 instead of $225,000. Accordingly, even though R Corporation's aggregate investment in United States property on December 31, 1965, of $250,000 exceeds the net amount ($100,000) taken into account under subparagraph (1)(i) of this paragraph as of December 31, 1964, by $150,000, there is no increase for taxable year 1965 in earnings invested in United States property because of the dividend limitation of paragraph (b)(1) of this section. Corporation R's aggregate investment in United States property on December 31, 1966, is unchanged ($250,000). Corporation R's current and accumulated earnings and profits on December 31, 1966, are $175,000, and, as a consequence, its aggregate investment in United States property which would constitute a dividend if distributed on that date is $175,000. Corporation R pays no amount during 1965 to which section 959(c)(1) applies. Corporation R's increase for the taxable year 1966 in earnings invested in United States property is $75,000, and A's pro rata share of that amount is $45,000 ($75,000 times 60 percent).

(d) *Date and basis of determinations.* The determinations made under paragraph (c)(1)(i) of this section with respect to the close of the preceding taxable year of a controlled foreign corporation and under paragraph (c)(1)(ii) with respect to the close of the current taxable year of such controlled foreign corporation, for purposes of determining the United States shareholder's pro rata share of such corporation's increased investment of earnings in United States property for the current taxable year, shall be made as of the last day of the current taxable year of such corporation but on the basis of stock owned, within the meaning of section 958(a) and the regulations thereunder, by such United States shareholder on the last day of the current taxable year of the foreign corporation on which such corporation is a controlled foreign corporation. See the last sentence of section 956(a)(2). The application of this paragraph may be illustrated from the following example:

Example. Domestic corporation M owns 60 percent of the only class of stock of A Corporation, a controlled foreign corporation during the entire period here involved. Both M Corporation and A Corporation use the calendar year as a taxable year. Corporation A's investment of earnings in

Reg. § 1.956-1(d)

United States property at the close of the taxable year 1963 is $100,000, as determined under paragraph (b) of this section, and M Corporation includes its pro rata share of such amount ($60,000) in gross income for its taxable year 1963. On June 1, 1964, M Corporation acquires an additional 25 percent of A Corporation's outstanding stock from a person who is not a United States person as defined in section 957(d). Corporation A's investment of earnings in United States property at the close of the taxable year 1964, as determined under paragraph (b) of this section, is unchanged ($100,000). Corporation A pays no amount during 1963 to which section 959(c)(1) applies. Corporation M is not required, by reason of the acquisition in 1964 of A Corporation's stock, to include an additional amount in its gross income with respect to A Corporation's investment of earnings in United States property even though the earnings invested in United States property by A Corporation attributable to the stock acquired by M Corporation were not previously taxed. The determination made under paragraph (c)(1)(i) of this section as well as the determination made under paragraph (c)(1)(ii) of this section with respect to A Corporation's investment for 1964 of earnings in United States property are made on the basis of stock owned by M Corporation (85 percent) at the close of 1964.

(e) *Amount attributable to property*—(1) *General rule.* Except as provided in subparagraph (2) of this paragraph, for purposes of paragraph (b)(1) of this section, the amount taken into account with respect to any United States property shall be its adjusted basis, as of the applicable determination date, reduced by any liability (other than a liability described in subparagraph (3) of this paragraph) to which such property is subject on such date. To be taken into account under this subparagraph, a liability must constitute a specific charge against the property involved. Thus, a liability evidenced by an open account or a liability secured only by the general credit of the controlled foreign corporation will not be taken into account. On the other hand, if a liability constitutes a specific charge against several items of property and cannot definitely be allocated to any single item of property, the liability shall be apportioned against each of such items of property in that ratio which the adjusted basis of such item on the applicable determination date bears to the adjusted basis of all such items at such time. A liability in excess of the adjusted basis of the property which is subject to such liability shall not be taken into account for the purpose of reducing the adjusted basis of other property which is not subject to such liability.

(2) *Rule for pledges and guarantees.* For the purposes of this section the amount taken into account with respect to any pledge or guarantee described in paragraph (c)(1) of § 1.956-2 shall be the unpaid principal amount on the applicable determination date of the obligation with respect to which the controlled foreign corporation is a pledgor or guarantor.

(3) *Excluded charges.* For purposes of subparagraph (1) of this paragraph, a specific charge created with respect to any item of property principally for the purpose of artificially increasing or decreasing the amount of a controlled foreign corporation's investment of earnings in United States property will not be recognized; whether a specific charge is created principally for such purpose will depend upon all the facts and circumstances of each case. One of the factors that will be considered in making such a determination with respect to a loan is whether the loan is from a related person, as defined in section 954(d)(3) and paragraph (e) of § 1.954-1.

(4) *Statement required.* If for purposes of this section a United States shareholder of a controlled foreign corporation reduces the adjusted basis of property which constitutes United States property on the ground that such property is subject to a liability, he shall attach to his return a statement setting forth the adjusted basis of the property before the reduction and the amount and nature of the reduction. [Reg. § 1.956-1.]

☐ [T.D. 6704, 2-19-64. *Amended by* T.D. 6795, 1-28-65, T.D. 7712, 8-6-80 *and* T.D. 8209, 6-13-88.]

[Reg. § 1.956-1T]

§ 1.956-1T. **Shareholder's pro rata share of a controlled foreign corporation's increase in earnings invested in United States property (temporary).**—(a) (reserved).

(b)(1)—(3) (reserved).

(b)(4) *Treatment of certain investments of earnings in United States property.* (i) *Special rule.* For purposes of § 1.956-1(b)(1) of the regulations, a controlled foreign corporation will be considered to hold indirectly (A) the investments in United States property held on its behalf by a trustee or a nominee or (B) at the discretion of the District Director, investments in U.S. property acquired by any other foreign corporation that is controlled by the controlled foreign corporation, if one of the principal purposes for creating, organizing, or funding (through capital contributions or debt) such other foreign corporation is to avoid the application of section 956 with respect to the controlled foreign corporation. For purposes of this paragraph (b), a foreign corporation will be controlled by the controlled foreign corporation if the foreign corporation and the controlled foreign corporation are related parties under section 267(b). In determining for purposes of this paragraph (b) whether two or more corporations are members of the same controlled group under section 267(b)(3), a person is considered to own stock owned directly by such person, stock owned with the application of section 1563(e)(1), and stock owned with the application of section 267(c). The following examples illustrate the application of this paragraph.

Example (1). P, a domestic corporation, owns all of the outstanding stock of FS1, a controlled foreign corporation, and all of the outstanding stock of FS2, also a controlled foreign corporation. FS1 sells products to FS2 in exchange for trade receivables due in 60 days. FS2 has no earnings and profits. FS1 has substantial accumulated earnings and profits. FS2 loans to P an amount equal to the debt it owes FS1. FS2 pays the trade receivables according to the terms of the receivables. FS1 will not be considered to hold indirectly the investment in United States property under this paragraph (b)(4), because there was no transfer of funds to FS2.

Example (2). The facts are the same as in Example (1), except that FS2 does not pay the receivables. FS1 is considered to hold indirectly the investment in United States property under this paragraph (b)(4), because there was a transfer of funds to FS2, a principal purpose of which was to avoid the application of section 956 to FS1.

(ii) *Effective date.* This section is effective June 14, 1988, with respect to investments made on or after June 14, 1988.

(c) (reserved).

(d) (reserved).

(e)(1)—(e)(4) (reserved).

(e)(5) *Excluded charges.* (i) *Special rule.* For purposes of § 1.956-1(e)(1) of the regulations, in the case of an investment in United States property consisting of an obligation of a related person, as defined in section 954(d)(3) and paragraph (e) of § 1.954-1, a liability will not be recognized as a specific charge if the liability representing the charge is with recourse with respect to the general credit or other assets of the investing controlled foreign corporation.

(ii) *Effective Date.* This section is effective June 14, 1988, with respect to investments made on or after June 14, 1988.

[Temporary Reg. § 1.956-1T.]

☐ [*T.D.* 8209, 6-13-88.]

[Reg. § 1.956-2]

§ 1.956-2. Definition of United States property.—(a) *Included property*—(1) *In general.* For purposes of section 956(a) and § 1.956-1, United States property is (except as provided in paragraph (b) of this section) any property acquired (within the meaning of paragraph (d)(1) of this section) by a foreign corporation (whether or not a controlled foreign corporation at the time) during any taxable year of such foreign corporation beginning after December 31, 1962, which is—

(i) Tangible property (real or personal) located in the United States;

(ii) Stock of a domestic corporation;

(iii) An obligation (as defined in paragraph (d)(2) of this section) of a United States person (as defined in section 957(d)); or

(iv) Any right to the use in the United States of—

(*a*) A patent or copyright,

(*b*) An invention, model, or design (whether or not patented),

(*c*) A secret formula or process, or

(*d*) Any other similar property right,

which is acquired or developed by the foreign corporation for use in the United States by any person. Whether a right described in this subdivision has been acquired or developed for use in the United States by any person is to be determined from all the facts and circumstances of each case. As a general rule, a right actually used principally in the United States will be considered to have been acquired or developed for use in the United States in the absence of affirmative evidence showing that the right was not so acquired or developed for such use.

(2) *Illustrations.* The application of the provisions of this paragraph may be illustrated by the following examples:

Example (1). Foreign corporation R uses as a taxable year a fiscal year ending on June 30. Corporation R acquires on June 1, 1963, and holds on June 30, 1963, $100,000 of tangible property (not described in section 956(b)(2)) located in the United States. Corporation R's aggregate investment in United States property at the close of its taxable year ending June 30, 1963, is zero since the property which is acquired on June 1, 1963, is not acquired during a taxable year of R Corporation beginning after December 31, 1962. Assuming no change in R Corporation's aggregate investment in United States property during its taxable year ending June 30, 1964, R Corporation's increase in earnings invested in United States property for such taxable year is zero.

Example (2). Foreign corporation S uses the calendar year as a taxable year and is a controlled foreign corporation for its entire taxable year 1965. Corporation S is not a controlled foreign corporation at any time during its taxable years 1963 and 1964. Corporation S owns on December 31, 1964, $100,000 of tangible property (not described in section 956(b)(2)) located in the United States which it acquires during taxable years beginning after December 31, 1962. Corporation S's aggregate investment in United States property on December 31, 1964, is $100,000. Corporation S's current and accumulated earnings and profits (determined as provided in paragraph (b) of § 1.956-1) as of December 31, 1964, are in excess of $100,000. Assuming no change in S Corporation's aggregate investment in United States property during its taxable year 1965, S Corporation's increase in earnings invested in United States property for such taxable year is zero.

Example (3). Foreign corporation T uses the calendar year as a taxable year and is a controlled foreign corporation for its entire taxable years 1963, 1964, and 1966. At December 31, 1964, T Corporation's investment in United States property is $100,000. Corporation T is not a controlled foreign corporation at any time during its taxable year 1965 in which it acquires $25,000 of tangible property (not described in section 956 (b)(2)) located in the United States. On December 31, 1965, T Corporation holds the United States property of $100,000 which it held on December 31, 1964, and, in addition, the United States property acquired in 1965. Corporation T's aggregate investment in United States property at December 31, 1965, is $125,000. Corporation T's current and accumulated earnings and profits (determined as provided in paragraph (b) of § 1.956-1) as of December 31, 1965, are in excess of $125,000, and T Corporation pays no amount during 1965 to which section 959(c)(1) applies. Assuming no change in T Corporation's aggregate investment in United States property during its taxable year 1966, T Corporation's increase in earnings invested in United States property for such taxable year is zero.

(b) *Exceptions*—(1) *Excluded property.* For purposes of section 956(a) and paragraph (a) of this section, United States property does not include the following types of property held by a foreign corporation:

(i) Obligations of the United States.

(ii) Money.

(iii) Deposits with persons carrying on the banking business, unless the deposits serve directly or indirectly as a pledge or guarantee within the meaning of paragraph (c) of this section. See paragraph (e)(2) of § 1.956-1.

(iv) Property located in the United States which is purchased in the United States for export to, or use in, foreign countries. For purposes of this subdivision, property to be used outside the United States will be considered property to be used in a foreign country. Whether property is of a type described in this subdivision is to be determined from all the facts and circumstances in each case. Property which constitutes export trade assets within the meaning of section 971(c)(2) and paragraph (c)(3) of § 1.971-1, will be considered property of a type described in this subdivision.

(v) Any obligation (as defined in paragraph (d)(2) of this section) of a United States person (as defined in section 957(d)) arising in connection with the sale or processing of property if the amount of such obligation outstanding at any time during the taxable year of the foreign corporation does not exceed an amount which is ordinary and necessary to carry on trade or business of both the other party to the sale or processing transaction and the United States person, or, if the sale or processing transaction occurs between related persons, would be ordinary and necessary to carry on the trade or business of both the other party to the sale or processing transaction and the United States person if such persons were unrelated persons. Whether the amount of an obligation described in this subdivision is ordinary and necessary is to be determined from all the facts and circumstances in each case.

(vi) Any aircraft, railroad rolling stock, vessel, motor vehicle, or container used in the transportation of persons or property in foreign commerce and used predominantly outside the United States. Whether transportation property described in this subdivision is used in foreign commerce and predominantly outside the United States is to be determined from all the facts and circumstances in each case. As a general rule, such transportation property will be considered to be used predominantly outside the United States if 70 percent or more of the miles traversed (during the taxable year at the close of which a determination is made under section 956(a)(2)) in the use of such property are traversed outside the United States or if such property is located outside the United States 70 percent of the time during such taxable year.

(vii) An amount of assets described in paragraph (a) of this section of an insurance company equivalent to the unearned premiums or reserves which are ordinary and necessary for the proper conduct of that part of its insurance busi-

Reg. § 1.956-2(b)(1)

ness which is attributable to contracts other than those described in section 953(a)(1) and the regulations thereunder. For purposes of this subdivision, a reserve will be considered ordinary and necessary for the proper conduct of an insurance business if, under the principles of paragraph (c) of § 1.953-4, such reserve would qualify as a reserve required by law. See paragraph (d)(3) of § 1.954-2 for determining, for purposes of this subdivision, the meaning of insurance company and of unearned premiums.

(viii) For taxable years beginning after December 31, 1975, the voting or nonvoting stock or obligations of an unrelated domestic corporation. For purposes of this subdivision, an unrelated domestic corporation is a domestic corporation which is neither a United States shareholder (as defined in section 951(b)) of the controlled foreign corporation making the investment, nor a corporation 25 percent or more of whose total combined voting power of all classes of stock entitled to vote is owned or considered as owned (within the meaning of section 958(b)) by United States shareholders of the controlled foreign corporation making the investment. The determination of whether a domestic corporation is an unrelated corporation is made immediately after each acquisition of stock or obligations by the controlled foreign corporations.

(ix) For taxable years beginning after December 31, 1975, movable drilling rigs or barges and other movable exploration and exploitation equipment (other than a vessel or an aircraft) when used on the Continental Shelf (as defined in section 638) of the United States in the exploration for, development, removal, or transportation of natural resources from or under ocean waters. Property used on the Continental Shelf includes property located in the United States which is being constructed or is in storage or in transit within the United States for use on the Continental Shelf. In general, the type of property which qualifies for the exception under this subdivision includes any movable property which would be entitled to the investment credit if used outside the United States in certain geographical areas of the Western Hemisphere pursuant to section 48(a)(2)(B)(x) (without reference to sections 49 and 50).

(x) An amount of—

(a) A controlled foreign corporation's assets described in paragraph (a) of this section equivalent to its earnings and profits which are accumulated after December 31, 1962, and are attributable to items of income described in section 952(b) and the regulations thereunder, reduced by the amount of

(b) The earnings and profits of such corporation which are applied in a taxable year of such corporation beginning after December 31, 1962, to discharge a liability on property, but only if the liability was in existence at the close of such corporation's taxable year immediately preceding its first taxable year beginning after December 31, 1962, and the property would have been United States property if it had been acquired by such corporation immediately before such discharge.

For purposes of this subdivision, distributions made by such corporation for any taxable year shall be considered first made out of earnings and profits for such year other than earnings and profits referred to in (a) of this subdivision.

(2) *Statement required.* If a United States shareholder of a controlled foreign corporation excludes any property from the United States property of such controlled foreign corporation on the ground that section 956(b)(2) applies to such excluded property, he shall attach to his return a statement setting forth, by categories described in paragraph (a)(1) of this section, the amount of United States property of the controlled foreign corporation and, by categories described in subparagraph (1) of this paragraph, the amount of such property which is excluded.

(c) *Treatment of pledges and guarantees*—(1) *General rule.* Except as provided in subparagraph (4) of this paragraph, any obligation (as defined in paragraph (d)(2) of this section) of a United States person (as defined in section 957(d)) with respect to which a controlled foreign corporation is a pledgor or guarantor shall be considered for purposes of section 956(a) and paragraph (a) of this section to be United States property held by such controlled foreign corporation.

(2) *Indirect pledge or guarantee.* If the assets of a controlled foreign corporation serve at any time, even though indirectly, as security for the performance of an obligation of a United States person, then, for purposes of paragraph (c)(1) of this section, the controlled foreign corporation will be considered a pledgor or guarantor of that obligation. For this purpose the pledge of stock of a controlled foreign corporation will be considered as the indirect pledge of the assets of the corporation if at least 66⅔ percent of the total combined voting power of all classes of stock entitled to vote is pledged and if the pledge of stock is accompanied by one or more negative covenants or similar restrictions on the shareholder effectively limiting the corporation's discretion with respect to the disposition of assets and the incurrence of liabilities other than in the ordinary course of business. This paragraph (c)(2) applies only to pledges and

Reg. § 1.956-2(c)(2)

guarantees which are made after September 8, 1980. For purposes of this paragraph (c)(2) a refinancing shall be considered as a new pledge or guarantee.

(3) *Illustrations.* The following examples illustrate the application of this paragraph (c):

Example (1). A, a United States person, borrows $100,000 from a bank in foreign country X on December 31, 1964. On the same date controlled foreign corporation R pledges its assets as security for A's performance of A's obligation to repay such loan. The place at which or manner in which A uses the money is not material. For purposes of paragraph (b) of § 1.956-1, R Corporation will be considered to hold A's obligation to repay the bank $100,000, and, under the provisions of paragraph (e)(2) of § 1.956-1, the amount taken into account in computing R Corporation's aggregate investment in United States property on December 31, 1964, is the unpaid principal amount of the obligation on that date ($100,000).

Example (2). The facts are the same as in example (1), except that R Corporation participates in the transaction, not by pledging its assets as security for A's performance of A's obligation to repay the loan, but by agreeing to buy for $100,000 at maturity the note representing A's obligation if A does not repay the loan. Separate arrangements are made with respect to the payment of the interest on the loan. The agreement of R Corporation to buy the note constitutes a guarantee of A's obligation. For purposes of paragraph (b) of § 1.956-1, R Corporation will be considered to hold A's obligation to repay the bank $100,000, and, under the provisions of paragraph (e)(2) of § 1.956-1, the amount taken into account in computing R Corporation's aggregate investment in United States property on December 31, 1964, is the unpaid principal amount of the obligation on that date ($100,000).

Example (3). A, a United States person, borrows $100,000 from a bank on December 10, 1981, pledging 70 percent of the stock of X, a controlled foreign corporation, as collateral for the loan. A and X use the calendar year as their taxable year. In the loan agreement, among other things, A agrees not to cause or permit X Corporation to do any of the following without the consent of the bank:

(a) Borrow money or pledge assets, except as to borrowings in the ordinary course of business of X Corporation;

(b) Guarantee, assume, or become liable on the obligation of another, or invest in or lend funds to another;

(c) Merge or consolidate with any other corporation or transfer shares of any controlled subsidiary;

(d) Sell or lease (other than in the ordinary course of business) or otherwise dispose of any substantial part of its assets;

(e) Pay or secure any debt owing by X Corporation to A; and

(f) Pay any dividends, except in such amounts as may be required to make interest or principal payments on A's loan from the bank.

A retains the right to vote the stock unless a default occurs by A. Under paragraph (c)(2) of this section, the assets of X Corporation serve indirectly as security for A's performance of A's obligation to repay the loan and X Corporation will be considered a pledgor or guarantor with respect to that obligation. For purposes of paragraph (b) of § 1.956-1, X Corporation will be considered to hold A's obligation to repay the bank $100,000 and under paragraph (e)(2) of § 1.956-1, the amount taken into account in computing X Corporation's aggregate investment in United States property on December 31, 1981, is the unpaid principal amount of the obligation on that date.

(4) *Special rule for certain conduit financing arrangements.* The rule contained in subparagraph (1) of this paragraph shall not apply to a pledge or a guarantee by a controlled foreign corporation to secure the obligation of a United States person if such United States person is a mere conduit in a financing arrangement. Whether the United States person is a mere conduit in a financing arrangement will depend upon all the facts and circumstances in each case. A United States person will be considered a mere conduit in a financing arrangement in a case in which a controlled foreign corporation pledges stock of its subsidiary corporation, which is also a controlled foreign corporation, to secure the obligation of such United States person, where the following conditions are satisfied:

(i) Such United States person is a domestic corporation which is not engaged in the active conduct of a trade or business and has no substantial assets other than those arising out of its relending of the funds borrowed by it on such obligation to the controlled foreign corporation whose stock is pledged; and

(ii) The assets of such United States person are at all times substantially offset by its obligation to the lender.

(d) *Definitions*—(1) *Meaning of "acquired"*— (i) *Applicable rules.* For purposes of this section—

Reg. § 1.956-2(c)(3)

Income from Sources Without the United States

See p. 20,601 for regulations not amended to reflect law changes

(a) Property shall be considered acquired by a foreign corporation when such corporation acquires an adjusted basis in the property;

(b) Property which is an obligation of a United States person with respect to which a controlled foreign corporation is a pledgor or guarantor (within the meaning of paragraph (c) of this section) shall be considered acquired when the corporation becomes liable as a pledgor or guarantor or is otherwise considered a pledgor or guarantor (within the meaning of paragraph (c)(2) of this section); and

(c) Property shall not be considered acquired by a foreign corporation if—

(1) Such property is acquired in a transaction in which gain or loss would not be recognized under this chapter to such corporation if such corporation were a domestic corporation;

(2) The basis of the property acquired by the foreign corporation is the same as the basis of the property exchanged by such corporation; and

(3) The property exchanged by the foreign corporation was not United States property (as defined in paragraph (a)(1) of this section) but would have been such property if it had been acquired by such corporation immediately before such exchange.

(ii) *Illustrations.* The application of the provisions of this subparagraph may be illustrated by the following examples:

Example (1). Foreign corporation R uses the calendar year as a taxable year and acquires before January 1, 1963, stock of domestic corporation M having as to R Corporation an adjusted basis of $10,000. The stock of M Corporation is not United States property of R Corporation on December 31, 1962, since it is not acquired in a taxable year of R Corporation beginning on or after January 1, 1963. On June 30, 1963, R Corporation sells the M Corporation stock for $15,000 in cash and expends such amount in acquiring stock of domestic corporation N which has as to R Corporation an adjusted basis of $15,000. For purposes of determining R Corporation's aggregate investment in United States property on December 31, 1963, R Corporation has, by virtue of acquiring the stock of N Corporation, acquired $15,000 of United States property.

Example (2). Foreign corporation S, a controlled foreign corporation for the entire period here involved, uses the calendar year as a taxable year and purchases for $100,000 on December 31, 1963, tangible property (not described in section 956(b)(2)) located in the United States and having a remaining estimated useful life of 10 years, subject to a mortgage of $80,000 payable in 5 annual installments. The property constitutes United States property as of December 31, 1963, and the amount taken into account for purposes of determining the aggregate amount of S Corporation's investment in United States property under paragraph (b) of § 1.956-1 is $20,000. No depreciation is sustained with respect to the property during the taxable year 1963. During the taxable year 1964, S Corporation pays $16,000 on the mortgage and sustains $10,000 of depreciation with respect to the property. As of December 31, 1964, the amount taken into account with respect to the property for purposes of determining the aggregate amount of S Corporation's investment in United States property under paragraph (b) of § 1.956-1 is $26,000, computed as follows:

Cost of property		$100,000
Less: Reserve for depreciation		10,000
Adjusted basis of property		90,000
Less: Liability to which property is subject:		
Gross amount of mortgage	$80,000	
Payment during 1964	16,000	$ 64,000
Amount taken into account (12/31/64)		$ 26,000

Example (3). Controlled foreign corporation T uses the calendar year as a taxable year and acquires on December 31, 1963, $10,000 of United States property not described in section 956(b)(2); no depreciation is sustained with respect to the property during 1963. Corporation T's current and accumulated earnings and profits (determined as provided in paragraph (b) of § 1.956-1) as of December 31, 1963, are in excess of $10,000, and T Corporation's United States shareholders include in their gross income under section 951(a)(1)(B) their pro rata share of T Corporation's increase ($10,000) for 1963 in earnings invested in United States property. On January 1, 1964, T Corporation acquires an additional $10,000 of United States property not described in section 956(b)(2). Each of the two items of property has an estimated useful life of 5 years, and T Corporation sustains $4,000 of depreciation with respect to such properties during its taxable year 1964. Corporation T's current and accumulated earnings and profits as of December 31,

Reg. § 1.956-2(d)(1)

1964, exceed $16,000, determined as provided in paragraph (b) of § 1.956-1. Corporation T pays no amounts during 1963 to which section 959(c)(1) applies. Corporation T's investment of earnings in United States property at December 31, 1964, is $16,000, and its increase for 1964 in earnings invested in United States property is $6,000.

Example (4). Foreign corporation U uses the calendar year as a taxable year and acquires before January 1, 1963, stock in domestic corporation M having as to U Corporation an adjusted basis of $10,000. On December 1, 1964, pursuant to a statutory merger described in section 368(a)(1), M Corporation merges into domestic corporation N, and U Corporation receives on such date one share of stock in N Corporation, the surviving corporation, for each share of stock it held in M Corporation. Pursuant to section 354 no gain or loss is recognized to U Corporation, and pursuant to section 358 the basis of the property received (stock of N Corporation) is the same as that of the property exchanged (stock of M Corporation). Corporation U is not considered for purposes of section 956 to have acquired United States property by reason of its receipt of the stock in N Corporation.

Example (5). The facts are the same as in example (4), except that U Corporation acquires the stock of M Corporation on February 1, 1963, rather than before January 1, 1963. For purposes of determining U Corporation's aggregate investment in United States property on December 31, 1963, U Corporation has, by virtue of acquiring the stock of M Corporation, acquired $10,000 of United States property. Corporation U pays no amount during 1963 to which section 959(c)(1) applies. The reorganization and resulting acquisition on December 1, 1964, by U Corporation of N Corporation's stock also represents an acquisition of United States property; however, assuming no other change in U Corporation's aggregate investment in United States property during 1964, U Corporation's increase for such year in earnings invested in United States property is zero.

(2) [Reserved.] [Reg. § 1.956-2.]

☐ [T.D. 6704, 2-19-64. *Amended by T.D.* 7712, 8-6-80, T.D. 7797, 11-24-81 *and* T.D. 8209, 6-13-88.]

[Reg. § 1.956-2T]

§ 1.956-2T. **Definition of United States property (temporary).**—(a) (reserved).

(b) (reserved).

(c) (reserved).

(d)(1) (reserved).

(d)(2) *Obligation defined.* (i) *Rule.* For purposes of § 1.956-2 of the regulations, the term "obligation" includes any bond, note, debenture, certificate, bill receivable, account receivable, note receivable, open account, or other indebtedness, whether or not issued at a discount and whether or not bearing interest, except that such term shall not include:

(A) Any indebtedness arising out of the involuntary conversion of property which is not United States property within the meaning of paragraph (a)(1) of § 1.956-2, or

(B) Any obligation of a United States person (as defined in section 957(c)) arising in connection with the provision of services by a controlled foreign corporation to the United States person if the amount of such obligation outstanding at any time during the taxable year of the controlled foreign corporation does not exceed an amount which would be ordinary and necessary to carry on the trade or business of the controlled foreign corporation and the United States person if they were unrelated. The amount of such obligations shall be considered to be ordinary and necessary to the extent of such receivables that are paid within 60 days.

See § 1.956-2(b)(1)(v) for the exclusion from United States property of obligations arising in connection with the sale or processing of property where such obligations are ordinary and necessary as to amount.

(ii) *Effective date.* This section is effective June 14, 1988, with respect to investments made on or after June 14, 1988. [Temporary Reg. § 1.956-2T.]

☐ [T.D. 8209, 6-13-88.]

[Reg. § 1.956-3T]

§ 1.956-3T. **Certain trade or service receivables acquired from United States persons (temporary).**—(a) *In general.* For purposes of section 956(a) and § 1.956-1, the term "United States property" also includes any trade or service receivable if the trade or service receivable is acquired (directly or indirectly) after March 1, 1984, from a related person who is a United States person (as defined in section 7701(a)(30)) (hereinafter referred to as a "related United States person") and the obligor under the receivable is a United States person. A trade or service receivable described in this paragraph shall be considered to be United States property notwithstanding the exceptions (other than subparagraph (H)) contained in section 956(b)(2). The terms "trade or service receivable" and "related person" have the respective meanings given to such terms by section 864(d) and the regulations thereunder. For purposes of this section, the exception contained in § 1.956-2T(d)(2)(i)(B) for short-term obligations shall not apply to service receivables described in this paragraph.

(b) *Acquisition of a trade or service receivable*—(1) *General rule.* The rules of § 1.864-8T(c)(1) shall be applied to determine whether a controlled foreign corporation has acquired a trade or service receivable.

(2) *Indirect acquisitions*—(i) *Acquisition through unrelated person.* A trade or service receivable will be considered to be acquired from a related person if it is acquired from an unrelated person who acquired (directly or indirectly) such receivable from a person who is a related person to the acquiring person.

(ii) *Acquisition by nominee or pass-through entity.* A controlled foreign corporation will be considered to have acquired a trade or service receivable of a related United States person held on its behalf:

(A) By a nominee or by a partnership, simple trust, S corporation or other pass-through entity to the extent the controlled foreign corporation owns (directly or indirectly) a beneficial interest in such partnership or other pass-through entity; or

(B) By another foreign corporation that is controlled by the controlled foreign corporation, if one of the principal purposes for creating, organizing, or funding such other foreign corporation (through capital contributions or debt) is to avoid the application of section 956. See § 1.956-1T.

The rule of this paragraph (b)(2)(ii) does not limit the application of paragraph (b)(2)(iii) of this section regarding the characterization of trade or service receivables of unrelated persons acquired pursuant to certain swap or pooling arrangements. The following examples illustrate the application of this paragraph (b)(2)(ii).

Example (1). FS1, a controlled foreign corporation with substantial accumulated earnings and profits, contributes $2,000,000 to PS, a partnership, in exchange for a 20 percent limited partnership interest in PS. PS purchases trade or service receivables of FS1's domestic parent, P. The obligors under the receivables are United States persons. PS does not purchase receivables of any person who is related to any other partner in PS. Under paragraph (b)(2)(ii)(A) of this section, there is an investment of the earnings of FS1 in United States property equal to 20 percent of PS's basis in the receivables of P.

Example (2). FS1, a controlled foreign corporation, has accumulated more than $3,000,000 in earnings and profits. It organizes a wholly-owned foreign corporation, FS2, with a $2,000,000 equity contribution. FS2 has no earnings and profits. FS2 uses the funds to purchase trade or service receivables of FS1's domestic parent, P. The obligors under the receivables are United States persons. Under paragraph (b)(2)(ii)(B) of this section, there is an investment of the earnings of FS1 in United States property equal to $2,000,000.

(iii) *Swap or pooling arrangements.* A trade or service receivable of an unrelated person will be considered to be a trade or service receivable acquired from a related United States person and subject to the rules of this section if it is acquired in accordance with an arrangement that involves two or more groups of related persons that are unrelated to each other and the effect of the arrangement is that one or more related persons in each group acquire (directly or indirectly) trade or service receivables of one or more unrelated United States persons who are also parties to the arrangement, in exchange for reciprocal purchases of receivables of United States persons in the first group. The following example illustrates the application of this paragraph (b)(2)(iii).

Example. Controlled foreign corporations A, B, C, and D are wholly-owned subsidiaries of domestic corporations M, N, O, and P, respectively. M, N, O, and P are not related persons. According to a prearranged plan, A, B, C, and D each acquire trade or service receivables of M, N, O, and/or P. The obligors under some or all of the receivables acquired by each of A, B, C, and D are United States persons. Because the effect of this arrangement is that the unrelated groups acquire each other's trade or service receivables of United States persons pursuant to the arrangement, there is an investment of the earnings of each of A, B, C, and D in United States property to the extent of the purchase price of those receivables under which the obligors are United States persons.

(iv) *Financing arrangements.* If a controlled foreign corporation participates (directly or indirectly) in a lending transaction that results in a loan to a United States person who purchases property described in section 1221(1) (hereinafter referred to as "inventory property") or services of a related United States person, or to any person who purchases trade or service receivables of a related United States person under which the obligor is a United States person, or to a person who is related to any such purchaser, and if the loan would not have been made or maintained on the same terms but for the corresponding purchase, then the controlled foreign corporation shall be considered to have indirectly acquired a

Reg. § 1.956-3T(b)(2)

trade or service receivable described in paragraph (a) of this section. For purposes of this paragraph (b)(2)(iv), it is immaterial that the sums lent are not, in fact, the sums used to finance the purchase of the inventory property or services or trade or service receivables of a related United States person. The amount to be taken into account with respect to the controlled foreign corporation's investment in United States property (resulting from application of this paragraph (b)(2)(iv)) shall be the amount lent pursuant to a lending transaction described in this paragraph (b)(2)(iv), if the amount lent is equal to or less than the purchase price of the inventory property, services, or trade or service receivables. If the amount lent is greater than the purchase price of the inventory property, services or receivables, the amount to be taken into account shall be the purchase price. The following examples illustrate the application of this paragraph (b)(2)(iv).

Example (1). P, a domestic corporation, owns all of the outstanding stock of FS1, a controlled foreign corporation. P sells equipment for $2,000,000 to X, an unrelated United States person. FS1 makes a $1,000,000 short-term loan to X, which loan would not have been made or maintained on the same terms but for X's purchase of P's equipment. Because FS1 directly participates in a lending transaction described in this paragraph (b)(2)(iv), FS1 is considered to have acquired the receivable of a related United States person. Thus, there is an investment of FS1's earnings and profits in United States property in the amount of $1,000,000.

Example (2). The facts are the same as in Example (1), except that instead of loaning money to X directly, FS1 deposits $3,000,000 with an unrelated financial institution that loans $2,000,000 to X in order for X to purchase P's equipment. The loan would not have been made or maintained on the same terms but for the corresponding deposit. Accordingly, the deposit and the loan are treated as a direct loan from FS1 to X. See Rev. Rul. 87-89, 1987-37 I.R.B. 16. Because FS1 indirectly participates in a lending transaction described in this paragraph (b)(2)(iv), FS1 is considered to have acquired the receivable of a related United States person. Thus, there is an investment of FS1's earnings and profits in United States property in the amount of $2,000,000.

Example (3). P, a domestic corporation, owns all of the outstanding stock of FS1, a controlled foreign corporation. FS1 makes a $3,000,000 loan to U, an unrelated foreign corporation, in connection with U's purchase for $2,000,000 of receivables from the sale of inventory property by P to United States obligors. Because FS1 directly participates in a lending transaction described in this paragraph (b)(2)(iv), FS1 is considered to have acquired receivables of a related United States person. Thus, there is an investment of FS1's earnings and profits in United States property in the amount of $2,000,000.

(c) *Substitution of obligor.* For purposes of this section, the substitution of another person for a United States obligor may be disregarded. Thus, if a purchaser who is a United States person arranges for a foreign person to pay a United States seller of inventory property or services and the seller transfers by sale or otherwise to its own controlled foreign corporation the foreign person's obligation for payment, then the acquisition of the foreign person's obligation shall constitute an investment in United States property by the seller's controlled foreign corporation, unless it can be demonstrated by the parties to the transaction that the primary purpose for the arrangement was not the avoidance of section 956. The following example illustrates the application of this paragraph.

Example. P, a domestic corporation, owns all of the outstanding stock of FS1, a controlled foreign corporation with substantial accumulated earnings and profits. P sells equipment to X, a domestic corporation unrelated to P. To pay for the equipment, X arranges for a foreign financing entity to issue a note to P. P then sells the note to FS1. FS1 has made an investment in United States property in the amount of the purchase price of the note. [Temporary Reg. § 1.956-3T.]

☐ [*T.D. 8209, 6-13-88.*]

[Reg. § 1.957-1]

§ 1.957-1. **Definition of controlled foreign corporation.**—(a) *In general.* The term *controlled foreign corporation* means any foreign corporation of which more than 50 percent (or such lesser amount as is provided in section 957(b) or section 953(c)) of either—

(1) The total combined voting power of all classes of stock of the corporation entitled to vote; or

(2) The total value of the stock of the corporation, is owned within the meaning of section 958(a), or (except for purposes of section 953(c)) is considered as owned by applying the rules of section 958(b) and § 1.958-2, by United States shareholders on any day during the taxable year of such foreign corporation. For the definition of the term *United States shareholder,* see sections 951(b) and 953(c)(1)(A). For the definition of the term *foreign corporation,* see § 301.7701-5 of this

Reg. § 1.957-1(a)(1)

chapter (Procedure and Administration Regulations). For the treatment of associations as corporations, see section 7701(a)(3) and §§ 301.7701-1 and 301.7701-2 of this chapter. For the definition of the term *stock*, see sections 958(a)(3) and 7701(a)(7). For the classification of a member in an association, joint stock company or insurance company as a shareholder, see section 7701(a)(8).

(b) *Percentage of total combined voting power owned by United States shareholders*—(1) *Meaning of combined voting power.* In determining for purposes of paragraph (a) of this section whether United States shareholders own the requisite percentage of total combined voting power of all classes of stock entitled to vote, consideration will be given to all the facts and circumstances of each case. In all cases, however, United States shareholders of a foreign corporation will be deemed to own the requisite percentage of total combined voting power with respect to such corporation—

(i) If they have the power to elect, appoint, or replace a majority of that body of persons exercising, with respect to such corporation, the powers ordinarily exercised by the board of directors of a domestic corporation;

(ii) If any person or persons elected or designated by such shareholders have the power, where such shareholders have the power to elect exactly one-half of the members of such governing body of such foreign corporation, either to cast a vote deciding an evenly divided vote of such body or, for the duration of any deadlock which may arise, to exercise the powers ordinarily exercised by such governing body; or

(iii) If the powers which would ordinarily be exercised by the board of directors of a domestic corporation are exercised with respect to such foreign corporation by a person whom such shareholders have the power to elect, appoint, or replace.

(2) *Shifting of formal voting power.* Any arrangement to shift formal voting power away from United States shareholders of a foreign corporation will not be given effect if in reality voting power is retained. The mere ownership of stock entitled to vote does not by itself mean that the shareholder owning such stock has the voting power of such stock for purposes of section 957. For example, if there is any agreement, whether express or implied, that any shareholder will not vote his stock or will vote it only in a specified manner, or that sharehlders owning stock having not more than 50 percent of the total combined voting power will exercise voting power normally possessed by a majority of stockholders, then the nominal ownership of the voting power will be disregarded in determining which shareholders actually hold such voting power, and this determination will be made on the basis of such agreement. Moreover, where United States shareholders own shares of one or more classes of stock of a foreign corporation which has another class of stock outstanding, the voting power ostensibly provided such other class of stock will be deemed owned by any person or persons on whose behalf it is exercised or, if not exercised, will be disregarded if the percentage of voting power of such other class of stock is substantially greater than its proportionate share of the corporate earnings, if the facts indicate that the shareholders of such other class of stock do not exercise their voting rights independently or fail to exercise such voting rights, and if a principal purpose of the arrangement is to avoid the classification of such foreign corporation as a controlled foreign corporation under section 957.

(c) *Illustrations.* The application of this section may be illustrated by the following examples:

Example (1). Foreign corporation R has two classes of capital stock outstanding, 60 shares of class A stock, and 40 shares of class B stock. Each share of each class of stock has one vote for all purposes. E, a United States person, owns 51 shares of class A stock. Corporation R is a controlled foreign corporation.

Example (2). Foreign corporation S has three classes of capital stock outstanding, consisting of 60 shares of class A stock, 40 shares of class B stock, and 200 shares of class C stock. The owners of a majority of class A stock are entitled to elect 6 of the 10 corporate directors, and the owners of a majority of the class B stock are entitled to elect the other 4 of the 10 directors. Class C stock has no voting rights. D, a United States person, owns all of the shares of the class C stock. He also owns 31 shares of class A stock and as such an owner can elect 6 members of the board of directors. None of the remaining shares of class A stock, or the 40 shares of class B stock, is owned, or considered as owned, within the meaning of section 958, by a United States person. Since, as owner of 31 shares of the class A stock, D has sufficient voting power to elect 6 directors, D has more than 50 percent of the total combined voting power of all classes of stock entitled to vote, and S Corporation is a controlled foreign corporation.

Example (3). M, a United States person, owns a 51-percent interest in R Company, a foreign company of which he is a member. The company, if it were domestic, would be taxable as a corporation. The remaining interest of 49 percent in the company is owned by seven other members none of whom is a United States person. The memorandum of association of R Company provides for

Reg. § 1.957-1(c)

only one manager, who with respect to the company exercises the powers ordinarily exercised by a board of directors of a domestic corporation. The manager is to be elected by unanimous agreement of all the members. Since M owns 51 percent of the company, he will be deemed to own more than 50 percent of the total combined voting power of all classes of stock of R Company entitled to vote, notwithstanding that he has power to elect a manager only with the agreement of the other members. Company R is a controlled foreign corporation.

Example (4). Domestic corporation M owns a 49-percent interest in S Company, a foreign company of which it is a member. The company, if it were domestic, would be taxable as a corporation. Company S is formed under the laws of foreign country Y. The remaining interest of 51 percent in S Company is owned by persons who are not United States persons. The organization contract of S Company provides for one manager, B, a citizen and resident of country Y who is an officer of M Corporation in charge of its foreign operations in such country, or any person M Corporation may at any time appoint to succeed B in such capacity. The manager has the sole authority with respect to S Company to exercise powers ordinarily exercised by a board of directors of a domestic corporation. Since M Corporation has the discretionary power to replace B and to appoint his successor as manager of S Company, the company is a controlled foreign corporation.

Example (5). N, a United States person, owns 50 percent of the outstanding shares of the only class of capital stock of foreign corporation R. An additional 48 percent of the outstanding shares is owned by foreign corporation S. The remaining 2 percent of shares is owned by P, a citizen and resident of foreign country T, who regularly acts as attorney for N in the conduct of N's business affairs in country T. All of the shares of the outstanding capital stock of R Corporation are bearer shares. At the time of the issuance of the shares to him, P places the certificates for such shares in a depository to which N has access. On several occasions N, with P's acquiescence, has taken such shares from the depository and, on one such occasion, used the shares as collateral in borrowing funds on a loan. Although dividends, when paid, are paid to P on his shares, his charges to N for legal fees are reduced by the amount of the dividends paid on such shares. Although P votes his shares at meetings of shareholders, the facts set forth above indicate an implied agreement between P and N that N is really to retain dominion over the stock. N is deemed to own the voting rights ostensibly attached to the stock owned by P, and R Corporation is a controlled foreign corporation.

Example (6). M, a domestic corporation which manufactures in the United States and distributes all of its production for foreign consumption through N, a person other than a related person or a United States person, forms foreign corporation S to purchase products from M Corporation and sell them to N. Corporations S and M have common directors. The outstanding capital stock of S Corporation consists of 10,000 shares of $100 par value class A stock, which has no voting rights except to vote for dissolution of the corporation on a share for share basis, and 500 shares of no par class B stock which has full voting rights. Each class of the outstanding stock is to participate on a share for share basis in any dividend. The class A stock has a preference as to assets on dissolution of the corporation to the extent of its par value as well as the right to participate with the class B stock in all other assets on a share for share basis. All of the shares of class A stock are issued to M Corporation in return for property having a value of $1 million. Of the class B stock, 300 of the shares are issued to N in return for $3,000 in cash and 200 shares are issued to M Corporation for $2,000 in cash. At stockholder meetings N never votes in opposition to M Corporation on important issues. Corporation S has average annual earnings of $200,000, all of which will be subpart F income if S Corporation is held to be a controlled foreign corporation. All such earnings are accumulated. Although N ostensibly has 60 percent of the voting power of S Corporation by virtue of his ownership of 300 shares of class B stock, he has the right to only approximately 3 percent of any dividends which may be paid by S Corporation; in addition, upon liquidation of S Corporation, N is entitled to share in the assets only after M Corporation has received the par value of its 10,000 shares of class A stock, or $1 million. Thus, the voting power owned by N is substantially greater than its proportionate share of the earnings of S Corporation. In addition, the facts set forth above indicate that N is not exercising his voting rights independently and that a principal purpose of the capitalization arrangement is to avoid classification of S Corporation as a controlled foreign corporation. For these reasons, the voting power ostensibly provided the class B stock will be deemed owned by M Corporation, and S Corporation is a controlled foreign corporation.

Example (7). Foreign corporation A, authorized to issue 100 shares of one class of capital stock, issues, for $1,000 per share, 45 shares to domestic corporation M, 45 shares to foreign corporation B, and 10 shares to foreign corporation C. Corpora-

Reg. § 1.957-1(c)

tion C, a bank, lends $3 million to finance the operations of A Corporation. In the course of negotiating these financial arrangements, D, an officer of C Corporation, and E, an officer of M Corporation, orally agree that C Corporation will vote its stock as M Corporation directs. By virtue of such oral agreement M Corporation possesses the voting power ostensibly owned by C Corporation, and A Corporation is a controlled foreign corporation.

Example 8. For its prior taxable year, JV, a foreign corporation, had outstanding 1000 shares of class A stock, which is voting common, and 1000 shares of class B stock, which is nonvoting preferred. DP, a domestic corporation, and FP, a foreign corporation, each owned precisely 500 shares of both class A and class B stock, and each elected 5 of the 10 members of JV's board of directors. The other facts and circumstances were such that JV was not a controlled foreign corporation on any day of the prior taxable year. On the first day of the current taxable year, DP purchased one share of class B stock from FP. JV was a controlled foreign corporation on the following day because over 50 percent of the total value in the corporation was held by a person that was a United States shareholder under section 951(b). See § 1.951-1(f).

Example 9. The facts are the same as in *Example 8* except that the stock of FP was publicly traded, FP had one class of stock, and on the first day of the current taxable year DP purchased one share of FP stock on the foreign stock exchange instead of purchasing one share of JV stock from FP. JV became a controlled foreign corporation on the following day because over 50 percent of the total value in the corporation was held by a person that was a United States shareholder under section 951(b).

Example 10. X, a foreign corporation, is incorporated under the laws of country Y. Under the laws of country Y, X is considered a mutual insurance company. X issues insurance policies that provide the policyholder with the right to vote for directors of the corporation, the right to a share of the assets upon liquidation in proportion to premiums paid, and the right to receive policyholder dividends in proportion to premiums paid. Only policyholders are provided with the right to vote for directors, share in assets upon liquidation, and receive distributions. United States policyholders contribute 25 percent of the premiums and have 25 percent of the outstanding rights to vote for the board of directors. Based on these facts, the United States policyholders are United States shareholders owning the requisite combined voting power and value. Thus, X is a controlled foreign corporation for purposes of taking into account related person insurance income under section 953(c).

(d) *Effective date.* Paragraphs (a) and (c) *Examples 8* through *10* of this section are effective for taxable years of a controlled foreign corporation beginning after March 7, 1996. [Reg. § 1.957-1.]

☐ [T.D. 6688, 10-30-63. Amended by T.D. 8216, 7-20-88; T.D. 8618, 9-6-95 and T.D. 8704, 12-31-96.]

[Reg. § 1.957-2]

§ 1.957-2. **Controlled foreign corporation deriving income from insurance of United States risks.**—(a) *In general.* For purposes of taking into account only the income derived from the insurance of United States risks under § 1.953-1, the term "controlled foreign corporation" means any foreign corporation of which more than 25 percent, but not more than 50 percent, of the total combined voting power of all classes of stock entitled to vote is owned within the meaning of section 958(a), or is considered as owned by applying the rules of ownership of section 958(b), by United States shareholders on any day of the taxable year of such foreign corporation, but only if the gross amount of premiums received by such foreign corporation during such taxable year which are attributable to the reinsuring and the issuing of insurance and annuity contracts in connection with United States risks, as defined in § 1.953-2 or 1.953-3, exceeds 75 percent of the gross amount of all premiums received by such foreign corporation during such year which are attributable to the reinsuring and the issuing of insurance and annuity contracts in connection with all risks. The subpart F income for a taxable year of a foreign corporation which is a controlled foreign corporation for such taxable year within the meaning of this paragraph shall, subject to the provisions of section 952(b), (c), and (d), and § 1.952-1, include only the income derived from the insurance of United States risks, as determined under § 1.953-1.

(b) *Gross amount of premiums defined.* For a foreign corporation which is engaged in the business of reinsuring or issuing insurance or annuity contracts and which, if it were a domestic corporation engaged only in such business, would be taxable as—

(1) A life insurance company to which part I (sections 801 through 820) of subchapter L of the Code applies,

(2) A mutual insurance company to which part II (sections 821 through 826) of subchapter L of the Code applies, or

(3) A mutual marine insurance or other insurance company to which part III (sections 831 and 832) of subchapter L of the Code applies,

the term "gross amount of premiums" means, for purposes of paragraph (a) of this section, the gross amount of premiums and other consideration which are taken into account by a life insurance company under section 809(c)(1). Determinations for purposes of this paragraph shall be made without regard to section 501(a). [Reg. § 1.957-2.]

☐ [T.D. 6795, 1-28-65.]

[Reg. § 1.957-3]

§ 1.957-3. Corporations organized in United States possessions.—(a) *General rule.* For purposes of sections 951 through 964, a corporation created or organized in a possession of the United States or under the laws of a possession of the United States shall not be treated as a controlled foreign corporation for any taxable year if—

(1) 80 percent or more of the gross income of such corporation for the 3-year period immediately preceding the close of the taxable year or for such part of such 3-year period as such corporation was in existence or for such part of such 3-year period as occurs on and after the beginning of such corporation's first annual accounting period beginning after December 31, 1962, whichever period is shortest, was derived from sources within a possession of the United States; and

(2) 50 percent or more of the gross income of such corporation for such period, or for such part of such period, was derived from the active conduct within a possession of the United States of one or more trades or businesses constituting—

(i) The manufacture or processing of goods, wares, merchandise, or other tangible personal property;

(ii) The processing of agricultural or horticultural products or commodities (including but not limited to livestock, poultry, or fur-bearing animals);

(iii) The catching or taking of any kind of fish, or any manufacturing or processing of any products or commodities obtained from such activities;

(iv) The mining or extraction of natural resources, or any manufacturing or processing of any products or commodities obtained from such activities; or

(v) The ownership or operation of hotels.

(b) *Special provisions.* For purposes of section 957(c) and this section—

(1) *United States defined.* The term "United States" includes only the States and the District of Columbia.

(2) *Possession of the United States defined.* The term "possession of the United States" includes Guam, the Midway Islands, the Panama Canal Zone, the Commonwealth of Puerto Rico, American Samoa, the Virgin Islands, and Wake Island.

(3) *Determination of source of gross income.* Whether gross income of a corporation referred to in paragraph (a) of this section is derived from sources within a possession of the United States shall be determined by the application of the provisions of § 1.955-6 except that, for purposes of making such determination, the term "produced", as used in paragraph (d)(2) of § 1.955-6, shall also include the activities described in paragraph (a)(2)(i) through (iv) of this section and the activities considered, under subparagraph (4) of this paragraph, to be qualifying trades or businesses.

(4) *Manufacturing or processing.* The trades or businesses which qualify under the provisions of paragraph (a)(2) of this section shall include, but not be limited to, the manufacture of tabulating cards, paper tablets or pads, facial tissues, and paper napkins from rolls of paper; the manufacture of such household products as liquid starch by mixing quantities of the ingredients which are used to produce liquid starch; and the manufacture of juices and drinks from fruit concentrates. In the application of paragraph (a)(2) of this section, proper regard shall be given to the classification of a trade or business as a manufacturing or processing activity under the applicable economic incentive law of the possession involved. The fact that an activity of a corporation qualifies as a trade or business for purposes of paragraph (a) of this section does not necessarily mean that such activity constitutes a substantial transformation of property within the meaning of paragraph (a)(4) of § 1.954-3 for purposes of determining any foreign base company income of such corporation. [Reg. § 1.957-3.]

☐ [T.D. 6683, 10-17-63.]

[Reg. § 1.957-4]

§ 1.957-4. United States person defined.—(a) *Basic rule*—(1) *In general.* The term "United States person" has the same meaning for purposes of sections 951 through 964 which it has under section 7701(a)(30) and in the regulations thereunder, except as provided in section 957(d) and paragraphs (b), (c), and (d) of this section which provide, with respect to corporations organized in possessions of the United States, that certain residents of such possessions are not United States persons. The effect of determining that an individual is not a United States person for such purposes is to exclude such individual in determining whether a foreign corporation created or

Reg. § 1.957-3(a)(1)

organized in, or under the laws of, Puerto Rico, the Virgin Islands, or any possession of the United States (other than Puerto Rico or the Virgin Islands) is a controlled foreign corporation. See § 1.957-1 for definition of the term "controlled foreign corporation"; § 1.957-2 for a special limitation on the amount of subpart F income of certain controlled foreign corporations deriving income from the insurance of United States risks; and § 1.957-3 for the exclusion of certain corporations organized in United States possessions from the definition of controlled foreign corporation.

(2) *Special provisions applicable to possessions of the United States.* For purposes of section 957(d) and this section—

(i) *Possession of the United States defined.* The term "possession of the United States" has the same meaning which it has under paragraph (b)(2) of § 1.957-3.

(ii) *Determination of residence in a possession.* Whether an individual is a bona fide resident of Puerto Rico, the Virgin Islands, or any other possession of the United States, shall be determined in general by applying to the facts and circumstances in each case the principles of §§ 1.871-2 through 1.871-5, relating to the determination of residence in the United States.

(b) *Puerto Rico corporation and resident.* With respect only to a foreign corporation created or organized in, or under the laws of, Puerto Rico—

(1) If an individual (who without regard to this paragraph, is a United States person) is a bona fide resident of Puerto Rico during his entire taxable year in which or with which the taxable year of such foreign corporation ends, and

(2) If 50 percent or more of the gross income of such foreign corporation is derived from sources within Puerto Rico, as determined under § 1.863-6, for the 3-year period (or for such part of such 3-year period as such foreign corporation has been in existence), ending with the close of the taxable year of such foreign corporation which—

(i) Ends with or within the taxable year next preceding such taxable year of such individual and at any time, during the period beginning with the beginning of such latter taxable year of such individual and ending not later than one year after the close of such taxable year of such foreign corporation, such individual directly owns stock in such foreign corporation, or

(ii) Ends within such taxable year of such individual and at any time, during the period beginning after the close of such taxable year of such foreign corporation and ending with the close of such taxable year of such individual, such individual directly owns stock in such foreign corporation, then, such individual shall not be considered a United States person with respect to such corporation for the taxable year of such corporation which ends with or within the taxable year of such person. The application of this paragraph may be illustrated by the following examples:

Example (1). Foreign corporation R, incorporated under the laws of Puerto Rico, is wholly owned by D, a United States citizen. D and corporation R use the calendar year as the taxable year. For 1961, 1962 and 1963, 60 percent of the gross income of R Corporation is derived from sources within Puerto Rico and 40 percent of the gross income of R Corporation is derived from sources within Panama, as determined under § 1.863-6. During all of 1964, D is a bona fide resident of Puerto Rico. D is not a United States person with respect to R Corporation for 1964. Accordingly, R Corporation is not a controlled foreign corporation at any time in 1964.

Example (2). Foreign corporation R is incorporated on January 1, 1962, under the laws of Puerto Rico. D, a United States citizen, owns all the one class of stock of R Corporation throughout 1962 and 1963. D and corporation R use the calendar year as the taxable year. For 1962, 55 percent of the gross income of R Corporation is derived from sources within Puerto Rico and 45 percent of the gross income of R Corporation is derived from sources within the Netherlands Antilles, as determined under § 1.863-6. For 1963, 40 percent of the gross income of R Corporation is derived from sources within Puerto Rico and 60 percent of the gross income of R Corporation is derived from sources within the Netherlands Antilles, as determined under § 1.863-6. During all of 1963, D is a bona fide resident of Puerto Rico. With respect to R Corporation, D is not a United States person for 1963 because D is a bona fide resident of Puerto Rico for all of 1963; 55 percent of the gross income of R Corporation for 1962 is derived from sources within Puerto Rico; and D owns stock in R Corporation at some time during 1963. Accordingly, R Corporation is not a controlled foreign corporation at any time in 1963. In making this determination, it is immaterial that R Corporation does not satisfy the 50-percent gross income test for 1963, the taxable year during all of which D is a resident of Puerto Rico.

Example (3). Foreign corporation R is incorporated on January 1, 1962, under the laws of Puerto Rico. D, a United States citizen, owns all the one class of stock of R Corporation throughout 1962 and 1963. D and corporation R use the calendar year as the taxable year. For 1962, 45 percent of the gross income of R Corporation is derived from sources within Puerto Rico and 55

Reg. § 1.957-4(b)(2)

percent of the gross income of R Corporation is derived from sources within the Netherlands Antilles, as determined under § 1.863-6. For 1963, 60 percent of the gross income of R Corporation is derived from sources within Puerto Rico and 40 percent of the gross income of R Corporation is derived from sources within the Netherlands Antilles, as determined under § 1.863-6. With respect to R Corporation, D is a United States person for 1963, since R Corporation does not satisfy the 50-percent gross income test for 1962. Accordingly, R Corporation is a controlled foreign corporation for all of 1963.

Example (4). Foreign corporation S is incorporated on July 1, 1962, under the laws of Puerto Rico. Corporation S uses the fiscal year ending on June 30 as the taxable year. For its fiscal year ending on June 30, 1963, 55 percent of the gross income of S Corporation is derived from sources within Puerto Rico and 45 percent of the gross income of S Corporation is derived from sources within Switzerland, as determined under § 1.863-6. For its fiscal years ending on June 30, 1964, and June 30, 1965, respectively, 40 percent of the gross income of S Corporation is derived from sources within Puerto Rico and 60 percent of the gross income of S Corporation is derived from sources within Switzerland, as determined under § 1.863-6. B, a United States citizen, who uses the calendar year as the taxable year, is a bona fide resident of Puerto Rico for all of 1964. On July 1, 1964, B acquires, and holds throughout the remainder of 1964, all of the one class of stock of S Corporation. With respect to S Corporation for its taxable year ending June 30, 1964, B is a United States person because—

(a) Although B is a bona fide resident of Puerto Rico for his entire year 1964 in which ends S Corporation's taxable year ending June 30, 1964, and S Corporation meets the 50-percent gross income test for the applicable part of the 3-year period ending June 30, 1963, B does not own stock in S Corporation during the period beginning January 1, 1964, and ending June 30, 1964, and

(b) Although B owns stock in S Corporation during the period beginning July 1, 1964, and ending December 31, 1964, S Corporation does not meet the 50-percent gross income test for the applicable part of the 3-year period ending June 30, 1964.

Accordingly, with respect to B, S Corporation is a controlled foreign corporation for its entire taxable year ending June 30, 1964.

Example (5). The facts are the same as in example (4), except B buys all of the stock of S Corporation on June 1, 1964, rather than on July 1, 1964. With respect to S Corporation for its taxable year ending June 30, 1964, B is not a United States person because B is a bona fide resident of Puerto Rico for his entire taxable year 1964 in which ends S Corporation's taxable year ending June 30, 1964; S Corporation meets the 50-percent gross income test for the applicable part of the 3-year period ending June 30, 1963; and B owns stock in S Corporation during the period beginning January 1, 1964, and ending June 30, 1964. Accordingly, with respect to B, S Corporation is not a controlled foreign corporation at any time during its taxable year ending June 30, 1964.

(c) *Virgin Islands corporation and resident.* With respect only to a foreign corporation created or organized in, or under the laws of, the Virgin Islands—

(1) If an individual (who, without regard to this paragraph, is a United States person) is a bona fide resident of the Virgin Islands as of the last day of his taxable year in which or with which the taxable year of such foreign corporation ends, and

(2) Such individual's income tax obligations under subtitle A (relating to income taxes) of the Code for his taxable year are satisfied, in accordance with section 28(a) of the Revised Organic Act of the Virgin Islands (48 U.S.C. 1642), by paying the tax on his income derived from all sources, both within and outside the Virgin Islands, into the treasury of the Virgin Islands,

then, such individual shall not be considered a United States person with respect to such corporation for the taxable year of such corporation which ends with or within the taxable year of such person. The application of this paragraph may be illustrated by the following examples:

Example (1). Foreign corporation S, incorporated under the laws of the Virgin Islands, is wholly owned by D, a United States citizen. Corporation S uses the fiscal year ending on June 30 as the taxable year, and D uses the calendar year as the taxable year. From September 1, 1963, to December 31, 1964, inclusive, D is a bona fide resident of the Virgin Islands. For 1963 and 1964, D satisfies his income tax obligations under section 28(a) of the Revised Organic Act of the Virgin Islands by paying the tax on his income derived from all sources, both within and outside the Virgin Islands, into the treasury of the Virgin Islands. With respect to S Corporation for its taxable years ending June 30, 1963, and 1964, D is not a United States person. Accordingly, S Corporation is not a controlled foreign corporation for such taxable years of such corporation.

Reg. § 1.957-4(c)(1)

Income from Sources Without the United States   49,347

See p. 20,601 for regulations not amended to reflect law changes

Example (2). The facts are the same as in example (1), except that from August 15, 1964, to December 31, 1964, inclusive, D is a bona fide resident of the United States. Thus, D does not satisfy his income tax obligations for 1964 under section 28(a) of the Revised Organic Act of the Virgin Islands. The result is the same as in example (1), except that with respect to S Corporation for its taxable year ending June 30, 1964, D is a United States person and, accordingly, S Corporation is a controlled foreign corporation for such taxable year of such corporation.

(d) *Corporation and resident of other United States possessions.* With respect only to a foreign corporation created or organized in, or under the laws of, any possession of the United States (other than Puerto Rico or the Virgin Islands)—

(1) If an individual (who, without regard to this paragraph, is a United States person) is a bona fide resident of such possession during his entire taxable year in which or with which the taxable year of such foreign corporation ends, and

(2) Any part or all of such individual's income (other than amounts includible in his gross income under section 951(a)) for his taxable year derived, in accordance with § 1.863-6, from sources within any possession of the United States (whether or not the possession of which such individual is a resident) is not, as a result of the application of section 931, included in his gross income for his taxable year,

then, such individual shall not be considered a United States person with respect to such corporation for the taxable year of such corporation which ends with or within the taxable year of such person. Subparagraph (2) of this paragraph shall apply only for purposes of determining whether an individual is a United States person; after such determination has been made, section 931 shall be applied to the gross income (including amounts includible in gross income under section 951(a)) of such individual to determine the amount to be excluded from such individual's gross income under section 931. The application of this paragraph may be illustrated by the following examples:

Example (1). Foreign corporation R, incorporated under the laws of Guam, is wholly owned by D, a United States citizen. D and corporation R use the calendar year as the taxable year and the cash receipts and disbursements method of accounting. D is a bona fide resident of Guam for all of 1963 and all of his income of $30,000 (determined without taking into account amounts includible in his gross income under section 951(a)) is derived from sources within Guam. Of such income, $24,000 is received in Guam and $6,000 is received in the United States. D meets the 3-year test of section 931(a) and, but for the application of section 931(b), all of his income of $30,000 would be excluded from gross income for 1963 under section 931. However, in accordance with section 931(b) and paragraph (c) of § 1.931-1, the $6,000 received in the United States is included in gross income. Nevertheless, since part ($24,000) of his income of $30,000 for 1963 derived, in accordance with § 1.863-6, from sources within Guam is not, as a result of the application of section 931, included in his gross income, D is not a United States person with respect to R Corporation for its taxable year 1963. Accordingly, R Corporation is not a controlled foreign corporation for its taxable year 1963.

Example (2). The facts are the same as in example (1), except that, instead of receiving the $6,000 in the United States, D receives $10,000 of the $30,000 in Guam for services performed for an agency of the United States. Under § 1.863-6, all of D's income for 1963 is income derived from sources within Guam. However, since D's income of $10,000 from the agency of the United States is deemed under section 931(i) to be derived from sources within the United States for purposes of section 931, at least 80 percent of his gross income for 1963, determined without the application of section 931, is not derived from sources within Guam. Accordingly, since no part of D's gross income of $30,000 for 1963 derived, in accordance with § 1.863-6, from sources within Guam is, as a result of the application of section 931, excluded from gross income for 1963, D is a United States person with respect to R Corporation for R Corporation's taxable year 1963. Accordingly, R Corporation is a controlled foreign corporation for its taxable year 1963. [Reg. § 1.957-4.]

☐ [T.D. 6775, 12-1-64.]

[Reg. § 1.958-1]

§ 1.958-1. **Direct and indirect ownership of stock.**—(a) *In general.* Section 958(a) provides that, for purposes of sections 951 to 964 (other than sections 955(b)(1)(A) and (B) and 955(c)(2)(A)(ii) (as in effect before the enactment of the Tax Reduction Act of 1975), and 960(a)(1)), stock owned means—

(1) Stock owned directly; and

(2) Stock owned with the application of paragraph (b) of this section.

The rules of section 958(a) and this section provide a limited form of stock attribution primarily for use in determining the amount taxable to a United States shareholder under section 951(a). These rules also apply for purposes of other provi-

Reg. § 1.958-1(a)(2)

sions of the Code and regulations which make express reference to section 958(a).

(b) *Stock ownership through foreign entities.* For purposes of paragraph (a)(2) of this section, stock owned, directly or indirectly, by or for a foreign corporation, foreign partnership, foreign trust (within the meaning of section 7701(a)(31)) described in sections 671 through 679, or other foreign trust or foreign estate (within the meaning of section 7701(a)(31)) shall be considered as being owned proportionately by its shareholders, partners, grantors or other persons treated as owners under sections 671 through 679 of any portion of the trust that includes the stock, or beneficiaries, respectively. Stock considered to be owned by reason of the application of this paragraph shall, for purposes of reapplying this paragraph, be treated as actually owned by such person. Thus, this rule creates a chain of ownership; however, since the rule applies only to stock owned by a foreign entity, attribution under the rule stops with the first United States person in the chain of ownership running from the foreign entity. The application of this paragraph may be illustrated by the following example:

Example. Domestic corporation M owns 75 percent of the one class of stock in foreign corporation R, which in turn owns 80 percent of the one class of stock in foreign corporation S, which in turn owns 90 percent of the one class of stock in foreign corporation T. Under this paragraph, R Corporation is considered as owning 80 percent of the 90 percent of the stock which S Corporation owns in T Corporation, or 72 percent. Corporation M is considered as owning 75 percent of such 72 percent of the stock in T Corporation, or 54 percent. Since M Corporation is a domestic corporation, the attribution under this paragraph stops with M Corporation, even though, illustratively, such corporation is wholly owned by domestic corporation N.

(c) *Rules of application*—(1) *Special rule for mutual insurance companies.* For purposes of applying paragraph (a) of this section in the case of a foreign mutual insurance company, the term "stock" shall include any certificate entitling the holder to voting power in the corporation.

(2) *Amount of interest in foreign corporation, foreign partnership, foreign trust, or foreign estate.* The determination of a person's proportionate interest in a foreign corporation, foreign partnership, foreign trust, or foreign estate will be made on the basis of all the facts and circumstances in each case. Generally, in determining a person's proportionate interest in a foreign corporation, the purpose for which the rules of section 958(a) and this section are being applied will be taken into account. Thus, if the rules of section 958 (a) are being applied to determine the amount of stock owned for purposes of section 951(a), a person's proportionate interest in a foreign corporation will generally be determined with reference to such person's interest in the income of such corporation. If the rules of section 958(a) are being applied to determine the amount of voting power owned for purposes of section 951(b) or 957, a person's proportionate interest in a foreign corporation will generally be determined with reference to the amount of voting power in such corporation owned by such person. However, any arrangement which artificially decreases a United States person's proportionate interest will not be recognized. See §§ 1.951-1 and 1.957-1.

(d) *Illustration.* The application of this section may be illustrated by the following examples:

Example (1). United States persons A and B own 25 percent and 50 percent, respectively, of the one class of stock in foreign corporation M. Corporation M owns 80 percent of the one class of stock in foreign corporation N, and N Corporation owns 60 percent of the one class of stock in foreign corporation P. Under paragraph (b) of this section, M Corporation is considered to own 48 percent (80% of 60%) of the stock in P Corporation; such 48 percent is treated as actually owned by M Corporation for the purpose of again applying paragraph (b) of this section. Thus, A and B are considered to own 12 percent (25% of 48%) and 24 percent (50% of 48%), respectively, of the stock in P Corporation.

Example (2). United States person C is a 60-percent partner in foreign partnership X. Partnership X owns 40 percent of the one class of stock in foreign corporation Q. Corporation Q is a 50-percent partner in foreign partnership Y, and partnership Y owns 100 percent of the one class of stock in foreign corporation R. By the application of paragraph (b) of this section, C is considered to own 12 percent (60% of 40% of 50% of 100%) of the stock in R Corporation.

Example (3). Foreign trust Z was created for the benefit of United States persons D, E, and F. Under the terms of the trust instrument, the trust income is required to be divided into three equal shares. Each beneficiary's share of the income may either be accumulated for him or distributed to him in the discretion of the trustee. In 1970, the trust is to terminate and there is to be paid over to each beneficiary the accumulated income applicable to his share and one-third of the corpus. The corpus of trust Z is composed of 90 percent of the one class of stock in foreign corporation S. By the application of this section, each of

Reg. § 1.958-1(b)

Income from Sources Without the United States

See p. 20,601 for regulations not amended to reflect law changes

D, E, and F is considered to own 30 percent (⅓ of 90 percent) of the stock in S Corporation.

Example (4). Among the assets of foreign estate W are Blackacre and a block of stock, consisting of 75 percent of the one class of stock of foreign corporation T. Under the terms of the will governing estate W, Blackacre is left to G, a nonresident alien, for life, remainder to H, a nonresident alien, and the block of stock is left to United States person K. By the application of this section, K is considered to own the 75 percent of the stock of T Corporation, and G and H are not considered to own any of such stock.

[Reg. § 1.958-1.]

☐ [T.D. 6889, 7-11-66. Amended by T.D. 7893, 5-11-83 and T.D. 8955, 7-19-2001.]

[Reg. § 1.958-2]

§ 1.958-2. Constructive ownership of stock.—(a) *In general.* Section 958(b) provides that, for purposes of sections 951(b), 954(d)(3), 956(b)(2), and 957, the rules of section 318(a) as modified by section 958(b) and this section shall apply to the extent that the effect is to treat a United States person as a United States shareholder within the meaning of section 951(b), to treat a person as a related person within the meaning of section 954(d)(3), to treat the stock of a domestic corporation as owned by a United States shareholder of a controlled foreign corporation under section 956(b)(2), or to treat a foreign corporation as a controlled foreign corporation under section 957.

The rules contained in this section also apply for purposes of other provisions of the Code and regulations which make express reference to section 958(b).

(b) *Members of family*—(1) *In general.* Except as provided in subparagraph (3) of this paragraph, an individual shall be considered as owning the stock owned, directly or indirectly, by or for—

(i) His spouse (other than a spouse who is legally separated from the individual under a decree of divorce or separate maintenance); and

(ii) His children, grandchildren, and parents.

(2) *Effect of adoption.* For purposes of subparagraph (1)(ii) of this paragraph, a legally adopted child of an individual shall be treated as a child of such individual by blood.

(3) *Stock owned by nonresident alien individual.* For purposes of this paragraph, stock owned by a nonresident alien individual (other than a foreign trust or foreign estate) shall not be considered as owned by a United States citizen or a resident alien individual. However, this limitation does not apply for purposes of determining whether the stock of a domestic corporation is owned or considered as owned by a United States shareholder under section 956(b)(2) and § 1.956-2(b)(1)(viii). See section 958(b)(1).

(c) *Attribution from partnerships, estates, trusts, and corporations*—(1) *In general.* Except as provided in subparagraph (2) of this paragraph—

(i) *From partnerships and estates.* Stock owned, directly or indirectly, by or for a partnership or estate shall be considered as owned proportionately by its partners or beneficiaries.

(ii) *From trusts*—(a) *To beneficiaries.* Stock owned, directly or indirectly, by or for a trust (other than employees' trust described in section 401(a) which is exempt from tax under section 501(a)) shall be considered as owned by its beneficiaries in proportion to the actuarial interest of such beneficiaries in such trust.

(b) *To owner.* Stock owned, directly or indirectly, by or for any portion of a trust of which a person is considered the owner under sections 671 to 679 (relating to grantors and others treated as substantial owners) shall be considered as owned by such person.

(iii) *From corporations.* If 10 percent or more in value of the stock in a corporation is owned, directly or indirectly, by or for any person, such person shall be considered as owning the stock owned, directly or indirectly, by or for such corporation, in that proportion which the value of the stock which such person so owns bears to the value of all the stock in such corporation. See section 958(b)(3).

(2) *Rules of application.* For purposes of subparagraph (1) of this paragraph, if a partnership, estate, trust, or corporation owns, directly or indirectly, more than 50 percent of the total combined voting power of all classes of stock entitled to vote in a corporation, it shall be considered as owning all the stock entitled to vote. See section 958(b)(2).

(d) *Attribution to partnerships, estates, trusts, and corporations*—(1) *In general.* Except as provided in subparagraph (2) of this paragraph—

(i) *To partnerships and estates.* Stock owned, directly or indirectly, by or for a partner or a beneficiary of an estate shall be considered as owned by the partnership or estate.

(ii) *To trusts*—(a) *From beneficiaries.* Stock owned, directly or indirectly, by or for a beneficiary of a trust (other than an employees' trust described in section 401(a) which is exempt from tax under section 501(a)) shall be considered as owned by the trust, unless such beneficiary's

Reg. § 1.958-2(d)(1)

interest in the trust is a remote contingent interest. For purposes of the preceding sentence, a contingent interest of a beneficiary in a trust shall be considered remote if, under the maximum exercise of discretion by the trustee in favor of such beneficiary, the value of such interest, computed actuarially, is 5 percent or less of the value of the trust property.

(b) *From owner.* Stock owned, directly or indirectly, by or for a person who is considered the owner of any portion of a trust under sections 671 to 678 (relating to grantors and others treated as substantial owners) shall be considered as owned by the trust.

(iii) *To corporations.* If 50 percent or more in value of the stock in a corporation is owned, directly or indirectly, by or for any person, such corporation shall be considered as owning the stock owned, directly or indirectly, by or for such person. This subdivision shall not be applied so as to consider a corporation as owning its own stock.

(2) *Limitation.* Subparagraph (1) of this paragraph shall not be applied so as to consider a United States person as owning stock which is owned by a person who is not a United States person. This limitation does not apply for purposes of determining whether the stock of a domestic corporation is owned or considered as owned by a United States shareholder under section 956(b)(2) and § 1.956-2(b)(1)(viii). See section 958(b)(4).

(e) *Options.* If any person has an option to acquire stock, such stock shall be considered as owned by such person. For purposes of the preceding sentence, an option to acquire such an option, and each one of a series of such options, shall be considered as an option to acquire such stock.

(f) *Rules of application.* For purposes of this section—

(1) *Stock treated as actually owned*—(i) *In general.* Except as provided in subdivisions (ii) and (iii) of this subparagraph, stock constructively owned by a person by reason of the application of paragraphs (b), (c), (d), and (e) of this section shall, for purposes of applying such paragraphs, be considered as actually owned by such person.

(ii) *Members of family.* Stock constructively owned by an individual by reason of the application of paragraph (b) of this section shall not be considered as owned by him for purposes of again applying such paragraph in order to make another the constructive owner of such stock.

(iii) *Partnerships, estates, trusts, and corporations.* Stock constructively owned by a partnership, estate, trust, or corporation by reason of the application of paragraph (d) of this section shall not be considered as owned by it for purposes of applying paragraph (c) of this section in order to make another the constructive owner of such stock.

(iv) *Option rule in lieu of family rule.* For purposes of this subparagraph, if stock may be considered as owned by an individual under paragraph (b) or (e) of this section, it shall be considered as owned by him under paragraph (e).

(2) *Coordination of different attribution rules.* For purposes of any one determination, stock which may be owned under more than one of the rules of § 1.958-1 and this section, or by more than one person, shall be owned under that attribution rule which imputes to the person, or persons, concerned the largest total percentage of such stock. The application of this subparagraph may be illustrated by the following examples:

Example (1). (a) United States persons A and B, and domestic corporation M, own 9 percent, 32 percent, and 10 percent, respectively, of the one class of stock in foreign corporation R. A also owns 10 percent of the one class of stock in M Corporation. For purposes of determining whether A is a United States shareholder with respect to R Corporation, 10 percent of the 10-percent interest of M Corporation in R Corporation is considered as owned by A. See paragraph (c)(1)(iii) of this section. Thus, A owns 10 percent (9% plus 10% of 10%) of the stock in R Corporation and is a United States shareholder with respect to such corporation. Corporations M and B, by reason of owning 10 percent and 32 percent, respectively, of the stock in R Corporation are United States shareholders with respect to such corporation.

(b) For purposes of determining whether R Corporation is a controlled foreign corporation, the 1 percent of the stock in R Corporation directly owned by M Corporation and considered as owned by A cannot be counted twice. Therefore, the total amount of stock in R Corporation owned by United States shareholders is 51 percent, determined as follows:

Stock ownership in R Corporation	(percent)
A	9
B	32
M Corporation	10
Total	51

Example (2). United States person C owns 10 percent of the one class of stock in foreign corporation N, which owns 60 percent of the one class of stock in foreign corporation S. Under paragraph (a)(2) of § 1.958-1, C is considered as owning 6 percent (10% of 60%) of the stock in S Corporation. Under paragraph (c)(1)(iii) and (2) of this

Reg. § 1.958-2(d)(2)

Income from Sources Without the United States

See p. 20,601 for regulations not amended to reflect law changes

section, N Corporation is considered as owning 100 percent of the stock in S Corporation and C is considered as owning 10 percent of such 100 percent, or 10 percent of the stock in S Corporation. Thus, for purposes of determining whether C is a United States shareholder with respect to S Corporation, the attribution rules of paragraph (c)(1)(iii) and (2) of this section are used inasmuch as C owns a larger total percentage of the stock of S Corporation under such rules.

(g) *Illustration.* The application of this section may be illustrated by the following examples:

Example (1). United States persons A and B own 5 percent and 25 percent, respectively, of the one class of stock in foreign corporation M. Corporation M owns 60 percent of the one class of stock in foreign corporation N. Under paragraph (a)(2) of § 1.958-1, A and B are considered as owning 3 percent (5% of 60%) and 15 percent (25% of 60%), respectively, of the stock in N Corporation. Under paragraph (c)(2) of this section, M Corporation is treated as owning all the stock in N Corporation, and, under paragraph (c)(1)(iii) of this section, B is considered as owning 25 percent of such 100 percent, or 25 percent of the stock in N Corporation. Inasmuch as A owns less than 10 percent of the stock in M Corporation, he is not considered as owning, under paragraph (c)(1)(iii) of this section, any of the stock in N Corporation owned by M Corporation. Thus, the attribution rules of paragraph (a)(2) of § 1.958-1 are used with respect to A inasmuch as he owns a larger total percentage of the stock of N Corporation under such rules; and the attribution rules of paragraph (c)(1)(iii) and (2) of this section are used with respect to B inasmuch as he owns a larger total percentage of the stock of N Corporation under such rules.

Example (2). United States person C owns 60 percent of the one class of stock in domestic corporation P; corporation P owns 60 percent of the one class of stock in foreign corporation Q; and corporation Q owns 60 percent of the one class of stock in foreign corporation R. Under paragraph (a)(2) of § 1.958-1, P Corporation is considered as owning 36 percent (60% of 60%) of the stock in R Corporation, and C is considered as owning none of the stock in R Corporation inasmuch as the chain of ownership stops at the first United States person and P Corporation is such a person. Under paragraph (c)(2) of this section, Q Corporation is treated as owning 100 percent of the stock in R Corporation, and under paragraph (c)(1)(iii) of this section, P Corporation is considered as owning 60 percent of such 100 percent, or 60 percent of the stock in R Corporation. For purposes of determining the amount of stock in R Corporation which C is considered as owning, P Corporation is treated under paragraph (c)(2) of this section as owning 100 percent of the stock in R Corporation; therefore, C is considered as owning 60 percent of the stock in R Corporation. Thus, the attribution rules of paragraph (c)(1)(iii) and (2) of this section are used with respect to C and P Corporation inasmuch as they each own a larger total percentage of the stock of R Corporation under such rules.

Example (3). United States person D owns 25 percent of the one class of stock in foreign corporation S. D is also a 40-percent partner in domestic partnership X, which owns 50 percent of the one class of stock in domestic corporation T. Under paragraph (d)(1)(i) of this section, the 25 percent of the stock in S Corporation owned by D is considered as being owned by partnership X; since such stock is treated as actually owned by partnership X under paragraph (f)(1)(i) of this section, such stock is in turn considered as being owned by T Corporation under paragraph (d)(1)(iii) of this section. Thus, under paragraphs (d)(1) and (f)(1)(i) of this section, T Corporation is considered as owning 25 percent of the stock in S Corporation.

Example (4). Foreign corporation U owns 100 percent of the one class of stock in domestic corporation V and also 100 percent of the one class of stock in foreign corporation W. By virtue of paragraph (d)(2) of this section, V Corporation may not be considered under paragraph (d)(1) of this section as owning the stock by its sole shareholder, U Corporation, in W Corporation.

Example (5). United States citizen E owns 15 percent of the one class of stock in foreign corporation Y, and United States citizen F, E's spouse, owns 5 percent of such stock. E and F's four nonresident alien grandchildren each own 20 percent of the stock in Y Corporation. Under paragraph (b)(1) of this section, E is considered as owning the stock owned by F in Y Corporation; however, by virtue of paragraph (b)(3) of this section, E may not be considered under paragraph (b)(1) of this section as owning any of the stock in Y Corporation owned by such grandchildren.

Example (6). United States person F owns 10 percent of the one class of stock in foreign corporation Z; corporation Z owns 10 percent of the one class of stock in foreign corporation K; and corporation K owns 100 percent of the one class of stock in foreign corporation L. United States person G, F's spouse, owns 9 percent of the stock in K Corporation. Under paragraph (c)(1)(iii) of this section or paragraph (a)(2) of § 1.958-1, F is considered as owning 1 percent (10% of 10% of 100%) of the stock in L Corporation by reason of his ownership of stock in Z Corporation, and, under

Reg. § 1.958-2(g)

paragraph (b)(1) of this section, G is considered as owning such 1 percent of the stock in L Corporation. Under paragraph (a)(2) of § 1.958-1, G is considered as owning 9 percent (9% of 100%) of the stock in L Corporation by reason of her ownership of stock in K Corporation, and, under paragraph (b)(1) of this section, F is considered as owning such 9 percent of the stock in L Corporation. Thus, for the purpose of determining whether F or G is a United States shareholder with respect to L Corporation, each of F and G is considered as owning a total of 10 percent of the stock in L Corporation by applying the rules of paragraph (a)(2) of § 1.958-1 and paragraphs (b)(1) and (c)(1)(iii) of this section.

[Reg. § 1.958-2.]

☐ [T.D. 6889, 7-11-66. Amended by T.D. 7712, 8-6-80 and T.D. 8955, 7-19-2001.]

[Reg. § 1.959-1]

§ 1.959-1. Exclusion from gross income of United States persons of previously taxed earnings and profits.—(a) *In general.* Sections 951 through 964 provide that certain types of income of controlled foreign corporations will be subject to United States income tax even though such amounts are not currently distributed to the United States shareholders of such corporations. The amounts so taxed to certain United States shareholders are described as subpart F income, previously excluded subpart F income withdrawn from investment in less developed countries, previously excluded subpart F income withdrawn from investment in foreign base company shipping operations, and increases in earnings invested in United States property. Section 959 provides that amounts taxed as subpart F income, as previously excluded subpart F income withdrawn from investment in less developed countries, or as previously excluded subpart F income withdrawn from investment in foreign base company shipping operations are not taxed again as increases in earnings invested in United States property. Section 959 also provides an exclusion whereby none of the amounts so taxed are taxed again when actually distributed directly, or indirectly through a chain of ownership described in section 958(a), to United States shareholders or to such shareholders' successors in interest. The exclusion also applies to amounts taxed to United States shareholders as income of one controlled foreign corporation and later distributed to another controlled foreign corporation in such a chain of ownership where such amounts would otherwise be again included in the income of such shareholders or their successors in interest as subpart F income of the controlled foreign corporation to which they are distributed. Section 959 also provides rules for the allocation of distributions to earnings and profits and for the non-dividend treatment of actual distributions which are excluded from gross income.

(b) *Actual distributions to United States persons.* The earnings and profits for a taxable year of a foreign corporation attributable to amounts which are, or have been, included in the gross income of a United States shareholder of such corporation under section 951(a) shall not, when such amounts are distributed to such shareholder directly, or indirectly through a chain of ownership described in section 958(a), be again included in the gross income of such United States shareholder. See section 959(a)(1). Thus, earnings and profits attributable to amounts which are, or have been, included in the gross income of a United States shareholder of a foreign corporation under section 951(a)(1)(A)(i) as subpart F income, under section 951(a)(1)(A)(ii) as previously excluded subpart F income withdrawn from investment in less developed countries, under section 951(a)(1)(A)(iii) as previously excluded subpart F income withdrawn from investment in foreign base company shipping operations, or under section 951(a)(1)(B) as earnings invested in United States property, shall not be again included in the gross income of such shareholder when such amounts are actually distributed, directly or indirectly, to such shareholder. See paragraph (d) of this section for exclusion applicable to such shareholder's successor in interest. The application of this paragraph may be illustrated by the following example:

Example. (a) A, a United States shareholder, owns 100 percent of the only class of stock of R Corporation, a corporation organized on January 1, 1963, which is a controlled foreign corporation throughout the period here involved. Both A and R Corporation use the calendar year as a taxable year.

(b) During 1964, R Corporation derives $100 of subpart F income, and A includes such amount in his gross income under section 951(a)(1)(A)(i). Corporation R's current and accumulated earnings and profits (before taking into account distributions made during 1964) are $150. Also, during 1964, R Corporation distributes $50 to A. The $50 distribution is excludable from A's gross income for 1964 under this paragraph and § 1.959-3 because such distribution represents earnings and profits attributable to amounts which are included in A's gross income for such year under section 951(a).

(c) If instead of deriving the $100 of subpart F income in 1964, R Corporation derives such amount during 1963 and has earnings and profits

Reg. § 1.959-1(a)

for 1963 in excess of $100, A must include $100 in his gross income for 1963 under section 951(a)(1)(A)(i). However, the $50 distribution made by R Corporation to A during 1964 is excludable from A's gross income for such year under this paragraph and § 1.959-3 because such distribution represents earnings and profits attributable to amounts which have been included in A's gross income for 1963 under section 951(a).

(d) If, with respect to 1964—

(1) Instead of owning the stock of R Corporation directly, A owns such stock through a chain of ownership described in section 958(a), that is, A owns 100 percent of M Corporation which owns 100 percent of N Corporation which owns 100 percent of R Corporation,

(2) Both M and N Corporations use the calendar year as a taxable year and are controlled foreign corporations throughout the period here involved,

(3) Corporation R derives $100 of subpart F income and has earnings and profits in excess of $100,

(4) Neither M Corporation nor N Corporation has earnings and profits or a deficit in earnings and profits, and

(5) The $50 distribution is from R Corporation to N Corporation to M Corporation to A,

A must include $100 in his gross income for 1964 under section 951(a)(1)(A)(i) by reason of his indirect ownership of R Corporation. However, the $50 distribution is excludable from A's gross income for 1964 under this paragraph and § 1.959-3 because such distribution represents earnings and profits attributable to amounts which are included in A's gross income for such year under section 951(a) and are distributed indirectly to A through a chain of ownership described in section 958(a).

(c) *Excludable investment of earnings in United States property.* The earnings and profits for a taxable year of a foreign corporation attributable to amounts which are, or have been, included in the gross income of a United States shareholder of such corporation under section 951(a)(1)(A) shall not, when such amounts would, but for section 959(a)(2) and this paragraph, be included under section 951(a)(1)(B) in the gross income of such shareholder directly, or indirectly through a chain of ownership described in section 958(a), be again included in the gross income of such United States shareholder. Thus, earnings and profits attributable to amounts which are, or have been, included in the gross income of a United States shareholder of a foreign corporation under section 951(a)(1)(A)(i) as subpart F income, under section 951(a)(1)(A)(ii) as previously excluded subpart F income withdrawn from investment in less developed countries, or under section 951(a)(1)(A)(iii) as previously excluded subpart F income withdrawn from investment in foreign base company shipping operations may be invested in United States property without being again included in such shareholder's income under section 951(a). Moreover, the first amounts deemed invested in United States property are amounts previously included in the gross income of a United States shareholder under section 951(a)(1)(A). See paragraph (d) of this section for exclusion applicable to such shareholder's successor in interest. The application of this paragraph may be illustrated by the following example:

Example. (a) A, a United States shareholder, owns 100 percent of the only class of stock of R Corporation, a corporation organized on January 1, 1963, which is a controlled foreign corporation throughout the period here involved. Both A and R Corporation use the calendar year as a taxable year.

(b) During 1964, R Corporation derives $35 of subpart F income, and A includes such amount in his gross income under section 951(a)(1)(A)(i). During 1964, R Corporation also invests $50 in tangible property (other than property described in section 956(b)(2)) located in the United States. Corporation R makes no distributions during the year, and its current earnings and profits are in excess of $50. Of the $50 investment of earnings in United States property, $35 is excludable from A's gross income for 1964 under section 959(a)(2) because such amount represents earnings and profits which are attributable to amounts which are included in A's gross income for such year under section 951(a)(1)(A)(i) and therefore may be invested in United States property without again being included in A's gross income. The remaining $15 is includible in A's gross income for 1964 under section 951(a)(1)(B).

(c) If, instead of deriving $35 of subpart F income in 1964, R Corporation has no subpart F income for 1964 but derives the $35 of subpart F income during 1963 and has earnings and profits for such year in excess of $35, A must include $35 in his gross income for 1963 under section 951(a)(1)(A)(i). However, of the $50 investment of earnings in United States property made by R Corporation during 1964, $35 is excludable from A's gross income for 1964 under section 959(a)(2) because such amount represents earnings and profits attributable to amounts which have been included in A's gross income for 1963 under section 951(a)(1)(A)(i). The remaining $15 is includ-

Reg. § 1.959-1(c)

ible in A's gross income for 1964 under section 951(a)(1)(B).

(d) *Application of exclusions to shareholder's successor in interest.* If a United States person (as defined in § 1.957-4) acquires from any person any portion of the interest in the foreign corporation of a United States shareholder referred to in paragraph (b) or (c) of this section, the rules of such paragraph shall apply to such acquiring person but only to the extent that the acquiring person establishes to the satisfaction of the district director the right to the exclusion provided by such paragraph. The information to be furnished by the acquiring person to the district director with his return for the taxable year to support such exclusion shall include:

(1) The name, address, and taxable year of the foreign corporation from which the distribution is received and of all other corporations, partnerships, trusts, or estates in any applicable chain of ownership described in section 958(a);

(2) The name, address, and (in the case of information required to be furnished after June 20, 1983) taxpayer identification number of the person from whom the stock interest was acquired;

(3) A description of the stock interest acquired and its relation, if any, to a chain of ownership described in section 958(a);

(4) The amount for which an exclusion under section 959(a) is claimed; and

(5) Evidence showing that the earnings and profits for which an exclusion is claimed are attributable to amounts which were included in the gross income of a United States shareholder under section 951(a), that such amounts were not previously excluded from the gross income of a United States person, and the identity of the United States shareholder including such amounts.

The acquiring person shall also furnish to the district director such other information as may be required by the district director in support of the exclusion.

Example. (a) A, a United States shareholder, owns 100 percent of the only class of stock of R Corporation, a corporation organized on January 1, 1964, and a controlled foreign corporation throughout the period here involved. Both A and R Corporation use the calendar year as a taxable year.

(b) During 1964, R Corporation has $100 of subpart F income and earnings and profits in excess of $100. A includes $100 in his gross income for 1964 under section 951(a)(1)(A)(i). During 1965, A sells 40 percent of his stock in R Corporation to B, a United States person who uses the calendar year as a taxable year. In 1965, R Corporation has no earnings and profits and experiences no increase in earnings invested in United States property. Corporation R distributes $40 to B on December 1, 1965. If B establishes his right to the exclusion to the satisfaction of the district director, he may exclude $40 from his gross income for 1965 under section 959(a)(1).

(c) If, instead of selling his 40-percent interest directly to B, A sells on February 1, 1965, 40 percent of his stock in R Corporation to C, a nonresident alien, and on October 1, 1965, B acquires the 40-percent interest in R Corporation from C, the result is the same as in paragraph (b) of this example, if B establishes his right to the exclusion to the satisfaction of the district director.

(d) If, instead of acquiring 40 percent, B acquires only 5 percent of A's stock in R Corporation and R Corporation distributes $5 to B during 1965, B is not a United States shareholder (within the meaning of section 951(b)) with respect to R Corporation since he owns only 5 percent of the stock of R Corporation. Notwithstanding, B may exclude the $5 distribution from his gross income for 1965 under section 959(a)(1) if he establishes his right to the exclusion to the satisfaction of the district director.

(e) If the facts are assumed to be the same as in paragraphs (a) and (b) of this example except that—

(1) A owns the stock of R Corporation indirectly through a chain of ownership described in section 958(a), that is, A owns 100 percent of M corporation which owns 100 percent of N Corporation which owns 100 percent of R Corporation,

(2) B acquires from N Corporation 40 percent of the stock in R Corporation,

(3) Both M Corporation and N Corporation are controlled foreign corporations which use the calendar year as a taxable year,

(4) Neither M Corporation nor N Corporation has any amount in 1964 or 1965 which is includible in gross income of United States shareholders under section 951(a), and

(5) Neither M Corporation nor N Corporation has a deficit in earnings and profits for 1964,

the result is the same as in paragraph (b) of this example if B establishes his right to the exclusion to the satisfaction of the district director. [Reg. § 1.959-1.]

□ [*T.D.* 6795, 1-28-65. Amended by *T.D.* 7893, 5-11-83.]

Reg. § 1.959-1(d)(1)

Income from Sources Without the United States

[Reg. § 1.959-2]

§ 1.959-2. Exclusion from gross income of controlled foreign corporations of previously taxed earnings and profits.—(a) *Applicable rule.* The earnings and profits for a taxable year of a controlled foreign corporation attributable to amounts which are, or have been, included in the gross income of a United States shareholder under section 951(a) shall not, when distributed through a chain of ownership described in section 958(a), be also included in the gross income of another controlled foreign corporation in such chain for purposes of the application of section 951(a) to such other controlled foreign corporation with respect to such United States shareholder. See section 959(b). The exclusion from the income of such other foreign corporation also applies with respect to any other United States shareholder who acquires from such United States shareholder or any other person any portion of the interest of such United States shareholder in the controlled foreign corporation, but only to the extent the acquiring shareholder establishes to the satisfaction of the district director the right to such exclusion. An acquiring shareholder claiming the exclusion under section 959(b) shall furnish to the district director with his return for the taxable year the information required under paragraph (d) of § 1.959-1 to support the exclusion under this paragraph.

(b) *Illustration.* The application of this section may be illustrated by the following example:

Example. (a) A, a United States shareholder, owns 100 percent of the only class of stock of M Corporation which in turn owns 100 percent of the only class of stock of N Corporation. A and corporations M and N use the calendar year as a taxable year and corporations M and N are controlled foreign corporations throughout the period here involved.

(b) During 1963, N Corporation invests $100 in tangible property (other than property described in section 956(b)(2)) located in the United States and has earnings and profits in excess of $100. A is required to include $100 in his gross income for 1963 under section 951(a)(1)(B) by reason of his indirect ownership of the stock of N Corporation. During 1963, M Corporation has no income or investments other than the income derived from a distribution of $100 from N Corporation. Corporation M has earnings and profits of $100 for 1963. Under paragraph (a) of § 1.954-2, the $100 distribution received by M Corporation from N Corporation would otherwise constitute subpart F income of M Corporation; however, by reason of section 959(b) and this section, this amount does not constitute gross income of M Corporation for purposes of determining amounts includible in A's gross income under section 951(a)(1)(A)(i).

(c) During 1964, N Corporation derives $100 of subpart F income and distributes $100 to M Corporation which has no subpart F income for 1964 but which invests the $100 distribution in tangible property (other than property described in section 956(b)(2)) located in the United States. Corporation N's earnings and profits for 1964 are in excess of $100, and M Corporation's current and accumulated earnings and profits (before taking into account distributions made during 1964) are in excess of $100. A is required with respect to N Corporation to include $100 in his gross income for 1964 under section 951(a)(1)(A)(i) by reason of his indirect ownership of the stock of N Corporation. The investment by M Corporation in United States property would otherwise constitute an investment of earnings in United States property to which section 956 applies; however, by reason of section 959(b) and this section, such amount does not constitute gross income of M Corporation for purposes of determining amounts includible in A's gross income under section 951(a)(1)(B).

(d) If during 1965, N Corporation invests $100 in tangible property (other than property described in section 956(b)(2)) located in the United States and has earnings and profits in excess of $100, A will be required with respect to N Corporation to include $100 in his gross income for 1965 under section 951(a)(1)(B), because the $100 of earnings and profits for 1964 attributable to N Corporation's subpart F income which was taxed to A in 1964 was distributed to M Corporation in such year.

(e) If, with respect to 1966—

(1) Corporation N owns 100 percent of the only class of stock of R Corporation,

(2) Corporation R derives $100 of subpart F income, has earnings and profits in excess of $100, and makes no distributions to N Corporation,

(3) Corporation N invests $25 in tangible property (other than property described in section 956(b)(2)) located in the United States and has current and accumulated earnings and profits in excess of $25, and

(4) Corporation M has no income or investments and does not have a deficit in earnings and profits,

the $100 of subpart F income derived by R Corporation is includible in A's gross income for 1966 under section 951(a)(1)(A)(i) and the $25 investment of earnings in United States property by N

Reg. § 1.959-2(b)

Corporation is includible in A's gross income for 1966 under section 951(a)(1)(B).

(f) If, however, the facts are the same as in paragraph (e) of this example except that—

(1) During 1966, R Corporation distributes $20 to N Corporation, and

(2) Corporation N makes no distributions during such year to M Corporation,

of the $25 investment in United States property by N Corporation, $20 is not includible in A's gross income for 1966 because such amount represents earnings and profits which are attributable to amounts included in A's gross income for such year under section 951(a)(1)(A)(i) with respect to R Corporation and which have been distributed to N Corporation by R Corporation. By reason of section 959(b) and this section, such $20 distribution to N Corporation does not constitute gross income of N Corporation for purposes of determining amounts includible in A's gross income under section 951(a)(1)(B); however, the remaining $5 of investment of earnings in United States property by N Corporation in 1966 is includible in A's gross income for such year under section 951(a)(1)(B). [Reg. § 1.959-2.]

☐ [T.D. 6795, 1-28-65.]

[Reg. § 1.959-3]

§ 1.959-3. **Allocation of distributions to earnings and profits of foreign corporations.**—(a) *In general.* For purposes of §§ 1.959-1 and 1.959-2, the source of the earnings and profits from which distributions are made by a foreign corporation as between earnings and profits attributable to increases in earnings invested in United States property, previously taxed subpart F income, previously excluded subpart F income withdrawn from investment in less developed countries, previously excluded subpart F income withdrawn from investment in foreign base company shipping operations, and other amounts shall be determined in accordance with section 959(c) and paragraphs (b) through (e) of this section.

(b) *Applicability of section 316(a).* For purposes of this section, section 316(a) shall be applied, in determining the source of distributions from the earnings and profits of a foreign corporation, by first applying section 316(a)(2) and then by applying section 316(a)(1)—

(1) First, as provided by section 959(c)(1), to earnings and profits attributable to amounts included in gross income of a United States shareholder under section 951(a)(1)(B) (or which would have been so included but for section 959(a)(2) and paragraph (c) of § 1.959-1),

(2) Secondly, as provided by section 959(c)(2), to earnings and profits attributable to amounts included in gross income of a United States shareholder under section 951(a)(1)(A) (but reduced by amounts not included in such gross income under section 951(a)(1)(B) because of the exclusion provided by section 959(a)(2) and paragraph (c) of § 1.959-1), and

(3) Finally, as provided by section 959(c)(3), to other earnings and profits.

Thus, distributions shall be considered first attributable to amounts, if any, described in subparagraph (1) of this paragraph (first for the current taxable year and then for prior taxable years beginning with the most recent prior taxable year), secondly to amounts, if any, described in subparagraph (2) of this paragraph (first for the current taxable year and then for prior taxable years beginning with the most recent prior taxable year), and finally to the amounts, if any, described in subparagraph (3) of this paragraph (first for the current taxable year and then for prior taxable years beginning with the most recent prior taxable year). See, however, paragraph (e) of § 1.963-3 (applied as if section 963 had not been repealed by the Tax Reduction Act of 1975) for a special rule for determination of the source of distributions counting as minimum distributions. Earnings and profits are classified as to year and as to section 959(c) amount in the year in which such amounts are included in gross income of a United States shareholder under section 951(a) and are reclassified as to section 959(c) amount in the year in which such amounts would be so included but for the provisions of section 959(a)(2); any subsequent distribution of such amounts to a higher tier in a chain of ownership described in section 958(a) does not of itself change such classifications. For example, earnings and profits of a foreign corporation attributable to amounts of previously excluded subpart F income withdrawn from investment in less developed countries (or from investments in export trade assets or foreign base company shipping operations) shall be reclassified as amounts to which subparagraph (2), rather than subparagraph (3), of this paragraph applies for purposes of determining priority of distribution, and such earnings and profits shall be considered attributable to the taxable year in which the withdrawal occurs. This paragraph shall apply to distributions by one foreign corporation to another foreign corporation and by a foreign corporation to a United States person. The application of this paragraph may be illustrated by the following example:

Example. (a) M, a controlled foreign corporation is organized on January 1, 1963, and is

Income from Sources Without the United States

100-percent owned by A, a United States shareholder. Both A and M Corporation use the calendar year as a taxable year, and M Corporation is a controlled foreign corporation throughout the period here involved. As of December 31, 1966, M Corporation's accumulated earnings and profits of $450 (before taking into account distributions made in 1966) applicable to A's interest in such corporation are classified for purposes of section 959(c) as follows:

Year	Classification of earnings and profits for purposes of sec. 959		
	(c)(1)	(c)(2)	(c)(3)
1963	$100		
1964	100	$75	
1965		75	$50
1966			50

(b) During 1966, M Corporation makes three separate distributions to A of $150 each, and the source of such distributions under section 959(c) is as follows:

	Amount	Year	Allocation of distributions under sec. 959
Distribution #1:	$100	1964	(c)(1)
	50	1963	(c)(1)
	150		
Distribution #2:	$50	1963	(c)(1)
	75	1965	(c)(2)
	25	1964	(c)(2)
	150		
Distribution #3:	$50	1964	(c)(2)
	50	1966	(c)(3)
	50	1965	(c)(3)
	150		

(c) If, in addition to the above facts—

(1) M Corporation owns throughout the period here involved 100 percent of the only class of stock of N Corporation, a controlled foreign corporation which uses the calendar year as a taxable year,

(2) Corporation N derives $60 of subpart F income for 1963 which A includes in his gross income for such year under section 951(a)(1)(A)(i),

(3) Corporation N has earnings and profits for 1963 of $60 but has neither earnings or profits nor a deficit in earnings and profits for 1964, 1965, or 1966, and

(4) During 1966, N Corporation invests $20 in tangible property (not described in section 956(b)(2)) located in the United States and distributes $45 to M Corporation,

the $20 investment of earnings in United States property is excludable from A's gross income for 1966, under section 959(a)(2) and paragraph (c) of § 1.959-1, with respect to N Corporation and the $45 dividend received by M Corporation does not, under section 959(b) and § 1.959-2, constitute gross income of M Corporation for 1966 for purposes of determining amounts includible in A's gross income under section 951(a)(1)(A)(i) with respect to M Corporation. However, the $45 dividend paid by N Corporation to M Corporation is allocated under section 959(c) and this paragraph to the earnings and profits of N Corporation as follows: $20 to 1963 earnings described in section 959(c)(1) and $25 to 1963 earnings described in section 959(c)(2). In such case, M Corporation's earnings and profits of $495 (before taking into account distributions made in 1966) would be classified as follows for purposes of section 959(c):

Year	Classification of earnings and profits for purposes of sec. 959		
	(c)(1)	(c)(2)	(c)(3)
1963	$120	$25	
1964	100	$75	
1965		75	$50
1966			50

Reg. § 1.959-3(b)(3)

(d) The three distributions to A in 1966 of $150 each would then have the following source under section 959(c):

	Amount	Year	Allocation of distributions under sec. 959
Distribution # 1:	$100	1964	(c)(1)
	50	1963	(c)(1)
	150		
Distribution # 2:	$ 70	1963	(c)(1)
	75	1965	(c)(2)
	5	1964	(c)(2)
	150		
Distribution # 3:	$ 70	1964	(c)(2)
	25	1963	(c)(2)
	50	1966	(c)(3)
	5	1965	(c)(3)
	150		

(c) *Treatment of deficits in earnings and profits.* For purposes of this section, a United States shareholder's pro rata share (determined in accordance with the principles of paragraph (e) of § 1.951-1) of a foreign corporation's deficit in earnings and profits, determined under section 964(a) and § 1.964-1, for any taxable year shall be applied only to earnings and profits described in paragraph (b)(3) of this section.

(d) *Treatment of certain foreign taxes.* For purposes of this section, any amount described in subparagraph (1), (2), or (3) of paragraph (b) of this section which is distributed by a foreign corporation through a chain of ownership described in section 958(a)(2) shall be reduced by any income, war profits, or excess profits taxes imposed on or with respect to such distribution by any foreign country or possession of the United States.

Example. (a) Domestic corporation M owns 100 percent of the only class of stock of foreign corporation A, which is incorporated under the laws of foreign country X and which, in turn, owns 100 percent of the only class of stock of foreign corporation B, which is incorporated under the laws of foreign country Y. All corporations use the calendar year as a taxable year and corporations A and B are controlled foreign corporations throughout the period here involved.

(b) During 1963, B Corporation (a less developed country corporation for 1963 within the meaning of § 1.955-5) derives $90 of subpart F income, after incurring $10 of foreign income tax allocable to such income under paragraph (c) of § 1.954-1, has earnings and profits in excess of $90, and makes no distributions. Corporation M must include $90 in its gross income for 1963 under section 951(a)(1)(A)(i). As of December 31, 1963, with respect to M Corporation, B Corporation has earnings and profits for 1963 described in section 959(c)(2) of $90.

(c) During 1964, B Corporation has neither earnings and profits nor a deficit in earnings and profits but distributes $90 to A Corporation, and, by reason of section 959(b) and § 1.959-2, such amount is not includible in the gross income of M Corporation for 1964 under section 951(a) with respect to A Corporation. Corporation A incurs a withholding tax of $13.50 on the $90 dividend distributed from B Corporation (15 percent of $90) and an additional foreign income tax of 10 percent or $7.65 by reason of the inclusion of the net distribution of $76.50 ($90 minus $13.50) in its taxable income for 1964. As of December 31, 1964, with respect to M Corporation, B Corporation's earnings and profits for 1963 described in section 959(c)(2) amount to zero ($90 minus $90); and A Corporation's earnings and profits for 1963 described in section 959(c)(2) amount to $68.85 ($90 minus $13.50 minus $7.65).

(e) *Determination of foreign tax credit.* For purposes of applying section 902 and section 960 in determining the foreign tax credit allowable under section 901 in a case in which distributions are made by a second-tier corporation or a first-tier corporation, as the case may be, from its earnings and profits for a taxable year which are attributable to an amount included in the gross income of a United States shareholder under section 951(a) or which are attributable to amounts excluded from the gross income of such foreign corporation under section 959(b) and § 1.959-2 with respect to a United States shareholder, the rules of paragraph (b) of this section shall apply except that in applying subparagraph (1) or (2) of such paragraph—

Reg. § 1.959-3(c)

(1) Distributions from the earnings and profits for such taxable year of the second-tier corporation shall be considered first attributable to its earnings and profits attributable to distributions from the earnings and profits of the foreign corporation, if any, next lower in the chain of ownership described in section 958(a), to the extent of such earnings and profits of the second-tier corporation, and then to the other earnings and profits of such second-tier corporation, and

(2) Distributions from the earnings and profits for such taxable year of the first-tier corporation shall be considered first attributable to its earnings and profits attributable to distributions from the earnings and profits of the second-tier corporation, to the extent of such earnings and profits of the first-tier corporation, and then to the other earnings and profits of such first-tier corporation.

For purposes of this paragraph, a second-tier corporation is a foreign corporation referred to in section 960(a)(1)(B), and a first-tier corporation is a foreign corporation referred to in section 960(a)(1)(A). The application of this paragraph may be illustrated by the following examples:

Example (1). (a) Domestic corporation A, a United States shareholder, owns 100 percent of the only class of stock of foreign corporation R which, in turn, owns 100 percent of the only class of stock of foreign corporation S. All corporations use the calendar year as a taxable year, and corporations R and S are controlled foreign corporations throughout the period here involved.

(b) Neither R Corporation nor S Corporation has subpart F income for 1963. During 1963, S Corporation increases by $100 its investment in tangible property (not described in section 956(b)(2)) located in the United States, makes no distributions, and has earnings and profits of $100. Corporation A must include $100 in its gross income for 1963 under section 951(a)(1)(B) with respect to S Corporation. During 1963, R Corporation also increases by $100 its investment in tangible property (not described in section 956(b)(2)) located in the United States, makes no distributions, and has earnings and profits of $100. Corporation A must include $100 in its gross income for 1963 under section 951(a)(1)(B) with respect to R Corporation.

(c) During 1964, S Corporation distributes $100 to R Corporation, and R Corporation distributes $100 to A Corporation. Neither corporation has any earnings or profits or deficit in earnings and profits for such year. At December 31, 1964, R Corporation has earnings and profits (computed before distributions to A Corporation made for the year) of $200, consisting of $100 of section 959(c)(1) amounts of R Corporation for 1963 and of $100 of section 959(c)(1) amounts of S Corporation for 1963. For purposes of determining the foreign tax credit under section 960 and the regulations thereunder, the $100 distribution by R Corporation shall be considered attributable to S Corporation's earnings and profits for 1963 described in section 959(c)(1).

Example (2). (a) Domestic corporation A, a United States shareholder, owns 100 percent of the only class of stock of foreign corporation T which, in turn, owns 100 percent of the only class of stock of foreign corporation U. All corporations use the calendar year as a taxable year, and corporations T and U are controlled foreign corporations throughout the period here involved.

(b) During 1964, T Corporation invests $100 in tangible property (not described in section 956(b)(2)) located in the United States. For 1964, T Corporation has no subpart F income and makes no distributions; A must include $100 in its gross income for 1964 under section 951(a)(1)(B) with respect to T Corporation. For 1964, U Corporation has no subpart F income or investment of earnings in United States property but U Corporation has $100 of earnings and profits which it distributes to T Corporation. At December 31, 1964, T Corporation has earnings and profits of $300, consisting of operating income of $100 for each of the years 1963 and 1964 and $100 in dividends received from the earnings and profits of U Corporation for 1964. These earnings and profits are classified as follows under section 959(c): $100 of section 959(c)(1) amounts of T Corporation for 1964, $100 of section 959(c)(3) amounts of U Corporation for 1964, and $100 of section 959(c)(3) amounts of T Corporation for 1963.

(c) During 1965 neither T Corporation nor U Corporation has any earnings and profits or deficit in earnings and profits or investment of earnings in United States property, but T Corporation distributes $100 to A Corporation. For purposes of determining the foreign tax credit under section 960 and the regulations thereunder, the $100 distribution of T Corporation shall be considered attributable to T Corporation's earnings and profits for 1964 described in section 959(c)(1).

(f) *Illustration.* The application of this section may be illustrated by the following example:

Example. (a) M, a controlled foreign corporation is organized on January 1, 1963, and is wholly owned by A, a United States shareholder. Both A and Corporation M use the calendar year as a taxable year.

(b) Corporation M's earnings and profits (before distributions) for 1963 are $200, $100 of which is attributable to subpart F income. Corporation M's earnings and profits for such year also

Reg. § 1.959-3(f)

include $25 attributable to subpart F income which is excluded from M Corporation's foreign base company income under section 954(b)(1) as dividends, interest, and gains invested in qualified investments in less developed countries. Corporation M's increase in earnings invested in tangible property (not described in section 956(b)(2)) located in the United States for 1963, is $50, and M Corporation makes a distribution of such property during such year of $20. For purposes of section 959, A's interest in M Corporation's earnings and profits as of December 31, 1963, determined after the distribution of $20, is classified as follows:

Sec. 959(c)(1) amounts:
Earnings for 1963 attributable to increased investment in United States property which would have been included in A's gross income but for application of sec. 959(a)(2) and § 1.959-1(c) .... $ 50
Less: Distribution for 1963 allocated under sec. 959(c)(1) and paragraph (b)(1) of this section to such amounts .... 20 $ 30

Sec. 959(c)(2) amounts:
Earnings for 1963 attributable to subpart F income included in A's gross income under sec. 951(a)(1)(A)(i) $100
Less: Earnings for 1963 attributable to increased investment in United States property which would have been included in A's gross income but for application of sec. 959(a)(2) and § 1.959-1(c) .... 50 $ 50

Sec. 959(c)(3) amounts:
Predistribution earnings for 1963 .... $200
Less: Earnings for 1963 classified as:
    Sec. 959(c)(1) amounts $50
    Sec. 959(c)(2) amounts 50   100 $100

A's total interest in M Corporation's earnings and profits $180

For 1963, A is required to include $100 of subpart F income in his gross income under section 951(a)(1)(A)(i). He would have been required to include $50 in his gross income under section 951(a)(1)(B) as M Corporation's increase in earnings invested in United States property, except that section 959(a)(2) and paragraph (c) of § 1.959-1 provide in effect that earnings and profits taxed to A under section 951(a)(1)(A) with respect to M Corporation (whether in the current taxable year or in prior years) may be invested in United States property without again being included in gross income under section 951(a). The $20 dividend from M Corporation is excluded from A's gross income under section 959(a)(1) and paragraph (b) of § 1.959-1, since such distribution is allocated under section 959(c)(1) and paragraph (b)(1) of this section to amounts described in section 959(c)(1).

(c) During 1964, M Corporation's earnings and profits (before distributions) are $300, $75 of which is attributable to subpart F income. Corporation M has no change in investments in United States property during such year and withdraws $15 of previously excluded subpart F income from investment in less developed countries. Corporation M makes a cash distribution of $250 to A during 1964. For purposes of section 959, A's interest in M Corporation's earnings and profits as of December 31, 1964, determined after the distribution of $250, is classified as follows:

Sec. 959(c)(1) amounts:
Sec. 959(c)(1) net amount for 1963 (as determined under paragraph (b) of this example) .... $ 30
Less: Distribution for 1964 allocated under sec. 959(c)(1) and paragraph (b)(1) of this section to such amount .... 30 $ 0

Sec. 959(c)(2) amounts:
Sec. 959(c)(2) net amount for 1963 (as determined under paragraph (b) of this example) .... $ 50
Plus: Earnings for 1964 attributable to:
    Subpart F income for 1964 included in A's gross income under sec. 951(a)(1)(A)(i) 75
    Previously excluded subpart F income withdrawn in 1964 from investment in less developed countries and included in A's gross income under sec. 951(a)(1)(A)(ii) 15
                                                                                  $140
Less: Distribution for 1964 allocated under sec. 959(c)(2) and paragraph (b)(2) of this section to such amounts $140   0

Reg. § 1.959-3(f)

Income from Sources Without the United States

See p. 20,601 for regulations not amended to reflect law changes

Sec. 959(c)(3) amounts:
Sec. 959(c)(3) net amount for 1963 (as determined under paragraph (b)
of this example) $100
Plus: Sec. 959(c)(3) net amount for 1964:
Predistribution earnings for 1964 .... $300
Less:
Earnings for 1964 classified as sec. 959(c)(1) amounts ($0)
and as sec. 959(c)(2) amounts ($75 + $15) $90
Distributions for 1964 allocated under sec. 959(c)(3) and
paragraph (b)(3) of this section $80 $170 $130 $230

A's total interest in M Corporation's earnings and profits $230

For 1964, A is required to include in his gross income under section 951(a)(1)(A)(i) $75 of subpart F income, and under section 951(a)(1)(A)(ii) $15 of previously excluded subpart F income withdrawn from investment in less developed countries. Of the $250 cash distribution, A may exclude $170 from his gross income under section 959(a)(1) and paragraph (b) of § 1.959-1 and $80 is includible in his gross income as a dividend.

(d) The source under section 959(c) of the 1964 distribution of $250 to A is as follows:

Year	Amount
1963 ... $30	(c)(1)
1964 ... 90	(c)(2)
1963 ... 50	(c)(2)
1964 ... 80	(c)(3)
Total ... $250	

[Reg. § 1.959-3.]

☐ [T.D. 6795, 1-28-65. Amended by T.D. 7334, 12-20-74, T.D. 7545, 5-5-78 and T.D. 7893, 5-11-83.]

[Reg. § 1.959-4]

§ 1.959-4. Distributions to United States persons not counting as dividends.—Except as provided in section 960(a)(3) and § 1.960-1 any distribution to a United States person which is excluded from the gross income of such person under section 959(a)(1) and § 1.959-1 shall be treated for purposes of chapter 1 (relating to normal taxes and surtaxes) of subtitle A (relating to income taxes) of the Code as a distribution which is not a dividend. However, see paragraph (b)(1) of § 1.956-1, relating to the dividend limitation on the amount of a controlled foreign corporation's investment of earnings in United States property. [Reg. § 1.959-4.]

☐ [T.D. 6795, 1-28-65. Amended by T.D. 7120, 6-3-71.]

[Reg. § 1.960-1]

§ 1.960-1. Foreign tax credit with respect to taxes paid on earnings and profits of controlled foreign corporations.—(a) *Scope of regulations under section 960.* This section prescribes rules for determining the foreign income taxes deemed paid under section 960(a)(1) by a domestic corporation which is required under section 951 to include in gross income an amount attributable to a first-, second-, or third-tier corporation's earnings and profits. Section 1.960-2 prescribes rules for applying section 902 to dividends paid by a third-, second-, or first-tier corporation from earnings and profits attributable to an amount which is, or has been, included in gross income under section 951. Section 1.960-3 provides special rules for the application of the gross-up provisions of section 78 where an amount is included in gross income under section 951. Section 1.960-4 prescribes rules for increasing the applicable foreign tax credit limitation under section 904(a) of the domestic corporation for the taxable year in which it receives a distribution of earnings and profits in respect of which it was required under section 951 to include an amount in its gross income for a prior taxable year. Section 1.960-5 prescribes rules for disallowing a deduction for foreign income taxes for such taxable year of receipt where the domestic corporation received the benefits of the foreign tax credit for such previous taxable year of inclusion. Section 1.960-6 provides that the excess of such an increase in the applicable limitation under section 904(a) over the tax liability of the domestic corporation for such taxable year of receipt results in an overpayment of tax. Section 1.960-7 prescribes the effective dates for application of these rules.

(b) *Definitions.* For purposes of section 960 and §§ 1.960-1 through 1.960-7—

(1) *First-tier corporation.* The term "first-tier corporation" means a foreign corporation at least 10 percent of the voting stock of which is owned

Reg. § 1.960-1(b)(1)

by the domestic corporation described in paragraph (a) of this section.

(2) *Second-tier corporation.* In the case of amounts included in the gross income of the taxpayer under section 951—

(i) For taxable years beginning before January 1, 1977, the term "second-tier corporation" means a foreign corporation at least 50 percent of the voting stock of which is owned by such first-tier corporation.

(ii) For taxable years beginning after December 31, 1976, the term "second-tier corporation" means a foreign corporation at least 10 percent of the voting stock of which is owned by such first-tier corporation.

(3) *Third-tier corporation.* In the case of amounts included in the gross income of a domestic shareholder under section 951 for taxable years beginning after December 31, 1976, the term "third-tier corporation" means a foreign corporation at least 10 percent of the voting stock of which is owned by such second-tier corporation.

(4) *Immediately lower-tier corporation.* In the case of a first-tier corporation the term "immediately lower-tier corporation" means a second-tier corporation. In the case of a second-tier corporation, the term "immediately lower-tier corporation" means a third-tier corporation. In the case of a third-tier corporation, the term "immediately lower-tier corporation" means a fourth-tier corporation.

(5) *Foreign income taxes.* The term "foreign income taxes" means income, war profits, and excess profits taxes, and taxes included in the term "income, war profits, and excess profits taxes" by reason of section 903, imposed by a foreign country or a possession of the United States.

(c) *Amount of foreign income taxes deemed paid by domestic corporation in respect of earnings and profits of foreign corporation attributable to amount included in income under section 951*—(1) *In general.* For purposes of section 901—

(i) If for the taxable year there is included in the gross income of a domestic corporation under section 951 an amount attributable to the earnings and profits of a first- or second-tier corporation for any taxable year, the domestic corporation shall be deemed to have paid the same proportion of the total foreign income taxes paid, accrued, or deemed (in accordance with paragraph (b) of § 1.960-2) to be paid by such foreign corporation on or with respect to its earnings and profits for its taxable year as the amount (in the case of a first-tier corporation, determined without regard to section 958(a)(2); in the case of a second-tier corporation, determined without regard to section 958(a)(1)(A) and, to the extent that stock of such second-tier corporation is owned by the domestic corporation through a foreign corporation other than the first-tier corporation, determined without regard to section 958(a)(2)) so included in the gross income of the domestic corporation under section 951 with respect to such foreign corporation bears to the total earnings and profits of such foreign corporation for its taxable year. This paragraph (c)(1)(i) shall not apply to amounts included in the gross income of the domestic corporation under section 951 with respect to the second-tier corporation unless the percentage-of-voting-stock requirement of section 902(b)(3)(A) is satisfied.

(ii) If for the taxable year there is included in the gross income of a domestic corporation under section 951 an amount attributable to the earnings and profits of a third-tier corporation for any taxable year, the domestic corporation shall be deemed to have paid the same proportion of the total foreign income taxes paid or accrued by such foreign corporation on or with respect to its earnings and profits for its taxable year as the amount (determined without regard to section 958(a)(1)(A) and, to the extent that stock of such third-tier corporation is owned by the domestic corporation through a foreign corporation other than the second-tier corporation, determined without regard to section 958(a)(2)) so included in the gross income of the domestic corporation under section 951 with respect to such foreign corporation bears to the total earnings and profits of such foreign corporation. This paragraph (c)(1)(ii) shall not apply unless the percentage-of-voting-stock requirement of section 902(b)(3)(B) is satisfied.

(iii) In applying paragraph (c)(1)(i) or (c)(1)(ii) of this section to a first-, second-, or third-tier corporation which for the taxable year has income excluded under section 959(b), paragraph (c)(3) of this section shall apply for purposes of excluding certain earnings and profits of such foreign corporation and foreign income taxes, if any, attributable to such excluded income.

(iv) This paragraph (c)(1) applies whether or not the first-, second-, or third-tier corporation makes a distribution for the taxable year of its earnings and profits which are attributable to the amount included in the gross income of the domestic corporation under section 951.

(v) This paragraph (c)(1) does not apply to an increase in current earnings invested in United States property which, but for paragraph (e) of § 1.963-3 (applied as if section 963 had not been

Income from Sources Without the United States

repealed by the Tax Reduction Act of 1975), would be included in the gross income of the domestic corporation under section 951(a)(1)(B) but which, pursuant to such paragraph, counts toward a minimum distribution for the taxable year. This subdivision shall apply in taxable years subsequent to the Tax Reduction Act of 1975 only in those cases where an adjustment is required as a result of an election made under section 963 prior to the Act.

(2) *Taxes paid or accrued on or with respect to earnings and profits of foreign corporation.* For purposes of paragraph (c)(1) of this section, the foreign income taxes paid or accrued by a first-, second-, or third-tier corporation on or with respect to its earnings and profits for its taxable year shall be the total amount of the foreign income taxes paid or accrued by such foreign corporation for such taxable year.

(3) *Exclusion of earnings and profits and taxes of a first-, second-, or third-tier corporation having income excluded under section 959(b).* If in the case of a first-, second-, or third-tier corporation to which paragraph (c)(1)(i) or (c)(1)(ii) of this section is applied—

(i) The earnings and profits of such foreign corporation for its taxable year consist of (A) earnings and profits attributable to dividends received from an immediately lower-tier corporation which are attributable to amounts included in the gross income of a domestic corporation under section 951 with respect to the immediately lower- or lower-tier corporations, and (B) other earnings and profits, and

(ii) The effective rate of foreign income taxes paid or accrued by such foreign corporation in respect to the dividends to which its earnings and profits described in paragraph (c)(3)(i)(A) of this section are attributable is higher or lower than the effective rate of foreign income taxes paid or accrued by such foreign corporation in respect to the income to which its earnings and profits described in paragraph (c)(3)(i)(B) of this section are attributable,

then, for purposes of applying paragraph (c)(1)(i) or (c)(1)(ii) of this section to the foreign income taxes paid, accrued, or deemed to be paid, by such foreign corporation on or with respect to its earnings and profits for such taxable year, the earnings and profits of such foreign corporation for such taxable year shall be considered not to include the earnings and profits described in paragraph (c)(3)(i)(A) of this section and only the foreign income taxes paid, accrued, or deemed to be paid, by such foreign corporation in respect to

the income to which its earnings and profits described in paragraph (c)(3)(i)(B) of this section are attributable shall be taken into account. For purposes of applying this paragraph (c)(3), the effective rate of foreign income taxes paid or accrued in respect to income shall be determined consistently with the principles of paragraphs (b)(3)(iv) and (viii) and (c) of § 1.954-1. Thus, for example, the effective rate of foreign income taxes paid or accrued in respect to dividends received by such foreign corporation shall be determined by taking into account any intercorporate dividends received deduction allowed to such corporation for such dividends.

(4) *Illustrations.* The application of this paragraph may be illustrated by the following examples:

Example (1). Domestic corporation N owns all the one class of stock of controlled foreign corporation A. Both corporations use the calendar year as the taxable year. For 1978, N Corporation is required under section 951 to include in gross income $50 attributable to the earnings and profits of A Corporation for such year, but A Corporation does not distribute any earnings and profits for such year. The foreign income taxes paid by A Corporation for 1978 which are deemed paid by N Corporation for such year under section 960(a)(1) are determined as follows upon the basis of the facts assumed:

Pretax earnings and profits of A Corporation	$100.00
Foreign income taxes (20%)	20.00
Earnings and profits	80.00
Amount required to be included in N Corporation's gross income under sec. 951	50.00
Dividends paid to N Corporation	none
Foreign income taxes paid on or with respect to earnings and profits of A Corporation	20.00
Foreign income taxes of A Corporation deemed paid by N Corporation under sec. 960(a)(1)($50/$80 × $20)	12.50

Example (2). Domestic corporation N owns all the one class of stock of controlled foreign corporation A, which owns all the one class of stock of controlled foreign corporation B. All such corporations use the calendar year as the taxable year. For 1978, N Corporation is required under section 951 to include in gross income $45 attributable to the earnings and profits of B Corporation for such year, but is not required to include any amount in gross income under section 951 attributable to the earnings and profits of A Corporation for such year. Neither B Corporation nor A Corporation distributes any earnings and profits for

Reg. § 1.960-1(c)(4)

1978. The foreign income taxes paid by B Corporation for 1978 which are deemed paid by N Corporation for such year under section 960(a)(1) are determined as follows upon the basis of the facts assumed:

Pretax earnings and profits of B Corporation	$100.00
Foreign income taxes (40%)	40.00
Earnings and profits	60.00
Amount required to be included in N Corporation's gross income under sec. 951 with respect to B Corporation	45.00
Dividends paid	none
Foreign income taxes paid on or with respect to earnings and profits of B Corporation	40.00
Foreign income taxes of B Corporation deemed paid by N Corporation under sec. 960(a)(1)($45/$60 × $40)	30.00

Example (3). Domestic corporation N owns all the one class of stock of controlled foreign corporation A, which owns all the one class of stock of controlled foreign corporation B, which owns all the one class of stock of foreign corporation C. All such corporations use the calendar year as the taxable year. For 1978, N Corporation is required under section 951 to include the gross income $80 attributable to the earnings and profits of C Corporation for such year, $45 attributable to the earnings and profits of B Corporation for such year and $50 attributable to the earnings and profits of A Corporation for such year. Neither C Corporation nor B Corporation distributes any earnings and profits for 1978. The foreign income taxes which are deemed paid by N Corporation for such year under section 960(a)(1) are determined as follows upon the basis of the facts assumed:

C Corporation (third-tier corporation):

Pretax earnings of C Corporation	$150.00
Foreign income taxes (40%)	60.00
Earnings and profits	90.00
Amounts required to be included in N Corporation's gross income under section 951	80.00
Dividends paid to B Corporation	0
Foreign income taxes paid on or with respect to earnings and profits of C Corporation	60.00

B Corporation (second-tier corporation):

Pretax earnings of B Corporation	$100.00
Foreign income taxes (40%)	40.00
Earnings and profits	60.00
Amount required to be included in N Corporation's gross income under section 951	45.00
Dividends paid to A Corporation	0
Foreign income taxes paid on or with respect to earnings and profits of B Corporation	40.00

A Corporation (first-tier corporation):

Pretax earnings and profits of A Corporation	$100.00
Foreign income taxes (20%)	20.00
Earnings and profits	80.00
Amount required to be included in N Corporation's gross income under section 951	50.00
Dividends paid to N Corporation	0
Foreign income taxes paid on or with respect to earnings and profits of A Corporation	20.00

N Corporation (domestic corporation):

Foreign income taxes deemed paid by N Corporation under section 960(a)(1):	
Taxes of C Corporation $80/$90 × $60	$ 53.33
Taxes of B Corporation $45/$60 × $40	30.00
Taxes of A Corporation $50/$80 × $20	12.50
Total taxes deemed paid under section 960(a)(1)	$ 95.83

Example (4). Domestic corporation N owns all the one class of stock of controlled foreign corporation A, which owns 5 percent of the one class of stock of controlled foreign corporation B. N Corporation also directly owns 95 percent of the one class of stock of B Corporation. (Under these facts, B Corporation is only a first-tier corporation with respect to N Corporation.) All such corporations use the calendar year as the taxable year. For 1978, N Corporation is required under section 951 to include in gross income $60 attributable to the earnings and profits of B Corporation and $79.20 attributable to the earnings and profits of A Corporation. For 1978, B Corporation distributes $19 to N Corporation and $1 to A Corporation, but A Corporation makes no distribution to N Corporation. The foreign income taxes paid by N Corporation for such year under section 960(a)(1) are determined as follows upon the basis of the facts assumed in accordance with § 1.960-1(c)(1)(i):

B Corporation (first-tier corporation):

Pretax earnings and profits	$100.00
Foreign income taxes (40%)	40.00
Earnings and profits	60.00
Amount required to be included in N Corporation's gross income under section 951 with respect to B Corporation	60.00

A Corporation (first-tier corporation):

Pretax earnings and profits (including $1 dividend from B Corporation)	$100.00
Foreign income taxes (20%)	20.00
Earnings and profits	80.00
Amount required to be included in N Corporation's gross income with respect to A Corporation ($99 − [$99 × 0.20])	79.20

N Corporation (domestic corporation):

Reg. § 1.960-1(c)(4)

Income from Sources Without the United States

Foreign income taxes deemed paid by N Corporation under section 960(a)(1) with respect to—
B Corporation ([$60 × 0.95/$60] × $40)	$ 38.00
A Corporation ($79.20/$80 × $20)	19.80
Total taxes deemed paid under section 960(a)(1)	$ 57.80

Example (5). Domestic corporation N owns all the one class of stock of controlled foreign corporation A, which owns all the one class of stock of controlled foreign corporation B. All such corporations use the calendar year as the taxable year. For 1978, N Corporation is required under section 951 to include in gross income $175 attributable to the earnings and profits of A Corporation for such year. For 1978, B Corporation has earnings and profits of $225, on which it pays foreign income taxes of $75. In 1978, B Corporation distributes $150, which, under paragraph (b) of § 1.960-2, consists of $100 to which section 902(b)(1) does not apply (from B Corporation's earnings and profits attributable to an amount required under section 951 to be included in N Corporation's gross income with respect to B Corporation) and $50 to which section 902(b)(1) applies (from B Corporation's other earnings and profits). The country under the laws of which A Corporation is incorporated imposes an income tax of 40 percent on all income but exempts from tax dividends received from a subsidiary corporation. A Corporation makes no distribution for 1978. Under paragraph (b) of § 1.960-2, A Corporation is deemed to have paid $25 ($50/$150 × $75) of the $75 foreign income taxes paid by B Corporation on its pretax earnings and profits of $225. The foreign income taxes deemed paid by N Corporation for 1978 under section 960(a)(1) with respect to A Corporation are determined as follows upon the basis of the following assumed facts:

Pretax earnings and profits of A Corporation:			
Dividends received from B Corporation		$150.00	
Other income		250.00	
Total pretax earnings and profits			$400.00
Foreign income taxes:			
On dividends received from B Corporation		0	
On other income ($250 × 0.40)		$100.00	
Total foreign income taxes			$100.00
Earnings and profits:			
Attributable to dividends received from B Corporation which are attributable to amounts included in N Corporation's gross income under section 951 with respect to B Corporation		100.00	
Attributable to other income:			
Attributable to dividends received from B Corporation which are attributable to amounts not included in N Corporation's gross income under 951 with respect to B Corporation	$ 50.00		
Attributable to other income ($250 − $100 [$250 × 0.40])	150.00	200.00	
Total earnings and profits			300.00
Foreign income taxes deemed paid by N Corporation under sec. 960(a)(1) with respect to A Corporation:			
Tax paid by A Corporation in respect to its income other than dividends received from B Corporation attributable to amounts included in N Corporation's gross income under section 951 with respect to B Corporation ($175/$200 × $100)			87.50
Tax of B Corporation deemed paid by A Corporation under sec. 902(b)(1) in respect to such income ($175/$200 × $25)			21.88
Total foreign income taxes deemed paid by N Corporation under sec. 960(a)(1) with respect to A Corporation			$109.38

(d) *Time for meeting stock ownership requirements*—(1) *In general.* For the purposes of applying paragraph (c) of this section to amounts included in the gross income of a domestic corporation attributable to the earnings and profits of a first-, second-, or third-tier corporation, the stock ownership requirements of paragraph (b)(1), (2), and (3) of this section and the percentage of voting stock requirements of paragraph (c)(1)(i) and (ii) of this section, if applicable, must be satisfied on the last day in the taxable year of such first-, second-, or third-tier corporation, as the case may be, on which such foreign corporation is a controlled foreign corporation. For paragraph (c) to apply to amounts included in a domestic corporation's gross income attributable to the earnings and profits of a second-tier corporation, the requirements of paragraph (b)(1) and (2) of this section and the percentage of voting stock requirement of paragraph (c)(1)(i) of this section must be met on such date. For paragraph (c) to apply to amounts included in a domestic

Reg. § 1.960-1(d)(1)

corporation's gross income attributable to the earnings and profits of a third-tier corporation, the requirements of paragraph (b)(1), (2), and (3) of this section and the percentage of voting stock requirement of paragraph (c)(1)(ii) of this section must be met on such date.

(2) *Illustrations.* The application of this paragraph may be illustrated by the following examples:

Example (1). Domestic corporation N is required for its taxable year ending June 30, 1978, to include in gross income under section 951 an amount attributable to the earnings and profits of controlled foreign corporation A for 1977 and another amount attributable to the earnings and profits of controlled foreign corporation B for such year. Corporations A and B use the calendar year as the taxable year. Such amounts are required to be included in N Corporation's gross income by reason of its ownership of stock in A Corporation and in turn by A Corporation's ownership of stock in B Corporation. Corporation A is a controlled foreign corporation throughout 1977, but B Corporation is a controlled foreign corporation only from January 1, 1977, through September 30, 1977. Corporation N may obtain credit under section 960(a)(1) for the year ending June 30, 1978, for foreign income taxes paid by A Corporation for 1977, only if N Corporation owns at least 10 percent of the voting stock of A Corporation on December 31, 1977. Corporation N may obtain credit under section 960(a)(1) for the year ending June 30, 1978, for foreign income taxes paid by B Corporation for 1977, only if on September 30, 1977, N Corporation owns at least 10 percent of the voting stock of A Corporation, A Corporation owns at least 10 percent of the voting stock of B Corporation, and the percentage of voting stock requirement of paragraph (c)(1)(i) of this section is met.

Example (2). The facts are the same as in example (1), except that A Corporation is a controlled foreign corporation only from January 1, 1977, through March 31, 1977. Corporation N may obtain credit under section 960(a)(1) for the year ending June 30, 1978, for foreign income taxes paid by A Corporation for 1977, only if N Corporation owns at least 10 percent of the voting stock of A Corporation on March 31, 1977. Corporation N may obtain credit under section 960(a)(1) for the year ending June 30, 1978, for foreign income taxes paid by B Corporation for 1977, only if on September 30, 1977, N Corporation owns at least 10 percent of the voting stock of A Corporation, A Corporation owns at least 10 percent of the voting stock of B Corporation, and the percentage of voting stock requirement of paragraph (c)(1)(i) of this section is met.

Example (3). Domestic Corporation N owns 100 percent of the stock of controlled foreign corporation A. A Corporation owns 20 percent of the stock of controlled foreign corporation B. B Corporation owns 10 percent of the voting stock of controlled foreign corporation C. For calendar year 1983, N Corporation is required to include amounts in its gross income attributable to the earnings and profits of A, B, and C Corporations. A, B, and C Corporations were all controlled foreign corporations throughout their respective taxable years ending as follows: A Corporation, December 31, 1983; B Corporation, November 30, 1983; and C Corporation, August 31, 1983. Paragraph (c) of this section applies to amounts included in gross income of N Corporation with respect to the earnings and profits of A Corporation because the 10 percent ownership requirement of paragraph (b)(1) of this section is met on December 31, 1983. Paragraph (c) of this section applies to amounts included in the gross income of N Corporation with respect to the earnings and profits of B Corporation because the 10 percent stock ownership requirements of paragraph (b)(1) and (2) of this section are met on November 30, 1983, and the percentage of voting stock requirement of paragraph (c)(1)(i) of this section (5 percent) is also met on such date. The percentage of voting stock in A Corporation owned by N Corporation (100 percent) multiplied by the percentage of voting stock in B Corporation owned by A Corporation (20 percent) is 20 percent. Paragraph (c) of this section will not apply to amounts included in N Corporation's gross income attributable to the earnings and profits of C Corporation even though on August 31, 1983, the 10 percent stock ownership requirements of paragraph (b)(1), (2), and (3) of this section are met, because the percentage of voting stock requirement of paragraph (c)(1)(ii) of this section (5 percent) is not met on such date. The percentage of voting stock of C Corporation owned by B Corporation (10 percent) multiplied by 20 percent (the percentage of voting stock of A Corporation owned by N Corporation multiplied by the percentage of voting stock of B Corporation owned by A Corporation) is 2 percent.

(e) *Information to be furnished.* If the credit for foreign income taxes claimed under section 901 includes taxes deemed paid under section 960(a)(1), the domestic corporation must furnish the same information with respect to the taxes so deemed paid as it is required to furnish with respect to the taxes actually paid or accrued by it and for which credit is claimed. See § 1.905-2. For other information required to be furnished by the domestic corporation for the annual accounting period of certain foreign corporations ending with or within such corporation's taxable year, see section 6038(a) and the regulations thereunder.

(f) *Reduction of foreign income taxes paid or deemed paid.* For reduction of the amount of foreign income taxes paid or deemed paid by a foreign corporation for purposes of section 960, see section 6038(c) (as amended by section 338 of the Tax Equity and Fiscal Responsibility Act of 1982) and the regulations thereunder, relating to failure to furnish information with respect to certain foreign corporations. For reduction of the foreign income taxes deemed paid by a domestic corporation under section 960 with respect to foreign oil and gas extraction income, see section 907(a).

(g) *Amounts under section 951 treated as distributions for purposes of applying effective dates.* For purposes of applying section 902 in determining the amount of credit allowed under section 960(a)(1) and paragraph (c) of this section, the effective date provisions of the regulations under section 902 shall apply, and for purposes of so applying the regulations under section 902, any amount attributable to the earnings and profits for the taxable year of a first-, second-, or third-tier corporation which is included in the gross income of a domestic corporation under section 951 shall be treated as a distribution received by such domestic corporation on the last day in such taxable year on which such foreign corporation is a controlled foreign corporation.

(h) *Source of income and country to which tax is deemed paid*—(1) *Source of income.* For purposes of section 904—

(i) The amount included in gross income of a domestic corporation under section 951 for the taxable year with respect to a first-, second-, or third-tier corporation, plus

(ii) Any section 78 dividend to which such section 951 amount gives rise by reason of taxes deemed paid by such domestic corporation under section 960(a)(1),

shall be deemed to be derived from sources within the foreign country or possession of the United States under the laws of which such first-tier corporation, or the first-tier corporation in the same chain of ownership as such second- or third-tier corporation, is created or organized.

(2) *Country to which taxes deemed paid.* For purposes of section 904, the foreign income taxes paid by the first-, second-, or third-tier corporation and deemed to be paid by the domestic corporation under section 960(a)(1) by reason of the inclusion of the amount described in paragraph (h)(1)(i) of this section in the gross income of such domestic corporation shall be deemed to be paid to the foreign country or possession of the United States under the laws of which such first-tier corporation, or the first-tier corporation in the same chain of ownership as such second- or third-tier corporation, is created or organized.

(3) *Illustration.* The application of this paragraph may be illustrated by the following example:

Example. Domestic corporation N owns all the one class of stock of controlled foreign corporation A, incorporated under the laws of foreign country X, which owns all the one class of stock of controlled foreign corporation B, incorporated under the laws of foreign country Y. All such corporations use the calendar year as the taxable year. For 1978, N Corporation is required under section 951 to include in gross income $45 attributable to the earnings and profits of B Corporation for such year and $50 attributable to the earnings and profits of A Corporation for such year. For 1978, because of the inclusion of such amounts in gross income, N Corporation is deemed under section 960(a)(1) and paragraph (c) of this section to have paid $15 of foreign income taxes paid by B Corporation for such year and $10 of foreign income taxes paid by A Corporation for such year. For purposes of section 904, the amount ($95) included in N Corporation's gross income under section 951 attributable to the earnings and profits of corporations A and B is deemed to be derived from sources within country X, and the section 78 dividend consisting of the foreign income taxes ($25) deemed paid by N Corporation under section 960(a)(1) with respect to such $95 is deemed to be derived from sources within country X. The $25 of foreign income taxes so deemed paid by N Corporation are deemed to be paid to country X for purposes of section 904.

(i) *Computation of deemed-paid taxes in post-1986 taxable years*—(1) *General rule.* If a domestic corporation is eligible to compute deemed-paid taxes under section 960(a)(1) with respect to an amount included in gross income under section 951(a), then, such domestic corporation shall be deemed to have paid a portion of the foreign corporation's post-1986 foreign income taxes determined under section 902 and the regulations under that section in the same manner as if the amount so included were a dividend paid by such foreign corporation (determined by applying section 902(c) in accordance with section 904(d)(3)(B)).

(2) *Ordering rule for computing deemed-paid taxes under sections 902 and 960.* If a domestic corporation computes deemed-paid taxes under both sections 902 and 960 in the same taxable

Reg. § 1.960-1(i)(2)

year, section 960 shall be applied first. After the deemed-paid taxes are computed under section 960 with respect to a deemed income inclusion, post-1986 undistributed earnings and post-1986 foreign income taxes in each separate category shall be reduced by the appropriate amounts before deemed-paid taxes are computed under section 902 with respect to a dividend distribution.

(3) *Computation of post-1986 undistributed earnings.* Post-1986 undistributed earnings (or an accumulated deficit in post-1986 undistributed earnings) are computed under section 902 and the regulations under that section.

(4) *Allocation of accumulated deficits.* For purposes of computing post-1986 undistributed earnings under sections 902 and 960, a post-1986 accumulated deficit in a separate category shall be allocated proportionately to reduce post-1986 undistributed earnings in the other separate categories. However, a deficit in any separate category shall not permanently reduce earnings in other separate categories, but after the deemed-paid taxes are computed the separate limitation deficit shall be carried forward in the same separate category in which it was incurred. In addition, because deemed-paid taxes may not exceed taxes paid or accrued by the controlled foreign corporation, in computing deemed-paid taxes with respect to an inclusion out of a separate category that exceeds post-1986 undistributed earnings in that separate category, the numerator of the deemed-paid credit fraction (deemed inclusion from the separate category) may not exceed the denominator (post-1986 undistributed earnings in the separate category).

(5) *Examples.* The application of this paragraph (i) may be illustrated by the following examples. See § 1.952-1(f)(4) for additional illustrations of these rules.

Example 1. (i) A, a U.S. person, is the sole shareholder of CFC, a controlled foreign corporation formed on January 1, 1998, whose functional currency is the u. In 1998 CFC earns 100u of general limitation income described in section 904(d)(1)(I) that is not subpart F income and 100u of foreign personal holding company income that is passive income described in section 904(d)(1)(A). In 1998 CFC also incurs a (50u) loss in the shipping category described in section 904(d)(1)(D). CFC's subpart F income for 1998, 100u, does not exceed CFC's current earnings and profits of 150u. Accordingly, all 100u of CFC's subpart F income is included in A's gross income under section 951(a)(1)(A). Under section 904(d)(3)(B) of the Internal Revenue Code and paragraph (i)(1) of this section, A includes 100u of passive limitation income in gross income for 1998.

(ii) For purposes of computing post-1986 undistributed earnings under sections 902, 904(d) and 960 with respect to the subpart F inclusion, the shipping limitation deficit of (50u) is allocated proportionately to reduce general limitation earnings of 100u and passive limitation earnings of 100u. Thus, general limitation earnings are reduced by 25u to 75u (100u general limitation earnings/200u total earnings in positive separate categories x (50u) shipping deficit = 25u reduction), and passive limitation earnings are reduced by 25u to 75u (100u passive earnings/200u total earnings in positive separate categories x (50u) shipping deficit = 25u reduction). All of CFC's post-1986 foreign income taxes with respect to passive limitation earnings are deemed paid by A under section 960 with respect to the 100u subpart F inclusion of passive income (75u inclusion (numerator limited to denominator under paragraph (i)(4) of this section)/75u passive earnings). After the inclusion and deemed-paid taxes are computed, at the close of 1998 CFC has 100u of general limitation earnings, 0 of passive limitation earnings (100u of foreign personal holding company income - 100u inclusion), and a (50u) deficit in shipping limitation earnings.

Example 2. (i) The facts are the same as in *Example 1* with the addition of the following facts. In 1999, CFC distributes 150u to A. CFC has 100u of previously-taxed earnings and profits described in section 959(c)(2) attributable to 1998, all of which is passive limitation earnings and profits. Under section 959(c), 100u of the 150u distribution is deemed to be made from earnings and profits described in section 959(c)(2). The remaining 50u is deemed to be made from earnings and profits described in section 959(c)(3). The entire dividend distribution of 50u is treated as made out of CFC's general limitation earnings and profits. See section 904(d)(3)(D).

(ii) For purposes of computing post-1986 undistributed earnings under section 902 with respect to the 1999 dividend of 50u, the shipping limitation accumulated deficit of (50u) reduces general limitation earnings and profits of 100u to 50u. Thus, 100% of CFC's post-1986 foreign income taxes with respect to general limitation earnings are deemed paid by A under section 902 with respect to the 1999 dividend of 50u (50u dividend/50u general limitation earnings). After the deemed-paid taxes are computed, at the close of 1999 CFC has 50u of general limitation earnings (100u opening balance - 50u distribution), 0

Reg. § 1.960-1(i)(3)

Income from Sources Without the United States

See p. 20,601 for regulations not amended to reflect law changes

of passive limitation earnings, and a (50u) deficit in shipping limitation earnings.

(6) *Effective date.* This paragraph (i) applies to taxable years of a controlled foreign corporation beginning after March 3, 1997. [Reg. § 1.960-1.]

☐ [T.D. 7120, 6-3-71. Amended by T.D. 7334, 12-20-74, T.D. 7481, 4-15-77, T.D. 7545, 5-5-78, T.D. 7649, 10-17-79, T.D. 7843, 11-5-82; T.D. 7961, 6-27-84 and T.D. 8704, 12-31-96.]

[Reg. § 1.960-2]

§ 1.960-2. Interrelation of section 902 and section 960 when dividends are paid by third-, second-, or first-tier corporation.—(a) *Scope of this section.* This section prescribes rules for the application of section 902 in a case where dividends are paid by a third-, second-, or first-tier corporation, as the case may be, from its earnings and profits for a taxable year when an amount attributable to such earnings and profits is included in the gross income of a domestic corporation under section 951, or when such earnings and profits are attributable to an amount excluded from the gross income of such foreign corporation under section 959(b) and § 1.959-2, with respect to the domestic corporation. In making determinations under this section, any portion of a distribution received from a first-tier corporation by the domestic corporation which is excluded from the domestic corporation's gross income under section 959(a) and § 1.959-1, or any portion of a distribution received from an immediately lower-tier corporation by the third-, second-, or first-tier corporation which is excluded from such foreign corporation's gross income under section 959(b) and § 1.959-2, shall be treated as a dividend for purposes of taking into account under section 902 any foreign income taxes paid by such third-, second-, or first-tier corporation which are not deemed paid by the domestic corporation under section 960(a)(1) and § 1.960-1.

(b) *Application of section 902(b) to dividends received from an immediately lower-tier corporation.* For purposes of paragraph (a) of this section and paragraph (c)(1)(i) of § 1.960-1, section 902(b) shall apply to all dividends received by the first- or second-tier corporation from the immediately lower-tier corporation other than dividends attributable to earnings and profits of such immediately lower-tier corporation in respect of which an amount is, or has been, included in the gross income of a domestic corporation under section 951 with respect to such immediately lower-tier corporation.

(c) *Application of section 902(a) to dividends received by domestic corporation from first-tier corporation.* For purposes of paragraph (a) of this section, section 902(a) shall apply to all dividends received by the domestic corporation for its taxable year from the first-tier corporation other than dividends attributable to earnings and profits of such first-tier corporation in respect of which an amount is, or has been, included in the gross income of a domestic corporation under section 951 with respect to such first-tier corporation.

(d) *Allocation of earnings and profits of a first- or second-tier corporation having income excluded under section 959(b)*—(1) *First-tier corporations.* If the first-tier corporation for its taxable year receives dividends from the second-tier corporation to which in accordance with paragraph (b) of this section 902(b)(1) or section 902(b)(2) applies and other dividends from the second-tier corporation to which such sections do not apply, then in applying section 902(a) pursuant to this section and in applying section 960(a)(1) pursuant to § 1.960-1(c)(1)(i), with respect to the foreign income taxes paid and deemed paid by the second-tier corporation which are deemed paid by the first-tier corporation for such taxable year under section 902(b)(1)—

(i) The earnings and profits of the first-tier corporation for such taxable year shall be considered not to include its earnings and profits which are attributable to the dividends to which section 902(b)(1) does not apply (in determining the domestic corporation's credit for the taxes paid by the second-tier corporation) or which are attributable to the dividends to which sections 902(b)(1) and 902(b)(2) do not apply (in determining the domestic corporation's credit for taxes deemed paid by the second-tier corporation) and

(ii) For the purposes of so applying section 902(a), distributions to the domestic corporation from such earnings and profits which are attributable to the dividends to which section 902(b)(1) does not apply (in determining the domestic corporation's credit for taxes paid by the second-tier corporation) or which are attributable to the dividends to which sections 902(b)(1) and 902(b)(2) do not apply (in determining the domestic corporation's credit for taxes deemed paid by the second-tier corporation) shall not be treated as a dividend.

(2) *Second-tier corporations.* If the second-tier corporation for its taxable year receives dividends from the third-tier corporation to which, in accordance with paragraph (b) of this section, section 902(b)(2) applies and other dividends from the third-tier corporation to which such section does not apply, then in applying section 902(b)(1) pursuant to this section, and in applying section 960(a)(1) pursuant to paragraph (c)(1)(i) of § 1.960-1, with respect to the foreign

Reg. § 1.960-2(d)(2)

taxes deemed paid by the second-tier corporation for such taxable year under section 902(b)(2)—

(i) The earnings and profits of the second-tier corporation for such taxable year shall be considered not to include its earnings and profits which are attributable to such other dividends from the third-tier corporation, and

(ii) For the purposes of so applying section 902(b)(1), distributions to the first-tier corporation from such earnings and profits which are attributable to such other dividends from the third-tier corporation shall not be treated as a dividend.

(e) *Separate determinations under sections 902(a), 902(b)(1), and 902(b)(2) in the case of a first-, second-, or third-tier corporation having income excluded under section 959(b).* If in the case of a first-, second-, or third-tier corporation to which paragraph (b) or (c) of this section is applied—

(1) The earnings and profits of such foreign corporation for its taxable year consist of—

(i) Dividends received from an immediately lower-tier corporation which are attributable to amounts included in the gross income of a domestic corporation under section 951 with respect to the immediately lower- or lower-tier corporations, and

(ii) Other earnings and profits, and

(2) The effective rate of foreign income taxes paid or accrued by such foreign corporation on the dividends described in paragraph (e)(1)(i) of this section is higher or lower than the effective rate of foreign income taxes attributable to its earnings and profits described in paragraph (e)(1)(ii) of this section,

then, for purposes of applying paragraphs (b) or (c) of this section to dividends paid by such foreign corporation to the domestic corporation or the first- or second-tier corporation, sections 902(a), 902(b)(1), and 902(b)(2) shall be applied separately to the portion of the dividend which is attributable to the earnings and profits described in paragraph (e)(1)(i) of this section and separately to the portion of the dividend which is attributable to the earnings and profits described in paragraph (e)(1)(ii) of this section. In making a separate determination with respect to the earnings and profits described in paragraph (e)(1)(i) or (e)(1)(ii) of this section, only the foreign income taxes paid or accrued (or, in the case of earnings and profits of a first- or second-tier corporation described in paragraph (e)(1)(ii) of this section, deemed to be paid) by such foreign corporation on the income attributable to such earnings and profits shall be taken into account. For purposes of applying this paragraph (e), no part of the foreign income taxes paid, accrued, or deemed to be paid which are attributable to the earnings and profits described in paragraph (e)(1)(ii) of this section shall be attributed to the dividend described in paragraph (e)(1)(i) of this section; and no part of the foreign income taxes paid or accrued on the dividend described in paragraph (e)(1)(i) of this section shall be attributed to the earnings and profits described in paragraph (e)(1)(ii) of this section. Furthermore, the effective rate of foreign income taxes paid or accrued shall be determined consistently with the principles of paragraph (b)(3)(iv) and (viii) and (c) of § 1.954-1. Thus, for example, the effective rate of foreign income taxes on dividends received by such foreign corporation shall be determined by taking into account any intercorporate dividends received deduction allowed to such corporation for such dividends.

(f) *Illustrations.* The application of this section may be illustrated by the following examples. In all of the examples other than examples (6), (7), (9) and (10), it is assumed that the effective rate of foreign income taxes paid or accrued by the first- or second-tier corporation, as the case may be, in respect to dividends received from the immediately lower-tier corporation is the same as the effective rate of foreign income taxes paid or accrued by the first- or second-tier corporation with respect to its other income:

Example (1). Domestic corporation N owns all the one class of stock of controlled foreign corporation A, which owns all the one class of stock of controlled foreign corporation B. All such corporations use the calendar year as the taxable year. For 1978, N Corporation is required under section 951 to include $50 in gross income attributable to the earnings and profits of A Corporation for such year, but is not required to include any amount in gross income under section 951 attributable to the earnings and profits of B Corporation. For such year, B Corporation distributes a dividend of $45, but A Corporation does not make any distributions. The foreign income taxes deemed paid by N Corporation for 1978 under section 960(a)(1), after applying section 902(b)(1) for such year of A Corporation, are determined as follows upon the basis of the facts assumed:

B Corporation (second-tier corporation):
Pretax earnings and profits	$100.00
Foreign income taxes (40%)	40.00
Earnings and profits	60.00
Dividends paid to A Corporation	45.00

Reg. § 1.960-2(e)(1)

Income from Sources Without the United States

Foreign income taxes paid by B Corporation on or with respect to its accumulated profits	40.00
Foreign income taxes of B Corporation deemed paid by A Corporation for 1978 under sec. 902(b)(1) ($45/$60 × $40)	30.00

A Corporation (first-tier corporation):
Pretax earnings and profits:

Dividends from B Corporation	$45.00	
Other income	100.00	
Total pretax earnings and profits		$145.00
Foreign income taxes (20%)		29.00
Earnings and profits		116.00
Foreign income taxes paid, and deemed to be paid, by A Corporation on or with respect to its earnings and profits ($29 + $30)		59.00
Amount required to be included in N Corporation's gross income under sec. 951 with respect to A Corporation		$ 50.00
Dividends paid to N Corporation		none

N Corporation (domestic corporation):

Foreign income taxes of A Corporation deemed paid by N Corporation for 1965 under sec. 960(a)(1) ($50/$116 × $59)	$ 25.43

Example (2). Domestic corporation N owns all the one class of stock of controlled foreign corporation A, which owns all the one class of stock of controlled foreign corporation B. All such corporations use the calendar year as the taxable year. For 1978, N Corporation is required under section 951 to include in gross income $150 attributable to the earnings and profits of B Corporation for such year, which B Corporation distributes during such year. Corporation N is not required for 1978 to include any amount in gross income under section 951 attributable to the earnings and profits of A Corporation, but A Corporation distributes for such year $135 from its earnings and profits attributable to B Corporation's dividend. The foreign income taxes deemed paid by N Corporation for 1978 under section 960(a)(1) and section 902(a) are determined as follows upon the basis of the facts assumed:

B Corporation (second-tier corporation):

Pretax earnings and profits	$250.00
Foreign income taxes (20%)	50.00
Earnings and profits	200.00
Amounts required to be included in N Corporation's gross income under sec. 951 with respect to B Corporation	150.00
Dividends paid to A Corporation	150.00
Foreign income taxes paid on or with respect to earnings and profits of B Corporation	50.00

A Corporation (first-tier corporation):
Pretax earnings and profits:

Dividends from B Corporation	$150.00	
Other income	200.00	
Total pretax earnings and profits		$350.00
Foreign income taxes (10%)		35.00
Earnings and profits		315.00
Dividends paid to N Corporation		135.00
Foreign income taxes paid by A Corporation on or with respect to its accumulated profits		35.00

N Corporation (domestic corporation):

Foreign income taxes of B Corporation deemed paid by N Corporation for 1978 under sec. 960(a)(1) ($150/$200 × $50)	$ 37.50
Foreign income taxes of A Corporation deemed paid by N Corporation for 1978 under sec. 902(a) ($135/$315 × $35)	15.00
Total foreign income taxes deemed paid by N Corporation under sec. 901	$ 52.50

Example (3). Domestic corporation N owns all the one class of stock of controlled foreign corporation A, which owns all the one class of stock of controlled foreign corporation B. All such corporations use the calendar year as the taxable year. For 1978, N Corporation is required under section 951 to include $180 in gross income attributable to the earnings and profits of A Corporation for such year, but is not required to include any amount in gross income under section 951 attributable to the earnings and profits of B Corporation. Corporation B distributes from its earnings and profits for 1978 a dividend of $50. For 1978, A Corporation distributes $180 from its earnings and profits attributable to the amount required under section 951 to be included in N Corporation's gross income for such year with respect to A Corporation and $20 from its other earnings and profits. The foreign income taxes deemed paid by N Corporation for 1978 under section 960(a)(1) and section 902(a) are determined as follows upon the basis of the facts assumed:

Reg. § 1.960-2(f)

Income from Sources Without the United States

See p. 20,601 for regulations not amended to reflect law changes

B Corporation (second-tier corporation):	
Pretax earnings and profits	$100.00
Foreign income taxes (40%)	40.00
Earnings and profits	60.00
Dividends paid to A Corporation	50.00
Foreign income taxes paid by B Corporation on or with respect to its accumulated profits	40.00
Foreign income taxes of B Corporation deemed paid by A Corporation for 1978 under sec. 902(b)(1) ($50/$60 × $40)	33.33
A Corporation (first-tier corporation):	
Pretax earnings and profits:	
Dividends from B Corporation ..... $ 50.00	
Other income 200.00	
Total pretax earnings and profits	250.00
Foreign income taxes (10%)	25.00
Earnings and profits	225.00
Foreign income taxes paid, and deemed to be paid, by A Corporation on or with respect to its earnings and profits ($25.00 + $33.33)	58.33
Amounts required to be included in N Corporation's gross income for 1978 under sec. 951 with respect to A Corporation	180.00
Dividends paid to N Corporation:	
Dividends to which sec. 902(a) does not apply (from A Corporation's earnings and profits in respect of which an amount is required under sec. 951 to be included in N Corporation's gross income with respect to A Corporation) $180.00	
Dividends to which sec. 902(a) applies (from A Corporation's other earnings and profits) 20.00	
Total dividends paid to N Corporation	200.00
N Corporation (domestic corporation):	
Foreign income taxes of corporations A and B deemed paid by N Corporation under sec. 960(a)(1) ($180/$225 × $58.33)	46.66
Foreign income taxes of corporations A and B deemed paid by N Corporation under sec. 902(a) ($20/$225 × $58.33)	5.18
Total foreign income taxes deemed paid by N Corporation under sec. 901	$ 51.84

Example (4). Domestic corporation N owns all the one class of stock of controlled foreign corporation A, which owns all the one class of stock of controlled foreign corporation B. All such corporations use the calendar year as the taxable year. For 1978, N Corporation is required under section 951 to include in gross income $150 attributable to the earnings and profits of B Corporation for such year and $22.50 attributable to the earnings and profits of A Corporation for such year. For 1978, B Corporation distributes $175, consisting of $150 from its earnings and profits attributable to amounts required under section 951 to be included in N Corporation's gross income with respect to B Corporation and $25 from its other earnings and profits. Corporation A does not distribute any dividends for 1978. The foreign income taxes deemed paid by N Corporation for 1978 under section 960(a)(1) are determined as follows upon the basis of the facts assumed:

B Corporation (second-tier corporation):	
Pretax earnings and profits	$250.00
Foreign income taxes (20%)	50.00
Earnings and profits	200.00
Amounts required to be included in N Corporation's gross income under sec. 951 for 1978 with respect to B Corporation	150.00
Dividends paid by B Corporation:	
Dividends to which sec. 902(b) does not apply (from B Corporation's earnings and profits in respect of which an amount is required under sec. 951 to be included in N Corporation gross income with respect to B Corporation) $150.00	
Dividends to which sec. 902(b)(1) applies (from B Corporation's other earnings and profits) 25.00	
Total dividends paid to A Corporation	175.00
Foreign income taxes paid by B Corporation on or with respect to its accumulated profits	50.00
Foreign income taxes of B Corporation deemed paid by A Corporation for 1978 under sec. 902(b)(1) ($25/$200 × $50)	6.25
A Corporation (first-tier corporation):	
Pretax earnings and profits	$175.00
Foreign income tax (10%)	17.50

Reg. § 1.960-2(f)

Income from Sources Without the United States

See p. 20,601 for regulations not amended to reflect law changes

Earnings and profits	157.50
Earnings and profits after exclusion of amounts attributable to dividends to which sec. 902(b) does not apply ($157.50 less [$150 − ($150 × .10)])	22.50
Amount required to be included in N Corporation's gross income for 1978 under sec. 951 with respect to A Corporation	22.50
Dividends paid to N Corporation	0

N Corporation (domestic corporation):
  Foreign income taxes deemed paid by N Corporation under sec. 960(a)(1) with respect to A Corporation:

Tax actually paid by A Corporation ($22.50/$157.50 × $17.50)	$ 2.50	
Tax of B Corporation deemed paid by A Corporation under sec. 902(b)(1) ($22.50/$22.50 × $6.25)	6.25	
		$ 8.75
Foreign income taxes deemed paid by N Corporation under sec. 960(a)(1)(C) with respect to B Corporation ($150/$200 × $50)		37.50
Total taxes deemed paid under sec. 960(a)(1)		$ 46.25

Example (5). Domestic corporation N owns all the one class of stock of controlled foreign corporation A, which owns all the one class of stock of controlled foreign corporation B. All such corporations use the calendar year as the taxable year. For 1978, N Corporation is required under section 951 to include in gross income $150 attributable to the earnings and profits of B Corporation for such year and $22.50 attributable to the earnings and profits of A Corporation for such year. For 1978, B Corporation distributes $175, consisting of $150 from its earnings and profits attributable to amounts required under section 951 to be included in N Corporation's gross income with respect to B Corporation and $25 from its other earnings and profits. For 1978, A Corporation distributes $225, consisting of $135 from its earnings and profits attributable to the amount required under section 951 to be included in N Corporation's gross income with respect to B Corporation, $22.50 from its earnings and profits attributable to the amount required under section 951 to be included in N Corporation's gross income with respect to A Corporation, and $67.50 from its other earnings and profits. The foreign income taxes deemed paid by N Corporation for 1978 under section 960(a)(1) and section 902(a) are determined as follows upon the basis of the facts assumed:

B Corporation (second-tier corporation):

Pretax earnings and profits		$250.00
Foreign income taxes (20%)		50.00
Earnings and profits		200.00
Amounts required to be included in N Corporation's gross income for 1978 under sec. 951 with respect to B Corporation		150.00
Dividends paid by B Corporation:		
Dividends to which sec. 902(b) does not apply (from B Corporation's earnings and profits in respect of which an amount is required under sec. 951 to be included in N Corporation's gross income with respect to B Corporation)	$150.00	
Dividends to which sec. 902(b)(1) applies (from B Corporation's other earnings and profits)	25.00	
Total dividends paid to A Corporation		175.00
Foreign income taxes paid by B Corporation on or with respect to its accumulated profits		50.00
Foreign income taxes of B Corporation deemed paid by A Corporation for 1978 under sec. 902(b)(1) ($25/$200 × $50)		6.25

A Corporation (first-tier corporation):

Pretax earnings and profits:		
Dividends received from B Corporation	$175.00	
Other income	100.00	
Total pretax earnings and profits		$275.00
Foreign income taxes (10%)		27.50
Earnings and profits		247.50
Earnings and profits after exclusion of amounts attributable to dividends to which sec. 902(b) does not apply ($247.50 less [$150 − ($150 × .10)])		112.50
Amount required to be included in N Corporation's gross income for 1978 under sec. 951 with respect to A Corporation		22.50

Reg. § 1.960-2(f)

49,374   Income from Sources Without the United States
See p. 20,601 for regulations not amended to reflect law changes

Distributions paid by A Corporation:
    Dividends to which sec. 902(a) does not apply (from A Corporation's
    earnings and profits in respect of which an amount is required under
    sec. 951 to be included in N Corporation's gross income with respect to
    A Corporation) .... $ 22.50
    Dividends to which sec. 902(a) applies (from A Corporation's other
    earnings and profits) 202.50

        Total dividends paid to N Corporation $225.00

N Corporation (domestic corporation):
    Foreign income taxes deemed paid by N Corporation under sec. 960(a)(1) with respect to—
        B Corporation ($150/$200 × $50) .... $ 37.50
    A Corporation:
        Tax paid by A Corporation ($22.50/$247.50 × $27.50) .... $ 2.50
        Tax of B Corporation deemed paid by A Corporation under sec.
        902(b)(1) ($22.50/$112.50 × $6.25) 1.25   3.75

        Total taxes deemed paid under sec. 960(a)(1) .... $ 41.25
    Foreign income taxes deemed paid by N Corporation under sec. 902(a) with
      respect to A Corporation:
        Tax paid by A Corporation ($202.50/$247.50 × $27.50) .... $ 22.50
        Tax of B Corporation deemed paid by A Corporation ($67.50/$112.50 ×
        $6.25) 3.75

        Total taxes deemed paid under sec. 902(a) .... $ 26.25

    Total foreign income taxes deemed paid by N Corporation under sec. 901 .... $ 67.50

Example (6). Domestic corporation N owns all the one class of stock of controlled foreign corporation A, which owns all the one class of stock of controlled foreign corporation B. All such corporations use the calendar year as the taxable year. A and B corporations are organized under the laws of foreign country X. All of B corporation's assets used in a trade or business are located in country X. Country X imposes an income tax of 20 percent on B corporation's income. For 1978, N Corporation is required under section 951 to include in gross income $100 attributable to the earnings and profits of B Corporation for such year. For 1978, B Corporation distributes $150, consisting of $100 from its earnings and profits attributable to the amount required under section 951 to be included in N Corporation's gross income with respect to B Corporation and $50 from its other earnings and profits. Country X imposes an income tax of 10 percent on A Corporation's income but exempts from tax dividends received from B Corporation. N is not required to include any amount in gross income under section 951 for 1978 attributable to the earnings and profits of A Corporation for such year. For 1978, A Corporation distributes $175, consisting of $100 from its earnings and profits attributable to the amount required under section 951 to be included in N Corporation's gross income with respect to B Corporation, and $75 from its other earnings and profits. The foreign income taxes deemed paid by N Corporation for 1978 under section 960(a)(1) and section 902(a) are determined as follows on the basis of the facts assumed:

B Corporation (second-tier corporation):
    Pretax earnings and profits $200.00
    Foreign income taxes (20%) 40.00
    Earnings and profits 160.00
    Amount required to be included in N Corporation's gross income for 1978 under sec. 951
      with respect to B Corporation 100.00
    Dividends paid by B Corporation:
        Dividends to which sec. 902(b) does not apply (from B Corporation's
        earnings and profits in respect of which an amount is required under
        sec. 951 to be included in N Corporation's gross income with respect to
        B Corporation) $100.00
        Dividends to which sec. 902(b)(1) applies (from B Corporation's other
        earnings and profits) 50.00

        Total dividends paid to A Corporation $150.00

Foreign income taxes of B Corporation deemed paid by A Corporation for 1978
    under sec. 902(b)(1) ($50/$160 × $40) .... $ 12.50

Reg. § 1.960-2(f)

Income from Sources Without the United States

A Corporation (first-tier corporation):

Pretax earnings and profits:		
Dividends received from B Corporation	$150.00	
Other income	100.00	
Total pretax earnings and profits		$250.00
Foreign income taxes:		
On dividends received from B Corporation	none	
On other income ($100 × .10)	$ 10.00	
Total foreign income taxes		$ 10.00
Earnings and profits:		
Attributable to dividends received from B Corporation to which sec. 902(b) does not apply		$100.00
Attributable to other income:		
Attributable to dividends received from B Corporation to which sec. 902(b)(1) applies	$50.00	
Attributable to other income ($100 − $10)	90.00	140.00
Total earnings and profits		$240.00
Earnings and profits after exclusion of amounts attributable to dividends to which sec. 902(b) does not apply ($240 − $100)		$140.00
Amount required to be included in N Corporation's gross income for 1978 under sec. 951 with respect to A Corporation		none
Dividends paid by A Corporation:		
Dividends to which sec. 902(a) does not apply (from A Corporation's earnings and profits in respect of which an amount is required under sec. 951 to be included in N Corporation's gross income with respect to A Corporation)		none
Dividends to which sec. 902(a) applies (from A Corporation's other earnings and profits)	$175.00	
Total dividends paid to N Corporation		$175.00

N Corporation (domestic corporation):

Foreign income taxes deemed paid by N Corporation under sec. 960(a)(1) with respect to B Corporation ($100/$160 × $40)		$ 25.00
Foreign income taxes deemed paid by N Corporation under sec. 902(a) with respect to A Corporation (allocation of earnings and profits being made under pars. (c)(2) and (d) of this section):		
Tax paid by A Corporation in respect to dividends received from B Corporation to which sec. 902(b) does not apply ($100/$100 × $0)	none	
Tax paid by A Corporation in respect to its other income ($75/$140 × $10)	$ 5.36	
Tax of B Corporation in respect to such other income ($75/$140 × $12.50)	6.70	
Total taxes deemed paid under sec. 902(a)		$ 12.06
Total foreign income taxes deemed paid by N Corporation under sec. 901		$ 37.06

Example (7). Domestic corporation N owns all the one class of stock of controlled foreign corporation A, which owns all the one class of stock of controlled foreign corporation B. All such corporations use the calendar year as the taxable year. For 1978, N Corporation is required under section 951 to include in gross income $150 attributable to the earnings and profits of B Corporation for such year and $47.50 attributable to the earnings and profits of A Corporation for such year. For 1978, B Corporation distributes $200, consisting of $150 from its earnings and profits attributable to the amount required under section 951 to be included in N Corporation's gross income with respect to B Corporation and $50 from its other earnings and profits. The country under the laws of which A Corporation is incorporated imposes an income tax of 5 percent on dividends received from a subsidiary corporation and 20 percent on other income. For 1978, A Corporation distributes $100 from its earnings and profits to N Corporation, such amount being attributable under paragraph (e) of § 1.959-3 to the amount required under section 951 to be included in N Corporation's gross income with respect to B Corporation. The foreign income taxes deemed paid by N Corporation for 1978 under section 960(a)(1) and section 902(a) are determined as follows on the basis of the facts assumed:

Reg. § 1.960-2(f)

49,376   Income from Sources Without the United States

See p. 20,601 for regulations not amended to reflect law changes

B Corporation (second-tier corporation):		
Pretax earnings and profits		$250.00
Foreign income taxes (20 percent)		50.00
Earnings and profits		200.00
Amount required to be included in N Corporation's gross income for 1978 under sec. 951 with respect to B Corporation		150.00
Dividends paid by B Corporation:		
Dividends to which sec. 902(b) does not apply (from B Corporation's earnings and profits in respect of which an amount is required under sec. 951 to be included in N Corporation's gross income with respect to B Corporation)	$150.00	
Dividends to which sec. 902(b)(1) applies (from B Corporation's other earnings and profits)	50.00	
Total dividends paid to A Corporation		200.00
Foreign income taxes of B Corporation deemed paid by A Corporation for 1978 under sec. 902(b)(1) ($50/$200 × $50)		12.50
A Corporation (first-tier corporation):		
Pretax earnings and profits:		
Dividends received from B Corporation	$200.00	
Other income	100.00	
Total pretax earnings and profits		$300.00
Foreign income taxes:		
On dividends received from B Corporation to which sec. 902(b) does not apply ($150 × .05)	$ 7.50	
On other income:		
Dividends received from B Corporation to which sec. 902(b)(1) applies ($50 × .05)	$ 2.50	
Other income of A Corporation ($100 × .20)	20.00	22.50
Total foreign income taxes		30.00
Earnings and Profits:		
Attributable to dividends received from B Corporation to which sec. 902(b) does not apply ($150 − $7.50)	$142.50	
Attributable to other income:		
Attributable to dividends received from B Corporation to which sec. 902(b)(1) applies ($50 − $2.50)	$47.50	
Attributable to other income ($100 − $20)	80.00	127.50
Total earnings and profits		$270.00
Earnings and profits after exclusion of amounts attributable to dividends to which sec. 902(b) does not apply ($270 less $142.50)		$127.50
Amount required to be included in N Corporation's gross income for 1978 under sec. 951 with respect to A Corporation		47.50
Dividends paid by A Corporation:		
Dividends to which sec. 902(a) does not apply (from A Corporation's earnings and profits in respect of which an amount is required under sec. 951 to be included in N Corporation's gross income with respect to A Corporation)	none	
Dividends to which sec. 902(a) applies (from A Corporation's other earnings and profits)	$100.00	
Total dividends paid to N Corporation		100.00
N Corporation (domestic corporation):		
Foreign income taxes deemed paid by N Corporation under sec. 960(a)(1) with respect to—		
B Corporation ($150/$200 × $50)		37.50
A Corporation (allocation of earnings and profits being made under § 1.960-1(c)(3) and par. (d) of this sec.):		
Tax paid by A Corporation ($47.50/$127.50 × $22.50)	$ 8.38	
Tax of B Corporation deemed paid by A Corporation under sec. 902(b)(1) ($47.50/$127.50 × $12.50)	4.66	$ 13.04
Total taxes deemed paid under sec. 960(a)(1)(C)		50.54
Foreign income taxes deemed paid by N Corporation under sec. 902(a) with respect to A Corporation (allocations of earnings and profits being made under pars. (c)(2) and (d) of this sec.) ($100/$142.50 × $7.50)		5.26
Total foreign income taxes deemed paid by N Corporation under sec. 901		$ 55.80

Reg. § 1.960-2(f)

Income from Sources Without the United States

See p. 20,601 for regulations not amended to reflect law changes

Example (8). Domestic corporation N owns all the one class of stock of controlled foreign corporation A, which owns all the one class of stock of controlled foreign corporation B, which owns all the one class of stock of controlled foreign corporation C. All such corporations use the calendar year as the taxable year. For 1978, N Corporation is required under section 951 to include $50 attributable to the earnings and profits of C Corporation and $15 attributable to the earnings and profits of B Corporation in its gross income. N Corporation is not required to include any amount in its gross income with respect to A Corporation under section 951 in 1978. For such year, C Corporation distributes $75 to B Corporation. B Corporation in turn distributes $60 of its earnings and profits to A Corporation. A Corporation has no other earnings and profits for 1978 and distributes $45 of its earnings and profits to N Corporation. The foreign income taxes deemed paid by N Corporation under section 960 (a)(1) and section 902(a) are determined as follows on the basis of the facts assumed:

C Corporation (third-tier corporation):

Pretax earnings and profits	$150.00
Foreign income taxes paid by C Corporation (30%)	45.00
Earnings and profits	105.00
Amount required to be included in gross income of N Corporation under section 951 with respect to C Corporation	50.00
Dividend to B Corporation	75.00
Dividend from earnings and profits to which section 902(b)(2) does not apply (attributable to amounts included in N Corporation's gross income under section 951 with respect to C Corporation)	$ 50.00
Dividend from earnings and profits to which section 902(b)(2) applies (attributable to amounts not included in N Corporation's gross income with respect to C Corporation)	25.00

Amount of foreign income taxes of C Corporation deemed paid by B Corporation under section 902(b)(2) and § 1.960-2(b):

$$\frac{\text{Dividend to B Corporation less portion of dividend from earnings included in N Corporation's gross income under section 951 with respect to C Corporation}}{\text{Earnings and profits of C Corporation}} \times \text{Taxes paid by C Corporation}$$

($25/$105 × $45) .... $ 10.71

B Corporation (second-tier corporation):

Pretax earnings and profits:		
Dividend from C Corporation	$75.00	
Other earnings and profits	225.00	
Total pretax earnings and profits		300.00
Foreign income taxes paid by B Corporation (40%)		120.00
Earnings and profits		180.00
Earnings and profits attributable to amounts to which section 902(b)(2) does not apply (amounts included in N Corporation's gross income under section 951 with respect to C Corporation) ($50 − ($50 × .40))	30.00	
Other earnings and profits	150.00	
Earnings and profits of B Corporation after exclusion for amounts to which section 902(b)(2) does not apply (amounts attributable to earnings and profits which are included in N Corporation's gross income under section 951 with respect to C Corporation) ($180 − $30)		150.00
Amount to be included in gross income under section 951 of N Corporation with respect to B Corporation		15.00
Amount of dividend to A Corporation		60.00
Dividend from earnings and profits to which section 902(b)(2) does not apply (attributable to amounts included in N Corporation's gross income under section 951 with respect to C Corporation)	30.00	
Dividend from earnings and profits to which section 902(b)(1) does not apply (attributable to amounts included in N Corporation's gross income under section 951 with respect to B Corporation)	15.00	
Dividend from other earnings and profits (attributable to amounts not included in N Corporation's gross income under section 951 with respect to B or C Corporation)	15.00	

Foreign income taxes of B Corporation deemed paid by A Corporation under section 902(b)(1) and § 1.960-2(b):

Reg. § 1.960-2(f)

49,378 Income from Sources Without the United States

See p. 20,601 for regulations not amended to reflect law changes

$$\frac{\text{Dividend to A Corporation less portion of dividend from earnings included in N Corporation's gross income under section 951 with respect to B Corporation}}{\text{Earnings and profits of B Corporation}} \times \text{Taxes paid by B Corporation}$$

($45/$180 × $120) 30.00

Foreign income taxes (of C Corporation) deemed paid by B Corporation deemed paid by A Corporation under section 902(b)(1) in accordance with § 1.960-2(b) and § 1.960-2(d)(2)(i) and (ii):

$$\frac{\text{Dividend to A Corporation less portion of dividend from earnings included in N Corporation's gross income under section 951 with respect to B Corporation and C Corporation}}{\text{Earnings and profits of B Corporation less earnings and profits attributable to amounts included in N Corporation's gross income with respect to C Corporation}} \times \text{Taxes paid by C Corporation which are deemed paid by B Corporation}$$

($15/$150 × $10.71) .... $ 1.07

A Corporation (first-tier corporation):

Pretax earnings and profits:
   Dividend from B Corporation .... $ 60.00
   Other earnings and profits.. 0

Total pretax earnings and profits 60.00
Foreign income taxes paid by A Corporation (10%) 6.00
Earnings and profits 54.00
   Earnings and profits attributable to amounts to which section 902 (b)(2) does not apply (attributable to amounts previously included in N Corporation's gross income under section 951 with respect to C Corporation)
   ($30 − ($30 × .10)).. $ 27.00
   Earnings and profits attributable to amounts to which section 902(b)(1) does not apply (attributable to amounts included in N Corporation's gross income under section 951 with respect to B Corporation)
   ($15 − ($15 × .10))... 13.50
   Other earnings and profits
   ($15 − ($15 × .10))... 13.50
Earnings and profits of A Corporation after exclusion for amounts to which section 902(b)(1) does not apply (attributable to amounts included in N Corporation's gross income under section 951 with respect to B Corporation)
($54.00 − $13.50)... $ 40.50
Earnings and profits of A Corporation after exclusion for amounts to which sections 902(b)(1) and (2) do not apply (attributable to amounts included in N Corporation's gross income under section 951 with respect to B or C Corporation)
($40.50 − $27.00)... 13.50
Dividend to N Corporation 45.00
   Dividend from earnings and profits to which section 902(b)(2) does not apply (attributable to amounts included in N Corporation's gross income under section 951 with respect to C Corporation)...................................... 27.00
   Dividend from earnings and profits to which section 902(b)(1) does not apply (attributable to amounts included in N Corporation's gross income under section 951 with respect to B Corporation)...................................... 13.50
   Dividend from earnings and profits to which section 902(a) does not apply (attributable to amounts included in N Corporation's gross income under section 951 with respect to A Corporation).. 0
   Dividend from other earnings and profits (attributable to amounts not included in N Corporation's gross income under section 951 with respect to A, B, or C Corporation).. $ 4.50

Reg. § 1.960-2(f)

N Corporation (domestic corporation):
Foreign income taxes deemed paid by N Corporation under section 960(a)(1) and § 1.960-1(c)(1)(ii) with respect to C Corporation:

$$\frac{\text{Amount included in N Corporation's gross income under section 951 with respect to C Corporation}}{\text{Earnings and profits of C Corporation } (\$50/\$105 \times \$45.00)} \times \text{Taxes paid by C Corporation} \quad \ldots \quad \$ 21.43$$

Foreign income taxes deemed paid by N Corporation under section 960(a)(1) and § 1.960-1(c)(1)(i) with respect to B Corporation 11.07
Taxes paid by B Corporation:

$$\frac{\text{Amount included in N Corporation's gross income under section 951 with respect to B Corporation}}{\text{Earnings and profits of B Corporation } (\$15/\$180 \times \$120)} \times \text{Taxes paid by B Corporation} \quad \ldots \quad \$ 10.00$$

Taxes deemed paid by B Corporation in accordance with § 1.960-2(d)(2)(i):

$$\frac{\text{Amount included in N Corporation's gross income under section 951 with respect to B Corporation}}{\text{Earnings and profits of B Corporation less earnings and profits attributable to amounts included in N Corporation's gross income with respect to C Corporation } (\$15/\$150 \times \$10.71)} \times \text{Taxes paid by C Corporation which are deemed paid by B Corporation} \quad \ldots \quad 1.07$$

Total taxes deemed paid by N Corporation under section 960(a)(1) .... $ 32.50
Foreign income taxes deemed paid by N Corporation under section 902(a):
Taxes paid by A Corporation in accordance with § 1.960-2(c):

$$\frac{\text{Dividend to N Corporation less portion of dividend from earnings included in N Corporation's gross income under section 951 with respect to A Corporation}}{\text{Earnings and profits of A Corporation } (\$45/\$54 \times \$6)} \times \text{Taxes paid by A Corporation} \quad \ldots \quad 5.00$$

Taxes paid by B Corporation deemed paid by A Corporation in accordance with § § 1.960-2(c) and 1.960-2(d)(1)(i) and (ii):

$$\frac{\text{Dividend to N Corporation less portion of dividend from earnings included in N Corporation's gross income under section 951 with respect to A and B Corporations}}{\text{Earnings and profits of A Corporation less earnings and profits attributable to amounts included in N Corporation's gross income under section 951 with respect to B Corporation } (\$31.50/\$40.50 \times \$30.00)} \times \text{Taxes paid by B Corporation which are deemed paid by A Corporation} \quad \ldots \quad 23.33$$

Taxes (of C Corporation) deemed paid by B Corporation deemed paid by A Corporation in accordance with § § 1.960-2(c) and 1.960-2(d)(1)(i) and (ii):

$$\frac{\text{Dividend to N Corporation less portion of dividend from earnings included in N Corporation's gross income under section 951 with respect to A, B, and C Corporations}}{\text{Earnings and profits of A Corporation less earnings and profits attributable to amounts included in N Corporation's gross income under section 951 with respect to B and C Corporations}} \times \text{Taxes deemed paid by B Corporation which are deemed paid by A Corporation}$$

Reg. § 1.960-2(f)

49,380 Income from Sources Without the United States
See p. 20,601 for regulations not amended to reflect law changes

($4.50/$13.50 × $1.07) .... .36
Total taxes deemed paid by N Corporation under section 902(a) .... $ 28.69
Total foreign income taxes deemed paid by N Corporation under section 901 .... $ 61.19

Example (9). Domestic corporation N owns all the one class of stock of controlled foreign corporation A, which owns all the one class of stock of controlled foreign corporation B, which owns all the one class of stock of controlled foreign corporation C. A and B Corporations are organized under the laws of foreign country X. C Corporation is organized under the laws of foreign country Y. All of B Corporation's assets used in a trade or business are located in country X. All such corporations use the calendar year as the taxable year. For 1978, N Corporation is required to include in its gross income under section 951, $50 attributable to the earnings and profits of C Corporation and $100 attributable to the earnings and profits of B Corporation. N Corporation is not required to include any amount in its gross income under section 951 with respect to A Corporation. Country X imposes an income tax of 10 percent on dividends from foreign subsidiaries, 20 percent on dividends from domestic subsidiaries, and 40 percent on other earnings and profits. For 1978, C Corporation distributes $75 to B Corporation. For such year, B Corporation distributes $175 of its earnings and profits to A Corporation. A Corporation has no other earnings and profits for 1978 and distributes $130 of its earnings and profits of N Corporation. The foreign income taxes deemed paid by N Corporation under sections 960(a)(1) and 902(a) are determined as follows on the basis of the facts assumed:

C Corporation (third-tier corporation):
    Pretax earnings and profits $150.00
    Foreign income taxes paid by C Corporation (30%) 45.00
    Earnings and profits 105.00
    Amount required to be included in gross income of N Corporation under section 951 with respect to C Corporation .... $ 50.00
    Dividend to B Corporation 75.00
    Dividend to which section 902(b)(2) does not apply (attributable to amounts included in N Corporation's gross income under section 951 with respect to C Corporation) .... $ 50.00
    Dividend to which section 902(b)(2) applies (attributable to amounts not included in N Corporation's gross income under section 951 with respect to C Corporation) 25.00
    Amount of foreign income taxes of C Corporation deemed paid by B Corporation under section 902(b)(2) and § 1.960-2(b) ($25/$105 × $45) 10.71
    (for formula see § 1.960-2(g)(1)(i)(A))

B Corporation (second-tier corporation):
    Pretax earnings and profits:
    Dividend from C Corporation 75.00
    Other earnings and profits 225.00

    Total pretax earnings and profits 300.00
    Foreign income taxes paid by B Corporation 97.50
    On dividends received from C Corporation to which section 902(b)(2) does not apply (attributable to amounts included in N Corporation's gross income under section 951 with respect to C Corporation) ($50 × .10) 5.00
    On dividend from C Corporation to which section 902(b)(2) applies (attributable to amounts not included in N Corporation's gross income under section 951 with respect to C Corporation) ($25 × .10) .... $ 2.50
    On other income of B Corporation ($225 × .40) 90.00
    Earnings and profits $202.50
    Attributable to dividend to which section 902(b)(2) does not apply (attributable to amounts included in N Corporation's gross income under section 951 with respect to C Corporation) ($50 − $5) 45.00
    Attributable to dividend to which section from C Corporation to which section 902(b)(2) applies (attributable to amounts not included in N Corporation's gross income under section 951 with respect to C Corporation) ($25 − $2.50) 22.50
    Attributable to other income of B Corporation ($225 − $90) 135.00
    Earnings and profits after exclusion of amounts attributable to dividend to which section 902(b)(2) does not apply (attributable to amounts included in N Corporation's gross income under section 951 with respect to C Corporation) ($202.50 − $45) 157.50

Reg. § 1.960-2(f)

Income from Sources Without the United States   49,381
See p. 20,601 for regulations not amended to reflect law changes

Amount required to be included in N Corporation's gross income under section 951 with respect to B Corporation	100.00
Dividend paid by B Corporation	$175.00
Dividend to which section 902(b)(2) does not apply (attributable to amounts included in N Corporation's gross income under section 951 with respect to C Corporation)	$ 45.00
Dividend to which section 902(b)(1) does not apply (attributable to amounts included in N Corporation's gross income under section 951 with respect to B Corporation)	100.00
Dividend from other earnings and profits (attributable to amounts not included in N Corporation's gross income with respect to B or C Corporation)	30.00

Foreign income taxes of B Corporation deemed paid by A Corporation under section 902(b)(1) (separate tax rate applicable to dividend received by B Corporation allocation in accordance with § 1.960-2(e)) (for formula see § 1.960-2(g)(1)(ii)(A)(*2*)(*i*) and (*ii*)):

Tax paid by B Corporation on earnings previously taxed with respect to C Corporation or lower-tiers which is deemed paid by A Corporation:

$$\frac{\text{Portion of dividend to A Corporation from earnings included in N Corporation's gross income under section 951 with respect to C Corporation or lower-tiers}}{\text{Earnings and profits of B Corporation included in N Corporation's gross income under section 951 with respect to C Corporation or lower-tiers}} \times \text{Tax paid by B Corporation on dividend received by B Corporation from earnings included in N Corporation's gross income with respect to C Corporation or lower-tiers}$$

($45/$45 × $5) .... $ 5.00

Tax paid by B Corporation on earnings not previously taxed with respect to C Corporation or lower-tiers which is deemed paid by A Corporation:

$$\frac{\text{Portion of dividend to A Corporation which is from earnings not included in N Corporation's gross income under section 951 with respect to B Corporation or lower-tiers}}{\text{Earnings and profits of B Corporation not included in N Corporation's gross income under section 951 with respect to C Corporation or lower-tiers}} \times \text{Tax paid by B Corporation on earnings not included in N Corporation's gross income with respect to C Corporation or lower-tiers}$$

($30/$157.50 × $92.50) 17.62

Foreign income taxes (of C Corporation) deemed paid by B Corporation deemed paid by A Corporation under section 902(b)(1)
($30/$157.50 × $10.71) 2.04
(for formula see § 1.960-2(g)(1)(ii)(B)(*1*))

A Corporation (first-tier corporation):

Pretax earnings and profits:		
Dividend from B Corporation	$175.00	
Other income	0	
Total pretax earnings and profits		175.00
Foreign income taxes paid by A Corporation (20%)		35.00
Earnings and profits		140.00
Attributable to dividend to which section 902(b)(2) does not apply (attributable to amounts included in N Corporation's gross income under section 951 with respect to C Corporation) ($45 − ($45 × .20))	$ 36.00	
Attributable to amounts to which section 902(b)(1) does not apply (attributable to amounts included in N Corporation's gross income under section 951 with respect to B Corporation) ($100 − ($100 × .20))	80.00	
Attributable to other earnings and profits (attributable to amounts not included in N Corporation's gross income with respect to B or C Corporation)	24.00	
Earnings and profits after exclusion for amounts to which section 902(b)(1) does not apply (attributable to amounts included in N Corporation's gross income under section 951 with respect to B Corporation) ($140 − $80)		60.00

Reg. § 1.960-2(f)

49,382   Income from Sources Without the United States
See p. 20,601 for regulations not amended to reflect law changes

Earnings and profits after exclusion for amounts to which sections 902(b)(1) and 902(b)(2) do not apply (attributable to amounts included in N Corporation's gross income under section 951 with respect to B or C Corporation) ($60 − $36)	24.00
Amount required to be included in N Corporation's gross income under section 951 with respect to A Corporation	None
Dividend to N Corporation	130.00
Dividend to which section 902(b)(2) does not apply (attributable to amounts included in N Corporation's gross income under section 951 with respect to C Corporation)	$ 36.00
Dividend to which section 902(b)(1) does not apply (attributable to amounts included in N Corporation's gross income under section 951 with respect to B Corporation)	80.00
Dividend to which section 902(a) does not apply (attributable to amounts included in N Corporation's gross income under section 951 with respect to A Corporation)	0
Dividend from other earnings and profits (attributable to amounts not included in N Corporation's gross income with respect to A,B, or C Corporation)	14.00

N Corporation (domestic corporation):

Foreign income taxes deemed paid by N Corporation under section 960(a)(1) and § 1.960-1(c) with respect to C Corporation ($50/$105 × $45) 21.43

(for formula see § 1.960-2(g)(2)(i)(A))

Foreign income taxes deemed paid by N Corporation under section 960(a)(1) with respect to B Corporation (allocation of earnings and profits being made in accordance with § 1.960-1(c)(3) and § 1.960-2(e)) (Separate tax rate applicable to dividend received by B Corporation) 65.53

Taxes paid by B corporation (for formula see § 1.960-2(g)(2)(ii)(A)(*2*))

$$\frac{\text{Amount included in N Corporation's gross income under section 951 with respect to B Corporation}}{\text{Earnings and profits of B Corporation not included in N Corporation's gross income under section 951 with respect to C Corporation or lower tiers}} \times \text{Tax paid by B Corporation on earnings not included in N Corporation's gross income with respect to C Corporation or lower tiers}$$

($100/$157.50 × $92.50) .... $ 58.73

Taxes (of C Corporation) deemed paid by B Corporation under section 902(b)(2) which are deemed paid by N Corporation under section 960(a)(1)($100/$157.50 × $10.71) 6.80
(for formula see § 1.960-2(g)(2)(ii)(B)(*1*))
Total taxes deemed paid by N Corporation under section 960(a)(1) .... $ 86.96
Foreign income taxes deemed paid by N Corporation under section 902(a):
Taxes paid by A Corporation ($130/$140 × $35) 32.50
(for formula see § 1.960-2(g)(1)(iii)(A)(*1*))
Taxes paid by B Corporation deemed paid by A Corporation (Separate tax rate applicable to dividend received by B Corporation allocation required by § 1.960-2(e)) (for formula see § 1.960-2(g)(1)(iii)(B)(*2*)(*i*) and (*ii*))

Tax paid by B Corporation on earnings previously taxed with respect to C Corporation or lower tiers which is deemed paid by N Corporation:

$$\frac{\text{Portion of dividend to N Corporation which is from earnings included in N Corporation's gross income under section 951 with respect to C Corporation or lower tiers}}{\text{Earnings and profits of A Corporation included in N Corporation's gross income under section 951 with respect to C Corporation or lower tiers}} \times \text{Tax paid by B Corporation on earnings previously taxed with respect to C Corporation or lower tiers which is deemed paid by A Corporation}$$

($36/$36 × $5) .... $ 5.00

Reg. § 1.960-2(f)

Income from Sources Without the United States 49,383
See p. 20,601 for regulations not amended to reflect law changes

Tax paid by B corporation on earnings not previously taxed with respect to C corporation or lower tiers which is deemed paid by N Corporation:

$$\frac{\text{Portion of dividend to N Corporation which is from earnings not included in N Corporation's gross income under section 951 with respect to A Corporation or lower tiers}}{\text{Earnings and profits of A Corporation not included in N Corporation's gross income under section 951 with respect to B Corporation or lower tiers}} \times \text{Tax paid by B Corporation on earnings not previously taxed with respect to C corporation or lower tiers which is deemed paid by A Corporation}$$

($14/$24 × $17.62) $10.28
Taxes (of C corporation) deemed paid by B Corporation deemed paid by A Corporation
($14/$24 × $2.04) 1.19

(for formula see § 1.960-2(g)(1)(iii)(C)(*1*))
Total taxes deemed paid by N Corporation under section 902(a) 48.97

Total foreign income taxes deemed paid by
N Corporation under section 901 .... $135.93

Example (10). The facts are the same as in example (9) except that A Corporation has other earnings and profits of $200 in 1978 and country X imposes a tax of 50 percent on A Corporation's other earnings and profits. A Corporation distributes $200 of its earnings and profits to N Corporation in 1978. The foreign income taxes paid by N Corporation under sections 960(a)(1) and 902(a) are determined as follows on the basis of the facts assumed:

C Corporation (third-tier corporation):
Pretax earnings and profits $150.00
Foreign incomes taxes paid by C Corporation (30%) 45.00
Earnings and profits 105.00
Amount required to be included in gross income of N Corporation under section 951 with respect
to C Corporation 50.00
Dividend to B Corporation 75.00
  Dividend to which section 902(b)(2) does not apply (attributable to amounts
  included in N Corporation's gross income under section 951 with respect to C
  Corporation) .... $ 50.00
  Dividend to which section 902(b)(2) applies attributable to amounts not included
  in N Corporation's gross income under section 951 with respect to C Corporation .. $ 25.00
Amount of foreign income taxes of C Corporation deemed paid by B Corporation under section
902(b)(2) and § 1.960-2(b) ($25/$105 × $45) 10.71
(for formula see § 1.960-2(g)(1)(i)(A))

B Corporation (second-tier corporation):
Pretax earnings and profits:
  Dividend from C Corporation 75.00
  Other earnings and profits 225.00

Total pretax earnings and profits 300.00
Foreign income taxes of B Corporation 97.50
  On dividends received from C Corporation to which section 902(b)(2) does not
  apply (attributable to amounts included in N Corporation's gross income under
  section 951 with respect to C Corporation) ($50 × .10) .... $ 5.00
  On dividend from C Corporation to which section 902(b)(2) applies (attributable to
  amounts not included in N Corporation's gross income under section 951 with
  respect to C Corporation) ($25 × .10) 2.50
  On other income of B Corporation ($225 × .40) 90.00
Earnings and profits 202.50
  Attributable to dividend to which section 902(b)(2) does not apply (attributable to
  amounts included in N Corporation's gross income under section 951 with respect
  to C Corporation) ($50 − $5) 45.00
  Attributable to dividend from C Corporation to which section 902(b)(2) applies
  (attributable to amounts not included in N Corporation's gross income under
  section 951 with respect to C Corporation) ($25 − $2.50) 22.50
  Attributable to other income of B Corporation ($225 − $90) 135.00
Earnings and profits after exclusion of amounts attributable to dividend to which section
902(b)(2) does not apply (attributable to amounts included in N Corporation's gross income
under section 951 with respect to C Corporation) ($202.50 − $45) 157.50

Reg. § 1.960-2(f)

49,384   Income from Sources Without the United States

See p. 20,601 for regulations not amended to reflect law changes

Amount required to be included in N Corporation's gross income under section 951 with respect to B Corporation	100.00
Dividend paid by B Corporation	175.00
Dividend to which section 902(b)(2) does not apply (attributable to amounts included in N Corporation's gross income under section 951 with respect to C Corporation)	$ 45.00
Dividend to which section 902(b)(1) does not apply (attributable to amounts included in N Corporation's gross income under section 951 with respect to B Corporation)	100.00
Dividend from other earnings and profits (attributable to amounts not included in N Corporation's gross income with respect to B or C Corporation)	30.00
Foreign income taxes of B Corporation deemed paid by A Corporation under section 902(b)(1) with allocation required by § 1.960-2(e):	
($45/$45 × $5)	5.00
($30/$157.50 × $92.50)	17.62
(for formula see § 1.960-2(g)(1)(ii)(A)(*2*)(*i*) and (*ii*))	
Foreign income taxes (of C Corporation) deemed paid by B Corporation deemed paid by A Corporation under section 902(b)(1) ($30/$157.50 × $10.71)	2.04
(for formula see § 1.960-2(g)(1)(ii)(B)(*1*))	

A Corporation (first-tier corporation):
Pretax earnings and profits:

Dividend from B Corporation	$175.00	
Other earnings and profits	200.00	
Total pretax earnings and profits		$375.00
Foreign income taxes paid by A Corporation		135.00
On dividend received from B Corporation to which section 902(b)(2) does not apply (attributable to amounts included in N Corporation's gross income under section 951 with respect to C Corporation) ($45 × .20)	$ 9.00	
On dividend received from B Corporation to which section 902(b)(1) does not apply (attributable to amounts included in N Corporation's gross income under section 951 with respect to B Corporation) ($100 × .20)	20.00	
On dividend from B Corporation attributable to B Corporation's other earnings and profits (attributable to amounts not included in N Corporation's gross income with respect to B or C Corporation) ($30 × .20)	6.00	
On other income of A Corporation ($200 × .50)	100.00	
Earnings and profits		$240.00
Attributable to dividend to which section 902(b)(2) does not apply (attributable to amounts included in N Corporation's gross income under section 951 with respect to C Corporation) ($45 − $9)	36.00	
Attributable to dividend to which section 902(b)(1) does not apply (attributable to amounts included in N Corporation's gross income with respect to B Corporation) ($100 − $20)	80.00	
Attributable to other earnings and profits of A Corporation (attributable to amounts not included in N Corporation's gross income with respect to A, B, or C Corporation) [($30 − $6) + ($200 − $100)]	$124.00	
Amount required to be included in N Corporation's gross income under section 951 with respect to A Corporation		None
Earnings and profits after exclusion of amounts attributable to dividend to which section 902(b)(1) does not apply (attributable to amounts included in N Corporation's gross income under section 951 with respect to B Corporation)		$160.00
Earnings and profits after exclusion of amounts attributable to dividend to which sections 902(b)(1) and 902(b)(2) do not apply (attributable to amounts included in N Corporation's gross income under section 951 with respect to B and C Corporation)		124.00
Dividend to N Corporation		200.00
Dividend attributable to amounts to which section 902(b)(2) does not apply (attributable to amounts included in N Corporation's gross income under section 951 with respect to C Corporation)	36.00	
Dividend attributable to amounts to which section 902(b)(1) does not apply (attributable to amounts included in N Corporation's gross income with respect to B Corporation)	80.00	
Dividend attributable to amounts to which section 902(a) does not apply (attributable to amounts included in N Corporation's gross income under section 951 with respect to A Corporation)	0	
Dividend attributable to A Corporation's other earnings and profits (attributable to amounts not included in N Corporation's gross income under section 951 with respect to A, B, or C Corporation)	$ 84.00	

Reg. § 1.960-2(f)

Income from Sources Without the United States 49,385
See p. 20,601 for regulations not amended to reflect law changes

N Corporation (domestic corporation)

Foreign income taxes deemed paid by N Corporation under section 960(a)(1) and § 1.960-1(c) with respect to C Corporation ($50/$150 × $45)		$ 21.43
(for formula see § 1.960-2(g)(2)(i)(A))		
Foreign income taxes deemed paid by N Corporation under section 960(a)(1) with respect to B Corporation (allocation of earning and profits being made in accordance with § 1.960-1(c)(3) and § 1.960-2(e))		65.53
Taxes paid by B Corporation ($100/$157.50 × $92.50)	58.73	
(for formula see § 1.960-2(g)(2)(ii)(A)(*2*))		
Taxes deemed paid by B Corporation ($100/$157.50 × $10.71)	6.80	
(for formula see § 1.960-2(g)(2)(ii)(B)(*1*))		
Total taxes deemed paid by N Corporation under section 960(a)(1)		86.96

Foreign income taxes deemed paid by N Corporation under section 902(a) (separate tax rate applicable to dividends received by A Corporation allocation required by § 1.960-2(e)) (for formula see § 1.960-2(g)(1)(iii)(A)(*2*)(*i*) and (*ii*)):

Tax paid by A Corporation on earnings previously taxed with respect to B Corporation or lower tiers which is deemed paid by N Corporation:

$$\frac{\text{Portion of dividend to N Corporation which is from earnings included in N Corporation's gross income under section 951 with respect to B Corporation or lower tiers}}{\text{Earnings and profits of A Corporation included in N Corporation's gross income under section 951 with respect to B Corporation or lower tiers}} \times \text{Tax paid by A Corporation on dividends received by A Corporation from earnings included in N Corporation's gross income with respect to B Corporation or lower tiers}$$

($116/$116 × $29) .... $ 29.00

Tax paid by A Corporation on earnings not previously taxed with respect to B Corporation or lower tiers which is deemed paid by N Corporation:

$$\frac{\text{Portion of dividend to N Corporation which is from earnings not included in N Corporation's gross income under section 951 with respect to A Corporation or lower tiers}}{\text{Earnings and profits of A Corporation not included in N Corporation's gross income under section 951 with respect to B Corporation or lower tiers}} \times \text{Tax paid by A Corporation on earnings not included in N Corporation's gross income with respect to B Corporation or lower tiers}$$

($84/$124 × $106)		$ 71.81
Taxes (paid by B Corporation) deemed paid by A Corporation allocation required by § 1.960-2(e):		
$36/$36 × $5)	$ 5.00	
($84/$124 × $17.62)	11.94	
(for formula see § 1.960-2(g)(1)(iii)(B)(*2*)(*i*) and (*ii*))		
Taxes (of C Corporation) deemed paid by B Corporation deemed paid by A Corporation		
($84/$124 × $2.04)	1.38	
(for formula see § 1.960-2(g)(1)(iii)(C)(*1*))		
Total taxes deemed paid by N Corporation under section 902(a) credit		$119.13
Total foreign income taxes deemed paid by N Corporation under section 901		$206.09

Reg. § 1.960-2(f)

(g) *Formulas.* This paragraph contains formulas for determining a domestic corporation's section 902 and 960 credits when amounts distributed through a chain of ownership have been included in whole or in part in the gross income of a domestic corporation under section 951 with respect to first-, second-, third-, or lower-tier corporations.

(1) *Determination of the section 902 credit.* (i) *Section 902(b)(2) credit.* If the second-tier corporation receives a dividend from a third-tier corporation attributable in whole or in part to amounts included in a domestic corporation's gross income under section 951 with respect to the third- or lower-tier corporations, the second-tier corporation's credit for taxes paid by the third-tier corporation under section 902(b)(2) is determined as follows:

(A) If the effective rate of tax on dividends received by the third-tier corporation is the same as the effective rate of tax on its other earnings and profits—

$$\frac{\text{Dividend to second-tier corporation less portion of dividend from earnings included in domestic corporation's gross income under section 951 with respect to third-tier corporation}}{\text{Earnings and profits of third-tier corporation}} \times \text{Taxes paid by third-tier corporation}$$

(B) If the effective rate of tax on dividends received by the third-tier corporation is higher or lower than the effective rate of tax on its other earnings and profits—

(*1*) Credit for tax paid by third-tier corporation on earnings included in domestic corporation's gross income with respect to fourth- or lower-tier corporations—

$$\frac{\text{Portion of dividends to second-tier corporation which is from earnings included in domestic corporation's gross income under section 951 with respect to fourth- or lower-tier corporations}}{\text{Earnings and profits of third-tier corporation included in domestic corporation's gross income under section 951 with respect to fourth- or lower-tier corporations}} \times \text{Tax paid by third-tier corporation on dividend received by third-tier corporation from earnings included in domestic corporation's gross income with respect to fourth- or lower-tier corporations}$$

(*2*) Credit for tax paid by third-tier corporation on earnings not included in domestic corporation's gross income with respect to fourth- or lower-tier corporations—

$$\frac{\text{Portion of dividend to second-tier corporation which is from earnings not included in domestic corporation's gross income under section 951 with respect to third- or lower-tier corporations}}{\text{Earnings and profits of third-tier corporation not included in domestic corporation's gross income under section 951 with respect to fourth- or lower-tier corporations}} \times \text{Tax paid by third-tier corporation on earnings not included in domestic corporation's gross income with respect to fourth- or lower-tier corporations}$$

(ii) *Section 902(b)(1) credit.* If the first-tier corporation receives a dividend from a second-tier corporation attributable in a whole or in part to amounts included in a domestic corporation's gross income under section 951 with respect to the second- or lower-tier corporations, the first-tier corporation's credit for taxes paid and deemed paid by the second-tier corporation under section 902(b)(1) is determined as follows:

(A) *Taxes paid by the second-tier corporation which are deemed paid by the first-tier corporation.*

(*1*) If the effective rate of tax on dividends received by the second-tier corporation is the same as the effective rate of tax on its other earnings and profits—

$$\frac{\text{Dividend to first-tier corporation less portion of dividend from earnings included in domestic corporation's gross income under section 951 with respect to second-tier corporation}}{\text{Earnings and profits of second-tier corporation}} \times \text{Taxes paid by second-tier corporation}$$

(*2*) If the effective rate of tax on dividends received by the second-tier corporation is higher or lower than the effective rate of tax on its other earnings and profits—

(*i*) Credit for tax paid by second-tier corporation on earnings previously taxed with respect to third- or lower-tier corporations—

Portion of dividend to first-tier corporation which is from earnings included in domestic corporation's gross income under section 951 with respect to third- or lower-tier corporations

———

Earnings and profits of second-tier corporation included in domestic corporation's gross income under section 951 with respect to third- or lower-tier corporations

× Tax paid by second-tier corporation on dividend received by second-tier corporation from earnings included in domestic corporation's gross income with respect to third- or lower-tier corporations

(*ii*) Credit for tax paid by second-tier corporation on earnings not previously taxed with respect to third- or lower-tier corporations—

Portion of dividend to first-tier corporation which is from earnings not included in domestic corporation's gross income under section 951 with respect to second- or lower-tier corporations

———

Earnings and profits of second-tier corporation not included in domestic corporation's gross income under section 951 with respect to third- or lower-tier corporations

× Tax paid by second-tier corporation on earnings not included in domestic corporation's gross income with respect to third- or lower-tier corporations

(B) *Taxes deemed paid by the second-tier corporation which are deemed paid by the first-tier corporation.*

(*1*) If the effective rate of tax on dividends received by the third-tier corporation is the same as the effective rate of tax on its other earnings and profits—

Dividend to first-tier corporation less portion of dividend from earnings included in domestic corporation's gross income under section 951 with respect to second- and third-tier corporations

———

Earnings and profits of second-tier corporation less earnings and profits attributable to amounts included in domestic corporation's gross income under section 951 with respect to third-tier corporation

× Taxes paid by third-tier corporation which are deemed paid by second-tier corporation

(*2*) If the effective rate of tax on dividends received by the third-tier corporation is higher or lower than the effective rate of tax on its other earnings and profits—

(*i*) Credit for tax paid by third-tier corporation on earnings previously taxed with respect to fourth- or lower-tier corporations—

Portion of dividend to first-tier corporation which is from earnings included in domestic corporation's gross income under section 951 with respect to fourth- or lower-tier corporations

———

Earnings and profits of second-tier corporations included in domestic corporation's gross income under section 951 with respect to fourth- or lower-tier corporations

× Tax paid by third-tier corporation on earnings previously taxed with respect to fourth- or lower-tier corporations which is deemed paid by second-tier corporation

(*ii*) Credit for tax paid by third-tier corporation on earnings not previously taxed with respect to fourth- or lower-tier corporations—

Reg. § 1.960-2(g)(1)

49,388 Income from Sources Without the United States

See p. 20,601 for regulations not amended to reflect law changes

$$\frac{\text{Portion of dividend to first-tier corporation which is from earnings not included in domestic corporation's gross income under section 951 with respect to second- or lower-tier corporations}}{\text{Earnings and profits of second-tier corporation not included in domestic corporation's gross income under section 951 with respect to third- or lower-tier corporations}}$$

$\times$ Tax paid by third-tier corporation on earnings not previously taxed with respect to fourth- or lower-tier corporations which is deemed paid by second-tier corporation

(iii) *Section 902(a) credit.* If the domestic corporation receives a dividend from a first-tier corporation attributable in whole or in part to amounts included in a domestic corporation's gross income under section 951 with respect to the first- or lower-tier corporations, the domestic corporation's credit for taxes paid and deemed paid by the first-tier corporation under section 902(a) is determined as follows:

(A) *Taxes paid by the first-tier corporation which are deemed paid by domestic corporation.*

(1) If the effective rate of tax on dividends received by the first-tier corporation is the same as the effective rate of tax on its other earnings and profits—

$$\frac{\text{Dividend to domestic corporation less portion of dividend from earnings included in domestic corporation's gross income under section 951 with respect to first-tier corporation}}{\text{Earnings and profits of first-tier corporation}}$$

$\times$ Taxes paid by first-tier corporation

(2) If the effective rate of tax on dividends received by the first-tier corporation is higher or lower than the effective rate of tax on its other earnings and profits—

(i) Credit for tax paid by first-tier corporation on earnings previously taxed with respect to second- or lower-tier corporations—

$$\frac{\text{Portion of dividend to domestic corporation which is from earnings included in domestic corporation's gross income under section 951 with respect to second- or lower-tier corporations}}{\text{Earnings and profits of first-tier corporation included in domestic corporation's gross income under section 951 with respect to second- or lower-tier corporations}}$$

$\times$ Tax paid by first-tier corporation on dividends received by first-tier corporation from earnings included in domestic corporation's gross income with respect to second- or lower-tier corporations

(ii) Credit for tax paid by first-tier corporation on earnings not previously taxed with respect to second- or lower-tier corporations—

$$\frac{\text{Portion of dividend to domestic corporation which is from earnings not included in domestic corporation's gross income under section 951 with respect to first- or lower-tier corporations}}{\text{Earnings and profits of first-tier corporation not included in domestic corporation's gross income under section 951 with respect to second- or lower-tier corporations}}$$

$\times$ Tax paid by first-tier corporation on earnings not included in domestic corporation's gross income with respect to second- or lower-tier corporations

Reg. § 1.960-2(g)(1)

(B) *Taxes (paid by second-tier corporation) deemed paid by first-tier corporation which are deemed paid by domestic corporation.*

(*1*) If the effective rate of tax on dividends received by the second-tier corporation is the same as its tax rate on other earnings and profits—

$$\frac{\text{Dividend to domestic corporation less portion of dividend from earnings included in domestic corporation's gross income under section 951 with respect to first- and second-tier corporations}}{\text{Earnings and profits of first-tier corporation less earnings and profits attributable to amounts included in domestic corporation's gross income under section 951 with respect to second-tier corporation}} \times \text{Taxes paid by second-tier corporation which are deemed paid by first-tier corporation}$$

(*2*) If the effective rate of tax on dividends received by the second-tier corporation is higher or lower than the effective rate of tax on its other earnings and profits—

(*i*) Credit for tax paid by second-tier corporation on earnings previously taxed with respect to third-tier or lower-tier corporations—

$$\frac{\text{Portion of dividend to domestic corporation which is from earnings included in domestic corporation's gross income under section 951 with respect to third- or lower-tier corporations}}{\text{Earnings and profits of first-tier corporation included in domestic corporation's gross income under section 951 with respect to third- or lower-tier corporations}} \times \text{Tax paid by second-tier corporation on earnings previously taxed with respect to third- or lower-tier corporations which is deemed paid by first-tier corporation}$$

(*ii*) Credit for tax paid by second-tier corporation on earnings not previously taxed with respect to third- or lower-tier corporations—

$$\frac{\text{Portion of dividend to domestic corporation which is from earnings not included in domestic corporation's gross income under section 951 with respect to first- or lower-tier corporations}}{\text{Earnings and profits of first-tier corporation not included in domestic corporation's gross income under section 951 with respect to second- or lower-tier corporations}} \times \text{Tax paid on second-tier corporation on earnings not previously taxed with respect to third- or lower-tier corporations which is deemed paid by first-tier corporation}$$

(C) *Taxes (of a third-tier corporation) deemed paid by first-tier corporation which are deemed paid by domestic corporation.*

(*1*) If the effective rate of tax on dividends received by the third-tier corporation is the same as the effective rate of tax on its other earnings and profits—

$$\frac{\text{Dividend to domestic corporation less portion of dividend from earnings included in domestic corporation's gross income under section 951 with respect to first-, second- and third-tier corporations}}{\text{Earnings and profits of first-tier corporation less earnings and profits attributable to amounts included in domestic corporation's gross income with respect to second- and third-tier corporations}} \times \text{Taxes deemed paid by second-tier corporation which are deemed paid by first-tier corporation}$$

(*2*) If the effective rate of tax on dividends received by the third-tier corporation is higher or lower than the effective rate of tax on its other earnings and profits—

(*i*) Credit for tax (of third-tier corporation) deemed paid by second-tier corporation on earnings previously taxed with respect to fourth- or lower-tier corporation—

Reg. § 1.960-2(g)(1)

49,390 Income from Sources Without the United States

See p. 20,601 for regulations not amended to reflect law changes

$$\frac{\text{Portion of dividend to domestic corporation which is from earnings included in domestic corporation's gross income under section 951 with respect to fourth- or lower-tier corporations}}{\text{Earnings and profits of first-tier corporation included in domestic corporation's gross income under section 951 with respect to fourth- or lower-tier corporations}}$$

$\times$ Tax deemed paid by second-tier corporation on earnings previously taxed with respect to fourth- or lower-tier corporations which is deemed paid by first-tier corporation

(ii) *Credit for tax (of third-tier corporation) deemed paid by second-tier on earnings not previously taxed with respect to fourth- or lower-tier corporations*—

$$\frac{\text{Portion of dividend to domestic corporation which is from earnings not included in domestic corporation's gross income under section 951 with respect to first- or lower-tier corporations}}{\text{Earnings and profits of first-tier corporation not included in domestic corporation's gross income under section 951 with respect to second- or lower-tier corporations}}$$

$\times$ Tax deemed paid by second-tier corporation on earnings not previously taxed with respect to fourth- or lower-tier corporations which is deemed paid by first-tier corporation

(2) *Determination of domestic corporation's section 960 credit for amounts included in its gross income with respect to a first-, second-, or third-tier corporation which has received a distribution previously included in the gross income of a domestic corporation under section 951.* (i) *Third-tier credit.* If a domestic corporation is required to include an amount in its gross income under section 951 with respect to a third-tier corporation which has received a distribution from a fourth-tier corporation of amounts included in a domestic corporation's gross income under section 951 with respect to the fourth- or lower-tier corporations, the domestic corporation's credit for taxes paid by the third-tier corporation under section 960(a)(1) is determined as follows:

(A) If the effective rate of tax on dividends received by the third-tier corporation is the same as the effective rate of tax on its other earnings and profits—

$$\frac{\text{Amount included in domestic corporation's gross income under section 951 with respect to third-tier corporation}}{\text{Earnings and profits of third-tier corporation}}$$

$\times$ Taxes paid by third-tier corporation

(B) If the effective rate of tax on dividends received by the third-tier corporation is higher or lower than the effective rate of tax on its other earnings and profits—

$$\frac{\text{Amount included in domestic corporation's gross income under section 951 with respect to third-tier corporation}}{\text{Earnings and profits of third-tier corporation not included in domestic corporation's gross income under section 951 with respect to fourth- or lower-tier corporations}}$$

$\times$ Tax paid by third-tier corporation on earnings not included in domestic corporation's gross income with respect to fourth- or lower-tier corporations

Reg. § 1.960-2(g)(2)

(ii) *Second-tier credit.* If a domestic corporation is required to include an amount in its gross income under section 951 with respect to a second-tier corporation which has received a distribution from a third-tier corporation of amounts included in a domestic corporation's gross income under section 951 with respect to the third- or lower-tier corporations, the domestic corporation's credit for taxes paid and deemed paid by the second-tier corporation under section 960(a)(1) is determined as follows:

$$\frac{\text{Amount included in domestic corporation's gross income under section 951 with respect to second-tier corporation}}{\text{Earnings and profits of second-tier corporation}}$$

(2) If the effective rate of tax on dividends received by the second-tier is higher or

$$\frac{\text{Amount included in domestic corporation's gross income under section 951 with respect to second-tier corporation}}{\text{Earnings and profits of second-tier corporation not included in domestic corporation's gross income under section 951 with respect to third- or lower-tier corporations}}$$

(B) *Credit for taxes (of the third-tier corporation) deemed paid by the second-tier corporation under section 902(b)(2).*

(1) If the effective rate of tax on dividends received by the third-tier corporation is

$$\frac{\text{Amount included in domestic corporation's gross income under section 951 with respect to second-tier corporation}}{\text{Earnings and profits of second-tier corporation less earnings and profits attributable to amounts included in domestic corporation's gross income with respect to third-tier corporation}}$$

(2) If the effective rate of tax on dividends received by the third-tier corporation is

$$\frac{\text{Amount included in domestic corporation's gross income under section 951 with respect to second-tier corporation}}{\text{Earnings and profits of second-tier corporation not included in domestic corporation's gross income under section 951 with respect to third- or lower-tier corporations}}$$

(iii) *First-tier credit.* If a domestic corporation is required to include amounts in its gross income under section 951 with respect to a first-tier corporation which has received a distribution from a second-tier corporation of amounts included in a domestic corporation's gross income under section 951 with respect to the second- or lower-tier corporations, the domestic corporation's credit for taxes paid and deemed paid by the first-

(A) *Credit for taxes paid by the second-tier corporation which are deemed paid by the domestic corporation.*

(1) If the effective rate of tax on dividends received by the second-tier corporation is the same as the effective rate of tax on its other earnings and profits—

$\times$ Taxes paid by second-tier corporation

lower than the effective rate of tax on its other earnings and profits—

$\times$ Tax paid by second-tier corporation on earnings not included in domestic corporation's gross income with respect to third- or lower-tier corporations

the same as the effective rate of tax on its other earnings and profits—

$\times$ Taxes paid by third-tier corporation which are deemed paid by second-tier corporation

higher or lower than the effective rate of tax on its other earnings and profits—

$\times$ Tax paid by third-tier corporation on earnings not previously taxed with respect to fourth- or lower-tier corporations which is deemed paid by second-tier corporation

tier corporation under section 960(a)(1) shall be determined as follows:

(A) *Credit for taxes paid by the first-tier corporation.*

(1) If the effective rate of tax on dividends received by the first-tier corporation is the same as the effective rate of tax on its other earnings and profits—

Reg. § 1.960-2(g)(2)

49,392   Income from Sources Without the United States
See p. 20,601 for regulations not amended to reflect law changes

$$\frac{\text{Amount included in domestic corporation's gross income under section 951 with respect to first-tier corporation}}{\text{Earnings and profits of first-tier corporation}} \times \text{Taxes paid by first-tier corporation}$$

(2) If the effective rate of tax on dividends received by the first-tier corporation is higher or lower than the effective rate of tax on its other earnings and profits—

$$\frac{\text{Amount included in domestic corporation's gross income under section 951 with respect to first-tier corporation}}{\text{Earnings and profits of first-tier corporation not included in domestic corporation's gross income under section 951 with respect to second- or lower-tier corporations}} \times \text{Tax paid by first-tier corporation on earnings not included in domestic corporation's gross income with respect to second- or lower-tier corporations}$$

(B) *Credit for taxes paid by the second-tier corporation deemed paid by the first-tier corporation under section 902(b)(1).*

(1) If the effective rate of tax on dividends received by the second-tier corporation is the same as the effective rate of tax on its other earnings and profits—

$$\frac{\text{Amount included in domestic corporation's gross income under section 951 with respect to first-tier corporation}}{\text{Earnings and profits of first-tier corporation less earnings and profits attributable to amounts included in domestic corporation's gross income under section 951 with respect to second-tier corporation}} \times \text{Taxes paid by second-tier corporation which are deemed paid by first-tier corporation}$$

(2) If the effective rate of tax on dividends received by the second-tier corporation is higher or lower than the effective rate of tax on its other earnings and profits—

$$\frac{\text{Amount included in domestic corporation's gross income under section 951 with respect to first-tier corporation}}{\text{Earnings and profits of first-tier corporation not included in domestic corporation's gross income under section 951 with respect to second- or lower-tier corporations}} \times \text{Tax paid by second-tier corporation on earnings not previously taxed with respect to third- or lower-tier corporations which is deemed paid by first-tier corporation}$$

(C) *Credit for taxes (of the third-tier corporation) deemed paid by the second-tier corporation which are deemed paid by first-tier corporation under section 902(b)(1).*

(1) If the effective rate of tax on dividends received by the third-tier corporation is the same as the effective rate of tax on its other earnings and profits—

$$\frac{\text{Amount included in domestic corporation's gross income under section 951 with respect to first-tier corporation}}{\text{Earnings and profits of first-tier corporation less earnings and profits attributable to amounts included in domestic corporation's gross income with respect to second- and third-tier corporation}} \times \text{Taxes deemed paid by second-tier corporation which are deemed paid by first-tier corporation}$$

(2) If the effective rate of tax on dividends received by the third-tier corporation is higher or lower than the effective rate of tax on its other earnings and profits—

$$\frac{\text{Amount included in domestic corporation's gross income under section 951 with respect to first-tier corporation}}{\text{Earnings and profits of first-tier corporation not included in domestic corporation's gross income under section 951 with respect to second- or lower-tier corporation}} \times \text{Tax deemed paid by second-tier corporation on earnings not previously taxed with respect to fourth- or lower-tier corporations which is deemed paid by first-tier corporation}$$

Reg. § 1.960-2(g)(2)

Income from Sources Without the United States

[Reg. § 1.960-2.]

☐ [T.D. 7120, 6-3-71. Amended by T.D. 7334, 12-20-74, T.D. 7649, 10-17-79 and T.D. 7843, 11-3-82.]

[Reg. § 1.960-3]

§ 1.960-3. Gross-up of amounts included in income under section 951.—(a) *General rule for including taxes in income.* Any taxes deemed paid by a domestic corporation for the taxable year pursuant to section 960(a)(1) shall, except as provided in paragraph (b) of this section, be included in the gross income of such corporation for such year as a dividend pursuant to section 78 and § 1.78-1. See also paragraph (a)(8) of § 1.902-3.

(b) *Certain taxes not included in income.* Any taxes deemed paid by a domestic corporation for the taxable year pursuant to section 902(a) or section 960(a)(1) shall not be included in the gross income of such corporation for such year as a dividend pursuant to section 78 and § 1.78-1 to the extent that such taxes are paid or accrued by the first-, second-, or third-tier corporation, as the case may be, on or with respect to an amount which is excluded from the gross income of such foreign corporation under section 959(b) and § 1.959-2 as distributions from the earnings and profits of another controlled foreign corporation attributable to an amount which is, or has been, required to be included in the gross income of the domestic corporation under section 951.

(c) *Illustrations.* The application of this section may be illustrated by the following examples:

Example (1). Domestic corporation N owns all the one class of stock of controlled foreign corporation A which owns all the one class of stock of controlled foreign corporation B. All such corporations use the calendar year as the taxable year. For 1978, B Corporation, after having paid $20 of foreign income taxes, has $80 in earnings and profits, which are attributable to the amount required to be included in N Corporation's gross income for such year under section 951 with respect to B Corporation and all of which are distributed to A Corporation in such year. The dividend so received from B Corporation is excluded from A Corporation's gross income under section 959(b) and § 1.959-2. An income tax of 10 percent is required to be withheld from such dividend by the foreign country under the laws of which B Corporation is created, and the foreign country under the laws of which A Corporation is created imposes an income tax of $22 on the dividend received from B Corporation. For 1978, A Corporation's earnings and profits are $50 ($80 − [.10 × $80] − $22), which it distributes in such year to N Corporation. For 1978, N Corporation is required under section 951 to include $80 in gross income with respect to B Corporation and also is required under the gross-up provisions of section 78 to include in gross income $20 ($80/$80 × $20), the amount equal to the foreign income taxes of B Corporation which are deemed paid by N Corporation under section 960(a)(1). Under paragraph (b) of this section N Corporation is not required to include in gross income the $30 ($8 + $22) of foreign income taxes which are paid by A Corporation in connection with the dividend received from B Corporation and which are deemed paid by N Corporation under section 902(a) and paragraph (c) of § 1.960-2.

Example (2). Domestic corporation N owns all the one class of stock of controlled foreign corporation A which owns all the one class of stock of controlled foreign corporation B, which in turn owns all the one class of stock of controlled foreign corporation C. All such corporations use the calendar year as the taxable year. For 1978, C Corporation, after having paid $20 of foreign income taxes, has $80 in earnings and profits, which are attributable to the amount required to be included in N Corporation's gross income for such year under section 951 with respect to C Corporation and all of which are distributed to B Corporation in such year. After having paid foreign income taxes of $10 on the dividend received from C Corporation, B Corporation distributes the balance of $70 to A Corporation. After having paid foreign income taxes of $5 on the dividend received from B Corporation, A Corporation distributes the balance of $65 to N Corporation. The dividend so received by B Corporation, and in turn by A Corporation, is excluded from the gross income of such corporations under section 959(b) and § 1.959-2. [Reg. § 1.960-3]

☐ [T.D. 7120, 6-3-71. Amended by T.D. 7481, 4-15-77, T.D. 7649, 10-17-79 and T.D. 7843, 11-3-82.]

[Reg. § 1.960-4]

§ 1.960-4. Additional foreign tax credit in year of receipt of previously taxed earnings and profits.—(a) *Increase in section 904(a) limitation for the taxable year of exclusion*—(1) *In general.* The applicable limitation under section 904(a) for a taxpayer's taxable year (hereinafter in this section referred to as the "taxable year of exclusion") in which he receives an amount which is excluded from gross income under section 959(a)(1) and which is attributable to a controlled foreign corporation's earnings and profits in respect of which an amount was required to be included in the gross income of such taxpayer under section 951(a) for a taxable year (hereinafter in this section referred to as the "taxable year

Reg. § 1.960-4(a)(1)

of inclusion") previous to the taxable year of exclusion shall be increased under section 960(b)(1) by the amount described in paragraph (b) of this section if the conditions described in subparagraph (2) of this paragraph are satisfied.

(2) *Conditions under which increase in limitation is allowed for the taxable year of exclusion.* The increase in limitation described in subparagraph (1) of this paragraph for the taxable year of exclusion shall be made only if the taxpayer—

(i) For the taxable year of inclusion either chose to claim a foreign tax credit as provided in section 901 or did not pay or accrue any foreign income taxes,

(ii) Chooses to claim a foreign tax credit as provided in section 901 for the taxable year of exclusion, and

(iii) For the taxable year of exclusion pays, accrues, or is deemed to have paid foreign income taxes with respect to the amount, described in subparagraph (1) of this paragraph, which is excluded from his gross income for such year under section 959(a)(1).

For purposes of determining the source of distributions in determining the foreign tax credit under section 960(b) and this section, see also paragraph (e) of § 1.959-3.

(b) *Amount of increase in limitation for the taxable year of exclusion.* The amount of increase under section 960(b)(1) in the applicable limitation under section 904(a) for the taxable year of exclusion shall be—

(1) The amount by which the applicable section 904(a) limitation for the taxable year of inclusion was increased, determined as provided in paragraph (c) of this section, by reason of the inclusion of the amount in the taxpayer's income for such year under section 951(a), reduced by

(2) The amount of foreign income taxes allowed as a credit under section 901 for such taxable year of inclusion and which were allowable to such taxpayer solely by reason of the inclusion of such amount in his gross income under section 951(a), as determined under paragraph (d) of this section, and then by

(3) The additional reduction for such taxable year of inclusion arising by reason of increases in limitation under section 960(b)(1) for taxable years intervening between such taxable year of inclusion and such taxable year of exclusion, as determined under paragraph (e) of this section in respect of such inclusion under section 951(a),

except that the amount of increase determined under this paragraph for the taxable year of exclusion shall in no case exceed the amount of foreign income taxes paid, accrued, or deemed to be paid by such taxpayer for such taxable year of exclusion with respect to the amount, described in paragraph (a)(1) of this section, which is excluded from gross income for such year under section 959(a)(1).

(c) *Determination of increase in limitation for the taxable year of inclusion.* The amount of the increase in the applicable limitation under section 904(a) for the taxable year of inclusion which arises by reason of the inclusion of the amount in gross income under section 951(a) shall be the amount of the applicable limitation under section 904(a) for such year reduced by the amount which would have been the applicable limitation under section 904(a) for such year if the amount had not been included in gross income for such year under section 951(a).

(d) *Determination of foreign income taxes allowed for taxable year of inclusion by reason of section 951(a) amount.* The amount of foreign income taxes allowed as a credit under section 901 for the taxable year of inclusion which were allowable solely by reason of the inclusion of the amount in gross income for such year under section 951(a) shall be the amount of foreign income taxes allowed as a credit under section 901 for such year reduced by the amount of foreign income taxes which would have been allowed as a credit under section 901 for such year if the amount had not been included in gross income for such year under section 951(a). For purposes of this paragraph, the term "foreign income taxes" includes foreign income taxes paid or accrued, and foreign income taxes deemed paid under section 902, section 904(d), and section 960(a), for the taxable year of inclusion.

(e) *Additional reduction for the taxable year of inclusion arising by reason of increases in limitation for intervening years.* The amount of increase in the applicable limitation under section 904(a) for the taxable year of inclusion shall also be reduced, after first deducting the foreign income taxes described in paragraph (b)(2) of this section, by any increases in limitation which arise under section 960(b)(1)—by reason of any earlier exclusions under section 959(a)(1) in respect of the same inclusion under section 951(a) for such taxable year of inclusion—for the first, second, third, fourth, etc., succeeding taxable years of exclusion, in that order, which follow such taxable year of inclusion and precede the taxable year of exclusion in respect of which the increase in limitation under section 960(b)(1) and paragraph (b) of this section is being determined. The amount of any increase in limitation which arises under section 960(b)(1) for any such succeeding taxable year of exclusion shall be the amount of foreign income

Reg. § 1.960-4(a)(2)

taxes allowed as a credit under section 901 for each such taxable year reduced by the amount of foreign income taxes which would have been allowed as a credit under section 901 for each such year if the limitation for each such year were not increased under section 960(b)(1). For any such succeeding taxable year of exclusion for which the taxpayer does not choose to claim a foreign tax credit as provided in section 901, the same increase in limitation under section 960(b)(1) shall be treated as having been made, for purposes of this paragraph, which would have been made for such taxable year if the taxpayer had chosen to claim the foreign tax credit for such year.

(f) *Illustrations.* The application of this section may be illustrated by the following examples:

Example (1). Domestic corporation N owns all of the one class of stock of controlled foreign corporation A. Corporation A, after paying foreign income taxes of $30, has earnings and profits for 1978 of $70, all of which are attributable to an amount required under section 951(a) to be included in N Corporation's gross income for 1978. Both corporations use the calendar year as the taxable year. For 1979 and 1980, A Corporation has no earnings and profits attributable to an amount required to be included in N Corporation's gross income under section 951(a); for each such year it makes a distribution of $35 (from its earnings and profits for 1978) from which a foreign income tax of $6 is withheld. For each of 1978, 1979, and 1980, N Corporation derives taxable income of $50 from sources within the United States and claims a foreign tax credit under section 901, determined by applying the overall limitation under section 904(a)(2). The United States tax payable by N Corporation is determined as follows, assuming a corporate tax rate of 48 percent:

1978

Taxable income of N Corporation:
U.S. sources .... $ 50.00
Sources without the U.S.:
    Amount required to be included in N Corporation's gross income under sec. 951(a) $70.00
    Foreign income taxes deemed paid by N Corporation under sec. 960(a)(1) and included in N Corporation's gross income under sec. 78 ($30 × $70/$70) .. 30.00   100.00

        Total taxable income $150.00

U.S. tax payable for 1978:
  U.S. tax before credit ($150 × .48) .... $ 72.00
  Credit: Foreign income taxes of $30, but not to exceed overall limitation of $48 for 1965 ($100/$150 × $72) 30.00

  U.S. tax payable .... $ 42.00

1979

Taxable income of N Corporation, consisting of income from U.S. sources .... $ 50.00
U.S. tax before credit ($50 × .48) 24.00
Section 904(a)(2) overall limitation for 1966:
  Limitation for 1966 before increase under sec. 960(b)(1) ($24 × $0/$50) 0
  Plus: Increase in overall limitation for 1979 under sec. 960(b)(1):
    Amount by which 1978 overall limitation was increased by reason of inclusion in N Corporation's gross income under sec. 951(a) for 1978 ($48 − [($50 × .48) × $0/$50]) $48.00
    Less: Foreign income taxes allowed as a credit for 1978 which were allowable solely by reason of such sec. 951(a) inclusion ($30 − $0) 30.00

      Balance 18.00
    But: Such balance not to exceed foreign income taxes paid by N Corporation for 1979 with respect to $35 distribution excluded under sec. 959(a)(1) ($6 tax withheld) .... 6.00 $ 6.00

Overall limitation for 1979 .... $ 6.00

U.S. tax payable for 1979:
  U.S. tax before credit ($50 × .48) .... $ 24.00
  Credit: Foreign income taxes of $6, but not to exceed overall limitation of $6 for 1966 ...... 6.00

  U.S. tax payable .... $ 18.00

Reg. § 1.960-4(f)

49,396 Income from Sources Without the United States

See p. 20,601 for regulations not amended to reflect law changes

1980

Taxable income of N Corporation, consisting of income from U.S. sources		$ 50.00
U.S. tax before credit ($50 × .48)		24.00
Section 904(a)(2) overall limitation for 1980:		
Limitation for 1980 before increase under sec. 960(b)(1) ($24 × $0/$50)		0
Plus: Increase in overall limitation for 1980 under sec. 960(b)(1):		
Amount by which 1978 overall limitation was increased by reason of inclusion in N Corporation's gross income under sec. 951(a) for 1978 ($48 − [($50 × .48) × $0/$50])	$48.00	
Less: Foreign income taxes allowed as a credit for 1978 which were allowable solely by reason of such sec. 951(a) inclusion ($30 − $0)	30.00	
Tentative balance	18.00	
Less: Increase in overall limitation under sec. 960(b)(1) for 1979 by reason of such sec. 951(a) inclusion	$ 6.00	
Balance	12.00	
But: Such balance not to exceed foreign income taxes paid by N Corporation for 1980 with respect to $35 distribution excluded under sec. 959(a)(1) ($6 tax withheld)	6.00	$ 6.00
Overall limitation for 1980		$ 6.00
U.S. tax payable for 1980:		
U.S. tax before credit ($50 × .48)		$ 24.00
Credit: Foreign income taxes of $6, but not to exceed overall limitation of $6 for 1980		6.00
U.S. tax payable		$ 18.00

Example (2). The facts for 1978, 1979, and 1980, are the same as in example (1), except that in 1977, to which the section 904(a)(2) overall limitation applies, N Corporation pays $18 of foreign income taxes in excess of the overall limitation and that such excess is not absorbed as a carryback to 1975 or 1976 under section 904(c). Therefore, there is no increase under section 960(b)(1) in the overall limitation for 1979 or 1980 since the amount ($48) by which the 1978 overall limitation was increased by reason of the inclusion in N Corporation's gross income for 1978 under section 951(a), less the foreign income taxes ($48) allowed as a credit which were allowable solely by reason of such inclusion, is zero. The foreign income taxes so allowed as a credit for 1978 which were allowable solely by reason of such section 951(a) inclusion consist of the $30 of foreign income taxes deemed paid for 1978 under section 960(a)(1) and the $18 of foreign income taxes for 1977 carried over and deemed paid for 1965 under section 904(c).

Example (3). (a) Domestic corporation N owns all the one class of stock of controlled foreign corporation A, which in turn owns all the one class of stock of controlled foreign corporation B. All corporations use the calendar year as the taxable year. Corporation B, after paying foreign income taxes of $30, has earnings and profits for 1978 of $70, all of which is attributable to an amount required under section 951(a) to be included in N Corporation's gross income for 1978, and $35 of which it distributes in such year to A Corporation. For 1978, A Corporation, after paying foreign income taxes of $5 on such dividend from B Corporation, has total earnings and profits of $30, all of which it distributes in such year to N Corporation, a foreign income tax of $3 being withheld therefrom.

(b) For 1966, B Corporation has no earnings and profits, but distributes in such year to A Corporation the $35 remaining of its earnings and profits for 1978. For 1979, A Corporation, after paying foreign income taxes of $5 on such dividend from B Corporation, has total earnings and profits of $30, all of which it distributes to N Corporation, a foreign income tax of $3 being withheld therefrom.

(c) For each of 1978 and 1979, N Corporation has taxable income of $100 from United States sources and claims a foreign tax credit under section 901, determined by applying the overall limitation under section 904(a)(2). The United States tax payable by N Corporation is determined as follows, assuming a corporate tax rate of 48 percent:

Reg. § 1.960-4(f)

Income from Sources Without the United States

See p. 20,601 for regulations not amended to reflect law changes

1978

Taxable income of N Corporation:		
U.S. sources		$100
Sources without the U.S.:		
Amount required to be included in N Corporation's gross income under sec. 951(a) with respect to B Corporation	$70	
Foreign income taxes deemed paid by N Corporation under sec. 960(a)(1) and included in N Corporation's gross income under sec. 78 ($30 × $70/$70)	30	100
Total taxable income		$200
U.S. tax payable for 1978:		
U.S. tax before credit ($200 × .48)		$ 96
Credit: Foreign income taxes of $38 ([$30 × $70/$70] + [$5 × $30/$30] + $3), but not to exceed overall limitation of $48 ($96 × $100/$200)		38
U.S. tax payable		$ 58

1979

Taxable income of N Corporation, consisting of income from U.S. sources			$100
U.S. tax before credit ($100 × .48)			48
Section 904(a)(2) overall limitation for 1979:			
Limitation for 1979 before increase under sec. 960(b)(1) ($48 × $0/$100)			0
Plus: Increase in overall limitation for 1979 under sec. 960(b)(1):			
Amount by which 1978 overall limitation was increased by reason of inclusion in N Corporation's gross income under sec. 951(a) for 1978 ($48 − [($100 × .48) × $0/$100])		$48	
Less: Foreign income taxes allowed as a credit for 1965 which were allowable solely by reason of such sec. 951(a) inclusion ($38 − $0)		38	
Balance		10	
But: Such balance not to exceed foreign income taxes paid and deemed paid by N Corporation for 1979 with respect to $30 distribution excluded under sec. 959(a)(1) ([$5 × $30/$30] + $3)		$ 8	$ 8
Overall limitation for 1979			$ 8
U.S. tax payable for 1979:			
U.S. tax before credit ($100 × .48)			$ 48
Credit: Foreign income taxes of $8 ($3 + $5), but not to exceed overall limitation of $8 for 1979			8
U.S. tax payable			$ 40

[Reg. § 1.960-4.]

☐ [T.D. 7120, 6-3-71. Amended by T.D. 7649, 10-17-79.]

[Reg. § 1.960-5]

§ 1.960-5. Credit for taxable year of inclusion binding for taxable year of exclusion.— (a) *Taxes not allowed as a deduction for taxable year of exclusion.* In the case of any taxpayer who—

(1) Chooses to claim a foreign tax credit as provided in section 901 for the taxable year for which he is required to include in gross income under section 951(a) an amount attributable to the earnings and profits of a controlled foreign corporation, and

(2) Does not choose to claim a foreign tax credit as provided in section 901 for a taxable year in which he receives an amount which is excluded from gross income under section 959(a)(1) and which is attributable to such earnings and profits of such controlled foreign corporation,

no deduction shall be allowed under section 164 for the taxable year of such exclusion for any foreign income taxes paid or accrued on or with respect to such excluded amount.

(b) *Illustration.* The application of this section may be illustrated by the following example:

Example. Domestic corporation N owns all the one class of stock of controlled foreign corporation A. Both corporations use the calendar year as the taxable year. All of A Corporation's earnings and profits of $80 for 1978 (after payment of foreign income taxes of $20 on its total income of $100 for such year) are attributable to an amount required under section 951(a) to be included in N Corporation's gross income for 1978. For 1978, N Corporation chooses to claim a foreign tax credit for the $20 of foreign income taxes which for such year are paid by A Corporation and deemed paid by N Corporation under section 960(a)(1) and paragraph (c)(1) of § 1.960-1. For 1979, A Corporation

Reg. § 1.960-5(b)

49,398   Income from Sources Without the United States
See p. 20,601 for regulations not amended to reflect law changes

distributes the entire $80 of 1978 earnings and profits, a foreign income tax of $8 being withheld therefrom. Although N Corporation does not choose to claim a foreign tax credit for 1966, it may not deduct such $8 of foreign income taxes under section 164. Corporation N may, however, deduct under such section a foreign income tax of $4 which is withheld from a distribution of $40 by A Corporation during 1979 from its 1979 earnings and profits. [Reg. § 1.960-5.]

☐ [T.D. 7120, 6-3-71. Amended by T.D. 7649, 10-17-79.]

[Reg. § 1.960-6]

§ 1.960-6. Overpayments resulting from increase in limitation for taxable year of exclusion.—(a) *Amount of overpayment.* If an increase in the limitation under section 960(b)(1) and § 1.960-4 for a taxable year of exclusion exceeds the tax (determined before allowance of any credits against tax) imposed by chapter 1 of the Code for such year, the amount of such excess shall be deemed an overpayment of tax for such year and shall be refunded or credited to the taxpayer in accordance with chapter 65 (section 6401 and following) of the Code.

(b) *Illustration.* The application of this section may be illustrated by the following example:

Example. Domestic corporation N owns all the one class of stock of controlled foreign corporation A. Both corporations use the calendar year as the taxable year. For 1978, A Corporation has total income of $100,000 on which it pays foreign income taxes of $20,000. All of A Corporation's earnings and profits for 1978 of $80,000 are attributable to an amount which is required under section 951(a) to be included in N Corporation's gross income for 1978. By reason of such income inclusion N Corporation is deemed for 1978 to have paid under section 960(a)(1), and is required under section 78 to include in gross income for such year, the $20,000 ($20,000 × $80,000/$80,000) of foreign income taxes paid by A Corporation for such year. Corporation N also derives $100,000 taxable income from sources within the United States for 1978. For 1979 N Corporation has $25,000 of taxable income, all of which is derived from sources within the United States. No part of A Corporation's earnings and profits for 1979 is attributable to an amount required under section 951(a) to be included in N Corporation's gross income. During 1979, A Corporation makes one distribution consisting of its $80,000 earnings and profits for 1978, all of which is excluded under section 959(a)(1) from N Corporation's gross income for 1979, and from which distribution foreign income taxes of $10,000 are withheld. For 1978 and 1979, N Corporation claims the foreign tax credit under section 901, determined by applying the overall limitation under section 904(a)(2). The United States tax of N Corporation is determined as follows for such years:

1978

Taxable income of N Corporation:		
U.S. sources		$100,000
Sources without the U.S.:		
Amount required to be included in N Corporation's gross income under sec. 951(a)	$80,000	
Foreign income taxes deemed paid by N Corporation under sec. 960(a)(1) and included in N Corporation's gross income under sec. 78 ($20,000 × $80,000/$80,000)	20,000	100,000
Total taxable income		$200,000
U.S. tax payable for 1978:		
U.S. tax before credit ([$200,000 × .22] + [$175,000 × .26])		$ 89,500
Credit: Foreign income taxes of $20,000, but not to exceed overall limitation of $44,750 ($89,500 × $100,000/$200,000)		20,000
U.S. tax payable		$ 69,500

1979

Taxable income of N Corporation, consisting of income from U.S. sources		$ 25,000
U.S. tax before credit ($25,000 × .22)		5,500
Section 904(a)(2) overall limitation for 1979:		
Limitation for 1979 before increase under sec. 960(b)(1) ($5,500 × $0/25,000)		0
Plus: Increase in overall limitation for 1979 under sec. 960(b)(1):		
Amount by which 1978 overall limitation was increased by reason of inclusion in N Corporation's gross income under sec. 951(a) for 1965 ($44,750 − [$41,500 × $0/$100,000])		$44,750
Less: Foreign income taxes allowed as a credit for 1965 which were allowable solely by reason of such sec. 951(a) inclusion ($20,000 − $0)		20,000
Balance		$24,750

Reg. § 1.960-6(a)

Income from Sources without the United States

See p. 20,601 for regulations not amended to reflect law changes

But: Such balance not to exceed foreign income taxes paid by N Corporation for 1966 with respect to $80,000 distribution excluded under sec. 959(a)(1) ($10,000 tax withheld)	$10,000	$ 10,000
Overall limitation for 1979		$ 10,000
U.S. tax payable for 1979:		
U.S. tax before credit ($25,000 × .22)		$ 5,500
Credit: Foreign income taxes of $10,000, but not to exceed overall limitation of $10,000 for 1979		10,000
U.S. tax payable		none
Overpayment of tax for 1979:		
Increase in limitation under sec. 960(b)(1) for 1979		$ 10,000
Less: Tax imposed for 1979 under chapter 1 of the Code		5,500
Excess treated as overpayment		$ 4,500

[Reg. § 1.960-6.]

☐ [T.D. 7120, 6-3-71. Amended by T.D. 7649, 10-17-79.]

[Reg. § 1.960-7]

§ 1.960-7. **Effective dates.**—(a) *General rule.* Except as provided in paragraph (b), the rules contained in §§ 1.960-1—1.960-6 shall apply to taxable years of foreign corporations beginning after December 31, 1962, and taxable years of U.S. corporate shareholders within which or with which the taxable year of such foreign corporation ends.

(b) *Exception for less developed country corporations.* If for any taxable year beginning after December 31, 1962, and before January 1, 1976, a first tier foreign corporation qualified as a less developed country corporation as defined in 26 CFR § 1.902-2 revised as of April 1, 1978, the rules pertaining to less developed country corporations contained in 26 CFR §§ 1.960-1—1.960-6 revised as of April 1, 1978, shall apply to any amounts required to be included in gross income under section 951 for such taxable year.

(c) *Third-tier credit.* The rules contained in §§ 1.960-1—1.960-6 shall apply to amounts included in the gross income of a domestic corporation under section 951 with respect to the earnings and profits of third-tier corporations (as defined in § 1.960-1) in taxable years beginning after December 31, 1976. [Reg. § 1.960-7.]

☐ [T.D. 7649, 10-17-79. Amended by T.D. 7843, 11-5-82.]

[Reg. § 1.961-1]

§ 1.961-1. **Increase in basis of stock in controlled foreign corporations and of other property.**—(a) *Increase in basis*—(1) *In general.* Except as provided in subparagraph (2) of this paragraph, the basis of a United States shareholder's—

(i) Stock in a controlled foreign corporation; or

(ii) Property (as defined in paragraph (b)(1) of this section) by reason of the ownership of which he is considered under section 958(a)(2) as owning stock in a controlled foreign corporation shall be increased under section 961(a), as of the last day in the taxable year of such corporation on which it is a controlled foreign corporation, by the amount required to be included with respect to such stock or such property in such shareholder's gross income under section 951(a) for his taxable year in which or with which such taxable year of such corporation ends. The increase in basis provided by the preceding sentence shall be made only to the extent to which such amount required to be included in gross income under section 951(a) was so included in gross income.

(2) *Limitation on amount of increase in case of election under section 962.* In the case of a United States shareholder who makes the election under section 962 for the taxable year, the amount of the increase in basis provided by subparagraph (1) of this paragraph shall not exceed the amount of United States tax paid in accordance with such election with respect to the amounts included in such shareholder's gross income under section 951(a) for such year (as determined under § 1.962-1).

(b) *Rules of application*—(1) *Property defined.* The property of a United States shareholder referred to in paragraph (a)(1)(ii) of this section shall consist of—

(i) Stock in a foreign corporation;

(ii) An interest in a foreign partnership; or

(iii) A beneficial interest in a foreign estate or trust (as defined in section 7701(a)(31)).

(2) *Increase with respect to each share of stock.* Any increase under paragraph (a) of this section in the basis of a United States shareholder's stock in a foreign corporation shall be

Reg. § 1.961-1(b)(2)

made in the amount included in gross income under section 951(a) or in the amount of United States tax paid in accordance with an election under section 962, as the case may be, with respect to each share of such stock.

(c) *Illustration.* The application of this section may be illustrated by the following examples:

Example (1). Domestic corporation M owns 800 of the 1,000 shares of the one class of stock in controlled foreign corporation R which owns all of the one class of stock in controlled foreign corporation S. Corporations M, R, and S use the calendar year as a taxable year. In 1964, S Corporation has $100,000 of earnings and profits after the payment of $11,250 of foreign income taxes, and $100,000 of subpart F income. Corporation R has no earnings and profits. With respect to S Corporation, M Corporation is required to include in gross income $80,000 (800/1,000 × $100,000) under section 951(a), and $9,000 ($80,000/$100,000 × $11,250) under section 78. On December 31, 1964, M Corporation must increase the basis of each share of its stock in R Corporation by $100 ($80,000/800).

Example (2). A, an individual United States shareholder, owns all of the 1,000 shares of the one class of stock in controlled foreign corporation T. Corporation T and A use the calendar year as a taxable year. In 1964, T Corporation has $80,000 of earnings and profits after the payment of $20,000 of foreign income taxes, and $80,000 of subpart F income. A makes the election under section 962 for 1964 and in accordance with such election pays a United States tax of $23,000 with respect to the $80,000 included in his gross income under section 951(a). On December 31, 1964, A must increase the basis of each share of his stock in T Corporation by $23 ($23,000/1,000). [Reg. § 1.961-1.]

☐ [T.D. 6850, 9-15-65.]

[Reg. § 1.961-2]

§ 1.961-2. **Reduction in basis of stock in foreign corporations and of other property.**—(a) *Reduction in basis*—(1) *In general.* Except as provided in subparagraph (2) of this paragraph, the adjusted basis of a United States person's—

(i) Stock in a foreign corporation;

(ii) Interest in a foreign partnership; or

(iii) Beneficial interest in a foreign estate or trust (as defined in section 7701(a)(31)),

with respect to which such United States person receives an amount which is excluded from gross income under section 959(a), shall be reduced under section 961(b), as of the time such person receives such excluded amount, by the sum of the amount so excluded and any income, war profits, or excess profits taxes imposed by any foreign country or possession of the United States on or with respect to the earnings and profits attributable to such excluded amount when such earnings and profits were actually distributed directly or indirectly through a chain or ownership described in section 958(a)(2).

(2) *Limitation on amount of reduction in case of election under section 962.* In the case of a distribution of earnings and profits attributable to amounts with respect to which an election under section 962 has been made, the amount of the reduction in basis provided by subparagraph (1) of this paragraph shall not exceed the sum of—

(i) The amount of such distribution which is excluded from gross income under section 959(a) after the application of section 962(d) and § 1.962-3; and

(ii) Any income, war profits, or excess profits taxes imposed by any foreign country or possession of the United States on or with respect to the earnings and profits attributable to such excluded amount when such earnings and profits were actually distributed directly or indirectly through a chain of ownership described in section 958(a)(2).

(b) *Reduction with respect to each share of stock.* Any reduction under paragraph (a) of this section in the adjusted basis of a United States person's stock in a foreign corporation shall be made with respect to each share of such stock in the sum of—

(1)(i) The amount excluded from gross income under section 959(a); or

(ii) The amount excluded from gross income under section 959(a) after the application of section 962(d) and § 1.962-3; and

(2) The amount of any income, war profits, or excess profits taxes imposed by any foreign country or possession of the United States on or with respect to the earnings and profits attributable to such excluded amount when such earnings and profits were actually distributed directly or indirectly through a chain of ownership described in section 958(a)(2).

(c) *Amount in excess of basis.* To the extent that the amount of the reduction in the adjusted basis of property provided by paragragh (a) of this section exceeds such adjusted basis, the amount shall be treated as gain from the sale or exchange of property.

(d) *Illustration.* The application of this section may be illustrated by the following examples:

Example (1). (a) Domestic corporation M owns all of the 1,000 shares of the one class of stock in

Income from Sources without the United States

controlled foreign corporation R, which owns all of the 500 shares of the one class of stock in controlled foreign corporation S. Each share of M Corporation's stock in R Corporation has a basis of $200. Corporations M, R, and S use the calendar year as a taxable year. In 1963, S Corporation has $100,000 of earnings and profits after the payment of $50,000 of foreign income taxes and $100,000 of subpart F income. For 1963, M Corporation includes $100,000 in gross income under section 951(a) with respect to S Corporation. In accordance with the provisions of § 1.961-1, M Corporation increases the basis of each of its 1,000 shares of stock in R Corporation to $300 ($200 + $100,000/1,000) as of December 31, 1963.

(b) On July 31, 1964, M Corporation sells 250 of its shares of stock in R Corporation to domestic corporation N at a price of $350 per share. Corporation N satisfies the requirements of paragraph (d) of § 1.959-1 so as to qualify as M Corporation's successor in interest. On September 30, 1964, the earnings and profits attributable to the $100,000 included in M Corporation's gross income under section 951(a) for 1963 are distributed to R Corporation which incurs a withholding tax of $10,000 on such distribution (10 percent of $100,000) and an additional foreign income tax of 33⅓ percent or $30,000 by reason of the inclusion of the net distribution of $90,000 ($100,000 minus $10,000) in its taxable income for 1964. On June 30, 1965, R Corporation distributes the remaining $60,000 of such earnings and profits to corporations M and N: Corporation M receives $45,000 (750/1000 × $60,000) and excludes such amount from gross income under section 959(a); Corporation N receives $15,000 (250/1,000 × $60,000) and, as M Corporation's successor in interest, excludes such amount from gross income under section 959(a). As of June 30, 1965, M Corporation must reduce the adjusted basis of each of its 750 shares of stock in R Corporation to $200 ($300 minus ($45,000/750 + $10,000/1,000 + $30,000/1,000)); and N Corporation must reduce the basis of each of its 250 shares of stock in R Corporation to $250 ($350 minus ($15,000/250 + $10,000/1,000 + $30,000/1,000)).

Example (2). The facts are the same as in paragraph (a) of example (1), except that in addition, on July 31, 1964, R Corporation sells its 500 shares of stock in S Corporation to domestic corporation P at a price of $600 per share. Corporation P satisfies the requirements of paragraph (d) of § 1.959-1 so as to qualify as M Corporation's successor in interest. On September 30, 1964, S Corporation distributes $100,000 of earnings and profits to P Corporation, which earnings and profits are attributable to the $100,000 included in M Corporation's gross income under section 951(a) for 1963. Corporation P incurs a withholding tax of $10,000 on the distribution from S Corporation (10 percent of $100,000). As M Corporation's successor in interest, P Corporation excludes the $90,000 it receives from gross income under section 959(a). As of September 30, 1964, P Corporation must reduce the basis of each of its 500 shares of stock in S Corporation to $400 ($600 minus ($90,000/500 + $10,000/500)). [Reg. § 1.961-2.]

☐ [*T.D.* 6850, 9-15-65.]

[Reg. § 1.962-1]

§ 1.962-1. **Limitation of tax for individuals on amounts included in gross income under section 951(a).**—(a) *In general.* An individual United States shareholder may, in accordance with § 1.962-2, elect to have the provisions of section 962 apply for his taxable year. In such case—

(1) The tax imposed under chapter 1 of the Internal Revenue Code on all amounts which are included in his gross income for such taxable year under section 951(a) shall (in lieu of the tax determined under section 1) be an amount equal to the tax which would be imposed under section 11 if such amounts were received by a domestic corporation (determined in accordance with paragraph (b)(1) of this section), and

(2) For purposes of applying section 960(a)(1) (relating to foreign tax credit) such amounts shall be treated as if received by a domestic corporation (as provided in paragraph (b)(2) of this section).

Thus, an individual United States shareholder may elect to be subject to tax at corporate rates on amounts included in his gross income under section 951(a) and to have the benefit of a credit for certain foreign tax paid with respect to the earnings and profits attributable to such amounts. Section 962 also provides rules for the treatment of an actual distribution of earnings and profits previously taxed in accordance with an election of the benefits of this section. See § 1.962-3. For transitional rules for certain taxable years, see § 1.962-4.

(b) *Rules of application.* For purposes of this section—

(1) *Application of section 11.* For purposes of applying section 11 for a taxable year as provided in paragraph (a)(1) of this section in the case of an electing United States shareholder—

(i) *Determination of taxable income.* The term "taxable income" as used in section 11 shall mean the sum of—

Reg. § 1.962-1(b)(1)

49,402 Income from Sources without the United States

See p. 20,601 for regulations not amended to reflect law changes

(a) All amounts required to be included in his gross income under section 951(a) for such taxable year; plus

(b) All amounts which would be required to be included in his gross income under section 78 for such taxable year with respect to the amounts referred to in (a) of this subdivision if such shareholder were a domestic corporation.

For purposes of this section, such sum shall not be reduced by any deduction of the United States shareholder even if such shareholder's deductions exceed his gross income.

(ii) *Limitation on surtax exemption.* The surtax exemption provided by section 11(c) shall not exceed an amount which bears the same ratio to $25,000 ($50,000 in the case of a taxable year ending after December 31, 1974, and before January 1, 1976) as the amounts included in his gross income under section 951(a) for the taxable year bear to his pro rata share of the earnings and profits for the taxable year of all controlled foreign corporations with respect to which such United States shareholder includes any amount in his gross income under section 951(a) for the taxable year.

(2) *Allowance of foreign tax credit* —(i) *In general.* Subject to the applicable limitation of section 904 and to the provisions of this subparagraph, there shall be allowed as a credit against the United States tax on the amounts described in subparagraph (1)(i) of this paragraph the foreign income, war profits, and excess profits taxes deemed paid under section 960(a)(1) by the electing United States shareholder with respect to such amounts.

(ii) *Application of section 960(a)(1).* In applying section 960 (a)(1) for purposes of this subparagraph in the case of an electing United States shareholder, the term "domestic corporation" as used in sections 960(a)(1) and 78, and the term "corporation" as used in section 901, shall be treated as referring to such shareholder with respect to the amounts described in subparagraph (1)(i) of this paragraph.

(iii) *Carryback and carryover of excess tax deemed paid.* For purposes of this subparagraph, any amount by which the foreign income, war profits, and excess profits taxes deemed paid by the electing United States shareholder for any taxable year under section 960(a)(1) exceed the limitation determined under subdivision (iv)(a) of this subparagraph shall be treated as a carryback and carryover of excess tax paid under section 904(d), except that in no case shall excess tax paid be deemed paid in a taxable year if an election under section 962 by such shareholders does not apply for such taxable year. Such carrybacks and carryovers shall be applied only against the United States tax on amounts described in subparagraph (1)(i) of this paragraph.

(iv) *Limitation on credit.* For purposes of determining the limitation under section 904 on the amount of the credit for foreign income, war profits, and excess profit taxes—

(a) Deemed paid with respect to amounts described in subparagraph (1)(i) of this paragraph, the electing United States shareholder's taxable income shall be considered to consist only of the amounts described in such subparagraph (1)(i), and

(b) Paid with respect to amounts other than amounts described in subparagraph (1)(i) of this paragraph, the electing United States shareholder's taxable income shall be considered to consist only of amounts other than the amounts described in such subparagraph (1)(i).

(v) *Effect of choosing benefits of sections 901 to 905.* The provisions of this subparagraph shall apply for a taxable year whether or not the electing United States shareholder chooses the benefits of subpart A of part III of subchapter N of chapter 1 (sections 901 to 905) of the Internal Revenue Code for such year.

(c) *Illustration.* The application of this section may be illustrated by the following example:

Example. Throughout his taxable year ending December 31, 1964, A, an unmarried individual who is not the head of a household, owns 60 of the 100 shares of the one class of stock in foreign corporation M and 80 of the 100 shares of the one class of stock in foreign corporation N. A and corporations M and N use the calendar year as a taxable year, corporations M and N are controlled foreign corporations throughout the period here involved, and neither corporation is a less developed country corporation. The earnings and profits and subpart F income of, and the foreign income taxes paid by, such corporations for 1964 are as follows:

	M	N
Pretax earnings and profits	$500,000	$1,200,000
Foreign income taxes	200,000	400,000
Earnings and profits	300,000	800,000
Subpart F income	150,000	750,000

Apart from his section 951(a) income, A has gross income of $200,600 and $100,000 of deductions attributable to such income. He is required to include $90,000 (.60 × $150,000) in gross income

Reg. § 1.962-1(b)(2)

under section 951(a) with respect to M Corporation and $600,000 (.80 × $750,000) with respect to N Corporation. A elects to have the provisions of section 962 apply for 1964 and computes his tax as follows:

Tax on amounts included under sec. 951(a):			
Income under sec. 951(a) from M Corporation	$ 90,000		
Gross-up under secs. 960(a)(1) and 78 ($90,000/$300,000 × $200,000)	60,000		
Income under sec. 951(a) from N Corporation	$600,000		
Gross-up under secs. 960(a)(1) and 78 ($600,000/$800,000 × $400,000)	300,000		
Taxable income under sec. 11	$1,050,000		
Normal tax (.22 × $1,050,000)		$231,000	
Surtax exemption ([$90,000+$600,000]/[.60 × $300,000 + (.80 × $800,000)] × $25,000)	21,036		
Subject to surtax under sec. 11 ($1,050,000 − $21,036)	1,028,964		
Surtax (.28 × $1,028,964)		288,110	
Tentative U.S. tax		$519,110	
Foreign tax credit ($60,000 + $300,000)		360,000	
Total U.S. tax payable on amounts included under sec. 951(a)			$159,110
Tax with respect to other income:			
Gross income		200,600	
Less:			
Personal exemption	$ 600		
Deductions	100,000	100,600	
Taxable income		$100,000	
Tax with respect to such other taxable income			59,340
Total tax ($159,110 + $59,340)			$218,450

[Reg. § 1.962-1.]

☐ [T.D. 6858, 10-27-65. Amended by T.D. 7413, 3-25-76.]

[Reg. § 1.962-2]

§ 1.962-2. Election of limitation of tax for individuals.—(a) *Who may elect.* The election under section 962 may be made only by a United States shareholder who is an individual (including a trust or estate).

(b) *Time and manner of making election.* Except as provided in § 1.962-4, a United States shareholder shall make an election under this section by filing a statement to such effect with his return for the taxable year with respect to which the election is made. The statement shall include the following information:

(1) The name, address, and taxable year of each controlled foreign corporation with respect to which the electing shareholder is a United States shareholder and of all other corporations, partnerships, trusts, or estates in any applicable chain of ownership described in section 958(a);

(2) The amounts, on a corporation-by-corporation basis, which are included in such shareholder's gross income for his taxable year under section 951(a);

(3) Such shareholder's pro rata share of the earnings and profits (determined under § 1.964-1) of each such controlled foreign corporation with respect to which such shareholder includes any amount in gross income for his taxable year under section 951(a) and the foreign income, war profits, excess profits, and similar taxes paid on or with respect to such earnings and profits;

(4) The amount of distributions received by such shareholder during his taxable year from each controlled foreign corporation referred to in subparagraph (1) of this paragraph from excludable section 962 earnings and profits (as defined in paragraph (b)(1)(i) of § 1.962-3), from taxable section 962 earnings and profits (as defined in paragraph (b)(1)(ii) of § 1.962-3), and from earnings and profits other than section 962 earnings and profits, showing the source of such amounts by taxable year; and

(5) Such further information as the Commissioner may prescribe by forms and accompanying instructions relating to such election.

(c) *Effect of election*—(1) *In general.* Except as provided in subparagraph (2) of this paragraph and § 1.962-4, an election under this section by a United States shareholder for a taxable year shall be applicable to all controlled foreign corporations with respect to which such shareholder includes any amount in gross income for his taxable year under section 951(a) and shall be binding for the taxable year for which such election is made.

(2) *Revocation.* Upon application by the United States shareholder, an election made

under this election may, subject to the approval of the Commissioner, be revoked. Approval will not be granted unless a material and substantial change in circumstances occurs which could not have been anticipated when the election was made. The application for consent to revocation shall be made by the United States shareholder's mailing a letter for such purpose to Commissioner of Internal Revenue, Attention: T.R., Washington, D.C. 20224 containing a statement of the facts upon which such shareholder relies in requesting such consent. [Reg. § 1.962-2.]

☐ [T.D. 6858, 10-27-65.]

[Reg. § 1.962-3]

§ 1.962-3. **Treatment of actual distributions.**—(a) *In general.* Section 962(d) provides that the earnings and profits of a foreign corporation attributable to amounts which are, or have been, included in the gross income of an individual United States shareholder under section 951(a) by reason of such shareholder's ownership (within the meaning of section 958(a)) of stock in such corporation and with respect to which amounts an election under § 1.962-2 applies or applied shall, when such earnings and profits are distributed to such shareholder with respect to such stock, notwithstanding the provisions of section 959(a)(1), be included in his gross income to the extent that such earnings and profits exceed the amount of income tax paid by such shareholder under this chapter on the amounts to which such election applies or applied. Thus, when such shareholder receives an actual distribution of section 962 earnings and profits (as defined in paragraph (b)(1) of this section) from a foreign corporation, only the excludable section 962 earnings and profits (as defined in paragraph (b)(1)(i) of this section) may be excluded from his gross income.

(b) *Rules of application.* For purposes of this section—

(1) *Section 962 earnings and profits defined.* With respect to an individual United States shareholder, the term "section 962 earnings and profits" means the earnings and profits of a foreign corporation referred to in paragraph (a) of this section. Such earnings and profits include—

(i) *Excludable section 962 earnings and profits.* Excludable section 962 earnings and profits which are the amount of the section 962 earnings and profits equal to the amount of income tax paid under this chapter by such shareholder on the amounts included in his gross income under section 951(a); and

(ii) *Taxable section 962 earnings and profits.* Taxable section 962 earnings and profits which are the excess of section 962 earnings and profits over the amount described in subdivision (i) of this subparagraph.

(2) *Determinations made separately for each taxable year.* If section 962 earnings and profits attributable to more than one taxable year are distributed by a foreign corporation, the determinations under this section shall be made separately with respect to each such taxable year.

(3) *Source of distributions*—(i) *In general.* Except as otherwise provided in this subparagraph, the provisions of paragraphs (a) through (d) of § 1.959-3 shall apply in determining the source of distributions of earnings and profits by a foreign corporation.

(ii) *Treatment of section 962 earnings and profits under § 1.959-3.* For purposes of a section 959(c) amount and year classification under paragraph (b) of § 1.959-3, a distribution of earnings and profits by a foreign corporation shall be first allocated to earnings and profits other than section 962 earnings and profits (as defined in subparagraph (1) of this paragraph) and then to section 962 earnings and profits. Thus, distributions shall be considered first attributable to amounts described in paragraph (b)(1) of § 1.959-3 which are not section 962 earnings and profits and then to amounts described in such paragraph (b)(1) which are section 962 earnings and profits (first for the current taxable year and then for prior taxable years beginning with the most recent prior taxable year), secondly to amounts described in paragraph (b)(2) of § 1.959-3 which are not section 962 earnings and profits and then to amounts described in such paragraph (b)(2) which are section 962 earnings and profits (first for the current taxable year and then for prior taxable years beginning with the most recent prior taxable year), and finally to the amounts described in paragraph (b)(3) of § 1.959-3 (first for the current taxable year and then for prior taxable years beginning with the most recent prior taxable year).

(iii) *Allocation to excludable section 962 earnings and profits.* A distribution of section 962 earnings and profits by a foreign corporation for any taxable year shall be considered first attributable to the excludable section 962 earnings and profits (as defined in subparagraph (1)(i) of this paragraph) and then to taxable section 962 earnings and profits.

(iv) *Allocation of deficits in earnings and profits.* A United States shareholder's pro rata share (determined in accordance with the principles of paragraph (e) of § 1.951-1) of a foreign corporation's deficit in earnings and profits (determined under § 1.964-1) for any taxable year

Income from Sources without the United States 49,405

See p. 20,601 for regulations not amended to reflect law changes

shall be applied in accordance with the provisions of paragraph (c) of § 1.959-3 except that such deficit shall also be applied to taxable section 962 earnings and profits (as defined in subparagraph (1)(ii) of this paragraph).

(4) *Distribution in exchange for stock.* The provisions of this section shall not apply to a distribution of section 962 earnings and profits which is treated as in part or full payment in exchange for stock under subchapter C of chapter 1 of the Internal Revenue Code. The application of this subparagraph may be illustrated by the following example:

Example. Individual United States shareholder A owns 60 percent of the only class of stock in foreign corporation M, the basis of which is $10,000. Both A and M Corporation use the calendar year as a taxable year. In each of the taxable years 1964, 1965, and 1966, M Corporation has $1,000 of earnings and profits and $1,000 of subpart F income. With respect to each such amount, A includes $600 in gross income under section 951(a), makes the election under section 962, and pays a United States tax of $132 (22 percent of $600). Accordingly, A increases the basis of his stock in M Corporation under section 961(a) by $132 in each of the years 1964, 1965, and 1966, and thus on December 31, 1966, the adjusted basis for A's stock in M Corporation is $10,396. In 1967, M Corporation is completely liquidated (in a transaction described in section 331) and A receives $13,800, consisting of $1,800 of earnings and profits attributable to the amounts which A included in gross income under section 951(a) in 1964, 1965, and 1966, and $12,000 attributable to the other assets of M Corporation. No amount of the $3,404 gain realized by A on such distribution ($13,800 minus $10,396) may be excluded from gross income under section 959(a)(1). However, section 962(d) will not prevent any part of such $3,404 from being treated as a capital gain under section 331.

(5) *Illustration.* The application of this paragraph may be illustrated by the following example:

Example. (a) M, a controlled foreign corporation is organized on January 1, 1963; A and B, individual United States shareholders, own 50 percent and 25 percent, respectively, of the only class of stock in M Corporation. Corporation M, A, and B use the calendar year as a taxable year, and M Corporation is a controlled foreign corporation throughout the period here involved. For the taxable years 1963, 1964, 1965, and 1966, A and B must include amounts in gross income under section 951(a) with respect to M Corporation. For the years 1963, 1965, and 1966, A makes the election under section 962. On January 1, 1967, B sells his 25-percent interest in M Corporation to A; A satisfies the requirements of paragraph (d) of § 1.959-1 so as to qualify as B's successor in interest. As of December 31, 1967, M Corporation's accumulated earnings and profits of $675 (before taking into account distributions made in 1967) applicable to A's interest (including his interest as B's successor in interest) in such corporation are classified under § 1.959-3 and this section for purposes of section 962(d) as follows:

Classification of earnings and profits for purposes of § 1.962-3.

Year	Sec. 959(c)(1) Non-sec. 962 earnings and profits	Sec. 959(c)(1) Excludable sec. 962 earnings and profits	Sec. 959(c)(1) Taxable sec. 962 earnings and profits	Sec. 959(c)(2) Non-sec. 962 earnings and profits	Sec. 959(c)(2) Excludable sec. 962 earnings and profits	Sec. 959(c)(2) Taxable sec. 962 earnings and profits	Sec. 959(c)(3)
1963	$ 25	$ 11	$ 39	....	....	....	....
1964	75	....	....	$ 60	....	....	$15
1965	....	....	....	75	$ 33	$117	....
1966	....	....	....	50	22	78	....
1967	....	....	....	....	....	....	75

(b) During 1967, M Corporation makes three separate distributions to A of $200, $208, and $267. The source of such distributions under § 1.959-3 and this section is as follows:

Reg. § 1.962-3(b)(5)

Income from Sources without the United States
See p. 20,601 for regulations not amended to reflect law changes

Amount	Year	Classification of distributions under secs. 959 and 962(d)
Distribution No. 1 .... $ 75	1964	(c)(1) non-sec. 962
25	1963	(c)(1) non-sec. 962
11	1963	(c)(1) excludable sec. 962
39	1963	(c)(1) taxable sec. 962
50	1966	(c)(2) non-sec. 962
200		
Distribution No. 2 .... $ 22	1966	(c)(2) excludable sec. 962
78	1966	(c)(2) taxable sec. 962
75	1965	(c)(2) non-sec. 962
33	1965	(c)(2) excludable sec. 962
208		
Distribution No. 3 .... $117	1965	(c)(2) taxable sec. 962
60	1964	(c)(2) non-sec. 962
75	1967	(c)(3)
15	1964	(c)(3)
267		

(c) A must include $324 in his gross income for 1967. The source of these amounts is as follows:

Distribution	Amount	Year	Classification
No. 1	$ 39	1963	(c)(1) taxable sec. 962
No. 2	78	1966	(c)(2) taxable sec. 962
No. 3	117	1965	(c)(2) taxable sec. 962
	75	1967	(c)(3)
	15	1964	(c)(3)
Total	$324		

(c) *Treatment of shareholder's successor in interest* —(1) *In general.* If a United States person (as defined in § 1.957-4) acquires from any person any portion of the interest in the foreign corporation of a United States shareholder referred to in this section, the rules of paragraphs (a) and (b) of this section shall apply to such acquiring person. However, no exclusion of section 962 earnings and profits under paragraph (a) of this section shall be allowed unless such acquiring person establishes to the satisfaction of the district director his right to such exclusion. The information to be furnished by the acquiring person to the district director with his return for the taxable year to support such exclusion shall include:

(i) The name, address, and taxable year of the foreign corporation from which a distribution of section 962 earnings and profits is received and of all other corporations, partnerships, trusts, or estates in any applicable chain of ownership described in section 958(a);

(ii) The name and address of the person from whom the stock interest was acquired;

(iii) A description of the stock interest acquired and its relation, if any, to a chain of ownership described in section 958(a);

(iv) The amount for which an exclusion under paragraph (a) of this section is claimed; and

(v) Evidence showing that the section 962 earnings and profits for which an exclusion is claimed are attributable to amounts which were included in the gross income of a United States shareholder under section 951(a) subject to an election under § 1.962-2, that such amounts were not previously excluded from the gross income of a United States person, and the identity of the United States shareholder including such amount.

The acquiring person shall also furnish to the district director such other information as may be required by the district director in support of the exclusion.

(2) *Taxes previously deemed paid by an individual United States shareholder.* If a corporate successor in interest of an individual United States shareholder receives a distribution of section 962 earnings and profits, the income, war profits, and excess profits taxes paid to any foreign country or to any possession of the United States in connection with such earnings and profits shall not be taken into account for purposes of section 902, to the extent such taxes were deemed paid by such individual United States shareholder under paragraph (b)(2) of § 1.962-1 and section

Reg. § 1.962-3(c)(1)

960(a)(1) for any prior taxable year. [Reg. § 1.962-3.]

☐ [T.D. 6858, 10-27-65.]

[Reg. § 1.962-4]

§ 1.962-4. Transitional rules for certain taxable years.—(a) *Extension of time for making or revoking election.* Paragraphs (b) and (c) of this section provide additional rules with respect to making or revoking an election under section 962 which apply only to a taxable year of a United States shareholder for which the last day prescribed by law for filing his return (including any extensions of time under section 6081) occurs or occurred on or before January 31, 1966.

(b) *Manner of making election not previously made.* If a United States shareholder who has not previously made an election under section 962 for any taxable year referred to in paragraph (a) of this section desires to make such an election, he may do so by filing his return or an amended return for such taxable year together with a statement setting forth the information required under paragraph (b) of § 1.962-2. Such return or amended return and statement shall be filed on or before January 31, 1966.

(c) *Revocation of election previously made.* If a United States shareholder who has made an election under section 962 on or before November 1, 1965, for any taxable year referred to in paragraph (a) of this section desires to revoke such election, he may do so by filing an amended return to which is attached a statement that the election previously made is revoked. Such amended return and statement shall be filed on or before January 31, 1966. [Reg. § 1.962-4.]

☐ [T.D. 6858, 10-27-65.]

[Reg. § 1.964-1]

§ 1.964-1. Determination of the earnings and profits of a foreign corporation.—(a) *In general.* For purposes of sections 951 through 964, the earnings and profits (or deficit in earnings and profits) of a foreign corporation for its taxable year shall, except as provided in paragraph (f) of this section, be computed substantially as if such corporation were a domestic corporation by—

(1) Preparing a profit and loss statement with respect to such year from the books of account regularly maintained by the corporation for the purpose of accounting to its shareholders;

(2) Making the adjustments necessary to conform such statement to the accounting principles described in paragraph (b) of this section;

(3) Making the further adjustments necessary to conform such statement to the tax accounting standards described in paragraph (c) of this section;

(4) Translating the amounts shown on such adjusted statement into United States dollars in accordance with paragraph (d) of this section; and

(5) Adjusting the amount of profit or loss shown on such translated and adjusted statement in accordance with paragraph (e) of this section to reflect any exchange gain or loss determined thereunder.

The computation described in the preceding sentence may be made by following the procedures described in subparagraphs (1) through (5) of this paragraph in an order other than the one listed, as long as the result so obtained would be the same. In determining earnings and profits, or the deficit in earnings and profits, of a foreign corporation under section 964, the amount of any illegal bribe, kickback, or other payment (within the meaning of section 162(c), as amended by section 288 of the Tax Equity and Fiscal Responsibility Act of 1982 in the case of payments made after September 3, 1982, and the regulations thereunder) paid after November 3, 1976, by or on behalf of the corporation during the taxable year of the corporation directly or indirectly to an official, employee, or agent in fact of a government shall not be taken into account to decrease such earnings and profits or to increase such deficit. No adjustment shall be required under subparagraph (2) or (3) of this paragraph unless it is material. Whether an adjustment is material depends on the facts and circumstances of the particular case, including the amount of the adjustment, its size relative to the general level of the corporation's total assets and annual profit or loss, the consistency with which the practice has been applied, and whether the item to which the adjustment relates is of a recurring or merely a nonrecurring nature. For the treatment of earnings and profits whose distribution is prevented by restrictions and limitations imposed by a foreign government, see section 964(b) and the regulations thereunder.

(b) *Accounting adjustments*—(1) *In general.* The accounting principles to be applied in making the adjustments required by paragraph (a)(2) of this section shall be those accounting principles generally accepted in the United States for purposes of reflecting in the financial statements of a domestic corporation the operations of its foreign affiliates, including the following:

(i) *Clear reflection income.* Any accounting practice designed for purposes other than the clear reflection on a current basis of income and expense for the taxable year shall not be given effect. For example, an adjustment will be required where an allocation is made to an arbitrary reserve out of current income.

(ii) *Physical assets, depreciation, etc.* All physical assets (as defined in paragraph (e)(5)(ii) of this section), including inventory when reflected at cost, shall be taken into account at historical cost computed either for individual assets or groups of similar assets. The historical cost of such an asset shall not reflect any appreciation or depreciation in its value or in the relative value of the currency in which its cost was incurred. Depreciation, depletion, and amortization allowances shall be based on the historical cost of the underlying asset and no effect shall be given to any such allowance determined on the basis of a factor other than historical cost. For special rules for determining historical cost where assets are acquired during a taxable year beginning before January 1, 1950, or a majority interest in the foreign corporation is acquired after December 31, 1949, but before October 27, 1964, see subparagraph (2) of this paragraph.

(iii) *Valuation of assets and liabilities.* Any accounting practice which results in the systematic undervaluation of assets or overvaluation of liabilities shall not be given effect, even though expressly permitted or required under foreign law, except to the extent allowable under paragraph (c) of this section. For example, an adjustment will be required where inventory is written down below market value. For the definition of market value, see paragraph (a) of § 1.471-4.

(iv) *Income equalization.* Income and expense shall be taken into account without regard to equalization over more than one accounting period; and any equalization reserve or similar provision affecting income or expense shall not be given effect, even though expressly permitted or required under foreign law, except to the extent allowable under paragraph (c) of this section.

(v) *Foreign currency.* If transactions effected in a foreign currency other than that in which the books of the corporation are kept are translated into the foreign currency reflected in the books, such translation shall be made in a manner substantially similar to that prescribed by paragraph (d) of this section for the translation of foreign currency amounts into United States dollars.

(2) *Historical cost.* For purposes of this section, the historical cost of an asset acquired by the foreign corporation during a taxable year beginning before January 1, 1963, shall be determined, if it is so elected by or on behalf of such corporation—

(i) In the event that the foreign corporation became a majority owned subsidiary of a United States person (within the meaning of section 7701(a)(30)) after December 31, 1949, but before October 27, 1964, and the asset was held by such foreign corporation at that time, as though the asset was purchased on the date during such period the foreign corporation first became a majority owned subsidiary at a price equal to its then fair market value, or

(ii) In the event that subdivision (i) of this subparagraph is inapplicable but the asset was acquired by the foreign corporation during a taxable year beginning before January 1, 1950, as though the asset were purchased on the first day of the first taxable year of the foreign corporation beginning after December 31, 1949, at a price equal to the undepreciated cost (cost or other basis minus book depreciation) of that asset as of that date as shown on the books of account of such corporation regularly maintained for the purpose of accounting to its shareholders.

For purposes of this subparagraph, a foreign corporation shall be considered a majority owned subsidiary of a United States person if, taking into account only stock acquired by purchase (as defined in section 334(b)(3)), the United States person owns (within the meaning of section 958(a)) more than 50 percent of the total combined voting power of all classes of stock of the foreign corporation entitled to vote. The election under this subparagraph shall be made for the first taxable year beginning after December 31, 1962, in which the foreign corporation is a controlled foreign corporation (within the meaning of section 957), or for which it is included in a chain or group under section 963(c)(2)(B) of 1975, (applied as if section 963 had not been repealed by the Tax Reduction Act of 1975) or has a deficit in earnings and profits sought to be taken into account under section 952(d), or pays a dividend that is included in the foreign base company shipping income of a controlled foreign corporation under § 1.954-6(f). Once made, such an election shall be irrevocable. For the time and manner in which an election may be made on behalf of a foreign corporation, see paragraph (c)(3) of this section.

(3) *Illustrations.* The application of this paragraph may be illustrated by the following examples:

Example (1). Corporation M is a controlled foreign corporation which regularly maintains books of account for the purpose of accounting to its shareholders in accordance with the accounting practices prevalent in country X, the country in which it operates. As a consequence of those practices, the profit and loss statement prepared from these books of account reflects an allocation to an arbitrary reserve out of current income and depreciation allowances based on replacement values which are greater than historical cost. Adjustments are necessary to conform such statement to accounting principles generally accepted in the United States. Assuming these adjustments to be material, the unacceptable practices will have to be eliminated from the statement, an increase in the amount of profit (or a decrease in the amount of loss) thereby resulting.

Example (2). In 1973, Corporation N is a foreign corporation which is not a controlled foreign corporation but which is included in a chain, for minimum distribution purposes, under section 963(c)(2)(B). Corporation N regularly maintains books of account for the purpose of accounting to its shareholders in accordance with the accounting practices of country Y, the country in which it operates. As a consequence of those practices, the profit and loss statement prepared from these books of account reflects the inclusion in income of stock dividends and of corporate distributions representing a return of capital. Adjustments are necessary to conform such statement to accounting principles generally accepted in the United States. Assuming these adjustments to be material, the unacceptable practices will have to be eliminated from the statement, a decrease in the amount of profit (or increase in the amount of loss) thereby resulting.

(c) *Tax adjustments*—(1) *In general.* The tax accounting standards to be applied in making the adjustments required by paragraph (a)(3) of this section shall be the following:

(i) *Accounting methods.* The method of accounting shall reflect the provisions of section 446 and the regulations thereunder.

(ii) *Inventories.* Inventories shall be taken into account in accordance with the provisions of sections 471 and 472 and the regulations thereunder.

(iii) *Depreciation.* Depreciation shall be computed as follows:

(a) For any taxable year beginning before July 1, 1972, depreciation shall be computed in accordance with section 167 and the regulations thereunder.

(b) If, for any taxable year beginning after June 30, 1972, 20 percent or more of the gross income from all sources of the corporation is derived from sources within the United States, then depreciation shall be computed in accordance with the provisions of § 1.312-15.

(c) If, for any taxable year beginning after June 30, 1972, less than 20 percent of the gross income from all sources of the corporation is derived from sources within the United States, then depreciation shall be computed in accordance with section 167 and the regulations thereunder.

(iv) *Elections.* Effect shall be given to any election made in accordance with an applicable provision of the Code and the regulations thereunder and these regulations. Except as provided in subparagraphs (2) and (3) of this paragraph, any requirements imposed by the Code or applicable regulations with respect to making an election or adopting or changing a method of accounting must be satisfied by or on behalf of the foreign corporation just as though it were a domestic corporation if such election or such adoption or change of method is to be taken into account in the computation of its earnings and profits.

(2) *Adoption of method.* For the first taxable year beginning after December 31, 1962, in which the foreign corporation is a controlled foreign corporation (within the meaning of section 957), or for which it is included in a chain or group under section 963(c)(2)(B) of 1975, (applied as if section 963 had not been repealed by the Tax Reduction Act of 1975) or has a deficit in earnings and profits sought to be taken into account under section 952(d), or pays a dividend that is included in the foreign base company shipping income of a controlled foreign corporation under § 1.954-6(f), there may be adopted or made by such corporation or on its behalf any method of accounting or election allowable under this section notwithstanding that, in previous years, its earnings and profits were computed, or its books or financial statements prepared, on a different basis and notwithstanding that such election is required by the Code or regulations to be made in a prior taxable year. For purposes of determining the amount of a deficit in earnings and profits taken into account pursuant to section 952(c)(1)(B), if a different basis is used in previous years, ratable adjustments shall be made in the earnings and profits attributable to such previous years to prevent any duplication or omission of amounts that would otherwise result from the adoption of such method or the making of such election. See subparagraph (3) of this paragraph for the manner in which a method of accounting or an election may be adopted or made on behalf of the foreign corporation.

(3) *Action on behalf of corporation*—(i) *In general.* An election shall be deemed made, or an adoption or change in method of accounting deemed effectuated, on behalf of the foreign corporation only if its controlling United States shareholders (as defined in subparagraph (5) of this paragraph)—

(a) Satisfy for such corporation any requirements imposed by the Code or applicable regulations with respect to such election or such adoption or change in method, such as the filing of forms, the execution of consents, securing the permission of the Commissioner, or maintaining books and records in a particular manner.

Reg. § 1.964-1(c)(3)

(b) File the written statement described in subdivision (ii) of this subparagraph at the time and in the manner prescribed therein, and

(c) Provide the written notice required by subdivision (iii) of this subparagraph at the time and in the manner prescribed therein.

For purposes of the preceding sentence, the books of the foreign corporation shall be considered to be maintained in a particular manner if the controlling United States shareholders or the foreign corporation regularly keep the records and accounts required by section 964(c) and the regulations thereunder in that manner. Any election required to be made or information required to be filed with a tax return shall be deemed made or furnished on behalf of the foreign corporation if its controlling United States shareholders file the written statement described in subdivision (ii) of this subparagraph with respect to such election within the period specified therein. For a special rule postponing the time for taking action by or on behalf of a foreign corporation until the amount of its earnings and profits becomes significant, see subparagraph (6) of this paragraph.

(ii) *Written statement.* The written statement required by subdivision (i) of this subparagraph shall be jointly executed by the controlling United States shareholders, shall be filed with the Director of Internal Revenue Service Center, 11601 Roosevelt Blvd., Philadelphia, Pennsylvania 19155, within 180 days after the close of the taxable year of the foreign corporation with respect to which the election is made or the adoption or change of method effected, or before May 1, 1965, whichever is later, and shall set forth the name and country of organization of the foreign corporation, the names, addresses, taxpayer identification numbers (in the case of statements required to be filed after June 20, 1983), and stock interests of the controlling United States shareholders, the nature of the action taken, the names, addresses, and (in the case of statements required to be filed after June 20, 1983) taxpayer identification numbers of all other United States shareholders notified of the election or adoption or change of method, and such other information as the Commissioner may by forms require.

(iii) *Notice.* Prior to the filing of the written statement described in subdivision (ii) of this subparagraph, the controlling United States shareholders shall provide written notice of the election made or the adoption or change of method effected to all other persons known by them to be United States shareholders who own (within the meaning of section 958(a)) stock of the foreign corporation. Such notice shall set forth the name and country of organization of the foreign corporation, the names, addresses, and stock interests of the controlling United States shareholders, the nature of the action taken, and such other information as the Commissioner may by forms require. However, the failure of the controlling United States shareholders to provide such notice to a person required to be notified thereunder shall not invalidate the election made or the adoption or change of method effected, if it is established to the satisfaction of the Commissioner that reasonable cause existed for such failure.

(4) *Effect of action by controlling United States shareholders.* Any action taken by the controlling United States shareholders on behalf of the foreign corporation pursuant to subparagraph (3) of this paragraph shall be reflected in the computation of the earnings and profits of such corporation under this section to the extent that it bears upon the tax liability of a United States shareholder who either—

(i) Was a controlling United States shareholder with respect to the action taken;

(ii) Received the written notice provided by subparagraph (3)(iii) of this paragraph;

(iii) Failed to file any of the returns required by section 6046 and the regulations thereunder within the period prescribed by section 6046(d); or

(iv) Was notified by the Director of the Philadelphia Service Center of the action taken—

(a) Within 61 days after the last day (including extensions of time) prescribed with respect to the taxable year of the foreign corporation by subparagraph (3)(ii) of this paragraph for filing the written statement described in such subparagraph, or

(b) Within 180 days after the close of the first taxable year in which such shareholder becomes a United States shareholder,

whichever is later.

To the extent that the computation of the earnings and profits of the foreign corporation bears upon the tax liability of any United States shareholder other than those enumerated in the preceding sentence, the computation shall reflect the action taken only if such shareholder assents to such treatment. Such assent may be given at any time, but not later than 90 days after the shareholder is first apprised of such action by the Director of the Philadelphia Service Center. The shareholder shall signify his assent by filing a written statement with the Director of the Internal Revenue Service Center, 11601 Roosevelt Blvd., Philadelphia, Pennsylvania 19155, setting forth the name and country of organization of the foreign corporation, his own name, address, and

Reg. § 1.964-1(c)(4)

stock interest in the corporation, the nature of the action being assented to, and such other information as the Commissioner may by forms require.

(5) *Controlling United States shareholders.* For purposes of this paragraph the controlling United States shareholders of a foreign corporation shall be those United States shareholders (as defined in section 951(b)), who, in the aggregate, own (within the meaning of section 958(a)) more than 50 percent of the total combined voting power of all classes of the stock of such corporation entitled to vote and who undertake to act on its behalf. In the event that the foreign corporation is not a controlled foreign corporation but is included in a chain or group under section 963(c)(2)(B) or (3)(B), the controlling United States shareholder with respect to such foreign corporation shall be deemed to be the domestic corporation which elects to receive the minimum distribution from such chain or group. In the event that the foreign corporation is neither a controlled foreign corporation nor included in a chain or group under section 963(c)(2)(B) or (3)(B) but has a deficit in earnings and profits sought to be taken into account under section 952(d), the controlling United States shareholder with respect to such foreign corporation shall be the shareholder seeking to take such deficit into account. In the event that the foreign corporation is a controlled foreign corporation but the United States shareholders (as defined in section 951(b)) do not, in the aggregate, own (within the meaning of section 958(a)) more than 50 percent of the total combined voting power of all classes of the stock of such corporation entitled to vote, the controlling United States shareholders of the foreign corporation shall be all those United States shareholders who own (within the meaning of section 958(a)) stock of such corporation. In the event that a foreign corporation is not a controlled foreign corporation but pays a dividend to a controlled foreign corporation that is attributable to foreign base company shipping income under § 1.954-6(f), the controlling United States shareholders (as defined in this subparagraph) of the controlled foreign corporation shall be considered the controlling United States shareholders of the foreign corporation.

(6) *Action not required until significant.* Notwithstanding any other provision of this paragraph, action by or on behalf of a foreign corporation (other than a foreign corporation subject to tax under section 882) to make an election or to adopt a method of accounting shall not be required until 180 days after the close of the first taxable year for which—

(i) An amount is includible in gross income with respect to such corporation under section 951(a);

(ii) It is sought to be established that such corporation is a less developed country corporation (within the meaning of section 955(c), as in effect before the enactment of the Tax Reduction Act of 1975);

(iii) An amount is excluded from subpart F income (within the meaning of section 952) by section 952(c), section 952(d), or section 970(a);

(iv) Such corporation is the subject of an election to secure an exclusion under section 963 (applied as if section 963 had not been repealed by the Tax Reduction Act of 1975); or

(v) It is sought to be established that the corporation has foreign base company shipping income (within the meaning of section 954(f)).

In the event that action by or on behalf of the foreign corporation is not undertaken by the time specified in the preceding sentence and such failure is shown to the satisfaction of the Commissioner to be due to inadvertence or a reasonable cause, such action may be undertaken during any period of at least 30 days occurring after such showing is made which the Commissioner may specify as appropriate for this purpose. Where the action necessary to make an election or to adopt a method of accounting is undertaken by or on behalf of the foreign corporation in accordance with this subparagraph, such election shall be deemed to have been made, or such adoption of accounting method effected, for the first taxable year of the foreign corporation beginning after December 31, 1962, in which such corporation is a controlled foreign corporation (within the meaning of section 957) or for which it is included in a chain or group under section 963(c)(2)(B) or (3)(B) (applied as if section 963 had not been repealed by the Tax Reduction Act of 1975) or has a deficit in earnings and profits sought to be taken into account under section 952(d), or pays a dividend that is included in the foreign base company shipping income of a controlled foreign corporation under § 1.954-6(f). For special rules for computing earnings and profits for purposes of section 1248 or income for purposes of applying an exclusion set forth in section 954(b) where the taxable year of the foreign corporation occurs prior to the making of elections or the adoption of methods of accounting under this subparagraph, see the regulations under section 952 and section 1248.

(7) *Revocation of election.* Notwithstanding any other provision of this section, any election made by or on behalf of a foreign corporation (other than a foreign corporation subject to tax

under section 882) may be modified or revoked by or on behalf of such corporation for the taxable year for which made whenever the consent of the Commissioner is secured for such modification or revocation, even though such election would be irrevocable but for this subparagraph.

(8) *Illustrations.* The application of this paragraph may be illustrated by the following examples:

Example (1). X Corporation is a controlled foreign corporation which maintains its books, in accordance with the laws of the country in which it operates, by taking inventoriable items into account under the "first-in, first-out" method. A, B, and C, the United States shareholders of X Corporation, own 45 percent, 30 percent, and 25 percent of its voting stock, respectively. For the first taxable year of X Corporation beginning after December 31, 1962, B and C adopt on its behalf the "last-in, first-out" inventory method, notifying A of the action taken. Even though A may object to such action, adjustments must be made to reflect the use of the LIFO method of inventorying in the computation of the earnings and profits of X Corporation with respect to him as well as with respect to B and C.

Example (2). Y Corporation is a controlled foreign corporation which maintains its books, in accordance with the laws of the country in which it operates, by employing the straight-line method of depreciation. D and E, the United States shareholders of Y Corporation, own 51 percent and 10 percent of its voting stock, respectively. For the first taxable year of Y Corporation beginning after December 31, 1962, D adopts on its behalf the declining balance method of depreciation. However, not knowing that E is a United States shareholder of the company, D fails to provide him with notice of the action taken. Assuming that E has filed the return required by section 6046 and the regulations thereunder within the period prescribed by section 6046(d), adjustments in the computation of earnings and profits will not be required with respect to him unless the Director of International Operations notifies him of the action taken within 240 days after the close of Y's taxable year. If notice is not provided to E within this period, he will not be compelled to make the adjustments. At his option, however, he may accept the action taken by assenting thereto not later than 90 days after he is first apprised of such action by the Director of International Operations.

(d) *Translation into United States dollars.*—(1) *In general.*—(i) *General rule.* Except as provided in subdivisions (ii), (iii), and (iv) of this subparagraph, the amounts to be shown on the profit and loss statement, adjusted pursuant to paragraphs (b) and (c) of this section, shall be translated into United States dollars (as required by paragraph (a)(4) of this section) at the appropriate exchange rate for the translation period (as defined in subparagraph (6) of this paragraph) to which they relate.

(ii) *Cost of goods sold.* Amounts representing items of inventory reflected in the cost of goods sold shall be translated—

(a) To the extent that such amounts represent items included in the opening inventory balance, so as to obtain the same amount of United States dollars which represented (after translation and adjustment) such items in the closing inventory balance for the preceding taxable year,

(b) To the extent that such amounts represent items purchased or otherwise first included in inventory during the taxable year, at the appropriate exchange rate for the translation period in which the historical cost of such items was incurred, and

(c) To the extent that such amounts represent items included in the closing inventory balance, at the appropriate exchange rate for the translation period in which the historical cost of such items was incurred, except that, if such amounts are written down to market value, such market value shall be determined at the year-end rate. Notwithstanding the preceding sentence, amounts representing items of inventory included in the closing inventory balance may be translated at the year-end rate even though not written down to market value; however, once such a rate is employed under those circumstances, translation may not be made for subsequent taxable years at the appropriate exchange rate for the translation period in which the historical cost of the items of inventory was incurred unless the permission of the Commissioner is secured.

(iii) *Depreciation, depletion, and amortization.* Amounts representing allowances for depreciation, depletion, or amortization shall be translated at the appropriate exchange rate for the translation period in which the historical cost of the underlying asset was incurred or is deemed to have been incurred. For purposes of this subdivision, if the historical cost of an asset is determined under paragraph (b)(2) of this section, such cost shall be deemed to have been incurred on the date the asset is considered to have been purchased under that paragraph.

(iv) *Prepaid expenses or income.* Amounts representing expenses or income paid or received in a prior taxable year shall be translated at the appropriate exchange rate for the translation pe-

Reg. § 1.964-1(c)(8)

riod during which they were paid or received. Notwithstanding the preceding sentence, amounts representing such prepaid income or expenses may be translated at the year-end rate; however, once such a rate is employed, translation may not be made for subsequent taxable years at the appropriate exchange rate for the translation period during which such income or expenses were paid or received unless the permission of the Commissioner is secured.

(2) *Appropriate exchange rate.*—(i) *In general.* Where the value of the foreign currency relative to the United States dollar does not fluctuate substantially during a translation period, a single exchange rate shall be appropriate for all amounts representing classes of items which relate to such period, such rate to be a simple average determined by dividing the sum of the closing rates for each of the calendar months ending with or within such period by the number of such months. On the other hand, where the value of the foreign currency relative to the United States dollar does fluctuate substantially during a translation period, the exchange rate appropriate to an amount representing a class of items which relates to such period shall be either (a) a simple average determined in accordance with the preceding sentence, or (b) a weighted average taking into account the volume of transactions (reflected by the amount being translated) for the calendar months ending with or within such period, depending upon which average would produce a result more representative of that which would have been obtained by translating the individual transactions reflected by that amount at the closing rate for the month to which each such transaction relates. Whether the value of the foreign currency relative to the United States dollar fluctuates substantially during the translation period is a question of fact, depending upon, among other things, the extent to which the volume of transactions varies from month to month. In general, however, the degree of fluctuation will be considered substantial if the closing rate for any calendar month ending with or within the translation period varies by more than 10 percent from the closing rate for any preceding calendar month ending within that period.

(ii) *Monthly rate.* Notwithstanding subdivision (i) of this subparagraph, if it is so elected by or on behalf of the foreign corporation, and if the closing rate for any calendar month ending with or within a translation period does not vary by more than 3 percent from the closing rate for any preceding calendar month ending within that period, the appropriate exchange rate for amounts representing all classes of items relating to such period shall be any exchange rate which is designated in the election and which does not vary by more than 3 percent from the closing rate for any calendar month ending with or within such period. An election under this subdivision may be made with respect to any translation period of any taxable year of the foreign corporation beginning after December 31, 1962. Such election shall be effective only with respect to the translation period for which it is made, and once made shall be irrevocable with respect to that period. See paragraph (c)(3) of this section for the time and manner in which an election may be made on behalf of the foreign corporation.

(iii) *Class of items.* For purposes of this subparagraph, the term "class of items" means any category which is reflected separately on books of account or financial statements. For example, sales is a class of items which is reflected separately on the profit and loss statement, and accounts receivable is a class of items which is reflected separately on the balance sheet.

(3) *Closing rate.* The closing rate for any calendar month shall be the exchange rate on the last day of that month determined by reference to a qualified source of exchange rates within the meaning of subparagraph (5) of this paragraph.

(4) *Year-end rate.* The year-end rate shall be the closing rate for the last calendar month of the taxable year.

(5) *Qualified source of exchange rates.* A qualified source of exchange rates shall be any source which is demonstrated to the satisfaction of the district director to reflect actual transactions conducted in a free market and involving representative amounts. In the absence of such a demonstration, the exchange rates taken into account in the computation of the earnings and profits of the foreign corporation shall be determined by reference to the free market rate set forth in the pertinent monthly issue of "International Financial Statistics" or a successor publication of the International Monetary Fund, or such other source of exchange rates reflecting actual transactions conducted in a free market and involving representative amounts as the Commissioner may designate as appropriate for this purpose.

(6) *Translation period*—(i) *In general.* Except as provided in subdivision (ii) of this subparagraph, the translation period shall be a taxable year.

(ii) *Currency fluctuations.* If it is so elected by or on behalf of the foreign corporation, the taxable year shall be divided into groups consisting of a calendar month or consecutive calendar months as specified in the election, each such group constituting a separate translation period. Where the value of the foreign currency relative

49,414 Income from Sources without the United States

See p. 20,601 for regulations not amended to reflect law changes

to the United States dollar fluctuates substantially during the taxable year, the use of the weighted average referred to in subparagraph (2)(i) of this paragraph ordinarily may be avoided by dividing the taxable year into translation periods so that the first translation period begins with the first day of such year and each subsequent translation period begins with the first day of the first calendar month thereafter ending with or within such year for which the closing rate varies by more than 10 percent from the closing rate for any month in the preceding translation period. An election under this subdivision may be made with respect to any taxable year of the foreign corporation beginning after December 31, 1962. Such an election shall be effective only with respect to the taxable year for which it is made, and once made shall be irrevocable with respect to such year. For the time and manner in which an election may be made on behalf of the foreign corporation, see paragraph (c)(3) of this section.

(7) *Actual transactions.* Notwithstanding any other provisions of this paragraph—

(i) *Dollar transactions.* Any transaction involving the payment or receipt of United States dollars shall be reflected in the profit and loss statement by the amount of United States dollars involved in such transaction.

(ii) *Conversion transactions.* Any transaction involving the conversion of a foreign currency into United States dollars, or the conversion of United States dollars into a foreign currency, shall be reflected in the profit and loss statement by an amount expressed in United States dollars and determined by translation at the exchange rate which conversion was effected if the foreign corporation knows, or reasonably should know, that exchange rate.

(iii) *Daily rate.* Any transaction other than one described in subdivision (i) or (ii) may be translated into United States dollars at the exchange rate for the day on which that transaction occurred, such rate to be determined by reference to a qualified source of exchange rates within the meaning of subparagraph (5) of this paragraph.

No transaction shall be required to be taken into account under subdivision (i) or (ii) unless the United States dollars involved are material in amount.

(8) *Other methods.* Notwithstanding the other provisions of this paragraph, translation into United States dollars may be made in accordance with a system or method not otherwise described in this paragraph, provided that such system or method (i) was employed by the corporation for purposes of accounting to its shareholders prior to January 1, 1963, and (ii) is shown to the satisfaction of the Commissioner to clearly reflect the earnings and profits of the corporation.

(9) *Illustrations.* The application of this paragraph may be illustrated by the following examples:

Example (1). M Corporation, a controlled foreign corporation organized on January 1, 1963, employs the calendar year as its taxable year and maintains its books of account in abbas, the currency of the country in which it operates. During 1963 M Corporation's monthly sales amounted to 100,000 abbas per month, its total payroll and other expenses for the year amounted to 180,000 abbas, and its total inventory purchases amounted to 1,050,000 abbas. Also during 1963, M Corporation purchased depreciable assets for 1,000,000 abbas. The value of the abba relative to the United States dollar fluctuated only slightly in 1963; the monthly closing rate moved between 19.8 abbas and 20.2 abbas per United States dollar and stood at 19.9 abbas per United States dollar for most of the year and at year-end. An election under subparagraph (2)(ii) of this paragraph is made on behalf of M Corporation to use the par rate of 20 abbas per United States dollar as the exchange rate appropriate for 1963. Assuming that none of the amounts shown therein reflects a transaction described in subparagraph (7) of this paragraph, M Corporation's adjusted profit and loss statement for 1963 would be translated into United States dollars as follows:

	Local Currency	Exchange Rate	U.S. Dollars
Sales	1,200,000	20:1	$60,000
Cost of Goods Sold:			
Purchases	1,050,000	20:1	52,500
Less—Closing Inventory	(350,000)	20:1	(17,500)
	700,000		35,000
Wages and Other Expenses	180,000	20:1	9,000
Depreciation	200,000	20:1	10,000
Total Costs and Expenses	1,080,000		54,000
Operating Profit	120,000		6,000

Reg. § 1.964-1(d)(7)

Income from Sources without the United States 49,415
See p. 20,601 for regulations not amended to reflect law changes

Example (2). The facts are the same as in example (1) and in addition during 1964 M Corporation had annual sales of 1,470,000 abbas, annual wages and other expenses of 252,000 abbas, and inventory purchases of 910,000 abbas. Also during 1964, M Corporation purchased additional depreciable assets for 430,000 abbas, the bulk of such purchases being made in the last half of the year. The value of the abba relative to the United States dollar gradually declined in 1964, the monthly closing rate moving from 19.9 abbas per United States dollar down to 22 abbas per United States dollar. For most classes of items, the appropriate exchange rate is a simple average of monthly closing rates or 21 abbas per United States dollar. However, since the bulk of the depreciable asset purchases were made in the last half of the year, the rate representative of those transactions is a weighted average of 21.5 abbas per United States dollar. Assuming that none of the amounts shown therein reflects a transaction described in subparagraph (7) of this paragraph and that closing inventory is translated at historical rates, M Corporation's adjusted profit and loss statement for 1964 would be translated into United States dollars as follows:

	Local Currency	Exchange Rate	U.S. Dollars
Sales	1,470,000	21:1	$70,000
Cost of Goods Sold:			
Opening Inventory	350,000	20:1	17,500
Purchases	910,000	21:1	43,333
Less—Closing Inventory	(418,000)	21:1	(19,905)
	842,000		40,928
Wages and Other Expenses	252,000	21:1	12,000
Depreciation (1963 assets)	150,000	20:1	7,500
Depreciation (1964 assets)	86,000	21.5:1	4,000
Total Costs and Expenses	1,330,000		64,428
Operating Profit	140,000		5,572

Example (3). The facts are the same as in examples (1) and (2) except that the 1964 sales of M Corporation amounted to 1,260,000 abbas plus $10,500 in United States dollars. Assuming that closing inventory is translated at historical rates, M Corporation's adjusted profit and loss statement for 1964 would be translated as follows:

	Local Currency	Exchange Rate	U.S. Dollars
Sales—Abbas	1,260,000	21:1	$60,000
Sales—U.S. Dollars	215,250	Transaction	10,500
Total Sales	1,475,250		70,500
Cost of Goods Sold:			
Opening Inventory	350,000	20:1	17,500
Purchases	910,000	21:1	43,333
Less—Closing Inventory	(418,000)	21:1	19,905
	842,000		40,928
Wages and Other Expenses	252,000	21:1	12,000
Depreciation (1963 assets)	150,000	20:1	7,500
Depreciation (1964 assets)	86,000	21.5:1	4,000
Total Costs and Expenses	1,330,000		64,428
Operating Profit	$ 145,250		$ 6,072

Example (4). The facts are the same as in examples (1) and (2). M Corporation continues to operate during 1965 and the value of the abba relative to the United States dollar declines materially during that year; the monthly closing rate drops from 22 abbas per United States dollar to 26 abbas per United States dollar, a decrease of more than 10 percent. An election under subparagraph (6)(ii) of this paragraph is made on behalf of M Corporation to divide the year into translation periods, the applicable periods being January 1 through July 31 and August 1 through December 31. For most classes of items, the appropriate exchange rate for each of these translation periods is a simple average of monthly closing rates, or 23 abbas and 25 abbas per United States dollar,

Reg. § 1.964-1(d)(9)

49,416 Income from Sources without the United States
See p. 20,601 for regulations not amended to reflect law changes

respectively. However, all of the depreciable asset purchases were made at the end of the first translation period—January 1 through July 31—and, therefore, the rate representative of those transactions is a weighted average of 24 abbas per United States dollar. The classes of items reflecting M Corporation's 1965 financial transactions and the representative rates of exchange for such classes of items are as follows:

	Local Currency	Exchange Rate
Sales (Jan. 1—July 31)	1,000,000	23:1
(Aug. 1—Dec. 31)	500,000	25:1
Inventory Purchases:		
(Jan. 1—July 31)	559,000	23:1
(Aug. 1—Dec. 31)	361,000	25:1
Expenses (Jan. 1—July 31)	115,000	23:1
(Aug. 1—Dec. 31)	145,000	25:1
Fixed Asset Purchases	216,000	24:1
Closing Inventory	430,000	Historical

Assuming that M Corporation uses the first-in, first-out method of inventory valuation, the closing inventory is assumed in normal circumstances to consist of purchases made during the most recent translation period as follows:

	Local Currency	Exchange Rate	U.S. Dollars
All of the August-December Purchases	361,000	25:1	$14,440
Balance from January-July Purchases	69,000	23:1	3,000
Total Closing Inventory	430,000		$17,440

Assuming that none of the amounts shown therein reflects a transaction described in subparagraph (7) of this paragraph, and that closing inventory is translated at historical rates, M Corporation's adjusted profit and loss statement for 1965 would be translated into United States dollars as follows:

	Local Currency	Exchange Rate	U.S. Dollars
Sales (Jan. 1—July 31)	1,000,000	23:1	$43,478
(Aug. 1—Dec. 31)	500,000	25:1	20,000
	1,500,000		$63,478
Cost of Goods Sold:			
Opening Inventory	418,000	21:1	19,905
Purchases			
(Jan. 1—July 31)	559,000	23:1	24,304
(Aug. 1—Dec. 31)	361,000	25:1	14,440
Less—Closing Inventory	(430,000)	Historical	(17,440)
	908,000		41,209
Wages and Other Expenses			
(Jan. 1—July 31)	115,000	23:1	5,000
(Aug. 1—Dec. 31)	145,000	25:1	5,800
Depreciation (1963 assets)	120,000	20:1	6,000
(1964 assets)	64,500	21.5:1	3,000
(1965 assets)	43,200	24:1	1,800
Total Costs and Expenses	1,395,700		62,809
Operating Profit	104,300		669

(e) *Exchange gain or loss*—(1) *In general.* The exchange gain or loss determined in accordance with subparagraph (2) of this paragraph shall be applied against and reduce, or applied to and increase, as the case may be, the amount of profit or loss shown on the profit and loss statement prepared pursuant to paragraph (a)(1) of this section, as adjusted and translated pursuant to paragraph (a)(2), (3), and (4) of this section. For the manner in which the exchange gain or loss is to be allocated to or applied against subpart F income, see section 952 and the regulations thereunder.

(2) *Determination of exchange gain or loss.* The exchange gain (or loss) for the taxable year shall be the amount which equals—

(i) The retained earnings for the taxable year as determined under subparagraph (3) of this paragraph, plus

Reg. § 1.964-1(e)(1)

(ii) The amount of any distributions made during the taxable year translated at the exchange rate appropriate to the translation period during which such distributions were made (or taken into account in accordance with paragraph (d)(7) of this section, if applicable), minus

(iii) The amount representing retained earnings for the preceding taxable year as determined under subparagraph (3) of this paragraph, minus

(iv) The amount of profit (or plus the amount of any loss) shown on the profit and loss statement for the taxable year prepared pursuant to paragraph (a)(1) of this section and adjusted and translated pursuant to paragraph (a)(2), (3), and (4) of this section.

(3) *Retained earnings.* The retained earnings for any taxable year shall be determined by first—

(i) Preparing a balance sheet as of the end of such year from the books of account regularly maintained by the foreign corporation for the purpose of accounting to its shareholders;

(ii) Making the adjustments necessary to conform such balance sheet to the accounting principles described in paragraph (b) of this section;

(iii) Making the further adjustments necessary to conform such balance sheet to the tax accounting standards described in paragraph (c) of this section; and

(iv) Translating the amounts shown on the balance sheet (other than amounts representing retained earnings) into United States dollars in accordance with subparagraph (4) of this paragraph.

The retained earnings shall be an amount equal to the excess of the aggregate amount representing assets on the balance sheet (as adjusted and translated under this subparagraph) over the aggregate amount representing liabilities, reserves (other than reserves out of current or accumulated earnings), and paid-in capital on the balance sheet (as adjusted and translated under this subparagraph).

(4) *Translation of balance sheet.* Amounts shown on the balance sheet as adjusted pursuant to subparagraph (3)(ii) and (iii) of this paragraph (other than amounts representing retained earnings) shall be translated into United States dollars as follows:

(i) *Financial assets.* Amounts representing financial assets shall be translated at the year-end rate.

(ii) *Physical assets.* Amounts representing physical assets (other than inventory) shall be translated at the appropriate exchange rate for the translation period in which the historical cost of the asset was incurred or is deemed to have been incurred. For special rules for determining date on which the historical cost of certain assets acquired during taxable years beginning before January 1, 1950, or owned at the time a majority interest in the corporation was acquired after December 31, 1949, but before October 27, 1964, is deemed to have been incurred, see paragraph (b)(2) of this section.

(iii) *Depreciation and similar reserves.* Amounts representing depreciation, depletion, and amortization reserves shall be translated at the appropriate exchange rate for the translation period in which the historical cost of the underlying asset was incurred or is deemed to have been incurred.

(iv) *Inventory.* Amounts representing items of inventory included in the closing inventory balance shall be translated in accordance with paragraph (d)(1)(ii) of this section.

(v) *Bad debt reserves.* Amounts representing bad debt reserves shall be translated at the year-end rate.

(vi) *Prepaid income or expense.* Amounts representing expenses or income paid or received in a prior taxable year shall be translated in accordance with paragraph (d)(1)(iv) of this section.

(vii) *Short-term liabilities.* Amounts representing short-term liabilities shall be translated at the year-end rate.

(viii) *Long-term liabilities.* Amounts representing long-term liabilities shall be translated at the appropriate exchange rate for the translation period in which such liabilities were incurred.

(ix) *Paid-in capital.* Amounts representing paid-in capital shall be translated at the appropriate exchange rate for the translation period in which such capital was paid in.

Notwithstanding any other provisions of this subparagraph, where the amount representing an item shown on the balance sheet reflects a transaction described in paragraph (d)(7) of this section, such transaction shall be taken into account in accordance with that paragraph.

(5) *Definitions.* For purposes of this paragraph—

(i) *Financial assets.* A financial asset shall be any asset reflecting a fixed amount of foreign currency, such as cash on hand, bank deposits, and loans and accounts receivable. Securities (within the meaning of section 1236(c)) shall be considered physical assets if they have been or are reasonably expected to be held for at least six

Reg. § 1.964-1(e)(5)

months; if not they shall be considered financial assets whether or not they reflect a fixed amount of foreign currency. Moreover, advances on open account to any corporation in which the foreign corporation and any related persons (within the meaning of section 954(d)(3) and the regulations thereunder) with respect thereto own at least 10 percent of the combined voting power of all classes of stock entitled to vote shall not be considered financial assets if such advances have remained open for more than one year.

(ii) *Physical assets.* A physical asset shall be any asset other than a financial asset and shall include goodwill, patents, and other intangibles.

(iii) *Short-term liabilities.* A short-term liability shall be any indebtedness of the foreign corporation which is due or overdue as of the date of the balance sheet or which will become due within one year thereafter.

(iv) *Long-term liabilities.* A long-term liability is any indebtedness of the foreign corporation other than a short-term liability.

For the definition of "appropriate exchange rate," "year-end rate," and "translation period," see paragraph (d)(2), (4) and (6), respectively, of this section.

(6) *Illustrations.* The application of this paragraph may be illustrated by the following examples:

Example (1). N Corporation is a controlled foreign corporation which uses the calendar year as its taxable year and which maintains its books in yuccas, the currency of the country in which it operates. For 1963, its operating profit is 140,000 yuccas or $55,720. At the end of the year, its balance sheet, as translated and adjusted pursuant to subparagraph (3) of this paragraph, is as follows:

	Local Currency	Exchange Rate	U.S. Dollars
Cash	77,000	2.20:1	$ 35,000
Accounts Receivable	209,000	2.20:1	95,000
Inventory	418,000	Historical	199,050
Fixed Assets	1,430,000	Historical	700,000
Less—Accumulated Depreciation	(436,000)	Historical	(215,000)
Total Assets	1,698,000		814,050
Current Liabilities	338,000	2.20:1	$153,640
Long-term Liabilities	300,000	Historical	150,000
Paid-in Capital	800,000	Historical	400,000
Retained Earnings	260,000		110,410
Total Liabilities and Net Worth	1,698,000		814,050

N Corporation's retained earnings for 1962 are determined on the basis of its balance sheet as of the end of that year, translated as follows:

	Local Currency	Exchange Rate	U.S. Dollars
Cash	70,000	2.00:1	$ 35,000
Accounts Receivable	180,000	2.00:1	90,000
Inventory	350,000	Historical	175,000
Fixed Assets	1,000,000	Historical	500,000
Less—Accumulated Depreciation	(200,000)	Historical	(100,000)
Total Assets	1,400,000		700,000
Current Liabilities	180,000	2.00:1	$ 90,000
Long-term Liabilities	300,000	Historical	150,000
Paid-in Capital	800,000	Historical	400,000
Retained Earnings	120,000		60,000
Total Liabilities and Net Worth	1,400,000		700,000

The exchange gain or loss of N Corporation for 1963 may be computed as follows:

Retained Earnings—1963			$110,410
Less—Retained Earnings—1962	$60,000		
Operating Profit—1963	55,720		115,720
Exchange Loss			(5,310)

Reg. § 1.964-1(e)(6)

Example (2). Assume the same facts as in example (1). For 1964, N Corporation's operating profit is 104,300 yuccas or $15,740. It pays a dividend of 26,000 yuccas during a translation period when the appropriate exchange rate is 2.60 yuccas per United States dollar. At year-end, its balance sheet, as translated and adjusted pursuant to subparagraph (3) of this paragraph, is as follows:

	Local Currency	Exchange Rate	U.S. Dollars
Cash	91,000	2.60:1	$ 35,000
Accounts Receivable	260,000	2.60:1	100,000
Inventory	430,000	Historical	174,400
Fixed Assets	1,646,000	Historical	790,000
Less—Accumulated Depreciation	(663,700)	Historical	(323,000)
Total Assets	1,763,300		776,400
Current Liabilities	325,000	2.60:1	$125,000
Long-term Liabilities	300,000	Historical	150,000
Paid-in Capital	800,000	Historical	400,000
Retained Earnings	338,300		101,400
Total Liabilities and Net Worth	1,763,300		776,400

The exchange gain or loss of N Corporation for 1964 would be computed as follows:

Retained Earnings—1964		$101,400
Add—Dividends—1964		10,000
Predistribution earnings		111,400
Less—Retained Earnings—1963	$110,410	
Operating Profit—1964	15,740	126,150
Exchange Loss		(14,750)

(f) *Determination of earnings and profits as if a domestic corporation*—(1) *In general.* If the books of account regularly maintained by a foreign corporation for the purpose of accounting to its shareholders are kept in U.S. dollars and in accordance with accounting principles generally accepted in the United States, and if it is so elected by or on behalf of such corporation, the earnings and profits of the foreign corporation for a taxable year shall, except as otherwise provided in paragraph (f)(2) of this section, be determined in every respect as if it were a domestic corporation. Such election shall be effective only for the taxable year with respect to which the election is made. Once made, such election shall be irrevocable. See paragraph (c)(3) of this section for the time and manner in which an election may be made on behalf of a foreign corporation.

(2) *Illegal payments.* The amount of any illegal bribe, kickback, or other payment (within the meaning of section 162(c), as amended by section 288 of the Tax Equity and Fiscal Responsibility Act of 1982 in the case of payments made after September 3, 1982, and the regulations thereunder) paid after November 3, 1976, by or on behalf of the corporation during the taxable year of the corporation directly or indirectly to an official, employee, or agent in fact of a government shall not be taken into account to decrease earnings and profits or increase the deficit in earnings and profits otherwise determined under paragraph (f)(1) of this section. [Reg. § 1.964-1.]

☐ [T.D. 6764, 10-26-64. Amended by T.D. 6787, 12-28-64, T.D. 6829, 6-22-65, T.D. 6995, 1-17-69, T.D. 7221, 11-20-72, T.D. 7322, 8-23-74, T.D. 7545, 5-5-78, T.D. 7862, 12-16-82 and T.D. 7893, 5-11-83.]

[Reg. § 1.964-1T]

§ 1.964-1T. **Special rules for computing earnings and profits of controlled foreign corporations in taxable years beginning after December 31, 1986 (temporary).**—

(a)-(f) [Reserved]

(g)(1) *Earnings and profits computed in functional currency*—(i) *Rule.* For taxable years of a controlled foreign corporation (within the meaning of section 957) beginning after December 31, 1986, earnings and profits shall be computed in the controlled foreign corporation's functional currency (determined under section 985 and the regulations thereunder) in accordance with § 1.964-1 as modified by this paragraph (g). Accordingly, § 1.964-1 (d), (e), and (f) and (to the extent inconsistent with this paragraph (g)) § 1.964-1(c) do not apply for taxable years of a controlled foreign corporation beginning after December 31, 1986. For purposes of this section, the term "earnings and profits" includes a deficit in earnings and profits.

(ii) *Cross reference.* In the case of a controlled foreign corporation with a functional currency other than the United States dollar (dollar), see sections 986(b) and 989(b) for rules regarding the time and manner of translating distributions or inclusions of the controlled foreign corporation's earnings and profits into dollars.

(2) *Election required when first significant.* Tax accounting methods or elections may be adopted or made by, or on behalf of, a controlled foreign corporation in the manner prescribed by the Code and regulations no later than 180 days after the close of the first taxable year of the controlled foreign corporation in which the computation of its earnings and profits is significant for United States income tax purposes with respect to its controlling United States shareholders (as defined in § 1.964-1(c)(5)). For taxable years of a controlled foreign corporation beginning before January 1, 1989, only the events listed in § 1.964-1(c)(6) are considered to cause a controlled foreign corporation's earnings and profits to have United States tax significance. For taxable years of a controlled foreign corporation beginning after December 31, 1988, events that cause a controlled foreign corporation's earnings and profits to have United States tax significance include, without limitation—

(i) The events listed in § 1.964-1(c)(6),

(ii) A distribution from the controlled foreign corporation to its shareholders with respect to their stock,

(iii) Any event making the controlled foreign corporation subject to tax under section 882,

(iv) An election by the controlled foreign corporation's controlling United States shareholders to use the tax book value method of allocating interest expense under section 864(e)(4), and

(v) A sale or exchange of the controlled foreign corporation's stock by the controlling United States shareholders.

The filing of the information return required by section 6038 shall not itself constitute a significant event.

(3) *Effect of failure to make required election.* If an accounting method or election is not timely adopted or made by, or on behalf of, a controlled foreign corporation, and such failure is not shown to the satisfaction of the Commissioner to be due to reasonable cause under § 1.964-1(c)(6), earnings and profits shall be computed in accordance with this section. Such computation shall be made as if no elections had been made and any permissible accounting methods not requiring an election and reflected in the books of account regularly maintained by the controlled foreign corporation for the purpose of accounting to its shareholders had been adopted. Thereafter, any change in a particular accounting method or methods may be made by, or on behalf of, the controlled foreign corporation only with the Commissioner's consent.

(4) *Computation of earnings and profits by a minority shareholder prior to majority election or significant event.* A minority United States shareholder (as defined in section 951(b)) of a controlled foreign corporation may be required to compute a controlled foreign corporation's earnings and profits before the controlled foreign corporation or its controlling United States shareholders make, or are required under this section to make, an election or adopt a method of accounting for United States tax purposes. In such a case, the minority United States shareholder must compute earnings and profits in accordance with this section. Such computation shall be made as if no elections had been made and any permissible accounting methods not requiring an election and reflected in the books of account regularly maintained by the controlled foreign corporation for the purpose of accounting to its shareholders had been adopted. However, a later, properly filed, and timely election or adoption of method by, or on behalf of, the controlled foreign corporation shall not be treated as a change in accounting method.

(5) *Binding effect.* For taxable years beginning after December 31, 1986, except as otherwise provided in the Code or regulations, earnings and profits of a controlled foreign corporation shall be computed consistently under the rules of sections 964(a) and 986(b) for all federal income tax purposes. An election or adoption of a method of accounting for United States tax purposes by a controlled foreign corporation, or on its behalf pursuant to § 1.964-1(c) or any other provision of the regulations (*e.g.,* § 1.985-2(c)(3)), shall bind both the controlled foreign corporation and its United States shareholders as to the computation of the controlled foreign corporation's earnings and profits under section 964 (a) for the year of the election or adoption and in subsequent taxable years unless the Commissioner consents to a change. The preceding sentence shall apply regardless of—

(i) Whether the election or adoption of a method of accounting was made in a pre-1987 or a post-1986 taxable year;

(ii) Whether the controlled foreign corporation was a controlled foreign corporation at the time of the election or adoption of method;

(iii) When ownership was acquired; or

(iv) Whether the United States shareholder received the written notice required by § 1.964-1(c)(3).

Adjustments to the appropriate separate category (as defined in § 1.904-5(a)(1)) of earnings and profits and income of the controlled foreign corporation shall be required using the principles of section 481 to prevent any duplication or omission of amounts attributable to previous years that would otherwise result from any such election or adoption.

(6) *Examples.* The following examples illustrate the rules of this section.

Example (1)—(i) P, a calendar year domestic corporation, owns all of the outstanding stock of FX, a calendar year controlled foreign corporation. None of the significant events specified in § 1.964-1(c)(6) or this section has occurred. In addition, neither P nor FX has ever made or adopted, or been required to make or adopt, an election or method of accounting for United States tax purposes with respect to FX. On June 1, 1990, FX makes a distribution to P. FX does not act to make any election or adopt a method of accounting for United States tax purposes.

(ii) P must compute FX's earnings and profits in order to determine if any portion of the distribution is taxable as a dividend and to determine P's foreign tax credit on such portion under section 902. P must satisfy the requirements of § 1.964-1(c)(3) and file the written statement and notice described therein within 180 days after the close of FX's 1990 taxable year in order to make an election or to adopt a method of accounting on behalf of FX. Any such election or adoption will govern the computation of earnings and profits of FX for all federal income tax purposes (including, *e.g.*, the determination of foreign tax credits on subpart F inclusions) in 1990 and subsequent taxable years unless the Commissioner consents to a change.

(iii) If P fails to satisfy the regulatory requirements in a timely manner and such failure is not shown to the satisfaction of the Commissioner to be due to reasonable cause, the earnings and profits of FX shall be computed as if no elections were made and any permissible methods of accounting not requiring an election and reflected in its books were adopted. Any subsequent attempt by FX or P to change an accounting method shall be effective only if the Commissioner consents to the change.

Example (2)—(i) The facts are the same as in *Example (1)*, except that P elects to allocate its interest expense under section 864(e)(4) for its 1989 taxable year under the tax book value method of § 1.861-12T(c) of the Temporary Income Tax Regulations.

(ii) P must compute the earnings and profits of FX in order to determine the adjustment to P's basis in the stock of FX for P's 1989 taxable year. P must satisfy the requirements of § 1.964-1(c)(3) and file the written statement and notice described therein within 180 days after the close of FX's 1989 taxable year in order to make an election or to adopt a method of accounting on behalf of FX. Any such election or adoption will govern the computation of FX's earnings and profits in 1989 and subsequent taxable years for all federal income tax purposes (including, *e.g.*, the characterization of the June 1, 1990 distribution and the determination of P's foreign tax credit, if any, with respect thereto) unless the Commissioner consents to a change.

(iii) If P fails to satisfy the regulatory requirements in a timely manner and such failure is not shown to the satisfaction of the Commissioner to be due to reasonable cause, the earnings and profits of FX shall be computed as if no elections were made and any permissible methods of accounting not requiring an election and reflected in its books were adopted. Any subsequent attempt by FX or P to change an accounting method shall be effective only if the Commissioner consents to the change.

Example (3)—(i) The facts are the same as in *Example (2)*, except that P elects to allocate its interest expense under section 864(e)(4) for its 1988 taxable year under the tax book value method of § 1.861-12T(c) of the Temporary Income Tax Regulations.

(ii) P must compute the earnings and profits of FX in order to determine the adjustment to P's basis in the stock of FX for P's 1988 taxable year. P must satisfy the requirements of § 1.964-1(c)(3) and file the written statement and notice described therein within 180 days after the close of FX's 1988 taxable year in order to make an election or to adopt a method of accounting on behalf of FX. Any such election or adoption will govern the computation of FX's earnings and profits in 1988 and subsequent taxable years for all federal income tax purposes (including, *e.g.*, P's basis adjustment for purposes of section 864(e)(4) in 1989 and the characterization of the June 1, 1990 distribution and the determination of P's foreign tax credit, if any, with respect thereto) unless the Commissioner consents to a change.

Reg. § 1.964-1T(g)(6)

(iii) If P fails to satisfy the regulatory requirements in a timely manner and such failure is not shown to the satisfaction of the Commissioner to be due to reasonable cause, the earnings and profits of FX for 1988 shall be computed as if no elections were made and any permissible methods of accounting not requiring an election and reflected in its books were adopted. However, a properly filed, timely election or adoption of method by, or on behalf of, FX with respect to its 1989 taxable year, when P's basis adjustment for purposes of section 864(e)(4) first constitutes a significant event, shall not be treated as a change in accounting method. No recomputation of P's basis adjustment for 1988 shall be required by reason of any such election or adoption of method with respect to FX's 1989 taxable year, but prospective adjustments to FX's earnings and profits and income shall be made to the extent required by § 1.964-1T(g)(5).

Example (4)—(i) The facts are the same as in *Example (3)*, except that FX had subpart F income taxable to P in 1986, and P computed FX's earnings and profits for purposes of determining the amount of the inclusion and the foreign taxes deemed paid by P in 1986 under section 960 pursuant to § 1.964-1(a) through (e).

(ii) Any election made or method of accounting adopted on behalf of FX by P pursuant to § 1.964-1(c) in 1986 is binding on P and FX for purposes of computing FX's earnings and profits in 1986 and subsequent taxable years. Thus, in determining P's basis adjustment for purposes of section 864(e)(4) in 1988 and 1989 and its deemed-paid credit with respect to the 1990 dividend, FX's earnings and profits must be computed consistently with the method used by P with regard to the 1986 subpart F inclusion. (However, § 1.964-1(d), (e), and (f) do not apply in computing FX's earnings and profits in post-1986 taxable years.)

Example (5)—(i) The facts are the same as in *Example (4)*, except that FX made a dividend distribution to P on June 1, 1985, and P computed FX's earnings and profits for purposes of computing the foreign taxes deemed paid by P in 1985 under section 902 with respect to the distribution under § 1.964-1 exclusive of paragraphs (d), (e), and (f) pursuant to a timely election under § 1.902-1(g)(1).

(ii) Any election made or method of accounting adopted on behalf of FX by P pursuant to § 1.964-1(c) in 1985 is binding on P and FX for purposes of computing FX's earnings and profits in 1985 and subsequent taxable years. Thus, in determining P's basis adjustment for purposes of section 864(e)(4) in 1988 and 1989 and its deemed-paid credit with respect to the 1986 subpart F inclusion and the 1990 dividend, FX's earnings and profits must be computed consistently with the method used by P with regard to the 1985 dividend. If, rather than choosing under § 1.902-1(g)(1) to use the section 964 rules, P computed FX's earnings and profits for purposes of section 902 in 1985 in all respects as if FX were a domestic corporation, then P would have been free to make elections or adopt a method of accounting on behalf of FX under § 1.964-1(c) with respect to the subpart F inclusion in 1986. Any such election or adoption would be binding on P and FX as to the computation of FX's earnings and profits in 1986 and subsequent taxable years. [Temporary Reg. § 1.964-1T.]

☐ [T.D. 8283, 1-24-90.]

[Reg. § 1.964-2]

§ 1.964-2. Treatment of blocked earnings and profits.—(a) *General rule.* If, in accordance with paragraph (d) of this section, it is established to the satisfaction of the district director that any amount of the earnings and profits of a controlled foreign corporation for the taxable year (determined under § 1.964-1) was subject to a currency or other restriction or limitation imposed under the laws of any foreign country (within the meaning of paragraph (b) of this section) on its distribution to United States shareholders who own (within the meaning of section 958(a)) stock of such corporation, such amount shall not be included in earnings and profits for purposes of sections 952, 955 (as in effect both before and after the enactment of the Tax Reduction Act of 1975), and 956 for such taxable year. For rules governing the treatment of amounts with respect to which such restriction or limitation is removed, see paragraph (c) of this section.

(b) *Rules of application.* For purposes of paragraph (a) of this section—

(1) *Period of restriction or limitation.* An amount of earnings and profits of a controlled foreign corporation for any taxable year shall not be included in earnings and profits for purposes of sections 952, 955 (as in effect both before and after the enactment of the Tax Reduction Act of 1975), and 956 only if such amount of earnings and profits is subject to a currency or other restriction or limitation (within the meaning of subparagraph (2) of this paragraph) throughout the 150-day period beginning 90 days before the close of the taxable year and ending 60 days after the close of such taxable year.

(2) *Restriction or limitation defined.* Whether earnings and profits of a controlled foreign corporation are subject to a currency or other

restriction or limitation imposed under the laws of a foreign country must be determined on the basis of all the facts and circumstances in each case. Generally, such a restriction or limitation must prevent—

(i) The ready conversion (directly or indirectly) of such currency into United States dollars or into property of a type normally owned by such corporation in the operation of its business or other money which is readily convertible into United States dollars; or

(ii) The distribution of dividends by such corporation to its United States shareholders.

For purposes of this subparagraph, if a United States shareholder owns (within the meaning of section 958(a)), or is considered as owning by applying the rules of ownership of section 958(b), 80 percent or more of the total combined voting power of all classes of stock of a foreign corporation in a chain of ownership described in section 958(a), the distribution of dividends by such corporation to such shareholder will not be considered prevented solely by reason of the existence of a currency or other restriction or limitation at an intermediate tier in such chain if dividends may be distributed directly to such shareholders.

(3) *Foreign laws.* A currency or other restriction or limitation on the distribution of earnings and profits may be imposed in a foreign country by express statutory provisions, executive orders or decrees, rules or regulations of a governmental agency, court decisions, the actions of appropriate officials who are acting within the scope of their authority, or by any similar official action. A currency restriction will not be considered to exist unless export restrictions are also imposed which prevent the exportation of property of a type normally owned by the controlled foreign corporation in the operation of its business which could be readily converted into United States dollars.

(4) *Voluntary restriction or limitation.* A currency or other restriction or limitation arising from the voluntary act of the controlled foreign corporation or its United States shareholders during a taxable year beginning after December 31, 1962, will not be taken into account. For example, if a controlled foreign corporation—

(i) Issues a stock dividend which has the effect of capitalizing earnings and profits;

(ii) Elects to restrict its earnings and profits or to make certain investments as a means of avoiding current tax or securing a reduced rate of tax; or

(iii) Allocates earnings and profits to an optional or arbitrary reserve;

such restriction is voluntary and will not be taken into account.

(5) *Treatment of earnings and profits in cases of certain mandatory reserves*—(i) *In general.* If a controlled foreign corporation is required under the laws of a foreign country to establish a reserve out of earnings and profits for the taxable year, such earnings and profits shall be considered subject to a restriction or limitation by reason of such requirement only to the extent that the amount required to be included in such reserve at the close of the taxable year exceeds the accumulated earnings and profits (determined in accordance with subdivision (ii) of this subparagraph) of such corporation at the close of the preceding taxable year,

(ii) *Determination of earnings and profits.* For purposes of determining the accumulated earnings and profits of a controlled foreign corporation under subdivision (i) of this subparagraph, such earnings and profits shall not include any amounts which are attributable to—

(*a*) Amounts which, for any prior taxable year, have been included in the gross income of a United States shareholder under section 951(a) and have not been distributed;

(*b*) Amounts which, for any prior taxable year, have been included in the gross income of a United States shareholder of such foreign corporation under section 551(b) and have not been distributed; or

(*c*) Amounts which become subject to a voluntary restriction or limitation (within the meaning of subparagraph (4) of this paragraph) during a taxable year beginning before January 1, 1963.

The rules of this subdivision apply only in determining the accumulated earnings and profits of a controlled foreign corporation for purposes of this subparagraph. See section 959 and the regulations thereunder for limitations on the exclusion from gross income of previously taxed earnings and profits.

(6) *Exhaustion of procedures for distributing earnings and profits.* Earnings and profits of a controlled foreign corporation for a taxable year will not be considered subject to a currency or other restriction or limitation on their distribution unless the United States shareholders of such corporation demonstrate either that the available procedures for distributing such earnings and profits have been exhausted or that the use of such procedures will be futile. As a general rule, such procedures will be considered to have been exhausted if the foreign corporation applies for dollars (or foreign currency readily convertible into dollars) at the appropriate rate of exchange

Reg. § 1.964-2(b)(6)

and complies with the applicable laws and regulations governing the acquisition and transfer of such currency including submission of the necessary documentation to the exchange authority. The fact that available procedures for distributing earnings and profits were exhausted without success with respect to a prior year is not, of itself, sufficient evidence that such procedures would not be successful with respect to the current taxable year.

(c) *Removal of restriction or limitation*—(1) *In general.* If, during any taxable year, a currency or other restriction or limitation (within the meaning of paragraph (b) of this section) imposed under the laws of a foreign country on the distribution of earnings and profits of a controlled foreign corporation to its United States shareholders is removed—

(i) *Treatment of deferred income.* Each United States shareholder of such corporation on the last day in such year that such corporation is a controlled foreign corporation shall include in his gross income for such taxable year the amounts attributable to such earnings and profits which would have been includible in his gross income under section 951(a) for prior taxable years but for the existence of the currency or other restriction or limitation except that the amounts included under this subdivision (i) shall not exceed his pro rata share of—

(*a*) The earnings and profits upon which the restriction was removed determined on the basis of his stock ownership on the last day of the immediately preceding taxable year, and

(*b*) The applicable limitations under paragraph (c) of § 1.952-1, paragraph (b)(2) of § 1.955-1, paragraph (b)(2) of § 1.955A-1, or paragraph (b) of § 1.956-1, determined as of the last day of the immediately preceding taxable year, taking into account the provisions of subdivision (ii) of this subparagraph.

(ii) *Treatment of earnings and profits.* For purposes of sections 952, 955 (as in effect both before and after the enactment of the Tax Reduction Act of 1975), and 956, the earnings and profits which are no longer subject to a currency or other restriction or limitation shall be treated as included in the corporation's earnings and profits for the year in which such earnings and profits were derived.

Amounts with respect to which a currency or other restriction or limitation is removed shall be translated into United States dollars at the appropriate exchange rate for the translation period during which such currency or other restriction or limitation is removed. See paragraph (d) of § 1.964-1. Amounts with respect to which a currency or other restriction or limitation is removed shall not be taken into account in determining whether a deficiency distribution (within the meaning of § 1.963-6 (applied as if section 963 had not been repealed by the Tax Reduction Act of 1975)) is required to be made for the year in which such earnings and profits were derived.

(2) *Removal of restriction or limitation defined.* An amount of earnings and profits shall be considered no longer subject to a limitation or restriction if and to the extent that—

(i) Money or property in such foreign country is readily convertible into United States dollars, or into other money or property of a type normally owned by such corporation in the operation of its business which is readily convertible into United States dollars;

(ii) Notwithstanding the existence of any laws or regulations forbidding the exchange of money or property into United States dollars, conversion is actually made into United States dollars, or other money or property of a type normally owned by such corporation in the operation of its business which is readily convertible into United States dollars; or

(iii) A mandatory reserve requirement (described in paragraph (b)(5) of this section) is removed either by a change in law of the foreign country imposing such requirement or by an accumulation of earnings and profits not subject to such requirement.

(3) *Distribution in foreign country.* If, during any taxable year, earnings and profits previously subject to a currency or other restriction or limitation are distributed in a foreign country to one or more United States shareholders of a controlled foreign corporation directly, or indirectly through a chain of ownership described in section 958(a), such earnings and profits shall be considered no longer subject to a restriction or limitation. However, distributed amounts may be excluded from such shareholder's gross income for the taxable year of receipt if such shareholder elects a method of accounting under which the reporting of blocked foreign income is deferred until the income ceases to be blocked.

(4) *Source of distribution.* If, during any taxable year, earnings and profits previously subject to a currency or other restriction or limitation are distributed to one or more United States shareholders of a controlled foreign corporation directly, or indirectly through a chain of ownership described in section 958(a), the source of such distribution shall be determined in accordance with the rules of § 1.959-3.

Reg. § 1.964-2(c)(1)

(5) *Illustration.* The provisions of this paragraph may be illustrated by the following example:

Example. (a) M, a United States person, owns all of the only class of stock of A Corporation, a foreign corporation incorporated under the laws of foreign country X on January 1, 1963. Both M and A Corporations use the calendar year as a taxable year and A Corporation is a controlled foreign corporation throughout the period here involved.

(b) During 1963, A Corporation derives income of $100,000 all of which is subpart F income and has earnings and profits of $100,000. Under the laws of X Country, currency cannot be exported without a license. During the last 90 days of 1963 and the first 60 days of 1964, A Corporation can obtain a license to distribute only an amount equivalent to $10,000. M must include $10,000 in his gross income for 1963 under section 951(a)(1)(A)(i) and $90,000 of A Corporation's earnings and profits for 1963 are not taken into account for purposes of sections 952, 955, and 956.

(c) During 1964, A Corporation has no income and no earnings and profits. On June 1, 1964, A Corporation converts an amount equivalent to $20,000 into property of a type normally owned by such corporation in the operation of its business which is readily convertible into United States dollars but does not distribute such amount. Corporation A must include $20,000 in its earnings and profits for 1963 for purposes of sections 952, 955, and 956. M must include $20,000 in his gross income for 1964.

(d) During 1965, A Corporation has no income and no earnings and profits. On December 15, 1965, A Corporation distributes an amount equivalent to $15,000 to M in X Country. Neither M nor A Corporation can obtain a license to export currency from X Country. In his return for the taxable year 1965, M elects a method of accounting under which the reporting of blocked foreign income is deferred until the income ceases to be blocked. Accordingly, M does not include the $15,000 in his gross income for 1965.

(e) During 1966, A Corporation has no income and no earnings and profits. On February 1, 1966, notwithstanding the laws and regulations of X Country which forbid the exchange of X Country's currency into United States dollars, M converts an amount equivalent to $15,000 into a currency which is readily convertible into United States dollars. Since the income has ceased to be blocked, M must include $15,000 in his gross income for 1966.

(d) *Manner of claiming existence of restriction or limitation on distribution of earnings and profits.* A United States shareholder claiming that an amount of the earnings and profits of a controlled foreign corporation for the taxable year was subject to a currency or other restriction or limitation imposed under the laws of a foreign country on its distribution shall file a statement with his return for the taxable year with or within which the taxable year of the foreign corporation ends which shall include—

(1) The name and address of the foreign corporation,

(2) A description of the classes of stock of the foreign corporation and a statement of the number of shares of each class owned (within the meaning of section 958(a)) or considered as owned (by applying the rules of ownership of section 958(b)) by the United States shareholder,

(3) A description of the currency or other restriction or limitation on the distribution of earnings and profits,

(4) The total earnings and profits of the foreign corporation for the taxable year (before any amount is excluded from earnings and profits under this section) and the United States shareholder's pro rata share of such total earnings and profits,

(5) The United States shareholder's pro rata share of the amount of earnings and profits subject to a restriction or limitation on distribution,

(6) The amounts which would be includible in the United States shareholder's gross income under section 951(a) but for the existence of the currency or other restriction or limitation,

(7) A description of the available procedures for distributing earnings and profits and a statement setting forth the steps taken to exhaust such procedures or a statement setting forth the reasons that the use of such procedures would be futile, and

(8) The amount of distributions made in a foreign country and a statement as to whether a method of accounting has been elected under which the reporting of blocked income is deferred until such income ceases to be blocked, including an identification of the taxable year and place of filing of such election.

In addition, such United States shareholder shall furnish to the district director such other information as he may require to verify the status of a currency or other restriction or limitation. [Reg. § 1.964-2.]

☐ [*T.D.* 6892, 8-22-66. *Amended by T.D.* 7545, 5-5-78 *and T.D.* 7893, 5-11-83.]

Reg. § 1.964-2(d)(8)

[Reg. § 1.964-3]

§ 1.964-3. Records to be provided by United States shareholders.—(a) *Shareholder's responsibility for providing records.* For purposes of verifying his income tax liability in respect of amounts includible in income under section 951 for the taxable year of a controlled foreign corporation each United States shareholder (as defined in section 951(b)) who owns (within the meaning of section 958(a)) stock of such corporation shall, within a reasonable time after demand by the district director, provide the district director—

(1) Such permanent books of account or records as are sufficient to satisfy the requirements of section 6001 and section 964(c), or true copies thereof, as are reasonably demanded, and

(2) If such books or records are not maintained in the English language, either (i) an accurate English translation of such books or records or (ii) the services of a qualified interpreter satisfactory to the district director. If such books or records are being used by another district director, the United States shareholder upon whom the district director has made a demand to provide such books or records shall file a statement of such fact with his district director, indicating the location of such books or records. For the length of time the United States shareholder of a controlled foreign corporation must cause such books or records as are under his control to be retained, see paragraph (e) of § 1.6001-1.

(b) *Records to be provided.* Except as otherwise provided in paragraph (c) of this section, the requirements of section 6001 and section 964(c) for record keeping shall be considered satisfied if the books or records produced are sufficient to verify for the taxable year—

(1) The subpart F income of the controlled foreign corporation and, if any part of such income is excluded from the income of the United States shareholder under section 963 or section 970(a), the application of such exclusion,

(2) The previously excluded subpart F income of such corporation withdrawn from investment in less developed countries,

(3) The previously excluded subpart F income of such corporation withdrawn from investment in foreign base company shipping operations,

(4) The previously excluded export trade income of such corporation withdrawn from investment, and

(5) The increase in earnings invested by such corporation in United States property.

(c) *Special rules.* Verification of the subpart F income of the controlled foreign corporation for the taxable year shall not be required if—

(1) It can be demonstrated to the satisfaction of the district director that—

(i) The locus and nature of such corporation's activities were such as to make it unlikely that the foreign base company income of such corporation (determined in accordance with paragraph (c)(3) of § 1.952-3) exceeded 5 percent of its gross income (determined in accordance with paragraph (b)(1) of § 1.952-3) for the taxable year (For taxable years to which § 1.952-3 does not apply, such amounts shall be determined under 26 CFR § § 1.954-1(d)(3)(i) and (ii) (Rev. as of April 1, 1975)), and

(ii) If such corporation reinsures or issues insurance or annuity contracts in connection with United States risks, the 5-percent minimum premium requirement prescribed in paragraph (b) of § 1.953-1 has not been exceeded for the taxable year, or

(2) The United States shareholder's pro rata share of such subpart F income is excluded in full from his income under section 963 and the books or records verify the application of such exclusion. [Reg. § 1.964-3.]

□ [T.D. 6824, 5-10-65. Amended by T.D. 7893, 5-11-83.]

[Reg. § 1.964-4]

§ 1.964-4. Verification of certain classes of income.—(a) *In general.* The provisions of this section shall apply for purposes of determining when books or records are sufficient for purposes of § 1.964-3 to verify the classes of income described in such section.

(b) *Subpart F income.* Books or records sufficient to verify the subpart F income of a controlled foreign corporation must establish for the taxable year—

(1) Its gross income and deductions,

(2) The income derived from the insurance of United States risks (as provided in paragraph (c) of this section),

(3) The foreign base company income (as provided in paragraph (d) of this section), and

(4) In the case of a United States shareholder claiming the benefit of the exclusion provided in section 952(b) or the limitation provided in section 952(c)—

(i) The items of income excluded from subpart F income by paragraph (b) of § 1.952-1 as income derived from sources within the United States, the United States income tax incurred with respect thereto, and the deductions properly allocable thereto and connected therewith, and

(ii) The earnings and profits, or deficit in earnings and profits, of any foreign corporation necessary for the determinations provided in paragraphs (c) and (d) of § 1.952-1.

(c) *Income from insurance of United States risks.* Books or records sufficient to verify the income of a controlled foreign corporation from the insurance of United States risks must establish for the taxable year—

(1) That the 5-percent minimum premium requirement prescribed in paragraph (b) of § 1.953-1 has not been exceeded, or

(2) The taxable income, as determined under § 1.953-4 or § 1.953-5, which is attributable to the reinsuring or the issuing of any insurance or annuity contracts in connection with United States risks, as defined in § 1.953-2 or § 1.953-3.

(d) *Foreign base company income and exclusions therefrom.* Books or records sufficient to verify the income of a controlled foreign corporation which is foreign base company income must establish for the taxable year the following items:

(1) *Foreign personal holding company income.* The foreign personal holding company income to which section 954(c) and § 1.954-2 apply, for which purpose there must be established the gross income from—

(i) All rents and royalties,

(ii) Rents and royalties received in the active conduct of a trade or business from an unrelated person, as determined under section 954(c)(3)(A) and paragraph (d)(1) of § 1.954-2,

(iii) Rents and royalties received from a related person for the use of property in the country of incorporation of the controlled foreign corporation, as determined under section 954(c)(4)(C) and paragraph (e)(3) of § 1.954-2,

(iv) All dividends, interest and, except where the controlled foreign corporation is a regular dealer in stock or securities, all gains and losses from the sale or exchange of stock or securities,

(v) Dividends, interest, and gains from the sale or exchange of stock or securities, received in the conduct of a banking, financing, or insurance business from an unrelated person, as determined under section 954(c)(3)(B) and paragraph (d)(2) and (3) of § 1.954-2,

(vi) Dividends and interest received from a related corporation organized in the country of incorporation of the controlled foreign corporation, as determined under section 954(c)(4)(A) and paragraph (e)(1) of § 1.954-2,

(vii) Interest received in the conduct of a banking or other financing business from a related person, as determined under section 954(c)(4)(B) and paragraph (e)(2) of § 1.954-2,

(viii) All annuities,

(ix) All gains from commodities transactions described in section 553(a)(3),

(x) All income from estates and trusts described in section 553(a)(4),

(xi) All income from personal service contracts described in section 553(a)(5), and

(xii) All compensation for the use of corporate property by shareholders described in section 553(a)(6).

(2) *Foreign base company sales income.* The foreign base company sales income to which section 954(d) and § 1.954-3 apply, for which purpose there must be established the gross income from—

(i) All sales by the controlled foreign corporation of its personal property and all purchases or sales of personal property by such corporation on behalf of another person,

(ii) Purchases and/or sales of personal property in connection with transactions not involving related persons (as defined in paragraph (e)(2) of § 1.954-1),

(iii) Purchases and/or sales of personal property manufactured, produced, etc., in the country of incorporation of the controlled foreign corporation, as determined under paragraph (a)(2) of § 1.954-3,

(iv) Purchases and/or sales of personal property for use, etc., in the country of incorporation of the controlled foreign corporation, as determined under paragraph (a)(3) of § 1.954-3, and

(v) Sales of personal property manufactured or produced by the controlled foreign corporation, as determined under paragraph (a)(4) of § 1.954-3.

Where an item of income falls within more than one of subdivisions (ii) through (v) of this subparagraph, it shall be sufficient to establish that it falls within any one of them. If a branch or similar establishment is treated as a wholly owned subsidiary corporation through the application of section 954(d)(2) and paragraph (b) of § 1.954-3, the requirements of this subparagraph shall be satisfied separately for each branch or similar establishment so treated and for the remainder of the controlled foreign corporation.

(3) *Foreign base company services income.* The foreign base company services income to which section 954(e) and § 1.954-4 apply, for

which purpose there must be established the gross income from—

(i) All services performed by the controlled foreign corporation,

(ii) Services other than those (as determined under paragraph (b) of § 1.954-4) performed for, or on behalf of, a related person,

(iii) Services performed in the country of incorporation of the controlled foreign corporation, as determined under paragraph (c) of § 1.954-4, and

(iv) Services performed in connection with the sale or exchange of, or with an offer or effort to sell or exchange, personal property manufactured, produced, etc., by the controlled foreign corporation, as determined under paragraph (d) of § 1.954-4.

Where an item of income falls within more than one of subdivisions (ii) through (iv) of this subparagraph, it shall be sufficient to establish that it falls within any one of them.

(4) *Foreign base company oil related income.*

(i) The foreign base company oil related income described in section 954(g) and § 1.954-8, for which purpose there must be established, with respect to each foreign country, the gross income derived from—

(A) The processing of minerals extracted (by the taxpayer or by any other person) from oil or gas wells into their primary products, as determined under section 907(c)(2)(A),

(B) The transportation of such minerals or primary products, as determined under section 907(c)(2)(B),

(C) The distribution or sale of such minerals or primary products, as determined under section 907(c)(2)(C),

(D) The disposition of assets used by the taxpayer in a trade or business described in subdivision (A), (B) or (C), as determined under section 907(c)(2)(D),

(E) Dividends, interests, partnership distributions, and other amounts, as determined under section 907(c)(3).

Where an item of income falls within more than one of the listings in paragraph (d)(4)(i)(A) through (E) of this section, it shall be sufficient to establish that it falls within any one of them.

(ii) If any of the items of income listed in paragraph (d)(4)(i) of this section arising from sources within a foreign country relates to oil, gas, or a primary product thereof and is described in section 954(g)(1)(A) or (B) and § 1.954-8(a)(1)(i) or (ii) (and, hence, is not foreign base company oil related income), then there must be established facts sufficient to verify the amount of such item of income which is not foreign base company oil related income. In this regard, the total quantities of oil, gas and primary products thereof which gave rise to such item of income and the portions of such quantities which were extracted or sold within the foreign country must be established.

(5) *Qualified investments in less developed countries.* For rules in effect for taxable years of foreign corporations beginning before January 1, 1976, see 26 CFR § 1.964-4(d)(4) (Rev. as of April 1, 1975).

(6) *Income derived from aircraft or ships.* For rules in effect for taxable years of foreign corporations beginning before January 1, 1976, see 26 CFR § 1.964-4(d)(5) (Rev. as of April 1, 1975).

(7) *Foreign base company shipping income.* The foreign base company shipping income to which section 954(f) and § 1.954-6 apply, for which purpose there must be established—

(i) Gross income derived from, or in connection with, the use (or hiring or leasing for use) of any aircraft or vessel in foreign commerce, as determined under § 1.954-6(c),

(ii) Gross income derived from, or in connection with, the performance of services directly related to the use of any aircraft or vessel in foreign commerce, as determined under § 1.954-6(d),

(iii) Gross income incidental to income described in subdivisions (i) and (ii) of this subparagraph, as determined under § 1.954-6(e),

(iv) Gross income derived from the sale, exchange, or other disposition of any aircraft or vessel used (by the seller or by a person related to the seller) in foreign commerce,

(v) Dividends, interest, and gains described in §§ 1.954-6(f) and 1.954-6(b)(1)(viii),

(vi) Income described in § 1.954-6(g) (relating to partnerships, trusts, etc.), and

(vii) Exchange gain, to the extent allocable to foreign base company shipping income, as determined under § 1.952-2(c)(2)(v)(*b*),

If the controlled foreign corporation has income derived from or in connection with, the use (or hiring or leasing for use) of any aircraft or vessel in foreign commerce, or derived from, or in connection with, the performance of services directly related to the use of any aircraft or vessel in foreign commerce, it shall be necessary to establish, from the books and records of the controlled foreign corporation, that such aircraft or vessel was used in foreign commerce within the meaning of subparagraphs (3) and (4) of § 1.954-6(b).

Reg. § 1.964-4(d)(4)

(8) *Income on which taxes are not substantially reduced.* The gross income excluded from foreign base company income under section 954(b)(4) and paragraph (b)(3) or (4) of § 1.954-1 in the case of a controlled foreign corporation not availed of to substantially reduce income taxes, the income or similar taxes incurred with respect thereto, and all other factors necessary to verify the application of such exclusion.

(9) *Qualified investments in foreign base company shipping operations.* The foreign base company shipping income that is excluded from foreign base company income under section 954(b)(2) and § 1.954-1(b)(1).

(10) *Special rule for shipping income.* The distributions received through a chain of ownership described in section 958(a) which are excluded from foreign base company income under section 954(b)(6)(B) and § 1.954-1(b)(2).

(11) *Deductions.* The deductions allocable, under paragraph (c) of § 1.954-1, to each of the classes and subclasses of gross income described in subparagraphs (1) through (9) of this paragraph.

(e) *Exclusion under section 963.* Books or records sufficient to verify the application of the exclusion provided by section 963 with respect to the subpart F income for the taxable year of a controlled foreign corporation must establish that the conditions set forth in paragraph (a)(2) of § 1.963-1 have been met.

(f) *Exclusion under section 970(a).* Books or records sufficient to verify the application for the taxable year of the exclusion provided by section 970(a) in respect of export trade income which is foreign base company income must establish for such year—

(1) That the controlled foreign corporation is an export trade corporation, as defined in section 971(a) and paragraph (a) of § 1.971-1,

(2) The export trade income, as determined under section 971(b) and paragraph (b) of § 1.971-1, which constitutes foreign base company income,

(3) The export promotion expenses, as determined under section 971(d) and paragraph (d) of § 1.971-1, which are allocable to the excludable export trade income,

(4) The gross receipts, and the gross amount on which is computed compensation included in gross receipts, from property in respect of which the excludable export trade income is derived, as described in section 970(a)(1)(B) and paragraph (b)(2)(ii) of § 1.970-1, and

(5) The increase in investments in export trade assets, as determined under section 970(c)(2) and paragraph (d)(2) of § 1.970-1.

(g-1) *Withdrawal of previously excluded subpart F income from qualified investment in less developed countries.* Books or records sufficient to verify the previously excluded subpart F income of the controlled foreign corporation withdrawn from investment in less developed countries for the taxable year must establish—

(1) The sum of the amounts of income excluded from foreign base company income under section 954(b)(1) and paragraph (b)(1) of § 1.954-1 (as in effect for taxable years beginning before January 1, 1976; see 26 CFR § 1.954-1(b)(1) (Rev. as of April 1, 1975)) for all prior taxable years,

(2) The sum of the amounts of previously excluded subpart F income withdrawn from investment in less developed countries for all prior taxable years, as determined under section 955(a) (as in effect before the enactment of the Tax Reduction Act of 1975) and paragraph (b) of § 1.955-1, and

(3) The amount withdrawn from investment in less developed countries for the taxable year as determined under section 955(a) (as in effect before the enactment of the Tax Reduction Act of 1975) and paragraph (b) of § 1.955-1.

(g-2) *Withdrawal of previously excluded subpart F income from investment in foreign base company shipping operations.* Books or records sufficient to verify the previously excluded subpart F income of the controlled foreign corporation withdrawn from investment in foreign base company shipping operations for the taxable year must establish—

(1) The sum of the amounts of income excluded from foreign base company income under section 954(b)(2) and paragraph (b)(1) of § 1.954-1 for all prior taxable years,

(2) The sum of the amounts of previously excluded subpart F income withdrawn from investment in foreign base company shipping operations for all prior taxable years, as determined under section 955(a) and paragraph (b) of § 1.955A-1,

(3) The amount withdrawn from investment in foreign base company shipping operations for the taxable year as determined under section 955(a) and paragraph (b) of § 1.955A-1, and

(4) If the carryover (as described in § 1.955A-1(b)(3)) of amounts relating to investments in less developed country shipping companies (as described in § 1.955-5(b)) is applicable, (i) the amount of the corporation's qualified investments (determined under § 1.955-2 other than paragraph (b)(5) thereof) in less developed country shipping companies at the close of the last

Reg. § 1.964-4(g)(4)

taxable year of the corporation beginning before January 1, 1976, and (ii) the amount of the limitation with respect to previously excluded subpart F income (determined under § 1.955-1(b)(2)(i)(*b*)) for the first taxable year of the corporation beginning after December 31, 1975.

(h) *Withdrawal of previously excluded export trade income from investment.* Books or records sufficient to verify the previously excluded export trade income of the controlled foreign corporation withdrawn from investment for the taxable year must establish the United States shareholder's proportionate share of—

(1) The sum of the amounts by which the subpart F income of such corporation was reduced for all prior taxable years under section 970(a) and paragraph (b) of § 1.970-1,

(2) The sum of the amounts described in section 970(b)(1)(B),

(3) The sum of the amounts of previously excluded export trade income of such corporation withdrawn from investment under section 970(b) and paragraph (c) of § 1.970-1 for all prior taxable years, and

(4) The amount withdrawn from investment under section 970(b) and paragraph (c) of § 1.970-1 for the taxable year.

(i) *Increase in earnings invested in United States property.* Books or records sufficient to verify the increase for the taxable year in earnings invested by the controlled foreign corporation in United States property must establish—

(1) The amount of such corporation's earnings invested in United States property (as defined in section 956(b)(1) and paragraph (a) of § 1.956-2) at the close of the current and preceding taxable years, as determined under paragraph (b) of § 1.956-1,

(2) The amount of excluded property described in section 956(b)(2) and paragraph (b) of § 1.956-2 held by such corporation at the close of such years,

(3) The earnings and profits, to which section 959(c)(1) and paragraph (b)(1) of § 1.959-3 apply, distributed by such corporation during the preceding taxable year, and

(4) The amount of increase in earnings invested by such corporation in United States property which is excluded from the United States shareholder's gross income for the taxable year under section 959(a)(2) and paragraph (c) of § 1.959-1. [Reg. § 1.964-4.]

☐ [*T.D.* 6824, 5-10-65. *Amended by T.D.* 7211, 10-5-72; *T.D.* 7893, 5-11-83 *and T.D.* 8331, 1-24-91.]

[Reg. § 1.964-5]

§ 1.964-5. **Effective date of subpart F.**—Sections 951 through 964 and §§ 1.951 through 1.964-4 shall apply with respect to taxable years of foreign corporations beginning after December 31, 1962, and to taxable years of United States shareholders within which or with which such taxable years of such corporations end. [Reg. § 1.964-5.]

☐ [*T.D.* 7120, 6-3-71.]

[The next page is 50,801.]

Income from Sources Without the United States

[Reg. § 1.970-1]

§ 1.970-1. Export trade corporations.—(a) *In general.* Sections 970 through 972 provide in general that if a controlled foreign corporation is an export trade corporation for any taxable year, the subpart F income of such corporation shall, subject to limitations provided by section 970(a) and paragraph (b) of this section, be reduced by so much of such corporation's export trade income as constitutes foreign base company income. To the extent subpart F income of an export trade corporation is reduced under section 970 and this section, an amount is required by section 970(b) and paragraph (c) of this section to be included in gross income of United States shareholders of the corporation if there is a subsequent decrease in such corporation's investments in export trade assets. See section 971(a) and paragraph (a) of § 1.971-1 for definition of the term "export trade corporation", section 971(b) and paragraph (b) of § 1.971-1 for definition of the term "export trade income", and section 971(c) and paragraph (c) of § 1.971-1 for definition of the term "export trade assets".

(b) *Amount by which export trade income shall reduce subpart F income*—(1) *Deductible amount.* The subpart F income, determined as provided in section 952 and the regulations thereunder but without regard to section 970 and this paragraph, of a controlled foreign corporation which is an export trade corporation for its taxable year shall be reduced by an amount equal to so much of its export trade income as constitutes foreign base company income for such taxable year, but only to the extent that such amount of export trade income does not exceed the limitation determined under subparagraph (2) of this paragraph for such taxable year. See section 972 and § 1.972-1 for rules relating to the consolidation of export trade corporations for purposes of determining the limitations described in subparagraph (2) of this paragraph.

(2) *Limitation on the amount of export trade income deductible from subpart F income.* The amount by which subpart F income of an export trade corporation may be reduced for any taxable year under subparagraph (1) of this paragraph may not exceed whichever of the following limitations is the smallest:

(i) The amount which is equal to 150 percent of the export promotion expenses, as defined in section 971(d) and paragraph (d) of § 1.971-1, of the export trade corporation paid or incurred during the taxable year which are properly allocable to the receipt or the production of so much of its export trade income as constitutes foreign base company income for such taxable year;

(ii) The amount which is equal to 10 percent of the gross receipts (other than from commissions, fees, or other compensation for services), plus 10 percent of the gross amount upon the basis of which are computed commissions, fees, or other compensation for services included in gross receipts, of the export trade corporation received or accrued during the taxable year from, or in connection with, the sale, installation, operation, maintenance, or use of property in respect of which such corporation derives export trade income which constitutes foreign base company income for such taxable year; or

(iii) The amount which bears the same ratio to the increase in investments in export trade assets, as defined in section 970(c)(2) and paragraph (d)(2) of this section, of the export trade corporation for its taxable year as the export trade income which constitutes foreign base company income of such corporation for such taxable year bears to the entire export trade income of the corporation for such year.

Under subdivision (ii) of this subparagraph, in the case of minimum or maximum fee arrangements, the determination shall be made on the basis of the actual gross amounts with respect to which such fees are paid, rather than on the basis of the amounts upon which such minimum or maximum fees are computed. All determinations of limitations under this subparagraph shall be made on an aggregate basis and not with respect to separate items or categories of income described in paragraph (b)(1) of § 1.971-1.

(3) *Determination of export promotion expense limitation.* For purposes of determining the limitation contained in subparagraph (2)(i) of this paragraph for any taxable year of the export trade corporation, there shall be taken into account with respect to those items or categories of export trade income which constitute foreign base company income the entire amount of those export promotion expenses which are directly related to such items or categories of income and a ratable part of any other export promotion expenses which are indirectly related to such items or categories of income, except that no export promotion expense shall be allocated to an item or category of income to which it clearly does not apply and no deduction allowable to such corporation under section 882(c) and the regulations thereunder shall be taken into account.

(4) *Application of section 482.* The limitations provided in section 970(a) and subparagraph (2) of this paragraph shall not affect the authority of the district director to apply the provisions of section 482 and the regulations thereunder, relat-

Reg. § 1.970-1(b)(4)

ing to allocation of income and deductions among taxpayers.

(5) *Illustrations.* The application of this paragraph may be illustrated by the following examples:

Example (1). Foreign corporation A is a wholly owned subsidiary of domestic corporation M. Both corporations use the calendar year as the taxable year. For 1963, A Corporation's subpart F income determined under section 952 and the regulations thereunder is $35, the total of its gross receipts and gross amounts referred to in subparagraph (2)(ii) of this paragraph is $310, its export promotion expenses properly allocable to its export trade income which constitutes foreign base company income are $18, its increase in investments in export trade assets is $32, and its export trade income is $40, of which $30 constitutes foreign base company income and $10 does not constitute foreign base company income. The subpart F income of A Corporation for 1963 as reduced under section 970(a) is $11, determined as follows:

(i) Subpart F income		$35
(ii) Less: $30 export trade income which constitutes foreign base company income, but deduction not to exceed the smallest of the following limitations (smallest of (a), (b), or (c)):		
(a) 150 percent of allocable export promotion expenses referred to in subparagraph (2)(i) of this paragraph (150% of $18)	$27	
(b) 10 percent of gross receipts and gross amounts referred to in subparagraph (2)(ii) of this paragraph (10% of $310)	31	
(c) Amount which bears to the increase in investments in export trade assets ($32) the same ratio as the export trade income which constitutes foreign base company income ($30) bears to total export trade income ($40) (75% [$30/$40] of $32)	24	$24
(iii) Subpart F income as reduced under sec. 970(a)		11

Example (2). The facts are the same as in example (1), except that A Corporation's export promotion expenses properly allocable to export trade income which constitutes foreign base company income are $14 instead of $18. The applicable limitation on the amount deductible from A Corporation's subpart F income for 1963 is $21 (150% of $14) instead of $24. The subpart F income as reduced under section 970(a) is $14 ($35 less $21).

Example (3). The facts are the same as in example (1), except that the total amount of A Corporation's gross receipts and gross amounts referred to in subparagraph (2)(ii) of this paragraph is $200 instead of $310. The applicable limitation on the amount deductible from A Corporation's subpart F income for 1963 is $20 (10 percent of $200) instead of $24. The subpart F income as reduced under section 970(a) is $15 ($35 less $20).

Example (4). The facts are the same as in example (1), except that A Corporation derives its export trade income which constitutes foreign base company income of $30 in a service arrangement with M Corporation under which it receives as a fee 5 percent of the gross receipts from M Corporation's sales or a minimum fee of $30. Such gross receipts are $220. The gross amounts taken into account in determining the limitation under subparagraph (2)(ii) of this paragraph are $220. The applicable limitation on the amount deductible from A Corporation's subpart F income for 1963 is $22 (10 percent of $220) instead of $24. The subpart F income as reduced under section 970(a) is $13 ($35 minus $22).

Example (5). The facts are the same as in example (1), except that A Corporation derives its export trade income which constitutes foreign base company income of $30 in a service arrangement with M Corporation under which it receives as a fee 9 percent of the gross receipts from M Corporation's sales or a maximum fee of $30. Such gross receipts are $400. In such instance, the limitation under (ii)(b) of example (1) is $40 (10 percent of $400 instead of $31. The applicable limitation on the amount deductible from A Corporation's subpart F income for 1963 is $24, the smallest of the three limitations. The subpart F income as reduced under section 970(a) is $11 ($35 less $24).

(c) *Withdrawal of previously excluded export trade income*—(1) *Inclusion of withdrawal in income of United States shareholders.* If—

(i) a controlled foreign corporation was an export trade corporation for any taxable year,

(ii) such corporation in any such taxable year derived subpart F income which, under the provisions of section 970(a) and paragraph (b) of this section, was reduced, and

(iii) such corporation has in a subsequent taxable year a decrease in investments in export trade assets,

every person who is a United States shareholder, as defined in section 951(b), of such corporation on the last day of such subsequent taxable year on which such corporation is a controlled foreign corporation shall include in his gross income, under section 951(a)(1)(A)(ii) and the regulations thereunder as an amount to which section 955 (as in

Reg. § 1.970-1(b)(5)

effect before the enactment of the Tax Reduction Act of 1975) applies, his pro rata share of the amount of such decrease in investments but only to the extent that such pro rata share does not exceed the limitations determined under subparagraph (2) of this paragraph. A United States shareholder's pro rata share of a controlled foreign corporation's decrease for any taxable year in investments in export trade assets shall be his pro rata share of such corporation's decrease for such year determined under section 970(c)(3) and paragraph (d)(3) of this section.

(2) *Limitations applicable in determining amount includible in income*—(i) *General.* A United States shareholder's pro rata share of a controlled foreign corporation's decrease in investments in export trade assets for any taxable year of such corporation shall, for purposes of determining an amount to be included in the gross income for any taxable year of such shareholder, not exceed the lesser of the limitations determined under *(a)* and *(b)* of this subdivision:

(a) Such shareholder's pro rata share of the sum of the controlled foreign corporation's earnings and profits (or deficit in earnings and profits) for the taxable year, computed as of the close of the taxable year without diminution by reason of any distributions made during the taxable year, plus his pro rata share of the sum of its earnings and profits (or deficits in earnings and profits) accumulated for prior taxable years beginning after December 31, 1962, or

(b)(1) Such shareholder's pro rata share of the sum of the amounts by which the subpart F income of such controlled foreign corporation for prior taxable years was reduced under section 970(a) and paragraph (b) of this section, plus

(2) Such shareholder's pro rata share of the sum of the amounts which were not included in the subpart F income of such controlled foreign corporation for such prior taxable years by reason of the application of section 972 and § 1.972-1, minus

(3) Such shareholder's pro rata share of the sum of the amounts which were previously included in his gross income for prior taxable years under section 951(a)(1)(A)(ii) by reason of the application of section 970(b) and this paragraph with respect to such controlled foreign corporation. The net amount determined under *(b)* of this subdivision with respect to any stock owned by the United States shareholder shall be determined without taking into account any amount attributable to a period prior to the date on which such shareholder acquired such stock. See section 1248 and the regulations thereunder for rules governing the treatment of gain from sales or exchanges of stock in certain foreign corporations.

(ii) *Treatment of earnings and profits.* For purposes of determining earnings and profits of a controlled foreign corporation under subdivision (i)*(a)* of this subparagraph, such earnings and profits shall be considered not to include any amounts which are attributable to—

(a) Amounts which are, or have been, included in the gross income of a United States shareholder of such controlled foreign corporation under section 951(a) (other than an amount included in the gross income of a United States shareholder under section 951(a)(1)(A)(ii) or section 951 (a)(1)(B) for the taxable year) and have not been distributed, or

(b)(1) Amounts which, for the current taxable year, are included in the gross income of a United States shareholder of such controlled foreign corporation under section 551(b) or would be so included under such section but for the fact that such amounts were distributed to such shareholder during the taxable year, or

(2) Amounts which, for any prior taxable year, have been included in the gross income of a United States shareholder of such controlled foreign corporation under section 551(b) and have not been distributed. The rules of this subdivision apply only in determining the limitation on a United States shareholder's pro rata share of a controlled foreign corporation's decrease in investments in export trade assets. See section 959 and the regulations thereunder for limitations on the exclusion of previously taxed earnings and profits.

(iii) *Rules of application.* The determinations made under subdivision (i) of this subparagraph for purposes of determining the United States shareholder's pro rata share of a controlled foreign corporation's decrease in investments in export trade assets for any taxable year shall be made on the basis of the stock such shareholder owns, within the meaning of section 958(a) and the regulations thereunder, in the controlled foreign corporation on the last day in the taxable year on which such corporation is a controlled foreign corporation even though such shareholder owned more or less stock in such corporation prior to that date. See section 972 and paragraph (b)(3) of § 1.972-1 for rules relating to the allocation of a decrease in investments in export trade assets of export trade corporations in a consolidated chain of such corporations. See section 951(a)(3) and the regulations thereunder for an additional limitation upon the amount of a United States shareholder's pro rata share determined under this paragraph.

(3) *Illustrations.* The application of this paragraph may be illustrated by the following examples:

Example (1). Foreign corporation A, which has one class of stock outstanding, is a wholly

Reg. § 1.970-1(c)(3)

50,804 Income from Sources Without the United States

See p. 20,601 for regulations not amended to reflect law changes

owned subsidiary of domestic corporation M throughout 1963 and 1964. Both corporations use the calendar year as the taxable year. For 1963, A Corporation qualifies as an export trade corporation and its subpart F income, determined in accordance with the provisions of section 952 and the regulations thereunder, is reduced by $20 under the provisions of section 970(a) and paragraph (b) of this section. Section 972 is assumed not to apply to A Corporation. For 1964, A Corporation has a decrease of $8 in investments in export trade assets. For 1963 and 1964, A Corporation has earnings and profits of $30 (determined under the provisions of subparagraph (2) of this paragraph). Corporation M's pro rata share of A Corporation's decrease in investments in export trade assets for 1964 which is includible in M Corporation's gross income for 1964 under section 951(a)(1)(A)(ii) by reason of the application of section 970(b) is $8, determined as follows:

(i) Corporation M's pro rata share of A Corporation's decrease in investments in export trade assets for 1964 (100% of $8) $8
(ii) Limitation on amount includible in gross income of M Corporation for 1964 (smaller of (a) or (b)):
  (a) Corporation M's pro rata share of A Corporation's earnings and profits for 1963 and 1964 determined under subparagraph (2) of this paragraph (100% of $30) $30
  (b) Corporation M's pro rata share of amounts by which the subpart F income of A Corporation for 1963 was reduced under sec. 970(a)(100% of $20) $20
  Plus: Corporation M's pro rata share of amounts which were not included in subpart F income of A Corporation for 1963 by reason of the application of sec. 972 0
    Total $20
  Less: Corporation M's pro rata share of the sum of amounts which were previously included in gross income of M Corporation under sec. 951(a)(1)(A)(ii) by reason of the application of sec. 970(b) with respect to A Corporation 0   20

(iii) Corporation M's pro rata share includible in gross income for 1964 under sec. 951(a)(1)(A)(ii) by reason of the application of sec. 970(b) (smaller of (i) or (ii)) $8

Example (2). Assume the same facts as in example (1), except that on February 14, 1965, M Corporation sells 25 percent of its stock in A Corporation to N Corporation. Corporation N is a domestic corporation which also uses the calendar year as a taxable year. For 1965, A Corporation has a decrease of $16 in investments in export trade assets. Corporation A's earnings and profits for 1963 and 1964 (determined under the provisions of subparagraph (2) of this paragraph) are $22 ($30 minus $8). Corporation A's earnings and profits for 1965 are $6 (determined under the provisions of subparagraph (2) of this paragraph). For 1965, M Corporation's pro rata share of A Corporation's decrease in investments in export trade assets which is includible in M Corporation's gross income under section 951(a)(1)(A)(ii) is $9, and N Corporation's pro rata share includible in gross income under such section is $0, determined as follows:

M CORPORATION

(i) Corporation M's pro rata share of A Corporation's decrease in investments in export trade assets for 1965 (75% of $16) $12
(ii) Limitation on amount includible in gross income of M Corporation for 1965 (smaller of (a) or (b)):
  (a) Corporation M's pro rata share of A Corporation's earnings and profits for 1963, 1964, and 1965 determined under subparagraph (2) of this paragraph (75% of $28) $21
  (b) Corporation M's pro rata share of amounts by which the subpart F income of A Corporation for 1963 was reduced under sec. 970(a) (75% of $20) $15
  Plus: Corporation M's pro rata share of amounts which were not included in subpart F income of A Corporation for 1963 and 1964 by reason of the application of sec. 972 .... $ 0
    Total $15

Reg. § 1.970-1(c)(3)

Income from Sources Without the United States

Less: Corporation M's pro rata share of the sum of amounts which were previously included in gross income of M Corporation under sec. 951(a)(1)(A)(ii) by reason of the application of sec. 970(b) with respect to A Corporation (75% of $8).................... $6

(iii) Corporation M's pro rata share includible in gross income for 1965 under sec. 951(a)(1)(A)(ii) by reason of the application of sec. 970(b) (smaller of (i) or (ii)) $9

N CORPORATION

(i) Corporation N's pro rata share of A Corporation's decrease in investments in export trade assets for 1965 (25% of $16) $4

(ii) Limitation on amount includible in gross income of N Corporation for 1965 (smaller of (a) or (b)):

(a) Corporation N's pro rata share of A Corporation's earnings and profits for 1963, 1964, and 1965 determined under subparagraph (2) of this paragraph (25% of $28)........................ $7

(b) Corporation N's pro rata share of amounts by which the subpart F income of A Corporation for 1963 was reduced under sec. 970(a) (amounts prior to 2/14/65 not being taken into account) $0

Plus: Corporation N's pro rata share of amounts which were not included in subpart F income of A Corporation for 1963 and 1964 by reason of the application of sec. 972 (amounts prior to 2/14/65 not being taken into account) $0

Total $0

Less: Corporation N's pro rata share of the sum of amounts which were previously included in gross income of N Corporation under sec. 951(a)(1)(A)(ii) by reason of the application of sec. 970(b) with respect to A Corporation (amounts prior to 2/14/65 not being taken into account) $0 $0

(iii) Corporation N's pro rata share includible in gross income for 1965 under sec. 951(a)(1)(A)(ii) by reason of the application of sec. 970(b) (smaller of (i) or (ii)) $0

$9

(d) *Investments in export trade assets*—(1) *Amount of investments.* For purposes of sections 970 through 972 and §§ 1.970-1 to 1.972-1, inclusive, export trade assets shall be taken into account on the following bases:

(i) *Working capital.* Working capital to which section 971(c)(1) applies shall be taken into account at the adjusted basis of current assets, determined as of the applicable determination date, less any current liabilities (except as provided in subdivision (iii) of this subparagraph).

(ii) *Other export trade assets.* Inventory to which section 971(c)(2) applies, facilities to which section 971(c)(3) applies, and evidences of indebtedness to which section 971(c)(4) applies, shall be taken into account at their adjusted bases as of the applicable determination date, reduced by any liabilities (except as provided in subdivision (iii) of this subparagraph) to which such property is subject on such date. To be taken into account under this subparagraph, a liability must constitute a specific charge against the property involved. Thus, a liability evidenced by an open account or a liability secured only by the general credit of the controlled foreign corporation will not be taken into account. On the other hand, if a liability constitutes a specific charge against several items of property and cannot definitely be allocated to any single item of property, the liability shall be apportioned against each of such items of property in that ratio which the adjusted basis of such item on the applicable determination date bears to the adjusted basis of all such items on such date. A liability in excess of the adjusted basis of the property which is subject to such liability will not be taken into account for the purpose of reducing the adjusted basis of other property which is not subject to such liability. See paragraph (c)(6) of § 1.971-1 for treatment of export trade assets which constitute working capital to which section 971(c)(1) applies and which also constitute inventory to which section 971(c)(2) applies or evidences of indebtedness to which section 971(c)(4) applies.

(iii) *Treatment of certain liabilities.* For purposes of subdivisions (i) and (ii) of this subparagraph, a current liability, or a specific charge created with respect to any item of property, principally for the purpose of artificially increasing or decreasing the amount of a controlled foreign corporation's investments in export trade assets shall be taken into account in such a manner as to properly reflect the controlled foreign corporation's investments in export trade assets; whether a specific charge or current liability is created principally for such purpose will depend upon all the facts and circumstances of each case. One of the factors that will be considered in making such a determination with respect to a loan is

Reg. § 1.970-1(d)(1)

whether the loan is from a related person, as defined in section 954(d)(3) and paragraph (e) of § 1.954-1.

(iv) *Statement required.* If for purposes of this section a United States shareholder of a controlled foreign corporation reduces the adjusted basis of property which constitutes an export trade asset on the ground that such property is subject to a liability, he shall attach to his return a statement setting forth the adjusted basis of the property before the reduction and the amount and nature of the reduction.

(2) *Increase in investments in export trade assets.* For purposes of section 970(a) and paragraph (b) of this section, the amount of increase in investments in export trade assets of a controlled foreign corporation for a taxable year shall be, except as provided in § 1.970-2, the amount by which—

(i) The amount of its investments in export trade assets at the close of such taxable year, exceeds

(ii) The amount of its investments in export trade assets at the close of the preceding taxable year.

(3) *Decrease in investments in export trade assets.* For purposes of section 970(b) and paragraph (c) of this section, the amount of the decrease in investments in export trade assets of a controlled foreign corporation for a taxable year shall be, except as provided in § 1.970-2, the amount by which—

(i) The amount of its investments in export trade assets at the close of the preceding taxable year, minus

(ii) An amount equal to the excess of recognized losses over recognized gains on sales, exchanges, involuntary conversions, or other dispositions, of export trade assets during the taxable year, exceeds

(iii) The amount of its investments in export trade assets at the close of the taxable year.

For purposes of subdivision (ii) of this subparagraph, recognized losses include a write-down of inventory to lower of cost or market in accordance with a method of inventory valuation established or adopted by or on behalf of such foreign corporation under paragraph (c) of § 1.964-1. [Reg. § 1.970-1.]

☐ [T.D. 6755, 9-8-64. *Amended by* T.D. 6795, 1-28-65, T.D. 6892, 8-22-66, T.D. 7293, 11-27-73 and T.D. 7893, 5-11-83.]

[Reg. § 1.970-2]

§ 1.970-2. Elections as to date of determining investments in export trade assets.—(a) *Nature of elections*—(1) *In general.* In lieu of determining the increase under the provisions of paragraph (d)(2) of § 1.970-1, or the decrease under the provisions of paragraph (d)(3) of § 1.970-1, in a controlled foreign corporation's investments in export trade assets for a taxable year in the manner provided in such provisions, a United States shareholder of such corporation may elect, under the provisions of section 970(c)(4) and this section, to determine such increase or decrease in accordance with the provisions of subparagraph (2) of this paragraph or, in the case of export trade assets which are facilities described in section 971(c)(3), in accordance with the provisions of subparagraph (3) of this paragraph. Separate elections may be made under subparagraph (2) and/or (3) of this paragraph with respect to each controlled foreign corporation with respect to which a person is a United States shareholder, within the meaning of section 951(b).

(2) *Election of 75-day rule.* A United States shareholder of a controlled foreign corporation may elect with respect to a taxable year of such corporation to make the determinations under subparagraphs (2)(i) and (3)(iii) of paragraph (d) of § 1.970-1 of the amount of such corporation's investments in export trade assets as of the 75th day after the close of the taxable year referred to in such subparagraphs of paragraph (d) of § 1.970-1. The election provided by this subparagraph may be made with respect to export trade assets other than facilities described in section 971(c)(3) or with respect to export trade assets which are facilities or with respect to both types of export trade assets (but the election under this paragraph with respect to export trade assets which are facilities or with respect to both types of export trade assets may be made only if the election provided by subparagraph (3) of this paragraph is not made). If the election provided by this subparagraph is made, the amount of export trade assets with respect to which such election is made at the close of the preceding taxable year which is described in subparagraphs (2)(ii) and (3)(i) of paragraph (d) of § 1.970-1 shall be the amount of export trade assets which was considered by application of the 75-day rule to be the amount of export trade assets at the close of such preceding taxable year; except that for the first taxable year of the controlled foreign corporation for which the 75-day rule is elected the amount of investments in export trade assets with respect to which such election is made at the close of such preceding year described in subparagraphs (2)(ii) and (3)(i) of paragraph (d) of § 1.970-1 shall be

Income from Sources Without the United States 50,807

See p. 20,601 for regulations not amended to reflect law changes

the amount of investments in export trade assets at the actual close of such preceding year. In the case of a taxable year of such corporation beginning after December 31, 1962, and before December 31, 1963, the amount of investments in export trade assets with respect to which such election is made alternatively may be determined by the United States shareholder as of the 75th day after the close of the preceding taxable year referred to in subparagraphs (2)(ii) and (3)(i) of paragraph (d) of § 1.970-1 rather than as of the close of such preceding taxable year.

(3) *Election for export trade assets which are facilities.* A United States shareholder of a controlled foreign corporation may elect with respect to a taxable year of such corporation to make the determinations under subparagraphs (2)(i) and (3)(iii) of paragraph (d) of § 1.970-1 of the amount of such corporation's investments in export trade assets which are facilities described in section 971(c)(3) as of the close of such corporation's taxable year following the taxable year referred to in such subparagraphs of paragraph (d) of § 1.970-1. The election provided by this subparagraph may be made only if the United States shareholder does not elect the 75-day rule of subparagraph (2) of this paragraph with respect to export trade assets which are facilities. If the election provided by this subparagraph is made, the amount of investments in export trade assets which are facilities at the close of the preceding taxable year which is described in subparagraphs (2)(ii) and (3)(i) of paragraph (d) of § 1.970-1 shall be the amount of export trade assets which are facilities which was considered, by reason of the application of the following-year rule provided in this subparagraph with respect to such preceding taxable year, to be the amount of export trade assets which are facilities at the close of such preceding taxable year; except that for the first taxable year of the controlled foreign corporation for which such following-year rule is elected the amount of investments in export trade assets which are facilities at the close of the preceding taxable year described in subparagraphs (2)(ii) and (3)(i) of paragraph (d) of § 1.970-1 shall be the amount of investments in export trade assets which are facilities at the actual close of such preceding taxable year.

(b) *Time and manner of making elections*—(1) *Without consent.* A United States shareholder may, with respect to any controlled foreign corporation, make one or both of the elections described in paragraph (a)(2) or (3) of this section without the consent of the Commissioner by filing a statement to such effect with his return for his taxable year in which or with which ends the first taxable year of such corporation in which—

(i) Such shareholder owns, within the meaning of section 958(a), or is considered as owning, by applying the rules of section 958(b), 10 percent or more of the total combined voting power of all classes of stock entitled to vote of such corporation, and

(ii) Such corporation realizes subpart F income which is reduced under section 970(a) and paragraph (b) of § 1.970-1.

The statement shall contain the name and address of the controlled foreign corporation, identification of such first taxable year of such corporation, and an indication as to which election or elections described in paragraph (a) of this section the United States shareholder is making. If such return has been filed on or before the 90th day after the date these regulations are published in the Federal Register, such United States shareholder shall file such statement with the district director with which the return was filed on or before such 90th day.

(2) *With consent.* A United States shareholder may make one or both of the elections described in paragraph (a)(2) or (3) of this section with respect to any controlled foreign corporation at any time with the consent of the Commissioner. Consent will not be granted unless the shareholder and the Commissioner agree to the terms, conditions, and adjustments under which the election will be effected. The application for consent to elect shall be made by the shareholder's mailing a letter for such purpose to the Commissioner of Internal Revenue, Washington, D.C. 20224. The application shall be mailed before the close of the first taxable year of the controlled foreign corporation with respect to which the shareholder desires to determine an exclusion under section 970(a) in accordance with one or both of the elections provided in paragraph (a) of this section. The application shall include the following information:

(i) The name, address, and taxable year of the United States shareholder;

(ii) The name, address, and taxable year of the controlled foreign corporation;

(iii) A statement indicating which of the elections the shareholder desires to make;

(iv) The amount of the foreign corporation's investments in export trade assets (by a category which includes export trade assets other than facilities and a category which includes only export trade assets which are facilities) at the close of its preceding taxable year;

(v) The shareholder's pro rata share of the sum of the amounts by which the subpart F income of the foreign corporation, for all prior taxa-

Reg. § 1.970-2(b)(2)

ble years during which such shareholder was a United States shareholder of such corporation, was reduced under section 970(a) and paragraph (b) of § 1.970-1;

(vi) The shareholder's pro rata share of the sum of the amounts which were not included in the subpart F income of the foreign corporation, for all prior taxable years during which such shareholder was a United States shareholder of such corporation, by reason of the application of section 972 and § 1.972-1; and

(vii) The shareholder's pro rata share of the sum of the amounts which were previously included in his gross income, for all prior taxable years during which such shareholder was a United States shareholder of such corporation, under section 951(a)(1)(A)(ii) by reason of the application of section 970(b) and paragraph (b) of § 1.970-1 to the foreign corporation.

(c) *Effect of elections*—(1) *General.* Except as provided in subparagraphs (3) and (4) of this paragraph, an election made under paragraph (a) of this section with respect to a controlled foreign corporation shall be binding on the United States shareholder and—

(i) In the case of the election described in paragraph (a)(2) of this section, shall apply to all investments in export trade assets with respect to which such election is made, acquired, or disposed of, by such corporation during the 75-day period following its taxable year for which subpart F income is first computed under the election and during all succeeding corresponding 75-day periods of such corporation, or

(ii) In the case of the election described in paragraph (a)(3) of this section, shall apply to all investments in export trade assets which are facilities acquired, or disposed of, by such corporation during the taxable year following its taxable year for which subpart F income is first computed under the election and during all succeeding corresponding taxable years of such corporation.

(2) *Returns.* Any return of a United States shareholder required to be filed before the completion of a period with respect to which determinations are to be made as to a controlled foreign corporation's investments in export trade assets for purposes of computing such shareholder's taxable income shall be filed on the basis of an estimate of the amount of such corporation's investments in export trade assets at the close of the period. If the actual amount of such investments is not the same as the amount of the estimate, the shareholder shall immediately notify the Commissioner. The Commissioner will thereupon redetermine the amount of such shareholder's tax for the year or years with respect to which the incorrect amount was taken into account. The amount of tax, if any, due upon such redetermination shall be paid by the shareholder upon notice and demand by the district director. The amount of tax, if any, shown by such redetermination to have been overpaid shall be credited or refunded to the shareholder in accordance with the provisions of sections 6402 and 6511 and the regulations thereunder.

(3) *Revocation*—(i) *In general*—(a) *Consent required.* Upon application by the United States shareholder, an election made under paragraph (a) of this section may, subject to the approval of the Commissioner, be revoked. Approval will not be granted unless the shareholder and the Commissioner agree to the terms, conditions, and adjustments under which the revocation will be effected.

(b) *Revocation of 75-day rule.* In the case of the revocation of an election described in paragraph (a)(2) of this section, the change in the controlled foreign corporation's investments in export trade assets with respect to which such election was made for its first taxable year for which subpart F income or a decrease in investments in export trade assets is computed without regard to the election previously made shall, unless the agreement with the Commissioner provides otherwise, be considered to be the amount by which—

(1) Such corporation's investments in export trade assets with respect to which such election was made at the close of such taxable year exceeds or, if applicable, is exceeded by

(2) Such corporation's investments in export trade assets with respect to which such election was made at the close of the 75th day after the close of the preceding taxable year of such corporation.

(c) *Revocation of following-year rule.* In the case of the revocation of an election described in paragraph (a)(3) of this section, the change in the controlled foreign corporation's investments in export trade assets which are facilities for its first taxable year for which subpart F income or a decrease in investments in export trade assets is computed without regard to the election previously made shall, unless the agreement with the Commissioner provides otherwise, be considered to be zero.

(ii) *Time and manner of applying for consent to revocation*—(a) *Application to Commissioner.* The application for consent to revocation of an election shall be made by the United States shareholder's mailing a letter for such purpose to the Commissioner of Internal Revenue, Washington, D.C., 20224. The application shall be mailed before the close of the first taxable year of the

Reg. § 1.970-2(c)(1)

Income from Sources Without the United States

controlled foreign corporation with respect to which the shareholder desires to determine an exclusion under section 970(a) or an inclusion under section 970(b) without regard to such election.

(*b*) *Information required.* The application shall include the following information:

(*1*) The name, address, and taxable year of the United States shareholder;

(*2*) The name, address, and taxable year of the controlled foreign corporation;

(*3*) A statement indicating the election the shareholder desires to revoke under this subparagraph;

(*4*) The information required under subdivisions (iv) through (vii) of paragraph (b)(2) of this section;

(*5*) In the case of an application for consent to revocation of an election made under paragraph (a)(2) of this section, the amount of the foreign corporation's investments in export trade assets with respect to which such election was made at the close of the 75th day after the close of such corporation's taxable year immediately preceding the taxable year of such corporation; and

(*6*) The reason for the request for consent to revocation.

(4) *Transfer of stock* —(i) *Election of 75-day rule in force.* (a) If during any taxable year of a controlled foreign corporation—

(*1*) A United States shareholder who has made the election described in paragraph (a)(2) of this section with respect to such corporation sells, exchanges, or otherwise disposes of all or part of his stock in such corporation, and

(*2*) The foreign corporation is a controlled foreign corporation immediately after the sale, exchange, or other disposition,

then, with respect to the stock so sold, exchanged, or disposed of, the successor in interest shall consider the controlled foreign corporation's change during the first 75 days of such taxable year in investments in export trade assets with respect to which such election is made to be zero.

(*b*) If the United States shareholder's successor in interest makes an election under paragraph (a)(2) of this section in order to determine an exclusion under section 970(a) for the taxable year of such corporation in which he acquires such stock, the amount of the controlled foreign corporation's investments in export trade assets with respect to which such election is made at the close of its preceding taxable year shall be considered, with respect to the stock so acquired, to be the amount of such corporation's investments in export trade assets with respect to which such election is made at the close of the 75th day after the close of such preceding taxable year.

(*c*) If the United States shareholder's successor in interest makes an election under paragraph (a)(2) of this section in order to determine an exclusion under section 970(a) for a taxable year of such corporation subsequent to the taxable year in which he acquired the stock, the amount of the controlled foreign corporation's investments in export trade assets with respect to which such election is made at the close of its taxable year immediately preceding such subsequent taxable year shall, with respect to the stock so acquired, be the amount of such corporation's investments in such assets at the actual close of such preceding taxable year.

(ii) *Election in force with respect to export trade assets which are facilities.* (a) If during any taxable year of a controlled foreign corporation—

(*1*) A United States shareholder who has made the election described in paragraph (a)(3) of this section with respect to such corporation sells, exchanges, or otherwise disposes of all or part of his stock in such corporation, and

(*2*) The foreign corporation is a controlled foreign corporation immediately after the sale, exchange or other disposition,

then, with respect to the stock so sold, exchanged, or disposed of, the successor in interest shall consider the controlled foreign corporation's change for such taxable year in investments in export trade assets which are facilities to be zero.

(*b*) If the United States shareholder's successor in interest makes an election under paragraph (a)(3) of this section in order to determine an exclusion under section 970(a) for the taxable year of such corporation in which he acquires such stock, the amount of the controlled foreign corporation's investments in export trade assets which are facilities at the close of its preceding taxable year shall be considered, with respect to the stock so acquired, to be the amount of such corporation's investments in export trade assets which are facilities at the close of the taxable year in which such stock is acquired.

(*c*) If the United States shareholder's successor in interest makes an election under paragraph (a)(3) of this section in order to determine an exclusion under section 970(a) for a taxable year of such corporation subsequent to the taxable year in which he acquired the stock, the amount of the controlled foreign corporation's investments in export trade assets which are facilities at the close of its taxable year immediately preceding such subsequent taxable year shall, with respect to the stock so acquired, be the amount of such

Reg. § 1.970-2(c)(4)

corporation's investments in such assets at the actual close of such preceding taxable year.

(d) *Illustrations.* The principles contained in this section are illustrated by the examples set forth in paragraph (d) of § 1.955-3. [Reg. § 1.970-2.]

☐ [T.D. 6755, 9-8-64.]

[Reg. § 1.970-3]

§ 1.970-3. **Effective date of subpart G.**—Sections 970 through 972 and §§ 1.970-1 through 1.972-1 shall apply with respect to taxable years of foreign corporations beginning after December 31, 1962, and to taxable years of United States shareholders within which or with which such taxable years of such corporations end. [Reg. § 1.970-3.]

☐ [T.D. 6755, 9-8-64.]

[Reg. § 1.971-1]

§ 1.971-1. **Definitions with respect to export trade corporations.**—(a) *Export trade corporations*—(1) *In general.* For purposes of sections 970 through 972 and §§ 1.970-1 to 1.972-1, inclusive, the term "export trade corporation" means a controlled foreign corporation which for the period specified in subparagraph (2) of this paragraph satisfies the conditions specified in subparagraph (3) of this paragraph. However, no controlled foreign corporation may qualify as an export trade corporation for any taxable year beginning after October 31, 1971, unless it qualified as an export trade corporation for any taxable year beginning before such date. In addition, if a corporation fails to qualify as an export trade corporation for a period of any 3 consecutive taxable years beginning after October 31, 1971, then for any taxable year beginning after such 3 year period, such corporation shall not be included within the term "export trade corporation".

(2) *Three-year period.* The period referred to in subparagraph (1) of this paragraph is the 3-year period ending with the close of the controlled foreign corporation's current taxable year, or such part of such 3-year period as occurs on and after the beginning of the corporation's first taxable year beginning after December 31, 1962, whichever period is shorter.

(3) *Gross income requirements.* The conditions referred to in subparagraph (1) of this paragraph are that the controlled foreign corporation derives—

(i) 90 percent or more of its gross income from sources without the United States, and

(ii) (a) 75 percent or more of its gross income from transactions, activities, or interest described in section 971(b) and paragraph (b) of this section, or

(b) 50 percent or more of its gross income from transactions, activities, or interest described in section 971(b) and paragraph (b) of this section in respect of agricultural products grown in the United States.

(4) *Determination of sources of gross income.* The sources of gross income of a controlled foreign corporation shall be determined for purposes of subparagraph (3)(i) of this paragraph in accordance with the rules for determining sources of gross income set forth in sections 861 through 864 and the regulations thereunder.

(b) *Export trade income*—(1) *General rule.* For purposes of sections 970 through 972 and §§ 1.970-1 to 1.972-1, inclusive, the term "export trade income" means the gross export trade income of a controlled foreign corporation derived from transactions, activities, or interest described in subdivisions (i) through (vii) of this subparagraph, less deductions allowed under subdivision (viii) of this subparagraph.

(i) *Sale of export property.* Gross export trade income of a controlled foreign corporation includes gross income it derives from the sale of export property (as defined in paragraph (e) of this section) which it purchases, if the sale is made to an unrelated person for use, consumption, or disposition outside the United States. See section 971(b)(1). As a general rule, property will be presumed to have been sold for use, consumption, or disposition in the country of destination of the sale. However, if at the time of the sale the controlled foreign corporation knows, or should have known from the facts and circumstances surrounding the sales transaction, that the property will probably be used, consumed, or disposed of in the United States, such property will be presumed to have been sold for use, consumption, or disposition in the United States unless the controlled foreign corporation establishes that such property was used, consumed, or disposed of outside the United States. For purposes of this subdivision, export property must be sold by a controlled foreign corporation in essentially the same form in which such property is purchased. Whether export property sold is in essentially the same form in which such property is purchased shall be determined on the basis of all the facts and circumstances in each case. Storage, handling, transportation, packaging, or servicing of property will be considered not to alter the form in which property is purchased. However, manufacture or production, within the meaning of paragraph (a)(4) of § 1.954-3, will be considered to alter the form in which property is purchased and no part of the gross income from the sale of such property will be treated as export trade income. The application of this subdivision may be illustrated by the following example:

Example. Controlled foreign corporation A, incorporated under the laws of foreign country Y, purchases articles manufactured in the United States from domestic corporation M and sells them in the form in which purchased to foreign corporation B, unrelated to A corporation, for use in foreign countries X, Y, and Z. The gross income of A Corporation from the purchase and sale of the articles constitutes gross export trade income.

(ii) *Commissions and other income derived in connection with the sale of export property.* Gross export trade income of a controlled foreign corporation includes gross commissions, fees, compensation, or other income derived by such corporation from the performance for any person of commercial, industrial, financial, technical, scientific, managerial, engineering, architectural, skilled, or other services in respect of a sale by such corporation in a transaction described in subdivision (i) of this subparagraph or in respect of the sale by any other person of export property to a person unrelated to the controlled foreign corporation for use, consumption, or disposition outside the United States. Such gross export trade income includes payments received for surveys made prior to, and in connection with, the sale of such export property (whether or not such sales are ultimately consummated). See section 971(b)(1). The term "any person" or "any other person" as used in this subdivision includes a related person as defined in section 954(d)(3) and paragraph (e) of § 1.954-1. The application of this subdivision may be illustrated by the following examples:

Example (1). Controlled foreign corporation A, incorporated under the laws of foreign country X, receives from M Corporation a commission equal to 6 percent of the gross selling price of all personal property shipped by M Corporation as a result of services performed by A Corporation in soliciting orders in foreign countries X, Y, and Z. In fulfillment of such orders, M Corporation ships products manufactured by it in the United States. Corporation A does not assume title to the property sold. Gross commissions received by A Corporation from M Corporation in connection with the sale of such property to persons unrelated to A Corporation for use, consumption, or disposition outside the United States constitute gross export trade income.

Example (2). Foreign corporation B, incorporated under the laws of foreign country X, is a wholly owned subsidiary of domestic corporation N. Corporation N is engaged in the business of manufacturing heavy duty electrical equipment in the United States. By contract, N Corporation engages B Corporation for the purpose of conducting engineering, technical, and financial studies required by N Corporation in the preparation of bids to supply foreign country Y with electrical equipment for a construction project to be undertaken by such country. Corporation N pays B Corporation a fee for the services, all of which are performed in country Y, which is based upon the number of hours of work performed without regard to whether a sale is ultimately consummated. Corporation N does not receive a contract from country Y on its bid to supply equipment. Income derived by B Corporation from performance of the service contract constitutes gross export trade income.

(iii) *Commissions and other income derived in connection with the installation or maintenance of export property.* Gross export trade income of a controlled foreign corporation includes gross commissions, fees, compensation, or other income derived by such corporation from the performance for any person or commercial, industrial, financial, technical, scientific, managerial, engineering, architectural, skilled, or other services in respect of the installation or maintenance of export property which has been sold by such corporation in a transaction described in subdivision (i) of this subparagraph or by any other person to a person unrelated to the controlled foreign corporation for use, consumption, or disposition outside the United States. See section 971(b)(1). The term "any person" or "any other person" as used in this subdivision includes a related person as defined in section 954(d)(3) and paragraph (e) of § 1.954-1.

(iv) *Commissions and other income derived in connection with the use of patents, copyrights, and other like property.* Gross export trade income of a controlled foreign corporation includes gross commissions, fees, compensation, or other income derived by such corporation from the performance for any person of commercial, industrial, financial, technical, scientific, managerial, engineering, architectural, skilled, or other services in connection with the use outside of the United States by an unrelated person of patents, copyrights, secret processes and formulas, goodwill, trademarks, trade brands, franchises, and other like property, including gross income derived from obtaining licensees for patents, but only if the patent, copyright, or other like property is acquired, or developed, and owned by the manufacturer, producer, grower, or extractor of any export property, in respect of which the controlled foreign corporation also derives gross ex-

Reg. § 1.971-1(b)(1)

50,812 Income from Sources Without the United States

See p. 20,601 for regulations not amended to reflect law changes

port trade income within the meaning of subdivision (i), (ii), or (iii) of this subparagraph. See section 971(b)(2). The application of this subdivision may be illustrated by the following example:

Example. Foreign corporation A incorporated under the laws of foreign country X, is a wholly owned subsidiary of domestic corporation M. Corporation M, the owner of a patent registered in foreign country X, grants B Corporation, a corporation unrelated to A Corporation, the right to use such patent in foreign country Y in exchange for payment of a royalty. By a separate contract with B Corporation, A Corporation agrees for a gross fee of $100,000 to furnish, by maintaining a staff of technical representatives at the offices of B Corporation, technical services to B Corporation in connection with B Corporation's use of the patent. Corporation A also derives export trade income from the sale of export property which it purchases from M Corporation, the manufacturer of such property, and sells to C Corporation, an unrelated person, for use in country Y by C Corporation. The gross fee of $100,000 received by A Corporation for the furnishing of technical services in connection with B Corporation's use of M Corporation's patent constitutes gross export trade income since the service for which the fee is paid is performed in connection with the use outside the United States by an unrelated person (B Corporation) of a patent owned by a manufacturer (M Corporation) of export property in respect of which the controlled foreign corporation (A Corporation) derives gross export trade income from the sale to an unrelated person (C Corporation) for use outside the United States of export property purchased by it from the manufacturer (M Corporation).

(v) *Income attributable to use of export property by an unrelated person.* Gross export trade income of a controlled foreign corporation includes gross commissions, fees, rents, compensation, or other income which is received by such corporation from an unrelated person and is attributable to the use of export property by such unrelated person. See section 971(b)(3). The application of this subdivision may be illustrated by the following example:

Example. Foreign corporation A, incorporated under the laws of foreign country X, is a wholly owned subsidiary of domestic corporation M. Corporation A acquires by purchase bottling machines manufactured in the United States and leases the machines to B Corporation, a corporation unrelated to A Corporation, for use by B Corporation in foreign country Y. Gross rental income of A Corporation from the lease of the machines to B Corporation constitutes gross export trade income.

(vi) *Income attributable to the use of export property in the rendition of technical, scientific, or engineering services*—(a) *General.* Gross export trade income of a controlled foreign corporation includes gross commissions, fees, compensation, or other income which is received by such corporation from an unrelated person and is attributable to the use of export property in the performance of technical, scientific, or engineering services to such unrelated person. See section 971(b)(3).

(b) *Rule of apportionment.* If a commission, fee, or other income received by a controlled foreign corporation from an unrelated person under a contract or arrangement for the performance of technical, scientific, or engineering services is not solely attributable to the use of export property in the performance of such services and the amount of the gross income attributable to such use of export property cannot be established by reference to transactions between other unrelated persons, such gross income shall be an amount which bears the same ratio to total gross income from the contract or arrangement as the cost of the export property consumed in the performance of such services, including a reasonable allowance for depreciation with respect to the export property so used, bears to the total costs and expenses attributable to the production of income under the contract or arrangement.

(c) *Illustration.* The application of this subdivision may be illustrated by the following example:

Example. Foreign corporation A, incorporated under the laws of foreign country X, is a wholly owned subsidiary of domestic corporation M. Corporation A is engaged in the seismograph service business in foreign country X. In an effort to establish the probable existence of oil in a concession area it owns in foreign country Y, B Corporation which is unrelated to A Corporation enters into a contract with A Corporation whereby A Corporation is required to make seismographic tests of the area in country Y for a fixed fee of $100,000. In performance of the contract, A Corporation hires a skilled crew to carry out the contract and utilizes equipment and supplies (for example, trucks, seismographic equipment, etc.) which constitute export property. Corporation A cannot establish by reference to transactions between other unrelated persons, the income attributable to the use of the export property in the performance of the contract. Corporation A's total costs and expenses (for example, salaries of the crew, administrative expenses, all

Reg. § 1.971-1(b)(1)

supplies, total depreciation on property used in performance of the contract, etc.) incurred in performance of the contract are $80,000. The cost of export property consumed in performance of the contract (for example, dynamite, motor oil, and other supplies which were produced in the United States, reasonable depreciation on trucks and seismographic equipment manufactured in the United States and used in performance of the contract, etc.) is $30,000. Corporation A's gross export trade income from the contract is $37,500, that is, the amount which bears the same ratio to total gross income from the contract ($100,000) as the cost of the export property consumed in the rendition of the services ($30,000) bears to total costs and expenses attributable to the contract ($80,000).

(vii) *Interest from export trade assets.* Gross export trade income of a controlled foreign corporation includes interest derived by it from export trade assets described in section 971(c)(4) and paragraph (c)(5) of this section. See section 971(b)(4).

(viii) *Deductions to be taken into account.* Export trade income of a controlled foreign corporation for any taxable year shall be the amount determined by deducting from the items or categories of gross income described in subdivisions (i) through (vii) of this subparagraph the entire amount of those expenses, taxes, and other deductions properly allocable to such items or categories of income. For purposes of this section, expenses, taxes, and other deductions shall first be allocated to items or categories of gross income to which they directly relate; then, expenses, taxes, and other deductions which cannot definitely be allocated to some item or category of gross income shall be ratably apportioned among all items or categories of gross income, except that no expense, tax, or other deduction shall be allocated to an item or category of income to which it clearly does not apply and no deduction allowable to such controlled foreign corporation under section 882(c) and the regulations thereunder shall be taken into account.

(2) *Cross reference.* For rules governing the determination of gross income and taxable income of a foreign corporation, see § 1.952-2.

(c) *Export trade assets*—(1) *In general.* For purposes of sections 970 through 972 and §§ 1.970-1 to 1.972-1, inclusive, the term "export trade assets" means—

(i) Working capital reasonably necessary for the production of export trade income,

(ii) Inventory of export property held for use, consumption, or disposition outside the United States,

(iii) Facilities located outside the United States for the storage, handling, transportation, packaging, servicing, sale, or distribution of export property, and

(iv) Evidences of indebtedness executed by unrelated persons in connection with payment for purchases of export property for use, consumption, or disposition outside the United States, or in connection with the payment for services described in section 971(b)(2) or (3) and paragraph (b)(1)(iv), (v), or (vi) of this section.

(2) *Working capital.* For purposes of subparagraph (1)(i) of this paragraph, working capital of a controlled foreign corporation is the excess of its current assets over its current liabilities. Liabilities maturing in one year or less shall be considered current liabilities. A determination of the amount of working capital of a controlled foreign corporation which is reasonably necessary for the production of export trade income will depend upon the nature and volume of the activities of the controlled foreign corporation which produce export trade income as they exist on the applicable determination date. In determining working capital which is reasonably necessary for the production of export trade income, the anticipated future needs of the business will be taken into account to the extent that such needs relate to the year of the controlled foreign corporation following the applicable determination date; anticipated future needs relating to a later period will not be taken into account unless it is clearly established that such needs are reasonably related to the production of export trade income as of the applicable determination date.

(3) *Inventory of export property.* For purposes of subparagraph (1)(ii) of this paragraph, the inclusion of items in inventory shall be determined in accordance with rules applicable to domestic corporations. See §§ 1.471-1 through 1.471-9. Inventory of export property of a controlled foreign corporation includes export property held for use, consumption, or disposition outside the United States regardless of where it is located on the applicable determination date. Thus, such property may be physically located in the United States on such date. However, for property physically located in the United States to constitute export property, it must have been acquired by the controlled foreign corporation with a clear intent that it would dispose of the property for use, consumption, or disposition outside the United States. As a general rule, if during the year following the applicable determination date export property which was physically located in the United States on such date is actually exported for use, consumption, or disposition

outside the United States, such property will be deemed held for such purpose on the applicable determination date. On the other hand, the indefinite warehousing of export property in the United States by the controlled foreign corporation, or the subsequent sale of export property by such corporation for use, consumption, or disposition in the United States, will evidence a lack of intent by such corporation on the applicable determination date to hold such property for use, consumption, or disposition outside the United States.

(4) *Facilities located outside the United States*—(i) *In general.* For purposes of subparagraph (1)(iii) of this paragraph, a facility, as defined in subdivision (ii)(a) of this subparagraph, will be considered an export trade asset only—

(a) If such facility is located outside the United States, and

(b) To the extent that such facility is used, within the meaning of subdivision (ii)(c) of this subparagraph, by the controlled foreign corporation for the storage, handling, transportation, packaging, servicing, sale, or distribution of export property in essentially the same form in which such property is acquired by such corporation.

Thus, a facility in which property is manufactured or produced, even though export property is used or consumed in the production or becomes a component part of the manufactured article, will not qualify as an export trade asset.

(ii) *Special rules*—(a) *Facility defined.* For purposes of subdivision (i) of this subparagraph, the term "facility" includes any asset or group of assets used for the storage, handling, transportation, packaging, servicing, sale, or distribution of export property. Thus, such term includes warehouse, storage, or sales facilities (for example, sales office equipment), transportation equipment (for example, motor trucks, vessels, etc.), and machinery and equipment (for example, packaging equipment, servicing equipment, cranes, fork lift trucks used in warehouses, etc.).

(b) *Determination of location of transportation facilities.* A transportation facility shall be considered to be located outside the United States for purposes of subdivision (i)(a) of this subparagraph if such property is predominantly located outside the United States. As a general rule, on an applicable determination date a transportation facility will be considered to be predominantly located outside the United States if 70 percent or more of the miles traversed (during the 12-month period immediately preceding such determination date or for such part of such period as such facility is owned by the controlled foreign corporation) in the use of such facility are traversed outside the United States or if such facility is located outside the United States at least 70 percent of the time during such period or such part thereof.

(c) *Determination of use.* For purposes of subdivision (i)(b) of this subparagraph, the extent to which a facility is used in carrying on the activities described in such subdivision depends on the use made of the facility for the 12-month period immediately preceding the applicable determination date or for such part of such period as such facility is owned by the controlled foreign corporation. The method of measuring such use will depend upon the facts and circumstances in each case. However, such determinations of use will generally be made for a facility as a whole and not on the basis of individual items used in the operation of a facility. Thus, a determination as to the use of a warehouse facility will generally be made with respect to the entire facility and not separately for the items used in such warehouse, such as fork lift trucks, storage bins, etc.

(5) *Evidences of indebtedness.* For purposes of subparagraph (1)(iv) of this paragraph, the term "evidence of indebtedness" shall mean a note, installment sales contract, a time bill of exchange evidencing a sale on credit, or similar written instrument executed by an unrelated person which evidences the obligation of an unrelated person to pay for export property which an unrelated person purchases for use, consumption, or disposition outside the United States or to pay for services described in section 971(b)(2) or (3) and paragraph (b)(1)(iv), (v), or (vi) of this section which are performed for an unrelated person. Receivables which arise out of the delivery of export property, or the performance of services, which are evidenced by invoices, bills of lading, bills of exchange which do not evidence a sale on credit, sales slips, and similar documents created by the unilateral act of a creditor shall not be considered evidences of indebtedness for purposes of section 971(c)(4).

(6) *Duplication of treatment and priority of application.* No asset which constitutes an export trade asset shall be taken into account more than once in determining the investments in export trade assets of a controlled foreign corporation. Assets which constitute working capital and also constitute inventory to which section 971(c)(2) applies or evidences of indebtedness to which section 971(c)(4) applies shall be taken into account in determining whether the amount of working capital of the controlled foreign corporation is reasonably necessary for the production of export trade income. However, to the extent that the

Reg. § 1.971-1(c)(4)

amount of inventory to which section 971(c)(2) applies or evidences of indebtedness to which section 971(c)(4) applies is not included in working capital to which section 971(c)(1) applies on the ground that such amount is not reasonably necessary for the production of export trade income, the amount shall be included under section 971(c)(2) or 971(c)(4), as the case may be, in a controlled foreign corporation's investments in export trade assets.

(d) *Export promotion expenses*—(1) *In general.* For purposes of sections 970 through 972, and §§ 1.970-1 to 1.972-1, inclusive, the term "export promotion expenses" means, subject to the provisions of subparagraph (2) of this paragraph, all the ordinary and necessary expenses paid or incurred during the taxable year by the controlled foreign corporation which are reasonably allocable to the receipt or production of export trade income including—

(i) A reasonable allowance for salaries or other compensation for personal services actually rendered for such purpose,

(ii) Rentals or other payments for the use of property actually used for such purpose, and

(iii) A reasonable allowance for the exhaustion, wear and tear, or obsolescence of property actually used for such purpose.

In determining for purposes of this subparagraph whether expenses are reasonably allocable to the receipt or production of export trade income, consideration shall be given to the facts and circumstances of each case. As a general rule, if export trade income results from the sale of export property, export promotion expenses allocable to such income shall include warehousing, advertising, selling, billing, collection, other administrative, and similar costs properly allocable to the marketing activity, but shall not include cost of goods sold, income or similar tax, any expense which does not advance the distribution or sale of export property for use, consumption, or disposition outside the United States, or any expense for which the controlled foreign corporation is reimbursed. If export trade income results from the rental of export property, export promotion expenses allocable to such income shall include a reasonable allowance for depreciation and servicing of such property, and the administrative and similar costs properly allocable to the rental activity. If export trade income results from the performance of services, export promotion expenses shall include a reasonable allowance for compensation of the persons performing services for the controlled foreign corporation in the execution of the service contract or arrangement and administrative expenses reasonably allocable to the service activity. In no case shall income taxes be included in export promotion expenses.

(2) *Expenses incurred within the United States.* No expense incurred within the United States shall be treated as an export promotion expense for purposes of section 971(d) and subparagraph (1) of this paragraph unless at least—

(i) 90 percent of all salaries and other personal service compensation incurred in the receipt or the production of export trade income,

(ii) 90 percent of rents and other payments for the use of property used in the receipt or the production of export trade income,

(iii) 90 percent of the allowances for the exhaustion, wear and tear, or obsolescence of property used in the receipt or the production of export trade income, and

(iv) 90 percent of all other ordinary and necessary expenses reasonably allocable to the receipt or the production of export trade income, is incurred outside the United States. For this purpose, personal service compensation will be considered incurred at the place where the service is performed (for example, salaries will be considered incurred at the place where the employee works; payments for art work will be considered incurred at the place where the art work is prepared, etc.); rent, depreciation, and other expenses related to real or personal property will be considered incurred at the place where the property is located; and expenses for media advertising will be considered incurred at the place where the advertising is consumed. For such purpose, newspaper or periodical advertising will be considered consumed where the newspaper or periodical is principally distributed, and television and radio advertising will be considered consumed at the place where the audience is primarily located. Technicalities of contract or payment, for example, the place where a contract is executed or the location of a bank account from which payment is made, shall not be determinative of the place where an expense is incurred.

(e) *Export property.* For purposes of sections 970 through 972 and §§ 1.970-1 to 1.972-1, inclusive, the term "export property" means property, or any interest in property, which is manufactured, produced, grown, or extracted in the United States. Whether property will be considered manufactured or produced in the United States will depend on the facts and circumstances of each case. As a general rule, if—

(1) The property sold, serviced, used, or rented by the controlled foreign corporation is substantially transformed in the United States prior to its export from the United States, or

Reg. § 1.971-1(e)(1)

Income from Sources Without the United States

See p. 20,601 for regulations not amended to reflect law changes

(2) The operations conducted in the United States with respect to the property sold, serviced, used, or rented by the controlled foreign corporation, whether performed in the United States by one person or a series of persons in a chain of distribution, are substantial in nature and are generally considered to constitute the manufacture or production of property,

then the property sold, serviced, used, or rented will be considered to have been manufactured or produced in the United States. The rules under paragraph (a)(4)(ii) of § 1.954-3, relating to the substantial transformation of property, and paragraph (a)(4)(iii) of such section, dealing with a substantive test for determining whether property will be treated as having been manufactured or produced, shall apply for purposes of making determinations under this paragraph.

(f) *Unrelated person.* For purposes of sections 970 through 972 and §§ 1.970-1 to 1.972-1, inclusive, the term "unrelated person" means a person other than a related person as defined in section 954(d)(3) and paragraph (e) of § 1.954-1. [Reg. § 1.971-1.]

☐ [T.D. 6755, 9-8-64. Amended by T.D. 7293, 11-27-73 and T.D. 7533, 2-14-78.]

[Reg. § 1.985-0]

§ 1.985-0. **Outline of regulations.**—This section lists the paragraphs contained in §§ 1.985-1 through 1.985-6.

§ 1.985-1. *Functional currency.*

(a) Applicability and effective date.

(b) Dollar functional currency.

(c) Functional currency of a QBU that is not required to use the dollar.

(d) Single functional currency for a foreign corporation.

(e) Translation of nonfunctional currency transactions.

(f) Examples.

§ 1.985-2. *Election to use the United States dollar as the functional currency of a QBU.*

(a) Background and scope.

(b) Eligible QBU.

(c) Time and manner for dollar election.

(d) Effect of dollar election.

§ 1.985-3. *United States dollar approximate separate transactions method.*

(a) Scope and effective date.

(b) Statement of method.

(c) Translation into United States dollars.

(d) Computation of DASTM gain or loss.

(e) Effect of DASTM gain or loss on gross income, taxable income, or earnings and profits.

§ 1.985-4. *Method of accounting.*

(a) Adoption or election.

(b) Condition for changing functional currencies.

(c) Relationship to certain other sections of the Code.

§ 1.985-5. *Adjustments required upon change in functional currency.*

(a) In general.

(b) Step 1—Taking into account exchange gain or loss on certain section 988 transactions.

(c) Step 2—Determining the new functional currency basis of property and the new functional currency amount of liabilities and any other relevant items.

(d) Step 3A—Additional adjustments that are necessary when a branch changes functional currency.

(e) Step 3B—Additional adjustments that are necessary when a taxpayer changes functional currency.

(f) Examples.

§ 1.985-6. *Transition rules for a QBU that uses the dollar approximate separate transactions method for its first taxable year beginning in 1987.*

(a) In general.

(b) Certain controlled foreign corporations.

(c) All other foreign corporations.

(d) Pre-1987 section 902 amounts.

(e) Net worth branch.

(f) Profit and loss branch.

[Reg. § 1.985-0.]

☐ [T.D. 8263, 9-19-89. Amended by T.D. 8464, 12-31-92 and T.D. 8556, 7-22-94.]

[Reg. § 1.985-1]

§ 1.985-1. **Functional currency.**—(a) *Applicability and effective date*—(1) *Purpose and scope.* These regulations provide guidance with respect to defining the functional currency of a taxpayer and each qualified business unit (QBU), as defined in section 989 (a). Generally, a taxpayer and each QBU must make all determinations under subtitle A of the Code (relating to income taxes) in its respective functional currency. This section sets forth rules for determining when the functional currency is the United States dollar (dollar) or a currency other than the dollar. Section 1.985-2 provides an election to use the dollar as the functional currency for certain QBUs that absent the election would have a functional cur-

Reg. § 1.985-0

rency that is a hyperinflationary currency, and explains the effect of making the election. Section 1.985-3 sets forth the dollar approximate separate transactions method that certain QBUs must use to compute their income or loss or earnings and profits. Section 1.985-4 provides that the adoption of a functional currency is a method of accounting and sets forth conditions for a change in functional currency. Section 1.985-5 provides adjustments that are required to be made upon a change in functional currency. Finally, § 1.985-6 provides transition rules for a QBU that uses the dollar approximate separate transactions method for its first taxable year beginning after December 31, 1986.

(2) *Effective date.* These regulations apply to taxable years beginning after December 31, 1986. However, any taxpayer desiring to apply temporary Income Tax Regulations § 1.985-0T through § 1.985-4T in lieu of these regulations to all taxable years beginning after December 31, 1986, and on or before OCT 20, 1989 may (on a consistent basis) so choose. For the text of the temporary regulations, see 53 Fed. Reg. 20308 (1988).

(b) *Dollar functional currency.*—(1) *In general.* The dollar shall be the functional currency of a taxpayer or QBU described in paragraph (b)(1)(i) through (v) of this section regardless of the currency used in keeping its books and records (as defined in § 1.989(a)-1(d)). The dollar shall be the functional currency of—

(i) A taxpayer that is not a QBU (e.g., an individual);

(ii) A QBU that conducts its activities primarily in dollars. A QBU conducts its activities primarily in dollars if the currency of the economic environment in which the QBU conducts its activities is primarily the dollar. The facts and circumstances test set forth in paragraph (c)(2) of this section shall apply in making this determination;

(iii) Except as otherwise provided by ruling or administrative pronouncement, a QBU that has the United States, or any possession or territory of the United States where the dollar is the standard currency, as its residence (as defined in section 988(a)(3)(B));

(iv) A QBU that does not keep books and records in the currency of any economic environment in which a significant part of its activities is conducted. Whether a QBU keeps such books and records is determined in accordance with paragraph (c)(3) of this section; or

(v) A QBU that produces income or loss that is, or is treated as, effectively connected with the conduct of a trade or business within the United States.

(2) *QBUs operating in a hyperinflationary environment*—(i) *Taxable years beginning on or before August 24, 1994.* For taxable years beginning on or before August 24, 1994, see § 1.985-2 with respect to a QBU that elects to use, or is otherwise required to use, the dollar as its functional currency.

(ii) *Taxable years beginning after August 24, 1994.*—(A) *In general.* For taxable years beginning after August 24, 1994, except as otherwise provided in paragraph (b)(2)(ii)(B) of this section, any QBU that otherwise would be required to use a hyperinflationary currency as its functional currency must use the dollar as its functional currency and compute income or loss or earnings and profits under the rules of § 1.985-3.

(B) *Exceptions*—(*1*) *Certain QBU branches.* The functional currency of a QBU that otherwise would be required to use a hyperinflationary currency as its functional currency and that is a branch of a foreign corporation having a non-dollar functional currency that is not hyperinflationary shall be the functional currency of the foreign corporation. Such QBU's income or loss or earnings and profits shall be determined under § 1.985-3 by substituting the functional currency of the foreign corporation for the dollar.

(*2*) *Corporation that is not a controlled foreign corporation.* A foreign corporation (or its QBU branch) operating in a hyperinflationary environment is not required to use the dollar as its functional currency pursuant to paragraph (b)(2)(ii)(A) of this section if that foreign corporation is not a controlled foreign corporation as defined in section 957 or 953(c)(1)(B). However, a noncontrolled section 902 corporation, as defined in section 904(d)(2)(E), may elect to use the dollar (or, if appropriate, the currency specified in paragraph (b)(2)(ii)(B)(*1*) of this section) as its (or its QBU branch's) functional currency under the procedures set forth in § 1.985-2(c)(3).

(C) *Change in functional currency.*— (*1*) *In general.* If a QBU is required to change its functional currency to the dollar under paragraph (b)(2)(ii)(A) of this section, or chooses or is required to change its functional currency to the dollar for any open taxable year (and all subsequent taxable years) under § 1.985-3(a)(2)(ii), the change is considered to be made with the consent of the Commissioner for purposes of § 1.985-4. A QBU changing functional currency must make adjustments described in § 1.985-7 if the year of change (as defined in § 1.481-1(a)(1)) begins after 1987, or the adjustments described in § 1.985-6 if the year of change begins in 1987. No adjustments under section 481 are required solely be-

Reg. § 1.985-1(b)(2)

cause of a change in functional currency described in this paragraph (b)(2)(ii)(C).

(2) *Effective date.* This paragraph (b)(2)(ii)(C) applies to taxable years beginning after April 6, 1998. However, a taxpayer may choose to apply this paragraph (b)(2)(ii)(C) to all open years after December 31, 1986, provided each person, and each QBU branch of a person, that is related (within the meaning of § 1.985-2(d)(3)) also applies to this paragraph (b)(2)(ii)(C).

(D) *Hyperinflationary currency.* For purposes of sections 985 through 989, the term hyperinflationary currency means the currency of a country in which there is cumulative inflation during the base period of at least 100 percent as determined by reference to the consumer price index of the country listed in the monthly issues of the "International Financial Statistics" or a successor publication of the International Monetary Fund. If a country's currency is not listed in the monthly issues of "International Financial Statistics," a QBU may use any other reasonable method consistently applied for determining the country's consumer price index. Base period means, with respect to any taxable year, the thirty-six calendar months immediately preceding the first day of the current calendar year. For this purpose, the cumulative inflation rate for the base period is based on compounded inflation rates. Thus, if for 1991, 1992, and 1993, a country's annual inflation rates are 29 percent, 25 percent, and 30 percent, respectively, the cumulative inflation rate for the three-year base period is 110 percent [((1.29 × 1.25 × 1.3) − 1.0 = 1.10) × 100 = 110%] and the currency of the country for the QBU's 1994 year is considered hyperinflationary. In making the determination whether a currency is hyperinflationary, the determination for purposes of United States generally accepted accounting principles may be used for income tax purposes provided the determination is based on criteria that is substantially similar to the rules previously set forth in this paragraph (b)(2)(ii)(D), the method of determination is applied consistently from year to year, and the same method is applied to all related persons as defined in § 1.985-3(e)(2)(vi).

(E) *Change in functional currency when currency ceases to be hyperinflationary*—(1) *In general.* A QBU that has been required to use the dollar as its functional currency under paragraph (b)(2) of this section, or has elected to use the dollar as its functional currency under paragraph (b)(2)(ii)(B)(*2*) of this section or § 1.985-2, must change its functional currency as of the first day of the first taxable year that follows three consecutive taxable years in which the currency of its economic environment, determined under paragraph (c)(2) of this section, is not a hyperinflationary currency. The functional currency of the QBU for such year shall be determined in accordance with paragraph (c) of this section. For purposes of § 1.985-4, the change is considered to be made with the consent of the Commissioner. See § 1.985-5 for adjustments that are required upon a change in functional currency.

(2) *Effective date.* This paragraph (b)(2)(ii)(E) of this section applies to taxable years beginning after April 6, 1998.

(c) *Functional currency of a QBU that is not required to use the dollar*—(1) *General rule.* The functional currency of a QBU that is not required to use the dollar under paragraph (b) of this section shall be the currency of the economic environment in which a significant part of the QBU's activities is conducted, if the QBU keeps, or is presumed under paragraph (c) (3) of this section to keep, its books and records in such currency.

(2) *Economic environment.* For purposes of section 985 and the regulations thereunder, the economic environment in which a significant part of a QBU's activities is conducted shall be determined by taking into account all the facts and circumstances.

(i) *Facts and circumstances.* The facts and circumstances that are considered in determining the economic environment in which a significant part of a QBU's activities is conducted include, but are not limited to, the following:

(A) The currency of the country in which the QBU is a resident as determined under section 988 (a)(3)(B);

(B) The currencies of the QBU's cash flows;

(C) The currencies in which the QBU generates revenues and incurs expenses;

(D) The currencies in which the QBU borrows and lends;

(E) The currencies of the QBU's sales markets;

(F) The currencies in which pricing and other financial decisions are made;

(G) The duration of the QBU's business operations; and

(H) The significance and/or volume of the QBU's independent activities.

(ii) *Rate of inflation.* The rate of inflation (regardless of how it is determined) shall not be a factor used to determine a QBU's economic environment.

Reg. § 1.985-1(c)(1)

(iii) *Consistency.* A taxpayer must consistently apply the facts and circumstances test set forth in this paragraph (c) (2) in evaluating the economic environment of its QBUs, e.g., its branches, that engage in the same or similar trades or businesses.

(3) *Books and records presumption.* A QBU shall be presumed to keep books and records in the currency of the economic environment in which a significant part of its activities are conducted. The presumption may be overcome only if the QBU can demonstrate to the satisfaction of the district director that a substantial nontax purpose exists for not keeping any books and records in such currency. A taxpayer may not use this presumption affirmatively in determining a QBU's functional currency.

(4) *Multiple currencies.* If a QBU has more than one currency that satisfies the requirements of paragraph (c) (1) of this section, the QBU may choose any such currency as its functional currency.

(5) *Relationship of United States accounting principles.* In making the functional currency determination under this paragraph (c), the currency of the QBU for purposes of United States generally accepted accounting principles (GAAP) will ordinarily be accepted as the functional currency of the QBU for income tax purposes, provided that the GAAP determination is based on facts and circumstances substantially similar to those set forth in paragraph (c) (2) of this section.

(6) *Effect of changed circumstances.* Regardless of any change in circumstances, a QBU may change its functional currency determined under this paragraph (c) only if the QBU complies with § 1.985-4 or the Commissioner's consent is considered to have been granted under § 1.985-2(d)(4) or § 1.985-3(a)(2)(ii). For special rules relating to the conversion to the euro, see § 1.985-8.

(d) *Single functional currency for a foreign corporation*—(1) *General rule.* This paragraph (d) applies to a foreign corporation that has two or more QBUs that do not have the same functional currency. The foreign corporation shall be treated as having a single functional currency for the corporation as a whole that is different from the functional currency of one or more of its QBUs. The determination of a foreign corporation's functional currency shall be made by first applying paragraph (d) (1) (i) and then paragraph (d) (1) (ii) of this section.

(i) *Step 1.* Each QBU of the foreign corporation determines its functional currency in accordance with the rules set forth in paragraphs (b) and (c) of this section and § 1.985-2.

(ii) *Step 2.* The foreign corporation determines its functional currency applying the principles of paragraphs (b) and (c) of this section to the corporation's activities as a whole. Thus, if a foreign corporation has two branches, the corporation shall determine its functional currency by applying the principles of paragraphs (b) and (c) of this section to the combined activities of the corporation and the branches.

For purposes of this paragraph (d)(1), if a QBU of a foreign corporation has the dollar as its functional currency under paragraph (b)(2) of this section, the QBU's activities shall be considered dollar activities of the corporation.

(2) *Translation of income or loss of QBUs having different functional currencies than the foreign corporation as a whole.* Where the functional currency of a foreign corporation as a whole differs from the functional currency of one or more of its QBUs, each such QBU shall determine the amount of its income or loss or earnings and profits (or deficit in earnings and profits) in its functional currency under the principles of section 987 (relating to branch transactions). The amount of income or loss or earnings and profits (or deficit in earnings and profits) of each QBU in its functional currency shall then be translated into the foreign corporation's functional currency using the appropriate exchange rate as defined in section 989 (b) (4) for purposes of determining the corporation's income or loss or earnings and profits (or deficit in earnings and profits).

(e) *Translation of nonfunctional currency transactions.* Except for a QBU using the dollar approximate separate transactions method described in § 1.985-3, see section 988 and the regulations thereunder for the treatment of nonfunctional currency transactions.

(f) *Examples.* The provisions of this section are illustrated by the following examples:

Example (1). P, a domestic corporation, operates exclusively through foreign branch X in Country A. X is a QBU within the meaning of section 989 (a) and its residence is Country A as determined under section 988 (a) (3) (B). The currency of Country A is the LC. All of X's purchases, sales, and expenses are in the LC. The laws of A require X to keep books and records in the LC. It is determined that the LC is the currency of X under United States generally accepted accounting principles. This determination is based on facts and circumstances substantially similar to those set forth in paragraph (c) (2) of this section. Under these facts, while the functional currency of P is the dollar since its residence is the United States, the functional currency of X is the LC.

Reg. § 1.985-1(f)

Example (2). P, a publicly-held domestic regulated investment company (as defined under section 851), operates exclusively through foreign branch B in Country R. B is a QBU within the meaning of section 989 (a) and its residence is Country R as determined under section 988 (a) (3) (B). The currency of Country R is the LC. B's principal activities consist of purchasing and selling stock and securities of Country R companies and securities issued by Country R. It is determined that the dollar is the currency of B under United States generally accepted accounting principles. This determination is not based on facts and circumstances substantially similar to those set forth in paragraph (c) (2) of this section. Under these facts, while the functional currency of P is the dollar since its residence is the United States, B may choose the LC as its functional currency because it has significant activities in the LC provided it keeps books and records in the LC. The fact that the dollar is the currency of B under generally accepted accounting principles is irrelevant for purposes of determining B's functional currency because the GAAP determination was not based on factors similar to those set forth in paragraph (c) (2) of this section.

Example (3). P, a domestic bank, operates through foreign branch X in Country R. X is a QBU within the meaning of section 989 (a) and its residence is Country R as determined under section 988 (a) (3) (B). The currency of Country R is the LC. The laws of R require X to keep books and records in the LC. The branch customarily loans dollars and LCs. In the case of its LC loans, X ordinarily fixes the terms of the loans by reference to a contemporary London Inter-Bank Offered Rate (LIBOR) on dollar deposits. For instance, the interest on the amount of the outstanding LC loan principal might equal LIBOR plus 2 percent and the amount of the outstanding LC loan principal would be adjusted to reflect changes in the dollar value of the LC. X is primarily funded with dollar-denominated funds borrowed from related and unrelated parties. X's only LC activities are paying local taxes, employee wages, and local expenses such as rent and electricity. Under these facts, X's activities are primarily conducted in dollars. Thus, although X keeps its books and records in LCs, X's functional currency is the dollar.

Example (4). S, a foreign corporation organized in Country U, is wholly-owned by P, a domestic corporation. The currency of Country U is the LC. S's sole function is acting as a financing vehicle for P and domestic corporations that are affiliated with P. All borrowing and lending transactions between S and P and its domestic affiliates are in dollars. Furthermore, primarily all of S's other borrowings are dollar-denominated or based on a dollar index. S's only LC activities are paying local taxes, employee wages, and local expenses such as rent and electricity. S keeps its books and records in the LC. Under these facts, S's activities are primarily conducted in dollars. Thus, although S keeps its books and records in LCs, S's functional currency is the dollar.

Example (5). D is a domestic corporation whose primary activity is the extraction of natural gas and oil through foreign branch X in Country Y. X is a QBU within the meaning of section 989 (a) and its residence is Country Y as determined under section 988 (a) (3) (B). The currency of Country Y is the LC. X bills a significant amount of its natural gas and oil sales in dollars and a significant amount in LCs. X also incurs significant LC and dollar expenses and liabilities. The laws of Country Y require X to keep its books and records in the LC. It is determined that the LC is the currency of X under United States generally accepted accounting principles. This determination is based on facts and circumstances substantially similar to those set forth in paragraph (c) (2) of this section. Absent other factors indicating that K primarily conducts its activities in the dollar, D could choose either the dollar or the LC as X's functional currency because X has significant activities in both the dollar and the LC, provided the books and records requirement is satisfied. If, instead, X's activities were determined to be primarily in the dollar, then X would have to use the dollar as its functional currency.

Example (6). S, a foreign corporation organized in Country U, is wholly-owned by P, a domestic corporation. The currency of U is the LC. S purchases the products it sells from related and unrelated parties, including P. These purchases are made in the LC. In addition, most of S's gross receipts are generated by transactions denominated in the LC. S attempts to determine its LC price for goods sold in such a manner as to obtain an LC equivalent of a certain dollar amount after reduction for all LC costs. However, local market conditions sometimes result in pricing adjustments. Thus, changes in the LC-dollar exchange rate from period to period generally result in corresponding changes in the LC price of S's products. S pays local taxes, employee wages, and other local expenses in the LC. It is determined that the dollar is the currency of S under United States generally accepted accounting principles. This determination is not based on facts and circumstances substantially similar to those set forth in paragraph (c) (2) of this section. Under these facts, S could choose either the dollar or the LC as its functional currency because S has significant activities in both the dollar and the LC, provided that the books and records requirement is satisfied.

Example (7). S, a foreign corporation organized in Country X, is wholly-owned by P, a domestic corporation. S conducts all of its operations through two branches. Branch A is located in Country F and branch B is located in Country G. S, A, and B are QBUs within the meaning of section 989 (a). Branch A's and branch B's residences are Country F and Country G respectively as determined under section 988 (a) (3) (B). The currency of Country F is the FC and the currency of Country G is the LC. The functional currencies of S, A, and B are determined in a two step procedure.

Step 1: The functional currency of branches A and B. Branch A and branch B both conduct all activities in their respective local currencies. The FC is the currency of branch A and the LC is the currency of branch B under United States generally accepted accounting principles. This determination is based on facts and circumstances substantially similar to those set forth in paragraph (c) (2) of this section. Under these facts, the functional currency of branch A is the FC and the functional currency of branch B is the LC.

Step 2: The functional currency of S. S's functional currency is determined by disregarding the fact that A and B are branches. When A's activities and B's activities are viewed as a whole, S determines that it only conducts significant activities in the LC. Therefore, S's functional currency is the LC. See Examples (9), (10), and (11) for how the earnings and profits of a foreign corporation, which has branches with different functional currencies, are determined.

Example (8). Assume the same facts as in Example (7), except that S does not exist and P conducts all of its operations through branch A and branch B. In this instance P's functional currency in Step 2 is the dollar, regardless of the fact that its branches' activities viewed as a whole are in the LC, because P is a taxpayer whose residence is the United States under section 988 (a) (3) (B) (i). Therefore, while the functional currency of branch A is the FC and the functional currency of branch B is the LC, the functional currency of P is the dollar because its residence is the United States.

Example (9). The facts are the same as in Example (7). In addition, assume that in 1987 branch A has earnings of 100 FC and branch B has earnings of 100 LC as determined under section 987. The weighted average exchange rate for the year is 1 FC/2 LC. Branch A's earnings are translated into 200 LC for purposes of computing S's earnings and profits in 1987. Thus, the total earnings and profits of S from branch A and branch B for 1987 is 300 LC.

Example (10). (i) X, a foreign corporation organized in Country W, is wholly-owned by P, a domestic corporation. Both X and P are calendar year taxpayers that began business during 1987. X operates exclusively through two branches, A and B both of which are located outside of Country W. The functional currency of X and A is the LC, while the functional currency of B is the DC as determined under section 985 and § 1.985-1. The earnings of B must be computed under section 987, relating to branch transactions. In 1987, A earns 900 LCs of nonsubpart F income and B earns 200 DCs of nonsubpart F income. Under section 904 (d) (2), A's income is financial service income and B's income is general limitation income. In order to determine X's earnings and profits, B's income must be translated into LCs (the functional currency of X). The weighted average exchange rate for 1987 is 1 LC/2 DC. Thus, in 1987 X's current earnings and profits (and its post-1986 undistributed earnings) are 1000 LCs consisting of 900 LCs of financial services income earned by A and 100 LCs (200 DC/2) of general limitation income earned by B. Neither A nor B makes any remittances during 1987.

(ii) In 1988, neither A nor B earns any income or generates any loss. On December 31, 1988, A remits 50 LCs directly to P. The remittance to P is considered to be remitted by A to X and then immediately distributed by X as a dividend. The 50 LC remittance does not result in an exchange gain or loss under section 987 to X because the functional currency of X and A is the LC. See section 987 (3). Under section 904 (d) (3) (D), the 50 LC dividend is treated as income in a separate category to the extent of the dividend's pro rata share of X's earnings and profits in each separate limitation category. Thus, 90 percent, or 45 LCs, is treated as financial services income, and 10 percent, or 5 LCs, is treated as general limitation income. After the dividend distribution, X has 950 LCs of accumulated earnings and profits (and post-1986 undistributed earnings) consisting of 855 LCs of financial service limitation income and 95 LCs of general limitation income.

Example (11). The facts are the same as in Example (10), except that A makes no remittance during 1988 but B remits 120 DCs to X on December 31, 1988, which X immediately converts into LCs, and X makes no dividend distribution during 1988. Assume that the appropriate exchange rate for the remittance is 1 LC/3 DCs. B's remittance triggers exchange loss to X. See section 987 (3). Under section 987, the exchange loss on the remittance is 20 LCs calculated as follows: 40

Reg. § 1.985-1(f)

LCs, which is the LC value of the 120 DC remittance (120 DCs/3), less 60 LCs, their LC basis (120 DCs/2). This loss is sourced and characterized under section 987 and regulations thereunder.

Example (12). F, a foreign corporation, has gain from the disposition of a United States real property interest (as defined in section 897 (c)). The gain is taken into account as if F were engaged in a trade or business within the United States during the taxable year and as if such gain were effectively connected with such trade or business. F's disposition activity shall be treated as a separate QBU with a dollar functional currency because such activity produced income that is treated as effectively connected with a trade or business within the United States. Therefore, F must compute its gain from the disposition by giving the United States real property interest an historic dollar basis. [Reg. § 1.985-1.]

☐ [T.D. 8263, 9-19-89. Amended by T.D. 8556, 7-22-94; T.D. 8765, 3-4-98 (corrected 3-31-98); T.D. 8776, 7-28-98 and T.D. 8927, 1-10-2001.]

[Reg. § 1.985-2]

§ 1.985-2. **Election to use the United States dollar as the functional currency of a QBU.**—(a) *Background and scope.*—(1) *In general.* This section permits an eligible QBU to elect to use the dollar as its functional currency for taxable years beginning on or before August 24, 1994. An election to use a dollar functional currency is not permitted for a QBU other than an eligible QBU. Paragraph (b) of this section defines an eligible QBU. Paragraph (c) of this section describes the time and manner for making the dollar election and paragraph (d) of this section describes the effect of making the election. For the definition of a QBU, see section 989(a). See § 1.985-1(b)(2)(ii) for rules requiring a QBU to use the dollar as its functional currency in taxable years beginning after August 24, 1994.

(2) *Exception.* Pursuant to § 1.985-1(b)(2)(ii)(B)(*2*), the rules of paragraph (c)(3) of this section shall apply with respect to the procedure required to be followed by a noncontrolled section 902 corporation as defined in section 904(d)(2)(E) to elect the dollar as its (or its QBU branch's) functional currency and the application of § 1.985-3.

(b) *Eligible QBU*—(1) *In general.* The term "eligible QBU" means a QBU that could have used a hyperinflationary currency as its functional currency absent the dollar election. See § 1.985-1 for how a QBU determines its functional currency absent the dollar election.

(2) *Hyperinflationary currency.* See § 1.985-1(b)(2)(ii)(D) for the definition of hyperinflationary currency.

(c) *Time and manner for dollar election*—(1) *QBUs that are branches of United States persons*—(i) *Rule.* If an eligible QBU is a branch of a United States person, the dollar election shall be made by attaching a completed Form 8819 to the United States person's timely filed (taking extensions into account) tax return for the first taxable year for which the election is to be effective.

(ii) *Procedure prior to the issuance of Form 8819.* In the absence of Form 8819, the election shall be made in accordance with § 1.985-2T(c)(1). Failure to file an amended return within the time period prescribed in § 1.985-2T(c)(1) shall not invalidate the dollar election if it is established to the satisfaction of the district director that reasonable cause existed for such failure. A subsequent election for 1988 will not prejudice the taxpayer with respect to such reasonable cause determination. Nevertheless, each United States person making an election under the § 1.985-2T(c)(1) must file a Form 8819 in the time and manner provided in the Form's instructions.

(2) *Eligible QBUs that are controlled foreign corporations or branches of controlled foreign corporations*—(i) *Rule.* If an eligible QBU is a controlled foreign corporation (as described in section 957), or a branch of a controlled foreign corporation, the election may be made either by the foreign corporation or by the controlling United States shareholders on behalf of the foreign corporation by—

(A) Filing a completed Form 8819 in the time and manner provided in the Form's instructions, and

(B) Providing the written notice required by paragraph (c)(2)(ii) of this section at the time and in the manner prescribed therein.

The term "controlling United States shareholders" means those United States shareholders (as defined in section 951(b)) who, in the aggregate, own (within the meaning of section 958(a)) greater than 50 percent of the total combined voting power of all classes of stock of the foreign corporation entitled to vote. If the foreign corporation is a controlled foreign corporation (as described in section 957) but the United States shareholders do not, in the aggregate, own the requisite voting power, the term "controlling United States shareholders" means all the United States shareholders (as defined in section 951(b)) who own (within the meaning of section 958(a)) stock of the controlled foreign corporation.

Reg. § 1.985-2(a)(1)

(ii) *Notice.* Prior to filing Form 8819, the controlling United States shareholders (or the foreign corporation, if the dollar election is made by the corporation) shall provide written notice that the dollar election will be made to all United States persons known to be shareholders who own (within the meaning of section 958(a)) stock of the foreign corporation. Such notice shall also include all information required in Form 8819.

(iii) *Reasonable cause exception.* Failure of the controlling United States shareholders (or the foreign corporation, if the dollar election is made by the corporation) to timely file Form 8819 or provide written notice to a United States person required to be notified by paragraph (c)(2)(ii) of this section shall not invalidate the dollar election, if it is established to the satisfaction of the district director that reasonable cause existed for such failure.

(iv) *Procedure prior to the issuance of Form 8819.* In the absence of Form 8819, an eligible QBU described in paragraph (c)(2)(i) of this section shall make the dollar election in accordance with § 1.985-2T(c)(2). Nevertheless, the person or persons that made such election must file a Form 8819 in the time and manner provided in the Form's instructions.

(3) *Eligible QBUs that are noncontrolled foreign corporations or branches of noncontrolled foreign corporations*—(i) *Rule.* If an eligible QBU is a noncontrolled foreign corporation (a foreign corporation not described in section 957), or a branch of a noncontrolled foreign corporation, the dollar election must be made by the corporation or the majority domestic corporate shareholders on behalf of the corporation by applying the rules provided in paragraph (c)(2)(i)(A) and (B), (ii), (iii), and (iv) of this section substituting "majority domestic corporate shareholders" for "controlling United States shareholders" wherever it appears therein. The term "majority domestic corporate shareholders" means those domestic corporate shareholders (as described in section 902(a)) who, in the aggregate, own (within the meaning of section 958(a) greater than 50 percent of the total combined voting stock of all classes of stock of the noncontrolled foreign corporation entitled to vote that is owned (within the meaning of section 958(a)) by all the domestic corporate shareholders.

(ii) *Procedure prior to the issuance of Form 8819.* In the absence of Form 8819, an eligible QBU described in paragraph (c)(3)(i) of this section shall make the dollar election in accordance with § 1.985-2T(c)(3). Nevertheless, the person or persons that made such election must file a Form 8819 in the time and manner provided in the Form's instructions.

(4) *Others.* Any other person making a dollar election under this section shall elect by filing Form 8819 and fulfilling any other notice requirements that may be required by the Commissioner.

(d) *Effect of dollar election*—(1) *General rule.* If a dollar election is made (or considered made under paragraph (d)(3) of this section) by or on behalf of an eligible QBU, the QBU shall be deemed to have the dollar as its functional currency. Each United States person that owns (within the meaning of section 958(a)) stock of a foreign corporation which has the dollar as its functional currency under § 1.985-2 must make all of its federal income tax calculations with respect to the foreign corporation using the dollar as the corporation's functional currency (regardless of when ownership was acquired or whether the United States person received the written notice required by paragraph (c)(2)(i)(B) of this section).

(2) *Computation*—(i) *In general.* Except as provided in paragraph (d)(2)(ii) of this section, any eligible QBU that pursuant to this § 1.985-2 has a dollar functional currency must compute income or loss or earnings and profits (or deficit in earnings and profits) in dollars using the dollar approximate separate transactions method described in § 1.985-3.

(ii) *Alternative method.* An eligible QBU that has a dollar functional currency pursuant to this § 1.985-2 may use a method other than the dollar approximate separate transactions method described in § 1.985-3 only if the QBU demonstrates to the satisfaction of the Commissioner that it can properly employ such method. Generally, the QBU must show that it could compute foreign currency gain or loss under the principles of section 988 with respect to each of its section 988 transactions. If subsequently the QBU can no longer demonstrate to the satisfaction of the district director that it can properly employ such an alternative method, then the QBU will be deemed to have changed its method of accounting to the dollar approximate separate transactions method described in § 1.985-3. This change in accounting will be treated as having been made with the consent of the Commissioner. No adjustments under either § 1.985-5T (or any succeeding final regulation) or section 481(a) shall be required solely because of the change. Rather the QBU shall begin accounting for its operations under § 1.985-3 based on its dollar books and records as of the time of the change.

(3) *Conformity*—(i) *General rule.* If a dollar election is made under this § 1.985-2 for an eligi-

Reg. § 1.985-2(d)(3)

ble QBU ("electing QBU"), then the dollar shall be the functional currency of any related person (regardless of when such person became related to the electing QBU) that is an eligible QBU, or any branch of any such related person that is an eligible QBU. For purposes of the preceding sentence, the term "related person" means any person with a relationship defined in section 267(b) to the electing QBU (or to the United States or foreign person of which the electing QBU is a part). In determining whether two or more corporations are members of the same controlled group under section 267(b)(3), a person is considered to own stock owned directly by such person, stock owned with the application of section 1563(e)(1), and stock owned with the application of section 267(c).

(ii) *Branches of United States and foreign persons.* If a dollar election is made for a QBU branch of any person, each eligible QBU branch of such person shall have the dollar as its functional currency.

(4) *Required adjustments.* If an eligible QBU's functional currency changes due to a dollar election, or due to the conformity requirements of paragraph (d)(3) of this section, such change shall be deemed for purposes of § 1.985-4 to be consented to by the Commissioner. No adjustments under section 481(a) shall be required solely because of the change. However, the QBU must make those adjustments required by § 1.985-5T (or any succeeding final regulation).

(5) *Taxable year conformity required.* Generally, the adjustments required by paragraph (d)(4) of this section shall be made for a related person's taxable year—

(i) that includes the date in which the electing QBU made the dollar election if the person was related to such electing QBU at any time during the QBU's taxable year that includes such date, or

(ii) during which the person first becomes related to any electing QBU, in all other cases.

For purposes of this paragraph (d)(5), the date in which the electing QBU makes the dollar election shall be the last day of the electing QBU's taxable year. The district director may permit the related party to make such adjustments beginning one taxable year later if, in the district director's sole judgment, reasonable cause exists for the related party not being able to make the required adjustments for the earlier year.

(6) *Availability of election.* A dollar election may be made by or on behalf of a QBU, or considered made under the conformity rule of paragraph (d)(3), in any year in which the QBU is an eligible QBU. If a dollar election is not made by or on behalf of a QBU for its first taxable year beginning after December 31, 1986 in which it is an eligible QBU, then any dollar election made by or on behalf of the QBU, or considered made under the conformity rules of paragraph (d)(3) of this section, that results in a change in the QBU's functional currency shall be treated as having been made with the consent of the Commissioner. In such a case, however, the taxpayer must make those adjustments required by § 1.985-5T (or any succeeding final regulation).

(7) *Effect of changed circumstances.* Regardless of any change in circumstances (e.g., a currency ceases to qualify as hyperinflationary), a QBU whose functional currency is the dollar under this section may change its functional currency only if the QBU complies with § 1.985-4.

(8) *Examples.* The provisions of this section are illustrated by the following examples.

Example (1). X is a calendar year domestic corporation that in 1987 establishes a branch, A, in Country Z. A's functional currency under section 985(b)(1) and (2) and § 1.985-1 is the "h", the currency of Country Z. The cumulative inflation in Country Z exceeds 100 percent for the thirty-six months prior to January 1987, as measured by the consumer price index of Country Z listed in the monthly issues of the "International Financial Statistics". Accordingly, A is an eligible QBU in 1987 because the h is a hyperinflationary currency. Thus, X may elect the dollar as the functional currency of A for 1987.

Example (2). The facts are the same as in Example (1). X does not elect the dollar as the functional currency of A for 1987. Rather, X elects the dollar as the functional currency of A for 1991, a year A is an eligible QBU. The election constitutes a change in A's functional currency that is made with the consent of the Commissioner. However, A must make the adjustments required under § 1.985-5T (or any succeeding final regulation).

Example (3). X is a domestic corporation that establishes A, an eligible QBU branch. X is wholly owned by domestic corporation Y. Y has an eligible QBU branch, B. Both X and Y are calendar year taxpayers. X makes a dollar election for A in 1987. Thus, A is an electing QBU. X and Y are related persons as defined in section 267(b) (i.e., Y has a relationship under section 267(b)(3) to X, the corporation of which A is a part). Therefore, the dollar election by X for A in 1987 results in B, the eligible QBU branch of Y, also having the dollar as its functional currency for 1987.

Example (4). The facts are the same as in Example (3), except that Y does not have an eligible QBU branch but owns all the stock of C, a calendar year controlled foreign corporation, which is not itself an eligible QBU but which has an eligible QBU branch, D. X and C are related persons as defined in section 267(b) (i.e., C has a relationship under section 267(b)(3) to X, the corporation of which A is a part). Therefore, the dollar election by X for A in 1987 results in D, the eligible QBU branch of C, also having the dollar as its functional currency for 1987.

Example (5). X, whose taxable year ends September 30, is an eligible QBU that does not use the dollar as its functional currency. X is wholly-owned by domestic corporation W. On January 1, 1989, X acquires all the stock of Y, an unrelated eligible QBU that made the dollar election under § 1.985-2. Y is a calendar year taxpayer. After the stock purchase, X and Y are related persons as defined in section 267(b). Under § 1.985-2(d)(3) and (5), the dollar shall be the functional currency of X, any person related to X, and any branch of such related person that is an eligible QBU beginning with the taxable year that includes December 31, 1989. Thus, X must change to the dollar for its taxable year beginning October 1, 1988. However, the district director may allow X to change to the dollar for its taxable year beginning October 1, 1989, provided reasonable cause exists. Those QBUs changing to the dollar as their functional currency as the result of the conformity requirements must make the adjustments required under § 1.985-5T (or any succeeding final regulation).

Example (6). The facts are the same as in Example (5), except that before X purchased the Y stock, X made the dollar election under § 1.985-2 but Y did not use the dollar as its functional currency. Under § 1.985-2(d)(3) and (5) the dollar shall be the functional currency of Y, any person related to Y, and any branch of such related person that is an eligible QBU beginning with the taxable year that includes September 30, 1989. Thus, Y must change to the dollar for its taxable year beginning January 1, 1989. However the district director may allow Y to change to the dollar for its taxable year beginning January 1, 1990, provided reasonable cause exists. Those QBUs changing to the dollar as their functional currency as the result of the conformity requirements must make the adjustments required under § 1.985-5T (or any succeeding final regulation). [Reg. § 1.985-2.]

☐ [T.D. 8263, 9-19-89. Amended by T.D. 8556, 7-22-94.]

[Reg. § 1.985-3]

§ 1.985-3. United States dollar approximate separate transactions method.—(a) *Scope and effective date*—(1) *Scope.* This section describes the United States dollar (dollar) approximate separate transactions method of accounting (DASTM). For all purposes of subtitle A, this method of accounting must be used to compute the gross income, taxable income or loss, or earnings and profits (or deficit in earnings and profits) of a QBU (as defined in section 989(a)) that has the dollar as its functional currency pursuant to § 1.985-1(b)(2).

(2) *Effective date*—(i) *In general.* This section is effective for taxable years beginning after August 24, 1994.

(ii) *DASTM prior-year election.* A taxpayer may elect to apply this section to any open taxable year beginning after December 31, 1986 (whether or not DASTM has been previously elected for some or all of those years). In order to make this election, the taxpayer must apply § 1.985-3 to that year and all subsequent years. In addition, each person that is related (within the meaning of § 1.985-3(e)(2)(vi)) to the taxpayer on the last day of any taxable year for which the election is effective and that would have been eligible to elect DASTM must also apply these rules to that year and all subsequent years. A taxpayer that has not previously elected to apply DASTM to its prior taxable years may make the DASTM election for the pertinent years by filing amended returns and complying with the applicable election procedures of § 1.985-2. Form 8819 shall be attached to the return for the first year for which the election is to be effective. A taxpayer that has elected DASTM for prior taxable years and applied the rules under § 1.985-3 (as contained in the April 1, 1994 edition of 26 CFR part 1 (1.908 to 1.1000)) may amend its returns to apply the rules of this § 1.985-3. In either case, the DASTM election for prior taxable years shall be deemed to be made with the consent of the Commissioner.

(b) *Statement of method.* Under DASTM, income or loss or earnings and profits (or a deficit in earnings and profits) of a QBU for its taxable year shall be determined in dollars by—

(1) Preparing an income or loss statement from the QBU's books and records (within the meaning of § 1.989(a)-1(d)) as recorded in the QBU's hyperinflationary currency (as defined in § 1.985-1(b)(2)(ii)(D));

(2) Making the adjustments necessary to conform such statement to United States generally accepted accounting principles and tax accounting principles (including reversing monetary cor-

Reg. § 1.985-3(b)(2)

rection adjustments required by local accounting principles);

(3) Translating the amounts of hyperinflationary currency as shown on such adjusted statement into dollars in accordance with paragraph (c) of this section; and

(4) Adjusting the resulting dollar income or loss or earnings and profits (or deficit in earnings and profits) and, where necessary, particular items of gross income, deductible expense or other amounts, in accordance with paragraph (e) of this section to reflect the amount of DASTM gain or loss as determined under paragraph (d) of this section.

(c) *Translation into United States dollars*—(1) *In general.* Except as otherwise provided in this paragraph (c), the amounts shown on the income or loss statement, as adjusted under paragraph (b)(2) of this section, shall be translated into dollars at the exchange rate (as defined in paragraph (c)(6) of this section) for the translation period (as defined in paragraph (c)(7) of this section) to which they relate. However, if the QBU previously changed its functional currency to the dollar, and the rules of § 1.985-5 (or, if applicable, § 1.985-5T, as contained in the April 1, 1993 edition of 26 CFR part 1 (1.908 to 1.1000)) applied in translating its balance sheet amounts into dollars, then the spot exchange rate applied under those rules shall be used to translate any amount that would otherwise be translated at a rate determined by reference to a translation period prior to the change in functional currency. For example, depreciation with respect to an asset acquired while the QBU had a nondollar functional currency shall be translated into dollars at the spot rate on the last day of the taxable year before the year of change to a dollar functional currency, rather than at the rate for the period in which the asset was acquired.

(2) *Cost of goods sold.* The dollar value of cost of goods sold shall equal the sum of the dollar values of beginning inventory and purchases less the dollar value of closing inventory as these amounts are determined under paragraph (c)(3) of this section.

(3) *Beginning inventory, purchases, and closing inventory*—(i) *Beginning inventory.* Amounts representing beginning inventory shall be translated so as to obtain the same amount of dollars which represented such items in the closing inventory balance for the preceding taxable year.

(ii) *Purchases.* Amounts representing items purchased or otherwise first included in inventory during the taxable year shall be translated at the exchange rate for the translation period in which the cost of such items was incurred.

(iii) *Closing inventory*—(A) *In general.* Amounts representing items included in the closing inventory balance shall be translated at the exchange rate for the translation period in which the cost of such items was incurred. However, if amounts representing items included in the closing inventory balance are either valued at market or written down to market value, they shall be translated at the exchange rate existing on the last day of the taxable year. For purposes of determining lower of cost or market, items of inventory included in the closing inventory balance shall be translated into dollars at the exchange rate for the translation period in which the cost of such items was incurred and compared with market as determined in the QBU's hyperinflationary currency translated into dollars at the exchange rate existing on the last day of the taxable year.

(B) *Determination of translation period.* The method used to determine the translation period of amounts representing items of closing inventory for purposes of paragraph (c)(3)(iii)(A) of this section may be based upon reasonable approximations and averages, including rates of turnover, provided that the method is used consistently from year to year.

(4) *Depreciation, depletion, and amortization.* Amounts representing allowances for depreciation, depletion, or amortization shall be translated at the exchange rate for the translation period in which the cost of the underlying asset was incurred, except as provided in paragraph (c)(1) of this section.

(5) *Prepaid expenses or income.* Amounts representing expense or income paid or received in a prior taxable year shall be translated at the exchange rate for the translation period during which they were paid or received.

(6) *Exchange rate.* The exchange rate for a translation period may be determined under any reasonable method, provided that the method is consistently applied to all translation periods and conforms to the taxpayer's method of financial accounting. Reasonable methods include the average of beginning and ending exchange rates for the translation period and the spot rate on the last day of the translation period. Once chosen, a method for determining an exchange rate can be changed only with the consent of the district director.

(7) *Translation period*—(i) *In general.* Except as provided in paragraphs (c)(3)(iii)(B) and (c)(7)(ii) of this section, a translation period shall be each month within a QBU's taxable year.

Reg. § 1.985-3(b)(3)

(ii) *Exception.* A taxpayer may divide its taxable year into translation periods of equal length (with not more than one short period annually) that are less than one month. Once such a translation period is established, it may not be changed without the consent of the district director.

(8) *Dollar transactions*—(i) *In general.* Except as provided in paragraph (c)(8)(ii) of this section, no DASTM gain or loss is realized with respect to dollar transactions since the dollar is the functional currency of the QBU. Thus, the amount of any payment or receipt of dollars shall be reflected in the income or loss statement by the amount of such dollars. Also, the income or loss attributable to any transaction in which the amount that a QBU is entitled to receive (or is required to pay) by reason of such transaction is denominated in terms of the dollar, or is determined by reference to the value of the dollar, must be computed transaction by transaction. For example, if a foreign corporation lends 20 LC when 20 LC = $20 and is entitled to receive the LC equivalent of $20 at maturity plus a market rate of interest in dollars (or its LC equivalent), the loan is a dollar transaction. Similarly, this paragraph applies to any transaction that is determined to be a dollar transaction under section 988.

(ii) *Non-dollar functional currency.* If pursuant to § 1.985-1(b)(2)(ii)(B)(*1*), a QBU is required to use a functional currency other than the dollar, then that currency shall be substituted for the dollar in applying paragraph (c)(8)(i) of this section.

(9) *Third currency transactions*—A taxpayer may use any reasonable method of accounting for transactions described in section 988(c)(1)(B) and (C) that are denominated in, or determined by reference to, a currency other than the QBU's hyperinflationary currency or the dollar (third currency transactions) so long as such method is consistent with its method of financial accounting.

(10) *Examples.* The provisions of this paragraph (c) are illustrated by the following examples:

Example 1. S is an accrual basis QBU that is required to use the dollar as its functional currency for its first taxable year beginning in 1994. S's hyperinflationary currency is the "h." During 1994, S accrues 100 dollars attributable to dollar-denominated sales. Because this is a dollar transaction under paragraph (c)(8) of this section, S's income or loss for 1994 shall reflect the 100 dollars (not the hyperinflationary value of such dollars when accrued).

Example 2. (i) S is an accrual basis QBU that is required to use the dollar as its functional currency for its first taxable year beginning in 1994. S's hyperinflationary currency is the "h." During 1994, S's sales amounted to 240,000,000h, its currently deductible expenses were 26,000,000h, and its total inventory purchases amounted to 100,000,000h. During January and February of 1994, S purchased depreciable assets for 80,000,000h and was allowed depreciation of 4,000,000h. At the end of 1994, S's closing inventory was 23,000,000h. No election to use a translation period other than the month is made, S had no transactions described in paragraph (c)(8) or (c)(9) of this section, and S's closing inventory was computed on the first-in, first-out inventory method. S's adjusted income or loss statement for 1994 is translated into dollars as follows:

	Hyperinflationary Currency	Exchange Rate	United States Dollars
Sales			
(Jan-Feb)	10,000,000h	20:1 [1]	$ 500,000
(Mar-Apr)	20,000,000	21:1	952,381
(May-June)	50,000,000	22:1	2,272,727
(July)	50,000,000	23:1	2,173,913
(August)	20,000,000	26:1	769,231
(Sept.)	20,000,000	28:1	714,286
(Oct.)	20,000,000	29:1	689,655
(Nov.)	20,000,000	30:1	666,667
(Dec.)	30,000,000	31:1	967,742
Total	240,000,000h		$9,706,602

Reg. § 1.985-3(c)(10)

50,828 Income from Sources Without the United States
See p. 20,601 for regulations not amended to reflect law changes

	Hyperinflationary Currency	Exchange Rate	United States Dollars
Cost of Goods Sold:			
Opening Inventory	–0–		–0–
Purchases:			
(Jan-Feb)	15,000,000h	20:1	$ 750,000
(Mar-Apr)	10,000,000	21:1	476,190
(May-June)	30,000,000	22:1	1,363,636
(July)	20,000,000	23:1	869,565
(August)	10,000,000	26:1	384,615
(Sept.)	5,000,000	28:1	178,571
(Oct.)	5,000,000	29:1	172,414
(Nov.)	2,500,000	30:1	83,333
(Dec.)	2,500,000	31:1	80,645
Less Closing Inventory	(23,000,000)	2	(822,655)
	77,000,000h		$3,536,314

[1] Where multiple months are indicated, the exchange rate applies for all months.
[2] See paragraph (ii) for this *Example*.

(ii) Since S uses the first-in, first-out inventory method, the closing inventory is assumed to consist of purchases made during the most recent translation period as follows:

	Hyperinflationary Currency	Exchange Rate	United States Dollars
December	2,500,000h	31:1	$ 80,645
November	2,500,000	30:1	83,333
October	5,000,000	29:1	172,414
September	5,000,000	28:1	178,571
August	8,000,000	26:1	307,692
Total	23,000,000h		$ 822,655

Non-Capitalized Expenses:			
(Jan-Feb)	4,000,000h	20:1	$ 200,000
(Mar-Apr)	2,500,000	21:1	119,048
(May-June)	2,500,000	22:1	113,636
(July)	2,000,000	23:1	86,957
(August)	3,000,000	26:1	115,385
(Sept.)	3,000,000	28:1	107,143
(Oct.)	2,000,000	29:1	68,966
(Nov.)	3,000,000	30:1	100,000
(Dec.)	4,000,000	31:1	129,032
Total	26,000,000h		$1,040,167
Depreciation	4,000,000h	20:1	$ 200,000
Total Cost & Expenses	107,000,000h		$4,776,481
Operating Profit	133,000,000h		$4,930,121

(d) *Computation of DASTM gain or loss*—(1) *Rule.* DASTM gain or loss of a QBU equals—

(i) The net worth of the QBU (as determined under paragraph (d)(2) of this section) at the end of the taxable year minus the net worth of the QBU at the end of the preceding taxable year; plus

(ii) The dollar amount of the items described in paragraph (d)(3) of this section and minus the dollar amount of the items described in paragraph (d)(4) of this section; minus

(iii) The amount of dollar income or earnings and profits (or plus the amount of any dollar loss or deficit in earnings and profits) as determined for the taxable year pursuant to paragraphs (b)(1) through (b)(3) of this section.

(2) *Net worth.* Net worth of a QBU at the end of any taxable year equals the aggregate dollar amount representing assets on the QBU's balance sheet at the end of the taxable year less the aggregate dollar amount representing liabilities on the balance sheet. Notwithstanding any other provision in this paragraph (d)(2), the district director may adjust the amount of any asset or liability if a purpose for acquiring (or disposing of) the asset or incurring (or discharging) the liability is to manipulate the composition of the balance sheet for any period during the taxable year in order to avoid tax. The taxpayer shall determine net worth by—

Reg. § 1.985-3(d)(1)

(i) Preparing a balance sheet as of the end of the taxable year from the QBU's books and records (within the meaning of § 1.989(a)-1(d)) as recorded in the QBU's hyperinflationary currency;

(ii) Making adjustments necessary to conform such balance sheet to United States generally accepted accounting principles and tax accounting principles (including reversing monetary correction adjustments required by local accounting principles); and

(iii) Translating the asset and liability amounts shown on the balance sheet into United States dollars in accordance with paragraph (d)(5) of this section.

(3) *Positive adjustments.* The items described in this paragraph (d)(3) are dividend distributions for the taxable year and any items that decrease net worth for the taxable year but that generally do not affect income or loss or earnings and profits (or a deficit in earnings and profits). Such items include a transfer to the home office of a QBU branch and a return of capital. Except as otherwise provided by ruling or administrative pronouncement, the amount of a transfer to the home office of a QBU branch, a dividend, or a distribution that is a return of capital shall be translated into dollars at the exchange rate on the date the amount is paid.

(4) *Negative adjustments.* The items described in this paragraph (d)(4) are items that increase net worth for the taxable year but that generally do not affect income or loss or earnings and profits (or a deficit in earnings and profits). Such items include a capital contribution or a transfer from a home office to a QBU branch. Except as otherwise provided by ruling or administrative pronouncement, if the contribution or transfer is not in dollars, the amount of a capital contribution or transfer shall be translated into dollars at the exchange rate on the date made.

(5) *Translation of balance sheet.* Asset and liability amounts shown on the balance sheet in hyperinflationary currency (adjusted pursuant to paragraph (d)(2)(ii) of this section) shall be translated into dollars as provided in this paragraph (d)(5). However, if the QBU previously changed its functional currency to the dollar and the rules of § 1.985-5 (or, if applicable, § 1.985-5T, as contained in the April 1, 1993 edition of 26 CFR part 1 (1.908 to 1.1000)) applied in translating its balance sheet amounts into dollars, then the spot exchange rate applied under those rules shall be used to translate any amount that would otherwise be translated at a rate determined by reference to a translation period prior to the change in functional currency. For example, the basis of real property acquired while the QBU had a nondollar functional currency shall be translated into dollars at the spot rate on the last day of the taxable year before the year of change to a dollar functional currency, rather than at the rate for the period in which the cost was incurred.

(i) *Closing inventory.* Amounts representing items of inventory included in the closing inventory balance shall be translated in accordance with paragraph (c)(3)(iii) of this section.

(ii) *Bad debt reserves.* Amounts representing bad debt reserves shall be translated at the exchange rate for the last translation period for the taxable year.

(iii) *Prepaid income or expense.* Amounts representing expenses or income paid or received in a prior taxable year shall be translated in accordance with paragraph (c)(5) of this section.

(iv) *Hyperinflationary currency.* Amounts of the hyperinflationary currency and hyperinflationary demand deposit balances shall be translated at the exchange rate for the last translation period of the taxable year.

(v) *Certain assets*—(A) *In general.* Amounts representing plant, real property, equipment, goodwill, and patents and other intangibles shall be translated at the exchange rate for the translation period in which the cost of the asset was incurred.

(B) *Adjustment to certain assets.* Amounts representing depreciation, depletion, and amortization reserves shall be translated in accordance with paragraph (c)(4) of this section.

(vi) *Hyperinflationary debt obligations.* Except as provided in paragraph (d)(5)(vii) of this section, amounts representing a hyperinflationary debt obligation (including accounts receivable and payable) shall be translated at the exchange rate for the last translation period for the taxable year.

(vii) *Accrued foreign income taxes.* Amounts representing an accrued but unpaid foreign income tax shall be translated at the exchange rate on the last day of the last translation period of the taxable year of accrual.

(viii) *Certain hyperinflationary financial instruments.* Amounts representing any item described in section 988(c)(1)(B)(iii) (relating to forward contracts, futures contracts, options, or similar financial instruments) denominated in or determined by reference to the hyperinflationary currency shall be translated at the exchange rate for the last translation period for the taxable year.

(ix) *Other assets and liabilities.* Amounts representing assets and liabilities, other than those described in paragraphs (d)(5)(i) through (viii) of this section, shall be translated at the exchange rate for the translation period in which

Reg. § 1.985-3(d)(5)

50,830 Income from Sources Without the United States

See p. 20,601 for regulations not amended to reflect law changes

the cost of the asset or the amount of the liability was incurred.

(6) *Dollar transactions.* Notwithstanding any other provisions of this paragraph (d), where the amount representing an item shown on the balance sheet reflects a dollar transaction (described in paragraph (c)(8) of this section), the transaction shall be taken into account in accordance with that paragraph.

(7) *Third currency transactions.* A taxpayer may use any reasonable method of accounting for transactions described in section 988(c)(1)(B) and (C) that are denominated in, or determined by reference to, a currency other than the QBU's hyperinflationary currency or the dollar (third currency transactions), so long as such method is consistent with its method of financial accounting.

(8) *Character.* The amount of DASTM gain or loss determined under paragraph (d)(1) of this section shall be ordinary income or loss.

(9) *Example.* The provisions of this paragraph (d) are illustrated by the following example:

Example. (i) S, an accrual method calendar year foreign corporation, uses DASTM. S's hyperinflationary currency is the "h." S's net worth at December 31, 1993 was $3,246,495. For 1994, S's operating profit is 81,340,000h, or $2,038,200. S made a 5,000,000h distribution in April and again in December of 1994. S's translation period is the month. None of S's assets or liabilities reflect a dollar or third currency transaction described in paragraph (c)(8) or (c)(9) of this section, respectively. The exchange rate for each month in 1994 is as follows:

January	32h:$1
Feb.-Mar.	33:1
April-May	34:1
June	35:1
July	36:1
Aug.-Sept.	37:1
Oct.	38:1
Nov.	39:1
Dec.	40:1

(ii) At the end of 1994, S's assets and liabilities, as adjusted and translated pursuant to paragraphs (d)(2) and (d)(5) of this section, are as follows:

	Hyper-inflationary	Exchange Rate	U.S.-Dollar
Hyperinflationary cash on hand	40,000h	40:1	$ 1,000
Checking account	400,000	40:1	10,000
Accounts Receivable- 30 Day Accounts	20,000,000	40:1[1]	500,000
60 Day Accounts	25,000,000	40:1	625,000
Inventory	65,000,000	[2]	2,500,000
Fixed assets--Property	90,000,000	27:1	3,333,333
Plant	190,000,000	[3]	6,785,714
Accumulated Depreciation	(600,000)	[3]	(21,428)
Equipment	10,000,000	[4]	340,000
Accumulated Depreciation	(400,000)	[4]	(13,333)
Common Stock--Stock A	500,000	34:1	14,706
Stock B	400,000	26:1	15,385
Preferred Stock	1,000,000	32:1	31,250
C.D.s	5,000,000	40:1	125,000
Total Assets	406,340,000		14,246,627
Accounts Payable	35,000,000	40:1	875,000
Long-term liabilities:			
Liability A	150,000,000	40:1	3,750,000
Liability B	80,000,000	40:1	2,000,000
Liability C	30,000,000	40:1	750,000
Total Liabilities	295,000,000h		$ 7,375,000

[1] S ages its accounts receivable and groups them into two categories - those outstanding for 30 days and those outstanding for 60 days.

[2] Translated the same as closing inventory under paragraph (c)(3)(iii).
[3] The cost of S's plant was incurred in several translation periods. Therefore, the dollar cost and dollar depreciation reflect several translation rates.
[4] S has a variety of equipment.

Reg. § 1.985-3(d)(6)

(iii) The DASTM gain of S for 1994 is computed as follows:

Net worth - 1994			$6,871,627
Less - Net worth - 1993			$3,246,495
Plus - 1994 Dividends	- April	$149,254	
	December	126,582[1]	275,836
Less Operating Profit - 1994			2,038,200
DASTM Gain			$1,862,768

[1] The exchange rates on the date of the April and December dividends were 33.5h:$1 and 39.5h:$1, respectively.

(iv) Thus, total profit = $2,038,200 + $1,862,768 = $3,900,968

(e) *Effect of DASTM gain or loss on gross income, taxable income, or earnings and profits*—(1) *In general.* For all purposes of subtitle A, the amount of DASTM gain or loss of a QBU determined under paragraph (d) of this section is taken into account by the QBU for purposes of determining the amount of its gross income, taxable income or loss, earnings and profits (or deficit in earnings and profits), and, where necessary, particular items of income, expense or other amounts. DASTM gain or loss is allocated under one of two methods. Certain small QBUs may elect the small QBU DASTM allocation described in paragraph (e)(2) of this section. All other QBUs must use the 9-step procedure described in paragraph (e)(3) of this section.

(2) *Small QBU DASTM allocation*—(i) *Election threshold.* A taxpayer may elect to use the small QBU DASTM allocation described in paragraph (e)(2)(iv) of this section with respect to a QBU that has an adjusted basis in assets (translated as provided in paragraph (d)(5) of this section) of $10 million or less at the end of any taxable year. In calculating the $10 million threshold, a QBU shall be treated as owning all of the assets of each related QBU (as defined in paragraph (e)(2)(vi) of this section) having its residence (as defined in section 988(a)(3)(B)) in the QBU's country of residence (related same-country QBU). For this purpose, appropriate adjustment shall be made to eliminate the double counting of assets created in transactions between related QBUs resident in the same country. For example, assume QBU-1, resident in country X, sells inventory to related QBU-2, also resident in country X, in exchange for an account receivable. For purposes of determining the assets of QBU-1 under this paragraph (e)(2)(i), the taxpayer shall take into account either the inventory shown on the books of QBU-2 or QBU-1's receivable from QBU-2 (but not both).

(ii) *Consent to election.* The election of the small QBU DASTM allocation or subsequent application of the rules of paragraph (e)(3) of this section due to an increase in the adjusted basis of the QBU's assets shall be deemed to have been made with the consent of the Commissioner. Once the election under paragraph (e)(2)(iii) of this section is made, it shall apply for all years in which the adjusted basis of the assets of the QBU (and any related same-country QBU) is $10 million or less, unless revoked with the Commissioner's consent. If the adjusted basis of the assets of the QBU (and any related same-country QBU) exceeds $10 million at the end of any taxable year, the rules of paragraph (e)(3) of this section shall apply to that QBU (and any related same-country QBU) for such year and each subsequent year unless such QBU again qualifies, and applies for and obtains the Commissioner's consent, to use the small QBU DASTM allocation. However, if a QBU acquires assets with a principal purpose of avoiding the application of paragraph (e)(2)(iv) of this section, the Commissioner may disregard the acquisition of such assets.

(iii) *Manner of making election*—(A) *QBUs that are branches of United States persons.* For the first year in which this election is effective, in the case of a QBU branch of a United States person, a statement shall be attached to the United States person's timely filed Federal income tax return (taking extensions into account). The statement shall identify the QBU (or QBUs) for which the election is being made by describing its business and its country of residence, state the adjusted basis of the assets of the QBU (and any related same-country QBUs) to which the election applies, and include a statement that the election is being made pursuant to § 1.985-3(e)(2).

(B) *Other QBUs.* In the case of a QBU other than one described in paragraph (e)(2)(iii)(A) of this section, an election must be made in the manner prescribed in § 1.964-1. The statement filed with the Internal Revenue Service as required under § 1.964-1 must include the information required under paragraph (e)(2)(iii)(A) of this section.

(iv) *Effect of election.* If a taxpayer elects under this paragraph (e)(2) to use the small QBU

DASTM allocation, DASTM gain or loss, as determined under paragraph (d) of this section, of a small QBU shall be allocated ratably to all items of the QBU's gross income (determined prior to adjustment for DASTM gain or loss). Therefore, for purposes of the foreign tax credit, DASTM gain or loss shall be allocated on the basis of the relative amounts of gross income in each separate category as defined in § 1.904-5(a)(1). In the case of a controlled foreign corporation (within the meaning of section 957 or 953(c)(1)(B)), for purposes of section 952, DASTM gain or loss shall be allocated to subpart F income in a separate category in the same ratio that the gross subpart F income in that category for the taxable year bears to its total gross income in that category for the taxable year.

(v) *Conformity.* If a person (or a QBU of such person) makes an election under this paragraph (e)(2) to use the small QBU DASTM allocation, then each QBU of any related person (as defined in paragraph (e)(2)(vi) of this section) that satisfies the threshold requirement of paragraph (e)(2)(i) of this section (after application of the aggregation rule of paragraph (e)(2)(i) of this section) shall be deemed to have made the election.

(vi) *Related person.* The term related person means any person with a relationship to the QBU (or to the United States or foreign person of which the electing QBU is a part) that is defined in section 267(b) or section 707(b).

(3) *DASTM 9-step procedure*—(i) *Step 1—prepare balance sheets.* The taxpayer shall prepare an opening and a closing balance sheet for the QBU for each balance sheet period during the taxable year. The balance sheet period is the most frequent period for which balance sheet data are reasonably available (but in no event less frequently than quarterly). The balance sheet period may not be changed without the consent of the district director. The balance sheets must be prepared under the principles of paragraph (d)(2) of this section.

(ii) *Step 2—identify certain assets and liabilities.* The taxpayer shall identify each item on the balance sheet that is described in section 988(c)(1)(B) or (C) and that would have been translated under paragraph (d)(5) of this section into dollars at the exchange rate for the last translation period for the taxable year (or the exchange rate on the last day of the last translation period of the taxable year in the case of an accrued foreign income tax liability).

(iii) *Step 3—characterize the assets.* The taxpayer shall characterize and group the assets identified in paragraph (e)(3)(ii) of this section

(Step 2) according to the source and the type of income that they generate, have generated, or may reasonably be expected to generate by applying the principles of § 1.861-9T(g)(3) or its successor regulation (relating to characterization of assets for purposes of interest expense allocation). If a purpose for a taxpayer's business practices is to manipulate asset characterization or groupings, the district director may allocate or apportion DASTM gain or loss attributable to the assets. Thus, if a taxpayer that previously did not separately state interest on accounts receivable begins to impose an interest charge and a purpose for the change was to manipulate tax characterizations or groupings, then the district director may require that none of the DASTM gain or loss attributable to those receivables be allocated or apportioned to interest income.

(iv) *Step 4—determine DASTM gain or loss attributable to certain assets*—(A) *General rule.* The taxpayer shall determine the dollar amount of DASTM gain or loss attributable to assets in each group identified in paragraph (e)(3)(iii) of this section (Step 3) as follows:

$$[(bb + eb) \div 2] \times [er - br]$$

where

bb = the hyperinflationary currency adjusted basis of the assets in the group at the beginning of the balance sheet period.

eb = the hyperinflationary currency adjusted basis of the assets in the group at the end of the balance sheet period.

er = one dollar divided by the number of hyperinflationary currency units that equal one dollar at the end of the balance sheet period.

br = one dollar divided by the number of hyperinflationary currency units that equal one dollar at the beginning of the balance sheet period.

(B) *Weighting to prevent distortion.* If averaging the adjusted basis of assets in a group at the beginning and end of a balance sheet period results in an allocation of DASTM gain or loss that does not clearly reflect income, as might be the case in the event of a purchase or disposition of an asset that is not in the normal course of business, the taxpayer must use a weighting method that reflects the time the assets are held by the QBU during the translation period.

(C) *Example.* The provisions of this paragraph (e)(3)(iv) are illustrated by the following example:

Example. S is a foreign corporation that operates in the hyperinflationary currency "h" and computes its income or loss or earnings and profits under DASTM. S's adjusted basis in a

Reg. § 1.985-3(e)(3)

group of assets described in section 988(c)(1)(B) or (C) that generate general limitation foreign source income (as characterized under paragraph (e)(3)(iii) of this section) at the beginning of the balance sheet period is 750,000h. S's basis in such assets at the end of the balance sheet period is 1,250,000h. The exchange rate at the beginning of the balance sheet period is $1 = 200h. The exchange rate at the end of the balance sheet period is $1 = 500h. The DASTM loss attributable to the assets described above is $3,000, determined as follows:

$[(750{,}000h + 1{,}250{,}000h) \div 2] \times [(\$1 \div 500h) - (\$1 \div 200h)] = (\$3000)$

(v) *Step 5—adjust dollar gross income by DASTM gain or loss from assets.* The taxpayer shall adjust the dollar amount of the QBU's gross income (computed under paragraphs (b)(1) through (b)(3) of this section) generated by each group of assets characterized in paragraph (e)(3)(iii) of this section (Step 3) by the amount of DASTM gain or loss attributable to those assets computed under paragraph (e)(3)(iv) of this section (Step 4). Thus, if a group of assets, such as accounts receivable, generates both a category of income described in section 904(d)(1)(I) (relating to general limitation income) that is not foreign base company income as defined in section 954 and a DASTM loss under paragraph (e)(3)(iv) of this section (Step 4), the amount of the DASTM loss would reduce the amount of the QBU's gross income in that category. Similarly, if a group of assets, such as short-term bank deposits, generates both foreign personal holding company income that is passive income (described in sections 954(c)(1)(A) and 904(d)(1)(A)) and a DASTM loss under paragraph (e)(3)(iv) of this section (Step 4), the amount of the DASTM loss would reduce the amount of the QBU's foreign personal holding company income and passive income. See section 904(f) and the regulations thereunder in the case where that section would apply and DASTM loss attributable to a group of assets exceeds the income generated by such assets.

(vi) *Step 6—determine DASTM gain or loss attributable to liabilities*—(A) *General rule.* The taxpayer shall determine the dollar amount of DASTM gain or loss attributable to liabilities identified in paragraph (e)(3)(ii) of this section (Step 2), and described in paragraph (e)(3)(vi)(B) of this section as follows:

$[(bl + el) \div 2] \times [br - er]$

where

bl = the hyperinflationary currency amount of liabilities at the beginning of the balance sheet period.

el = the hyperinflationary currency amount of liabilities at the end of the balance sheet translation period.

br = one dollar divided by the number of hyperinflationary currency units that equal one dollar at the beginning of the balance sheet period.

er = one dollar divided by the number of hyperinflationary currency units that equal one dollar at the end of the balance sheet period.

(B) *Separate calculation.* The calculation shall be made separately for interest-bearing liabilities described in paragraph (e)(3)(vii) of this section (Step 7) and for each of the classes of non-interest-bearing liabilities described in paragraph (e)(3)(viii) of this section (Step 8).

(C) *Weighting to prevent distortion.* Where a distortion would result from averaging the amount of liabilities at the beginning and end of a balance sheet period, as might be the case where a taxpayer incurs or retires a substantial liability, the taxpayer must use a different method that more clearly reflects the average amount of liabilities weighted to reflect the time the liability was outstanding during the balance sheet period.

(vii) *Step 7—adjust dollar income and expense by DASTM gain or loss from interest-bearing liabilities*—(A) *In general.* The taxpayer shall apply the amount of DASTM gain on interest-bearing liabilities computed under paragraph (e)(3)(vi) of this section (Step 6) to reduce interest expense generated by such liabilities (e.g., prior to the application of § 1.861-9T or its successor regulation). To the extent DASTM gain on such liabilities exceeds interest expense, it shall be sourced or otherwise classified in the same manner that interest expense is allocated and apportioned under § 1.861-9T or its successor regulation. The amount of DASTM loss on interest-bearing liabilities computed under paragraph (e)(3)(vi) of this section (Step 6) shall be allocated and apportioned in the same manner that interest expense is allocated and apportioned under § 1.861-9T or its successor regulation (without regard to the exceptions to fungibility in § 1.861-10T or its successor regulation). For purposes of this section, an interest-bearing liability is a liability that requires payment of periodic interest (whether fixed or variable), has original issue discount, or would have interest imputed under subtitle A.

(B) *Allocation of DASTM gain or loss from interest-bearing liabilities that generate related person interest expense.* DASTM gain or loss from interest-bearing liabilities that generate related person interest expense (as provided in section 954(b)(5)) shall be allocated for purposes of

Reg. § 1.985-3(e)(3)

subtitle A (including sections 904 and 952) in the same manner that the related person interest expense of that debt is required to be allocated under the rules of section 954(b)(5) and § 1.904-5(c)(2).

(C) *Modified gross income method.* In applying the modified gross income method described in § 1.861-9T(j) or its successor regulation, gross income shall be adjusted for any DASTM gain or loss from assets as provided in paragraph (e)(3)(v) of this section (Step 5) and any DASTM gain or loss with respect to short-term, non-interest-bearing trade payables as provided in paragraph (e)(3)(viii)(A) of this section.

(viii) *Step 8—adjust dollar income and expense by DASTM gain or loss from non-interest bearing liabilities*—(A) *Short-term, non-interest-bearing trade payables.* The taxpayer shall allocate DASTM gain or loss on short-term non-interest-bearing trade payables for purposes of subtitle A (including sections 904 and 952) to the same category or type of gross income as the cost or expense to which the trade payable relates. For this purpose, a short-term, non-interest-bearing trade payable is a non-interest-bearing liability with a term of 183 days or less that is incurred to purchase property or services to be used by the obligor in an active trade or business.

(B) *Excise tax payables.* The taxpayer shall allocate DASTM gain or loss on excise tax payables for purposes of subtitle A (including sections 904 and 952) to the same category or type of gross income as would be derived from the activity to which the excise tax relates.

(C) *Other non-interest-bearing liabilities*—(*1*) *In general.* Except as provided in paragraphs (e)(3)(viii)(A), (e)(3)(viii)(B), and (e)(3)(viii)(C)(*2*) of this section, DASTM gain or loss on non-interest-bearing liabilities shall be allocated under paragraph (e)(3)(ix) of this section (Step 9).

(*2*) *Tracing if substantial distortion of income.* DASTM gains and losses on liabilities described in paragraph (e)(3)(viii)(C)(*1*) of this section may be attributed to the same section 904(d) separate category or subpart F category as the transaction to which the liability relates if the taxpayer demonstrates to the satisfaction of the district director, or it is determined by the district director, that application of paragraph (e)(3)(viii)(C)(*1*) of this section results in a substantial distortion of income.

(ix) *Step 9—allocate residual DASTM gain or loss.* If there is a difference between the net DASTM gain or loss determined under paragraphs (e)(3)(i) through (viii) of this section (Steps 1 through 8) and the DASTM gain or loss determined under paragraph (d) of this section, the amount of the difference must be allocated for purposes of subtitle A (including sections 904 and 952) to the QBU's gross income (computed under paragraphs (b)(1) through (3) of this section, as adjusted under paragraphs (e)(3)(i) through (viii) of this section (Steps 1 through 8)) on the basis of the relative amounts of each category or type of gross income. [Reg. § 1.985-3.]

☐ [T.D.8263, 9-19-89. Amended by T.D. 8556, 7-22-94.]

[Reg. § 1.985-4]

§ 1.985-4. Method of accounting.—(a) *Adoption or election.* The adoption of, or the election to use, a functional currency shall be treated as a method of accounting. The functional currency shall be used for the year of adoption (or election) and for all subsequent taxable years unless permission to change is granted, or considered to be granted under § 1.985-2 or 1.985-8, by the Commissioner.

(b) *Condition for changing functional currencies.* Generally, permission to change functional currencies shall not be granted unless significant changes in the facts and circumstances of the QBU's economic environment occur. If the determination of the functional currency of the QBU for purposes of United States generally accepted accounting principles (GAAP) is based on facts and circumstances substantially similar to those set forth in § 1.985-1(c)(2), then ordinarily the Commissioner will grant a taxpayer's request to change its functional currency (or the functional currency of its branch that is a QBU) to a new functional currency only if the taxpayer (or its QBU) also changes to the new functional currency for purposes of GAAP. However, permission to change will not necessarily be granted merely because the new functional currency will conform to the taxpayer's GAAP functional currency.

(c) *Relationship to certain other sections of the Code.* Nothing in this section shall be construed to override the provisions of any other sections of the Code or regulations that require the use of consistent accounting methods. Such provisions must be independently satisfied separate and apart from the identification of a functional currency. For instance, while separate geographical divisions of a taxpayer's trade or business may have different functional currencies, such geographical divisions may nevertheless be required to consistently use other methods of accounting. [Reg. § 1.985-4.]

☐ [T.D. 8263, 9-19-89. Amended by T.D. 8776, 7-28-98 and T.D. 8927, 1-10-2001.]

[Reg. § 1.985-5]

§ 1.985-5. Adjustments required upon change in functional currency.—(a) *In general.* This section applies in the case of a QBU that changes from one functional currency (old functional currency) to another functional currency (new functional currency). A taxpayer or QBU subject to the rules of this section shall make the adjustments set forth in the 3-step procedure described in paragraphs (b) through (e) of this section. The adjustments shall be made on the last day of the taxable year ending before the year of change as defined in § 1.481-1(a)(1). Gain or loss required to be recognized under paragraphs (b), (d)(2), and (e)(2) of this section is not subject to section 481 and, therefore, the full amount of the gain or loss must be included in income or earnings and profits on the last day of the taxable year ending before the year of change. Except as provided in § 1.985-6, a QBU with a functional currency for its first taxable year beginning in 1987 that is different from the currency in which it had kept its books and records for United States accounting and tax accounting purposes for its prior taxable year shall apply the principles of this § 1.985-5 for purposes of computing the relevant functional currency items, such as earnings and profits, basis of an asset, and amount of a liability, as of the first day of a taxpayer's first taxable year beginning in 1987. However, a QBU that changes to the dollar pursuant to § 1.985-1(b)(2) after 1987 shall apply § 1.985-7.

(b) *Step 1—Taking into account exchange gain or loss on certain section 988 transactions.* The QBU shall recognize or otherwise take into account for all purposes of the Code the amount of any unrealized exchange gain or loss attributable to a section 988 transaction (as defined in section 988(c)(1)(A), (B), and (C)) that, after applying section 988(d), is denominated in terms of or determined by reference to the new functional currency. The amount of such gain or loss shall be determined without regard to the limitations of section 988(b) (*i.e.*, whether any gain or loss would be realized on the transaction as a whole). The character and source of such gain or loss shall be determined under section 988.

(c) *Step 2—Determining the new functional currency basis of property and the new functional currency amount of liabilities and any other relevant items.* The new functional currency adjusted basis of property and the new functional currency amount of liabilities and any other relevant items (*e.g.*, items described in section 988(c)(1)(B)(iii)) shall equal the product of the amount of the old functional currency adjusted basis or amount multiplied by the new functional currency/old functional currency spot exchange rate on the last day of the taxable year ending before the year of change (spot rate).

(d) *Step 3A—Additional adjustments that are necessary when a branch changes functional currency*—(1) *Branch changing to a functional currency other than the taxpayer's functional currency*—(i) *Rule.* If a QBU that is a branch of a taxpayer changes to a functional currency other than the taxpayer's functional currency, the branch shall make the adjustments set forth in either paragraph (d)(1)(ii) or (d)(1)(iii) of this section for purposes of section 987. See § 1.987-5(d) for rules for computing the branch's equity pool and basis pool.

(ii) *Where prior to the change the branch and taxpayer had different functional currencies.* If the branch and the taxpayer had different functional currencies prior to the change, the branch's new functional currency equity pool shall equal the product of the old functional currency amount of the equity pool multiplied by the spot rate. No adjustment to the basis pool is necessary.

(iii) *Where prior to the change the branch and taxpayer had the same functional currency.* If the branch and the taxpayer had the same functional currency prior to the change, the branch's basis pool shall equal the difference between the branch's total old functional currency basis of its assets and its total old functional currency amount of its liabilities. The branch's equity pool shall equal the product of the basis pool multiplied by the spot rate.

(2) *Branch changing to the taxpayer's functional currency.* If a branch changes its functional currency to the taxpayer's functional currency, the branch shall be treated as if it terminated on the last day of the taxable year ending before the year of change. In such a case, the taxpayer shall realize gain or loss attributable to the branch's equity pool under the principles of section 987.

(e) *Step 3B—Additional adjustments that are necessary when a taxpayer changes functional currency*—(1) *Corporations.* The amount of a corporation's new functional currency earnings and profits and the amount of its new functional currency paid-in capital shall equal the product of the old functional currency amounts of such items multiplied by the spot rate. The foreign income taxes and accumulated profits or deficits in accumulated profits of a foreign corporation that were maintained in foreign currency for purposes of section 902 and that are attributable to taxable years of the foreign corporation beginning before January 1, 1987, also shall be translated into the new functional currency at the spot rate.

Reg. § 1.985-5(e)

50,836 Income from Sources Without the United States

See p. 20,601 for regulations not amended to reflect law changes

(2) *Collateral consequences to a United States shareholder of a corporation changing to the United States dollar as its functional currency.* A United States shareholder (within the meaning of section 951(b) or section 953(c)(1)(A)) of a controlled foreign corporation (within the meaning of section 957 or section 953(c)(1)(B)) changing its functional currency to the dollar shall recognize foreign currency gain or loss computed under section 986(c) as if all previously taxed earnings and profits, if any, (including amounts attributable to pre-1987 taxable years that were translated from dollars into functional currency in the foreign corporation's first post-1986 taxable year) were distributed immediately prior to the change. Such a shareholder shall also recognize gain or loss attributable to the corporation's paid-in capital to the same extent, if any, that such gain or loss would be recognized under the regulations under section 367(b) if the corporation was liquidated completely.

(3) *Taxpayers that are not corporations.* [Reserved]

(4) *Adjustments to a branch's accounts when a taxpayer changes functional currency*—(i) *Taxpayer changing to a functional currency other than the branch's functional currency.* If a taxpayer changes to a functional currency that differs from the functional currency of a branch of the taxpayer, the branch shall adjust its basis pool in the manner prescribed in paragraph (d)(1)(ii) of this section for adjusting the equity pool, if the taxpayer's old functional currency was different from the branch's functional currency. If the taxpayer's old functional currency was the same as the branch's functional currency, the branch shall determine its equity pool and basis pool in the manner set forth in paragraph (d)(1)(iii) of this section for determining the basis pool and equity pool, respectively.

(ii) *Taxpayer changing to the same functional currency as the branch.* If a taxpayer changes to the same functional currency as a branch of the taxpayer, the taxpayer shall realize gain or loss as set forth in paragraph (d)(2) of this section.

(f) *Examples.* The provisions of this section are illustrated by the following examples.

Example 1. S, a calendar year foreign corporation, is wholly owned by domestic corporation P. The Commissioner granted permission to change S's functional currency from the LC to the FC beginning January 1, 1993. The LC/FC exchange rate on December 31, 1992 is 1 LC/2 FC. The following shows how S must convert the items on its balance sheet from the LC to the FC.

LC	1:2	FC
Assets:		
Cash on hand	40,000	80,000
Accounts Receivable	10,000	20,000
Inventory	100,000	200,000
100,000 FC Bond (100,000 LC historical basis)	50,000 [1]	100,000
Fixed assets:		
Property	200,000	400,000
Plant	500,000	1,000,000
Accumulated Depreciation	(200,000)	(400,000)
Equipment	1,000,000	2,000,000
Accumulated Depreciation	(400,000)	(800,000)
Total Assets	1,300,000	2,600,000
Liabilities:		
Accounts Payable	50,000	100,000
Long-term Liabilities.....	400,000	800,000
Paid-in-Capital	800,000	1,600,000
Retained Earnings.......	50,000 [2]	100,000
Total Liabilities and Equity	1,300,000	2,600,000

Example 2. P, a domestic corporation, operates a foreign branch, S. The Commissioner granted permission to change S's functional currency from the LC to the FC beginning January 1, 1993. As of December 31, 1992, S's equity pool was 2,000 LC and its basis pool was $4,000. The LC/FC exchange rate on December 31, 1992 is 1 LC/2 FC. On January 1, 1993, the new functional currency amount of S's equity pool is 4,000 FC. The basis pool is not affected. [Reg. § 1.985-5.]

☐ [T.D. 8464, 12-31-92. Amended by T.D. 8765, 3-4-98.]

[Reg. § 1.985-6]

§ 1.985-6. Transition rules for a QBU that uses the dollar approximate separate transactions method for its first taxable year beginning in 1987.—(a) *In general.* This section sets forth transition rules for a QBU that used the dollar approximate separate transactions method of accounting set forth in § 1.985-3 or § 1.985-3T (as contained in the April 1, 1989 edition of 26 CFR part 1 (1.908 to 1.1000)) for its first taxable year beginning in 1987 (DASTM QBU). A DASTM QBU must determine the dollar and hyperinflationary currency basis of its assets and

---

[1] Under § 1.985-5(b), S will recognize a 50,000 LC loss (100,000 LC basis − 50,000 LC value) on the bond resulting from the change in functional currency. Thus, immediately before the change, S's basis in the PC bond (taking into account the loss) is 50,000 LC.

[2] The amount of S's LC retained earnings reflects the 50,000 LC loss on the bond.

Reg. § 1.985-6(a)

the dollar and hyperinflationary currency amount of its liabilities that were acquired or incurred in taxable years beginning before January 1, 1987. In addition, a DASTM QBU must determine its net worth, including its retained earnings, at the end of the QBU's last taxable year beginning before January 1, 1987. This section provides rules for controlled foreign corporations (as defined in section 957 or section 953(c)(1)(B)), other foreign corporations, and branches of United States persons that must make these determinations.

(b) *Certain controlled foreign corporations.* If a DASTM QBU was a controlled foreign corporation for its last taxable year beginning before January 1, 1987, and it had a significant event as described in § 1.964-1(c)(6) in a taxable year beginning before January 1, 1987, then the rules of this paragraph (b) shall apply.

(1) *Basis in assets and amount of liabilities.* The hyperinflationary currency adjusted basis of the QBU's assets and the hyperinflationary currency amount of the QBU's liabilities acquired or incurred by the QBU in a taxable year beginning before January 1, 1987, shall be the basis or the amount as determined under § 1.964-1(e) prior to translation under § 1.964-1(e)(4). The dollar adjusted basis of such assets and the dollar amount of such liabilities shall be the adjusted basis or the amount as determined under the rules of § 1.964-1(e) after translation under § 1.964-1(e)(4).

(2) *Retained earnings.* The dollar amount of the QBU's retained earnings at the end of its last taxable year beginning before January 1, 1987, shall be the dollar amount determined under § 1.964-1(e)(3).

(c) *All other foreign corporations.* If a foreign corporation is a DASTM QBU that is not described in paragraph (b) of this section, then the hyperinflationary currency and dollar adjusted basis in the QBU's assets acquired in taxable years beginning before January 1, 1987, the hyperinflationary currency and dollar amount of the QBU's liabilities acquired or incurred in taxable years beginning before January 1, 1987, and the dollar amount of the QBU's net worth, including its retained earnings, at the end of its last taxable year beginning before January 1, 1987, shall be determined by applying the principles of § 1.985-3T or § 1.985-3. Thus, for example, the dollar basis of plant and equipment shall be determined using the appropriate historical exchange rate.

(d) *Pre-1987 section 902 amounts*—(1) *Translation of pre-1987 section 902 accumulated profits and taxes into United States dollars.* The foreign income taxes and accumulated profits or deficits in accumulated profits of a foreign corporation that were maintained in foreign currency for purposes of section 902 and that are attributable to taxable years of the foreign corporation beginning before January 1, 1987, shall be translated into dollars at the spot exchange rate on the first day of its first taxable year beginning after December 31, 1986. Once translated into dollars, these accumulated profits and taxes shall (absent a change in functional currency) remain in dollars for all federal income tax purposes.

(2) *Carryforward of accumulated deficits in accumulated profits from pre-1987 taxable years to post-1986 taxable years.* For purposes of sections 902 and 960, the post-1986 undistributed earnings of a foreign corporation that is subject to the rules of this section shall be reduced by the dollar amount of the corporation's deficit in accumulated profits, if any, determined under section 902 and the regulations thereunder, that was accumulated at the end of the corporation's last taxable year beginning before January 1, 1987. The dollar amount of the accumulated deficit shall be determined by multiplying the foreign currency amount of such deficit by the spot exchange rate on the last day of the corporation's last taxable year beginning before January 1, 1987, and shall be taken into account on the first day of the corporation's first taxable year beginning after December 31, 1986. Post-1986 undistributed earnings may not be reduced by the dollar amount of a pre-1987 deficit in retained earnings determined under § 1.964-1(e).

(e) *Net worth branch.* If a DASTM QBU is a branch of a United States person and the QBU used a net worth method of accounting for its last taxable year beginning before January 1, 1987, then the rules of this paragraph (e) shall apply. A net worth method of accounting is any method of accounting under which the taxpayer calculates the taxable income of a QBU based on the net change in the dollar value of the QBU's equity (assets minus liabilities) during the course of a taxable year, taking into account any contributions or remittances made during the year. *See, e.g.,* Rev. Rul. 75-106, 1975-1 C.B. 31. (See § 601.601(d)(2)(ii)(*b*) of this chapter).

(1) *Basis in assets and amount of liabilities*— (i) *Hyperinflationary amounts.* For the first taxable year beginning in 1987, the hyperinflationary currency adjusted basis of a QBU's assets or the hyperinflationary currency amounts of its liabilities acquired or incurred in a taxable year beginning before January 1, 1987 is the hyperinflationary currency basis or amount at the date when acquired or incurred, as adjusted ac-

Reg. § 1.985-6(e)(1)

cording to United States generally accepted accounting and tax accounting principles. If a hyperinflationary currency basis or amount was not determined at such date, the dollar basis or amount, as adjusted according to United States generally accepted accounting and tax accounting principles, shall be translated into hyperinflationary currency at the spot exchange rate on the date when the asset or liability was acquired or incurred.

(ii) *Dollar amounts.* For the first taxable year beginning in 1987, the dollar adjusted basis of the QBU's assets and the amounts of its liabilities shall be those amounts reflected on the QBU's dollar books and records at the end of the taxpayer's last taxable year beginning before January 1, 1987, after adjusting the books and records according to United States generally accepted accounting and tax accounting principles.

(2) *Ending net worth.* The dollar amount of the QBU's net worth at the end of its last taxable year beginning before January 1, 1987 shall equal the QBU's net worth at that date as determined under paragraph (e)(1)(ii) of this section.

(f) *Profit and loss branch.* If a DASTM QBU is a branch of a United States person and the QBU used a profit and loss method of accounting for its last taxable year beginning before January 1, 1987, then the United States person shall first apply the transition rules of § 1.987-5 in order to determine the beginning amount and dollar basis of the branch's EQ pool, the hyperinflationary currency basis of the branch's assets, and the hyperinflationary currency amounts of its liabilities. A profit and loss method of accounting is any method of accounting under which the taxpayer calculates the profits of a QBU by computing the QBU's profits in its functional currency and translating the net result into dollars. See, e.g., Rev. Rul. 75-107, 1975-1 C.B. 32. (See § 601.601(d)(2)(ii)(*b*) of this chapter). The QBU and the taxpayer must then make the adjustments required by § 1.985-5, *e.g.,* the QBU must take into account unrealized exchange gain or loss on dollar-denominated section 988 transactions, the taxpayer must account for the deemed termination of the branch, and the taxpayer must translate the QBU's balance sheet items from hyperinflationary currency into dollars at the spot rate. [Reg. § 1.985-6.]

☐ [*T.D.* 8464, 12-31-92.]

[Reg. § 1.985-7]

§ 1.985-7. Adjustments required in connection with a change to DASTM.—(a) *In general.* If a QBU begins to use the dollar approximate separate transactions method of accounting set forth in § 1.985-3 (DASTM) in a taxable year beginning after April 6, 1998, adjustments shall be made as provided by this section. For the rules with respect to foreign corporations, see paragraph (b) of this section. For the rules with respect to adjustments to the income of United States shareholders of controlled foreign corporations, see paragraph (c) of this section. For the rules with respect to adjustments relating to QBU branches, see paragraph (d) of this section. For the effective date of this section, see paragraph (e). For purposes of applying this section, the look-back period shall be the period beginning with the first taxable year after the transition date and ending on the last day prior to the taxable year of change. The term transition date means the later of the last day of the last taxable year ending before the base period as defined in § 1.985-1(b)(2)(ii)(D) or the last day of the taxable year in which the QBU last applied DASTM. The taxable year of change shall mean the taxable year of change as defined in § 1.481-1(a)(1). The application of this paragraph may be illustrated by the following examples:

Example 1. A calendar year QBU that has not previously used DASTM operates in a country in which the functional currency of the country is hyperinflationary as defined under § 1.985-1(b)(2)(ii)(D) for the QBU's 1999 tax year. The look-back period is the period from January 1, 1996 through December 31, 1998, the transition date is December 31, 1995, and the taxable year of change is the taxable year beginning January 1, 1999.

Example 2. A QBU that has not previously used DASTM with a taxable year ending June 30, operates in a country in which the functional currency of the country is hyperinflationary for the QBU's tax year beginning July 1, 1999 as defined under § 1.985-1(b)(2)(ii)(D) (where the base period is the thirty-six calendar months immediately preceding the first day of the current calendar year 1999). The look-back period is the period from July 1, 1995 through June 30, 1999, the transition date is June 30, 1995, and the taxable year of change is the taxable year beginning July 1, 1999.

(b) *Adjustments to foreign corporations*—(1) *In general.* In the case of a foreign corporation, the corporation shall make the adjustments set forth in paragraphs (b)(2) through (4) of this section. The adjustments shall be made on the first day of the taxable year of change.

(2) *Treatment of certain section 988 transactions*—(i) *Exchange gain or loss from section 988 transactions unrealized as of the transition date.* A foreign corporation shall adjust earnings and

Reg. § 1.985-7(a)

profits by the amount of any unrealized exchange gain or loss that was attributable to a section 988 transaction (as defined in sections 988(c)(1)(A), (B), and (C)) that was denominated in terms of (or determined by reference to) the dollar and was held by the corporation on the transition date. Such gain or loss shall be computed as if recognized on the transition date and shall be reduced by any gain and increased by any loss recognized by the corporation with respect to such transaction during the look-back period. The amount of such gain or loss shall be determined without regard to the limitations of section 988(b) (i.e., whether any gain or loss would be realized on the transaction as a whole). The character and source of such gain or loss shall be determined under section 988. Proper adjustments shall be made to account for gain or loss taken into account by reason of this paragraph (b)(2). See § 1.985-5(f) Example 1, footnote 1.

(ii) *Treatment of a section 988 transaction entered into and terminated during the look-back period.* A foreign corporation shall reduce earnings and profits by the amount of any gain, and increase earnings and profits by the amount of any loss, that was recognized with respect to any dollar denominated section 988 transactions entered into and terminated during the look-back period.

(3) *Opening balance sheet.* The opening balance sheet of a foreign corporation for the taxable year of change shall be determined as if the corporation had changed its functional currency to the dollar by applying § 1.985-5(c) on the transition date and had translated its assets and liabilities acquired and incurred during the look-back period under § 1.985-3.

(4) *Earnings and profits adjustments*—(i) *Pre-1987 accumulated profits.* The foreign income taxes and accumulated profits or deficits in accumulated profits of a foreign corporation that are attributable to taxable years beginning before January 1, 1987, as stated on the transition date, and that were maintained for purposes of section 902 in the old functional currency, shall be translated into dollars at the spot rate in effect on the transition date. The applicable accumulated profits shall be reduced on a last-in, first-out basis by the aggregate dollar amount (translated from functional currency in accordance with the rules of section 989(b)) attributable to earnings and profits that were distributed (or treated as distributed) during the look-back period to the extent such amounts distributed exceed the earnings and profits calculated under (b)(4)(ii) or (b)(4)(iii), as applicable. See § 1.902-1(b)(2)(ii). Once translated into dollars, these pre-1987 taxes and accumulated profits or deficits in accumulated profits shall (absent a change in functional currency) remain in dollars for all federal income tax purposes.

(ii) *Post-1986 undistributed earnings of a CFC.* In the case of a controlled foreign corporation (within the meaning of section 957 or section 953(c)(1)(B)) (CFC) or a foreign corporation subject to the rules of § 1.904-6(a)(2), the corporation's post-1986 undistributed earnings in each separate category as defined in § 1.904-5(a)(1) as of the first day of the taxable year of change (and prior to adjustment under paragraph (c)(1) of this section) shall equal the sum of—

(A) The corporation's post-1986 undistributed earnings and profits (or deficit in earnings and profits) in each separate category as defined in § 1.904-5(a)(1) as stated on the transition date translated into dollars at the spot rate in effect on the transition date; and

(B) The sum of the earnings and profits (or deficit in earnings and profits) in each separate category determined under § 1.985-3 for each post-transition date taxable year prior to the taxable year of change.

Such amount shall be reduced by the aggregate dollar amount (translated from functional currency in accordance with the rules of section 989(b)) attributable to earnings and profits that were distributed (or treated as distributed) during the look-back period out of post-1986 earnings and profits in such separate category. For purposes of applying this paragraph (b)(4)(ii)(B), the opening balance sheet for calculating earnings and profits under § 1.985-3 for the first post-transition year shall be translated into dollars pursuant to § 1.985-5(c).

(iii) *Post-1986 undistributed earnings of other foreign corporations.* In the case of a foreign corporation that is not a CFC or subject to the rules of § 1.904-6(a)(2), the corporation's post-1986 undistributed earnings shall equal the sum of—

(A) The corporation's post-1986 undistributed earnings (or deficit) on the transition date translated into dollars at the spot rate in effect on the transition date; and

(B) The sum of the earnings and profits (or deficit in earnings and profits) determined under § 1.985-3 for each post-transition date taxable year (or such later year determined under section 902(c)(3)(A)) prior to the taxable year of change.

Such amount shall be reduced by the aggregate dollar amount (translated from functional currency in accordance with the rules of section

Reg. § 1.985-7(b)(4)

989(b)) that was distributed (or treated as distributed) during the look-back period out of post-1986 earnings and profits. For purposes of applying this paragraph (b)(4)(iii)(B), the opening balance sheet for calculating earnings and profits under § 1.985-3 for the first post-transition year shall be translated into dollars pursuant to § 1.985-5(c).

(c) *United States shareholders of controlled foreign corporations*—(1) *In general.* A United States shareholder (within the meaning of section 951(b) or section 953(c)(1)(B)) of a CFC that changes to DASTM shall make the adjustments set forth in paragraphs (c)(2) through (5) of this section on the first day of the taxable year of change. Adjustments under this section shall be taken into account by the shareholder (or such shareholder's successor in interest) ratably over four taxable years beginning with the taxable year of change. Similar rules shall apply in determining adjustments to income of United States persons who have made an election under section 1295 to treat a passive foreign investment company as a qualified electing fund.

(2) *Treatment under subpart F of income recognized on section 988 transactions.* The character of amounts taken into account under paragraph (b)(2) of this section for purposes of sections 951 through 964, shall be determined on the transition date and to the extent characterized as subpart F income shall be taken into account in accordance with the rules of paragraph (c)(1) of this section. Such amounts shall retain their character for all federal income tax purposes (including sections 902, 959, 960, 961, 1248, and 6038).

(3) *Recognition of foreign currency gain or loss on previously taxed earnings and profits on the transition date.* Gain or loss is recognized under section 986(c) as if all previously taxed earnings and profits as determined on the transition date, if any, were distributed on such date. Such gain or loss shall be reduced by any foreign currency gain and increased by any foreign currency loss that was recognized under section 986(c) with respect to distributions of previously taxed earnings and profits during the look-back period. Such amount shall be characterized in accordance with section 986(c) and taken into account in accordance with the rules of paragraph (c)(1) of this section.

(4) *Subpart F income adjustment.* Subpart F income in a separate category shall be determined under § 1.985-3 for each look-back year. For this purpose, the opening DASTM balance sheet shall be determined under § 1.985-5. The sum of the difference (positive or negative) between the amount computed pursuant to § 1.985-3 and amount that was included in income for each year shall be taken into account in the taxable year of change pursuant to paragraph (c)(1) of this section. Such amounts shall retain their character for all federal income tax purposes (including sections 902, 959, 960, 961, 1248, and 6038). For rules applicable if an adjustment under this section results in a loss for the taxable year in a separate category, see section 904(f) and the regulations thereunder. The amount of previously taxed earnings and profits as determined under section 959(c)(2) shall be adjusted (positively or negatively) by the amount taken into account under this paragraph (c)(4) as of the first day of the taxable year of change.

(5) *Foreign tax credit.* A United States shareholder of a CFC shall compute an amount of foreign taxes deemed paid under section 960 with respect to any positive adjustments determined under paragraph (c) of this section. The amount of foreign tax deemed paid shall be computed with reference to the full amount of the adjustment and to the post-1986 undistributed earnings determined under paragraph (b)(4)(i) and (ii) of this section and the post-1986 foreign income taxes of the CFC on the first day of the taxable year of change (i.e., without taking into account earnings and taxes for the taxable year of change). For purposes of section 960, the associated taxes in each separate category shall be allocated pro rata among, and deemed paid in, the shareholder's taxable years in which the income is taken into account. (No adjustment to foreign taxes deemed paid in prior years is required solely by reason of a negative adjustment to income under paragraph (c)(1) of this section).

(d) *QBU branches*—(1) *In general.* In the case of a QBU branch, the taxpayer shall make the adjustments set forth in paragraphs (d)(2) through (d)(4) of this section. Adjustments under this section shall be taken into account by the taxpayer ratably over four taxable years beginning with the taxable year of change.

(2) *Treatment of certain section 988 transactions*—(i) *Exchange gain or loss from section 988 transactions unrealized as of the transition date.* A QBU branch shall adjust income by the amount of any unrealized exchange gain or loss that was attributable to a section 988 transaction (as defined in sections 988(c)(1)(A), (B), and (C)) that was denominated in terms of (or determined by reference to) the dollar and was held by the QBU branch on the transition date. Such gain or loss shall be computed as if recognized on the transition date and shall be reduced by any gain and increased by any loss recognized by the QBU branch with respect to such transaction during the look-back period. The amount of such gain or

loss shall be determined without regard to the limitations of section 988(b) (i.e., whether any gain or loss would be realized on the transaction as a whole). The character and source of such gain or loss shall be determined under section 988. Proper adjustments shall be made to account for gain or loss taken into account by reason of this paragraph (d)(2). See § 1.985-5(f) *Example 1, footnote 1.*

(ii) *Treatment of a section 988 transaction entered into and terminated during the look-back period.* A QBU branch shall reduce income by the amount of any gain, and increase income by the amount of any loss, that was recognized with respect to any dollar denominated section 988 transactions entered into and terminated during the look-back period.

(3) *Deemed termination income adjustment.* The taxpayer shall realize gain or loss attributable to the QBU branch's equity pool (as stated on the transition date) under the principles of section 987, computed as if the branch terminated on the transition date. Such amount shall be reduced by section 987 gain and increased by section 987 loss that was recognized by such taxpayer with respect to remittances during the look-back period.

(4) *Branch income adjustment.* Branch income in a separate category shall be determined under § 1.985-3 for each look-back year. For this purpose, the opening DASTM balance sheet shall be determined under § 1.985-5. The sum of the difference (positive or negative) between the amount computed pursuant to § 1.985-3 and amount taken into account for each year shall be taken into account in the taxable year of change pursuant to paragraph (d)(1) of this section. Such amounts shall retain their character for all federal income tax purposes.

(5) *Opening balance sheet.* The opening balance sheet of a QBU branch for the taxable year of change shall be determined as if the branch had changed its functional currency to the dollar by applying § 1.985-5(c) on the transition date and had translated its assets and liabilities acquired and incurred during the look-back period under § 1.985-3.

(e) *Effective date.* This section is effective for taxable years beginning after April 6, 1998. However, a taxpayer may choose to apply this section to all open taxable years beginning after December 31, 1986, provided each person, and each QBU branch of a person, that is related (within the meaning of § 1.985-2(d)(3)) to the taxpayer also applies this section. [Reg. § 1.985-7.]

☐ [*T.D. 8765, 3-4-98 (corrected 3-31-98).*]

[Reg. § 1.985-8]

§ 1.985-8. Special rules applicable to the European Monetary Union (conversion to euro).—(a) *Definitions*—(1) *Legacy currency.* A legacy currency is the former currency of a Member State of the European Community which is substituted for the euro in accordance with the Treaty establishing the European Community signed February 7, 1992. The term legacy currency shall also include the European Currency Unit.

(2) *Conversion rate.* The conversion rate is the rate at which the euro is substituted for a legacy currency.

(b) *Operative rules*—(1) *Initial adoption.* A QBU (as defined in § 1.989(a)-1(b)) whose first taxable year begins after the euro has been substituted for a legacy currency may not adopt a legacy currency as its functional currency.

(2) *QBU with a legacy currency as its functional currency*—(i) *Required change.* A QBU with a legacy currency as its functional currency is required to change its functional currency to the euro beginning the first day of the first taxable year—

(A) That begins on or after the day that the euro is substituted for that legacy currency (in accordance with the Treaty on European Union); and

(B) In which the QBU begins to maintain its books and records (as described in § 1.989(a)-1(d)) in the euro.

(ii) Notwithstanding paragraph (b)(2)(i) of this section, a QBU with a legacy currency as its functional currency is required to change its functional currency to the euro no later than the last taxable year beginning on or before the first day such legacy currency is no longer valid legal tender.

(3) *QBU with a non-legacy currency as its functional currency*—(i) *In general.* A QBU with a non-legacy currency as its functional currency may change its functional currency to the euro pursuant to this § 1.985-8 if—

(A) Under the rules set forth in § 1.985-1(c), the euro is the currency of the economic environment in which a significant part of the QBU's activities are conducted;

(B) After conversion, the QBU maintains its books and records (as described in § 1.989(a)-1(d)) in the euro; and

(C) The QBU is not required to use the dollar as its functional currency under § 1.985-1(b).

(ii) *Time period for change.* A QBU with a non-legacy currency as its functional currency

Reg. § 1.985-8(b)(3)

may change its functional currency to the euro under this section only if it does so within the period set forth in paragraph (b)(2) of this section as if the functional currency of the QBU was a legacy currency.

(4) *Consent of Commissioner.* A change made pursuant to paragraph (b) of this section shall be deemed to be made with the consent of the Commissioner for purposes of § 1.985-4. A QBU changing its functional currency to the euro pursuant to paragraph (b)(2) of this section must make adjustments as provided in paragraph (c) of this section. A QBU changing its functional currency to the euro pursuant to paragraph (b)(3) must make adjustments as provided in § 1.985-5.

(5) *Statement to file upon change.* With respect to a QBU that changes its functional currency to the euro under paragraph (b) of this section, an affected taxpayer shall attach to its return for the taxable year of change a statement that includes the following: "TAXPAYER CERTIFIES THAT A QBU OF THE TAXPAYER HAS CHANGED ITS FUNCTIONAL CURRENCY TO THE EURO PURSUANT TO TREAS. REG. § 1.985-8." For purposes of this paragraph (b)(5), an affected taxpayer shall be in the case where the QBU is: a QBU of an individual U.S. resident (as a result of the activities of such individual), the individual; a QBU branch of a U.S. corporation, the corporation; a controlled foreign corporation (as described in section 957) (or QBU branch thereof), each United States shareholder (as described in section 951(b)); a partnership, each partner separately; a noncontrolled section 902 corporation (as described in section 904(d)(2)(E)) (or branch thereof), each domestic shareholder as described in § 1.902-1(a)(1); or a trust or estate, the fiduciary of such trust or estate.

(c) *Adjustments required when a QBU changes its functional currency from a legacy currency to the euro pursuant to paragraph (b)(2) of this section*—(1) *In general.* A QBU that changes its functional currency from a legacy currency to the euro pursuant to paragraph (b)(2) of this section must make the adjustments described in paragraphs (c)(2) through (5) of this section. Section 1.985-5 shall not apply.

(2) *Determining the euro basis of property and the euro amount of liabilities and other relevant items.* The euro basis in property and the euro amount of liabilities and other relevant items shall equal the product of the legacy functional currency adjusted basis or amount of liabilities multiplied by the applicable conversion rate.

(3) *Taking into account exchange gain or loss on legacy currency section 988 transactions*—(i) *In general.* Except as provided in paragraphs (c)(3)(iii) and (iv) of this section, a legacy currency denominated section 988 transaction (determined after applying section 988(d)) outstanding on the last day of the taxable year immediately prior to the year of change shall continue to be treated as a section 988 transaction after the change and the principles of section 988 shall apply.

(ii) *Examples.* The application of this paragraph (c)(3) may be illustrated by the following examples:

Example 1. X, a calendar year QBU on the cash method of accounting, uses the deutschmark as its functional currency. X is not described in section 1281(b). On July 1, 1998, X converts 10,000 deutschmarks (DM) into Dutch guilders (fl) at the spot rate of fl1 = DM1 and loans the 10,000 guilders to Y (an unrelated party) for one year at a rate of 10% with principal and interest to be paid on June 30, 1999. On January 1, 1999, X changes its functional currency to the euro pursuant to this section. Assume that the euro/deutschmark conversion rate is set by the European Council at €1 = DM2. Assume further that the euro/guilder conversion rate is set at €1 = fl2.25. Accordingly, under the terms of the note, on June 30, 1999, X will receive €4444.44 (fl10,000/2.25) of principal and €4444.44 (fl1,000/2.25) of interest. Pursuant to this paragraph (c)(3), X will realize an exchange loss on the principal computed under the principles of § 1.988-2(b)(5). For this purpose, the exchange rate used under § 1.988-2(b)(5)(i) shall be the guilder/euro conversion rate. The amount under § 1.988-2(b)(5)(ii) is determined by translating the fl10,000 at the guilder/deutschmark spot rate on July 1, 1998, and translating that deutschmark amount into euros at the deutschmark/euro conversion rate. Thus, X will compute an exchange loss for 1999 of €555.56 determined as follows: [€4444.44 (fl10,000/2.25) − €5000 ((fl10,000/1) /2) = -€555.56]. Pursuant to this paragraph (c)(3), the character and source of the loss are determined pursuant to section 988 and regulations thereunder. Because X uses the cash method of accounting for the interest on this debt instrument, X does not realize exchange gain or loss on the receipt of that interest.

Example 2. (i) X, a calendar year QBU on the accrual method of accounting, uses the deutschmark as its functional currency. On February 1, 1998, X converts 12,000 deutschmarks into Dutch guilders at the spot rate of fl1 = DM1 and loans the 12,000 guilders to Y (an unrelated party) for one year at a rate of 10% with principal and interest to be paid on January 31, 1999. In

Reg. § 1.985-8(b)(4)

addition, assume the average rate (deutschmark/guilder) for the period from February 1, 1998, through December 31, 1998 is fl1.07 = DM1. Pursuant to § 1.988-2(b)(2)(ii)(C), X will accrue eleven months of interest on the note and recognize interest income of DM1028.04 (fl1100/1.07) in the 1998 taxable year.

(ii) On January 1, 1999, the euro will replace the deutschmark as the national currency of Germany pursuant to the Treaty on European Union signed February 7, 1992. Assume that on January 1, 1999, X changes its functional currency to the euro pursuant to this section. Assume that the euro/deutschmark conversion rate is set by the European Council at €1 = DM2. Assume further that the euro/guilder conversion rate is set at €1 = fl2.25. In 1999, X will accrue one month of interest equal to €44.44 (fl100/2.25). On January 31, 1999, pursuant to the note, X will receive interest denominated in euros of €533.33 (fl1200/2.25). Pursuant to this paragraph (c)(3), X will realize an exchange loss in the 1999 taxable year with respect to accrued interest computed under the principles of § 1.988-2(b)(3). For this purpose, the exchange rate used under § 1.988-2(b)(3)(i) is the guilder/euro conversion rate and the exchange rate used under § 1.988-2(b)(3)(ii) is the deutschmark/euro conversion rate. Thus, with respect to the interest accrued in 1998, X will realize exchange loss of €25.13 under § 1.988-2(b), (3) as follows: [€488.89 (fl1100/2.25) − €514.02 (DM1028.04/2) = -€25.13]. With respect to the one month of interest accrued in 1999, X will realize no exchange gain or loss since the exchange rate when the interest accrued and the spot rate on the payment date are the same.

(iii) X will realize exchange loss of €666.67 on repayment of the loan principal computed in the same manner as in Example 1 [€5333.33 (fl12,000/2.25) − €6000 fl12,000/1)/2)]. The losses with respect to accrued interest and principal are characterized and sourced under the rules of section 988.

(iii) *Special rule for legacy nonfunctional currency.* The QBU shall realize or otherwise take into account for all purposes of the Internal Revenue Code the amount of any unrealized exchange gain or loss attributable to nonfunctional currency (as described in section 988(c)(1)(C)(ii)) that is denominated in a legacy currency as if the currency were disposed of on the last day of the taxable year immediately prior to the year of change. The character and source of the gain or loss are determined under section 988.

(iv) *Legacy currency denominated accounts receivable and payable*—(A) *In general.* A QBU may elect to realize or otherwise take into account for all purposes of the Internal Revenue Code the amount of any unrealized exchange gain or loss attributable to a legacy currency denominated item described in section 988(c)(1)(B)(ii) as if the item were terminated on the last day of the taxable year ending prior to the year of change.

(B) *Time and manner of election.* With respect to a QBU that makes an election described in paragraph (c)(3)(iv)(A) of this section, an affected taxpayer (as described in paragraph (b)(5) of this section) shall attach a statement to its tax return for the taxable year ending immediately prior to the year of change which includes the following: "TAXPAYER CERTIFIES THAT A QBU OF THE TAXPAYER HAS ELECTED TO REALIZE CURRENCY GAIN OR LOSS ON LEGACY CURRENCY DENOMINATED ACCOUNTS RECEIVABLE AND PAYABLE UPON CHANGE OF FUNCTIONAL CURRENCY TO THE EURO." A QBU making the election must do so for all legacy currency denominated items described in section 988(c)(1)(B)(ii).

(4) *Adjustments when a branch changes its functional currency to the euro*—(i) *Branch changing from a legacy currency to the euro in a taxable year during which taxpayer's functional currency is other than the euro.* If a branch changes its functional currency from a legacy currency to the euro for a taxable year during which the taxpayer's functional currency is other than the euro, the branch's euro equity pool shall equal the product of the legacy currency amount of the equity pool multiplied by the applicable conversion rate. No adjustment to the basis pool is required.

(ii) *Branch changing from a legacy currency to the euro in a taxable year during which taxpayer's functional currency is the euro.* If a branch changes its functional currency from a legacy currency to the euro for a taxable year during which the taxpayer's functional currency is the euro, the taxpayer shall realize gain or loss attributable to the branch's equity pool under the principles of section 987, computed as if the branch terminated on the last day prior to the year of change. Adjustments under this paragraph (c)(4)(ii) shall be taken into account by the taxpayer ratably over four taxable years beginning with the taxable year of change.

(5) *Adjustments to a branch's accounts when a taxpayer changes to the euro*—(i) *Taxpayer changing from a legacy currency to the euro in a taxable year during which a branch's functional currency is other than the euro.* If a taxpayer changes its functional currency to the euro for a taxable year during which the functional currency

Reg. § 1.985-8(c)(5)

of a branch of the taxpayer is other than the euro, the basis pool shall equal the product of the legacy currency amount of the basis pool multiplied by the applicable conversion rate. No adjustment to the equity pool is required.

(ii) *Taxpayer changing from a legacy currency to the euro in a taxable year during which a branch's functional currency is the euro.* If a taxpayer changes its functional currency from a legacy currency to the euro for a taxable year during which the functional currency of a branch of the taxpayer is the euro, the taxpayer shall take into account gain or loss as determined under paragraph (c)(4)(ii) of this section.

(6) *Additional adjustments that are necessary when a corporation changes its functional currency to the euro.* The amount of a corporation's euro currency earnings and profits and the amount of its euro paid-in capital shall equal the product of the legacy currency amounts of these items multiplied by the applicable conversion rate. The foreign income taxes and accumulated profits or deficits in accumulated profits of a foreign corporation that were maintained in foreign currency for purposes of section 902 and that are attributable to taxable years of the foreign corporation beginning before January 1, 1987, also shall be translated into the euro at the conversion rate.

(d) *Treatment of legacy currency section 988 transactions with respect to a QBU that has the euro as its functional currency*—(1) *In general.* This § 1.985-8(d) applies to a QBU that has the euro as its functional currency and that holds a section 988 transaction denominated in, or determined by reference to, a currency that is substituted by the euro. For example, this paragraph (d) will apply to a German QBU with the euro as its functional currency if the QBU is holding Country X currency or other section 988 transactions denominated in such currency on the day in the year 2005 when the euro is substituted for the Country X currency.

(2) *Principles of paragraph (c)(3) of this section shall apply.* With respect to a QBU described in paragraph (d) of this section, the principles of paragraph (c)(3) of this section shall apply. For example, if a German QBU with the euro as its functional currency is holding a Country X currency denominated debt instrument on the day in the year 2005 when the euro is substituted for the Country X currency, the instrument shall continue to be treated as a section 988 transaction pursuant to the principles of paragraph (c)(3)(i) of this section. However, if such QBU holds Country X currency, the QBU shall take into account any unrealized exchange gain or loss pursuant to the principles of paragraph (c)(3)(iii) of this section as if the currency was disposed of on the day prior to the day the euro is substituted for the Country X currency. Similarly, if the QBU makes an election under the principles of paragraph (c)(3)(iv) of this section, the QBU shall take into account for all purposes of the Internal Revenue Code the amount of any unrealized exchange gain or loss attributable to a legacy currency denominated item described in section 988(c)(1)(B)(ii) as if the item were terminated on the day prior to the day the euro is substituted for the Country X currency.

(e) *Effective date.* This section applies to tax years ending after July 29, 1998. [Reg. § 1.985-8.]

☐ [T.D. 8927, 1-10-2001.]

[Reg. § 1.987-1]

§ 1.987-1. **Profit and loss method of accounting for a qualified business unit of a taxpayer having a different functional currency from the taxpayer.** [RESERVED]

[Reg. § 1.987-2]

§ 1.987-2. **Accounting for gain or loss on certain transfers of property.** [RESERVED]

[Reg. § 1.987-3]

§ 1.987-3. **Termination.** [RESERVED]

[Reg. § 1.987-4]

§ 1.987-4. **Special rules relating to QBU branches of foreign taxpayers.** [RESERVED]

[Reg. § 1.987-5]

§ 1.987-5. **Transition rules for certain qualified business units using a profit and loss method of accounting for taxable years beginning before January 1, 1987.**—(a) *Applicability*—(1) *In general.* This section applies to qualified business unit (QBU) branches of United States persons, whose functional currency (as defined in section 985 of the Code and the regulations thereunder) is other than the United States dollar (dollar) and that used a profit and loss method of accounting for their last taxable year beginning before January 1, 1987. Generally, a profit and loss method of accounting is any method of accounting under which the taxpayer calculates the profits of a QBU branch in its functional currency and translates the net result into dollars. For all taxable years beginning after December 31, 1986, such QBU branches must use the profit and loss method of accounting as described in section 987, except to the extent otherwise provided in regulations under section 985 or any other provision of the Code. See § 1.989(c)-1 regarding transition rules for QBU branches of

Income from Sources Without the United States

United States persons that have a nondollar functional currency and that used a net worth method of accounting for their last taxable year beginning before January 1, 1987.

(2) *Insolvent QBU branches.* A taxpayer may apply the principles of this section to a QBU branch that used a profit and loss method of accounting for its last taxable year beginning before January 1, 1987, whose $E pool (as defined in paragraph (d)(3)(i) of this section) is negative. For taxable years beginning on or after October 25, 1991, the principles of this section shall apply to insolvent QBU branches.

(b) *General rules.* Generally, section 987 gain or loss occurs when a QBU branch makes a remittance. A remittance is considered to be made from one or more functional currency pools under rules provided in paragraph (c) of this section. In general, the amount of section 987 gain or loss from a remittance equals the difference between the dollar value of the functional currency adjusted basis of the property remitted and the portion of the dollar basis in the applicable pool. Section 987 gain or loss is calculated under a 4-step procedure described in paragraph (d) of this section. Section 987 gain or loss attributable to a remittance is realized and must be recognized in the taxable year of the remittance except to the extent otherwise provided in regulations.

(c) *Determining the pool(s) from which a remittance is made*—(1) *Remittances made during taxable years beginning after December 31, 1986, and before October 25, 1991.* A remittance made during taxable years beginning after December 31, 1986 and before October 25, 1991, first represents an amount of the QBU branch's post-86 profits pool (including functional currency profits for the current taxable year determined without regard to remittances made during the current year). To the extent the functional currency amount of the remittance exceeds the post-86 profits pool, it is considered to come out of the EQ pool. Paragraph (d)(2) of this section describes the EQ pool and the post-86 profits pool.

(2) *Remittances made in taxable years beginning on or after October 25, 1991.* For remittances made in taxable years beginning on or after October 25, 1991, the post-86 profits and EQ pools are combined into one pool called the equity pool. Therefore, remittances made during those taxable years will only come from the equity pool. The dollar basis of, and section 987 gain or loss on, such remittances shall be calculated utilizing the principles set forth in paragraph (d)(4) and (5) of this section.

(d) *Calculation of section 987 gain or loss*—(1) *In general.* This paragraph (d) describes the 4-step procedure for calculating section 987 gain or loss.

(2) *Step 1—Calculate the amount of the functional currency pools*—(i) *EQ pool.* (A) *Beginning pool.* The beginning amount of the EQ pool is equal to the functional currency adjusted bases of a QBU branch's assets less the functional currency amount of the QBU branch's liabilities at the end of the taxpayer's last taxable year beginning before January 1, 1987, as these amounts are determined under the rules of paragraphs (e) and (f) of this section. The district director may allow for additional adjustments to the beginning amount of the EQ pool to prevent the recognition of section 987 gain or loss due to factors unrelated to the movement of exchange rates.

(B) *Adjusting the EQ pool.* The EQ pool is increased by the functional currency amount of any transfer (as determined under section 987) to the QBU branch made during the current taxable year or any prior taxable year beginning after December 31, 1986. If the transfer is made in a nonfunctional currency, this amount is translated into the QBU branch's functional currency at the spot rate (determined under the principles of section 988 and the regulations thereunder) on the date of the transfer. The method for determining the rate must be applied consistently each quarter. The EQ pool is decreased by the functional currency amount of any remittance (as determined under section 987) made during a prior taxable year beginning after December 31, 1986, that is considered remitted from the EQ pool under paragraph (c) of this section. The EQ pool must also be decreased by any transfer from the QBU branch that is not a remittance.

(ii) *Post-86 profits pool.* The amount of a QBU branch's post-86 profits pool is calculated at the end of each taxable year beginning after December 31, 1986. The opening balance of the post-86 profits pool at the beginning of the first taxable year beginning after December 31, 1986, is zero. The post-86 profits pool is increased by the functional currency amount of the QBU branch's profits (determined under section 987) for the taxable year. The post-86 profits pool is decreased by the functional currency amount of the QBU branch's losses (determined under section 987) for the taxable year and the amount of any remittances by the QBU branch during the taxable year from the post-86 profits pool as provided under paragraph (c) of this section.

(iii) *Adjustments to the equity pool.* For remittances made in taxable years beginning on or after October 25, 1991 under paragraph (c)(2) of this section, the post-86 profits and EQ pools are combined into one pool called the equity pool.

Reg. § 1.987-5(d)(2)

50,846 Income from Sources Without the United States

See p. 20,601 for regulations not amended to reflect law changes

Additions to and subtractions from the equity pool shall be made utilizing the principles of paragraphs (d)(2)(i)(B) and (ii) of this section. For example, remittances shall reduce the equity pool.

(3) *Step 2—Calculate the dollar basis of the pools*—(i) *Dollar basis of the EQ pool*—(A) *Beginning dollar basis.* The beginning dollar basis of the EQ pool (hereinafter referred to as the $E pool) equals:

(*1*) The dollar amount of all the QBU branch's profits reported on the taxpayer's income tax returns for taxable years beginning before January 1, 1987, plus the total dollar amount of all transfers to the QBU branch during that period (properly reflected on the taxpayer's books), less

(*2*) The dollar amount of all the QBU branch's losses reported on the taxpayer's income tax returns for such years, and the total dollar basis of all remittances and all transfers made by the QBU branch during that period (properly reflected on the taxpayer's books).

A QBU branch's profits and losses shall be properly adjusted for foreign taxes of the QBU branch.

(B) *Adjusting the $E pool.* The $E pool is increased by the dollar amount of any transfers to the QBU branch made during the current taxable year or any prior taxable year beginning after December 31, 1986. If a transfer is made in a currency other than the dollar, the amount of the currency is translated into dollars at the spot rate (determined under the principles of section 988 and the regulations thereunder) on the date of the transfer. The $E pool is decreased by the dollar basis of any remittance made during a prior taxable year beginning after December 31, 1986, that is considered remitted from the $E pool under paragraphs (c) and (d)(4) of this section. The $E pool is also reduced by the amount of a transfer (other than a remittance) from the QBU branch translated into dollars at the spot rate (determined under the principles of section 988 and the regulations thereunder) on the date of the transfer. The method for determining the spot rate must be applied consistently to all transfers to and from a QBU branch.

(ii) *Dollar basis of the post-86 profits pool.* The amount of a QBU branch's dollar basis in the post-86 profits pool (the $P pool) is calculated at the end of each taxable year beginning after December 31, 1986. The opening balance of the $P pool at the beginning of the first taxable year beginning after December 31, 1986, is zero. The $P pool is increased by the functional currency amount of the QBU branch's profits (determined under section 987) for the taxable year translated into dollars at the weighted average exchange rate (as defined in § 1.989(b)-1) for the year. The $P pool is decreased by the functional currency amount of the QBU branch's losses (determined under section 987) for the taxable year translated into dollars at the weighted average exchange rate for the year and by the dollar basis of any remittances made by the QBU branch during the taxable year from the post-86 profits pool under paragraph (c)(1) of this section.

(iii) *Combination of the $E and the $P pools.* For taxable years beginning on or after October 25, 1991 the $P and the $E pools are combined into one pool called the basis pool. Additions to and subtractions from the basis pool shall be made utilizing the principles set forth in paragraph (d)(3)(i) and (ii) of this section.

(4) *Step 3—Calculation of the dollar basis of a remittance.* For all taxable years beginning after December 31, 1986, the dollar basis of a remittance is calculated using the following formula:

$$\frac{\text{amount of remittance (in QBU branch's functional currency) from the applicable pool (EQ, post-86 profits, or equity pool)}}{\text{Balance of the applicable pool (EQ, post-86 profits, or equity pool) reduced by prior remittances}} \times \text{The dollar basis of the applicable pool (\$E, \$P, or basis pool) reduced by prior remittances}$$

(5) *Step 4—Calculation of the section 987 gain or loss on a remittance.* Section 987 gain or loss equals the difference between—

(i) The dollar amount of the remittance, and

(ii) The dollar basis of the remittance as calculated under paragraph (d)(4) of this section.

(e) *Functional currency adjusted basis of QBU branch assets acquired in taxable years beginning before January 1, 1987*—(1) *Basis of asset.* For taxable years beginning after December 31, 1986, the functional currency adjusted basis of a QBU branch asset acquired in a taxable year beginning before January 1, 1987, is the functional currency basis of the asset at the date of acquisition, as adjusted according to United States tax principles. The functional currency adjusted basis of an asset for which a functional currency basis was not determined at the date of acquisition is the nonfunctional currency basis of the asset at the date of acquisition multiplied by the spot ex-

Reg. § 1.987-5(d)(3)

change rate on the date of acquisition, as adjusted according to United States tax principles.

(2) *Adjustment to basis of asset.* Any future adjustments to the functional currency adjusted basis of such an asset are determined with respect to the appropriate functional currency adjusted basis of the asset as determined under this paragraph (e).

(f) *Functional currency amount of QBU branch liabilities acquired in taxable years beginning before January 1, 1987.* For the first taxable year beginning after December 31, 1986, the amount of a QBU branch liability incurred in a taxable year beginning before January 1, 1987, is the functional currency amount of the liability at the date incurred, as adjusted according to United States tax principles. The functional currency amount of a liability for which a functional currency amount was not determined at the date incurred is the nonfunctional currency amount of the liability at the date incurred multiplied by the spot exchange rate on the date incurred, as adjusted according to United States tax principles.

(g) *Examples.* The provisions of this section are illustrated by the following examples.

Example 1—(i) *Facts.* U.S. is a domestic corporation. B, a QBU branch of U.S., operates in country X and was established in 1985. B's functional currency is the FC. U.S. is on a calendar taxable year and, prior to January 1, 1987, accounted for the operations of B by the profit and loss method of accounting as set forth in Rev. Rul. 75-107, 1975-1 C.B. 32. B's books and records were kept according to United States tax principles. B received a transfer of $2,000 in 1985, and had profits of $3,000 in 1985 and $5,000 in 1986. B made a remittance in 1986, the dollar basis of which was $1,000. As of December 31, 1986, the adjusted basis of B's functional currency assets exceeded the functional currency amount of its liabilities by 15,000 FC (the beginning pool of EQ). Under section 987, B has profits of 8,000 FC in 1987, which are worth $1,000 when translated at the weighted average exchange rate for 1987 as required by sections 987(2) and 989(b)(4). B has no profits or loss in 1988. There are no transfers to B in 1987 and 1988. B remits 18,000 FC in 1988. Under section 987, the appropriate exchange rate for the 1988 remittance is 10 FC/$1.

(ii) *Calculation of section 987 loss on remittance*—(A) *Post-86 profits.* Under paragraph (c)(i) of this section, the 18,000 FC remittance comes first out of the post-86 profits pool (8,000 FC) and second out of EQ (10,000 FC). The loss on the 1988 remittance out of the post-86 profits pool equals:

$$\text{Dollar value of post-86 profits remitted} - \text{Dollar basis of post-86 profit remitted}$$
$$= (8{,}000 \text{ FC} \times 10 \text{ FC}/\$1) - \$1{,}000$$
$$= \$800 - \$1{,}000$$
$$= <\$200> \text{ loss}$$

(B) *EQ.* Under paragraph (d) of this section, U.S. calculates 987 gain or loss on the 10,000 FC remittance of EQ from B as follows:

Step 1. The total EQ pool equals 15,000 FC (the functional currency adjusted bases of its assets less the functional currency amount of its liabilities as of December 31, 1986). There are no adjustments necessary under paragraph (d)(2)(i)(B) of this section.

Step 2. The $E pool is $9,000 (the $2,000 transfer in 1985 plus profits of $3,000 in 1985 and $5,000 in 1986 and less the $1,000 basis of the 1986 remittance). There are no adjustments necessary under paragraph (d)(3)(i)(B) of this section.

Step 3. The entire 10,000 FC remittance is deemed to come out of EQ.

Step 4. The dollar basis of the EQ remitted equals:

$$N \times \$E \text{ determined under paragraph (d)(3)(i)}$$
$$= \frac{10{,}000 \text{ FC}}{15{,}000 \text{ FC}} \times \$9{,}000$$
$$= \$6{,}000$$

Where:

$$N = \frac{\text{Portion of remittance out of EQ}}{\text{EQ balance determined under paragraph (d)(2)(i) of this section}}$$

Step 5. Section 987 loss of U.S. on remittance equals:

$$= (10{,}000 \text{ FC} \times 10 \text{ FC}/\$1) - \$6{,}000$$
$$= \$1{,}000 - \$6{,}000$$
$$= <\$5{,}000> \text{ loss}$$

(C) *Total loss on remittance.* The total combined loss on the remittance is <$5,200>. The total of amounts determined in paragraphs (ii)(A) and (B) of this Example 1.

Example 2—(i) *Facts.* D is a domestic corporation. B, a QBU branch of D, operates in country X. B's functional currency is the FC. At the end of B's last taxable year beginning before October 25, 1991 B's EQ pool equals 15,000 FC and B's post-86 profits pool equals 8,000 FC. B's $E amount equals $9,000, and the $P pool equals $1,000. In B's first taxable year beginning on or after October 25, 1991 B remits 18,000 FC. Under section 987, the appropriate exchange rate for this remittance is 10FC:$1.

(ii) *Computation of the equity pool.*

$$\underset{\text{(EQ pool)}}{15{,}000 \text{ FC}} + \underset{\text{(post-86 profits pool)}}{8{,}000 \text{ FC}} = \underset{\text{(equity pool)}}{23{,}000 \text{ FC}}$$

(iii) *Computation of the basis pool.*

$$\underset{(\$E \text{ amount})}{\$9{,}000} + \underset{(\$P \text{ amount})}{\$1{,}000} = \$10{,}000$$

(iv) *Dollar basis in remittance.*

$$\frac{\underset{\text{(amount of remittance)}}{18{,}000 \text{ FC}}}{\underset{\text{(equity pool)}}{23{,}000 \text{ FC}}} \times \$10{,}000 = \$7{,}826$$

(v) *Computation of section 987 loss by U.S. on remittance.*

$$\underset{\text{(dollar value of remittance)}}{\$1{,}800} - \underset{\text{(dollar basis in remittance)}}{\$7{,}826} = \underset{\text{(loss on remittance)}}{<\$6{,}026>}$$

(h) *Character and source of section 987 gain or loss.* Section 987 gain or loss is sourced and characterized as provided by section 987 and regulations issued under that section. [Reg. § 1.987-5.]

☐ [*T.D. 8367, 9-24-91.*]

[Reg. § 1.988-0T]

§ 1.988-0T. **Taxation of gain or loss from a section 988 transaction; Table of Contents (Temporary regulations).**—[This section listed captioned paragraphs contained in §§ 1.988-0T through 1.988-5T, temporary regulations under section 988 of the Internal Revenue Code. T.D. 8400 removed Temporary Reg. §§ 1.988-1T through 1.988-5T, but did not officially remove § 1.988-0T. The text of Temporary Reg. § 1.988-0T has been removed to conform to T.D. 8400 and the addition of Reg. § 1.988-0.—CCH.]

[Reg. § 1.988-0]

§ 1.988-0. **Taxation of gain or loss from a section 988 transaction; Table of Contents.**—This section lists captioned paragraphs contained in §§ 1.988-1 through 1.988-5.

§ 1.988-1. *Certain definitions and special rules.*

(a) Section 988 transaction.

(1) In general.

(2) Description of transactions.

(3)-(5) [Reserved]

(6) Examples.

(7) Special rules for regulated futures contracts and non-equity options.

(8) Special rules for qualified funds.

(9) Exception for certain transactions entered into by an individual.

(10) Intra-taxpayer transactions.

(11) Authority of Commissioner to include or exclude transactions from section 988.

(b) Spot contract.

(c) Nonfunctional currency.

(d) Spot rate.

(1) In general.

(2) Consistency required in valuing transactions subject to section 988.

(3) Use of certain spot rate conventions for payables and receivables denominated in nonfunctional currency.

(4) Currency where an official government established rate differs from a free market rate.

(e) Exchange gain or loss.

(f) Hyperinflationary currency.

(g) Fair market value.

Reg. § 1.988-0T

(h) Interaction with sections 1092 and 1256 in examples.

(i) Effective date.

§ 1.988-2. Recognition and computation of exchange gain or loss.

(a) Disposition of nonfunctional currency.

(1) Recognition of exchange gain or loss.

(2) Computation of exchange gain or loss.

(b) Translation of interest income or expense and determination of exchange gain or loss with respect to debt instruments.

(1) Translation of interest income received with respect to a nonfunctional currency demand account.

(2) Translation of nonfunctional currency interest income or expense received or paid with respect to a debt instrument described in § 1.988-1(a)(1)(ii) and (2)(i).

(3) Exchange gain or loss recognized by the holder with respect to accrued interest income.

(4) Exchange gain or loss recognized by the obligor with respect to accrued interest expense.

(5) Exchange gain or loss recognized by the holder of a debt instrument with respect to principal.

(6) Exchange gain or loss recognized by the obligor of a debt instrument with respect to principal.

(7) Payment ordering rules.

(8) Limitation of exchange gain or loss on payment or disposition of a debt instrument.

(9) Examples.

(10) Treatment of bond premium.

(11) Market discount.

(12) Tax exempt bonds.

(13) Nonfunctional currency debt exchanged for stock of obligor.

(14) [Reserved]

(15) Debt instruments and deposits denominated in hyperinflationary currencies.

(16) Coordination with section 267 regarding debt instruments.

(17) Coordination with installment method under section 453.

(c) Item of expense or gross income or receipts which is to be paid or received after the date accrued.

(1) In general.

(2) Determination of exchange gain or loss with respect to an item of gross income or receipts.

(3) Determination of exchange gain or loss with respect to an item of expense.

(4) Examples.

(d) Exchange gain or loss with respect to forward contracts, futures contracts and option contracts.

(1) Scope.

(2) Realization of exchange gain or loss.

(3) Recognition of exchange gain or loss.

(4) Determination of exchange gain or loss.

(5) Hyperinflationary contracts.

(e) Currency swaps and notional principal contracts.

(1) Notional principal contract denominated in a single nonfunctional currency.

(2) Special rules for currency swaps.

(3) Amortization of swap premium or discount in the case of off market swaps.

(4) Treatment of taxpayer disposing of a currency swap.

(5) Examples.

(6) Special effective date for rules regarding currency swaps.

(7) Special rules for currency swap contracts in hyperinflationary currencies.

(f) Substance over form.

(1) In general.

(2) Example.

(g) Effective date.

§ 1.988-3. Character of exchange gain or loss.

(a) In general.

(b) Election to characterize exchange gain or loss on certain identified forward contracts, futures contracts and option contracts as capital gain or loss.

(1) In general.

(2) Special rule for contracts that become part of a straddle after the election is made.

(3) Requirements for making the election.

(4) Verification.

(5) Independent verification.

(6) Effective date.

(c) Exchange gain or loss treated as interest.

(1) In general.

(2) Exchange loss realized by the holder on nonfunctional currency tax exempt bonds.

(d) Effective date.

§ 1.988-4. Source of gain of [or] loss realized on a section 988 transaction.

(a) In general.

(b) Qualified business unit.

Reg. § 1.988-0

50,850 Income from Sources Without the United States

See p. 20,601 for regulations not amended to reflect law changes

(1) In general.

(2) Proper reflection on the books of the taxpayer or qualified business unit.

(c) Effectively connected exchange gain or loss.

(d) Residence.

(1) In general.

(2) Exception.

(3) Partner in a partnership not engaged in a U.S. trade or business under section 864(b)(2).

(e) Special rule for certain related party loans.

(1) In general.

(2) United States person.

(3) Loans by related person.

(4) 10 percent owned foreign corporation.

(f) Exchange gain or loss treated as interest under § 1.988-3.

(g) Exchange gain or loss allocated in the same manner as interest under § 1.861-9T.

(h) Effective date.

§ 1.988-5. Section 988(d) hedging transactions.

(a) Integration of a nonfunctional currency debt instrument and a § 1.988-5(a) hedge.

(1) In general.

(2) Exception.

(3) Qualifying debt instrument.

(4) Section 1.988-5(a) hedge.

(5) Definition of integrated economic transaction.

(6) Special rules for legging in and legging out of integrated treatment.

(7) Transactions part of a straddle.

(8) Identification requirements.

(9) Taxation of qualified hedging transactions.

(10) Transition rules and effective dates.

(b) Hedged executory contracts.

(1) In general.

(2) Definitions.

(3) Identification rules.

(4) Effect of hedged executory contract.

(5) References to this paragraph (b).

(c) Hedges of period between trade date and settlement date on purchase or sale of publicly traded stock or security.

(d) [Reserved]

(e) Advance rulings regarding net hedging and anticipatory hedging systems.

(f) [Reserved]

(g) General effective date.

[Reg. § 1.988-0.]

☐ [T.D. 8400, 3-16-92. Amended by T.D. 8860, 1-12-2000.]

[Reg. § 1.988-1]

§ 1.988-1. Certain definitions and special rules.—(a) *Section 988 transaction*—(1) *In general.* The term "section 988 transaction" means any of the following transactions—

(i) A disposition of nonfunctional currency as defined in paragraph (c) of this section;

(ii) Any transaction described in paragraph (a)(2) of this section if any amount which the taxpayer is entitled to receive or is required to pay by reason of such transaction is denominated in terms of a nonfunctional currency or is determined by reference to the value of one or more nonfunctional currencies.

A transaction described in this paragraph (a) need not require or permit payment with a nonfunctional currency as long as any amount paid or received is determined by reference to the value of one or more nonfunctional currencies. The acquisition of nonfunctional currency is treated as a section 988 transaction for purposes of establishing the taxpayer's basis in such currency and determining exchange gain or loss thereon.

(2) *Description of transactions.* The following transactions are described in this paragraph (a)(2).

(i) *Debt instruments.* Acquiring a debt instrument or becoming an obligor under a debt instrument. The term "debt instrument" means a bond, debenture, note, certificate or other evidence of indebtedness.

(ii) *Payables, receivables, etc.* Accruing, or otherwise taking into account, for purposes of subtitle A of the Internal Revenue Code, any item of expense or gross income or receipts which is to be paid or received after the date on which so accrued or taken into account. A payable relating to cost of goods sold, or a payable or receivable relating to a capital expenditure or receipt, is within the meaning of this paragraph (a)(2)(ii). Generally, a payable relating to foreign taxes (whether or not claimed as a credit under section 901) is within the meaning of this paragraph (a)(2)(ii). However, a payable of a domestic person relating to accrued foreign taxes of its qualified business unit (QBU branch) is not within the meaning of this paragraph (a)(2)(ii) if the QBU branch's functional currency is the U.S. dollar and the foreign taxes are claimed as a credit under section 901.

(iii) *Forward contract, futures contract, option contract, or similar financial instrument.* Except as otherwise provided in this paragraph (a)(2)(iii) and paragraph (a)(4)(i) of this section,

Reg. § 1.988-1(a)(1)

entering into or acquiring any forward contract, futures contract, option, warrant, or similar financial instrument.

(A) *Limitation for certain derivative instruments.* A forward contract, futures contract, option, warrant, or similar financial instrument is within this paragraph (a)(2)(iii) only if the underlying property to which the instrument ultimately relates is a nonfunctional currency or is otherwise described in paragraph (a)(1)(ii) of this section. Thus, if the underlying property of an instrument is another financial instrument (*e.g.*, an option on a futures contract), then the underlying property to which such other instrument (*e.g.*, the futures contract) ultimately relates must be a nonfunctional currency. For example, a forward contract to purchase wheat denominated in a nonfunctional currency, an option to enter into a forward contract to purchase wheat denominated in a nonfunctional currency, or a warrant to purchase stock denominated in a nonfunctional currency is not described in this paragraph (a)(2)(iii). On the other hand, a forward contract to purchase a nonfunctional currency, an option to enter into a forward contract to purchase a nonfunctional currency, an option to purchase a bond denominated in or the payments of which are determined by reference to the value of a nonfunctional currency, or a warrant to purchase nonfunctional currency is described in this paragraph (a)(2)(iii).

(B) *Nonfunctional currency notional principal contracts*—(*1*) *In general.* The term "similar financial instrument" includes a notional principal contract only if the payments required to be made or received under the contract are determined with reference to a nonfunctional currency.

(*2*) *Definition of notional principal contract.* The term "notional principal contract" means a contract (*e.g.*, a swap, cap, floor or collar) that provides for the payment of amounts by one party to another at specified intervals calculated by reference to a specified index upon a notional principal amount in exchange for specified consideration or a promise to pay similar amounts. For this purpose, a "notional principal contract" shall only include an instrument where the underlying property to which the instrument ultimately relates is money (*e.g.*, functional currency), nonfunctional currency, or property the value of which is determined by reference to an interest rate. Thus, the term "notional principal contract" includes a currency swap as defined in § 1.988-2(e)(2)(ii), but does not include a swap referenced to a commodity or equity index.

(C) *Effective date with respect to certain contracts.* This paragraph (a)(2)(iii) does not apply to any forward contract, futures contract, option, warrant, or similar financial instrument entered into or acquired on or before October 21, 1988, if such instrument would have been marked to market under section 1256 if held on the last day of the taxable year.

(3)-(5) [Reserved]

(6) *Examples.* The following examples illustrate the application of paragraph (a) of this section. The examples assume that X is a U.S. corporation on an accrual method with the calendar year as its taxable year. Because X is a U.S. corporation the U.S. dollar is its functional currency under section 985. The examples also assume that section 988(d) does not apply.

Example 1. On January 1, 1989, X acquires 10,000 Canadian dollars. On January 15, 1989, X uses the 10,000 Canadian dollars to purchase inventory. The acquisition of the 10,000 Canadian dollars is a section 988 transaction for purposes of establishing X's basis in such Canadian dollars. The disposition of the 10,000 Canadian dollars is a section 988 transaction pursuant to paragraph (a)(1) of this section.

Example 2. On January 1, 1989, X acquires 10,000 Canadian dollars. On January 15, 1989, X converts the 10,000 Canadian dollars to U.S. dollars. The acquisition of the 10,000 Canadian dollars is a section 988 transaction for purposes of establishing X's basis in such Canadian dollars. The conversion of the 10,000 Canadian dollars to U.S. dollars is a section 988 transaction pursuant to paragraph (a)(1) of this section.

Example 3. On January 1, 1989, X borrows 100,000 British pounds (£) for a period of 10 years and issues a note to the lender with a face amount of £100,000. The note provides for payments of interest at an annual rate of 10% paid quarterly in pounds and has a stated redemption price at maturity of £100,000. X's becoming the obligor under the note is a section 988 transaction pursuant to paragraphs (a)(1)(ii) and (2)(i) of this section. Because X is an accrual basis taxpayer, the accrual of interest expense under X's note is a section 988 transaction pursuant to paragraphs (a)(1)(ii) and (2)(ii) of this section. In addition, the acquisition of the British pounds to make payments under the note is a section 988 transaction for purposes of establishing X's basis in such pounds, and the disposition of such pounds is a section 988 transaction under paragraph (a)(1)(i) of this section. See § 1.988-2(b) with respect to the translation of accrued interest expense and the determination of exchange gain or loss upon payment of accrued interest expense.

Example 4. On January 1, 1989, X purchases at original issue for 74,621.54 British pounds (£) a

Reg. § 1.988-1(a)(6)

50,852 Income from Sources Without the United States

See p. 20,601 for regulations not amended to reflect law changes

3-year bond maturing on December 31, 1991, at a stated redemption price of £100,000. The bond provides for no stated interest. The bond has a yield to maturity of 10% compounded semiannually and has £25,378.46 of original issue discount. The acquisition of the bond is a section 988 transaction as provided in paragraphs (a)(1)(ii) and (2)(i) of this section. The accrual of original issue discount with respect to the bond is a section 988 transaction under paragraphs (a)(1)(ii) and (2)(ii) of this section. See § 1.988-2(b) with respect to the translation of original issue discount and the determination of exchange gain or loss upon receipt of such amounts.

Example 5. On January 1, 1989, X sells and delivers inventory to Y for 10,000,000 Italian lira for payment on April 1, 1989. Under X's method of accounting, January 1, 1989 is the accrual date. Because X is an accrual basis taxpayer, the accrual of a nonfunctional currency denominated item of gross receipts on January 1, 1989, for payment after the date of accrual is a section 988 transaction under paragraphs (a)(1)(ii) and (2)(ii) of this section.

Example 6. On January 1, 1989, X agrees to purchase a machine from Y for delivery on March 1, 1990 for 1,000,000 yen. The agreement calls for X to pay Y for the machine on June 1, 1990. Under X's method of accounting, the expenditure for the machine does not accrue until delivery on March 1, 1990. The agreement to purchase the machine is not a section 988 transaction. In particular, the agreement to purchase the machine is not described in paragraph (a)(2)(ii) of this section because the agreement is not an item of expense taken into account under subtitle A (but rather is an agreement to purchase a capital asset in the future). However, the payable that will arise on the delivery date is a section 988 transaction under paragraphs (a)(1)(ii) and (2)(ii) of this section even though the payable relates to a capital expenditure. In addition, the disposition of yen to satisfy the payable on June 1, 1990, is a section 988 transaction under paragraph (a)(1)(i) of this section.

Example 7. On January 1, 1989, X purchases and takes delivery of inventory for 10,000 French francs with payment to be made on April 1, 1989. Under X's method of accounting, the expense accrues on January 1, 1989. On January 1, 1989, X also enters into a forward contract with a bank to purchase 10,000 French francs for $2,000 on April 1, 1989. Because X is an accrual basis taxpayer, the accrual of a nonfunctional currency denominated item of expense on January 1, 1989, for payment after the date of accrual is a section 988 transaction under paragraphs (a)(1)(ii) and (2)(ii) of this section. Entering into the forward contract to purchase the 10,000 French francs is a section 988 transaction under paragraphs (a)(1)(ii) and (2)(iii) of this section.

Example 8. On January 1, 1989, X acquires 100,000 Norwegian krone. On January 15, 1989, X purchases and takes delivery of 1,000 shares of common stock with the 100,000 krone acquired on January 1, 1989. On August 1, 1989, X sells the 1,000 shares of common stock and receives 120,000 krone in payment. On August 30, 1989, X converts the 120,000 krone to U.S. dollars. The acquisition of the 100,000 krone on January 1, 1989, and the acquisition of the 120,000 krone on August 1, 1989, are section 988 transactions for purposes of establishing the basis of such krone. The disposition of the 100,000 krone on January 15, 1989, and the 120,000 krone on August 30, 1989, are section 988 transactions as provided in paragraph (a)(1)(i) of this section. Neither the acquisition on January 15, 1989, nor the disposition on August 1, 1989, of the stock is a section 988 transaction.

Example 9. On May 11, 1989, X purchases a one year note at original issue for its issue price of $1,000. The note pays interest in dollars at the rate of 4 percent compounded semiannually. The amount of principal received by X upon maturity is equal to $1,000 plus the equivalent of the excess, if any, of (a) the Financial Times One Hundred Stock Index (an index of stocks traded on the London Stock Exchange hereafter referred to as the FT100) determined and translated into dollars on the last business day prior to the maturity date, over (b) £2,150, the "stated value" of the FT100, which is equal to 110% of the average value of the index for the six months prior to the issue date, translated at the exchange rate of £1 = $1.50. The purchase by X of the instrument described above is not a section 988 transaction because the index used to compute the principal amount received upon maturity is determined with reference to the value of stock and not nonfunctional currency.

Example 10. On April 9, 1989, X enters into an interest rate swap that provides for the payment of amounts by X to its counterparty based on 4% of a 10,000 yen principal amount in exchange for amounts based on yen LIBOR rates. Pursuant to paragraphs (a)(1)(ii) and (2)(iii) of this section, this yen for yen interest rate swap is a section 988 transaction.

Example 11. On August 11, 1989, X enters into an option contract for sale of a group of stocks traded on the Japanese Nikkei exchange. The contract is not a section 988 transaction within the meaning of § 1.988-1(a)(2)(iii) because

Reg. § 1.988-1(a)(6)

Income from Sources Without the United States

the underlying property to which the option relates is a group of stocks and not nonfunctional currency.

(7) *Special rules for regulated futures contracts and non-equity options*—(i) *In general.* Except as provided in paragraph (a)(7)(ii) of this section, paragraph (a)(2)(iii) of this section shall not apply to any regulated futures contract or non-equity option which would be marked to market under section 1256 if held on the last day of the taxable year.

(ii) *Election to have paragraph (a)(2)(iii) of this section apply.* Notwithstanding paragraph (a)(7)(i) of this section, a taxpayer may elect to have paragraph (a)(2)(iii) of this section apply to regulated futures contracts and non-equity options as provided in paragraph (a)(7)(iii) and (iv) of this section.

(iii) *Procedure for making the election.* A taxpayer shall make the election provided in paragraph (a)(7)(ii) of this section by sending to the Internal Revenue Service Center, Examination Branch, Stop Number 92, Kansas City, MO 64999 a statement titled "ELECTION TO TREAT REGULATED FUTURES CONTRACTS AND NON-EQUITY OPTIONS AS SECTION 988 TRANSACTIONS UNDER SECTION 988(c)(1)(D)(ii)" that contains the following:

(A) The taxpayer's name, address, and taxpayer identification number;

(B) The date the notice is mailed or otherwise delivered to the Internal Revenue Service Center;

(C) A statement that the taxpayer (including all members of such person's affiliated group as defined in section 1504 or in the case of an individual all persons filing a joint return with such individual) elects to have section 988(c)(1)(D)(i) and § 1.988-1(a)(7)(i) not apply;

(D) The date of the beginning of the taxable year for which the election is being made;

(E) If the election is filed after the first day of the taxable year, a statement regarding whether the taxpayer has previously held a contract described in section 988(c)(1)(D)(i) or § 1.988-1(a)(7)(i) during such taxable year, and if so, the first date during the taxable year on which such contract was held; and

(F) The signature of the person making the election (in the case of individuals filing a joint return, the signature of all persons filing such return).

The election shall be made by the following persons: in the case of an individual, by such individual; in the case of a partnership, by each partner separately; effective for taxable years beginning after March 17, 1992, in the case of tiered partnerships, each ultimate partner; in the case of an S corporation, by each shareholder separately; in the case of a trust (other than a grantor trust) or estate, by the fiduciary of such trust or estate; in the case of any corporation other than an S corporation, by such corporation (in the case of a corporation that is a member of an affiliated group that files a consolidated return, such election shall be valid and binding only if made by the common parent, as that term is used in § 1.1502-77(a)); in the case of a controlled foreign corporation, by its controlling United States shareholders under § 1.964-1(c)(3). With respect to a corporation (other than an S corporation), the election, when made by the common parent, shall be binding on all members of such corporation's affiliated group as defined in section 1504 that file a consolidated return. The election shall be binding on any income or loss derived from the partner's share (determined under the principles of section 702(a)) of all contracts described in section 988(c)(1)(D)(i) or paragraph (a)(7)(i) of this section in which the taxpayer holds a direct interest or indirect interest through a partnership or S corporation; however, the election shall not apply to any income or loss of a partnership for any taxable year if such partnership made an election under section 988(c)(1)(E)(iii)(V) for such year or any preceding year. Generally, a copy of the election must be attached to the taxpayer's income tax return for the first year it is effective. It is not required to be attached to subsequent returns. However, in the case of a partner, a copy of the election must be attached to the taxpayer's income tax return for every year during which the taxpayer is a partner in a partnership that engages in a transaction that is subject to the election.

(iv) *Time for making the election*—(A) *In general.* Unless the requirements for making a late election described in paragraph (a)(7)(iv)(B) of this section are satisfied, an election under section 988(c)(1)(D)(ii) and paragraph (a)(7)(ii) of this section for any taxable year shall be made on or before the first day of the taxable year or, if later, on or before the first day during such taxable year on which the taxpayer holds a contract described in section 988(c)(1)(D)(ii) and paragraph (a)(7)(ii) of this section. The election under section 988(c)(1)(D)(ii) and paragraph (a)(7)(ii) of this section shall apply to contracts entered into or acquired after October 21, 1988, and held on or after the effective date of the election. The election shall be effective as of the beginning of the taxable year and shall be binding with respect to all succeeding taxable years unless revoked with the prior consent of the Commissioner. In

Reg. § 1.988-1(a)(7)

determining whether to grant revocation of the election, recapture of the tax benefit derived from the election in previous taxable years will be considered.

(B) *Late elections.* A taxpayer may make an election under section 988(c)(1)(D)(ii) and paragraph (a)(7)(ii) of this section within 30 days after the time prescribed in the first sentence of paragraph (a)(7)(iv)(A) of this section. Such a late election shall be effective as of the beginning of the taxable year; however, any losses recognized during the taxable year with respect to contracts described in section 988(c)(1)(D)(ii) or paragraph (a)(7)(ii) of this section which were entered into or acquired after October 21, 1988, and held on or before the date on which the late election is mailed or otherwise delivered to the Internal Revenue Service Center shall not be treated as derived from a section 988 transaction. A late election must comply with the procedures set forth in paragraph (a)(7)(iii) of this section.

(v) *Transition rule.* An election made prior to September 21, 1989 which satisfied the requirements of Notice 88-124, 1988-51 I.R.B. 6, shall be deemed to satisfy the requirements of paragraphs (a)(7)(iii) and (iv) of this section.

(vi) *General effective date provision.* This paragraph (a)(7) shall apply with respect to futures contracts and options entered into or acquired after October 21, 1988.

(8) *Special rules for qualified funds*—(i) *Definition of qualified fund.* The term "qualified fund" means any partnership if—

(A) At all times during the taxable year (and during each preceding taxable year to which an election under section 988(c)(1)(E)(iii)(V) applied) such partnership has at least 20 partners and no single partner owns more than 20 percent of the interests in the capital or profits of the partnership;

(B) The principal activity of such partnership for such taxable year (and each such preceding taxable year) consists of buying and selling options, futures, or forwards with respect to commodities;

(C) At least 90 percent of the gross income of the partnership for the taxable year (and each such preceding year) consists of income or gains described in subparagraph (A), (B), or (G) of section 7704(d)(1) or gain from the sale or disposition of capital assets held for the production of interest or dividends;

(D) No more than a de minimis amount of the gross income of the partnership for the taxable year (and each such preceding taxable year) was derived from buying and selling commodities; and

(E) An election under section 988(c)(1)(E)(iii)(V) as provided in paragraph (a)(8)(iv) of this section applies to the taxable year.

(ii) *Special rules relating to paragraph (a)(8)(i)(A) of this section*—(A) *Certain general partners.* The interest of a general partner in the partnership shall not be treated as failing to meet the 20 percent ownership requirement of paragraph (a)(8)(i)(A) of this section for any taxable year of the partnership if, for the taxable year of the partner in which such partnership's taxable year ends, such partner (and each corporation filing a consolidated return with such partner) had no ordinary income or loss from a section 988 transaction (other than income from the partnership) which is exchange gain or loss (as the case may be).

(B) *Treatment of incentive compensation.* For purposes of paragraph (a)(8)(i)(A) of this section, any income allocable to a general partner as incentive compensation based on profits rather than capital shall not be taken into account in determining such partner's interest in the profits of the partnership.

(C) *Treatment of tax exempt partners.* The interest of a partner in the partnership shall not be treated as failing to meet the 20 percent ownership requirements of paragraph (a)(5)(8)(A) of this section if none of the income of such partner from such partnership is subject to tax under chapter 1 of subtitle A of the Internal Revenue Code (whether directly or through one or more pass-through entities).

(D) *Look-through rule.* In determining whether the 20% ownership requirement of paragraph (a)(8)(i)(A) of this section is met with respect to any partnership, any interest in such partnership held by another partnership shall be treated as held proportionately by the partners in such other partnership.

(iii) *Other special rules*—(A) *Related persons.* Interests in the partnership held by persons related to each other (within the meaning of section 267(b) or 707(b)) shall be treated as held by one person.

(B) *Predecessors.* Reference to any partnership shall include a reference to any predecessor thereof.

(C) *Treatment of certain debt instruments.* Solely for purposes of paragraph (a)(8)(i)(D) of this section, any debt instrument which is described in both paragraph (a)(1)(ii)

Reg. § 1.988-1(a)(8)

and (2)(i) of this section shall be treated as a commodity.

(iv) *Procedure for making the election provided in section 988(c)(1)(E)(iii)(V)*. A partnership shall make the election provided in section 988(c)(1)(E)(iii)(V) by sending to the Internal Revenue Service Center, Examination Branch, Stop Number 92, Kansas City, MO 64999 a statement titled "QUALIFIED FUND ELECTION UNDER SECTION 988(c)(1)(E)(iii)(V)" that contains the following:

(A) The partnership's name, address, and taxpayer identification number;

(B) The name, address and taxpayer identification number of the general partner making the election on behalf of the partnership;

(C) The date the notice is mailed or otherwise delivered to the Internal Revenue Service Center;

(D) A brief description of the activity of the partnership;

(E) A statement that the partnership is making the election provided in section 988(c)(1)(E)(iii)(V);

(F) The date of the beginning of the taxable year for which the election is being made;

(G) If the election is filed after the first day of the taxable year, then a statement regarding whether the partnership previously held an instrument referred to in section 988(c)(1)(E)(i) during such taxable year and, if so, the first date during the taxable year on which such contract was held; and

(H) The signature of the general partner making the election.

The election shall be made by a general partner with management responsibility of the partnership's activities and a copy of such election shall be attached to the partnership's income tax return (Form 1065) for the first taxable year it is effective. It is not required to be attached to subsequent returns.

(v) *Time for making the election*. The election under section 988(c)(1)(E)(iii)(V) for any taxable year shall be made on or before the first day of the taxable year or, if later, on or before the first day during such year on which the partnership holds an instrument described in section 988(c)(1)(E)(i). The election under section 988(c)(1)(E)(iii)(V) shall apply to the taxable year for which made and all succeeding taxable years. Such election may only be revoked with the consent of the Commissioner. In determining whether to grant revocation of the election, recapture by the partners of the tax benefit derived from the election in previous taxable years will be considered.

(vi) *Operative rules applicable to qualified funds*—(A) *In general*. In the case of a qualified fund, any bank forward contract or any foreign currency futures contract traded on a foreign exchange which is not otherwise a section 1256 contract shall be treated as a section 1256 contract for purposes of section 1256.

(B) *Gains and losses treated as short-term*. In the case of any instrument treated as a section 1256 contract under paragraph (a)(8)(vi)(A) of this section, subparagraph (A) of section 1256(a)(3) shall be applied by substituting "100 percent" for "40 percent" (and subparagraph (B) of such section shall not apply).

(vii) *Transition rule*. An election made prior to September 21, 1989, which satisfied the requirements of Notice 88-124, 1988-51 I.R.B. 6, shall be deemed to satisfy the requirements of § 1.988-1(a)(8)(iv) and (v).

(viii) *General effective date rules*—(A) The requirements of subclause (IV) of section 988(c)(1)(E)(iii) shall not apply to contracts entered into or acquired on or before October 21, 1988.

(B) In the case of any partner in an existing partnership, the 20 percent ownership requirements of subclause (I) of section 988(c)(1)(E)(iii) shall be treated as met during any period during which such partner does not own a percentage interest in the capital or profits of such partnership greater than 33 1/3 percent (or, if lower, the lowest such percentage interest of such partner during any period after October 21, 1988, during which such partnership is in existence). For purposes of the preceding sentence, the term "existing partnership" means any partnership if—

(*1*) such partnership was in existence on October 21, 1988, and principally engaged on such date in buying and selling options, futures, or forwards with respect to commodities; or

(*2*) a registration statement was filed with respect to such partnership with the Securities and Exchange Commission on or before such date and such registration statement indicated that the principal activity of such partnership will consist of buying and selling instruments referred to in paragraph (a)(8)(viii)(B)(*1*) of this section.

(9) *Exception for certain transactions entered into by an individual*—(i) *In general*. A transaction entered into by an individual which otherwise qualifies as a section 988 transaction shall be considered a section 988 transaction only

Reg. § 1.988-1(a)(9)

to the extent expenses properly allocable to such transaction meet the requirements of section 162 or 212 (other than the part of section 212 dealing with expenses incurred in connection with taxes).

(ii) *Examples.* The following examples illustrate the application of paragraph (a)(9) of this section.

Example 1. X is a U.S. citizen who therefore has the U.S. dollar as his functional currency. On January 1, 1990, X enters into a spot contract to purchase 10,000 British pounds (£) for $15,000 for delivery on January 3, 1990. Immediately upon delivery, X acquires at original issue a pound denominated bond with an issue price of £10,000. The bond matures on January 3, 1993, pays interest in pounds at a rate of 10% compounded semiannually, and has no original issue discount. Assume that all expenses properly allocable to these transactions would meet the requirements of section 212. Under § 1.988-2(d)(1)(ii), entering into the spot contract on January 1, 1990, is not a section 988 transaction. The acquisition of the pounds on January 3, 1990, under the spot contract is a section 988 transaction for purposes of establishing X's basis in the pounds. The disposition of the pounds and the acquisition of the bond by X are section 988 transactions. These transactions are not excluded from the definition of a section 988 transaction under paragraph (a)(9) of this section because expenses properly allocable to such transactions meet the requirements of section 212.

Example 2. X is a U.S. citizen who therefore has the dollar as his functional currency. In preparation for X's vacation, X purchases 1,000 British pounds (£) from a bank on June 1, 1989. During the period of X's vacation in the United Kingdom beginning June 10, 1989, and ending June 20, 1989, X spends £500 for hotel rooms, £300 for food and £200 for miscellaneous vacation expenses. The expenses properly allocable to such dispositions do not meet the requirements of section 162 or 212. Thus, the disposition of the pounds by X on his vacation are not section 988 transactions.

(10) *Intra-taxpayer transactions*—(i) *In general.* Except as provided in paragraph (a)(10)(ii) of this section, transactions between or among the taxpayer and/or qualified business units of that taxpayer ("intra-taxpayer transactions") are not section 988 transactions. See section 987 and the regulations thereunder.

(ii) *Certain transfers.* Exchange gain or loss with respect to nonfunctional currency or any item described in paragraph (a)(2) of this section entered into with another taxpayer shall be realized upon an intra-taxpayer transfer of such currency or item where as the result of the transfer the currency or other such item—

(A) Loses its character as nonfunctional currency or an item described in paragraph (a)(2) of this section; or

(B) Where the source of the exchange gain or loss could be altered absent the application of this paragraph (a)(10)(ii).

Such exchange gain or loss shall be computed in accordance with § 1.988-2 (without regard to § 1.988-2(b)(8)) as if the nonfunctional currency or item described in paragraph (a)(2) of this section had been sold or otherwise transferred at fair market value between unrelated taxpayers. For purposes of the preceding sentence, a taxpayer must use the translation rate that it uses for purposes of computing section 987 gain or loss with respect to the QBU branch that makes the transfer. In the case of a gain or loss incurred in a transaction described in this paragraph (a)(10)(ii) that does not have a significant business purpose, the Commissioner, may defer such gain or loss.

(iii) *Example.* The following example illustrates the provisions of this paragraph (a)(10).

Example. (A) X, a corporation with the U.S. dollar as its functional currency, operates through foreign branches Y and Z. Y and Z are qualified business units as defined in section 989(a) with the LC as their functional currency. X computes Y's and Z's income under section 987 (relating to branch transactions). On November 12, 1988, Y transfers $25 to the home office of X when the fair market value of such amount equals LC120. Y has a basis of LC100 in the $25. Under paragraph (a)(10)(ii) of this section, Y realizes foreign source exchange gain of LC20 (LC120 − LC100) as the result of the $25 transfer. For purposes of determining whether the transfer is a remittance resulting in additional gain or loss, see section 987 and the regulations thereunder.

(B) If instead Y transfers the $25 to Z, exchange gain is not realized because the $25 is nonfunctional currency with respect to Z and if Z were to immediately convert the $25 into LCs, the gain would be foreign source. For purposes of determining whether the transfer is a remittance resulting in additional gain or loss, see section 987 and the regulations thereunder.

(11) *Authority to include or exclude transactions from section 988*—(i) *In general.* The Commissioner may recharacterize a transaction (or series of transactions) in whole or in part as a section 988 transaction if the effect of such transaction (or series of transactions) is to avoid section 988. In addition, the Commissioner may exclude a transaction (or series of transactions) which in form is a section 988 transaction from the provi-

sions of section 988 if the substance of the transaction (or series of transactions) indicates that it is not properly considered a section 988 transaction.

(ii) *Example.* The following example illustrates the provisions of this paragraph (a)(11).

Example. B is an individual with the U.S. dollar as its functional currency. B holds 500,000 Swiss francs which have a basis of $100,000 and a fair market value of $400,000 as of October 15, 1989. On October 16, 1989, B transfers the 500,000 Swiss francs to a newly formed U.S. corporation, X, with the dollar as its functional currency. On October 16, 1989, B sells the stock of X for $400,000. Assume the transfer to X qualified for nonrecognition under section 351. Because the sale of the stock of X is a substitute for the disposition of an asset subject to section 988, the Commissioner may recharacterize the sale of the stock as a section 988 transaction. The same result would obtain if B transferred the Swiss francs to a partnership and then sold the partnership interest.

(b) *Spot contract.* A spot contract is a contract to buy or sell nonfunctional currency on or before two business days following the date of the execution of the contract. See § 1.988-2(d)(1)(ii) for operative rules regarding spot contracts.

(c) *Nonfunctional currency.* The term "nonfunctional currency" means with respect to a taxpayer or a qualified business unit (as defined in section 989(a)) a currency (including the European Currency Unit) other than the taxpayer's or the qualified business unit's functional currency as defined in section 985 and the regulations thereunder. For rules relating to nonrecognition of exchange gain or loss with respect to certain dispositions of nonfunctional currency, see § 1.988-2(a)(1)(iii).

(d) *Spot rate*—(1) *In general.* Except as otherwise provided in this paragraph, the term "spot rate" means a rate demonstrated to the satisfaction of the District Director or the Assistant Commissioner (International) to reflect a fair market rate of exchange available to the public for currency under a spot contract in a free market and involving representative amounts. In the absence of such a demonstration, the District Director or the Assistant Commissioner (International), in his or her sole discretion, shall determine the spot rate from a source of exchange rate information reflecting actual transactions conducted in a free market. For example, the taxpayer or the District Director or the Assistant Commissioner (International) may determine the spot rate by reference to exchange rates published in the pertinent monthly issue of "International Financial Statistics" or a successor publication of the International Monetary Fund; exchange rates published by the Board of Governors of the Federal Reserve System pursuant to 31 U.S.C. section 5151; exchange rates published in newspapers, financial journals or other daily financial news sources; or exchange rates quoted by electronic financial news services.

(2) *Consistency required in valuing transactions subject to section 988.* If the use of inconsistent sources of spot rate quotations results in the distortion of income, the District Director or the Assistant Commissioner (International) may determine the appropriate spot rate.

(3) *Use of certain spot rate conventions for payables and receivables denominated in nonfunctional currency.* If consistent with the taxpayer's financial accounting, a taxpayer may utilize a spot rate convention determined at intervals of one quarter year or less for purposes of computing exchange gain or loss with respect to payables and receivables denominated in a nonfunctional currency that are incurred in the ordinary course of business with respect to the acquisition or sale of goods or the obtaining or performance of services. For example, if consistent with the taxpayer's financial accounting, a taxpayer may accrue all payables and receivables incurred during the month of January at the spot rate on December 31 or January 31 (or at an average of any spot rates occurring between these two dates) and record the payment or receipt of amounts in satisfaction of such payables and receivables consistent with such convention. The use of a spot rate convention cannot be changed without the consent of the Commissioner.

(4) *Currency where an official government established rate differs from a free market rate*—(i) *In general.* If a currency has an official government established rate that differs from a free market rate, the spot rate shall be the rate which most clearly reflects the taxpayer's income. Generally, this shall be the free market rate.

(ii) *Examples.* The following examples illustrate the application of this paragraph (d)(4).

Example 1. X is an accrual method U.S. corporation with the dollar as its functional currency. X owns all the stock of a Country L subsidiary, CFC. CFC has the currency of Country L, the LC, as its functional currency. Country L imposes restrictions on the remittance of dividends. On April 1, 1990, CFC pays a dividend to X in the amount of LC100. Assume that the official government established rate is $1 = LC1 and the free market rate, which takes into account the remittance restrictions and which is the rate that most clearly reflects income, is $1 =

Reg. § 1.988-1(d)(4)

LC4. On April 1, 1990, X donates the LC100 in a transaction that otherwise qualifies as a charitable contribution under section 170(c). Both the amount of the dividend income and the deduction under section 170 is $25 (LC100 × the free market rate, $.25).

Example 2. X, a corporation with the U.S. dollar as its functional currency, operates in foreign country L through branch Y. Y is a qualified business unit as defined in section 989(a). X computes Y's income under the dollar approximate separate transactions method as described in § 1.985-3. The currency of L is the LC. X can purchase legally United States dollars ($) in L only from the L government. In order to take advantage of an arbitrage between the official and secondary dollar to LC exchange rates in L:

(i) X purchases LC100 for $60 in L on the secondary market when the official exchange rate is $1 = LC1;

(ii) X transfers the LC100 to Y;

(iii) Y purchases $100 for LC100; and

(iv) Y transfers $65 ($100 less an L tax withheld of $35 on the transfer) to the home office of X.

Under paragraph (a)(7) of this section, the transfer of the LC100 by X to Y is a realization event. X has a basis of $60 in the LC100. Under these facts, the appropriate dollar to LC exchange rate for computing the amount realized by X is the official exchange rate. Therefore, X realizes $40 ($100 − $60) of U.S. source gain from the transfer to Y. The same result would obtain if Y rather than X purchased the LC100 on the secondary market in L with $60 supplied by X, because the substance of this transaction is that X is performing the arbitrage.

(e) *Exchange gain or loss.* The term "exchange gain or loss" means the amount of gain or loss realized as determined in § 1.988-2 with respect to a section 988 transaction. Except as otherwise provided in these regulations (*e.g.*, § 1.988-5), the amount of exchange gain or loss from a section 988 transaction shall be separately computed for each section 988 transaction, and such amount shall not be integrated with gain or loss recognized on another transaction (whether or not such transaction is economically related to the section 988 transaction). See § 1.988-2(b)(8) for a special rule with respect to debt instruments.

(f) *Hyperinflationary currency*—(1) *Definition*—(i) *General rule.* For purposes of section 988, a hyperinflationary currency means a currency described in § 1.985-1(b)(2)(ii)(D). Unless otherwise provided, the currency in any example used in § § 1.988-1 through 1.988-5 is not a hyperinflationary currency.

(ii) *Special rules for determining base period.* In determining whether a currency is hyperinflationary under § 1.985-1(b)(2)(ii)(D) for purposes of this paragraph (f), the following rules will apply:

(A) The base period means the thirty-six calendar month period ending on the last day of the taxpayer's (or qualified business unit's) current taxable year. Thus, for example, if for 1996, 1997, and 1998, a country's annual inflation rates are 6 percent, 11 percent, and 90 percent, respectively, the cumulative inflation rate for the three-year base period is 124% [((1.06 × 1.11 × 1.90) − 1.0 = 1.24) × 100 = 124%]. Accordingly, assuming the QBU has a calendar year as its taxable year, the currency of the country is hyperinflationary for the 1998 taxable year. This change in the § 1.985-1(b)(2)(ii)(D) base period shall not apply to any section 988 transaction of an entity described in section 851 (regulated investment company (RIC)) or section 856 (real estate investment trust (REIT)). The Service may, by notice, provide that the foregoing change in the § 1.985-1(b)(2)(ii)(D) base period does not apply to any section 988 transaction of an entity with distribution requirements similar to a RIC or REIT.

(B) The last sentence of § 1.985-1(b)(2)(ii)(D) shall not apply to alter the base period for purposes of this paragraph (f) in determining whether a currency is hyperinflationary for purposes of section 988. Accordingly, generally accepted accounting principles may not apply to alter the base period for purposes of this paragraph (f).

(2) *Effective date.* Paragraph (f)(1) of this section shall apply to transactions entered into after February 14, 2000.

(g) *Fair market value.* The fair market value of an item shall, where relevant, reflect an appropriate premium or discount for the time value of money (*e.g.*, the fair market value of a forward contract to buy or sell nonfunctional currency shall reflect the present value of the difference between the units of nonfunctional currency times the market forward rate at the time of valuation and the units of nonfunctional currency times the forward rate set forth in the contract). However, if consistent with the taxpayer's method of financial accounting (and consistently applied from year to year), the preceding sentence shall not apply to a financial instrument that matures within one year from the date of issuance or acquisition. Unless otherwise provided, the fair market value given in any example used in

§§ 1.988-1 through 1.988-5 is deemed to reflect appropriately the time value of money. If the use of inconsistent sources of forward or other market rate quotations results in the distortion of income, the District Director or the Assistant Commissioner (International) may determine the appropriate rate.

(h) *Interaction with sections 1092 and 1256.* Unless otherwise provided, it is assumed for purposes of §§ 1.988-1 through 1.988-5 that any contract used in any example is not a section 1256 contract and is not part of a straddle as defined in section 1092. No inference is intended regarding the application of section 1092 or 1256 unless expressly stated.

(i) *Effective date.* Except as otherwise provided in this section, this section shall be effective for taxable years beginning after December 31, 1986. Thus, except as otherwise provided in this section, any payments made or received with respect to a section 988 transaction in taxable years beginning after December 31, 1986, are subject to this section. [Reg. § 1.988-1.]

☐ [*T.D.* 8400, 3-16-92. Amended by *T.D.* 8914, 12-29-2000.]

[Reg. § 1.988-2]

§ 1.988-2. **Recognition and computation of exchange gain or loss.**—(a) *Disposition of nonfunctional currency*—(1) *Recognition of exchange gain or loss*—(i) *In general.* Except as otherwise provided in this section, § 1.988-1(a)(7)(ii), and § 1.988-5, the recognition of exchange gain or loss upon the sale or other disposition of nonfunctional currency shall be governed by the recognition provisions of the Internal Revenue Code which apply to the sale or disposition of property (*e.g.,* section 1001 or, to the extent provided in regulations, section 1092). The disposition of nonfunctional currency in settlement of a forward contract, futures contract, option contract, or similar financial instrument is considered to be a sale or disposition of the nonfunctional currency for purposes of the preceding sentence.

(ii) *Clarification of section 1031.* An amount of one nonfunctional currency is not "property of like kind" with respect to an amount of a different nonfunctional currency.

(iii) *Coordination with section 988(c)(1)(C)(ii).* No exchange gain or loss is recognized with respect to the following transactions—

(A) An exchange of units of nonfunctional currency for different units of the same nonfunctional currency;

(B) The deposit of nonfunctional currency in a demand or time deposit or similar instrument (including a certificate of deposit) issued by a bank or other financial institution if such instrument is denominated in such currency;

(C) The withdrawal of nonfunctional currency from a demand or time deposit or similar instrument issued by a bank or other financial institution if such instrument is denominated in such currency;

(D) The receipt of nonfunctional currency from a bank or other financial institution from which the taxpayer purchased a certificate of deposit or similar instrument denominated in such currency by reason of the maturing or other termination of such instrument; and

(E) The transfer of nonfunctional currency from a demand or time deposit or similar instrument issued by a bank or other financial institution to another demand or time deposit or similar instrument denominated in the same nonfunctional currency issued by a bank or other financial institution.

The taxpayer's basis in the units of nonfunctional currency or other property received in the transaction shall be the adjusted basis of the units of nonfunctional currency or other property transferred. See paragraph (b) of this section with respect to the timing of interest income or expense and the determination of exchange gain or loss thereon.

(iv) *Example.* The following example illustrates the provisions of paragraph (a)(1)(iii) of this section.

Example. X is a corporation on the accrual method of accounting with the U.S. dollar as its functional currency. On January 1, 1989, X acquires 1,500 British pounds (£) for $2,250 (£1 = $1.50). On January 3, 1989, when the spot rate is £1 = $1.49, X deposits the £1,500 with a British financial institution in a non-interest bearing demand account. On February 1, 1989, when the spot rate is £1 = $1.45, X withdraws the £1,500. On February 5, 1989, when the spot rate is £1 = $1.42, X purchases inventory in the amount of £1,500. Pursuant to paragraph (a)(1)(iii) of this section, no exchange loss is realized until February 5, 1989, when X disposes of the £1,500 for inventory. At that time, X realizes exchange loss in the amount of $120 computed under paragraph (a)(2) of this section. The loss is not an adjustment to the cost of the inventory.

(2) *Computation of gain or loss*—(i) *In general.* Exchange gain realized from the sale or other disposition of nonfunctional currency shall be the excess of the amount realized over the adjusted basis of such currency, and exchange loss realized shall be the excess of the adjusted basis of such currency over the amount realized.

Reg. § 1.988-2(a)(2)

50,860 Income from Sources Without the United States

See p. 20,601 for regulations not amended to reflect law changes

(ii) *Amount realized*—(A) *In general.* The amount realized from the disposition of nonfunctional currency shall be determined under section 1001(b). A taxpayer that uses a spot rate convention under § 1.988-1(d)(3) to determine exchange gain or loss with respect to a payable shall determine the amount realized upon the disposition of nonfunctional currency paid in satisfaction of the payable in a manner consistent with such convention.

(B) *Exchange of nonfunctional currency for property.* For purpose of paragraph (a)(2) of this section, the exchange of nonfunctional currency for property (other than nonfunctional currency) shall be treated as—

(*1*) An exchange of the units of nonfunctional currency for units of functional currency at the spot rate on the date of the exchange, and

(*2*) The purchase or sale of the property for such units of functional currency.

(C) *Example.* The following example illustrates the provisions of paragraph (a)(2)(ii)(B) of this section.

Example. G is a U.S. corporation with the U.S. dollar as its functional currency. On January 1, 1989, G enters into a contract to purchase a paper manufacturing machine for 10,000,000 British pounds (£) for delivery on January 1, 1991. On January 1, 1991, when G exchanges £10,000,000 (which G purchased for $12,000,000) for the machine, the fair market value of the machine is £17,000,000. On January 1, 1991, the spot exchange rate is £1 = $1.50. Under paragraph (a)(2)(ii)(B) of this section, the transaction is treated as an exchange of £10,000,000 for $15,000,000 and the purchase of the machine for $15,000,000. Accordingly, in computing G's exchange gain of $3,000,000 on the disposition of the £10,000,000, the amount realized is $15,000,000. G's basis in the machine is $15,000,000. No gain is recognized on the bargain purchase of the machine.

(iii) *Adjusted basis*—(A) *In general.* Except as provided in paragraph (a)(2)(iii)(B) of this section, the adjusted basis of nonfunctional currency is determined under the applicable provisions of the Internal Revenue Code (*e.g.,* sections 1011 through 1023). A taxpayer that uses a spot rate convention under § 1.988-1(d)(3) to determine exchange gain or loss with respect to a receivable shall determine the basis of nonfunctional currency received in satisfaction of such receivable in a manner consistent with such convention.

(B) *Determination of the basis of nonfunctional currency withdrawn from an account with a bank or other financial institution*—(*1*) *In general.* The basis of nonfunctional currency withdrawn from an account with a bank or other financial institution shall be determined under any reasonable method that is consistently applied from year to year by the taxpayer to all accounts denominated in a nonfunctional currency. For example, a taxpayer may use a first in first out method, a last in first out method, a prorata method (as illustrated in the example below), or any other reasonable method that is consistently applied. However, a method that consistently results in units of nonfunctional currency with the highest basis being withdrawn first shall not be considered reasonable.

(*2*) *Example.* The following example illustrates the provisions of this paragraph (a)(2)(iii)(B).

Example. (i) X, a cash basis individual with the dollar as his functional currency, opens a demand account with a Swiss bank. Assume expenses associated with the demand account are deductible under section 212. The following chart indicates Swiss franc deposits to the account, Swiss franc interest credited to the account, the dollar basis of each deposit, and the determination of the aggregate dollar basis of all Swiss francs in the account. Assume that the taxpayer has properly translated all the amounts specified in the chart and that all transactions are subject to section 988.

Date	Swiss francs Deposited	Interest Received	U.S. dollar Basis	Aggregate U.S. dollar Basis
1/01/89	1000 Sf		$500	$500
3/31/89		50 Sf	$ 25	$525
6/30/89		50 Sf	$ 24	$549
9/30/89		50 Sf	$ 25	$574
12/31/89		50 Sf	$ 26	$600

(ii) On January 1, 1990, X withdraws 500 Swiss francs from the account. X may determine his basis in the Swiss francs by multiplying the aggregate U.S. dollar basis of Swiss francs in the account by a fraction the numerator of which is the number of Swiss francs withdrawn from the account and the denominator is the total number of Swiss francs in the account. Under this method, X's basis in the 500 Swiss francs is $250 computed as follows:

$$\frac{500 \text{ Sf}}{1200 \text{ Sf}} \times \$600 = \$250$$

(iii) X's basis in the Swiss francs remaining in the account is $350 ($600 − $250). X must use this method consistently from year to year with respect to withdrawals of nonfunctional currency from all of X's accounts.

Reg. § 1.988-2(a)(2)

(iv) *Purchase and sale of stock or securities traded on an established securities market by cash basis taxpayer*—(A) *Amount realized.* If stock or securities traded on an established securities market are sold by a cash basis taxpayer for nonfunctional currency, the amount realized with respect to the stock or securities (as determined on the trade date) shall be computed by translating the units of nonfunctional currency received into functional currency at the spot rate on the settlement date of the sale. This rule applies notwithstanding that the stock or securities are treated as disposed of on a date other than the settlement date under another section of the Code. See section 453(k).

(B) *Basis.* If stock or securities traded on an established securities market are purchased by a cash basis taxpayer for nonfunctional currency, the basis of the stock or securities shall be determined by translating the units of nonfunctional currency paid into functional currency at the spot rate on the settlement date of the purchase.

(C) *Example.* The following example illustrates the provisions of this paragraph (a)(2)(iv).

Example. On November 1, 1989 (the trade date), X, a calendar year cash basis U.S. individual, purchases stock for £100 for settlement on November 5, 1989. On November 1, 1989, the spot value of the £100 is $140. On November 5, 1989, X purchases £100 for $141 which X uses to pay for the stock. X's basis in the stock is $141. On December 30, 1990 (the trade date), X sells the stock for £110 for settlement on January 5, 1991. On December 30, 1990, the spot value of £110 is $165. On January 5, 1991, X transfers the stock and receives £110 which, translated at the spot rate, equal $166. Under section 453(k), the stock is considered disposed of on December 30, 1990. The amount realized with respect to such disposition is the value of the £110 on January 5, 1991 ($166). Accordingly, X's gain realized on December 30, 1990, from the disposition of the stock is $25 ($166 amount realized less $141 basis). X's basis in the £110 received from the sale of the stock is $166.

(v) *Purchase and sale of stock or securities traded on an established securities market by accrual basis taxpayer.* For taxable years beginning after March 17, 1992, an accrual basis taxpayer may elect to apply the rules of paragraph (a)(2)(iv) of this section. The election shall be made by filing a statement with the taxpayer's first return in which the election is effective clearly indicating that the election has been made. A method so elected must be applied consistently from year to year and cannot be changed without the consent of the Commissioner.

(b) *Translation of interest income or expense and determination of exchange gain or loss with respect to debt instruments*—(1) *Translation of interest income received with respect to a nonfunctional currency demand account.* Interest income received with respect to a demand account with a bank or other financial institution which is denominated in (or the payments of which are determined by reference to) a nonfunctional currency shall be translated into functional currency at the spot rate on the date received or accrued or pursuant to any reasonable spot rate convention consistently applied by the taxpayer to all taxable years and to all accounts denominated in nonfunctional currency in the same financial institution. For example, a taxpayer may translate interest income received with respect to a demand account on the last day of each month of the taxable year, on the last day of each quarter of the taxable year, on the last day of each half of the taxable year, or on the last day of the taxable year. No exchange gain or loss is realized upon the receipt or accrual of interest income with respect to a demand account subject to this paragraph (b)(1).

(2) *Translation of nonfunctional currency interest income or expense received or paid with respect to a debt instrument described in § 1.988-1(a)(1)(ii) and (2)(i)*—(i) *Scope*—(A) *In general.* Paragraph (b) of this section only applies to debt instruments described in § 1.988-1(a)(1)(ii) and (2)(i) where all payments are denominated in, or determined with reference to, a single nonfunctional currency. Except as provided in paragraph (b)(2)(i)(B) of this section, this paragraph (b) shall not apply to contingent payment debt instruments.

(B) *Nonfunctional currency contingent payment debt instruments*—(*1*) *Operative rules.* [RESERVED]

(*2*) *Certain instruments are not contingent payment debt instruments.* For purposes of section 1275(d), a debt instrument denominated in, or all payments of which are determined with reference to, a single nonfunctional currency (with no contingencies) is not a contingent payment debt instrument. See § 1.988-1(a)(4) and (5) for the treatment of dual currency and multicurrency debt instruments.

(ii) *Determination and translation of interest income or expense*—(A) *In general.* Interest income or expense on a debt instrument described in paragraph (b)(2)(i) of this section (including original issue discount determined in accordance with sections 1271 through 1275 and 163(e) as adjusted for acquisition premium under section

1272(a)(7), and acquisition discount determined in accordance with sections 1281 through 1283) shall be determined in units of nonfunctional currency and translated into functional currency as provided in paragraphs (b)(2)(ii)(B) and (C) of this section. For purposes of sections 483, 1273(b)(5) and 1274, the nonfunctional currency in which an instrument is denominated (or by reference to which payments are determined) shall be considered money.

(B) *Translation of interest income or expense that is not required to be accrued prior to receipt or payment.* With respect to an instrument described in paragraph (b)(2)(i) of this section, interest income or expense received or paid that is not required to be accrued by the taxpayer prior to receipt or payment shall be translated at the spot rate on the date of receipt or payment. No exchange gain or loss is realized with respect to the receipt or payment of such interest income or expense (other than the exchange gain or loss that might be realized under paragraph (a) of this section upon the disposition of the nonfunctional currency so received or paid).

(C) *Translation of interest income or expense that is required to be accrued prior to receipt or payment.* With respect to an instrument described in paragraph (b)(2)(i) of this section, interest income or expense that is required to be accrued prior to receipt or payment (*e.g.*, under section 1272, 1281 or 163(e) or because the taxpayer uses an accrual method of accounting) shall be translated at the average rate (or other rate specified in paragraph (b)(2) (iii)(B) of this section) for the interest accrual period or, with respect to an interest accrual period that spans two taxable years, at the average rate (or other rate specified in paragraph (b)(2)(iii)(B) of this section) for the partial period within the taxable year. See paragraphs (b)(3) and (4) of this section for the determination of exchange gain or loss on the receipt or payment of accrued interest income or expense.

(iii) *Determination of average rate or other accrual convention*—(A) *In general.* For purposes of this paragraph (b), the average rate for an accrual period (or partial period) shall be a simple average of the spot exchange rates for each business day of such period or other average exchange rate for the period reasonably derived and consistently applied by the taxpayer.

(B) *Election to use spot accrual convention.* For taxable years beginning after March 17, 1992, a taxpayer may elect to translate interest income and expense at the spot rate on the last day of the interest accrual period (and in the case of a partial accrual period, the spot rate on the last day of the taxable year). If the last day of the interest accrual period is within five business days of the date of receipt or payment, the taxpayer may translate interest income or expense at the spot rate on the date of receipt or payment. The election shall be made by filing a statement with the taxpayer's first return in which the election is effective clearly indicating that the election has been made. A method so elected must be applied consistently to all debt instruments from year to year and cannot be changed without the consent of the Commissioner.

(3) *Exchange gain or loss recognized by the holder with respect to accrued interest income.* The holder of a debt instrument described in paragraph (b)(2)(i) of this section shall realize exchange gain or loss with respect to accrued interest income on the date such accrued interest income is received or the instrument is disposed of (including a deemed disposition under section 1001 that results from a material change in terms of the instrument). Except as otherwise provided in this paragraph (b) (*e.g.*, paragraph (b)(8) of this section), exchange gain or loss realized with respect to accrued interest income shall be recognized in accordance with the applicable recognition provisions of the Internal Revenue Code. The amount of exchange gain or loss so realized with respect to accrued interest income is determined for each accrual period by—

(i) Translating the units of nonfunctional currency interest income received with respect to such accrual period (as determined under the ordering rules of paragraph (b)(7) of this section) into functional currency at the spot rate on the date the interest income is received or the instrument is disposed of (or deemed disposed of), and

(ii) Subtracting from such amount the amount computed by translating the units of nonfunctional currency interest income accrued with respect to such income received at the average rate (or other rate specified in paragraph (b)(2) (iii)(B) of this section) for the accrual period.

(4) *Exchange gain or loss recognized by the obligor with respect to accrued interest expense.* The obligor under a debt instrument described in paragraph (b)(2)(i) of this section shall realize exchange gain or loss with respect to accrued interest expense on the date such accrued interest expense is paid or the obligation to make payments is transferred or extinguished (including a deemed disposition under section 1001 that results from a material change in terms of the instrument). Except as otherwise provided in this paragraph (b) (*e.g.*, paragraph (b)(8) of this section), exchange gain or loss realized with respect to accrued interest expense shall be recognized in

Income from Sources Without the United States

See p. 20,601 for regulations not amended to reflect law changes

accordance with the applicable recognition provisions of the Internal Revenue Code. The amount of exchange gain or loss so realized with respect to accrued interest expense is determined for each accrual period by—

(i) Translating the units of nonfunctional currency interest expense accrued with respect to the amount of interest paid into functional currency at the average rate (or other rate specified in paragraph (b)(2)(iii)(B) of this section) for such accrual period; and

(ii) Subtracting from such amount the amount computed by translating the units of nonfunctional currency interest paid (or, if the obligation to make payments is extinguished or transferred, the units accrued) with respect to such accrual period (as determined under the ordering rules in paragraph (b)(7) of this section) into functional currency at the spot rate on the date payment is made or the obligation is transferred or extinguished (or deemed extinguished).

(5) *Exchange gain or loss recognized by the holder of a debt instrument with respect to principal.* The holder of a debt instrument described in paragraph (b)(2)(i) of this section shall realize exchange gain or loss with respect to the principal amount of such instrument on the date principal (determined under the ordering rules of paragraph (b)(7) of this section) is received from the obligor or the instrument is disposed of (including a deemed disposition under section 1001 that results from a material change in terms of the instrument). For purposes of computing exchange gain or loss, the principal amount of a debt instrument is the holder's purchase price in units of nonfunctional currency. See paragraph (b)(10) of this section for rules regarding the amortization of that part of the principal amount that represents bond premium and the computation of exchange gain or loss thereon. If, however, the holder acquired the instrument in a transaction in which exchange gain or loss was realized but not recognized by the transferor, the nonfunctional currency principal amount of the instrument with respect to the holder shall be the same as that of the transferor. Except as otherwise provided in this paragraph (b) (*e.g.*, paragraph (b)(8) of this section), exchange gain or loss realized with respect to such principal amount shall be recognized in accordance with the applicable recognition provisions of the Internal Revenue Code. The amount of exchange gain or loss so realized by the holder with respect to principal is determined by—

(i) Translating the units of nonfunctional currency principal at the spot rate on the date payment is received or the instrument is disposed of (or deemed disposed of); and

(ii) Subtracting from such amount the amount computed by translating the units of nonfunctional currency principal at the spot rate on the date the holder (or a transferor from whom the nonfunctional principal amount is carried over) acquired the instrument (is deemed to acquire the instrument).

(6) *Exchange gain or loss recognized by the obligor of a debt instrument with respect to principal.* The obligor under a debt instrument described in paragraph (b)(2)(i) of this section shall realize exchange gain or loss with respect to the principal amount of such instrument on the date principal (determined under the ordering rules of paragraph (b)(7) of this section) is paid or the obligation to make payments is transferred or extinguished (including a deemed disposition under section 1001 that results from a material change in terms of the instrument). For purposes of computing exchange gain or loss, the principal amount of a debt instrument is the amount received by the obligor for the debt instrument in units of nonfunctional currency. See paragraph (b)(10) of this section for rules regarding the amortization of that part of the principal amount that represents bond premium and the computation of exchange gain or loss thereon. If, however, the obligor became the obligor in a transaction in which exchange gain or loss was realized but not recognized by the transferor, the nonfunctional currency principal amount of the instrument with respect to such obligor shall be the same as that of the transferor. Except as otherwise provided in this paragraph (b) (*e.g.*, paragraph (b)(8) of this section), exchange gain or loss realized with respect to such principal shall be recognized in accordance with the applicable recognition provisions of the Internal Revenue Code. The amount of exchange gain or loss so realized by the obligor is determined by—

(i) Translating the units of nonfunctional currency principal at the spot rate on the date the obligor (or a transferor from whom the principal amount is carried over) became the obligor (or is deemed to have become the obligor); and

(ii) Subtracting from such amount the amount computed by translating the units of nonfunctional currency principal at the spot rate on the date payment is made or the obligation is transferred or extinguished (or deemed extinguished).

(7) *Payment ordering rules*—(i) *Debt instruments subject to the rules of sections 163(e), or 1271 through 1288.* In the case of a debt instrument described in paragraph (b)(2)(i) of this section that is subject to the rules of sections 163(e), or 1272 through 1288, units of nonfunctional cur-

Reg. § 1.988-2(b)(7)

rency (or an amount determined with reference to nonfunctional currency) received or paid with respect to such debt instrument shall be treated first as a receipt or payment of periodic interest under the principles of section 1273 and the regulations thereunder, second as a receipt or payment of original issue discount to the extent accrued as of the date of the receipt or payment, and finally as a receipt or payment of principal. Units of nonfunctional currency (or an amount determined with reference to nonfunctional currency) treated as a receipt or payment of original issue discount under the preceding sentence are attributed to the earliest accrual period in which original issue discount has accrued and to which prior receipts or payments have not been attributed. No portion thereof shall be treated as prepaid interest. These rules are illustrated by *Example 10* of paragraph (b)(9) of this section.

(ii) *Other debt instruments.* In the case of a debt instrument described in paragraph (b)(2)(i) of this section that is not subject to the rules of section 163(e) or 1272 through 1288, whether units of nonfunctional currency (or an amount determined with reference to nonfunctional currency) received or paid with respect to such debt instrument are treated as interest or principal shall be determined under section 163 or other applicable section of the Code.

(8) *Limitation of exchange gain or loss on payment or disposition of a debt instrument.* When a debt instrument described in paragraph (b)(2)(i) of this section is paid or disposed of, or when the obligation to make payments thereunder is satisfied by another person, or extinguished or assumed by another person, exchange gain or loss is computed with respect to both principal and any accrued interest (including original issue discount), as provided in paragraph (b)(3) through (7) of this section. However, pursuant to section 988(b)(1) and (2), the sum of any exchange gain or loss with respect to the principal and interest of any such debt instrument shall be realized only to the extent of the total gain or loss realized on the transaction. The gain or loss realized shall be recognized in accordance with the general principles of the Code. See *Examples 3, 4* and *6* of paragraph (b)(9) of this section.

(9) *Examples.* The preceding provisions are illustrated in the following examples. The examples assume that any transaction involving an individual is a section 988 transaction.

Example 1. (i) X is an individual on the cash method of accounting with the dollar as his functional currency. On January 1, 1992, X converts $13,000 to 10,000 British pounds (£) at the spot rate of £1 = $1.30 and loans the £10,000 to Y for 3 years. The terms of the loan provide that Y will make interest payments of £1,000 on December 31 of 1992, 1993, and 1994, and will repay X's £10,000 principal on December 31, 1994. Assume the spot rates for the pertinent dates are as follows:

Date	Spot rate (pounds to dollars)
January 1, 1992	£1 = $1.30
December 31, 1992	£1 = $1.35
December 31, 1993	£1 = $1.40
December 31, 1994	£1 = $1.45

(ii) Under paragraph (b)(2)(ii)(B) of this section, X will translate the £1,000 interest payments at the spot rate on the date received. Accordingly, X will have interest income of $1,350 in 1992, $1,400 in 1993, and $1,450 in 1994. Because X is a cash basis taxpayer, X does not realize exchange gain or loss on the receipt of interest income.

(iii) Under paragraph (b)(5) of this section, X will realize exchange gain upon repayment of the £10,000 principal amount determined by translating the £10,000 at the spot rate on the date it is received (£10,000 × $1.45 = $14,500) and subtracting from such amount, the amount determined by translating the £10,000 at the spot rate on the date the loan was made (£10,000 × $1.30 = $13,000). Accordingly, X will realize an exchange gain of $1,500 on the repayment of the loan on December 31, 1994.

Example 2. (i) Assume the same facts as in *Example 1* except that X is an accrual method taxpayer and that average rates are as follows:

Accrual Period	Average rate (pounds to dollars)
1992	£1 = $1.32
1993	£1 = $1.37
1994	£1 = $1.42

(ii) Under paragraph (b)(2)(ii)(C) of this section, X will accrue the £1,000 interest payments at the average rate for the accrual period. Accordingly, X will have interest income of $1,320 in 1992, $1,370 in 1993, and $1,420 in 1994. Because X is an accrual basis taxpayer, X determines exchange gain or loss for each interest accrual period by translating the units of nonfunctional currency interest income received with respect to such accrual period at the spot rate on the date received and subtracting the amounts of interest income accrued for such period. Thus, X will realize $90 of exchange gain with respect to interest received under the loan, computed as follows:

Reg. § 1.988-2(b)(8)

Income from Sources Without the United States

See p. 20,601 for regulations not amended to reflect law changes

Year	Spot Value Interest Received	Accrued Interest @ Avg. Rate	Exch. Gain
1992	$1,350	$1,320	$30
1993	$1,400	$1,370	$30
1994	$1,450	$1,420	$30
TOTAL			$90

(iii) Under paragraph (b)(5) of this section, X will realize exchange gain upon repayment of the £10,000 loan principal determined in the same manner as in *Example 1*. Accordingly, X will realize an exchange gain of $1,500 on the repayment of the loan principal on December 31, 1994.

Example 3. Assume the same facts as in *Example 1* except that X is a calendar year taxpayer on the accrual method of accounting that elects to use a spot rate convention to translate interest income as provided in § 1.988-2(b)(2)(iii)(B). Interest income is received by X on the last day of each accrual period. Under paragraph (b)(2)(ii)(C), X will translate the interest income at the spot rate on the last day of each interest accrual period. Accordingly, X will have interest income of $1,350 in 1992, and $1,400 in 1993, $1,450 in 1994. Because the rate at which the interest income is translated is the same as the rate on the day of receipt, X will not realize any exchange gain or loss with respect to the interest income. Under paragraph (b)(5) of this section, X will realize exchange gain upon repayment of the £10,000 loan principal determined in the same manner as in *Example 1*. Accordingly, X will realize an exchange gain of $1,500 on the repayment of the loan principal on December 31, 1994.

Example 4. Assume the same facts as in *Example 1* except that on December 31, 1993, X sells Y's note for 9,821.13 British pounds (£) after the interest payment. Under paragraph (b)(8) of this section, X will compute exchange gain on the £10,000 principal. The exchange gain is $1,000 [(£10,000 × $1.40) − (£10,000 × $1.30)]. This exchange gain, however, is only realized to the extent of the total gain on the disposition. X's total gain is $749.58 [(£9,821.13 × $1.40) − (£10,000 × $1.30)]. Thus, X will realize $749.58 of exchange gain (and will realize no market loss).

Example 5. (i) The facts are the same as in *Example 1* except that Y becomes insolvent and fails to repay the full £10,000 principal when due. Instead, X and Y agree to compromise the debt for a payment of £8,000 on December 31, 1994. Under paragraph (b)(8) of this section, X will compute exchange gain on the £10,000 originally booked. The exchange gain is $1,500 [(£10,000 × $1.45) − (£10,000 × $1.30) = $1,500]. This exchange gain, however, is only realized to the extent of the total gain on the disposition. X realizes an overall loss on the disposition of $1,400 [(£8,000 × $1.45) − (£10,000 × $1.30) = ($1,400)]. Thus, X will realize no exchange gain (and a $1400 market loss).

(ii) If the exchange rate on December 31, 1994, were £1 = $1.25, rather than £1 = $1.45, X would compute exchange loss under paragraph (b)(8) of this section, on the £10,000 originally booked. The exchange loss would be $500 [(£10,000 × $1.25) − (£10,000 × $1.30) = ($500)]. X's total loss on the disposition would be $3,000 [(£8,000 × $1.25) − (£10,000 × $1.30) = ($3,000)]. Thus, X would realize $500 of exchange loss and a $2,500 market loss on the disposition.

Example 6. (i) X is an individual with the dollar as his functional currency. X is on the cash method of accounting. On January 1, 1989, X borrows 10,000 British pounds (£) from Y, an unrelated person. The terms of the loan provide that X will make interest payments of £1,200 on December 31 of 1989 and 1990 and will repay Y's £10,000 principal on December 31, 1990. The spot rates for the pertinent dates are as follows:

DATE	SPOT RATE (pounds to dollars)
January 1, 1989	1 = $1.50
December 31, 1989	1 = $1.60
December 31, 1990	1 = $1.70

Assume that the basis of the £1,200 paid as interest by X on December 31, 1989 is $2,000, the basis of the £1,200 paid as interest by X on December 31, 1990, is $2,020 and the basis of the £10,000 principal paid by X on December 31, 1990 is $16,000.

(ii) Under paragraph (b)(2)(ii)(B) of this section, X translates the £1,200 interest payments at the spot rate on the day paid. Thus, X paid $1,920 (£1,200 × $1.60) of interest on December 31, 1989 and $2,040 (£1,200 × $1.70) of interest on December 31, 1990. In addition, X will realize exchange gain or loss on the disposition of the £1,200 on December 31, 1989 and 1990, under paragraph (a) of this section. Pursuant to paragraph (a)(2) of this section, X will realize an exchange loss of $80 [(£1,200 × $1.60) − $2,000] on December 31, 1989 and exchange gain of $20 [(£1,200 × $1.70) − $2,020] on December 31, 1990.

(iii) Under paragraph (b)(6) of this section, X will realize exchange loss on December 31, 1990 upon repayment of the £10,000 principal amount determined by translating the £10,000 received at the spot rate on January 1, 1989 (£10,000 × $1.50 = $15,000) and subtracting from such amount, the amount determined by translating the £10,000 paid at the spot rate on December 31, 1990 (£10,000 × $1.70 = $17,000). Thus, under paragraph (b)(6) of this section, X has an ex-

Reg. § 1.988-2(b)(9)

change loss with respect to the £10,000 principal of $2,000. Further, under paragraph (a)(2) of this section, X will realize an exchange gain upon disposition of the £10,000 on December 31, 1990. Under paragraph (a)(2) of this section, X will subtract his adjusted basis in the £10,000 ($16,000) from the amount realized upon the disposition of the £10,000 (£10,000 × $1.70 = $17,000) resulting in a gain of $1,000. Accordingly, X's combined exchange gain and loss realized on December 31, 1990 with respect to the repayment of the £10,000 is a $1,000 exchange loss.

Example 7. (i) X is a calendar year corporation on the accrual method of accounting and with the dollar as its functional currency. On January 1, 1989, X purchases at original issue for 82.64 Canadian dollars (C$) M corporation's 2 year note maturing on December 31, 1990, at a stated redemption price of C$ 100. The yield to maturity in Canadian dollars is 10 percent and the accrual period is the one year period beginning January 1 and ending December 31. The note has C$17.36 of original issue discount. Assume that the spot rates are as follows: C$1 = U.S.$.72 on January 1, 1989; C$1 = U.S.$.80 on January 1, 1990; C$1 = U.S.$.82 on December 31, 1990. Assume further that the average rate for 1989 is C$1 = U.S.$.76 and for 1990 is C$1 = U.S.$.81.

(ii) Under paragraph (b)(2)(ii)(A) of this section, X will determine its interest income in Canadian dollars. Accordingly, under section 1272, X must take into account original issue discount in the amount of C$8.26 on December 31, 1989 and C$9.10 on December 31, 1990. Pursuant to paragraph (b)(2)(ii)(C) of this section, X will translate these amounts into U.S. dollars at the average exchange rate for the relevant accrual period. Thus, the amount of interest income taken into account in 1989 is U.S.$6.28 (C$8.26 × U.S.$.76) and in 1990 is U.S.$7.37 (C$9.10 × U.S.$.81). Pursuant to paragraph (b)(3)(ii) of this section, X will realize exchange gain or loss with respect to the accrued interest determined for each accrual period by translating the Canadian dollars received with respect to such accrual period into U.S. dollars at the spot rate on the date the interest is received and subtracting from that amount the amount accrued in U.S. dollars. Thus, the amount of exchange gain realized on December 31, 1990, is U.S.$.58 (U.S.$.49 from 1989 + U.S.$.09 from 1990). Pursuant to paragraph (b)(5) of this section, X shall realize exchange gain or loss with respect to the principal (C$82.64) on December 31, 1990, computed by translating the C$82.64 at the spot rate on December 31, 1990 (U.S.$67.76) and subtracting the C$82.64 translated at the spot rate on January 1, 1989 (U.S.$59.50) for an exchange gain of U.S.$8.26. Thus, X's combined exchange gain is U.S.$8.84 (U.S.$.49 + U.S.$.09 + U.S.$8.26).

(iii) Assume instead that on January 1, 1990, X sells the note for C$86.95, which it immediately converts to U.S. dollars. X's exchange gain is computed under paragraph (b)(8) of this section with reference to the nonfunctional currency denominated principal amount (C$82.64) and the nonfunctional currency denominated accrued original issue discount (C$8.26). X will compute an exchange gain of U.S.$6.61 with respect to the issue price [(C$82.64 × U.S.$.80) − (C$82.64 × U.S.$.72)] and an exchange gain of U.S.$.33 with respect to the accrued original issue discount [(C$8.26 × U.S.$.80) − (C$8.26 × U.S.$.76)]. Accordingly, prior to the application of paragraph (b)(8) of this section, X's total exchange gain is U.S.$6.94 (U.S.$6.61 + U.S.$.33), and X's market loss is U.S.$3.16 [(C$90.90 − C$86.95) × U.S.$.80]. Pursuant to paragraph (b)(8) of this section, however, X's market loss on the note of U.S.$3.16 is netted against X's exchange gain of U.S.$6.94, resulting in a realized exchange gain of U.S.$3.78 and no market loss.

Example 8. (i) The facts are the same as in *Example 7* (i) except that on January 1, 1990, X contributes the M corporation note to Y, a wholly-owned U.S. subsidiary of X with the dollar as its functional currency, and Y collects C$100 from M corporation at maturity on December 31, 1990, when the spot rate is C$1= U.S.$.82. The transfer of the note from X to Y qualifies for nonrecognition of gain under section 351(a). On December 31, 1990, Y includes C$9.10 of accrued interest in income which translated at the average exchange rate of C$1 = U.S.$.81 for the year results in U.S.$7.37 of interest income.

(ii) Y's exchange gain is computed under paragraph (b)(3) of this section with respect to accrued interest income and paragraph (b)(5) of this section with respect to the nonfunctional currency principal amount. Under paragraph (b)(3) of this section, Y will realize exchange gain or loss for each accrual period computed by translating the units of nonfunctional currency interest income received with respect to such accrual period at the spot rate on the day received and subtracting the amounts of interest income accrued for such period. Thus, Y will realize $.49 of exchange gain with respect to original issue discount accrued in 1989 [(C$8.26 × U.S.$.82) − (C$8.26 × U.S.$.76) = U.S.$.49] and $.09 of exchange gain with respect to original issue discount accrued in 1990 [(C$9.10 × U.S.$.82) − (C$9.10 × U.S.$.81) = $.09].

(iii) Pursuant to paragraph (b)(5) of this section, the nonfunctional currency principal

Reg. § 1.988-2(b)(9)

amount of the M bond in the hands of Y is C$82.64, the amount carried over from X, the transferor. Y's exchange gain with respect to the nonfunctional currency principal amount is $8.26 [(C$82.64 × U.S.$.82) − (C$82.64 × U.S.$.72) = U.S.$8.26]. Accordingly, Y's combined exchange gain is U.S.$8.84 ($.49 + $.09 + $8.26). Because the amount realized in Canadian dollars equals the adjusted issue price (C$100) on retirement of the M note, there is no market loss, and the netting rule of paragraph (b)(8) of this section does not limit realization of the exchange gain.

Example 9. (i) X is a calendar year corporation on the accrual method of accounting and with the dollar as its functional currency. X elects to use the spot rate convention to translate interest income as provided in paragraph (b)(2)(iii)(B) of this section. On January 31, 1992, X loans £1000 to Y, an unrelated person. Under the terms of the loan, Y will pay X interest of £50 on July 31, 1992, and January 31, 1993, and will repay the £1000 principal on January 31, 1993. Assume the following spot exchange rates:

DATE	SPOT RATE (pounds to dollars)
January 31, 1992	£1 = $1.50
July 31, 1992	£1 = $1.55
December 31, 1992	£1 = $1.60
January 31, 1993	£1 = $1.61

(ii) Under paragraph (b)(2)(ii)(C) of this section, X will translate the interest income at the spot rate on the last day of each interest accrual period (and in the case of a partial accrual period, at the spot rate on the last day of the taxable year). Accordingly, X will have interest income of $77.50 (£50 × $1.55) on July 31, 1992. Assuming under X's method of accounting that interest is accrued daily, X will accrue $66.50 (153/184 × £50) × $1.60) of interest income on December 31, 1992. On January 31, 1993, X will have interest income of $13.60 ((31/184 × £50) × $1.61). Because the rate at which the interest income is translated is the same as the rate on the day of receipt, X will not realize any exchange gain or loss with respect to the interest income received on July 31, 1992. However, X will realize exchange gain on the £41.50 (153/184 × £50) of accrued interest income of $.41 [(£41.50 × $1.61) − (£41.50 × $1.60) = $.41].

(iii) Under paragraph (b)(5) of this section, X will realize exchange gain upon repayment of the £100 principal amount determined by translating the £100 at the spot rate on the date it is received (£100 × $1.61 = $161.00) and subtracting from such amount, the amount determined by translating the £100 at the spot rate on the date the loan was made (£100 × $1.50 = $150.00). Accordingly, X will realize an exchange gain of $11 on the repayment of the loan on January 31, 1993.

Example 10. (i) X, a cash basis taxpayer with the dollar as its functional currency, has the calendar year as its taxable year. On January 1, 1992, X purchases at original issue for 65.88 British pounds (£) M corporation's 5-year bond maturing on December 31, 1996, having a stated redemption price at maturity of £100. The bond provides for annual payments of interest in pounds of 1 pound per year on December 31 of each year. The bond has 34.12 British pounds of original issue discount. The yield to maturity is 10 percent in British pounds and the accrual period is the one year period beginning January 1 and ending December 31 of each calendar year. The amount of original issue discount is determined in pounds for each accrual period by multiplying the adjusted issue price expressed in pounds by the yield and subtracting from such amount the periodic interest payments expressed in pounds for such period. The periodic interest payments are translated at the spot rate on the payment date (December 31 of each year). The original issue discount is translated at the average rate for the accrual period (January 1 through December 31). The following chart describes the determination of interest income with respect to the facts presented and provides other pertinent information.

Reg. § 1.988-2(b)(9)

50,868 Income from Sources Without the United States

See p. 20,601 for regulations not amended to reflect law changes

Table 1

1	2	3	4	5	6	7	8	9	10
Year (Dec. 31)	Periodic interest payments in pounds for the accrual period	Original issue discount in pounds for the accrual period	Issue price or adjusted issue price in pounds	Assumed spot rate on Dec. 31 (pounds to dollars)	Assumed average rate for accrual period (pounds to dollars)	Periodic interest payments in pounds multiplied by spot rate on the date of payment (column 2 times column 5)	Original issue discount in pounds multiplied by the average rate for the accrual period (column 3 times column 6)	Total interest income in dollars (column 7 plus column 8)	Adjusted issue price in dollars
Issue Date			65.88	1 = $1.20					$79.06
1992	1	5.59	71.47	1 = $1.30	1 = $1.25	$1.30	$6.99	$8.29	$86.05
1993	1	6.15	77.62	1 = $1.40	1 = $1.35	$1.40	$8.30	$9.70	$94.35
1994	1	6.76	84.38	1 = $1.50	1 = $1.45	$1.50	$9.80	$11.30	$104.15
1995	1	7.44	91.82	1 = $1.60	1 = $1.55	$1.60	$11.53	$13.13	$115.68
1996	1	8.18	100.00	1 = $1.70	1 = $1.65	$1.70	$13.50	$15.20	$129.18

(ii) Because X is a cash basis taxpayer, X does not realize exchange gain or loss on the receipt of the £1 periodic interest payments. However, X will realize exchange gain on December 31, 1996 totaling $7.88 with respect to the original issue discount. Exchange gain is determined for each interest accrual period by translating the units of nonfunctional currency interest income received with respect to such accrual period at the spot rate on the date received and subtracting from such amount, the amount computed by translating the units of nonfunctional currency interest income accrued for such period at the average rate for the period. The following chart illustrates this computation:

Table 2

1	2	3	4	5	6	7
Year	OID accrued in pounds for each accrual period	Assumed spot rate on date payment received (pounds to dollars)	Interest received times spot rate on the date received (col. 2 times col. 3)	Assumed average rate for accrual period (pounds to dollars)	OID in pounds times the average rate for the accrual period (col. 2 times col. 5)	Exchange gain or loss (col. 4 less col. 6)
1992	5.59	1 = $1.70	$9.50	1 = $1.25	$6.99	$2.51
1993	6.15	1 = $1.70	$10.46	1 = $1.35	$8.30	$2.16
1994	6.76	1 = $1.70	$11.49	1 = $1.45	$9.80	$1.69
1995	7.44	1 = $1.70	$12.65	1 = $1.55	$11.53	$1.12
1996	8.18	1 = $1.70	$13.90	1 = $1.65	$13.50	$.40
					TOTAL	$7.88

(iii) X will also realize exchange gain with respect to the principal of the loan (*i.e.*, the issue price of 65.88 British pounds) on December 31, 1996 computed by translating the units of nonfunctional currency principal received at the spot rate on the date principal is received (65.88 British pounds × $1.70 = $112.00) and subtracting from such amount, the units of nonfunctional currency principal received translated at the spot rate on the date the instrument was acquired (65.88 British pounds × $1.20 = $79.06). Accordingly, X's exchange gain on the principal is $32.94

Reg. § 1.988-2(b)(9)

Income from Sources Without the United States   50,869
See p. 20,601 for regulations not amended to reflect law changes

and X's total exchange gain with respect to the accrued interest and principal is $40.82. It should be noted that, under this fact pattern, the total exchange gain may be determined in an alternative fashion. Exchange gain may be computed by subtracting the adjusted issue price in dollars at maturity ($129.18—see column 10 of Table 1) from the amount computed by multiplying the stated redemption price at maturity in pounds times the spot rate on the maturity date (£100 × $1.70 = $170), which equals $40.82.

Example 11. (i) The facts are the same as in *Example 10* except that X makes an election under paragraph (b)(2)(iii) of this section to translate accrued interest on the last day of the accrual period. Accordingly, columns 8, 9 and 10 in Table 1 would change as follows:

1 Year (Dec. 31)	8 Original issue discount in pounds multiplied by the spot rate on last day of accrual period (Dec. 31)	9 Total interest income in dollars (column 7 plus column 8)	10 Adjusted issue price in dollars
			$ 79.06
1992	$ 7.27	$ 8.57	$ 87.63
1993	$ 8.61	$10.01	$ 97.64
1994	$10.14	$11.64	$109.28
1995	$11.90	$13.50	$122.78
1996	$13.91	$15.61	$138.39

(ii) Because X is a cash basis taxpayer, X does not realize exchange gain or loss on the receipt of the £1 periodic interest payments. However, X will realize exchange gain on December 31, 1993 totaling $6.18 with respect to the original issue discount. Exchange gain is determined for each interest accrual period by translating the units of nonfunctional currency interest income received with respect to such accrual period at the spot rate on the date received and subtracting from such amount, the amount computed by translating the units of nonfunctional currency interest income accrued for such period at the spot rate on the last day of the accrual period. Accordingly, columns 5, 6 and 7 of Table 2 would change as follows:

1 Year	5 Spot rate on last day of accrual period	6 OID in pounds times the spot rate on the last day of the accrual period (col. 2 times col. 3)	7 Exchange gain or loss (col. 4 less col. 6)
1992	$1.30	$ 7.27	$2.23
1993	$1.40	$ 8.61	$1.85
1994	$1.50	$10.14	$1.35
1995	$1.60	$11.90	$0.75
1996	$1.70	$13.90	$0.00
			$6.18

(iii) X will realize exchange gain with respect to the principal amount of the loan as provided in the preceding example.

Example 12. (i) C is a corporation that is a calendar year accrual method taxpayer with the dollar as its functional currency. On January 1, 1989, C lends 100 British pounds (£) in exchange for a note under the terms of which C will receive two equal payments of £57.62 on December 31, 1989, and December 31, 1990. Each payment of £57.62 represents the annual payment necessary to amortize the £100 principal amount at a rate of 10% compounded annually over a two year period. The following tables reflect the amounts of principal and interest that compose each payment and assumptions as to the relevant exchange rates:

Date	Principal	Interest
12/31/89	£47.62	£10.00
12/31/90	£52.38	£ 5.24

Date	Spot Rate £1 =	Average Rate for Year Ending
1/01/89	$1.30	
12/31/89	$1.40	$1.35
12/31/90	$1.50	$1.45

(ii) Because each interest payment is equal to the product of the outstanding principal balance of the obligation and a single fixed rate of interest, each stated interest payment constitutes periodic interest under the principles of section 1273. Accordingly, there is no original issue discount.

(iii) Because C is an accrual basis taxpayer, C will translate the interest income at the average rate for the annual accrual period pursuant to paragraph (b)(2)(ii)(C) of this section. Thus, C's interest income is $13.50 (£10.00 × $1.35) in 1989, and $7.60 (£5.24 × $1.45) in 1990. C will realize exchange gain or loss upon receipt of ac-

Reg. § 1.988-2(b)(9)

crued interest computed in accordance with paragraph (b)(3) of this section. Thus, C will realize exchange gain in the amount of $.50 [(£10.00 × $1.40) − $13.50] in 1989, and $.26 [(£5.24 × $1.50) − $7.60] in 1990.

(iv) In addition, C will realize exchange gain or loss upon the receipt of principal each year computed under paragraph (b)(5) of this section. Thus, C will realize exchange gain in the amount of $4.76 [(£47.62 × $1.40) − (£47.62 × $1.30)] in 1989, and $10.48 [(£52.38 × $1.50) − (£52.38 × $1.30)] in 1990.

(10) *Treatment of bond premium*—(i) *In general.* Amortizable bond premium on a bond described in paragraph (b)(2)(i) of this section shall be computed in the units of nonfunctional currency in which the bond is denominated (or in which the payments are determined). Amortizable bond premium properly taken into account under section 171 or § 1.61-12 (or the successor provision thereof) shall reduce interest income or expense in units of nonfunctional currency. Exchange gain or loss is realized with respect to bond premium described in the preceding sentence by treating the portion of premium amortized with respect to any period as a return of principal. With respect to a holder that does not elect to amortize bond premium under section 171, the amount of bond premium will constitute a market loss when the bond matures. See paragraph (b)(8) of this section. The principles set forth in this paragraph (b)(10) shall apply to determine the treatment of acquisition premium described in section 1272(a)(7).

(ii) *Example.* The following example illustrates the provisions of this paragraph (b)(10).

Example. (A) X is an individual on the cash method of accounting with the dollar as his functional currency. On January 1, 1989, X purchases Y corporation's note for 107.99 British pounds (£) from Z, an unrelated party. The note has an issue price of £100, a stated redemption price at maturity of £100, pays interest in pounds at the rate of 10% compounded annually, and matures on December 31, 1993. X elects to amortize the bond premium of £7.99 under the rules of section 171. Pursuant to paragraph (b)(10)(i) of this section, bond premium is determined and amortized in British pounds. Assume the amortization schedule is as follows:

Year Ending 12/31	Bond Premium Amortized	Unamortized Premium Plus Principal	Interest
		£107.99	
1989	£1.36	£106.63	£8.64
1990	£1.47	£105.16	£8.53
1991	£1.59	£103.57	£8.41
1992	£1.71	£101.86	£8.29
1993	£1.85	£100.00	£8.25

(B) The bond premium reduces X's pound interest income under the note. For example, the £10 stated interest payment made in 1989 is reduced by £1.36 of bond premium, and the resulting £8.64 interest income is translated into dollars at the spot rate on December 31, 1989. Exchange gain or loss is realized on the £1.36 bond premium based on the difference between the spot rates on January 1, 1989, the date the premium is paid to acquire the bond, and December 31, 1989, the date the bond premium is returned as part of the stated interest. The £1.36 bond premium reduces the unamortized premium plus principal to £106.63 (£107.99 − £1.36). On December 31, 1993, when the bond matures and the £7.99 of bond premium has been fully amortized, X will realize exchange gain or loss with respect to the remaining purchase price of £100.

(11) *Market discount*—(i) *In general.* Market discount as defined in section 1278(a)(2) shall be determined in units of nonfunctional currency in which the market discount bond is denominated (or in which the payments are determined). Accrued market discount (other than market discount currently included in income pursuant to section 1278(b)) shall be translated into functional currency at the spot rate on the date the market discount bond is disposed of. No part of such accrued market discount is treated as exchange gain or loss. Accrued market discount currently includible in income pursuant to section 1278(b) shall be translated into functional currency at the average exchange rate for the accrual period. Exchange gain or loss with respect to accrued market discount currently includible in income under section 1278(b) shall be determined in accordance with paragraph (b)(3) of this section relating to accrued interest income.

(ii) *Example.* The following example illustrates the provisions of this paragraph (b)(11).

Example—(A) X is a calendar year corporation with the U.S. dollar as its functional currency. On January 1, 1990, X purchases a bond of M corporation for 96,530 British pounds (£). The bond, which was issued on January 1, 1989, has an issue price of £100,000, a stated redemption price at maturity of £100,000, and provides for annual pound payments of interest at 8 percent. The bond matures on December 31, 1991. X purchased the bond at a market discount of 3,470 pounds and did not elect to include the market discount currently in income under section 1278(b). X holds the bond to maturity and on December 31, 1991, receives payment of £100,000 (plus £8,000 interest) when the exchange rate is £1 = $1.50.

Reg. § 1.988-2(b)(10)

(B) Pursuant to paragraph (b)(11) of this section, X computes market discount in units of nonfunctional currency. Thus, the market discount as defined under section 1278(a)(2) is £3,470. Accrued market discount (other than market discount currently included in income pursuant to section 1278(b)) is translated at the spot rate on the date the market discount bond is disposed of. Accordingly, X will translate the accrued market discount of £3,470 at the spot rate on December 31, 1991 (£3,470 × $1.50 = $5,205). No exchange gain or loss is realized with respect to the £3,470 of accrued market discount. See paragraphs (b)(3) and (5) of this section for the realization and recognition of exchange gain or loss with respect to accrued interest and principal.

(12) *Tax exempt bonds.* See § 1.988-3(c)(2), which characterizes exchange loss realized with respect to a nonfunctional currency tax exempt bond as a reduction of interest income.

(13) *Nonfunctional currency debt exchanged for stock of obligor*—(i) *In general.* Notwithstanding any other section of the Code other than section 267, 1091 or 1092, exchange gain or loss shall be realized and recognized by the holder and the obligor in accordance with the rules of paragraphs (b)(3) through (7) of this section with respect to the principal and accrued interest of a debt instrument described in paragraph (b)(2)(i) of this section that is acquired by the obligor in exchange for its stock, provided however, that such gain or loss shall be recognized only to the extent of the total gain or loss on the exchange (regardless of whether such gain or loss would otherwise be recognized). This rule shall apply whether the debt instrument is converted into stock according to its terms or exchanged pursuant to a separate agreement between the obligor and the holder. A debt instrument that is acquired by the obligor from a shareholder as a contribution to capital shall be treated for purposes of this section as exchanged for stock, whether or not additional stock is issued.

(ii) *Coordination with section 108.* Section 988 and this section shall apply before section 108. Exchange gain realized by the obligor on an exchange described in paragraph (b)(13)(i) of this section shall not be treated as discharge of indebtedness income, but shall be considered to reduce the amount of the liability for purposes of computing the obligor's income on the exchange under section 108(e)(4), section 108(e)(6) or section 108(e)(10).

(iii) *Effective date.* This paragraph (b)(13) shall be effective for exchanges of debt for stock effected after September 21, 1989.

(iv) *Examples.* The following examples illustrate the operation of this paragraph (b)(13). In each such example, assume that sections 267, 1091 and 1092 do not apply.

Example 1. (i) X is a calendar year U.S. corporation with the U.S. dollar as its functional currency. On January 1, 1990 (the issue date), X acquired a convertible bond maturing on December 31, 1998, issued by Y corporation, a U.K. corporation with the British pound (£) as its functional currency. The issue price of the bond is £100,000, the stated redemption price at maturity is £100,000, and the bond provides for annual pound interest payments at the rate of 10%. The terms of the bond also provide that at any time prior to December 31, 1998, the holder may surrender all of his interest in the bond in exchange for 20 shares of Y common stock. On January 1, 1994, X surrenders his interest in the bond for 20 shares of Y common stock. Assume the following: (a) The spot rate on January 1, 1990, is £1 = $1.30, (b) The spot rate on January 1, 1994, is £1 = $1.50, and (c) The 20 shares of Y common stock have a market value of £200,000 on January 1, 1994.

(ii) Pursuant to paragraph (b)(13) of this section, X will realize and recognize exchange gain with respect to the issue price (£100,000) of the bond on January 1, 1994, when the bond is converted to stock. X will compute exchange gain pursuant to paragraph (b)(5) of this section by translating the issue price at the spot rate on the conversion date (£100,000 × $1.50 = $150,000) and subtracting from such amount the issue price translated at the spot rate on the date X acquired the bond (£100,000 × $1.30 = $130,000). Thus, X will realize and recognize $20,000 of exchange gain. X's basis in the 20 shares of Y common stock is $150,000 ($130,000 substituted basis + $20,000 recognized gain).

Example 2. (i) X, a foreign corporation with the British pound (£) as its functional currency, lends £100 at a market rate of interest to Y, its wholly-owned U.S. subsidiary, on January 1, 1990, on which date the spot exchange rate is £1 = $1. Y's functional currency is the U.S. dollar. On January 1, 1992, when the spot exchange rate is £1 = $.50, X cancels the debt as a contribution to capital. Pursuant to paragraph (b)(13) of this section, Y will realize and recognize exchange gain with respect to the £100 issue price of the debt instrument on January 1, 1992. Y will compute exchange gain pursuant to paragraph (b)(6) of this section by translating the issue price at the spot rate on the date Y became the obligor (£100 × $1 = $100) and subtracting from such amount the issue price translated at the spot rate on the

Reg. § 1.988-2(b)(13)

date of extinguishment (£100 × $.50 = $50). Thus, Y will realize and recognize $50 of exchange gain.

(ii) Under section 108(e)(6), on the acquisition of its indebtedness from X as a contribution to capital Y is treated as having satisfied the debt with an amount of money equal to X's adjusted basis in the debt (£100). For purposes of section 108(e)(6), X's adjusted basis is translated into United States dollars at the spot rate on the date Y acquires the debt (£1 = $.50). Therefore, Y is treated as having satisfied the debt for $50. Pursuant to paragraph (b)(13) of this section, for purposes of section 108 the amount of the indebtedness is considered to be reduced by the exchange gain from $100 to $50. Accordingly, Y recognizes $50 of exchange gain and no discharge of indebtedness income on the extinguishment of its debt to X.

(iii) If X were a United States taxpayer with a dollar functional currency and a $100 basis in Y's obligation, X would realize and recognize an exchange loss of $50 under paragraph (b)(5) of this section on the contribution of the debt to Y. The recognized loss would reduce X's adjusted basis in the debt from $100 to $50, so that for purposes of applying section 108(e)(6) Y is treated as having satisfied the debt for $50. Accordingly, under these facts as well Y would recognize $50 of exchange gain and no discharge of indebtedness income.

Example 3. (i) X and Y are unrelated calendar year U.S. corporations with the U.S. dollar as their functional currency. On January 1, 1990 (the issue date), X acquires Y's bond maturing on December 31, 1999. The issue price of the bond is £100,000, the stated redemption price at maturity is £100,000, and the bond provides for annual pound interest payments at the rate of 10%. On January 1, 1994, X and Y agree that Y will redeem its bond from X in exchange for 20 shares of Y common stock. Assume the following:

(a) The spot rate on January 1, 1990, is £1 = $1.00,

(b) The spot rate on January 1, 1994, is £1 = $.50,

(c) Interest rates on equivalent bonds have increased so that as of January 1, 1994, the value of Y's bond has declined to £90,000, and

(d) The 20 shares of Y common stock have a market value of £90,000 as of January 1, 1994.

(ii) Pursuant to paragraph (b)(13) of this section, X will realize and recognize exchange loss with respect to the issue price (£100,000) of the bond on January 1, 1994, when the bond is exchanged for stock. X will compute exchange loss pursuant to paragraph (b)(5) of this section by translating the issue price at the spot rate on the exchange date (£100,000 × $.50 = $50,000) and subtracting from such amount the issue price translated at the spot rate on the date X acquired the bond (£100,000 × $1.00 = $100,000). Thus, X will compute $50,000 of exchange loss, all of which will be realized and recognized because it does not exceed the total $55,000 realized loss on the exchange ($45,000 worth of stock received less $100,000 basis in the exchanged bond).

(iii) Pursuant to paragraph (b)(13) of this section, Y will realize and recognize exchange gain with respect to the issue price, computed under paragraph (b)(6) of this section by translating the issue price at the spot rate on the date Y became the obligor (£100,000 × $1.00 = $100,000) and subtracting from such amount the issue price translated at the spot rate on the exchange date (£100,000 × $.50 = $50,000). Thus, Y will realize and recognize $50,000 of exchange gain. Under section 108(e)(10), on the transfer of stock to X in satisfaction of its indebtedness Y is treated as having satisfied the indebtedness with an amount of money equal to the fair market value of the stock (£90,000 × $.50 = $45,000). Pursuant to paragraph (b)(13) of this section, for purposes of section 108 the amount of the indebtedness is considered to be reduced by the recognized exchange gain from $100,000 to $50,000. Accordingly, Y recognizes an additional $5,000 of discharge of indebtedness income on the exchange.

Example 4. (i) The facts are the same as in *Example 3* except that interest rates on equivalent bonds have declined, rather than increased, so that the value of Y's bond on January 1, 1994, has risen to £112,500; and X and Y agree that Y will redeem its bond from X on that date in exchange for 25 shares of Y common stock worth £112,500. Pursuant to paragraphs (b)(13) and (b)(5) of this section, X will compute $50,000 of exchange loss on the exchange with respect to the £100,000 issue price of the bond. See Example 3. However, because X's total loss on the exchange is only $43,750 ($56,250 worth of stock received less $100,000 basis in the exchanged bond), under the netting rule of paragraph (b)(13) of this section the realized exchange loss is limited to $43,750.

(ii) Pursuant to paragraphs (b)(13) and (b)(6) of this section, Y will compute $50,000 of exchange gain with respect to the issue price. See *Example 3.* Under section 108(e)(10), Y is treated as having satisfied the $100,000 indebtedness with an amount of money equal to the fair market value of the stock (£112,500 × $.50 = $56,250), resulting in a total gain on the exchange of $43,750. Accordingly, under paragraph (b)(13) of this section Y's realized (and recognized) exchange gain on the exchange is limited to $43,750. Also pursuant to paragraph (b)(13) of this section, for purposes of section 108 the amount of the indebtedness is considered to be reduced by the recognized exchange gain from $100,000 to

Reg. § 1.988-2(b)(13)

Income from Sources Without the United States

$56,250. Accordingly, Y recognizes no discharge of indebtedness income on the exchange.

(14) [Reserved]

(15) *Debt instruments and deposits denominated in hyperinflationary currencies*—(i) *In general.* If a taxpayer issues, acquires, or otherwise enters into or holds a hyperinflationary debt instrument (as defined in paragraph (b)(15)(vi)(A) of this section) or a hyperinflationary deposit (as defined in paragraph (b)(15)(vi)(B) of this section) on which interest is paid or accrued that is denominated in (or determined by reference to) a nonfunctional currency of the taxpayer, then the taxpayer shall realize exchange gain or loss with respect to such instrument or deposit for its taxable year determined by reference to the change in exchange rates between—

(A) The later of the first day of the taxable year, or the date the instrument was entered into (or an amount deposited); and

(B) The earlier of the last day of the taxable year, or the date the instrument (or deposit) is disposed of or otherwise terminated.

(ii) *Only exchange gain or loss is realized.* No gain or loss is realized under paragraph (b)(15)(i) by reason of factors other than movement in exchange rates, such as the creditworthiness of the debtor.

(iii) *Special rule for synthetic, non-hyperinflationary currency debt instruments*—(A) *General rule.* Paragraph (b)(15)(i) does not apply to a debt instrument that has interest and principal payments that are to be made by reference to a currency or item that does not reflect hyperinflationary conditions in a country (within the meaning of § 1.988-1(f)).

(B) *Example.* Paragraph (b)(15)(iii)(A) is illustrated by the following example:

Example. When the Turkish lira (TL) is a hyperinflationary currency, A, a U.S. corporation with the U.S. dollar as its functional currency, makes a 5 year, 100,000 TL-denominated loan to B, an unrelated corporation, at a 10% interest rate when 1,000 TL equals $1. Under the terms of the debt instrument, B must pay interest annually to A in amount of Turkish lira that is equal to $100. Also under the terms of the debt instrument, B must pay A upon maturity of the debt instrument an amount of Turkish lira that is equal to $1,000. Although the principal and interest are payable in a hyperinflationary currency, the debt instrument is a synthetic dollar debt instrument and is not subject to paragraph (b)(15)(i) of this section.

(iv) *Source and character of gain or loss*—
(A) *General rule for hyperinflationary conditions.*

The rules of this paragraph (b)(15)(iv)(A) shall apply to any taxpayer that is either an issuer of (or obligor under) a hyperinflationary debt instrument or deposit and has currency gain on such debt instrument or deposit, or a holder of a hyperinflationary debt instrument or deposit and has currency loss on such debt instrument or deposit. For purposes of subtitle A of the Internal Revenue Code, any exchange gain or loss realized under paragraph (b)(15)(i) of this section is directly allocable to the interest expense or interest income, respectively, from the debt instrument or deposit (computed under this paragraph (b)), and therefore reduces or increases the amount of interest income or interest expense paid or accrued during that year with respect to that instrument or deposit. With respect to a debt instrument or deposit during a taxable year, to the extent exchange gain realized under paragraph (b)(15)(i) of this section exceeds interest expense of an issuer, or exchange loss realized under paragraph (b)(15)(i) of this section exceeds interest income of a holder or depositor, the character and source of such excess amount shall be determined under §§ 1.988-3 and 1.988-4.

(B) *Special rule for subsiding hyperinflationary conditions.* If the taxpayer is an issuer of (or obligor under) a hyperinflationary debt instrument or deposit and has currency loss, or if the taxpayer is a holder of a hyperinflationary debt instrument or deposit and has currency gain, then for purposes of subtitle A of the Internal Revenue Code, the character and source of the currency gain or loss is determined under §§ 1.988-3 and 1.988-4. Thus, if an issuer has both interest expense and currency loss, the currency loss is sourced and characterized under section 988, and does not affect the determination of interest expense.

(v) *Adjustment to principal or basis.* Any exchange gain or loss realized under paragraph (b)(15)(i) of this section is an adjustment to the functional currency principal amount of the issuer, functional currency basis of the holder, or the functional currency amount of the deposit. This adjusted amount or basis is used in making subsequent computations of exchange gain or loss, computing the basis of assets for purposes of allocating interest under §§ 1.861-9T through 1.861-12T and 1.882-5, or making other determinations that may be relevant for computing taxable income or loss.

(vi) *Definitions*—(A) *Hyperinflationary debt instrument.* A hyperinflationary debt instrument is a debt instrument that provides for—

(*1*) Payments denominated in or determined by reference to a currency that is hyper-

Reg. § 1.988-2(b)(15)

inflationary (as defined in § 1.988-1(f)) at the time the taxpayer enters into or otherwise acquires the debt instrument; or

(*2*) Payments denominated in or determined by reference to a currency that is hyperinflationary (as defined in § 1.988-1(f)) during the taxable year, and the terms of the instrument provide for the adjustment of principal or interest payments in a manner that reflects hyperinflation. For example, a debt instrument providing for a variable interest rate based on local conditions and generally responding to changes in the local consumer price index will reflect hyperinflation.

(B) *Hyperinflationary deposit.* A hyperinflationary deposit is a demand or time deposit or similar instrument issued by a bank or other financial institution that provides for—

(*1*) Payments denominated in or determined by reference to a currency that is hyperinflationary (as defined in § 1.988-1(f)) at the time the taxpayer enters into or otherwise acquires the deposit; or

(*2*) Payments denominated in or determined by reference to a currency that is hyperinflationary (as defined in § 1.988-1(f)) during the taxable year, and the terms of the deposit provide for the adjustment of the deposit amount or interest payments in a manner that reflects hyperinflation.

(vii) *Interaction with other provisions*—(A) *Interest allocation rules.* In determining the amount of interest expense, this paragraph (b)(15) applies before §§ 1.861-9T through 1.861-12T, and 1.882-5.

(B) *DASTM.* With respect to a qualified business unit that uses the United States dollar approximate separate transactions method of accounting described in § 1.985-3, paragraph (b)(15)(i) of this section does not apply.

(C) *Interaction with section 988(a)(3)(C).* Section 988(a)(3)(C) does not apply to a debt instrument subject to the rules of paragraph (b)(15)(i) of this section.

(D) *Hedging rules.* To the extent § 1.446-4 or 1.988-5 apply, the rules of paragraph (b)(15)(i) of this section will not apply. This paragraph (b)(15)(vii)(D) does not apply if the application of § 1.988-5 results in hyperinflationary debt instrument or deposit described in paragraph (b)(15)(vi)(A) or (B) of this section.

(viii) *Effective date.* This paragraph (b)(15) applies to transactions entered into after February 14, 2000.

(16) *Coordination with section 267 regarding debt instruments*—(i) *Treatment of a creditor.*

For rules applicable to a corporation included in a controlled group that is a creditor under a debt instrument see § 1.267(f)-1(h).

(ii) *Treatment of a debtor.* [Reserved]

(17) *Coordination with installment method under section 453.* [Reserved]

(c) *Item of expense or gross income or receipts which is to be paid or received after the date accrued*—(1) *In general.* Except as provided in § 1.988-5, exchange gain or loss with respect to an item described in § 1.988-1(a)(1)(ii) and (2)(ii) (other than accrued interest income or expense subject to paragraph (b) of this section) shall be realized on the date payment is made or received. Except as provided in the succeeding sentence, such exchange gain or loss shall be recognized in accordance with the applicable recognition provisions of the Internal Revenue Code. If the taxpayer's right to receive income, or obligation to pay an expense, is transferred or modified in a transaction in which gain or loss would otherwise be recognized, exchange gain or loss shall be realized and recognized only to the extent of the total gain or loss on the transaction.

(2) *Determination of exchange gain or loss with respect to an item of gross income or receipts.* Exchange gain or loss realized on an item of gross income or receipts described in paragraph (c)(1) of this section shall be determined by multiplying the units of nonfunctional currency received by the spot rate on the payment date, and subtracting from such amount the amount determined by multiplying the units of nonfunctional currency received by the spot rate on the booking date. The term "spot rate on the payment date" means the spot rate determined under § 1.988-1(d) on the date payment is received or otherwise taken into account. Pursuant to § 1.988-1(d)(3), a taxpayer may use a spot rate convention for purposes of determining the spot rate on the payment date. The term "spot rate on the booking date" means the spot rate determined under § 1.988-1(d) on the date the item of gross income or receipts is accrued or otherwise taken into account. Pursuant to § 1.988-1(d)(3), a taxpayer may use a spot rate convention for purposes of determining the spot rate on the booking date.

(3) *Determination of exchange gain or loss with respect to an item of expense.* Exchange gain or loss realized on an item of expense described in paragraph (c)(1) of this section shall be determined by multiplying the units of nonfunctional currency paid by the spot rate on the booking date and subtracting from such amount the amount determined by multiplying the units of nonfunctional currency paid by the spot rate on the payment date. The term "spot rate on the

Reg. § 1.988-2(b)(16)

booking date" means the spot rate determined under § 1.988-1(d) on the date the item of expense is accrued or otherwise taken into account. Pursuant to § 1.988-1(d)(3), a taxpayer may use a spot rate convention for purposes of determining the spot rate on the booking date. The term "spot rate on the payment date" means the spot rate determined under § 1.988-1(d) on the date payment is made or otherwise taken into account. Pursuant to § 1.988-1(d)(3), a taxpayer may use a spot rate convention for purposes of determining the spot rate on the payment date.

(4) *Examples.* The following examples illustrate the application of paragraph (c) of this section.

Example 1. X is a calendar year corporation with the dollar as its functional currency. X is on the accrual method of accounting. On January 15, 1989, X sells inventory for 10,000 Canadian dollars (C$). The spot rate on January 15, 1989, is C$1 = U.S. $.55. On February 23, 1989, when X receives payment of the C$10,000, the spot rate is C$1 = U.S. $.50. On February 23, 1989, X will realize exchange loss. X's loss is computed by multiplying the C$10,000 by the spot rate on the date the C$10,000 are received (C$10,000 × .50 = U.S. $5,000) and subtracting from such amount, the amount computed by multiplying the C$10,000 by the spot rate on the booking date (C$10,000 × .55 = U.S. $5,500). Thus, X's exchange loss on the transaction is U.S. $500 (U.S. $5,000 − U.S. $5,500).

Example 2. The facts are the same as in *Example 1* except that X uses a spot rate convention to determine the spot rate as provided in § 1.988-1(d)(3). Pursuant to X's spot rate convention, the spot rate at which a payable or receivable is booked is determined monthly for each nonfunctional currency payable or receivable by adding the spot rate at the beginning of the month and the spot rate at the end of the month and dividing by two. All payables and receivables in a nonfunctional currency booked during the month are translated into functional currency at the rate described in the preceding sentence. Further, the translation of nonfunctional currency paid with respect to a payable, and nonfunctional currency received with respect to a receivable, is also performed pursuant to the spot rate convention. Assume the spot rate determined under the spot rate convention for the month of January is C$1 = U.S. $.54 and for the month of February is C$1 = U.S. $.51. On the last date in February, X will realize exchange loss. X's loss is computed by multiplying the C$10,000 by the spot rate convention for the month of February (C$10,000 × U.S. $.51 = U.S. $5,100) and subtracting from such amount, the amount computed by multiplying the C$10,000 by the spot rate convention for the month of January (C$10,000 × U.S. $.54 = $5,400). Thus, X's exchange loss on the transaction is U.S. $300 (U.S. $5,100 − U.S. $5,400). X's basis in the C$10,000 is U.S. $5,400.

Example 3. The facts are the same as in *Example 2* except that X has a standing order with X's bank for the bank to convert any nonfunctional currency received in satisfaction of a receivable into U.S. dollars on the day received and to deposit those U.S. dollars in X's U.S. dollar bank account. X may use its convention to translate the amount booked into U.S. dollars, but must use the U.S. dollar amounts received from the bank with respect to such receivables to determine X's exchange gain or loss. Thus, if X receives payment of the C$10,000 on February 23, 1989, when the spot rate is C$1 = U.S.$ .50, X determines exchange gain or loss by subtracting the amount booked under X's convention (U.S.$5,400) from the amount of U.S. dollars received from the bank under the standing conversion order (assume $5,000). X's exchange loss is U.S.$400.

(d) *Exchange gain or loss with respect to forward contracts, futures contracts and option contracts*—(1) *Scope*—(i) *In general.* This paragraph (d) applies to forward contracts, futures contracts and option contracts described in § 1.988-1(a)(1)(ii) and (2)(iii). For rules applicable to currency swaps and notional principal contracts described in § 1.988-1(a)(1)(ii) and (2)(iii), see paragraph (e) of this section.

(ii) *Treatment of spot contracts.* Solely for purposes of this paragraph (d), a spot contract as defined in § 1.988-1(b) to buy or sell nonfunctional currency is not considered a forward contract or similar transaction described in § 1.988-1(a)(2)(iii) unless such spot contract is disposed of (or otherwise terminated) prior to making or taking delivery of the currency. For example, if a taxpayer with the dollar as its functional currency enters into a spot contract to purchase British pounds, and takes delivery of such pounds under the contract, the delivery of the pounds is not a realization event under section 988(c)(5) and paragraph (e)(4)(ii) of this section because the contract is not considered a forward contract or similar transaction described in § 1.988-1(a)(2)(iii). However, if the taxpayer sells or otherwise terminates the contract before taking delivery of the pounds, exchange gain or loss shall be realized and recognized in accordance with paragraphs (d)(2) and (3) of this section.

(2) *Realization of exchange gain or loss*—(i) *In general.* Except as provided in § 1.988-5, exchange gain or loss on a contract described in

Reg. § 1.988-2(d)(2)

§ 1.988-2(d)(1) shall be realized in accordance with the applicable realization section of the Internal Revenue Code (*e.g.*, sections 1001, 1092, and 1256). See also section 988(c)(5). For purposes of determining the timing of the realization of exchange gain or loss, sections 1092 and 1256 shall take precedence over section 988(c)(5).

(ii) *Realization by offset*—(A) *In general.* Except as provided in paragraphs (d)(2)(ii)(B) and (C) of this section, exchange gain or loss with respect to a transaction described in § 1.988-1(a)(1)(ii) and (2)(iii) shall not be realized solely because such transaction is offset by another transaction (or transactions).

(B) *Exception where economic benefit is derived.* If a transaction described in § 1.988-1(a)(1)(ii) and (2)(iii) is offset by another transaction or transactions, exchange gain shall be realized to the extent the taxpayer derives, by pledge or otherwise, an economic benefit (*e.g.*, cash, property or the proceeds from a borrowing) from any gain inherent in such offsetting positions. Proper adjustment shall be made in the amount of any gain or loss subsequently realized for gain taken into account by reason of the preceding sentence. This paragraph (d)(2)(ii)(B) shall apply to transactions creating an offset after September 21, 1989.

(C) *Certain contracts traded on an exchange.* If a transaction described in § 1.988-1(a)(1)(ii) and (2)(iii) is traded on an exchange and it is the general practice of the exchange to terminate offsetting contracts, entering into an offsetting contract shall be considered a termination of the contract being offset.

(iii) *Clarification of section 988(c)(5).* If the delivery date of a contract subject to section 988(c)(5) and paragraph (d)(4)(ii) of this section is different than the date the contract expires, then for purposes of determining the date exchange gain or loss is realized, the term delivery date shall mean expiration date.

(iv) *Examples.* The following examples illustrate the rules of this paragraph (d)(1) and (2).

Example 1. On August 1, 1989, X, a calendar year corporation with the dollar as its functional currency, enters into a forward contract with Bank A to buy 100 New Zealand dollars for $80 for delivery on January 31, 1990. (The forward purchase contract is not a section 1256 contract.) On November 1, 1989, the market price for the purchase of 100 New Zealand dollars for delivery on January 31, 1990, is $76. On November 1, 1989, X cancels its obligation under the forward purchase contract and pays Bank A $3.95 (the present value of $4 discounted at 12% for the period) in cancellation of such contract. Under section 1001(a), X realizes an exchange loss of $3.95 on November 1, 1989, because cancellation of the forward purchase contract for cash results in the termination of X's contract.

Example 2. X is a corporation with the dollar as its functional currency. On January 1, 1989, X enters into a currency swap contract with Bank A under which X is obligated to make a series of Japanese yen payments in exchange for a series of dollar payments. On February 21, 1992, X has a gain of $100,000 inherent in such contract as a result of interest rate and exchange rate movements. Also on February 21, 1992, X enters into an offsetting swap with Bank A to lock in such gain. If on February 21, 1992, X pledges the gain inherent in such offsetting positions as collateral for a loan, X's initial swap contract is treated as being terminated on February 21, 1992, under paragraph (d)(2)(ii)(B) of this section. Proper adjustment is made in the amount of any gain or loss subsequently realized for the gain taken into account by reason of paragraph (d)(2)(ii)(B) of this section.

Example 3. X is a calendar year corporation with the dollar as its functional currency. On October 1, 1989, X enters into a forward contract to buy 100,000 Swiss francs (Sf) for delivery on March 1, 1990, for $51,220. Assume that the contract is a section 1256 contract under section 1256(g)(2) and that section 1256(e) does not apply. Pursuant to section 1256(a)(1), the forward contract is treated as sold for its fair market value on December 31, 1989. Assume that the fair market value of the contract is $1,000 determined under § 1.988-1(g). Thus X will realize an exchange gain of $1,000 on December 31, 1989. Such gain is subject to the character rules of § 1.988-3 and the source rules of § 1.988-4.

(v) *Extension of the maturity date of certain contracts.* An extension of time for making or taking delivery under a contract described in paragraph (d)(1) of this section (*e.g.*, a historical rate rollover as defined in § 1.988-5(b)(2)(iii)(C)) shall be considered a sale or exchange of the contract for its fair market value on the date of the extension and the establishment of a new contract on such date. If, under the terms of the extension, the time value of any gain or loss recognized pursuant to the preceding sentence adjusts the price of the currency to be bought or sold under the new contract, the amount attributable to such time value shall be treated as interest income or expense for all purposes of the Code. However, the preceding sentence shall not apply and the amount attributable to the time value of any gain or loss recognized shall be treated as exchange gain or loss if the period beginning on the first

Reg. § 1.988-2(d)(2)

date the contract is rolled over and ending on the date payment is ultimately made or received with respect to such contract does not exceed 183 days.

(3) *Recognition of exchange gain or loss.* Except as provided in § 1.988-5 (relating to section 988 hedging transactions), exchange gain or loss realized with respect to a contract described in paragraph (d)(1) of this section shall be recognized in accordance with the applicable recognition provisions of the Internal Revenue Code. For example, a loss realized with respect to a contract described in paragraph (d)(1) of this section which is part of a straddle shall be recognized in accordance with the provisions of section 1092 to the extent such section is applicable.

(4) *Determination of exchange gain or loss*— (i) *In general.* Exchange gain or loss with respect to a contract described in § 1.988-2(d)(1) shall be determined by subtracting the amount paid (or deemed paid), if any, for or with respect to the contract (including any amount paid upon termination of the contract) from the amount received (or deemed received), if any, for or with respect to the contract (including any amount received upon termination of the contract). Any gain or loss determined according to the preceding sentence shall be treated as exchange gain or loss.

(ii) *Special rules where taxpayer makes or takes delivery.* If the taxpayer makes or takes delivery in connection with a contract described in paragraph (d)(1) of this section, any gain or loss shall be realized and recognized in the same manner as if the taxpayer sold the contract (or paid another person to assume the contract) on the date on which he took or made delivery for its fair market value on such date. See paragraph (d)(2)(iii) of this section regarding the definition of the term "delivery date." This paragraph (d)(4)(ii) shall not apply in any case in which the taxpayer makes or takes delivery before June 11, 1987.

(iii) *Examples.* The following examples illustrate the application of paragraph (d)(4) of this section.

Example 1. X is a calendar year corporation with the dollar as its functional currency. On October 1, 1989, when the six month forward rate is $.4907, X enters into a forward contract to buy 100,000 New Zealand dollars (NZD) for delivery on March 1, 1990. On March 1, 1990, when X takes delivery of the 100,000 NZD, the spot rate is 1NZD equals $.48. Pursuant to section 988(c)(5) and paragraph (d)(4)(ii) of this section, a taxpayer that takes delivery of nonfunctional currency under a forward contract that is subject to section 988 is treated as if the taxpayer sold the contract for its fair market value on the date delivery is taken. If X sold the contract on March 1, 1990, the transferee would require a payment of $1,070 [($.48 × 100,000NZD) − ($.4907 × 100,000NZD)] to compensate him for the loss in value of the 100,000NZD. Therefore, X realizes an exchange loss of $1,070. X has a basis in the 100,000NZD of $48,000.

Example 2. Assume the same facts as in Example 1 except that the contract is for Swiss francs and is a section 1256 contract. Assume further that on December 31, 1989, the value to X of the contract as marked to market is $1,000. Pursuant to section 1256(a), X realizes an exchange gain of $1,000. Such gain, however, is characterized as ordinary income under § 1.988-3 and will be sourced under § 1.988-4.

Example 3. X is a calendar year corporation with the dollar as its functional currency. On May 2, 1989, X enters into an option contract with Bank A to purchase 50,000 Canadian dollars (C$) for U.S. $42,500 (C$1 = U.S. $.85) for delivery on or before September 18, 1989. X pays a $285 premium to Bank A to obtain the option contract. On September 18, 1989, when X exercises the option and takes delivery of the C$50,000, the spot rate is C$1 equals U.S. $.90. Pursuant to section 988(c)(5) and paragraph (d)(4)(ii) of this section, a taxpayer that takes delivery under an option contract that is subject to section 988 is treated as if the taxpayer sold the contract for its fair market value on the date delivery is taken. If X sold the contract for its fair market value on September 18, 1989, X would receive U.S. $2,500 [(C$50,000 × U.S. $.90) − (C$50,000 × U.S. $.85)]. Accordingly, X is deemed to have received U.S. $2,500 on the sale of the contract at its fair market value. X will realize U.S. $2,215 ($2,500 deemed received less $285 paid) of exchange gain with respect to the delivery of Canadian dollars under the option contract. X's basis in the 50,000 Canadian dollars is U.S. $45,000.

(5) *Hyperinflationary contracts*—(i) *In general.* If a taxpayer acquires or otherwise enters into a hyperinflationary contract (as defined in paragraph (d)(5)(ii) of this section) that has payments to be made or received that are denominated in (or determined by reference to) a nonfunctional currency of the taxpayer, then the taxpayer shall realize exchange gain or loss with respect to such contract for its taxable year determined by reference to the change in exchange rates between—

(A) The later of the first day of the taxable year, or the date the contract was acquired or entered into; and

Reg. § 1.988-2(d)(5)

(B) The earlier of the last day of the taxable year, or the date the contract is disposed of or otherwise terminated.

(ii) *Definition of hyperinflationary contract.* A hyperinflationary contract is a contract described in paragraph (d)(1) of this section that provides for payments denominated in or determined by reference to a currency that is hyperinflationary (as defined in § 1.988-1(f)) at the time the taxpayer acquires or otherwise enters into the contract.

(iii) *Interaction with other provisions*—(A) *DASTM.* With respect to a qualified business unit that uses the United States dollar approximate separate transactions method of accounting described in § 1.985-3, this paragraph (d)(5) does not apply.

(B) *Hedging rules.* To the extent § 1.446-4 or 1.988-5 apply, this paragraph (d)(5) does not apply.

(C) *Adjustment for subsequent transactions.* Proper adjustments must be made in the amount of any gain or loss subsequently realized for gain or loss taken into account by reason of this paragraph (d)(5).

(iv) *Effective date.* This paragraph (d)(5) is applicable to transactions acquired or otherwise entered into after February 14, 2000.

(e) *Currency swaps and other notional principal contracts*—(1) *In general.* Except as provided in paragraph (e)(2) of this section or in § 1.988-5, the timing of income, deduction and loss with respect to a notional principal contract that is a section 988 transaction shall be governed by section 446 and the regulations thereunder. Such income, deduction and loss is characterized as exchange gain or loss (except as provided in another section of the Internal Revenue Code (or regulations thereunder), § 1.988-5, or in paragraph (f) of this section).

(2) *Special rules for currency swaps*—(i) *In general.* Except as provided in paragraph (e)(2)(iii)(B) of this section, the provisions of this paragraph (e)(2) shall apply solely for purposes of determining the realization, recognition and amount of exchange gain or loss with respect to a currency swap contract, and not for purposes of determining the source of such gain or loss, or characterizing such gain or loss as interest. Except as provided in § 1.988-3(c), any income or loss realized with respect to a currency swap contract shall be characterized as exchange gain or loss (and not as interest income or expense). Any exchange gain or loss realized in accordance with this paragraph (e)(2) shall be recognized unless otherwise provided in an applicable section of the Code. For purposes of this paragraph (e)(2), a currency swap contract is a contract defined in paragraph (e)(2)(ii) of this section. With respect to a contract which requires the payment of swap principal prior to maturity of such contract, see paragraph (f) of this section. For purposes of this paragraph (e), the rules of paragraph (d)(2)(ii) of this section (regarding realization by offset) apply. See Example 2 of paragraph (d)(2)(iv) of this section.

(ii) *Definition of currency swap contract*—(A) *In general.* A currency swap contract is a contract involving different currencies between two or more parties to—

(*1*) Exchange periodic interim payments, as defined in paragraph (e)(2)(ii)(C) of this section, on or prior to maturity of the contract; and

(*2*) Exchange the swap principal amount upon maturity of the contract.

A currency swap contract may also require an exchange of the swap principal amount upon commencement of the agreement.

(B) *Swap principal amount.* The swap principal amount is an amount of two different currencies which, under the terms of the currency swap contract, is used to determine the periodic interim payments in each currency and which is exchanged upon maturity of the contract. If such amount is not clearly set forth in the contract, the Commissioner may determine the swap principal amount.

(C) *Exchange of periodic interim payments.* An exchange of periodic interim payments is an exchange of one or more payments in one currency specified by the contract for one or more payments in a different currency specified by the contract where the payments in each currency are computed by reference to an interest index applied to the swap principal amount. A currency swap contract must clearly indicate the periodic interim payments, or the interest index used to compute the periodic interim payments, in each currency.

(iii) *Timing and computation of periodic interim payments*—(A) *In general.* Except as provided in paragraph (e)(2)(iii)(B) of this section and § 1.988-5, the timing and computation of the periodic interim payments provided in a currency swap agreement shall be determined by treating—

(*1*) Payments made under the swap as payments made pursuant to a hypothetical borrowing that is denominated in the currency in which payments are required to be made (or are determined with reference to) under the swap, and

Reg. § 1.988-2(e)(1)

(2) Payments received under the swap as payments received pursuant to a hypothetical loan that is denominated in the currency in which payments are received (or are determined with reference to) under the swap.

Except as provided in paragraph (e)(2)(v) of this section, the hypothetical issue price of such hypothetical borrowing and loan shall be the swap principal amount. The hypothetical stated redemption price at maturity is the total of all payments (excluding any exchange of the swap principal amount at the inception of the contract) provided under the hypothetical borrowing or loan other than periodic interest payments under the principles of section 1273. For purposes of determining economic accrual under the currency swap, the number of hypothetical interest compounding periods of such hypothetical borrowing and loan shall be determined pursuant to a semi-annual compounding convention unless the currency swap contract indicates otherwise. For purposes of determining the timing and amount of the periodic interim payments, the principles regarding the amortization of interest (see generally, sections 1272 through 1275 and 163(e)) shall apply to the hypothetical interest expense and income of such hypothetical borrowing and loan. However, such principles shall not apply to determine the time when principal is deemed to be paid on the hypothetical borrowing and loan. See paragraph (d)(2)(iii) of this section and *Example 2* of paragraph (d)(5) of this section with respect to the time when principal is deemed to be paid. With respect to the translation and computation of exchange gain or loss on any hypothetical interest income or expense, see § 1.988-2(b). The amount treated as exchange gain or loss by the taxpayer with respect to the periodic interim payments for the taxable year shall be the amount of hypothetical interest income and exchange gain or loss attributable to such interest income from the hypothetical borrowing and loan for such year less the amount of hypothetical interest expense and exchange gain or loss attributable to the interest expense from such hypothetical borrowing and loan for such year.

(B) *Effect of prepayment for purposes of section 956.* For purposes of section 956, the Commissioner may treat any prepayment of a currency swap as a loan.

(iv) *Timing and determination of exchange gain or loss with respect to the swap principal amount.* Exchange gain or loss with respect to the swap principal amount shall be realized on the day the units of swap principal in each currency are exchanged. (See paragraph (e)(2)(ii)(A)(*2*) of this section which requires that the entire swap principal amount be exchanged upon maturity of the contract.) Such gain or loss shall be determined on the date of the exchange by subtracting the value (on such date) of the units of swap principal paid from the value of the units of swap principal received. This paragraph (e)(2)(iv) does not apply to an equal exchange of the swap principal amount at the commencement of the agreement at a market exchange rate.

(v) *Anti-abuse rules*—(A) *Method of accounting does not clearly reflect income.* If the taxpayer's method of accounting for income, expense, gain or loss attributable to a currency swap does not clearly reflect income, or if the present value of the payments to be made is not equivalent to that of the payments to be received (including the swap premium or discount, as defined in paragraph (e)(3)(ii) of this section) on the day the taxpayer enters into or acquires the contract, the Commissioner may apply principles analogous to those of section 1274 or such other rules as the Commissioner deems appropriate to clearly reflect income. For example, in order to clearly reflect income the Commissioner may determine the hypothetical issue price, the hypothetical stated redemption price at maturity, and the amounts required to be taken into account within a taxable year. Further, if the present value of the payments to be made is not equivalent to that of the payments to be received (including the swap premium or discount, as defined in paragraph (e)(3)(ii) of this section) on the day the taxpayer enters into or acquires the contract, the Commissioner may integrate the swap with another transaction (or transactions) in order to clearly reflect income.

(B) *Terms must be clearly stated.* If the currency swap contract does not clearly set forth the swap principal amount in each currency, and the periodic interim payments in each currency (or the interest index used to compute the periodic interim payments in each currency), the Commissioner may defer any income, deduction, gain or loss with respect to such contract until termination of the contract.

(3) *Amortization of swap premium or discount in the case of off-market currency swaps*— (i) *In general.* An "off-market currency swap" is a currency swap contract under which the present value of the payments to be made is not equal to that of the payments to be received on the day the taxpayer enters into or acquires the contract (absent the swap premium or discount, as defined in paragraph (e)(3)(ii) of this section). Generally, such present values may not be equal if the swap exchange rate (as defined in paragraph (e)(3)(iii) of this section) is not the spot rate, or the interest

Reg. § 1.988-2(e)(3)

indices used to compute the periodic interim payments do not reflect current values, on the day the taxpayer enters into or acquires the currency swap.

(ii) *Treatment of taxpayer entering into or acquiring an off-market currency swap.* If a taxpayer that enters into or acquires a currency swap makes a payment (that is, the taxpayer pays a premium, "swap premium," to enter into or acquire the currency swap) or receives a payment (that is, the taxpayer enters into or acquires the currency swap at a discount, "swap discount") in order to make the present value of the amounts to be paid equal the amounts to be received, such payment shall be amortized in a manner which places the taxpayer in the same position it would have been in had the taxpayer entered into a currency swap contract under which the present value of the amounts to be paid equal the amounts to be received (absent any swap premium or discount). Thus, swap premium or discount shall be amortized as follows—

(A) The amount of swap premium or discount that is attributable to the difference between the swap exchange rate (as defined in paragraph (e)(3)(iii) of this section) and the spot rate on the date the contract is entered into or acquired shall be taken into account as income or expense on the date the swap principal amounts are taken into account; and

(B) The amount of swap premium or discount attributable to the difference in values of the periodic interim payments shall be amortized in a manner consistent with the principles of economic accrual. Cf., section 171.

Any amount taken into account pursuant to this paragraph (e)(3)(ii) shall be treated as exchange gain or loss.

(iii) *Definition of swap exchange rate.* The swap exchange rate is the single exchange rate set forth in the contract at which the swap principal amounts are determined. If the swap exchange rate is not clearly set forth in the contract, the Commissioner may determine such rate.

(iv) *Coordination with § 1.446-3(g)(4) regarding swaps with significant nonperiodic payments.* The rules of § 1.446-3(g)(4) apply to any currency swap with a significant nonperiodic payment. Section 1.446-3(g)(4) applies before this paragraph (e)(3). Thus, if § 1.446-3(g)(4) applies, currency gain or loss may be realized on the loan. This paragraph (e)(3)(iv) applies to transactions entered into after February 14, 2000.

(4) *Treatment of taxpayer disposing of a currency swap.* Any gain or loss realized on the disposition or the termination of a currency swap is exchange gain or loss.

(5) *Examples.* The following examples illustrate the application of this paragraph (e).

Example 1. (i) C is an accrual method calendar year corporation with the dollar as its functional currency. On January 1, 1989, C enters into a currency swap with J with the following terms:

(1) the principal amount is $150 and 100 British pounds (£) (the equivalent of $150 on the effective date of the contract assuming a spot rate of £1 = $1.50 on January 1, 1989);

(2) C will make payments equal to 10% of the dollar principal amount on December 31, 1989, and December 31, 1990;

(3) J will make payments equal to 12% of the pound principal amount on December 31, 1989, and December 31, 1990; and

(4) on December 31, 1990, C will pay to J the $150 principal amount and J will pay to C the £100 principal amount.

Assume that the spot rate is £1 = $1.50 on January 1, 1989, £1 = $1.40 on December 31, 1989, and £1 = $1.30 on December 31, 1990. Assume further that the average rate for 1989 is £1 = $1.45 and for 1990 is £1 = $1.35.

(ii) Solely for determining the realization of gain or loss in accordance with paragraph (e)(2) of this section (and not for purposes of determining whether any payments are treated as interest), C will treat the dollar payments made by C as payments made pursuant to a dollar borrowing with an issue price of $150, a stated redemption price at maturity of $150, and yield to maturity of 10%. C will treat the pound payments received as payments received pursuant to a pound loan with an issue price of £100, a stated redemption price at maturity of £100, and a yield of 12% to maturity. Pursuant to § 1.988-2(b), C is required to compute hypothetical accrued pound interest income at the average rate for the accrual period and then determine exchange gain or loss on the day payment is received with respect to such accrued amount. Accordingly, C will accrue $17.40 (£12 × $1.45) in 1989 and $16.20 (£12 × $1.35) in 1990. C also will compute hypothetical exchange loss of $.60 on December 31, 1989 [(£12 × $1.40) − (£12 × $1.45)] and hypothetical exchange loss of $.60 on December 31, 1990 [£12 × $1.30) − (£12 × $1.35)]. All such hypothetical interest income and exchange loss are characterized and sourced as exchange gain and loss. Further, C is treated as having paid $15 ($150 × 10%) of hypothetical interest on December 31, 1989, and again on December 31, 1990. Such hypothetical interest expense is characterized and sourced as exchange loss. Thus, C will have a net exchange gain of $1.80 ($17.40 − $.60 − $15.00) with respect to the periodic interim payments in

Reg. § 1.988-2(e)(4)

Income from Sources Without the United States

See p. 20,601 for regulations not amended to reflect law changes

1989 and a net exchange gain of $.60 ($16.20 − $.60 − $15.00) with respect to the periodic interim payments in 1990. Finally, C will realize an exchange loss on December 31, 1990 with respect to the exchange of the swap principal amount. This loss is determined by subtracting the value of the units of swap principal paid ($150) from the value of the units of swap principal received ($100 × $1.30 = $130) resulting in a $20 exchange loss.

Example 2. (i) C is an accrual method calendar year corporation with the dollar as its functional currency. On January 1, 1989, when the spot rate is £1 = $1.50, C enters into a currency swap contract with J under which C agrees to make and receive the following payments:

Date	C Pays	J Pays
December 31, 1989	$ 15.00	£12.00
December 31, 1990	$ 41.04	£12.00
December 31, 1991	$ 0.00	£12.00
December 31, 1992	$150.00	£112.00

(ii) Under paragraph (e)(2)(iii) of this section, C must treat the dollar periodic interim payments under the swap as made pursuant to a hypothetical dollar borrowing. The hypothetical issue price is $150 and the stated redemption price at maturity is $206.04. The amount of hypothetical interest expense must be amortized in accordance with economic accrual. Thus J must include and C must deduct periodic interim payment amounts as follows:

	Amount Taken into Account	Adjusted Issue Price
December 31, 1989	$15.00	150.00
December 31, 1990	$15.00	123.96
December 31, 1991	$12.40	136.36
December 31, 1992	$13.64	

(iii) Gain or loss with respect to the periodic interim payments of the currency swap is determined under paragraph (e)(2)(iii)(A) of this section with respect to the dollar cash flow amortized as set forth above and the corresponding pound cash flow as stated in the currency swap contract. Gain or loss with respect to the principal payments (*i.e.*, $150 and £100) exchanged on December 31, 1992, is determined under paragraph (e)(2)(iv) of this section on December 31, 1992, notwithstanding that under the principles regarding amortization of interest $26.04 would have been regarded as a payment of principal on December 31, 1990.

Example 3. (i) X is a corporation on the accrual method of accounting with the dollar as its functional currency and the calendar year as its taxable year. On January 1, 1989, X enters into a three year currency swap contract with Y with the following terms. The swap principal amount is $100 and the Swiss franc (Sf) equivalent of such amount which equals Sf200 translated at the swap exchange rate of $1 = Sf2. There is no initial exchange of the swap principal amount. The interest rates used to compute the periodic interim payments are 10% compounded annually for U.S. dollar payments and 5% compounded annually for Swiss franc payments. Thus, under the currency swap, X agrees to pay Y $10 (10% × $100) on December 31st of 1989, 1990 and 1991 and to pay Y the swap principal amount of $100 on December 31, 1991. Y agrees to pay X Sf10 (5% × Sf200) on December 31st of 1989, 1990 and 1991 and to pay X the swap principal amount of Sf200 on December 31, 1991. Assume that the average rate for 1989 and the spot rate on December 31, 1989, is $1 = Sf2.5.

(ii) Under paragraph (e)(2)(iii) of this section, on December 31, 1989, X will realize an exchange loss of $6 (the sum of $10 of loss by reason of the $10 periodic interim payment paid to Y and $4.00 of gain, the value of Sf10 on December 31, 1989, from the receipt of Sf10 on such date).

(iii) On January 1, 1990, X transfers its rights and obligations under the swap contract to Z, an unrelated corporation. Z has the dollar as its functional currency, is on the accrual method of accounting, and has the calendar year as its taxable year. On January 1, 1990, the exchange rate is $1 = Sf2.50. The relevant dollar interest rate is 8% compounded annually and the relevant Swiss franc interest rate is 5% compounded annually. Because of the movement in exchange and interest rates, the agreement between X and Z to transfer the currency swap requires X to pay Z $23.56 (the swap discount as determined under paragraph (e)(3) of this section).

(iv) Pursuant to paragraph (e)(4) of this section, X may deduct the loss of $23.56 in 1990. The loss is characterized under § 1.988-3 and sourced under § 1.988-4.

(v) Pursuant to paragraph (e)(3)(ii) of this section, Z is required to amortize the $23.56 received as follows. The amount of the $23.56 pay-

Reg. § 1.988-2(e)(5)

ment that is attributable to movements in exchange rates ($20) is taken into account on December 31, 1991, the date the swap principal amounts are exchanged, under paragraph (e)(3)(ii)(A) of this section. This amount is the present value (discounted at 10%, the rate under the currency swap contract used to compute the dollar periodic interim payments) of the financial asset required to compensate Z for the loss in value of the hypothetical Swiss franc loan resulting from movements in exchange rates between January 1, 1989 and January 1, 1990. This amount is determined by assuming that interest rates did not change from the date the swap originally was entered into (January 1, 1989), but that the exchange rate is $1 = Sf2.50. Under this assumption, a taxpayer undertaking the obligation to pay dollars under the currency swap on January 1, 1990, would only agree to pay $8 for Sf10 on December 31, 1990 and $88 for Sf210 on December 31, 1991, because the exchange rates have moved from $1 = Sf2 to $1 = Sf2.50. Thus, Z requires $2 on December 31, 1990 and $22 on December 31, 1991 to compensate for the amount of dollar payments Z is required to make in exchange for the Swiss francs received on December 31, 1990 and 1991. The present value of $2 on December 31, 1990 and $22 on December 31, 1991 discounted at the rate for U.S. dollar payments of 10% is $20 ($1.82 + $18.18). This amount is discounted at the rate for U.S. dollar payments (i.e., at the historic rate) because the amount of the $23.56 payment received by Z that is attributable to movements in interest rates is computed and amortized separately as provided in the following paragraph.

(vi) Pursuant to paragraph (e)(3)(ii)(B) of this section, Z is required to amortize the portion of the $23.56 payment attributable to movements in interest rates under principles of economic accrual over the term of the currency swap agreement. The amount of the $23.56 payment that is attributable to movements in interest rates (assuming that exchange rates have not changed) is the present value ($3.56) of the excess ($2.00 in 1990 and $2.00 in 1991) of the periodic interim payments Z is required to pay under the currency swap agreement ($10 in 1990 and $10 in 1991) over the amount Z would be required to pay if the currency swap agreement reflected current interest rates on the day Z acquired the swap contract ($8 in 1990 and $8 in 1991) discounted at the appropriate dollar interest rate on January 1, 1990. Thus, under principles of economic accrual (e.g., see section 171 of the Code), Z will include in income $1.72 on December 31, 1990, the amount that, when added to the interest ($.28) on the $3.56 computed at the 8% rate on the date Z acquired the currency swap contract, will equal the $2.00 needed to compensate Z for the movement in interest rates between January 1, 1989 and January 1, 1990. Z also will include in income $1.85 on December 31, 1991, the amount that, when added to the interest ($.15) on the $1.85 (the remaining balance of the $3.56 payment) computed at the 8% rate on the date Z acquired the currency swap contract, will equal the $2.00 needed to compensate Z for the movement in interest rates between January 1, 1990 and January 1, 1991. This amount is computed assuming exchange rates have not changed because the amount attributable to movements in exchange rates is computed and amortized separately under the preceding paragraph.

(6) *Special effective date for rules regarding currency swaps.* Paragraph (e)(3) of this section regarding amortization of swap premium or discount in the case of off-market currency swaps shall be effective for transactions entered into after September 21, 1989, unless such swap premium or discount was paid or received pursuant to a binding contract with an unrelated party that was entered into prior to such date. For transactions entered into prior to this date, see Notice 89-21, 1989-8 I.R.B. 23.

(7) *Special rules for currency swap contracts in hyperinflationary currencies*—(i) *In general.* If a taxpayer enters into a hyperinflationary currency swap (as defined in paragraph (e)(7)(iv) of this section), then the taxpayer realizes exchange gain or loss for its taxable year with respect to such instrument determined by reference to the change in exchange rates between—

(A) The later of the first day of the taxable year, or the date the instrument was entered into (by the taxpayer); and

(B) The earlier of the last day of the taxable year, or the date the instrument is disposed of or otherwise terminated.

(ii) *Adjustment to principal or basis.* Proper adjustments are made in the amount of any gain or loss subsequently realized for gain or loss taken into account by reason of this paragraph (e)(7).

(iii) *Interaction with DASTM.* With respect to a qualified business unit that uses the United States dollar approximate separate transactions method of accounting described in § 1.985-3, this paragraph (e)(7) does not apply.

(iv) *Definition of hyperinflationary currency swap contract.* A hyperinflationary currency swap contract is a currency swap contract that provides for—

Reg. § 1.988-2(e)(6)

(A) Payments denominated in or determined by reference to a currency that is hyperinflationary (as defined in § 1.988-1(f)) at the time the taxpayer enters into or otherwise acquires the currency swap; or

(B) Payments that are adjusted to take into account the fact that the currency is hyperinflationary (as defined in § 1.988-1(f)) during the current taxable year. A currency swap contract that provides for periodic payments determined by reference to a variable interest rate based on local conditions and generally responding to changes in the local consumer price index is an example of this latter type of currency swap contract.

(v) *Special effective date for nonfunctional hyperinflationary currency swap contracts.* This paragraph (e)(7) applies to transactions entered into after February 14, 2000.

(f) *Substance over form*—(1) *In general.* If the substance of a transaction described in § 1.988-1(a)(1) differs from its form, the timing, source, and character of gains or losses with respect to such transaction may be recharacterized by the Commissioner in accordance with its substance. For example, if a taxpayer enters into a transaction that it designates a "currency swap contract" that requires the prepayment of all payments to be made or to be received (but not both), the Commissioner may recharacterize the contract as a loan. In applying the substance over form principle, separate transactions may be integrated where appropriate. See also § 1.861-9T(b)(1).

(2) *Example.* The following example illustrates the provisions of this paragraph (f).

Example. (i) On January 1, 1990, X, a U.S. corporation with the dollar as its functional currency, enters into a contract with Y under which X will pay Y $100 and Y will pay X LC100 on January 1, 1990, and X will pay Y LC109.3 and Y will pay X $133 on December 31, 1992. On January 1, 1990, the spot exchange rate is LC1 = $1 and the 3 year forward rate is LC1 = $.8218. X's cash flows are summarized below:

Date	Dollar	LC
1/1/90	(100)	100
12/31/90	0	0
12/31/91	0	0
12/31/92	133	(109.3)

(ii) X and Y designate this contract as a "currency swap." Notwithstanding this designation, for purposes of determining the timing, source, and character with respect to the transaction, the transaction is characterized by the Commissioner in accordance with its substance. Thus, the January 1, 1990, exchange by X of $100 for LC 100 is treated as a spot purchase of LCs by X and the December 31, 1992, exchange by X at 109.3 LC for $133 is treated as a forward sale of LCs by X. Under such treatment there would be no tax consequences to X under paragraph (e)(2) of this section in 1990, 1991, and 1992 with respect to this transaction other than the realization of exchange gain or loss on the sale of the LC109.3 on December 31, 1992. Calculation of such gain or loss would be governed by the rules of paragraph (d) of this section.

(g) *Effective date.* Except as otherwise provided in this section, this section shall be effective for taxable years beginning after December 31, 1986. Thus, except as otherwise provided in this section, any payments made or received with respect to a section 988 transaction in taxable years beginning after December 31, 1986, are subject to this section.

(h) *Timing of income and deductions from notional principal contracts.* Except as otherwise provided (e.g., in § 1.988-5 or 1.446-3(g)), income or loss from a notional principal contract described in § 1.988-1(a)(2)(iii)(B) (other than a currency swap) is exchange gain or loss. For the rules governing the timing of income and deductions with respect to notional principal contracts, see § 1.446-3. See paragraph (e)(2) of this section with respect to currency swaps. [Reg. § 1.988-2.]

☐ [T.D. 8400, 3-16-92. *Amended by T.D.* 8491, 10-8-93 *and T.D.* 8860, 1-12-2000.]

[Reg. § 1.988-3]

§ 1.988-3. **Character of exchange gain or loss.**—(a) *In general.* The character of exchange gain or loss recognized on a section 988 transaction is governed by section 988 and this section. Except as otherwise provided in section 988(c)(1)(E), section 1092, § 1.988-5 and this section, exchange gain or loss realized with respect to a section 988 transaction (including a section 1256 contract that is also a section 988 transaction) shall be characterized as ordinary gain or loss. Accordingly, unless a valid election is made under paragraph (b) of this section, any section providing special rules for capital gain or loss treatment, such as sections 1233, 1234, 1234A, 1236 and 1256(f)(3), shall not apply.

(b) *Election to characterize exchange gain or loss on certain identified forward contracts, futures contracts and option contracts as capital* gain or loss—(1) *In general.* Except as provided in paragraph (b)(2) of this section, a taxpayer may elect, subject to the requirements of paragraph (b)(3) of this section, to treat any gain or loss recognized on a contract described in § 1.988-2(d)(1) as capital gain or loss, but only if the contract—

(i) Is a capital asset in the hands of the taxpayer;

(ii) Is not part of a straddle within the meaning of section 1092(c) (without regard to subsections (c) (4) or (e)); and

(iii) Is not a regulated futures contract or nonequity option with respect to which an election under section 988(c)(1)(D)(ii) is in effect.

If a valid election under this paragraph (b) is made with respect to a section 1256 contract, section 1256 shall govern the character of any gain or loss recognized on such contract.

(2) *Special rule for contracts that become part of a straddle after an election is made.* If a contract which is the subject of an election under paragraph (b)(1) of this section becomes part of a straddle within the meaning of section 1092(c) (without regard to subsections (c)(4) or (e)) after the date of the election, the election shall be invalid with respect to gains from such contract and the Commissioner, in his sole discretion, may invalidate the election with respect to losses.

(3) *Requirements for making the election.* A taxpayer elects to treat gain or loss on a transaction described in paragraph (b)(1) of this section as capital gain or loss by clearly identifying such transaction on its books and records on the date the transaction is entered into. No specific language or account is necessary for identifying a transaction referred to in the preceding sentence. However, the method of identification must be consistently applied and must clearly identify the pertinent transaction as subject to the section 988(a)(1)(B) election. The Commissioner, in his sole discretion, may invalidate any purported election that does not comply with the preceding sentence.

(4) *Verification.* A taxpayer that has made an election under § 1.988-3(b)(3) must attach to his income tax return a statement which sets forth the following:

(i) A description and the date of each election made by the taxpayer during the taxpayer's taxable year;

(ii) A statement that each election made during the taxable year was made before the close of the date the transaction was entered into;

(iii) A description of any contract for which an election was in effect and the date such contract expired or was otherwise sold or exchanged during the taxable year;

(iv) A statement that the contract was never part of a straddle as defined in section 1092; and

(v) A statement that all transactions subject to the election are included on the statement attached to the taxpayer's income tax return.

In addition to any penalty that may otherwise apply, the Commissioner, in his sole discretion, may invalidate any or all elections made during the taxable year under § 1.988-3(b)(1) if the taxpayer fails to verify each election as provided in this § 1.988-3(b)(4). The preceding sentence shall not apply if the taxpayer's failure to verify each election was due to reasonable cause or bona fide mistake. The burden of proof to show reasonable cause or bona fide mistake made in good faith is on the taxpayer.

(5) *Independent verification*—(i) *Effect of independent verification.* If the taxpayer receives independent verification of the election in paragraph (b)(3) of this section, the taxpayer shall be presumed to have satisfied the requirements of paragraphs (b)(3) and (4) of this section. A contract that is a part of a straddle as defined in section 1092 may not be independently verified and shall be subject to the rules of paragraph (b)(2) of this section.

(ii) *Requirements for independent verification.* A taxpayer receives independent verification of the election in paragraph (b)(3) of this section if—

(A) The taxpayer establishes a separate account(s) with an unrelated broker(s) or dealer(s) through which all transactions to be independently verified pursuant to this paragraph (b)(5) are conducted and reported.

(B) Only transactions entered into on or after the date the taxpayer establishes such account may be recorded in the account.

(C) Transactions subject to the election of paragraph (b)(3) of this section are entered into such account on the date such transactions are entered into.

(D) The broker or dealer provides the taxpayer a statement detailing the transactions conducted through such account and includes on such statement the following: "Each transaction identified in this account is subject to the election set forth in section 988(a)(1)(B)."

(iii) *Special effective date for independent verification.* The rules of this paragraph (b)(5) shall be effective for transactions entered into after March 17, 1992.

Reg. § 1.988-3(b)(2)

(6) *Effective date.* Except as otherwise provided, this paragraph (b) is effective for taxable years beginning on or after September 21, 1989. For prior taxable years, any reasonable contemporaneous election meeting the requirements of section 988(a)(1)(B) shall satisfy this paragraph (b).

(c) *Exchange gain or loss treated as interest—*(1) *In general.* Except as provided in this paragraph (c)(1), exchange gain or loss realized on a section 988 transaction shall not be treated as interest income or expense. Exchange gain or loss realized on a section 988 transaction shall be treated as interest income or expense as provided in paragraph (c)(2) of this section with regard to tax exempt bonds, § 1.988-2(e)(2)(ii)(B), § 1.988-5, and in administrative pronouncements. See § 1.861-9T(b), providing rules for the allocation of certain items of exchange gain or loss in the same manner as interest expense.

(2) *Exchange loss realized by the holder on nonfunctional currency tax exempt bonds.* Exchange loss realized by the holder of a debt instrument the interest on which is excluded from gross income under section 103(a) or any similar provision of law shall be treated as an offset to and reduce total interest income received or accrued with respect to such instrument. Therefore, to the extent of total interest income, no exchange loss shall be recognized. This paragraph (c)(2) shall be effective with respect to debt instruments acquired on or after June 24, 1987.

(d) *Effective date.* Except as otherwise provided in this section, this section shall be effective for taxable years beginning after December 31, 1986. Thus, except as otherwise provided in this section, any payments made or received with respect to a section 988 transaction in taxable years beginning after December 31, 1986, are subject to this section. Thus, for example, a payment made prior to January 1, 1987, under a forward contract that results in the deferral of a loss under section 1092 to a taxable year beginning after December 31, 1986, is not characterized as an ordinary loss by virtue of paragraph (a) of this section because payment was made prior to January 1, 1987. [Reg. § 1.988-3.]

☐ [*T.D.* 8400, 3-16-92.]

[Reg. § 1.988-4]

§ 1.988-4. **Source of gain or loss realized on a section 988 transfer.**—(a) *In general.* Except as otherwise provided in § 1.988-5 and this section, the source of exchange gain or loss shall be determined by reference to the residence of the taxpayer. This rule applies even if the taxpayer has made an election under § 1.988-3(b) to characterize exchange gain or loss as capital gain or loss. This section takes precedence over section 865.

(b) *Qualified business unit—*(1) *In general.* The source of exchange gain or loss shall be determined by reference to the residence of the qualified business unit of the taxpayer on whose books the asset, liability, or item of income or expense giving rise to such gain or loss is properly reflected.

(2) *Proper reflection on the books of the taxpayer or qualified business unit—*(i) *In general.* Whether an asset, liability, or item of income or expense is properly reflected on the books of a qualified business unit is a question of fact.

(ii) *Presumption if booking practices are inconsistent.* It shall be presumed that an asset, liability, or item of income or expense is not properly reflected on the books of the qualified business unit if the taxpayer and its qualified business units employ inconsistent booking practices with respect to the same or similar assets, liabilities, or items of income or expense. If not properly reflected on the books, the Commissioner may allocate any asset, liability, or item of income or expense between or among the taxpayer and its qualified business units to properly reflect the source (or realization) of exchange gain or loss.

(c) *Effectively connected exchange gain or loss.* Notwithstanding paragraphs (a) and (b) of this section, exchange gain or loss that under principles similar to those set forth in § 1.864-4(c) arises from the conduct of a United States trade or business shall be sourced in the United States and such gain or loss shall be treated as effectively connected to the conduct of a United States trade or business for purposes of sections 871(b) and 882(a)(1).

(d) *Residence—*(1) *In general.* Except as otherwise provided in this paragraph (d), for purposes of sections 985 through 989, the residence of any person shall be—

(i) In the case of an individual, the country in which such individual's tax home (as defined in section 911(d)(3)) is located;

(ii) In the case of a corporation, partnership, trust or estate which is a United States person (as defined in section 7701(a)(30)), the United States; and

(iii) In the case of a corporation, partnership, trust or estate which is not a United States person, a country other than the United States.

If an individual does not have a tax home (as defined in section 911(d)(3)), the residence of such individual shall be the United States if such individual is a United States citizen or a resident alien and shall be a country other than the United

States if such individual is not a United States citizen or resident alien. If the taxpayer is a U.S. person and has no principal place of business outside the United States, the residence of the taxpayer is the United States. Notwithstanding paragraph (d)(1)(ii) of this section, if a partnership is formed or availed of to avoid tax by altering the source of exchange gain or loss, the source of such gain or loss shall be determined by reference to the residence of the partners rather than the partnership.

(2) *Exception.* In the case of a qualified business unit of any taxpayer (including an individual), the residence of such unit shall be the country in which the principal place of business of such qualified business unit is located.

(3) *Partner in a partnership not engaged in a U.S. trade or business under section 864(b)(2).* The determination of residence shall be made at the partner level (without regard to whether the partnership is a qualified business unit of the partners) in the case of partners in a partnership that are not engaged in a U.S. trade or business by reason of section 864(b)(2).

(e) *Special rule for certain related party loans*—(1) *In general.* In the case of a loan by a United States person or a related person to a 10 percent owned foreign corporation, or a corporation that meets the 80 percent foreign business requirements test of section 861(c)(1), other than a corporation subject to § 1.861-11T(e)(2)(i), which is denominated in, or determined by reference to, a currency other than the U.S. dollar and bears interest at a rate at least 10 percentage points higher than the Federal mid-term rate (as determined under section 1274(d)) at the time such loan is entered into, the following rules shall apply—

(i) For purposes of section 904 only, such loan shall be marked to market annually on the earlier of the last business day of the United States person's (or related person's) taxable year or the date the loan matures; and

(ii) Any interest income earned with respect to such loan for the taxable year shall be treated as income from sources within the United States to the extent of any notional loss attributable to such loan under paragraph (d)(1)(i) of this section.

(2) *United States person.* For purposes of this paragraph (e), the term "United States person" means a person described in section 7701(a)(30).

(3) *Loans by related foreign persons*—(i) *In general.* [Reserved]

(ii) *Definition of related person.* For purposes of this paragraph (e), the term "related person" has the meaning given such term by section 954(d)(3) except that such section shall be applied by substituting "United States person" for "controlled foreign corporation" each place such term appears.

(4) *10 percent owned foreign corporation.* For purposes of this paragraph (e), the term "10 percent owned foreign corporation" means any foreign corporation in which the United States person owns directly or indirectly (within the meaning of section 318(a)) at least 10 percent of the voting stock.

(f) *Exchange gain or loss treated as interest under § 1.988-3.* Notwithstanding the provisions of this section, any gain or loss realized on a section 988 transaction that is treated as interest income or expense under § 1.988-3(c)(1) shall be sourced or allocated and apportioned pursuant to section 861(a)(1), 862(a)(1), or 864(e) as the case may be.

(g) *Exchange gain or loss allocated in the same manner as interest under § 1.861-9T.* The allocation and apportionment of exchange gain or loss under § 1.861-9T shall not affect the source of exchange gain or loss for purposes of sections 871(a), 881, 1441, 1442 and 6049.

(h) *Effective date.* This section shall be effective for taxable years beginning after December 31, 1986. Thus, any payments made or received with respect to a section 988 transaction in taxable years beginning after December 31, 1986, are subject to this section. [Reg. § 1.988-4.]

☐ [*T.D. 8400, 3-16-92.*]

[Reg. § 1.988-5]

§ 1.988-5. Section 988(d) hedging transactions.—(a) *Integration of a nonfunctional currency debt instrument and a § 1.988-5(a) hedge*—(1) *In general.* This paragraph (a) applies to a qualified hedging transaction as defined in this paragraph (a)(1). A qualified hedging transaction is an integrated economic transaction, as provided in paragraph (a)(5) of this section, consisting of a qualifying debt instrument as defined in paragraph (a)(3) of this section and a § 1.988-5(a) hedge as defined in paragraph (a)(4) of this section. If a taxpayer enters into a transaction that is a qualified hedging transaction, no exchange gain or loss is recognized by the taxpayer on the qualifying debt instrument or on the § 1.988-5(a) hedge for the period that either is part of a qualified hedging transaction, and the transactions shall be integrated as provided in paragraph (a)(9) of this section. However, if the qualified hedging transaction results in a synthetic nonfunctional currency denominated debt instrument, such instrument shall be subject to the rules of § 1.988-2(b).

(2) *Exception.* This paragraph (a) does not apply with respect to a qualified hedging transaction that creates a synthetic asset or liability denominated in, or determined by reference to, a currency other than the U.S. dollar if the rate that approximates the Federal short-term rate in such currency is at least 20 percentage points higher than the Federal short term rate (determined under section 1274(d)) on the date the taxpayer identifies the transaction as a qualified hedging transaction.

(3) *Qualifying debt instrument*—(i) *In general.* A qualifying debt instrument is a debt instrument described in § 1.988-1(a)(2)(i), regardless of whether denominated in, or determined by reference to, nonfunctional currency (including dual currency debt instruments, multi-currency debt instruments and contingent payment debt instruments). A qualifying debt instrument does not include accounts payable, accounts receivable or similar items of expense or income.

(ii) *Special rule for debt instrument of which all payments are proportionately hedged.* If a debt instrument satisfies the requirements of paragraph (a)(3)(i) of this section, and all principal and interest payments under the instrument are hedged in the same proportion, then for purposes of this paragraph (a), that portion of the instrument that is hedged is eligible to be treated as a qualifying debt instrument, and the rules of this paragraph (a) shall apply separately to such qualifying debt instrument. See Example 8 in paragraph (a)(9)(iv) of this section.

(4) *Section 1.988-5(a) hedge*—(i) *In general.* A § 1.988-5(a) hedge (hereinafter referred to in this paragraph (a) as a "hedge") is a spot contract, futures contract, forward contract, option contract, notional principal contract, currency swap contract, similar financial instrument, or series or combination thereof, that when integrated with a qualifying debt instrument permits the calculation of a yield to maturity (under principles of section 1272) in the currency in which the synthetic debt instrument is denominated (as determined under paragraph (a) (9)(ii)(A) of this section).

(ii) *Retroactive application of definition of currency swap contract.* A taxpayer may apply the definition of currency swap contract set forth in § 1.988-2(e)(2)(ii) in lieu of the definition of swap agreement in section 2(e)(5) of Notice 87-11, 1987-1 C.B. 423 to transactions entered into after December 31, 1986 and before September 21, 1989.

(5) *Definition of integrated economic transaction.* A qualifying debt instrument and a hedge are an integrated economic transaction if all of the following requirements are satisfied—

(i) All payments to be made or received under the qualifying debt instrument (or amounts determined by reference to a nonfunctional currency) are fully hedged on the date the taxpayer identifies the transaction under paragraph (a) of this section as a qualified hedging transaction such that a yield to maturity (under principles of section 1272) in the currency in which the synthetic debt instrument is denominated (as determined under paragraph (a)(9)(ii)(A) of this section) can be calculated. Any contingent payment features of the qualifying debt instrument must be fully offset by the hedge such that the synthetic debt instrument is not classified as a contingent payment debt instrument. See *Examples 6* and *7* of paragraph (a)(9)(iv) of this section.

(ii) The hedge is identified in accordance with paragraph (a)(8) of this section on or before the date the acquisition of the financial instrument (or instruments) constituting the hedge is settled or closed.

(iii) None of the parties to the hedge are related. The term "related" means the relationships defined in section 267(b) or section 707(b).

(iv) In the case of a qualified business unit with a residence, as defined in section 988(a)(3)(B), outside of the United States, both the qualifying debt instrument and the hedge are properly reflected on the books of such qualified business unit throughout the term of the qualified hedging transaction.

(v) Subject to the limitations of paragraph (a)(5) of this section, both the qualifying debt instrument and the hedge are entered into by the same individual, partnership, trust, estate, or corporation. With respect to a corporation, the same corporation must enter into both the qualifying debt instrument and the hedge whether or not such corporation is a member of an affiliated group of corporations that files a consolidated return.

(vi) With respect to a foreign person engaged in a U.S. trade or business that enters into a qualifying debt instrument or hedge through such trade or business, all items of income and expense associated with the qualifying debt instrument and the hedge (other than interest expense that is subject to § 1.882-5), would have been effectively connected with such U.S. trade or business throughout the term of the qualified hedging transaction had this paragraph (a) not applied.

Reg. § 1.988-5(a)(5)

(6) *Special rules for legging in and legging out of integrated treatment*—(i) *Legging in.* "Legging in" to integrated treatment under this paragraph (a) means that a hedge is entered into after the date the qualifying debt instrument is entered into or acquired, and the requirements of this paragraph (a) are satisfied on the date the hedge is entered into ("leg in date"). If a taxpayer legs into integrated treatment, the following rules shall apply—

(A) Exchange gain or loss shall be realized with respect to the qualifying debt instrument determined solely by reference to changes in exchange rates between—

(*1*) The date the instrument was acquired by the holder, or the date the obligor assumed the obligation to make payments under the instrument; and

(*2*) The leg in date.

(B) The recognition of such gain or loss will be deferred until the date the qualifying debt instrument matures or is otherwise disposed of.

(C) The source and character of such gain or loss shall be determined on the leg in date as if the qualifying debt instrument was actually sold or otherwise terminated by the taxpayer.

(ii) *Legging out.* With respect to a qualifying debt instrument and hedge that are properly identified as a qualified hedging transaction, "legging out" of integrated treatment under this paragraph (a) means that the taxpayer disposes of or otherwise terminates all or a part of the qualifying debt instrument or hedge prior to maturity of the qualified hedging transaction, or the taxpayer changes a material term of the qualifying debt instrument (*e.g.,* exercises an option to change the interest rate or index, or the maturity date) or hedge (*e.g.,* changes the interest or exchange rates underlying the hedge, or the expiration date) prior to maturity of the qualified hedging transaction. A taxpayer that disposes of or terminates a qualified hedging transaction (*i.e.,* disposes of or terminates both the qualifying transaction and the hedge on the same day) shall be considered to have disposed of or otherwise terminated the synthetic debt instrument rather than as legging out. If a taxpayer legs out of integrated treatment, the following rules shall apply—

(A) The transaction will be treated as a qualified hedging transaction during the time the requirements of this paragraph (a) were satisfied.

(B) If the hedge is disposed of or otherwise terminated, the qualifying debt instrument shall be treated as sold for its fair market value on the date the hedge is disposed of or otherwise terminated (the "leg-out date"), and any gain or loss (including gain or loss resulting from factors other than movements in exchange rates) from the identification date to the leg-out date is realized and recognized on the leg-out date. The spot rate on the leg-out date shall be used to determine exchange gain or loss on the debt instrument for the period beginning on the leg-out date and ending on the date such instrument matures or is disposed of or otherwise terminated. Proper adjustment to the principal amount of the debt instrument must be made to reflect any gain or loss taken into account. The netting rule of § 1.988-2(b)(8) shall apply.

(C) If the qualifying debt instrument is disposed of or otherwise terminated, the hedge shall be treated as sold for its fair market value on the date the qualifying debt instrument is disposed of or otherwise terminated (the "leg-out date"), and any gain or loss from the identification date to the leg-out date is realized and recognized on the leg-out date. The spot rate on the leg-out date shall be used to determine exchange gain or loss on the hedge for the period beginning on the leg-out date and ending on the date such hedge is disposed of or otherwise terminated.

(D) Except as provided in paragraph (a)(8)(iii) of this section (regarding identification by the Commissioner), that part of the qualified hedging transaction that has not been terminated (*i.e.,* the remaining debt instrument in its entirety even if partially hedged, or hedge) cannot be part of a qualified hedging transaction for any period subsequent to the leg out date.

(E) If a taxpayer legs out of a qualified hedging transaction and realizes a gain with respect to the terminated instrument, then paragraph (a)(6)(ii)(B) or (C) of this section, as appropriate, shall not apply if during the period beginning 30 days before the leg-out date and ending 30 days after that date the taxpayer enters into another transaction that hedges at least 50% of the remaining currency flow with respect to the qualifying debt instrument which was part of the qualified hedging transaction (or, if appropriate, an equivalent amount under the § 1.988-5 hedge which was part of the qualified hedging transaction).

(7) *Transactions part of a straddle.* At the discretion of the Commissioner, a transaction shall not satisfy the requirements of paragraph (a)(5) of this section if the debt instrument making up the qualified hedging transaction is part of a straddle as defined in section 1092(c) prior to the time the qualified hedging transaction is identified.

(8) *Identification requirements*—(i) *Identification by the taxpayer.* A taxpayer must establish

Reg. § 1.988-5(a)(6)

Income from Sources Without the United States

a record and before the close of the date the hedge is entered into, the taxpayer must enter into the record for each qualified hedging transaction the following information—

(A) The date the qualifying debt instrument and hedge were entered into;

(B) The date the qualifying debt instrument and the hedge are identified as constituting a qualified hedging transaction;

(C) The amount that must be deferred, if any, under paragraph (a)(6) of this section and the source and character of such deferred amount;

(D) A description of the qualifying debt instrument and the hedge; and

(E) A summary of the cash flow resulting from treating the qualifying debt instrument and the hedge as a qualified hedging transaction.

(ii) *Identification by trustee on behalf of beneficiary.* A trustee of a trust that enters into a qualified hedging transaction may satisfy the identification requirements described in paragraph (a)(8)(i) of this section on behalf of a beneficiary of such trust.

(iii) *Identification by the Commissioner.* If—

(A) A taxpayer enters into a qualifying debt instrument and a hedge but fails to comply with one or more of the requirements of this paragraph (a), and

(B) On the basis of all the facts and circumstances, the Commissioner concludes that the qualifying debt instrument and the hedge are, in substance, a qualified hedging transaction,

then the Commissioner may treat the qualifying debt instrument and the hedge as a qualified hedging transaction. The Commissioner may identify a qualifying debt instrument and a hedge as a qualified hedging transaction regardless of whether the qualifying debt instrument and the hedge are held by the same taxpayer.

(9) *Taxation of qualified hedging transactions*—(i) *In general*—(A) *General rule.* If a transaction constitutes a qualified hedging transaction, the qualifying debt instrument and the hedge are integrated and treated as a single transaction with respect to the taxpayer that has entered into the qualified hedging transaction during the period that the transaction qualifies as a qualified hedging transaction. Neither the qualifying debt instrument nor the hedge that makes up the qualified hedging transaction shall be subject to section 263(g), 1092 or 1256 for the period such transactions are integrated. However, the qualified hedging transaction may be subject to section 263(g) or 1092 if such transaction is part of a straddle.

(B) *Special rule for income or expense of foreign persons effectively connected with a U.S. trade or business.* Interest income of a foreign person resulting from a qualified hedging transaction entered into by such foreign person that satisfies the requirements of paragraph (a)(5)(vii) of this section shall be treated as effectively connected with a U.S. trade or business. Interest expense of a foreign person resulting from a qualified hedging transaction entered into by such foreign person that satisfies the requirements of paragraph (a)(5)(vii) of this section shall be allocated and apportioned under § 1.882-5 of the regulations.

(C) *Special rule for foreign persons that enter into qualified hedging transactions giving rise to U.S. source income not effectively connected with a U.S. trade or business.* If a foreign person enters into a qualified hedging transaction that gives rise to U.S. source interest income (determined under the source rules for synthetic asset transactions as provided in this section) not effectively connected with a U.S. trade or business of such foreign person, for purposes of sections 871(a), 881, 1441, 1442 and 6049, the provisions of this paragraph (a) shall not apply and such sections of the Internal Revenue Code shall be applied separately to the qualifying debt instrument and the hedge. To the extent relevant to any foreign person, if the requirements of this paragraph (a) are otherwise met, the provisions of this paragraph (a) shall apply for all other purposes of the Internal Revenue Code (*e.g.*, for purposes of calculating the earnings and profits of a controlled foreign corporation that enters into a qualified hedging transaction through a qualified business unit resident outside the United States, income or expense with respect to such qualified hedging transaction shall be calculated under the provisions of this paragraph (a)).

(ii) *Income tax effects of integration.* The effect of integrating and treating a transaction as a single transaction is to create a synthetic debt instrument for income tax purposes, which is subject to the original issue discount provisions of sections 1272 through 1288 and 163(e), the terms of which are determined as follows:

(A) *Denomination of synthetic debt instrument.* In the case where the qualifying debt instrument is a borrowing, the denomination of the synthetic debt instrument is the same as the currency paid under the terms of the hedge to acquire the currency used to make payments under the qualifying debt instrument. In the case where the qualifying debt instrument is a lending, the denomination of the synthetic debt instrument is the same as the currency received under

Reg. § 1.988-5(a)(9)

the terms of the hedge in exchange for amounts received under the qualifying debt instrument. For example, if the hedge is a forward contract to acquire British pounds for dollars, and the qualifying debt instrument is a borrowing denominated in British pounds, the synthetic debt instrument is considered a borrowing in dollars.

(B) *Term and accrual periods.* The term of the synthetic debt instrument shall be the period beginning on the identification date and ending on the date the qualifying debt instrument matures or such earlier date that the qualifying debt instrument or hedge is disposed of or otherwise terminated. Unless otherwise clearly indicated by the payment interval under the hedge, the accrual period shall be a six month period which ends on the dates determined under section 1272(a)(5).

(C) *Issue price.* The issue price of the synthetic debt instrument is the adjusted issue price of the qualifying debt instrument translated into the currency in which the synthetic debt instrument is denominated at the spot rate on the identification date.

(D) *Stated redemption price at maturity.* In the case where the qualifying debt instrument is a borrowing, the stated redemption price at maturity shall be determined under section 1273(a)(2) on the identification date by reference to the amounts to be paid under the hedge to acquire the currency necessary to make interest and principal payments on the qualifying debt instrument. In the case where the qualifying debt instrument is a lending, the stated redemption price at maturity shall be determined under section 1273(a)(2) on the identification date by reference to the amounts to be received under the hedge in exchange for the interest and principal payments received pursuant to the terms of the qualifying debt instrument.

(iii) *Source of interest income and allocation of expense.* Interest income from a synthetic debt instrument described in paragraph (a)(9)(ii) of this section shall be sourced by reference to the source of income under sections 861(a)(1) and 862(a)(1) of the qualifying debt instrument. The character for purposes of section 904 of interest income from a synthetic debt instrument shall be determined by reference to the character of the interest income from qualifying debt instrument. Interest expense from a synthetic debt instrument described in paragraph (a)(9)(ii) of this section shall be allocated and apportioned under §§ 1.861-8T through 1.861-12T or the successor sections thereof or under § 1.882-5.

(iv) *Examples.* The following examples illustrate the application of this paragraph (a)(9).

Example 1. (i) K is a U.S. corporation with the U.S. dollar as its functional currency. On December 24, 1989, K agrees to close the following transaction on December 31, 1989. K will borrow from an unrelated party on December 31, 1989, 100 British pounds (£) for 3 years at a 10 percent rate of interest, payable annually, with no principal payment due until the final installment. K will also enter into a currency swap contract with an unrelated counterparty under the terms of which—

(a) K will swap, on December 31, 1989, the £100 obtained from the borrowing for $100; and

(b) K will exchange dollars for pounds pursuant to the following table in order to obtain the pounds necessary to make payments on the pound borrowing:

DATE	U.S. Dollars	Pounds
December 31, 1990	8	10
December 31, 1991	8	10
December 31, 1992	108	110

(ii) The interest rate on the borrowing is set and the exchange rates on the swap are fixed on December 24, 1989. On December 31, 1989, K borrows the £100 and swaps such pounds for $100. Assume K has satisfied the identification requirements of paragraph (a)(8) of this section.

(iii) The pound borrowing (which constitutes a qualifying debt instrument under paragraph (a)(3) of this section) and the currency swap contract (which constitutes a hedge under paragraph (a)(4) of this section) are a qualified hedging transaction as defined in paragraph (a)(1) of this section. Accordingly, the pound borrowing and the swap are integrated and treated as one transaction with the following consequences:

(A) The integration of the pound borrowing and the swap results in a synthetic dollar borrowing with an issue price of $100 under section 1273(b)(2).

(B) The total amount of interest and principal of the synthetic dollar borrowing is equal to the dollar payments made by K under the currency swap contract (i.e., $8 in 1990, $8 in 1991, and $108 in 1992).

(C) The stated redemption price at maturity (defined in section 1273(a)(2)) is $100. Because the stated redemption price equals the issue price, there is no OID on the synthetic dollar borrowing.

Reg. § 1.988-5(a)(9)

(D) K may deduct the annual interest payments of $8 under section 163(a) (subject to any limitations on deductibility imposed by other provisions of the Code) according to its regular method of accounting. K has also paid $100 as a return of principal in 1992.

(E) K must allocate and apportion its interest expense with respect to the synthetic dollar borrowing under the rules of §§ 1.861-8T through 1.861-12T.

Example 2. (i) K, a U.S. corporation, has the U.S. dollar as its functional currency. On December 24, 1989, when the spot rate for Swiss francs (Sf) is Sf1 = $1, K enters into a forward contract to purchase Sf100 in exchange for $100.04 for delivery on December 31, 1989. The Sf100 are to be used for the purchase of a franc denominated debt instrument on December 31, 1989. The instrument will have a term of 3 years, an issue price of Sf100, and will bear interest at 6 percent, payable annually, with no repayment of principal until the final installment. On December 24, 1989, K also enters into a series of forward contracts to sell the franc interest and principal payments that will be received under the terms of the franc denominated debt instrument for dollars according to the following schedule:

Date	U.S. Dollars	Francs
December 31, 1990	6.12	6
December 31, 1991	6.23	6
December 31, 1992	112.16	106

(ii) On December 31, 1989, K takes delivery of the Sf100 and purchases the franc denominated debt instrument. Assume K satisfies the identification requirements of paragraph (a)(8) of this section. The purchase of the franc debt instrument (which constitutes a qualifying debt instrument under paragraph (a)(3) of this section) and the series of forward contracts (which constitute a hedge under paragraph (a)(4) of this section) are a qualified hedging transaction under paragraph (a)(1) of this section. Accordingly, the franc debt instrument and all the forward contracts are integrated and treated as one transaction with the following consequences:

(A) The integration of the franc debt instrument and the forward contracts results in a synthetic dollar debt instrument in an amount equal to the dollars exchanged under the forward contract to purchase the francs necessary to acquire the franc debt instrument. Accordingly, the issue price is $100.04 (section 1273(b)(2) of the Code).

(B) The total amount of interest and principal received by K with respect to the synthetic dollar debt instrument is equal to the dollars received under the forward sales contracts (i.e., $6.12 in 1990, $6.23 in 1991, and $112.16 in 1992).

(C) The synthetic dollar debt instrument is an installment obligation and its stated redemption price at maturity is $106.15 (i.e., $6.12 of the payments in 1990, 1991, and 1992 are treated as periodic interest payments under the principles of section 1273). Because the stated redemption price at maturity exceeds the issue price, under section 1273(a)(1) the synthetic dollar debt instrument has OID of $6.11.

(D) The yield to maturity of the synthetic dollar debt instrument is 8.00 percent, compounded annually. Assuming K is a calendar year taxpayer, it must include interest income of $8.00 in 1990 (of which $1.88 constitutes OID), $8.15 in 1991 (of which $2.03 constitutes OID), and $8.32 in 1992 (of which $2.20 constitutes OID). The amount of the final payment received by K in excess of the interest income includible is a return of principal and a payment of previously accrued OID.

(E) The source of the interest income shall be determined by applying sections 861(a)(1) and 862(a)(1) with reference to the franc interest income that would have been received had the transaction not been integrated.

Example 3. (i) K is an accrual method U.S. corporation with the U.S. dollar as its functional currency. On January 1, 1992, K borrows 100 British pounds (£) for 3 years at a 10% rate of interest payable on December 31 of each year with no principal payment due until the final installment. The spot rate on January 1, 1992, is £1 = $1.50. On January 1, 1993, when the spot rate is £1 = $1.60, K enters into a currency swap contract with an unrelated counterparty under the terms of which K will exchange dollars for pounds pursuant to the following table in order to obtain the pounds necessary to make the remaining payments on the pound borrowing:

DATE	U.S. Dollars	Pounds
December 31, 1993	12.80	10
December 31, 1994	12.80	10
December 31, 1994	160.00	100

Reg. § 1.988-5(a)(9)

(ii) Assume that British pound interest rates are still 10% and that K properly identifies the pound borrowing and the currency swap contract as a qualified hedging transaction as provided in paragraph (a)(8) of this section. Under paragraph (a)(6)(i) of this section, K must realize exchange gain or loss with respect to the pound borrowing determined solely by reference to changes in exchange rates between January 1, 1992 and January 1, 1993. (Thus, gain or loss from other factors such as movements in interest rates or changes in credit quality of K are not taken into account). Recognition of such gain or loss is deferred until K terminates its pound borrowing. Accordingly, K must defer exchange loss in the amount of $10 [(£100 × 1.50) − (£100 × 1.60)].

(iii) Additionally, the qualified hedging transaction is treated as a synthetic U.S. dollar debt instrument with an issue date of January 1, 1993, and a maturity date of December 31, 1994. The issue price of the synthetic debt instrument is $160 (£100 × 1.60, the spot rate on January 1, 1993) and the total amount of interest and principal is $185.60. The accrual period is the one year period beginning on January 1 and ending December 31 of each year. The stated redemption price at maturity is $160. Thus, K is treated as paying $12.80 of interest in 1993, $12.80 of interest in 1994, and $160 of principal in 1994. The interest expense from the synthetic instrument is allocated and apportioned in accordance with the rules of §§ 1.861-8T through 1.861-12T. Sections 263(g), 1092, and 1256 do not apply to the positions comprising the synthetic dollar borrowing.

Example 4. (i) K is an accrual method U.S. corporation with the U.S. dollar as its functional currency. On January 1, 1990, K borrows 100 British pounds (£) for 3 years at a 10% rate of interest payable on December 31 of each year with no principal payment due until the final installment. The spot rate on January 1, 1990, is £1 = $1.50. Also on January 1, 1990, K enters into a currency swap contract with an unrelated counterparty under the terms of which K will exchange dollars for pounds pursuant to the following table in order to obtain the pounds necessary to make the remaining payments on the pound borrowing:

DATE	U.S. Dollars	Pounds
December 31, 1990	12.00	10
December 31, 1991	12.00	10
December 31, 1992	162.00	110

(ii) Assume that K properly identifies the pound borrowing and the currency swap contract as a qualified hedging transaction as provided in paragraph (a)(1) of this section.

(iii) The pound borrowing (which constitutes a qualifying debt instrument under paragraph (a)(3) of this section) and the currency swap contract (which constitutes a hedge under paragraph (a)(4) of this section) are a qualified hedging transaction as defined in paragraph (a)(1) of this section. Accordingly, the pound borrowing and the swap are integrated and treated as one transaction with the following consequences:

(A) The integration of the pound borrowing and the swap results in a synthetic dollar borrowing with an issue price of $150 under section 1273(b)(2).

(B) The total amount of interest and principal of the synthetic dollar borrowing is equal to the dollar payments made by K under the currency swap contract (i.e., $12 in 1990, $12 in 1991, and $162 in 1992).

(C) The stated redemption price at maturity (defined in section 1273(a)(2)) is $150. Because the stated redemption price equals the issue price, there is no OID on the synthetic dollar borrowing.

(D) K may deduct the annual interest payments of $12 under section 163(a) (subject to any limitations on deductibility imposed by other provisions of the Code) according to its regular method of accounting. K has also paid $150 as a return of principal in 1992.

(E) K must allocate and apportion its interest expense from the synthetic instrument under the rules of §§ 1.861-8T through 1.861-12T.

(iv) Assume that on January 1, 1991, the spot exchange rate is £1 = $1.60, interest rates have not changed since January 1, 1990, (accordingly, assume that the market value of K's bond in pounds has not changed) and that K transfers its rights and obligations under the currency swap contract in exchange for $10. Under § 1.988-2(e)(3)(iii), K will include in income as exchange gain $10 on January 1, 1991. Pursuant to paragraph (a)(6)(ii) of this section, the pound borrowing and the currency swap contract are treated as a qualified hedging transaction for 1990. The loss inherent in the pound borrowing from January 1, 1990, to January 1, 1991, is realized and recognized on January 1, 1991. Such loss is exchange loss in the amount of $10.00 [(£100 × $1.50, the spot rate on January 1, 1990) − (£100 × $1.60, the spot rate on January 1, 1991)]. For purposes of determining exchange gain or loss on the £100 principal amount of the debt instrument for the period January 1, 1991, to December 31, 1992, the spot rate on January 1, 1991 is used rather than the spot rate on the issue date. Thus, assuming that the spot rate on December 31, 1992, the maturity date, is £1 = $1.80, K realizes exchange loss in the amount of $20 [(£100 × $1.60) − (£100 × $1.80)]. Except as provided in paragraph (a)(8)(iii) (regarding identification by the Commissioner), the pound borrowing cannot be part of a qualified hedging transaction for any period subsequent to the leg out date.

Example 5. (i) K, a U.S. corporation, has the U.S. dollar as its functional currency. On January 1, 1990, when the spot rate for Swiss francs (Sf) is Sf1 = $.50, K converts $100 to Sf200 and purchases a franc denominated debt instrument. The instrument has a term of 3 years, an adjusted issue price of Sf200, and will bear interest at 5 percent, payable annually, with no repayment of principal until the final installment. The U.S. dollar interest rate on an equivalent instrument is 8% on January 1, 1990, compounded annually. On January 1, 1990, K also enters into a series of forward contracts to sell the franc interest and principal payments that will be received under the terms of the franc denominated debt instrument for dollars according to the following schedule:

DATE	U.S. Dollars	Francs
December 31, 1990	5.14	10
December 31, 1991	5.29	10
December 31, 1992	114.26	210

(ii) Assume K satisfies the identification requirements of paragraph (a)(8) of this section. Assume further that on January 1, 1991, the spot exchange rate is Sf1 = U.S.$ .5143, the U.S. dollar interest rate is 10%, compounded annually, and the Swiss franc interest rate is the same as on January 1, 1990 (5%, compounded annually). On January 1, 1991, K disposes of the forward contracts that were to mature on December 31, 1991, and December 31, 1992 and incurs a loss of $3.62 (the present value of $.10 with respect to the 1991 contract and $4.27 with respect to the 1992 contract).

(iii) The purchase of the franc debt instrument (which constitutes a qualifying debt instrument under paragraph (a)(3) of this section) and the series of forward contracts (which constitute a hedge under paragraph (a)(4) of this section) are a qualified hedging transaction under paragraph (a)(1) of this section. Accordingly, the franc debt instrument and all the forward contracts are integrated for the period beginning January 1, 1990, and ending January 1, 1991.

(A) The integration of the franc debt instrument and the forward contracts results in a synthetic dollar debt instrument with an issue price of $100.

(B) The total amount of interest and principal to be received by K with respect to the synthetic dollar debt instrument is equal to the dollars to be received under the forward sales contracts (i.e., $5.14 in 1990, $5.29 in 1991, and $114.26 in 1992).

(C) The synthetic dollar debt instrument is an installment obligation and its stated redemption price at maturity is $109.27 (i.e., $5.14 of the payments in 1990, 1991, and 1992 is treated as periodic interest payments under the principles of section 1273). Because the stated redemption price at maturity exceeds the issue price, under section 1273(a)(1) the synthetic dollar debt instrument has OID of $9.27.

(D) The yield to maturity of the synthetic dollar debt instrument is 8.00 percent, compounded annually. Assuming K is a calendar year taxpayer, it must include interest income of $8.00 in 1990 (of which $2.86 constitutes OID).

(E) The source of the interest income is determined by applying sections 861(a)(1) and 862(a)(1) with reference to the franc interest income that would have been received had the transaction not been integrated.

(iv) Because K disposed of the forward contracts on January 1, 1991, the rules of paragraph (a)(6)(ii) of this section shall apply. Accordingly, the $3.62 loss from the disposition of the forward contracts is realized and recognized on January 1, 1991. Additionally, K is deemed to have sold the franc debt instrument for $102.86, its fair market value in dollars on January 1, 1991. K will compute gain or loss with respect to the deemed sale of the franc debt instrument by subtracting its adjusted basis in the instrument ($102.86—the value of the Sf200 issue price at the spot rate on the identification date plus $2.86 of original issue discount accrued on the synthetic dollar debt instrument for 1990) from the amount realized on the deemed sale of $102.86. Thus K realizes and recognizes no gain or loss from the deemed sale of the debt instrument. The dollar amount used to determine exchange gain or loss with respect to the franc debt instrument is the Sf200 issue price on January 1, 1991, translated into dollars at the spot rate on January 1, 1991, of Sf1 = U.S.$ .5143. Except as provided in paragraph (a)(8)(iii) of this section (regarding identification by the Commissioner), the franc borrowing cannot be part of a qualified hedging transaction for any period subsequent to the leg out date.

Example 6. (i) K is a U.S. corporation with the dollar as its functional currency. On January 1, 1992, K issues a debt instrument with the following terms: the issue price is $1,000, the instrument pays interest annually at a rate of 8% on the $1,000 principal amount, the instrument matures on December 31, 1996, and the amount paid at maturity is the greater of zero or $2,000 less the U.S. dollar value (determined on December 31, 1996) of 150,000 Japanese yen.

(ii) Also on January 1, 1992, K enters into the following hedges with respect to the instrument described in the preceding paragraph: a forward contract under which K will sell 150,000 yen for $1,000 on December 31, 1996 (note that this forward rate assumes that interest rates in yen and dollars are equal); and an option contract that expires on December 31, 1996, under which K has the right (but not the obligation) to acquire 150,000 yen for $2,000. K will pay for the option by making payments to the writer of the option equal to $5 each December 31 from 1992 through 1996.

(iii) The net economic effect of these transactions is that K has created a liability with a principal amount and amount paid at maturity of $1,000, with an interest cost of 8.5% (8% on debt instrument, 0.5% option price) compounded annually. For example, if on December 31, 1996, the spot exchange rate is $1 = 100 yen, K pays $500 on the bond [$2,000 − (150,000 yen/$100)], and $500 in satisfaction of the forward contract [$1,000 − (150,000 yen/$100)]. If instead the spot exchange rate on December 31, 1996 is $1 = 200 yen, K pays $1,250 on the bond [$2,000 − (150,000 yen/$200)] and K receives $250 in satisfaction of the forward contract [$1,000 − (150,000 yen/$200)]. Finally, if the spot exchange rate on December 31, 1996 is $1 = 50 yen, K pays $0 on the bond [$2,000 − (150,000 yen/$50)], but the bond holder is not required under the terms of the instrument to pay additional principal]; K exercises the option to buy 150,000 yen for $2,000; and K then delivers the 150,000 yen as required by the forward contract in exchange for $1,000.

(iv) Assume K satisfies the identification requirements of paragraph (a)(8) of this section. The debt instrument described in paragraph (i) of this *Example 6* (which constitutes a qualifying debt instrument under paragraph (a)(3) of this section) and the forward contract and option contract described in paragraph (ii) of this example (which constitute a hedge under paragraph (a)(4) of this section and are collectively referred to hereafter as "the contracts") together are a qualified hedging transaction under paragraph (a)(1) of this section. Accordingly, with respect to K, the debt instrument and the contracts are integrated, resulting in a synthetic dollar debt instrument with an issue price of $1000, a stated redemption price at maturity of $1000 and a yield to maturity of 8.5% compounded annually (with no original issue discount). K must allocate and apportion its annual interest expense of $85 under the rules of §§ 1.861-8T through 1.861-12T.

Example 7. (i) R is a U.S. corporation with the dollar as its functional currency. On January 1, 1995, R issues a debt instrument with the following terms: the issue price is 504 British pounds (£), the instrument pays interest at a rate of 3.7% (compounded semi-annually) on the £504 principal amount, the instrument matures on December 31, 1999, with a repayment at maturity of the £504 principal plus the proportional gain, if any, in the "Financial Times" 100 Stock Exchange (FTSE) index (determined by the excess of the value of the FTSE index on the maturity date over the value of the FTSE on the issue date, divided by the value of the FTSE index on the issue date, multiplied by the number of FTSE index contracts that could be purchased on the issue date for £504).

(ii) Also on January 1, 1995, R enters into a contract with a bank under which on January 1, 1995, R will swap the £504 for $1,000 (at the current spot rate). R will make U.S. dollar payments to the bank equal to 8.15% on the notional principal amount of $1,000 (compounded semiannually) for the period beginning January 1, 1995 and ending December 31, 1999. R will receive pound payments from the bank equal to 3.7% on the notional principal amount of £504 (compounded semi-annually) for the period beginning January 1, 1995 and ending December 31, 1999. On December 31, 1999, R will swap with the bank $1,000 for £504 plus the proportional gain, if any, in the FTSE index (computed as provided above).

(iii) Economically, both the indexed debt instrument and the hedging contract are hybrid instruments with the following components. The indexed debt instrument is composed of a par pound debt instrument that is assumed to have a 10.85% coupon (compounded semi-annually) plus an embedded FTSE equity index option for which the investor pays a premium of 7.15% (amortized semi-annually) on the pound principal amount. The combined effect is that the premium paid by the investor partially offsets the coupon payments resulting in a return of 3.7% (10.85% − 7.15%). Similarly, the dollar payments under the hedging

Reg. § 1.988-5(a)(9)

contract to be made by R are computed by multiplying the dollar notional principal amount by an 8.00% rate (compounded semi-annually) which the facts assume would be the rate paid on a conventional currency swap plus a premium of 0.15% (amortized semi-annually) on the dollar notional principal amount for an embedded FTSE equity index option.

(iv) Assume R satisfies the identification requirements of paragraph (a)(8) of this section. The indexed debt instrument described in paragraph (i) of this *Example 7* constitutes a qualifying debt instrument under paragraph (a)(3) of this section. The hedging contract described in paragraph (ii) of this *Example 7* constitutes a hedge under paragraph (a)(4) of this section. Since both the pound exposure of the indexed debt instrument and the exposure to movements of the FTSE embedded in the indexed debt instrument are hedged such that a yield to maturity can be determined in dollars, the transaction satisfies the requirement of paragraph (a)(5)(i) of this section. Assuming the transactions satisfy the other requirements of paragraph (a)(5) of this section, the indexed debt instrument and hedge are a qualified hedging transaction under paragraph (a)(1) of this section. Accordingly, with respect to R, the debt instrument and the contracts are integrated, resulting in a synthetic dollar debt instrument with an issue price of $1000, a stated redemption price at maturity of $1000 and a yield to maturity of 8.15% compounded semi-annually (with no original issue discount). K must allocate and apportion its interest expense from the synthetic instrument under the rules §§ 1.861-8T through 1.861-12T.

Example 8. (i) K is a U.S. corporation with the U.S. dollar as its functional currency. On December 24, 1992, K agrees to close the following transaction on December 31, 1992. K will borrow from an unrelated party on December 31, 1992, 200 British pounds (£) for 3 years at a 10 percent rate of interest, payable annually, with no principal payment due until the final installment. K will also enter into a currency swap contract with an unrelated counterparty under the terms of which—

(A) K will swap, on December 31, 1992, £100 obtained from the borrowing for $100; and

(B) K will exchange dollars for pounds pursuant to the following table:

DATE	U.S. Dollars	Pounds
December 31, 1993	8	10
December 31, 1994	8	10
December 31, 1995	108	110

(ii) The interest rate on the borrowing is set and the exchange rates on the swap are fixed on December 24, 1992. On December 31, 1992, K borrows the £200 and swaps £100 for $100. Assume K has satisfied the identification requirements of paragraph (a)(8) of this section.

(iii) The £200 debt instrument satisfies the requirements of paragraph (a)(3)(i) of this section. Because all principal and interest payments under the instrument are hedged in the same proportion (50% of all interest and principal payments are hedged), 50% of the payments under the £200 instrument (principal amount of £100 and annual interest of £10) are treated as a qualifying debt instrument for purposes of paragraph (a) of this section. Thus, the distinct £100 borrowing and the currency swap contract (which constitutes a hedge under paragraph (a)(4) of this section) are a qualified hedging transaction as defined in paragraph (a)(1) of this section. Accordingly, £100 of the pound borrowing and the swap are integrated and treated as one synthetic dollar transaction with the following consequences:

(A) The integration of £100 of the pound borrowing and the swap results in a synthetic dollar borrowing with an issue price of $100 under section 1273(b)(2).

(B) The total amount of interest and principal of the synthetic dollar borrowing is equal to the dollar payments made by K under the currency swap contract (i.e., $8 in 1993, $8 in 1994, and $108 in 1995).

(C) The stated redemption price at maturity (defined in section 1273(a)(2)) is $100. Because the stated redemption price equals the issue price, there is no OID on the synthetic dollar borrowing.

(D) K may deduct the annual interest payments of $8 under section 163(a) (subject to any limitations on deductibility imposed by other provisions of the Code) according to its regular method of accounting. K has also paid $100 as a return of principal in 1995.

(E) K must allocate and apportion its interest expense from the synthetic instrument under the rules of §§ 1.861-8T through 1.861-12T.

That portion of the £200 pound debt instrument that is not hedged (i.e., £100) is treated as a separate debt instrument subject to the rules of § 1.988-2(b) and §§ 1.861-8T through 1.861-12T.

Reg. § 1.988-5(a)(9)

Example 9. (i) K is an accrual method U.S. corporation with the U.S. dollar as its functional currency. On January 1, 1992, K borrows 100 British pounds (£) for 3 years at a 10% rate of interest payable on December 31 of each year with no principal payment due until the final installment. On the same day, K enters into a currency swap agreement with an unrelated bank under which K agrees to the following:

(A) On January 1, 1992, K will exchange the £100 borrowed for $150.

(B) For the period beginning January 1, 1992 and ending December 31, 1994, K will pay at the end of each month an amount determined by multiplying $150 by one month LIBOR less 65 basis points and receive from the bank on December 31st of 1992, 1993, and 1994, £10.

(C) On December 31, 1994, K will exchange $150 for £100.

Assume K satisfies the identification requirements of paragraph (a)(8) of this section.

(ii) The pound borrowing (which constitutes a qualifying debt instrument under paragraph (a)(3) of this section) and the currency swap contract (which constitutes a hedge under paragraph (a)(4) of this section) are a qualified hedging transaction as defined in paragraph (a)(1) of this section. Accordingly, the pound borrowing and the swap are integrated and treated as one transaction with the following consequences:

(A) The integration of the pound borrowing and the swap results in a synthetic dollar borrowing with an issue price of $150 under section 1273(b)(2).

(B) The total amount of interest and principal of the synthetic dollar borrowing is equal to the dollar payments made by K under the currency swap contract.

(C) The stated redemption price at maturity (defined in section 1273(a)(2)) is $150. Because the stated redemption price equals the issue price, there is no OID on the synthetic dollar borrowing.

(D) K may deduct the monthly variable interest payments under section 163(a) (subject to any limitations on deductibility imposed by other provisions of the Code) according to its regular method of accounting. K has also paid $150 as a return of principal in 1994.

(E) K must allocate and apportion its interest expense from the synthetic instrument under the rules of §§ 1.861-8T through 1.861-12T.

Example 10. (i) K is an accrual method U.S. corporation with the U.S. dollar as its functional currency. On January 1, 1992, K loans 100 British pounds (£) for 3 years at a 10% rate of interest payable on December 31 of each year with no principal payment due until the final installment. The spot rate on January 1, 1992, is £1 = $1.50. Also on January 1, 1992, K enters into a currency swap contract with an unrelated counterparty under the terms of which K will exchange pounds for dollars pursuant to the following table:

DATE	Pounds	Dollars
December 31, 1992	10	12
December 31, 1993	10	12
December 31, 1994	110	162

(ii) Assume that K properly identifies the pound borrowing and the currency swap contract as a qualified hedging transaction as provided in paragraph (a)(1) of this section.

(iii) The pound loan (which constitutes a qualifying debt instrument under paragraph (a)(3) of this section) and the currency swap contract (which constitutes a hedge under paragraph (a)(4) of this section) are a qualified hedging transaction as defined in paragraph (a)(1) of this section. Accordingly, the pound loan and the swap are integrated and treated as one transaction with the following consequences:

(A) The integration of the pound loan and the swap results in a synthetic dollar loan with an issue price of $150 under section 1273(b)(2).

(B) The total amount of interest and principal of the synthetic dollar loan is equal to the dollar payments received by K under the currency swap contract (i.e., $12 in 1992, $12 in 1993, and $162 in 1994).

(C) The stated redemption price at maturity (defined in section 1273(a)(2)) is $150. Because the stated redemption price equals the issue price, there is no OID on the synthetic dollar loan.

(D) K must include in income as interest $12 in 1992, 1993, and 1994.

(E) The source of the interest income shall be determined by applying sections 861(a)(1) and 862(a)(1) with reference to the pound interest income that would have been received had the transaction not been integrated.

(iv) On January 1, 1993, K transfers both the pound loan and the currency swap to B, its wholly owned U.S. subsidiary, in exchange for B stock in a transfer that satisfies the requirements of section 351. Under paragraph (a)(6) of this section, the transfer of both instruments is not "legging out." Rather, K is considered to have

Reg. § 1.988-5(a)(9)

Income from Sources Without the United States 50,897
See p. 20,601 for regulations not amended to reflect law changes

transferred the synthetic dollar loan to B in a transaction in which gain or loss is not recognized. B's basis in the loan under section 362 is $100.

(10) *Transition rules and effective dates for certain provisions*—(i) *Coordination with Notice 87-11.* Any transaction entered into prior to September 21, 1989 which satisfied the requirements of Notice 87-11, 1987-1 C.B. 423, shall be deemed to satisfy the requirements of paragraph (a) of this section.

(ii) *Prospective application to contingent payment debt instruments.* In the case of a contingent payment debt instrument, the definition of qualifying debt instrument set forth in paragraph (a)(3)(i) of this section applies to transactions entered into after March 17, 1992.

(iii) *Prospective application of partial hedging rule.* Paragraph (a)(3)(ii) of this section is effective for transactions entered into after March 17, 1992.

(iv) *Effective date for paragraph (a)(6)(i) of this section.* The rules of paragraph (a)(6)(i) of this section are effective for qualified hedging transactions that are legged into after March 17, 1992.

(b) *Hedged executory contracts*—(1) *In general.* If the taxpayer enters into a hedged executory contract as defined in paragraph (b)(2) of this section, the executory contract and the hedge shall be integrated as provided in paragraph (b)(4) of this section.

(2) *Definitions*—(i) *Hedged executory contract.* A hedged executory contract is an executory contract as defined in paragraph (b)(2)(ii) of this section that is the subject of a hedge as defined in paragraph (b)(2)(iii) of this section, provided that the following requirements are satisfied—

(A) The executory contract and the hedge are identified as a hedged executory contract as provided in paragraph (b)(3) of this section.

(B) The hedge is entered into (*i.e.*, settled or closed, or in the case of nonfunctional currency deposited in an account with a bank or other financial institution, such currency is acquired and deposited) on or after the date the executory contract is entered into and before the accrual date as defined in paragraph (b)(2)(iv) of this section.

(C) The executory contract is hedged in whole or in part throughout the period beginning with the date the hedge is identified in accordance with paragraph (b)(3) of this section and ending on or after the accrual date.

(D) None of the parties to the hedge are related. The term related means the relationships defined in section 267(b) and section 707(c)(1).

(E) In the case of a qualified business unit with a residence, as defined in section 988(a)(3)(B), outside of the United States, both the executory contract and the hedge are properly reflected on the books of the same qualified business unit.

(F) Subject to the limitations of paragraph (b)(2)(i)(E) of this section, both the executory contract and the hedge are entered into by the same individual, partnership, trust, estate, or corporation. With respect to a corporation, the same corporation must enter into both the executory contract and the hedge whether or not such corporation is a member of an affiliated group of corporations that files a consolidated return.

(G) With respect to a foreign person engaged in a U.S. trade or business that enters into an executory contract or hedge through such trade or business, all items of income and expense associated with the executory contract and the hedge would have been effectively connected with such U.S. trade or business throughout the term of the hedged executory contract had this paragraph (b) not applied.

(ii) *Executory contract*—(A) *In general.* Except as provided in paragraph (b)(2)(ii)(B) of this section, an executory contract is an agreement entered into before the accrual date to pay nonfunctional currency (or an amount determined with reference thereto) in the future with respect to the purchase of property used in the ordinary course of the taxpayer's business, or the acquisition of a service (or services), in the future, or to receive nonfunctional currency (or an amount determined with reference thereto) in the future with respect to the sale of property used or held for sale in the ordinary course of the taxpayer's business, or the performance of a service (or services), in the future. Notwithstanding the preceding sentence, a contract to buy or sell stock shall be considered an executory contract. (Thus, for example, a contract to sell stock of an affiliate is an executory contract for this purpose.) On the accrual date, such agreement ceases to be considered an executory contract and is treated as an account payable or receivable.

(B) *Exceptions.* An executory contract does not include a section 988 transaction. For example, a forward contract to purchase nonfunctional currency is not an executory contract. An executory contract also does not include a transaction described in paragraph (c) of this section.

(C) *Effective date for contracts to buy or sell stock.* That part of paragraph (b)(2)(ii)(A)

Reg. § 1.988-5(b)(2)

of this section which provides that a contract to buy or sell stock shall be considered an executory contract applies to contracts to buy or sell stock entered into on or after March 17, 1992.

(iii) *Hedge*—(A) *In general.* For purposes of this paragraph (b), the term hedge means a deposit of nonfunctional currency in a hedging account (as defined in paragraph (b)(3)(iii)(D) of this section), a forward or futures contract described in § 1.988-1(a)(1)(ii) and (2)(iii), or combination thereof, which reduces the risk of exchange rate fluctuations by reference to the taxpayer's functional currency with respect to nonfunctional currency payments made or received under an executory contract. The term hedge also includes an option contract described in § 1.988-1(a)(1)(ii) and (2)(iii), but only if the option's expiration date is on or before the accrual date. The premium paid for an option that lapses shall be integrated with the executory contract.

(B) *Special rule for series of hedges.* A series of hedges as defined in paragraph (b)(3)(iii)(A) of this section shall be considered a hedge if the executory contract is hedged in whole or in part throughout the period beginning with the date the hedge is identified in accordance with paragraph (b)(3)(i) of this section and ending on or after the accrual date. A taxpayer that enters into a series of hedges will be deemed to have satisfied the preceding sentence if the hedge that succeeds a hedge that has been terminated is entered into no later than the business day following such termination.

(C) *Special rules for historical rate rollovers*—(*1*) *Definition.* A historical rate rollover is an extension of the maturity date of a forward contract where the new forward rate is adjusted on the rollover date to reflect the taxpayer's gain or loss on the contract as of the rollover date plus the time value of such gain or loss through the new maturity date.

(*2*) *Certain historical rate rollovers considered a hedge.* A historical rate rollover is considered a hedge if the rollover date is before the accrual date.

(*3*) *Treatment of time value component of certain historical rate rollovers that are hedges.* Interest income or expense determined under § 1.988-2(d)(2)(v) with respect to a historical rate rollover shall be considered part of a hedge if the period beginning on the first date a hedging contract is rolled over and ending on the date payment is made or received under the executory contract does not exceed 183 days. Such interest income or expense shall not be recognized and shall be an adjustment to the income from, or expense of, the services performed or received under the executory contract, or to the amount realized or basis of the property sold or purchased under the executory contract. For the treatment of such interest income or expense that is not considered part of a hedge, see § 1.988-2(d)(2)(v).

(D) *Special rules regarding deposits of nonfunctional currency in a hedging account.* A hedging account is an account with a bank or other financial institution used exclusively for deposits of nonfunctional currency used to hedge executory contracts. For purposes of determining the basis of units in such account that comprise the hedge, only those units in the account as of the accrual date shall be taken into consideration. A taxpayer may adopt any reasonable convention (consistently applied to all hedging accounts) to determine which units comprise the hedge as of the accrual date and the basis of the units as of such date.

(E) *Interest income on deposit of nonfunctional currency in a hedging account.* Interest income on a deposit of nonfunctional currency in a hedging account may be taken into account for purposes of determining the amount of a hedge if such interest is accrued on or before the accrual date. However, such interest income shall be included in income as provided in section 61. For example, if a taxpayer with the dollar as its functional currency enters into an executory contract for the purchase and delivery of a machine in one year for 100 British pounds (£), and on such date deposits £90.91 in a properly identified bank account that bears interest at the rate of 10%, the interest that accrues prior to the accrual date shall be included in income and may be considered a hedge.

(iv) *Accrual date.* The accrual date is the date when the item of income or expense (including a capital expenditure) that relates to an executory contract is required to be accrued under the taxpayer's method of accounting.

(v) *Payment date.* The payment date is the date when payment is made or received with respect to an executory contract or the subsequent corresponding account payable or receivable.

(3) *Identification rules*—(i) *Identification by the taxpayer.* A taxpayer must establish a record and before the close of the date the hedge is entered into, the taxpayer must enter into the record a clear description of the executory contract and the hedge and indicate that the transaction is being identified in accordance with paragraph (b)(3) of this section.

(ii) *Identification by the Commissioner.* If a taxpayer enters into an executory contract and a hedge but fails to satisfy one or more of the requirements of paragraph (b) of this section and,

Reg. § 1.988-5(b)(3)

based on the facts and circumstances, the Commissioner concludes that the executory contract in substance is hedged, then the Commissioner may apply the provisions of paragraph (b) of this section as if the taxpayer had satisfied all of the requirements therein, and may make appropriate adjustments. The Commissioner may apply the provisions of paragraph (b) of this section regardless of whether the executory contract and the hedge are held by the same taxpayer.

(4) *Effect of hedged executory contract*—(i) *In general.* If a taxpayer enters into a hedged executory contract, amounts paid or received under the hedge by the taxpayer are treated as paid or received by the taxpayer under the executory contract, or any subsequent account payable or receivable, or that portion to which the hedge relates. Also, the taxpayer recognizes no exchange gain or loss on the hedge. If an executory contract, on the accrual date, becomes an account payable or receivable, the taxpayer recognizes no exchange gain or loss on such payable or receivable for the period covered by the hedge.

(ii) *Partially hedged executory contracts.* The effect of integrating an executory contract and a hedge that partially hedges such contract is to treat the amounts paid or received under the hedge as paid or received under the portion of the executory contract being hedged, or any subsequent account payable or receivable. The income or expense of services performed or received under the executory contract, or the amount realized or basis of property sold or purchased under the executory contract, that is attributable to that portion of the executory contract that is not hedged shall be translated into functional currency on the accrual date. Exchange gain or loss shall be realized when payment is made or received with respect to any payable or receivable arising on the accrual date with respect to such unhedged amount.

(iii) *Disposition of a hedge or executory contract prior to the accrual date*—(A) *In general.* If a taxpayer identifies an executory contract as part of a hedged executory contract as defined in paragraph (b)(2) of this section, and disposes of (or otherwise terminates) the executory contract prior to the accrual date, the hedge shall be treated as sold for its fair market value on the date the executory contract is disposed of and any gain or loss shall be realized and recognized on such date. Such gain or loss shall be an adjustment to the amount received or expended with respect to the disposition or termination, if any. The spot rate on the date the hedge is treated as sold shall be used to determine subsequent exchange gain or loss on the hedge. If a taxpayer identifies a hedge as part of a hedged executory contract as defined in paragraph (b)(2) of this section, and disposes of the hedge prior to the accrual date, any gain or loss realized on such disposition shall not be recognized and shall be an adjustment to the income from, or expense of, the services performed or received under the executory contract, or to the amount realized or basis of the property sold or purchased under the executory contract.

(B) *Certain events in a series of hedges treated as a termination of the hedged executory contract.* If the rules of paragraph (b)(2)(iii)(B) of this section are not satisfied, the hedged executory contract shall be terminated and the provisions of paragraph (b)(4)(iii)(A) of this section shall apply to any gain or loss previously realized with respect to such hedge. Any subsequent hedging contracts entered into to reduce the risk of exchange rate movements with respect to such executory contract shall not be considered a hedge as defined in paragraph (b)(2)(iii) of this section.

(C) *Executory contracts between related persons.* If an executory contract is between related persons as defined in section 267(b) and 707(b), and the taxpayer disposes of the hedge or terminates the executory contract prior to the accrual date, the Commissioner may redetermine the timing, source, and character of gain or loss from the hedge or the executory contract if he determines that a significant purpose for disposing of the hedge or terminating the executory contract prior to the accrual date was to affect the timing, source, or character of income, gain, expense, or loss for Federal income tax purposes.

(iv) *Disposition of a hedge on or after the accrual date.* If a taxpayer identifies a hedge as part of a hedged executory contract as defined in paragraph (b)(2) of this section, and disposes of the hedge on or after the accrual date, no gain or loss is recognized on the hedge and the booking date as defined in § 1.988-2(c)(2) of the payable or receivable for purposes of computing exchange gain or loss shall be the date such hedge is disposed of. See *Example 3* of paragraph (b)(4)(iv) of this section.

(v) *Sections 263(g), 1092, and 1256 do not apply.* Sections 263(g), 1092, and 1256 do not apply with respect to an executory contract or hedge which comprise a hedged executory contract as defined in paragraph (b)(2) of this section. However, sections 263(g), 1092 and 1256 may apply to the hedged executory contract if such transaction is part of a straddle.

(vi) *Examples.* The principles set forth in paragraph (b) of this section are illustrated in the following examples. The examples assume that K

Reg. § 1.988-5(b)(4)

is an accrual method, calendar year U.S. corporation with the dollar as its functional currency.

Example 1. (i) On January 1, 1992, K enters into a contract with JPF, a Swiss machine manufacturer, to pay 500,000 Swiss francs for delivery of a machine on June 1, 1993. Also on January 1, 1992, K enters into a foreign currency forward agreement to purchase 500,000 Swiss francs for $250,000 for delivery on June 1, 1993. K properly identifies the executory contract and the hedge in accordance with paragraph (b)(3)(i) of this section. On June 1, 1993, K takes delivery of the 500,000 Swiss francs (in exchange for $250,000) under the forward contract and makes payment of 500,000 Swiss francs to JPF in exchange for the machine. Assume that the accrual date is June 1, 1993.

(ii) Under paragraph (b)(1) of this section, the hedge is integrated with the executory contract. Therefore, K is deemed to have paid $250,000 for the machine and there is no exchange gain or loss on the foreign currency forward contract. K's basis in the machine is $250,000. Section 1256 does not apply to the forward contract.

Example 2. (i) On January 1, 1992, K enters into a contract with S, a Swiss machine manufacturer, to pay 500,000 Swiss francs for delivery of a machine on June 1, 1993. Under the contract, K is not obligated to pay for the machine until September 1, 1993. On February 1, 1992, K enters into a foreign currency forward agreement to purchase 500,000 Swiss francs for $250,000 for delivery on September 1, 1993. K properly identifies the executory contract and the hedge in accordance with paragraph (b)(3) of this section. On June 1, 1993, K takes delivery of [the] machine. Assume that under K's method of accounting the delivery date is the accrual date. On September 1, 1993, K takes delivery of the 500,000 Swiss francs (in exchange for $250,000) under the forward contract and makes payment of 500,000 Swiss francs to S.

(ii) Under paragraph (b)(1) of this section, the hedge is integrated with the executory contract. Therefore K is deemed to have paid $250,000 for the machine and there is no exchange gain or loss on the foreign currency forward contract. Thus K's basis in the machine is $250,000. In addition, no exchange gain or loss is recognized on the payable in existence from June 1, 1993, to September 1, 1993. Section 1256 does not apply to the forward contract.

Example 3. The facts are the same as in Example 2 except that K disposed of the forward contract on August 1, 1993 for $10,000. Pursuant to paragraph (b)(4)(iv) of this section, K does not recognize the $10,000 gain. K's basis in the machine is $250,000 (the amount fixed by the forward contract), regardless of the amount in dollars that K actually pays to acquire the Sf500,000 when K pays for the machine. K has a payable with a booking date of August 1, 1993, payable on September 1, 1993 for 500,000 Swiss francs. Thus, K will realize exchange gain or loss on the difference between the amount booked on August 1, 1993 and the amount paid on September 1, 1993 under § 1.988-2(c).

Example 4. (i) On January 1, 1992, K enters into a contract with S, a Swiss machine repair firm, to pay 500,000 Swiss francs for repairs to be performed on June 1, 1992. Under the contract, K is not obligated to pay for the repairs until September 1, 1992. On February 1, 1992, K enters into a foreign currency forward agreement to purchase 500,000 Swiss francs for $250,000 for delivery on August 1, 1992. K properly identifies the executory contract and the hedge in accordance with paragraph (b)(3) of this section. On June 1, 1992, S performs the repair services. Assume that under K's method of accounting this date is the accrual date. On August 1, 1992, K takes delivery of the 500,000 Swiss francs (in exchange for $250,000) under the forward contract. On the same day, K deposits the Sf500,000 in a separate account with a bank and properly identifies the transaction as a continuation of the hedged executory contract. On September 1, 1992, K makes payment of the Sf500,000 in the account to S.

(ii) Under paragraph (b)(1) of this section, the hedge is integrated with the executory contract. Therefore K is deemed to have paid $250,000 for the services and there is no exchange gain or loss on the foreign currency forward contract or on the disposition of Sf500,000 in the account. Any interest on the Swiss francs in the account is included in income but is not considered part of the hedge (because the amount paid for the services must be set on or before the accrual date). In addition, no exchange gain or loss is recognized on the payable in existence from June 1, 1992, to September 1, 1992. Section 1256 does not apply to the forward contract.

Example 5. (i) On January 1, 1992, K enters into a contract with S, a Swiss machine manufacturer, to pay 500,000 Swiss francs for delivery of a machine on June 1, 1993. Under the contract, K is not obligated to pay for the machine until September 1, 1993. On February 1, 1992, K enters into a foreign currency forward agreement to purchase 250,000 Swiss francs for $125,000 for delivery on September 1, 1993. K properly identifies the executory contract and the hedge in accordance with paragraph (b)(3) of this section. On June 1, 1993, K takes delivery of the machine. Assume that under K's method of accounting the delivery date is the accrual date. Assume further that the exchange rate is Sf1 = $.50 on June 1, 1993. On August 30, 1993, K purchases Sf250,000 for $135,000. On September 1, 1993, K takes delivery of the 250,000 Swiss francs (in exchange for $125,000) under the forward contract and makes payment of 500,000 Swiss francs (the Sf250,000 received under the contract plus the Sf250,000 purchased on August 30, 1993) to S. Assume the spot rate on September 1, 1993, is 1 Sf1 = $.5420 (Sf250,000 equal $135,500).

(ii) Under paragraph (b)(1) of this section, the partial hedge is integrated with the executory contract. K is deemed to have paid $250,000 for the machine [$125,000 on the hedged portion of the Sf500,000 and $125,000 ($.50, the spot rate on June 1, 1993, times Sf250,000) on the unhedged portion of the Sf500,000]. K's basis in the machine therefore is $250,000. K recognizes no exchange gain or loss on the foreign currency forward contract but K will realize exchange gain of $500 on the disposition of the Sf250,000 purchased on August 30, 1993 under § 1.988-2(a). In addition, exchange loss is realized on the unhedged portion of the payable in existence from June 1, 1993, to September 1, 1993. Thus, K will realize exchange loss of $10,500 ($125,000 booked less $135,500 paid) under § 1.988-2 (c) on the payable. Section 1256 does not apply to the forward contract.

Example 6. (i) On January 1, 1990, K enters into a contract with S, a Swiss steel manufacturer, to buy steel for 1,000,000 Swiss francs (Sf) for delivery and payment on December 31, 1990. On January 1, 1990, the spot rate is Sf1 = $.50, the U.S. dollar interest rate is 10% compounded annually, and the Swiss franc rate is 5% compounded annually. Under K's method of accounting, the delivery date is the accrual date.

(ii) Assume that on January 1, 1990, K enters into a foreign currency forward contract to buy Sf1,000,000 for $523,800 for delivery on December 31, 1990. K properly identifies the executory contract and the hedge in accordance with paragraph (b)(3) of this section. Pursuant to paragraph (b)(2)(iii) of this section, the forward contract constitutes a hedge. Assuming that the requirements of paragraph (b)(2)(i) of this section are satisfied, the executory contract to buy steel and the forward contract are integrated under paragraph (b)(1) of this section. Thus, K is deemed to have paid $523,800 for the steel and will have a basis in the steel of $523,800. No gain or loss is realized with respect to the forward contract and section 1256 does not apply to such contract.

(iii) Assume instead that on January 1, 1990, K enters into a foreign currency forward contract to buy Sf1,000,000 for $512,200 for delivery on July 1, 1990. K properly identifies the executory contract and the hedge in accordance with paragraph (b)(3) of this section. On July 1, 1990, when the spot rate is Sf1 = $.53, K cancels the forward contract in exchange for $17,800 ($530,000 − $512,200). On July 1, 1990, K enters into a second forward agreement to buy Sf1,000,000 for $542,900 for delivery on December 31, 1990. K properly identifies the second forward agreement as a hedge in accordance with paragraph (b)(3) of this section. Pursuant to paragraph (b)(2)(iii) of this section, the forward contract entered into on January 1, 1990, and the forward contract entered into on July 1, 1990, constitute a hedge. Assuming that the requirements of paragraph (b)(2)(i) of this section are satisfied, the executory contract to buy steel and the forward agreements are integrated under paragraph (b)(1) of this section. Thus, K is deemed to have paid $525,100 for the steel (the forward price in the second forward agreement of $542,900 less the gain on the first forward agreement of $17,800) and will have a basis in the steel of $525,100. No gain is realized with respect to the forward contracts and section 1256 does not apply to such contracts.

(iv) Assume instead that on January 1, 1990, K enters into a foreign currency forward contract to buy Sf1,000,000 for $512,200 for delivery on July 1, 1990. K properly identifies the executory contract and the hedge in accordance with paragraph (b)(3) of this section. On July 1, 1990, when the spot rate is Sf1 = $.53, K enters into a historical rate rollover of its $17,800 gain ($530,000 − $512,200) on the forward agreement. Thus, K enters into a second foreign currency forward agreement to buy Sf1,000,000 for $524,210 for delivery on December 31, 1990. (The forward price of $524,210 is the market forward price on July 1, 1990 for the purchase of Sf1,000,000 for delivery on December 31, 1990 of $542,900 less the $17,800 gain on January 1, 1990 contract and less the time value of such gain of $890.) K properly identifies the second forward agreement as a hedge in accordance with paragraph (b)(3) of this section. On December 31, 1990, when the spot rate is Sf1 = $.54, K takes delivery of the Sf1,000,000 (in exchange for $524,210) and purchases the steel for Sf1,000,000. Pursuant to paragraph (b)(2)(iii) of this section, the forward contract entered into on January 1, 1990, and the forward contract entered into on

Reg. § 1.988-5(b)(4)

July 1, 1990, which incorporates the rollover of K's gain on the January 1, 1990 contract, constitute a hedge. Assuming that the requirements of paragraph (b)(2)(i) of this section are satisfied, the executory contract to buy steel and the forward agreements are integrated under paragraph (b)(1) of this section. Because the period from the rollover date to the date payment is made under the executory contract does not exceed 183 days, the $890 of interest income is considered part of the hedge and is not recognized. Thus, K is deemed to have paid $524,210 for the steel and will have a basis in the steel of $524,210. No gain is realized with respect to the forward contracts and section 1256 does not apply to such contracts.

(v) Assume instead that on January 1, 1990, K purchases Sf952,380.95 (the present value of Sf1,000,000 to be paid on December 31, 1990) for $476,190.48 and on the same day deposits the Swiss francs in a separate bank account that bears interest at a rate of 5%, compounded annually. K properly identifies the transaction as a hedged executory contract. Over the period beginning January 1, 1990, and ending December 31, 1990, K receives Sf47,619.05 in interest on the account that is included in income and that has a basis of $25,714.29. (Assume that under § 1.988-2(b)(1), K uses the spot rate of Sf1 = $.54 to translate the interest income). On December 31, 1990, K makes payment of the Sf1,000,000 principal and accrued interest in the account to S. Pursuant to paragraph (b)(2)(iii) of this section, the principal in the bank account and the interest constitute a hedge. Under paragraph (b)(1) of this section, the hedge is integrated with the executory contract. Therefore K is deemed to have paid $501,904.77 (the basis of the principal deposited plus the basis of the interest) for the steel and there is no exchange gain or loss on the disposition of the Sf1,000,000. K's basis in the steel therefore is $501,904.77.

(5) *References to this paragraph (b).* If the rules of this paragraph (b) are referred to in another paragraph of this section (*e.g.*, paragraph (c) of this section), then the rules of this paragraph (b) shall be applied for purposes of such other paragraph by substituting terms appropriate for such other paragraph. For example, paragraph (c)(2) of this section refers to the identification rules of paragraph (b)(3) of this section. Accordingly, for purposes of paragraph (c)(2), the rules of paragraph (b)(3) will be applied by substituting the term "stock or security" for "executory contract".

(c) *Hedges of period between trade date and settlement date on purchase or sale of publicly traded stock or security.* If a taxpayer purchases or sells stocks or securities which are traded on an established securities market and—

(1) Hedges all or part of such purchase or sale for any part of the period beginning on the trade date and ending on the settlement date; and

(2) Identifies the hedge and the underlying stock or securities as an integrated transaction under the rules of paragraph (b)(3) of this section;

then any gain or loss on the hedge shall be an adjustment to the amount realized or the adjusted basis of the stock or securities sold or purchased (and shall not be taken into account as exchange gain or loss). The term hedge means a deposit of nonfunctional currency in a hedging account (within the meaning of paragraph (b)(2)(iii)(D) of this section), or a forward or futures contract described in § 1.988-1(a)(1)(ii) and (2)(iii), or combination thereof, which reduces the risk of exchange rate fluctuations for any portion of the period beginning on the trade date and ending on the settlement date. The provisions of paragraphs (b)(2)(i)(D) through (G), and (b)(2)(iii)(D) and (E) of this section shall apply. Sections 263(g), 1092, and 1256 do not apply with respect to stock or securities and a hedge which are subject to this paragraph (c).

(d) [Reserved]

(e) *Advance rulings regarding net hedging and anticipatory hedging systems.* In his sole discretion, the Commissioner may issue an advance ruling addressing the income tax consequences of a taxpayer's system of hedging either its net nonfunctional currency exposure or anticipated nonfunctional currency exposure. The ruling may address the character, source, and timing of both the section 988 transaction(s) making up the hedge and the underlying transactions being hedged. The procedures for obtaining a ruling shall be governed by such pertinent revenue procedures and revenue rulings as the Commissioner may provide. The Commissioner will not issue a ruling regarding hedges of a taxpayer's investment in a foreign subsidiary.

(f) [Reserved]

(g) *General effective date.* Except as otherwise provided in this section, the rules of this section shall apply to qualified hedging transactions, hedged executory contracts and transactions described in paragraph (c) of this section entered into on or after September 21, 1989. This section shall apply even if the transaction being hedged (*e.g.*, the debt instrument) was entered into or acquired prior to such date. The effective date regarding advance rulings for net and anticipatory hedging shall be governed by such revenue procedures that the Commissioner may publish. [Reg. § 1.988-5.]

☐ [T.D. 8400, 3-16-92.]

Income from Sources Without the United States

[Reg. § 1.989(a)-1]

§ 1.989(a)-1. **Definition of a Qualified Business Unit.**—(a) *Applicability*—(1) *In general.* This section provides rules relating to the definition of the term "qualified business unit" (QBU) within the meaning of section 989.

(2) *Effective date.* These rules shall apply to taxable years beginning after December 31, 1986. However, any person may apply on a consistent basis § 1.989(a)-lT(c) of the Temporary Income Tax Regulations in lieu of § 1.989(a)-1(c) to all taxable years beginning after December 31, 1986, and on or before February 3, 1990. For the text of the temporary regulation, see 53 FR 20612 (June 8, 1988).

(b) *Definition of a qualified business unit*—(1) *In general.* A QBU is any separate and clearly identified unit of a trade or business of a taxpayer provided that separate books and records are maintained.

(2) *Application of the QBU definition*—

(i) *Persons.* A corporation is a QBU. An individual is not a QBU. A partnership, trust, or estate is a QBU of a partner or beneficiary.

(ii) *Activities.* Activities of a corporation, partnership, trust, estate, or individual qualify as a QBU if—

(A) The activities constitute a trade or business; and

(B) A separate set of books and records is maintained with respect to the activities.

(3) *Special rule.* Any activity (wherever conducted and regardless of its frequency) that produces income or loss that is, or is treated as, effectively connected with the conduct of a trade or business within the United States shall be treated as a separate QBU, provided the books and records requirement of paragraph (d)(2) of this section is satisfied.

(c) *Trade or business.*—The determination as to whether activities constitute a trade or business is ultimately dependent upon an examination of all the facts and circumstances. Generally, a trade or business for purposes of section 989(a) is a specific unified group of activities that constitutes (or could constitute) an independent economic enterprise carried on for profit, the expenses related to which are deductible under section 162 or 212 (other than that part of section 212 dealing with expenses incurred in connection with taxes). To constitute a trade or business, a group of activities must ordinarily include every operation which forms a part of, or a step in, a process by which an enterprise may earn income or profit. Such group of activities must ordinarily include the collection of income and the payment of expenses. It is not necessary that the activities carried out by a QBU constitute a different trade or business from those carried out by other QBUs of the taxpayer. A vertical, functional, or geographic division of the same trade or business may be a trade or business for this purpose provided that the activities otherwise qualify as a trade or business under this paragraph (c). However, activities that are merely ancillary to a trade or business will not constitute a trade or business under this paragraph (c). Activities of an individual as an employee are not considered by themselves to constitute a trade or business under this paragraph (c).

(d) *Separate books and records*—(1) *General rule.* Except as provided in paragraph (d)(2) of this section, a separate set of books and records shall include books of original entry and ledger accounts, both general and subsidiary, or similar records. For example, in the case of a taxpayer using the cash receipts and disbursements method of accounting, the books of original entry include a cash receipts and disbursements journal where each receipt and each disbursement is recorded. Similarly, in the case of a taxpayer using an accrual method of accounting, the books of original entry include a journal to record sales (accounts receivable) and a journal to record expenses incurred (accounts payable). In general, a journal represents a chronological account of all transactions entered into by an entity for an accounting period. A ledger account, on the other hand, chronicles the impact during an accounting period of the specific transactions recorded in the journal for that period upon the various items shown on the entity's balance sheet (*i.e.*, assets, liabilities, and capital accounts) and income statement (*i.e.*, revenues and expenses).

(2) *Special rule.* For purposes of paragraph (b)(3) of this section, books and records include books and records used to determine income or loss that is, or is treated as, effectively connected with the conduct of a trade or business within the United States.

(e) *Examples.* The provisions of this section may be illustrated by the following examples:

Example (1). Corporation X is a domestic corporation. Corporation X manufactures widgets in the U.S. for export. Corporation X sells widgets in the United Kingdom through a branch office in London. The London office has its own employees and solicits and processes orders. Corporation X maintains in the U.S. a separate set of books and records for all transactions conducted by the London office. Corporation X is a QBU under

Reg. § 1.989(a)-1(e)

paragraph (b)(2)(i) of this section because of its corporate status. The London branch office is a QBU under paragraph (b)(2)(ii) of this section because (1) the sale of widgets is a trade or business as defined in paragraph (c) of this section; and (2) a complete and separate set of books and records (as described in paragraph (d) of this section) is maintained with respect to its sales operations.

Example (2). A domestic corporation incorporates a wholly-owned subsidiary in Switzerland. The domestic corporation is a manufacturer that markets its product abroad primarily through the Swiss subsidiary. To facilitate sales of the parent's product in Europe, the Swiss subsidiary has branch offices in France and West Germany that are responsible for all marketing operations in those countries. Each branch has its own employees, solicits and processes orders, and maintains a separate set of books and records. The domestic corporation and the Swiss subsidiary are both QBUs under paragraph (b)(2)(i) of this section because of their corporate status. The French and West German branches are QBUs of the Swiss subsidiary. They satisfy paragraph (b)(2)(ii) because each constitutes a trade or business (as defined in paragraph (c) of this section) and because separate sets of books and records (as described in paragraph (d) of this section) of their respective operations is maintained. Each branch is considered to have a trade or business although each is a geographical division of the same trade or business.

Example (3). W is a domestic corporation that manufactures product X in the United States for sale worldwide. All of W's sales functions are conducted exclusively in the United States. W employs individual Q to work in France. Q's sole function is to act as a courier to deliver sales documents to customers in France. With respect to Q's activities in France, a separate set of books and records as described in paragraph (d) is maintained. Under paragraph (c) of this section, Q's activities in France do not constitute a QBU since they are merely ancillary to W's manufacturing and selling business. Q is not considered to have a QBU because an individual's activities as an employee are not considered to constitute a trade or business of the individual under paragraph (c).

Example (4). The facts are the same as in example (3) except that the courier function is the sole activity of a wholly-owned French subsidiary of W. Under paragraph (b)(2)(i) of this section, the French subsidiary is considered to be a QBU.

Example (5). A corporation incorporated in the Netherlands is a subsidiary of a domestic corporation and a holding company for the stock of one or more subsidiaries incorporated in other countries. The Dutch corporation's activities are limited to paying its directors and its administrative expenses, receiving capital contributions from its United States parent corporation, contributing capital to its subsidiaries, receiving dividend distributions from its subsidiaries, and distributing dividends to its domestic parent corporation. Under paragraph (b)(2)(i) of this section, the Netherlands corporation is considered to be a QBU.

Example (6). Taxpayer A, an individual resident of the United States, is engaged in a trade or business wholly unrelated to any type of investment activity. A also maintains a portfolio of foreign currency-denominated investments through a foreign broker. The broker is responsible for all activities necessary to the management of A's investments and maintains books and records as described in paragraph (d) of this section, with respect to all investment activities of A. A's investment activities qualify as a QBU under paragraph (b)(2)(ii) of this section to the extent the activities engaged in by A generate expenses that are deductible under section 212 (other than that part of section 212 dealing with expenses incurred in connection with taxes).

Example (7). Taxpayer A, an individual resident of the United States, is the sole shareholder of foreign corporation (FC) whose activities are limited to trading in stocks and securities. FC is a QBU under paragraph (b)(2)(i) of this section.

Example (8). Taxpayer A, an individual resident of the United States, markets and sells in Spain and in the United States various products produced by other United States manufacturers. A has an office and employs a salesman to manage A's activities in Spain, maintains a separate set of books and records with respect to his activities in Spain, and is engaged in a trade or business as defined in paragraph (c) of this section. Therefore, under paragraph (b)(2)(ii) of this section, the activities of A in Spain are considered to be a QBU.

Example (9). Foreign corporation FX is incorporated in Mexico and is wholly owned by a domestic corporation. The domestic corporation elects to treat FX as a domestic corporation under section 1504(d). FX operates entirely in Mexico and maintains a separate set of books and records with respect to its activities in Mexico. FX is a QBU under paragraph (b)(2)(i) of this section. The activities of FX in Mexico also constitute a QBU under paragraph (b)(2)(ii) of this section.

Example (10). F, a foreign corporation, computes a gain of $100 from the disposition of a United States real property interest (as defined in

Reg. § 1.989(a)-1(e)

section 897(c)). The gain is taken into account as if F were engaged in a trade or business in the United States and as if such gain were effectively connected with such trade or business. F is a QBU under paragraph (b)(2)(i) of this section because of its corporate status. F's disposition activity constitutes a separate QBU under paragraph (b)(3) of this section. [Reg. § 1.989(a)-1.]

☐ [T.D. 8279, 1-3-90.]

[Reg. § 1.989(b)-1]

§ 1.989(b)-1. Definition of weighted average exchange rate.—For purposes of section 989(b)(3) and (4), the term "weighted average exchange rate" means the simple average of the daily exchange rates (determined by reference to a qualified source of exchange rates within the meaning of § 1.964-1(d)(5), excluding weekends, holidays and any other nonbusiness days for the taxable year. [Reg. § 1.989(b)-1.]

☐ [T.D. 8263, 9-19-89. Amended by T.D. 8367, 9-24-91.]

[Reg. § 1.989(c)-1]

§ 1.989(c)-1. Transition rules for certain branches of United States persons using a net worth method of accounting for taxable years beginning before January 1, 1987.—(a) *Applicability*—(1) *In general.* This section applies to qualified business units (QBU) branches of United States persons, whose functional currency (as defined in section 985 of the Code and regulations issued thereunder) is other than the United States dollar (dollar) and that used a net worth method of accounting for their last taxable year beginning before January 1, 1987. Generally, a net worth method of accounting is any method of accounting under which the taxpayer calculates the taxable income of a QBU branch based on the net change in the dollar value of the QBU branch's equity over the course of a taxable year, taking into account any remittance made during the year. QBU branch equity is the excess of QBU branch assets over QBU branch liabilities. For all taxable years beginning after December 31, 1986, such QBU branches must use the profit and loss method of accounting as described in section 987, except to the extent otherwise provided in regulations under section 985 or any other provision of the Code.

(2) *Insolvent QBU branches.* A taxpayer may apply the principles of this section to a QBU branch that used a net worth method of accounting for its last taxable year beginning before January 1, 1987, whose $E pool (as defined in paragraph (d)(3)(i) of this section) is negative. For taxable years beginning on or after October 25, 1991 the principles of this section shall apply to insolvent QBU branches.

(b) *General rules.* For the general rules, see § 1.987-5(b).

(c) *Determining the pool(s) from which a remittance is made.* To determine from which pool(s) a remittance is made, see § 1.987-5(c).

(d) *Calculation of Section 987 gain or loss*—(1) *In general.* See § 1.987-5(d)(1) for rules to make this calculation.

(2) *Step 1—Calculate the amount of the functional currency pools.* For calculation of the amount of the functional currency pools, see § 1.987-5(d)(2).

(3) *Step 2—Calculate the dollar basis pools*—(i) *Dollar basis of the EQ pool*—(A) *Beginning dollar basis.* The beginning dollar basis of the EQ pool (hereinafter referred to as the $E pool) equals the final net worth of the QBU branch. Final net worth of the QBU branch equals the QBU branch's equity value (assets less liabilities) measured in dollars at the end of the taxpayer's last taxable year beginning before January 1, 1987, determined on the basis of the QBU branch's books and records as adjusted according to United States tax principles.

(B) *Adjusting the $E pool.* For adjustments to be made to the $E pool, see § 1.987-5(d)(3)(i)(B).

(ii) *Dollar basis of the post-86 profits pool.* To calculate the dollar basis of the post-86 profits pool, see § 1.987-5(d)(3)(ii).

(iii) *Dollar basis of the equity pool.* To calculate the dollar basis of the equity pool, see § 1.987-5(d)(3)(iii).

(4) *Step 3—Calculation of the dollar basis of a remittance.* To calculate the dollar basis of the EQ remitted, see § 1.987-5(d)(4).

(5) *Step 4—Calculation of the section 987 gain or loss on a remittance.* To calculate 987 gain or loss determined on a remittance, see § 1.987-5(d)(5).

(e) *Functional currency adjusted basis of QBU branch assets acquired in taxable years beginning before January 1, 1987.* To determine the functional currency adjusted basis of QBU branch assets acquired in taxable years beginning before January 1, 1987, see § 1.987-5(e).

(f) *Functional currency amount of QBU branch liabilities acquired in taxable years beginning before January 1, 1987.* To determine the functional currency amount of QBU branch liabilities acquired in taxable years beginning before January 1, 1987, see § 1.987-5(f). [Reg. § 1.989(c)-1.]

☐ [T.D. 8367, 9-24-91.]

Domestic International Sales Corporation

[Reg. § 1.991-1]

§ 1.991-1. Taxation of a domestic international sales corporation.—(a) *In general.* A corporation which is a DISC for a taxable year is not subject to any tax imposed by subtitle A of the Code (sections 1 through 1564) for such taxable year, except for the tax imposed by chapter 5 thereof (sections 1491 through 1494) on certain transfers to avoid tax. Thus, for example, a corporation which is a DISC for a taxable year is not subject for such year to the corporate income tax (section 11), the minimum tax on tax preferences (sections 56 through 58), or the accumulated earnings tax (sections 531 through 537). A DISC is liable for the payment of all taxes payable by corporations under other subtitles of the Code, such as, for example, income taxes withheld at the source and other employment taxes under subtitle C and the interest equalization tax and other miscellaneous excise taxes imposed by subtitle D. In addition, a DISC is subject to the provisions of chapter 3 of subtitle A (including section 1461), relating to withholding of tax on nonresident aliens and foreign corporations and tax-free covenant bonds. See § 1.992-1 for the definition of the term "DISC".

(b) *Determination of taxable income*—(1) *In general.* Although a DISC is not subject to tax under subtitle A of the Code (other than chapter 5 thereof), a DISC's taxable income shall be determined for each taxable year in order to determine, for example, the amount deemed distributed for that taxable year to its shareholders pursuant to § 1.995-2. Except as otherwise provided in the Code and the regulations thereunder, the taxable income of a DISC shall be determined in the same manner as if the DISC were a domestic corporation which had not elected to be treated as a DISC. Thus, for example, a DISC chooses its method of depreciation, inventory method, and annual accounting period in the same manner as if it were a corporation which had not elected to be treated as a DISC. Any elections affecting the determination of taxable income shall be made by the DISC. Thus, as a further example, a DISC which makes an installment sale described in section 453 is able to avail itself of the benefits of section 453: *Provided,* The DISC complies with the election requirements of such section. See § 1.995-2(e) and § 1.996-8 and the regulations thereunder for rules relating to the application for a taxable year of a DISC of a deduction under section 172 for a net operating loss carryback or carryover or of a capital loss carryback or carryover under section 1212.

(2) *Choice of method of accounting.* A DISC may, generally, choose any method of accounting permissible under section 446(c) and the regulations thereunder. However, if a DISC is a member of a controlled group (as defined in § 1.993-1(k)), the DISC may not choose a method of accounting which, when applied to transactions between the DISC and other members of the controlled group, will result in a material distortion of the income of the DISC or any other member of the controlled group. Such a material distortion of income would occur, for example, if a DISC chooses to use the cash method of accounting where the DISC acts as commission agent in a substantial volume of sales of property by a related corporation which uses the accrual method of accounting and which customarily pays commissions to the DISC more than 2 months after such sales. As a further example, a material distortion of income would occur if a DISC chooses to use the accrual method of accounting where the DISC leases a substantial amount of property from a related corporation which uses the cash method of accounting, if the DISC customarily accrues any portion of the rent on such property more than 2 months before the rent is paid. Changes in the method of accounting of a DISC are subject to the requirements of section 446(e) and the regulations thereunder.

(3) *Choice of annual accounting period*—(i) *In general.* A DISC may choose its annual accounting period without regard to the annual accounting period of any of its stockholders. In general, changes in the annual accounting period of a DISC are subject to the requirements of section 442 and the regulations thereunder.

(ii) *Transition rule for change in taxable year in order to become a DISC.* A corporation may, without the consent of the Commissioner, change its annual accounting period and adopt a new taxable year beginning on the first day of any month in 1972, provided that—

(a) Such change has the effect of accelerating the time as of which such corporation can become a DISC,

(b) The Commissioner is notified of such change by means of a statement filed (with the regional service center with which such corporation files its election to be treated as a DISC) not later than the end of the period during which such corporation may file an election to be treated as a DISC for such new taxable year, and

(c) The short period required to effect such change is not a taxable year in which such corporation has a net operating loss as defined in section 172.

Reg. § 1.991-1(a)

Thus, for example, if a corporation which uses the calendar year for its taxable year does not complete arrangements to become a DISC until May 15, 1972, such corporation can, pursuant to this subdivision, change its annual accounting period and adopt a taxable year beginning on the first day of any month in 1972 after May. A change to a new annual accounting period made pursuant to this subdivision is effective only if the corporation which makes such change qualifies as a DISC for such new period. A corporation may change its annual accounting period and adopt a new taxable year pursuant to this subdivision without regard to the provisions of § 1.1502-76 (relating to the taxable year of members of a group). A copy of the statement described in (b) of this subdivision shall be attached to the return of a corporation for the new taxable year to which such corporation changes pursuant to this subdivision. A corporation which changes its annual accounting period pursuant to this subparagraph will not be permitted under section 442 to change its annual accounting period at any time before 1982, except with the consent of the Commissioner as provided in § 1.442-1(b)(1) or pursuant to subparagraph (4) of this paragraph.

(4) *Transition rule for change of taxable year of certain DISC's.* In the case of a DISC all of the shares of which are held by a single shareholder or by members of a group who file a consolidated return, such DISC may (without the consent of the Commissioner) change its annual accounting period and adopt a taxable year beginning in 1972 which is the same as the taxable year of such shareholder or the members of such group. A change to a new annual accounting period may be made by a DISC pursuant to this subparagraph even if such DISC has changed its annual accounting period pursuant to subparagraph (3)(ii) of this paragraph.

(5) *Transition rule for beginning of first taxable year of certain corporations.* If a corporation organized before January 1, 1972, neither acquires assets (other than cash or other property acquired as consideration for the issuance of stock) nor begins doing business prior to January 1, 1972, the first taxable year of such corporation is deemed to begin at the time such corporation acquires any asset (other than cash or other property acquired as consideration for the issuance of stock) or begins doing business, whichever is earlier: *Provided,* That such corporation is a DISC for such first taxable year. For purposes of § 1.6012-2(a), such corporation is treated as not coming into existence until the beginning of such first taxable year.

(c) *Effective date.* The provisions of this section and the regulations under sections 992 through 997 apply with respect to taxable years ending after December 31, 1971, except that a corporation may not be a DISC for any taxable year beginning before January 1, 1972.

(d) *Related statutes.* For rules relating to the transfer, during a taxable year beginning before January 1, 1976, to a DISC of assets of an export trade corporation (as defined in section 971), where a parent owns all the outstanding stock of both such DISC and such export trade corporation, see section 505(b) of the Revenue Act of 1971 (85 Stat. 551). For rules regarding limitations on the qualification of a corporation as an export trade corporation for any taxable year beginning after October 31, 1971, see section 971(a)(3). [Reg. § 1.991-1.]

☐ [T.D. 7323, 9-24-74. Amended by T.D. 7854, 11-15-82.]

[Reg. § 1.992-1]

§ 1.992-1. Requirements of a DISC.—(a) *"DISC" defined.* The term "DISC" refers to a domestic international sales corporation. The term "DISC" means a corporation which, for a taxable year—

(1) Is duly incorporated and existing under the laws of any State or the District of Columbia,

(2) Satisfies the gross receipts test described in paragraph (b) of this section,

(3) Satisfies the assets test described in paragraph (c) of this section,

(4) Satisfies the capitalization requirement described in paragraph (d) of this section,

(5) Satisfies the requirement that an election to be treated as a DISC be in effect for such year, as described in paragraph (e) of this section,

(6) [Reserved],

(7) Maintains separate books and records, and

(8) Is not an ineligible corporation described in paragraph (f) of this section.

A corporation which satisfies the requirements described in subparagraphs (1) through (8) of this paragraph for a taxable year is treated as a separate corporation for Federal tax purposes and qualifies as a DISC, even though such corporation would not be treated (if it were not a DISC) as a corporate entity for Federal income tax purposes. An association cannot qualify as a DISC even if such association is taxable as a corporation pursuant to section 7701(a)(3). In addition, a corporation created or organized in, or under the law of, a possession of the United States cannot qualify as a DISC. The rules contained in this paragraph

Reg. § 1.992-1(a)(8)

constitute a relaxation of the general rules of corporate substance otherwise applicable under the Code. The separate incorporation of a DISC is required under section 992(a)(1) to make it possible to keep a better record of the income which is subject to the special treatment provided by sections 991 through 996, but this does not necessitate in all other respects the separate relationships which otherwise would be required between a parent corporation and its subsidiary. However, this relaxation of the general rules of corporate substance does not apply with respect to other corporations in other contexts. In the case of a transaction between a DISC and a person related to such DISC for purposes of section 482, see § 1.993-1(l) for rules for determining whether income is income of a DISC to which the intercompany pricing rules authorized by section 994 apply.

(b) *Gross receipts test.* In order for a corporation described in paragraph (a)(1) of this section to be a DISC for a taxable year, 95 percent or more of its gross receipts (as defined in § 1.993-6) for such year must consist of qualified export receipts (as defined in § 1.993-1). Gross receipts for a taxable year are determined in accordance with the method of accounting adopted by the corporation pursuant to § 1.991-1(b)(2). However, for rules regarding gross receipts in the case of a commission sale by such corporation, see § 1.993-6. See § 1.992-3 with respect to distributions to meet qualification requirements in the event the requirements of this paragraph are not satisfied for the taxable year.

(c) *Assets test*—(1) *In general.* In order for a corporation described in paragraph (a)(1) of this section to be a DISC for a taxable year, the adjusted basis (determined under section 1011) of its qualified export assets (as defined in § 1.993-2) at the close of such year must equal or exceed 95 percent of the sum of the adjusted bases (determined under section 1011) of all assets of such corporation at the close of such year. See § 1.992-3 with respect to distributions to meet qualification requirements in the event the requirements of this paragraph are not satisfied for the taxable year.

(2) *Assets acquired to meet assets test.* For purposes of determining whether the requirements of subparagraph (1) of this paragraph are satisfied by a corporation at the end of a taxable year, an asset which is a qualified export asset (as defined in § 1.993-2) is treated as not being an asset of such corporation at such time if such asset is held for a total of 60 days or less and is acquired directly or indirectly through borrowing, unless the acquisition of such asset is established to the satisfaction of the Commissioner or his delegate to have been for bona fide purposes. Such acquisition is deemed to have been for bona fide purposes if, for example, it is made in the usual course of the corporation's trade or business.

(d) *Capitalization requirement*—(1) *In general.* To qualify as a DISC for a taxable year, a corporation must have, on each day of that taxable year, only one class of stock. The par value (or, in the case of stock without par value, the stated value) of the corporation's outstanding stock must be on each day of the taxable year at least $2,500. In the case of a corporation which elects to be treated as a DISC for its first taxable year, the requirements of this paragraph (d)(1) are satisfied if the corporation has no more than one class of stock at any time during the year and if the par value (or, in the case of stock without par value, the stated value) of the corporation's outstanding stock is at least $2,500 on the last day of the period within which the election must be made and on each succeeding day of the year. For purposes of this paragraph (d)(1), the stated value of shares is the aggregate amount of the consideration paid for such shares which is not allotted to paid in surplus, or other surplus. The law of the State of incorporation of the DISC determines what consideration may be used to capitalize the DISC. A corporation will not be a qualified DISC unless at least $2,500 of valid consideration was used for this purpose. If a corporation has a realized or unrealized loss during a taxable year which results in the impairment of all or part of the capital required under this paragraph (d)(1), that impairment does not result in disqualification under this paragraph (d)(1), provided that the corporation does not take any legal or formal action under State law to reduce capital for that year below the amount required under this paragraph (d)(1).

(2) *Treatment of debt payable to shareholders*—(i) *In general.* Purported debt of a DISC payable to any person, whether or not such person is a shareholder or a member of a controlled group (as defined in § 1.993-1(k)) of which such DISC is a member, is treated as debt for all purposes of the Code, provided that such purported debt—

(a) Would qualify as debt for purposes of the Code if the DISC were a corporation which did not qualify as a DISC.

(b) Qualifies under subdivision (ii) of this subparagraph, or

(c) Are trade accounts payable described in subdivision (iii) of this subparagraph.

Such debt is not treated as stock, and interest payable by the DISC on such debt is treated as interest by both the DISC and the holder of such debt. Payment of the principal of such debt by a

Reg. § 1.992-1(b)

DISC does not constitute the payment of a dividend by such DISC. The provisions of this subparagraph apply for a taxable year of a DISC, even though debt described in this subparagraph would be treated as stock of the corporation if such corporation did not qualify as a DISC for such year.

(ii) *Safe harbor rule.* Purported debt of a DISC will in no event be treated as other than debt for purposes of subdivision (i) of this subparagraph if—

(a) It is a written obligation to pay a sum certain on or before a fixed maturity date,

(b) Interest is payable on such purported debt at an arm's length interest rate (as determined under § 1.482-2(a)(2)), expressed as a fixed dollar amount or a fixed percentage of principal,

(c) Such purported debt is not convertible into stock or into other purported debt unless such purported debt qualifies under this subparagraph as debt of the DISC,

(d) Such purported debt does not confer voting rights upon its holder, except in the event of default thereon, and

(e) Interest and principal are paid in accordance with the terms of such purported debt or with any modification of such terms consistent with (a) through (d) of this subdivision.

The determination of whether purported debt of a DISC constitutes debt described in this subdivision is made without regard to the proportion of debt of the DISC held by any of its shareholders, to the ratio of the outstanding debt of the DISC to its equity, or to the amount of outstanding debt of such DISC. The provisions of (e) of this subdivision do not prevent the modification of the terms of debt of a DISC where, for example, a DISC becomes unable to make timely payments of principal required under such terms, provided that such modification is consistent with (a) through (d) of this subdivision.

(iii) *Trade accounts payable.* Trade accounts payable of a DISC which arise in the normal course of its trade or business (such as in consideration for inventory or supplies) constitute debt of the DISC (whether or not such accounts payable are debt described in subdivision (i)(a) or (b) of this subparagraph), provided that such accounts are payable within 15 months after they arise. If such accounts are payable more than 15 months after they arise, they are debt of such DISC only if they are debt described in subdivision (i)(a) or (b) of this subparagraph.

(iv) *Relation of subparagraph to other corporations.* The provisions of this subparagraph generally constitute a relaxation of the ordinary rules used in determining whether purported debt of a corporation is debt or equity. This relaxation is in recognition of the principle that a corporation may qualify as a DISC even though it has relatively little capital. This relaxation does not apply with respect to purported debt of other corporations in other contexts. The provisions of subdivisions (i), (ii), and (iii) of this subparagraph apply only for taxable years for which a corporation qualifies (or is treated as) a DISC.

(3) *Classes of stock.* [Reserved]

(e) *Election in effect.* In order for a corporation to be a DISC for a taxable year, an election to be treated as a DISC must be made by such corporation pursuant to § 1.992-2 and must be in effect for such taxable year. A corporation does not become or remain a DISC solely by making such an election. A corporation is a DISC for a taxable year only if such an election is in effect for that year and the corporation also satisfies the requirements of paragraphs (a) through (d) of this section. See § 1.992-2 for rules regarding the time and manner of making such an election.

(f) *Ineligible corporations.* The following corporations shall not be eligible to be treated as a DISC—

(1) A corporation exempt from tax by reason of section 501,

(2) A personal holding company (as defined in section 542),

(3) A financial institution to which section 581 or 593 applies,

(4) An insurance company subject to the tax imposed by Subchapter L,

(5) A regulated investment company (as defined in section 851(a)),

(6) A China Trade Act corporation receiving the special deduction provided in section 941(a), or

(7) An electing small business corporation (as defined in section 1371(b)).

(g) *Status as DISC after having filed return as a DISC.* Under section 992(a)(2), notwithstanding the failure of a corporation to meet the requirements of paragraph (a) of this section for a taxable year, such corporation will be treated as a DISC for purposes of the Code for such taxable year (and thus, will not be able to claim that it is not eligible to be a DISC) if—

(1) Such corporation files a return as a DISC for such taxable year,

(2) Such corporation does not notify the district director, more than 30 days before the expiration of the period of limitation (including

Reg. § 1.992-1(g)(2)

extensions thereof) on assessment for underpayment of tax for such taxable year (as determined under section 6501 and the regulations thereunder), that it is not a DISC for such taxable year, and

(3) The Internal Revenue Service has not issued, within such period of limitation (including extensions thereof) on assessment for underpayment of tax for such taxable year, a notice of deficiency based on a determination that such corporation is not a DISC for such taxable year.

A corporation is treated as a DISC, for all purposes, pursuant to the provisions of this paragraph for any taxable year for which it meets the requirements of this paragraph, even if such corporation is an ineligible corporation described in paragraph (f) of this section for such taxable year. Thus, for example, a corporation which is treated as a DISC for a taxable year pursuant to this paragraph is treated as a DISC for that taxable year for purposes of § 1.992-2(e)(3) (relating to the termination of a DISC election if a corporation is not a DISC for each of any 5 consecutive taxable years). If a corporation is treated as a DISC for a taxable year pursuant to this paragraph, persons who held stock of such corporation at any time during such taxable year are treated, with respect to such stock, as holders of stock in a DISC for the period or periods during which they held such stock within such taxable year.

(h) *Definition of "former DISC".* Under section 992(a)(3), the term "former DISC" refers to a corporation which is not a DISC for a taxable year but which was (or was treated as) a DISC for a prior taxable year. However, a corporation is not a former DISC for a taxable year unless such corporation has, at the beginning of such taxable year, undistributed previously taxed income (as defined in § 1.996-3(c)) or accumulated DISC income (as defined in § 1.996-3(b)). A corporation which is a former DISC for a taxable year is a former DISC for all purposes of the Code. [Reg. § 1.992-1].

☐ [T.D. 7323, 9-24-74. Amended by T.D. 7420, 5-19-76; T.D. 7747, 12-29-80; T.D. 7920, 11-3-83 and T.D. 8371, 10-24-91.]

[Reg. § 1.992-2]

§ 1.992-2. **Election to be treated as a DISC.**—(a) *Manner and time of election*—(1) *Manner*—(i) *In general.* A corporation can elect to be treated as a DISC for a taxable year beginning after December 31, 1971. Except as provided in subdivision (ii) of this subparagraph, the election is made by the corporation filing Form 4876 with the service center with which it would file its income tax return if it were subject for such taxable year to all the taxes imposed by subtitle A of the Internal Revenue Code of 1954. The form shall be signed by any person authorized to sign a corporation return under section 6062, and shall contain the information required by such form. Except as provided in paragraphs (b)(3) and (c) of this section, such election to be treated as a DISC shall be valid only if the consent of every person who is a shareholder of the corporation as of the beginning of the first taxable year for which such election is effective is on or attached to such Form 4876 when filed with the service center.

(ii) *Transitional rule for corporations electing during 1972.* If the first taxable year for which an election by a corporation to be treated as a DISC is a taxable year beginning after December 31, 1971, and on or before December 31, 1972, such election may be made either in the manner prescribed in subdivision (i) of this subparagraph or by filing, at the place prescribed in subdivision (i) of this subparagraph, a statement captioned "Election to be Treated as a DISC." Such statement of election shall be valid only if the consent of each shareholder is filed with the service center in the form, and at the time, prescribed in paragraph (b) of this section. Such statement shall be signed by any person authorized to sign a corporation return under section 6062 and shall include the name, address, and employer identification number (if known) of the corporation, the beginning date of the first taxable year for which the election is effective, the number of shares of stock of the corporation issued and outstanding as of the earlier of the beginning of the first taxable year for which the election is effective or the time the statement is filed, the number of shares held by each shareholder as of the earlier of such dates, and the date and place of incorporation. As a condition of the election being effective, a corporation which elects to become a DISC by filing a statement in accordance with this subdivision must furnish (to the service center with which the statement was filed) such additional information as is required by Form 4876 by March 31, 1973.

(2) *Time of making election*—(i) *In general.* In the case of a corporation making an election to be treated as a DISC for its first taxable year, such election shall be made within 90 days after the beginning of such taxable year. In the case of a corporation which makes an election to be treated as a DISC for any taxable year beginning after March 31, 1972 (other than the first taxable year of such corporation), the election shall be made during the 90-day period immediately preceding the first day of such taxable year.

(ii) *Transitional rules for certain corporations electing during 1972.* In the case of a corporation which makes an election to be treated as a DISC for a taxable year beginning after December 31, 1971, and on or before March 31, 1972 (other than its first taxable year), the election shall be made within 90 days after the beginning of such taxable year.

(b) *Consent by shareholders*—(1) *In general* — (i) *Time and manner of consent.* Under paragraph (a)(1)(i) of this section, subject to certain exceptions, the election to be treated as a DISC is not valid unless each person who is a shareholder as of the beginning of the first taxable year for which the election is effective signs either the statement of consent on Form 4876 or a separate statement of consent attached to such form. A shareholder's consent is binding on such shareholder and all transferees of his shares and may not be withdrawn after a valid election is made by the corporation. In the case of a corporation which files an election to become a DISC for a taxable year beginning after December 31, 1972, if a person who is a shareholder as of the beginning of the first taxable year for which the election is effective does not consent by signing the statement of consent set forth on Form 4876, such election shall be valid (except in the case of an extension of the time for filing granted under the provisions of subparagraph (3) of this paragraph or paragraph (c) of this section) only if the consent of such shareholder is attached to the Form 4876 upon which such election is made.

(ii) *Form of consent.* A consent other than the statement of consent set forth on Form 4876 shall be in the form of a statement which is signed by the shareholder and which sets forth *(a)* the name and address of the corporation and of the shareholder and *(b)* the number of shares held by each such shareholder as of the time the consent is made and (if the consent is made after the beginning of the corporation's taxable year for which the election is effective) as of the beginning of such year. If the consent is made by a recipient of transferred shares pursuant to paragraph (c) of this section, the statement of consent shall also set forth the name and address of the person who held such shares as of the beginning of such taxable year and the number of such shares. Consent shall be made in the following form: "I (insert name of shareholder), a shareholder of (insert name of corporation seeking to make the election) consent to the election of (insert name of corporation seeking to make the election) to be treated as a DISC under section 992(b) of the Internal Revenue Code. The consent so made by me is irrevocable and is binding upon all transferees of my shares in (insert name of corporation seeking to make the election)." The consents of all shareholders may be incorporated in one statement.

(iii) *Who may consent.* Where stock of the corporation is owned by a husband and wife as community property (or the income from such stock is community property), or is owned by tenants in common, joint tenants, or tenants by the entirety, each person having a community interest in such stock or the income therefrom and each tenant in common, joint tenant, and tenant by the entirety must consent to the election. The consent of a minor shall be made by his legal guardian or by his natural guardian if no legal guardian has been appointed. The consent of an estate shall be made by the executor or administrator thereof. The consent of a trust shall be made by the trustee thereof. The consent of an estate or trust having more than one executor, administrator, or trustee, may be made by any executor, administrator, or trustee, authorized to make a return of such estate or trust pursuant to section 6012(b)(5). The consent of a corporation or partnership shall be made by an officer or partner authorized pursuant to section 6062 or 6063, as the case may be, to sign the return of such corporation or partnership. In the case of a foreign person, the consent may be signed by any individual (whether or not a U.S. person) who would be authorized under sections 6061 through 6063 to sign the return of such foreign person if he were a U.S. person.

(2) *Transitional rule for corporations electing during 1972.* In the case of a corporation which files an election to be treated as a DISC for a taxable year beginning after December 31, 1971, and on or before December 31, 1972, such election shall be valid only if the consent of each person who is a shareholder as of the beginning of the first taxable year for which such election is effective is filed with the service center with which the election was filed within 90 days after the first day of such taxable year or within the time granted for an extension of time for filing such consent. The form of such consent shall be the same as that prescribed in subparagraph (1) of this paragraph. Such consent shall be attached to the statement of election or shall be filed separately (with such service center) with a copy of the statement of election. An extension of time for filing a consent may be granted in the manner, and subject to the conditions, described in subparagraph (3) of this paragraph.

(3) *Extension of time to consent.* An election which is timely filed and would be valid except for the failure to attach the consent of any shareholder to the Form 4876 upon which the election was made or to comply with the 90-day requirement in subparagraph (2) of this paragraph or paragraph (c)(1) of this section, as the case may be, will not be invalid for such reason if it is shown

Reg. § 1.992-2(b)(3)

to the satisfaction of the service center that there was reasonable cause for the failure to file such consent, and if such shareholder files a proper consent to the election within such extended period of time as may be granted by the Internal Revenue Service. In the case of a late filing of a consent, a copy of the Form 4876 or statement of election shall be attached to such consent and shall be filed with the same service center as the election. The form of such consent shall be the same as that set forth in paragraph (b)(1)(ii) of this section. In no event can any consent be made pursuant to this paragraph on or after the last day of the first taxable year for which a corporation elects to be treated as a DISC.

(c) *Consent by holder of transferred shares*—(1) *In general.* If a shareholder of a corporation transfers—

(i) Prior to the first day of the first taxable year for which such corporation elects to be treated as a DISC, some or all of the shares held by him without having consented to such election, or

(ii) On or before the 90th day after the first day of the first taxable year for which such corporation elects to be treated as a DISC, some or all of the shares held by him as of the first day of such year (or if later, held by him as of the time such shares are issued) without having consented to such election, then consent may be made by any recipient of such shares on or before the 90th day after the first day of such first taxable year. If such recipient fails to file his consent on or before such 90th day, an extension of time for filing such consent may be granted in the manner, and subject to the conditions, described in paragraph (b)(3) of this section. In addition, if the transfer occurs more than 90 days after the first day of such taxable year, an extension of time for filing such consent may be granted to such recipient only if it is determined under paragraph (b)(3) of this section that an extension of time would have been granted the transferor for the filing of such consent if the transfer had not occurred. A consent which is not attached to the original Form 4876 or statement of election (as the case may be) shall be filed with the same service center as the original Form 4876 or statement of election and shall have attached a copy of such original form or statement of election. The form of such consent shall be the same as that set forth in paragraph (b)(1)(ii) of this section. For the purposes of this paragraph, a transfer of shares includes any sale, exchange, or other disposition, including a transfer by gift or at death.

(2) *Requirement for the filing of an amended Form 4876 or statement of election.* In any case in which a consent to a corporation's election to be treated as a DISC is made pursuant to subparagraph (1) of this paragraph, such corporation must file an amended Form 4876 or statement of election (as the case may be) reflecting all changes in ownership of shares. Such form must be filed with the same service center with which the original Form 4876 or statement of election was filed by such corporation.

(d) *Effect of election*—(1) *Effect on corporation.* A valid election to be treated as a DISC remains in effect (without regard to whether the electing corporation qualifies as a DISC for a particular year) until terminated by any of the methods provided in paragraph (e) of this section. While such election is in effect, the electing corporation is subject to sections 991 through 997 and other provisions of the Code applicable to DISC's for any taxable year for which it qualifies as a DISC (or is treated as qualifying as a DISC pursuant to § 1.992-1(g)). Such corporation is also subject to such provisions for any taxable year for which it is treated as a former DISC as a result of qualifying or being treated as a DISC for any taxable year for which such election was in effect.

(2) *Effect on shareholders.* A valid election by a corporation to be treated as a DISC subjects the shareholders of such corporation to the provisions of section 995 (relating to the taxation of the shareholders of a DISC or former DISC) and to all other provisions of the Code relating to the shareholders of a DISC or former DISC. Such provisions of the Code apply to any person who is a shareholder of a DISC or former DISC whether or not such person was a shareholder at the time the corporation elected to become a DISC.

(e) *Termination of election*—(1) *In general.* An election to be treated as a DISC is terminated only as provided in subparagraph (2) or (3) of this paragraph.

(2) *Revocation of election*—(i) *Manner of revocation.* An election by a corporation to be treated as a DISC may be revoked by the corporation for any taxable year of the corporation after the first taxable year for which the election is effective. Such revocation shall be made by the corporation filing a statement that the corporation revokes its election under section 992(b) to be treated as a DISC. Such statement shall indicate the corporation's name, address, employer identification number, and the first taxable year of the corporation for which the revocation is to be effective. The statement shall be signed by any person authorized to sign a corporation return under section 6062. Such revocation shall be filed with the service center with which the corporation filed its election, except that, if it filed an annual informa-

Reg. § 1.992-2(c)(1)

tion return under section 6011(e)(2), the revocation shall be filed with the service center with which it filed its last such return.

(ii) *Years for which revocation is effective.* If a corporation files a statement revoking its election to be treated as a DISC during the first 90 days of a taxable year (other than the first taxable year for which such election is effective), such revocation will be effective for such taxable year and all taxable years thereafter. If the corporation files a statement revoking its election to be treated as a DISC after the first 90 days of a taxable year, the revocation will be effective for all taxable years following such taxable year.

(3) *Continued failure to be a DISC.* If a corporation which has elected to be treated as a DISC does not qualify as a DISC (and is not treated as a DISC pursuant to § 1.992-1(g)) for each of any 5 consecutive taxable years, such election terminates and will not be effective for any taxable year after such fifth taxable year. Such termination will be effective automatically, without notice to such corporation or to the Internal Revenue Service. If, during any 5-year period for which an election is effective, the corporation should qualify as a DISC (or be treated as a DISC pursuant to § 1.992-1(g)) for a taxable year, a new 5-year period shall automatically start at the beginning of the following taxable year.

(4) *Election after termination.* If a corporation has made a valid election to be treated as a DISC and such election terminates in either manner described in subparagraph (2) or (3) of this paragraph, such corporation is eligible to reelect to be treated as a DISC at any time by following the procedures described in paragraphs (a) through (c) of this section. If a corporation terminates its election and subsequently reelects to be treated as a DISC, the corporation and its shareholders continue to be subject to sections 995 and 996 with respect to the period during which its first election was in effect. Thus, for example, distributions upon disqualification includible in the gross incomes of shareholders of a corporation pursuant to section 995(b)(2) continue to be so includible for taxable years for which a second election of such corporation is in effect without regard to the second election. [Reg. § 1.992-2.]

☐ [T.D. 7323, 9-24-74. Amended by T.D. 7420, 5-19-76.]

[Reg. § 1.992-3]

§ 1.992-3. **Deficiency distributions to meet qualification requirements.**—(a) *In general.* A corporation which meets the requirements described in § 1.992-1 for treatment as a DISC for a taxable year, other than the 95 percent of gross receipts test described in § 1.992-1(b) or the 95-percent assets test described in § 1.992-1(c), or both tests, may nevertheless qualify as a DISC for such year by making deficiency distributions (attributable to its gross receipts other than qualified export receipts and its assets other than qualified export assets) if all of the following requirements are satisfied:

(1) The corporation distributes the amount determined under paragraph (b) of this section as a deficiency distribution. The amount of a deficiency distribution is determined without regard to the amount by which the corporation fails to meet either test.

(2) The reasonable cause requirements prescribed in paragraph (c)(1) of this section are satisfied with respect to both the corporation's failure to meet either test and its failure to make a deficiency distribution prior to the time the distribution is made.

(3) The corporation makes such deficiency distribution pro rata to all its shareholders.

(4) The corporation designates the distribution, at the time of the distribution, as a deficiency distribution, pursuant to section 992(c), to meet the qualification requirements to be a DISC. Such designation shall be in the form of a communication sent at the time of such distribution to each shareholder and to the service center with which the corporation has filed or will file its return for the taxable year to which the distribution relates. A corporation may not retroactively designate a prior distribution as a deficiency distribution to meet qualification requirements. Subject to the limitation described in paragraph (c)(3) of this section, a corporation may make a deficiency distribution with respect to a taxable year at any time after the close of such taxable year or, in the case of a deficiency distribution made on or before September 29, 1975, at any time during or after such taxable year.

See sections 246(d), 904(f), 995, and 996 for rules regarding the treatment of a deficiency distribution to meet qualification requirements by the shareholders and the corporation.

(b) *Amount of deficiency distribution*—(1) *In general.* In order to meet the requirements of paragraph (a) of this section, the amount of a deficiency distribution must be, if the corporation fails to meet—

(i) The 95 percent of gross receipts test, the amount determined in subparagraph (2) of this paragraph,

(ii) The 95-percent assets test, the amount determined in subparagraph (3) of this paragraph, and

Reg. § 1.992-3(b)(1)

(iii) Both such tests, except as provided in subparagraph (4) of this paragraph, the sum of the amounts determined in subparagraphs (2) and (3) of this paragraph.

(2) *Computation of deficiency distribution to meet 95 percent of gross receipts test.*—(i) *In general.* If a corporation fails to meet the 95 percent of gross receipts test described in § 1.992-1(b) for its taxable year, the amount of the deficiency distribution required by this subparagraph is an amount equal to the sum of its taxable income (if any) from each transaction giving rise to gross receipts (as defined in § 1.993-6) which are not qualified export receipts (as defined in § 1.993-1). A corporation's taxable income from a transaction shall be the amount of such gross receipts from such transaction reduced only by (a) its cost of goods sold attributable to such gross receipts, and by (b) its expenses, losses, and other deductions properly apportioned or allocated thereto in a manner consistent with the rules set forth in § 1.861-8. For purposes of this subdivision, however, any expenses, losses, or other deductions which cannot definitely be allocated to some item or class of gross income in such manner shall not reduce such gross receipts. If the corporation is a commission agent for a principal in a transaction, the corporation's taxable income is the amount of the commission from such transaction reduced only by the amounts described in (b) of this subdivision.

(ii) *Example.* The provisions of this subparagraph may be illustrated by the following example:

Example. (a) X and Y are calendar year taxpayers. X, a domestic manufacturing company, owns all the stock of Y, which seeks to qualify as a DISC for 1973. During 1973, X manufactures a machine which is eligible to be export property as defined in § 1.993-3. Y is made a commission agent with respect to exporting such machine. Thereafter, during 1973 Y is considered to receive gross receipts of $100,000, as determined under section 993(f), attributable to X's sale of the machine in a manner which causes the gross receipts to be excluded receipts pursuant to section 993(a)(2) and, therefore, not qualified export receipts. Y's total gross receipts for 1973 are $1 million of which $900,000 (i.e., 90 percent) are qualified export receipts. Therefore, Y does not satisfy the 95 percent of gross receipts test for 1973 because less than 95 percent of its gross receipts are qualified export receipts. Y has $9,000 of expenses properly apportioned or allocated to its gross income from such sale and $1,000 of other expenses which cannot definitely be allocated to some item or class of gross income,

Reg. § 1.992-3(b)(2)

determined in a manner consistent with the rules set forth in § 1.861-8. In order to satisfy the 95 percent of gross receipts test for 1973, if the commission due from X to Y were $15,000, Y must make a deficiency distribution of $6,000 computed as follows:

Y's commission (gross income) from the transaction	$15,000
Less: Y's expenses apportioned or allocated to its gross income from the transaction	9,000
Required deficiency distribution by reason of $100,000 of gross receipts which are not qualified export receipts	6,000

(b) If the commission due from X to Y were $9,400, resulting in a net loss of $600 to Y ($9,400 to $10,000), Y must make a deficiency distribution of $400 computed as follows:

Y's commissions (gross income) from the transaction	$ 9,400
Less: Y's expenses apportioned or allocated to its gross income from the transaction	9,000
Required deficiency distribution by reason of $100,000 of gross receipts which are not qualified export receipts	400

(c) If the commission due from X to Y were $8,500, Y would not be required to make a deficiency distribution since, under this subparagraph, there would be no taxable income attributable to gross receipts from the sale.

(3) *Computation of deficiency distribution to meet 95 percent assets test.*—(i) *In general.* If a corporation fails to meet the 95 percent assets test described in § 1.992-1(c) for its taxable year, the amount of the deficiency distribution required by this subparagraph is an amount equal to the fair market value as of the last day of such taxable year of the assets which are not qualified export assets held by such corporation on such last day.

(ii) *Asset held for more than 1 year.* In the case of a corporation which holds continuously an asset which is not a qualified export asset at the close of more than 1 taxable year, it must distribute an amount equal to its fair market value (or, if greater, the amount determined under subparagraph (4) of this paragraph) only once if, at the close of the first such taxable year, such corporation reasonably believed that such asset was a qualified export asset. This subdivision shall not apply for any taxable year beginning after the date the corporation knows (or a reasonable man would have known) that an asset is not a qualified export asset and in order to qualify for each such year, the corporation must distribute the fair market value of such asset for each such year.

(4) *Computation in the case of a failure to meet both tests as a result of a single transaction.*

If a corporation fails to meet both the 95 percent of gross receipts test and the 95 percent assets test for a taxable year, and if the corporation holds at the end of such year assets (other than cash or qualified export assets) which were received as proceeds of a sale or exchange during such year which resulted in gross receipts other than qualified export receipts, then the amount of the deficiency distribution required by this paragraph with respect to such sale or exchange and assets held is the larger of the amount required by subparagraph (2) of this paragraph with respect to the sale or exchange or the amount required by subparagraph (3) of this paragraph with respect to such assets held. Thus, for example, if a corporation sells property which is not a qualified export asset for $100, receives $85 in cash and a note for $15, and derives $25 of taxable income from the sale as determined under subparagraph (2) of this paragraph, it must distribute $25. If the provisions of this subparagraph are applied with respect to assets of a DISC, (other than qualified export assets), such provisions do not apply to any property received as proceeds from a sale or exchange of such assets.

(c) *Reasonable cause for failure*—(1) *In general.* If for a taxable year, a corporation has failed to meet the 95 percent of gross receipts test, the 95 percent assets test, or both tests, such corporation may satisfy any such test for such year by means of a deficiency distribution in the amount determined under paragraph (b) of this section only if the reasonable cause requirements of this subparagraph are satisfied. Such reasonable cause requirements are satisfied if—

(i) There is reasonable cause (as determined in accordance with subparagraph (2) of this paragraph) for such corporation's failure to satisfy such test and to make such distribution prior to the date on which it was made, the time limit in subparagraph (3) of this paragraph for making the distribution is satisfied, and interest (if required) is paid in the amount and in the manner prescribed by subparagraph (4) of this paragraph, or

(ii) The time and "70-percent" requirements of the reasonable cause test of paragraph (d) of this section are satisfied.

(2) *Determination of reasonable cause.* In general, whether a corporation's failure to meet the 95 percent of gross receipts test, the 95 percent assets test, or both tests for a taxable year and its failure to make a pro rata distribution prior to the date on which it was made will be considered for reasonable cause where the action or inaction which resulted in such failure occurred in good faith, such as failure to meet the 95 percent assets test resulting from blocked currency or expropriation, or failure to meet either test because of reasonable uncertainty as to what constitutes a qualified export receipt or a qualified export asset. For further examples, if a corporation's reasonable determination of the percentage of its total gross receipts that are qualified export receipts is subsequently redetermined to be less than 95 percent as a result of a price adjustment by the Internal Revenue Service under section 482, or if the corporation has a casualty loss for which it receives an unanticipated insurance recovery which causes its qualified export receipts to be less than 95 percent of its gross receipts, then the failure to satisfy the 95 percent of gross receipts test is considered to be due to reasonable cause.

(3) *Time limit for deficiency distribution.* Except as otherwise provided in this subparagraph, the time limit prescribed by this subparagraph for making a deficiency distribution is satisfied if the amount of the distribution required by paragraph (b) of this section is made within 90 days from the date of the first written notification to the corporation by the Internal Revenue Service that it had not satisfied the 95 percent of gross receipts test or the 95 percent assets test or both tests, for a taxable year. Upon a showing by the corporation that an extension of the 90-day time limit is reasonable and necessary, the Commissioner may grant such extension of such time limit. In any case in which a corporation contests the decision of the Internal Revenue Service that such corporation has not met the 95 percent of gross receipts test, the 95 percent assets test, or both tests, an extension of the 90-day time limit will be allowed until 30 days after the final determination of such contest. The date of the final determination of such contest shall, for purposes of section 992(c), be established in the manner specified in subdivisions (i) through (iv) of this subparagraph:

(i) The date of final determination by a decision of the United States Tax Court is the date upon which such decision becomes final, as prescribed in section 7481.

(ii) The date of final determination in a case which is contested in a court (and upon which there is a judgment) other than the Tax Court is the date upon which the judgment becomes final and will be determined on the basis of the facts and circumstances of each particular case. For example, ordinarily a judgment of a United States district court becomes final upon the expiration of the time allowed for taking an appeal, if no such appeal is duly taken within such time; and a judgment of the United States

Reg. § 1.992-3(c)(3)

Court of Claims becomes final upon the expiration of the time allowed for filing a petition for certiorari if no such petition is duly filed within such time.

(iii) The date of a final determination by a closing agreement, made under section 7121, is the date such agreement is approved by the Commissioner.

(iv) A final determination under section 992(c) may be made by an agreement signed by the district director or director of the service center with which the corporation files its annual return or by such other official to which authority to sign has been delegated, and by or on behalf of the taxpayer. The agreement shall set forth the total amount of the deficiency distribution to be paid to the shareholders of the DISC for the taxable year or years. An agreement under this subdivision shall be sent to the taxpayer at his last known address by either registered or certified mail. For further guidance regarding the definition of last known address, see § 301.6212-2 of this chapter. If registered mail is used for such purpose, the date of registration is considered the date of final determination; if certified mail is used for such purpose, the date of postmark on the sender's receipt for such mail is considered the date of final determination. If the corporation makes a deficiency distribution before such registration or postmark date but on or after the date the district director or director of the service center or other official has signed the agreement, the date of signature by the district director or director of the service center or other official is considered the date of final determination. If the corporation makes a deficiency distribution before the district director or director of the service center or other official signs the agreement, the date of final determination is considered to be the date of the making of the deficiency distribution. During any extension of time the interest charge provided in subparagraph (4) of this paragraph will continue to accrue at the rate provided for in such subparagraph.

(4) *Payment of interest for delayed distribution*—(i) *In general.* If a corporation makes a deficiency distribution after the 15th day of the ninth month after the close of the taxable year with respect to which such distribution is made, such distribution will not be deemed to satisfy the 95 percent of gross receipts test or the 95 percent assets test for such year unless such corporation pays to the Internal Revenue Service a charge determined by multiplying *(a)* an amount equal to 4½ percent of such distribution by *(b)* the number of its taxable years which begin *(1)* after the taxable year with respect to which the distribution is made and (2) before such distribution is made. Such charge must be paid, within the 30-day period beginning with the day on which such distribution is made, to the service center with which the corporation files its annual information return for its taxable year in which the distribution is made. For purposes of the Internal Revenue Code, such charge is considered interest.

(ii) *Example.* The provisions of subdivision (i) of this subparagraph may be illustrated by the following example:

Example. X corporation, which uses the calendar year as its taxable year, meets the 95 percent assets test but fails to meet the 95 percent of gross receipts test for 1972 and does not by September 15, 1973, make the deficiency distribution required by reason of its failure to meet such test. Assume that reasonable cause exists for the corporation's failure to meet the 95 percent of gross receipts test and failure to make the required deficiency distribution. If X makes the required deficiency distribution, in the amount of $10,000, on April 1, 1976, X must pay on or before April 30, 1976, to the service center with which it files its annual information return a charge of $1,800, computed as follows:

Deficiency distribution made by X	$10,000
Multiplied by 4½ percent	.045
Intermediate product	450
Multiplied by: Number of X's taxable years beginning after 1972 and before April 1, 1976	4
Charge to be paid service center because of late deficiency distribution (which is considered interest)	1,800

(d) *Certain distributions deemed for reasonable cause.* If a corporation makes a distribution in the amount required by paragraph (b) of this section with respect to a taxable year on or before the 15th day of the ninth month after the close of such year, it will be deemed to have acted with reasonable cause with respect to its failure to satisfy the 95 percent of gross receipts test, the 95 percent assets test, or both tests, for such year and its failure to make such distribution prior to the date on which the distribution was made if—

(1) At least 70 percent of the gross receipts of such corporation for such taxable year consist of qualified export receipts; and

(2) The sum of the adjusted bases of the qualified export assets held by such corporation on the last day of each month of the taxable year equals or exceeds 70 percent of the sum of the adjusted bases of all assets held by the corporation on each such day. [Reg. § 1.992-3.]

Reg. § 1.992-3(c)(4)

☐ [T.D. 7323, 9-24-74. Amended by T.D. 7420, 5-19-76; T.D. 7854, 11-15-82 and T.D. 8939, 1-11-2001.]

[Reg. § 1.992-4]

§ 1.992-4. Coordination with personal holding company provisions in case of certain produced film rents.—(a) *In general.* Section 992(d)(2) provides that a personal holding company is not eligible to be treated as a DISC. Section 543(a)(5)(B) provides that, for purposes of section 543, the term "produced film rents" means payments received with respect to an interest in a film for the use of, or the right to use, such film, but only to the extent that such interest was acquired before substantial completion of production of such film. Under section 992(e), if such produced film rents are included in the ordinary gross income (as defined in section 543(b)(1)) of a qualified subsidiary for a taxable year of such subsidiary, and such interest was acquired by such subsidiary from its parent, such interest is deemed (for purposes of the application of sections 541, 543(b)(1), and 992(d)(2), and § 1.992-1(f) for such taxable year) to have been acquired by such subsidiary at the time such interest was acquired by such parent. Thus, for example, if a parent acquires an interest in a film before it is substantially completed, then substantially completes such film prior to transferring an interest in such motion picture to a qualified subsidiary, the qualified subsidiary is considered as having acquired such interest prior to substantial completion of such motion picture for purposes of determining whether payments from the rental of such motion picture will be classified as produced film rents of such subsidiary. The provisions of section 992(e) and this section are not applicable in determining whether payments received with respect to an interest in a film are included in the ordinary gross income of a parent or a qualified subsidiary. Thus, even though a qualified subsidiary is treated pursuant to this section as having acquired an interest in a film at the time such interest was acquired by such subsidiary's parent, payments received by such parent with respect to such interest prior to the transfer of such interest to such subsidiary are includible in the ordinary gross income of such parent and not includible in the ordinary gross income of such subsidiary.

(b) *Definitions*—(1) *"Qualified subsidiary".* For purposes of this section, a corporation is a qualified subsidiary for a taxable year if—

(i) Such corporation was established for the purpose of becoming a DISC,

(ii) Such corporation would qualify (or be treated) as a DISC for such taxable year if it is not a personal holding company, and

(iii) On every day of such taxable year on which shares of such corporation are outstanding, at least 80 percent of such shares are held directly by a second corporation.

(2) *"Parent".* For purposes of this section, the term "parent" means a second corporation referred to in subparagraph (1)(iii) of this paragraph. [Reg. § 1.992-4.]

☐ [T.D. 7323, 9-24-74.]

[Reg. § 1.993-1]

§ 1.993-1. Definition of qualified export receipts.—(a) *In general.* For a corporation to qualify as a DISC, at least 95 percent of its gross receipts for a taxable year must consist of qualified export receipts. Under section 993(a), the term "qualified export receipts" means any of the eight amounts described in paragraphs (b) through (i) of this section, except to the extent that any of the eight amounts is an excluded receipt within the meaning of paragraph (j) of this section. For purposes of this section and §§ 1.993-2 through 1.993-6—

(1) *DISC.* All references to a DISC mean a DISC, except when the context indicates that such term means a corporation in the process of meeting the conditions necessary for that corporation to become a DISC, or a corporation being tested as to whether it qualifies as a DISC.

(2) *Sale, lease, and license.* The term "sale" includes an exchange or other disposition and the term "lease" includes a rental or a sublease. The term "license" includes a sublicense. All rules under this section and §§ 1.993-2 through 1.993-6 applicable to leases of export property apply in the same manner to licenses of export property. See § 1.993-3(f)(3) for a description of intangible property which cannot be export property.

(3) *Gross receipts.* The term "gross receipts" is defined by section 993(f) and § 1.993-6.

(4) *Qualified export assets.* The term "qualified export assets" is defined by section 993(b) and § 1.993-2.

(5) *Export property.* The term "export property" is defined by section 993(c) and § 1.993-3.

(6) *Related person.* The term "related person" means a person who is related to another person if either immediately before or after a transaction—

(i) The relationship between such persons would result in a disallowance of losses under section 267 (relating to disallowance of losses, etc., between related taxpayers), or section 707(b) (relating to losses disallowed, etc., between partners and controlled partnerships), and the regulations thereunder, or

Reg. § 1.993-1(a)(6)

(ii) Such persons are members of the same controlled group of corporations, as defined in section 1563(a) (relating to definition of controlled group of corporations), except that (a) "more than 50 percent" shall be substituted for "at lease 80 percent" each place it appears in section 1563(a) and the regulations thereunder, and (b) the provisions of section 1563(b) shall not apply in determining whether such persons are members of the same controlled group.

(7) *Related supplier.* The term "related supplier" is defined by § 1.994-1(a)(3)(ii).

(8) *Controlled group.* The term "controlled group" is defined by paragraph (k) of this section.

(b) *Sales of export property.* Qualified export receipts of a DISC include gross receipts from the sale of export property by such DISC, or by any principal for whom such DISC acts as a commission agent (whether or not such principal is a related supplier), pursuant to the terms of a contract entered into with a purchaser by such DISC or by such principal at any time or by any other person and assigned to such DISC or such principal at any time prior to the shipment of such property to the purchaser. Any agreement, oral or written, which constitutes a contract at law, satisfies the contractual requirement of this paragraph. Gross receipts from the sale of export property, whenever received, do not constitute qualified export receipts unless the seller (or the corporation acting as commission agent for the seller) is a DISC at the time of the shipment of such property to the purchaser. For example, if a corporation which sells export property under the installment method is not a DISC for the taxable year in which the property is shipped to the purchaser, gross receipts from such sale do not constitute qualified export receipts for any taxable year of the corporation.

(c) *Leases of export property*—(1) *In general.* Qualified export receipts of a DISC include gross receipts from the lease of export property provided that—

(i) Such property is held by such DISC (or by a principal for whom such DISC acts as commission agent with respect to the lease) either as an owner or lessee at the beginning of the term of such lease, and

(ii) Such DISC qualified (or was treated) as a DISC for its taxable year in which the term of such lease began.

(2) *Prepayment of lease receipts.* If part or all of the gross receipts from a lease of property are prepaid, then—

(i) All such prepaid gross receipts are qualified export receipts of a DISC if it is reasonably expected at the time of such prepayment that throughout the term of such lease they would be qualified export receipts if received not as a prepayment; or

(ii) If it is reasonably expected at the time of such prepayment that throughout the term of such lease they would not be qualified export receipts if received not as a prepayment, then only those prepaid receipts, for the taxable years of the DISC for which they would be qualified export receipts, are qualified export receipts.

Thus, for example, if a lessee makes a prepayment of the first and last years' rent, and it is reasonably expected that the leased property will be export property for the first half of the lease period but not the second half of such period, the amount of the prepayment which represents the first year's rent will be considered qualified export receipts if it would otherwise qualify, whereas the amount of the prepayment which represents the last year's rent will not be considered qualified export receipts.

(d) *Related and subsidiary services*—(1) *In general.* Qualified export receipts of a DISC include gross receipts from services furnished by such DISC which are related and subsidiary to any sale or lease (as described in paragraph (b) or (c) of this section) of export property by such DISC or with respect to which such DISC acts as a commission agent, provided that such DISC derives qualified export receipts from such sale or lease. Such services may be performed within or without the United States.

(2) *Services furnished by DISC.* Services are considered to be furnished by a DISC for purposes of this paragraph if such services are provided by—

(i) The person who sold or leased the export property to which such services are related and subsidiary, provided that the DISC acts as a commission agent with respect to the sale or lease of such property and with respect to such services,

(ii) The DISC as principal, or any other person pursuant to a contract between such person and such DISC, provided the DISC acted as principal or commission agent with respect to the sale or lease of such property, or

(iii) A member of the same controlled group as the DISC where the sale or lease of the export property is made by another member of such controlled group provided, however, that the DISC act as principal or commission agent with respect to such sale or lease and as commission agent with respect to such services.

(3) *Related services.* A service is related to a sale or lease of export property if—

Reg. § 1.993-1(a)(7)

(i) Such service is of the type customarily and usually furnished with the type of transaction in the trade or business in which such sale or lease arose and

(ii) The contract to furnish such service—

(a) Is expressly provided for in or is provided for by implied warranty under the contract of sale or lease,

(b) Is entered into on or before the date which is 2 years after the date on which the contract under which such sale or lease was entered into, provided that the person described in subparagraph (2) of this paragraph which is to furnish such service delivers to the purchaser or lessor a written offer or option to furnish such services on or before the date on which the first shipment of goods with respect to which the service is to be performed is delivered, or

(c) Is a renewal of the services contract described in (a) or (b) of this subdivision. Services which may be related to a sale or lease of export property include but are not limited to warranty service, maintenance service, repair service, and installation service. Transportation (including insurance related to such transportation) may be related to a sale or lease of export property, provided that the cost of such transportation is included in the sale price or rental of the property or, if such cost is separately stated, is paid by the DISC (or its principal) which sold or leased the property to the person furnishing the transportation service. Financing or the obtaining of financing for a sale or lease is not a related service for purposes of this paragraph.

(4) *Subsidiary services*—(i) *In general.* Services related to a sale or lease of export property are subsidiary to such sale or lease only if it is reasonably expected at the time of such sale or lease that the gross receipts from all related services furnished by the DISC (as defined in subparagraphs (2) and (3) of this paragraph) will not exceed 50 percent of the sum of (a) the gross receipts from such sale or lease and (b) the gross receipts from related services furnished by the DISC (as described in subparagraph (2) of this paragraph). In the case of a sale, reasonable expectations at the time of the sale are based on the gross receipts from all related services which may reasonably be expected to be performed at any time before the end of the 10-year period following the date of such sale. In the case of a lease, reasonable expectations at the time of the lease are based on the gross receipts from all related services which may reasonably be expected to be performed at any time before the end of the term of such lease (determined without regard to renewal options).

(ii) *Allocation of gross receipts from services.* In determining whether the services related to a sale or lease of export property are subsidiary to such sale or lease, the gross receipts to be treated as derived from the furnishing of services may not be less than the amount of gross receipts reasonably allocated to such services as determined under the facts and circumstances of each case without regard to whether—

(a) Such services are furnished under a separate contract or under the same contract pursuant to which such sale or lease occurs or

(b) The cost of such services is specified in the contract of sale or lease.

(iii) *Transactions involving more than one item of export property.* If more than one item of export property is sold or leased in a single transaction pursuant to one contract, the total gross receipts from such transaction and the total gross receipts from all services related to such transaction are each taken into account in determining whether such services are subsidiary to such transaction. However, the provisions of this subdivision apply only if such items could be included in the same product line, as determined under § 1.994-1(c)(7).

(iv) *Renewed service contracts.* If under the terms of a contract for related services, such contract is renewable within 10 years after a sale of export property, or during the term of a lease of export property, related services to be performed under the renewed contract are subsidiary to such sale or lease if it is reasonably expected at the time of such renewal that the gross receipts from all related services which have been and which are to be furnished by the DISC (as described in subparagraph (2) of this paragraph) will not exceed 50 percent of the sum of (a) the gross receipts from such sale or lease and (b) the gross receipts from related services furnished by the DISC (as so described). Reasonable expectations are determined as provided in subdivision (i) of this subparagraph.

(v) *Parts used in services.* If a services contract described in subparagraph (3) of this paragraph provides for the furnishing of parts in connection with the furnishing of related services, gross receipts from the furnishing of such parts are not taken into account in determining whether under this subparagraph the services are subsidiary. See paragraph (b) or (c) of this section to determine whether the gross receipts from the furnishing of parts constitute qualified export receipts. See § 1.993-3(c)(2)(iv) and (e)(3) for rules regarding the treatment of such parts with respect to the manufacture of export property and the foreign content of such property, respectively.

Reg. § 1.993-1(d)(4)

(5) *Relation to leases.* If the gross receipts for services which are related and subsidiary to a lease of property have been prepaid at any time for all such services which are to be performed before the end of the term of such lease, then as of the time of the prepayment the rules in paragraph (c)(2) of this section (relating to prepayment of lease receipts) will determine whether prepaid services under this subdivision are qualified export receipts. Thus, for example, if it is reasonably expected that leased property will be export property for the first year of the term of the lease but will not be export property for the second year of the term, prepaid gross receipts for related and subsidiary services to be furnished in the first year may be qualified export receipts. However, any prepaid gross receipts for such services to be furnished in the second year cannot be qualified export receipts.

(6) *Relation with export property determination.* The determination as to whether gross receipts from the sale or lease of export property constitute qualified export receipts does not depend upon whether services connected with such sale or lease are related and subsidiary to such sale or lease. Thus, for example, assume that a DISC receives gross receipts of $1,000 from the sale of export property and gross receipts of $1,100 from installation and maintenance services which are to be furnished by such DISC within 10 years after the sale and which are related to such sale. The $1,100 which the DISC receives for such services would not be qualified export receipts since the gross receipts from the services exceed 50 percent of the sum of the gross receipts from the sale and the gross receipts from the related services furnished by such DISC. The $1,000 which the DISC receives from the sale of export property would, however, be a qualified export receipt if the sale met the requirements of paragraph (b) of this section.

(e) *Gains from sales of certain qualified export assets.* Qualified export receipts of a DISC include gross receipts from the sale by such DISC of any assets (wherever located) which, as of the date of such sale, are qualified export assets as defined in § 1.993-2 even though such assets are not export property (as defined in § 1.993-3). Gross receipts are derived from the sale of such assets only where such sale results in recognized gain (see § 1.993-6(a)). For purposes of this paragraph, losses from the sale of such qualified export assets shall not be taken into account for purposes of determining the DISC's qualified export receipts.

(f) *Dividends.* Qualified export receipts of a DISC for a taxable year include all dividends includible in the gross income of such DISC for such taxable year with respect to the stock of related foreign export corporations (as defined in § 1.993-5) and all amounts includible in the gross income of such DISC with respect to such corporations pursuant to section 951 (relating to amounts included in the gross income of U.S. shareholders of controlled foreign corporations).

(g) *Interest on obligations which are qualified export assets.* Qualified export receipts of a DISC include interest on any obligation which is a qualified export asset of such DISC, including any amount includible in gross income as interest (such as, for example, an amount treated as original issue discount pursuant to section 1232) or as imputed interest under section 483. Gain from the sale of obligations described in this paragraph is treated (to the extent such gain is not treated as interest on such obligations) as qualified export receipts pursuant to paragraph (e) of this section.

(h) *Engineering and architectural services*—(1) *In general.* Qualified export receipts of a DISC include gross receipts from engineering services (as described in subparagraph (5) of this paragraph) or architectural services (as described in subparagraph (6) of this paragraph) furnished by such DISC (as described in subparagraph (7) of this paragraph) for a construction project (as defined in subparagraph (8) of this paragraph) located, or proposed for location, outside the United States. Such services may be performed within or without the United States.

(2) *Services included.* Engineering and architectural services include feasibility studies for a proposed construction project whether or not such project is ultimately initiated.

(3) *Excluded services.* Engineering and architectural services do not include—

(i) Services connected with the exploration for minerals or

(ii) Technical assistance or know-how.

For purposes of this paragraph, the term "technical assistance or know-how" includes activities or programs designed to enable business, commerce, industrial establishments, and governmental organizations to acquire or use scientific, architectural, or engineering information.

(4) *Other services.* Receipts from the performance of construction activities other than engineering and architectural services constitute qualified export receipts to the extent that such activities are related and subsidiary services (within the meaning of paragraph (d) of this section) with respect to a sale or lease of export property.

(5) *Engineering services.* For purposes of this paragraph, engineering services in connection

Reg. § 1.993-1(d)(5)

with any construction project (within the meaning of subparagraph (8) of this paragraph) include any professional services requiring engineering education, training, and experience and the application of special knowledge of the mathematical, physical, or engineering sciences to such professional services as consultation, investigation, evaluation, planning, design, or responsible supervision of construction for the purpose of assuring compliance with plans, specifications, and design.

(6) *Architectural services.* For purposes of this paragraph, architectural services include the offering or furnishing of any professional services such as consultation, planning, aesthetic, and structural design, drawings and specifications, or responsible supervision of construction (for the purpose of assuring compliance with plans, specifications, and design) or erection, in connection with any construction project (within the meaning of subparagraph (8) of this paragraph).

(7) *Definition of "furnished by such DISC".* For purposes of this paragraph, architectural and engineering services are considered furnished by a DISC if such services are provided—

(i) By the DISC,

(ii) By another person (whether or not a United States person) pursuant to a contract entered into by such person with the DISC at any time prior to the furnishing of such services, provided that the DISC acts as principal with respect to the furnishing of such services, or

(iii) By another person (whether or not a United States person) pursuant to a contract for the furnishing of such services entered into at any time prior to the furnishing of such services provided that the DISC acts as commission agent with respect to such services.

(8) *Definition of "construction project".* For purposes of this paragraph, the term "construction project" includes the erection, expansion, or repair (but not including minor remodeling or minor repairs) of new or existing buildings or other physical facilities including, for example, roads, dams, canals, bridges, tunnels, railroad tracks, and pipelines. The term also includes site grading and improvement and installation of equipment necessary for the construction. Gross receipts from the sale or lease of construction equipment are not qualified export receipts unless such equipment is export property (as defined in § 1.993-3).

(i) *Managerial services*—(1) *In general.* Qualified export receipts of a first DISC for its taxable year include gross receipts from the furnishing of managerial services provided for another DISC, which is not a related person, to aid such unrelated DISC in deriving qualified export receipts, provided that at least 50 percent of the gross receipts of the first DISC for such year consists of qualified export receipts derived from the sale or lease of export property and the furnishing of related and subsidiary services, as described in paragraphs (b), (c), and (d) of this section, respectively. For purposes of this paragraph, managerial services are considered furnished by a DISC if such services are provided—

(i) By the first DISC,

(ii) By another person (whether or not a United States person) pursuant to a contract entered into by such person with the first DISC at any time prior to the furnishing of such services, provided that the first DISC acts as principal with respect to the furnishing of such services, or

(iii) By another person (whether or not a United States person) pursuant to a contract for the furnishing of such services entered into at any time prior to the furnishing of such services provided that the DISC acts as commission agent with respect to such services.

(2) *Definition of "managerial services".* The term "managerial services" as used in this paragraph means activities relating to the operation of another unrelated DISC which derives qualified export receipts from the sale or lease of export property and from the furnishing of services related and subsidiary to such sales or leases. Such term includes staffing and operational services necessary to operate such other DISC, but does not include legal, accounting, scientific, or technical services. Examples of managerial services are: (i) Export market studies, (ii) making shipping arrangements, and (iii) contacting potential foreign purchasers.

(3) *Status of recipient of managerial services*—(i) *In general.* Qualified export receipts of a first DISC include receipts from the furnishing of managerial services during any taxable year of a recipient if such recipient qualifies as a DISC (within the meaning of § 1.992-1(a)) for such taxable year.

(ii) *Recipient deemed to qualify as a DISC.* For purposes of subdivision (i) of this subparagraph, a recipient is deemed to qualify as a DISC for its taxable year if the first DISC obtains from such recipient a copy of such recipient's election to be treated as a DISC as described in § 1.992-2(a) together with such recipient's sworn statement that such election has been filed with the Internal Revenue Service Center. The recipient may mark out the names of its shareholders on a copy of its election to be treated as a DISC before submitting it to the first DISC. The copy of the election and the sworn statement of such

Reg. § 1.993-1(i)(3)

recipient must be received by the first DISC within 6 months after the beginning of the first taxable year of the recipient during which such first DISC furnishes managerial services for such recipient. The copy of the election and the sworn statement of the recipient need not be obtained by the first DISC for subsequent taxable years of the recipient.

(iii) *Recipient not treated as a DISC.* For purposes of subdivision (i) of this subparagraph, a recipient of managerial services is not treated as a DISC with respect to such services performed during a taxable year for which such recipient does not qualify as a DISC if the DISC performing such services does not believe or if a reasonable person would not believe (taking into account the furnishing DISC's managerial relationship with such recipient DISC) at the beginning of such taxable year that the recipient will qualify as a DISC for such taxable year.

(j) *Excluded receipts*—(1) *In general.* Notwithstanding the provisions of paragraphs (b) through (i) of this section, qualified export receipts of a DISC do not include any of the five amounts described in subparagraphs (2) through (6) of this paragraph.

(2) *Sales and leases of property for ultimate use in the United States.* Property which is sold or leased for ultimate use in the United States does not constitute export property (relating to determination of where the ultimate use of the property occurs). See § 1.993-3(d)(4). Thus, qualified export receipts of a DISC described in paragraph (b) or (c) of this section do not include gross receipts of the DISC from the sale or lease of such property.

(3) *Sales of export property accomplished by subsidy.* Qualified export receipts of a DISC do not include gross receipts described in paragraph (b) of this section if the sale of export property (whether or not such property consists of agricultural products) is pursuant to any of the following:

(i) The development loan program, or grants under the technical cooperation and development grants program of the Agency for International Development, or grants under the military assistance program administered by the Department of Defense, pursuant to the Foreign Assistance Act of 1961, as amended (22 U.S.C. 2151), unless the DISC shows to the satisfaction of the district director that, under the conditions existing at the time of the sale, the purchaser had a reasonable opportunity to purchase, on competitive terms and from a seller who was not a U.S. person, goods which were substantially identical to such property and which were not manufactured, produced, grown, or extracted (as described in § 1.993-3(c)) in the United States,

(ii) The Public Law 480 program authorized under Title I of the Agricultural Trade Development and Assistance Act of 1954, as amended (7 U.S.C. 1691, 1701-1710).

(iii) For taxable years ending before January 1, 1974, the Barter program of the Commodity Credit Corporation authorized by section 4(h) of the Commodity Credit Corporation Charter Act, as amended (15 U.S.C. 714b(h)), and section 303 of the Agricultural Trade Development and Assistance Act of 1954, as amended (7 U.S.C. 1692) but only if the taxpayer treats such sales as sales giving rise to excluded receipts,

(iv) The Export Payment Program of the Commodity Credit Corporation authorized by sections 5(d) and (f) of the Commodity Credit Corporation Charter Act, as amended (15 U.S.C. 714c(d) and (f)),

(v) The section 32 export payment programs authorized by section 32 of the Act of August 24, 1935, as amended (7 U.S.C. 612c), and

(vi) For taxable years beginning after November 3, 1972, the Export Sales program of the Commodity Credit Corporation authorized by sections 5(d) and (f) of the Commodity Credit Corporation Charter Act, as amended (15 U.S.C. 714c(d) and (f)), other than the GSM-4 program provided under 7 CFR 1488, and section 407 of the Agricultural Act of 1949, as amended (7 U.S.C. 1427), for the purpose of disposing of surplus agricultural commodities and exporting or causing to be exported agricultural commodities, except that for taxable years beginning on or before November 3, 1972, the taxpayer may treat such sales as sales giving rise to excluded receipts.

(4) *Sales or leases of export property and furnishing of engineering or architectural services for use by the United States*—(i) *In general.* Qualified export receipts of a DISC do not include gross receipts described in paragraph (b), (c), or (h) of this section if a sale or lease of export property, or the furnishing of engineering or architectural services, is for use by the United States or an instrumentality thereof in any case in which any law or regulation requires in any manner the purchase or lease of property manufactured, produced, grown, or extracted in the United States or requires the use of engineering or architectural services performed by a U.S. person. For example, a sale by a DISC of export property to the Department of Defense for use outside the United States would not produce qualified export receipts for such DISC if the Department of Defense purchased such property from appropriated funds subject to any provisions of the Armed

Forces Procurement Regulations (32 CFR Subchapter A, Part 6, Subpart A) or any appropriations act for the Department of Defense for the applicable year which restricts the availability of such appropriated funds to the procurement of items which are grown, reprocessed, reused, or produced in the United States.

(ii) *Direct or indirect sales or leases.* Any sale or lease of export property is for use by the United States or an instrumentality thereof if such property is sold or leased by a DISC (or by a principal for whom such DISC acts as commission agent) to—

(a) A person who is a related person with respect to such DISC or such principal and who sells or leases such property for use by the United States or an instrumentality thereof or

(b) A person who is not a related person with respect to such DISC or such principal if, at the time of such sale or lease, there is an agreement or understanding that such property will be sold or leased for use by the United States or an instrumentality thereof (or if a reasonable person would have known at the time of such sale or lease that such property would be sold or leased for use by the United States or an instrumentality thereof) within 3 years after such sale or lease.

(iii) *Excluded programs.* The provisions of subdivisions (i) and (ii) of this subparagraph do not apply in the case of a purchase by the United States or an instrumentality thereof if such purchase is pursuant to—

(a) The Foreign Military Sales Act, as amended (22 U.S.C. § 2751 et seq.), or a program under which the U.S. Government purchases property for resale, on commercial terms, to a foreign government or agency or instrumentality thereof, or

(b) A program (whether bilateral or multi-lateral) under which sales to the U.S. Government are open to international competitive bidding.

(5) *Services.* Qualified export receipts of a DISC do not include gross receipts described in paragraph (d) of this section (concerning related and subsidiary services) if the services from which such gross receipts are derived are related and subsidiary to the sale or lease of property which results in excluded receipts pursuant to this paragraph.

(6) *Receipts within controlled group*—(i) *In general.* Gross receipts of a corporation do not constitute qualified export receipts for any taxable year of such corporation if—

(a) At the time of the sale, lease, or other transaction resulting in such gross receipts, such corporation and the person from whom such receipts are directly or indirectly derived (whether or not such corporation and such person are the same person) are members of the same controlled group (as defined in paragraph (k) of this section) and

(b) Such corporation and such person each qualifies (or is treated under section 992(a)(2)) as a DISC for its taxable year in which its receipts arise.

Thus, for example, assume that R, S, X, and Y are members of the same controlled group and that X and Y are DISC's. If R sells property to S and pays X a commission relating to that sale and if S sells the same property to an unrelated foreign party and pays Y a commission relating to that sale, the receipts received by X from the sale of such property by R to S will be considered to be derived from Y, a DISC which is a member of the same controlled group as X, and thus will not result in qualified export receipts to X. The receipts received by Y from the sale to an unrelated foreign party may, however, result in qualified export receipts to Y. For another example, if R and S both assign the commissions to X, receipts derived from the sale from R to S will be considered to be derived from X acting as commission agent for S and will not result in qualified export receipts to X. Receipts derived by X from the sale of property by S to an unrelated foreign party, may, however, constitute qualified export receipts.

(ii) *Leased property.* See § 1.993-3(f)(2) regarding property not constituting export property in certain cases where such property is leased to any corporation which is a member of the same controlled group as the lessor.

(k) *Definition of "controlled group."* For purposes of sections 991 through 996 and the regulations thereunder, the term "controlled group" has the same meaning as is assigned to the term "controlled group of corporations" by section 1563(a), except that (1) the phrase "more than 50 percent" is substituted for the phrase "at least 80 percent" each place the latter phrase appears in section 1563(a), and (2) section 1563(b) shall not apply. Thus, for example, a foreign corporation subject to tax under section 881 may be a member of a controlled group. Furthermore, two or more corporations (including a foreign corporation) are members of a controlled group at any time such corporations meet the requirements of section 1563(a) (as modified by this paragraph).

(l) *DISC's entitlement to income*—(1) *Application of section 994.* A corporation which meets the requirements of § 1.992-1(a) to be treated as a DISC for a taxable year is entitled to income, and

Reg. § 1.993-1(l)(1)

the intercompany pricing rules of section 994(a)(1) or (2) apply, in the case of any transactions described in § 1.994-1(b) between such DISC and its related supplier (as defined in § 1.994-1(a)(3)). For purposes of this subparagraph, such DISC need not have employees or perform any specific function.

(2) *Other transactions.* In the case of a transaction to which the provisions of subparagraph (1) of this paragraph do not apply but from which a DISC derives gross receipts, the income to which the DISC is entitled as a result of the transaction is determined pursuant to the terms of the contract for such transaction and, if applicable, section 482 and the regulations thereunder.

(3) *Examples.* The provisions of this paragraph may be illustrated by the following examples:

Example (1). P Corporation forms S Corporation as a wholly-owned subsidiary. S qualifies as a DISC for its taxable year. S has no employees on its payroll. S is granted a franchise with respect to specified exports of P. P will sell such exports to S for resale by S. Such exports are of a type which produce qualified export receipts as defined in paragraph (b) of this section. P's sales force will solicit orders in the name of S using S's order forms. S places orders with P only when S itself has received orders. No inventory is maintained by S. P makes shipments directly to customers of S. Employees of P will act for S and billings and collections will be handled by P in the name of S. Under these facts, the income derived by S for such taxable year from the purchase and resale of the specified export is treated for Federal income tax purposes as the income of S, and the amount of income allocable to S will be determined under section 994 of the Code.

Example (2). P Corporation forms S Corporation as a wholly-owned subsidiary. S qualifies as a DISC for its taxable year. S has no employees on its payroll. S is granted a sales franchise with respect to specified exports of P and will receive commissions with respect to such exports. Such exports are of a type which will produce gross receipts for S which are qualified export receipts as defined in paragraph (b) of this section. P's sales force will solicit orders in the name of P. Billings and collections are handled directly by P. Under these facts, the commissions paid to S for such taxable year with respect to the specified exports shall be treated for Federal income tax purposes as the income of S, and the amount of income allocable to S is determined under section 994 of the Code. [Reg. § 1.993-1.]

☐ [T.D. 7514, 10-14-77. Amended by T.D. 7854, 11-15-82.]

[Reg. § 1.993-2]

§ 1.993-2. **Definition of qualified export assets.**—(a) *In general.* For a corporation to qualify as a DISC, at the close of its taxable year it must have qualified export assets with adjusted bases equal to at least 95 percent of the sum of the adjusted bases of all its assets. An asset which is a qualified export asset under more than one paragraph of this section shall be taken into account only once in determining the sum of the adjusted bases of all qualified export assets. Under section 993(b), the qualified export assets held by a corporation are—

(1) Export property as defined in § 1.993-3 (see paragraph (b) of this section),

(2) Business assets described in paragraph (c) of this section,

(3) Trade receivables described in paragraph (d) of this section,

(4) Temporary investments to the extent described in paragraph (e) of this section,

(5) Producer's loans as defined in § 1.993-4 (see paragraph (f) of this section),

(6) Stock or securities (described in paragraph (g) of this section) of related foreign export corporations as defined in § 1.993-5,

(7) Export-Import Bank and other obligations described in paragraph (h) of this section,

(8) Financing obligations described in paragraph (i) of this section, and

(9) Funds awaiting investment described in paragraph (j) of this section.

(b) *Export property.* In general, export property is certain property held for sale or lease which meets the requirements of § 1.993-3.

(c) *Business assets.* For purposes of this section, business assets are assets used by a DISC (other than as a lessor) primarily in connection with—

(1) The sale, lease, storage, handling, transportation, packaging, assembly, or servicing of export property, or

(2) The performance of engineering or architectural services (described in § 1.993-1(h)) or managerial services (described in § 1.993-1(i)) in furtherance of the production of qualified export receipts.

Assets used primarily in the manufacture, production, growth, or extraction (within the meaning of § 1.993-3(c)) of property are not business assets.

(d) *Trade receivables*—(1) *In general.* For purposes of this section, trade receivables are accounts receivable and evidences of indebtedness which arise by reason of transactions of such corporation or of another corporation which is a DISC and which is a member of a controlled group which includes such corporation described in subparagraph (A), (B), (C), (D), (G), or (H), of section 993(a)(1) and which are due the DISC (or, if it acts as an agent, due its principal) and held by the DISC.

(2) *Trade receivables representing commissions.* If a DISC acts as commission agent for a principal in a transaction described in § 1.993-1(b), (c), (d), (e), (h), or (i) which results in qualified export receipts for the DISC, and if an account receivable or evidence of indebtedness held by the DISC and representing the commission payable to the DISC as a result of the transaction arises (and, in the case of an evidence of indebtedness, designated on its face as representing such commission), such account receivable or evidence of indebtedness shall be treated as a trade receivable. If, however, the principal is a related supplier (as defined in § 1.994-1(a)(3)) with respect to the DISC, such account receivable or evidence or indebtedness will not be treated as a trade receivable unless it is payable and paid in a time and manner which satisfy the requirements of § 1.994-1(e)(3) or (5) (relating to initial payment of transfer price or commission and procedure for adjustments to transfer price or commission, respectively), as the case may be. However, see subparagraph (3) of this paragraph for rules regarding certain accounts receivable representing commissions payable to a DISC by its related supplier.

(3) *Indebtedness arising under § 1.994-1(e).* An indebtedness arising under § 1.994-1(e)(3)(iii) (relating to initial payment of transfer price of commission) in favor of a DISC is not a qualified export asset. An indebtedness arising under § 1.994-1(e)(5)(i) (relating to procedure for adjustments to transfer price or commission) in favor of a DISC is a trade receivable if it is paid in the time and manner described in § 1.994-1(e)(5)(i) and (ii) and if it otherwise satisfies the requirements of subparagraph (2) of this paragraph. If such an indebtedness is not paid in the time and manner described in § 1.994-1(e)(5)(i) and (ii), it is not a qualified export asset.

(e) *Temporary investments*—(1) *In general.* For purposes of this section, temporary investments are money, bank deposits (not including time deposits of more than 1 year), and other similar temporary investments to the extent maintained by a DISC as reasonably necessary to meet its requirements for working capital. For purposes of this paragraph, a temporary investment is an obligation, including an evidence of indebtedness as defined in paragraph (d)(1) of this section, which is a demand obligation or has a period remaining to maturity of not more than 1 year at the date it is acquired by the DISC. A temporary investment does not include trade receivables.

(2) *Determination of amount of working capital maintained.* For purposes of this paragraph—

(i) The working capital of a DISC is the excess of its current assets over current liabilities,

(ii) Current assets are cash and other assets (other than trade receivables) which may reasonably be expected to be converted into cash or sold or consumed during the current normal operating cycle of the DISC's trade or business,

(iii) Current liabilities are obligations (or portions of obligations) due within the current normal operating cycle of the trade or business of the DISC whose satisfaction when due is reasonably expected to require the use of current assets,

(iv) Generally accepted financial accounting treatments will be accepted, and

(v) Current assets (other than temporary investments) are taken into account before temporary investments, and trade receivables are never taken into account, in determining whether such temporary investments are maintained by the DISC as reasonably necessary to meet its current liabilities and its requirements for working capital.

(3) *Determination of amount of working capital reasonably required.* For purposes of this paragraph, a determination of the amount of money, bank deposits, and other similar temporary investments reasonably necessary to meet the requirements of the DISC for working capital will depend upon the nature and volume of the activities of the DISC existing at the end of the DISC's taxable year for which such determination is made, such as, for example—

(i) In the case of a DISC which purchases and sells inventory, the amount of working capital reasonably required is limited to an amount reasonably necessary to meet the ordinary operating expenses during the current normal operating cycle of the trade or business of the DISC, an amount reasonably needed to meet specific and definite plans for expansion and any amounts necessary for reasonably anticipated extraordinary business expenses.

(ii) In the case of a DISC which actively conducts a trade or business (including the employment of a sales force) and receives commissions in respect of goods to which such DISC does not have title, the amount of working capital required will depend upon the nature and volume of the activities of the DISC which produce such income as they exist on the applicable determination date. In determining the amount of working

Reg. § 1.993-2(e)(3)

capital which is reasonably required for the production of such income, the anticipated future needs of the business will be taken into account to the extent that such needs relate to the year of the DISC following the applicable determination date. Anticipated future needs relating to a later period will not be taken into account unless it is clearly established that such needs are reasonably related to the production of such income as of the applicable determination date.

(iii) In the case of a DISC which does not actively conduct a trade or business, and which receives commissions solely by reason of section 994(a)(1), (a)(2), or (b) with respect to goods to which such DISC does not have title, no working capital would be required beyond a *de minimis* amount unless it appears from the facts and circumstances that additional working capital will be required.

(iv) In the case of a DISC deriving income from the leasing of property, the amount of working capital required will be determined on the basis of the facts and circumstances in such case.

(4) *Relationship of working capital to other qualified export assets.* If a temporary investment is a qualified export asset under any provisions of this section (other than this paragraph), this paragraph shall not affect its status as a qualified export asset. However, any such temporary investment is taken into account before other temporary investments in determining whether such other temporary investments are maintained by a DISC as reasonably necessary to meet its requirements for working capital. Current assets (other than temporary investments) are taken into account before temporary investments, and trade receivables are never taken into account, in determining whether such temporary investments are maintained by the DISC as reasonably necessary requirements for working capital. An obligation issued or incurred by a member of a controlled group (as defined in § 1.993-1(k)) of which the DISC is a member is not a qualified export asset under this paragraph. For rules regarding working capital as of the end of each month of a taxable year for purposes of the 70-percent reasonableness standard with respect to certain deficiency distributions, see paragraph (j)(3) of this section.

(f) *Producer's loans.* For purposes of this section, a producer's loan is an evidence of indebtedness arising in connection with producer's loans which are made by a DISC and which meet the requirements of § 1.993-4. If a producer's loan is a qualified export asset, interest accrued with respect to the producer's loan will also be treated as a qualified export asset provided that payment is made in the form of money, property (valued at its fair market value on its date of transfer and including accounts receivable for sales by or through a DISC), a written obligation which qualifies as a debt under the safe harbor rule of § 1.992-1(d)(2)(ii), or an accounting entry offsetting the account receivable against an existing debt owed by the person in whose favor the account receivable was established to the person with whom it engaged in the transaction and that payment is made no later than 60 days following the close of the taxable year of accrual of the interest. This paragraph (f) is effective for taxable years beginning after January 10, 1985 except that the taxpayer may at its option apply the provisions of this paragraph to taxable years ending after December 31, 1971.

(g) *Stock or securities of related foreign export corporations.* For purposes of this section, the term "stock or securities", with respect to a related foreign export corporation (as defined in § 1.993-5), has the same meaning of such term has as used in section 351 (relating to transfers to controlled corporations), except that the term "securities" does not include obligations which are repaid, in whole or in part, at any time during the taxable year of the DISC following the taxable year of the DISC during which such obligations were acquired by the DISC or were issued, unless the DISC demonstrates to the satisfaction of the district director that the repayment was for bona fide business purposes and not for the purpose of avoidance of Federal income taxes.

(h) *Export-Import Bank obligations.* For purposes of this section, the term "Export-Import Bank obligations" means obligations issued, guaranteed, insured, or reinsured (in whole or in part) by the Export-Import Bank of the United States or by the Foreign Credit Insurance Association, but only if such obligations are acquired by the DISC—

(1) From the Export-Import Bank of the United States,

(2) From the Foreign Credit Insurance Association, or

(3) From the person selling or purchasing the goods or services by reason of which such obligations arose, or from any corporation which is a member of the same controlled group (as defined in § 1.993-1(k)) as such person.

For purposes of this paragraph, obligations issued by a person described in subparagraphs (1), (2), and (3) of this paragraph are treated as acquired from such person by the DISC if acquired from any person not more than 90 days after the date of original issue (as defined in § 1.1232-3(b)(3)). Examples of specific types of Export-Import Bank

Reg. § 1.993-2(e)(4)

obligations include debentures issued by such bank and certificates of loan participation.

(i) *Financing obligations.* For purposes of this section, financing obligations are obligations (held by a DISC) of a domestic corporation organized solely for the purpose of financing sales of export property pursuant to an agreement with the Export-Import Bank of the United States under which such corporation makes export loans guaranteed by such Bank.

(j) *Funds awaiting investment* —(1) *In general.* For purposes of this section, subject to the limitation described in subparagraph (2) of this paragraph, if, at the close of a DISC's taxable year, the sum of the DISC's money, bank deposits, and other similar temporary investments is determined under paragraph (e) of this section to exceed an amount reasonably necessary to meet the DISC's requirements for working capital, the amount of the DISC's bank deposits in the United States to the extent of the amount of this excess are funds awaiting investments at the close of such taxable year.

(2) *Limitation.* Bank deposits described in subparagraph (1) of this paragraph are funds awaiting investment only if, by the last day of each of the sixth, seventh, and eighth months after the close of such taxable year, the sum of the adjusted bases of the qualified export assets of the DISC (other than such bank deposits) equals or exceeds 95 percent of the sum of the adjusted bases of all assets of the DISC (including such bank deposits) it held on the last day of such taxable year. For purposes of this subparagraph, the adjusted bases of assets of a DISC are determined as of the end of each of the months referred to in this subparagraph. Funds awaiting investment as described in this paragraph need not be traceable to any of the qualified export assets held by the DISC at the end of any of the months referred to in this subparagraph.

(3) *Coordination with certain deficiency distribution provisions.* Under section 992(c)(3) and § 1.992-3(d), a deficiency distribution made on or before the 15th day of the ninth month after the end of a corporation's taxable year is deemed to be for reasonable cause if certain requirements are met, including the requirement (described in section 992(c)(3)(B) and § 1.992-3(d)(2)) that the sum of the adjusted bases of the qualified export assets held by the corporation on the last day of each month of such year equals or exceeds 70 percent of the sum of the adjusted bases of all assets held by the corporation on each such last day. If, on any such last day, the sum of a DISC's money, bank deposits, and other similar temporary investments is determined under paragraph (e) of this section to exceed an amount reasonably necessary to meet the DISC's requirements for working capital, the amount of the DISC's bank deposits to the extent of the amount of this excess are funds awaiting investment on such last day, if either—

(i) The requirements of subparagraph (2) of this paragraph are satisfied with respect to the taxable year of the DISC which includes such month or

(ii) At the close of such taxable year the sum of the DISC's money, bank deposits, and other similar temporary investments is determined under paragraph (e) of this section not to exceed an amount reasonably necessary to meet the DISC's requirements for working capital. [Reg. § 1.993-2.]

☐ [T.D. 7514, 10-14-77. Amended by T.D. 7854, 11-15-82 and T.D. 7984, 10-11-84.]

[Reg. § 1.993-3]

§ 1.993-3. **Definition of export property.**—(a) *General rule.* Under section 993(c), except as otherwise provided with respect to excluded property in paragraph (f) of this section and with respect to certain short supply property in paragraph (i) of this section, export property is property in the hands of any person (whether or not a DISC)—

(1) Manufactured, produced, grown, or extracted in the United States by any person or persons other than a DISC (see paragraph (c) of this section),

(2) Held primarily for sale or lease in the ordinary course of a trade or business to any person for direct use, consumption, or disposition outside the United States (see paragraph (d) of this section),

(3) Not more than 50 percent of the fair market value of which is attributable to articles imported into the United States (see paragraph (e) of this section), and

(4) Which is not sold or leased by a DISC, or with a DISC as commission agent, to another DISC which is a member of the same controlled group (as defined in § 1.993-1(k)) as the DISC.

(b) *Services.* For purposes of this section, services (including the written communication of services in any form) are not export property. Whether an item is property or services shall be determined on the basis of the facts and circumstances attending the development and disposition of the item. Thus, for example, the preparation of a map of a particular construction site would constitute services and not export property, but standard maps prepared for sale to customers generally would not constitute services

Reg. § 1.993-3(b)

and would be export property if the requirements of this section were otherwise met.

(c) *Manufacture, production, growth, or extraction of property*—(1) *By a person other than a DISC.* Export property may be manufactured, produced, grown, or extracted in the United States by any person, provided that such person does not qualify (and is not treated) as a DISC. Property held by a DISC which was manufactured, produced, grown, or extracted by it at a time when it did not qualify (and was not treated) as a DISC is not export property of the DISC. Property which sustains further manufacture or production outside the United States prior to sale or lease by a person but after manufacture or production in the United States will not be considered as manufactured, produced, grown, or extracted in the United States by such person.

(2) *Manufactured or produced*—(i) *In general.* For purposes of this section, property which is sold or leased by a person is considered to be manufactured or produced by such person if such property is manufactured or produced (within the meaning of either subdivision (ii), (iii), or (iv) of this subparagraph) by such person or by another person pursuant to a contract with such person. Except as provided in subdivision (iv) of this subparagraph, manufacture or production of property does not include assembly or packaging operations with respect to property.

(ii) *Substantial transformation.* Property is manufactured or produced by a person if such property is substantially transformed by such person. Examples of substantial transformation of property would include the conversion of woodpulp to paper, steel rods to screws and bolts, and the canning of fish.

(iii) *Operations generally considered to constitute manufacturing.* Property is manufactured or produced by a person if the operations performed by such person in connection with such property are substantial in nature and are generally considered to constitute the manufacture or production of property.

(iv) *Value added to property.* Property is manufactured or produced by a person if with respect to such property conversion costs (direct labor and factory burden including packaging or assembly) of such person account for 20 percent or more of—

(a) The cost of goods sold or inventory amount of such person for such property if such property is sold or held for sale, or

(b) The adjusted basis of such person for such property, as determined in accordance with the provisions of section 1011, if such property is held for lease or leased.

The value of parts provided pursuant to a services contract, as described in § 1.993-1(d)(4)(v), is not taken into account in applying this subdivision.

(d) *Primary purpose for which property is held*—(1) *In general*—(i) *General rule.* Under paragraph (a)(2) of this section, export property (a) must be held primarily for the purpose of sale or lease in the ordinary course of a trade or business to a DISC, or to any other person, and (b) such sale or lease must be for direct use, consumption, or disposition outside the United States. Thus, property cannot qualify as export property unless it is sold or leased for direct use, consumption, or disposition outside the United States. Property is sold or leased for direct use, consumption, or disposition outside the United States if such sale or lease satisfies the destination test described in subparagraph (2) of this paragraph, the proof of compliance requirements described in subparagraph (3) of this paragraph, and the use-outside-the-United States test described in subparagraph (4) of this paragraph.

(ii) *Factors not taken into account.* In determining whether property which is sold or leased to a DISC is sold or leased for direct use, consumption, or disposition outside the United States, the fact that the acquiring DISC holds the property in inventory or for lease prior to the time it sells or leases it for direct use, consumption, or disposition outside the United States will not affect the characterization of the property as export property. Export property need not be physically segregated from other property.

(2) *Destination test.* (i) For purposes of subparagraph (1) of this paragraph, the destination test in this subparagraph is satisfied with respect to property sold or leased by a seller or lessor only if it is delivered by such seller or lessor (or an agent of such seller or lessor) regardless of the F.O.B. point or the place at which title passes or risk of loss shifts from the seller or lessor—

(a) Within the United States to a carrier or freight forwarder for ultimate delivery outside the United States to a purchaser or lessee (or to a subsequent purchaser or sublessee),

(b) Within the United States to a purchaser or lessee, if such property is ultimately delivered, directly used, or directly consumed outside the United States (including delivery to a carrier or freight forwarder for delivery outside the United States) by the purchaser or lessee (or a subsequent purchaser or sublessee) within 1 year after such sale or lease,

(c) Within or outside the United States to a purchaser or lessee which, at the time of the sale or lease, is a DISC and is not a member of the

Reg. § 1.993-3(c)(1)

same controlled group (as defined in § 1.993-1(k)) as the seller or lessor,

(d) From the United States to the purchaser or lessee (or a subsequent purchaser or sublessee) at a point outside the United States by means of a ship, aircraft, or other delivery vehicle, owned, leased, or chartered by the seller or lessor,

(e) Outside the United States to a purchaser or lessee from a warehouse, a storage facility, or assembly site located outside the United States, if such property was previously shipped by such seller or lessor from the United States, or

(f) Outside the United States to a purchaser or lessee if such property was previously shipped by such seller or lessor from the United States and if such property is located outside the United States pursuant to a prior lease by the seller or lessor, and either

(1) Such prior lease terminated at the expiration of its term (or by the action of the prior lessee acting alone),

(2) The sale occurred or the term of the subsequent lease began after the time at which the term of the prior lease would have expired, or

(3) The lessee under the subsequent lease is not a related person (as defined in § 1.993-1(a)(6)) with respect to the lessor and the prior lease was terminated by the action of the lessor (acting alone or together with the lessee).

(ii) For purposes of this subparagraph (other than (c) and (f) (3) of subdivision (i) thereof), any relationship between the seller or lessor and any purchaser, subsequent purchaser, lessee, or sublessee is immaterial.

(iii) In no event is the destination test of this subparagraph satisfied with respect to property which is subject to any use (other than a resale or sublease), manufacture, assembly, or other processing (other than packaging) by any person between the time of the sale or lease by such seller or lessor and the delivery or ultimate delivery outside the United States described in this subparagraph.

(iv) If property is located outside the United States at the time it is purchased by a person or leased by a person as lessee, such property may be export property in the hands of such purchaser or lessee only if it is imported into the United States prior to its further sale or lease (including a sublease) outside the United States. Paragraphs (a)(3) and (e) of this section (relating to 50 percent foreign content test) are applicable in determining whether such property is export property. Thus, for example, if such property is not subjected to manufacturing or production (as defined in paragraph (c) of this section) within the United States after such importation, it does not qualify as export property.

(3) *Proof of compliance with destination test*—(i) *Delivery outside the United States*. For purposes of subparagraph (2) of this paragraph (other than subdivision (i)(c) thereof), a seller or lessor shall establish ultimate delivery, use, or consumption of property outside the United States by providing—

(a) A facsimile or carbon copy of the export bill of lading issued by the carrier who delivers the property,

(b) A certificate of an agent or representative of the carrier disclosing delivery of the property outside the United States,

(c) A facsimile or carbon copy of the certificate of lading for the property executed by a customs officer of the country to which the property is delivered,

(d) If such contract has no customs administration, a written statement by the person to whom delivery outside the United States was made,

(e) A facsimile or carbon copy of the shipper's export declaration, a monthly shipper's summary declaration filed with the Bureau of Customs, or a magnetic tape filed in lieu of the Shipper's Export Declaration, covering the property, or

(f) Any other proof (including evidence as to the nature of the property or the nature of the transaction) which establishes to the satisfaction of the Commissioner that the property was ultimately delivered, or directly sold, or directly consumed outside the United States within 1 year after the sale or lease.

(ii) The requirements of subdivision (i) (a), (b), (c), or (e) of this subparagraph will be considered satisfied even though the name of the ultimate consignee and the price paid for the goods is marked out provided that, in the case of a Shipper's Export Declaration or other document listed in such subdivision (e) or a document such as an export bill of lading such document still indicates the country in which delivery to the ultimate consignee is to be made and, in the case of a certificate of an agent or representative of the carrier, that such document indicates that the property was delivered outside the United States.

(iii) A seller or lessor shall also establish the meeting of the requirement of subparagraph (2)(i) of this paragraph (other than subdivision (c) thereof), that the property was delivered outside the United States without further use, manufac-

Reg. § 1.993-3(d)(3)

ture, assembly, or other processing within the United States.

(iv) *Sale or lease to an unrelated DISC.* For purposes of subparagraph (2)(i)(c) of this paragraph, a purchaser or lessee of property is deemed to qualify as a DISC for its taxable year if the seller or lessor obtains from such purchaser or lessee a copy of such purchaser's or lessee's election to be treated as a DISC as described in § 1.992-2(a) together with such purchaser's or lessee's sworn statement that such election has been filed with the Internal Revenue Service Center. The copy of the election and the sworn statement of such purchaser or lessee must be received by the seller or lessor within 6 months after the sale or lease. A purchaser or lessee is not treated as a DISC with respect to a sale or lease during a taxable year for which such purchaser or lessee does not qualify as a DISC if the seller or lessor does not believe or if a reasonable person would not believe at the time such sale or lease is made that the purchaser or lessee will qualify as a DISC for such taxable year.

(v) *Failure of proof.* If a seller or lessor fails to provide proof of compliance with the destination test as required by this subparagraph, the property sold or leased is not export property.

(4) *Sales and leases of property for ultimate use in the United States*—(i) *In general.* For purposes of subparagraph (1) of this paragraph, the use test in this subparagraph is satisfied with respect to property which—

(a) Under subdivisions (ii) through (iv) of this subparagraph is not sold for ultimate use in the United States or

(b) Under subdivision (v) of this subparagraph is leased for ultimate use outside the United States.

(ii) *Sales of property for ultimate use in the United States.* For purposes of subdivision (i) of this subparagraph, a purchaser of property (including components, as defined in subdivision (vii) of this subparagraph) is deemed to use such property ultimately in the United States if any of the following conditions exists:

(a) Such purchaser is a related person (as defined in § 1.993-1(a)(6)) with respect to the seller and such purchaser ultimately uses such property, or a second product into which such property is incorporated as a component, in the United States.

(b) At the time of the sale, there is an agreement or understanding that such property, or a second product into which such property is incorporated as a component, will be ultimately used by the purchaser in the United States.

(c) At the time of the sale, a reasonable person would have believed that such property or such second product would be ultimately used by such purchaser in the United States unless, in the case of a sale of components, the fair market value of such components at the time of delivery to the purchaser constitutes less than 20 percent of the fair market value of the second product into which such components are incorporated (determined at the time of completion of the production, manufacture, or assembly of such second product).

For purposes of (b) of this subdivision, there is an agreement or understanding that property will ultimately be used in the United States if, for example, a component is sold abroad under an express agreement with the foreign purchaser that the component is to be incorporated into a product to be sold back to the United States. As a further example, there would also be such an agreement or understanding if the foreign purchaser indicated at the time of the sale or previously that the component is to be incorporated into a product which is designed principally for the United States market. However, such an agreement or understanding does not result from the mere fact that a second product, into which components exported from the United States have been incorporated and which is sold on the world market, is sold in substantial quantities in the United States.

(iii) *Use in the United States.* For purposes of subdivision (ii) of this subparagraph, property (including components incorporated into a second product) is or would be ultimately used in the United States by such purchaser if, at any time within 3 years after the purchase of such property or components, either such property or components (or the second product into which such components are incorporated) is resold by such purchaser for use by a subsequent purchaser within the United States or such purchaser or subsequent purchaser fails, for any period of 365 consecutive days, to use such property or second product predominantly outside the United States as defined in subdivision (vi) of this subparagraph.

(iv) *Sales to retailers.* For purposes of subdivision (ii)(c) of this subparagraph property sold to any person whose principal business consists of selling from inventory to retail customers at retail outlets outside the United States will be considered as property for ultimate use outside the United States.

(v) *Leases of property for ultimate use outside the United States.* For purposes of subdivision (i) of this subparagraph, a lessee of prop-

Reg. § 1.993-3(d)(4)

erty is deemed to use such property ultimately outside the United States during a taxable year of the lessor if such property is used predominantly outside the United States (as defined in subdivision (vi) of this subparagraph) by the lessee during the portion of the lessor's taxable year which is included within the term of the lease. A determination as to whether the ultimate use of leased property satisfies the requirements of this subdivision is made for each taxable year of the lessor. Thus, leased property may be used predominantly outside the United States for a taxable year of the lessor (and thus, constitute export property if the remaining requirements of this section are met) even if the property is not used predominantly outside the United States in earlier taxable years or later taxable years of the lessor.

(vi) *Predominant use outside the United States.* For purposes of this subparagraph, property is used predominantly outside the United States for any period if, during such period, such property is located outside the United States more than 50 percent of the time. An aircraft, railroad rolling stock, vessel, motor vehicle, container, or other property used for transportation purposes is deemed to be used predominantly outside the United States for any period if, during such period, either such property is located outside the United States more than 50 percent of the time or more than 50 percent of the miles traversed in the use of such property are traversed outside the United States. However, any such property is deemed to be within the United States at all times during which it is engaged in transport between any two points within the United States except where such transport constitutes uninterrupted international air transportation within the meaning of section 4262(c)(3) and the regulations thereunder (relating to tax on air transportation of persons). For purposes of applying section 4262(c)(3) to this subdivision, the term "United States" has the same meaning as in § 1.993-7.

(vii) *Component.* For purposes of this subparagraph, a component is property which is (or is reasonably expected to be) incorporated into a second product by the purchaser of such component by means of production, manufacture, or assembly.

(e) *Foreign content of property*—(1) *The 50 percent test.* Under paragraph (a)(3) of this section, no more than 50 percent of the fair market value of export property may be attributable to the fair market value of articles which were imported into the United States. For purposes of this paragraph, articles imported into the United States are referred to as "foreign content." The fair market value of the foreign content of export property is computed in accordance with subparagraph (4) of this paragraph. The fair market value of export property which is sold to a person who is not a related person with respect to the seller is the sale price for such property (not including interest, finance or carrying charges, or similar charges).

(2) *Application of 50 percent test.* The 50 percent test described in subparagraph (1) of this paragraph is applied on an item-by-item basis. If, however, a person sells or leases a substantial volume of substantially identical export property in a taxable year and if all of such property contains substantially identical foreign content in substantially the same proportion, such person may determine the portion of foreign content contained in such property on an aggregate basis.

(3) *Parts and services.* If, at the time property is sold or leased the seller or lessor agrees to furnish parts pursuant to a services contract (as provided in § 1.993-1(d)(4)(v)) and the price for the parts is not separately stated, the 50 percent test described in subparagraph (1) of this paragraph is applied on an aggregate basis to the property and parts. If the price for the parts is separately stated, the 50 percent test described in subparagraph (1) of this paragraph is applied separately to the property and to the parts.

(4) *Computation of foreign content*—(i) *Valuation.* For purposes of applying the 50 percent test described in subparagraph (1) of this paragraph, it is necessary to determine the fair market value of all articles which constitute foreign content of the property being tested to determine if it is export property. The fair market value of such imported articles is determined as of the time such articles are imported into the United States. With respect to articles imported into the United States before July 1, 1980, the fair market value of such articles is their appraised value as determined under section 402 or 402a of the Tariff Act of 1930 (19 U.S.C. 1401a or 1402) in connection with their importation. With respect to articles imported into the United States on or after July 1, 1980, the fair market value of such articles in their appraised value as determined under section 402 of the Tariff Act of 1930 (19 U.S.C. 1401a) in connection with their importation. The appraised value of such articles is the full dutiable value of such articles, determined, however, without regard to any special provision in the United States tariff laws which would result in a lower dutiable value. Thus, an article which is imported into the United States is treated as entirely imported even if all or a portion of such article was originally manufactured, produced, grown, or extracted in the United States.

Reg. § 1.993-3(e)(4)

(ii) *Evidence of fair market value.* For purposes of subdivision (i) of this subparagraph, the fair market value of imported articles constituting foreign content may be evidenced by the customs invoice issued on the importation of such articles into the United States. If the holder of such articles is not the importer (or a related person with respect to the importer), the fair market value of such articles may be evidenced by a certificate based upon information contained in the customs invoice and furnished to the holder by the person from whom such articles (or property incorporating such articles) were purchased. If a customs invoice or certificate described in the preceding sentence is not available to a person purchasing property, such person shall establish that no more than 50 percent of the fair market value of such property is attributable to the fair market value of articles which were imported into the United States.

(iii) *Interchangeable component articles.* (a) Where identical or similar component articles can be incorporated interchangeably into property and a person acquires some such component articles that are imported into the United States and other such component articles that are not imported into the United States, the determination whether imported component articles were incorporated in such property as is exported from the United States shall be made on a substitution basis as in the case of the rules relating to drawback accounts under the customs laws. See section 313(b) of the Tariff Act of 1930, as amended (19 U.S.C. 1313(b)).

(b) The provisions of (a) of this subdivision may be illustrated by the following example:

Example. Assume that a manufacturer produces a total of 20,000 electronic devices. The manufacturer exports 5,000 of the devices and subsequently sells 11,000 of the devices to a DISC which exports the 11,000 devices. The major single component article in each device is a tube which represents 60 percent of the fair market value of the device at the time the device is sold by the manufacturer. The manufacturer imports 8,000 of the tubes and produces the remaining 12,000 tubes. For purposes of this subdivision, in accordance with the substitution principle used in the customs drawback laws, the 5,000 devices exported by the manufacturer are each treated as containing an imported tube because the devices were exported prior to the sale to the DISC. The remaining 3,000 imported tubes are treated as being contained in the first 3,000 devices purchased and exported by the DISC. Thus, since the 50 percent test is not met with respect to the first 3,000 devices purchased and exported by the DISC, those devices are not export property. The remaining 8,000 devices purchased and exported by the DISC are treated as containing tubes produced in the United States, and those devices are export property (if they otherwise meet the requirements of this section).

(f) *Excluded property*—(1) *In general.* Notwithstanding any other provision of this section, the following property is not export property—

(i) Property described in subparagraph (2) of this paragraph (relating to property leased to a member of a controlled group),

(ii) Property described in subparagraph (3) of this paragraph (relating to certain types of intangible property),

(iii) Products described in paragraph (g) of this section (relating to depletable products), and

(iv) Products described in paragraph (h) of this section (relating to certain export controlled products).

(2) *Property leased to member of controlled group.* (i) *In general.* Property leased to a person (whether or not a DISC) which is a member of the same controlled group (as defined in § 1.993-1(k)) as the lessor constitutes export property for any period of time only if during the period—

(a) Such property is held for sublease, or is subleased, by such person to a third person for the ultimate use of such third person;

(b) Such third person is not a member of the same controlled group; and

(c) Such property is used predominantly outside the United States by such third person.

(ii) *Predominant use.* The provisions of paragraph (d)(4)(vi) of this section apply in determining under subdivision (i)(c) of this subparagraph whether such property is used predominantly outside the United States by such third person.

(iii) *Leasing rule.* For purposes of this subparagraph, leased property is deemed to be ultimately used by a member of the same controlled group as the lessor if such property is leased to a person which is not a member of such controlled group but which subleases such property to a person which is a member of such controlled group. Thus, for example, if X, a DISC for the taxable year, leases a movie film to Y, a foreign corporation which is not a member of the same controlled group as X, and Y then subleases the film to persons which are members of such group for showing to the general public, the film is not export property. On the other hand, if X, a DISC for the taxable year, leases a movie film to Z, a foreign corporation which is a member of the same controlled group as X, and Z then subleases the

Reg. § 1.993-3(f)(1)

film to Y, another foreign corporation, which is not a member of the same controlled group for showing to the general public, the film is not disqualified under this subparagraph from being export property.

(iv) *Certain copyrights.* With respect to a copyright which is not excluded by subparagraph (3) of this paragraph from being export property, the ultimate use of such property is the sale or exhibition of such property to the general public. Thus, if A, a DISC for the taxable year, leases recording tapes to B, a foreign corporation which is a member of the same controlled group as A, and if B makes records from the recording tape and sells the records to C, another foreign corporation, which is not a member of the same controlled group, for sale by C to the general public, the recording tape is not disqualified under this subparagraph from being export property, notwithstanding the leasing of the recording tape by A to a member of the same controlled group, since the ultimate use of the tape is the sale of the records (*i.e.*, property produced from the recording tape).

(3) *Intangible property.* Export property does not include any patent, invention, model, design, formula, or process, whether or not patented, or any copyright (other than films, tapes, records, or similar reproductions, for commercial or home use), goodwill, trademark, tradebrand, franchise, or other like property. Although a copyright such as a copyright on a book does not constitute export property, a copyrighted article (such as a book) if not accompanied by a right to reproduce it is export property if the requirements of this section are otherwise satisfied. However, a license of a master recording tape for reproduction outside the United States is not disqualified under this subparagraph from being export property.

(g) *Depletable products*—(1) *In general.* Under section 993(c)(2)(C), a product or commodity which is a depletable product (as defined in subparagraph (2) of this paragraph) or contains a depletable product is not export property if—

(i) It is a primary product from oil, gas, coal, or uranium (as described in subparagraph (3) of this paragraph), or

(ii) It does not qualify as a 50-percent manufactured or processed product (as described in subparagraph (4) of this paragraph).

(2) *Definition of "depletable product".* For purposes of this paragraph, the term "depletable product" means any product or commodity of a character with respect to which a deduction for depletion is allowable under section 613 or 613A. Thus, the term depletable product includes any mineral extracted from a mine, an oil or gas well, or any other natural deposit, whether or not the DISC or related supplier is allowed a deduction, or is eligible to take a deduction, for depletion with respect to the mineral in computing its taxable income. Thus, for example, iron ore purchased by a DISC from a broker is a depletable product in the hands of the DISC for purposes of this paragraph even though the DISC is not eligible to take a deduction for depletion under section 613 or 613A.

(3) *Primary product from oil, gas, coal, or uranium.* A primary product from oil, gas, coal, or uranium is not export property. For purposes of this paragraph—

(i) *Primary product from oil.* The term "primary product from oil" means crude oil and all products derived from the destructive distillation of crude oil, including—

(A) Volatile products,

(B) Light oils such as motor fuel and kerosene,

(C) Distillates such as naphtha,

(D) Lubricating oils,

(E) Greases and waves, and

(F) Residues such as fuel oil.

For purposes of this paragraph, a product or commodity derived from shale oil which would be a primary product from oil if derived from crude oil is considered a primary product from oil.

(ii) *Primary product from gas.* The term "primary product from gas" means all gas and associated hydrocarbon components from gas wells or oil wells, whether recovered at the lease or upon further processing, including—

(A) Natural gas,

(B) Condensates,

(C) Liquefied petroleum gases such as ethane, propane, and butane, and

(D) Liquid products such as natural gasoline.

(iii) *Primary product from coal.* The term "primary product from coal" means coal and all products recovered from the carbonization of coal including—

(*a*) Coke,

(*b*) Coke-oven gas,

(*c*) Gas liquor,

(*d*) Crude light oil, and

(*e*) Coal tar.

(iv) *Primary product from uranium.* The term "primary product from uranium" means uranium ore and uranium concentrates (known in the industry as "yellow cake"), and nuclear materials derived from the refining of uranium

Reg. § 1.993-3(g)(3)

ore and uranium concentrates, or produced in a nuclear reaction, including—

(A) Uranium hexafluoride,

(B) Enriched uranium hexafluoride,

(C) Uranium metal,

(D) Uranium compounds, such as uranium carbide,

(E) Uranium dioxide, and

(F) Plutonium fuels.

(v) *Primary products and changing technology.* The primary products from oil, gas, coal, or uranium described in paragraphs (g)(3)(i) through (iv) of this section and the processes described in those subdivisions are not intended to represent either the only primary products from oil, gas, coal, or uranium, or the only processes from which primary products may be derived under existing and future technologies, such as the gasification and liquefaction of coal.

(vi) *Petrochemicals.* For purposes of this paragraph, petrochemicals are not considered primary products from oil, gas, or coal.

(4) *50-percent manufactured or processed product*—(i) *In general.* A product or commodity (other than a primary product from oil, gas, coal, or uranium) which is or contains a depletable product is not excluded from the term "export property" by reason of section 993(c)(2)(C) if it is a 50-percent manufactured or processed product. Such a product or commodity is a "50-percent manufactured or processed product" if, after the cutoff point of the depletable product, it is manufactured or processed (as defined in paragraph (g)(4)(ii) of this section) and either the cost test described in paragraph (g)(4)(iv) of this section or the fair market value test described in paragraph (g)(4)(v) of this section is satisfied. To determine cutoff point, see paragraphs (g)(4)(vi) and (vii) of this section.

(ii) *Manufactured or processed.* A product is manufactured or processed if it is manufactured or produced within the meaning of paragraph (c)(2) of this section, except that for purposes of this subparagraph the term manufacturing or processing does not include any excluded process (as defined in paragraph (g)(4)(iii) of this section) and the term conversion costs (as used in subparagraph (iv) of such paragraph (c)(2)) does not include any costs attributable to any excluded process.

(iii) *Excluded processes.* For purposes of this paragraph, excluded processes are extracting (*i.e.*, all processes which are applied before the cutoff point of the mineral to which such processes are applied), and handling, packing, packaging, grading, storing, and transporting.

(iv) *Cost test.* A product or commodity will qualify as a 50-percent manufactured or processed product if—

(A) Its manufacturing and processing costs (that is, the portion of the cost of goods sold or inventory amount of the product or commodity attributable to the aggregate cost of manufacturing or processing each mineral contained therein) equal or exceed

(B) An amount equal to either of the following:

(*1*) 50 percent of its cost of goods sold or inventory amount (decreased, at the DISC's option, by the portion of such cost or amount the DISC establishes is allocable to the difference between each prior owner's selling price for each depletable product contained in such product or commodity and such prior owner's cost of goods sold with respect thereto).

(*2*) The aggregate of the cost at the cutoff point (see paragraphs (9)(4)(vi) and (vii) of this section) properly attributable to each mineral contained in such product or commodity. However, if this subparagraph (*2*) is applied, then the amount in (A) of this subparagraph (iv) shall be decreased and the amount in this subparagraph (*2*) shall be increased, by so much of the cost of goods sold or inventory amount of the product or commodity as is properly allocable to any process other than transportation applied after the cutoff point of such mineral which would be a mining process (within the meaning of § 1.613-4) were it applied before such point.

(v) *Fair market value test.* A product or commodity will qualify as a 50-percent manufactured or processed product if—

(A) The excess of its fair market value on the date it is sold, exchanged, or otherwise disposed of (or, if not sold, exchanged, or otherwise disposed of, the last day of the DISC's taxable year) over the portion thereof properly allocable to excluded processes other than extracting is equal to or greater than

(B) Twice the aggregate of the fair market value at the cutoff point for each mineral contained in such product or commodity.

For purposes of this subparagraph (v), the fair market value of a product or commodity on the date it is sold, exchanged, or otherwise disposed of is the price at which it is disposed of, subject to any adjustment that may be required under the arm's length standard of section 482 and the regulations thereunder. If such product or commodity is not sold, exchanged, or otherwise disposed of, then, for purposes of section 992(a)(1)(B) (relating to the 95-percent test with respect to

Reg. § 1.993-3(g)(4)

qualified export assets), the fair market value of a product or commodity on the last day of the DISC's taxable year is the arm's length price at which such product or commodity would have been sold on such date, determined by applying the principles of section 482 and the regulations thereunder.

(vi) *Cutoff point of a mineral.* For purposes of this subparagraph—

(A) The cutoff point is the point at which gross income from the property (within the meaning of section 613(a)) was in fact determined.

(B) The cost at the cutoff point is deemed to be the amount of the gross income from the property of the taxpayer eligible for a depletion deduction with respect to the mineral.

(C) The fair market value at the cutoff point is deemed to be the amount of the gross income from the property of the taxpayer eligible for a depletion deduction with respect to the mineral, except that, if (1) the fair market value of a product or commodity on the date specified in paragraph (g)(4)(v)(A) of this section exceeds the aggregate of the fair market value at the cutoff point for each mineral contained therein and (2) 10 percent or more of such excess is attributable to a net increase in the fair market values of such minerals by reason of factors other than manufacturing or processing or the application of excluded processes (such as, for example, increases in the fair market values of some minerals by reason of inflation or speculation exceed decreases in such values of other minerals by reason of deflation or speculation), then the aggregate of the fair market value at the cutoff point for each such mineral shall be increased to reflect the net excess so attributable.

(D) The provisions of this subparagraph (vi) are illustrated by the following example.

Example. An integrated manufacturer, X, on February 1, 1976, had gross income from the property (within the meaning of section 613(a)) of $50 with respect to a specified volume of a mineral. Thus, the cost at the cutoff point of the mineral was $50. X converted the mineral into a product which it sold on July 15, 1976, for $75. Of the $25 excess of the selling price over the gross income from the property, $23 was attributable to manufacturing, processing, and the application of excluded processes, and $2 was attributable to an increase in the fair market value of the mineral due to inflation between February 1 and July 15, 1976. Since only 8 percent of such excess ($2/$25) was attributable to factors other than manufacturing, processing, and the application of excluded processes, the fair market value at the cutoff point of the mineral is $50. However, had $3 of the $25 excess, or 12 percent, been attributable to an increase in the fair market value of the mineral due to inflation, then the fair market value at the cutoff point of the mineral would be $53.

(vii) *Cutoff point of timber.* [Reserved.]

(viii) *Special rule for certain used products, and scrap products.* If a product or commodity is a used 50-percent manufactured or processed product, or is recovered as scrap from a 50-percent manufactured or processed product, such product or commodity will be treated as a 50-percent manufactured or processed product.

(ix) *Special rule for byproducts and waste products.* For purposes of applying the cost test or fair market value test of paragraphs (g)(4)(iv) or (v) of this section if a depletable product is recovered from a manufacturing process as a byproduct or waste product, then the cost and fair market value at the cutoff point are each deemed to be the lesser of—

(A) The fair market value of the waste product or byproduct containing the depletable product, determined as of the date the byproduct or waste product is recovered, or

(B) The amount the cost at the cutoff point would be for a depletable product of like kind and grade which is extracted, determined as of the date the byproduct or waste product is recovered.

For purposes of (B) of this subparagraph, the cutoff point for the depletable product of like kind and grade is deemed to be the point at which gross income from the property would be determined if such depletable product were sold by the taxpayer eligible to take a deduction for depletion after the completion of all mining processes applied to the depletable product and before the application of any nonmining process.

(x) *Proof of satisfaction of 50-percent manufactured or processed test.* (A) No substantiation is required to establish that either the cost test or the fair market value test of paragraphs (g)(4)(iv) or (v) of this section is satisfied or that a product or commodity qualifies under paragraph (g)(4)(viii) of this section as either a used 50-percent manufactured or processed product or as scrap from a 50-percent manufactured or processed product as long as it is reasonably obvious, on the basis of all relevant facts and circumstances, that either the cost test or fair market value test is satisfied, or that the product or commodity qualifies either as used 50-percent manufactured or processed product or as scrap from a 50-percent manufactured or processed product. Thus, for example, in the case of a DISC

Reg. § 1.993-3(g)(4)

exporting a high precision lens at least 50 percent of the fair market value of which is obviously attributable to grinding, no substantiation of gross income from the property properly allocable to the depletable products contained in the lens, costs, or fair market values will be required.

(B) In cases in which satisfaction of either the cost test or the fair market value test is not reasonably obvious, a DISC will be required to substantiate the gross income from the property properly allocable to each depletable product in a product or commodity and either all costs or fair market values relied upon the DISC.

(C) For purposes of substantiating (1) gross income from the property properly allocable to a depletable product, (2) costs, and (3) fair market values, the DISC and related supplier shall each identify items in (or that were in) inventory in the same manner each used to identify items in inventory for purposes of computing Federal income tax.

(xi) *Application of 50-percent test.* The 50-percent test described in this subparagraph is applied on an item-by-item basis. If, however, a DISC sells a substantial volume of substantially identical products or commodities and if all or a group of such products or commodities contain substantially identical depletable products in substantially the same proportions and have cost or fair market value relationships (as the case may be) that are in substantially the same proportions, such DISC may apply the 50-percent test on an aggregate basis with respect to all such products or commodities, or group, as the case may be.

(5) Effective dates. Except as provided in subparagraph (6) of this paragraph, section 993(c)(2)(C) applies—

(i) With respect to any product or commodity not owned by a DISC, to sales, exchanges, or other dispositions made after March 18, 1975, with respect to which the DISC derives gross receipts.

(ii) With respect to any product or commodity acquired by a DISC after March 18, 1975.

(iii) With respect to any product or commodity owned by a DISC on March 18, 1975, to sales, exchanges, or other dispositions made after March 18, 1976, and to owning such product or commodity after such date.

For purposes of this subparagraph and subparagraph (6) of this paragraph, the date of a sale, exchange, or other disposition of a product or commodity is the date as of which title to such product or commodity passes. The accounting method of a person is not determinative of the date of a sale, exchange, or other disposition.

(6) *Fixed contracts.* Section 1101(f) of the Tax Reform Act of 1976 provides an exception to the effective date rules in this paragraph and in paragraph (h) of this section. Section 1101(f)(2) of the Act provides that section 993(c)(2)(C) and (D) shall not apply to sales, exchanges, and other dispositions made after March 18, 1975, but before March 19, 1980, if they are made pursuant to a fixed contract. Section 1101(f)(2) also defines fixed contract. Under that definition, if the seller can vary the price of the product for unspecified cost increases (which could include tax cost increases), or if the quantity of products or commodities to be sold can be increased or decreased under the contract by the seller without penalty, the contract is not to be considered a fixed contract with respect to the amount over which the seller has discretion. For example, if a contract calls for a minimum delivery of x amount of a product but allows the seller to refuse to deliver goods beyond that minimum amount (or allows a renegotiation of the sales price of goods beyond that amount), then with respect to the amount above the minimum the contract is not a fixed quantity contract.

(h) *Export controlled products*—(1) *In general.* An export controlled product is not export property. A product or commodity may be an export controlled product at one time but not an export controlled product at another time. For purposes of this paragraph, a product or commodity is an "export controlled product" at a particular time if at that time the export of such product or commodity is prohibited or curtailed under section 4(b) of the Export Administration Act of 1969 or section 7(a) of the Export Administration Act of 1979, to effectuate the policy relating to the protection of the domestic economy set forth in such Acts (paragraph (2)(A) of section 3 of the Export Administration Act of 1969 and paragraph (2)(C) of section 3 of the Export Administration Act of 1979). Such policy is to use export controls to the extent necessary "to protect the domestic economy from the excessive drain of scarce materials and to reduce the serious inflationary impact of foreign demand."

(2) *Products considered export controlled products*—(i) *In general.* For purposes of this paragraph, an export controlled product is a product or commodity which is subject to short supply export controls under 15 CFR Part 377. A product or commodity is considered an export controlled product for the duration of each control period which applies to such product or commodity. A control period of a product or commodity begins on and includes the initial control date (as defined in paragraph (o)(2)(ii) of this section) and ends on

Reg. § 1.993-3(g)(5)

and includes the final control date (as defined in paragraph (n)(2)(iii) of this section).

(ii) *Initial control date.* The initial control date of a product or commodity which was subject to short supply export controls on March 19, 1975, is March 19, 1975. The initial control date of a product or commodity which is subject to short supply export controls after March 19, 1975, is the effective date stated in the regulations to 15 CFR Part 377 which subjects such product or commodity to short supply export controls. If there is no effective date stated in such regulations, the initial control date of such product or commodity is the date on which such regulations are filed for publication in the FEDERAL REGISTER.

(iii) *Final control date.* The final control date of a product or commodity is the effective date stated in the regulations to 15 CFR Part 377 which removes such product or commodity from short supply export controls. If there is no effective date stated in such regulations, then the final control date of such product or commodity is the date on which such regulations are filed for publication in the FEDERAL REGISTER.

(iv) *Expiration of Export Administration Act.* An initial control date and a final control date cannot occur after the expiration date of the export administration act under the authority of which the short supply export controls were issued.

(3) *Effective dates*—(i) *Products controlled on March 19, 1975.* Except as provided in paragraph (g)(6) of this section, if a product or commodity was subject to short supply export controls on March 19, 1975, this paragraph applies—

(A) With respect to any such product or commodity not owned by a DISC, to sales, exchanges, other dispositions, or leases made after March 18, 1975, with respect to which the DISC derives gross receipts.

(B) With respect to any such product or commodity acquired by a DISC after March 18, 1975, and

(C) With respect to any such product or commodity owned by a DISC on March 18, 1975, to sales, exchanges, other dispositions, and leases made after March 18, 1976, and to owning such product or commodity after such date.

(ii) *Products first controlled after March 19, 1975.* If a product or commodity becomes subject to short supply export controls after March 19, 1975, this paragraph applies to sales, exchanges, other dispositions, or leases of such product or commodity made on or after the initial control date of such product or commodity, and to owning such product or commodity on or after such date.

(iii) *Date of sale, exchange, lease, or other disposition.* For purposes of this subparagraph, the date of sale, exchange, or other disposition of a product or commodity is the date as of which title to such product or commodity passes. The date of a lease is the date as of which the lessee takes possession of a product or commodity. The accounting method of a person is not determinative of the date of sale, exchange, other disposition, or lease.

(i) *Property in short supply.* Except as provided in paragraph (g)(6) of this section, if the President determines that the supply of any property which is otherwise export property as defined in this section is insufficient to meet the requirements of the domestic economy, he may by Executive order designate such property as in short supply. Any property so designated will be treated as property which is not export property during the period beginning with the date specified in such Executive order and ending with the date specified in an Executive order setting forth the President's determination that such property is no longer in short supply. [Reg. § 1.993-3.]

☐ [T.D. 7514, 10-14-77. Amended by T.D. 7513, 10-14-77 and T.D. 7854, 11-15-82.]

[Reg. § 1.993-4]

§ 1.993-4. Definition of producer's loans.—(a) *General rule*—(1) *Definition.* Under section 993(d), a loan made by a DISC to a person, referred to in this section as the "borrower," is a producer's loan if—

(i) The loan is made out of accumulated DISC income within the meaning of subparagraph (3) of this paragraph,

(ii) The loan is evidenced by an obligation described in subparagraph (4) of this paragraph,

(iii) The requirement as to the trade or business of the borrower described in subparagraph (5) of this paragraph is satisfied.

(iv) At the time the loan is made, the obligation referred to in subdivision (ii) of this subparagraph bears a legend stating "This Obligation Is Designated A Producer's Loan Within The Meaning of Section 993(d) of the Internal Revenue Code" or words of substantially the same meaning,

(v) The limitation as to the export-related assets of the borrower described in paragraph (b) of this section is satisfied,

(vi) The requirement as to the increased investment of the borrower in export-related as-

Reg. § 1.993-4(a)(1)

sets described in paragraph (c) of this section is satisfied, and

(vii) The requirement of paragraph (d) of this section as to proof of compliance with paragraphs (b) and (c) of this section is satisfied.

(2) *Application of this section*—(i) *In general.* A loan which is a producer's loan is a qualified export asset of the DISC (see § 1.993-2(a)(5) and (f)). The interest on a producer's loan is a qualified export receipt of the DISC (see § 1.993-1(g)). A producer's loan is not a dividend to a borrower which is also a shareholder of the DISC making the loan. For rules with respect to deemed distributions by reason of the amount of foreign investment attributable to producer's loans, see section 995(b)(1)(G) and (d) and the regulations thereunder.

(ii) *No tracing of loan proceeds.* For purposes of applying this section, in order to qualify as a producer's loan, the proceeds of the loan need not be traced to an investment in any specific asset.

(iii) *Unrelated borrower.* For purposes of applying this section, it is not necessary for a borrower to be a related person with respect to the DISC from which it receives a producer's loan or a member of the same controlled group as the DISC.

(iv) *Unpaid balance of producer's loans.* For purposes of applying this section, the unpaid balance of producer's loans does not include the unpaid balance of any producer's loan to the extent the loan has been deducted or charged off by the DISC as totally or partially worthless under section 165 or 166.

(v) *Refinancing, renewal, and extension.* For purposes of applying this section, the refinancing, renewal, or extension of a producer's loan shall be treated as the making of a new loan which may qualify as a producer's loan only if the requirements of subparagraph (1) of this paragraph are met.

(vi) *Events subsequent to time loan is made.* The determination as to whether a loan qualifies as a producer's loan is made on the basis of the relevant facts taken into account for purposes of determining whether the loan was a producer's loan when made. Thus, for example, if the accumulated DISC income of the lender is later reduced below the unpaid balance of all producer's loans previously made by the DISC, such subsequent decrease in the amount of accumulated DISC income will not result in later disqualification of such loan (or part thereof) as a producer's loan. Similarly, if a loan (or part of a loan) does not qualify as a producer's loan because of an insufficient amount of accumulated DISC income at the time the loan is made, a subsequent increase in the amount of accumulated DISC income will not result in later qualification of such loan (or part thereof) as a producer's loan. As a further example, for purposes of applying the borrower's export related assets limitation described in paragraph (b) of this section, a loan which qualifies as a producer's loan when made will not later be disqualified if property, the gross receipts from the sale or lease of which were includible in the numerator of the fraction described in paragraph (b)(3)(i) of this section at the time of sale or lease by the borrower, is later characterized as excluded property (as defined in § 1.993-3(f)).

(vii) *Application of tests under paragraphs (b) and (c) on controlled group bases.* If the borrower is a member of a controlled group (as defined in § 1.993-1(k)) at the time a loan is made, all amounts that must be determined for purposes of applying the limitation and increased investment requirement with respect to the export-related assets of the borrower (described in paragraphs (b) and (c), respectively, of this section) may be determined at the election of the borrower by aggregating such amounts for all members of the controlled group, determined for the taxable year of each member of the controlled group during which the loan is made, excluding only such members of the group as are DISC's or foreign corporations for such year. However, such amounts may be included only to the extent that such amounts have not already been taken into account in applying the limitation and increased investment requirement with respect to any other borrower. The borrower may make such election by causing its written statement of election to be attached to the lending DISC's return under section 6011(e)(2) for the first taxable year of the lending DISC within which or with which the borrower's taxable year for which the election is to apply ends. An election once made is binding on all members of the controlled group which includes the borrower with respect to all taxable years of the borrower beginning with its first taxable year for which the election is made. A borrower who makes such election may revoke it only if it secures the consent of the Commissioner to such revocation upon application made through the lending DISC.

(3) *Loan out of accumulated DISC income*— (i) *In general.* A loan is a producer's loan only to the extent that it is made out of accumulated DISC income. A loan is made out of accumulated DISC income only if the amount of the loan, when added to the unpaid balance at the time such loan is made of all other producer's loans made by a DISC, does not exceed the amount of accumulated DISC income of the DISC at the beginning of the

Reg. § 1.993-4(a)(2)

month in which the loan is made. The amount of accumulated DISC income at the beginning of any month is determined as if the DISC's taxable year closed at the end of the immediately preceding month.

(ii) *Presumption.* A loan made during a taxable year shall be deemed under subdivision (i) of this subparagraph to have been made out of accumulated DISC income if the balance of producer's loans at the beginning of the year and those made during the year do not exceed accumulated DISC income at the end of the year.

(iii) *Deemed distributions.* For purposes of this subparagraph, accumulated DISC income as of the end of any taxable year (or month) shall be determined without regard to deemed distributions under section 995(b)(1)(G) for the amount of foreign investment attributable to producer's loans for such year (or for the taxable year for which such month is a part) but actual distributions shall be taken into account.

(4) *Evidence and terms of obligation.* A loan is a producer's loan only if the loan is evidenced by a note or other evidence of indebtedness which is made by the borrower and which has a stated maturity date not more than 5 years from the date the loan is made. Accordingly, a loan which does not have a stated maturity date or which has a stated maturity date more than 5 years from the date such loan is made can never meet the 5-year requirement of this subparagraph. Thus, for example, even if there is a period of less than 5 years remaining to the stated maturity date of a loan, the loan can never be a producer's loan if it had a stated maturity date more than 5 years from the date it was made. For a further example, if a loan having a period remaining to maturity of 2 years is extended for a further period of 3 years (making a total of 5 years to maturity from the date of the extension), the extension of the loan would under subparagraph (2)(v) of this paragraph constitute the making of a new producer's loan and the original producer's loan would terminate. If, however, a loan having a period remaining to maturity of 2 years is extended for a further period of 4 years (making a total of 6 years to maturity from the date of the extension), the original producer's loan will terminate and the new loan will not be a producer's loan. If a producer's loan is not paid in full at its maturity date and is not formally refinanced, renewed, or extended, such loan shall be deemed to be a new loan which does not have a stated maturity date and, thus, will not be a producer's loan. For purposes of this subparagraph, an evidence of indebtedness is a written instrument of indebtedness. Section 482 and the regulations thereunder are applicable to determine in the case of a loan by the DISC to a borrower which is owned or controlled directly or indirectly by the same interests as the DISC within the meaning of section 482, whether the interest charged on such loan is at an arm's length rate.

(5) *Borrower's trade or business.* A loan is a producer's loan only if the loan is made to a person engaged in the United States in the manufacture, production, growth, or extraction (within the meaning of § 1.993-3(c)) of export property determined without regard to § 1.993-3(f)(1)(iii) and (iv). The borrower may also be engaged in other trades or businesses and the loan need not be traceable to specific investments in export property.

(b) *Borrower's export related assets limitation*—(1) *General rule.* A loan to a borrower is a producer's loan only to the extent that the amount of the loan, when added to the unpaid balance of all other producer's loans made by all DISC's to the borrower which are outstanding at the time the loan is made, does not exceed an amount equal to the amount of the borrower's export-related assets (determined under subparagraph (2) of this paragraph) multiplied by the fraction set forth in subparagraph (3) of this paragraph.

(2) *Amount of export-related assets*—(i) *In general.* For purposes of subparagraph (1) of this paragraph, the amount of the borrower's export-related assets is the sum of the amounts described in subdivisions (ii), (iii) and (iv) of this subparagraph.

(ii) *Borrower's plant and equipment.* The amount described in this subdivision is the sum of the borrower's adjusted bases (determined as of the beginning of the borrower's taxable year in which a loan is made to it) for plant, machinery, equipment, and supporting production facilities, which are located in the United States. Supporting production facilities are all property used primarily in connection with the manufacture, production, growth, or extraction (within the meaning of § 1.993-3(c)) or storage, handling, transportation, or assembly of property by the borrower.

(iii) *Borrower's property held primarily for sale or lease.* The amount described in this subdivision is the amount of the borrower's property (at the beginning of the taxable year of the borrower in which a loan is made to it) held primarily for sale or lease to customers in the ordinary course of its trade or business. The amount of such property held for sale is determined under the methods of identifying and valuing inventory normally used by the borrower. The amount of such property held for lease or leased is the borrower's adjusted

Reg. § 1.993-4(b)(2)

basis, determined under section 1011, for such property.

(iv) *Borrower's research and experimental expenditures.* The amount described in this subdivision is the aggregate amount, whether or not charged to capital account, of research and experimental expenditures (within the meaning of section 174) incurred in the United States by the borrower during each of its taxable years which begin after December 31, 1971, and precede the taxable year in which the loan is made to the borrower. Such research and experimental expenditures need bear no relationship to export property (as defined in § 1.993-3) of the borrower. The aggregate amount of all such expenditures for each of such preceding taxable years is taken into account for purposes of this subparagraph, regardless of whether all or any portion of the aggregate amount has been taken into account with respect to producer's loans made to the borrower by any DISC in preceding taxable years. The aggregate amount of all such expenditures shall include such expenditures of a corporation, the assets of which were acquired by the borrower in a distribution or a transfer described in section 381(a)(1) or (2) (relating to carryovers in certain corporate acquisitions).

(3) *Fraction referred to in subparagraph (1) of this paragraph*—(i) *Numerator of fraction.* The numerator of the fraction set forth in this subparagraph is the sum of the borrower's gross receipts for each of its 3 taxable years immediately preceding the taxable year in which the loan is made (but not including any taxable year beginning before January 1, 1972) from the sale or lease of export property (determined without regard to § 1.993-3(f)(1)(iii) and (iv)) which is manufactured, produced, grown, or extracted (within the meaning of § 1.993-3(c)) by the borrower whether or not sold or leased directly or through a related domestic person (notwithstanding § 1.993-3(a)(4) and (f)(2)). For purposes of the preceding sentence, with respect to a sale or lease to a related DISC in which the transfer price is determined under section 994(a)(1) or (2), the rules under § 1.994-1(c)(5) (relating to incomplete transactions) shall be applied, and with respect to all other sales and leases the rules under § 1.994-1(c)(5) other than subdivision (i)(*d*) thereof shall be applied.

(ii) *Denominator of fraction.* The denominator of the fraction set forth in this subparagraph is the sum of the amount included in the numerator and all other gross receipts of the borrower, for each of its taxable years for which gross receipts are included in the numerator of the fraction, from all sales or leases of all property

held by the borrower primarily for sale or lease to customers in the ordinary course of its trade or business.

For purposes of subdivision (i) of this subparagraph and this subdivision, if such property is sold or leased to a domestic related person which resells or subleases such property, the borrower's gross receipts shall be the gross receipts derived by the domestic related person from the resale or sublease of the export property.

(iii) *Taxable years.* If the borrower has not engaged in the sale or lease of property (as described in this subparagraph) for the 3 immediately preceding taxable years, or if 3 taxable years beginning after December 31, 1971, have not elapsed, the fraction will be computed on the basis of such gross receipts for its taxable years immediately preceding the loan and beginning after December 31, 1971, during which the borrower has so engaged. No producer's loans can be made to a borrower until after the end of the first taxable year of the borrower beginning after December 31, 1971.

(c) *Requirement for increased investment in export-related assets*—(1) *In general.* A loan to a borrower is a producer's loan only to the extent that the amount of the loan, when added to the unpaid balance of all other producer's loans made by all DISC's to the borrower during the borrower's taxable year during which such loan is made, does not exceed the amount of the borrower's increase for the year in investment in export-related assets. Such increase for any taxable year is the sum of—

(i) The increase (if any) in the borrower's adjusted basis of certain types of assets as determined under subparagraph (2) of this paragraph and

(ii) The amount (if any) during the year of its research and experimental expenditures as determined under paragraph (b)(2)(iv) of this section.

(2) *Increase in adjusted basis.* The amount under this subparagraph is the amount (not less than zero) by which—

(i) The borrower's adjusted basis (determined as of the end of its taxable year in which the producer's loan is made) in all of its property which is described in paragraph (b)(2)(ii) (plant and equipment), and (iii) (property held primarily for sale or lease) of this section, including any such property acquired by it during such taxable year, exceeds

(ii) Its adjusted bases in all such property (determined as of the beginning of such year).

Reg. § 1.993-4(b)(3)

(3) *Ordering rule.* If during the borrower's taxable year the amount of increase in investment in export-related assets determined under this subparagraph is exceeded by amounts loaned to the borrower during such year that would otherwise qualify as producer's loans such loans shall be applied in the order made against the amount of such increase in order to determine which loans qualify as producer's loans.

(d) *Proof of borrower's compliance with paragraphs (b) and (c) of this section.* For purposes of paragraphs (b) and (c) of this section, a DISC shall be prepared to establish initially the compliance of the borrower with the requirements of such paragraphs by providing the written statement of the borrower, certified by a certified public accountant, stating that the borrower has complied with the limitation and increased investment requirement in section 993(d)(2) and (3) of the Internal Revenue Code of 1954. In lieu of certification by a certified public accountant, the DISC may attach to its return a statement signed by the borrower under penalties of perjury on a form provided by the Internal Revenue Service certifying that the borrower has complied with the limitation and increased investment requirement in section 993(d)(2) and (3) of the Internal Revenue Code of 1954. For taxable years ending after October 17, 1977 the DISC must attach either the certification by the certified public accountant or the certification by the borrower to its return. Additional full substantiation of the borrower's compliance with the requirements of such paragraphs may be required by the district director. If full substantiation of such compliance is not provided by the DISC (or the borrower) when required, the loan shall be deemed not to be a producer's loan.

(e) *Special limitation in the case of domestic film maker*—(1) *General rule.* The limitation of paragraph (b) of this section as to the export-related assets of the borrower will be considered satisfied if the DISC—

(i) Is engaged in the trade or business of selling or leasing films which are export property, or is acting as a commission agent for a person who is so engaged.

(ii) Makes a loan to a borrower which is a domestic film maker (as defined in subparagraph (5) of this paragraph) for the purpose of making a film, and

(iii) The amount of such loan, when added to the unpaid balance of all other producer's loans made by all DISC's to the borrower which are outstanding at the time the loan is made, does not exceed an amount determined by multiplying—

(a) The sum of (1) the amount of the export-related assets of the borrower (determined under paragraph (b)(2)(i) of this section as of the beginning of the borrower's taxable year in which the loan is made), plus (2) the amount of a reasonable estimate of the amount of such export-related assets obtained or to be obtained by the borrower during such year and subsequent years with respect to films as to which filming begins within such year by

(b) The percentage which, based on the experience of other film makers of similar films for the 5 calendar years preceding the calendar year in which the loan is made, the annual gross receipts (as described in § 1.993-6(a)(1), whether or not such films constitute property described therein) of such other film makers from the sale or lease of such films outside the United States is of the annual gross receipts of such other film makers from all sales or leases of such films.

(2) *Purpose of loan.* A loan by a DISC will be deemed to be for the making of a film if there exists a written agreement between the DISC and the borrower, executed at or before the time the loan is made, stating that the loan is made or to be made to enable the borrower to make such film.

(3) *Reasonable estimate of amounts.* For purposes of subparagraph (1)(iii) (a)(2) of this paragraph, a reasonable estimate shall be based on the conditions known by the DISC and borrower to exist at the time a loan is made (or which the DISC and borrower have reason to know to exist at such time).

(4) *Experience of film makers.* For purposes of subparagraph (1)(iii)(b) of this paragraph, the experience of other film makers of similar films for the 5 calendar years preceding the calendar year in which the loan is made shall be derived from such records and statistics as are acknowledged in the trade as reasonably reliable.

(5) *Domestic film maker.* For purposes of this section, a borrower is a domestic film maker with respect to a film if—

(i) The borrower is a U.S. person within the meaning of section 7701(a)(30), except that (a) with respect to a partnership all of the partners must be U.S. persons and (b) with respect to a corporation all of its officers and at least a majority of its directors must be U.S. persons,

(ii) The borrower is engaged in the trade or business of making the film with respect to which the loan is made,

(iii) Each studio, if any, used or to be used for filming or for recording sound incorporated into such film is located in the United States (as defined in section 7701(a)(9)),

Reg. § 1.993-4(e)(5)

(iv) At least 80 percent of the aggregate playing time of the film is or will be photographed within the United States (as defined in section 7701(a)(9)), and

(v) At least 80 percent of the total amount (not including any amount which is contingent upon receipts or profits of such film and which is fully taxable by the United States) paid or to be paid for services performed in the making of the film is either paid or to be paid to persons who are U.S. persons at the time such services are performed or consists of amounts which are fully taxable by the United States.

(6) *Amounts as fully taxable.* For purposes of subparagraph (5)(v) of this paragraph, an amount is considered fully taxable by the United States if the entire amount is included in gross income under section 61 or is subject to withholding under any provision of U.S. law or treaty to which the United States is a party and is not exempt from taxation under any provision of such law or treaty. Where a nonresident alien individual is engaged for the making of a film or where a foreign corporation is engaged to furnish the services of one of its officers or employees for the making of a film, the amount paid such individual or corporation will be considered as fully taxable by the United States only if it meets the test of this subparagraph. [Reg. § 1.993-4.]

☐ [T.D. 7513, 10-14-77. Amended by T.D. 7513, 10-14-77 and T.D. 7854, 11-15-82.]

[Reg. § 1.993-5]

§ 1.993-5. **Definition of related foreign export corporation.**—(a) *General rule*—(1) *Definition.* Under section 993(e), a foreign corporation is a related foreign export corporation with respect to a DISC if—

(i) It is a foreign international sales corporation described in paragraph (b) of this section,

(ii) It is a real property holding company described in paragraph (c) of this section, or

(iii) It is an associated foreign corporation described in paragraph (d) of this section.

(2) *Application of this section.* It is necessary to determine whether a foreign corporation is a related foreign export corporation with respect to a DISC for the following two purposes:

(i) *Qualified export assets.* Under § 1.993-2(g), the stock or securities of a related foreign export corporation held by the DISC are qualified export assets.

(ii) *Qualified export receipts.* Under § 1.993-1(e), (f), and (g), certain receipts of the DISC with respect to stock or securities of a related foreign export corporation held by the DISC are qualified export receipts.

(b) *Foreign international sales corporation*—(1) *In general.* A foreign corporation is a foreign international sales corporation with respect to a taxable year of a DISC if—

(i) On each day during such taxable year of the DISC on which the foreign corporation has stock issued and outstanding, the DISC owns directly stock of the foreign corporation possessing more than 50 percent of the total combined voting power of all classes of stock of the foreign corporation entitled to vote as determined under the principles of § 1.957-1(b) (relating to definition of controlled foreign corporation),

(ii) 95 percent or more of such foreign corporation's gross receipts (as defined in § 1.993-6) for its taxable year ending with or within such taxable year of the DISC consists of qualified export receipts described in § 1.993-1(b) through (e) or interest described in § 1.993-1(g) derived from any obligations described in § 1.993-2(d) or (e), and

(iii) The sum of the adjusted bases of the assets of the foreign corporation which are qualified export assets described in § 1.993-2(b) through (e) and which are held by the foreign corporation at the close of its taxable year which ends with or within such taxable year of the DISC equals or exceeds 95 percent of the sum of the adjusted bases of all assets held by the foreign corporation at the close of such taxable year.

(2) *Certain determinations.* The determinations as to whether gross receipts are qualified export receipts described in subparagraph (1)(ii) of this paragraph and as to whether assets are qualified export assets described in subparagraph (1)(iii) of this paragraph are made by applying the requirements of §§ 1.993-1 and 1.993-2 to the foreign corporation as if it were a domestic corporation being tested to determine whether it is a DISC. For purposes of making either of such determinations, the principles of accounting applicable for purposes of computing earnings and profits under § 1.964-1 (relating to a controlled foreign corporation's earnings and profits) shall apply.

(c) *Real property holding company*—(1) *In general.* A foreign corporation is a real property holding company with respect to a taxable year of a DISC if—

(i) On each day during such taxable year of the DISC on which the foreign corporation has stock issued and outstanding, the DISC owns directly stock of the foreign corporation possessing more than 50 percent of the total combined voting power of all classes of stock of the foreign corpora-

Reg. § 1.993-5(a)(1)

tion entitled to vote as determined under the principles of § 1.957-1(b) and

(ii) The sole function of the foreign corporation is to hold title to real property situated outside the United States for the exclusive use of the DISC, title to which may not be held by the DISC (and, if the DISC subleases such property to a related supplier, as described in subparagraph (3) of this paragraph, by such related supplier) under the law of the country in which such property is situated.

(2) *Activities of the foreign corporation.* For purposes of subparagraph (1)(ii) of this paragraph, a foreign corporation which holds title to real property situated outside the United States may also perform activities with respect to such property (such as management, maintenance, and payment of taxes) which are ancillary to its function of holding title to such property.

(3) *Exclusive use by the DISC.* Real property held by the foreign corporation must be used exclusively by the DISC whether under a lease or any other arrangement. Real property is not so used by the DISC if the DISC subleases such property to any other person. If, however, during a taxable year of the DISC—

(i) 90 percent or more of the qualified export receipts of the DISC for such year are derived from transactions with respect to which it is a commission agent for a related supplier (as defined in § 1.994-1(a)(3)(ii), and

(ii) The DISC subleases such property to such related supplier then such property will be considered as used exclusively by the DISC during such year if such related supplier does not sublease such property.

(d) *Associated foreign corporation*—(1) *In general.* A foreign corporation is an associated foreign corporation with respect to a taxable year of the DISC if—

(i) On each day during such taxable year of the DISC on which the foreign corporation has stock issued and outstanding, the DISC, or one or more members of the same controlled group of corporations (as defined in subparagraph (2) of this paragraph) as the DISC, owns (within the meaning of sec. 1563 (d) and (e)) stock of the foreign corporation possessing less than 10 percent of the total combined voting power of all classes of stock of the foreign corporation entitled to vote, as determined under the principles of § 1.957-1(b), or owns no stock of such corporation, and

(ii) The ownership of stock, or of securities (as defined in § 1.993-2(g)), of the foreign corporation by the DISC or by one or more members of such controlled group of corporations reasonably furthers a transaction or transactions giving rise to qualified export receipts for the DISC.

(2) *Controlled group of corporations.* For purposes of this paragraph, the term "controlled group of corporations" has the same meaning assigned to the term in section 1563(a) and not section 993(a)(3) and § 1.993-1(k). Thus, for purposes of this paragraph, the test of control is 80 percent control and, since the rules of section 1563(b) apply, only domestic members are considered to be members of the controlled group.

(3) *Furtherance of qualified export receipts.* Ownership of stock or securities of a foreign corporation will be considered as reasonably furthering a transaction or transactions giving rise to qualified export receipts for a DISC if—

(i) The ownership is necessary to obtain or maintain the foreign corporation as a customer of the DISC or of a related supplier, as defined in § 1.994-1(a)(3)(ii) of the DISC or to aid the sales distribution system of the DISC or of such related supplier, and

(ii) The amount of the investment in the foreign corporation bears a reasonable relationship to the amount of the DISC's annual net profit from transactions in its trade or business which it may reasonably expect to derive on account of such ownership.

In determining whether the amount of the investment is reasonable, there shall be taken into account any stock or securities of the foreign corporation owned by any other foreign corporation which, if it were a domestic corporation, would be a member of the same controlled group of corporations as the DISC. [Reg. § 1.993-5.]

☐ [T.D. 7514, 10-14-77.]

[Reg. § 1.993-6]

§ 1.993-6. Definition of gross receipts.—(a) *General rule.* Under section 993(f), for purposes of sections 991 through 996, the gross receipts of a person for a taxable year are—

(1) The total amounts received or accrued by the person from the sale or lease of property held primarily for sale or lease in the ordinary course of a trade or business, and

(2) Gross income recognized from all other sources, such as, for example, from—

(i) The furnishing of services (whether or not related to the sale or lease of property described in subparagraph (1) of this paragraph),

(ii) Dividends and interest,

(iii) The sale at a gain of any property not described in subparagraph (1) of this paragraph, and

Reg. § 1.993-6(a)(2)

(iv) Commission transactions as and to the extent described in paragraph (e) of this section.

(b) *Nongross receipts items.* For purposes of paragraph (a) of this section, gross receipts do not include amounts received or accrued by a person from—

(1) The proceeds of a loan or of the repayment of a loan, or

(2) A receipt of property in a transaction to which section 118 (relating to contribution to capital) or 1032 (relating to exchange of stock for property) applies.

(c) *Nonreduction of total amounts.* For purposes of paragraph (a) of this section, the total amounts received or accrued by a person are not reduced by returns and allowances, costs of goods sold, expenses, losses, a deduction for dividends received under section 243, or any other deductible amounts.

(d) *Method of accounting.* For purposes of paragraph (a) of this section, the total amounts received or accrued by a person shall be determined under the method of accounting used in computing its taxable income. If, for example, a DISC receives advance or installment payments for the sale or lease of property described in paragraph (a)(1) of this section, for the furnishing of services, or which represent recognized gain from the sale of property not described in paragraph (a)(1) of this section, any amount of such advance payments is considered to be gross receipts of the DISC for the taxable year for which such amount is included in the gross income of the DISC.

(e) *Commission transactions.* (1) In the case of transactions which give rise to a commission on the sale or lease of property or the furnishing of services by a principal, the amount recognized by the commission agent as gross income from all such transactions shall be the gross receipts derived by the principal from the sale or lease of the property, or the gross income derived by the principal from the furnishing of services, with respect to which the commissions are derived. In the case of a commission agent for a related supplier (as defined in § 1.994-1(a)(3)(ii)), the gross receipts or gross income of such agent shall be determined as if it used the same method of accounting as its related supplier. In the case of a commission agent for a principal other than a related supplier, the gross receipts or gross income of such principal shall be determined as if such principal used the same method of accounting as its agent.

(2) If the commission arrangement provides that the commission agent will receive a commission only with respect to sales or leases of export property, or the furnishing of services, which result in qualified export receipts, the commission agent will not take into account the gross receipts or gross income, as the case may be, derived by the principal from any transaction for which the commission agent would not be entitled to a commission under the commission arrangement.

(f) *Example.* The provisions of this section may be illustrated by the following example:

Example. During 1973, M, a related supplier (as defined in § 1.994-1(a)(3)(ii)) of N, is engaged in the manufacture of machines in the United States. N, a calendar year taxpayer, is engaged in the sale and lease of such machines in foreign countries. N furnishes services which are related and subsidiary to its sale and lease of such machines. N also acts as a commission agent in foreign countries for Z, an unrelated supplier, with respect to Z's sale of products. N receives dividends on stock owned by it in a related foreign export corporation (as defined in § 1.993-5), interest on producer's loans made to M, and proceeds from sales of business assets located outside the United States resulting in a recognized gains and losses. N's gross receipts for 1973 are $3,550, computed on the basis of the additional facts assumed in the table below:

(1) N's sales receipts for machines manufactured by M (without reduction for cost of goods sold and selling expenses)	$1,500
(2) N's lease receipts for machines manufactured by M (without reduction for depreciation and leasing expenses)	500
(3) N's gross income from services for machines manufactured by M (without reduction for service expenses)	400
(4) Z's sale receipts for products manufactured by Z (without reduction for Z's cost of goods sold, commissions on sales, and commission sales expenses)	550
(5) Dividends received by N	150
(6) Interest received by N on producer's loans	200
(7) Proceeds received by N representing recognized gain (but not losses) from sales of business assets located outside the United States ...	250
(8) N's gross receipts	$3,550

[Reg. § 1.993-6.]

[Reg. § 1.993-7]

§ 1.993-7. Definition of United States.— Under section 993(g), the term "United States" includes the States, the District of Columbia, the Commonwealth of Puerto Rico, and possessions of the United States. For the requirement that a DISC must be incorporated and existing under

Reg. § 1.993-7

the laws of a State or the District of Columbia, see § 1.992-1(a)(1). [Reg. § 1.993-7.]

☐ [*T.D.* 7514, 10-14-77.]

[Reg. § 1.994-1]

§ 1.994-1. Inter-company pricing rules for DISC's.—(a) *In general*—(1) *Scope.* In the case of a transaction described in paragraph (b) of this section, section 994 permits a person related to a DISC to determine the allowable transfer price charged the DISC (or commission paid the DISC) by its choice of three methods described in paragraph (c)(2), (3), and (4) of this section: The "4 percent" gross receipts method, the "50-50" combined taxable income method, and the section 482 method. Under the first two methods, the DISC is entitled to 10 percent of its export promotion expenses as additional taxable income. When the gross receipts method or combined taxable income method is applied to a transaction, the Commissioner may not make distributions, apportionments, or allocations as provided by section 482 and the regulations thereunder. For rules as to certain "incomplete transactions" and for computing combined taxable income, see paragraphs (c)(5) and (6) of this section. Grouping of transactions for purposes of applying the method chosen is provided by paragraph (c)(7) of this section. The rules in paragraph (c) of this section are directly applicable only in the case of sales or exchanges of export property to a DISC for resale, and are applicable by analogy to leases, commissions, and services as provided in paragraph (d) of this section. For rules limiting the application of the gross receipts method and combined taxable income method so that the supplier related to the DISC will not incur a loss on transactions, see paragraph (e)(1) of this section. Paragraph (e)(2) of this section provides for the applicability of section 482 to resales by the DISC to related persons. Paragraph (e)(3) of this section provides for the time by which a reasonable estimate of the transfer price (including commissions and other payments) should be paid. The subsequent determination and further adjustments to transfer prices are set forth in paragraph (e)(4) of this section. Export promotion expenses are defined in paragraph (f) of this section. Paragraph (g) of this section has several examples illustrating the provisions of this section. Section 1.994-2 prescribes the marginal costing rules authorized by section 994(b)(2).

(2) *Performance of substantial economic functions.* The application of section 994(a)(1) or (2) does not depend on the extent to which the DISC performs substantial economic functions (except with respect to export promotion expenses). See paragraph (1) of § 1.993-1.

(3) *Related party and related supplier.* For the purposes of this section—

(i) The term "related party" means a person which is owned or controlled directly or indirectly by the same interests as the DISC within the meaning of section 482 and § 1.482-1(a).

(ii) The term "related supplier" means a related party which singly engages in a transaction directly with the DISC which is subject to the rules of section 994 and this section. However, a DISC may have different related suppliers with respect to different transactions. If, for example, X owns all the stock of Y, a corporation, and of Z, a DISC, and sells a product to Y which is resold to Z, only Y is the related supplier of Z, and, thus, only the resale from Y to Z is subject to section 994 and this section. If, however, X sells directly to Z and Y also sells directly to Z, then, as to the transactions involving direct sales to Z, each of X and Y is a related supplier of Z.

(b) *Transactions to which section 994 applies.* Section 994(a)(3) may be applied, as described in paragraph (a) of this section, to any transaction between a related supplier and a DISC. Sections 994(a)(1) or (2) may be applied, as described in paragraph (a) of this section, to a transaction between a related supplier and a DISC only in the following cases:

(1) Where the related supplier sells export property to the DISC for resale or where the DISC is commission agent for the related supplier on sales by the related supplier of export property to third parties whether or not related parties. For purposes of this section, references to sales include exchanges.

(2) Where the related supplier leases export property to the DISC for sublease for a comparable period with comparable terms of payment or where the DISC is commission agent for the related supplier on leases by the related supplier of export property to third parties whether or not related parties.

(3) Where services are furnished by a related supplier which are related and subsidiary to any sale or lease by the DISC, acting as principal or commission agent, of export property under subparagraph (1) or (2) of this paragraph.

(4) Where engineering or architectural services for construction projects located (or proposed for location) outside of the United States are furnished by a related supplier where the DISC is acting as principal or commission agent with respect to the furnishing of such services to a third party whether or not a related party.

(5) Where the related supplier furnishes managerial services in furtherance of the produc-

Reg. § 1.994-1(b)(5)

tion of qualified export receipts of an unrelated DISC where the related DISC is acting as principal or commission agent with respect to the furnishing of such services to an unrelated DISC.

Transactions are included, for purposes of this paragraph, only if they give rise to qualified export receipts (within the meaning of section 993(a)) in the hands of the related DISC. If a transaction is not included in subparagraph (1), (2), (3), (4), or (5) of this paragraph, the rules of section 994(a)(1) or (2) do not apply. Thus, for example, the rules of section 994(a)(1) or (2) would not apply if a DISC purchased export property from its related supplier and leased such property to a third party.

(c) *Transfer price for sales of export property*— (1) *In general.* Under this paragraph, rules are prescribed for computing the allowable price for the transfer from a related supplier to a DISC in the case of a sale of export property described in paragraph (b)(1) of this section.

(2) *The "4-percent" gross receipts method.* Under the gross receipts method of pricing, the transfer price for a sale by the related supplier to the DISC is the price as a result of which the taxable income derived by the DISC from the sale will not exceed the sum of (i) 4 percent of the qualified export receipts of the DISC derived from the sale of the export property (as defined in section 993(c)) and (ii) 10 percent of the export promotion expenses (as defined in paragraph (f) of this section) of the DISC attributable to such qualified export receipts.

(3) *The "50-50" combined taxable income method.* Under the combined taxable income method of pricing, the transfer price for a sale by the related supplier to the DISC is the price as a result of which the taxable income derived by the DISC from the sale will not exceed the sum of (i) 50 percent of the combined taxable income (as defined in subparagraph (6) of this paragraph) of the DISC and its related supplier attributable to the qualified export receipts from such sale and (ii) 10 percent of the export promotion expenses (as defined in paragraph (f) of this section) of the DISC attributable to such qualified export receipts.

(4) *Section 482 method.* If the rules of subparagraphs (2) and (3) of this paragraph are inapplicable to a sale or a taxpayer does not choose to use them, the transfer price for a sale by the related supplier to the DISC is to be determined on the basis of the sale price actually charged but subject to the rules provided by section 482 and the regulations thereunder.

(5) *Incomplete transactions.* (i) For purposes of the gross receipts and combined taxable income methods, where property encompassed within a transaction or group chosen under subparagraph (7) of this paragraph is transferred by a related supplier to a DISC during a taxable year of either the DISC or related supplier, but some or all of such property is not sold by the DISC during such year—

(a) The transfer price of such property sold by the DISC during such year shall be computed separately from the transfer price of the property not sold by the DISC during such year.

(b) With respect to such property not sold by the DISC during such year, the transfer price paid by the DISC for such year shall be the related supplier's cost of goods sold (see subparagraph (6)(ii) of this paragraph) with respect to the property, except that, with respect to such taxable years ending on or before [date which is 30 days after publication of this Treasury decision], the transfer price paid by the DISC shall be at least (but need not exceed) the related supplier's cost of goods sold with respect to the property.

(c) For the subsequent taxable year during which such property is resold by the DISC, an additional amount shall be paid by the DISC (to be treated as income for such year by the related supplier) equal to the excess of the amount which would have been the transfer price under this section had the transfer to the DISC by the related supplier and the resale by the DISC taken place during the taxable year of the DISC during which it resold the property over the amount already paid under (b) of this subdivision.

(d) The time and manner of payment of transfer prices required by (b) and (c) of this subdivision shall be determined under paragraph (e)(3), (4), and (5) of this section.

(ii) For purposes of this paragraph, a DISC may determine the year in which it receives property from a related supplier and the year in which it sells property in accordance with the method of identifying goods in its inventory properly used under section 471 or 472 (relating respectively to general rule for inventories and to LIFO inventories). Transportation expense of the related supplier in connection with a transaction to which this subparagraph applies shall be treated as an item of cost of goods sold with respect to the property if the related supplier includes the cost of intracompany transportation between its branches, divisions, plants, or other units in its cost of goods sold (see subparagraph (6)(ii) of this paragraph).

(6) *Combined taxable income.* For purposes of this section, the combined taxable income of a DISC and its related supplier from a sale of ex-

Reg. § 1.994-1(c)(1)

port property is the excess of the gross receipts (as defined in section 993(f)) of the DISC from such sale over the total costs of the DISC and related supplier which relate to such gross receipts. Gross receipts from a sale do not include interest with respect to the sale. Combined taxable income under this paragraph shall be determined after taking into account under paragraph (e)(2) of this section all adjustments required by section 482 with respect to transactions to which such section is applicable. In determining the gross receipts of the DISC and the total costs of the DISC and related supplier which relate to such gross receipts, the following rules shall be applied:

(i) Subject to subdivisions (ii) through (v) of this subparagraph, the taxpayer's method of accounting used in computing taxable income will be accepted for purposes of determining amounts and the taxable year for which items of income and expense (including depreciation) are taken into account. See § 1.991-1(b)(2) with respect to the method of accounting which may be used by a DISC.

(ii) Cost of goods sold shall be determined in accordance with the provisions of § 1.61-3. See sections 471 and 472 and the regulations thereunder with respect to inventories. With respect to property to which an election under section 631 applies (relating to cutting of timber considered as a sale or exchange), cost of goods sold shall be determined by applying § 1.631-1(d)(3) and (e) (relating to fair market value as of the beginning of the taxable year of the standing timber cut during the year considered as its cost).

(iii) Costs (other than cost of goods sold) which shall be treated as relating to gross receipts from sales of export property are (a) the expenses, losses, and other deductions definitely related, and therefore allocated and apportioned, thereto, and (b) a ratable part of any other expenses, losses, or other deductions which are not definitely related to a class of gross income, determined in a manner consistent with the rules set forth in § 1.861-8.

(iv) The taxpayer's choice in accordance with subparagraph (7) of this paragraph as to the grouping of transactions shall be controlling, and costs deductible in a taxable year shall be allocated and apportioned to the items or classes of gross income of such taxable year resulting from such grouping.

(v) If an account receivable arising with respect to a sale of export property is transferred by the related supplier to a DISC which is a member of the same controlled group within the meaning of § 1.993-1(k) for an amount reflecting a discount from the selling price taken into account in computing (without regard to this subdivision) combined taxable income of the DISC and its related supplier, then the combined taxable income from such sale shall be reduced by the amount of the discount.

(7) *Grouping transactions.* (i) Generally, the determinations under this section are to be made on a transaction-by-transaction basis. However, at the annual choice of the taxpayer some or all of these determinations may be made on the basis of groups consisting of products or product lines.

(ii) A determination by a taxpayer as to a product or a product line will be accepted by a district director if such determination conforms to any one of the following standards: (*a*) a recognized industry or trade usage, or (*b*) the two-digit major groups (or any inferior classifications or combinations thereof, with a major group) of the Standard Industrial Classification as prepared by the Statistical Policy Division of the Office of Management and Budget, Executive Office of the President.

(iii) A choice by the taxpayer to group transactions for a taxable year on a product or product line basis shall apply to all transactions with respect to that product or product line consummated during the taxable year. However, the choice of a product or product line grouping applies only to transactions covered by the grouping and, as to transactions not encompassed by the grouping, the determinations are made on a transaction-by-transaction basis. For example, the taxpayer may choose a product grouping with respect to one product and use the transaction-by-transaction method for another product within the same taxable year.

(iv) For rules as to grouping certain related and subsidiary services, see paragraph (d)(3)(ii) of this section.

(d) *Rules under section 994(a)(1) and (2) for transactions other than sales.* The following rules are prescribed for purposes of applying the gross receipts method or combined taxable income method to transactions other than sales:

(1) *Leases.* In the case of a lease of export property by a related supplier to a DISC for sublease by the DISC to produce gross receipts, for any taxable year the amount of rent the DISC must pay to the related supplier shall be determined under the DISC's lease with its related supplier but must be computed in a manner consistent with the rules in paragraph (c) of this section for computing the transfer price in the case of sales and resales of export property under the gross receipts method or combined taxable income method. For purposes of applying this subparagraph, transactions may not be so

Reg. § 1.994-1(d)(1)

grouped on a product or product line basis under the rules of paragraph (c)(7) of this section as to combine in any one group of transactions both lease transactions and sale transactions involving the same product or product line.

(2) *Commissions.* If any transaction to which section 994 applies is handled on a commission basis for a related supplier by a DISC and such commissions give rise to qualified export receipts under section 993(a)—

(i) The amount of the income that may be earned by the DISC in any year is the amount, computed in a manner consistent with paragraph (c) of this section, which the DISC would have been permitted to earn under the gross receipts method, the combined taxable income method, or section 482 method if the related supplier had sold (or leased) the property or service to the DISC and the DISC in turn sold (or subleased) to a third party, whether or not a related party, and

(ii) The maximum commission the DISC may charge the related supplier is the sum of the amount of income determined under subdivision (i) of this subparagraph plus the DISC's total costs for the transaction as determined under paragraph (c)(6) of this section.

(3) *Receipts from services*—(i) *Related and subsidiary services attributable to the year of the export transaction.* The gross receipts for related and subsidiary services described in paragraph (b)(3) of this section shall be treated as part of the receipts from the export transaction to which such services are related and subsidiary, but only if, under the arrangement between the DISC and its related supplier and the accounting method otherwise employed by the DISC, the income from such services is includible for the same taxable year as income from such export transaction.

(ii) *Other services.* In the case of related and subsidiary services to which subdivision (i) of this subparagraph does not apply and other services described in paragraph (b)(4) or (5) of this section performed by a related supplier (relating respectively to engineering and architectural services and certain managerial services), the amount of taxable income which the DISC may derive for any taxable year shall be determined under the arrangement between the DISC and its related supplier and shall be computed in a manner consistent with the rules in paragraph (c) of this section for computing the transfer price in the case of sales for resale of export property under the gross receipts method or combined taxable income method. Related and subsidiary services to which subdivision (i) of this subparagraph does not apply may be grouped, under the rules for grouping of transactions in paragraph (c)(7) of this section, with the products or product lines to which they are related and subsidiary, so long as the grouping of services chosen is consistent with the grouping of products or product lines chosen for the taxable year in which either the products or product lines were sold or in which payment for such services is received or accrued. The rules for grouping of transaction in paragraph (c)(7) of this section shall not apply with respect of the determination of taxable income which the DISC may derive from other services described in paragraph (b)(4) or (5) of this section performed by a related supplier or commissions on such services, and such determination shall be made only on a transaction-by-transaction basis.

(e) *Methods of applying paragraphs (c) and (d) of this section*—(1) *Limitation on DISC income ("no loss" rule)*—(i) *In general.* Except as otherwise provided in this subparagraph, neither the gross receipts method nor the combined taxable income method may be applied to cause in any taxable year a loss to the related supplier, but either method may be applied to the extent it does not cause a loss. A loss to a related supplier would result if the taxable income of the DISC would exceed the combined taxable income of the related supplier and the DISC. If, however, there is no combined taxable income of the DISC and the related supplier (because, for example, a combined loss is incurred), a transfer price (or commission) will not be deemed to cause a loss to the related supplier if it allows the DISC to recover an amount not in excess of its costs (if any).

(ii) *Special rule for applying "4 percent" gross receipts method to sales.* A transfer price or commission, determined under the "4 percent" gross receipts method (determined without regard to subdivision (i) of this subparagraph), for a sale of export property referred to in paragraph (b)(1) of this section, will not be considered to cause a loss for the related supplier if for the DISC's taxable year, the ratio that (*a*) the taxable income of the DISC derived from such sale by using such price or commission bears to (*b*) the DISC's gross receipts from such sale is not greater than the ratio that (*c*) all of the taxable income of the related supplier and the DISC from all sales of the same product or product line (domestic and foreign) to third parties whether or not related parties bears to (*d*) the total gross receipts of the related supplier and the DISC from such sales. For purposes of the preceding sentence, sales between the DISC and its related suppliers shall not be taken into account under (*c*) or (*d*) of this subdivision. For example, assume that for a taxable year of a DISC the total costs of the related supplier and the DISC with respect to all sales ($150 for domestic and $44 for foreign) of a prod-

Reg. § 1.994-1(d)(2)

uct line are $194 and the total gross receipts of the related supplier and the DISC with respect to such sales are $200 so that the total taxable income of the related supplier and the DISC with respect to such sales is $6. The parties would thus be entitled to compute a transfer price determined under the gross receipts method on any given sale of product A of such product line by the related supplier to the DISC which would allocate to the DISC taxable income equal to not more than 3 percent (i.e., $6/$200) of its gross receipts derived from its resale of such product. If the DISC were to resell an item of product A for $10, the transfer price paid by the DISC to the related supplier determined under the gross receipts method could be as low as $9.70.

(iii) *Grouping transactions.* For purposes of subdivision (i) of this subparagraph, the basis for grouping transactions chosen by the taxpayer under paragraph (c)(7) of this section for the taxable year shall be applied. For purposes of making the computations of subdivision (ii)(c) and (d) of this subparagraph, however, the taxpayer may choose any basis for grouping transactions permissible under paragraph (c)(7) of this section, even though it may not be the same basis as that already chosen under paragraph (c)(7) of this section for computing transfer prices or commissions to a DISC. If, for example, the taxpayer has chosen to group transactions on a product basis for computing transfer prices or commissions to a DISC for a taxable year, the taxpayer may still group transactions on a product line basis for purposes of computing taxable income and total gross receipts under subdivision (ii)(c) and (d) of this subparagraph. For a further example, if the taxpayer computes taxable income for one group of transactions under the gross receipts method and computes taxable income for a second group of transactions under the combined taxable income method, the taxpayer may aggregate these transactions for purposes of computing taxable income and total gross receipts under subdivision (ii)(c) and (d) of this subparagraph.

(2) *Relationship to section 482.* In applying the rules under section 994, it may be necessary to first take into account the price of a transfer (or other transaction) between the DISC (or related supplier), and a related party which is subject to the arm's length standard of section 482. Thus, for example, where a related supplier sells export property to a DISC which the related supplier purchased from related parties, the costs taken into account in computing the combined taxable income of the DISC and the related supplier are determined after any necessary adjustment under section 482 of the price paid by the related supplier to the related parties. In applying section 482 to a transfer by a DISC, however, the DISC and its related supplier are treated as if they were a single entity carrying on all the functions performed by the DISC and the related supplier with respect to the transaction and the DISC shall be allowed to receive under the section 482 standard the amount the related supplier would have received had there been no DISC.

(3) *Initial payment of transfer price or commission.* (i) The amount of a transfer price (or reasonable estimate thereof) actually charged by a related supplier to a DISC or a sales commission (or reasonable estimate thereof) actually charged by a DISC to a related supplier, in a transaction to which section 994 applies must be paid no later than 60 days following the close of the taxable year of the DISC during which the transaction occurred.

(ii) Payment must be in the form of money, property (including accounts receivable from sales by or through the DISC), a written obligation which qualifies as debt under the safe harbor rule of § 1.992-1(d)(2)(ii), or an accounting entry offsetting the account receivable against an existing debt owed by the person in whose favor the account receivable was established to the person with whom it engaged in the transaction. The form of the payment to a DISC need not be a qualified export asset under § 1.993-2. However, for the requirement that the adjusted basis of the qualified export assets of the DISC at the close of its taxable year must equal or exceed 95 percent of the sum of the adjusted bases of all assets of the DISC at the close of its taxable year, see section 992(a)(1)(B).

(iii) If the district director can demonstrate, based upon the data available as of the 60th day after the close of such taxable year, that the amount actually paid did not represent a reasonable estimate of the transfer price or commission (as the case may be) to be determined under section 994 and this section, an indebtedness will be deemed to arise, from the person required to make the payment in favor of the person to whom the payment is required to be made, in an amount equal to the difference between the amount of the transfer price or commission determined under section 994 and this section and the amount (if any) actually paid and received. Such indebtedness will be deemed to arise as of the date the transaction occurred which gave rise to the indebtedness, except that, if such transaction occurred in a taxable year of the DISC ending on or before August 15, 1975, at the taxpayer's option, the indebtedness will be deemed to arise as of the date by which payment was required under subdivision (i) of this para-

Reg. § 1.994-1(e)(3)

graph (e)(3). Such indebtedness owed to a DISC shall be treated as an asset but shall not be treated as a trade receivable or other qualified export asset (see § 1.993-2(d)(3)) as of the end of the taxable year of the DISC in which the indebtedness is deemed to arise.

(iv) (a) Except with respect to incomplete transactions to which paragraph (c)(5)(i)(b) of this section applies, if the amount actually paid results in the DISC realizing at least 50 percent of the DISC's taxable income from the transaction as reported in its tax return for the taxable year the transaction is completed, then the amount actually paid shall be deemed to be a reasonable estimate of such transfer price or commission.

(b) With respect to incomplete transactions to which paragraph (c)(5)(i)(b) of this section applies and which were initiated during a taxable year ending after August 15, 1975, the amount actually paid shall be deemed to be a reasonable estimate of such transfer price if any one of the following three tests is met:

(1) The amount actually paid by the DISC to the related supplier in respect to the property does not exceed the related supplier's cost of goods sold (see paragraph (c)(6)(ii) of this section) with respect to the property.

(2) If the transaction is completed by the date on which the DISC's return is required to be filed for the year in which the transaction was initiated, the amount actually paid by the DISC to the related supplier in respect of the property results in the DISC realizing at least 50 percent of the DISC's taxable income from the transaction when completed.

(3) The percentage that (i) an amount equal to (a) the amount actually paid by the DISC to the related supplier in respect of the property minus (b) the related supplier's cost of goods sold with respect to the property, bears to (ii) the related supplier's cost of goods sold in respect of the property, is not greater than 50 percent of the percentage that (iii) the combined taxable income for completed transactions of the same group as the property during the DISC's taxable year in which the incomplete transaction was initiated, bears to (iv) the cost of goods sold of the related supplier and DISC with respect to such transactions.

(c) For purposes of this subdivision (iv), whether the transfer price or commission actually paid is deemed a reasonable estimate may be determined on the basis of grouping transactions chosen by the taxpayer under paragraph (c)(5) and (7) of this section.

(v) An indebtedness arising under subdivision (iii) of this subparagraph shall bear interest at an arm's length rate, computed in the manner provided by § 1.482-2(a)(2) from the 61st day after the close of the DISC's taxable year in which the transaction occurred which gave rise to the indebtedness to the date of payment. The interest so computed shall be accrued and included in the taxable income of the person to whom the indebtedness is owed for each taxable year during which the indebtedness is unpaid.

(4) *Subsequent determination of transfer price or commission.* The DISC and its related supplier would ordinarily determine under section 994 and this section the transfer price payable by the DISC (or the commission payable to the DISC) for a transaction before the DISC files its return for the taxable year of the transaction. After the DISC has filed its return, a redetermination of the transfer price (or commission) may only be made if permitted by the Code and regulations thereunder. Such a redetermination would include a redetermination by reason of an adjustment under section 482 and the regulations thereunder or section 861 and § 1.861-8 which affects the amounts which entered into the determination of the transfer price or commission.

(5) *Procedure for adjustments to transfer price or commission.* (i)(a) If the transfer price (or commission) for a transaction determined under section 994 is different from the price (or commission) actually charged, the person who received too small a transfer price (or commission) or paid too large a transfer price (or commission) shall establish (or be deemed to have established), at the date of the determination or redetermination under subparagraph (4) of this paragraph of the transfer price (or commission) under section 994, an account receivable from the person with whom it engaged in the transaction equal to the difference in amount between the transfer price (or commission) so determined and the transfer price (or commission) previously paid and received. If the account receivable due the DISC is paid within 90 days after the date it is established (or deemed established), then as of the end of the taxable year of the DISC in which the transaction occurred which gave rise to the indebtedness, the account receivable shall be treated as an asset and, under § 1.993-2(d)(3) as a trade receivable, and thus as a qualified export asset.

(b) If, for example, during 1972, a DISC which uses the calendar year as its taxable year sold a product which it purchased that year from its related supplier and paid a price of $10,000 which price is a reasonable estimate under subparagraph (3)(iii) of this paragraph but is later determined under section 994 to be $8,000 immediately before the DISC filed its return for

Reg. § 1.994-1(e)(4)

1972, the DISC must be paid $2,000 (*i.e.*, $10,000 − $8,000) by its related supplier or establish an account receivable from its related supplier of $2,000. The account receivable may be paid without tax consequences, provided that such account receivable is paid within 90 days after the date it is established (or deemed established). Such account receivable paid within such 90 days will be considered to relate to the taxable year in which the transaction occurred which gave rise thereto rather than the taxable year during which it is established or paid.

(ii) Payment must be in a form specified in subparagraph (3) of this paragraph.

(iii) If an account receivable of a DISC described in subdivision (i) of this paragraph (e)(5) is not paid within 90 days of the date it is established (or deemed established), then, as of the end of the taxable year of the DISC in which the transaction occurred which gives rise to the indebtedness, the account receivable shall be treated as an asset except that, if the account receivable is established (or deemed established) in a taxable year of the DISC ending on or before August 15, 1975, at the taxpayer's option, the account receivable shall be treated as an asset as of the end of such taxable year. However, under § 1.993-2(d)(3), an account receivable referred to in the preceding sentence shall not be treated as a trade receivable or other qualified export asset.

(iv) An account receivable established in accordance with subdivision (i) of this subparagraph shall bear interest at an arm's length rate, computed in the manner provided by § 1.482-2(a)(2) from the day after the date the account receivable is deemed established to the date of payment. The interest so computed shall be accrued and included in the taxpayer's taxable income for each taxable year during which the account receivable is outstanding.

(v)(*a*) In lieu of establishing an account receivable in accordance with subdivision (i) of this subparagraph for all or part of an amount due a related supplier, the related supplier and DISC are permitted to treat all or part of any distribution which was made by the DISC out of its previously taxed income with respect to the year to which the determination or redetermination relates as an additional payment of transfer price or repayment of commission (and not as a distribution) made as of the date the distribution was made. Any additional amount arising on the determination or redetermination due the related supplier after this treatment shall be represented by an account receivable established under subdivision (i) of this subparagraph. To the extent that a distribution is so treated under this subdivision

(v), it shall cease to qualify as distribution for any Federal income tax purpose, and the DISC's account for previously taxed income shall be adjusted accordingly. If all or part of any distribution made to a shareholder other than the related supplier is recharacterized under this subdivision (v), the related supplier shall establish an account receivable from that shareholder for the amount so recharacterized. Such account receivable shall be paid in the time and manner set forth in this paragraph (e)(5). In order to obtain the relief provided by this subdivision (v), the conditions and procedures prescribed by Revenue Procedure 84-3 must be met. The provisions of this paragraph (e)(5)(v) shall apply to all open taxable years ending after December 31, 1971.

(*b*) If, for example, during 1982, a DISC commission from a related supplier with respect to a transaction completed in 1980 was redetermined to be $1,000 less than the commission actually charged by, and paid to, the DISC, the amount of any distribution previously made by the DISC from its 1980 previously taxed income to the related supplier as a shareholder may, to the extent of $1,000, be treated not as a distribution but as a repayment of commission.

(vi) The procedure for adjustments to transfer price provided by this subparagraph does not apply to incomplete transactions described in paragraph (c)(5)(i)(*b*) of this section. Such procedure will, however, be applied to any such transaction with respect to the taxable year in which the transaction is completed.

(6) *Examples.* The provisions of this paragraph may be illustrated by the following examples:

Example (1). (i) During 1975, a DISC which uses the calendar year as its taxable year purchased a product from its related supplier and made an initial payment of $8,500. If $8,500 were determined to be the transfer price under section 994, the DISC's taxable income from the transaction would be $1,000. Immediately before the DISC filed its return for 1975, under section 994 it is determined that the transfer price is $8,000 and the DISC's taxable income is $1,500. Thus, the requirement of a reasonable estimate under subparagraph (3) of this paragraph was met because the amount ($8,500) actually paid resulted in the DISC realizing taxable income of $1,000 which is not less than 50 percent of the DISC's taxable income ($1,500) from the transaction as determined under section 994.

(ii) Pursuant to subparagraph (5) of this paragraph, an account receivable due the DISC for $500, *i.e.*, $8,500-$8,000, is established on September 15, 1976, the date the DISC files its re-

Reg. § 1.994-1(e)(6)

turn for 1975, and is paid on December 1, 1976. The account receivable for $500 will be considered to relate to the taxable year (1975) in which the transaction occurred which gave rise thereto and will be a qualified export asset under § 1.993-2(d)(3) for the last day of such year.

Example (2). Assume the same facts as in example (1) except that the account receivable for $500 is paid on January 1, 1977. The account receivable for $500 will still be considered to relate to the taxable year (1975) in which the transaction occurred which gave rise thereto. However, such account receivable will be treated as an asset which is not a qualified export asset under § 1.993-2(d)(3) for the last day of such year.

(f) *Export promotion expenses*—(1) *Purpose of expense.* (i) In order for an expense or cost of a type described in subparagraph (2) of this paragraph to be an export promotion expense, the expense or cost must be incurred or treated as incurred by the DISC (under subparagraph (7) of this paragraph) to advance the sale, lease, or other distribution of export property for use, consumption, or distribution outside the United States. Costs of services in performing installation (but not assembly) on the site and for meeting warranty commitments if such services are related and subsidiary (within the meaning of § 1.993-1(d)) to any qualified sale, lease, or other distribution of export property by the DISC (or with respect to which the DISC received a commission) will be considered to advance the sale, lease, or other distribution of export property. General and administrative expenses attributable to billing customers, other clerical functions of the DISC, or generally operating the DISC, will also be considered to advance the sale, lease, or other distribution of export property.

(ii) Where an expense or cost incurred or treated as incurred by the DISC qualifies only in part as an export promotion expense, such expense or cost must be allocated between the qualified portion and such other portion on a reasonable basis. See § 1.994-2(b)(2) for the option of the related supplier not to claim expenses as export promotion expenses.

(2) *Types of expenses.* The only expenses or costs which may be export promotion expenses are those expenses or costs meeting the test of subparagraph (1) of this paragraph which constitute—

(i) Ordinary and necessary expenses of the DISC paid or incurred during the DISC's taxable year in carrying on any trade or business, allowable as deductions under section 162, such as expenses for market studies, advertising, salaries and wages (including contributions or compensations deductible under section 404) of sales, clerical, and other personnel, rentals on property, sales commissions, warehousing, and other selling expenses,

(ii) A reasonable allowance under section 167 for exhaustion, wear and tear, or obsolescence of the property of the DISC,

(iii) Costs of freight (subject to the limitations of subparagraph (4) of this paragraph),

(iv) Costs of packaging for export (as defined in subparagraph (5) of this paragraph), or

(v) Costs of designing and labeling packages exclusively for export markets (under subparagraph (6) of this paragraph).

(3) *Ineligible expenses.* Items ineligible to be export promotion expenses include, for example, interest expenses, bad debt expenses, freight insurance, State and local income and franchise taxes, the cost of manufacture or assembly operations, and items of cost of goods sold (except as otherwise provided in this paragraph in the case of certain freight, packaging, and designing and labeling expenses). Income or similar taxes eligible for a foreign tax credit under sections 901 and 903 are also not eligible to be export promotion expenses.

(4) *Freight expenses*—(i) *In general.* Export promotion expenses include one-half of the freight expense (not including insurance) for shipping export property aboard a United States flag carrier in those cases where law or regulation of the United States or of any State or political subdivision thereof or of any agency or instrumentality of any of these does not require that the export property be shipped aboard a United States flag carrier. For purposes of this paragraph, the term "freight expense" includes charges paid for C.O.D. service, miscellaneous ground charges, such as charges incurred for services normally performed by United States flag carriers, charges for services of loading aboard United States flag carriers normally performed by such carriers, freight forwarders, or independent contractors engaged in loading property, and charges attributable to a freight consolidation function normally performed by freight forwarders. In order for one-half of freight expenses paid to the owner (or the agent of the owner) of a United States flag carrier to be claimed as an export promotion expense, the DISC must obtain a written statement (such as, for example, a bill of lading) from the owner (or the agent) disclosing that the export property was shipped aboard the owner's United States flag carrier or another United States flag carrier, and the DISC must have no reasonable basis for disbelieving such statement of the owner (or the agent). For the requirement of a written state-

Reg. § 1.994-1(f)(1)

ment from a freight forwarder, see subdivision (iv) of this subparagraph.

(ii) *U.S.-flag carrier defined.* For purposes of this paragraph, the term "U.S.-flag carrier" is an airplane owned and operated by a U.S. person or persons (as defined in section 7701(a)(30)) or a ship documented under the laws of the United States. Shipment initiated by delivery to the U.S. Postal Service shall be considered shipment aboard a U.S.-flag carrier, but not if shipped to a place to which mail shipments from the United States are ordinarily accomplished by land transportation, such as to Canada or Mexico, unless airmail is specified.

(iii) *Shipment pursuant to law or regulation.* Shipment pursuant to law or regulation includes instances where a U.S.-flag carrier must be used in order to obtain permission from the Government to make the export. If the law or regulation requires a fixed portion of the export property to be shipped aboard a U.S.-flag carrier, the freight expense on that portion of such export property that was so shipped in order to satisfy such requirement cannot qualify as an export promotion expense.

(iv) *Freight forwarders.* A payment to a freight forwarder shall be considered freight expense within the meaning of this paragraph to the extent the forwarder utilizes a United States flag carrier. For purposes of this paragraph, the term "freight forwarder" includes air freight consolidators and carriers owned and operated by United States persons utilizing United States flag carriers such as non-vessel-owning common carriers. In order for one-half of freight expenses paid to a freight forwarder to be claimed as export promotion expenses, the DISC must obtain a written statement (such as, for example, a bill of lading) from the freight forwarder that the export property was shipped aboard a United States flag carrier, and the DISC must have no reasonable basis for disbelieving such statements of the freight forwarder.

(v) *Freight within the United States.* A DISC may not claim as export promotion expense any amount that is attributable to carriage of export property between points within the United States. If, however, export property is carried from the United States to a foreign country on a through shipment pursuant to a single bill of lading or similar document aboard one or more United States flag carriers, the freight expense of such carriage shall not be apportioned between the domestic and foreign portions of such carriage, even though a carrier may stop en route within the United States or the export property may be shifted from one carrier to another, and one-half of such freight expense may be claimed as an export promotion expense. Freight expense does not include the cost of transporting the export property to the depot of the United States flag carrier or freight forwarder for shipment abroad. The expense of shipment of export property initiated by delivery to the United States Postal Service for ultimate delivery outside the United States shall be considered as attributable entirely to carriage of such property outside the United States.

(5) *Packaging for export.* (i) Export promotion expenses include the direct and indirect cost of packaging export property (including the cost of the package) for export whether or not the packaging is the same as domestic packaging. Such packaging costs do not include costs of manufacturing (as defined in the regulations under section 993) and assembly. Thus, if a DISC buys and packages export property for resale, its costs of packaging the export property are export promotion expenses. If, however, the process of such packaging by the DISC is physically integrated with the process of manufacturing the export property by the related supplier, the costs of such packaging are not export promotion expenses.

(ii) The cost of containers leased from a shipping company to which the DISC also pays freight for the property packaged is not a cost of packaging. However, in such circumstances, one-half of the rental charge may be allowable as a freight expense if permitted under subparagraph (4) of this paragraph.

(6) *Designing and labeling packages.* Export promotion expenses include the direct and indirect costs of designing and labeling packages, including bottles, cans, jars, boxes, cartons, or containers, to the extent incurred for export markets. Thus, for example, to the extent incurred for supplying export markets, the cost of designing labels in a foreign language and the cost of printing such labels are export promotion expenses.

(7) *DISC must incur export promotion expenses*—(i) *In general.* In order for an expense to be an export promotion expense it must be incurred or treated as incurred under this subparagraph by the DISC. For example, an expense is incurred by a DISC if the expense results from (*a*) the DISC incurring an obligation to pay compensation to its employees, (*b*) depreciation of property owned by the DISC and used by its employees, (*c*) the DISC incurring an obligation to pay for office supplies used by its employees, (*d*) the DISC incurring an obligation to pay space costs for use by its employees, or (*e*) the DISC incurring an obligation to pay other costs supporting efforts by its employees.

Reg. § 1.994-1(f)(7)

(ii) *Payments to independent contractors.* A payment to an independent contractor, directly or indirectly, is treated as incurred by the DISC if the cost of performing the function performed by the independent contractor would be considered an export promotion expense described in subparagraphs (1) and (2) of this paragraph if performed by the DISC, and if, in a case where the services of the independent contractor were engaged by a party related to the DISC, such related party and such DISC agreed in writing before the contract was entered into that a specified portion or all of the contract was for the benefit of the DISC and that all of the expenses of the contract (eligible to be considered as export promotion expenses) with respect to such portion would be borne by the DISC.

(iii) *Expenses incurred by related parties.* Reimbursements or other payments by a DISC to a related party are export promotion expenses only if the expenses of the related person for which reimbursement is made are for space in a building actually used by employees of the DISC or for export property owned by the DISC. Except as otherwise provided in the preceding sentence, expenses incurred by a foreign international sales corporation (FISC) or a real property holding company (as defined in section 993(e)(1) and (2), respectively) shall not be treated as export promotion expenses of its DISC.

(iv) *Selling commissions paid by a DISC.* A commission paid by a DISC to a person other than a related person, with respect to a transaction which gives rise to qualified export receipts of the DISC, is an export promotion expense of the DISC. A commission paid by a DISC to a related person is not an export promotion expense.

(v) *Sales of promotional material.* If a DISC sells promotional material to a buyer of export property from the DISC at a price which is greater than the costs of the DISC for such material, such costs are not export promotion expenses. If, however, the DISC sells promotional material at a price which is less than its costs for such material, the excess of such costs over such price is an export promotion expense. For rules relating to the status of promotional material as qualified export assets and export property, see § 1.993-2 and § 1.993-3, respectively.

(vi) An expense may be incurred by the DISC under subdivisions (i) through (v) of this subparagraph even if the accounting for and payment of such expense is handled by a related party and the DISC reimburses the related party for such expenses.

(8) *Incomplete transactions.* Expenses eligible to be treated as export promotion expenses which are attributable to the sale, lease, or other distribution of export property and which are incurred prior to the taxable year of sale, lease, or other distribution by the DISC are not treated as export promotion expenses until the taxable year of sale, lease, or other distribution or until the taxable year in which it is first determined that no transaction is reasonably expected to result from the expense incurred (whether or not a transaction subsequently results). Thus, for example, if a DISC incurs a packaging cost which is otherwise eligible to be treated as an export promotion expense, the DISC may not include such charge as an export promotion expense until the year in which the export property with respect to which the packaging cost was incurred is actually sold by the DISC. If no transaction is reasonably expected to result from the packaging cost, such cost should be allocated as an export promotion expense to the group of transactions to which such cost is most closely related.

(g) *Examples.* The provisions of this section may be illustrated by the following examples:

Example (1). J and K are calendar year taxpayers. J, a domestic manufacturing company, owns all the stock of K, a DISC for the taxable year. During 1972, J manufactures only 100 units of a product (which is eligible to be export property as defined in section 933(c)). J enters into a written agreement with K whereby K is granted a sales franchise with respect to exporting such property and K will receive commissions with respect to such exports equal to the maximum amount permitted to be received under the intercompany pricing rules of section 994. Thereafter, the 100 units are sold for $1,000. J's cost of goods sold attributable to the 100 units is $650. J's direct selling expenses so attributable are $100. Although J has other deductible expenses, for purposes of this example assume that J has no other deductible expenses. K pays $230 to independent contractors which qualify as export promotion expenses under paragraph (f)(7)(ii) of this section. K does not perform functions substantial enough to entitle it to an allocation of income which meets the arm's length standard of section 482. The income which K may earn under section 994 under the franchise is $20, computed as follows:

(1) Combined taxable income:

(a) K's sales price	$1,000
(b) Less deductions:	
J's cost of goods sold	$650
J's direct selling expenses	100
K's export promotion expenses	230
Total deductions .	980
(c) Combined taxable income .	20

Reg. § 1.994-1(f)(8)

Domestic International Sales Corporation

See p. 20,601 for regulations not amended to reflect law changes

(2) K's profit under combined taxable income method (before application of loss limitation):

(a) 50 percent of combined taxable income	$10
(b) Plus: 10 percent of K's export promotion expenses (10% of $230)	23
(c) K's profit	33

(3) K's profit under gross receipts method (before application of loss limitation):

(a) 4 percent of K's sales price (4% of $1,000)	$40
(b) Plus: 10 percent of K's export promotion expenses (10% of $230)	23
(c) K's profit	63

Since combined taxable income ($20) is lower than both K's profit under the combined taxable income method ($33) and under the gross receipts method ($63), the maximum income K may earn is $20. Accordingly, the commissions K may receive from J are $250, i.e., K's expenses ($230) plus K's profit ($20).

Example (2). M and N are calendar year taxpayers. M, a domestic manufacturing company, owns all the stock of N, a DISC for the taxable year. During 1972, M produces and sells a particular product line of export property to N for $75, a price which can be justified as satisfying the standard of arm's length price of section 482. N performs substantial functions with respect to the transaction and resells the export property for $100. M's cost of goods sold attributable to the export property is $60. M's direct selling expenses so attributable (relating to advertising of the product line in foreign markets) are $12. Although M has other deductible expenses, for purposes of this example, assume that M has no other deductible expenses. N's expenses attributable to resale of the export property are $22 of which $20 are export promotion expenses. The maximum profit which N may earn with respect to the product line is $6, computed as follows:

(1) Combined taxable income:

(a) N's sales price	$100
(b) Less deductions:	
M's cost of goods sold	60
M's direct selling expenses	12
N's expenses	22
Total deductions	94
(c) Combined taxable income	6

(2) N's profit under combined taxable income method (before application of loss limitation):

(a) 50 percent of combined taxable income	3
(b) Plus: 10 percent of N's export promotion expenses (10% of $20)	2
(c) N's profit	5

(3) N's profit under gross receipts method (before application of loss limitation):

(a) 4 percent of N's sales price (4% of $100)	4
(b) Plus: 10 percent of N's export promotion expenses (10% of $20)	2
(c) N's profit	6

(4) N's profit under section 482 method:

(a) N's sales price	100
(b) Less deductions:	
N's cost of goods sold (price paid by N to M)	75
N's expenses	22
Total deductions	97
(c) N's profit	3

Since the gross receipts method results in greater profit to N ($6) than does the combined taxable income method ($5) or section 482 method ($3), and does not exceed combined taxable income ($6), N may earn a maximum profit of $6. Accordingly, the transfer price from M to N may be readjusted as long as the transfer price is not readjusted below $72, computed as follows:

Reg. § 1.994-1(g)

50,956   Domestic International Sales Corporation
See p. 20,601 for regulations not amended to reflect law changes

(5) Transfer price from M to N:

(a) N's sales price		$100
(b) Less:		
N's expenses	22	
N's profit	6	
Total subtractions		28
(c) Transfer price		72

Example (3). Q and R are calendar year taxpayers. Q, a domestic manufacturing company, owns all the stock of R, a DISC for the taxable year. During 1972, Q produces and sells a product line of export property to R for $170, a price which can be justified as satisfying the standards of arm's length price of section 482, and R resells the export property for $200. Q's cost of goods sold attributable to the export property is $115 so that the combined gross income from the sale of the export property is $85 (*i.e.*, $200 minus $115). Q's expenses incurred in connection with the property sold are $35. Q's deductible overhead and other supportive expenses allocable to all gross income are $6. Apportionment of these supportive expenses on the basis of gross income does not result in a material distortion of income and is a reasonable method of apportionment. Q's gross income from sources other than the transaction is $170 making total gross income of Q and R (excluding the transfer price paid by R) $255 (*i.e.*, $85 plus $170). R's expenses attributable to resale of the export property are $20, all of which are export promotion expenses. The maximum profit which R may earn with respect to the product line is $16, computed as follows:

(1) Combined taxable income:
  (a) R's sales price $200
  (b) Less deductions:
    (i) Q's cost of goods sold $115
    (ii) Q's expenses incurred in connection with the property sold 35
    (iii) Apportionment of Q's supportive expenses:
      Q's supportive expenses .... $ 6
      Combined gross income from sale of export property: 85
      Total gross income of Q and R: 255
      Apportionment

$$\left\{ \$6 \times \frac{\$85}{\$255} \right\} : \ldots\ldots\ldots\ldots\ldots\ldots\ldots\ldots\ 2$$

    (iv) R's expenses 20

      Total deductions 172

  (c) Combined taxable income .... $ 28

(2) R's profit under combined taxable income method (before application of loss limitation):
  (a) 50 percent of combined taxable income .... $ 14
  (b) Plus: 10 percent of R's export promotion expenses (10% of $20) 2
  (c) R's profit .... $ 16

(3) R's profit under gross receipts method (before application of loss limitation):
  (a) 4 percent of R's sales price (4% of $200) .... $ 8
  (b) Plus: 10 percent of R's export promotion expenses (10% of $20) 2
  (c) R's profit .... $ 10

(4) R's profit under section 482 method:
  (a) R's sales price $200
  (b) Less deductions:
    R's cost of goods sold (price paid by R to Q) $170
    R's expenses 20
      Total deductions $190
  (c) R's profit .... $ 10

Reg. § 1.994-1(g)

Since the combined taxable income method results in greater profit to R ($16) than does the gross receipts method ($10) or section 482 method ($10), and does not exceed combined taxable income ($28), R may earn a maximum profit of $16. Accordingly, the transfer price from Q to R may be readjusted as long as the transfer price is not readjusted below $164 computed as follows:

(5) Transfer price from Q to R:
 (a) R's sales price $200
 (b) Less: R's expenses $20
  R's profit 16
                                                                          36
 (c) Transfer price $164

Example (4). S and T are calendar year taxpayers. S, a domestic manufacturing company, owns all the stock of T, a DISC for the taxable year. During 1972, S produces and sells 100 units of a particular product to T under a written agreement which provides that the transfer price between S and T shall be that price which allocates to T the maximum permitted to be received under the intercompany pricing rules of section 994. Thereafter, the 100 units are sold by T for $950. S's cost of goods sold attributable to the 100 units is $650. S's other deductible expenses so attributable are $300. Although S has other deductible expenses, for purposes of this example, assume that S has no deductible expenses not definitely allocable to any item of gross income. T's expenses attributable to the resale of the 100 units are $50. S chooses not to apply the section 482 method. T may not earn any income under the gross receipts or combined taxable income method with respect to resale of the 100 units because combined taxable income is a negative figure, computed as follows:

(1) Combined taxable income:
 (a) T's sales price .... $ 950
 (b) Less deductions:
  S's cost of goods sold $650
  S's expenses 300
  T's expenses 50
   Total deductions 1,000
 (c) Combined taxable income (loss) .... ($ 50)

Under paragraph (e)(1)(i) of this section, T is permitted to recover its expenses attributable to the 100 units ($50) even though such recovery results in a loss or increased loss to the related supplier. Accordingly, the transfer price from S to T may be readjusted as long as the transfer price is not readjusted below $900, computed as follows:

(2) Transfer price from S to T:
 (a) T's sales price $950
 (b) Less: T's expenses 50
 (c) Transfer price $900

Example (5). Assume the same facts as in example (4) except that S chooses to apply the section 482 method and that under arm's length dealings T would have derived $10 of income. Accordingly, the transfer price from S to T may be set at an amount not less than $890, computed as follows:

(1) Transfer price from S to T:
 (a) T's sales price $950
 (b) Less: T's expenses $50
  T's profit 10
   Total deductions 60
 (c) Transfer price $890

Example (6). X and Y are calendar year taxpayers. X, a domestic manufacturing company, owns all the stock of Y, a DISC for the taxable year. During March 1972, X manufactures a particular product of export property which it leases on April 1, 1972, to Y for a term of 1 year at a monthly rental of $1,000, a rent which satisfies the standard of arm's length rental under section

Reg. § 1.994-1(g)

50,958   Domestic International Sales Corporation

See p. 20,601 for regulations not amended to reflect law changes

482. Y subleases the product on April 1, 1972, for a term of 1 year at a monthly rental of $1,200. X's cost for the product leased is $40,000. X's other deductible expenses attributable to the product are $900, all of which are incurred in 1972. Although X has other deductible expenses, for purposes of this example, assume that X has no other deductible expenses. Y's expenses attributable to sublease of the export property are $450, all of which are incurred in 1972 and are export promotion expenses. X depreciates the property on a straight line basis without the use of an averaging convention, assuming a useful life of 8 years and no salvage value. The profit which Y may earn with respect to the transaction is $2,895 for 1972 and $1,175 for 1973, computed as follows:

COMPUTATION FOR 1972

(1) Combined taxable income:
    (a) Y's sublease rental receipts for year ($1,200 × 9 months) $10,800

    (b) Less deductions:
        X's depreciation ($40,000 × 1/8 × 9/12)............................ 3,750
        X's other expenses 900
        Y's expenses 450
            Total deductions 5,100
    (c) Combined taxable income .... $ 5,700

(2) Y's profit under combined taxable income method (before application of loss limitation):
    (a) 50 percent of combined taxable income.................................. $ 2,850
    (b) Plus: 10 percent of Y's export promotion expenses (10% of $450) 45
    (c) Y's profit 2,895

(3) Y's profit under gross receipts method (before application of loss limitation):
    (a) 4 percent of Y's sublease rental receipts for year (4% of $10,800) .... $ 432
    (b) Plus: 10 percent of Y's export promotion expenses (10% of $450) 45
    (c) Y's profit 477

(4) Y's profit under section 482 method:
    (a) Y's sublease rental receipts for year $10,800

    (b) Less deductions:
        Y's lease rental payments for year 9,000
        Y's expenses.. 450
            Total deductions 9,450
    (c) Y's profit 1,350

Since the combined taxable income method results in greater profit to Y ($2,895) than does the gross receipts method ($477) or section 482 method ($1,350), Y may earn a profit of $2,895 for 1971. Accordingly, the monthly rental payable by Y to X for 1972 may be readjusted as long as the monthly rental payable is not readjusted below $828.33, computed as follows:

(5) Monthly rental payable by Y to X for 1972:
    (a) Y's sublease rental receipts for year..................................... $10,800.00

    (b) Less:
        Y's expenses 450.00
        Y's profit.. 2,895.00
            Total 3,345.00
    (c) Rental payable for 1972 .... 7,455.00

    (d) Rental payable each month ($7,455 ÷ 9 months) 828.33

COMPUTATION FOR 1973

(1) Combined taxable income:
    (a) Y's sublease rental receipts for year ($1,200 × 3 months) $3,600

    (b) Less: X's depreciation ($40,000 × 1/8 × 3/12) 1,250
    (c) Combined taxable income... 2,350

(2) Y's profit under combined taxable income method (before application of loss limitation):
    (a) 50 percent of combined taxable income $1,175

    (b) Y's profit 1,175

Reg. § 1.994-1(g)

(3) Y's profit under gross receipts method (before application of loss limitation):
   (a) 4 percent of Y's sublease rental receipts for year (4% of $3,600) 144
   (b) Y's profit .... $ 144

(4) Y's profit under section 482 method:
   (a) Y's sublease rental receipts for year $3,600
   (b) Less: Y's lease rental payments for year 3,000
   (c) Y's profit .... $ 600

Since the combined taxable income method results in greater profit to Y ($1,175) than does the gross receipts method ($144) or section 482 method ($600), Y may earn a profit of $1,175 for 1973.

Accordingly, the monthly rental payable by Y to X for 1973 may be readjusted as long as the monthly rental payable is not readjusted below $808.33, computed as follows:

(5) Monthly rental payable by Y to X for 1973:
   (a) Y's sublease rental receipts for year $3,600.00
   (b) Less: Y's profit 1,175.00
   (c) Rental payable for 1973 .... 2,425.00
   (d) Rental payable for each month ($2,425 ÷ 3 months) .... $ 808.33

[Reg. § 1.994-1.]

☐ [T.D. 7364, 7-15-75. Amended by T.D. 7435, 9-29-76, T.D. 7854, 11-6-82 and T.D. 7984, 10-11-84.]

[Reg. § 1.994-2]

§ 1.994-2. **Marginal costing rules.**—(a) *In general.* This section prescribes the marginal costing rules authorized by section 994(b)(2). If under paragraph (c)(1) of this section a DISC is treated for its taxable year as seeking to establish or maintain a foreign market for sales of an item, product, or product line of export property (as defined in § 1.993-3) from which qualified export receipts are derived, the marginal costing rules prescribed in paragraph (b) of this section may be applied to allocate costs between gross receipts derived from such sales and other gross receipts for purposes of computing, under the "50-50" combined taxable income method of § 1.994-1(c)(3), the combined taxable income of the DISC and related supplier derived from such sales. Such marginal costing rules may be applied whether or not the related supplier manufactures, produces, grows, or extracts (within the meaning of § 1.993-3(c)) the export property sold. Such marginal costing rules do not apply to sales of export property which in the hands of a purchaser related under section 954(d)(3) to the seller give rise to foreign base company sales income as described in section 954(d) unless, for the purchaser's year in which it resells the export property, section 954(b)(3)(A) is applicable or such income is under the exceptions in section 954(b)(4). Such marginal costing rules do not apply to leases of property or the performance of any services whether or not related and subsidiary services (as defined in § 1.994-1(b)(3)).

(b) *Marginal costing rules for allocations of costs*—(1) *In general.* Marginal costing is a method under which only marginal or variable costs of producing and selling a particular item, product, or product line are taken into account for purposes of section 994. Where this section is applicable, costs attributable to deriving qualified export receipts for the DISC's taxable year from sales of an item, product, or product line may be determined in any manner the related supplier (as defined in § 1.994-1(a)(3)(ii)) chooses, provided that the requirements of both subparagraphs (2) and (3) of this paragraph are met.

(2) *Variable costs taken into account.* There are taken into account in computing the combined taxable income of the DISC and its related supplier from sales of an item, product, or product line the following costs: (i) Direct production costs (as defined in § 1.471-11(b)(2)(i)) and (ii) costs which are export promotion expenses, but only if they are claimed as export promotion expenses in determining taxable income derived by the DISC under the combined taxable income method of § 1.994-1(c)(3). At the taxpayer's option, all, a part, or none of the costs which qualify as export promotion expenses may be so claimed as export promotion expenses.

(3) *Overall profit percentage limitation.* As a result of such determination of costs attributable to such qualified export receipts for the DISC's taxable year, the combined taxable income of the DISC and its related supplier from sales of such item, product, or product line for the DISC's taxable year does not exceed gross receipts (determined under § 1.993-6) of the DISC derived from such sales, multiplied by the overall profit percentage (determined under paragraph (c)(2) of this section).

(c) *Definitions*—(1) *Establishing or maintaining a foreign market.* A DISC shall be treated for its taxable year as seeking to establish or maintain a foreign market with respect to sales of an item, product, or product line of export property from which qualified export receipts are derived if the combined taxable income computed under paragraph (b) of this section is greater than the combined taxable income computed under § 1.994-1(c)(6).

(2) *Overall profit percentage.* (i) For purposes of this section, the overall profit percentage for a taxable year of the DISC for a product or product line is the percentage which—

(*a*) The combined taxable income of the DISC and its related supplier plus all other taxable income of its related supplier from all sales (domestic and foreign) of such product or product line during the DISC's taxable year, computed under the full costing method, is of

(*b*) The total gross receipts (determined under § 1.993-6) from all such sales.

(ii) At the annual option of the related supplier, the overall profit percentage for the DISC's taxable year for all products and product lines may be determined by aggregating the amounts described in subdivision (i)(*a*) and (*b*) of this subparagraph of the DISC, and all domestic members of the controlled group (as defined in § 1.993-1(k)) of which the DISC is a member, for the DISC's taxable year and for taxable years of such members ending with or within the DISC's taxable year.

(iii) For purposes of determining the amounts in subdivisions (i)(*b*) and (ii) of this subparagraph, a sale of property between a DISC and its related supplier or between domestic members of the controlled group shall be taken into account only during the DISC's taxable year (or taxable year of the member ending within the DISC's taxable year) during which the property is ultimately sold to a person which is neither the DISC nor such a domestic member.

(3) *Grouping of transactions.* (i) In general, for purposes of this section, an item, product, or product line is the item or group consisting of the product or product line pursuant to § 1.994-1(c)(7) used by the taxpayer for purposes of applying the intercompany pricing rules of § 1.994-1.

(ii) However, for purposes of determining the overall profit percentage under subparagraph (2) of this paragraph, any product or product line grouping permissible under § 1.994-1(c)(7) may be used at the annual choice of the taxpayer, even though it may not be the same item or grouping referred to in subdivision (i) of this subparagraph, as long as the grouping chosen for determining the overall profit percentage is at least as broad as the grouping referred to in such subdivision (i).

(4) *Full costing method.* For purposes of this section, the term "full costing method" is the method for determining combined taxable income set forth in § 1.994-1(c)(6).

(d) *Application of limitation on DISC income ("no loss" rule).* If the marginal costing rules of this section are applied, the combined taxable income method of § 1.994-1(c)(3) may not be applied to cause in any taxable year a loss to the related supplier, but such method may be applied to the extent it does not cause a loss. For purposes of the preceding sentence, a loss to a related supplier would result if the taxable income of the DISC would exceed the combined taxable income of the related supplier and the DISC determined in accordance with paragraph (b) of this section. If, however, there is no combined taxable income (so determined), see the last sentence of § 1.994-1(e)(1)(i).

(e) *Examples.* The provisions of this section may be illustrated by the following examples:

Example (1). X and Y are calendar year taxpayers. X, a domestic manufacturing company, owns all the stock of Y, a DISC for the taxable year. During 1973, X manufactures a product line which is eligible to be export property (as defined in § 1.993-3). X enters into a written agreement with Y whereby Y is granted a sales franchise with respect to exporting such product line from which qualified export receipts will be derived and Y will receive commissions with respect to such exports equal to the maximum amount permitted to be received under the intercompany pricing rules of section 994. Commissions are computed using the combined taxable income method under § 1.994-1(c)(3). For purposes of applying the combined taxable income method, X and Y compute their combined taxable income attributable to the product line of export property under the marginal costing rules in accordance with the additional facts assumed in the table below:

(1) Maximum combined taxable income (determined under paragraph (b)(2) of this section):

(a) Y's gross receipts from export sales	$95.00
(b) Less:	
(i) Direct materials..........	40.00
(ii) Direct labor	20.00
(iii) Y's export promotion expenses claimed in determining Y's DISC taxable income	$ 5.00
(iv) Total deductions	65.00

Reg. § 1.994-2(c)(1)

(c) Maximum combined taxable income 30.00

(2) Overall profit percentage limitation (determined under paragraph (b)(3) of this section):

(a) Gross receipts of X and Y from all domestic and foreign sales	400.00
(b) Less deductions:	
(i) Direct materials.........	160.00
(ii) Direct labor...........	80.00
(iii) Other costs (of which $8 are costs of the DISC including $5 of export promotion expenses claimed in determining Y's taxable income).....	40.00
(c) Total deductions	280.00
(d) Total taxable income from all sales computed on a full costing method	120.00
(e) Overall profit percentage (line (d) ($120) divided by line (a) ($400)) (percent)	30
(f) Multiply by gross receipts from Y's export sales (line (1)(a))	$ 95.00
(g) Overall profit percentage limitation	28.50

Since the overall profit percentage limitation under line (2)(g) ($28.50) is less than the maximum combined taxable income under line (1)(c) ($30), combined taxable income under marginal costing is limited to $28.50. Since under the franchise agreement Y is to earn the maximum commission permitted under the interecompany pricing rules of section 994, combined taxable income on the transactions is $28.50. Accordingly, the costs attributable to export sales (other than for direct material, direct labor, and export promotion expenses) are $1.50, i.e., line (1)(c) ($30) minus line (2)(g) ($28.50). Under the combined taxable income method of § 1.994-1(c)(3), Y will have taxable income attributable to the sales of $14.75, i.e., the sum of ½ of combined taxable income (½ of $28.50) and 10 percent of Y's export promotion expenses claimed in determining Y's taxable income (10 percent of $5). Accordingly, the commissions Y receives from X are $22.75, i.e., Y's costs ($8, see line (2)(b)(iii)) plus Y's profit ($14.75).

Example (2). (1) Assume the same facts as in example (1), except that gross receipts from export sales are only $85 and gross receipts from all sales remain at $400. For purposes of applying the combined taxable income method, X and Y may compute their combined taxable income attributable to the product line of export property under the marginal costing rules as follows:

(1) Maximum combined taxable income (determined under paragraph (b)(2) of this section):

(a) Y's gross receipts from export sales............................	$85.00
(b) Less:	
(i) Direct materials	$40.00
(ii) Direct labor	20.00
(iii) Y's export promotion expenses claimed in determining Y's taxable income.....................	5.00
(iv) Total deductions	65.00
(c) Maximum combined taxable income	20.00

(2) Overall profit percentage limitation (determined under paragraph (b)(3) of this section):

(a) Gross receipts from Y's export sales (line (1)(a))	85.00
(b) Multiply by overall profit percentage (as determined in example (1)) (percent).....................	30
(c) Overall profit percentage limitation	25.50

Since maximum combined taxable income under line (1)(c) ($20) is less than the overall profit percentage limitation under line (2)(c) ($25.50), combined taxable income under marginal costing is limited to $20. Since under the franchise agreement Y is to earn the maximum commission permitted under the intercompany pricing rules of section 994, combined taxable income on the transactions is $20. Accordingly, no costs (other than for direct material, direct labor, and export promotion expenses) will be attributed to export sales. Under the combined taxable income method of § 1.994-1(c)(3), Y will have taxable income attributable to the sales of $10.50, i.e., the sum of ½ of combined taxable income (½ of $20) and 10 percent of Y's export promotion expenses claimed in determining Y's taxable income (10 percent of $5). Accordingly, the Commissions Y receives from X are $18.50, i.e., Y's costs ($8, see line (2)(b)(iii) of example (1)) plus Y's profit ($10.50).

(2) If export promotion expenses are not claimed in determining taxable income of Y under the combined taxable income method, the taxable income of Y would be increased to $12.50 and commissions payable to Y would be increased to $20.50, computed as follows:

(3) Maximum combined taxable income (determined under paragraph (b)(2) of this section):

Reg. § 1.994-2(e)

(a) Y's gross receipts from export sales	$85.00
(b) Less:	
(i) Direct materials	40.00
(ii) Direct labor	20.00
(iii) Total deductions	60.00
(c) Maximum combined taxable income	25.00
(4) Overall profit percentage limitation (line (2)(c))	25.50

Since maximum combined taxable income under line (3)(c) ($25) is less than the overall profit percentage under line (4) ($25.50), combined taxable income under marginal costing is limited to $25. Since under the franchise agreement Y is to earn the maximum commission permitted under the intercompany pricing rules of section 994, combined taxable income on the transactions is $25. Accordingly, no costs (other than for direct material and direct labor) will be attributed to export sales. Under the combined taxable income method of § 1.994-1(c)(3), Y will have taxable income attributable to the sales of $12.50, i.e., ½ of combined taxable income (½ of $25). Accordingly, the commissions Y receives from X are $20.50, i.e., Y's costs ($8, see line (2)(b)(iii) of example (1)) plus Y's profit ($12.50).

Example (3). (1) Assume the same facts as in example (1), except that gross receipts from export sales are only $85, gross receipts from all sales remain at $400, and Y has costs of $40 consisting of Y's export promotion expenses of $35 and costs of $5 other than for direct material, direct labor, or export promotion expenses. For purposes of applying the combined taxable income method, X and Y may compute their combined taxable income attributable to the product line of export property under the marginal costing rules as follows:

(1) Maximum combined taxable income (determined under paragraph (b)(2) of this section):	
(a) Y's gross receipts from export sales	$85.00
(b) Less:	
(i) Direct materials	40.00
(ii) Direct labor	20.00
(iii) Y's export promotion expenses claimed in determining Y's taxable income	35.00
(iv) Total deductions	95.00
(c) Maximum combined taxable income (loss)	(10.00)
(2) Overall profit percentage limitation (as determined in example (2))	25.50

Reg. § 1.995-1(a)(2)

Since maximum combined taxable income under line (1)(c) (which is a loss of $10) is less than the overall profit percentage limitation under line (2)(c) ($25.50), combined taxable income under marginal costing is a loss of $10 and under the combined taxable income method of § 1.994-1(c)(3), Y will have no taxable income or loss attributable to the sales. Accordingly, the commissions Y receives from X are $40, i.e., Y's costs ($40).

(2) If export promotion expenses are not claimed in determining Y's taxable income under the combined taxable income method, the taxable income of Y would be increased to $12.50 and commissions payable to Y would be increased to $52.50 computed as follows:

(3) Maximum combined taxable income (determined under paragraph (b)(2) of this section) (line (3)(c) of example (2))	$25.00
(4) Overall profit percentage limitation (as determined in example (2))	25.50

The results would be the same as in part (2) of example (2), except that the commissions Y receives from X are $52.50, i.e., Y's cost ($40) plus Y's profit ($12.50). [Reg. § 1.994-2.]

☐ [T.D. 7364, 7-15-75.]

[Reg. § 1.995-1]

§ 1.995-1. Taxation of DISC income to shareholders.—(a) *In general.* (1) Under § 1.991-1(a), a corporation which is a DISC for a taxable year is not subject to any tax imposed by subtitle A of the Code (sections 1 through 1564) for the taxable year, except for the tax imposed by chapter 5 thereof (sections 1491 through 1494) on certain transfers to avoid tax.

(2) Under section 995(a), the shareholders of a DISC, or a former DISC, are subject to taxation on the earnings and profits of the DISC in accordance with the provisions of chapter 1 of the Code generally applicable to shareholders, but subject to the modifications provided in sections 995, 996, and 997.

(3) Under § 1.996-3, three divisions of earnings and profits of a DISC, or former DISC, are defined: "accumulated DISC income", "previously taxed income", and "other earnings and profits". Under § 1.995-2, certain amounts of the DISC's earnings and profits are deemed to be distributed as dividends to shareholders of the DISC at the close of the DISC's taxable year in which such earnings were derived. Such deemed distributions do not cause a reduction in the DISC's earnings and profits, but are taken into account in § 1.996-3(c) as an increase in previously taxed income. To the extent the DISC's earnings and profits are paid out in a subsequent

distribution which is, under § 1.996-1, treated as made out of such "previously taxed income," they will not be taxable to the shareholders a second time.

(4) In general, "accumulated DISC income" is the earnings and profits of the DISC which have not been deemed distributed and which may be deferred from taxation so long as they are not actually distributed with respect to its stock. However, deferral of taxation on "accumulated DISC income" may be terminated, in whole or in part, in the event of: (i) Certain foreign investment attributable to producer's loans (see § 1.995-2(a)(5) and § 1.995-5); (ii) revocation of the election to be treated as a DISC or other disqualification (see § 1.995-3); and (iii) certain dispositions of DISC stock in which gain is realized (see § 1.995-4).

(5) Since a DISC is not taxed on its taxable income, section 246(d) and § 1.246-4 provide that the deduction otherwise allowed under section 243 shall not be allowed with respect to a dividend from a DISC, or former DISC, paid or treated as paid out of accumulated DISC income or previously taxed income or with respect to a deemed distribution in a qualified year under § 1.995-2(a).

(b) *Amounts and character of amounts includible in shareholder's gross income.* Each shareholder of a corporation which is a DISC, or former DISC, shall include in his gross income—

(1) Amounts actually distributed to him that are includible in his gross income in accordance with paragraph (c) of this section,

(2) Amounts which, pursuant to § 1.995-2, he is deemed to receive as a distribution taxable as a dividend on the last day of each of the corporation's taxable years for which it qualifies as a DISC,

(3) Amounts which, pursuant to § 1.995-3, he is deemed to receive as a distribution taxable as a dividend in the event the corporation revokes its election to be treated as a DISC or otherwise is disqualified as a DISC, and

(4) Gain realized on certain dispositions of stock in the corporation which, under § 1.995-4, is includible in his gross income as a dividend.

(c) *Treatment of actual distributions.* (1) Except as provided in subparagraph (3) of this paragraph, amounts actually distributed to a shareholder of a DISC, or former DISC, with respect to his stock are includible in his gross income in accordance with section 301.

(2) Since a deemed distribution does not reduce the earnings and profits of a DISC, it does not affect the determination as to whether a subsequent actual distribution is a "dividend" under section 316(a). Since, however, the amount of a deemed distribution increases "previously taxed income", it does affect the determination as to whether a subsequent actual distribution is excluded (as described in subparagraph (3) of this paragraph) from gross income.

(3) Under § 1.996-1(c), the amount of any actual distribution (including a deficiency distribution made pursuant to § 1.992-3), with respect to stock in a DISC, or former DISC, which is treated under § 1.996-1 as made out of previously taxed income, is excluded by the distributee from gross income, but only to the extent that such amount does not exceed the adjusted basis of the distributee's stock. Under § 1.996-5(b), that portion of any actual distribution which is treated as made out of previously taxed income shall be applied against and reduce the adjusted basis of the stock and, to the extent that it exceeds the adjusted basis of the stock, it shall be treated as gain from the sale or exchange of property.

(4) A deficiency distribution pursuant to § 1.992-3 may be made after the close of the DISC's taxable year with respect to which it is made. The determinations as to whether such deficiency distribution is a dividend under section 301 and as to which division of earnings and profits is the source thereof depend upon the status of the DISC's earnings and profits account and divisions thereof at the time the distribution is actually made. See § 1.996-1(d) for the priority of such deficiency distribution over other actual distributions made during the same taxable year.

(d) *Personal holding company income.* (1) Any amount includible in a shareholder's gross income as a dividend with respect to the stock of a DISC, or former DISC, pursuant to paragraph (b) of this section shall be treated as a dividend for all purposes of the Code, except that for purposes of determining whether such shareholder is a personal holding company within the meaning of section 542 any amount deemed distributed for qualified years under § 1.995-2 or upon disqualification under § 1.995-3, any amount of gain on certain dispositions of DISC stock to which § 1.995-4 applies, and any amount treated under § 1.996-1 as distributed out of accumulated DISC income or previously taxed income shall not be treated as a dividend or any other kind of income described in section 543(a).

(2) Notwithstanding subparagraph (1) of this paragraph, the shareholder may treat as an item of income described under section 543 (for example, rents) any amount to which the exception in such subparagraph (1) applies, if it establishes to the satisfaction of the district director that such amount is attributable to earnings and profits derived from such item of income. [Reg. § 1.995-1.]

☐ [T.D. 7324, 9-27-74.]

Reg. § 1.995-1(d)(2)

[Reg. § 1.995-2]

§ 1.995-2. Deemed distributions in qualified years.—(a) *General rule.* Under section 995(b)(1), each shareholder of a DISC shall be treated as having received a distribution taxable as a dividend with respect to his stock on the last day of each taxable year of the DISC, in an amount which is equal to his pro rata share of the sum (as limited by paragraph (b) of this section), of the following seven items:

(1) An amount equal to the gross interest derived by the DISC during such year from producer's loans (as defined in § 1.993-4).

(2) An amount equal to the lower of—

(i) Any gain recognized by the DISC during such year on the sale or exchange of property (other than property which in the hands of the DISC is a qualified export asset) which was previously transferred to it in a transaction in which the transferor realized gain which was not recognized in whole or in part, or

(ii) The amount of the transferor's gain which was not recognized on the previous transfer of the property to the DISC.

For purposes of this subparagraph, each item of property shall be considered separately. See paragraph (d) of this section for special rules with respect to certain tax-free acquisitions of property by the DISC.

(3) An amount equal to the lower of—

(i) Any gain recognized by the DISC during such year on the sale or exchange of property which in the hands of the DISC is a qualified export asset (other than stock in trade or property described in section 1221(1)) and which was previously transferred to the DISC in a transaction in which the transferor realized gain which was not recognized in whole or in part, or

(ii) The amount of the transferor's gain which was not recognized on the previous transfer of the property to the DISC and which would have been includible in the transferor's gross income as ordinary income if its entire realized gain had been recognized upon the transfer.

For purposes of this subparagraph, each item of property shall be considered separately. See paragraph (d) of this section for special rules with respect to certain tax-free acquisitions of property by the DISC.

(4) For taxable years beginning after December 31, 1975, an amount equal to 50 percent of the taxable income of the DISC for the taxable years attributable to military property (as defined in § 1.995-6).

(5) For taxable years beginning after December 31, 1975, the taxable income for the taxable year attributable to base period export gross receipts (as defined in § 1.995-7).

(6) The sum of—

(i)(A) In the case of a corporate shareholder, an amount equal to 57.5 percent of the excess (if any) (one-half for DISCs' taxable years beginning before January 1, 1983) of the taxable income of the DISC for such year (computed as provided in § 1.991-1(b)(1)) over the sum of the amounts deemed distributed for the taxable year in accordance with subparagraph (1), (2), (3), (4) and (5) of this paragraph, or

(B) In the case of a non-corporate shareholder, an amount equal to one-half of the excess (if any) of the taxable income of the DISC for such year (computed as provided in § 1.991-1(b)(1)) over the sum of the amounts deemed distributed for the taxable year in accordance with subparagraphs (1), (2), (3), (4), and (5) of this paragraph.

(ii)(A) An amount equal to the amount under subdivision (i) of paragraph (a)(6) of this section multiplied by the international boycott factor as determined under section 999(c)(1), or

(B) In lieu of the amount determined under subdivision (ii)(A) of paragraph (a)(6) of this section, the amount described under section 999(c)(2) of such international boycott income, and

(iii) An amount equal to the sum of any illegal bribes, kickbacks, or other payments paid by or on behalf of the DISC directly or indirectly to an official, employee, or agent in fact of a government. An amount is paid by a DISC where it is paid by any officer, director, employee, shareholder, or agent of the DISC for the benefit of such DISC. For purposes of this section, the principles of section 162(c) and the regulations thereunder shall apply. The fair market value of an illegal payment made in the form of property or services shall be considered the amount of such illegal payment.

(7) The amount of foreign investment attributable to producer's loans of the DISC, as of the close of the "group taxable year" ending with such taxable year of the DISC, determined in accordance with § 1.995-5. The amount of such foreign investment attributable to producer's loans so determined for any taxable year of a former DISC shall be deemed distributed as a dividend to the shareholders of such former DISC on the last day of such taxable year. See § 1.995-3(e) for the effect that such deemed distribution has on scheduled installments of deemed distributions of accumu-

Reg. § 1.995-2(a)(1)

lated DISC income under § 1.995-3(a) upon disqualification.

(b) *Limitation on amount of deemed distributions under section 995(b)(1).* (1) The sum of the amounts described in paragraph (a)(1) through (a)(6) of this section which is deemed distributed pro rata to the DISC's shareholders a dividend for any taxable year of the corporation shall not exceed the DISC's earnings and profits for such year.

(2) The amount of foreign investment attributable to producer's loans of the DISC (as described in paragraph (a)(7) of this section) which is deemed to be distributed pro rata to the DISC's shareholders as dividends for any taxable year of the corporation shall not exceed the lower of the corporation's accumulated DISC income at the beginning of such year or the corporation's accumulated earnings and profits at the beginning of such year (but not less than zero)—

 (i) Increased by any DISC income of the corporation for such year as defined in § 1.996-3(b)(2) (*i.e.*, any excess of the DISC's earnings and profits for such year over the sum of the amounts described in paragraph (a)(1) through (a)(6) of this section), or

 (ii) Decreased by any deficit in the corporation's earnings and profits for such year.

Thus, for example, if a DISC has a deficit in accumulated earnings and profits at the beginning of a taxable year of $10,000, current earnings and profits of $12,000, no amounts described in paragraph (a)(1) through (a)(6) of this section for the year, and foreign investment attributable to producer's loans for the taxable year of $5,000, the DISC would have a deemed distribution described in paragraph (a)(7) of this section of $5,000 for the taxable year. On the other hand, suppose the DISC had accumulated earnings and profits of $13,000 at the beginning of the taxable year, accumulated DISC income of $10,000 at the beginning of the taxable year, a deficit in earnings and profits for the taxable year of $12,000, no amounts described in paragraph (a)(1) through (a)(6) of this section for the taxable year, and foreign investment attributable to producer's loans for the taxable year of $5,000. Under these facts the DISC would have no deemed distribution described in paragraph (a)(7) of this section because the corporation had no DISC income for the taxable year and the current year's deficit in earnings and profits subtracted from the DISC's accumulated DISC income at the beginning of the year produces a negative amount. For rules relating to the carryover to a subsequent year of the $5,000 of foreign investment attributable to producer's loans, see § 1.995-5(a)(6).

(3) If, by reason of the limitation in subparagraph (1) of this paragraph, less than the sum of the amounts described in paragraph (a)(1) through (a)(6) of this section is deemed distributed, then the portion of such sum which is deemed distributed shall be attributed first to the amount described in subparagraph (1) of such paragraph, to the extent thereof; second to the amount described in subparagraph (2) of such paragraph, to the extent thereof; third to the amount described in subparagraph (3) of such paragraph, to the extent thereof; and so forth, and finally to the amount described in paragraph (b)(6) of this paragraph.

(c) *Examples.* Paragraphs (a) and (b) of this section may be illustrated by the following examples:

Example (1). Y is a corporation which uses the calendar year as its taxable year and which elects to be treated as a DISC beginning with 1972. X is its sole shareholder. In 1972, X transfers certain property to Y in exchange for Y's stock in a transaction in which X does not recognize gain or loss by reason of the application of section 351(a). Included in the property transferred to Y is depreciable property described in paragraph (a)(3) of this section on which X realizes, but does not recognize by reason of the application of section 1245(b)(3), a gain of $20,000. If X had sold such property for cash, the $20,000 gain would have been recognized as ordinary income under section 1245. Also included in the transfer of Y is 100 shares of stock in a third corporation (which is not a related foreign export corporation) on which X realizes, but does not recognize, a gain of $5,000. In 1973, Y sells such property and recognizes a gain of $25,000 on the depreciable property and $8,000 on the 100 shares of stock. Y has accumulated earnings and profits at the beginning of 1973 of $5,000, earnings and profits for 1973 of $72,000, and taxable income for 1973 of $100,000. At the beginning of 1973, Y has $6,000 of accumulated DISC income, no previously taxed income, and a deficit of $1,000 of other earnings and profits. Under these facts and the additional facts assumed in the table below, X is treated as having received a deemed distribution taxable as a dividend of $76,000 on December 31, 1973, determined as follows:

(1) Gross interest derived by Y in 1973 from producer's loans .... $ 7,000
(2) Amount of gain on depreciable property (lower of Y's recognized gain ($25,000) or X's gain not recognized on section 1245 property ($20,000)) 20,000
(3) Amount of gain on stock (lower of X's gain not recognized ($5,000) or Y's recognized gain ($8,000)) 5,000

Reg. § 1.995-2(c)

(4) One-half excess of taxable income for 1973 over the sum of lines (1), (2), and (3) (½ of ($100,000 minus $32,000))	34,000
(5) Limitation on lines (1) through (4):	
(a) Sum of lines (1) through (4)	66,000
(b) Earnings and profits for 1973	72,000
(c) Lower of lines (a) and (b)	$66,000
(6) Amount under paragraph (a)(5) of this section:	
(a) Foreign investment attributable to producer's loans under § 1.995-5	10,000
(b) Sum of the lower of accumulated earnings and profits at beginning of 1973 ($5,000) or accumulated DISC income at beginning of 1973 ($6,000) and excess of earnings and profits for 1973 over line (5)(c) ($72,000 minus $66,000)	11,000
(c) Lower of lines (a) and (b)	10,000
(7) Total deemed distribution (sum of lines (5)(c) and (6)(c))	76,000

Example (2). Assume the facts are the same as in example (1), except that earnings and profits for 1973 amount to only $60,000. Under these facts, X is treated as receiving a deemed distribution taxable as a dividend of $65,000 on December 31, 1973, determined as follows:

(5) Limitation on lines (1) through (4):	
(a) Line (5)(a) of example (1)	$66,000
(b) Earnings and profits for 1973	60,000
(c) Lower of lines (a) and (b)	60,000
(6) Amount under paragraph (a)(5) of this section:	
(a) Line (6)(a) of example (1)	10,000
(b) Sum of the lower of accumulated earnings and profits at beginning of 1973 ($5,000) or accumulated DISC income at beginning of 1973 ($6,000) plus excess of earnings and profits for 1973 over line (5)(c) ($60,000 minus $60,000)	5,000
(c) Lower of lines (a) and (b)	5,000
(7) Total deemed distribution (sum of lines (5)(c) and (6)(c))	65,000

Example (3). Assume the facts are the same as in example (1), except that Y has a deficit in accumulated earnings and profits at the beginning of 1973 of $4,000. Such deficit is comprised of accumulated DISC income of $1,000, no previously taxed income, and a deficit in other earnings and profits of $5,000. Under these facts, X is treated as receiving a deemed distribution taxable as a dividend in the amount of $72,000 on December 31, 1973, determined as follows:

(5) Limitation on lines (1) through (4):	
(a) Line (5)(a) of example (1)	$66,000
(b) Earnings and profits for 1973	72,000
(c) Lower of lines (a) and (b)	66,000
(6) Amount under paragraph (a)(5) of this section:	
(a) Line (6)(a) of example (1)	10,000
(b) Sum of accumulated earnings and profits at beginning of 1973 (not less than $0), and excess of earnings and profits for 1973 over amount in line (5)(c) ($72,000 minus $66,000)	6,000
(c) Lower of lines (a) and (b)	6,000
(7) Total deemed distribution (sum of lines (5)(c) and (6)(c))	72,000

(d) *Special rules for certain tax-free acquisitions of property by the DISC.* (1) For purposes of paragraph (a)(2)(i) and (3)(i) of this section, if—

(i) A DISC acquires property in a first transaction and in a second transaction it disposes of such property in exchange for other property, and

(ii) By reason of the application of section 1031 (relating to like-kind exchanges) or section 1033 (relating to involuntary conversions), the basis in the DISC's hands of the other property acquired in such second transaction is determined in whole or in part with reference to the basis of the property acquired in the first transaction,

then upon a disposition of such other property in a third transaction by the DISC such other property shall be treated as though it had been transferred to the DISC in the first transaction. Thus, if the first transaction is a purchase of the property for cash, then paragraph (a)(2) and (3) of this section will not apply to a sale by the DISC of the other property acquired in the second transaction.

(2) For purposes of paragraph (a)(2)(i) and (3)(i) of this section, if a DISC acquires property in a first transaction and it transfers such property to a transferee DISC in a second transaction in which the transferor DISC's gain is not recognized in whole or in part, then such property shall be treated as though it had been transferred to the transferee DISC in the same manner in which it was acquired in the first transaction by the transferor DISC. For example, if X and Y both qualify as DISC's and X transfers property to Y in a second transaction in which gain or loss is not recognized, paragraph (a)(2) or (3) of this section does not apply to a sale of such property by Y in a third transaction if X had acquired the property in a first transaction by a purchase for cash. If,

however, X acquired the property from a transferor other than a DISC in the first transaction in which the transferor's realized gain was not recognized, then paragraph (a)(2) or (3) of this section may apply to the sale by Y if the other conditions of such paragraph (a)(2) or (3) are met.

(3) If a DISC acquires property in a second transaction described in subparagraph (1) or (2) of this paragraph in which it (or, in the case of a second transaction described in subparagraph (2) of this paragraph, the transferor DISC) recognizes a portion (but not all) of the realized gain, then the amount described in paragraph (a)(2)(ii) or (a)(3)(ii) of this section with respect to a disposition by the DISC of such acquired property in a third transaction shall not exceed the transferor's gain which was not recognized on the first transaction minus the amount of gain recognized by the DISC (or transferor DISC) on the second transaction.

(4) The provisions of this paragraph may be illustrated by the following examples:

Example (1). X and Y are corporations each of which qualifies as a DISC and uses the calendar year as its taxable year. In 1972, X acquires section 1245 property in a first transaction in which the transferor's entire realized gain of $17 is not recognized. In 1973, X transfers such property to Y in a second transaction in which X realizes a gain of $20 of which only $4 is recognized. (On December 31, 1973, X's shareholders are treated as having received a deemed distribution of a dividend which includes such $4 under paragraph (a)(3) of this section, provided the limitation in paragraph (b) of this section is met.) In a third transaction in 1974, Y sells such property and recognizes a gain of $25. With respect to Y's shareholders on December 31, 1974, the amount described in paragraph (a)(3)(ii) of this section would be limited to $13, which is the amount of the transferor's gain which was not recognized on the first transaction ($17) minus the amount of gain recognized by X on the second transaction ($4).

Example (2). Z is a DISC using the calendar year as its taxable year. In a first transaction in 1972, in exchange for its stock, Z acquires section 1245 property from A, an individual who is its sole shareholder, in a transaction in which A's realized gain of $30 is not recognized by reason of the application of section 351(a). In a second transaction in 1973, Z exchanges such property for other property in a like-kind exchange to which section 1031 (b) applies and recognizes $10 of a realized gain of $35. (On December 31, 1973, A is treated as having received a deemed distribution of a dividend which includes such $10 under paragraph (a)(3) of this section, provided the limitation in paragraph (b) of this section is met.) In a third transaction in 1974, Z sells the property acquired in the like-kind exchange and recognizes a gain of $25. With respect to A on December 31, 1974, the amount described in paragraph (a)(3)(ii) of this section is limited to $20, which is the amount of A's gain which was not recognized on the first transaction ($30) minus the amount of gain recognized by Z on the second transaction ($10).

(e) *Carryback of net operating loss and capital loss to prior DISC taxable year.* For purposes of sections 991, 995, and 996, the amount of the deduction for the taxable year under section 172 for a net operating loss carryback or carryover or under section 1212 for a capital loss carryback or carryover shall be determined in the same manner as if the DISC were a domestic corporation which had not elected to be treated as a DISC. Thus, the amount of the deduction will be the same whether or not the corporation was a DISC in the year of the loss or in the year to which the loss is carried. For provisions setting forth adjustments to the DISC's, or former DISC's, deemed distributions, adjustments to its divisions of earnings and profits, and other tax consequences arising from such carrybacks, see § 1.996-8. [Reg. § 1.995-2.]

☐ [T.D. 7324, 9-27-74. Amended by T.D. 7862, 12-16-82 and T.D. 7984, 10-11-84.]

[Reg. § 1.995-3]

§ 1.995-3. Distributions upon disqualification.—(a) *General rule.* Under section 995(b)(2), a shareholder of a corporation which is disqualified from being a DISC, either because pursuant to § 1.992-2(e)(2) it revoked its election to be treated as a DISC or because it has failed to satisfy the requirements as set forth in § 1.992-1 to be a DISC for a taxable year, shall be deemed to have received (at the times specified in paragraph (b) of this section) distributions taxable as dividends aggregating an amount equal to his pro rata share of the accumulated DISC income (as defined in § 1.996-3(b)) of such corporation which was accumulated during the immediately preceding consecutive taxable years for which the corporation was a DISC. The pro rata share referred to in the preceding sentence shall be determined as of the close of the last of such consecutive taxable years for which the corporation was a DISC. See § 1.996-7(c) for rules relating to the carryover of, and maintaining a separate account for, such accumulated DISC income in certain reorganizations.

(b) *Time of receipt of deemed distributions.* Distributions described in paragraph (a) of this section shall be deemed to be received in equal

Reg. § 1.995-3(b)

installments on the last day of each of the 10 taxable years of the corporation following the year of the disqualification described in paragraph (a) of this section, except that in no case may the number of equal installments exceed the number of the immediately preceding consecutive taxable years for which the corporation was a DISC.

(c) *Transfer of shares.* Deemed distributions are includible under paragraphs (a) and (b) of this section in a shareholder's gross income as a dividend only so long as he continues to hold the shares with respect to which the distribution is deemed made. Thus, the transferee of such shareholder will include in his gross income under paragraphs (a) and (b) of this section the remaining installments of the deemed distribution which the transferor would have included in his gross income as a dividend had he not transferred the shares. However, if the transferee acquires the shares in a transaction in which the transferor's gain is treated under § 1.995-4 in whole or in part as a dividend, then under § 1.996-4(a) such transferee does not include subsequent installments in his gross income to the extent that the transferee treats such subsequent installments as made out of previously taxed income.

(d) *Effect of requalification.* Deemed distributions under paragraphs (a) and (b) of this section continue and are includible in gross income as dividends by the shareholders whether or not the corporation subsequently requalifies and is treated as a DISC.

(e) *Effect of actual distributions and deemed distributions under section 995(b)(1)(G).* If, during the period a shareholder of a DISC, or former DISC, is taking into account deemed distributions under paragraphs (a) and (b) of this section, an actual distribution is made to him out of accumulated DISC income or a deemed distribution because of foreign investment attributable to producer's loans is made under § 1.995-2(a)(5) out of accumulated DISC income, such actual or deemed distribution shall first reduce the last installment of the deemed distributions scheduled to be included in the shareholder's gross income as a dividend, and then the preceding scheduled installments in reverse order. If deemed distributions are scheduled to be included in gross income for two or more disqualifications, an actual distribution or a deemed distribution under § 1.995-2(a)(5) which is treated as made out of accumulated DISC income reduces the deemed distributions resulting from the earlier disqualification first.

(f) *Examples.* This section may be illustrated by the following examples:

Example (1). X Corporation, which uses the calendar year as its taxable year, elects to be treated as a DISC beginning with 1972. X qualifies as a DISC for taxable years 1972 through 1975, but, pursuant to § 1.992-2(e)(2), revokes its election as of January 1, 1976, and is disqualified as a DISC. On that date, X has $24,000 of accumulated DISC income. X's shareholders will be deemed to receive $6,000 in distributions taxable as a dividend on the last day of each of X's four succeeding taxable years (1977, 1978, 1979, and 1980).

Example (2). Assume the same facts as in example (1), except that in 1978 X makes an actual distribution of $22,000 to its shareholders of which $10,000 is treated under § 1.996-1 as made out of accumulated DISC income. (The remaining $12,000 of such distribution is treated as made out of previously taxed income.) The actual distribution would first reduce the $6,000 deemed distribution scheduled for 1980 to zero and then reduce the $6,000 deemed distribution scheduled for 1979 to $2,000. Thus, X's shareholders include in 1978 $16,000 in gross income as dividends ($10,000 of actual distributions and the $6,000 deemed distribution scheduled for that year) and $2,000 as a dividend in 1979.

Example (3). Assume the same facts as in example (2), except that X requalifies as a DISC for taxable year 1977 during which it derives $7,000 of DISC income (computed after taking into account a deemed distribution under § 1.995-2(a)(4) of $7,000), but is again disqualified in 1978. In addition, X makes an actual distribution in 1977 equal to the deemed distribution of $7,000. Such actual distribution is excluded from gross income under § 1.996-1(c). In 1977, X's shareholders include in gross income as dividends the $6,000 deemed distribution upon disqualification (in addition to the deemed distributions of $7,000 under § 1.995-2 for 1977 when it was treated as a DISC). The actual distribution in 1978 still reduces the installments resulting from the earlier disqualification. Thus, in 1978, X's shareholders include $16,000 in gross income as dividends. In 1979, X's shareholders include $9,000 in gross income as dividends (the final installment of $2,000 from the earlier disqualification plus the single deemed distribution of $7,000 resulting from the later disqualification). [Reg. § 1.995-3.]

☐ [T.D. 7324, 9-27-74. Amended by T.D. 7854, 11-15-82.]

[Reg. § 1.995-4]

§ 1.995-4. **Gain on certain dispositions of stock in a DISC.**—(a) *Disposition in which gain is recognized* —(1) *In general.* If a shareholder disposes, or is treated as disposing, of stock in a

DISC, or former DISC, then any gain recognized on such disposition shall be included in the shareholder's gross income as a dividend, notwithstanding any other provision of the Code, to the extent of the accumulated DISC income amount (described in paragraph (d) of this section). To the extent the recognized gain exceeds the accumulated DISC income amount, it is taxable as gain from the sale or exchange of the stock.

(2) *Nonapplication of subparagraph (1).* The provisions of subparagraph (1) of this paragraph do not apply (i) to the extent gain is not recognized (such as, for example, in the case of a gift or an exchange of stock to which section 354 applies) and (ii) to the amount of any recognized gain which is taxable as a dividend (such as, for example, under section 301 or 356(a)(2)) or as gain from the sale or exchange of property which is not a capital asset. The amount taxable as a dividend under section 301 or 356(a)(2) is subject to the rules provided in § 1.995-1(c) for the treatment of actual distributions by a DISC.

(b) *Disposition in which separate corporate existence of DISC is terminated*—(1) *General.* If stock in a corporation that is a DISC, or former DISC, is disposed of in a transaction in which its separate corporate existence as a DISC, or former DISC, is terminated, then, notwithstanding any other provision of the Code, an amount of realized gain shall be recognized and included in the transferor's gross income as a dividend. The realized gain shall be recognized to the extent that such gain—

(i) Would not have been recognized but for the provisions of this paragraph, and

(ii) Does not exceed the accumulated DISC income amount (described in paragraph (d) of this section).

(2) *Cessation of separate corporate existence as a DISC, or former DISC.* For purposes of subparagraph (1) of this paragraph, separate corporate existence as a DISC, or former DISC, will be treated as having ceased if, as a result of the transaction, there is no separate entity which is a DISC and to which is carried over the accumulated DISC income and other tax attributes of the DISC, or former DISC, the stock of which is disposed of. Thus, for example, if stock in a DISC, or former DISC, is exchanged in a transaction described in section 381(a) (relating to carryovers in certain corporate acquisitions), the gain realized on the transfer of such stock will not be recognized under subparagraph (1) of this paragraph if the assets of such DISC, or former DISC, are acquired by a corporation which immediately after the acquisition qualifies as a DISC. For a further example, if a DISC, or former DISC, is liquidated in a transaction to which section 332 (relating to complete liquidations of subsidiaries) applies, the transaction will be subject to subparagraph (1) of this paragraph if the basis to the transferee corporation of the assets acquired on the liquidation is determined under section 334(b)(2) (as in effect prior to amendment by the Tax Equity and Fiscal Responsibility Act of 1982) or if immediately after such liquidation the transferee of such assets does not qualify as a DISC. However, separate corporate existence as a DISC, or former DISC, will not be treated as having ceased in the case of a mere change in place of organization, however effected. See § 1.996-7 for rules for the carryover of the divisions of a DISC's earnings and profits to one or more DISC's.

(c) *Disposition to which section 311, 336, or 337 applies*—(1) *In general.* If, after December 31, 1976, a shareholder distributes, sells, or exchanges stock in a DISC, or former DISC, in a transaction to which section 311, 336, or 337 applies, then an amount equal to the excess of the fair market value of such stock over its adjusted basis in the hands of the shareholder shall, notwithstanding any other provision of the Code, be included in gross income of the shareholder as a dividend to the extent of the accumulated DISC income amount (described in paragraph (d) of this section).

(2) *Nonapplication of subparagraph (1).* Subparagraph (1) shall not apply if the person receiving the stock in the disposition has a holding period for the stock which includes the period for which the stock was held by the shareholder disposing of such stock.

(d) *Accumulated DISC income amount*—(1) *General.* For purposes of this section, the accumulated DISC income amount is the accumulated DISC income of the DISC or former DISC which is attributable to the stock disposed of and which was accumulated in taxable years of such DISC or former DISC during the period or periods such stock was held by the shareholder who disposed of such stock.

(2) *Period during which a shareholder has held stock.* For purposes of this section, the period during which a shareholder has held stock includes the period he is considered to have held it by reason of the application of section 1223 and, if his basis is determined in whole or in part under the provisions of section 1014(d) (relating to special rule for DISC stock acquired from decedent), the holding period of the decedent. Such holding period is to exclude the day of acquisition but include the day of disposition. Thus, for example, if A purchases stock in a DISC on December 31,

Reg. § 1.995-4(d)(2)

1972, and makes a gift of such stock to B on June 30, 1973, then on December 31, 1974, B will be treated as having held the stock for 2 full years. If the basis of the stock in C's hands is determined under section 1014(d) upon a transfer from B's estate on December 31, 1976 by reason of B's death on June 30, 1974, then on December 31, 1976, C will be treated as having held the stock for 4 full years.

(e) *Accumulated DISC income allocable to shareholder under section 995(c)(2)* —(1) *In general.* Under this paragraph, rules are prescribed for purposes of paragraph (d) of this section as to the manner of determining, with respect to the stock of a DISC, a former DISC, disposed of, the amount of accumulated DISC income which is attributable to such stock and which was accumulated in taxable years of the corporation during the period or periods the stock disposed of was held or treated under paragraph (d)(2) of this section as held by the transferor. Subparagraphs (2), (3), and (4) of this paragraph set forth a method of computation which may be employed to determine such amount. Any other method may be employed so long as the result obtained would be the same as the result obtained under such method.

(2) *Step 1.* Determine the increase (or decrease) in accumulated DISC income for each taxable year of the DISC, or former DISC, by subtracting from the amount of accumulated DISC income (as defined in § 1.996-3(b)) at the close of each taxable year the amount thereof as of the close of the immediately preceding taxable year.

(3) *Step 2.* (i) Determine for each taxable year of the DISC, or former DISC, the increase (or decrease) in accumulated DISC income per share by dividing such increase (or decrease) for the year by the number of shares outstanding or deemed outstanding on each day of such year.

(ii) If the number of shares of stock in the corporation outstanding on each day of a taxable year of the DISC, or former DISC, is not constant, then the number of such shares deemed outstanding on each day of such year shall be the sum of the fractional amounts in respect of each share which was outstanding on any day of the taxable year. The fractional amount in respect of a share shall be determined by dividing the number of days in the taxable year on which such share was outstanding (excluding the day the share became outstanding, but including the day the share ceased to be outstanding), by the total number of days in such taxable year.

(iii) If for any taxable year of a DISC, or former DISC, the share disposed of was not held (or treated under paragraph (d)(2) of this section as held) by the disposing shareholder for the entire year, then the amount of increase (or decrease) in accumulated DISC income attributable to such share for such year is the amount determined as if he held the share until the end of such year multiplied by a fraction the numerator of which is the number of days in the taxable year on which the shareholder held (or under paragraph (d)(2) of this section is treated as having held) such share and the denominator of which is the total number of days in the taxable year.

(4) *Step 3.* Add the amounts computed in step 2 for each taxable year of the DISC, or former DISC, in which the shareholder held such share of stock.

(5) *Examples.* This paragraph may be illustrated by the following examples:

Example (1). X Corporation uses the calendar year as its taxable year and elects to be a DISC for the first time for 1973. On January 1, 1973, X has 20 shares issued and outstanding. A and B each own 10 shares. On July 1, 1976, X issues 10 shares to C. On December 31, 1977, A sells his 10 shares to D and recognizes a gain of $120. Under these facts and other facts assumed in the table below, A includes in his gross income for 1977 a dividend under paragraph (b) of this section of $61.30 and long-term capital gain of $58.70.

Year	(a) Year end accumulated DISC income	(b) Increase (decrease) in accumulated DISC income	(c) Shares outstanding	(d) Increase (decrease) per share (column (b) ÷ column (c))
1973	$ 80	$80	20	$4.00
1974	50	(30)	20	(1.50)
1975	80	30	20	1.50
1976	100	20	25 [1]	.80
1977	140	40	30	1.33

[1] Under subparagraph (3)(ii) of this paragraph, the aggregate fractional amount of the 10 shares issued on July 1, 1976, is 5 shares, *i.e.,* 10 shares, multiplied by (183 days/366 days). Thus, the number of shares deemed outstanding for 1976 is 25 shares, *i.e.,* 20 shares plus 5 shares.

Reg. § 1.995-4(e)(1)

(1)	Total increase in accumulated DISC income for each share disposed of (sum of amounts in column (d))	$ 6.13
	Multiply by number of shares disposed of	10
(2)	Total amount of accumulated DISC income attributable to A's shares disposed of	$ 61.30
(3)	A's gain	120.00
(4)	Portion of A's gain taxable as a dividend (lower of lines (2) and (3))	61.30
(5)	Portion of A's gain taxable as long-term capital gain (line (3) minus line (4))	$ 58.70

Example (2). Assume the same facts as in example (1), except that A sells his 10 shares to D on July 1, 1977. Under subparagraph (3)(iii) of this paragraph, the amount of increase in accumulated DISC income for 1977 which is attributable to each share disposed of is limited to $.67, i.e., $1.33 multiplied by 182 days/365 days. Therefore, the sum of the yearly increases (and decreases) in accumulated DISC income for each share is reduced by $.66 (i.e., $1.33 minus $.67). The total increase in accumulated DISC income for each share disposed of is $5.47 (i.e., $6.13 minus $.66). Under these facts, A would include in his gross income for 1977 a dividend of $54.70 and long-term capital gain of $65.30 determined as follows:

(1)	Total increase in accumulated DISC income for each share disposed of	$ 5.47
	Multiplied by number of shares disposed of	10
(2)	Total amount of accumulated DISC income attributable to all shares disposed of	54.70
(3)	A's gain	120.00
(4)	Portion of A's gain taxable as a dividend (lower of lines (2) and (3))	54.70
(5)	Portion of A's gain taxable as long-term capital gain (line (3) minus line (4))	65.30

[Reg. § 1.995-4.]

☐ [T.D. 7324, 9-27-74. Amended by T.D. 7854, 11-15-82.]

[Reg. § 1.995-5]

§ 1.995-5. Foreign investment attributable to producer's loans.—(a) *In general*—(1) *Limitation.* Under section 995(d), the amount as of the close of a "group taxable year" (as defined in subparagraph (3) of this paragraph) of foreign investment attributable to producer's loans of a DISC for purposes of section 995(b)(1)(G) shall be the excess (as of the close of such year) of—

(i) The smallest of—

(a) The amount of the net increase in foreign assets (as defined in paragraph (b) of this section) by domestic and foreign members of the controlled group which includes the DISC,

(b) The amount of the actual foreign investment by the domestic members of such group (as determined under paragraph (c) of this section), or

(c) The amount of outstanding producer's loans (as determined under § 1.993-4) by such DISC to members of such controlled group, over

(ii) The amount (determined under § 1.995-2(a)(5) and (b)(2)) of foreign investment attributable to producer's loans treated under section 995(b)(1)(G) as deemed distributions by the particular DISC taxable as dividends for prior taxable years of that particular DISC.

Thus, for example, if the shareholders of a DISC which uses the calendar year as its taxable year (and which is a member of a controlled group in which all of the members use the calendar year as their taxable year) are treated under section 995(b)(1)(G) as receiving foreign investment attributable to producer's loans of a DISC of $0 in 1972, $10 in 1973, and $30 in 1974, or a total of $40, and if the smallest of the amounts described in subdivision (i) of this subparagraph at the end of 1975 is $90, then the amount of the foreign investment attributable to producer's loans of a DISC at the end of 1975 is $50, i.e., the excess (as of the close of 1975) of the smallest of the amounts described in subdivision (i) of this subparagraph ($90) over the sum of the amounts of foreign investment attributable to producer's loans treated under section 995(b)(1)(G) as deemed distributions by the DISC taxable as dividends for prior taxable years of the DISC ($40). If the separate corporate existence of the DISC as to which the amount described in subdivision (ii) of this subparagraph relates ceases to exist within the meaning of § 1.995-4(c)(2), then such amount shall no longer be taken into account by the group for any purpose. For inclusion of amounts because of certain corporate acquisitions, see paragraph (d) of this section.

(2) *Controlled group; domestic and foreign member.* For purposes of this section—

(i) The term "controlled group" has the meaning assigned to such term by § 1.993-1(k).

(ii) The term "domestic member" means a domestic corporation which is a member of a controlled group, and the term "foreign member" means a foreign corporation which is a member of a controlled group.

(3) *Group taxable year.* (i) The term "group taxable year" refers collectively to the taxable year of the DISC and to the taxable year of each

Reg. § 1.995-5(a)(3)

corporation in the controlled group which includes the DISC ending with or within the taxable year of the DISC. Thus, for example, if a corporation has a subsidiary which uses the calendar year as its taxable year and which elects to be treated as a DISC, and if the parent has a taxable year ending on October 31, the "group taxable year" for 1973 would refer to calendar year 1973 for the DISC and to the parent's taxable year ending October 31, 1973.

(ii) In cases in which the DISC makes a return for a short taxable year, that is, for a taxable year consisting of a period of less than 12 months, pursuant to section 443 and the regulations thereunder, or § 1.991-1(b)(3), the following rules shall apply—

(a) In the case of a change in the annual accounting period of the DISC resulting in a short taxable year, the "group taxable year" refers collectively to the short taxable year and to the taxable year of each corporation in the controlled group which includes the DISC ending with or within the short taxable year.

(b) In the case of a DISC which is in existence during only part of what would otherwise be its taxable year, the "group taxable year" refers collectively to the short period during which the DISC was in existence and to the taxable year of each corporation in the controlled group which includes the DISC ending with or within the 12-month period ending on the last day of the short period.

(iii) With respect to periods prior to the first taxable year for which a member of the group qualified (or is treated) as a DISC, each group taxable year shall be determined under subdivision (i) of this subparagraph as if such member was in existence, it qualified as a DISC, and its taxable year ended on that date corresponding to the date such member's first taxable year ended after it qualified (or is treated) as a DISC whether or not the corporation which qualifies (or is treated) as a DISC used the same taxable year before it so qualified (or is so treated). Thus, for example, if a corporation which is organized on March 3, 1975, uses the calendar year as its taxable year, and is a member of a controlled group which does not include a DISC, first qualifies (or is treated) as a DISC for calendar year 1975, then the term "group taxable year" with respect to years prior to 1975 refers collectively to such prior calendar years and to the taxable year of each corporation in the group ending with or within such prior calendar years.

(iv) For special rules in the case of a group which includes more than one DISC, see paragraph (g) of this section.

(4) *Amounts determined for prior years.* Unless the 3-year limitation is properly elected under subparagraph (5) of this paragraph, the amounts described in paragraphs (b) (relating to net increase in foreign assets) and (c) (relating to actual foreign investments by domestic members) of this section reflect, as of the close of a group taxable year, amounts for all taxable years of members of the group beginning after December 31, 1971 (and amounts arising after December 31, 1971, or such other date prescribed in paragraph (b)(7) of this section), provided that such amounts relate to such group taxable year and preceding group taxable years. Thus, for example, if all members of a controlled group use the calendar year as the taxable year, and 1980 is the first taxable year for which any member of the group qualifies (or is treated) as a DISC, then, unless the 3-year limitation is elected under subparagraph (5) of this paragraph, the amounts described in paragraphs (b) and (c) of this section will be taken into account beginning with the dates specified in the preceding sentence. For rules as to carryovers on certain corporate acquisitions and reorganizations, see paragraph (d) of this section.

(5) *Three-year elective limitation.* (i) A DISC may elect to take into account only amounts described in paragraphs (b) (relating to net increase in foreign assets) and (c) (relating to actual foreign investment by domestic members) of this section for the 3 taxable years of each member immediately preceding its taxable year included in that first group taxable year which includes a member's first taxable year during which it qualifies (or is treated) as a DISC. For purposes of the preceding sentence, determinations shall be made by reference to the taxable year of the issuer or transferor (as the case may be). If an election is made under this subdivision, the offset for uncommitted transitional funds under paragraph (b)(7) of this section is not allowed. If an election is made under this subdivision, the 3-year limitation applies to amounts described in paragraphs (b)(4) and (c)(1) and (2) of this section.

(ii) An election under subdivision (i) of this subparagraph shall not apply with respect to amounts which must be carried over under paragraph (d) of this section in the case of certain corporate acquisitions and reorganizations.

(iii) An election under subdivision (i) of this subparagraph shall be made by the DISC attaching to its first return, filed under section 6011(e)(2), a statement to the effect that the 3-year limitation is being elected under § 1.995-5(a)(5)(i).

(6) *Cumulative basis.* Pursuant to section 995(d)(5), all determinations of amounts specified

Reg. § 1.995-5(a)(4)

in this section are to be made on a cumulative basis from the 1st year (or date) provided for in this section. Thus, each such determination shall take into account a net increase or a net decrease during the year, as the case may be. However, if the 3-year limitation is elected under subparagraph (5) of this paragraph, then only amounts with respect to periods specified in such subparagraph (5) are amounts taken into account for years before a member of the group qualifies (or is treated) as a DISC. The computations described in this section may be made in any way chosen by the DISC (including a corporation being tested as to whether it qualifies as a DISC), provided such method results in the amount prescribed by this section.

(7) *Example.* The provisions of this paragraph may be illustrated by the following example:

Example. X Corporation, which uses the calendar year as its taxable year, is a member of a controlled group (within the meaning of subparagraph (2) of this paragraph). X elects to be treated as a DISC beginning with 1972. The amount of foreign investment attributable to X's producer's loans treated under section 995(b)(1)(G) as a distribution taxable as a dividend as of the close of each group taxable year with respect to each taxable year of X from 1972 through 1975 are set forth in the table below, computed on the basis of the facts assumed (the amounts on lines (1), (2), (3), and (5) being running balances):

Taxable year of X	1972	1973	1974	1975
(1) Net increase (or decrease) in foreign assets since January 1, 1972, at close of group taxable year	$(30)	$10	$100	$150
(2) Actual foreign investment at close of group taxable year	20	60	80	140
(3) Outstanding producer's loans of X (the DISC) as of the close of group taxable year	0	40	90	120
(4) Smallest of lines (1), (2), or (3) (not less than zero)	0	10	80	120
(5) Less section 995(b)(1)(G) deemed distributions for prior taxable years (sum of lines (5) and (6) from prior year)	0	0	10	80
(6) Section 995(b)(1)(G) deemed distribution as of close of taxable year	0	10	70	40

(b) *Net increase in foreign assets*—(1) *In general.* (i) The term "net increase in foreign assets" when used in this section means the excess for the controlled group (as of the close of the group taxable year) of *(a)* the investment in foreign assets to be taken into account under subparagraph (2) of this paragraph over *(b)* the aggregate of the five offsets allowed by subparagraphs (3) through (7) of this paragraph.

(ii) No amount described in this paragraph (other than amounts described in subparagraphs (4) and (7) of this paragraph) with respect to a member of the group (or foreign branch of a member) shall be taken into account unless it is attributable to a taxable year of such member beginning after December 31, 1971. For a 3-year elective limitation with respect to the first taxable year for which a member qualifies (or is treated) as a DISC, see paragraph (a)(5) of this section. For manner of determining amounts on a cumulative basis, see paragraph (a)(6) of this section.

(2) *Investments made in foreign assets.* (i) For purposes of subparagraph (1) of this paragraph, there shall be taken into account as investment in foreign assets the aggregate of the amounts expended (within the meaning of subdivision (ii) of this subparagraph) during the period described in subparagraph (1)(ii) of this paragraph by all members of the controlled group which includes the DISC to acquire assets described in section 1231(b) (determined without regard to any holding period therein provided) which are located outside the United States (as defined in § 1.993-7) reduced by the aggregate of the amounts received by all such members of the controlled group from the sale, exchange, or involuntary conversion of such assets described in section 1231(b) which are located outside the United States. For purposes of this section, amounts expended for assets which are qualified export assets (as defined in § 1.993-2) of a DISC (or which would be qualified export assets if owned by a DISC) shall not be taken into account. Thus, for example, if a DISC acquires a qualified export asset located outside the United States, the asset is not to be taken into account for purposes of determining the net increase in foreign assets.

(ii) As used in subdivision (i) of this subparagraph, the term "amounts expended" (or amounts received) means the amount of any money or the fair market value (on the date of acquisition, sale, exchange, or involuntary conversion) of any property (other than money) used to acquire (or received for) the assets described in such subdivision (i).

Reg. § 1.995-5(b)(2)

(iii) For purposes of this subparagraph, an asset (other than an aircraft or vessel) is considered as located outside the United States if it was used predominantly outside the United States during the group taxable year. The determination as to whether such an asset is used predominantly outside the United States during the group taxable year in which it was acquired or sold, exchanged, or involuntarily converted shall be made by applying the rules of § 1.993-3(d) except that an aircraft described in section 48(a)(2)(B)(i) or a vessel described in section 48(a)(2)(B)(iii) shall be considered located in the United States and all other aircraft or vessels shall be considered located outside the United States. Thus, for example, if a member of a controlled group which includes a DISC acquires a vessel which is documented under the laws of a foreign country, the amount expended to acquire that vessel is an amount described in subdivision (i) of this subparagraph.

(iv) *Examples.* The provisions of this subparagraph may be illustrated by the following examples:

Example (1). X Corporation, which uses the calendar year as its taxable year, is a domestic member of a controlled group (within the meaning of paragraph (a)(2) of this section). During 1972, in a transaction to which section 1031 applies, X acquires a warehouse located outside the United States and having a fair market value of $100. As consideration, X transfers $20 in cash and a warehouse located within the United States and having a fair market value of $80. Under these facts, $100 will be taken into account as investment in foreign assets.

Example (2). The facts are the same as in example (1), except that the warehouse transferred by X as consideration is located outside the United States. Under these facts, only $20 will be taken into account as investment in foreign assets because the amount expended for such assets (*i.e.,* $100) is reduced by the fair market value of any property located outside the United States received in exchange for such assets (*i.e.,* $80).

(3) *Depreciation with respect to all foreign assets of a controlled group.* (i) An offset allowed by this subparagraph is the depreciation (determined under subdivision (ii) of this subparagraph) or depletion (determined under subdivision (iii) of this subparagraph) attributable to taxable years of the member beginning after December 31, 1971, with respect to all of the group's foreign assets described in subparagraph (2) of this paragraph including such assets acquired prior to the date provided in such subparagraph (2), and without regard to whether the 3-year election in paragraph (a)(5) of this section is made. Thus, for example, depreciation for a taxable year of a member beginning after December 31, 1971, with respect to an asset described in section 1231(b) which is located outside of the United States and which was acquired during a taxable year of the member beginning before January 1, 1972, is an offset allowed by this subparagraph. For a further example, depreciation with respect to a qualified export asset is not such an offset.

(ii) The depreciation taken into account under subdivision (i) of this subparagraph shall be—

(a) In the case of an asset owned by a domestic member, only the amount allowed under section 167(b)(1) (relating to the allowance of the straight-line method of depreciation) and § 1.162-11(b) (relating to amortization in lieu of depreciation), but not the amount allowed under section 179 (relating to the additional first-year depreciation allowance).

(b) In the case of an asset owned by a foreign member, the depreciation and amortization (referred to in *(a)* of this subdivision) allowable for purposes of computing earnings and profits under subparagraph (5)(i) of this paragraph.

(iii) The depletion taken into account under subdivision (i) of this subparagraph shall be limited to cost depletion computed under sections 611 and 612 and the regulations thereunder. Thus, percentage depletion is not to be taken into account in computing the offset under this subparagraph.

(4) *Amount of outstanding stock or debt.* (i) An offset allowed by this subparagraph is the outstanding amount of stock (including treasury stock) or debt obligations of any member of the group issued, sold, or exchanged after December 31, 1971, by any member (whether or not the same member) to persons who (on the date of such issuance, sale, or exchange) were neither United States persons (within the meaning of section 7701(a)(30)) nor members of the group, provided that, in the case of a debt obligation, such obligation is not repaid within 12 months after such issuance, sale, or exchange. Thus, for example, if stock is issued to a member of the group before January 1, 1972, and after December 31, 1971, it is sold to a person who is neither a United States person nor a member of the group, an offset allowed by this subparagraph includes the outstanding amount of such stock. For purposes of this subparagraph, foreign branches of United States banks are not considered to be United States persons.

Reg. § 1.995-5(b)(3)

(ii) The outstanding amount of stock or debt obligations shall be determined in accordance with the following provisions:

(a) The outstanding amount of stock or debt obligations described in subdivision (i) of this subparagraph is equal to the net amount described in (b) of this subdivision reduced (but not below zero) by the amount described in (c) of this subdivision.

(b) The net amount described in this subdivision (b) is the excess of (1) the aggregate of the amount of money and the fair market value of property (other than money) transferred by persons who are not members of the group and who are not U.S. persons as consideration for such stock and debt obligations over (2) fees and commission expenses borne by the issuer or transferor with respect to their issuance, sale, or exchange.

(c) The amount described in this subdivision (c) is the aggregate amount of money and fair market value of property (other than money) distributed to such persons on distributions in respect of such stock from other than earnings and profits or on distributions in redemption of such stock and the amount of principal paid pursuant to such debt obligations.

(d) For purposes of this subdivision (ii), in the case of a redemption, the stock or debt redeemed shall be charged against the earliest of such stock or debt issued, sold, or exchanged in order to determine the amount by which the balance of outstanding stock or debt is to be reduced. For purposes of this subparagraph, the fair market value of property received as consideration shall be determined as of the date the transaction occurs, and a contribution to capital within the meaning of section 118 shall be treated as the issuance of stock.

(iii) The provisions of subdivision (i) of this subparagraph apply regardless of the treatment under the Code of the transaction in which the stock or debt was issued, sold, or exchanged. Thus, for example, if X Corporation, a member of a controlled group which includes a DISC, acquires from a nonresident alien individual in exchange solely for X's voting stock all of the stock of Y Corporation pursuant to a reorganization as defined in section 368 (a)(1)(B), the fair market value of the Y stock on the date of the exchange would be an offset allowed by this subparagraph.

(iv) The provisions of this subparagraph may be illustrated by the following example:

Example. X Corporation is a member of a controlled group (within a meaning of paragraph (a)(2) of this section) every member of which uses the calendar year as its taxable year. On January 1, 1972, X issues in a public offering its stock to persons described in subdivision (i) of this subparagraph who, in the aggregate, pay $1,000 as consideration. X pays $100 in underwriting fees. On the same date, X receives $425 upon issuing a $500 debt obligation to such persons at a discount of $75 and pays $25 in underwriting fees. On December 31, 1972, the offset allowed under this subparagraph is $1,300 *i.e.,* ($1,000 minus $100) plus ($425 minus $25). If, during 1973, X makes a distribution of $150 (not in redemption) from other than earnings and profits with respect to such stock, then the offset is reduced to $1,150.

(5) *Earnings and profits.* (i) An offset allowed by this subparagraph is one-half the aggregate of the earnings and profits accumulated for all taxable years beginning after December 31, 1971, computed (without regard to any distributions from earnings and profits by a foreign corporation to a domestic corporation) in accordance with § 1.964-1 (relating to a controlled foreign corporation's earnings and profits), of each foreign member of the group which is controlled directly or indirectly (as determined under the principles of section 958 and the regulations thereunder) by a domestic member of the group and each foreign branch of a domestic member of the group (computed as if the branch were a foreign corporation). The DISC is bound by any action on behalf of a foreign member that was taken pursuant to § 1.964-1(c)(3) or by any failure to take action by or on behalf of a foreign member within the time specified in § 1.964-1(c)(6). With respect to a foreign member for which action was not previously required under § 1.964-1(c)(6) to be taken, the DISC may take action on behalf of such member by attaching a statement to that effect to the return of the DISC under section 6011(e)(2) for the first taxable year during which it qualifies (or is treated) as a DISC and there is outstanding a producer's loan made by such DISC to a member of the controlled group which includes the DISC.

(ii) If the aggregate of the accumulated earnings and profits described in subdivision (i) of this subparagraph is a deficit, the amount allowable as an offset under this subparagraph is zero.

(6) *Royalties and fees.* An offset allowed by this subparagraph is one-half the royalties and fees paid by foreign members of the group to domestic members of the group and by foreign branches of domestic members of the group to domestic members of the group during the taxable years of such members beginning after December 31, 1971.

(7) *Uncommitted transitional funds.* (i) An offset allowed by this subparagraph for the uncommitted transitional funds of the group is the sum described in subdivision (ii) of this subpara-

Reg. § 1.995-5(b)(7)

graph of the amount of certain capital raised under the foreign direct investment program and the amounts described in subdivision (iv) of this subparagraph of certain foreign excess working capital held on October 31, 1971.

(ii) The amount described in this subdivision of certain capital raised under the foreign direct investment program is the excess (if any) of—

(a) The amount of the offset allowed by subparagraph (4) of this paragraph, determined, however, with respect to the stock and debt obligations of domestic members of the group outstanding on December 31, 1971 (including amounts treated as stock outstanding by reason of a contribution to capital), whether or not outstanding after such date which were issued, sold, or exchanged on or after January 1, 1968, by any member (whether or not the same member) to persons who (on the date of such issuance, sale, or exchange) were neither United States persons (within the meaning of section 7701(a)(30)) nor members of the group, but only to the extent the taxpayer establishes that such amount constitutes a long-term borrowing (see 15 CFR § 1000.324) for purposes of the foreign direct investment program (see 15 CFR Part 1000), over

(b) The amount (determined under paragraph (c) of this section) of actual foreign investment by the domestic members of the group during the portion of the period such stock or debt obligations have been outstanding prior to January 1, 1972, such determination to be made by substituting January 1, 1968, for the December 31, 1971, date specified in such paragraph (c) and by not taking into account the earnings and profits described in paragraph (c)(3) of this section.

For purposes of this subparagraph, foreign branches of United States banks are not considered to be United States persons.

(iii)(a) A taxpayer may establish that an amount under subdivision (ii)(a) of this subparagraph constitutes a long-term borrowing for purposes of the foreign direct investment program by keeping records sufficient to demonstrate that appropriate reports were filed with the Office of Foreign Direct Investment of the Department of Commerce with respect to the foreign borrowing or by any other method satisfactory to the district director.

(b) The amounts described in subdivision (ii)(a) of this subparagraph include amounts with respect to which an election under section 4912(c), to subject certain obligations of a United States person to the interest equalization tax, has been made, provided that the obligations to which such amounts relate were issued by an "overseas financing subsidiary" described in 15 CFR Part 1000 N and were assumed by a United States person from such overseas financing subsidiary. Thus, for example, if an overseas financing subsidiary issues its notes to a foreign person in 1968, and such notes are assumed by its United States parent in 1973, which parent elects under section 4912(c) to have the notes subject to the interest equalization tax, then the amount of money received by the subsidiary is an amount described in subdivision (ii)(a) of this subparagraph.

(iv) The amount described in this subdivision of foreign excess working capital is the amount of liquid assets held by the foreign members of such group and foreign branches of domestic members of such group on October 31, 1971 (whether or not so held after such date) in excess of their reasonable working capital needs (as defined in § 1.993-2(e)) on that date, but only to the extent not included in subdivision (ii) of this subparagraph. For purposes of this subdivision, the term "liquid assets" means money, bank deposits (not including time deposits), and indebtedness of any kind (including time deposits) which on the day acquired had a maturity of 2 years or less.

(8) *Example.* The provisions of this paragraph may be illustrated by the following example:

Example. X Corporation, which uses the calendar year as its taxable year is a member of a controlled group (within the meaning of paragraph (a)(2) of this section). X elects to be treated as a DISC beginning with 1972. The amount of net increase in foreign assets of the group at the close of each group taxable year with respect to each taxable year of X from 1972 through 1975 are set forth in the table below, computed on the basis of the facts assumed (the amounts on each line being running balances):

Taxable Year of X	1972	1973	1974	1975
(1) Investment in foreign assets	$150	$165	$260	$300
(2) Depreciation with respect to foreign assets of group	20	40	60	80
(3) Amount of stock or debt outstanding issued after December 31, 1971	30	30	30	30
(4) One-half earnings and profits of foreign members	40	70	100	130
(5) Royalties and fees paid by foreign members to domestic members	10	15	20	20
(6) Uncommitted transitional funds	10	10	10	10

Reg. § 1.995-5(b)(8)

(7) Sum of lines (2) through (6)	110	165	220	270
(8) Net increase in foreign assets (line (1) minus line (6))	$ 40	$ 0	$ 40	$ 30

(c) *Actual foreign investment by domestic members.* For purposes of determining the limitation in paragraph (a) of this section, the amount of the actual foreign investment by domestic members of a controlled group is the sum (as of the close of the group taxable year) determined on a cumulative basis (see paragraph (a)(6) of this section) of—

(1) *Outstanding stock or debt (including contributions to capital).* The outstanding amount (determined in accordance with the principles of paragraph (b)(4)(ii) of this section, applied with respect to stock or debt obligations described in this subparagraph) of stock (including treasury stock) or debt obligations (other than normal trade indebtedness) of foreign members of the group issued, sold, or exchanged after December 31, 1971, by any person (whether or not a member) which is not a domestic member to domestic members of the group, provided that the outstanding amount of debt obligations of any foreign member shall be the greater of such amount outstanding at the close of the taxable year of such member or the highest such amount outstanding at any time during the immediately preceding 90 days,

(2) *Transfers to foreign branches.* The amount of money or the fair market value of property (other than money) transferred by domestic members of the group after December 31, 1971, to foreign branches of such members in transactions which would, if the branch were a corporation, be in consideration for the sale of stock or debt obligations of (or a contribution of capital to) such foreign branches (as determined under subparagraph (1) of this paragraph), and

(3) *Earnings and profits of foreign members.* One-half of the earnings and profits (computed in accordance with paragraph (b)(5) of this section for purposes of computing net increase in foreign assets) of foreign members of the group which are controlled directly or indirectly (as determined under the principles of section 958 and the regulations thereunder) by a domestic member of the group and foreign branches (treated for this purpose as a corporation) of domestic members of the group accumulated during the taxable years of such foreign members (or branches) beginning after December 31, 1971, or, if later, the taxable year referred to in paragraph (a)(5)(i) of this section if the 3-year election provided for in such paragraph (a)(5)(i) is made.

(d) *Carryovers on certain corporate acquisitions and reorganizations*—(1) *Certain corporate acquisitions.* (i) If—

(a) A member of a controlled group ("first controlled group") acquires in a transaction to which section 381 applies the assets of a corporation which is a member of a second controlled group or acquires stock in such a corporation pursuant to a reorganization as defined in section 368(a)(1)(B) to which section 361 applies, or

(b) A member or combination of members of the first controlled group acquire in a transaction not described in (a) of this subdivision a majority interest (as defined in paragraph (e)(2) of this section) in the stock of a corporation which is a member of a second controlled group which includes a DISC so that such DISC after the acquisition is a member of the new controlled group,

then, for purposes of computing foreign investment attributable to producer's loans with respect to the new controlled group as constituted after such acquisition, all amounts described in paragraphs (a) through (c) of this section, including the amount specified in paragraph (a)(1)(ii) of this section (relating to amounts treated under section 995(b)(1)(G) as deemed distributions by the DISC taxable as dividends for prior taxable years of the DISC), with respect to members of the second controlled group which become members of the new controlled group shall carry over to such new controlled group. For purposes of this subdivision (i), a controlled group may consist of only one member. With respect to certain transactions involving foreign corporations, see section 367.

(ii) If a member or combination of members of a controlled group, immediately after an acquisition of stock to which subdivision (i) of this subparagraph applies, do not control the total combined voting power (determined under § 1.957-1(b)) of the corporation whose stock was acquired, proper apportionment consistent with the principles of paragraph (e)(5) of this section shall be made with respect to amounts to which paragraphs (a) through (c) of this section apply.

(iii)(a) If subdivision (i) of this subparagraph applies, then for purposes of determining the application of the 3-year elective limitation provided for in paragraph (a)(5) of this section, the rules in *(b), (c),* and *(d)* of this subdivision (iii) apply.

Reg. § 1.995-5(d)(1)

(b) If both the "first controlled group" and the "second controlled group" (as those terms are defined in subdivision (i) of this subparagraph) include a DISC, and a DISC in either group has elected the 3-year limitation provided in paragraph (a)(5) of this section, then only those amounts taken into account under such paragraph (a)(5) by the electing DISC or DISC's shall be taken into account.

(c) If one of the groups includes a DISC and the other does not, and if the DISC has elected the 3-year limitation provided in paragraph (a)(5) of this section, then, for purposes of computing foreign investment attributable to producer's loans with respect to the new controlled group as constituted after the acquisition, all amounts described in paragraphs (a) through (c) of this section with respect to members of the controlled group which did not include the DISC shall carry over to such new controlled group, but only to the extent provided in such paragraph (a)(5), computed as if the group taxable year in which the acquisition occurred was the first group taxable year which includes a member's first taxable year during which it qualifies (or is treated) as a DISC.

(d) If (c) of this subdivision (iii) applies, except that the DISC has not elected the 3-year limitation provided in paragraph (a)(5) of this section, then the DISC in the new controlled group as constituted after the acquisition may, with respect to members of the controlled group which did not include the DISC, make the election provided in such paragraph (a)(5), and treat the year in which the acquisition occurred as if it were the first group taxable year which includes a member's first taxable year during which it qualifies (or is treated) as a DISC.

(iv) If a majority interest, or an interest in addition to a majority interest, is acquired in a transaction other than a transaction described in subdivision (i) of this subparagraph, then the rules in paragraph (e) of this section (relating to the acquisition of the foreign assets of a corporation) apply.

(2) *Corporation ceasing to be a member.* As of the date a corporation which is a member of a controlled group ceases to be a member of such group, the amounts of such group described in paragraphs (a) through (c) of this section will be reduced by such amounts which are attributable to the corporation which is no longer a member of the group.

(e) *Acquisition of a majority interest in a corporation.*—(1) *In general.* If paragraph (d)(1)(i) of this section (relating to certain corporate acquisitions in which all amounts described in paragraphs (a) through (c) of this section carry over) does not apply, then, for purposes of determining under paragraph (b)(2) of this section the investments made in foreign assets by a controlled group, the acquisition of a majority interest (as defined in subparagraph (2) of this paragraph) or an interest in addition to a majority interest in a corporation by any member or combination of members of the controlled group is considered an acquisition of the assets (to the extent provided in subparagraph (5) of this paragraph) of the acquired corporation by the group, including the assets of any foreign corporation in which the acquired corporation owns a majority interest (to the extent provided in subparagraph (5) of this paragraph). For the rules concerning the date upon which an acquisition of a majority interest is considered to have occurred, see subparagraph (3) of this paragraph.

(2) *Majority interest.* For purposes of this section, a majority interest is more than 50 percent of the total combined voting power of all classes of a corporation's stock entitled to vote, as determined under § 1.957-1(b).

(3) *Acquisition date.* For purposes of this paragraph, an acquisition of a majority interest shall be considered to have occurred on the day on which the combined voting power of the group first reached the percentage required in subparagraph (2) of this paragraph.

(4) *Valuation of assets.* For purposes of this section, the amount of a corporation's assets deemed acquired is the fair market value of the assets on the date of a majority interest, or an interest in addition to a previously held majority interest, is acquired.

(5) *Apportionment in the case of the acquisition of less than all of the voting stock.* (i) If the acquisition described in subparagraph (1) of this paragraph of a majority interest is of less than 100 percent of the total combined voting power of all classes of stock of the acquired corporation entitled to vote, then for purposes of subparagraph (1) of this paragraph the amount of the foreign assets of the corporation deemed acquired as of the day the majority interest is considered acquired shall be an amount equal to the fair market value of all of the corporation's foreign assets described in paragraph (b)(2) of this section as of such day multiplied by the percentage of the total combined voting power (determined under § 1.957-1(b)) held by members of the group on the day the majority interest is considered acquired.

(ii) If any member or combination of members of the controlled group hold a majority interest in a corporation, then for purposes of subparagraph (1) of this paragraph the acquisi-

Reg. § 1.995-5(d)(2)

tion of additional combined voting power by members of the controlled group shall be considered an acquisition of its foreign assets described in paragraph (b)(2) of this section in an amount equal to the fair market value of all such assets held by the foreign corporation on the date of the acquisition, multiplied by the increase (expressed in percentage points) in total combined voting power (as determined under § 1.957-1(b)) which occurred.

(6) *Examples.* The application of this paragraph may be illustrated by the following examples:

Example (1). M Corporation uses the calendar year as its taxable year. On November 18, 1973, M acquires from A, an individual United States person, for $1 million cash all 10,000 shares of the voting stock of N, a foreign corporation. N's only asset is a warehouse located in France with a fair market value on the date of acquisition of $1 million. Under subparagraph (1) of this paragraph, the controlled group of which M is a member is considered to have expended $1 million for the acquisition of foreign assets described in paragraph (b)(2) of this section.

Example (2). The facts are the same as in example (1), except that on November 18, 1973, M acquires only 80 percent of N's voting stock. M is considered to have expended $800,000 for the acquisition of assets described in paragraph (b)(2) of this section, computed as follows:

(1) Fair market value of N's foreign assets described in paragraph (b)(2) of this section $1,000,000
(2) Multiply by percentage of total combined voting power of all classes of N stock entitled to vote acquired by M 8
(3) Amount considered expended .... $ 800,000

Example (3). The facts are the same as in example (2), except that individual A is not a United States person, and M acquires the 80 percent of N voting stock in exchange for cash of $100,000 and M stock having a fair market value on the date of the acquisition of $700,000. M is considered to have acquired assets described in paragraph (b)(2) of this section in the amount of $800,000 (see computations in example (2)) and to have an offset under paragraph (b)(4) of this section (relating to outstanding stock or debt) of $700,000 (the fair market value of the M stock transferred to A who is not a United States person). However, the controlled group of which M is a member is not considered to have acquired any other amounts described in paragraphs (a) through (c) of this section with respect to N for taxable years prior to the taxable year of N during which the acquisition occurred.

Example (4). P Corporation, which uses the calendar year as its taxable year, is a member of a controlled group which includes a DISC. During 1973, P acquires from B, an individual United States person, for cash, 30 percent of the total combined voting power of all classes of stock entitled to vote of Q, a foreign corporation. All of Q's assets are assets described in paragraph (b)(2) of this section. No additional interest in Q is acquired by members of the group during 1973. The controlled group of which Q is a member is not considered to have made any investments in foreign assets described in such paragraph (b)(2) as of the close of 1973.

Example (5). Assume the same facts as in example (4). Assume further that during 1974, R Corporation, a member of the controlled group which includes P, acquires for cash 40 percent of the total combined voting power of all classes of stock of Q entitled to vote as follows: 20 percent on July 31, and 20 percent on December 31. Thus, on December 31, 1974, members of the controlled group own 70 percent of Q's voting power (30 + 20 + 20) and on that date are considered to have acquired a majority interest in Q. The fair market value of Q's assets on December 31, 1974, is $5 million. The group is considered to have expended $3,500,000 for the acquisition of assets described in paragraph (b)(2) of this section computed as follows:

(1) Fair market value of Q's foreign assets described in paragraph (b)(2) of this section as of the date the acquisition is deemed to have occurred under subparagraph (3) of this paragraph (December 31, 1974) $5,000,000
(2) Multiply by percentage of total combined voting power of all classes of Q stock entitled to vote held by members of the group on such date 7
3,500,000

Example (6). The facts are the same as in example (5). Assume further that on July 15, 1975, P acquires the remaining 30 percent of the total combined voting power of all classes of Q stock entitled to vote, and on such date the fair market value of Q's assets is $5,500,000. The group is considered to have expended $5,150,000 for the acquisition of assets described in paragraph (b)(2) of this section as of the close of 1975, computed as follows:

Reg. § 1.995-5(e)(6)

(1) Amount of prior years' investment $3,500,000
(2) Investment during 1975:
  (a) Fair market value of Q's foreign assets described in paragraph (b)(2) of this section on July 15, 1975 ..... $5,500,000
  (b) Multiply by additional percentage acquired of total combined voting power of all classes of Q stock entitled to vote 3
  (c) Investment during 1975..... $1,650,000
(3) Amount considered expended for foreign assets described in paragraph (b)(2) of this section by reason of the acquisition of Q stock....................... $5,150,000

(f) *Records.* A DISC shall keep or be readily able to produce such permanent books of account or records as are sufficient to establish the transactions and amounts described in this section. Where applicable, such books of account or records shall be cumulative and shall show transactions and amounts of the members of the controlled group which includes the DISC which occurred prior to the date the DISC qualified (or is treated) as a DISC.

(g) *Multiple DISC's*—(1) *Allocation amoung DISC's.* In the case of a controlled group which includes more than one DISC, the amounts described in paragraphs (b) and (c) of this section shall be allocated among the DISC's in order to determine the limitation in paragraph (a) of this section. Each DISC's allocable portion of these amounts shall be equal to the total of such amounts multiplied by a fraction the numerator of which is the individual DISC's outstanding producer's loans to members of the group, and the denominator of which is the aggregate amounts of outstanding producer's loans to members of the group by all DISC's which are members of the group.

(2) *Different taxable years.* If all of the DISC's which are members of the controlled group do not have the same taxable year, then one such DISC shall on behalf of all such DISC's elect to make all computations under section 995(d) as if all DISC's that are members of the group use the same taxable year as the actual taxable year of any one of the DISC's. The election as to which DISC's taxable year is to be used shall be made by the electing DISC attaching to its first return, filed under section 6011(e)(2), a statement indicating which such taxable year will be used. Once such an election is made it may not be revoked until such time as all of the DISC's which are members of the group use the same taxable year. If this subparagraph applies, books and records must be kept by the group which are adequate to show the necessary computations under section 995(d).

(3) This paragraph may be illustrated by the following example:

Example. Corporation X and Corporation Y are members of the same controlled group and each has elected to be treated as a DISC. X uses a taxable year ending March 31, and Y uses a taxable year ending November 30. Notwithstanding the fact that all other members of the group use the calendar year as their taxable year, all computations for purposes of determining the amount of foreign investment attributable to producer's loans under section 995(d) must be made as if both DISC's use a taxable year ending either March 31 (X's taxable year) or November 30 (Y's taxable year). [Reg. § 1.995-5.]

☐ [T.D. 7324, 9-27-74. *Amended by* T.D. 7420, 5-19-76 and T.D. 7854, 11-6-82.]

[Reg. § 1.995-6]

§ 1.995-6. **Taxable income attributable to military property.**—(a) *Gross income attributable to military property.* For purposes of section 995(b)(3)(A)(i), the term "gross income which is attributable to military property" includes income from the sale, exchange, lease, or rental of military property (as described in paragraph (c) of this section). The term also includes gross income from the performance of services which are related and subsidiary (as defined in § 1.993-1(d)) to any qualified sale, exchange, lease, or rental of military property. Where gross income cannot be determined on an item by item basis, the gross income with respect to those items not so determinable shall be apportioned. Such apportionment shall be accomplished using appropriate facts and circumstances, so that the gross income apportioned to sale of military property bears a reasonably close factual relationship to the actual gross income earned on such sales. The apportionment shall be based on methods which include the fair market value of property sold or exchanged, the fair rental value of any leaseholds granted, the fair market value of any related or subsidiary services performed in connection with such sale or leases or methods based on gross receipts or costs of goods sold, where appropriate.

(b) *Deductions.* For purposes of section 995(b)(3)(A)(ii), deductions shall be properly allocated and apportioned to gross income, described in paragraph (a) of this section, in accordance with the rules of § 1.861-8. These deductions include all applicable deductions from gross income provided under part VI of subchapter B of chapter 1 of the Code.

(c) *Military property.* For purposes of this section, the term "military property" means any property which is an arm, ammunition, or implement of war designated in the munitions list published pursuant to section 38 of the International Security Assistance and Arms Export Control Act of 1976 (22 U.S.C. 2778 which superseded 22 U.S.C. 1934) and the regulations thereunder (22 CFR 121.01).

(d) *Illustration.* The principles of this section may be illustrated by the following example:

Example. X Corporation elects to be a DISC for the first time in 1976. X has taxable income of $50,000, of which $30,000 is attributable to military property and $10,000 to interest on producer's loans. The total deemed distributions with respect to X are as follows:

(1) Gross interest from Producer's loans in 1976	$10,000
(2) 50 percent of the taxable income of the DISC attributable to military property in 1976	15,000
(3) One-half of the excess of taxable income for 1976 over the sum of lines (1) and (2) (½ of ($50,000 minus $25,000))	12,500
(4) Total deemed distributions (sum of total lines (1), (2), and (3))	37,500

[Reg. § 1.995-6.]

☐ [T.D. 7984, 10-11-84.]

[Reg. § 1.996-1]

§ 1.996-1. **Rules for actual distributions and certain deemed distributions.**—(a) *General rule.* Under section 996(a)(1), any actual distribution (other than a distribution described in paragraph (b) of this section or to which § 1.995-4 applies) to a shareholder by a DISC, or former DISC, which is made out of earnings and profits shall be treated as made—

(1) First, out of "previously taxed income" (as defined in § 1.996-3(c)) to the extent thereof,

(2) Second, out of "accumulated DISC income" (as defined in § 1.996-3(b)) to the extent thereof, and

(3) Third, out of "other earnings and profits" (as defined in § 1.996-3(d)) to the extent thereof.

(b) *Rules for qualifying distributions and deemed distributions under section 995(b)(1)(G)*—(1) *In general.* Except as provided in subparagraph (2), any actual distribution to meet qualification requirements made pursuant to § 1.992-3 and any deemed distribution pursuant to § 1.995-2(a)(5) (relating to foreign investment attributable to producer's loans) which is made out of earnings and profits shall be treated as made—

(i) First, out of "accumulated DISC income" (as defined in § 1.996-3(b)) to the extent thereof,

(ii) Second, out of "other earnings and profits" (as defined in § 1.996-3(d)) to the extent thereof, and

(iii) Third, out of "previously taxed income" (as defined in § 1.996-3(c)) to the extent thereof.

(2) *Special rule.* For taxable years beginning after December 31, 1975, paragraph (b)(1) of this section shall apply to one-half of the amount of an actual distribution made pursuant to § 1.992-3 to satisfy the condition of § 1.992-1(b) (the gross receipts test) and paragraph (a) of this section shall apply to the remaining one-half of such amount.

(c) *Exclusion from gross income.* Under section 996(a)(3), amounts distributed out of previously taxed income shall be excluded by the distributee from gross income. However, see § 1.996-5(b) for treatment as gain from the sale or exchange of property of the portion of an actual distribution out of previously taxed income to the extent it exceeds the adjusted basis of the stock with respect to which the distribution is made.

(d) *Priority of distributions.* Under section 996(c), for purposes of determining their treatment under paragraphs (a), (b), and (c) of this section, distributions made during a taxable year shall be treated as being made in the following order—

(1) Deemed distributions under §§ 1.995-2 and 1.995-3.

(2) Actual distributions to meet qualification requirements made pursuant to § 1.992-3 in the order in which they are made, and

(3) Other actual distributions in the order in which they are made.

Thus, the treatment of any distribution shall be determined after the divisions of earnings and profits have been properly adjusted by taking into account distributions of higher priority which are made or deemed made during the same taxable year.

(e) *Examples.* The provisions of this section may be illustrated by the following examples:

Example (1). Y Corporation, which uses the calendar year as its taxable year elects to be treated as a DISC beginning with 1972. During 1973, Y makes a cash distribution of $100 to X Corporation, Y's sole shareholder. For 1973, Y has no earnings and profits. As of the beginning of 1973, Y has $300 of accumulated earnings and profits, which consist of $70 of accumulated DISC income, $40 of previously taxed income, and $190 of other earnings and profits. The entire $100 distribution is a dividend under section 316. However, $40 thereof is treated as made out of previously taxed income and is thus excluded from gross income. Accordingly, only $60 is treated as distributed out of accumulated DISC income and includible in gross income. See § 1.246-4 for the inapplicability of the dividend received deduction with respect to the entire distribution of $100.

Example (2). Assume the same facts as in example (1), except that the cash distribution is designated as a distribution to meet qualification requirements made pursuant to § 1.992-3. Under these facts, X includes the entire distribution in its gross income as a dividend. Of the $100 distributed, $70 is treated as made out of accumulated DISC income and the remaining $30 is treated as made out of other earnings and profits. The dividend received deduction under section 243 is available only with respect to such $30.

Example (3). Y Corporation, which uses the calendar year as its taxable year, elects to be treated as a DISC beginning with 1972. As of the end of 1975, Y had failed to meet the gross receipts test for that year. In 1975 Y had $100 of taxable income, $80 of which was attributable to qualified export receipts and $20 of which was attributable to receipts that did not qualify as qualified export receipts. As of the beginning of 1976, Y had $300 of accumulated earnings and profits, which consisted of $70 of accumulated DISC income, $40 of previously taxed income, and $190 of other earnings and profits. In 1976 Y makes a cash distribution of $20 pursuant to § 1.992-3 in order to satisfy the gross receipts test for 1975. For 1976 Y has no earnings and profits and no deemed distributions. The entire $20 distribution is a dividend under section 316. Under § 1.996-1(b)(2), half of the $20 cash distribution is treated pursuant to § 1.996-1(b)(1) and half is treated pursuant to § 1.996-1(a). Thus, $10 is treated as distributed out of accumulated DISC income and is includible in gross income. The other $10 is treated as made out of previously taxed income and is thus excluded from gross income. As of the beginning of 1977, Y has $280 of accumulated earnings and profits, which consists of $60 of accumulated DISC income, $30 of previously taxed income, and $190 of other earnings and profits. [Reg. § 1.996-1.]

☐ [T.D. 7324, 9-27-74. Amended by T.D. 7854, 11-6-82.]

[Reg. § 1.996-2]

§ 1.996-2. Ordering rules for losses.—(a) *In general.* Under section 996(b), if for any taxable year a DISC, or a former DISC, incurs a deficit in earnings and profits, such deficit shall be charged—

(1) First, to other earnings and profits (as defined in § 1.996-3(d)) to the extent thereof,

(2) Second, to accumulated DISC income (as defined in § 1.996-3(b)) to the extent thereof, subject to the special rule in paragraph (b) of this section,

(3) Third, to previously taxed income (as defined in § 1.996-3(c)) to the extent thereof, and

(4) To the extent that the amount of such deficit exceeds the sum of the amounts charged in accordance with subparagraphs (1), (2), and (3) of this paragraph, to other earnings and profits (as defined in § 1.996-3(d)). Thus, the excess deficit charged to other earnings and profits under subparagraph (4) of this paragraph will create a deficit therein in the amount of such excess. To determine the amount of any division of earnings and profits for the purpose of determining under § 1.996-1 the treatment of any actual and certain deemed distributions, the portion of a deficit in earnings and profits chargeable under this paragraph to such division prior to such distribution shall be determined in a manner consistent with the rules in § 1.316-2(b) for determining the amount of earnings and profits available on the date of any distribution.

(b) *Deficits subsequent to a disqualification.* A deficit in earnings and profits of a DISC, or former DISC, shall not be charged to accumulated DISC income which has been determined is to be deemed distributed to the shareholders pursuant to § 1.995-3 as a result of a revocation of election or other disqualification. Thus, in accordance with paragraph (a) of this section as modified by this paragraph, a deficit incurred by a former DISC following such a revocation or disqualification shall be charged first to other earnings and profits and then to previously taxed income with any balance being charged to other earnings and profits and creating a deficit therein. The preceding sentence shall also apply in the case of a deficit incurred by a DISC which has no accumulated DISC income accumulated during its current taxable year and all immediately preceding consecutive taxable years for which it was a DISC. If as a result of the application of this paragraph the amount of a deficit in other earnings and profits exceeds the amount of a deficit in accumulated earnings and profits, then upon any subsequent actual distribution the deficit in other earnings and profits shall be reduced by the lower of (1) the amount of such actual distribution chargeable to accumulated DISC income or previously taxed income or (2) the amount of such excess.

(c) *Examples.* The provisions of this section may be illustrated by the following examples:

Domestic International Sales Corporation

See p. 20,601 for regulations not amended to reflect law changes

Example (1). X Corporation, which uses the calendar year as its taxable year, becomes a DISC beginning with 1976. In addition to other facts assumed in the table below, X incurs a deficit in earnings and profits for 1979 of $70. Such deficit is charged to the divisions of X's earnings and profits pursuant to paragraph (a) of this section in the manner set forth in such table.

	Accumulated DISC income	Previously taxed income	Other earnings and profits
Balance Jan. 1, 1976	...	...	$50
Increase for 1976	$10	$ 8	...
Increase for 1977	10	8	...
Increase for 1978	10	8	...
Balance Jan. 1, 1979	30	24	50
Deficit for 1979 of $70:			
Charge No. 1	...	...	(50)
Charge No. 2	(20)	...	...
Balance Jan. 1, 1980	10	24	0

Example (2). Assume the same facts as in example (1), except that effective for taxable years beginning with 1979, X revokes its election to be treated as a DISC. Under § 1.995-3, X has $30 of accumulated DISC income which is to be deemed distributed $10 per year in 1980, 1981, and 1982. The deficit in earnings and profits for 1979 is charged to the divisions of X's earnings and profits pursuant to paragraph (b) of this section in the manner set forth in the table below:

	Accumulated DISC income	Previously taxed income	Other earnings and profits
Balance Jan. 1, 1979	$30	$24	$50
Deficit for 1979 of $70:			
Charge No. 1	.....	.....	(50)
Charge No. 2	.....	(20)	.....
Balance Jan. 1, 1980	30	4	0

Example (3). Assume the same facts as in example (2), except that the deficit in earnings and profits for 1979 is $120. Assume further that for 1980, 1981, and 1982, during which years X's shareholders are receiving scheduled installments of the deemed distributions of accumulated DISC income under § 1.995-3, X, a former DISC, has neither earnings and profits nor a deficit in earnings and profits. The $120 deficit for 1979 is charged to the divisions of X's earnings and profits pursuant to paragraph (b) of this section in the manner set forth in the table below:

	Accumulated DISC income	Previously taxed income	Other earnings and profits	Accumulated earnings and profits
Balance Jan. 1, 1979	$30	$24	$50	$104
Deficit for 1979 of $120	.....	...	...	(120)
Charge No. 1	.....	...	(50)	.....
Charge No. 2	.....	(24)	...	.....
Charge No. 3	.....	...	(46)	.....
Balance Jan. 1, 1980	$30	$ 0	($46)	($16)
Deemed distributions in 1980 under § 1.995-3	(10)	10	..	..
Balance Jan. 1, 1981	20	10	(46)	(16)

Example (4). Assume the same facts as in example (3), except that on December 31, 1980, X makes an actual distribution of $10 out of previously taxed income. On January 1, 1981, X has $20 of accumulated DISC income, no previously taxed income, and a deficit of $36 in other earnings and profits. The deficit of $16 in accumulated earnings and profits remains the same. [Reg. § 1.996-2.]

□ [T.D. 7324, 9-27-74.]

Reg. § 1.996-2(c)

[Reg. § 1.996-3]

§ 1.996-3. Divisions of earnings and profits.—(a) *In general.* For purposes of sections 991 through 997, the earnings and profits of a DISC, or former DISC, shall be treated as composed of the following three divisions:

(1) Accumulated DISC income (as defined in paragraph (b) of this section),

(2) Previously taxed income (as defined in paragraph (c) of this section), and

(3) Other earnings and profits (as defined in paragraph (d) of this section).

(b) *Accumulated DISC income defined.* (1) Accumulated DISC income is that portion of a corporation's earnings and profits which were derived during taxable years for which it qualified as a DISC and which were deferred from taxation. Accumulated DISC income as of the close of each taxable year of the corporation is—

(i) The amount of accumulated DISC income as of the close of the immediately preceding taxable year increased by

(ii) The amount of DISC income for the year (as determined in subparagraph (2) of this paragraph) and reduced (but not below zero) by

(iii) The items enumerated in subparagraph (3) of this paragraph.

(2) Under section 966(f)(1), DISC income is (i) the earnings and profits derived by the corporation during a taxable year for which such corporation is a DISC minus (ii) amounts deemed distributed under § 1.995-2 other than the amount of foreign investment attributable to producer's loans described in § 1.995-2(a)(5). For example, the earnings and profits of a DISC for a taxable year include any amounts includible in such DISC's gross income pursuant to section 951(a) (relating to controlled foreign corporations). Deemed distributions under § 1.995-2(a)(5) are taken into account under subparagraph (3) of this paragraph as a reduction in computing accumulated DISC income.

(3) The accumulated DISC income (as increased by DISC income for the year determined under subparagraph (2) of this paragraph) is reduced by each of the following items in the following order:

(i) Any amount deemed distributed for such year under § 1.995-3 (relating to deemed distributions upon disqualification),

(ii) Any amount of foreign investment attributable to producer's loans deemed distributed for such year under § 1.995-2(a)(5) to the extent it is charged to accumulated DISC income under § 1.996-1(b)(1)(i),

(iii) The amount of any adjustment to accumulated DISC income for such year under § 1.996-4(b)(1), and

(iv) To the extent they are treated, under § 1.996-1(a) or (b) (relating to ordering rules for distributions), as made out of accumulated DISC income, the amounts of any actual qualifying distributions pursuant to § 1.992-3 in the order in which they are made, and thereafter by the amounts of any other actual distributions in the order in which they are made, except that, prior to each actual distribution, accumulated DISC income shall be reduced by the portion of any deficit in earnings and profits for the taxable year chargeable at that time under § 1.996-2(a)(2) to accumulated DISC income.

(4) Every distribution or other reduction in accumulated DISC income pursuant to subparagraph (3) of this paragraph shall be charged to the most recently accumulated DISC income.

(c) *Previously taxed income.* Under section 996(f)(2), previously taxed income as of the close of each taxable year of the corporation is an amount equal to—

(1) The sum of—

(i) The amount of previously taxed income as of the close of the immediately preceding taxable year,

(ii) Amounts deemed distributed for the current year under § 1.995-2 (relating to deemed distributions in qualified years),

(iii) Amounts deemed distributed for the current year under § 1.995-3 (relating to deemed distributions upon disqualification),

(iv) With respect to a distribution in redemption to which § 1.996-4(b)(1) applies, an amount equal to the excess (if any) of (*a*) the amount of the reduction under § 1.996-4(b)(1) in accumulated DISC income over (*b*) the reduction in the corporation's earnings and profits (see section 312(e)), and

(v) Any amount by which accumulated DISC income is reduced under paragraph (b)(3)(ii) of this section by reason of a deemed distribution as a dividend, under § 1.995-2(a)(5), of an amount of foreign investment attributable to producer's loans,

(2) Decreased (but not below zero), to the extent they are treated, under § 1.996-1(a) or (b) (relating to ordering rules for distributions), as made out of previously taxed income, by the amounts of any actual qualifying distributions pursuant to § 1.992-3 in the order in which they are made, and thereafter by the amounts of any other actual distributions in the order in which they are made, except that, prior to any actual distribution, previously taxed income shall be re-

Domestic International Sales Corporation 50,985

See p. 20,601 for regulations not amended to reflect law changes

duced by the portion of any deficit in earnings and profits for the taxable year chargeable at that time under § 1.996-2(a)(3) to previously taxed income.

(d) *Other earnings and profits.* Under section 996(f)(3), other earnings and profits consist of earnings and profits other than accumulated DISC income and previously taxed income described respectively in paragraphs (b) and (c) of this section. Other earnings and profits as of the close of each taxable year of the corporation is (subject to paragraph (e) of this section) an amount equal to the amount of other earnings and profits as of the close of the immediately preceding taxable year decreased (if necessary, below zero) in the following order by—

(1) To the extent they are treated, under § 1.996-1(a) or (b) (relating to ordering rules for distributions), as made out of other earnings and profits, the amounts of any actual qualifying distributions pursuant to § 1.992-3 in the order in which they are made, and thereafter the amount of any other actual distributions in the order in which they are made, except that, prior to any actual distribution, other earnings and profits shall be reduced by the portion of any deficit in earnings and profits for the taxable year chargeable at that time under § 1.996-2(a)(1) to other earnings and profits, and

(2) With respect to a distribution in redemption to which § 1.996-4(b)(1) applies, an amount equal to the excess (if any) of (*a*) the reduction in the corporation's earnings and profits (see section 312(e)) over (*b*) the amount of the reduction under § 1.996-4(b)(1) in accumulated DISC income.

(e) *Distributions in kind.* (1) For purposes of determining, under paragraphs (b), (c), and (d) of this section, the amount by which any division of earnings and profits is reduced by reason of a distribution of property (other than money or the DISC's, or former DISC's, own obligations), the amount of such distribution is the fair market value of such property at the time of the distribution.

(2) For any taxable year in which the DISC makes a distribution of such property, the amount of other earnings and profits determined under paragraph (d) of this section (without regard to this subparagraph) shall be—

(i) Increased by the excess (if any) of the amount of such distribution treated as a dividend under section 316(a) over the adjusted basis of such property, and

(ii) Decreased by the excess (if any) of the adjusted basis of such property over the amount of such distribution treated as a dividend under section 316(a).

Each item of property shall be considered separately for purposes of making the adjustment under this subparagraph.

(f) *Examples.* The provisions of §§ 1.996-1, 1.996-2, and this section may be illustrated by the following examples:

Example (1). M Corporation, which uses the calendar year as its taxable year, elects to be treated as a DISC beginning with 1974. During 1975, M derives no earnings and profits and makes no deemed or actual distributions, except that on December 31, 1975, M's shareholders are treated as having received a dividend distribution of $100 under § 1.995-2(a)(5) (relating to foreign investment attributable to producer's loans). M's earnings and profits are adjusted as shown on line (2) of the table below on the basis of facts assumed therein.

	Accumulated earnings and profits	Accumulated DISC income	Previously taxed income	Other earnings and profits
(1) Balance Jan. 1, 1975	$450	$100	$250	$100
(2) Adjustments (see paragraphs (b)(3)(ii) and (c)(1)(v) of this section)	0	(100)	100	0
(3) Balance Jan. 1, 1976	450	0	350	100

Example (2). N Corporation, which uses the calendar year as its taxable year, elects to be treated as a DISC beginning with 1972. During 1973, N derives no earnings and profits for the year and makes no deemed or actual distributions, except that A, a shareholder, realized $200 of gain upon receiving an actual cash distribution of $300 in redemption of N stock having an adjusted basis of $100 in his hands. The redemption is treated as an exchange under section 302(a) but, under section 995(c), A includes the $200 of gain in his gross income as a dividend. Assuming that, under section 312(e), $240 is properly chargeable to capital account of N and that, under § 1.996-4(b), accumulated DISC income is reduced by $200, N's accounts are adjusted on line (2) of the table below on the basis of facts assumed therein.

Reg. § 1.996-3(f)

Domestic International Sales Corporation

See p. 20,601 for regulations not amended to reflect law changes

	Capital	Accumulated earnings and profits	Accumulated DISC income	Previously taxed income	Other earnings and profits
(1) Balance Jan. 1, 1973	$2,000	$400	$300	$100	0
(2) Adjustments (see § 1.996-4(b) and paragraph (c)(1)(iv) of this section)	(240)	(60)	(200)	140	0
(3) Balance Jan. 1, 1974	1,760	340	100	240	0

Example (3). P Corporation, which uses the calendar year as its taxable year, elects to be treated as a DISC beginning with 1973. During 1974, P derives no earnings and profits for the year and makes no deemed or actual distributions, except for a distribution to B, its sole shareholder, of property with a fair market value of $100 and an adjusted basis in P's hands of $40. Under § 1.996-1(a)(1), B treats the entire amount of the distribution as being made out of previously taxed income and, under § 1.996-1(c), excludes it from his gross income. P's earnings and profits' divisions are adjusted on lines (2) and (3) of the table below on the basis of facts assumed therein.

	Accumulated earnings and profits	Accumulated DISC income	Previously taxed income	Other earnings and profits
(1) Balance January 1, 1974	$200	$80	$120	$0
(2) Adjustment under paragraphs (c)(2) and (e)(1) this section	(40)	0	(100)	0
(3) Adjustment under paragraph (e)(2)(i) of this section	0	0	0	60
(4) Balance January 1, 1975	160	80	20	60

Example (4). Q Corporation, which uses the calendar year as its taxable year, elects to be treated as a DISC beginning with 1974. On January 1, 1975, Q has accumulated earnings and profits of $1,200 and, during 1975, Q incurs a deficit in earnings and profits of $365. The amount of such deficit incurred as of any date before the close of 1975 cannot be shown. On July 1, 1975, Q makes a cash distribution of $650, with respect to its stock to C, Q's sole shareholder. C subsequently transfers by gift all of his Q stock to D. On December 31, 1975, Q makes a cash distribution of $650, with respect to its stock, to D. Under these facts and additional facts assumed in the table below, C is treated as having received a dividend of $650 of which $320 is treated as distributed out of previously taxed income and excluded from gross income. D is treated as receiving a dividend of $186. Adjustments to Q's earnings and profits accounts are illustrated in the table below.

	Accumulated earnings and profits	Accumulated DISC income	Previously taxed income	Other earnings and profits
(1) Balance January 1, 1975	$1,200	$800	$320	$80
(2) Portion of 1975 deficit of $365 chargeable as of June 30, 1975, pursuant to § 1.996-2(a)	(181)	(101)	0	(80)
(3) Balance July 1, 1975	1,019	699	320	0
(4) $650 distributed to C on July 1, 1975	(650)	(330)	(320)	0
(5) Portion of 1975 deficit of $365 chargeable as of December 30, 1975, pursuant to § 1.996-2(a)	(183)	(183)	0	0
(6) Balance December 31, 1975	186	186	0	0
(7) $650 distributed to D on December 31, 1975 [1]	(186)	(186)	0	0
(8) Balance January 1, 1976	0	0	0	0

[1] $60 treated as return of capital pursuant to section 301(c)(2).

Example (5)—(1) *Facts.* R Corporation, which uses the calendar year as its taxable year, elects to be treated as a DISC beginning with 1972. X Corporation is its sole shareholder. At the beginning of 1974, R has a deficit in earnings and profits of $60 all of which is composed of "other earnings and profits". For 1974, R has earnings and profits of $80 before reduction for any distributions and taxable income of $70. On June 15, 1974, R makes a cash distribution to X of $60, with respect to its stock, to which section 301 applies. On August 15, 1974, R makes a cash distribution to X of $30 designated as a distribution to meet qualification requirements pursuant to § 1.992-3. Under § 1.995-2(a), X is deemed to receive, on December 31, 1974, a distribution of a dividend of $35, *i.e.,* one-half of R's taxable income of $70. The tax consequences of these facts to X and their effect on R's earnings and profits are set forth in the subsequent subparagraphs of this example.

Reg. § 1.996-3(f)

(2) *Dividend treatment of actual distributions.* Since R had $80 of earnings and profits for 1974 and a deficit in accumulated earnings and profits at the beginning of 1974, only $80 of the actual distributions ($90) are treated as dividends under sections 301(c)(1) and 316(a)(2). ($10 of the actual distribution, which is not treated as a dividend is treated in the manner specified in section 301(c)(2) and (3).) Thus, under § 1.316-2(b), $26.67 of the actual qualifying distribution made on August 15, 1974 ($30 × $80/$90), and $53.33 of the actual distribution made on June 15, 1974 ($60 × $80/$90), are considered made out of earnings and profits.

(3) *Priority of distributions.* Under § 1.996-1(d), for purposes of adjusting the divisions of R's earnings and profits and determining the treatment of subsequent distributions, the sequence in which each distribution is treated as having been made is—

(i) First, the deemed distribution of $35,

(ii) Second, the actual qualifying distribution of $30 made on August 15, 1974, pursuant to § 1.992-3, and

(iii) Finally, the actual distribution of $60 made on June 15, 1974.

(4) *Treatment and effect of deemed distribution.* Under § 1.995-2(a), on December 31, 1974, X includes the deemed distribution of $35 in its gross income as a dividend. Under paragraph (c)(1)(ii) of this section, R's previously taxed income is increased by $35 as shown on line (3) of the table in subparagraph (7) of this example. Under paragraph (b)(1)(ii) and (2) of this section, accumulated DISC income is increased by $45 of DISC income, *i.e.*, R's earnings and profits for 1974, $80, minus the deemed distribution of $35, as shown on line (4) of the table.

(5) *Treatment and effect of actual qualifying distribution of $30.* As indicated in subparagraph (2) of this example, $26.67 of the $30 qualifying distribution on August 15, 1974, is treated as made out of earnings and profits for 1974. Under § 1.996-1(b)(1)(i), the entire $26.67 is treated as distributed out of accumulated DISC income. Thus, on August 15, 1974, X includes $26.67 in its gross income as a dividend. No deduction is allowable under section 243. Under paragraph (b)(3)(iv) of this section, R's accumulated DISC income is reduced by $26.67 as shown on line (6) of the table in subparagraph (7) of this example.

(6) *Treatment and effect of actual distribution of $60.* As indicated in subparagraph (2) of this example, $53.33 of the $60 distribution on June 15, 1974, is treated as made out of earnings and profits for 1974. Under § 1.996-1(a), the $53.33 is treated as distributed out of previously taxed income to the extent thereof, $35, and then out of accumulated DISC income, $18.33. Thus, on June 15, 1974, X includes $18.33 in its gross income as a dividend. Under § 1.996-1(c), the distribution of $35 out of previously taxed income is excluded from gross income. No deduction is allowable under section 243 with respect to the actual distribution of $53.33. Under paragraph (b)(3)(iv) of this section, accumulated DISC income is reduced by $18.33 and, under paragraph (c)(2) of this section, previously taxed income is reduced by $35, as shown on line (7) of the table in subparagraph (7) of this example.

(7) *Summary.* The effects on earnings and profits and the divisions of earnings and profits are summarized in the following table:

	Earnings and profits for year	Accumulated earnings and profits	Accumulated DISC income	Previously taxed income	Other earnings and profits
(1) Balance Jan. 1, 1974	......	($60.00)	......	......	($60.00)
(2) Earnings and profits for year before reduction for distributions	$80.00	......	......	......	......
(3) Deemed distribution of $35 to X on Dec. 31, 1974, under § 1.995-2(a)	......	......	......	$35.00	......
(4) DISC income for 1974 of $45 as defined in paragraph (b)(2) of this section (line 2 ($80) minus line 3 ($35))	......	......	$45.00	......	......
(5) Balance before actual distributions	80.00	(60.00)	45.00	35.00	(60.00)
(6) Qualifying distribution of $30 to X on Aug. 15, 1974, pursuant to § 1.992-3	(26.67)	......	(26.67)	......	......
(7) Actual distribution to P of $60 on June 15, 1974	(53.33)	......	(18.33)	(35.00)	......
(8) Balance Jan. 1, 1975	0	($60.00)	0	......	($60.00)

Example (6). Assume the facts are the same as in example (5), except that at the beginning of 1974 R's accumulated earnings and profits amount to $60 consisting of accumulated DISC income of $20, previously taxed income of $10, and other earnings and profits of $30. In addition, on August 1, 1974, X transfers all R's stock to Y Corporation in a reorganization described in section 368(a)(1)(B) in which under section 354 X recognizes no gain or loss. Under these facts, X

Reg. § 1.996-3(f)

includes in its gross income for 1974 a dividend of $15 which is attributable to the actual distribution of $60 paid out of earnings and profits on June 15, 1974. X excludes from gross income the balance of the $60 distribution ($45) paid out of earnings and profits because, under § 1.996-1(a), it is treated as paid out of previously taxed income. Y includes in its gross income for 1974 a dividend of $65 of which $35 is attributable to the deemed distribution of a dividend to Y on December 31, 1974, under § 1.995-2(a) and $30 is attributable to the qualifying distribution paid out of earnings and profits to Y on August 15, 1974. The adjustments to R's earnings and profits are summarized in the following table:

	Earnings and profits for year	Accumulated earnings and profits	Accumulated DISC income	Previously taxed income	Other earnings and profits
(1) Balance Jan. 1, 1974	.....	$60.00	$20.00	$10.00	$30.00
(2) Earnings and profits for year before reduction for distributions	$80.00	.....	.....	.....	.....
(3) Deemed distribution of $35 to Y on Dec. 31, 1974, under § 1.995-2(a)	.....	.....	.....	$35.00	.....
(4) DISC income for 1974 of $45 as defined in paragraph (b)(2) of this section (line 2 ($80) minus line 3 ($35))	.....	.....	$45.00	.....	.....
(5) Balance before actual distributions	$80.00	$60.00	65.00	45.00	$30.00
(6) Qualifying distribution of $30 to Y on Aug. 15, 1974, pursuant to § 1.992-3	(26.67)	(3.33)	(30.00)	.....	.....
(7) Actual distribution to X of $60 on June 15, 1974	(53.33)	(6.67)	(15.00)	(45.00)	.....
(8) Balance Jan. 1, 1975	.....	50.00	20.00	0	30.00

(g) *DISCs having corporate and noncorporate shareholders.* In the case of a DISC having one or more corporate shareholders but less than all of its shareholders subject to the special rules of section 291(a)(4), relating to certain deferred DISC income as a corporate preference item, accumulated DISC income and previously taxed income of the DISC are divided between the corporate shareholders, as a class, and the other shareholders, as a class, in proportion to amounts of DISC income not deemed distributed and amounts deemed distributed to each class. Subsequent taxation of actual and qualifying distributions shall be based upon this division. Thus, if a DISC is owned 50 percent by corporate shareholders and 50 percent by individual shareholders and has undistributed taxable income of $2,000 for its year, the division is made as follows:

Corporate shareholders:
 Previously taxed income (57.5% of $2,000 ÷ 2) $575
 Accumulated DISC income (42.5% of $2,000 ÷ 2) 425
Individual shareholders:
 Previously taxed income (50% of $2,000 ÷ 2) 500
 Accumulated DISC income (50% of $2,000 ÷ 2) 500

[Reg. § 1.996-3.]

☐ [T.D. 7324, 9-27-74. Amended by T.D. 7854, 11-15-82 and T.D. 7984, 10-11-84.]

Reg. § 1.996-4(a)(1)

[Reg. § 1.996-4]

§ 1.996-4. Subsequent effect of previous disposition of DISC stock.—(a) *Shareholder adjustment for previously taxed income.*—(1) Under section 996(d)(1), except as provided in subparagraph (2) of this paragraph, if—

 (i) Gain with respect to a share of stock of a DISC, or former DISC, is treated under § 1.995-4 as a dividend, and

 (ii) With respect to such share, any person subsequently receives an actual distribution made out of accumulated DISC income, or a deemed distribution made, pursuant to § 1.995-3, by reason of disqualification, out of accumulated DISC income,

then such person shall treat such distribution in the same manner as a distribution from previously taxed income (and thus excludable from gross income under § 1.996-1(c)) to the extent that the gain referred to in subdivision (i) of this subparagraph exceeds the aggregate amount of any other distributions with respect to such share which were treated under this subparagraph as made from previously taxed income.

 (2) In applying subparagraph (1) of this paragraph with respect to a share of stock in a DISC, or former DISC, the gain referred to in subparagraph (1)(i) of this paragraph does not include any gain to a shareholder on a redemption of such share which qualifies as an exchange under section 302(a) or any gain on a disposition of such share prior to such redemption. Distributions de-

scribed in subparagraph (1)(ii) of this paragraph do not include a distribution in a redemption which qualifies as an exchange under section 302(a). For adjustments to accumulated DISC income by reason of dividend treatment under § 1.995-4 with respect to gain upon a redemption of DISC stock to which section 302(a) applies and upon a prior disposition of such stock, see paragraph (b) of this section.

(3) *Example.* The provisions of this paragraph may be illustrated by the following example:

Example. In 1974, under § 1.995-4, A, a shareholder of a DISC, on the sale of his DISC stock to B, is required to treat $20 of his gain as a dividend. The DISC has no previously taxed income and $40 of accumulated DISC income. Subsequently in the same year, B, the purchaser of the stock, receives an actual dividend distribution of $15 with respect to such stock which, under § 1.996-1(a), is treated as made out of accumulated DISC income. The amounts of the DISC's previously taxed income and accumulated DISC income were not adjusted by reason of the $20 treated as a dividend on the prior sale. However, even though the DISC had no previously taxed income, the purchaser would treat the $15 as though it had been paid out of previously taxed income and, therefore would not include the $15 in gross income. If in 1975, B receives another actual distribution of $9 with respect to such stock, $5 (i.e., $20 dividend on A's sale less the $15 distribution to B in 1974 which was treated under subparagraph (1) of this paragraph as made from previously taxed income) is treated as made from previously taxed income and excluded from gross income. The result would be the same if, on January 1, 1975, B had transferred such stock to C by gift and the $9 distribution had been made to C.

(b) *Corporate adjustment upon redemption.* (1) Under section 996(d)(2), if by reason of § 1.995-4 gain on a redemption of stock in a DISC, or former DISC, is included in the shareholder's gross income as a dividend, then the accumulated DISC income shall be reduced by an amount equal to the sum of—

    (i) The amount of gain on such redemption which, under § 1.995-4, is treated as a dividend, and

    (ii) The amount of any gain with respect to such redeemed stock which, under § 1.995-4, was treated as a dividend on a disposition prior to such redemption minus the amount of distributions with respect to such stock which have been treated as made out of previously taxed income by reason of the application of paragraph (a)(1) of this section.

(2) The provisions of this paragraph may be illustrated by the following examples:

Example (1). The entire stock of a DISC, which uses the calendar year as its taxable year, has been owned equally by A, B, C, and D since it was organized. At the close of 1976, when the DISC has $100 of accumulated DISC income, it redeems all of A's shares in a transaction qualifying as an exchange under section 302(a) and A, under § 1.995-4, includes $25 in his gross income as a dividend. The redemption has the effect of reducing accumulated DISC income by $25 to $75.

Example (2). Assume the same facts as in example (1) except that the stock of the DISC has not been held equally by A, B, C, and D since its organization. A purchased his shares from X in 1974 in a transaction in which X, under § 1.995-4, included in his gross income $30 as a dividend. In 1975, A receives a distribution of $10 out of accumulated DISC income which, under paragraph (a)(1) of this section, is treated as made out of previously taxed income. Under these facts, the redemption of A's stock in 1976 has the effect of reducing accumulated DISC income by $45 to $55 determined as follows:

(a) Accumulated DISC income $100
(b) Minus sum of
  (1) Dividend on redemption of A's stock $25
  (2) Excess of dividend on X's sale ($30) over distribution to A treated as made out of previously taxed income ($10)   20

    Total 45

(c) Accumulated DISC income on 12/31/76 .... $ 55

[Reg. § 1.996-4.]

☐ [T.D. 7324, 9-27-74.]

[Reg. § 1.996-5]

§ 1.996-5. Adjustment to basis.—(a) *Addition to basis.* Under section 996(e)(1) amounts representing deemed distributions as provided in section 995(b) shall increase the basis of the stock with respect to which the distribution is made.

(b) *Reductions of basis.* Under section 996(e)(2), the portion of an actual distribution treated as made out of previously taxed income shall reduce the basis of the stock with respect to which it is made and, to the extent that it exceeds the adjusted basis of such stock, shall be treated as gain from the sale or exchange of property. In the case of stock includible in the gross estate of a decedent for which an election is made under section 2032 (relating to alternate valuation), this paragraph shall not apply to any distribution made after the date of the decedent's death and before the alternate valuation date provided by section 2032. See section 1014(d) for a special rule for determining the basis of stock in a DISC, or former DISC, acquired from a decedent. [Reg. § 1.996-5.]

☐ [T.D. 7324, 9-27-74.]

[Reg. § 1.996-6]

§ 1.996-6. Effectively connected income.—In the case of a shareholder who is a nonresident alien individual or a foreign corporation, trust, or estate, amounts taxable as dividends by reason of the application of § 1.995-4 (relating to gain on disposition of stock in a DISC), amounts treated under § 1.996-1 as distributed out of accumulated DISC income, and amounts deemed distributed under § 1.995-2(a)(1) through (4) shall be treated as gains and distributions which are effectively connected with the conduct of a trade or business conducted through a permanent establishment of such shareholder within the United States, and shall be subject to tax in accordance with the provisions of section 871(b) and the regulations thereunder in the case of nonresident alien individuals, trusts, or estates, or section 882 and the regulations thereunder in the case of foreign corporations. In no case, however, shall other income of such shareholder be taxable as effectively connected with the conduct of a trade or business through a permanent establishment in the United States solely because of the application of this section. [Reg. § 1.996-6.]

☐ [T.D. 7324, 9-27-74.]

[Reg. § 1.996-7]

§ 1.996-7. Carryover of DISC tax attributes.—(a) *In general.* Carryover of a DISC's divisions of earnings and profits to acquiring corporations in nontaxable transactions shall be subject to rules generally applicable to other corporate tax attributes. For example, a DISC which acquires the assets of another DISC in a transaction to which section 381(a) applies shall succeed to, and take into account, the divisions of the earnings and profits of the transferor DISC in accordance with section 381(c)(2).

(b) *Allocation of divisions of earnings and profits in corporate separations.* (1) If one DISC transfers part of its assets to a controlled DISC in a transaction to which section 368(a)(1)(D) applies and immediately thereafter the stock of the controlled DISC is distributed in a distribution or exchange to which section 355 (or so much of section 356 as relates to section 355) applies, then—

(i) The earnings and profits of the distributing DISC immediately before the transaction shall be allocated between the distributing DISC and the controlled DISC in accordance with the provisions of § 1.312-10.

(ii) Each of the divisions of such earnings and profits, namely previously taxed income, accumulated DISC income, and other earnings and profits, shall be allocated between the distributing DISC and the controlled DISC on the same basis as the earnings and profits are allocated.

(iii) Any assets of the distributing DISC whose status as qualified export assets is limited by its accumulated DISC income (*e.g.,* producer's loans described in § 1.993-4, Export-Import Bank and other obligations described in § 1.993-2(h), and financing obligations described in § 1.993-2(i)) shall be treated as having been allocated, for the purpose of determining the classification of such assets in the hands of the distributing DISC or the controlled DISC, on the same basis as the earnings and profits are allocated regardless of how such assets are actually allocated.

(2) *Example.* The provisions of this paragraph may be illustrated by the following example:

Example. On January 1, 1974, P Corporation transfers part of its assets to S Corporation, a newly organized subsidiary of P, in a transaction described in section 368(a)(1)(D) and distributes all the S stock in a transaction which qualifies under section 355. Immediately before such transfer, P had earnings and profits of $120,000 of which $100,000 constitutes accumulated DISC income. The unpaid balance of P's producer's loans is $80,000 all of which is retained by P. Pursuant to § 1.312-10, 25 percent of P's accumulated DISC income is allocated to S (*i.e.,* $25,000). P's producer's loans will be treated as allocated to S in the same proportion. Accordingly, for purposes of determining, under § 1.993-4(a)(3), the amount of producer's loans which S is entitled to make, S is treated as having an unpaid balance of producer's loans of $20,000 (*i.e.,* 25% × $80,000) and P is treated as having an unpaid balance of $60,000 (*i.e.,* 75% × $80,000).

(c) *Accumulated DISC income accounts of separate DISC's maintained after corporate combination.* If two or more DISC's combine to form a new DISC, or if the assets of one DISC are acquired by another DISC, in a transaction described in section 381(a), accumulated DISC income of the acquired DISC or DISC's shall carry over and be taken into account by the acquiring or new DISC, except that a separate account shall be maintained for the accumulated DISC income of any DISC scheduled to be received as a deemed distribution by its shareholders under § 1.995-3 (relating to deemed distributions upon disqualification). If, as a part of such transaction, the stock of the DISC which has accumulated DISC income scheduled to be deemed distributed is exchanged for stock of the acquiring or new DISC to which such accumulated DISC income is carried over and which maintains a separate account, then such accumulated DISC income shall be deemed distributed pro rata to shareholders of the acquiring or new DISC on the basis of stock ownership immediately after the exchange. [Reg. § 1.996-7.]

☐ [T.D. 7324, 9-27-74.]

[Reg. § 1.996-8]

§ 1.996-8. **Effect of carryback of capital loss or net operating loss to prior DISC taxable year.**—(a) Under § 1.995-2(e), the deduction under section 172 for a net operating loss carryback or under section 1212 for a capital loss carryback is determined as if the DISC were a domestic corporation which had not elected to be treated as a DISC. A carryback of a net operating loss or of a capital loss of any corporation which reduces its taxable income for a preceding taxable year for which it qualified as a DISC will have the consequences enumerated in paragraphs (b) through (e) of this section.

(b) For such preceding taxable year, the amount of a deemed distribution of one-half of certain taxable income described in § 1.995-2(a)(4) will ordinarily be reduced in effect (but not below zero) by one-half of the sum of the amount of the deduction under section 172 for such year for net operating loss carrybacks and the amount of the deduction under section 1212 for such year for capital loss carrybacks.

(c) The amount of reduction in the deemed distribution under paragraph (b) of this section will have the effect of increasing the limitation, provided in § 1.995-2(b)(2), on the amount of foreign investment attributable to producer's loans which is deemed distributed under § 1.995-2(a)(5).

(d) If the amount of a deemed distribution for a preceding taxable year is reduced as described in paragraph (b) of this section, then for such preceding taxable year the previously taxed income (as defined in § 1.996-3(c)) shall be decreased by the amount of such reduction and the accumulated DISC income (as defined in § 1.996-3(b)) shall be increased by the amount of such reduction. Such adjustments shall be made as of the time the deemed distribution for such preceding taxable year is treated as having occurred. See § 1.996-1(d) for the priority of such deemed distribution in relation to other distributions made in that preceding taxable year.

(e) The amount and treatment of any actual distribution made in such preceding taxable year or a year subsequent to such preceding year, and the treatment of gain on a disposition (in any such year) of the DISC's stock to which § 1.995-4 applies, shall be properly adjusted to reflect the adjustments to previously taxed income and accumulated DISC income described in paragraph (d) of this section. [Reg. § 1.996-8.]

☐ [T.D. 7324, 9-27-74.]

[Reg. § 1.997-1]

§ 1.997-1. **Special rules for subchapter C of the Code.**—(a) For purposes of applying the provisions of sections 301 through 395 of the Code, any distribution in property to a corporation by a DISC, or former DISC, which is made out of previously taxed income or accumulated DISC income shall be treated as a distribution in the same amount as if such distribution of property were made to an individual, and have a basis, in the hands of the recipient corporation, equal to such amount treated as having been distributed.

(b) This section may be illustrated by the following example:

Example. X corporation is the sole shareholder of Y corporation which is a DISC. Y makes an actual distribution of property to X with respect to X's stock in Y. The property has a basis of $50 and a fair market value of $100. The distribution is treated as made out of accumulated DISC income under section 996(a) and is taxable as a dividend under section 301(c)(1). Even though X is a corporation, the amount of the distribution is $100 notwithstanding the provisions of section 301(b)(1)(B) and the basis of the property in X's hands is $100 notwithstanding the provisions of section 301(d)(2). [Reg. § 1.997-1.]

☐ [T.D. 7324, 9-27-74.]

International Boycott Determinations

[Reg. § 7.999-1]

§ 7.999-1. Computation of the international boycott factor (Temporary).—(a) *In general.* Sections 908(a), 952(a)(3), and 995(b)(1)(F) provide that certain benefits of the foreign tax credit, deferral of earnings of foreign corporations, and DISC are denied if a person or a member of a controlled group (within the meaning of section 993(a)(3)) that includes that person participates in or cooperates with an international boycott (within the meaning of section 999(b)(3)). The loss of tax benefits may be determined by multiplying the otherwise allowable tax benefits by the "international boycott factor." Section 999(c)(1) provides that the international boycott factor is to be determined under regulations prescribed by the Secretary. The method of computing the international boycott factor is set forth in paragraph (c) of this section. A special rule for computing the international boycott factor of a person that is a member of two or more controlled groups is set forth in paragraph (d). Transitional rules for making adjustments to the international boycott factor for years affected by the effective dates are set forth in paragraph (e). The definitions of the terms used in this section are set forth in paragraph (b).

(b) *Definitions.* For purposes of this section:

(1) *Boycotting country.* In respect of a particular international boycott, the term "boycotting country" means any country described in section 999(a)(1)(A) or (B) that requires participation in or cooperation with that particular international boycott.

(2) *Participation in or cooperation with an international boycott.* For the definition of the term "participation in or cooperation with an international boycott", see section 999(b)(3) and Parts H through M of the Treasury Department's International Boycott Guidelines.

(3) *Operations in or related to a boycotting country.* For the definitions of the terms "operations", "operations in a boycotting country", "operations related to a boycotting country", and "operations with the government, a company, or a national of a boycotting country", see Part B of the Treasury Department's International Boycott Guidelines.

(4) *Clearly demonstrating clearly separate and identifiable operations.* For the rules for "clearly demonstrating clearly separate and identifiable operations", see Part D of the Treasury Department's International Boycott Guidelines.

(5) *Purchase made from a country.* The terms "purchase made from a boycotting country" and "purchases made from any country other than the United States" mean, in respect of any particular country, the gross amount paid in connection with the purchase of, the use of, or the right to use:

(i) Tangible personal property (including money) from a stock of goods located in that country,

(ii) Intangible property (other than securities) in that country,

(iii) Securities by a dealer to a beneficial owner that is a resident of that country (but only if the dealer knows or has reason to know the country of residence of the beneficial owner),

(iv) Real property located in that country, or

(v) Services performed in, and the end product of services performed in, that country (other than payroll paid to a person that is an officer or employee of the payor).

(6) *Sales made to a country.* The terms "sales made to a boycotting country" and "sales made to any country other than the United States" mean, in respect of any particular country, the gross receipts from the sale, exchange, other disposition, or use of:

(i) Tangible personal property (including money) for direct use, consumption, or disposition in that country,

(ii) Services performed in that country.

(iii) The end product of services (wherever performed) for direct use, consumption, or disposition in that country,

(iv) Intangible property (other than securities) in that country,

(v) Securities by a dealer to a beneficial owner that is a resident of the country (but only if the dealer knows or has reason to know the country of residence of the beneficial owner), or

(vi) Real property located in that country.

To determine the country of direct use, consumption, or disposition of tangible personal property and the end product of services, see paragraph (b)(10) of this section.

(7) *Sales made from a country.* The terms "sales made from a boycotting country" and "sales made from any country other than the United States" mean, in respect of a particular country, the gross receipts from the sale, exchange, other disposition, or use of:

(i) Tangible personal property (including money) from a stock of goods located in that country,

Reg. § 7.999-1(a)

(ii) Intangible property (other than securities) in that country, or

(iii) Services performed in, and the end product of services performed in, that country.

However, gross receipts from any such sale, exchange, other disposition, or use by a person that are included in the numerator of that person's international boycott factor by reason of paragraph (b)(6) of this section shall not again be included in the numerator by reason of this subparagraph.

(8) *Payroll paid or accrued for services performed in a country.* The terms "payroll paid or accrued for services performed in a boycotting country" and "payroll paid or accrued for services performed in any country other than the United States" mean, in respect of a particular country, the total amount paid or accrued as compensation to officers and employees, including wages, salaries, commissions, and bonuses, for services performed in that country.

(9) *Services performed partly within and partly without a country.* (i) *In general.* Except as provided in paragraph (b)(9)(ii) of this section, for purposes of allocating to a particular country:

(A) The gross amount paid in connection with the purchase or use of,

(B) The gross receipts from the sale, exchange, other disposition or use of, and

(C) The payroll paid or accrued

for services performed, or the end product of services performed, partly within and partly without that country, the amount paid, received, or accrued to be allocated to that country, unless the facts and circumstances of a particular case warrant a different amount, will be that amount that bears the same relation to the total amount paid, received, or accrued as the number of days of performance of the services within that country bears to the total number of days of performance of services for which the total amount is paid, received, or accrued.

(ii) *Transportation, telegraph, and cable services.* Transportation, telegraph, and cable services performed partly within one country and partly within another country are allocated between the two countries as follows:

(A) In the case of a purchase of such services performed from Country A to Country B, fifty percent of the gross amount paid is deemed to be a purchase made from Country A and the remaining fifty percent is deemed to be a purchase made from Country B.

(B) In the case of a sale of such services performed from Country A to Country B, fifty percent of the gross receipts is deemed to be a sale made from Country B and the remaining fifty percent is deemed to be a sale made to Country B.

(10) *Country of use, consumption, or disposition.* As a general rule, the country of use, consumption, or disposition of tangible personal property (including money) and the end product of services (wherever performed) is deemed to be the country of destination of the tangible personal property or the end product of the services. (Thus, if legal services are performed in one country and an opinion is given for use by a client in a second country, the end product of the legal services is used, consumed, or disposed of in the second country.) The occurrence in a country of a temporary interruption in the shipment of the tangible personal property or the delivery of the end product of services shall not constitute such country the country of destination. However, if at the time of the transaction the person providing the tangible personal property or the end product of services knew, or should have known from the facts and circumstances surrounding the transaction, that the tangible personal property or the end product of services probably would not be used, consumed, or disposed of in the country of destination, that person must determine the country of ultimate use, consumption or disposition of the tangible personal property or the end product of services. Notwithstanding the preceding provisions of this subparagraph, a person that sells, exchanges, otherwise disposes of, or makes available for use, tangible personal property to any person all of whose business except for an insubstantial part consists of selling from inventory to retail customers at retail outlets all within one country may assume at the time of such sale to such person that the tangible personal property will be used, consumed, or disposed of within such country.

(11) *Controlled group taxable year.* The term "controlled group taxable year" means the taxable year of the controlled group's common parent corporation. In the event that no common parent corporation exists, the members of the group shall elect the taxable year of one of the members of the controlled group to serve as the controlled group taxable year. The taxable year election is a binding election to be changed only with the approval of the Secretary or his delegate. The election is to be made in accordance with the procedures set forth in the instructions to Form 5713, the International Boycott Report.

(c) *Computation of international boycott factor.* (1) *In general.* The method of computing the international boycott factor of a person that is not a member of a controlled group is set forth in paragraph (c)(2) of this section. The method of computing the international boycott factor of a

Reg. § 7.999-1(c)

person that is a member of a controlled group is set forth in paragraph (c)(3) of this section. For purposes of paragraphs (c)(2) and (3), purchases and sales made by, and payroll paid or accrued by, a partnership are deemed to be made or paid or accrued by a partner in that proportion that the partner's distributive share bears to the purchases and sales made by, and the payroll paid or accrued by, the partnership. Also for purposes of paragraphs (c)(2) and (3), purchases and sales made by, and payroll paid or accrued by, a trust referred to in section 671 are deemed to be made both by the trust (for purposes of determining the trust's international boycott factor), and by a person treated under section 671 as the owner of the trust (but only in that proportion that the portion of the trust that such person is considered as owning under sections 671 through 679 bears to the purchases and sales made by, and the payroll paid and accrued by, the trust).

(2) *International boycott factor of a person that is not a member of a controlled group.* The international boycott factor to be applied by a person that is not a member of a controlled group (within the meaning of section 993(a)(3)) is a fraction.

    (i) The numerator of the fraction is the sum of the—

       (A) Purchases made from all boycotting countries associated in carrying out a particular international boycott,

       (B) Sales made to or from all boycotting countries associated in carrying out a particular international boycott, and

       (C) Payroll paid or accrued for services performed in all boycotting countries associated in carrying out a particular international boycott by that person during that person's taxable year, minus the amount of such purchases, sales, and payroll that is clearly demonstrated to be attributable to clearly separate and identifiable operations in connection with which there was no participation in or cooperation with that international boycott.

    (ii) The denominator of the fraction is the sum of the—

       (A) Purchases made from any country other than the United States,

       (B) Sales made to or from any country other than the United States, and

       (C) Payroll paid or accrued for services performed in any country other than the United States

by that person during that person's taxable year.

(3) *International boycott factor of a person that is a member of a controlled group.* The international boycott factor to be applied by a person that is a member of a controlled group (within the meaning of section 993(a)(3)) shall be computed in the manner described in paragraph (c)(2) of this section, except that there shall be taken into account the purchases and sales made by, and the payroll paid or accrued by, each member of the controlled group during each member's own taxable year that ends with or within the controlled group taxable year that ends with or within that person's taxable year.

(d) *Computation of the international boycott factor of a person that is a member of two or more controlled groups.* The international boycott factor to be applied under sections 908(a), 953(a)(3), and 995(b)(1)(F) by a person that is a member of two or more controlled groups shall be determined in the manner described in paragraph (c)(3), except that the purchases, sales, and payroll included in the numerator and denominator shall include the purchases, sales, and payroll of that person and of all other members of the two or more controlled groups of which that person is a member.

(e) *Transitional rules.* (1) *Pre-November 3, 1976 boycotting operations.* The international boycott factor to be applied under sections 908(a), 952(a)(3), and 995(b)(1)(F) by a person that is not a member of a controlled group, for that person's taxable year that includes November 3, 1976, or a person that is a member of a controlled group, for the controlled group taxable year that includes November 3, 1976, shall be computed in the manner described in paragraphs (c)(2) and (c)(3), respectively, of this section. However, that the following adjustments shall be made:

    (i) There shall be excluded from the numerators described in paragraphs (c)(2)(i) and (c)(3)(i) of this section purchases, sales, and payroll clearly demonstrated to be attributable to clearly separate and identifiable operations—

       (A) That were completed on or before November 3, 1976, or

       (B) In respect of which it is demonstrated that the agreements constituting participation in or cooperation with the international boycott were renounced, the renunciations were communicated on or before November 3, 1976, to the governments or persons with which the agreements were made, and the agreements have not been reaffirmed after November 3, 1976, and

    (ii) The international boycott factor resulting after the numerator has been modified in accordance with paragraph (e)(1)(i) of this section shall be further modified by multiplying it by a fraction. The numerator of that fraction shall be the number of days in that person's taxable year

Reg. § 7.999-1(c)(2)

(or, if applicable, in that person's controlled group taxable year) remaining after November 3, 1976, and the denominator shall be 366.

The principles of this subparagraph are illustrated in the following example:

Example. Corporation A, a calendar year taxpayer, is not a member of a controlled group. During the 1976 calendar year, Corporation A had three operations in a boycotting country under three separate contracts, each of which contained agreements constituting participation in or cooperation with an international boycott. Each contract was entered into on or after September 2, 1976. Operation (1) was completed on November 1, 1976. The sales made to a boycotting country in connection with Operation (1) amounted to $10. Operation (2) was not completed during the taxable year, but on November 1, 1976, Corporation A communicated a renunciation of the boycott agreement covering that operation to the government of the boycotting country. The sales made to a boycotting country in connection with Operation (2) amounted to $40. Operation (3) was not completed during the taxable year, nor was any renunciation of the boycott agreement made. The sales made to a boycotting country in connection with Operation (3) amounted to $25. Corporation A had no purchases made from, sales made from, or payroll paid or accrued for services performed in, a boycotting country. Corporation A had $500 of purchases made from, sales made from, sales made to, and payroll paid or accrued for services performed in, countries other than the United States. Company A's boycott factor for 1976, computed under paragraph (c)(2) of this section (before the application of this subparagraph) would be:

$$\frac{\$10 + \$40 + \$25}{\$500} = \frac{\$75}{\$500}$$

However, the $10 is eliminated from the numerator by reason of paragraph (e)(j)(1)(A) of this section, and the $40 is eliminated from the numerator by reason of paragraph (e)(j)(1)(B) of this section. Thus, before the application of paragraph (e)(1)(ii) of this section, Corporation A's international boycott factor is $25/$500. After the application of paragraph (e)(1)(ii), Corporation A's international boycott factor is:

$$\frac{\$25}{\$500} = \frac{58}{366}$$

(2) *Pre-December 31, 1977 boycotting operations.* The international boycott factor to be applied under sections 908(a), 952(a)(3), and 995(b)(1)(P) by a person that is not a member of a controlled group, for that person's taxable year that includes December 31, 1977, or by a person that is a member of a controlled group, for the controlled group taxable year that includes December 31, 1977, shall be computed in the manner described in paragraphs (c)(2) and (c)(3), respectively, of this section. However, the following adjustments shall be made:

(i) There shall be excluded from the numerators described in paragraphs (c)(2)(i) and (c)(3)(i) of this section purchases, sales, and payroll clearly demonstrated to be attributable to clearly separate and identifiable operations that were carried out in accordance with the terms of binding contracts entered into before September 3, 1976, and—

(A) That were completed on or before December 31, 1977, or

(B) In respect of which it is demonstrated that the agreements constituting participation in or cooperation with the international boycott were renounced, the renunciations were communicated on or before December 31, 1977, to the governments or persons with which the agreements were made, and the agreements were not reaffirmed after December 31, 1977, and

(ii) In the case of clearly separate and identifiable operations that are carried out in accordance with the terms of binding contracts entered into before September 2, 1976, but that do not meet the requirements of paragraph (e)(2)(i) of this section, the numerators described in paragraphs (e)(2)(i) and (e)(3)(i) of this section shall be adjusted by multiplying the purchases, sales, and payroll clearly demonstrated to be attributable to those operations by a fraction, the numerator of which is the number of days in such person's taxable year (or, if applicable, in such person's controlled group taxable year) remaining after December 31, 1977, and the denominator of which is 365.

The principles of this subparagraph are illustrated in the following example:

Example. Corporation A is not a member of a controlled group and reports on the basis of a July 1-June 30 fiscal year. During the 1977-1978 fiscal year, Corporation A had 2 operations carried out pursuant to the terms of separate contracts, each of which had a clause that constituted participation in or cooperation with an international boycott. Neither operation was completed during the fiscal year, nor were either of the boycotting clauses renounced. Operation (1) was carried out in accordance with the terms of a contract entered into on November 15, 1976. Operation (2) was carried out in accordance with the terms of a binding contract entered into before September 2, 1976. Corporation A had sales made to a boycotting country in connection with Opera-

Reg. § 7.999-1(e)(2)

tion (1) in the amount of $50, and in connection with Operation (2) in the amount of $100. Corporation A had sales made to countries other than the United States in the amount of $500. Corporation A had no purchases made from, sales made from, or payroll paid or accrued for services performed in, any country other than the United States. In the absence of this subparagraph, Corporation A's international boycott factor would be

$$\frac{\$50 + \$100}{\$500}$$

However, by reason of the application of this subparagraph, Corporation A's international boycott factor is reduced to

$$\frac{\$50 + \$100 \left(\frac{181}{365}\right)}{\$500}$$

(3) *Incomplete controlled group taxable year.* If, at the end of the taxable year of a person that is a member of a controlled group, the controlled group taxable year that includes November 3, 1976 has not ended, or the taxable year of one or more members of the controlled group that includes November 3, 1976 has not ended, then the international boycott factor to be applied under sections 908(a), 952(a)(3) and 955(b)(1)(P) by such person for the taxable year shall be computed in the manner described in paragraph (c)(3) of this section. However, the numerator and the denominator in that paragraph shall include only the purchases, sales, and payroll of those members of the controlled group whose taxable years ending after November 3, 1976 have ended as the end of the taxable year of such person.

(f) *Effective date.* This section applies to participation in or cooperation with an international boycott after November 3, 1976. In the case of operations which constitute participation in or cooperation with an international boycott and which are carried out in accordance with the terms of a binding contract entered into before September 2, 1976, this section applies to such participation or cooperation after December 31, 1977. [Temporary Reg. § 7.999-1.]

☐ [T.D. 7467, 2-24-77.]

[The next page is 51,901.]

GAIN OR LOSS ON DISPOSITION OF PROPERTY
Determination and Recognition of Gain or Loss

[Reg. § 1.1001-1]

§ 1.1001-1. Computation of gain or loss.—(a) *General Rule.* Except as otherwise provided in subtitle A of the Code, the gain or loss realized from the conversion of property into cash, or from the exchange of property for other property differing materially either in kind or in extent, is treated as income or as loss sustained. The amount realized from a sale or other disposition of property is the sum of any money received plus the fair market value of any property (other than money) received. The fair market value of property is a question of fact, but only in rare and extraordinary cases will property be considered to have no fair market value. The general method of computing such gain or loss is prescribed by section 1001(a) through (d) which contemplates that from the amount realized upon the sale or exchange there shall be withdrawn a sum sufficient to restore the adjusted basis prescribed by section 1011 and the regulations thereunder (i.e., the cost or other basis adjusted for receipts, expenditures, losses, allowances, and other items chargeable against and applicable to such cost or other basis). The amount which remains after the adjusted basis has been restored to the taxpayer constitutes the realized gain. If the amount realized upon the sale or exchange is insufficient to restore to the taxpayer the adjusted basis of the property, a loss is sustained to the extent of the difference between such adjusted basis and the amount realized. The basis may be different depending upon whether gain or loss is being computed. For example, see section 1015(a) and the regulations thereunder. Section 1001(e) and paragraph (f) of this section prescribe the method of computing gain or loss upon the sale or other disposition of a term interest in property the adjusted basis (or a portion) of which is determined pursuant, or by reference, to section 1014 (relating to the basis of property acquired from a decedent) or section 1015 (relating to the basis of property acquired by gift or by a transfer in trust).

(b) *Real estate taxes as amounts received.* (1) Section 1001(b) and section 1012 state rules applicable in making an adjustment upon a sale of real property with respect to the real property taxes apportioned between seller and purchaser under section 164(d). Thus, if the seller pays (or agrees to pay) real property taxes attributable to the real property tax year in which the sale occurs, he shall not take into account, in determining the amount realized from the sale under section 1001(b), any amount received as reimbursement for taxes which are treated under section 164(d) as imposed upon the purchaser. Similarly, in computing the cost of the property under section 1012, the purchaser shall not take into account any amount paid to the seller as reimbursement for real property taxes which are treated under section 164(d) as imposed upon the purchaser. These rules apply whether or not the contract of sale calls for the purchaser to reimburse the seller for such real property taxes paid or to be paid by the seller.

(2) On the other hand, if the purchaser pays (or is to pay) an amount representing real property taxes which are treated under section 164(d) as imposed upon the seller, that amount shall be taken into account both in determining the amount realized from the sale under section 1001(b) and in computing the cost of the property under section 1012. It is immaterial whether or not the contract of sale specifies that the sale price has been reduced by, or is in any way intended to reflect, the taxes allocable to the seller. See also paragraph (b) of § 1.1012-1.

(3) Subparagraph (1) of this paragraph shall not apply to a seller who, in a taxable year prior to the taxable year of sale, pays an amount representing real property taxes which are treated under section 164(d) as imposed on the purchaser, if such seller has elected to capitalize such amount in accordance with section 266 and the regulations thereunder (relating to election to capitalize certain carrying charges and taxes).

(4) The application of this paragraph may be illustrated by the following examples:

Example (1). Assume that the contract price on the sale of a parcel of real estate is $50,000 and that real property taxes thereon in the amount of $1,000 for the real property tax year in which occurred the date of sale were previously paid by the seller. Assume further that $750 of the taxes are treated under section 164(d) as imposed upon the purchaser and that he reimburses the seller in that amount in addition to the contract price. The amount realized by the seller is $50,000. Similarly, $50,000 is the purchaser's cost. If, in this example, the purchaser made no payment other than the contract price of $50,000, the amount realized by the seller would be $49,250, since the sales price would be deemed to include $750 paid to the seller in reimbursement for real property taxes imposed upon the purchaser. Similarly, $49,250 would be the purchaser's cost.

Reg. § 1.1001-1(b)(4)

51,902 Determination and Recognition of Gain or Loss
See p. 20,601 for regulations not amended to reflect law changes

Example (2). Assume that the purchaser in example (1) above, paid all of the real property taxes. Assume further that $250 of the taxes are treated under section 164(d) as imposed upon the seller. The amount realized by the seller is $50,250. Similarly, $50,250 is the purchaser's cost, regardless of the taxable year in which the purchaser makes actual payment of the taxes.

Example (3). Assume that the seller described in the first part of example (1), above, paid the real property taxes of $1,000 in the taxable year prior to the taxable year of sale and elected under section 266 to capitalize the $1,000 of taxes. In such a case, the amount realized is $50,750. Moreover, regardless of whether the seller elected to capitalize the real property taxes, the purchaser in that case could elect under section 266 to capitalize the $750 of taxes treated under section 164(d) as imposed upon him, in which case his adjusted basis would be $50,750 (cost of $50,000 plus capitalized taxes of $570 [$750]).

(c) *Other rules.* (1) Even though property is not sold or otherwise disposed of, gain is realized if the sum of all the amounts received which are required by section 1016 and other applicable provisions of subtitle A of the Code to be applied against the basis of the property exceeds such basis. Except as otherwise provided in section 301(c)(3)(B) with respect to distributions out of increase in value of property accrued prior to March 1, 1913, such gain is includible in gross income under section 61 as "income from whatever source derived". On the other hand, a loss is not ordinarily sustained prior to the sale or other disposition of the property, for the reason that until such sale or other disposition occurs there remains the possibility that the taxpayer may recover or recoup the adjusted basis of the property. Until some identifiable event fixes the actual sustaining of a loss and the amount thereof, it is not taken into account.

(2) The provisions of subparagraph (1) of this paragraph may be illustrated by the following example:

Example. A, an individual on a calendar year basis, purchased certain shares of stock subsequent to February 28, 1913, for $10,000. On January 1, 1954, A's adjusted basis for the stock had been reduced to $1,000 by reason of receipts and distributions described in sections 1016(a)(1) and 1016(a)(4). He received in 1954 a further distribution of $5,000, being a distribution covered by section 1016(a)(4), other than a distribution out of increase of value of property accrued prior to March 1, 1913. This distribution applied against the adjusted basis as required by section 1016(a)(4) exceeds that basis by $4,000. The $4,000 excess is a gain realized by A in 1954 and is includible in gross income in his return for that calendar year. In computing gain from the stock, as in adjusting basis, no distinction is made between items of receipts or distributions described in section 1016. If A sells the stock in 1955 for $5,000, he realizes in 1955 a gain of $5,000, since the adjusted basis of the stock for the purpose of computing gain or loss from the sale is zero.

(d) *Installment sales.* In the case of property sold on the installment plan, special rules for the taxation of the gain are prescribed in section 453.

(e) *Transfers in part a sale and in part a gift.* (1) Where a transfer of property is in part a sale and in part a gift, the transferor has a gain to the extent that the amount realized by him exceeds his adjusted basis in the property. However, no loss is sustained on such a transfer if the amount realized is less than the adjusted basis. For determination of basis of the property in the hands of the transferee, see § 1.1015-4. For the allocation of the adjusted basis of property in the case of a bargain sale to a charitable organization, see § 1.1011-2.

(2) *Examples.* The provisions of subparagraph (1) may be illustrated by the following examples:

Example (1). A transfers property to his son for $60,000. Such property in the hands of A has an adjusted basis of $30,000 (and a fair market value of $90,000). A's gain is $30,000, the excess of $60,000, the amount realized, over the adjusted basis, $30,000. He has made a gift of $30,000, the excess of $90,000, the fair market value, over the amount realized, $60,000.

Example (2). A transfers property to his son for $30,000. Such property in the hands of A has an adjusted basis of $60,000 (and a fair market value of $90,000). A has no gain or loss, and has made a gift of $60,000, the excess of $90,000, the fair market value, over the amount realized, $30,000.

Example (3). A transfers property to his son for $30,000. Such property in A's hands has an adjusted basis of $30,000 (and a fair market value of $60,000). A has no gain and has made a gift of $30,000, the excess of $60,000, the fair market value, over the amount realized, $30,000.

Example (4). A transfers property to his son for $30,000. Such property in A's hands has an adjusted basis of $90,000 (and a fair market value of $60,000). A has sustained no loss, and has made a gift of $30,000, the excess of $60,000, the fair market value, over the amount realized, $30,000.

Reg. § 1.1001-1(c)(2)

(f) *Sale or other disposition of a term interest in property*—(1) *General rule.* Except as otherwise provided in subparagraph (3) of this paragraph, for purposes of determining gain or loss from the sale or other disposition after October 9, 1969, of a term interest in property (as defined in subparagraph (2) of this paragraph), a taxpayer shall not take into account that portion of the adjusted basis of such interest which is determined pursuant to, or by reference, to section 1014 (relating to the basis of property acquired from a decedent) or section 1015 (relating to the basis of property acquired by gift or by a transfer in trust) to the extent that such adjusted basis is a portion of the adjusted uniform basis of the entire property (as defined in § 1.1014-5). Where a term interest in property is transferred to a corporation in connection with a transaction to which section 351 applies and the adjusted basis of the term interest (i) is determined pursuant to section 1014 or 1015 and (ii) is also a portion of the adjusted uniform basis of the entire property, a subsequent sale or other disposition of such term interest by the corporation will be subject to the provisions of section 1001(e) and this paragraph to the extent that the basis of the term interest so sold or otherwise disposed of is determined by reference to its basis in the hands of the transferor as provided by section 362(a). See subparagraph (2) of this paragraph for rules relating to the characterization of stock received by the transferor of a term interest in property in connection with a transaction to which section 351 applies. That portion of the adjusted uniform basis of the entire property which is assignable to such interest at the time of its sale or other disposition shall be determined under the rules provided in § 1.1014-5. Thus, gain or loss realized from a sale or other disposition of a term interest in property shall be determined by comparing the amount of the proceeds of such sale with that part of the adjusted basis of such interest which is not a portion of the adjusted uniform basis of the entire property.

(2) *Term interest defined.* For purposes of section 1001(e) and this paragraph, a "term interest in property" means—

(i) A life interest in property,

(ii) An interest in property for a term of years, or

(iii) An income interest in a trust.

Generally subdivisions (i), (ii), and (iii) refer to an interest, present or future, in the income from property or the right to use property which will terminate or fail on the lapse of time, on the occurrence of an event or contingency, or on the failure of an event or contingency to occur. Such divisions do not refer to remainder or reversionary interests in the property itself or other interests in the property which will ripen into ownership of the entire property upon termination or failure of a preceding term interest. A "term interest in property" also includes any property received upon a sale or other disposition of a life interest in property, an interest in property for a term of years, or an income interest in a trust by the original holder of such interest, but only to the extent that the adjusted basis of the property received is determined by reference to the adjusted basis of the term interest so transferred.

(3) *Exception.* Paragraph (1) of section 1001(e) and subparagraph (1) of this paragraph shall not apply to a sale or other disposition of a term interest in property as a part of a single transaction in which the entire interest in the property is transferred to a third person or to two or more other persons, including persons who acquire such entire interest as joint tenants, tenants by the entirety, or tenants in common. See § 1.1014-5 for computation of gain or loss upon such a sale or other disposition where the property has been acquired from a decedent or by gift or transfer in trust.

(4) *Illustrations.* For examples illustrating the application of this paragraph, see paragraph (c) of § 1.1014-5.

(g) *Debt instruments issued in exchange for property*—(1) *In general.* If a debt instrument is issued in exchange for property, the amount realized attributable to the debt instrument is the issue price of the debt instrument as determined under § 1.1273-2 or § 1.1274-2; whichever is applicable. If, however, the issue price of the debt instrument is determined under section 1273(b)(4), the amount realized attributable to the debt instrument is its stated principal amount reduced by any unstated interest (as determined under section 483).

(2) *Certain debt instruments that provide for contingent payments*—(i) *In general.* Paragraph (g)(1) of this section does not apply to a debt instrument subject to either § 1.483-4 or § 1.1275-4(c) (certain contingent payment debt instruments issued for nonpublicly traded property).

(ii) *Special rule to determine amount realized.* If a debt instrument subject to § 1.1275-4(c) is issued in exchange for property, and the income from the exchange is not reported under the installment method of section 453, the amount realized attributable to the debt instrument is the issue price of the debt instrument as determined under § 1.1274-2(g), increased by the fair market value of the contingent payments payable on the

Reg. § 1.1001-1(g)(2)

debt instrument. If a debt instrument subject to § 1.483-4 is issued in exchange for property, and the income from the exchange is not reported under the installment method of section 453, the amount realized attributable to the debt instrument is its stated principal amount, reduced by any unstated interest (as determined under section 483), and increased by the fair market value of the contingent payments payable on the debt instrument. This paragraph (g)(2)(ii), however, does not apply to a debt instrument if the fair market value of the contingent payments is not reasonably ascertainable. Only in rare and extraordinary cases will the fair market value of the contingent payments be treated as not reasonably ascertainable.

(3) *Coordination with section 453.* If a debt instrument is issued in exchange for property, and the income from the exchange is not reported under the installment method of section 453, this paragraph (g) applies rather than § 15a.453-1(d)(2) to determine the taxpayer's amount realized attributable to the debt instrument.

(4) *Effective date.* This paragraph (g) applies to sales or exchanges that occur on or after August 13, 1996. [Reg. § 1.1001-1.]

☐ [*T.D.* 6265, 11-6-57. *Amended by T.D.* 7142, 9-23-71; *T.D.* 7207, 10-3-72; *T.D.* 7213, 10-17-72; *T.D.* 8517, 1-27-94 *and T.D.* 8674, 6-11-96.]

[Reg. § 1.1001-2]

§ 1.1001-2. **Discharge of liabilities.**—(a) *Inclusion in amount realized.*—(1) *In general.* Except as provided in paragraph (a)(2) and (3) of this section, the amount realized from a sale or other disposition of property includes the amount of liabilities from which the transferor is discharged as a result of the sale or disposition.

(2) *Discharge of indebtedness.* The amount realized on a sale or other disposition of property that secures a recourse liability does not include amounts that are (or would be if realized and recognized) income from the discharge of indebtedness under section 61(a)(12). For situations where amounts arising from the discharge of indebtedness are not realized and recognized, see section 108 and § 1.61-12(b)(1).

(3) *Liability incurred on acquisition.* In the case of a liability incurred by reason of the acquisition of the property, this section does not apply to the extent that such liability was not taken into account in determining the transferor's basis for such property.

(4) *Special rules.* For purposes of this section—

(i) The sale or other disposition of property that secures a nonrecourse liability discharges the transferor from the liability;

(ii) The sale or other disposition of property that secures a recourse liability discharges the transferor from the liability if another person agrees to pay the liability (whether or not the transferor is in fact released from liability);

(iii) A disposition of property includes a gift of the property or a transfer of the property in satisfaction of liabilities to which it is subject;

(iv) Contributions and distributions of property between a partner and a partnership are not sales or other dispositions of property; and

(v) The liabilities from which a transferor is discharged as a result of the sale or disposition of a partnership interest include the transferor's share of the liabilities of the partnership.

(b) *Effect of fair market value of security.* The fair market value of the security at the time of sale or disposition is not relevant for purposes of determining under paragraph (a) of this section the amount of liabilities from which the taxpayer is discharged or treated as discharged. Thus, the fact that the fair market value of the property is less than the amount of the liabilities it secures does not prevent the full amount of those liabilities from being treated as money received from the sale or other disposition of the property. However, see paragraph (a)(2) of this section for a rule relating to certain income from discharge of indebtedness.

(c) *Examples.* The provisions of this section may be illustrated by the following examples. In each example assume the taxpayer uses the cash receipts and disbursements method of accounting, makes a return on the basis of the calendar year, and sells or disposes of all property which is security for a given liability.

Example (1). In 1976 A purchases an asset for $10,000. A pays the seller $1,000 in cash and signs a note payable to the seller for $9,000. A is personally liable for repayment with the seller having full recourse in the event of default. In addition, the asset which was purchased is pledged as security. During the years 1976 and 1977, A takes depreciation deductions on the asset in the amount of $3,100. During this same time period A reduces the outstanding principal on the note to $7,600. At the beginning of 1978 A sells the asset. The buyer pays A $1,600 in cash and assumes personal liability for the $7,600 outstanding liability. A becomes secondarily liable for repayment of the liability. A's amount realized is $9,200 ($1,600 + $7,600). Since A's adjusted basis in the asset is $6,900 ($10,000 − $3,100) A realizes a gain of $2,300 ($9,200 − $6,900).

Reg. § 1.1001-2(a)(1)

Determination and Recognition of Gain or Loss

Example (2). Assume the same facts as in example (1) except that A is not personally liable on the $9,000 note given to the seller and in the event of default the seller's only recourse is to the asset. In addition, on the sale of the asset by A, the purchaser takes the asset subject to the liability. Nevertheless, A's amount realized is $9,200 and A's gain realized is $2,300 on the sale.

Example (3). In 1975 L becomes a limited partner in partnership GL. L contributes $10,000 in cash to GL and L's distributive share of partnership income and loss is 10 percent. L is not entitled to receive any guaranteed payments. In 1978 M purchases L's entire interest in partnership GL. At the time of the sale L's adjusted basis in the partnership interest is $20,000. At that time L's proportionate share of liabilities, of which no partner has assumed personal liability, is $15,000. M pays $10,000 in cash for L's interest in the partnership. Under section 752(d) and this section, L's share of partnership liabilities, $15,000, is treated as money received. Accordingly, L's amount realized on the sale of the partnership interest is $25,000 ($10,000 + $15,000). L's gain realized on the sale is $5,000 ($25,000 − $20,000).

Example (4). In 1976 B becomes a limited partner in partnership BG. In 1978 B contributes B's entire interest in BG to a charitable organization described in section 170(c). At the time of the contribution all of the partnership liabilities are liabilities for which neither B nor G has assumed any personal liability and B's proportionate share of which is $9,000. The charitable organization does not pay any cash or other property to B, but takes the partnership interest subject to the $9,000 of liabilities. Assume that the contribution is treated as a bargain sale to a charitable organization and that under section 1011 (b) $3,000 is determined to be the portion of B's basis in the partnership interest allocable to the sale. Under section 752(d) and this section, the $9,000 of liabilities is treated by B as money received, thereby making B's amount realized $9,000. B's gain realized is $6,000 ($9,000 − $3,000).

Example (5). In 1975 C, an individual, creates T, an irrevocable trust. Due to certain powers expressly retained by C, T is a "grantor trust" for purposes of subpart E of part 1 of subchapter J of the Code and therefore C is treated as the owner of the entire trust. T purchases an interest in P, a partnership. C, as owner of T, deducts the distributive share of partnership losses attributable to the partnership interest held by T. In 1978, when the adjusted basis of the partnership interest held by T is $1,200, C renounces the powers previously and expressly retained that initially resulted in T being classified as a grantor trust. Consequently, T ceases to be a grantor trust and C is no longer considered to be the owner of the trust. At the time of the renunciation all of J's liabilities are liabilities on which none of the partners have assumed any personal liability and the proportionate share of which of the interest held by T is $11,000. Since prior to the renunciation C was the owner of the entire trust, C was considered the owner of all the trust property for Federal income tax purposes, including the partnership interest. Since C was considered to be the owner of the partnership interest, C not T, was considered to be the partner in P during the time T was a "grantor trust." However, at the time C renounced the powers that gave rise to T's classification as a grantor trust, T no longer qualified as a grantor trust with the result that C was no longer considered to be the owner of the trust and trust property for Federal income tax purposes. Consequently, at that time, C is considered to have transferred ownership of the interest in P to T, now a separate taxable entity, independent of its grantor C. On the transfer, C's share of partnership liabilities ($11,000) is treated as money received. Accordingly, C's amount realized is $11,000 and C's gain realized is $9,800 ($11,000 − $1,200).

Example (6). In 1977 D purchases an asset for $7,500. D pays the seller $1,500 in cash and signs a note payable to the seller for $6,000. D is not personally liable for repayment but pledges as security the newly purchased asset. In the event of default, the seller's only recourse is to the asset. During the years 1977 and 1978 D takes depreciation deductions on the asset totaling $4,200 thereby reducing D's basis in the asset to $3,300 ($7,500 − $4,200). In 1979 D transfers the asset to a trust which is not a "grantor trust" for purposes of subpart E of part 1 of subchapter J of the Code. Therefore D is not treated as the owner of the trust. The trust takes the asset subject to the liability and in addition pays D $750 in cash. Prior to the transfer D had reduced the amount outstanding on the liability to $4,700. D's amount realized on the transfer is $5,450 ($4,700 + $750). Since D's adjusted basis is $3,300, D's gain realized is $2,150 ($5,450 − $3,300).

Example (7). In 1974 E purchases a herd of cattle for breeding purposes. The purchase price is $20,000 consisting of $1,000 cash and a $19,000 note. E is not personally liable for repayment of the liability and the seller's only recourse in the event of default is to the herd of cattle. In 1977 E transfers the herd back to the original seller thereby satisfying the indebtedness pursuant to a provision in the original sales agreement. At the time of the transfer the fair market value of the

Reg. § 1.1001-2(c)

herd is $15,000 and the remaining principal balance on the note is $19,000. At the time E's adjusted basis in the herd is $16,500 due to a deductible loss incurred when a portion of the herd died as a result of a disease. As a result of the indebtedness being satisfied, E's amount realized is $19,000 notwithstanding the fact that the fair market value of the herd was less than $19,000. E's realized gain is $2,500 ($19,000 − $16,500).

Example (8). In 1980, F transfers to a creditor an asset with a fair market value of $6,000 and the creditor discharges $7,500 of indebtedness for which F is personally liable. The amount realized on the disposition of the asset is its fair market value ($6,000). In addition, F has income from the discharge of indebtedness of $1,500 ($7,500 − $6,000). [Reg. § 1.1001-2.]

☐ [*T.D.* 7741, 12-11-80.]

[Reg. § 1.1001-3]

§ 1.1001-3. Modifications of debt instruments.—(a) *Scope*—(1) *In general.* This section provides rules for determining whether a modification of the terms of a debt instrument results in an exchange for purposes of § 1.1001-1(a). This section applies to any modification of a debt instrument, regardless of the form of the modification. For example, this section applies to an exchange of a new instrument for an existing debt instrument, or to an amendment of an existing debt instrument. This section also applies to a modification of a debt instrument that the issuer and holder accomplish indirectly through one or more transactions with third parties. This section, however, does not apply to exchanges of debt instruments between holders.

(2) *Qualified tender bonds.* This section does not apply for purposes of determining whether tax-exempt bonds that are qualified tender bonds are reissued for purposes of sections 103 and 141 through 150.

(b) *General rule.* For purposes of § 1.1001-1(a), a significant modification of a debt instrument, within the meaning of this section, results in an exchange of the original debt instrument for a modified instrument that differs materially either in kind or in extent. A modification that is not a significant modification is not an exchange for purposes of § 1.1001-1(a). Paragraphs (c) and (d) of this section define the term *modification* and contain examples illustrating the application of the rule. Paragraphs (e) and (f) of this section provide rules for determining when a modification is a significant modification. Paragraph (g) of this section contains examples illustrating the application of the rules in paragraphs (e) and (f) of this section.

(c) *Modification defined*—(1) *In general*—(i) *Alteration of terms.* A *modification* means any alteration, including any deletion or addition, in whole or in part, of a legal right or obligation of the issuer or a holder of a debt instrument, whether the alteration is evidenced by an express agreement (oral or written), conduct of the parties, or otherwise.

(ii) *Alterations occurring by operation of the terms of a debt instrument.* Except as provided in paragraph (c)(2) of this section, an alteration of a legal right or obligation that occurs by operation of the terms of a debt instrument is not a modification. An alteration that occurs by operation of the terms may occur automatically (for example, an annual resetting of the interest rate based on the value of an index or a specified increase in the interest rate if the value of the collateral declines from a specified level) or may occur as a result of the exercise of an option provided to an issuer or a holder to change a term of a debt instrument.

(2) *Exceptions.* The alterations described in this paragraph (c)(2) are modifications, even if the alterations occur by operation of the terms of a debt instrument.

(i) *Change in obligor or nature of instrument.* An alteration that results in the substitution of a new obligor, the addition or deletion of a co-obligor, or a change (in whole or in part) in the recourse nature of the instrument (from recourse to nonrecourse or from nonrecourse to recourse) is a modification.

(ii) *Property that is not debt.* An alteration that results in an instrument or property right that is not debt for federal income tax purposes is a modification unless the alteration occurs pursuant to a holder's option under the terms of the instrument to convert the instrument into equity of the issuer (notwithstanding paragraph (c)(2)(iii) of this section).

(iii) *Certain alterations resulting from the exercise of an option.* An alteration that results from the exercise of an option provided to an issuer or a holder to change a term of a debt instrument is a modification unless—

(A) The option is unilateral (as defined in paragraph (c)(3) of this section); and

(B) In the case of an option exercisable by a holder, the exercise of the option does not result in (or, in the case of a variable or contingent payment, is not reasonably expected to result in) a deferral of, or a reduction in, any scheduled payment of interest or principal.

(3) *Unilateral option.* For purposes of this section, an option is unilateral only if, under the terms of an instrument or under applicable law—

(i) There does not exist at the time the option is exercised, or as a result of the exercise, a right of the other party to alter or terminate the instrument or put the instrument to a person who is related (within the meaning of section 267(b) or section 707(b)(1)) to the issuer;

(ii) The exercise of the option does not require the consent or approval of—

(A) The other party;

(B) A person who is related to that party (within the meaning of section 267(b) or section 707(b)(1)), whether or not that person is a party to the instrument; or

(C) A court or arbitrator; and

(iii) The exercise of the option does not require consideration (other than incidental costs and expenses relating to the exercise of the option), unless, on the issue date of the instrument, the consideration is a de minimis amount, a specified amount, or an amount that is based on a formula that uses objective financial information (as defined in § 1.446-3(c)(4)(ii)).

(4) *Failure to perform*—(i) *In general.* The failure of an issuer to perform its obligations under a debt instrument is not itself an alteration of a legal right or obligation and is not a modification.

(ii) *Holder's temporary forbearance.* Notwithstanding paragraph (c)(1) of this section, absent a written or oral agreement to alter other terms of the debt instrument, an agreement by the holder to stay collection or temporarily waive an acceleration clause or similar default right (including such a waiver following the exercise of a right to demand payment in full) is not a modification unless and until the forbearance remains in effect for a period that exceeds—

(A) Two years following the issuer's initial failure to perform; and

(B) Any additional period during which the parties conduct good faith negotiations or during which the issuer is in a title 11 or similar case (as defined in section 368(a)(3)(A)).

(5) *Failure to exercise an option.* If a party to a debt instrument has an option to change a term of an instrument, the failure of the party to exercise that option is not a modification.

(6) *Time of modification*—(i) *In general.* Except as provided in this paragraph (c)(6), an agreement to change a term of a debt instrument is a modification at the time the issuer and holder enter into the agreement, even if the change in the term is not immediately effective.

(ii) *Closing conditions.* If the parties condition a change in a term of a debt instrument on reasonable closing conditions (for example, shareholder, regulatory, or senior creditor approval, or additional financing), a modification occurs on the closing date of the agreement. Thus, if the reasonable closing conditions do not occur so that the change in the term does not become effective, a modification does not occur.

(iii) *Bankruptcy proceedings.* If a change in a term of a debt instrument occurs pursuant to a plan of reorganization in a title 11 or similar case (within the meaning of section 368(a)(3)(A)), a modification occurs upon the effective date of the plan. Thus, unless the plan becomes effective, a modification does not occur.

(d) *Examples.* The following examples illustrate the provisions of paragraph (c) of this section:

Example 1. Reset bond. A bond provides for the interest rate to be reset every 49 days through an auction by a remarketing agent. The reset of the interest rate occurs by operation of the terms of the bond and is not an alteration described in paragraph (c)(2) of this section. Thus, the reset of the interest rate is not a modification.

Example 2. Obligation to maintain collateral. The original terms of a bond provide that the bond must be secured by a certain type of collateral having a specified value. The terms also require the issuer to substitute collateral if the value of the original collateral decreases. Any substitution of collateral that is required to maintain the value of the collateral occurs by operation of the terms of the bond and is not an alteration described in paragraph (c)(2) of this section. Thus, such a substitution of collateral is not a modification.

Example 3. Alteration contingent on an act of a party. The original terms of a bond provide that the interest rate is 9 percent. The terms also provide that, if the issuer files an effective registration statement covering the bonds with the Securities and Exchange Commission, the interest rate will decrease to 8 percent. If the issuer registers the bond, the resulting decrease in the interest rate occurs by operation of the terms of the bond and is not an alteration described in paragraph (c)(2) of this section. Thus, such a decrease in the interest rate is not a modification.

Example 4. Substitution of a new obligor occurring by operation of the terms of the debt instrument. Under the original terms of a bond issued by a corporation, an acquirer of substantially all of the corporation's assets may assume the corporation's obligations under the bond. Substantially all of the corporation's assets are acquired by another corporation and the acquiring corporation

Reg. § 1.1001-3(d)

becomes the new obligor on the bond. Under paragraph (c)(2)(i) of this section, the substitution of a new obligor, even though it occurs by operation of the terms of the bond, is a modification.

Example 5. Defeasance with release of covenants. (i) A corporation issues a 30-year, recourse bond. Under the terms of the bond, the corporation may secure a release of the financial and restrictive covenants by placing in trust government securities as collateral that will provide interest and principal payments sufficient to satisfy all scheduled payments on the bond. The corporation remains obligated for all payments, including the contribution of additional securities to the trust if necessary to provide sufficient amounts to satisfy the payment obligations. Under paragraph (c)(3) of this section, the option to defease the bond is a unilateral option.

(ii) The alterations occur by operation of the terms of the debt instrument and are not described in paragraph (c)(2) of this section. Thus, such a release of the covenants is not a modification.

Example 6. Legal defeasance. Under the terms of a recourse bond, the issuer may secure a release of the financial and restrictive covenants by placing in trust government securities that will provide interest and principal payments sufficient to satisfy all scheduled payments on the bond. Upon the creation of the trust, the issuer is released from any recourse liability on the bond and has no obligation to contribute additional securities to the trust if the trust funds are not sufficient to satisfy the scheduled payments on the bond. The release of the issuer is an alteration described in paragraph (c)(2)(i) of this section, and thus is a modification.

Example 7. Exercise of an option by a holder that reduces amounts payable. (i) A financial institution holds a residential mortgage. Under the original terms of the mortgage, the financial institution has an option to decrease the interest rate. The financial institution anticipates that, if market interest rates decline, it may exercise this option in lieu of the mortgagor refinancing with another lender.

(ii) The financial institution exercises the option to reduce the interest rate. The exercise of the option results in a reduction in scheduled payments and is an alteration described in paragraph (c)(2)(iii) of this section. Thus, the change in interest rate is a modification.

Example 8. Conversion of adjustable rate to fixed rate mortgage. (i) The original terms of a mortgage provide for a variable interest rate, reset annually based on the value of an objective index. Under the terms of the mortgage, the mortgagor may, upon the payment of a fee equal to a specified percentage of the outstanding principal amount of the mortgage, convert to a fixed rate of interest as determined based on the value of a second objective index. The exercise of the option does not require the consent or approval of any person or create a right of the holder to alter the terms of, or to put, the instrument.

(ii) Because the required consideration to exercise the option is a specified amount fixed on the issue date, the exercise of the option is unilateral as defined in paragraph (c)(3) of this section. The conversion to a fixed rate of interest is not an alteration described in paragraph (c)(2) of this section. Thus, the change in the type of interest rate occurs by operation of the terms of the instrument and is not a modification.

Example 9. Holder's option to increase interest rate. (i) A corporation issues an 8-year note to a bank in exchange for cash. Under the terms of the note, the bank has the option to increase the rate of interest by a specified amount upon a certain decline in the corporation's credit rating. The bank's right to increase the interest rate is a unilateral option as described in paragraph (c)(3) of this section.

(ii) The credit rating of the corporation declines below the specified level. The bank exercises its option to increase the rate of interest. The increase in the rate of interest occurs by operation of the terms of the note and does not result in a deferral or a reduction in the scheduled payments or any other alteration described in paragraph (c)(2) of this section. Thus, the change in interest rate is not a modification.

Example 10. Issuer's right to defer payment of interest. A corporation issues a 5-year note. Under the terms of the note, interest is payable annually at the rate of 10 percent. The corporation, however, has an option to defer any payment of interest until maturity. For any payments that are deferred, interest will compound at a rate of 12 percent. The exercise of the option, which results in the deferral of payments, does not result from the exercise of an option by the holder. The exercise of the option occurs by operation of the terms of the debt instrument and is not a modification.

Example 11. Holder's option to grant deferral of payment. (i) A corporation issues a 10-year note to a bank in exchange for cash. Interest on the note is payable semi-annually. Under the terms of the note, the bank may grant the corporation the right to defer all or part of the interest payments. For any payments that are deferred, interest will compound at a rate 150 basis points greater than the stated rate of interest.

Reg. § 1.1001-3(d)

(ii) The corporation encounters financial difficulty and is unable to satisfy its obligations under the note. The bank exercises its option under the note and grants the corporation the right to defer payments. The exercise of the option results in a right of the corporation to defer scheduled payments and, under paragraph (c)(3)(i) of this section, is not a unilateral option. Thus, the alteration is described in paragraph (c)(2)(iii) of this section and is a modification.

Example 12. Alteration requiring consent. The original terms of a bond include a provision that the issuer may extend the maturity of the bond with the consent of the holder. Because any extension pursuant to this term requires the consent of both parties, such an extension does not occur by the exercise of a unilateral option (as defined in paragraph (c)(3) of this section) and is a modification.

Example 13. Waiver of an acceleration clause. Under the terms of a bond, if the issuer fails to make a scheduled payment, the full principal amount of the bond is due and payable immediately. Following the issuer's failure to make a scheduled payment, the holder temporarily waives its right to receive the full principal for a period ending one year from the date of the issuer's default to allow the issuer to obtain additional financial resources. Under paragraph (c)(4)(ii) of this section, the temporary waiver in this situation is not a modification. The result would be the same if the terms provided the holder with the right to demand the full principal amount upon the failure of the issuer to make a scheduled payment and, upon such a failure, the holder exercised that right and then waived the right to receive the payment for one year.

(e) *Significant modifications.* Whether the modification of a debt instrument is a significant modification is determined under the rules of this paragraph (e). Paragraph (e)(1) of this section provides a general rule for determining the significance of modifications not otherwise addressed in this paragraph (e). Paragraphs (e)(2) through (6) of this section provide specific rules for determining the significance of certain types of modifications. Paragraph (f) of this section provides rules of application, including rules for modifications that are effective on a deferred basis or upon the occurrence of a contingency.

(1) *General rule.* Except as otherwise provided in paragraphs (e)(2) through (e)(6) of this section, a modification is a significant modification only if, based on all facts and circumstances, the legal rights or obligations that are altered and the degree to which they are altered are economically significant. In making a determination under this paragraph (e)(1), all modifications to the debt instrument (other than modifications subject to paragraphs (e)(2) through (6) of this section) are considered collectively, so that a series of such modifications may be significant when considered together although each modification, if considered alone, would not be significant.

(2) *Change in yield*—(i) *Scope of rule.* This paragraph (e)(2) applies to debt instruments that provide for only fixed payments, debt instruments with alternative payment schedules subject to § 1.1272-1(c), debt instruments that provide for a fixed yield subject to § 1.1272-1(d) (such as certain demand loans), and variable rate debt instruments. Whether a change in the yield of other debt instruments (for example, a contingent payment debt instrument) is a significant modification is determined under paragraph (e)(1) of this section.

(ii) *In general.* A change in the yield of a debt instrument is a significant modification if the yield computed under paragraph (e)(2)(iii) of this section varies from the annual yield on the unmodified instrument (determined as of the date of the modification) by more than the greater of—

(A) 1/4 of one percent (25 basis points); or

(B) 5 percent of the annual yield of the unmodified instrument (.05 x annual yield).

(iii) *Yield of the modified instrument*—(A) *In general.* The yield computed under this paragraph (e)(2)(iii) is the annual yield of a debt instrument with—

(*1*) an issue price equal to the adjusted issue price of the unmodified instrument on the date of the modification (increased by any accrued but unpaid interest and decreased by any accrued bond issuance premium not yet taken into account, and increased or decreased, respectively, to reflect payments made to the issuer or to the holder as consideration for the modification); and

(*2*) payments equal to the payments on the modified debt instrument from the date of the modification.

(B) *Prepayment penalty.* For purposes of this paragraph (e)(2)(iii), a commercially reasonable prepayment penalty for a pro rata prepayment (as defined in § 1.1275-2(f)) is not consideration for a modification of a debt instrument and is not taken into account in determining the yield of the modified instrument.

(iv) *Variable rate debt instruments.* For purposes of this paragraph (e)(2), the annual yield of a variable rate debt instrument is the annual yield of the equivalent fixed rate debt instrument

Reg. § 1.1001-3(e)(2)

(as defined in § 1.1275-5(e)) which is constructed based on the terms of the instrument (either modified or unmodified, whichever is applicable) as of the date of the modification.

(3) *Changes in timing of payments*—(i) *In general.* A modification that changes the timing of payments (including any resulting change in the amount of payments) due under a debt instrument is a significant modification if it results in the material deferral of scheduled payments. The deferral may occur either through an extension of the final maturity date of an instrument or through a deferral of payments due prior to maturity. The materiality of the deferral depends on all the facts and circumstances, including the length of the deferral, the original term of the instrument, the amounts of the payments that are deferred, and the time period between the modification and the actual deferral of payments.

(ii) *Safe-harbor period.* The deferral of one or more scheduled payments within the safe-harbor period is not a material deferral if the deferred payments are unconditionally payable no later than at the end of the safe-harbor period. The safe-harbor period begins on the original due date of the first scheduled payment that is deferred and extends for a period equal to the lesser of five years or 50 percent of the original term of the instrument. For purposes of this paragraph (e)(3)(ii), the term of an instrument is determined without regard to any option to extend the original maturity and deferrals of de minimis payments are ignored. If the period during which payments are deferred is less than the full safe-harbor period, the unused portion of the period remains a safe-harbor period for any subsequent deferral of payments on the instrument.

(4) *Change in obligor or security*—(i) *Substitution of a new obligor on recourse debt instruments*—(A) *In general.* Except as provided in paragraph (e)(4)(i)(B), (C), or (D) of this section, the substitution of a new obligor on a recourse debt instrument is a significant modification.

(B) *Section 381(a) transaction.* The substitution of a new obligor is not a significant modification if the acquiring corporation (within the meaning of section 381) becomes the new obligor pursuant to a transaction to which section 381(a) applies, the transaction does not result in a change in payment expectations, and the transaction (other than a reorganization within the meaning of section 368(a)(1)(F)) does not result in a significant alteration.

(C) *Certain asset acquisitions.* The substitution of a new obligor is not a significant modification if the new obligor acquires substantially all of the assets of the original obligor, the transaction does not result in a change in payment expectations, and the transaction does not result in a significant alteration.

(D) *Tax-exempt bonds.* The substitution of a new obligor on a tax-exempt bond is not a significant modification if the new obligor is a related entity to the original obligor as defined in section 168(h)(4)(A) and the collateral securing the instrument continues to include the original collateral.

(E) *Significant alteration.* For purposes of this paragraph (e)(4), a significant alteration is an alteration that would be a significant modification but for the fact that the alteration occurs by operation of the terms of the instrument.

(F) *Section 338 election.* For purposes of this section, an election under section 338 following a qualified stock purchase of an issuer's stock does not result in the substitution of a new obligor.

(G) *Bankruptcy proceedings.* For purposes of this section, the filing of a petition in a title 11 or similar case (as defined in section 368(a)(3)(A)) by itself does not result in the substitution of a new obligor.

(ii) *Substitution of a new obligor on nonrecourse debt instruments.* The substitution of a new obligor on a nonrecourse debt instrument is not a significant modification.

(iii) *Addition or deletion of co-obligor.* The addition or deletion of a co-obligor on a debt instrument is a significant modification if the addition or deletion of the co-obligor results in a change in payment expectations. If the addition or deletion of a co-obligor is part of a transaction or series of related transactions that results in the substitution of a new obligor, however, the transaction is treated as a substitution of a new obligor (and is tested under paragraph (e)(4)(i)) of this section rather than as an addition or deletion of a co-obligor.

(iv) *Change in security or credit enhancement*—(A) *Recourse debt instruments.* A modification that releases, substitutes, adds or otherwise alters the collateral for, a guarantee on, or other form of credit enhancement for a recourse debt instrument is a significant modification if the modification results in a change in payment expectations.

(B) *Nonrecourse debt instruments.* A modification that releases, substitutes, adds or otherwise alters a substantial amount of the collateral for, a guarantee on, or other form of credit enhancement for a nonrecourse debt instrument is a significant modification. A substitution of collateral is not a significant modification, however,

Reg. § 1.1001-3(e)(3)

if the collateral is fungible or otherwise of a type where the particular units pledged are unimportant (for example, government securities or financial instruments of a particular type and rating). In addition, the substitution of a similar commercially available credit enhancement contract is not a significant modification, and an improvement to the property securing a nonrecourse debt instrument does not result in a significant modification.

(v) *Change in priority of debt.* A change in the priority of a debt instrument relative to other debt of the issuer is a significant modification if it results in a change in payment expectations.

(vi) *Change in payment expectations*—(A) *In general.* For purposes of this section, a change in payment expectations occurs if, as a result of a transaction—

(1) There is a substantial enhancement of the obligor's capacity to meet the payment obligations under a debt instrument and that capacity was primarily speculative prior to the modification and is adequate after the modification; or

(2) There is a substantial impairment of the obligor's capacity to meet the payment obligations under a debt instrument and that capacity was adequate prior to the modification and is primarily speculative after the modification.

(B) *Obligor's capacity.* The obligor's capacity includes any source for payment, including collateral, guarantees, or other credit enhancement.

(5) *Changes in the nature of a debt instrument*—(i) *Property that is not debt.* A modification of a debt instrument that results in an instrument or property right that is not debt for federal income tax purposes is a significant modification. For purposes of this paragraph (e)(5)(i), any deterioration in the financial condition of the obligor between the issue date of the unmodified instrument and the date of modification (as it relates to the obligor's ability to repay the debt) is not taken into account unless, in connection with the modification, there is a substitution of a new obligor or the addition or deletion of a co-obligor.

(ii) *Change in recourse nature*—(A) *In general.* Except as provided in paragraph (e)(5)(ii)(B) of this section, a change in the nature of a debt instrument from recourse (or substantially all recourse) to nonrecourse (or substantially all nonrecourse) is a significant modification. Thus, for example, a legal defeasance of a debt instrument in which the issuer is released from all liability to make payments on the debt instrument (including an obligation to contribute additional securities to a trust if necessary to provide sufficient funds to meet all scheduled payments on the instrument) is a significant modification. Similarly, a change in the nature of the debt instrument from nonrecourse (or substantially all nonrecourse) to recourse (or substantially all recourse) is a significant modification. If an instrument is not substantially all recourse or not substantially all nonrecourse either before or after a modification, the significance of the modification is determined under paragraph (e)(1) of this section.

(B) *Exceptions*—(1) *Defeasance of tax-exempt bonds.* A defeasance of a tax-exempt bond is not a significant modification even if the issuer is released from any liability to make payments under the instrument if the defeasance occurs by operation of the terms of the original bond and the issuer places in trust government securities or tax-exempt government bonds that are reasonably expected to provide interest and principal payments sufficient to satisfy the payment obligations under the bond.

(2) *Original collateral.* A modification that changes a recourse debt instrument to a nonrecourse debt instrument is not a significant modification if the instrument continues to be secured only by the original collateral and the modification does not result in a change in payment expectations. For this purpose, if the original collateral is fungible or otherwise of a type where the particular units pledged are unimportant (for example, government securities or financial instruments of a particular type and rating), replacement of some or all units of the original collateral with other units of the same or similar type and aggregate value is not considered a change in the original collateral.

(6) *Accounting or financial covenants.* A modification that adds, deletes, or alters customary accounting or financial covenants is not a significant modification.

(f) *Rules of application*—(1) *Testing for significance*—(i) *In general.* Whether a modification of any term is a significant modification is determined under each applicable rule in paragraphs (e)(2) through (6) of this section and, if not specifically addressed in those rules, under the general rule in paragraph (e)(1) of this section. For example, a deferral of payments that changes the yield of a fixed rate debt instrument must be tested under both paragraphs (e)(2) and (3) of this section.

(ii) *Contingent modifications.* If a modification described in paragraphs (e)(2) through (5) of this section is effective only upon the occurrence of a substantial contingency, whether or not the change is a significant modification is deter-

Reg. § 1.1001-3(f)(1)

51,912 Determination and Recognition of Gain or Loss

See p. 20,601 for regulations not amended to reflect law changes

mined under paragraph (e)(1) of this section rather than under paragraphs (e)(2) through (5) of this section.

(iii) *Deferred modifications.* If a modification described in paragraphs (e)(4) and (5) of this section is effective on a substantially deferred basis, whether or not the change is a significant modification is determined under paragraph (e)(1) of this section rather than under paragraphs (e)(4) and (5) of this section.

(2) *Modifications that are not significant.* If a rule in paragraphs (e)(2) through (4) of this section prescribes a degree of change in a term of a debt instrument that is a significant modification, a change of the same type but of a lesser degree is not a significant modification under that rule. For example, a 20 basis point change in the yield of a fixed rate debt instrument is not a significant modification under paragraph (e)(2) of this section. Likewise, if a rule in paragraph (e)(4) of this section requires a change in payment expectations for a modification to be significant, a modification of the same type that does not result in a change in payment expectations is not a significant modification under that rule.

(3) *Cumulative effect of modifications.* Two or more modifications of a debt instrument over any period of time constitute a significant modification if, had they been done as a single change, the change would have resulted in a significant modification under paragraph (e) of this section. Thus, for example, a series of changes in the maturity of a debt instrument constitutes a significant modification if, combined as a single change, the change would have resulted in a significant modification. The significant modification occurs at the time that the cumulative modification would be significant under paragraph (e) of this section. In testing for a change of yield under paragraph (e)(2) of this section, however, any prior modification occurring more than 5 years before the date of the modification being tested is disregarded.

(4) *Modifications of different terms.* Modifications of different terms of a debt instrument, none of which separately would be a significant modification under paragraphs (e)(2) through (6) of this section, do not collectively constitute a significant modification. For example, a change in yield that is not a significant modification under paragraph (e)(2) of this section and a substitution of collateral that is not a significant modification under paragraph (e)(4)(iv) of this section do not together result in a significant modification. Although the significance of each modification is determined independently, in testing a particular modification it is assumed that all other simultaneous modifications have already occurred.

(5) *Definitions.* For purposes of this section:

(i) *Issuer* and *obligor* are used interchangeably and mean the issuer of a debt instrument or a successor obligor.

(ii) *Variable rate debt instrument* and *contingent payment debt instrument* have the meanings given those terms in section 1275 and the regulations thereunder.

(iii) *Tax-exempt bond* means a state or local bond that satisfies the requirements of section 103(a).

(iv) *Conduit loan* and *conduit borrower* have the same meanings as in § 1.150-1(b).

(6) *Certain rules for tax-exempt bonds*—(i) *Conduit loans.* For purposes of this section, the obligor of a tax-exempt bond is the entity that actually issues the bond and not a conduit borrower of bond proceeds. In determining whether there is a significant modification of a tax-exempt bond, however, transactions between holders of the tax-exempt bond and a borrower of a conduit loan may be an indirect modification under paragraph (a)(1) of this section. For example, a payment by the holder of a tax-exempt bond to a conduit borrower to waive a call right may result in an indirect modification of the tax-exempt bond by changing the yield on that bond.

(ii) *Recourse nature*—(A) *In general.* For purposes of this section, a tax-exempt bond that does not finance a conduit loan is a recourse debt instrument.

(B) *Proceeds used for conduit loans.* For purposes of this section, a tax-exempt bond that finances a conduit loan is a recourse debt instrument unless both the bond and the conduit loan are nonrecourse instruments.

(C) *Government securities as collateral.* Notwithstanding paragraphs (f)(6)(ii)(A) and (B) of this section, for purposes of this section a tax-exempt bond that is secured only by a trust holding government securities or tax-exempt government bonds that are reasonably expected to provide interest and principal payments sufficient to satisfy the payment obligations under the bond is a nonrecourse instrument.

(g) *Examples.* The following examples illustrate the provisions of paragraphs (e) and (f) of this section:

Example 1. Modification of call right. (i) Under the terms of a 30-year, fixed-rate bond, the issuer can call the bond for 102 percent of par at the end of ten years or for 101 percent of par at the end of 20 years. At the end of the eighth year, the holder of the bond pays the issuer to waive the issuer's

Reg. § 1.1001-3(f)(2)

right to call the bond at the end of the tenth year. On the date of the modification, the issuer's credit rating is approximately the same as when the bond was issued, but market rates of interest have declined from that date.

(ii) The holder's payment to the issuer changes the yield on the bond. Whether the change in yield is a significant modification depends on whether the yield on the modified bond varies from the yield on the original bond by more than the change in yield as described in paragraph (e)(2)(ii) of this section.

(iii) If the change in yield is not a significant modification, the elimination of the issuer's call right must also be tested for significance. Because the specific rules of paragraphs (e)(2) through (e)(6) of this section do not address this modification, the significance of the modification must be determined under the general rule of paragraph (e)(1) of this section.

Example 2. Extension of maturity and change in yield. (i) A zero-coupon bond has an original maturity of ten years. At the end of the fifth year, the parties agree to extend the maturity for a period of two years without increasing the stated redemption price at maturity (i.e., there are no additional payments due between the original and extended maturity dates, and the amount due at the extended maturity date is equal to the amount due at the original maturity date).

(ii) The deferral of the scheduled payment at maturity is tested under paragraph (e)(3) of this section. The safe-harbor period under paragraph (e)(3)(ii) of this section starts with the date the payment that is being deferred is due. For this modification, the safe-harbor period starts on the original maturity date, and ends five years from this date. All payments deferred within this period are unconditionally payable before the end of the safe-harbor period. Thus, the deferral of the payment at maturity for a period of two years is not a material deferral under the safe-harbor rule of paragraph (e)(3)(ii) of this section and thus is not a significant modification.

(iii) Even though the extension of maturity is not a significant modification under paragraph (e)(3)(ii) of this section, the modification also decreases the yield of the bond. The change in yield must be tested under paragraph (e)(2) of this section.

Example 3. Change in yield resulting from reduction of principal. (i) A debt instrument issued at par has an original maturity of ten years and provides for the payment of $100,000 at maturity with interest payments at the rate of 10 percent payable at the end of each year. At the end of the fifth year, and after the annual payment of interest, the issuer and holder agree to reduce the amount payable at maturity to $80,000. The annual interest rate remains at 10 percent but is payable on the reduced principal.

(ii) In applying the change in yield rule of paragraph (e)(2) of this section, the yield of the instrument after the modification (measured from the date that the parties agree to the modification to its final maturity date) is computed using the adjusted issue price of $100,000. With four annual payments of $8,000, and a payment of $88,000 at maturity, the yield on the instrument after the modification for purposes of determining if there has been a significant modification under paragraph (e)(2)(i) of this section is 4.332 percent. Thus, the reduction in principal is a significant modification.

Example 4. Deferral of scheduled interest payments. (i) A 20-year debt instrument issued at par provides for the payment of $100,000 at maturity with annual interest payments at the rate of 10 percent. At the beginning of the eleventh year, the issuer and holder agree to defer all remaining interest payments until maturity with compounding. The yield of the modified instrument remains at 10 percent.

(ii) The safe-harbor period of paragraph (e)(3)(ii) of this section begins at the end of the eleventh year, when the interest payment for that year is deferred, and ends at the end of the sixteenth year. However, the payments deferred during this period are not unconditionally payable by the end of that 5-year period. Thus, the deferral of the interest payments is not within the safe-harbor period.

(iii) This modification materially defers the payments due under the instrument and is a significant modification under paragraph (e)(3)(i) of this section.

Example 5. Assumption of mortgage with increase in interest rate. (i) A recourse debt instrument with a 9 percent annual yield is secured by an office building. Under the terms of the instrument, a purchaser of the building may assume the debt and be substituted for the original obligor if the purchaser has a specified credit rating and if the interest rate on the instrument is increased by one-half percent (50 basis points). The building is sold, the purchaser assumes the debt, and the interest rate increases by 50 basis points.

(ii) If the purchaser's acquisition of the building does not satisfy the requirements of paragraphs (e)(4)(i)(B) or (C) of this section, the substitution of the purchaser as the obligor is a significant modification under paragraph (e)(4)(i)(A) of this section.

Reg. § 1.1001-3(g)

(iii) If the purchaser acquires substantially all of the assets of the original obligor, the assumption of the debt instrument will not result in a significant modification if there is not a change in payment expectations and the assumption does not result in a significant alteration.

(iv) The change in the interest rate, if tested under the rules of paragraph (e)(2) of this section, would result in a significant modification. The change in interest rate that results from the transaction is a significant alteration. Thus, the transaction does not meet the requirements of paragraph (e)(4)(i)(C) of this section and is a significant modification under paragraph (e)(4)(i)(A) of this section.

Example 6. Assumption of mortgage. (i) A recourse debt instrument is secured by a building. In connection with the sale of the building, the purchaser of the building assumes the debt and is substituted as the new obligor on the debt instrument. The purchaser does not acquire substantially all of the assets of the original obligor.

(ii) The transaction does not satisfy any of the exceptions set forth in paragraph (e)(4)(i)(B) or (C) of this section. Thus, the substitution of the purchaser as the obligor is a significant modification under paragraph (e)(4)(i)(A) of this section.

(iii) Section 1274(c)(4), however, provides that if a debt instrument is assumed in connection with the sale or exchange of property, the assumption is not taken into account in determining if section 1274 applies to the debt instrument unless the terms and conditions of the debt instrument are modified in connection with the sale or exchange. Because the purchaser assumed the debt instrument in connection with the sale of property and the debt instrument was not otherwise modified, the debt instrument is not retested to determine whether it provides for adequate stated interest.

Example 7. Substitution of a new obligor in section 381(a) transaction. (i) The interest rate on a 30-year debt instrument issued by a corporation provides for a variable rate of interest that is reset annually on June 1st based on an objective index.

(ii) In the tenth year, the issuer merges (in a transaction to which section 381(a) applies) into another corporation that becomes the new obligor on the debt instrument. The merger occurs on June 1st, at which time the interest rate is also reset by operation of the terms of the instrument. The new interest rate varies from the previous interest rate by more than the greater of 25 basis points and 5 percent of the annual yield of the unmodified instrument. The substitution of a new obligor does not result in a change in payment expectations.

(iii) The substitution of the new obligor occurs in a section 381(a) transaction and does not result in a change in payment expectations. Although the interest rate changed by more than the greater of 25 basis points and 5 percent of the annual yield of the unmodified instrument, this alteration did not occur as a result of the transaction and is not a significant alteration under paragraph (e)(4)(i)(E) of this section. Thus, the substitution meets the requirements of paragraph (e)(4)(i)(B) of this section and is not a significant modification.

Example 8. Substitution of credit enhancement contract. (i) Under the terms of a recourse debt instrument, the issuer's obligations are secured by a letter of credit from a specified bank. The debt instrument does not contain any provision allowing a substitution of a letter of credit from a different bank. The specified bank, however, encounters financial difficulty and rating agencies lower its credit rating. The issuer and holder agree that the issuer will substitute a letter of credit from another bank with a higher credit rating.

(ii) Under paragraph (e)(4)(iv)(A) of this section, the substitution of a different credit enhancement contract is not a significant modification of a recourse debt instrument unless the substitution results in a change in payment expectations. While the substitution of a new letter of credit by a bank with a higher credit rating does not itself result in a change in payment expectations, such a substitution may result in a change in payment expectations under certain circumstances (for example, if the obligor's capacity to meet payment obligations is dependent on the letter of credit and the substitution substantially enhances that capacity from primarily speculative to adequate).

Example 9. Improvement to collateral securing nonrecourse debt. A parcel of land and its improvements, a shopping center, secure a nonrecourse debt instrument. The obligor expands the shopping center with the construction of an additional building on the same parcel of land. After the construction, the improvements that secure the nonrecourse debt include the new building. The building is an improvement to the property securing the nonrecourse debt instrument and its inclusion in the collateral securing the debt is not a significant modification under paragraph (e)(4)(iv)(B) of this section.

(h) *Effective date.* This section applies to alterations of the terms of a debt instrument on or after September 24, 1996. Taxpayers, however, may rely on this section for alterations of the

Reg. § 1.1001-3(g)

Determination and Recognition of Gain or Loss

terms of a debt instrument after December 2, 1992, and before September 24, 1996. [Reg. § 1.1001-3.]

☐ [T.D. 8675, 6-25-96.]

[Reg. § 1.1001-4]

§ 1.1001-4. **Modifications of certain notional principal contracts.**—(a) *Dealer assignments.* For purposes of § 1.1001-1(a), the substitution of a new party on an interest rate or commodity swap, or other notional principal contract (as defined in § 1.446-3(c)(1)), is not treated as a deemed exchange by the nonassigning party of the original contract for a modified contract that differs materially either in kind or in extent if—

(1) The party assigning its rights and obligations under the contract and the party to which the rights and obligations are assigned are both dealers in notional principal contracts, as defined in § 1.446-3(c)(4)(iii); and

(2) The terms of the contract permit the substitution.

(b) *Effective date.* This section applies to assignments of interest rate swaps, commodity swaps, and other notional principal contracts occurring on or after September 23, 1996. [Reg. § 1.1001-4.]

☐ [T.D. 8763, 1-28-98.]

[Reg. § 1.1001-5]

§ 1.1001-5. **European Monetary Union (conversion to the euro).**—(a) *Conversion of currencies.* For purposes of § 1.1001-1(a), the conversion to the euro of legacy currencies (as defined in § 1.985-8(a)(1)) is not the exchange of property for other property differing materially in kind or extent.

(b) *Effect of currency conversion on other rights and obligations.* For purposes of § 1.1001-1(a), if, solely as the result of the conversion of legacy currencies to the euro, rights or obligations denominated in a legacy currency become rights or obligations denominated in the euro, that event is not the exchange of property for other property differing materially in kind or extent. Thus, for example, when a debt instrument that requires payments of amounts denominated in a legacy currency becomes a debt instrument requiring payments of euros, that alteration is not a modification within the meaning of § 1.1001-3(c).

(c) *Effective date.* This section applies to tax years ending after July 29, 1998. [Reg. § 1.1001-5.]

☐ [T.D. 8927, 1-10-2001.]

[Reg. § 1.1002-1]

§ 1.1002-1. **Sales or exchanges.**—(a) *General rule.* The general rule with respect to gain or loss realized upon the sale or exchange of property as determined under section 1001 is that the entire amount of such gain or loss is recognized except in cases where specific provisions of subtitle A of the Code provide otherwise.

(b) *Strict construction of exceptions from general rule.* The exceptions from the general rule requiring the recognition of all gains and losses, like other exceptions from a rule of taxation of general and uniform application, are strictly construed and do not extend either beyond the words or the underlying assumptions and purposes of the exception. Nonrecognition is accorded by the Code only if the exchange is one which satisfies both (1) the specific description in the Code of an excepted exchange, and (2) the underlying purpose for which such exchange is excepted from the general rule. The exchange must be germane to, and a necessary incident of, the investment or enterprise in hand. The relationship of the exchange to the venture or enterprise is always material, and the surrounding facts and circumstances must be shown. As elsewhere, the taxpayer claiming the benefit of the exception must show himself within the exception.

(c) *Certain exceptions to general rule.* Exceptions to the general rule are made, for example, by sections 351(a), 354, 361(a), 371(a)(1), 371(b)(1), 721, 1031, 1035 and 1036. These sections describe certain specific exchanges of property in which at the time of the exchange particular differences exist between the property parted with and the property acquired, but such differences are more formal than substantial. As to these, the Code provides that such differences shall not be deemed controlling, and that gain or loss shall not be recognized at the time of the exchange. The underlying assumption of these exceptions is that the new property is substantially a continuation of the old investment still unliquidated; and, in the case of reorganizations, that the new enterprise, the new corporate structure, and the new property are substantially continuations of the old still unliquidated.

(d) *Exchange.* Ordinarily, to constitute an exchange, the transaction must be a reciprocal transfer of property, as distinguished from a transfer of property for a money consideration only. [Reg.§ 1.1002-1.]

☐ [T.D. 6265, 11-6-57.]

Reg. § 1.1002-1(d)

Basis Rules of General Application

[Reg. § 1.1011-1]

§ 1.1011-1. Adjusted basis.—The adjusted basis for determining the gain or loss from the sale or other disposition of property is the cost or other basis prescribed in section 1012 or other applicable provisions of subtitle A of the Code, adjusted to the extent provided in sections 1016, 1017, and 1018 or as otherwise specifically provided for under applicable provisions of internal revenue laws. [Reg. § 1.1011-1.]

☐ [T.D. 6265, 11-6-57.]

[Reg. § 1.1011-2]

§ 1.1011-2. Bargain sale to a charitable organization.—(a) *In general.* (1) If for the taxable year a charitable contributions deduction is allowable under section 170 by reason of a sale or exchange of property, the taxpayer's adjusted basis of such property for purposes of determining gain from such sale or exchange must be computed as provided in section 1011(b) and paragraph (b) of this section. If after applying the provisions of section 170 for the taxable year, including the percentage limitations of section 170(b), no deduction is allowable under that section by reason of the sale or exchange of the property, section 1011(b) does not apply and the adjusted basis of the property is not required to be apportioned pursuant to paragraph (b) of this section. In such case the entire adjusted basis of the property is to be taken into account in determining gain from the sale or exchange, as provided in § 1.1011-1(e). In ascertaining whether or not a charitable contributions deduction is allowable under section 170 for the taxable year for such purposes, that section is to be applied without regard to this section and the amount by which the contributed portion of the property must be reduced under section 170(e)(1) is the amount determined by taking into account the amount of gain which would have been ordinary income or long-term capital gain if the contributed portion of the property had been sold by the donor at its fair market value at the time of the sale or exchange.

(2) If in the taxable year there is a sale or exchange of property which gives rise to a charitable contribution which is carried over under section 170(b)(1)(D)(ii) or section 170(d) to a subsequent taxable year or is postponed under section 170(a)(3) to a subsequent taxable year, section 1011(b) and paragraph (b) of this section must be applied for purposes of apportioning the adjusted basis of the property for the year of the sale or exchange, whether or not such contribution is allowable as a deduction under section 170 in such subsequent year.

(3) If property is transferred subject to an indebtedness, the amount of the indebtedness must be treated as an amount realized for purposes of determining whether there is a sale or exchange to which section 1011(b) and this section apply, even though the transferee does not agree to assume or pay the indebtedness.

(4)(i) Section 1011(b) and this section apply where property is sold or exchanged in return for an obligation to pay an annuity and a charitable contributions deduction is allowable under section 170 by reason of such sale or exchange.

(ii) If in such case the annuity received in exchange for the property is nonassignable, or is assignable but only to the charitable organization to which the property is sold or exchanged, and if the transferor is the only annuitant or the transferor and a designated survivor annuitant or annuitants are the only annuitants, any gain on such exchange is to be reported as provided in example (8) in paragraph (c) of this section. In determining the period over which gain may be reported as provided in such example, the life expectancy of the survivor annuitant may not be taken into account. The fact that the transferor may retain the right to revoke the survivor's annuity or relinquish his own right to the annuity will not be considered, for purposes of this subdivision, to make the annuity assignable to someone other than the charitable organization. Gain on an exchange of the type described in this subdivision pursuant to an agreement which is entered into after December 19, 1969, and before May 3, 1971, may be reported as provided in example (8) in paragraph (c) of this section, even though the annuity is assignable.

(iii) In the case of an annuity to which subdivision (ii) of this subparagraph applies, the gain unreported by the transferor with respect to annuity payments not yet due when the following events occur is not required to be included in gross income of any person where—

(*a*) The transferor dies before the entire amount of gain has been reported and there is no surviving annuitant, or

(*b*) The transferor relinquishes the annuity to the charitable organization. If the transferor dies before the entire amount of gain on a two-life annuity has been reported, the unreported gain is required to be reported by the surviving annuitant or annuitants with respect to the annuity payments received by them.

Reg. § 1.1011-1

Basis Rules of General Application

See p. 20,601 for regulations not amended to reflect law changes

(b) *Apportionment of adjusted basis.* For purposes of determining gain on a sale or exchange to which this paragraph applies, the adjusted basis of the property which is sold or exchanged shall be that portion of the adjusted basis of the entire property which bears the same ratio to the adjusted basis as the amount realized bears to the fair market value of the entire property. The amount of such gain which shall be treated as ordinary income (or long-term capital gain) shall be that amount which bears the same ratio to the ordinary income (or long-term capital gain) which would have been recognized if the entire property had been sold by the donor at its fair market value at the time of the sale or exchange as the amount realized on the sale or exchange bears to the fair market value of the entire property at such time. The terms "ordinary income" and "long-term capital gain", as used in this section, have the same meaning as they have in paragraph (a) of § 1.170A-4. For determining the portion of the adjusted basis, ordinary income, and long-term capital gain allocated to the contributed portion of the property for purposes of applying section 170(e)(1) and paragraph (a) of § 1.170A-4 to the contributed portion of the property, and for determining the donee's basis in such contributed portion, see paragraph (c)(2) and (4) of § 1.170A-4. For determining the holding period of such contributed portion, see section 1223(2) and the regulations thereunder.

(c) *Illustrations.* The application of this section may be illustrated by the following examples, which are supplemented by other examples in paragraph (d) of § 1.170A-4:

Example (1). In 1970, a calendar-year individual taxpayer, sells to a church for $4,000 stock held for more than 6 months which has an adjusted basis of $4,000 and a fair market value of $10,000. A's contribution base for 1970, as defined in section 170(b)(1)(F), is $100,000, and during that year he makes no other charitable contributions. Thus, A makes a charitable contribution to the church of $6,000 ($10,000 value − $4,000 amount realized). Without regard to this section, A is allowed a deduction under section 170 of $6,000 for his charitable contribution to the church, since there is no reduction under section 170(e)(1) with respect to the long-term capital gain. Accordingly, under paragraph (b) of this section the adjusted basis for determining gain on the bargain sale is $1,600 ($4,000 adjusted basis × $4,000 amount realized/$10,000 value of property). A has recognized long-term capital gain of $2,400 ($4,000 amount realized − $1,600 adjusted basis) on the bargain sale.

Example (2). The facts are the same as in Example (1) except that A also makes a charitable contribution in 1970 of $50,000 cash to the church. By reason of section 170(b)(1)(A), the deduction allowed under section 170 for 1970 is $50,000 for the amount of cash contributed to the church; however, the $6,000 contribution of property is carried over to 1971 under section 170(d). Under paragraphs (a)(2) and (b) of this section the adjusted basis for determining gain for 1970 on the bargain sale in that year is $1,600 ($4,000 × $4,000/$10,000). A has a recognized long-term capital gain for 1970 of $2,400 ($4,000 − $1,600) on the sale.

Example (3). In 1970, C, a calendar-year individual taxpayer, makes a charitable contribution of $50,000 cash to a church. In addition, he sells for $4,000 to a private foundation not described in section 170(b)(1)(E) stock held for more than 6 months which has an adjusted basis of $4,000 and a fair market value of $10,000. Thus, C makes a charitable contribution of $6,000 of such property to the private foundation ($10,000 value − $4,000 amount realized). C's contribution base for 1970, as defined in section 170(b)(1)(F), is $100,000, and during that year he makes no other charitable contributions. By reason of section 170(b)(1)(A), the deduction allowed under section 170 for 1970 is $50,000 for the amount of cash contributed to the church. Under section 170(e)(1)(B)(ii) and paragraphs (a)(1) and (c)(2)(i) of § 1.170A-4, the $6,000 contribution of stock is reduced to $4,800 ($6,000 − [50% × ($6,000 value of contributed portion of stock − $3,600 adjusted basis)]). However, by reason of section 170(b)(1)(B)(ii), applied without regard to section 1011(b), no deduction is allowed under section 170 for 1970 or any other year for the reduced contribution of $4,800 to the private foundation. Accordingly, paragraph (b) of this section does not apply for purposes of apportioning the adjusted basis of the stock sold to the private foundation, and under section 1.1011-1(e) the recognized gain on the bargain sale is $0 ($4,000 amount realized − $4,000 adjusted basis).

Example (4). In 1970, B, a calendar-year individual taxpayer, sells to a church for $2,000 stock held for not more than 6 months which has an adjusted basis of $4,000 and a fair market value of $10,000. B's contribution base for 1970, as defined in section 170(b)(1)(F), is $20,000 and during such year B makes no other charitable contributions. Thus, he makes a charitable contribution to the church of $8,000 ($10,000 value − $2,000 amount realized). Under paragraph (b) of this section the adjusted basis for determining gain on the bargain sale is $800 ($4,000 adjusted

Reg. § 1.1011-2(c)

basis × $2,000 amount realized/$10,000 value of stock). Accordingly, B has a recognized short-term capital gain of $1,200 ($2,000 amount realized − $800 adjusted basis) on the bargain sale. After applying section 1011(b) and paragraphs (a)(1) and (c)(2)(i) of § 1.170A-4, B is allowed a charitable contributions deduction for 1970 of $3,200 ($8,000 value of gift − [$8,000 − ($4,000 adjusted basis of property × $8,000 value of gift/$10,000 value of property)]).

Example (5). The facts are the same as in Example (4) except that B sells the property to the church for $4,000. Thus, B makes a charitable contribution to the church of $6,000 ($10,000 value − $4,000 amount realized). Under paragraph (b) of this section the adjusted basis for determining gain on the bargain sale is $1,600 ($4,000 adjusted basis × $4,000 amount realized/$10,000 value of stock). Accordingly, B has a recognized short-term capital gain of $2,400 ($4,000 amount realized − $1,600 adjusted basis) on the bargain sale. After applying section 1011(b) and paragraphs (a)(1) and (c)(2)(i) of § 1.170A-4, B is allowed a charitable contributions deduction for 1970 of $2,400 ($6,000 value of gift − [$6,000 − ($4,000 adjusted basis of property × $6,000 value of gift/$10,000 value of property)]).

Example (6). The facts are the same as in Example (4) except that B sells the property to the church for $6,000. Thus, B makes a charitable contribution to the church of $4,000 ($10,000 value − $6,000 amount realized). Under paragraph (b) of this section the adjusted basis for determining gain on the bargain sale is $2,400 ($4,000 adjusted basis × $6,000 amount realized/$10,000 value of stock). Accordingly, B has a recognized short-term capital gain of $3,600 ($6,000 amount realized − $2,400 adjusted basis) on the bargain sale. After applying section 1011(b) and paragraphs (a)(1) and (c)(2)(i) of § 1.170A-4, B is allowed a charitable contributions deduction for 1970 of $1,600 ($4,000 value of gift − [$4,000 − ($4,000 adjusted basis of property × $4,000 value of gift/$10,000 value of property)]).

Example (7). In 1970, C, a calendar-year individual taxpayer, sells to a church for $4,000 tangible personal property used in his business for more than 6 months which has an adjusted basis of $4,000 and a fair market value of $10,000. Thus, C makes a charitable contribution to the church of $6,000 ($10,000 value − $4,000 adjusted basis). C's contribution base for 1970, as defined in section 170(b)(1)(F), is $100,000 and during such year he makes no other charitable contributions. If C had sold the property at its fair market value at the time of its contribution, it is assumed that under section 1245 $4,000 of the gain of $6,000 ($10,000 value − $4,000 adjusted basis) would have been treated as ordinary income. Thus, there would have been long-term capital gain of $2,000. It is also assumed that the church does not put the property to an unrelated use, as defined in paragraph (b)(3) of § 1.170A-4. Under paragraph (b) of this section the adjusted basis for determining gain on the bargain sale is $1,600 ($4,000 adjusted basis × $4,000 amount realized/$10,000 value of property). Accordingly, C has a recognized gain of $2,400 ($4,000 amount realized − $1,600 adjusted basis) on the bargain sale, consisting of ordinary income of $1,600 ($4,000 ordinary income × $4,000 amount realized/$10,000 value of property) and of long-term capital gain of $800 ($2,000 long-term gain × $4,000 amount realized/$10,000 value of property). After applying section 1011(b) and paragraphs (a) and (c)(2)(i) of § 1.170A-4, C is allowed a charitable contributions deduction for 1970 of $3,600 ($6,000 gift − [$4,000 ordinary income × $6,000 value of gift/$10,000 value of property]).

Example (8). (a) On January 1, 1970, A, a male of age 65, transfers capital assets consisting of securities held for more than 6 months to a church in exchange for a promise by the church to pay A a nonassignable annuity of $5,000 per year for life. The annuity is payable monthly with the first payment to be made on February 1, 1970. A's contribution base for 1970, as defined in section 170(b)(1)(F), is $200,000, and during that year he makes no other charitable contributions. On the date of transfer the securities have a fair market value of $100,000 and an adjusted basis to A of $20,000.

(b) The present value of the right of a male age 65 to receive a life annuity of $5,000 per annum, payable in equal installments at the end of each monthly period, is $59,755 ($5,000 × [11.469 + 0.482]), determined in accordance with section 101(b) of the Code, paragraph (e)(1)(iii)(b)(2) of § 1.101-2, and section 3 of Rev. Rul. 62-216, C.B. 1962-2, 30. Thus, A makes a charitable contribution to the church of $40,245 ($100,000 − $59,755). See Rev. Rul. 84-162, 1984-2 C.B. 200, for transfers for which the valuation date falls after November 23, 1984. (See § 601.601(d)(2)(ii)(b) of this chapter). For the applicable valuation tables in connection therewith, see § 20.2031-7(d)(6) of this chapter. See, however, § 1.7520-3(b) (relating to exceptions to the use of standard actuarial factors in certain circumstances).

(c) Under paragraph (b) of this section, the adjusted basis for determining gain on the bargain

Reg. § 1.1011-2(c)

sale is $11,951 ($20,000 × $59,775/$100,000). Accordingly, A has a recognized long-term capital gain of $47,804 ($59,755 − $11,951) on the bargain sale. Such gain is to be reported by A ratably over the period of years measured by the expected return multiple under the contract but only from that portion of the annual payments which is a return of his investment in the contract under section 72 of the Code. For such purposes, the investment in the contract is $59,755, that is, the present value of the annuity.

(*d*) The computation and application of the exclusion ratio, the gain, and the ordinary annuity income are as follows, determined by using the expected return multiple of 15.0 applicable under Table I of § 1.72-9:

A's expected return (annual payments of $5,000 × 15)....	$75,000.00
Exclusion ratio ($59,755 investment in contract divided by expected return of $75,000)	79.7%
Annual exclusion (annual payments of $5,000 × 79.7%).	3,985.00
Ordinary annuity income ($5,000 − $3,985)	1,015.00
Long-term capital gain per year ($47,804/15) with respect to the annual exclusion	3,186.93

(*e*) The exclusion ratio of 79.7 percent applies throughout the life of the contract. During the first 15 years of the annuity, A is required to report ordinary income of $1,015 and long-term capital gain of $3,186.93 with respect to the annuity payments he receives. After the total long-term capital gain of $47,804 has been reported by A, he is required to report only ordinary income of $1,015.00 per annum with respect to the annuity payments he receives.

(d) *Effective date.* This section applies only to sales and exchanges made after December 19, 1969.

(e) *Cross reference.* For rules relating to the treatment of liabilities in a bargain sale transaction, see § 1.1001-2. [Reg. § 1.1011-2.]

☐ [T.D. 7207, 10-3-72. Amended by T.D. 7741, 12-11-80, T.D. 8176, 2-24-88 and T.D. 8540, 6-9-94.]

[Reg. § 1.1012-1]

§ 1.1012-1. **Basis of property.**—(a) *General rule.* In general, the basis of property is the cost thereof. The cost is the amount paid for such property in cash or other property. This general rule is subject to exceptions stated in subchapter O (relating to gain or loss on the disposition of property), subchapter C (relating to corporate distributions and adjustments), subchapter K (relating to partners and partnerships), and subchapter P (relating to capital gains and losses), chapter 1 of the Code.

(b) *Real estate taxes as part of cost.* In computing the cost of real property, the purchaser shall not take into account any amount paid to the seller as reimbursement for real property taxes which are treated under section 164(d) as imposed upon the purchaser. This rule applies whether or not the contract of sale calls for the purchaser to reimburse the seller for such real estate taxes paid or to be paid by the seller. On the other hand, where the purchaser pays (or assumes liability for) real estate taxes which are treated under section 164(d) as imposed upon the seller, such taxes shall be considered part of the cost of the property. It is immaterial whether or not the contract of sale specifies that the sale price has been reduced by, or is in any way intended to reflect, real estate taxes allocable to the seller under section 164(d). For illustrations of the application of the paragraph, see paragraph (b) of § 1.1001-1.

(c) *Sale of stock* —(1) *In general.* If shares of stock in a corporation are sold or transferred by a taxpayer who purchased or acquired lots of stock on different dates or at different prices, and the lot from which the stock was sold or transferred cannot be adequately identified, the stock sold or transferred shall be charged against the earliest of such lots purchased or acquired in order to determine the cost or other basis of such stock and in order to determine the holding period of such stock for purposes of subchapter P chapter 1 of the Code. If, on the other hand, the lot from which the stock is sold or transferred can be adequately identified, the rule stated in the preceding sentence is not applicable. As to what constitutes "adequate identification," see subparagraphs (2), (3), and (4) of this paragraph.

(2) *Identification of stock.* An adequate identification is made if it is shown that certificates representing shares of stock from a lot which was purchased or acquired on a certain date or for a certain price were delivered to the taxpayer's transferee. Except as otherwise provided in subparagraph (3) or (4) of this paragraph, such stock certificates delivered to the transferee constitute the stock sold or transferred by the taxpayer. Thus, unless the requirements of subparagraph (3) or (4) of this paragraph are met, the stock sold or transferred is charged to the lot to which the certificates delivered to the transferee belong, whether or not the taxpayer intends, or instructs his broker or other agent, to sell or transfer stock from a lot purchased or acquired on a different date or for a different price.

(3) *Identification on confirmation document.* (i) Where the stock is left in the custody of a broker or other agent, an adequate identification is made if—

(*a*) At the time of the sale or transfer, the taxpayer specifies to such broker or other agent having custody of the stock the particular stock to be sold or transferred, and

(*b*) Within a reasonable time thereafter, confirmation of such specification is set forth in a written document from such broker or other agent.

Stock identified pursuant to this subdivision is the stock sold or transferred by the taxpayer, even though stock certificates from a different lot are delivered to the taxpayer's transferee.

(ii) Where a single stock certificate represents stock from different lots, where such certificate is held by the taxpayer rather than his broker or other agent, and where the taxpayer sells a part of the stock represented by such certificate through a broker or other agent, an adequate identification is made if—

(*a*) At the time of the delivery of the certificate to the broker or other agent, the taxpayer specifies to such broker or other agent the particular stock to be sold or transferred, and

(*b*) Within a reasonable time thereafter, confirmation of such specification is set forth in a written document from such broker or agent.

Where part of stock represented by a single certificate is sold or transferred directly by the taxpayer to the purchaser or transferee instead of through a broker or other agent, an adequate identification is made if the taxpayer maintains a written record of the particular stock which he intended to sell or transfer.

(4) *Stock held by a trustee, executor, or administrator.* Where stock is held by a trustee or by an executor or administrator of an estate (and not left in the custody of a broker or other agent) an adequate identification is made if at the time of a sale, transfer, or distribution, the trustee, executor, or administrator—

(i) Specifies in writing in the books and records of the trust or estate the particular stock to be sold, transferred, or distributed, and

(ii) In the case of a distribution, also furnishes the distributee with a written document setting forth the particular stock distributed to him. Stock identified pursuant to this subparagraph is the stock sold, transferred, or distributed by the trust or estate, even though stock certificates from a different lot are delivered to the purchaser, transferee, or distributee.

(5) *Subsequent sales.* If stock identified under subparagraph (3) or (4) of this paragraph as belonging to a particular lot is sold, transferred, or distributed, the stock so identified shall be deemed to have been sold, transferred, or distributed, and such sale, transfer, or distribution will be taken into consideration in identifying the taxpayer's remaining stock for purposes of subsequent sales, transfers, or distributions.

(6) *Bonds.* The provisions of subparagraphs (1) through (5) of this paragraph shall apply to the sale or transfer of bonds after July 13, 1965.

(7) *Book-entry securities.* (i) In applying the provisions of subparagraph (3)(i)(*a*) of this paragraph in the case of a sale or transfer of a book-entry security (as defined in subdivision (iii)(*a*) of this subparagraph) which is made after December 31, 1970, pursuant to a written instruction by the taxpayer, a specification by the taxpayer of the unique lot number which he has assigned to the lot which contains the securities being sold or transferred shall constitute specification as required by such subparagraph. The specification of the lot number shall be made either—

(*a*) In such written instruction, or

(*b*) In the case of a taxpayer in whose name the book entry by the Reserve Bank is made, in a list of lot numbers with respect to all book-entry securities on the books of the Reserve Bank sold or transferred on that date by the taxpayer, provided such list is mailed to or received by the Reserve Bank on or before the Reserve Bank's next business day.

This subdivision shall apply only if the taxpayer assigns lot numbers in numerical sequence to successive purchases of securities of the same loan title (series) and maturity date, except that securities of the same loan title (series) and maturity date which are purchased at the same price on the same date may be included within the same lot.

(ii) In applying the provisions of subparagraph (3)(i)(*b*) of this paragraph in the case of a sale or transfer of a book-entry security which is made pursuant to a written instruction by the taxpayer, a confirmation as required by such subparagraph shall be deemed made by—

(*a*) In the case of a sale or transfer made after December 31, 1970, the furnishing to the taxpayer of a written advice of transaction, by the Reserve Bank or the person through whom the taxpayer sells or transfers the securities, which specifies the amount and description of the securities sold or transferred and the date of the transaction, or

(*b*) In the case of a sale or transfer made before January 1, 1971, the furnishing of a

Reg. § 1.1012-1(c)(3)

serially numbered advice of transaction by a Reserve Bank.

(iii) For purposes of this subparagraph:

(a) The term "book-entry security" means—

(1) In the case of a sale or transfer made after December 31, 1970, a transferable Treasury bond, note, certificate of indebtedness, or bill issued under the Second Liberty Bond Act (31 U.S.C. 774(2)), as amended, or other security of the United States (as defined in (b) of this subdivision (iii)) in the form of an entry made as prescribed in 31 CFR Part 306, or other comparable Federal regulations, on the records of a Reserve Bank, or

(2) In the case of a sale or transfer made before January 1, 1971, a transferable Treasury bond, note, certificate of indebtedness, or bill issued under the Second Liberty Bond Act, as amended, in the form of an entry made as prescribed in 31 CFR Part 306, Subpart O, on the records of a Reserve Bank which is deposited in an account with a Reserve Bank (i) as collateral pledged to a Reserve Bank (in its individual capacity) for advances by it, (ii) as collateral pledged to the United States under Treasury Department Circular No. 92 or 176, both as revised and amended, (iii) by a member bank of the Federal Reserve System for its sole account for safekeeping by a Reserve Bank in its individual capacity, (iv) in lieu of a surety or sureties upon the bond required by section 61 of the Bankruptcy Act, as amended (11 U.S.C. 101), of a banking institution designated by a judge of one of the several courts of bankruptcy under such section as a depository for the moneys of a bankrupt's estate, (v) pursuant to 6 U.S.C. 15, in lieu of a surety or sureties required in connection with any recognizance, stipulation, bond, guaranty, or undertaking which must be furnished under any law of the United States or regulations made pursuant thereto, (vi) by a banking institution, pursuant to a State or local law, to secure the deposit in such banking institution of public funds by a State, municipality, or other political subdivision, (vii) by a State bank or trust company or a national bank, pursuant to a State or local law, to secure the faithful performance of trust or other fiduciary obligations by such State bank or trust company or national bank, or (viii) to secure funds which are deposited or held in trust by a State bank or trust company or a national bank and are awaiting investment, but which are used by such State bank or trust company or national bank in the conduct of its business;

(b) The term "other security of the United States" means a bond, note, certificate of indebtedness, bill, debenture, or similar obligation which is subject to the provisions of 31 CFR Part 306 or other comparable Federal regulations and which is issued by (1) any department or agency of the Government of the United States, or (2) the Federal National Mortgage Association, the Federal Home Loan Banks, the Federal Home Loan Mortgage Corporation, the Federal Land Banks, the Federal Intermediate Credit Banks, the Banks for Cooperatives, or the Tennessee Valley Authority;

(c) The term "serially-numbered advice of transaction" means the confirmation (prescribed in 31 CFR 306.116) issued by the Reserve Bank which is identifiable by a unique number and indicates that a particular written instruction to the Reserve Bank with respect to the deposit or withdrawal of a specified book-entry security (or securities) has been executed; and

(d) The term "Reserve Bank" means a Federal Reserve Bank and its branches acting as Fiscal Agent of the United States.

(d) *Obligations issued as part of an investment unit.* For purposes of determining the basis of the individual elements of an investment unit (as defined in paragraph (b)(2)(ii)(a) of § 1.1232-3) consisting of an obligation and an option (which is not an excluded option under paragraph (b)(1)(iii)(c) of § 1.1232-3), security, or other property, the cost of such investment unit shall be allocated to such individual elements on the basis of their respective fair market values. In the case of the initial issuance of an investment unit consisting of an obligation and an option, security, or other property, where neither the obligation nor the option, security, or other property has a readily ascertainable fair market value, the portion of the cost of the unit which is allocable to the obligation shall be an amount equal to the issue price of the obligation as determined under paragraph (b)(2)(ii)(a) of § 1.1232-3.

(e) *Election as to certain regulated investment company stock* —(1) *General rule*—(i) *In general.* Notwithstanding paragraph (c) of this section, and except as provided in subdivision (ii) of this subparagraph, if—

(a) Shares of stock of a regulated investment company (as defined in subparagraph (5) of this paragraph) are left by a taxpayer in the custody of a custodian or agent in an account maintained for the acquisition or redemption of shares of such company, and

(b) The taxpayer purchased or acquired shares of stock held in the account at different prices or bases,

the taxpayer may elect to determine the cost or other basis of shares of stock he sells or transfers

Reg. § 1.1012-1(e)(1)

from such account by using one of the methods described in subparagraphs (3) and (4) of this paragraph. The cost or other basis determined in accordance with either of such methods shall be known as the "average basis." For purposes of this paragraph, securities issued by unit investment trusts shall be treated as shares of stock and the term "share" or "shares" shall include fractions of a share.

(ii) *Certain gift shares.* (*a*) Except as provided in subdivision (*b*) of this subdivision (ii), this paragraph shall not apply to any account which contains shares which were acquired by the taxpayer by gift after December 31, 1920, if the basis of such shares (adjusted for the period before the date of the gift as provided in section 1016) in the hands of the donor or the last preceding owner by whom it was not acquired by gift was greater than the fair market value of such shares at the time of the gift. However, shares acquired by a taxpayer as a result of a taxable dividend or a capital gain distribution from such an account may be included in an account to which this paragraph applies.

(*b*) Notwithstanding the provisions of subdivision (*a*) of this subdivision (ii), this paragraph shall apply with respect to accounts containing gift shares described in such subdivision (*a*) if, at the time the election described in this paragraph is made in the manner prescribed in subparagraph (6) of this paragraph, the taxpayer includes a statement, in writing, indicating that the basis of such gift shares shall be the fair market value of such gift shares at the time they were acquired by the taxpayer by gift and that such basis shall be used in computing average basis in the manner described in subparagraph (3) or (4) of this paragraph. Such statement shall be effective with respect to gift shares acquired prior to making such election and with respect to gift shares after such time and shall remain in effect so long as such election remains in effect.

(2) *Determination of average basis.* Average basis shall be determined using either the method described in subparagraph (3) of this paragraph (the double-category method) or the method described in subparagraph (4) of this paragraph (the single-category method). The taxpayer shall specify, in the manner described in subparagraph (6) of this paragraph, the method used. Such method shall be used with respect to an account until such time as the election is revoked with the consent of the Commissioner. Although a taxpayer may specify different methods with respect to accounts in different regulated investment companies, the same method shall be used with respect to all of the taxpayer's accounts in the same regulated investment company.

(3) *Double-category method* —(i) *In general.* In determining average basis using the double category method, all shares in an account at the time of each sale or transfer shall be divided into two categories. The first category shall include all shares in such account having, at the time of the sale or transfer, a holding period of more than 1 year (6 months for taxable years beginning before 1977; 9 months for taxable years beginning in 1977) (the "more-than-1-year (6-month for taxable years beginning before 1977; 9-month for taxable years beginning in 1977)" category), and the second category shall include all shares in such account having, at such time, a holding period of 1 year (6 months for taxable years beginning before 1977; 9 months for taxable years beginning in 1977) or less (the "1-year (6-month for taxable years beginning before 1977; 9-month for taxable years beginning in 1977) -or-less" category). The cost or other basis of each share in a category shall be an amount equal to the remaining aggregate cost or other basis of all shares in that category at the time of the sale or transfer divided by the aggregate number of shares in that category at such time.

(ii) *Order of disposition of shares sold or transferred.* Prior to a sale or transfer of shares from such an account, the taxpayer may specify, to the custodian or agent having custody of the account, from which category (described in subdivision (i) of this subparagraph) the shares are to be sold or transferred. Shares shall be deemed sold or transferred from the category specified without regard to the stock certificates, if any, actually delivered if, within a reasonable time thereafter, confirmation of such specification is set forth in a written document from the custodian or agent having custody of the account. In the absence of such specification or confirmation, shares sold or transferred shall be charged against the more-than-1-year (6-month for taxable years beginning before 1977; 9-month for taxable years beginning in 1977) category. However, if the number of shares sold or transferred exceeds the number in such category, the additional shares sold or transferred shall be charged against the shares in the 1-year (6-month for taxable years beginning before 1977; 9-month for taxable years beginning in 1977) -or-less category. Any gain or loss attributable to a sale or transfer which is charged against shares in the more-than-1-year (6-month for taxable years beginning before 1977; 9-month for taxable years beginning in 1977) category shall constitute long-term gain or loss, and any gain or loss attributable to a sale or transfer which is charged against shares in the 1-year (6-month

Reg. § 1.1012-1(e)(2)

Basis Rules of General Application

for taxable years beginning before 1977; 9-month for taxable years beginning in 1977) -or-less category shall constitute short-term gain or loss. As to adjustments from wash sales, see section 1091(d) and subdivisions (iii)(c) and (d) of this subparagraph.

(iii) *Special rules with respect to shares from the 1-year-or-less category.* (a) After the taxpayer's holding period with respect to a share is more than 1 year (6 months for taxable years beginning before 1977; 9 months for taxable years beginning in 1977), such share shall be changed from the 1-year (6-month for taxable years beginning before 1977; 9-month for taxable years beginning in 1977) -or-less category to the more-than-1-year (6-month for taxable years beginning before 1977; 9-month for taxable years beginning in 1977) category. For purposes of such change, the basis of a changed share shall be its actual cost or other basis to the taxpayer or its basis determined in accordance with the rules contained in subdivision (b)(2) of this subdivision (ii) if the rules of such subdivision (b)(2) are applicable.

(b) If, during the period that shares are in the 1-year (6-month for taxable years beginning before 1977; 9-month for taxable years beginning in 1977) -or-less category some but not all of the shares in such category are sold or transferred, then—

(1) The shares sold or transferred (the basis of which was determined in the manner prescribed by subdivision (i) of this subparagraph) shall be assumed to be those shares in such category which were earliest purchased or acquired, and

(2) The basis of those shares which are not sold or transferred and which are changed from the 1-year (6-month for taxable years beginning before 1977; 9-month for taxable years beginning in 1977) -or-less category to the more-than-1-year (6-month for taxable years beginning before 1977; 9-month for taxable years beginning in 1977) category shall be the average basis of the shares in the 1-year (6-month for taxable years beginning before 1977; 9-month for taxable years beginning in 1977) -or-less category at the time of the most recent sale or transfer of shares from such category. For such purposes, the average basis shall be determined in the manner prescribed in subdivision (i) of this subparagraph.

(c) Paragraph (a) of § 1.1091-2 contains examples which illustrate the general application of section 1091(d), relating to unadjusted basis in the case of a wash sale of stock. However, in the case of certain wash sales of stock from the 1-year (6-month for taxable years beginning before 1977; 9-month for taxable years beginning in 1977) -or-less category, the provisions of section 1091(d) shall be applied in the manner described in subdivision (d) of this subdivision (iii).

(d) In the case of a wash sale of stock (determined in accordance with the provisions of section 1091 from the 1-year (6-month for taxable years beginning before 1977; 9-month for taxable years beginning in 1977) -or-less category which occurs after the acquisition of shares of stock into such category, the aggregate cost or other basis of all shares remaining in the 1-year (6-month for taxable years beginning before 1977; 9-month for taxable years beginning in 1977) -or-less category after such sale shall be increased by the amount of the loss which is not deductible because of the provisions of section 1091 and the regulations thereunder. The provisions of this subdivision may be illustrated by the following example:

Example. Assume the following acquisitions to, and sale from, the 1 year (6-month for taxable years beginning before 1977; 9-month for taxable years beginning in 1977) -or-less category:

1-YEAR (6-MONTH FOR TAXABLE YEARS BEGINNING BEFORE 1977; 9-MONTH FOR TAXABLE YEARS BEGINNING IN 1977) -OR-LESS CATEGORY

Date	Action	Number Shares	Price/Share	Aggregate
1-5-71	Purchase	10	$110	$1,100
2-5-71	Purchase	10	100	1,000
3-5-71	Purchase	10	90	900
Average		30	100	3,000
3-15-71	Sale	10	90	900
Loss		10	10	100

In this example, the unadjusted basis of the shares remaining in the account after the sale is $2,000 (aggregate basis of $3,000 before the sale, less $1,000, the aggregate basis of the shares sold after the averaging of costs). The adjusted basis of the shares remaining in the 1-year (6-month for taxable years beginning before 1977; 9-month for taxable years beginning in 1977) -or-less category after the sale and after adjustment

Reg. § 1.1012-1(e)(3)

is $2,100 (the unadjusted basis of $2,000, plus the $100 loss resulting from the sale).

(4) *Single-category method* —(i) *In general.* In determining average basis using the single-category method, the cost or other basis of all shares in an account at the time of each sale or transfer (whether such shares have a holding period of more than 1 year (6 months for taxable years beginning before 1977; 9 months for taxable years beginning in 1977) or 1 year (6 months for taxable years beginning before 1977; 9 months for taxable years beginning in 1977) or less) shall be used in making the computation. The cost or other basis of each share in such account shall be an amount equal to the remaining aggregate cost or other basis of all shares in such account at the time of the sale or transfer divided by the aggregate number of shares in such account at such time.

(ii) *Order of disposition of shares sold or transferred.* In the case of the sale or transfer of shares from an account to which the election provided by this paragraph applies, and with respect to which the taxpayer has specified that he uses the single-category method of determining average basis, shares sold or transferred shall be deemed to be those shares first acquired. Thus, when shares are sold or transferred from an account such shares will be those with a holding period of more than 1 year (6 months for taxable years beginning before 1977; 9 months for taxable years beginning in 1977) to the extent that such account contains shares with a holding period of more than 1 year (6 months for taxable years beginning before 1977; 9 months for taxable years beginning in 1977). If the number of shares sold or transferred exceeds the number of shares in the account with a holding period of more than 1 year (6 months for taxable years beginning before 1977; 9 months for taxable years beginning in 1977), any such excess shares sold or transferred will be deemed to be shares with a holding period of 1 year (6 months for taxable years beginning before 1977; 9 months for taxable years beginning in 1977) or less. Any gain or loss attributable to shares held for more than 1 year (6 months for taxable years beginning before 1977; 9 months for taxable years beginning in 1977) shall constitute long-term gain or loss, and any gain or loss attributable to shares held for 1 year (6 months for taxable years beginning before 1977; 9 months for taxable years beginning in 1977) or less shall constitute short-term gain or loss. For example, if a taxpayer sells or transfers 50 shares from an account containing 100 shares with a holding period of more than 1 year (6 months for taxable years beginning before 1977; 9 months for taxable years beginning in 1977) and 100 shares with a holding period of 1 year (6 months for taxable years beginning before 1977; 9 months for taxable years beginning in 1977) or less, all of the shares sold or transferred will be deemed to be shares with a holding period of more than 1 year (6 months for taxable years beginning before 1977; 9 months for taxable years beginning in 1977). If, however, the account contains 40 shares with a holding period of more than 1 year (6 months for taxable years beginning before 1977; 9 months for taxable years beginning in 1977) and 100 shares with a holding period of 1 year (6 months for taxable years beginning before 1977; 9 months for taxable years beginning in 1977) or less, the taxpayer will be deemed to have sold or transferred 40 shares with a holding period of more than 1 year (6 months for taxable years beginning before 1977; 9 months for taxable years beginning in 1977) and 10 shares with a holding period of 1 year (6 months for taxable years beginning before 1977; 9 months for taxable years beginning in 1977) or less.

(iii) *Restriction on use of single-category method.* The single-category method of determining average basis shall not be used where it appears from the facts and circumstances that a purpose of using such single-category method is to convert long-term capital gains or losses to short-term capital gains or losses or to convert short-term capital gains or losses to long-term capital gains or losses.

(iv) *Wash sales.* The provisions of section 1091(d) (relating to unadjusted basis in the case of a wash sale of stock) and the regulations thereunder shall apply in the case of wash sales of stock from an account with respect to which the single-category method of determining average basis is being used.

(5) *Definition.* (i) For purposes of this paragraph, a "regulated investment company" means any domestic corporation (other than a personal holding company as defined in section 542) which meets the limitations of section 851(b) and § 1.851-2, and which is registered at all times during the taxable year under the Investment Company Act of 1940, as amended (15 U.S.C. 80a-1 to 80b-2), either as a management company, or as a unit investment trust.

(ii) Notwithstanding subdivision (i), this paragraph shall not apply in the case of a unit investment trust unless it is one—

(a) Substantially all of the assets of which consist (1) of securities issued by a single management company (as defined in such Act) and securities acquired pursuant to subdivision (b) of this subdivision (ii), or (2) securities issued by a single other corporation, and

Reg. § 1.1012-1(e)(4)

Basis Rules of General Application

See p. 20,601 for regulations not amended to reflect law changes

(b) Which has no power to invest in any other securities except securities issued by a single other management company, when permitted by such Act or the rules and regulations of the Securities and Exchange Commission.

(6) *Election.* (i) An election to adopt one of the methods described in this paragraph shall be made in an income tax return for the first taxable year ending on or after December 31, 1970, for which the taxpayer desires the election to apply. If the taxpayer does not file a timely return (taking into account extensions of the time for filing) for such taxable year the election shall be filed at the time the taxpayer files his first return for such year. The election may be made with an amended return only if such amended return is filed no later than the time prescribed by law (including extensions thereof) for filing the return for such taxable year. If the election is made, the taxpayer shall clearly indicate on his income tax return for each year to which the election is applicable that an average basis has been used in reporting gain or loss from the sale or transfer of shares sold or transferred. In addition, the taxpayer shall specify on such return the method (either the single-category method or the double-category method) used in determining average basis. The taxpayer shall also indicate in a statement described in subparagraph (1)(ii)(b) of this paragraph if the election is to apply to accounts described in subparagraph (1)(ii) of this paragraph. Such statement shall be attached to, or incorporated in, such return. A taxpayer making the election shall maintain such records as are necessary to substantiate the average basis (or bases) used on his income tax return.

(ii) An election made with respect to some of the shares of a regulated investment company sold or transferred from an account described in subparagraph (1)(i) of this paragraph applies to all such shares in the account. Such election also applies to all shares of that regulated investment company held in other such accounts (*i.e.*, those described in subparagraph (1)(i) of this paragraph) by the electing taxpayer for his own benefit. Thus, the election shall apply to all shares of the regulated investment company held by the electing taxpayer (for his own benefit) in such accounts on or after the first day of the first taxable year for which the election is made. Such election does not apply to shares held in account described in subparagraph (1)(ii) of this paragraph unless the taxpayer indicates, in the manner described in subdivision (i) of this subparagraph, that the election is to apply to shares held in such accounts. An election made pursuant to the provisions of this paragraph may not be revoked without the prior written permission of the Commissioner.

(7) *Examples.* The provisions of this paragraph may be illustrated by the following examples:

Example (1). (i) On January 11, 1971, taxpayer A, who files his income tax return on a calendar year basis, enters into an agreement with the W Bank establishing an account for the periodic acquisition of shares of the Y Company, an open-end mutual fund. The agreement provides (1) that the bank is to purchase, for A, shares of Y stock as A may from time to time direct, (2) that all shares in the account are to be left in the custody of the bank, and (3) that the bank is to reinvest any dividends paid by Y (including capital gain dividends) in additional shares of Y stock. Pursuant to the agreement, on January 11, 1971, February 1, 1971, and March 1, 1971, respectively, the bank purchases, at A's direction, 100 shares of Y stock for a total of $1,880, 20 shares of Y stock for a total of $400, and 20 shares of Y stock for a total of $410. On March 15, 1971, the bank reinvests a $1-per-share capital gain dividend (that is, a total of $140) in seven additional shares of Y stock. The acquisitions to A's account, are, therefore, as follows:

Date	Number of shares	Basis
Jan. 11, 1971	100	$1,880
Feb. 1, 1971	20	400
Mar. 1, 1971	20	410
Mar. 15, 1971	7	140

On August 20, 1971, at A's direction, the bank redeems (*i.e.*, sells) 40 shares of Y stock, and on September 20, 1971, 30 shares. A elects to determine the gain or loss from the sales of the stock by reference to its average basis using the double-category method of determining average basis. A did not specify from which category the sales were to take place, and therefore, each sale is deemed to have been made from the more-than-6-months category.

(ii) The average basis for the shares sold on August 20, 1971, is $19.00, and the total average basis for the 40 shares which are sold is $760.00, computed as follows:

Reg. § 1.1012-1(e)(7)

51,926 Basis Rules of General Application

See p. 20,601 for regulations not amended to reflect law changes

Number of shares in the more-than-6-months category at the time of sale	Basis
100	$1,880
20	400
Total 120	$2,280

Average cost or other basis: $2,280 ÷ 120 = $19. 40 shares × $19 each = $760, total average basis. Therefore, after the sale on August 20, 1971, 80 shares remain in the more-than-6-months category, and their remaining aggregate cost is $1,520.

(iii) The average basis for the shares sold on September 20, 1971, must reflect the sale which was made on August 20, 1971. Accordingly, such average basis would be $19.35 and may be computed as follows:

Number of shares in the more-than-6-months category at the time of sale	Basis
80	$1,520
20	410
7	140
Total 107	$2,070

Average cost or other basis: $2,070 ÷ 107 shares = $19.35 (to the nearest cent).

Example (2). Taxpayer B, who files his income tax returns on a calendar year basis, enters into an agreement with the X Bank establishing an account for the periodic acquisition of shares of the Z Company, an open-end mutual fund. X acquired for B's account shares of Z on the following dates in the designated amounts:

January 15, 1971	50 shares.
February 16, 1971	30 shares.
March 15, 1971	25 shares.

Pursuant to B's direction, the bank redeemed (i.e., sold) 25 shares from the account on February 1, 1971, and 20 shares on April 1, 1971, for a total of 45 shares. All of such shares had been held for less than 6 months. B elects to determine the gain or loss from the sales of the stock by reference to its average basis using the double-category method of determining average basis. Thus, the 45 shares which were sold are assumed to be from the 50 shares which were purchased on January 15, 1971. Accordingly, on July 16, 1971, only five shares from those shares which had been purchased on January 15, 1971, remain to be transferred from the 6-months-or-less category to the more-than-6-months category. The basis of such five shares for purposes of the change to the more-than-6-months category would be the average basis of the shares in the 6-months-or-less category at the time of the sale on April 1, 1971.

Example (3). Assume the same facts as in example (2), except that an additional sale of 18 shares was made on May 3, 1971. There were, therefore, a total of 63 shares sold during the 6-month period beginning on January 15, 1971, the date of the earliest purchase. Fifty of the shares which were sold during such period shall be assumed to be the shares purchased on January 15, 1971, and the remaining 13 shares shall be assumed to be from the shares which were purchased on February 16, 1971. Thus, none of the shares which were purchased on January 15, 1971, remain to be changed from the 6-months-or-less category to the more-than-6-months category. In the absence of further dispositions of shares during the 6-months holding period for the shares purchased on February 16, 1971, there would be 17 of such shares to be changed over after the expiration of that period since 13 of the shares sold on May 3, 1971, were assumed to be from the shares purchased on February 16, 1971. The basis of the 17 shares for purposes of the change to the more-than-6-months category would be the average basis of the shares in the 6-months-or-less category at the time of the sale on May 3, 1971.

Example (4). Taxpayer C, who files his income tax returns on a calendar year basis, enters into an agreement with Y bank establishing an account for the periodic acquisition of XYZ Company, a closed-end mutual fund. Y acquired for B's account shares of XYZ on the following dates in the designated amounts:

Date	Number of Shares	Cost
January 8, 1971	25 shares	$200
February 8, 1971	24 shares	200
March 8, 1971	23 shares	200
April 8, 1971	23 shares	200

Reg. § 1.1012-1(e)(7)

Pursuant to C's direction, the bank redeemed (*i.e.*, sold) 40 shares from the account on July 15, 1971, for $10 per share or a total of $400. C elects to determine the gain or loss from the sale of the stock by reference to its average basis using the single-category method of determining average basis. The average basis for the shares sold on July 15, 1971 (determined by dividing the total number of shares in the account at such time (95) into the aggregate cost of such shares ($800)) is $8.42 (to the nearest cent). Under the rules of subparagraph (4) of this paragraph the shares sold would be deemed to be those first acquired. Thus, C would realize a $39.50 ($1.58 × 25) long-term capital gain with respect to the 25 shares acquired on January 8, 1971, and he would realize a $23.70 ($1.58 × 15) short-term capital gain with respect to 15 of the shares acquired on February 8, 1971. The next sale occurred on August 16, 1971. At that time, absent further intervening acquisitions or dispositions, the account contained 9 shares (the 24 shares acquired on February 8, 1971, less 15 of such shares which were sold on July 15, 1971) with a holding period of more than six months, and 46 shares with a holding period of six months or less.

Example (5). Taxpayer D owns four separate accounts (D-1, D-2, D-3, and D-4) for the periodic acquisition of shares of the Y Company, an open-end mutual fund. Account D-4 contains shares which D acquired by gift on April 15, 1970. These shares had an adjusted basis in the hands of the donor which was greater than the fair market value of the donated shares on such date. For his taxable year ending on December 31, 1971, D elects to use an average basis for shares sold from account D-1 during such year using the single-category method of determining average basis. Under the provisions of subparagraph (1)(ii) of this paragraph, D may use an average basis for shares sold or transferred from account D-4 if he includes with his statement of election a statement, in writing, indicating that the basis of such gift shares in account D-4 shall be the fair market value of such shares at the time he acquired such shares and that such basis shall be used in computing the average basis of shares in account D-4. In addition, since D elected to use an average basis for shares sold from account D-1, he must also use an average basis for all shares sold or transferred from accounts D-2 and D-3 (as well as account D-1) for his taxable year ending on December 31, 1971, and for all subsequent years until he revokes (with the consent of the Commissioner) his election to use an average basis for such accounts. Further, D must use the single-category method of determining average basis with respect to accounts D-2, D-3 (and D-4 if the above-mentioned statement is filed).

(f) *Special rules.* For special rules for determining the basis for gain or loss in the case of certain vessels acquired through the Maritime Commission (or its successors) or pursuant to an agreement with the Secretary of Commerce, see sections 510, 511, and 607 of the Merchant Marine Act, 1936, as amended (46 U.S.C. 1160, 1161) and 26 CFR Parts 2 and 3. For special rules for determining the unadjusted basis of property recovered in respect of war losses, see section 1336. For special rules with respect to taxable years beginning before January 1, 1964, for determining the basis for gain or loss in the case of a disposition of a share of stock acquired pursuant to the timely exercise of a restricted stock option where the option price was between 85 percent and 95 percent of the fair market value of the stock at the time the option was granted, see paragraph (b) of § 1.421-5. See sections 423(c)(1) or 424(c)(1), whichever is applicable, for special rules with respect to taxable years ending after December 31, 1963, for determining the basis for gain or loss in the case of the disposition of a share of stock acquired pursuant to the timely exercise of a stock option described in such sections. See section 422(c)(1) for special rules with respect to taxable years ending after December 31, 1963, for determining the basis for gain or loss in the case of an exercise of a qualified stock option.

(g) *Debt instruments issued in exchange for property*—(1) *In general.* For purposes of paragraph (a) of this section, if a debt instrument is issued in exchange for property, the cost of the property that is attributable to the debt instrument is the issue price of the debt instrument as determined under § 1.1273-2 or § 1.1274-2, whichever is applicable. If, however, the issue price of the debt instrument is determined under section 1273(b)(4), the cost of the property attributable to the debt instrument is its stated principal amount reduced by any unstated interest (as determined under section 483).

(2) *Certain tax-exempt obligations.* This paragraph (g)(2) applies to a tax-exempt obligation (as defined in section 1275(a)(3)) that is issued in exchange for property and that has an issue price determined under § 1.1274-2(j) (concerning tax-exempt contingent payment obligations and certain tax-exempt variable rate debt instruments subject to section 1274). Notwithstanding paragraph (g)(1) of this section, if this paragraph (g)(2) applies to a tax-exempt obligation, for purposes of paragraph (a) of this section, the cost of the property that is attributable to the obligation is the sum of the present values of the noncontin-

Reg. § 1.1012-1(g)(2)

Basis Rules of General Application

See p. 20,601 for regulations not amended to reflect law changes

gent payments (as determined under § 1.1274-2(c)).

(3) *Effective date.* This paragraph (g) applies to sales or exchanges that occur on or after August 13, 1996. [Reg. § 1.1012-1.]

☐ [T.D. 6265, 11-6-57. *Amended by* T.D. 6311, 9-10-58; T.D. 6837, 7-12-65; T.D. 6887, 6-23-66; T.D. 6934, 11-13-67; T.D. 6984, 12-23-68; T.D. 7015, 6-19-69; T.D. 7081, 12-30-70; T.D. 7129, 7-6-71; T.D. 7154, 12-27-71; T.D. 7213, 10-17-72; T.D. 7568, 10-11-78; T.D. 7728, 10-31-80; T.D. 8517, 1-27-94 *and* T.D. 8674, 6-11-96.]

[Reg. § 1.1012-2]

§ 1.1012-2. Transfers in part a sale and in part a gift.—For rules relating to basis of property acquired in a transfer which is in part a gift and in part a sale, see § 1.170A-4(c), § 1.1011-2(b), and § 1.1015-4. [Reg. § 1.1012-2.]

☐ [T.D. 6265, 11-6-57. *Amended by* T.D. 7207, 10-3-72.]

[Reg. § 1.1013-1]

§ 1.1013-1. Property included in inventory.—The basis of property required to be included in inventory is the last inventory value of such property in the hands of the taxpayer. The requirements with respect to the valuation of an inventory are stated in subpart D (sections 471 and following), part II, or subchapter E, chapter 1 of the Code, and the regulations thereunder. [Reg. § 1.1013-1.]

☐ [T.D. 6265, 11-6-57.]

[Reg. § 1.1014-1]

§ 1.1014-1. Basis of property acquired from a decedent.—(a) *General rule.* The purpose of section 1014 is, in general, to provide a basis for property acquired from a decedent which is equal to the value placed upon such property for purposes of the Federal estate tax. Accordingly, the general rule is that the basis of property acquired from a decedent is the fair market value of such property at the date of the decedent's death, or, if the decedent's executor so elects, at the alternate valuation date prescribed in section 2032, or in section 811(j) of the Internal Revenue Code of 1939. Property acquired from a decedent includes, principally, property acquired by bequest, devise, or inheritance, and, in the case of decedents dying after December 31, 1953, property required to be included in determining the value of the decedent's gross estate under any provision of the Internal Revenue Code of 1954 or the Internal Revenue Code of 1939. The general rule governing basis of property acquired from a decedent, as well as other rules prescribed elsewhere in this section, shall have no application if the property is sold, exchanged, or otherwise disposed of before the decedent's death by the person who acquired the property from the decedent. For general rules on the applicable valuation date where the executor of a decedent's estate elects under section 2032, or under section 811(j) of the Internal Revenue Code of 1939, to value the decedent's gross estate at the alternate valuation date prescribed in such sections, see paragraph (e) of § 1.1014-3.

(b) *Scope and application.* With certain limitations, the general rule described in paragraph (a) of this section is applicable to the classes of property described in paragraphs (a) and (b) of § 1.1014-2, including stock in a DISC or former DISC. In the case of stock in a DISC or former DISC, the provisions of this section and §§ 1.1014-2 through 1.1014-8 are applicable, except as provided in § 1.1014-9. Special basis rules with respect to the basis of certain other property acquired from a decedent are set forth in paragraph (c) of § 1.1014-2. These special rules concern certain stock or securities of a foreign personal holding company and the surviving spouse's one-half share of community property held with a decedent dying after October 21, 1942, and on or before December 31, 1947. In this section and §§ 1.1014-2 to 1.1014-6, inclusive, whenever the words "property acquired from a decedent" are used, they shall also mean "property passed from a decedent", and the phrase "person who acquired it from the decedent" shall include the "person to whom it passed from the decedent."

(c) *Property to which section 1014 does not apply.* Section 1014 shall have no application to the following classes of property:

(1) Property which constitutes a right to receive an item of income in respect of a decedent under section 691; and

(2) Restricted stock options described in section 421 which the employee has not exercised at death if the employee died before January 1, 1957. In the case of employees dying after December 31, 1956, see paragraph (d)(4) of § 1.421-5. In the case of employees dying in a taxable year ending after December 31, 1963, see paragraph (c)(4) of § 1.421-9 with respect to an option described in part II of subchapter D. [Reg. § 1.1014-1.]

☐ [T.D. 6265, 11-6-57. *Amended by* T.D. 6527, 1-18-61, T.D. 6887, 6-23-66 *and* T.D. 7283, 8-2-73.]

Reg. § 1.1012-2

[Reg. § 1.1014-2]

§ 1.1014-2. **Property acquired from a decedent.**—(a) *In general.* The following property, except where otherwise indicated, is considered to have been acquired from a decedent and the basis thereof is determined in accordance with the general rule in § 1.1014-1:

(1) Without regard to the date of the decedent's death, property acquired by bequest, devise, or inheritance, or by the decedent's estate from the decedent, whether the property was acquired under the decedent's will or under the law governing the descent and distribution of the property of decedents. However, see paragraph (c)(1) of this section if the property was acquired by bequest or inheritance from a decedent dying after August 26, 1937, and if such property consists of stock or securities of a foreign personal holding company.

(2) Without regard to the date of the decedent's death, property transferred by the decedent during his lifetime in trust to pay the income for life to or on the order or direction of the decedent, with the right reserved to the decedent at all times before his death to revoke the trust.

(3) In the case of decedents dying after December 31, 1951, property transferred by the decedent during his lifetime in trust to pay the income for life to or on the order or direction of the decedent with the right reserved to the decedent at all times before his death to make any change in the enjoyment thereof through the exercise of a power to alter, amend, or terminate the trust.

(4) Without regard to the date of the decedent's death, property passing without full and adequate consideration under a general power of appointment exercised by the decedent by will. (See section 2041(b) for definition of general power of appointment.)

(5) In the case of decedents dying after December 31, 1947, property which represents the surviving spouse's one-half share of community property held by the decedent and the surviving spouse under the community property laws of any State, Territory, or possession of the United States or any foreign country, if at least one-half of the whole of the community interest in that property was includible in determining the value of the decedent's gross estate under part III, chapter 11 of the Internal Revenue Code of 1954 (relating to the estate tax) or section 811 of the Internal Revenue Code of 1939. It is not necessary for the application of this subparagraph that an estate tax return be required to be filed for the estate of the decedent or that an estate tax be payable.

(6) In the case of decedents dying after December 31, 1950, and before January 1, 1954, property which represents the survivor's interest in a joint and survivor's annuity if the value of any part of that interest was required to be included in determining the value of the decedent's gross estate under section 811 of the Internal Revenue Code of 1939. It is necessary only that the value of a part of the survivor's interest in the annuity be includible in the gross estate under section 811. It is not necessary for the application of this subparagraph that an estate tax return be required to be filed for the estate of the decedent or that an estate tax be payable.

(b) *Property acquired from a decedent dying after December 31, 1953*—(1) *In general.* In addition to the property described in paragraph (a) of this section, and except as otherwise provided in subparagraph (3) of this paragraph, in the case of a decedent dying after December 31, 1953, property shall also be considered to have been acquired from the decedent to the extent that both of the following conditions are met: (i) the property was acquired from the decedent by reason of death, form of ownership, or other conditions (including property acquired through the exercise or non-exercise of a power of appointment), and (ii) the property is includible in the decedent's gross estate under the provisions of the Internal Revenue Code of 1954, or the Internal Revenue Code of 1939, because of such acquisition. The basis of such property in the hands of the person who acquired it from the decedent shall be determined in accordance with the general rule in § 1.1014-1. See, however, § 1.1014-6 for special adjustments if such property is acquired before the death of the decedent. See also subparagraph (3) of this paragraph for a description of property not within the scope of this paragraph.

(2) *Rules for the application of subparagraph (1) of this paragraph.* Except as provided in subparagraph (3) of this paragraph, this paragraph generally includes all property acquired from a decedent, which is includible in the gross estate of the decedent if the decedent died after December 31, 1953. It is not necessary for the application of this paragraph that an estate tax return be required to be filed for the estate of the decedent or that an estate tax be payable. Property acquired prior to the death of a decedent which is includible in the decedent's gross estate, such as property transferred by a decedent in contemplation of death, and property held by a taxpayer and the decedent as joint tenants or as tenants by the entireties is within the scope of this paragraph. Also, this paragraph includes property acquired through the exercise or non-exercise of a power of

appointment where such property is includible in the decedent's gross estate. It does not include property not includible in the decedent's gross estate such as property not situated in the United States acquired from a nonresident who is not a citizen of the United States.

(3) *Exceptions to application of this paragraph.* The rules of this paragraph are not applicable to the following property:

(i) Annuities described in section 72;

(ii) Stock or securities of a foreign personal holding company as described in section 1014(b)(5) (see paragraph (c)(1) of this section);

(iii) Property described in any paragraph other than paragraph (9) of section 1014(b). See paragraphs (a) and (c) of this section.

In illustration of subdivision (ii), assume that A acquired by gift stock of a character described in paragraph (c)(1) of this section from a donor and upon the death of the donor the stock was includible in the donor's estate as being a gift in contemplation of death. A's basis in the stock would not be determined by reference to its fair market value at the donor's death under the general rule in section 1014(a). Furthermore, the special basis rules prescribed in paragraph (c)(1) are not applicable to such property acquired by gift in contemplation of death. It will be necessary to refer to the rules in section 1015(a) to determine the basis.

(c) *Special basis rules with respect to certain property acquired from a decedent* —(1) *Stock or securities of a foreign personal holding company.* The basis of certain stock or securities of a foreign corporation which was a foreign personal holding company with respect to its taxable year next preceding the date of the decedent's death is governed by a special rule. If such stock was acquired from a decedent dying after August 26, 1937, by bequest or inheritance, or by the decedent's estate from the decedent, the basis of the property in the hands of the person who so acquired it (notwithstanding any other provision of section 1014) shall be the fair market value of such property at the date of the decedent's death or the adjusted basis of the stock in the hands of the decedent, whichever is lower.

(2) *Spouse's interest in community property of decedent dying after October 21, 1942, and on or before December 31, 1947.* In the case of a decedent dying after October 21, 1942, and on or before December 31, 1947, a special rule is provided for determining the basis of such part of any property, representing the surviving spouse's one-half share of property held by the decedent and the surviving spouse under the community property laws of any State, Territory, or possession of the United States or any foreign country, as was included in determining the value of the decedent's gross estate, if a tax under chapter 3 of the Internal Revenue Code of 1939 was payable upon the decedent's net estate. In such case the basis shall be the fair market value of such part of the property at the date of death (or the optional valuation elected under section 811(j) of the Internal Revenue Code of 1939) or the adjusted basis of the property determined without regard to this subparagraph, whichever is the higher. [Reg. § 1.1014-2.]

☐ [*T.D.* 6265, 11-6-57.]

[Reg. § 1.1014-3]

§ 1.1014-3. Other basis rules.—(a) *Fair market value.* For purposes of this section and § 1.1014-1, the value of property as of the date of the decedent's death as appraised for the purpose of the Federal estate tax or the alternate value as appraised for such purpose, whichever is applicable, shall be deemed to be its fair market value. If no estate tax return is required to be filed under section 6018 (or under section 821 or 864 of the Internal Revenue Code of 1939), the value of the property appraised as of the date of the decedent's death for the purpose of State inheritance or transmission taxes shall be deemed to be its fair market value and no alternative valuation date shall be applicable.

(b) *Property acquired from a decedent dying before March 1, 1913.* If the decedent died before March 1, 1913, the fair market value on that date is taken in lieu of the fair market value on the date of death, but only to the same extent and for the same purposes as the fair market value on March 1, 1913, is taken under section 1053.

(c) *Reinvestments by a fiduciary.* The basis of property acquired after the death of the decedent by a fiduciary as an investment is the cost or other basis of such property to the fiduciary, and not the fair market value of such property at the death of the decedent. For example, the executor of an estate purchases stock of X company at a price of $100 per share with the proceeds of the sale of property acquired from a decedent. At the date of the decedent's death the fair market value of such stock was $98 per share. The basis of such stock to the executor or to a legatee, assuming the stock is distributed, is $100 per share.

(d) *Reinvestments of property transferred during life.* Where property is transferred by a decedent during life and the property is sold, exchanged, or otherwise disposed of before the decedent's death by the person who acquired the property from the decedent, the general rule stated in paragraph (a) of § 1.1014-1 shall not apply to such property. However, in such a case, the basis of any property acquired by such donee in exchange for the original property, or of any property acquired by the donee through reinvesting the proceeds of the sale of the original prop-

Reg. § 1.1014-3(a)

Basis Rules of General Application

See p. 20,601 for regulations not amended to reflect law changes

erty, shall be the fair market value of the property thus acquired at the date of the decedent's death (or applicable alternate valuation date) if the property thus acquired is properly included in the decedent's gross estate for Federal estate tax purposes. These rules also apply to property acquired by the donee in any further exchanges or in further reinvestments. For example, on January 1, 1956, the decedent made a gift of real property to a trust for the benefit of his children, reserving to himself the power to revoke the trust at will. Prior to the decedent's death, the trustee sold the real property and invested the proceeds in stock of the Y company at $50 per share. At the time of the decedent's death, the value of such stock was $75 per share. The corpus of the trust was required to be included in the decedent's gross estate owing to his reservation of the power of revocation. The basis of the Y company stock following the decedent's death is $75 per share. Moreover, if the trustee sold the Y company stock before the decedent's death for $65 a share and reinvested the proceeds in Z company stock which increased in value to $85 per share at the time of the decedent's death, the basis of the Z company stock following the decedent's death would be $85 per share.

(e) *Alternate valuation dates.* Section 1014(a) provides a special rule applicable in determining the basis of property described in § 1.1014-2 where—

(1) The property is includible in the gross estate of a decedent who died after October 21, 1942, and

(2) The executor elects for estate tax purposes under section 2032, or section 811(j) of the Internal Revenue Code of 1939, to value the decedent's gross estate at the alternate valuation date prescribed in such sections.

In those cases, the value applicable in determining the basis of the property is not the value at the date of the decedent's death but (with certain limitations) the value at the date one year after his death if not distributed, sold, exchanged, or otherwise disposed of in the meantime. If such property was distributed, sold, exchanged, or otherwise disposed of within one year after the date of the decedent's death by the person who acquired it from the decedent, the value applicable in determining the basis is its value as of the date of such distribution, sale, exchange, or other disposition. For illustrations of the operation of this paragraph, see the estate tax regulations under section 2032. [Reg. § 1.1014-3.]

☐ [*T.D.* 6265, 11-6-57.]

[Reg. § 1.1014-4]

§ 1.1014-4. Uniformity of basis; adjustment to basis.—(a) *In general.*—(1) The basis of property acquired from a decedent, as determined under section 1014(a), is uniform in the hands of every person having possession or enjoyment of the property at any time under the will or other instrument or under the laws of descent and distribution. The principle of uniform basis means that the basis of the property (to which proper adjustments must, of course, be made) will be the same, or uniform, whether the property is possessed or enjoyed by the executor or administrator, the heir, the legatee or devisee, or the trustee or beneficiary of a trust created by a will or an inter vivos trust. In determining the amount allowed or allowable to a taxpayer in computing taxable income as deductions for depreciation or depletion under section 1016(a)(2), the uniform basis of the property shall at all times be used and adjusted. The sale, exchange, or other disposition by a life tenant or remainderman of his interest in property will, for purposes of this section, have no effect upon the uniform basis of the property in the hands of those who acquired it from the decedent. Thus, gain or loss on sale of trust assets by the trustee will be determined without regard to the prior sale of any interest in the property. Moreover, any adjustment for depreciation shall be made to the uniform basis of the property without regard to such prior sale, exchange, or other disposition.

(2) Under the law governing wills and the distribution of the property of decedents, all titles to property acquired by bequest, devise, or inheritance relate back to the death of the decedent, even though the interest of the person taking the title was, at the date of death of the decedent, legal, equitable, vested, contingent, general, specific, residual, conditional, executory, or otherwise. Accordingly, there is a common acquisition date for all titles to property acquired from a decedent within the meaning of section 1014, and, for this reason, a common or uniform basis for all such interests. For example, if distribution of personal property left by a decedent is not made until one year after his death, the basis of such property in the hands of the legatee is its fair market value at the time when the decedent died, and not when the legatee actually received the property. If the bequest is of the residue to trustees in trust, and the executors do not distribute the residue to such trustees until five years after the death of the decedent, the basis of each piece of property left by the decedent and thus received, in the hands of the trustees, is its fair market value at the time when the decedent dies. If the bequest is to trustees in trust to pay to A

Reg. § 1.1014-4(a)(2)

during his lifetime the income of the property bequeathed, and after his death to distribute such property to the survivors of a class, and upon A's death the property is distributed to the taxpayer as the sole survivor, the basis of such property, in the hands of the taxpayer, is its fair market value at the time when the decedent died. The purpose of the Code in prescribing a general uniform basis rule for property acquired from a decedent is, on the one hand, to tax the gain, in respect of such property, to him who realizes it (without regard to the circumstance that at the death of the decedent it may have been quite uncertain whether the taxpayer would take or gain anything); and, on the other hand, not to recognize as gain any element of value resulting solely from the circumstance that the possession or enjoyment of the taxpayer was postponed. Such postponement may be, for example, until the administration of the decedent's estate is completed, until the period of the possession or enjoyment of another has terminated, or until an uncertain event has happened. It is the increase or decrease in the value of property reflected in a sale or other disposition which is recognized as the measure of gain or loss.

(3) The principles stated in subparagraphs (1) and (2) of this paragraph do not apply to property transferred by an executor, administrator or trustee, to an heir, legatee, devisee or beneficiary under circumstances such that the transfer constitutes a sale or exchange. In such a case, gain or loss must be recognized by the transferor to the extent required by the revenue laws, and the transferee acquires a basis equal to the fair market value of the property on the date of the transfer. Thus, for example, if the trustee of a trust created by will transfers to a beneficiary, in satisfaction of a specific bequest of $10,000, securities which had a fair market value of $9,000 on the date of the decedent's death (the applicable valuation date) and $10,000 on the date of the transfer, the trust realizes a taxable gain of $1,000 and the basis of the securities in the hands of the beneficiary would be $10,000. As a further example, if the executor of an estate transfers to a trust property worth $200,000, which had a fair market value of $175,000 on the date of the decedent's death (the applicable valuation date), in satisfaction of the decedent's bequest in trust for the benefit of his wife of cash or securities to be selected by the executor in an amount sufficient to utilize the marital deduction to the maximum extent authorized by law (after taking into consideration any other property qualifying for the marital deduction), capital gain in the amount of $25,000 would be realized by the estate and the basis of the property in the hands of the trustees would be $200,000. If, on the other hand, the decedent bequeathed a fraction of his residuary estate to a trust for the benefit of his wife, which fraction will not change regardless of any fluctuations in value of property in the decedent's estate after his death, no gain or loss would be realized by the estate upon transfer of property to the trust, and the basis of the property in the hands of the trustee would be its fair market value on the date of the decedent's death or on the alternate valuation date.

(b) *Multiple interests.* Where more than one person has an interest in property acquired from a decedent, the basis of such property shall be determined and adjusted without regard to the multiple interests. The basis for computing gain or loss on the sale of any one of such multiple interests shall be determined under § 1.1014-5. Thus, the deductions for depreciation and for depletion allowed or allowable, under sections 167 and 611, to a legal life tenant as if the life tenant were the absolute owner of the property, constitute an adjustment to the basis of the property not only in the hands of the life tenant, but also in the hands of the remainderman and every other person to whom the same uniform basis is applicable. Similarly, the deductions allowed or allowable under sections 167 and 611, both to the trustee and to the trust beneficiaries, constitute an adjustment to the basis of the property not only in the hands of the trustee, but also in the hands of the trust beneficiaries and every other person to whom the uniform basis is applicable. See, however, section 262. Similarly, adjustments in respect of capital expenditures or losses, tax-free distributions, or other distributions applicable in reduction of basis, or other items for which the basis is adjustable are made without regard to which one of the persons to whom the same uniform basis is applicable makes the capital expenditures or sustains the capital losses, or to whom the tax-free or other distributions are made, or to whom the deductions are allowed or allowable. See § 1.1014-6 for adjustments in respect of property acquired from a decedent prior to his death.

(c) *Records.* The executor or other legal representative of the decedent, the fiduciary of a trust under a will, the life tenant and every other person to whom a uniform basis under this section is applicable, shall maintain records showing in detail all deductions, distributions, or other items for which adjustment to basis is required to be made by sections 1016 and 1017, and shall furnish to the district director such information with respect to those adjustments as he may require. [Reg. § 1.1014-4.]

☐ [*T.D.* 6265, 11-6-57.]

Reg. § 1.1014-4(a)(3)

[Reg. § 1.1014-5]

§ 1.1014-5. Gain or loss.—(a) *Sale or other disposition of a life interest, remainder interest, or other interest in property acquired from a decedent.* (1) Except as provided in paragraph (b) of this section with respect to the sale or other disposition after October 9, 1969, of a term interest in property, gain or loss from a sale or other disposition of a life interest, remainder interest, or other interest in property acquired from a decedent is determined by comparing the amount of the proceeds with the amount of that part of the adjusted uniform basis which is assignable to the interest so transferred. The adjusted uniform basis is the uniform basis of the entire property adjusted to the date of sale or other disposition of any such interest as required by sections 1016 and 1017. The uniform basis is the unadjusted basis of the entire property determined immediately after the decedent's death under the applicable sections of part II of subchapter O of chapter 1 of the Code.

(2) Except as provided in paragraph (b) of this section, the proper measure of gain or loss resulting from a sale or other disposition of an interest in property acquired from a decedent is so much of the increase or decrease in the value of the entire property as is reflected in such sale or other disposition. Hence, in ascertaining the basis of a life interest, remainder interest, or other interest which has been so transferred, the uniform basis rule contemplates that proper adjustments will be made to reflect the change in relative value of the interests on account of the passage of time.

(3) The factors set forth in the tables contained in § 20.2031-7 or, for certain prior periods, § 20.2031-7A of Part 20 of this chapter (Estate Tax Regulations) shall be used in the manner provided therein in determining the basis of the life interest, the remainder interest, or the term certain interest in the property on the date such interest is sold. The basis of the life interest, the remainder interest, or the term certain interest is computed by multiplying the uniform basis (adjusted to the time of the sale) by the appropriate factor. In the case of the sale of a life interest or a remainder interest, the factor used is the factor (adjusted where appropriate) which appears in the life interest or the remainder interest column of the table opposite the age (on the date of the sale) of the person at whose death the life interest will terminate. In the case of the sale of a term certain interest, the factor used is the factor (adjusted where appropriate) which appears in the term certain column of the table opposite the number of years remaining (on the date of sale) before the term certain interest will terminate.

(b) *Sale or other disposition of certain term interests.* In determining gain or loss from the sale or other disposition after October 9, 1969, of a term interest in property (as defined in paragraph (f)(2) of § 1.1001-1) the adjusted basis of which is determined pursuant, or by reference, to section 1014 (relating to the basis of property acquired from a decedent) or section 1015 (relating to the basis of property acquired by gift or by a transfer in trust), that part of the adjusted uniform basis assignable under the rules of paragraph (a) of this section to the interest sold or otherwise disposed of shall be disregarded to the extent and in the manner provided by section 1001(e) and paragraph (f) of § 1.1001-1.

(c) *Illustrations.* The application of this section may be illustrated by the following examples, in which references are made to the actuarial tables contained in Part 20 of this chapter (Estate Tax Regulations):

Example (1). Securities worth $500,000 at the date of decedent's death on January 1, 1971, are bequeathed to his wife, W, for life, with remainder over to his son, S. W is 48 years of age when the life interest is acquired. The estate does not elect the alternate valuation allowed by section 2032. By reference to § 20.2031-7A(c), the life estate factor for age 48, female, is found to be 0.77488 and the remainder factor for such age is found to be 0.22512. Therefore, the present value of the portion of the uniform basis assigned to W's life interest is $387,440 ($500,000 × 0.77488), and the present value of the portion of the uniform basis assigned to S's remainder interest is $112,560 ($500,000 × 0.22512). W sells her life interest to her nephew, A, on February 1, 1971, for $370,000, at which time W is still 48 years of age. Pursuant to section 1001(e), W realizes no loss; her gain is $370,000, the amount realized from the sale. A has a basis of $370,000 which he can recover by amortization deductions over W's life expectancy.

Example (2). The facts are the same as in example (1) except that W retains the life interest for 12 years, until she is 60 years of age, and then sells it to A on February 1, 1983, when the fair market value of the securities has increased to $650,000. By reference to § 20.2031-7A(c), the life estate factor for age 60, female, is found to be 0.63226 and the remainder factor for such age is found to be 0.36774. Therefore, the present value on February 1, 1983, of the portion of the uniform basis assigned to W's life interest is $316,130 ($500,000 × 0.63226) and the present value on that date of the portion of the uniform basis assigned to S's remainder interest is $183,870 ($500,000 × 0.36774). W sells her life interest for

Reg. § 1.1014-5(c)

$410,969, that being the commuted value of her remaining life interest in the securities as appreciated ($650,000 × 0.63226). Pursuant to section 1001(e), W's gain is $410,969, the amount realized. A has a basis of $410,969 which he can recover by amortization deductions over W's life expectancy.

Example (3). Unimproved land having a fair market value of $18,800 at the date of the decedent's death on January 1, 1970, is devised to A, a male, for life, with remainder over to B, a female. The estate does not elect the alternate valuation allowed by section 2032. On January 1, 1971, A sells his life interest to S for $12,500. S is not related to A or B. At the time of the sale, A is 39 years of age. By reference to § 20.2031-7A(c), the life estate factor for age 39, male, is found to be 0.79854. Therefore, the present value of the portion of the uniform basis assigned to A's life interest is $15,012.55 ($18,800 × 0.79854). This portion is disregarded under section 1001(e). A realized no loss; his gain is $12,500, the amount realized. S has a basis of $12,500 which he can recover by amortization deductions over A's life expectancy.

Example (4). The facts are the same as in example (3) except that on January 1, 1971, A and B jointly sell the entire property to S for $25,000 and divide the proceeds equally between them. A and B are not related, and there is no element of gift or compensation in the transaction. By reference to § 20.2031-7A(c), the remainder factor for age 39, male, is found to be 0.20146. Therefore, the present value of the uniform basis assigned to B's remainder interest is $3,787.45 ($18,800 × 0.20146). On the sale A realizes a loss of $2,512.55 ($15,012.55 less $12,500), the portion of the uniform basis assigned to his life interest not being disregarded by reason of section 1001(e)(3). B's gain on the sale is $8,712.55 ($12,500 less $3,787.45). S has a basis in the entire property of $25,000, no part of which, however, can be recovered by amortization deductions over A's life expectancy.

Example (5). (a) Nondepreciable property having a fair market value of $54,000 at the date of decedent's death on January 1, 1971, is devised to her husband, H, for life and, after his death, to her daughter, D, for life, with remainder over to her grandson, G. The estate does not elect the alternate valuation allowed by section 2032. On January 1, 1973, H sells his life interest to D for $32,000. At the date of the sale, H is 62 years of age, and D is 45 years of age. By reference to § 20.2031-7A(c), the life estate factor for age 62, male, is found to be 0.52321. Therefore, the present value on January 1, 1973, of the portion of the adjusted uniform basis assigned to H's life interest is $28,253 ($54,000 × 0.52321). Pursuant to section 1001(e), H realizes no loss; his gain is $32,000, the amount realized from the sale. D has a basis of $32,000 which she can recover by amortization deductions over H's life expectancy.

(b) On January 1, 1976, D sells both life estates to G for $40,000. During each of the years 1973 through 1975, D is allowed a deduction for the amortization of H's life interest. At the date of the sale H is 65 years of age, and D is 48 years of age. For purposes of determining gain or loss on the sale by D, the portion of the adjusted uniform basis assigned to H's life interest and the portion assigned to D's life interest are not taken into account under section 1001(e). However, pursuant to § 1.1001-1(f)(1), D's cost basis in H's life interest, minus deductions for the amortization of such interest, is taken into account. On the sale, D realizes gain of $40,000 minus an amount which is equal to the $32,000 cost basis (for H's life estate) reduced by amortization deductions. G is entitled to amortize over H's life expectancy that part of the $40,000 cost which is attributable to H's life interest. That part of the $40,000 cost which is attributable to D's life interest is not amortizable by G until H dies.

Example (6). Securities worth $1,000,000 at the date of decedent's death on January 1, 1971, are bequeathed to his wife, W, for life, with remainder over to his son, S. W is 48 years of age when the life interest is acquired. The estate does not elect the alternate valuation allowed by section 2032. By reference to § 20.2031-7A(c), the life estate factor for age 48, female, is found to be 0.77488, and the remainder factor for such age is found to be 0.22512. Therefore, the present value of the portion of the uniform basis assigned to W's life interest is $774,880 ($1,000,000 × 0.77488), and the present value of the portion of the uniform basis assigned to S's remainder interest is $225,120 ($1,000,000 × 0.22512). On February 1, 1971, W transfers her life interest to Corporation X in exchange for all of the stock of X pursuant to a transaction in which no gain or loss is recognized by reason of section 351. On February 1, 1972, W sells all of her stock in X to S for $800,000. Pursuant to section 1001(e) and § 1.1001-1(f)(2), W realizes no loss; her gain is $800,000, the amount realized from the sale. On February 1, 1972, X sells to N for $900,000 the life interest transferred to it by W. Pursuant to section 1001(e) and § 1.1001-1(f)(1), X realizes no loss; its gain is $900,000, the amount realized from the sale. N has a basis of $900,000 which he can recover by amortization deductions over W's life expectancy. [Reg. § 1.1014-5.]

☐ [T.D. 6265, 11-6-57. Amended by T.D. 7142, 9-23-71 and T.D. 8540, 6-9-94.]

Reg. § 1.1014-5(b)

Basis Rules of General Application

[Reg. § 1.1014-6]

§ 1.1014-6. **Special rule for adjustments to basis where property is acquired from a decedent prior to his death.**—(a) *In general.* (1) The basis of property described in section 1014(b)(9) which is acquired from a decedent prior to his death shall be adjusted for depreciation, obsolescence, amortization, and depletion allowed the taxpayer on such property for the period prior to the decedent's death. Thus, in general, the adjusted basis of such property will be its fair market value at the decedent's death, or the applicable alternate valuation date, less the amount allowed (determined with regard to section 1016(a)(2)(B)) to the taxpayer as deductions for exhaustion, wear and tear, obsolescence, amortization and depletion for the period held by the taxpayer prior to the decedent's death. The deduction allowed for a taxable year in which the decedent dies shall be an amount properly allocable to that part of the year prior to his death. For a discussion of the basis adjustment required by section 1014(b)(9) where property is held in trust, see paragraph (c) of this section.

(2) Where property coming within the purview of subparagraph (1) of this paragraph was held by the decedent and his surviving spouse as tenants by the entirety or as joint tenants with right of survivorship, and joint income tax returns were filed by the decedent and the surviving spouse in which the deductions referred to in subparagraph (1) were taken, there shall be allocated to the surviving spouse's interest in the property that proportion of the deductions allowed for each period for which the joint returns were filed which her income from the property bears to the total income from the property. Each spouse's income from the property shall be determined in accordance with local law.

(3) The application of this paragraph may be illustrated by the following examples:

Example (1). The taxpayer acquired income-producing property by gift on January 1, 1954. The property had a fair market value of $50,000 on the date of the donor's death, January 1, 1956, and was included in his gross estate at that amount for estate tax purposes as a transfer in contemplation of death. Depreciation in the amount of $750 per year was allowable for each of the taxable years 1954 and 1955. However, the taxpayer claimed depreciation in the amount of $500 for each of these years (resulting in a reduction in his taxes) and his income tax returns were accepted as filed. The adjusted basis of the property as of the date of the decedent's death is $49,000 ($50,000, the fair market value at the decedent's death, less $1,000, the total of the amounts actually allowed as deductions).

Example (2). On July 1, 1952, H purchased for $30,000 income-producing property which he conveyed to himself and W, his wife, as tenants by the entirety. Under local law each spouse was entitled to one-half of the income therefrom. H died on January 1, 1955, at which time the fair market value of the property was $40,000. The entire value of the property was included in H's gross estate. H and W filed joint income tax returns for the years 1952, 1953, and 1954. The total depreciation allowance for the year 1952 was $500 and for each of the other years 1953 and 1954 was $1,000. One-half of the $2,500 depreciation will be allocated to W. The adjusted basis of the property in W's hands [as] of January 1, 1955, was $38,750 ($40,000, value on the date of H's death, less $1,250, depreciation allocated to W for periods before H's death). However, if, under local law, all of the income from the property was allocable to H, no adjustment under this paragraph would be required and W's basis for the property as of the date of H's death would be $40,000.

(b) *Multiple interests in property described in section 1014(b)(9) and acquired from a decedent prior to his death.* (1) Where more than one person has an interest in property described in section 1014(b)(9) which was acquired from a decedent before his death, the basis of such property and of each of the several interests therein shall, in general, be determined and adjusted in accordance with the principles contained in §§ 1.1014-4 and 1.1014-5, relating to the uniformity of basis rule. Application of these principles to the determination of basis under section 1014(b)(9) is shown in the remaining subparagraphs of this paragraph in connection with certain commonly encountered situations involving multiple interests in property acquired from a decedent before his death.

(2) Where property is acquired from a decedent before his death, and the entire property is subsequently included in the decedent's gross estate for estate tax purposes, the uniform basis of the property, as well as the basis of each of the several interests in the property, shall be determined by taking into account the basis adjustments required by section 1014(a) owing to such inclusion of the entire property in the decedent's gross estate. For example, suppose that the decedent transfers property in trust, with a life estate to A, and the remainder to B or his estate. The transferred property consists of 100 shares of the common stock of X Corporation, with a basis of

Reg. § 1.1014-6(b)(2)

$10,000 at the time of the transfer. At the time of the decedent's death the value of the stock is $20,000. The transfer is held to have been made in contemplation of death and the entire value of the trust is included in the decedent's gross estate. Under section 1014(a), the uniform basis of the property in the hands of the trustee, the life tenant, and the remainderman, is $20,000. If immediately prior to the decedent's death, A's share of the uniform basis of $10,000 was $6,000, and B's share was $4,000, then, immediately after the decedent's death, A's share of the uniform basis of $20,000 is $12,000, and B's share is $8,000.

(3)(i) In cases where, due to the operation of the estate tax, only a portion of property acquired from a decedent before his death is included in the decedent's gross estate, as in cases where the decedent retained a reversion to take effect upon the expiration of a life estate in another, the uniform basis of the entire property shall be determined by taking into account any basis adjustments required by section 1014(a) owing to such inclusion of a portion of the property in the decedent's gross estate. In such cases the uniform basis is the adjusted basis of the entire property immediately prior to the decedent's death increased (or decreased) by an amount which bears the same relation to the total appreciation (or diminution) in value of the entire property (over the adjusted basis of the entire property immediately prior to the decedent's death) as the value of the property included in the decedent's gross estate bears to the value of the entire property. For example, assume that the decedent creates a trust to pay the income to A for life, remainder to B or his estate. The trust instrument further provides that if the decedent should survive A, the income shall be paid to the decedent for life. Assume that the decedent predeceases A, so that, due to the operation of the estate tax, only the present value of the remainder interest is included in the decedent's gross estate. The trust consists of 100 shares of the common stock of X Corporation with an adjusted basis immediately prior to the decedent's death of $10,000 (as determined under section 1015). At the time of the decedent's death the value of the stock is $20,000, and the value of the remainder interest in the hands of B is $8,000. The uniform basis of the entire property following the decedent's death is $14,000, computed as follows:

Uniform basis prior to decedent's death $10,000
plus
Increase in uniform basis (determined by the following formula) 4,000

$$\frac{\text{Increase in uniform basis (to be determined)}}{\$10{,}000 \text{ (total appreciation)}} = \frac{\$8{,}000 \text{ (value of property included in gross estate)}}{\$20{,}000 \text{ (value of entire property)}}$$

Uniform basis under section 1014(a) $14,000

(ii) In cases of the type described in subdivision (i) of this subparagraph, the basis of any interest which is included in the decedent's gross estate may be ascertained by adding to (or subtracting from) the basis of such interest determined immediately prior to the decedent's death the increase (or decrease) in the uniform basis of the property attributable to the inclusion of the interest in the decedent's gross estate. Where the interest is sold or otherwise disposed of at any time after the decedent's death, proper adjustment must be made in order to reflect the change in value of the interest on account of the passage of time, as provided in § 1.1014-5. For an illustration of the operation of this subdivision, see step 6 of the example in § 1.1014-7.

(iii) In cases of the type described in subdivision (i) of this subparagraph (cases where, due to the operation of the estate tax, only a portion of the property is included in the decedent's gross estate), the basis for computing the depreciation, amortization, or depletion allowance shall be the uniform basis of the property determined under section 1014(a). However, the manner of taking into account such allowance computed with respect to such uniform basis is subject to the following limitations:

(a) In cases where the value of the life interest is not included in the decedent's gross estate, the amount of such allowance to the life tenant under section 167(h) (or section 611(b)) shall not exceed (or be less than) the amount which would have been allowable to the life tenant if no portion of the basis of the property was determined under section 1014(a). Proper adjustment shall be made for the amount allowable to the life tenant, as required by section 1016. Thus, an appropriate adjustment shall be made to the uniform basis of the property in the hands of the trustee, to the basis of the life interest in the hands of the life tenant, and to the basis of the remainder in the hands of the remainderman.

(b) Any remaining allowance (that is, the increase in the amount of depreciation, amor-

Reg. § 1.1014-6(b)(3)

Basis Rules of General Application 51,937

See p. 20,601 for regulations not amended to reflect law changes

tization, or depletion allowable resulting from any increase in the uniform basis of the property under section 1014(a)) shall not be allowed to the life tenant. The remaining allowance shall, instead, be allowed to the trustee to the extent that the trustee both (1) is required or permitted, by the governing trust instrument (or under local law), to maintain a reserve for depreciation, amortization, or depletion, and (2) actually maintains such a reserve. If, in accordance with the preceding sentence, the trustee does maintain such a reserve, the remaining allowance shall be taken into account, under section 1016, in adjusting the uniform basis of the property in the hands of the trustee and in adjusting the basis of the remainder interest in the hands of the remainderman, but shall not be taken into account, under section 1016, in determining the basis of the life interest in the hands of the life tenant. For an example of the operation of this subdivision, see paragraph (b) of § 1.1014-7.

(4) In cases where the basis of any interest in property is not determined under section 1014(a), as where such interest (i) is not included in the decedent's gross estate, or (ii) is sold, exchanged or otherwise disposed of before the decedent's death, the basis of such interest shall be determined under other applicable provisions of the Code. To illustrate, in the example shown in subparagraph (3)(i) of this paragraph the basis of the life estate in the hands of A shall be determined under section 1015, relating to the basis of property acquired by gift. If, on the other hand, A had sold his life interest prior to the decedent's death, the basis of the life estate in the hands of A's transferee would be determined under section 1012.

(c) *Adjustments for deductions allowed prior to the decedent's death.* (1) As stated in paragraph (a) of this section, section 1014(b)(9) requires a reduction in the uniform basis of property acquired from a decedent before his death for certain deductions allowed in respect of such property during the decedent's lifetime. In general, the amount of the reduction in basis required by section 1014(b)(9) shall be the aggregate of the deductions allowed in respect of the property, but shall not include deductions allowed in respect of the property to the decedent himself. In cases where, owing to the operation of the estate tax, only a part of the value of the entire property is included in the decedent's gross estate, the amount of the reduction required by section 1014(b)(9) shall be an amount which bears the same relation to the total of all deductions (described in paragraph (a) of this section) allowed in respect of the property as the value of the property included in the decedent's gross estate bears to the value of the entire property.

(2) The application of this paragraph may be illustrated by the following examples:

Example (1). The decedent creates a trust to pay the income to A for life, remainder to B or his estate. The property transferred in trust consists of an apartment building with a basis of $50,000 at the time of the transfer. The decedent dies 2 years after the transfer is made and the gift is held to have been made in contemplation of death. Depreciation on the property was allowed in the amount of $1,000 annually. At the time of the decedent's death the value of the property is $58,000. The uniform basis of the property in the hands of the trustee, the life tenant, and the remainderman, immediately after the decedent's death is $56,000 ($58,000, fair market value of the property immediately after the decedent's death, reduced by $2,000, deductions for depreciation allowed prior to the decedent's death).

Example (2). The decedent creates a trust to pay the income to A for life, remainder to B or his estate. The trust instrument provides that if the decedent should survive A, the income shall be paid to the decedent for life. The decedent predeceases A and the present value of the remainder interest is included in the decedent's gross estate for estate tax purposes. The property transferred consists of an apartment building with a basis of $110,000 at the time of the transfer. Following the creation of the trust and during the balance of the decedent's life, deductions for depreciation were allowed on the property in the amount of $10,000. At the time of decedent's death the value of the entire property is $150,000, and the value of the remainder interest is $100,000. Accordingly, the uniform basis of the property in the hands of the trustee, the life tenant, and the remainderman, as adjusted under section 1014(b)(9), is $126,666, computed as follows:

Uniform basis prior to decedent's death $100,000
plus
Increase in uniform basis—before reduction (determined by the following formula) 33,333

Reg. § 1.1014-6(c)(2)

Basis Rules of General Application

See p. 20,601 for regulations not amended to reflect law changes

$$\frac{\text{Increase in uniform basis (to be determined)}}{\$50,000 \text{ (total appreciation of property since time of transfer)}} = \frac{\$100,000 \text{ (value of property included in gross estate)}}{\$150,000 \text{ (value of entire property)}}$$

	$133,333
less Deductions allowed prior to decedent's death—taken into account under section 1014(b)(9) (determined by the following formula)	6,667

$$\frac{\text{Prior deductions taken into account (to be determined)}}{\$10,000 \text{ (total deductions allowed prior to decedent's death)}} = \frac{\$100,000 \text{ (value of property included in gross estate)}}{\$150,000 \text{ (value of entire property)}}$$

Uniform basis under section 1014	$126,666

[Reg. § 1.1014-6.]

☐ [T.D. 6265, 11-6-57. Amended by T.D. 6712, 3-23-64 and T.D. 7142, 9-23-71.]

[Reg. § 1.1014-7]

§ 1.1014-7. Example applying rules of §§ 1.1014-4 through 1.1014-6 to case involving multiple interests.—(a) On January 1, 1950, the decedent creates a trust to pay the income to A for life, remainder to B or his estate. The trust instrument provides that if the decedent should survive A, the income shall be paid to the decedent for life. The decedent, who died on January 1, 1955, predeceases A, so that, due to the operation of the estate tax, only the present value of the remainder interest is included in the decedent's gross estate. The trust consists of an apartment building with a basis of $30,000 at the time of transfer. Under the trust instrument the trustee is required to maintain a reserve for depreciation. During the decedent's lifetime depreciation is allowed in the amount of $800 annually. At the time of the decedent's death the value of the apartment building is $45,000. A, the life tenant, is 43 years of age at the time of the decedent's death. Immediately after the decedent's death, the uniform basis of the entire property under section 1014(a) is $32,027; A's basis for the life interest is $15,553; and B's basis for the remainder interest is $16,474, computed as follows:

Step 1. Uniform basis (adjusted) immediately prior to decedent's death:	
Basis at time of transfer	$30,000
less	
Depreciation allowed under section 1016 before decedent's death ($800 × 5)	4,000
	$26,000
Step 2. Value of property included in decedent's gross estate:	
0.40180 (remainder factor, age 43) × $45,000 (value of entire property)	$18,081
Step 3. Uniform basis of property under section 1014(a), before reduction required by section 1014(b)(9):	
Uniform basis (adjusted) prior to decedent's death	26,000
Increase in uniform basis (determined by the following formula)	7,634

$$\frac{\text{Increase in uniform basis (to be determined)}}{\$19,000 \text{ (total appreciation, \$45,000—\$26,000)}} = \frac{\$18,081 \text{ (value of property included in gross estate)}}{\$45,000 \text{ (value of entire propery)}}$$

	$33,634
Step 4. Uniform basis reduced as required by section 1014(b)(9) for deductions allowed prior to death:	
Uniform basis before reduction	33,634
less	
Deductions allowed prior to decedent's death—taken into account under section 1014(b)(9) (determined by the following formula)	1,607

Reg. § 1.1014-7(a)

Basis Rules of General Application

See p. 20,601 for regulations not amended to reflect law changes

$$\frac{\text{Prior deductions taken into account (to be determined)}}{\$4{,}000 \text{ (total deductions allowed prior to decedent's death)}} = \frac{\$18{,}081 \text{ (value of property included in gross estate)}}{\$45{,}000 \text{ (value of entire property)}}$$

$32,027

Step 5. A's basis for the life interest at the time of the decedent's death, determined under section 1015:
0.59820 (life factor, age 43) × $26,000 15,553

Step 6. B's basis for the remainder interest, determined under section 1014(a):
Basis prior to the decedent's death:
0.40180 (remainder factor, age 43) × $26,000 10,447
plus
Increase in uniform basis owing to decedent's death:
Increase in uniform basis $7,634
Reduction required by section 1014(b)(9) $1,607 $6,027

$16,474

(b) Assume the same facts as in (a) of this section. Assume further, that following the decedent's death depreciation is allowed in the amount of $1,000 annually. As of January 1, 1964, when A's age is 52, the adjusted uniform basis of the entire property is $23,027; A's basis for the life interest is $9,323; and B's basis for the remainder interest is $13,704, computed as follows:

Step 7. Uniform basis (adjusted) as of January 1, 1964:
Uniform basis determined under section 1014(a), reduced as required by section 1014(b)(9)............................... $32,027
Depreciation allowed since decedent's death ($1,000 × 9) 9,000

$23,027

Step 8. Allocable share of adjustment for depreciation allowable in the nine years since the decedent's death:
A's interest
0.49587 (life factor, age 52) × $7,200 ($800, depreciation attributable to uniform basis before increase under section 1014(a), × 9) 3,570

B's interest
0.50413 (remainder factor, age 52) × $7,200 ($800, depreciation attributable to uniform basis before increase under section 1014(a), × 9) 3,630
plus
$200 (annual depreciation attributable to increase in uniform basis under section 1014(a))
× 9 1,800

$5,430

Step 9. Tentative bases of A's and B's interests as of January 1, 1964 (before adjustment for depreciation).
A's interest
0.49587 (life factor, age 52) × $26,000 (adjusted uniform basis immediately before decedent's death) 12,893

B's interest
0.50413 (remainder factor, age 52) × $26,000 (adjusted uniform basis immediately before decedent's death) 13,107
plus
Increase in uniform basis owing to inclusion of remainder in decedent's gross estate..................................... 6,027

$19,134

Step 10. Bases of A's and B's interests as of January 1, 1964
A
Tentative basis (Step 9)..................................... $12,893
less
Allocable depreciation (Step 8) 3,570

$9,323

Reg. § 1.1014-7(b)

51,940 Basis Rules of General Application

See p. 20,601 for regulations not amended to reflect law changes

	B	
Tentative basis (Step 9)		$19,134
less		
Allocable depreciation (Step 8)		5,430
		$13,704

[Reg. § 1.1014-7.]

☐ [T.D. 6265, 11-6-57.]

[Reg. § 1.1014-8]

§ 1.1014-8. Bequest, devise, or inheritance of a remainder interest.—(a)(1) Where property is transferred for life, with remainder in fee, and the remainderman dies before the life tenant, no adjustment is made to the uniform basis of the property on the death of the remainderman (see paragraph (a) of § 1.1014-4). However, the basis of the remainderman's heir, legatee, or devisee for the remainder interest is determined by adding to (or subtracting from) the part of the adjusted uniform basis assigned to the remainder interest (determined in accordance with the principles set forth in §§ 1.1014-4 through 1.1014-6) the difference between—

(i) The value of the remainder interest included in the remainderman's estate, and

(ii) The basis of the remainder interest immediately prior to the remainderman's death.

(2) The basis of any property distributed to the heir, legatee, or devisee upon termination of a trust (or legal life estate) or at any other time (unless included in the gross income of the legatee or devisee) shall be determined by adding to (or subtracting from) the adjusted uniform basis of the property thus distributed the difference between—

(i) The value of the remainder interest in the property included in the remainderman's estate, and

(ii) The basis of the remainder interest in the property immediately prior to the remainderman's death.

(b) The provisions of paragraph (a) of this section are illustrated by the following examples:

Example (1). Assume that, under the will of a decedent, property consisting of common stock with a value of $1,000 at the time of the decedent's death is transferred in trust, to pay the income to A for life, remainder to B or to B's estate. B predeceases A and bequeaths the remainder interest to C. Assume that B dies on January 1, 1956, and that the value of the stock originally transferred is $1,600 at B's death. A's age at that time is 37. The value of the remainder interest included in B's estate is $547 (0.34185, remainder factor age 37, × $1,600), and hence $547 is C's basis for the remainder interest immediately after B's death. Assume that C sells the remainder interest on January 1, 1961, when A's age is 42. C's basis for the remainder interest at the time of such sale is $596, computed as follows:

Basis of remainder interest computed with respect to uniform basis of entire property (0.39131, remainder factor age 42, × $1,000, uniform basis of entire property)		$391
plus		
Value of remainder interest included in B's estate	$547	
less		
Basis of remainder interest immediately prior to B's death (0.34185, remainder factor of age 37, × $1,000)	342	205
Basis of C's remainder interest at the time of sale		$596

Example (2). Assume the same facts as in example (1), except that C does not sell the remainder interest. Upon A's death terminating the trust, C's basis for the stock distributed to him is computed as follows:

Uniform basis of the property, adjusted to date of termination of the trust		$1,000
plus		
Value of remainder interest in the property at the time of B's death	$547	
less		
B's share of uniform basis of the property at the time of his death	342	205
C's basis for the stock distributed to him upon the termination of the trust		$1,205

Reg. § 1.1014-8(a)(2)

Example (3). Assume the same facts as in example (2), except that the property transferred is depreciable. Assume further that $100 of depreciation was allowed prior to B's death and that $50 of depreciation is allowed between the time of B's death and the termination of the trust. Upon A's death terminating the trust, C's basis for the property distributed to him is computed as follows:

Uniform basis of the property, adjusted to date of termination of the trust:		
Uniform basis immediately after decedent's death	$1,000	
Depreciation allowed following decedent's death	150	$850
plus		
Value of remainder interest in the property at the time of B's death		$547
less		
B's share of uniform basis of the property at the time of his death (0.34185 × $900, uniform basis at B's death)	$308	$239
C's basis for the property distributed to him upon the termination of the trust		$1,089

(c) The rules stated in paragraph (a) of this section do not apply where the basis of the remainder interest in the hands of the remainderman's transferee is determined by reference to its cost to such transferee. See, also, paragraph (a) of § 1.1014-4. Thus, if, in example *(1)* of paragraph (b) of this section, B sold his remainder interest to C for $547 in cash, C's basis for the stock distributed to him upon the death of A terminating the trust is $547. [Reg. § 1.1014-8.]

☐ [*T.D.* 6265, 11-6-57.]

[Reg. § 1.1014-9]

§ 1.1014-9. Special rule with respect to DISC stock.—(a) *In general.* If property consisting of stock of a DISC or former DISC (as defined in section 992(a)(1) or (3) as the case may be) is considered to have been acquired from a decedent (within the meaning of paragraph (a) or (b) of § 1.1014-2), the uniform basis of such stock under section 1014, as determined pursuant to §§ 1.1014-1 through 1.1014-8 shall be reduced as provided in this section. Such uniform basis shall be reduced by the amount (hereinafter referred to in this section as the amount of reduction), if any, which the decedent would have included in his gross income under section 995(c) as a dividend if the decedent had lived and sold such stock at its fair market value on the estate tax valuation date. If the alternate valuation date for Federal estate tax purposes is elected under section 2032, in computing the gain which the decedent would have had if he had lived and sold the stock on the alternate valuation date, the decedent's basis shall be determined with reduction for any distributions with respect to the stock which may have been made, after the date of the decedent's death and on or before the alternate valuation date, from the DISC's previously taxed income (as defined in section 996(f)(2)). For this purpose, the last sentence of section 996(e)(2) (relating to reductions of basis of DISC stock) shall not apply. For purposes of this section, if the corporation is not a DISC or former DISC at the date of the decedent's death but is a DISC for a taxable year which begins after such date and on or before the alternate valuation date, the corporation will be considered to be a DISC or former DISC only if the alternate valuation date is elected. The provisions of this paragraph apply with respect to stock of a DISC or former DISC which is included in the gross estate of the decedent, including but not limited to property which—

(1) Is acquired from the decedent before his death, and the entire property is subsequently included in the decedent's gross estate for estate tax purposes, or

(2) Is acquired property described in paragraph (d) of § 1.1014-3.

(b) *Portion of property acquired from decedent before his death included in decedent's gross estate*—(1) *In general.* In cases where, due to the operation of the estate tax, only a portion of property which consists of stock of a DISC or former DISC and which is acquired from a decedent before his death is included in the decedent's gross estate, the uniform basis of such stock under section 1014, as determined pursuant to § 1.1014-1 through § 1.1014-8, shall be reduced by an amount which bears the same ratio to the amount of reduction which would have been determined under paragraph (a) of this section if the entire property consisting of such stock were included in the decedent's gross estate as the value of such property included in the decedent's gross estate bears to the value of the entire property.

(2) *Example.* The provisions of this paragraph may be illustrated by the following example:

Reg. § 1.1014-9(b)(2)

Basis Rules of General Application
See p. 20,601 for regulations not amended to reflect law changes

Example. The decedent creates a trust during his lifetime to pay the income to A for life, remainder to B or his estate. The trust instrument further provides that if the decedent should survive A, the income shall be paid to the decedent for life. The decedent predeceases A, so that, due to the operation of the estate tax, only the present value of the remainder interest is included in the decedent's gross estate. The trust consists of 100 shares of the stock of X Corporation (which is a DISC at the time the shares are transferred to the trust and at the time of the decedent's death) with an adjusted basis immediately prior to the decedent's death of $10,000 (as determined under section 1015). At the time of the decedent's death the value of the stock is $20,000, and the value of the remainder interest in the hands of B is $8,000. Applying the principles of paragraph (b)(3)(i) of § 1.1014-6, the uniform basis of the entire property following the decedent's death, prior to reduction pursuant to this paragraph, is $14,000. The amount of reduction which would have been determined under paragraph (a) of this section if the entire property consisting of such stock of X Corporation were included in the decedent's gross estate is $5,000. The uniform basis of the entire property following the decedent's death, as reduced pursuant to this paragraph, is $12,000, computed as follows:

Uniform basis under section 1014(a), prior to reduction pursuant to this paragraph	$14,000
Less decrease in uniform basis (determined by the following formula)	2,000

$$\frac{\text{Reduction in uniform basis (to be determined)}}{\$5,000 \text{ (amount of reduction if paragraph (a) applied)}} = \frac{\$8,000 \text{ (value of property included in gross estate)}}{\$20,000 \text{ (value of entire property)}}$$

Uniform basis under section 1014(a) reduced pursuant to this paragraph . . $12,000

(c) *Estate tax valuation date.* For purposes of section 1014(d) and this section, the estate tax valuation date is the date of the decedent's death or, in the case of an election under section 2032, the applicable valuation date prescribed by that section.

(d) *Examples.* The provisions of this section may be illustrated by the following examples:

Example (1). At the date of A's death, his DISC stock has a fair market value of $100. The estate does not elect the alternate valuation allowed by section 2032, and A's basis in such stock is $60 at the date of his death. The person who acquires such stock from the decedent will take as a basis for such stock its fair market value at A's death ($100), reduced by the amount which would have been included in A's gross income under section 995(c) as a dividend if A had sold stock on the date he died. Thus, if the amount that would have been treated as a dividend under section 995(c) were $30, such person will take a basis of $70 for such stock ($100, reduced by $30). If such person were immediately to sell the DISC stock so received for $100, $30 of the proceeds from the sale would be treated as a dividend by such person under section 995(c).

Example (2). Assume the same facts as in example (1) except that the estate elects the alternate valuation allowed by section 2032, the DISC stock has a fair market value of $140 on the alternate valuation date, the amount that would have been treated as a dividend under section 995(c) in the event of a sale on such date is $50 and the DISC has $20 of previously taxed income which accrued after the date of the decedent's death and before the alternate valuation date. The basis of the person who acquires such stock will be $90 determined as follows:

(1) Fair market value of DISC stock at alternate valuation date	$140
(2) Less: Amount which would have been treated as a dividend under section 995(c)	50
(3) Basis of person who acquires DISC stock	$ 90

If a distribution of $20 attributable to such previously taxed income had been made by the DISC on or before the alternate valuation date (with the DISC stock having a fair market value of $120 after such distribution), the basis of the person who acquires such stock will be $70 determined as follows:

(1) Fair market value of DISC stock at alternate valuation date	$120
(2) Less: Amount which would have been treated as a dividend under section 995(c)	50
(3) Basis of person who acquires DISC stock	$ 70

[Reg. § 1.1014-9.]

☐ [T.D. 7283, 8-2-73.]

[Reg. § 1.1015-1]

§ 1.1015-1. Basis of property acquired by gift after December 31, 1920.—(a) *General rule.* (1) In the case of property acquired by gift after December 31, 1920 (whether by a transfer in trust or otherwise), the basis of the property for the purpose of determining gain is the same as it

Reg. § 1.1015-1(a)

Basis Rules of General Application

See p. 20,601 for regulations not amended to reflect law changes

would be in the hands of the donor or the last preceding owner by whom it was not acquired by gift. The same rule applies in determining loss unless the basis (adjusted for the period prior to the date of gift in accordance with sections 1016 and 1017) is greater than the fair market value of the property at the time of the gift. In such case, the basis for determining loss is the fair market value at the time of the gift.

(2) The provisions of subparagraph (1) of this paragraph may be illustrated by the following example.

Example. A acquires by gift income-producing property which has an adjusted basis of $100,000 at the date of gift. The fair market value of the property at the date of gift is $90,000. A later sells the property for $95,000. In such case there is neither gain nor loss. The basis for determining loss is $90,000; therefore, there is no loss. Furthermore, there is no gain, since the basis for determining gain is $100,000.

(3) If the facts necessary to determine the basis of property in the hands of the donor or the last preceding owner by whom it was not acquired by gift are unknown to the donee, the district director shall, if possible, obtain such facts from such donor or last preceding owner, or any other person cognizant thereof. If the district director finds it impossible to obtain such facts, the basis in the hands of such donor or last preceding owner shall be the fair market value of such property as found by the district director as of the date or approximate date at which, according to the best information the district director is able to obtain, such property was acquired by such donor or last preceding owner. See paragraph (e) of this section for rules relating to fair market value.

(b) *Uniform basis; proportionate parts of.* Property acquired by gift has a single or uniform basis although more than one person may acquire an interest in such property. The uniform basis of the property remains fixed subject to proper adjustment for items under sections 1016 and 1017. However, the value of the proportionate parts of the uniform basis represented, for instance, by the respective interests of the life tenant and remainderman are adjustable to reflect the change in the relative values of such interest on account of the lapse of time. The portion of the basis attributable to an interest at the time of its sale or other disposition shall be determined under the rule provided in § 1.1014-5. In determining gain or loss from the sale or other disposition after October 9, 1969, of a term interest in property (as defined in § 1.1001-1(f)(2)) the adjusted basis of which is determined pursuant, or by reference, to section 1015, that part of the adjusted uniform basis assignable under the rules of § 1.1014-5(a) to the interest sold or otherwise disposed of shall be disregarded to the extent and in the manner provided by section 1001(e) and § 1.1001-1(f).

(c) *Time of acquisition.* The date that the donee acquires an interest in property by gift is when the donor relinquishes dominion over the property and not necessarily when title to the property is acquired by the donee. Thus, the date that the donee acquires an interest in property by gift where he is a successor in interest, such as in the case of a remainderman of a life estate or a beneficiary of the distribution of the corpus of a trust, is the date such interests are created by the donor and not the date the property is actually acquired.

(d) *Property acquired by gift from a decedent dying after December 31, 1953.* If an interest in property was acquired by the taxpayer by gift from a donor dying after December 31, 1953, under conditions which require the inclusion of the property in the donor's gross estate for estate tax purposes, and the property had not been sold, exchanged, or otherwise disposed of by the taxpayer before the donor's death, see the rules prescribed in section 1014 and the regulations thereunder.

(e) *Fair market value.* For the purposes of this section, the value of property as appraised for the purpose of the Federal gift tax, or, if the gift is not subject to such tax, its value as appraised for the purpose of a State gift tax, shall be deemed to be the fair market value of the property at the time of the gift.

(f) *Reinvestments by fiduciary.* If the property is an investment by the fiduciary under the terms of the gift (as, for example, in the case of a sale by the fiduciary of property transferred under the terms of the gift, and the reinvestment of the proceeds), the cost or other basis to the fiduciary is taken in lieu of the basis specified in paragraph (a) of this section.

(g) *Records.* To insure a fair and adequate determination of the proper basis under section 1015, persons making or receiving gifts of property should preserve and keep accessible a record of the facts necessary to determine the cost of the property and, if pertinent, its fair market value as of March 1, 1913, or its fair market value as of the date of the gift. [Reg. § 1.1015-1.]

☐ [*T.D.* 6265, 11-6-57. *Amended by T.D.* 6693, 12-2-63 *and T.D.* 7142, 9-23-71.]

[Reg. § 1.1015-2]

§ 1.1015-2. **Transfer of property in trust after December 31, 1920.**—(a) *General rule.* (1) In the case of property acquired after December 31,

1920, by transfer in trust (other than by a transfer in trust by a gift, bequest, or devise) the basis of property so acquired is the same as it would be in the hands of the grantor increased in the amount of gain or decreased in the amount of loss recognized to the grantor upon such transfer under the law applicable to the year in which the transfer was made. If the taxpayer acquired the property by a transfer in trust, this basis applies whether the property be in the hands of the trustee, or the beneficiary, and whether acquired prior to the termination of the trust and distribution of the property, or thereafter.

(2) The principles stated in paragraph (b) of § 1.1015-1 concerning the uniform basis are applicable in determining the basis of property where more than one person acquires an interest in property by transfer in trust after December 31, 1920.

(b) *Reinvestment by fiduciary.* If the property is an investment made by the fiduciary (as, for example, in the case of a sale by the fiduciary of property transferred by the grantor, and the reinvestment of the proceeds), the cost or other basis to the fiduciary is taken in lieu of the basis specified in paragraph (a) of this section. [Reg. § 1.1015-2.]

☐ [*T.D. 6265,* 11-6-57.]

[Reg. § 1.1015-3]

§ 1.1015-3. Gift or transfer in trust before January 1, 1921.—(a) In the case of property acquired by gift or transfer in trust before January 1, 1921, the basis of such property is the fair market value thereof at the time of the gift or at the time of the transfer in trust.

(b) The principles stated in paragraph (b) of § 1.1015-1 concerning the uniform basis are applicable in determining the basis of property where more than one person acquires an interest in property by gift or transfer in trust before January 1, 1921. In addition, if an interest in such property was acquired from a decedent and the property had not been sold, exchanged, or otherwise disposed of before the death of the donor, the rules prescribed in section 1014 and the regulations thereunder are applicable in determining the basis of such property in the hands of the taxpayer. [Reg. § 1.1015-3.]

☐ [*T.D. 6265,* 11-6-57.]

[Reg. § 1.1015-4]

§ 1.1015-4. Transfers in part a gift and in part a sale.—(a) *General rule.* Where a transfer of property is in part a sale and in part a gift, the unadjusted basis of the property in the hands of the transferee is the sum of—

(1) Whichever of the following is the greater:

(i) The amount paid by the transferee for the property, or

(ii) The transferor's adjusted basis for the property at the time of the transfer, and

(2) The amount of increase, if any, in basis authorized by section 1015(d) for gift tax paid (see § 1.1015-5).

For determining loss, the unadjusted basis of the property in the hands of the transferee shall not be greater than the fair market value of the property at the time of such transfer. For determination of gain or loss of the transferor, see § 1.1001-1(e) and § 1.1011-2. For special rule where there has been a charitable contribution of less than a taxpayer's entire interest in property, see section 170(e)(2) and § 1.170A-4(c).

(b) *Examples.* The rule of paragraph (a) of this section is illustrated by the following examples:

Example (1). If A transfers property to his son for $30,000, and such property at the time of the transfer has an adjusted basis of $30,000 in A's hands (and a fair market value of $60,000), the unadjusted basis of the property in the hands of the son is $30,000.

Example (2). If A transfers property to his son for $60,000, and such property at the time of transfer had an adjusted basis of $30,000 in A's hands (and a fair market value of $90,000), the unadjusted basis of such property in the hands of the son is $60,000.

Example (3). If A transfers property to his son for $30,000, and such property at the time of transfer has an adjusted basis in A's hands of $60,000 (and a fair market value of $90,000), the unadjusted basis of such property in the hands of the son is $60,000.

Example (4). If A transfers property to his son for $30,000 and such property at the time of transfer has an adjusted basis of $90,000 in A's hands (and a fair market value of $60,000), the unadjusted basis of the property in the hands of the son is $90,000. However, since the adjusted basis of the property in A's hands at the time of the transfer was greater than the fair market value at that time, for the purpose of determining any loss on a later sale or other disposition of the property by the son its unadjusted basis in his hands is $60,000. [Reg. § 1.1015-4.]

☐ [*T.D. 6265,* 11-6-57. Amended by *T.D. 6693,* 12-2-63 and *T.D. 7207,* 10-3-72.]

[Reg. § 1.1015-5]

§ 1.1015-5. Increased basis for gift tax paid.—(a) *General rule in the case of gifts made on or before December 31, 1976.*—(1)(i) Subject to the conditions and limitations provided in section

Reg. § 1.1015-3(a)

1015(d), as added by the Technical Amendments Act of 1958, the basis (as determined under section 1015(a) and paragraph (a) of § 1.1015-1) of property acquired by gift is increased by the amount of gift tax paid with respect to the gift of such property. Under section 1015(d)(1)(A), such increase in basis applies to property acquired by gift on or after September 2, 1958 (the date of enactment of the Technical Amendments Act of 1958). Under section 1015(d)(1)(B), such increase in basis applies to property acquired by gift before September 2, 1958, and not sold, exchanged, or otherwise disposed of before such date. If section 1015(d)(1)(A) applies, the basis of the property is increased as of the date of the gift regardless of the date of payment of the gift tax. For example, if the property was acquired by gift on September 8, 1958, and sold by the donee on October 15, 1958, the basis of the property would be increased (subject to the limitation of section 1015(d)) as of September 8, 1958 (the date of the gift), by the amount of gift tax applicable to such gift even though such tax was not paid until March 1, 1959. If section 1015 (d)(1)(B) applies, any increase in the basis of the property due to gift tax paid (regardless of date of payment) with respect to the gift is made as of September 2, 1958. Any increase in basis under section 1015(d) can be no greater than the amount by which the fair market value of the property at the time of the gift exceeds the basis of such property in the hands of the donor at the time of the gift. See paragraph (b) of this section for rules for determining the amount of gift tax paid in respect of property transferred by gift.

(ii) With respect to property acquired by gift before September 2, 1958, the provisions of section 1015(d) and this section do not apply if, before such date, the donee has sold, exchanged, or otherwise disposed of such property. The phrase "sold, exchanged, or otherwise disposed of" includes the surrender of a stock certificate for corporate assets in complete or partial liquidation of a corporation pursuant to section 331. It also includes the exchange of property for property of a like kind such as the exchange of one apartment house for another. The phrase does not, however, extend to transactions which are mere changes in form. Thus, it does not include a transfer of assets to a corporation in exchange for its stock in a transaction with respect to which no gain or loss would be recognizable for income tax purposes under section 351. Nor does it include an exchange of stock or securities in a corporation for stock or securities in the same corporation or another corporation in a transaction such as a merger, recapitalization, reorganization, or other transaction described in section 368(a) or 355, with respect to which no gain or loss is recognizable for income tax purposes under section 354 or 355. If a binding contract for the sale, exchange, or other disposition of property is entered into, the property is considered as sold, exchanged, or otherwise disposed of on the effective date of the contract, unless the contract is not subsequently carried out substantially in accordance with its terms. The effective date of a contract is normally the date it is entered into (and not the date it is consummated, or the date legal title to the property passes) unless the contract specifies a different effective date. For purposes of this subdivision, in determining whether a transaction comes within the phrase "sold, exchanged, or otherwise disposed of", if a transaction would be treated as a mere change in the form of the property if it occurred in a taxable year subject to the Internal Revenue Code of 1954, it will be so treated if the transaction occurred in a taxable year subject to the Internal Revenue Code of 1939 or prior revenue law.

(2) Application of the provisions of subparagraph (1) of this paragraph may be illustrated by the following examples:

Example (1). In 1938, A purchased a business building at a cost of $120,000. On September 2, 1958, at which time the property had an adjusted basis in A's hands of $60,000, he gave the property to his nephew, B. At the time of the gift to B, the property had a fair market value of $65,000 with respect to which A paid a gift tax in the amount of $7,545. The basis of the property in B's hands at the time of the gift, as determined under section 1015(a) and § 1.1015-1, would be the same as the adjusted basis in A's hands at the time of the gift, or $60,000. Under section 1015(d) and this section, the basis of the building in B's hands as of the date of the gift would be increased by the amount of the gift tax paid with respect to such gift, limited to an amount by which the fair market value of the property at the time of the gift exceeded the basis of the property in the hands of A at the time of gift, or $5,000. Therefore, the basis of the property in B's hands immediately after the gift, both for determining gain or loss on the sale of the property, would be $65,000.

Example (2). C purchased property in 1938 at a cost of $100,000. On October 1, 1952, at which time the property had an adjusted basis of $72,000 in C's hands, he gave the property to his daughter, D. At the date of the gift to D, the property had a fair market value of $85,000 with respect to which C paid a gift tax in the amount of $11,745. On September 2, 1958, D still held the property which then had an adjusted basis in her hands of $65,000. Since the excess of the fair

Reg. § 1.1015-5(a)(2)

market value of the property at the time of the gift to D over the adjusted basis of the property in C's hands at such time is greater than the amount of gift tax paid, the basis of the property in D's hands would be increased as of September 2, 1958, by the amount of the gift tax paid, or $11,745. The adjusted basis of the property in D's hands, both for determining gain or loss on the sale of the property, would then be $76,745 ($65,000 plus $11,745).

Example (3). On December 31, 1951, E gave to his son, F, 500 shares of common stock of the X Corporation which shares had been purchased earlier by E at a cost of $100 per share, or a total cost of $50,000. The basis in E's hands was still $50,000 on the date of the gift to F. On the date of the gift, the fair market value of the 500 shares was $80,000 with respect to which E paid a gift tax in the amount of $10,695. In 1956, the 500 shares of X Corporation stock were exchanged for 500 shares of common stock of the Y Corporation in a reorganization with respect to which no gain or loss was recognized for income tax purposes under section 354. F still held the 500 shares of Y Corporation stock on September 2, 1958. Under such circumstances, the 500 shares of X Corporation stock would not, for purposes of section 1015(d) and this section, be considered as having been "sold, exchanged, or otherwise disposed of" by F before September 2, 1958. Therefore, the basis of the 500 shares of Y Corporation stock held by F as of such date would, by reason of section 1015(d) and this section, be increased by $10,695, the amount of gift tax paid with respect to the gift to F of the X Corporation stock.

Example (4). On November 15, 1953, G gave H property which had a fair market value of $53,000 and a basis in the hands of G of $20,000. G paid gift tax of $5,250 on the transfer. On November 16, 1956, H gave the property to J who still held it on September 2, 1958. The value of the property on the date of the gift to J was $63,000 and H paid gift tax of $7,125 on the transfer. Since the property was not sold, exchanged, or otherwise disposed of by J before September 2, 1958, and the gift tax paid on the transfer to J did not exceed $43,000 ($63,000, fair market value of property at time of gift to J, less $20,000, basis of property in H's hands at that time), the basis of property in his hands is increased on September 2, 1958, by $7,125, the amount of gift tax paid by H on the transfer. No increase in basis is allowed for the $5,250 gift tax paid by G on the transfer to H, since H had sold, exchanged, or otherwise disposed of the property before September 2, 1958.

(b) *Amount of gift tax paid with respect to gifts made on or before December 31, 1976.*—(1)(i) If only one gift was made during a certain "calendar period" (as defined in § 25.2502-1(c)(1)), the entire amount of the gift tax paid under chapter 12 or the corresponding provisions of prior revenue laws for that calendar period is the amount of the gift tax paid with respect to the gift.

(ii) If more than one gift was made during a certain calendar period, the amount of the gift tax paid under chapter 12 or the corresponding provisions of prior revenue laws with respect to any specified gift made during that calendar period is an amount, A, which bears the same ratio to B (the total gift tax paid for that calendar period) as C (the "amount of the gift," computed as described in this paragraph (b)(1)(ii)) bears to D (the total taxable gifts for the calendar period computed without deduction for the gift tax specific exemption under section 2521 (as in effect prior to its repeal by the Tax Reform Act of 1976) or the corresponding provisions of prior revenue laws).

(iii) If a gift consists of more than one item of property, the gift tax paid with respect to each item shall be computed by allocating to each item a proportionate part of the gift tax paid with respect to the gift, computed in accordance with the provisions of this paragraph.

(2) For purposes of this paragraph, it is immaterial whether the gift tax is paid by the donor or the donee. Where more than one gift of a present interest in property is made to the same donee during a "calendar period" (as defined in § 25.2502-1(c)(1)), the annual exclusion shall apply to the earliest of such gifts in point of time.

(3) Where the donor and his spouse elect under section 2513 or the corresponding provisions of prior law to have any gifts made by either of them considered as made one-half by each, the amount of gift tax paid with respect to such a gift is the sum of the amounts of tax (computed separately) paid with respect to each half of the gift by the donor and his spouse.

(4) The method described in section 1015(d)(2) and this paragraph for computing the amount of gift tax paid in respect of a gift may be illustrated by the following examples:

Example (1). Prior to 1959 H made no taxable gifts. On July 1, 1959, he made a gift to his wife, W, of land having a value for gift tax purposes of $60,000 and gave to his son, S, certain securities valued at $60,000. During the year 1959, H also contributed $5,000 in cash to a charitable organization described in section 2522. H filed a timely gift tax return for 1959 with

Reg. § 1.1015-5(b)(1)

Basis Rules of General Application

respect to which he paid gift tax in the amount of $6,000, computed as follows:

Value of land given to W		$60,000
Less: Annual exclusion	$3,000	
Marital deduction	30,000	33,000
Included amount of gift		$27,000
Value of securities given to S		$60,000
Less: Annual exclusion		3,000
Included amount of gift		57,000
Gift to charitable organization		$5,000
Less: Annual exclusion	$3,000	
Charitable deduction	2,000	5,000
Included amount of gift		None
Total included gifts		84,000
Less: Specific exemption allowed		30,000
Taxable gifts for 1959		54,000
Gift tax on $54,000		$ 6,000

In determining the gift tax paid with respect to the land given to W, amount C of the ratio set forth in subparagraph (1)(ii) of this paragraph is $60,000, value of property given to W, less $33,000 (the sum of $3,000, the amount excluded under section 2503(b), and $30,000, the amount deducted under section 2523), or $27,000. Amount D of the ratio is $84,000 (the amount of taxable gifts, $54,000, plus the gift tax specific exemption, $30,000). The gift tax paid with respect to the land given to W is $1,928.57, computed as follows:

$$\frac{\$27,000 \; (C)}{\$84,000 \; (D)} \times \$6,000 \; (B)$$

Example (2). The facts are the same as in example (1) except that H made his gifts to W and S on July 1, 1971, and that prior to 1971, H made no taxable gifts. Furthermore, H made his charitable contribution on August 12, 1971. These were the only gifts made by H during 1971. H filed his gift tax return for the third quarter of 1971 on November 15, 1971, as required by section 6075(b). With respect to the above gifts, H paid a gift tax in the amount of $6,000, on total taxable gifts of $54,000 for the third quarter of 1971. The gift tax paid with respect to the land given to W is $1,928.57. The computations for these figures are identical to those used in example (1).

Example (3). On January 15, 1956, A made a gift to his nephew, N, of land valued at $86,000, and on June 30, 1956, gave N securities valued at $40,000. On July 1, 1956, A gave to his sister, S, $46,000 in cash. A and his wife, B, were married during the entire calendar year 1956. The amount of A's taxable gifts for prior years was zero although in arriving at that amount A had used in full the specific exemption authorized by section 2521. B did not make any gifts before 1956. A and B elected under section 2513 to have all gifts made by either during 1956 treated as made one-half by A and one-half by B. Pursuant to that election, A and B each filed a gift tax return for 1956. A paid gift tax of $11,325 and B paid gift tax of $5,250, computed as follows:

	A	B
Value of land given to N	$43,000	$43,000
Less: exclusion	3,000	3,000
Included amount of gift	$40,000	$40,000
Value of securities given to N	$20,000	$20,000
Less: exclusion	none	none
Included amount of gift	20,000	20,000
Cash gift to S	23,000	23,000
Less: exclusion	3,000	3,000
Included amount of gift	20,000	20,000
Total included gifts	80,000	80,000
Less: specific exemption	none	30,000
Taxable gifts for 1956	80,000	50,000
Gift tax for 1956	11,325	5,250

The amount of the gift tax paid by A with respect to the land given to N is computed as follows:

$$\frac{\$40,000 \; (C)}{\$80,000 \; (D)} \times \$11,325 \; (B) = \$5,662.50$$

The amount of the gift tax paid by B with respect to the land given to N is computed as follows:

Reg. § 1.1015-5(b)(4)

$$\frac{\$40,000 \text{ (C)}}{\$80,000 \text{ (D)}} \times \$5,250 \text{ (B)} = \$2,625$$

The amount of the gift tax paid with respect to the land is $5,662.50 plus $2,625, or $8,287.50. Computed in a similar manner, the amount of gift tax paid by A with respect to the securities given to N is $2,831.25, and the amount of gift tax paid by B with respect thereto is $1,312.50, or a total of $4,143.75.

Example (4). The facts are the same as in example (3) except that A gave the land to N on January 15, 1972, the securities to N on February 3, 1972, and the cash to S on March 7, 1972. As in example (3), the amount of A's taxable gifts for taxable years prior to 1972 was zero, although in arriving at that amount A had used in full the specific exemption authorized by section 2521. B did not make any gifts before 1972. Pursuant to the election under section 2513, A and B treated all gifts made by either during 1972 as made one-half by A and one-half by B. A and B each filed a gift tax return for the first quarter of 1972 on May 15, 1972, as required by section 6075(b). A paid gift tax of $11,325 on taxable gifts of $80,000 and B paid gift tax of $5,250 on taxable gifts of $50,000. The amount of the gift tax paid by A and B with respect to the land given to N is $5,662.50 and $2,625, respectively. The computations for these figures are identical to those used in example (3).

(c) *Special rule for increased basis for gift tax paid in the case of gifts made after December 31, 1976*—(1) *In general.* With respect to gifts made after December 31, 1976 (other than gifts between spouses described in section 1015(e)), the increase in basis for gift tax paid is determined under section 1015(d)(6). Under section 1015(d)(6)(A), the increase in basis with respect to gift tax paid is limited to the amount (not in excess of the amount of gift tax paid) that bears the same ratio to the amount of gift tax paid as the net appreciation in value of the gift bears to the amount of the gift.

(2) *Amount of gift.* In general, for purposes of section 1015(d)(6)(A)(ii), the amount of the gift is determined in conformance with the provisions of paragraph (b) of this section. Thus, the amount of the gift is the amount included with respect to the gift in determining (for purposes of section 2503(a)) the total amount of gifts made during the calendar year (or calendar quarter in the case of a gift made on or before December 31, 1981), reduced by the amount of any annual exclusion allowable with respect to the gift under section 2503(b), and any deductions allowed with respect to the gift under section 2522 (relating to the charitable deduction) and section 2523 (relating to the marital deduction). Where more than one gift of a present interest in property is made to the same donee during a calendar year, the annual exclusion shall apply to the earliest of such gifts in point of time.

(3) *Amount of gift tax paid with respect to the gift.* In general, for purposes of section 1015(d)(6), the amount of gift tax paid with respect to the gift is determined in conformance with the provisions of paragraph (b) of this section. Where more than one gift is made by the donor in a calendar year (or quarter in the case of gifts made on or before December 31, 1981), the amount of gift tax paid with respect to any specific gift made during that period is the amount which bears the same ratio to the total gift tax paid for that period (determined after reduction for any gift tax unified credit available under section 2505) as the amount of the gift (computed as described in paragraph (c)(2) of this section) bears to the total taxable gifts for the period.

(4) *Qualified domestic trusts.* For purposes of section 1015(d)(6), in the case of a qualified domestic trust (QDOT) described in section 2056A(a), any distribution during the noncitizen surviving spouse's lifetime with respect to which a tax is imposed under section 2056A(b)(1)(A) is treated as a transfer by gift, and any estate tax paid on the distribution under section 2056A(b)(1)(A) is treated as a gift tax. The rules under this paragraph apply in determining the extent to which the basis in the assets distributed is increased by the tax imposed under section 2056A(b)(1)(A).

(5) *Examples.* Application of the provisions of this paragraph (c) may be illustrated by the following examples:

Example 1. (i) Prior to 1995, X exhausts X's gift tax unified credit available under section 2505. In 1995, X makes a gift to X's child Y, of a parcel of real estate having a fair market value of $100,000. X's adjusted basis in the real estate immediately before making the gift was $70,000. Also in 1995, X makes a gift to X's child Z, of a painting having a fair market value of $70,000. X timely files a gift tax return for 1995 and pays gift tax in the amount of $55,500, computed as follows:

Value of real estate transferred to Y	$100,000	
Less: Annual exclusion	10,000	
Included amount of gift (C)		$ 90,000

Reg. § 1.1015-5(c)(2)

Basis Rules of General Application

See p. 20,601 for regulations not amended to reflect law changes

Value of painting transferred to Z	$ 70,000	
Less: annual exclusion	10,000	
Included amount of gift		60,000
Total included gifts (D)		$150,000
Total gift tax liability for 1995 gifts (B)		$ 55,500

(ii) The gift tax paid with respect to the real estate transferred to Y, is determined as follows:

$$\frac{\$90,000(C)}{\$150,000(D)} \times \$55,500 = \$33,300$$

(iii) (A) The amount by which Y's basis in the real property is increased is determined as follows:

$$\frac{\$30,000 \text{ (net appreciation)}}{\$90,000 \text{ (amount of gift)}} \times \$33,300 = \$11,000$$

(B) Y's basis in the real property is $70,000 plus $11,100, or $81,100. If X had not exhausted any of X's unified credit, no gift tax would have been paid and, as a result, Y's basis would not be increased.

$$\frac{\$20,000 \text{ (net appreciation)}}{\$70,000 \text{ (distribution)}} \times \$38,500 \text{ (section 2056a estate tax)} = \$11,000$$

(ii) Y's basis in the stock is $50,000 plus $11,000, or $61,000.

(6) *Effective date.* The provisions of this paragraph (c) are effective for gifts made after August 22, 1995.

(d) *Treatment as adjustment to basis.* Any increase in basis under section 1015(d) and this section shall for purposes of section 1016(b) (relating to adjustments to a substituted basis), be treated as an adjustment under section 1016(a) to the basis of the donee's property to which such increase applies. See paragraph (p) of § 1.1016-5. [Reg. § 1.1015-5.]

☐ [T.D. 6693, 12-2-63. Amended by T.D. 7238, 12-28-72; T.D. 7910, 9-6-83 and T.D. 8612, 8-21-95.]

[Reg. § 1.1016-1]

§ 1.1016-1. **Adjustments to basis; scope of section.**—Section 1016 and §§ 1.1016-2 to 1016-10, inclusive, contain the rules relating to the adjustments to be made to the basis of property to determine the adjusted basis as defined in section 1011. However, if the property was acquired from a decedent before his death, see § 1.1014-6 for adjustments on account of certain deductions allowed the taxpayer for the period between the date of acquisition of the property and the date of death of the decedent. If an election has been made under the Retirement-Straight Line Adjustment Act of 1958 (26 U.S.C. 1016 note), see § 1.9001-1 for special rules for

Example 2. (i) X dies in 1995. X's spouse, Y, is not a United States citizen. In order to obtain the marital deduction for property passing to X's spouse, X established a QDOT in X's will. In 1996, the trustee of the QDOT makes a distribution of principal from the QDOT in the form of shares of stock having a fair market value of $70,000 on the date of distribution. The trustee's basis in the stock (determined under section 1014) is $50,000. An estate tax is imposed on the distribution under section 2056A(b)(1)(A) in the amount $38,500, and is paid. Y's basis in the shares of stock is increased by a portion of the section 2056A estate tax paid determined as follows:

determining adjusted basis in the case of a taxpayer who has changed from the retirement to the straight-line method of computing depreciation allowances. [Reg. § 1.1016-1.]

☐ [T.D. 6265, 11-6-57. Amended by T.D. 6418, 10-9-59.]

[Reg. § 1.1016-2]

§ 1.1016-2. **Items properly chargeable to capital account.**—(a) The cost or other basis shall be properly adjusted for any expenditure, receipt, loss, or other item, properly chargeable to capital account, including the cost of improvements and betterments made to the property. No adjustment shall be made in respect of any item which, under any applicable provision of law or regulation, is treated as an item not properly chargeable to capital account but is allowable as a deduction in computing net or taxable income for the taxable year. For example, in the case of oil and gas wells no adjustment may be made in respect of any intangible drilling and development expense allowable as a deduction in computing net or taxable income. See the regulations under section 263(c).

(b) The application of the foregoing provisions may be illustrated by the following example:

Example. A, who makes his returns on the calendar year basis, purchased property in 1941 for $10,000. He subsequently expended $6,000 for improvements. Disregarding, for the purpose of this example, the adjustments required for depre-

Reg. § 1.1016-2(b)

ciation, the adjusted basis of the property is $16,000. If A sells the property in 1954 for $20,000, the amount of his gain will be $4,000.

(c) Adjustment to basis shall be made for carrying charges such as taxes and interest, with respect to property (whether real or personal, improved or unimproved, and whether productive or unproductive), which the taxpayer elects to treat as chargeable to capital account under section 266, rather than as an allowable deduction. The term "taxes" for this purpose includes duties and excise taxes but does not include income taxes.

(d) Expenditures described in section 173 to establish, maintain, or increase the circulation of a newspaper, magazine, or other periodical are chargeable to capital account only in accordance with and in the manner provided in the regulations under section 173. [Reg. § 1.1016-2.]

☐ [T.D. 6265, 11-6-57.]

[Reg. § 1.1016-3]

§ 1.1016-3. Exhaustion, wear and tear, obsolescence, amortization, and depletion for periods since February 28, 1913.—(a) *In general* — (1) *Adjustment where deduction is claimed.* (i) For taxable periods beginning on or after January 1, 1952, the cost or other basis of property shall be decreased for exhaustion, wear and tear, obsolescence, amortization, and depletion by the greater of the following two amounts: (a) the amount allowed as deductions in computing taxable income, to the extent resulting in a reduction of the taxpayer's income taxes, or (b) the amount allowable for the years involved. See paragraph (b) of this section. Where the taxpayer makes an appropriate election the above rule is applicable for periods since February 28, 1913, and before January 1, 1952. See paragraph (d) of this section. For rule for such periods where no election is made, see paragraph (c) of this section.

(ii) The determination of the amount properly allowable for exhaustion, wear and tear, obsolescence, amortization, and depletion shall be made on the basis of facts reasonably known to exist at the end of the taxable year. A taxpayer is not permitted to take advantage in a later year of his prior failure to take any such allowance or his taking an allowance plainly inadequate under the known facts in prior years. In the case of depreciation, if in prior years the taxpayer has consistently taken proper deductions under one method, the amount allowable for such prior years shall not be increased even though a greater amount would have been allowable under another proper method. For rules governing losses on retirement of depreciable property, including rules for determining basis, see § 1.167(a)-8. This subdivision may be illustrated by the following example:

Example. An asset was purchased January 1, 1950, at a cost of $10,000. The useful life of the asset is 10 years. It has no salvage value. Depreciation was deducted and allowed for 1950 to 1954 as follows:

1950	$ 500
1951	.....
1952	1,000
1953	1,000
1954	1,000
Total amount allowed	$3,500

The correct reserve as of December 31, 1954, is computed as follows:

Dec. 31:
1950 ($10,000 ÷ 10)	$1,000
1951 ($9,000 ÷ 9)	1,000
1952 ($8,000 ÷ 8)	1,000
1953 ($7,000 ÷ 7)	1,000
1954 ($6,000 ÷ 6)	1,000
Reserve Dec. 31, 1954	$5,000

Depreciation for 1955 is computed as follows:

Cost	$10,000
Reserve as of December 31, 1954	5,000
Unrecovered cost	5,000
Depreciation allowable for 1955 ($5,000 ÷ 5)	1,000

(2) *Adjustment for amount allowable where no depreciation deduction claimed.* (i) If the taxpayer has not taken a depreciation deduction either in the taxable year or for any prior taxable year, adjustments to basis of the property for depreciation allowable shall be determined by using the straight-line method of depreciation. (See § 1.1016-4 for adjustments in the case of persons exempt from income taxation.)

(ii) For taxable years beginning after December 31, 1953, and ending after August 16, 1954, if the taxpayer with respect to any property has taken a deduction for depreciation properly under one of the methods provided in section 167(b) for one or more years but has omitted the deduction in other years, the adjustment to basis for the depreciation allowable in such a case will be the deduction under the method which was used by the taxpayer with respect to that property. Thus, if A acquired property in 1954 on which he properly computed his depreciation deduction under the method described in section 167(b)(2) (the declining-balance method) for the first year of its useful life but did not take a deduction in the second and third year of the asset's life, the adjustment to basis for depreciation allowable for the second and third year will be likewise computed under the declining-balance method.

(3) *Adjustment for depletion deductions with respect to taxable years before 1932.* Where for any taxable year before the taxable year 1932 the depletion allowance was based on discovery value or a percentage of income, then the adjustment for depletion for such year shall not exceed a depletion deduction which would have been allowable for such year if computed without reference to discovery value or a percentage of income.

(b) *Adjustment for periods beginning on or after January 1, 1952.* The decrease required by paragraph (a) of this section for deductions in respect of any period beginning on or after January 1, 1952, shall be whichever is the greater of the following amounts:

(1) The amount allowed as deductions in computing taxable income under subtitle A of the Code or prior income tax laws and resulting (by reason of the deductions so allowed) in a reduction for any taxable year of the taxpayer's taxes under subtitle A of the Code (other than chapter 2, relating to tax on self-employment income) or prior income, war-profits, or excess-profits tax laws; or

(2) The amount properly allowable as deductions in computing taxable income under subtitle A of the Code or prior income tax laws (whether or not the amount properly allowable would have caused a reduction for any taxable year of the taxpayer's taxes).

(c) *Adjustment for periods since February 28, 1913, and before January 1, 1952, where no election made.* If no election has been properly made under section 1020, or under section 113(d) of the Internal Revenue Code of 1939 (see paragraph (d) of this section), the decrease required by paragraph (a) of this section for deductions in respect of any period since February 28, 1913, and before January 1, 1952, shall be whichever of the following amounts is the greater:

(1) The amount allowed as deductions in computing net income under chapter 1 of the Internal Revenue Code of 1939 or prior income tax laws;

(2) The amount properly allowable in computing net income under chapter 1 of the Internal Revenue Code of 1939 or prior income tax laws.

For the purpose of determining the decrease required by this paragraph, it is immaterial whether or not the amount under subparagraph (1) of this paragraph or the amount under subparagraph (2) of this paragraph would have resulted in a reduction for any taxable year of the taxpayer's taxes.

(d) *Adjustment for periods since February 28, 1913, and before January 1, 1952, where election made.* If an election has been properly made under section 1020, or under section 113(d) of the Internal Revenue Code of 1939, the decrease required by paragraph (a) of this section for deductions in respect of any period since February 28, 1913, and before January 1, 1952, shall be whichever is the greater of the following amounts:

(1) The amount allowed as deductions in computing net income under chapter 1 of the Internal Revenue Code of 1939 or prior income tax laws and resulting (by reason of the deductions so allowed) in a reduction for any taxable year of the taxpayer's taxes under such chapter 1 (other than subchapter E, relating to tax on self-employment income), subchapter E, chapter 2, of the Internal Revenue Code of 1939, or prior income, war-profits, or excess-profits tax laws;

(2) The amount properly allowable as deductions in computing net income under chapter 1 of the Internal Revenue Code of 1939 or prior income tax laws (whether or not the amount properly allowable would have caused a reduction for any taxable year of the taxpayer's taxes).

(e) *Determination of amount allowed which reduced taxpayer's taxes.* (1) As indicated in paragraphs (b) and (d) of this section, there are situations in which it is necessary to determine (for the purpose of ascertaining the basis adjustment required by paragraph (a) of this section) the extent to which the amount allowed as deductions resulted in a reduction for any taxable year of the taxpayer's taxes under subtitle A (other than chapter 2 relating to tax on self-employment income) of the Internal Revenue Code of 1954, or prior income, war-profits, or excess-profits tax laws. This amount (amount allowed which resulted in a reduction of the taxpayer's taxes) is hereinafter referred to as the "tax-benefit amount allowed." For the purpose of determining whether the tax-benefit amount allowed exceeded the amount allowable, a determination must be made of that portion of the excess of the amount allowed over the amount allowable which, if disallowed, would not have resulted in an increase in any such tax previously determined. If the entire excess of the amount allowed over the amount allowable could be disallowed without any such increase in tax, the tax-benefit amount allowed shall not be considered to have exceeded the amount allowable. In such a case (if paragraph (b) or (d) of this section is applicable) the reduction in basis required by paragraph (a) of this section would be the amount properly allowable as a deduction. If only part of such excess could be disallowed without any such increase in tax, the tax-benefit

Reg. § 1.1016-3(e)

amount allowed shall be considered to exceed the amount allowable to the extent of the remainder of such excess. In such a case (if paragraph (b) or (d) of this section is applicable) the reduction in basis required by paragraph (a) of this section would be the amount of the tax-benefit amount allowed.

(2) For the purpose of determining the tax-benefit amount allowed the tax previously determined shall be determined under the principles of section 1314. The only adjustments made in determining whether there would be an increase in tax shall be those resulting from the disallowance of the amount allowed. The taxable years for which the determination is made shall be the taxable year for which the deduction was allowed and any other taxable year which would be affected by the disallowance of such deduction. Examples of such other taxable years are taxable years to which there was a carryover or carryback of a net operating loss from the taxable year for which the deduction was allowed, and taxable years for which a computation under section 111 or section 1333 was made by reference to the taxable year for which the deduction was allowed. In determining whether the disallowance of any part of the deduction would not have resulted in an increase in any tax previously determined, proper adjustment must be made for previous determinations under section 1311, or section 3801 of the Internal Revenue Code of 1939, and for any previous application of section 1016(a)(2)(B), or section 113(b)(1)(B)(ii) of the Internal Revenue Code of 1939.

(3) If a determination under section 1016(a)(2)(B) must be made with respect to several properties for each of which the amount allowed for the taxable year exceeded the amount allowable, the tax-benefit amount allowed with respect to each of such properties shall be an allocated portion of the tax-benefit amount allowed determined by reference to the sum of the amounts allowed and the sum of the amounts allowable with respect to such several properties.

(4) In the case of property held by a partnership or trust, the computation of the tax-benefit amount allowed shall take into account the tax benefit of the partners or beneficiaries, as the case may be, from the deduction by the partnership or trust of the amount allowed to the partnership or the trust. For this purpose, the determination of the amount allowed which resulted in a tax benefit to the partners or beneficiaries shall be made in the same manner as that provided above with respect to the taxes of the person holding the property.

(5) A taxpayer seeking to limit the adjustment to basis to the tax-benefit amount allowed for any period, in lieu of the amount allowed, must establish the tax-benefit amount allowed. A failure of adequate proof as to the tax-benefit amount allowed with respect to one period does not preclude the taxpayer from limiting the adjustment to basis to the tax-benefit amount allowed with respect to another period for which adequate proof is available.

For example, a corporate transferee may have available adequate records with respect to the tax effect of the deduction of erroneous depreciation for certain taxable years, but may not have available adequate records with respect to the deduction of excessive depreciation for other taxable years during which the property was held by its transferor. In such case the corporate transferee shall not be denied the right to apply this section with respect to the erroneous depreciation for the period for which adequate proof is available.

(f) *Determination of amount allowable in prior taxable years.*—(1) One of the factors in determining the adjustment to basis as of any date is the amount of depreciation, depletion, etc., allowable for periods prior to such date. The amount allowable for such prior periods is determined under the law applicable to such prior periods; all adjustments required by the law applicable to such periods are made in determining the adjusted basis of the property for the purpose of determining the amount allowable. Provisions corresponding to the rules in section 1016(a)(2)(B) described in paragraphs (d) and (e) of this section, which limit adjustments to the "tax-benefit amount allowed" where an election is properly exercised, were first enacted by Act of July 14, 1952 (66 Stat. 629). That law provided that corresponding rules are deemed to be includible in all revenue laws applicable to taxable years ending after December 31, 1931. Accordingly, those rules shall be taken into account in determining the amount of depreciation, etc., allowable for any taxable year ending after December 31, 1931. For example, if the adjusted basis of property held by the taxpayer since January 1, 1930, is determined as of January 1, 1955, and if an election was properly made under section 1020, or section 113(d) of the Internal Revenue Code of 1939, then the amount allowable which is taken into account in computing the adjusted basis as of January 1, 1955, shall be determined by taking those rules into account for all taxable years ending after December 31, 1931. Public Law 539 made no change in the law applicable in determining the amount allowable for taxable years ending before January 1, 1932. If there was a final decision of a court prior to the enactment of the Act of July 14,

Reg. § 1.1016-3(e)(2)

Basis Rules of General Application

1952, determining the amount allowable for a particular taxable year, such determination shall be adjusted. In such case the adjustment shall be made only for the purpose of taking the provision of that law into account and only to the extent made necessary by such provisions.

(2) Although the Act of July 14, 1952, amended the law applicable to all taxable years ending after December 31, 1931, the amendment does not permit refund, credit, or assessment of a deficiency for any taxable year for which such refund, credit, or assessment was barred by any law or rule of law.

(g) *Property with transferred basis.* The following rules apply in the determination of the adjustments to basis of property in the hands of a transferee, donee, or grantee which are required by section 1016(b), or section 113(b)(2) of the Internal Revenue Code of 1939, with respect to the period the property was held by the transferor, donor, or grantor:

(1) An election or a revocation of an election under section 1020, or section 113(d) of the Internal Revenue Code of 1939, by a transferor, donor, or grantor, which is made after the date of the transfer, gift, or grant of the property shall not affect the basis of such property in the hands of the transferee, donee, or grantee. An election or a revocation of an election made before the date of the transfer, gift, or grant of the property shall be taken into account in determining under section 1016(b) the adjustments to basis of such property as of the date of the transfer, gift, or grant, whether or not an election or a revocation of an election under section 1020, or section 113(d) of the Internal Revenue Code of 1939, was made by the transferee, donee, or grantee.

(2) An election by the transferee, donee, or grantee, or a revocation of such an election shall be applicable in determining the adjustments to basis for the period during which the property was held by the transferor, donor, or grantor, whether or not the transferor, donor, or grantor had made an election or a revocation of an election, provided that the property was held by the transferee, donee, or grantee at any time on or before the date on which the election or revocation was made.

(h) *Examples.* The application of section 1016(a)(1) and (2) may be illustrated by the following examples:

Example (1). The case of Corporation A discloses the following facts:

(1) Year	(2) Amount allowed	(3) Amount allowed which reduced taxpayer's taxes	(4) Amount allowable	(5) Amount allowable but not less than amount allowed	(6) Amount allowable but not less than amount allowed which reduced taxpayer's taxes
1949	$6,000	$5,500	$5,000	$ 6,000	$ 5,500
1950	7,000	7,000	6,500	7,000	7,000
1951	5,000	4,000	6,500	6,500	6,500
Total, 1949-51	.....	.....	.....	19,500	19,000
1952	$6,500	$6,500	$6,000	......	$ 6,500
1953	5,000	4,000	4,000	......	4,000
1954	4,500	4,500	6,000	......	6,000
Total, 1952-54	.....	.....	.....	......	$16,500

The cost or other basis is to be adjusted by $16,500 with respect to the years 1952-54, that is, by the amount allowable but not less than the amount allowed which reduced the taxpayer's taxes. An adjustment must also be made with respect to the years 1949-1951, the amount of such adjustment depending upon whether an election was properly made under section 1020, or section 113(d) of the Internal Revenue Code of 1939. If no such election was made, the amount of the adjustment with respect to the years 1949-1951 is $19,500, that is, the amount allowed but not less than the amount allowable. If an election was properly made, the amount of the adjustment with respect to the years 1949-1951 is $19,000, that is, the amount allowable but not less than the amount allowed which reduced the taxpayer's taxes.

Example (2). Corporation A, which files its returns on the basis of a calendar year, purchased a building on January 1, 1950, at a cost of $100,000. On the basis of the facts reasonably

Reg. § 1.1016-3(h)

51,954   Basis Rules of General Application

See p. 20,601 for regulations not amended to reflect law changes

known to exist at the end of 1950, a period of 50 years should have been used as the correct useful life of the building; nevertheless, depreciation was computed by Corporation A on the basis of a useful life of 25 years, and was allowed for 1950 through 1953 as a deduction in an annual amount of $4,000. The building was sold on January 1, 1954. Corporation A did not make an election under section 1020, or section 113(d) of the Internal Revenue Code of 1939. No part of the amount allowed Corporation A for any of the years 1950 through 1953 resulted in a reduction of Corporation A's taxes. The adjusted basis of the building as of January 1, 1954, is $88,166, computed as follows:

Taxable year	Adjustments to basis as of beginning of taxable year	Adjusted basis on Jan. 1	Remaining life on Jan. 1	Depreciation allowable	Depreciation allowed
1950	.....	$100,000	50	$2,000	$4,000
1951	$ 4,000	96,000	49	1,959	4,000
1952	8,000	92,000	48	1,917	4,000
1953	9,917	90,083	47	1,917	4,000
1954	11,834	88,166	.....	.....	.....

Example (3). The facts are the same as in example (2), except that Corporation A made a proper election under section 1020. In such case, the adjusted basis of the building as of January 1, 1954, is $92,000, computed as follows:

Taxable year	Adjustments to basis as of beginning of taxable year	Adjusted basis on Jan. 1	Remaining life on Jan. 1	Depreciation allowable	Depreciation allowed
1950	.....	$100,000	50	$2,000	$4,000
1951	$2,000	98,000	49	2,000	4,000
1952	4,000	96,000	48	2,000	4,000
1953	6,000	94,000	47	2,000	4,000
1954	8,000	92,000	.....	.....	.....

Example (4). If it is assumed that in example (2), or in example (3), all of the deduction allowed Corporation A for 1953 had resulted in a reduction of A's taxes, the adjustment to the basis of the building for depreciation for 1953 would reflect the entire $4,000 deduction. In such case, the adjusted basis of the building as of January 1, 1954, would be $86,083 in example (2), and $90,000 in example (3).

Example (5). The facts are the same as in example (2), except that for the year 1950 all of the $4,000 amount allowed Corporation A as a deduction for depreciation for that year resulted in a reduction of A's taxes. In such case, the adjustments to the basis of the building remain the same as those set forth in example (2).

Example (6). The facts are the same as in example (3) except that for the year 1950 all of the $4,000 amount allowed Corporation A as a deduction for depreciation resulted in a reduction of A's taxes. In such case, the adjusted basis of the building as of January 1, 1954, is $90,123, computed as follows:

Taxable year	Adjustments to basis as of beginning of taxable year	Adjusted basis on Jan. 1	Remaining life on Jan. 1	Depreciation allowable	Depreciation allowed
1950	.....	$100,000	50	$2,000	$4,000
1951	$4,000	96,000	49	1,959	4,000
1952	5,959	94,041	48	1,959	4,000
1953	7,918	92,082	47	1,959	4,000
1954	9,877	90,123	.....	.....	.....

[Reg. § 1.1016-3.]   ☐ [T.D. 6265, 11-6-57.]

Reg. § 1.1016-3(h)

Basis Rules of General Application

[Reg. § 1.1016-4]

§ 1.1016-4. Exhaustion, wear and tear, obsolescence, amortization, and depletion; periods during which income was not subject to tax.—(a) Adjustments to basis must be made for exhaustion, wear and tear, obsolescence, amortization, and depletion to the extent actually sustained in respect of:

(1) Any period before March 1, 1913,

(2) Any period since February 28, 1913, during which the property was held by a person or organization not subject to income taxation under chapter 1 of the Code or prior income tax laws,

(3) Any period since February 28, 1913, and before January 1, 1958, during which the property was held by a person subject to tax under part I, subchapter L, chapter 1 of the Code, or prior income tax law, to the extent that section 1016(a)(2) does not apply, or

(4) Any period since February 28, 1913, during which such property was held by a person subject to tax under part II of subchapter L, chapter 1 of the Code, or prior income tax law, to the extent that section 1016(a)(2) does not apply.

(b) The amount of the adjustments described in paragraph (a) of this section actually sustained is that amount charged off on the books of the taxpayer where such amount is considered by the Commissioner to be reasonable. Otherwise, the amount actually sustained will be the amount that would have been allowable as a deduction:

(1) During the period described in paragraph (a)(1) or (2) of this section, had the taxpayer been subject to income tax during those periods, or

(2) During the period described in paragraph (a)(3) or (4) of this section, with respect to property held by a taxpayer described in that paragraph, to the extent that section 1016(a)(2) was inapplicable to such property during that period.

In the case of a taxpayer subject to the adjustment required by subparagraph (1) or (2) of this paragraph, depreciation shall be determined by using the straight line method. [Reg. § 1.1016-4.]

☐ [T.D. 6265, 1-6-57. Amended by T.D. 6610, 8-30-62 and T.D. 6681, 10-16-63.]

[Reg. § 1.1016-5]

§ 1.1016-5. Miscellaneous adjustments to basis.—(a) *Certain stock distributions.* (1) In the case of stock, the cost or other basis must be diminished by the amount of distributions previously made which, under the law applicable to the year in which the distribution was made, either were tax free or were applicable in reduction of basis (not including distributions made by a corporation which was classified as a personal service corporation under the provisions of the Revenue Act of 1918 (40 Stat. 1057) or the Revenue Act of 1921 (42 Stat. 227), out of its earnings or profits which were taxable in accordance with the provisions of section 218 of the Revenue Act of 1918 or the Revenue Act of 1921). For adjustments to basis in the case of certain corporate distributions, see section 301 and the regulations thereunder.

(2) The application of subparagraph (1) of this paragraph may be illustrated by the following example:

Example. A, who makes his returns upon the calendar year basis, purchased stock in 1923 for $5,000. He received in 1924 a distribution of $2,000 paid out of earnings and profits of the corporation accumulated before March 1, 1913. The adjusted basis for determining the gain or loss from the sale or other disposition of the stock in 1954 is $5,000 less $2,000, or $3,000, and the amount of the gain or loss from the sale or other disposition of the stock is the difference between $3,000 and the amount realized from the sale or other disposition.

(b) *Amortizable bond premium*—(1) *In general.* A holder's basis in a bond is reduced by the amount of bond premium used to offset qualified stated interest income under § 1.171-2. This reduction occurs when the holder takes the qualified stated interest into account under the holder's regular method of accounting.

(2) *Special rules for taxable bonds.* A holder's basis in a taxable bond is reduced by the amount of bond premium allowed as a deduction under § 1.171-3(c)(5)(ii) (relating to the issuer's call of a taxable bond) or under § 1.171-2(a)(4)(i)(A) (relating to excess bond premium).

(3) *Special rule for tax-exempt obligations.* A holder's basis in a tax-exempt obligation is reduced by the amount of excess bond premium that is treated as a nondeductible loss under § 1.171-2(a)(4)(ii).

(c) *Municipal bonds.* In the case of a municipal bond (as defined in section 75(b)), basis shall be adjusted to the extent provided in section 75 or as provided in section 22(o) of the Internal Revenue Code of 1939, and the regulations thereunder.

(d) *Sale or exchange of residence.* Where the acquisition of a new residence results in the nonrecognition of any part of the gain on the sale, exchange, or involuntary conversion of the old residence, the basis of the new residence shall be reduced by the amount of the gain not so recognized pursuant to section 1034(a), or section 112(n) of the Internal Revenue Code of 1939, and the regulations thereunder. See section 1034(e) and the regulations thereunder.

(e) *Loans from Commodity Credit Corporation.* In the case of property pledged to the Commodity

Reg. § 1.1016-5(e)

Credit Corporation, the basis of such property shall be increased by the amount received as a loan from such corporation and treated by the taxpayer as income for the year in which received under section 77, or under section 123 of the Internal Revenue Code of 1939. The basis of such property shall be reduced to the extent of any deficiency on such loan with respect to which the taxpayer has been relieved from liability.

(f) *Deferred development and exploration expenses.* Expenditures for development and exploration of mines or mineral deposits treated as deferred expenses under sections 615 and 616, or under the corresponding provisions of prior income tax laws, are chargeable to capital account and shall be an adjustment to the basis of the property to which they relate. The basis so adjusted shall be reduced by the amount of such expenditures allowed as deductions which results in a reduction for any taxable year of the taxpayer's taxes under subtitle A (other than chapter 2 relating to tax on self-employment income) of the Code, or prior income, war-profits, or excess-profits tax laws, but not less than the amounts allowable under such provisions for the taxable year and prior years. This amount is considered as the "tax-benefit amount allowed" and shall be determined in accordance with paragraph (e) of § 1.1016-3. For example, if a taxpayer purchases unexplored and undeveloped mining property for $1,000,000 and at the close of the development stage has incurred exploration and development costs of $9,000,000 treated as deferred expenses, the basis of such property at such time for computing gain or loss will be $10,000,000. Assuming that the taxpayer in this example has operated the mine for several years and has deducted allowable percentage depletion in the amount of $2,000,000 and has deducted allowable deferred exploration and development expenditures of $2,000,000, the basis of the property in the taxpayer's hands for purposes of determining gain or loss from a sale will be $6,000,000.

(g) *Sale of land with unharvested crop.* In the case of an unharvested crop which is sold, exchanged, or involuntarily converted with the land and which is considered as property used in the trade or business under section 1231, the basis of such crop shall be increased by the amount of the items which are attributable to the production of such crop and which are disallowed, under section 268, as deductions in computing taxable income. The basis of any other property shall be decreased by the amount of any such items which are attributable to such other property, notwithstanding any provisions of section 1016 or of this section to the contrary. For example, if the items attributable to the production of an unharvested crop consist only of fertilizer costing $100 and $50 depreciation on a tractor used only to cultivate such crop, and such items are disallowed under section 268, the adjustments to the basis of such crop shall include an increase of $150 for such items and the adjustments to the basis of the tractor shall include a reduction of $50 for depreciation.

(h) *Consent dividends.*—(1) In the case of amounts specified in a shareholder's consent to which section 28 of the Internal Revenue Code of 1939 applies, the basis of the consent stock shall be increased to the extent provided in subsection (h) of such section.

(2) In the case of amounts specified in a shareholder's consent to be treated as a consent dividend to which section 565 applies, the basis of the consent stock shall be increased by the amount which, under section 565(c)(2), is treated as contributed to the capital of the corporation.

(i) *Stock in foreign personal holding company.* In the case of the stock of a United States shareholder in a foreign personal holding company, basis shall be adjusted to the extent provided in section 551(f) or corresponding provisions of prior income tax laws.

(j) *Research and experimental expenditures.* Research and experimental expenditures treated as deferred expenses under section 174(b) are chargeable to capital account and shall be an adjustment to the basis of the property to which they relate. The basis so adjusted shall be reduced by the amount of such expenditures allowed as deductions which results in a reduction for any taxable year of the taxpayer's taxes under subtitle A (other than chapter 2 relating to tax on self-employment income) of the Code, or prior income, war-profits, or excess-profits tax laws, but not less than the amounts allowable under such provisions for the taxable year and prior years. This amount is considered as the "tax-benefit amount allowed" and shall be determined in accordance with paragraph (e) of § 1.1016-3.

(k) *Deductions disallowed in connection with disposal of coal or domestic iron ore.* Basis shall be adjusted by the amount of the deductions disallowed under section 272 with respect to the disposal of coal or domestic iron ore covered by section 631.

(l) *Expenditures attributable to grants or loans covered by section 621.* In the case of expenditures attributable to a grant or loan made to a taxpayer by the United States for the encouragement of exploration for, or development or mining of, critical and strategic minerals or metals, basis shall be adjusted to the extent provided in section 621, or in section 22(b)(15) of the Internal Revenue Code of 1939.

Reg. § 1.1016-5(f)

Basis Rules of General Application

See p. 20,601 for regulations not amended to reflect law changes

(m) *Trademark and trade name expenditures.* Trademark and trade name expenditures treated as deferred expenses under section 177 are chargeable to capital account and shall be an adjustment to the basis of the property to which they relate. The basis so adjusted shall be reduced by the amount of such expenditures allowed as deductions which results in a reduction for any taxable year of the taxpayer's taxes under subtitle A (other than chapter 2, relating to tax on self-employment income) of the Code, but not less than the amounts allowable under such section for the taxable year and prior years. This amount is considered as the "tax-benefit amount allowed" and shall be determined in accordance with paragraph (e) of § 1.1016-3.

(n) *Life insurance companies.* In the case of any evidence of indebtedness referred to in section 818(b), the basis shall be adjusted to the extent of the adjustments required under section 818(b) (or the corresponding provisions of prior income tax laws) for the taxable year and all prior taxable years. The basis of any such evidence of indebtedness shall be reduced by the amount of the adjustment required under section 818(b) (or the corresponding provision of prior income tax laws) on account of amortizable premium and shall be increased by the amount of the adjustment required under section 818(b) on account of accruable discounts.

(o) *Stock and indebtedness of electing small business corporation.* In the case of a shareholder of an electing small business corporation, as defined in section 1371(b), the basis of the shareholder's stock in such corporation, and the basis of any indebtedness of such corporation owing to the shareholder, shall be adjusted to the extent provided in §§ 1.1375-4, 1.1376-1, and 1.1376-2.

(p) *Gift tax paid on certain property acquired by gift.* Basis shall be adjusted by that amount of the gift tax paid in respect of property acquired by gift which, under section 1015(d), is an increase in the basis of such property.

(q) *Section 38 property.* In the case of property which is or has been section 38 property (as defined in section 48(a)), the basis shall be adjusted to the extent provided in section 48(g) and in section 203(a)(2) of the Revenue Act of 1964.

(r) *Stock in controlled foreign corporations and other property.* In the case of stock in controlled foreign corporations (or foreign corporations which were controlled foreign corporations) and of property by reason of which a person is considered as owning such stock, the basis shall be adjusted to the extent provided in section 961.

(s) *Original issue discount.* In the case of certain corporate obligations issued at a discount after May 27, 1969, the basis shall be increased under section 1232(a)(3)(E) by the amount of original issue discount included in the holder's gross income pursuant to section 1232(a)(3).

(t) *Section 23 credit.* In the case of property with respect to which a credit has been allowed under section 23 or former section 44C (relating to residential energy credit), basis shall be adjusted as provided in paragraph (k) of § 1.23-3. [Reg. § 1.1016-5.]

☐ [T.D. 6265, 11-6-57. Amended by T.D. 6452, 2-3-60, T.D. 6610, 9-30-62, T.D. 6647, 4-10-63, T.D. 6693, 12-2-63, T.D. 6795, 1-28-65, T.D. 6841, 7-26-65, T.D. 7154, 12-27-71, T.D. 7717, 8-26-80; T.D. 8146, 7-15-87 and T.D. 8746, 12-30-97.]

[Reg. § 1.1016-6]

§ 1.1016-6. **Other applicable rules.**—(a) Adjustments must always be made to eliminate double deductions or their equivalent. Thus, in the case of the stock of a subsidiary company, the basis thereof must be properly adjusted for the amount of the subsidiary company's losses for the years in which consolidated returns were made.

(b) In determining basis, and adjustments to basis, the principles of estoppel apply, as elsewhere under the Code, and prior internal revenue laws. [Reg. § 1.1016-6.]

☐ [T.D. 6265, 11-6-57.]

[Reg. § 1.1016-10]

§ 1.1016-10. **Substituted basis.**—(a) Whenever it appears that the basis of property in the hands of the taxpayer is a substituted basis, as defined in section 1016(b), the adjustments indicated in §§ 1.1016-1 to 1.1016-6, inclusive, shall be made after first making in respect of such substituted basis proper adjustments of a similar nature in respect of the period during which the property was held by the transferor, donor, or grantor, or during which the other property was held by the person for whom the basis is to be determined. In addition, whenever it appears that the basis of property in the hands of the taxpayer is a substituted basis, as defined in section 1016(b)(1), the adjustments indicated in §§ 1.1016-7 to 1.1016-9, inclusive, and in section 1017 shall also be made, whenever necessary, after first making in respect of such substituted basis a proper adjustment of a similar nature in respect of the period during which the property was held by the transferor, donor, or grantor. Similar rules shall also be applied in the case of a series of substituted bases.

(b) The application of this section may be illustrated by the following example:

Reg. § 1.1016-10(b)

Example. A, who makes his returns upon the calendar year basis, in 1935 purchased the X Building and subsequently gave it to his son B. B exchanged the X Building for the Y Building in a tax-free exchange, and then gave the Y Building to his wife C. C, in determining the gain from the sale or disposition of the Y Building in 1954, is required to reduce the basis of the building by deductions for depreciation which were successively allowed (but not less than the amount allowable) to A and B upon the X Building and to B upon the Y Building, in addition to the deductions for depreciation allowed (but not less than the amount allowable) to herself during her ownership of the Y Building. [Reg. § 1.1016-10.]

☐ [*T.D.* 6265, 11-6-57.]

[Reg. § 1.1017-1]

§ 1.1017-1. **Basis reductions following a discharge of indebtedness.**—(a) *General rule for section 108(b)(2)(E).* This paragraph (a) applies to basis reductions under section 108(b)(2)(E) that are required by section 108(a)(1)(A) or (B) because the taxpayer excluded discharge of indebtedness (COD income) from gross income. A taxpayer must reduce in the following order, to the extent of the excluded COD income (but not below zero), the adjusted bases of property held on the first day of the taxable year following the taxable year that the taxpayer excluded COD income from gross income (in proportion to adjusted basis)—

(1) Real property used in a trade or business or held for investment, other than real property described in section 1221(1), that secured the discharged indebtedness immediately before the discharge;

(2) Personal property used in a trade or business or held for investment, other than inventory, accounts receivable, and notes receivable, that secured the discharged indebtedness immediately before the discharge;

(3) Remaining property used in a trade or business or held for investment, other than inventory, accounts receivable, notes receivable, and real property described in section 1221(1);

(4) Inventory, accounts receivable, notes receivable, and real property described in section 1221(1); and

(5) Property not used in a trade or business nor held for investment.

(b) *Operating rules*—(1) *Prior tax-attribute reduction.* The amount of excluded COD income applied to reduce basis does not include any COD income applied to reduce tax attributes under sections 108(b)(2)(A) through (D) and, if applicable, section 108(b)(5). For example, if a taxpayer excludes $100 of COD income from gross income under section 108(a) and reduces tax attributes by $40 under sections 108(b)(2)(A) through (D), the taxpayer is required to reduce the adjusted bases of property by $60 ($100 − $40) under section 108(b)(2)(E).

(2) *Multiple discharged indebtednesses.* If a taxpayer has COD income attributable to more than one discharged indebtedness resulting in the reduction of tax attributes under sections 108(b)(2)(A) through (D) and, if applicable, section 108(b)(5), paragraph (b)(1) of this section must be applied by allocating the tax-attribute reductions among the indebtednesses in proportion to the amount of COD income attributable to each discharged indebtedness. For example, if a taxpayer excludes $20 of COD income attributable to secured indebtedness A and excludes $80 of COD income attributable to unsecured indebtedness B (a total exclusion of $100), and if the taxpayer reduces tax attributes by $40 under sections 108(b)(2)(A) through (D), the taxpayer must reduce the amount of COD income attributable to secured indebtedness A to $12 ($20 − ($20 / $100 × $40)) and must reduce the amount of COD income attributable to unsecured indebtedness B to $48 ($80 − ($80 / $100 × $40)).

(3) *Limitation on basis reductions under section 108(b)(2)(E) in bankruptcy or insolvency.* If COD income arises from a discharge of indebtedness in a title 11 case or while the taxpayer is insolvent, the amount of any basis reduction under section 108(b)(2)(E) shall not exceed the excess of—

(i) The aggregate of the adjusted bases of property and the amount of money held by the taxpayer immediately after the discharge; over

(ii) The aggregate of the liabilities of the taxpayer immediately after the discharge.

(c) *Modification of ordering rules for basis reductions under sections 108(b)(5) and 108(c)*—(1) *In general.* The ordering rules prescribed in paragraph (a) of this section apply, with appropriate modifications, to basis reductions under sections 108(b)(5) and (c). Thus, a taxpayer that elects to reduce basis under section 108(b)(5) may, to the extent that the election applies, reduce only the adjusted basis of property described in paragraphs (a)(1), (2), and (3) of this section and, if an election is made under paragraph (f) of this section, paragraph (a)(4) of this section. Within paragraphs (a)(1),(2), (3) and (4) of this section, such a taxpayer may reduce only the adjusted bases of depreciable property. A taxpayer that elects to apply section 108(c) may reduce only the adjusted basis of property described in paragraphs (a)(1) and (3) of this section and,

Reg. § 1.1017-1(a)(1)

within paragraphs (a)(1) and (3) of this section, may reduce only the adjusted bases of depreciable real property. Furthermore, for basis reductions under section 108(c), a taxpayer must reduce the adjusted basis of the qualifying real property to the extent of the discharged qualified real property business indebtedness before reducing the adjusted bases of other depreciable real property. The term *qualifying real property* means real property with respect to which the indebtedness is qualified real property business indebtedness within the meaning of section 108(c)(3). See paragraphs (f) and (g) of this section for elections relating to section 1221(1) property and partnership interests.

(2) *Partial basis reductions under section 108(b)(5).* If the amount of basis reductions under section 108(b)(5) is less than the amount of the COD income excluded from gross income under section 108(a), the taxpayer must reduce the balance of its tax attributes, including any remaining adjusted bases of depreciable and other property, by following the ordering rules under section 108(b)(2). For example, if a taxpayer excludes $100 of COD income from gross income under section 108(a) and elects to reduce the adjusted bases of depreciable property by $10 under section 108(b)(5), the taxpayer must reduce its remaining tax attributes by $90, starting with net operating losses under section 108(b)(2).

(3) *Modification of fresh start rule for prior basis reductions under section 108(b)(5).* After reducing the adjusted bases of depreciable property under section 108(b)(5), a taxpayer must compute the limitation on basis reductions under section 1017(b)(2) using the aggregate of the remaining adjusted bases of property. For example, if, immediately after the discharge of indebtedness in a title 11 case, a taxpayer's adjusted bases of property is $100 and its undischarged indebtedness is $70, and if the taxpayer elects to reduce the adjusted bases of depreciable property by $10 under section 108(b)(5), section 1017(b)(2) limits any further basis reductions under section 108(b)(2)(E) to $20 (($100 − $10) − $70).

(d) *Changes in security.* If any property is added or eliminated as security for an indebtedness during the one-year period preceding the discharge of that indebtedness, such addition or elimination shall be disregarded where a principal purpose of the change is to affect the taxpayer's basis reductions under section 1017.

(e) *Depreciable property.* For purposes of this section, the term *depreciable property* means any property of a character subject to the allowance for depreciation or amortization, but only if the basis reduction would reduce the amount of depreciation or amortization which otherwise would be allowable for the period immediately following such reduction. Thus, for example, a lessor cannot reduce the basis of leased property where the lessee's obligation in respect of the property will restore to the lessor the loss due to depreciation during the term of the lease, since the lessor cannot take depreciation in respect of such property.

(f) *Election to treat section 1221(1) real property as depreciable*—(1) *In general.* For basis reductions under section 108(b)(5) and basis reductions relating to qualified farm indebtedness, a taxpayer may elect under sections 1017(b)(3)(E) and (4)(C), respectively, to treat real property described in section 1221(1) as depreciable property. This election is not available, however, for basis reductions under section 108(c).

(2) *Time and manner.* To make an election under section 1017(b)(3)(E) or (4)(C), a taxpayer must enter the appropriate information on Form 982, *Reduction of Tax Attributes Due to Discharge of Indebtedness (and Section 1082 Basis Adjustment)*, and attach the form to a timely filed (including extensions) Federal income tax return for the taxable year in which the taxpayer has COD income that is excluded from gross income under section 108(a). An election under this paragraph (f) may be revoked only with the consent of the Commissioner.

(g) *Partnerships*—(1) *Partnership COD income.* For purposes of paragraph (a) of this section, a taxpayer must treat a distributive share of a partnership's COD income as attributable to a discharged indebtedness secured by the taxpayer's interest in that partnership.

(2) *Partnership interest treated as depreciable property*—(i) *In general.* For purposes of making basis reductions, if a taxpayer makes an election under section 108(b)(5) (or 108(c)), the taxpayer must treat a partnership interest as depreciable property (or depreciable real property) to the extent of the partner's proportionate share of the partnership's basis in depreciable property (or depreciable real property), provided that the partnership consents to a corresponding reduction in the partnership's basis (inside basis) in depreciable property (or depreciable real property) with respect to such partner.

(ii) *Request by partner and consent of partnership*—(A) *In general.* Except as otherwise provided in this paragraph (g)(2)(ii), a taxpayer may choose whether or not to request that a partnership reduce the inside basis of its depreciable property (or depreciable real property) with respect to the taxpayer, and the partnership may grant or withhold such consent, in its sole discre-

Reg. § 1.1017-1(g)(2)

tion. A request by the taxpayer must be made before the due date (including extensions) for filing the taxpayer's Federal income tax return for the taxable year in which the taxpayer has COD income that is excluded from gross income under section 108(a).

(B) *Request for consent required.* A taxpayer must request a partnership's consent to reduce inside basis if, at the time of the discharge, the taxpayer owns (directly or indirectly) a greater than 50 percent interest in the capital and profits of the partnership, or if reductions to the basis of the taxpayer's depreciable property (or depreciable real property) are being made with respect to the taxpayer's distributive share of COD income of the partnership.

(C) *Granting of request required.* A partnership must consent to reduce its partners' shares of inside basis with respect to a discharged indebtedness if consent is requested with respect to that indebtedness by partners owning (directly or indirectly) an aggregate of more than 80 percent of the capital and profits interests of the partnership or five or fewer partners owning (directly or indirectly) an aggregate of more than 50 percent of the capital and profits interests of the partnership. For example, if there is a cancellation of partnership indebtedness that is secured by real property used in a partnership's trade or business, and if partners owning (in the aggregate) 90 percent of the capital and profits interests of the partnership elect to exclude the COD income under section 108(c), the partnership must make the appropriate reductions in those partners' shares of inside basis.

(iii) *Partnership consent statement*—(A) *Partnership requirement.* A consenting partnership must include with the Form 1065, U.S. Partnership Return of Income, for the taxable year following the year that ends with or within the taxable year the taxpayer excludes COD income from gross income under section 108(a), and must provide to the taxpayer on or before the due date of the taxpayer's return (including extensions) for the taxable year in which the taxpayer excludes COD income from gross income, a statement that—

(*1*) Contains the name, address, and taxpayer identification number of the partnership; and

(*2*) States the amount of the reduction of the partner's proportionate interest in the adjusted bases of the partnership's depreciable property or depreciable real property, whichever is applicable.

(B) *Taxpayer's requirement.* Statements described in paragraph (g)(2)(iii)(A) of this section must be attached to a taxpayer's timely filed (including extensions) Federal income tax return for the taxable year in which the taxpayer has COD income that is excluded from gross income under section 108(a).

(iv) *Partner's share of partnership basis*—(A) *In general.* For purposes of this paragraph (g), a partner's proportionate share of the partnership's basis in depreciable property (or depreciable real property) is equal to the sum of—

(*1*) The partner's section 743(b) basis adjustments to items of partnership depreciable property (or depreciable real property); and

(*2*) The common basis depreciation deductions (but not including remedial allocations of depreciation deductions under § 1.704-3(d)) that, under the terms of the partnership agreement effective for the taxable year in which the discharge of indebtedness occurs, are reasonably expected to be allocated to the partner over the property's remaining useful life. The assumptions made by a partnership in determining the reasonably expected allocation of depreciation deductions must be consistent for each partner. For example, a partnership may not treat the same depreciation deductions as being reasonably expected by more than one partner.

(B) *Effective date.* This paragraph (g)(2)(iv) applies to elections made under sections 108(b)(5) and 108(c) on or after December 15, 1999.

(v) *Treatment of basis reduction*—(A) *Basis adjustment.* The amount of the reduction to the basis of depreciable partnership property constitutes an adjustment to the basis of partnership property with respect to the partner only. No adjustment is made to the common basis of partnership property. Thus, for purposes of income, deduction, gain, loss, and distribution, the partner will have a special basis for those partnership properties the bases of which are adjusted under section 1017 and this section.

(B) *Recovery of adjustments to basis of partnership property.* Adjustments to the basis of partnership property under this section are recovered in the manner described in § 1.743-1.

(C) *Effect of basis reduction.* Adjustments to the basis of partnership property under this section are treated in the same manner and have the same effect as an adjustment to the basis of partnership property under section 743(b). The following example illustrates this paragraph (g)(2)(v):

Example. (i) A, B, and C are equal partners in partnership PRS, which owns (among other things) Asset 1, an item of depreciable property with a basis of $30,000. A's basis in its partnership interest is $20,000. Under the terms of the partnership agreement, A's share of the depreciation deductions from Asset 1 over its remaining useful life will be $10,000. Under section 1017, A requests, and PRS agrees, to decrease the basis of Asset 1 with respect to A by $10,000.

(ii) In the year following the reduction of basis under section 1017, PRS amends its partnership agreement to provide that items of depreciation and loss from Asset 1 will be allocated equally between B and C. In that year, A's distributive share of the partnership's common basis depreciation deductions from Asset 1 is now $0. Under § 1.743-1(j)(4)(ii)(B), the amount of the section 1017 basis adjustment that A recovers during the year is $1,000. A will report $1,000 of ordinary income because A's distributive share of the partnership's common basis depreciation deductions from Asset 1 ($0) is insufficient to offset the amount of the section 1017 basis adjustment recovered by A during the year ($1,000).

(iii) In the following year, PRS sells Asset 1 for $15,000 and recognizes a $12,000 loss. This loss is allocated equally between B and C, and A's share of the loss is $0. Upon the sale of Asset 1, A recovers its entire remaining section 1017 basis adjustment ($9,000). A will report $9,000 of ordinary income.

(D) *Effective date.* This paragraph (g)(2)(v) applies to elections made under sections 108(b)(5) and 108(c) on or after December 15, 1999.

(3) *Partnership basis reduction.* The rules of this section (including this paragraph (g)) apply in determining the properties to which the partnership's basis reductions must be made.

(h) *Special allocation rule for cases to which section 1398 applies.* If a bankruptcy estate and a taxpayer to whom section 1398 applies (concerning only individuals under Chapter 7 or 11 of title 11 of the United States Code) hold property subject to basis reduction under section 108(b)(2)(E) or (5) on the first day of the taxable year following the taxable year of discharge, the bankruptcy estate must reduce all of the adjusted bases of its property before the taxpayer is required to reduce any adjusted bases of property.

(i) *Effective date.* This section applies to discharges of indebtedness occurring on or after October 22, 1998. [Reg. § 1.1017-1.]

☐ [T.D. 6158, 1-6-56. *Amended by* T.D. 8787, 10-21-98 *and* T.D. 8847, 12-14-99.]

[Reg. § 1.1019-1]

§ 1.1019-1. **Property on which lessee had made improvements.**—In any case in which a lessee of real property has erected buildings or made other improvements upon the leased property and the lease is terminated by forfeiture or otherwise resulting in the realization by such lessor of income which, were it not for the provisions of section 109, would be includible in gross income of the lessor, the amount so excluded from gross income shall not be taken into account in determining the basis or the adjusted basis of such property or any portion thereof in the hands of the lessor. If, however, in any taxable year beginning before January 1, 1942, there has been included in the gross income of the lessor an amount representing any part of the value of such property attributable to such buildings or improvements, the basis of each portion of such property shall be properly adjusted for the amount so included in gross income. For example, A leased in 1930 to B for a period of 25 years unimproved real property and in accordance with the terms of the lease B erected a building on the property. It was estimated that upon expiration of the lease the building would have a depreciated value of $50,000, which value the lessor elected to report (beginning in 1931) as income over the term of the lease. This method of reporting was used until 1942. In 1952 B forfeits the lease. The amount of $22,000 reported as income by A during the years 1931 to 1941, inclusive, shall be added to the basis of the property represented by the improvements in the hands of A. If in such case A did not report during the period of the lease any income attributable to the value of the building erected by the lessee and the lease was forfeited in 1940 when the building was worth $75,000, such amount, having been included in gross income under the law applicable to that year, is added to the basis of the property represented by the improvements in the hands of A. As to treatment of such property for the purposes of capital gains and losses, see subchapter P (sections 1201 and following), chapter 1 of the Code. [Reg. § 1.1019-1.]

☐ [T.D. 6265, 11-6-57.]

[Reg. § 1.1021-1]

§ 1.1021-1. **Sale of annuities.**—In the case of a transfer for value of an annuity contract to which section 72(g) and paragraph (a) of § 1.72-10 apply, the transferor shall adjust his basis in such contract as of the time immediately prior to such transfer by subtracting from the premiums or other consideration he has paid or is deemed to have paid for such contract all amounts he has received or is deemed to have received under such annuity contract to the extent that such amounts were not includible in the gross income of the transferor or other recipient under the applicable income tax law. In any case where the amounts which were not includible in the gross income of the recipient were received or deemed to have been received by such transferor exceed the amounts paid or deemed paid by him, the adjusted basis of the contract shall be zero. The income realized by the transferor on such a transfer shall not exceed the total of the amounts received as consideration for the transfer. [Reg. § 1.1021-1.]

☐ [T.D. 6211, 11-14-56.]

Common Nontaxable Exchanges

[Reg. § 1.1031-0]

§ 1.1031-0. **Table of contents.**

This section lists the captions that appear in the regulations under section 1031.

§ 1.1031(a)-1 *Property held for productive use in a trade or business or for investment.*

(a) In general.

(b) Definition of "like kind."

(c) Examples of exchanges of property of a "like kind."

(d) Examples of exchanges not solely in kind.

(e) Effective date.

§ 1.1031(a)-2 *Additional rules for exchanges of personal property.*

(a) Introduction.

(b) Depreciable tangible personal property.

(c) Intangible personal property and nondepreciable personal property.

§ 1.1031(b)-1 *Receipt of other property or money in tax-free exchange.*

§ 1.1031(b)-2 *Safe harbor for qualified intermediaries.*

§ 1.1031(c)-1 *Nonrecognition of loss.*

§ 1.1031(d)-1 *Property acquired upon a tax-free exchange.*

§ 1.1031(d)-1T *Coordinatin of section 1060 with section 1031 (temporary).*

§ 1.1031(d)-2 *Treatment of assumption of liabilities.*

§ 1.1031(e)-1 *Exchanges of livestock of different sexes.*

§ 1.1031(j)-1 *Exchanges of multiple properties.*

(a) Introduction.

(b) Computation of gain recognized.

(c) Computation of basis of properties received.

(d) Examples.

(e) Effective date.

§ 1.1031(k)-1 *Treatment of deferred exchanges.*

(a) Overview.

(b) Identification and receipt requirements.

(c) Identification of replacement property before the end of the identification period.

(d) Receipt of identified replacement property.

(e) Special rules for identification and receipt of replacement property to be produced.

(f) Receipt of money or other property.

(g) Safe harbors.

(h) Interest and growth factors.

(i) [Reserved]

(j) Determination of gain or loss recognized and the basis of property received in a deferred exchange.

(k) Definition of disqualified person.

(l) [Reserved]

(m) Definition of fair market value.

(n) No inference with respect to actual or constructive receipt rules outside of section 1031.

(o) Effective date. [Reg. § 1.1031-0.]

☐ [T.D. 8346, 4-25-91.]

[Reg. § 1.1031(a)-1]

§ 1.1031(a)-1. **Property held for productive use in trade or business or for investment.—** (a) *In general*—(1) *Exchanges of property solely for property of a like kind.* Section 1031(a)(1) provides an exception from the general rule requiring the recognition of gain or loss upon the sale or exchange of property. Under section 1031(a)(1), no gain or loss is recognized if property held for productive use in a trade or business or for investment is exchanged solely for property of a like kind to be held either for productive use in a trade or business or for investment. Under section 1031(a)(1), property held for productive use in trade or business may be exchanged for property held for investment. Similarly, under section 1031(a)(1), property held for investment may be exchanged for property held for productive use in a trade or business. However, section 1031(a)(2) provides that section 1031(a)(1) does not apply to any exchange of—

(i) Stock in trade or other property held primarily for sale;

(ii) Stocks, bonds, or notes;

(iii) Other securities or evidences of indebtedness or interest;

(iv) Interests in a partnership;

(v) Certificates of trust or beneficial interests; or

(vi) Choses in action.

Reg. § 1.1031-0

Section 1031(a)(1) does not apply to any exchange of interests in a partnership regardless of whether the interests exchanged are general or limited partnership interests or are interests in the same partnership or in different partnerships. An interest in a partnership that has in effect a valid election under section 761(a) to be excluded from the application of all of subchapter K is treated as an interest in each of the assets of the partnership and not as an interest in a partnership for purposes of section 1031(a)(2)(D) and paragraph (a)(1)(iv) of this section. An exchange of an interest in such a partnership does not qualify for nonrecognition of gain or loss under section 1031 with respect to any asset of the partnership that is described in section 1031(a)(2) or to the extent the exchange of assets of the partnership does not otherwise satisfy the requirements of section 1031(a).

(2) *Exchanges of property not solely for property of a like kind.* A transfer is not within the provisions of section 1031(a) if, as part of the consideration, the taxpayer receives money or property which does not meet the requirements of section 1031(a), but the transfer, if otherwise qualified, will be within the provisions of either section 1031(b) or (c). Similarly, a transfer is not within the provisions of section 1031(a) if, as part of the consideration, the other party to the exchange assumes a liability of the taxpayer (or acquires property from the taxpayer that is subject to a liability), but the transfer, if otherwise qualified, will be within the provisions of either section 1031(b) or (c). A transfer of property meeting the requirements of section 1031(a) may be within the provisions of section 1031(a) even though the taxpayer transfers in addition property not meeting the requirements of section 1031(a) or money. However, the nonrecognition treatment provided by section 1031(a) does not apply to the property transferred which does not meet the requirements of section 1031(a).

(b) *Definition of "like kind."* As used in section 1031(a), the words "like kind" have reference to the nature or character of the property and not to its grade or quality. One kind or class of property may not, under that section, be exchanged for property of a different kind or class. The fact that any real estate involved is improved or unimproved is not material, for that fact relates only to the grade or quality of the property and not to its kind or class. Unproductive real estate held by one other than a dealer for future use or future realization of the increment in value is held for investment and not primarily for sale. For additional rules for exchanges of personal property, see § 1.1031(a)-2.

(c) *Examples of exchanges of property of a "like kind."* No gain or loss is recognized if (1) a taxpayer exchanges property held for productive use in his trade or business, together with cash, for other property of like kind for the same use, such as a truck for a new truck or a passenger automobile for a new passenger automobile to be used for a like purpose; or (2) a taxpayer who is not a dealer in real estate exchanges city real estate for a ranch or farm, or exchanges a leasehold of a fee with 30 years or more to run for real estate, or exchanges improved real estate for unimproved real estate; or (3) a taxpayer exchanges investment property and cash for investment property of a like kind.

(d) *Examples of exchanges not solely in kind.* Gain or loss is recognized if, for instance, a taxpayer exchanges (1) Treasury bonds maturing March 15, 1958, for Treasury bonds maturing December 15, 1968, unless section 1037(a) (or so much of section 1031 as relates to section 1037(a)) applies to such exchange, or (2) a real estate mortgage for consolidated farm loan bonds.

(e) *Effective date relating to exchanges of partnership interests.* The provisions of paragraph (a)(1) of this section relating to exchanges of partnership interests apply to transfers of property made by taxpayers on or after April 25, 1991. [Reg. § 1.1031(a)-1.]

☐ [T.D. 6210, 11-6-56. *Amended by* T.D. 6935, 11-16-67; T.D. 8343, 4-11-91 *and* T.D. 8346, 4-25-91.]

[Reg. § 1.1031(a)-2]

§ 1.1031(a)-2. **Additional rules for exchanges of personal property.**—(a) *Introduction.* Section 1.1031(a)-1(b) provides that the nonrecognition rules of section 1031 do not apply to an exchange of one kind or class of property for property of a different kind or class. This section contains additional rules for determining whether personal property has been exchanged for property of a like kind or like class. Personal properties of a like class are considered to be of a "like kind" for purposes of section 1031. In addition, an exchange of properties of a like kind may qualify under section 1031 regardless of whether the properties are also of a like class. In determining whether exchanged properties are of a like kind, no inference is to be drawn from the fact that the properties are not of a like class. Under paragraph (b) of this section, depreciable tangible personal properties are of a like class if they are either within the same General Asset Class (as defined in paragraph (b)(2) of this section) or within the same Product Class (as defined in paragraph (b)(3) of this section). Paragraph (c) of this section pro-

Reg. § 1.1031(a)-2(a)

vides rules for exchanges of intangible personal property and nondepreciable personal property.

(b) *Depreciable tangible personal property*—(1) *General rule.* Depreciable tangible personal property is exchanged for property of a "like kind" under section 1031 if the property is exchanged for property of a like kind or like class. Depreciable tangible personal property is of a like class to other depreciable tangible personal property if the exchanged properties are either within the same General Asset Class or within the same Product Class. A single property may not be classified within more than one General Asset Class or within more than one Product Class. In addition, property classified within any General Asset Class may not be classified within a Product Class. A property's General Asset Class or Product Class is determined as of the date of the exchange.

(2) *General Asset Classes.* Except as provided in paragraphs (b)(4) and (b)(5) of this section, property within a General Asset Class consists of depreciable tangible personal property described in one of asset classes 00.11 through 00.28 and 00.4 of Rev. Proc. 87-56, 1987-2 C.B. 674. These General Asset Classes describe types of depreciable tangible personal property that frequently are used in many businesses. The General Asset Classes are as follows:

(i) Office furniture, fixtures, and equipment (asset class 00.11),

(ii) Information systems (computers and peripheral equipment) (asset class 00.12),

(iii) Data handling equipment, except computers (asset class 00.13),

(iv) Airplanes (airframes and engines), except those used in commercial or contract carrying of passengers or freight, and all helicopters (airframes and engines) (asset class 00.21),

(v) Automobiles, taxis (asset class 00.22),

(vi) Buses (asset class 00.23),

(vii) Light general purpose trucks (asset class 00.241),

(viii) Heavy general purpose trucks (asset class 00.242),

(ix) Railroad cars and locomotives, except those owned by railroad transportation companies (asset class 00.25),

(x) Tractor units for use over-the-road (asset class 00.26),

(xi) Trailers and trailer-mounted containers (asset class 00.27),

(xii) Vessels, barges, tugs, and similar water-transportation equipment, except those used in marine construction (asset class 00.28), and

(xiii) Industrial steam and electric generation and/or distribution systems (asset class 00.4).

(3) *Product Classes.* Except as provided in paragraphs (b)(4) and (b)(5) of this section, property within a Product Class consists of depreciable tangible personal property that is listed in a 4-digit product class within Division D of the Standard Industrial Classification codes, set forth in Executive Office of the President, Office of Management and Budget, *Standard Industrial Classification Manual* (1987) ("*SIC Manual*"). Copies of the *SIC Manual* may be obtained from the National Technical Information Service, an agency of the U.S. Department of Commerce. Division D of the *SIC Manual* contains a listing of manufactured products and equipment. For this purpose, any 4-digit product class ending in a "9" (*i.e.*, a miscellaneous category) will not be considered a Product Class. If a property is listed in more than one product class, the property is treated as listed in any one of those product classes. A property's 4-digit product classification is referred to as the property's "SIC Code."

(4) *Modifications of Rev. Proc. 87-56 and SIC Manual.* The asset classes of Rev. Proc. 87-56 and the product classes of the *SIC Manual* may be updated or otherwise modified from time to time. In the event Rev. Proc. 87-56 is modified, the General Asset Classes will follow the modification, and the modification will be effective for exchanges occurring on or after the date the modification is published in the Internal Revenue Bulletin, unless otherwise provided. Similarly, in the event the *SIC Manual* is modified, the Product Classes will follow the modification, and the modification will be effective for exchanges occurring on or after the effective date of the modification. However, taxpayers may rely on the unmodified *SIC Manual* for exchanges occurring during the one-year period following the effective date of the modification. The *SIC Manual* generally is modified every five years, in years ending in a 2 or 7 (e.g., 1987 and 1992). The effective date of the modified *SIC Manual* is announced in the Federal Register and generally is January 1 of the year the *SIC Manual* is modified.

(5) *Modified classification through published guidance.* The Commissioner may, by guidance published in the Internal Revenue Bulletin, supplement the guidance provided in this section relating to classification of properties. For example, the Commissioner may determine not to follow, in whole or in part, any modification of Rev. Proc. 87-56 or the *SIC Manual.* The Commissioner may also determine that two types of property that are listed in separate product classes each ending in a "9" are of a like class, or that a type

Reg. § 1.1031(a)-2(b)(1)

of property that has a SIC Code is of a like class to a type of property that does not have a SIC Code.

(6) *No inference outside of Section 1031.* The rules provided in this section concerning the use of Rev. Proc. 87-56 and the *SIC Manual* are limited to exchanges under section 1031. No inference is intended with respect to the classification of property for other purposes, such as depreciation.

(7) *Examples.* The application of this paragraph (b) may be illustrated by the following examples:

Example 1. Taxpayer A transfers a personal computer (asset class 00.12) to B in exchange for a printer (asset class 00.12). With respect to A, the properties exchanged are within the same General Asset Class and therefore are of a like class.

Example 2. Taxpayer C transfers an airplane (asset class 00.21) to D in exchange for a heavy general purpose truck (asset class 00.242). The properties exchanged are not of a like class because they are within different General Asset Classes. Because each of the properties is within a General Asset Class, the properties may not be classified within a Product Class. The airplane and heavy general purpose truck are also not of a like kind. Therefore, the exchange does not qualify for nonrecognition of gain or loss under section 1031.

Example 3. Taxpayer E transfers a grader to F in exchange for a scraper. Neither property is within any of the General Asset Classes, and both properties are within the same Product Class (SIC Code 3533). With respect to E, therefore, the properties exchanged are of a like class.

Example 4. Taxpayer G transfers a personal computer (asset class 00.12), an airplane (asset class 00.21) and a sanding machine (SIC Code 3553), to H in exchange for a printer (asset class 00.12), a heavy general purpose truck (asset class 00.242) and a lathe (SIC Code 3553). The personal computer and the printer are of a like class because they are within the same General Asset Class; the sanding machine and the lathe are of a like class because neither property is within any of the General Asset Classes and they are within the same Product Class. The airplane and the heavy general purpose truck are neither within the same General Asset Class nor within the same Product Class, and are not of a like kind.

(c) *Intangible personal property and nondepreciable personal property*—(1) *General rule.* An exchange of intangible personal property or nondepreciable personal property qualifies for nonrecognition of gain or loss under section 1031 only if the exchanged properties are of a like kind. No like classes are provided for these properties. Whether intangible personal property is of a like kind to other intangible personal property generally depends on the nature or character of the rights involved (*e.g.*, a patent or a copyright) and also on the nature or character of the underlying property to which the intangible personal property relates.

(2) *Goodwill and going concern value.* The goodwill or going concern value of a business is not of a like kind to the goodwill or going concern value of another business.

(3) *Examples.* The application of this paragraph (c) may be illustrated by the following examples:

Example (1). Taxpayer K exchanges a copyright on a novel for a copyright on a different novel. The properties exchanged are of a like kind.

Example (2). Taxpayer J exchanges a copyright on a novel for a copyright on a song. The properties exchanged are not of a like kind.

(d) *Effective date.* Section 1.1031(a)-2 is effective for exchanges occurring on or after April 11, 1991. [Reg. § 1.1031(a)-2.]

☐ [*T.D.* 8343, 4-11-91.]

[Reg. § 1.1031(b)-1]

§ 1.1031(b)-1. **Receipt of other property or money in tax-free exchange.**—(a) If the taxpayer receives other property (in addition to property permitted to be received without recognition of gain) or money—

(1) In an exchange described in section 1031(a) of property held for investment or productive use in trade or business for property of like kind to be held either for productive use or for investment,

(2) In an exchange described in section 1035(a) of insurance policies or annuity contracts,

(3) In an exchange described in section 1036(a) of common stock for common stock, or preferred stock for preferred stock, in the same corporation and not in connection with a corporate reorganization, or

(4) In an exchange described in section 1037(a) of obligations of the United States, issued under the Second Liberty Bond Act (31 U.S.C. 774(2)), solely for other obligations issued under such Act,

the gain, if any, to the taxpayer will be recognized under section 1031(b) in an amount not in excess of the sum of the money and the fair market value of the other property, but the loss, if any, to the taxpayer from such an exchange will not be recognized under section 1031(c) to any extent.

(b) The application of this section may be illustrated by the following examples:

Common Nontaxable Exchanges

Example (1). A, who is not a dealer in real estate, in 1954 exchanges real estate held for investment, which he purchased in 1940 for $5,000, for other real estate (to be held for productive use in trade or business) which has a fair market value of $6,000, and $2,000 in cash. The gain from the transaction is $3,000, but is recognized only to the extent of the cash received of $2,000.

Example (2). (a) B, who uses the cash receipts and disbursements method of accounting and the calendar year as his taxable year, has never elected under section 454(a) to include in gross income currently the annual increase in the redemption price of non-interest-bearing obligations issued at a discount. In 1943, for $750 each, B purchased four $1,000 series E United States savings bonds bearing an issue date of March 1, 1943.

(b) On October 1, 1963, the redemption value of each such bond was $1,396, and the total redemption value of the four bonds was $5,584. On that date B submitted the four $1,000 series E bonds to the United States in a transaction in which one of such $1,000 bonds was reissued by issuing four $100 series E United States savings bonds bearing an issue date of March 1, 1943, and by considering six $100 series E bonds bearing an issue date of March 1, 1943, to have been issued. The redemption value of each such $100 series E bond was $139.60 on October 1, 1963. Then, as part of the transaction, the six $100 series E bonds so considered to have been issued and the three $1,000 series E bonds were exchanged, in an exchange qualifying under section 1037(a), for five $1,000 series H United States savings bonds plus $25.60 in cash.

(c) The gain realized on the exchange qualifying under section 1037(a) is $2,325.60, determined as follows:

Amount realized:		
Par value of five series H bonds		$5,000.00
Cash received		25.60
Total realized		5,025.60
Less: Adjusted basis of series E bonds surrendered in the exchange:		
Three $1,000 series E bonds	$2,250	
Six $100 series E bonds at $75 each	450	2,700.00
Gain realized		$2,325.60

(d) Pursuant to section 1031(b), only $25.60 (the money received) of the total gain of $2,325.60 realized on the exchange is recognized at the time of exchange and must be included in B's gross income for 1963. The $2,300 balance of the gain ($2,325.60 less $25.60) must be included in B's gross income for the taxable year in which the series H bonds are redeemed or disposed of, or reach final maturity, whichever is earlier, as provided in paragraph (c) of § 1.454-1.

(e) The gain on the four $100 series E bonds, determined by using $75 as a basis for each such bond, must be included in B's gross income for the taxable year in which such bonds are redeemed or disposed of, or reach final maturity, whichever is earlier.

Example (3). (a) The facts are the same as in example (2), except that, as part of the transaction, the $1,000 series E bond is reissued by considering ten $100 series E bonds bearing an issue date of March 1, 1943, to have been issued. Six of the $100 series E bonds so considered to have been issued are surrendered to the United States as part of the exchange qualifying under section 1037(a) and the other four are immediately redeemed.

(b) Pursuant to section 1031(b), only $25.60 (the money received) of the total gain of $2,325.60 realized on the exchange qualifying under section 1037(a) is recognized at the time of the exchange and must be included in B's gross income for 1963. The $2,300 balance of the gain ($2,325.60 less $25.60) realized on such exchange must be included in B's gross income for the taxable year in which the series H bonds are redeemed or disposed of, or reach final maturity, whichever is earlier, as provided in paragraph (c) of § 1.454-1.

(c) The redemption on October 1, 1963, of the four $100 series E bonds considered to have been issued at such time results in gain of $258.40, which is then recognized and must be included in B's gross income for 1963. This gain of $258.40 is the difference between the $558.40 redemption value of such bonds on the date of the exchange and the $300 (4 × $75) paid for such series E bonds in 1943.

Example (4). On November 1, 1963, C purchased for $91 a marketable United States bond which was originally issued at its par value of $100 under the Second Liberty Bond Act. On February 1, 1964, in an exchange qualifying under section 1037(a), C surrendered the bond to the United States for another marketable United States bond, which then had a fair market value of $92, and $1.85 in cash, $0.85 of which was

Reg. § 1.1031(b)-1(b)

Common Nontaxable Exchanges

interest. The $0.85 interest received is includible in gross income for the taxable year of the exchange, but the $2 gain ($93 less $91) realized on the exchange is recognized for such year under section 1031(b) to the extent of $1 (the money received). Under section 1031(d), C's basis in the bond received in exchange is $91 (his basis of $91 in the bond surrendered, reduced by the $1 money received and increased by the $1 gain recognized).

(c) Consideration received in the form of an assumption of liabilities (or a transfer subject to a liability) is to be treated as "other property or money" for the purposes of section 1031(b). Where, on an exchange described in section 1031(b), each party to the exchange either assumes a liability of the other party or acquires property subject to a liability, then, in determining the amount of "other property or money" for purposes of section 1031(b), consideration given in the form of an assumption of liabilities (or a receipt of property subject to a liability) shall be offset against consideration received in the form of an assumption of liabilities (or a transfer subject to a liability). See § 1.1031(d)-2, examples (1) and (2). [Reg. § 1.1031(b)-1.]

☐ [T.D. 6210, 11-6-56. Amended by T.D. 6935, 11-16-67.]

[Reg. § 1.1031(b)-2]

§ 1.1031(b)-2. Safe harbor for qualified intermediaries.—(a) In the case of simultaneous transfers of like-kind properties involving a qualified intermediary (as defined in § 1.1031(k)-1(g)(4)(iii)), the qualified intermediary is not considered the agent of the taxpayer for purposes of section 1031(a). In such a case, the transfer and receipt of property by the taxpayer is treated as an exchange.

(b) In the case of simultaneous exchanges of like-kind properties involving a qualified intermediary (as defined in § 1.1031(k)-1(g)(4)(iii)), the receipt by the taxpayer of an evidence of indebtedness of the transferee of the qualified intermediary is treated as the receipt of an evidence of indebtedness of the person acquiring property from the taxpayer for purposes of section 453 and § 15a.453-1(b)(3)(i) of this chapter.

(c) Paragraph (a) of this section applies to transfers of property made by taxpayers on or after June 10, 1991.

(d) Paragraph (b) of this section applies to transfers of property made by taxpayers on or after April 20, 1994. A taxpayer may choose to apply paragraph (b) of this section to transfers of property made on or after June 10, 1991. [Reg. § 1.1031(b)-2.]

☐ [T.D. 8346, 4-25-91. Amended by T.D. 8535, 4-19-94.]

[Reg. § 1.1031(c)-1]

§ 1.1031(c)-1. Nonrecognition of loss.—Section 1031(c) provides that a loss shall not be recognized from an exchange of property described in section 1031(a), 1035(a), 1036(a), or 1037(a) where there is received in the exchange other property or money in addition to property permitted to be received without recognition of gain or loss. See example (4) of paragraph (a)(3) of § 1.1037-1 for an illustration of the application of this section in the case of an exchange of United States obligations described in section 1037(a). [Reg. § 1.1031(c)-1.]

☐ [T.D. 6210, 11-6-56. Amended by T.D. 6935, 11-16-67.]

[Reg. § 1.1031(d)-1]

§ 1.1031(d)-1. Property acquired upon a tax-free exchange.—(a) If, in an exchange of property solely of the type described in section 1031, section 1035(a), section 1036(a), or section 1037(a), no part of the gain or loss was recognized under the law applicable to the year in which the exchange was made, the basis of the property acquired is the same as the basis of the property transferred by the taxpayer with proper adjustments to the date of the exchange. If additional consideration is given by the taxpayer in the exchange, the basis of the property acquired shall be the same as the property transferred increased by the amount of additional consideration given (see section 1016 and the regulations thereunder).

(b) If, in an exchange of properties of the type indicated in section 1031, section 1035(a), section 1036(a), or section 1037(a), gain to the taxpayer was recognized under the provisions of section 1031(b) or a similar provision of a prior revenue law, on account of the receipt of money in the transaction, the basis of the property acquired is the basis of the property transferred (adjusted to the date of the exchange), decreased by the amount of money received and increased by the amount of gain recognized on the exchange. The application of this paragraph may be illustrated by the following example:

Example. A, an individual in the moving and storage business, in 1954 transfers one of his moving trucks with an adjusted basis in his hands of $2,500 to B in exchange for a truck (to be used in A's business) with a fair market value of $2,400 and $200 in cash. A realizes a gain of $100 upon the exchange, all of which is recognized under section 1031(b). The basis of the truck acquired by A is determined as follows:

Common Nontaxable Exchanges

Adjusted basis of A's former truck	$2,500
Less: Amount of money received	200
Difference	2,300
Plus: Amount of gain recognized	100
Basis of truck acquired by A	$2,400

(c) If, upon an exchange of properties of the type described in section 1031, section 1035(a), section 1036(a), or section 1037(a), the taxpayer received other property (not permitted to be received without the recognition of gain) and gain from the transaction was recognized as required under section 1031(b), or a similar provision of a prior revenue law, the basis (adjusted to the date of the exchange) of the property transferred by the taxpayer, decreased by the amount of any money received and increased by the amount of gain recognized, must be allocated to and is the basis of the properties (other than money) received on the exchange. For the purpose of the allocation of the basis of the properties received, there must be assigned to such other property an amount equivalent to its fair market value at the date of the exchange. The application of this paragraph may be illustrated by the following example:

Example. A, who is not a dealer in real estate, in 1954 transfers real estate held for investment which he purchased in 1940 for $10,000 in exchange for other real estate (to be held for investment) which has a fair market value of $9,000, an automobile which has a fair market value of $2,000, and $1,500 in cash. A realizes a gain of $2,500, all of which is recognized under section 1031(b). The basis of the property received in exchange is the basis of the real estate A transfers ($10,000) decreased by the amount of money received ($1,500) and increased in the amount of gain that was recognized ($2,500), which results in a basis for the property received of $11,000. This basis of $11,000 is allocated between the automobile and the real estate received by A, the basis of the automobile being its fair market value at the date of the exchange, $2,000, and the basis of the real estate received being the remainder, $9,000.

(d) Section 1031(c) and, with respect to section 1031 and section 1036(a), similar provisions of prior revenue laws provide that no loss may be recognized on an exchange of properties of a type described in section 1031, section 1035(a), section 1036(a), or section 1037(a), although the taxpayer receives other property or money from the transaction. However, the basis of the property or properties (other than money) received by the taxpayer is the basis (adjusted to the date of the exchange) of the property transferred, decreased by the amount of money received. This basis must be allocated to the properties received, and for this purpose there must be allocated to such other property an amount of such basis equivalent to its fair market value at the date of the exchange.

(e) If, upon an exchange of properties of the type described in section 1031, section 1035(a), section 1036(a), or section 1037(a), the taxpayer also exchanged other property (not permitted to be transferred without the recognition of gain or loss) and gain or loss from the transaction is recognized under section 1002 or a similar provision of a prior revenue law, the basis of the property acquired is the total basis of the properties transferred (adjusted to the date of the exchange) increased by the amount of gain and decreased by the amount of loss recognized on the other property. For purposes of this rule, the taxpayer is deemed to have received in exchange for such other property an amount equal to its fair market value on the date of the exchange. The application of this paragraph may be illustrated by the following example:

Example. A exchanges real estate held for investment plus stock for real estate to be held for investment. The real estate transferred has an adjusted basis of $10,000 and a fair market value of $11,000. The stock transferred has an adjusted basis of $4,000 and a fair market value of $2,000. The real estate acquired has a fair market value of $13,000. A is deemed to have received a $2,000 portion of the acquired real estate in exchange for the stock, since $2,000 is the fair market value of the stock at the time of the exchange. A $2,000 loss is recognized under section 1002 on the exchange of the stock for real estate. No gain or loss is recognized on the exchange of the real estate since the property received is of the type permitted to be received without recognition of gain or loss. The basis of the real estate acquired by A is determined as follows:

Adjusted basis of real estate transferred	$10,000
Adjusted basis of stock transferred	4,000
	14,000
Less: Loss recognized on transfer of stock	2,000
Basis of real estate acquired upon the exchange	12,000

[Reg. § 1.1031(d)-1.]

☐ [T.D. 6210, 11-6-56. *Amended by T.D.* 6453, 2-16-60 *and T.D.* 6935, 11-16-67.]

[Reg. § 1.1031(d)-1T]

§ 1.1031(d)-1T. **Coordination of section 1060 with section 1031 (temporary).**—If the properties exchanged under section 1031 are part of a group of assets which constitute a trade or business under section 1060, the like-kind property and other property or money which are treated as

Common Nontaxable Exchanges

See p. 20,601 for regulations not amended to reflect law changes

transferred in exchange for the like-kind property shall be excluded from the allocation rules of section 1060. However, section 1060 shall apply to property which is not like-kind property or other property or money which is treated as transferred in exchange for the like-kind property. For application of the section 1060 allocation rules to property which is not part of the like-kind exchange, see § 1.1060-1(b), (c), and (d) *Example (1)*. [Temporary Reg. § 1.1031(d)-1T.]

☐ [T.D. 8215, 7-15-88. *Amended by* T.D. 8858, 1-5-2000 *and* T.D. 8940, 2-12-2001.]

[Reg. § 1.1031(d)-2]

§ 1.1031(d)-2. Treatment of assumption of liabilities.—For the purposes of section 1031(d), the amount of any liabilities of the taxpayer assumed by the other party to the exchange (or of any liabilities to which the property exchanged by the taxpayer is subject) is to be treated as money received by the taxpayer upon the exchange, whether or not the assumption resulted in a recognition of gain or loss to the taxpayer under the law applicable to the year in which the exchange was made. The application of this section may be illustrated by the following examples:

Example (1). B, an individual, owns an apartment house which has an adjusted basis in his hands of $500,000, but which is subject to a mortgage of $150,000. On September 1, 1954, he transfers the apartment house to C, receiving in exchange therefor $50,000 in cash and another apartment house with a fair market value on that date of $600,000. The transfer to C is made subject to the $150,000 mortgage. B realizes a gain of $300,000 on the exchange, computed as follows:

Value of property received	$600,000
Cash	50,000
Liabilities subject to which old property was transferred	150,000
Total consideration received	800,000
Less: Adjusted basis of property transferred	500,000
Gain realized	300,000

Under section 1031(b), $200,000 of the $300,000 gain is recognized. The basis of the apartment house acquired by B upon the exchange is $500,000, computed as follows:

Adjusted basis of property transferred		$500,000
Less: Amount of money received:		
Cash	$ 50,000	
Amount of liabilities subject to which property was transferred	150,000	
		200,000
Difference		300,000
Plus: Amount of gain recognized upon the exchange		200,000
Basis of property acquired upon the exchange		$500,000

Example (2). (a) D, an individual, owns an apartment house. On December 1, 1955, the apartment house owned by D has an adjusted basis in his hands of $100,000, a fair market value of $220,000, but is subject to a mortgage of $80,000. E, an individual, also owns an apartment house. On December 1, 1955, the apartment house owned by E has an adjusted basis of $175,000, a fair market value of $250,000, but is subject to a mortgage of $150,000. On December 1, 1955, D transfers his apartment house to E, receiving in exchange therefor $40,000 in cash and the apartment house owned by E. Each apartment house is transferred subject to the mortgage on it.

(b) D realizes a gain of $120,000 on the exchange, computed as follows:

Value of property received		$250,000
Cash		40,000
Liabilities subject to which old property was transferred		80,000
Total consideration received		370,000
Less: Adjusted basis of property transferred	$100,000	
Liabilities to which new property is subject	150,000	$250,000
Gain realized		$120,000

For purposes of section 1031(b), the amount of "other property or money" received by D is $40,000. (Consideration received by D in the form of a transfer subject to a liability of $80,000 is offset by consideration given in the form of a receipt of property subject to a $150,000 liability. Thus, only the consideration received in the form of cash, $40,000, is treated as "other property or money" for purposes of section 1031(b).) Accordingly, under section 1031(b), $40,000 of the $120,000 gain is recognized. The basis of the apartment house acquired by D is $170,000, computed as follows:

Adjusted basis of property transferred		$100,000
Liabilities to which new property is subject		150,000
Total		$250,000
Less: Amount of money received:		
Cash	$40,000	
Amount of liabilities subject to which property was transferred	80,000	
		$120,000

Reg. § 1.1031(d)-2

Difference	$130,000
Plus: Amount of gain recognized upon the exchange	40,000
Basis of property acquired upon the exchange	$170,000

(c) E realizes a gain of $75,000 on the exchange, computed as follows:

Value of property received		$220,000
Liabilities subject to which old property was transferred		$150,000
Total consideration received		370,000
Less: Adjusted basis of property transferred	$175,000	
Cash	40,000	
Liabilities to which new property is subject	80,000	
		$295,000
Gain realized		$ 75,000

For purposes of section 1031(b), the amount of "other property or money" received by E is $30,000. (Consideration received by E in the form of a transfer subject to a liability of $150,000 is offset by consideration given in the form of a receipt of property subject to an $80,000 liability and by the $40,000 cash paid by E. Although consideration received in the form of cash or other property is not offset by consideration given in the form of an assumption of liabilities or a receipt of property subject to a liability, consideration given in the form of cash or other property is offset against consideration received in the form of an assumption of liabilities or a transfer of property subject to a liability.) Accordingly, under section 1031(b), $30,000 of the $75,000 gain is recognized. The basis of the apartment house acquired by E is $175,000, computed as follows:

Adjusted basis of property transferred	$175,000
Cash	40,000
Liabilities to which new property is subject	80,000
Total	295,000
Less: Amount of money received: Amount of liabilities subject to which property was transferred	$150,000
	150,000
Difference	$145,000
Plus: Amount of gain recognized upon the exchange	30,000
Basis of property acquired upon the exchange	$175,000

[Reg. § 1.1031(d)-2.]

☐ [T.D. 6210, 11-6-56.]

[Reg. § 1.1031(e)-1]

§ 1.1031(e)-1. **Exchanges of livestock of different sexes.**—Section 1031(e) provides that livestock of different sexes are not property of like kind. Section 1031(e) and this section are applicable to taxable years to which the Internal Revenue Code of 1954 applies. [Reg. § 1.1031(e)-1.]

☐ [T.D. 7141, 9-21-71.]

[Reg. § 1.1031(j)-1]

§ 1.1031(j)-1. **Exchanges of multiple properties.**—(a) *Introduction*—(1) *Overview.* As a general rule, the application of section 1031 requires a property-by-property comparison for computing the gain recognized and basis of property received in a like-kind exchange. This section provides an exception to this general rule in the case of an exchange of multiple properties. An exchange is an exchange of multiple properties if, under paragraph (b)(2) of this section, more than one exchange group is created. In addition, an exchange is an exchange of multiple properties if only one exchange group is created but there is more than one property being transferred or received within that exchange group. Paragraph (b) of this section provides rules for computing the amount of gain recognized in an exchange of multiple properties qualifying for nonrecognition of gain or loss under section 1031. Paragraph (c) of this section provides rules for computing the basis of properties received in an exchange of multiple properties qualifying for nonrecognition of gain or loss under section 1031.

(2) *General Approach.* (i) In general, the amount of gain recognized in an exchange of multiple properties is computed by first separating the properties transferred and the properties received by the taxpayer in the exchange into exchange groups in the manner described in paragraph (b)(2) of this section. The separation of the properties transferred and the properties received in the exchange into exchange groups involves matching up properties of a like kind or like class to the extent possible. Next, all liabilities assumed by the taxpayer as part of the transaction are offset by all liabilities of which the taxpayer is relieved as part of the transaction, with the excess liabilities assumed or relieved allocated in accordance with paragraph (b)(2)(ii) of this section. Then, the rules of section 1031 and the regulations thereunder are applied separately to each exchange group to determine the amount of gain recognized in the exchange. See §§ 1.1031(b)-1 and 1.1031(c)-1. Finally, the rules of section 1031 and the regulations thereunder are applied separately to each exchange group to determine the basis of the properties received in the exchange. See §§ 1.1031(d)-1 and 1.1031(d)-2.

(ii) For purposes of this section, the exchanges are assumed to be made at arms' length, so that the aggregate fair market value of the property received in the exchange equals the aggregate fair market value of the property transferred. Thus, the amount realized with respect to the properties transferred in each exchange group is assumed to equal their aggregate fair market value.

(b) *Computation of gain recognized*—(1) *In general.* In computing the amount of gain recognized in an exchange of multiple properties, the fair market value must be determined for each property transferred and for each property received by the taxpayer in the exchange. In addition, the adjusted basis must be determined for each property transferred by the taxpayer in the exchange.

(2) *Exchange groups and residual group.* The properties transferred and the properties received by the taxpayer in the exchange are separated into exchange groups and a residual group to the extent provided in this paragraph (b)(2).

(i) *Exchange groups.* Each exchange group consists of the properties transferred and received in the exchange, all of which are of a like kind or like class. If a property could be included in more than one exchange group, the taxpayer may include the property in any of those exchange groups. Property eligible for inclusion within an exchange group does not include money or property described in section 1031(a)(2) (*i.e.*, stock in trade or other property held primarily for sale, stocks, bonds, notes, other securities or evidences of indebtedness or interest, interests in a partnership, certificates of trust or beneficial interests, or choses in action). For example, an exchange group may consist of all exchanged properties that are within the same General Asset Class or within the same Product Class (as defined in § 1.1031(a)-2(b)). Each exchange group must consist of at least one property transferred and at least one property received in the exchange.

(ii) *Treatment of liabilities.* (A) All liabilities assumed by the taxpayer as part of the exchange are offset against all liabilities of which the taxpayer is relieved as part of the exchange, regardless of whether the liabilities are recourse or nonrecourse and regardless of whether the liabilities are secured by or otherwise relate to specific property transferred or received as part of the exchange. See §§ 1.1031(b)-1(c) and 1.1031(d)-2. For purposes of this section, liabilities assumed by the taxpayer as part of the exchange consist of liabilities of the other party to the exchange assumed by the taxpayer and liabilities subject to which the exchange. Similarly, liabilities of which the taxpayer is relieved as part of the exchange consist of liabilities of the taxpayer assumed by the other party to the exchange and liabilities subject to which the taxpayer's property is transferred.

(B) If there are excess liabilities assumed by the taxpayer as part of the exchange (*i.e.*, the amount of liabilities assumed by the taxpayer exceeds the amount of liabilities of which the taxpayer is relieved), the excess is allocated among the exchange groups (but not to the residual group) in proportion to the aggregate fair market value of the properties received by the taxpayer in the exchange groups. The amount of excess liabilities assumed by the taxpayer that are allocated to each exchange group may not exceed the aggregate fair market value of the properties received in the exchange group.

(C) If there are excess liabilities of which the taxpayer is relieved as part of the exchange (*i.e.*, the amount of liabilities of which the taxpayer is relieved exceeds the amount of liabilities assumed by the taxpayer), the excess is treated as a Class I asset for purposes of making allocations to the residual group under paragraph (b)(2)(iii) of this section.

(D) Paragraphs (b)(2)(ii)(A), (B), and (C) of this section are applied in the same manner even if section 1031 and this section apply to only a portion of a larger transaction (such as a transaction described in section 1060(c) and § 1.1060-1T(b)). In that event, the amount of excess liabilities assumed by the taxpayer or the amount of excess liabilities of which the taxpayer is relieved is determined based on all liabilities assumed by the taxpayer and all liabilities of which the taxpayer is relieved as part of the larger transaction.

(iii) *Residual group.* If the aggregate fair market value of the properties transferred in all of the exchange groups differs from the aggregate fair market value of the properties received in all of the exchange groups (taking liabilities into account in the manner described in paragraph (b)(2)(ii) of this section), a residual group is created. The residual group consists of an amount of money or other property having an aggregate fair market value equal to that difference. The residual group consists of either money or other property transferred in the exchange or money or other property received in the exchange, but not both. For this purpose, other property includes property described in section 1031(a)(2) (*i.e.*, stock in trade or other property held primarily for sale, stocks, bonds, notes, other securities or evidences of indebtedness or interest, interests in a partnership, certificates of trust or beneficial interests, or choses in action), property transferred that is not of a like kind or like class with any property received, and property received that is

Reg. § 1.1031(j)-1(b)(2)

Common Nontaxable Exchanges

See p. 20,601 for regulations not amended to reflect law changes

not of a like kind or like class with any property transferred. The money and properties that are allocated to the residual group are considered to come from the following assets in the following order: first from Class I assets, then from Class II assets, then from Class III assets, and then from Class IV assets. The terms Class I assets, Class II assets, Class III assets, and Class IV assets have the same meanings as in § 1.338-6(b), to which reference is made by § 1.1060-1(c)(2). Within each Class, taxpayers may choose which properties are allocated to the residual group.

(iv) *Exchange group surplus and deficiency.* For each of the exchange groups described in this section, an "exchange group surplus" or "exchange group deficiency," if any, must be determined. An exchange group surplus is the excess of the aggregate fair market value of the properties received (less the amount of any excess liabilities assumed by the taxpayer that are allocated to that exchange group) in an exchange group over the aggregate fair market value of the properties transferred in that exchange group. An exchange group deficiency is the excess of the aggregate fair market value of the properties transferred in an exchange group over the aggregate fair market value of the properties received (less the amount of any excess liabilities assumed by the taxpayer that are allocated to that exchange group) in that exchange group.

(3) *Amount of gain recognized.*—(i) For purposes of this section, the amount of gain or loss realized with respect to each exchange group and the residual group is the difference between the aggregate fair market value of the properties transferred in that exchange group or residual group and the properties' aggregate adjusted basis. The gain realized with respect to each exchange group is recognized to the extent of the lesser of the gain realized and the amount of the exchange group deficiency, if any. Losses realized with respect to an exchange group are not recognized. See section 1031(a) and (c). The total amount of gain recognized under section 1031 in the exchange is the sum of the amount of gain recognized with respect to each exchange group. With respect to the residual group, the gain or loss realized (as determined under this section) is recognized as provided in section 1001 or other applicable provision of the Code.

(ii) The amount of gain or loss realized and recognized with respect to properties transferred by the taxpayer that are not within any exchange group or the residual group is determined under section 1001 and other applicable provisions of the Code, with proper adjustments made for all liabilities not allocated to the exchange groups or the residual group.

(c) *Computation of basis of properties received.* In an exchange of multiple properties qualifying for nonrecognition of gain or loss under section 1031 and this section, the aggregate basis of properties received in each of the exchange groups is the aggregate adjusted basis of the properties transferred by the taxpayer within that exchange group, increased by the amount of gain recognized by the taxpayer with respect to that exchange group, increased by the amount of the exchange group surplus or decreased by the amount of the exchange group deficiency, and increased by the amount, if any, of excess liabilities assumed by the taxpayer that are allocated to that exchange group. The resulting aggregate basis of each exchange group is allocated proportionately to each property received in the exchange group in accordance with its fair market value. The basis of each property received within the residual group (other than money) is equal to its fair market value.

(d) *Examples.* The application of this section may be illustrated by the following examples:

Example 1. (i) K exchanges computer A (asset class 00.12) and automobile A (asset class 00.22), both of which were held by K for productive use in its business, with W for printer B (asset class 00.12) and automobile B (asset class 00.22), both of which will be held by K for productive use in its business. K's adjusted basis and the fair market value of the exchanged properties are as follows:

	Adjusted Basis	Fair Market Value
Computer A	$ 375	$1000
Automobile A	1500	4000
Printer B	—	2050
Automobile B	—	2950

(ii) Under paragraph (b)(2) of this section, the properties exchanged are separated into exchange groups as follows:

(A) The first exchange group consists of computer A and printer B (both are within the same General Asset Class) and, as to K, has an exchange group surplus of $1050 because the fair market value of printer B ($2050) exceeds the fair market value of computer A ($1000) by that amount.

(B) The second exchange group consists of automobile A and automobile B (both are within the same General Asset Class) and, as to K, has an exchange group deficiency of $1050 because the fair market value of automobile A ($4000) exceeds the fair market value of automobile B ($2950) by that amount.

Reg. § 1.1031(j)-1(b)(3)

(iii) K recognizes gain on the exchange as follows:

(A) With respect to the first exchange group, the amount of gain realized is the excess of the fair market value of computer A ($1000) over its adjusted basis ($375), or $625. The amount of gain recognized is the lesser of the gain realized ($625) and the exchange group deficiency ($0), or $0.

(B) With respect to the second exchange group, the amount of gain realized is the excess of the fair market value of automobile A ($4000) over its adjusted basis ($1500), or $2500. The amount of gain recognized is the lesser of the gain realized ($2500) and the exchange group deficiency ($1050), or $1050.

(iv) The total amount of gain recognized by K in the exchange is the sum of the gains recognized with respect to both exchange groups ($0 + $1050), or $1050.

(v) The basis of the property received by K in the exchange, printer B and automobile B, are determined in the following manner:

(A) The basis of the property received in the first exchange group is the adjusted basis of the property transferred within that exchange group ($375), increased by the amount of gain recognized with respect to that exchange group ($0), increased by the amount of the exchange group surplus ($1050), and increased by the amount of excess liabilities assumed allocated to that exchange group ($0), or $1425. Because printer B was the only property received within the first exchange group, the entire basis of $1425 is allocated to printer B.

(B) The basis of the property received in the second exchange group is the adjusted basis of the property transferred within that exchange group ($1500), increased by the amount of gain recognized with respect to that exchange group ($1050), decreased by the amount of the exchange group deficiency ($1050), and increased by the amount of excess liabilities assumed allocated to that exchange group ($0), or $1500. Because automobile B was the only property received within the second exchange group, the entire basis of $1500 is allocated to automobile B.

Example 2. (i) F exchanges computer A (asset class 00.12) and automobile A (asset class 00.22), both of which were held by F for productive use in its business, with G for printer B (asset class 00.12) and automobile B (asset class 00.22), both of which will be held by F for productive use in its business, and corporate stock and $500 cash. The adjusted basis and fair market value of the properties are as follows:

	Adjusted Basis	Fair Market Value
Computer A	$ 375	$1000
Automobile A	3500	4000
Printer B	—	800
Automobile B	—	2950
Corporate Stock	—	750
Cash	—	500

(ii) Under paragraph (b)(2) of this section, the properties exchanged are separated into exchange groups as follows:

(A) The first exchange group consists of computer A and printer B (both are within the same General Asset Class) and, as to F, has an exchange group deficiency of $200 because the fair market value of computer A ($1000) exceeds the fair market value of printer B ($800) by that amount.

(B) The second exchange group consists of automobile A and automobile B (both are within the same General Asset Class) and, as to F, has an exchange group deficiency of $1050 because the fair market value of automobile A ($4000) exceeds the fair market value of automobile B ($2950) by that amount.

(C) Because the aggregate fair market value of the properties transferred by F in the exchange groups ($5,000) exceeds the aggregate fair market value of the properties received by F in the exchange groups ($3750) by $1250, there is a residual group in that amount consisting of the $500 cash and the $750 worth of corporate stock.

(iii) F recognizes gain on the exchange as follows:

(A) With respect to the first exchange group, the amount of gain realized is the excess of the fair market value of computer A ($1000) over its adjusted basis ($375), or $625. The amount of gain recognized is the lesser of the gain realized ($625) and the exchange group deficiency ($200), or $200.

(B) With respect to the second exchange group, the amount of gain realized is the excess of the fair market value of automobile A ($4000) over its adjusted basis ($3500), or $500. The amount of gain recognized is the lesser of the gain realized ($500) and the exchange group deficiency ($1050), or $500.

(C) No property transferred by F was allocated to the residual group. Therefore, F does not recognize gain or loss with respect to the residual group.

(iv) The total amount of gain recognized by F in the exchange is the sum of the gains recognized with respect to both exchange groups ($200 + $500), or $700.

(v) The bases of the properties received by F in the exchange (printer B, automobile B, and the

Reg. § 1.1031(j)-1(d)

corporate stock) are determined in the following manner:

(A) The basis of the property received in the first exchange group is the adjusted basis of the property transferred within that exchange group ($375), increased by the amount of gain recognized with respect to that exchange group ($200), decreased by the amount of the exchange group deficiency ($200), and increased by the amount of excess liabilities assumed allocated to that exchange group ($0), or $375. Because printer B was the only property received within the first exchange group, the entire basis of $375 is allocated to printer B.

(B) The basis of the property received in the second exchange group is the adjusted basis of the property transferred within that exchange group ($3500), increased by the amount of gain recognized with respect to that exchange group ($500), decreased by the amount of the exchange group deficiency ($1050), and increased by the amount of excess liabilities assumed allocated to that exchange group ($0), or $2950. Because automobile B was the only property received within the second exchange group, the entire basis of $2950 is allocated to automobile B.

(C) The basis of the property received within the residual group (the corporate stock) is equal to its fair market value or $750. Cash of $500 is also received within the residual group.

Example 3. (i) J and H enter into an exchange of the following properties. All of the property (except for the inventory) transferred by J was held for productive use in J's business. All of the property received by J will be held by J for productive use in its business.

J Transfers:

	Adjusted Basis	Fair Market Value
Computer A	$1500	$ 5000
Computer B	500	3000
Printer C	2000	1500
Real Estate D	1200	2000
Real Estate E	0	1800
Scraper F	3300	2500
Inventory	1000	1700
Total	$9500	$17,500

H Transfers:

Property		Fair Market Value
Computer Z		$ 4500
Printer Y		2500
Real Estate X		1000
Real Estate W		4000
Grader V		2000
Truck T		1700
Cash		1800
Total		$17,500

(ii) Under paragraph (b)(2) of this section, the properties exchanged are separated into exchange groups as follows:

(A) The first exchange group consists of computer A, computer B, printer C, computer Z, and printer Y (all are within the same General Asset Class) and, as to J, has an exchange group deficiency of $2500 (($5000 + $3000 + $1500) − ($4500 + $2500)).

(B) The second exchange group consists of real estate D, E, X and W (all are of a like kind) and, as to J, has an exchange group surplus of $1200 (($1000 + $4000) − ($2000 + $1800)).

(C) The third exchange group consists of scraper F and grader V (both are within the same Product Class (SIC Code 3531)) and, as to J, has an exchange group deficiency of $500 ($2500 − $2000).

(D) Because the aggregate fair market value of the properties transferred by J in the exchange groups ($15,800) exceeds the aggregate fair market value of the properties received by J in the exchange groups ($14,000) by $1800, there is a residual group in that amount consisting of the $1800 cash (a Class I asset).

(E) The transaction also includes a taxable exchange of inventory (which is property described in section 1031(a)(2)) for truck T (which is not of a like kind or like class to any property transferred in the exchange).

(iii) J recognizes gain on the transaction as follows:

(A) With respect to the first exchange group, the amount of gain realized is the excess of the aggregate fair market value of the properties transferred in the exchange group ($9500) over the aggregate adjusted basis ($4000), or $5500. The amount of gain recognized is the lesser of the gain realized ($5500) and the exchange group deficiency ($2500), or $2500.

(B) With respect to the second exchange group, the amount of gain realized is the excess of the aggregate fair market value of the properties transferred in the exchange group ($3800) over the aggregate adjusted basis ($1200), or $2600. The amount of gain recognized is the lesser of the gain realized ($2600) and the exchange group deficiency ($0), or $0.

(C) With respect to the third exchange group, a loss is realized in the amount of $800 because the fair market value of the property transferred in the exchange group ($2500) is less than its adjusted basis ($3300). Although a loss of

Reg. § 1.1031(j)-1(d)

$800 was realized, under section 1031(a) and (c) losses are not recognized.

(D) No property transferred by J was allocated to the residual group. Therefore, J does not recognize gain or loss with respect to the residual group.

(E) With respect to the taxable exchange of inventory for truck T, gain of $700 is realized and recognized by J (amount realized of $1700 (the fair market value of truck T) less the adjusted basis of the inventory ($1000)).

(iv) The total amount of gain recognized by J in the transaction is the sum of the gains recognized under section 1031 with respect to each exchange group ($2500 + $0 + $0) and any gain recognized outside of section 1031 ($700), or $3200.

(v) The basis of the property received by J in the exchange are determined in the following manner:

(A) The aggregate basis of the properties received in the first exchange group is the adjusted basis of the properties transferred within that exchange group ($4000), increased by the amount of gain recognized with respect to that exchange group ($2500), decreased by the amount of the exchange group deficiency ($2500), and increased by the amount of excess liabilities assumed allocated to that exchange group ($0), or $4000. This $4000 of basis is allocated proportionately among the assets received within the first exchange group in accordance with their fair market values: computer Z's basis is $2571 ($4000 × $4500/$7000); printer Y's basis is $1429 ($4000 × $2500/$7000).

(B) The aggregate basis of the properties received in the second exchange group is the adjusted basis of the properties transferred within that exchange group ($1200), increased by the amount of gain recognized with respect to that exchange group ($0), increased by the amount of the exchange group surplus ($1200), and increased by the amount of excess liabilities assumed allocated to that exchange group ($0), or $2400. This $2400 of basis is allocated proportionately among the assets received within the second exchange group in accordance with their fair market values: real estate X's basis is $480 ($2400 × $1000/$5000); real estate W's basis is $1920 ($2400 × $4000/$5000).

(C) The basis of the property received in the third exchange group is the adjusted basis of the property transferred within that exchange group ($3300), increased by the amount of gain recognized with respect to that exchange group ($0), decreased by the amount of the exchange group deficiency ($500), and increased by the amount of excess liabilities assumed allocated to that exchange group ($0), or $2800. Because grader V was the only property received within the third exchange group, the entire basis of $2800 is allocated to grader V.

(D) Cash of $1800 is received within the residual group.

(E) The basis of the property received in the taxable exchange (truck T) is equal to its cost of $1700.

Example 4. (i) B exchanges computer A (asset class 00.12), automobile A (asset class 00.22) and truck A (asset class 00.241), with C for computer R (asset class 00.12), automobile R (asset class 00.22), truck R (asset class 00.241) and $400 cash. All properties transferred by either B or C were held for productive use in the respective transferor's business. Similarly, all properties to be received by either B or C will be held for productive use in the respective recipient's business. Automobile A, automobile R and truck R are each secured by a nonrecourse liability and are transferred subject to such liability. The adjusted basis, fair market value, and liability secured by each property, if any, are as follows:

	Adjusted Basis	Fair Market Value	Liability
B Transfers:			
Computer A	$ 800	$ 1500	$ 0
Automobile A	900	2500	500
Truck A	700	2000	0
C Transfers:			
Computer R	$1100	$ 1600	$ 0
Automobile R	2100	3100	750
Truck R	600	1400	250
Cash		400	

(ii) The tax treatment to B is as follows:

(A)(*1*) The first exchange group consists of computers A and R (both are within the same General Asset Class).

(*2*) The second exchange group consists of automobiles A and R (both are within the same General Asset Class).

(*3*) The third exchange group consists of trucks A and R (both are in the same General Asset Class).

(B) Under paragraph (b)(2)(ii) of this section, all liabilities assumed by B ($1000) are offset by all liabilities of which B is relieved ($500), resulting in excess liabilities assumed of $500. The excess liabilities assumed of $500 is allocated among the exchange groups in proportion to the fair market value of the properties received by B in the exchange groups as follows:

(*1*) $131 of excess liabilities assumed ($500 × $1600/$6100) is allocated to the first exchange

Reg. § 1.1031(j)-1(d)

group. The first exchange group has an exchange group deficiency of $31 because the fair market value of computer A ($1500) exceeds the fair market value of computer R less the excess liabilities assumed allocated to the exchange group ($1600 − $131) by that amount.

(2) $254 of excess liabilities assumed ($500 × $3100/$6100) is allocated to the second exchange group. The second exchange group has an exchange group surplus of $346 because the fair market value of automobile R less the excess liabilities assumed allocated to the exchange group ($3100 − $254) exceeds the fair market value of automobile A ($2500) by that amount.

(3) $115 of excess liabilities assumed ($500 × $1400/$6100) is allocated to the third exchange group. The third exchange group has an exchange group deficiency of $715 because the fair market value of truck A ($2000) exceeds the fair market value of truck R less the excess liabilities assumed allocated to the exchange group ($1400 − $115) by that amount.

(4) The difference between the aggregate fair market value of the properties transferred in all of the exchange groups, $6000, and the aggregate fair market value of the properties received in all of the exchange groups (taking excess liabilities assumed into account), $5600, is $400. Therefore there is a residual group in that amount consisting of $400 cash received.

(C) B recognizes gain on the exchange as follows:

(1) With respect to the first exchange group, the amount of gain realized is the excess of the fair market value of computer A ($1500) over its adjusted basis ($800), or $700. The amount of gain recognized is the lesser of the gain realized ($700) and the exchange group deficiency ($31), or $31.

(2) With respect to the second exchange group, the amount of gain realized is the excess of the fair market value of automobile A ($2500) over its adjusted basis ($900), or $1600. The amount of gain recognized is the lesser of the gain realized ($1600) and the exchange group deficiency ($0), or $0.

(3) With respect to the third exchange group, the amount of gain realized is the excess of the fair market value of truck A ($2000) over its adjusted basis ($700), or $1300. The amount of gain recognized is the lesser of gain realized ($1300) and the exchange group deficiency ($715), or $715.

(4) No property transferred by B was allocated to the residual group. Therefore, B does not recognize gain or loss with respect to the residual group.

(D) The total amount of gain recognized by B in the exchange is the sum of the gains recognized under section 1031 with respect to each exchange group ($31 + $0 + $715), or $746.

(E) The basis of the property received by B in the exchange (computer R, automobile R, and truck R) are determined in the following manner:

(1) The basis of the property received in the first exchange group is the adjusted basis of the property transferred within that exchange group ($800), increased by the amount of gain recognized with respect to that exchange group ($31), decreased by the amount of the exchange group deficiency ($31), and increased by the amount of excess liabilities assumed allocated to that exchange group ($131), or $931. Because computer R was the only property received within the first exchange group, the entire basis of $931 is allocated to computer R.

(2) The basis of the property received in the second exchange group is the adjusted basis of the property transferred within that exchange group ($900), increased by the amount of gain recognized with respect to that exchange group ($0), increased by the amount of the exchange group surplus ($346), and increased by the amount of excess liabilities assumed allocated to that exchange group ($254), or $1500. Because automobile R was the only property received within the second exchange group, the entire basis of $1500 is allocated to automobile R.

(3) The basis of the property received in the third exchange group is the adjusted basis of the property transferred within that exchange group ($700), increased by the amount of gain recognized with respect to that exchange group ($715), decreased by the amount of the exchange group deficiency ($715), and increased by the amount of excess liabilities assumed allocated to that exchange group ($115), or $815. Because truck R was the only property received within the third exchange group, the entire basis of $815 is allocated to truck R.

(F) Cash of $400 is also received by B.

(iii) The tax treatment to C is as follows:

(A)(1) The first exchange group consists of computers R and A (both are within the same General Asset Class).

(2) The second exchange group consists of automobiles R and A (both are within the same General Asset Class).

(3) The third exchange group consists of trucks R and A (both are in the same General Asset Class).

Reg. § 1.1031(j)-1(d)

Common Nontaxable Exchanges

(B) Under paragraph (b)(2)(ii) of this section, all liabilities of which C is relieved ($1000) are offset by all liabilities assumed by C ($500), resulting in excess liabilities relieved of $500. This excess liabilities relieved is treated as cash received by C.

(1) The first exchange group has an exchange group deficiency of $100 because the fair market value of computer R ($1600) exceeds the fair market value of computer A ($1500) by that amount.

(2) The second exchange group has an exchange group deficiency of $600 because the fair market value of automobile R ($3100) exceeds the fair market value of automobile A ($2500) by that amount.

(3) The third exchange group has an exchange group surplus of $600 because the fair market value of truck A ($2000) exceeds the fair market value of truck R ($1400) by that amount.

(4) The difference between the aggregate fair market value of the properties transferred by C in all of the exchange groups, $6100, and the aggregate fair market value of the properties received by C in all of the exchange groups, $6000, is $100. Therefore, there is a residual group in that amount, consisting of excess liabilities relieved of $100, which is treated as cash received by C.

(5) The $400 cash paid by C and $400 of the excess liabilities relieved which is treated as cash received by C are not within the exchange groups or the residual group.

(C) C recognizes gain on the exchange as follows:

(1) With respect to the first exchange group, the amount of gain realized is the excess of the fair market value of computer R ($1600) over its adjusted basis ($1100), or $500. The amount of gain recognized is the lesser of the gain realized ($500) and the exchange group deficiency ($100), or $100.

(2) With respect to the second exchange group, the amount of gain realized is the excess of the fair market value of automobile R ($3100) over its adjusted basis ($2100), or $1000. The amount of gain recognized is the lesser of the gain realized ($1000) and the exchange group deficiency ($600), or $600.

(3) With respect to the third exchange group, the amount of gain realized is the excess of the fair market value of truck R ($1400) over its adjusted basis ($600), or $800. The amount of gain recognized is the lesser of gain realized ($800) and the exchange group deficiency ($0), or $0.

(4) No property transferred by C was allocated to the residual group. Therefore, C does not recognize any gain with respect to the residual group.

(D) The total amount of gain recognized by C in the exchange is the sum of the gains recognized under section 1031 with respect to each exchange group ($100 + $600 + $0), or $700.

(E) The basis of the properties received by C in the exchange (computer A, automobile A, and truck A) are determined in the following manner:

(1) The basis of the property received in the first exchange group is the adjusted basis of the property transferred within that exchange group ($1100), increased by the amount of gain recognized with respect to that exchange group ($100), decreased by the amount of the exchange group deficiency ($100), and increased by the amount of excess liabilities assumed allocated to that exchange group ($0), or $1100. Because computer A was the only property received within the first exchange group, the entire basis of $1100 is allocated to computer A.

(2) The basis of the property received in the second exchange group is the adjusted basis of the property transferred within that exchange group ($2100), increased by the amount of gain recognized with respect to that exchange group ($600), decreased by the amount of the exchange group deficiency ($600), and increased by the amount of excess liabilities assumed allocated to that exchange group ($0), or $2100. Because automobile A was the only property received within the second exchange group, the entire basis of $2100 is allocated to automobile A.

(3) The basis of the property received in the third exchange group is the adjusted basis of the property transferred within that exchange group ($600), increased by the amount of gain recognized with respect to that exchange group ($0), increased by the amount of the exchange group surplus ($600), and increased by the amount of excess liabilities assumed allocated to that exchange group ($0), or $1200. Because truck A was the only property received within the third exchange group, the entire basis of $1200 is allocated to truck A.

Example 5. (i) U exchanges real estate A, real estate B, and grader A (SIC Code 3531) with V for real estate R and railroad car R (General Asset Class 00.25). All properties transferred by either U or V were held for productive use in the respective transferor's business. Similarly, all properties to be received by either U or V will be held for productive use in the respective recipient's business. Real estate R is secured by a recourse liability and is transferred subject to that

Reg. § 1.1031(j)-1(d)

liability. The adjusted basis, fair market value, and liability secured by each property, if any, are as follows:

	Adjusted Basis	Fair Market Value	Liability
U Transfers:			
Real Estate A	$ 2000	$ 5000	
Real Estate B	8000	13,500	
Grader A	500	2000	
V Transfers:			
Real Estate R	$20,000	$26,500	$7000
Railroad Car R	1200	1000	

(ii) The tax treatment to U is as follows:

(A) The exchange group consists of real estate A, real estate B, and real estate R.

(B) Under paragraph (b)(2)(ii) of this section, all liabilities assumed by U ($7000) are excess liabilities assumed. The excess liabilities assumed of $7000 is allocated to the exchange group.

(1) The exchange group has an exchange group surplus of $1000 because the fair market value of real estate R less the excess liabilities assumed allocated to the exchange group ($26,500 − $7000) exceeds the aggregate fair market value of real estate A and B ($18,500) by that amount.

(2) The difference between the aggregate fair market value of the properties received in the exchange group (taking excess liabilities assumed into account), $19,500, and the aggregate fair market value of the properties transferred in the exchange group, $18,500, is $1000. Therefore, there is a residual group in that amount consisting of $1000 (or 50 percent of the fair market value) of grader A.

(3) The transaction also includes a taxable exchange of the 50 percent portion of grader A not allocated to the residual group (which is not of a like kind or like class to any property received by U in the exchange) for railroad car R (which is not of a like kind or like class to any property transferred by U in the exchange).

(C) U recognizes gain on the exchange as follows:

(1) With respect to the exchange group, the amount of the gain realized is the excess of the aggregate fair market value of real estate A and B ($18,500) over the aggregate adjusted basis ($10,000), or $8500. The amount of the gain recognized is the lesser of the gain realized ($8500) and the exchange group deficiency ($0), or $0.

(2) With respect to the residual group, the amount of gain realized and recognized is the excess of the fair market value of the 50 percent portion of grader A that is allocated to the residual group ($1000) over its adjusted basis ($250), or $750.

(3) With respect to the taxable exchange of the 50 percent portion of grader A not allocated to the residual group for railroad car R, gain of $750 is realized and recognized by U (amount realized of $1000 (the fair market value of railroad car R) less the adjusted basis of the 50 percent portion of grader A not allocated to the residual group ($250)).

(D) The total amount of gain recognized by U in the transaction is the sum of the gain recognized under section 1031 with respect to the exchange group ($0), any gain recognized with respect to the residual group ($750), and any gain recognized with respect to property transferred that is not in the exchange group or the residual group ($750), or $1500.

(E) The basis of the property received by U in the exchange (real estate R and railroad car R) are determined in the following manner:

(1) The basis of the property received in the exchange group is the aggregate adjusted basis of the property transferred within that exchange group ($10,000), increased by the amount of gain recognized with respect to that exchange group ($0), increased by the amount of the exchange group surplus ($1000), and increased by the amount of excess liabilities assumed allocated to that exchange group ($7000), or $18,000. Because real estate R is the only property received within the exchange group, the entire basis of $18,000 is allocated to real estate R.

(2) The basis of railroad car R is equal to its cost of $1000.

(iii) The tax treatment to V is as follows:

(A) The exchange group consists of real estate R, real estate A, and real estate B.

(B) Under paragraph (b)(2)(ii) of this section, the liabilities of which V is relieved ($7000) results [sic] in excess liabilities relieved of $7000 and is [sic] treated as cash received by V.

(1) The exchange group has an exchange group deficiency of $8000 because the fair market value of real estate R ($26,500) exceeds the aggregate fair market value of real estate A and B ($18,500) by that amount.

(2) The difference between the aggregate fair market value of the properties transferred by V in the exchange group, $26,500, and the aggregate fair market value of the properties received by V in the exchange group, $18,500, is $8000. Therefore, there is a residual group in that amount, consisting of the excess liabilities relieved of $7000, which is treated as cash received by V, and

Reg. § 1.1031(j)-1(d)

$1000 (or 50 percent of the fair market value) of grader A.

(*3*) The transaction also includes a taxable exchange of railroad car R (which is not of a like kind or like class to any property received by V in the exchange) for the 50 percent portion of grader A (which is not of a like kind or like class to any property transferred by V in the exchange) not allocated to the residual group.

(C) V recognizes gain on the exchange as follows:

(*1*) With respect to the exchange group, the amount of the gain realized is the excess of the fair market value of real estate R ($26,500) over its adjusted basis ($20,000), or $6500. The amount of the gain recognized is the lesser of the gain realized ($6500) and the exchange group deficiency ($8000), or $6500.

(*2*) No property transferred by V was allocated to the residual group. Therefore, V does not recognize gain or loss with respect to the residual group.

(*3*) With respect to the taxable exchange of railroad car R for the 50 percent portion of grader A not allocated to the exchange group or the residual group, a loss is realized and recognized in the amount of $200 (the excess of the $1200 adjusted basis of railroad car R over the amount realized of $1000 (fair market value of the 50 percent portion of grader A)).

(D) The basis of the property received by V in the exchange (real estate A, real estate B, and grader A) are determined in the following manner:

(*1*) The basis of the property received in the exchange group is the adjusted basis of the property transferred within that exchange group ($20,000), increased by the amount of gain recognized with respect to that exchange group ($6500), and decreased by the amount of the exchange group deficiency ($8000), or $18,500. This $18,500 of basis is allocated proportionately among the assets received within the exchange group in accordance with their fair market values: real estate A's basis is $5000 ($18,500 × $5000/$18,500); real estate B's basis is $13,500 ($18,500 × $13,500/$18,500).

(*2*) The basis of grader A is $2000.

(e) *Effective date.* Section 1.1031(j)-1 is effective for exchanges occurring on or after April 11, 1991. [Reg. § 1.1031(j)-1.]

☐ [*T.D. 8343, 4-11-91. Amended by T.D. 8858, 1-5-2000 and T.D. 8940, 2-12-2001.*]

[Reg. § 1.1031(k)-1]

§ 1.1031(k)-1. **Treatment of deferred exchanges.**—(a) *Overview.* This section provides rules for the application of section 1031 and the regulations thereunder in the case of a "deferred exchange." For purposes of section 1031 and this section, a deferred exchange is defined as an exchange in which, pursuant to an agreement, the taxpayer transfers property held for productive use in a trade or business or for investment (the "relinquished property") and subsequently receives property to be held either for productive use in a trade or business or for investment (the "replacement property"). In the case of a deferred exchange, if the requirements set forth in paragraphs (b), (c), and (d) of this section (relating to identification and receipt of replacement property) are not satisfied, the replacement property received by the taxpayer will be treated as property which is not of a like kind to the relinquished property. In order to constitute a deferred exchange, the transaction must be an exchange (i.e., a transfer of property for property, as distinguished from a transfer of property for money). For example, a sale of property followed by a purchase of property of a like kind does not qualify for nonrecognition of gain or loss under section 1031 regardless of whether the identification and receipt requirements of section 1031(a)(3) and paragraphs (b), (c), and (d) of this section are satisfied. The transfer of relinquished property in a deferred exchange is not within the provisions of section 1031(a) if, as part of the consideration, the taxpayer receives money or property which does not meet the requirements of section 1031(a), but the transfer, if otherwise qualified, will be within the provisions of either section 1031(b) or (c). See § 1.1031(a)-1(a)(2). In addition, in the case of a transfer of relinquished property in a deferred exchange, gain or loss may be recognized if the taxpayer actually or constructively receives money or property which does not meet the requirements of section 1031(a) before the taxpayer actually receives like-kind replacement property. If the taxpayer actually or constructively receives money or property which does not meet the requirements of section 1031(a) in the full amount of the consideration for the relinquished property, the transaction will constitute a sale, and not a deferred exchange, even though the taxpayer may ultimately receive like-kind replacement property. For purposes of this section, property which does not meet the requirements of section 1031(a)(whether by being described in section 1031(a)(2) or otherwise) is referred to as "other property." For rules regarding actual and constructive receipt, and safe harbors therefrom, see paragraphs (f) and (g), respectively, of this section. For rules regarding the determination of gain or loss recognized and the basis of property received in a deferred exchange, see paragraph (j) of this section.

(b) *Identification and receipt requirements*— (1) *In general.* In the case of a deferred exchange, any replacement property received by the taxpayer will be treated as property which is not of a like kind to the relinquished property if—

(i) The replacement property is not "identified" before the end of the "identification period," or

(ii) The identified replacement property is not received before the end of the "exchange period."

(2) *Identification period and exchange period.* (i) The identification period begins on the date the taxpayer transfers the relinquished property and ends at midnight on the 45th day thereafter.

(ii) The exchange period begins on the date the taxpayer transfers the relinquished property and ends at midnight on the earlier of the 180th day thereafter or the due date (including extensions) for the taxpayer's return of the tax imposed by chapter 1 of subtitle A of the Code for the taxable year in which the transfer of the relinquished property occurs.

(iii) If, as part of the same deferred exchange, the taxpayer transfers more than one relinquished property and the relinquished properties are transferred on different dates, the identification period and the exchange period are determined by reference to the earliest date on which any of the properties are transferred.

(iv) For purposes of this paragraph (b)(2), property is transferred when the property is disposed of within the meaning of section 1001(a).

(3) *Example.* This paragraph (b) may be illustrated by the following example.

Example. (i) M is a corporation that files its Federal income tax return on a calendar year basis. M and C enter into an agreement for an exchange of property that requires M to transfer property X to C. Under the agreement, M is to identify like-kind replacement property which C is required to purchase and to transfer to M. M transfers property X to C on November 16, 1992.

(ii) The identification period ends at midnight on December 31, 1992, the day which is 45 days after the date of transfer of property X. The exchange period ends at midnight on March 15, 1993, the due date for M's Federal income tax return for the taxable year in which M transferred property X. However, if M is allowed the automatic six-month extension for filing its tax return, the exchange period ends at midnight on May 15, 1993, the day which is 180 days after the date of transfer of property X.

(c) *Identification of replacement property before the end of the identification period*—(1) *In general.* For purposes of paragraph (b)(1)(i) of this section (relating to the identification requirement), replacement property is identified before the end of the identification period only if the requirements of this paragraph (c) are satisfied with respect to the replacement property. However, any replacement property that is received by the taxpayer before the end of the identification period will in all events be treated as identified before the end of the identification period.

(2) *Manner of identifying replacement property.* Replacement property is identified only if it is designated as replacement property in a written document signed by the taxpayer and hand delivered, mailed, telecopied, or otherwise sent before the end of the identification period to either—

(i) The person obligated to transfer the replacement property to the taxpayer (regardless of whether that person is a disqualified person as defined in paragraph (k) of this section); or

(ii) Any other person involved in the exchange other than the taxpayer or a disqualified person (as defined in paragraph (k) of this section).

Examples of persons involved in the exchange include any of the parties to the exchange, an intermediary, an escrow agent, and a title company. An identification of replacement property made in a written agreement for the exchange of properties signed by all parties thereto before the end of the identification period will be treated as satisfying the requirements of this paragraph (c)(2).

(3) *Description of replacement property.* Replacement property is identified only if it is unambiguously described in the written document or agreement. Real property generally is unambiguously described if it is described by a legal description, street address, or distinguishable name (e.g., the Mayfair Apartment Building). Personal property generally is unambiguously described if it is described by a specific description of the particular type of property. For example, a truck generally is unambiguously described if it is described by a specific make, model, and year.

(4) *Alternative and multiple properties.* (i) The taxpayer may identify more than one replacement property. Regardless of the number of relinquished properties transferred by the taxpayer as part of the same deferred exchange, the maximum number of replacement properties that the taxpayer may identify is—

Reg. § 1.1031(k)-1(b)(1)

(A) Three properties without regard to the fair market values of the properties (the "3-property rule"), or

(B) Any number of properties as long as their aggregate fair market value as of the end of the identification period does not exceed 200 percent of the aggregate fair market value of all the relinquished properties as of the date the relinquished properties were transferred by the taxpayer (the "200-percent rule").

(ii) If, as of the end of the identification period, the taxpayer has identified more properties as replacement properties than permitted by paragraph (c)(4)(i) of this section, the taxpayer is treated as if no replacement property had been identified. The preceding sentence will not apply, however, and an identification satisfying the requirements of paragraph (c)(4)(i) of this section will be considered made, with respect to—

(A) Any replacement property received by the taxpayer before the end of the identification period, and

(B) Any replacement property identified before the end of the identification period and received before the end of the exchange period, but only if the taxpayer receives before the end of the exchange period identified replacement property the fair market value of which is at least 95 percent of the aggregate fair market value of all identified replacement properties (the "95-percent rule").

For this purpose, the fair market value of each identified replacement property is determined as of the earlier of the date the property is received by the taxpayer or the last day of the exchange period.

(iii) For purposes of applying the 3-property rule, the 200-percent rule, and the 95-percent rule, all identifications of replacement property, other than identifications of replacement property that have been revoked in the manner provided in paragraph (c)(6) of this section, are taken into account. For example, if, in a deferred exchange, B transfers property X with a fair market value of $100,000 to C and B receives like-kind property Y with a fair market value of $50,000 before the end of the identification period, under paragraph (c)(1) of this section, property Y is treated as identified by reason of being received before the end of the identification period. Thus, under paragraph (c)(4)(i) of this section, B may identify either two additional replacement properties of any fair market value or any number of additional replacement properties as long as the aggregate fair market value of the additional replacement properties does not exceed $150,000.

(5) *Incidental property disregarded.* (i) Solely for purposes of applying this paragraph (c), property that is incidental to a larger item of property is not treated as property that is separate from the larger item of property. Property is incidental to a larger item of property if—

(A) In standard commercial transactions, the property is typically transferred together with the larger item of property, and

(B) The aggregate fair market value of all of the incidental property does not exceed 15 percent of the aggregate fair market value of the larger item of property.

(ii) This paragraph (c)(5) may be illustrated by the following examples.

Example 1. For purposes of paragraph (c) of this section, a spare tire and tool kit will not be treated as separate property from a truck with a fair market value of $10,000, if the aggregate fair market value of the spare tire and tool kit does not exceed $1,500. For purposes of the 3-property rule, the truck, spare tire, and tool kit are treated as 1 property. Moreover, for purposes of paragraph (c)(3) of this section (relating to the description of replacement property), the truck, spare tire, and tool kit are all considered to be unambiguously described if the make, model, and year of the truck are specified, even if no reference is made to the spare tire and tool kit.

Example 2. For purposes of paragraph (c) of this section, furniture, laundry machines, and other miscellaneous items of personal property will not be treated as separate property from an apartment building with a fair market value of $1,000,000 if the aggregate fair market value of the furniture, laundry machines, and other personal property does not exceed $150,000. For purposes of the 3-property rule, the apartment building, furniture, laundry machines, and other personal property are treated as 1 property. Moreover, for purposes of paragraph (c)(3) of this section (relating to the description of replacement property), the apartment building, furniture, laundry machines, and other personal property are all considered to be unambiguously described if the legal description, street address, or distinguishable name of the apartment building is specified, even if no reference is made to the furniture, laundry machines, and other personal property.

(6) *Revocation of identification.* An identification of replacement property may be revoked at any time before the end of the identification period. An identification of replacement property is revoked only if the revocation is made in a written document signed by the taxpayer and hand delivered, mailed, telecopied, or otherwise sent before the end of the identification period to the person

Reg. § 1.1031(k)-1(c)(6)

to whom the identification of the replacement property was sent. An identification of replacement property that is made in a written agreement for the exchange of properties is treated as revoked only if the revocation is made in a written amendment to the agreement or in a written document signed by the taxpayer and hand delivered, mailed, telecopied, or otherwise sent before the end of the identification period to all of the parties to the agreement.

(7) *Examples.* This paragraph (c) may be illustrated by the following examples. Unless otherwise provided in an example, the following facts are assumed: B, a calendar year taxpayer, and C agree to enter into a deferred exchange. Pursuant to their agreement, B transfers real property X to C on May 17, 1991. Real property X, which has been held by B for investment, is unencumbered and has a fair market value on May 17, 1991, of $100,000. On or before July 1, 1991 (the end of the identification period), B is to identify replacement property that is of a like kind to real property X. On or before November 13, 1991 (the end of the exchange period), C is required to purchase the property identified by B and to transfer that property to B. To the extent the fair market value of the replacement property transferred to B is greater or less than the fair market value of real property X, either B or C, as applicable, will make up the difference by paying cash to the other party after the date the replacement property is received by B. No replacement property is identified in the agreement. When subsequently identified, the replacement property is described by legal description and is of a like kind to real property X (determined without regard to section 1031(a)(3) and this section). B intends to hold the replacement property received for investment.

Example 1. (i) On July 2, 1991, B identifies real property E as replacement property by designating real property E as replacement property in a written document signed by B and personally delivered to C.

(ii) Because the identification was made after the end of the identification period, pursuant to paragraph (b)(1)(i) of this section (relating to the identification requirement), real property E is treated as property which is not of a like kind to real property X.

Example 2. (i) C is a corporation of which 20 percent of the outstanding stock is owned by B. On July 1, 1991, B identifies real property F as replacement property by designating real property F as replacement property in a written document signed by B and mailed to C.

(ii) Because C is the person obligated to transfer the replacement property to B, real property F is identified before the end of the identification period. The fact that C is a "disqualified person" as defined in paragraph (k) of this section does not change this result.

(iii) Real property F would also have been treated as identified before the end of the identification period if, instead of sending the identification to C, B had designated real property F as replacement property in a written agreement for the exchange of properties signed by all parties thereto on or before July 1, 1991.

Example 3. (i) On June 3, 1991, B identifies the replacement property as "unimproved land located in Hood County with a fair market value not to exceed $100,000." The designation is made in a written document signed by B and personally delivered to C. On July 8, 1991, B and C agree that real property G is the property described in the June 3, 1991 document.

(ii) Because real property G was not unambiguously described before the end of the identification period, no replacement property is identified before the end of the identification period.

Example 4. (i) On June 28, 1991, B identifies real properties H, J, and K as replacement properties by designating these properties as replacement properties in a written document signed by B and personally delivered to C. The written document provides that by August 1, 1991, B will orally inform C which of the identified properties C is to transfer to B. As of July 1, 1991, the fair market values of real properties H, J, and K are $75,000, $100,000, and $125,000, respectively.

(ii) Because B did not identify more than three properties as replacement properties, the requirements of the 3-property rule are satisfied, and real properties H, J, and K are all identified before the end of the identification period.

Example 5. (i) On May 17, 1991, B identifies real properties L, M, N, and P as replacement properties by designating these properties as replacement properties in a written document signed by B and personally delivered to C. The written document provides that by July 2, 1991, B will orally inform C which of the identified properties C is to transfer to B. As of July 1, 1991, the fair market values of real properties L, M, N, and P are $30,000, $40,000, $50,000, and $60,000, respectively.

(ii) Although B identified more than three properties as replacement properties, the aggregate fair market value of the identified properties as of the end of the identification period ($180,000) did not exceed 200 percent of the aggregate fair market value of real property X (200% × $100,000 = $200,000). Therefore, the requirements of the 200-percent rule are satisfied, and real properties L, M, N, and P are all identified before the end of the identification period.

Example 6. (i) On June 21, 1991, B identifies real properties Q, R, and S as replacement properties by designating these properties as replacement properties in a written document signed by B and mailed to C. On June 24, 1991, B identifies real properties T and U as replacement properties in a written document signed by B and mailed to C. On June 28, 1991, B revokes the identification of real properties Q and R in a written document signed by B and personally delivered to C.

(ii) B has revoked the identification of real properties Q and R in the manner provided by paragraph (c)(6) of this section. Identifications of replacement property that have been revoked in the manner provided by paragraph (c)(6) of this section are not taken into account for purposes of applying the 3-property rule. Thus, as of June 28, 1991, B has identified only replacement properties S, T, and U for purposes of the 3-property rule. Because B did not identify more than three properties as replacement properties for purposes of the 3-property rule, the requirements of that rule are satisfied, and real properties S, T, and U are all identified before the end of the identification period.

Example 7. (i) On May 20, 1991, B identifies real properties V and W as replacement properties by designating these properties as replacement properties in a written document signed by B and personally delivered to C. On June 4, 1991, B identifies real properties Y and Z as replacement properties in the same manner. On June 5, 1991, B telephones C and orally revokes the identification of real properties V and W. As of July 1, 1991, the fair market values of real properties V, W, Y, and Z are $50,000, $70,000, $90,000, and $100,000, respectively. On July 31, 1991, C purchases real property Y and Z and transfers them to B.

(ii) Pursuant to paragraph (c)(6) of this section (relating to revocation of identification), the oral revocation of the identification of real properties V and W is invalid. Thus, the identification of real properties V and W is taken into account for purposes of determining whether the requirements of paragraph (c)(4) of this section (relating to the identification of alternative and multiple properties) are satisfied. Because B identified more than three properties and the aggregate fair market value of the identified properties as of the end of the identification period ($310,000) exceeds 200 percent of the fair market value of real property X (200% × $100,000 = $200,000), the requirements of paragraph (c)(4) of this section are not satisfied, and B is treated as if B did not identify any replacement property.

(d) *Receipt of identified replacement property*—(1) *In general.* For purposes of paragraph (b)(1)(ii) of this section (relating to the receipt requirement), the identified replacement property is received before the end of the exchange period only if the requirements of this paragraph (d) are satisfied with respect to the replacement property. In the case of a deferred exchange, the identified replacement property is received before the end of the exchange period if—

(i) The taxpayer receives the replacement property before the end of the exchange period, and

(ii) The replacement property received is substantially the same property as identified.

If the taxpayer has identified more than one replacement property, section 1031(a)(3)(B) and this paragraph (d) are applied separately to each replacement property.

(2) *Examples.* This paragraph (d) may be illustrated by the following examples. The following facts are assumed: B, a calendar year taxpayer, and C agree to enter into a deferred exchange. Pursuant to their agreement, B transfers real property X to C on May 17, 1991. Real property X, which has been held by B for investment, is unencumbered and has a fair market value on May 17, 1991, of $100,000. On or before July 1, 1991 (the end of the identification period), B is to identify replacement property that is of a like kind to real property X. On or before November 13, 1991 (the end of the exchange period), C is required to purchase the property identified by B and to transfer that property to B. To the extent the fair market value of the replacement property transferred to B is greater or less than the fair market value of real property X, either B or C, as applicable, will make up the difference by paying cash to the other party after the date the replacement property is received by B. The replacement property is identified in a manner that satisfies paragraph (c) of this section (relating to identification of replacement property) and is of a like kind to real property X (determined without regard to section 1031(a)(3) and this section). B intends to hold any replacement property received for investment.

Example 1. (i) In the agreement, B identifies real properties J, K, and L as replacement properties. The agreement provides that by July 26, 1991, B will orally inform C which of the properties C is to transfer to B.

(ii) As of July 1, 1991, the fair market values of real properties J, K, and L are $75,000, $100,000, and $125,000, respectively. On July 26,

Reg. § 1.1031(k)-1(d)(2)

1991, B instructs C to acquire real property K. On October 31, 1991, C purchases real property K for $100,000 and transfers the property to B.

(iii) Because real property K was identified before the end of the identification period and was received before the end of the exchange period, the identification and receipt requirements of section 1031(a)(3) and this section are satisfied with respect to real property K.

Example 2. (i) In the agreement, B identifies real property P as replacement property. Real property P consists of two acres of unimproved land. On October 15, 1991, the owner of real property P erects a fence on the property. On November 1, 1991, C purchases real property P and transfers it to B.

(ii) The erection of the fence on real property P subsequent to its identification did not alter the basic nature or character of real property P as unimproved land. B is considered to have received substantially the same property as identified.

Example 3. (i) In the agreement, B identifies real property Q as replacement property. Real property Q consists of a barn on two acres of land and has a fair market value of $250,000 ($187,500 for the barn and underlying land and $87,500 for the remaining land). As of July 26, 1991, real property Q remains unchanged and has a fair market value of $250,000. On that date, at B's direction, C purchases the barn and underlying land for $187,500 and transfers it to B, and B pays $87,500 to C.

(ii) The barn and underlying land differ in basic nature or character from real property Q as a whole. B is not considered to have received substantially the same property as identified.

Example 4. (i) In the agreement, B identifies real property R as replacement property. Real property R consists of two acres of unimproved land and has a fair market value of $250,000. As of October 3, 1991, real property R remains unimproved and has a fair market value of $250,000. On that date, at B's direction, C purchases 1½ acres of real property R for $187,500 and transfers it to B, and B pays $87,500 to C.

(ii) The portion of real property R that B received does not differ from the basic nature or character of real property R as a whole. Moreover, the fair market value of the portion of real property R that B received ($187,500) is 75 percent of the fair market value of real property R as of the date of receipt. Accordingly, B is considered to have received substantially the same property as identified.

(e) *Special rules for identification and receipt of replacement property to be produced*—(1) *In general.* A transfer of relinquished property in a deferred exchange will not fail to qualify for nonrecognition of gain or loss under section 1031 merely because the replacement property is not in existence or is being produced at the time the property is identified as replacement property. For purposes of this paragraph (e), the terms "produced" and "production" have the same meanings as provided in section 263A(g)(1) and the regulations thereunder.

(2) *Identification of replacement property to be produced.* (i) In the case of replacement property that is to be produced, the replacement property must be identified as provided in paragraph (c) of this section (relating to identification of replacement property). For example, if the identified replacement property consists of improved real property where the improvements are to be constructed, the description of the replacement property satisfies the requirements of paragraph (c)(3) of this section (relating to description of replacement property) if a legal description is provided for the underlying land and as much detail is provided regarding construction of the improvements as is practicable at the time the identification is made.

(ii) For purposes of paragraphs (c)(4)(i)(B) and (c)(5) of this section (relating to the 200-percent rule and incidental property), the fair market value of replacement property that is to be produced is its estimated fair market value as of the date it is expected to be received by the taxpayer.

(3) *Receipt of replacement property to be produced.* (i) For purposes of paragraph (d)(1)(ii) of this section (relating to receipt of the identified replacement property), in determining whether the replacement property received by the taxpayer is substantially the same property as identified where the identified replacement property is property to be produced, variations due to usual or typical production changes are not taken into account. However, if substantial changes are made in the property to be produced, the replacement property received will not be considered to be substantially the same property as identified.

(ii) If the identified replacement property is personal property to be produced, the replacement property received will not be considered to be substantially the same property as identified unless production of the replacement property received is completed on or before the date the property is received by the taxpayer.

(iii) If the identified replacement property is real property to be produced and the production of the property is not completed on or before the date the taxpayer receives the property, the property received will be considered to be substantially the same property as identified only if, had production been completed on or before the date the taxpayer receives the replacement property, the property received would have been considered to be substantially the same property as identified. Even so, the property received is considered to be substantially the same property as identified only to the extent the property received constitutes real property under local law.

(4) *Additional rules.* The transfer of relinquished property is not within the provisions of section 1031(a) if the relinquished property is transferred in exchange for services (including production services). Thus, any additional production occurring with respect to the replacement property after the property is received by the taxpayer will not be treated as the receipt of property of a like kind.

(5) *Example.* This paragraph (e) may be illustrated by the following example.

Example. (i) B, a calendar year taxpayer, and C agree to enter into a deferred exchange. Pursuant to their agreement, B transfers improved real property X and personal property Y to C on May 17, 1991. On or before November 13, 1991 (the end of the exchange period), C is required to transfer to B real property M, on which C is constructing improvements, and personal property N, which C is producing. C is obligated to complete the improvements and production regardless of when properties M and N are transferred to B. Properties M and N are identified in a manner that satisfies paragraphs (c)(relating to identification of replacement property) and (e)(2) of this section. In addition, properties M and N are of a like kind, respectively, to real property X and personal property Y (determined without regard to section 1031(a)(3) and this section). On November 13, 1991, when construction of the improvements to property M is 20 percent completed and the production of property N is 90 percent completed, C transfers to B property M and property N. If construction of the improvements had been completed, property M would have been considered to be substantially the same property as identified. Under local law, property M constitutes real property to the extent of the underlying land and the 20 percent of the construction that is completed

(ii) Because property N is personal property to be produced and production of property N is not completed before the date the property is received by B, property N is not considered to be substantially the same property as identified and is treated as property which is not of a like kind to property Y.

(iii) Property M is considered to be substantially the same property as identified to the extent of the underlying land and the 20 percent of the construction that is completed when property M is received by B. However, any additional construction performed by C with respect to property M after November 13, 1991, is not treated as the receipt of property of a like kind.

(f) *Receipt of money or other property*—(1) *In general.* A transfer of relinquished property in a deferred exchange is not within the provisions of section 1031(a) if, as part of the consideration, the taxpayer receives money or other property. However, such a transfer, if otherwise qualified, will be within the provisions of either section 1031(b) or (c). See § 1.1031(a)-1(a)(2). In addition, in the case of a transfer of relinquished property in a deferred exchange, gain or loss may be recognized if the taxpayer actually or constructively receives money or other property before the taxpayer actually receives like-kind replacement property. If the taxpayer actually or constructively receives money or other property in the full amount of the consideration for the relinquished property before the taxpayer actually receives like-kind replacement property, the transaction will constitute a sale and not a deferred exchange, even though the taxpayer may ultimately receive like-kind replacement property.

(2) *Actual and constructive receipt.* Except as provided in paragraph (g) of this section (relating to safe harbors), for purposes of section 1031 and this section, the determination of whether (or the extent to which) the taxpayer is in actual or constructive receipt of money or other property before the taxpayer actually receives like-kind replacement property is made under the general rules concerning actual and constructive receipt and without regard to the taxpayer's method of accounting. The taxpayer is in actual receipt of money or property at the time the taxpayer actually receives the money or property or receives the economic benefit of the money or property. The taxpayer is in constructive receipt of money or property at the time the money or property is credited to the taxpayer's account, set apart for the taxpayer, or otherwise made available so that the taxpayer may draw upon it at any time or so that the taxpayer can draw upon it if notice of intention to draw is given. Although the taxpayer is not in constructive receipt of money or property if the taxpayer's control of its receipt is subject to substantial limitations or restrictions, the taxpayer is in constructive receipt of the money or property at the time the limitations or restrictions lapse, expire, or are waived. In addition, actual or constructive receipt of money or property by an agent of the taxpayer (determined without regard

to paragraph (k) of this section) is actual or constructive receipt by the taxpayer.

(3) *Example.* This paragraph (f) may be illustrated by the following example.

Example. (i) B, a calendar year taxpayer, and C agree to enter into a deferred exchange. Pursuant to the agreement, on May 17, 1991, B transfers real property X to C. Real property X, which has been held by B for investment, is unencumbered and has a fair market value on May 17, 1991, of $100,000. On or before July 1, 1991 (the end of the identification period), B is to identify replacement property that is of a like kind to real property X. On or before November 13, 1991 (the end of the exchange period), C is required to purchase the property identified by B and to transfer that property to B. At any time after May 17, 1991, and before C has purchased the replacement property, B has the right, upon notice, to demand that C pay $100,000 in lieu of acquiring and transferring the replacement property. Pursuant to the agreement, B identifies replacement property, and C purchases the replacement property and transfers it to B.

(ii) Under the agreement, B has the unrestricted right to demand the payment of $100,000 as of May 17, 1991. B is therefore in constructive receipt of $100,000 on that date. Because B is in constructive receipt of money in the full amount of the consideration for the relinquished property before B actually receives the like-kind replacement property, the transaction constitutes a sale, and the transfer of real property X does not qualify for nonrecognition of gain or loss under section 1031. B is treated as if B received the $100,000 in consideration for the sale of real property X and then purchased the like-kind replacement property.

(iii) If B's right to demand payment of the $100,000 were subject to a substantial limitation or restriction (e.g., the agreement provided that B had no right to demand payment before November 14, 1991 (the end of the exchange period)), then, for purposes of this section, B would not be in actual or constructive receipt of the money unless (or until) the limitation or restriction lapsed, expired, or was waived.

(g) *Safe harbors*—(1) *In general.* Paragraphs (g)(2) through (g)(5) of this section set forth four safe harbors the use of which will result in a determination that the taxpayer is not in actual or constructive receipt of money or other property for purposes of section 1031 and this section. More than one safe harbor can be used in the same deferred exchange, but the terms and conditions of each must be separately satisfied. For purposes of the safe harbor rules, the term "taxpayer" does not include a person or entity utilized in a safe harbor (e.g., a qualified intermediary). See paragraph (g)(8), *Example 3(v),* of this section.

(2) *Security or guarantee arrangements.* (i) In the case of a deferred exchange, the determination of whether the taxpayer is in actual or constructive receipt of money or other property before the taxpayer actually receives like-kind replacement property will be made without regard to the fact that the obligation of the taxpayer's transferee to transfer the replacement property to the taxpayer is or may be secured or guaranteed by one or more of the following—

(A) A mortgage, deed of trust, or other security interest in property (other than cash or a cash equivalent),

(B) A standby letter of credit which satisfies all of the requirements of § 15A.453-1(b)(3)(iii) and which may not be drawn upon in the absence of a default of the transferee's obligation to transfer like-kind replacement property to the taxpayer, or

(C) A guarantee of a third party.

(ii) Paragraph (g)(2)(i) of this section ceases to apply at the time the taxpayer has an immediate ability or unrestricted right to receive money or other property pursuant to the security or guarantee arrangement.

(3) *Qualified escrow accounts and qualified trusts.* (i) In the case of a deferred exchange, the determination of whether the taxpayer is in actual or constructive receipt of money or other property before the taxpayer actually receives like-kind replacement property will be made without regard to the fact that the obligation of the taxpayer's transferee to transfer the replacement property to the taxpayer is or may be secured by cash or a cash equivalent if the cash or cash equivalent is held in a qualified escrow account or in a qualified trust.

(ii) A qualified escrow account is an escrow account wherein—

(A) The escrow holder is not the taxpayer or a disqualified person (as defined in paragraph (k) of this section), and

(B) The escrow agreement expressly limits the taxpayer's rights to receive, pledge, borrow, or otherwise obtain the benefits of the cash or cash equivalent held in the escrow account as provided in paragraph (g)(6) of this section.

(iii) A qualified trust is a trust wherein—

(A) The trustee is not the taxpayer or a disqualified person (as defined in paragraph (k) of this section, except that for this purpose the relationship between the taxpayer and the trustee created by the qualified trust will not be considered a relationship under section 267(b)), and

(B) The trust agreement expressly limits the taxpayer's rights to receive, pledge, borrow, or otherwise obtain the benefits of the cash or cash equivalent held by the trustee as provided in paragraph (g)(6) of this section.

(iv) Paragraph (g)(3)(i) of this section ceases to apply at the time the taxpayer has an immediate ability or unrestricted right to receive, pledge, borrow, or otherwise obtain the benefits of the cash or cash equivalent held in the qualified escrow account or qualified trust. Rights conferred upon the taxpayer under state law to terminate or dismiss the escrow holder of a qualified escrow account or the trustee of a qualified trust are disregarded for this purpose.

(v) A taxpayer may receive money or other property directly from a party to the exchange, but not from a qualified escrow account or a qualified trust, without affecting the application of paragraph (g)(3)(i) of this section.

(4) *Qualified intermediaries.* (i) In the case of a taxpayer's transfer of relinquished property involving a qualified intermediary, the qualified intermediary is not considered the agent of the taxpayer for purposes of section 1031(a). In such a case, the taxpayer's transfer of relinquished property and subsequent receipt of like-kind replacement property is treated as an exchange, and the determination of whether the taxpayer is in actual or constructive receipt of money or other property before the taxpayer actually receives like-kind replacement property is made as if the qualified intermediary is not the agent of the taxpayer.

(ii) Paragraph (g)(4)(i) of this section applies only if the agreement between the taxpayer and the qualified intermediary expressly limits the taxpayer's rights to receive, pledge, borrow, or otherwise obtain the benefits of money or other property held by the qualified intermediary as provided in paragraph (g)(6) of this section.

(iii) A qualified intermediary is a person who—

(A) Is not the taxpayer or a disqualified person (as defined in paragraph (k) of this section), and

(B) Enters into a written agreement with the taxpayer (the "exchange agreement") and, as required by the exchange agreement, acquires the relinquished property from the taxpayer, transfers the relinquished property, acquires the replacement property, and transfers the replacement property to the taxpayer.

(iv) Regardless of whether an intermediary acquires and transfers property under general tax principals [principles], solely for purposes of paragraph (g)(4)(iii)(B) of this section—

(A) An intermediary is treated as acquiring and transferring property if the intermediary acquires and transfers legal title to that property,

(B) An intermediary is treated as acquiring and transferring the relinquished property if the intermediary (either on its own behalf or as the agent of any party to the transaction) enters into an agreement with a person other than the taxpayer for the transfer of the relinquished property to that person and, pursuant to that agreement, the relinquised property is transferred to that person, and

(C) An intermediary is treated as acquiring and transferring replacement property if the intermediary (either on its own behalf or as the agent of any party to the transaction) enters into an agreement with the owner of the replacement property for the transfer of that property and, pursuant to that agreement, the replacement property is transferred to the taxpayer.

(v) Solely for purposes of paragraphs (g)(4)(iii) and (g)(4)(iv) of this section, an intermediary is treated as entering into an agreement if the rights of a party to the agreement are assigned to the intermediary and all parties to that agreement are notified in writing of the assignment on or before the date of the relevant transfer of property. For example, if a taxpayer enters into an agreement for the transfer of relinquished property and thereafter assigns its rights in that agreement to an intermediary and all parties to that agreement are notified in writing of the assignment on or before the date of the transfer of the relinquished property, the intermediary is treated as entering into that agreement. If the relinquished property is transferred pursuant to that agreement, the intermediary is treated as having acquired and transferred the relinquished property.

(vi) Paragraph (g)(4)(i) of this section ceases to apply at the time the taxpayer has an immediate ability or unrestricted right to receive, pledge, borrow, or otherwise obtain the benefits of money or other property held by the qualified intermediary. Rights conferred upon the taxpayer under state law to terminate or dismiss the qualified intermediary are disregarded for this purpose.

(vii) A taxpayer may receive money or other property directly from a party to the transaction other than the qualified intermediary with-

Reg. § 1.1031(k)-1(g)(4)

out affecting the application of paragraph (g)(4)(i) of this section.

(5) *Interest and growth factors.* In the case of a deferred exchange, the determination of whether the taxpayer is in actual or constructive receipt of money or other property before the taxpayer actually receives the like-kind replacement property will be made without regard to the fact that the taxpayer is or may be entitled to receive any interest or growth factor with respect to the deferred exchange. The preceding sentence applies only if the agreement pursuant to which the taxpayer is or may be entitled to the interest or growth factor expressly limits the taxpayer's rights to receive the interest or growth factor as provided in paragraph (g)(6) of this section. For additional rules concerning interest or growth factors, see paragraph (h) of this section.

(6) *Additional restrictions on safe harbors under paragraphs (g)(3) through (g)(5).* (i) An agreement limits a taxpayer's rights as provided in this paragraph (g)(6) only if the agreement provides that the taxpayer has no rights, except as provided in paragraphs (g)(6)(ii) and (g)(6)(iii) of this section, to receive, pledge, borrow, or otherwise obtain the benefits of money or other property before the end of the exchange period.

(ii) The agreement may provide that if the taxpayer has not identified replacement property by the end of the identification period, the taxpayer may have rights to receive, pledge, borrow, or otherwise obtain the benefits of money or other property at any time after the end of the identification period.

(iii) The agreement may provide that if the taxpayer has identified replacement property, the taxpayer may have rights to receive, pledge, borrow, or otherwise obtain the benefits of money or other property upon or after—

(A) The receipt by the taxpayer of all of the replacement property to which the taxpayer is entitled under the exchange agreement, or

(B) The occurrence after the end of the identification period of a material and substantial contingency that—

(1) Relates to the deferred exchange,

(2) Is provided for in writing, and

(3) Is beyond the control of the taxpayer and of any disqualified person (as defined in paragraph (k) of this section), other than the person obligated to transfer the replacement property to the taxpayer.

(7) *Items disregarded in applying safe harbors under paragraphs (g)(3) through (g)(5).* In determining whether a safe harbor under paragraphs (g)(3) through (g)(5) of this section ceases to apply and whether the taxpayer's rights to receive, pledge, borrow, or otherwise obtain the benefits of money or other property are expressly limited as provided in paragraph (g)(6) of this section, the taxpayer's receipt of or right to receive any of the following items will be disregarded—

(i) Items that a seller may receive as a consequence of the disposition of property and that are not included in the amount realized from the disposition of property (e.g., prorated rents), and

(ii) Transactional items that relate to the disposition of the relinquished property or to the acquisition of the replacement property and appear under local standards in the typical closing statement as the responsibility of a buyer or seller (e.g., commissions, prorated taxes, recording or transfer taxes, and title company fees).

(8) *Examples.* This paragraph (g) may be illustrated by the following examples. Unless otherwise provided in an example, the following facts are assumed: B, a calendar year taxpayer, and C agree to enter into a deferred exchange. Pursuant to their agreement, B is to transfer real property X to C on May 17, 1991. Real property X, which has been held by B for investment, is unencumbered and has a fair market value on May 17, 1991, of $100,000. On or before July 1, 1991 (the end of the identification period), B is to identify replacement property that is of a like kind to real property X. On or before November 13, 1991 (the end of the exchange period), C is required to purchase the property identified by B and to transfer that property to B. To the extent the fair market value of the replacement property transferred to B is greater or less than the fair market value of real property X, either B or C, as applicable, will make up the difference by paying cash to the other party after the date the replacement property is received by B. The replacement property is identified as provided in paragraph (c) of this section (relating to identification of replacement property) and is of a like kind to real property X (determined without regard to section 1031(a)(3) and this section). B intends to hold any replacement property received for investment.

Example 1. (i) On May 17, 1991, B transfers real property X to C. On the same day, C pays $10,000 to B and deposits $90,000 in escrow as security for C's obligation to perform under the agreement. The escrow agreement provides that B has no rights to receive, pledge, borrow, or otherwise obtain the benefits of the money in escrow before November 14, 1991, except that:

(A) if B fails to identify replacement property on or before July 1, 1991, B may demand the

Reg. § 1.1031(k)-1(g)(5)

funds in escrow at any time after July 1, 1991; and

(B) if B identifies and receives replacement property, then B may demand the balance of the remaining funds in escrow at any time after B has received the replacement property.

The funds in escrow may be used to purchase the replacement property. The escrow holder is not a disqualified person as defined in paragraph (k) of this section. Pursuant to the terms of the agreement, B identifies replacement property, and C purchases the replacement property using the funds in escrow and transfers the replacement property to B.

(ii) C's obligation to transfer the replacement property to B was secured by cash held in a qualified escrow account because the escrow holder was not a disqualified person and the escrow agreement expressly limited B's rights to receive, pledge, borrow, or otherwise obtain the benefits of the money in escrow as provided in paragraph (g)(6) of this section. In addition, B did not have the immediate ability or unrestricted right to receive money or other property in escrow before B actually received the like-kind replacement property. Therefore, for purposes of section 1031 and this section, B is determined not to be in actual or constructive receipt of the $90,000 held in escrow before B received the like-kind replacement property. The transfer of real property X by B and B's acquisition of the replacement property qualify as an exchange under section 1031. See paragraph (j) of this section for determining the amount of gain or loss recognized.

Example 2. (i) On May 17, 1991, B transfers real property X to C, and C deposits $100,000 in escrow as security for C's obligation to perform under the agreement. Also on May 17, B identifies real property J as replacement property. The escrow agreement provides that no funds may be paid out without prior written approval of both B and C. The escrow agreement also provides that B has no rights to receive, pledge, borrow, or otherwise obtain the benefits of the money in escrow before November 14, 1991, except that:

(A) B may demand the funds in escrow at any time after the later of July 1, 1991, and [or] the occurrence of any of the following events—

(*1*) real property J is destroyed, seized, requisitioned, or condemned, or

(*2*) a determination is made that the regulatory approval necessary for the transfer of real property J cannot be obtained in time for real property J to be transferred to B before the end of the exchange period;

(B) B may demand the funds in escrow at any time after August 14, 1991, if real property J has not been rezoned from residential to commercial use by that date; and

(C) B may demand the funds in escrow at the time B receives real property J or any time thereafter.

Otherwise, B is entitled to all funds in escrow after November 13, 1991. The funds in escrow may be used to purchase the replacement property. The escrow holder is not a disqualified person as described in paragraph (k) of this section. Real property J is not rezoned from residential to commercial use on or before August 14, 1991.

(ii) C's obligation to transfer the replacement property to B was secured by cash held in a qualified escrow account because the escrow holder was not a disqualified person and the escrow agreement expressly limited B's rights to receive, pledge, borrow, or otherwise obtain the benefits of the money in escrow as provided in paragraph (g)(6) of this section. From May 17, 1991, until August 15, 1991, B did not have the immediate ability or unrestricted right to receive money or other property before B actually received the like-kind replacement property. Therefore, for purposes of section 1031 and this section, B is determined not to be in actual or constructive receipt of the $100,000 in escrow from May 17, 1991, until August 15, 1991. However, on August 15, 1991, B had the unrestricted right, upon notice, to draw upon the $100,000 held in escrow. Thus, the safe harbor ceased to apply and B was in constructive receipt of the funds held in escrow. Because B constructively received the full amount of the consideration ($100,000) before B actually received the like-kind replacement property, the transaction is treated as a sale and not as a deferred exchange. The result does not change even if B chose not to demand the funds in escrow and continued to attempt to have real property J rezoned and to receive the property on or before November 13, 1991.

(iii) If real property J had been rezoned on or before August 14, 1991, and C had purchased real property J and transferred it to B on or before November 13, 1991, the transaction would have qualified for nonrecognition of gain or loss under section 1031(a).

Example 3. (i) On May 1, 1991, D offers to purchase real property X for $100,000. However, D is unwilling to participate in a like-kind exchange. B thus enters into an exchange agreement with C whereby B retains C to facilitate an exchange with respect to real property X. C is not a disqualified person as described in paragraph (k) of this section. The exchange agreement between

Reg. § 1.1031(k)-1(g)(8)

B and C provides that B is to execute and deliver a deed conveying real property X to C who, in turn, is to execute and deliver a deed conveying real property X to D. The exchange agreement expressly limits B's rights to receive, pledge, borrow, or otherwise obtain the benefits of money or other property held by C as provided in paragraph (g)(6) of this section. On May 3, 1991, C enters into an agreement with D to transfer real property X to D for $100,000. On May 17, 1991, B executes and delivers to C a deed conveying real property X to C. On the same date, C executes and delivers to D a deed conveying real property X to D, and D deposits $100,000 in escrow. The escrow holder is not a disqualified person as defined in paragraph (k) of this section and the escrow agreement expressly limits B's rights to receive, pledge, borrow, or otherwise obtain the benefits of money or other property in escrow as provided in paragraph (g)(6) of this section. However, the escrow agreement provides that the money in escrow may be used to purchase replacement property. On June 3, 1991, B identifies real property K as replacement property. On August 9, 1991, E executes and delivers to C a deed conveying real property K to C and $80,000 is released from the escrow and paid to E. On the same date, C executes and delivers to B a deed conveying real property K to B, and the escrow holder pays B $20,000, the balance of the $100,000 sale price of real property X remaining after the purchase of real property K for $80,000.

(ii) B and C entered into an exchange agreement that satisfied the requirements of paragraph (g)(4)(iii) (B) of this section. Regardless of whether C may have acquired and transferred real property X under general tax principles, C is treated as having acquired and transferred real property X because C acquired and transferred legal title to real property X. Similarly, C is treated as having acquired and transferred real property X because C acquired and transferred legal title to real property K. Thus, C was a qualified intermediary. This result is reached for purposes of this section regardless of whether C was B's agent under state law.

(iii) Because the escrow holder was not a disqualified person and the escrow agreement expressly limited B's rights to receive, pledge, borrow, or otherwise obtain the benefits of money or other property in escrow as provided in paragraph (g)(6) of this section, the escrow account was a qualified escrow account. For purposes of section 1031 and this section, therefore, B is determined not to be in actual or constructive receipt of the funds in escrow before B received real property K.

(iv) The exchange agreement between B and C expressly limited B's rights to receive, pledge, borrow, or otherwise obtain the benefits of any money held by C as provided in paragraph (g)(6) of this section. Because C was a qualified intermediary, for purposes of section 1031 and this section B is determined not to be in actual or constructive receipt of any funds held by C before B received real property K. In addition, B's transfer of real property X and acquisition of real property K qualify as an exchange under section 1031. See paragraph (j) of this section for determining the amount of gain or loss recognized.

(v) If the escrow agreement had expressly limited C's rights to receive, pledge, borrow, or otherwise obtain the benefits of money or other property in escrow as provided in paragraph (g)(6) of this section, but had not expressly limited B's rights to receive, pledge, borrow, or otherwise obtain the benefits of that money or other property, the escrow account would not have been a qualified escrow account. Consequently, paragraph (g)(3)(i) of this section would not have been applicable in determining whether B was in actual or constructive receipt of that money or other property before B received real property X.

Example 4. (i) On May 1, 1991, B enters into an agreement to sell real property X to D for $100,000 on May 17, 1991. However, D is unwilling to participate in a like-kind exchange. B thus enters into an exchange agreement with C whereby B retains C to facilitate an exchange with respect to real property X. C is not a disqualified person as described in paragraph (k) of this section. In the exchange agreement between B and C, B assigns to C all of B's rights in the agreement with D. The exchange agreement expressly limits B's rights to receive, pledge, borrow, or otherwise obtain the benefits of money or other property held by C as provided in paragraph (g)(6) of this section. On May 17, 1991, B notifies D in writing of the assignment. On the same date, B executes and delivers to D a deed conveying real property X to D. D pays $10,000 to B and $90,000 to C. On June 1, 1991, B identifies real property L as replacement property. On July 5, 1991, B enters into an agreement to purchase real property L from E for $90,000, assigns its rights in that agreement to C, and notifies E in writing of the assignment. On August 9, 1991, C pays $90,000 to E, and E executes and delivers to B a deed conveying real property L to B.

(ii) The exchange agreement entered into by B and C satisfied the requirements of paragraph (g)(4)(iii) (B) of this section. Because B's rights in its agreements with D and E were assigned to C, and D and E were notified in writing of the assignment on or before the transfer of real properties X and L, respectively, C is treated as entering into those agreements. Because C is treated as entering into an agreement with D for the transfer of real property X and, pursuant to that agreement, real property X was transferred to D, C is treated as acquiring and transferring real property X. Similarly, because C is treated as entering into an agreement with E for the transfer of real property K and, pursuant to that agreement, real property K was transferred to B, C is treated as acquiring and transferring real property K. This result is reached for purposes of this section regardless of whether C was B's agent under state law and regardless of whether C is considered, under general tax principles, to have acquired title or beneficial ownership of the properties. Thus, C was a qualified intermediary.

(iii) The exchange agreement between B and C expressly limited B's rights to receive, pledge, borrow, or otherwise obtain the benefits of the money held by C as provided in paragraph (g)(6) of this section. Thus, B did not have the immediate ability or unrestricted right to receive money or other property held by C before B received real property L. For purposes of section 1031 and this section, therefore, B is determined not to be in actual or constructive receipt of the $90,000 held by C before B received real property L. In addition, the transfer of real property X by B and B's acquisition of real property L qualify as an exchange under section 1031. See paragraph (j) of this section for determining the amount of gain or loss recognized.

Example 5. (i) On May 1, 1991, B enters into an agreement to sell real property X to D for $100,000. However, D is unwilling to participate in a like-kind exchange. B thus enters into an agreement with C whereby B retains C to facilitate an exchange with respect to real property X. C is not a disqualified person as described in paragraph (k) of this section. The agreement between B and C expressly limits B's rights to receive, pledge, borrow, or otherwise obtain the benefits of money or other property held by C as provided in paragraph (g)(6) of this section. C neither enters into an agreement with D to transfer real property X to D nor is assigned B's rights in B's agreement to sell real property X to D. On May 17, 1991, B transfers real property X to D and instructs D to transfer the $100,000 to C. On June 1, 1991, B identifies real property M as replacement property. On August 9, 1991, C purchases real property L from E for $100,000, and E executes and delivers to C a deed conveying real property M to C. On the same date, C executes and delivers to B a deed conveying real property M to B.

(ii) Because B transferred real property X directly to D under B's agreement with D, C did not acquire real property X from B and transfer real property X to D. Moreover, because C did not acquire legal title to real property X, did not enter into an agreement with D to transfer real property X to D, and was not assigned B's rights in B's agreement to sell real property X to D, C is not treated as acquiring and transferring real property X. Thus, C was not a qualified intermediary and paragraph (g)(4)(i) of this section does not apply.

(iii) B did not exchange real property X for real property M. Rather, B sold real property X to D and purchased, through C, real property M. Therefore, the transfer of real property X does not qualify for nonrecognition of gain or loss under section 1031.

(h) *Interest and growth factors*—(1) *In general.* For purposes of this section, the taxpayer is treated as being entitled to receive interest or a growth factor with respect to a deferred exchange if the amount of money or property the taxpayer is entitled to receive depends upon the length of time elapsed between transfer of the relinquished property and receipt of the replacement property.

(2) *Treatment as interest.* If, as part of a deferred exchange, the taxpayer receives interest or a growth factor, the interest or growth factor will be treated as interest, regardless of whether it is paid to the taxpayer in cash or in property (including property of a like kind). The taxpayer must include the interest or growth factor in income according to the taxpayer's method of accounting.

(i) [Reserved]

(j) *Determination of gain or loss recognized and the basis of property received in a deferred exchange*—(1) *In general.* Except as otherwise provided, the amount of gain or loss recognized and the basis of property received in a deferred exchange is determined by applying the rules of section 1031 and the regulations thereunder. See §§ 1.1031(b)-1, 1.1031(c)-1, 1.1031(d)-1, 1.1031(d)-1T, 1.1031(d)-2, and 1.1031(j)-1.

(2) *Coordination with section 453*—(i) *Qualified escrow accounts and qualified trusts.* Subject to the limitations of paragraphs (j)(2)(iv) and (v) of this section, in the case of a taxpayer's transfer of relinquished property in which the obligation of the taxpayer's transferee to transfer replacement property to the taxpayer is or may be secured by cash or a cash equivalent, the determination of whether the taxpayer has received a payment for purposes of section 453 and § 15a.453-1(b)(3)(i) of this chapter will be made without regard to the fact that the obligation is or may be so secured if

Reg. § 1.1031(k)-1(j)(2)

the cash or cash equivalent is held in a qualified escrow account or a qualified trust. This paragraph (j)(2)(i) ceases to apply at the earlier of—

(A) The time described in paragraph (g)(3)(iv) of this section; or

(B) The end of the exchange period.

(ii) *Qualified intermediaries.* Subject to the limitations of paragraphs (j)(2)(iv) and (v) of this section, in the case of a taxpayer's transfer of relinquished property involving a qualified intermediary, the determination of whether the taxpayer has received a payment for purposes of section 453 and § 15a.453-1(b)(3)(i) of this chapter is made as if the qualified intermediary is not the agent of the taxpayer. For purposes of this paragraph (j)(2)(ii), a person who otherwise satisfies the definition of a qualified intermediary is treated as a qualified intermediary even though that person ultimately fails to acquire identified replacement property and transfer it to the taxpayer. This paragraph (j)(2)(ii) ceases to apply at the earlier of—

(A) The time described in paragraph (g)(4)(vi) of this section; or

(B) The end of the exchange period.

(iii) *Transferee indebtedness.* In the case of a transaction described in paragraph (j)(2)(ii) of this section, the receipt by the taxpayer of an evidence of indebtedness of the transferee of the qualified intermediary is treated as the receipt of an evidence of indebtedness of the person acquiring property from the taxpayer for purposes of section 453 and § 15a.453-1(b)(3)(i) of this chapter.

(iv) *Bona fide intent requirement.* The provisions of paragraphs (j)(2)(i) and (ii) of this section do not apply unless the taxpayer has a bona fide intent to enter into a deferred exchange at the beginning of the exchange period. A taxpayer will be treated as having a bona fide intent only if it is reasonable to believe, based on all the facts and circumstances as of the beginning of the exchange period, that like-kind replacement property will be acquired before the end of the exchange period.

(v) *Disqualified property.* The provisions of paragraphs (j)(2)(i) and (ii) of this section do not apply if the relinquished property is disqualified property. For purposes of this paragraph (j)(2), *disqualified property* means property that is not held for productive use in a trade or business or for investment or is property described in section 1031(a)(2).

(vi) *Examples.* This paragraph (j)(2) may be illustrated by the following examples. Unless otherwise provided in an example, the following facts are assumed: B is a calendar year taxpayer who agrees to enter into a deferred exchange. Pursuant to the agreement, B is to transfer real property X. Real property X, which has been held by B for investment, is unencumbered and has a fair market value of $100,000 at the time of transfer. B's adjusted basis in real property X at that time is $60,000. B identifies a single like-kind replacement property before the end of the identification period, and B receives the replacement property before the end of the exchange period. The transaction qualifies as a like-kind exchange under section 1031.

Example 1. (i) On September 22, 1994, B transfers real property X to C and C agrees to acquire like-kind property and deliver it to B. On that date B has a bona fide intent to enter into a deferred exchange. C's obligation, which is not payable on demand or readily tradable, is secured by $100,000 in cash. The $100,000 is deposited by C in an escrow account that is a qualified escrow account under paragraph (g)(3) of this section. The escrow agreement provides that B has no rights to receive, pledge, borrow, or otherwise obtain the benefits of the cash deposited in the escrow account until the earlier of the date the replacement property is delivered to B or the end of the exchange period. On March 11, 1995, C acquires replacement property having a fair market value of $80,000 and delivers the replacement property to B. The $20,000 in cash remaining in the qualified escrow account is distributed to B at that time.

(ii) Under section 1031(b), B recognizes gain to the extent of the $20,000 in cash that B receives in the exchange. Under paragraph (j)(2)(i) of this section, the qualified escrow account is disregarded for purposes of section 453 and § 15a.453-1(b)(3)(i) of this chapter in determining whether B is in receipt of payment. Accordingly, B's receipt of C's obligation on September 22, 1994, does not constitute a payment. Instead, B is treated as receiving payment on March 11, 1995, on receipt of the $20,000 in cash from the qualified escrow account. Subject to the other requirements of sections 453 and 453A, B may report the $20,000 gain in 1995 under the installment method. See section 453(f)(6) for special rules for determining total contract price and gross profit in the case of an exchange described in section 1031(b).

Example 2. (i) D offers to purchase real property X but is unwilling to participate in a like-kind exchange. B thus enters into an exchange agreement with C whereby B retains C to facilitate an exchange with respect to real property X. On September 22, 1994, pursuant to the agree-

Reg. § 1.1031(k)-1(j)(2)

ment, B transfers real property X to C who transfers it to D for $100,000 in cash. On that date B has a bona fide intent to enter into a deferred exchange. C is a qualified intermediary under paragraph (g)(4) of this section. The exchange agreement provides that B has no rights to receive, pledge, borrow, or otherwise obtain the benefits of the money held by C until the earlier of the date the replacement property is delivered to B or the end of the exchange period. On March 11, 1995, C acquires replacement property having a fair market value of $80,000 and delivers it, along with the remaining $20,000 from the transfer of real property X, to B.

(ii) Under section 1031(b), B recognizes gain to the extent of the $20,000 cash B receives in the exchange. Under paragraph (j)(2)(ii) of this section, any agency relationship between B and C is disregarded for purposes of section 453 and § 15a.453-1(b)(3)(i) of this chapter in determining whether B is in receipt of payment. Accordingly, B is not treated as having received payment on September 22, 1994, on C's receipt of payment from D for the relinquished property. Instead, B is treated as receiving payment on March 11, 1995, on receipt of the $20,000 in cash from C. Subject to the other requirements of sections 453 and 453A, B may report the $20,000 gain in 1995 under the installment method.

Example 3. (i) D offers to purchase real property X but is unwilling to participate in a like-kind exchange. B enters into an exchange agreement with C whereby B retains C as a qualified intermediary to facilitate an exchange with respect to real property X. On December 1, 1994, pursuant to the agreement, B transfers real property X to C who transfers it to D for $100,000 in cash. On that date B has a bona fide intent to enter into a deferred exchange. The exchange agreement provides that B has no rights to receive, pledge, borrow, or otherwise obtain the benefits of the cash held by C until the earliest of the end of the identification period if B has not identified replacement property, the date the replacement property is delivered to B, or the end of the exchange period. Although B has a bona fide intent to enter into a deferred exchange at the beginning of the exchange period, B does not identify or acquire any replacement property. In 1995, at the end of the identification period, C delivers the entire $100,000 from the sale of real property X to B.

(ii) Under section 1001, B realizes gain to the extent of the amount realized ($100,000) over the adjusted basis in real property X ($60,000), or $40,000. Because B has a bona fide intent at the beginning of the exchange period to enter into a deferred exchange, paragraph (j)(2)(iv) of this section does not make paragraph (j)(2)(ii) of this section inapplicable even though B fails to acquire replacement property. Further, under paragraph (j)(2)(ii) of this section, C is a qualified intermediary even though C does not acquire and transfer replacement property to B. Thus, any agency relationship between B and C is disregarded for purposes of section 453 and § 15a.453-1(b)(3)(i) of this chapter in determining whether B is in receipt of payment. Accordingly, B is not treated as having received payment on December 1, 1994, on C's receipt of payment from D for the relinquished property. Instead, B is treated as receiving payment at the end of the identification period in 1995 on receipt of the $100,000 in cash from C. Subject to the other requirements of sections 453 and 453A, B may report the $40,000 gain in 1995 under the installment method.

Example 4. (i) D offers to purchase real property X but is unwilling to participate in a like-kind exchange. B thus enters into an exchange agreement with C whereby B retains C to facilitate an exchange with respect to real property X. C is a qualified intermediary under paragraph (g)(4) of this section. On September 22, 1994, pursuant to the agreement, B transfers real property X to C who then transfers it to D for $80,000 in cash and D's 10-year installment obligation for $20,000. On that date B has a bona fide intent to enter into a deferred exchange. The exchange agreement provides that B has no rights to receive, pledge, borrow, or otherwise obtain the benefits of the money or other property held by C until the earlier of the date the replacement property is delivered to B or the end of the exchange period. D's obligation bears adequate stated interest and is not payable on demand or readily tradable. On March 11, 1995, C acquires replacement property having a fair market value of $80,000 and delivers it, along with the $20,000 installment obligation, to B.

(ii) Under section 1031(b), $20,000 of B's gain (i.e., the amount of the installment obligation B receives in the exchange) does not qualify for nonrecognition under section 1031(a). Under paragraphs (j)(2)(ii) and (iii) of this section, B's receipt of D's obligation is treated as the receipt of an obligation of the person acquiring the property for purposes of section 453 and § 15a.453-1(b)(3)(i) of this chapter in determining whether B is in receipt of payment. Accordingly, B's receipt of the obligation is not treated as a payment. Subject to the other requirements of sections 453 and 453A, B may report the $20,000 gain under the installment method on receiving payments from D on the obligation.

Reg. § 1.1031(k)-1(j)(2)

Example 5. (i) B is a corporation that has held real property X to expand its manufacturing operations. However, at a meeting in November 1994, B's directors decide that real property X is not suitable for the planned expansion, and authorize a like-kind exchange of this property for property that would be suitable for the planned expansion. B enters into an exchange agreement with C whereby B retains C as a qualified intermediary to facilitate an exchange with respect to real property X. On November 28, 1994, pursuant to the agreement, B transfers real property X to C, who then transfers it to D for $100,000 in cash. The exchange agreement does not include any limitations or conditions that make it unreasonable to believe that like-kind replacement property will be acquired before the end of the exchange period. The exchange agreement provides that B has no rights to receive, pledge, borrow, or otherwise obtain the benefits of the cash held by C until the earliest of the end of the identification period, if B has not identified replacement property, the date the replacement property is delivered to B, or the end of the exchange period. In early January 1995, B's directors meet and decide that it is not feasible to proceed with the planned expansion due to a business downturn reflected in B's preliminary financial reports for the last quarter of 1994. Thus, B's directors instruct C to stop seeking replacement property. C delivers the $100,000 cash to B on January 12, 1995, at the end of the identification period. Both the decision to exchange real property X for other property and the decision to cease seeking replacement property because of B's business downturn are recorded in the minutes of the directors' meetings. There are no other facts or circumstances that would indicate whether, on November 28, 1994, B had a bona fide intent to enter into a deferred like-kind exchange.

(ii) Under section 1001, B realizes gain to the extent of the amount realized ($100,000) over the adjusted basis of real property X ($60,000), or $40,000. The directors' authorization of a like-kind exchange, the terms of the exchange agreement with C, and the absence of other relevant facts, indicate that B had a bona fide intent at the beginning of the exchange period to enter into a deferred like-kind exchange. Thus, paragraph (j)(2)(iv) of this section does not make paragraph (j)(2)(ii) of this section inapplicable, even though B fails to acquire replacement property. Further, under paragraph (j)(2)(ii) of this section, C is a qualified intermediary, even though C does not transfer replacement property to B. Thus, any agency relationship between B and C is disregarded for purposes of section 453 and § 15a.453-1(b)(3)(i) of this chapter in determining whether B is in receipt of payment. Accordingly, B is not treated as having received payment until January 12, 1995, on receipt of the $100,000 cash from C. Subject to the other requirements of sections 453 and 453A, B may report the $40,000 gain in 1995 under the installment method.

Example 6. (i) B has held real property X for use in its trade or business, but decides to transfer that property because it is no longer suitable for B's planned expansion of its commercial enterprise. B and D agree to enter into a deferred exchange. Pursuant to their agreement, B transfers real property X to D on September 22, 1994, and D deposits $100,000 cash in a qualified escrow account as security for D's obligation under the agreement to transfer replacement property to B before the end of the exchange period. D's obligation is not payable on demand or readily tradable. The agreement provides that B is not required to accept any property that is not zoned for commercial use. Before the end of the identification period, B identifies real properties J, K, and L, all zoned for residential use, as replacement properties. Any one of these properties, rezoned for commercial use, would be suitable for B's planned expansion. In recent years, the zoning board with jurisdiction over properties J, K, and L has rezoned similar properties for commercial use. The escrow agreement provides that B has no rights to receive, pledge, borrow, or otherwise obtain the benefits of the money in the escrow account until the earlier of the time that the zoning board determines, after the end of the identification period, that it will not rezone the properties for commercial use or the end of the exchange period. On January 5, 1995, the zoning board decides that none of the properties will be rezoned for commercial use. Pursuant to the exchange agreement, B receives the $100,000 cash from the escrow on January 5, 1995. There are no other facts or circumstances that would indicate whether, on September 22, 1994, B had a bona fide intent to enter into a deferred like-kind exchange.

(ii) Under section 1001, B realizes gain to the extent of the amount realized ($100,000) over the adjusted basis of real property X ($60,000), or $40,000. The terms of the exchange agreement with D, the identification of properties J, K, and L, the efforts to have those properties rezoned for commercial purposes, and the absence of other relevant facts, indicate that B had a bona fide intent at the beginning of the exchange period to enter into a deferred exchange. Moreover, the limitations imposed in the exchange agreement on acceptable replacement property do not make it unreasonable to believe that like-kind replacement property would be acquired before the end of the exchange period. Therefore, paragraph (j)(2)(iv) of this section does not make paragraph (j)(2)(i) of this section inapplicable even though B fails to acquire replacement property. Thus, for purposes of section 453 and § 15a.453-1(b)(3)(i) of this chapter, the qualified escrow account is disregarded in determining whether B is in receipt of payment. Accordingly, B is not treated as having received payment on September 22, 1994, on D's deposit of the $100,000 cash into the qualified escrow account. Instead, B is treated as receiving payment on January 5, 1995. Subject to the other requirements of sections 453 and 453A, B may report the $40,000 gain in 1995 under the installment method.

(vii) *Effective date.* This paragraph (j)(2) is effective for transfers of property occurring on or after April 20, 1994. Taxpayers may apply this paragraph (j)(2) to transfers of property occurring before April 20, 1994 but on or after June 10, 1991, if those transfers otherwise meet the requirements of § 1.1031(k)-1. In addition, taxpayers may apply this paragraph (j)(2) to transfers of property occurring before June 10, 1991, but on or after May 16, 1990, if those transfers otherwise meet the requirements of § 1.1031(k)-1 or follow the guidance of IA-237-84 published in 1990-1, C.B. See § 601.601(d)(2)(ii)(*b*) of this chapter.

(3) *Examples.* This paragraph (j) may be illustrated by the following examples. Unless otherwise provided in an example, the following facts are assumed: B, a calendar year taxpayer, and C agree to enter into a deferred exchange. Pursuant to their agreement, B is to transfer real property X to C on May 17, 1991. Real property X, which has been held by B for investment, is unencumbered and has a fair market value on May 17, 1991, of $100,000. B's adjusted basis in real property X is $40,000. On or before July 1, 1991 (the end of the identification period), B is to identify replacement property that is of a like kind to real property X. On or before November 13, 1991 (the end of the exchange period), C is required to purchase the property identified by B and to transfer that property to B. To the extent the fair market value of the replacement property transferred to B is greater or less than the fair market value of real property X, either B or C, as applicable, will make up the difference by paying cash to the other party after the date the replacement property is received. The replacement property is identified as provided in paragraph (c) of this section and is of a like kind to real property X (determined without regard to section 1031(a)(3) and this section). B intends to hold any replacement property received for investment.

Example 1. (i) On May 17, 1991, B transfers real property X to C and identifies real property R as replacement property. On June 3, 1991, C transfers $10,000 to B. On September 4, 1991, C purchases real property R for $90,000 and transfers real property R to B.

(ii) The $10,000 received by B is "money or other property" for purposes of section 1031 and the regulations thereunder. Under section 1031(b), B recognizes gain in the amount of $10,000. Under section 1031(d), B's basis in real property R is $40,000 (i.e., B's basis in real property X ($40,000), decreased in the amount of money received ($10,000), and increased in the amount of gain recognized ($10,000) in the deferred exchange).

Example 2. (i) On May 17, 1991, B transfers real property X to C and identifies real property S as replacement property, and C transfers $10,000 to B. On September 4, 1991, C purchases real property S for $100,000 and transfers real property S to B. On the same day, B transfers $10,000 to C.

(ii) The $10,000 received by B is "money or other property" for purposes of section 1031 and the regulations thereunder. Under section 1031(b), B recognizes gain in the amount of $10,000. Under section 1031 (d), B's basis in real property S is $50,000 (i.e., B's basis in real property X ($40,000), decreased in the amount of money received ($10,000), increased in the amount of gain recognized ($10,000), and increased in the amount of the additional consideration paid by B ($10,000) in the deferred exchange).

Example 3. (i) Under the exchange agreement, B has the right at all times to demand $100,000 in cash in lieu of replacement property. On May 17, 1991, B transfers real property X to C and identifies real property T as replacement property. On September 4, 1991, C purchases real property T for $100,000 and transfers real property T to B.

(ii) Because B has the right on May 17, 1991, to demand $100,000 in cash in lieu of replacement property, B is in constructive receipt of the $100,000 on that date. Thus, the transaction is a sale and not an exchange, and the $60,000 gain realized by B in the transaction (i.e., $100,000 amount realized less $40,000 adjusted basis) is recognized. Under section 1031(d), B's basis in real property T is $100,000.

Example 4. (i) Under the exchange agreement, B has the right at all times to demand up to $30,000 in cash and the balance in replacement property instead of receiving replacement property in the amount of $100,000. On May 17, 1991,

Reg. § 1.1031(k)-1(j)(3)

B transfers real property X to C and identifies real property U as replacement property. On September 4, 1991, C purchases real property U for $100,000 and transfers real property U to B.

(ii) The transaction qualifies as a deferred exchange under section 1031 and this section. However, because B had the right on May 17, 1991, to demand up to $30,000 in cash, B is in constructive receipt of $30,000 on that date. Under section 1031(b), B recognizes gain in the amount of $30,000. Under section 1031(d), B's basis in real property U is $70,000 (i.e., B's basis in real property X ($40,000), decreased in the amount of money that B received ($30,000), increased in the amount of gain recognized ($30,000), and increased in the amount of additional consideration paid by B ($30,000) in the deferred exchange).

Example 5. (i) Assume real property X is encumbered by a mortgage of $30,000. On May 17, 1991, B transfers real property X to C and identifies real property V as replacement property, and C assumes the $30,000 mortgage on real property X. Real property V is encumbered by a $20,000 mortgage. On July 5, 1991, C purchases real property V for $90,000 by paying $70,000 and assuming the mortgage and transfers real property V to B with B assuming the mortgage.

(ii) The consideration received by B in the form of the liability assumed by C ($30,000) is offset by the consideration given by B in the form of the liability assumed by B ($20,000). The excess of the liability assumed by C over the liability assumed by B, $10,000, is treated as "money or other property." See § 1.1031(b)-1 (c). Thus, B recognizes gain under section 1031(b) in the amount of $10,000. Under section 1031(d), B's basis in real property V is $40,000 (i.e., B's basis in real property X ($40,000), decreased in the amount of money that B is treated as receiving in the form of the liability assumed by C ($30,000), increased in the amount of money that B is treated as paying in the form of the liability assumed by B ($20,000), and increased in the amount of the gain recognized ($10,000) in the deferred exchange).

(k) *Definition of disqualified person.* (1) For purposes of this section, a disqualified person is a person described in paragraph (k)(2), (k)(3), or (k)(4) of this section.

(2) The person is the agent of the taxpayer at the time of the transaction. For this purpose, a person who has acted as the taxpayer's employee, attorney, accountant, investment banker or broker, or real estate agent or broker within the 2-year period ending on the date of the transfer of the first of the relinquished properties is treated as an agent of the taxpayer at the time of the transaction. Solely for purposes of this paragraph (k)(2), performance of the following services will not be taken into account—

(i) Services for the taxpayer with respect to exchanges of property intended to qualify for nonrecognition of gain or loss under section 1031; and

(ii) Routine financial, title insurance, escrow, or trust services for the taxpayer by a financial institution, title insurance company, or escrow company.

(3) The person and the taxpayer bear a relationship described in either section 267(b) or section 707(b) (determined by substituting in each section "10 percent" for "50 percent" each place it appears).

(4) The person and a person described in paragraph (k) (2) of this section bear a relationship described in either section 267(b) or section 707(b) (determined by substituting in each section "10 percent" for "50 percent" each place it appears).

(5) This paragraph (k) may be illustrated by the following examples. Unless otherwise provided, the following facts are assumed: On May 1, 1991, B enters into an exchange agreement (as defined in paragraph (g)(4)(iii) (B) of this section) with C whereby B retains C to facilitate an exchange with respect to real property X. On May 17, 1991, pursuant to the agreement, B executes and delivers to C a deed conveying real property X to C. C has no relationship to B described in paragraphs (k)(2), (k) (3), or (k)(4) of this section.

Example 1. (i) C is B's accountant and has rendered accounting services to B within the 2-year period ending on May 17, 1991, other than with respect to exchanges of property intended to qualify for nonrecognition of gain or loss under section 1031.

(ii) C is a disqualified person because C has acted as B's accountant within the 2-year period ending on May 17, 1991.

(iii) If C had not acted as B's accountant within the 2-year period ending on May 17, 1991, or if C had acted as B's accountant within that period only with respect to exchanges intended to qualify for nonrecognition of gain or loss under section 1031, C would not have been a disqualified person.

Example 2. (i) C, which is engaged in the trade or business of acting as an intermediary to facilitate deferred exchanges, is a wholly owned subsidiary of an escrow company that has performed routine escrow services for B in the past. C

Reg. § 1.1031(k)-1(k)(2)

has previously been retained by B to act as an intermediary in prior section 1031 exchanges.

(ii) C is not a disqualified person notwithstanding the intermediary services previously provided by C to B (see paragraph (k)(2)(i) of this section) and notwithstanding the combination of C's relationship to the escrow company and the escrow services previously provided by the escrow company to B (see paragraph (k)(2)(ii) of this section).

Example 3. (i) C is a corporation that is only engaged in the trade or business of acting as an intermediary to facilitate deferred exchanges. Each of 10 law firms owns 10 percent of the outstanding stock of C. One of the 10 law firms that owns 10 percent of C is M. J is the managing partner of M and is the president of C. J, in his capacity as a partner in M, has also rendered legal advice to B within the 2-year period ending on May 17, 1991, on matters other than exchanges intended to qualify for nonrecognition of gain or loss under section 1031.

(ii) J and M are disqualified persons. C, however, is not a disqualified person because neither J nor M own, directly or indirectly, more than 10 percent of the stock of C. Similarly, J's participation in the management of C does not make C a disqualified person.

(1) [Reserved]

(m) *Definition of fair market value.* For purposes of this section, the fair market value of property means the fair market value of the property without regard to any liabilities secured by the property.

(n) *No inference with respect to actual or constructive receipt rules outside of section 1031.* The rules provided in this section relating to actual or constructive receipt are intended to be rules for determining whether there is actual or constructive receipt in the case of a deferred exchange. No inference is intended regarding the application of these rules for purposes of determining whether actual or constructive receipt exists for any other purpose.

(o) *Effective date.* This section applies to transfers of property made by a taxpayer on or after June 10, 1991. However, a transfer of property made by a taxpayer on or after May 16, 1990, but before June 10, 1991, will be treated as complying with section 1031(a)(3) and this section if the deferred exchange satisfies either the provisions of this section or the provisions of the notice of proposed rulemaking published in the *Federal Register* on May 16, 1990 (55 F.R. 20278). [Reg. § 1.1031(k)-1.]

☐ [T.D. 8346, 4-25-91. Amended by T.D. 8535, 4-19-94.]

[Reg. § 1.1032-1]

§ 1.1032-1. Disposition by a corporation of its own capital stock.—(a) The disposition by a corporation of shares of its own stock (including treasury stock) for money or other property does not give rise to taxable gain or deductible loss to the corporation regardless of the nature of the transaction or the facts and circumstances involved. For example, the receipt by a corporation of the subscription price of shares of its stock upon their original issuance gives rise to neither taxable gain nor deductible loss, whether the subscription or issue price be equal to, in excess of, or less than, the par or stated value of such stock. Also, the exchange or sale by a corporation of its own shares for money or other property does not result in taxable gain or deductible loss, even though the corporation deals in such shares as it might in the shares of another corporation. A transfer by a corporation of shares of its own stock (including treasury stock) as compensation for services is considered, for purposes of section 1032(a), as a disposition by the corporation of such shares for money or other property.

(b) Section 1032(a) does not apply to the acquisition by a corporation of shares of its own stock except where the corporation acquires such shares in exchange for shares of its own stock (including treasury stock). See paragraph (e) of § 1.311-1, relating to treatment of acquisition of a corporation's own stock. Section 1032(a) also does not relate to the tax treatment of the recipient of a corporation's stock.

(c) Where a corporation acquires shares of its own stock in exchange for shares of its own stock (including treasury stock) the transaction may qualify not only under section 1032(a), but also under section 368(a)(1)(E)(recapitalization) or section 305(a) (distribution of stock and stock rights).

(d) For basis of property acquired by a corporation in connection with a transaction to which section 351 applies or in connection with a reorganization, see section 362. For basis of property acquired by a corporation in a transaction to which section 1032 applies but which does not qualify under any other nonrecognition provision, see section 1012. [Reg. § 1.1032-1.]

☐ [T.D. 6210, 11-6-56.]

[Reg. § 1.1032-2]

§ 1.1032-2. Disposition by a corporation of stock of a controlling corporation in certain triangular reorganizations.—(a) *Scope.* This section provides rules for certain triangular reorganizations described in § 1.358-6(b) when the acquiring corporation (S) acquires property or stock of another corporation (T) in exchange for stock of the corporation (P) in control of S.

(b) *General nonrecognition of gain or loss.* For purposes of § 1.1032-1(a), in the case of a forward triangular merger, a triangular C reorganization, or a triangular B reorganization (as described in § 1.358-6(b)), P stock provided by P to S, or directly to T or T's shareholders on behalf of S, pursuant to the plan of reorganization is treated as a disposition by P of shares of its own stock for T's assets or stock, as applicable. For rules governing the use of P stock in a reverse triangular merger, see section 361.

(c) *Treatment of S.* S must recognize gain or loss on its exchange of P stock as consideration in a forward triangular merger, a triangular C reorganization, or a triangular B reorganization (as described in § 1.358-6(b)), if S did not receive the P stock from P pursuant to the plan of reorganization. See § 1.358-6(d) for the effect on P's basis in its S or T stock, as applicable. For rules governing S's use of P stock in a reverse triangular merger, see section 361.

(d) *Examples.* The rules of this section are illustrated by the following examples. For purposes of these examples, P, S, and T are domestic corporations, P and S do not file consolidated returns P owns all of the only class of S stock, the P stock exchanged in the transaction satisfies the requirements of the applicable reorganization provisions, and the facts set forth the only corporate activity.

Example 1. *Forward triangular merger solely for P stock.* (a) *Facts.* T has assets with an aggregate basis of $60 and fair market value of $100 and no liabilities. Pursuant to a plan, P forms S by transferring $100 of P stock to S and T merges into S. In the merger, the T shareholders receive, in exchange for their T stock, the P stock that P transferred to S. The transaction is a reorganization to which sections 368(a)(1)(A) and (a)(2)(D) apply.

(b) *No gain or loss recognized on the use of P stock.* Under paragraph (b) of this section, the P stock provided by P pursuant to the plan of reorganization is treated for purposes of § 1.1032-1 (a) as disposed of by P for the T assets acquired by S in the merger. Consequently, neither P nor S has taxable gain or deductible loss on the exchange.

Example 2. *Forward triangular merger solely for P stock provided in part by S.* (a) *Facts.* T has assets with an aggregate basis of $60 and fair market value of $100 and no liabilities. S is an operating company with substantial assets that has been in existence for several years. S also owns P stock with a $20 adjusted basis and $30 fair market value. S acquired the P stock in an unrelated transaction several years before the reorganization. Pursuant to a plan, P transfers additional P stock worth $70 to S and T merges into S. In the merger, the T shareholders receive $100 of P stock ($70 of P stock provided by P to S as part of the plan and $30 of P stock held by S previously). The transaction is a reorganization to which sections 368(a)(1)(A) and (a)(2)(D) apply.

(b) *Gain or loss recognized by S on the use of its P stock.* Under paragraph (b) of this section, the $70 of P stock provided by P pursuant to the plan of reorganization is treated as disposed of by P for the T assets acquired by S in the merger. Consequently, neither P nor S has taxable gain or deductible loss on the exchange of those shares. Under paragraph (c) of this section, however, S recognizes $10 of gain on the exchange of its P stock in the reorganization because S did not receive the P stock from P pursuant to the plan of reorganization. See § 1.358-6(d) for the effect on P's basis in its S stock.

(e) *Stock options.* The rules of this section shall apply to an option to buy or sell P stock issued by P in the same manner as the rules of this section apply to P stock.

(f) *Effective dates.* This section applies to triangular reorganizations occurring on or after December 23, 1994, except for paragraph (e) of this section, which applies to transfers of stock options occurring on or after May 16, 2000. [Reg. § 1.1032-2.]

☐ [T.D. 8648, 12-20-95. Amended by T.D. 8883, 5-11-2000.]

[Reg. § 1.1032-3]

§ 1.1032-3. **Disposition of stock or stock options in certain transactions not qualifying under any other nonrecognition provision.—** (a) *Scope.* This section provides rules for certain transactions in which a corporation or a partnership (the acquiring entity) acquires money or other property (as defined in § 1.1032-1) in exchange, in whole or in part, for stock of a corporation (the issuing corporation).

(b) *Nonrecognition of gain or loss*—(1) *General rule.* In a transaction to which this section applies; no gain or loss is recognized on the disposition of the issuing corporation's stock by the acquiring entity. The transaction is treated as if, immediately before the acquiring entity disposes of the stock of the issuing corporation, the acquiring entity purchased the issuing corporation's stock from the issuing corporation for fair market value with cash contributed to the acquiring entity by the issuing corporation (or, if necessary, through intermediate corporations or partnerships). For rules that may apply in determining the issuing corporation's adjustment to basis in the acquiring entity (or, if necessary, in determining the adjustment to basis in intermediate entities), see sections 358, 722, and the regulations thereunder.

(2) *Special rule for actual payment for stock of the issuing corporation.* If the issuing corporation receives money or other property in payment for its stock, the amount of cash deemed contributed under paragraph (b)(1) of this section is the difference between the fair market value of the issuing corporation stock and the amount of money or the fair market value of other property that the issuing corporation receives as payment.

(c) *Applicability.* The rules of this section apply only if, pursuant to a plan to acquire money or other property—

(1) The acquiring entity acquires stock of the issuing corporation directly or indirectly from the issuing corporation in a transaction in which, but for this section, the basis of the stock of the issuing corporation in the hands of the acquiring entity would be determined, in whole or in part, with respect to the issuing corporation's basis in the issuing corporation's stock under section 362(a) or 723 (provided that, in the case of an indirect acquisition by the acquiring entity, the transfers of issuing corporation stock through intermediate entities occur immediately after one another);

(2) The acquiring entity immediately transfers the stock of the issuing corporation to acquire money or other property (from a person other than an entity from which the stock was directly or indirectly acquired);

(3) The party receiving stock of the issuing corporation in the exchange specified in paragraph (c)(2) of this section from the acquiring entity does not receive a substituted basis in the stock of the issuing corporation within the meaning of section 7701(a)(42); and

(4) The issuing corporation stock is not exchanged for stock of the issuing corporation.

(d) *Stock options.* The rules of this section shall apply to an option issued by a corporation to buy or sell its own stock in the same manner as the rules of this section apply to the stock of an issuing corporation.

(e) *Examples.* The following examples illustrate the application of this section:

Example 1. (i) X, a corporation, owns all of the stock of Y corporation. Y reaches an agreement with C, an individual, to acquire a truck from C in exchange for 10 shares of X stock with a fair market value of $100. To effectuate Y's agreement with C, X transfers to Y the X stock in a transaction in which, but for this section, the basis of the X stock in the hands of Y would be determined with respect to X's basis in the X stock under section 362(a). Y immediately transfers the X stock to C to acquire the truck.

(ii) In this *Example 1*, no gain or loss is recognized on the disposition of the X stock by Y. Immediately before Y's disposition of the X stock, Y is treated as purchasing the X stock from X for $100 of cash contributed to Y by X. Under section 358, X's basis in its Y stock is increased by $100.

Example 2. (i) Assume the same facts as *Example 1*, except that, rather than X stock, X transfers an option with a fair market value of $100 to purchase X stock.

(ii) In this *Example 2*, no gain or loss is recognized on the disposition of the X stock option by Y. Immediately before Y's disposition of the X stock option, Y is treated as purchasing the X stock option from X for $100 of cash contributed to Y by X. Under section 358, X's basis in its Y stock is increased by $100.

Example 3. (i) X, a corporation, owns all of the outstanding stock of Y corporation. Y is a partner in partnership Z. Z reaches an agreement with C, an individual, to acquire a truck from C in exchange for 10 shares of X stock with a fair market value of $100. To effectuate Z's agreement with C, X transfers to Y the X stock in a transaction in which, but for this section, the basis of the X stock in the hands of Y would be determined with respect to X's basis in the X stock under section 362(a). Y immediately transfers the X stock to Z in a transaction in which, but for this section, the basis of the X stock in the hands of Z would be determined under section 723. Z immediately transfers the X stock to C to acquire the truck.

(ii) In this *Example 3*, no gain or loss is recognized on the disposition of the X stock by Z. Immediately before Z's disposition of the X stock, Z is treated as purchasing the X stock from X for $100 of cash indirectly contributed to Z by X through an intermediate corporation, Y. Under section 722, Y's basis in its Z partnership interest is increased by $100, and, under section 358, X's basis in its Y stock is increased by $100.

Example 4. (i) X, a corporation, owns all of the outstanding stock of Y corporation. B, an individual, is an employee of Y. Pursuant to an agreement between X and Y to compensate B for services provided to Y, X transfers to B 10 shares of X stock with a fair market value of $100. Under § 1.83-6(d), but for this section, the transfer of X stock by X to the would be treated as a

Reg. § 1.1032-3(e)

52,000   Common Nontaxable Exchanges

See p. 20,601 for regulations not amended to reflect law changes

contribution of the X stock by X to the capital of Y, and immediately thereafter, a transfer of the X stock by Y to B. But for this section, the basis of the X stock in the hands of Y would be determined with respect to X's basis in the X stock under section 362(a).

(ii) In this *Example 4*, no gain or loss is recognized on the deemed disposition of the X stock by Y. Immediately before Y's deemed disposition of the X stock, Y is treated as purchasing the X stock from X for $100 of cash contributed to Y by X. Under section 358, X's basis in its Y stock is increased by $100.

Example 5. (i) X, a corporation, owns all of the outstanding stock of Y corporation. B, an individual, is an employee of Y. To compensate B for services provided to Y, B is offered the opportunity to purchase 10 shares of X stock with a fair market value of $100 at a reduced price of $80. B transfers $80 and Y transfers $10 to X as partial payment for the X stock.

(ii) In this *Example 5*, no gain or loss is recognized on the deemed disposition of the X stock by Y. Immediately before Y's deemed disposition of the X stock, Y is treated as purchasing the X stock from X for $100, $80 of which Y is deemed to have received from B, $10 of which originated with Y, and $10 of which is deemed to have been contributed to Y by X. Under section 358, X's basis in its Y stock is increased by $10.

Example 6. (i) X, a corporation, owns stock of Y. To compensate Y's employee, B, for services provided to Y, X issues 10 shares of X stock to B, subject to a substantial risk of forfeiture. B does not have an election under section 83(b) in effect with respect to the X stock. X retains the only reversionary interest in the X stock in the event that B forfeits the right to the stock. Several years after X's transfer of the X shares, the stock vests. At the time the stock vests, the 10 shares of X stock have a fair market value of $100. Under § 1.83-6(d), but for this section, the transfer of the X stock by X to B would be treated, at the time the stock vests, as a contribution of the X stock by X to the capital of Y, and immediately thereafter, a disposition of the X stock by Y to B. The basis of the X stock in the hands of Y, but for this section, would be determined with respect to X's basis in the X stock under section 362(a).

(ii) In this *Example 6*, no gain or loss is recognized on the deemed disposition of X stock by Y when the stock vests Immediately before Y's deemed disposition of the X stock, Y is treated as purchasing X's stock from X for $100 of cash contributed to Y by X. Under section 358, X's basis in its Y stock is increased by $100.

Example 7. (i) Assume the same facts as in *Example 6*, except that Y (rather than X) retains a reversionary interest in the X stock in the event that B forfeits the right to the stock. Several years after X's transfer of the X shares, the stock vests.

(ii) In this *Example 7*, this section does not apply to Y's deemed disposition of the X shares because Y is not deemed to have transferred the X stock to B immediately after receiving the stock from X. For the tax consequences to Y on the deemed disposition of the X stock, see § 1.83-6(b).

Example 8. (i) X, a corporation, owns all of the outstanding stock of Y corporation. In Year 1, X issues to Y's employee, B, a nonstatutory stock option to purchase 10 shares of X stock as compensation for services provided to Y. The option is exercisable against X and does not have a readily ascertainable fair market value (determined under § 1.83-7(b)) at the time the option is granted. In Year 2, B exercises the option by paying X the strike price of $80 for the X stock, which then has a fair market value of $100.

(ii) In this *Example 8*, because, under section 83(e)(3), section 83(a) does not apply to the grant of the option, paragraph (d) of this section also does not apply to the grant of the option. Section 83 and § 1.1032-3 apply in Year 2 when the option is exercised; thus, no gain or loss is recognized on the deemed disposition of X stock by Y in Year 2. Immediately before Y's deemed disposition of the X stock in Year 2, Y is treated as purchasing the X stock from X for $100, $80 of which Y is deemed to have received from B and the remaining $20 of which is deemed to have been contributed to Y by X. Under section 358, X's basis in its Y stock is increased by $20.

Example 9. (i) A, an individual, owns a majority of the stock of X. X owns stock of Y constituting control of Y within the meaning of section 368(c). A transfers 10 shares of its X stock to B, a key employee of Y. The fair market value of the 10 shares on the date of transfer was $100.

(ii) In this *Example 9*, A is treated as making a nondeductible contribution of the 10 shares of X to the capital of X, and no gain or loss is recognized by A as a result of this transfer. See *Commissioner v. Fink*, 483 U.S. 89 (1987). A must allocate his basis in the transferred shares to his remaining shares of X stock. No gain or loss is recognized on the deemed disposition of the X stock by Y. Immediately before Y's disposition of the X stock, Y is treated as purchasing the X stock from X for $100 of cash contributed to Y by X. Under section 358, X's basis in its Y stock is increased by $100.

Example 10. (i) In Year 1, X, a corporation, forms a trust which will be used to satisfy de-

Reg. § 1.1032-3(e)

ferred compensation obligations owed by Y, X's wholly owned subsidiary, to Y's employees. X funds the trust with X stock, which would revert to X upon termination of the trust, subject to the employees' rights to be paid the deferred compensation due to them. The creditors of X can reach all the trust assets upon the insolvency of X. Similarly, Y's creditors can reach all the trust assets upon the insolvency of Y. In Year 5, the trust transfers X stock to the employees of Y in satisfaction of the deferred compensation obligation.

(ii) In this *Example 10*, X is considered to be the grantor of the trust, and, under section 677, X is also the owner of the trust. Any income earned by the trust would be reflected on X's income tax return. Y is not considered a grantor or owner of the trust corpus at the time X transfers X stock to the trust. In Year 5, when employees of Y receive X stock in satisfaction of the deferred compensation obligation, no gain or loss is recognized on the deemed disposition of the X stock by Y. Immediately before Y's deemed disposition of the X stock, Y is treated as purchasing the X stock from X for fair market value using cash contributed to Y by X. Under section 358, X's basis in its Y stock increases by the amount of cash deemed contributed.

(f) *Effective date.* This section applies to transfers of stock or stock options of the issuing corporation occurring on or after May 16, 2000. [Reg. § 1.1032-3.]

☐ [T.D. 8883, 5-11-2000 (*corrected* 6-14-2000).]

[Reg. § 1.1033(a)-1]

§ 1.1033(a)-1. **Involuntary conversion; nonrecognition of gain.**—(a) *In general.* Section 1033 applies to cases where property is compulsorily or involuntarily converted. An "involuntary conversion" may be the result of the destruction of property in whole or in part, the theft of property, the seizure of property, the requisition or condemnation of property, or the threat or imminence of requisition or condemnation of property. An "involuntary conversion" may be a conversion into similar property or into money or into dissimilar property. Section 1033 provides that, under certain specified circumstances, any gain which is realized from an involuntary conversion shall not be recognized. In cases where property is converted into other property similar or related in service or use to the converted property, no gain shall be recognized regardless of when the disposition of the converted property occurred and regardless of whether or not the taxpayer elects to have the gain not recognized. In other types of involuntary conversion cases, however, the proceeds arising from the disposition of the converted property must (within the time limits specified) be reinvested in similar property in order to avoid recognition of any gain realized. Section 1033 applies only with respect to gains; losses from involuntary conversions are recognized or not recognized without regard to this section.

(b) *Special rules.* For rules relating to the application of section 1033 to involuntary conversions of a principal residence with respect to which an election has been made under section 121 (relating to gain from sale or exchange of residence of individual who has attained age 65), see paragraph (g) of § 1.121-5. For rules applicable to involuntary conversions of a principal residence occurring before January 1, 1951, see § 1.1033(a)-3. For rules applicable to involuntary conversions of a principal residence occurring after December 31, 1950, and before January 1, 1954, see paragraph (h)(1) of § 1.1034-1. For rules applicable to involuntary conversions of a personal residence occurring after December 31, 1953, see § 1.1033(a)-3. For special rules relating to the election to have section 1034 apply to certain involuntary conversions of a principal residence occurring after December 31, 1957, see paragraph (h) (2) of § 1.1034-1. For special rules relating to certain involuntary conversions of real property held either for productive use in trade or business or for investment and occurring after December 31, 1957, see § 1.1033(g)-1. See also special rules applicable to involuntary conversions of property sold pursuant to reclamation laws, livestock destroyed by disease, and livestock sold on account of drought provided in § § 1.1033(c)-1, 1.1033(d)-1, and 1.1033(e)-1, respectively. For rules relating to basis of property acquired through involuntary conversions, see § 1.1033(b)-1. For determination of the period for which the taxpayer has held property acquired as a result of certain involuntary conversions, see section 1223 and regulations issued thereunder. For treatment of gains from involuntary conversions as capital gains in certain cases, see section 1231(a) and regulations issued thereunder. For portion of war loss recoveries treated as gain on involuntary conversion, see section 1332(b)(3) and regulations issued thereunder. [Reg. § 1.1033(a)-1.]

☐ [T.D. 6222, 1-9-57. Amended by T.D. 6338, 12-11-58, T.D. 6453, 2-6-60, T.D. 6856, 10-19-65, T.D. 7625, 5-29-79 and T.D. 7758, 1-16-81.]

[Reg. § 1.1033(a)-2]

§ 1.1033(a)-2. **Involuntary conversion into similar property, into money or into dissimilar property.**—(a) *In general.* The term "disposition of the converted property" means the destruction, theft, seizure, requisition, or condemnation of the converted property, or the sale or exchange of such property under threat or imminence of requisition or condemnation.

(b) *Conversion into similar property.* If property (as a result of its destruction in whole or in part, theft, seizure, or requisition or condemnation or threat or imminence thereof) is compulsorily or involuntarily converted only into property similar or related in service or use to the property so converted, no gain shall be recognized. Such nonrecognition of gain is mandatory.

(c) *Conversion into money or into dissimilar property.* (1) If property (as a result of its destruction in whole or in part, theft, seizure, or requisition or condemnation or threat or imminence thereof) is compulsorily or involuntarily converted into money or into property not similar or related in service or use to the converted property, the gain, if any, shall be recognized, at the election of the taxpayer, only to the extent that the amount realized upon such conversion exceeds the cost of other property purchased by the taxpayer which is similar or related in service or use to the property so converted, or the cost of stock of a corporation owning such other property which is purchased by the taxpayer in the acquisition of control of such corporation, if the taxpayer purchased such other property, or such stock, for the purpose of replacing the property so converted and during the period specified in subparagraph (3) of this paragraph. For the purposes of section 1033 the term "control" means the ownership of stock possessing at least 80 percent of the total combined voting power of all classes of stock entitled to vote and at least 80 percent of the total number of shares of all other classes of stock of the corporation.

(2) All of the details in connection with an involuntary conversion of property at a gain (including those relating to the replacement of the converted property, or a decision not to replace, or the expiration of the period for replacement) shall be reported in the return for the taxable year or years in which any of such gain is realized. An election to have such gain recognized only to the extent provided in subparagraph (1) of this paragraph shall be made by including such gain in gross income for such year or years only to such extent. If, at the time of filing such a return, the period within which the converted property must be replaced has expired, or if such an election is not desired, the gain should be included in gross income for such year or years in the regular manner. A failure to so include such gain in gross income in the regular manner shall be deemed to be an election by the taxpayer to have such gain recognized only to the extent provided in subparagraph (1) of this paragraph even though the details in connection with the conversion are not reported in such return. If, after having made an election under section 1033(a)(2), the converted property is not replaced within the required period of time, or replacement is made at a cost lower than was anticipated at the time of the election, or a decision is made not to replace, the tax liability for the year or years for which the election was made shall be recomputed. Such recomputation should be in the form of an "amended return". If a decision is made to make an election under section 1033(a)(2) after the filing of the return and the payment of the tax for the year or years in which any of the gain on an involuntary conversion is realized and before the expiration of the period within which the converted property must be replaced, a claim for credit or refund for such year or years should be filed. If the replacement of the converted property occurs in a year or years in which none of the gain on the conversion is realized, all of the details in connection with such replacement shall be reported in the return for such year or years.

(3) The period referred to in subparagraphs (1) and (2) of this paragraph is the period of time commencing with the date of the disposition of the converted property, or the date of the beginning of the threat or imminence of requisition or condemnation of the converted property, whichever is earlier, and ending two years (or, in the case of a disposition occurring before December 31, 1969, one year) after the close of the first taxable year in which any part of the gain upon the conversion is realized, or at the close of such later date as may be designated pursuant to an application of the taxpayer. Such application shall be made prior to the expiration of two years (or, in the case of a disposition occurring before December 31, 1969, one year) after the close of the first taxable year in which any part of the gain from the conversion is realized, unless the taxpayer can show to the satisfaction of the district director—

(i) reasonable cause for not having filed the application within the required period of time, and

(ii) the filing of such application was made within a reasonable time after the expiration of the required period of time.

See section 1033(g)(4) and § 1.1033(g)-1 for the circumstances under which, in the case of the conversion of real property held either for productive use in trade or business or for investment, the 2-year period referred to in this paragraph (c)(3) shall be extended to 3 years.

Reg. § 1.1033(a)-2(b)

Common Nontaxable Exchanges

The application shall contain all of the details in connection with the involuntary conversion. Such application shall be made to the district director for the internal revenue district in which the return is filed for the first taxable year in which any of the gain from the involuntary conversion is realized. No extension of time shall be granted pursuant to such application unless the taxpayer can show reasonable cause for not being able to replace the converted property within the required period of time.

(4) Property or stock purchased before the disposition of the converted property shall be considered to have been purchased for the purpose of replacing the converted property only if such property or stock is held by the taxpayer on the date of the disposition of the converted property. Property or stock shall be considered to have been purchased only if, but for the provisions of section 1033(b), the unadjusted basis of such property or stock would be its cost to the taxpayer within the meaning of section 1012. If the taxpayer's unadjusted basis of the replacement property would be determined, in the absence of section 1033(b), under any of the exceptions referred to in section 1012, the unadjusted basis of the property would not be its cost within the meaning of section 1012. For example, if property similar or related in service or use to the converted property is acquired by gift and its basis is determined under section 1015, such property will not qualify as a replacement for the converted property.

(5) If a taxpayer makes an election under section 1033(a)(2), any deficiency, for any taxable year in which any part of the gain upon the conversion is realized, which is attributable to such gain may be assessed at any time before the expiration of three years from the date the district director with whom the return for such year has been filed is notified by the taxpayer of the replacement of the converted property or of an intention not to replace, or of a failure to replace, within the required period, notwithstanding the provisions of section 6212(c) or the provisions of any other law or rule of law which would otherwise prevent such assessment. If replacement has been made, such notification shall contain all of the details in connection with such replacement. Such notification should be made in the return for the taxable year or years in which the replacement occurs, or the intention not to replace is formed, or the period for replacement expires, if this return is filed with such district director. If this return is not filed with such district director, then such notification shall be made to such district director at the time of filing this return. If the taxpayer so desires, he may, in either event, also notify such district director before the filing of such return.

(6) If a taxpayer makes an election under section 1033(a)(2) and the replacement property or stock was purchased before the beginning of the last taxable year in which any part of the gain upon the conversion is realized, any deficiency, for any taxable year ending before such last taxable year, which is attributable to such election may be assessed at any time before the expiration of the period within which a deficiency for such last taxable year may be assessed, notwithstanding the provisions of section 6212(c) or 6501 or the provisions of any law or rule of law which would otherwise prevent such assessment.

(7) If the taxpayer makes an election under section 1033(a)(2), the gain upon the conversion shall be recognized to the extent that the amount realized upon such conversion exceeds the cost of the replacement property or stock, regardless of whether such amount is realized in one or more taxable years.

(8) The proceeds of a use and occupancy insurance contract, which by its terms insured against actual loss sustained of net profits in the business, are not proceeds of an involuntary conversion but are income in the same manner that the profits for which they are substituted would have been.

(9) There is no investment in property similar in character and devoted to a similar use if—

(i) The proceeds of unimproved real estate, taken upon condemnation proceedings, are invested in improved real estate.

(ii) The proceeds of conversion of real property are applied in reduction of indebtedness previously incurred in the purchase of a leasehold.

(iii) The owner of a requisitioned tug uses the proceeds to buy barges.

(10) If, in a condemnation proceeding, the Government retains out of the award sufficient funds to satisfy special assessments levied against the remaining portion of the plot or parcel of real estate affected for benefits accruing in connection with the condemnation, the amount so retained shall be deducted from the gross award in determining the amount of the net award.

(11) If, in a condemnation proceeding, the Government retains out of the award sufficient funds to satisfy liens (other than liens due to special assessments levied against the remaining portion of the plot or parcel of real estate affected for benefits accruing in connection with the condemnation) and mortgages against the property, and itself pays the same, the amount so retained shall not be deducted from the gross award in

Reg. § 1.1033(a)-2(c)(11)

determining the amount of the net award. If, in a condemnation proceeding, the Government makes an award to a mortgagee to satisfy a mortgage on the condemned property, the amount of such award shall be considered as a part of the "amount realized" upon the conversion regardless of whether or not the taxpayer was personally liable for the mortgage debt. Thus, if a taxpayer has acquired property worth $100,000 subject to a $50,000 mortgage (regardless of whether or not he was personally liable for the mortgage debt) and, in a condemnation proceeding, the Government awards the taxpayer $60,000 and awards the mortgagee $50,000 in satisfaction of the mortgage, the entire $110,000 is considered to be the "amount realized" by the taxpayer.

(12) An amount expended for replacement of an asset, in excess of the recovery for loss, represents a capital expenditure and is not a deductible loss for income tax purposes. [Reg. § 1.1033(a)-2.]

☐ [T.D. 6222, 1-9-57. Amended by T.D. 6679, 9-30-63, T.D. 7075, 11-23-70, T.D. 7625, 5-29-79 and T.D. 7758, 1-16-81.]

[Reg. § 1.1033(a)-3]

§ 1.1033(a)-3. **Involuntary conversion of principal residence.**—Section 1033 shall apply in the case of property used by the taxpayer as his principal residence if the destruction, theft, seizure, requisition, or condemnation of such residence, or the sale or exchange of such residence under threat or imminence thereof, occurs before January 1, 1951, or after December 31, 1953. However, section 1033 shall not apply to the seizure, requisition, or condemnation (but not destruction), or the sale or exchange under threat or imminence thereof, of such residence property if the seizure, requisition, condemnation, sale, or exchange occurs after December 31, 1957, and if the taxpayer properly elects under section 1034(i) to treat the transaction as a sale (see paragraph (h)(2)(ii) of § 1.1034-1). See section 121 and paragraphs (d) and (g) of § 1.121-5 for special rules relating to the involuntary conversion of a principal residence of individuals who have attained age 65. [Reg. § 1.1033(a)-3.]

☐ [T.D. 6222, 1-9-57. Amended by T.D. 6453, 2-16-60, T.D. 6856, 10-19-65 and T.D. 7625, 5-29-79.]

[Reg. § 1.1033(b)-1]

§ 1.1033(b)-1. **Basis of property acquired as a result of an involuntary conversion.**—(a) The provisions of the first sentence of section 1033(b) may be illustrated by the following example:

Example. A's vessel which has an adjusted basis of $100,000 is destroyed in 1950 and A receives in 1951 insurance in the amount of $200,000. If A invests $150,000 in a new vessel, taxable gain to the extent of $50,000 would be recognized. The basis of the new vessel is $100,000; that is, the adjusted basis of the old vessel ($100,000) minus the money received by the taxpayer which was not expended in the acquisition of the new vessel ($50,000) plus the amount of gain recognized upon the conversion ($50,000). If any amount in excess of the proceeds of the conversion is expended in the acquisition of the new property, such amount may be added to the basis otherwise determined.

(b) The provisions of the last sentence of section 1033(b) may be illustrated by the following example:

Example. A taxpayer realizes $22,000 from the involuntary conversion of his barn in 1955; the adjusted basis of the barn to him was $10,000, and he spent in the same year $20,000 for a new barn which resulted in the nonrecognition of $10,000 of the $12,000 gain on the conversion. The basis of the new barn to the taxpayer would be $10,000—the cost of the new barn ($20,000) less the amount of the gain not recognized on the conversion ($10,000). The basis of the new barn would not be a substituted basis in the hands of the taxpayer within the meaning of section 1016(b)(2). If the replacement of the converted barn had been made by the purchase of two smaller barns which, together, were similar or related in service or use to the converted barn and which cost $8,000 and $12,000, respectively, then the basis of the two barns would be $4,000 and $6,000, respectively, the total basis of the purchased property ($10,000) allocated in proportion to their respective costs (8,000/20,000 of $10,000 or $4,000; and 12,000/20,000 of $10,000, or $6,000). [Reg. § 1.1033(b)-1.]

☐ [T.D. 6222, 1-9-57. Amended by T.D. 7625, 5-29-79.]

[Reg. § 1.1033(c)-1]

§ 1.1033(c)-1. **Disposition of excess property within irrigation project deemed to be involuntary conversion.**—(a) The sale, exchange, or other disposition occurring in a taxable year to which the Internal Revenue Code of 1954 applies, of excess lands lying within an irrigation project or division in order to conform to acreage limitations of the Federal reclamation laws effective with respect to such project or division shall be treated as an involuntary conversion to which the provisions of section 1033 and the regulations thereunder shall be applicable. The term "excess lands" means irrigable lands within an irrigation project or division held by one owner in excess of the amount of irrigable land held by such owner entitled to receive water under the Federal reclamation laws applicable to such owner in such project or division. Such excess lands may be either (1) lands receiving no water from the project or division, or (2) lands receiving water only because the owner thereof has executed a valid recordable contract agreeing to sell such lands under terms and conditions satisfactory to the Secretary of the Interior.

(b) If a disposition in order to conform to the acreage limitation provisions of Federal reclamation laws includes property other than excess lands (as, for example, where the excess lands alone do not constitute a marketable parcel) the provisions of section 1033(c) shall apply only to the part of the disposition that relates to excess lands.

(c) The provisions of § 1.1033(a)-2 shall be applicable in the case of dispositions treated as involuntary conversions under this section. The details in connection with such a disposition required to be reported under paragraph (c)(2) of § 1.1033(a)-2 shall include the authority whereby the lands disposed of are considered "excess lands", as defined in this section, and a statement that such disposition is not part of a plan contemplating the disposition of all or any nonexcess land within the irrigation project or division.

(d) The term "involuntary conversion," where it appears in subtitle A of the Code or the regulations thereunder, includes dispositions of excess property within irrigation projects described in this section. (See, e.g., section 1231 and the regulations thereunder.) [Reg. § 1.1033(c)-1.]

☐ [T.D. 6222, 1-9-57. Amended by T.D. 7625, 5-29-79.]

[Reg. § 1.1033(d)-1]

§ 1.1033(d)-1. Destruction or disposition of livestock because of disease.—(a) The destruction occurring in a taxable year to which the Internal Revenue Code of 1954 applies, of livestock by, or on account of, disease, or the sale or exchange, in such a year, of livestock because of disease, shall be treated as an involuntary conversion to which the provisions of section 1033 and the regulations thereunder shall be applicable. Livestock which are killed either because they are diseased or because of exposure to disease shall be considered destroyed on account of disease. Livestock which are sold or exchanged because they are diseased or have been exposed to disease, and would not otherwise have been sold or exchanged at that particular time shall be considered sold or exchanged because of disease.

(b) The provisions of § 1.1033(a)-2 shall be applicable in the case of a disposition treated as an involuntary conversion under this section. The details in connection with such a disposition required to be reported under paragraph (c)(2) of § 1.1033(a)-2 shall include a recital of the evidence that the livestock were destroyed by or on account of disease, or sold or exchanged because of disease.

(c) The term "involuntary conversion," where it appears in subtitle A of the Code or the regulations thereunder, includes disposition of livestock described in this section. (See, e.g., section 1231 and the regulations thereunder.) [Reg. § 1.1033(d)-1.]

☐ [T.D. 6222, 1-9-57. Amended by T.D. 7625, 5-29-79.]

[Reg. § 1.1033(e)-1]

§ 1.1033(e)-1. Sale or exchange of livestock solely on account of drought.—(a) The sale or exchange of livestock (other than poultry) held for draft, breeding, or dairy purposes in excess of the number the taxpayer would sell or exchange during the taxable year if he followed his usual business practices shall be treated as an involuntary conversion to which section 1033 and the regulations thereunder are applicable if the sale or exchange of such livestock by the taxpayer is solely on account of drought. Section 1033(e) and this section shall apply only to sales and exchanges occurring after December 31, 1955.

(b) To qualify under section 1033(e) and this section, the sale or exchange of the livestock need not take place in a drought area. While it is not necessary that the livestock be held in a drought area, the sale or exchange of the livestock must be solely on account of drought conditions the existence of which affected the water, grazing, or other requirements of the livestock so as to necessitate their sale or exchange.

(c) The total sales or exchanges of livestock held for draft, breeding, or dairy purposes occurring in any taxable year which may qualify as an involuntary conversion under section 1033(e) and this section is limited to the excess of the total number of such livestock sold or exchanged during the taxable year over the number that the taxpayer would have sold or exchanged if he had followed his usual business practices, that is, the number he would have been expected to sell or exchange under ordinary circumstances if there had been no drought. For example, if in the past it has been a taxpayer's practice to sell or exchange annually one-half of his herd of dairy cows, only the number sold or exchanged solely on account of drought conditions which is in excess of one-half of his herd may qualify as an involuntary conversion under section 1033(e) and this section.

Reg. § 1.1033(e)-1(c)

(d) The replacement requirements of section 1033 will be satisfied only if the livestock sold or exchanged is replaced within the prescribed period with livestock which is similar or related in service or use to the livestock sold or exchanged because of drought, that is, the new livestock must be functionally the same as the livestock involuntarily converted. This means that the new livestock must be held for the same useful purpose as the old was held. Thus, although dairy cows could be replaced by dairy cows, a taxpayer could not replace draft animals with breeding or dairy animals.

(e) The provisions of § 1.1033(a)-2 shall be applicable in the case of a sale or exchange treated as an involuntary conversion under this section. The details in connection with such a disposition required to be reported under paragraph (c)(2) of § 1.1033(a)-2 shall include:

(1) Evidence of the existence of the drought conditions which forced the sale or exchange of the livestock;

(2) A computation of the amount of gain realized on the sale or exchange;

(3) The number and kind of livestock sold or exchanged; and

(4) The number of livestock of each kind that would have been sold or exchanged under the usual business practice in the absence of the drought.

(f) The term "involuntary conversion", where it appears in subtitle A of the Code or the regulations thereunder, includes the sale or exchange of livestock described in this section.

(g) The provisions of section 1033(e) and this section apply to taxable years ending after December 31, 1955, but only in the case of sales or exchange of livestock after December 31, 1955. [Reg. § 1.1033(e)-1.]

☐ [T.D. 6338, 12-11-58. Amended by T.D. 7625, 5-29-79.]

[Reg. § 1.1033(g)-1]

§ 1.1033(g)-1. Condemnation of real property held for productive use in trade or business or for investment.—(a) *Special rule in general.* This section provides special rules for applying section 1033 with respect to certain dispositions, occurring after December 31, 1957, of real property held either for productive use in trade or business or for investment (not including stock in trade or other property held primarily for sale). For this purpose, disposition means the seizure, requisition, or condemnation (but not destruction) of the converted property, or the sale or exchange of such property under threat or imminence of seizure, requisition, or condemnation. In such cases, for purposes of applying section 1033, the replacement of such property with property of like kind to be held either for productive use in trade or business or for investment shall be treated as property similar or related in service or use to the property so converted. For principles in determining whether the replacement property is property of like kind, see paragraph (b) of § 1.1031(a)-1.

(b) *Election to treat outdoor advertising displays as real property*—(1) *In general.* Under section 1033(g)(3) of the Code, a taxpayer may elect to treat property which constitutes an outdoor advertising display as real property for purposes of chapter 1 of the Code. The election is available for taxable years beginning after December 31, 1970. In the case of an election made on or before July 21, 1981, the election is available whether or not the period for filing a claim for credit or refund under section 6511 has expired. No election may be made with respect to any property for which (i) the investment credit under section 38 has been claimed, or (ii) an election to expense certain depreciable business assets under section 179(a) is in effect. The election once made applies to all outdoor advertising displays of the taxpayer which may be made the subject of an election under this paragraph, including all outdoor advertising displays acquired or constructed by the taxpayer in a taxable year after the taxable year for which the election is made. The election applies with respect to disposition during the taxable year for which made and all subsequent taxable years (unless an effective revocation is made pursuant to paragraph (b)(2)(ii) or (iii)).

(2) *Election*—(i) *Time and manner of making election*—(A) *In general.* Unless otherwise provided in the return or in the instructions for a return for a taxable year, any election made under section 1033(g)(3) shall be made by attaching a statement to the return (or amended return if filed on or before July 21, 1981) for the first taxable year to which the election is to apply. Any election made under this paragraph must be made not later than the time, including extensions thereof, prescribed by law for filing the income tax return for such taxable year or July 21, 1981, whichever occurs last. If a taxpayer makes an election (or revokes an election under subdivision (ii) or (iii) of this subparagraph (b)(2)) for a taxable year for which he or she has previously filed a return, the return for that taxable year and all other taxable years affected by the election (or revocation) must be amended to reflect any tax consequences of the election (or revocation). However, no return for a taxable year for which the period for filing a claim for credit or refund under

section 6511 has expired may be amended to make any changes other than those resulting from the election (or revocation). In order for the election (or revocation) to be effective, the taxpayer must remit with the amended return any additional tax due resulting from the election (or revocation), notwithstanding the provisions of section 6212(c) or 6501 or the provisions of any other law or rule of law which would prevent assessment or collection of such tax.

(B) *Statement required when making election.* The statement required when making the election must clearly indicate that the election to treat outdoor advertising displays as real property is being made.

(ii) *Revocation of election by Commissioner's consent.* Except as otherwise provided in paragraph (b)(2)(iii) of this section, an election under section 1033(g)(3) shall be irrevocable unless consent to revoke is obtained from the Commissioner. In order to secure the Commissioner's consent to revoke an election, the taxpayer must file a request for revocation of election with the Commissioner of Internal Revenue, Washington, D.C. 20224. The request for revocation shall include—

(A) The taxpayer's name, address, and taxpayer identification number,

(B) The date on which and taxable year for which the election was made and the Internal Revenue Service office with which it was filed,

(C) Identification of all outdoor advertising displays of the taxpayer to which the revocation would apply (including the location, date of purchase, and adjusted basis in such property),

(D) The effective date desired for the revocation, and

(E) The reasons for requesting the revocation.

The Commissioner may require such other information as may be necessary in order to determine whether the requested revocation will be permitted. The Commissioner may prescribe administrative procedures (subject to such limitations, terms and conditions as he deems necessary) to obtain his consent to permit the taxpayer to revoke the election. The taxpayer may submit a request for revocation for any taxable year for which the period of limitations for filing a claim for credit or refund for overpayment of tax has not expired.

(iii) *Revocation where election was made on or before December 11, 1979.* In the case of an election made on or before December 11, 1979, the taxpayer may revoke such election provided such revocation is made not later than March 23, 1981. The request for revocation shall be made in conformity with the requirements of paragraph (b)(2)(ii), except that, in lieu of the information required by paragraph (b)(2)(ii)(E), the taxpayer shall state that the revocation is being made pursuant to this paragraph. In addition, the taxpayer must forward, with the statement of revocation, copies of his or her tax returns, including both the original return and any amended returns, for the taxable year in which the original election was made and for all subsequent years and must remit any additional tax due as a result of the revocation.

(3) *Definition of outdoor advertising display.* The term "outdoor advertising display" means a rigidly assembled sign, display, or device that constitutes, or is used to display, a commercial or other advertisement to the public and is permanently affixed to the ground or permanently attached to a building or other inherently permanent structure. The term includes highway billboards affixed to the ground with wood or metal poles, pipes, or beams, with or without concrete footings.

(4) *Character of replacement property.* For purposes of section 1033(g), an interest in real property purchased as replacement property for a compulsorily or involuntarily converted outdoor advertising display (with respect to which an election under this section is in effect) shall be considered property of a like kind as the property converted even though a taxpayer's interest in the replacement property is different from the interest held in the property converted. Thus, for example, a fee simple interest in real estate acquired to replace a converted billboard and a 5-year leasehold interest in the real property on which the billboard was located qualifies as property of a like kind under this section.

(c) *Special rule for period within which property must be replaced.* In the case of a disposition described in paragraph (a) of this section, section 1033(a)(2)(B) and § 1.1033(a)-2(c)(3) (relating to the period within which the property must be replaced) shall be applied by substituting 3 years for 2 years. This paragraph shall apply to any disposition described in section 1033(f)(1) and paragraph (a) of this section occurring after December 31, 1974, unless a condemnation proceeding with respect to the property was begun before October 4, 1976. Thus, regardless of when the property is disposed of, the taxpayer will not be eligible for the 3-year replacement period if a condemnation proceeding was begun before October 4, 1976. However, if the property is disposed of after December 31, 1974, and the condemnation proceeding was begun (if at all) after October 3, 1976, then the taxpayer is eligible for the

Reg. § 1.1033(g)-1(c)

3-year replacement period. For the purposes of this paragraph, whether a condemnation proceeding is considered as having begun is determined under the applicable State or Federal procedural law.

(d) *Limitation on application of special rule.* This section shall not apply to the purchase of stock in the acquisition of control of a corporation described in section 1033(a)(2)(A). [Reg. § 1.1033(g)-1.]

☐ [*T.D.* 6453, 2-16-60. Amended by *T.D.* 7625, 5-29-79, *T.D.* 7758, 1-16-81 *and T.D.* 8121, 1-5-87.]

[Reg. § 1.1033(h)-1]

§ 1.1033(h)-1. **Effective date.**—Except as provided otherwise in § 1.1033(e)-1 and § 1.1033(g)-1, the provisions of section 1033 and the regulations thereunder are effective for taxable years beginning after December 31, 1953, and ending after August 16, 1954. [Reg. § 1.1033(h)-1.]

☐ [*T.D.* 6222, 1-9-57. Amended by *T.D.* 6338, 12-11-58, *T.D.* 6453, 1-16-60, *T.D.* 7625, 5-29-79 *and T.D.* 7758, 1-16-81.]

[Reg. § 1.1034-1]

§ 1.1034-1. **Sale or exchange of residence.**—(a) *Nonrecognition of gain; general statement.* Section 1034 provides rules for the nonrecognition of gain in certain cases where a taxpayer sells one residence after December 31, 1953, and buys or builds, and uses as his principal residence, another residence within specific time limits before or after such sale. In general, if the taxpayer invests in a new residence an amount at least as large as the adjusted sales price of his old residence, no gain is recognized on the sale of the old residence (see paragraph (b) of this section for definitions of "adjusted sales price", "new residence", and "old residence"). On the other hand, if the new residence costs the taxpayer less than the adjusted sales price of the old residence, gain is recognized to the extent of the difference. Thus, if an amount equal to or greater than the adjusted sales price of an old residence is invested in a new residence, according to the rules stated in section 1034, none of the gain (if any) realized from the sale shall be recognized. If an amount less than such adjusted sales price is so invested, gain shall be recognized, but only to the extent provided in section 1034. If there is no investment in a new residence, section 1034 is inapplicable and all of the gain shall be recognized. Whenever, as a result of the application of section 1034, any or all of the gain realized on the sale of an old residence is not recognized, a corresponding reduction must be made in the basis of the new residence. The provisions of section 1034 are mandatory, so that the taxpayer cannot elect to have gain recognized under circumstances where this section is applicable. Section 1034 applies only to gains; losses are recognized or not recognized without regard to the provisions of this section. Section 1034 affects only the amount of gain recognized, and not the amount of gain realized (see also section 1001 and regulations issued thereunder). Any gain realized upon disposition of other property in exchange for the new residence is not affected by section 1034. For special rules relating to the sale or exchange of a principal residence by a taxpayer who has attained age 65, see section 121 and paragraph (g) of § 1.121-5. For special rules relating to a case where real property with respect to the sale of which gain is not recognized under this section is reacquired by the seller in partial or full satisfaction of the indebtedness arising from such sale and resold by him within 1 year after the date of such reacquisition, see § 1.1038-2.

(b) *Definitions.* The following definitions of frequently used terms are applicable for purposes of section 1034 (other definitions and detailed explanations appear in subsequent paragraphs of this regulation):

(1) "Old residence" means property used by the taxpayer as his principal residence which is the subject of a sale by him after December 31, 1953 (section 1034(a); for detailed explanation see paragraph (c)(3) of this section).

(2) "New residence" means property used by the taxpayer as his principal residence which is the subject of a purchase by him (section 1034(a); for detailed explanation and limitations see paragraphs (c)(3) and (d)(1) of this section).

(3) "Adjusted sales price" means the amount realized reduced by the fixing-up expenses (section 1034(b)(1); for special rule applicable in some cases to husband and wife see paragraph (f) of this section).

(4) "Amount realized" is to be computed by subtracting

(i) The amount of the items which, in determining the gain from the sale of the old residence, are properly an offset against the consideration received upon the sale (such as commissions and expenses of advertising the property for sale, of preparing the deed, and of other legal services in connection with the sale); from

(ii) The amount of the consideration so received, determined (in accordance with section 1001(b) and regulations issued thereunder) by adding to the sum of any money so received, the fair market value of the property (other than money) so received. If, as part of the consideration for the sale, the purchaser either assumes a

Reg. § 1.1033(h)-1

Common Nontaxable Exchanges

liability of the taxpayer or acquires the old residence subject to a liability (whether or not the taxpayer is personally liable on the debt), such assumption or acquisition, in the amount of the liability, shall be treated as money received by the taxpayer in computing the "amount realized."

(5) "Gain realized" is the excess (if any) of the amount realized over the adjusted basis of the old residence (see also section 1001(a) and regulations issued thereunder).

(6) "Fixing-up expenses" mean the aggregate of the expenses for work performed (in any taxable year, whether beginning before, on, or after January 1, 1954) on the old residence in order to assist in its sale, provided that such expenses (i) are incurred for work performed during the 90-day period ending on the day on which the contract to sell the old residence is entered into; and (ii) are paid on or before the 30th day after the date of the sale of the old residence; and (iii) are neither (a) allowable as deductions in computing taxable income under section 63(a), nor (b) taken into account in computing the amount realized from the sale of the old residence (section 1034(b)(2) and (3)). "Fixing-up expenses" does not include expenditures which are properly chargeable to capital account and which would, therefore, constitute adjustments to the basis of the old residence (see section 1016 and regulations issued thereunder).

(7) "Cost of purchasing the new residence" means the total of all amounts which are attributable to the acquisition, construction, reconstruction, and improvements constituting capital expenditures, made during the period beginning 18 months (one year in the case of a sale of an old residence prior to January 1, 1975) before the date of sale of the old residence and ending either (i) 18 months (one year in the case of a sale of an old residence prior to January 1, 1975), after such date in the case of a new residence purchased but not constructed by the taxpayer, or (ii) two years (18 months in the case of a sale of an old residence prior to Janaury 1, 1975) after such date in the case of a new residence the construction of which was commenced by the taxpayer before the expiration of 18 months (one year in the case of a sale of an old residence prior to January 1, 1975) after such date (section 1034(a), (c)(2) and (c)(5); for detailed explanation, see paragraph (c)(4) of this section; for special rule applicable in some cases to husband and wife, see paragraph (f) of this section; see also paragraph (b)(9) of this section for definition of "purchase").

(8) "Sale" (of a residence) means a sale or an exchange (of a residence) for other property which occurs after December 31, 1953, an involuntary conversion (of a residence) which occurs after December 31, 1950, and before January 1, 1954, or certain involuntary conversions where the disposition of the property occurs after December 31, 1957, in respect of which a proper election is made under section 1034(i)(2) (see sections 1034(c)(1), 1034(i)(1)(A), and 1034(i)(2); for detailed explanation concerning involuntary conversions, see paragraph (h) of this section).

(9) "Purchase" (of a residence) means a purchase or an acquisition (of a residence) on the exchange of property or the partial or total construction or reconstruction (of a residence) by the taxpayer (section 1034(c)(1) and (2)). However, the mere improvement of a residence, not amounting to reconstruction, does not constitute "purchase" of a residence.

(c) *Rules for application of section 1034* —(1) *General rule; limitations on applicability.* Gain realized from the sale (after December 31, 1953) of an old residence will be recognized only to the extent that the taxpayer's adjusted sales price of the old residence exceeds the taxpayer's cost of purchasing the new residence, provided that the taxpayer either (i) within a period beginning 18 months (one year in the case of a sale of an old residence prior to January 1, 1975) before the date of such sale and ending 18 months (one year in the case of a sale of an old residence prior to January 1, 1975) after such date purchases property and uses it as his principal residence, or (ii) within a period beginning 18 months (one year in the case of a sale of an old residence prior to January 1, 1975) before the date of such sale and ending two years (18 months in the case of a sale of an old residence prior to January 1, 1975) after such date uses as his principal residence a new residence the construction of which was commenced by him at any time before the expiration of 18 months (one year in the case of a sale of an old residence prior to January 1, 1975) after the date of the sale of the old residence (section 1034(a) and (c)(5); for detailed explanation of use as "principal residence" see subparagraph (3) of this paragraph). The rule stated in the preceding sentence applies to a new residence purchased by the taxpayer before the date of sale of the old residence provided the new residence is still owned by him on such date (section 1034(c)(3)). Whether the construction of a new residence was commenced by the taxpayer before the expiration of 18 months (one year in the case of sale of an old residence prior to January 1, 1975) after the date of the sale of the old residence will depend upon the facts and circumstances of each case. Section 1034 is not applicable to the sale of a residence if within the previous 18 months (previous year in the case of a sale of an old residence prior to January 1, 1975) the taxpayer made another sale

Reg. § 1.1034-1(c)(1)

52,010 Common Nontaxable Exchanges

See p. 20,601 for regulations not amended to reflect law changes

of residential property on which gain was realized but not recognized (section 1034(d)). For further details concerning limitations on the application of section 1034, see paragraph (d) of this section.

(2) *Computation and examples.* In applying the general rule stated in subparagraph (1) of this paragraph, the taxpayer should first subtract the commissions and other selling expenses from the selling price of his old residence, to determine the amount realized. A comparison of the amount realized with the cost or other basis of the old residence will then indicate whether there is any gain realized on the sale. Unless the amount realized is greater than the cost or other basis, no gain is realized and section 1034 does not apply. If the amount realized exceeds the cost or other basis, the amount of such excess constitutes the gain realized. The amount realized should then be reduced by the fixing-up expenses (if any), to determine the adjusted sales price. A comparison of the adjusted sales price of the old residence with the cost of purchasing the new residence will indicate how much (if any) of the realized gain is to be recognized. If the cost of purchasing the new residence is the same as, or greater than, the adjusted sales price of the old residence, then none of the realized gain is to be recognized. On the other hand, if the cost of purchasing the new residence is smaller than the adjusted sales price of the old residence, the gain realized is to be recognized to the extent of the difference. (It should be noted that any amount of gain realized but not recognized is to be applied as a downward adjustment to the basis of the new residence (for details see paragraph (e) of this section).) The application of the general rule stated above may be illustrated by the following examples:

Example (1). A taxpayer decides to sell his residence, which has a basis of $17,500. To make it more attractive to buyers, he paints the outside at a cost of $300 in April, 1954. He pays for the painting when the work is finished. In May, 1954, he sells the house for $20,000. Brokers' commissions and other selling expenses are $1,000. In October, 1954, the taxpayer buys a new residence for $18,000. The amount realized, the gain realized, the adjusted sales price, and the gain to be recognized are computed as follows:

Selling price	$20,000
Less: Commissions and other selling expenses	1,000
Amount realized	19,000
Less: Basis	17,500
Gain realized	1,500
Amount realized	$19,000
Less: Fixing-up expenses	300
Adjusted sales price	18,700
Cost of purchasing new residence	18,000
Gain recognized	700
Gain realized but not recognized	800
Adjusted basis of new residence (see paragraph (e) of this section)	$17,200

Example (2). The facts are the same as in example (1), except that the selling price of the old residence is $18,500. The computations are as follows:

Selling price	$18,500
Less: Commissions and other selling expenses	1,000
Amount realized	17,500
Less: Basis	17,500
Gain realized	0

Note: Since no gain is realized, section 1034 is inapplicable; it is, therefore, unnecessary to compute the adjusted sales price of the old residence and compare it with the cost of purchasing the new residence. No adjustment to the basis of the new residence is to be made.

Example (3). The facts are the same as in example (1), except that the cost of purchasing the new residence is $17,000. The computations are as follows:

Selling price	$20,000
Less: Commissions and other selling expenses	1,000
Amount realized	19,000
Less: Basis	17,500
Gain realized	1,500
Amount realized	$19,000
Less: Fixing-up expenses	300
Adjusted sales price	18,700
Cost of purchasing the new residence	17,000
Gain recognized	1,500

Note: Since the adjusted sales price of the old residence exceeds the cost of purchasing the new residence by $1,700, which is more than the gain realized, all of the gain realized is recognized. No adjustment to the basis of the new residence is to be made.

Gain realized but not recognized	$ 0

Example (4). The facts are the same as in example (1), except that the fixing-up expenses are $1,100. The computations are as follows:

Selling price	$20,000
Less: Commissions and other selling expenses	1,000
Amount realized	19,000
Less: Basis	17,500
Gain realized	1,500

Reg. § 1.1034-1(c)(2)

Common Nontaxable Exchanges

See p. 20,601 for regulations not amended to reflect law changes

Amount realized	$19,000
Less: Fixing-up expenses	1,100
Adjusted sales price	17,900
Cost of purchasing the new residence	18,000
Gain recognized	0

Note: Since the cost of purchasing the new residence exceeds the adjusted sales price, none of the gain realized is recognized.

Gain realized but not recognized	$ 1,500
Adjusted basis of new residence (see paragraph (e) of this section)	16,500

(3) *Property used by the taxpayer as his principal residence.* (i) Whether or not property is used by the taxpayer as his residence, and whether or not property is used by the taxpayer as his principal residence (in the case of a taxpayer using more than one property as a residence), depends upon all the facts and circumstances in each case, including the good faith of the taxpayer. The mere fact that property is, or has been, rented is not determinative that such property is not used by the taxpayer as his principal residence. For example, if the taxpayer purchases his new residence before he sells his old residence, the fact that he temporarily rents out the new residence during the period before he vacates the old residence may not, in the light of all the facts and circumstances in the case, prevent the new residence from being considered as property used by the taxpayer as his principal residence. Property used by the taxpayer as his principal residence may include a houseboat, a house trailer, or stock held by a tenant-stockholder in a cooperative housing corporation (as those terms are defined in section 216(b)(1) and (2)), if the dwelling which the taxpayer is entitled to occupy as such stockholder is used by him as his principal residence (section 1034(f)). Property used by the taxpayer as his principal residence does not include personal property such as a piece of furniture, a radio, etc., which, in accordance with the applicable local law, is not a fixture.

(ii) Where part of a property is used by the taxpayer as his principal residence and part is used for other purposes, an allocation must be made to determine the application of this section. If the old residence is used only partially for residential purposes, only that part of the gain allocable to the residential portion is not to be recognized under this section and only an amount allocable to the selling price of such portion need be invested in the new residence in order to have the gain allocable to such portion not recognized under this section. If the new residence is used only partially for residential purposes only so much of its cost as is allocable to the residential portion may be counted as the cost of purchasing the new residence.

(4) *Cost of purchasing new residence.* (i) The taxpayer's cost of purchasing the new residence includes not only cash but also any indebtedness to which the property purchased is subject at the time of purchase whether or not assumed by the taxpayer (including purchase-money mortgages, etc.) and the face amount of any liabilities of the taxpayer which are part of the consideration for the purchase. Commissions and other purchasing expenses paid or incurred by the taxpayer on the purchase of the new residence are to be included in determining such cost. In the case of an acquisition of a residence upon an exchange which is considered as a "purchase" under this section, the fair market value of the new residence on the date of the exchange shall be considered as the taxpayer's cost of purchasing the new residence. Where any part of the new residence is acquired by the taxpayer other than by "purchase", the value of such part is not to be included in determining the taxpayer's cost of the new residence (see paragraph (b)(9) of this section for definition of "purchase"). For example, if the taxpayer acquires a residence by gift or inheritance, and spends $20,000 in reconstructing such residence, only such $20,000 may be treated as his cost of purchasing the new residence.

(ii) The taxpayer's cost of purchasing the new residence includes only so much of such cost as is attributable to acquisition, construction, reconstruction, or improvements made within the period of three years or 42 months (two years or 30 months in the case of a sale of an old residence prior to January 1, 1975), as the case may be, in which the purchase and use of the new residence must be made in order to have gain on the sale of the old residence not recognized under this section. Thus, if the construction of the new residence is begun three years before the date of sale of the old residence and completed on the date of sale of the old residence, only that portion of the cost which is attributable to the last 18 months (last year in the case of a sale of an old residence prior to January 1, 1975) of such construction constitutes the taxpayer's cost of purchasing the new residence, for purposes of section 1034. Furthermore, the taxpayer's cost of purchasing the new residence includes only such amounts as are properly chargeable to capital account rather than to current expense. As to what constitutes capital expenditures, see section 263.

(iii) The provisions of this subparagraph may be illustrated by the following example:

Example. M began the construction of a new residence on January 15, 1974, and com-

Reg. § 1.1034-1(c)(4)

pleted it on October 14, 1974. The cost of $45,000 was incurred ratably over the 9-month period of construction. On December 14, 1975, M sold his old residence and realized a gain. In determining the extent to which the realized gain is not to be recognized under section 1034, M's cost of constructing the new residence shall include only the $20,000 which was attributable to the June 15—October 14, 1974, period (4 months at $5,000). The $25,000 balance of the cost of constructing the new residence was not attributable to the period beginning 18 months before the date of the sale of the old residence and ending two years after such date and, under section 1034, is not properly a part of M's cost of constructing the new residence.

(d) *Limitations on application of section 1034.* (1) If a residence is purchased by the taxpayer prior to the date of the sale of the old residence, the purchased residence shall, in no event, be treated as a new residence if such purchased residence is sold or otherwise disposed of by him prior to the date of the sale of the old residence (section 1034(c)(3)). And, if the taxpayer, during the period within which the purchase and use of the new residence must be made in order to have any gain on the sale of the old residence not recognized under this section, purchases more than one property which is used by him as his principal residence during the 18 months (or two years in the case of the construction of the new residence) succeeding the date of the sale of the old residence, only the last of such properties shall be considered a new residence (section 1034(c)(4)). In the case of a sale of an old residence prior to January 1, 1975, the period of 18 months (or two years) referred to in the preceding sentence shall be one year (or 18 months). If within 18 months (one year in the case of a sale of an old residence prior to January 1, 1975) before the date of the sale of the old residence, the taxpayer sold other property used by him as his principal residence at a gain, and any part of such gain was not recognized under this section or section 112(n) of the Internal Revenue Code of 1939, this section shall not apply with respect to the sale of the old residence (section 1034(d)).

(2) The following example will illustrate the rules of subparagraph (1) of this paragraph:

Example. A taxpayer sells his old residence on January 15, 1954, and purchases another residence on February 15, 1954. On March 15, 1954, he sells the residence which he bought on February 15, 1954, and purchases another residence on April 15, 1954. The gain on the sale of the old residence on January 15, 1954, will not be recognized except to the extent to which the taxpayer's adjusted sales price of the old residence exceeds the cost of purchasing the residence which he purchased on April 15, 1954. Gain on the sale of the residence which was bought on February 15, 1954, and sold on March 15, 1954, will be recognized.

(e) *Basis of new residence.* (1) Where the purchase of a new residence results, under this section, in the nonrecognition of any part of the gain realized upon the sale of an old residence, then, in determining the adjusted basis of the new residence as of any time following the sale of the old residence, the adjustments to basis shall include a reduction by an amount equal to the amount of the gain which was not recognized upon the sale of the old residence (section 1034(e); for special rule applicable in some cases to husband and wife, see paragraph (f) of this section). Such a reduction is not to be made for the purpose of determining the adjusted basis of the new residence as of any time preceding the sale of the old residence. For the purpose of this determination, the amount of the gain not recognized under this section upon the sale of the old residence includes only so much of the gain as is not recognized because of the taxpayer's cost, up to the date of the determination of the adjusted basis, of purchasing the new residence.

(2) The following example will illustrate the rule of subparagraph (1) of this paragraph:

Example. On January 1, 1954, the taxpayer buys a new residence for $10,000. On March 1, 1954, he sells for an adjusted sales price of $15,000 his old residence, which has an adjusted basis to him of $5,000 (no fixing-up expenses are involved, so that $15,000 is the "amount realized" as well as the "adjusted sales price"). Between April 1 and April 15 a wing is constructed on the new house at a cost of $5,000. Between May 1 and May 15 a garage is constructed at a cost of $2,000. The adjusted basis of the new residence is $10,000 during January and February, $5,000 during March, $5,000 following the completion of the construction in April, and $7,000 following the completion of the construction in May. Since the old residence was not sold until March 1, no adjustment to the basis of the new residence is made during January and February. Computations for March, April, and May are as follows:

Amount realized on sale of old residence ... $15,000
Less: Adjusted basis of old residence 5,000

Gain realized on sale of old residence 10,000

March 1, 1954

Adjusted sales price of old residence $15,000
Less: Cost of purchasing new residence 10,000

Gain recognized 5,000

Reg. § 1.1034-1(d)(2)

Common Nontaxable Exchanges

Gain realized but not recognized	$ 5,000
Cost of purchasing new residence	$10,000
Less: Gain realized but not recognized	5,000
Adjusted basis of new residence	5,000

April 15, 1954

Gain realized on sale of old residence	$10,000
Adjusted sales price of old residence	15,000
Less: Cost of purchasing new residence	15,000
Gain recognized	0
Gain realized but not recognized	10,000
Cost of purchasing new residence	$15,000
Less: Gain realized but not recognized	10,000
Adjusted basis of new residence	5,000

May 15, 1954

Gain realized on sale of old residence	$10,000
Adjusted sales price of old residence	15,000
Less: Cost of purchasing new residence	17,000
Gain recognized	0
Gain realized but not recognized	10,000
Cost of purchasing new residence	$17,000
Less: Gain realized but not recognized	10,000
Adjusted basis of new residence	7,000

(f) *Husband and wife.* (1) If the taxpayer and his spouse file the consent referred to in this paragraph, then the "taxpayer's adjusted sales price of the old residence" shall mean the taxpayer's, or the taxpayer's and his spouse's, adjusted sales price of the old residence, and the "taxpayer's cost of purchasing the new residence" shall mean the cost to the taxpayer, or to his spouse, or to both of them, of purchasing the new residence, whether such new residence is held by the taxpayer, or his spouse, or both (section 1034(g)). Such consent may be filed only if the old residence and the new residence are each used by the taxpayer and his same spouse as their principal residence. If the taxpayer and his spouse do not file such a consent, the recognition of gain upon sale of the old residence shall be determined under this section without regard to the foregoing.

(2) The consent referred to in subparagraph (1) of this paragraph is a consent by the taxpayer and his spouse to have the basis of the interest of either of them in the new residence reduced from what it would have been but for the filing of such consent by an amount by which the gain of either of them on the sale of his interest in the old residence is not recognized solely by reason of the filing of such consent. Such reduction in basis is applicable to the basis of the new residence, whether such basis is that of the husband, of the wife, or divided between them. If the basis is divided between the husband and wife, the reduction in basis shall be divided between them in the same proportion as the basis (determined without regard to such reduction) is divided. Such consent shall be filed with the district director with whom the taxpayer filed the return for the taxable year or years in which the gain from the sale of the old residence was realized.

(3) The following examples will illustrate the application of this rule:

Example (1). A taxpayer, in 1954, sells for an adjusted sales price of $10,000 the principal residence of himself and his wife, which he owns individually and which has an adjusted basis to him of $5,000 (no fixing-up expenses are involved, so that $10,000 is the "amount realized" as well as the "adjusted sales price"). Within a year after such sale he and his wife contribute $5,000 each from their separate funds for the purchase of their new principal residence which they hold as tenants in common, each owning an undivided one-half interest therein. If the taxpayer and his wife file the required consent, the gain of $5,000 upon the sale of the old residence will not be recognized to the taxpayer, and the adjusted basis of the taxpayer's interest in the new residence will be $2,500 and the adjusted basis of his wife's interest in such property will be $2,500.

Example (2). A taxpayer and his wife, in 1954, sell for an adjusted sales price of $10,000 their principal residence, which they own as joint tenants and which has an adjusted basis of $2,500 to each of them ($5,000 together) (no fixing-up expenses are involved, so that $10,000 is the "amount realized" as well as the "adjusted sales price"). Within a year after such sale, the wife spends $10,000 of her own funds in the purchase of a principal residence for herself and the taxpayer and takes title in her name only. If the taxpayer and his wife file the required consent, the adjusted basis to the wife of the new residence will be $5,000, and the gain of the taxpayer of $2,500 upon the sale of the old residence will not be recognized. The wife, as a taxpayer herself, will have her gain of $2,500 on the sale of the old residence not recognized under the general rule.

(g) *Members of Armed Forces.* (1) Section 1034(h) provides a special rule for members of the Armed Forces with respect to the period after the sale of the old residence within which the acquisition of a new residence may result in a nonrecognition of gain on such sale. The running of the period of 18 months (one year in the case of a sale of an old residence prior to January 1, 1975) after the sale of the old residence in the case of the purchase of a new residence, or the period of two years (18 months in the case of a sale of an old residence prior to January 1, 1975) after such sale in the case of the construction of a new residence,

Reg. § 1.1034-1(g)

is suspended during any time that the taxpayer serves on extended active duty with the Armed Forces of the United States. (This paragraph applies to time served on extended active duty prior to July 1, 1973, only if such extended active duty occurred during an induction period as defined in section 112(c)(5) as in effect prior to July 1, 1973.) However, in no event may such suspension extend for more than four years after the date of the sale of the old residence the period within which the purchase or construction of a new residence may result in a nonrecognition of gain. For example, if the taxpayer is on extended active duty with the Army from January 1, 1975, to June 30, 1976, and if he sold his old residence on January 10, 1975, the latest date on which the taxpayer may use a new residence constructed by him and have any part of the gain on the sale of his old residence not recognized under this section is June 30, 1978 (the date two years following the taxpayer's termination of active duty). However, if this taxpayer were on extended active duty with the Army from January 1, 1975, to December 31, 1978, the latest date on which he might use a new residence constructed by him and have any part of the gain on the sale of his old residence not recognized under this section would be January 10, 1979 (the date four years following the date of the sale of the old residence).

(2) This suspension covers not only the Armed Forces service of the taxpayer but if the taxpayer and his same spouse used both the old and the new residences as their principal residence, then the extension applies in like manner to the time the taxpayer's spouse is on extended active duty with the Armed Forces of the United States.

(3) The time during which the running of the period is suspended is part of such period. Thus, construction costs during such time are includible in the cost of purchasing the new residence under paragraph (c)(4) of this section.

(4) The running of the period of 18 months (or two years) after the date of sale of the old residence referred to in section 1034(c)(4) and in paragraph (d) of this section is not suspended. The running of the 18-month period prior to the date of the sale of the old residence within which the new residence may be purchased in order to have gain on the sale of the old residence not recognized under this section is also not suspended. In the case of a sale of an old residence prior to Janaury 1, 1975, the periods of 18 months (or two years) referred to in each of the two preceding sentences shall be one year (or 18 months).

(5) The term "extended active duty" means any period of active duty which is served pursuant to a call or order to such duty for a period in excess of 90 days or for an indefinite period. If the call or order is for a period of more than 90 days it is immaterial that the time served pursuant to such call or order is less than 90 days, if the reason for such shorter period of service occurs after the beginning of such duty. As to what constitutes active service as a member of the Armed Forces of the United States, see paragraph (i) of §1.112-1. As to who are members of the Armed Forces of the United States, see section 7701(a)(15) and the regulations in Part 301 of this chapter (Regulations on Procedure and Administration).

(h) *Special rules for involuntary conversions*—(1) *In general.* Except as provided in subparagraph (2) of this paragraph, section 1034 is inapplicable to involuntary conversions of personal residences occurring after December 31, 1953 (section 1034(i)(1)(B)). For purposes of section 1034, an involuntary conversion of a personal residence occurring after December 31, 1950, and before January 1, 1954, is treated as a sale of such residence (section 1034(i)(1)(A); see paragraph (b)(8) of this section). For purposes of this paragraph, an involuntary conversion is defined as the destruction in whole or in part, theft, seizure, requisition, or condemnation of property, or the sale or exchange of property under threat or imminence thereof. See section 1033 and §1.1033(a)-3 for treatment of residences involuntarily converted after December 31, 1953.

(2) *Election to treat condemnation of personal residence as sale.* (i) Section 1034(i)(2) provides a special rule which permits a taxpayer to elect to treat the seizure, requisition, or condemnation of his principal residence, or the sale or exchange of such residence under threat or imminence thereof, if occurring after December 31, 1957, as the sale of such residence for purposes of section 1034 (relating to sale or exchange of residence). A taxpayer may thus elect to have section 1034 apply, rather than section 1033 (relating to involuntary conversions), in determining the amount of gain realized on the disposition of his old residence that will not be recognized and the extent to which the basis of his new residence acquired in lieu thereof shall be reduced. Once made, the election shall be irrevocable.

(ii) If the taxpayer elects to be governed by the provisions of section 1034, section 1033 will have no application. Thus, a taxpayer who elects under section 1034(i)(2) to treat the seizure, requisition, or condemnation of his principal residence (but not the destruction), or the sale

Reg. § 1.1034-1(g)(2)

Common Nontaxable Exchanges 52,015
See p. 20,601 for regulations not amended to reflect law changes

or exchange of such residence under threat or imminence thereof, as a sale for the purposes of section 1034 must satisfy the requirements of section 1034 and this section. For example, under section 1034 a taxpayer generally must replace his old residence with a new residence which he uses as his principal residence, within a period beginning 18 months (one year in the case of a sale of an old residence prior to January 1, 1975) before the date of disposition of his old residence, and ending 18 months (one year in the case of a sale of an old residence prior to January 1, 1975) after such date. However, in the case of a new residence the construction of which was commenced by the taxpayer within such period, the replacement period shall not expire until 2 years (18 months in the case of a sale of an old residence prior to January 1, 1975) after the date of disposition of the old residence.

(iii) *Time and manner of making election.* The election under section 1034(i)(2) shall be made in a statement attached to the taxpayer's income tax return, when filed, for the taxable year during which the disposition of his old residence occurs. The statement shall indicate that the taxpayer elects under section 1034(i)(2) to treat the disposition of his old residence as a sale for purposes of section 1034, and shall also show—

(a) The basis of the old residence;

(b) The date of its disposition;

(c) The adjusted sales price of the old residence, if known; and

(d) The purchase price, date of purchase, and date of occupancy of the new residence if it has been acquired prior to the time of making the election.

(i) *Statute of limitations.* (1) Whenever a taxpayer sells property used as his principal residence at a gain, the statutory period prescribed in section 6501(a) for the assessment of a deficiency attributable to any part of such gain shall not expire prior to the expiration of three years from the date of receipt, by the district director with whom the return was filed for the taxable year or years in which the gain from the sale of the old residence was realized (section 1034(j)), of a written notice from the taxpayer of—

(i) The taxpayer's cost of purchasing the new residence which the taxpayer claims results in nonrecognition of any part of such gain,

(ii) The taxpayer's intention not to purchase a new residence within the period when such a purchase will result in nonrecognition of any part of such gain, or

(iii) The taxpayer's failure to make such a purchase within such period.

Any gain from the sale of the old residence which is required to be recognized shall be included in gross income for the taxable year or years in which such gain was realized. Any deficiency attributable to any portion of such gain may be assessed before the expiration of the 3-year period described in this paragraph, notwithstanding the provisions of any law or rule of law which might otherwise bar such assessment.

(2) The notification required by the preceding subparagraph shall contain all pertinent details in connection with the sale of the old residence and, where applicable, the purchase price of the new residence. The notification shall be in the form of a written statement and shall be accompanied, where appropriate, by an amended return for the year in which the gain from the sale of the old residence was realized, in order to reflect the inclusion in gross income for that year of gain required to be recognized in connection with such sale.

(j) *Effective date.* Pursuant to section 7851(a)(1)(C), paragraphs (a), (b), (c), (d), (f), (g), and (i) of this section apply in the case of any "sale" (as defined in subparagraph (8) of paragraph (b) of this section) made after December 31, 1953, although such sale may occur in a taxable year subject to the Internal Revenue Code of 1939. Similarly, the rule in paragraph (h) of this section that involuntary conversions of personal residences are not to be treated as sales for purposes of section 1034 but are governed by section 1033 applies to any such involuntary conversion made after December 31, 1953, although such involuntary conversion may occur in a taxable year subject to the Internal Revenue Code of 1939. The rule in paragraph (e) of this section requiring an adjustment to the basis of a new residence, the purchase of which results (under section 1034, or section 112(n) of the Internal Revenue Code of 1939) in the nonrecognition of gain on the sale of an old residence, applies in determining the adjusted basis of the new residence at any time following such sale, although such sale may occur in a taxable year subject to the Internal Revenue Code of 1939. [Reg. § 1.1034-1.]

☐ [T.D. 6179, 6-1-56. *Amended by* T.D. 6453, 2-16-60; T.D. 6856, 10-19-65; T.D. 6916, 4-12-67; T.D. 7404, 2-12-76 and T.D. 7625, 5-29-79.]

[Reg. § 1.1035-1]

§ 1.1035-1. Certain exchanges of insurance policies.—Under the provisions of section 1035 no gain or loss is recognized on the exchange of:

Reg. § 1.1035-1

(a) A contract of life insurance for another contract of life insurance or for an endowment or annuity contract (section 1035 (a)(1));

(b) A contract of endowment insurance for another contract of endowment insurance providing for regular payments beginning at a date not later than the date payments would have begun under the contract exchanged, or an annuity contract (section 1035(a)(2)); or

(c) An annuity contract for another annuity contract (section 1035 (a)(3)),

but section 1035 does not apply to such exchanges if the policies exchanged do not relate to the same insured. The exchange, without recognition of gain or loss, of an annuity contract for another annuity contract under section 1035(a)(3) is limited to cases where the same person or persons are the obligee or obligees under the contract received in exchange as under the original contract. This section and section 1035 do not apply to transactions involving the exchange of an endowment contract or annuity contract for a life insurance contract, nor an annuity contract for an endowment contract. In the case of such exchanges, any gain or loss shall be recognized. In the case of exchanges which would be governed by section 1035 except for the fact that the property received in exchange consists not only of property which could otherwise be received without the recognition of gain or loss, but also of other property or money, see section 1031(b) and (c) and the regulations thereunder. Such an exchange does not come within the provisions of section 1035. Determination of the basis of property acquired in an exchange under section 1035(a) shall be governed by section 1031(d) and the regulations thereunder. [Reg. § 1.1035-1.]

☐ [T.D. 6211, 11-14-56.]

[Reg. § 1.1036-1]

§ 1.1036-1. Stock for stock of the same corporation.—(a) Section 1036 permits the exchange, without the recognition of gain or loss, of common stock for common stock, or of preferred stock for preferred stock, in the same corporation. Section 1036 applies even though voting stock is exchanged for nonvoting stock or nonvoting stock is exchanged for voting stock. It is not limited to an exchange between two individual stockholders; it includes a transaction between a stockholder and the corporation. However, a transaction between a stockholder and the corporation may qualify not only under section 1036(a), but also under section 368(a)(1)(E) (recapitalization) or section 305(a) (distribution of stock and stock rights). The provisions of section 1036(a) do not apply if stock is exchanged for bonds, or preferred stock is exchanged for common stock, or common stock is exchanged for preferred stock, or common stock in one corporation is exchanged for common stock in another corporation. See paragraph (1) of § 1.301-1 for certain transactions treated as distributions under section 301. See paragraph (e)(5) of § 1.368-2 for certain transactions which result in deemed distributions under section 305(c) to which sections 305(b)(4) and 301 apply.

(b) For rules relating to recognition of gain or loss where an exchange is not wholly in kind, see subsections (b) and (c) of section 1031. For rules relating to the basis of property acquired in an exchange described in paragraph (a) of this section, see subsection (d) of section 1031.

(c) A transfer is not within the provisions of section 1036(a) if as part of the consideration the other party to the exchange assumes a liability of the taxpayer (or if the property transferred is subject to a liability), but the transfer, if otherwise qualified, will be within the provisions of section 1031(b).

(d) *Nonqualified preferred stock.* See § 1.356-7(a) for the applicability of the definition of nonqualified preferred stock in section 351(g)(2) for stock issued prior to June 9, 1997, and for stock issued in transactions occurring after June 8, 1997, that are described in section 1014(f)(2) of the Taxpayer Relief Act of 1997, Public Law 105-34 (111 Stat. 788, 921). [Reg. § 1.1036-1.]

☐ [T.D. 6210, 11-6-56. *Amended by T.D.* 7281, 7-11-73 *and T.D.* 8904, 9-29-2000.]

[Reg. § 1.1037-1]

§ 1.1037-1. Certain exchanges of United States obligations.—(a) *Nonrecognition of gain or loss*—(1) *In general.* Section 1037 (a) provides for the nonrecognition of gain or loss on the surrender to the United States of obligations of the United States issued under the Second Liberty Bond Act (31 U.S.C. 774 (2)) when such obligations are exchanged solely for other obligations issued under that Act and the Secretary provides by regulations promulgated in connection with the issue of such other obligations that gain or loss is not to be recognized on such exchange. It is not necessary that at the time of the exchange the obligation which is surrendered to the United States be a capital asset in the hands of the taxpayer. For purposes of section 1037(a) and this subparagraph, a circular of the Treasury Department which offers to exchange obligations of the United States issued under the Second Liberty Bond Act for other obligations issued under that Act shall constitute regulations promulgated by the Secretary in connection with the issue of the

Reg. § 1.1036-1(a)

Common Nontaxable Exchanges

obligations offered to be exchanged if such circular contains a declaration by the Secretary that no gain or loss shall be recognized for Federal income tax purposes on the exchange or grants the privilege of continuing to defer the reporting of the income on the bonds exchanged until such time as the bonds received in the exchange are redeemed or disposed of, or have reached final maturity, whichever is earlier. See, for example, regulations of the Bureau of the Public Debt, 31 CFR Part 339, or Treasury Department Circular 1066, 26 F.R. 8647. The application of section 1037(a) and this subparagraph will not be precluded merely because the taxpayer is required to pay money on the exchange. See section 1031 and the regulations thereunder if the taxpayer receives money on the exchange.

(2) *Recognition of gain or loss postponed.* Gain or loss which has been realized but not recognized on the exchange of a United States obligation for another such obligation because of the provisions of section 1037(a) (or so much of section 1031(b) or (c) as relates to section 1037(a)) shall be recognized at such time as the obligation received in the exchange is disposed of, or redeemed, in a transaction other than an exchange described in section 1037(a) (or so much of section 1031 (b) or (c) as relates to section 1037(a)) or reaches final maturity, whichever is earlier, to the extent gain or loss is realized on such later transaction.

(3) *Illustrations.* The application of this paragraph may be illustrated by the following examples, in which it is assumed that the taxpayer uses the cash receipts and disbursements method of accounting and has never elected under section 454(a) to include in gross income currently the annual increase in the redemption price of non-interest-bearing obligations issued at a discount. In addition, it is assumed that the old obligations exchanged are capital assets transferred in an exchange in respect of which regulations are promulgated pursuant to section 1037(a):

Example (1). A, the owner of a $1,000 series E United States savings bond purchased for $750 and bearing an issue date of May 1 1945, surrenders the bond to the United States in exchange solely for series H United States savings bonds on February 1, 1964, when the series E bond has a redemption value of $1,304.80. If in the exchange A pays an additional $195.20 and obtains three $500 series H bonds, none of the $554.80 gain ($1,304.80 less $750) realized by A on the series E bond is recognized at the time of the exchange.

Example (2). In 1963, B purchased for $97 a marketable United States bond which was originally issued at its par value of $100. In 1964 he surrenders the bond to the United States in exchange solely for another marketable United States bond which then has a fair market value of $95. B's loss of $2 on the old bond is not recognized at the time of the exchange, and his basis for the new bond is $97 under section 1031(d). If it had been necessary for B to pay $1 additional consideration in the exchange, his basis in the new bond would be $98.

Example (3). The facts are the same as in example (2) except that B also receives $1 interest on the old bond for the period which has elapsed since the last interest payment date and that B does not pay any additional consideration on the exchange. As in example (2), B has a loss of $2 which is not recognized at the time of the exchange and his basis in the new bond is $97. In addition, the $1 of interest received on the old bond is includible in gross income. B holds the new bond 1 year and sells it in the market for $99 plus interest. At this time he has a gain of $2, the difference between his basis of $97 in the new bond and the sales price of such bond. In addition, the interest received on the new bond is includible in gross income.

Example (4). The facts are the same as in example (2), except that in addition to the new bond B also receives $1.85 in cash, $0.85 of which is interest. The $0.85 interest received is includible in gross income. B's loss of $1 ($97 less $96) on the old bond is not recognized at the time of the exchange by reason of section 1031(c). Under section 1031(d) B's basis in the new bond is $96 (his basis of $97 in the old bond, reduced by the $1 cash received in the exchange.)

Example (5). (a) For $975 D subscribes to a marketable United States obligation which has a face value of $1,000. Thereafter, he surrenders this obligation to the United States in exchange solely for a 10-year marketable $1,000 obligation which at the time of exchange has a fair market value of $930, at which price such obligation is initially offered to the public. At the time of issue of the new obligation there was no intention to call it before maturity. Five years after the exchange D sells the new obligation for $960.

(b) On the exchange of the old obligation for the new obligation D sustains a loss of $45 ($975 less $930), none of which is recognized pursuant to section 1037(a).

(c) The basis of the new obligation in D's hands, determined under section 1031(d), is $975 (the same basis as that of the old obligation).

(d) On the sale of the new obligation D sustains a loss of $15 ($975 less $960), all of which is recognized by reason of section 1002.

Reg. § 1.1037-1(a)(3)

Common Nontaxable Exchanges

Example (6). (a) The facts are the same as in example (5), except that five years after the exchange D sells the new obligation for $1,020.

(b) On the exchange of the old obligation for the new obligation D sustains a loss of $45 ($975 less $930), none of which is recognized pursuant to section 1037(a).

(c) The basis of the new obligation in D's hands, determined under section 1031(d), is $975 (the same basis as that of the old obligation). The issue price of the new obligation under section 1232(b)(2) is $930.

(d) On the sale of the new obligation D realizes a gain of $45 ($1,020 less $975), all of which is recognized by reason of section 1002. Of this gain of $45, the amount of $35 is treated as ordinary income and $10 is treated as long-term capital gain, determined as follows:

(1) Ordinary income under first sentence of sec. 1232(a)(2)(B) on sale of new obligation:
Stated redemption price of new obligation at maturity $1,000
Less: Issue price of new obligation under sec. 1232(b)(2) 930

Original issue discount on new obligation 70

Proration under sec. 1232 (a)(2)(B) (ii): ($70 × 60 months/120 months) 35
(2) Long-term capital gain ($45 less $35) $10

Example (7). (a) The facts are the same as in example (5), except that D retains the new obligation and redeems it at maturity for $1,000.

(b) On the exchange of the old obligation for the new obligation D sustains a loss of $45 ($975 less $930), none of which is recognized pursuant to section 1037(a).

(c) The basis of the new obligation in D's hands, determined under section 1031(d), is $975 (the same basis as that of the old obligation). The issue price of the new obligation is $930 under section 1232(b)(2).

(d) On the redemption of the new obligation D realizes a gain of $25 ($1,000 less $975), all of which is recognized by reason of section 1002. Of this gain of $25, the entire amount is treated as ordinary income, determined as follows:

Ordinary income under first sentence of sec. 1232(a)(2)(B) on redemption of new obligation:
Stated redemption price of new obligation at maturity $1,000
Less: Issue price of new obligation under sec. 1232(b)(2) 930

Original issue discount on new obligation 70

Proration under sec. 1232(a)(2)(B)(ii): ($70 × 120 months/120 months), but such amount not to exceed the $25 gain recognized on redemption $25

(b) *Application of section 1232 upon disposition or redemption of new obligation*—(1) *Exchanges involving nonrecognition of gain on obligations issued at a discount.* If an obligation, the gain on which is subject to the first sentence of section 1232(a)(2)(B) because the obligation was originally issued at a discount, is surrendered to the United States in exchange for another obligation and any part of the gain realized on the exchange is not then recognized because of the provisions of section 1037(a) (or because of so much of section 1031(b) as relates to section 1037(a)), the first sentence of section 1232(a)(2)(B) shall apply to so much of such unrecognized gain as is later recognized upon the disposition or redemption of the obligation which is received in the exchange as though the obligation so disposed of or redeemed were the obligation surrendered, rather than the obligation received, in such exchange. See the first sentence of section 1037(b)(1). Thus, in effect that portion of the gain which is unrecognized on the exchange but is recognized upon the later disposition or redemption of the obligation received from the United States in the exchange shall be considered as ordinary income in an amount which is equal to the gain which, by applying the first sentence of section 1232(a)(2)(B) upon the earlier surrender of the old obligation to the United States, would have been considered as ordinary income if the gain had been recognized upon such earlier exchange. Any portion of the gain which is recognized under section 1031(b) upon the earlier exchange and is treated at such time as ordinary income shall be deducted from the gain which is treated as ordinary income by applying the first sentence of section 1232(a)(2)(B) pursuant to this subparagraph upon the disposition or redemption of the obligation which is received in the earlier exchange. This subparagraph shall apply only in a case where on the exchange of United States obligations there was some gain not recognized by reason of section 1037(a) (or so much of section 1031(b) as relates to section 1037(a)); it shall not apply where only loss was unrecognized by reason of section 1037(a).

(2) *Rules to apply when a nontransferable obligation is surrendered in the exchange.* For purposes of applying both section 1232(a)(2)(B) and subparagraph (1) of this paragraph to the total gain realized on the obligation which is later disposed of or redeemed, if the obligation surrendered to the United States in the earlier exchange

Reg. § 1.1037-1(b)(1)

is a nontransferable obligation described in section 454(a) or (c)—

(i) The aggregate amount considered, with respect to the obligation so surrendered in the earlier exchange, as ordinary income shall not exceed the difference between the issue price of the surrendered obligation and the stated redemption price of the surrendered obligation which applied at the time of the earlier exchange, and

(ii) The issue price of the obligation which is received from the United States in the earlier exchange shall be considered to be the stated redemption price of the surrendered obligation which applied at the time of the earlier exchange, increased by the amount of other consideration (if any) paid to the United States as part of the earlier exchange.

If the obligation received in the earlier exchange is a nontransferable obligation described in section 454(c) and such obligation is partially redeemed before final maturity, or partially disposed of by being partially reissued to another owner, the amount determined by applying subdivision (i) of this subparagraph shall be determined on a basis proportional to the total denomination of obligations redeemed or disposed of. See paragraph (c) of § 1.454-1.

(3) *Long-term capital gain.* If, in a case where both subparagraphs (1) and (2) of this paragraph are applied, the total gain realized on the redemption or disposition of the obligation which is received from the United States in the exchange to which section 1037(a) (or so much of section 1031(b) as relates to section 1037(a)) applies exceeds the amount of gain which, by applying such subparagraphs, is treated as ordinary income, the gain in excess of such amount shall be treated as long-term capital gain.

(4) *Illustrations.* The application of this paragraph may be illustrated by the following examples, in which it is assumed that the taxpayer uses the cash receipts and disbursements method of accounting and has never elected under section 454(a) to include in gross income currently the annual increase in the redemption price of non-interest-bearing obligations issued at a discount. In addition, it is assumed that the old obligations exchanged are capital assets transferred in an exchange in respect of which regulations are promulgated pursuant to section 1037(a):

Example (1). (a) A purchased a non-interest-bearing nontransferable United States bond for $74 which was issued after December 31, 1954, and redeemable in 10 years for $100. Several years later, when the stated redemption value of such bond is $94.50, A surrenders it to the United States in exchange for $1 in cash and a 10-year marketable bond having a face value of $100. On the date of exchange the bond received in the exchange has a fair market value of $96. Less than one month after the exchange, A sells the new bond for $96.

(b) On the exchange of the old bond for the new bond A realizes a gain of $23, determined as follows:

Amount realized (a new bond worth $96 plus $1 cash)	$97
Less: Adjusted basis of old bond	74
Gain realized	$23

Pursuant to so much of section 1031(b) as applies to section 1037(a), the amount of such gain which is recognized is $1 (the money received). Such recognized gain of $1 is treated as ordinary income. On the exchange of the old bond a gain of $22 ($23 less $1) is not recognized.

(c) The basis of the new bond in A's hands, determined under section 1031(d), is $74 (the basis of the old bond, decreased by the $1 received in cash and increased by the $1 gain recognized on the exchange).

(d) On the sale of the new bond A realizes a gain of $22 ($96 less $74), all of which is recognized by reason of section 1002. Of this gain of $22, the amount of $19.50 is treated as ordinary income and $2.50 is treated as long-term capital gain, determined as follows:

(1) Ordinary income treating sale of new bond as though a sale of old bond and applying sec. 1037(b)(1)(A):	
Stated redemption price of old bond	$94.50
Less: Issue price of old bond	74.00
Aggregate gain under sec. 1037(b)(1)(A) (not to exceed $22 not recognized at time of exchange)	$20.50
Less: Amount of such gain recognized at time of exchange	$ 1.00
Ordinary income	$19.50

Reg. § 1.1037-1(b)(4)

52,020   Common Nontaxable Exchanges

See p. 20,601 for regulations not amended to reflect law changes

(2) Ordinary income under first sentence of sec. 1232(a)(2)(B), applying sec. 1037(b)(1)(B) to sale of new bond:
    Stated redemption price of new bond at maturity $100.00
    Less: Issue price of new bond under sec. 1037(b)(1)(B) ($94.50 plus $0 additional consideration paid on exchange) 94.50

    Original issue discount on new bond............................. $ 5.50

    Proration under sec. 1232(a)(2)(B)(ii): ($5.50 × 0 months/120 months) ... 0

(3) Total ordinary income (sum of subparagraphs (1) and (2)) $19.50
(4) Long-term capital gain ($22 less $19.50) 2.50

    Example (2). (a) The facts are the same as in example (1), except that, less than one month after the exchange of the old bond, the new bond is sold for $92.

    (b) On the sale of the new bond A realizes a gain of $18 ($92 less $74), all of which is recognized by reason of section 1002. Of this gain, the entire amount of $18 is treated as ordinary income. This amount is determined as provided in paragraph (d)(1) of example (1) except that the ordinary income of $19.50 is limited to the $18 recognized on the sale of the new bond.

    Example (3). (a) The facts are the same as in example (1), except that 2 years after the exchange of the old bond A sells the new bond for $98.

    (b) On the sale of the new bond A realizes a gain of $24 ($98 less $74), all of which is recognized by reason of section 1002. Of this gain of $24, the amount of $20.60 is treated as ordinary income and $3.40 is treated as long-term capital gain, determined as follows:

(1) Ordinary income applicable to old bond (determined as provided in paragraph (d)(1) of example (1))............... $19.50
(2) Ordinary income applicable to new bond (determined as provided in paragraph (d)(2) of example (1), except that the proration of the original issue discount under sec. 1232(a)(2)(B)(ii) amounts to $1.10 ($5.50 × 24 months/120 months))........................ 1.10

(3) Total ordinary income (sum of subparagraphs (1) and (2)) $20.60
(4) Long-term capital gain ($24 less $20.60) . 3.40

    Example (4). (a) The facts are the same as in example (1), except that A retains the new bond and redeems it at maturity for $100.

    (b) On the redemption of the new bond A realizes a gain of $26 ($100 less $74), all of which is recognized by reason by section 1002. Of this gain of $26, the amount of $25 is treated as ordinary income and $1 is treated as long-term capital gain, determined as follows:

(1) Ordinary income applicable to old bond (determined as provided in paragraph (d)(1) of example (1))............... $19.50

(2) Ordinary income applicable to new bond (determined as provided in paragraph (d)(2) of example (1), except that the proration of the original issue discount under sec. 1232(a)(2)(B)(ii) amounts to $5.50 ($5.50 × 120 months/120 months)) 5.50

(3) Total ordinary income (sum of subparagraphs (1) and (2)) 25.00
(4) Long-term capital gain ($26 less $25) ... 1.00

    Example (5). (a) In 1958 B purchased for $7,500 a series E United States savings bond having a face value of $10,000. In 1965 when the stated redemption value of the series E bond is $9,760, B surrenders it to the United States in exchange solely for a $10,000 series H United States savings bond, after paying $240 additional consideration. B retains the series H bond and redeems it at maturity in 1975 for $10,000, after receiving all the semi-annual interest payments thereon.

    (b) On the exchange of the series E bond for the series H bond, B realizes a gain of $2,260 ($9,760 less $7,500), none of which is recognized at such time by reason of section 1037(a).

    (c) The basis of the series H bond in B's hands, determined under section 1031(d), is $7,740 (the $7,500 basis of the series E bond, plus $240 additional consideration paid for the series H bond).

    (d) On the redemption of the series H bond, B realizes a gain of $2,260 ($10,000 less $7,740), all of which is recognized by reason of section 1002. This entire gain is treated as ordinary income by treating the redemption of the series H bond as though it were a redemption of the series E bond and by applying section 1037(b)(1)(A).

    (e) Under section 1037(b)(1)(B) the issue price of the series H bond is $10,000 ($9,760 stated redemption price of the series E bond at time of exchange, plus $240 additional consideration paid). Thus, with respect to the series H bond, there is no original issue discount to which section 1232(a)(2)(B) might apply.

    Example (6). (a) The facts are the same as in example (5), except that in 1970 B submits the $10,000 series H bond to the United States for partial redemption in the amount of $3,000 and for reissuance of the remainder in $1,000 series H savings bonds registered in his name. On this transaction B receives $3,000 cash and seven

Reg. § 1.1037-1(b)(4)

Common Nontaxable Exchanges

$1,000 series H bonds bearing the original issue date of the $10,000 bond which is partially redeemed. The $1,000 series H bonds are redeemed at maturity in 1975 for $7,000.

(b) On the partial redemption of the $10,000 series H bond in 1970 B realizes a gain of $678 ($3,000 less $2,322 [$7,740 × $3,000/$10,000]), all of which is recognized at such time by reason of section 1002 and paragraph (c) of § 1.454-1. This entire gain is treated as ordinary income, by treating the partial redemption of the series H bond as though it were a redemption of the relevant denominational portion of the series E bond and by applying section 1037(b)(1)(A).

(c) On the redemption at maturity in 1975 of the seven $1,000 series H bonds B realizes a gain of $1,582 ($7,000 less $5,418 [$7,740 × $7,000/$10,000]), all of which is recognized at such time by reason of section 1002 and paragraph (c) of § 1.454-1. This entire gain is treated as ordinary income, determined in the manner described in paragraph (b) of this example.

Example (7). (a) The facts are the same as in example (5), except that in 1970 B requests the United States to reissue the $10,000 series H bond by issuing two $5,000 series H bonds bearing the original issue date of such $10,000 bond. One of such $5,000 bonds is registered in B's name, and the other is registered in the name of C, who is B's son. Each $5,000 series H bond is redeemed at maturity in 1975 for $5,000.

(b) On the issuing in 1970 of the $5,000 series H bond to C, B realizes a gain of $1,130 ($5,000 less $3,870 [$7,740 × $5,000/$10,000]), all of which is recognized at such time by reason of section 1002 and paragraph (c) of § 1.454-1. This entire gain is treated as ordinary income by treating the transaction as though it were a redemption of the relevant denominational portion of the series E bond and by applying section 1037(b)(1)(A).

(c) On the redemption at maturity in 1975 of the $5,000 series H bond registered in his name B realizes a gain of $1,130 ($5,000 less $3,870 [$7,740 × $5,000/$10,000]), all of which is recognized at such time by reason of section 1002 and paragraph (c) of § 1.454-1. This entire gain is treated as ordinary income, determined in the manner described in paragraph (b) of this example.

(d) On the redemption at maturity in 1975 of the $5,000 series H bond registered in his name C does not realize any gain, since the amount realized on redemption does not exceed his basis in the property, determined as provided in section 1015.

(5) *Exchanges involving nonrecognition of gain or loss on transferable obligations issued at not less than par*—(i) *In general.* If a transferable obligation of the United States which was originally issued at not less than par is surrendered to the United States for another transferable obligation in an exchange to which the provisions of section 1037(a) (or so much of section 1031(b) or (c) as relates to section 1037(a)) apply, the issue price of the obligation received from the United States in the exchange shall be considered for purposes of applying section 1232 to gain realized on the disposition or redemption of the obligation so received, to be the same as the issue price of the obligation which is surrendered to the United States in the exchange, increased by the amount of other consideration, if any, paid to the United States as part of the exchange. This subparagraph shall apply irrespective of whether there is gain or loss unrecognized on the exchange and irrespective of the fair market value, at the time of the exchange, of either the obligation surrendered to, or the obligation received from, the United States in the exchange.

(ii) *Illustrations.* The application of this subparagraph may be illustrated by the following examples, in which it is assumed that the taxpayer uses the cash receipts and disbursements method of accounting and that the old obligations exchanged are capital assets transferred in an exchange in respect of which regulations are promulgated pursuant to section 1037(a):

Example (1). (a) A purchases in the market for $85 a marketable United States bond which was originally issued at its par value of $100. Three months later, A surrenders this bond to the United States in exchange solely for another $100 marketable United States bond which then has a fair market value of $88. He holds the new bond for 5 months and then sells it on the market for $92.

(b) On the exchange of the old bond for the new bond A realizes a gain of $3 ($88 less $85), none of which is recognized by reason of section 1037(a).

(c) The basis of the new bond in A's hands, determined under section 1031(d), is $85 (the same as that of the old bond). The issue price of the new bond for purposes of section 1232(a)(2)(B) is considered under section 1037(b)(2) to be $100 (the same issue price as that of the old bond).

(d)(1) Ordinary income under first sentence of sec. 1232(a)(2)(B), applicable to old bond:

Reg. § 1.1037-1(b)(5)

Stated redemption price of old bond at
maturity $100
Less: Issue price of old bond 100
Original issue discount on old bond........... 0

(2) Ordinary income under first sentence of sec. 1232(a)(2)(B), applying sec. 1037(b)(2) to sale of new bond:

Stated redemption price of new bond at
maturity $100
Less: Issue price of new bond under sec.
1037(b)(2) 100
Original issue discount on new bond.......... 0

Example (2). The facts are the same as in example (1), except that A retains the new bond and redeems it at maturity for $100. On the redemption of the new bond, A realizes a gain of $15 ($100 less $85), all of which is recognized under section 1002. This entire gain is treated as long-term capital gain, determined in the same manner as provided in paragraph (d) of example (1).

Example (3). (a) For $1,000 B subscribes to a marketable United States bond which has a face value of $1,000. Thereafter, he surrenders this bond to the United States in exchange solely for a 10-year marketable $1,000 bond which at the time of exchange has a fair market value of $930, at which price such bond is initially offered to the public. Five years after the exchange, B sells the new bond for $950.

(b) On the exchange of the old bond for the new bond, B sustains a loss of $70 ($1,000 less $930), none of which is recognized pursuant to section 1037(a).

(c) The basis of the new bond in A's hands, determined under section 1031(d), is $1,000 (the same basis as that of the old bond).

(d) On the sale of the new bond B sustains a loss of $50 ($1,000 less $950), all of which is recognized by reason of section 1002.

Example (4). (a) The facts are the same as in example (3), except that five years after the exchange B sells the new bond for $1,020.

(b) On the exchange of the old bond for the new bond B sustains a loss of $70 ($1,000 less $930), none of which is recognized pursuant to section 1037(a).

(c) The basis of the new bond in B's hands, determined under section 1031(d), is $1,000 (the same basis as that of the old bond). The issue price of the new bond for purposes of section 1232(a)(2)(B) is considered under section 1037(b)(2) to be $1,000 (the same issue price as that of the old bond).

(d) On the sale of the new bond B realizes a gain of $20 ($1,020 less $1,000), all of which is recognized by reason of section 1002. This entire gain is treated as long-term capital gain, determined in the same manner as provided in paragraph (d) of example (1).

(6) *Other rules for applying section 1232.* To the extent not specifically affected by the provisions of section 1037(b) and subparagraphs (1) through (5) of this paragraph, any gain realized on the disposition or redemption of any obligation received from the United States in an exchange to which section 1037(a) (or so much of section 1031(b) or (c) as relates to section 1037(a)) applies shall be treated in the manner provided by section 1232 if the facts and circumstances relating to the acquisition and disposition or redemption of such obligation require the application of section 1232.

(c) *Holding period of obligation received in the exchange.* The holding period of an obligation received from the United States in an exchange to which the provisions of section 1037(a) (or so much of section 1031(b) or (c) as relates to section 1037(a)) apply shall include the period for which the obligation which was surrendered to the United States in the exchange was held by the taxpayer, but only if the obligation so surrendered was at the time of the exchange a capital asset in the hands of the taxpayer. See section 1223 and the regulations thereunder.

(d) *Basis.* The basis of an obligation received from the United States in an exchange to which the provisions of section 1037(a) (or so much of section 1031(b) or (c) as relates to section 1037(a)) apply shall be determined as provided in section 1031(d) and the regulations thereunder.

(e) *Effective date.* Section 1.1037 and this section shall apply only for taxable years ending after September 22, 1959. [Reg. § 1.1037-1.]

☐ [T.D. 6935, 11-16-67. Amended by T.D. 7154, 12-27-71.]

[Reg. § 1.1038-1]

§ 1.1038-1. Reacquisitions of real property in satisfaction of indebtedness.—(a) *Scope of section 1038*—(1) *General rule on gain or loss.* If a sale of real property gives rise to indebtedness to the seller which is secured by the real property which is sold, and the seller of such property reacquires such property in a taxable year beginning after September 2, 1964, in partial or full satisfaction of such indebtedness, then, except as provided in paragraphs (b) and (f) of this section, no gain or loss shall result to the seller from such reacquisition. The treatment so provided is mandatory; however, see § 1.1038-3 for an elec-

Reg. § 1.1038-1(a)(1)

tion to apply the provisions of this section to certain taxable years beginning after December 31, 1957. It is immaterial, for purposes of applying this subparagraph, whether the seller realized a gain or sustained a loss on the sale of the real property, or whether it can be ascertained at the time of the sale whether gain or loss occurs as a result of the sale. It is also immaterial what method of accounting the seller used in reporting gain or loss from the sale of the real property or whether at the time of reacquisition such property has depreciated or appreciated in value since the time of the original sale. Moreover, the character of the gain realized on the original sale of the property is immaterial for purposes of applying this subparagraph. The provisions of this section shall apply, except as provided in § 1.1038-2, to the reacquisition of real property which was used by the seller as his principal residence and with respect to the sale of which an election under section 121 is in effect or with respect to the sale of which gain was not recognized under section 1034.

(2) *Sales giving rise to indebtedness*—(i) *Sale defined.* For purposes of this section, it is not necessary for title to the property to have passed to the purchaser in order to have a sale. Ordinarily, a sale of property has occurred in a transaction in which title to the property has not passed to the purchaser, if the purchaser has a contractual right to retain possession of the property so long as he performs his obligations under the contract and to obtain title to the property upon the completion of the contract. However, a sale may have occurred even if the purchaser does not have the right to possession until he partially or fully satisfies the terms of the contract. For example, if S contracts to sell real property to P, and if S promises to convey title to P upon the completion of all of the payments due under the contract and to allow P to obtain possession of the property after 10 percent of the purchase price has been paid, there has been a sale on the date of the contract for purposes of this section. This section shall not apply to a disposition of real property which constituted an exchange of property or was treated as a sale under section 121(d)(4) or section 1034(i); nor shall it apply to a sale of stock in a cooperative housing corporation described in section 121(d)(3) or section 1034(f).

(ii) *Secured indebtedness defined.* An indebtedness to the seller is secured by the real property for purposes of this section whenever the seller has the right to take title or possession of the property or both if there is a default with respect to such indebtedness. A sale of real property may give rise to an indebtedness to the seller although the seller is limited in his recourse to the property for payment of the indebtedness in the case of a default.

(3) *Reacquisitions in partial or full satisfaction of indebtedness*—(i) *Purpose of reacquisition.* This section applies only where the seller reacquires the real property in partial or full satisfaction of the indebtedness to him that arose from the sale of the real property and was secured by the property. That is, the reacquisition must be in furtherance of the seller's security rights in the property with respect to indebtedness to him that arose at the time of the sale. Accordingly, if the seller in reacquiring the real property does not pay consideration in addition to discharging the purchaser's indebtedness to him that arose from the sale and was secured by such property, this section shall apply to the reacquisition even though the purchaser has not defaulted in his obligations under the contract or such a default is not imminent. If in addition to discharging the purchaser's indebtedness to him that arose from the sale the seller pays consideration in reacquiring the real property, this section shall generally apply to the reacquisition if the reacquisition and the payment of additional consideration is provided for in the original contract for the sale of the property. This section generally shall apply to a reacquisition of real property if the seller reacquires the property either when the purchaser has defaulted in his obligations under the contract or when such a default is imminent. This section generally shall not apply to a reacquisition of real property where the seller pays consideration in addition to discharging the purchaser's indebtedness to him that arose from the sale if the reacquisition and payment of additional consideration was not provided for in the original contract for the sale of the property and if the purchaser has not defaulted in his obligations under the contract or such a default is not imminent. Thus, for example, if the purchaser is in arrears on the payment of interest or principal or has in any other way defaulted on his contract for the purchase of the property, or if the facts of the case indicate that the purchaser is unable satisfactorily to perform his obligations under the contract, and the seller reacquires the property from the purchaser in a transaction in which the seller pays consideration in addition to discharging the purchaser's indebtedness to him that arose from the sale and was secured by the property, this section shall apply to the reacquisition. Additional consideration paid by the seller includes money and other property paid or transferred by the seller. Also, the reacquisition by the seller of real property subject to an indebtedness (or the assumption, upon the reacquisition, of indebtedness) which arose subsequent to the original sale shall be considered as a pay-

Reg. § 1.1038-1(a)(3)

ment by the seller of additional consideration. However, the reacquisition by the seller of real property subject to an indebtedness (or the assumption, upon the reacquisition, of an indebtedness) which arose prior to or arose out of the original sale shall not be considered as a payment by the seller of additional consideration.

(ii) *Manner of reacquisition.* For purposes of applying section 1038 and this section there must be a reacquisition by the seller of the real property itself, but the manner in which the seller so reduces the property to ownership or possession, as the case may be, shall generally be immaterial. Thus, the seller may reduce the real property to ownership or possession or both, as the case may require, by agreement or by process of law. The reduction of the real property to ownership or possession by agreement includes, where valid under local law, such methods as voluntary conveyance from the purchaser and abandonment to the seller. The reduction of the real property to ownership or possession by process of law includes foreclosure proceedings in which a competitive bid is entered, such as foreclosure by judicial sale or by power of sale contained in the loan agreement without recourse to the courts, as well as those types of foreclosure proceedings in which a competitive bid is not entered, such as strict foreclosure and foreclosure by entry and possession, by writ of entry, or by publication or notice.

(4) *Persons from whom real property may be reacquired.* The real property reacquired in satisfaction of the indebtedness need not be reacquired from the purchaser but may be required from the purchaser's transferee or assignee, or from a trustee holding title to such property pending the purchaser's satisfaction of the terms of the contract, so long as the indebtedness that is partially or completely satisfied in the reacquisition of such property arose in the original sale of the property and was secured by the property so reacquired. In such a case, a reference in this section to the purchaser shall, where appropriate, include the purchaser's transferee or assignee. Thus, for example, this section will apply if the seller reacquires the property from a purchaser from the original purchaser and either the property is subject to, or the subsequent purchaser assumes, the liability to the seller on the indebtedness.

(5) *Reacquisitions not included.* This section shall not apply to reacquisitions of real property by mutual savings banks, domestic building and loan associations, and cooperative banks, described in section 593(a). However, for rules respecting the reacquisition of real property by such organizations, see § 1.595-1.

(b) *Amount of gain resulting from a reacquisition*—(1) *Determination of amount*—(i) *In general.* As a result of a reacquisition to which paragraph (a) of this section applies gain shall be derived by the seller to the extent that the amount of money and the fair market value of other property (other than obligations of the purchaser arising with respect to the sale) which are received by the seller, prior to such reacquisition, with respect to the sale of the property exceed the amount of the gain derived by the seller on the sale of such property which is returned as income for periods prior to the reacquisition. However, the amount of gain so determined shall in no case exceed the amount determined under paragraph (c) of this section with respect to such reacquisition.

(ii) *Amount of gain returned as income for prior periods.* For purposes of this subparagraph and paragraph (c)(1) of this section, the amount of gain on the sale of the property which is returned as income for periods prior to the reacquisition of the real property does not include any amount of income determined under paragraph (f)(2) of this section which is considered to be received at the time of the reacquisition of the property. However, the amount of gain on the sale of the property which is returned as income for such periods does include gain on the sale resulting from payments received in the taxable year in which the date of reacquisition occurs if such payments are received prior to such reacquisition. The application of this subdivision may be illustrated by the following example:

Example. In 1965 S, who uses the calendar year as the taxable year, sells to P for $10,000 real property which has an adjusted basis of $3,000. S properly elects under section 453 to report the income from the sale on the installment method. In 1965 and 1966, S receives a total of $4,000 on the contract. On May 15, 1967, S receives $1,000 on the contract. Because of P's default, S reacquires the property on August 31, 1967. The gain on the sale which is returned as income for periods prior to the reacquisition is $3,500 ($5,000 × $7,000/$10,000).

(2) *Amount of money and other property received with respect to the sale*—(i) *In general.* Amounts of money and other property received by the seller with respect to the sale of the property include payments made by the purchaser for the seller's benefit, as well as payments made and other property transferred directly to the seller. If the purchaser of the real property makes payments on a mortgage or other indebtedness to which the property is subject at the time of the sale of such property to him, or on which the seller

Reg. § 1.1038-1(a)(4)

was personally liable at the time of such sale, such payments are considered amounts received by the seller with respect to the sale. However, if after the sale the purchaser borrows money and uses the property as security for the loan, payments by the purchaser in satisfaction of the indebtedness are not considered as amounts received by the seller with respect to the sale, although the seller does in fact receive some indirect benefit when the purchaser makes such payments.

(ii) *Payments by purchaser at time of reacquisition.* All payments made by the purchaser at the time of the reacquisition of the real property that are with respect to the original sale of the property shall be treated, for purposes of subparagraph (1) of this paragraph, by the seller as having been received prior to the reacquisition with respect to such sale. For example, if the purchaser, at the time of the reacquisition by the seller, pays money or other property to the seller in partial or complete satisfaction of the purchaser's indebtedness on the original sale, the seller shall treat such amounts as having been received prior to the reacquisition with respect to the sale.

(iii) *Interest received.* For purposes of this subparagraph and paragraph (c)(1) of this section any amounts received by the seller as interest, stated or unstated, are excluded from the computation of gain on the sale of the property and are not considered amounts of money or other property received with respect to the sale.

(iv) *Amounts received on sale of purchaser's indebtedness.* Money or other property received by the seller on the sale of the purchaser's indebtedness that arose at the time of the sale of the real property are amounts received by the seller with respect to the sale of such real property, except that the amounts so received from the sale of such indebtedness shall be reduced by the amount of money and the fair market value of other property paid or transferred by the seller, before the reacquisition of the real property, to reacquire such indebtedness. For example, if S sells real property to P for $25,000, and under the contract receives $10,000 down and a note from P for $15,000, S would receive $22,000 with respect to the sale if he were to discount the note for $12,000. If before the reacquisition of the real property S were to reacquire the discounted note for $8,000, he would receive $14,000 with respect to the sale.

(3) *Obligations of the purchaser arising with respect to the sale.* The term "obligations of the purchaser arising with respect to the sale" of the real property includes, for purposes of subparagraph (1) of this paragraph, only that indebtedness on which the purchaser is liable to the seller and which arises out of the sale of such property. Thus, the term does not include any indebtedness in respect of the property that the seller owes to a third person which the purchaser assumes, or to which the property is subject, at the time of the sale of the property to the purchaser. Nor does the term include any indebtedness on which the purchaser is liable to the seller if such indebtedness arises subsequent to the sale of such property.

(c) *Limitation upon amount of gain*—(1) *In general.* Except as provided by subparagraph (2) of this paragraph, the amount of gain on a reacquisition of real property, as determined under paragraph (b) of this section, shall in no case exceed—

(i) The amount by which the price at which the real property was sold exceeded its adjusted basis at the time of the sale, as determined under § 1.1011-1, reduced by

(ii) The amount of gain on the sale of such real property which is returned as income for periods prior to the reacquisition, and by

(iii) The amount of money and the fair market value of other property (other than obligations of the purchaser to the seller which are secured by the real property) paid or transferred by the seller in connection with the reacquisition of such real property.

(2) *Cases where limitation does not apply.* The limitation provided by subparagraph (1) of this paragraph shall not apply in a case where the selling price of property is indefinite in amount and cannot be ascertained at the time of the reacquisition of such property, as, for example, where the selling price is stated as a percentage of the profits to be realized from the development of the property which is sold. Moreover, the limitation so provided shall not apply to a reacquisition of real property occurring in a taxable year beginning before September 3, 1964, to which the provisions of this section are applied pursuant to an election under § 1.1038-3.

(3) *Determination of sales price.* The price at which the real property was sold shall be, for purposes of subparagraph (1) of this paragraph, the gross sales price reduced by the selling commissions, legal fees, and other expenses incident to the sale of such property which are properly taken into account in determining gain or loss on the sale. For example, the amount of selling commissions paid by a nondealer will be deducted from the gross sales price in determining the price at which the real property was sold; on the other hand, selling commissions paid by a real estate dealer will be deducted as a business expense. Examples of other expenses incident to the sale of

Reg. § 1.1038-1(c)(3)

the property are expenses for appraisal fees, advertising expense, cost of preparing maps, recording fees, and documentary stamp taxes. Payments on indebtedness to the seller which are for interest, stated or unstated, are not included in determining the price at which the property was sold. See paragraph (b)(2)(iii) of this section.

(4) *Determination of amounts paid or transferred in connection with a reacquisition*—(i) *In general.* Amounts of money or property paid or transferred by the seller of the real property in connection with the reacquisition of such property include payments of money, or transfers of property, to persons from whom the real property is reacquired as well as to other persons. Payments or transfers in connection with the reacquisition of the property do not include money or property paid or transferred by the seller to reacquire obligations of the purchaser to the seller which were received by the seller with respect to the sale of the property or which arose subsequent to the sale. Amounts of money or property paid or transferred by the seller in connection with the reacquisition of the property include payments or transfers for such items as court costs and fees for services of an attorney, master, trustee, or auctioneer, or for publication, acquiring title, clearing liens, or filing and recording.

(ii) *Assumption of indebtedness.* The assumption by the seller, upon reacquisition of the real property, of any indebtedness to another person which at such time is secured by such property will be considered a payment of money by the seller in connection with the reacquisition. Also, if at the time of reacquisition such property is subject to an indebtedness which is not an indebtedness of the purchaser to the seller, the seller shall be considered to have paid money, in an amount equal to such indebtedness, in connection with the reacquisition of the property. Thus, for example, if at the time of the sale the purchaser executes in connection with the sale a first mortgage to a bank and a second mortgage to the seller and at the time of reacquisition the seller reacquires the property subject to the first mortgage which he does not assume, the seller will be considered to have paid money, in an amount equal to the unpaid amount of the first mortgage, in connection with the reacquisition.

(d) *Character of gain resulting from a reacquisition.* Paragraphs (b) and (c) of this section set forth the extent to which gain shall be derived from a reacquisition to which paragraph (a) of this section applies, but the rules provided by section 1038 and this section do not affect the character of the gain so derived. The character of the gain resulting from such a reacquisition is determined on the basis of whether the gain on the original sale was returned on the installment method or, if not, on the basis of whether title to the real property was transferred to the purchaser; and, if title was transferred to the purchaser in a deferred-payment sale, whether the reconveyance of the property to the seller was voluntary. For example, if the gain on the original sale of the reacquired property was returned on the installment method, the character of the gain on reacquisition by the seller shall be determined in accordance with the rules provided in paragraph (a) of § 1.453-9. If the original sale was not on the installment method but was a deferred-payment sale, as described in § 1.453-6(a), where title to the real property was transferred to the purchaser and the seller accepts a voluntary reconveyance of the property, the gain on the reacquisition shall be ordinary income; however, if the obligations satisfied are securities (as defined in section 165(g)(2)(C)), any gain resulting from the reacquisition is capital gain subject to the provisions of subchapter P of chapter 1 of the Code.

(e) *Recognition of gain.* The entire amount of the gain determined under paragraphs (b) and (c) of this section with respect to a reacquisition to which paragraph (a) of this section applies shall be recognized notwithstanding any other provision of subtitle A (relating to income taxes) of the Code.

(f) *Special rules applicable to worthless indebtedness*—(1) *Worthlessness resulting from reacquisition.* No debt of the purchaser to the seller which was secured by the reacquired real property shall be considered as becoming worthless or partially worthless as a result of a reacquisition of such real property to which paragraph (a) of this section applies. Accordingly, no deduction for a bad debt and no charge against a reserve for bad debts shall be allowed, as a result of the reacquisition, in order to reflect the noncollectibility of any indebtedness of the purchaser to the seller which at the time of reacquisition was secured by such real property.

(2) *Indebtedness treated as worthless prior to reacquisition*—(i) *Prior taxable years.* If for any taxable year ending before the taxable year in which occurs a reacquisition of real property to which paragraph (a) of this section applies the seller of such property has treated any indebtedness of the purchaser which is secured by such property as having become worthless or partially worthless by taking a bad debt deduction under section 166(a), he shall be considered as receiving, at the time of such reacquisition, income in an amount equal to the amount of such indebtedness previously treated by him as having become

worthless. The amount so treated as income received shall be treated as a recovery of a bad debt previously deducted as worthless or partially worthless. Accordingly, the amount of such income shall be excluded from gross income, as provided in § 1.111-1, to the extent of the "recovery exclusion" with respect to such item. For purposes of § 1.111-1, if the indebtedness was treated as partially worthless in a prior taxable year, the amount treated under this subparagraph as a recovery shall be considered to be with respect to the part of the indebtedness that was previously deducted as worthless. The seller shall not be considered to have treated an indebtedness as worthless in any taxable year for which he took the standard deduction under section 141 or paid the tax imposed by section 3 if a deduction in respect of such indebtedness was not allowed in determining adjusted gross income for such year under section 62.

(ii) *Current taxable year.* No deduction shall be allowed under section 166(a), for the taxable year in which occurs a reacquisition of real property to which paragraph (a) of this section applies, in respect of any indebtedness of the purchaser secured by such property which has been treated by the seller as having become worthless or partially worthless in such taxable year but prior to the date of such reacquisition.

(3) *Basis adjustment.* The basis of any indebtedness described in subparagraph (2)(i) of this paragraph shall be increased (as of the date of the reacquisition) by an amount equal to the amount which, under such subparagraph of this paragraph, is treated as income received by the seller with respect to such indebtedness, but only to the extent the amount so treated as received is not excluded from gross income by reason of the application of § 1.111-1.

(g) *Rules for determining gain or loss on disposition of reacquired property*—(1) *Basis of reacquired real property.* The basis of any real property acquired in a reacquisition to which paragraph (a) of this section applies shall be the sum of the following amounts, determined as of the date of such reacquisition:

(i) The amount of the adjusted basis, determined under sections 453 and 1011, and the regulations thereunder, of all indebtedness of the purchaser to the seller which at the time of reacquisition was secured by such property, including any increase by reason of paragraph (f)(3) of this section,

(ii) The amount of gain determined under paragraphs (b) and (c) of this section with respect to such reacquisition, and

(iii) The amount of money and the fair market value of other property (other than obligations of the purchaser to the seller which are secured by the real property) paid or transferred by the seller in connection with the reacquisition of such real property, determined as provided in paragraph (c) of this section even though such paragraph does not apply to the reacquisition.

(2) *Basis of undischarged indebtedness.* The basis of any indebtedness of the purchaser to the seller which was secured by the reacquired real property described in subparagraph (1) of this paragraph, to the extent that such indebtedness is not discharged upon the reacquisition of such property, shall be zero. Therefore, to the extent not discharged upon the reacquisition of the real property, indebtedness on the original obligation of the purchaser, a substituted obligation of the purchaser, a deficiency judgment entered in a court of law into which the purchaser's obligation has merged, or any other obligation of the purchaser to the seller, shall be zero if such indebtedness constitutes an indebtedness to the seller which was secured by such property.

(3) *Holding period of reacquired property.* Since the reacquisition described in subparagraph (1) of this paragraph is in a sense considered a nullification of the original sale of the real property, for purposes of determining gain or loss on a disposition of such property after its reacquisition the period for which the seller has held the real property at the time of such disposition shall include the period for which such property is held by him prior to the original sale. However, the holding period shall not include the period of time commencing with the date following the date on which the property is originally sold to the purchaser and ending with the date on which the property is reacquired by the seller. The period for which the property was held by the seller prior to the original sale shall be determined as provided in § 1.1223-1. For example, if under paragraph (a) of § 1.1223-1 real property, which was acquired as the result of an involuntary conversion, has been held for five months on January 1, 1965, the date of its sale, and such property is reacquired on July 2, 1965, and resold on July 3, 1965, the seller will be considered to have held such property for five months and one day for purposes of this subparagraph.

(h) *Illustrations.* The application of this section may be illustrated by the following examples in which it is assumed that the reacquisition is in satisfaction of secured indebtedness arising out of the sale of the real property:

Example (1). (a) S purchases real property for $20 and sells it to P for $100, the property not

Reg. § 1.1038-1(h)

Common Nontaxable Exchanges

See p. 20,601 for regulations not amended to reflect law changes

being mortgaged at the time of sale. Under the contract P pays $10 down and executes a note for $90, with stated interest at 6 percent, to be paid in nine annual installments. S properly elects to report the gain on the installment method. After the second $10 annual payment P defaults and S accepts a voluntary reconveyance of the property in complete satisfaction of the indebtedness. S pays $5 in connection with the reacquisition of the property. The fair market value of the property at the time of the reacquisition is $110.

(b) The gain derived by S on the reacquisition of the property is $6, determined as follows:

Gain before application of limitation:		
Money with respect to the sale received by S prior to the reacquisition		$30
Less: Gain returned by S as income for periods to the reacquisition ($30 × [($100 − $20)/$100])		24
Gain before application of limitation		6
Limitation on amount of gain:		
Sales price of real property		$100
Less:		
Adjusted basis of the property at the time of sale	$20	
Gain returned by S as income for periods prior to the reacquisition	24	
Amount of money paid by S in connection with the reacquisition	5	49
Limitation on amount of gain		51
Gain resulting from the reacquisition of the property		$6

(c) The basis of the reacquired real property at the date of the reacquisition is $25, determined as follows:

Adjusted basis of P's indebtedness to S ($70 − [$70 × $80/$100])	$14
Gain resulting from the reacquisition of the property	6
Amount of money paid by S in connection with the reacquisition	5
Basis of reacquired property	25

Example (2). (a) The facts are the same as in example (1) except that S purchased the property for $80.

(b) The gain derived by S on the reacquisition of the property is $9, determined as follows:

Gain before application of limitation:		
Money with respect to the sale received by S prior to the reacquisition		$30
Less: Gain returned by S as income for periods prior to the reacquisition ($30 × [($100 − $80)/$100])		6
Gain before application of limitation		24
Limitation on amount of gain:		
Sales price of real property		$100
Less:		
Adjusted basis of the property at the time of sale	$80	
Gain returned by S as income for periods prior to the reacquisition	6	
Amount of money paid by S in connection with the reacqusition	5	91
Limitation on amount of gain		9
Gain resulting from the reacquisition of the property		$9

(c) The basis of the reacquired real property at the date of reacquisition is $70, determined as follows:

Adjusted basis of P's indebtedness to S ($70 − [$70 × $20/$100])	$56
Gain resulting from the reacquisition of the property	9
Amount of money paid by S in connection with the reacquisition	5
Basis of reacquired property	70

Example (3). (a) S purchases real property for $70 and sells it to P for $100, the property not being mortgaged at the time of sale. Under the contract P pays $10 down and executes a note for $90, with stated interest at 6 percent, to be paid in nine annual installments. S properly elects to report the gain on the installment method. After the first $10 annual payment P defaults and S

Reg. § 1.1038-1(h)

Common Nontaxable Exchanges

52,029

See p. 20,601 for regulations not amended to reflect law changes

accepts a voluntary reconveyance of the property in complete satisfaction of the indebtedness. S pays $5 in connection with the reacquisition of the property. The fair market value of the property at the time of the reacquisition is $50.

Gain before application of limitation:		
Money with respect to the sale received by S prior to the reacquisition		$ 20
Less: Gain returned by S as income for periods prior to the reacquisition ($20 × [($100 − $70)/$100])		6
Gain before application of limitation		14
Limitation on amount of gain:		
Sales price of real property		$100
Less:		
Adjusted basis of the property at time of sale	$70	
Gain returned by S as income for periods prior to the reacquisition	6	
Amount paid by S in connection with the reacquisition	5	$ 81
Limitation on amount of gain		19
Gain resulting from the reacquisition of the property		$ 14

(c) The basis of the reacquired real property at the date of the reacquisition is $75, determined as follows:

Adjusted basis of P's indebtedness to S ($80 − [$80 × $30/$100])	$56
Gain resulting from the reacquisition of the property	14
Amount of money paid by S in connection with the reacquisition	5
Basis of reacquired property	75

Example (4). (a) S purchases real property for $20 and sells it to P for $100, the property not being mortgaged at the time of sale. Under the contract P pays $10 down and executes a note for $90, with stated interest at 6 percent, to be paid in nine annual installments. S properly elects to report gain on the installment method. After the second $10 annual payment P defaults and S accepts from P in complete satisfaction of the indebtedness a voluntary reconveyance of the property plus cash in the amount of $20. S does not pay any amount in connection with the reacquisition of the property. The fair market value of the property at the time of the reacquisition is $30.

(b) The gain derived by S on the reacquisition of the property is $10, determined as follows:

Gain before application of the limitation:		
Money with respect to the sale received by S prior to the reacquisition ($30 + $20)	$ 50	
Less: Gain returned by S as income for periods prior to the reacquisition ($50 × [($100 − $20)/$100])	40	
Gain before application of limitation		10
Limitation on amount of gain:		

(b) The gain derived by S on the reacquisition of the property is $14, determined as follows:

Sales price of real property		$100
Less:		
Adjusted basis of the property at time of sale	$20	
Gain returned by S as income for periods prior to the reacquisition	40	60
Limitation on amount of gain		40
Gain resulting from the reacquisition of the property		$ 10

(c) The basis of the reacquired real property at the date of the reacquisition is $20, determined as follows:

Adjusted basis of P's indebtedness to S ($50 − [$50 × $80/$100])	$ 10
Gain resulting from the reacquisition of the property	10
Basis of reacquired property	20

Example (5). (a) S purchases real property for $80 and sells it to P for $100, the property not being mortgaged at the time of sale. Under the contract P pays $10 down and executes a note for $90, with stated interest at 6 percent, to be paid in nine annual installments. At the time of sale P's note has a fair market value of $90. S does not elect to report the gain on the installment method but treats the transaction as a deferred-payment sale. After the third $10 annual payment P defaults and S forecloses. Under the foreclosure sale S bids in the property at $70, cancels P's obligation of $60, and pays $10 to P. There are no other amounts paid by S in connection with the reacquisition of the property. The fair market value of the property at the time of the reacquisition is $70.

(b) The gain derived by S on the reacquisition of the property is $0, determined as follows:

Reg. § 1.1038-1(h)

Gain before application of the limitation:
Money with respect to the sale received by S prior to the reacquisition .... $ 40
Less: Gain returned by S as income for periods prior to the reacquisition ([$10 + $90] − $80) .... $ 20
Gain before application of limitation 20

Limitation on amount of gain:
Sales price of real property $100
Less:
Adjusted basis of the property at time of sale $80
Gain returned by S as income for periods prior to the reacquisition 20
Amount of money paid by S in connection with the reacquisition 10   110
Limitation on amount of gain (not to be less than zero) 0

Gain resulting from the reacquisition of the property 0

(c) The basis of the reacquired real property at the date of the reacquisition is $70, determined as follows:

Adjusted basis of P's indebtedness to S (face value at time of reacquisition) .... $ 60
Gain resulting from the reacquisition of the property 0
Amount of money paid by S in connection with the reacquisition 10
Basis of reacquired property 70

[Reg. § 1.1038-1.]

☐ [T.D. 6916, 4-12-67.]

[Reg. § 1.1038-2]

§ 1.1038-2. Reacquisition and resale of property used as a principal residence.—(a) *Application of special rules*—(1) *In general.* If paragraph (a) of § 1.1038-1 applies to the reacquisition of real property which was used by the seller as his principal residence and with respect to the sale of which an election under section 121 is in effect or with respect to the sale of which gain was not recognized under section 1034, the provisions of § 1.1038-1 (other than paragraph (a) thereof) shall not, and this section shall, apply to the reacquisition of such property if the property is resold by the seller within one year after the date of the reacquisition. For purposes of this section an election under section 121 shall be considered to be in effect with respect to the sale of the property if, at the close of the last day for making such an election under section 121(c) with respect to such sale, an election under section 121

has been made and not revoked. Thus, a taxpayer who properly elects, subsequent to the reacquisition, to have section 121 apply to a sale of his residence may be eligible for the treatment provided in this section. The treatment provided by this section is mandatory; however, see § 1.1038-3 for an election to apply the provisions of this section to certain taxable years beginning after December 31, 1957.

(2) *Sale and resale treated as one transaction.* In the case of a reacquisition to which this section applies, the resale of the reacquired property shall be treated, for purposes of applying sections 121 and 1034, as part of the transaction constituting the original sale of such property. In effect, the reacquisition is generally disregarded pursuant to this section and, for purposes of applying sections 121 and 1034, the resale of the property is considered to constitute a sale of such property occurring on the date of the original sale of such property.

(b) *Transactions not included.* (1) If with respect to the original sale of the property there was no nonrecognition of gain under section 1034 and an election under section 121 is not in effect, the provisions of § 1.1038-1, and not this section, shall apply to the reacquisition. Thus, for example, if in the case of a taxpayer not entitled to the benefit of section 121 there is no gain on the original sale of the property, the provisions of § 1.1038-1, and not this section, shall apply even though a redetermination of gain under this section would result in the nonrecognition of gain on the sale under section 1034. Also, if in the case of such a taxpayer there was gain on the original sale of the property but after the application of section 1034 all of such gain was recognized, the provisions of § 1.1038-1, and not this section, shall apply to the reacquisition.

(2) If the original sale of the property was not eligible for the treatment provided by section 121 and section 1034, the provisions of § 1.1038-1, and not this section, shall apply to the reacquisition of the property even though the resale of such property is eligible for the treatment provided by either or both of sections 121 and 1034.

(c) *Redetermination of gain required*—(1) *Sale of old residence.* The amount of gain excluded under section 121 on the sale of the property and the amount of gain recognized under section 1034 on the sale of the property shall be redetermined under this section by recomputing the adjusted sales price and the adjusted basis of the property, and any adjustments resulting from the redetermination of the gain on the sale of such property shall be reflected in the income of the seller for his

Reg. § 1.1038-2(a)(1)

taxable year in which the resale of the property occurs.

(2) *Sale of new residence.* If gain was not recognized under section 1034 on the original sale of the property, the adjusted basis of the new residence shall be redetermined under this section. If the new residence has been sold, the amount of gain returned on such sale of the new residence which is affected by the redetermination of the recognized gain on the sale of the old residence shall be redetermined under this section, and any adjustments resulting from the redetermination of the gain on the sale of the new residence shall be reflected in income of the seller for his taxable year in which the resale of the old residence occurs.

(d) *Redetermination of adjusted sales price.* For purposes of applying sections 121 and 1034 pursuant to this section, the adjusted sales price of the reacquired real property shall be redetermined by taking into account both the sale and the resale of the property and shall be—

(1) The amount realized, which for purposes of section 1001 shall be—

(i) The amount realized on the resale of the property, as determined under paragraph (b)(4) of § 1.1034-1, plus

(ii) The amount realized on the original sale of the property, determined as provided in paragraph (b)(4) of § 1.1034-1, less that portion of any obligations of the purchaser arising with respect to such sale which at the time of reacquisition is secured by such property and is unpaid, less

(iii) The amount of money and the fair market value of other property (other than obligations of the purchaser to the seller secured by the real property) paid or transferred by the seller in connection with the reacquisition of such real property,

reduced by

(2) The total of the fixing-up expenses (as defined in paragraph (b)(6) of § 1.1034-1) incurred for work performed on such real property to assist in both its original sale and its resale.

For purposes of applying paragraph (b)(6) of § 1.1034-1, there shall be two 90-day periods, the first ending on the day on which the contract to sell is entered into in connection with the original sale of the property, and the second ending on the day on which the contract to sell is entered into in connection with the resale of the property. There shall also be two 30-day periods for such purposes, the first ending on the 30th day after the date of the original sale, and the second ending on the 30th day after the date of the resale. For determination of the obligations of the purchaser arising with respect to the original sale of the property, see paragraph (b)(3) of § 1.1038-1. For determination of amounts paid or transferred by the seller in connection with the reacquisition of the property, see paragraph (c)(4) of § 1.1038-1.

(e) *Determination of adjusted basis at time of resale.* For purposes of applying sections 121 and 1034 pursuant to this section, the adjusted basis of the reacquired real property at the time of its resale shall be—

(1) The sum of—

(i) The adjusted basis of such property at the time of the original sale, with proper adjustment under section 1016(a) in respect of such property for the period occurring after the reacquisition of such property, and

(ii) Any indebtedness of the purchaser to the seller which arose subsequent to the original sale of such property and which at the time of reacquisition was secured by such property,

reduced by

(2) Any indebtedness of the purchaser to the seller which at the time of reacquisition was secured by the reacquired real property and which, for any taxable year ending before the taxable year in which occurs the reacquisition of such property, was treated by the seller as having become worthless or partially worthless by taking a bad debt deduction under section 166(a). The reduction under the preceding sentence by reason of having treated indebtedness as worthless or partially worthless shall not exceed the amount by which there would be an increase in the basis of such indebtedness under paragraph (f)(3) of § 1.1038-1 if section 1038(d) had been applicable to the reacquisition of such property.

(f) *Treatment of indebtedness secured by the property*—(1) *Year of reacquisition.* No debt of the purchaser to the seller which was secured by the reacquired real property shall be considered as becoming worthless or partially worthless as a result of a reacquisition of such real property to which this section applies. Accordingly, no deduction for a bad debt shall be allowed, as a result of the reacquisition, in order to reflect the noncollectibility of any indebtedness of the purchaser to the seller which at the time of reacquisition was secured by such real property. In addition, no deduction shall be allowed, for the taxable year in which occurs a reacquisition of real property to which this section applies, in respect of any indebtedness of the purchaser secured by such property which has been treated by the seller as having become worthless or partially worthless in such taxable year but prior to the date of such reacquisition.

Reg. § 1.1038-2(f)(1)

Common Nontaxable Exchanges

(2) *Prior taxable years.* For reduction of the basis of the real property for indebtedness treated as worthless or partially worthless for taxable years ending before the taxable year in which occurs the reacquisition, see paragraph (e) of this section.

(3) *Basis of indebtedness.* The basis of any indebtedness of the purchaser to the seller which was secured by the reacquired real property, to the extent that such indebtedness is not discharged upon the reacquisition of such property, shall be zero.

(g) *Date of sale.* Since the resale of the property, by being treated as part of the transaction constituting the original sale of the property, is treated as having occurred on the date of the original sale, in determining whether any of the time requirements of section 121 or section 1034 are satisfied for purposes of this section the date of the original sale is used, except to the extent provided in paragraph (d)(2) of this section.

(h) *Illustrations.* The application of this section may be illustrated by the following examples:

Example (1). (a) On June 30, 1964, S, a single individual over 65 years of age, sells his principal residence to P for $25,000, the property not being mortgaged at the time of sale. S properly elects to apply the provisions of section 121 to the sale. Under the contract, P pays $5,000 down and executes a note for $20,000, with stated interest at 6 percent, the principal being payable in installments of $5,000 each on January 1 of each year and the note being secured by the real property which is sold. At the time of sale P's note has a fair market value of $20,000. S does not elect to report the gain on the installment method but treats the transaction as a deferred-payment sale, title to the property being transferred to P at the time of sale. S uses the calendar year as the taxable year and the cash receipts and disbursements method of accounting. After making two annual payments of $5,000 each on the note, P defaults on the contract, and on March 1, 1967, S reacquires the real property in full satisfaction of P's indebtedness, title to the property being voluntarily reconveyed to S. On November 1, 1967, S sells the property to T for $35,000. The assumption is made that no fixing-up expenses are incurred for work performed on the principal residence in order to assist in the sale of the property in 1964 or in the resale of the property in 1967. At the time of sale in 1964 the property has an adjusted basis of $15,000. S does not treat any indebtedness with respect to the sale in 1964 as being worthless or partially worthless or make any capital expenditures with respect to the property after such sale. In his return for 1964, S includes in income $2,000 capital gain from the sale of his residence.

(b) The results obtained before and after the reacquisition of the property are as follows:

	Before Reacquisition	After Reacquisition
Adjusted sales price:		
$5,000 + $20,000	$25,000	
$15,000 + $35,000		$50,000
Less: Adjusted basis of property at time of sale	15,000	15,000
Gain on sale	10,000	35,000
Gain excluded from income under sec. 121:		
$10,000 × $20,000/$25,000	8,000	
$35,000 × $20,000/$50,000		14,000
Gain included in income after applying sec. 121:		
$10,000 − $8,000	$ 2,000	
$35,000 − $14,000		$21,000

(c) S is required to show the additional inclusion of $19,000 capital gain ($21,000 − $2,000) in income on his return for 1967.

Example (2). (a) The facts are the same as in example (1) except that on April 1, 1965, S purchases a new residence at a cost of $30,000 and qualifies for the nonrecognition of gain under section 1034 in respect of the sale of his principal residence on June 30, 1964. In his return for 1964, S does not include any capital gain in income as a result of the sale of the old residence.

(b) The results obtained before and after the reacquisition of the property are as follows:

Reg. § 1.1038-2(f)(2)

Common Nontaxable Exchanges

See p. 20,601 for regulations not amended to reflect law changes

	Before Reacquisition	After Reacquisition
Application of sec. 121 (see example (1)):		
Adjusted sales price	$25,000	$50,000
Less: Adjusted basis of property at time of sale	15,000	15,000
Gain on sale	10,000	35,000
Gain excluded from income under sec. 121	8,000	14,000
Gain not excluded from income under sec. 121	2,000	21,000
Application of sec. 1034:		
Adjusted sales price:		
$25,000 − $ 8,000	$17,000	......
$50,000 − $14,000	......	$36,000
Less: Cost of new residence	30,000	30,000
Gain recognized under sec. 1034 on sale of old residence	0	6,000
Gain not recognized under sec. 1034 on sale of old residence:		
($10,000 − [$8,000 + $0])	$ 2,000	......
($35,000 − [$14,000 + $6,000])	......	$15,000
Adjusted basis of new residence on April 1, 1965:		
$30,000 − $ 2,000	28,000	......
$30,000 − $15,000	......	15,000

(c) The $6,000 of capital gain on the sale of the old residence is required to be included in income on the return for 1967. The adjusted basis on April 1, 1965, for determining gain on a sale or exchange of the new residence at any time on or after that date is $15,000, after taking into account the reacquisition and resale of the old residence.

Example (3). The facts are the same as in example (2) except that S sells the new residence on June 20, 1965, for $40,000 and includes $12,000 of capital gain ($40,000 − $28,000) on its sale in his income on the return for 1965. S is required to include the additional capital gain of $13,000 ([$40,000 − $15,000] − $12,000) on the sale of the new residence in his income on the return for 1967. For this purpose, the assumption is also made that there are no additional adjustments to the basis of the new residence after April 1, 1965. [Reg. § 1.1038-2.]

☐ [T.D. 6916, 4-12-67.]

[Reg. § 1.1038-3]

§ 1.1038-3. Election to have section 1038 apply for taxable years beginning after December 31, 1957.—(a) *In general.* If an election is made in the manner provided by paragraph (b) of this section, the applicable provisions of § 1.1038-1 and § 1.1038-2 shall apply to all reacquisitions of real property occurring in each and every taxable year beginning after December 31, 1957, and before September 3, 1964, for which the assessment of a deficiency, or the credit or refund of an overpayment, is not prevented on September 2, 1964, by the operation of any law or rule of law. The election so made shall apply to all taxable years beginning after December 31, 1957, and before September 3, 1964, for which the assessment of a deficiency, or the credit or refund of an overpayment, is not prevented on September 2, 1964, by the operation of any law or rule of law and shall apply to every reacquisition occurring in such taxable years. The fact that the assessment of a deficiency, or the credit or refund of an overpayment, is prevented for any other taxable year or years affected by the election will not prohibit the making of an election under this section. For example, if an individual who uses the calendar year as the taxable year were to sell in 1960 real property used as his principal residence in respect of the sale of which gain is not recognized under section 1034, and if such property were reacquired by the seller in 1962 and resold within one year, he would be permitted to make an election under this section with respect to such reacquisition even though on September 2, 1964, the period of limitations on assessment or refund has run for 1960. An election under this section shall be deemed a consent to the application of the provisions of this section.

(b) *Time and manner of making election*—(1) *In general.* (i) An election to have the provisions of § 1.1038-2 apply to reacquisitions of real property occurring in taxable years beginning after December 31, 1957, and before September 3, 1964, shall be made by filing on or before September 3, 1965, a return, an amended return, or a claim for refund, whichever is proper, for each taxable year in which the resale of such real property occurs. If the return for any such year is not due on or before such date and has not been filed, the election with respect to such taxable year shall be made by filing on or before such date the statement described in subparagraph (2) of this paragraph.

(ii) An election to have the provisions of § 1.1038-1 apply to reacquisitions of real property occurring in taxable years beginning after December 31, 1957, and before September 3, 1964, shall be made by filing on or before September 3, 1965, a return, an amended return, or a claim for refund, whichever is proper, for each taxable year in which such reacquisitions occur. If the return for

Reg. § 1.1038-3(b)(1)

any such year is not due on or before such date and has not been filed, the election with respect to such taxable year shall be made by filing on or before such date the statement described in subparagraph (2) of this paragraph.

(iii) If the facts are such that § 1.1038-2 applies to a reacquisition of property except that the reacquisition occurs in a taxable year beginning after December 31, 1957, and before September 3, 1964, an election may not be made under this paragraph to have the provisions of § 1.1038-1 apply to such reacquisition.

(iv) Once made, an election under this paragraph may not be revoked after September 3, 1965. To any return, amended return, or claim for refund filed under this subparagraph there shall be attached the statement described in subparagraph (2) of this paragraph.

(2) *Statement to be attached.* The statement described in subparagraph (1) of this paragraph shall indicate—

(i) The name, address and account number of the taxpayer, and the fact that the taxpayer is electing to have the provisions of section 1038 apply to the reacquisitions of real property,

(ii) The taxable years in which the reacquisitions of property occur and any other taxable year or years the tax for which is affected by the application of section 1038 to such reacquisitions,

(iii) The office of the district director where the return or returns for such taxable year or years were or will be filed,

(iv) The dates on which such return or returns were filed and on which the tax for such taxable year or years was paid,

(v) The type of real property reacquired, the terms under which such property was sold and reacquired, and an indication of whether the taxpayer is applying the provisions of § 1.1038-2 to the reacquisition of such property,

(vi) If § 1.1038-2 is being applied to the reacquisition, the terms under which the old residence was resold and, if applicable, the terms under which the new residence was sold, and

(vii) The office where, and the date when, the election to apply section 121 in respect of any sale of such property was or will be made.

(3) *Place for filing.* Any claim for refund, amended return, or statement, filed under this paragraph in respect of any taxable year, whether the taxable year in which occurs the reacquisition of property or the taxable year in which occurs the resale of the old residence, shall be filed in the office of the district director in which the return for such taxable year was or will be filed.

(c) *Extension of period of limitations on assessment or refund*—(1) *Assessment of tax.* If an election is properly made under paragraph (b) of this section and the assessment of a deficiency for the taxable years to which such election applies is not prevented on September 2, 1964, by the operation of any law or rule of law, the period within which a deficiency for such taxable years may be assessed shall, to the extent such deficiency is attributable to the application of section 1038, not expire prior to one year after the date on which such election is made.

(2) *Refund of tax.* If an election is properly made under paragraph (b) of this section and the credit or refund of any overpayment for the taxable years to which such election applies is not prevented on September 2, 1964, by the operation of any law or rule of law, the period within which a claim for credit or refund of an overpayment for such taxable years may be filed shall, to the extent such overpayment is attributable to the application of section 1038, not expire prior to one year after the date on which such election is made.

(d) *Payment of interest for period prior to September 2, 1964.* No interest shall be payable with respect to any deficiency attributable to the application of the provisions of section 1038, and no interest shall be allowed with respect to any credit or refund of any overpayment attributable to the application of such section, for any period prior to September 2, 1964. See section 2(c)(3) of the Act of September 2, 1964 (Public Law 88-570, 78 Stat. 856). [Reg. § 1.1038-3.]

☐ [T.D. 6916, 4-12-67.]

[Reg. § 1.1039-1]

§ 1.1039-1. **Certain sales of low-income housing projects.**—(a) *Nonrecognition of gain.* Section 1039 provides rules under which the taxpayer may elect not to recognize gain in certain cases where a qualified housing project is sold or disposed of after October 9, 1969, in an approved disposition and another such qualified housing project or projects (referred to as the "replacement project") is acquired, constructed, or reconstructed within a specified reinvestment period. If the requirements of section 1039 are met, and if the taxpayer makes an election in accordance with the provisions of paragraph (b)(4) of this section, then the gain realized upon the sale or disposition is recognized only to the extent that the net amount realized on such sale or disposition exceeds the cost of the replacement project. However, notwithstanding section 1039, gain may be recognized by reason of the application of section 1245 or 1250 to the sale or disposition. (See § 1.1245-6(b) and § 1.1250-3(h).) The terms

Reg. § 1.1039-1(a)

"qualified housing project," "approved disposition," "reinvestment period," and "net amount realized" are defined in paragraph (c) of this section.

(b) *Rules of application*—(1) *In general.* The election under section 1039 (a) may be made only by the taxpayer owning the qualified housing project disposed of. Thus, if the qualified housing project disposed of is owned by a partnership, the partnership must make the election. (See section 703(b).) Similarly, if the qualified housing project disposed of is owned by a corporation or trust, the corporation or trust must make the election. In addition, the reinvestment of the taxpayer must be in such a manner that the taxpayer would be entitled to a deduction for depreciation on the replacement project. Thus, if the qualified housing project disposed of is owned by individual A, the purchase by A of stock in a corporation owning or constructing such a project or of an interest in a partnership owning or constructing such a project will not be considered as the purchase or construction by A of such a project.

(2) *Special rules.* (i) The cost of a replacement project acquired before the approved disposition of a qualified housing project shall be taken into account under section 1039 only if such property is held by the taxpayer on the date of the approved disposition.

(ii) Except as provided in section 1039(d), no property acquired by the taxpayer shall be taken into account for purposes of section 1039(a)(2) unless the unadjusted basis of such property is its cost within the meaning of section 1012. For example, if a qualified housing project is acquired in an exchange under section 1031, relating to exchange of property held for productive use or investment, such property will not be taken into account under section 1039(a)(2) because its basis is determined by reference to the basis of the property exchanged. (See section 1031(d).)

(3) *Cost of replacement project.* The taxpayer's cost for the replacement project includes only amounts properly treated as capital expenditures by the taxpayer that are attributable to acquisition, construction, or reconstruction made within the reinvestment period (as defined in paragraph (c)(4) of this section). See section 263 for rules as to what constitutes capital expenditures. Thus, assume that a calendar year taxpayer realizes gain in 1970 upon the approved disposition of a qualified housing project occurring on January 1, 1970. If the taxpayer had begun construction of another qualified housing project on January 1, 1969, and completes such construction on June 1, 1972, only that portion of the cost attributable to the period before January 1, 1972, constitutes the cost of the replacement project for purposes of section 1039. For purposes of determining the cost of a replacement project attributable to a particular period, the total cost of the project may be allocated to such period on the basis of the portion of the total project actually constructed during such period.

(4) *Election.* (i) An election not to recognize the gain realized upon an approved disposition of a qualified housing project to the extent provided in section 1039(a) may be made by attaching a statement to the income tax return filed for the first taxable year in which any portion of the gain on such disposition is realized. Such a statement shall contain the information required by subdivision (iii) of this subparagraph. If the taxpayer does not file such a statement for the first taxable year in which any portion of the gain is realized, but fails to report a portion of the gain realized upon the approved disposition as income for such year or for any subsequent taxable year, then an election shall be deemed to be made under section 1039(a) with respect to that portion of the gain not reported as income.

(ii) An election may be made under section 1039(a) even though the replacement project has not been acquired or constructed at the time of election. However, if an election has been made and *(a)* a replacement project is not constructed, reconstructed, or acquired, *(b)* the cost of the replacement project is lower than the net amount realized from the approved disposition, or *(c)* a decision is made not to construct, reconstruct, or acquire a replacement project, then the tax liability for the year or years for which the election was made shall be recomputed and an amended return filed. An election may be made even though the taxpayer has filed his return and recognized gain upon the disposition provided that the period of limitation on filing claims for credit or refund prescribed by section 6511 has not expired. In such case, a statement containing the information required by subdivision (iii) of this subparagraph should be filed together with a claim for credit or refund for the taxable year or years in which gain was recognized.

(iii) The statement referred to in subdivisions (i) and (ii) of this subparagraph shall contain the following information:

(a) The date of the approved disposition;

(b) If a replacement project has been acquired, the date of acquisition and cost of the project;

(c) If a replacement project has been constructed or reconstructed by or for the taxpayer, the date construction was begun, the date

Reg. § 1.1039-1(b)(4)

construction was completed, and the percentage of construction completed within the reinvestment period;

(d) If no replacement project has been constructed, reconstructed, or acquired prior to the time of filing of the statement, the estimated cost of such construction, reconstruction, or acquisition;

(e) The adjusted basis of the project disposed of; and

(f) The amount realized upon the approved disposition and a description of the expenses directly connected with the disposition and the taxes (other than income taxes) attributable to the disposition.

(c) *Definitions*—(1) *General.* The definitions contained in subparagraphs (2) through (5) of this paragraph shall apply for purposes of this section.

(2) *Qualified housing project.* The term "qualified housing project" means a rental or cooperative housing project for lower income families that has been constructed, reconstructed, or rehabilitated pursuant to a mortgage which is insured under section 221(d)(3) or 236 of the National Housing Act, provided that with respect to the housing project disposed of and the replacement project constructed, reconstructed, or acquired, the owner of the project at the time of the approved disposition and prior to the close of the reinvestment period is, under such sections or regulations issued thereunder,

(i) Limited as to rate of return on his investment in the project, and

(ii) Limited as to rentals or occupancy charges for units in the project.

If the owner of the project is organized and operated as a nonprofit cooperative or other nonprofit organization, then such owner shall be considered to meet the requirement of subdivision (i) of this subparagraph.

(3) *Approved disposition.* The term "approved disposition" means a sale or other disposition of a qualified housing project to the tenants or occupants of units in such project, or to a nonprofit cooperative or other nonprofit organization formed and operated solely for the benefit of such tenants or occupants, provided that it is approved by the Secretary of Housing and Urban Development or his delegate under section 221(d)(3) or 236 of the National Housing Act or regulations issued under such sections. Evidence of such approval should be attached to the tax return or statement in which the election under section 1039 is made.

(4) *Reinvestment period.* (i) The term "reinvestment period" means the period beginning 1 year before the date of the disposition and ending 1 year after the close of the first taxable year in which any part of the gain from such disposition is realized, or at such later date as may be designated pursuant to an application made by the taxpayer. Such application shall be made before the expiration of 1 year after the close of the first taxable year in which any part of the gain from such disposition is realized, unless the taxpayer can show to the satisfaction of the district director that—

(a) Reasonable cause exists for not having filed the application within the required period, and

(b) The filing of such application was made within a reasonable time after the expiration of the required period.

The application shall contain all the information required by paragraph (b)(4) of this section and shall be made to the district director for the internal revenue district in which the return is filed for the first taxable year in which any of the gain from the approved disposition is realized.

(ii) Ordinarily, requests for extension of the reinvestment period will not be granted until near the end of such period and any extension will usually be limited to a period not exceeding 1 year. Although granting of an extension depends upon the facts and circumstances of a particular case, if a predominant portion of the construction of the replacement project has been completed or is reasonably expected to be completed within the reinvestment period (determined without regard to any extension thereof), an extension of the reinvestment period will ordinarily be granted. The fact that there is a scarcity of replacement property for acquisition will not be considered sufficient grounds for granting an extension.

(5) *Net amount realized.* (i) The "net amount realized" from the approved disposition of a qualified housing project is the amount realized from such disposition, reduced by—

(a) The expenses paid or incurred by the taxpayer which are directly connected with the approved disposition, and

(b) The amount of taxes (other than income taxes) paid or incurred by the taxpayer which are attributable to the approved disposition.

(ii) Examples of expenses directly connected with an approved disposition of a qualified housing project include amounts paid for sales or other commissions, advertising, and for the preparation of a deed or other legal services in connection with the disposition. An amount paid for a repair to the building will be considered as an expense directly connected with the approved disposition under subdivision (i)(a) of this subparagraph only if such repair is required as a condition of sale, or is required by the Secretary of Housing and Urban Development or his delegate as a condition of approval of the disposition.

(iii) *Examples* of taxes that are attributable to the approved disposition include local property transfer taxes and stamp taxes. A local real property tax is not so attributable.

(d) *Basis and holding period of replacement project* —(1) *Basis.* If the taxpayer makes an election under section 1039, the basis of the replacement housing project shall be its cost (including costs incurred subsequent to the reinvestment period) reduced by the amount of gain not recognized under section 1039(a). If the replacement consists of more than one housing project, the basis determined under this subparagraph shall be allocated to the properties in proportion to their respective costs.

(2) *Holding period.* The holding period of the replacement housing project shall begin on the date the taxpayer acquires such project, that is, on the date the taxpayer first acquires possession or control of such project and bears the burdens and enjoys the benefits of ownership of the project. (For special rule regarding the holding period of property for purposes of section 1250, see section 1250(e)(4).)

(e) *Assessment of deficiencies*—(1) *Deficiency attributable to gain.* If a taxpayer makes an election under section 1039(a) with respect to an approved disposition, any deficiency attributable to the gain on such disposition, for any taxable year in which any part of such gain is realized, may be assessed at any time before the expiration of 3 years after the date the district director or director of the regional service center with whom the return for such year has been filed is notified by the taxpayer of the acquisition or the completion of construction or reconstruction of the replacement qualified housing project or of the failure to acquire, construct, or reconstruct a replacement qualified housing project, as the case may be. Such a deficiency may be assessed before the expiration of such 3-year period notwithstanding the provisions of section 6212(c) or the provisions of any other law or rule of law which would otherwise prevent such assessment. If replacement has been made, such notification shall contain the information required by paragraph (b)(4)(iii) of this section. Such notification shall be attached to the return filed for the taxable year or years in which the replacement occurs, or in which the period for the replacement expires, and a copy of such notification shall be filed with the district director or director of regional service center with whom the election under section 1039(a) was required to be filed, if the return is not filed with such director.

(2) *Deficiency attributable to election.* If gain upon an approved disposition is realized in two (or more) taxable years, and the replacement qualified housing project was acquired, constructed, or reconstructed before the beginning of the last such year, any deficiency, for any taxable year before such last year, which is attributable to an election by the taxpayer under section 1039(a) may be assessed at any time before the expiration of the period within which a deficiency for such last taxable year may be assessed, notwithstanding the provisions of section 6212(c) or 6501 or the provisions of any law or rule of law which would otherwise prevent such assessment. Thus, if gain upon an approved disposition is realized in 1971 and 1975, and if a replacement project is purchased in 1971, any deficiency for 1971 may be assessed within the period for assessing a deficiency for 1975. [Reg. § 1.1039-1.]

☐ [T.D. 7191, 6-29-72. Amended by T.D. 7400, 2-3-76.]

[Reg. § 1.1041-1T]

§ 1.1041-1T. **Treatment of transfer of property between spouses or incident to divorce (temporary).—**

Q-1. How is the transfer of property between spouses treated under section 1041?

A-1. Generally, no gain or loss is recognized on a transfer of property from an individual to (or in trust for the benefit of) a spouse or, if the transfer is incident to a divorce, a former spouse. The following questions and answers describe more fully the scope, tax consequences and other rules which apply to transfers of property under section 1041.

(a) *Scope of section 1041 in general.*

Q-2. Does section 1041 apply only to transfers of property incident to divorce?

A-2. No. Section 1041 is not limited to transfers of property incident to divorce. Section 1041 applies to any transfer of property between spouses regardless of whether the transfer is a gift or is a sale or exchange between spouses acting at arm's length (including a transfer in exchange for the relinquishment of property or marital rights or an exchange otherwise governed by another nonrecognition provision of the Code). A divorce or legal separation need not be contemplated between the spouses at the time of the transfer nor must a divorce or legal separation ever occur.

Example (1). A and B are married and file a joint return. A is the sole owner of a condominium unit. A sale or gift of the condominium from A to B is a transfer which is subject to the rules of section 1041.

Example (2). A and B are married and file separate returns. A is the owner of an independent sole proprietorship, X Company. In the ordinary course of business, X Company makes a sale of property to B. This sale is a transfer of property between spouses and is subject to the rules of section 1041.

Example (3). Assume the same facts as in example (2), except that X Company is a corporation wholly owned by A. This sale is not a sale between spouses subject to the rules of section 1041. However, in appropriate circumstances, general tax principles, including the step-transaction doctrine, may be applicable in recharacterizing the transaction.

Q-3. Do the rules of section 1041 apply to a transfer between spouses if the transferee spouse is a nonresident alien?

A-3. No. Gain or loss (if any) is recognized (assuming no other nonrecognition provision applies) at the time of a transfer of property if the property is transferred to a spouse who is a nonresident alien.

Q-4. What kinds of transfers are governed by section 1041?

A-4. Only transfers of property (whether real or personal, tangible or intangible) are governed by section 1041. Transfers of services are not subject to the rules of section 1041.

Q-5. Must the property transferred to a former spouse have been owned by the transferor spouse during the marriage?

A-5. No. A transfer of property acquired after the marriage ceases may be governed by section 1041.

(b) *Transfer incident to the divorce.*

Q-6. What is a transfer of property "incident to the divorce"?

A-6. A transfer of property is "incident to the divorce" in either of the following 2 circumstances—

(1) the transfer occurs not more than one year after the date on which the marriage ceases, or

(2) the transfer is related to the cessation of the marriage.

Thus, a transfer of property occurring not more than one year after the date on which the marriage ceases need not be related to the cessation of the marriage to qualify for section 1041 treatment. (See A-7 for transfers occurring more than one year after the cessation of the marriage.)

Q-7. When is a transfer of property "related to the cessation of the marriage"?

A-7. A transfer of property is treated as related to the cessation of the marriage if the transfer is pursuant to a divorce or separation instrument, as defined in section 71(b)(2), and the transfer occurs not more than 6 years after the date on which the marriage ceases. A divorce or separation instrument includes a modification or amendment to such decree or instrument. Any transfer not pursuant to a divorce or separation instrument and any transfer occurring more than 6 years after the cessation of the marriage is presumed to be not related to the cessation of the marriage. This presumption may be rebutted only by showing that the transfer was made to effect the division of property owned by the former spouses at the time of the cessation of the marriage. For example, the presumption may be rebutted by showing that (a) the transfer was not made within the one- and six-year periods described above because of factors which hampered an earlier transfer of the property, such as legal or business impediments to transfer or disputes concerning the value of the property owned at the time of the cessation of the marriage, and (b) the transfer is effected promptly after the impediment to transfer is removed.

Q-8. Do annulments and the cessations of marriages that are void *ab initio* due to violations of state law constitute divorces for purposes of section 1041?

A-8. Yes.

(c) *Transfers on behalf of a spouse.*

Q-9. May transfers of property to third parties on behalf of a spouse (or former spouse) qualify under section 1041?

A-9. Yes. There are three situations in which a transfer of property to a third party on behalf of a spouse (or former spouse) will qualify under section 1041, provided all other requirements of the section are satisfied. The first situation is where the transfer to the third party is required by a divorce or separation instrument. The second situation is where the transfer to the third party is pursuant to the written request of the other spouse (or former spouse). The third situation is where the transferor receives from the other spouse (or former spouse) a written consent or ratification of the transfer to the third party. Such consent or ratification must state that the parties intend the transfer to be treated as a transfer to the nontransferring spouse (or former spouse) subject to the rules of section 1041 and must be received by the transferor prior to the date of filing of the transferor's first return of tax for the taxable year in which the transfer was

Reg. § 1.1041-1T(b)

made. In the three situations described above, the transfer of property will be treated as made directly to the nontransferring spouse (or former spouse) and the nontransferring spouse will be treated as immediately transferring the property to the third party. The deemed transfer from the nontransferring spouse (or former spouse) to the third party is not a transaction that qualifies for nonrecognition of gain under section 1041.

(d) *Tax consequences of transfers subject to section 1041.*

Q-10. How is the transferor of property under section 1041 treated for income tax purposes?

A-10. The transferor of property under section 1041 recognizes no gain or loss on the transfer even if the transfer was in exchange for the release of marital rights or other consideration. This rule applies regardless of whether the transfer is of property separately owned by the transferor or is a division (equal or unequal) of community property. Thus, the result under section 1041 differs from the result in *United States v. Davis*, 370 U.S. 65 (1962).

Q-11. How is the transferee of property under section 1041 treated for income tax purposes?

A-11. The transferee of property under section 1041 recognizes no gain or loss upon receipt of the transferred property. In all cases, the basis of the transferred property in the hands of the transferee is the adjusted basis of such property in the hands of the transferor immediately before the transfer. Even if the transfer is a bona fide sale, the transferee does not acquire a basis in the transferred property equal to the transferee's cost (the fair market value). This carryover basis rule applies whether the adjusted basis of the transferred property is less than, equal to, or greater than its fair market value at the time of transfer (or the value of any consideration provided by the transferee) and applies for purposes of determining loss as well as gain upon the subsequent disposition of the property by the transferee. Thus, this rule is different from the rule applied in section 1015(a) for determining the basis of property acquired by gift.

Q-12. Do the rules described in A-10 and A-11 apply even if the transferred property is subject to liabilities which exceed the adjusted basis of the property?

A-12. Yes. For example, assume A owns property having a fair market value of $10,000 and an adjusted basis of $1,000. In contemplation of making a transfer of this property incident to a divorce from B, A borrows $5,000 from a bank, using the property as security for the borrowing. A then transfers the property to B and B assumes, or takes the property subject to, the liability to pay the $5,000 debt. Under section 1041, A recognizes no gain or loss upon the transfer of the property, and the adjusted basis of the property in the hands of B is $1,000.

Q-13. Will a transfer under section 1041 result in a recapture of investment tax credits with respect to the property transferred?

A-13. In general, no. Property transferred under section 1041 will not be treated as being disposed of by, or ceasing to be section 38 property with respect to, the transferor. However, the transferee will be subject to investment tax credit recapture if, upon or after transfer, the property is disposed of by, or ceases to be section 38 property with respect to, the transferee. For example, as part of a divorce property settlement, B receives a car from A that has been used in A's business for two years and for which an investment tax credit was taken by A. No part of A's business is transferred to B and B's use of the car is solely personal. B is subject to recapture of the investment tax credit previously taken by A.

(e) *Notice and recordkeeping requirement with respect to transactions under section 1041.*

Q-14. Does the transferor of property in a transaction described in section 1041 have to supply, at the time of the transfer, the transferee with records sufficient to determine the adjusted basis and holding period of the property at the time of the transfer and (if applicable) with notice that the property transferred under section 1041 is potentially subject to recapture of the investment tax credit?

A-14. Yes. A transferor of property under section 1041 must, at the time of the transfer, supply the transferee with records sufficient to determine the adjusted basis and holding period of the property as of the date of the transfer. In addition, in the case of a transfer of property which carries with it a potential liability for investment tax credit recapture, the transferor must, at the time of the transfer, supply the transferee with records sufficient to determine the amount and period of such potential liability. Such records must be preserved and kept accessible by the transferee.

(f) *Property settlements—effective dates, transitional periods and elections.*

Q-15. When does section 1041 become effective?

A-15. Generally, section 1041 applies to all transfers after July 18, 1984. However, it does not apply to transfers after July 18, 1984 pursuant to instruments in effect on or before July 18, 1984. (See A-16 with respect to exceptions to the general rule.)

Q-16. Are there any exceptions to the general rule stated in A-15 above?

Reg. § 1.1041-1T(f)

A-16. Yes. Two transitional rules provide exceptions to the general rule stated in A-15. First, section 1041 will apply to transfers after July 18, 1984 under instruments that were in effect on or before July 18, 1984 if both spouses (or former spouses) elect to have section 1041 apply to such transfers. Second, section 1041 will apply to all transfers after December 31, 1983 (including transfers under instruments in effect on or before July 18, 1984) if both spouses (or former spouses) elect to have section 1041 apply. (See A-18 relating to the time and manner of making the elections under the first or second transitional rule.)

Q-17. Can an election be made to have section 1041 apply to some, but not all, transfers made after December 31, 1983, or to some, but not all, transfers made after July 18, 1984 under instruments in effect on or before July 18, 1984?

A-17. No. Partial elections are not allowed. An election under either of the two elective transitional rules applies to all transfers governed by that election whether before or after the election is made, and is irrevocable.

(g) *Property settlements—time and manner of making the elections under section 1041.*

Q-18. How do spouses (or former spouses) elect to have section 1041 apply to transfers after December 31, 1983, or to transfers after July 18, 1984 under instruments in effect on or before July 18, 1984?

A-18. In order to make an election under section 1041 for property transfers after December 31, 1983, or property transfers under instruments that were in effect on or before July 18, 1984, both spouses (or former spouses) must elect the application of the rules of section 1041 by attaching to the transferor's first filed income tax return for the taxable year in which the first transfer occurs, a statement signed by both spouses (or former spouses) which includes each spouse's social security number and is in substantially the form set forth at the end of this answer.

In addition, the transferor must attach a copy of such statement to his or her return for each subsequent taxable year in which a transfer is made that is governed by the transitional election. A copy of the signed statement must be kept by both parties.

The election statements shall be in substantially the following form:

In the case of an election regarding transfers after 1983:

Section 1041 Election

The undersigned hereby elect to have the provisions of section 1041 of the Internal Revenue Code apply to all qualifying transfers of property after December 31, 1983. The undersigned understand that section 1041 applies to all property transferred between spouses, or former spouses incident to divorce. The parties further understand that the effects for Federal income tax purposes of having section 1041 apply are that (1) no gain or loss is recognized by the transferor spouse or former spouse as a result of this transfer; and (2) the basis of the transferred property in the hands of the transferee is the adjusted basis of the property in the hands of the transferor immediately before the transfer, whether or not the adjusted basis of the transferred property is less than, equal to, or greater than its fair market value at the time of the transfer. The undersigned understand that if the transferee spouse or former spouse disposes of the property in a transaction in which gain is recognized, the amount of gain which is taxable may be larger than it would have been if this election had not been made.

In the case of an election regarding preexisting decrees:

Section 1041 Election

The undersigned hereby elect to have the provisions of section 1041 of the Internal Revenue Code apply to all qualifying transfers of property after July 18, 1984 under any instrument in effect on or before July 18, 1984. The undersigned understand that section 1041 applies to all property transferred between spouses, or former spouses incident to the divorce. The parties further understand that the effects for Federal income tax purposes of having section 1041 apply are that (1) no gain or loss is recognized by the transferor spouse or former spouse as a result of this transfer; and (2) the basis of the transferred property in the hands of the transferee is the adjusted basis of the property in the hands of the transferor immediately before the transfer, whether or not the adjusted basis of the transferred property is less than, equal to, or greater than its fair market value at the time of the transfer. The undersigned understand that if the transferee spouse or former spouse disposes of the property in a transaction in which gain is recognized, the amount of gain which is taxable may be larger than it would have been if this election had not been made. [Temp. Reg. § 1.1041-1T.]

☐ [*T.D.* 7973, 8-30-84.]

[Reg. § 1.1042-1T]

§ 1.1042-1T. **Questions and answers relating to the sales of stock to employee stock ownership plans or certain cooperatives (Temporary).—**

Q-1: What does section 1042 provide?

A-1: (a) Section 1042 provides rules under which a taxpayer may elect not to recognize gain in certain cases where "qualified securities" are sold to a qualifying employee stock ownership plan or worker-owned cooperative in taxable years of the seller beginning after July 18, 1984, and "qualified replacement property" is purchased by the taxpayer within the "replacement period." If the requirements of Q&A-2 of this section are met, and if the taxpayer makes an election under section 1042(a) in accordance with Q&A-3 of this section, the gain realized by the taxpayer on the sale of the qualified securities is recognized only to the extent that the amount realized on such sale exceeds the cost to the taxpayer of the qualified replacement property.

(b) Under section 1042, the term "qualified securities" means employer securities (as defined in section 409(l)) with respect to which each of the following requirements is satisfied: (1) the employer securities were issued by a domestic corporation; (2) for at least one year before and immediately after the sale, the domestic corporation that issued the employer securities (and each corporation that is a member of a "controlled group of corporations" with such corporation for purposes of section 409(l)) has no stock outstanding that is readily tradable on an established market; (3) as of the time of the sale, the employer securities have been held by the taxpayer for more than 1 year; and (4) the employer securities were not received by the taxpayer in a distribution from a plan described in section 401(a) or in a transfer pursuant to an option or other right to acquire stock to which section 83, 422, 422A, 423, or 424 applies.

(c) The term "replacement period" means the period which begins 3 months before the date on which the sale of qualified securities occurs and which ends 12 months after the date of such sale. A replacement period may include any period which occurs prior to July 19, 1984.

(d) The term "qualified replacement property" means any securities (as defined in section 165(g)(2)) issued by a domestic corporation which does not, for the taxable year of such corporation in which the securities are purchased by the taxpayer, have passive investment income (as defined in section 1362(d)(3)(D)) that exceeds 25 percent of the gross receipts of such corporation for the taxable year preceding the taxable year of purchase. In addition, securities of the domestic corporation that issued the employer securities qualifying under section 1042 (and of any corporation that is a member of a "controlled group of corporations" with such corporation for purposes of section 409(l)) will not qualify as "qualified replacement property."

(e) For purposes of section 1042(a), there is a "purchase" of qualified replacement property only if the basis of such property is determined by reference to its cost to the taxpayer. If the basis of the qualified replacement property is determined by reference to its basis in the hands of the transferor thereof or another person, or by reference to the basis of property (other than cash or its equivalent) exchanged for such property, then the basis of such property is not determined solely by reference to its cost to the taxpayer.

Q-2: What is a sale of qualified securities for purposes of section 1042(b)?

A-2: (a) Under section 1042(b), a sale of qualified securities is one under which all of the following requirements are met:

(1) The qualified securities are sold to an employee stock ownership plan (as defined in section 4975(e)(7)) maintained by the corporation that issued the qualified securities (or by a member of the "controlled group of corporations" with such corporation for purposes of section 409(l)) or to an eligible worker-owned cooperative (as defined in section 1042(c)(2));

(2) The employee stock ownership plan or eligible worker-owned cooperative owns, immediately after the sale, 30 percent or more of the total value of the employer securities (within the meaning of section 409(l)) outstanding as of such time;

(3) No portion of the assets of the employee stock ownership plan or eligible worker-owned cooperative attributable to qualified securities that are sold to the plan or cooperative by the taxpayer or by any other person in a sale with respect to which an election under section 1042(a) is made accrue under the plan or are allocated by the cooperative, either directly or indirectly and either concurrently with or at any time thereafter, for the benefit of (i) the taxpayer; (ii) any person who is a member of the family of the taxpayer (within the meaning of section 267(c)(4)); or (iii) any person who owns (after the application of section 318(a)), at any time after July 18, 1984, and until immediately after the sale, more than 25 percent of in value of the outstanding portion of any class of stock of the corporation that issued the qualified securities (or of any member of the "controlled group of corporations" with such corporation for purposes of section 409(l)). For purposes of this calculation, stock that is owned, directly or indirectly, by or for a qualified plan shall not be treated as outstanding.

(4) The taxpayer files with the Secretary (as part of the required election described in Q&A-3

Reg. § 1.1042-1T

of this section) a verified written statement of the domestic corporation (or corporations) whose employees are covered by the plan acquiring the qualified securities or of any authorized officer of the eligible worker-owned cooperative, consenting to the application of section 4978(a) with respect to such corporation or cooperative.

(b) For purposes of determining whether paragraph (a)(2) above is satisfied, sales of qualified securities by two or more taxpayers may be treated as a single sale if such sales are made as part of a single, integrated transaction under a prearranged agreement between the taxpayers.

(c) For purposes of determining whether paragraph (a)(3) above is satisfied with respect to the prohibition against an accrual or allocation of qualified securities, the accrual or allocation of any benefits or contributions or other assets that are not attributable to qualified securities sold to the employee stock ownership plan or eligible worker-owned cooperative in a sale with respect to which an election under section 1042(a) is made (including any accrual or allocation under any other plan or arrangement maintained by the corporation or any member of the "the controlled group of corporations" with such corporation for purposes of section 409(l)) must be made without regard to the allocation of such qualified securities. Paragraph (a)(3) above may be illustrated in part by the following example: Individuals A, B, and C own 50, 25, and 25, respectively, of the 100 outstanding shares of common stock of Corporation X. Such shares constitute qualified securities as defined in Q&A-1 of this section. A and B, but not C, are employees of Corporation X. For the benefit of all its employees, Corporation X establishes an employee stock ownership plan that obtains a loan meeting the exemption requirements of section 4975(d)(3). The loan proceeds are used by the plan to purchase the 100 shares of qualified securities from A, B, and C, all of whom elect nonrecognition treatment under section 1042(a) with respect to the gain realized on their sale of such securities. Under the requirements of paragraph (a)(3) above, no part of the assets of the plan attributable to the 100 shares of qualified securities may accrue under the plan (or under any other plan or arrangement maintained by Corporation X) for the benefit of A or B or any person who is a member of the family of A or B (as determined under section 267(c)(4)). Furthermore, no other assets of the plan or assets of the employer may accrue for the benefit of such individuals in lieu of the receipt of assets attributable to such qualified securities.

(d) A sale under section 1042(a) shall not include any sale of securities by a dealer or underwriter in the ordinary course of its trade or business as a dealer or underwriter, whether or not guaranteed.

Q-3: What is the time and manner for making the election under section 1042(a)?

A-3: (a) The election not to recognize the gain realized upon the sale of qualified securities to the extent provided under section 1042(a) shall be made in a "statement of election" attached to the taxpayer's income tax return filed on or before the due date (including extensions of time) for the taxable year in which the sale occurs. If a taxpayer does not make a timely election under this section to obtain section 1042(a) nonrecognition treatment with respect to the sale of qualified securities, it may not subsequently make an election on an amended return or otherwise. Also, an election once made is irrevocable.

(b) The statement of election shall provide that the taxpayer elects to treat the sale of securities as a sale of qualified securities under section 1042(a), and shall contain the following information:

(1) A description of the qualified securities sold, including the type and number of shares;

(2) The date of the sale of the qualified securities;

(3) The adjusted basis of the qualified securities;

(4) The amount realized upon the sale of the qualified securities;

(5) The identity of the employee stock ownership plan or eligible worker-owned cooperative to which the qualified securities were sold; and

(6) If the sale was part of a single, interrelated transaction under a prearranged agreement between taxpayers involving other sales of qualified securities, the names and taxpayer identification numbers of the other taxpayers under the agreement and the number of shares sold by the other taxpayers. See Q&A-2 of this section.

If the taxpayer has purchased qualified replacement property at the time of the election, the taxpayer must attach as part of the statement of election a "statement of purchase" describing the qualified replacement property, the date of the purchase, and the cost of the property, and declaring such property to be the qualifed replacement property with respect to the sale of qualified securities. Such statement of purchase must be notarized by the later of thirty days after the purchase or March 6, 1986. In addition, the statement of election must be accompanied by the verified written statement of consent required under Q&A-2 of this section with respect to the qualified securities sold.

Reg. § 1.1042-1T

(c) If the taxpayer has not purchased qualified replacement property at the time of the filing of the statement of election, a timely election under this Q&A shall not be considered to have been made unless the taxpayer attaches the notarized statement of purchase described above to the taxpayer's income tax return filed for the taxable year following the year for which the election under section 1042(a) was made. Such notarized statement of purchase shall be filed with the district director or the director of the regional service center with whom such election was originally filed, if the return is not filed with such director.

Q-4: What is the basis of qualified replacement property?

A-4: If a taxpayer makes an election under section 1042(a), the basis of the qualified replacement property purchased by the taxpayer during the replacement period shall be reduced by an amount equal to the amount of gain which was not recognized. If more than one item of qualified replacement property is purchased, the basis of each of such items shall be reduced by an amount determined by multiplying the total gain not recognized by reason of the application of section 1042(a) by a fraction, the numerator of which is the cost of such item of property and the denominator of which is the total cost of all such items of property. For the rule regarding the holding period of qualified replacement property, see section 1223(13).

Q-5: What is the statute of limitations for the assessment of a deficiency relating to the gain on the sale of qualified securities?

A-5: (a) If any gain is realized by the taxpayer on the sale of any qualified securities and such gain has not been recognized under section 1042(a) in accordance with the requirements of this section, the statutory period provided in section 6501(a) for the assessment of any deficiency with respect to such gain shall not expire prior to the expiration of 3 years from the date of receipt, by the district director or director of the regional service center with whom the statement of election under 1042(a) was originally filed, of:

(1) a notarized statement of purchase as described in Q&A-3;

(2) a written statement of the taxpayer's intention not to purchase qualified replacement property within the replacement period; or

(3) a written statement of the taxpayer's failure to purchase qualified replacement property within the replacement period.

In those situations when a taxpayer is providing a written statement of an intention not to purchase or of a failure to purchase qualified replacement property, the statement shall be accompanied, where appropriate, by an amended return for the taxable year in which the gain from the sale of the qualified securities was realized, in order to reflect the inclusion in gross income for that year of gain required to be recognized in connection with such sale.

(b) Any gain from the sale of qualified securities which is required to be recognized due to a failure to meet the requirements under section 1042 shall be included in the gross income for the taxable year in which the gain was realized. If any gain from the sale of qualified securities is not recognized under section 1042(a) in accordance with the requirements of this section, any deficiency attributable to any portion of such gain may be assessed at any time before the expiration of the 3-year period described in this Q&A, notwithstanding the provision of any law or rule of law which would otherwise prevent such assessment.

Q-6: When does section 1042 become effective?

A-6: Section 1042 applies to sales of qualified securities in taxable years of sellers beginning after July 18, 1984. [Temporary Reg. § 1.1042-1T.]

☐ [T.D. 8073, 1-29-86.]

[Reg. § 1.1044(a)-1]

§ 1.1044(a)-1. Time and manner for making election under the Omnibus Budget Reconciliation Act of 1993.—(a) *Description.* Section 1044(a), as added by section 13114 of the Omnibus Budget Reconciliation Act of 1993 (Public Law 10366, 107 Stat. 430), generally allows individuals and C corporations that sell publicly traded securities after August 9, 1993, to elect not to recognize certain gain from the sale if the taxpayer purchases common stock or a partnership interest in a specialized small business investment company (SSBIC) within the 60-day period beginning on the date the publicly traded securities are sold.

(b) *Time and manner for making the election.* The election under section 1044(a) must be made on or before the due date (including extensions) for the income tax return for the year in which the publicly traded securities are sold. The election is to be made by reporting the entire gain from the sale of publicly traded securities on Schedule D of the income tax return in accordance with instructions for Schedule D, and by attaching a statement to Schedule D showing—

(1) How the nonrecognized gain was calculated;

(2) The SSBIC in which common stock or a partnership interest was purchased;

Special Rules

(3) The date the SSBIC stock or partnership interest was purchased; and

(4) The basis of the SSBIC stock or partnership interest.

(c) *Revocability of election.* The election described in this section is revocable with the consent of the Commissioner.

(d) *Effective date.* The rules set forth in this section are effective December 12, 1996. [Reg. § 1.1044(a)-1.]

☐ [T.D. 8688, 12-11-96.]

Special Rules

[Reg. § 1.1051-1]

§ 1.1051-1. **Basis of property acquired during affiliation.**—(a)(1) The basis of property acquired by a corporation during a period of affiliation from a corporation with which it was affiliated shall be the same as it would be in the hands of the corporation from which acquired. This rule is applicable if the basis of the property is material in determining tax liability for any year, whether a separate return or a consolidated return is made in respect of such year. For the purpose of this section, the term "period of affiliation" means the period during which such corporations were affiliated (determined in accordance with the law applicable thereto), but does not include any taxable year beginning on or after January 1, 1922, unless a consolidated return was made, nor any taxable year after the taxable year 1928.

(2) The application of subparagraph (1) of this paragraph may be illustrated by the following example:

Example. The X Corporation, the Y Corporation, and the Z Corporation were affiliated for the taxable year 1920. During that year the X Corporation transferred assets to the Y Corporation for $120,000 cash, and the Y Corporation in turn transferred the assets during the same year to the Z Corporation for $130,000 cash. The assets were acquired by the X Corporation in 1916 at a cost of $100,000. The basis of the assets in the hands of the Z Corporation is $100,000.

(b) The basis of property acquired by a corporation during any period, in the taxable year 1929 or any subsequent taxable year, in respect of which a consolidated return was made or was required under the regulations governing the making of consolidated returns, shall be determined in accordance with such regulations. The basis in the case of property held by a corporation during any period, in the taxable year 1929 or any subsequent taxable year, in respect of which a consolidated return is made or is required under the regulations governing the making of consolidated returns, shall be adjusted in respect of any items relating to such period in accordance with such regulations.

(c) Except as otherwise provided in the regulations promulgated under section 141 of the Internal Revenue Code of 1939 or the Revenue Acts of section 1502 of the Internal Revenue Code of 1954 or the regulations under 1938 (52 Stat. 447), 1936 (49 Stat. 1652), 1934 (48 Stat. 683), 1932 (47 Stat. 169), or 1928 (45 Stat. 791), the basis of property after a consolidated return period shall be the same as the basis immediately prior to the close of such period. [Reg. § 1.1051-1.]

☐ [T.D. 6178, 6-1-56.]

[Reg. § 1.1052-1]

§ 1.1052-1. **Basis of property established by Revenue Act of 1932.**—Section 1052(a) provides that if property was acquired after February 28, 1913, in any taxable year beginning before January 1, 1934, and the basis of the property, for the purposes of the Revenue Act of 1932 (47 Stat. 169), was prescribed by section 113(a)(6), (7), or (9) of that Act, then for purposes of subtitle A of the Code, the basis shall be the same as the basis prescribed in the Revenue Act of 1932. For the rules applicable in determining the basis of stocks or securities under section 113(a)(9) of the Revenue Act of 1932 in case of certain distributions after December 31, 1923, and in any taxable year beginning before January 1, 1934, see 26 CFR (1939) 39.113(a)(12)-1 (Regulations 118). [Reg. § 1.1052-1.]

☐ [T.D. 6178, 6-1-56.]

[Reg. § 1.1052-2]

§ 1.1052-2. **Basis of property established by Revenue Act of 1934.**—Section 1052(b) provides that if property was acquired after February 28, 1913, in any taxable year beginning before January 1, 1936, and the basis of the property for the purposes of the Revenue Act of 1934 (48 Stat. 683) was prescribed by section 113(a)(6), (7), or (8) of that Act, then for purposes of subtitle A of the Code the basis shall be the same as the basis prescribed in the Revenue Act of 1934. For example, if after December 31, 1920, and in any taxable year beginning before January 1, 1936, property was acquired by a corporation by the issuance of its stock or securities in connection with a transaction which is not described in section 112(b)(5) of the Internal Revenue Code of 1939 but which is described in section 112(b)(5) of the Revenue Act of 1934, the basis of the property so acquired shall be the same as it would be in the hands of the transferor, with proper adjustments to the date of the exchange. [Reg. § 1.1052-2.]

☐ [T.D. 6178, 6-1-56.]

[Reg. § 1.1052-3]

§ 1.1052-3. Basis of property established by the Internal Revenue Code of 1939.—Section 1052(c) provides that if property was acquired after February 28, 1913, in a transaction to which the Internal Revenue Code of 1939 applied and the basis thereof was prescribed by section 113(a)(6), (7), (8), (13), (15), (18), (19) or (23) of such code, then for purposes of subtitle A the basis shall be the same as the basis prescribed in the Internal Revenue Code of 1939. In such cases see section 113(a) of the Internal Revenue Code of 1939 and the regulations thereunder. [Reg. § 1.1052-3.]

☐ [T.D. 6178, 6-1-56.]

[Reg. § 1.1053-1]

§ 1.1053-1. Property acquired before March 1, 1913.—(a) *Basis for determining gain.* In the case of property acquired before March 1, 1913, the basis as of March 1, 1913, for determining gain is the cost or other basis, adjusted as provided in section 1016 and other applicable provisions of chapter 1 of the Code, or its fair market value as of March 1, 1913, whichever is greater.

(b) *Basis for determining loss.* In the case of property acquired before March 1, 1913, the basis as of March 1, 1913, for determining loss is the basis determined in accordance with part II (section 1011 and following), subchapter O, chapter 1 of the Code, or other applicable provisions of chapter 1 of the Code, without reference to the fair market value as of March 1, 1913.

(c) *Example.* The application of paragraphs (a) and (b) of this section may be illustrated by the following example:

Example. (i) On March 1, 1908, a taxpayer purchased for $100,000, property having a useful life of 50 years. Assuming that there were no capital improvements to the property, the depreciation sustained on the property before March 1, 1913, was $10,000 (5 years @ $2,000), so that the original cost adjusted, as of March 1, 1913, for depreciation sustained prior to that date is $90,000. On that date the property had a fair market value of $94,500 with a remaining life of 45 years.

(ii) For the purpose of determining gain from the sale or other disposition of the property on March 1, 1954, the basis of the property is the fair market value of $94,500 as of March 1, 1913, adjusted for depreciation allowed or allowable after February 28, 1913, computed on $94,500. Thus, the substituted basis, $94,500, is reduced by the depreciation adjustment from March 1, 1913, to February 28, 1954, in the aggregate of $86,100 (41 years @ $2,100), leaving an adjusted basis for determining gain of $8,400 ($94,500 less $86,100).

(iii) For the purpose of determining loss from the sale or other disposition of such property on March 1, 1954, the basis of the property is its cost, adjusted for depreciation sustained before March 1, 1913, computed on cost, and the amount of depreciation allowed or allowable after February 28, 1913, computed on the fair market value of $94,500 as of March 1, 1913. In this example, the amount of depreciation sustained before March 1, 1913, is $10,000 and the amount of depreciation determined for the period after February 28, 1913, is $86,100. Therefore, the aggregate amount of depreciation for which the cost ($100,000) should be adjusted is $96,100 ($10,000 plus $86,100), and the adjusted basis for determining loss on March 1, 1954, is $3,900 ($100,000 less $96,100).

(d) *Fair market value.* The determination of the fair market value of property on March 1, 1913, is generally a question of fact and shall be established by competent evidence. In determining the fair market value of stock or other securities, due regard shall be given to the fair market value of the corporate assets as of such date, and other pertinent factors. In the case of property traded in on public exchanges, actual sales on or near the basic date afford evidence of value. In general, the fair market value of a block or aggregate of a particular kind of property is not to be determined by a forced-sale price, or by an estimate of what a whole block or aggregate would bring if placed upon the market at one and the same time. In such a case the value should be determined by ascertaining as the basis the fair market value of each unit of the property. All relevant facts and elements of value as of the basic date should be considered in each case. [Reg. § 1.1053-1.]

☐ [T.D. 6178, 6-1-56.]

[Reg. § 1.1054-1]

§ 1.1054-1. Certain Stock of Federal National Mortgage Association.—(a) *In general.* The basis in the hands of the initial holder of a share of stock which is issued pursuant to section 303(c) of the Federal National Mortgage Association Charter Act (12 U.S.C., sec. 1718) in a taxable year beginning after December 31, 1959, shall

Reg. § 1.1054-1(a)

be an amount equal to the issuance price of the stock reduced by the amount, if any, required by section 162(d) to be treated (with respect to such share) as an ordinary and necessary business expense. See section 162(d) and § 1.162-19. For purposes of this section the initial holder is the original purchaser who is issued stock of the Federal National Mortgage Association (FNMA) pursuant to section 303(c) of the Act and who appears on the books of FNMA as the initial holder. See § 1.162-19.

(b) *Example.* The provisions of this section may be illustrated by the following example:

Example. Pursuant to section 303(c) of the Federal National Mortgage Association Charter Act a certificate of FNMA stock is issued to A as of January 1, 1961. The issuance price of the stock was $100 and the fair market value of the stock on the date of issue was $69. A was required by section 162(d) to treat $31 as a business expense for the year 1961. The basis of the share of stock in the hands of A, the initial holder, shall be $69, the amount paid for the stock ($100) reduced by $31. [Reg. § 1.1054-1.]

☐ [*T.D.* 6690, 11-18-83.]

[Reg. § 1.1055-1]

§ 1.1055-1. **General rule with respect to redeemable ground rents.**—(a) *Character of a redeemable ground rent.* For purposes of subtitle A of the Code (1) a redeemable ground rent (as defined in section 1055(c) and paragraph (b) of this section) shall be treated as being in the nature of a mortgage, and (2) real property held subject to liabilities under such a redeemable ground rent shall be treated as held subject to liabilities under a mortgage. Thus, under section 1055(a) and this paragraph, the transfer of property subject to a redeemable ground rent has the same effect as the transfer of property subject to a mortgage, the acquisition of property subject to a redeemable ground rent is to be treated the same as the acquisition of property subject to a mortgage, and the holding of property subject to a redeemable ground rent is to be treated in the same manner as the holding of property subject to a mortgage. See section 163(c) for the treatment of any annual or periodic rental payment under a redeemable ground rent as interest.

(b) *Definition of redeemable ground rent.* For purposes of subtitle A of the Code, the term "redeemable ground rent" means only a ground rent with respect to which all the following conditions are met:

(1) There is a lease of land which is assignable by the lessee without the consent of the lessor.

(2) The term of the lease is for a period in excess of 15 years, taking into account all periods for which the lease may be renewed at the option of the lessee.

(3) The lessee has a present or future right to terminate the lease and to acquire the lessor's interest in the land (*i.e.*, to redeem the ground rent) by the payment of a determined or determinable amount, which amount is referred to in §§ 1.1055-2, 1.1055-3, and 1.1055-4 as a "redemption price". Such right must exist by virtue of State or local law. If the lessee's right to terminate the lease and to acquire the lessor's interest is not granted by State or local law but exists solely by virtue of a private agreement or privately created condition, the ground rent is not a "redeemable ground rent".

(4) The lessor's interest in the land subject to the lease is primarily a security interest to protect the payment to him of the annual or periodic rental payments due under the lease.

(c) *Effective date.* In general, the provisions of section 1055 and paragraph (a) of this section take effect on April 11, 1963, and apply with respect to taxable years ending on or after such date. See § 1.1055-3 for rules for determining the basis of real property acquired subject to liabilities under a redeemable ground rent regardless of when such property was acquired. See also § 1.1055-4 for rules for determining the basis of a redeemable ground rent in the hands of a holder who reserved or created such ground rent in connection with a transfer, occurring before April 11, 1963, of the right to hold real property subject to liabilities under such ground rent. [Reg. § 1.1055-1.]

☐ [*T.D.* 6821, 5-3-65.]

[Reg. § 1.1055-2]

§ 1.1055-2. **Determination of amount realized on the transfer of the right to hold real property subject to liabilities under a redeemable ground rent.**—In determining the amount realized from a transfer, occurring on or after April 11, 1963, of the right to hold real property subject to liabilities under a redeemable ground rent, such ground rent shall be accounted for in the same manner as a mortgage for an amount of money equal to the redemption price of the ground rent. The provisions of this section apply in respect of any such transfer even though such ground rent was created prior to April 11, 1963. For provisions relating to the determination of the amount of and recognition of gain or loss from the sale or other disposition of property, see section 1001 and the regulations thereunder. [Reg. § 1.1055-2.]

☐ [*T.D.* 6821, 5-3-65.]

Reg. § 1.1055-1(a)

Special Rules

See p. 20,601 for regulations not amended to reflect law changes

[Reg. § 1.1055-3]

§ 1.1055-3. Basis of real property held subject to liabilities under a redeemable ground rent.—(a) *In general.* The provisions of section 1055(a) and paragraph (a) of § 1.1055-1 are applicable in determining the basis of real property held on or after April 11, 1963, in any case where the property at the time of acquisition was subject to liabilities under a redeemable ground rent. (See section 1055(b)(2).) Thus, if on or after April 11, 1963, a taxpayer holds real property which was subject to liabilities under a redeemable ground rent at the time he acquired it, the basis of such property in the hands of such taxpayer, regardless of when the property was acquired, will include the redeemable ground rent in the same manner as if it were a mortgage in an amount equal to the redemption price of such ground rent. Likewise, if on or after April 11, 1963, a taxpayer holds real property which was subject to liabilities under a redeemable ground rent at the time he acquired it and which has a substituted basis in his hands, the basis of the property in the hands of the taxpayer's predecessor in interest is to be determined by treating the redeemable ground rent in the same manner as a mortgage in an amount equal to the redemption price of such ground rent.

(b) *Illustrations.* The provisions of this section may be illustrated by the following examples:

Example (1). On April 11, 1963, taxpayer A held residential property which he acquired on January 15, 1963, for a purchase price of $10,000 and which, at the time he acquired it, was subject to a ground rent redeemable for a redemption price of $1,600. A's basis for the property includes the purchase price ($10,000) plus the redeemable ground rent in the same manner as if it were a mortgage for $1,600.

Example (2). In 1962, taxpayer X, a corporation, acquired real property subject to a redeemable ground rent in a transfer to which section 351 (relating to transfer of property to corporation controlled by transferor) applied and in which the basis of the property to X was the transferor's basis. X still held the property on April 11, 1963. The transferor's basis in the property is to be determined by treating the redeemable ground rent to which it was subject in the transferor's hands as if it were a mortgage. [Reg. § 1.1055-3.]

☐ [T.D. 6821, 5-3-65.]

[Reg. § 1.1055-4]

§ 1.1055-4. Basis of redeemable ground rent reserved or created in connection with transfers of real property before April 11, 1963.—(a)

In general. In the case of a redeemable ground rent created or reserved in connection with a transfer, occurring before April 11, 1963, of the right to hold real property subject to liabilities under such ground rent, the basis of such ground rent on or after April 11, 1963, in the hands of the person who reserved or created the ground rent is the amount which was taken into account in respect of such ground rent in computing the amount realized from the transfer of such real property. Thus, if no such amount was taken into account, such basis shall be determined without regard to section 1055. (See section 1055(b)(3).)

(b) The provisions of this section may be illustrated by the following examples:

Example (1). The taxpayer, who was in the business of building houses, purchased an undeveloped lot of land for $500 and built a house thereon at a cost of $10,000. Subsequently, he transferred the right to hold the lot improved by the house for a consideration of $12,000, and an annual ground rent for such property of $120 which was redeemable for a redemption price of $2,000. The taxpayer reported a $2,000 gain on the transfer, treating the amount realized as $12,000 and his cost allocable to the interest transferred as $10,000. Since the builder did not take the redeemable ground rent into account in computing gain on the transfer, his basis for such ground rent is $500 (the cost of the land not offset against the consideration received for the transfer). Thus, if he subsequently sells the redeemable ground rent (or if it is redeemed from him) for $2,000, he has a gain of $1,500 in the year of sale (or redemption).

Example (2). Assume the same facts as in Example (1) except that the builder reported a gain of $3,500 on the transfer, treating the amount realized as $14,000 ($12,000 cash plus $2,000 for the redeemable ground rent) and his costs as $10,500 ($10,000 for the house and $500 for the lot). Since the taxpayer took the entire amount of the redeemable ground rent into account in computing his gain, his basis for such ground rent is $2,000. Thus, if he subsequently sells the redeemable ground rent (or if it is redeemed from him) for $2,000, he has no gain or loss on the transaction.

Example (3). Assume the same facts as in Example (1) except that the builder reported a gain of $3,000 on the transfer. He computed this gain by treating the amount realized as $12,000 but treating his cost allocable to the interest transferred as $12,000/$14,000ths of his total $10,500 cost, or $9,000. Since the builder still has remaining $1,500 of unallocated cost, his basis for the redeemable ground rent is $1,500. Thus, if he subsequently sells the redeemable ground rent (or if it is redeemed from him) for $2,000, he has a gain of $500 in the year of sale (or redemption). [Reg. § 1.1055-4.]

☐ [*T.D.* 6821, 5-3-65.]

[Reg. § 1.1059(e)-1]

§ 1.1059(e)-1. **Non-pro rata redemptions.**—(a) *In general.* Section 1059(d)(6) (exception where stock held during entire existence of corporation) and section 1059(e)(2) (qualifying dividends) do not apply to any distribution treated as an extraordinary dividend under section 1059(e)(1). For example, if a redemption of stock is not pro rata as to all shareholders, any amount treated as a dividend under section 301 is treated as an extraordinary dividend regardless of whether the dividend is a qualifying dividend.

(b) *Reorganizations.* For purposes of section 1059(e)(1), any exchange under section 356 is treated as a redemption and, to the extent any amount is treated as a dividend under section 356(a)(2), it is treated as a dividend under section 301.

(c) *Effective date.* This section applies to distributions announced (within the meaning of section 1059(d)(5)) on or after June 17, 1996. [Reg. § 1.1059(e)-1.]

☐ [*T.D.* 8724, 7-15-97.]

[Reg. § 1.1059A-1]

§ 1.1059A-1. **Limitation on taxpayer's basis or inventory cost in property imported from related persons.**—(a) *General rule.* In the case of property imported into the United States in a transaction (directly or indirectly) by a controlled taxpayer from another member of a controlled group of taxpayers, except for the adjustments permitted by paragraph (c)(2) of this section, the amount of any costs taken into account in computing the basis or inventory cost of the property by the purchasing U.S. taxpayer and which costs are also taken into account in computing the valuation of the property for customs purposes may not, for purposes of the basis or inventory cost, be greater than the amount of the costs used in computing the customs value. For purposes of this section, the terms "controlled taxpayer" and "group of controlled taxpayers" shall have the meaning set forth in § 1.482-1(a).

(b) *Definitions*—(1) *Import.* For purposes of section 1059A and this section only, the term "import" means the filing of the entry documentation required by the U.S. Customs Service to secure the release of imported merchandise from custody of the U.S. Customs Service.

(2) *Indirectly.* For purposes of this section, "indirectly" refers to a transaction between a controlled taxpayer and another member of the controlled group whereby property is imported through a person acting as an agent of, or otherwise on behalf of, either or both related persons, or as a middleman or conduit for transfer of the property between a controlled taxpayer and another member of the controlled group. In the case of the importation of property indirectly, an adjustment shall be permitted under paragraph (c)(2) of this section for a commission or markup paid to the person acting as agent, middleman, or conduit, only to the extent that the commission or markup: is otherwise properly included in cost basis or inventory cost; was actually incurred by the taxpayer and not remitted, directly or indirectly, to the taxpayer or related party; and there is a substantial business reason for the use of a middleman, agent, or conduit.

(c) *Customs value*—(1) *Definition.* For purposes of this section only, the term "customs value" means the value required to be taken into account for purposes of determining the amount of any customs duties or any other duties which may be imposed on the importation of any property. Where an item or a portion of an item is not subject to any customs duty or is subject to a free rate of duty, such item or portion of such item shall not be subject to the provisions of section 1059A or this section. Thus, for example, the portion of an item that is an American good returned and not subject to duty (items 806.20 and 806.30, Tariff Schedules of the United States, 19 U.S.C. 1202); imports on which no duty is imposed that are valued by customs for statistical purposes only; and items subject to a zero rate of duty (19 U.S.C. 1202, General Headnote 3) are not subject to section 1059A or this section. Also, items subject only to the user fee under 19 U.S.C. 58(c), or the harbor maintenance tax imposed by 26 U.S.C. 4461, or only to both, are not subject to section 1059A or this section. This section imposes no limitation on a claimed basis or inventory cost in property which is less than the value used to compute the customs duty with respect to the same property. Section 1059A and this section have no application to imported property not subject to any customs duty based on value, including property subject only to a per item duty or a duty based on volume, because there is no customs value, within the meaning of this paragraph, with respect to such property.

(2) *Adjustments to customs value.* To the extent not otherwise included in customs value, a

Reg. § 1.1059(e)-1(a)

taxpayer, for purposes of determining the limitation on claimed basis or inventory cost of property under this section, may increase the customs value of imported property by the amounts incurred by it and properly included in inventory cost for—

    (i) Freight charges,

    (ii) Insurance charges,

    (iii) The construction, erection, assembly, or technical assistance provided with respect to, the property after is importation into the United States, and

    (iv) Any other amounts which are not taken into account in determining the customs value, which are not properly includible in customs value, and which are appropriately included in the cost basis or inventory cost for income tax purposes. See § 1.471-11 and section 263A.

Appropriate adjustments may also be made to customs values when the taxpayer has not allocated the value of assists to individual articles but rather has reported the value of assists on a periodic basis in accordance with 19 CFR § 152.103(e). When 19 CFR § 152.103(e) has been utilized for customs purposes, the taxpayer may adjust his customs values by allocating the value of the assists to all imported articles to which the assists relate. To the extent that an amount attributable to an adjustment permitted by this section is paid by a controlled taxpayer to another member of the group of controlled taxpayers, an adjustment is permitted under this section only to the extent that the amount incurred represents an arm's length charge within the meaning of § 1.482-1(d)(3).

    (3) *Offsets to adjustments.* To the extent that a customs value is adjusted under paragraph (c)(2) of this section for purposes of calculating the limitation on claimed cost basis or inventory cost under this section, the amount of the adjustments must be offset (reduced) by amounts that properly reduce the cost basis of inventory and that are not taken into account in determining customs value, such as rebates and other reductions in the price actually incurred, effected between the purchaser and related seller after the date of importation of the property.

    (4) *Application of section 1059A to property having dutiable and nondutiable portions.* When an item of imported property is subject to a duty upon the full value of the imported article, less the cost or value of American goods returned, and the taxpayer claims a basis or inventory cost greater than the customs value reported for the item, the claimed tax basis or inventory cost in the dutiable portion of the item is limited under section 1059A and this section to the customs value of the dutiable portion under paragraph (c)(1). The claimed tax basis or inventory cost in the nondutiable portion of the item is determined by multiplying the customs value of the nondutiable portion by a fraction the numerator of which is the amount by which the claimed basis or inventory cost of the item exceeds the customs value of the item and the denominator of which is the customs value of the item and adding this amount to the customs value of the nondutiable portion of the item. The claimed tax basis or inventory cost in the dutiable portion is determined by multiplying the customs value of the dutiable portion by a fraction the numerator of which is the amount by which the claimed basis or inventory cost of the item exceeds the customs value of the item and the denominator of which is the customs value of the item and adding this amount to the customs value of the dutiable portion of the item. However, the taxpayer may not claim a tax basis or inventory cost in the dutiable portion greater than the customs value of this portion of the item.

    (5) *Allocation of adjustments to property having dutiable and nondutiable portions.* When an item of imported property is subject to a duty upon the full value of the imported article, less the cost or value of American goods returned, and the taxpayer establishes that the customs value may be increased by adjustments permitted under paragraph (c)(2) of this section for purposes of the section 1059A limitation, the taxpayer's basis or inventory cost of the dutiable portion of the item is determined by multiplying the customs value of the dutiable portion times the percentage that the adjustments represent of the total customs value of the item and adding this amount to the customs value of the dutiable portion of the item. The taxpayer's basis or inventory cost of the nondutiable portion of the item is determined in the same manner. The amount so determined for the dutiable portion of the item is the section 1059A limitation for this portion of the item.

    (6) *Alternative method of demonstrating compliance.* In lieu of calculating all adjustments and offsets to adjustments to customs value for an item of property pursuant to paragraph (c)(2) and (3) of this section, a taxpayer may demonstrate compliance with this section and section 1059A by comparing costs taken into account in computing basis or inventory costs of the property and the costs taken into account in computing customs value at any time after importation, provided that in any such comparison the same costs are included both in basis or inventory costs and in customs value. If, on the basis of such comparison, the basis or inventory cost is equal to or less than the customs value, the taxpayer shall be deemed

Reg. § 1.1059A-1(c)(6)

52,050 — Special Rules

to have met the requirements of this section and section 1059A.

(7) *Relationship of section 1059A to section 482.* Neither this section nor section 1059A limits in any way the authority of the Commissioner to increase or decrease the claimed basis or inventory cost under section 482 or any other appropriate provision of law. Neither does this section or section 1059A permit a taxpayer to adjust upward its cost basis or inventory cost for property appropriately determined under section 482 because such basis or inventory cost is less than the customs value with respect to such property.

(8) *Illustrations.* The application of this section may be illustrated by the following examples:

Example (1). Corporation X, a United States taxpayer, and Y Corporation are members of a group of controlled corporations. X pays $2,000 to Y for merchandise imported into the United States and an additional $150 for ocean freight and insurance. The customs value of the shipment is determined to be the amount actually paid by X ($2,000) and does not include the charges for ocean freight and insurance. For purposes of computing the limitation on its inventory cost for the merchandise under section 1059A and this section, X is permitted, under paragraph (c)(2) of this section, to increase the customs value ($2,000) by amounts it paid for ocean freight and insurance charges ($150). Thus, the inventory cost claimed by X in the merchandise may not exceed $2,150.

Example (2). Assume the same facts as in Example (1) except that, subsequent to the date of importation of the merchandise, Y grants to X a rebate of $200 of the purchase price. At the time of sale, the rebate was contingent upon the volume of merchandise ultimately bought by X from Y. The value of the merchandise, for customs purposes, is not decreased by the rebate paid to X by Y. Therefore, the customs value, for customs purposes, of the merchandise remains the same ($2,000). For purposes of computing its inventory cost, X was permitted, under paragraph (c)(2) of this section, to increase the customs value for purposes of section 1059A of $2,000 by the amounts it paid for ocean freight and insurance charges ($150). However, under paragraph (c)(3) of this section, X is required to reduce the amount of the customs value by the lesser of the amount of the rebate or the amount of any positive adjustments to the original customs value. The inventory price claimed by X may not exceed $2,000 ($2,000 customs value, plus $150 transportation adjustment, less $150 offsetting rebate adjustment). While X's limitation under section 1059A is $2,000, X may not claim a basis or inventory cost in the merchandise in excess of $1,950. See I.R.C. § 1012; and § 1.471-2.

Example (3). Corporation X, a United States taxpayer, and Y Corporation are members of a group of controlled corporations. X pays $10,000 to Y for merchandise imported into the United States. The merchandise is composed, in part, of American goods returned. The customs value of the merchandise, on which a customs duty is imposed, is determined to be $8,000 ($10,000, the amount declared by X, less $2,000, the value of the American goods returned). For income tax purposes, X claims a cost basis in the merchandise of $11,000. None of the adjustments permitted by paragraph (c)(2) of this section is applicable. The portion of the merchandise constituting American goods returned represented 20 percent of the total customs value of the merchandise. Since the cost basis claimed by X for income tax purposes represents a 10 percent increase over the customs valuation (before reduction for American goods returned), the claimed tax basis in the dutiable content is considered to be $8,800 and in the portion constituting American goods returned is $2,200. Since a customs duty was imposed only on the dutiable content of the merchandise, the limitation in section 1059A and this section is applicable only to the claimed tax basis in this portion of the merchandise. Accordingly, under paragraph (a) of this section, X is limited to a cost basis of $10,200 in the merchandise. This amount represents a cost basis of $8,000 in the dutiable content and of $2,200 in the portion of the merchandise constituting American goods returned.

Example (4). Assume the same facts as in Example (3) except that X establishes that it is entitled to increase its customs value by $1,000 in adjustments permitted by paragraph (c)(2) of this section. Since the adjustments to customs value that X is entitled to under paragraph (c)(2) of this section are 10 percent of the customs value, for purposes of determining the limitation under section 1059A and this section, both the dutiable content and the portion of the merchandise constituting American goods returned shall be increased to an amount 10 percent greater than the respective values determined for customs purposes, or $8,800 for the dutiable content and $2,200 for the portion of the merchandise constituting American goods returned. Accordingly, under paragraph (a) of this section, X is limited to a cost basis of $11,000 in the merchandise.

Example (5). Corporation X, a United States taxpayer, and Y Corporation are members of a group of controlled corporations. X pays $10,000 to Y for merchandise imported into the United States. The customs value of the merchandise, on

Reg. § 1.1059A-1(c)(7)

Special Rules

See p. 20,601 for regulations not amended to reflect law changes

which a customs duty is imposed, is determined to be $10,000. Subsequent to the date of importation of the merchandise, Y grants to X a rebate of $1,000 of the purchase price. The value of the merchandise, for customs purposes, is not decreased by the rebate paid to X by Y. Notwithstanding the fact that X correctly reported and paid customs duty on a value of $10,000 and that its limitation on basis or inventory cost under this section is $10,000, X may not claim a basis or inventory cost in the merchandise in excess of $9,000. See I.R.C. § 1012; and § 1.471-2.

Example (6). Corporation X, a United States taxpayer, and Y Corporation are members of a group of controlled corporations. X pays $5,000 to Y for merchandise imported into the United States. The merchandise is not subject to a customs duty or is subject to a free rate of duty and is valued by customs solely for statistical purposes. Accordingly, pursuant to paragraph (c)(1) of this section, the merchandise is not subject to the provisions of section 1059A or this section.

Example (7). Assume the same facts as in Example 6, except that the merchandise is subject to a customs duty based on value and that the customs value (taking into account no costs other than the value of the goods) is determined to be $5,000. Assume further that the $5,000 payment is only for the value of the goods, no other cost is reflected in that payment, and only the $5,000 payment to Y is reflected in X's inventory cost or basis prior to inclusion of any other amounts properly included in inventory or cost basis. Pursuant to paragraph (c)(6) of this section, X, by demonstrating these facts is deemed to meet the requirements of this section and section 1059A.

Example (8). Corporation X, a United States taxpayer, and Y Corporation are members of a group of controlled corporations. X pays $9 to Y for merchandise imported into the United States and an additional $1 for ocean freight. The customs value of the article does not include the $1 paid for ocean freight. Furthermore, for customs purposes the value is calculated pursuant to computed value and is determined to be $8. For purposes of computing the limitation on its inventory cost for the article under section 1059A and this section, X is permitted, under paragraph (c)(2) of this section, to increase the customs value ($8) by the amount it paid for ocean freight ($1). Thus, the inventory cost claimed by X in the article may not exceed $9.

(9) *Averaged customs values.* In cases of transactions in which (i) an appropriate transfer price is properly determined for tax purposes by reference to events occurring after importation, (ii) the value for customs purposes of one article is higher and of a second article is lower than the actual transaction values, (iii) the relevant articles have been appraised on the basis of a value estimated at the time of importation in accordance with customs regulations, and (iv) the entries have been liquidated upon importation, the section 1059A limitation on the undervalued article may be increased up to the amount of actual transaction value by the amount of the duty overpaid on the overvalued article times a fraction the numerator of which is "1" and the denominator of which is the rate of duty on the undervalued article. This paragraph (c)(9) applies exclusively to cases of property imported in transactions that are open for tax purposes in which the actual transaction value cannot be determined and the entry has been liquidated for customs purposes on the basis of a value estimated at the time of importation in accordance with customs regulations; in these cases, the property is appropriately valued for tax purposes by reference to a formula, in existence at the time of importation, based on subsequent events and valued for customs purposes by a different formula. This paragraph (c)(9) does not apply where customs value is correctly determined for purposes of liquidating the entry and where the customs value is subsequently adjusted for tax purposes, for example by a rebate, under paragraph (c)(2) of this section. The application of paragraph (c)(9) may be illustrated by the following example:

Example. Corporation X, a United States taxpayer, and Y Corporation are members of a group of controlled corporations. X purchases Articles A and B from Y on consignment and imports the Articles into the United States. The purchase price paid by X will be determined as a percentage of the sale prices that X realizes. Rather than deferring liquidation, customs liquidates the entry on the basis of estimated values and the customs duties are paid by X. Ultimately, it is determined that Article A was undervalued and Article B was overvalued by X for customs purposes. The section 1059A limitation for Article A is computed as follows:

	Article A	Article B
Finally-determined customs value	$9	$9
Transaction value	$10	$5
Duty rate	10%	5%
Customs duty paid	$.90	$.45
Duty overpaid or (underpaid)	($.10)	$.20

The section 1059A limitation on Article A may be increased by the amount of the duty overpaid on Article B, $.20, times 1/.10, up to the amount of the transaction value. Therefore, the section 1059A limitation on Article A is $9.00 plus $1.00, or a total of $10.00. The section 1059A

Reg. § 1.1059A-1(c)(9)

limitation on Article B is reduced (but never below transaction value) by $2.00 to $7.00.

(d) *Finality of customs value and of other determinations of the U.S. Customs Service.* For purposes of section 1059A and this section, a taxpayer is bound by the finally-determined customs value and by every final determination made by the U.S. Customs Service, including, but not limited to, dutiable value, the value attributable to the cost or value of products of the United States, and classification of the product for purposes of imposing any duty. The customs value is considered to be finally determined, and all U.S. Customs Service determinations are considered final, when liquidation of the entry becomes final. For this purpose, the term "liquidation" means the ascertainment of the customs duties occurring on the entry of the property, and liquidation of the entry is considered to become final after 90 days following notice of liquidation to the importer, unless a protest is filed. If the importer files a protest, the customs value will be considered finally determined and all other U.S. Customs Service determinations will be considered final either when a decision by the Customs Service on the protest is not contested after expiration of the period allowed to contest the decision or when a judgment of the Court of International Trade becomes final. For purposes of this section, any adjustments to the customs value resulting from a petition under 19 U.S.C. section 1516 (requests by interested parties unrelated to the importer for redetermination of the appraised value, classification, or the rate of duty imposed on imported merchandise) or reliquidation under 19 U.S.C. section 1521 (reliquidation by the Customs Service upon a finding that fraud was involved in the original liquidation) will not be taken into account. However, reliquidation under 19 U.S.C. section 1501 (voluntary reliquidation by the Customs Service within 90 days of the original liquidation to correct errors in appraisement, classification, or any element entering into a liquidation or reliquidation) or reliquidation under 19 U.S.C. section 1520(c)(1) (to correct a clerical error, mistake of fact, or other inadvertance within one year of a liquidation or reliquidation) will be taken into account in the same manner as, and take the place of, the original liquidation in determining customs value.

(e) *Drawbacks.* For purposes of this section, a drawback, that is, a refund or remission (in whole or in part) of a customs duty because of a particular use made (or to be made) of the property on which the duty was assessed or collected, shall not affect the determination of the customs value of the property.

(f) *Effective date.* Property imported by a taxpayer is subject to section 1059A and this section if the entry documentation required to be filed to obtain the release of the property from the custody of the United States Customs Service was filed after March 18, 1986. Section 1059A and this section will not apply to imported property where (1) the entry documentation is filed prior to September 3, 1987; and (2) the importation was liquidated under the circumstances described in paragraph (c)(9) of this section. [Reg. § 1.1059A-1.]

☐ [*T.D.* 8260, 9-7-89.]

[Reg. § 1.1060-1]

§ 1.1060-1. Special allocation rules for certain asset acquisitions.—(a) *Scope*—(1) *In general.* This section prescribes rules relating to the requirements of section 1060, which, in the case of an applicable asset acquisition, requires the transferor (the seller) and the transferee (the purchaser) each to allocate the consideration paid or received in the transaction among the assets transferred in the same manner as amounts are allocated under section 338(b)(5) (relating to the allocation of adjusted grossed-up basis among the assets of the target corporation when a section 338 election is made). In the case of an applicable asset acquisition described in paragraph (b)(1) of this section, sellers and purchasers must allocate the consideration under the residual method as described in §§ 1.338-6 and 1.338-7 in order to determine, respectively, the amount realized from, and the basis in, each of the transferred assets. For rules relating to distributions of partnership property or transfers of partnership interests which are subject to section 1060(d), see § 1.755-2T.

(2) *Effective date.* The provisions of this section apply to any asset acquisition occurring after March 15, 2001. For rules applicable to asset acquisitions on or before March 15, 2001, see § 1.1060-1T in effect prior to March 16, 2001 (see 26 CFR part 1 revised April 1, 2000).

(3) *Outline of topics.* In order to facilitate the use of this section, this paragraph (a)(3) lists the major paragraphs in this section as follows:

(a) Scope.

(1) In general.

(2) Effective date.

(3) Outline of topics.

(b) Applicable asset acquisition.

(1) In general.

(2) Assets constituting a trade or business.

(i) In general.

(ii) Goodwill or going concern value.

Reg. § 1.1060-1(a)(1)

Special Rules

(iii) Factors indicating goodwill or going concern value.

(3) Examples.

(4) Asymmetrical transfers of assets.

(5) Related transactions.

(6) More than a single trade or business.

(7) Covenant entered into by the seller.

(8) Partial non-recognition exchanges.

(c) Allocation of consideration among assets under the residual method.

(1) Consideration.

(2) Allocation of consideration among assets.

(3) Certain costs.

(4) Effect of agreement between parties.

(d) Examples.

(e) Reporting requirements.

(1) Applicable asset acquisitions.

(i) In general.

(ii) Time and manner of reporting.

(A) In general.

(B) Additional reporting requirement.

(2) Transfers of interests in partnerships.

(b) *Applicable asset acquisition*—(1) *In general.* An applicable asset acquisition is any transfer, whether direct or indirect, of a group of assets if the assets transferred constitute a trade or business in the hands of either the seller or the purchaser and, except as provided in paragraph (b)(8) of this section, the purchaser's basis in the transferred assets is determined wholly by reference to the purchaser's consideration.

(2) *Assets constituting a trade or business*—(i) *In general.* For purposes of this section, a group of assets constitutes a trade or business if—

(A) The use of such assets would constitute an active trade or business under section 355; or

(B) Its character is such that goodwill or going concern value could under any circumstances attach to such group.

(ii) *Goodwill or going concern value.* Goodwill is the value of a trade or business attributable to the expectancy of continued customer patronage. This expectancy may be due to the name or reputation of a trade or business or any other factor. Going concern value is the additional value that attaches to property because of its existence as an integral part of an ongoing business activity. Going concern value includes the value attributable to the ability of a trade or business (or a part of a trade or business) to continue functioning or generating income without interruption notwithstanding a change in ownership. It also includes the value that is attributable to the immediate use or availability of an acquired trade or business, such as, for example, the use of the revenues or net earnings that otherwise would not be received during any period if the acquired trade or business were not available or operational.

(iii) *Factors indicating goodwill or going concern value.* In making the determination in this paragraph (b)(2), all the facts and circumstances surrounding the transaction are taken into account. Whether sufficient consideration is available to allocate to goodwill or going concern value after the residual method is applied is not relevant in determining whether goodwill or going concern value could attach to a group of assets. Factors to be considered include—

(A) The presence of any intangible assets (whether or not those assets are section 197 intangibles), provided, however, that the transfer of such an asset in the absence of other assets will not be a trade or business for purposes of section 1060;

(B) The existence of an excess of the total consideration over the aggregate book value of the tangible and intangible assets purchased (other than goodwill and going concern value) as shown in the financial accounting books and records of the purchaser; and

(C) Related transactions, including lease agreements, licenses, or other similar agreements between the purchaser and seller (or managers, directors, owners, or employees of the seller) in connection with the transfer.

(3) *Examples.* The following examples illustrate paragraphs (b)(1) and (2) of this section:

Example 1. S is a high grade machine shop that manufactures microwave connectors in limited quantities. It is a successful company with a reputation within the industry and among its customers for manufacturing unique, high quality products. Its tangible assets consist primarily of ordinary machinery for working metal and plating. It has no secret formulas or patented drawings of value. P is a company that designs, manufactures, and markets electronic components. It wants to establish an immediate presence in the microwave industry, an area in which it previously has not been engaged. P is acquiring assets of a number of smaller companies and hopes that these assets will collectively allow it to offer a broad product mix. P acquires the assets of S in order to augment its product mix and to promote its presence in the microwave industry. P will not use the assets acquired from S to manufacture microwave connectors. The assets transferred are assets that constitute a trade or

Reg. § 1.1060-1(b)(3)

business in the hands of the seller. Thus, P's purchase of S's assets is an applicable asset acquisition. The fact that P will not use the assets acquired from S to continue the business of S does not affect this conclusion.

Example 2. S, a sole proprietor who operates a car wash, both leases the building housing the car wash and sells all of the car wash equipment to P. S's use of the building and the car wash equipment constitute a trade or business. P begins operating a car wash in the building it leases from S. Because the assets transferred together with the asset leased are assets which constitute a trade or business, P's purchase of S's assets is an applicable asset acquisition.

Example 3. S, a corporation, owns a retail store business in State X and conducts activities in connection with that business enterprise that meet the active trade or business requirement of section 355. P is a minority shareholder of S. S distributes to P all the assets of S used in S's retail business in State X in complete redemption of P's stock in S held by P. The distribution of S's assets in redemption of P's stock is treated as a sale or exchange under sections 302(a) and 302(b)(3), and P's basis in the assets distributed to it is determined wholly by reference to the consideration paid, the S stock. Thus, S's distribution of assets constituting a trade or business to P is an applicable asset acquisition.

Example 4. S is a manufacturing company with an internal financial bookkeeping department. P is in the business of providing a financial bookkeeping service on a contract basis. As part of an agreement for P to begin providing financial bookkeeping services to S, P agrees to buy all of the assets associated with S's internal bookkeeping operations and provide employment to any of S's bookkeeping department employees who choose to accept a position with P. In addition to selling P the assets associated with its bookkeeping operation, S will enter into a long term contract with P for bookkeeping services. Because assets transferred from S to P, along with the related contract for bookkeeping services, are a trade or business in the hands of P, the sale of the bookkeeping assets from S to P is an applicable asset acquisition.

(4) *Asymmetrical transfers of assets.* A purchaser is subject to section 1060 if—

    (i) Under general principles of tax law, the seller is not treated as transferring the same assets as the purchaser is treated as acquiring;

    (ii) The assets acquired by the purchaser constitute a trade or business; and

    (iii) Except as provided in paragraph (b)(8) of this section, the purchaser's basis in the transferred assets is determined wholly by reference to the purchaser's consideration.

(5) *Related transactions.* Whether the assets transferred constitute a trade or business is determined by aggregating all transfers from the seller to the purchaser in a series of related transactions. Except as provided in paragraph (b)(8) of this section, all assets transferred from the seller to the purchaser in a series of related transactions are included in the group of assets among which the consideration paid or received in such series is allocated under the residual method. The principles of § 1.338-1(c) are also applied in determining which assets are included in the group of assets among which the consideration paid or received is allocated under the residual method.

(6) *More than a single trade or business.* If the assets transferred from a seller to a purchaser include more than one trade or business, then, in applying this section, all of the assets transferred (whether or not transferred in one transaction or a series of related transactions and whether or not part of a trade or business) are treated as a single trade or business.

(7) *Covenant entered into by the seller.* If, in connection with an applicable asset acquisition, the seller enters into a covenant (e.g., a covenant not to compete) with the purchaser, that covenant is treated as an asset transferred as part of a trade or business.

(8) *Partial non-recognition exchanges.* A transfer may constitute an applicable asset acquisition notwithstanding the fact that no gain or loss is recognized with respect to a portion of the group of assets transferred. All of the assets transferred, including the non-recognition assets, are taken into account in determining whether the group of assets constitutes a trade or business. The allocation of consideration under paragraph (c) of this section is done without taking into account either the non-recognition assets or the amount of money or other property that is treated as transferred in exchange for the non-recognition assets (together, the non-recognition exchange property). The basis in and gain or loss recognized with respect to the non-recognition exchange property are determined under such rules as would otherwise apply to an exchange of such property. The amount of the money and other property treated as exchanged for non-recognition assets is the amount by which the fair market value of the non-recognition assets transferred by one party exceeds the fair market value of the non-recognition assets transferred by the other (to the extent of the money and the fair market value of property transferred in the exchange). The money and other property that are treated as

transferred in exchange for the non-recognition assets (and which are not included among the assets to which section 1060 applies) are considered to come from the following assets in the following order: first from Class I assets, then from Class II assets, then from Class III assets, then from Class IV assets, then from Class V assets, then from Class VI assets, and then from Class VII assets. For this purpose, liabilities assumed (or to which a non-recognition exchange property is subject) are treated as Class I assets. See *Example 1* in paragraph (d) of this section for an example of the application of section 1060 to a single transaction which is, in part, a non-recognition exchange.

(c) *Allocation of consideration among assets under the residual method*—(1) *Consideration.* The seller's consideration is the amount, in the aggregate, realized from selling the assets in the applicable asset acquisition under section 1001(b). The purchaser's consideration is the amount, in the aggregate, of its cost of purchasing the assets in the applicable asset acquisition that is properly taken into account in basis.

(2) *Allocation of consideration among assets.* For purposes of determining the seller's amount realized for each of the assets sold in an applicable asset acquisition, the seller allocates consideration to all the assets sold by using the residual method under §§ 1.338-6 and 1.338-7, substituting consideration for ADSP. For purposes of determining the purchaser's basis in each of the assets purchased in an applicable asset acquisition, the purchaser allocates consideration to all the assets purchased by using the residual method under §§ 1.338-6 and 1.338-7, substituting consideration for AGUB. In allocating consideration, the rules set forth in paragraphs (c)(3) and (4) of this section apply in addition to the rules in §§ 1.338-6 and 1.338-7.

(3) *Certain costs.* The seller and purchaser each adjusts the amount allocated to an individual asset to take into account the specific identifiable costs incurred in transferring that asset in connection with the applicable asset acquisition (e.g., real estate transfer costs or security interest perfection costs). Costs so allocated increase, or decrease, as appropriate, the total consideration that is allocated under the residual method. No adjustment is made to the amount allocated to an individual asset for general costs associated with the applicable asset acquisition as a whole or with groups of assets included therein (e.g., non-specific appraisal fees or accounting fees). These latter amounts are taken into account only indirectly through their effect on the total consideration to be allocated.

(4) *Effect of agreement between parties.* If, in connection with an applicable asset acquisition, the seller and purchaser agree in writing as to the allocation of any amount of consideration to, or as to the fair market value of, any of the assets, such agreement is binding on them to the extent provided in this paragraph (c)(4). Nothing in this paragraph (c)(4) restricts the Commissioner's authority to challenge the allocations or values arrived at in an allocation agreement. This paragraph (c)(4) does not apply if the parties are able to refute the allocation or valuation under the standards set forth in *Commissioner v. Danielson*, 378 F.2d 771 (3d Cir.), *cert. denied*, 389 U.S. 858 (1967) (a party wishing to challenge the tax consequences of an agreement as construed by the Commissioner must offer proof that, in an action between the parties to the agreement, would be admissible to alter that construction or show its unenforceability because of mistake, undue influence, fraud, duress, etc.).

(d) *Examples.* The following examples illustrate this section:

Example 1. (i) On January 1, 2001, A transfers assets X, Y, and Z to B in exchange for assets D, E, and F plus $1,000 cash.

(ii) Assume the exchange of assets constitutes an exchange of like-kind property to which section 1031 applies. Assume also that goodwill or going concern value could under any circumstances attach to each of the DEF and XYZ groups of assets and, therefore, each group constitutes a trade or business under section 1060.

(iii) Assume the fair market values of the assets and the amount of money transferred are as follows:

By A

Asset	Fair Market Value
X	$ 400
Y	400
Z	200
Total	$1,000

By B

Asset	Fair Market Value
D	$ 40
E	30
F	30
Cash (amount)	1,000
Total	$1,100

Reg. § 1.1060-1(d)

(iv) Under paragraph (b)(8) of this section, for purposes of allocating consideration under paragraph (c) of this section, the like-kind assets exchanged and any money or other property that are treated as transferred in exchange for the like-kind property are excluded from the application of section 1060.

(v) Since assets X, Y, and Z are like-kind property, they are excluded from the application of the section 1060 allocation rules.

(vi) Since assets D, E, and F are like-kind property, they are excluded from the application of the section 1060 allocation rules. Thus, the allocation rules of section 1060 do not apply in determining B's gain or loss with respect to the disposition of assets D, E, and F, and the allocation rules of section 1060 and paragraph (c) of this section are not applied to determine A's bases of assets D, E, and F. In addition, $900 of the $1,000 cash B gave to A for A's like-kind assets (X, Y, and Z) is treated as transferred in exchange for the like-kind property in order to equalize the fair market values of the like-kind assets. Therefore, $900 of the cash is excluded from the application of the section 1060 allocation rules.

(vii) $100 of the cash is allocated under section 1060 and paragraph (c) of this section.

(viii) A received $100 that must be allocated under section 1060 and paragraph (c) of this section. Since A transferred no Class I, II, III, IV, V, or VI assets to which section 1060 applies, in determining its amount realized for the part of the exchange to which section 1031 does not apply, the $100 is allocated to Class VII assets (goodwill and going concern value).

(ix) B gave A $100 that must be allocated under section 1060 and paragraph (c) of this section. Since B received from A no Class I, II, III, IV, V, or VI assets to which section 1060 applies, the $100 consideration is allocated by B to Class VII assets (goodwill and going concern value).

Example 2. (i) On January 1, 2001, S, a sole proprietor, sells to P, a corporation, a group of assets that constitutes a trade or business under paragraph (b)(2) of this section. S, who plans to retire immediately, also executes in P's favor a covenant not to compete. P pays S $3,000 in cash and assumes $1,000 in liabilities. Thus, the total consideration is $4,000.

(ii) On the purchase date, P and S also execute a separate agreement that states that the fair market values of the Class II, Class III, Class V, and Class VI assets S sold to P are as follows:

Asset Class	Asset	Fair Market Value
II	Actively traded securities	$ 500
	Total Class II	500
III	Accounts receivable	200
	Total Class III	200
V	Furniture and fixtures	800
	Building	800
	Land	200
	Equipment	400
	Total Class V	2,200
VI	Covenant not to compete	900
	Total Class VI	900

(iii) P and S each allocate the consideration in the transaction among the assets transferred under paragraph (c) of this section in accordance with the agreed upon fair market values of the assets, so that $500 is allocated to Class II assets, $200 is allocated to the Class III asset, $2,200 is allocated to Class V assets, $900 is allocated to Class VI assets, and $200 ($4,000 total consideration less $3,800 allocated to assets in Classes II, III, V, and VI) is allocated to the Class VII assets (goodwill and going concern value).

(iv) In connection with the examination of P's return, the Commissioner, in determining the fair market values of the assets transferred, may disregard the parties' agreement. Assume that the Commissioner correctly determines that the fair market value of the covenant not to compete was $500. Since the allocation of consideration among Class II, III, V, and VI assets results in allocation up to the fair market value limitation, the $600 of unallocated consideration resulting from the Commissioner's redetermination of the value of the covenant not to compete is allocated to Class VII assets (goodwill and going concern value).

(e) *Reporting requirements*—(1) *Applicable asset acquisitions*—(i) *In general.* Unless otherwise excluded from this requirement by the Commissioner, the seller and the purchaser in an applicable asset acquisition each must report information concerning the amount of consideration in the

Reg. § 1.1060-1(ix)

transaction and its allocation among the assets transferred. They also must report information concerning subsequent adjustments to consideration.

(ii) *Time and manner of reporting*—(A) *In general.* The seller and the purchaser each must file asset acquisition statements on Form 8594, "Asset Allocation Statement," with their income tax returns or returns of income for the taxable year that includes the first date assets are sold pursuant to an applicable asset acquisition. This reporting requirement applies to all asset acquisitions described in this section. For reporting requirements relating to asset acquisitions occurring before March 16, 2001, as described in paragraph (a)(2) of this section, see the temporary regulations under section 1060 in effect prior to March 16, 2001 (see 26 CFR part 1 revised April 1, 2000).

(B) *Additional reporting requirement.* When an increase or decrease in consideration is taken into account after the close of the first taxable year that includes the first date assets are sold in an applicable asset acquisition, the seller and the purchaser each must file a supplemental asset acquisition statement on Form 8594 with the income tax return or return of income for the taxable year in which the increase (or decrease) is properly taken into account.

(2) *Transfers of interests in partnerships.* For reporting requirements relating to the transfer of a partnership interest, see § 1.755-2T(c). [Reg. § 1.1060-1.]

☐ [T.D. 8940, 2-12-2001.]

Changes to Effectuate F.C.C. Policy
[Reg. § 1.1071-1]

§ 1.1071-1. Gain from sale or exchange to effectuate policies of Federal Communications Commission.—(a)(1) At the election of the taxpayer, section 1071 postpones the recognition of the gain upon the sale or exchange of property if the Federal Communications Commission grants the taxpayer a certificate with respect to the ownership and control of radio broadcasting stations which is in accordance with subparagraph (2) of this paragraph. Any taxpayer desiring to obtain the benefits of section 1071 shall file such certificate with the Commissioner of Internal Revenue, or the district director for the internal revenue district in which the income tax return of the taxpayer is required to be filed.

(2)(i) In the case of a sale or exchange before January 1, 1958, the certificate from the Federal Communications Commission must clearly identify the property and show that the sale or exchange is necessary or appropriate to effectuate the policies of such Commission with respect to the ownership and control of radio broadcasting stations.

(ii) In the case of a sale or exchange after December 31, 1957, the certificate from the Federal Communications Commission must clearly identify the property and show that the sale or exchange is necessary or appropriate to effectuate a change in a policy of, or the adoption of a new policy by, such Commission with respect to the ownership and control of radio broadcasting stations.

(3) The certificate shall be accompanied by a detailed statement showing the kind of property, the date of acquisition, the cost or other basis of the property, the date of sale or exchange, the name and address of the transferee, and the amount of money and the fair market value of the property other than money received upon such sale or exchange.

(b) Section 1071 applies only in the case of a sale or exchange made necessary by reason of the Federal Communications Commission's policies as to ownership or control of radio facilities. Section 1071 does not apply in the case of a sale or exchange made necessary as a result of other matters, such as the operation of a broadcasting station in a manner determined by the Commission to be not in the public interest or in violation of Federal or State law.

(c) An election to have the benefits of section 1071 shall be made in the manner prescribed in § 1.1071-4.

(d) For purposes of section 1071, the term "radio broadcasting" includes telecasting. [Reg. § 1.1071-1.]

☐ [T.D. 6178, 6-1-56. Amended by T.D. 6453, 2-16-60.]

[Reg. § 1.1071-2]

§ 1.1071-2. Nature and effect of election—(a) *Alternative elections.* (1) A taxpayer entitled to the benefits of section 1071 in respect of a sale or exchange of property may elect—

(i) To treat such sale or exchange as an involuntary conversion under the provisions of section 1033; or

(ii) To treat such sale or exchange as an involuntary conversion under the provisions of section 1033, and in addition elect to reduce the basis of property, in accordance with the regulations prescribed in § 1.1071-3, by all or part of the

Reg. § 1.1071-2(a)

gain that would otherwise be recognized under section 1033; or

(iii) To reduce the basis of property, in accordance with the regulations prescribed in § 1.1071-3, by all or part of the gain realized upon the sale or exchange.

(2) The effect of the provisions of subparagraph (1) of this paragraph is, in general, to grant the taxpayer an election to treat the proceeds of the sale or exchange as the proceeds of an involuntary conversion subject to the provisions of section 1033, and a further election to reduce the basis of certain property owned by the taxpayer by the amount of the gain realized upon the sale or exchange to the extent of that portion of the proceeds which is not treated as the proceeds of an involuntary conversion.

(3) An election in respect to a sale or exchange under section 1071 shall be irrevocable and binding for taxable year in which the sale or exchange takes place and for all subsequent taxable years.

(b) *Application of section 1033.* (1) If the taxpayer elects, under either paragraph (a)(1)(i) or (ii) of this section, to treat the sale or exchange as an involuntary conversion, the provisions of section 1033, as modified by section 1071, together with the regulations prescribed under such sections, shall be applicable in determining the amount of recognized gain and the basis of property acquired as a result of such sale or exchange. For the purposes of section 1071 and the regulations thereunder, stock of a corporation operating a radio broadcasting station shall be treated as property similar or related in service or use to the property sold or exchanged. Securities of such a corporation other than stock, or securities of a corporation not operating a radio broadcasting station, do not constitute property similar or related in service or use to the property sold or exchanged. If the taxpayer exercises the election referred to in paragraph (a)(1)(i) of this section, the gain realized upon such sale or exchange shall be recognized to the extent of that part of the money received upon the sale or exchange which is not expended in the manner prescribed in section 1033 and the regulations thereunder. If, however, the taxpayer exercises the elections referred to in paragraph (a)(1)(ii) of this section, the amount of the gain which would be recognized, determined in the same manner as in the case of an election under paragraph (a)(1)(i) of this section, shall not be recognized but shall be applied to reduce the basis of property, remaining in the hands of the taxpayer after such sale or exchange or acquired by him during the same taxable year, which is of a character subject to the allowance for depreciation under section 167. Such reduction of basis shall be made in accordance with and under the conditions prescribed by § 1.1071-3.

(2) In the application of section 1033 to determine the recognized gain and the basis of property acquired as a result of a sale or exchange pursuant to an election under paragraph (a)(1)(i) or (ii) of this section, the entire amount of the proceeds of such sale or exchange shall be taken into account.

(c) *Example.* The application of the provisions of section 1071 may be illustrated by the following example:

Example. A, who makes his return on a calendar year basis, sold in 1954, for $100,000 cash, stock of X Corporation, which operates a radio broadcasting station. A's basis of this stock was $75,000. The sale was certified by the Federal Communications Commission as provided in section 1071. Soon after, in the same taxable year, A used $50,000 of the proceeds of the sale to purchase stock in Y Corporation, which operates a radio broadcasting station. A elected in his 1954 return to treat such sale and purchase as an involuntary conversion subject to the provisions of section 1033. He also elected at the same time to reduce the basis of depreciable property by the amount of the gain that otherwise would be recognized under the provisions of section 1033, as made applicable by section 1071. The sale results in a recognized gain of $25,000 under section 1033. However, this gain is not recognized in this case because the taxpayer elected to reduce the basis of other property by the amount of the gain. This may be shown as follows:

(1) Sale price of X Corporation stock	$100,000
Basis for gain or loss	75,000
Gain realized	25,000
Proceeds of sale	$100,000
Amount expended to replace property sold	50,000
Amount not expended in manner prescribed in section 1033	50,000
Realized gain, recognized under section 1033 (not to exceed the unexpended portion of proceeds of sale)	$ 25,000
Less: Amount applied as a reduction of basis of depreciable property	25,000
Recognized gain for tax purposes	None

(2) The basis of Y Corporation stock in the hands of A is $50,000, computed in accordance with section 1033 and the regulations prescribed under that section. The $50,000 basis is computed as follows:

Reg. § 1.1071-2(a)(2)

Changes to Effectuate F.C.C. Policy

See p. 20,601 for regulations not amended to reflect law changes

Basis of property sold (converted)	$ 75,000
Less: Amount of proceeds not expended	50,000
Balance	25,000
Plus amount of gain recognized under section 1033	25,000
Basis of Y Corporation stock in A's hands	50,000

[Reg. § 1.1071-2.]

☐ [*T.D.* 6178, 6-1-56.]

[Reg. § 1.1071-3]

§ 1.1071-3. Reduction of basis of property pursuant to election under section 1071.—(a) *General rule.* (1) In addition to the adjustments provided in section 1016 and other applicable provisions of chapter 1 of the Code, which adjustments are required to be made with respect to the cost or other basis of property, a further adjustment shall be made in the amount of the unrecognized gain under section 1071, if the taxpayer so elects. Such further adjustment shall be made only with respect to the cost or other basis of property which is of a character subject to the allowance for depreciation under section 167 (whether or not used in connection with a broadcasting business), and which remains in the hands of the taxpayer immediately after the sale or exchange in respect of which the election is made, or which is acquired by the taxpayer in the same taxable year in which such sale or exchange occurs. If the property is in the hands of the taxpayer immediately after the sale or exchange, the time of reduction of the basis is the date of the sale or exchange; in all other cases the time of reduction of the basis is the date of acquisition.

(2) The reduction of basis under section 1071 in the amount of the unrecognized gain shall be made in respect of the cost or other basis, as of the time prescribed, of all units of property of the specified character. The cost or other basis of each unit shall be decreased in an amount equal to such proportion of the unrecognized gain as the adjusted basis (for determining gain, determined without regard to this section) of such unit bears to the aggregate of such adjusted bases of all units of such property, but the amount of the decrease shall not be more than the amount of such adjusted basis. If in the application of such rule the adjusted basis of any unit is reduced to zero, the process shall be repeated to reduce the adjusted basis of the remaining units of property by the portion of the unrecognized gain which is not absorbed in the first application of the rule. For such purpose the "adjusted basis" of the remaining units shall be the adjusted basis for determining gain reduced by the amount of the adjustment previously made under this section. The process shall be repeated until the entire amount of the unrecognized gain has been absorbed.

(3) The application of the provisions of this section may be illustrated by the following example:

Example. Using the facts given in the example set forth in § 1.1071-2(c), except that the taxpayer elects to reduce the basis of depreciable property in accordance with paragraph (a)(1)(iii) of § 1.1071-2, the computation may be illustrated as follows:

Sale price of X Corporation stock	$100,000
Basis for gain or loss	75,000
Realized gain (recognized except for the election under § 1.1071-1)	$ 25,000

Adjusted basis of other depreciable property in hands of A immediately after sale:

Building	$ 80,000
Transmitter	16,000
Fixtures	4,000
TOTAL	$100,000

Computation of reduction:

Building	$\dfrac{80,000}{100,000} \times \$25,000$ (gain)	$ 20,000
Transmitter	$\dfrac{16,000}{100,000} \times \$25,000$	4,000
Fixtures	$\dfrac{4,000}{100,000} \times \$25,000$	1,000
Total Reduction		$ 25,000

New basis of assets:

Building ($80,000 minus $20,000)	$ 60,000
Transmitter ($16,000 minus $4,000)	12,000
Fixtures ($4,000 minus $1,000)	3,000

Reg. § 1.1071-3(a)(3)

52,060 Exchanges in Obedience to S.E.C. Orders

See p. 20,601 for regulations not amended to reflect law changes

Total adjusted basis after reduction under section 1071	$ 75,000
Realized gain upon sale of X Corporation stock	25,000
Less: Amount applied as a reduction to basis of depreciable property	25,000
Recognized gain for tax purposes	None

(b) *Special cases.* With the consent of the Commissioner, the taxpayer may, however, have the basis of the various units of property of the class specified in section 1071 and this section adjusted in a manner different from the general rule set forth in paragraph (a) above. Variations from such general rule may, for example, involve adjusting the basis of only certain units of such property. The request for variations from such general rule should be filed by the taxpayer with his return for the taxable year in which he elects to have the basis of property reduced under section 1071. Agreement between the taxpayer and the Commissioner as to any variations from such general rule shall be effective only if incorporated in a closing agreement entered into under the provisions of section 7121. [Reg. § 1.1071-3.]

☐ [*T.D.* 6178, 6-1-56.]

[Reg. § 1.1071-4]

§ 1.1071-4. Manner of election.—(a) An election under the provisions of section 1071 shall be in the form of a written statement and shall be executed and filed in duplicate. Such statement shall be signed by the taxpayer or his authorized representative. In the case of a corporation, the statement shall be signed with the corporate name, followed by the signature and title of an officer of the corporation empowered to sign for the corporation, and the corporate seal must be affixed. An election under section 1071 to reduce the basis of property and an election under such section to treat the sale or exchange as an involuntary conversion under section 1033 may be exercised independently of each other. An election under section 1071 must be filed with the return for the taxable year in which the sale or exchange occurs. Where practicable, the certificate of the Federal Communications Commission required by § 1.1071-1 should be filed with the election.

(b) If, in pursuance of an election to have the basis of its property adjusted under section 1071, the taxpayer desires to have such basis adjusted in any manner different from the general rule set forth in paragraph (a) of § 1.1071-3, the precise method (including allocation of amounts) should be set forth in detail on separate sheets accompanying the election. Consent by the Commissioner to any departure from such general rule shall be effected only by a closing agreement entered into under the provisions of section 7121. [Reg. § 1.1071-4.]

☐ [*T.D.* 6178, 6-1-56.]

Exchanges in Obedience to S.E.C. Orders

[Reg. § 1.1081-1]

§ 1.1081-1. Terms used.—The following terms, when used in this section and §§ 1.1081-2 to 1.1083-1, inclusive, shall have the meanings assigned to them in section 1083: "Order of the Securities and Exchange Commission"; "registered holding company"; "holding company system"; "associate company"; "majority-owned subsidiary company"; "system group"; "nonexempt property"; and "stock or securities". Any other term used in this section and §§ 1.1081-2 to 1.1083-1, inclusive, which is defined in the Internal Revenue Code of 1954, shall be given the respective definition contained in such Code. [Reg. § 1.1081-1.]

☐ [*T.D.* 6178, 6-1-56.]

[Reg. § 1.1081-2]

§ 1.1081-2. Purpose and scope of exception.—(a) The general rule is that the entire amount of gain or loss from the sale or exchange of property is to be recognized (see section 1002) and that the entire amount received as a dividend is to be included in gross income. (See sections 61 and 301.) Exceptions to the general rule are provided elsewhere in subchapters C and O, chapter 1 of the Code, one of which is that made by section 1081 with respect to exchanges, sales, and distributions specifically described in section 1081. Section 1081 provides the extent to which gain or loss is not to be recognized on (1) the receipt of a distribution described in section 1081(c)(2), or (2) an exchange or sale, or the receipt of a distribution, made in obedience to an order of the Securities and Exchange Commission, which is issued to effectuate the provisions of section 11(b) of the Public Utility Holding Company Act of 1935 (15 U.S.C. 79k(b)). Section 331 provides that a distribution in liquidation of a corporation shall be treated as an exchange. Such distribution is to be treated as an exchange under the provisions of sections 1081 to 1083, inclusive. The order of the Securities and Exchange Commission must be one requiring or approving action which the Commission finds to be necessary or appropriate to effect a simplification or geographical integration of a particular public utility hold-

Reg. § 1.1071-4(a)

Exchanges in Obedience to S.E.C. Orders   **52,061**

See p. 20,601 for regulations not amended to reflect law changes

ing company system. For specific requirements with respect to an order of the Securities and Exchange Commission, see section 1081(f).

(b) The requirements for nonrecognition of gain or loss as provided in section 1081 are precisely stated with respect to the following general types of transactions:

(1) The exchange that is provided for in section 1081(a), in which stock or securities in a registered holding company or a majority-owned subsidiary company are exchanged for stock or securities.

(2) The exchange that is provided for in section 1081(b), in which a registered holding company or an associate company of a registered holding company exchanges property for property.

(3) The distribution that is provided for in section 1081(c)(1), in which stock or securities are distributed to a shareholder in a corporation which is a registered holding company or a majority-owned subsidiary company, or the distribution that is provided for in section 1081(c)(2), in which a corporation distributes to a shareholder, rights to acquire common stock in a second corporation.

(4) The transfer that is provided for in section 1081(d), in which a corporation which is a member of a system group transfers property to another member of the same system group.

Certain rules with respect to the receipt of nonexempt property on an exchange described in section 1081(a) are prescribed in section 1081(e).

(c) These exceptions to the general rule are to be strictly construed. Unless both the purpose and the specific requirements of sections 1081 to 1083, inclusive, are clearly met, the recognition of gain or loss upon the exchange, sale, or distribution will not be postponed under those sections. Moreover, even though a taxable transaction occurs in connection or simultaneously with a realization of gain or loss to which nonrecognition is accorded, nevertheless, nonrecognition will not be accorded to such taxable transaction. In other words, the provisions of section 1081 do not extend in any case to gain or loss other than that realized from and directly attributable to a disposition of property as such, or the receipt of a corporate distribution as such, in an exchange, sale, or distribution specifically described in section 1081.

(d) The application of the provisions of part VI (section 1081 and following), subchapter O, chapter 1 of the Code, is intended to result only in postponing the recognition of gain or loss until a disposition of property is made which is not covered by such provisions, and, in the case of an exchange or sale subject to the provisions of section 1081(b), in the reduction of basis of certain property. The provisions of section 1082 with respect to the continuation of basis and the reduction in basis are designed to effect these results. Although the time of recognition may be shifted, there must be a true reflection of income in all cases, and it is intended that the provisions of such part VI, inclusive, shall not be constructed or applied in such a way as to defeat this purpose. [Reg. § 1.1081-2.]

☐ [*T.D.* 6178, 6-1-56.]

[Reg. § 1.1081-3]

§ 1.1081-3. Exchanges of stock or securities solely for stock or securities.—The exchange, without the recognition of gain or loss, that is provided for in section 1081(a) must be one in which stock or securities in a corporation which is a registered holding company or a majority-owned subsidiary company are exchanged solely for stock or securities other than stock or securities which constitute nonexempt property. An exchange is not within the provisions of section 1081(a) unless the stock or securities transferred and those received are stock or securities as defined by section 1083(f). The stock or securities which may be received without the recognition or gain or loss are not limited to stock or securities in the corporation from which they are received. An exchange within the provisions of section 1081(a) may be a transaction between the holder of stock or securities and the corporation which issued the stock or securities. Also the exchange may be made by a holder of stock or securities with an associate company (i.e., a corporation in the same holding company system with the issuing corporation) which is a registered holding company or a majority-owned subsidiary company. In either case, the nonrecognition provisions of section 1081(a) apply only to the holder of the stock or securities. However, the transferee corporation must be acting in obedience to an order of the Securities and Exchange Commission directed to such corporation, if no gain or loss is to be recognized to the holder of the stock or securities who makes the exchange with such corporation. See also section 1081(b), in case the holder of the stock or securities is a registered holding company or an associate company of a registered holding company. An exchange is not within the provisions of section 1081(a) if it is within the provisions of section 1081(d), relating to transfers within a system group. For treatment when nonexempt property is received, see section 1081(e); for further limitations, see section 1081(f). [Reg. § 1.1081-3.]

☐ [*T.D.* 6178, 6-1-56.]

Reg. § 1.1081-3

Exchanges in Obedience to S.E.C. Orders

See p. 20,601 for regulations not amended to reflect law changes

[Reg. § 1.1081-4]

§ 1.1081-4. **Exchanges of property for property by corporations.**—(a) *Application of section 1081(b).* Section 1081(b) applies only to the transfers specified therein with respect to which section 1081(d) is inapplicable, and deals only with such transfers if gain is realized upon the sale or other disposition effected by such transfers. If loss is realized section 1081(b) is inapplicable and the application of other provisions of subtitle A of the Code must be determined. See section 1081(g). If section 1081(b) is applicable, the other provisions of subchapters C and O, chapter 1 of the Code, relating to the nonrecognition of gain are inapplicable, and the conditions under which, and the extent to which, the realized gain is not recognized are set forth in paragraphs (b), (c), (d), (e), and (f) of this section.

(b) *Nonrecognition of gain; no nonexempt proceeds.* No gain is recognized to a transferor corporation upon the sale or other disposition of property transferred by such transferor corporation in exchange solely for property other than nonexempt property, as defined in section 1083(e), but only if all of the following requirements are satisfied:

(1) The transferor corporation is, under the definition in section 1083(b), a registered holding company or an associate company of a registered holding company;

(2) Such transfer is in obedience to an order of the Securities and Exchange Commission (as defined in section 1083(a)) and such order satisfies the requirements of section 1081(f);

(3) The transferor corporation has filed the required consent to the regulations under section 1082(a)(2) (see paragraph (g) of this section); and

(4) The entire amount of the gain, as determined under section 1001, can be applied in reduction of basis under section 1082(a)(2).

(c) *Nonrecognition of gain; nonexempt proceeds.* If the transaction would be within the provisions of paragraph (b) of this section if it were not for the fact that the property received in exchange consists in whole or in part of nonexempt property (as defined in section 1083(e)), then no gain is recognized if such nonexempt property, or an amount equal to the fair market value of such nonexempt property at the time of the transfer,

(1) Is expended within the required 24-month period for property other than nonexempt property; or

(2) Is invested within the required 24-month period as a contribution to the capital, or as paid-in surplus, of another corporation;

but only if the expenditure or investment is made

(3) In accordance with an order of the Securities and Exchange Commission (as defined in section 1083(a)) which satisfies the requirements of section 1081(f) and which recites that such expenditure or investment by the transferor corporation is necessary or appropriate to the integration or simplification of the holding company system of which the transferor corporation is a member; and

(4) The required consent, waiver, and bond have been executed and filed. See paragraphs (g) and (h) of this section.

(d) *Recognition of gain in part; insufficient expenditure or investment in case of nonexempt proceeds.* If the transaction would be within the provisions of paragraph (c) of this section if it were not for the fact that the amount expended or invested is less than the fair market value of the nonexempt property received in exchange, then the gain, if any, is recognized, but in an amount not in excess of the amount by which the fair market value of such nonexempt property at the time of the transfer exceeds the amount so expended and invested.

(e) *Items treated as expenditures for the purpose of paragraphs (c) and (d) of this section.* For the purposes of paragraphs (c) and (d) of this section, the following are treated as expenditures for property other than nonexempt property:

(1) A distribution in cancellation or redemption (except a distribution having the effect of a dividend) of the whole or a part of the transferor's own stock (not acquired on the transfer);

(2) A payment in complete or partial retirement or cancellation of securities representing indebtedness of the transferor or a complete or partial retirement or cancellation of such securities which is a part of the consideration for the transfer; and

(3) If, on the transfer, a liability of the transferor is assumed, or property of the transferor is transferred subject to a liability, the amount of such liability.

(f) *Recognition of gain in part; inability to reduce basis.* If the transaction would be within the provisions of paragraph (b) or (c) of this section, if it were not for the fact that an amount of gain cannot be applied in reduction of basis under section 1082(a)(2), then the gain, if any, is recognized, but in an amount not in excess of the amount which cannot be so applied in reduction of basis. If the transaction would be within the provisions of paragraph (d) of this section, if it were not for the fact that an amount of gain cannot be applied in reduction of basis under section 1082(a)(2), then the gain, if any, is recognized,

Reg. § 1.1081-4(a)

but in an amount not in excess of the aggregate of—

(1) The amount of gain which would be recognized under paragraph (d) of this section if there were no inability to reduce basis under section 1082(a)(2); and

(2) The amount of gain which cannot be applied in reduction of basis under section 1082(a)(2).

(g) *Consent to regulations under section 1082(a)(2).* To be entitled to the benefits of the provisions of section 1081(b), a corporation must file with its return for the taxable year in which the transfer occurs a consent to have the basis of its property adjusted under section 1082(a)(2) (see § 1.1082-3), in accordance with the provisions of the regulations in effect at the time of filing of the return for the taxable year in which the transfer occurs. Such consent shall be made on Form 982 in accordance with these regulations and instructions on the form or issued therewith.

(h) *Requirements with respect to expenditure or investment.* If the full amount of the expenditure or investment required for the application of paragraph (c) of this section has not been made by the close of the taxable year in which such transfer occurred, the taxpayer shall file with the return for such year an application for the benefit of the 24-month period for expenditure and investment, reciting the nature and time of the proposed expenditure or investment. When requested by the district director, the taxpayer shall execute and file (at such time and in such form) such waiver of the statute of limitations with respect to the assessment of deficiencies (for the taxable year of the transfer and for all succeeding taxable years in any of which falls any part of the period beginning with the date of the transfer and ending 24 months thereafter) as the district director may specify, and such bond with such surety as the district director may require, in an amount not in excess of double the estimated maximum income tax which would be payable if the corporation does not make the required expenditure or investment within the required 24-month period. [Reg. § 1.1081-4.]

☐ [*T.D.* 6178, 6-1-56. *Amended by T.D.* 6751, 8-5-64 *and T.D.* 7517, 11-11-77.]

[Reg. § 1.1081-5]

§ 1.1081-5. **Distribution solely of stock or securities.**—(a) *In general.* If, without any surrender of his stock or securities as defined in section 1083(f), a shareholder in a corporation which is a registered holding company or a majority-owned subsidiary company receives stock or securities in such corporation or owned by such corporation, no gain to the shareholder will be recognized with respect to the stock or securities received by such shareholder which do not constitute nonexempt property, if the distribution to such shareholder is made by the distributing corporation in obedience to an order of the Securities and Exchange Commission directed to such corporation. A distribution is not within the provisions of section 1081(c)(1) if it is within the provisions of section 1081(d), relating to transfers within a system group. A distribution is also not within the provisions of section 1081(c)(1) if it involves a surrender by the shareholder of stock or securities or a transfer by the shareholder of property in exchange for the stock or securities received by the shareholder. For further limitations, see section 1081(f).

(b) *Special rule.* (1) If there is distributed to a shareholder in a corporation rights to acquire common stock in a second corporation, no gain to the shareholder from the receipt of the rights shall be recognized, but only if all the following requirements are met:

(i) The rights are received by the shareholder without the surrender by the shareholder of any stock in the distributing corporation,

(ii) Such distribution is in accordance with an arrangement forming a ground for an order of the Securities and Exchange Commission issued pursuant to section 3 of the Public Utility Holding Company Act of 1935 (15 U.S.C. 79c) that the distributing corporation is exempt from any provision or provisions of such act, and

(iii) Before January 1, 1958, the distributing corporation disposes of all the common stock in the second corporation which it owns.

(2) The distributing corporation shall, as soon as practicable, notify the district director in whose district the corporation's income tax return and supporting data was filed (see paragraph (g) of § 1.1081-11), as to whether or not requirement of subparagraph (1)(iii) of this paragraph has been met. If such requirement has not been met, the periods of limitation (sections 6501 and 6502) with respect to any deficiency, including interest and additions to the tax, resulting solely from the receipt of such rights to acquire stock, shall include one year immediately following the date of such notification; and assessment and collection shall be made notwithstanding any provisions of law or rule of law which would otherwise prevent such assessment and collection. [Reg. § 1.1081-5.]

☐ [*T.D.* 6178, 6-1-56.]

[Reg. § 1.1081-6]

§ 1.1081-6. **Transfers within system group.**—(a) The nonrecognition of gain or loss

Reg. § 1.1081-6(a)

provided for in section 1081(d)(1) is applicable to an exchange of property for other property (including money and other nonexempt property) between corporations which are all members of the same system group. The term "system group" is defined in section 1083(d).

(b) Section 1081(d)(1) also provides for nonrecognition of gain to a corporation which is a member of a system group if property (including money or other nonexempt property) is distributed to such corporation as a shareholder in a corporation which is a member of the same system group, without the surrender by such shareholder of stock or securities in the distributing corporation.

(c) As stated in § 1.1081-2, nonrecognition of gain or loss will not be accorded to a transaction not clearly provided for in part VI (section 1081 and following), subchapter O, chapter 1 of the Code, even though such transaction occurs simultaneously or in connection with an exchange, sale, or distribution to which nonrecognition is specifically accorded. Therefore, nonrecognition will not be accorded to any gain or loss realized from the discharge, or the removal of the burden, of the pecuniary obligations of a member of a system group, even though such obligations are acquired upon a transfer or distribution specifically described in section 1081(d)(1); but the fact that the acquisition of such obligations was upon a transfer or distribution specifically described in section 1081(d)(1) will, because of the basis provisions of section 1082(d), affect the cost to the member of such discharge or its equivalent. Thus, section 1081(d)(1) does not provide for the nonrecognition of any gain or loss realized from the discharge of the indebtedness of a member of a system group as the result of the acquisition in exchange, sale, or distribution of its own bonds, notes, or other evidences of indebtedness which were acquired by another member of the same system group for a consideration less or more than the issuing price thereof (with proper adjustments for amortization of premiums or discounts).

(d) The provisions of paragraph (c) of this section may be illustrated by the following example:

Example. Suppose that the A Corporation and the B Corporation are both members of the same system group; that the A Corporation holds at a cost of $900 a bond issued by the B Corporation at par, $1,000; and that the A Corporation and the B Corporation enter into an exchange subject to the provisions of section 1081(d)(1) in which the $1,000 bond of the B Corporation is transferred from the A Corporation to the B Corporation. The $900 basis reflecting the cost to the A Corporation which would have been the basis available to the B Corporation if the property transferred to it had been something other than its own securities (see § 1.1082-6) will, in this type of transaction, reflect the cost to the B Corporation of effecting a retirement of its own $1,000 bond. The $100 gain of the B Corporation reflected in the retirement will therefore be recognized.

(e) No exchange or distribution may be made without the recognition of gain or loss as provided for in section 1081(d)(1), unless all the corporations which are parties to such exchange or distribution are acting in obedience to an order of the Securities and Exchange Commission. If an exchange or distribution is within the provisions of section 1081(d)(1) and also may be considered to be within some other provisions of section 1081, it shall be considered that only the provisions of section 1081(d)(1) apply and that the nonrecognition of gain or loss upon such exchange or distribution is by virtue of that section. [Reg. § 1.1081-6.]

☐ [T.D. 6178, 6-1-56.]

[Reg. § 1.1081-7]

§ 1.1081-7. **Sale of stock or securities received upon exchange by members of system group.**—(a) Section 1081(d)(2) provides that to the extent that property received upon an exchange by corporations which are members of the same system group consists of stock or securities issued by the corporation from which such property was received, such stock or securities may, under certain specifically described circumstances, be sold to a party not a member of the system group, without the recognition of gain or loss to the selling corporation. The nonrecognition of gain or loss is limited, in the case of stock, to a sale of stock which is preferred as to both dividends and assets. The stock or securities must have been received upon an exchange with respect to which section 1081(d)(1) operated to prevent recognition of gain or loss to any party to the exchange. Nonrecognition of gain or loss upon the sale of such stock or securities is permitted only if the proceeds derived from the sale are applied in retirement or cancellation of stock or securities of the selling corporation which were outstanding at the time the exchange was made. It is also essential to nonrecognition of gain or loss upon the sale that both the sale of the stock or securities and the application of the proceeds derived therefrom be made in obedience to an order of the Securities and Exchange Commission. If any part of the proceeds derived from the sale is not applied in making the required retirement or cancellation of stock or securities and if the sale is otherwise within the provisions of section 1081(d)(2), the gain resulting from the sale shall be recognized, but in an amount not in excess of the proceeds which are not so applied. In any event, if the proceeds derived from the sale of the stock or securities exceed the fair market value of such stock or securities at the time of the exchange through which they were acquired by the selling corporation, the gain resulting from the sale is to be recognized to the extent of such excess. Section 1081(d)(2) does not provide for the nonrecognition of any gain resulting from the retirement of bonds, notes, or other evidences of indebtedness for a consideration less than the issuing price thereof. Also, that section does not provide for the nonrecognition of gain or loss upon the sale of any stock or securities received upon a distribution or otherwise than upon an exchange.

(b) The application of paragraph (a) of this section may be illustrated by the following example:

Example. The X Corporation and the Y Corporation, both of which make their income tax returns on a calendar year basis, are members of the same system group. As part of an exchange to which section 1081(d)(1) is applicable the Y Corporation on June 1, 1954, issued to the X Corporation 1,000 shares of class A stock, preferred as to both dividends and assets. The fair market value of such stock at the time of issuance was $90,000 and its basis to the X Corporation was $75,000. On December 1, 1954, in obedience to an appropriate order of the Securities and Exchange Commission, the X Corporation sells all of such stock to the public for $100,000 and applies $95,000 of this amount to the retirement of its own bonds, which are outstanding on June 1, 1954. The remaining $5,000 is not used to retire any of the X Corporation's stock or securities. Of the total gain of $25,000 realized on the disposition of the Y Corporation stock, only $10,000 is recognized (the difference between the fair market value of the stock when acquired and the amount for which it was sold), since such amount is greater than the portion ($5,000) of the proceeds not applied to the retirement of the X Corporation's stock or securities. If in this example the stock acquired by the X Corporation had not been stock of the Y Corporation issued to the X Corporation or if it had been stock not preferred as to both dividends and assets, the full amount of the gain ($25,000) realized upon its disposition would have been recognized, regardless of what was done with the proceeds. [Reg. § 1.1081-7.]

☐ [*T.D.* 6178, 6-1-56.]

[Reg. § 1.1018-8]

§ 1.1081-8. Exchanges in which money or other nonexempt property is received.—(a) Under section 1081(e)(1), if in any exchange (not within any of the provisions of section 1081(d)), in which stock or securities in a corporation which is a registered holding company or a majority-owned subsidiary are exchanged for stock or securities as provided for in section 1081(a), there is received by the taxpayer money or other nonexempt property (in addition to property permitted to be received without recognition of gain), then—

(1) The gain, if any, to the taxpayer is to be recognized in an amount not in excess of the sum of the money and the fair market value of the other nonexempt property, but

(2) The loss, if any, to the taxpayer from such an exchange is not to be recognized to any extent.

(b) If money or other nonexempt property is received from a corporation in an exchange described in paragraph (a) of this section and if the distribution of such money or other nonexempt property by or on behalf of such corporation has the effect of the distribution of a taxable dividend, then, as provided in section 1081(e)(2), there shall be taxed to each distributee (1) as a dividend, such an amount of the gain recognized on the exchange as is not in excess of the distributee's ratable share of the undistributed earnings and profits of the corporation accumulated after February 28, 1913, and (2) the remainder of the gain so recognized shall be taxed as a gain from the exchange of property. [Reg. § 1.1081-8.]

☐ [*T.D.* 6178, 6-1-56.]

[Reg. § 1.1081-9]

§ 1.1081-9. Requirements with respect to order of Securities and Exchange Commission.—The term "order of the Securities and Exchange Commission" is defined in section 1083(a). In addition to the requirements specified in that definition, section 1081(f) provides that, except in the case of a distribution described in section 1081(c)(2), the provisions of section 1081 shall not apply to an exchange, expenditure, investment, distribution, or sale unless each of the following requirements is met:

(a) The order of the Securities and Exchange Commission must recite that the exchange, expenditure, investment, distribution, or sale is necessary or appropriate to effectuate the provisions of section 11(b) of the Public Utility Holding Company Act of 1935 (15 U.S.C. 79k(b)).

(b) The order shall specify and itemize the stocks and securities and other property (including money) which are ordered to be acquired, transferred, received, or sold upon such exchange, acquisition, expenditure, distribution, or sale and, in the case of an investment, the investment to be made, so as clearly to identify such property.

Reg. § 1.1081-9(b)

Exchanges in Obedience to S.E.C. Orders

(c) The exchange, acquisition, expenditure, investment, distribution, or sale shall be made in obedience to such order and shall be completed within the time prescribed in such order.

These requirements were not designed merely to simplify the administration of the provisions of section 1081, and they are not to be considered as pertaining only to administrative matters. Each one of the three requirements is essential and must be met if gain or loss is not to be recognized from the transaction. [Reg. § 1.1081-9.]

□ [T.D. 6178, 6-1-56.]

[Reg. § 1.1081-10]

§ 1.1081-10. **Nonapplication of other provisions of the Internal Revenue Code of 1954.**—The effect of section 1081(g) is that an exchange, sale, or distribution which is within section 1081 shall, with respect to the nonrecognition of gain or loss and the determination of basis, be governed only by the provisions of part VI (section 1081 and following), subchapter O, chapter 1 of the Code, the purpose being to prevent overlapping of the provisions of such sections and other provisions of subtitle A of the Code. In other words, if by virtue of section 1081 any portion of a person's gain or loss on any particular exchange, sale, or distribution is not to be recognized, then the gain or loss of such person shall be nonrecognized only to the extent provided in section 1081, regardless of what the result might have been if part VI (section 1081 and following), subchapter O, chapter 1 of the Code, had not been enacted; and similarly, the basis in the hands of such person of the property received by him in such transaction shall be the basis provided by section 1082, regardless of what the basis of such property might have been under section 1011 if such part VI had not been enacted. On the other hand, if section 1081 does not provide for the nonrecognition of any portion of a person's gain or loss (whether or not such person is another party to the same transaction referred to above), then the gain or loss of such person shall be recognized or nonrecognized to the extent provided for by other provisions of subtitle A of the Code as if such part VI had not been enacted; and similarly, the basis in his hands of the property received by him in such transaction shall be the basis provided by other provisions of subtitle A of the Code as if such part VI had not been enacted. [Reg. § 1.1081-10.]

□ [T.D. 6178, 6-1-56.]

[Reg. § 1.1081-11]

§ 1.1081-11. **Records to be kept and information to be filed with returns.**—(a) *Exchanges; holders of stock or securities.* Every holder of stock or securities who receives stock or securities and other property (including money) upon an exchange shall, if the exchange is made with a corporation acting in obedience to an order of the Securities and Exchange Commission, file as a part of his income tax return for the taxable year in which the exchange takes place a complete statement of all facts pertinent to the nonrecognition of gain or loss upon such exchange, including—

(1) A clear description of the stock or securities transferred in the exchange, together with a statement of the cost or other basis of such stock or securities.

(2) The name and address of the corporation from which the stock or securities were received in the exchange.

(3) A statement of the amount of stock or securities and other property (including money) received from the exchange. The amount of each kind of stock or securities and other property received shall be set forth upon the basis of the fair market value thereof at the date of the exchange.

(b) *Exchanges; corporations subject to S.E.C. orders.* Each corporation which is a party to an exchange made in obedience to an order of the Securities and Exchange Commission directed to such corporation shall file as a part of its income tax return for its taxable year in which the exchange takes place a complete statement of all facts pertinent to the nonrecognition of gain or loss upon such exchange, including—

(1) A copy of the order of the Securities and Exchange Commission directed to such corporation, in obedience to which the exchange was made.

(2) A certified copy of the corporate resolution authorizing the exchange.

(3) A clear description of all property, including all stock or securities, transferred in the exchange, together with a complete statement of the cost or other basis of each class property.

(4) The date of acquisition of any stock or securities transferred in the exchange, and, if any of such stock or securities were acquired by the corporation in obedience to an order of the Securities and Exchange Commission, a copy of such order.

(5) The name and address of all persons to whom any property was transferred in the exchange.

(6) If any property transferred in the exchange was transferred to another corporation, a copy of any order of the Securities and Exchange Commission directed to the other corporation, in

obedience to which the exchange was made by such other corporation.

(7) If the corporation transfers any nonexempt property, the amount of the undistributed earnings and profits of the corporation accumulated after February 28, 1913, to the time of the exchange, computed in accordance with the last sentence in paragraph (b) of § 1.316-2.

(8) A statement of the amount of stock or securities and other property (including money) received upon the exchange, including a statement of all distributions or other dispositions made thereof. The amount of each kind of stock or securities and other property received shall be stated on the basis of the fair market value thereof at the date of the exchange.

(9) A statement showing as to each class of its stock the number of shares and percentage owned by any other corporation, the voting rights and voting power, and the preference (if any) as to both dividends and assets.

(10) The term "exchange" shall, whenever occurring in this paragraph, be read as "exchange, expenditure, or investment".

(c) *Distributions; shareholders.* Each shareholder who receives stock or securities or other property (including money) upon a distribution made by a corporation in obedience to an order of the Securities and Exchange Commission shall file as a part of his income tax return for the taxable year in which such distribution is received a complete statement of all facts pertinent to the nonrecognition of gain upon such distribution, including—

(1) The name and address of the corporation from which the distribution is received.

(2) A statement of the amount of stock or securities or other property received upon the distribution, including (in case the shareholder is a corporation) a statement of all distributions or other disposition made of such stock or securities or other property by the shareholder. The amount of each class of stock or securities and each kind of property shall be stated on the basis of the fair market value thereof at the date of the distribution.

(3) If the shareholder is a corporation, a statement showing as to each class of its stock the number of shares and percentage owned by a registered holding company or a majority-owned subsidiary company of a registered holding company, the voting rights and voting power, and the preference (if any) as to both dividends and assets.

(d) *Distributions; distributing corporations subject to S.E.C. orders.* Every corporation making a distribution in obedience to an order of the Securities and Exchange Commission shall file as a part of its income tax return for its taxable year in which the distribution is made a complete statement of all facts pertinent to the nonrecognition of gain to the distributee upon such distribution including—

(1) A copy of the order of the Securities and Exchange Commission, in obedience to which the distribution was made.

(2) A certified copy of the corporate resolution authorizing the distribution.

(3) A statement of the amount of stock or securities or other property (including money) distributed to each shareholder. The amount of each kind of stock or securities or other property shall be stated on the basis of the fair market value thereof at the date of the distribution.

(4) The date of acquisition of the stock or securities distributed, and, if any of such stock or securities were acquired by the distributing corporation in obedience to an order of the Securities and Exchange Commission, a copy of such order.

(5) The amount of the undistributed earnings and profits of the corporation accumulated after February 28, 1913, to the time of the distribution, computed in accordance with the last sentence in paragraph (b) of § 1.316-2.

(6) A statement showing as to each class of its stock the number of shares and percentage owned by any other corporation, the voting rights and voting power, and the preference (if any) as to both dividends and assets.

(e) *Sales by members of system groups.* Each corporation which is a member of a system group and which in obedience to an order of the Securities and Exchange Commission sells stock or securities received upon an exchange (made in obedience to an order of the Securities and Exchange Commission) and applies the proceeds derived therefrom in retirement or cancellation of its own stock or securities shall file as a part of its income tax return for the taxable year in which the sale is made a complete statement of all facts pertaining to the nonrecognition of gain or loss upon such sale, including—

(1) A copy of the order of the Securities and Exchange Commission in obedience to which the sale was made.

(2) A copy of the order of the Securities and Exchange Commission in obedience to which the proceeds derived from the sale were applied in whole or in part in the retirement or cancellation of its stock or securities.

(3) A certified copy of the corporate resolutions authorizing the sale of the stock or securities

Reg. § 1.1081-11(e)(3)

and the application of the proceeds derived therefrom.

(4) A clear description of the stock or securities sold, including the name and address of the corporation by which they were issued.

(5) The date of acquisition of the stock or securities sold, together with a statement of the fair market value of such stock or securities at the date of acquisition, and a copy of all orders of the Securities and Exchange Commission in obedience to which such stock or securities were acquired.

(6) The amount of the proceeds derived from such sale.

(7) The portion of the proceeds of such sale which was applied in retirement or cancellation of its stock or securities, together with a statement showing how long such stock or securities were outstanding prior to retirement or cancellation.

(8) The issuing price of its stock or securities which were retired or canceled.

(f) *Section 1081(c)(2) distributions; shareholders.* Each shareholder who receives a distribution described in section 1081(c)(2) (concerning rights to acquire common stock) shall file as a part of his income tax return for the taxable year in which such distribution is received a complete statement of all the facts pertinent to the nonrecognition of gain upon such distribution, including—

(1) The name and address of the corporation from which the distribution is received.

(2) A statement of the amount of the rights received upon the distribution, stated on the basis of their fair market value at the date of the distribution.

(g) *Section 1081(c)(2) distributions; distributing corporations.* Every corporation making a distribution described in section 1081(c)(2) (concerning rights to acquire common stock) shall file as a part of its income tax return for its taxable year in which the distribution is made a complete statement of all facts pertinent to the nonrecognition of gain to the distributees upon such distribution including—

(1) A copy of the arrangement forming the basis for the issuance of the order by the Securities and Exchange Commission.

(2) A copy of the order issued by the Securities and Exchange Commission pursuant to section 3 of the Public Utility Holding Company Act of 1935.

(3) A certified copy of the corporate resolution authorizing the arrangement and the distribution.

(4) A statement of the amount of the rights distributed to each shareholder, stated on the basis of their fair market value at the date of the distribution.

(5) The date of acquisition of the stock with respect to which such rights are distributed, and, if any were acquired by the distributing corporation in obedience to an order of the Securities and Exchange Commission, a copy of such order.

(6) The amount of undistributed earnings and profits of the distributing corporation accumulated after February 28, 1913, to the time of the distribution, computed in accordance with the last sentence in paragraph (b) of § 1.316-2.

(h) *General requirements.* Permanent records in substantial form shall be kept by every taxpayer who participates in an exchange or distribution to which sections 1081 to 1083, inclusive, are applicable, showing the cost or other basis of the property transferred and the amount of stock or securities and other property (including money) received, in order to facilitate the determination of gain or loss from a subsequent disposition of such stock or securities and other property received on the exchange or distribution. [Reg. § 1.1081-11.]

☐ [*T.D.* 6178, 6-1-56.]

[Reg. § 1.1082-1]

§ 1.1082-1. **Basis for determining gain or loss.**—(a) For determining the basis of property acquired in a taxable year beginning before January 1, 1942, in any manner described in section 372 of the Internal Revenue Code of 1939 prior to its amendment by the Revenue Act of 1942 (56 Stat. 798), see such section (before its amendment by such Act).

(b) If the property was acquired in a taxable year beginning after December 31, 1941, in any manner described in section 1082 (other than subsection (a)(2)), or section 372 (other than subsection (a)(2)) of the Internal Revenue Code of 1939 after its amendments, the basis shall be that prescribed in section 1082 with respect to such property. However, in the case of property acquired in a transaction described in section 1081(c)(2), this paragraph is applicable only if the property was acquired in a distribution made in a taxable year subject to the Internal Revenue Code of 1954.

(c) Section 1082 makes provisions with respect to the basis of property acquired in a transfer in connection with which the recognition of gain or loss is prohibited by the provisions of section 1081 with respect to the whole or any part of the property received. In general, and except as provided in § 1.1082-3, it is intended that the basis for determining gain or loss pertaining to the property prior to its transfer, as well as the basis for determining the amount of depreciation or

Reg. § 1.1082-1(a)

depletion deductible and the amount of earnings or profits available for distribution, shall continue notwithstanding the nontaxable conversion of the asset in form or its change in ownership. The continuance of the basis may be reflected in a shift thereof from one asset to another in the hands of the same owner, or in its transfer with the property from one owner into the hands of another. See also § 1.1081-2. [Reg. § 1.1082-1.]

☐ [T.D. 6178, 6-1-56.]

[Reg. § 1.1082-2]

§ 1.1082-2. Basis of property acquired upon exchanges under section 1081(a) or (e).—(a) In the case of an exchange of stock or securities for stock or securities as described in section 1081(a), if no part of the gain or loss upon such exchange was recognized under section 1081, the basis of the property acquired is the same as the basis of the property transferred by the taxpayer with proper adjustments to the date of the exchange.

(b) If, in an exchange of stock or securities as described in section 1081(a), gain to the taxpayer was recognized under section 1081(e) on account of the receipt of money, the basis of the property acquired is the basis of the property transferred (adjusted to the date of the exchange), decreased by the amount of money received and increased by the amount of gain recognized upon the exchange. If, upon such exchange, there were received by the taxpayer money and other nonexempt property (not permitted to be received without the recognition of gain), and gain from the transaction was recognized under section 1081(e), the basis (adjusted to the date of the exchange) of the property transferred by the taxpayer, decreased by the amount of money received and increased by the amount of gain recognized, must be apportioned to and is the basis of the properties (other than money) received on the exchange. For the purpose of the allocation of such basis to the properties received, there must be assigned to the nonexempt property (other than money) an amount equivalent to its fair market value at the date of the exchange.

(c) Section 1081(e) provides that no loss may be recognized on an exchange of stock or securities for stock or securities as described in section 1081(a), although the taxpayer receives money or other nonexempt property from the transaction. However, the basis of the property (other than money) received by the taxpayer is the basis (adjusted to the date of the exchange) of the property transferred, decreased by the amount of money received. This basis must be apportioned to the properties received, and for this purpose there must be allocated to the nonexempt property (other than money) an amount of such basis equivalent to the fair market value of such nonexempt property at the date of the exchange.

(d) Section 1082(a) does not apply in ascertaining the basis of property acquired by a corporation by the issuance of its stock or securities as the consideration in whole or in part for the transfer of the property to it. For the rule in such cases, see section 1082(b).

(e) For purposes of this section, any reference to section 1081 shall be deemed to include a reference to corresponding provisions of prior internal revenue laws. [Reg. § 1.1082-2.]

☐ [T.D. 6178, 6-1-56.]

[Reg. § 1.1082-3]

§ 1.1082-3. Reduction of basis of property by reason of gain not recognized under section 1081(b).—(a) *Introductory.* In addition to the adjustments provided in section 1016 and other applicable provisions of chapter 1 of the Code, and the regulations relating thereto, which are required to be made with respect to the cost or other basis of property, section 1082(a)(2) provides that a further adjustment shall be made in any case in which there shall have been a nonrecognition of gain under section 1081(b). Such further adjustment shall be made with respect to the basis of the property in the hands of the transferor immediately after the transfer and of the property acquired within 24 months after such transfer by an expenditure or investment to which section 1081(b) relates, and on account of which expenditure or investment gain is not recognized. If the property is in the hands of the transferor immediately after the transfer, the time of reduction is the day of the transfer; in all other cases the time of reduction is the date of acquisition. The effect of applying an amount in reduction of basis of property under section 1081(b) is to reduce by such amount the basis for determining gain upon sale or other disposition, the basis for determining loss upon sale or other disposition, the basis for depreciation and for depletion, and any other amount which the Code prescribes shall be the same as any of such bases. For the purposes of the application of an amount in reduction of basis under section 1081(b), property is not considered as having a basis capable of reduction if—

(1) It is money, or

(2) If its adjusted basis for determining gain at the time the reduction is to be made is zero, or becomes zero at any time in the application of section 1081(b).

(b) *General rule.* (1) Section 1082(a)(2) sets forth seven categories of property, the basis of which for determining gain or loss shall be reduced in the order stated.

Reg. § 1.1082-3(b)

Exchanges in Obedience to S.E.C. Orders

See p. 20,601 for regulations not amended to reflect law changes

(2) If any of the property in the first category has a basis capable of reduction, the reduction must first be made before applying an amount in reduction of the basis of any property in the second or in a succeeding category, to each of which in turn a similar rule is applied.

(3) In the application of the rule to each category, the amount of the gain not recognized shall be applied to reduce the cost or other basis of all the property in the category as follows: The cost or other basis (at the time immediately after the transfer or, if the property is not then held but is thereafter acquired, at the time of such acquisition) of each unit of property in the first category shall be decreased (but the amount of the decrease shall not be more than the amount of the adjusted basis at such time for determining gain, determined without regard to this section) in an amount equal to such proportion of the unrecognized gain as the adjusted basis (for determining gain, determined without regard to this section) at such time of each unit of property of the taxpayer in that category bears to the aggregate of the adjusted basis (for determining gain, computed without regard to this section) at such time of all the property of the taxpayer in that category. When such adjusted basis of the property in the first category has been thus reduced to zero, a similar rule shall be applied, with respect to the portion of such gain which is unabsorbed in such reduction of the basis of the property in such category, in reducing the basis of property in the second category. A similar rule with respect to the remaining unabsorbed gain shall be applied in reducing the basis of the property in the next succeeding category.

(c) *Special cases.* (1) With the consent of the Commissioner, the taxpayer may, however, have the basis of the various units of property within a particular category specified in section 1082(a)(2) adjusted in a manner different from the general rule set forth in paragraph (b) of this section. Variations from such general rule may, for example, involve adjusting the basis of only certain units of the taxpayer's property within a given category. A request for variations from the general rule should be filed by the taxpayer with its income tax return for the taxable year in which the transfer of property has occurred.

(2) Agreement between the taxpayer and the Commissioner as to any variations from such general rule shall be effective only if incorporated in a closing agreement entered into under the provisions of section 7121. If no such agreement is entered into by the taxpayer and the Commissioner, then the consent filed on Form 982 shall (except as otherwise provided in this subparagraph) be deemed to be a consent to the application of such general rule, and such general rule shall apply in the determination of the basis of the taxpayer's property. If, however, the taxpayer specifically states on such form that it does not consent to the application of the general rule, then, in the absence of a closing agreement, the document filed shall not be deemed a consent within the meaning of section 1081(b)(4). [Reg. § 1.1082-3.]

☐ [T.D. 6178, 6-1-56. Amended by T.D. 7517, 11-11-77.]

[Reg. § 1.1082-4]

§ 1.1082-4. **Basis of property acquired by corporation under section 1081(a), 1081(b) or 1081(e) as contribution of capital or surplus, or in consideration for its own stock or securities.**—If, in connection with an exchange of stock or securities for stock or securities as described in section 1081(a), or an exchange of property for property as described in section 1081(b), or an exchange as described in section 1081(e), property is acquired by a corporation by the issuance of its stock or securities, the basis of such property shall be determined under section 1082(b). If the corporation issued its stock or securities as part or sole consideration for the property acquired, the basis of the property in the hands of the acquiring corporation is the basis (adjusted to the date of the exchange) which the property would have had in the hands of the transferor if the transfer had not been made, increased in the amount of gain or decreased in the amount of loss recognized under section 1081 to the transferor upon the transfer. If any property is acquired by a corporation from a shareholder as paid-in surplus, or from any person as a contribution to capital, the basis of the property to the corporation is the basis (adjusted to the date of acquisition) of the property in the hands of the transferor. [Reg. § 1.1082-4.]

☐ [T.D. 6178, 6-1-56.]

[Reg. § 1.1082-5]

§ 1.1082-5. **Basis of property acquired by shareholder upon tax-free distribution under section 1081(c)(1) or (2).**—(a) *Stock or securities.* If there was distributed to a shareholder in a corporation which is a registered holding company or a majority-owned subsidiary company, stock or securities (other than stock or securities which are nonexempt property), and if by virtue of section 1081(c)(1) no gain was recognized to the shareholder upon such distribution, then the basis of the stock in respect of which the distribution was made must be apportioned between such stock and the stock or securities so distributed to the shareholder. The basis of the old shares and the

Reg. § 1.1082-4

stock or securities received upon the distribution shall be determined in accordance with the following rules:

(1) If the stock or securities received upon the distribution consist solely of stock in the distributing corporation and the stock received is all of substantially the same character and preference as the stock in respect of which the distribution is made, the basis of each share will be the quotient of the cost or other basis of the old shares of stock divided by the total number of the old and the new shares.

(2) If the stock or securities received upon the distribution are in whole or in part stock in a corporation other than the distributing corporation, or are in whole or in part stock of a character or preference materially different from the stock in respect of which the distribution is made, or if the distribution consists in whole or in part of securities other than stock, the cost or other basis of the stock in respect of which the distribution is made shall be apportioned between such stock and the stock or securities distributed in proportion, as nearly as may be, to the respective values of each class of stock or security, old and new, at the time of such distribution, and the basis of each share of stock or unit of security will be the quotient of the cost or other basis of the class of stock or security to which such share or unit belongs, divided by the number of shares or units in the class. Within the meaning of this subparagraph, stocks or securities in one corporation are different in class from stocks or securities in another corporation, and, in general, any material difference in character or preference or terms sufficient to distinguish one stock or security from another stock or security, so that different values may properly be assigned thereto, will constitute a difference in class.

(b) *Stock rights.* If there was distributed to a shareholder in a corporation rights to acquire common stock in a second corporation, and if by virtue of section 1081(c)(2) no gain was recognized to the shareholder upon such distribution, then the basis of the stock in respect of which the distribution was made must be apportioned between such stock and the stock rights so distributed to the shareholder. The basis of such stock and the stock rights received upon the distribution shall be determined in accordance with the following:

(1) The cost or other basis of the stock in respect of which the distribution is made shall be apportioned between such stock and the stock rights distributed, in proportion to the respective values thereof at the time the rights are issued.

(2) The basis for determining gain or loss from the sale of a right, or from the sale of a share of stock in respect of which the distribution is made, will be the quotient of the cost or other basis, properly adjusted, assigned to the rights or the stock, divided, as the case may be, by the number of rights acquired or by the number of shares of such stock held.

(c) *Cross reference.* As to the basis of stock or securities distributed by one member of a system group to another member of the same system group, see § 1.1082-6. [Reg. § 1.1082-5.]

☐ [*T.D.* 6178, 6-1-56.]

[Reg. § 1.1082-6]

§ 1.1082-6. **Basis of property acquired under section 1081(d) in transactions between corporations of the same system group.**—(a) If property was acquired by a corporation which is a member of a system group, from a corporation which is a member of the same system group, upon a transfer or distribution described in section 1081(d)(1), then as a general rule the basis of such property in the hands of the acquiring corporation is the basis which such property would have had in the hands of the transferor if the transfer or distribution had not been made. Except as otherwise indicated in this section, this rule will apply equally to cases in which the consideration for the property acquired consists of stock or securities, money, and other property, or any of them, but it is contemplated that an ultimate true reflection of income will be obtained in all cases, notwithstanding any peculiarities in form which the various transactions may assume. See the example in § 1.1081-6.

(b) An exception to the general rule is provided for in case the property acquired consists of stock or securities issued by the corporation from which such stock or securities were received. If such stock or securities were the sole consideration for the property transferred to the corporation issuing such stock or securities, then the basis of the stock or securities shall be (1) the same as the basis (adjusted to the time of the transfer) of the property transferred for such stock or securities, or (2) the fair market value of such stock or securities at the time of their receipt, whichever is the lower. If such stock or securities constituted only part consideration for the property transferred to the corporation issuing such stock or securities, then the basis shall be an amount which bears the same ratio to the basis of the property transferred as the fair market value of such stock or securities on their receipt bears to the total fair market value of the entire consideration received, except that the fair market value of such stock or securities at the time of their receipt shall be the basis therefor, if such value is lower than such amount.

Reg. § 1.1082-6(b)

(c) The application of paragraph (b) of this section may be illustrated by the following examples:

Example (1). Suppose the A Corporation has property with an adjusted basis of $600,000 and, in an exchange in which section 1081(d)(1) is applicable, transfers such property to the B Corporation in exchange for a total consideration of $1,000,000, consisting of (1) cash in the amount of $100,000, (2) tangible property having a fair market value of $400,000 and an adjusted basis in the hands of the B Corporation of $300,000, and (3) stock or securities issued by the B Corporation with a par value and a fair market value as of the date of their receipt in the amount of $500,000. The basis to the B Corporation of the property received by it is $600,000, which is the adjusted basis of such property in the hands of the A Corporation. The basis to the A Corporation of the assets (other than cash) received by it is as follows: Tangible property, $300,000, the adjusted basis of such property to the B Corporation, the former owner; stock or securities issued by the B Corporation, $300,000, an amount equal to 500,000/1,000,000ths of $600,000.

Example (2). Suppose that in example (1) the property of the A Corporation transferred to the B Corporation had an adjusted basis of $1,100,000 instead of $600,000, and that all other factors in the example remain the same. In such case, the basis to the A Corporation of the stock or securities in the B Corporation is $500,000, which was the fair market value of such stock or securities at the time of their receipt by the A Corporation, because this amount is less than the amount established as 500,000/1,000,000ths of $1,100,000 or $550,000. [Reg. § 1.1082-6.]

☐ [T.D. 6178, 6-1-56.]

[Reg. § 1.1083-1]

§ 1.1083-1. *Definitions.*—(a) *Order of the Securities and Exchange Commission.* (1) An order of the Securities and Exchange Commission as defined in section 1083(a) must be issued after May 28, 1938 (the date of the enactment of the Revenue Act of 1938 (52 Stat. 447)), and must be issued under the authority of section 11(b) or 11(e) of the Public Utility Holding Company Act of 1935 (15 U.S.C. 79k(b), (e)), to effectuate the provisions of section 11(b) of such Act. In all cases the order must become or have become final in accordance with law; i.e., it must be valid, outstanding, and not subject to further appeal. See further sections 1083(a) and 1081(f).

(2) Section 11(b) of the Public Utility Holding Company Act of 1935 provides:

Section 11. *Simplification of holding company systems.* * * *

(b) It shall be the duty of the Commission, as soon as practicable after January 1, 1938:

(1) To require by order, after notice and opportunity for hearing, that each registered holding company, and each subsidiary company thereof, shall take such action as the Commission shall find necessary to limit the operations of the holding-company system of which such company is a part to a single integrated public-utility system, and to such other businesses as are reasonably incidental, or economically necessary or appropriate to the operations of such integrated public-utility system: *Provided, however,* That the Commission shall permit a registered holding company to continue to control one or more additional integrated public-utility systems, if, after notice and opportunity for hearing, it finds that—

(A) Each of such additional systems cannot be operated as an independent system without the loss of substantial economies which can be secured by the retention of control by such holding company of such system;

(B) All of such additonal systems are located in one State, or in adjoining States, or in a contiguous foreign country; and

(C) The continued combination of such systems under the control of such holding company is not so large (considering the state of the art and the area or region affected) as to impair the advantages of localized management, efficient operation, or the effectiveness of regulation.

The Commission may permit as reasonably incidental, or economically necessary or appropriate to the operations of one or more integrated public-utility systems the retention of an interest in any business (other than the business of a public-utility company as such) which the Commission shall find necessary or appropriate in the public interest or for the protection of investors or consumers and not detrimental to the proper functioning of such system or systems.

(2) To require by order, after notice and opportunity for hearing, that each registered holding company, and each subsidiary company thereof, shall take such steps as the Commission shall find necessary to ensure that the corporate structure or continued existence of any company in the holding-company system does not unduly or unnecessarily complicate the structure, or unfairly or inequitably distribute voting power among security holders, of such holding-company system. In carrying out the provisions of this paragraph the Commission

shall require each registered holding company (and any company in the same holding-company system with such holding company) to take such action as the Commission shall find necessary in order that such holding company shall cease to be a holding company with respect to each of its subsidiary companies which itself has a subsidiary company which is a holding company. Except for the purpose of fairly and equitably distributing voting power among the security holders of such company, nothing in this paragraph shall authorize the Commission to require any change in the corporate structure or existence of any company which is not a holding company, or of any company whose principal business is that of a public-utility company.

The Commission may by order revoke or modify any order previously made under this subsection, if, after notice and opportunity for hearing, it finds that the conditions upon which the order was predicated do not exist. Any order made under this subsection shall be subject to judicial review as provided in section 24.

(3) Section 11(e) of the Public Utility Holding Company Act of 1935 provides:

Sec. 11. *Simplification of holding company systems.* * * *

(e) In accordance with such rules and regulations or order as the Commission may deem necessary or appropriate in the public interest or for the protection of investors or consumers, any registered holding company may, at any time after January 1, 1936, submit a plan to the Commission for the divestment of control, securities, or other assets, or for other action by such company or any subsidiary company of a registered holding company or any subsidiary company thereof for the purpose of enabling such company or any subsidiary company thereof to comply with the provisions of subsection (b). If, after notice and opportunity for hearing, the Commission shall find such plan, as submitted or as modified, necessary to effectuate the provisions of subsection (b) and fair and equitable to the persons affected by such plan, the Commission shall make an order approving such plan; and the Commission, at the request of the company, may apply to a court, in accordance with the provisions of subsection (f) of section 18, to enforce and carry out the terms and provisions of such plan. If, upon any such application, the court, after notice and opportunity for hearing, shall approve such plan as fair and equitable and as appropriate to effectuate the provisions of section 11, the court as a court of equity may, to such extent as it deems necessary for the purpose of carrying out the terms and provisions of such plan, take exclusive jurisdiction and possession of the company or companies and the assets thereof, wherever located; and the court shall have jurisdiction to appoint a trustee, and the court may constitute and appoint the Commission as sole trustee, to hold or administer, under the direction of the court and in accordance with the plan theretofore approved by the court and the Commission, the assets so possessed.

(b) *Registered holding company, holding-company system, and associate company.* (1) Under section 5 of the Public Utility Holding Company Act of 1935 (15 U.S.C. 79e), any holding company may register by filing with the Securities and Exchange Commission a notification of registration, in such form as the Commission may by rules and regulations prescribe as necessary or appropriate in the public interest or for the protection of investors or consumers. A holding company shall be deemed to be registered upon receipt by the Securities and Exchange Commission of such notification of registration. As used in this part, the term "registered holding company" means a holding company whose notification of registration has been so received and whose registration is still in effect under section 5 of the Public Utility Holding Company Act of 1935. Under section 2(a)(7) of the Public Utility Holding Company Act of 1935 (15 U.S.C. 79b(a)(7)), a corporation is a holding company (unless it is declared not to be such by the Securities and Exchange Commission), if such corporation directly or indirectly owns, controls, or holds with power to vote 10 percent or more of the outstanding voting securities of a public-utility company (i.e., an electric utility company or a gas utility company as defined by such act) or of any other holding company. A corporation is also a holding company if the Securities and Exchange Commission determines, after notice and opportunity for hearing, that such corporation directly or indirectly exercises (either alone or pursuant to an arrangement or understanding with one or more other persons) such a controlling influence over the management or policies of any public-utility company (i.e., an electric utility company or a gas utility company as defined by such act) or holding company as to make it necessary or appropriate in the public interest or for the protection of investors or consumers that such corporation be subject to the obligations, duties and liabilities imposed upon holding companies by the Public Utility Holding Company Act of 1935 (15 U.S.C. ch. 2 C). An electric utility company is defined by section 2(a)(3) of the Public Utility Holding Company Act of 1935 (15 U.S.C. 79b(a)(3)) to mean a

Reg. § 1.1083-1(b)

company which owns or operates facilities used for the generation, transmission, or distribution of electrical energy for sale, other than sale to tenants or employees of the company operating such facilities for their own use and not for resale; and a gas utility company is defined by section 2(a)(4) of such act (15 U.S.C. 79b(a)(4)), to mean a company which owns or operates facilities used for the distribution at retail (other than distribution only in enclosed portable containers, or distribution to tenants or employees of the company operating such facilities for their own use and not for resale) of natural or manufactured gas for heat, light, or power. However, under certain conditions the Securities and Exchange Commission may declare a company not to be an electric utility company or gas utility company, as the case may be, in which event the company shall not be considered an electric utility company or a gas utility company.

(2) The term "holding company system" has the meaning assigned to it by section 2(a)(9) of the Public Utility Holding Company Act of 1935 (15 U.S.C. 79b(a)(9)), and hence means any holding company, together with all its subsidiary companies (i.e., subsidiary companies within the meaning of section 2(a)(8) of such act (15 U.S.C. 79b(a)(8)), which in general include all companies 10 percent of whose outstanding voting securities is owned directly or indirectly by such holding company) and all mutual service companies of which such holding company or any subsidiary company thereof is a member company. The term "mutual service company" means a company approved as a mutual service company under section 13 of the Public Utility Holding Company Act of 1935 (15 U.S.C. 79m). The term "member company" is defined by section 2(a)(14) of such act (15 U.S.C. 79b(a)(14)), to mean a company which is a member of an association or group of companies mutually served by a mutual service company.

(3) The term "associate company" has the meaning assigned to it by section 2(a)(10) of the Public Utility Holding Company Act of 1935 (15 U.S.C. 79b(a)(10)), and hence an associate company of a company is any company in the same holding-company system with such company.

(c) *Majority-owned subsidiary company.* The term "majority-owned subsidiary company" is defined in section 1083(c). Direct ownership by a registered holding company of more than 50 percent of the specified stock of another corporation is not necessary to constitute such corporation a majority-owned subsidiary company. To illustrate, if the H Corporation, a registered holding company, owns 51 percent of the common stock of the A Corporation and 31 percent of the common stock of the B Corporation, and the A Corporation owns 20 percent of the common stock of the B Corporation (the common stock in each case being the only stock entitled to vote), both the A Corporation and the B Corporation are majority-owned subsidiary companies.

(d) *System group.* The term "system group" is defined in section 1083(d) to mean one or more chains of corporations connected through stock ownership with a common parent corporation, if at least 90 percent of each class of stock (other than (1) stock which is preferred as to both dividends and assets, and (2) stock which is limited and preferred as to dividends but which is not preferred as to assets but only if the total value of such stock is less than 1 percent of the aggregate value of all classes of stock which are not preferred as to both dividends and assets) of each of the corporations (except the common parent corporation) is owned directly by one or more of the other corporations, and if the common parent corporation owns directly at least 90 percent of each class of stock (other than stock preferred as to both dividends and assets) of at least one of the other corporations; but no corporation is a member of a system group unless it is either a registered holding company or a majority-owned subsidiary company. While the type of stock which must, for the purpose of this definition, be at least 90 percent owned may be different from the voting stock which must be more than 50 percent owned for the purpose of the definition of a majority-owned subsidiary company under section 1083(c), as a general rule both types of ownership tests must be met under section 1083(d), since a corporation, in order to be a member of a system group, must also be a registered holding company or a majority-owned subsidiary company.

(e) *Nonexempt property.* The term "nonexempt property" is defined by section 1083(e) to include—

(1) The amount of any consideration in the form of a cancellation or assumption of debts or other liabilities of the transferor (including a continuance of encumbrances subject to which the property was transferred). To illustrate, if in obedience to an order of the Securities and Exchange Commission the X Corporation, a registered holding company, transfers property to the Y Corporation in exchange for property (not nonexempt property) with a fair market value of $500,000, the X Corporation receives $100,000 of nonexempt property, if for example—

(i) The Y Corporation cancels $100,000 of indebtedness owed to it by the X Corporation;

Reg. § 1.1083-1(b)(2)

Wash Sales; Straddles

See p. 20,601 for regulations not amended to reflect law changes

(ii) The Y Corporation assumes an indebtedness of $100,000 owed by the X Corporation to another company, the A Corporation; or

(iii) The Y Corporation takes over the property conveyed to it by the X Corporation subject to a mortgage of $100,000.

(2) *Short-term obligations* (including notes, drafts, bills of exchange, and bankers' acceptances) having a maturity at the time of issuance of not exceeding 24 months, exclusive of days of grace.

(3) Securities issued or guaranteed as to principal or interest by a government or subdivision thereof (including those issued by a corporation which is an instrumentality of a government or subdivision thereof).

(4) Stock or securities which were acquired from a registered holding company which acquired such stock or securities after February 28, 1938, or an associate company of a registered holding company which acquired such stock or securities after February 28, 1938, unless such stock or securities were acquired in obedience to an order of the Securities and Exchange Commission (as defined in section 1083(a)) or were acquired with the authorization or approval of the Securities and Exchange Commission under any section of the Public Utility Holding Company Act of 1935, and are not nonexempt property within the meaning of section 1083(e)(1), (2), or (3).

(5) Money, and the right to receive money not evidenced by a security other than an obligation described as nonexempt property in section 1083(e)(2) or (3). The term "the right to receive money" includes, among other items, accounts receivable, claims for damages, and rights to refunds of taxes.

(f) *Stock or securities.* The term "stock or securities" is defined in section 1083(f) for the purposes of part VI (section 1081 and following), subchapter O, chapter 1 of the Code. As therein defined, the term includes voting trust certificates and stock rights or warrants. [Reg. § 1.1083-1.]

☐ [T.D. 6178, 6-1-56.]

Wash Sales; Straddles

[Reg. § 1.1091-1]

§ 1.1091-1. **Losses from wash sales of stock or securities.**—(a) A taxpayer cannot deduct any loss claimed to have been sustained from the sale or other disposition of stock or securities if, within a period beginning 30 days before the date of such sale or disposition and ending 30 days after such date (referred to in this section as the 61-day period), he has acquired (by purchase or by an exchange upon which the entire amount of gain or loss was recognized by law), or has entered into a contract or option so to acquire, substantially identical stock or securities. However, this prohibition does not apply (1) in the case of a taxpayer, not a corporation, if the sale or other disposition of stock or securities is made in connection with the taxpayer's trade or business, or (2) in the case of a corporation, a dealer in stock or securities, if the sale or other disposition of stock or securities is made in the ordinary course of its business as such dealer.

(b) Where more than one loss is claimed to have been sustained within the taxable year from the sale or other disposition of stock or securities, the provisions of this section shall be applied to the losses in the order in which the stock or securities the disposition of which resulted in the respective losses were disposed of (beginning with the earliest disposition). If the order of disposition of stock or securities disposed of at a loss on the same day cannot be determined, the stock or securities will be considered to have been disposed of in the order in which they were originally acquired (beginning with the earliest acquisition).

(c) Where the amount of stock or securities acquired within the 61-day period is less than the amount of stock or securities sold or otherwise disposed of, then the particular shares of stock or securities the loss from the sale or other disposition of which is not deductible shall be those with which the stock or securities acquired are matched in accordance with the following rule: The stock or securities acquired will be matched in accordance with the order of their acquisition (beginning with the earliest acquisition) with an equal number of the shares of stock or securities sold or otherwise disposed of.

(d) Where the amount of stock or securities acquired within the 61-day period is not less than the amount of stock or securities sold or otherwise disposed of, then the particular shares of stock or securities the acquisition of which resulted in the nondeductibility of the loss shall be those with which the stock or securities disposed of are matched in accordance with the following rule: The stock or securities sold or otherwise disposed of will be matched with an equal number of the shares of stock or securities acquired in accordance with the order of acquisition (beginning with the earliest acquisition) of the stock or securities acquired.

(e) The acquisition of any share of stock or any security which results in the nondeductibility of a loss under the provisions of this section shall be disregarded in determining the deductibility of any other loss.

(f) The word "acquired" as used in this section means acquired by purchase or by an exchange upon which the entire amount of gain or loss was recognized by law, and comprehends cases where the taxpayer has entered into a contract or option within the 61-day period to acquire by purchase or by such an exchange.

(g) For purposes of determining under this section the 61-day period applicable to a short sale of stock or securities, the principles of paragraph (a) of § 1.1233-1 for determining the consummation of a short sale shall generally apply except that the date of entering into the short sale shall be deemed to be the date of sale if, on the date of entering into the short sale, the taxpayer owns (or on or before such date has entered into a contract or option to acquire) stock or securities identical to those sold short and subsequently delivers such stock or securities to close the short sale.

(h) The following examples illustrate the application of this section:

Example (1). A, whose taxable year is the calendar year, on December 1, 1954, purchased 100 shares of common stock in the M Company for $10,000 and on December 15, 1954, purchased 100 additional shares for $9,000. On January 3, 1955, he sold the 100 shares purchased on December 1, 1954, for $9,000. Because of the provisions of section 1091, no loss from the sale is allowable as a deduction.

Example (2). A, whose taxable year is the calendar year, on September 21, 1954, purchased 100 shares of the common stock of the M Company for $5,000. On December 21, 1954, he purchased 50 shares of substantially identical stock for $2,750, and on December 27, 1954, he purchased 25 additional shares of such stock for $1,125. On January 3, 1955, he sold for $4,000 the 100 shares purchased on September 21, 1954. There is an indicated loss of $1,000 on the sale of the 100 shares. Since, within the 61-day period, A purchased 75 shares of substantially identical stock, the loss on the sale of 75 of the shares ($3,750 − $3,000, or $750) is not allowable as a deduction because of the provisions of section 1091. The loss on the sale of the remaining 25 shares ($1,250 − $1,000, or $250) is deductible subject to the limitations provided in sections 267 and 1211. The basis of the 50 shares purchased December 21, 1954, the acquisition of which resulted in the nondeductibility of the loss ($500) sustained on 50 of the 100 shares sold on January 3, 1955, is $2,500 (the cost of 50 of the shares sold on January 3, 1955) + $750 (the difference between the purchase price ($2,750) of 50 of the shares acquired on December 21, 1954, and the selling price ($2,000) of the 50 shares sold on January 3, 1955, or $3,250). Similarly, the basis of the 25 shares purchased on December 27, 1954, the acquisition of which resulted in the nondeductibility of the loss ($250) sustained on 25 of the shares sold on January 3, 1955, is $1,250 + $125, or $1,375. See § 1.1091-2.

Example (3). A, whose taxable year is the calendar year, on September 15, 1954, purchased 100 shares of the stock of the M Company for $5,000. He sold these shares on February 1, 1956, for $4,000. On each of the four days from February 15, 1956, to February 18, 1956, inclusive, he purchased 50 shares of substantially identical stock for $2,000. There is an indicated loss of $1,000 from the sale of the 100 shares on February 1, 1956, but, since within the 61-day period A purchased not less than 100 shares of substantially identical stock, the loss is not deductible. The particular shares of stock the purchase of which resulted in the nondeductibility of the loss are the first 100 shares purchased within such period, that is, the 50 shares purchased on February 15, 1956, and the 50 shares purchased on February 16, 1956. In determining the period for which the 50 shares purchased on February 15, 1956, and the 50 shares purchased on February 16, 1956, were held, there is to be included the period for which the 100 shares purchased on September 15, 1954, and sold on February 1, 1956, were held. [Reg. § 1.1091-1.]

☐ [T.D. 6178, 6-1-56. *Amended by T.D. 6926, 8-8-67.*]

[Reg. § 1.1091-2]

§ 1.1091-2. **Basis of stock or securities acquired in "wash sales".**—(a) *In general.* The application of section 1091(d) may be illustrated by the following examples:

Example (1). A purchased a share of common stock of the X Corporation for $100 in 1935, which he sold January 15, 1955, for $80. On February 1, 1955, he purchased a share of common stock of the same corporation for $90. No loss from the sale is recognized under section 1091. The basis of the new share is $110; that is, the basis of the old share ($100) increased by $10, the excess of the price at which the new share was acquired ($90) over the price at which the old share was sold ($80).

Example (2). A purchased a share of common stock of the Y Corporation for $100 in 1935, which he sold January 15, 1955, for $80. On February 1, 1955, he purchased a share of common stock of the same corporation for $70. No loss from the sale is recognized under section 1091.

Reg. § 1.1091-2(a)

The basis of the new share is $90; that is, the basis of the old share ($100) decreased by $10, the excess of the price at which the old share was sold ($80) over the price at which the new share was acquired ($70).

(b) *Special rule.* For a special rule as to the adjustment to basis required under section 1091(d) in the case of wash sales involving certain regulated investment company stock for which there is an average basis, see paragraph (e)(3)(iii)*(c)* and *(d)* of § 1.1012-1. [Reg. § 1.1091-2.]

☐ [T.D. 6178, 6-1-56. *Amended by T.D. 7129, 7-6-71.*]

[Reg. § 1.1092(b)-1T]

§ 1.1092(b)-1T. **Coordination of loss deferral rules and wash sale rules (temporary).**—(a) *In general.* Except as otherwise provided, in the case of the disposition of a position or positions of a straddle, the rules of paragraph (a)(1) of this section apply before the application of the rules of paragraph (a)(2) of this section.

(1) Any loss sustained from the disposition of shares of stock or securities that constitute positions of a straddle shall not be taken into account for purposes of this subtitle if, within a period beginning 30 days before the date of such disposition and ending 30 days after such date, the taxpayer has acquired (by purchase or by an exchange on which the entire amount of gain or loss was recognized by law), or has entered into a contract or option so to acquire, substantially identical stock or securities.

(2) Except as otherwise provided, if a taxpayer disposes of less than all of the positions of a straddle, any loss sustained with respect to the disposition of that position or positions (hereinafter referred to as "loss position") shall not be taken into account for purposes of this subtitle to the extent that the amount of unrecognized gain as of the close of the taxable year in one or more of the following positions—

(i) Successor positions,

(ii) Offsetting positions to the loss position, or

(iii) Offsetting positions to any successor position,

exceeds the amount of loss disallowed under paragraph (a)(1) of this section. See § 1.1092(b)-5T relating to definitions.

(b) *Carryover of disallowed loss.* Any loss that is disallowed under paragraph (a) of this section shall, subject to any further application of paragraph (a)(1) of this section and the limitations under paragraph (a)(2) of this section, be treated as sustained in the succeeding taxable year. However, a loss disallowed in Year 1, for example, under paragraph (a)(1) of this section will not be allowed in Year 2 unless the substantially identical stock or securities, the acquisition of which caused the loss to be disallowed in Year 1, are disposed of during Year 2 and paragraphs (a)(1) and (a)(2) of this section do not apply in Year 2 to disallow the loss.

(c) *Treatment of disallowed loss*—(1) *Character.* If the disposition of a loss position would (but for the application of this section) result in a capital loss, the loss allowed under paragraph (b) of this section with respect to the disposition of the loss position shall be treated as a capital loss. In any other case, a loss allowed under paragraph (b) of this section shall be treated as an ordinary loss. For example, if the disposition of a loss position would, but for the application of paragraph (a) of this section, give rise to a capital loss, that loss when allowed pursuant to paragraph (b) of this section will be treated as a capital loss on the date the loss is allowed regardless of whether any gain or loss with respect to one or more successor positions would be treated as ordinary income or loss.

(2) *Section 1256 contracts.* If the disposition of a loss position would (but for the application of this section) result in 60 percent long-term capital loss and 40 percent short-term capital loss, the loss allowed under paragraph (b) of this section with respect to the disposition of the loss position shall be treated as 60 percent long-term capital loss and 40 percent short-term capital loss regardless of whether any gain or loss with respect to one or more successor positions would be treated as 100 percent long-term or short-term capital gain or loss.

(d) *Exceptions.*—(1) This section shall not apply to losses sustained—

(i) With respect to the disposition of one or more positions that constitute part of a hedging transaction;

(ii) With respect to the disposition of a loss position included in a mixed straddle account (as defined in paragraph (b) of § 1.1092(b)-4T); and

(iii) With respect to the disposition of a position that is part of a straddle consisting only of section 1256 contracts.

(2) Paragraph (a)(1) of this section shall not apply to losses sustained by a dealer in stock or securities if such losses are sustained in a transaction made in the ordinary course of such business.

(e) *Coordination with section 1091.* Section 1092(b) applies in lieu of section 1091 to losses sustained from the disposition of positions in a straddle. See example (18) of paragraph (g) of this section.

(f) *Effective date.* The provisions of this section apply to dispositions of loss positions on or after January 24, 1985.

(g) *Examples.* This section may be illustrated by the following examples. It is assumed in each example that the following positions are the only positions held directly or indirectly (through a related person or flowthrough entity) by an individual calendar year taxpayer during the taxable year and none of the exceptions contained in paragraph (d) of this section apply.

Example (1). On December 1, 1985, A enters into offsetting long and short positions. On December 10, 1985, A disposes of the short position at an $11 loss, at which time there is $5 of unrealized gain in the offsetting long position. At year-end there is still $5 of unrecognized gain in the offsetting long position. Under these circumstances, $5 of the $11 loss will be disallowed for 1985 because there is $5 of unrecognized gain in the offsetting long position; the remaining $6 of loss, however, will be taken into account in 1985.

Example (2). Assume the facts are the same as in example (1), except that at year-end there is $11 of unrecognized gain in the offsetting long position. Under these circumstances, the entire $11 loss will be disallowed for 1985 because there is $11 of unrecognized gain at year-end in the offsetting long position.

Example (3). Assume the facts are the same as in example (1), except that at year-end there is no unrecognized gain in the offsetting long position. Under these circumstances, the entire $11 loss will be allowed for 1985.

Example (4). On November 1, 1985, A enters into offsetting long and short positions. On November 10, 1985, A disposes of the long position at a $10 loss, at which time there is $10 of unrealized gain in the short position. On November 11, 1985, A enters into a new long position (successor position) that is offsetting with respect to the retained short position but is not substantially identical to the long position disposed of on November 10, 1985. A holds both positions through year-end, at which time there is $10 of unrecognized gain in the successor long position and no unrecognized gain in the offsetting short position. Under these circumstances, the entire $10 loss will be disallowed for 1985 because there is $10 of unrecognized gain in the successor long position.

Example (5). Assume the facts are the same as in example (4), except that at year-end there is $4 of unrecognized gain in the successor long position and $6 of unrecognized gain in the offsetting short position. Under these circumstances, the entire $10 loss will be disallowed for 1985 because there is a total of $10 of unrecognized gain in both the successor long position and offsetting short position.

Example (6). Assume the facts are the same as in example (4), except that at year-end A disposes of the offsetting short position at a $2 loss. Under these circumstances, $10 of the total $12 loss will be disallowed because there is $10 of unrecognized gain in the successor long position.

Example (7). Assume the facts are the same as in example (4), and on January 10, 1986, A disposes of the successor long position at no gain or loss. A holds the offsetting short position until year-end, at which time there is $10 of unrecognized gain. Under these circumstances, the $10 loss will be disallowed for 1986 because there is $10 of unrecognized gain in an offsetting position at year-end.

Example (8). Assume the facts are the same as in example (4), except at year-end there is $8 of unrecognized gain in the successor long position and $8 of unrecognized loss in the offsetting short position. Under these circumstances, $8 of the total $10 realized loss will be disallowed because there is $8 of unrecognized gain in the successor long position.

Example (9). On October 1, 1985, A enters into offsetting long and short positions. Neither the long nor the short position is stock or securities. On October 2, 1985, A disposes of the short position at a $10 loss and the long position at a $10 gain. On October 3, 1985, A enters into a long position identical to the original long position. At year-end, there is $10 of unrecognized gain in the second long position. Under these circumstances, the $10 loss is allowed because the second long position is not a successor position or offsetting position to the short loss position.

Example (10). On November 1, 1985, A enters into offsetting long and short positions. On November 10, 1985, there is $20 of unrealized gain in the long position and A disposes of the short position at a $20 loss. By November 15, 1985, the value of the long position has declined eliminating all unrealized gain in the position. On November 15, 1985, A establishes a second short position (successor position) that is offsetting with respect to the long position but is not substantially identical to the short position disposed of on November 10, 1985. At year-end there is no unrecognized gain in the offsetting long position or in the successor short position. Under these circumstances, the $20 loss sustained with respect to the short loss position will be allowed for 1985 because at year-end there is no unrecognized gain in the

Reg. § 1.1092(b)-1T(f)

successor short position or the offsetting long position.

Example (11). Assume the facts are the same as in example (10) except that the second short position was established on November 8, 1985, and there is $20 of unrecognized gain in the second short position at year-end. Since the second short position was entered into within 30 days before the disposition of the loss position, the second short position is considered a successor position of the loss position. Under these circumstances, the $20 loss will be disallowed because there is $20 of unrecognized gain in a successor position.

Example (12). Assume the facts are the same as in example (10), except that at year-end there is $18 of unrecognized gain in the offsetting long position and $18 of unrecognized gain in the successor short position. Under these circumstances, the entire loss will be disallowed because there is more than $20 of unrecognized gain in both the successor short position and offsetting long position.

Example (13). Assume the facts are the same as in example (10), except that there is $20 of unrecognized gain in the successor short position and no unrecognized gain in the offsetting long position at year-end. Under these circumstances, the entire $20 loss will be disallowed because there is $20 of unrecognized gain in the successor short position.

Example (14). On January 2, 1986, A enters into offsetting long and short positions. Neither the long nor the short position is stock or securities. On March 3, 1986, A disposes of the long position at a $10 gain. On March 10, 1986, A disposes of the short position at a $10 loss. On March 14, 1986, A enters into a new short position. On April 10, 1986, A enters into an offsetting long position. A holds both positions to year-end, at which time there is $10 of unrecognized gain in the offsetting long position and no unrecognized gain or loss in the short position. Under these circumstances, the $10 loss will be allowed because (1) the rules of paragraph (a)(1) of this section are not applicable; and (2) the rules of paragraph (a)(2) of this section do not apply, since all positions of the straddle that contained the loss position were disposed of.

Example (15). On December 1, 1985, A enters into offsetting long and short positions. On December 4, 1985, A disposes of the short position at a $10 loss. On December 5, 1985, A establishes a new short position that is offsetting to the long position, but is not substantially identical to the short position disposed of on December 4, 1985. On December 6, 1985, A disposes of the long position at a $10 gain. On December 7, 1985, A enters into a second long position that is offsetting to the new short position, but is not substantially identical to the long position disposed of on December 6, 1985. A holds both positions to year-end at which time there is no unrecognized gain in the second short position and $10 of unrecognized gain in the offsetting long position. Under these circumstances, the entire $10 loss will be disallowed for the 1985 taxable year because the second long position is an offsetting position with respect to the second short position which is a successor position.

Example (16). On September 1, 1985, A enters into offsetting positions consisting of a long section 1256 contract and short non-section 1256 position. No elections under sections 1256(d)(1) or 1092(b)(2)(A), relating to mixed straddles, are made. On November 1, 1985, at which time there is $20 of unrecognized gain in the short non-section 1256 position, A disposes of the long section 1256 contract at a $20 loss and on the same day acquires a long non-section 1256 position (successor position) that is offsetting with respect to the short non-section 1256 position. But for the application of this section, A's disposition of the section 1256 contract would give rise to a capital loss. At year-end there is $20 of unrecognized gain in the offsetting short non-section 1256 position and no unrecognized gain in the successor long position. Under these circumstances, the entire $20 loss will be disallowed for 1985 because there is $20 unrecognized gain in the offsetting short position. In 1986, A disposes of the successor long non-section 1256 position and there is no unrecognized gain at year-end in the offsetting short position. Under these circumstances, the $20 loss disallowed in 1985 with respect to the section 1256 contract will be treated in 1986 as 60 percent long-term capital loss and 40 percent short-term capital loss.

Example (17). On January 2, 1986, A, not a dealer in stock or securities, acquires stock in X Corporation (X stock) and an offsetting put option. On March 3, 1986, A disposes of the X stock at a $10 loss. On March 10, 1986, A disposes of the put option at a $10 gain. On March 14, 1986, A acquires new X stock that is substantially identical to the X stock disposed of on March 3, 1986. A holds the X stock to year-end. Under these circumstances, the $10 loss will be disallowed for 1986 under paragraph (a)(1) of this section because A, within a period beginning 30 days before March 3, 1986 and ending 30 days after such date, acquired stock substantially identical to the X stock disposed of.

Example (18). On June 2, 1986, A, not a dealer in stock or securities, acquires stock in X Corpora-

Reg. § 1.1092(b)-1T(g)

tion (X stock). On September 2, 1986, A disposes of the X stock at a $100 loss. On September 15, 1986, A acquires new X stock that is substantially identical to the X stock disposed of on September 2, 1986, and an offsetting put option. A holds these straddle positions to year-end. Under these circumstances, section 1091, rather than section 1092(b), will apply to disallow the $100 loss for 1986 because the loss was not sustained from the disposition of a position that was part of a straddle. See paragraph (e) of this section.

Example (19). On November 1, 1985, A, not a dealer in stock or securities, acquires stock in Y Corporation (Y stock) and an offsetting put option. On November 12, 1985, there is $20 of unrealized gain in the put option and A disposes of the Y stock at a $20 loss. By November 15, 1985, the value of the put option has declined eliminating all unrealized gain in the position. On November 15, 1985, A acquires a second Y stock position that is substantially identical to the Y stock disposed of on November 12, 1985. At year-end there is no unrecognized gain in the put option or in the Y stock. Under these circumstances, the $20 loss will be disallowed for 1985 under paragraph (a)(1) of this section because A, within a period beginning 30 days before November 12, 1985 and ending 30 days after such date, acquired stock substantially identical to the Y stock disposed of.

Example (20). Assume the facts are the same as in example (19), and that on December 31, 1986, A disposes of the put option at a $40 gain and there is $20 of unrecognized loss in the Y stock. Under these circumstances, the $20 loss which was disallowed in 1985 also will be disallowed for 1986 under the rules of paragraph (a)(1) of this section because A has not disposed of the stock substantially identical to the Y stock disposed of on November 12, 1985.

Example (21). Assume the facts are the same as in example (19), except that on December 31, 1986, A disposes of the Y stock at a $20 loss and there is $40 of unrecognized gain in the put option. Under these circumstances, A will not recognize in 1986 either the $20 loss disallowed in 1985 or the $20 loss sustained with respect to the December 31, 1986 disposition of Y stock. Paragraph (a)(1) of this section does not apply to disallow the losses in 1986 since the substantially identical Y stock was disposed of during the year (and no substantially identical stock or securities was acquired by A within the 61 day period). However, paragraph (a)(2) of this section applies to disallow for 1986 the $40 of losses sustained with respect to the dispositions of positions in the straddle because there is $40 of unrecognized gain in the put option, an offsetting position to the loss positions.

Example (22). On January 2, 1986, A, not a dealer in stock or securities, acquires stock in X Corporation (X stock) and an offsetting put option. On March 3, 1986, A disposes of the X stock at a $10 loss. On March 17, 1986, A acquires new X stock that is substantially identical to the X stock disposed of on March 3, 1986. On December 31, 1986, A disposes of the X stock at a $5 gain, at which time there is $5 of unrecognized gain in the put option. Under these circumstances, the $10 loss sustained with respect to the March 3, 1986, disposition of X stock will be allowed under paragraph (a)(1) of this section since the substantially identical X stock acquired on March 17, 1986, was disposed of by year-end (and no substantially identical stock or securities were acquired by A within the 61 day period). However, $5 of the $10 loss will be disallowed under paragraph (a)(2) of this section because there is $5 of unrecognized gain in the put option, an offsetting position to the loss position.

Example (23). Assume the facts are the same as in example (22), except that on December 31, 1986, A disposes of the offsetting put option at a $5 loss and there is $5 of unrecognized gain in the X stock acquired on March 17, 1986. Under these circumstances, the $10 loss sustained with respect to the X stock disposed of on March 3, 1986, will be disallowed for 1986 under paragraph (a)(1) of this section. The $5 loss sustained upon the disposition of the put option will be allowed because (1) the rules of paragraph (a)(1) of this section are not applicable; and (2) the rules of paragraph (a)(2) of this section allow the loss, since the unrecognized gain in the X stock ($5) is not in excess of the loss ($10) disallowed under paragraph (a)(1) of this section.

Example (24). On January 2, 1986, A, not a dealer in stock or securities, acquires 200 shares of Z Corporation stock (Z stock) and 2 put options on Z stock (giving A the right to sell 200 shares of Z stock). On September 2, 1986, there is $200 of unrealized gain in the put option positions and A disposes of the 200 shares of Z stock at a $200 loss. On September 10, 1986, A acquires 100 shares of Z stock (substantially identical to the Z stock disposed of on September 2, 1986), and a call option that is offsetting to the put options on Z stock and that is not an option to acquire property substantially identical to the Z stock disposed of on September 2, 1986. At year-end, there is $80 of unrecognized gain in the Z stock position, $80 of unrecognized gain in the call option position, and no unrecognized gain or loss in the offsetting put option positions. Under these

Reg. § 1.1092(b)-1T(g)

Wash Sales; Straddles

circumstances, $40 of the $200 loss sustained with respect to the September 2, 1986 disposition of Z stock will be recognized by A in 1986 under paragraph (a) of this section, as set forth below. Paragraph (a)(1) of this section applies first to disallow $100 of the loss (1/2 of the loss), since 100 shares of substantially identical Z stock (1/2 of the stock) were acquired within the 61 day period. Paragraph (a)(2) of this section then applies to disallow that portion of the loss allowed under paragraph (a)(1) of this section ($200 − $100 = $100) equal to the excess of the total unrecognized gain in the Z stock and call option positions (successor positions to the loss position) ($80 + $80 = $160) over the $100 loss disallowed under paragraph (a)(1) of this section ($160 − $100 = $60; $100 − $60 = $40).

Example (25). Assume the facts are the same as in example (24), except that at year-end there is $110 of unrecognized gain in the Z stock position, $78 of unrecognized gain in the call option position, and $10 of unrecognized gain in the offsetting put option positions. Under these circumstances, $2 of the $200 loss sustained with respect to the September 2, 1986 disposition of Z stock will be allowed in 1986 under paragraph (a) of this section, as set forth below. Paragraph (a)(1) of this section applies first to disallow $100 of the loss (½ of the loss) since 100 shares of substantially identical Z stock (½ of the stock) were acquired within the 61 day period. Paragraph (a)(2) of this section then applies to disallow that portion of the loss allowed under paragraph (a)(1) of this section ($200 − $100 = $100) equal to the excess of the total unrecognized gain in the Z stock and call option positions (successor positions to the loss position) and the put option positions (offsetting positions to the loss position) ($110 + $78 + $10 = $198) over the $100 loss disallowed under paragraph (a)(1) of this section ($198 − $100 = $98; $100 − $98 = $2).

Example (26). Assume the facts are the same as in example (24), except that at year-end there is $120 of unrecognized gain in the Z stock position, $88 of unrecognized gain in the call option position, and $10 of unrecognized loss in one of the offsetting put option positions. At year-end A disposes of the other put option position at a $10 loss. Under these circumstances, $2 of the $210 loss sustained with respect to the September 2, 1986 disposition of Z stock ($200) and the year-end disposition of a put option ($10) will be allowed in 1986 under paragraph (a) of this section, as set forth below. Paragraph (a)(1) of this section applies first to disallow $100 of the loss from the disposition of Z stock (½ of the loss), since 100 shares of substantially identical Z stock (½ of the stock) were acquired within the 61 day period. Paragraph (a)(2) of this section then applies to disallow that portion of the loss allowed under paragraph (a)(1) of this section ($210 − $100 = $110) equal to the excess of the total unrecognized gain in the Z stock and call option positions (successor positions to the Z stock loss position, and offsetting positions to the put option loss position) ($120 + $88 = $208) over the $100 loss disallowed under paragraph (a)(1) of this section ($208 − $100 = $108; $110 − $108 = $2).

Example (27). On January 27, 1986, A enters into offsetting long (L1) and short (S1) positions. Neither L1 nor S1 nor any other positions entered into by A in 1986 are stock or securities. On February 3, 1986, A disposes of L1 at a $10 loss. On February 5, 1986, A enters into a new long position (L2) that is offsetting to S1. On October 15, 1986, A disposes of S1 at an $11 loss. On October 17, 1986, A enters into a new short position (S2) that is offsetting to L2. On December 30, 1986, A disposes of L2 at a $12 loss. On December 31, 1986, A enters into a new long position (L3) that is offsetting to S2. At year-end, S2 has an unrecognized gain of $33. Paragraph (a)(1) of this section does not apply since none of the positions were shares of stock or securities. However, all $33 ($10 + $11 + $12) of the losses sustained with respect to L1, S1 and L2 will be disallowed under paragraph (a)(2) because there is $33 of unrecognized gain in S2 at year-end. The $10 loss from the disposition of L1 is disallowed because S2 is or was an offsetting position to a successor long position (L2 or L3). The $11 loss from the disposition of S1 is disallowed because S2 is a successor position to S1. The $12 loss from the disposition of L2 is disallowed because S2 was an offsetting position to L2. [Temporary Reg. § 1.1092(b)-1T.]

☐ [T.D. 8007, 1-18-85. Amended by T.D. 8070, 1-13-86.]

[Reg. § 1.1092(b)-2T]

§ 1.1092(b)-2T. Treatment of holding periods and losses with respect to straddle positions (Temporary).—(a) *Holding period*—(1) *In general.* Except as otherwise provided in this section, the holding period of any position that is part of a straddle shall not begin earlier than the date the taxpayer no longer holds directly or indirectly (through a related person or flowthrough entity) an offsetting position with respect to that position. See § 1.1092(b)-5T relating to definitions.

(2) *Positions held for the long-term capital gain holding period (or longer) prior to establishment of the straddle.* Paragraph (a)(1) of this section shall not apply to a position held by a taxpayer for the long-term capital gain holding

period (or longer) before a straddle that includes such position is established. The determination of whether a position has been held by a taxpayer for the long-term capital gain holding period (or longer) shall be made by taking into account the application of paragraph (a)(1) of this section. See section 1222(3) relating to the holding period for long-term capital gains.

(b) *Treatment of loss*—(1) *In general.* Except as provided in paragraph (b)(2) of this section, loss on the disposition of one or more positions ("loss position") of a straddle shall be treated as a long-term capital loss if—

(i) On the date the taxpayer entered into the loss position the taxpayer held directly or indirectly (through a related person or flow-through entity) one or more offsetting positions with respect to the loss position; and

(ii) All gain or loss with respect to one or more positions in the straddle would be treated as long-term capital gain or loss if such positions were disposed of on the day the loss position was entered into.

(2) *Special rules for non-section 1256 positions in a mixed straddle.* Loss on the disposition of one or more positions ("loss position") that are part of a mixed straddle and that are non-section 1256 positions shall be treated as 60 percent long-term capital loss and 40 percent short-term capital loss if—

(i) Gain or loss from the disposition of one or more of the positions of the straddle that are section 1256 contracts would be considered gain or loss from the sale or exchange of a capital asset;

(ii) The disposition of no position in the straddle (other than a section 1256 contract) would result in a long-term capital gain or loss; and

(iii) An election under section 1092(b)(2)(A)(i)(I) (relating to straddle-by-straddle identification) or 1092(b)(2)(A)(i)(II) (relating to mixed straddle accounts) has not been made.

(c) *Exceptions*—(1) *In general.* This section shall not apply to positions that—

(i) Constitute part of a hedging transaction;

(ii) Are included in a straddle consisting only of section 1256 contracts; or

(iii) Are included in a mixed straddle account (as defined in paragraph (b) of § 1.1092(b)-4T).

(2) *Straddle-by-straddle identification.* Paragraphs (a)(2) and (b) of this section shall not apply to positions in a section 1092(b)(2) identified mixed straddle. See § 1.1092(b)-3T.

(d) *Special rule for positions held by regulated investment companies.* For purposes of section 851(b)(3) (relating to the definition of a regulated investment company), the holding period rule of paragraph (a) of this section shall not apply to positions of a straddle. However, if section 1233(b) (without regard to sections 1233(e)(2)(A) and 1092(b)) would have applied to such positions, then for purposes of section 851(b)(3) the rules of section 1233(b) shall apply. Similarly, the effect of daily marking-to-market provided under § 1.1092(b)-4T(c) will be disregarded for purposes of section 851(b)(3).

(e) *Effective date*—(1) *In general.* Except as provided in paragraph (e)(2) of this section, the provisions of this section apply to positions in a straddle established after June 23, 1981, in taxable years ending after such date.

(2) *Special effective date for mixed straddle positions.* The provisions of paragraph (b)(2) of this section shall apply to positions in a mixed straddle established on or after January 1, 1984.

(f) *Examples.* Paragraphs (a) through (e) may be illustrated by the following examples. It is assumed in each example that the following positions are the only positions held directly or indirectly (through a related person or flowthrough entity) by an individual calendar year taxpayer during the taxable year and none of the exceptions in paragraph (c) of this section apply.

Example (1). On October 1, 1984, A acquires gold. On January 1, 1985, A enters into an offsetting short gold forward contract. On April 1, 1985, A disposes of the short gold forward contract at no gain or loss. On April 10, 1985, A sells the gold at a gain. Since the gold had not been held for more than 6 months before the offsetting short position was entered into, the holding period for the gold begins no earlier than the time the straddle is terminated. Thus, the holding period of the original gold purchased on October 1, 1984, and sold on April 10, 1985, begins on April 1, 1985, the date the straddle was terminated. Consequently, gain recognized with respect to the gold will be treated as short-term capital gain.

Example (2). On January 1, 1985, A enters into a long gold forward contract. On May 1, 1985, A enters into an offsetting short gold regulated futures contract. A does not make an election under section 1256(d) or 1092(b)(2)(A). On August 1, 1985, A disposes of the gold forward contract at a gain. Since the forward contract had not been held by A for more than 6 months prior to the establishment of the straddle, the holding period for the forward contract begins no earlier than the time the straddle is terminated. Thus, the gain recog-

Reg. § 1.1092(b)-2T(b)(1)

nized on the closing of the gold forward contract will be treated as short-term capital gain.

Example (3). Assume the facts are the same as in example (2), except that A disposes of the short gold regulated futures contract on July 1, 1985, at no gain or loss and the forward contract on November 1, 1985. Since the forward contract had not been held for more than 6 months before the mixed straddle was established, the holding period for the forward contract begins July 1, 1985, the date the straddle terminated. Thus, the gain recognized on the closing of the forward contract will be treated as short-term capital gain.

Example (4). On January 1, 1985, A enters into a long gold forward contract and on August 4, 1985, A enters into an offsetting short gold forward contract. On September 1, 1985, A disposes of the short position at a loss. Since an offsetting long position had been held by A for more than 6 months prior to the acquisition of the offsetting short position, the loss with respect to the closing of the short position will be treated as long-term capital loss.

Example (5). On March 1, 1985, A enters into a long gold forward contract and on July 17, 1985, A enters into an offsetting short gold regulated futures contract. A does not make an election under section 1256(d) or 1092(b)(2)(A). On August 10, 1985, A disposes of the long gold forward contract at a loss. Since the gold forward contract was part of a mixed straddle, and the disposition of no position in the straddle (other than the regulated futures contract) would give rise to a long-term capital loss, the loss recognized on the termination of the gold forward contract will be treated as 40 percent short-term capital loss and 60 percent long-term capital loss.

Example (6). Assume the facts are the same as in example (5), except that on August 11, 1985, A disposes of the short gold regulated futures contract at a gain. Under these circumstances, the gain will be treated as 60 percent long-term capital gain and 40 percent short-term capital gain since the holding period rules of paragraph (a) of this section are not applicable to section 1256 contracts.

Example (7). Assume the facts are the same as in example (5), except that A enters into the long gold forward contract on January 1, 1985, and does not dispose of the long gold forward contract but instead on August 10, 1985, disposes of the short gold regulated futures contract at a loss. Under these circumstances, the loss will be treated as a long-term capital loss since A held an offsetting non-section 1256 position for more than 6 months prior to the establishment of the straddle. However, such loss may be subject to the rules of § 1.1092(b)-1T. [Temporary Reg. § 1.1092(b)-2T.]

☐ [T.D. 8007, 1-18-85. *Amended by* T.D. 8070, 1-13-86.]

[Reg. § 1.1092(b)-3T]

§ 1.1092(b)-3T. Mixed straddles; straddle-by-straddle identification under section 1092(b)(2)(A)(i)(I) (Temporary).—(a) *In general.* Except as otherwise provided, a taxpayer shall treat in accordance with paragraph (b) of this section gains and losses on positions that are part of a mixed straddle for which the taxpayer has made an election under paragraph (d) of this section (hereinafter referred to as a "section 1092(b)(2) identified mixed straddle"). No election may be made under this section for any straddle composed of one or more positions that are includible in a mixed straddle account (as defined in paragraph (b) of § 1.1092(b)-4T) or for any straddle for which an election under section 1256(d) has been made. See § 1.1092(b)-5T relating to definitions.

(b) *Treatment of gains and losses from positions included in a section 1092(b)(2) identified mixed straddle*—(1) *In general.* Gains and losses from positions that are part of a section 1092(b)(2) identified mixed straddle shall be determined and treated in accordance with the rules of paragraph (b)(2) through (7) of this section.

(2) *All positions of a section 1092(b)(2) identified mixed straddle are disposed of on the same day.* If all positions of a section 1092(b)(2) identified mixed straddle are disposed of (or deemed disposed of) on the same day, gains and losses from section 1256 contracts in the straddle shall be netted, and gains and losses from non-section 1256 positions in the straddle shall be netted. Net gain or loss from the section 1256 contracts shall then be offset against net gain or loss from the non-section 1256 positions to determine the net gain or loss from the straddle. If net gain or loss from the straddle is attributable to the positions of the straddle that are section 1256 contracts, such gain or loss shall be treated as 60 percent long-term capital gain or loss and 40 percent short-term capital gain or loss. If net gain or loss from the straddle is attributable to the positions of the straddle that are non-section 1256 positions, such gain or loss shall be treated as short-term capital gain or loss. This paragraph (b)(2) may be illustrated by the following examples. It is assumed in each example that the positions are the only positions held directly or indirectly (through a related person or flowthrough entity) by an individual calendar year taxpayer during the taxable year.

Reg. § 1.1092(b)-3T(b)(2)

Example (1). On April 1, 1985, A enters into a non-section 1256 position and an offsetting section 1256 contract and makes a valid election to treat such straddle as a section 1092(b)(2) identified mixed straddle. On April 10, 1985, A disposes of the non-section 1256 position at a $600 loss and the section 1256 contract at a $600 gain. Under these circumstances, the $600 loss on the non-section 1256 position will be offset against the $600 gain on the section 1256 contract and the net gain or loss from the straddle will be zero.

Example (2). Assume the facts are the same as in example (1), except that the gain on the section 1256 contract is $800. Under these circumstances, the $600 loss on the non-section 1256 position will be offset against the $800 gain on the section 1256 contract. The net gain of $200 from the straddle will be treated as 60 percent long-term capital gain and 40 percent short-term capital gain because it is attributable to the section 1256 contract.

Example (3). Assume the facts are the same as in example (1), except that the loss on the non-section 1256 position is $800. Under these circumstances, the $600 gain on the section 1256 contract will be offset against the $800 loss on the non-section 1256 position. The net loss of $200 from the straddle will be treated as short-term capital loss because it is attributable to the non-section 1256 position.

Example (4). On May 1, 1985, A enters into a straddle consisting of two non-section 1256 positions and two section 1256 contracts and makes a valid election to treat the straddle as a section 1092(b)(2) identified mixed straddle. On May 10, 1985, A disposes of the non-section 1256 positions, one at a $700 loss and the other at a $500 gain, and disposes of the section 1256 contracts, one at a $400 gain and the other at a $300 loss. Under these circumstances, the gain and losses from the section 1256 contracts and non-section 1256 positions will first be netted, resulting in a net gain of $100 ($400 − $300) on the section 1256 contracts and a net loss of $200 ($700 − $500) on the non-section 1256 positions. The net gain of $100 from the section 1256 contracts will then be offset against the $200 net loss on the non-section 1256 positions. The net loss of $100 from the straddle will be treated as short-term capital loss because it is attributable to the non-section 1256 positions.

Example (5). On December 30, 1985, A enters into a section 1256 contract and an offsetting non-section 1256 position and makes a valid election to treat such straddle as a section 1092(b)(2) identified mixed straddle. On December 31, 1985, A disposes of the non-section 1256 position at a $2,000 gain. A also realizes a $2,000 loss on the section 1256 contract because it is deemed disposed of under section 1256(a)(1). Under these circumstances, the $2,000 gain on the non-section 1256 position will be offset against the $2,000 loss on the section 1256 contract, and the net gain or loss from the straddle will be zero.

Example (6). Assume the facts are the same as in example (5), except that the section 1092(b)(2) identified mixed straddle was entered into on November 12, 1985, A realizes a $2,200 loss on the section 1256 contract, and on December 15, 1985, A enters into a non-section 1256 position that is offsetting to the non-section 1256 gain position of the section 1092(b)(2) identified mixed straddle. At year-end there is $200 of unrecognized gain in the non-section 1256 position that was entered into on December 15. Under these circumstances, the $2,200 loss on the section 1256 contract will be offset against the $2,000 gain on the non-section 1256 position. The net $200 loss from the straddle will be treated as 60 percent long-term capital loss and 40 percent short-term capital loss because it is attributable to the section 1256 contract. The net loss of $200 from the straddle will be disallowed in 1985 under the loss deferral rules of section 1092(a) because there is $200 of unrecognized gain in a successor position (as defined in paragraph (n) of § 1.1092(b)-5T) at year-end. See paragraph (c) of this section.

(3) *All of the non-section 1256 positions of a section 1092(b)(2) identified mixed straddle disposed of on the same day.* This paragraph (b)(3) applies if all of the non-section 1256 positions of a section 1092(b)(2) identified mixed straddle are disposed of on the same day or if this paragraph (b)(3) is made applicable by paragraph (b)(5) of this section. In the case to which this paragraph (b)(3) applies, gain and loss realized from non-section 1256 positions shall be netted. Realized and unrealized gain and loss with respect to the section 1256 contracts of the straddle also shall be netted on that day. Realized net gain or loss from the non-section 1256 positions shall then be offset against net gain or loss from the section 1256 contracts to determine the net gain or loss from the straddle on that day. Net gain or loss from the straddle that is attributable to the non-section 1256 positions shall be realized and treated as short-term capital gain or loss on that day. Net gain or loss from the straddle that is attributable to realized gain or loss with respect to section 1256 contracts shall be realized and treated as 60 percent long-term capital gain or loss and 40 percent short-term capital gain or loss. Any gain or loss subsequently realized on the section 1256 contracts shall be adjusted (through an adjustment to basis or otherwise) to take into account

the extent to which gain or loss was offset by unrealized gain or loss on the section 1256 contracts on that day. This paragraph (b)(3) may be illustrated by the following examples. It is assumed in each example that the positions are the only positions held directly or indirectly (through a related person or flowthrough entity) by an individual calendar year taxpayer during the taxable year.

Example (1). On July 20, 1985, A enters into a section 1256 contract and an offsetting non-section 1256 position and makes a valid election to treat such straddle as a section 1092(b)(2) identified mixed straddle. On July 27, 1985, A disposes of the non-section 1256 position at a $1,500 loss, at which time there is $1,500 of unrealized gain in the section 1256 contracts. A holds the section 1256 contract at year-end at which time there is $1,800 of gain. Under these circumstances, on July 27, 1985, A offsets the $1,500 loss on the non-section 1256 position against the $1,500 gain on the section 1256 contract and realizes no gain or loss. On December 31, 1985, A realizes a $300 gain on the section 1256 contract because the position is deemed disposed of under section 1256(a)(1). The $300 gain is equal to $1,800 of gain less a $1,500 adjustment for unrealized gain offset against the loss realized on the non-section 1256 position on July 27, 1985, and the gain will be treated as 60 percent long-term capital gain and 40 percent short-term capital gain.

Example (2). Assume the facts are the same as in example (1), except that on July 27, 1985, A realized a $1,700 loss on the non-section 1256 position. Under these circumstances, on July 27, 1985, A offsets the $1,700 loss on the non-section 1256 position against the $1,500 gain on the section 1256 contract. A realizes a $200 loss from the straddle on July 27, 1985, which will be treated as short-term capital loss because it is attributable to the non-section 1256 position. On December 31, 1985, A realizes a $300 gain on the section 1256 contract, computed as in example (1), which will be treated as 60 percent long-term capital gain and 40 percent short-term capital gain.

Example (3). On March 1, 1985, A enters into a straddle consisting of two non-section 1256 positions and two section 1256 contracts and makes a valid election to treat such straddle as a section 1092(b)(2) identified mixed straddle. On March 11, 1985, A disposes of the non-section 1256 positions, one at a $100 loss and the other at a $150 loss, and disposes of one section 1256 contract at a $100 loss. On that day there is $100 of unrealized gain on the section 1256 contract retained by A. A holds the remaining section 1256 contract at year-end, at which time there is $150 of gain. Under these circumstances, on March 11, 1985, A will first net the gains and losses from the section 1256 contracts and net the gains and losses from the non-section 1256 positions resulting in no gain or loss on the section 1256 contracts and a net loss of $250 on the non-section 1256 positions. Since there is no gain or loss to offset against the non-section 1256 positions, the net loss of $250 will be treated as short-term capital loss because it is attributable to the non-section 1256 positions. On December 31, 1985, A realizes a $50 gain on the remaining section 1256 contract because the position is deemed disposed of under section 1256(a)(1). The $50 gain is equal to $150 gain less a $100 adjustment to take into account the $100 unrealized gain that was offset against the $100 loss realized on the section 1256 contract on March 11, 1985.

Example (4). Assume the facts are the same as in example (3), except that A disposes of the section 1256 contract at a $500 gain. As in example (3), A has a net loss of $250 on the non-section 1256 positions disposed of. In this example, however, A has a net gain of $600 ($500 + $100) on the section 1256 contracts on March 11, 1985. Therefore, of the net gain from the straddle of $350 ($600 − $250), $250 ($500 − $250) is treated as 60 percent long-term capital gain and 40 percent short-term capital gain because only $250 is attributable to the realized gain from the section 1256 contract. In addition, because none of the $100 unrealized gain from the remaining section 1256 contract was offset against gain or loss on the non-section 1256 positions, no adjustment is made under paragraph (b)(3) of this section and the entire $150 gain on December 31 with respect to that contract is realized on that date.

(4) *All of the section 1256 contracts of a section 1092(b)(2) identified mixed straddle disposed of on the same day.* This paragraph (b)(4) applies if all of the section 1256 contracts of a section 1092(b)(2) identified mixed straddle are disposed of (or deemed disposed of) on the same day or if this paragraph (b)(4) is made applicable by paragraph (b)(5) of this section. In the case to which this paragraph (b)(4) applies, gain and loss realized from section 1256 contracts shall be netted. Realized and unrealized gain and loss with respect to the non-section 1256 positions of the straddle also shall be netted on that day. Realized net gain or loss from the section 1256 contracts shall be treated as short-term capital gain or loss to the extent of net gain or loss on the non-section 1256 positions on that day. Net gain or loss with respect to the section 1256 contracts that exceeds the net gain or loss with respect to the non-section

Reg. § 1.1092(b)-3T(b)(4)

1256 positions of the straddle shall be treated as 60 percent long-term capital gain or loss and 40 percent short-term capital gain or loss. See paragraph (b)(7) of this section relating to the gain or loss on such non-section 1256 positions. This paragraph (b)(4) may be illustrated by the following examples. It is assumed in each example that the positions are the only positions held directly or indirectly (through a related person or flow-through entity) by an individual calendar year taxpayer during the taxable year.

Example (1). On December 30, 1985, A enters into a section 1256 contract and an offsetting non-section 1256 position and makes a valid election to treat such straddle as a section 1092(b)(2) identified mixed straddle. On December 31, 1985, A disposes of the section 1256 contract at a $1,000 gain, at which time there is $1,000 of unrealized loss in the non-section 1256 position. Under these circumstances, the $1,000 gain realized on the section 1256 contract will be treated as short-term capital gain because there is a $1,000 loss on the non-section 1256 position.

Example (2). Assume the facts are the same as in example (1), except that A realized a $1,500 gain on the disposition of the section 1256 contract. Under these circumstances, $1,000 of the gain realized on the section 1256 contract will be treated as short-term capital gain because there is a $1,000 loss on the non-section 1256 position. The net gain of $500 from the straddle will be treated as 60 percent long-term capital gain and 40 percent short-term capital gain because it is attributable to the section 1256 contract.

Example (3). Assume the facts are the same as in example (1), except that A realized a $1,000 loss on the section 1256 contract and there is $1,000 of unrecognized gain on the non-section 1256 position. Under these circumstances, the $1,000 loss on the section 1256 contract will be treated as short-term capital loss because there is a $1,000 gain on the non-section 1256 position. Such loss, however, will be disallowed in 1985 under the loss deferral rules of section 1092(a) because there is $1,000 of unrecognized gain in an offsetting position at year-end. See paragraph (c) of this section.

Example (4). Assume the facts are the same as in example (1), except that the section 1256 contract and non-section 1256 position were entered into on December 1, 1985, and the section 1256 contract is disposed of on December 19, 1985, for a $1,000 gain, at which time there is $1,000 of unrealized loss on the non-section 1256 position. At year-end there is only $800 of unrealized loss in the non-section 1256 position. Under these circumstances, the result is the same as in example (1) because there was $1,000 of unrealized loss on the non-section 1256 position at the time of the disposition of the section 1256 contract.

Example (5). On July 15, 1985, A enters into a straddle consisting of two non-section 1256 positions and two section 1256 contracts and makes a valid election to treat such straddle as a section 1092(b)(2) identified mixed straddle. On July 20, 1985, A disposes of one non-section 1256 position at a gain of $1,000 and both section 1256 contracts at a net loss of $1,000. On the same day there is $200 of unrealized loss on the non-section 1256 position retained by A. Under these circumstances, realized and unrealized gain and loss with respect to the non-section 1256 positions is [sic] netted, resulting in a net gain of $800. Thus, $800 of the net loss on the section 1256 contracts disposed of will be treated as short-term capital loss because there is $800 of net gain on the non-section 1256 positions. In addition, the net loss of $200 from the straddle will be treated as 60 percent long-term capital loss and 40 percent short-term capital loss because it is attributable to the section 1256 contract.

(5) *Disposition of one or more, but not all, positions of a section 1092(b)(2) identified mixed straddle on the same day.* If one or more, but not all, of the positions of a section 1092(b)(2) identified mixed straddle are disposed of on the same day, and paragraph (b)(3) and (4) of this section are not applicable (without regard to this paragraph (b)(5)), the gain and loss from the non-section 1256 positions that are disposed of on that day shall be netted, and the gain and loss from the section 1256 contracts that are disposed of on that day shall be netted. In order to determine whether the rules of paragraph (b)(3) or (b)(4) of this section apply, net gain or loss from the section 1256 contracts disposed of shall then be offset against net gain or loss from the non-section 1256 positions disposed of to determine net gain or loss from such positions of the straddle. If net gain or loss from the disposition of such positions of the straddle is attributable to the non-section 1256 positions disposed of, the rules prescribed in paragraph (b)(3) of this section apply. If net gain or loss from the disposition of such positions is attributable to the section 1256 contracts disposed of, the rules prescribed in paragraph (b)(4) of this section apply. If the net gain or loss from the netting of non-section 1256 positions disposed of and the netting of section 1256 contracts disposed of are either both gains or losses, the rules prescribed in paragraph (b)(3) of this section shall apply to net gain or loss from such non-section 1256 positions, and the rules prescribed in paragraph (b)(4) of this section shall apply to net gain

Reg. § 1.1092(b)-3T(b)(5)

or loss from such section 1256 contracts. However, for purposes of determining the treatment of gain or loss subsequently realized on a position of such straddle, to the extent that unrealized gain or loss on other positions was used to offset realized gain or loss on a non-section 1256 position under paragraph (b)(3) of this section, or was used to treat realized gain or loss on a section 1256 contract as short-term capital gain or loss under paragraph (b)(4) of this section, such amount shall not be used for such purposes again. This paragraph (b)(5) may be illustrated by the following examples. It is assumed that the positions are the only positions held directly or indirectly (through a related person or flow-through entity) by an individual calendar year taxpayer during the taxable year.

Example (1). On July 15, 1985, A enters into a straddle consisting of four non-section 1256 positions and four section 1256 contracts and makes a valid election to treat such straddle as a section 1092(b)(2) identified mixed straddle. On July 20, 1985, A disposes of one non-section 1256 position at a gain of $800 and one section 1256 contract at a loss of $300. On the same day there is $400 of unrealized net loss on the section 1256 contracts retained by A and $100 of unrealized net loss on the non-section 1256 positions retained by A. Under these circumstances, the loss of $300 on the section 1256 contract disposed of will be offset against the gain of $800 on the non-section 1256 position disposed of. The net gain of $500 is attributable to the non-section 1256 position. Therefore, the rules of paragraph (b)(3) of this section apply. Under the rules of paragraph (b)(3) of this section, the net loss of $700 on the section 1256 contracts is offset against the net gain of $800 attributable to the non-section 1256 position disposed of. The net gain of $100 will be treated as short-term capital gain because it is attributable to the non-section 1256 position disposed of. Gain or loss subsequently realized on the section 1256 contracts will be adjusted to take into account the unrealized loss of $400 that was offset against the $800 gain attributable to the non-section 1256 position disposed of.

Example (2). Assume the facts are the same as in example (1), except that A disposes of the non-section 1256 position at a gain of $300 and the section 1256 contract at a loss of $800, and there is $200 of unrealized net gain in the non-section 1256 positions retained by A. Under these circumstances, the gain of $300 on the non-section 1256 position disposed of will be offset against the loss of $800 on the section 1256 contract disposed of. The net loss of $500 is attributable to the section 1256 contract. Therefore, the rules of paragraph (b)(4) of this section apply. Under the rules of paragraph (b)(4) of this section, $500 of the net loss realized on the section 1256 contract will be treated as short-term capital loss because there is $500 of realized and unrealized gain in the non-section 1256 positions. The remaining net loss of $300 will be treated as 60 percent long-term capital loss and 40 percent short-term capital loss because it is attributable to a section 1256 contract disposed of. In addition, A realizes a $300 short-term capital gain attributable to the disposition of the non-section 1256 position.

Example (3). (i) Assume the facts are the same as in example (1), except that the section 1256 contract was disposed of at a $500 gain. Under these circumstances, there is gain of $500 attributable to the section 1256 contract disposed of and a gain of $800 attributable to the non-section 1256 position. Therefore, the rules of both paragraphs (b)(3) and (4) of this § 1.1092(b)-3T apply.

(ii) Under paragraph (b)(3) of this section, the realized and unrealized gains and losses on the section 1256 contracts are netted, resulting in a net gain of $100 ($500 − $400). The section 1256 contract net gain does not offset the gain on the non-section 1256 position disposed of. Therefore, the gain of $800 on the non-section 1256 position disposed of will be treated as a short-term capital gain because there is no net loss on the section 1256 contracts.

(iii) Under paragraph (b)(4) of this section, the realized and unrealized gains and losses on the non-section 1256 positions are netted, resulting in a non-section 1256 position net gain of $700 ($800 − $100). Because there is no net loss on the non-section 1256 positions, the $500 gain realized on the section 1256 contract will be treated as 60 percent long-term capital gain and 40 percent short-term capital gain.

(6) *Accrued gain and loss with respect to positions of a section 1092(b)(2) identified mixed straddle.* If one or more positions of a section 1092(b)(2) identified mixed straddle were held by the taxpayer on the day prior to the day the section 1092(b)(2) identified mixed straddle is established, such position or positions shall be deemed sold for their fair market value as of the close of the last business day preceding the day such straddle is established. See §§ 1.1092(b)-1T and 1.1092(b)-2T for application of the loss deferral and wash sale rules and for treatment of holding periods and losses with respect to such positions. An adjustment (through an adjustment to basis or otherwise) shall be made to any subsequent gain or loss realized with respect to such position or positions for any gain or loss recognized under this paragraph (b)(6). This paragraph

Reg. § 1.1092(b)-3T(b)(6)

(b)(6) may be illustrated by the following examples. It is assumed in each example that the positions are the only positions held directly or indirectly (through a related person or flow-through entity) by an individual calendar year taxpayer during the taxable year.

Example (1). On January 1, 1985, A enters into a non-section 1256 position. As of the close of the day on July 9, 1985, there is $500 of unrealized long-term capital gain in the non-section 1256 position. On July 10, 1985, A enters into an offsetting section 1256 contract and makes a valid election to treat the straddle as a section 1092(b)(2) identified mixed straddle. Under these circumstances, on July 9, 1985, A will recognize $500 of long-term capital gain on the non-section 1256 position.

Example (2). On February 1, 1985, A enters into a section 1256 contract. As of the close of the day on February 4, 1985, there is $500 of unrealized gain on the section 1256 contract. On February 5, 1985, A enters into an offsetting non-section 1256 position and makes a valid election to treat the straddle as a section 1092(b)(2) identified mixed straddle. Under these circumstances, on February 4, 1985, A will recognize a $500 gain on the section 1256 contract, which will be treated as 60 percent long-term capital gain and 40 percent short-term capital gain.

Example (3). Assume the facts are the same as in example (2) and that on February 10, 1985, there is $2,000 of unrealized gain in the section 1256 contract. A disposes of the section 1256 contract at a $2,000 gain and disposes of the offsetting non-section 1256 position at a $1,000 loss. Under these circumstances, the $2,000 gain on the section 1256 contract will be reduced to $1,500 to take into account the $500 gain recognized when the section 1092(b)(2) identified mixed straddle was established. The $1,500 gain on the section 1256 contract will be offset against the $1,000 loss on the non-section 1256 position. The net $500 gain from the straddle will be treated as 60 percent long-term capital gain and 40 percent short-term capital gain because it is attributable to the section 1256 contract.

Example (4). On March 1, 1985, A enters into a non-section 1256 position. As of the close of the day on March 2, 1985, there is $400 of unrealized short-term capital gain in the non-section 1256 position. On March 3, 1985, A enters into an offsetting section 1256 contract and makes a valid election to treat the straddle as a section 1092(b)(2) identified mixed straddle. On March 10, 1985, A disposes of the section 1256 contract at a $500 loss and the non-section 1256 position at a $500 gain. Under these circumstances, on March 2, 1985, A will recognize $400 of short-term capital gain attributable to the gain accrued on the non-section 1256 position prior to the day the section 1092(b)(2) identified mixed straddle was established. On March 10, 1985, the gain of $500 on the non-section 1256 position will be reduced to $100 to take into account the $400 of gain recognized when the section 1092(b)(2) identified mixed straddle was established. The $100 gain on the non-section 1256 position will be offset against the $500 loss on the section 1256 contract. The net loss of $400 from the straddle will be treated as 60 percent long-term capital loss and 40 percent short-term capital loss because it is attributable to the section 1256 contract.

(7) *Treatment of gain and loss from non-section 1256 positions after disposition of all section 1256 contracts.* Gain or loss on a non-section 1256 position that is part of a section 1092(b)(2) identified mixed straddle and that is held after all section 1256 contracts in the straddle are disposed of shall be treated as short-term capital gain or loss to the extent attributable to the period when the positions were part of such straddle. See § 1.1092(b)-2T for rules concerning the holding period of such positions. This paragraph (b)(7) may be illustrated by the following example. It is assumed that the positions are the only positions held directly or indirectly (through a related person or flowthrough entity) during the taxable years.

Example. On December 1, 1985, A, an individual calendar year taxpayer, enters into a section 1256 contract and an offsetting non-section 1256 position and makes a valid election to treat such straddle as a section 1092(b)(2) identified mixed straddle. On December 31, 1985, A disposes of the section 1256 contract at a $1,000 loss. On the same day, there is $1,000 of unrecognized gain in the non-section 1256 position. The $1,000 loss on the section 1256 contract is treated as short-term capital loss because there is a $1,000 gain on the non-section 1256 position, but the $1,000 loss is disallowed in 1985 because there is $1,000 of unrecognized gain in the offsetting non-section 1256 position. See section 1092(a) and § 1.1092(b)-1T. On July 10, 1986, A disposes of the non-section 1256 position at a $1,500 gain, $500 of which is attributable to the post-straddle period. Under these circumstances, $1,000 of the gain on the non-section 1256 position will be treated as short-term capital gain because that amount of the gain is attributable to the period when the position was part of a section 1092(b)(2) identified mixed straddle. The remaining $500 of the gain will be treated as long-term capital gain because the position was held for more than six months after the straddle was terminated. In ad-

Reg. § 1.1092(b)-3T(b)(7)

dition, the $1,000 short-term capital loss disallowed in 1985 will be taken into account at this time.

(c) *Coordination with loss deferral and wash sale rules of § 1.1092(b)-1T.* This section shall apply prior to the application of the loss deferral and wash sale rules of § 1.1092(b)-1T.

(d) *Identification required*—(1) *In general.* To elect the provisions of this section, a taxpayer must clearly identify on a reasonable and consistently applied economic basis each position that is part of the section 1092(b)(2) identified mixed straddle before the close of the day on which the section 1092(b)(2) identified mixed straddle is established. If the taxpayer disposes of a position that is part of a section 1092(b)(2) identified mixed straddle before the close of the day on which the straddle is established, such identification must be made at or before the time that the taxpayer disposes of the position. In the case of a taxpayer who is an individual, the close of the day is midnight (local time) in the location of the taxpayer's principal residence. In the case of all other taxpayers, the close of the day is midnight (local time) in the location of the taxpayer's principal place of business. Only the person or entity that directly holds all positions of a straddle may make the election under this section.

(2) *Presumptions.* A taxpayer is presumed to have identified a section 1092(b)(2) identified mixed straddle by the time prescribed in paragraph (d)(1) of this section if the taxpayer receives independent verification of the identification (within the meaning of paragraph (d)(4) of this section). The presumption referred to in this paragraph (d)(2) may be rebutted by clear and convincing evidence to the contrary.

(3) *Corroborating evidence.* If the presumption of paragraph (d)(2) of this section does not apply, the burden shall be on the taxpayer to establish that an election under paragraph (d)(1) of this section was made by the time specified in paragraph (d)(1) of this section. If the taxpayer has no evidence of the time when the identification required by paragraph (d)(1) of this section is made, other than the taxpayer's own testimony, the election is invalid unless the taxpayer shows good cause for failure to have evidence other than the taxpayer's own testimony.

(4) *Independent verification.* For purposes of this section, the following constitute independent verification:

(i) *Separate Account.* Placement of one or more positions of a section 1092(b)(2) identified mixed straddle in a separate account designated as a "section 1092(b)(2) identified mixed straddle account" that is maintained by a broker (as defined in § 1.6045-1(a)(1)), futures commission merchant (as defined in 7 U.S.C. 2 and 17 CFR 1.3 (p)), or similar person and in which notations are made by such person identifying all positions of the section 1092(b)(2) identified mixed straddle and stating the date the straddle is established.

(ii) *Confirmation.* A written confirmation from a person referred to in paragraph (d)(4)(i) of this section, or from the party from which one or more positions of the section 1092(b)(2) identified mixed straddle are acquired, stating the date the straddle is established and identifying the other positions of the straddle.

(iii) *Other methods.* Such other methods of independent verification as the Commissioner may approve at the Commissioner's discretion.

(5) *Section 1092(b)(2) identified mixed straddles established before February 25, 1985.* Notwithstanding the provisions of paragraph (d)(1) of this section, relating to the time of identification of a section 1092(b)(2) identified mixed straddle, a taxpayer may identify straddles that were established before February 25, 1985, as section 1092(b)(2) identified mixed straddles after the time specified in paragraph (d)(1) of this section if the taxpayer adopts a reasonable and consistent economic basis for identifying the positions of such straddles.

(e) *Effective date*—(1) *In general.* The provisions of this section shall apply to straddles established on or after January 1, 1984.

(2) *Pre-1984 accrued gain.* If the last business day referred to in paragraph (b)(6) of this section is contained in a period to which paragraph (b)(6) does not apply, the gains and losses from the deemed sale shall be included in the first period to which paragraph (b)(6) applies. [Temporary Reg. § 1.1092(b)-3T.]

☐ [T.D. 8008, 1-18-85.]

[Reg. § 1.1092(b)-4T]

§ 1.1092(b)-4T. **Mixed straddles; mixed straddle account (Temporary).**—(a) *In general.* A taxpayer may elect (in accordance with paragraph (f) of this section) to establish one or more mixed straddle accounts (as defined in paragraph (b) of this section). Gains and losses from positions includible in a mixed straddle account shall be determined and treated in accordance with the rules set forth in paragraph (c) of this section. A mixed straddle account is treated as established as of the first day of the taxable year for which the taxpayer makes the election or January 1, 1984, whichever is later. See § 1.1092(b)-5T relating to definitions.

(b) *Mixed straddle account defined*—(1) *In general.* The term "mixed straddle account" means an account for determining gains and losses from all positions held as capital assets in a designated class of activities by the taxpayer at the time the taxpayer elects to establish a mixed straddle account. A separate mixed straddle account must be established for each separate designated class of activities.

(2) *Permissible designations.* Except as otherwise provided in this section, a taxpayer may designate as a class of activities the types of positions that a reasonable person, on the basis of all the facts and circumstances, would ordinarily expect to be offsetting positions. This paragraph (b)(2) may be illustrated by the following example. It is assumed in the example that the positions are the only positions held directly or indirectly (through a related person or flowthrough entity) during the taxable year, and that gain or loss from the positions is treated as gain or loss from a capital asset.

Example. B engages in transactions in dealer equity options on XYZ Corporation stock, stock in XYZ Corporation, dealer equity options on UVW Corporation stock, and stock in UVW Corporation. A reasonable person, on the basis of all the facts and circumstances, would not expect dealer equity options on XYZ Corporation stock and stock in XYZ Corporation to offset any dealer equity options on UVW Corporation stock or any stock in UVW Corporation. If B makes the mixed straddle account election under this section for all such positions, B must designate two separate classes of activities, one consisting of transactions in dealer equity options on XYZ Corporation stock and stock in XYZ Corporation, and the other consisting of transactions in dealer equity options on UVW Corporation stock and stock in UVW Corporation, and maintain two separate mixed straddle accounts.

(3) *Positions that offset positions in more than one mixed straddle account.* Gains and losses from positions that a reasonable person, on the basis of all the facts and circumstances, ordinarily would expect to be offsetting with respect to positions in more than one mixed straddle account shall be allocated among such accounts under a reasonable and consistent method that clearly reflects income. This paragraph (b)(2) may be illustrated by the following example. It is assumed that the positions are the only positions held directly or indirectly (through a related person or flowthrough entity) during the taxable year, and that gain or loss from the positions is treated as gain or loss from a capital asset.

Example. B holds stock in XYZ Corporation, UVW Corporation, and RST Corporation, and options on a broad based stock index future. A reasonable person, on the basis of all the facts and circumstances, would expect the stock in XYZ Corporation, UVW Corporation, and RST Corporation to be offsetting positions with respect to the options on the broad based stock index future. A reasonable person, on the basis of all the facts and circumstances, would not expect that stock in XYZ Corporation, UVW Corporation, or RST Corporation would be offsetting positions with respect to each other. If B makes the mixed straddle account election under this section for all such positions, B must designate three separate classes of activities: one consisting of stock in XYZ Corporation; one consisting of stock in UVW Corporation; and one consisting of stock in RST Corporation, and maintain three separate mixed straddle accounts. Options on the broad based stock index future must be designated as part of all three classes of activities and gains and losses from such options must be allocated among such accounts under a reasonable and consistent method that clearly reflects income, because such options are a type of position expected to be offsetting with respect to the positions in all three mixed straddle accounts.

(4) *Impermissible designations*—(i) *Types of positions that are not offsetting included in designated class of activities.* If the Commissioner determines, on the basis of all the facts and circumstances, that a class of activities designated by a taxpayer includes types of positions that a reasonable person, on the basis of all the facts and circumstances, ordinarily would not expect to be offsetting positions with respect to other types of positions in the account, the Commissioner may—

(A) Amend the class of activities designated by the taxpayer and remove positions from the account that are not within the amended designated class of activities; or

(B) Amend the class of activities designated by the taxpayer to establish two or more mixed straddle accounts.

(ii) *Types of positions that are offsetting not included in designated class of activities.* If the Commissioner determines, on the basis of all the facts and circumstances, that a designated class of activities does not include types of positions that are offsetting with respect to types of positions within the designated class, the Commissioner may—

(A) Amend the class of activities designated by the taxpayer to include types of positions that are offsetting with respect to the types of positions within the designated class and place such positions in the account; or

Reg. § 1.1092(b)-4T(b)(2)

(B) Amend the class of activities designated by the taxpayer to exclude types of positions that are offsetting with respect to the types of positions that are not in the account.

(iii) *Treatment of positions removed from or included in the account.* (A) Positions removed from a mixed straddle account will be subject to the rules of taxation generally applicable to such positions. Thus, for example, if the positions removed from the account are offsetting positions with respect to other positions outside the account, the rules of §§ 1.1092(b)-1T and 1.1092(b)-2T apply.

(B) If the taxpayer acted consistently and in good faith in designating the class of activities of the account and in placing positions in the account, the rules of § 1.1092(b)-2T(b)(2) shall not apply to any mixed straddles resulting from the removal of such positions from the account and the Commissioner, at the Commissioner's discretion, may identify such mixed straddles as section 1092(b)(2) identified mixed straddles and apply the rules of § 1.1092(b)-3T(b) to such straddles.

(C) If positions are placed in a mixed straddle account, such positions shall be treated as if they were originally included in the mixed straddle account in which they are placed.

(5) *Positions included in a mixed straddle account that are not within the designated class of activities.* The Commissioner may remove one or more positions from a mixed straddle account if, on the basis of all the facts and circumstances, the Commissioner determines that such positions are not within the designated class of activities of the account. See paragraph (b)(4)(iii) of this section for rules concerning the treatment of such positions.

(6) *Positions outside a mixed straddle account that are within the designated class of activities.* If a taxpayer holds types of positions outside of a mixed straddle account (including positions in another mixed straddle account) that are within the designated class of activities of a mixed straddle account, the Commissioner may require the taxpayer to include such types of positions in the mixed straddle account, move positions from one account to another, or remove from the mixed straddle account types of positions that are offsetting with respect to the types of positions held outside the account. See paragraph (b)(4)(iii) of this section for the treatment of such positions.

(c) *Treatment of gains and losses from positions in a mixed straddle account*—(1) *Daily account net gain or loss.* Except as provided in paragraphs (d) and (e) of this section (relating to positions in a mixed straddle account before January 1, 1985) as of the close of each business day of the taxable year, gain or loss shall be determined for each position in a mixed straddle account that is disposed of during the day. Positions in a mixed straddle account that have not been disposed of as of the close of the day shall be treated as if sold for their fair market value at the close of each business day. Gains and losses for each business day from non-section 1256 positions in each mixed straddle account shall be netted to determine "net non-section 1256 position gain or loss" for the account, and gains and losses for each business day from section 1256 contracts in each mixed straddle account shall be netted to determine "net section 1256 contract gain or loss" for the account. Net non-section 1256 position gain or loss from the account is then offset against net section 1256 contract gain or loss from the same mixed straddle account to determine the "daily account net gain or loss" for the account. If daily account net gain or loss is attributable to the net non-section 1256 position gain or loss, daily account net gain or loss for such account shall be treated as short-term capital gain or loss. If daily account net gain or loss is attributable to the net section 1256 contract gain or loss, daily account net gain or loss for such account shall be treated as 60 percent long-term capital gain or loss and 40 percent short-term capital gain or loss. If net non-section 1256 position gain or loss and net section 1256 contract gain or loss are either both gains or both losses, that portion of the daily account net gain or loss attributable to net non-section 1256 position gain or loss shall be treated as short-term capital gain or loss and that portion of the daily account net gain or loss attributable to net section 1256 contract gain or loss shall be treated as 60 percent long-term capital gain or loss and 40 percent short-term capital gain or loss. An adjustment (through an adjustment to basis or otherwise) shall be made to any subsequent gain or loss determined under this paragraph (c)(1) to take into account any gain or loss determined for prior business days under this paragraph (c)(1).

(2) *Annual account net gain or loss; total annual account net gain or loss.* On the last business day of the taxable year, the "annual account net gain or loss" for each mixed straddle account established by the taxpayer shall be determined by netting the daily account net gain or loss for each business day in the taxable year for each account. Annual account net gain or loss for each mixed straddle account shall be adjusted pursuant to paragraph (c)(3) of this section. The "total annual account net gain or loss" shall be determined by netting the annual account net gain or loss for all mixed straddle accounts established by

Reg. § 1.1092(b)-4T(c)(2)

the taxpayer, as adjusted pursuant to paragraph (c)(3) of this section. Total annual account net gain or loss is subject to the limitations of paragraph (c)(4) of this section. See paragraphs (d) and (e) of this section for determining the annual account net gain or loss for mixed straddle accounts established for taxable years beginning before January 1, 1985.

(3) *Application of section 263(g) to mixed straddle accounts.* No deduction shall be allowed for interest and carrying charges (as defined in section 263(g)(2)) properly allocable to a mixed straddle account. Interest and carrying charges properly allocable to a mixed straddle account means the excess of—

(i) The sum of—

(A) Interest on indebtedness incurred or continued during the taxable year to purchase or carry any position in the account; and

(B) All other amounts (including charges to insure, store, or transport the personal property) paid or incurred to carry any position in the account; over

(ii) The sum of—

(A) The amount of interest (including original issue discount) includible in gross income for the taxable year with respect to all positions in the account;

(B) Any amount treated as ordinary income under section 1271(a)(3)(A), 1278, or 1281(a) with respect to any position in the account for the taxable year; and

(C) The excess of any dividends includible in gross income with respect to positions in the account for the taxable year over the amount of any deduction allowable with respect to such dividends under section 243, 244, or 245.

For purposes of paragraph (c)(3)(i) of this section, the term "interest" includes any amount paid or incurred in connection with positions in the account used in a short sale. Any interest and carrying charges disallowed under this paragraph (c)(3) shall be capitalized by treating such charges as an adjustment to the annual account net gain or loss and shall be allocated pro rata between net short-term capital gain or loss and net long-term capital gain or loss.

(4) *Limitation on total annual account net gain or loss.* No more than 50 percent of total annual account net gain for the taxable year shall be treated as long-term capital gain. Any long-term capital gain in excess of the 50 percent limit shall be treated as short-term capital gain. No more than 40 percent of total annual account net loss for the taxable year shall be treated as short-term capital loss. Any short-term capital loss in excess of the 40 percent limit shall be treated as long-term capital loss.

(5) *Accrued gain and loss with respect to positions includible in a mixed straddle account.* Positions includible in a mixed straddle account that are held by a taxpayer on the day prior to the day the mixed straddle account is established shall be deemed sold for their fair market value as of the close of the last business day preceding the day such mixed straddle account is established. See §§ 1.1092(b)-1T and 1.1092(b)-2T for application of the loss deferral and wash sale rules and for treatment of holding periods and losses with respect to such positions. An adjustment (through an adjustment to basis or otherwise) shall be made to any subsequent gain or loss realized with respect to such positions for any gain or loss recognized under this paragraph (c)(5).

(6) *Examples.* This paragraph (c) may be illustrated by the following examples. It is assumed in each example that the positions are the only positions held directly or indirectly (through a related person or flow-through entity) by an individual calendar year taxpayer during the taxable year, and that gain or loss from the positions is treated as gain or loss from a capital asset.

Example (1). A establishes a mixed straddle account for a class of activities consisting of transactions in stock of XYZ Corporation and dealer equity options on XYZ Corporation stock. Assume that A enters into no transactions in XYZ Corporation stock or dealer equity options on XYZ Corporation stock prior to December 26, 1985. Thus, the net non-section 1256 position gain or loss and the net section 1256 contract gain or loss for the account are zero for each business day except the following days:

	Net non-section 1256 position gain or loss (XYZ Corporation stock)	Net section 1256 contract gain or loss (XYZ Corporation dealer equity options)
December 26, 1985	$1,000	$20,000
December 27, 1985	(9,000)	3,000
December 30, 1985	(5,000)	15,000
December 31, 1985	7,000	(2,000)

Reg. § 1.1092(b)-4T(c)(3)

Wash Sales; Straddles

See p. 20,601 for regulations not amended to reflect law changes

The daily account net gain or loss is as follows:

	Daily account net gain or loss	Treatment of daily account net gain or loss	Long-term	Short-term
December 26, 1985	$21,000	$1,000 short-term capital gain, $20,000 60 percent long-term capital gain and 40 percent short-term capital gain	$12,000	$9,000
December 27, 1985	(6,000)	short-term capital loss	....	(6,000)
December 30, 1985	10,000	60 percent long-term capital gain and 40 percent short-term capital gain	6,000	4,000
December 31, 1985	5,000	short-term capital gain	....	5,000

The annual account net gain or loss is $18,000 of long-term capital gain and $12,000 of short-term capital gain. Because A has no other mixed straddle accounts, total annual account net gain or loss is also $18,000 long-term capital gain and $12,000 short-term capital gain. Because more than 50 percent of the total annual account net gain is long-term capital gain, $3,000 of the $18,000 long-term capital gain will be treated as short-term capital gain.

Example (2). Assume the facts are the same as in example (1), except that interest and carrying charges in the amount of $6,000 are allocable to the mixed straddle account and are capitalized under paragraph (c)(3) of this section. Under these circumstances, $3,600 (($18,000/$30,000) × $6,000) of the interest and carrying charges will reduce the $18,000 long-term capital gain to $14,400 long-term capital gain and $2,400 (($12,000/$30,000) × $6,000) of the interest and carrying charges will reduce the $12,000 short-term capital gain to $9,600 short-term capital gain. Because more than 50 percent of the total annual account net gain is long-term capital gain, $2,400 of the $14,400 long-term capital gain will be treated as short-term capital gain.

Example (3). Assume the facts are the same as in example (1), except that A has a second mixed straddle account, which has an annual account net loss of $14,000 of long-term capital loss and $6,000 of short-term capital loss. Under these circumstances, the total annual account net gain is $4,000 ($18,000 − $14,000) of long-term capital gain and $6,000 ($12,000 − $6,000) of short-term capital gain. Because not more than 50 percent of the total annual account net gain is long-term capital gain, none of the long-term capital gain will be treated as short-term capital gain.

Example (4). Assume the facts are the same as in example (3), except that interest and carrying charges in the amount of $4,000 are allocable to the second mixed straddle account and are capitalized under paragraph (c)(3) of this section. Under these circumstances, $2,800 (($14,000/$20,000) × $4,000) of the interest and carrying charges will increase the $14,000 long-term capital loss to $16,800 of long-term capital loss and $1,200 (($6,000/$20,000) × $4,000) of the interest and carrying charges will increase the $6,000 short-term capital loss to $7,200 short-term capital loss. The total annual account net gain is $1,200 of long-term capital gain ($18,000 − $16,800) and $4,800 ($12,000 − $7,200) of short-term capital gain. Because not more than 50 percent of the total annual account net gain is long-term capital gain, none of the $1,200 long-term capital gain will be treated as short-term capital gain.

Example (5). Assume the facts are the same as in example (1), except that A has a second mixed straddle account, which has an annual account net loss of $20,000 of long-term capital loss and $15,000 of short-term capital loss. Under these circumstances, the total annual account net loss is $2,000 ($20,000 − $18,000) of long-term capital loss and $3,000 ($15,000 − $12,000) of short-term capital loss. Because more than 40 percent of the total annual account net loss is short-term capital loss, $1,000 of the short-term capital loss will be treated as long-term capital loss.

Example (6). A establishes two mixed straddle accounts. Account 1 has an annual account net gain of $5,000 short-term capital gain, which results from netting $5,000 of long-term capital loss and $10,000 of short-term capital gain. Account 2 has an annual account net loss of $2,000 long-term capital loss, which results from netting $3,000 of long-term capital loss against $1,000 of short-term capital gain. The total annual account net gain is $3,000 short-term capital gain, which results from netting the annual account net gain of $5,000 short-term capital gain from Account 1 against the annual account net loss of $2,000 long-term capital loss from Account 2.

(d) *Treatment of gains and losses from positions in a mixed straddle account established on or before December 31, 1984, in taxable years ending after December 31, 1984; pre-1985 account net gain or loss.* For mixed straddle accounts es-

Reg. § 1.1092(b)-4T(d)

tablished on or before December 31, 1984, in taxable years ending after December 31, 1984, the taxpayer on December 31, 1984, shall determine gain or loss for each position in the mixed straddle account that has been disposed of on any day during the period beginning on the first day of the taxpayer's taxable year that includes December 31, 1984, and ending on December 31, 1984. Positions in the mixed straddle account that have not been disposed of as of the close of December 31, 1984, shall be treated as if sold for their fair market value as of the close of December 31, 1984. Gains and losses for such period from non-section 1256 positions in each mixed straddle account shall be netted to determine "pre-1985 net non-section 1256 position gain or loss" and gains and losses for such period from section 1256 contracts in each mixed straddle account shall be netted to determine "pre-1985 net section 1256 contract gain or loss." Pre-1985 net non-section 1256 position gain or loss is then offset against pre-1985 net section 1256 contract gain or loss from the same mixed straddle account to determine the "pre-1985 account net gain or loss" for the period. If the pre-1985 account net gain or loss is attributable to pre-1985 net non-section 1256 position gain or loss, the pre-1985 account net gain or loss from such account shall be treated as short-term capital gain or loss. If the pre-1985 account net gain or loss is attributable to pre-1985 net section 1256 contract gain or loss, the pre-1985 account net gain or loss from such account shall be treated as 60 percent long-term capital gain or loss and 40 percent short-term capital gain or loss. If pre-1985 net non-section 1256 position gain or loss and pre-1985 net section 1256 contract gain or loss are either both gains or losses, that portion of the pre-1985 account net gain or loss attributable to pre-1985 net non-section 1256 position gain or loss shall be treated as short-term capital gain or loss and that portion of the pre-1985 account net gain or loss attributable to pre-1985 net section 1256 contract gain or loss shall be treated as 60 percent long-term capital gain or loss and 40 percent short-term capital gain or loss. An adjustment (through an adjustment to basis or otherwise) shall be made to any subsequent gain or loss realized with respect to such positions for any gain or loss recognized under this paragraph (d). To determine the annual account net gain or loss for such account, the pre-1985 account net gain or loss shall be treated as daily account net gain or loss for purposes of paragraph (c)(2) of this section. See paragraph (c)(5) of this section for treatment of accrued gain or loss with respect to positions includible in a mixed straddle account.

(e) *Treatment of gains and losses from positions in a mixed straddle account for taxable years ending on or before December 31, 1984*—(1) *In general.* For mixed straddle accounts established on or before December 31, 1984, in taxable years ending on or before December 31, 1984, the taxpayer at the close of the taxable year shall determine gain or loss for each position in the mixed straddle account that has been disposed of on any day during the period beginning on the later of the first day of the taxable year or January 1, 1984, and ending on the last day of the taxable year. Positions in the mixed straddle account that have not been disposed of as of the close of the last business day of the taxable year shall be treated as if sold for their fair market value at the close of such day. Gains and losses from non-section 1256 positions in each mixed straddle account shall be netted to determine "1984 net non-section 1256 position gain or loss" for the account and gains and losses from section 1256 contracts shall be netted to determine "1984 net section 1256 contract gain or loss" for the account. The 1984 net non-section 1256 position gain or loss is then offset against 1984 net section 1256 contract gain or loss from the same mixed straddle account to determine "annual account net gain or loss" for the account. If annual account net gain or loss is attributable to 1984 net non-section 1256 position gain or loss, annual account net gain or loss shall be treated as short-term capital gain or loss. If annual account net gain or loss is attributable to 1984 net section 1256 contract gain or loss, annual account net gain or loss shall be treated as 60 percent long-term capital gain or loss and 40 percent short-term capital gain or loss. If 1984 net non-section 1256 position gain or loss and 1984 net section 1256 contract gain or loss are either both gains or both losses, that portion of annual account net gain or loss attributable to 1984 net non-section 1256 position gain or loss shall be treated as short-term capital gain or loss and that portion of annual account net gain or loss attributable to 1984 net section 1256 contract gain or loss shall be treated as 60 percent long-term capital gain or loss and 40 percent short-term capital gain or loss. An adjustment (through an adjustment to basis or otherwise) shall be made to any subsequent gain or loss realized with respect to such positions for any gain or loss recognized under this paragraph (e). See paragraph (c)(2) through (5) of this section relating to determining the total annual account net gain or loss, application of section 263(g) to mixed straddle accounts, the limitation on the total annual account net gain or loss, and treatment of accrued gain or loss with respect to positions includible in a mixed straddle account.

Reg. § 1.1092(b)-4T(e)

(2) *Pre-1984 accrued gain.* If the last business day referred to in paragraph (c)(5) of this section is contained in a period to which such paragraph (c)(5) does not apply, the gains and losses from the deemed sale shall be included in the first period to which paragraph (c)(5) applies.

(f) *Election*—(1) *Time for making the election.* Except as otherwise provided, the election under this section to establish one or more mixed straddle accounts for a taxable year must be made by the due date (without regard to automatic and discretionary extensions) of the taxpayer's income tax return for the immediately preceding taxable year (or part thereof). For example, an individual taxpayer on a calendar year basis must make the election by April 15, 1986, to establish one or more mixed straddle accounts for taxable year 1986. Similarly, a calendar year corporate taxpayer must make its election by March 15, 1986, to establish one or more mixed straddle accounts for 1986. If a taxpayer begins trading or investing in positions in a new class of activities during a taxable year, the election under this seciton with respect to the new class of activities must be made by the taxpayer by the later of the due date of the taxpayer's income tax return for the immediately preceding taxable year (without regard to automatic and discretionary extensions), or 60 days after the first mixed straddle in the new class of activities is entered into. Similarly, if on or after the date the election is made with respect to an account, the taxpayer begins trading or investing in positions that are includible in such account but were not specified in the original election, the taxpayer must make an amended election as prescribed in paragraph (f)(2)(ii) of this section by the later of the due date of the taxpayer's income tax return for the immediately preceding taxable year (without regard to automatic and discretionary extensions), or 60 days after the acquisition of the first of the positions. If an election is made after the times specified in this paragraph (f)(1), the election will be permitted only if the Commissioner concludes that the taxpayer had reasonable cause for failing to make a timely election. For example, if a calendar year taxpayer holds few positions in one class of activities prior to April 15 of a taxable year, and the taxpayer greatly increases trading activity with respect to positions in the class of activities after April 15, then the Commissioner may conclude that the taxpayer had reasonable cause for failing to make a timely election and allow the taxpayer to make a mixed straddle account election for the taxable year. See paragraph (f)(2) of this section for rules relating to the manner for making these elections.

(2) *Manner for making the election*—(i) *In general.* A taxpayer must make the election on Form 6781 in the manner prescribed by such Form, and by attaching the Form to the taxpayer's income tax return for the immediately preceding taxable year (or request for an automatic extension). In addition, the taxpayer must attach a statement to Form 6781 designating with specificity the class of activities for which a mixed straddle account is established. The designation must describe the class of activities in sufficient detail so that the Commissioner may determine, on the basis of the designation, whether specific positions are includible in the mixed straddle account. In the case of a taxpayer who elects to establish more than one mixed straddle account, the Commissioner must be able to determine, on the basis of the designations, that specific positions are placed in the appropriate account. The election applies to all positions in the designated class of activities held by the taxpayer during the taxable year.

(ii) *Elections for new classes of activities and expanded elections.* Amended elections and elections made with respect to a new class of activities that the taxpayer has begun trading or investing in during a taxable year, shall be made on Form 6781 within the times prescribed in paragraph (f)(1) of this section. A statement must be attached to the Form containing the information required in paragraph (f)(2)(i) of this section, with respect to the new or expanded designated class of activities.

(iii) *Special rule.* The Commissioner may disregard a mixed straddle account election if the Commissioner determines, on the basis of all the facts and circumstances, that the principal purpose for making the mixed straddle account election with respect to a class of activities was to avoid the rules of § 1.1092(b)-1T(a). For example, if a taxpayer holds stock that is not part of a straddle and that would generate a loss if sold or otherwise disposed of, and the taxpayer both acquires offsetting option positions with respect to the stock and makes a mixed straddle account election with respect to the stock and stock options near the end of a taxable year, the Commissioner may disregard the mixed straddle account election.

(3) *Special rule for taxable years ending after 1983 and before September 1, 1986.* An election under this section to establish one or more mixed straddle accounts for any taxable year that includes July 17, 1984, and any taxable year that ends before September 1, 1986 (or, in the case of a corporation, October 1, 1986), must be made by the later of—

Reg. § 1.1092(b)-4T(f)(3)

(i) December 31, 1985, or

(ii) The due date (without regard to automatic and discretionary extensions) of the return for the taxpayer's taxable year that begins in 1984 if the due date of the taxpayer's return for such year (without regard to automatic and discretionary extensions) is after December 31, 1985.

The election shall be made by attaching Form 6781 together with a statement to the taxpayer's income tax return, amended return, or other appropriate form that is filed on or before the deadline determined in the preceding sentence. The attached statement must designate with specificity, in accordance with paragraph (f)(2)(i) of this section, the class of activities for which a mixed straddle account is established. For example, if a fiscal year taxpayer's return (for its taxable year ending September 30, 1985) is due (without regard to extensions) on January 15, 1986, and the taxpayer intends to obtain an automatic extension to file the return, the election under this section for any or all of the fiscal years ending in 1984, 1985 or 1986 must be made on or before January 15, 1986, with the request for an automatic extension. Similarly, a calendar year taxpayer (whether or not such taxpayer has obtained an automatic extension of time to file) who has filed its 1984 income tax return before October 15, 1985, without making a mixed straddle account election for either 1984 or 1985, or both, may make the mixed straddle account election under this section for either or for both of such years with an amended return filed on or before December 31, 1985. The mixed straddle account elected on this amended return will be effective for all positions in the designated class of activities even if the taxpayer had elected straddle-by-straddle identification as provided under § 1.1092(b)-3T for purposes of the previously filed 1984 income tax return. For taxable years beginning in 1984 and 1985, the election under this paragraph (f)(3) is effective for the entire taxable year. For taxable years beginning in 1983, an election shall be effective for that part of the year beginning after December 31, 1983, for which the election under § § 1.1256(h)-1T or 1.1256(h)-2T is made. See § 1.6081-1T regarding an extension of time to file certain individual income tax returns.

(4) *Period for which election is effective.* For taxable years beginning on or after January 1, 1984, an election under this section, including an amendment to the election pursuant to paragraph (f)(1) of this section, shall be effective only for the taxable year for which the election is made. This election may be revoked during the taxable year for the remainder of the taxable year only with the consent of the Commissioner. An application for consent to revoke the election shall be filed with the service center with which the election was filed and shall—

(i) Contain the name, address, and taxpayer identification number of the taxpayer;

(ii) Show that the volume or nature of the taxpayer's activities has changed substantially since the election was made, and that the taxpayer's activities no longer warrant the use of such mixed straddle account; and

(iii) Any other relevant information.

If a taxpayer's election for a taxable year is revoked, the taxpayer may not make a new election for the same class of activities under paragraph (f)(1) of this section during the same taxable year.

(g) *Effective date.* The provisions of this section apply to positions held on or after January 1, 1984. [Temporary Reg. § 1.1092(b)-4T.]

☐ [T.D. 8008, 1-18-85. Amended by T.D. 8058, 10-11-85.]

[Reg. § 1.1092(b)-5T]

§ 1.1092(b)-5T. Definitions (Temporary).—The following definitions apply for purposes of § § 1.1092(b)-1T through 1.1092(b)-4T.

(a) *Disposing, disposes, or disposed.* The term "disposing," "disposes," or "disposed" includes the sale, exchange, cancellation, lapse, expiration, or other termination of a right or obligation with respect to personal property (as defined in section 1092(d)(1)).

(b) *Hedging transaction.* The term "hedging transaction" means a hedging transaction as defined in section 1256(e).

(c) *Identified straddle.* The term "identified straddle" means an identified straddle as defined in section 1092(a)(2)(B).

(d) *Loss.* The term "loss" means a loss otherwise allowable under section 165(a) (without regard to the limitation contained in section 165(f)) and includes a write-down in inventory.

(e) *Mixed straddle.* The term "mixed straddle" means a straddle—

(1) All of the positions of which are held as capital assets;

(2) At least one (but not all) of the positions of which is a section 1256 contract;

(3) For which an election under section 1256(d) has not been made; and

(4) Which is not part of a larger straddle.

(f) *Non-section 1256 position.* The term "non-section 1256 position" means a position that is not a section 1256 contract.

Reg. § 1.1092(b)-5T(a)

(g) *Offsetting position.* The term "offsetting position" means an offsetting position as defined in section 1092(c)(2).

(h) *Position.* The term "position" means a position as defined in section 1092(d)(2).

(i) [Reserved]

(j) *Related person or flowthrough entity.* The term "related person or flowthrough entity" means a related person or flowthrough entity as defined in sections 1092(d)(4)(B) and (C), respectively.

(k) *Section 1256 contract.* The term "section 1256 contract" means a section 1256 contract as defined in section 1256(b).

(l) [Reserved]

(m) *Straddle.* The term "straddle" means a straddle as defined in section 1092(c)(1).

(n) *Successor position.* The term "successor position" means a position ("P") that is or was at any time offsetting to a second position if—

(1) The second position was offsetting to any loss position disposed of; and

(2) P is entered into during a period commencing 30 days prior to, and ending 30 days after, the disposition of the loss position referred to in paragraph (n)(1) of this section.

(3) P is entered into no later than 30 days after the loss position is no longer included in a straddle.

(o) *Unrecognized gain.* The term "unrecognized gain" means unrecognized gain as defined in section 1092(a)(3)(A).

(p) *Substantially identical.* The term "substantially identical" has the same meaning as substantially identical in section 1091(a).

(q) *Securities.* The term "security" means a security as defined in section 1236(c). [Temporary Reg. § 1.1092(b)-5T.]

☐ [T.D. 8007, 1-18-85. Amended by T.D. 8070, 1-13-86.]

[Reg. § 1.1092(c)-1]

§ 1.1092(c)-1. **Equity options with flexible terms.**—(a) *In general.* Section 1092(c)(4) provides an exception to the general rule that a straddle exists if a taxpayer holds stock and writes a call option on that stock. Under section 1092(c)(4), the ownership of stock and the issuance of a call option meeting certain requirements result in a qualified covered call, which is exempted from the general straddle rules of section 1092. This section addresses the consequences of the availability of equity options with flexible terms under the qualified covered call rules.

(b) *No effect on lowest qualified bench mark for standardized options.* The availability of strike prices for equity options with flexible terms does not affect the determination of the lowest qualified bench mark, as defined in section 1092(c)(4)(D), for an option that is not an equity option with flexible terms.

(c) [Reserved].

(d) *Definitions.* For purposes of this section—

(1) *Equity option with flexible terms* means an equity option—

(i) That is described in any of the following Securities Exchange Act Releases—

(A) Self-Regulatory Organizations; Order Approving Proposed Rule Changes and Notice of Filing and Order Granting Accelerated Approval of Amendments by the Chicago Board Options Exchange, Inc. and the Pacific Stock Exchange, Inc., Relating to the Listing of Flexible Equity Options on Specified Equity Securities, Securities Exchange Act Release No. 34-36841 (Feb. 21, 1996); or

(B) Self-Regulatory Organizations; Order Approving Proposed Rule Changes and Notice of Filing and Order Granting Accelerated Approval of Amendment Nos. 2 and 3 to the Proposed Rule Change by the American Stock Exchange, Inc., Relating to the Listing of Flexible Equity Options on Specified Equity Securities, Securities Exchange Act Release No. 34-37336 (June 27, 1996); or

(C) Self-Regulatory Organizations; Order Approving Proposed Rule Change and Notice of Filing and Order Granting Accelerated Approval of Amendment Nos. 2, 4 and 5 to the Proposed Rule Change by the Philadelphia Stock Exchange, Inc., Relating to the Listing of Flexible Exchange Traded Equity and Index Options, Securities Exchange Act Release No. 34-39549 (Jan. 23, 1998); or

(D) Any changes to the SEC releases described in paragraphs (d)(1)(i)(A) through (C) of this section that are approved by the Securities and Exchange Commission; or

(ii) That is traded on any national securities exchange which is registered with the Securities and Exchange Commission (other than those described in the SEC Releases set forth in paragraph (d)(1)(i) of this section) or other market which the Secretary determines has rules adequate to carry out the purposes of section 1092 and is—

(A) Substantially identical to the equity options described in paragraph (d)(1)(i) of this section; and

(B) Approved by the Securities and Exchange Commission in a Securities Exchange Act Release.

(2) *Securities Exchange Act Release* means a release issued by the Securities and Exchange Commission. To determine identifying information for releases referenced in paragraph (d)(1) of this section, including release titles, identification numbers, and issue dates, contact the Office of the Secretary, Securities and Exchange Commission, 450 5th Street, NW., Washington, DC 20549. To obtain a copy of a Securities Exchange Act Release, submit a written request, including the specific release identification number, title, and issue date, to Securities and Exchange Commission, Attention Public Reference, 450 5th Street, NW., Washington, DC 20549.

(e) *Effective date.* These regulations apply to equity options with flexible terms entered into on or after January 25, 2000. [Reg. § 1.1092(c)-1.]

☐ [T.D. 8866, 1-21-2000.]

[Reg. § 1.1092(d)-1]

§ 1.1092(d)-1. Definitions and special rules.—(a) *Actively traded.* Actively traded personal property includes any personal property for which there is an established financial market.

(b) *Established financial market*—(1) *In general.* For purposes of this section, an established financial market includes—

(i) A national securities exchange that is registered under section 6 of the Securities Exchange Act of 1934 (15 U.S.C. 78f);

(ii) An interdealer quotation system sponsored by a national securities association registered under section 15A of the Securities Exchange Act of 1934;

(iii) A domestic board of trade designated as a contract market by the Commodities Futures Trading Commission;

(iv) A foreign securities exchange or board of trade that satisfies analogous regulatory requirements under the law of the jurisdiction in which it is organized (such as the London International Financial Futures Exchange, the Marche a Terme International de France, the International Stock Exchange of the United Kingdom and the Republic of Ireland, Limited, the Frankfurt Stock Exchange, and the Tokyo Stock Exchange);

(v) An interbank market;

(vi) An interdealer market (as defined in paragraph (b)(2)(i) of this section); and

(vii) Solely with respect to a debt instrument, a debt market (as defined in paragraph (b)(2)(ii) of this section).

(2) *Definitions*—(i) *Interdealer market.* An interdealer market is characterized by a system of general circulation (including a computer listing disseminated to subscribing brokers, dealers, or traders) that provides a reasonable basis to determine fair market value by disseminating either recent price quotations (including rates, yields, or other pricing information) of one or more identified brokers, dealers, or traders or actual prices (including rates, yields, or other pricing information) of recent transactions. An interdealer market does not include a directory or listing of brokers, dealers, or traders for specific contracts (such as yellow sheets) that provides neither price quotations nor actual prices of recent transactions.

(ii) *Debt market.* A debt market exists with respect to a debt instrument if price quotations for the instrument are readily available from brokers, dealers, or traders. A debt market does not exist with respect to a debt instrument if—

(A) No other outstanding debt instrument of the issuer (or of any person who guarantees the debt instrument) is traded on an established financial market described in paragraph (b)(1)(i), (ii), (iii), (iv), (v), or (vi) of this section (other traded debt);

(B) The original stated principal amount of the issue that includes the debt instrument does not exceed $25 million;

(C) The conditions and covenants relating to the issuer's performance with respect to the debt instrument are materially less restrictive than the conditions and covenants included in all of the issuer's other traded debt (e.g., the debt instrument is subject to an economically significant subordination provision whereas the issuer's other traded debt is senior); or

(D) The maturity date of the debt instrument is more than 3 years after the latest maturity date of the issuer's other traded debt.

(c) *Notional principal contracts.* For purposes of section 1092(d)—

(1) A notional principal contract (as defined in § 1.446-3(c)(1)) constitutes personal property of a type that is actively traded if contracts based on the same or substantially similar specified indices are purchased, sold, or entered into on an established financial market within the meaning of paragraph (b) of this section; and

(2) The rights and obligations of a party to a notional principal contract are rights and obligations with respect to personal property and constitute an interest in personal property.

(d) *Effective dates.* Paragraph (b)(1)(vii) of this section applies to positions entered into on or after October 14, 1993. Paragraph (c) of this section applies to positions entered into on or after July 8, 1991. [Reg. § 1.1092(d)-1.]

☐ [T.D. 8491, 10-8-93.]

[Reg. § 1.1092(d)-2]

§ 1.1092(d)-2. **Personal property.**—(a) *Special rules for stock.* Under section 1092(d)(3)(B), personal property includes any stock that is part of a straddle, at least one of the offsetting positions of which is a position with respect to substantially similar or related property (other than stock). For purposes of this rule, the term *substantially similar or related property* is defined in § 1.246-5 (other than § 1.246-5(b)(3)). The rule in § 1.246-5(c)(6) does not narrow the related party rule in section 1092(d)(4).

(b) *Effective date*—(1) *In general.* This section applies to positions established on or after March 17, 1995.

(2) *Special rule for certain straddles.* This section applies to positions established after March 1, 1984, if the taxpayer substantially diminished its risk of loss by holding substantially similar or related property involving the following types of transactions—

(i) Holding offsetting positions consisting of stock and a convertible debenture of the same corporation where the price movements of the two positions are related; or

(ii) Holding a short position in a stock index regulated futures contract (or alternatively an option on such a regulated futures contract or an option on the stock index) and stock in an investment company whose principal holdings mimic the performance of the stocks included in the stock index (or alternatively a portfolio of stocks whose performance mimics the performance of the stocks included in the stock index). [Reg. § 1.1092(d)-2.]

☐ [T. D. 8590, 3-17-95.]

[The next page is 53,401.]

Reg. § 1.1092(d)-2(b)(2)

Capital Gains and Losses Treatment of Capital Gains
[Reg. § 1.1201-1]

§ 1.1201-1. **Alternative tax.**—(a) *Corporations*—(1) *In general.* (i) If for any taxable year a corporation has net capital gain (net section 1201 gain for taxable years beginning before January 1, 1977) (as defined in section 1222 (11)), section 1201(a) imposes an alternative in lieu of the tax imposed by sections 11 and 511, but only if such alternative tax is less than the tax imposed by sections 11 and 511. The alternative tax is not in lieu of the personal holding company tax imposed by section 541 or of any other tax not specifically set forth in section 1201(a).

(ii) In the case of an insurance company, the alternative tax imposed by section 1201(a) is also in lieu of the tax imposed by sections 821(a) or (c) and 831(a), except that for taxable years beginning before January 1, 1963, the reference to section 821(a) or (c) is to be read as reference to section 821(a)(1) or (b). For taxable years beginning after December 31, 1954, and before January 1, 1958, the alternative tax imposed by section 1201(a) shall also be in lieu of the tax imposed by section 802(a), as amended by the Life Insurance Company Tax Act for 1955 (70 Stat. 38), if such alternative tax is less than the tax imposed by such section. See section 802(e), as added by the Life Insurance Company Tax Act for 1955 (70 Stat. 39). However, for taxable years beginning after December 31, 1958, and before January 1, 1962, section 802(a)(2), as amended by the Life Insurance Company Income Tax Act of 1959 (73 Stat. 115), imposes a separate tax equal to 25 percent of the amount by which the net long-term capital gain of any life insurance company (as defined in section 801(a) and paragraph (b) of § 1.801-3) exceeds its net short-term capital loss. See paragraph (f) of § 1.802-3. For alternative tax for life insurance companies in the case of taxable years beginning after December 31, 1961, see section 802(a)(2) and the regulations thereunder.

(iii) See section 56 and the regulations thereunder for provisions relating to the minimum tax for tax preferences.

(2) *Alternative tax.* The alternative tax is the sum of—

(i) A partial tax computed at the rates provided in sections 11, 511, 821(a) or (c), and 831(a), on the taxable income of the taxpayer reduced by the amount of the net capital gain (net section 1201 gain for taxable years beginning before January 1, 1977), and

(ii) An amount equal to the tax determined under subparagraph (3) of this paragraph.

For taxable years beginning after December 31, 1954, and before January 1, 1958, the partial tax under subdivision (i) of this subparagraph shall also be computed at the rates provided in section 802(a). For taxable years beginning before January 1, 1963, the reference in such subdivision to section 821(a) or (c) is to be read as a reference to section 821(a) or (b).

(3) *Tax on capital gains.* For purposes of subparagraph (2)(ii) of this paragraph, the tax shall be—

(i) In the case of a taxable year beginning after December 31, 1974, a tax of 30 percent of the net section 1201 gain (net capital gain for taxable years beginning before December 31, 1976),

(ii) In the case of a taxable year beginning after December 31, 1969, and before January 1, 1975—

(*a*) A tax of 25 percent of the lesser of the amount of the subsection (d) gain (as defined in section 1201(d) and paragraph (f) of this section) or the amount of the net section 1201 gain (net capital gain for taxable years beginning before December 31, 1976), plus

(*b*) A tax of 30 percent (28 percent in the case of a taxable year beginning after December 31, 1969, and before January 1, 1971) of the excess, if any, of the net section 1201 gain (net capital gain for taxable years beginning before December 31, 1976) over the subsection (d) gain,

(iii) In the case of a taxable year beginning before January 1, 1970, and after March 31, 1954, a tax of 25 percent of the net section 1201 gain (net capital gain for taxable years beginning before December 31, 1976), or

(iv) In the case of a taxable year beginning before April 1, 1954, a tax of 26 percent of the net section 1201 gain (net capital gain for taxable years beginning before December 31, 1976).

(4) *Determination of special deductions.* In the computation of the partial tax described in subparagraph (2)(i) of this paragraph the special deductions provided for in sections 243, 244, 245, 247, 922, and 941 shall not be recomputed as the result of the reduction of taxable income by the net capital gain (net section 1201 gain for taxable years beginning before January 1, 1977).

(b) *Other taxpayers*—(1) *In general.* If for any taxable year a taxpayer (other than a corporation) has net capital gain (net section 1201 gain for taxable years beginning before January 1, 1977) (as defined in section 1222(11)), section 1201(b) imposes an alternative tax in lieu of the tax imposed by sections 1 and 511, but only if such

Reg. § 1.1201-1(b)(1)

alternative tax is less than the tax imposed by sections 1 and 511. The alternative tax is not in lieu of any other tax not specifically set forth in section 1201(b). See section 56 and the regulations thereunder for provisions relating to the minimum tax for tax preferences.

(2) *Alternative tax.* The alternative tax is the sum of—

(i) A partial tax computed at the rates provided by sections 1 and 511 on the taxable income reduced by an amount equal to 50 percent of the net capital gain (net section 1201 gain for taxable years beginning before January 1, 1977), and

(ii) In the case of a taxable year beginning after December 31, 1969—

(a) A tax of 25 percent of the lesser of the amount of the subsection (d) gain (as defined in section 1201(d) and paragraph (f) of this section) or the amount of the net capital gain (net section 1201 gain for taxable years beginning before January 1, 1977), plus

(b) A tax computed as provided in section 1201(c) and paragraph (e) of this section on the excess, if any, of the net capital gain (net section 1201 gain for taxable years beginning before January 1, 1977) over the subsection (d) gain, or

(iii) In the case of a taxable year beginning before January 1, 1970, a tax of 25 percent of the net section 1201 gain (net capital gain for taxable years beginning before December 31, 1976).

(3) *Cross references.* See § 1.1-2(a) for rule relating to the computation of the limitation on tax in cases where the alternative tax is imposed. See § 1.34-2(a) for rule relating to the computation of the dividend received credit under section 34 (for dividends received on or before December 31, 1964), and § 1.35-1(a) for rule relating to the computation of credit for partially tax-exempt interest under section 35 in cases where the alternative tax is imposed.

(c) *Tax-exempt trusts and organizations.* In applying section 1201 in the case of tax-exempt trusts or organizations subject to the tax imposed by section 511, the only amount which is taken into account as capital gain or loss is that which is taken into account in computing unrelated business taxable income under section 512. Under section 512, the only amount taken into account as capital gain or loss is that resulting from the application of section 631(a), relating to the election to treat the cutting of timber as a sale or exchange.

(d) *Joint returns.* In the case of a joint return, the excess of any net long-term capital gain over any net short-term capital loss is to be determined by combining the long-term capital gains and losses and the short-term capital gains and losses of the spouses.

(e) *Computation of tax on capital gain in excess of subsection (d) gain*—(1) *In general.* The tax computed for purposes of section 1201(b)(3) and paragraph (b)(2)(ii)(b) of this section shall be the amount by which a tax determined under section 1 or 511 on an amount equal to the taxable income (but not less than 50 percent of the net capital gain (net section 1201 gain for taxable years beginning before January 1, 1977) for the taxable year exceeds a tax determined under section 1 or 511 on an amount equal to the sum of (i) the amount subject to tax under section 1201(b)(1) and paragraph (b)(2)(i) of this section for such year plus (ii) an amount equal to 50 percent of the subsection (d) gain for such year.

(2) *Limitation.* Notwithstanding subparagraph (1) of this paragraph, the tax computed for purposes of section 1201(b)(3) and paragraph (b)(2)(ii) (b) of this section shall not exceed an amount equal to the following percentage of the excess of the net capital gain (net section 1201 gain for taxable years beginning before January 1, 1977) over the subsection (d) gain for the taxable year:

(i) 29½ percent, in the case of a taxable year beginning after December 31, 1969, and before January 1, 1971, or

(ii) 32½ percent, in the case of a taxable year beginning after December 31, 1970, and before January 1, 1972.

(f) *Definition of subsection (d) gain*—(1) *In general.* For purposes of section 1201 and this section, the term "subsection (d) gain" means the sum of the long-term capital gains for the taxable year arising—

(i) In the case of amounts received or accrued, as the case may be, before January 1, 1975 (other than any gain from a transaction described in section 631 or 1235), from—

(a) Sales or other dispositions on or before October 9, 1969, including sales or other dispositions the income from which is returned as provided in section 453(a)(1) or (b)(1), or

(b) Sales or other dispositions after October 9, 1969, pursuant to binding contracts entered into on or before that date, including sales or other dispositions the income from which is returned as provided in section 453(a)(1) or (b)(1),

(ii) From liquidating distributions made by a corporation which are made (a) before October 10, 1970, and (b) pursuant to a plan of complete liquidation adopted on or before October 9, 1969, or

(iii) In the case of a taxpayer (other than a corporation), from any other source not described in subdivision (i) or (ii) of this subparagraph, but the amount taken into account from such other sources shall be limited to the amount, if any, by which $50,000 ($25,000 in the case of a married individual filing a separate return) exceeds the sum of the gains to which subdivisions (i) and (ii) of this subparagraph apply.

(2) *Special rules.* For purposes of subparagraph (1) of this paragraph—

(i) A binding contract entered into on or before October 9, 1969, means a contract, whether written or unwritten, which on or before that date was legally enforceable against the taxpayer under applicable law. If on or before October 9, 1969, a taxpayer grants an irrevocable option or irrevocable contractual right to another party to buy certain property and such other party exercises that option or right after October 9, 1969, the sale of such property is a sale pursuant to a binding contract entered into on or before October 9, 1969. The application of this subdivision may be illustrated by the following example:

Example. During 1964, A, B, and C formed a closely-held corporation, and A was appointed as president of the organization. On July 1, 1964, A received for consideration 100 shares of common stock in the corporation subject to the agreement that, if A should retire from the management of the corporation or die, A or his estate would first offer his shares of stock to the corporation for purchase and that, if the corporation did not buy the stock within 60 days, the stock could be sold to any party other than the corporation. On September 1, 1970, A retired from the management of the corporation and offered his shares to the corporation for purchase. Pursuant to the agreement, the corporation purchased A's stock on September 30, 1970. A's sale of such stock was pursuant to a binding contract entered into on or before October 9, 1969.

(ii) A contract which pursuant to subdivision (i) of this subparagraph constitutes a binding contract entered into on or before October 9, 1969, does not cease to qualify as such a contract by reason of the fact that after October 9, 1969, there is a modification of the terms of the contract, such as a change in the time of performance, or in the amount of the debt or in the terms and mode of payment, or in the rate of interest, or there is a change in the form or nature of the obligation or the character of the security, so long as the taxpayer is at all times on and after October 9, 1969, legally bound by such contract. The application of this subdivision may be illustrated by the following examples:

Example (1). On August 1, 1969, A sold certain capital assets to B on the installment plan and elected to return the gain therefrom under section 453, the agreement providing for payments over a period of 2 years. At the time of the sale these assets had been held by A for more than 6 months. On July 31, 1970, A and B agreed to a modification of the terms of payment under the sales agreement, the only change in the contract being that the installment payments due after July 31, 1970, would be paid over a 3-year period. For purposes of this paragraph the payments received by A after July 31, 1970, are considered amounts received from the sale on August 1, 1969. (See section 483 for rules with respect to interest on deferred payments.)

Example (2). On April 1, 1969, A sold certain capital assets to B on the installment plan and elected to return the gain therefrom under section 453, the agreement providing for payments over a period of 3 years. At the time of the sale these assets had been held by A for more than 6 months. On March 31, 1970, C assumed B's obligation to pay the balance of the installments which were due after that date. For purposes of this paragraph any installment payments received by A after March 31, 1970, from C are considered amounts received from a sale made on or before October 9, 1969.

Example (3). On May 1, 1969, A offers to sell certain capital assets to B if B accepts the offer within one year, unless it is previously withdrawn by A. B accepts the offer on November 1, 1969, and the transaction is consummated shortly thereafter. For purposes of this paragraph, any payment received by A pursuant to the sale is not considered an amount received from a sale made on or before October 9, 1969, or from a sale pursuant to a binding contract entered into on or before that date.

(iii) An amount which is considered under section 402(a)(2) or 403(a)(2) as gain of the taxpayer from the sale or exchange of a capital asset held for more than 6 months shall be treated as gain subject to the provisions of section 1201(d)(1) and subdivision (i) of such subparagraph, but only if on or before October 9, 1969, (a) the employee with respect to whom such amount is distributed or paid died or was otherwise separated from the service and (b) the terms of the plan required, or the employee elected, that the total distributions or amounts payable be paid to the taxpayer within one taxable year.

(iv) Gain described in section 1201(d)(1) or (2) with respect to a partnership, estate, or trust, which is required to be included in the gross

Reg. § 1.1201-1(f)(2)

income of a partner in such partnership, or of a beneficiary of such estate or trust, shall be treated as such gain with respect to such partner or beneficiary. Thus, for example, if during 1974 a partnership which uses the calendar year as its taxable year receives amounts which give rise to section 1201(d)(1) gain, a partner who uses the fiscal year ending June 30 as his taxable year shall treat his distributive share of such gain as subsection (d) gain for his taxable year ending June 30, 1975, even though such share is distributed to him after December 31, 1974. See § 1.706-1.

(v) An individual shall be considered married for purposes of subdivision (iii) of such subparagraph if for the taxable year he may elect with his spouse to make a joint return under section 6013(a).

(vi) In applying such subparagraph for purposes of section 21(a)(1) long-term capital gains arising from amounts received before January 1, 1970, shall be taken into account if such amounts are received during the taxable year.

(g) *Illustrations.* The application of this section may be illustrated by the following examples in which the assumption is made that section 56 (relating to minimum tax for tax preferences) does not apply:

Example (1). A, a single individual, has for the calendar year 1954 taxable income (exclusive of capital gains and losses) of $99,400. He realizes in 1954 a gain of $50,000 on the sale of a capital asset held for 19 months and sustains a loss of $20,000 on the sale of a capital asset held for five months. He has no other capital gains or losses. Since the alternative tax is less than the tax otherwise computed under section 1, the tax payable is the alternative tax, that is $74,298. The tax is computed as follows:

Tax Under Section 1

Taxable income exclusive of capital gains and losses		$ 99,400
Net long-term capital gain (100 percent of $50,000)	$50,000	
Net short-term capital loss (100 percent of $20,000)	20,000	
Excess of net long-term capital gain over the net short-term capital loss		30,000
		$129,400
Deduction of 50 percent of excess of net long-term capital gain over the net short-term capital loss (section 1202)		15,000
Taxable income		$114,400
Tax under section 1		$ 80,136

Alternative Tax Under Section 1201(b)

Taxable income	$114,400
Less 50 percent of excess of net long-term capital gain over net short-term capital loss (section 1201(b)(1))	15,000
Taxable income exclusive of capital gains and losses	$ 99,400
Partial tax (tax on $99,400)	$ 66,798
Plus 25 percent of $30,000	7,500
Alternative tax under section 1201(b)	$ 74,298

Example (2). A husband and wife, who file a joint return for the calendar year 1970, have taxable income (exclusive of capital gains and losses) of $100,000. In 1970 they realize $200,000 of net long-term capital gain in excess of net short-term capital loss, including long-term capital gains of $100,000 arising from sales consummated in 1968 the income from which is returned on the installment method under section 453, and long-term capital gains of $50,000 arising in respect of distributions from X corporation made before October 10, 1970, which were pursuant to a plan of complete liquidation adopted on October 9, 1969. Since the alternative tax under section 1201(b) is less than the tax otherwise computed under section 1, the tax payable for 1970 is the alternative tax, that is, $97,430 plus the tax surcharge under section 51. The tax (without regard to the tax surcharge) is computed as follows:

Tax Under Section 1

Taxable income exclusive of capital gains and losses	$100,000
Net section 1201 gain (net capital gain for taxable years beginning before December 31, 1976) (excess of net long-term capital gain over the net short-term capital loss)	200,000
Total	$300,000
Deduction of 50 percent of net section 1201 gain (section 1202)	100,000
Taxable income	$200,000
Tax under sec. 1	$110,980

Reg. § 1.1201-1(g)

Treatment of Capital Gains

See p. 20,601 for regulations not amended to reflect law changes

Alternative Tax Under Section 1201(b)

(1) Net section 1201 gain (net capital gain for taxable years beginning before December 31, 1976)		$200,000
(2) Subsection (d) gain:		
Sec. 1201(d)(1)		$100,000
Sec. 1201(d)(2)		50,000
Total subsection (d) gain		$150,000
(3) Net section 1201 gain (net capital gain for taxable years beginning before December 31, 1976) in excess of subsection (d) gain ($200,000 less $150,000)		$ 50,000
(4) Tax under sec. 1201(b)(1):		
(i) Taxable income	$200,000	
(ii) Less: 50% of item (1)	100,000	
(iii) Amount subject to tax under sec. 1201(b)(1)	$100,000	
Partial tax (computed under sec. 1)		$ 45,180
(5) Tax under sec. 1201(b)(2):		
(25% of item (1) or of item (2), whichever is lesser [25% of $150,000])		37,500
(6) Tax under sec. 1201(b)(3) on item (3):		
Tax under sec. 1 on taxable income ($200,000)	$110,980	
Less: Tax under sec. 1 on sum of item (4)(iii) ($100,000) plus 50% of item (2) ($75,000) (Total $175,000)	93,780	
Tax under sec. 1201(c)(1)	$ 17,200	
Limitation under sec. 1201(c)(2)(A) (29½% of item (3))	$ 14,750	14,750
(7) Alternative tax under sec. 1201(b)		$ 97,430

Example (3). A husband and wife, who file a joint return for the calendar year 1971, have taxable income (exclusive of capital gains and losses) of $80,000. In 1971 they realize long-term capital gain of $30,000 arising from a sale consummated on July 1, 1969, the income from which is returned on the installment method under section 453. From securities transactions in 1971 they have long-term capital gains of $60,000 and a short-term capital loss of $10,000. Since the alternative tax under section 1201(b) is less than the tax otherwise computed under section 1, the tax payable is the alternative tax, that is, $55,140. The tax is computed as follows:

Tax Under Section 1

Taxable income exclusive of capital gains and losses		$ 80,000
Net long-term capital gains (100% of $90,000)	$ 90,000	
Net short-term capital loss (100% of $10,000)	10,000	
Net section 1201 gain (net capital gain for taxable years beginning before December 31, 1976)		80,000
Total		$160,000
Deduction of 50% of net section 1201 gain (net capital gain for taxable years beginning before December 31, 1976) (sec. 1202)		40,000
Taxable income		$120,000
Tax under sec. 1		$ 57,580

Alternative Tax Under Section 1201(b)

(1) Net section 1201 gain (net capital gain for taxable years beginning before December 31, 1976)		$ 80,000
(2) Subsection (d) gain:		
Sec. 1201(d)(1)		$ 30,000
Sec. 1201(d)(2)		
Sec. 1201(d)(3) ($50,000 less $30,000)		20,000
Total subsection (d) gain		$ 50,000
(3) Net section 1201 gain (net capital gain for taxable years beginning before December 31, 1976) in excess of subsection (d) gain ($80,000 less $50,000)		$ 30,000
(4) Tax under sec. 1201(b)(1):		
(i) Taxable income	$120,000	
(ii) Less: 50% of item (1)	40,000	
(iii) Amount subject to tax under sec. 1201(b)(1)	$ 80,000	
Partial tax (computed under sec. 1)		$ 33,340

Reg. § 1.1201-1(g)

Treatment of Capital Gains

See p. 20,601 for regulations not amended to reflect law changes

(5) Tax under sec. 1201(b)(2):
    (25% of item (1) or of item (2), whichever is lesser [25% of $50,000]) 12,500
(6) Tax under sec. 1201(b)(3) on item (3):
    Tax under sec. 1 on taxable income ($120,000)......................... $ 57,580
    Less: Tax under sec. 1 on sum of item (4)(iii) ($80,000) plus 50% of item
        (2) ($25,000) (Total $105,000).................................. 48,280

        Tax under sec. 1201(c)(1) .... $ 9,300

        Limitation under sec. 1201(c)(2)(B) (32½% of item (3)) .... $ 9,750 $ 9,300

(7) Alternative tax under sec. 1201(b) .... $ 55,140

Example (4). A husband and wife, who file a joint return for the calendar year 1973, have taxable income (exclusive of capital gains and losses) of $250,000. In 1973 they realize long-term capital gains (not described in section 1201(d)(1) or (2)) of $140,000 and a short-term capital loss of $50,000. Since the alternative tax under section 1201(b) is less than the tax otherwise computed under section 1, the tax payable is the alternative tax, that is, $172,480. The tax is computed as follows:

Tax Under Section 1

Taxable income exclusive of capital gains and losses $250,000
Net long-term capital gains (100% of $140,000) $140,000
Net short-term capital loss (100% of $50,000) 50,000

Net section 1201 gain (net capital gain for taxable years beginning before
    December 31, 1976)... 90,000
    Total.. $340,000
Deduction of 50% of net section 1201 gain (sec. 1202) 45,000

    Taxable income $295,000

Tax under sec. 1.. $177,480

Alternative Tax Under Section 1201(b)

(1) Net section 1201 gain (net capital gain for taxable years beginning before December 31,
    1976) .... $ 90,000
(2) Subsection (d) gain:
    Sec. 1201(d)(1) .... $
    Sec. 1201(d)(2) ....
    Sec. 1201(d)(3) ($50,000) ....

    Total subsection (d) gain .... $ 50,000

(3) Net section 1201 gain (net capital gain for taxable years beginning before December 31,
    1976) in excess of subsection (d) gain ($90,000 less $50,000) .... $ 40,000
(4) Tax under sec. 1201(b)(1):
    (i) Taxable income $295,000
    (ii) Less: 50% of item (1) 45,000

    (iii) Amount subject to tax under sec. 1201(b)(1) $250,000

    Partial tax (computed under sec. 1) $145,980
(5) Tax under sec. 1201(b)(2):
    (25% of item (1) or of item (2), whichever is lesser [25% of $50,000]) 12,500
(6) Tax under sec. 1201(b)(3) on item (3):
    Tax under sec. 1 on taxable income ($295,000)........................ $177,480
    Less: Tax under sec. 1 on sum of item (4)(iii) ($250,000) plus 50% of item
        (2) ($25,000) (Total $275,000).................................. 163,480   14,000

(7) Alternative tax under sec. 1201(b) $172,480

[Reg. § 1.1201-1.]

☐ [T.D. 6243, 7-23-57. Amended by T.D. 6610, 8-30-62; T.D. 6681, 10-16-63; T.D. 6777, 12-15-64; T.D. 7337, 12-26-74 and T.D. 7728, 10-31-80.]

[Reg. § 1.1202-0]

§ 1.1202-0. Table of contents.—This section lists the major captions that appear in the regulations under § 1.1202-2.

§ 1.1202-2. *Qualified small business stock; effect of redemptions.*

(a) Redemptions from taxpayer or related person.

Treatment of Capital Gains

See p. 20,601 for regulations not amended to reflect law changes

(1) In general.

(2) De minimis amount.

(b) Significant redemptions.

(1) In general.

(2) De minimis amount.

(c) Transfers by shareholders in connection with the performance of services not treated as purchases.

(d) Exceptions for termination of services, death, disability or mental incompetency, or divorce.

(1) Termination of services.

(2) Death.

(3) Disability or mental incompetency.

(4) Divorce.

(e) Effective date.

[Reg. § 1.1202-0.]

☐ [T.D. 8749, 12-30-97.]

[Reg. § 1.1202-1]

§ 1.1202-1. Deduction for capital gains.—(a) In computing gross income, adjusted gross income, taxable income, capital gain net income (net capital gain for taxable years beginning before January 1, 1977) and net capital loss, 100 percent of any gain or loss (computed under section 1001, recognized under section 1002, and taken into account without regard to subchapter P (section 1201 and following), chapter 1 of the Code), upon the sale or exchange of a capital asset shall be taken into account regardless of the period for which the capital asset has been held. Nevertheless, the net short-term capital gain or loss and the net long-term capital gain or loss must be separately computed. In computing the adjusted gross income or the taxable income of a taxpayer other than a corporation, if for any taxable year the net long-term capital gain exceeds the net short-term capital loss, 50 percent of the amount of the excess is allowable as a deduction from gross income under section 1202.

(b) For the purpose of computing the deduction allowable under section 1202 in the case of an estate or trust, any long-term or short-term capital gains which, under section 652 and 662, are includible in the gross income of its income beneficiaries as gains derived from the sale or exchange of capital assets must be excluded in determining whether, for the taxable year of the estate or trust, its net long-term capital gain exceeds its net short-term capital loss. To determine the extent to which such gains are includible in the gross income of a beneficiary, see the regulations under sections 652 and 662. For example, during 1954 a trust realized a gain of $1,000 upon the sale of stock held for 10 months. Under the terms of the trust instrument all of such gain must be distributed during the taxable year to A, the sole income beneficiary. Assuming that under section 652 or 662 A must include all of such gain in his gross income, the trust is not entitled to any deduction with respect to such gain under section 1202. Assuming A had no other capital gains or losses for 1954, he would be entitled to a deduction of $500 under section 1202. For purposes of this section, an income beneficiary shall be any beneficiary to whom an amount is required to be distributed, or is paid or credited, which is includible in his gross income.

(c) The provisions of this section may be illustrated by the following example:

Example. A, an individual, had the following transactions in 1954:

Long-term capital gain		$6,000
Long-term capital loss		4,000
Net long-term capital gain		$2,000
Short-term capital loss	1,800	
Short-term capital gain	300	
Net short-term capital loss		1,500
Excess of net long-term capital gain over net short-term capital loss		$ 500

Since the net long-term capital gain exceeds the net short-term capital loss by $500, 50 percent of the excess, or $250, is allowable as a deduction under section 1202. [Reg. § 1.1202-1.]

☐ [T.D. 6243, 7-23-57. Amended by T.D. 7728, 10-31-80.]

[Reg. § 1.1202-2]

§ 1.1202-2. Qualified small business stock; effect of redemptions.—(a) *Redemptions from taxpayer or related person*—(1) *In general.* Stock acquired by a taxpayer is not qualified small business stock if, in one or more purchases during the 4-year period beginning on the date 2 years before the issuance of the stock, the issuing corporation purchases (directly or indirectly) more than a de minimis amount of its stock from the taxpayer or from a person related (within the meaning of section 267(b) or 707(b)) to the taxpayer.

(2) *De minimis amount.* For purposes of this paragraph (a), stock acquired from the taxpayer or a related person exceeds a de minimis amount only if the aggregate amount paid for the stock

Reg. § 1.1202-2(a)(2)

exceeds $10,000 and more than 2 percent of the stock held by the taxpayer and related persons is acquired. The following rules apply for purposes of determining whether the 2-percent limit is exceeded. The percentage of stock acquired in any single purchase is determined by dividing the stock's value (as of the time of purchase) by the value (as of the time of purchase) of all stock held (directly or indirectly) by the taxpayer and related persons immediately before the purchase. The percentage of stock acquired in multiple purchases is the sum of the percentages determined for each separate purchase.

(b) *Significant redemptions*—(1) *In general.* Stock is not qualified small business stock if, in one or more purchases during the 2-year period beginning on the date 1 year before the issuance of the stock, the issuing corporation purchases more than a de minimis amount of its stock and the purchased stock has an aggregate value (as of the time of the respective purchases) exceeding 5 percent of the aggregate value of all of the issuing corporation's stock as of the beginning of such 2-year period.

(2) *De minimis amount.* For purposes of this paragraph (b), stock exceeds a de minimis amount only if the aggregate amount paid for the stock exceeds $10,000 and more than 2 percent of all outstanding stock is purchased. The following rules apply for purposes of determining whether the 2-percent limit is exceeded. The percentage of the stock acquired in any single purchase is determined by dividing the stock's value (as of the time of purchase) by the value (as of the time of purchase) of all stock outstanding immediately before the purchase. The percentage of stock acquired in multiple purchases is the sum of the percentages determined for each separate purchase.

(c) *Transfers by shareholders in connection with the performance of services not treated as purchases.* A transfer of stock by a shareholder to an employee or independent contractor (or to a beneficiary of an employee or independent contractor) is not treated as a purchase of the stock by the issuing corporation for purposes of this section even if the stock is treated as having first been transferred to the corporation under § 1.836(d)(1) (relating to transfers by shareholders to employees or independent contractors).

(d) *Exceptions for termination of services, death, disability or mental incompetency, or divorce.* A stock purchase is disregarded if the stock is acquired in the following circumstances:

(1) *Termination of services*—(i) *Employees and directors.* The stock was acquired by the seller in connection with the performance of services as an employee or director and the stock is purchased from the seller incident to the seller's retirement or other bona fide termination of such services;

(ii) *Independent contractors.* [Reserved];

(2) *Death.* Prior to a decedent's death, the stock (or an option to acquire the stock) was held by the decedent or the decedent's spouse (or by both), by the decedent and joint tenant, or by a trust revocable by the decedent or the decedent's spouse (or by both), and—

(i) The stock is purchased from the decedent's estate, beneficiary (whether by bequest or lifetime gift), heir, surviving joint tenant, or surviving spouse, or from a trust established by the decedent or decedent's spouse; and

(ii) The stock is purchased within 3 years and 9 months from the date of the decedent's death;

(3) *Disability or mental incompetency.* The stock is purchased incident to the disability or mental incompetency of the selling shareholder; or

(4) *Divorce.* The stock is purchased incident to the divorce (within the meaning of section 1041(c)) of the selling shareholder.

(e) *Effective date.* This section applies to stock issued after August 10, 1993. [Reg. § 1.1202-2.]

□ [T.D. 8749, 12-30-97.]

Treatment of Capital Losses

[Reg. § 1.1211-1]

§ 1.1211-1. Limitation on capital losses.—(a) *Corporations*—(1) *General rule.* In the case of a corporation, there shall be allowed as a deduction an amount equal to the sum of—

(i) Losses sustained during the taxable year from sales or exchanges of capital assets, plus

(ii) The aggregate of all losses sustained in other taxable years which are treated as a short-term capital loss in such taxable year pursuant to section 1212(a)(1),

but only to the extent of gains from such sales or exchanges of capital assets in such taxable year.

(2) *Banks.* See section 582(c) for modification of the limitation under section 1211(a) in the case of a bank, as defined in section 581.

(b) *Taxpayers other than corporations*—(1) *General rule.* In the case of a taxpayer other than

Reg. § 1.1211-1(a)(1)

a corporation, there shall be allowed as a deduction an amount equal to the sum of—

(i) Losses sustained during the taxable year from sales or exchanges of capital assets, plus

(ii) The aggregate of all losses sustained in other taxable years which are treated either as a short-term capital loss or as a long-term capital loss in such taxable year pursuant to section 1212(b),

but only to the extent of gains from sales or exchanges of capital assets in such taxable year, plus (if such losses exceed such gains) the additional allowance or transitional additional allowance deductible under section 1211(b) from ordinary income for such taxable year. The additional allowance deductible under section 1211(b) shall be determined by application of subparagraph (2) of this paragraph, and the transitional additional allowance by application of subparagraph (3) of this paragraph.

(2) *Additional allowance.* Except as otherwise provided by subparagraph (3) of this paragraph, the additional allowance deductible under section 1211(b) for taxable years beginning after December 31, 1969, shall be the least of—

(i) The taxable income for the taxable year reduced, but not below zero, by the zero bracket amount (in the case of taxable years beginning before January 1, 1977, the taxable income for the taxable year);

(ii) $3,000 ($2,000 for taxable years beginning in 1977; $1,000 for taxable years beginning before January 1, 1977); or

(iii) The sum of the excess of the net short-term capital loss over the net long-term capital gain, plus one-half of the excess of the net long-term capital loss over the net short-term capital gain.

(3) *Transitional additional allowance*—(i) *In general.* If, pursuant to the provisions of § 1.1212-1(b) and subdivision (iii) of this subparagraph, there is carried to the taxable year from a taxable year beginning before January 1, 1970, a long-term capital loss, and if for the taxable year there is an excess of net long-term capital loss over net short-term capital gain, then, in lieu of the additional allowance provided by subparagraph (2) of this paragraph, the transitional additional allowance deductible under section 1211(b) shall be the least of—

(a) The taxable income for the taxable year reduced, but not below zero, by the zero bracket amount (in the case of taxable years beginning before January 1, 1977, the taxable income for the taxable year);

(b) $3,000 ($2,000 for taxable years beginning in 1977; $1,000 for taxable years beginning before January 1, 1977); or

(c) The sum of the excess of the net short-term capital loss over the net long-term capital gain; that portion of the excess of the net long-term capital loss over the net short-term capital gain computed as provided in subdivision (ii) of this subparagraph; plus one-half of the remaining portion of the excess of the net long-term capital loss over the net short-term capital gain.

(ii) *Computation of specially treated portion of excess long-term capital loss over net short-term capital gain.* In determining the transitional additional allowance deductible as provided by this subparagraph, there shall be applied thereto in full on a dollar-for-dollar basis the excess of net long-term capital loss over net short-term capital gain (computed with regard to capital losses carried to the taxable year) to the extent that the long-term capital losses carried to the taxable year from taxable years beginning before January 1, 1970, as provided by § 1.1212-1(b) and subdivision (iii) of this subparagraph, exceed the sum of (a) the portion of the capital gain net income (net capital gain for taxable years beginning before January 1, 1977) actually realized in the taxable year (*i.e.,* computed without regard to capital losses carried to the taxable year) which consists of net long-term capital gain actually realized in the taxable year, plus (b) the amount by which the portion of the capital gain net income (net capital gain for taxable years beginning before January 1, 1977) actually realized in the taxable year (*i.e.,* computed without regard to capital losses carried to the taxable year) which consists of net short-term capital gain actually realized in the taxable year exceeds the total of short-term capital losses carried to the taxable year from taxable years beginning before January 1, 1970, as provided by § 1.1212-1(b) and subdivision (iv) of this subparagraph. The amount by which the net long-term capital losses carried to the taxable year from taxable years beginning before January 1, 1970, exceeds the sum of (a) plus (b) shall constitute the "transitional net long-term capital loss component" for the taxable year for the purpose of this subparagraph.

(iii) *Carryover of certain long-term capital losses not utilized in computation of transitional additional allowance.* If for a taxable year beginning after December 31, 1969, the transitional net

Reg. § 1.1211-1(b)(3)

long-term capital loss component determined as provided in subdivision (ii) of this subparagraph exceeds the amount of such component applied to the transitional additional allowance for the taxable year as provided by subdivision (i) of this subparagraph and subparagraph (4)(ii) of this paragraph, then such excess shall for the purposes of this subparagraph be carried to the succeeding taxable year as long-term capital losses from taxable years beginning before January 1, 1970, for utilization in the computation of the transitional additional allowance in the succeeding taxable year as provided in subdivisions (i) and (ii) of this subparagraph. In no event, however, shall the amount of such component carried to the following taxable year as otherwise provided by this subdivision exceed the total of net long-term capital losses actually carried to such succeeding taxable year pursuant to section 1212(b) and § 1.1212-1(b).

(iv) *Carryover of certain short-term capital losses not utilized in computation of additional allowance or transitional additional allowance.* If for a taxable year beginning after December 31, 1969, the total short-term capital losses carried to such year from taxable years beginning before January 1, 1970, as provided by § 1.1212-1(b) and this subdivision exceed the sum of—

(a) The portion of the capital gain net income (net capital gain for taxable years beginning before January 1, 1977) actually realized in the taxable year (*i.e.*, computed without regard to capital losses carried to the taxable year) which consists of net short-term capital gain actually realized in the taxable year, plus

(b) The amount by which the portion of the capital gain net income (net capital gain for taxable years beginning before January 1, 1977) actually realized in the taxable year (*i.e.*, computed without regard to capital losses carried to the taxable year) which consists of net long-term capital gain actually realized in the taxable year exceeds the total long-term capital losses carried to the taxable year from taxable years beginning before January 1, 1970, as provided in § 1.1212-1(b) and subdivision (iii) of this subparagraph, then such excess shall constitute the "transitional net short-term capital loss component" for the taxable year, and to the extent such component also exceeds the net short-term capital loss applied to the additional allowance (as provided in subparagraphs (2) and (4)(i) of this paragraph) or the transitional additional allowance (as provided by subdivision (i) of this subparagraph and subparagraph (4)(i) of this paragraph) for the taxable year shall be carried to the succeeding taxable year as short-term capital losses from tax-

able years beginning before January 1, 1970, for utilization in such succeeding taxable year in the computation of the additional allowance (as provided by subparagraph (2) of this paragraph) or the transitional additional allowance (as provided by subdivision (i) and (ii) of this subparagraph). In no event, however, shall the amount of such component so carried to the following taxable year as otherwise provided by this subdivision exceed the total of net short- term capital losses actually carried to such succeeding taxable year pursuant to section 1212(b) and § 1.1212-1(b).

(v) *Scope of rules.* The rules provided by this subparagraph are for the purpose of computing the amount of the transitional additional allowance deductible for the taxable year pursuant to the provisions of section 1212(b)(3) and this subparagraph. More specifically, their operation permits the limited use of a long-term capital loss carried to the taxable year from a taxable year beginning before December 31, 1969, in full on a dollar-for-dollar basis in computing the transitional additional allowance deductible for the taxable year. These rules have no application to, or effect upon, a determination of the character or amount of capital gain net income (net capital gains for taxable years beginning before January 1, 1977) reportable in the taxable year. See paragraph (b)(1) of this section and § 1.1212-1 for the determination of the amount and character of capital gains and losses reportable in the taxable year. Further, except to the extent that their application may affect the amount of the transitional additional allowance deductible for the taxable year and thus the amount to be treated as short-term capital loss for carryover purposes under section 1212(b) and § 1.1212-1(b)(2), these rules have no effect upon a determination of the character or amount of capital losses carried to or from the taxable year pursuant to section 1212(b) and § 1.1212-1(b).

(4) *Order of application of capital losses to additional allowance or transitional additional allowance.* In applying the excess of the net short-term capital loss over the net long-term capital gain and the excess of the net long-term capital loss over the net short-term capital gain to the additional allowance or transitional additional allowance deductible under section 1211(b) and this paragraph, such excesses shall, subject to the limitations of subparagraph (2) or (3) of this paragraph, be used in the following order:

(i) First, there shall be applied to the additional allowance or transitional additional allowance the excess, if any, of the net short-term capital loss over the net long-term capital gain.

Reg. § 1.1211-1(b)(4)

Treatment of Capital Losses

See p. 20,601 for regulations not amended to reflect law changes

(ii) Second, if such transitional additional allowance exceeds the amount so applied thereto as provided in subdivision (i) of this subparagraph, there shall next be applied thereto as provided in subparagraph (3) of this paragraph the excess, if any, of the net long-term capital loss over the net short-term capital gain to the extent of the transitional net long-term capital loss component for the taxable year computed as provided by subdivision (ii) of subparagraph (3) of this paragraph.

(iii) Third, if such additional allowance or transitional additional allowance exceeds the sum of the amounts so applied thereto as provided in subdivisions (i) and (ii) of this subparagraph, there shall be applied thereto one-half of the balance, if any, of the excess net long-term capital loss not applied pursuant to the provisions of subdivision (ii) of this subparagraph.

(5) *Taxable years beginning prior to January 1, 1970.* For any taxable year beginning prior to January 1, 1970, subparagraphs (2) and (3) of this paragraph shall not apply and losses from sales or exchanges of capital assets shall be allowed as a deduction only to the extent of gains from such sales or exchanges, plus (if such losses exceed such gains) the taxable income of the taxpayer or $1,000, whichever is smaller.

(6) *Special rules.* (i) For purposes of section 1211(b) and this paragraph, taxable income is to be computed without regard to gains or losses from sales or exchanges of capital assets and without regard to the deductions provided in section 151 (relating to personal exemptions) or any deduction in lieu thereof. For example, the deductions available to estates and trusts under section 642(b) are in lieu of the deductions allowed under section 151, and, in the case of estates and trusts, are to be added back to taxable income for the purposes of section 1211(b) and this paragraph.

(ii) For taxable years beginning before January 1, 1976, in case the tax is computed under section 3 and the regulations thereunder (relating to optional tax tables for individuals), the term "taxable income" as used in section 1211(b) and this paragraph shall be read as "adjusted gross income."

(iii) In the case of a joint return, the limitation under section 1211(b) and this paragraph, relating to the allowance of losses from sales or exchanges of capital assets, is to be computed and the net capital loss determined with respect to the combined taxable income and the combined capital gains and losses of the spouses.

(7) *Married taxpayers filing separate returns*—(i) *In general.* In the case of a husband or a wife who files a separate return for a taxable year beginning after December 31, 1969, the $3,000, $2,000, and $1,000 amounts specified in subparagraphs (2)(ii) and (3)(i)(*b*) of this paragraph shall instead be $1,500, $1,000, and $500, respectively.

(ii) *Special rule.* If, pursuant to the provisions of § 1.1212-1(b) and subparagraph (3)(iii) or (iv) of this paragraph, there is carried to the taxable year from a taxable year beginning before January 1, 1970, a short-term capital loss or a long-term capital loss, the $1,500, $1,000, and $500 amounts specified in subdivision (i) of this subparagraph shall instead be maximum amounts of $3,000, $2,000, and $1,000, respectively, equal to $1,500, $1,000, and $500, respectively, plus the total of the transitional net long-term capital loss component for the taxable year computed as provided by subparagraph (3)(ii) of this paragraph and the transitional net short-term capital loss component for the taxable year computed as provided by subparagraph (3)(iv) of this paragraph.

(8) *Examples.* The provisions of section 1211(b) may be illustrated by the following examples:

Example (1). A, an unmarried individual with one exemption allowable as a deduction under section 151, has the following transactions in 1970:

Taxable income exclusive of capital gains and losses	$4,400
Deduction provided by section 151	625
Taxable income for purposes of section 1211(b)	$5,025
Long-term capital gain .... $ 1,200	
Long-term capital loss .... (5,300)	
Net long-term capital loss	($ 4,100)
Losses to the extent of gains	($ 1,200)
Additional allowance deductible under section 1211(b)	$1,000

The net long-term capital loss of $4,100 is deductible in 1970 only to the extent of an additional allowance of $1,000 which is smaller than the taxable income of $5,025. Under section 1211(b) and subparagraph (2) of this paragraph, $2,000 of excess net long-term capital loss was required to produce the $1,000 additional allowance. Therefore, a net long-term capital loss of $2,100 ($4,100 minus $2,000) is carried over under section 1212(b) to the succeeding taxable year. If A had

Reg. § 1.1211-1(b)(8)

Treatment of Capital Losses

See p. 20,601 for regulations not amended to reflect law changes

the same taxable income for purposes of section 1211(b) (after reduction by the zero bracket amount) and the same transactions in 1977, the additional allowance would be $2,000, and a net long-term capital loss of $100 would be carried over. For a taxable year beginning in 1978 or thereafter, these facts would give rise to a $2,050 additional allowance and no carryover.

Example (2). B, an unmarried individual with one exemption allowable as a deduction under section 151, has the following transactions in 1970:

Taxable income exclusive of capital gains and losses		$ 90
Deduction provided by section 151		625
Taxable income for purposes of section 1211(b)		$715
Long-term capital gain	$1,200	
Long-term capital loss	(5,200)	
Net long-term capital loss	($4,000)	
Losses to the extent of gains	($1,200)	
Additional allowance deductible under section 1211(b)		$715

The net long-term capital loss of $4,000 is deductible in 1970 only to the extent of an additional allowance of $715, since the $715 of taxable income for purposes of section 1211(b) is smaller than $1,000. Under section 1211(b) and subparagraph (2) of this paragraph, $1,430 of net long-term capital loss was required to produce the $715 additional allowance. Therefore a net long-term capital loss of $2,570 ($4,000 minus $1,430) is carried over under section 1212(b) to the succeeding taxable year. For illustration of the result if the net capital loss for the taxable year is smaller than both $1,000 and taxable income for the purposes of section 1211(b), see examples (3) and (4) of this subparagraph. For carryover of a net capital loss, see § 1.1212-1. Assuming the same taxable income for purposes of section 1211(b) (after reduction by the zero bracket amount) and the same transactions for taxable years beginning in 1977 or thereafter, the same result would be reached.

Example (3). A, an unmarried individual with one exemption allowable as a deduction under section 151, has the following transactions in 1971:

Taxable income exclusive of capital gains and losses		$13,300
Deduction provided by section 151		675
Taxable income for purposes of section 1211(b)		$13,975
Long-term capital gain	$ 400	
Long-term capital loss	(600)	
Net long-term capital loss	($ 200)	
Short-term capital gain	$ 900	
Short-term capital loss	(1,400)	
Net short-term capital loss	($ 500)	
Losses to extent of gains	($1,300)	
Additional allowance deductible under section 1211(b)		$ 600

The $600 additional allowance deductible under section 1211(b) is the least of: (i) taxable income of $13,975, (ii) $1,000, or (iii) the sum of the excess of the net short-term capital loss of $500 over the net long-term capital gain, plus one-half of the excess of the net long-term capital loss of $200 over the net short-term capital gain. The $600 additional allowance, therefore, consists of the net short-term capital loss of $500, plus $100 (one-half of the net long-term capital loss of $200), the total of which is smaller than both $1,000 and taxable income for purposes of section 1211(b). No amount of net capital loss remains to be carried over under section 1212(b) to the succeeding taxable year since the entire amount of the net short-term capital loss of $500 plus the entire amount of the net long-term capital loss of $200 required to produce $100 of the deduction was absorbed by the additional allowance deductible under section 1211(b) for 1971. Assuming the same taxable income for purposes of section 1211(b) (after reduction by the zero bracket amount) and the same transactions for taxable years beginning in 1977 or thereafter, the result would remain unchanged.

Example (4). A, a married individual filing a separate return with one exemption allowable as a deduction under section 151, has the following transactions in 1971:

Reg. § 1.1211-1(b)(8)

Treatment of Capital Losses

Taxable income exclusive of capital gains and losses		$12,000
Deduction provided by section 151		675
Taxable income for purposes of section 1211(b)		$12,675
Long-term capital loss	($800)	
Long-term capital gain	300	
Net long-term capital loss	($500)	
Short-term capital loss	($500)	
Short-term capital gain	600	
Net short-term capital gain	$100	
Losses to the extent of gains		($900)
Additional allowance deductible under section 1211(b)		$200

The excess net long-term capital loss of $400 (net long-term capital loss of $500 minus net short-term capital gain of $100) is deductible in 1971 only to the extent of an additional allowance of $200 (one-half of $400) which is smaller than both $500 (married taxpayer filing a separate return for a taxable year beginning after December 31, 1969) and taxable income for purposes of section 1211(b). Since there is no net short-term capital loss in excess of net long-term capital gains for the taxable year, the $200 additional allowance deductible under section 1211(b) consists entirely of excess net long-term capital loss. No amount of net capital loss remains to be carried over under section 1212(b) to the succeeding taxable year. Assuming the same taxable income for purposes of section 1211(b) (after reduction by the zero bracket amount) and the same transactions for taxable years beginning in 1977 or thereafter, the result would remain unchanged.

Example (5). A, an unmarried individual with one exemption allowable as a deduction under section 151, has the following transactions in 1970:

Taxable income exclusive of capital gains and losses		$13,300
Deduction provided by section 151		625
Taxable income for purposes of section 1211(b)		$13,925
Long-term capital loss	($6,000)	
Long-term capital gain	$2,000	
Net long-term capital loss	($4,000)	
Short-term capital gain	$3,000	
Short-term capital loss carried to 1970 from 1969 under section 1212(b)(1)	($3,000)	
Net short-term capital loss	—0—	
Losses to the extent of gains	($5,000)	
Additional allowance deductible under section 12(b)	$1,000	

The $1,000 additional allowance deductible under section 1211(b) is the least of (i) taxable income of $13,925, (ii) $1,000, or (iii) the sum of the net short-term capital loss ($0) plus one-half the net long-term capital loss of $4,000. The $1,000 additional allowance, therefore, consists of net long-term capital loss. Since $2,000 of the net long-term capital loss of $4,000 was required to produce the $1,000 additional allowance, the $2,000 balance of the net long-term capital loss is carried over under section 1212(b) to 1971. Assuming the same taxable income for purposes of section 1211(b) (after reduction by the zero bracket amount) and the same transactions for taxable years beginning in 1977 or thereafter, the additional allowance would be $2,000, and there would be no carryover.

Example (6). A, an unmarried individual with one exemption allowable as a deduction under section 151, has the following transactions in 1970:

Taxable income exclusive of capital gains and losses		$13,300
Deduction provided by section 151		625
Taxable income for purposes of section 1211(b)		$13,925
Long-term capital gain	$5,000	
Long-term capital loss	($7,000)	

Reg. § 1.1211-1(b)(8)

Treatment of Capital Losses

See p. 20,601 for regulations not amended to reflect law changes

Long-term capital loss carried to 1970 from 1969 under section 1212(b)(1)	($ 500)
Net long-term capital loss	($2,500)
Short-term capital gain	$1,100
Short-term capital loss	(1,400)
Net short-term capital loss	($ 300)
Losses to extent of gains	($6,100)
Transitional additional allowance deductible under section 1211(b)	$1,000

Because a component of the net long-term capital loss for 1970 is a $500 long-term capital loss carried to 1970 from 1969, the transitional additional allowance deductible under section 1211(b) and subparagraph (3) of this paragraph is the least of (i) taxable income of $13,925, (ii) $1,000, or (iii) the sum of the net short-term capital loss of $300, plus the net long-term capital loss for 1970 to the extent of the $500 long-term capital loss carried to 1970 from 1969 and one-half of the $2,000 balance of the net long-term capital loss. The entire $500 long-term capital loss carried to 1970 from 1969 is applicable in full to the transitional additional allowance because there was no net capital gain (capital gain net income for taxable years beginning after December 31, 1976) actually realized in 1970. The $1,000 transitional additional allowance, therefore, consists of the net short-term capital loss of $300, the $500 long-term capital loss carried to 1970 from 1969, plus one-half of enough of the balance of the 1970 net long-term capital loss ($400) to make up the $200 balance of the $1,000 transitional additional allowance. A long-term capital loss of $1,600 ($2,500 minus $900), all of which is attributable to 1970, is carried over under section 1212(b) to 1971. Assuming the same taxable income for purposes of section 1211(b) (after reduction by the zero bracket amount) and the same transactions for taxable years beginning in 1977 or thereafter, the transitional additional allowance would be $1,800. No amount would remain to be carried over to the succeeding taxable year.

Example (7). A, an unmarried individual with one exemption allowable as a deduction under section 151, has the following transactions in 1970:

Taxable income exclusive of capital gains and losses		$13,300
Deduction provided by section 151		625
Taxable income for purposes of section 1211(b)		$13,925
Long-term capital loss	($2,000)	
Long-term capital loss carried to 1970 from 1969 under section 1212(b)(1)	(500)	
Net long-term capital loss		($2,500)
Short-term capital gain	$2,600	
Short-term capital loss carried to 1970 from 1969 under section 1211(b)(1)	($3,000)	
Net short-term capital loss		($ 400)
Losses to the extent of gains		($2,600)
Transitional additional allowance deductible under section 1211(b)		$1,000

Because a component of the net long-term capital loss for 1970 is a $500 long-term capital loss carried to 1970 from 1969, the transitional additional allowance deductible under section 1211(b) and subparagraph (3) of this paragraph is the least of (i) taxable income of $13,925, (ii) $1,000, or (iii) the sum of the net short-term capital loss of $400, plus the net long-term capital loss for 1970 to the extent of the $500 long-term capital loss carried to 1970 from 1969, and one-half of the $2,000 balance of the net long-term capital loss. The entire $500 long-term capital loss carried to 1970 from 1969 is applicable in full to the transitional additional allowance because the net capital gain (capital gain net income for taxable years beginning after December 31, 1976) for the taxable year (computed without regard to capital losses carried to the taxable year) consisted entirely of net short-term capital gain not in excess of the short-term capital loss carried to 1970 from 1969. The $1,000 transitional additional allowance, therefore, consists of the net short-term capital loss of $400, the $500 long-term capital loss carried to 1970 from 1969, plus one-half of enough of the balance of the 1970 net long-term capital loss ($200) to make up the $100 balance of the

Reg. § 1.1211-1(b)(8)

Treatment of Capital Losses

See p. 20,601 for regulations not amended to reflect law changes

$1,000 transitional additional allowance. A long-term capital loss of $1,800 ($2,500 minus $700), all of which is attributable to 1970, is carried over under section 1212(b) to 1971. Assuming the same taxable income for purposes of section 1211(b) (after reduction by the zero bracket amount) and the same transactions for taxable years beginning in 1977 or thereafter, the transitional additional allowance would be $1,900. No amount would remain to be carried over to the succeeding taxable year.

Example (8). Assume the facts in Example (7) but assume that the individual with one exemption allowable as a deduction under section 151 is married and files a separate return for 1970. The maximum transitional additional allowance to which the individual would be entitled for 1970 pursuant to subparagraph (7)(ii) of this paragraph would be the sum of $500 plus (i) $2,400 of the short-term capital loss of $3,000 carried to 1970 from 1969 (the amount by which such carryover exceeds the $600 net capital gain (capital gain net income for taxable years beginning after December 31, 1976) actually realized in 1970, all of which is net short-term capital gain) and (ii) the $500 long-term capital loss carried to 1970 from 1969. However, since this sum ($3,400) exceeds $1,000, the maximum transitional additional allowance to which the individual is entitled for 1970 is limited to $1,000. If for 1971, the same married individual had taxable income of $13,925 for purposes of section 1211(b) and no capital transactions, and filed a separate return, the additional allowance deductible under section 1211(b) for 1971 would be limited to $500 by reason of subdivision (i) of subparagraph (7) of this paragraph, since, as illustrated in Example (7), no part of the capital loss carried over to 1971 under section 1212(b) is attributable to 1969. Assuming the same taxable income for purposes of section 1211(b) (after reduction by the zero bracket amount) and the same transactions as in example (7) for a married individual filing a separate return for a taxable year beginning in 1977 or thereafter, the transitional additional allowance would be $1,900. No amount would remain to be carried over to the succeeding taxable year.

Example (9). B, an unmarried individual with one exemption allowable as a deduction under section 151, has the following transactions in 1971:

Taxable income exclusive of capital gains and losses	$10,000
Deductions provided by section 151	675
Taxable income for purposes of section 1211(b)	$10,675
Long-term capital gain	$2,500
Long-term capital loss treated under § 1.1211-1(b)(3)(iii) as carried over from 1969	(5,000)
Net long-term capital loss	($2,500)
Short-term capital gain	$2,700
Short-term capital loss carried to 1971 from 1970 under section 1212(b)(1)	(1,000)
Short-term capital loss treated under § 1.1211-1(b)(3)(iv) as carried over from 1969	(2,000)
Net short-term capital loss	($ 300)
Losses to extent of gain	($5,200)
Transitional additional allowance deductible under section 1211(b)	$1,000

Because a component of the net long-term capital loss for 1971 is a long-term capital loss treated under subparagraph (3)(iii) of this paragraph as carried over from 1969, the rules for computation of the transitional additional allowance under subparagraph (3)(i) and (ii) of this paragraph apply. The "transitional net long-term capital loss component" for 1971 under subparagraph (3)(ii) of this paragraph is $1,800, that is, the amount by which the $5,000 long-term loss treated as carried over from 1969 to 1971 exceeds (*a*) the net long-term capital gain of $2,500 actually realized in 1971 plus (*b*) the $700 excess of the $2,700 net short-term capital gain actually realized in 1971 over the $2,000 short-term capital loss treated as carried over to 1971 from 1969. The transitional additional allowance for 1971 consists of the $300 net short-term capital loss plus $700 of the net long-term capital loss attributable to 1969. A net long-term capital loss of $1,800 ($2,500 minus $700) is carried over to 1972 under section 1212(b). Only $1,100 of the $1,800 will be treated in 1972 as carried over from 1969 since under subparagraph (3)(iii) of this paragraph the "transitional net long-term capital loss component" of $1,800 is reduced by the amount ($700) applied to the transitional additional allowance for 1971. Assuming the same taxable income for purposes of

Reg. § 1.1211-1(b)(8)

Treatment of Capital Losses

section 1211(b) (after reduction by the zero bracket amount) and the same transactions for a taxable year beginning in 1977, the transitional additional allowance would be $2,000. A net long-term capital loss of $800 would remain to be carried over. Of this amount $100 would be treated as carried over from 1969. Assuming the original facts for a taxable year beginning in 1978, the transitional additional allowance would be $2,450. No amount would remain to be carried over to the succeeding taxable year. [Reg. § 1.1211-1.]

☐ [T.D. 6243, 7-23-57. Amended by T.D. 7301, 1-3-74, T.D. 7597, 3-6-79 and T.D. 7728, 10-31-80.]

[Reg. § 1.1212-1]

§ 1.1212-1. **Capital loss carryovers and carrybacks.**—(a) *Corporations; other taxpayers for taxable years beginning before January 1, 1964* — (1) *Regular net capital loss sustained for taxable years beginning before January 1, 1970.* (i) A corporation sustaining a net capital loss for any taxable year beginning before January 1, 1970, and a taxpayer other than a corporation sustaining a net capital loss for any taxable year beginning before January 1, 1964, shall carry over such net loss to each of the five succeeding taxable years and treat it in each of such five succeeding taxable years as a short-term capital loss to the extent not allowed as a deduction against any net capital gains (capital gain net income for taxable years beginning after December 31, 1976) of any taxable years intervening between the taxable year in which the net capital loss was sustained and the taxable year to which carried. The carryover is thus applied in each succeeding taxable year to offset any net capital gain (capital gain net income for taxable years beginning after December 31, 1976) in such succeeding taxable year. The amount of the capital loss carryover may not be included in computing a new net capital loss of a taxable year which can be carried over to the next five succeeding taxable years. For purposes of this subparagraph, a net capital gain (capital gain net income for taxable years beginning after December 31, 1976) shall be computed without regard to capital loss carryovers or carrybacks. In the case of nonresident alien individuals, see section 871 for special rules on capital loss carryovers. For the rules applicable to the portion of a net capital loss of a corporation which is attributable to a foreign expropriation capital loss sustained in taxable years beginning after December 31, 1958, see subparagraph (2) of this paragraph. For the rules applicable to a taxpayer other than a corporation in the treatment of that amount of a net capital loss which may be carried over under section 1212 and this subparagraph as a short-term capital loss to the first taxable year beginning after December 31, 1963, see paragraph (b) of this section.

(ii) The practical operation of the provisions of this subparagraph may be illustrated by the following example:

Example. (a) For the taxable years 1952 to 1956, inclusive, an individual with one exemption allowable under section 151 (or corresponding provision of prior law) is assumed to have a net short-term capital loss, net short-term capital gain, net long-term capital loss, net long-term capital gain, and taxable income (net income for 1952 and 1953) as follows:

	1952	1953	1954	1955	1956
Carryover from prior years:					
From 1952		($50,000)	($29,500)	($29,500)	
From 1954				(19,500)	($13,000)
Net short-term loss (computed without regard to the carryovers)	($30,000)	(5,000)	(10,000)		
Net short-term gain (computed without regard to the carryovers)				40,000	
Net long-term loss	(20,500)		(10,000)	(5,000)	
Net long-term gain		(25,000)			15,000
Net income or taxable income, computed without regard to capital gains and losses, and, after 1953, without regard to the deduction provided by section 151	500	500	500	1,000	500
Net capital gain (capital gain net income for taxable years beginning after December 31, 1976) (computed without regard to the carryovers)		20,500		36,000	
Net capital loss	(50,000)		(19,500)		
Deduction allowable under section 1202					1,000
Taxable income (after deductions allowable under sections 151 and 1202)					900

Reg. § 1.1212-1(a)(1)

(b) *Net capital loss of 1952.* The net capital loss is $50,000. This figure is the excess of the losses from sales or exchanges of capital assets over the sum of (1) gains (in this case, none) from sales or exchanges of capital assets, and (2) net income (computed without regard to capital gains and losses) of $500. This amount may be carried forward in full as a short-term loss to 1953. However, in 1953 there was a net capital gain (capital gain net income for taxable years beginning after December 31, 1976) of $20,500, as defined by section 117(a)(10)(B) of the Internal Revenue Code of 1939, and limited by section 117(e)(1) of the 1939 Code, against which this net capital loss of $50,000 is allowed in part. The remaining portion—$29,500—may be carried forward to 1954 and 1955 since there was no net capital gain (capital gain net income for taxable years beginning after December 31, 1976) in 1954. In 1955 this $29,500 is allowed in full against net capital gain (capital gain net income for taxable years beginning after December 31, 1976) of $36,000, as defined by paragraph (d) of § 1.1222-1 and limited by subdivision (i) of this subparagraph.

(c) *Net capital loss of 1954.* The net capital loss is $19,500. This figure is the excess of the losses from sales or exchanges of capital assets over the sum of (1) gains (in this case, none) from sales or exchanges of capital assets and (2) taxable income (computed without regard to capital gains and losses and the deductions provided in section 151) of $500. This amount may be carried forward in full as a short-term loss to 1955. The net capital gain (capital gain net income for taxable years beginning after December 31, 1976) in 1955, before deduction of any carryovers, is $36,000. (See sections 1222(9)(B) and 1212 of the Internal Revenue Code of 1954, as it existed prior to the enactment of the Revenue Act of 1964.) The $29,500 balance of the 1952 loss is first applied against the $36,000, leaving a balance of $6,500. Against this amount the $19,500 loss arising in 1954 is applied, leaving a loss of $13,000, which may be carried forward to 1956. Since this amount is treated as a short-term capital loss in 1956 under subdivision (i) of this subparagraph, the excess of the net long-term capital gain over the net short-term capital loss is $2,000 ($15,000 minus $13,000). Half of this excess is allowable as a deduction under section 1202. Thus, after also deducting the exemption allowed as a deduction under section 151 ($600), the taxpayer has a taxable income of $900 ($2,500 minus $1,600) for 1956.

(2) *Corporations sustaining foreign expropriation capital losses for taxable years ending after December 31, 1958* —(i) *In general.* A corporation sustaining a net capital loss for any taxable year ending after December 31, 1958, any portion of which is attributable to a foreign expropriation capital loss, shall carry over such portion of the loss to each of the ten succeeding taxable years and treat it in each of such succeeding taxable years as a short-term capital loss to the extent and consistent with the manner provided in subparagraph (1) of this paragraph. For such purposes, the portion of any net capital loss for any taxable year which is attributable to a foreign expropriation capital loss is the amount, not in excess of the net capital loss for such year, of the foreign expropriation capital loss for such year. The portion of a net capital loss for any taxable year which is attributable to a foreign expropriation capital loss shall be treated as a separate net capital loss for that year and shall be applied, after first applying the remaining portion of such net capital loss, to offset any capital gain net income (net capital gain(s) for taxable years beginning before January 1, 1977) in a succeeding taxable year. In applying net capital losses of two or more taxable years to offset the capital gain net income (net capital gain(s) for taxable years beginning before January 1, 1977) of a subsequent taxable year, such net capital losses shall be offset against such capital gain net income (net capital gain(s) for taxable years beginning before January 1, 1977) in the order of the taxable years in which the losses were sustained, beginning with the loss for the earliest preceding taxable year, even though one or more of such net capital losses are attributable in whole or in part to a foreign expropriation capital loss.

(ii) *Foreign expropriation capital loss defined.* For purposes of this subparagraph the term "foreign expropriation capital loss" means, for any taxable year, the sum of the losses taken into account in computing the net capital loss for such year which are—

(*a*) Losses sustained directly by reason of the expropriation, intervention, seizure, or similar taking of property by the government of any foreign country, any political subdivision thereof, or any agency or instrumentality of the foregoing, or

(*b*) Losses (treated under section 165(g)(1) as losses from the sale or exchange of capital assets) from securities which become worthless by reason of the expropriation, intervention, seizure, or similar taking of property by the government of any foreign country, any political subdivision thereof, or any agency or instrumentality of the foregoing.

(iii) *Illustrations.* The application of this subparagraph may be illustrated by the following examples:

Reg. § 1.1212-1(a)(2)

Example 1. X, a domestic corporation which uses the calendar year as the taxable year, owns as a capital asset 75 percent of the outstanding stock of Y, a foreign corporation operating in a foreign country. In 1961, the foreign country seizes all of the assets of Y, rendering X's stock in Y worthless and thus causing X to sustain a $40,000 foreign expropriation capital loss for such year. In 1961, X has $30,000 of other losses from the sale or exchange of capital assets and $50,000 of gains from the sale or exchange of capital assets. X's net capital loss for 1961 is $20,000 ($70,000 − $50,000). Since the foreign expropriation capital loss exceeds this amount, the entire $20,000 is a foreign expropriation capital loss for 1961.

Example 2. Z, a domestic corporation which uses the calendar year as the taxable year, has a net capital loss of $50,000 for 1961, $30,000 of which is attributable to a foreign expropriation capital loss. Pursuant to the provisions of this paragraph, $30,000 of such net capital loss shall be carried over as a short-term capital loss to each of the 10 taxable years succeeding 1961, and the remaining $20,000 of the net capital loss shall be carried over as a short-term capital loss to each of the 5 taxable years succeeding 1961. Z has a $35,000 net capital gain (capital gain net income for taxable years beginning after December 31, 1976) (determined without regard to any capital loss carryover) for 1962. In offsetting the $50,000 capital loss carryover from 1961 against the $35,000 net capital gain (capital gain net income for taxable years beginning after December 31, 1976) for 1962, the $30,000 portion of such carryover which is attributable to the foreign expropriation capital loss for 1961 is applied against the 1962 net capital gain (capital gain net income for taxable years beginning after December 31, 1976) after applying the $20,000 remaining portion of the carryover. Thus, there is a capital loss carryover of $15,000 to 1963, all of which is attributable to the foreign expropriation capital loss for 1961. Z has a net capital loss for 1963 of $10,000, no portion of which is attributable to a foreign expropriation capital loss. For 1964, Z has a net capital gain (capital gain net income for taxable years beginning after December 31, 1976) of $22,000 (determined without regard to the capital loss carryovers from 1961 and 1963). In offsetting the capital loss carryovers from 1961 and 1963 against Z's $22,000 net capital gain for 1964, the $15,000 carryover from 1961 is applied against the 1964 net capital gain (capital gain net income for taxable years beginning after December 31, 1976) before the $10,000 capital loss carryover from 1963 is applied against such gain. Thus, $3,000 of the 1963 net capital loss remains to be carried over to 1965.

(3) *Regular net capital loss sustained by a corporation for taxable years beginning after December 31, 1969*—(i) *General rule.* A corporation sustaining a net capital loss for any taxable year beginning after December 31, 1969 (hereinafter in this paragraph referred to as the "loss year"), shall—

(a) Carry back such net capital loss to each of the three taxable years preceding the loss year, but only to the extent that such net capital loss is not attributable to a foreign expropriation capital loss and the carryback of such net capital loss does not increase or produce a net operating loss (as defined in section 172(c)) for the taxable year to which it is carried back; and

(b) Carry over such net capital loss to each of the five taxable years succeeding the loss year,

and, subject to subdivision (ii) of this subparagraph, treat such net capital loss in each of such three preceding and five succeeding taxable years as a short-term capital loss.

(ii) *Amount treated as a short-term capital loss in each year.* The entire amount of the net capital loss for any loss year shall be carried to the earliest of the taxable years to which such net capital loss may be carried, and the portion of such net capital loss which shall be carried to each of the other taxable years to which such net capital loss may be carried shall be the excess, if any, of such net capital loss over the total of the capital gain net income (net capital gain(s) for taxable years beginning before January 1, 1977) (computed without regard to the capital loss carryback from the loss year or any taxable year thereafter) for each of the prior taxable years to which such net capital loss may be carried.

(iii) *Special rules.* (a) In the case of a net capital loss which is not a foreign expropriation capital loss and which cannot be carried back in full to a preceding taxable year by reason of section 1212(a)(1)(A)(ii) and subdivision (i)(a) of this subparagraph because such loss would produce or increase a net operating loss in such preceding taxable year, the capital gain net income (net capital gain(s) for taxable years beginning before January 1, 1977) for such preceding taxable year shall in no case be treated as greater than the amount of such net capital loss which can be carried back to such preceding taxable year upon the application of section 1212(a)(1)(A)(ii) and subdivision (i)(a) of this subparagraph.

(b) For the rules applicable to the portion of a net capital loss of a corporation which is attributable to a foreign expropriation capital loss sustained in a taxable year beginning after December 31, 1958, see section 1212(a)(2) and subparagraph (2) of this paragraph.

(c) Section 1212(a)(1)(A) and subdivision (i)(a) of this subparagraph shall not apply to (and no carryback shall be allowed with respect to) the net capital loss of a corporation for any taxable year for which such corporation is an electing small business corporation under subchapter S. See § 1.1372-1.

(d) A net capital loss of a corporation for a year for which it is not an electing small business corporation under subchapter S shall not be carried back under section 1212(a)(1)(A) and subdivision (i)(a) of this subparagraph to a taxable year for which such corporation is an electing small business corporation. See section 1212(a)(3).

(e) A net capital loss of a corporation shall not be carried back under section 1212(a)(1)(A) and subdivision (i)(a) of this subparagraph to a taxable year for which the corporation was a foreign personal holding company, a regulated investment company, or a real estate investment trust, or for which an election made by the corporation under section 1247 is applicable. See section 1212(a)(4).

(f) A taxable year to which a net capital loss of a corporation cannot, by reason of (d) or (e) of this subdivision, be carried back under section 1212(a)(1)(A) and subdivision (i)(a) of this subparagraph shall nevertheless be treated as one of the 3 taxable years preceding the loss year for purposes of section 1212(a)(1)(A) and such subdivision (i)(a); but any capital gain net income (net capital gain for taxable years beginning before January 1, 1977) for such taxable year to which such net capital loss cannot be carried back shall be disregarded for purposes of subdivision (ii) of this subparagraph.

(g) A regulated investment company (as defined in section 851) sustaining a net capital loss shall carry over that loss to each of the 8 taxable years succeeding the loss year. However, the 8-year period prescribed in the preceding sentence shall be reduced (but not to less than 5 years) by the sum of (1) the number of taxable years to which the net capital loss must be carried back pursuant to subdivision (i)(a) of this subparagraph (as limited by subdivision (iii)(e) of this subparagraph) and (2) the number of taxable years, of the 8 taxable years succeeding the loss year, that the corporation failed to qualify as a regulated investment company as defined in section 851. This subdivision shall not extend the carryover period prescribed in subdivision (i)(b) of this subparagraph to a year in which a corporation is not a regulated investment company as defined in section 851.

(iv) The application of this subparagraph may be illustrated by the following examples, in each of which it is assumed that the corporation is not, and never has been, a corporation described in subdivision (iii)(c) or (d) of this subparagraph, that the corporation files its tax returns on a calendar year basis, and that no capital loss sustained is a foreign expropriation capital loss:

Example (1). A corporation has a net capital loss for 1970 which section 1212(a)(1)(A) permits to be carried back. The entire net capital loss for 1970 may be carried back to 1967, but only to the extent that a net operating loss for 1967 would not be produced or increased. The amount of the carryback to 1968 is the excess of the net capital loss for 1970 over the net capital gain (capital gain net income for taxable years beginning after December 31, 1976) for 1967, computed without regard to a capital loss carryback from 1970 or any taxable year thereafter. The amount of the carryback to 1969 is the excess of the net capital loss for 1970 over the sum of the net capital gains (capital gain net income for taxable years beginning after December 31, 1976) for 1967 and 1968, computed without regard to a capital loss carryback from 1970 or any taxable year thereafter. The amount of the carryover to 1971 is the excess of the net capital loss for 1970 over the sum of the net capital gains (capital gain net income for taxable years beginning after December 31, 1976) for 1967, 1968 and 1969, computed without regard to a capital loss carryback from 1970 or any taxable year thereafter. Similarly, the amount of the carryover to 1972, 1973, 1974 and 1975, respectively, is the excess of the net capital loss for 1970 over the sum of the net capital gains (capital gain net income for taxable years beginning after December 31, 1976) for taxable years prior to 1972, 1973, 1974, or 1975, as the case may be, to which the net capital loss for 1970 may be carried, computed without regard to a capital loss carryback from 1970 or any year thereafter.

Example (2). For the taxable years 1967 to 1975, inclusive, a corporation is assumed to have net capital loss, net capital gain, and taxable income (computed without regard to capital gains and losses) as follows [reproduced on page 53,752]:

The net capital loss of 1969, under the rules of subparagraph (1) of this paragraph, may not be carried back. Thus, the net capital loss for 1970 is carried back and partially absorbed by the net capital gain (capital gain net income for taxable years beginning after December 31, 1976) for 1967, and a portion of the net capital losses of

Reg. § 1.1212-1(a)(3)

both 1970 and 1971 are carried back to 1968. The net capital loss for 1969 is the oldest that may be carried to 1973, and thus, it is the first carried over and absorbed by the net capital gain (capital gain net income for taxable years beginning after December 31, 1976) for 1973. The net capital loss for 1972 (which is not carried back because of the net capital losses in the three years preceding 1972) may be carried over to 1973.

Example (3). For the taxable years 1967 to 1970, inclusive, a corporation which was organized on January 1, 1967, realized operating income and net capital gains (capital gain net income for taxable years beginning after December 31, 1976) and sustained operating losses and net capital losses as follows:

	Operating Income or Loss (Exclusive of Capital Gain or Loss)	Capital Gain or Loss
1967	$20,000	$24,000
1968	$20,000	—0—
1969	$20,000	—0—
1970	($25,000)	($20,000)

The net capital loss of $20,000 for 1970 is carried back to 1967 and applied against the $24,000 net capital gain (capital gain net income for taxable years beginning after December 31, 1976) realized in that year, reducing such net capital gain (capital gain net income for taxable years beginning after December 31, 1976) to $4,000. The net operating loss of $25,000 for 1970 is then carried back to 1967 and applied first to eliminate the $20,000 of operating income for that year and then to eliminate the net capital gain (capital gain net income for taxable years beginning after December 31, 1976) for that year of $4,000 (as reduced by the 1970 capital loss carryback).

Example (4). Assume the same facts as in Example (3) but substitute the following figures:

	Operating Income or Loss (Exclusive of Capital Gain or Loss)	Capital Gain or Loss
1967	($20,000)	$24,000
1968	$20,000	—0—
1969	$20,000	—0—
1970	($25,000)	($20,000)

The net capital loss of $20,000 for 1970 is carried back to 1967 and applied against the $24,000 net capital gain (capital gain net income for taxable years beginning after December 31, 1976) realized in that year only to the extent of $4,000, the maximum amount to which the 1970 capital loss carryback can be applied without producing a net operating loss for 1967. The unused $16,000 balance of the 1970 net long-term capital loss can be carried forward to 1971 and subsequent taxable years to the extent provided in subdivision (i)(b) of this subparagraph.

Example (5). Assume the same facts as in Example (3) but substitute the following figures:

	Operating Income or Loss (Exclusive of Capital Gain or Loss)	Capital Gain or Loss
1967	—0—	—0—
1968	($20,000)	—0—
1969	—0—	$24,000
1970	$20,000	($24,000)

The net capital loss of $24,000 for 1970 is carried back to 1969 and applied against the $24,000 net capital gain (capital gain net income for taxable years beginning after December 31, 1976) realized in that year to the extent of $24,000. The application of the capital loss carryback is not limited as it was in Example (4) because such carryback neither increases nor produces a net operating loss, as such, for 1969. The $20,000 net operating loss for 1968 is then carried forward to 1970 to eliminate the $20,000 of operating income for that year.

Reg. § 1.1212-1(a)(3)

Treatment of Capital Losses

See p. 20,601 for regulations not amended to reflect law changes

	1967	1968	1969	1970	1971	1972	1973	1974	1975
Taxable income (computed without regard to capital gains or losses)	$25,000	$25,000	$25,000	$25,000	$25,000	$25,000	$25,000	$25,000	$25,000
Net capital loss			($1,000)	($29,500)	($16,000)	($500)			
Net capital gain (capital gain net income for taxable years beginning after December 31, 1976) (computed without regard to carrybacks or carryovers)	$14,000	$16,000					$8,000	$7,500	$6,500
Carryback or carryover:									
From 1969:	($14,000)	($15,500)							
From 1970:		($500)					($1,000)		
From 1971:							($7,000)	($7,500)	($1,000)
From 1972:									($500)

Reg. § 1.1212-1(a)(3)

Example (6). Assume the same facts as in Example (3) but substitute the following figures:

	Operating Income or Loss (Exclusive of Capital Gain or Loss)	Capital Gain or Loss
1967	—0—	—0—
1968	—0—	—0—
1969	($20,000)	($24,000)
1970	$20,000	$20,000

The net capital loss of $24,000 for 1969 is carried forward to 1970 and applied against the $20,000 net capital gain realized in that year. The unused $4,000 balance of the 1969 net capital loss can be carried forward to 1971 and subsequent taxable years to the extent provided in subdivision (i)(*b*) of this subparagraph.

(b) *Taxpayers other than corporations for taxable years beginning after December 31, 1963* — (1) *In general.* If a taxpayer other than a corporation sustains a net capital loss for any taxable year beginning after December 31, 1963, the portion thereof which is a short-term capital loss carryover shall be carried over to the succeeding taxable year and treated as a short-term capital loss sustained in such succeeding taxable year, and the portion thereof which constitutes a long-term capital loss carryover shall be carried over to the succeeding taxable year and treated as a long-term capital loss sustained in such succeeding taxable year. The carryovers are included in the succeeding taxable year in the determination of the amount of the short-term capital loss, the net short-term capital gain or loss, the long-term capital loss, and the net long-term capital gain or loss in such year, the net capital loss in such year, and the capital loss carryovers from such year. For purposes of this subparagraph—

(i) A short-term capital loss carryover is the excess of the net short-term capital loss for the taxable year over the net long-term capital gain for such year, and

(ii) A long-term capital loss carryover is the excess of the net long-term capital loss for the taxable year over the net short-term capital gain for such year.

(2) *Special rules for determining a net short-term capital gain or loss for purposes of carryovers*—(i) *Taxable years beginning after December 31, 1963, and before January 1, 1970.* In determining a net short-term capital gain or loss of a taxable year beginning after December 31, 1963, and before January 1, 1970, for purposes of computing a short-term or long-term capital loss carryover to the succeeding taxable year, an amount equal to the additional allowance deductible under section 1211(b) for the taxable year (determined as provided in section 1211(b), as in effect for taxable years beginning before January 1, 1970 and § 1.1211-1(b)(5)) is treated as a short-term capital gain occurring in such year.

(ii) *Taxable years beginning after December 31, 1969.* In determining a net short-term capital gain or loss of a taxable year beginning after December 31, 1969—

(*a*) For purposes of computing a short-term capital loss carryover to the succeeding taxable year, an amount equal to the additional allowance for the taxable year (determined as provided in section 1211(b) and § 1.1211-1(b)(2)) is treated as a short-term capital gain occurring in such year, and

(*b*) For purposes of computing a long-term capital loss carryover to the succeeding taxable year, an amount equal to the sum of the additional allowance for the taxable year (determined as provided in section 1211(b) and § 1.1211-1(b)(2)), plus the excess of such additional allowance over the net short-term capital loss (determined without regard to section 1212(b)(2) for such year) is treated as a short-term capital gain in such year.

The rules provided in this subdivision are for the purpose of taking into account the additional allowance deductible for the current taxable year under section 1211(b) and § 1.1211-1(b)(2) in determining the amount and character of capital loss carryovers from the current taxable year to the succeeding taxable year. Their practical application to a determination of the amount and character of capital loss carryovers from the current taxable year to the succeeding taxable year involves identification of the net long-term and net short-term capital loss components of the additional allowance deductible in the current taxable year as provided by § 1.1211-1(b)(2)(iii). To the extent that the additional allowance is composed of net short-term capital losses, such losses are treated as a short-term capital gain in the current taxable year in determining the capital loss carryovers to the succeeding year. To the extent that the additional allowance is composed of net long-term capital losses applied pursuant to the provisions of § 1.1211-1(b)(2)(iii), an amount equal to twice the amount of such component of the additional allowance is treated as a short-term capital gain in the current taxable year. See paragraph (4) of this section for transitional rules if any part of the additional allowance is composed of net long-term capital losses carried to the current taxable year from a taxable year beginning before January 1, 1970.

(3) *Transitional rule for net capital losses sustained in a taxable year beginning before January 1, 1964.* A taxpayer other than a corporation

Reg. § 1.1212-1(b)(2)

Treatment of Capital Losses

See p. 20,601 for regulations not amended to reflect law changes

sustaining a net capital loss for any taxable year beginning before January 1, 1964, shall treat as a short-term capital loss in the first taxable year beginning after December 31, 1963, any amount which would be treated as a short-term capital loss in such year under subchapter P of chapter 1 of the Code as in effect immediately before the enactment of the Revenue Act of 1964.

(4) *Transitional rule for net long-term capital losses sustained in a taxable year beginning before January 1, 1970.* In the case of a net long-term capital loss sustained by a taxpayer other than a corporation in a taxable year beginning prior to January 1, 1970 (referred to in this section as a "pre-1970 taxable year") which is carried over and treated as a long-term capital loss in the first taxable year beginning after December 31, 1969 (referred to in this section as a "post-1969 taxable year"), the transitional additional allowance deductible under section 1211(b) for the taxable year shall be determined by application of section 1211(b) as in effect for pre-1970 taxable years and § 1.1211-1(b)(3), and the amount of such long-term capital loss carried over and treated as a long-term capital loss in the succeeding taxable year shall be determined by application of section 1212(b)(1) as in effect for pre-1970 taxable years and subparagraph (2)(i) of this paragraph (instead of under sections 1211(b) and 1212(b)(1) as in effect for post-1969 taxable years and § 1.1211-1(b)(2) and subparagraph (2)(ii) of this paragraph, respectively) but only to the extent that such pre-1970 long-term capital loss constitutes a "transitional net long-term capital loss component" (determined as provided in § 1.1211-1(b)(3)(ii)) in the taxable year to which such pre-1970 long-term capital loss is carried. Thus, for purposes of paragraph (2) of this section, to the extent that a component of the transitional additional allowance deductible for a post-1969 taxable year under section 1211(b) and § 1.1211-1(b)(3)(i) is a transitional net long-term capital loss component carried over to such post-1969 taxable year, such component shall be treated as a short-term capital gain in determining the amount and character of capital loss carryovers from such post-1969 taxable year to the succeeding taxable year. Such component shall be so treated as a short-term capital gain in full on a dollar-for-dollar basis and shall not be doubled for this purpose as is provided by subdivision (ii) of paragraph (2) of this section in the case of a component of the additional allowance made up of net long-term capital losses applied pursuant to the provisions of § 1.1211-1(b)(2)(iii). The transitional rule provided in this paragraph does not apply to a determination of the character of capital losses (as long-term or short-term) actually deductible for the current taxable year under section 1211(b) and § 1.1211-1(b).

(5) *Examples.* The application of this paragraph can be illustrated by the following examples:

Example (1). For the taxable year 1971, an unmarried individual has taxable income for purposes of section 1211(b) of $8,000, a long-term capital loss of $2,000, and no other capital gains or losses. $1,000 (one-half) of the net long-term capital loss is deductible in 1971 as the additional allowance deductible under section 1211(b). No amount of capital loss remains to be carried over to the succeeding taxable year.

Example (2). For the taxable year 1972, the same unmarried individual has taxable income for purposes of section 1211(b) of $8,000, a long-term capital loss of $3,000 and no other capital gains or losses. $1500 (one-half of the excess net capital loss) is deductible in 1972, but limited to the $1,000 maximum additional allowance deductible under section 1211(b). By application of section 1212(b)(1), he will carry over to 1973 a long-term capital loss of $1,000 determined as follows:

Net long-term capital loss	($3,000)
Additional allowance deductible under section 1211(b)	$1,000
Excess of additional allowance over net short-term capital loss (determined without regard to section 1212(b)(2)(B)(i))	$1,000
Total amount treated as short-term capital gain under 1212(b)(2)(B) for purposes of determining carryover	$2,000
Long-term capital loss carryover to 1973	($1,000)

If, in 1973, he had taxable income for purposes of section 1211(b) of $8,000, but no capital gains or losses, $500 (one-half) of the net long-term capital loss carryover from 1972 would be deductible in 1973 as the additional allowance deductible under section 1211(b). No amount of capital loss would be carried over to 1974.

Example (3). For the taxable year 1971, an unmarried individual has taxable income for purposes of section 1211(b) of $9,000, a $500 short-term capital gain, a $700 short-term capital loss, a $1,000 long-term capital gain and a $1,700 long-term capital loss. He will offset $1,500 of capital losses against capital gains. The excess net capital loss of $900 is deductible in 1971 to the extent of a $550 additional allowance deductible under 1211(b) which is smaller than both $1,000 and taxable income for purposes of section 1211(b), determined as follows:

Reg. § 1.1212-1(b)(5)

53,424   Treatment of Capital Losses
See p. 20,601 for regulations not amended to reflect law changes

Losses allowed to the extent of gains	($1,500)
Amount allowed under section 1211(b)(1)(C)	
(i) excess of net short-term capital loss over net long-term capital gain	($ 200)
(ii) one-half of the excess of net long-term capital loss over net short-term capital gain	(350)
Additional allowance deductible under section 1211(b)	$ 550

The total amount treated as short-term capital gain under section 1212(b)(2)(B) for purposes of determining any carryover to the succeeding taxable year exceeds $900. No amount of net capital loss remains to be carried over to the succeeding taxable year.

Example (4). If in example (3) above, the long-term capital loss had been $2,800, the taxpayer would carry over $200 of long-term capital loss to 1972, determined as follows:

Losses allowed to extent of gains	($1,500)
Amount allowed under section 1211(b)(1)(B) and (C):	
(i) excess of net short-term capital loss over net long-term capital gain	(200)
(ii) one-half the excess of net long-term capital loss over net short-term capital gain	(900)
as limited by 1211(b)(1)(B) to an additional allowance of $1,000.	
Carryover under section 1212(b)(1):	
Net long-term capital loss for 1971	($1,800)
Additional allowance under section 1211(b)(1)(B)	$1,000
Excess of additional allowance deductible under section 1211(b) over net short-term capital loss determined without regard to section 1212(b)(2)(B)(i) ($1,000 less $200)	$ 800
Total amount treated as short-term capital gain under section 1212(b)(2)(B) for purposes of determining carryover	$1,800
Short-term capital gain for 1971	500
Total short-term capital gain	$2,300
Short-term capital loss for 1971	($ 700)
Net short-term capital gain	$1,600
Long-term capital loss carryover ($1,800 less $1,600)	$ 200

Example (5). For 1969, an unmarried individual has taxable income for purposes of section 1211(b) of $8,000, a long-term capital loss of $3,000, and no other capital gains or losses. He is allowed to deduct in 1969 $1,000 as the additional allowance deductible under section 1211(b) (as in effect for pre-1970 taxable years) and to carry over to 1970, a long-term capital loss of $2,000 under section 1212(b) (as in effect for pre-1970 taxable years).

If, in 1970, the same unmarried individual with taxable income for purposes of section 1211(b) of $8,000, has no capital gains or losses, he would deduct $1,000 of his pre-1970 capital loss carryover as the transitional additional allowance deductible under section 1211(b) (as in effect for pre-1970 years) and carry over under section 1212(b)(1) (as in effect for pre-1970 taxable years) to 1971 the remaining $1,000 as a pre-1970 long-term capital loss.

If, in 1970, the same individual instead has a long-term capital gain of $2,500, and a long-term capital loss of $1,500, he would net these two items with the $2,000 carried to 1970 as a long-term capital loss. Thus, he would have a net long-term capital loss for 1970 of $1,000 which is deductible in 1970 as the transitional additional allowance deductible under section 1211(b). He would have no amount to carry over under section 1212(b)(1) to 1971.

If, in 1970, the same individual instead has a long-term capital loss of $1,200, and a long-term capital gain of $200, resulting in a net long-term capital loss of $3,000 when netted with the $2,000 carried to 1970 as a long-term capital loss, he would deduct $1,000 in respect of his pre-1970 long-term capital loss carryover as the transitional additional allowance deductible under section 1211(b) (as in effect for pre-1970 taxable years) and carry over under section 1212(b)(1) (as in effect for pre-1970 taxable years) to 1971 the remaining $1,000 of the pre-1970 component of his long-term capital loss carryover, and the $1,000 net long-term capital loss actually sustained in 1970 as the second component of his long-term capital loss carryover.

Example (6). For 1970 a married individual filing a separate return has taxable income of $8,000, a long-term capital loss of $3,500 and a short-term capital gain of $3,000. He also has a pre-1970 short-term capital loss of $2,000 which is carried to 1970. The $3,000 short-term capital gain realized in 1970 would first be reduced by the $2,000 short-term capital loss carryover, and then the remaining $1,000 balance of the short-term capital gain would be offset against the $3,500 long-term capital loss, producing a net long-term capital loss of $2,500, no part of which is a net long-term capital loss carried over from 1969. However, under the special rule in § 1.1211-1(b)(7)(ii) in 1970, the taxpayer would deduct as the additional allowance deductible under section 1211(b), the $500 limitation in § 1.1211-1(b)(2)(ii) in the case of a married taxpayer filing a separate return in a taxable year

Reg. § 1.1212-1(b)(5)

Treatment of Capital Losses

See p. 20,601 for regulations not amended to reflect law changes

ending after December 31, 1969, plus the "transitional net short-term capital loss component" of $2,000 computed under § 1.1211-1(b)(3)(iv), but limited to a total deduction of $1,000. The $1,000 additional allowance deductible under section 1211(b) would absorb $2,000 of the $2,500 net long-term capital loss, and he would carry the unused $500 balance of such loss to 1971 for use in that year.

Example (7). For 1970, an unmarried individual filing a separate return has taxable income for purposes of section 1211(b) of $8,000, and a long-term capital loss of $2,000. He also has a pre-1970 long-term capital loss of $2,500 which is carried to 1970. In 1970, the taxpayer would deduct as the transitional additional allowance deductible under section 1211(b) $1,000, absorbing $1,000 of the pre-1970 long-term capital loss of $2,500. He would carry to 1971 the unused $1,500 balance of his pre-1970 long-term capital loss plus the 1970 long-term capital loss of $2,000, or a total of $3,500, for use in 1971.

For 1971, the same taxpayer filing a separate return with taxable income for purposes of section 1211(b) of $8,000, has a $3,600 long-term capital gain and a $2,200 long-term capital loss. When these gains and losses are combined with the long-term capital loss carryover from 1970 of $3,500, a net long-term capital loss of $2,100 results. He would deduct $1,000 as the transitional additional allowance deductible under section 1211(b). The $1,000 additional allowance would absorb $100 of the unused pre-1970 long-term capital loss carryover of $1,500 plus $1,800 of the unused post-1969 long-term capital loss carryover of $2,100 (the amount of the 1971 net long-term capital loss necessary to make up the remaining $900 balance of the additional allowance). Although a component of the 1971 net long-term capital loss is the unused pre-1970 long-term capital loss carryover of $1,500, only $100 of this carryover is available for use in full on a dollar-for-dollar basis in computing the transitional additional allowance for 1971 since it only exceeds by that amount the $1,400 net capital gain (capital gain net income for taxable years beginning after December 31, 1976) actually realized in 1971 all of which is net long-term capital gain (long-term capital gain of $3,600 reduced by long-term capital loss of $2,200). See § 1.1211-1(b)(3)(ii). The taxpayer would carry over to 1972 as a long-term capital loss the remaining $200 of the 1971 long-term capital loss.

Example (8). For 1970, an unmarried individual has taxable income for purposes of section 1211(b) of $8,000 and a short-term capital loss of $700. He also has a pre-1970 long-term capital loss carryover of $1,200. He would deduct $1,000 as the transitional additional allowance deductible under section 1211(b). The $1,000 transitional additional allowance would be composed of the 1970 short-term capital loss of $700 and $300 of the pre-1970 long-term capital loss carryover. He would carry over to 1971 the unused $900 balance of his $1,200 pre-1970 long-term capital loss carryover for use in 1971.

(c) *Husband and wife*—(1) The following rules shall be applied in computing net capital loss carryovers by husband and wife:

(i) If a husband and wife making a joint return for any taxable year made separate returns for the preceding year, any capital loss carryovers of each spouse from such preceding taxable year may be carried forward to the taxable year in accordance with paragraph (a) or (b) of this section.

(ii) If a joint return was made for the preceding taxable year, any capital loss carryover from such preceding taxable year may be carried forward to the taxable year in accordance with paragraph (a) or (b) of this section.

(iii) If a husband and wife make separate returns for the first taxable year beginning after December 31, 1963, or any prior taxable year, and they made a joint return for the preceding taxable year, any capital loss carryover from such preceding taxable year shall be allocated to the spouses on the basis of their individual net capital loss which gave rise to such capital loss carryover. The capital loss carryover so allocated to each spouse may be carried forward by such spouse to the taxable year in accordance with paragraph (a) or (b) of this section.

(iv) If a husband and wife making separate returns for any taxable year following the first taxable year beginning after December 31, 1963, made a joint return for the preceding taxable year, any long-term or short-term capital loss carryovers shall be allocated to the spouses on the basis of their individual net long-term and net short-term capital losses for the preceding taxable year which gave rise to such capital loss carryovers, and the portions of the long-term or short-term capital loss carryovers so allocated to each spouse may be carried forward by such spouse to the taxable year in accordance with paragraph (b) of this section.

(v) If separate returns are made both for the taxable year and the preceding taxable year, any capital loss carryover of each spouse may be carried forward by such spouse in accordance with paragraph (a) or (b) of this section.

Reg. § 1.1212-1(c)(1)

53,426 Rules for Determining Capital Gains and Losses

See p. 20,601 for regulations not amended to reflect law changes

(2) The provisions of subparagraph (1)(i), (iii), and (iv) of this paragraph may be illustrated by the following examples:

Example (1). If H and W, husband and wife, make a joint return for 1955, having made separate returns for 1954 in which H had a net capital loss of $3,000 and W had a net capital loss of $2,000, in their joint return for 1955 they would have a short-term capital loss of $5,000 (the sum of their separate capital loss carryovers from 1954), allowable in accordance with paragraph (a) of this section. If, on the other hand, they make separate returns in 1955 following a joint return in 1954 in which their net capital loss was $5,000 allocable $3,000 to H and $2,000 to W, the carryover of H as a short-term capital loss for the purpose of his 1955 separate return would be $3,000 and that of W for her separate return would be $2,000, each allowable in accordance with paragraph (a) of this section.

Example (2). H and W, husband and wife, make separate returns for 1966 following a joint return for 1965. The capital gains and losses incurred by H and W in 1965, including those carried over by them to 1965, were as follows:

	H	W
Long-term capital gains	$ 8,000	$9,000
Long-term capital losses	(15,000)	(6,000)
Short-term capital gains	10,000	4,000
Short-term capital losses	(19,000)	(5,000)

Thus, in 1965 H and W had a net capital loss of $14,000 on their joint return. Of this amount, $4,000 was a long-term capital loss carryover, and $10,000 was a short-term capital loss carryover, determined in accordance with paragraph (b) of this section. H's net long-term capital loss was $7,000 for 1965. This amount was offset on the joint return by W's net long-term capital gain of $3,000. Thus, H may carry over to his separate return for 1966, a long-term capital loss carryover of $4,000. H and W may carry over to their separate returns for 1966, as short-term capital loss carryovers, the amounts of their respective net short-term losses from 1965, $9,000 and $1,000. [Reg. § 1.1212-1.]

☐ [T.D. 6243, 7-23-57. Amended by T.D. 6828, 6-16-65, T.D. 6867, 12-6-65, T.D. 7301, 1-3-74, T.D. 7659, 12-14-79 and T.D. 7728, 10-31-80.]

General Rules for Determining Capital Gains and Losses

[Reg. § 1.1221-1]

§ 1.1221-1. **Meaning of terms.**—(a) The term "capital assets" includes all classes of property not specifically excluded by section 1221. In determining whether property is a "capital asset", the period for which held is immaterial.

(b) Property used in the trade or business of a taxpayer of a character which is subject to the allowance for depreciation provided in section 167 and real property used in the trade or business of a taxpayer is excluded from the term "capital assets". Gains and losses from the sale or exchange of such property are not treated as gains and losses from the sale or exchange of capital assets, except to the extent provided in section 1231. See § 1.1231-1. Property held for the production of income, but not used in a trade or business of the taxpayer, is not excluded from the term "capital assets" even though depreciation may have been allowed with respect to such property under section 23(l) of the Internal Revenue Code of 1939 before its amendment by section 121(c) of the Revenue Act of 1942 (56 Stat. 819). However, gain or loss upon the sale or exchange of land held by a taxpayer primarily for sale to customers in the ordinary course of his business, as in the case of a dealer in real estate, is not subject to the provisions of subchapter P (section 1201 and following), chapter 1 of the Code.

(c)(1) A copyright, a literary, musical, or artistic composition, and similar property are excluded from the term "capital assets" if held by a taxpayer whose personal efforts created such property, or if held by a taxpayer in whose hands the basis of such property is determined, for purposes of determining gain from a sale or exchange, in whole or in part by reference to the basis of such property in the hands of a taxpayer whose personal efforts created such property. For purposes of this subparagraph, the phrase "similar property" includes, for example, such property as a theatrical production, a radio program, a newspaper cartoon strip, or any other property eligible for copyright protection (whether under statute or common law), but does not include a patent or an invention, or a design which may be protected only under the patent law and not under the copyright law.

(2) In the case of sales and other dispositions occurring after July 25, 1969, a letter, a memorandum, or similar property is excluded from the term "capital asset" if held by (i) a taxpayer whose personal efforts created such property, (ii) a taxpayer for whom such property was prepared or produced, or (iii) a taxpayer in whose hands the basis of such property is determined, for purposes of determining gain from a sale or exchange, in whole or in part by reference to the basis of such property in the hands of a taxpayer described in

Reg. § 1.1221-1(a)

Rules for Determining Capital Gains and Losses

See p. 20,601 for regulations not amended to reflect law changes

subdivision (i) or (ii) of this subparagraph. In the case of a collection of letters, memorandums, or similar property held by a person who is a taxpayer described in subdivision (i), (ii), or (iii) of this subparagraph as to some of such letters, memorandums, or similar property but not as to others, this subparagraph shall apply only to those letters, memorandums, or similar property as to which such person is a taxpayer described in such subdivision. For purposes of this subparagraph, the phrase "similar property" includes, for example, such property as a draft of a speech, a manuscript, a research paper, an oral recording of any type, a transcript of an oral recording, a transcript of an oral interview or of dictation, a personal or business diary, a log or journal, a corporate archive, including a corporate charter, office correspondence, a financial record, a drawing, a photograph, or a dispatch. A letter, memorandum, or property similar to a letter or memorandum, addressed to a taxpayer shall be considered as prepared or produced for him. This subparagraph does not apply to property, such as a corporate archive, office correspondence, or a financial record, sold or disposed of as part of a going business if such property has no significant value separate and apart from its relation to and use in such business; it also does not apply to any property to which subparagraph (1) of this paragraph applies (i.e., property to which section 1221(3) applied before its amendment by section 514(a) of the Tax Reform Act of 1969 (83 Stat. 643).

(3) For purposes of this paragraph, in general property is created in whole or in part by the personal efforts of a taxpayer if such taxpayer performs literary, theatrical, musical, artistic, or other creative or productive work which affirmatively contributes to the creation of the property, or if such taxpayer directs and guides others in the performance of such work. A taxpayer, such as corporate executive, who merely has administrative control of writers, actors, artists, or personnel and who does not substantially engage in the direction and guidance of such persons in the performance of their work, does not create property by his personal efforts. However, for purposes of subparagraph (2) of this paragraph, a letter or memorandum, or property similar to a letter or memorandum, which is prepared by personnel who are under the administrative control of a taxpayer, such as a corporate executive, shall be deemed to have been prepared or produced for him whether or not such letter, memorandum, or similar property is reviewed by him.

(4) For the application of section 1231 to the sale or exchange of property to which this paragraph applies, see § 1.1231-1. For the application of section 170 to the charitable contribution of property to which this paragraph applies, see section 170(e) and the regulations thereunder.

(d) Section 1221(4) excludes from the definition of "capital asset" accounts or notes receivable acquired in the ordinary course of trade or business for services rendered or from the sale of stock in trade or inventory or property held for sale to customers in the ordinary course of trade or business. Thus, if a taxpayer acquires a note receivable for services rendered, reports the fair market value of the note as income, and later sells the note for less than the amount previously reported, the loss is an ordinary loss. On the other hand, if the taxpayer later sells the note for more than the amount originally reported, the excess is treated as ordinary income.

(e) Obligations of the United States or any of its possessions, or of a State or Territory, or any political subdivision thereof, or of the District of Columbia, issued on or after March 1, 1941, on a discount basis and payable without interest at a fixed maturity date not exceeding one year from the date of issue, are excluded from the term "capital assets." An obligation may be issued on a discount basis even though the price paid exceeds the face amount. Thus, although the Second Liberty Bond Act (31 U.S.C. 754) provides that United States Treasury bills shall be issued on a discount basis, the issuing price paid for a particular bill may, by reason of competitive bidding, actually exceed the face amount of the bill. Since the obligations of the type described in this paragraph are excluded from the term "capital assets", gains or losses from the sale or exchange of such obligations are not subject to the limitations provided in such subchapter P. It is, therefore, not necessary for a taxpayer (other than a life insurance company taxable under part I (section 801 and following), subchapter L, chapter 1 of the Code, as amended by the Life Insurance Company Tax Act of 1955 (70 Stat. 36), and, in the case of taxable years beginning before January 1, 1955, subject to taxation only on interest, dividends, and rents) to segregate the original discount accrued and the gain or loss realized upon the sale or other disposition of any such obligation. See section 454(b) with respect to the original discount accrued. The provisions of this paragraph may be illustrated by the following examples:

Example (1). A (not a life insurance company) buys a $100,000, 90-day Treasury bill upon issuance for $99,998. As of the close of the forty-fifth day of the life of such bill, he sells it to B (not a life insurance company) for $99,999.50. The entire net gain to A of $1.50 may be taken into

Reg. § 1.1221-1(e)

account as a single item of income, without allocating $1 to interest and $0.50 to gain. If B holds the bill until maturity his net gain of $0.50 may similarly be taken into account as a single item of income, without allocating $1 to interest and $0.50 to loss.

Example (2). The facts in this example are the same as in example (1) except that the selling price to B is $99,998.50. The net gain to A of $0.50 may be taken into account without allocating $1 to interest and $0.50 to loss, and, similarly, if B holds the bill until maturity his entire net gain of $1.50 may be taken into account as a single item of income without allocating $1 to interest and $0.50 to gain. [Reg. § 1.1221-1.]

☐ [T.D. 6243, 7-23-57. Amended by T.D. 7369, 7-15-75.]

[Reg. § 1.1221-2]

§ 1.1221-2. **Hedging transactions.**—(a) *Treatment of hedging transactions*—(1) *In general.* This section governs the treatment of hedging transactions under section 1221. Except as provided in paragraph (f)(2) of this section (and notwithstanding the provisions of § 1.1221-1(a)), the term capital asset does not include property that is part of a hedging transaction (as defined in paragraph (b) of this section).

(2) *Short sales and options.* This section also governs the character of gain or loss from a short sale or option that is part of a hedging transaction. See §§ 1.1233-2 and 1.1234-4. Except as provided in paragraph (f)(2) of this section, gain or loss on a short sale or option that is part of a hedging transaction (as defined in paragraph (b) of this section) is ordinary income or loss.

(3) *Exclusivity.* If a transaction is not a hedging transaction as defined in paragraph (b) of this section, gain or loss from the transaction is not made ordinary on the grounds that property involved in the transaction is a surrogate for a noncapital asset, that the transaction serves as insurance against a business risk, that the transaction serves a hedging function, or that the transaction serves a similar function or purpose.

(4) *Coordination with other sections*—(i) *Section 988.* This section does not apply to determine the character of gain or loss realized on a section 988 transaction as defined in section 988(c)(1) or realized with respect to a qualified fund as defined in section 988(c)(1)(E)(iii). This section does apply, however, to transactions or payments that would be subject to section 988 but for the date that the transactions were entered into or the date that the payments were made.

(ii) *Sections 864(e) and 954(c).* Except as otherwise provided in regulations issued pursuant to sections 864(e) and 954(c), the definition of hedging transaction in paragraph (b) of this section does not apply for purposes of section 864(e) and 954(c).

(b) *Hedging transaction defined.* A hedging transaction is a transaction that a taxpayer enters into in the normal course of the taxpayer's trade or business primarily—

(1) To reduce risk of price changes or currency fluctuations with respect to ordinary property (as defined in paragraph (c)(5) of this section) that is held or to be held by the taxpayer; or

(2) To reduce risk of interest rate or price changes or currency fluctuations with respect to borrowings made or to be made, or ordinary obligations incurred or to be incurred, by the taxpayer.

(c) *Rules of application.* The rules of this paragraph (c) apply for purposes of the definition of the term hedging transaction in paragraph (b) of this section. These rules must be interpreted reasonably and consistently with the purposes of this section. Where no specific rules of application control, the definition of hedging transaction must be interpreted reasonably and consistently with the purposes of this section.

(1) *Reducing risk*—(i) *Transactions that reduce risk.* Whether a transaction reduces a taxpayer's risk is determined based on all of the facts and circumstances surrounding the taxpayer's business and the transaction. In general, a taxpayer's hedging strategies and policies as reflected in the taxpayer's minutes or other records are evidence of whether particular transactions reduce the taxpayer's risk.

(ii) *Micro and macro hedges*—(A) *In general.* A taxpayer has risk of a particular type only if it is at risk when all of its operations are considered. Nonetheless, a hedge of a particular asset or liability generally will be respected as reducing risk if it reduces the risk attributable to the asset or liability and if it is reasonably expected to reduce the overall risk of the taxpayer's operations. If a taxpayer hedges particular assets or liabilities, or groups of assets or liabilities, and the hedges are undertaken as part of a program that, as a whole, is reasonably expected to reduce the overall risk of the taxpayer's operations, the taxpayer generally does not have to demonstrate that each hedge that was entered into pursuant to the program reduces its overall risk.

(B) *Fixed-to-floating hedges.* Under the principles of paragraph (c)(1)(ii)(A) of this section, a transaction that economically converts an interest rate or price from a fixed price or rate to a floating price or rate may reduce risk. For

Rules for Determining Capital Gains and Losses

example, if a taxpayer's income varies with interest rates, the taxpayer may be at risk if it has a fixed rate liability. Similarly, a taxpayer with a fixed cost for its inventory may be at risk if the price at which the inventory can be sold varies with a particular factor. Thus, a transaction that converts an interest rate or price from fixed to floating may be a hedging transaction.

(iii) *Written options.* A written option may reduce risk. For example, in appropriate circumstances, a written call option with respect to assets held by a taxpayer or a written put option with respect to assets to be acquired by a taxpayer may be a hedging transaction. See also paragraph (c)(1)(v) of this section.

(iv) *Extent of risk reduction.* A taxpayer may hedge all or any portion of its risk for all or any part of the period during which it is exposed to the risk.

(v) *Transactions that counteract hedging transactions.* If a transaction is entered into primarily to counteract all or any part of the risk reduction effected by one or more hedging transactions, the transaction is a hedging transaction. For example, if a written option is used to reduce or eliminate the risk reduction obtained from another position such as a purchased option, then it may be part of a hedging transaction.

(vi) *Number of transactions.* The fact that a taxpayer frequently enters into and terminates positions (even if done on a daily or more frequent basis) is not relevant to whether these transactions are hedging transactions. Thus, for example, a taxpayer hedging the risk associated with an asset or liability may frequently establish and terminate positions that hedge that risk, depending on the extent the taxpayer wishes to be hedged. Similarly, if a taxpayer maintains its level of risk exposure by entering into and terminating a large number of transactions in a single day, its transactions may nonetheless qualify as hedging transactions.

(vii) *Transactions that do not reduce risk.* A transaction that is not entered into to reduce a taxpayer's risk is not a hedging transaction. For example, assume that a taxpayer produces a commodity for sale, sells the commodity, and enters into a long futures or forward contract in that commodity in the hope that the price will increase. Because the long position does not reduce risk, the transaction is not a hedging transaction. Moreover, gain or loss on the contract is not made ordinary on the grounds that it is a surrogate for inventory. See paragraph (a)(3) of this section.

(2) *Entering into a hedging transaction.* A taxpayer may enter into a hedging transaction by using a position that was a hedge of one asset or liability to hedge another asset or liability (recycling).

(3) *No investments as hedging transactions.* If an asset (such as an investment) is not acquired primarily to reduce risk, the purchase or sale of that asset is not a hedging transaction even if the terms of the asset limit or reduce the taxpayer's risk with respect to other assets or liabilities. For example, a taxpayer's interest rate risk from a floating rate borrowing may be reduced by the purchase of debt instruments that bear a comparable floating rate. The acquisition of the debt instruments, however, is not a hedging transaction because the transaction is not entered into primarily to reduce the taxpayer's risk. Similarly, borrowings generally are not made primarily to reduce risk.

(4) *Normal course.* Solely for purposes of paragraph (b) of this section, if a transaction is entered into in furtherance of a taxpayer's trade or business, the transaction is entered into in the normal course of the taxpayer's trade or business. This rule applies even if the risk to be reduced relates to the expansion of an existing business or the acquisition of a new trade or business.

(5) *Ordinary property and obligations*—(i) *In general.* Except as provided in paragraph (g)(3) of this section (which contains transition rules), property is ordinary property to a taxpayer only if a sale or exchange of the property by the taxpayer could not produce capital gain or loss regardless of the taxpayer's holding period when the sale or exchange occurs. Thus, for example, property used in a trade or business within the meaning of section 1231(b) (determined without regard to the holding period specified in that section) is not ordinary property. An obligation is an ordinary obligation if performance or termination of the obligation by the taxpayer could not produce capital gain or loss. For purposes of the preceding sentence, termination has the same meaning as in section 1234A.

(ii) *Hedges of noninventory supplies.* Notwithstanding paragraph (c)(5)(i) of this section, if a taxpayer sells only a negligible amount of a noninventory supply, then, only for purposes of determining whether a transaction to hedge the purchase of that noninventory supply is a hedging transaction, the supply is treated as ordinary property. A noninventory supply is a supply that a taxpayer purchases for consumption in its trade or business and that is not an asset described in sections 1221(1) through (5).

(6) *Borrowings.* Whether hedges of a taxpayer's debt issuances (borrowings) are hedging transactions is determined without regard to the use of the proceeds of the borrowing.

Reg. § 1.1221-2(c)(6)

53,430 Rules for Determining Capital Gains and Losses

See p. 20,601 for regulations not amended to reflect law changes

(7) *Hedging an aggregate risk.* The term hedging transaction includes a transaction that reduces an aggregate risk of interest rate changes, price changes, and/or currency fluctuations only if all of the risk, or all but a de minimis amount of the risk, is with respect to ordinary property, ordinary obligations, and borrowings.

(d) *Hedging by members of a consolidated group*—(1) *General rule: single-entity approach.* For purposes of this section, the risk of one member of a consolidated group is treated as the risk of the other members as if all of the members of the group were divisions of a single corporation. For example, if any member of a consolidated group hedges the risk of another member of the group by entering into a transaction with a third party, that transaction may potentially qualify as a hedging transaction. Conversely, intercompany transactions are not hedging transactions because, when considered as transactions between divisions of a single corporation, they do not reduce the risk of that single corporation.

(2) *Separate-entity election.* In lieu of the single-entity approach specified in paragraph (d)(1) of this section, a consolidated group may elect separate-entity treatment of its hedging transactions. If a group makes this separate-entity election, the following rules apply.

(i) *Risk of one member not risk of other members.* Notwithstanding paragraph (d)(1) of this section, the risk of one member is not treated as the risk of other members.

(ii) *Intercompany transactions.* An intercompany transaction is a hedging transaction (an intercompany hedging transaction) with respect to a member of a consolidated group if and only if it meets the following requirements—

(A) The position of the member in the intercompany transaction would qualify as a hedging transaction with respect to the member (taking into account paragraph (d)(2)(i) of this section) if the member had entered into the transaction with an unrelated party; and

(B) The position of the other member (the marking member) in the transaction is marked to market under the marking member's method of accounting.

(iii) *Treatment of intercompany hedging transactions.* An intercompany hedging transaction (that is, a transaction that meets the requirements of paragraphs (d)(2)(ii)(A) and (B) of this section) is subject to the following rules—

(A) The character and timing rules of § 1.1502-13 do not apply to the income, deduction, gain, or loss from the intercompany hedging transaction; and

(B) Except as provided in paragraph (f)(3) of this section, the character of the marking member's gain or loss from the transaction is ordinary.

(iv) *Making and revoking the election.* Unless the Commissioner otherwise prescribes, the election described in this paragraph (d)(2) must be made in a separate statement saying "[Insert Name and Employer Identification Number of Common Parent] HEREBY ELECTS THE APPLICATION OF SECTION 1.1221-2(d)(2) (THE SEPARATE-ENTITY APPROACH)." The statement must also indicate the date as of which the election is to be effective. The election must be signed by the common parent and filed with the group's federal income tax return for the taxable year that includes the first date for which the election is to apply. The election applies to all transactions entered into on or after the date so indicated. The election may be revoked only with the consent of the Commissioner.

(3) *Definitions.* For definitions of consolidated group, divisions of a single corporation, group, intercompany transactions, and member, see section 1502 and the regulations thereunder.

(4) *Examples.* The following examples illustrate this paragraph (d):

General Facts. In these examples, O and H are members of the same consolidated group. O's business operations give rise to interest rate-risk "A," which O wishes to hedge. O enters into an intercompany transaction with H that transfers the risk to H. O's position in the intercompany transaction is "B," and H's position in the transaction is "C." H enters into position "D" with a third party to reduce the interest rate risk it has with respect to its position C. D would be a hedging transaction with respect to risk A if O's risk A were H's risk.

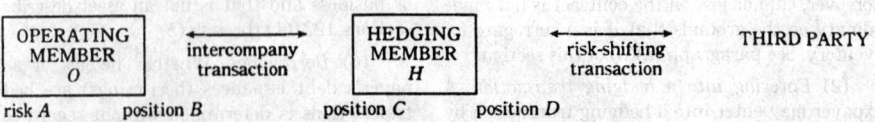

Reg. § 1.1221-2(c)(7)

Rules for Determining Capital Gains and Losses 53,431

See p. 20,601 for regulations not amended to reflect law changes

Example 1. Single-entity treatment—(i) *General rule.* Under paragraph (d)(1) of this section O's risk A is treated as H's risk, and therefore D is a hedging transaction with respect to risk A. Thus, the character of D is determined under the rules of this section, and the income, deduction, gain, or loss from D must be accounted for under a method of accounting that satisfies § 1.446-4. The intercompany transaction B-C is not a hedging transaction and is taken into account under § 1.1502-13.

(ii) *Identification.* D must be identified as a hedging transaction under paragraph (e)(1) of this section, and A must be identified as the hedged item under paragraph (e)(2) of this section. Under paragraph (e)(5) of this section, the identification of A as the hedged item can be accomplished by identifying the positions in the intercompany transaction as hedges or hedged items, as appropriate. Thus, substantially contemporaneous with entering into D, H may identify C as the hedged item and O may identify B as a hedge and A as the hedged item.

Example 2. Separate-entity election; counterparty that does not mark to market. In addition to the *General Facts* stated above, assume that the group makes a separate-entity election under paragraph (d)(2) of this section. If H does not mark C to market under its method of accounting, then B is not a hedging transaction, and the B-C intercompany transaction is taken into account under the rules of section 1502. D is not a hedging transaction with respect to A, but D may be a hedging transaction with respect to C if C is ordinary property or an ordinary obligation and if the other requirements of paragraph (b) of this section are met. If D is not part of a hedging transaction, then D may be part of a straddle for purposes of section 1092.

Example 3. Separate-entity election; counterparty that marks to market. The facts are the same as in *Example 2* above, except that H marks C to market under its method of accounting. Also assume that B would be a hedging transaction with respect to risk A if O had entered into that transaction with an unrelated party. Thus, for O, the B-C transaction is an intercompany hedging transaction with respect to O's risk A, the character and timing rules of § 1.1502-13 do not apply to the B-C transaction, and H's income, deduction, gain, or loss from C is ordinary. However, other attributes of the items from the B-C transaction are determined under § 1.1502-13. D is a hedging transaction with respect to C if it meets the requirements of paragraph (b) of this section.

(e) *Identification and recordkeeping*—(1) *Same-day identification of hedging transactions.* A taxpayer that enters into a hedging transaction (including recycling an existing hedge) must identify it as a hedging transaction. This identification must be made before the close of the day on which the taxpayer enters into the transaction.

(2) *Substantially contemporaneous identification of hedged item*—(i) *Content of the identification.* A taxpayer that enters into a hedging transaction must identify the item, items, or aggregate risk being hedged. Identification of an item being hedged generally involves identifying a transaction that creates risk, and the type of risk that the transaction creates. For example, if a taxpayer is hedging the price risk with respect to its June purchases of corn inventory, the transaction being hedged is the June purchase of corn and the risk is price movements in the market where the taxpayer buys its corn. For additional rules concerning the content of this identification, see paragraph (e)(3) of this section.

(ii) *Timing of the identification.* The identification required by this paragraph (e)(2) must be made substantially contemporaneously with entering into the hedging transaction. An identification is not substantially contemporaneous if it is made more than 35 days after entering into the hedging transaction.

(3) *Identification requirements for certain hedging transactions.* In the case of the hedging transactions described in this paragraph (e)(3), the identification under paragraph (e)(2) of this section must include the information specified.

(i) *Anticipatory asset hedges.* If the hedging transaction relates to the anticipated acquisition of assets by the taxpayer, the identification must include the expected date or dates of acquisition and the amounts expected to be acquired.

(ii) *Inventory hedges.* If the hedging transaction relates to the purchase or sale of inventory by the taxpayer, the identification is made by specifying the type or class of inventory to which the transaction relates. If the hedging transaction relates to specific purchases or sales, the identification must also include the expected dates of the purchases or sales and the amounts to be purchased or sold.

(iii) *Hedges of debt of the taxpayer*—(A) *Existing debt.* If the hedging transaction relates to accruals or payments under an issue of existing debt of the taxpayer, the identification must specify the issue and, if the hedge is for less than the full adjusted issue price or the full term of the debt, the amount and the term covered by the hedge.

Reg. § 1.1221-2(e)(3)

(B) *Debt to be issued.* If the hedging transaction relates to the expected issuance of debt by the taxpayer or to accruals or payments under debt that is expected to be issued by the taxpayer, the identification must specify the following information: the expected date of issuance of the debt; the expected maturity or maturities; the total expected issue price of the issue; and the expected interest provisions. If the hedge is for less than the entire expected issue price of the debt or the full expected term of the debt, the identification must also include the amount or the term being hedged. The identification may indicate a range of dates, terms, and amounts, rather than specific dates, terms, or amounts. For example, a taxpayer might identify a transaction as hedging the yield on an anticipated issuance of fixed rate debt during the second half of its fiscal year, with the anticipated amount of the debt between $75 million and $125 million, and an anticipated term of approximately 20 to 30 years.

(iv) *Hedges of aggregate risk*—(A) *Required identification.* If a transaction hedges aggregate risk as described in paragraph (c)(7) of this section, the identification under paragraph (e)(2) of this section must include a description of the risk being hedged and of the hedging program under which the hedging transaction was entered. This requirement may be met by placing in the taxpayer's records a description of the hedging program and by establishing a system under which individual transactions are identified as being entered into pursuant to the program.

(B) *Description of hedging program.* A description of a hedging program must include an identification of the type of risk being hedged, a description of the type of items giving rise to the risk being aggregated, and sufficient additional information to demonstrate that the program is designed to reduce aggregate risk of the type identified. If the program contains controls on speculation (for example, position limits), the description of the hedging program must also explain how the controls are established, communicated, and implemented.

(4) *Manner of identification and records to be retained*—(i) *Inclusion of identification in tax records.* The identification required by this paragraph (e) must be made on, and retained as part of, the taxpayer's books and records.

(ii) *Presence or absence of identification must be unambiguous.* The presence or absence of an identification for purposes of this paragraph (e) must be unambiguous. The identification of a hedging transaction for financial accounting or regulatory purposes does not satisfy this requirement unless the taxpayer's books and records indicate that the identification is also being made for tax purposes. The taxpayer may indicate that individual hedging transactions, or a class or classes of hedging transactions, that are identified for financial accounting or regulatory purposes are also being identified as hedging transactions for purposes of this section.

(iii) *Manner of identification.* The taxpayer may separately and explicitly make each identification, or, so long as paragraph (e)(4)(ii) of this section is satisfied, the taxpayer may establish a system pursuant to which the identification is indicated by the type of transaction or by the manner in which the transaction is consummated or recorded. An identification under this system is made at the later of the time that the system is established or the time that the transaction satisfies the terms of the system by being entered, or by being consummated or recorded, in the designated fashion.

(iv) *Examples.* The following examples illustrate the principles of paragraph (e)(4)(iii) of this section and assume that the other requirements of paragraph (e) of this section are satisfied.

(A) A taxpayer can make an identification by designating a hedging transaction for (or placing it in) an account that has been identified as containing only hedges of a specified item (or of specified items or specified aggregate risk).

(B) A taxpayer can make an identification by including and retaining in its books and records a statement that designates all future transactions in a specified derivative product as hedges of a specified item, items, or aggregate risk.

(C) A taxpayer can make an identification by placing a designated mark on a record of the transaction (for example, trading ticket, purchase order, or trade confirmation) or by using a designated form or a record that contains a designated legend.

(5) *Identification of hedges involving members of a consolidated group*—(i) *General rule: single-entity approach.* A member of a consolidated group must satisfy the requirements of this paragraph (e) as if all of the members of the group were divisions of a single corporation. Thus, the member entering into the hedging transaction with a third party must identify the hedging transaction under paragraph (e)(1) of this section. Under paragraph (e)(2) of this section, that member must also identify the item, items, or aggregate risk that is being hedged, even if the item, items, or aggregate risk relates primarily or entirely to other members of the group. If the members of a group use intercompany transactions to

Reg. § 1.1221-2(e)(4)

Rules for Determining Capital Gains and Losses

See p. 20,601 for regulations not amended to reflect law changes

transfer risk within the group, the requirements of paragraph (e)(2) of this section may be met by identifying the intercompany transactions, and the risks hedged by the intercompany transactions, as hedges or hedged items, as appropriate. Because identification of the intercompany transaction as a hedge serves solely to identify the hedged item, the identification is timely if made within the period required by paragraph (e)(2) of this section. For example, if a member transfers risk in an intercompany transaction, it may identify under the rules of this paragraph (e) both its position in that transaction and the item, items, or aggregate risk being hedged. The member that hedges the risk outside the group may identify under the rules of this paragraph (e) both its position with the third party and its position in the intercompany transaction. Paragraph (d)(4) *Example 1* of this section illustrates this identification.

(ii) *Rule for consolidated groups making the separate-entity election.* If a consolidated group makes the separate-entity election under paragraph (d)(2) of this section, each member of the group must satisfy the requirements of this paragraph (e) as though it were not a member of a consolidated group.

(6) *Consistency with section 1256(e)(2)(C).* Any identification for purposes of section 1256(e)(2)(C) is also an identification for purposes of paragraph (e)(1) of this section.

(f) *Effect of identification and non-identification*—(1) *Transactions identified*—(i) *In general.* If a taxpayer identifies a transaction as a hedging transaction for purposes of paragraph (e)(1) of this section, the identification is binding with respect to gain, whether or not all of the requirements of paragraph (e) of this section are satisfied. Thus, gain from that transaction is ordinary income. If the transaction is not in fact a hedging transaction described in paragraph (b) of this section, however, paragraphs (a)(1) and (a)(2) of this section do not apply and the character of loss is determined without reference to whether the transaction is a surrogate for a noncapital asset, serves as insurance against a business risk, serves a hedging function, or serves a similar function or purpose. Thus, the taxpayer's identification of the transaction as a hedging transaction does not itself make loss from the transaction ordinary.

(ii) *Inadvertent identification.* Notwithstanding paragraph (f)(1)(i) of this section, if the taxpayer identifies a transaction as a hedging transaction for purposes of paragraph (e) of this section, the character of the gain is determined as if the transaction had not been identified as a hedging transaction if—

(A) The transaction is not a hedging transaction (as defined in paragraph (b) of this section);

(B) The identification of the transaction as a hedging transaction was due to inadvertent error; and

(C) All of the taxpayer's transactions in all open years are being treated on either original or, if necessary, amended returns in a manner consistent with the principles of this section.

(2) *Transactions not identified*—(i) *In general.* Except as provided in paragraphs (f)(2)(ii) and (iii) of this section, the absence of an identification that satisfies the requirements of paragraph (e)(1) of this section is binding and establishes that a transaction is not a hedging transaction. Thus, subject to the exceptions, the rules of paragraphs (a)(1) and (2) of this section do not apply, and the character of gain or loss is determined without reference to whether the transaction is a surrogate for a noncapital asset, serves as insurance against a business risk, serves a hedging function, or serves a similar function or purpose.

(ii) *Inadvertent error.* If a taxpayer does not make an identification that satisfies the requirements of paragraph (e) of this section, the taxpayer may treat gain or loss from the transaction as ordinary income or loss under paragraph (a)(1) or (a)(2) of this section if—

(A) The transaction is a hedging transaction (as defined in paragraph (b) of this section);

(B) The failure to identify the transaction was due to inadvertent error; and

(C) All of the taxpayer's hedging transactions in all open years are being treated on either original or, if necessary, amended returns as provided in paragraphs (a)(1) and (a)(2) of this section.

(iii) *Anti-abuse rule.* If a taxpayer does not make an identification that satisfies all the requirements of paragraph (e) of this section but the taxpayer has no reasonable grounds for treating the transaction as other than a hedging transaction, then gain from the transaction is ordinary. Thus, a taxpayer may not elect to treat gain or loss from a hedging transaction as capital gain or loss. The reasonableness of the taxpayer's failure to identify a transaction is determined by taking into consideration not only the requirements of paragraph (b) of this section but also the taxpayer's treatment of the transaction for financial accounting or other purposes and the taxpayer's identification of similar transactions as hedging transactions.

Reg. § 1.1221-2(f)(2)

(3) *Transactions by members of a consolidated group*—(i) *Single-entity approach.* If a consolidated group is under the general rule of paragraph (d)(1) of this section (the single-entity approach), the rules of this paragraph (f) apply only to transactions that are not intercompany transactions.

(ii) *Separate-entity election.* If a consolidated group has made the election under paragraph (d)(2) of this section, then, in addition to the rules of paragraphs (f)(1) and (2) of this section, the following rules apply.

(A) If an intercompany transaction is identified as a hedging transaction but does not meet the requirements of paragraphs (d)(2)(B)(A) and (B) of this section, then, notwithstanding any contrary provision in § 1.1502-13, each party to the transaction is subject to the rules of paragraph (f)(1) of this section with respect to the transaction as though it had incorrectly identified its position in the transaction as a hedging transaction.

(B) If a transaction meets the requirements of paragraphs (d)(2)(ii)(A) and (B) of this section but the transaction is not identified as a hedging transaction, each party to the transaction is subject to the rules of paragraph (f)(2) of this section. (Because the transaction is an intercompany hedging transaction, the character and timing rules of § 1.1502-13 do not apply. See paragraph (d)(2)(iii)(A) of this section.)

(g) *Effective dates and transition rules*—(1) *Effective date for identification requirements*—(i) *In general.* Paragraph (e) of this section applies to transactions that—

(A) Are entered into on or after January 1, 1994; or

(B) Are entered into before that date and remain in existence on March 31, 1994.

(ii) *Transition rule.* In the case of a hedging transaction that is entered into before January 1, 1994, and remains in existence on March 31, 1994, an identification is timely if it is made before the close of business on March 31, 1994.

(iii) *Special rules for hedging transactions not described in § 1.1221-2T(b).* In the case of a transaction that is entered into before October 1, 1994, that is a hedging transaction within the meaning of paragraph (b) of this section (or is treated as a hedging transaction under paragraph (g)(3) of this section), and that the taxpayer reasonably treated as not being a hedging transaction within the meaning of paragraph (b) of § 1.1221-2T (26 CFR part 1 revised as of April 1, 1994)—

(A) If the transaction does not remain in existence on October 1, 1994, paragraph (e) of this section does not apply; and

(B) If the transaction remains in existence on October 1, 1994, paragraph (e) of this section applies, and an identification is timely if it is made before the close of business on October 1, 1994.

(2) *Reliance on § 1.1221-2T*—(i) *General rule.* A taxpayer may rely on any paragraph in § 1.1221-2T (26 CFR part 1 revised as of April 1, 1994), for transactions entered into prior to October 1, 1994, provided that the taxpayer applies the paragraph reasonably and consistently.

(ii) *Identification.* In the case of a transaction entered into before October 1, 1994, an identification is deemed to satisfy paragraph (e) of this section if it satisfies § 1.1221-2T(c) (26 CFR part 1 revised as of April 1, 1994). For this purpose, identification of the hedged item is timely if it is made within the period specified in paragraph (e)(2)(ii) of this section.

(3) *Transition rules for hedges of certain property*—(i) *Transition rule for section 1231 assets.* For all taxable years that ended prior to July 18, 1994, and that, as of September 1, 1994, were still open for assessment under section 6501, a taxpayer may treat as hedging transactions all transactions that were entered into during those years and that hedge property used in the trade or business within the meaning of section 1231(b) (a section 1231 asset) if the taxpayer can establish that, during those years—

(A) Sales of section 1231 assets did not give rise to net gain treated as capital gain (after application of section 1231(c));

(B) All of the hedges of section 1231 assets would be hedging transactions under paragraph (b) of this section if section 1231 assets were ordinary property; and

(C) On original or amended returns, the taxpayer consistently treats all of the hedges of section 1231 assets as hedging transactions.

(ii) *Transition rule for noninventory supplies.* For all taxable years that ended prior to July 18, 1994, and that, as of September 1, 1994, were still open for assessment under section 6501, a taxpayer may treat as hedging transactions all hedges of purchases of noninventory supplies (as defined in paragraph (c)(5)(ii) of this section) that would not otherwise qualify as hedging transactions and that were entered into during those years if the taxpayer can establish that, during those years—

(A) The taxpayer did not sell in any of those years more than 15 percent of the greater of

Reg. § 1.1221-2(f)(3)

Rules for Determining Capital Gains and Losses

the total amount of the supply held at the beginning of the year or the total amount of the supply acquired during that year;

(B) All of the hedges would be hedging transactions under paragraph (b) of this section if noninventory supplies were ordinary property; and

(C) On original or amended returns, the taxpayer consistently treats all of the hedges of noninventory supplies as hedging transactions.

(4) *Effective date and transition rules for hedges by members of a consolidated group.* Paragraphs (d), (e)(5), and (f)(3) of this section apply to transactions entered into on or after March 8, 1996.

(5) *Elections to accelerate the effective date of the regulations*—(i) *Election to apply the single-entity approach retroactively.* A consolidated group may elect to begin to apply paragraphs (d)(1) and (3), (e)(5)(i), and (f)(3)(i) of this section to all transactions entered into in any taxable year (the election year) beginning prior to March 8, 1996. This election must be made in the manner, and at the time, prescribed by the Commissioner. A group may make the election only if the election year, and each subsequent taxable year, are still open for assessment under section 6501 on July 1, 1996 (or such earlier date as the Commissioner may allow). The election applies to all transactions entered into in the election year and in all subsequent consolidated return years until the date, if any, as of which the group makes a separate-entity election under paragraph (d)(2) of this section. The rules of paragraph (g)(6) of this section apply to all transactions that were entered into before March 8, 1996 in taxable years subject to an election under this paragraph (g)(5)(i). The election may be revoked only with the consent of the Commissioner.

(ii) *Ability to apply the separate-entity approach retroactively.* Notwithstanding paragraph (g)(4) of this section, the separate-entity election described in paragraph (d)(2) of this section may be made for any taxable year beginning on or after July 12, 1995. If that election is made for a taxable year beginning before March 8, 1996, then paragraphs (d)(2) and (3), (e)(5)(ii), and (f)(3)(ii) of this section apply to all transactions entered into on or after the beginning of that taxable year and while the election is in effect, and the rules of paragraph (g)(6) of this section (other than paragraph (g)(6)(i)) apply to all transactions that were entered into on or after the first day of the first year for which the election is made and before March 8, 1996.

(6) *Transitional identification rules.* To allow a consolidated group to conform to paragraphs (g)(5)(i) and (ii) of this section, this paragraph (g)(6) nullifies certain hedge identifications and permits a member of a consolidated group to add certain hedge identifications. This paragraph (g)(6) applies only to the extent provided in paragraph (g)(5) of this section.

(i) *Intercompany transactions previously identified.* Notwithstanding paragraph (f)(1)(i) of this section, if, for purposes of paragraph (e)(1) of this section, a member identified as a hedging transaction an intercompany transaction (or a transaction that would qualify as an intercompany transaction under § 1.1502-13(b)(1) if the taxable year in which the transaction was entered into were described in § 1.1502-13(*l*)), the character of the gain on the intercompany transaction is determined as if it had not been identified as a hedging transaction. The identification may, however, serve to identify the hedged item under paragraph (e)(5)(i) of this section.

(ii) *Additional identifications of hedging transactions.* A member of a consolidated group must identify under paragraph (e)(5) of this section a transaction that—

(A) Was entered into before March 8, 1996,

(B) When entered into was not a hedging transaction (as defined in paragraph (b) of this section),

(C) Solely as a result of the group's election under paragraph (g)(5)(i) or (ii) of this section, is a hedging transaction (as defined in paragraph (b) of this section), and

(D) Remains in existence on March 8, 1996.

(iii) *Additional identification of hedged items.* In the case of transactions described in paragraph (g)(6)(ii) of this section, the hedging member must identify under paragraph (e)(5) of this section the item, items, or aggregate risk being hedged.

(iv) *Consistency requirement for hedge identifications.* In identifying transactions as hedging transactions under paragraph (g)(6)(ii) of this section, all of the members of the group must treat similar or identical transactions consistently within the same year and from year to year. If paragraph (g)(6)(ii) of this section requires a member to identify a transaction, and the member fails to identify a transaction as a hedging transaction, but it or another member of the group identifies similar or identical hedging transactions in the same or a subsequent year, then for purposes of paragraphs (f)(2)(iii) and (3) of this section, the member entering into the transaction is treated as having no reasonable grounds for

Reg. § 1.1221-2(g)(6)

treating the transaction as other than a hedging transaction.

(v) *Extension of time for making additional identifications.* If an identification of a hedging transaction would not be required but for the rules of paragraph (g)(6)(ii) of this section, the identification is timely for purposes of paragraph (e)(1) of this section if made before the close of business on May 7, 1996. If an identification of a hedged item would not be required but for the rules of paragraph (g)(6)(iii) of this section, it is timely for purposes of paragraph (e)(2) of this section if made before the close of business on the later of May 7, 1996 or the last day of the period specified in paragraph (e)(2)(ii) of this section. [Reg. § 1.1221-2.]

☐ [T.D. 8555, 7-13-94. Amended by T.D. 8653, 1-5-96.]

[Reg. § 1.1222-1]

§ 1.1222-1. **Other terms relating to capital gains and losses.**—(a) The phrase "short-term" applies to the category of gains and losses arising from the sale or exchange of capital assets held for 1 year (6 months for taxable years beginning before 1977; 9 months for taxable years beginning in 1977) or less; the phrase "long-term" to the category of gains and losses arising from the sale or exchange of capital assets held for more than 1 year (6 months for taxable years beginning before 1977; 9 months for taxable years beginning in 1977). The fact that some part of a loss from the sale or exchange of a capital asset may be finally disallowed because of the operation of section 1211 does not mean that such loss is not "taken into account in computing taxable income" within the meaning of that phrase as used in sections 1222(2) and 1222(4).

(b) (1) In the definition of "net short-term capital gain", as provided in section 1222(5), the amounts brought forward to the taxable year under section 1212 (other than section 1212 (b)(1)(B)) are short-term capital losses for such taxable year.

(2) In the definition of "net long-term capital gain", as provided in section 1222(7), the amounts brought forward to the taxable year under section 1212(b)(1)(B) are long-term capital losses for such taxable year.

(c) Gains and losses from the sale or exchange of capital assets held for not more than 1 year (6 months for taxable years beginning before 1977; 9 months for taxable years beginning in 1977) (described as short-term capital gains and short-term capital losses) shall be segregated from gains and losses arising from the sale or exchange of such assets held for more than 1 year (6 months for taxable years beginning before 1977; 9 months for taxable years beginning in 1977) (described as long-term capital gains and long-term capital losses).

(d)(1) The term "capital gain net income" (net capital gain for taxable years beginning before January 1, 1977) means the excess of the gains from sales or exchanges of capital assets over the losses from sales or exchanges of capital assets, which losses include any amounts carried to the taxable year pursuant to section 1212(a) or section 1212(b).

(2) Notwithstanding subparagraph (1) of this paragraph, in the case of a taxpayer other than a corporation for taxable years beginning before January 1, 1964, the term "net capital gain" means the excess of (i) the sum of the gains from sales or exchanges of capital assets, plus the taxable income (computed without regard to gains and losses from sales or exchanges of capital assets and without regard to the deductions provided by section 151, relating to personal exemptions, or any deductions in lieu thereof) of the taxpayer or $1,000, whichever is smaller, over (ii) the losses from sales or exchanges of capital assets, which losses include amounts carried to the taxable year by such taxpayer under paragraph (a)(1) of § 1.1212-1. Thus, in the case of estates and trusts for taxable years beginning before January 1, 1964, taxable income for the purposes of this paragraph shall be computed without regard to gains and losses from sales or exchanges of capital assets and without regard to the deductions allowed by section 642(b) to estates and trusts in lieu of personal exemptions. The term "net capital gain" is not applicable in the case of a taxpayer other than a corporation for taxable years beginning after December 31, 1963, and before January 1, 1970. In the case of a taxpayer whose tax liability is computed under section 3 for taxable years beginning before January 1, 1964, the term "taxable income", for purposes of this paragraph, shall be read as "adjusted gross income".

(e) The term "net capital loss" means the excess of the losses from sales or exchanges of capital assets over the sum allowed under section 1211. However, in the case of a corporation, amounts which are short-term capital losses under § 1.1212-1(a) are excluded in determining such "net capital loss".

(f) See section 165(g) and section 166(e), under which losses from worthless stocks, bonds, and other securities (if they constitute capital assets) are required to be treated as losses under subchapter P (section 1201 and following), chapter 1 of the Code, from the sale or exchange of capital assets, even though such securities are not actu-

Reg. § 1.1222-1(a)

ally sold or exchanged. See also section 1231 and § 1.1231-1 for the determination of whether or not gains and losses from the involuntary conversion of capital assets and from the sale, exchange, or involuntary conversion of certain property used in the trade or business shall be treated as gains and losses from the sale or exchange of capital assets. See also section 1236 and § 1.1236-1 for the determination of whether or not gains from the sale or exchange of securities by a dealer in securities shall be treated as capital gains, or whether losses from such sales or exchanges shall be treated as ordinary losses.

(g) In the case of nonresident alien individuals not engaged in trade or business within the United States, see section 871 and the regulations thereunder for the determination of the net amount of capital gains subject to tax.

(h) The term "net capital gain" ("net section 1201 gain" for taxable years beginning before January 1, 1977) means the excess of the net long-term capital gain for the taxable year over the net short-term capital loss for such year. [Reg. § 1.1222-1.]

☐ [T.D. 6243, 7-23-57. Amended by T.D. 6828, 6-16-65; T.D. 6867, 12-6-65; T.D. 7301, 1-3-74; T.D. 7337, 12-26-74 and T.D. 7728, 10-31-80.]

[Reg. § 1.1223-1]

§ 1.1223-1. Determination of period for which capital assets are held.—(a) The holding period of property received in an exchange by a taxpayer includes the period for which the property which he exchanged was held by him, if the property received has the same basis in whole or in part for determining gain or loss in the hands of the taxpayer as the property exchanged. However, this rule shall apply, in the case of exchanges after March 1, 1954, only if the property exchanged was at the time of the exchange a capital asset in the hands of the taxpayer or property used in his trade or business as defined in section 1231(b). For the purposes of this paragraph the term "exchange" includes the following transactions: (1) An involuntary conversion described in section 1033, and (2) a distribution to which section 355 (or so much of section 356 as relates to section 355) applies. Thus, if property acquired as the result of a compulsory or involuntary conversion of other property of the taxpayer has under section 1033(c) the same basis in whole or in part in the hands of the taxpayer as the property so converted, its acquisition is treated as an exchange and the holding period of the newly acquired property shall include the period during which the converted property was held by the taxpayer. Thus, also, where stock of a controlled corporation is received by a taxpayer pursuant to a distribution to which section 355 (or so much of section 356 as relates to section 355) applies, the distribution is treated as an exchange and the period for which the taxpayer has held the stock of the controlled corporation shall include the period for which he held the stock of the distributing corporation with respect to which such distribution was made.

(b) The holding period of property in the hands of a taxpayer shall include the period during which the property was held by any other person, if such property has the same basis in whole or in part in the hands of the taxpayer for determining gain or loss from a sale or exchange as it would have in the hands of such other person. For example, the period for which property acquired by gift after December 31, 1920, was held by the donor must be included in determining the period for which the property was held by the taxpayer if, under the provisions of section 1015, such property has, for the purpose of determining gain or loss from the sale or exchange, the same basis in the hands of the taxpayer as it would have in the hands of the donor.

(c) In determining the period for which the taxpayer has held stock or securities received upon a distribution where no gain was recognized to the distributee under section 1081(c) (or under section 112(g) of the Revenue Act of 1928 (45 Stat. 818) or the Revenue Act of 1932 (47 Stat. 197)), there shall be included the period for which he held the stock or securities in the distributing corporation before the receipt of the stock or securities on such distribution.

(d) If the acquisition of stock or securities resulted in the nondeductibility (under section 1091, relating to wash sales) of the loss from the sale or other disposition of substantially identical stock or securities, the holding period of the newly acquired securities shall include the period for which the taxpayer held the securities with respect to which the loss was not allowable.

(e) The period for which the taxpayer has held stock, or stock subscription rights, received on a distribution shall be determined as though the stock dividend, or stock right, as the case may be, were the stock in respect of which the dividend was issued if the basis for determining gain or loss upon the sale or other disposition of such stock dividend or stock right is determined under section 307. If the basis of stock received by a taxpayer pursuant to a spin-off is determined under so much of section 1052(c) as refers to section 113(a)(23) of the Internal Revenue Code of 1939, and such stock is sold or otherwise disposed of in a taxable year which is subject to the Internal Revenue Code of 1954, the period for which the tax-

Reg. § 1.1223-1(e)

payer has held the stock received in such spin-off shall include the period for which he held the stock of the distributing corporation with respect to which such distribution was made.

(f) The period for which the taxpayer has held stock or securities issued to him by a corporation pursuant to the exercise by him of rights to acquire such stock or securities from the corporation will, in every case and whether or not the receipt of taxable gain was recognized in connection with the distribution of the rights, begin with and include the day upon which the rights to acquire such stock or securities were exercised. A taxpayer will be deemed to have exercised rights received from a corporation to acquire stock or securities therein where there is an expression of assent to the terms of such rights made by the taxpayer in the manner requested or authorized by the corporation.

(g) The period for which the taxpayer has held a residence, the acquisition of which resulted under the provisions of section 1034 in the nonrecognition of any part of the gain realized on the sale or exchange of another residence, shall include the period for which such other residence had been held as of the date of such sale or exchange. See § 1.1034-1. For purposes of this paragraph, the term "sale or exchange" includes an involuntary conversion occurring after December 31, 1950, and before January 1, 1954.

(h) If a taxpayer accepts delivery of a commodity in satisfaction of a commodity futures contracts, the holding period of the commodity shall include the period for which the taxpayer held the commodity futures contract, if such futures contract was a capital asset in his hands.

(i) If shares of stock in a corporation are sold from lots purchased at different dates or at different prices and the identity of the lots cannot be determined, the rules prescribed by the regulations under section 1012 for determining the cost or other basis of such stocks so sold or transferred shall also apply for the purpose of determining the holding period of such stock.

(j) In the case of a person acquiring property, or to whom property passed, from a decedent (within the meaning of section 1014(b)) dying after December 31, 1970, such person shall be considered to have held the property for more than 6 months if the property—

(1) Has a basis in the hands of such person which is determined in whole or in part under section 1014, and

(2) Is sold or otherwise disposed of by such person within 6 months after the decedent's death.

The provisions of this paragraph apply to sales of such property included in the decedent's gross estate for the purposes of the estate tax by the executor or administrator of the estate and to sales of such property by other persons who have acquired property from the decedent. The provisions of this paragraph may also be applicable to cases involving joint tenancies, community property, and properties transferred in contemplation of death. Thus, if a surviving joint tenant, who acquired property by right of survivorship, sells or otherwise disposes of such property within 1 year (6 months for taxable years beginning before 1977; 9 months for taxable years beginning in 1977) after the date of the decedent's death, and the basis of the property in his hands is determined in whole or in part under section 1014, the property shall be considered to have been held by the surviving joint tenant for more than 1 year (6 months for taxable years beginning before 1977; 9 months for taxable years beginning in 1977). Similarly, a surviving spouse's share of community property shall be considered to have been held by her for more than 1 year (6 months for taxable years beginning before 1977; 9 months for taxable years beginning in 1977) if it is sold or otherwise disposed of within 1 year (6 months for taxable years beginning before 1977; 9 months for taxable years beginning in 1977) after the date of the decedent's death, regardless of when the property was actually acquired by the marital community. For the purposes of this paragraph, it is immaterial that the sale or other disposition produces gain or loss. If property is considered to have been held for more than 1 year (6 months for taxable years beginning before 1977; 9 months for taxable years beginning in 1977) by reason of this paragraph, it also is considered to have been held for that period for purposes of section 1231 (if that section is otherwise applicable).

(k) Any reference in section 1223 or this section to another provision of the Internal Revenue Code of 1954 is, where applicable, to be deemed a reference to the corresponding provision of the Internal Revenue Code of 1939, or prior internal revenue laws. The provisions of prior internal revenue laws here intended are the sections referred to in the sections of the 1939 Code which correspond to the sections of the Internal Revenue Code of 1954 referred to in section 1223. Thus, the sections corresponding to section 1081(c) are section 371(c) of the Revenue Act of 1938 (52 Stat. 553) and section 371(c) of the Internal Revenue Code of 1939. The sections corresponding to section 1091 are section 118 of each of the following: The Revenue Acts of 1928 (45 Stat. 826), 1932 (47 Stat. 208), 1934 (48 Stat. 715), 1936 (49 Stat.

Reg. § 1.1223-1(f)

1692), and 1938 (52 Stat. 503), and the Internal Revenue Code of 1939. [Reg. § 1.1223-1.]

☐ [T.D. 6243, 7-23-57. Amended by T.D. 7238, 12-28-72 and T.D. 7728, 10-31-80.]

[Reg. § 1.1223-3]

§ 1.1223-3. Rules relating to the holding periods of partnership interests.—(a) *In general.* A partner shall not have a divided holding period in an interest in a partnership unless—

(1) The partner acquired portions of an interest at different times; or

(2) The partner acquired portions of the partnership interest in exchange for property transferred at the same time but resulting in different holding periods (e.g., section 1223).

(b) *Accounting for holding periods of an interest in a partnership*—(1) *General rule.* The portion of a partnership interest to which a holding period relates shall be determined by reference to a fraction, the numerator of which is the fair market value of the portion of the partnership interest received in the transaction to which the holding period relates, and the denominator of which is the fair market value of the entire partnership interest (determined immediately after the transaction).

(2) *Special rule.* For purposes of applying paragraph (b)(1) of this section to determine the holding period of a partnership interest (or portion thereof) that is sold or exchanged (or with respect to which gain or loss is recognized upon a distribution under section 731), if a partner makes one or more contributions of cash to the partnership and receives one or more distributions of cash from the partnership during the one-year period ending on the date of the sale or exchange (or distribution with respect to which gain or loss is recognized under section 731), the partner may reduce the cash contributions made during the year by cash distributions received on a last-in-first-out basis, treating all cash distributions as if they were received immediately before the sale or exchange (or at the time of the distribution with respect to which gain or loss is recognized under section 731).

(3) *Deemed contributions and distributions.* For purposes of paragraphs (b)(1) and (2) of this section, deemed contributions of cash under section 752(a) and deemed distributions of cash under section 752(b) shall be disregarded to the same extent that such amounts are disregarded under § 1.704-1(b)(2)(iv)(c).

(4) *Adjustment with respect to contributed section 751 assets.* For purposes of applying paragraph (b)(1) of this section to determine the holding period of a partnership interest (or portion thereof) that is sold or exchanged, if a partner receives a portion of the partnership interest in exchange for property described in section 751(c) or (d) (section 751 assets) within the one-year period ending on the date of the sale or exchange of all or a portion of the partner's interest in the partnership, and the partner recognizes ordinary income or loss on account of such a section 751 asset in a fully taxable transaction (either as a result of the sale of all or part of the partner's interest in the partnership or the sale by the partnership of the section 751 asset), the contribution of the section 751 asset during the one-year period shall be disregarded. However, if, in the absence of this paragraph, a partner would not be treated as having held any portion of the interest for more than one year (e.g., because the partner's only contributions to the partnership are contributions of section 751 assets or section 751 assets and cash within the prior one-year period), this adjustment is not available.

(5) *Exception.* The Commissioner may prescribe by guidance published in the Internal Revenue Bulletin (see § 601.601(d)(2) of this chapter) a rule disregarding certain cash contributions (including contributions of a de minimis amount of cash) in applying paragraph (b)(1) of this section to determine the holding period of a partnership interest (or portion thereof) that is sold or exchanged.

(c) *Sale or exchange of all or a portion of an interest in a partnership*—(1) *Sale or exchange of entire interest in a partnership.* If a partner sells or exchanges the partner's entire interest in a partnership, any capital gain or loss recognized shall be divided between long-term and short-term capital gain or loss in the same proportions as the holding period of the interest in the partnership is divided between the portion of the interest held for more than one year and the portion of the interest held for one year or less.

(2) *Sale or exchange of a portion of an interest in a partnership*—(i) *Certain publicly traded partnerships.* A selling partner in a publicly traded partnership (as defined under section 7704(b)) may use the actual holding period of the portion of a partnership interest transferred if—

(A) The ownership interest is divided into identifiable units with ascertainable holding periods;

(B) The selling partner can identify the portion of the partnership interest transferred; and

(C) The selling partner elects to use the identification method for all sales or exchanges of interests in the partnership after September 21, 2000. The selling partner makes the election referred to in this paragraph (c)(2)(i)(C) by using the actual holding period of the portion of the partner's interest in the partnership first transferred after September 21, 2000 in reporting the transaction for federal income tax purposes.

(ii) *Other partnerships.* If a partner has a divided holding period in a partnership interest, and paragraph (c)(2)(i) of this section does not apply, then the holding period of the transferred interest shall be divided between long-term and short-term capital gain or loss in the same proportions as the long-term and short-term capital gain or loss that the transferor partner would realize if the entire interest in the partnership were transferred in a fully taxable transaction immediately before the actual transfer.

(d) *Distributions*—(1) *In general.* Except as provided in paragraph (b)(2) of this section, a partner's holding period in a partnership interest is not affected by distributions from the partnership.

(2) *Character of capital gain or loss recognized as a result of a distribution from a partnership.* If a partner is required to recognize capital gain or loss as a result of a distribution from a partnership, then the capital gain or loss recognized shall be divided between long-term and short-term capital gain or loss in the same proportions as the long-term and short-term capital gain or loss that the distributee partner would realize if such partner's entire interest in the partnership were transferred in a fully taxable transaction immediately before the distribution.

(e) *Section 751(c) assets.* For purposes of this section, properties and potential gain treated as unrealized receivables under section 751(c) shall be treated as separate assets that are not capital assets as defined in section 1221 or property described in section 1231.

(f) *Examples.* The provisions of this section are illustrated by the following examples:

Example 1. Division of holding period—contribution of money and a capital asset. (i) *A* contributes $5,000 of cash and a nondepreciable capital asset *A* has held for two years to a partnership (*PRS*) for a 50 percent interest in *PRS*. *A*'s basis in the capital asset is $5,000, and the fair market value of the asset is $10,000. After the exchange, *A*'s basis in *A*'s interest in *PRS* is $10,000, and the fair market value of the interest is $15,000. *A* received one-third of the interest in *PRS* for a cash payment of $5,000 ($5,000/$15,000). Therefore, *A*'s holding period in one-third of the interest received (attributable to the contribution of money to the partnership) begins on the day after the contribution. *A* received two-thirds of the interest in *PRS* in exchange for the capital asset ($10,000/$15,000). Accordingly, pursuant to section 1223(1), *A* has a two-year holding period in two-thirds of the interest received in *PRS*.

(ii) Six months later, when *A*'s basis in *PRS* is $12,000 (due to a $2,000 allocation of partnership income to *A*), *A* sells the interest in *PRS* for $17,000. Assuming *PRS* holds no inventory or unrealized receivables (as defined under section 751(c)) and no collectibles or section 1250 property, *A* will realize $5,000 of capital gain. As determined above, one-third of *A*'s interest in *PRS* has a holding period of one year or less, and two-thirds of *A*'s interest in *PRS* has a holding period equal to two years and six months. Therefore, one-third of the capital gain will be short-term capital gain, and two-thirds of the capital gain will be long-term capital gain.

Example 2. Division of holding period—contribution of section 751 asset and a capital asset. *A* contributes inventory with a basis of $2,000 and a fair market value of $6,000 and a capital asset which *A* has held for more than one year with a basis of $4,000 and a fair market value of $6,000, and *B* contributes cash of $12,000 to form a partnership (*AB*). As a result of the contribution, one-half of *A*'s interest in *AB* is treated as having been held for more than one year under section 1223(1). Six months later. *A* transfers one-half of *A*'s interest in *AB* to *C* for $6,000, realizing a gain of $3,000. If *AB* were to sell all of its section 751 property in a fully taxable transaction immediately before *A*'s transfer of the partnership interest, *A* would be allocated $4,000 of ordinary income on account of the inventory. Accordingly, *A* will recognize $2,000 of ordinary income and $1,000 of capital gain ($3,000 − $2,000) on account of the transfer to *C*. Because *A* recognizes ordinary income on account of the inventory that was contributed to *AB* within the one year period ending on the date of the sale, the inventory will be disregarded in determining the holding period of *A*'s interest in *AB*. All of the capital gain will be long-term.

Example 3. Netting of cash contributions and distributions. (i) On January 1, 2000,*A* holds a 50 percent interest in the capital and profits of a partnership (*PS*). The value of *A*'s *PS* interest is $900, and *A*'s holding period in the entire interest is long-term. On January 2, 2000, when the value of *A*'s *PS* interest is still $900, *A* contributes $100 to *PS*. On June 1, 2000, *A* receives a distribution of $40 cash from the partnership. On September 1, 2000, when the value of *A*'s interest in *PS* is $1,350, *A* contributes an additional $230 cash to *PS*, and on October 1, 2000, *A* receives another $40 cash distribution from *PS*. *A* sells *A*'s entire partnership interest on November 1, 2000, for

Reg. § 1.1223-3(d)(1)

$1,600. A's adjusted basis in the PS interest at the time of the sale is $1,000.

(ii) For purposes of netting cash contributions and distributions in determining the holding period of A's interest in PS, A is treated as having received a distribution of $80 on November 1, 2000. Applying that distribution on a last-in-first-out basis to reduce prior contributions during the year, the contribution made on September 1, 2000, is reduced to $150 ($230 − $80). The holding period then is determined as follows: Immediately after the contribution of $100 on January 2, 2000, A's holding period in A's PS interest is 90 percent long-term ($900 ÷ ($900 + $100)) and 10 percent short-term ($100 ÷ ($900 + $100)). The contribution of $150 on September 1, 2000, causes 10 percent of A's partnership interest ($150 ÷ ($1,350 + $150)) to have a short-term holding period. Accordingly, immediately after the contribution on September 1, 2000, A's holding period in A's PS interest is 81 percent long-term (.90 × .90) and 19 percent short-term ((.10 × .90) + .10). Accordingly, $486 ($600 × .81) of the gain from A's sale of the PS interest is long-term capital gain, and $114 ($600 × .19) is short-term capital gain.

Example 4. Division of holding period when capital account is increased by contribution. A, B, C, and D are equal partners in a partnership (PRS), and the fair market value of a 25 percent interest in PRS is $100. A, B, C, and D each contribute an additional $100 to partnership capital, thereby increasing the fair market value of each partner's interest to $200. As a result of the contribution, each partner has a new holding period in the portion of the partner's interest in PRS that is attributable to the contribution. That portion equals 50 percent ($100 ÷ $200) of each partners interest in PRS.

Example 5. Sale or exchange of a portion of an interest in a partnership. (i) A, B, and C form an equal partnership (PRS). In connection with the formation, A contributes $5,000 in cash and a capital asset (capital asset 1) with a fair market value of $5,000 and a basis of $2,000; B contributes $7,000 in cash and a capital asset (capital asset 2) with a fair market value of $3,000 and a basis of $3,000; and C contributes $10,000 in cash. At the time of the contribution, A had held the contributed property for two years. Six months later, when A's basis in PRS is $7,000, A transfers one-half of A's interest in PRS to T for $7,000 at a time when PRS's balance sheet (reflecting a cash receipts and disbursements method of accounting) is as follows:

ASSETS

	Adjusted Basis	Market Value
Cash	$22,000	$22,000
Unrealized Receivables	0	6,000
Capital Asset 1	2,000	5,000
Capital Asset 2	3,000	9,000
Capital Assets	5,000	14,000
Total	$27,000	$42,000

(ii) Although at the time of the transfer A has not held A's interest in PRS for more than one year, 50 percent of the fair market value of A's interest in PRS was received in exchange for a capital asset with a long-term holding period. Therefore, 50 percent of A's interest in PRS has a long-term holding period.

(iii) If PRS were to sell all of its section 751 property in a fully taxable transaction immediately before A's transfer of the partnership interest, A would be allocated $2,000 of ordinary income. One-half of that amount ($1,000) is attributable to the portion of A's interest in PRS transferred to T. Accordingly, A will recognize $1,000 ordinary income and $2,500 ($3,500 − $1,000) of capital gain on account of the transfer to T of one-half of A's interest in PRS. Fifty percent ($1,250) of that gain is long-term capital gain and 50 percent ($1,250) is short-term capital gain.

Example 6. Sale of units of interests in a partnership. A publicly traded partnership (PRS) has ownership interests that are segregated into identifiable units of interest. A owns 10 limited partnership units in PRS for which A paid $10,000 on January 1, 1999. On August 1, 2000, A purchases five additional units for $10,000. At the time of purchase, the fair market value of each unit has increased to $2,000. A's holding period for one-third ($10,000/$30,000) of the interest in PRS begins on the day after the purchase of the five additional units. Less than one year later, A sells five units of ownership in PRS for $11,000. At the time, A's basis in the 15 units PRS is $20,000, and A's capital gain on the sale of 5 units is $4,333 (amount realized of $11,000 − one-third of the adjusted basis or $6,667). For purposes of determining the holding period, A can designate the specific units of PRS sold. If A properly identifies the five units sold as five of the ten units for

Reg. § 1.1223-3(f)

which A has a long-term holding period and elects to use the identification method for all subsequent sales or exchanges of interests in the partnership by using the actual holding period in reporting the transaction on A's federal income tax return, the capital gain realized will be long-term capital gain.

Example 7. Disproportionate distribution. In 1997, A and B each contribute cash of $50,000 to form and become equal partners in a partnership (PRS). More than one year later, A receives a distribution worth $22,000 from PRS, which reduces A's interest in PRS to 36 percent. After the distribution, B owns 64 percent of PRS. The holding periods of A and B in their interests in PRS are not affected by the distribution.

Example 8. Gain or loss as a result of a distribution—(i) On January 1, 1996, A contributes property with a basis of $10 and a fair market value of $10,000 in exchange for an interest in a partnership (ABC). On September 30, 2000, when A's interest in ABC is worth $12,000 (and the basis of A's partnership interest is still $10), A contributes $12,000 cash in exchange for an additional interest in ABC. A is allocated a loss equal to $10,000 by ABC for the taxable year ending December 31, 2000, thereby reducing the basis of A's partnership interest to $2,010. On February 1, 2001, ABC makes a cash distribution to A of $10,000. ABC holds no inventory or unrealized receivables. (Assume that A is allocated no gain or loss for the taxable year ending December 31, 2001, so that the basis of A's partnership interest does not increase or decrease as a result of such allocations.)

(ii) The netting rule contained in paragraph (b)(2) of this section provides that, in determining the holding period of A's interest in ABC, the cash contribution made on September 30, 2000, must be reduced by the distribution made on February 1, 2001. Accordingly, for purposes of determining the holding period of A's interest in ABC, A is treated as having made a cash contribution of $2,000 ($12,000 − $10,000) to ABC on September 30, 2000. A's holding period in one-seventh of A's interest in ABC ($2,000 cash contributed over the $14,000 value of the entire interest (determined as if only $2,000 were contributed rather than $12,000)) begins on the day after the cash contribution. A recognizes $7,990 of capital gain as a result of the distribution. See section 731(a)(1). One-seventh of the capital gain recognized as a result of the distribution is short-term capital gain, and six-sevenths of the capital gain is long-term capital gain. After the distribution, A's basis in the interest in PRS is $0, and the holding period for the interest in PRS continues to be divided in the same proportions as before the distribution.

(g) *Effective date.* This section applies to transfers of partnership interests and distributions of property from a partnership that occur on or after September 21, 2000. [Reg. § 1.1223-3.]

☐ [T.D. 8902, 9-20-2000.]

Special Rules for Determining Capital Gains and Losses
[Reg. § 1.1231-1]

§ 1.1231-1. **Gains and losses from the sale or exchange of certain property used in the trade or business.**—(a) *In general.* Section 1231 provides that, subject to the provisions of paragraph (e) of this section, a taxpayer's gains and losses from the disposition (including involuntary conversion) of assets described in that section as "property used in the trade or business" and from the involuntary conversion of capital assets held for more than 1 year (6 months for taxable years beginning before 1977; 9 months for taxable years beginning in 1977) shall be treated as long-term capital gains and losses if the total gains exceed the total losses. If the total gains do not exceed the total losses, all such gains and losses are treated as ordinary gains and losses. Therefore, if the taxpayer has no gains subject to section 1231, a recognized loss from the condemnation (or from a sale or exchange under threat of condemnation) of even a capital asset held for more than 1 year (6 months for taxable years beginning before 1977; 9 months for taxable years beginning in 1977) is an ordinary loss. Capital assets subject to section 1231 treatment include only capital assets involuntarily converted. The noncapital assets subject to section 1231 treatment are (1) depreciable business property and business real property held for more than 1 year (6 months for taxable years beginning before 1977; 9 months for taxable years beginning in 1977), other than stock in trade and certain copyrights and artistic property and, in the case of sales and other dispositions occurring after July 25, 1969, other than a letter, memorandum, or property similar to a letter or memorandum; (2) timber, coal, and iron ore which do not otherwise meet the requirements of section 1231 but with respect to which section 631 applies; and (3) certain livestock and unharvested crops. See paragraph (c) of this section.

(b) *Treatment of gains and losses.* For the purpose of applying section 1231, a taxpayer must aggregate his recognized gains and losses from—

(1) The sale, exchange, or involuntary conversion of property used in the trade or business (as defined in section 1231(b)), and

Reg. § 1.1231-1(a)

Rules for Determining Capital Gains and Losses

See p. 20,601 for regulations not amended to reflect law changes

(2) The involuntary conversion (but not sale or exchange) of capital assets held for more than 1 year (6 months for taxable years beginning before 1977; 9 months for taxable years beginning in 1977).

If the gains to which section 1231 applies exceed the losses to which the section applies, the gains and losses are treated as long-term capital gains and losses and are subject to the provisions of parts I and II (section 1201 and following), subchapter P, chapter 1, of the Code, relating to capital gains and losses. If the gains to which section 1231 applies do not exceed the losses to which the section applies, the gains and losses are treated as ordinary gains and losses. Therefore, in the latter case, a loss from the involuntary conversion of a capital asset held for more than 1 year (6 months for taxable years beginning before 1977; 9 months for taxable years beginning in 1977) is treated as an ordinary loss and is not subject to the limitation on capital losses in section 1211. The phrase "involuntary conversion" is defined in paragraph (e) of this section.

(c) *Transactions to which section applies.* Section 1231 applies to recognized gains and losses from the following:

(1) The sale, exchange, or involuntary conversion of property held for more than 1 year (6 months for taxable years beginning before 1977; 9 months for taxable years beginning in 1977) and used in the taxpayer's trade or business, which is either real property or is of a character subject to the allowance for depreciation under section 167 (even though fully depreciated), and which is not—

(i) Property of a kind which would properly be includible in the inventory of the taxpayer if on hand at the close of the taxable year, or property held by the taxpayer primarily for sale to customers in the ordinary course of business;

(ii) A copyright, a literary, musical, or artistic composition, or similar property, or (in the case of sales and other dispositions occurring after July 25, 1969) a letter, memorandum, or property similar to a letter or memorandum, held by a taxpayer described in section 1221(3); or

(iii) Livestock held for draft, breeding, dairy, or sporting purposes, except to the extent included under subparagraph (4) of this paragraph, or poultry.

(2) The involuntary conversion of capital assets held for more than 1 year (6 months for taxable years beginning before 1977; 9 months for taxable years beginning in 1977).

(3) The cutting or disposal of timber, or the disposal of coal or iron ore, to the extent considered arising from a sale or exchange by reason of the provisions of section 631 and the regulations thereunder.

(4) The sale, exchange, or involuntary conversion of livestock if the requirements of § 1.1231-2 are met.

(5) The sale, exchange, or involuntary conversion of unharvested crops on land which is (i) used in the taxpayer's trade or business and held for more than 1 year (6 months for taxable years beginning before 1977; 9 months for taxable years beginning in 1977), and (ii) sold or exchanged at the same time and to the same person. See paragraph (f) of this section. For purposes of section 1231, the phrase "property used in the trade or business" means property described in this paragraph (other than property described in subparagraph (2) of this paragraph). Notwithstanding any of the provisions of this paragraph, section 1231(a) does not apply to gains and losses under the circumstances described in paragraph (e)(2) or (3) of this section.

(d) *Extent to which gains and losses are taken into account.* All gains and losses to which section 1231 applies must be taken into account in determining whether and to what extent the gains exceed the losses. For the purpose of this computation, the provisions of section 1211 limiting the deduction of capital losses do not apply, and no losses are excluded by that section. With that exception, gains are included in the computations under section 1231 only to the extent that they are taken into account in computing gross income, and losses are included only to the extent that they are taken into account in computing taxable income. The following are examples of gains and losses not included in the computations under section 1231:

(1) Losses of a personal nature which are not deductible by reason of section 165(c) or (d), such as losses from the sale of property held for personal use;

(2) Losses which are not deductible under section 267 (relating to losses with respect to transactions between related taxpayers) or section 1091 (relating to losses from wash sales);

(3) Gain on the sale of property (to which section 1231 applies) reported for any taxable year on the installment method under section 453, except to the extent the gain is to be reported under section 453 for the taxable year; and

(4) Gains and losses which are not recognized under section 1002, such as those to which sections 1031 through 1036, relating to common nontaxable exchanges, apply.

Reg. § 1.1231-1(d)(4)

53,444 Rules for Determining Capital Gains and Losses
See p. 20,601 for regulations not amended to reflect law changes

(e) *Involuntary conversion*—(1) *General rule.* For purposes of section 1231, the terms "compulsory or involuntary conversion" and "involuntary conversion" of property mean the conversion of property into money or other property as a result of complete or partial destruction, theft or seizure, or an exercise of the power of requisition or condemnation, or the threat of imminence thereof. Losses upon the complete or partial destruction, theft, seizure, requisition, or condemnation of property are treated as losses upon an involuntary conversion whether or not there is a conversion of the property into other property or money and whether or not the property is uninsured, partially insured, or totally insured. For example, if a capital asset held for more than 1 year (6 months for taxable years beginning before 1977; 9 months for taxable years beginning in 1977), with an adjusted basis of $400, but not held for the production of income, is stolen, and the loss which is sustained in the taxable year 1956 is not compensated for by insurance or otherwise, section 1231 applies to the $400 loss. For certain exceptions to this subparagraph, see subparagraphs (2) and (3) of this paragraph.

(2) *Certain uninsured losses.* Notwithstanding the provisions of subparagraph (1) of this paragraph, losses sustained during a taxable year beginning after December 31, 1957, and before January 1, 1970, with respect to both property used in the trade or business and any capital asset held for more than 6 months and held for the production of income, which losses arise from fire, storm, shipwreck, or other casualty, or from theft, and which are not compensated for by insurance in any amount, are not losses to which section 1231(a) applies. Such losses shall not be taken into account in applying the provisions of this section.

(3) *Exclusion of gains and losses from certain involuntary conversions.* Notwithstanding the provisions of subparagraph (1) of this paragraph, if for any taxable year beginning after December 31, 1969, the recognized losses from the involuntary conversion as a result of fire, storm, shipwreck, or other casualty, or from theft, of any property used in the trade or business or of any capital asset held for more than 1 year (6 months for taxable years beginning before 1977; 9 months for taxable years beginning in 1977) exceed the recognized gains from the involuntary conversion of any such property as a result of fire, storm, shipwreck, or other casualty, or from theft, such gains and losses are not gains and losses to which section 1231 applies and shall not be taken into account in applying the provisions of this section. The net loss, in effect, will be treated as an ordinary loss. This subparagraph shall apply whether such property is uninsured, partially insured, or totally insured and, in the case of a capital asset held for more than 1 year (6 months for taxable years beginning before 1977; 9 months for taxable years beginning in 1977), whether the property is property used in the trade or business, property held for the production of income, or a personal asset.

(f) *Unharvested crops.*—Section 1231 does not apply to a sale, exchange or involuntary conversion of an unharvested crop if the taxpayer retains any right or option to reacquire the land the crop is on, directly or indirectly (other than a right customarily incident to a mortgage or other security transaction). The length of time for which the crop, as distinguished from the land, is held is immaterial. A leasehold or estate for years is not "land" for the purpose of section 1231.

(g) *Examples.* The provisions of this section may be illustrated by the following examples:

Example (1). A, an individual, makes his income tax return on the calendar year basis. A's recognized gains and losses for 1957 of the kind described in section 1231 are as follows:

	Gains	Losses
1. Gain on sale of machinery, used in the business and subject to an allowance for depreciation, held for more than 6 months	$4,000	
2. Gain reported in 1957 (under sec. 453) on installment sale in 1956 of factory premises used in the business (including building and land, each held for more than 6 months)	6,000	
3. Gain reported in 1957 (under sec. 453) on installment sale in 1957 of land held for more than 6 months, used in the business as a storage lot for trucks	2,000	
4. Gain on proceeds from requisition by Government of boat, held for more than 6 months, used in the business and subject to an allowance for depreciation	500	
5. Loss upon the destruction by fire of warehouse, held for more than 6 months and used in the business (excess of adjusted basis of warehouse over compensation by insurance, etc.)		$3,000
6. Loss upon theft of unregistered bearer bonds, held for more than 6 months		5,000
7. Loss in storm of pleasure yacht, purchased in 1950 for $1,800 and having a fair market value of $1,000 at the time of the storm		1,000
8. Total gains	$12,500	
9. Total losses		$9,000
10. Excess of gains over losses	$3,500	

Reg. § 1.1231-1(e)(1)

Rules for Determining Capital Gains and Losses 53,445
See p. 20,601 for regulations not amended to reflect law changes

Since the aggregate of the recognized gains ($12,500) exceeds the aggregate of the recognized losses ($9,000), such gains and losses are treated under section 1231 as gains and losses from the sale or exchange of capital assets held for more than six months. For any taxable year ending after December 31, 1957, and before January 1, 1970, the $5,000 loss upon theft of bonds (item 6) would not be taken into account under section 1231. See paragraph (e)(2) of this section.

Example (2). If in example (1), A also had a loss of $4,000 from the sale under threat of condemnation of a capital asset acquired for profit and held for more than six months, then the gains ($12,500) would not exceed the losses ($9,000 plus $4,000 or $13,000). Neither the loss on that sale nor any of the other items set forth in example (1) would then be treated as gains and losses from the sale or exchange of capital assets, but all of such items would be treated as ordinary gains and losses. Likewise, if A had no other gain or loss, the $4,000 loss would be treated as an ordinary loss.

Example (3). A's yacht, used for pleasure and acquired for that use in 1945 at a cost of $25,000, was requisitioned by the Government in 1957 for $15,000. A sustained no loss deductible under section 165(c) and since no loss with respect to the requisition is recognizable, the loss will not be included in the computations under section 1231.

Example (4). A, an individual, makes his income tax return on a calendar year basis. During 1970 trees on A's residential property which were planted in 1950 after the purchase of such property were destroyed by fire. The loss, which was in the amount of $2,000 after applying section 165(c)(3), was not compensated for by insurance or otherwise. During the same year A also recognized a $1,500 gain from insurance proceeds compensating him for the theft sustained in 1970 of a diamond brooch purchased in 1960 for personal use. A has no other gains or losses for 1970 from the involuntary conversion of property. Since the recognized losses exceed the recognized gains from the involuntary conversion for 1970 as a result of fire, storm, shipwreck, or other casualty, or from theft, of any property used in the trade or business or of any capital asset held for more than 6 months, neither the gain nor loss is included in making the computations under section 1231.

Example (5). The facts are the same as in example (4), except that A also recognized a gain of $1,000 from insurance proceeds compensating him for the total destruction by fire of a truck, held for more than 6 months, used in A's business and subject to an allowance for depreciation. A has no other gains or losses for 1970 from the involuntary conversion of property. Since the recognized losses ($2,000) do not exceed the recognized gains ($2,500) from the involuntary conversion for 1970 as a result of fire, storm, shipwreck, or other casualty, or from theft, of any property used in the trade or business or of any capital asset held for more than 6 months, such gains and losses are included in making the computations under section 1231. Thus, if A has no other gains or losses for 1970 to which section 1231 applies, the gains and losses from these involuntary conversions are treated under section 1231 as gains and losses from the sale or exchange of capital assets held for more than 6 months.

Example (6). The facts are the same as in example (5) except that A also has the following recognized gains and losses for 1970 to which section 1231 applies:

	Gains	Losses
Gain on sale of machinery, used in the business and subject to an allowance for depreciation, held for more than 6 months	$4,000	
Gain reported in 1970 (under sec. 453) on installment sale in 1969 of factory premises used in the business (including building and land, each held for more than 6 months)	6,000	
Gain reported in 1970 (under sec. 453) on installment sale in 1970 of land held for more than 6 months, used in the business as a storage lot for trucks	2,000	
Loss upon the sale in 1970 of warehouse, used in the business and subject to an allowance for depreciation, held for more than 6 months		$5,000
Total gains	12,000	
Total losses		5,000

Since the aggregate of the recognized gains ($14,500) exceeds the aggregate of the recognized losses ($7,000), such gains and losses are treated under section 1231 as gains and losses from the sale or exchange of capital assets held for more than 6 months.

Example (7). B, an individual, makes his income tax return on the calendar year basis. During 1970 furniture used in his business and held for more than 6 months was destroyed by fire. The recognized loss, after compensation by insurance, was $2,000. During the same year B recognized a

Reg. § 1.1231-1(g)

53,446 Rules for Determining Capital Gains and Losses

See p. 20,601 for regulations not amended to reflect law changes

$1,000 gain upon the sale of a parcel of real estate used in his business and held for more than 6 months, and a $6,000 loss upon the sale of stock held for more than 6 months. B has no other gains or losses for 1970 from the involuntary conversion, or the sale or exchange of, property. The $6,000 loss upon the sale of stock is not a loss to which section 1231 applies since the stock is not property used in the trade or business, as defined in section 1231(b). The $2,000 loss upon the destruction of the furniture is not a loss to which section 1231 applies since the recognized losses ($2,000) exceed the recognized gains ($0) from the involuntary conversion for 1970 as a result of fire, storm, shipwreck, or other casualty, or from theft, of any property used in the trade or business or of any capital asset held for more than 6 months. Accordingly, the $1,000 gain upon the sale of real estate is considered to be gain from the sale or exchange of a capital asset held for more than 6 months since the gains ($1,000) to which section 1231 applies exceed the losses ($0) to which such section applies.

Example (8). The facts are the same as in example (7) except that B also recognized a gain of $4,000 from insurance proceeds compensating him for the total destruction by fire of a freighter, held for more than 6 months, used in B's business and subject to an allowance for depreciation. Since the recognized losses ($2,000) do not exceed the recognized gains ($4,000) from the involuntary conversion for 1970 as a result of fire, storm, shipwreck, or other casualty, or from theft, of any property used in the trade or business or of any capital asset held for more than 6 months, such gains and losses are included in making the computations under section 1231. Since the aggregate of the recognized gains to which section 1231 applies ($5,000) exceeds the aggregate of the recognized losses to which such section applies ($2,000), such gains and losses are treated under section 1231 as gains and losses from the sale or exchange of capital assets held for more than 6 months. The $6,000 loss upon the sale of stock is not taken into account in making such computation since it is not a loss to which section 1231 applies. [Reg. § 1.1231-1.]

☐ [T.D. 6253, 9-25-57. Amended by T.D. 6394, 7-1-59; T.D. 6841, 7-26-65; T.D. 7141, 9-21-71; T.D. 7369, 7-15-75; T.D. 7728, 10-31-80 and T.D. 7829, 8-31-82.]

[Reg. § 1.1231-2]

§ 1.1231-2. **Livestock held for draft, breeding, dairy, or sporting purposes.**—(a) (1) In the case of cattle, horses, or other livestock acquired by the taxpayer after December 31, 1969, section 1231 applies to the sale, exchange, or involuntary conversion of such cattle, horses, or other livestock, regardless of age, held by the taxpayer for draft, breeding, dairy, or sporting purposes, and held by him—

(i) For 24 months or more from the date of acquisition in the case of cattle or horses, or

(ii) For 12 months or more from the date of acquisition in the case of such other livestock.

(2) In the case of livestock (including cattle or horses) acquired by the taxpayer on or before December 31, 1969, section 1231 applies to the sale, exchange, or involuntary conversion of such livestock, regardless of age, held by the taxpayer for draft, breeding, or dairy purposes, and held by him for 12 months or more from the date of acquisition.

(3) For the purposes of section 1231, the term "livestock" is given a broad, rather than a narrow, interpretation and includes cattle, hogs, horses, mules, donkeys, sheep, goats, fur-bearing animals, and other mammals. However, it does not include poultry, chickens, turkeys, pigeons, geese, other birds, fish, frogs, reptiles, etc.

(b)(1) Whether or not livestock is held by the taxpayer for draft, breeding, dairy, or sporting purposes depends upon all of the facts and circumstances in each case. The purpose for which the animal is held is ordinarily shown by the taxpayer's actual use of the animal. However, a draft, breeding, dairy, or sporting purpose may be present if an animal is disposed of within a reasonable time after its intended use for such purpose is prevented or made undesirable by reason of accident, disease, drought, unfitness of the animal for such purpose, or a similar factual circumstance. Under certain circumstances, an animal held for ultimate sale to customers in the ordinary course of the taxpayer's trade or business may be considered as held for draft, breeding, dairy, or sporting purposes. However, an animal is not held by the taxpayer for draft, breeding, dairy, or sporting purposes merely because it is suitable for such purposes or merely because it is held by the taxpayer for sale to other persons for use by them for such purposes. Furthermore, an animal held by the taxpayer for other purposes is not considered as held for draft, breeding, dairy, or sporting purposes merely because of a negligible use of the animal for such purposes or merely because of the use of the animal for such purposes as an ordinary or necessary incident to the other purposes for which the animal is held. See paragraph (c) of this section for the rules to be used in determining when horses are held for racing purposes and, therefore, are considered as held for sporting purposes.

Reg. § 1.1231-2(a)(2)

Rules for Determining Capital Gains and Losses

(2) The application of this paragraph is illustrated by the following examples:

Example (1). An animal intended by the taxpayer for use by him for breeding purposes is discovered to be sterile or unfit for the breeding purposes for which it was held, and is disposed of within a reasonable time thereafter. This animal is considered as held for breeding purposes.

Example (2). The taxpayer retires from the breeding or dairy business and sells his entire herd, including young animals which would have been used by him for breeding or dairy purposes if he had remained in business. These young animals are considered as held for breeding or dairy purposes. The same would be true with respect to young animals which would have been used by the taxpayer for breeding or dairy purposes but which are sold by him in reduction of his breeding or dairy herd, because of, for example, drought.

Example (3). A taxpayer in the business of raising hogs for slaughter customarily breeds sows to obtain a single litter to be raised by him for sale, and sells these brood sows after obtaining the litter. Even though these brood sows are held for ultimate sale to customers in the ordinary course of the taxpayer's trade or business, they are considered as held for breeding purposes.

Example (4). A taxpayer in the business of raising horses for sale to others for use by them as draft horses uses them for draft purposes on his own farm in order to train them. This use is an ordinary or necessary incident to the purpose of selling the animals, and, accordingly, these horses are not considered as held for draft purposes.

Example (5). The taxpayer is in the business of raising registered cattle for sale to others for use by them as breeding cattle. It is the business practice of this particular taxpayer to breed the offspring of his herd which he is holding for sale to others prior to sale in order to establish their fitness for sale as registered breeding cattle. In such case, the taxpayer's breeding of such offspring is an ordinary and necessary incident to his holding them for the purpose of selling them as bred heifers or proven bulls and does not demonstrate that the taxpayer is holding them for breeding purposes. However, those cattle held by the taxpayer as additions or replacements to his own breeding herd to produce calves are considered to be held for breeding purposes, even though they may not actually have produced calves.

Example (6). A taxpayer, engaged in the business of buying cattle and fattening them for slaughter, purchased cows with calf. The calves were born while the cows were held by the taxpayer. These cows are not considered as held for breeding purposes.

(c)(1) For purposes of paragraph (b) of this section, a horse held for racing purposes shall be considered as held for sporting purposes. Whether a horse is held for racing purposes shall be determined in accordance with the following rules:

(i) A horse which has actually been raced at a public race track shall, except in rare and unusual circumstances, be considered as held for racing purposes.

(ii) A horse which has not been raced at a public track shall be considered as held for racing purposes if it has been trained to race and other facts and circumstances in the particular case also indicate that the horse was held for this purpose. For example, assume that the taxpayer maintains a written training record on all horses he keeps in training status, which shows that a particular horse does not meet objective standards (including, but not limited to, such considerations as failure to achieve predetermined standards of performance during training, or the existence of a physical or other defect) established by the taxpayer for determining the fitness and quality of horses to be retained in his racing stable. Under such circumstances, if the taxpayer disposes of the horse within a reasonable time after he determined that it did not meet his objective standards for retention, the horse shall be considered as held for racing purposes.

(iii) A horse which has neither been raced at a public track nor trained for racing shall not, except in rare and unusual circumstances, be considered as held for racing purposes.

(2) This paragraph may be illustrated by the following examples:

Example (1). The taxpayer breeds, raises, and trains horses for the purpose of racing. Every year he culls some horses from his racing stable. In 1971, the taxpayer decided that in order to prevent his racing stable from getting too large to be effectively operated he must cull six horses from it. All six of the horses culled by the taxpayer had been raced at public tracks in 1970. Under subparagraph (1)(i) of this paragraph, all these horses are considered as held for racing purposes.

Example (2). Assume the same facts as in example (1). Assume further that the taxpayer decided to cull four more horses from his racing stable in 1971. All these horses had been trained to race but had not been raced at public tracks. The taxpayer culled these four horses because the training log which the taxpayer maintains on all the horses he trains showed these horses to be unfit to remain in his racing stable. Horse A was culled because it developed shin splints during training. Horses B and C were culled because of

Reg. § 1.1231-2(c)(2)

poor temperament. B bolted every time a rider tried to mount it, and C became extremely nervous when it was placed in the starting gate. Horse D was culled because it did not qualify for retention under one of the objective standards the taxpayer had established for determining which horses to retain since it was unable to run a specified distance in a minimum time. These four horses were disposed of within a reasonable time after the taxpayer determined that they were unfit to remain in his stable. Under subparagraph (1)(ii) of this paragraph, all these horses are considered as held for racing purposes. [Reg. § 1.1231-2.]

☐ [T.D. 6253, 9-25-57. Amended by T.D. 7141, 9-21-71.]

[Reg. § 1.1232-1]

§ 1.1232-1. Bonds and other evidences of indebtedness; scope of section.—(a) *In general.* Section 1232 applies to any bond, debenture, note, or certificate or other evidence of indebtedness (referred to in this section and §§ 1.1232-2 through 1.1232-4 as an obligation) (1) which is a capital asset in the hands of the taxpayer, and (2) which is issued by any corporation, or by any government or political subdivision thereof. In general, section 1232(a)(1) provides that the retirement of an obligation, other than certain obligations issued before January 1, 1955, is considered to be an exchange and, therefore, is usually subject to capital gain or loss treatment. In general, section 1232(a)(2)(B) provides that in the case of a gain realized on the sale or exchange of certain obligations issued at a discount after December 31, 1954, which are either corporate bonds issued on or before May 27, 1969, or government bonds, the amount of gain equal to such discount or, under certain circumstances, the amount of gain equal to a specified portion of such discount, constitutes ordinary income. In the case of certain corporate obligations issued after May 27, 1969, in general, section 1232(a)(3) provides for the inclusion as interest in gross income of a ratable portion of original issue discount for each taxable year over the life of the obligation, section 1232(a)(3)(E) provides for an increase in basis equal to the original issue discount included in gross income, and section 1232(a)(2)(A) provides that any gain realized on such an obligation held more than 1 year (6 months for taxable years beginning before 1977; 9 months for taxable years beginning in 1977) shall be considered gain from the sale or exchange of a capital asset held more than 1 year (6 months for taxable years beginning before 1977; 9 months for taxable years beginning in 1977). For the requirements for reporting original issue discount on certain obligations issued after May 27, 1969, see section 6049(a) and the regulations thereunder. Section 1232(c) treats as ordinary income a portion of any gain realized upon the disposition of (i) coupon obligations which were acquired after August 16, 1954, and before January 1, 1958, without all coupons maturing more than 12 months after purchase attached, and (ii) coupon obligations which were acquired after December 31, 1957, without all coupons maturing after the date of purchase attached.

(b) *Requirement that obligations be capital assets.* In order for section 1232 to be applicable, an obligation must be a capital asset in the hands of the taxpayer. See section 1221 and the regulations thereunder. Obligations held by a dealer in securities (except as provided in section 1236) or obligations arising from the sale of inventory or personal services by the holder are not capital assets. However, obligations held by a financial institution, as defined in section 582(c) (relating to treatment of losses and gains on bonds of certain financial institutions) for investment and not primarily for sale to customers in the ordinary course of the financial institution's trade or business, are capital assets. Thus, with respect to obligations held as capital assets by such a financial institution which are corporate obligations to which section 1232(a)(3) applies, there is ratable inclusion of original issue discount as interest in gross income under paragraph (a) of § 1.1232-3A, and gain on a sale or exchange (including retirement) may be subject to ordinary income treatment under section 582(c) and paragraph (a)(1) of § 1.1232-3.

(c) *Face-amount certificates*—(1) *In general.* For purposes of section 1232, this section and §§ 1.1232-2 through 1.1232-4, the term "other evidence of indebtedness" includes "face amount certificates" as defined in section 2(a)(15) and (4) of the Investment Company Act of 1940 (15 U.S.C. 80a-2 and 80a-4).

(2) *Amounts received in taxable years beginning prior to January 1, 1964.* Amounts received in taxable years beginning prior to January 1, 1964 under face-amount certificates which were issued after December 31, 1954, are subject to the limitation on tax under section 72(e)(3). See paragraph (g) of § 1.72-11 (relating to limit on tax attributable to receipt of a lump sum received as an annuity payment). However, section 72(e)(3) does not apply to any such amounts received in taxable years beginning after December 31, 1963.

(3) *Certificates issued after December 31, 1975.* In the case of a face-amount certificate issued after December 31, 1975 (other than such a certificate issued pursuant to a written commitment which was binding on such date and at all

Reg. § 1.1232-1(a)

Rules for Determining Capital Gains and Losses

times thereafter), the provisions of section 1232(a)(3) (relating to the ratable inclusion of original issue discount in gross income) shall apply. See § 1.1232-3A(f). For treatment of any increase in basis under section 1232(a)(3)(A) as consideration paid for purposes of computing the investment in the contract under section 72, see § 1.72-6(c)(4).

(d) *Certain deposits in financial institutions.* For purposes of section 1232, this section and §§ 1.1232-2 through 1.1232-4, the term "other evidence of indebtedness" includes certificates of deposit, time deposits, bonus plans, and other deposit arrangements with banks, domestic building and loan associations, and similar financial institutions. For application of section 1232 to such deposits, see paragraph (e) of § 1.1232-3A. However, section 1232, this section, and §§ 1.1232-2 through 1.1232-4 shall not apply to such deposits made prior to January 1, 1971. For treatment of renewable certificates of deposit, see paragraph (e)(4) of § 1.1232-3A. [Reg. § 1.1232-1.]

☐ [*T.D.* 6253, 9-25-57. *Amended by T.D.* 6468, 6-6-60, *T.D.* 7154, 12-27-71, *T.D.* 7311, 3-29-74, *T.D.* 7336, 12-19-74; *T.D.* 7365, 6-30-75 and *T.D.* 7728, 10-31-80.]

[Reg. § 1.1232-2]

§ 1.1232-2. **Retirement.**—Section 1232(a)(1) provides that any amount received by the holder upon the retirement of an obligation shall be considered as an amount received in exchange therefor. However, section 1232(a)(1) does not apply in the case of an obligation issued before January 1, 1955, which was not issued with interest coupons or in registered form on March 1, 1954. For treatment of gain on an obligation held by certain financial institutions, see section 582(c) and paragraph (a)(1)(iii) of § 1.1232-3. [Reg. § 1.1232-2.]

☐ [*T.D.* 6253, 9-25-57. *Amended by T.D.* 7154, 12-27-71.]

[Reg. § 1.1232-3]

§ 1.1232-3. **Gain upon sale or exchange of obligations issued at a discount.**—(a) *General rule; sale or exchange*—(1) *Obligations issued by a corporation after May 27, 1969*—(i) *General rule.* Under section 1232(a)(2)(A), in the case of gain realized upon the sale or exchange of an obligation issued at a discount by a corporation after May 27, 1969 (other than an obligation subject to the transitional rule of subparagraph (4) of this paragraph), and held by the taxpayer for more than 1 year (6 months for taxable years beginning before 1977; 9 months for taxable years beginning in 1977)—

(a) If at the time of original issue there was no intention to call the obligation before maturity, such gain shall be considered as long-term capital gain, or

(b) If at the time of original issue there was an intention to call the obligation before maturity, such gain shall be considered ordinary income to the extent it does not exceed the excess of—

(1) An amount equal to the entire "original issue discount", over

(2) An amount equal to the entire "original issue discount" multiplied by a fraction the numerator of which is the sum of the number of complete months and any fractional part of a month elapsed since the date of original issue and the denominator of which is the number of complete months and any fractional part of a month from the date of original issue to the stated maturity date.

The balance, if any, of the gain shall be considered as long-term capital gain. The amount described in (2) of this subdivision (b) in effect reduces the amount of original issue discount to be treated as ordinary income under this subdivision (b) by the amounts previously includible (regardless of whether included) by all holders (computed, however, as to any holder without regard to any purchase allowance under paragraph (a)(2)(ii) of § 1.1232-3A and without regard to whether any holder purchased at a premium as defined in paragraph (d)(2) of § 1.1232-3).

(ii) *Cross references.* For definition of the terms "original issue discount" and "intention to call before maturity", see paragraph (b)(1) and (4) respectively of this section. For definition of the term "date of original issue", see paragraph (b)(3) of this section. For computation of the number of complete months and any fractional portion of a month, see paragraph (a)(3) of § 1.1232-3A.

(iii) *Effect of section 582(c).* Gain shall not be considered to be long-term capital gain under subdivision (i) of this subparagraph if section 582(c) (relating to treatment of losses and gains on bonds of certain financial institutions) applies.

(2) *Examples.* The provisions of subparagraph (1) of this paragraph may be illustrated by the following examples:

Example (1). On January 1, 1970, A, a calendar-year taxpayer, purchases at original issue for cash of $7,600, M Corporation's 10-year, 5 percent bond which has a stated redemption price at maturity of $10,000. On January 1, 1972, A sells the bond to B, for $9,040. A has previously included $480 of the original issue discount in his

Reg. § 1.1232-3(a)(2)

53,450 Rules for Determining Capital Gains and Losses

See p. 20,601 for regulations not amended to reflect law changes

gross income (see example (1) of paragraph (d) of § 1.1232-3A) and increased his basis in the bond by that amount to $8,080 (see paragraph (c) of § 1.1232-3A). Thus, if at the time of original issue there was no intention to call the bond before maturity, A's gain of $960 (amount realized, $9,040, less adjusted basis, $8,080) is considered long-term capital gain.

Example (2). (i) Assume the same facts as in example (1), except that at the time of original issue there was an intention to call the bond before maturity. The amount of the entire gain includible by A as ordinary income under subparagraph (1)(ii) of this paragraph is determined as follows:

(1) Entire original issue discount (stated redemption price at maturity, $10,000, minus issue price, $7,600) . . $2,400
(2) Less: Line (1), $2,400, multiplied by months elapsed since date of original issue, 24, divided by months from such date to stated maturity date, 120 . . . . $ 480
(3) Maximum amount includible by A as ordinary income $1,920

Since the amount in line (3) is greater than A's gain, $960, A's entire gain is includible as ordinary income.

(ii) On January 1, 1979, B, a calendar-year taxpayer, sells the bond to C for $10,150. Assume that B has included $120 of original issue discount in his gross income for each taxable year he held the bond (see example (2) of paragraph (d) of § 1.1232-3A) and therefore increased his basis by $840 (*i.e.*, $120 each year × 7 years) to $9,880. B's gain is therefore $270 (amount realized, $10,150, less basis, $9,880). The amount of such gain includible by B as ordinary income under subparagraph (1)(ii) of this paragraph is determined as follows:

(1) Entire original issue discount (as determined in part (i) of this example) $2,400
(2) Less: Line (1), $2,400, multiplied by months elapsed since date of original issue, 108, divided by months from such date to stated maturity date, 120 . . . . $2,160
(3) Maximum amount includible by B as ordinary income . . . . $ 240

Since the amount in line (3) is less than B's gain, $270, only $240 of B's gain is includible as ordinary income. The remaining portion of B's gain, $30, is considered long-term capital gain.

(3) *Obligations issued by a corporation on or before May 27, 1969, and government obligations.*
Under section 1232(a)(2)(B), if gain is realized on the sale or exchange after December 31, 1957, of an obligation held by the taxpayer more than 6 months, and if the obligation either was issued at a discount after December 31, 1954, and on or before May 27, 1969, by a corporation or was issued at a discount after December 31, 1954, by or on behalf of the United States or a foreign country, or a political subdivision of either, then such gain shall be considered ordinary income to the extent it does not exceed—

(i) An amount equal to the entire "original issue discount," or

(ii) If at the time of original issue there was no intention to call the obligation before maturity, a portion of the "original issue discount" determined in accordance with paragraph (c) of this section,

and the balance, if any, of the gain shall be considered as long-term capital gain. For the definition of the terms "original issue discount" and "intention to call before maturity," see paragraph (b)(1) and (4) respectively of this section. See section 1037(b) and paragraph (b) of § 1.1037-1 for special rules which are applicable in applying section 1232(a)(2)(B) and this subparagraph to gain realized on the disposition or redemption of obligations of the United States which were received from the United States in an exchange upon which gain or loss is not recognized because of section 1037(a) (or so much of section 1031(b) or (c) as relates to section 1037(a)).

(4) *Transitional rule.* Subparagraph (3) of this paragraph (in lieu of subparagraph (1) thereof) shall apply to an obligation issued by a corporation pursuant to a written commitment which was binding on May 27, 1969, and at all times thereafter.

(5) *Obligations issued after December 31, 1954, and sold or exchanged before January 1, 1958.* Gain realized upon the sale or exchange before January 1, 1958, of an obligation issued at a discount after December 31, 1954, and held by the taxpayer for more than 6 months, shall be considered ordinary income to the extent it equals a specified portion of the "original issue discount," and the balance, if any, of the gain shall be considered as long-term capital gain. The term "original issue discount" is defined in paragraph (b)(1) of this section. The computation of the amount of gain which constitutes ordinary income is illustrated in paragraph (c) of this section.

(6) *Obligations issued before January 1, 1955.* Whether gain representing original issue discount realized upon the sale or exchange of obligations issued at a discount before January 1,

Reg. § 1.1232-3(a)(3)

Rules for Determining Capital Gains and Losses

See p. 20,601 for regulations not amended to reflect law changes

1955, is capital gain or ordinary income shall be determined without reference to section 1232.

(b) *Definitions*—(1) *Original issue discount* — (i) *In general.* For purposes of section 1232, the term "original issue discount" means the difference between the issue price and the stated redemption price at maturity. The stated redemption price is determined without regard to optional call dates.

(ii) *De minimis rule.* If the original issue discount is less than one-fourth of 1 percent of the stated redemption price at maturity multiplied by the number of full years from the date of original issue to maturity, then the discount shall be considered to be zero. For example, a 10-year bond with a stated redemption price at maturity of $100 issued at $98 would be regarded as having an original issue discount of zero. Thus, any gain realized by the holder would be a long-term capital gain if the bond was a capital asset in the hands of the holder and held by him for more than 1 year (6 months for taxable years beginning before 1977; 9 months for taxable years beginning in 1977). However, if the bond were issued at $97.50 or less, the original issue discount would not be considered zero.

(iii) *Stated redemption price at maturity*—(*a*) *Definition.* Except as otherwise provided in this subdivision (iii), the term "stated redemption price at maturity" means the amount fixed by the last modification of the purchase agreement, including dividends, interest, and any other amounts, however designated, payable at that time. If any amount based on a fixed rate of simple or compound interest is actually payable or will be treated as constructively received under section 451 and the regulations thereunder either—

(*1*) At fixed periodic intervals of one year or less during the entire term of an obligation, or

(*2*) Except as provided in subdivision (e) of this paragraph (b)(1)(iii), at maturity in the case of an obligation with a term of one year or less,

any such amount payable at maturity shall not be included in determining the stated redemption price at maturity. For purposes of subdivision (*a*)(*2*) of this paragraph (b)(1)(iii), the term of an obligation shall include any renewal period with respect to which, under the terms of the obligation, the holder may either take action or refrain from taking action which would prevent the actual or constructive receipt of any interest on such obligation until the expiration of any such renewal period. To illustrate this paragraph (b)(1)(iii), assume that a note which promises to pay $1,000 at the end of three years provides for additional amounts labeled as interest to be paid at the rate of $50 at the end of the first year, $50 at the end of the second year, and $120 at the end of the third year. The stated redemption price at maturity will be $1,070 since only $50 of the $120 payable at the end of the third year is based on a fixed rate of simple or compound interest. If, however, the $120 were payable at the end of the second year, so that only $50 in addition to principal would be payable at the end of the third year, then under the rule for serial obligations contained in subparagraph (2)(iv)(c) of this paragraph, the $1,000 note is treated as consisting of two series. The first series is treated as maturing at the end of the second year at a stated redemption price of $70. The second series is treated as maturing at the end of the third year at a stated redemption price of $1,000. For the calculation of issue price and the allocation of original issue discount with respect to each such series, see example (3) of subparagraph (2)(iv)(*f*) of this paragraph.

(*b*) *Special rules.* In the case of face-amount certificates, the redemption price at maturity is the price as modified through changes such as extensions of the purchase agreement and includes any dividends which are payable at maturity. In the case of an obligation issued as part of an investment unit consisting of such obligation and an option (which is not excluded by (*c*) of this subdivision (iii)), security, or other property, the term "stated redemption price at maturity" means the amount payable on maturity in respect of the obligation, and does not include any amount payable in respect of the option, security, or other property under a repurchase agreement or option to buy or sell the option, security, or other property. For application of this subdivision to certain deposits in financial institutions, see paragraph (e) of § 1.1232-3A.

(*c*) *Excluded option.* An option is excluded by this subdivision (*c*) if it is an option to which paragraph (a) of § 1.61-15 applies or if it is an option, referred to in paragraph (a) of § 1.83-7, granted in connection with performance of services to which section 421 does not apply.

(*d*) *Obligation issued in installments.* If an obligation is issued by a corporation under terms whereby the holder makes installment payments, then the stated redemption price for each installment payment shall be computed in a manner consistent with the rules contained in subparagraph (2)(iv) of this paragraph for computing the issue price for each series of a serial obligation. For application of this subdivision (*d*) to certain

Reg. § 1.1232-3(b)(1)

open account deposit arrangements, see examples (1) and (2) of paragraph (e)(5)(ii) of § 1.1232-3A.

(e) *Application of definition.* Subdivision (a)(2) of this paragraph (b)(1)(iii) shall not apply—

(*1*) For taxable years beginning before September 19, 1979, if for the issuer's last taxable year beginning before September 19, 1978, the rules of § 1.163-4 were properly applied by the issuer, or

(*2*) In the case of an obligation with a term of six months or less held by a nonresident alien individual or foreign corporation, but only for purposes of the application of sections 871 and 881.

(iv) *Carryover of original issue discount.* If in pursuance of a plan of reorganization an obligation is received in an exchange for another obligation, and if gain or loss is not recognized in whole or in part on such exchange of obligations by reason, for example, of section 354 or 356, then the obligation received shall be considered to have the same original issue discount as the obligation surrendered reduced by the amount of gain (if any) recognized as ordinary income upon such exchange of obligations, and by the amount of original issue discount with respect to the obligation surrendered which was included as interest income under the ratable inclusion rules of section 1232(a)(3) and § 1.1232-3A. If inclusion as interest of the ratable monthly portion of original issue discount is required under section 1232(a)(3) with respect to the obligation received, see paragraph (a)(2)(iii) of § 1.1232-3A for computation of the ratable monthly portion of original issue discount. For special rules in connection with certain exchanges of U.S. obligations, see section 1037.

(2) *Issue price defined*—(i) *In general.* The term "issue price" in the case of obligations registered with the Securities and Exchange Commission means the initial offering price to the public at which price a substantial amount of such obligations were sold. For this purpose, the term "the public" does not include bond houses and brokers, or similar persons or organizations acting in the capacity of underwriters or wholesalers. Ordinarily, the issue price will be the first price at which the obligations were sold to the public, and the issue price will not change if, due to market developments, part of the issue must be sold at a different price. When obligations are privately placed, the issue price of each obligation is the price paid by the first buyer of the particular obligation, irrespective of the issue price of the remainder of the issue. In the case of an obligation issued by a foreign obligor, the issue price shall be increased by the amount, if any, of interest equalization tax paid under section 4911 (and not credited, refunded, or reimbursed) on the acquisition of the obligation by the first buyer. In the case of an obligation which is convertible into stock or another obligation, the issue price includes any amount paid in respect of the conversion privilege. However, in the case of an obligation issued as part of an investment unit (as defined in subdivision (ii) (*a*) of this subparagraph), the issue price of the obligation includes only that portion of the initial offering price or price paid by the first buyer properly allocable to the obligation under the rules prescribed in subdivision (ii) of this subparagraph. The terms "initial offering price" and "price paid by the first buyer" include the aggregate payments made by the purchaser under the purchase agreement, including modifications thereof. Thus, all amounts paid by the purchaser under the purchase agreement or a modification of it are included in the issue price (but in the case of an obligation issued as part of an investment unit, only to the extent allocable to such obligation under subdivision (ii) of this subparagraph), such as amounts paid upon face-amount certificates or installment trust certificates in which the purchaser contracts to make a series of payments which will be returnable to the holder with an increment at a later date.

(ii) *Investment units consisting of obligations and property*—(*a*) *In general.* An investment unit, within the meaning of this subdivision (ii) and for purposes of section 1232, consists of an obligation and an option, security, or other property. For purposes of this subparagraph, the initial offering price of an investment unit shall be allocated to the individual elements of the unit on the basis of their respective fair market values. However, if the fair market value of the option, security, or other property is not readily ascertainable (within the meaning of paragraph (c) of § 1.421-6), then the portion of the initial offering price or price paid by the first buyer of the unit which is allocable to the obligation issued as part of such unit shall be ascertained as of the time of acquisition of such unit by reference to the assumed price at which such obligation would have been issued had it been issued apart from such unit. The assumed price of the obligation shall be ascertained by comparison to the yields at which obligations of a similar character which are not issued as part of an investment unit are sold in arm's length transactions, and by adjusting the price of the obligation in question to this yield. This adjustment may be made by subtracting from the face amount of the obligation the total present value of the interest foregone by the purchaser as a result of purchasing the obligation at a lower yield as part of an investment unit. In most

Rules for Determining Capital Gains and Losses

See p. 20,601 for regulations not amended to reflect law changes

cases, assumed price may also be determined in a similar manner through the use of standard bond tables. Any reasonable method may be used in selecting the obligation for comparative purposes. Obligations of the same grade and classification shall be used to the extent possible, and proper regard shall be given, with respect to both the obligation in question and the comparative obligation, to the solvency of the issuer, the nature of the issuer's trade or business, the presence and nature of security for the obligation, the geographic area in which the loan is made, and all other factors relevant to the circumstances. An obligation which is convertible into stock or another obligation must not be used as a comparative obligation (except where the investment unit contains an obligation convertible into stock or another obligation), since such an obligation would not reflect the yield attributable solely to the obligation element of the investment unit.

(b) *Agreement as to assumed price.* In the case of an investment unit which is privately placed, the assumed price at which the obligation would have been issued had it been issued apart from such unit may be agreed to by the issuer and the original purchaser of the investment unit in writing on or before the date of purchase. Alternatively, an agreement between the issuer and original purchaser may specify the rate of interest which would have been paid on the obligation if the transaction were one not involving the issuance of options, and an assumed price may be determined (in the manner described in (a) of this subdivision) from such agreed assumed rate of interest. An assumed price based upon such an agreement between the parties will generally be presumed to be the issue price of the obligation with respect to the issuer, original purchaser and all subsequent holders: *Provided,* That the agreement was made in arm's-length negotiations between parties having adverse interests: *And provided further,* That such price does not, under the rules stated in (a) of this subdivision, appear to be clearly erroneous. An assumed issue price agreed to by the parties as provided herein will not be considered clearly erroneous if it is not less than the face value adjusted (in the manner described in (a) of this subdivision) to a yield which is one percentage point greater than the actual rate of interest payable on the obligation. Similarly, if the agreement between the parties specifies an agreed assumed rate of interest (in lieu of an agreed assumed issue price) and such agreed rate is not more than 1 percentage point greater than the actual rate payable on the obligation, an adjusted issue price based upon such agreed assumed rate of interest will not be considered clearly erroneous.

(c) *Cross references.* For rules relating to the deductibility by the issuing corporation of bond discount resulting from an allocation under the rule stated in (a) of this subdivision, see §§ 1.163-3 and 1.163-4. For rules relating to the basis of obligations and options, securities, or other property acquired in investment units, see § 1.1012-1(d). For rules relating to certain reporting requirements with respect to options acquired in connection with evidences of indebtedness and for the tax treatment of such options, see § 1.61-15, and section 1234 and the regulations thereunder. With respect to the tax consequences to the issuing corporation upon the exercise of options issued in connection with evidences of indebtedness to which this section applies, see section 1032 and the regulations thereunder.

(d) *Examples.* The application of the principles set forth in this subdivision (ii) may be illustrated by the following examples in each of which it is assumed that there was no intention to call the note before maturity:

Example (1). M Corporation is a small manufacturer of electronic components located in the southwestern United States. On January 1, 1969, in consideration for the payment of $41,500, M issues to X its unsecured note for $40,000 together with warrants to purchase 3,000 shares of M stock at $10 per share at any time during the term of the note. The note is payable in 4 years and provides for interest at the rate of 5 percent per year, payable semiannually. The fair market values of the note and the warrants are not readily ascertainable. Assume that companies in the same industry as M Corporation, and similarly situated both financially and geographically, are generally able to borrow money on their unsecured notes at an annual interest rate of 6 percent. Using a present value table, the calculation of the issue price of a 5 percent, 4 year, $40,000 note, discounted to yield 6 percent compounded semiannually is made as follows:

(1) Semiannual interest period	(2) Amount payable at 5%	(3) Factor for present value discounted at 3% per period	(2) × (3) Present value of payment
1	$1,000	0.9709	$ 970.90
2	1,000	.9426	942.60
3	1,000	.9151	915.10
4	1,000	.8885	888.50

Reg. § 1.1232-3(b)(2)

Rules for Determining Capital Gains and Losses
See p. 20,601 for regulations not amended to reflect law changes

5	1,000	.8626	862.60
6	1,000	.8375	837.50
7	1,000	.8131	813.10
8	1,000	.7894	789.40
8	40,000	.7894	31,576.00

Total present value of note discounted
at 6%, compounded semiannually $38,595.70

The same result may be reached through the use of a standard bond table or by the following present value calculation:

Present value of annuity of $1,000 payable over 8 periods at 3 percent per
period = 1000 × 7.0197 = ... $ 7,019.70
Add: Present value of principal (as calculated above) 31,576.00

Total .... $ 38,595.70

Accordingly, the assumed price at which M's note would have been issued had it been issued without stock purchase warrants, i.e., that portion of the $41,500 price paid by X which is allocable to M's note, is $38,596 (rounded). Since the price payable on redemption of M's note at maturity is $40,000, the original issue discount on M's note is $1,404 ($40,000 minus $38,596). Under the rules stated in § 1.163-3, M is entitled to a deduction, to be prorated or amortized over the life of the note, equal to this original issue discount on the note. The excess of the price for the unit over the portion of such price allocable to the note, $2,904 ($41,500 minus $38,596), is allocable to and is the basis of the stock purchase warrants acquired by X in connection with M's note. Upon the exercise of X's warrants, M will be allowed no deduction and will have no income. Upon maturity of the note X will receive $40,000 from M, of which $1,404, the amount of the original issue discount, will be taxable as ordinary income. If X were to transfer the note at its face amount to A 2 years after the issue date, X would realize, under section 1232(a)(2)(B), ordinary income of $702 (one-half of $1,404).

Example (2). (1) On January 1, 1969, N Corporation negotiates with Y, a small business investment company, for a loan in the amount of $51,500 in consideration of which N Corporation issues to Y its unsecured 5-year note for $50,000, together with warrants to purchase 2,000 shares of N stock at $5 per share at any time during the term of the note. The note provides for interest of 6 percent, payable semiannually. The fair market values of the note and warrants are not readily ascertainable. The loan agreement between Y and N contains a provision, agreed to in arms-length bargaining between the parties, that a rate of 7 percent payable semiannually would have been applied to the loan if warrants were not issued as part of the consideration for the loan. The issue price of the note is $47,921 (rounded), determined with the use of a standard bond table, or computed in the manner illustrated in Example (1) or in the following alternative manner:

(1) Interest period	(2) Interest rate differential	(3) Principal	(4) Interest foregone for period (1/2%)	(5) Factor for present value discounted at 3½% per period	(4) × (5) Present value of interest foregone
1	1% (7% − 6%)	$50,000	250	0.9662	$ 241.55
2	1%	50,000	250	.9335	233.38
3	1%	50,000	250	.9019	225.48
4	1%	50,000	250	.8714	217.85
5	1%	50,000	250	.8420	210.50
6	1%	50,000	250	.8135	203.38
7	1%	50,000	250	.7860	196.50
8	1%	50,000	250	.7594	189.85
9	1%	50,000	250	.7337	183.43
10	1%	50,000	250	.7089	177.23

Total present value of interest foregone .... $ 2,079.15

Principal $50,000.00
Less: Total present value of interest foregone 2,079.00

Issue price $47,921.00

Reg. § 1.1232-3(b)(2)

Rules for Determining Capital Gains and Losses

See p. 20,601 for regulations not amended to reflect law changes

The calculation of present value of interest foregone may also be made as follows:

Present value of annuity of $250 discounted for 10 periods at 3½ percent per period = $250 × 8.3166 = $2,079.15.

The total present value of interest foregone, $2,079, is also the original issue discount attributable to the note ($50,000 − $47,921). Under (b) of this subdivision, since the agreed assumed rate of interest of 7 percent is not more than 1 percentage point greater than the actual rate payable on the note, determination of the issue price of the note (and original issue discount) based upon such assumed rate will be presumed to be correct and will not be considered clearly erroneous, provided that both N and Y adhere to such determination. Under the rules in § 1.163-3, N is entitled to a deduction, to be prorated or amortized over the life of the note, equal to the original issue discount on the note. The excess of the price paid for the unit over the portion of such price allocable to the note, $3,579 ($51,500 minus $47,921) is allocable to and is the basis of the stock purchase warrants acquired by Y in connection with N's note. Upon the exercise or sale of the warrants by Y, N will be allowed no deduction and will have no income. Upon maturity of the note Y will receive $50,000 from N, of which $2,079, the amount of the original issue discount, will be taxable as ordinary income. If Y were to transfer the note at its face value to B 2½ years after the issue date, Y would realize, under section 1232(a)(2)(B), ordinary income of $1,039.50 (one-half of $2,079).

(2) Assume that instead of the parties agreeing on as assumed interest rate at which the obligation would have been issued without the warrants, the parties agreed that the obligation at the actual 6 percent rate would have been issued without the warrants at a discounted price of $48,000. In this situation the agreed assumed issue price is presumed to be correct since it is not less than the face value adjusted (in the manner illustrated in part (1) of this example) to a yield which is one percentage point greater than the actual rate of interest payable on the obligation ($47,921).

Example (3). O Corporation is a small advertising company located in the northeastern United States. Z is a tax-exempt organization. In consideration for the payment of $60,000, O issues to Z, in a transaction not within the scope of section 503(c), its unsecured 5-year note for $60,000, together with warrants to purchase 6,000 shares of O stock at $10 per share at any time during the term of the note. The note is subject to quarterly amortization at the rate of $3,000 per quarter, and provides for interest on the outstanding unpaid balance at an annual rate of 6 percent payable quarterly (1½ percent per quarter). The fair market values of the notes and warrants are not readily ascertainable. The loan agreement between O and Z contains a recital that if the $60,000 note had been issued without the warrants only $45,000 would have been paid for it. An examination of relevant facts indicates that companies in the same industry as O Corporation, and similarly situated both financially and geographically, are able to borrow money on their unsecured notes at an annual interest cost of 8½ percent payable quarterly (2⅛ percent per quarter). By reference to a present value table, it is found that the present value of O's note discounted to yield 8½ percent compounded quarterly is $56,608 (rounded). The computation is as follows:

(1) Quarterly interest period	(2) Principal payable	(3) Interest payable (1½%)	(4) Total amount payable (2) + (3)	(5) Factor for present value discounted at 2⅛% per quarter	(6) Present value of total payment (4) × (5)
1	$3,000	$900	$3,900	0.9792	$3,818.88
2	3,000	855	3,855	.9588	3,696.17
3	3,000	810	3,810	.9389	3,577.21
4	3,000	765	3,765	.9193	3,461.16
5	3,000	720	3,720	.9002	3,348.74
6	3,000	675	3,675	.8815	3,239.51
7	3,000	630	3,630	.8631	3,133.05
8	3,000	585	3,585	.8452	3,030.04
9	3,000	540	3,540	.8276	2,929.70
10	3,000	495	3,495	.8104	2,832.35
11	3,000	450	3,450	.7935	2,737.58
12	3,000	405	3,405	.7770	2,645.69
13	3,000	360	3,360	.7608	2,556.29
14	3,000	315	3,315	.7450	2,469.68
15	3,000	270	3,270	.7295	2,385.47
16	3,000	225	3,225	.7143	2,303.62

Reg. § 1.1232-3(b)(2)

53,456 Rules for Determining Capital Gains and Losses
See p. 20,601 for regulations not amended to reflect law changes

17	3,000	180	3,180	.6994	2,224.09
18	3,000	135	3,135	.6849	2,147.16
19	3,000	90	3,090	.6706	2,072.15
20	3,000	45	3,045	.6567	1,999.65
					$56,608.19

This amount ($56,609) is the assumed price at which the note would have been issued had it been issued without stock purchase warrants. The assumed price of $45,000 agreed to by the parties is not presumed to be correct since it is less than the face value adjusted to a yield which is one percentage point greater than the actual rate of interest payable on the obligation. The parties did not have adverse interests in agreeing upon an assumed price (since an excessively large amount of original issue discount would benefit O, the borrower, without adversely affecting Z, an exempt organization which would pay no tax on original issue discount income), and the price agreed to appears to be clearly erroneous when compared to the $56,608 assumed issue price determined under the principles of (a) of this subdivision. Since the maturity value of O's note is $60,000, the original issue discount on O's note is $3,392 ($60,000 minus $56,608). Under the rules in § 1.163-3, O is entitled to a deduction, to be prorated or amortized over the life of the note, equal to this original issue discount on the note. The excess of the price paid for the unit over the portion of such price allocable to the note, $3,392 ($60,000 minus $56,608), is allocable to and is the basis of the stock purchase warrants acquired by Z in connection with O's note. Upon the exercise or sale of the warrants by Z, O will be allowed no deduction and will have no income.

(iii) *Issuance for property after May 27, 1969*—(a) *In general.* Except as provided in (b) of this subdivision, if an obligation or an investment unit is issued for property other than money, the issue price of such obligation shall be the stated redemption price at maturity and, therefore, no original issue discount is created as a result of the exchange. However, in such case, there may be an amount treated as interest under section 483. In the case of certain exchanges of obligations of the United States for other such obligations, see section 1037 for the determination of the amount of original issue discount on the obligation acquired in the exchange. For carryover of original issue discount in the case of certain exchanges of obligations, see subparagraph (1)(iv) of this paragraph.

(b) *Exceptions for original issue discount.* If an obligation or investment unit is issued for property in an exchange which is not pursuant to a plan of reorganization referred to in (d) of this subdivision, and if—

(1) The obligation, investment unit, or an element of the investment unit is part of an issue a portion of which is traded on an established securities market, or

(2) The property for which such obligation or investment unit is issued is stock or securities which are traded on an established securities market,

then the issue price of the obligation or investment unit shall be the fair market value of the property for which such obligation or investment unit is issued, as determined under (c) of this subdivision. Such issue price shall control for purposes of determining the amount realized by the person exchanging the property for the obligation or unit issued and the basis of the property acquired by the holder and the issuer. An obligation which is not traded on an established securities market and which is not part of an issue or investment unit a portion of which is so traded shall not be treated as property described in (1) of this subdivision (b) even though the obligation is convertible into property so traded. For purposes of this subdivision (b), an obligation, investment unit, or element of an investment unit shall be treated as traded on an established securities market if it is so traded on or within ten "trading" days after the date it is issued. "Trading" days shall mean those days on which an established securities market is open. For purposes of this subdivision (iii), the term "established securities market" shall have the same meaning as in paragraph (d)(4) of § 1.453-3 (relating to limitations on installment method for purchaser evidences of indebtedness payable on demand or readily tradable).

(c) *Determination of fair market value in cases to which (b) of this subdivision applies.* In general, for purposes of (b) of this subdivision, the fair market value of property for which an obligation or investment unit is issued shall be deemed to be the same as the fair market value of such obligation or investment unit, determined by reference to the fair market value of that portion of the issue, of which such obligation or unit is a part, which is traded on an established securities market. The fair market value of such obligation or unit shall be determined as of the first date after the date of issue (within the meaning of section 1232(b)(3)) that such obligation or unit is traded on an established securities market. If, however, the obligation or investment unit is not part of an issue a portion of which is traded on an

Reg. § 1.1232-3(b)(2)

Rules for Determining Capital Gains and Losses

established securities market, but the property for which the obligation or investment unit is issued is stock or securities which are traded on an established securities market, the fair market value of such property shall be the fair market value of such stock or securities on the date such obligation or unit is issued for such property. The fair market value of property for purposes of this subdivision (c) shall be determined as provided in § 20.2031-2 of this chapter (Estate Tax Regulations) but without applying the blockage and other special rules contained in paragraph (e) thereof.

(d) *Not in reorganization.* An exchange which is not pursuant to a reorganization referred to in this subdivision (d) is an exchange in which the obligation or investment unit is not issued pursuant to a plan of reorganization within the meaning of section 368(a)(1) or pursuant to an insolvency reorganization within the meaning of section 371, 373, or 374. Thus, for example, no original issue discount is created on an obligation issued in a recapitalization within the meaning of section 368(a)(1)(E). Similarly, no original issue discount is created on an obligation issued in an exchange, pursuant to a plan of reorganization, to which section 361 applies regardless of the income tax consequences to any person who pursuant to such plan is the ultimate recipient of the obligation. The application of section 351 shall not preclude the creation of original issue discount. For carryover of original issue discount in the case of an exchange of obligations pursuant to a plan of reorganization, see subparagraph (1)(iv) of this paragraph.

(e) *Effective date.* Determinations with respect to obligations issued on or before May 27, 1969, or pursuant to a written commitment which was binding on that date and at all times thereafter, shall be made without regard to this subdivision (iii).

(iv) *Serial obligations*—(a) *In general.* If an issue of obligations which matures serially is issued by a corporation, and if on the basis of the facts and circumstances in such case an independent issue price for each particular maturity can be established, then the obligations with each particular maturity shall be considered a separate series, and the obligations of each such series shall be treated as a separate issue with a separate issue price, maturity date, and stated redemption price at maturity. The ratable monthly portion of original issue discount attributable to each obligation within a particular series shall be determined and ratably included as interest in gross income under the rules of § 1.1232-3A.

(b) *Issue price not independently established.* If a separate issue price cannot be established with respect to each series of an issue of obligations which matures serially, the issue price for each obligation of each series shall be its stated redemption price at maturity minus the amount of original issue discount allocated thereto in accordance with (d) of this subdivision. The amount of original issue discount so allocated shall be ratably included as interest in gross income under rules of § 1.1232-3A.

(c) *Single obligation rule.* If a single corporate obligation provides for payments (other than payments which would not be included in the stated redemption price at maturity under subparagraph (1)(iii) of this paragraph) in two or more installments, the provisions of (b) of this subdivision shall be applied by treating such obligation as an issue of obligations consisting of more than one series each of which matures on the due date of each such installment payment.

(d) *Allocation of discount.* For purposes of (b) and (c) of this subdivision, the original issue discount with respect to each series of an issue shall be the total original issue discount for the issue multiplied by a fraction—

(1) The numerator of which is the product of (i) the stated redemption price of such series and (ii) the number of complete years (and any fraction thereof) constituting the period for such series from the date of original issue (as defined in paragraph (b)(3) of this section) to its stated maturity date, and

(2) The denominator of which is the sum of the products determined in (1) of this subdivision (d) with respect to each such series.

If a series consists of more than one obligation, the original issue discount allocated to such series shall be apportioned to such obligations in proportion to the stated redemption price of each. Computations under this subdivision (d) may be made using periods other than years, such as, for example, months or periods of 3 months.

(e) *Effective date.* The provisions of this subdivision (iv) shall apply with respect to corporate obligations issued after [insert date on which notice of proposed rule making is published in Federal Register]. However, no inference shall be drawn from the preceding sentence with respect to serial obligations issued prior to such date.

(f) *Examples.* The provisions of this subdivision (iv) may be illustrated by the following examples:

Example (1). On January 1, 1972, P Corporation issued a note with a total face value of $100,000 to B for cash of $94,000. The terms of

Reg. § 1.1232-3(b)(2)

53,458 Rules for Determining Capital Gains and Losses
See p. 20,601 for regulations not amended to reflect law changes

the note provide that $50,000 is payable on December 31, 1973, and the other $50,000 on December 31, 1975. Each payment is treated as the stated redemption price of a series, and the total original issue discount with respect to the note, $6,000, is allocated to each such series as follows:

Year of maturity	1973	1975	Total
(1) Stated redemption price	$ 50,000	$ 50,000	
(2) Multiply by years outstanding	2	4	
(3) Product of bond years	$100,000	$200,000	
(4) Sum of products			$300,000
(5) Fractional portion of discount	$100,000 / $300,000	$200,000 / $300,000	
(6) Multiply line (5) by discount for entire issue	6,000	6,000	
(7) Discount for each series	$ 2,000	$ 4,000	
(8) Issue price (line (1), minus line (7))	$ 48,000	$ 46,000	

Example (2). Assume the same facts as in example (1) except that a separate note is issued for each payment. The result is the same as in example (1).

Example (3). On January 1, 1971, Y Bank, a corporation, issues a note to C for $1,000 cash. The terms of the note provide that $50 will be paid at the end of the first year, $120 at the end of the second year, and $1,050 at the end of the third year. Under (c) of this subdivision (iv), the $1,000 note is treated as consisting of two series, the first of which matures at the end of the second year, and the second of which matures at the end of the third year. The issue price and the allocation of original issue discount with respect to each series is computed as follows:

Year of maturity	1973	1975	Total
(1) Stated redemption price	$ 70	$ 1,000	
(2) Multiply by years outstanding	2	3	
(3) Product of bond years	$ 140	$ 3,000	
(4) Sum of products			$3,140
(5) Fractional portion of discount	140 / $3,140	3,000 / $ 3,140	
(6) Multiply line (5) by discount for entire issue	70	70	
(7) Discount for each series	$ 3.12	$ 66.88	
(8) Issue price (line (1) minus line (7))	$66.88	$933.12	

(3) *Date of original issue.* In the case of issues of obligations which are registered with the Securities and Exchange Commission, the term "date of original issue" means the date on which the issue was first sold to the public at the issue price. In the case of issues which are privately placed, the term "date of original issue" means the date on which each obligation was sold to the original purchaser.

(4) *Intention to call before maturity*—(i) *Meaning of term.* For purposes of section 1232, the term "intention to call the bond or other evidence of indebtedness before maturity" means an understanding between (a) the issuing corporation (such corporation is hereinafter referred to as the "issuer"), and (b) the original purchaser of such obligation (or, in the case of obligations constituting part of an issue, any of the original purchasers of such obligations) that the issuer will redeem the obligation before maturity. For purposes of this subparagraph, the term "original purchaser" does not include persons or organizations acting in the capacity of underwriters or dealers, who purchased the obligation for resale in the ordinary course of their trade or business. It is not necessary that the issuer's intention to call the obligation before maturity be communicated directly to the original purchaser by the issuer. The understanding to call before maturity need not be unconditional; it may, for example, be dependent upon the financial condition of the issuer on the proposed early call date.

(ii) *Proof of intent*—(a) *In general.* Ordinarily the existence or non-existence of an understanding at the time of original issue that the obligation will be redeemed before maturity shall be determined by an examination of all of the circumstances under which the obligation was issued and held. The fact that the obligation is issued with provisions on its face giving the issuer the privilege of redeeming the obligation before maturity is not determinative of an intention to call before maturity; likewise, the absence of such provision is not determinative of the absence of an intention to call before maturity. However, such provision, or the absence of such provision, is one of the circumstances to be given consideration along with other factors in determining whether

Reg. § 1.1232-3(b)(3)

Rules for Determining Capital Gains and Losses

See p. 20,601 for regulations not amended to reflect law changes

an understanding existed. If the obligation was part of an issue registered with the Securities and Exchange Commission and was sold to the public (whether or not sold directly to the public by the obligor) without representation to the public that the obligor intends to call the obligation before maturity, there shall be a presumption that no intention to call the obligation before maturity was in existence at the time of original issue. The existence of a provision on the face of an obligation giving the issuer the privilege of redeeming the obligation before maturity shall not in and of itself overcome the presumption set forth in the preceding sentence.

(*b*) *Circumstances indicating absence of understanding.* Examples of circumstances which would be evidence that there was no understanding at the time of original issue to redeem the obligation before maturity are—

(*1*) The issue price and term of the obligation appear to be reasonable, taking into account the interest rate, if any, on the obligation, for a corporation in the financial condition of the issuer at the time of issue.

(*2*) The original purchaser and the issuer are not related within the meaning of section 267(b) and have not engaged in transactions with each other (other than concerning the obligation).

(*3*) The original purchaser is not related within the meaning of section 267(b) to any of the officers or directors of the issuer, and he has not engaged in transactions with such officers or directors (other than concerning the obligation).

(*4*) The officers and directors of the issuer at the time of issue of the obligation are different from those in control at the time the obligation is called or the taxpayer disposes of it.

(c) *Gain treated as ordinary income in certain cases; computation.* The amount of gain treated as ordinary income under paragraph (a)(3)(ii) or (5) of this section is computed by multiplying the original issue discount by a fraction, the numerator of which is the number of full months the obligation was held by the holder and the denominator of which is the number of full months from the date of original issue to the date specified as the redemption date at maturity. (See paragraph (b)(3) of this section for definition of "date of original issue".) The period that the obligation was held by the taxpayer shall include any period that it was held by another person if, under chapter 1 of the Code, for the purpose of determining gain or loss from a sale or exchange, the obligation has the same basis, in whole or in part, in the hands of the taxpayer as it would have in the hands of such other person. This computation is illustrated by the following examples:

Example (1). An individual purchases a 10-year, 3 percent coupon bond for $900 on original issue on February 1, 1955, and sells it on February 20, 1960 for $940. The redemption price is $1,000. At the time of original issue, there was no intention to call the bond before maturity. The bond has been held by the taxpayer for 60 full months. (The additional days amounting to less than a full month are not taken into account.) The number of complete months from date of issue to date of maturity is 120 (10 years). The fraction 60/120 multiplied by the discount of $100 is equal to $50, which represents the proportionate part of the original issue discount attributable to the period of ownership by the taxpayer. Accordingly, any part of the gain up to $50 will be treated as ordinary income. Therefore, in this case the entire gain of $40 is treated as ordinary income.

Example (2). Assume the same facts in the preceding example, except that the selling price of the bond is $970. In this case $50 of the gain of $70 is treated as ordinary income and the balance of $20 is treated as long-term capital gain.

Example (3). Assume the same facts as in example (1), except that the selling price of the bond is $800. In this case, the individual has a long-term capital loss of $100.

Example (4). Assume the same facts as in example (1), except that the bond is purchased by the second holder February 1, 1960, for $800. The second holder keeps it to the maturity date (February 1, 1965) when it is redeemed for $1,000. Since that holder has held the bond for 60 full months, he will, upon redemption, have $50 in ordinary income and $150 in long-term capital gain.

(d) *Exceptions to the general rule*—(1) *In general.* Section 1232(a)(2)(C) provides that section 1232(a)(2) does not apply (i) to obligations the interest on which is excluded from gross income under section 103 (relating to certain government obligations), or (ii) to any holder who purchases an obligation at a premium.

(2) *Premium.* For purposes of section 1232, this section, and § 1.1232-3A, "premium" means a purchase price which exceeds the stated redemption price of an obligation at its maturity. For purposes of the preceding sentence, if an obligation is acquired as part of an investment unit consisting of an option, security, or other property and an obligation, the purchase price of the obligation is that portion of the price paid or payable for the unit which is allocable to the obligation. The price paid for the unit shall be allocated to

Reg. § 1.1232-3(d)(2)

53,460 Rules for Determining Capital Gains and Losses
See p. 20,601 for regulations not amended to reflect law changes

the individual elements of the unit on the basis of their respective fair market values. However, if the fair market value of the option, security, or other property is not readily ascertainable (within the meaning of paragraph (c) of § 1.421-6), then the price paid for the unit shall be allocated in accordance with the rules under paragraph (b)(2)(ii) of this section for allocating the initial offering price of an investment unit to its elements. If, under chapter 1 of the Code, the basis of an obligation in the hands of the holder is the same, in whole or in part, for the purposes of determining gain or loss from a sale or exchange, as the basis of the obligation in the hands of another person who purchased the obligation at a premium, then the holder shall be considered to have purchased the obligation at a premium. Thus, the donee of an obligation purchased at a premium by the donor will be considered a holder who purchased the obligation at a premium.

(e) *Amounts previously includible in income.* Nothing in section 1232(a)(2) shall require the inclusion of any amount previously includible in gross income. Thus, if an amount was previously includible in a taxpayer's income on account of obligations issued at a discount and redeemable for fixed amounts increasing at stated intervals, or, under section 818(b) (relating to accrual of discount on bonds and other evidences of indebtedness held by life insurance companies), such amount is not again includible in the taxpayer's gross income under section 1232(a)(2). For example, amounts includible in gross income by a cash receipts and disbursements method taxpayer who has made an election under section 454(a) or (c) (relating to accounting rules for certain obligations issued at a discount to which section 1232(a)(3) does not apply) are not includible in gross income under section 1232(a)(2). In the case of a gain which would include, under section 1232(a)(2), an amount considered to be ordinary income and a further amount considered long-term capital gain, any amount to which this paragraph applies is first used to offset the amount considered ordinary income. For example, on January 1, 1955, A purchases a ten-year bond which is redeemable for fixed amounts increasing at stated intervals. At the time of original issue, there was no intention to call the bond before maturity. The purchase price of the bond is $75, which is also the issue price. The stated redemption price at maturity of the bond is $100. A elects to treat the annual increase in the redemption price of the bond as income pursuant to section 454(a). On January 1, 1960, A sells the bond for $90. The total stated increase in the redemption price of the bond which A has reported annually as income for the taxable year 1955 through 1959 is $7. The portion of the original issue discount of $25 attributable to this period is $12.50, computed as follows:

$$\frac{60 \text{ (months bond is held by A)}}{120 \text{ (months from date of original issue to redemption date)}} \times \$25 \text{ (original issue discount)}$$

However, $7, which represents the annual stated increase taken into income, is offset against the amount of $12.50, leaving $5.50 of the gain from the sale to be treated as ordinary income.

(f) *Record keeping requirements.* In the case of any obligation held by a taxpayer which was issued at an original issue discount after December 31, 1954, the taxpayer shall keep a record of the issue price and issue date upon or with each such obligation (if known to or reasonably ascertainable by him). If the obligation held by the taxpayer is an obligation of the United States received from the United States in an exchange upon which gain or loss is not recognized because of section 1037(a) (or so much of section 1031(b) or (c) as relates to section 1037(a)), the taxpayer shall keep sufficient records to determine the issue price of such obligation for purposes of applying section 1037(b) and paragraphs (a) and (b) of § 1.1037-1 upon the disposition or redemption of such obligation. The issuer (or in the case of obligations first sold to the public through an underwriter or wholesaler, the underwriter or wholesaler) shall mark the issue price and issue date upon every obligation which is issued at an original issue discount after September 26, 1957, but only if the period between the date of original issue (as defined in paragraph (b)(3) of this section) and the stated maturity date is more than 6 months. [Reg. § 1.1232-3.]

☐ [*T.D.* 6253, 9-25-57. *Amended by T.D.* 6468, 6-6-60, *T.D.* 6935, 11-16-67, *T.D.* 6984, 12-23-68, *T.D.* 7154, 12-27-71, *T.D.* 7213, 10-7-72, *T.D.* 7663, 12-21-79 *and T.D.* 7728, 10-31-80.]

Reg. § 1.1232-3(e)

Rules for Determining Capital Gains and Losses

See p. 20,601 for regulations not amended to reflect law changes

[Reg. § 1.1232-3A]

§ 1.1232-3A. Inclusion as interest of original issue discount on certain obligations issued after May 27, 1969.—(a) *Ratable inclusion as interest* —(1) *General rule.* Under section 1232(a)(3), the holder of any obligation issued by a corporation after May 27, 1969 (other than an obligation issued by or on behalf of the United States or a foreign country, or a political subdivision of either) shall include as interest in his gross income an amount equal to the ratable monthly portion of original issue discount multiplied by the sum of the number of complete months and any fractional part of a month such holder held the obligation during the taxable year. For increase in basis for amounts included as interest in gross income pursuant to this paragraph, see paragraph (c) of this section. For requirements for reporting original issue discount, see section 6049(a) and the regulations thereunder.

(2) *Ratable monthly portion of original issue discount* —(i) *General rule.* Except when subdivision (ii) of this subparagraph applies, the term "ratable monthly portion of original issue discount" means an amount equal to the original issue discount divided by the sum of the number of complete months (plus any fractional part of a month) beginning on the date of original issue and ending the day before the stated maturity date of such obligation.

(ii) *Reduction for purchase allowance.* With respect to an obligation which has been acquired by purchase (within the meaning of subparagraph (4) of this paragraph), the term "ratable monthly portion of original issue discount" means the lesser of the amount determined under subdivision (i) of this subparagraph or an amount equal to—

(*a*) the excess (if any) of the stated redemption price of the obligation at maturity over its cost to the purchaser divided by

(*b*) The sum of the number of complete months (plus any fractional part of a month) beginning on the date of such purchase and ending the day before the stated maturity date of such obligation.

The amount of the ratable monthly portion within the meaning of this subdivision reflects a purchase allowance provided under section 1232(a)(3)(B) where a purchase is made at a price in excess of the sum of the issue price plus the portion of original issue discount previously includible (regardless of whether included) in the gross income of all previous holders (computed, however, as to such previous holders without regard to any purchase allowance under this subdivision and without regard to whether any previous holder purchased at a premium).

(iii) *Ratable monthly portion upon carryover to new obligation.* In any case in which there is a carryover of original issue discount under paragraph (b)(1)(iv) of § 1.1232-3 from an obligation exchanged to an obligation received in such exchange, the ratable monthly portion of original issue discount in respect of the obligation received shall be computed by dividing the amount of original issue discount carried over by the sum of the number of complete months (plus any fractional part of a month) beginning on the date of the exchange and ending the day before the stated maturity date of the obligation received.

(iv) *Cross references.* For definitions of the terms "original issue discount" and "date of original issue", see subparagraphs (1) and (3), respectively, of § 1.1232-3(b). For definition of the term "premium," see paragraph (d)(2) of § 1.1232-3.

(3) *Determination of number of complete months*—(i) *In general.* For purposes of this section—

(*a*) A complete month and a fractional part of a month commence with the date of original issue and the corresponding day of each succeeding calendar month (or the last day of a calendar month in which there is no corresponding day),

(*b*) If an obligation is acquired on any day other than the date a complete month commences, the ratable monthly portion of original issue discount for the complete month in which the acquisition occurs shall be allocated between the transferor and the transferee in accordance with the number of days in such complete month each held the obligation,

(*c*) In determining the allocation under (*b*) of this subdivision, any holder may treat each month as having 30 days,

(*d*) The transferee, and not the transferor, shall be deemed to hold the obligation during the entire day on the date of acquisition, and

(*e*) The obligor will be treated as the transferee on the date of redemption.

(ii) *Example.* The provisions of this subparagraph may be illustrated by the following example:

Example. On February 22, 1970, A acquires an obligation of X Corporation for which February 1, 1970, is the date of original issue. B acquires the obligation on June 16, 1970. A does not choose to treat each month as having 30 days. Thus, A held the obligation for 3¾ months during 1970, *i.e.*, ¼ of February (7/28 days), March, April, May, ½ of June (15/30 days). The ratable

53,462 Rules for Determining Capital Gains and Losses

See p. 20,601 for regulations not amended to reflect law changes

monthly portion of original issue discount for the obligation is multiplied by 3¾ months to determine the amount included in A's gross income for 1970 pursuant to this paragraph.

(4) *Purchase.* For purposes of this section, the term "purchase" means any acquisition (including an acquisition upon original issue) of an obligation to which this section applies, but only if the basis of such obligation is not determined in whole or in part by reference to the adjusted basis of such obligation in the hands of the person from whom it was acquired or under section 1014(a) (relating to property acquired from a decedent).

(b) *Exceptions*—(1) *Binding commitment.* Section 1232(a)(3) shall not apply to any obligation issued pursuant to a written commitment which was binding on May 27, 1969, and at all times thereafter.

(2) *Exception for one-year obligations.* Section 1232(a)(3) shall not apply to any obligation in respect of which the period between the date of original issue (as defined in paragraph (b)(3) of § 1.1232-3) and the stated maturity date is one year or less. In such case, gain on the sale or exchange of such obligation shall be included in gross income as interest to the extent the gain does not exceed an amount equal to the ratable monthly portion of original issue discount multiplied by the sum of the number of complete months and any fractional part of a month such taxpayer held such obligation.

(3) *Purchase at a premium.* Section 1232(a)(3) shall not apply to any holder who purchased the obligation at a premium (within the meaning of paragraph (d)(2) of § 1.1232-3).

(4) *Life insurance companies.* Section 1232(a)(3) shall not apply to any holder which is a life insurance company to which section 818(b) applies. However, ratable inclusion of original issue discount as interest under section 1232(a)(3) is required by an insurance company which is subject to the tax imposed by section 821 or 831.

(c) *Basis adjustment.* The basis of an obligation in the hands of the holder thereof shall be increased by any amount of original issue discount with respect thereto included as interest in his gross income pursuant to paragraph (a) of this section. See section 1232(a)(3)(E). However, the basis of an obligation shall not be increased by any amount that was includible as interest in gross income under paragraph (a) of this section, but was not actually included by the holder in his gross income.

(d) *Examples.* The provisions of paragraphs (a) through (c) of this section may be illustrated by the following examples:

Example (1). On January 1, 1970, A, a calendar-year taxpayer, purchases at original issue, for cash of $7,600, M Corporation's 10-year, 5-percent bond which has a stated redemption price of $10,000. The ratable monthly portion of original issue discount, as determined under section 1232(a)(3) and this section, to be included as interest in A's gross income for each month he holds such bond is $20, computed as follows:

Original issue discount (stated redemption price, $10,000, minus issue price, $7,600)	$2,400
Divide by: Number of months from date of original issue to stated maturity date	120 months
Ratable monthly portion	$ 20

Assume that A holds the bond for all of 1970 and 1971 and includes as interest in his gross income for each such year an amount equal to the ratable monthly portion, $20, multiplied by the number of months he held the bond each such year, 12 months, or $240. Accordingly, on January 1, 1972, A's basis in the bond will have increased under paragraph (c) of this section by the amount so included, $480 (*i.e.*, $240 × 2), from his cost, $7,600, to $8,080. For results if A sells the bond on that date, see examples (1) and (2) paragraph (a)(2) of § 1.1232-3.

Example (2). Assume the same facts as in example (1). Assume further that on January 1, 1972, A sells the bond to B, a calendar-year taxpayer for $9,040.

Since B purchased the bond, he determines under paragraph (a)(2)(ii) of this section the amount of the ratable monthly portion he must include as interest in his gross income in order to reflect the amount of his purchase allowance (if any). B determines that his ratable monthly portion is $10, computed as follows:

(1) Stated redemption price at maturity	$10,000
(2) Minus: B's cost	9,040
(3) Excess	$ 960
(4) Divide by: Number of months from date of purchase to stated maturity date	96 months
(5) Tentative ratable monthly portion	$ 10
(6) Ratable monthly portion as computed in example (1)	20

Since line (5) is lower than line (6), B's ratable monthly portion is $10. Accordingly, if B holds the bond for all of 1972, he must include $120 (*i.e.*, ratable monthly portion, $10, × 12 months) as interest in his gross income.

Reg. § 1.1232-3A(a)(4)

Rules for Determining Capital Gains and Losses 53,463

See p. 20,601 for regulations not amended to reflect law changes

Example (3). (1) Assume the same facts as in example (1). Assume further that on January 1, 1975, A sells the bond to B for $10,150. Under the exception of paragraph (b)(3) of this section, B is not required to include any amount in respect of original issue discount as interest in his gross income since he has purchased the bond at a premium.

(2) On January 1, 1979, B sells the bond to C, a calendar-year taxpayer, for $9,940. Since C is now the holder of the bond (and no exception applies to him), he must include as interest in his gross income the ratable monthly portion of original issue determined under section 1232(a)(3) and this section. Since C purchased the bond he determines under paragraph (a)(2)(ii) of this section the amount of the ratable monthly portion he must include as interest in his gross income in order to reflect the amount of his purchase allowance (if any). C determines that his ratable monthly portion is $5, computed as follows:

(1) Stated redemption price at maturity	$10,000
(2) Minus: C's cost	9,940
(3) Excess	$ 60
(4) Divide by: Number of months from date of purchase to stated maturity date	12 months
(5) Tentative ratable monthly portion..................	$ 5
(6) Ratable monthly portion as computed in example (1) ..	20

Since line (5) is lower than line (6), C's ratable monthly portion is $5. Accordingly, if C holds the bond for all of 1979, he must include $60 (*i.e.*, ratable monthly portion, $5, × 12 months) as interest in his gross income. Upon maturity of the bond on January 1, 1980, C will receive $10,000 from M, which under paragraph (c) of this section will equal his adjusted basis (the sum of his cost, $9,940, plus original issue discount included as interest in his gross income, $60).

Example (4). On January 1, 1968, D, a calendar year taxpayer, purchases at original issue, for cash of $8,000, P Corporation's 20-year, 6 percent bond which has a stated redemption price of $10,000 and which will mature on January 1, 1988. The original issue discount with respect to such bond is $2,000. However, the ratable inclusion rules of section 1232(a)(3) do not apply to D, since the bond was issued by P before May 28, 1969. On January 1, 1973, pursuant to a plan of reorganization as defined in section 368(a)(1)(E), and in which no gain or loss is recognized by D under section 354, D's 20-year bond is exchanged for a 10-year, 6 percent bond which also has a stated redemption price of $10,000 but will mature on January 1, 1983. Under paragraph (b)(1)(iv) of § 1.1232-3, the $2,000 of original issue discount is carried over to the new 10-year bond received in such exchange. Since the new bond is an obligation issued after May 27, 1969, D is required to begin ratable inclusion of the $2,000 of discount as interest in his gross income for 1973. The ratable monthly portion of original issue discount, as determined under section 1232(a)(3) to be included as interest in gross income is computed as follows:

Amount of original issue discount carried over	$2,000
Divide by: Number of complete months beginning on January 1, 1973, and ending on December 31, 1982	120 months
Ratable monthly portion	$16.67

(e) *Application of section 1232 to certain deposits in financial institutions and similar arrangements*—(1) *In general.* Under paragraph (d) of § 1.1232-1, the term "other evidence of indebtedness" includes certificates of deposit, time deposits, bonus plans, and other deposit arrangements with banks, domestic building and loan associations, and similar financial institutions.

(2) *Adjustments where obligation redeemed before maturity*—(i) *In general.* If an obligation described in subparagraph (1) of this paragraph is redeemed for a price less than the stated redemption price at maturity from a taxpayer who acquired the obligation upon original issue, such taxpayer shall be allowed as a deduction, in computing adjusted gross income, the amount of the original issue discount he included in gross income but did not receive (as determined under subdivision (ii) of this subparagraph). The taxpayer's basis of such obligation (determined after any increase in basis for the taxable year under section 1232(a)(3)(E) by the amount of original issue discount included in the holder's gross income under section 1232(a)(3)) shall be decreased by the amount of such adjustment.

(ii) *Computation.* The amount of the adjustment under subdivision (i) of this subparagraph shall be an amount equal to the excess (if any) of (*a*) the ratable monthly portion of the original issue discount included in the holder's gross income under section 1232(a)(3) for the period he held the obligation, over (*b*) the excess (if any) of the amount received upon the redemption over the issue price. Under paragraph (b)(1)(iii)(*a*) of § 1.1232-3, if any amount based on a fixed rate of simple or compound interest is actually payable or will be treated as constructively received under section 451 and the regulations thereunder at fixed periodic intervals of one

Reg. § 1.1232-3A(e)(2)

53,464 Rules for Determining Capital Gains and Losses
See p. 20,601 for regulations not amended to reflect law changes

year or less during the term of the obligation, any such amount payable upon redemption shall not be included in determining the amount received upon such redemption.

(iii) *Partial redemption.* (*a*) In the case of an obligation (other than a single obligation having serial maturity dates), if a portion of the obligation is redeemed prior to the stated maturity date of the entire obligation, the provisions of this subdivision shall be applied and not the provisions of subdivision (ii) of this subparagraph. In such case, the adjusted basis of the unredeemed portion of the obligation on the date of the partial redemption shall be an amount equal to the adjusted basis of the entire obligation on that date minus the amount paid upon the redemption.

(*b*) If the adjusted basis of the unredeemed portion (as computed under (*a*) of this subdivision) is equal to or in excess of the amount to be received for the unredeemed portion at maturity, no gain or loss shall be recognized at the time of the partial redemption but the holder shall be allowed a deduction, in computing adjusted gross income for the taxable year during which such partial redemption occurs, equal to the amount of such excess (if any), and no further original issue discount will be includible in the holder's gross income under section 1232(a)(3) over the remaining term of the unredeemed portion. In such case, the holder shall decrease his basis in the unredeemed portion (as computed under (*a*) of this subdivision) by the amount of such adjustment.

(*c*) If the adjusted basis of the unredeemed portion (as computed under (*a*) of this subdivision) is less than the redemption price of the unredeemed portion at maturity, a new computation shall be made under paragraph (a) of this section (without regard to the exception for one-year obligations in paragraph (b)(2) of this section) of the ratable monthly portion of original issue discount to be included as interest in the gross income of the holder over the remaining term of the unredeemed portion. For purposes of such computation, the adjusted basis of the unredeemed portion shall be treated as the issue price, the date of the partial redemption shall be treated as the issue date, and the amount to be paid for the unredeemed portion at maturity shall be treated as the stated redemption price.

(3) *Examples.* The application of section 1232 to obligations to which this paragraph applies may be illustrated by the following examples:

Example (1). A is a cash method taxpayer who uses the calendar year as his taxable year. On January 1, 1971, he purchases a certificate of deposit from X bank, a corporation, for $10,000. The certificate of deposit is not redeemable until December 31, 1975, except in an emergency as defined in, and subject to the qualifications provided by, Regulation Q of the Board of Governors of the Federal Reserve. See 12 C.F.R. § 217.4(d). The stated redemption price at maturity is $13,382.26. The terms of the certificate do not expressly refer to any amount as interest. A's certificate of deposit is an obligation to which section 1232 and this paragraph apply. A shall include the ratable portion of original issue discount in gross income for 1971 as determined under section 1232(a)(3). Thus, if A holds the certificate of deposit for the full calendar year 1971, the amount to be included in A's gross income for 1971 is $676.45, that is, 12/60 months, multiplied by the excess of the stated redemption price ($13,382.26) over the issue price ($10,000).

Example (2). Assume the same facts as in example (1), except that the certificate of deposit provides for payment upon redemption at December 31, 1975, of an amount equal to "$10,000, plus 6 percent compound interest from January 1, 1971, to December 31, 1975." Thus, the total amount payable upon redemption in both example (1) and this example is $13,382.26. The certificate of deposit is an obligation to which section 1232 and this paragraph apply and, since the substance of the deposit arrangement is identical to that contained in example (1), A must include the same amount in gross income.

Example (3). Assume the same facts as in example (1), except that the certificate provides for the payment of interest in the amount of $200 on December 31 of each year and $2,000 plus $10,000 (the original amount) payable upon redemption at December 31, 1975. Thus, if A holds the certificate of deposit for the full calendar year 1971, A must include in his gross income for 1971 the $200 interest payable on December 31, 1971, and $400 of original issue discount, that is 12/60 months multiplied by the excess of the stated redemption price ($12,000) over the issue price ($10,000).

Example (4). B is a cash method taxpayer who uses the calendar year as his taxable year. On January 1, 1971, B purchases a 4-year savings certificate from the Y Building and Loan Corporation for $4,000, redeemable on December 31, 1974, for $5,000. On December 31, 1973, Y redeems the certificate for $4,660. Under section 1232(a)(3), B included $250 of original issue discount in his gross income for 1971, $250 for 1972, and includes $250 in his gross income for 1973 for a total of $750. Since the excess of (i) the amount received upon the redemption, $4,660, over (ii)

Reg. § 1.1232-3A(e)(3)

Rules for Determining Capital Gains and Losses 53,465
See p. 20,601 for regulations not amended to reflect law changes

the issue price, $4,000, or $660, is lower than the total amount of original issue discount ($750) included in B's gross income for the period he held the certificate by $90, the $90 will be treated under subparagraph (2) of this paragraph as a deduction in computing adjusted gross income, and accordingly, will decrease the basis of his certificate by such amount. B has no gain or loss upon the redemption, as determined in accordance with the following computation:

Adjusted basis 1/1/73	$4,500
Increase under section 1232(a)(3)(E)	250
Subtotal	$4,750
Decrease under subparagraph (b)(2) of this paragraph	90
Basis upon redemption	$4,660
Amount realized upon redemption	4,660
Gain or loss	$ 0

Example (5). On January 1, 1971, C, a cash method taxpayer who uses the calendar year as his taxable year, opens a savings account in Z bank with a $10,000 deposit. Under the terms of the account, interest is made available semi-annually at 6 percent annual interest, compounded semi-annually. Since all of the interest on C's account in Z Bank is made available semi-annually, the stated redemption price at maturity under paragraph (b)(1)(iii)(a) of § 1.1232-3 equals the issue price, and, therefore, no original issue discount is reportable by C under section 1232(a)(3). However, C must include the sum of $300 (*i.e.*, 1/2 × 6% × $10,000) plus $309 (*i.e.*, 1/2 × 6% × $10,300), or $609, of interest made available during 1971 in his gross income for 1971.

Example (6). (i) D is a cash method taxpayer who uses the calendar year as his taxable year. On January 1, 1971, D purchases a $10,000 deferred income certificate from M Bank. Under the terms of the certificate, interest accrues at 6 percent per annum, compounded quarterly. The period of the account is 10 years. In addition, the holder is permitted to withdraw the entire amount of the purchase price at any time (but not interest prior to the expiration of the 10 year term), and upon such a withdrawal of the purchase price, no further interest accrues. If the certificate is held to maturity, the issue price plus accrued interest will aggregate $18,140.18.

(ii) In respect of the certificate, the original issue discount is $8,140.18, determined by subtracting the issue price of the certificate ($10,000) from the stated redemption price at maturity ($18,140.18). Thus, under section 1232(a)(3) the ratable monthly portion of original issue discount is $67,835 (*i.e.*, 1/120 months, multiplied by $8,140.18). Under section 1232(a)(3), D includes $814.02 (*i.e.*, 12 months, multiplied by $67,835) in his gross income for each calendar year the certificate remains outstanding and under section 1232(a)(3)(E) increases his basis by that amount. Thus, on December 31, 1975, D's basis for the certificate is $14,070.10 (*i.e.*, issue price, $10,000, increased by product of $814.02 × 5 years).

(iii) On December 31, 1975, D withdraws the $10,000. Under the terms of the certificate $3,468.55 cannot be withdrawn until December 31, 1980. Under the provisions of subparagraph (2)(iii) of this paragraph, the $10,000 partial redemption shall be treated as follows:

(1) Adjusted basis of obligation at time of partial redemption	$14,070.10
(2) Amount paid upon redemption	$10,000.00
(3) Adjusted basis of unredeemed portion (line (1) less line (2))	$ 4,070.10
(4) Amount to be paid for unredeemed portion at maturity (December 31, 1980)	$ 3,468.55
(5) Adjustment in computing adjusted gross income (excess of line (3) over line (4))	$ 601.55

Since the adjusted basis of the unredeemed portion exceeds the amount to be received for the unredeemed portion at maturity, D is allowed a deduction, in computing adjusted gross income, of $601.25 in 1975 and no further original issue discount is includible as interest in his gross income. In addition, D will decrease his basis in the unredeemed portion by $601.25, the amount of such adjustment, from $4,070.10 to $3,468.55.

Example (7). E is a cash method taxpayer who uses the calendar year as his taxable year. On January 1, 1971, E purchases a $10,000 "Bonus Savings Certificate" from N Building and Loan Corporation. Under the terms of the certificate, interest is payable at 5 percent per annum, compounded quarterly, and the period of the account is 3 years. In addition, the certificate provides that if the holder makes no withdrawals of principal or interest during the term of the certificate, a bonus payment equal to 5 percent of the purchase price of the certificate will be paid to the holder of the certificate at maturity. Thus, the amount of the bonus payment is $500 (*i.e.*, 5 percent multiplied by $10,000). Since the 5 percent annual interest is payable quarterly, the amount of such interest is not included in determining the stated redemption price at maturity under paragraph (b)(1)(iii) of § 1.1232-3. However, since the bonus payment is only payable at maturity, the amount of such bonus is included as part of the stated redemption price at maturity. Thus, the stated redemption price at maturity equals $10,500 (purchase price, $10,000, plus bonus payment,

Reg. § 1.1232-3A(e)(3)

53,466   Rules for Determining Capital Gains and Losses
See p. 20,601 for regulations not amended to reflect law changes

$500). Accordingly, the original issue discount attributable to such certificate equals $500 (stated redemption price at maturity $10,500, minus issue price, $10,000). Therefore, E must include as interest $166.67 (*i.e.*, 12/36 months multiplied by the original issue discount, $500) in his gross income for each taxable year he holds the certificate.

(4) *Renewable certificates of deposit*—(i) *In general.* The renewal of a certificate of deposit shall be treated as a purchase of the certificate on the date the renewal period begins regardless of any requirement pursuant to the terms of the certificate that the holder give notice of an intention to renew or not to renew. Thus, for example, in the case of a certificate of deposit for which a renewal period begins after December 31, 1970, such renewal shall be treated as a purchase after such date whether or not the initial period began before such date.

(ii) *Computation.* For purposes of computing the amount of original issue discount to be ratably included as interest in gross income under section 1232(a)(3) in respect of a renewable certificate of deposit for the initial period or any renewal period, the following rules apply:

(*a*) The issue price on the date any renewal period begins is considered to be in the case of a certificate of deposit initially purchased—

(*1*) After December 31, 1970, the adjusted basis of the certificate on the date such period begins,

(*2*) Before January 1, 1971, the amount the adjusted basis would have been on the date such period begins had the holder included all amounts of original issue discount as interest in gross income that would have been includible if section 1232(a)(3) had applied to the certificate from the date of original purchase.

Thus, if under the terms of the certificate, no amount is forfeited upon a failure to renew, then the issue price on the date any renewal period begins is considered to be the amount which would have been received by the holder on such date had it not been renewed.

(*b*) The date of original issue for any renewal period shall be considered to be the date it begins.

(*c*) The date of maturity for the initial period or any renewal period shall be considered to be the date it ends.

(*d*) The stated redemption price at maturity for the initial period or any renewal period shall be considered to be the maximum amount which would be received at the end of any such period, without regard to any reduction resulting from withdrawal prior to maturity or failure to renew at any renewal date.

(iii) *Application of one-year rule.* For purposes of paragraph (b)(2) of this section (relating to nonapplication of section 1232(a)(3) to any obligation having a term of one year or less), the period between the date of original issue (as defined in paragraph (b)(3) of § 1.1232-3) of a renewable certificate of deposit and its stated maturity date shall include all renewal periods with respect to which, under the terms of the certificate, the holder may either take action or refrain from taking action which would prevent the actual or constructive receipt of any interest on such certificate until the expiration of any such renewal period whether or not the original date of issue is prior to January 1, 1971.

(iv) *Example.* The provisions of this subparagraph may be illustrated by the following example:

Example. (*a*) On May 1, 1969, A purchases a 2-year renewable certificate of deposit from M bank, a corporation, for $10,000. Interest will be compounded semiannually at 6 percent on May 1 and November 1. The terms of the certificate provide that such certificate will be automatically renewed on the anniversary date every 2 years if the holder does not notify M of an intention not to renew prior to 60 days before the particular anniversary date. Thus, on May 1, 1971, and May 1, 1973, the certificate may be redeemed for $11,255.09 and $12,667.60, respectively. However, in no event shall the initial period and the renewal periods exceed 10 years. A does not notify M of an intention not to renew by March 1, 1971, and the certificate is automatically renewed for an additional 2-year period on May 1, 1971.

(*b*) Under subdivision (i) of this subparagraph, the May 1, 1971, renewal shall be treated as the purchase of a certificate of deposit on that date, *i.e.*, after December 31, 1970. Under subdivision (ii) of this subparagraph, the issue price is considered to be $11,255.09 and the date of maturity is considered to be May 1, 1973. Since the stated redemption price at maturity is $12,667.60, A must include $58.85 as interest in gross income for each month he holds the certificate during the renewal period beginning May 1, 1971, computed as follows:

Original issue discount (stated redemption price, $12,667.60, minus issue price, $11,255.09)	$ 1,412.51
Divide by: Number of months from renewal to maturity date	24 months
Ratable monthly portion	$ 58.85

Reg. § 1.1232-3A(e)(4)

Rules for Determining Capital Gains and Losses

See p. 20,601 for regulations not amended to reflect law changes

(5) *Time deposit open account arrangements*—(i) *In general.* The term "time deposit open account arrangement" means an arrangement with a fixed maturity date where deposits may be made from time to time and ordinarily no interest will be paid or constructively received until such fixed maturity date. All deposits pursuant to such an arrangement constitute parts of a single obligation. The amount of original issue discount to be ratably included as interest in the gross income of the depositor for any taxable year shall be the sum of the amounts separately computed for each deposit. For this purpose, the issue price for a deposit is the amount thereof and the stated redemption price at maturity is computed under paragraph (b)(1)(iii)(*d*) of § 1.1232-3.

(ii) *Obligations redeemed before maturity.* In the event of a partial redemption of a time deposit open account before maturity, the following rules, in addition to subparagraph (2) of this paragraph, shall apply:

(*a*) If, pursuant to the terms of the withdrawal, the amount received by the depositor is determined with reference to the principal amount of a specific deposit and interest earned from the date of such deposit, then such terms shall control for the purpose of determining which deposit was withdrawn.

(*b*) If (*a*) of this subdivision (ii) does not apply, then the withdrawal shall be deemed to be of specific deposits together with interest earned from the date of such deposits, on a first-in, first-out basis.

(iii) *Examples.* The provisions of this subparagraph may be illustrated by the following examples:

Example (1). (i) F is a cash method taxpayer who uses the calendar year as his taxable year. On December 1, 1970, F enters into a 5-year deposit open account arrangement with M Savings and Loan Corporation. The terms of the arrangement provide that F will deposit $100 each month for a period of 5 years, and that interest will be compounded semiannually (on June 1 and December 1) at 6 percent, but will be paid only at maturity. Thus, assuming F makes deposits of $100 on the first of each month beginning with December 1, 1970, the account will have a stated redemption price of $6,998.20 at maturity on December 1, 1975. Since, however, section 1232 applies only to deposits made after December 31, 1970 (see paragraph (d) of § 1.1232-1), the $34.39 of compound interest to be earned on the first deposit of $100 over the term of the arrangement will not be subject to the ratable inclusion rules of section 1232(a)(3). F must include such $34.39 of interest in his gross income on December 1, 1975, the date it is paid.

(ii) For 1971, F must include $44.19 of original issue discount as interest in gross income, to be computed as follows:

(1)	(2)	(3)	(4)	(5)	(6)	(7)
Date of $100 deposit	Months to Maturity	Redemption price at maturity	Original issue discount (Col.3 − $100)	Ratable monthly portion (Col.4 ÷ Col. 2)	Months on deposit in 1971	1971 original issue discount (Col.5 × Col. 6)
1/1/71	59	$133.73	$33.73	$0.5717	12	$6.86
2/1/71	58	133.07	33.07	0.5702	11	6.27
3/1/71	57	132.42	32.42	0.5688	10	5.69
4/1/71	56	131.77	31.77	0.5673	9	5.11
5/1/71	55	131.12	31.12	0.5658	8	4.53
6/1/71	54	130.48	30.48	0.5644	7	3.95
7/1/71	53	129.84	29.84	0.5630	6	3.38
8/1/71	52	129.20	29.20	0.5615	5	2.81
9/1/71	51	128.56	28.56	0.5600	4	2.24
10/1/71	50	127.93	27.93	0.5586	3	1.68
11/1/71	49	127.30	27.30	0.5571	2	1.11
12/1/71	48	126.68	26.68	0.5558	1	0.56

Total original issue discount to be included as interest in F's gross income for 1971 .... $44.19

Example (2). (i) G is a cash method taxpayer who uses the calendar year as his taxable year. On February 1, 1971, G enters into a 4-year deposit open account arrangement with T Bank, a corporation. The terms of the deposit arrangement provide that G may deposit any amount from time to time in multiples of $50 for a period of 4 years. The terms also provide that G may not redeem any amount until February 1, 1975, except in an emergency as defined in, and subject to the qualifications provided by, Regulation Q of the Board of Governors of the Federal Reserve System. See 12 CFR § 217.4(d). Interest will be compounded semiannually (on February 1 and

53,468 Rules for Determining Capital Gains and Losses
See p. 20,601 for regulations not amended to reflect law changes

August 1) at 6 percent, providing there is no redemption prior to February 1, 1975. However, if there is a redemption prior to such date, interest will be compounded semiannually at 5½ percent.

(ii) The schedule of deposits made by G pursuant to the arrangement, and computation of ratable monthly portion for each deposit, are set forth in the table below:

(1) Date of deposit	(2) Months to maturity	(3) Amount of deposit	(4) Redemption price at maturity	(5) Original issue discount (Col. 4 − Col. 3)	(6) Ratable monthly portion (Col. 5 ÷ Col. 2)
2/1/71	48	$100	$126.68	$26.68	$0.5558
6/1/71	44	200	248.42	48.42	1.1005
12/1/71	38	500	602.95	102.95	2.7092
2/1/72	36	800	955.24	155.24	4.3122
3/1/72	35	800	950.56	150.56	4.3017
7/1/72	31	600	699.00	99.00	3.1935
8/1/72	30	250	289.82	39.82	1.3273

(iii) With respect to amounts on deposit pursuant to the arrangement, the amounts of original issue discount G must include as interest in his gross income for 1971 and 1972 are computed in the table below:

(1) Date of deposit	(2) Ratable monthly portion	(3) Months on deposit in 1971	(4) 1971 original issue discount (Col. 2 × Col.3)	(5) Months on deposit in 1972	(6) 1972 original issue discount (Col. 2 × Col.5)
2/1/71	$0.5558	11	$6.11	12	$ 6.67
6/1/71	1.1005	7	7.70	12	13.21
12/1/71	2.7092	1	2.71	12	32.51
2/1/72	4.3122			11	47.43
3/1/72	4.3017			10	43.02
7/1/72	3.1935			6	19.16
8/1/72	1.3273			5	6.64
Total original issue discount includible as interest in gross income for taxable year			$16.52		$168.64

(6) *Certain contingent interest arrangements*—(i) *In general.* If under the terms of a deposit arrangement—

(a) The holder cannot receive payment of any interest or constructively receive any interest prior to a fixed maturity date,

(b) Interest is earned at a guaranteed minimum rate of compound interest,

(c) Additional contingent interest may be earned for any year at a rate not to exceed one percentage point above such guaranteed minimum rate, and

(d) Any additional contingent interest is credited at least annually to the depositor's account then any contingent interest credited to the depositor shall be treated as creating a separate obligation subject to the rules of subdivision (ii) of this subparagraph.

(ii) *Computation.* For purposes of computing the original issue discount to be included as interest in the depositor's gross income under section 1232(a)(3) with respect to such separate obligation—

(a) The issue price shall be zero,

(b) The date of original issue shall be the date on which the contingent interest is credited to the depositor's account and begins to earn interest,

(c) The date of maturity shall be the fixed maturity date of the deposit, and

(d) The stated redemption price at maturity is the sum of the amount of such contingent interest plus interest to be earned thereon at the guaranteed minimum rate of compound interest between such dates of original issue and maturity.

(7) *Contingent interest arrangements other than those described in subparagraph (6)*—(i) *In general.* If under the terms of a deposit arrangement, contingent interest may be earned and credited to a depositor's account, but is neither actually or constructively received before a fixed maturity date nor treated under subparagraph (6)(i) of this paragraph as creating a separate obligation, then the redemption price shall include the amount which would be credited to such account assuming the issuer, during the term of such account, credits contingent interest at the greater of the rate—

Reg. § 1.1232-3A(e)(6)

Rules for Determining Capital Gains and Losses

(*a*) Last credited on a similar account, or

(*b*) Equal to the average rate credited for the preceding five calendar years on a similar account.

(ii) *Adjustments for additional interest.* The rate taken into account under this subparagraph in computing the redemption price shall be treated as the guaranteed minimum rate for purposes of applying subparagraph (6) of this paragraph in the event the rate at which contingent interest is actually credited to the depositor's account exceeds such rate previously taken into account. If for any period the actual rate at which contingent interest is credited to the account exceeds by more than one percentage point the rate for the previous period taken into account under this subparagraph in computing the redemption price, a new computation shall be made to determine the ratable monthly portion of original issue discount to be included as interest in the gross income of the depositor over the remaining term of the account. For purposes of such computation, the date that interest is first so credited to the account shall be treated as the issue date, the adjusted basis of the account on such date shall be the issue price, and the redemption price shall equal the amount actually on deposit in the account on such date plus the amount which would be credited to such account assuming the issuer, during the remaining term of such account, continues to credit contingent interest at the new rate.

(iii) *Adjustment for reduced interest.* If for any period the actual rate of interest at which contingent interest is credited to the depositor's account is less than the rate for the previous period taken into account under this subparagraph in computing the redemption price, the difference between the amount of interest which would have been credited to the account at the rate for such previous period and the amount actually credited shall be allowed as a deduction against the amount of original issue discount with respect to such account required to be included in the gross income of the depositor. If an account is redeemed for a price less than the adjusted basis of the account, the depositor shall be allowed as a deduction, in computing adjusted gross income, the amount of the original issue discount he included in gross income but did not receive.

(f) *Application of section 1232(a)(3) to face-amount certificates*—(1) *In general.* Under paragraph (c)(3) of § 1.1232-1, the provisions of section 1232 (a)(3) and this section apply in the case of a face-amount certificate issued after December 31, 1975 (other than such a certificate issued pursuant to a written commitment which was binding on such date and at all times thereafter).

(2) *Relationship with paragraph (e) of this section.* Determinations with regard to the inclusion as interest of original issue discount on, and certain adjustments with respect to, face-amount certificates to which this section applies shall be made in a manner consistent with the rules of paragraph (e) of this section (relating to the application of section 1232 to certain deposits in financial institutions and similar arrangements). Thus, for example, if a face-amount certificate is redeemed before maturity, the holder shall be allowed a deduction in computing adjusted gross income computed in a manner consistent with the rules of paragraph (e)(2) of this section. For a further example, if under the terms of a face-amount certificate, the issuer may grant additional credits to be paid at a fixed maturity date, computations with respect to such additional credits shall be made in a manner consistent with the rules of paragraph (e)(6) and (7) of this section (as applicable) relating to contingent interest arrangements. [Reg. § 1.1232-3A.]

☐ [*T.D. 7154, 12-27-71. Amended by T.D. 7213, 10-13-72, T.D. 7311, 3-29-74, T.D. 7336, 12-19-74 and T.D. 7365, 6-30-75.*]

[Reg. § 1.1233-1]

§ 1.1233-1. **Gains and losses from short sales.**—(a) *General.* (1) For income tax purposes a short sale is not deemed to be consummated until delivery of property to close the short sale. Whether the recognized gain or loss from a short sale is capital gain or loss or ordinary gain or loss depends upon whether the property so delivered constitutes a capital asset in the hands of the taxpayer.

(2) Thus, if a dealer in securities makes a short sale of X Corporation stock, ordinary gain or loss results on closing of the short sale if the stock used to close the short sale was stock which he held primarily for sale to customers in the ordinary course of his trade or business. If the stock used to close the short sale was a capital asset in his hands, or if the taxpayer in this example was not a dealer, a capital gain or loss would result.

(3) Generally, the period for which a taxpayer holds property delivered to close a short sale determines whether long-term or short-term capital gain or loss results.

(4) Thus, if a taxpayer makes a short sale of shares of stock and covers the short sale by purchasing and delivering shares which he held for not more than 1 year (6 months for taxable years beginning before 1977; 9 months for taxable years beginning in 1977), the recognized gain or

53,470 Rules for Determining Capital Gains and Losses
See p. 20,601 for regulations not amended to reflect law changes

loss would be considered short-term capital gain or loss. If the short sale is made through a broker and the broker borrows property to make a delivery, the short sale is not deemed to be consummated until the obligation of the seller created by the short sale is finally discharged by delivery of property to the broker to replace the property borrowed by the broker.

(5) For rules for determining the date of sale for purposes of applying under section 1091 the 61-day period applicable to a short sale of stock or securities at a loss, see paragraph (g) of § 1.1091-1.

(b) *Hedging transactions.* Under section 1233(g), the provisions of section 1233 and this section shall not apply to any bona fide hedging transaction in commodity futures entered into by flour millers, producers of cloth, operators of grain elevators, etc., for the purpose of their business. Gain or loss from a short sale of commodity futures which does not qualify as a hedging transaction shall be considered gain or loss from the sale or exchange of a capital asset if the commodity future used to close the short sale constitutes a capital asset in the hands of the taxpayer as explained in paragraph (a) of this section.

(c) *Special short sales*—(1) *General.* Section 1233 provides rules as to the tax consequences of a short sale of property if gain or loss from the short sale is considered as gain or loss from the sale or exchange of a capital asset under section 1233(a) and paragraph (a) of this section and if, at the time of the short sale or on or before the date of the closing of the short sale, the taxpayer holds property substantially identical to that sold short. The term "property" is defined for purposes of such rules to include only stocks and securities (including stocks and securities dealt with on a "when issued" basis) and commodity futures, which are capital assets in the hands of the taxpayer. Certain restrictions on the application of the section to commodity futures are provided in section 1233(e) and paragraph (d)(2) of this section. Section 1233(f) contains special provisions governing the operation of rule (2) in subparagraph (2) of this paragraph in the case of a purchase and short sale of stocks or securities in a transaction qualifying as an arbitrage operation. See paragraph (f) of this section for detailed rules relating to arbitrage operations in stocks and securities.

(2) *Treatment of special short sales.* The first two rules, which are set forth in section 1233(b), are applicable whenever property substantially identical to that sold short has been held by the taxpayer on the date of the short sale for not more than 1 year (6 months for taxable years beginning before 1977; 9 months for taxable years beginning in 1977) (determined without regard to rule (2), contained in this subparagraph, relating to the holding period) or is acquired by him after the short sale and on or before the date of the closing thereof. These rules are:

Rule (1). Any gain upon the closing of such short sale shall be considered as a gain upon the sale or exchange of a capital asset held for not more than 1 year (6 months for taxable years beginning before 1977; 9 months for taxable years beginning in 1977) (notwithstanding the period of time any property used to close such short sale has been held); and

Rule (2). The holding period of such substantially identical property shall be considered to begin (notwithstanding the provisions of section 1233) on the date of the closing of such short sale or on the date of a sale, gift, or other disposition of such property, whichever date occurs first.

(3) *Options to sell.* For the purpose of rule (1) and rule (2) in paragraph (2) of this paragraph, the acquisition of an option to sell property at a fixed price shall be considered a short sale, and the exercise or failure to exercise such option shall be considered as a closing of such short sale, except that any option to sell property at a fixed price acquired on or after August 17, 1954 (the day after enactment of the Internal Revenue Code of 1954), shall not be considered a short sale and the exercise or failure to exercise such option shall not be considered as the closing of a short sale provided that the option and property identified as intended to be used in its exercise are acquired on the same date. This exception shall not apply, if the option is exercised, unless it is exercised by the sale of the property so identified. In the case of any option not exercised which falls within this exception, the cost of such option shall be added to the basis of the property with which such option is identified. If the option itself does not specifically identify the property intended to be used in exercising the option, then the identification of such property shall be made by appropriate entries in the taxpayer's records within 15 days after the date such property is acquired or before November 17, 1956, whichever expiration date later occurs.

(4) *Treatment of losses.* The third rule, which is set forth in section 1233(d), is applicable whenever property substantially identical to that sold short has been held by the taxpayer on the date of the short sale for more than 1 year (6 months for taxable years beginning before 1977; 9 months for taxable years beginning in 1977). This rule is:

Rule (3). Any loss upon the closing of such short sale shall be considered as a loss upon the

Reg. § 1.1233-1(a)(5)

Rules for Determining Capital Gains and Losses

See p. 20,601 for regulations not amended to reflect law changes

sale or exchange of a capital asset held for more than 1 year (6 months for taxable years beginning before 1977; 9 months for taxable years beginning in 1977), notwithstanding the period of time any property used to close such short sale has been held. For the purpose of this rule, the acquisition of an option to sell property at a fixed price is not considered a short sale, and the exercise or failure to exercise such option is not considered as a closing of a short sale.

(5) *Application of rules.* Rules (1) and (3) contained in subparagraphs (2) and (4) of this paragraph do not apply to the gain or loss attributable to so much of the property sold short as exceeds in quantity the substantially identical property referred to in sections 1233(b) and (d), respectively. Except as otherwise provided in section 1233(f), rule (2) in subparagraph (2) of this paragraph applies to the substantially identical property referred to in section 1233(b) in the order of the dates of the acquisition of such property, but only to so much of such property as does not exceed the quantity sold short. If property substantially identical to that sold short has been held by the taxpayer on the date of the short sale for not more than 1 year (6 months for taxable years beginning before 1977; 9 months for taxable years beginning in 1977), or is acquired by him after the short sale and on or before the date of the closing thereof, and if property substantially identical to that sold short has been held by the taxpayer on the date of the short sale for more than 1 year (6 months for taxable years beginning before 1977; 9 months for taxable years beginning in 1977), all three rules are applicable.

(6) *Examples.* The following examples illustrate the application of these rules to short sales of stock in the case of a taxpayer who makes his return on the basis of the calendar year:

Example (1). A buys 100 shares of X stock at $10 per share on February 1, 1955, sells short 100 shares of X stock at $16 per share on July 1, 1955, and closes the short sale on August 2, 1955, by delivering the 100 shares of X stock purchased on February 1, 1955, to the lender of the stock used to effect the short sale. Since 100 shares of X stock had been held by A on the date of the short sale for not more than 6 months, the gain of $600 realized upon the closing of the short sale is, by application of rule (1) in subparagraph (2) of this paragraph, a short-term capital gain.

Example (2). A buys 100 shares of X stock at $10 per share on February 1, 1955, sells short 100 shares of X stock at $16 per share on July 1, 1955, closes the short sale on August 1, 1955, with 100 shares of X stock purchased on that date at $18 per share, and on August 2, 1955, sells at $18 per share the 100 shares of X stock purchased on February 1, 1955. The $200 loss sustained upon the closing of the short sale is a short-term capital loss to which section 1233(d) has no application. By application of rule (2) in subparagraph (2) of this paragraph, however, the holding period of the 100 shares of X stock purchased on February 1, 1955, and sold on August 2, 1955 is considered to begin on August 1, 1955, the date of the closing of the short sale. The $800 gain realized upon the sale of such stock is, therefore, a short-term capital gain.

Example (3). A buys 100 shares of X stock at $10 per share on February 1, 1955, sells short 100 shares of X stock at $16 per share on September 1, 1955, sells on October 1, 1955, at $18 per share the 100 shares of X stock purchased on February 1, 1955, and closes the short sale on October 1, 1955, with 100 shares of X stock purchased on that date at $18 per share. The $800 gain realized upon the sale of the 100 shares of X stock purchased on February 1, 1955, is a long-term capital gain to which section 1233(b) has no application. Since A had held 100 shares of X stock on the date of the short sale for more than 6 months, the $200 loss sustained upon the closing of the short sale is, by application of rule (3) in subparagraph (4) of this paragraph, a long-term capital loss. If, instead of purchasing 100 shares of X stock on October 1, 1955, A closed the short sale with the 100 shares of stock purchased on February 1, 1955, the $600 gain realized on the closing of the short sale would be a long-term capital gain to which section 1233(b) has no application.

Example (4). A sells short 100 shares of X stock at $16 per share on February 1, 1955. He buys 250 shares of X stock on March 1, 1955, at $10 per share and holds the latter stock until September 2, 1955 (more than 6 months), at which time, 100 shares of the 250 shares of X stock are delivered to close the short sale made on February 1, 1955. Since substantially identical property was acquired by A after the short sale and before it was closed, the $600 gain realized on the closing of the short sale is, by application of rule (1) in subparagraph (2) of this paragraph, a short-term capital gain. The holding period of the remaining 150 shares of X stock is not affected by section 1233 since this amount of the substantially identical property exceeds the quantity of the property sold short.

Example (5). A buys 100 shares of X stock at $10 per share on February 1, 1955, buys an additional 100 shares of X stock at $20 per share on July 1, 1955, sells short 100 shares of X stock at $30 per share on September 1, 1955, and closes the short sale on February 1, 1956, by delivering

Reg. § 1.1233-1(c)(6)

the 100 shares of X stock purchased on February 1, 1955, to the lender of the stock used to effect the short sale. Since 100 shares of X stock had been held by A on the date of the short sale for not more than 6 months, the gain of $2,000 realized upon the closing of the short sale is, by application of rule (1) in subparagraph (2) of this paragraph a short-term capital gain and the holding period of the 100 shares of X stock purchased on July 1, 1955, is considered, by application of rule (2) in subparagraph (2) of this paragraph to begin on February 1, 1956, the date of the closing of the short sale. If, however, the 100 shares of X stock purchased on July 1, 1955, had been used by A to close the short sale, then, since 100 shares of X stock had been held by A on the date of the short sale for not more than 6 months, the gain of $1,000 realized upon the closing of the short sale would be, by application of rule (1) in subparagraph (2) of this paragraph, a short-term capital gain, but the holding period of the 100 shares of X stock purchased on February 1, 1955, would not be affected by section 1233. If, on the other hand, A purchased an additional 100 shares of X stock at $40 per share on February 1, 1956, and used such shares to close the short sale at that time, then, since 100 shares of X stock had been held by A on the date of the short sale for more than 6 months, the loss of $1,000 sustained upon the closing of the short sale would be, by application of rule (3) in subparagraph (4) of this paragraph, a long-term capital loss, and since 100 shares of X stock had been held by A on the date of the short sale for not more than 6 months, the holding period of the 100 shares of X stock purchased on July 1, 1955, would be considered by application of rule (2) in subparagraph (2) of this paragraph, to begin on February 1, 1956, but the holding period of the 100 shares of X stock purchased on February 1, 1955, would not be affected by section 1233.

Example (6). A buys 100 shares of X preferred stock at $10 per share on February 1, 1955. On July 1, 1955, he enters into a contract to sell 100 shares of XY common stock at $16 per share when, as, and if issued pursuant to a particular proposed plan of reorganization. On August 2, 1955, he receives 100 shares of XY common stock in exchange for the 100 shares of X perferred stock purchased on February 1, 1955, and delivers such common shares in performance of his July 1, 1955, contract. Assume that the exchange of the X preferred stock for the XY common stock is a tax-free exchange pursuant to section 354(a)(1), and that on the basis of all of the facts and circumstances existing on July 1, 1955, the "when issued" XY common stock is substantially identical to the X preferred stock. Since 100 shares of substantially identical property had been held by A for not more than 6 months on the date of entering into the July 1, 1955, contract of sale, the gain of $600 realized upon the closing of the contract of sale is, by application of rule (1) in subparagraph (2) of this paragraph, a short-term capital gain.

(d) *Other rules for the application of section 1233*—(1) *Substantially identical property.* The term "substantially identical property" is to be applied according to the facts and circumstances in each case. In general, as applied to stocks or securities, the term has the same meaning as the term "substantially identical stock or securities" used in section 1091, relating to wash sales of stocks or securities. For certain restrictions on the term as applied to commodity futures see subparagraph (2) of this paragraph. Ordinarily, stocks or securities of one corporation are not considered substantially identical to stocks or securities of another corporation. In certain situations they may be substantially identical; for example, in the case of a reorganization the facts and circumstances may be such that the stocks and securities of predecessor and successor corporations are substantially identical property. Similarly, bonds or preferred stock of a corporation are not ordinarily considered substantially identical to the common stock of the same corporation. However, in certain situations, as, for example, where the preferred stock or bonds are convertible into common stock of the same corporation, the relative values, price changes, and other circumstances may be such as to make such bonds or preferred stock and the common stock substantially identical property. Similarly, depending on the facts and circumstances, the term may apply to the stocks and securities to be received in a corporate reorganization or recapitalization, traded in on a when issued basis, as compared with the stocks or securities to be exchanged in such reorganization or recapitalization.

(2) *Commodity futures.* (i) As provided in section 1233(e)(2)(B), in the case of futures transactions in any commodity on or subject to the rules of a board of trade or commodity exchange, a commodity future requiring delivery in one calendar month shall not be considered as property substantially identical to another commodity future requiring delivery in a different calendar month. For example, commodity futures in May wheat and July wheat are not considered, for the purpose of section 1233, substantially identical property.

Similarly, futures in different commodities which are not generally through custom of the trade used as hedges for each other (such as corn and

Rules for Determining Capital Gains and Losses

See p. 20,601 for regulations not amended to reflect law changes

wheat, for example) are not considered substantially identical property. If commodity futures are otherwise substantially identical property, the mere fact that they were procured through different brokers will not remove them from the scope of the term "substantially identical property". Commodity futures procured on different markets may come within the term "substantially identical property" depending upon the facts and circumstances in the case, with the historical similarity in the price movements in the two markets as the primary factor to be considered.

(ii) Section 1233(e)(3), relating to so-called "arbitrage" transactions in commodity futures, provides that where a taxpayer enters into two commodity futures transactions on the same day, one requiring delivery by him in one market and the other requiring delivery to him of the same (or substantially identical) commodity in the same calendar month in a different market, and the taxpayer subsequently closes both such transactions on the same day, section 1233 shall have no application to so much of the commodity involved in either such transaction as does not exceed in quantity the commodity involved in the other. Section 1233(f), relating to arbitrage operations in stocks or securities, has no application to arbitrage transactions in commodity futures.

(iii) The following example indicates the application of section 1233 to a commodity futures transaction:

Example. A who makes his return on the basis of the calendar year, on February 1, 1955, enters into a contract through broker X to purchase 10,000 bushels of December wheat on the Chicago market at $2 per bushel. On July 1, 1955, he enters into a contract through broker Y to sell 10,000 bushels of December wheat on the Chicago market at $2.25 per bushel. On August 2, 1955, he closes both transactions at $2.50 per bushel. The $2,500 loss sustained on the closing of the short sale is a short-term capital loss to which section 1233(d) has no application. By application of rule (2) in paragraph (c)(2) of this section, however, the holding period of the futures contract entered into on February 1, 1955, is considered to begin on August 2, 1955, the date of the closing of the short sale. The $5,000 gain realized upon the closing of such contract is, therefore, a short-term capital gain.

(3) *Husband and wife.* Section 1233(e)(2)(C) provides that, in the case of a short sale of property by an individual, the term "taxpayer" in the application of subsections (b), (d), and (e) shall be read as "taxpayer or his spouse". Thus, if the spouse of a taxpayer holds or acquires property substantially identical to that sold short by the taxpayer, and other conditions of subsections (b), (d), and (e) are met, then the rules set forth therein are applicable to the same extent as if the taxpayer held or acquired the substantially identical property. For this purpose, an individual who is legally separated from the taxpayer under a decree of divorce or of separate maintenance shall not be considered as the spouse of the taxpayer.

(e) *Special rule for short sales by dealers in securities under certain circumstances.* In the case of a short sale of stock (as defined in subparagraph (3) of this paragraph) after December 31, 1957, by a dealer in securities, section 1233(e)(4)(A) provides that the holding period of substantially identical stock which he has held as an investment for not more than 1 year (6 months for taxable years beginning before 1977; 9 months for taxable years beginning in 1977) shall be determined in accordance with section 1233(b)(2) unless such short sale is closed within 20 days of the date on which it was made. See rule (2) in paragraph (c)(2) of this section for the purpose of determining the holding period of such substantially identical stock. In addition, section 1233(e)(4)(B) provides that for the purpose of the special rule of section 1233(e)(4)(A), the acquisition of an option to sell property at a fixed price shall be considered a short sale, and the exercise or failure to exercise such option shall be considered a closing of such short sale. For purposes of this paragraph—

(1) Whether or not a taxpayer is a "dealer in securities" shall be determined in accordance with the meaning of the term for purposes of section 1236;

(2) Whether or not stock is "substantially identical" with other property shall be determined in accordance with the provisions of paragraph (d)(1) of this section; and

(3) The term "stock" means—

(i) Any share or certificate of stock,

(ii) Any bond or other evidence of indebtedness which is convertible into a share or certificate of stock, and

(iii) Any evidence of an interest in, or right to subscribe to or purchase, any of the items described in subdivision (i) or (ii) of this subparagraph.

(f) *Arbitrage operations in stocks and securities and holding periods*—(1) *General rule.* (i) In the case of a short sale entered into as part of an arbitrage operation, rule (2) of paragraph (c)(2) of this section shall apply first to substantially identical property acquired for arbitrage operations and held by the taxpayer at the close of business on the day of the short sale. The holding period of

Reg. § 1.1233-1(f)(1)

53,474 Rules for Determining Capital Gains and Losses

See p. 20,601 for regulations not amended to reflect law changes

substantially identical property not acquired for arbitrage operations shall be affected only to the extent that the amount of property sold short exceeds the amount of substantially identical property acquired for arbitrage operations and held by the taxpayer at the close of business on the day of the short sale.

(ii) If the substantially identical property acquired for arbitrage operations is disposed of without closing the short sale so that a net short position in assets acquired for arbitrage operations is created, a short sale in the amount of such net short position will be deemed to have been made on the day such net short position is created. Rule (2) of paragraph (c)(2) of this section will then apply to substantially identical property not acquired for arbitrage operations to the same extent as if the taxpayer, on the day such net short position is created, sold short an amount equal to the amount of the net short position in a transaction not entered into as part of an arbitrage operation.

(iii) The following examples illustrate the application of rule (2) of paragraph (c)(2) of this section to arbitrage operations:

Example (1). On August 13, 1957, A buys 100 bonds of X Corporation for purposes other than arbitrage operations. The bonds are convertible at the option of the bondholders into common stock of X Corporation on the basis of one bond for one share of stock. On November 1, 1957, A sells short 100 shares of common stock of X Corporation in a transaction identified and intended to be part of an arbitrage operation and on the same day buys another 100 bonds of X Corporation in a transaction identified and intended to be part of the same arbitrage operation. The bonds acquired on both August 13, 1957, and November 1, 1957, are, on the basis of all the facts and circumstances, substantially identical to the common stock of X Corporation. On December 1, 1957, A closes the short sale with 100 shares of common stock of X Corporation acquired on that day. The holding period of the bonds acquired on November 1, by application of rule (2) of paragraph (c)(2) of this section, will be deemed to begin on December 1 and the holding period of the bonds acquired on August 13 will be unaffected. If, instead of purchasing the 100 shares of common stock of X Corporation on December 1, 1957, A had converted the bonds acquired on November 1 into common stock and, on December 1, 1957, used the stock so acquired to close the short sale, rule (2) of paragraph (c)(2) of this section would similarly have no effect on the holding period of the bonds acquired on August 13.

Example (2). Assume the same facts as in example (1), except that A, on December 1, sells the bonds acquired on November 1 (or converts such bonds into common stock and sells the stock), but does not close the short sale. The sale of the bonds (or stock) creates a net short position in assets acquired for arbitrage operations which is deemed to be a short sale made on December 1. Accordingly, the holding period of the bonds acquired on August 13 will, by application of rule (2) of paragraph (c)(2) of this section, begin on the date such short sale is closed or on the date of sale, gift, or other disposition of such bonds, whichever date occurs first.

(2) *Right to receive or acquire property.* (i) For purposes of section 1233(f)(1) and (2) and subparagraph (1) of this paragraph, a taxpayer will be deemed to hold substantially identical property acquired for arbitrage operations at the close of any business day if, by virtue of the ownership of other property acquired for arbitrage operations (whether or not substantially identical) or because of any contract entered into by the taxpayer in an arbitrage operation, he then has the right to receive or acquire such substantially identical property.

(ii) The application of section 1233(f)(3) and subdivision (i) of this subparagraph may be illustrated by the following example:

Example. A acquires on August 13, 1957, 100 shares of common stock of X Corporation for purposes other than arbitrage operations. On November 1, A sells short, in a transaction identified and intended to be part of an arbitrage operation, 100 shares of X common stock. On the same day, in a transaction also identified and intended to be part of the same arbitrage operation, A contracts to purchase 100 shares of preferred stock of X. The preferred stock of X may be converted into common stock of X on the basis of one share of preferred stock for one share of common stock. The preferred stock is not actually delivered to A until November 3. Since A has contracted before the close of business on the date of the short sale, as part of an arbitrage operation, to purchase property by virtue of which he has the right to receive or acquire substantially identical property to that sold short, he will be deemed, for purposes of section 1233(f)(1) and (2), to hold such substantially identical property at the close of business on the date of the short sale. For purposes of this subparagraph, it is immaterial whether, on the basis of all the facts and circumstances, the preferred stock of X is substantially identical to the common stock of X. The short sale on November 1 does not affect the holding period of the 100 shares of X Corporation common stock purchased

Reg. § 1.1233-1(f)(2)

on August 13, 1957. Because of the operation of rule (2) of paragraph (c)(2) of this section, the holding period of the preferred stock acquired as the result of A's contract to purchase it as part of an arbitrage operation (or the common stock which A acquires by conversion of such preferred stock into common stock) will not begin until the short sale entered into in the arbitrage operation is closed.

(3) *Definition of arbitrage operations.* For the purpose of section 1233(f), arbitrage operations are transactions involving the purchase and sale of property entered into for the purpose of profiting from a current difference between the price of the property purchased and the price of the property sold. Assets acquired for arbitrage operations include only stocks and securities and rights to acquire stocks and securities. The property purchased may be either identical to the property sold or, if not so identical, such that its acquisition will entitle the taxpayer to acquire property which is so identical. Thus, the purchase of bonds or preferred stock convertible, at the holder's option, into common stock and the short sale of the common stock which may be acquired therefor, or the purchase of stock rights and the short sale of the stock to be acquired on the exercise of such rights, may qualify as arbitrage operations. A transaction will qualify as an arbitrage operation under section 1233(f) only if the taxpayer properly identifies the transaction as an arbitrage operation on his records as soon as he is able to do so. Such identification must ordinarily be entered in the taxpayer's records on the day of the transaction. Property acquired in a transaction properly identified as part of an arbitrage operation is the only property which will be deemed acquired for an arbitrage operation. The provisions of section 1233(f) and this paragraph shall continue to apply to property acquired in a transaction properly identified as an arbitrage operation although, because of subsequent events, e.g., a change in the value of bonds so acquired or of stock into which such bonds may be converted, the taxpayer sells such property outright rather than using it to complete the arbitrage operation.

(4) *Effective date of section 1233(f).* Section 1233(f), relating to arbitrage operations involving short sales of property, is effective only with respect to taxable years ending after August 12, 1955, and only with respect to short sales made after such date. [Reg. § 1.1233-1.]

☐ [*T.D.* 6207, 10-17-56. *Amended by T.D.* 6494, 9-29-60; *T.D.* 6926, 8-8-67 and *T.D.* 7728, 10-31-80.]

[Reg. § 1.1233-2]

§ 1.1233-2. **Hedging transactions.**—The character of gain or loss on a short sale that is (or is identified as being) part of a hedging transaction is determined under the rules of § 1.1221-2. [Reg. § 1.1233-2.]

☐ [*T.D.* 8555, 7-13-94.]

[Reg. § 1.1234-1]

§ 1.1234-1. **Options to buy or sell.**—(a) *Sale or exchange*—(1) *Capital assets.* Gain or loss from the sale or exchange of an option (or privilege) to buy or sell property which is (or if acquired would be) a capital asset in the hands of the taxpayer holding the option is considered as gain or loss from the sale or exchange of a capital asset (unless, under the provisions of subparagraph (2) of this paragraph, the gain or loss is subject to the provisions of section 1231). The period for which the taxpayer has held the option determines whether the capital gain or loss is short-term or long-term.

(2) *Section 1231 transactions.* Gain or loss from the sale or exchange of an option to buy or sell property is considered a gain or loss subject to the provisions of section 1231 if, had the sale or exchange been of the property subject to the option, held by the taxpayer for the length of time he held the option, the sale or exchange would have been subject to the provisions of section 1231.

(3) *Other property.* Gain or loss from the sale or exchange of an option to buy or sell property which is not (or if acquired would not be) a capital asset in the hands of the taxpayer holding the option is considered ordinary income or loss (unless under the provisions of subparagraph (2) of this paragraph the gain or loss is subject to the provisions of section 1231).

(b) *Failure to exercise option.* If the holder of an option to buy or sell property incurs a loss on failure to exercise the option, the option is deemed to have been sold or exchanged on the date that it expired. Any such loss to the holder of an option is treated under the general rule provided in paragraph (a) of this section. Any gain to the grantor of an option arising from the failure of the holder to exercise it is ordinary income. In addition, any gain or loss realized by the grantor of an option as a result of a closing transaction, such as repurchasing the option from the holder, is considered ordinary income or loss. However, for the treatment of gain or loss from a closing transaction with respect to, or gain on the lapse of, an option granted in stock, securities, commodities, or commodity futures, see section 1234(b) and § 1.1234-3. For special rules for grantors of straddles applicable to certain options granted on or before September 1, 1976, see § 1.1234-2.

(c) *Certain options to sell property at a fixed price.* Section 1234 does not apply to a loss on the failure to exercise an option to sell property at a fixed price which is acquired on the same day on which the property identified as intended to be used in exercising the option is acquired. Such a loss is not recognized, but the cost of the option is added to the basis of the property with which it is identified. See section 1233(c) and the regulations thereunder.

(d) *Dealers in options to buy or sell.* Any gain or loss realized by a dealer in options from the sale or exchange of an option to buy or sell property is considered ordinary income or loss under paragraph (a)(3) of this section. A dealer in options to buy or sell property is considered a dealer in the property subject to the option.

(e) *Other exceptions.* Section 1234 does not apply to gain resulting from the sale or exchange of an option—

(1) To the extent that the gain is in the nature of compensation (see sections 61 and 421, and the regulations thereunder, relating to employee stock options);

(2) If the option is treated as section 306 stock (see section 306 and the regulations thereunder, relating to dispositions of certain stock); or

(3) To the extent that the gain is a distribution of earnings or profits taxable as a dividend (see section 301 and the regulations thereunder, relating to distributions of property);

(4) Acquired by the taxpayer before March 1, 1954, if in the hands of the taxpayer such option is a capital asset (whether or not the property to which the option relates is, or would be if acquired by the taxpayer, a capital asset in the hands of the taxpayer).

(f) *Limitations on effect of section.* Losses to which section 1234 applies are subject to the limitations on losses under sections 165(c) and 1211 when applicable. Section 1234 does not permit the deduction of any loss which is disallowed under any other provision of law. In addition, section 1234 does not apply to an option to lease property, but does apply to an option to buy or sell a lease. Thus, an option to obtain all the right, title, and interest of a lessee in leased property is subject to the provisions of section 1234, but an option to obtain a sublease from the lessee is not. Furthermore, if section 1234 applies to an option to buy or sell a lease, it is the character the lease itself, if acquired, would have in the hands of the taxpayer, and not the character of the property leased, which determines the treatment of gain or loss experienced by the taxpayer with respect to such an option.

(g) *Examples.* The rules set forth in this section may be illustrated by the following examples:

Example (1). A taxpayer is considering buying a new house for his residence and acquires an option to buy a certain house at a fixed price. Although the property goes up in value, the taxpayer decides he does not want the house for his residence and sells the option for more than he paid for it. The gain which taxpayer realized is a capital gain since the property, if acquired, would have been a capital asset in his hands.

Example (2). Assume the same facts as in example (1), except that the property goes down in value, and the taxpayer decides not to purchase the house. He sells the option at a loss. While this is a capital loss under section 1234, it is not a deductible loss because of the provisions of section 165(c).

Example (3). A dealer in industrial property acquires an option to buy an industrial site and fails to exercise the option. The loss is an ordinary loss since he would have held the property for sale to customers in the ordinary course of his trade or business if he had acquired it. [Reg. § 1.1234-1.]

☐ [T.D. 6253, 9-25-57. Amended by T.D. 6394, 7-1-59; T.D. 7152, 12-22-71 and T.D. 7652, 10-29-79.]

[Reg. § 1.1234-2]

§ 1.1234-2. **Special rules for grantors of straddles applicable to certain options granted on or before September 1, 1976.**—(a) *In general.* Section 1234(c)(1) provides a special rule applicable in the case of gain on the lapse of an option granted by the taxpayer as part of a straddle. In such a case, the gain shall be deemed to be gain from the sale or exchange of a capital asset held for not more than 1 year (6 months for taxable years beginning before 1977; 9 months for taxable years beginning in 1977) on the day that the option expired. Thus, such gain shall be treated as a short-term capital gain, as defined in section 1222(1). Section 1234(c)(1) does not apply to any person who holds securities (including options to acquire or sell securities) for sale to customers in the ordinary course of his trade or business.

(b) *Definitions.* The following definitions apply for purposes of section 1234(c) and this section.

(1) *Straddle.* The term "straddle" means a simultaneously granted combination of an option to buy (i.e., a "call") and an option to sell (i.e., a "put") the same quantity of a security at the same price during the same period of time.

Rules for Determining Capital Gains and Losses

(2) *Security.* The term "security" has the meaning assigned to such term by section 1236(c) and the regulations thereunder. Thus, for example, the term "security" does not include commodity futures.

(3) *Grantor.* The term "grantor" means the writer or issuer of the option contracts making up the straddle.

(4) *Multiple option.* The term "multiple option" means a simultaneously granted combination of an option to buy plus an option to sell plus one or more additional options to buy or sell a security.

(c) *Special rules in the case of a multiple option.* (1) If, in the case of a multiple option, the number of the options to sell and the number of the options to buy are the same and if the terms of all of the options are identical (as to the quantity of the security, price, and period of time), then each of the options contained in the multiple option shall be deemed to be a component of a straddle for purposes of section 1234(c)(1) and paragraph (a) of this section.

(2) If, in the case of a multiple option, the number of the options to sell and the number of the options to buy are not the same or if the terms of all of the options are not identical (as to the quantity of the security, price, and period of time), then section 1234(c)(1) applies to gain on the lapse of an option granted as part of the multiple option only if—

    (i) The grantor of the multiple option identified the two options which comprise each straddle contained in the multiple option in the manner prescribed in subparagraph (3) of this paragraph; or

    (ii) It is clear from the facts and circumstances that the lapsed option was part of a straddle. See example (6) of paragraph (f) of this section. A multiple option to which this subdivision applies may not be regarded as consisting of a number of straddles which exceeds the lesser of the options to sell or the options to buy as the case may be. For example, if a multiple option of five puts and four calls is granted it may not be regarded as consisting of more than four straddles, although the particular facts and circumstances could dictate that the option consist of less than four straddles.

(3) The identification required under subparagraph (2)(i) of this paragraph shall be made by the grantor indicating in his records, to the extent feasible, the individual serial number of, or other characteristic symbol imprinted upon, each of the two individual options which comprise the straddle, or by adopting any other method of identification satisfactory to the Commissioner. Such identification must be made before the expiration of the fifteenth day after the day on which the multiple option is granted. The preceding sentence shall apply only with respect to multiple options granted after [the 30th day following the date of publication in the *Federal Register* of the Treasury decision]. In computing the 15-day period prescribed by this paragraph, the first day of such period is the day following the day on which the multiple option is granted.

(d) *Allocation of premium.* The allocation of a premium received for a straddle or a multiple option between or among the component options thereof shall be made on the basis of the relative market value of such component options at the time of their issuance or on any other reasonable and consistently applied basis which is acceptable to the Commissioner.

(e) *Effective date*—(1) *In general.* This section, relating to special rules for grantors of straddles, shall apply only with respect to straddle transactions entered into after January 25, 1965, and before September 2, 1976.

(2) *Special rule.* For a special rule with respect to the identification of a straddle granted as part of a multiple option, see paragraph (c).

(f) *Illustrations.* The application of section 1234(c) and this section may be illustrated by the following examples:

    Example (1). On February 1, 1971, taxpayer A, who files his income tax returns on a calendar year basis, issues a straddle for 100 shares of X Corporation stock and receives a premium of $1,000. The options comprising the straddle were to expire on August 10, 1971. A has allocated $450 (45 percent of $1,000) of the premium to the put and $550 (55 percent of $1,000) to the call. On March 1, 1971, B, the holder of the put, exercises his option. C, the holder of the call, fails to exercise his option prior to its expiration. As a result of C's failure to exercise his option, A realizes a short-term capital gain of $550 (that part of the premium allocated to the call) on August 10, 1971.

    Example (2). Assume the same facts as in example (1), except that C exercises his call on March 1, 1971, and B fails to exercise his put prior to its expiration. As a result of B's failure to exercise his option, A realizes a short-term capital gain of $450 (that part of the premium allocated to the put) on August 10, 1971.

    Example (3). Assume the same facts as in example (1), except that both B and C fail to exercise their respective options. As a result of the failure of B and C to exercise their options, A realizes short-term capital gains of $1,000 (the

Reg. § 1.1234-2(f)

premium for granting the straddle) on August 10, 1971.

Example (4). On March 1, 1971, taxpayer D issues a multiple option containing five puts and five calls. Each put and each call is for the same number of shares of Y Corporation stock, at the same price, and for the same period of time. Thus, each of the puts and calls is deemed to be a component part of a straddle. The puts and calls comprising the multiple option were to expire on September 10, 1971. All of the puts are exercised, and all of the calls lapse. As a result of the lapse of the calls, D realizes a short-term capital gain on September 10, 1971, in the amount of that part of the premium for the multiple option which is allocable to all of the calls.

Example (5). Assume the same facts as in example (4) except that one of the puts and two of the calls lapse and the remaining puts and calls are exercised. As a result, on September 10, 1971, D realizes a short-term capital gain in the amount of that part of the premium for the multiple option which is allocable to both of the lapsed calls and the lapsed put.

Example (6). On March 1, 1971, taxpayer E issues a multiple option containing five puts and four calls. Each put and call is for the same number of shares of Y Corporation stock at the same price and for the same period of time. E does not identify the puts and calls as parts of straddles in the manner prescribed in paragraph (c)(3) of this section. However, because the terms of all of the puts and all of the calls are identical four of the puts and four of the calls are deemed to be a component part of a straddle. The puts and calls comprising the multiple option were to expire on September 10, 1971. Four of the puts are exercised and the four calls and one of the puts lapse. As a result, on September 10, 1971, E realizes short-term capital gain in the amount of that part of the premium for the multiple option which is allocable to the four lapsed calls and realizes ordinary income in the amount of that part of such premium which is allocable to the lapsed put. If E had identified four of the puts and four of the calls as constituting parts of straddles in the manner prescribed in paragraph (c)(3) of this section and the put that lapsed constituted part of a straddle, then the gain on the lapse of the put would also be short-term capital gain.

Example (7). Assume the same facts as in example (6) except that two of the puts are for Y Corporation stock at a price which is greater than that of the other puts and the other calls and that two of the calls expire on October 10, 1971. Additionally, assume that the put which lapses is at the lower price. The two puts offering the Y Corporation stock at the greater price and the two calls with the later expiration date cannot be deemed to be component parts of a straddle. Thus, only two of the puts and two of the calls are deemed to be a component part of a straddle. As a result, E realizes income as follows:

(i) On September 10, 1971, short-term capital gain in the amount of that part of the premium for the multiple option which is allocable to the two lapsed calls with the expiration date of September 10, 1971, and ordinary income in the amount of that part of such premium which is allocable to the lapsed put. If E had identified two of the puts at the lower price and the two calls with the expiration date of September 10, 1971, as constituting parts of straddles in the manner prescribed in paragraph (c)(3) of this section and if the put that lapsed was one of those identified as constituting a part of a straddle, then the gain on the lapse of that put would also be short-term capital gain.

(ii) On October 10, 1971, ordinary income in the amount of that part of the premium for the multiple option which is allocable to the lapsed calls with an expiration date of October 10, 1971. [Reg. § 1.1234-2.]

☐ [T.D. 7152, 12-22-71. Amended by T.D. 7210, 10-2-72; T.D. 7652, 10-29-79 and T.D. 7728, 10-31-80.]

[Reg. § 1.1234-3]

§ 1.1234-3. **Special rules for the treatment of grantors of certain options granted after September 1, 1976.**—(a) *In general.* In the case of the grantor of an option (including an option granted as part of a straddle or multiple option), gain or loss from any closing transaction with respect to, and gain on the lapse of, an option in property shall be treated as a gain or loss from the sale or exchange of a capital asset held not more than 1 year (6 months for taxable years beginning before 1977; 9 months for taxable years beginning in 1977).

(b) *Definitions.* The following definitions apply for purposes of this section.

(1) The term "closing transaction" means any termination of a grantor's obligation under an option to buy property (a "call") or an option to sell property (a "put") other than through the exercise or lapse of the option. For example, the grantor of a call may effectively terminate his obligation under the option by either (i) repurchasing the option from the holder or (ii) purchasing from an options exchange a call with terms identical to the original option granted and designating the purchase as a closing transaction. A put or call purchased to make a closing transac-

Rules for Determining Capital Gains and Losses

See p. 20,601 for regulations not amended to reflect law changes

tion is identical as to striking price and expiration date. Such put or call need not match the granted option in time of creation, date of acquisition, cost of the entire option or units therein, or number of units subject to the option. If such put or call terminates only part of a grantor's obligation under the granted option, a closing transaction is made as to that part.

(2) The term "property" means stocks and securities (including stocks and securities dealt with on a "when issued" basis), commodities, and commodity futures.

(3) The term "grantor" means the writer or issuer of an option.

(4) The term "straddle" means a simultaneously granted combination of an option to buy and an option to sell the same quantity of property at the same price during the same period of time.

(5) The term "multiple option" means a simultaneously granted combination of an option to buy plus an option to sell plus one or more additional options to buy or sell property.

(c) *Nonapplicability to broker-dealers.* The provisions of this section do not apply to any option granted in the ordinary course of the taxpayer's trade or business of granting options. However, the provisions of this section do apply to—

(1) Gain from any closing transaction with respect to an option and gain on lapse of an option if gain on the sale or exchange of the option would be considered capital gain by a dealer in securities under section 1236(a) and the regulations thereunder, and

(2) Loss from any closing transaction with respect to an option if loss on the sale or exchange of the option would not be considered ordinary loss by a dealer in securities under section 1236(b) and the regulations thereunder.

The preceding sentence shall be applied with respect to dealers in "property" (as defined in paragraph (b)(2) of this section) and without regard to the limitation of the applicability of section 1236 to dealers in securities.

(d) *Nonapplicability to compensatory options.* Section 1234 does not apply to options to purchase stock or other property which are issued as compensation for services, as described in sections 61, 83, and 421 and the regulations thereunder.

(e) *Premium allocation for simultaneously granted options.* The allocation of a premium received for a straddle or multiple option between or among the component options thereof shall be made on the basis of the relative market value of the component options at the time of their issuance or on any other reasonable and consistently applied basis which is acceptable to the Commissioner.

(f) *Effective date.* This section, relating to special rules for the treatment of grantors of certain options, shall apply to options granted after September 1, 1976. [Reg. § 1.1234-3.]

☐ [T.D. 7652, 10-29-79.]

[Reg. § 1.1234-4]

§ **1.1234-4. Hedging transactions.**—The character of gain or loss on an acquired or a written option that is (or is identified as being) part of a hedging transaction is determined under the rules of § 1.1221-2. [Reg. § 1.1234-4.]

☐ [T.D. 8555, 7-13-94.]

[Reg. § 1.1235-1]

§ **1.1235-1. Sale or exchange of patents.**—(a) *General rule.* Section 1235 provides that a transfer (other than by gift, inheritance, or devise) of all substantial rights to a patent, or of an undivided interest in all such rights to a patent, by a holder to a person other than a related person constitutes the sale or exchange of a capital asset held for more than 1 year (6 months for taxable years beginning before 1977; 9 months for taxable years beginning in 1977), whether or not payments therefor are—

(1) Payable periodically over a period generally coterminous with the transferee's use of the patent, or

(2) Contingent on the productivity, use, or disposition of the property transferred.

(b) *Scope of section 1235.* If a transfer is not one described in paragraph (a) of this section, section 1235 shall be disregarded in determining whether or not such transfer is the sale or exchange of a capital asset. For example, a transfer by a person other than a holder or a transfer by a holder to a related person is not governed by section 1235. The tax consequences of such transfers shall be determined under other provisions of the internal revenue laws.

(c) *Special rules*—(1) *Payments for infringement.* If section 1235 applies to the transfer of all substantial rights to a patent (or an undivided interest therein), amounts received in settlement of, or as the award of damages in, a suit for compensatory damages for infringement of the patent shall be considered payments attributable to a transfer to which section 1235 applies to the extent that such amounts relate to the interest transferred. For taxable years beginning before January 1, 1964, see section 1304, as in effect before such date, and § 1.1304a-1 for treatment of compensatory damages for patent infringement.

Reg. § 1.1235-1(c)(1)

(2) *Payments to an employee.* Payments received by an employee as compensation for services rendered as an employee under an employment contract requiring the employee to transfer to the employer the rights to any invention by such employee are not attributable to a transfer to which section 1235 applies. However, whether payments received by an employee from his employer (under an employment contract or otherwise) are attributable to the transfer by the employee of all substantial rights to a patent (or an undivided interest therein) or are compensation for services rendered the employer by the employee is a question of fact. In determining which is the case, consideration shall be given not only to all the facts and circumstances of the employment relationship but also to whether the amount of such payments depends upon the production, sale, or use by, or the value to, the employer of the patent rights transferred by the employee. If it is determined that payments are attributable to the transfer of patent rights, and all other requirements under section 1235 are met, such payments shall be treated as proceeds derived from the sale of a patent.

(3) *Successive transfers.* The applicability of section 1235 to transfers of undivided interest in patents, or to successive transfers of such rights, shall be determined separately with respect to each transfer. For example, X, who is a holder, and Y, who is not a holder, transfer their respective two-thirds and one-third undivided interests in a patent to Z. Assume the transfer by X qualifies under section 1235 and that X in a later transfer acquires all the rights with respect to Y's interest, including the rights to payments from Z. One-third of all the payments thereafter received by X from Z are not attributable to a transfer to which section 1235 applies.

(d) *Payor's treatment of payments in a transfer under section 1235.* Payments made by the transferee of patent rights pursuant to a transfer satisfying the requirements of section 1235 are payments of the purchase price for the patent rights and are not the payment of royalties.

(e) *Effective date.* Amounts received or accrued, and payments made or accrued, during any taxable year beginning after December 31, 1953 and ending after August 16, 1954, pursuant to a transfer satisfying the requirements of section 1235, whether such transfer occurred in a taxable year to which the Internal Revenue Code of 1954 applies, or in a year prior thereto, are subject to the provisions of section 1235.

(f) *Nonresident aliens.* For the special rule relating to nonresident aliens who have gains arising from a transfer to which section 1235 applies,

see section 871 and the regulations thereunder. For withholding of tax from income of nonresident aliens, see section 1441 and the regulations thereunder [Reg. § 1.1235-1.]

☐ [T.D. 6263, 11-5-57. Amended by T.D. 6885, 6-1-66 and T.D. 7728, 10-31-80.]

[Reg. § 1.1235-2]

§ 1.1235-2. Definition of terms.—For the purposes of section 1235 and § 1.1235-1—

(a) *Patent.* The term "patent" means a patent granted under the provisions of title 35 of the United States Code, or any foreign patent granting rights generally similar to those under a United States patent. It is not necessary that the patent or patent application for the invention be in existence if the requirements of section 1235 are otherwise met.

(b) *All substantial rights to a patent.* (1) The term "all substantial rights to a patent" means all rights (whether or not then held by the grantor) which are of value at the time the rights to the patent (or an undivided interest therein) are transferred. The term "all substantial rights to a patent" does not include a grant of rights to a patent—

(i) Which is limited geographically within the country of issuance;

(ii) Which is limited in duration by the terms of the agreement to a period less than the remaining life of the patent;

(iii) Which grants rights to the grantee, in fields of use within trades or industries, which are less than all the rights covered by the patent, which exist and have value at the time of the grant; or

(iv) Which grants to the grantee less than all the claims or inventions covered by the patent which exist and have value at the time of the grant.

The circumstances of the whole transaction, rather than the particular terminology used in the instrument of transfer, shall be considered in determining whether or not all substantial rights to a patent are transferred in a transaction.

(2) Rights which are not considered substantial for purposes of section 1235 may be retained by the holder. Examples of such rights are:

(i) The retention by the transferor of legal title for the purpose of securing performance or payment by the transferee in a transaction involving transfer of an exclusive license to manufacture, use, and sell for the life of the patent;

(ii) The retention by the transferor of rights in the property which are not inconsistent with the passage of ownership, such as the reten-

Reg. § 1.1235-2(a)

tion of a security interest (such as a vendor's lien), or a reservation in the nature of a condition subsequent (such as a provision for forfeiture on account of nonperformance).

(3) Examples of rights which may or may not be substantial, depending upon the circumstances of the whole transaction in which rights to a patent are transferred, are:

(i) The retention by the transferor of an absolute right to prohibit sublicensing or subassignment by the transferee;

(ii) The failure to convey to the transferee the right to use or to sell the patent property.

(4) The retention of a right to terminate the transfer at will is the retention of a substantial right for the purposes of section 1235.

(c) *Undivided interest.* A person owns an "undivided interest" in all substantial rights to a patent when he owns the same fractional share of each and every substantial right to the patent. It does not include, for example, a right to the income from a patent, or a license limited geographically, or a license which covers some, but not all, of the valuable claims or uses covered by the patent. A transfer limited in duration by the terms of the instrument to a period less than the remaining life of the patent is not a transfer of an undivided interest in all substantial rights to a patent.

(d) *Holder.* (1) The term "holder" means any individual—

(i) Whose efforts created the patent property and who would qualify as the "original and first" inventor, or joint inventor, within the meaning of title 35 of the United States Code, or

(ii) Who has acquired his interest in the patent property in exchange for a consideration paid to the inventor in money or money's worth prior to the actual reduction of the invention to practice (see paragraph (e) of this section), provided that such individual was neither the employer of the inventor nor related to him (see paragraph (f) of this section). The requirement that such individual is neither the employer of the inventor nor related to him must be satisfied at the time when the substantive rights as to the interest to be acquired are determined, and at the time when the consideration in money or money's worth to be paid is definitely fixed. For example, if prior to the actual reduction to practice of an invention an individual who is neither the employer of the inventor nor related to him agrees to pay the inventor a sum of money definitely fixed as to amount in return for an undivided one-half interest in rights to a patent and at a later date, when such individual has become the employer of the inventor, he pays the definitely fixed sum of money pursuant to the earlier agreement, such individual will not be denied the status of a holder because of such employment relationship.

(2) Although a partnership cannot be a holder, each member of a partnership who is an individual may qualify as a holder as to his share of a patent owned by the partnership. For example, if an inventor who is a member of a partnership composed solely of individuals uses partnership property in the development of his invention with the understanding that the patent when issued will become partnership property, each of the inventor's partners during this period would qualify as a holder. If, in this example, the partnership were not composed solely of individuals, nevertheless, each of the individual partners' distributive shares of income attributable to the transfer of all substantial rights to the patent or an undivided interest therein, would be considered proceeds from the sale or exchange of a capital asset held for more than 1 year (6 months for taxable years beginning before 1977; 9 months for taxable years beginning in 1977).

(3) An individual may qualify as a holder whether or not he is in the business of making inventions or in the business of buying and selling patents.

(e) *Actual reduction to practice.* For the purposes of determining whether an individual is a holder under paragraph (d) of this section, the term "actual reduction to practice" has the same meaning as it does under section 102(g) of title 35 of the United States Code. Generally, an invention is reduced to actual practice when it has been tested and operated successfully under operating conditions. This may occur either before or after application for a patent but cannot occur later than the earliest time that commercial exploitation of the invention occurs.

(f) *Related person.* (1) The term "related person" means one whose relationship to another person at the time of the transfer is described in section 267(b), except that the term does not include a brother or sister, whether of the whole or the half blood. Thus, if a holder transfers all his substantial rights to a patent to his brother or sister, or both, such transfer is not to a related person.

(2) If, prior to September 3, 1958, a holder transferred all his substantial rights to a patent to a corporation in which he owned more than 50 percent in value of the outstanding stock, he is considered as having transferred such rights to a related person for the purpose of section 1235. On the other hand, if a holder, prior to September 3, 1958, transferred all his substantial rights to a

Reg. § 1.1235-2(f)(2)

patent to a corporation in which he owned 50 percent or less in value of the outstanding stock and his brother owned the remaining stock, he is not considered as having transferred such rights to a related person since the brother relationship is to be disregarded for purposes of section 1235.

(3) If, subsequent to September 2, 1958, a holder transfers all his substantial rights to a patent to a corporation in which he owns 25 percent or more in value of the outstanding stock, he is considered as transferring such rights to a related person for the purpose of section 1235. On the other hand if a holder, subsequent to September 2, 1958, transfers all his substantial rights to a patent to a corporation in which he owns less than 25 percent in value of the outstanding stock and his brother owns the remaining stock, he is not considered as transferring such rights to a related person since the brother relationship is to be disregarded for purposes of section 1235.

(4) If a relationship described in section 267(b) exists independently of family status, the brother-sister exception, described in subparagraphs (1), (2), and (3) of this paragraph, does not apply. Thus, if a holder transfers all his substantial rights to a patent to the fiduciary of a trust of which the holder is the grantor, the holder and the fiduciary are related persons for purposes of section 1235(d). (See section 267(b)(4).) The transfer, therefore, would not qualify under section 1235(a). This result obtains whether or not the fiduciary is the brother or sister of the holder since the disqualifying relationship exists because of the grantor-fiduciary status and not because of family status. [Reg. § 1.1235-2.]

☐ [*T.D.* 6263, 11-5-57. *Amended by T.D.* 6394, 7-1-59, *T.D.* 6852, 10-5-65 *and T.D.* 7728, 10-31-80.]

[Reg. § 1.1236-1]

§ 1.1236-1. **Dealers in securities.**—(a) *Capital gains.* Section 1236(a) provides that gain realized by a dealer in securities from the sale or exchange of a security (as defined in paragraph (c) of this section) shall not be considered as gain from the sale or exchange of a capital asset unless—

(1) The security is, before the expiration of the thirtieth day after the date of its acquisition, clearly identified in the dealer's records as a security held for investment, or if acquired before October 20, 1951, was so identified before November 20, 1951; and

(2) The security is not held by the dealer primarily for sale to customers in the ordinary course of his trade or business at any time after the identification referred to in subparagraph (1) of this paragraph has been made. Unless both of these requirements are met, the gain is considered as gain from the sale of assets held by the dealer primarily for sale to customers in the course of his business.

(b) *Ordinary losses.* Section 1236(b) provides that a loss sustained by a dealer in securities from the sale or exchange of a security shall not be considered a loss from the sale or exchange of property which is not a capital asset if at any time after November 19, 1951, the security has been clearly identified in the dealer's records as a security held for investment. Once a security has been identified after November 19, 1951, as being held by the dealer for investment, it shall retain that character for purposes of determining loss on its ultimate disposition, even though at the time of its disposition the dealer holds it primarily for sale to his customers in the ordinary course of business. However, section 1236 has no application to the extent that section 582(c) applies to losses of banks.

(c) *Definitions*—(1) *Security.* For the purposes of this section, the term "security" means any share of stock in any corporation, any certificate of stock or interest in any corporation, any note, bond, debenture, or other evidence of indebtedness, or any evidence of any interest in, or right to subscribe to or purchase, any of the foregoing.

(2) *Dealer in securities.* For definition of a "dealer in securities," see the regulations under section 471.

(d) *Identification of security in dealer's records.* (1) A security is clearly identified in the dealer's records as a security held for investment when there is an accounting separation of the security from other securities, as by making appropriate entries in the dealer's books of account to distinguish the security from inventories and to designate it as an investment and by (i) indicating with such entries, to the extent feasible, the individual serial number of, or other characteristic symbol imprinted upon, the individual security, or (ii) adopting any other method of identification satisfactory to the Commissioner.

(2) In computing the 30-day period prescribed by section 1236(a), the first day of the period is the day following the date of acquisition. Thus, in the case of a security acquired on March 18, 1957, the 30-day period expires at midnight on April 17, 1957. [Reg. § 1.1236-1.]

☐ [*T.D.* 6253, 9-25-57. *Amended by T.D.* 6726, 4-28-64.]

[Reg. § 1.1237-1]

§ 1.1237-1. **Real property subdivided for sale.**—(a) *General rule*—(1) *Introductory.* This section provides a special rule for determining

Reg. § 1.1236-1(a)(1)

Rules for Determining Capital Gains and Losses

whether the taxpayer holds real property primarily for sale to customers in the ordinary course of his business under section 1221(1). This rule is to permit taxpayers qualifying under it to sell real estate from a single tract held for investment without the income being treated as ordinary income merely because of subdividing the tract or of active efforts to sell it. The rule is not applicable to dealers in real estate or to corporations, except a corporation making such sales in a taxable year beginning after December 31, 1954, if such corporation qualifies under the provisions of paragraph (c)(5)(iv) of this section.

(2) *When subdividing and selling activities are to be disregarded.* When its conditions are met, section 1237 provides that if there is no other substantial evidence that a taxpayer holds real estate primarily for sale to customers in the ordinary course of his business, he shall not be considered a real estate dealer holding it primarily for sale merely because he has (i) subdivided the tract into lots (or parcels) and (ii) engaged in advertising, promotion, selling activities or the use of sales agents in connection with the sale of lots in such subdivision. Such subdividing and selling activities shall be disregarded in determining the purpose for which the taxpayer held real property sold from a subdivision whenever it is the only substantial evidence indicating that the taxpayer has ever held the real property sold primarily for sale to customers in the ordinary course of his business.

(3) *When subdividing and selling activities are to be taken into account.* When other substantial evidence tends to show that the taxpayer held real property for sale to customers in the ordinary course of his business, his activities in connection with the subdivision and sale of the property sold shall be taken into account in determining the purpose for which the taxpayer held both the subdivided property and any other real property. For example, such other evidence may consist of the taxpayer's selling activities in connection with other property in prior years during which he was engaged in subdividing or selling activities with respect to the subdivided tract, his intention in prior years (or at the time of acquiring the property subdivided) to hold the tract primarily for sale in his business, his subdivision of other tracts in the same year, his holding other real property for sale to customers in the same year, or his construction of a permanent real estate office which he could use in selling other real property. On the other hand, if the only evidence of the taxpayer's purpose in holding real property consisted of not more than one of the following, in the year in question, such fact would not be considered substantial other evidence:

(i) Holding a real estate dealer's license;

(ii) Selling other real property which was clearly investment property;

(iii) Acting as a salesman for a real estate dealer, but without any financial interest in the business; or

(iv) Mere ownership of other vacant real property without engaging in any selling activity whatsoever with respect to it.

If more than one of the above exists, the circumstances may or may not constitute substantial evidence that the taxpayer held real property for sale in his business, depending upon the particular facts in each case.

(4) *Section 1237 not exclusive.* (i) The rule in section 1237 is not exclusive in its application. Section 1237 has no application in determining whether or not real property is held by a taxpayer primarily for sale in his business if any requirement under the section is not met. Also, even though the conditions of section 1237 are met, the rules of section 1237 are not applicable if without regard to section 1237 the real property sold would not have been considered real property held primarily for sale to customers in the ordinary course of his business. Thus, the district director may at all times conclude from convincing evidence that the taxpayer held the real property solely as an investment. Furthermore, whether or not the conditions of section 1237 are met, the section has no application to losses realized upon the sale of realty from subdivided property.

(ii) If, owing solely to the application of section 1237, the real property sold is deemed not to have been held primarily for sale in the ordinary course of business, any gain realized upon such sale shall be treated as ordinary income to the extent provided in section 1237(b)(1) and (2) and paragraph (e) of this section. Any additional gain realized upon the sale shall be treated as gain arising from the sale of a capital asset or, if the circumstances so indicate, as gain arising from the sale of real property used in the trade or business as defined in section 1231(b)(1). For the relationship between sections 1237 and 1231, see paragraph (f) of this section.

(5) *Principal conditions of qualification.* Before section 1237 applies, the taxpayer must meet three basic conditions, more fully explained later: He cannot have held any part of the tract at any time previously for sale in the ordinary course of his business, nor in the year of sale held any other real estate for sale to customers; he cannot make substantial improvements on the tract which increase the value of the lot sold substantially; and he must have owned the property 5 years, unless he inherited it. However, the tax-

Reg. § 1.1237-1(a)(5)

payer may make certain improvements if they are necessary to make the property marketable if he elects neither to add their cost to the basis of the property, or of any other property, nor to deduct the cost as an expense, and he has held the property at least 10 years. If the requirements of section 1237 are met, gain (but not more than 5 percent of the selling price of each lot) shall be treated as ordinary income in and after the year in which the sixth lot or parcel is sold.

(b) *Disqualification arising from holding real property primarily for sale*—(1) *General rule.* Section 1237 does not apply to any transaction if the taxpayer either—

(i) Held the lot sold (or the tract of which it was a part) primarily for sale in the ordinary course of his business in a prior year, or

(ii) Holds other real property primarily for sale in the ordinary course of his business in the same year in which such lot is sold.

Where either of these elements is present, section 1237 shall be disregarded in determining the proper treatment of any gain arising from such sale.

(2) *Method of applying general rule.* For purposes of this paragraph, in determining whether the lot sold was held primarily for sale in the ordinary course of business in a prior year, the principles of section 1237 shall be applied, whether or not section 1237 was effective for such prior year, if the sale of the lot occurs after December 31, 1953, or, in the case of a corporation meeting the requirements of paragraph (c)(5)(iv) of this section, if the sale of the lot occurs in a taxable year beginning after December 31, 1954. Whether, on the other hand, the taxpayer holds other real property for sale in the ordinary course of his business in the same year such lot was sold shall be determined without regard to the application of section 1237 to such other real property.

(3) *Attribution rules with respect to the holding of property.* The taxpayer is considered as holding property which he owns individually, jointly, or as a member of a partnership. He is not generally considered as holding property owned by members of his family, an estate or trust, or a corporation. See, however, paragraph (c)(5)(iv)(c) of this section for an exception to this rule. The purpose for which a prior owner held the lot or tract, or his activities, are immaterial except to the extent they indicate the purpose for which the taxpayer has held the lot or tract. See paragraph (d) of this section for rules relating to the determination of the period for which the property is held. The principles of this subparagraph may be illustrated by the following example:

Example. A dealer in real property held a tract of land for sale to customers in the ordinary course of his business for 5 years. He then made a gift of it to his son. As a result of the operation of section 1223(2) the son will have held the property for the period of time required by section 1237. However, he will not qualify for the benefits of section 1237 because, there being no evidence to the contrary, the circumstances involved establish that the son holds the property for sale to customers, as did his father.

(c) *Disqualification arising from substantial improvements*—(1) *General rule.* Section 1237 will not apply if the taxpayer or certain others make improvements on the tract which are substantial and which substantially increase the value of the lot sold. Certain improvements are not substantial within the meaning of section 1237(a)(2) if they are necessary to make the lot marketable at the prevailing local price and meet the other conditions of section 1237(b)(3). See subparagraph (5) of this paragraph.

(2) *Improvements made or deemed to be made by the taxpayer.* Certain improvements made by the taxpayer or made under a contract of sale between the taxpayer and the buyer make section 1237 inapplicable.

(i) For the purposes of section 1237(a)(2) the taxpayer is deemed to have made any improvements on the tract while he held it which are made by:

(*a*) The taxpayer's whole or half brothers and sisters, spouse, ancestors, and lineal descendants.

(*b*) A corporation controlled by the taxpayer. A corporation is controlled by the taxpayer if he controls, as the result of direct ownership, constructive ownership, or otherwise, more than 50 percent of the corporation's voting stock.

(*c*) A partnership of which the taxpayer was a member at the time the improvements were made.

(*d*) A lessee if the improvement takes the place of a payment of rental income. See section 109 and the regulations thereunder.

(*e*) A Federal, State, or local government, or political subdivision thereof, if the improvement results in an increase in the taxpayer's basis for the property, as it would, for example, from a special tax assessment for paving streets.

(ii) The principles of subdivision (i) of this subparagraph may be illustrated by the following example:

Example. A held a tract of land for 3 years during which he made substantial improvements thereon which substantially enhanced the value of

Reg. § 1.1237-1(b)(1)

Rules for Determining Capital Gains and Losses

every lot on the tract. A then made a gift of the tract to his son. The son made no further improvements on the tract, but held it for 3 years and then sold several lots therefrom. The son is not entitled to the benefits of section 1237 since under section 1237(a)(2) he is deemed to have made the substantial improvements made by his father, and under section 1223(2) he is treated as having held the property for the period during which his father held it. Thus, the disqualifying improvements are deemed to have been made by the son while the tract was held by him. See paragraph (d) of this section for rules relating to the determination of the period for which the property is held.

(iii) The taxpayer is also charged with making any improvements made pursuant to a contract of sale entered into between the taxpayer and the buyer. Therefore, the buyer, as well as the taxpayer, may make improvements which prevent the application of section 1237.

(a) If a contract of sale obligates either the taxpayer or the buyer to make a substantial improvement which would substantially increase the value of the lot, the taxpayer may not claim the application of section 1237 unless the obligation to improve the lot ceases (for any reason other than that the improvement has been made) before or within the period, prescribed by section 6511, within which the taxpayer may file a claim for credit or refund of an overpayment of his tax on the gain from the sale of the lot. The following example illustrates this rule:

Example. In 1956, A sells several lots from a tract he has subdivided for sale. Section 1237 would apply to the sales of these lots except that in the contract of sale A agreed to install sewers, hard surface roads, and other utilities which would increase the value of the lots substantially. If in 1957, instead of requiring the improvements, the buyer releases A from this obligation, A may then claim the application of section 1237 to the sale of lots in 1956 in computing his income tax for 1956, since the period of limitations in which A may file a claim for credit or refund of an overpayment of his 1956 income tax has not expired.

(b) An improvement is made pursuant to a contract if the contract imposes an obligation on either party to make the improvement, but not if the contract merely places restrictions on the improvements, if any, either party may make. The following example illustrates this rule:

Example. B sells several lots from a tract which he has subdivided. Each contract of sale prohibits the purchaser from building any structure on his lot except a personal residence costing $15,000 or more. Even if the purchasers build such residences, that does not preclude B from applying section 1237 to the sales of such lots, since the contracts did not obligate the purchasers to make any improvements.

(iv) Improvements made by a bona fide lessee (other than as rent) or by others not described in section 1237(a)(2) do not preclude the use of section 1237.

(3) *When improvements substantially enhance the value of the lot sold.* Before a substantial improvement will preclude the use of section 1237, it must substantially enhance the value of the lot sold.

(i) The increase in value to be considered is only the increase attributable to the improvement or improvements. Other changes in the market price of the lot, not arising from improvements made by the taxpayer, shall be disregarded. The difference between the value of the lot, including improvements, when the improvement has been completed and an appraisal of its value if unimproved at that time, will disclose the value added by the improvements.

(ii) Whether improvements have substantially increased the value of a lot depends upon the circumstances in each case. If improvements increase the value of a lot by 10 percent or less, such increase will not be considered as substantial, but if the value of the lot is increased by more than 10 percent, then all relevant factors must be considered to determine whether, under such circumstances, the increase is substantial.

(iii) Improvements may increase the value of some lots in a tract without equally affecting other lots in the same tract. Only the lots whose value was substantially increased are ineligible for application of the rule established by section 1237.

(4) *When an improvement is substantial.* To prevent the application of section 1237, the improvement itself must be substantial in character. Among the improvements considered substantial are shopping centers, other commercial or residential buildings, and the installation of hard surface roads or utilities such as sewers, water, gas, or electric lines. On the other hand a temporary structure used as a field office, surveying, filling, draining, leveling and clearing operations, and the construction of minimum all-weather access roads, including gravel roads where required by the climate, are not substantial improvements.

(5) *Special rules relating to substantial improvements.* Under certain conditions a taxpayer, including a corporation to which subdivision (iv) of this subparagraph applies, may obtain the benefits of section 1237 whether or not substantial improvements have been made. In addition, an

Reg. § 1.1237-1(c)(5)

individual taxpayer may, under certain circumstances, elect to have substantial improvements treated as necessary and not substantial.

(i) *When an improvement is not considered substantial.* An improvement will not be considered substantial if all of the following conditions are met:

(a) The taxpayer has held the property for 10 years. The full 10-year period must elapse, whether or not the taxpayer inherited the property. Although the taxpayer must hold the property 10 years, he need not hold it for 10 years after subdividing it. See paragraph (d) of this section for rules relating to the determination of the period for which the property is held.

(b) The improvement consists of the building or installation of water, sewer, or drainage facilities (either surface, sub-surface, or both) or roads, including hard surface roads, curbs, and gutters.

(c) The district director with whom the taxpayer must file his return is satisfied that, without such improvement, the lot sold would not have brought the prevailing local price for similar building sites.

(d) The taxpayer elects, as provided in subdivision (iii) of this subparagraph, not to adjust the basis of the lot sold or any other property held by him for any part of the cost of such improvement attributable to such lot and not to deduct any part of such cost as an expense.

(ii) *Meaning of "similar building site".* A "similar building site" is any real property in the immediate vicinity whose size, terrain, and other characteristics are comparable to the taxpayer's property. For the purpose of determining whether a tract is marketable at the prevailing local price for similar building sites, the taxpayer shall furnish the district director with sufficient evidence to enable him to compare (a) the value of the taxpayer's property in an unimproved state with (b) the amount for which similar building sites, improved by the installation of water, sewer, or drainage facilities or roads, have recently been sold, reduced by the present cost of such improvements. Such comparison may be made and expressed in terms of dollars per square foot, dollars per acre, or dollars per front foot, or in any other suitable terms depending upon the practice generally followed by real estate dealers in the taxpayer's locality. The taxpayer shall also furnish evidence, where possible, of the best bona fide offer received for the tract or a lot thereof just before making the improvement, to assist the district director in determining the value of the tract or lot if it had been sold in its unimproved state. The operation of this subdivision and subdivision (i) of this subparagraph may be illustrated by the following examples:

Example (1). A has been offered $500 per acre for a tract without roads, water, or sewer facilities which he has owned for 15 years. The adjacent tract has been subdivided and improved with water facilities and hard surface roads, and has sold for $4,000 per acre. The estimated cost of roads and water facilities on the adjacent tract is $2,500 per acre. The prevailing local price for similar building sites in the vicinity would be $1,500 per acre (i.e., $4,000 less $2,500). If A installed roads and water facilities at a cost of $2,500 per acre, his tract would sell for approximately $4,000 per acre. Under section 1237 (b)(3) the installation of roads and water facilities does not constitute a substantial improvement if A elects to disregard the cost of such improvements ($2,500 per acre) in computing his cost or other basis for the lots sold from the tract, and in computing his basis for any other property owned by him.

Example (2). Assume the same facts as in example (1) of this subdivision, except that A can obtain $1,600 per acre for his property without improvements. The installation of any substantial improvements would not constitute a necessary improvement under section 1237(b)(3), since the prevailing local price could have been obtained without any improvement.

Example (3). Assume the same facts as in Example (1) of this subdivision, except that the adjacent tract has also been improved with sewer facilities, the present cost of which is $1,200 per acre. The installation of the substantial improvements would not constitute a necessary improvement under section 1237(b)(3) on A's part, since the prevailing local price ($4,000 less the sum of $1,200 plus $2,500, or $300) could have been obtained by A without any improvement.

(iii) *Manner of making election.* The election required by section 1237(b)(3)(C) shall be made as follows:

(a) The taxpayer shall submit:

(1) A plat showing the subdivision and all improvements attributable to him.

(2) A list of all improvements to the tract, showing:

(i) The cost of such improvements.

(ii) Which of the improvements, without regard to the election, he considers "substantial" and which he considers not "substantial."

(iii) Those improvements which are substantial to which the election is to apply, with a fair allocation of their cost to each lot they affect, and the amount by which they have increased the values of such lots.

(iv) The date on which each lot was acquired and its basis for determining gain or loss, exclusive of the cost of any improvements listed in subdivision (iii) of this subdivision.

(3) A statement that he will neither deduct as an expense nor add to the basis of any lot sold, or of any other property, any portion of the cost of any substantial improvement which substantially increased the value of any lot in the tract and which either he listed pursuant to subdivision (2)(iii) of this subdivision or which the district director deems substantial.

(b) The election and the information required under subdivision (a) of this subdivision shall be submitted to the district director—

(1) With the taxpayer's income tax return for the taxable year in which the lots subject to the election were sold, or

(2) In the case of a return filed prior to August 14, 1957, either with a timely claim for refund, where the benefits of section 1237 have not been claimed on such return, or, independently, before November 13, 1957, where such benefits have been claimed, or

(3) If there is an obligation to make disqualifying improvements outstanding when the taxpayer files his return, with a formal claim for refund at the time of the release of the obligation, if it is then still possible to file a timely claim.

(c) Once made, the election as to the necessary improvement costs attributable to any lot sold shall be irrevocable and binding on the taxpayer unless the district director assesses an income tax as to such lot as if it were held for sale in the ordinary course of taxpayer's business. Under such circumstances, in computing gain, the cost or other basis shall be computed without regard to section 1237.

(iv) *Exceptions with respect to "necessary" improvements and certain corporations.* For taxable years beginning after December 31, 1954, individual taxpayers and certain corporations may obtain the benefits of section 1237 without complying with the provisions of subdivisions (i)(c) and (d), (ii), and (iii) of this subparagraph if the requirements of section 1237 are otherwise met and if—

(a) The property in question was acquired by the taxpayer through the foreclosure of a lien thereon,

(b) The lien foreclosed secured the payment of an indebtedness to the taxpayer or (in the case of a corporation) secured the payment of an indebtedness to a creditor who has transferred the foreclosure bid to the taxpayer in exchange for all of the stock of the corporation and other consideration, and

(c) In the case of a corporate taxpayer, no shareholder of the corporation holds real property for sale to customers in the ordinary course of his trade or business or holds a controlling interest in another corporation which actually so holds real property, or which, but for the application of this subdivision, would be considered to so hold real property. Thus, in the case of such property, it is not necessary for the taxpayer to satisfy the district director that the property would not have brought the prevailing local price without improvements or to elect not to add the cost of the improvements to his basis. In addition, if 80 percent or more of the real property owned by a taxpayer is property to which this subdivision applies, the requirements of (a) and (b) of this subdivision need not be met with respect to property adjacent to such property which is also owned by the taxpayer.

(d) *Holding period required*—(1) *General rules.* To apply section 1237, the taxpayer must either have inherited the lot sold or have held it for 5 years. Generally, the provisions of section 1223 are applicable in determining the period for which the taxpayer has held the property. The provisions of this subparagraph may be illustrated by the following examples:

Example (1). A held a tract of land for 3 years under circumstances otherwise qualifying for section 1237 treatment. He made a gift of the tract to B at a time when the fair market value of the tract exceeded A's basis for the tract. B held the tract for 2 more years under similar circumstances. B then sold 4 lots from the tract. B is entitled to the benefits of section 1237 since under section 1223(2) he held the lots for 5 years and all the other requirements of section 1237 are met.

Example (2). C purchased all the stock in a corporation in 1955. The corporation purchased an unimproved tract of land in 1957. In 1961 the corporation was liquidated under section 333 and C acquired the tract of land. For purposes of section 1237, C's holding period commenced on the date the corporation actually acquired the land in 1957 and not on the date C purchased the stock.

(2) *Rules relating to property acquired upon death.* If the taxpayer inherited the property there is no 5-year holding period required under section 1237. However, any holding period required by any other provision of the Code, such as section 1222, is nevertheless applicable. For purposes of section 1237, neither the survivor's one-half of community property, nor property ac-

Reg. § 1.1237-1(d)(2)

Rules for Determining Capital Gains and Losses

See p. 20,601 for regulations not amended to reflect law changes

quired by survivorship in a joint tenancy, is property acquired by devise or inheritance. The holding period for the surviving joint tenant begins on the date the property was originally acquired.

(e) *Tax consequences if section 1237 applies*—(1) *Introductory.* Where there is no substantial evidence other than subdivision and related selling activities that real property is held for sale in the ordinary course of taxpayer's business and section 1237 applies, section 1237(b)(1) provides a special rule for computing taxable gain. For the relationship between sections 1237 and 1231, see paragraph (f) of this section.

(2) *Characterization of gain and its relation to selling expenses.* (i) When the taxpayer has sold less than 6 lots or parcels from the same tract up to the end of his taxable year, the entire gain will be capital gain. (Where the land is used in a trade or business, see paragraph (f) of this section.) In computing the number of lots or parcels sold, two or more contiguous lots sold to a single buyer in a single sale will be counted as only one parcel. The following example illustrates this rule:

Example. A meets all the conditions of section 1237 in subdividing and selling a single tract. In 1956 he sells 4 lots to B, C, D, and E. In the same year F buys 3 adjacent lots. Since A has sold only 5 lots or parcels from the tract, any gain A realizes on the sales will be capital gain.

(ii) If the taxpayer has sold the sixth lot or parcel from the same tract within the taxable year, then the amount, if any, by which 5 percent of the selling price of each lot exceeds the expenses incurred in connection with its sale or exchange, shall, to the extent it represents gain, be ordinary income. Any part of the gain not treated as ordinary income will be treated as capital gain. (Where the land is used in a trade or business, see paragraph (f) of this section.) Five percent of the selling price of each lot sold from the tract in the taxable year the sixth lot is sold and thereafter is, to the extent it represents gain, considered ordinary income. However, all expenses of sale of the lot are to be deducted first from the 5 percent of the gain which would otherwise be considered ordinary income, and any remainder of such expenses shall reduce the gain upon the sale or exchange which would otherwise be considered capital gain. Such expenses cannot be deducted as ordinary business expenses from other income. The 5-percent rule applies to all lots sold from the tract in the year the sixth lot or parcel is sold. Thus, if the taxpayer sells the first 6 lots of a single tract in one year, 5 percent of the selling price of each lot sold shall be treated as ordinary income and reduced by the selling expenses. On the other hand, if the taxpayer sells the first 3 lots of a single tract in 1955, and the next 3 lots in 1956, only the gain realized from the sales made in 1956 shall be so treated. For the effect of a 5-year interval between sales, see paragraph (g)(2) of this section. The operation of this subdivision may be illustrated by the following examples:

Example (1). Assume the selling price of the sixth lot of a tract is $10,000, the basis of the lot in the hands of the taxpayer is $5,000, and the expenses of sale are $750. The amount of gain realized by the taxpayer is $4,250, of which the amount of ordinary income attributable to the sale is zero, computed as follows:

Selling price		$10,000
Basis		5,000
Excess over basis		5,000
5 percent of selling price	$500	
Expenses of sale	750	
Amount of gain realized treated as ordinary income		0
Excess over basis		5,000
5 percent of selling price	500	
Excess of expenses over 5 percent of selling price	250	750
Amount of gain realized from sale of property not held for sale in ordinary course of business		$4,250

Example (2). Assume the same facts as in Example (1), except that the expenses of sale of such sixth lot are $300. The amount of gain realized by the taxpayer is $4,700, of which the amount of ordinary income attributable to the sale is $200, computed as follows:

Reg. § 1.1237-1(e)(1)

Rules for Determining Capital Gains and Losses

See p. 20,601 for regulations not amended to reflect law changes

Selling price		$10,000
Basis		5,000
Excess over basis		5,000
5 percent of selling price	$500	
Expenses of sale	300	
Amount of gain realized treated as ordinary income		$ 200
Excess over basis		5,000
5 percent of selling price	$500	
Excess of expenses over 5 percent of selling price	0	500
Amount of gain realized from sale of property not held for sale in ordinary course of business		$ 4,500

(iii) In the case of an exchange, the term "selling price" shall mean the fair market value of property received plus any sum of money received in exchange for the lot. See section 1031 for those exchanges in which no gain is recognized. For the purpose of subsections (b) and (c) of section 1237 and paragraphs (e) and (g) of this section, an exchange shall be treated as a sale or exchange whether or not gain or loss is recognized with respect to such exchange.

(f) *Relationship of section 1237 and section 1231.* Application of section 1237 to a sale of real property may, in some cases, result in the property being treated as real property used in the trade or business, as described in section 1231(b)(1). Thus, assuming section 1237 is otherwise applicable, if the lot sold would be considered property described in section 1231(b)(1) except for the fact that the taxpayer subdivided the tract of which it was a part, then evidence of such subdivision and connected sales activities shall be disregarded and the lot sold shall be considered real property used in the trade or business. Under such circumstances, any gain or loss realized from the sale shall be treated as gain or loss arising from the sale of real property used in the trade or business.

(g) *Definition of "tract"*—(1) *Aggregation of properties.* For the purposes of section 1237, the term "tract" means either (i) a single piece of real property or (ii) two or more pieces of real property if they were contiguous at any time while held by the taxpayer, or would have been contiguous but for the interposition of a road, street, railroad, stream, or similar property. Properties are contiguous if their boundaries meet at one or more points. The single piece or contiguous properties need not have been conveyed by a single deed. The taxpayer may have assembled them over a period of time and may hold them separately, jointly, or as a partner, or in any combination of such forms of ownership.

(2) *When a subdivision will be considered a new tract.* If the taxpayer sells or exchanges no lots from the tract for a period of 5 years after the sale or exchange of at least 1 lot in the tract, then the remainder of the tract shall be deemed a new tract for the purpose of counting the number of lots sold from the same tract under section 1237(b)(1). The pieces in the new tract need not be contiguous. The 5-year period is measured between the dates of the sales or exchanges.

(h) *Effective date.* This section shall apply only to gain realized on sales made after December 31, 1953, or, in the case of a person meeting the requirements of paragraph (c)(5)(iv) of this section, if the sale of the lot occurs in a taxable year beginning after December 31, 1954. Pursuant to section 7851 (a)(1)(C), the regulations prescribed in this section (other than subdivision (iv) of paragraph (c)(5)) shall also apply to taxable years beginning before January 1, 1954, and ending after December 31, 1953, and to taxable years beginning after December 31, 1953, and ending before August 17, 1954, although such years are subject to the Internal Revenue Code of 1939. Irrespective of whether the taxable year involved is subject to the Internal Revenue Code of 1939 or the Internal Revenue Code of 1954, sales or exchanges made before January 1, 1954, shall be taken into account to determine whether: (1) No sales or exchanges have been made for 5 years, under section 1237(c), and (2) more than 5 lots or parcels have been sold or exchanged from the same tract, under Section 1237(b)(1). Thus, if the taxpayer sold 5 lots from a single tract in 1950, and another lot is sold in 1954, the lot sold in 1954 constitutes the "sixth lot" sold from the original tract. On the other hand, if the first 5 lots were sold in 1948, the sale made in 1954 shall be deemed to have been made from a new tract. [Reg. § 1.1237-1.]

☐ [T.D. 6247, 8-13-57.]

[Reg. § 1.1238-1]

§ 1.1238-1. **Amortization in excess of depreciation.**—(a) *In general.* Section 1238 provides that if a taxpayer is entitled to a deduction for amortization of an emergency facility under sec-

Reg. § 1.1238-1(a)

tion 168, and if the facility is later sold or exchanged, any gain realized shall be considered as ordinary income to the extent the amortization deduction exceeds normal depreciation. Thus, under section 1238 gain from a sale or exchange of property shall be considered as ordinary income to the extent that its adjusted basis is less than its adjusted basis would be if it were determined without regard to section 168. If an entire facility is certified under section 168(e), the taxpayer may use allowances for depreciation based on any rate and method which would have been proper if the basis of the facility were not subject to amortization under section 168, in determining what the adjusted basis of the facility would be if it were determined without regard to section 168. If only a portion of a facility is certified under section 168(e), allowances for depreciation based on the rate and method properly used with respect to the uncertified part of the facility are used in determining what the adjusted basis of the facility would be if it were determined without regard to section 168. The principles of this paragraph may be illustrated by the following examples:

Example (1). On December 31, 1954, a taxpayer making his income tax returns on a calendar year basis acquires at a cost of $20,000 an emergency facility (used in his business) 50 percent of the adjusted basis of which has been certified under section 168(e). The facility would normally have a useful life of 20 years and a salvage value of $2,000 allocable equally between the certified and uncertified portions. Under section 168 the taxpayer elects to begin the 60-month amortization period on January 1, 1955. He takes amortization deductions with respect to the certified portion in the amount of $4,000 for the years 1955 and 1956 (24 months). On December 31, 1956, he sells the facility for a price of $19,000 which is allocable equally between the certified and uncertified portions. The adjusted basis of the certified portion on that date is $6,000 ($10,000 cost, less $4,000 amortization). With respect to the uncertified portion, the straight line method of depreciation is used and a deduction for depreciation in the amount of $450 is claimed and allowed for the year 1955. The adjusted basis of the uncertified portion on January 1, 1956, is $9,550 ($10,000 cost, less $450 depreciation). The depreciation allowance for the uncertified portion for the year 1956 would be limited to $50, the amount by which the adjusted basis of such portion at the beginning of the year exceeded its aliquot portion of the sales price. Thus, on December 31, 1956, the adjusted basis of the uncertified portion would be $9,500. Without regard to section 168, and using the rate and method the taxpayer properly applied to the uncertified portion of the facility, the adjusted basis of the certified portion on December 31, 1956, would be $9,500, computed in the same manner as the adjusted basis of the uncertified portion. The difference between the facility's actual adjusted basis ($15,500) and its adjusted basis determined without regard to section 168 ($19,000), is $3,500. Accordingly, the entire $3,500 gain on the sale of the facility ($19,000 sale price, less $15,500 adjusted basis) is treated as ordinary income.

Example (2). Assume that the entire facility in example (1) had been certified under section 168(e) and that, therefore, the adjusted basis of the facility on December 31, 1956, is $12,000. Assume further that the taxpayer adopts straight line depreciation as a proper method of depreciation for determining the adjusted basis of the facility without regard to section 168. Thus, the adjusted basis, without regard to section 168, would be $19,000. This amount is $7,000 more than the $12,000 adjusted basis under section 168. Hence, the entire $7,000 gain on the sale of the facility ($19,000 sale price less $12,000 adjusted basis) is treated as ordinary income.

(b) *Substituted basis.* If a taxpayer acquires other property in an exchange for an emergency facility with respect to which amortization deductions have been allowed or allowable, and if the basis in his hands of the other property is determined by reference to the basis of the emergency facility, then the basis of the other property is determined with regard to section 168, and therefore the provisions of section 1238 apply with respect to gain realized on a subsequent sale or exchange of the other property. The provisions of section 1238 also apply to gain realized on the sale or exchange of an emergency facility (or other property acquired, as described in the preceding sentence, in exchange for an emergency facility) by a taxpayer in whose hands the basis of the facility (or other property) is determined by reference to its basis in the hands of another person to whom deductions were allowable or allowed with respect to the facility under section 168. [Reg. § 1.1238-1.]

☐ [T.D. 6253, 9-25-57. Amended by T.D. 6825, 6-1-65.]

[Reg. § 1.1239-1]

§ 1.1239-1. **Gain from sale or exchange of depreciable property between certain related taxpayers after October 4, 1976.**—(a) *In general.* In the case of a sale or exchange of property, directly or indirectly, between related persons after October 4, 1976 (other than a sale or exchange made under a binding contract entered into on or before that date), any gain recognized by the transferor shall be treated as ordinary income if

Reg. § 1.1239-1(a)

Rules for Determining Capital Gains and Losses

See p. 20,601 for regulations not amended to reflect law changes

such property is, in the hands of the transferee, subject to the allowance for depreciation provided in section 167. This rule also applies to property which would be subject to the allowance for depreciation provided in section 167 except that the purchaser has elected a different form of deduction, such as those allowed under sections 169, 188, and 191.

(b) *Related persons.* For purposes of paragraph (a), the term "related persons" means—

(1) A husband and wife,

(2) An individual and a corporation 80 percent or more in value of the outstanding stock of which is owned, directly or indirectly, by or for such individual, or

(3) Two or more corporations 80 percent or more in value of the outstanding stock of each of which is owned, directly or indirectly, by or for the same individual.

(c) *Rules of construction*—(1) *Husband and wife.* For purposes of paragraph (b)(1), if on the date of the sale or exchange a taxpayer is legally separated from his spouse under an interlocutory decree of divorce, the taxpayer and his spouse shall not be treated as husband and wife, provided the sale or exchange is made pursuant to the decree and the decree subsequently becomes final. Thus, if pursuant to an interlocutory decree of divorce, an individual transfers depreciable property to his spouse and, because of this section, the gain recognized on the transfer of the property is treated as ordinary income, the individual may, if the interlocutory decree becomes final after his tax return has been filed, file a claim for a refund.

(2) *Sales between commonly controlled corporations.* In general, in the case of a sale or exchange of depreciable property between related corporations (within the meaning of paragraph (b)(3) of this section), gain which is treated as ordinary income by reason of this section shall be taxable to the transferor corporation rather than to a controlling shareholder. However, such gain shall be treated as ordinary income taxable to a controlling shareholder rather than the transferor corporation if the transferor corporation is used by a controlling shareholder as a mere conduit to make a sale to another controlled corporation, or the entity of the corporate transferor is otherwise properly disregarded for tax purposes. Sales between two or more corporations that are related within the meaning of paragraph (b)(3) of this section may also be subject to the rules of section 482 (relating to allocation of income between or among organizations, trades, or businesses which are commonly owned or controlled), and to rules requiring constructive dividend treatment to the controlling shareholder in appropriate circumstances.

(3) *Relationship determination for transfers made after January 6, 1983—taxpayer and an 80-percent owned entity.* For purposes of paragraph (b)(2) of this section with respect to transfers made after January 6, 1983—

(i) If the transferor is an entity, the transferee and such entity are related if the entity is an 80-percent owned entity with respect to such transferee either immediately before or immediately after the sale or exchange of depreciable property, and

(ii) If the transferor is not an entity, the transferee and such transferor are related if the transferee is an 80-percent owned entity with respect to such transferor immediately after the sale or exchange of depreciable property.

(4) *Relationship determination for transfers made after January 6, 1983—two 80-percent owned entities.* For purposes of paragraph (b)(3) of this section, with respect to transfers made after January 6, 1983, two entities are related if the same shareholder both owns 80 percent or more in value of the stock of the transferor before the sale or exchange of depreciable property and owns 80 percent or more in value of the stock of the transferee immediately after the sale or exchange of depreciable property.

(5) *Ownership of stock.* For purposes of determining the ownership of stock under this section, the constructive ownership rules of section 318 shall be applied, except that section 318(a)(2)(C) (relating to attribution of stock ownership from a corporation) and section 318(a)(3)(C) (relating to attribution of stock ownership to a corporation) shall be applied without regard to the 50-percent limitation contained therein. The application of the constructive ownership rules of section 318 to section 1239 is illustrated by the following examples:

Example (1). A, an individual, owns 79 percent of the stock (by value) of Corporation X, and a trust for A's children owns the remaining 21 percent of the stock. A's children are deemed to own the stock owned for their benefit by the trust in proportion to their actuarial interests in the trust (section 318(a)(2)(B)). A, in turn, constructively owns the stock so deemed to be owned by his children (section 318(a)(1)(A)(ii)). Thus, A is treated as owning all the stock of Corporation X, and any gain A recognizes from the sale of depreciable property to Corporation X is treated under section 1239 as ordinary income.

Example (2). Y Corporation owns 100% in value of the stock of Z Corporation. Y Corporation sells depreciable property at a gain to Z Corpora-

Reg. § 1.1239-1(c)(5)

Rules for Determining Capital Gains and Losses

See p. 20,601 for regulations not amended to reflect law changes

tion. P and his daughter, D, own 80 percent in value of the Y Corporation stock. Under the constructive ownership rules of section 318, as applied to section 1239, P and D are each considered to own the stock in Z Corporation owned by Y Corporation. Also, P and D are each considered to own the stock in Y Corporation owned by the other. As a result, both P and D constructively own 80 percent or more in value of the stock of both Y and Z Corporations. Thus, the sale between Y and Z is governed by section 1239 and produces ordinary income to Y. [Reg. § 1.1239-1.]

☐ [T.D. 7569, 11-2-78. Amended by T.D. 8106, 11-25-86.]

[Reg. § 1.1239-2]

§ 1.1239-2. Gain from sale or exchange of depreciable property between certain related taxpayers on or before October 4, 1976.—Section 1239 provides in general that any gain from the sale or exchange of depreciable property between a husband and wife or between an individual and a controlled corporation on or before October 4, 1976 (and in the case of a sale or exchange occurring after that date if made under a binding contract entered into on or before that date), shall be treated as ordinary income. Thus, any gain recognized to the transferor from a sale or exchange after May 3, 1951, and on or before October 4, 1976 (or thereafter if pursuant to a binding contract entered into on or before that date), directly or indirectly, between a husband and wife or between an individual and a controlled corporation, of property which, in the hands of the transferee, is property of a character subject to an allowance for depreciation provided in section 167 (including such property on which a deduction for amortization is allowable under sections 168 and 169) shall be considered as gain from the sale or exchange of property which is neither a capital asset nor property described in section 1231. For the purpose of section 1239, a corporation is controlled when more than 80 percent in value of all outstanding stock of the corporation is beneficially owned by the taxpayer, his spouse, and his minor children and minor grandchildren. For the purpose of this section, the terms "children" and "grandchildren" include legally adopted children and their children. The provisions of section 1239(a)(2) are applicable whether property is transferred from a corporation to a shareholder or from a shareholder to a corporation. [Reg. § 1.1239-2.]

☐ [T.D. 6253, 9-25-57. Redesignated and amended by T.D. 7569, 11-2-78.]

[Reg. § 1.1241-1]

§ 1.1241-1. Cancellation of lease or distributor's agreement.—(a) *In general.* Section 1241 provides that proceeds received by lessees or distributors from the cancellation of leases or of certain distributorship agreements are considered as amounts received in exchange therefor. Section 1241 applies to leases of both real and personal property. Distributorship agreements to which section 1241 applies are described in paragraph (c) of this section. Section 1241 has no application in determining whether or not a cancellation not qualifying under that section is a sale or exchange. Further, section 1241 has no application in determining whether or not a lease or a distributorship agreement is a capital asset, even though its cancellation qualifies as an exchange under section 1241.

(b) *Definition of "cancellation".* The term "cancellation" of a lease or a distributor's agreement, as used in section 1241, means a termination of all the contractual rights of a lessee or distributor with respect to particular premises or a particular distributorship, other than by the expiration of the lease or agreement in accordance with its terms. A payment made in good faith for a partial cancellation of a lease or a distributorship agreement is recognized as an amount received for cancellation under section 1241 if the cancellation relates to a severable economic unit, such as a portion of the premises covered by a lease, a reduction in the unexpired term of a lease or distributorship agreement, or a distributorship in one of several areas or of one of several products. Payments made for other modifications of leases or distributorship agreements, however, are not recognized as amounts received for cancellation under section 1241.

(c) *Amounts received upon cancellation of a distributorship agreement.* Section 1241 applies to distributorship agreements only if they are for marketing or marketing and servicing of goods. It does not apply to agreements for selling intangible property or for rendering personal services as, for example, agreements establishing insurance agencies or agencies for the brokerage of securities. Further, it applies to a distributorship agreement only if the distributor has made a substantial investment of capital in the distributorship. The substantial capital investment must be reflected in physical assets such as inventories of tangible goods, equipment, machinery, storage facilities, or similar property. An investment is not considered substantial for purposes of section 1241 unless it consists of a significant fraction or more of the facilities for storing, transporting, processing, or otherwise dealing with the goods distributed, or

Reg. § 1.1239-2

consists of a substantial inventory of such goods. The investment required in the maintenance of an office merely for clerical operations is not considered substantial for purposes of this section. Furthermore, section 1241 shall not apply unless a substantial amount of the capital or assets needed for carrying on the operations of a distributorship are acquired by the distributor and actually used in carrying on the distributorship at some time before the cancellation of the distributorship agreement. It is immaterial for the purposes of section 1241 whether the distributor acquired the assets used in performing the functions of the distributorship before or after beginning his operations under the distributorship agreement. It is also immaterial whether the distributor is a retailer, wholesaler, jobber, or other type of distributor. The application of this paragraph may be illustrated by the following examples:

Example (1). Taxpayer is a distributor of various food products. He leases a warehouse including cold storage facilities and owns a number of motor trucks. In 1955 he obtains the exclusive rights to market certain frozen food products in his State. The marketing is accomplished by using the warehouse and trucks acquired before he entered into the agreement and entails no additional capital. Payments received upon the cancellation of the agreement are treated under section 1241 as though received upon the sale or exchange of the agreement.

Example (2). Assume that the taxpayer in example (1) entered into an exclusive distributorship agreement with the producer under which the taxpayer merely solicits orders through his staff of salesmen, the goods being shipped direct to the purchasers. Payments received upon the cancellation of the agreement would not be treated under section 1241 as though received upon the sale or exchange of the agreement.

Example (3). Taxpayer is an exclusive distributor for M city of certain frozen food products which he distributes to frozen-food freezer and locker customers. The terms of his distributorship do not make it necessary for him to have any substantial investment in inventory. Taxpayer rents a loading platform for a nominal amount, but has no warehouse space. Orders for goods from customers are consolidated by the taxpayer and forwarded to the producer from time to time. Upon receipt of these goods, taxpayer allocates them to the individual orders of customers and delivers them immediately by truck. Although it would require a fleet of fifteen or twenty trucks to carry out this operation, the distributor uses only one truck of his own and hires cartage companies to deliver the bulk of the merchandise to the customers. Payments received upon the cancellation of the distributorship agreement in such a case would not be considered received upon the sale or exchange of the agreement under section 1241 since the taxpayer does not have facilities for the physical handling of more than a small fraction of the goods involved in carrying on the distributorship and, therefore, does not have a substantial capital investment in the distributorship. On the other hand, if the taxpayer had acquired and used a substantial number of the trucks necessary for the deliveries to his customers, payments received upon the cancellation of the agreement would be considered received in exchange therefor under section 1241. [Reg. § 1.1241-1.]

☐ [T.D. 6253, 9-25-57.]

[Reg. § 1.1242-1]

§ 1.1242-1. **Losses on small business investment company stock.**—(a) *In general.* Any taxpayer who sustains a loss for a taxable year beginning after September 2, 1958, as a result of the worthlessness, or from the sale or exchange, of the stock of a small business investment company (whether or not such stock was originally issued to such taxpayer) shall treat such loss as a loss from the sale or exchange of property which is not a capital asset, if at the time of such loss—

(1) The company which issued the stock is licensed to operate as a small business investment company pursuant to regulations promulgated by the Small Business Administration (13 CFR Part 107), and

(2) Such loss would, but for the provisions of section 1242, be a loss from the sale or exchange of a capital asset.

(b) *Treatment of losses for purposes of section 172.* For the purposes of section 172 (relating to the net operating loss deduction), any amount of loss treated by reason of section 1242 as a loss from the sale or exchange of property which is not a capital asset shall be treated as attributable to the trade or business of the taxpayer. Accordingly, the limitation of section 172(d)(4) on the allowance of nonbusiness deductions in computing a net operating loss shall not apply to any loss with respect to the stock of a small business investment company as described in paragraph (a) of this section. See section 172(d) and § 1.172-3.

(c) *Statement to be filed with return.* A taxpayer claiming a deduction for a loss on the stock of a small business investment company shall file with his income tax return a statement containing: the name and address of the small business investment company which issued the stock, the number of shares, basis, and selling price of the

Reg. § 1.1242-1(c)

stock with respect to which the loss is claimed, the respective dates of purchase and sale of such stock, or the reason for its worthlessness and approximate date thereof. For the rules applicable in determining the worthlessness of securities, see section 165 and the regulations thereunder. [Reg. § 1.1242-1.]

☐ [T.D. 6449, 1-27-60.]

[Reg. § 1.1243-1]

§ 1.1243-1. Loss of small business investment company.—(a) *In general.*—(1) *Taxable years beginning after July 11, 1969.* For taxable years beginning after July 11, 1969, a small business investment company to which section 582(c) applies, and which sustains a loss as a result of the worthlessness, or on the sale or exchange, of the stock of a small business concern (as defined in section 103(5) of the Small Business Investment Act of 1958, as amended (15 U.S.C. 662(5)) and in 13 CFR 107.3), shall treat such loss as a loss from the sale or exchange of property which is not a capital asset if—

(i) The stock was issued pursuant to the conversion privilege of the convertible debentures acquired in accordance with the provisions of section 304 of the Small Business Investment Act of 1958 (15 U.S.C. 684) and the regulations thereunder,

(ii) Such loss would, but for the provisions of section 1243, be a loss from the sale or exchange of a capital asset, and

(iii) At the time of the loss, the company is licensed to operate as a small business investment company pursuant to regulations promulgated by the Small Business Administration (13 CFR Part 107).

If section 582(c) does not apply for the taxable year, see subparagraph (2) of this paragraph.

(2) *Taxable years beginning before July 11, 1974.* For taxable years beginning after September 2, 1958, but before July 11, 1974, a small business investment company to which section 582(c) does not apply, and which sustains a loss as a result of the worthlessness, or on the sale or exchange, of the securities of a small business concern (as defined in section 103(5) of the Small Business Investment Act of 1958, as amended (15 U.S.C. 662(5)) and in 13 CFR 107.3), shall treat such loss as a loss from the sale or exchange of property which is not a capital asset if—

(i) The securities are either the convertible debentures, or the stock issued pursuant to the conversion privilege thereof, acquired in accordance with the provisions of section 304 of the Small Business Investment Act of 1958 (15 U.S.C. 684) and the regulations thereunder,

(ii) Such loss would, but for the provisions of this subparagraph, be a loss from the sale or exchange of a capital asset, and

(iii) At the time of the loss, the company is licensed to operate as a small business investment company pursuant to regulations promulgated by the Small Business Administration (13 CFR Part 107).

If section 582(c) applies for the taxable year, see subparagraph (1) of this paragraph.

(b) *Material to be filed with return.* A small business investment company which claims a deduction for a loss on the convertible debentures (pursuant to paragraph (a)(2) of this section) or stock (pursuant to paragraph (a)(1) or (a)(2) of this section) of a small business concern shall submit with its income tax return a statement that it is a Federal licensee under the Small Business Investment Act of 1958 (15 U.S.C. ch. 14B). The statement shall also set forth: the name and address of the small business concern with respect to whose securities the loss was sustained, the number of shares of stock or the number and denomination of debentures with respect to which the loss is claimed, the basis and selling price thereof, and the respective dates of purchase and sale of the securities, or the reason for their worthlessness and the approximate date thereof. For the rules applicable in determining the worthlessness of securities, see section 165 and the regulations thereunder. [Reg. § 1.1243-1.]

☐ [T.D. 6449, 1-27-60. Amended by T.D. 7171, 3-16-72.]

[Reg. § 1.1244(a)-1]

§ 1.1244(a)-1. Loss on small business stock treated as ordinary loss.—(a) *In general.* Subject to certain conditions and limitations, section 1244 provides that a loss on the sale or exchange (including a transaction treated as a sale or exchange, such as worthlessness) of "section 1244 stock" which would otherwise be treated as loss from the sale or exchange of a capital asset shall be treated as a loss from the sale or exchange of an asset which is not a capital asset (referred to in this section and §§ 1.1244(b)-1 to 1.1244(e)-1, inclusive, as an "ordinary loss"). Such a loss shall be allowed as a deduction from gross income in arriving at adjusted gross income. The requirements that must be satisfied in order that stock may be considered section 1244 stock are described in §§ 1.1244(c)-1 and 1.1244(c)-2. These requirements relate to the stock itself and the corporation issuing such stock. In addition, the taxpayer who claims an ordinary loss deduction pursuant to section 1244 must satisfy the requirements of paragraph (b) of this section.

Reg. § 1.1243-1(a)(1)

Rules for Determining Capital Gains and Losses

(b) *Taxpayers entitled to ordinary loss.* The allowance of an ordinary loss deduction for a loss on section 1244 stock is permitted only to the following two classes of taxpayers:

(1) An individual sustaining the loss to whom the stock was issued by a small business corporation, or

(2) An individual who is a partner in a partnership at the time the partnership acquired the stock in an issuance from a small business corporation and whose distributive share of partnership items reflects the loss sustained by the partnership. The ordinary loss deduction is limited to the lesser of the partner's distributive share at the time of the issuance of the stock or the partner's distributive share at the time the loss is sustained. In order to claim a deduction under section 1244 the individual, or the partnership, sustaining the loss must have continuously held the stock from the date of issuance. A corporation, trust, or estate is not entitled to ordinary loss treatment under section 1244 regardless of how the stock was acquired. An individual who acquires stock from a shareholder by purchase, gift, devise, or in any other manner is not entitled to an ordinary loss under section 1244 with respect to this stock. Thus, ordinary loss treatment is not available to a partner to whom the stock is distributed by the partnership. Stock acquired through an investment banking firm, or other person, participating in the sale of an issue may qualify for ordinary loss treatment only if the stock is not first issued to the firm or person. Thus, for example, if the firm acts as a selling agent for the issuing corporation the stock may qualify. On the other hand, stock purchased by an investment firm and subsequently resold does not qualify as section 1244 stock in the hands of the person acquiring the stock from the firm.

(c) *Examples.* The provisions of paragraph (b) of this section may be illustrated by the following examples:

Example (1). A and B, both individuals, and C, a trust, are equal partners in a partnership to which a small business corporation issues section 1244 stock. The partnership sells the stock at a loss. A's and B's distributive share of the loss may be treated as an ordinary loss pursuant to section 1244, but C's distributive share of the loss may not be so treated.

Example (2). The facts are the same as in example (1) except that the section 1244 stock is distributed by the partnership to partner A and he subsequently sells the stock at a loss. Section 1244 is not applicable to the loss since A did not acquire the stock by issuance from the small business corporation. [Reg. § 1.1244(a)-1.]

☐ [T.D. 6495, 10-7-60. Amended by T.D. 7779, 6-1-81.]

[Reg. § 1.1244(b)-1]

§ 1.1244(b)-1. Annual limitation.—(a) *In general.* Subsection (b) of section 1244 imposes a limitation on the aggregate amount of loss that for any taxable year may be treated as an ordinary loss by a taxpayer by reason of that section. In the case of a partnership, the limitation is determined separately as to each partner. Any amount of loss in excess of the applicable limitation is treated as loss from the sale or exchange of a capital asset.

(b) *Amount of loss*—(1) *Taxable years beginning after December 31, 1978.* For any taxable year beginning after December 31, 1978, the maximum amount that may be treated as an ordinary loss under section 1244 is—

(i) $50,000, or

(ii) $100,000, if a husband and wife file a joint return under section 6013.

These limitations on the maximum amount of ordinary loss apply whether the loss or losses are sustained on pre-November 1978 stock (as defined in § 1.1244(c)-1(a)(1)), post-November 1978 stock (as defined in § 1.1244(c)-1(a)(2)), or on any combination of pre-November 1978 stock and post-November 1978 stock. The limitation referred to in (ii) applies to a joint return whether the loss or losses are sustained by one or both spouses.

(2) *Taxable years ending before November 6, 1978.* For any taxable year ending before November 6, 1978, the maximum amount that may be treated as an ordinary loss under section 1244 is—

(i) $25,000 or

(ii) $50,000, if a husband and wife file a joint return under section 6013.

The limitation referred to in (ii) applies to a joint return whether the loss or losses are sustained by one or both spouses.

(3) *Taxable years including November 6, 1978.* For a taxable year including November 6, 1978, the maximum amount that may be treated as ordinary loss under section 1244 is the sum of—

(i) The amount calculated by applying the limitations described in subparagraph (1) of this paragraph (b) to the amount of loss, if any, sustained during the taxable year on post-November 1978 stock, plus

(ii) The amount calculated by applying the limitations described in subparagraph (2) of this paragraph (b) to the amount of loss, if any, sustained during the taxable year on pre-November 1978 stock.

to the extent this sum does not exceed $50,000, or, if a husband and wife file a joint return under section 6013 for the taxable year, $100,000.

(4) *Examples.* The provisions of this section may be illustrated by the following examples:

Example (1). A, a married taxpayer who files a joint return for the taxable year ending December 31, 1977, sustains a $50,000 loss qualifying under section 1244 on pre-November 1978 stock in Corporation X and an equal amount of loss qualifying under section 1244 on pre-November 1978 stock in Corporation Y. A is limited to $50,000 of ordinary loss under paragraph (b)(2)(ii). The remaining $50,000 of loss is treated as loss from the sale or exchange of a capital asset.

Example (2). For the taxable year ending December 31, 1979, B, a married taxpayer who files a joint return, sustains a $90,000 loss on post-November 1978 stock in Corporation X. In the same taxable year, C, B's spouse, sustains a $25,000 loss on post-November 1978 stock in Corporation Y. Both losses qualify under section 1244. B and C's ordinary loss is limited to $100,000 under paragraph (b)(1)(ii). The remaining $15,000 of loss is treated as loss from the sale or exchange of a capital asset.

Example (3). D, a married taxpayer who files a joint return and reports income on a fiscal year basis for the taxable year ending November 30, 1978, sustains a $60,000 loss qualifying under section 1244 on pre-November 1978 stock and a $40,000 loss qualifying under section 1244 on post-November 1978 stock. D's ordinary loss on pre-November 1978 stock is limited to $50,000 under subparagraph (3)(ii) of this paragraph (b). D's $40,000 loss on post-November 1978 stock is within the limit of subparagraph (3)(i) of this paragraph (b). The total of these losses, $90,000, is the aggregate amount deductible by D as ordinary loss under section 1244. The remaining $10,000 of loss is treated as loss from the sale or exchange of a capital asset.

Example (4). E, a married taxpayer who files a joint return for the taxable year ending December 31, 1980, sustains a $75,000 loss qualifying under section 1244 on pre-November 1978 stock and a $10,000 loss qualifying under section 1244 on post-November 1978 stock. E may deduct the total of these losses, $85,000, as ordinary loss under paragraph (b)(1)(ii).

Example (5). Assume the same facts as in the preceding example, except that the losses are sustained in the taxable year beginning January 1, 1978, and ending December 31, 1978. E is limited to $60,000 of ordinary loss ($50,000 on pre-November 1978 stock plus $10,000 on post-November 1978 stock) under paragraph (b)(3). The remaining $25,000 of loss is treated as loss from the sale or exchange of a capital asset.

Example (6). F, a married taxpayer who files a joint return for the taxable year beginning January 1, 1978, and ending December 31, 1978, sustains a $75,000 loss qualifying under section 1244 on pre-November 1978 stock and a $125,000 loss qualifying under section 1244 on post-November 1978 stock. F's loss on pre-November 1978 stock is limited to $50,000 of ordinary loss under subparagraph (3)(ii) of this paragraph (b). F's loss on post-November 1978 stock is limited to $100,000 of ordinary loss under subparagraph (3)(i) of this paragraph (b). The total of these losses, $150,000, is limited to $100,000 of ordinary loss under paragraph (b)(3). F's aggregate amount of ordinary loss under section 1244 is $100,000. The remaining $100,000 of loss is treated as loss from the sale or exchange of a capital asset. [Reg. § 1.1244(b)-1.]

☐ [T.D. 6495, 10-7-60. Amended by T.D. 7779, 6-1-81.]

[Reg. § 1.1244(c)-1]

§ 1.1244(c)-1. **Section 1244 stock defined.**—(a) *In general.* For purposes of §§ 1.1244(a)-1 to 1.1244(e)-1, inclusive—

(1) The term "pre-November 1978 stock" means stock issued after June 30, 1958, and on or before November 6, 1978.

(2) The term "post-November 1978 stock" means stock issued after November 6, 1978.

In order that stock may qualify as section 1244 stock, the requirements described in paragraphs (b) through (e) of this section must be satisfied. In addition, the requirements of paragraph (f) of this section must be satisfied in the case of pre-November 1978 stock. Whether these requirements have been met is determined at the time the stock is issued, except for the requirement in paragraph (e) of this section. Whether the requirement in paragraph (e) of this section, relating to gross receipts of the corporation, has been satisfied is determined at the time a loss is sustained. Therefore, at the time of issuance it cannot be said with certainty that stock will qualify for the benefits of section 1244.

(b) *Common stock.* Only common stock, either voting or nonvoting, in a domestic corporation may qualify as section 1244 stock. For purposes of section 1244, neither securities of the corporation convertible into common stock nor common stock convertible into other securities of the corporation are treated as common stock. An increase in the basis of outstanding stock as a result of a contribution to capital is not treated as an issuance of stock under section 1244. For definition of domes-

Rules for Determining Capital Gains and Losses 53,497
See p. 20,601 for regulations not amended to reflect law changes

tic corporation, see section 7701(a)(4) and the regulations under that section.

(c) *Small business corporation.* At the time the stock is issued (or, in the case of pre-November 1978 stock, at the time of adoption of the plan described in paragraph (f)(1) of this section) the corporation must be a "small business corporation". See § 1.1244(c)-2 for the definition of a small business corporation.

(d) *Issued for money or other property.* (1) The stock must be issued to the taxpayer for money or other property transferred by the taxpayer to the corporation. However, stock issued in exchange for stock or securities, including stock or securities of the issuing corporation, cannot qualify as section 1244 stock, except as provided in § 1.1244(d)-3, relating to certain cases where stock is issued in exchange for section 1244 stock. Stock issued for services rendered or to be rendered to, or for the benefit of, the issuing corporation does not qualify as section 1244 stock. Stock issued in consideration for cancellation of indebtedness of the corporation shall be considered issued in exchange for money or other property unless such indebtedness is evidenced by a security, or arises out of the performance of personal services.

(2) The following examples illustrate situations where stock fails to qualify as section 1244 stock as a result of the rules in subparagraph (1) of this paragraph:

Example (1). A taxpayer owns stock of Corporation X issued to him prior to July 1, 1958. Under a plan adopted in 1977, he exchanges his stock for a new issuance of stock of Corporation X. The stock received by the taxpayer in the exchange may not qualify as section 1244 stock even if the corporation has adopted a valid plan and is a small business corporation.

Example (2). A taxpayer owns stock in Corporation X. Corporation X merges into Corporation Y. In exchange for his stock, Corporation Y issues shares of its stock to the taxpayer. The stock in Corporation Y does not qualify as section 1244 stock even if the stock exchanged by the taxpayer did qualify.

Example (3). Corporation X transfers part of its business assets to Corporation Y, a new corporation, and all of the stock of Corporation Y is issued directly to the shareholders of Corporation X. Since the Corporation Y stock was not issued to the shareholders for a transfer by them of money or other property, none of the Corporation Y stock in the hands of the shareholders can qualify.

(e) *Gross receipts.* (1)(i)(a) Except as provided in subparagraph (2) of this paragraph, stock will not qualify under section 1244 if 50 percent or more of the gross receipts of the corporation, for the period consisting of the five most recent taxable years of the corporation ending before the date the loss on such stock is sustained by the shareholders is derived from royalties, rents, dividends, interest, annuities, and sales or exchanges of stock or securities. If the corporation has not been in existence for five taxable years ending before such date, the percentage test referred to in the preceding sentence applies to the period of the taxable years ending before such date during which the corporation has been in existence; and if the loss is sustained during the first taxable year of the corporation such test applies to the period beginning with the first day of such taxable year and ending on the day before the loss is sustained. The test under this paragraph shall be made on the basis of total gross receipts, except that gross receipts from the sales or exchanges of stock or securities shall be taken into account only to the extent of gains therefrom. The term "gross receipts" as used in section 1244(c)(1)(C) is not synonymous with "gross income". Gross receipts means the total amount received or accrued under the method of accounting used by the corporation in computing its taxable income. Thus, the total amount of receipts is not reduced by returns and allowances, cost, or deductions. For example, gross receipts will include the total amount received or accrued during the corporation's taxable year from the sale or exchange (including a sale or exchange to which section 337 applies) of any kind of property, from investments, and for services rendered by the corporation. However, gross receipts does not include amounts received in nontaxable sales or exchanges (other than those to which section 337 applies), except to the extent that gain is recognized by the corporation, nor does that term include amounts received as a loan, as repayment of a loan, as a contribution to capital, or on the issuance by the corporation of its own stock.

(b) The meaning of the term "gross receipts" as used in section 1244(c)(1)(C) may be further illustrated by the following examples:

Example (1). A corporation on the accrual method sells property (other than stock or securities) and receives payment partly in money and partly in the form of a note payable at a future time. The amount of the money and the face amount of the note would be considered gross receipts in the taxable year of the sale and would not be reduced by the adjusted basis of the property, the costs of sale, or any other amount.

Example (2). A corporation has a long-term contract as defined in paragraph (a) of § 1.451-3 with respect to which it reports income

Reg. § 1.1244(c)-1(e)

according to the percentage-of-completion method as described in paragraph (b)(1) of § 1.451-3. The portion of the gross contract price which corresponds to the percentage of the entire contract which has been completed during the taxable year shall be included in gross receipts for such year.

Example (3). A corporation which regularly sells personal property on the installment plan elects to report its taxable income from the sale of property (other than stock or securities) on the installment method in accordance with section 453. The installment payments actually received in a given taxable year of the corporation shall be included in gross receipts for such year.

(ii) The term "royalties" as used in subdivision (i) of this subparagraph means all royalties, including mineral, oil, and gas royalties (whether or not the aggregate amount of such royalties constitutes 50 percent or more of the gross income of the corporation for the taxable year), and amounts received for the privilege of using patents, copyrights, secret processes and formulas, good will, trademarks, trade brands, franchises, and other like property. The term "royalties" does not include amounts received upon the disposal of timber, coal, or domestic iron ore with a retained economic interest to which the special rules of section 631(b) and (c) apply or amounts received from the transfer of patent rights to which section 1235 applies. For the definition of "mineral, oil, or gas royalties," see paragraph (b)(11)(ii) and (iii) of § 1.543-1. For purposes of this subdivision, the gross amount of royalties shall not be reduced by any part of the cost of the rights under which they are received or by any amount allowable as a deduction in computing taxable income.

(iii) The term "rents" as used in subdivision (i) of this subparagraph means amounts received for the use of, or right to use, property (whether real or personal) of the corporation, whether or not such amounts constitute 50 percent or more of the gross income of the corporation for the taxable year. The term "rents" does not include payments for the use or occupancy of rooms or other space where significant services are also rendered to the occupant, such as for the use or occupancy of rooms or other quarters in hotels, boarding houses, or apartment houses furnishing hotel services, or in tourist homes, motor courts, or motels. Generally, services are considered rendered to the occupant if they are primarily for his convenience and are other than those usually or customarily rendered in connection with the rental of rooms or other space for occupancy only. The supplying of maid service, for example, constitutes such services; whereas the furnishing of heat and light, the cleaning of public entrances, exits, stairways, and lobbies, the collection of trash, etc., are not considered as services rendered to the occupant. Payments for the use or occupancy of entire private residences or living quarters in duplex or multiple housing units, of offices in an office building, etc., are generally "rents" under section 1244(c)(1)(C). Payments for the parking of automobiles ordinarily do not constitute rents. Payments for the warehousing of goods or for the use of personal property do no constitute rents if significant services are rendered in connection with such payments.

(iv) The term "dividends" as used in subdivision (i) of this subparagraph includes dividends as defined in section 316, amounts required to be included in gross income under section 551 (relating to foreign personal holding company income taxed to United States shareholders), and consent dividends determined as provided in section 565.

(v) The term "interest" as used in subdivision (i) of this subparagraph means any amounts received for the use of money (including tax-exempt interest).

(vi) The term "annuities" as used in subdivision (i) of this subparagraph means the entire amount received as an annuity under an annuity, endowment, or life insurance contract, regardless of whether only part of such amount would be includible in gross income under section 72.

(vii) For purposes of subdivision (i) of this subparagraph, gross receipts from the sales or exchanges of stock or securities are taken into account only to the extent of gains therefrom. Thus, the gross receipts from the sale of a particular share of stock will be the excess of the amount realized over the adjusted basis of such share. If the adjusted basis should equal or exceed the amount realized on the sale or exchange of a certain share of stock, bond, etc., there would be no gross receipts resulting from the sale of such security. Losses on sales or exchanges of stock or securities do not offset gains on the sales or exchanges of other stock or securities for purposes of computing gross receipts from such sales or exchanges. Gross receipts from the sale or exchange of stocks and securities include gains received from such sales or exchanges by a corporation even though such corporation is a regular dealer in stocks and securities. For the meaning of the term "stocks or securities," see paragraph (b)(5)(i) of § 1.543-1.

(2) The requirement of subparagraph (1) of this paragraph need not be satisfied if for the applicable period the aggregate amount of deductions allowed to the corporation exceeds the aggregate amount of its gross income. But for this

Reg. § 1.1244(c)-1(e)(2)

purpose the deductions allowed by section 172, relating to the net operating loss deduction, and by sections 242, 243, 244, and 245, relating to certain special deductions for corporations, shall not be taken into account. Notwithstanding the provisions of this subparagraph and of subparagraph (1) of this paragraph, pursuant to the specific delegation of authority granted in section 1244(e) to prescribe such regulations as may be necessary to carry out the purposes of section 1244, ordinary loss treatment will not be available with respect to stock of a corporation which is not largely an operating company within the five most recent taxable years (or such lesser period as the corporation is in existence) ending before the date of the loss. Thus, for example, assume that a person who is not a dealer in real estate forms a corporation which issues stock to him which meets all the formal requirements of section 1244 stock. The corporation then acquires a piece of unimproved real estate which it holds as an investment. The property declines in value and the stockholder sells his stock at a loss. The loss does not qualify for ordinary loss treatment under section 1244 but must be treated as a capital loss.

(3) In applying subparagraphs (1) and (2) of this paragraph to a successor corporation in a reorganization described in section 368(a)(1)(F), such corporation shall be treated as the same corporation as its predecessor. See paragraph (d)(2) of § 1.1244(d)-3.

(f) *Special rules applicable to pre-November 1978 stock.* (1)(i) Pre-November 1978 common stock must have been issued under a written plan adopted by the corporation after June 30, 1958, and on or before November 6, 1978, to offer only this stock during a period specified in the plan ending not later than 2 years after the date the plan is adopted. The 2-year requirement referred to in the preceding sentence is met if the period specified in the plan is based upon the date when, under the rules or regulations of a Government agency relating to the issuance of the stock, the stock may lawfully be sold, and it is clear that this period will end, and in fact does end, within 2 years after the plan is adopted. The plan must specifically state, in terms of dollars, the maximum amount to be received by the corporation in consideration for the stock to be issued under the plan. See § 1.1244(c)-2 for the limitation on the amount that may be received by the corporation under the plan.

(ii) To qualify, the pre-November 1978 stock must be issued during the period of the offer, which period must end not later than two years after the date the plan is adopted. Pre-November 1978 stock which is subscribed for during the period of the plan but not issued during this period cannot qualify as section 1244 stock. Pre-November 1978 stock issued on the exercise of a stock right, stock warrant, or stock option (which right, warrant, or option was not outstanding at the time the plan was adopted) will be treated as issued under a plan only if the right, warrant, or option is applicable solely to unissued stock offered under the plan and is exercised during the period of the plan.

(iii) Pre-November 1978 stock subscribed for prior to the adoption of the plan, including stock subscribed for prior to the date the corporation comes into existence, may be considered issued under a plan adopted by the corporation if the stock is not in fact issued prior to the adoption of the plan.

(iv) Pre-November 1978 stock issued for a payment which, alone or together with prior payments, exceeds the maximum amount that may be received under the plan, is not considered issued under the plan, and none of the stock can qualify as section 1244 stock. See § 1.1244(c)-2(b) for a different rule with respect to post-November 1978 stock.

(2) Pre-November 1978 stock does not qualify as section 1244 stock if at the time of the adoption of the plan under which it is issued there remains unissued any portion of a prior offering of stock. Thus, if any portion of an outstanding offering of common or preferred stock is unissued at the time of the adoption of the plan, stock issued under the plan will not qualify as section 1244 stock. An offer is outstanding unless and until it is withdrawn by affirmative action before the plan is adopted. Stock rights, stock warrants, stock options, or securities convertible into stock, that are outstanding at the time the plan is adopted, are considered prior offerings. The authorization in the corporate charter to issue stock different from stock offered under the plan or in excess of stock offered under the plan is not of itself a prior offering.

(3)(i) Even though the plan satisfies the requirements of subparagraph (1) of this paragraph (f), if another offering of pre-November 1978 stock is made by the corporation subsequent to, or simultaneous with, the adoption of the plan, pre-November 1978 stock issued under the plan after the other offering does not qualify as section 1244 stock. The issuance of stock options, stock rights, or stock warrants, at any time during the period of the plan, that are exercisable on stock other than stock offered under the plan, is considered a subsequent offering. Similarly, the issuance of pre-November 1978 stock other than that offered under the plan is considered a subsequent offer-

Reg. § 1.1244(c)-1(f)(3)

53,500 Rules for Determining Capital Gains and Losses
See p. 20,601 for regulations not amended to reflect law changes

ing. Because stock issued upon exercise of a conversion privilege is stock issued for a security, and stock issued under a stock option granted in whole or in part for services is not issued for money or other property, the issuance of securities with a conversion privilege and the issuance of such a stock option are subsequent offerings, because the conversion privilege and the stock option are exercisable with respect to stock other than that which may properly be offered under the plan. Pre-November 1978 stock issued under the plan before a subsequent offering is not disqualified because of the subsequent offering. The rule of the subparagraph, together with the rule of subparagraph (2) of this paragraph (f), relating to offers prior to the adoption of the plan, limits pre-November 1978 section 1244 stock to stock issued by the corporation during a period when any stock issued by it must have been issued under the plan.

(ii) Any modification of a plan that changes the offering to include preferred stock, or that increases the amount of pre-November 1978 stock that may be issued under the plan to such an extent that the requirements of paragraph (c) of this section would not have been satisfied if determined with reference to this amount as of the date the plan was initially adopted, or that extends the period of time during which stock may be issued under the plan to more than 2 years from the date the plan was initially adopted, is considered a subsequent offering, and no stock issued after this offering may qualify. However, a corporation may withdraw a plan and adopt a new plan to issue stock. To determine whether stock issued under this new plan may qualify, this paragraph (f) must be applied with respect to the new plan as of the date of its adoption. For example, amounts received for stock under the prior plan must be taken into account in determining whether the statutory requirements relating to definition of small business corporation are satisfied. In applying the requirements of paragraph (c) of this section, reference should be made to equity capital as of the date the new plan is adopted. The same principles apply if the period of the initial plan expires and the corporation adopts a new plan. [Reg. § 1.1244(c)-1.]

☐ [T.D. 6495, 10-7-60 and T.D. 6508, 12-1-60. Amended by T.D. 6637, 2-25-63, T.D. 6841, 7-26-65 and T.D. 7779, 6-1-81.]

[Reg. § 1.1244(c)-2]

§ 1.1244(c)-2. **Small business corporation defined.**—(a) *In general.* A corporation is treated as a small business corporation if it is a domestic corporation that satisfies the requirements described in paragraph (b) or (c) of this section. The requirements of paragraph (b) of this section apply if a loss is sustained on post-November 1978 stock. The requirements of paragraph (c) of this section apply if a loss is sustained on pre-November 1978 stock. If losses are sustained on both pre-November 1978 stock and post-November 1978 stock in the same taxable year, the requirements of paragraph (b) of this section are applied to the corporation at the time of the issuance of the stock (as required by paragraph (b) in the case of a loss on post-November 1978 stock) in order to determine whether the loss on post-November 1978 stock qualifies as a section 1244 loss, and the requirements of paragraph (c) of this section are applied to the corporation at the time of the adoption of the plan (as required by paragraph (c) in the case of a loss on pre-November 1978 stock) in order to determine whether the loss on pre-November 1978 stock qualifies as a section 1244 loss. For definition of domestic corporation, see section 7701(a)(4) and the regulations under that section.

(b) *Post-November 1978 stock*—(1) *Amount received by corporation for stock.* Capital receipts of a small business corporation may not exceed $1,000,000. For purposes of this paragraph the term "capital receipts" means the aggregate dollar amount received by the corporation for its stock, as a contribution to capital, and as paid-in surplus. If the $1,000,000 limitation is exceeded, the rules of subparagraph (2) of this paragraph (b) apply. In making these determinations, (i) property is taken into account at its adjusted basis to the corporation (for determining gain) as of the date received by the corporation, and (ii) this aggregate amount is reduced by the amount of any liability to which the property was subject and by the amount of any liability assumed by the corporation at the time the property was received. Capital receipts are not reduced by distributions to shareholders, even though the distributions may be capital distributions.

(2) *Requirement of designation in event $1,000,000 limitation exceeded.* (i) If capital receipts exceed $1,000,000, the corporation shall designate as section 1244 stock certain shares of post-November 1978 common stock issued for money or other property in the transitional year. For purposes of this paragraph, the term "transitional year" means the first taxable year in which capital receipts exceed $1,000,000 and in which the corporation issues stock. This designation shall be made in accordance with the rules of subdivision (iii) of this paragraph (b)(2). The amount received for designated stock shall not exceed $1,000,000, less amounts received—

Reg. § 1.1244(c)-2(a)

Rules for Determining Capital Gains and Losses

See p. 20,601 for regulations not amended to reflect law changes

(A) In exchange for stock in years prior to the transitional year;

(B) As contributions to capital in years prior to the transitional year; and

(C) As paid-in surplus in years prior to the transitional year.

(ii) Post-November 1978 common stock issued for money or other property before the transitional year qualifies as section 1244 stock without affirmative designation by the corporation. Post-November 1978 common stock issued after the transitional year does not qualify as section 1244 stock.

(iii) The corporation shall make the designation required by subdivision (i) of this paragraph (b)(2) not later than the 15th day of the third month following the close of the transitional year. However, in the case of post-November 1978 common stock issued on or before June 2, 1981 the corporation shall make the required designation by August 3, 1981 or by the 15th day of the 3rd month following the close of the transitional year, whichever is later. The designation shall be made by entering the numbers of the qualifying share certificates on the corporation's records. If the shares do not bear serial numbers or other identifying numbers or letters, or are not represented by share certificates, the corporation shall make an alternative designation in writing at the time of issuance, or, in the case of post-November 1978 common stock issued on or before June 2, 1981 by August 3, 1981. This alternative designation may be made in any manner sufficient to identify the shares qualifying for section 1244 treatment. If the corporation fails to make a designation by share certificate number or an alternative written designation as described, the rules of subparagraph (3) of this paragraph (b) apply.

(3) *Allocation of section 1244 benefit in event corporation fails to designate qualifying shares.* If a corporation issues post-November 1978 stock in the transitional year and fails to designate certain shares of post-November 1978 common stock as section 1244 stock in accordance with the rules of subparagraph (2) of this paragraph (b), the following rules apply:

(i) Section 1244 treatment is extended to losses sustained on post-November 1978 common stock issued for money or other property in taxable years before the transitional year and is withheld from losses sustained on post-November 1978 stock issued in taxable years after the transitional year.

(ii) Post-1958 capital received before the transitional year is subtracted from $1,000,000.

(iii) Subject to the annual limitation described in § 1.1244(b)-1, an ordinary loss on post-November 1978 common stock issued for money or other property in the transitional year is allowed in an amount which bears the same ratio to the total loss sustained by the individual as—

(A) The amount described in § 1.1244(c)-2(b)(3)(ii) bears to

(B) The total amount of money and other property received by the corporation in exchange for stock, as a contribution to capital, and as paid-in surplus in the transitional year.

(4) *Examples.* The provisions of this paragraph (b) may be illustrated by the following examples:

Example (1). On December 1, 1978, Corporation W, a newly-formed corporation, issues 10,000 shares of common stock at $125 a share for an amount (determined under subparagraph (1) of this paragraph (b)) of money and other property totaling $1,250,000. The board of directors specifies that 8,000 shares are section 1244 stock and records the certificate numbers of the qualifying shares in its minutes. Because Corporation W issued post-November 1978 common stock in exchange for money and other property exceeding $1,000,000, but has designated shares of stock as section 1244 stock and the designated shares were issued in exchange for money and other property not exceeding $1,000,000 (8,000 shares × $125 price per share = $1,000,000), the 8,000 designated shares qualify as section 1244 stock.

Example (2). Corporation X comes into existence on June 1, 1979. On June 10, 1979, Corporation X issues 2,500 shares of common stock at $250 per share to shareholder A and 2,500 shares of common stock at $250 per share to shareholder B. By written agreement dated September 1, 1981, shareholder A and shareholder B determine that 1,500 of shareholder A's shares and all of shareholder B's shares will be treated as section 1244 stock. Although shareholder A's 1,500 shares and shareholder B's 2,500 shares were issued for money and other property not exceeding $1,000,000 (4,000 shares × $250 price per share = $1,000,000), these 4,000 shares do not qualify as section 1244 stock under the rules of subparagraph (2) of this paragraph (b) for three reasons: The agreement of September 1, 1979, (i) did not identify which 1,500 of shareholder A's 2,500 shares were intended to qualify for section 1244 treatment, (ii) was made by the shareholders and not by Corporation X, and (iii) was made later than the 15th day of the third month following the close of the transitional year. However, certain of the shares issued by Corporation X may qualify as section 1244 stock under the rules of

Reg. § 1.1244(c)-2(b)(4)

53,502 Rules for Determining Capital Gains and Losses

See p. 20,601 for regulations not amended to reflect law changes

subparagraph (3) of this paragraph (b). See example (4).

Example (3). On December 1, 1980, Corporation Y issues common stock to shareholder A in exchange for $500,000 in cash. On August 1, 1981, Corporation Y issues common stock to shareholder B in exchange for property having an adjusted basis to Corporation Y of $500,000. On December 1, 1981, B transfers a tract of land having a basis in B's hands of $250,000 to Corporation Y as a contribution to capital. Under section 362(a)(2) of the Code, Corporation Y takes a basis of $250,000 in the tract of land. Corporation Y is a calendar year corporation. On February 15, 1982, it designates all of shareholder B's stock as section 1244 stock by entering the numbers of the qualifying certificates on the corporation's records. The designation made by Corporation Y is effective because it identifies which shares of its stock qualify for section 1244 treatment, was made in writing before the 15th day of the 3rd month following the close of the transitional year (1981), and because of the amount received for designated stock does not exceed $1,000,000, less amounts received (i) in exchange for stock in years prior to the transitional year; (ii) as contributions to capital in years prior to the transitional year; and (iii) as paid-in surplus in years prior to the transitional year. Nevertheless, in the event of B's sale of his stock at a loss, the increase in basis attributable to his December, 1981, contribution to capital will be treated as allocable to stock that is not section 1244 stock under § 1.1244(d)-2.

Example (4). Corporation Z, a newly-formed corporation, issues 10,000 shares of common stock at $200 per share on July 1, 1979. In exchange for its stock Corporation Z receives property (other than stock or securities) having a basis to the corporation of $400,000, and $1,600,000 in cash, for a total of $2,000,000. Corporation Z fails to designate any of the issued shares as section 1244 stock. Shareholder C purchases 2,500 shares of the 10,000 shares of Corporation Z stock for $500,000 on July 1, 1979. Subsequently, shareholder C sells the 2,500 shares for $400,000. Shareholder C may treat $50,000 of the $100,000 loss as an ordinary loss under section 1244. The amount of that loss is computed under the rule of subparagraph (3) of this paragraph (b) as follows:

$$\frac{X \text{ (C's section 1244 loss)}}{\$100,000 \text{ (C's total loss)}} = \frac{\$1,000,000 \ (\$1,000,000 - 0 = \$1,000,000)}{\$2,000,000 \text{ (total amount received by Corporation Z)}}$$

$$X = \$50,000$$

The remaining $50,000 is not treated as an ordinary loss under section 1244.

Example (5). (i) Corporation V, a newly-formed corporation, issues common stock to shareholder A and shareholder B on June 15, 1980, in exchange for $800,000 in cash ($400,000 from A and $400,000 from B). On September 15, 1981, the corporation issues common stock to shareholder C in exchange for $600,000 in cash. On January 1, 1982, common stock is issued to shareholder D in exchange for $100,000 in cash. Corporation V fails to designate any of the issued share as section 1244 stock. A, B, C, and D subsequently sell their Corporation Y stock at a loss.

(ii) Subject to the annual limitation discussed in § 1.1244(b)-1, A and B may treat their entire loss as an ordinary loss under section 1244. D may not treat any part of his loss as an ordinary loss under section 1244. Subject to the annual limitation, one-third of the loss sustained by shareholder C is treated as an ordinary loss under section 1244. These results are calculated under the rules of subparagraph (3) of this paragraph (b) as follows: First, section 1244 treatment is extended to post-November 1978 stock issued to A and B in 1980, a taxable year before the transitional year (1981); section 1244 treatment is withheld from the stock issued to D in 1982, a taxable year after the transitional year. Second, $800,000 the amount of post-1958 capital received in taxable years before the transitional year, is subtracted from $1,000,000 to leave $200,000. Third, subject to the annual limitation, an ordinary loss is allowed to C in an amount which bears the same ratio to his total loss as the amount calculated in the preceding sentence ($200,000) bears to the total amount received by the corporation in the transitional year in exchange for stock, as a contribution to capital, or as paid-in surplus ($600,000).

Example (6). Corporation V comes into existence on July 1, 1982. On that date it issues 10 shares of voting common stock to shareholder A in exchange for $500,000 and 5 shares of voting common stock to shareholder B in exchange for $250,000, designating the shares issued to both A and B as section 1244 stock. On September 15, 1982, Corporation V receives a contribution to capital from shareholders A and B having a basis in their hands of $225,000. On February 1, 1983, Corporation V issues one share of stock to shareholder C in exchange for $50,000. Corporation V may designate one-half of the share issued to shareholder C as section 1244 stock under

Reg. § 1.1244(c)-2(b)(4)

Rules for Determining Capital Gains and Losses

See p. 20,601 for regulations not amended to reflect law changes

§ 1.1244(c)-2(b)(2). In 1982 the corporation received $750,000 for stock ($500,000 from A and $250,000 from B) and $225,000 as a capital contribution, totaling $975,000 in capital receipts. The receipt of $50,000 from shareholder C in exchange for stock in 1983 causes capital receipts to exceed $1,000,000 and 1983 thus becomes Corporation V's transitional year. Corporation V may receive only $25,000 for designated stock in 1983 under the rule set forth in § 1.1244(c)-2(b)(2)(i), which states that the amount received for designated stock shall not exceed $1,000,000, less amounts received (i) in exchange for stock in years prior to the transitional year ($750,000 from A and B), (ii) as contributions to capital in years prior to the transitional year ($225,000), and (iii) as paid-in surplus in years prior to the transitional year ($0). Thus, one-half of C's share (representing the receipt of $25,000) may be designated as section 1244 stock by Corporation V. In the event of the sale of A's stock or B's stock at a loss, the increase in basis attributable to their contribution to capital will be treated as allocable to stock that is not section 1244 stock under § 1.1244(d)-2.

(c) *Pre-November 1978 stock* —(1) *Amount received by corporation for stock.* At the time of the adoption of the plan, the sum of the aggregate dollar amount to be paid for pre-November 1978 stock that may be offered under the plan plus the aggregate amount of money and other property that has been received by the corporation after June 30, 1958, and on or before November 6, 1978, for its stock, as a contribution to capital by its shareholders, and as paid-in surplus must not exceed $500,000. In making these determinations (i) property is taken into account at its adjusted basis to the corporation (for determining gain) as of the date received by the corporation, and (ii) this aggregate amount is reduced by the amount of any liability to which the property was subject and by the amount of any liability assumed by the corporation at the time the property was received. For purposes of the $500,000 test, the total amount of money and other property received for stock, as a contribution to capital, and as paid-in surplus is not reduced by distributions to shareholders, even though the distributions may be capital distributions. Thus, once the total amount of money and other property received after June 30, 1958, reaches $500,000, the corporation is precluded from subsequently issuing pre-November 1978 stock. For a different rule that applies to post-November 1978 stock, see § 1.1244(c)-2(b).

(2) *Equity capital.* The sum of the aggregate dollar amount to be paid for pre-November 1978 stock that may be offered under the plan plus the equity capital of the corporation (determined on the date of the adoption of the plan may not exceed $1,000,000. For this purpose, equity capital is the sum of the corporation's money and other property (in an amount equal to its adjusted basis for determining gain) less the amount of the corporation's indebtedness to persons other than its shareholders.

(3) *Examples.* The provisions of this paragraph (c) may be illustrated by the following examples:

Example (1). Corporation W comes into existence on December 1, 1958. On that date the corporation may adopt a plan to issue common stock for an amount (determined under subparagraph (1) of this paragraph (c)) not in excess of $500,000 during a period ending not later than November 30, 1960. Such corporation will qualify as a small business corporation as of the date that the plan is adopted. However, if the corporation adopts a plan to issue stock for an amount in excess of $500,000 it is not a small business corporation at the time the plan is adopted and no stock issued under the plan may qualify as section 1244 stock. If the cost of organizing Corporation W amounted to $1,000 and constituted paid-in surplus or a contribution to capital, such amount must be taken into account in determining the amount that may be received under the plan, with the result that only $499,000 may be so received.

Example (2). On December 1, 1958, Corporation X, a newly formed corporation, adopts a plan to issue common stock for an amount (determined under subparagraph (1) of this paragraph (c)) not in excess of $500,000 during a period ending not later than November 30, 1960. By January 1, 1960, the corporation has, pursuant to the plan, issued at par, stock having an aggregate par value of $400,000, $200,000 of which was issued for $200,000 cash, and $200,000 of which was issued for property (other than stock or securities) having a basis to the corporation of $100,000 and a fair market value of $200,000. The corporation may, prior to November 30, 1960, issue stock for an amount not in excess of $200,000 cash or property having a basis to it not in excess of $200,000. Stock issued for any payment which, alone or together with any payments received after January 1, 1960, exceeds such $200,000 amount would not qualify as section 1244 stock because it would not be issued pursuant to the plan.

Example (3). Assume that on December 1, 1958, Corporation Y, a newly formed corporation, adopts a plan to issue common stock for an amount (determined under subparagraph (1) of

Reg. § 1.1244(c)-2(c)(3)

53,504   Rules for Determining Capital Gains and Losses

See p. 20,601 for regulations not amended to reflect law changes

this paragraph (c)) not in excess of $500,000 during a period ending not later than November 30, 1960. By January 1960 the corporation has received $400,000 cash for stock issued pursuant to the plan, but due to business successes the equity capital of the corporation exceeds $1,000,000. Since the equity capital test is made as of the date that the plan is adopted, the corporation may still, prior to November 30, 1960, issue section 1244 stock pursuant to the plan until the full amount specified in the plan has been received.

Example (4). Subsequent to June 30, 1958, Corporation Z receives a total of $600,000 cash on the issuance of its stock. In 1960 Corporation Z redeems shares of its stock for the total amount of $300,000 and the redemptions reduce Corporation Z's capital to substantially less than $500,000. Notwithstanding the redemptions, pre-November 1978 stock subsequently issued by Corporation Z will not qualify as section 1244 stock because the $500,000 limitation has been previously exceeded. [Reg. § 1.1244(c)-2.]

☐ [T.D. 6495, 10-7-60. Amended by T.D. 7779, 6-1-81 and T.D. 7837, 9-28-82.]

[Reg. § 1.1244(d)-1]

§ 1.1244(d)-1. Contributions of property having basis in excess of value.—(a) *In general.* (1) Section 1244(d)(1)(A) provides a special rule which limits the amount of loss on section 1244 stock that may be treated as an ordinary loss. This rule applies only when section 1244 stock is issued by a corporation in exchange for property that, immediately before the exchange, has an adjusted basis (for determining loss) in excess of its fair market value. If section 1244 stock is issued in exchange for such property and the basis of such stock in the hands of the taxpayer is determined by reference to the basis of such property, then for purposes of section 1244, the basis of such stock shall be reduced by an amount equal to the excess, at the time of the exchange, of the adjusted basis of the property over its fair market value.

(2) The provisions of section 1244(d)(1)(A) do not affect the basis of stock for purposes other than section 1244. Such provisions are to be used only in determining the portion of the total loss sustained that may be treated as an ordinary loss pursuant to section 1244.

(b) *Transfer of more than one item.* If a taxpayer exchanges several items of property for stock in a single transaction so that the basis of the property transferred is allocated evenly among the shares of stock received, the computation under this section should be made by reference to the aggregate fair market value and the aggregate basis of the property transferred.

(c) *Examples.* The provisions of this section may be illustrated by the following examples:

Example (1). B transfers property with an adjusted basis of $1,000 and a fair market value of $250 to a corporation for 10 shares of section 1244 stock in an exchange that qualifies under section 351. The basis of B's stock is $1,000 ($100 per share), but, solely for purposes of section 1244, the total basis of the stock must be reduced by $750, the excess of the adjusted basis of the property exchanged over its fair market value. Thus, the basis of such stock for purposes of section 1244 is $250 and the basis of each share for such purposes is $25. If B sells his 10 shares for $250, he will recognize a loss of $750, all of which must be treated as a capital loss. If he sells the 10 shares for $200, then $50 of his total loss of $800 will be treated as an ordinary loss under section 1244, assuming the various requirements of such section are satisfied, and the remaining $750 will be a capital loss.

Example (2). B owns property with a basis of $20,000. The fair market value of the property unencumbered is $15,000 but the property is subject to a $2,000 mortgage. B transfers the encumbered property to a corporation for 100 shares of section 1244 stock in an exchange that qualifies under section 351. The basis of the shares, determined in accordance with section 358, is $18,000 or $180 per share, but solely for purposes of section 1244 the basis is $13,000 ($130 per share), which is its basis for purposes other than section 1244, reduced by $5,000, the excess of the adjusted basis, immediately before the exchange, of the property transferred over its fair market value.

Example (3). C transfers business assets to a corporation for 100 shares of section 1244 stock in an exchange that qualifies under section 351. The assets transferred are as follows:

	Basis	Fair Market Value
Cash	$ 10,000	$10,000
Inventory	15,000	30,000
Depreciable property	50,000	20,000
Land	25,000	10,000
	$100,000	$70,000

The basis for the shares received by C is $100,000, which is applied $1,000 to each share. However, the basis of the shares for purposes of section 1244 is $70,000 ($700 per share), the basis for general purposes reduced by $30,000, the excess of the aggregate adjusted basis of the property transferred over the aggregate fair market value of such property. [Reg. § 1.1244(d)-1.]

☐ [T.D. 6495, 10-7-60.]

Reg. § 1.1244(d)-1(a)(2)

Rules for Determining Capital Gains and Losses

See p. 20,601 for regulations not amended to reflect law changes

[Reg. § 1.1244(d)-2]

§ 1.1244(d)-2. Increases in basis of section 1244 stock.—(a) *In general.* If subsequent to the time of its issuance there is for any reason, including the operation of section 1376(a), an increase in the basis of section 1244 stock, such increase shall be treated as allocable to stock which is not section 1244 stock. Therefore, a loss on stock, the basis of which has been increased subsequent to its issuance, must be apportioned between the part that qualifies as section 1244 stock and the part that does not so qualify. Only the loss apportioned to the part that so qualifies may be treated as an ordinary loss pursuant to section 1244. The amount of loss apportioned to the part that qualifies is the amount which bears the same ratio to the total loss as the basis of the stock which is treated as allocated to section 1244 stock bears to the total basis of the stock.

(b) *Example.* The provisions of paragraph (a) of this section may be illustrated by the following example:

Example. For $10,000 a corporation issues 100 shares of section 1244 stock to X. X later contributes $2,000 to the capital of the corporation and this increases the total basis of his 100 shares to $12,000. Subsequently, he sells the 100 shares for $9,000. Of the $3,000 loss, $2,500 is allocated to the portion of the stock that qualifies as section 1244 stock

$$\left(\frac{\$10,000}{\$12,000} \text{ of } \$3,000 \right)$$

and the remaining $500 is allocated to the portion of the stock that does not so qualify. Therefore, to the extent of $2,500, the loss may be treated as an ordinary loss assuming the various requirements of section 1244 stock are satisfied. However, the remaining $500 loss must be treated as a capital loss. [Reg. § 1.1244(d)-2.]

☐ [*T.D.* 6495, 10-7-60.]

[Reg. § 1.1244(d)-3]

§ 1.1244(d)-3. Stock dividend, recapitalization, changes in name, etc.—(a) *In general.* Section 1244(c)(1) provides that stock may not qualify for the benefits of section 1244 unless it is issued to the taxpayer for money or other property not including stock or securities. However, section 1244(d)(2) authorizes exceptions to this rule. The exceptions may apply in three situations: (1) The receipt of a stock dividend; (2) the exchange of stock for stock pursuant to a reorganization described in section 368(a)(1)(E); and (3) the exchange of stock for stock pursuant to a reorganization described in section 368(a)(1)(F).

(b) *Stock dividends.* (1) If common stock is received by an individual or partnership in a nontaxable distribution under section 305(a) made solely with respect to stock owned by such individual or partnership which meets the requirements of section 1244 stock determinable at the time of the distribution, then the common stock so received will also be treated as meeting such requirements. For purposes of this paragraph and paragraphs (c) and (d) of this section, the requirements of section 1244 stock determinable at the time of the distribution or exchange are all of the requirements of section 1244(c)(1) other than the one described in subparagraph (C) thereof, relating to the gross receipts test.

(2) If, however, such stock dividend is received by such individual or partnership partly with respect to stock meeting the requirements of section 1244 stock determinable at the time of the distribution, and partly with respect to stock not meeting such requirements, then only part of the stock received as a stock dividend will be treated as meeting such requirements. Assuming all the shares with respect to which the dividend is received have equal rights to dividends, such part is the number of shares which bears the same ratio to the total number of shares received as the number of shares owned immediately before the stock dividend which meets such qualifications bears to the total number of shares with respect to which the stock dividend is received. In determining the basis of shares received in the stock dividend and of the shares held before the stock dividend, section 307 shall apply as if two separate nontaxable stock dividends were made, one with respect to the shares that meet the requirements and the other with respect to shares that do not meet the requirements.

(3) The provisions of subparagraphs (1) and (2) of this paragraph may be illustrated by the following examples:

Example (1). Corporation X issues 100 shares of its common stock to B for $1,000. Subsequently, in a nontaxable stock dividend B receives 5 more shares of common stock of Corporation X. If the 100 shares meet all the requirements of section 1244 stock determinable at the time of the distribution of the stock dividend, the 5 additional shares shall also be treated as meeting such requirements.

Example (2). In 1959, Corporation Y issues 100 shares of its common stock to C for $1,000 and these shares meet the requirements of section 1244 stock determinable at the time of the issuance. In 1960, C purchases an additional 200 shares of such stock from another shareholder for $3,000; however, these shares do not meet the requirements of section 1244 stock because they were not originally issued to C by the corporation. In 1961, C receives 15 shares of Corporation Y common stock as a stock dividend. Of the shares received, 5 shares, the number received with respect to the 100 shares of stock which met the requirements of section 1244 at the time of the distribution, i.e.,

$$\frac{100}{300} \times 15,$$

shall also be treated as meeting such requirements. The remaining 10 shares do not meet such requirements as they are not received with respect to section 1244 stock. The basis of such 5 shares is determined by applying section 307 as if the 5 shares were received as a separate stock dividend made solely with respect to shares that meet the requirements of section 1244 stock at the time of the distribution. Thus, the basis of the 5 shares is $47.61

$$\left(\frac{5}{105} \text{ of } \$1,000\right).$$

(c) *Recapitalizations.* (1) If, pursuant to a recapitalization described in section 368(a)(1)(E), common stock of a corporation is received by an individual or partnership in exchange for stock of such corporation meeting the requirements of section 1244 stock determinable at the time of the exchange, such common stock shall be treated as meeting such requirements.

(2) If common stock is received pursuant to such a recapitalization partly in exchange for stock meeting the requirements of section 1244 stock determinable at the time of the exchange and partly in exchange for stock not meeting such requirements, then only part of such common stock will be treated as meeting such requirements. Such part is the number of shares which bears the same ratio to the total number of shares of common stock so received as the basis of the shares transferred which meet such requirements bears to the basis of all the shares transferred for such common stock. The basis allocable, pursuant to section 358, to the common stock which is treated as meeting such requirements is limited to the basis of stock that meets such requirements transferred in the exchange.

(3) The provisions of subparagraphs (1) and (2) of this paragraph may be illustrated by the following examples:

Example (1). A owns 500 shares of voting common stock of Corporation X. Corporation X revises its capital structure to provide for two classes of common stock: Class A voting and Class B nonvoting. In a recapitalization described in subparagraph (E) of section 368(a)(1), A exchanges his 500 shares for 750 shares of Class B nonvoting stock. If the 500 shares meet all the requirements of section 1244 stock determinable at the time of the exchange, the 750 shares received in the exchange are treated as meeting such requirements.

Example (2). B owns 500 shares of common stock of Corporation X with a basis of $5,000, and 100 shares of preferred stock of that corporation with a basis of $2,500. Pursuant to a recapitalization described in section 368(a)(1)(E), B exchanges all of his shares for 900 shares of common stock of Corporation X. The 500 common shares meet the requirements of section 1244 stock determinable at the time of the exchange, but the 100 preferred shares do not meet such requirements since only common stock may qualify. Of the 900 common shares received, 600 shares

$$\left(\frac{\$5,000}{\$7,500} \times 900 \text{ shares}\right)$$

are treated as meeting the requirements of section 1244 at the time of the exchange, because they are deemed to be received in exchange for the 500 common shares which met such requirements. The remaining 300 shares do not meet such requirements as they are not deemed to be received in exchange for section 1244 stock. The basis of the 600 shares is $5,000, the basis of the relinquished shares meeting the requirements of section 1244.

(d) *Change of name, etc.* (1) If, pursuant to a reorganization described in section 368(a)(1)(F), common stock of a successor corporation is received by an individual or partnership in exchange for stock of the predecessor corporation meeting the requirements of section 1244 stock determinable at the time of the exchange, such common stock shall be treated as meeting such requirements. If common stock is received pursuant to such a reorganization partly in exchange for stock meeting the requirements of section 1244 stock determinable at the time of the exchange and partly in exchange for stock not meeting such requirements, the principles of paragraph (c)(2) of this section apply in determining the number of shares received which are treated as meeting the requirements of section 1244 stock and the basis of those shares.

(2) For purposes of paragraphs (1)(C) and (3)(A) of section 1244(c), a successor corporation in a reorganization described in section 368(a)(1)(F) shall be treated as the same corporation as its predecessor. [Reg. § 1.1244(d)-3.]

☐ [T.D. 6495, 10-7-60. Amended by T.D. 7779, 6-1-81.]

[Reg. § 1.1244(d)-4]

§ 1.1244(d)-4. **Net operating loss deduction.**—(a) *General rule.* For purposes of section 172, relating to the net operating loss deduction, any amount of loss that is treated as an ordinary loss under section 1244 (taking into account the annual dollar limitation of that section) shall be treated as attributable to the trade or business of the taxpayer. Therefore, this loss is allowable in determining the taxpayer's net operating loss for a taxable year and is not subject to the application of section 172(d)(4), relating to nonbusiness deductions. A taxpayer may deduct the maximum of ordinary loss permitted under section 1244(b) even though all or a portion of the taxpayer's net operating loss carryback or carryover for the taxable year was, when incurred, a loss on section 1244 stock.

(b) *Example.* The provisions of this section may be illustrated by the following example:

Example. A, a single individual, computes a net operating loss of $15,000 for 1980 in accordance with the rules of § 1.172-3, relating to net operating loss in case of a taxpayer other than a corporation. Included within A's computation of this net operating loss is a deduction arising under section 1244 for a loss on a small business stock. A had no taxable income in 1977, 1978, or 1979. Assume that A can carry over the entire $15,000 loss under the rules of section 172. In 1981 A has gross income of $75,000 and again sustains a loss on section 1244 stock. The amount of A's 1981 loss on section 1244 stock is $50,000. A may deduct the full $50,000 as an ordinary loss under section 1244 and the full $15,000 as a net operating loss carryover in 1981. [Reg. § 1.1244(d)-4.]

☐ [T.D. 6495, 10-7-60. Amended by T.D. 7779, 6-1-81.]

[Reg. § 1.1244(e)-1]

§ 1.1244(e)-1. Records to be kept.—(a) *By the corporation*—(1) *Mandatory records.* A plan to issue pre-November 1978 stock must appear upon the records of the corporation. Any designation of post-November 1978 stock under § 1.1244(c)-2(b)(2) also must appear upon the records of the corporation.

(2) *Discretionary records.* In order to substantiate an ordinary loss deduction claimed by its shareholders, the corporation should maintain records showing the following:

(i) The persons to whom stock was issued, the date of issuance to these persons, and a description of the amount and type of consideration received from each;

(ii) If the consideration received is property, the basis in the hands of the shareholder and the fair market value of the property when received by the corporation;

(iii) The amount of money and the basis in the hands of the corporation of other property received for its stock, as a contribution to capital, and as paid-in surplus;

(iv) Financial statements of the corporation, such as its income tax returns, that identify the source of the gross receipt of the corporation for the period consisting of the five most recent taxable years of the corporation, or, if the corporation has not been in existence for 5 taxable years, for the period of the corporation's existence;

(v) Information relating to any tax-free stock dividend made with respect to section 1244 stock and any reorganization in which stock is transferred by the corporation in exchange for section 1244 stock; and

(vi) With respect to pre-November 1978 stock:

(A) Which certificates represent stock issued under the plan;

(B) The amount of money and the basis in the hands of the corporation of other property received after June 30, 1958, and before the adoption of the plan, for its stock, as a contribution to capital, and as paid-in surplus; and

(C) The equity capital of the corporation on the date of adoption of the plan.

(b) *By the taxpayer.* A person who claims an ordinary loss with respect to stock under section 1244 must have records sufficient to establish that the taxpayer is entitled to the loss and satisfies the requirements of section 1244. See also section 6001, requiring records to be maintained. [Reg. § 1.1244(e)-1.]

☐ [T.D. 6495, 10-7-60. Amended by T.D. 7779, 6-1-81 and T.D. 8594, 4-27-95.]

[Reg. § 1.1245-1]

§ 1.1245-1. General rule for treatment of gain from dispositions of certain depreciable property.—(a) *General.*—(1) In general, section 1245(a)(1) provides that, upon a disposition of an item of section 1245 property, the amount by which the lower of (i) the "recomputed basis" of the property, or (ii) the amount realized on a sale, exchange, or involuntary conversion (or the fair market value of the property on any other disposition), exceeds the adjusted basis of the property shall be treated as gain from the sale or exchange of property which is neither a capital asset nor property described in section 1231 (that is, shall be recognized as ordinary income). The amount of such gain shall be determined separately for each item of section 1245 property. In general, the term "recomputed basis" means the adjusted basis of property plus all adjustments reflected in such adjusted basis on account of depreciation allowed or allowable for all periods after December 31, 1961. See section 1245(a)(2) and § 1.1245-2. Generally, the ordinary income treatment applies even though in the absence of section 1245 no gain would be recognized under the Code. For example, if a corporation distributes section 1245 property as a dividend, gain may be recognized as ordinary income to the corporation even though, in the absence of section 1245, section 311(a) would preclude any recognition of gain to the corporation. For the definition of "section 1245 property," see section 1245(a)(3) and § 1.1245-3. For exceptions and limitations to the application of section 1245(a)(1), see section 1245(b) and § 1.1245-4.

(2) Section 1245(a)(1) applies to dispositions of section 1245 property in taxable years beginning after December 31, 1962, except that—

(i) In respect of section 1245 property which is an elevator or escalator, section 1245(a)(1) applies to dispositions after December 31, 1963, and

(ii) In respect of section 1245 property which is livestock (described in subparagraph (4) of § 1.1245-3(a)), section 1245(a)(1) applies to dispositions made in taxable years beginning after December 31, 1969, and

(iii) [reserved].

(3) For purposes of this section and §§ 1.1245-2 through 1.1245-6, the term "disposition" includes a sale in a sale-and-leaseback transaction and a transfer upon the foreclosure of a security interest, but such term does not include a mere transfer of title to a creditor upon creation of a security interest or to a debtor upon termination of a security interest. Thus, for example, a disposition occurs upon a sale of property pursuant to a conditional sales contract even though the seller retains legal title to the property for purposes of security but a disposition does not occur when the seller ulitmately gives up his security interest following payment by the purchaser.

(4) For purposes of applying section 1245, the facts and circumstances of each disposition shall be considered in determining what is the appropriate item of section 1245 property. A taxpayer may treat any number of units of section 1245 property in any particular depreciation account (as defined in § 1.167(a)-7) as one time of section 1245 property as long as it is reasonably clear, from the best estimates obtainable on the basis of all the facts and circumstances, that the amount of gain to which section 1245(a)(1) applies is not less than the total of the gain under section 1245(a)(1) which would be computed separately for each unit. Thus, for example, if 50 units of section 1245 property X, 25 units of section 1245 property Y, and other property are accounted for in one depreciation account, and if each such unit is sold at a gain in one transaction in which the total gain realized on the sale exceeds the sum of the adjustments reflected in the adjusted basis (as defined in paragraph (a)(2) of § 1.1245-2) of each such unit on account of depreciation allowed or allowable for periods after December 31, 1961, all 75 units may be treated as one item of section 1245 property. If, however, 5 such units of section 1245 property Y were sold at a loss, then only 70 of such units (50 of X plus the 20 of Y sold at a gain) may be treated as one item of section 1245 property.

(5) In case of a sale, exchange, or involuntary conversion of section 1245 and nonsection 1245 property in one transaction, the total amount realized upon the disposition shall be allocated between the section 1245 property and the nonsection 1245 property in proportion to their respective fair market values. In general, if a buyer and seller have adverse interests as to the allocation of the amount realized between the section 1245 property and the nonsection 1245 property, any arm's length agreement between the buyer and the seller will establish the allocation. In the absence of such an agreement, the allocation shall be made by taking into account the appropriate facts and circumstances. Some of the facts and circumstances which shall be taken into account to the extent appropriate include, but are not limited to, a comparison between the section 1245 property and all the property disposed of in such transaction of (i) the original cost and reproduction cost of construction, erection, or production, (ii) the remaining economic useful life, (iii) state of obsolescence, and (iv) anticipated expenditures to maintain, renovate, or to modernize.

(b) *Sale, exchange, or involuntary conversion.*— (1) In the case of a sale, exchange, or involuntary conversion of section 1245 property, the gain to which section 1245(a)(1) applies is the amount by which (i) the lower of the amount realized upon the disposition of the property or the recomputed basis of the property, exceeds (ii) the adjusted basis of the property.

(2) The provisions of this paragraph may be illustrated by the following examples:

Example (1). On January 1, 1964, Brown purchases section 1245 property for use in his

Reg. § 1.1245-1(a)(2)

manufacturing business. The property has a basis for depreciation of $3,300. After taking depreciation deductions of $1,300 (the amount allowable), Brown realizes after selling expenses the amount of $2,900 upon sale of the property on January 1, 1969. Brown's gain is $900 ($2,900 amount realized minus $2,000 adjusted basis). Since the amount realized upon disposition of the property ($2,900) is lower than its recomputed basis ($3,300, i.e., $2,000 adjusted basis plus $1,300 in depreciation deductions), the entire gain is treated as ordinary income under section 1245(a)(1) and not as gain from the sale or exchange of property described in section 1231.

Example (2). Assume the same facts as in example (1) except that Brown exchanges the section 1245 property for land which has a fair market value of $3,700, thereby realizing a gain of $1,700 ($3,700 amount realized minus $2,000 adjusted basis). Since the recomputed basis of the property ($3,300) is lower than the amount realized upon its disposition ($3,700), the excess of recomputed basis over adjusted basis, or $1,300, is treated as ordinary income under section 1245(a)(1). The remaining $400 of the gain may be treated as gain from the sale or exchange of property described in section 1231.

(c) *Other dispositions.* (1) In the case of a disposition of section 1245 property other than by way of a sale, exchange, or involuntary conversion, the gain to which section 1245(a)(1) applies is the amount by which (i) the lower of the fair market value of the property on the date of disposition or the recomputed basis of the property, exceeds (ii) the adjusted basis of the property. If property is transferred by a corporation to a shareholder for an amount less than its fair market value in a sale or exchange, for purposes of applying section 1245 such transfer shall be treated as a disposition other than by way of a sale, exchange, or involuntary conversion.

(2) The provisions of this paragraph may be illustrated by the following examples:

Example (1). X Corporation distributes section 1245 property to its shareholders as a dividend. The property has an adjusted basis of $2,000 to the corporation, a recomputed basis of $3,300, and a fair market value of $3,100. Since the fair market value of the property ($3,100) is lower than its recomputed basis ($3,300), the excess of fair market value over adjusted basis, or $1,100, is treated under section 1245(a)(1) as ordinary income to the corporation even though, in the absence of section 1245, section 311(a) would preclude recognition of gain to the corporation.

Example (2). Assume the same facts as in example (1) except that X Corporation distributes the section 1245 property to its shareholders in complete liquidation of the corporation. Assume further that section 1245(b)(3) does not apply and that the fair market value of the property is $3,800 at the time of the distribution. Since the recomputed basis of the property ($3,300) is lower than its fair market value ($3,800), the excess of recomputed basis over adjusted basis, or $1,300, is treated under section 1245(a)(1) as ordinary income to the corporation even though, in the absence of section 1245, section 336 would preclude recognition of gain to the corporation.

(d) *Losses.* Section 1245(a)(1) does not apply to losses. Thus, section 1245(a)(1) does not apply if a loss is realized upon a sale, exchange, or involuntary conversion of property, all of which is considered section 1245 property, nor does the section apply to a disposition of such property other than by way of sale, exchange, or involuntary conversion if at the time of the disposition the fair market value of such property is not greater than its adjusted basis.

(e) *Treatment of partnership and partners.*— (1) The manner of determining the amount of gain recognized under section 1245(a)(1) to a partnership may be illustrated by the following example:

Example. A partnership sells for $63 section 1245 property which has an adjusted basis to the partnership of $30 and a recomputed basis to the partnership of $60. The partnership recognizes under section 1245(a)(1) gain of $30, i.e., the lower of the amount realized ($63) or recomputed basis ($60), minus adjusted basis ($30). This result would not be changed if one or more partners had, in respect of the property, a special basis adjustment described in section 743(b) or had taken depreciation deductions in respect of such special basis adjustment.

(2)(i) Unless paragraph (e)(3) of this section applies, a partner's distributive share of gain recognized under section 1245(a)(1) by the partnership is equal to the lesser of the partner's share of total gain from the disposition of the property (gain limitation) or the partner's share of depreciation or amortization with respect to the property (as determined under paragraph (e)(2)(ii) of this section). Any gain recognized under section 1245(a)(1) by the partnership that is not allocated under the first sentence of this paragraph (e)(2)(i) (excess depreciation recapture) is allocated among the partners whose shares of total gain from the disposition of the property exceed their shares of depreciation or amortization with respect to the property. Excess depreciation recapture is allocated among those partners in proportion to their relative shares of the total gain

Reg. § 1.1245-1(e)(2)

(including gain recognized under section 1245(a)(1)) from the disposition of the property that is allocated to the partners who are not subject to the gain limitation. See *Example 2* of paragraph (e)(2)(iii) of this section.

(ii)(A) Subject to the adjustments described in paragraphs (e)(2)(ii)(B) and (e)(2)(ii)(C) of this section, a partner's share of depreciation or amortization with respect to property equals the total amount of allowed or allowable depreciation or amortization previously allocated to that partner with respect to the property.

(B) If a partner transfers a partnership interest, a share of depreciation or amortization must be allocated to the transferee partner as it would have been allocated to the transferor partner. If the partner transfers a portion of the partnership interest, a share of depreciation or amortization proportionate to the interest transferred must be allocated to the transferee partner.

(C)(*1*) A partner's share of depreciation or amortization with respect to property contributed by the partner includes the amount of depreciation or amortization allowed or allowable to the partner for the period before the property is contributed.

(*2*) A partner's share of depreciation or amortization with respect to property contributed by a partner is adjusted to account for any curative allocations. (See § 1.704-3(c) for a description of the traditional method with curative allocations.) The contributing partner's share of depreciation or amortization with respect to the contributed property is decreased (but not below zero) by the amount of any curative allocation of ordinary income to the contributing partner with respect to that property and by the amount of any curative allocation of deduction or loss (other than capital loss) to the noncontributing partners with respect to that property. A noncontributing partner's share of depreciation or amortization with respect to the contributed property is increased by the noncontributing partner's share of any curative allocation of ordinary income to the contributing partner with respect to that property and by the amount of any curative allocation of deduction or loss (other than capital loss) to the noncontributing partner with respect to that property. The partners' shares of depreciation or amortization with respect to property from which curative allocations of depreciation or amortization are taken is determined without regard to those curative allocations. See *Example 3*(iii) of paragraph (e)(2)(iii) of this section.

(*3*) A partner's share of depreciation or amortization with respect to property contributed by a partner is adjusted to account for any remedial allocations. (See § 1.704-3(d) for a description of the remedial allocation method.) The contributing partner's share of depreciation or amortization with respect to the contributed property is decreased (but not below zero) by the amount of any remedial allocation of income to the contributing partner with respect to that property. A noncontributing partner's share of depreciation or amortization with respect to the contributed property is increased by the amount of any remedial allocation of depreciation or amortization to the noncontributing partner with respect to that property. See *Example 3*(iv) of paragraph (e)(2)(iii) of this section.

(*4*) If, under paragraphs (e)(2)(ii)(C)(*2*) and (e)(2)(ii)(C)(*3*) of this section, the partners' shares of depreciation or amortization with respect to a contributed property exceed the adjustments reflected in the adjusted basis of the property under § 1.1245-2(a) at the partnership level, then the partnership's gain recognized under section 1245(a)(1) with respect to that property is allocated among the partners in proportion to their relative shares of depreciation or amortization (subject to any gain limitation that might apply).

(*5*) This paragraph (e)(2)(ii)(C) also applies in determining a partner's share of depreciation or amortization with respect to property for which differences between book value and adjusted tax basis are created when a partnership revalues partnership property pursuant to § 1.704-1(b)(2)(iv)(*f*).

(iii) *Examples.* The application of this paragraph (e)(2) may be illustrated by the following examples:

Example 1. Recapture allocations. (i) *Facts.* A and B each contribute $5,000 cash to form AB, a general partnership. The partnership agreement provides that depreciation deductions will be allocated 90 percent to A and 10 percent to B, and, on the sale of depreciable property, A will first be allocated gain to the extent necessary to equalize A's and B's capital accounts. Any remaining gain will be allocated 50 percent to A and 50 percent to B. In its first year of operations, AB purchases depreciable equipment for $5,000. AB depreciates the equipment over its 5-year recovery period and elects to use the straight-line method. In its first year of operations, AB's operating income equals its expenses (other than depreciation). (To simplify this example, AB's depreciation deductions are determined without regard to any first-year depreciation conventions.)

(ii) *Year 1.* In its first year of operations, AB has $1,000 of depreciation from the partner-

Rules for Determining Capital Gains and Losses 53,511
See p. 20,601 for regulations not amended to reflect law changes

ship equipment. In accordance with the partnership agreement, AB allocates 90 percent ($900) of the depreciation to A and 10 percent ($100) of the depreciation to B. At the end of the year, AB sells the equipment for $5,200, recognizing $1,200 of gain ($5,200 amount realized less $4,000 adjusted tax basis). In accordance with the partnership agreement, the first $800 of gain is allocated to A to equalize the partners' capital accounts, and the remaining $400 of gain is allocated $200 to A and $200 to B.

(iii) *Recapture allocations.* $1,000 of the gain from the sale of the equipment is treated as section 1245(a)(1) gain. Under paragraph (e)(2)(i) of this section, each partner's share of the section 1245(a)(1) gain is equal to the lesser of the partner's share of total gain recognized on the sale of the equipment or the partner's share of total depreciation with respect to the equipment. Thus, A's share of the section 1245(a)(1) gain is $900 (the lesser of A's share of the total gain ($1,000) and A's share of depreciation ($900)). B's share of the section 1245(a)(1) gain is $100 (the lesser of B's share of the total gain ($200) and B's share of depreciation ($100)). Accordingly, $900 of the $1,000 of total gain allocated to A is treated as ordinary income and $100 of the $200 of total gain allocated to B is treated as ordinary income.

Example 2. Recapture allocation subject to gain limitation. (i) *Facts.* A, B, and C form general partnership ABC. The partnership agreement provides that depreciation deductions will be allocated equally among the partners, but that gain from the sale of depreciable property will be allocated 75 percent to A and 25 percent to B. ABC purchases depreciable personal property for $300 and subsequently allocates $100 of depreciation deductions each to A, B, and C, reducing the adjusted tax basis of the property to $0. ABC then sells the property for $440. ABC allocates $330 of the gain to A (75 percent of $440) and allocates $110 of the gain to B (25 percent of $440). No gain is allocated to C.

(ii) *Application of gain limitation.* Each partner's share of depreciation with respect to the property is $100. C's share of the total gain from the disposition of the property, however, is $0. As a result, under the gain limitation provision in paragraph (e)(2)(i) of this section, C's share of section 1245(a)(1) gain is limited to $0.

(iii) *Excess depreciation recapture.* Under paragraph (e)(2)(i) of this section, the $100 of section 1245(a)(1) gain that cannot be allocated to C under the gain limitation provision (excess depreciation recapture) is allocated to A and B (the partners not subject to the gain limitation at the time of the allocation) in proportion to their relative shares of total gain from the disposition of the property. A's relative share of the total gain allocated to A and B is 75 percent ($330 of $440 total gain). B's relative share of the total gain allocated to A and B is 25 percent ($110 of $440 total gain). However, under the gain limitation provision of paragraph (e)(2)(i) of this section, B cannot be allocated 25 percent of the excess depreciation recapture ($25) because that would result in a total allocation of $125 of depreciation recapture to B (a $100 allocation equal to B's share of depreciation plus a $25 allocation of excess depreciation recapture), which is in excess of B's share of the total gain from the disposition of the property ($110). Therefore, only $10 of excess depreciation recapture is allocated to B and the remaining $90 of excess depreciation recapture is allocated to A. A is not subject to the gain limitation because A's share of the total gain ($330) still exceeds A's share of section 1245(a)(1) gain ($190). Accordingly, all $110 of the total gain allocated to B is treated as ordinary income ($100 share of depreciation allocated to B plus $10 of excess depreciation recapture) and $190 of the total gain allocated to A is treated as ordinary income ($100 share of depreciation allocated to A plus $90 of excess depreciation recapture).

Example 3. Determination of partners' shares of depreciation with respect to contributed property. (i) *Facts.* C and D form partnership CD as equal partners. C contributes depreciable personal property C1 with an adjusted tax basis of $800 and a fair market value of $2,800. Prior to the contribution, C claimed $200 of depreciation from C1. At the time of the contribution, C1 is depreciable under the straight-line method and has four years remaining on its 5-year recovery period. D contributes $2,800 cash, which CD uses to purchase depreciable personal property D1, which is depreciable over seven years under the straight-line method. (To simplify the example, all depreciation is determined without regard to any first-year depreciation conventions.)

(ii) *Traditional method.* C1 generates $700 of book depreciation (1/4 of $2,800 book value) and $200 of tax depreciation (1/4 of $800 adjusted tax basis) each year. C and D will each be allocated $350 of book depreciation from C1 in year 1. Under the traditional method of making section 704(c) allocations, D will be allocated the entire $200 of tax depreciation from C1 in year 1. D1 generates $400 of book and tax depreciation each year (1/7 of $2,800 book value and adjusted tax basis). C and D will each be allocated $200 of book and tax depreciation from D1 in year 1. As a result, after the first year of partnership operations, C's share of depreciation with respect to C1 is $200 (the depreciation taken by C prior to

Reg. § 1.1245-1(e)(2)

contribution) and D's share of depreciation with respect to C1 is $200 (the amount of tax depreciation allocated to D). C and D each have a $200 share of depreciation with respect to D1. At the end of four years, C's share of depreciation with respect to C1 will be $200 (the depreciation taken by C prior to contribution) and D's share of depreciation with respect to C1 will be $800 (four years of $200 depreciation per year). At the end of four years, C and D will each have an $800 share of depreciation with respect to D1 (four years of $200 depreciation per year).

(iii) *Effect of curative allocations.* (A) *Year 1.* If the partnership elects to make curative allocations under § 1.704-3(c) using depreciation from D1, the results will be the same as under the traditional method, except that $150 of the $200 of tax depreciation from D1 that would be allocated to C under the traditional method will be allocated to D as additional depreciation with respect to C1. As a result, after the first year of partnership operations, C's share of depreciation with respect to C1 will be reduced to $50 (the total depreciation taken by C prior to contribution ($200) decreased by the amount of the curative allocation to D ($150)). D's share of depreciation with respect to C1 will be $350 (the depreciation allocated to D under the traditional method ($200) increased by the amount of the curative allocation to D ($150)). C and D will each have a $200 share of depreciation with respect to D1.

(B) *Year 4.* At the end of four years, C's share of depreciation with respect to C1 will be reduced to $0 (the total depreciation taken by C prior to contribution ($200) decreased, but not below zero, by the amount of the curative allocations to D ($600)), and D's share of depreciation with respect to C1 will be $1,400 (the total depreciation allocated to D under the traditional method ($800) increased by the amount of the curative allocations to D ($600)). However, CD's section 1245(a)(1) gain with respect to C1 will not be more than $1,000 (CD's tax depreciation ($800) plus C's tax depreciation prior to contribution ($200)). Under paragraph (e)(2)(ii)(C)(4) of this section, because the partners' shares of depreciation with respect to C1 exceed the adjustments reflected in the property's adjusted basis, CD's section 1245(a)(1) gain will be allocated in proportion to the partners' relative shares of depreciation with respect to C1. Because C's share of depreciation with respect to C1 is $0, and D's share of depreciation with respect to C1 is $1,400, all of CD's $1,000 of section 1245(a)(1) gain will be allocated to D. At the end of four years, C and D will each have an $800 share of depreciation with respect to D1 (four years of $200 depreciation per year).

(iv) *Effect of remedial allocations.* (A) *Year 1.* If the partnership elects to make remedial allocations under § 1.704-3(d), there will be $600 of book depreciation from C1 in year 1. (Under the remedial allocation method, the amount by which C1's book basis ($2,800) exceeds its tax basis ($800) is depreciated over a 5-year life, rather than a 4-year life.) C and D will each be allocated one-half ($300) of the total book depreciation. As under the traditional method, D will be allocated all $200 of tax depreciation from C1. Because the ceiling rule would cause a disparity of $100 between D's book and tax allocations of depreciation, D will also receive a $100 remedial allocation of depreciation with respect to C1, and C will receive a $100 remedial allocation of income with respect to C1. As a result, after the first year of partnership operations, D's share of depreciation with respect to C1 is $300 (the depreciation allocated to D under the traditional method ($200) increased by the amount of the remedial allocation ($100)). C's share of depreciation with respect to C1 is $100 (the total depreciation taken by C prior to contribution ($200) decreased by the amount of the remedial allocation of income ($100)). C and D will each have a $200 share of depreciation with respect to D1.

(B) *Year 5.* At the end of five years, C's share of depreciation with respect to C1 will be $0 (the total depreciation taken by C prior to contribution ($200) decreased, but not below zero, by the total amount of the remedial allocations of income to C ($600)). D's share of depreciation with respect to C1 will be $1,400 (the total depreciation allocated to D under the traditional method ($800) increased by the total amount of the remedial allocations of depreciation to D ($600)). However, CD's section 1245(a)(1) gain with respect to C1 will not be more than $1,000 (CD's tax depreciation ($800) plus C's tax depreciation prior to contribution ($200)). Under paragraph (e)(2)(ii)(C)(4) of this section, because the partners' shares of depreciation with respect to C1 exceed the adjustments reflected in the property's adjusted basis, CD's section 1245(a)(1) gain will be allocated in proportion to the partners' relative shares of depreciation with respect to C1. Because C's share of depreciation with respect to C1 is $0, and D's share of depreciation with respect to C1 is $1,400, all of CD's $1,000 of section 1245(a)(1) gain will be allocated to D. At the end of five years, C and D will each have a $1,000 share of depreciation with respect to D1 (five years of $200 depreciation per year).

Reg. § 1.1245-1(e)(2)

Rules for Determining Capital Gains and Losses

See p. 20,601 for regulations not amended to reflect law changes

(iv) *Effective date*. This paragraph (e)(2) is effective for properties acquired by a partnership on or after August 20, 1997. However, partnerships may rely on this paragraph (e)(2) for properties acquired before August 20, 1997, and disposed of on or after August 20, 1997.

(3)(i) If (*a*) a partner had a special basis adjustment under section 743(b) in respect of section 1245 property, or (*b*) on the date he acquired his partnership interest by way of a sale or exchange (or upon death of another partner) the partnership owned section 1245 property and an election under section 754 (relating to optional adjustment to basis of partnership property) was in effect with respect to the partnership, then the amount of gain recognized under section 1245(a)(1) by him upon a disposition by the partnership of such property shall be determined under this subparagraph.

(ii) There shall be allocated to such partner, in the same proportion as the partnership's total gain is allocated to him as his distributive share under section 704, a portion of (*a*) the common partnership adjusted basis for the property, and (*b*) the amount realized by the partnership upon the disposition, or, if nothing is realized, the fair market value of the property. There shall also be allocated to him, in the same proportion as the partnership's gain recognized under section 1245(a)(1) is allocated under subparagraph (2) of this paragraph as his distributive share of such gain, a portion of "the adjustments reflected in the adjusted basis" (as defined in paragraph (a)(2) of § 1.1245-2) of such property. If on the date he acquired his partnership interest by way of a sale or exchange the partnership owned such property and an election under section 754 was in effect, then for purposes of the preceding sentence the amount of the adjustments reflected in the adjusted basis of such property on such date shall be deemed to be zero. For special rules relating to the amount of adjustments reflected in the adjusted basis of property after partnership transactions, see paragraph (c)(6) of § 1.1245-2.

(iii) The partner's adjusted basis in respect of the property shall be deemed to be (*a*) the portion of the partnership's adjusted basis for the property allocated to the partner under subdivision (ii) of this subparagraph, (*b*) increased by the amount of any special basis adjustment described in section 743(b)(1) (or decreased by the amount of any special basis adjustment described in section 743(b)(2)) which the partner may have in respect of the property on the date the partnership disposed of the property.

(iv) The partner's recomputed basis in respect of the property shall be deemed to be (*a*) the sum of the partner's adjusted basis for the property, as determined in subdivision (iii) of this subparagraph, plus the amount of "the adjustments reflected in the adjusted basis" (as defined in paragraph (a)(2) of § 1.1245-2) for the property allocated to the partner under subdivision (ii) of this subparagraph, (*b*) increased by the amount by which any special basis adjustment described in section 743(b)(1) (or decreased by the amount by which any special basis adjustment described in section 743(b)(2)) in respect of the property was reduced, but only to the extent such amount was applied to adjust the amount of the deductions allowed or allowable to the partner for depreciation or amortization of section 1245 property attributable to periods referred to in paragraph (a)(2) of § 1.1245-2. The terms "allowed or allowable," "depreciation or amortization," and "attributable to periods" shall have the meanings assigned to those terms in paragraph (a) of § 1.1245-2.

(4) The application of subparagraph (3) of this paragraph may be illustrated by the following example:

Example. A, B, and C each hold a one-third interest in calendar year partnership ABC. On December 31, 1962, the firm holds section 1245 property which has an adjusted basis of $30,000 and a recomputed basis of $33,000. Depreciation deductions in respect of the property for 1962 were $3,000. On January 1, 1963, when D purchases C's partnership interest, the election under section 754 is in effect and a $5,000 special basis adjustment is made in respect of D to his one-third share of the common partnership adjusted basis for the property. For 1963 and 1964 the partnership deducts $6,000 as depreciation in respect of the property, thereby reducing its adjusted basis to $24,000, and D deducts $2,800, *i.e.*, his distributive share of partnership depreciation ($2,000) plus depreciation in respect of his special basis adjustment ($800). On March 15, 1965, the partnership sells the property for $48,000. Since the partnership's recomputed basis for the property ($33,000, i.e., $24,000 adjusted basis plus $9,000 in depreciation deductions) is lower than the amount realized upon the sale ($48,000), the excess of recomputed basis over adjusted basis, or $9,000, is treated as partnership gain under section 1245(a)(1). D's distributive share of such gain is $3,000 (⅓ of $9,000). However, the amount of gain recognized by D under section 1245(a)(1) is only $2,800, determined as follows:

Reg. § 1.1245-1(e)(4)

53,514 Rules for Determining Capital Gains and Losses

See p. 20,601 for regulations not amended to reflect law changes

(1) Adjusted basis:
D's portion of partnership adjusted basis (⅓ of $24,000)	$ 8,000	
D's special basis adjustment as of December 31, 1964 ($5,000 minus $800)	4,200	
D's adjusted basis		$12,200

(2) Recomputed basis:
D's adjusted basis	$12,200	
D's portion of partnership depreciation for 1963 and 1964, *i.e.*, for periods after he acquired his partnership interest (⅓ of $6,000)	2,000	
Depreciation for 1963 and 1964 in respect of D's special basis adjustment	800	
D's recomputed basis		$15,000

(3) D's portion of amount realized by partnership (⅓ of $48,000) $16,000
(4) Gain recognized to D under section 1245(a)(1), *i.e.*, the lower of (2) or (3), minus (1) .... $ 2,800

[Reg. § 1.1245-1.]

☐ [T.D. 6832, 7-6-65. Amended by T.D. 7084, 1-7-71; T.D. 7141, 9-21-71 and T.D. 8730, 8-19-97.]

[Reg. § 1.1245-2]

§ 1.1245-2. **Definition of recomputed basis.**—(a) *General rule*—(1) *Recomputed basis defined.* The term "recomputed basis" means, with respect to any property, an amount equal to the sum of—

(i) The adjusted basis of the property, as defined in section 1011, plus

(ii) The amount of the adjustments reflected in the adjusted basis.

(2) *Definition of adjustments reflected in adjusted basis.* The term "adjustments reflected in the adjusted basis" means—

(i) with respect to any property other than property described in subdivision (ii), (iii), or (iv) of this subparagraph, the amount of the adjustments attributable to periods after December 31, 1961,

(ii) with respect to an elevator or escalator, the amount of the adjustments attributable to periods after June 30, 1963,

(iii) with respect to livestock (described in subparagraph (4) of § 1.1245-3(a)), the amount of the adjustments attributable to periods after December 31, 1969, or

(iv) [reserved]

which are reflected in the adjusted basis of such property on account of deductions allowed or allowable for depreciation or amortization (within the meaning of subparagraph (3) of this paragraph). For cases where the taxpayer can establish that the amount allowed for any period was less than the amount allowable, see subparagraph (7) of this paragraph. For determination of adjusted basis of property in a multiple asset account, see paragraph (c)(3) of § 1.167(a)-8.

(3) *Meaning of "depreciation or amortization."* (i) For purposes of subparagraph (2) of this paragraph, the term "depreciation or amortization" includes allowances (and amounts treated as allowances) for depreciation (or amortization in lieu thereof), and deductions for amortization of emergency facilities under section 168. Thus, for example, such term includes a reasonable allowance for exhaustion, wear and tear (including a reasonable allowance for obsolescence) under section 167, an expense allowance (additional first-year depreciation allowance for property placed in service before January 1, 1981) under section 179, an expenditure treated as an amount allowed under section 167 by reason of the application of section 182(d)(2)(B) (relating to expenditures by farmers for clearing land), and a deduction for depreciation of improvements under section 611 (relating to depletion). For further examples, the term "depreciation or amortization" includes periodic deductions referred to in § 1.162-11 in respect of a specified sum paid for the acquisition of a leasehold and in respect of the cost to a lessee of improvements on property of which he is the lessee. However, such term does not include deductions for the periodic payment of rent.

(ii) The provisions of this subparagraph may be illustrated by the following example:

Example. On January 1, 1966, Smith purchases for $1,000, and places in service, an item of property described in section 1245(a)(3)(A). Smith deducts an additional first-year allowance for depreciation under section 179 of $200. Accordingly, the basis of the property for purposes of depreciation is $800 on January 1, 1966. Between that date and January 1, 1974, Smith deducts $640 in depreciation (the amount allowable) with respect to the property, thereby reducing its adjusted basis to $160. Since this adjusted basis reflects deductions for depreciation and amortization (within the meaning of this subparagraph) amounting to $840 ($200 plus $640), the recomputed basis of the property is $1,000 ($160 plus $840).

Reg. § 1.1245-2(a)(1)

Rules for Determining Capital Gains and Losses 53,515
See p. 20,601 for regulations not amended to reflect law changes

(4) *Adjustments of other taxpayers or in respect of other property.* (i) For purposes of subparagraph (2) of this paragraph, the adjustments reflected in adjusted basis on account of depreciation or amortization which must be taken into account in determining recomputed basis are not limited to those adjustments on account of depreciation or amortization with respect to the property disposed of, nor are such adjustments limited to those on account of depreciation or amortization allowed or allowable to the taxpayer disposing of such property. Except as provided in subparagraph (7) of this paragraph, all such adjustments are taken into account, whether the deductions were allowed or allowable in respect of the same or other property and whether to the taxpayer or to any other person. For manner of determining the amount of adjustments reflected in the adjusted basis of property immediately after certain dispositions, see paragraph (c) of this section.

(ii) The provisions of this subparagraph may be illustrated by the following example:

Example. On January 1, 1966, Jones purchases machine X for use in his trade or business. The machine, which is section 1245 property, has a basis for depreciation of $10,000. After taking depreciation deductions of $2,000 (the amount allowable), Jones transfers the machine to his son as a gift on January 1, 1968. Since the exception for gifts in section 1245(b)(1) applies, Jones does not recognize gain under section 1245(a)(1). The son's adjusted basis for the machine is $8,000. On January 1, 1969, after taking a depreciation deduction of $1,000 (the amount allowable), the son exchanges machine X for machine Y in a like kind exchange described in section 1031. Since the exception for like kind exchanges in section 1245(b)(4) applies, the son does not recognize gain under section 1245(a)(1). The son's adjusted basis for machine Y is $7,000. In 1969, the son takes a depreciation deduction of $1,000 (the amount allowable) in respect of machine Y. The son sells machine Y on June 30, 1970. No depreciation was allowed or allowable for 1970, the year of the sale. The recomputed basis of machine Y on June 30, 1970, is determined in the following manner:

Adjusted basis		$ 6,000
Adjustments reflected in the adjusted basis:		
Depreciation deducted by Jones for 1966 and 1967 on machine X	$2,000	
Depreciation deducted by son for 1968 on machine X	$1,000	
Depreciation deducted by son for 1969 on machine Y	$1,000	
Total adjustments reflected in the adjusted basis		$ 4,000
Recomputed basis		$10,000

(5) *Adjustments reflected in adjusted basis of property described in section 1245(a)(3)(B).* For purposes of subparagraph (2) of this paragraph, the adjustments reflected in the adjusted basis of property described in section 1245(a)(3)(B), on account of depreciation or amortization which must be taken into account in determining recomputed basis, may include deductions attributable to periods during which the property is not used as an integral part of an activity, or does not constitute a facility, specified in section 1245(a)(3)(B)(i) or (ii). Thus, for example, if depreciation deductions taken with respect to such property after December 31, 1961, amount to $10,000 (the amount allowable), of which $6,000 is attributable to periods during which the property is used as an integral part of a specified activity or constitutes a specified facility, then the entire $10,000 of depreciation deductions are adjustments reflected in the adjusted basis for purposes of determining recomputed basis. Moreover, if the property was never so used but was acquired in a transaction to which section 1245(b)(4) (relating to like kind exchanges and involuntaray conversions) applies, and if by reason of the application of paragraph (d)(3) of § 1.1245-4 the property is considered as section 1245 property described in section 1245(a)(3)(B), then the entire $10,000 of depreciation deductions would also be adjustments reflected in the adjusted basis for purposes of determining recomputed basis.

(6) *Allocation of adjustments attributable to periods after certain dates.* (i) For purposes of determining recomputed basis, the amount of adjustments reflected in the adjusted basis of property other than property described in subparagraph (2)(ii), (iii), or (iv) of this paragraph are limited to adjustments attributable to periods after December 31, 1961. Accordingly, if depreciation deducted with respect to such property of a calendar year taxpayer is $1,000 a year (the amount allowable) for each of 10 years beginning with 1956, only the depreciation deducted in 1962 and succeeding years shall be treated as reflected in the adjusted basis for purposes of

Reg. § 1.1245-2(a)(6)

determining recomputed basis. With respect to a taxable year beginning in 1961 and ending in 1962, the deduction for depreciation or amortization shall be ascertained by applying the principles stated in paragraph (c)(3) of § 1.167(a)-8 (relating to determination of adjusted basis of retired asset). The amount of the deduction, determined in such manner, shall be allocated on a daily basis in order to determine the portion thereof which is attributable to a period after December 31, 1961. Thus, for example, if a taxpayer, whose fiscal year ends on May 31, 1962, acquires section 1245 property on November 12, 1961, and the deduction for depreciation attributable to the property for such fiscal year is ascertained (under the principles of paragraph (c)(3) of § 1.167(a)-8) to be $400, then the portion thereof attributable to a period after December 31, 1961, is $302 (151/200 of $400). If, however, the property were acquired by such taxpayer after December 31, 1961, the entire deduction for depreciation attributable to the property for such fiscal year would be allocable to a period after December 31, 1961. For treatment of certain normal retirements described in paragraph (e)(2) of § 1.167(a)-8, see paragraph (c) of § 1.1245-6. For principles of determining the amount of adjustments for depreciation or amortization reflected in the adjusted basis of property upon an abnormal retirement of property in a multiple asset account, see paragraph (c)(3) of § 1.167(a)-8.

(ii) For purposes of determining recomputed basis, the amount of adjustments reflected in the adjusted basis of an elevator or escalator are limited to adjustments attributable to periods after June 30, 1963.

(iii) For purposes of determining recomputed basis, the amount of adjustments reflected in the adjusted basis of livestock (described in subparagraph (2)(iii) of this paragraph) are limited to adjustments attributable to periods after December 31, 1969.

(7) *Depreciation or amortization allowed or allowable.* For purposes of determining recomputed basis, generally all adjustments (for periods after Dec. 31, 1961, or, in the case of property described in subparagraph (2)(ii), (iii), or (iv) of this paragraph, for periods after the applicable date, 1969, as the case may be) attributable to allowed or allowable depreciation or amortization must be taken into account. See section 1016(a)(2) and the regulations thereunder for the meaning of "allowed" and "allowable". However, if a taxpayer can establish by adequate records or other sufficient evidence that the amount allowed for depreciation or amortization for any period was less than the amount allowable for such period, the amount to be taken into account for such period shall be the amount allowed. No adjustment is to be made on account of the tax imposed by section 56 (relating to the minimum tax for tax preferences). See paragraph (b) of this section (relating to records to be kept and information to be filed). For example, assume that in the year 1967 it becomes necessary to determine the recomputed basis of property, the $500 adjusted basis of which reflects adjustments of $1,000 with respect to depreciation deductions allowable for periods after December 31, 1961. If the taxpayer can establish by adequate records or other sufficient evidence that he had been allowed deductions amounting to $800 for the period, then in determining recomputed basis the amount added to adjusted basis with respect to the $1,000 adjustments to basis for the period will be only $800.

(8) *Exempt organizations.* In respect of property disposed of by an organization which is or was exempt from income taxes (within the meaning of section 501(a)), adjustments reflected in the adjusted basis (within the meaning of subparagraph (2) of this paragraph) shall include only depreciation or amortization allowed or allowable (i) in computing unrelated business taxable income (as defined in section 512(a)), or (ii) in computing taxable income of the organization (or a predecessor organization) for a period during which it was not exempt or, by reason of the application of section 502, 503, or 504, was denied its exemption.

(b) *Records to be kept.* In any case in which it is necessary to determine recomputed basis of an item of section 1245 property, the taxpayer shall have available permanent records of all the facts necessary to determine with reasonable accuracy the amount of such recomputed basis, including the following—

(1) The date, and the manner in which, the property was acquired,

(2) The taxpayer's basis on the date the property was acquired and the manner in which the basis was determined,

(3) The amount and the date of all adjustments to the basis of the property allowed or allowable to the taxpayer for depreciation or amortization and the amount and date of any other adjustments by the taxpayer to the basis of the property,

(4) In the case of section 1245 property which has an adjusted basis reflecting adjustments for depreciation or amortization taken by the taxpayer with respect to other property, or by another taxpayer with respect to the same or other property, the information described in subparagraphs (1), (2), and (3) of this paragraph

Rules for Determining Capital Gains and Losses

See p. 20,601 for regulations not amended to reflect law changes

with respect to such other property or such other taxpayer.

(c) *Adjustments reflected in adjusted basis immediately after certain acquisitions*—(1) *Zero.* (i) If on the date a person acquires property his basis for the property is determined solely by reference to its cost (within the meaning of section 1012), then on such date the amount of the adjustments reflected in his adjusted basis for the property is zero.

(ii) If on the date a person acquires property his basis for the property is determined solely by reason of the application of section 301(d) (relating to basis of property received in corporate distribution) or section 334(a) (relating to basis of property received in a liquidation in which gain or loss is recognized), then on such date the amount of the adjustments reflected in his adjusted basis for the property is zero.

(iii) If on the date a person acquires property his basis for the property is determined solely under the rules of section 334(b)(2) or (c) (relating to basis of property received in certain corporate liquidations), then on such date the amount of the adjustments reflected in his adjusted basis for the property is zero.

(iv) If as of the date a person acquires property from a decedent such person's basis is determined, by reason of the application of section 1014(a), solely by reference to the fair market value of the property on the date of the decedent's death or on the applicable date provided in section 2032 (relating to alternate valuation date), then on such date the amount of the adjustments reflected in his adjusted basis for the property is zero.

(2) *Gifts and certain tax-free transactions.* (i) If property is disposed of in a transaction described in subdivision (ii) of this subparagraph, then the amount of the adjustments reflected in the adjusted basis of the property in the hands of a transferee immediately after the disposition shall be an amount equal to—

(*a*) The amount of the adjustments reflected in the adjusted basis of the property in the hands of the transferor immediately before the disposition, minus

(*b*) The amount of any gain taken into account under section 1245(a)(1) by the transferor upon the disposition.

(ii) The transactions referred to in subdivision (i) of this subparagraph are—

(*a*) A disposition which is in part a sale or exchange and in part a gift (see paragraph (a)(3) or § 1.1245-4),

(*b*) A disposition (other than a disposition to which section 1245(b)(6)(A) applies) which is described in section 1245(b)(3) (relating to certain tax-free transactions), or

(*c*) An exchange described in paragraph (e)(2) of § 1.1245-4 (relating to transfers described in section 1081(d)(1)(A)).

(iii) The provisions of this subparagraph may be illustrated by the following example:

Example. Jones transfers section 1245 property to a corporation in exchange for stock of the corporation and $1,000 cash in a transaction which qualifies under section 351 (relating to transfer to a corporation controlled by a transferor). Before the exchange the amount of the adjustments reflected in the adjusted basis of the property is $3,000. Upon the exchange $1,000 gain is recognized under section 1245(a)(1). Immediately after the exchange, the amount of the adjustments reflected in the adjusted basis of the property in the hands of the corporation is $2,000 (that is, $3,000 minus $1,000).

(3) *Certain transfers at death.* (i) If property is acquired in transfer at death to which section 1245(b)(2) applies, the amount of the adjustments reflected in the adjusted basis of property in the hands of the transferee immediately after the transfer shall be the amount (if any) of depreciation or amortization deductions allowed the transferee before the decedent's death, to the extent that the basis of the property (determined under section 1014(a)) is required to be reduced under the second sentence of section 1014(b)(9) (relating to adjustments to basis where property is acquired from a decedent prior to his death).

(ii) The provisions of this subparagraph may be illustrated by the following example:

Example. H purchases section 1245 property in 1965 which he immediately conveys to himself and W, his wife, as tenants by the entirety. Under local law each spouse is entitled to one-half the income from the property. H and W file joint income tax returns for calendar years 1965, 1966, and 1967. Over the 3 years, depreciation deductions amounting to $4,000 (the amount allowable) are allowed in respect of the property of which one-half thereof, or $2,000, is allocable to W. On January 1, 1968, H dies and the entire value of the property at the date of death is included in H's gross estate. Since W's basis for the property (determined under section 1014(a)) is reduced (under the second sentence of section 1014(b)(9)) by the $2,000 depreciation deductions allowed W before H's death, the adjustments reflected in the adjusted basis of the property in the hands of W immediately after H's death amount to $2,000.

Reg. § 1.1245-2(c)(3)

(4) *Property received in a like kind exchange, involuntary conversion, or F.C.C. transaction.* (i) If property is acquired in a transaction described in subdivision (ii) of this subparagraph, then immediately after the acquisition (and before applying subparagraph (5) of this paragraph, if applicable) the amount of the adjustments reflected in the adjusted basis of the property acquired shall be an amount equal to—

(a) The amount of the adjustments reflected in the adjusted basis of the property disposed of immediately before the disposition, minus

(b) The sum of (1) the amount of any gain recognized under section 1245(a)(1) upon the disposition, plus (2) the amount of gain (if any) referred to in subparagraph (5)(ii) of this paragraph.

(ii) The transactions referred to in subdivision (i) of this subparagraph are—

(a) A disposition which is a like kind exchange or an involuntary conversion to which section 1245(b)(4) applies, or

(b) A disposition to which the provisions of section 1071 and paragraph (e)(1) of § 1.1245-4 apply.

(iii) The provisions of subdivisions (i) and (ii) of this subparagraph may be illustrated by the following examples:

Example (1). Smith exchanges machine A for machine B and $1,000 cash in a like kind exchange. Gain of $1,000 is recognized under section 1245 (a)(1). If before the exchange the amount of the adjustments reflected in the adjusted basis of machine A was $5,000, the amount of adjustments reflected in the adjusted basis of machine B after the exchange is $4,000 (that is, $5,000 minus $1,000).

Example (2). Assume the same facts as in example (1) except that machine A is destroyed by fire, that $5,000 in insurance proceeds are received of which $4,000 is used to purchase machine B, and that Smith properly elects under section 1033(a)(3)(A) to limit recognition of gain. The result is the same as in example (1), that is, the amount of adjustments reflected in the adjusted basis of machine B is $4,000 ($5,000 minus $1,000).

(iv) If more than one item of section 1245 property is acquired in a transaction referred to in subdivision (i) of this subparagraph, the total amount of the adjustments reflected in the adjusted bases of the items acquired shall be allocated to such items in proportion to their respective adjusted bases.

(5) *Property after a reduction in basis pursuant to election under section 1071 or application of section 1082(a)(2).* If the basis of section 1245 property is reduced pursuant to an election under section 1071 (relating to gain from sale or exchange to effectuate policies of F.C.C.), or the application of section 1082(a)(2) (relating to sale or exchange in obedience to order of S.E.C.), then immediately after the basis reduction the amount of the adjustments reflected in the adjusted basis of the property shall be the sum of—

(i) The amount of the adjustments reflected in the adjusted basis of the property immediately before the basis reduction (but after applying subparagraph (4) of this paragraph, if applicable), plus

(ii) The amount of gain which was not recognized under section 1245(a)(1) by reason of the reduction in the basis of the property. See paragraph (e)(1) of § 1.1245-4.

(6) *Partnership property after certain transactions.* (i) For the amount of adjustments reflected in the adjusted basis of property immediately after certain distributions of the property by a partnership to a partner, see section 1245(b)(6)(B).

(ii) If under paragraph (b)(3) of § 1.751-1 (relating to certain distributions of partnership property other than section 751 property treated as sales or exchanges) a partnership is treated as purchasing section 1245 property (or a portion thereof) from a distributee who relinquishes his interest in such property (or portion), then on the date of such purchase the amount of adjustments reflected in the adjusted basis of such purchased property (or portion) shall be zero.

(iii) See paragraph (e)(3)(ii) of § 1.1245-1 for the amount of adjustments reflected in the adjusted basis of partnership property in respect of a partner who acquired his partnership interest in certain transactions when an election under section 754 (relating to optional adjustments to basis of partnership property) was in effect. [Reg. § 1.1245-2.]

☐ [T.D. 6832, 7-6-65. Amended by T.D. 7084, 1-7-71; T.D. 7141, 9-21-71; T.D. 7564, 9-18-78; and T.D. 8121, 1-5-87.]

[Reg. § 1.1245-3]

§ 1.1245-3. Definition of section 1245 property.—(a) *In general.* (1) The term "section 1245 property" means any property (other than livestock excluded by the effective date limitation in subparagraph (4) of this paragraph) which is or has been property of a character subject to the allowance for depreciation provided in section 167 and which is either—

Reg. § 1.1245-3(a)

Rules for Determining Capital Gains and Losses

(i) Personal property (within the meaning of paragraph (b) of this section),

(ii) Property described in section 1245(a)(3)(B) (see paragraph (c) of this section), or

(iii) An elevator or an escalator within the meaning of subparagraph (C) of section 48(a)(1) (relating to the definition of "section 38 property" for purposes of the investment credit), but without regard to the limitations in such subparagraph (C).

(2) If property is section 1245 property under a subdivision of subparagraph (1) of this paragraph, a leasehold of such property is also section 1245 property under such subdivision. Thus, for example, if A owns personal property which is section 1245 property under subparagraph (1)(i) of this paragraph, and if A leases the personal property to B, B's leasehold is also section 1245 property under such provision. For a further example, if C owns and leases to D for a single lump-sum payment of $100,000 property consisting of land and a fully equipped factory building thereon, and if 40 percent of the fair market value of such property is properly allocable to section 1245 property, then 40 percent of D's leasehold is also section 1245 property. A leasehold of land is not section 1245 property.

(3) Even though property may not be of a character subject to the allowance for depreciation in the hands of the taxpayer, such property may nevertheless be section 1245 property if the taxpayer's basis for the property is determined by reference to its basis in the hands of a prior owner of the property and such property was of a character subject to the allowance for depreciation in the hands of such prior owner, or if the taxpayer's basis for the property is determined by reference to the basis of other property which in the hands of the taxpayer was property of a character subject to the allowance for depreciation. Thus, for example, if a father uses an automobile in his trade or business during a period after December 31, 1961, and then gives the automobile to his son as a gift for the son's personal use, the automobile is section 1245 property in the hands of the son.

(4) Section 1245 property includes livestock, but only with respect to taxable years beginning after December 31, 1969. For purposes of section 1245, the term "livestock" includes horses, cattle, hogs, sheep, goats, and mink and other furbearing animals, irrespective of the use to which they are put or the purpose for which they are held.

(b) *Personal property defined.* The term "personal property" means—

(1) Tangible personal property (as defined in paragraph (c) of § 1.48-1, relating to the definition of "section 38 property" for purposes of the investment credit), and

(2) Intangible personal property.

(c) *Property described in section 1245(a)(3)(B).* (1) The term "property described in section 1245(a)(3)(B)" means tangible property of the requisite depreciable character other than personal property (and other than a building and its structural components), but only if there are adjustments reflected in the adjusted basis of the property (within the meaning of paragraph (a)(2) of § 1.1245-2) for a period during which such property (or other property)—

(i) Was used as an integral part of manufacturing, production, or extraction, or as an integral part of furnishing transportation, communications, electrical energy, gas, water, or sewage disposal services by a person engaged in a trade or business of furnishing any such service, or

(ii) Constituted a research or storage facility used in connection with any of the foregoing activities.

Thus, even though during the period immediately preceding its disposition the property is not used as an integral part of an activity specified in subdivision (i) of this subparagraph and does not constitute a facility specified in subdivision (ii) of this subparagraph, such property is nevertheless property described in section 1245(a)(3)(B) if, for example, there are adjustments reflected in the adjusted basis of the property for a period during which the property was used as an integral part of manufacturing by the taxpayer or another taxpayer, or for a period during which other property (which was involuntarily converted into, or exchanged in a like kind exchange for, the property) was so used by the taxpayer or another taxpayer. For rules applicable to involuntary conversions and like kind exchanges, see paragraph (d)(3) of § 1.1245-4.

(2) The language used in subparagraph (1)(i) and (ii) of this paragraph shall have the same meaning as when used in paragraph (a) of § 1.48-1, and the terms "building" and "structural components" shall have the meanings assigned to those terms in paragraph (e) of § 1.48-1. [Reg. § 1.1245-3.]

☐ [*T.D. 6832, 7-6-65. Amended by T.D. 7141, 9-21-71.*]

[Reg. § 1.1245-4]

§ 1.1245-4. **Exceptions and limitations.**—(a) *Exception for gifts.*—(1) *General rule.* Section 1245(b)(1) provides that no gain shall be recognized under section 1245(a)(1) upon a disposition by gift. For purposes of this paragraph, the term "gift" means, except to the extent that subpara-

Reg. § 1.1245-4(a)(1)

graph (3) of this paragraph applies, a transfer of property which, in the hands of the transferee, has a basis determined under the provisions of section 1015(a) or (d) (relating to basis of property acquired by gifts). For reduction in amount of charitable contribution in case of a gift of section 1245 property, see section 170(e) and the regulations thereunder.

(2) *Examples.* The provisions of subparagraph (1) of this paragraph may be illustrated by the following examples:

Example (1). A places section 1245 property in trust to pay the income from the property to B for his life, and after B's death to distribute the property to C. If the basis of the property to the fiduciary and to C is determined under the uniform basis rules prescribed in paragraph (b) of § 1.1015-1, and under paragraph (c) of § 1.1015-1 the time the fiduciary and C acquire their interests in the property is the time the donor relinquished dominion over the property, then section 1245(a)(1) does not apply to the transfer by A to the trust or to the distribution to C.

Example (2). Assume the same facts as in example (1), except that the fiduciary sells the section 1245 property and reinvests the proceeds in other section 1245 property which is distributed to C upon B's death. Assume further that under paragraph (f) of § 1.1015-1 C's basis for the distributed property is the cost or other basis to the fiduciary. Section 1245(a)(1) applies to the sale but not to the distribution.

(3) *Disposition in part a sale or exchange and in part a gift.* Where a disposition of property is in part a sale or exchange and in part a gift, the gain to which section 1245(a)(1) applies is the amount by which (i) the lower of the amount realized upon the disposition of the property or the recomputed basis of the property, exceeds (ii) the adjusted basis of the property. For determination of the recomputed basis of the property in the hands of the transferee, see paragraph (c)(2) of § 1.1245-2.

(4) *Example.* The provisions of subparagraph (3) of this paragraph may be illustrated by the following example:

Example. (i) Smith transfers section 1245 property, which he has held in excess of 1 year (6 months for taxable years beginning before 1977; 9 months for taxable years beginning in 1977), to his son for $60,000. Immediately before the transfer the property in the hands of Smith has an adjusted basis of $30,000, a fair market value of $90,000, and a recomputed basis of $110,000. Since the amount realized upon disposition of the property ($60,000) is lower than its recomputed basis ($110,000), the excess of the amount realized over adjusted basis, or $30,000, is treated as ordinary income under section 1245(a)(1) and not as gain from the sale or exchange of property described in section 1231. Smith has made a gift of $30,000 ($90,000 fair market value minus $60,000 amount realized) to which section 1245(a)(1) does not apply.

(ii) Immediately before the transfer, the amount of adjustments reflected in the adjusted basis of the property was $80,000. Under paragraph (c)(2) of § 1.1245-2, $50,000 of adjustments are reflected in the adjusted basis of the property immediately after the transfer, that is, $80,000 of such adjustments immediately before the transfer, minus $30,000 gain taken into account under section 1245(a)(1) upon the transfer. Thus, the recomputed basis of the property in the hands of the son is $110,000.

(b) *Exception for transfers at death* —(1) *General rule.* Section 1245(b)(2) provides that, except as provided in section 691 (relating to income in respect of a decedent), no gain shall be recognized under section 1245(a)(1) upon a transfer at death. For purposes of this paragraph, the term "transfer at death" means a transfer of property which, in the hands of the transferee, has a basis determined under the provisions of section 1014(a) (relating to basis of property acquired from a decedent) because of the death of the transferor. For recomputed basis of property acquired in a transfer at death, see paragraph (c)(1)(iv) of § 1.1245-2.

(2) *Examples.* The provisions of this paragraph may be illustrated by the following examples:

Example (1). Smith owns section 1245 property which, upon Smith's death, is inherited by his son. Since the property is described in section 1014(b)(1), its basis in the hands of the son is determined under the provisions of section 1014(a). Therefore, section 1245(a)(1) does not apply to the transfer at Smith's death.

Example (2). H purchases section 1245 property which he conveys to himself and W, his wife, as tenants by the entirety. Upon H's death in 1970 the property (including W's share) is included in his gross estate. Since the entire property is described in section 1014(b)(1) and (9), its basis in the hands of W is determined under the provisions of section 1014(a). Therefore, section 1245(a)(1) does not apply to the transfer at H's death. For determination of the recomputed basis of the property in the hands of W, see paragraph (c)(3) of § 1.1245-2.

Example (3). Green's will provides for the bequest of section 1245 property to trustees to pay the income from the property to his wife for

Reg. § 1.1245-4(a)(2)

Rules for Determining Capital Gains and Losses

See p. 20,601 for regulations not amended to reflect law changes

her lifetime, and upon her death to distribute the property to his son. If under paragraph (a)(2) of § 1.1014-4 the son's unadjusted basis for the property is its fair market value at the time the decedent died, section 1245(a)(1) does not apply to the distribution of the property to the son.

Example (4). The trustee of a trust created by will transfers section 1245 property to a beneficiary in satisfaction of a specific bequest of $10,000. If under the principles of paragraph (a)(3) of § 1.1014-4 the trust realizes a taxable gain upon the transfer, section 1245(a)(1) applies to the transfer.

(c) *Limitation for certain tax-free transactions*—(1) *Limitation on amount of gain.* Section 1245(b)(3) provides that upon a transfer of property described in subparagraph (2) of this paragraph, the amount of gain taken into account by the transferor under section 1245(a)(1) shall not exceed the amount of gain recognized to the transferor on the transfer (determined without regard to section 1245). For purposes of this subparagraph, in case of a transfer of both section 1245 property and non-section 1245 property in one transaction, the amount realized from the disposition of the section 1245 property (as determined under paragraph (a)(5) of § 1.1245-1) shall be deemed to consist of that portion of the fair market value of each property acquired which bears the same ratio to the fair market value of such acquired property as the amount realized from the disposition of the section 1245 property bears to the total amount realized. The preceding sentence shall be applied solely for purposes of computing the portion of the total gain (determined without regard to section 1245) which shall be recognized as ordinary income under section 1245(a)(1). For determination of the recomputed basis of the section 1245 property in the hands of the transferee, see paragraph (c)(2) of § 1.1245-2. Section 1245(b)(3) does not apply to a disposition of property to an organization (other than a cooperative described in section 521) which is exempt from the tax imposed by chapter 1 of the Code.

(2) *Transfers covered.* The transfers referred to in subparagraph (1) of this paragraph are transfers of property which the basis of the property in the hands of the transferee is determined by reference to its basis in the hands of the transferor by reason of the application of any of the following provisions:

(i) Section 332 (relating to distributions in complete liquidation of an 80-percent-or-more controlled subsidiary corporation). See subparagraph (3) of this paragraph.

(ii) Section 351 (relating to transfer to a corporation controlled by transferor).

(iii) Section 361 (relating to exchanges pursuant to certain corporate reorganizations).

(iv) Section 371(a) (relating to exchanges pursuant to certain receivership and bankruptcy proceedings).

(v) Section 374(a) (relating to exchanges pursuant to certain railroad reorganizations).

(vi) Section 721 (relating to transfers to a partnership in exchange for a partnership interest).

(vii) Section 731 (relating to distributions by a partnership to a partner). For special carryover basis rule, see section 1245(b)(6)(A) and paragraph (f)(1) of this section.

(3) *Complete liquidation of subsidiary.* In the case of a distribution in complete liquidation of an 80-percent-or-more controlled subsidiary to which section 332 applies, the limitation provided in section 1245(b)(3) is confined to instances in which the basis of the property in the hands of the transferee is determined, under section 334(b)(1), by reference to its basis in the hands of the transferor. Thus, for example, the limitation of section 1245(b)(3) may apply in respect of a liquidating distribution of section 1245 property by an 80-percent-or-more controlled corporation to the parent corporation, but does not apply in respect of a liquidating distribution of section 1245 property to a minority shareholder. Section 1245(b)(3) does not apply to a liquidating distribution of property by an 80-percent-or-more controlled subsidiary to its parent if the parent's basis for the property is determined, under section 334(b)(2), by reference to its basis for the stock of the subsidiary.

(4) *Examples.* The provisions of this paragraph may be illustrated by the following examples:

Example (1). Section 1245 property, which is owned by Smith, has a fair market value of $10,000, a recomputed basis of $8,000, and an adjusted basis of $4,000. Smith transfers the property to a corporation in exchange for stock in the corporation worth $9,000 plus $1,000 in cash in a transaction qualifying under section 351. Without regard to section 1245, Smith would recognize $1,000 gain under section 351(b), and the corporation's basis for the property would be determined under section 362(a) by reference to its basis in the hands of Smith. Since the recomputed basis of the property disposed of ($8,000) is lower than the amount realized ($10,000), the excess of recomputed basis over adjusted basis ($4,000), or $4,000, would be treated as ordinary income under section 1245(a)(1) if the provisions of section 1245(b)(3) did not apply. However, section 1245(b)(3) limits the gain taken into account by

Reg. § 1.1245-4(c)(4)

Smith under section 1245(a)(1) to $1,000. If, instead, Smith transferred the property to the corporation solely in exchange for stock of the corporation worth $10,000, then, because of the application of section 1245(b)(3), Smith would not take any gain into account under section 1245(a)(1). If, however, Smith transferred the property to the corporation for stock worth $5,000 and $5,000 cash, only $4,000 of the $5,000 gain under section 351(b) would be treated as ordinary income under section 1245(a)(1).

Example (2). Assume the same facts as in example (1) except that Smith contributes the property to a new partnership in which he has a one-half interest. Since, without regard to section 1245, no gain would be recognized to Smith under section 721, and by reason of the application of section 721 the partnership's basis for the property would be determined under section 723 by reference to its basis in the hands of Smith, the application of section 1245(b)(3) results in no gain being taken into account by Smith under section 1245(a)(1).

Example (3). Assume the same facts as in example (2) except that the property is subject to a $9,000 mortgage. Since under section 752(b) (relating to decrease in partner's liabilities) Smith is treated as receiving a distribution in money of $4,500 (one-half) of liability assumed by partnership), and since the basis of Smith's partnership interest is $4,000 (the adjusted basis of the contributed property), the $4,500 distribution results in his realizing $500 gain under section 731(a) (relating to distributions by a partnership), determined without regard to section 1245. Accordingly, the application of section 1245(b)(3) limits the gain taken into account by Smith under section 1245(a)(1) to $500.

(d) *Limitation for like kind exchanges and involuntary conversions*—(1) *General rule.* Section 1245(b)(4) provides that if property is disposed of and gain (determined without regard to section 1245) is not recognized in whole or in part under section 1031 (relating to like kind exchanges) or section 1033 (relating to involuntary conversions), then the amount of gain taken into account by the transferor under section 1245(a)(1) shall not exceed the sum of—

(i) The amount of gain recognized on such disposition (determined without regard to section 1245), plus

(ii) The fair market value of property acquired which is not section 1245 property and which is not taken into account under subdivision (i) of this subparagraph (that is, the fair market value of non-section 1245 property acquired which is qualifying property under section 1031 or 1033, as the case may be).

(2) *Examples.* The provisions of subparagraph (1) of this paragraph may be illustrated by the following examples:

Example (1). Smith exchanges machine A for machine B in a like kind exchange as to which no gain is recognized under section 1031(a). Both machines are section 1245 property. No gain is recognized under section 1245(a)(1) because of the limitation contained in section 1245(b)(4). The result would be the same if machine A were involuntarily converted into machine B in a transaction as to which no gain is recognized under section 1033(a)(1).

Example (2). Jones owns property A, which is section 1245 property, with an adjusted basis of $100,000 and a recomputed basis of $116,000. The property is destroyed by fire and Jones receives $117,000 of insurance proceeds. Thus, the amount of gain under section 1245(a)(1), determined without regard to section 1245(b)(4), would be $16,000. He uses $105,000 of the proceeds to purchase section 1245 property similar or related in service or use to property A, and $9,000 of the proceeds to purchase stock in the acquisition of control of a corporation owning property similar or related in service or use to property A. Both acquisitions qualify under section 1033(a)(3)(A). Jones properly elects under section 1033(a)(3)(A) and the regulations thereunder to limit recognition of gain to the amount by which the amount realized from the conversion exceeds the cost of the stock and other property acquired to replace the converted property. Since $3,000 of the gain is recognized (without regard to section 1245) under section 1033(a)(3) (that is, $117,000 minus $114,000), and since the stock purchased for $9,000 is not section 1245 property and was not taken into account in determining the gain under section 1033, section 1245(b)(4) limits the amount of the gain taken into account under section 1245(a)(1) to $12,000 (that is, $3,000 plus $9,000). If, instead of purchasing $9,000 in stock, Jones purchases $9,000 worth of property which is section 1245 property similar or related in use to the destroyed property, section 1245(b)(4) would limit the amount of gain taken into account under section 1245(a)(1) to $3,000.

(3) *Certain tangible property.* If—

(i) A person disposes of section 1245 property in a transaction to which section 1245(b)(4) applies,

(ii) Adjustments are reflected in the adjusted basis (within the meaning of paragraph (a)(2) of § 1.1245-2) of such property which are attributable to the use of such property (or other

Reg. § 1.1245-4(d)(1)

Rules for Determining Capital Gains and Losses

property) as an integral part of an activity, or as a facility, specified in section 1245(a)(3)(B)(i) or (ii), and

(iii) Property is acquired in the transaction which would be considered as section 1245 property described in section 1245(a)(3)(B) if such person used the acquired property as an integral part of such an activity, or as such a facility,

then (regardless of the use of the acquired property) the acquired property shall be considered as section 1245 property described in section 1245(a)(3)(B). For definition of property described in section 1245(a)(3)(B), see paragraph (c) of § 1.1245-3. Thus, for example, if a person's section 1245 property (which is personal property) is involuntarily converted into property A which would qualify as section 1245 property only if it were devoted to a specified use, and if the person had so devoted the section 1245 property disposed of, then the acquired property is considered as section 1245 property described in section 1245(a)(3)(B) and therefore its fair market value is not taken into account under subparagraph (1)(ii) of this paragraph. For recomputed basis of property A, see paragraph (a)(5) of § 1.1245-2. Moreover, if property A is not devoted to a specified use and is subsequently involuntarily converted into property B which would qualify as section 1245 property only if it were so devoted, then property B is also considered as section 1245 property described in section 1245(a)(3)(B).

(4) *Application to disposition of section 1245 property and non-section 1245 property in one transaction.* For purposes of this paragraph, if both section 1245 property and non-section 1245 property are acquired as the result of one disposition in which both section 1245 property and non-section 1245 property are disposed of, then except as provided in subparagraph (7) of this paragraph—

(i) The total amount realized upon the disposition shall be allocated (in a manner consistent with the principles of paragraph (a)(5) of § 1.1245-1) between the section 1245 property and the non-section 1245 property disposed of in proportion to their respective fair market values.

(ii) The amount realized upon the disposition of the section 1245 property shall be deemed to consist of so much of the fair market value of the section 1245 property acquired as is not in excess of the amount realized from the section 1245 property disposed of, and the remaining portion (if any) of the amount realized upon the disposition of the section 1245 property shall be deemed to consist of so much of the fair market value of the non-section 1245 property acquired as is not in excess of the amount of such remaining portion, and

(iii) The amount realized upon the disposition of the non-section 1245 property shall be deemed to consist of so much of the fair market value of all the property acquired which was not taken into account in subdivision (ii) of this subparagraph.

(5) *Example.* The provisions of subparagraph (4) of this paragraph may be illustrated by the following example:

Example. (i) Smith owns section 1245 property A with a fair market value of $30,000, and non-section 1245 property X with a fair market value of $20,000. Properties A and X are destroyed by fire and Smith receives insurance proceeds of $40,000. He uses all the proceeds, plus additional cash of $10,000, to purchase in a single transaction properties B and Y which qualify under section 1033(a)(3)(A), and he properly elects under section 1033(a)(3)(A) and the regulations thereunder to limit recognition of gain to the excess of the amount realized from the conversion over the costs of the qualifying properties acquired. Thus no gain would be recognized (without regard to section 1245) under section 1033(a)(3)(A). Property B is section 1245 property with a fair market value of $15,000, and property Y is nonsection 1245 property with a fair market value of $35,000.

(ii) The amount realized upon the disposition of A and X ($40,000) is allocated between A and X in proportion to their respective fair market values. Thus, the amount considered realized in respect of A is $24,000 (that is, 30/50 of $40,000). (The amount considered realized in respect of X is $16,000 (that is, 20/50 of $40,000).)

(iii) The $24,000 realized upon the disposition of A is deemed to consist of the fair market value of B ($15,000) and $9,000 of the fair market value of Y. (The $16,000 realized upon the disposition of X is deemed to consist of $16,000 of the fair market value of Y. Also, $10,000 of the fair market value of Y is attributable to the additional cash of $10,000.)

(iv) Assume that A has an adjusted basis of $5,000, and a recomputed basis of $40,000. Since the amount considered realized upon the disposition of A ($24,000) is lower than its recomputed basis ($40,000), the amount of gain which would be recognized under section 1245(a)(1), determined without regard to section 1245(b)(4), is $19,000, that is, the amount realized ($24,000), minus the adjusted basis ($5,000). Since no gain is recognized (without regard to section 1245) under section 1033(a)(3), and since $9,000 of the property acquired in exchange for section 1245 prop-

Reg. § 1.1245-4(d)(5)

erty A is nonsection 1245 property Y, section 1245(b)(4) limits the amount of gain taken into account under section 1245(a)(1) to $9,000.

(6) *Cross references.* For the manner of determining the recomputed basis of property acquired in a transaction to which section 1245(b)(4) applies, see paragraph (c)(4) of § 1.1245-2. For the manner of determining the basis of such property, see paragraph (a) of § 1.1245-5.

(7) *Coordination with section 1250.* For purposes of this paragraph, if section 1245 property and section 1250 property are disposed of in one transaction in which the property acquired includes section 1250 property, the allocation rules of paragraph (d)(6) of § 1.1250-3 shall apply.

(e) *Limitation for section 1071 and 1081 transactions*—(1) *Section 1071 and 1081(b) transactions.* If property is disposed of and gain (determined without regard to section 1245) is not recognized in whole or in part because of the application of section 1071 (relating to gain from sale or exchange to effectuate policies of F.C.C.) or section 1081(b) (relating to gain from sale or exchange in obedience to order of S.E.C.), then the amount of gain taken into account by the transferor under section 1245(a)(1) shall not exceed the sum of—

(i) The amount of gain recognized on such disposition (determined without regard to section 1245),

(ii) In the case of a transaction to which section 1071 applies, the fair market value of property acquired which is not section 1245 property and which is not taken into account under subdivision (i) of this subparagraph, plus

(iii) The amount by which the basis of property, other than section 1245 property, is reduced (pursuant to an election under section 1071 or pursuant to the application of section 1082(a)(2)), and which is not taken into account under subdivision (i) or (ii) of this subparagraph.

(2) *Section 1081(d)(1)(A) transaction.* No gain shall be recognized under section 1245(a)(1) upon an exchange of property as to which gain would not be recognized (without regard to section 1245) because of the application of section 1081(d)(1)(A) (relating to transfers within system group). For recomputed basis of property acquired in a transaction referred to in this subparagraph, see paragraph (c)(2) of § 1.1245-2.

(3) *Examples.* The provisions of this paragraph may be illustrated by the following examples:

Example (1). Corporation X elects under section 1071 to treat a sale of section 1245 property for $100,000 as an involuntary conversion subject to the provisions of section 1033, but does not elect to reduce the basis of depreciable property pursuant to an election under section 1071. The corporation uses $35,000 of the proceeds to purchase section 1245 property and $40,000 to purchase other property. Both properties qualify as replacement property under section 1033. Assuming that the amount of gain under section 1245(a)(1) (determined without regard to this paragraph) would be $70,000, and that $25,000 of gain would be recognized (without regard to section 1245) upon the application of section 1071, the amount of gain taken into account under section 1245(a)(1) is $65,000 ($25,000 plus $40,000).

Example (2). (i) Assume the same facts as in example (1) except that the corporation elects under section 1071 to reduce its basis for property of a character subject to the allowance for depreciation under section 167 by the amount of gain which would be recognized without regard to the application of section 1245, that is, by $25,000. Assume further that under section 1071 the corporation may reduce the basis of depreciable property consisting of property A, which is section 1245 property with an adjusted basis of $30,000, and property B, which is property other than section 1245 property with an adjusted basis of $20,000. Under paragraph (a)(2) of § 1.1071-3, the $25,000 of unrecognized gain is applied to reduce the basis of property A by $15,000 (30,000/50,000 of $25,000) and the basis of property B by $10,000 (20,000/50,000 of $25,000).

(ii) The amount of gain which would be recognized (determined without regard to section 1245) under section 1071 is zero, i.e., the amount determined in example (1) ($25,000), minus the amount of the reduction in basis of depreciable property pursuant to the election ($25,000). The amount of gain taken into account under section 1245(a)(1) is $50,000, i.e., the sum of *(a)* the gain which would be recognized without regard to section 1245 (zero), *(b)* the cost of property acquired which is not section 1245 property ($40,000), plus, *(c)* the amount by which the basis of property B is reduced ($10,000). For method of increasing basis of property B, see paragraph (b)(2) of § 1.1245-5, and for recomputed basis of property A, see paragraph (c)(5) of § 1.1245-2.

(f) *Limitation for property distributed by a partnership*—(1) *In general.* For purposes of section 1245(b)(3) (relating to certain tax-free transactions), the basis of section 1245 property distributed by a partnership to a partner shall be deemed to be determined by reference to the adjusted basis of such property to the partnership.

Reg. § 1.1245-4(d)(6)

Rules for Determining Capital Gains and Losses

See p. 20,601 for regulations not amended to reflect law changes

(2) *Adjustments reflected in the adjusted basis.* If section 1245 property is distributed by a partnership to a partner, then, for purposes of determining the recomputed basis of the property in the hands of the distributee, the amount of the adjustments reflected in the adjusted basis of the property immediately after the distribution shall be an amount equal to—

(i) The potential section 1245 income (as defined in paragraph (c)(4) of § 1.751-1) of the partnership in respect of the property immediately before the distribution, reduced by

(ii) The portion of such potential section 1245 income which is recognized as ordinary income to the partnership under paragraph (b)(2)(ii) of § 1.751-1.

(3) *Examples.* The provisions of this paragraph may be illustrated by the following examples:

Example (1). (i) A machine, which is section 1245 property owned by partnership ABC, has an adjusted basis of $9,000, a recomputed basis of $18,000, and a fair market value of $15,000. Since the fair market value of the machine is lower than its recomputed basis, the potential section 1245 income in respect of the machine is the excess of fair market value over adjusted basis, or $6,000. The partnership distributes the machine to C in a complete liquidation of his partnership interest to which section 736(a) does not apply. C, who had originally contributed the machine to the partnership, has a basis for his partnership interest of $10,000. Since section 751(b)(2)(A) provides that section 751(b)(1) does not apply to a distribution of property to the partner who contributed the property, no gain would be recognized to the partnership under section 731(b) (without regard to the application of section 1245). By reason of the application of section 731, C's basis for the property would, under section 732(b), be equal to his basis for his interest in the partnership, or $10,000.

(ii) Since section 731 applies to the distribution, and since subparagraph (1) of this paragraph provides that, for purposes of section 1245(b)(3), C's basis for the property is deemed to be determined by reference to the adjusted basis of the property to the partnership, the gain taken into account under section 1245(a)(1) by the partnership is limited by section 1245(b)(3) so as not to exceed the amount of gain which would be recognized to the partnership if section 1245 did not apply. Accordingly, the partnership does not recognize any gain under section 1245(a)(1) upon the distribution.

(iii) Immediately after the distribution, the amount of the adjustments reflected in the adjusted basis of the property is equal to $6,000 (that is, the potential section 1245 income of the partnership in respect of the property before the distribution, $6,000, minus the gain recognized by the partnership under section 751(b), zero). Accordingly, C's recomputed basis for the property is $16,000 (that is, adjusted basis, $10,000, plus adjustments reflected in the adjusted basis, $6,000).

Example (2). Assume the same facts as in example (1) except that the machine had been purchased by the partnership. Assume further that upon the distribution, the partnership recognizes $4,000 gain as ordinary income under section 751(b). Under section 1245(b)(3), gain to be taken into account under section 1245(a)(1) by the partnership is limited to $4,000. Immediately after the distribution, the amount of adjustments reflected in the adjusted basis of the property is $2,000 (that is, potential section 1245 income of the partnership, $6,000, minus gain recognized to the partnership under section 751(b), $4,000). Thus, if the adjusted basis of the machine in the hands of C were $11,333 (see, for example, the computation in paragraph (d)(2) of example (6) of paragraph (g) of § 1.751-1), the recomputed basis of the machine would be $13,333 ($11,333 plus $2,000).

(g) [Reserved]

(h) *Timber property subject to amortization under section 194* —(1) *In general.* For purposes of section 1245(a)(2), in determining the recomputed basis of property with respect to which a deduction under section 194 was allowed for any taxable year, a taxpayer shall not take into account amortization deductions claimed under section 194 to the extent such deductions are attributable to the amortizable basis (within the meaning of section 194(c)(2)) of the taxpayer acquired before the tenth taxable year preceding the taxable year in which gain with respect to the property is recognized.

(2) *Example.* The principles of paragraph (h)(1) of this section are illustrated by the following example:

Example. Assume A owns qualified timber property (as defined in section 194(c)(1)) with a basis of $30,000. In 1981, A incurs $12,000 of qualifying reforestation expenditures and elects to amortize the maximum $10,000 of such expenses under section 194. The $10,000 of deductions are taken during the 8-year period from 1981 to 1988. If A sells the property in 1990 for $60,000 a gain of $28,000 ($60,000 − adjusted basis of $32,000) is recognized on the sale. Since the sale took place within 10 years of the taxable year in which the reforestation expenditures were made, $10,000 of

Reg. § 1.1245-4(h)(2)

the gain is treated as ordinary income, and the remaining $18,000 of gain would be capital gain, if it otherwise qualifies for capital gain treatment. In order to avoid ordinary income treatment of the gain attributable to the reforestation expenditures incurred in 1981, A would have to wait until 1992 to dispose of the property. [Reg. § 1.1245-4.]

☐ [*T.D. 6832, 7-6-65. Amended by T.D. 7084, 1-7-71, T.D. 7207, 10-3-72; T.D. 7728, 10-31-80 and T.D. 7927, 12-15-83.*]

[Reg. § 1.1245-5]

§ 1.1245-5. Adjustments to basis.—In order to reflect gain recognized under section 1245(a)(1), the following adjustments to the basis of property shall be made:

(a) *Property acquired in like kind exchange or involuntary conversion.*—(1) If property is acquired in a transaction to which section 1245(b)(4) applies, its basis shall be determined under the rules of section 1031(d) or 1033(c).

(2) The provisions of this paragraph may be illustrated by the following example:

Example. Jones exchanges property A, which is section 1245 property with an adjusted basis of $10,000, for property B, which has a fair market value of $9,000, and property C, which has a fair market value of $3,500, in a like kind exchange as to which no gain would be recognized under section 1031(a). Upon the exchange $2,500 gain is recognized under section 1245(a)(1), since property C is not section 1245 property. See section 1245(b)(4). Under the rules of section 1031(d), the basis of the properties received in the exchange is $12,500 (i.e., the basis of property transferred, $10,000, plus the amount of gain recognized, $2,500), of which the amount allocated to property C is $3,500 (the fair market value thereof), and the residue, $9,000, is allocated to property B.

(b) *Section 1071 and 1081 transactions.* (1) If property is acquired in a transaction to which section 1071 and paragraph (e)(1) of § 1.1245-4 (relating to limitation for section 1071 transactions, etc.) apply, its basis shall be determined in accordance with the principles of paragraph (a) of this section.

(2) If the basis of property, other than section 1245 property, is reduced pursuant to either an election under section 1071 or the application of section 1082(a)(2), then the basis of the property shall be increased to the extent of the gain recognized under section 1245(a)(1) by reason of the application of paragraph (e)(1)(iii) of § 1.1245-4. [Reg. § 1.1245-5.]

☐ [*T.D. 6832, 7-6-65.*]

Reg. § 1.1245-5(a)(1)

[Reg. § 1.1245-6]

§ 1.1245-6. Relation of section 1245 to other sections.—(a) *General.* The provisions of section 1245 apply notwithstanding any other provision of subtitle A of the Code. Thus, unless an exception or limitation under section 1245 (b) applies, gain under section 1245(a)(1) is recognized notwithstanding any contrary nonrecognition provision or income characterizing provision. For example, since section 1245 overrides section 1231 (relating to property used in the trade or business), the gain recognized under section 1245(a)(1) upon a disposition will be treated as ordinary income and only the remaining gain, if any, from the disposition may be considered as gain from the sale or exchange of a capital asset if section 1231 is applicable. See example (2) of paragraph (b)(2) of § 1.1245-1. For effect of section 1245 on basis provisions of the Code, see § 1.1245-5.

(b) *Nonrecognition sections overridden.* The nonrecognition provisions of subtitle A of the Code which section 1245 overrides include, but are not limited to, sections 267(d), 311(a), 336, 337, 501(a), 512(b)(5), and 1039. See section 1245(b) for the extent to which section 1245(a)(1) overrides sections 332, 351, 361, 371(a), 374(a), 721, 731, 1031, 1033, 1071, and 1081(b)(1) and (d)(1)(A). For limitation on amount of adjustments reflected in adjusted basis of property disposed of by an organization exempt from income taxes (within the meaning of section 501(a)), see paragraph (a)(8) of § 1.1245-2.

(c) *Normal retirement of asset in multiple asset account.* Section 1245(a)(1) does not require recognition of gain upon normal retirements of section 1245 property in a multiple asset account as long as the taxpayer's method of accounting, as described in paragraph (e)(2) of § 1.167(a)-8 (relating to accounting treatment of asset retirements), does not require recognition of such gain.

(d) *Installment method.* (1) Gain from a disposition to which section 1245(a)(1) applies may be reported under the installment method if such method is otherwise available under section 453 of the Code. In such case, the income (other than interest) on each installment payment shall be deemed to consist of gain to which section 1245(a)(1) applies until all such gain has been reported, and the remaining portion (if any) of such income shall be deemed to consist of gain to which section 1245(a)(1) does not apply. For treatment of amounts as interest on certain deferred payments, see section 483.

(2) The provisions of this paragraph may be illustrated by the following example:

Rules for Determining Capital Gains and Losses 53,527
See p. 20,601 for regulations not amended to reflect law changes

Example. Jones contracts to sell an item of section 1245 property for $10,000 to be paid in 10 equal payments of $1,000 each, plus a sufficient amount of interest so that section 483 does not apply. He properly elects under section 453 to report under the installment method gain of $2,000 to which section 1245(a)(1) applies and gain of $1,000 to which section 1231 applies. Accordingly, $300 of each of the first 6 installment payments and $200 of the seventh installment payment is ordinary income under section 1245(a)(1), and $100 of the seventh installment payment and $300 of each of the last 3 installment payments is gain under section 1231.

(e) *Exempt income.* The fact that section 1245 provides for recognition of gain as ordinary income does not change into taxable income any income which is exempt under section 115 (relating to income of states, etc.), 892 (relating to income of foreign governments), or 894 (relating to income exempt under treaties).

(f) *Treatment of gain not recognized under section 1245.* Section 1245 does not prevent gain which is not recognized under section 1245 from being considered as gain under another provision of the Code, such as, for example, section 311(c) (relating to liability in excess of basis), section 341(f) (relating to collapsible corporations), section 357(c) (relating to liabilities in excess of basis), section 1238 (relating to amortization in excess of depreciation), or section 1239 (relating to gain from sale of depreciable property between certain related persons). Thus, for example, if section 1245 property, which has an adjusted basis of $1,000 and a recomputed basis of $1,500, is sold for $1,750 in a transaction to which section 1239 applies, $500 of the gain would be recognized under section 1245(a)(1) and the remaining $250 of the gain would be treated as ordinary income under section 1239. [Reg. § 1.1245-6.]

☐ [T.D. 6832, 7-6-65. *Amended by* T.D. 7084, 1-7-71 *and* T.D. 7400, 2-3-76.]

[Reg. § 1.1247-1]

§ 1.1247-1. **Election by foreign investment companies to distribute income currently.—** (a) *Election by foreign investment company*—(1) *In general.* If a registered foreign investment company (as defined in paragraph (b) of this section) elects, on or before December 31, 1962, with respect to each of its taxable years beginning after December 31, 1962, to comply with the requirements of subparagraph (2) of this paragraph, then section 1246 (relating to gain on foreign investment company stock) shall not apply with respect to a qualified shareholder (as defined in paragraph (b) of § 1.1247-3) of such company who disposes of his stock during any taxable year of the company to which such election applies. See section 1247(a)(1).

(2) *Requirements.* A registered foreign investment company which makes an election under section 1247(a) shall, with respect to each of its taxable years beginning after December 31, 1962, comply with the following requirements:

(i) Under section 1247(a)(1)(A), the company shall distribute to its shareholders, during the taxable year, 90 percent or more of what its taxable income would be for such taxable year if it were a domestic corporation. To the extent elected by the company under section 1247(a)(2)(B), a distribution of taxable income made not later than 2 months and 15 days after the close of the taxable year shall be treated as distributed during such taxable year. For rules relating to computation of taxable income for a taxable year and distributions of such taxable income, see § 1.1247-2.

(ii) Under section 1247(a)(1)(B), the company shall designate to each shareholder the amount of his pro rata share of the excess of the net long-term capital gain over the net short-term capital loss for the taxable year and the amount thereof which is being distributed. For the manner of designating and the computation of such amounts, see § 1.1247-3.

(iii) Under section 1247(a)(1)(C), the company shall provide the information and maintain the records required by § 1.1247-5.

(b) *Definition of registered foreign investment company.* The term "registered foreign investment company" means a foreign corporation which is registered within the time specified in this paragraph under the Investment Company Act of 1940, as amended (15 U.S.C. 80a-1 to 80b-2), either as a management company or as a unit investment trust. Under such Act, a company is deemed registered upon receipt by the Securities and Exchange Commission of Form N-8A entitled "Notification of Registration Filed Pursuant to section 8(a) of the Investment Company Act of 1940". See section 8(a) of such Act (15 U.S.C. 80a-8(a)) and 17 CFR 274.10. A company which computes its income on the basis of a calendar year must have registered on or before December 31, 1962, and a company which computes its income on the basis of a fiscal year must have registered on or before the last day of its fiscal year beginning in 1962 and ending in 1963.

(c) *Time and manner of making election*—(1) *In general.* The election provided by paragraph (a) of this section must have been made on or before December 31, 1962, by means of a letter addressed to the Director of International Opera-

Reg. § 1.1247-1(c)(1)

tions, Internal Revenue Service, Washington 25, D.C., which clearly stated that the company elects to comply with the provisions of section 1247. The letter must have been signed by an officer of the foreign investment company who was a resident of the United States and who was duly authorized to act on behalf of the company.

(2) *Information furnished.* The following information must have been submitted in connection with the election:

(i) The name, address, and employer identification number, if any, and the taxable year of the company;

(ii) The principal place of business of the company;

(iii) The date and the country under whose laws the company was incorporated;

(iv) The date of filing with the Securities and Exchange Commission, and the file number, of Form N-8A;

(v) The names and addresses of all of the company's directors and officers and of any custodian or agent of the company located in the United States; and

(vi) The name and address of the person (or persons) in the United States having custody of the books of account, records, and other documents of the company, and the location of such books, records, and other documents if different from such address.

(3) *Time information furnished.* (i) If a foreign investment company was registered with the Securities and Exchange Commission on the date of election, all the information required by subparagraph (2) of this paragraph must have been submitted with the election.

(ii) If a foreign investment company made its election before it was so registered, the information required by subparagraph (2)(i), (ii), and (iii) of this paragraph must have been submitted with the election and the information required by subparagraph (2)(iv), (v), and (vi) of this paragraph must have been submitted within 60 days following receipt by the Securities and Exchange Commission of Form N-8A.

(d) *Termination of election*—(1) *General.* Section 1247(b) provides that the election of a foreign investment company under section 1247(a) shall permanently terminate as of the close of the taxable year preceding its first taxable year in which any of the following occurs:

(i) The company fails to comply with the provisions of section 1247(a)(1)(A), (B), or (C), unless it is shown that such failure is due to reasonable cause and not due to willful neglect;

(ii) The company is a foreign personal holding company as defined in section 552; or

(iii) The company ceases to be a registered foreign investment company which is described in paragraph (b) of this section. A company ceases to be a registered company, for example, as of the time the Securities and Exchange Commission revokes its order permitting registration of the company.

(2) *Reasonable cause.* Whether a failure by a foreign investment company to comply with the provisions of section 1247(a)(1)(A), (B), or (C) is due to reasonable cause and not due to willful neglect depends on whether the company exercised ordinary business care and prudence. For example, if in determining its taxable income under section 1247(a) the company relied in good faith upon estimates and opinions of independent certified public accountants or other experts which are also used for purposes of its financial statements filed with the Securities and Exchange Commission under the Investment Company Act of 1940, such reliance would constitute reasonable cause for purposes of this paragraph. In such a case, the company's election under section 1247(a) for the taxable year would not be terminated nor would the company be required to make an additional distribution for such taxable year in order to comply with the provisions of section 1247(a)(1)(A). [Reg. § 1.1247-1].

☐ [T.D. 6798, 2-3-65.]

[Reg. § 1.1247-2]

§ 1.1247-2. **Computation and distribution of taxable income.**—(a) *In general.* Taxable income of a foreign investment company means taxable income as defined in section 63(a), computed without regard to subchapter N, chapter 1 of the Code, and in accordance with the following rules:

(1) There shall be excluded the excess, if any, of the company's net long-term capital gain over the net short-term capital loss. See § 1.1247-3 for the manner of computing such excess.

(2) The deduction provided in section 172 (relating to net operating losses) shall not be allowed.

(3) Except for the deduction provided in section 248 (relating to organizational expenditures), the special deductions provided for corporations in part VIII (sections 241 and following), subchapter B, chapter 1 of the Code shall not be allowed.

(4) In computing the amount of the deduction allowed under section 164 there shall be included taxes paid or accrued during the taxable year which are imposed by the United States or by the country under the laws of which the com-

Rules for Determining Capital Gains and Losses

See p. 20,601 for regulations not amended to reflect law changes

pany is created or organized. See, however, § 1.1247-4.

(b) *Election to distribute taxable income after close of taxable year.* A company may elect under section 1247(a)(2)(B), in respect of taxable income for a taxable year, to treat a distribution made not later than 2 months and 15 days after the close of such taxable year as a distribution made during such taxable year of such taxable income. The company shall make the election by attaching to the information return required by paragraph (c)(1) of § 1.1247-5 for such taxable year a statement setting forth the amount of each distribution (or portion thereof) to which the election applies and the date of each such distribution. The election shall be irrevocable after the expiration of the time for filing such information return. The distribution (or portion thereof) to which the election applies shall be considered as paid out of the earnings and profits of the taxable year for which such election is made, and not out of the earnings and profits of the taxable year in which the distribution is actually made. A distribution to which this paragraph applies shall be includible in the gross income of a shareholder of the foreign investment company for his taxable year in which received or accrued. [Reg. § 1.1247-2.]

☐ [*T.D.* 6798, 2-3-65.]

[Reg. § 1.1247-3]

§ 1.1247-3. **Treatment of capital gains.**—(a) *Treatment by the company*—(1) *In general.* If an election to distribute income currently pursuant to section 1247(a) is in effect for a taxable year of a foreign investment company, the company shall designate (in the manner described in subparagraph (3) of this paragraph) to each shareholder his pro rata amount of the excess of the net long-term capital gain over the net short-term capital loss for the company's taxable year, and the portion thereof which is being distributed to each such shareholder. See section 1247(a)(1)(B). Except as provided in subparagraph (2) of this paragraph, the company shall compute such excess (hereinafter referred to as "excess capital gains") as if such company were a domestic corporation, but without regard to subchapter N, chapter 1 of the Code. See paragraph (d) of § 1.1247-1 for rules relating to termination of election under section 1247(a) for failure to properly compute or to properly designate excess capital gains. A company may make an irrevocable election (by notifying its shareholders as provided in subparagraph (3) of this paragraph) to distribute, on or before the 45th day following the close of its taxable year, all or a portion of the excess capital gains and have any such distribution treated as if made during such taxable year.

(2) *Rules for computing capital gains and losses.* Generally, the adjusted basis of property held by a foreign investment company shall be its cost adjusted in accordance with the applicable provisions of the Code. However, in respect of property held by a foreign investment company on the first day of the first taxable year for which the election under section 1247(a) applies, the amounts shown on such day in the permanent books of account, records, and other documents of the company shall, at the option of the company, be accepted as the adjusted basis of such property, if on such day such books, records, and other documents were being maintained in the manner prescribed by regulations under section 30 of the Investment Company Act of 1940 (15 U.S.C. 80a-30). In computing capital gains and losses of a foreign investment company under section 1247, the provisions of section 1212 (relating to allowance of capital loss carryover) shall not apply to any capital loss incurred in or with respect to taxable years before the first taxable year for which the election under section 1247(a) applies. See section 1247(a)(2)(C).

(3) *Notice to shareholders.* The company shall designate by written notice, mailed on or before the 45th day following the close of its taxable year—

(i) To each person who is a shareholder at the close of such taxable year, his pro rata amount of the portion of the excess capital gains for such year which was not distributed, and

(ii) To each person who received a distribution of excess capital gains with respect to such taxable year, the amount and the date of each such distribution.

Each notice shall show the name and address of the foreign investment company and the taxable year of the company for which the designation is made.

(b) *Treatment of capital gains by qualified shareholder*—(1) *Definition of qualified shareholder.* (i) The term "qualified shareholder" means any shareholder of a registered foreign investment company who is a United States person (as defined in section 7701(a)(30)), other than a shareholder described in subdivision (ii) of this subparagraph.

(ii) A United States person shall not be treated as a qualified shareholder for a taxable year if in his return for such taxable year (or for any prior taxable year) he did not include, in computing his long-term capital gains, his pro rata amount of the undistributed portion of the excess capital gains which the company designated for its taxable year ending within or with such taxable year of the shareholder. Thus, for

Reg. § 1.1247-3(b)(1)

53,530 Rules for Determining Capital Gains and Losses

See p. 20,601 for regulations not amended to reflect law changes

example, if a shareholder fails to include as long-term capital gain in his return for his taxable year ending December 31, 1966, the amount designated by the company as his pro rata amount of undistributed excess capital gains for the company's taxable year ending June 30, 1966, he would not be a qualified shareholder for his taxable year ending December 31, 1966, or for any subsequent taxable year. However, if the shareholder can show that his failure to include his pro rata amount of the undistributed portion of the excess capital gains in his return was due to reasonable cause and not due to willful neglect, he will continue to be a qualified shareholder. Such shareholder shall, for the year with respect to which such failure occurred, include in his taxable income his previously omitted pro rata amount of the undistributed portion of excess capital gains.

(2) *Treatment of excess capital gains.* A qualified shareholder of a foreign investment company, for any taxable year of the company for which the election under section 1247(a) is in effect, shall include in his return in computing his long-term capital gains—

(i) For his taxable year in which received, his pro rata amount of the distributed portion of the excess capital gains for such taxable year of the company, and

(ii) For his taxable year in which or with which the taxable year of the company ends, his pro rata amount of the undistributed portion of the excess capital gains for such taxable year of the company.

(3) *Sales at end of company's taxable year.* For purposes of determining whether the purchaser or seller of a share of foreign investment company stock is the shareholder at the close of such company's taxable year who is required to include an amount of undistributed excess capital gains in gross income, the amount of the undistributed excess capital gains shall be treated in the same manner as a cash dividend payable to shareholders of record at the close of the company's taxable year. Thus, if a cash dividend paid to shareholders of record as of the close of the foreign investment company's taxable year would be considered income to the purchaser, then the purchaser is also considered to be the shareholder of such company at the close of its taxable year for purposes of including an amount of undistributed excess capital gains in gross income. For rules for determining whether a dividend is income to the purchaser or seller of a share of stock, see paragraph (c) of § 1.61-9.

(4) *Partners and partnerships.* If the shareholder required to include an amount of undistributed excess capital gains in gross income under section 1247(d)(2) and subparagraph (2)(ii) of this paragraph is a partnership, such amount shall be taken into account by the partnership for the taxable year of the partnership in which occurs the last day of the taxable year of the foreign investment company in respect of which the undistributed portion of the excess capital gains were designated. The amount so includible by the partnership shall be taken into account by the partners as distributive shares of the partnership gains and losses from sales or exchanges of capital assets held for more than 1 year (6 months for taxable years beginning before 1977; 9 months for taxable years beginning in 1977) pursuant to section 702(a)(2) and paragraph (a)(2) of § 1.702-1. The partners shall increase the basis of their partnership interests under section 705(a)(1) by their distributive shares of such gains.

(5) *Effect on earnings and profits of corporate shareholder.* If a shareholder required to include an amount of undistributed excess capital gains in gross income under section 1247(d)(2) and subparagraph (2)(ii) of this paragraph is a corporation, such corporation, in computing its earnings and profits for the taxable year for which such amount is so includible, shall treat such amount as if it had actually been received in that year.

(6) *Example.* The application of this paragraph may be illustrated by the following example:

Example. Smith owns one share of stock in a foreign investment company which he purchased in 1964. In respect of the company's taxable year ending June 30, 1966, during which the election under section 1247(a) was in effect, Smith receives from the company on July 15, 1966, a distribution in the amount of $8. He also receives a notice stating that for such taxable year $9 was being designated as his pro rata amount of the excess capital gains, $8 of which was distributed on July 15, 1966, and $1 of which was being designated as the undistributed portion. In order for Smith to be a qualified shareholder for his taxable year ending December 31, 1966, he must include in computing his long-term capital gains in his return for 1966, his pro rata amount of the undistributed portion of the excess capital gains, that is, $1. Smith must also include in such return his pro rata amount of the distributed portion of excess capital gains, that is, $8. If, however, Smith does not include in income his pro rata amount of the undistributed portion of excess capital gains, he is not a qualified shareholder for 1966 (or for any subsequent year). In such a case, the $8 is not treated under the provisions of section 1247(d)(1) as a distribution of long-term

Reg. § 1.1247-3(b)(2)

capital gains for such year but as a corporate distribution taxable as ordinary income to the extent provided in subchapter C, chapter 1 of the Code.

(c) *Adjustments relating to undistributed capital gains*—(1) *Adjustments in earnings and profits of the company.* If a foreign investment company, to which the election under section 1247(a) applies, designates an amount as the undistributed portion of excess capital gains for its taxable year, the earnings and profits of the company (within the meaning of subchapter C, chapter 1 of the Code) shall be reduced, and its capital account shall be increased, by such amount.

(2) *Increase in basis of qualified shareholder's stock.* A qualified shareholder, who computes his long-term capital gains for a taxable year by including (in respect of each share of stock which he owns in a foreign investment company) the pro rata amount of the undistributed portion of the excess capital gains which was designated by the company for its taxable year ending with or within such taxable year of the shareholder, shall, as of the day following the close of such taxable year of the company, increase the adjusted basis of each share by such pro rata amount.

(d) *Loss on sale or exchange of certain stock held 1 year or less*—(1) *In general.* If—

(i) A qualified shareholder of a foreign investment company to which the election under section 1247(a) applies treats any amount designated under section 1247(a)(1)(B) with respect to a share of stock as long-term capital gain, and

(ii) Such share is held by the taxpayer for 1 year (6 months for taxable years beginning before 1977; 9 months for taxable years beginning in 1977) or less,

then any loss on the sale or exchange of such share shall, to the extent of the amount described in subdivision (i) of this subparagraph, be treated under section 1247(i) as loss from the sale or exchange of a capital asset held for more than 1 year (6 months for taxable years beginning before 1977; 9 months for taxable years beginning in 1977).

(2) *Example.* The application of this paragraph may be illustrated by the following example:

Example. On October 1, 1966, B, a calendar year taxpayer, purchases for $100 a share of stock in a foreign investment company to which the election under section 1247(a) applies. On January 20, 1967, the company, in a notice to B, designates for its taxable year ending December 31, 1966, $8 per share as excess capital gains of which $6 was distributed on December 1, 1966, and $2 was designated as undistributed. B includes the $8 in computing his long-term capital gains in his return for 1966 and, under paragraph (c)(2) of this section, B's basis for the share is increased to $102 as of January 1, 1967. On February 1, 1967, B sells the share for $93, incurring a $9 loss of which $8 is treated as a long-term capital loss under section 1247(i) and $1 is treated as a short-term capital loss. [Reg. § 1.1247-3.]

☐ [*T.D.* 6798, 2-3-65. Amended by *T.D.* 7728, 10-31-80.]

[Reg. § 1.1247-4]

§ 1.1247-4. **Election by foreign investment company with respect to foreign tax credit.**— (a) *In general*—(1) *Election.* If an election to distribute income currently pursuant to section 1247(a) is in effect for a taxable year of a foreign investment company, and if at the close of such taxable year more than 50 percent of the value of the total assets of the company consists of stock or securities in foreign corporations, then the company may elect for such taxable year, in the manner provided in paragraph (d) of this section, the application of section 1247(f) in respect of foreign taxes referred to in subparagraph (2) of this paragraph which are paid during such taxable year. For purposes of this section, the term "value" shall have the same meaning as assigned to such term in section 851(c)(4) (relating to definition of regulated investment company). For definition of foreign corporation, see section 7701(a).

(2) *Taxes affected.* The election under section 1247(f) for a taxable year applies with respect to income, war profits, and excess profits taxes described in section 901(b)(1) which are paid by the company to foreign countries and possessions of the United States. A tax paid by a foreign investment company does not include a tax which is paid by the shareholders of the company. Whether a tax is paid by the company, and whether a tax is an income, war profits, or excess profits tax described in section 901(b)(1), shall be determined under the principles of chapter 1 of the Code without regard to the law of any foreign country and without regard to any income tax convention, including any income tax convention to which the United States is a party. Section 1247(f) does not apply with respect to foreign taxes which would be deemed to have been paid by the company under section 902 if the company were a domestic corporation. For purposes of this paragraph, taxes paid to the United States are not considered foreign taxes.

(b) *Effect of election*—(1) *Effect on company.* If a valid election under section 1247(f) is made for a taxable year of a foreign investment company, then, for purposes of determining under section 1247(a)(1)(A) whether the company has distributed to its shareholders with respect to such taxable year 90 percent or more of what the company's taxable income would be for such year if the company were a domestic corporation, the following rules shall apply:

(i) The company shall compute such taxable income without any deduction for the foreign taxes referred to in paragraph (a)(2) of this section which were paid or accrued during the taxable year.

(ii) If the amount of taxable income (computed without regard to subdivision (i) of this subparagraph) is more than zero, the company shall treat the foreign taxes referred to in paragraph (a)(2) of this section which were paid during such taxable year of the company as distributed to its shareholders to the extent of the amount which bears the same ratio to the amount of such foreign taxes as (a) the amount actually distributed (or treated as distributed pursuant to an election under section 1247(a)(2)(B)) during such taxable year from such taxable income (determined without regard to subdivision (i) of this subparagraph), bears to (b) the amount of such taxable income (also determined without regard to such subdivision (i)). Thus, for example, if for a taxable year a foreign investment company has taxable income of $1,000 (determined after deducting foreign taxes paid of $100), and if $600 of such taxable income is distributed during the taxable year and $350 of such taxable income is distributed not later than 2 months and 15 days after the close of the taxable year, then $950 is treated as distributed for purposes of satisfying the 90-percent distribution requirement of section 1247(a)(1)(A), and the amount of foreign taxes treated as distributed under this subdivision is $95 (that is, $100 multiplied by $950/$1,000).

(iii) If the amount of taxable income (computed without regard to subdivision (i) of this subparagraph) is zero, then all foreign taxes referred to in paragraph (a)(2) of this section which were paid during the taxable year shall be treated as distributed by the company on the last day of such taxable year. Thus, for example, if for a taxable year a foreign investment company has taxable income of $500 (computed without deducting $800 of foreign taxes paid during such year), the amount of taxable income computed without regard to subdivision (i) of this paragraph is zero, and the $800 of foreign taxes is treated as distributed under this subdivision on the last day of the company's taxable year.

(2) *Effect on qualified shareholders.* The following rules apply to a qualified shareholder of a foreign investment company which makes a valid election under section 1247(f) for a taxable year:

(i) The qualified shareholder shall include in his gross income (in addition to taxable dividends actually received) his proportionate share of the foreign taxes referred to in paragraph (a)(2) of this section which were paid during such taxable year of the company, and shall treat such proportionate share as paid by him for purposes of the deduction under section 164(a) and the foreign tax credit under section 901. See, however, paragraph (c)(1) of this section for a limitation on the amount a shareholder may treat as his proportionate share of foreign taxes.

(ii) In respect of any distribution made (or treated as made under section 1247(a)(2)(B)) during the taxable year of the company and which is received by a qualified shareholder, the term "proportionate share of foreign taxes" means, for purposes of this section, an amount which bears the same ratio to (a) the amount of the foreign taxes referred to in paragraph (a)(2) of this section which were paid during such taxable year of the company, as (b) the amount of such distribution to the shareholder out of the company's taxable income for such taxable year (determined without regard to subparagraph (1)(i) of this paragraph), bears to (c) the amount of such taxable income (also determined without regard to such subparagraph (1)(i)).

(iii) In respect of any distribution of foreign taxes treated as made under subparagraph (1)(iii) of this paragraph on the last day of the taxable year of the company, the term "proportionate share of foreign taxes" means, for purposes of this section, an amount which bears the same ratio to (a) the amount of foreign taxes referred to in paragraph (a)(2) of this section which were paid during such taxable year of the company, as (b) the fair market value of all shares of stock of the company held by such qualified shareholder on the last day of such taxable year, bears to (c) the fair market value of all such shares outstanding on such last day.

(iv) For purposes of the foreign tax credit, the qualified shareholder shall treat his proportionate share of foreign taxes as having been paid by him to the country in which the foreign investment company is created or organized.

(v) For purposes of the foreign tax credit, the qualified shareholder shall treat as gross income from sources within the country in which the foreign investment company is created or organized the sum of (a) his proportionate share of foreign taxes, (b) any dividend paid to him by such foreign investment company, and (c) his pro rata amount of distributed and undistributed por-

Reg. § 1.1247-4(b)(2)

Rules for Determining Capital Gains and Losses

See p. 20,601 for regulations not amended to reflect law changes

tions of excess capital gains referred to in paragraph (a) of § 1.1247-3.

(vi) (a) In respect of a distribution made (or treated as made under section 1247(a)(2)(B)) during a taxable year of the company, a qualified shareholder shall consider his proportionate share of foreign taxes as having been received, and as having been paid, by him during his taxable year in which the distribution is includible in his gross income.

(b) In respect of an amount of foreign taxes treated as distributed under subparagraph (1)(iii) of this paragraph on the last day of a taxable year of the company, the qualified shareholder shall consider his proportionate share of foreign taxes as having been received, and as having been paid, by him during his taxable year in which such last day falls.

(vii) If the qualified shareholder is a corporation, it shall not be deemed under section 902 to have paid any taxes paid by the foreign investment company to which the election under section 1247(f) applied.

(3) *Effect on nonqualified shareholders.* A shareholder who is not a qualified shareholder shall not include his proportionate share of foreign taxes in gross income, and shall not be entitled to treat such proportionate share as having been paid by him to a foreign country for purposes of the deduction under section 164(a) or, except to the extent that section 902 is applicable, for purposes of the foreign tax credit under section 901.

(4) *Example.* The application of paragraph (a) of this section and this paragraph may be illustrated by the following examples:

Example (1). (i) X Corporation, a foreign investment company incorporated in country C with 100,000 shares of stock outstanding, uses the calendar year as its taxable year. For 1964, X Corporation has the following income and pays the following foreign taxes:

Dividend income, minus operating expenses	$675,000
Foreign income taxes paid:	
Withheld by country A	$25,000
Withheld by country B	50,000
Income tax of country C	90,000
Total foreign income tax paid	165,000
Taxable income for purposes of section 1247(a)(1)(A), determined without regard to section 1247(f)	$510,000

X Corporation distributes to its shareholders the amount of $459,000 (i.e., 90 percent of $510,000).

(ii) Assume that X Corporation validly elects the application of section 1274(f). Accordingly, X Corporation determines that its taxable income for purposes of section 1247(a)(1)(A) without any deduction for foreign income taxes paid or accrued is $675,000 ($510,000, plus $165,000).

(iii) Assume that X Corporation intends to distribute the least amount which would satisfy the requirements of section 1247(a)(1)(A), as modified by the election under section 1247(f). Thus, the total amount X distributes is $607,500, which consists of the sum of (a) $459,000 actually distributed, that is, 90 percent of $510,000 of taxable income (determined after the deduction for foreign taxes), plus (b) foreign taxes paid of $148,500 which are treated as distributed, that is, 90 percent of $165,000 of foreign taxes paid by X Corporation.

Example (2). Assume the same facts as in example (1) except that X Corporation distributes the entire $510,000 in the following manner: On December 15, 1964, X Corporation distributes $170,000 as a dividend of $1.70 per share. On February 25, 1965, X Corporation distributes the remaining $340,000 as a dividend of $3.40 per share pursuant to an election under section 1247(a)(2)(B) to treat such distribution as if made in 1964. Assume that Brown, a qualified shareholder, uses the calendar year as his taxable year. The amount of $0.55 per share (that is, $165,000, multiplied by $1.70/$510,000) must be treated by Brown as foreign taxes paid by him in 1964 to country C and the amount of $1.10 per share (that is, $165,000 multiplied by $3.40/$510,000) must be similarly treated by Brown in 1965. The amount of $2.25 per share ($1.70 of dividends actually received plus $0.55 representing foreign taxes paid) must be reported by Brown as income considered received in 1964 from country C, and the amount of $4.50 per share ($3.40 of dividends actually received plus $1.10 representing foreign taxes paid) must be so reported by Brown in 1965.

Example (3). A foreign investment company organized under the laws of country C receives a dividend of $1,000 from X Corporation, which is also organized under the laws of country C. Under the laws of country C, the foreign investment company would, if it so elects, be considered as having paid income tax in the amount of $150 which X Corporation paid to country C with respect to the earnings from which the dividend was

Reg. § 1.1247-4(b)(4)

paid. If the foreign investment company were a domestic corporation, however, it would not be considered for purposes of section 901(b)(1) as having paid the tax actually paid by X Corporation. Accordingly, the election under section 1247(f) does not apply in respect of the $150. The result would be the same if X Corporation was organized under the laws of any other foreign country to which it paid taxes and if the laws of country C permitted the foreign investment company to be considered as the payor of such taxes.

(c) *Notice to shareholders*—(1) *In general.* If, in the manner provided in paragraph (d) of this section, a foreign investment company makes an election with respect to the foreign tax credit under section 1247(f), the company shall furnish to each shareholder a written notice mailed not later than 45 days after the close of the taxable year of the company for which the election is made, designating the shareholder's proportionate share of the foreign taxes referred to in paragraph (a)(2) of this section which were paid by the company during such taxable year. This notice may be combined with the written notice to shareholders described in paragraph (a)(3) of § 1.1247-3 relating to excess capital gains.

(2) *Application to shareholder.* For purposes of paragraph (b)(2) of this section, the amount which a shareholder may treat as his proportionate share of foreign taxes paid by the company shall not exceed the amounts so designated by the company in such written notice. If, however, an amount designated by the company in a notice exceeds the shareholder's proper proportionate share of such foreign taxes, the shareholder is limited to the amount correctly determined.

(d) *Manner of making election*—(1) *In general.* The election of a foreign investment company to have section 1247(f) apply for a taxable year shall be made by filing as part of its information return required by paragraph (c)(1) of § 1.1247-5 a Form 1118 modified so that it becomes a statement in support of the election made by the company under section 1247(f).

(2) *Irrevocability of election.* An election under section 1247(f) for a taxable year of a foreign investment company shall be made with respect to all foreign taxes referred to in paragraph (a)(2) of this section which were paid during such taxable year, and must be made not later than the time prescribed for filing the information return under paragraph (c)(1) of § 1.1247-5. Such election, if made, shall be irrevocable with respect to the distributions, and the foreign taxes with respect thereto, to which the election applies. [Reg. § 1.1247-4.]

☐ [*T.D.* 6798, 2-3-65.]

Reg. § 1.1247-5(a)

[Reg. § 1.1247-5]

§ 1.1247-5. Information and record keeping requirements.—(a) *General.* In order to carry out the purposes of section 1247, a foreign investment company shall keep the records and comply with the information requirements prescribed by this section for each taxable year of the company for which the election under section 1247(a) is in effect. See section 1247(a)(1)(C).

(b) *Record keeping requirements.* The company shall maintain and preserve such permanent books of account, records, and other documents as are sufficient to establish in accordance with the provisions of § 1.1247-2 what its taxable income would be if it were a domestic corporation. Generally, if the books and records of the company are maintained in the manner prescribed by regulations under section 30 of the Investment Company Act of 1940 (15 U.S.C. 80a-30), the requirements of the preceding sentence shall be considered satisfied. Such books, records, and other documents shall be available for inspection in the United States by authorized internal revenue officers or employees, and shall be maintained so long as the contents thereof may be material in the administration of section 1247.

(c) *Information returns.* The company shall file, for each taxable year during which the election under section 1247(a) is in effect, on or before the 15th day of the third month following the close of its taxable year or on or before May 1, 1965, whichever is later, with the Director of International Operations, Internal Revenue Service, Washington, D.C. 20225—

(1) Form 1120, modified so as to be an annual information return, establishing the amount of its taxable income referred to in paragraph (b) of this section, and

(2) Form 2438, modified so as to be an annual information return, establishing the amount of the company's excess capital gains (referred to in paragraph (a)(1) of § 1.1247-3) for the taxable year, the distributed portion thereof, and the amount of the undistributed portion thereof. [Reg. § 1.1247-5.]

☐ [*T.D.* 6798, 2-3-65.]

[Reg. § 1.1248-1]

§ 1.1248-1. Treatment of gain from certain sales or exchanges of stock in certain foreign corporations.—(a) *In general.* (1) If a United States person (as defined in section 7701(a)(30)) recognizes gain on a sale or exchange after December 31, 1962, of stock in a foreign corporation, and if in respect of such person the conditions of subparagraph (2) of this paragraph are satisfied, then the gain shall be included in the gross income

Rules for Determining Capital Gains and Losses

of such person as a dividend to the extent of the earnings and profits of such corporation attributable to such stock under § 1.1248-2 or 1.1248-3, whichever is applicable, which were accumulated in taxable years of such foreign corporation beginning after December 31, 1962, during the period or periods such stock was held (or was considered as held by reason of the application of section 1223) by such person while such corporation was a controlled foreign corporation. See section 1248(a). For computation of earnings and profits attributable to such stock if there are any "lower tier" corporations, see paragraph (a)(3) and (4) of § 1.1248-2 or paragraph (a) of § 1.1248-3, whichever is applicable. In general, the amount of gain to be included in a person's gross income as a dividend under section 1248(a) shall be determined separately for each share of stock sold or exchanged. However, such determination may be made in respect of a block of stock if earnings and profits attributable to the block are computed under § 1.1248-2 or 1.1248-3. See paragraph (b) of § 1.1248-2 and paragraph (a)(5) of § 1.1248-3. For the limitation on the tax attributable to an amount included in an individual's gross income as a dividend under section 1248(a), see section 1248(b) and § 1.1248-4. For the treatment, under certain circumstances, of the sale or exchange of stock in a domestic corporation as the sale or exchange of stock held by the domestic corporation in a foreign corporation, see section 1248(e) and § 1.1248-6. For the nonapplication of section 1248 in certain circumstances, see section 1248(f) and paragraph (e) of this section. For the requirement that the person establish the amount of earnings and profits attributable to the stock sold or exchanged and, for purposes of section 1248(b), the amount of certain taxes, see section 1248(g) and § 1.1248-7.

(2) In respect of a United States person who sells or exchanges stock in a foreign corporation, the conditions referred to in subparagraph (1) of this paragraph are satisfied only if (i) such person owned, within the meaning of section 958(a), or was considered as owning by applying the rules of ownership of section 958(b), 10 percent or more of the total combined voting power of all classes of stock entitled to vote of such foreign corporation at any time during the 5-year period ending on the date of the sale or exchange, and (ii) at such time such foreign corporation was a controlled foreign corporation (as defined in section 957).

(3) For purposes of subparagraph (2) of this paragraph, (i) a foreign corporation shall not be considered to be a controlled foreign corporation at any time before the first day of its first taxable year beginning after December 31, 1962, and (ii) the percentage of the total combined voting power of stock of a foreign corporation owned (or considered as owned) by a United States person shall be determined in accordance with the principles of section 951(b) and the regulations thereunder.

(4) The application of this paragraph may be illustrated by the following examples:

Example (1). Corporation F is a foreign corporation which has outstanding 100 shares of one class of stock. F was a controlled foreign corporation for the period beginning on January 1, 1963, and ending on June 30, 1965, but was not a controlled foreign corporation at any time thereafter. On December 31, 1965, Brown, a United States person who has owned 15 shares of F stock since 1962, sells 7 of his 15 shares and recognizes gain with respect to each share sold. Since Brown owned stock representing at least 10 percent of the total combined voting power of F at a time during the 5-year period ending on December 31, 1965, while F was a controlled foreign corporation, the conditions of subparagraph (2) of this paragraph are satisfied. Therefore, section 1248(a) applies to the gain recognized by Brown to the extent of the earnings and profits attributable under § 1.1248-3 to such shares.

Example (2). Assume the same facts as in example (1). Assume further that on February 1, 1970, Brown sells the remainder of his shares in F Corporation and recognizes gain with respect to each share sold. Even though Brown did not own stock representing at least 10 percent of the total combined voting power of F on February 1, 1970, nevertheless, in respect of each of the 8 shares of F stock which he sold on such date, the conditions of subparagraph (2) of this paragraph are satisfied since Brown owned stock representing at least 10 percent of such voting power at a time during the 5-year period ending on February 1, 1970, while F was a controlled foreign corporation. Therefore, section 1248(a) applies to the gain recognized by Brown to the extent of the earnings and profits attributable under § 1.1248-3 to such shares. If, however, Brown had sold the remainder of his shares in F on July 1, 1970, since the last date on which Brown owned stock representing at least 10 percent of the total combined voting power of F while F was a controlled foreign corporation was June 30, 1965, a date which is not within the 5-year period ending July 1, 1970, the conditions of subparagraph (2) of this paragraph would not be satisfied and section 1248(a) would not apply.

Example (3). Corporation G, a foreign corporation created in 1950, has outstanding 100 shares of one class of stock and uses the calendar year as its taxable year. Corporation X, a United States person, owns 60 shares of G stock and has owned

Reg. § 1.1248-1(a)(4)

such stock since G was created. Corporation Y, a United States person, owned 15 shares of the G stock from 1950 until December 1, 1962, on which date it sold 10 of such shares. On December 31, 1963, Y sells its remaining 5 shares of the G stock and recognizes gain on the sale. Since G is not considered to be a controlled foreign corporation at any time before January 1, 1963, and since Y did not own stock representing at least 10 percent of the total combined voting power of G at any time on or after such date, the conditions of subparagraph (2) of this paragraph are not satisfied and section 1248(a) does not apply.

(b) *Sale or exchange.* For purposes of this section and §§ 1.1248-2 through 1.1248-7, the term "sale or exchange" includes the receipt of a distribution which is treated as in exchange for stock under section 302(a) (relating to distributions in redemption of stock), section 331(a)(1) (relating to distributions in complete liquidation of a corporation), or section 331(a)(2) (relating to distributions in partial liquidation of a corporation).

(c) *Gain recognized.* Section 1248(a) applies to a sale or exchange of stock in a foreign corporation only if gain is recognized in whole or in part upon such sale or exchange. Thus, for example, if a United States person exchanges stock in a foreign corporation, and if under section 332, 351, 354, 355, or 361 no gain is recognized as a result of a determination by the Commissioner under section 367 that the exchange is not in pursuance of a plan having as one of its principal purposes the avoidance of Federal income taxes, then no amount is includible in the gross income of such person as a dividend under section 1248(a).

(d) *Credit for foreign taxes.* (1) If a domestic corporation includes an amount in its gross income as a dividend under section 1248(a) upon a sale or exchange of stock in a foreign corporation (referred to as a "first tier" corporation), and if on the date of the sale or exchange the domestic corporation owns directly at least 10 percent of the voting stock of the first tier corporation—

(i) The foreign tax credit provisions of sections 901 through 908 shall apply in the same manner and subject to the same conditions and limitations as if the first tier corporation on such date distributed to the domestic corporation as a dividend that portion of the amount included in gross income under section 1248(a) which does not exceed the earnings and profits of the first tier corporation attributable to the stock under § 1.1248-2 or § 1.1248-3, as the case may be, and

(ii) If on such date such first tier corporation owns directly 50 percent or more of the voting stock of a "lower tier" corporation described in paragraph (a)(3) of § 1.1248-2 or paragraph (a)(3) of § 1.1248-3, as the case may be (referred to as a "second tier" corporation), then the foreign tax credit provisions of sections 901 through 905 shall apply in the same manner and subject to the same conditions and limitations as if on such date (a) the domestic corporation owned directly that percentage of the stock in the second tier corporation which such domestic corporation is considered to own by reason of the application of section 958(a)(2), and (b) the second tier corporation had distributed to the domestic corporation as a dividend that portion of the amount included in gross income under section 1248(a) which does not exceed the earnings and profits of the second tier corporation attributable to such stock under § 1.1248-2 or § 1.1248-3, as the case may be.

(2) A credit shall not be allowed under subparagraph (1) of this paragraph in respect of taxes which are not actually paid or accrued. For the inclusion as a dividend in the gross income of a domestic corporation of an amount equal to the taxes deemed paid by such corporation under section 902(a)(1), see section 78.

(3) If subparagraph (1)(ii) of this paragraph applies, and if the amount included in gross income under section 1248(a) upon the sale or exchange of the stock in a first tier corporation described in subparagraph (1)(ii) of this paragraph is less than the sum of the earnings and profits of the first tier corporation attributable to such stock under § 1.1248-2 or § 1.1248-3, as the case may be, plus the earnings and profits of the second tier corporation attributable to such stock under § 1.1248-2 or 1.1248-3, as the case may be, then the amount considered distributed to the domestic corporation as a dividend shall be determined by multiplying the amount included in gross income under section 1248(a) by—

(i) For purposes of applying subparagraph (1)(i) of this paragraph, the percentage that (a) the earnings and profits of the first tier corporation attributable to such stock under § 1.1248-2 or § 1.1248-3, as the case may be, bears to (b) the sum of the earnings and profits of the first tier corporation attributable to such stock under § 1.1248-2 or § 1.1248-3, as the case may be, plus the earnings and profits of the second tier corporation attributable to such stock under § 1.1248-2 or § 1.1248-3, as the case may be, and

(ii) For purposes of applying subparagraph (1)(ii) of this paragraph, the percentage that (a) the earnings and profits of the second tier corporation attributable to such stock under § 1.1248-2 or 1.1248-3, as the case may be, bears to (b) the sum referred to in subdivision (i)(b) of this subparagraph.

Reg. § 1.1248-1(b)

Rules for Determining Capital Gains and Losses

(4) The provisions of this paragraph may be illustrated by the following examples:

Example (1). On June 30, 1964, domestic corporation D owns 10 percent of the voting stock of controlled foreign corporation X. On such date, D sells a share of X stock and includes $200 of the gain on the sale in its gross income as a dividend under section 1248(a). X does not own any stock of a lower tier corporation referred to in paragraph (a)(3) of § 1.1248-3. D uses the calendar year as its taxable year and instead of deducting foreign taxes under section 164, D chooses the benefits of the foreign tax credit provisions for 1964. If D had included $200 in its gross income as a dividend with respect to a distribution from X on June 30, 1964, the amount of the foreign income taxes paid by X which D would be deemed to have paid under section 902(a) in respect of such distribution would be $60. Thus, in respect of the $200 included in D's gross income as a dividend under section 1248(a), and subject to the applicable limitations and conditions of sections 901 through 905, D is entitled under this paragraph to a foreign tax credit of $60 for 1964.

Example (2). On June 30, 1965, domestic corporation D owns all of the voting stock of foreign corporation Y, and Y (the first tier corporation) owns all of the voting stock of foreign corporation Z (a second tier corporation). On such date, D sells a block of Y stock and includes $400 of the gain on the sale in its gross income as a dividend under section 1248(a). The earnings and profits attributable under § 1.1248-3 to the block are $600 from Y and $1,800 from Z. D uses the calendar year as its taxable year and instead of deducting foreign taxes under section 164, D chooses the benefits of the foreign tax credit provisions for 1965. For purposes of applying the foreign tax credit provisions, Y is considered under subparagraph (3) of this paragraph to have distributed to D a dividend of $100 ($400 × 600/2400) and Z is considered to have so distributed to D a dividend of $300 ($400 × 1800/2400). If D had included $100 in its gross income as a dividend with respect to a distribution from Y on June 30, 1965, the amount of foreign income taxes paid by Y which D would be deemed to have paid under section 902(a) in respect of such distribution is $80. If D had owned the stock in Z directly, and if D had included $300 in its gross income as a dividend with respect to a distribution from Z, the amount of foreign income taxes paid by Z which D would be deemed to have paid under section 902(a) in respect of such distribution is $120. Thus, in respect of the $400 included in D's gross income as a dividend under section 1248(a), and subject to the applicable limitations and conditions of sections 901 through 905, D is entitled under this paragraph to a foreign tax credit of $200 ($80 plus $120) for 1965.

(e) *Exceptions.* Under section 1248(f), this section and § § 1.1248-2 through 1.1248-7 shall not apply to—

(1) Distributions to which section 303 (relating to distributions in redemption of stock to pay death taxes) applies;

(2) Gain realized on exchanges to which section 356 (relating to receipt of additional consideration in certain reorganizations) applies; or

(3) Any amount to the extent that such amount is, under any other provision of the Code, treated as (i) a dividend, (ii) gain from the sale of an asset which is not a capital asset, or (iii) gain from the sale of an asset held for not more than 1 year (6 months for taxable years beginning before 1977; 9 months for taxable years beginning in 1977).

(f) *Installment method.* (1) Gain from a sale or exchange to which section 1248 applies may be reported under the installment method if such method is otherwise available under section 453 of the Code. In such case, the income (other than interest) in each installment payment shall be deemed to consist of gain which is included in gross income under section 1248 as a dividend until all such gain has been reported, and the remaining portion (if any) of such income shall be deemed to consist of gain to which section 1248 does not apply. For treatment of amounts as interest on certain deferred payments, see section 483.

(2) The application of this paragraph may be illustrated by the following example:

Example. Jones contracts to sell stock in a controlled foreign corporation for $5,000 to be paid in 10 equal payments of $500 each, plus a sufficient amount of interest so that section 483 does not apply. He properly elects under section 453 to report under the installment method gain of $1,000 which is includible in gross income under section 1248 as a dividend and gain of $500 which is a long-term capital gain. Accordingly, $150 of each of the first 6 installment payments and $100 of the seventh installment payment are included in gross income under section 1248 as a dividend, and $50 of the seventh installment payment and $150 of each of the last 3 installment payments are long-term capital gain. [Reg. § 1.1248-1.]

☐ [T.D. 6779, 12-21-64. Amended by T.D. 7728, 10-31-80 *and* T.D. 7961, 6-20-84.]

Reg. § 1.1248-1(f)(2)

[Reg. § 1.1248-2]

§ 1.1248-2. Earnings and profits attributable to a block of stock in simple cases.—(a) *General*—(1) *Manner of computation.* For purposes of paragraph (a)(1) of § 1.1248-1, if a United States person sells or exchanges a block of stock (as defined in paragraph (b) of this section) in a foreign corporation, and if the conditions of paragraph (c) of this section are satisfied in respect of the block, then the earnings and profits attributable to the block which were accumulated in taxable years of the corporation beginning after December 31, 1962, during the period such block was held (or was considered to be held by reason of the application of section 1223) by such person while such corporation was a controlled foreign corporation, shall be computed in accordance with the steps set forth in subparagraphs (2), (3), and (4) of this paragraph.

(2) *Step 1.* (i) For each taxable year of the corporation beginning after December 31, 1962, the earnings and profits accumulated for each such taxable year by the corporation shall be computed in the manner prescribed in paragraph (d) of this section, and (ii) for the period the person held (or is considered to have held by reason of the application of section 1223) the block, the amount of earnings and profits attributable to the block shall be computed in the manner prescribed in paragraph (e) of this section.

(3) *Step 2.* If the conditions of paragraph (c)(5)(ii) of this section must be satisfied in respect of stock in a "lower tier" foreign corporation which such person owns within the meaning of section 958(a)(2), then (i) the earnings and profits accumulated for each such taxable year by such lower tier corporation shall be computed in the manner prescribed in paragraph (d) of this section, and (ii) for the period the person held (or is considered to have held by reason of the application of section 1223) the block, the amount of earnings and profits of the lower tier corporation attributable to the block shall be computed in the manner prescribed in paragraph (e) of this section applied as if such person owned directly the percentage of such stock in such lower tier corporation which such person owns within the meaning of section 958(a)(2).

(4) *Step 3.* The amount of earnings and profits attributable to the block shall be the sum of the amounts computed under steps 1 and 2.

(b) *Block of stock.* For purposes of this section, the term "block of stock" means a group of shares sold or exchanged in one transaction, but only if—

(1) The amount realized, basis, and holding period are identical for each such share, and

(2) In case, during the period the person held (or is considered to have held by reason of the application of section 1223) such shares, any amount was included under section 951 in the gross income of the person (or another person) in respect of the shares, the excess under paragraph (e)(3)(ii) of this section (computed as if each share were a block) is identical for each such share.

(c) *Conditions to application.* This section shall apply only if the following conditions are satisfied:

(1) (i) On each day of the period during which the block of stock was held (or is considered as held by reason of the application of section 1223) by the person during taxable years of the corporation beginning after December 31, 1962, the corporation is a controlled foreign corporation, and (ii) on no such day is the corporation a foreign personal holding company (as defined in section 552) or a foreign investment company (as defined in section 1246(b)).

(2) The corporation had only one class of stock, and the same number of shares of such stock were outstanding, on each day of each taxable year of the corporation beginning after December 31, 1962, any day of which falls within the period referred to in subparagraph (1) of this paragraph.

(3) For each taxable year referred to in subparagraph (2) of this paragraph, the corporation is not a less developed country corporation (as defined in section 902(d)).

(4) For each taxable year referred to in subparagraph (2) of this paragraph, the corporation does not make any distributions out of its earnings and profits other than distributions which, under section 316 (as modified by section 959), are considered to be out of earnings and profits accumulated in taxable years beginning after December 31, 1962, during the period such person held (or is considered to have held by reason of the application of section 1223) the block while such corporation was a controlled foreign corporation.

(5) (i) If (a) on the date of the sale or exchange such person, by reason of his ownership of such block, owns within the meaning of section 958(a)(2) stock in another foreign corporation (referred to as a "lower tier" corporation), and (b) the conditions of paragraph (a)(2) of § 1.1248-1 would be satisfied by such person in respect of such stock in the lower tier corporation if such person were deemed to have sold or exchanged such stock in the lower tier corporation on the date he actually sold or exchanged such block in the first tier corporation, then the conditions of subdivision (ii) of this subparagraph must be satisfied.

(ii) In respect of stock in such lower tier corporation, (a) the conditions set forth in subparagraphs (1) through (4) of this paragraph (applied as if such person owned directly such stock in such lower tier corporation) must be met and (b) such person must own within the meaning of section 958(a)(2) the same percentage of the shares of such stock on each day which falls within the period referred to in subparagraph (1) of this paragraph.

(d) *Earnings and profits accumulated for a taxable year*—(1) *General.* For purposes of this section, the earnings and profits accumulated for a taxable year of a foreign corporation shall be the earnings and profits for such year computed in accordance with the rules prescribed in § 1.964-1 (relating to determination of earnings and profits for a taxable year of a controlled foreign corporation) and reduced by any distributions therefrom. If the stock in the corporation is sold or exchanged before any action is taken by or on behalf of the corporation under paragraph (c) of § 1.964-1, the computation of earnings and profits under § 1.964-1 for purposes of this section shall be made as if no elections had been made and no accounting method had been adopted.

(2) *Special rules.* (i) The earnings and profits of the corporation accumulated—

(a) For any taxable year beginning before January 1, 1967 (computed without any reduction for distributions), shall not include the excess of any item includible in gross income of the foreign corporation under section 882(b) as gross income derived from sources within the United States, and

(b) For any taxable year beginning after December 31, 1966 (computed without any reduction for distributions), shall not include the excess of any item includible in gross income of the foreign corporation under section 882(b)(2) as income effectively connected for that year with the conduct by such corporation of a trade or business in the United States, whether derived from sources within or from sources without the United States,

over any deductions allocable to such item under section 882(c). However, if the sale or exchange of stock in the foreign corporation by the United States person occurs before January 1, 1967, the provisions of (a) of this subdivision apply with respect to such sale or exchange even though the taxable year begins after December 31, 1966. See section 1248(d)(4). Any item which is required to be excluded from gross income, or which is taxed at a reduced rate, under an applicable treaty obligation of the United States shall not be excluded under this subdivision from earnings and profits accumulated for a taxable year (computed without any reduction for distributions).

(ii) If a foreign corporation adopts a plan of complete liquidation in a taxable year of the corporation beginning after December 31, 1962, and if because of the application of section 337(a) gain or loss would not be recognized by the corporation from the sale or exchange of property if the corporation were a domestic corporation, then the earnings and profits of the corporation accumulated for the taxable year (computed without any reduction for distributions) shall be determined without regard to the amount of such gain or loss. See section 1248(d)(2). For the nonapplication of section 337(a) to a liquidation by a collapsible corporation (as defined in section 341) and to certain other liquidations, see section 337(c).

(e) *Earnings and profits attributable to block*—(1) *General.* Except as provided in subparagraph (3) of this paragraph, the earnings and profits attributable to a block of stock of a controlled foreign corporation for the period a United States person held (or is considered to have held by reason of the application of section 1223) the block are an amount equal to—

(i) The sum of the earnings and profits accumulated for each taxable year of the corporation beginning after December 31, 1962 (computed under paragraph (d) of this section) during such period, multiplied by

(ii) The percentage that (a) the number of shares in the block, bears to (b) the total number of shares of the corporation outstanding during such period.

(2) *Special rule.* For purposes of computing the sum referred to in subparagraph (1)(i) of this paragraph, in case the block was held (or is considered as held by reason of the application of section 1223) during a taxable year beginning after December 31, 1962, but not on each day of such taxable year, there shall be included in such sum only that portion which bears the same ratio to (i) the total earnings and profits for such taxable year computed under paragraph (d) of this section), as (ii) the number of days during such taxable year the block was held (or is considered as so held), bears to (iii) the total number of days in such taxable year.

(3) *Amounts included in gross income under section 951.* (i) If, during the period the person held (or is considered to have held by reason of the application of section 1223) the block, any amount was included under section 951 in the gross income of such person (or of another person whose holding of the stock sold or exchanged is, by reason of the application of section 1223, attributed to such person) in respect of the block, then

Reg. § 1.1248-2(e)(3)

53,540 Rules for Determining Capital Gains and Losses
See p. 20,601 for regulations not amended to reflect law changes

the earnings and profits attributable to the block for such period shall be an amount equal to (a) the earnings and profits attributable to the block which would have been computed under subparagraph (1) of this paragraph if this subparagraph did not apply, reduced by (b) the excess computed under subdivision (ii) of this subparagraph. See section 1248(d)(1).

(ii) The excess computed under this subdivision is the excess (if any) of (a) amounts included under section 951 in the gross income of such person (or such other person) in respect of the block during such period, over (b) the portion of such amounts which, in any taxable year of such person (or such other person), resulted in an exclusion from the gross income of such person (or such other person) under section 959(a)(1) (relating to exclusion from gross income of distributions of previously taxed earnings and profits).

(iii) This subparagraph shall apply notwithstanding an election under section 962 by such person to be subject to tax at corporate rates.

(4) *Example.* The application of this paragraph may be illustrated by the following examples:

Example (1). On May 26, 1965, Green, a United States person, purchases at its fair market value a block of 25 of the 100 outstanding shares of the only class of stock of controlled foreign corporation F. He sells the block on January 1, 1968. In respect of the block, Green did not include any amount in his gross income under section 951. F uses the calendar year as its taxable year and does not own stock in any lower tier corporation referred to in paragraph (c)(5)(i) of this section. All of the conditions of paragraph (c) of this section are satisfied in respect of the block. The earnings and profits accumulated by F (computed under paragraph (d) of this section) are $10,000 for 1965, $13,000 for 1966, and $11,000 for 1967. The earnings and profits of F attributable to the block are $7,500, determined as follows:

Sum of earnings and profits accumulated by F during period block was held:

For 1965 (219/365 × $10,000)	$ 6,000
For 1966	13,000
For 1967	11,000
Sum	$30,000
Multiplied by: Number of shares in block (25), divided by total number of shares outstanding (100)	25%
Earnings and profits attributable to block	$ 7,500

Example (2). Assume the same facts as in example (1) except that in respect of the block Green includes in his gross income under section 951 the total amount of $2,800 for 1965 and 1966, and because of such inclusion the amount of $2,300 which was distributed to Green by F on January 15, 1967, is excluded from his gross income under section 959(a)(1). Accordingly, the earnings and profits of F attributable to the block are $7,000, determined as follows:

Earnings and profits attributable to the block, as computed in example (1)	$7,500
Minus: Excess of amount included in Green's gross income under section 951 ($2,800), over portion thereof which resulted in an exclusion under section 959(a)(1) ($2,300)	$ 500
Earnings and profits attributable to block	$7,000

Example (3). Assume the same facts as in example (1) except that on each day beginning on January 1, 1966 (the date controlled foreign corporation G was organized) through January 1, 1968, F owns 80 of the 100 outstanding shares of the only class of G stock. Since, by reason of his ownership of 25 shares of F stock, Green owns within the meaning of section 958(a)(2) the equivalent of 20 shares of G stock (25/100 of 80 shares), G is a lower tier corporation referred to in paragraph (c)(5)(i)(a) of this section. If Green had sold the 20 shares of G stock on January 1, 1968, the date he actually sold the block of F stock, the conditions of paragraph (a)(2) of § 1.1248-1 would be satisfied in respect of the G stock, and, accordingly, the conditions of paragraph (c)(5)(ii) of this section must be satisfied. Assume further that such conditions are satisfied, that G uses the calendar year as its taxable year, and that the earnings and profits accumulated by G (computed under paragraph (d) of this section) are $19,000 for 1966 and $21,000 for 1967. The earnings and profits of F and of G attributable to the block are $15,500, determined as follows:

Reg. § 1.1248-2(e)(4)

Rules for Determining Capital Gains and Losses

See p. 20,601 for regulations not amended to reflect law changes

Sum of earnings and profits accumulated by G for period Green owned G stock within the meaning of section 958(a)(2) ($19,000 plus $21,000)	$40,000
Multiplied by: Number of G shares deemed owned within the meaning of section 958(a)(2) by Green (20), divided by total number of G shares outstanding (100)	20%
Earnings and profits of G attributable to block	$ 8,000
Earnings and profits of F attributable to block, as determined in example (1)	7,500
Total earnings and profits attributable to block	$15,500

[Reg. § 1.1248-2.]

☐ [T.D. 6779, 12-21-64. Amended by T.D. 7293, 11-27-73.]

[Reg. § 1.1248-3]

§ 1.1248-3. Earnings and profits attributable to stock in complex cases.—(a) *General*—(1) *Manner of computation.* For purposes of paragraph (a)(1) of § 1.1248-1, if a United States person sells or exchanges stock in a foreign corporation, and if the provisions of § 1.1248-2 do not apply, then the earnings and profits attributable to the stock which were accumulated in taxable years of the corporation beginning after December 31, 1962, during the period or periods such stock was held (or was considered to be held by reason of the application of section 1223) by such person while such corporation was a controlled foreign corporation, shall be computed in accordance with the steps set forth in subparagraphs (2), (3), and (4) of this paragraph.

(2) *Step 1.* For each taxable year of the corporation beginning after December 31, 1962, (i) the earnings and profits accumulated for such taxable year by the corporation shall be computed in the manner prescribed in paragraph (b) of this section, (ii) the person's "tentative ratable share" of such earnings and profits shall be computed in the manner prescribed in paragraph (c) or (d) (whichever is applicable) of this section, and (iii) the person's "ratable share" of such earnings and profits shall be computed by adjusting the tentative ratable share in the manner prescribed in paragraph (e) of this section.

(3) *Step 2.* If the provisions of paragraph (f) of this section (relating to earnings and profits of "lower tier" foreign corporations) apply, the amount of the person's ratable share of the earnings and profits accumulated by each "lower tier" corporation attributable to any such taxable year (i) shall be computed in the manner prescribed by paragraph (f) of this section,, and (ii) shall be added to such person's ratable share for such taxable year determined in step 1.

(4) *Step 3.* The amount of earnings and profits attributable to the share shall be the sum of the ratable shares computed for each such taxable year in the manner prescribed in steps 1 and 2.

(5) *Share or block.* In general, the computation under this paragraph shall be made separately for each share of stock sold or exchanged, except that if a group of shares constitute a block of stock the computation may be made in respect of the block. For purposes of this section, the term "block of stock" means a group of shares sold or exchanged in one transaction, but only if (i) the amount realized, basis, and holding period are identical for each such share, and (ii) the adjustments (if any) under paragraphs (e) and (f)(5) of this section of the tentative ratable shares would be identical for each such share if such adjustments were computed separately for each such share.

(6) *Deficit in earnings and profits.* For purposes of this section and §§ 1.1248-4 through 1.1248-7, in respect of a taxable year, the term "earnings and profits accumulated" for a taxable year (but only if computed under paragraph (b) of this section) includes a deficit in earnings and profits accumulated for such taxable year. Similarly, a tentative ratable share, or a ratable share, may be a deficit.

(7) *Examples.* The application of the provisions of this paragraph may be illustrated by the following examples:

Example (1). On December 31, 1967, Brown sells 10 shares of stock in foreign corporation X, which uses the calendar year as its taxable year. The 10 shares constitute a block of stock under subparagraph (5) of this paragraph. Under step 1, Brown's ratable shares of the earnings and profits of X attributable to the block are as follows:

Taxable year of X	Ratable shares
1963	$100
1964	150
1965	−50(deficit)
1966	50
1967	100
Sum	$350

The amount of the earnings and profits attributable to such block under step 3 is $350.

Example (2). Assume the same facts as in example (1), except that in respect of X there are "lower tier" corporations Y and Z to which the provisions of paragraph (f) of this section apply. Brown's ratable shares of the earnings and profits of X, Y, and Z attributable to the block under

Reg. § 1.1248-3(a)(7)

53,542 Rules for Determining Capital Gains and Losses
See p. 20,601 for regulations not amended to reflect law changes

steps 1 and 2 for each taxable year of X are as follows:

Taxable year of X	X	Ratable shares Y	Z	Total
1963	$100	$40	$20	$160
1964	150	40	−60	130
1965	−50	30	50	30
1966	50	50	30	130
1967	100	−40	40	100
Sum	$350	$120	$80	$550

The amount of the earnings and profits attributable to such block under step 3 is $550.

(b) *Earnings and profits accumulated for a taxable year*—(1) *General.* For purposes of this section, the earnings and profits accumulated for a taxable year of a foreign corporation shall be the earnings and profits for such year, computed in accordance with the rules prescribed in § 1.964-1 (relating to determination of earnings and profits for a taxable year of a controlled foreign corporation), except that (i) the special rules of subparagraph (2) of this paragraph shall apply, and (ii) adjustments shall be made under subparagraph (3) of this paragraph for distributions made by the corporation during such taxable year. If the stock in the corporation is sold or exchanged before any action is taken by or on behalf of the corporation under paragraph (c) of § 1.964-1, the computation of earnings and profits under § 1.964-1 for purposes of this section shall be made as if no elections had been made and no accounting method had been adopted. The amount of earnings and profits accumulated for a taxable year of a foreign corporation, as computed under this paragraph, is not necessarily the same amount as the earnings and profits of the taxable year computed under section 316(a)(2) or paragraph (d) of § 1.1248-2. Thus, for example, if a distribution with respect to stock is in excess of the amount of earnings and profits of the taxable year computed under section 316(a)(2), such excess is treated under section 316(a)(1) or paragraph (d) of § 1.1248-2 as made out of any earnings and profits accumulated in prior taxable years, whereas the amount of such excess may create, or increase, a deficit in the earnings and profits accumulated for the taxable year as computed under this paragraph. See subparagraph (3) of this paragraph.

(2) *Special rules.* (i) The earnings and profits of the corporation accumulated—

(a) For any taxable year beginning before January 1, 1967, shall not include the excess of any item includible in gross income of the foreign corporation under section 882(b) as gross income derived from sources within the United States, and

(b) For any taxable year beginning after December 31, 1966, shall not include the excess of any item includible in gross income of the foreign corporation under section 882(b)(2) as income effectively connected for that year with the conduct by such corporation of a trade or business in the United States, whether derived from sources within or from sources without the United States,

over any deductions allocable to such item under section 882(c). However, if the sale or exchange of stock in the foreign corporation by the U.S. person occurs before January 1, 1967, the provisions of (a) of this subdivision apply with respect to such sale or exchange even though the taxable year begins after December 31, 1966. See section 1248(d)(4). Any item which is required to be excluded from gross income, or which is taxed at a reduced rate, under an applicable treaty obligation of the United States shall not be excluded under this subdivision from earnings and profits accumulated for a taxable year.

(ii) If a foreign corporation adopts a plan of complete liquidation in a taxable year of the corporation beginning after December 31, 1962, and if because of the application of section 337(a) gain or loss would not be recognized by the corporation from the sale or exchange of property if the corporation were a domestic corporation, then the earnings and profits of the corporation accumulated for the taxable year shall be determined without regard to the amount of such gain or loss. See section 1248(d)(2). For the nonapplication of section 337(a) to a liquidation by a collapsible corporation (as defined in section 341) and to certain other liquidations, see section 337(c).

(3) *Adjustment for distributions.* (i) The earnings and profits of a foreign corporation accumulated for a taxable year (computed without regard to this subparagraph) shall be reduced (if necessary below zero so as to create a deficit), or a deficit in such earnings and profits shall be increased, by the amount of the distributions (other than in redemption of stock under section 302(a) or 303) made by the corporation in respect of its stock during such taxable year (a) out of such earnings and profits, or (b) out of earnings and profits accumulated for prior taxable years beginning after December 31, 1962 (computed under this paragraph). Except for purposes of applying this subparagraph, the application of the preceding sentence shall not affect the amount of earnings and profits accumulated for any such prior taxable year.

(ii) The application of this subparagraph may be illustrated by the following examples:

Example (1). X Corporation, which uses the calendar year as its taxable year, was organ-

Reg. § 1.1248-3(b)(1)

Rules for Determining Capital Gains and Losses

See p. 20,601 for regulations not amended to reflect law changes

ized on January 1, 1965, and was a controlled foreign corporation on each day of 1965. The amount of X's earnings and profits accumulated for 1965 (computed under this paragraph without regard to the adjustment for distributions under this subparagraph) is $400,000, of which $100,000 is distributed by X as dividends during 1965. The amount of X's earnings and profits accumulated for 1965 (computed under this paragraph) is $300,000 (that is, $400,000 minus $100,000). The result would be the same even if X was not a controlled foreign corporation on each day of 1965.

Example (2). Assume the same facts as in example (1). Assume further that the amount of X's earnings and profits accumulated for 1966 (computed under this paragraph without regard to the adjustment for distributions under this subparagraph) is $150,000, and that X distributes the amount of $260,000 as dividends during 1966. Since $150,000 of the distribution is from earnings and profits accumulated for 1966 (computed without regard to the adjustment for distributions under this subparagraph), and since $110,000 is from earnings and profits accumulated for 1965, the earnings and profits of X accumulated for 1966 are a deficit of $110,000 (that is, $150,000 minus $260,000). However, the earnings and profits accumulated for 1965 are still $300,000 for purposes of computing in the manner prescribed in paragraph (c) of this section a person's tentative ratable share.

(c) *Tentative ratable share if earnings and profits accumulated for a taxable year not less than zero*—(1) *General rule.* For purposes of paragraph (a)(2)(ii) of this section, in respect of a share (or block) of stock in a foreign corporation, if the amount of the earnings and profits accumulated for a taxable year of the corporation (computed under paragraph (b) of this section), beginning after December 31, 1962, is not less than zero, then the person's tentative ratable share for such taxable year shall be equal to—

(i) *(a)* Such amount (if the computation is made in respect of a block, multiplied by the number of shares in the block), divided by *(b)* the number of shares in the corporation outstanding, or deemed under subparagraph (2) of this paragraph to be outstanding, on each day of such taxable year, multiplied by

(ii) The percentage that *(a)* the number of days in such taxable year of the corporation during the period the person held (or was considered to have held by reason of the application of section 1223) the share (or block) while the corporation was a controlled foreign corporation, bears to *(b)* the total number of days in such taxable year.

(2) *Shares deemed outstanding for a taxable year.* For purposes of this section and §§ 1.1248-4 through 1.1248-7, if the number of shares of stock in a foreign corporation outstanding on each day of a taxable year of the corporation is not constant, then the number of such shares deemed outstanding on each such day shall be the sum of the fractional amounts in respect of each share outstanding on any day of the taxable year. The fractional amount in respect of a share shall be determined by dividing (i) the number of days in the taxable year during which such share was outstanding (excluding the day the share became outstanding, but including the day the share ceased to be outstanding), by (ii) the total number of days in such taxable year.

(3) *Examples.* The application of subparagraphs (1) and (2) of this paragraph may be illustrated by the following examples:

Example (1). On each day of 1964, S owns a block consisting of 30 of the 100 shares of the only class of stock outstanding in F Corporation, and on each such day F is a controlled foreign corporation. F uses the calendar year as its taxable year and F's earnings and profits accumulated for 1964 (computed under paragraph (b) of this section) are $10,000. S's tentative ratable share with respect to the block is $3,000, computed as follows:

Earnings and profits accumulated for taxable year $10,000
Multiplied by:
Number of shares in block (30), divided by number of shares outstanding (100) . 30%
Multiplied by:
Number of days in 1964 S held block while F was a controlled foreign corporation (365), divided by number of days in 1964 (365) 100%

    Tentative ratable share for block ...... $ 3,000

Example (2). On December 31, 1964, X Corporation, a controlled foreign corporation which uses the calendar year as its taxable year, had 100 shares of one class of stock outstanding, 15 of which were owned by T. T's 15 shares were redeemed by X on March 14, 1965. On December 31, 1965, in addition to the remaining 85 shares, 10 new shares of stock (which were issued on May 26, 1965) were outstanding. Thus, during 1965, 15 shares were outstanding for 73 days, 10 for 219 days, and 85 for 365 days. The earnings and profits (computed under paragraph (b) of this section) accumulated for X's taxable year ending on December 31, 1965, are $18,800. T's tentative ratable share with respect to one share of stock is $40, computed as follows:

Reg. § 1.1248-3(c)(3)

53,544 Rules for Determining Capital Gains and Losses
See p. 20,601 for regulations not amended to reflect law changes

Earnings and profits accumulated for taxable year	$18,800

Divided by:
Number of shares deemed outstanding on each day of 1965:

15 for 73 days (15 × 73/365)	3
10 for 219 days (10 × 219/365)	6
85 for 365 days (85 × 365/365)	85
Total number of shares deemed outstanding each day of 1965	94

Earnings and profits accumulated per share	$ 200

Multiplied by:

Number of days in 1965 T held his share while X was a controlled foreign corporation (73), divided by number of days in 1965 (365)	20%
T's tentative ratable share per share of stock	$ 40

Example (3). Assume the same facts as in example (2) except that X was not a controlled foreign corporation after January 31, 1965. T's tentative ratable share with respect to one share of stock for 1965 is $17, computed as follows:

Earnings and profits accumulated per share, determined in example (2)	$200

Multiplied by:

Number of days in 1965 T held X stock while X was a controlled foreign corporation (31), divided by number of days in 1965 (365)	8.5%
Tentative ratable share	$ 17

(4) *More than one class of stock.* If a foreign corporation for a taxable year has more than one class of stock outstanding, then before applying subparagraphs (1) and (2) of this paragraph the earnings and profits accumulated for the taxable year of the corporation (computed under paragraph (b) of this section) shall be allocated to each class of stock in accordance with the principles of paragraph (e)(2) and (3) of § 1.951-1, applied as if the corporation were a controlled foreign corporation on each day of such taxable year.

(d) *Tentative ratable share if deficit in earnings and profits accumulated for taxable year*—(1) *General rule.* For purposes of paragraph (a)(2)(ii) of this section, in respect of a share (or block) of stock in a foreign corporation, if there is a deficit in the earnings and profits accumulated for a taxable year of the corporation (computed under paragraph (b) of this section) beginning after December 31, 1962, the person's tentative ratable share for such taxable year shall be an amount equal to the sum of the partial tentative ratable shares computed under subparagraphs (2) and (3) of this paragraph.

(2) *Operating deficit.* The partial tentative ratable share under this subparagraph is computed in 2 steps. First, compute (under paragraph (b) of this section without regard to the adjustment for distributions under subparagraph (3) thereof) the deficit (if any) in earnings and profits accumulated for such taxable year. Second, compute the partial tentative ratable share in the same manner as the tentative ratable share for such taxable year would be computed under paragraph (c) of this section if such deficit were the amount referred to in paragraph (c)(1)(i)(a) of this section.

(3) *Deficit from distributions.* The partial tentative ratable share under this subparagraph is computed in 2 steps. First, compute and treat as a deficit only that portion of the adjustment for distributions under paragraph (b)(3) of this section for such taxable year which is attributable under subparagraph (4) of this paragraph to distributions out of earnings and profits accumulated during prior taxable years of the corporation beginning after December 31, 1962, during the period or periods the corporation was a controlled foreign corporation and the share (or block) of stock was owned by a United States shareholder (as defined in section 951(b) and the regulations thereunder). Second, compute the partial tentative ratable share for such taxable year in the same manner as the tentative ratable share for such taxable year would be computed under paragraph (c) of this section if (i) such deficit were the amount referred to in paragraph (c)(1)(i)(a) of this section, and (ii) the corporation were a controlled foreign corporation on each day of such taxable year.

(4) *Order of distributions.* For purposes of applying subparagraph (3) of this paragraph only, the adjustment for distributions under paragraph (b)(3) of this section for a taxable year of a foreign corporation shall be treated as attributable first to distributions of earnings and profits for the taxable year (computed under paragraph (b) of this section without regard to such adjustment) to the extent thereof, and then to distributions out of the most recent of earnings and profits accumulated during prior taxable years beginning after December 31, 1962 (computed under paragraph (b) of this section). If the foreign corporation was a controlled foreign corporation during a prior taxable year for a period or periods which was only part of such prior taxable year, then for purposes of the preceding sentence (i) such taxable year shall be divided into periods the corporation was or was not a controlled foreign corporation, (ii) distributions of the earnings and profits accumulated during such prior taxable year shall be considered made from the most re-

Reg. § 1.1248-3(c)(4)

cent period first, and (iii) the earnings and profits accumulated during such prior taxable year shall be allocated to a period during such year in the same proportion as the number of days in the period bears to the number of days in such year. Except for purposes of applying subparagraph (3) of this paragraph, the application of this subparagraph shall not affect the amount of earnings and profits accumulated for any such prior taxable year (computed under paragraph (b) of this section).

(5) *Examples.* The application of this paragraph may be illustrated by the following examples:

Example (1). On each day of 1965 X Corporation, which uses the calendar year as its taxable year, was a controlled foreign corporation having 100 shares of one class of stock outstanding, a block of 25 of which were owned by T, who acquired them in 1962 and sold them in 1967. The deficit in X's earnings and profits accumulated for 1965 (computed under paragraph (b) of this section without regard to the adjustment for distributions under subparagraph (3) thereof) is $100,000, and thus in respect of the block T's partial tentative ratable share computed under subparagraph (2) of this paragraph is a deficit of $25,000 (that is, $100,000 × 25/100). During 1965 X does not make any distributions in respect of its stock, and thus in respect of the block T's partial tentative ratable share computed under subparagraph (3) of this paragraph is zero. Accordingly, T's tentative ratable share in respect of the block of X stock for 1965 is a deficit of $25,000. If, however, X was a controlled foreign corporation for only 292 days during 1965, T's tentative ratable share in respect of the block for 1965 would be a deficit of $20,000 (that is, $25,000 × 292/365).

Example (2). (i) Assume the same facts as in example (1) except that at no time during 1965 is X a controlled foreign corporation and that during 1965 X distributes $80,000 with respect to its stock. Assume further that X was a controlled foreign corporation on each day of 1964, but only for the first 146 days of 1963, and that X's earnings and profits accumulated for prior taxable years computed under paragraph (b) of this section are $70,000 for 1964 and $20,000 for 1963.

(ii) Since X was not a controlled foreign corporation on any day of 1965, in respect of the block T's partial tentative ratable share computed under subparagraph (2) of this paragraph is zero.

(iii) The partial tentative ratable share under subparagraph (3) of this paragraph is computed in the following manner: For 1965 the adjustment for distributions under paragraph (b)(3) of this section is $80,000. Under subparagraph (4) of this paragraph $70,000 of such adjustment is attributable to the distribution of all of the earnings and profits accumulated during 1964, on every day of which X was a controlled foreign corporation, and $10,000 of the adjustment is attributable to the distribution of $10,000 of the earnings and profits accumulated for 1963. The portion of the earnings and profits accumulated by X in 1963 attributable to the first 146 days in 1963 during which X was a controlled foreign corporation is $8,000 (that is, $20,000 × 146/365), and the portion attributable to the period in 1963 during which X was not a controlled foreign corporation is $12,000 (that is, $20,000 × 219/365). Under subparagraph (4)(ii) of this paragraph, the distribution in 1965 of $10,000 of earnings and profits accumulated during 1963 is attributable to the more recent period in 1963, that is, the period X was not a controlled foreign corporation. Accordingly, the portion of the adjustment for distributions under paragraph (b)(3) of this section attributable to earnings and profits accumulated during periods X was a controlled foreign corporation is $70,000, and in respect of the block T's partial tentative ratable share under subparagraph (3) of this paragraph is a deficit of $17,500 (that is, $70,000 × 25/100).

(iv) T's tentative ratable share in respect of the block of X stock for 1965 is a deficit of $17,500 (that is, the sum of the partial tentative ratable share for the block computed under subparagraph (2) of this paragraph, zero, plus the partial tentative ratable share for the block computed under subparagraph (3) of this paragraph, a deficit of $17,500).

(v) Assume that X had 100 shares of one class of stock outstanding on each day of 1964 and 1963. Notwithstanding the distributions in 1965 of earnings and profits accumulated during 1964 and 1963 (computed under paragraph (b) of this section), nevertheless, in respect of the block T's tentative ratable share for 1964 is $17,500 (that is, earnings and profits accumulated during 1964 so computed of $70,000, multiplied by 25 shares/100 shares) and in respect of the block T's tentative ratable share for 1963 is $2,000 (that is, earnings and profits accumulated during 1963 so computed of $20,000, multiplied by 25 shares/100 shares, and multiplied by the percentage that the number of days in 1963 on which X was a controlled foreign corporation bears to the total number of days in 1963, 146/365).

Example (3). Assume the same facts as in example (2) except that X was a controlled foreign corporation on each day of 1965. The tentative ratable share with respect to the block of stock for 1965 is a deficit of $42,500, that is, the

Reg. § 1.1248-3(d)(5)

53,546 Rules for Determining Capital Gains and Losses

See p. 20,601 for regulations not amended to reflect law changes

sum of the partial tentative ratable share under subparagraph (2) of this paragraph (as determined in example (1)), a deficit of $25,000, plus the partial tentative ratable share under subparagraph (3) of this paragraph (as determined in example (2)), a deficit of $17,500.

(6) *More than one class of stock.* If a foreign corporation for a taxable year has more than one class of stock outstanding, then before applying subparagraph (1) of this paragraph the earnings and profits accumulated for the taxable year of the corporation (computed under paragraph (b) of this section) shall be allocated to each class of stock in accordance with the principles of paragraph (e)(2) and (3) of § 1.951-1, applied as if the corporation were a controlled foreign corporation on each day of such taxable year.

(e) *Ratable share of earnings and profits accumulated for a taxable year*—(1) *In general.* For purposes of paragraph (a)(2)(iii) of this section, in respect of a share (or block) of stock in a foreign corporation, the person's ratable share of the earnings and profits accumulated for a taxable year beginning after December 31, 1962, shall be an amount equal to the tentative ratable share computed under paragraph (c) or (d) (as the case may be) of this section, adjusted in the manner prescribed in subparagraphs (2) through (6) of this paragraph.

(2) *Amounts included in gross income under section 951.* (i) In respect of a share (or block) of stock in a foreign corporation, a person's tentative ratable share for a taxable year of the corporation (computed under paragraph (c) of this section) shall be reduced (but not below zero) by the excess of *(a)* the amount, if any, included (in respect of such corporation for such taxable year) under section 951 in the gross income of such person or (during the period such share, or block, was considered to be held by such person by reason of the application of section 1223) in the gross income of any other person who held such share (or block), over *(b)* the portion of such amount which, in any taxable year of such person or such other person, resulted in an exclusion from the gross income of such person or such other person of an amount under section 959(a)(1) (relating to exclusion from gross income of distributions of previously taxed earnings and profits). See section 1248(d)(1). This subdivision shall apply notwithstanding an election under section 962 by such person to be subject to tax at corporate rates.

(ii) The application of this subparagraph may be illustrated by the following example:

Example. On December 31, 1975, Brown sells one share of stock in X Corporation, a controlled foreign corporation which has never been a less developed country corporation (as defined in section 902(d)). Both Brown and X use the calendar year as the taxable year. In respect of his share, Brown's tentative ratable share for 1971 (computed under paragraph (c) of this section) is $35. In respect of his share, Brown included $4 in his gross income for 1971 under section 951, and the amount of $3, which was distributed to him by X on January 15, 1972, is excluded from Brown's gross income under section 959(a)(1). In respect of the stock, Brown's ratable share for 1971 is $34, determined as follows:

Tentative ratable share	$35
Minus:	
Excess of amount of tentative ratable share included in Brown's gross income under section 951 ($4), over portion thereof which resulted in exclusion under section 959(a)(1)($3)	1
Ratable share	$34

(3) *Amounts included in gross income under section 551.* In respect of a share (or block) of stock in a foreign corporation, a person's tentative ratable share for a taxable year of the corporation (computed under paragraph (c) of this section) shall be reduced (but not below zero) by the amount, if any, included (in respect of such corporation for such taxable year) under section 551 in the gross income of such person or (during the period such share, or block, was considered to be held by such person by reason of the application of section 1223) in the gross income of any other person who held such share (or block).

(4) *Less developed country corporations.* (i) If the foreign corporation was a less developed country corporation as defined in section 902(d) for a taxable year of the corporation, and if the person who sold or exchanged a share (or block) of stock in such corporation satisfies the requirements of paragraph (a) of § 1.1248-5 in respect of such stock, then his ratable share for such taxable year shall be zero. See section 1248(d)(3).

(ii) The application of this subparagraph may be illustrated by the following example:

Example. Assume the same facts as in the example in subparagraph (2)(ii) of this paragraph except that X was a less developed country corporation for 1971. Assume further that Brown satisfies the requirements of paragraph (a) of § 1.1248-5. Brown's ratable share in respect of the stock for 1971 is zero.

Reg. § 1.1248-3(d)(6)

(5) *Qualified shareholder of foreign investment company.* In respect of a share (or block) of stock in a foreign corporation which was a foreign investment company described in section 1246(b)(1), if the election under section 1247(a) to distribute income currently was in effect for a taxable year of the company, and if the person who sold or exchanged the stock (or another person who actually owned the stock during such taxable year and whose holding of the stock is attributed by reason of the application of section 1223 to the person who sold or exchanged the stock) was a qualified shareholder (as defined in section 1247(c)) for his taxable year in which or with which such taxable year of the company ends, then the ratable share in respect of the share (or block) for such taxable year of the company shall be zero. See section 1248(d)(5). In case gain is recognized under section 1246 in respect of a share (or block), see section 1248(f)(3)(B).

(6) *Adjustment for certain distributions.* If (i) the person who sold or exchanged the share or block (or another person who actually owned the share or block and whose holding of the share or block is attributed by reason of the application of section 1223 to such person) received a distribution during a taxable year of the corporation, and (ii) such distribution was not included in the gross income of such person (or such other person) by reason of the application of section 959(a)(1) to amounts which were included under section 951(a)(1) in the gross income of a United States shareholder whose holding of the share or block is not attributed by reason of the application of section 1223 to such person (or such other person), then the amount of such distribution shall be added to such person's tentative ratable share for such taxable year. Thus, for example, such tentative ratable share may be increased, or a deficit reduced, by the amount of such distribution.

(f) *Earnings and profits of subsidiaries of foreign corporations*—(1) *Application of paragraph.* (i) In respect of a person who sells or exchanges stock in a foreign corporation (referred to as a "first tier" corporation), the provisions of this paragraph shall apply if the following 3 conditions exist:

(a) The conditions of paragraph (a)(2) of § 1.1248-1 are satisfied by the person in respect of such stock;

(b) By reason of his ownership of such stock, on the date of such sale or exchange such person owned, within the meaning of section 958(a)(2), stock in another foreign corporation (referred to as a "lower tier" corporation); and

(c) The conditions of paragraph (a)(2) of § 1.1248-1 would be satisfied by such person in respect of such stock in the lower tier corporation if such person were deemed to have sold or exchanged such stock in the lower tier corporation on the date he actually sold or exchanged such stock in the first tier corporation.

(ii) If the provisions of this paragraph apply, (a) the person's tentative ratable share (or shares) of the earnings and profits accumulated by the lower tier corporation attributable to a taxable year of the first tier corporation shall be computed under subparagraph (2) or (4) of this paragraph, whichever is applicable, and (b) such person's ratable share (or shares) for the lower tier corporation attributable to a taxable year of the first tier corporation shall be computed under subparagraph (5) of this paragraph. For the manner of taking into account the ratable share for a lower tier corporation, see paragraph (a)(3) of this section.

(iii) The application of this subparagraph may be illustrated by the following example:

Example. On each day of 1964 and 1965 corporations X and Y are controlled foreign corporations, and each has outstanding 100 shares of one class of stock. On January 15, 1965, T, a United States person, owns one share of stock in X and X directly owns 20 shares of stock in Y. Thus, T owns, within the meaning of section 958(a)(2), stock in Y. On that date, T sells his share in X and satisfies the conditions of paragraph (a)(2) of § 1.1248-1 in respect of his stock in X. Assuming that the conditions of paragraph (a)(2) of § 1.1248-1 would be satisfied by T in respect of the stock he indirectly owns in Y if, on January 15, 1965, he were deemed to have sold such stock in Y, the provisions of this paragraph apply.

(2) *Tentative ratable share (of lower tier corporation attributable to a taxable year of first tier corporation) not less than zero.* If the provisions of this paragraph apply to a sale or exchange by a United States person of a share (or block) of stock in a first tier corporation, and if the amount of earnings and profits accumulated (computed under paragraph (b) of this section) for a taxable year (beginning after December 31, 1962) of the lower tier corporation is not less than zero, then in respect of the share (or block) such person's tentative ratable share of the earnings and profits accumulated for such taxable year of the lower tier corporation attributable to any taxable year (beginning after December 31, 1962) of such first tier corporation shall be an amount equal to—

(i)(a) Such amount of earnings and profits accumulated for such taxable year of the lower tier corporation (if the computation is made in respect of a block in the first tier corporation, multiplied by the number of shares in the block),

Reg. § 1.1248-3(f)(2)

53,548 Rules for Determining Capital Gains and Losses

See p. 20,601 for regulations not amended to reflect law changes

divided by *(b)* the number of shares in the first tier corporation outstanding, or deemed under paragraph (c)(2) of this section to be outstanding, on each day of such taxable year of the first tier corporation, multiplied by

    (ii) The percentage that *(a)* the number of days during the period or periods in such taxable year of the first tier corporation on which such person held (or was considered to have held by reason of the application of section 1223) the share (or block) in the first tier corporation while the first tier corporation owned (within the meaning of section 958(a)) stock of such lower tier corporation at times while such lower tier corporation was a controlled foreign corporation, bears to *(b)* the total number of days in such taxable year of the first tier corporation, multiplied by

    (iii) The percentage that *(a)* the average number of shares in the lower tier corporation which were owned within the meaning of section 958(a) by the first tier corporation during such period or periods (referred to in subdivision (ii)*(a)* of this subparagraph), bears to *(b)* the total number of such shares outstanding, or deemed under the principles of paragraph (c)(2) of this section to be outstanding, during such period or periods, multiplied by

    (iv) The percentage that *(a)* the number of days in such taxable year of the lower tier corporation which fall within the taxable year of the first tier corporation, bears to *(b)* the total number of days in such taxable year of the lower tier corporation.

    (3) *Examples.* The application of subparagraph (2) of this paragraph may be illustrated by the following examples:

    Example (1). In a year subsequent to 1969, Brown, a United States person, sells 5 of his shares of stock in X Corporation in a transaction as to which the provisions of this paragraph apply. Brown had purchased the 5 shares prior to 1969. On each day of 1969 X Corporation actually had 100 shares of one class of stock outstanding. On each such day X Corporation directly owned all of the shares of stock in Y Corporation, and Y Corporation directly owned all of the shares of stock in Z Corporation. Z Corporation on each such day was a controlled foreign corporation. Both X and Z use the calendar year as the taxable year. Z's earnings and profits accumulated for 1969 (computed under paragraph (b) of this section) are $2,000. Brown's tentative ratable share of the earnings and profits accumulated by Z attributable to the 1969 calendar year of X is $20 per share, computed as follows:

    (i) Z's earnings and profits for 1969 ($2,000), divided by the number of shares in X deemed outstanding each day of 1969 (100) .. $20

Multiplied by:

    (ii) Since on each day of 1969 Brown (by reason of owning directly his shares in X) owned, within the meaning of section 958(a)(2), stock in Z while Z was a controlled foreign corporation, the percentage determined under subparagraph (2)(ii) of this paragraph equals 100%

Multiplied by:

    (iii) Since on each day of 1969 X owned 100 percent of the stock of Y while Y owned 100 percent of the stock in Z, the percentage determined under subparagraph (2)(iii) equals .. 100%

Multiplied by:

    (iv) Since X and Z each use the same taxable year, the percentage determined under subparagraph (2)(iv) of this paragraph equals
.... 100%

Total $20

    Example (2). Assume the same facts as in example (1), except that Brown sold his stock in X on October 19, 1969. Brown's tentative ratable share of the earnings and profits accumulated by Z attributable to the 1969 calendar year of X is $16 per share, computed as follows:

    (i) The amount determined in subdivision (i) of example (1) $20
        Multiplied by:
    (ii) The number of days in the period during 1969 Brown (by reason of owning directly his stock in X) owned, within the meaning of section 958(a)(2), his stock in Z while Z was a controlled foreign corporation (292), divided by the number of days in 1969 (365), equals 80%
        Multiplied by:
    (iii) The percentage determined in subdivision (iii) of example (1) ... 100%
        Multiplied by:
    (iv) The percentage determined in subdivision (iv) of example (1) 100%

        Total $16

    Example (3). Assume the same facts as in examples (1) and (2), except that on each day during 1969 Y owned (within the meaning of section 958(a)(2)) 81 of the 100 shares of Z's outstanding stock. Brown's tentative ratable share of the earnings and profits accumulated by Z attributable to the 1969 calendar year of X is $12.96 per share, computed as follows:

Reg. § 1.1248-3(f)(3)

Rules for Determining Capital Gains and Losses

See p. 20,601 for regulations not amended to reflect law changes

(i) The amount determined in subdivision (i) of example (1)	$20
Multiplied by:	
(ii) The percentage determined in subdivision (ii) of example (2)	80%
Multiplied by:	
(iii) The average number of shares in Z which were owned (within the meaning of section 958(a)) by X during the applicable period (81), divided by the total number of shares in Z during such period (100)	81%
Multiplied by:	
(iv) The percentage determined in subdivision (iv) of example (1)	100%
Total	$12.96

The result would be the same if X owned (within the meaning of section 958(a)(2)) 81 percent of the stock in Y while Y so owned 100 percent of the stock in X, or if X so owned 90 percent of the stock in Y while Y so owned 90 percent of the stock in Z.

Example (4). Assume the same facts as in example (3), except that Z Corporation uses a fiscal year ending June 30 as its taxable year. Assume further that Z's earnings and profits accumulated for its fiscal year ending June 30, 1969, and for its fiscal year ending June 30, 1970, are $3,000 and $2,000, respectively. Brown's tentative ratable share of the earnings and profits accumulated by Z attributable to the 1969 calendar year of X is $16.17 per share, computed as follows:

	In respect of Z's taxable year ending	
	June 30, 1969	June 30, 1970
(i) Z's earnings and profits, divided by the number of shares in X deemed outstanding on each day of 1969:		
$3,000/100	$30	
$2,000/100		$20
Multiplied by:		
(ii) The percentage determined in subdivision (ii) of example (2)	80%	80%
Multiplied by:		
(iii) The percentage determined in subdivision (iii) of example (3)	81%	81%
Multiplied by:		
(iv) Number of days in Z's taxable year which fall within 1969, divided by total number of days in Z's taxable year:		
181/365	49.6%	
184/365		50.4%
Totals	$9.64	$6.53

(v) Sum of tentative ratable shares of Z attributable to X's 1969 calendar year:

For Z's taxable year ending	
June 30, 1969	$ 9.64
June 30, 1970	6.53
Sum	$16.17

(4) *Deficit in tentative ratable share of lower tier corporation attributable to a taxable year of first tier corporation.* (i) If there is a deficit in the earnings and profits accumulated for a taxable year of a lower tier corporation beginning after December 31, 1962 (computed under paragraph (b) of this section), the person's tentative ratable share for such taxable year of such lower tier corporation attributable to a taxable year of a first tier corporation shall not be computed under subparagraph (2) of this paragraph but shall be an amount equal to the sum of the partial tentative ratable shares computed under subdivisions (ii) and (iii) of this subparagraph.

(ii) The partial tentative ratable share under this subdivision is computed in 2 steps. First, compute (under paragraph (b) of this section without regard to the adjustments for distributions under subparagraph (3) thereof) the deficit (if any) in earnings and profits accumulated for such taxable year of such lower tier corporation. Second, compute the partial tentative ratable share in the same manner as such tentative ratable share would be computed under

Reg. § 1.1248-3(f)(4)

subparagraph (2) of this paragraph if such deficit were the amount referred to in subparagraph (2)(i)(a) of this paragraph.

(iii) The partial tentative ratable share under this subdivision is computed in 2 steps. First, compute and treat as a deficit the portion of the adjustment for distributions under paragraph (b)(3) of this section for such taxable year which is attributable under paragraph (d)(4) of this section to distributions of earnings and profits accumulated during prior taxable years of the lower tier corporation beginning after December 31, 1962, during the period or periods such lower tier corporation was a controlled foreign corporation and the percentage of the stock of such lower tier corporation (which the person owns within the meaning of section 958(a)(2)) was owned within the meaning of section 958(a) by a United States shareholder (as defined in section 951(b) and the regulations thereunder). Second, compute the partial tentative ratable share in the same manner as such tentative ratable share would be computed under subparagraph (2) of this paragraph if (a) such deficit were the amount referred to in subparagraph (2)(i)(a) of this paragraph, and (b) such lower tier corporation were a controlled foreign corporation on each day of such taxable year.

(5) *Ratable share of lower tier corporation attributable to a first tier corporation.* (i) If the provisions of this paragraph apply in respect of a share of stock in a first tier corporation, a person's ratable share of the earnings and profits accumulated by the lower tier corporation attributable to a taxable year of the first tier corporation shall be an amount equal to the tentative ratable share computed under subparagraph (2) or (4) of this paragraph, adjusted in the manner prescribed in this subparagraph.

(ii) If the first tier corporation and the lower tier corporation use the same taxable year, then in respect of a share (or block) of stock in the first tier corporation the person's tentative ratable share of the accumulated earnings and profits of the lower tier corporation attributable to the taxable year of the first tier corporation (computed under subparagraph (2) of this paragraph) shall be reduced (but not below zero) by the excess of (a) the amount, if any, included (in respect of such lower tier corporation for its taxable year) under section 951 in the gross income of such person or (during the period such stock was considered to be held by such person by reason of the application of section 1223) in the gross income of any other person who held such stock, over (b) the portion of such amount which, in any taxable year of such person or such other person, resulted in an exclusion from the gross income of such person or such other person of an amount under section 959(a)(1). For an illustration of the principles in the preceding sentence, see the example in paragraph (e)(2)(ii) of this section.

(iii) If the first tier corporation and the lower tier corporation do not use the same taxable year, and if there would be an excess computed under subdivision (ii) of this subparagraph in respect of a taxable year of the lower tier corporation (were the taxable years of such corporations the same), then such person's tentative ratable share of the accumulated earnings and profits for a taxable year of the lower tier corporation attributable to such taxable year of the first tier corporation shall be reduced (but not below zero) by an amount which bears the same ratio to (a) such excess, as (b) the number of days in the taxable year of the lower tier corporation which fall within the taxable year of the first tier corporation, bears to (c) the total number of days in the taxable year of the first tier corporation.

(iv) If the first tier corporation and the lower tier corporation use the same taxable year, then in respect of a share (or block) of stock in the first tier corporation the person's tentative ratable share of the accumulated earnings and profits of the lower tier corporation attributable to the taxable year of the first tier corporation (computed under subparagraph (2) of this paragraph) shall be reduced (but not below zero) by the amount, if any, included (in respect of such corporation for such taxable year) under section 551, by reason of the application of section 555(b), in the gross income of such person or (during the period such share (or block) was considered to be held by such person by reason of the application of section 1223) in the gross income of any other person who held such share (or block).

(v) If the first tier corporation and the lower tier corporation do not use the same taxable year, and if there would be a reduction in the person's tentative ratable share of the accumulated earnings and profits of the lower tier corporation attributable to the taxable year of the first tier corporation by an amount computed under subdivision (iv) of this subparagraph in respect of a taxable year of the lower tier corporation (were the taxable years of such corporations the same), then such person's tentative ratable share of the accumulated earnings and profits for a taxable year of the lower tier corporation attributable to such taxable year of the first tier corporation shall be reduced by an amount which bears the same ratio to (a) such amount, as (b) the number of days in the taxable year of the lower tier corporation which fall within the taxable year of the first tier corporation, bears to (c) the total number of

Rules for Determining Capital Gains and Losses

See p. 20,601 for regulations not amended to reflect law changes

days in the taxable year of the first tier corporation.

(vi) If the lower tier corporation was a less developed country corporation as defined in section 902(d) for a taxable year of the corporation, see paragraph (g) of this section.

(g) *Lower tier corporation a less developed country corporation*—(1) *General.* If the lower tier corporation was a less developed country corporation as defined in section 902(d) for a taxable year of such corporation, and if the person who sold or exchanged a share (or block) of stock in the first tier corporation satisfies on the date of such sale or exchange—

(i) The requirements of paragraph (a)(1) of § 1.1248-5 with respect to such stock, and

(ii) The requirements of paragraph (d)(1) of § 1.1248-5 with respect to any stock of the lower tier corporation which such person, by reason of his direct ownership of such stock in the first tier corporation, owned within the meaning of section 958(a)(2),

then such person's ratable share (or a deficit in such ratable share) for such taxable year of the lower tier corporation attributable to a taxable year of the first tier corporation (determined without regard to this paragraph) shall be reduced by an amount computed by multiplying such ratable share (so determined without regard to this paragraph) by the percentage computed under either subparagraph (2) or (4) of this paragraph, whichever is applicable.

(2) *Percentage for second tier corporation.* For purposes of subparagraph (1) of this paragraph, if stock of a lower tier corporation (hereinafter referred to as a "second tier" corporation) is owned directly by the first tier corporation on the date of the sale or exchange referred to in such subparagraph (1), the percentage under this subparagraph shall be computed by dividing (i) the number of shares of stock of the second tier corporation which the first tier corporation has owned directly for an uninterrupted 10-year period ending on such date, by (ii) the total number of shares of the stock of such second tier corporation owned directly by such first tier corporation on such date.

(3) *Examples.* The provisions of subparagraph (2) of this paragraph may be illustrated by the following examples:

Example (1). On January 1, 1966, Smith, a United States person, recognizes gain upon the sale of one share of the only class of stock of F Corporation, which he has owned continuously since 1955. He includes a portion of the gain in his gross income as a dividend under section 1248(a). On January 1, 1966, F owns directly 60 shares of the 100 outstanding shares of the only class of stock of G Corporation, which F acquired in 1955 and owned continuously until such sale. F uses a taxable year ending June 30, and G uses the calendar year as the taxable year. For 1964, G was a less developed country corporation, and on each day of 1964 G was a controlled foreign corporation. Smith's ratable share for G's taxable year ending December 31, 1964, attributable to F's taxable year ending June 30, 1965 (determined without regard to this paragraph) is $6.00. Since the percentage computed under subparagraph (2) of this paragraph is 100 percent (60 shares divided by 60 shares), Smith's ratable share for G's taxable year ending December 31, 1964, attributable to F's taxable year ending June 30, 1965 (after the application of subparagraph (2) of this paragraph) is zero (that is, $6.00 reduced by 100 percent of $6.00).

Example (2). Assume the same facts as in example (1) except that of the 60 shares of G Corporation which F Corporation owned on January 1, 1966, 20 shares were acquired in 1961. The percentage computed under subparagraph (2) of this paragraph is 66⅔ percent (40 shares divided by 60 shares). Accordingly, Smith's ratable share for G's taxable year ending December 31, 1964, attributable to F's taxable year ending June 30, 1965 (after the application of subparagraph (2) of this paragraph) is $2.00 (that is, $6.00 reduced by 66⅔ percent of $6.00).

(4) *Percentage for lower tier corporations other than second tier corporation.* For purposes of subparagraph (1) of this paragraph, if stock of a lower tier corporation (other than a second tier corporation) is owned within the meaning of section 958(a)(2) by the first tier corporation on the date of the sale or exchange referred to in such subparagraph (1), the percentage under this subparagraph shall be computed in the following manner:

(i) First, determine the percentage for the second tier corporation in accordance with subparagraph (2) of this paragraph.

(ii) Second, determine a partial percentage for each other lower tier corporation in the same manner as the percentage for the second tier corporation is determined. Thus, for example, the partial percentage for a third tier corporation is determined by dividing *(a)* the number of shares of stock of the third tier corporation which the second tier corporation has owned directly for an uninterrupted 10-year period ending on the date of the sale or exchange referred to in subparagraph (1) of this paragraph, by *(b)* the total number of shares of stock of such third tier corporation owned directly by such second tier corporation on such date.

Reg. § 1.1248-3(g)(4)

53,552 Rules for Determining Capital Gains and Losses
See p. 20,601 for regulations not amended to reflect law changes

(iii) Third, the percentage for a third tier corporation is the percentage for the second tier corporation multiplied by the partial percentage for the third tier corporation. The percentage for a fourth tier corporation is the percentage for the third tier corporation (as determined in the preceding sentence) multiplied by the partial percentage for the fourth tier corporation. In a similar manner, the percentage for any other lower tier corporation may be determined.

(5) *Example.* The application of subparagraph (4) of this paragraph may be illustrated by the following example:

(1) Corporation	(2) Shares directly owned by preceding tier— For uninterrupted 10-year period ending 1/1/67	(3) On 1/1/67	(4) Col. (2) divided by Col. (3) (percent)
X	40	60	66 2/3
Y	30	40	75
Z	20	30	66 2/3

For 1964, the percentage referred to in subparagraph (4) of this paragraph for Z is 33 1/3 percent (66 2/3% × 75% × 66 2/3%).

(6) *Special rule.* For purposes of applying the provisions of this paragraph, a lower tier corporation may be treated as a second tier corporation with respect to any of its stock which is owned directly by a first tier corporation whereas such lower tier corporation may be treated as a lower tier corporation other than a second tier corporation with respect to other stock in such lower tier corporation which is owned (within the meaning of section 958(a)(2)) by such first tier corporation. Thus, for example, if corporations X, Y, and Z are foreign corporations, X is a first tier corporation owning directly 100 percent of the stock of Y and 40 percent of the stock of Z, and in addition Y owns directly 60 percent of the stock of Z, then the 40 percent of the Z stock (which X owns directly) is considered to be stock in a second tier corporation and the 60 percent of the Z stock (which Y owns directly and which X is considered to own within the meaning of section 958(a)(2)) is considered to be stock in a third tier corporation. [Reg. § 1.1248-3.]

☐ [T.D. 6779, 12-21-64. Amended by T.D. 7293, 11-27-73 and T.D. 7545, 5-5-78.]

[Reg. § 1.1248-4]

§ 1.1248-4. Limitation on tax applicable to individuals.—(a) *General rule*—(1) *Limitation on tax.* Under section 1248(b), if during a taxable year an individual sells or exchanges stock in a foreign corporation, then in respect of the stock the increase in the individual's income tax liability for such taxable year which is attributable

Example. On January 1, 1967, Brown, a United States person recognizes gain upon the sale of one share of the only class of stock of W Corporation, which he has owned continuously since 1955. He includes a portion of the gain in his gross income as a dividend under section 1248(a). W is the first tier corporation of a chain of foreign corporations W, X, Y, and Z. W and Z each use the calendar year as the taxable year. For 1964, Z was a less developed country corporation and on each day of 1964 Z was a controlled foreign corporation. Additional facts are set forth in the table below:

(under paragraph (b) of this section) to the amount included in his gross income as a dividend under section 1248(a) shall not be greater than an amount equal to the sum of—

(i) The excess, computed under paragraph (c) of this section in respect of the stock, of the United States taxes which would have been paid by the corporation over the taxes (including United States taxes) actually paid by the corporation, plus

(ii) An amount equal to the increase in the individual's income tax liability which would be attributable to the inclusion in his gross income for such taxable year, as long-term capital gain, of an amount equal to the excess of *(a)* the amount included in the individual's gross income as a dividend under section 1248(a) in respect of such stock, over *(b)* the excess referred to in subdivision (i) of this subparagraph.

(2) *Share or block.* In general, the limitation on tax attributable (under paragraph (b) of this section) to the amount included in an individual's gross income as a dividend under section 1248(a) shall be determined separately for each share of stock sold or exchanged. However, such determination may be made in respect of a block of stock if earnings and profits attributable to the block are computed under § 1.1248-2 or 1.1248-3. See paragraph (b) of § 1.1248-2 and paragraph (a)(5) of § 1.1248-3.

(3) *Application of limitation.* The provisions of subparagraph (1) of this paragraph shall not apply unless the individual establishes—

(i) In the manner prescribed in § 1.1248-7, the amount of the earnings and profits of the

Reg. § 1.1248-4(a)(1)

Rules for Determining Capital Gains and Losses 53,553
See p. 20,601 for regulations not amended to reflect law changes

corporation attributable under paragraph (a)(1) of § 1.1248-2 or under paragraph (a)(1) of § 1.1248-3, whichever is applicable, to the stock, and

(ii) The amount equal to the sum described in subparagraph (1) of this paragraph, computed in accordance with the provisions of this section.

(4) *Example.* The provisions of this paragraph may be illustrated by the following example:

Example. On December 31, 1966, Smith, a United States person, sells a share of stock of X Corporation which he has owned continuously since December 31, 1965, and includes $100 of the gain on the sale in his gross income as a dividend under section 1248(a). Both X and Smith use the calendar year as the taxable year. The increase in Smith's income tax liability for 1966 which is attributable (under paragraph (b) of this section) to the inclusion of the $100 in his gross income as a dividend is $70. X was a controlled foreign corporation on each day of 1966. The excess, computed under paragraph (c) of this section in respect of the share, of the United States taxes which X would have paid over the taxes (including United States taxes) actually paid by X is $49. Under section 1248(b), the limitation on the tax attributable to the $100 included by Smith in his gross income as a dividend under section 1248(a) is $61.75, computed as follows:

(i) Excess, computed under paragraph (c) of this section, of United States taxes which X Corporation would have paid in 1966 over the taxes actually paid by X in 1966 .... $49.00
(ii) The amount determined under subparagraph (1)(ii) of this paragraph:
The amount Smith included in his gross income as a dividend under section 1248(a) $100.00
Less the excess referred to in subdivision (i) of this example .... $ 49.00

Difference .... $ 51.00

Increase in Smith's tax liability attributable to including $51 in his gross income as long-term capital gain (25 percent of $51) $12.75

(iii) Limitation on tax $61.75

(b) *Tax attributable to amount treated as dividend* —(1) *General.* For purposes of paragraph (a)(1) of this section, in respect of a share (or block) of stock in a foreign corporation sold or exchanged by an individual during a taxable year, the tax attributable to the amount included in his gross income as a dividend under section 1248(a) shall be the amount which bears the same ratio to (i) the excess of *(a)* his income tax liability for the taxable year determined without regard to section 1248(b) over *(b)* such tax liability determined as if the portion of the total gain recognized during the taxable year which is treated as a dividend under section 1248(a) had not been recognized, as (ii) the amount included as a dividend under section 1248(a) in respect of the share (or block), bears to (iii) the total amount included as a dividend under section 1248(a) in the individual's gross income for such taxable year.

(2) *Examples.* The application of this paragraph may be illustrated by the following examples:

Example (1). (i) During 1963, Brown, an unmarried United States person, sells a block of stock in a controlled foreign corporation. On the sale, he recognizes $22,000 gain, of which $18,000 is treated as a dividend under section 1248(a) and $4,000 as long-term capital gain. Brown computes his income tax liability for his taxable year ending December 31, 1963, under section 1201 (relating to alternative tax) in accordance with the additional facts assumed in the following table:

	Computation of income tax liability without regard to section 1248(b)	Computation of income tax liability as if the gain treated as a dividend under section 1248(a) had not been recognized
Income from salary	$300,000	$300,000
Long-term capital gain resulting from sale of stock, less deduction for capital gains under section 1202 ($4,000 less $2,000)	2,000	2,000
Amount treated as a dividend under section 1248(a)	$18,000	0
Adjusted gross income	$320,000	$302,000
Charitable contribution of $100,000 to church (limited under section 170(b) to 30 percent of adjusted gross income) ...	(96,000)	(90,600)

Reg. § 1.1248-4(b)(2)

Other itemized deductions and personal exemption	(7,700)	(7,700)
Taxable income	$216,300	$203,700
Less 50 percent of $4,000	2,000	2,000
Amount subject to partial tax under section 1201(b)(1)	$214,300	$201,700
Partial tax	$169,833	$158,367
25 percent of $4,000	1,000	1,000
Tax liability	$170,833	$159,367

(ii) The tax attributable to the $18,000 treated as a dividend under section 1248(a) is $11,466 ($170,833 minus $159,367).

Example (2). Assume the same facts as in example (1) except that the $18,000 treated as a dividend under section 1248(a) is attributable to the sale of a block of stock in X Corporation and a block of stock in Y Corporation. Assume further that $10,000 of the gain on the block of X stock was treated as a dividend and that $8,000 of the gain on the block of Y stock was treated as a dividend. Thus, the tax attributable to the amount treated as a dividend in respect of the block of X stock is $6,370 ($10,000/$18,000 of $11,466) and the amount in respect of the block of Y stock is $5,096 ($8,000/$18,000 of $11,466). The result would be the same if both blocks of stock were blocks of stock in the same corporation.

(c) *Excess (of United States taxes which would have been paid over taxes actually paid) attributable to a share*—(1) *General.* For purposes of paragraph (a)(1)(i) of this section—

(i) The term "taxes" means income, war profits, or excess profits taxes, and

(ii) The excess (and the portion of such excess attributable to an individual's share or block of stock in a foreign corporation) of the United States taxes which would have been paid by the corporation over the taxes (including United States taxes) actually paid by the corporation, for the period or periods the stock was held (or was considered to be held by reason of the application of section 1223) by the individual in taxable years of the corporation beginning after December 31, 1962, while the corporation was a controlled foreign corporation, shall be computed in accordance with the steps set forth in subparagraphs (2), (3), and (4) of this paragraph.

(2) *Step 1.* For each taxable year of the corporation beginning after December 31, 1962, in respect of the individual's share (or block) of such stock (i) the taxable income of the corporation shall be computed in the manner prescribed in paragraph (d) of this section, and (ii) the excess (and the portion of such excess attributable to the stock) of the United States taxes which would have been paid by the corporation on such taxable income over the taxes (including United States taxes) actually paid by the corporation shall be computed in the manner prescribed in paragraph (e) of this section.

(3) *Step 2.* If during such taxable year the corporation is a first tier corporation to which paragraph (f) of this section applies, (i) the excess (and the portion of such excess attributable to the individual's share, or block, of stock in the first tier corporation) of the United States taxes which would have been paid by any lower tier corporation over the taxes (including United States taxes) actually paid by such lower tier corporation shall be computed under paragraph (f) of this section, and (ii) such portion shall be added to the portion of the excess attributable to the individual's share (or block) of such stock as determined in step 1 for such taxable year.

(4) *Step 3.* The excess, in respect of the individual's share (or block), of the United States taxes which would have been paid by the corporation over the taxes actually paid by the corporation shall be the sum of the portions computed for each such taxable year in the manner prescribed in steps 1 and 2.

(d) *Taxable income.* For purposes of paragraph (c)(2)(i) of this section, taxable income shall be computed in respect of an individual's share (or block) in accordance with the following rules:

(1) *Application of principles of § 1.952-2.* Except as otherwise provided in this paragraph, the principles of paragraphs (a)(1), (b)(1), and (c) of § 1.952-2 (other than subparagraphs (2)(iii)(b), (2)(v), (5)(i), and (6) of such paragraph (c)) shall apply.

(2) *Effect of elections.* In respect of a taxable year of a foreign corporation, no effect shall be given to an election or an adoption of accounting method unless for such taxable year effect is given to such election or adoption of accounting method under paragraph (d)(1) of § 1.1248-2 or paragraph (b)(1) of § 1.1248-3, whichever is applicable.

(3) The deductions for certain dividends received provided in sections 243, 244, and 245 shall not be allowed.

(4) *Deduction for taxes.* In computing the amount of the deduction allowed under section 164, there shall be excluded income, war profits, or excess profits taxes paid or accrued which are imposed by the authority of any foreign country or possession of the United States.

Reg. § 1.1248-4(c)(2)

Rules for Determining Capital Gains and Losses 53,555

See p. 20,601 for regulations not amended to reflect law changes

(5) *Capital loss carryover.* In determining the amount of a net capital loss to be carried forward under section 1212 to the taxable year—

(i) No net capital loss shall be carried forward from a taxable year beginning before January 1, 1963.

(ii) The portion of a net capital loss or a capital gain net income (net capital gain for taxable years beginning before January 1, 1977) for a taxable year beginning after December 31, 1962, which shall be taken into account shall be the amount of such loss or gain (as the case may be), multiplied by the percentage which *(a)* the number of days in such taxable year during which the individual held (or was considered to have held by reason of the application of section 1223) the share (or block) of stock sold or exchanged while the corporation was a controlled foreign corporation, bears to *(b)* the total number of days in such taxable year.

(iii) The application of this subparagraph may be illustrated by the following examples:

Example (1). Corporation X is a foreign corporation which was created on January 1, 1963, and which uses the calendar year as its taxable year. X was a controlled foreign corporation on each day of the period March 15, 1963, through December 31, 1965, but was not a controlled foreign corporation on any day during the period January 1, 1963, through March 14, 1963. On December 31, 1965, Smith, a United States person, sells a share of X stock which he has owned continuously since January 1, 1963. A portion of the gain recognized on the sale is includible in Smith's gross income as a dividend under section 1248(a). X had a net capital loss (determined without regard to subchapter N, chapter 1 of the Code) of $200 for 1963. Since, however, X was a controlled foreign corporation for only 292 days in 1963, for purposes of determining the net capital loss carryover to 1964 the portion of the net capital loss of $200 for 1963 which Smith takes into account under subdivision (ii) of this subparagraph is $160 (292/365 of $200), and, accordingly, the amount of the net capital loss carryover to 1964 is $160.

Example (2). Assume the same facts as in example (1), except that X was not a controlled foreign corporation on any day of the period May 26, 1964, through June 30, 1965. Assume further that X had a net capital gain (capital gain net income for taxable years beginning after December 31, 1976) (determined without regard to subchapter N, chapter 1, of the Code) of $160 for 1964. In computing X's taxable income for 1964 under this paragraph, Smith applies the net capital loss carryover of $160 from 1963 to reduce the net capital gain (capital gain net income for taxable years beginning after December 31, 1976) of $160 for 1964 to zero. Since, however, X was a controlled foreign corporation for only 146 days in 1964, for purposes of computing the portion of the 1963 capital loss of $160 which is a net capital loss carryover to 1965, the portion of the 1964 capital gain which Smith takes into account under subdivision (ii) of this subparagraph is $63.83 (146/366 of $160). Thus, the net capital loss carryover to 1965 is $96.17 ($160 minus $63.83).

(6) *Net operating loss deduction.* (i) The individual shall reduce the taxable income (computed under subparagraphs (1) through (5) of this paragraph) of the corporation for the taxable year by the amount of the net operating loss deduction of the corporation computed under section 172, as modified in the manner prescribed in this subparagraph.

(ii) The rules of subparagraphs (1) through (5) of this paragraph shall apply for purposes of determining the excess referred to in section 172(c) and the taxable income referred to in section 172(b)(2).

(iii) A net operating loss shall not be carried forward from, or carried back to, a taxable year beginning before January 1, 1963.

(iv) The portion of a net operating loss incurred, or of taxable income earned, in a taxable year beginning after December 31, 1962, which shall be taken into account under section 172(b)(2) shall be the amount of such loss or income (as the case may be), multiplied by the percentage which *(a)* the number of days in such taxable year during which the individual held (or was considered to have held by reason of the application of section 1223) the share (or block) of stock sold or exchanged while the corporation was a controlled foreign corporation, bears to *(b)* the total number of days in such taxable year.

(v) For illustrations of the principles of this subparagraph, see the examples relating to net capital loss carryovers in subparagraph (5)(iii) of this paragraph.

(7) *Adjustment for amount previously included in gross income of United States shareholders.* In respect of the individual's share (or block) of stock sold or exchanged, the taxable income of the corporation for the taxable year (determined without regard to this subparagraph and subparagraph (8) of this paragraph) shall be reduced (but not below zero) by an amount equal to the sum of the amounts included under section 951 in the gross income of United States shareholders (as defined in section 951(b)) of the corporation for the taxable year.

(8) *Adjustment for distributions.* In respect of the individual's share (or block) of stock sold or exchanged, the taxable income of the corporation

Reg. § 1.1248-4(d)(8)

Rules for Determining Capital Gains and Losses

for the taxable year (determined without regard to this subparagraph) shall be reduced (but not below zero) by the amount of the distributions (other than in redemption of stock under section 302(a) or 303) made by the corporation out of earnings and profits of such taxable year (within the meaning of section 316(a)(2)). For purposes of the preceding sentence, distributions shall be taken into account only to the extent not excluded from the gross income of the United States shareholders of the corporation under section 959.

(e) *Excess attributable to a share (or block) of stock* —(1) *Excess of United States taxes which would have been paid over taxes actually paid.* For purposes of paragraph (c)(2)(ii) of this section, in respect of a taxable year of a foreign corporation, the portion of the excess under this subparagraph which is attributable to an individual's share (or block) of such stock shall be an amount equal to—

(i) The excess (if any) of (a) the United States taxes which would have been paid by the corporation on its taxable income (computed under paragraph (d) of this section) for the taxable year had it been taxed as a domestic corporation under chapter 1 of the Code (but without regard to subchapters F, G, H, L, M, N, S, and T thereof) for such taxable year, over (b) the income, war profits, or excess profits taxes actually paid by the corporation during such taxable year (including such taxes paid to the United States),

(ii) Multiplied by the percentage that (a) the number of days in such taxable year of the corporation during the period or periods the share (or block) was held (or was considered as held by reason of the application of section 1223) by the individual while the corporation was a controlled foreign corporation, bears to (b) the total number of days in such taxable year,

(iii) If the computation is made in respect of a block, multiplied by the number of shares in the block, and

(iv) Divided by the number of shares in the corporation outstanding, or deemed under paragraph (c)(2) of § 1.1248-3 to be outstanding, on each day of such taxable year.

(2) *Example.* The provisions of this paragraph may be illustrated by the following example:

Example. (i) Jones, a United States person, owns on each day of 1963 10 shares of the 100 shares of the only class of outstanding stock of X Corporation. He sells one of such shares on December 31, 1963. X Corporation is a controlled foreign corporation on each day of 1963 and Jones and X each use the calendar year as the taxable year. For 1963, the excess of the United States taxes which would have been paid by X had it been taxable as a domestic corporation over the taxes (including United States taxes) actually paid by X is $23,500, computed as follows:

Amount subject to partial tax under section 1201 (a)(1), as computed by Jones:

Taxable income		$300,000
Less excess of net long-term capital gain over net short-term capital loss		100,000
Amount subject to partial tax		$200,000
Excess determined under subparagraph (1)(i) of this paragraph:		
30 percent × $25,000	$ 7,500	
52 percent × $175,000	91,000	
Partial tax		$ 98,500
25 percent × $100,000		25,000
United States taxes X would have paid (alternative tax computed under section 1201(a))		$123,500
Less income taxes X actually paid to: United States	$10,000	
foreign countries	90,000	
Total		$100,000
Excess		$ 23,500
Multiplied by:		
Percentage determined under subparagraph (1)(ii) of this paragraph:		
Since on each day of 1963, Jones held the share of X stock while X was a controlled foreign corporation, the percentage equals		100%
Total		$ 23,500

(ii) The portion of the excess determined in subdivision (i) of this example which is attributable to the share held by Jones is $235, that is, the amount of such excess ($23,500), divided by the number of shares of X deemed to be outstanding on each day of 1963 (100).

(3) *More than one class of stock.* If a foreign corporation for a taxable year has more than one class of stock outstanding, then before applying subparagraph (1) of this paragraph the excess (if any) which would be determined under subparagraph (1)(i) of this paragraph shall be allocated to each class of stock in accordance with the princi-

Reg. § 1.1248-4(e)(1)

ples of paragraph (e)(2) and (3) and § 1.951-1, applied as if the corporation were a controlled foreign corporation on each day of such taxable year.

(f) *Subsidiaries of foreign corporations*—(1) *Excess for lower tier corporation attributable to taxable year of first tier corporation.* For purposes of paragraph (c)(3) of this section, if the provisions of paragraph (a)(3) of § 1.1248-2 or paragraph (f) of § 1.1248-3 apply in the case of the sale or exchange by an individual of a share (or block) of stock in a first tier corporation, then in respect of a taxable year of a lower tier corporation (beginning after December 31, 1962) which includes at least one day which falls within a taxable year of the first tier corporation (beginning after December 31, 1962), the portion of the excess under this subparagraph attributable to the share shall be an amount equal to—

(i) The excess (if any) of *(a)* the United States taxes which would have been paid by the lower tier corporation on its taxable income (computed under paragraph (g) of this section) for such taxable year of the lower tier corporation had it been taxed as a domestic corporation under chapter 1 of the Code (but without regard to subchapters F, G, H, L, M, N, and T thereof) for such taxable year of the lower tier corporation, over *(b)* the income, war profits, or excess profits taxes actually paid by the lower tier corporation during such taxable year (including such taxes paid to the United States),

(ii) Multiplied by each of the percentages described under paragraph (f)(2)(ii), (iii), and (iv) of § 1.1248-3 in respect of such taxable year of the first tier corporation,

(iii) If the computation is made in respect of a block of stock, multiplied by the number of shares in the block, and

(iv) Divided by the number of shares in the first tier corporation outstanding, or deemed under paragraph (c)(2) of § 1.1248-3 to be outstanding, on each day of such taxable year of the first tier corporation.

(2) *More than one class of stock.* If a foreign corporation for a taxable year has more than one class of stock outstanding, then before applying subparagraph (1) of this paragraph the principles of paragraph (e)(3) of this section shall apply.

(g) *Taxable income of lower tier corporations*— (1) *General.* For purposes of paragraph (f)(1)(i) of this section, in respect of the individual's share (or block) the taxable income of a lower tier corporation shall be computed in the manner provided in paragraph (d) of this section, except as provided in this paragraph.

(2) *Capital loss carryover.* For purposes of subparagraph (1) of this paragraph, the provisions of paragraph (d)(5)(ii) of this section shall not apply. In determining the amount of a net capital loss to be carried forward under section 1212 to the taxable year of a lower tier corporation, the portion of a net capital loss or a capital gain net income (net capital gain for taxable years beginning before January 1, 1977) for a taxable year of the lower tier corporation beginning after December 31, 1962, which shall be taken into account shall be the amount of such loss or gain (as the case may be), multiplied by the percentage which (i) the number of days in such taxable year during the period or periods the individual held (or was considered to have held by reason of the application of section 1223) the share (or block) of stock in the first tier corporation sold or exchanged while the first tier corporation owned (within the meaning of section 958(a)) stock in the lower tier corporation while the lower tier corporation was a controlled foreign corporation, bears to (ii) the total number of days in such taxable year.

(3) *Net operating loss deduction.* For purposes of subparagraph (1) of this paragraph, the provisions of paragraph (d)(6)(iv) of this section shall not apply. In determining the amount of the net operating loss deduction for a taxable year of a lower tier corporation, the portion of a net operating loss incurred, or of taxable income earned, in a taxable year of the lower tier corporation beginning after December 31, 1962, which shall be taken into account under section 172(b)(2) shall be the amount of such loss or income (as the case may be) multiplied by the percentage described in subparagraph (2) of this paragraph for such taxable year. [Reg. § 1.1248-4.]

☐ [T.D. 6779, 12-21-64. Amended by T.D. 7545, 5-5-78 and T.D. 7728, 10-31-80.]

[Reg. § 1.1248-5]

§ 1.1248-5. Stock ownership requirements for less developed country corporations.—(a) *General rule*—(1) *Requirements.* For purposes of paragraph (e)(4) of § 1.1248-3, a United States person shall be considered as satisfying the requirements of this paragraph with respect to a share (or block) of stock of a foreign corporation if on the date he sells or exchanges such share (or block)—

(i) The 10-year stock ownership requirement of paragraph (b) of this section is met with respect to such share (or block), and

(ii) In the case of a United States person which is a domestic corporation, the requirement of paragraph (c) of this section, if applicable, is met.

(2) *Ownership of stock.* For purposes of this section—

(i) The rules for determining ownership of stock prescribed by section 958(a) and (b) shall apply.

(ii) Stock owned by a United States person who is an individual, estate, or trust which was acquired by reason of the death of the predecessor in interest of such United States person shall be considered as owned by such United States person during the period such stock was owned by such predecessor in interest, and during the period such stock was owned by any other predecessor in interest if between such United States person and such other predecessor in interest there was no transfer other than by reason of the death of an individual.

(b) *10-year stock ownership requirement* —(1) *General.* A United States person meets the 10-year stock ownership requirement with respect to a share (or block) of stock in a foreign corporation which he sells or exchanges only if the share (or block) was owned (under the rules of paragraph (a)(2) of this section) by such person for a continuous period of at least 10 years ending on the date of the sale or exchange. See the first sentence of section 1248(d)(3). Thus, for example, if Jones, a United States person, sells a share of stock in a foreign corporation on January 1, 1965, the 10-year stock ownership requirement is met with respect to the share only if the share was owned (under the rules of paragraph (a)(2) of this section) by Jones continuously from January 1, 1955, to January 1, 1965. If a foreign corporation has not been in existence for at least 10 years on the date of the sale or exchange of the share, the 10-year stock ownership requirement cannot be met.

(2) *Special rule.* For purposes of this paragraph, a United States person shall be considered to have owned stock during the period he was considered to have held the stock by reason of the application of section 1223.

(c) *Disqualification of domestic corporation as a result of changes in ownership of its stock* —(1) *General.* (i) For purposes of paragraph (a)(1)(ii) of this section, the requirement of this paragraph must be met only if, on at least one day during the 10-year period ending on the date of the sale or exchange by a domestic corporation of a share of stock in a foreign corporation, one or more noncorporate United States shareholders (as defined in subdivision (iii) of this subparagraph) own more than 50 percent of the total combined voting power of all classes of stock entitled to vote of the domestic corporation.

(ii) The requirement of this paragraph is that if one or more persons are noncorporate United States shareholders on the first such day (referred to in subdivision (i) of this subparagraph), such person or persons continue after such first day, at all times during the remainder of such 10-year period, to own in the aggregate more than 50 percent of the total combined voting power of all classes of stock entitled to vote of the domestic corporation. For purposes of determining whether a domestic corporation meets the requirement of this paragraph, the stock owned by a United States person who is a noncorporate United States shareholder of a domestic corporation on such first day shall not be counted at any time after he ceases during such ten-year period to be a noncorporate United States shareholder of such corporation.

(iii) For purposes of this paragraph, the term "noncorporate United States shareholder" means, with respect to a domestic corporation, a United States person who is an individual, estate, or trust and who owns 10 percent or more of the total combined voting power of all classes of stock of such domestic corporation.

(iv) For purposes of this paragraph, the percentage of the total combined voting power of stock of a foreign corporation owned by a United States person shall be determined in accordance with the principles of section 951(b) and the regulations thereunder.

(2) *Examples.* The application of this paragraph may be illustrated by the following examples:

Example (1). During the entire period beginning December 31, 1954, and ending December 31, 1964, domestic corporation N owns all the stock of controlled foreign corporation X, a less developed country corporation. On December 31, 1964, N recognizes gain upon the sale of all its X stock. A, B, and C, who are unrelated individuals, were the only United States persons owning, or considered as owning, 10 percent or more of the total combined voting power of all classes of stock entitled to vote of N at any time during the 10-year period December 31, 1954, through December 31, 1964. The percentages of the total combined voting power in N, which A, B, and C owned during such 10-year period, are as follows:

Reg. § 1.1248-5(a)(2)

Owner	Dec. 31, 1954-Apr. 1, 1957 Percent	Apr. 2, 1957-Oct. 1, 1959 Percent	Oct. 2, 1959-Dec. 31, 1964 Percent
A	20	20	20
B	9	30	30
C	30	15	9

Domestic corporation N does not meet the requirement of this paragraph with respect to the stock of controlled foreign corporation X for the following reasons:

(i) April 2, 1957, is the first day (during the 10-year period ending on December 31, 1964, the date N sells the X stock) on which noncorporate United States shareholders of N own more than 50 percent of the total combined voting power in N, and thus the requirement of this paragraph must be met. See subparagraph (1)(i) of this paragraph. Although A, B, and C did own, in the aggregate, more than 50 percent of such voting power before April 2, 1957, the voting power owned by B is not counted because B was not a noncorporate United States shareholder of N before such date.

(ii) Although C is a noncorporate United States shareholder on April 2, 1957, C ceases to own 10 percent or more of the total combined voting power in N on October 2, 1959. Thus, after October 1, 1959, the N stock which C owns is not counted for purposes of determining whether the more-than-50-percent stock ownership test is met. See subparagraph (1)(ii) of this paragraph. Accordingly, after October 1, 1959, the requirement of this paragraph is not met.

Example (2). Assume the same facts as in example (1), except that B's wife owns directly 5 percent of the total combined voting power in N from December 31, 1954, to December 31, 1964. On the basis of the assumed facts, N meets the requirement of this paragraph with respect to the stock of controlled foreign corporation X for the following reasons:

(i) December 31, 1954, is the first day (of the 10-year period ending on the date N sells the X stock) on which noncorporate United States shareholders of N own more than 50 percent of the total combined voting power in N. B is a noncorporate United States shareholder on such date because he owns, and is considered as owning, 14 percent of the total combined voting power in N (9 percent directly, and, under section 958(b), 5 percent constructively). Thus, on December 31, 1954, noncorporate United States shareholders A, B, and C own, in the aggregate, more than 50 percent of the total combined voting power in N.

(ii) A, B, and C, the noncorporate United States shareholders of N on December 31, 1954, own, and are considered as owning, more than 50 percent of the total voting power of N from December 31, 1954, to October 1, 1959. Since beginning on October 2, 1959, A owns 20 percent and B owns, and is considered as owning, 35 percent of the total combined voting power in N, A and B own, and are considered as owning, more than 50 percent of the total combined voting power in N from October 2, 1959, to December 31, 1964. Therefore, the requirement of this paragraph is met.

(d) *Application of section to lower tier corporation*—(1) *General.* For purposes of paragraph (g)(1)(ii) of § 1.1248-3, a United States person satisfies the requirements of this subparagraph in respect of stock of a lower tier corporation which such person, by reason of his direct ownership of the share (or block) of the first tier corporation sold or exchanged, owned within the meaning of section 958(a)(2) on the date he sold or exchanged such share (or block), if on such date—

(i) The 10-year stock ownership requirement of paragraph (b) of this section is met by such person with respect to any stock in the lower tier corporation which such person so owned, and

(ii) In the case of a United States person which is a domestic corporation, the requirement of paragraph (c) of this section, if applicable, is met.

(2) *Special rule.* For purposes of this paragraph, in applying paragraphs (b) and (c) of this section, the sale or exchange of a share (or block) of stock in a first tier corporation by a United States person shall be deemed to be the sale or exchange of any stock in a lower tier corporation which the person, by reason of his direct ownership of such share (or block) of the first tier corporation, owned within the meaning of section 958(a)(2) on the date he actually sold or exchanged such share (or block) in the first tier corporation. [Reg. § 1.1248-5.]

☐ [T.D. 6779, 12-21-64.]

[Reg. § 1.1248-6]

§ 1.1248-6. Sale or exchange of stock in certain domestic corporations.—(a) *General rule.* If a United States person recognizes gain upon the sale or exchange of a share (or block) of stock of a domestic corporation which was formed or availed of principally for the holding, directly or indirectly, of stock of one or more foreign corporations, and if the conditions of paragraph (a)(2) of § 1.1248-1 would be met by such person in respect

53,560 Rules for Determining Capital Gains and Losses

See p. 20,601 for regulations not amended to reflect law changes

of the share (or block) if the domestic corporation were a foreign corporation, then section 1248 shall apply in respect of such gain in accordance with the rules provided in paragraph (b) of this section.

(b) *Application.* (1) The gain referred to in paragraph (a) of this section shall be included in the gross income of the United States person as a dividend under section 1248(a) to the extent of the earnings and profits attributable under § 1.1248-2 or § 1.1248-3, whichever is applicable, to the share (or block), computed, however, in accordance with the following rules:

(i) The domestic corporation shall be treated as if it were a first tier foreign corporation;

(ii) If, after the application of subdivision (i) of this subparagraph, the provisions of paragraph (a)(3) of § 1.1248-2 or paragraph (f) of § 1.1248-3 (as the case may be) would apply in respect of a foreign corporation the stock of which is owned (within the meaning of section 958(a)) by the domestic corporation treated as the first tier corporation, such foreign corporation shall be considered a lower tier corporation;

(iii) Except to the extent provided in subdivision (iv) of this subparagraph, the earnings and profits of the domestic corporation treated as the first tier corporation accumulated for a taxable year, as computed under paragraph (d) of § 1.1248-2 or paragraph (b) of § 1.1248-3 (as the case may be), shall be considered to be zero; and

(iv) If, during a taxable year, a domestic corporation treated as the first tier corporation realizes gain upon the sale or exchange of stock in a foreign corporation, and solely by reason of the application of section 337 (relating to certain liquidations) the gain was not recognized, then the earnings and profits of such domestic corporation accumulated for the taxable year as computed under paragraph (d) of § 1.1248-2 or paragraph (b) of § 1.1248-3 (as the case may be), shall be considered to be an amount equal to the portion of such gain realized during the taxable year which, if section 337 had not applied, would have been treated as a dividend under section 1248(a).

(2) If the person selling or exchanging the stock in the domestic corporation is an individual, the limitation on tax attributable to the amount included in his gross income as a dividend under subparagraph (1) of this paragraph shall be determined, in accordance with the principles of paragraph (f) of § 1.1248-4, by treating the domestic corporation as a first tier corporation.

(3)(i) If the earnings and profits of the foreign corporation or corporations (or of the domestic corporation treated as a first tier corporation) to be taken into account under subparagraph (1) of this paragraph are not established in the manner provided in paragraph (a)(1) of § 1.1248-7, all of the gain from the sale or exchange of the share (or block) of the domestic corporation shall be treated as a dividend.

(ii) To the extent that the person does not establish, in the manner provided in paragraph (c) of § 1.1248-7, the foreign taxes paid by such foreign corporation or corporations to be taken into account for purposes of computing the limitation on tax attributable to a share, such foreign taxes shall not be taken into account for purposes of such computation.

(c) *Corporation formed or availed of principally for holding stock of foreign corporations.* Whether or not a domestic corporation is formed or availed of principally for the holding, directly or indirectly, of stock of one or more foreign corporations shall be determined on the basis of all the facts and circumstances of each particular case. [Reg. § 1.1248-6.]

☐ [*T.D.* 6779, 12-21-64.]

[Reg. § 1.1248-7]

§ 1.1248-7. Taxpayer to establish earnings and profits and foreign taxes.—(a) *In general*—(1) *Earnings and profits.* If a taxpayer sells or exchanges stock in a foreign corporation which was a controlled foreign corporation and the Commissioner determines that the taxpayer has not established the amount of the earnings and profits of the corporation attributable to the stock under § 1.1248-2 or § 1.1248-3, whichever is applicable, all the gain from such sale or exchange shall be treated as a dividend under section 1248(a). See section 1248(g). A taxpayer shall be considered to have established such amount if—

(i) He attaches to his income tax return, filed on or before the last day prescribed by law (including extensions thereof) for his taxable year in which he sold or exchanged the stock, the schedule prescribed by paragraph (b) of this section or, if such last day is before April 1, 1965, he files such schedule before such date with the district director with whom such return was filed, and

(ii) He establishes in the manner prescribed by paragraph (d) of this section the correctness of each amount shown on such schedule.

(2) Notwithstanding an omission of information from, or an error with respect to an amount shown on, the schedule referred to in subparagraph (1)(i) of this paragraph, a taxpayer shall be considered to have complied with such subparagraph (1)(i) if—

(i) He establishes that such omission or error was inadvertent, or due to reasonable cause

Reg. § 1.1248-7(a)(1)

and not due to willful neglect, and that he has substantially complied with the requirements of this section, and

(ii) The taxpayer corrects such omission or error at the time when he complies with paragraph (d) of this section.

(3) For the requirement to establish the amount of foreign taxes to be taken into account for purposes of section 1248(b), see paragraph (c) of this section.

(b) *Schedule attached to return.* (1) The taxpayer shall attach to his income tax return for his taxable year in which he sold or exchanged the stock, a schedule showing his name, address, and identifying number. Except to the extent provided in paragraph (e) of this section, the schedule shall also show the amount of the earnings and profits attributable under paragraph (a) of § 1.1248-2 or paragraph (a) of § 1.1248-3 (as the case may be) to the stock, and, in order to support the computation of such amount, any additional information required by subparagraphs (2), (3), (4), and (5) of this paragraph.

(2) The schedule shall also show for the first tier corporation, and for each lower tier corporation as to which information is required under subparagraph (4) of this paragraph, (i) the name of the corporation, (ii) the country under whose laws the corporation is created or organized, and (iii) the last day of the taxable year which the corporation regularly uses in computing its income.

(3) If the amount of earnings and profits attributable to a block of stock sold or exchanged are computed under § 1.1248-2, the schedule shall also show—

(i) For each taxable year of the corporation, beginning after December 31, 1962, during the period the taxpayer held (or was considered to have held by reason of the application of section 1223) the block, (a) the earnings and profits accumulated for each such taxable year computed under paragraph (d) of § 1.1248-2, and (b) the sum thereof computed under paragraph (e)(1)(i) and (2) of § 1.1248-2,

(ii) The number of shares in the block and the total number of shares of the corporation outstanding during such period,

(iii) If during the period the person held (or is considered to have held by reason of the application of section 1223) the block any amount was included under section 951 in the gross income of such person (or another person) in respect of the block, the computation of the excess referred to in paragraph (e)(3)(ii) of § 1.1248-2, and

(iv) If the amount of earnings and profits of a lower tier corporation attributable to the block are computed under paragraph (a)(3) of § 1.1248-2, (a) the number of shares in the lower tier corporation which the taxpayer owns within the meaning of section 958(a)(2), (b) the total number of shares of such lower tier corporation outstanding during such period, and (c) in respect of such lower tier corporation, the information prescribed in subdivisions (i) and (iii) of this subparagraph.

(4) If the amount of earnings and profits attributable to a share (or block) sold or exchanged are computed under § 1.1248-3, the schedule shall also show for each taxable year of the corporation beginning after December 31, 1962, any day of which falls in a period or periods the taxpayer held (or was considered to have held by reason of the application of section 1223) the stock while the corporation was a controlled foreign corporation—

(i) The number of days in such period or periods, but only if such number is less than the total number of days in such taxable year,

(ii) The earnings and profits accumulated for the taxable year computed under paragraph (b) of § 1.1248-3,

(iii) The number of shares in the corporation outstanding, or deemed under paragraph (c)(2) of § 1.1248-3 to be outstanding, on each day of the taxable year,

(iv) The taxpayer's tentative ratable share computed under paragraph (c) or (d) (as the case may be) of § 1.1248-3,

(v) The amount of, and a short description of each adjustment to, the tentative ratable share under paragraph (e) of § 1.1248-3, and

(vi) The amount of the ratable share referred to in paragraph (e)(1) of § 1.1248-3.

(5) In respect of a taxable year referred to in subparagraph (4) of this paragraph of a first tier corporation, if the taxpayer is required to compute under paragraph (f)(5) of § 1.1248-3 his ratable share of the earnings and profits for a taxable year of the lower tier corporation attributable to such taxable year of such first tier corporation, then for such taxable year of the lower tier corporation the schedule shall show—

(i) The earnings and profits accumulated for the taxable year of the lower tier corporation, computed under paragraph (b) of § 1.1248-3,

(ii) Each percentage described in paragraph (f)(2)(ii), (iii), and (iv) of § 1.1248-3,

(iii) The amount of the taxpayer's tentative ratable share computed under paragraph (f)(2) or (4) (as the case may be) of § 1.1248-3,

Reg. § 1.1248-7(b)(5)

(iv) The amount of, and a short description of each adjustment to, the tentative ratable share under paragraph (f)(5) of § 1.1248-3, and

(v) The amount of the ratable share referred to in paragraph (f)(5)(i) of § 1.1248-3.

(c) *Foreign taxes.* (1) If the taxpayer fails to establish any portion of the amount of any foreign taxes which he is required to establish by subparagraph (2) of this paragraph, then such portion shall not be taken into account under section 1248(b)(1)(B).

(2) The taxpayer shall establish in respect of the stock he sells or exchanges the amount of the foreign taxes described in section 1248(b)(1)(B) paid by the first tier corporation for each taxable year of such corporation for which the information is required under paragraph (b)(3) or (4) of this section, and the amount of such taxes paid by each lower tier corporation for each taxable year (as to which information is required under paragraph (b)(3)(iv) or (5) of this section) of each such lower tier corporation. A taxpayer shall be considered to have established the amount of such foreign taxes if—

(i) He attaches to the schedule described in paragraph (b) of this section a supplementary schedule which, except to the extent provided in paragraph (e) of this section, sets forth the amount of such foreign taxes for each taxable year (of the first tier corporation and of each such lower tier corporation) as to which such amount must be established under this subparagraph, and

(ii) He establishes in the manner prescribed by paragraph (d)(2) of this section the correctness of each amount shown on such supplementary schedule.

(d) *Establishing amounts on schedules.* (1) A taxpayer shall be considered to have established, in respect of the stock he sold or exchanged, the correctness of an amount shown on a schedule described in paragraph (b) of this section only if he produces or provides within 180 days after demand by the district director (or within such longer period to which such director consents)—

(i) The books of original entry, or similar systematic accounting records maintained by any person or persons on a current basis as supplements to such books, which establish to the satisfaction of the district director the correctness of each such amount, and

(ii) In respect of any such books or records which are not in the English language, either an accurate English translation of any such records as are demanded, or the services of a qualified interpreter satisfactory to such director.

(2) A shareholder shall be considered to have established in respect of such stock the correctness of an amount shown on a supplementary schedule described in paragraph (c) of this section only if he produces or provides within 180 days after demand by the district director (or within such longer period to which such director consents)—

(i) Evidence described in paragraph (a)(2) of § 1.905-2 of such amount, or

(ii) Secondary evidence of such amount, in the same manner and to the same extent as would be permissible under paragraph (b) of § 1.905-2 in the case of a taxpayer who claimed the benefits of the foreign tax credit in respect of such amount

(e) *Insufficient information at time return is filed.* If stock in a foreign corporation, which was a controlled foreign corporation, is sold or exchanged by a taxpayer during a taxable year of the corporation (or of a lower tier corporation) which ends after the last day of the taxpayer's taxable year in which the sale or exchange occurs, and if—

(1) For the taxpayer's taxable year, the last day referred to in paragraph (a)(1) of this section for filing his income tax return with a schedule prescribed in paragraph (b) of this section, and, if applicable, with a supplemental schedule prescribed in paragraph (c) of this section, or

(2) The last day referred to in paragraph (a)(1) of this section (that is, April 1, 1965) for filing any such schedule or schedules with the district director with whom such return was filed,

is not later than 90 days after the close of such taxable year of any such corporation, then such return with such schedule or schedules may be filed, or any such schedule or schedules may be filed, on the basis of estimates of amounts or percentages (for any such taxable year of any such corporation) required to be shown on any such schedule or schedules. If any such estimate differs from the actual amount or percentage, the taxpayer shall, within 90 days after the close of any such taxable year of any such corporation, file

Reg. § 1.1248-7(c)(2)

(or attach to a claim for refund or amended return filed) at the office of the district director with whom he filed the return a new schedule or schedules showing the actual amounts or percentages. [Reg. § 1.1248-7.]

☐ [T.D. 6779, 12-21-64.]

[Reg. § 1.1249-1]

§ 1.1249-1. Gain from certain sales or exchanges of patents, etc., to foreign corporations.—(a) *General rule.* Section 1249 provides that if gain is recognized from the sale or exchange after December 31, 1962, of a patent, an invention, model, or design (whether or not patented), a copyright, a secret formula or process, or any other similar property right (not including property such as goodwill, a trademark, or a trade brand) to any foreign corporation by any United States person (as defined in section 7701(a)(30)) which controls such foreign corporation, and if such gain would (but for the provisions of section 1249) be gain from the sale or exchange of a capital asset or of property described in section 1231, then such gain shall be considered as gain from the sale or exchange of property which is neither a capital asset nor property described in section 1231. Section 1249 applies only to gain recognized in taxable years beginning after December 31, 1962.

(b) *Control.* For purposes of paragraph (a) of this section, the term "control" means, with respect to any foreign corporation, the ownership, directly or indirectly, of stock possessing more than 50 percent of the total combined voting power of all classes of stock entitled to vote. For purposes of the preceding sentence, the rules for determining ownership of stock provided by section 958(a) and (b), and the principles for determining percentage of total combined voting power owned by United States shareholders provided by paragraphs (b) and (c) of § 1.957-1, shall apply. [Reg. § 1.1249-1.]

☐ [T.D. 6765, 11-2-64.]

[Reg. § 1.1250-1]

§ 1.1250-1. Gain from dispositions of certain depreciable realty.—(a) *Dispositions after December 31, 1969*—(1) *Ordinary income.* (i) In general, section 1250(a)(1) provides that, upon a disposition of an item of section 1250 property after December 31, 1969, the applicable percentage of the lower of—

(a) The additional depreciation (as defined in § 1.1250-2) attributable to periods after December 31, 1969 in respect of the property, or

(b) The excess of the amount realized on a sale, exchange, or involuntary conversion (or the fair market value of the property on any other disposition) over the adjusted basis of the property,

shall be treated as gain from the sale or exchange of property which is neither a capital asset nor property described in section 1231 (that is, shall be recognized as ordinary income). The amount of such gain shall be determined separately for each item (see subparagraph (2)(ii) of this paragraph) of section 1250 property. If the amount determined under (b) of this subdivision exceeds the amount determined under (a) of this subdivision, then such excess shall be treated as provided in subdivision (ii) of this subparagraph. For relation of section 1250 to other provisions, see paragraph (c) of this section.

(ii) If the amount determined under subdivision (i)(b) of this subparagraph exceeds the amount determined under subdivision (i)(a) of this subparagraph, then the applicable percentage of the lower of—

(a) The additional depreciation attributable to periods before January 1, 1970, or

(b) Such excess,

shall also be recognized as ordinary income.

(iii) If gain would be recognized upon a disposition of an item of section 1250 property under subdivisions (i) and (ii) of this subparagraph, and if section 1250(d) applies, then the gain recognized shall be considered as recognized first under subdivision (i) of this subparagraph. (See example (3)(i) of paragraph (c)(4) of § 1.1250-3.)

(2) *Meaning of terms.* (i) For purposes of section 1250, the term "disposition" shall have the same meaning as in paragraph (a)(3) of § 1.1245-1. "Section 1250 property" is, in general, depreciable real property other than section 1245 property. See paragraph (e) of this section. See paragraph (d)(1) of this section for meaning of the term "applicable percentage." If, however, the property is considered to have 2 or more elements with separate periods (for example, because units thereof are placed in service on different dates, improvements are made to the property, or because of the application of paragraph (h) of § 1.1250-3), see the special rules of § 1.1250-5.

(ii) For purposes of applying section 1250, the facts and circumstances of each disposition shall be considered in determining what is the appropriate item of section 1250 property. In general, a building is an item of section 1250 property, but in an appropriate case more than one building may be treated as a single item. For example, if two or more buildings or structures on a single tract or parcel (or contiguous tracts or

Reg. § 1.1250-1(a)(2)

parcels) of land are operated as an integrated unit (as evidenced by their actual operation, management, financing, and accounting), they may be treated as a single item of section 1250 property. For the manner of determining whether an expenditure shall be treated as an addition to capital account of an item of section 1250 property or as a separate item of section 1250 property, see paragraph (d)(2)(iii) of § 1.1250-5.

(3) *Sale, exchange, or involuntary conversion after December 31, 1969.* (i) In the case of a disposition of section 1250 property by sale, exchange, or involuntary conversion after December 31, 1969, the gain to which section 1250(a)(1) applies is the applicable percentage for the property (determined under paragraph (d)(1) of this section) multiplied by the lower of (*a*) the additional depreciation in respect of the property attributable to periods after December 31, 1969, or (*b*) the excess (referred to as "gain realized") of the amount realized over the adjusted basis of the property.

(ii) In addition to gain recognized under section 1250(a)(1) and subdivision (i) of this subparagraph, gain may also be recognized under section 1250(a)(2) and this subdivision if the gain realized exceeds the additional depreciation attributable to periods after December 31, 1969. In such a case, the amount of gain recognized under section 1250(a)(2) and this subdivision is the applicable percentage for the property (determined under paragraph (d)(2) of this section) multiplied by the lower of (*a*) the additional depreciation attributable to periods before January 1, 1970, or (*b*) the excess (referred to as "remaining gain") of the gain realized over the additional depreciation attributable to periods after December 31, 1969.

(iii) The provisions of this subparagraph may be illustrated by the following examples:

Example (1). Section 1250 property which has an adjusted basis of $500,000 is sold for $650,000 after December 31, 1969, and thus the gain realized is $150,000. At the time of the sale the additional depreciation in respect of the property attributable to periods after December 31, 1969, is $190,000 and the applicable percentage is 100 percent (paragraph (d)(1)(i)(e) of this section). Since the gain realized ($150,000), is lower than the additional depreciation ($190,000), the amount of gain recognized as ordinary income under section 1250(a)(1) is $150,000 (that is, 100 percent of $150,000). No gain is recognized under section 1250(a)(2).

Example (2). Section 1250 property which has an adjusted basis of $440,000 is sold for $500,000 on December 31, 1974, and thus the gain realized is $60,000. The property was acquired on March 31, 1966. At the time of the sale, the additional depreciation attributable to periods after December 31, 1969, is $20,000, and the additional depreciation attributable to periods before January 1, 1970, is $60,000. The property qualified as residential rental property for each taxable year ending after December 31, 1969, and the applicable percentage is 95 percent (paragraph (d)(1)(i)(c) of this section). The applicable percentage under paragraph (d)(2) of this section is 15 percent. Since the additional depreciation attributable to periods after December 31, 1969 ($20,000), is lower than the gain realized ($60,000), the amount of gain recognized as ordinary income under section 1250(a)(1) is $19,000 (that is, 95 percent of $20,000). In addition, gain is recognized under section 1250(a)(2) since there is remaining gain of $40,000 (that is, the gain realized ($60,000) minus the additional depreciation attributable to periods after December 31, 1969 ($20,000)). Since the remaining gain of $40,000 is lower than the additional depreciation attributable to periods before January 1, 1970 ($60,000), the amount of gain recognized as ordinary income under section 1250(a)(2) is $6,000 (that is, 15 percent of $40,000). The remaining $35,000 (that is, gain realized $60,000, minus gain recognized under section 1250(a), $25,000) of the gain may be treated as gain from the sale or exchange of property described in section 1231.

(4) *Other dispositions after December 31, 1969.* (i) In the case of a disposition of section 1250 property after December 31, 1969, other than by way of sale, exchange, or involuntary conversion, the gain to which section 1250(a)(1) applies is the applicable percentage for the property (determined under paragraph (d)(1) of this section) multiplied by the lower of (*a*) the additional depreciation in respect of the property attributable to periods after December 31, 1969, or (*b*) the excess (referred to as "potential gain") of the fair market value of the property over its adjusted basis. In addition, if the potential gain exceeds the additional depreciation attributable to periods after December 31, 1969, then the gain to which section 1250(a)(2) applies is the applicable percentage for the property (determined under paragraph (d)(2) of this section) multiplied by the lower of (*c*) the additional depreciation attributable to periods before January 1, 1970, or (*d*) the excess (referred to as "remaining potential gain") of the potential gain over the additional depreciation attributable to periods after December 31, 1969. If property is transferred by a corporation to a shareholder for an amount less than its fair market value in a sale or exchange, for purposes of applying section 1250 such transfer shall be

Reg. § 1.1250-1(a)(3)

treated as a dispositon other than by way of a sale, exchange, or involuntary conversion.

(ii) The provisions of this subparagraph may be illustrated by the following examples:

Example (1). Section 1250 property having an adjusted basis of $500,000 and a fair market value of $550,000 is distributed by a corporation to a stockholder in complete liquidation of the corporation after December 31, 1969, and thus the potential gain is $50,000. At the time of the liquidation, the additional depreciation for the property attributable to periods after December 31, 1969, is $80,000 and the applicable percentage is 100 percent (paragraph (d)(1)(i)(e) of this section). Since the potential gain of $50,000 is lower than the additional depreciation attributable to periods after December 31, 1969 ($80,000), the amount of gain recognized as ordinary income under section 1250(a)(1) is $50,000 (that is, 100 percent of $50,000) even though in the absence of section 1250, section 336 would preclude recognition of gain to the corporation.

Example (2). The facts are the same as in example (1) except that the fair market value of the property is $650,000, and thus the potential gain is $150,000. Since the additional depreciation attributable to periods after December 31, 1969 ($80,000), is lower than the potential gain of $150,000, the amount of gain recognized as ordinary income under section (a)(1) is $80,000 (that is, 100 percent of $80,000). In addition, section 1250 (a)(2) applies since there is remaining potential gain of $70,000, that is, potential gain ($150,000) minus additional depreciation attributable to periods after December 31, 1969 ($80,000). The additional depreciation attributable to periods before January 1, 1970, is $90,000 and the applicable percentage under paragraph (d)(2) of this section is 50 percent. Since the remaining potential gain of $70,000 is lower than the additional depreciation attributable to periods before January 1, 1970 ($90,000), the amount of gain recognized as ordinary income under section 1250(a)(2) is $35,000 (that is, 50 percent of $70,000). Thus under section 1250(a), $115,000 (that is, $80,000 under section 1250(a)(1), plus $35,000 under section 1250(a)(2)) is recognized as ordinary income, even though in the absence of section 1250, section 336 would preclude recognition of gain to the corporation.

(5) *Instances of nonapplication.* (i) Section 1250(a)(1) does not apply to losses. Thus, section 1250(a)(1) does not apply if a loss is realized upon a sale, exchange, or involuntary conversion of property, all of which is considered section 1250 property, nor does the section apply to a disposition of such property other than by way of sale, exchange, or involuntary conversion if at the time of the disposition the fair market value of such property is not greater than its adjusted basis.

(ii) In general, in the case of section 1250 property with a holding period under section 1223 of more than one year, section 1250(a)(1) does not apply if for periods after December 31, 1969, there are no "depreciation adjustments in excess of straight line" (as computed under section 1250(b) and paragraph (b) of § 1.1250-2).

(6) *Allocation rules.* (i) In the case of the sale, exchange, or involuntary conversion of section 1250 property and nonsection 1250 property in one transaction after December 31, 1969, the total amount realized upon the disposition shall be allocated between the section 1250 property and the other property in proportion to their respective fair market values. Such allocation shall be made in accordance with the principles set forth in paragraph (a)(5) of § 1.1245-1 (relating to allocation between section 1245 property and nonsection 1245 property).

(ii) If an item of section 1250 property has two (or more) applicable percentages because one subdivision of paragraph (d)(1)(i) of this section applies to one portion of the taxpayer's holding period (determined under § 1.1250-4) and another subdivision of such paragraph applies with respect to another such portion, then the gain realized on a sale, exchange, or involuntary conversion, or the potential gain in the case of any other disposition, shall be allocated to each such portion of the taxpayer's holding period after December 31, 1969, in the same proportion as the additional depreciation with respect to such item for such portion bears to the additional depreciation with respect to such item for the entire holding period after December 31, 1969.

(b) *Dispositions before January 1, 1970*—(1) *Ordinary income.* In general, section 1250(a)(2) provides that, upon a disposition of an item of section 1250 property after December 31, 1963, and before January 1, 1970, the applicable percentage of the lower of—

(i) The additional depreciation (as defined in § 1.1250-2) attributable to periods before January 1, 1970 in respect of the property, or

(ii) The excess of the amount realized on a sale, exchange, or involuntary conversion (or the fair market value of the property on any other disposition) over the adjusted basis of the property,

shall be treated as gain from the sale or exchange of property which is neither a capital asset nor property described in section 1231 (that is, shall be recognized as ordinary income). The amount of such gain shall be determined separately for each

Reg. § 1.1250-1(b)(1)

item (see subparagraph (2)(ii) of this paragraph) of section 1250 property. For relation of section 1250 to other provisions, see paragraph (c) of this section.

(2) *Meaning of terms.* (i) For purposes of section 1250, the term "disposition" shall have the same meaning as in paragraph (a)(3) of § 1.1245-1. "Section 1250 property" is, in general, depreciable real property other than section 1245 property. See paragraph (e) of this section. For purposes of this paragraph, the term "applicable percentage" means 100 percent minus 1 percentage point for each full month the property was held after the date on which the property was held 20 full months. See paragraph (d)(2) of this section. If, however, the property is considered to have two or more elements with separate holding periods (for example, because units thereof are placed in service on different dates, or improvements are made to the property), see the special rules of § 1.1250-5.

(ii) For purposes of applying section 1250, the facts and circumstances of each disposition shall be considered in determining what is the appropriate item of section 1250 property. In general, a building is an item of section 1250 property, but in an appropriate case more than one building may be treated as a single item. For manner of determining whether an expenditure shall be treated as an addition to the capital account of an item of section 1250 property or as a separate item of section 1250 property, see paragraph (d)(2)(iii) of § 1.1250-5.

(3) *Sale, exchange, or involuntary conversion before January 1, 1970.* (i) In the case of a disposition of section 1250 property by a sale, exchange, or involuntary conversion before January 1, 1970, the gain to which section 1250(a)(2) applies is the applicable percentage for the property multiplied by the lower of (*a*) the additional depreciation in respect of the property or (*b*) the excess (referred to as "gain realized") of the amount realized over the adjusted basis of the property.

(ii) The provisions of this subparagraph may be illustrated by the following example:

Example. Section 1250 property, which has an adjusted basis of $200,000, is sold for $290,000 before January 1, 1970. At the time of the sale the additional depreciation in respect of the property is $130,000 and the applicable percentage is 60 percent. Since the gain realized ($90,000, that is, amount realized, $290,000, minus adjusted basis, $200,000) is lower than the additional depreciation ($130,000), the amount of gain recognized as ordinary income under section 1250(a)(2) is $54,000 (that is, 60 percent of $90,000). The remaining $36,000 ($90,000 minus $54,000) of the gain may be treated as gain from the sale or exchange of property described in section 1231.

(4) *Other dispositions before January 1, 1970.* (i) In the case of a disposition of section 1250 property before January 1, 1970, other than by way of a sale, exchange, or involuntary conversion, the gain to which section 1250(a)(2) applies is the applicable percentage for the property multiplied by the lower of (*a*) the additional depreciation in respect of the property, or (*b*) the excess (referred to as "potential gain") of the fair market value of the property on the date of disposition over its adjusted basis. If property is transferred by a corporation to a shareholder for an amount less than its fair market value in a sale or exchange, for purposes of applying section 1250 such transfer shall be treated as a disposition other than by way of a sale, exchange, or involuntary conversion.

(ii) The provisions of this subparagraph may be illustrated by the following example:

Example. Assume the same facts as in the example in subparagraph (3)(ii) of this paragraph except that the property is distributed by a corporation to a stockholder before January 1, 1970, in complete liquidation of the corporation, and that at the time of the distribution the fair market value of the property is $370,000. Since the additional depreciation ($130,000) is lower than the potential gain of $170,000 (that is, fair market value, $370,000, minus adjusted basis, $200,000), the amount of gain recognized as ordinary income under section 1250(a)(2) is $78,000 (that is, 60 percent of $130,000) even though, in the absence of section 1250, section 336 would preclude recognition of gain to the corporation.

(5) *Instances of nonapplication.* (i) Section 1250(a)(2) does not apply to losses. Thus, section 1250(a)(2) does not apply if a loss is realized upon a sale, exchange, or involuntary conversion of property, all of which is considered section 1250 property, nor does the section apply to a disposition of such property other than by way of sale, exchange, or involuntary conversion if at the time of the disposition the fair market value of such property is not greater than its adjusted basis.

(ii) In general, in the case of section 1250 property with a holding period under section 1223 of more than one year, section 1250(a)(2) does not apply if for periods after December 31, 1963, there are no "depreciation adjustments in excess of straight line" (as computed under section 1250(b) and paragraph (b) of § 1.1250-2).

(iii) In a case in which section 1250 property (including each element thereof, if any) has a holding period under § 1.1250-4 (or paragraph

Reg. § 1.1250-1(b)(2)

(a)(2)(ii) of § 1.1250-5) of at least 10 years, section 1250(a)(2) does not apply. If within the 10-year period preceding the date the property is disposed of, an element is added to the property by reason, for example, of an addition to capital account, see § 1.1250-5.

(6) *Allocation rule.* In the case of a sale, exchange, or involuntary conversion of section 1250 property and nonsection 1250 property in one transaction before January 1, 1970, the total amount realized upon the disposition shall be allocated between the section 1250 property and the other property in proportion to their respective fair market values. Such allocation shall be made in accordance with the principles set forth in paragraph (a)(5) of § 1.1245-1 (relating to allocation between section 1245 property and nonsection 1245 property).

(c) *Relation of section 1250 to other provisions*—(1) *General.* The provisions of section 1250 apply notwithstanding any other provision of subtitle A of the Code. See section 1250(i). Thus, unless an exception or limitation under section 1250(d) and § 1.1250-3 applies, gain under section 1250(a) is recognized notwithstanding any contrary nonrecognition provision or income characterizing provision. For example, since section 1250 overrides section 1231 (relating to property used in the trade or business), the gain recognized under section 1250(a) upon a disposition will be treated as ordinary income and only the remaining gain, if any, from the disposition may be considered as gain from the sale or exchange of a capital asset if section 1231 is applicable. See the example in paragraph (b)(3)(ii) of this section.

(2) *Nonrecognition sections overridden.* The nonrecognition provisions of subtitle A of the Code which section 1250 overrides include, but are not limited to, sections 267(d), 311(a), 336, 337, 501(a), and 512(b)(5). See section 1250(d) for the extent to which section 1250(a) overrides sections 332, 351, 361, 371(a), 374(a), 721, 731, 1031, 1033, 1039, 1071, and 1081(b)(1) and (d)(1)(A). For amount of additional depreciation in respect of property disposed of by an organization exempt from income taxes (within the meaning of section 501 (a)), see paragraph (d)(6) of § 1.1250-2.

(3) *Exempt income.* The fact that section 1250 provides for recognition of gain as ordinary income does not change into taxable income any income which is exempt under section 115 (relating to income of States, etc.), 892 (relating to income of foreign governments), or 894 (relating to income exempt under treaties).

(4) *Treatment of gain not recognized under section 1250.* Section 1250 does not prevent gain which is not recognized under section 1250 from being considered as gain under another provision of the Code, such as, for example, section 1239 (relating to gain from sale of depreciable property between certain related persons). Thus, for example, if section 1250 property which has an adjusted basis of $10,000 is sold for $17,500 in a transaction to which section 1239 applies, and if $5,000 of the gain would be recognized under section 1250(a), then the remaining $2,500 of the gain would be treated as ordinary income under section 1239.

(5) *Normal retirement of asset in multiple asset account.* Section 1250 (a) does not require recognition of gain upon normal retirements of section 1250 property in a multiple asset account as long as the taxpayer's method of accounting, as described in paragraph (e)(2) of § 1.167(a)-8 (relating to accounting treatment of asset retirements), does not require recognition of such gain.

(6) *Installment method.* Gain from a disposition to which section 1250(a) applies may be reported under the installment method if such method is otherwise available under section 453 of the Code. In such case, the income (other than interest) on each installment payment shall be deemed to consist of gain to which section 1250(a) applies until all such gain has been reported, and the remaining portion (if any) of such income shall be deemed to consist of other gain. For treatment of amounts as interest on certain deferred payments, see section 483.

(d) *Applicable percentage*—(1) *Definition for purposes of section 1250(a)(1).* (i) For purposes of section 1250(a)(1), the term "applicable percentage" means—

(*a*) In the case of property disposed of pursuant to a written contract which was, on July 24, 1969, and at all times thereafter binding on the owner of the property, 100 percent minus 1 percentage point for each full month the property was held after the date on which the property was held 20 full months;

(*b*) In the case of property constructed, reconstructed, or acquired by the taxpayer before January 1, 1975, with respect to which a mortgage is insured under section 221(d)(3) or 236 of the National Housing Act, or housing is financed or assisted by direct loan or tax abatement under similar provisions of State or local laws, and with respect to which the owner is subject to the restrictions described in section 1039(b)(1)(B) (relating to approved dispositions of certain Government-assisted housing projects), 100 percent minus one percentage point for each full month of the taxpayer's holding period for the property (determined under § 1.1250-4) during which the property qualified under this sentence,

Reg. § 1.1250-1(d)(1)

beginning after the date on which the property so qualified for 20 full months.

(c) In the case of residential rental property (as defined in section 167(j)(2)(B)) other than that covered by (a) and (b) of this subdivision, 100 percent minus 1 percentage point for each full month of the taxpayer's holding period for the property (determined under § 1.1250-4) included within a taxable year for which the property qualified as residential rental property, beginning after the date on which the property so qualified for 100 full months.

(d) In the case of property with respect to which a deduction was allowed under section 167(k) (relating to depreciation of expenditures to rehabilitate low-income rental housing), 100 percent minus 1 percentage point for each full month of the taxpayer's holding period (determined under § 1.1250-4) beginning 100 full months after the date on which the property was placed in service.

(e) In the case of all other property, 100 percent.

The provisions of (a), (b), and (c) of this subdivision shall not apply with respect to additional depreciation described in section 1250(b)(4). If the taxpayer's holding period under § 1.1250-4 includes a period before January 1, 1970, such period shall be taken into account in applying each provision of this subdivision.

(ii) A single item of property may have two (or more) applicable percentages under the provisions of subdivision (i) of this subparagraph. For example, if the provision of subdivision (i) which applies to an item of section 1250 property (or to an element of such property if the property is treated as consisting of more than one element under § 1.1250-5) in the taxable year in which the item (or element) is disposed of did not apply to the item (or element) in a prior taxable year which is included within the taxpayer's holding period under § 1.1250-4 and which ends after December 31, 1969, then each provision of subdivision (i) of this subparagraph shall apply only for the period during which the property qualified under such provision.

(iii) If the taxpayer makes rehabilitation expenditures and elects to compute depreciation under section 167(k) with respect to the property attributable to the rehabilitation expenditures, such property will generally constitute a separate improvement under paragraph (c) of § 1.1250-5 and therefore will constitute an element of section 1250 property. For computation of applicable percentage and gain recognized under section 1250(a) in such a case, see paragraph (a) of § 1.1250-5.

(iv) The principles of this subparagraph may be illustrated by the following examples:

Example (1). Section 1250 property is sold on December 31, 1970, pursuant to a written contract which was binding on the owner of the property on July 24, 1969, and at all times thereafter. The property was acquired on July 31, 1968. The applicable percentage for the property under subdivision (i)(a) of this subparagraph is 91 percent, since the property was held for 29 full months.

Example (2). Section 1250 property is sold on June 30, 1978. The property was acquired by a calendar year taxpayer on June 30, 1966. Subdivision (i)(e) of this subparagraph applies to the property in 1977 and 1978. However, subdivision (i)(c) of this subparagraph applied to the property for the taxable years of 1970 through 1976. Thus, the property has two applicable percentages under this subparagraph. The period before January 1, 1970 (42 full months), and the period from 1970 through 1976 (84 full months) are both taken into account in determining the applicable percentage under subdivision (i)(c) of this subparagraph. Thus, the applicable percentage is 74 percent (that is, 100 percent minus the excess of the holding period taken into account (126 full months) over 100 full months). The applicable percentage for the years 1977 and 1978 is 100 percent under subdivision (i)(e) of this subparagraph.

Example (3). Section 1250 property is sold on December 31, 1968. The property was acquired by a calendar year taxpayer on December 31, 1969. The taxpayer made rehabilitation expenditures in 1973 and properly elected to compute depreciation under section 167(k) on the property attributable to the expenditures for the 60-month period beginning on January 1, 1974, the date such property was placed in service. Subdivision (i)(c) applies to the property (other than the property with respect to which a deduction was allowed under section 167(k)) for the taxable years of 1970 through 1978 (108 full months) and the applicable percentage for such property is 92 percent. The applicable percentage for the property with respect to which a deduction under section 167(k) was allowed is 100 percent under subdivision (i)(d) of this subparagraph, since the holding period for purposes of such subdivision begins on the date such property is placed in service.

Example (4). Section 1250 property is sold by a calendar year taxpayer on March 31, 1974. The property was transferred to the taxpayer by gift on December 31, 1970, and under section 1250(e)(2), the taxpayer's holding period for the

Reg. § 1.1250-1(d)(1)

Rules for Determining Capital Gains and Losses

property for purposes of computing the applicable percentage includes the transferor's holding period of 80 full months. Subdivision (i)(c) of this subparagraph applies to the property in the years 1970 through 1974. The applicable percentage under subdivision (i)(c) of this subparagraph is 81 percent, since the period before January 1, 1970 (68 full months), and that portion of the period after December 31, 1969, during which such subdivision applied (51 full months) are taken into account.

(2) *Definition for purposes of section 1250(a)(2).* For purposes of section 1250(a)(2), the term "applicable percentage" means—

 (i) In case of property with a holding period of 20 full months or less, 100 percent;

 (ii) In case of property with a holding period of more than 20 full months but less than 10 years, 100 percent minus 1 percentage point for each full month the property is held after the date on which the property is held 20 full months; and

 (iii) In case of property with a holding period of at least 10 years, zero.

(3) *Holding period.* For purposes of this paragraph, the holding period of property shall be determined under the rules of § 1.1250-4, and not under the rules of section 1223, notwithstanding that the property was acquired on or before December 31, 1963. In the case of a disposition of section 1250 property which consists of 2 or more elements (within the meaning of paragraph (c) of § 1.1250-5), the holding period for each element shall be determined under the rules of paragraph (a)(2)(ii) of § 1.1250-5.

(4) *Full month.* For purposes of this paragraph, the term "full month" (or "full months") means the period beginning on a date in 1 month and terminating on the date before the corresponding date in the next succeeding month (or in another succeeding month), or, if a particular succeeding month does not have such a corresponding date, terminating on the last day of such particular succeeding month.

(5) *Examples.* The provisions of this paragraph may be illustrated by the following examples:

Example (1). Property is purchased on January 17, 1959. Under paragraph (b)(1) of § 1.1250-4, its holding period begins on January 18, 1959, and thus at any time during the period beginning on October 17, 1960, and ending on November 16, 1960, the property is considered held 21 full months and has an applicable percentage under section 1250(a)(2) of 99 percent. On and after January 17, 1969, the property has a holding period of at least 120 full months (10 years) and, therefore, the applicable percentage under section 1250(a)(2) for the property is zero. Accordingly, no gain would be recognized under section 1250(a)(2) upon disposition of the property. If, however, the property consists of two or more elements, see the special rules of § 1.1250-5.

Example (2). Property is purchased on January 31, 1968. Under paragraph (b)(1) of § 1.1250-4 its holding period begins on February 1, 1968, and thus at any time during the period beginning on February 29, 1968, and ending on March 30, 1968, the property is considered held 1 full month. At any time during the period beginning on March 31, 1970, and ending on April 29, 1970, the property is considered held 26 full months. At any time during the period beginning on April 30, 1970, and ending on May 30, 1970, the property is considered held 27 full months.

(e) *Section 1250 property*—(1) *Definition.* The term "section 1250 property" means any real property (other than section 1245 property, as defined in section 1245(a)(3) and § 1.1245-3) which is or has been property of a character subject to the allowance for depreciation provided in section 167. See section 1250(c).

(2) *Character of property.* For purposes of subparagraph (1) of this paragraph, the term "is or has been property of a character subject to the allowance for depreciation provided in section 167" shall have the same meaning as when used in paragraph (a)(1) and (3) of § 1.1245-3. Thus, if a father uses a house in his trade or business during a period after December 31, 1963, and then gives the house to his son as a gift for the son's personal use, the house is section 1250 property in the hands of the son. For exception to the application of section 1250(a) upon disposition of a principal residence, see section 1250(d)(7).

(3) *Real property.* (i) For purposes of subparagraph (1) of this paragraph, the term "real property" means any property which is not personal property within the meaning of paragraph (b) of § 1.1245-3. The term section 1250 property includes three types of depreciable real property. The first type is intangible real property. For purposes of this paragraph, a leasehold of land or of section 1250 property is intangible real property, and accordingly such a leasehold is section 1250 property. However, a fee simple interest in land is not depreciable, and therefore is not section 1250 property. The second type is a building or its structural components within the meaning of paragraph (c) of § 1.1245-3. The third type is all other tangible real property except (a) "property described in section 1245(a)(3)(B)" as defined in paragraph (c)(1) of § 1.1245-3 (relating to

Reg. § 1.1250-1(e)(3)

53,570 Rules for Determining Capital Gains and Losses

See p. 20,601 for regulations not amended to reflect law changes

property used as an integral part of a specified activity or as a specified facility), and (b) property described in section 1245(a)(3)(D). An elevator or escalator (within the meaning of section 1245(a)(3)(C)) is not section 1250 property.

(ii) The provisions of this subparagraph may be illustrated by the following example:

Example. A owns and leases to B for a single lump-sum payment of $100,000 property consisting of land and a fully equipped factory building thereon. If 30 percent of the fair market value of such property is properly allocable to the land, 25 percent to section 1250 property (the building and its structural components), and 45 percent to section 1245 property (the equipment), then 55 percent of B's leasehold is section 1250 property.

(4) *Coordination with definition of section 1245 property.* (i) Property may lose its character as section 1250 property and become section 1245 property. Thus, for example, if section 1250 property of the third type described in subparagraph (3)(i)(a) of this paragraph is converted to use as an integral part of manufacturing, the property would lose its character as section 1250 property and would become section 1245 property. However, once property in the hands of a taxpayer is section 1245 property, it can never become section 1250 property in the hands of such taxpayer. See also paragraph (a)(4) and (5) of § 1.1245-2.

(ii) [Reserved]

(f) *Treatment of partnerships and partners.* If a partnership disposes of section 1250 property, the amount of gain recognized under section 1250(a) by the partnership and by a partner shall be determined in a manner consistent with the principles provided in paragraph (e) of § 1.1245-1. Thus, for example, a partner's distributive share of gain recognized by the partnership under section 1250(a) shall be determined in the same manner as his distributive share of gain recognized by the partnership under section 1245(a)(1) is determined, and, if required, additional depreciation in respect of section 1250 property shall be allocated to the partner in the same manner as the adjustments reflected in the adjusted basis of section 1245 property are allocated to the partner. For a further example, if on the date a partner acquires his partnership interest by way of a sale or exchange the partnership owns section 1250 property and an election under section 754 (relating to optional adjustment to basis of partnership property) is in effect with respect to the partnership, then such partner's additional depreciation in respect of such property on such date is deemed to be zero. For limitation on the amount of gain recognized under section 1250(a) in respect of a partnership and for the amount of additional depreciation in respect of partnership property after certain transactions, see paragraph (f) of § 1.1250-3. For treatment of section 1250 property as an unrealized receivable, see section 751(c).

(g) *Examples.* The principles of this section may be illustrated by the following examples:

Example (1). Section 1250 property which has an adjusted basis of $350,000 is sold for $630,000 on December 31, 1984. The property was acquired by a calendar year taxpayer on December 31, 1969. For the taxable years from 1970 through 1980, the property qualified as residential rental property and the applicable percentage for those years is 68 percent (paragraph (d)(1)(i)(c) of this section). For taxable years from 1981 through 1984, the property did not qualify as residential rental property and the applicable percentage for those years is 100 percent (paragraph (d)(1)(i)(e) of this section). The additional depreciation for the years from 1970 through 1980 is $120,000. The additional depreciation for the years from 1981 through 1984 is $20,000. The gain realized is $280,000 (that is, amount realized, $630,000, minus adjusted basis $350,000). The gain recognized as ordinary income under section 1250(a)(1) is computed in two steps. First, since the additional depreciation attributable to the years 1970 through 1980 ($120,000) is lower than the gain realized attributable to such years determined under paragraph (a)(6) of this section ($240,000, that is, gain realized, $280,000 multiplied by 12/14), the gain recognized as ordinary income under section 1250(a)(1) in the first step is $81,600, that is, 68 percent of $120,000. Second, since the additional depreciation attributable to the years 1981 through 1984 ($20,000) is lower than the gain realized attributable to those years ($40,000, that is, gain realized, $280,000, multiplied by 12/14), the gain recognized as ordinary income under section 1250(a)(1) for the years from 1981 through 1984 is $20,000 (that is, 100 percent of $20,000). The total gain recognized under section 1250(a)(1) is $101,600 (that is, $81,600 plus $20,000).

Example (2). Section 1250 property which has an adjusted basis of $400,000 is sold for $472,000 on December 31, 1978. The property was acquired on December 31, 1966. The additional depreciation attributable to periods before January 1, 1970, is $40,000 and the applicable percentage under paragraph (d)(2) of this section is zero percent. The property qualifies as residential rental property for the years 1970 through 1976, but fails to qualify for 1977 and 1978. Under paragraph (d)(1) of this section, the appli-

Reg. § 1.1250-1(e)(4)

cable percentage for the years 1970 through 1976 is 80 percent (paragraph (d)(1)(i)(c) of this section), and the applicable percentage for the years 1977 and 1978 is 100 percent (paragraph (d)(1)(i)(e) of this section). The additional depreciation attributable to the years 1970 through 1976 is $50,000, and the additional depreciation attributable to the years 1977 and 1978 is $10,000. The gain recognized as ordinary income under section 1250(a)(1) is computed in two steps. First, since the additional depreciation attributable to the years 1970 through 1976 ($50,000) is lower than the gain realized attributable to such years ($60,000, that is, $72,000 multiplied by 5/6), the gain recognized under section 1250(a)(1) in the first step is $40,000 (that is, 80 percent of $50,000). Second, since the additional depreciation attributable to 1977 and 1978 ($10,000) is lower than the gain realized attributable to 1977 and 1978 ($10,000) is lower than the gain realized attributable to such years ($12,000, that is, $72,000 multiplied by 1/6), the gain realized under section 1250(a)(1) in the second step is $10,000 (that is, 100 percent of $10,000). In addition, section 1250(a)(2) applies. However, since the applicable percentage is zero percent, none of the gain is recognized as ordinary income under section 1250(a)(2). Thus, the remaining $22,000 (that is, gain realized, $72,000, minus gain recognized under section 1250(a), $50,000) of the gain may be treated as gain from the sale or exchange of property described in section 1231.

Example (3). The facts are the same as in example (2) except that the property is disposed of on December 31, 1980. The property qualifies as residential rental property for the years 1979 and 1980. Thus, the applicable percentage for years 1970 through 1976, 1979, and 1980 is 56 percent (paragraph (d)(1)(i)(c) of this section). The applicable percentage for the years 1977 and 1978 is 100 percent (paragraph (d)(1)(i)(e) of this section). The additional depreciation for the years 1979 and 1980 is $8,000. The gain recognized under section 1250(a)(1) is computed in two steps. First, since the additional depreciation attributable to the years 1970 through 1976, 1979, and 1980 ($58,000) is lower than the gain realized attributable to such years ($61,412, that is, $72,000 multiplied by $58,000/$68,000), the gain recognized under section 1250(a)(1) in the first step is $32,480 (that is, 56 percent of $58,000). Second, since the additional depreciation attributable to 1977 and 1978 ($10,000) is lower than the gain realized attributable to such years ($10,588, that is, $72,000 multiplied by $10,000/$68,000) the gain recognized under section 1250(a)(1) in the second step is $10,000 (that is, 100 percent of $10,000). In addition section 1250(a)(2) applies. However, since the applicable percentage is zero percent, none of the gain is recognized as ordinary income under section 1250(a)(2). Thus, the remaining $29,520 (that is, gain realized, $72,000, minus gain recognized under section 1250(a), $42,480) of the gain may be treated as gain from the sale or exchange of property described in section 1231. [Reg. § 1.1250-1.]

☐ [T.D. 7084, 1-7-71. Amended by T.D. 7193, 6-29-72.]

[Reg. § 1.1250-2]

§ 1.1250-2. Additional depreciation defined.—(a) *In general*—(1) *Definition for purposes of section 1250(b)(1).* Except as otherwise provided in paragraph (e) of this section, for purposes of section 1250(b)(1), the term "additional depreciation" means—

(i) In case of property which at the time of disposition has a holding period under section 1223 of not more than 1 year, the "depreciation adjustments" (as defined in paragraph (d) of this section) in respect of such property for periods after December 31, 1963, and

(ii) In the case of property which at the time of disposition has a holding period under section 1223 of more than 1 year, the depreciation adjustments in excess of straight line for periods after December 31, 1963, computed under paragraph (b)(1) of this section.

(2) *Definition for purposes of section 1250(b)(4).* Except as otherwise provided in paragraph (e) of this section, for purposes of section 1250(b)(4), the term "additional depreciation" means—

(i) In the case of property with respect to which a deduction under section 167(k) (relating to depreciation of expenditures to rehabilitate low-income rental housing) was allowed, which at the time of disposition has a holding period under section 1223 of not more than 1 year from the time the rehabilitation expenditures were incurred, the "depreciation adjustments" (as defined in paragraph (d) of this section) in respect of the property, and

(ii) In the case of property with respect to which a deduction under section 167(k) (relating to depreciation of expenditures to rehabilitate low-income rental housing) was allowed, which at the time of disposition has a holding period under section 1223 of more than 1 year from the time the rehabilitation expenditures were incurred, the depreciation adjustments in excess of straight line for the property, computed under paragraph (b)(2) of this section.

For purposes of this subparagraph, all rehabilitation expenditures which are incurred in connection with the rehabilitation of an element of section 1250 property shall be considered incurred on the date the last such expenditure is considered incurred under the accrual method of accounting, regardless of the method of accounting used by the taxpayer with regard to other items of income and expense. If the property consists of two or more elements (for example, if the property is placed in service at different times), then each element shall be treated as if it were a separate property and the expenditures attributable to each such element shall be considered incurred on the date the last such expenditure is considered incurred.

(3) *Allocation to certain periods.* With respect to a taxable year beginning in 1963 and ending in 1964, or beginning in 1969 and ending in 1970, the amount of depreciation adjustments or of depreciation adjustments in excess of straight line (as the case may be) shall be ascertained by applying the principles of paragraph (c)(3) of § 1.167(a)-8 (relating to determination of adjusted basis of retired asset), and the amount determined in such manner shall be allocated on a daily basis in order to determine the portion thereof which is attributable to a period after December 31, 1963, or after December 31, 1969, as the case may be.

(b) *Computation of depreciation adjustments in excess of straight line*—(1) *General rule.* For purposes of paragraph (a)(1) of this section, depreciation adjustments in excess of straight line shall be, in the case of any property, the excess of (i) the sum of the "depreciation adjustments" (as defined in paragraph (d) of this section) in respect of the property attributable to periods after December 31, 1963, over (ii) the sum such adjustments would have been for such periods if such adjustments had been determined for the entire period the property was held under the straight line method of depreciation (or, if applicable, under the lease-renewal-period provision in paragraph (c) of this section). Depreciation in excess of straight line may arise, for example, if the declining balance method, the sum of the years-digits method, or the units of production method is used, or for another example, if the cost of a leasehold improvement or of a leasehold is depreciated over a period which does not take into account certain renewal periods referred to in paragraph (c) of this section. For computations of depreciation adjustments in excess of straight line (or a deficit therein) both on an annual basis and on the basis of the entire period the property was held, see subparagraph (6) of this paragraph.

(2) *Depreciation under section 167(k).* For purposes of paragraph (a)(2) of this section, depreciation adjustments in excess of straight line shall be, in the case of any property with respect to which a deduction was allowed under section 167(k) (relating to depreciation of expenditures to rehabilitate low-income rental housing), the excess of (i) the sum of the "depreciation adjustments" (as defined in paragraph (d) of this section) allowed in respect of the property, over (ii) the sum such adjustments would have been if such adjustments had been determined for the entire period the property was held under the straight line method of depreciation permitted by section 167(b)(1).

(3) *General rule for computing useful life and salvage value.* For purposes of computing under subparagraph (1)(ii) of this paragraph the sum the depreciation adjustments would have been under the straight line method, if a useful life (or salvage value) was used in determining the amount allowed as a depreciation adjustment for any taxable year, such life (or value) shall be used in determining the amount such depreciation adjustment would have been for such taxable year under the straight line method. If, however, for any taxable year a method of depreciation was used as to which a useful life was not taken into account such as, for example, the units of production method, or as to which salvage value was not taken into account in determining the annual allowances, such as, for example, the declining balance method or the amortization of a leasehold improvement over the term of a lease, then, for the purpose of determining the amount such depreciation adjustment would have been under the straight line method for such taxable year—

(i) There shall be used the useful life (or salvage value) which would have been proper if depreciation had actually been determined under the straight line method throughout the period the property was held, and

(ii) Such useful life (or such salvage value) shall be determined by taking into account for each taxable year the same facts and circumstances as would have been taken into account if the taxpayer had used such method throughout the period the property was held.

(4) *Special rule for computing useful life and salvage value (section 167(k)).* For purposes of computing under subparagraph (2)(ii) of this paragraph the sum the depreciation adjustments would have been under the straight line method, the useful life and salvage value permitted under section 167(k) shall not apply, the useful life of the property shall be determined under paragraph (b) of § 1.167(a)-1 (or, if applicable, under the lease-renewal-period provision of paragraph (c) of this section), and the salvage value of the prop-

Reg. § 1.1250-2(a)(3)

Rules for Determining Capital Gains and Losses 53,573
See p. 20,601 for regulations not amended to reflect law changes

erty shall be determined under paragraph (c) of § 1.167(a)-1. Such useful life or salvage value shall be determined by taking into account for each taxable year the same facts and circumstances as would have been taken into account if the taxpayer had used the straight line method permitted under section 167(b)(1) throughout the period the property was held.

(5) *Property held before January 1, 1964.* In the case of property held before January 1, 1964—

(i) For purposes of computing under subparagraph (1)(ii) of this paragraph the sum the depreciation adjustments would have been under the straight line method, the adjusted basis of the property on such date shall be allowed or allowable before such date had been determined under the straight line method computed in accordance with subparagraph (3) of this paragraph, and

(ii) The depreciation adjustments in excess of straight line in respect of the property computed under subparagraph (1) of this paragraph, but without regard to this subdivision, shall be reduced by the amount of depreciation adjustments less than straight line for periods before January 1, 1964, that is, by the excess (if any) of the sum the depreciation adjustments would have been for periods before January 1, 1964, under the straight line method, over the sum of the depreciation adjustments attributable to periods before such date.

(6) *Determination of additional depreciation in certain cases.* If an item of section 1250 property is subject to two (or more) applicable percentages, a separate computation of additional depreciation shall be made for the portion of the taxpayer's holding period subject to each such percentage. That is, a separate computation shall be made to determine the excess of (i) the depreciation adjustments (as defined in paragraph (d) of this section) for each such portion of the taxpayer's holding period after December 31, 1963, over (ii) the amount such adjustments would have been for each such portion if such adjustments were determined under the straight line method of depreciation (or, if applicable, under the lease-renewal-period provision in paragraph (c) of this section). Thus, for example, in the case of an item of section 1250 property acquired on January 1, 1968, and disposed of on January 1, 1973, if the applicable percentage for the period before January 1, 1970, were determined under paragraph (d)(2) of § 1.1250-1 and the applicable percentage for the period after December 31, 1969, were determined under paragraph (d)(1)(i)(e) of § 1.1250-1, the additional depreciation would be computed separately for the period before January 1, 1970, and for the period after December 31, 1969. If the additional depreciation attributable to any such portion of the taxpayer's holding period is a deficit (that is, if the depreciation adjustments for that portion are less than the amount such adjustments would have been for that portion if depreciation adjustments were determined for the entire period the property was held under the straight line method of depreciation, or, if applicable, under the lease-renewal-period provision in paragraph (c) of this section), then such deficit will be applied to reduce the additional depreciation for the other portion (or portions) of the taxpayer's holding period. (See examples (4) and (5) of subparagraph (7) of this paragraph.)

(7) *Examples.* The provisions of this paragraph may be illustrated by the following examples:

Example (1). A calendar year taxpayer sells section 1250 property on January 1, 1968, which he purchased for $10,000 on January 1, 1963. For the period of 1963 through 1967 he computed depreciation deductions in respect of the property under the declining balance method using a rate of 200 percent of the straight line rate and a proper useful life of 10 years. Under such method salvage value is not taken into account in computing annual allowances. For purposes of applying subparagraph (3) of this paragraph, if the taxpayer had used the straight line method for such period, he would have used a salvage value of $1,000, and the depreciation under the straight line method would have been $900 each year, that is, one-tenth of $10,000 minus $1,000. As of January 1, 1968, the additional depreciation for the property is $1,123, as computed in the table below:

Year	Actual depreciation	Straight line	Additional depreciation (deficit)
1963	$2,000	$ 900	....
1964	1,600	900	$ 700
1965	1,280	900	380
1966	1,024	900	124
1967	819	900	(81)
Sum for periods after Dec. 31, 1963	$4,723	$3,600	$1,123

Reg. § 1.1250-2(b)(7)

53,574 Rules for Determining Capital Gains and Losses

See p. 20,601 for regulations not amended to reflect law changes

Example (2). Assume the same facts as in example (1) except that the taxpayer sells the section 1250 property on January 1, 1970. Assume further that as of January 1, 1968, the taxpayer elects under section 167(e)(1) to change to the straight line method. On that date the adjusted basis of the property is $3,277 ($10,000 minus $6,723). He redetermines the remaining useful life of the property to be 8 years and its salvage value to be $77, and thus takes depreciation deductions for 1968 and 1969 of $400 (the amount allowable) for each such year, that is, one-eighth of $3,200 (that is, $3,277 minus $77). For purposes of applying subparagraph (3) of this paragraph, if he had used the straight line method throughout the period he held the property, the adjusted basis of the property on January 1, 1968, would have been $5,500 ($10,000 minus $4,500), and the depreciation which would have resulted under such method for 1968 and 1969 would have been $678 for each such year, that is, one-eighth of $5,423 ($5,500 minus $77). As of January 1, 1970, the additional depreciation for the property is $567, as computed in the table below:

Years	Depreciation	Straight line	Additional depreciation (deficit)
1964 through 1967	$4,723	$3,600	$1,123
1968	400	678	(278)
1969	400	678	(278)
Sum for periods after Dec. 31, 1963	$5,523	$4,956	$ 567

Example (3). On January 1, 1978, a calendar year taxpayer sells section 1250 property. The property, which is attributable to rehabilitation expenditures of $50,000 incurred in 1970, was placed in service on January 1, 1971. The taxpayer elected to compute depreciation for the period of 1971 through 1975 under section 167(k). Under such section salvage value is not taken into account in computing annual allowances, and the useful life of the property is deemed to be 5 years. For purposes of applying subparagraph (4) of this paragraph, if the taxpayer had used the straight line method permitted under section 167(b)(1) for such period, he would have used a salvage value of $5,000 and a useful life of 15 years. Depreciation under the straight line method would thus have been $3,000 each year, 1/15 of $45,000 (that is, $50,000 minus $5,000). As of January 1, 1978, the additional depreciation for the property is $29,000, as computed in the table below:

Year	Actual depreciation	Straight line	Additional depreciation (deficit)
1971	$10,000	$ 3,000	$ 7,000
1972	10,000	3,000	7,000
1973	10,000	3,000	7,000
1974	10,000	3,000	7,000
1975	10,000	3,000	7,000
1976	......	3,000	(3,000)
1977	......	3,000	(3,000)
Total	$50,000	$21,000	$29,000

Example (4). Section 1250 property which has an adjusted basis of $108,000 is sold for $146,000 on December 31, 1972, and thus the gain realized is $38,000. The property was acquired on December 31, 1963. The applicable percentage for the period before January 1, 1970, is 12 percent (paragraph (d)(2) of § 1.1250-1) and the applicable percentage for the period after December 31, 1969, is 100 percent (paragraph (d)(1)(i)(e) of § 1.1250-1). The additional depreciation must be computed separately for the period before January 1, 1970, and for the period after December 31, 1969. Assume that the additional depreciation for the period before January 1, 1970, is $32,000 and that there is a deficit in additional depreciation of $2,000 for the period after December 31, 1969. Accordingly, the additional depreciation for the period before January 1, 1970 ($32,000) is reduced to $30,000 by the $2,000 deficit in additional depreciation for the period after December 31, 1969. Although section 1250(a)(1) applies to the property, none of the gain is recognized as ordinary income under that section since there is a deficit in additional depreciation for the period after December 31, 1969. Gain is recognized under section 1250(a)(2) since there is remaining gain of $38,000 (that is, gain realized, $38,000, minus the additional depreciation attributable to periods after December 31, 1969, zero). Since the additional depreciation attributable to the period before January 1, 1970 ($30,000), is lower than the gain realized ($38,000), the amount of gain recognized under

Reg. § 1.1250-2(b)(7)

Rules for Determining Capital Gains and Losses

See p. 20,601 for regulations not amended to reflect law changes

section 1250(a)(2) is $3,600 (that is, 12 percent of $30,000).

Example (5). Section 1250 property which has an adjusted basis of $207,000 is sold for $267,000 on February 24, 1988, and thus the gain realized is $60,000. The property was acquired on April 30, 1970. The applicable percentage for the period from April 30, 1970, through December 31, 1981, is 60 percent (paragraph (d)(1)(i)(c) of § 1.1250-1) and the applicable percentage for the period from January 1, 1982, through February 24, 1988, is 100 percent (paragraph (d)(1)(i)(e) of § 1.1250-1). The additional depreciation must be computed separately for the period before January 1, 1982, and for the period after December 31, 1981. Assume that the additional depreciation for the period before January 1, 1982, is $43,000 and that there is a deficit in additional depreciation of $6,000 for the period after December 31, 1981. Accordingly, the addition depreciation for the period before January 1, 1982 ($43,000), is reduced to $37,000 by the $6,000 deficit for the period after December 31, 1981. There is no gain recognized under section 1250(a)(1) for the period after December 31, 1981, since there is a deficit in additional depreciation for that period. The gain recognized under section 1250(a)(1) for the period before January 1, 1982, is $22,200, that is, the lower of the gain realized attributable to that period ($60,000) or the additional depreciation attributable to that period ($37,000), or $37,000, multiplied by 60 percent, the applicable percentage.

(c) *Property held by lessee*—(1) *Amount depreciation would have been.* For purposes of paragraph (b) of this section, in case of a leasehold which is section 1250 property, in determining the amount the depreciation adjustments would have been under the straight line method in respect of any building or other improvement (which is section 1250 property) erected or made on the leased property, or in respect of any cost of acquiring the lease, the lease period shall be treated as including all renewal periods. See section 1250(b)(2). For determination of the extent to which a leasehold is section 1250 property, see paragraph (e)(3) of § 1.1250-1.

(2) *Renewal period.* (i) For purposes of this paragraph, the term "renewal period" means any period for which the lease may be renewed, extended, or continued pursuant to an option or options exercisable by the lessee (whether or not specifically provided for in the lease) except that the inclusion of one or more renewal periods shall not extend the period taken into account by more than two-thirds of the period on the basis of which the depreciation adjustments were allowed.

(ii) In respect of the cost of any building erected (or other improvement made) on the leased property by the lessee, or in respect of the portion of the cost of acquiring a leasehold which is attributable to an existing building (or other improvement) on the leasehold at the time the lessee acquires the leasehold, the inclusion of one or more renewal periods shall not extend the period taken into account to a period which exceeds the useful life remaining, at the time the leasehold is disposed of, of such building (or such other improvement). Determinations under this subdivision shall be made without regard to the proper period under section 167 or 178 for depreciating or amortizing a leasehold acquisition cost or improvement.

(iii) The provisions of this subparagraph may be illustrated by the following example:

Example. Assume that a leasehold improvement with a useful life of 30 years is properly amortized on the basis of a 10-year initial lease term. The lease is renewable for an additional 9 years. The period taken into account is $16 2/3$ years, that is, 10 years plus $2/3$ of 10 years. If, however, the leasehold improvement were disposed of at the end of 12 years, and if its remaining useful life were only 3 years, then the period taken into account would be 15 years.

(d) *Depreciation adjustments*—(1) *General.* For purposes of this section, the term "depreciation adjustments" means, in respect of any property, all adjustments reflected in the adjusted basis of such property on account of deductions described in subparagraph (2) of this paragraph allowed or allowable (whether in respect of the same or other property) to the taxpayer or to any other person. For cases where the taxpayer can establish that the amount allowed for any period was less than the amount allowable, see subparagraph (4) of this paragraph. For determination of adjusted basis of property in a multiple asset account, see paragraph (c)(3) of § 1.167(a)-8. The term "depreciation adjustments" as used in this section does not have the same meaning as the term "adjustments reflected in the adjusted basis" as defined in paragraph (a)(2) of § 1.1245-2.

(2) *Deductions.* The deductions described in this subparagraph are allowances (and amounts treated as allowances) for depreciation or amortization (other than amortization under section 168, 169 (as enacted by section 704(a), Tax Reform Act of 1969 (83 Stat. 667)), or 185). Thus, for example, such deductions include a reasonable allowance for exhaustion, wear, and tear (including a reasonable allowance for obsolescence) under section 167, the periodic deductions referred to in § 1.162-11 in respect of a specified sum paid for

Reg. § 1.1250-2(d)(2)

the acquisition of a leasehold and in respect of the cost to a lessee of improvements on property of which he is the lessee. However, such deductions do not include deductions for the periodic payment of rent.

(3) *Depreciation of other taxpayers or in respect of other property.* (i) The depreciation adjustments (reflected in the adjusted basis) referred to in subparagraph (1) of this paragraph (*a*) are not limited to adjustments with respect to the property disposed of, nor to those allowed or allowable to the taxpayer disposing of such property, and (*b*) except as provided in subparagraph (4) of this paragraph, are taken into account, whether allowed or allowable in respect of the same or other property and whether to the taxpayer or to any other person. For manner of determining the amount of additional depreciation after certain dispositions, see paragraph (e) of this section.

(ii) The provisions of this subparagraph may be illustrated by the following example:

Example. On January 1, 1966, a calendar year taxpayer purchases for $100,000 a building for use in his trade or business. He takes depreciation deductions of $20,000 (the amount allowable), of which $3,000 is additional depreciation, and transfers the building to his son as a gift on January 1, 1968. Since the exception for gifts in section 1250(d)(1) applies, the taxpayer does not recognize gain under section 1250(a)(2). In the son's adjusted basis of $80,000 for the building there is reflected $3,000 of additional depreciation. On January 1, 1969, after taking a depreciation deduction of $10,000 (the amount allowable), of which $1,000 is additional depreciation, the son sells the building. At the time of the sale the additional depreciation is $4,000 ($3,000 allowed the father plus $1,000 allowed the son).

(4) *Depreciation allowed or allowable.* (i) For purposes of subparagraph (1) of this paragraph, generally all deductions (described in subparagraph (2) of this paragraph) allowed or allowable shall be taken into account. See section 1016(a)(2) and the regulations thereunder for the meaning of "allowed" and "allowable." However, if a taxpayer can establish by adequate records or other sufficient evidence that the amount allowed for any period was less than the amount allowable for such period, the amount to be taken into account for such period shall be the amount allowed. The preceding sentence shall not apply for purposes of computing under paragraph (b)(1)(ii) of this section the amount such deductions would have been under the straight line method.

(ii) The provisions of subdivision (i) of this subparagraph may be illustrated by the following example:

Example. In the year 1969 it becomes necessary to determine the additional depreciation in respect of section 1250 property, the adjusted basis of which reflects a depreciation adjustment of $1,000 with respect to depreciation deductions allowable for the calendar year 1965 under the sum of the years-digits method. Under paragraph (b)(1)(ii) of this section, the depreciation which would have resulted under the straight line method for 1965 is $800. If the taxpayer can establish by adequate records or other sufficient evidence that he did not take, and was not allowed, any deduction for depreciation in respect of the property in 1965, then, for purposes of computing the depreciation adjustments in excess of straight line in respect of the property, the amount to be taken into account for 1965 as allowed or allowable is zero, and the amount to be taken into account in computing deductions which would have resulted under the straight line method in 1965 is $800. Thus, in effect, there is a deficit in additional depreciation for 1965 of $800.

(5) *Retired or demolished property.* Depreciation adjustments referred to in subparagraph (1) of this paragraph generally do not include adjustments in respect of retired or demolished portions of an item of section 1250 property. If a retired or demolished portion is replaced in a disposition described in section 1250(d)(4)(A) (relating to like kind exchanges and involuntary conversions), see paragraph (d)(7) of § 1.1250-3.

(6) *Exempt organization.* In respect of property disposed of by an organization which is or was exempt from income taxes (within the meaning of section 501(a)), the depreciation adjustments (reflected in the adjusted basis) referred to in subparagraph (1) of this paragraph shall include only adjustments allowed or allowable (i) in computing unrelated business taxable income (as defined in section 512(a)), or (ii) in computing taxable income of the organization for a period during which it was not exempt or, by reason of the application of section 502, 503, or 504, was denied its exemption.

(e) *Additional depreciation immediately after certain acquisitions*—(1) *Zero.* If on the date a person acquires property his basis for the property is determined solely (i) by reference to its cost (within the meaning of sec. 1012), (ii) by reason of the application of section 301(d) (relating to basis of property received in corporate distribution) or section 334(a) (relating to basis of property received in a liquidation in which gain or loss is recognized), or (iii) under the rules of sec-

Reg. § 1.1250-2(d)(3)

tion 334(b)(2) or (c) (relating to basis of property received in certain corporate liquidations), then on such date the additional depreciation for the property is zero.

(2) *Transactions referred to in section 1250(d)*. In the case of property acquired in a disposition described in section 1250(d) (relating to exceptions and limitations to application of section 1250), additional depreciation shall be computed in accordance with the rules prescribed in § 1.1250-3.

(f) *Records to be kept and information to be filed*—(1) *Records to be kept.* In any case in which it is necessary to determine the additional depreciation of an item of section 1250 property, the taxpayer shall have available permanent records of all the facts necessary to determine with reasonable accuracy the amount of such additional depreciation, including the following—

(i) The date, and the manner in which, the property was acquired,

(ii) The taxpayer's basis on the date the property was acquired and the manner in which the basis was determined,

(iii) The amount and date of all adjustments to the basis of the property allowed or allowable to the taxpayer for depreciation adjustments referred to in paragraph (d)(1) of this section and the amount and date of any other adjustments by the taxpayer to the basis of the property, and

(iv) In the case of section 1250 property which has an adjusted basis reflecting depreciation adjustments referred to in paragraph (d)(1) of this section taken by the taxpayer with respect to other property, or by another taxpayer with respect to the same or other property, the information described in subdivisions (i), (ii), and (iii) of this subparagraph with respect to such other property or such other taxpayer.

(2) *Information to be filed.* If a taxpayer acquires in a transaction (other than a like kind exchange or involuntary conversion described in section 1250(d)(4)) section 1250 property which has a basis reflecting depreciation adjustments referred to in paragraph (d)(1) of this section allowed or allowable to another taxpayer, then the taxpayer shall file with its income tax return or information return for the taxable year in which the property is acquired a statement showing all information described in subparagraph (1) of this paragraph. See section 6012 (relating to person required to make returns of income) and part III of subchapter A of chapter 61 of the Code (relating to information returns). [Reg. § 1.1250-2.]

☐ [T.D. 7084, 1-7-71. Amended by T.D. 7193, 6-29-72.]

[Reg. § 1.1250-3]

§ 1.1250-3. Exceptions and limitations.—(a) *Exception for gifts*—(1) *General rule.* Section 1250(d)(1) provides that no gain shall be recognized under section 1250(a) upon a disposition by gift. For purposes of this paragraph, the term "gift" shall have the same meaning as in paragraph (a) of § 1.1245-4. For reduction in amount of charitable contribution in case of a gift of section 1250 property, see section 170(e) and paragraph (c)(3) of § 1.170-1.

(2) *Disposition in part a sale or exchange and in part a gift.* Where a disposition of property is in part a sale or exchange and in part a gift, the disposition shall be subject to the provisions of § 1.1250-1 and the gain to which section 1250(a) applies, shall be computed under that section.

(3) *Treatment of property in hands of transferee.* If property is disposed of in a transaction which is a gift—

(i) The additional depreciation for the property in the hands of the transferee immediately after the disposition shall be an amount equal to (*a*) the amount of the additional depreciation for the property in the hands of the transferor immediately before the disposition, minus (*b*) the amount of any gain (in case the disposition is in part a sale or exchange and in part a gift) which would have been taken into account under section 1250(a) by the transferor upon the disposition if the applicable percentage had been 100 percent,

(ii) For purposes of computing the applicable percentage, the holding period under section 1250(e)(2) of property received as a gift in the hands of the transferee includes the transferor's holding period,

(iii) In case of a disposition which is in part a sale or exchange and in part a gift, if the adjusted basis of the property in the hands of the transferee exceeds its adjusted basis immediately before the transfer, the excess is an addition to capital account under paragraph (d)(2)(ii) of § 1.1250-5 (relating to property with two or more elements), and

(iv) If the property disposed of consists of two or more elements within the meaning of paragraph (c) of § 1.1250-5, see paragraph (e)(1) of § 1.1250-5 for the amount of additional depreciation and holding period for each element in the hands of the transferee.

(4) *Examples.* The provisions of this paragraph may be illustrated by the following examples:

Example (1). (i) On May 15, 1967, Smith transfers section 1250 property to his son for $45,000. In the hands of Smith the property had an adjusted basis of $40,000 and a fair market value of $70,000. Thus, the gain realized is $5,000 (amount realized, $45,000, minus adjusted basis, $40,000), and Smith has made a gift of $25,000 (fair market value, $70,000, minus amount realized, $45,000).

(ii) Smith's holding period for the property is 80 full months and, thus, the applicable percentage under section 1250(a)(2) is 40 percent. The additional depreciation for the property is $10,000. Since the gain realized ($5,000) is lower than the additional depreciation ($10,000), Smith recognized as ordinary income under section 1250(a)(2) gain of $2,000 (that is, applicable percentage, 40 percent, multiplied by gain realized, $5,000) and the $3,000 remaining portion of the gain realized may be treated as gain from the sale of property described in section 1231.

(iii) On the date the son receives the property, the additional depreciation for the property in his hands is $5,000, that is, the additional depreciation for the property in the hands of the father immediately before the transfer ($10,000), minus the gain which would have been recognized under section 1250(a)(2) upon the transfer if the applicable percentage had been 100 percent ($5,000); for purposes of computing applicable percentage his holding period is his father's holding period of 80 full months; and under § 1.1015-4 his unadjusted basis for the property is $45,000, that is, the amount he paid ($45,000) plus the excess (zero) of his father's adjusted basis over such amount.

(iv) The son sells the property for $80,000 on March 15, 1968, 10 full months after he received it from his father. Thus, his holding period is 90 full months (his father's holding period of 80 full months plus the 10 full months the son actually owned the property) and the applicable percentage under section 1250(a)(2) is 30 percent. Assume that no depreciation was allowed or allowable to the son. Thus, the son's adjusted basis and additional depreciation for the property on the date of the sale is the same as on the date he received it. Accordingly, the gain realized is $35,000 (selling price of $80,000, minus adjusted basis of $45,000). Since the additional depreciation ($5,000) is lower than the gain realized ($35,000), the son recognizes as ordinary income under section 1250(a)(2) gain of $1,500, that is, applicable percentage (30 percent) multiplied by additional depreciation ($5,000).

Example (2). Assume the same facts as in example (1), except that the son sells the property on June 15, 1969, 25 full months after he received it from his father. Thus, his holding period is 105 full months (his father's holding period of 80 full months plus the 25 full months the son actually owned the property) and the applicable percentage under section 1250(a)(2) is 15 percent. Assume further that on the date of the sale the adjusted basis of the property is $39,000, and that for the period the son actually owned the property there is a deficit in additional depreciation of $2,000. Accordingly, the gain realized is $41,000 (selling price of $80,000, minus adjusted basis of $39,000), and the additional depreciation for the property is $3,000 (that is, the additional depreciation for the property in the hands of the son on the date he received it, as determined in example (1), $5,000, minus the amount of the deficit in additional depreciation for the period the son actually owned the property, $2,000). Since the additional depreciation ($3,000) is lower than the gain realized ($41,000), the son recognizes as ordinary income under section 1250(a)(2) gain of $450, that is, applicable percentage (15 percent) multiplied by additional depreciation ($3,000).

(b) *Exception for transfers at death*—(1) *General rule.* Section 1250(d)(2) provides that, except as provided in section 691 (relating to income in respect of a decedent), no gain shall be recognized under section 1250(a) upon a transfer at death. For purposes of this paragraph, the term "transfer at death" shall have the same meaning as in paragraph (b) of § 1.1245-4.

(2) *Treatment of transferee.* (i) If as of the date a person acquires property from a decedent such person's basis is determined, by reason of the application of section 1014(a), solely by reference to the fair market value of the property on the date of the decedent's death or on the applicable date provided in section 2032 (relating to alternate valuation date), then (*a*) on the date of death the additional depreciation for the property is zero, and (*b*) for purposes of computing applicable percentage the holding period of the property under section 1250(e)(1)(A) is deemed to begin on the day after the date of death.

(ii) If property is acquired in a transfer at death to which section 1250(d)(2) applies, the amount of the additional depreciation for the property in the hands of the transferee immediately after the transfer shall be the amount (if any) of the additional depreciation in respect of the property allowed the transferee before the decedent's death, but only to the extent that the basis of the property (determined under section 1014(a)) is required to be reduced under the second sentence of section 1014(b)(9) (relating to adjustments to basis where property is acquired

Rules for Determining Capital Gains and Losses

from a decedent prior to his death) by depreciation adjustments referred to in paragraph (d)(1) of § 1.1250-2 which give rise to such additional depreciation. For treatment of such property as having a special element with additional depreciation so computed, see paragraph (c)(5)(i) of § 1.1250-5 (relating to property with two or more elements). For purposes of determining applicable percentage, such special element shall have a holding period which includes the transferee's holding period for such property for the period before the decedent's death.

(3) *Examples.* The provisions of this paragraph may be illustrated by the following examples:

Example (1). On March 6, 1966, Smith dies owning an item of section 1250 property. On March 7, 1968, the executor distributes the property to Smith's son pursuant to a specific bequest of the property in Smith's will. Under section 1014(a)(2) and paragraph (a)(2) of § 1.1014-4, the unadjusted basis of the property in the hands of the son is its fair market value on March 6, 1966 (the date Smith died), and the son is considered to have acquired the property on such date. Under section 1250(e)(1)(A), the son's holding period for the property begins on March 7, 1966 (the day after the day he is considered to have acquired the property). Thus, on March 7, 1968 (the date the property was distributed to the son), the holding period for the property is 24 full months, and the applicable percentage under section 1250 (a)(2) is 96 percent. On such date, the additional depreciation for the property includes any additional depreciation in respect of the property for the period the property was possessed by the estate.

Example (2). H purchases section 1250 property in 1965 which he immediately conveys to himself and W, his wife, as tenants by the entirety. Under local law each spouse is entitled to one-half the income from the property. H and W file joint income tax returns for calendar years 1965, 1966, and 1967. Over the 3 years, depreciation allowed in respect of the property was $4,000 (the amount allowable) of which $500 is additional depreciation. One-half of these amounts are allocable to W. Thus, depreciation deductions of $2,000, of which $250 is additional depreciation, are allowable to W. On January 1, 1968, H dies and the entire value of the property at the date of death is included in H's gross estate. Since W's basis for the property (determined under section 1014(a)) is reduced (under the second sentence of section 1014(b)(9)) by the $2,000 depreciation deductions allowed W before H's death of which $250 is additional depreciation, the additional depreciation for the property in the hands of W immediately after H's death is $250.

(c) *Limitations for certain tax-free transactions*—(1) *General.* Section 1250(d)(3) provides that upon a transfer of property described in subparagraph (2) of this paragraph, the amount of gain taken into account by the transferor under section 1250(a) shall not exceed the amount of gain recognized to the transferor on the transfer (determined without regard to section 1250). For purposes of this subparagraph, in case of a transfer of both section 1250 property and nonsection 1250 property in one transaction, the amount realized from the disposition of the section 1250 property shall be deemed to consist of that portion of the fair market value of each property acquired which bears the same ratio to the fair market value of such acquired property as the amount realized from the disposition of the section 1250 property bears to the total amount realized. The preceding sentence shall be applied solely for purposes of computing the portion of the total gain (determined without regard to section 1250) which shall be recognized as ordinary income under section 1250(a). Section 1250(d)(3) does not apply to a disposition of property to an organization (other than a cooperative described in section 521) which is exempt from the tax imposed by chapter 1 of the Code.

(2) *Transfers covered.* The transfers described in this subparagraph are transfers of property in which the basis of the property in the hands of the transferee is determined by reference to its basis in the hands of the transferor by reason of the application of any of the following provisions:

(i) Section 332 (relating to distributions in complete liquidation of an 80 percent or more controlled subsidiary corporation). For application of section 1250(d)(3) to such a complete liquidation, the principles of paragraph (c)(3) of § 1.1245-4 shall apply.

(ii) Section 351 (relating to transfer to a corporation controlled by transferor).

(iii) Section 361 (relating to exchanges pursuant to certain corporate reorganizations).

(iv) Section 371(a) (relating to exchanges pursuant to certain receivership and bankruptcy proceedings).

(v) Section 374(a) (relating to exchanges pursuant to certain railroad reorganizations).

(vi) Section 721 (relating to transfers to a partnership in exchange for a partnership interest).

(vii) Section 731 (relating to distributions by a partnership to a partner). For special carry-

Reg. § 1.1250-3(c)(2)

over basis rule, see section 1250(d)(6)(A) and paragraph (f)(1) of this section.

(3) *Treatment of property in hands of transferee.* In the case of a transfer described in subparagraph (2) (other than subdivision (vii) thereof) of this paragraph—

(i) The additional depreciation for the property in the hands of the transferee immediately after the disposition shall be an amount equal to (a) the amount of the additional depreciation for the property in the hands of the transferor immediately before the disposition, minus (b) the amount of additional depreciation necessary to produce an amount equal to the gain taken into account under section 1250(a) by the transferor upon the disposition (taking into account the applicable percentage for the property),

(ii) For purposes of computing applicable percentage, the holding period under section 1250(e)(2) of the property in the hands of the transferee includes the transferor's holding period,

(iii) If the adjusted basis of the property in the hands of the transferee exceeds its adjusted basis immediately before the transfer, the excess is an addition to capital account under paragraph (d)(2)(ii) of § 1.1250-5 (relating to property with 2 or more elements), and

(iv) If the property disposed of consists of 2 or more elements within the meaning of paragraph (c) of § 1.1250-5, see paragraph (e)(1) of § 1.1250-5 for the amount of additional depreciation and the holding period for each element in the hands of the transferee.

(4) *Examples.* The provisions of this paragraph may be illustrated by the following examples:

Example (1). (i) Green transfers section 1250 property on March 1, 1968 to a corporation, which is not exempt from taxation, in exchange for cash of $9,000 and stock in the corporation worth $91,000, in a transaction qualifying under section 351. Thus the amount realized is $100,000 ($9,000 plus $91,000). The property has an applicable percentage under section 1250(a)(2) of 60 percent, an adjusted basis of $40,000, and additional depreciation of $20,000. The gain realized is $60,000, that is, amount realized ($100,000) minus adjusted basis ($40,000). Since the additional depreciation ($20,000) is lower than the gain realized ($60,000), the amount of gain which would be treated as ordinary income under section 1250(a)(2) would be $12,000 (60 percent of $20,000) if the limitation provided in section 1250(d)(3) did not apply. Since under section 351(b) gain in the amount of $9,000 would be recognized to the transferor without regard to section 1250, the limitation provided in section 1250(d)(3) limits the gain taken into account by the transferor under section 1250(a)(2) to $9,000.

(ii) The amount of additional depreciation for the property in the hands of the transferee immediately after the transfer is $5,000, that is, the amount of additional depreciation before the transfer ($20,000) minus the amount of additional depreciation necessary to produce an amount equal to the gain recognized under section 1250(a)(2) upon the transfer ($15,000, that is, $9,000 gain recognized divided by 60 percent, the applicable percentage). (If the property is subsequently disposed of, and for the period after the initial transfer there is additional depreciation in respect of the property, then at the time of the subsequent disposition the additional depreciation will exceed $5,000. If, however, for the period after the initial transfer there was a deficit in additional depreciation, then at the time of the subsequent disposition the additional depreciation would be less than $5,000.)

Example (2). (i) Assume the same facts as in example (1) except that the additional depreciation is $10,000. Since additional depreciation ($10,000) is lower than the gain realized ($60,000), the amount of gain which would be treated as ordinary income under section 1250(a)(2) would be $6,000 (60 percent of $10,000) if the limitation provided in section 1250(d)(3) did not apply. Since under section 351(b) gain in the amount of $9,000 would be recognized to the transferor without regard to section 1250, the limitation under section 1250(d)(3) does not prevent treatment of the entire $6,000 as ordinary income under section 1250(a)(2). The $3,000 remaining portion of the $9,000 gain may be treated as gain from the sale of property described in section 1231.

(ii) Immediately after the transfer, the amount of additional depreciation is zero, that is, the amount of additional depreciation before the transfer ($10,000) minus the amount of additional depreciation necessary to produce an amount equal to the gain taken into account under section 1250(a)(2) upon the transfer ($10,000), that is, $6,000 divided by 60 percent.

Example (3). (i) Miller transfers section 1250 property after December 31, 1969, to a corporation, which is not exempt from taxation, in exchange for cash of $9,000 and stock in the corporation worth $31,000, in a transaction qualifying under section 351. Thus, the amount realized is $40,000 ($9,000 plus $31,000). The property has an applicable percentage under paragraph (d)(1)(i)(e) of this section of 100 percent and an applicable percentage under paragraph (d)(2) of this section of 50 percent. The adjusted

Reg. § 1.1250-3(c)(3)

Rules for Determining Capital Gains and Losses 53,581
See p. 20,601 for regulations not amended to reflect law changes

basis of the property on the date of the transfer is $24,000, and the gain realized is $16,000 (that is, amount realized, $40,000, minus adjusted basis, $24,000). The additional depreciation attributable to periods after December 31, 1969, is $8,000 and the additional depreciation attributable to periods before January 1, 1970, is $12,000. Since the additional depreciation attributable to periods after December 31, 1969 ($8,000), is lower than the gain realized ($16,000), the amount of gain which would be recognized as ordinary income under section 1250(a)(1) would be $8,000 (100 percent of $8,000) if the limitation provided in section 1250(d)(3) did not apply. In addition, gain is recognized under section 1250(a)(2) since there is a remaining potential gain of $8,000 (that is, gain realized, $16,000, minus additional depreciation attributable to periods after December 31, 1969 ($8,000)). Since the remaining potential gain ($8,000) is lower than the additional depreciation attributable to periods before January 1, 1970 ($12,000), the amount of gain which would be recognized under section 1250(a)(2) would be $4,000 (50 percent of $8,000) if the limitation in section 1250(d)(3) did not apply. Since under section 351(b) gain in the amount of $9,000 would be recognized to the transferor without regard to section 1250, the limitation in section 1250(d)(3) limits the gain taken into account by the transferor under section 1250(a) to $9,000. Since the section 1250(a)(1) gain is considered as recognized first under paragraph (a)(1)(iii) of § 1.1250-1, of the $9,000 of gain recognized, $8,000 is recognized under section 1250(a)(1) and $1,000 is recognized under section 1250(a)(2).

(ii) The amount of additional depreciation for the property in the hands of the transferee immediately after the transfer is $10,000, the amount of additional depreciation immediately before the transfer ($20,000), minus the sum of (a) the amount of additional depreciation necessary to produce an amount equal to the gain recognized under section 1250(a)(1) upon the transfer, $8,000 (that is, gain recognized under section 1250(a)(1), $8,000, divided by 100 percent, the applicable percentage under section 1250(a)(1)), plus (b) the amount of additional depreciation necessary to produce an amount equal to the gain recognized under section 1250(a)(2) upon the transfer, $2,000 (that is, gain recognized under section 1250(a)(2), $1,000, divided by 50 percent, the applicable percentage under section 1250(a)(2)). Of this amount, zero (that is, $8,000 minus $8,000) is attributable to periods after December 31, 1969, and $10,000 ($12,000 minus $2,000) is attributable to periods before January 1, 1970.

(d) *Limitation for like kind exchanges and involuntary conversions*—(1) *Limitation on gain.* (i) Under section 1250(d)(4)(A), if property is disposed of and gain (determined without regard to section 1250) is not recognized in whole or in part under section 1031 (relating to like kind exchanges) or section 1033 (relating to involuntary conversions), then the amount of gain taken into account by the transferor under section 1250(a) shall not exceed the greater of the two limitations set forth in subdivisions (ii) and (iii) of this subparagraph. Immediately after the transfer the basis of the acquired property shall be determined under subparagraph (2), (3), or (4) (whichever is applicable) of this paragraph, and its additional depreciation shall be computed under subparagraph (5) of this paragraph. The holding period of the acquired property for purposes of computing applicable percentage, which is determined under section 1250(e)(1), does not include the holding period of the property disposed of. In the case of a disposition of section 1250 property and other property in one transaction, see subparagraph (6) of this paragraph. In case of a disposition described in section 1250(d)(4)(A) of a portion of this item of property, see subparagraph (7) of this paragraph.

(ii) For purposes of this subparagraph, the first limitation is the sum of—

(a) The amount of gain recognized on the disposition under section 1031 or 1033 (determined without regard to section 1250), plus

(b) An amount equal to the cost of any stock purchased in a corporation which (without regard to section 1250) would result in nonrecognition of gain under section 1033(a)(3)(A).

(iii) For purposes of this subparagraph, the second limitation is the excess (if any) of—

(a) The amount of gain which would (without regard to section 1250(d)(4)) be taken into account under section 1250(a), over

(b) The fair market value (or cost in the case of a transaction described in section 1033(a)(3)) of the section 1250 property acquired in the transaction.

(iv) The provisions of this subparagraph may be illustrated by the following example:

Example. A taxpayer receives $96,000 of insurance proceeds upon the destruction of section 1250 property by fire. If section 1250(d)(4)(A) did not apply to the disposition, $16,000 of gain would be recognized under section 1250(a). In acquisitions qualifying under section 1033(a)(3)(A), he uses $90,000 of the proceeds to purchase property similar or related in service or use to the property destroyed, of which $42,000 is

Reg. § 1.1250-3(d)(1)

Rules for Determining Capital Gains and Losses

See p. 20,601 for regulations not amended to reflect law changes

for one item of section 1250 property and $48,000 is for one piece of land, and $5,000 of the proceeds to purchase stock in the acquisition of control of a corporation owning property similar or related in service or use to the property destroyed. The taxpayer properly elects under section 1033(a)(3)(A) and the regulations thereunder to limit recognition of gain (determined without regard to section 1250) to $1,000, that is, the excess of the amount realized from the conversion ($96,000) over the cost of the property acquired in acquisitions qualifying under section 1033(a)(3)(A) ($95,000, that is, $90,000 plus $5,000). The amount of gain recognized under section 1250(a) is $6,000, determined in the following manner:

The first limitation:
(a) Amount of gain recognized under section 1033(a)(3), determined without regard to section 1250(a) .... $ 1,000
(b) Fair market value of stock in a corporation which qualifies under section 1033(a)(3)(A) 5,000
(c) Sum of (a) plus (b) .... $ 6,000

The second limitation:
(d) Amount of gain which would be recognized under section 1250(a) if section 1250(d)(4) did not apply $16,000
(e) Cost of section 1250 property acquired in transaction 42,000
(f) Excess of (d) over (e) .... $ 0

Since the first limitation ($6,000) exceeds the second limitation (zero), the amount of gain recognized under section 1250(a) is $6,000. The balance ($10,000) of the gain realized ($16,000) is not recognized.

(2) *Basis of property purchased upon involuntary conversion into money.* (i) If section 1250 property is purchased in a compulsory or involuntary conversion to which section 1033(a)(3) applies, and if by reason of the application of section 1250(d)(4)(A) all or part of the gain computed under section 1250(a) is not taken into account, then the basis of the section 1250 property and other purchased property shall be determined under the rules prescribed in this subparagraph. See section 1250(d)(4)(D).

(ii) The total basis of all purchased property, the acquisition of which results in the nonrecognition of any part of the gain realized upon the transaction, shall be (a) its cost, reduced by (b) the portion of the total gain realized which was not recognized. To the extent that section 1250(d)(4)(A)(i) prevents the purchase of stock from resulting in nonrecognition of gain, the basis of purchased stock is its cost.

(iii) If purchased property consists of both section 1250 property and other property, the total basis computed under subdivision (ii) of this subparagraph shall be allocated between the section 1250 property (treated as a class) and the other property (treated as a class) in proportion to their respective costs, except that for purposes of this subdivision (but not subdivision (iv) of this subparagraph) the cost of the section 1250 property shall be deemed to be the excess of (a) its actual cost, over (b) the gain not taken into account under section 1250(a) by reason of the application of section 1250(d)(4)(A).

(iv) If the property acquired consists of more than one item of section 1250 property (or of more than one item of other property), the total basis of the section 1250 property (or of the other property), as computed under subdivisions (ii) and (iii) of this subparagraph, shall be allocated to each item of section 1250 property (or other property) in proportion to their respective actual costs.

(v) The provisions of this subparagraph may be illustrated by the following examples:

Example (1). Assume the same facts as in the example in subparagraph (1)(iv) of this paragraph. Assume further that the portion of the gain realized which was not recognized under section 1033(a)(3) or 1250(a) upon the transaction is $60,000, of which the gain computed under section 1250(a) which is not taken into account by reason of the application of section 1250(d)(4)(A) is $10,000, that is, the excess of the gain which would have been recognized under section 1250(a) if section 1250(d)(4)(A) did not apply ($16,000) over the gain recognized under section 1250(a) ($6,000). In such example $95,000 of proceeds were used to purchase property in acquisitions qualifying under section 1033(a)(3)(A) of which $42,000 was for section 1250 property, $48,000 for land, and $5,000 for stock in a corporation. The basis of each acquired property is determined in the following manner:

(a) Under subdivision (ii) of this subparagraph, the total basis of the acquired properties (other than the stock) is $30,000, that is, their cost ($90,000, of which $42,000 is for section 1250 property and $48,000 is for land), reduced by the

Reg. § 1.1250-3(d)(2)

Rules for Determining Capital Gains and Losses

portion of the total gain realized which was not recognized ($60,000).

(b) Under subdivision (iii) of this subparagraph, such total basis is allocated between the section 1250 property and the land in proportion to their respective costs, and for this purpose the cost of the section 1250 property is considered to be $32,000, that is, its actual cost ($42,000) minus the gain not recognized under section 1250(a) by reason of the application of section 1250(d)(4)(A) ($10,000). Thus, the basis of the section 1250 property is $12,000 (32/80 of $30,000), and the basis of the land is $18,000 (48/80 of $30,000).

(c) The basis of the purchased stock is its cost of $5,000. See last sentence of subdivision (ii) of this subparagraph.

Example (2). Assume the same facts as in example (1) except that the section 1250 property purchased for $42,000 consists of 2 items of such property ($10,500 for C, and $31,500 for D), and that the land purchased for $48,000 consists of 2 pieces of land ($12,000 for X, and $36,000 for Y). Under subdivision (iv) of this subparagraph, the total basis for each class of property is allocated between the individual properties of such class in proportion to their respective actual costs. Thus, the total basis of $12,000, as determined in example (1), for the section 1250 property is allocated as follows:

To C: $12,000 × ($10,500/$42,000)	$ 3,000
To D: $12,000 × ($31,500/$42,000)	9,000
Total	$12,000

The total basis of $18,000, as determined in example (1), for the land is allocated as follows:

To X: $18,000 × ($12,000/$48,000)	$ 4,500
To Y: $18,000 × ($36,000/$48,000)	13,500
Total	$18,000

(3) *Basis of property acquired upon involuntary conversion into similar property.* If property is involuntarily converted into property similar or related in service or use in a transaction to which section 1033(a)(1) applies, and if by reason of the application of section 1250(d)(4)(A) all or part of the gain computed under section 1250(a) is not taken into account, then—

(i) The total basis of the acquired property shall be determined under the first sentence of section 1033(c), and

(ii) If more than one item of property is acquired, such total basis shall be allocated to the individual items of property acquired in accordance with the principles prescribed in subparagraph (2)(iii) and (iv) of this paragraph, except that an amount equivalent to the fair market value of each item of property on the date acquired shall be treated as its actual cost.

(4) *Basis of property acquired in like kind exchange.* If section 1250 property is transferred in an exchange described in section 1031(a) or (b), and if by reason of the application of section 1250(d)(4)(A) all or part of the gain computed under section 1250(a) is not taken into account, then—

(i) The total basis of the property (including nonsection 1250 property) acquired of the type permitted to be received under section 1031 without recognition of gain or loss shall be determined under section 1031(d), and

(ii) If more than one item of property of such type was received, such total basis shall be allocated to the individual items of property of such type in accordance with the principles prescribed in subparagraph (2)(iii) and (iv) of this paragraph, except that an amount equivalent to the fair market value of each such item of property on the date received shall be treated as its actual cost.

(5) *Additional depreciation for property acquired in like kind exchange or involuntary conversion.* (i) If property is disposed of in a transaction described in section 1031 or 1033, and if by reason of the application of section 1250(d)(4)(A) all or part of the gain computed under section 1250(a) is not taken into account, then the additional depreciation for the acquired property immediately after the transaction (as computed under section 1250(d)(4)(E)) shall be an amount equal to the amount of gain computed under section 1250(a) which was not taken into account by reason of the application of section 1250(d)(4)(A).

(ii) In case more than one item of section 1250 property is acquired in the transaction, the additional depreciation computed under subdivision (i) of this subparagraph shall be allocated to each such item of section 1250 property in proportion to their respective adjusted bases.

(iii) The provisions of this subparagraph may be illustrated by the following examples:

Example (1). (a) On January 15, 1969, section 1250 property X is condemned and proceeds of $100,000 are received. On such date, X's adjusted basis is $25,000, the additional depreciation is $10,000, and the applicable percentage under section 1250(a)(2) is 70 percent. Since the additional depreciation ($10,000) is less than the gain realized ($75,000, that is, $100,000 minus $25,000) the amount of gain computed under section 1250(a)(2) (without regard to section 1250(d)(4)(A)) is $7,000, that is, 70 percent of $10,000.

Reg. § 1.1250-3(d)(5)

53,584 Rules for Determining Capital Gains and Losses

See p. 20,601 for regulations not amended to reflect law changes

(b) On March 1, 1969, all the proceeds are used to purchase section 1250 property Y in a transaction qualifying under section 1033(a)(3)(A) for nonrecognition of gain. Accordingly, the gain not recognized by reason of the application of section 1033(a)(3)(A) is $75,000, of which $7,000 is gain computed under section 1250(a)(2) which is not taken into account by reason of the application of section 1250(d)(4)(A). See subparagraph (1) of this paragraph.

(c) Immediately after the transaction, Y's basis is $25,000, that is, its cost ($100,000) minus the total gain realized which was not recognized ($75,000), and the additional depreciation (as computed under section 1250(d)(4)(E)) is $7,000, that is, the amount of gain not taken into account under section 1250(a)(2) by reason of the application of section 1250(d)(4)(A).

(d) On December 15, 1969, before any depreciation deductions were allowed or allowable in respect of Y, Y is sold for $90,000. Under section 1250(e)(1), the holding period of Y is 9 months, and thus, under section 1250(a)(2), the applicable percentage is 100 percent. Since the additional depreciation ($7,000) is less than the gain realized ($65,000, that is, $90,000 minus $25,000), the amount of gain recognized under section 1250(a)(2) as ordinary income is $7,000, that is, 100 percent of $7,000.

Example (2). Assume the same facts as in example (1), except that property Y was purchased on June 15, 1962, and that 90 full months thereafter, or December 15, 1969, it is sold for $35,000. Thus the applicable percentage under section 1250(a)(2) is 30 percent. Assume further that at the time of such sale Y's adjusted basis is $5,000 and additional depreciation in respect of Y for periods after it was acquired is $2,500. Thus, the additional depreciation at the time of the sale is $9,500, that is, the sum of the additional depreciation in respect of Y attributable to X as computed under section 1250(d)(4)(E) in (c) of example (1) ($7,000), plus the additional depreciation attributable to periods after Y was acquired ($2,500). Since the additional depreciation ($9,500) is less than the gain realized ($30,000, that is, $35,000 minus $5,000), the gain recognized under section 1250(a)(2) as ordinary income is $2,850, that is, 30 percent of $9,500.

(6) *Single disposition of section 1250 property and property of different class.* (i) For purposes of this subparagraph—

(a) Section 1250 property, section 1245 property (as defined in section 1245(a)(3)), and other property shall each be treated as a separate class of property, and

(b) The term "qualifying property" means property which may be acquired without recognition of gain under the applicable provision of section 1031 or 1033 (applied without regard to section 1250 or 1245) upon the disposition of property.

(ii) If upon a sale of section 1250 property gain would be recognized under section 1250(a), and if such section 1250 property together with property of a different class or classes are disposed of in one transaction in which gain is not recognized in whole or in part under section 1031 or 1033 (without regard to sections 1245 and 1250), then—

(a) The total amount realized shall be allocated between the different classes of property disposed of in proportion to their respective fair market values,

(b) The amount realized upon the disposition of property of a class shall be deemed to consist of so much of the fair market value of qualifying property of the same class acquired as is not in excess of the amount realized from the property of such class disposed of,

(c) The remaining portion (if any) of the amount realized upon the disposition of property of such class shall be deemed to consist of so much of the fair market value of any other property acquired as is not in excess of such remaining portion, and

(d) For purposes of applying (c) of this subdivision, the fair market value of acquired property shall be taken into account only once and in such manner as the taxpayer determines.

(iii) The amounts determined under this subparagraph in respect of property shall apply for all purposes of the Code.

(iv) The application of this subparagraph may be illustrated by the following example:

Example. (a) Green owns property consisting of land and a fully equipped factory building thereon. The property is condemned and proceeds of $100,000 are received. If the property were sold for $100,000, gain of $40,000 would be recognized of which $10,000 would be recognized as ordinary income under section 1250(a). Proceeds of $95,000 are used to purchase property similar or related in service or use to the condemned property and under section 1033(a)(3)(A) (without regard to sections 1245 and 1250) recognition of gain is limited to $5,000. The fair market values by classes of the property disposed of, and of the property acquired, are summarized in the table below:

Reg. § 1.1250-3(d)(6)

Rules for Determining Capital Gains and Losses

See p. 20,601 for regulations not amended to reflect law changes

	Fair market value of property Disposed of	Acquired
Section 1245 property	$ 35,000	$ 55,000
Section 1250 property	45,000	28,000
Land	20,000	12,000
Cash		5,000
	$100,000	$100,000

(b) The allocations under subdivision (ii) of this subparagraph are summarized in the table below:

Property disposed of	Property acquired Sec. 1245 property	Sec. 1250 property	Land	Cash remaining
$35,000 of sec. 1245 property	$35,000	...	...	...
$45,000 of sec. 1250 property	[1] 17,000	$28,000	...	...
$20,000 of land	[1] 3,000	...	$12,000	[1] $5,000
Total	$55,000	$28,000	$12,000	$5,000

[1] Determined by taxpayer pursuant to subdivision (ii)(d) of this subparagraph

(c) Upon the disposition of the section 1245 property, only section 1245 property is acquired, and thus gain (if any) would not be recognized under section 1245(a)(1). See section 1245(b)(4). Upon the disposition of the section 1250 property gain under section 1250(a) would not be recognized by reason of the application of section 1250(d)(4)(A). See subparagraph (1) of this paragraph. If the gain realized on the disposition of the land is not less than $5,000, then under section 1033(a)(3)(A) the gain recognized would be $5,000, that is, an amount equal to the portion of the proceeds from the disposition of the land ($5,000) not invested in qualifying property.

(7) *Disposition of portion of property.* A disposition described in section 1250(d)(4)(A) of a portion of an item of property gives rise to an addition to capital account described in the last sentence of paragraph (d)(2)(i) of § 1.1250-5 (relating to property with 2 or more elements). If the addition to capital account is a separate improvement within the meaning of paragraph (d) of § 1.1250-5, and thus an element, then immediately after the addition is made the amount of additional depreciation for such separate improvement shall be computed under subparagraph (5) of this paragraph by treating such portion and such addition as separate properties. If the addition is not a separate improvement, then immediately after the addition is made such property is considered under paragraph (c)(5)(ii) of § 1.1250-5 as having a special element with the same amount of additional depreciation so computed. For purposes of computing applicable percentage, the holding period of the separate improvement or special element (as the case may be), which is determined under section 1250(c)(1), does not include the holding period of the property disposed of.

(e) *Sections 1071 and 1081 transactions*—(1) *General.* This paragraph prescribes regulations under section 1250(d)(5) which apply in the case of a disposition of section 1250 property in a transaction in which gain (determined without regard to section 1250) is not recognized in whole or in part by reason of the application of section 1071 (relating to gain from sale or exchange to effectuate policies of FCC) or section 1081 (relating to gain from sale or exchange in obedience to order of SEC).

(2) *Involuntary conversion treatment under section 1071.* If section 1250 property is disposed of and gain (determined without regard to section 1250) is not recognized in whole or in part solely by reason of an election under the first sentence of section 1071(a) to treat the transaction as an involuntary conversion, the consequences of the transaction shall be determined under the principles of paragraph (d) of this section.

(3) *Basis reduction under section 1071 or 1082(a)(2).* (i) If section 1250 property is disposed of and gain (determined without regard to section 1250) is not recognized in whole or in part by reason of a reduction in basis of property pursuant to an election under section 1071(a) or the application of section 1082(a)(2), then the amount of gain taken into account by the transferor under section 1250(a) shall not exceed the sum of—

(a) The amount of gain recognized on such disposition (determined without regard to section 1250), plus

(b) In case involuntary conversion treatment was also elected under section 1071(a),

Reg. § 1.1250-3(e)(3)

an amount equal to the cost of any stock purchased in a corporation which (without regard to section 1250) would result in nonrecognition of gain under section 1033(a)(3), as modified by section 1071(a), plus

(c) The portion of the gain computed under section 1250 (a) (without regard to this paragraph) which is neither taken into account under (a) or (b) of this subdivision nor applied under subdivision (ii) of this subparagraph to reduce the basis of section 1250 property.

(ii)(a) The amount of gain computed under section 1250(a) (without regard to this paragraph) which is not taken into account under subdivision (i)(a) or (b) of this subparagraph shall be applied to the amount by which the basis of the section 1250 property was reduced under section 1071(a) or 1082(a)(2), as the case may be, before other gain (which is not gain computed under section 1250(a)) is so applied.

(b) If the basis of more than one item of section 1250 property was so reduced, the gain applied under (a) of this subdivision to all such section 1250 properties shall be applied to such items in proportion to the amounts of their respective basis reductions.

(c) Any gain not applied under (a) of this subdivision shall be applied to the amount by which the basis of the non-section 1250 property was reduced.

(iii) If gain computed under section 1250 is applied under subdivision (ii) of this subparagraph to reduce the basis of section 1250 property, the amount so applied shall be treated as additional depreciation in respect of such section 1250 property. For treatment of such section 1250 property as having a special element with additional depreciation consisting of such amount, see paragraph (c)(5)(i) of § 1.1250-5. For purposes of computing applicable percentage, such special element shall have a holding period beginning on the day after the date as of which the property's basis was so reduced.

(4) *Section 1081(d)(1)(A) transaction.* No gain shall be recognized under section 1250(a) upon an exchange of property as to which gain is not recognized (without regard to section 1250) because of the application of section 1081(d)(1)(A) (relating to transfers within system group). For treatment of property in the hands of a transferee, the principles of paragraph (c)(3) of this section shall apply.

(f) *Property distributed by a partnership to a partner*—(1) *General.* For purposes of section 1250(d)(3) and (e)(2), the basis of section 1250 property distributed by a partnership to a partner shall be determined by reference to the adjusted basis of such property to the partnership. Thus, if section 731 applies to a distribution of section 1250 property by a partnership to a partner, then even though the partner's basis is not determined for other purposes by reference to the partnership's basis, (i) the amount of gain taken into account by the partnership under section 1250(a) is limited by section 1250(d)(3) to the amount of gain recognized to the partnership upon the distribution (determined without regard to section 1250), and (ii) the holding period of the property in the hands of the partner shall, under section 1250(e)(2), include the holding period of the property in the hands of the partnership. For nonapplication of section 1250(d)(3) to a disposition to an organization (other than a cooperative described in section 521) which is exempt from the tax imposed by chapter 1 of the Code, see paragraph (c)(1) of this section.

(2) *Treatment of property distributed by partnership.* (i) If section 1250 property is distributed by a partnership to a partner in a distribution in which no part of the partnership's "potential section 1250 income" in respect of the property was recognized as ordinary income to the partnership under paragraph (b)(2)(ii) of § 1.751-1, the additional depreciation for the property in the hands of the distributee attributable to periods before the distribution shall be an amount equal to the total potential section 1250 income of the partnership in respect of the property immediately before the distribution, recomputed as if the applicable percentage for the property had been 100 percent. Under paragraph (c)(4) of § 1.751-1, the potential section 1250 income is, in effect, the gain to which section 1250(a) would have applied if the property had been sold by the partnership immediately before the distribution at its fair market value at such time.

(ii) If upon the distribution any potential section 1250 income in respect of the property was recognized to the partnership under paragraph (b)(2)(ii) of § 1.751-1, then after the distribution the additional depreciation shall be an amount equal to (a) the total potential section 1250 income in respect of the property, as recomputed in subdivision (i) of this subparagraph, minus (b) the amount of potential section 1250 income which would have been recognized to the partnership under paragraph (b)(2)(ii) of § 1.751-1 if the applicable percentage for the property had been 100 percent.

(iii) If the partner's basis for the property immediately after the transaction exceeds the partnership's adjusted basis for the property immediately before the transaction, the excess may

Reg. § 1.1250-3(e)(4)

be an addition to capital account under paragraph (d)(2)(ii) of § 1.1250-5 (relating to property with two or more elements).

(3) *Examples.* The provisions of subparagraphs (1) and (2) of this paragraph may be illustrated by the following examples:

Example (1). (i) A partnership distributes a building to Smith on January 1, 1969, in a complete liquidation of his partnership interest to which section 736(a) does not apply. On the date of the distribution, the partnership's holding period for the property is 40 full months and, accordingly, the applicable percentage under section 1250(a)(2) is 80 percent. On such date, the partnership's additional depreciation for the building ($6,250) is lower than the excess ($40,000) of its fair market value of ($140,000) over adjusted basis ($100,000). Thus, under paragraph (c)(4) of § 1.751-1, the partnership's potential section 1250 income in respect of the building is $5,000 (80 percent of $6,250). Assume that section 751(b) does not apply to the distribution. Accordingly, no gain would be recognized to the partnership under section 731(b) (without regard to the application of section 1250). Smith's basis for his partnership interest was $150,000, and under section 732(b) Smith's basis for the building is equal to his basis for his partnership interest. Thus, Smith's basis for the building is not determined by reference to the partnership's basis for the building. Nevertheless, under subparagraph (1) of this paragraph, no gain is recognized to the partnership under section 1250(a)(2) and Smith's holding period for the property includes the partnership's holding period.

(ii) Six full months after Smith receives the building in the distribution, or July 1, 1969, he sells it for $153,000. Assume that no depreciation was allowed or allowable to Smith for the building, and that the special rules under § 1.1250-5 for property with two or more elements do not apply. Since Smith's holding period for the building includes its holding period in the hands of the partnership, his holding period is 46 full months (40 full months for the partnership plus 6 full months for Smith) and the applicable percentage under section 1250(a)(2) is 74 percent.

(iii) Since no potential section 1250 income was recognized to the partnership under paragraph (b)(2)(ii) of § 1.751-1, the additional depreciation for the building attributable to periods before the distribution is determined under the provisions of subparagraph (2)(i) of this paragraph. Under such provisions, the potential section 1250 income to the partnership which was actually $5,000 (that is, 80 percent of $6,250), is recomputed as if the applicable percentage were 100 percent, and thus such additional depreciation is $6,250 (that is, 100 percent of $6,250). Since no depreciation was allowed or allowable for the building in Smith's hands, the additional depreciation for the building attributable to Smith's total holding period (46 full months) is $6,250. Since the gain realized ($3,000, that is, amount realized, $153,000, minus adjusted basis, $150,000) is lower than the additional depreciation ($6,250), the gain recognized to Smith under section 1250(a)(2) is $2,220 (that is, 74 percent of $3,000).

Example (2). Assume the facts as in example (1) except that as a result of the distribution the partnership recognizes under paragraph (b)(2)(ii) of § 1.751-1 potential section 1250 income of $1,000 (that is, 80 percent of $1,250). The additional depreciation attributable to periods before the distribution, as determined under the provisions of subparagraph (2)(ii) of this paragraph, is $5,000, that is, (a) the total potential section 1250 income in respect of the property, recomputed, in example (1) as if the applicable percentage were 100 percent ($6,250), minus (*b*) the amount of potential section 1250 income which would have been recognized to the partnership under paragraph (b)(2)(ii) of § 1.751-1 if the applicable percentage for the property had been 100 percent of ($1,250, that is, 100 percent of $1,250).

(4) *Treatment of partnership property after certain transactions.* If under paragraph (b)(3) of § 1.751-1 (relating to certain distributions of partnership property other than section 751 property treated as sales or exchanges) a partnership is treated as purchasing section 1250 property (or a portion thereof) from a distributee who relinquishes his interest in such property (or portion), then after the date of such purchase the following rules shall apply:

(i) If only a portion of the property is treated as purchased, there shall be excluded from the additional depreciation for the remaining portion any additional depreciation in respect of the purchased portion for periods before such purchase.

(ii) In respect of the purchased property (or portion), (*a*) as of the date of purchase the amount of additional depreciation shall be zero, and (*b*) for purposes of computing applicable percentage the holding period shall begin on the day after the date of such purchase.

(5) *Cross reference.* See paragraph (f) of § 1.1250-1 for the amount of additional depreciation for partnership property in respect of a partner who acquired his partnership interest in certain transactions when an election under sec-

Reg. § 1.1250-3(f)(5)

53,588 Rules for Determining Capital Gains and Losses
See p. 20,601 for regulations not amended to reflect law changes

tion 754 (relating to optional adjustments to basis of partnership property) was in effect.

(g) *Disposition of principal residence*—(1) *In general.* (i) Section 1250(d)(7)(A) provides that section 1250(a) shall not apply to a disposition of property by a taxpayer to the extent the property is used by the taxpayer as his principal residence (within the meaning of section 1034(a) and the regulations thereunder, relating to a sale or exchange of residence). Thus, for example, if a doctor sells a house, of which one portion was used as his principal residence within the meaning of section 1034(a) and the other portion was properly subject to the allowance for depreciation as property used in his trade or business, then, by reason of the application of section 1250(d)(7)(A), section 1250(a) does not apply in respect of the disposition of the portion used as his principal residence. The provisions of this subparagraph shall apply regardless of whether section 1034 applies. Thus, for example, if section 1034 did not apply to the sale because the doctor did not invest in a new principal residence within the period specified in section 1034, nevertheless section 1250(a) would not apply to the disposition of the portion used as a principal residence.

(ii) Section 1250(d)(7)(B) provides that section 1250(a) shall not apply to a disposition of section 1250 property by a taxpayer who, in respect of the property, satisfies the age and ownership requirements of section 121 (relating to exclusion from gross income of gain on sale or exchange of residence of individual who has attained age 65), but only to the extent the taxpayer satisfies the use requirements of section 121 in respect of such property. Thus, if a taxpayer has attained the age of 65 before the date on which he disposes of section 1250 property, and if during the 8-year period ending on the date of the disposition the property has been owned and used by the taxpayer solely as his principal residence for periods aggregating 5 years or more, then section 1250(a) does not apply in respect to the disposition. This result would not be changed even if the taxpayer does not or cannot make the election provided for in section 121 and even if section 121 applies to only a portion of the gain because the adjusted sales price exceeds the $20,000 limitation in section 121(b)(1). If, however, only a portion of the property has been used as his principal residence for such periods aggregating 5 years or more, then, by reason of the application of section 1250(d)(7)(B), section 1250(a) is inapplicable only to the portion so used. For special rules for determining whether the age, ownership, and use requirements of section 121 are treated as satisfied, and for the manner of applying such requirements, see section 121(d) and the regulations thereunder.

(2) *Concurrent operation of section 1250(d)(7) with other provisions.* Upon the disposition of a principal residence, gain computed under section 1250(a) may not be recognized in whole or in part by reason of the application of both the provisions of section 1250(d)(7) and the provisions of one of the other exceptions or limitations enumerated in section 1250(d). Thus, for example, if an entire house is transferred as a gift, and if section 1250(d)(7) applies to only a portion of the house, then section 1250(d)(1) excepts the disposition of the entire house from the application of section 1250(a).

(3) *Special rule.* If by reason of section 1250(d)(7) a disposition is partially excepted from the application of section 1250(a), and if no other paragraph of section 1250(d) excepts the disposition entirely from such application, then the gain to which section 1250(a) applies shall be an amount which bears the same ratio to (i) the gain computed under section 1250(a) (without regard to section 1250(d)(7)), as (ii) the fair market value of the portion of the property to which the exception in section 1250(d)(7) does not apply, bears to (iii) the total fair market value of the property. Thus, for example, if under paragraph (a)(2) of this section gain of $300 would be recognized as ordinary income under section 1250(a) (without regard to section 1250(d)(7)) upon a combined sale and gift of section 1250 property, and if the property has a fair market value of $25,000 of which $10,000 is properly allocable to a portion not used as a principal residence, then the amount of gain recognized as ordinary income under section 1250(a) would be $120 (10/25 of $300).

(4) *Treatment of property in hands of transferee.* If property is disposed of in a transaction to which section 1250(d)(7) applies, and if its basis in the hands of the transferee is determined by reference to its basis in the hands of the transferor by reason of the application of section 1250(d)(1) (relating to gifts) or section 1250(d)(3) (relating to certain tax-free transactions), then the treatment of the property in the hands of the transferee shall be determined under paragraph (a)(3) or (c)(3) (whichever is applicable) of this section.

(5) *Treatment of property acquired in like kind exchange or involuntary conversion.* If property is disposed of in a transaction to which section 1250(d)(7) (relating to principal residence) and section 1250(d)(4) (relating to like kind exchanges and involuntary conversions) apply, then—

Reg. § 1.1250-3(g)(1)

Rules for Determining Capital Gains and Losses

(i) The basis of the property acquired shall be determined under the applicable provisions of paragraph (d)(2), (3), or (4) of this section applied as if all gain computed under section 1250(a) (except any gain not recognized solely by reason of the application of section 1250(d)(7)) were not taken into account by reason of section 1250(d)(4)(A),

(ii) The additional depreciation for the property acquired shall be determined in the manner prescribed in paragraph (d)(5) of this section, so applied, and

(iii) For purposes of computing the applicable percentage, the holding period of the acquired property shall be determined under section 1250(e)(1).

(6) *Treatment of property acquired in section 1034 transaction.* If a principal residence is disposed of in a transaction to which section 1250(d)(7) applies, and if by reason of the application of section 1034 (relating to sale or exchange of residence) the basis of property acquired in the transaction is determined by reference to the basis in the hands of the taxpayer of the property disposed of, then—

(i) The additional depreciation for the acquired property immediately after the transaction shall be an amount equal to (*a*) the amount of the additional depreciation for the property disposed of, minus (*b*) the amount of any gain which would have been taken into account under section 1250(a) by the transferor upon the disposition if the applicable percentage for the property had been 100 percent,

(ii) For purposes of computing the applicable percentage, the holding period of the acquired property includes the holding period of the disposed of property (see section 1250(e)(3)),

(iii) If the adjusted basis of the acquired property exceeds the adjusted basis immediately before the transfer of the property disposed of, the excess is an addition to capital account under paragraph (d)(2)(ii) of § 1.1250-5 (relating to property with more than one element), and

(iv) If the property disposed of consisted of 2 or more elements within the meaning of paragraph (c) of § 1.1250-5, see paragraph (e)(3) of § 1.1250-5 for the amount of additional depreciation and the holding period for each element in the hands of the transferee.

(h) *Limitation for disposition of qualified low-income housing*—(1) *Limitation on gain.* (i) Under section 1250(d)(8)(A), if section 1250 property is disposed of and gain (determined without regard to section 1250) is not recognized in whole or in part under section 1039 (relating to certain sales of low income housing projects), then the amount of gain recognized by the transferor under section 1250(a) shall not exceed the greater of—

(*a*) The amount of gain recognized under section 1039 (determined without regard to section 1250), or

(*b*) The excess, if any, of the amount of gain which would, but for section 1250(d)(8)(A), be taken into account under section 1250(a), over the cost of the section 1250 property acquired in the transaction.

For purposes of this paragraph the term "qualified housing project", "approved disposition", "reinvestment period", and "net amount realized" shall have the same meaning as in section 1039 and § 1.1039-1.

(ii) The principles of this subparagraph may be illustrated by the following examples:

Example (1). (i) Taxpayer A owns a qualified housing project and makes an approved disposition of the project on January 1, 1971. The net amount realized upon the disposition is $550,000, of which $475,000 is attributable to section 1250 property. The adjusted basis of the section 1250 property is $250,000 and the gain realized on the disposition of section 1250 property is $225,000. The additional depreciation for the property is $100,000, the applicable percentage is 48 percent, and if section 1250(d)(8)(A) did not apply to the disposition, $48,000 of gain would be recognized under section 1250(a). Within the reinvestment period, A purchases a replacement qualified housing project at a cost of $525,000, of which $425,000 is attributable to section 1250 property. A properly elects under section 1039(a) and the regulations thereunder to limit the recognition of gain (determined without regard to section 1250) to $25,000, that is, the excess of the net amount realized ($550,000) over the cost of the replacement housing project ($525,000).

(ii) The amount of gain recognized under section 1250(a) is limited to $25,000, that is, the greater of (*a*) the amount of gain recognized without regard to section 1250(a) ($25,000), or (*b*) the excess of (*1*) the amount of gain which would be taken into account under section 1250(a) if section 1250(d)(8)(A) did not apply ($225,000) over (*2*) the cost of the replacement section 1250 property ($425,000), or zero.

Example (2). The facts are the same as in example (1) except that only $180,000 of the cost of the replacement housing project is attributable to section 1250 property. Thus, the gain recognized under section 1250(a) is limited to $45,000, the greater of (*a*) the excess of (*1*) the amount of gain which would be taken into account under section 1250(a) if section 1250(d)(8)(A) did not

Reg. § 1.1250-3(h)(1)

apply ($225,000), over (*2*) the cost of the replacement section 1250 property ($180,000), or (*b*) the amount of gain recognized without regard to section 1250 ($25,000).

(2) *Replacement project consisting of more than one element.* (i) If (*a*) section 1250 property is disposed of, (*b*) any portion of the gain which would have been recognized under section 1250(a) is not recognized by reason of section 1250(d)(8)(A), and (*c*) the cost of the replacement section 1250 property constructed, reconstructed, or acquired during the reinvestment period exceeds the net amount realized attributable to the section 1250 property disposed of, then the section 1250 property shall consist of two elements. For purposes of this paragraph, the "reinvestment element" is that portion of the section 1250 property constructed, reconstructed, or acquired during the reinvestment period the cost of which does not exceed the net amount realized attributable to the section 1250 property disposed of, reduced by any gain recognized with respect to such property. The "additional cost element" is that portion of the section 1250 property constructed, reconstructed, or acquired during the reinvestment period whose cost exceeds the net amount realized attributable to the section 1250 property disposed of.

(ii) The principles of this subparagraph may be illustrated by the following example:

Example. (1)(i) Taxpayer B disposes of a qualified housing project consisting of section 1250 property with an adjusted basis of $500,000 and land with a basis of $100,000. The amount realized on the disposition is $750,000 of which $650,000 is attributable to the section 1250 property. B constructs a replacement housing project at a cost of $1,000,000 of which $850,000 is attributable to section 1250 property. B elects in accordance with the provisions of section 1039(a) and the regulations thereunder not to recognize the $150,000 gain realized.

(ii) Under section 1250(d)(8)(A) no gain is recognized under section 1250(a). The replacement section 1250 property consists of the two elements. The reinvestment element has a cost of $650,000, *i.e.*, that portion of the replacement section 1250 property the cost of which does not exceed the amount realized attributable to the section 1250 property disposed of ($650,000), reduced by any gain recognized with respect to such property (zero). The additional cost element has a cost of $200,000, that is, the excess of the cost of the replacement section 1250 property ($850,000) over the amount realized attributable to the section 1250 property disposed of ($650,000).

(3) *Basis of property acquired.* (i) If section 1250 property is disposed of and gain (determined without regard to section 1250) is not recognized in whole or in part under section 1039 (relating to certain sales of low-income housing projects), then the basis of the section 1250 property and other property acquired in the transaction shall be determined in accordance with the rules of this subparagraph. Generally, the basis of the property acquired in a transaction to which section 1039(a) applies is its cost reduced by the amount of any gain not recognized attributable to the property disposed of (see section 1039(d)). In a case where the replacement section 1250 property constructed, reconstructed, or acquired within the reinvestment period is treated as consisting of more than one element under section 1250(d)(8)(E), the aggregate basis of the property determined under section 1039(d) shall be allocated as follows: first, to the reinvestment element of the section 1250 property, in an amount equal to the amount determined under section 1250(d)(8)(E)(i) reduced by the amount of any gain not recognized attributable to the section 1250 property disposed of; second, to the other replacement property (other than section 1250 property) in an amount equal to the amount of its cost reduced (but not below zero) by any remaining amount of gain not recognized; and finally, to the additional cost element of the section 1250 property, in an amount equal to the amount determined under section 1250(d)(8)(E)(ii) reduced by any amount of gain not recognized which has not taken into account in determining the basis of the reinvestment element and the other replacement property that is not section 1250 property. See paragraph (h)(2) of this section for definition of the terms "reinvestment element" and "additional cost element".

(ii) The principles of this subparagraph may be illustrated by the following examples:

Example (1). The facts are the same as in example (1) of subparagraph (1)(ii) of this paragraph. The basis of the replacement section 1250 property is $225,000, the amount of the reinvestment element ($425,000) minus the gain not recognized attributable to the section 1250 property disposed of ($200,000).

Example (2). Taxpayer C disposes of a qualified housing project on January 1, 1971. The adjusted basis for the project is $3,800,000, of which $3,000,000 is attributable to section 1250 property and $800,000 is attributable to land. The amount realized on the disposition is $5,000,000, of which $4,000,000 is attributable to the section 1250 property and $1,000,000 is attributable to the land. The gain realized upon the

Reg. § 1.1250-3(h)(2)

disposition is $1,200,000, that is, amount realized ($5,000,000) minus adjusted basis ($3,800,000), of which $1,000,000 is attributable to the section 1250 property disposed of. Within the reinvestment period, C purchases another qualified housing project at a cost of $5,500,000, of which $4,000,000 is attributable to section 1250 property and $1,500,000 is attributable to other property. C makes an election under section 1039(a) and the regulations thereunder and none of the $1,200,000 gain realized on the disposition is recognized (determined without regard to section 1250). Under section 1250(d)(8)(A), none of the gain realized is recognized under section 1250(a). The basis of the replacement section 1250 property is $3,000,000, that is, the amount of the reinvestment element ($4,000,000) less the amount of gain not recognized attributable to section 1250 property disposed of ($1,000,000). The basis of the other property acquired is $1,300,000, that is, its cost ($1,500,000) reduced by the remaining gain not recognized ($200,000).

Example (3). The facts are the same as in example (2) except that the cost of the replacement section 1250 property is $4,500,000 and the cost of the other property is $1,000,000. Thus, the replacement section 1250 property consists of two elements under section 1250(d)(8)(E). The reinvestment element (section 1250(d)(8)(E)(i)) has a basis of $3,000,000, that is, $4,000,000 (that portion of the section 1250 property acquired the cost of which does not exceed the net amount realized attributable to the section 1250 property disposed of), reduced by $1,000,000 (the gain not recognized attributable to the section 1250 property disposed of). The basis of the other property is $800,000, that is, its cost ($1,000,000) reduced by the remaining gain not recognized ($200,000). The additional cost element (section 1250(d)(8)(E)(ii)) has a basis of $500,000, that is, the portion of the section 1250 property acquired the cost of which exceeds the net amount realized attributable to the section 1250 property disposed of. This amount ($500,000) is not reduced by any amount of gain not recognized because all of the gain not recognized has already been taken into account in determining the basis of the reinvestment element and the other replacement property that is not section 1250 property.

(4) *Additional depreciation for property acquired.* (i) If a qualified housing project is disposed of in a transaction to which section 1039(a) applies, the additional depreciation for the replacement property immediately after the transaction shall be an amount equal to (*a*) the amount of additional depreciation for the property disposed of, minus (*b*) the amount of additional depreciation necessary to produce the amount of gain recognized under section 1250(a). Thus, if no gain is recognized upon a disposition of a qualified housing project, the additional depreciation for the property acquired will be the same as for the property disposed of. On the other hand, if upon disposition of a project, gain of $40,000 was recognized under section 1250(a), and if the additional depreciation for the project and the applicable percentage were $100,000 and 80 percent, respectively, the additional depreciation for the replacement housing project would be $50,000, that is, $100,000 minus $50,000, the amount of additional depreciation necessary to produce $40,000 of recognized gain where the applicable percentage is 80 percent.

(ii) If the property acquired in the transaction consists of more than one element of section 1250 property by reason of section 1250(d)(8)(E), the additional depreciation under subdivision (i) of this subparagraph shall be allocated solely to the reinvestment element.

(5) *Additional limitation.* If, in a transaction to which section 1039(a) applies, gain is recognized by the taxpayer, the amount of gain recognized which is attributable to section 1250 property disposed of is, under section 1250(d)(8)(F)(i), limited to an amount equal to the net amount realized attributable to the section 1250 property disposed of reduced by the greater of (i) the adjusted basis of the section 1250 property disposed of or (ii) the cost of the section 1250 property acquired. The limitation of section 1250(d)(8)(F)(i) may be illustrated by the following example:

Example. Taxpayer D owns property constituting a qualified housing project under section 1039(b)(1). In an approved disposition, the project is sold for $225,000. The net amount realized on the disposition is $225,000 of which $175,000 is attributable to the section 1250 property disposed of. The adjusted basis of such property is $150,000 and thus the gain realized upon the disposition of the section 1250 property is $25,000. Assume that the total gain realized upon disposition of the project is $45,000. Within the reinvestment period, D purchases another qualified housing project at a cost of $200,000, of which $160,000 is attributable to section 1250 property. D elects, in accordance with section 1039(a) and the regulations thereunder, to limit the recognition of gain to $25,000, that is, the net amount realized ($225,000), minus the cost of the replacement housing project ($200,000). Under this subparagraph, $15,000 of the $25,000 gain recognized is attributable to the section 1250 property disposed of, that is, the net amount realized attributable to the section 1250 property

Reg. § 1.1250-3(h)(5)

53,592 Rules for Determining Capital Gains and Losses

See p. 20,601 for regulations not amended to reflect law changes

disposed of ($175,000), reduced by $160,000, the greater of the adjusted basis of the section 1250 property disposed of ($150,000) or the cost of the section 1250 property acquired ($160,000).

(6) *Allocation rule.* (i) If, in a transaction to which paragraph (h)(1) of this section applies, the section 1250 property disposed of is treated as consisting of more than one element by reason of the application of section 1250(d)(8)(E) with respect to a prior transaction, then the amount of gain recognized, the net amount realized, and the additional depreciation with respect to each such element shall be allocated to the elements of the replacement section 1250 property in accordance with the provisions of this subparagraph.

(ii) The portion of the net amount realized upon such a disposition which shall be allocated to each element of the section 1250 property disposed of is that amount which bears the same ratio to the net amount realized attributable to all the section 1250 property disposed of in the transaction as the additional depreciation for that element bears to the total additional depreciation for all elements disposed of. If any gain is recognized upon disposition of the section 1250 property, such gain shall be allocated to each element in the same proportion as the gain realized for that element bears to the gain realized for all elements disposed of. The additional depreciation for each reinvestment element of the replacement section 1250 property shall be the same as for the corresponding element of the property disposed of, decreased by the amount of additional depreciation necessary to produce the amount of gain recognized for such element. The additional depreciation for any additional cost element shall be zero.

(iii) The principles of this subparagraph may be illustrated by the following example:

Example. Taxpayer E disposes of a qualified housing project in an approved disposition. The net amount realized is $1,090,000 of which $900,000 is attributable to section 1250 property. The section 1250 property consists of (1) a reinvestment element with an adjusted basis of $300,000, additional depreciation of $100,000, and an applicable percentage of 50 percent, and (2) an additional cost element with an adjusted basis of $200,000, additional depreciation of $50,000, and an applicable percentage of 80 percent. Gain of $400,000 is realized on the disposition of the section 1250 property, that is, amount realized ($900,000) minus adjusted basis ($500,000). Within the reinvestment period, E purchases another qualified housing project at a cost of $1,000,000 of which $840,000 is attributable to section 1250 property. E elects, in accordance with section 1039 and the regulations thereunder, to limit recognition of gain (determined without regard to section 1250) to $90,000, that is, the excess of the net amount realized ($1,090,000) over the cost of the replacement project ($1,000,000). Under section 1250(d)(8)(A), the amount of gain recognized under section 1250(a) is limited to $90,000 (see subparagraph (1) of this paragraph). Under section 1250(d)(8)(F)(ii) and this subparagraph, $600,000 of the $900,000 net amount realized attributable to the section 1250 property is allocated to the reinvestment element, that is, additional depreciation for the element ($100,000) over total additional depreciation ($150,000) times the net amount realized ($900,000). The remaining $300,000 is allocated to the additional cost element. Thus, the gain realized attributable to the reinvestment element is $300,000, that is, net amount realized ($600,000) minus adjusted basis ($300,000). The gain realized attributable to the additional cost element is $100,000, that is, net amount realized ($300,000) minus adjusted basis ($200,000). Under subparagraph (5) of this paragraph, the gain recognized attributable to the section 1250 property is limited to $60,000, that is, the net amount realized attributable to the section 1250 property disposed of ($900,000) minus the greater of the adjusted basis of such property ($500,000) or the cost of the section 1250 property acquired in the transaction ($840,000). Under section 1250(d)(8)(F)(ii) and this subparagraph, $45,000, of the $60,000 gain recognized is attributable to the reinvestment element, that is, $60,000 multiplied by a fraction whose numerator is the gain realized attributable to the reinvestment element ($300,000) and whose denominator is the total gain realized attributable to all the section 1250 property ($400,000). The remaining $15,000 of the gain recognized is attributable to the additional cost element. The new property acquired has no additional cost element. The reinvestment element of the new property acquired consists of 2 subelements corresponding to the reinvestment element and additional cost element of the property disposed of. The subelement corresponding to the reinvestment element has additional depreciation of $10,000, that is, its additional depreciation immediately before the disposition ($100,000), minus $90,000, the amount of additional depreciation necessary to produce $45,000 of section 1250(a) gain where the applicable percentage is 50 percent. The subelement corresponding to the additional cost element has additional depreciation of $31,250, that is, its additional depreciation immediately before the disposition ($50,000), minus $18,750, the amount of additional deprecia-

Reg. § 1.1250-3(h)(6)

tion necessary to produce $15,000 of section 1250(a) gain where the applicable percentage is 80 percent. [Reg. § 1.1250-3.]

☐ [T.D. 7084, 1-7-71. Amended by T.D. 7193, 6-29-72 and T.D. 7400, 2-3-76.]

[Reg. § 1.1250-4]

§ 1.1250-4. Holding period.—(a) *General.* In general, for purposes only of determining the applicable percentage (as defined in sec. 1250(1)(C) and (2)(B)) of section 1250 property, the holding period of the property shall be determined under the rules of section 1250(e) and this section and not under the rules of section 1223. If the property is treated as consisting of two or more elements (within the meaning of paragraph (c)(1) of § 1.1250-5), see paragraph (a)(2)(ii) of § 1.1250-5 for application of this section to determination of holding period of each element. Section 1250(e) does not affect the determination of the amount of additional depreciation in respect of section 1250 property.

(b) *Beginning of holding period.* (1) For the purpose of determining the applicable percentage, in the case of property acquired by the taxpayer (other than by means of a transaction referred to in paragraph (c) or (d) of this section), the holding period of the property shall begin on the day after the date of its acquisition. See section 1250(e)(1)(A). Thus, for example, if a taxpayer purchases section 1250 property on January 1, 1965, the holding period of the property begins on January 2, 1965. If he sells the property on October 1, 1966, the holding period on the day of the sale is 21 full months, and, accordingly, the applicable percentage is 99 percent. This result would not be changed even if the property initially had been used solely as the taxpayer's residence for a portion of the 21-month period. If, however, the property were sold on September 30, 1966, the holding period would be only 20 full months.

(2) For the purpose of determining the applicable percentage in the case of property constructed, reconstructed, or erected by the taxpayer, the holding period of the property shall begin on the first day of the month during which the property is placed in service. See section 1250(e)(1)(B). Thus, for example, if a taxpayer constructs section 1250 property and places it in service on January 15, 1965, its holding period begins on January 1, 1965. If the taxpayer sells the property on December 31, 1966, its holding period on the day of sale is 24 full months, and, accordingly, the applicable percentage is 96 percent. For purposes of this subparagraph, property is placed in service on the date on which it is first used, whether in a trade or business, in the production of income, or in a personal activity. Thus, for example, a residence constructed by a taxpayer for his personal use is placed in service on the date it is occupied as a residence. For purposes of determining the date property is placed in service, it is immaterial when the period begins for depreciation with respect to the property under any depreciation practice under which depreciation begins in any month other than the month in which the property is placed in service. If one or more units of a single property are placed in service on different dates before the completion of the property, see paragraph (c)(3) of § 1.1250-5 (relating to treatment of each such unit as an element).

(c) *Property with transferred basis.* Under section 1250(e)(2), if the basis of property acquired in a transaction described in this subparagraph is determined by reference to its basis in the hands of the transferor, then the holding period of the property in the hands of the transferee shall include the holding period of the property in the hands of the transferor. The transactions described in this subparagraph are:

(1) A gift described in section 1250(d)(1).

(2) Certain transfers at death to the extent provided in paragraph (b)(2)(ii) of § 1.1250-3.

(3) Certain tax-free transactions to which section 1250(d)(3) applies. For application of section 1250(d)(3) and (e)(2) to a distribution by a partnership to a partner, see paragraph (f)(1) of § 1.1250-3.

(4) A transfer described in paragraph (e)(4) of § 1.1250-3 (relating to transaction under section 1081(d)(1)(A)).

(d) *Principal residence acquired in certain transactions.* The holding period of a principal residence acquired in a transaction to which section 1034 and paragraph (g)(6) of § 1.1250-3 apply includes the holding period of the principal residence disposed of in such transaction. See section 1250(e)(3). The holding period of a principal residence acquired does not include the period beginning on the day after the date of the disposition and ending on the date of the acquisition.

(e) *Application of transferred basis and principal residence rules.* The determination of holding period under this section shall be made without regard to whether a transaction occurred prior to the effective date of section 1250 and without regard to whether there was any gain upon the transaction. Thus, for example, under paragraph (c) of this section a donee's holding period for property includes his donor's holding period notwithstanding that the gift occurred on or before December 31, 1963, or that there was no additional depreciation in respect of the property at the time of the gift.

Reg. § 1.1250-4(e)

53,594 Rules for Determining Capital Gains and Losses

See p. 20,601 for regulations not amended to reflect law changes

(f) *Qualified low-income housing project acquired in certain transactions.* The holding period of a "reinvestment element" (and of subelements thereof) of section 1250 property (as defined in paragraph (h)(2) of § 1.1250-3) acquired in a transaction to which sections 1039(a) and 1250(d)(8)(A) apply includes the holding period of the corresponding element of the section 1250 property disposed of. See section 1250(e)(4). The holding period of the "additional cost element" (as defined in paragraph (h)(2) of § 1.1250-3) begins on the date the replacement project is acquired. The holding period of a "reinvestment element" of section 1250 property does not include the period beginning on the day after the date of the disposition and ending (1) on the date of the acquisition of the replacement housing project, or (2) on the date the replacement housing project constructed or reconstructed by the taxpayer is placed in service.

(g) *Cross reference.* If the adjusted basis of the property in the hands of the transferee immediately after a transaction to which paragraph (c) or (d) of this section applies exceeds its adjusted basis in the hands of the transferor immediately before the transaction, the excess is an addition to capital account under paragraph (d)(2)(ii) of § 1.1250-5 (relating to property with two or more elements). [Reg. § 1.1250-4.]

☐ [T.D. 7084, 1-7-71. Amended by T.D. 7400, 2-3-76.]

[Reg. § 1.1250-5]

§ 1.1250-5. **Property with two or more elements.**—(a) *Dispositions before January 1, 1970*—(1) *Amount treated as ordinary income.* If section 1250 property consisting of two or more elements (described in paragraph (c) of this section) is disposed of before January 1, 1970, the amount of gain taken into account under section 1250(a)(2) shall be the sum, determined in three steps under subparagraphs (2), (3), and (4) of this paragraph, of the amounts of gain for each element.

(2) *Step 1.* The first step is to make the following computations:

(i) In respect of the property as a whole, compute the additional depreciation (as defined in section 1250(b)), and the gain realized. For purposes of this paragraph, in the case of a transaction other than a sale, exchange or involuntary conversion, the gain realized shall be considered to be the excess of the fair market value of the property over its adjusted basis.

(ii) In respect of each element as if it were a separate property, compute the additional depreciation for the element, and the applicable percentage (as defined in section 1250(a)(2)) for the element. For additional depreciation in respect of an element of property acquired in certain transactions, see paragraph (e) of this section. For purposes of determining additional depreciation, the holding period of an element shall be determined under section 1223, applied by treating the element as a separate property. However, for the purpose of determining applicable percentage, the holding period for an element shall, except to the extent provided in paragraphs (c)(5), (e), and (f) of this section, be determined in accordance with the rules prescribed in § 1.1250-4.

(3) *Step 2.* The second step is to determine the amount of gain for each element in the following manner:

(i) If the amount of additional depreciation in respect of the property as a whole is equal to the sum of the additional depreciation in respect of each element having additional depreciation, and if such amount is not more than the gain realized, then the amount of gain to be taken into account for an element is the product of the additional depreciation for the element, multiplied by the applicable percentage for the element.

(ii) If subdivision (i) of this subparagraph does not apply, the amount of gain to be taken into account for an element is the product of—

(a) The additional depreciation for the element, multiplied by

(b) The applicable percentage for the element, and multiplied by

(c) A ratio, computed by dividing (1) the lower of the additional depreciation in respect of the property as a whole or the gain realized, by (2) the sum of the additional depreciation in respect of each element having additional depreciation.

(4) *Step 3.* The third step is to compute the sum of the amounts of gain for each element, as determined in step 2.

(5) *Examples.* The provisions of this subparagraph may be illustrated by the following examples:

Example (1). Gain of $35,000 is realized upon a sale, before January 1, 1970, of section 1250 property which consists of four elements (W, X, Y, and Z). Since on the date of the sale the amount of additional depreciation in respect of the property as a whole ($24,000) is equal to the sum of the additional depreciation in respect of each element having additional depreciation and is less than the gain realized, the additional depreciation for each element is determined under sub-

Reg. § 1.1250-5(a)(1)

paragraph (3)(i) of this paragraph. The amount of gain taken into account under section 1250(a)(2) is $7,500, as determined in the following table in accordance with the additional facts assumed.

Element	Additional depreciation		Applicable percentage		Gain for element
W	$12,000	×	0	=	$ 0
X	6,000	×	50	=	3,000
Y	0	×	63	=	0
Z	6,000	×	75	=	4,500
Totals	$24,000				$7,500

Example (2). Assume the same facts as in example (1), except that in respect of the property as a whole the additional depreciation is $20,000 because with respect to element Y additional depreciation allowed was $4,000 less than straight line. Accordingly, the sum of the additional depreciation for each element having additional depreciation is $24,000, that is, $4,000 greater than the additional depreciation in respect of the property as a whole. Thus, the additional depreciation for each element is determined under subparagraph (3)(ii) of this paragraph. The ratio referred to in subparagraph (3)(ii)(c) of this paragraph is twenty twenty-fourths, that is, the lower of additional depreciation in respect of the property as a whole ($20,000) or the gain realized ($35,000), divided by the sum of the additional depreciation in respect of each element having additional depreciation ($24,000). The amount of gain taken into account under section 1250(a)(2) is $6,250, as determined in the following table:

Element	Additional depreciation		Applicable percentage		Ratio		Gain for element
W	$12,000	×	0	×	20:24	=	$ 0
X	6,000	×	50	×	20:24	=	2,500
Y	0	×	63	×	20:24	=	0
Z	6,000	×	75	×	20:24	=	3,750
Totals	$24,000						$6,250

(b) *Dispositions after December 31, 1969*—(1) *Amount treated as ordinary income.* If section 1250 property consisting of two or more elements (described in paragraph (c) of this section) is disposed of after December 31, 1969, the amount of gain taken into account under section 1250(a) shall be the sum, determined in 5 steps under subparagraphs (2), (3), (4), (5), and (6) of this paragraph, of the amount of gain for each element. Steps 3 and 4 are used only if the gain realized exceeds the additional depreciation attributable to periods after December 31, 1969, in respect of the property as a whole.

(2) *Step 1.* The first step is to make the following computations:

(i) In respect of the property as a whole, compute the additional depreciation (as defined in section 1250(b)) attributable to periods after December 31, 1969, and the gain realized. For purposes of this paragraph, in the case of a transaction other than a sale, exchange, or involuntary conversion, the gain realized shall be considered to be the excess of the fair market value of the property over its adjusted basis.

(ii) In respect of each element as if it were a separate property, compute the additional depreciation for the element attributable to periods after December 31, 1969, and the applicable percentage (as defined in section 1250(a)(1)) for the element. For additional depreciation in respect of an element of property acquired in certain transactions, see paragraph (e) of this section. For purposes of determining additional depreciation, the holding period of an element shall be determined under section 1223, applied by treating the element as a separate property. However, for the purpose of determining applicable percentage, the holding period for an element shall, except to the extent provided in paragraphs (c)(5), (e), and (f) of this section, be determined in accordance with the rules prescribed in § 1.1250-4.

(3) *Step 2.* The second step is to determine the amount of gain recognized for each element under section 1250(a)(1) in the following manner:

(i) If the amount of additional depreciation in respect of the property as a whole attributable to periods after December 31, 1969, is equal to the sum of the additional depreciation in respect of each element having such additional depreciation, and if such amount is not more than the gain realized, then the amount of gain to be taken into account for an element under section 1250(a)(1) is the product of the additional depreciation attributable to periods after December 31, 1969, for the element multiplied by the applicable percentage for the element determined under section 1250(a)(1).

Reg. § 1.1250-5(b)(3)

53,596 Rules for Determining Capital Gains and Losses

See p. 20,601 for regulations not amended to reflect law changes

(ii) If subdivision (i) of this subparagraph does not apply, the amount of gain to be taken into account under section 1250(a)(1) for an element is the product of—

(a) The additional depreciation attributable to periods after December 31, 1969, for the element multiplied by

(b) The applicable percentage for the element determined under section 1250(a)(1) for the element, and multiplied by

(c) A ratio, computed by dividing (1) the lower of the additional depreciation in respect of the property as a whole which is attributable to periods after December 31, 1969, or the gain realized, by (2) the sum of the additional depreciation attributable to periods after December 31, 1969, in respect of each element having such additional depreciation.

(4) *Step (3)*. If the gain realized exceeds the additional depreciation in respect of the property as a whole attributable to periods after December 31, 1969,

(i) Compute the additional depreciation attributable to periods before January 1, 1970, and the remaining gain (or remaining potential gain in the case of a transaction other than a sale, exchange, or involuntary conversion), in respect of the property as a whole.

(ii) Compute the additional depreciation attributable to periods before January 1, 1970, and the applicable percentage determined under section 1250(a)(2) in respect of each element as if it were a separate property. For additional depreciation in respect of an element of property acquired in certain transactions, see paragraph (e) of this section. For purposes of determining additional depreciation, the holding period of an element shall be determined under section 1223, applied by treating the element as a separate property. However, for the purpose of determining applicable percentage, the holding period of an element shall, except to the extent provided in paragraphs (c)(5), (e), and (f) of this section, be determined in accordance with the rules prescribed in § 1.1250-4.

(5) *Step (4)*. The fourth step is to compute the gain recognized under section 1250(a)(2) for each element (if computation was required under step (3)) in the following manner:

(i) If the amount of additional depreciation in respect of the property as a whole attributable to periods before January 1, 1970, is equal to the sum of the additional depreciation in respect of each element having such additional depreciation, and if such amount is not more than the remaining gain (or remaining potential gain), then the amount of gain to be taken into account for an element under section 1250(a)(2) is the product of the additional depreciation attributable to periods before January 1, 1970, for the element, multiplied by the applicable percentage determined under section 1250(a)(2) for the element.

(ii) If subdivision (i) of this subparagraph does not apply, the amount of gain to be taken into account for an element under section 1250(a)(2) is the product of—

(a) The additional depreciation attributable to periods before January 1, 1970, for the element, multiplied by

(b) The applicable percentage for the element determined under section 1250(a)(2), and multiplied by

(c) A ratio, computed by dividing (1) the lower of the additional depreciation in respect of the property as a whole which is attributable to periods before January 1, 1970, or the remaining gain (or remaining potential gain), by (2) the sum of the additional depreciation attributable to periods before January 1, 1970, in respect of each element having additional depreciation.

(6) *Step (5)*. The fifth step is to compute the sum of the amount of gain for each element, as determined in steps (2) and (4).

(7) *Examples*. The provisions of this subparagraph may be illustrated by the following examples:

Example (1). Gain of $60,000 is realized upon a sale, after December 31, 1969, of section 1250 property which was constructed by the taxpayer after such date. The property consists of 4 elements (W, X, Y, and Z). Since on the date of sale the amount of additional depreciation attributable to periods after December 31, 1969, in respect of the property as a whole ($32,000), is equal to the sum of the additional depreciation in respect of each element having such additional depreciation and is less than the gain realized, the gain recognized for each element is determined under subparagraph (3)(i) of this paragraph. The amount of gain taken into account under section 1250(a)(1) is $28,500, as determined in the following table in accordance with the additional facts assumed:

Element	Additional depreciation after 12/31/69		Applicable percentage (1250(a)(1))		Gain for element
W	$14,000	×	80	=	$11,200
X	6,000	×	90	=	5,400

Reg. § 1.1250-5(b)(4)

Rules for Determining Capital Gains and Losses

See p. 20,601 for regulations not amended to reflect law changes

Y	2,000	×	95	=	1,900
Z	10,000	×	100	=	10,000
Total	$32,000				$28,500

Example (2). Assume the same facts as in example (1), except that the property was acquired by the taxpayer before January 1, 1970. Since the gain realized ($60,000) exceeds the additional depreciation attributable to periods after December 31, 1969 ($32,000), section 1250(a)(2) applies to the remaining gain of $28,000. Since the additional depreciation in respect of the property as a whole attributable to periods before January 1, 1970 ($21,000), is equal to the sum of the additional depreciation in respect of each element having such additional depreciation and is less than the remaining gain ($28,000), the amount of gain recognized for each element under section 1250(a)(2) is determined under subparagraph (5)(i) of this paragraph. The amount of gain taken into account under section 1250(a)(1) is $28,500 the same as in example (1). The amount of gain taken into account under section 1250(a)(2) is $3,900, as determined in the following table in accordance with the additional facts assumed:

Element	Additional depreciation before 1/1/70		Applicable percentage (1250(a)(2))		Gain for element (1250(a)(2))
W	$ 8,000	×	0	=	$ 0
X	6,000	×	10	=	600
Y	2,000	×	15	=	300
Z	5,000	×	60	=	3,000
Total	$21,000				$ 3,900

Example (3). (i) The facts are the same as in example (2) except that element Y has a deficit in additional depreciation attributable to periods after December 31, 1969, of $6,000 and thus the additional depreciation attributable to periods after December 31, 1969, in respect of the property as a whole is $24,000. The sum of the additional depreciation for each element having additional depreciation is $30,000, or $6,000 more than the additional depreciation in respect of the property as a whole. Thus, the gain recognized for each element under section 1250(a)(1) is determined under subparagraph (3)(ii) of this paragraph. The ratio referred to in subparagraph (3)(ii)(c) of this paragraph is 24/30, that is, the lower of the additional depreciation in respect of the property as a whole attributable to periods after December 31, 1969 ($24,000), or the gain realized ($60,000), divided by the sum of the additional depreciation in respect of each element having such additional depreciation ($30,000). The amount of gain taken into account under section 1250(a)(1) is $21,280, as determined in the following table:

Element	Additional depreciation after 12/31/69		Applicable percentage (1250(a)(1))		Ratio		Gain for element
W	$14,000	×	80	×	24/30	=	$ 8,960
X	6,000	×	90	×	24/30	=	4,320
Y	(6,000)	×	95	×	24/30	=	0
Z	10,000	×	100	×	24/30	=	8,000
Total	$24,000						$21,280

(ii) In addition, gain is recognized under section 1250(a)(2) since there is a remaining potential gain of $36,000, that is, gain realized ($60,000) minus the additional depreciation attributable to periods after December 31, 1969 ($24,000). The gain recognized in respect of each element and the gain recognized under section 1250(a)(2) ($3,900) are the same as in example (2), since the additional depreciation attributable to periods before January 1, 1970 ($21,000) is less than the remaining gain ($36,000).

(c) *Element* —(1) *General.* For purposes of this section, in the case of section 1250 property there shall be treated as separate elements the separate improvements, units, remaining property, special elements, and low-income housing elements which are respectively referred to in paragraphs (c)(2), (3), (4), (5) and (6) of this section.

(2) *Separate improvements.* There shall be treated as an element each "separate improvement" (as defined in paragraph (d)(1) of this section) to the property.

(3) *Units.* If before completion of section 1250 property one or more units thereof are placed in service, each such unit of the section 1250 property shall be treated as an element.

(4) *Remaining property.* The remaining property which is not taken into account under

Reg. § 1.1250-5(c)(4)

53,598 Rules for Determining Capital Gains and Losses

See p. 20,601 for regulations not amended to reflect law changes

subparagraph (2) or (3) of this paragraph shall be treated as an element.

(5) *Special elements.* (i) If the basis of section 1250 property is reduced in the manner described in paragraph (b)(2)(ii) of § 1.1250-3 (relating to property acquired from a decedent prior to his death) or in paragraph (e)(3)(iii) of § 1.1250-3 (relating to basis reduction under section 1071 or 1082(a)(2)), then such property shall be considered as having a special element with additional depreciation equal to the amount of additional depreciation included in the depreciation adjustments (referred to in paragraph (d)(1) of § 1.1250-2) to which the basis reduction is attributable. For purposes of computing applicable percentage, the holding period of a special element under this subdivision shall be determined under paragraph (b)(2)(ii) or (e)(3)(iii) (whichever is applicable) of § 1.1250-3.

(ii) If a disposition described in section 1250(d)(4)(A) (relating to like kind exchanges and involuntary conversions) of a portion of an item of property gives rise to an addition to capital account (described in the last sentence of paragraph (d)(2)(i) of this section) which is not a separate improvement, then such property shall be considered as having a special element with additional depreciation and, for purposes of computing applicable percentage, a holding period determined under paragraph (d)(7) of § 1.1250-3.

(6) *Low-income housing elements.* If, in an approved disposition of a qualified housing project, a replacement qualified housing project is treated as consisting of more than one element of section 1250 property by reason of section 1250(d)(8)(E) (see paragraph (h)(2) of § 1.1250-3), the elements determined under such section shall be treated as elements for purposes of this section. For definition of the terms "qualified housing project" and "approved disposition," see section 1039(b) and the regulations thereunder.

(7) *Examples.* The provisions of this paragraph may be illustrated by the following examples:

Example (1). A taxpayer constructs an apartment house which he places in service in three stages. The total cost is $1 million of which $350,000 is allocable to the first stage, $500,000 to the second stage, and $150,000 to the third stage. The first stage, which is placed in service on January 1, 1965, consists of 300 apartments and certain facilities including a central heating system and a common lobby. The second stage, which is placed in service on July 15, 1965, consists of 550 apartments and certain facilities including the motor for a central air-conditioning system. The third stage, which is placed in service on January 19, 1966, consists of the residue of the apartment house. On December 31, 1968, the taxpayer disposes of the apartment house. On such date, the apartment house has three elements which are described in the table below:

Stage	Kind of element	Cost	Full months in holding period	Applicable percentage
1	unit	$350,000	48	72
2	unit	500,000	42	78
3	remaining property	150,000	36	84

Example (2). Assume the same facts as in example (1) except that on January 1, 1969, two new floors, which were added after the apartment house was completed, are placed in service and that on July 1, 1972, the taxpayer disposes of the building. Assume further that the two new floors are one separate improvement (within the meaning of paragraph (d) of this section). On the date disposed of, the property consists of four elements, that is, the three elements described in example (1) and the separate improvement.

(d) *Separate improvement* —(1) *Definition.* For purposes of this section, with respect to any section 1250 property, the term "separate improvement" means an "addition to capital account" described in subparagraph (2) of this paragraph which qualifies as an "improvement" under the one-year test prescribed in subparagraph (3) of this paragraph and which satisfies the 36-month test prescribed in subparagraph (4) of this paragraph.

(2) *Addition to capital account.* (i) In the case of any section 1250 property, an addition to capital account described in this subparagraph is any addition to capital account in respect of such property after its initial acquisition or completion by the taxpayer or by any person who held the property during a period included in the taxpayer's holding period (see § 1.1250-4) for the property. An addition to the capital account of section 1250 property may arise, for example, if there is an expenditure for section 1250 property which is an improvement, replacement, addition, or alteration to such property (regardless of whether the cost thereof is capitalized or charged against the depreciation reserve). In such a case, the "addition to capital account" is the gross addition, unreduced by amounts attributable to replaced property, to the net capital account and

Reg. § 1.1250-5(c)(5)

Rules for Determining Capital Gains and Losses

not the net addition to such account. Thus, if a roof has an adjusted basis of $20,000, and is replaced by constructing a new roof at a cost of $50,000, the gross addition of $50,000 is an addition to capital account. (The adjusted basis of the old roof is no longer included in the capital account for the property.) For purposes of this section, the status of an addition to capital account is not affected by whether or not it is treated as a separate property for purposes of determining depreciation adjustments. In case of an addition to the capital account of property arising after December 31, 1963, upon a disposition referred to in section 1250(d)(4) (relating to like kind exchanges and involuntary conversions) of a portion of an item of such property, the amount of such addition (and its basis for all purposes of the Code) shall be the basis thereof determined under paragraph (d)(2), (3), or (4) (whichever is applicable) of § 1.1250-3, applied by treating such portion and such addition as separate properties.

(ii) An addition to capital account may be attributable to an excess of the adjusted basis of section 1250 property in the hands of a transferee immediately after a transaction referred to in section 1250(e)(2) (relating to holding period of property with transferred basis) over its adjusted basis in the hands of the transferor immediately before the transaction. Thus, for example, such excess may arise from a gift which is in part a sale or exchange (see paragraph (a)(2) of § 1.1250-3), from an increase in basis due to gift tax paid (see section 1015(d)), from a transfer referred to in paragraph (c)(2) of § 1.1250-3 (relating to certain tax-free transactions) in which gain is partially recognized, or from a distribution by a partnership to a partner in which no gain is recognized by reason of the application of section 731. Similarly, an addition to capital account may be attributable to an excess of the adjusted basis of a principal residence acquired in a transaction referred to in section 1250(e)(3) over the adjusted basis of the principal residence disposed of, as well as to any increase in the adjusted basis of section 1250 property of a partnership by reason of an optional basis adjustment under section 734(b) or 743(b).

(iii) Whether or not an expenditure shall be treated as an addition to capital account described in this subparagraph, as distinguished from a separate item of property, may depend on how the property or properties are disposed of. Thus, for example, if a taxpayer, who owns a motel consisting of 10 buildings with common heating and plumbing systems, adds to the motel three new buildings which are connected to the common systems, and if the taxpayer sells the motel to one person in one transaction, then for purposes of this subparagraph the cost of the three new buildings shall be treated as an addition to the capital account of the motel and, if the 1-year and 36-month tests of subparagraphs (3) and (4) of this paragraph are satisfied, the motel consists of at least two elements. If, however, the 10-building group and the three-building group were individually sold in separate transactions to two different people each of whom would operate his group as a separate business, the motel would consist of two items of property.

(3) *One-year test for improvement.* (i) An addition to capital account of section 1250 property for any taxable year (including a short taxable year and the entire taxable year in which the disposition occurs) shall be treated as an improvement only if the sum of all additions to the capital account of such property for such taxable year exceeds the greater of—

(*a*) $2,000, or

(*b*) One percent of the unadjusted basis of the property, determined as of the beginning (*1*) of such taxable year, or (*2*) of the holding period (within the meaning of § 1.1250-4) of the property, whichever is the later.

(ii) For purposes of this section, the term "unadjusted basis" means the adjusted basis of the property, determined without regard to the adjustments provided in section 1016(a)(2) and (3) (relating to adjustments for depreciation, amortization, and depletion). For purposes of this paragraph, as of any particular date the unadjusted basis of section 1250 property (*a*) includes the cost of any addition to capital account for the property which arises prior to such date (regardless of whether such addition qualified under this subparagraph as an improvement), and (*b*) does not include the cost of a component retired before such date.

(iii) In respect of a particular disposition of section 1250 property by a person—

(*a*) There shall not be taken into account under the 1-year test for improvements in this subparagraph any addition to capital account which arises by reason of (or after) such disposition or which arises before the beginning of the holding period under § 1.1250-4 of such person for the property, and

(*b*) Such test shall be made in respect of each taxable year of such person (and of any prior transferor) any day of which is included under § 1.1250-4 in such person's holding period for the property, except that (*1*) such test shall be made for a taxable year of such person only if such person actually owned the property on at least 1 day of such taxable year, and (*2*) such test shall be made for a taxable year of such prior transferor

Reg. § 1.1250-5(d)(3)

only if such prior transferor actually owned the property on at least 1 day of such taxable year.

(iv) The provisions of this subpararaph may be illustrated by the following examples:

Example (1). The unadjusted basis of section 1250 property as of the beginning of January 1, 1960, is $300,000. During the taxable year ending on December 31, 1960, the only additions to the capital account for the property are addition A on January 1, 1960, costing $1,000, and addition B on July 1, 1960, costing $600. Since the sum of the amounts added to capital account for such taxable year is less than $2,000, A and B are not treated as improvements. This result would not be changed if addition C, costing $600, were added on December 15, 1960, since although the sum of the additions ($1,000 plus $600 plus $600, or $2,200) exceeds $2,000, such sum is less than 1 percent of the unadjusted basis of the property as of the beginning of 1960 ($3,000, that is, 1 percent of $300,000). If however, C cost $1,500, then A, B, and C would each be considered an improvement since the sum of the amounts added to capital account ($3,100) would exceed $3,000.

Example (2). Green and his son both use the calendar year as the taxable year. On February 1, 1965, Green makes addition A to a piece of section 1250 property. On June 15, 1965, Green transfers such property to his son as a gift which is in part a sale (see paragraph (a) of § 1.1250-3). Addition B arises by reason of the transfer. On August 1, 1965, the son makes addition C to the property. For purposes of determining the amount of gain recognized under section 1250(a) to Green upon the transfer, the determination of whether addition A is an improvement is made without taking into account additions B and C. For purposes of determining the amount of gain recognized under section 1250(a) upon a subsequent disposition of the property by the son, additions B and C would be taken into account in the determination of whether A is an improvement, and A would be taken into account in the determination of whether B and C are improvements.

Example (3). Assume the same facts as in example (2). Assume further that on September 15, 1965, the son transfers the property to a corporation in exchange for cash and stock in the corporation in a transaction qualifying under section 351 (see paragraph (c) of § 1.1250-3), and that the corporation uses a fiscal year ending November 30. For purposes of determining the amount of gain recognized under section 1250(a) upon a subsequent disposition by the corporation, the one-year test under subdivision (i) of this subparagraph is made for the entire taxable year of Green and of the son ending on December 31, 1965, and in respect of the corporation's taxable year ending November 30, 1965. Accordingly, if on December 7, 1965, addition D is made by the corporation, then, upon a subsequent disposition by the corporation, D is taken into account for purposes of the determination in respect of the entire taxable year of Green and of the son ending on December 31, 1965, and for the corporation's taxable year ending November 30, 1966, but not for purposes of the corporation's taxable year ending November 30, 1965. If D were made on January 3, 1966, D would still be taken into account for purposes of the determination in respect of the corporation's taxable year ending November 30, 1966. However, since neither Green nor his son actually owned the property on any day of the taxable year ending December 31, 1966, no determination is made in respect of such taxable year of Green or of the son.

(4) *36-month test for separate improvement.* (i) If, during the 36-month period ending on the last day of any taxable year (including a short taxable year and the entire taxable year in which the disposition occurs), the sum of the amounts treated under subparagraph (3) of this paragraph as improvements for such period exceeds the greatest of—

(*a*) 25 percent of the adjusted basis of the property,

(*b*) 10 percent of the unadjusted basis (determined under subparagraph (3)(ii) of this paragraph) of the property, or

(*c*) $5,000,

then each such improvement during such period shall be treated as a separate improvement, and thus as an element. For purposes of (*a*) and (*b*) of this subdivision, the adjusted basis (or unadjusted basis) of section 1250 property shall be determined as of the beginning of the 36-month period, or as of the beginning of the holding period of the property (within the meaning of § 1.1250-4), whichever is the later.

(ii) In respect of a particular disposition of section 1250 property by a person—

(*a*) There shall not be taken into account under the 36-month test for separate improvements in this subparagraph any amount treated under subparagraph (3) of this paragraph as an improvement which arises by reason of (or after) the disposition or which arises before the beginning of the holding period under § 1.1250-4 of such person for the property, and

(*b*) Such test shall be made in respect of each 36-month period ending on the last day of each taxable year of such person (and of any prior transferor) if at least 1 day of such period is

Reg. § 1.1250-5(d)(4)

Rules for Determining Capital Gains and Losses 53,601
See p. 20,601 for regulations not amended to reflect law changes

included under § 1.1250-4 in such person's holding period for the property, except that (*1*) such test shall be made for a 36-month period ending on the last day of a taxable year of such person only if such person actually owned the property on at least 1 day of such period, and (*2*) such test shall be made for a 36-month period ending on the last day of a taxable year of such prior transferor only if such prior transferor actually owned the property on at least 1 day of such period.

(iii) For illustration of the principles of subdivision (ii) of this subparagraph, see examples (2) and (3) in subparagraph (3)(iv) of this paragraph.

(5) *Example.* The application of this paragraph may be illustrated by the following example:

Example. (i) On December 31, 1967, X, a calendar year taxpayer, purchases an item of section 1250 property at a cost of $100,000. In the table below, the adjusted basis and unadjusted basis of the property are shown for the beginning of January 1 of each taxable year and it is assumed that each addition to capital was added on January 1 of the year shown.

Year	Adjusted basis	Unadjusted basis	1 percent of unadjusted basis		Addition
1969	$94,000	$100,000	$1,000	A	$10,000
1970	97,030	110,000	1,100	B	4,000
1971	94,041	114,000	1,140	C	6,000
1972	92,799	120,000	1,200		......
1973	86,158	120,000	1,200	D	18,000

(ii) Since each addition to capital account for the property exceeds the greater of $2,000 or one percent of unadjusted basis, determined as of the beginning of the taxable year in which made, each addition to capital account qualifies as an improvement under subparagraph (2) of this paragraph.

(iii) Since the beginning of the holding period of the property under § 1.1250-4 (Jan. 1, 1968) is later than the beginning of the 36-month period ending on December 31, 1969, the determination as to whether there are any separate improvements on the property as of December 31, 1969, is made by examining the adjusted basis (or unadjusted basis) of the property as of the beginning of January 1, 1968. As of December 31, 1969, there were no separate improvements on the property since the only amount treated as an improvement for the period beginning on January 1, 1968, and ending on December 31, 1969, is addition A (costing $10,000), which is less than $25,000, that is, 25 percent of the adjusted basis ($100,000) of the property as of the beginning of January 1, 1968.

(iv) As of December 31, 1970, there were no separate improvements on the property since the sum of the amounts treated as improvements for the 36-month period ending on December 31, 1970, is $14,000 (that is, $10,000 for A, plus $4,000 for B), and this sum is less than $25,000, that is, 25 percent of the adjusted basis ($100,000) of the property as of the beginning of January 1, 1968.

(v) As of December 31, 1971, there were no separate improvements on the property since the sum of the amounts treated as improvements for the 36-month period ending on December 31, 1971, is $20,000 (that is, $10,000 for A, plus $4,000 for B, plus $6,000 for C), and this sum is less than $23,500, that is, 25 percent of the adjusted basis ($94,000) of the property as of the beginning of January 1, 1969.

(vi) As of December 31, 1972, there were no separate improvements on the property since the sum of the amounts treated as improvements for the 36-month period ending on December 31, 1972, is $10,000 (that is, $4,000 for B plus $6,000 for C), and this sum is less than $24,258 that is, 25 percent of the adjusted basis ($97,030) of the property as of the beginning of January 1, 1970.

(vii) As of December 31, 1973, C and D are separate improvements (notwithstanding that as of December 31, 1971 and 1972, C was not a separate improvement) since the sum of the amounts added for the 36-month period ending December 31, 1973, is $24,000 (that is, $6,000 for C plus $18,000 for D), and this sum exceeds the greatest of—

(*a*) $23,510, that is, 25 percent of the adjusted basis ($94,041) of the section 1250 property as of the beginning of January 1, 1971,

(*b*) $11,400, that is, 10 percent of the unadjusted basis ($114,000) of the property as of the beginning of such first day, or

(*c*) $5,000.

(e) *Additional depreciation and holding period of property acquired in certain transactions*—(1) *Transferred basis.* If property consisting of two or more elements is disposed of, and if the holding period of the property in the hands of the transferee for purposes of computing applicable per-

Reg. § 1.1250-5(e)(1)

centage includes the holding period of the transferor by reason of the application of paragraph (c) (other than subparagraph (2) thereof) of § 1.1250-4, then the additional depreciation for each element of the property in the hands of the transferee immediately after the transfer shall be computed in the manner set forth in this subparagraph. First, any element having a deficit in additional depreciation in the hands of the transferor immediately before such transfer shall be considered to have the same deficit in the hands of the transferee. Second, elements having additional depreciation in the hands of the transferor immediately before the transfer shall be considered to have additional depreciation in the hands of the transferee. The sum of the transferee's additional depreciation for all elements of the property having additional depreciation in the hands of the transferor shall be an amount equal to the additional depreciation in respect of the property as a whole immediately after the transfer increased by the sum of the deficits in additional depreciation for all elements having such deficits. In case there is more than one element having additional depreciation, the additional depreciation for any such element in the hands of the transferee shall be computed by multiplying (i) the amount computed under the preceding sentence by (ii) the additional depreciation for such element in the hands of the transferor divided by the sum of the additional depreciation for all such elements having additional depreciation in the hands of the transferor. For purposes of computing applicable percentage, the holding period for an element of such property in the hands of the transferee shall include the holding period of such element in the hands of the transferor.

(2) *Example.* The provisions of subparagraph (1) of this paragraph may be illustrated by the following example:

Example. Section 1250 property has additional depreciation of $16,000 of which $12,000 is additional depreciation for element X and $4,000 for element Y. The property is transferred to a corporation in exchange for cash of $6,000 and for stock in the corporation. Assume that recognition of gain under section 1250(a) is limited to $6,000 (the amount of cash received) by reason of the application of section 351(b) (relating to transfer to corporation controlled by transferor) and section 1250(d)(3) (relating to limitation on application of section 1250 in certain tax-free transactions). Under paragraph (c)(3)(i) of § 1.1250-3, the additional depreciation for the property in the hands of the corporation immediately after the transfer is $10,000, that is, the additional depreciation for the property in the hands of the transferor immediately before the transfer ($16,000) minus the gain under section 1250 (a) recognized upon the transfer ($6,000). Under subparagraph (1) of this paragraph, in the hands of the corporation immediately after the transfer element X has additional depreciation of $7,500 (12/16 of $10,000) and element Y has additional depreciation of $2,500 (4/16 of $10,000). Under paragraph (d)(2)(ii) of this section there is an addition of $6,000 to the capital account for the property.

(3) *Principal residence.* If a principal residence consisting of two or more elements is disposed of, and if for purposes of computing applicable percentage the holding period of the principal residence acquired includes the holding period of the principal residence disposed of by reason of the application of paragraph (d) of § 1.1250-4, then the additional depreciation (or a deficit in additional depreciation) for an element of the principal residence acquired immediately after the transaction shall be determined in a manner consistent with the principles of subparagraph (1) of this paragraph. For purposes of computing applicable percentage, the holding period for an element of the principal residence acquired includes the holding period of such element of the principal residence disposed of, but not the period beginning on the day after the date of the disposition and ending on the date of the acquisition.

(4) [Reserved]

(f) *Holding period for small separate improvements*—(1) *General.* This paragraph prescribes a special holding period solely for the purpose of computing the applicable percentage of a separate improvement (as defined in paragraph (d) of this section) which is treated as an element. See paragraph (a)(2)(ii) of this section for determination of holding period under section 1223 for purposes of computing additional depreciation. In respect of section 1250 property, if the amount of a separate improvement does not exceed the greater of—

(i) $2,000, or

(ii) One percent of the unadjusted basis (within the meaning of paragraph (d)(3)(ii) of this section) of such property, determined as of the beginning of the taxable year in which such separate improvement was made,

then such separate improvement shall be treated for purposes of computing applicable percentage as placed in service on the first day, of a calendar month, which is the closest such first day to the middle of the taxable year. See the last sentence of section 1250(f)(4)(B). If two such first days are equally close to the middle of the taxable year, the earliest of such days is the applicable day.

Reg. § 1.1250-5(e)(2)

Rules for Determining Capital Gains and Losses

(2) *Example.* The application of this paragraph may be illustrated by the following example:

Example. (i) The unadjusted basis of section 1250 property as of the beginning of January 1, 1960, is $100,000. During the taxable year ending on December 31, 1960, the only additions to the capital account for the property are addition A on March 10, 1960, costing $1,200 and addition B on September 16, 1960, costing $1,400. Since the sum of the additions ($2,600) exceeds the greater of $2,000 and one percent of unadjusted basis ($1,000, that is, one percent of $100,000), each addition is an improvement under the 1-year test of paragraph (d)(3) of this section. Assume that the 36-month test of paragraph (d)(4) of this section is satisfied and, therefore, each addition is a separate improvement treated as an element.

(ii) Since each element is less than $2,000, the provisions of this paragraph apply. Since there are 366 days in 1960, the middle of the year is at the end of 183 days, or July 1. Thus, that first day of a calendar month in 1960, which is the closest first day (of a calendar month) to the middle of the taxable year, is July 1, 1960. Accordingly, for purposes of computing applicable percentage, elements A and B are each treated as placed in service on July 1, 1960. [Reg. § 1.1250-5.]

☐ [T.D. 7084, 1-7-71. Amended by T.D. 7193, 6-29-72 and T.D. 7400, 2-3-76.]

[Reg. § 1.1252-1]

§ 1.1252-1. **General rule for treatment of gain from disposition of farm land.**—(a) *Ordinary income*—(1) *General rule.* (i) Except as otherwise provided in this section and § 1.1252-2, if farm land is disposed of during a taxable year beginning after December 31, 1969, then under section 1252(a)(1) there shall be treated as gain from the sale or exchange of property which is neither a capital asset nor property described in section 1231 (that is, shall be recognized as ordinary income) the lower of—

(a) The applicable percentage of the amount computed in subdivision (ii) of this subparagraph, or

(b) The amount computed in subdivision (iii) of this subparagraph.

(ii) The amount computed in this subdivision is an amount equal to—

(a) The aggregate of the deductions allowed, in any taxable year any day of which falls within the period the taxpayer held (or is considered to have held) the farm land, under sections 175 (relating to soil and water conservation expenditures) and 182 (relating to expenditures by farmers for clearing land) for expenditures paid or incurred after December 31, 1969, with respect to the farm land disposed of, minus

(b) The amount of gain recognized as ordinary income under section 1251(c)(1) (relating to gain from disposition of property used in farming where farm losses offset nonfarm income) upon such disposition of such land.

(iii) The amount computed in this subdivision is an amount equal to—

(a) The gain realized, that is, the excess of the amount realized (in the case of a sale, exchange, or involuntary conversion) or the fair market value of the farm land (in the case of any other disposition), over the adjusted basis of the farm land, minus

(b) The amount of gain recognized as ordinary income under section 1251(c)(1) upon such disposition of such land.

(iv) If a deduction under section 175 is allowed in respect of the farm land disposed of for a taxable year every day of which falls within the period after the taxpayer held (or is considered to have held) the farm land, and if the deduction is attributable to expenditures paid or incurred after December 31, 1969, with respect to such land during the period the taxpayer held (or is considered to have held) the land, then the amount of such deduction shall be applied to increase the amount computed (without regard to this subdivision) under subdivision (ii)(a) of this subparagraph.

(2) *Application of section.* Any gain treated as ordinary income under section 1252(a)(1) shall be recognized as ordinary income notwithstanding any other provision of subtitle A of the Code. For special rules with respect to the application of section 1252, see § 1.1252-2. For the relation of section 1252 to other provisions see paragraph (d) of this section.

(3) *Meaning of terms.* For purpose of section 1252—

(i) The term "farm land" means any land with respect to which deductions have been allowed under section 175 or 182. See section 1252(a)(2).

(ii) The period for which farm land shall be considered to be held shall be determined under section 1223.

(iii) The term "disposition" shall have the same meaning as in paragraph (a)(3) of § 1.1245-1.

(iv) The applicable percentage shall be determined as follows:

Reg. § 1.1252-1(a)(3)

53,604 Rules for Determining Capital Gains and Losses

See p. 20,601 for regulations not amended to reflect law changes

If the farm land is disposed of—	The applicable percentage is—
Within 5 years after the date it was acquired	100 percent
Within the sixth year after it was acquired	80 percent
Within the seventh year after it was acquired	60 percent
Within the eighth year after it was acquired	40 percent
Within the ninth year after it was acquired	20 percent
Within the tenth year after it was acquired and thereafter	0 percent

(4) *Portion of parcel.* The amount of gain to be recognized as ordinary income under section 1252(a)(1) shall be determined separately for each parcel of farm land in a manner consistent with the principles of subparagraphs (4) and (5) of § 1.1245-1(a) (relating to gain from disposition of certain depreciable property). If (i) only a portion of a parcel of farm land is disposed of in a transaction, or if two or more portions of a single parcel are disposed of in one transaction, and (ii) the aggregate of the deductions allowed under sections 175 and 182 with respect to any such portion cannot be established to the satisfaction of the Commissioner or his delegate, then the aggregate of the deductions in respect of the entire parcel shall be allocated to each portion in proportion to the fair market value of each at the time of the disposition.

(b) *Instances of non-application*—(1) *In general.* Section 1252 does not apply if a taxpayer disposes of farm land for which the holding period is in excess of 9 years or with respect to which no deductions have been allowed under sections 175 and 182.

(2) *Losses.* Section 1252(a)(1) does not apply to losses. Thus, section 1252(a)(1) does not apply if a loss is realized upon a sale, exchange, or involuntary conversion of property, all of which is farm land, nor does the section apply to a disposition of such property other than by way of sale, exchange, or involuntary conversion if at the time of the disposition the fair market value of such property is not greater than its adjusted basis.

(c) *Treatment of partnerships and partners.* [Reserved.]

(d) *Relation of section 1252 to other provisions*—(1) *General.* The provisions of section 1252 apply notwithstanding any other provision of subtitle A of the Code. Thus, unless an exception or limitation under § 1.1252-2 applies, gain under section 1252 (a)(1) is recognized notwithstanding any contrary nonrecognition provision or income characterizing provision. For example, since section 1252 overrides section 1231 (relating to property used in the trade or business), the gain recognized under section 1252(a)(1) upon a disposition of farm land will be treated as ordinary income and only the remaining gain, if any, from the disposition may be considered as gain from the sale or exchange of a capital asset if section 1231 is applicable. See example (1) of paragraph (e) of this section.

(2) *Nonrecognition sections overridden.* The nonrecognition of gain provisions of subtitle A of the Code which section 1252 overrides include, but are not limited to, sections 267(d), 311(a), 336, 337, and 512(b)(5). See § 1.1252-2 for the extent to which section 1252(a)(1) overrides sections 332, 351, 361, 371(a), 374(a), 721, 731, 1031, and 1033.

(3) *Installment method.* Gain from a disposition to which section 1252 (a)(1) applies may be reported under the installment method if such method is otherwise available under section 453 of the Code. In such case, the income (other than interest) on each installment payment shall (*a*) first be deemed to consist of gain to which section 1251(c)(1) applies (if applicable) until all such gain has been reported, (*b*) the next portion (if any) of such income shall be deemed to consist of gain to which section 1252(a)(1) applies until all such gain has been reported, and (*c*) finally the remaining portion (if any) of such income shall be deemed to consist of gain to which neither section 1251(c)(1) nor 1252(a)(1) applies. For treatment of amounts as interest on certain deferred payments, see section 483.

(4) *Exempt income.* With regard to exempt income, the principles of paragraph (e) of § 1.1245-6 shall be applicable.

(5) *Treatment of gain not recognized under section 1252(a)(1).* For treatment of gain not recognized under this section, the principles of paragraph (f) of § 1.1245-6 shall be applicable.

(e) *Examples.* The provisions of this section may be illustrated by the following examples:

Example (1). Individual A uses the calendar year as his taxable year. On April 10, 1975 he sells for $75,000 a parcel of farm land which he had acquired on January 5, 1970, with an adjusted basis of $52,500 for a realized gain of $22,500. The aggregate of the deductions allowed under sections 175 and 182 with respect to such land is $18,000 and all of such amount was allowed for 1970. Under the stated facts, none of the $22,500 gain realized is recognized as ordinary income under section 1251(c)(1) as there is no potential gain (as defined in section 1251(e)(5)) with re-

Reg. § 1.1252-1(a)(4)

Rules for Determining Capital Gains and Losses

spect to the farm land. Since no gain is recognized as ordinary income under section 1251(c)(1), and since the applicable percentage, 80 percent, of the aggregate of the deductions allowed under sections 175 and 182, $18,000, or $14,400, is lower than the gain realized, $22,500, the amount of gain recognized as ordinary income under section 1252(a)(1) is $14,400. The remaining $8,100 of the gain may be treated as gain from the sale or exchange of property described in section 1231.

Example (2). Assume the same facts as in example (2) of paragraph (b)(6) of § 1.1251-1. Assume further that the aggregate of the amount of section 175 and 182 deductions allowable to the M corporation is equal to the amount allowed. Under paragraph (a)(1) of this section, $5,000 is recognized as ordinary income under section 1252(a)(1) upon the disposition of the land as a dividend, computed as follows:

(1) Aggregate of deductions allowed under sections 175 and 182	$18,000
(2) Minus: Gain recognized as ordinary income under section 1251(c)(1)	13,000
(3) Difference	$ 5,000
(4) Multiply: Applicable percentage for property disposed of within the fifth year after it was acquired	100%
(5) Amount in paragraph (a)(1)(i)(*a*) of this section	$ 5,000
(6) Gain realized (fair market value $67,500, less adjusted basis, $45,000)	$22,500
(7) Minus: Amount in line (2)	13,000
(8) Amount in paragraph (a)(1)(i)(*b*) of this section	$ 9,500
(9) Lower of line (5) or line (8)	$ 5,000

The "gain realized", $22,500, minus the sum of the gain recognized as ordinary income under section 1251(c)(1), $13,000, and under section 1252(a)(1), $5,000, equals $4,500. Assuming section 311(d) (relating to certain distributions of appreciated property to redeem stock) does not apply, under section 311(a) the corporation does not recognize gain on account of the $4,500.

Example (3). Assume the same facts as in example (2) of this paragraph, except that M contracted to sell the land for $67,500 which would be paid in 10 equal payments of $6,750 each, plus a sufficient amount of interest so that section 483 does not apply. Assume further that the remaining gain of $4,500 is treated as gain from the sale or exchange of property described in section 1231. M properly elects under section 453 to report under the installment method gain of $13,000 to which section 1251(c)(1) applies, gain of $5,000 to which section 1252(a)(1) applies, and gain of $4,500 to which section 1231 applies. Since the total gain realized on the sale was $22,500, the gross profit realized on each installment payment is $2,250, *i.e.*, $6,750 × ($22,500/$67,500). Accordingly, the treatment of the income to be reported on each installment payment is as follows:

Payment No.	Applicable sections		
	1251	1252	1231
(1)	$ 2,250	...	...
(2)	2,250	...	...
(3)	2,250	...	...
(4)	2,250	...	...
(5)	2,250	...	...
(6)	1,750	$ 500	...
(7)	...	2,250	...
(8)	...	2,250	...
(9)	...	...	$2,250
(10)	...	...	2,250
Totals	$13,000	$5,000	$4,500

☐ [T.D. 7418, 5-6-76.]

[Reg. § 1.1252-2]

§ 1.1252-2. Special rules.—(a) *Exception for gifts*—(1) *General rule.* In general, no gain shall be recognized under section 1252(a)(1) upon a disposition of farm land by gift. For purposes of section 1252 and this paragraph, the term "gift" shall have the same meaning as in paragraph (a) of § 1.125-4 and, with respect to the application of this paragraph, principles illustrated by the examples of paragraph (a)(2) of § 1.1245-4 shall apply. For reduction in amount of charitable contribution in case of a gift of farm land, see section 170(e) and § 1.170A-4.

(2) *Disposition in part a sale or exchange and in part a gift.* Where a disposition of farm land is

53,606 Rules for Determining Capital Gains and Losses

See p. 20,601 for regulations not amended to reflect law changes

in part a sale or exchange and in part a gift, the amount of gain which shall be recognized as ordinary income under section 1252(a)(1) shall be computed under paragraph (a)(1) of § 1.1252-1, applied by treating the gain realized (for purposes of paragraph (a)(1)(iii)(a) of § 1.1252-1) as the excess of the amount realized over the adjusted basis of the farm land.

(3) *Treatment of farm land in hands of transferee.* See paragraph (f) of this section for treatment of the transferee in the case of a disposition to which this paragraph applies.

(4) *Examples.* The provisions of this paragraph may be illustrated by the following examples:

Example (1). On March 2, 1976, A, a calendar year taxpayer, makes a gift to B of a parcel of land having an adjusted basis of $40,000, a fair market value of $65,000, and a holding period of 6 years (A, having purchased the land on January 15, 1971). On the date of such gift, the aggregate of the deductions allowed to A under sections 175 and 182 with respect to the land is $24,000 with $21,000 of such amount attributable to 1971. Upon making the gift, A recognizes no gain under section 1251(c)(1) or section 1252(a)(1). See paragraph (a)(1) of § 1.1251-4 and subparagraph (1) of this paragraph. For treatment of the farm land in the hands of B, see example (1) of paragraph (f)(3) of this section. For effect of the gift on the excess deductions accounts of A and of B, see paragraph (e)(2) of § 1.1251-2.

Example (2). (i) Assume the same facts as in example (1), except that A transfers the land to B for $50,000. Thus, the gain realized is $10,000 (amount realized, $50,000, minus adjusted basis, $40,000), and A has made a gift of $15,000 (fair market value, $65,000, minus amount realized, $50,000).

(ii) Upon the transfer of the land to B, A recognizes $3,000 of gain under section 1251(c)(1). See example (2) of paragraph (a)(4) of § 1.1251-4. Thus, A recognizes $7,000 as ordinary income under section 1252(a)(1), computed under subparagraph (2) of this paragraph as follows:

(1) Aggregate of deductions allowed under sections 175 and 182	$24,000
(2) Minus: Gain recognized as ordinary income under section 1251(c)(1)	3,000
(3) Difference	$21,000
(4) Multiply: Applicable percentage for land disposed of within sixth year after it was acquired	80%
(5) Amount in paragraph (a)(1)(i)(a) of § 1.1252-1	$16,800
(6) Gain realized (see subdivision (i) of this example)	$10,000
(7) Minus: Amount in line (2)	3,000
(8) Amount in paragraph (a)(1)(i)(b) of § 1.1252-1, applied in accordance with subparagraph (2) of this paragraph	$ 7,000
(9) Lower of line (5) or line (8)	$ 7,000

Thus, the entire gain realized on the transfer, $10,000, is recognized as ordinary income since that amount is equal to the sum of the gain recognized as ordinary income under section 1251(c)(1), $3,000, and under section 1252(a)(1), $7,000. For treatment of the farm land in the hands of B, see example (2) of paragraph (f)(3) of this section.

(b) *Exceptions for transfers at death*—(1) *In general.* Except as provided in section 691 (relating to income in respect of a decedent), no gain shall be recognized under section 1252(a)(1) upon a transfer at death. For purposes of section 1252 and this paragraph, the term "transfer at death" shall have the same meaning as in paragraph (b) of § 1.1245-4 and, with respect to the application of this paragraph, principles illustrated by the examples of paragraph (b)(2) of § 1.1245-4 shall apply.

(2) *Treatment of farm land in hands of transferee.* If as of the date a person acquires farm land from a decedent such person's basis is determined, by reason of the application of section 1014(a), solely by reference to the fair market value of the property on the date of the decedent's death or on the applicable date provided in section 2032 (relating to alternative valuation date), then on such date the aggregate of the section 175 and 182 deductions allowed with respect to the farm land in the hands of such transferee is zero.

(c) *Limitation for certain tax-free transactions*—(1) *Limitation on amount of gain.* Upon a transfer of farm land described in subparagraph (2) of this paragraph, the amount of gain recognized as ordinary income under section 1252(a)(1) shall not exceed an amount equal to the excess (if any) of (i) the amount of gain recognized to the transferor on the transfer (determined without regard to section 1252) over (ii) the amount (if

Reg. § 1.1252-2(a)(3)

Rules for Determining Capital Gains and Losses

any) of gain recognized as ordinary income under section 1251(c)(1). For purposes of this subparagraph, the principles of paragraph (c)(1) of § 1.1245-4 shall apply. Thus, in the case of a transfer of farm land and property other than farm land in one transaction, the amount realized from the disposition of the farm land (as determined in a manner consistent with the principles of paragraph (a)(5) of § 1.1245-1) shall be deemed to consist of that portion of the fair market value of each property acquired which bears the same ratio to the fair market value of such acquired property as the amount realized from the disposition of the farm land bears to the total amount realized. The preceding sentence shall be applied solely for purposes of computing the portion of the total gain (determined without regard to section 1252) which is eligible to be recognized as ordinary income under section 1252(a)(1). The provisions of this paragraph do not apply to a disposition of property to an organization (other than a cooperative described in section 521) which is exempt from the tax imposed by chapter 1 of the Code.

(2) *Transfers covered.* The transfers referred to in subparagraph (1) of this paragraph are transfers of farm land in which the basis of such property in the hands of the transferee is determined by reference to its basis in the hands of the transferor by reason of the application of any of the following provisions:

(i) Section 332 (relating to distributions in complete liquidation of an 80-percent-or-more controlled subsidiary corporation). For application of subparagraph (1) of this paragraph to such a complete liquidation, the principles of paragraph (c)(3) of § 1.1245-4 shall apply. Thus, for example, the provisions of subparagraph (1) of this paragraph do not apply to a liquidating distribution of farm land by an 80-percent-or-more controlled subsidiary to its parent if the parent's basis for the property is determined, under section 334(b)(2), by reference to its basis for the stock of the subsidiary.

(ii) Section 351 (relating to transfer to a corporation controlled by transferor).

(iii) Section 361 (relating to exchanges pursuant to certain corporate reorganizations).

(iv) Section 371(a) (relating to exchanges pursuant to certain receivership and bankruptcy proceedings).

(v) Section 374(a) (relating to exchanges pursuant to certain railroad reorganizations).

(vi) Section 721 (relating to transfers to a partnership in exchange for a partnership interest). See paragraph (e) of this section.

(vii) Section 731 (relating to distributions by a partnership to a partner). For special carryover of basis rule, see paragraph (e) of this section.

(3) *Treatment of farm land in the hands of transferee.* See paragraph (f) of this section for treatment of the transferee in the case of a disposition to which this paragraph applies.

(4) *Examples.* The provisions of this paragraph may be illustrated by the following examples:

Example (1). On January 4, 1975, A, an individual calendar year taxpayer, owns a parcel of farm land, which he acquired on March 25, 1970, having an adjusted basis of $15,000 and a fair market value of $40,000. On that date he transfers the parcel to corporation M in exchange for stock in the corporation worth $40,000 in a transaction qualifying under section 351. On the date of such transfer, the aggregate of the deductions allowed under section 175 and 182 with respect to the land is $18,000. Without regard to section 1252, A would recognize no gain under section 351 upon the transfer and M's basis for the land would be determined under section 362(a) by reference to its basis in the hands of A. Thus, as a result of the disposition, no gain is recognized as ordinary income under section 1251(c)(1) or section 1252(a)(1) by A since the amount of gain recognized under such sections is limited to the amount of gain which is recognized under section 351 (determined without regard to sections 1251 and 1252). See paragraph (c)(1) of § 1.1251-4 and subparagraph (1) of this paragraph. For treatment of the farm land in the hands of B, see paragraph (f)(1) of this section. For effect of the transfer on the excess deductions account of A and of B, see paragraph (e)(1) of § 1.1251-2.

Example (2). Assume the same facts in example (1), except that A transferred the land to M for stock in the corporation worth $32,000 and $8,000 cash. The gain realized is $25,000 (amount realized, $40,000, minus adjusted basis, $15,000). Without regard to section 1252, A would recognize $8,000 of gain under section 351(b). Assume further that no gain is recognized as ordinary income under section 1251(c)(1). Therefore, since the applicable percentage, 100 percent, of the aggregate of the deductions allowed under sections 175 and 182, $18,000, is lower than the gain realized, $25,000, the amount of gain to be recognized as ordinary income under section 1252(a)(1) would be $18,000 if the provisions of subparagraph (1) of this paragraph do not apply. Since under section 351(b) gain in the amount of $8,000 would be recognized to the transferor without

Reg. § 1.1252-2(c)(4)

53,608 Rules for Determining Capital Gains and Losses

See p. 20,601 for regulations not amended to reflect law changes

regard to section 1252, the limitation provided in subparagraph (1) of this paragraph limits the gain taken into account by A under section 1252(a)(1) to $8,000.

Example (3). Assume the same facts as in example (2), except that $5,000 of gain is recognized as ordinary income under section 1251(c)(1). The amount of gain recognized as ordinary income under section 1252(a)(1) is $3,000 computed as follows:

(1) Amount of gain under section 1252(a)(1) (determined without regard to subparagraph (1) of this paragraph):	
(a) Aggregate of deductions allowed under sections 175 and 182	$18,000
(b) Minus: Gain recognized as ordinary income under section 1251(c)(1)	5,000
(c) Difference	$13,000
(d) Multiply: Applicable percentage for property disposed of within the fifth year after it was acquired	100%
(e) Amount in paragraph (a)(1)(i)(*a*) of § 1.1252-1	$13,000
(f) Gain realized (amount realized, $40,000, less adjusted basis, $15,000)	$25,000
(g) Minus: Amount in line (b)	5,000
(h) Amount in paragraph (a)(1)(i)(*b*) of § 1.1252-1	$20,000
(i) Lower of line (e) or (h)	$13,000
(2) Limitation in subparagraph (1) of this paragraph:	
(a) Gain recognized (determined without regard to section 1252)	$ 8,000
(b) Minus: Gain recognized as ordinary income under section 1251(c)(1)	5,000
(c) Difference	$ 3,000
(3) Lower of line (1)(i) or line (2)(c)	$ 3,000

Thus, the entire gain recognized under section 351(b) (determined without regard to sections 1251 and 1252), $8,000, is recognized as ordinary income since that amount is equal to the sum of the gain recognized as ordinary income under section 1251(c)(1), $5,000, and under section 1252(a)(1), $3,000.

(d) *Limitation for like kind exchanges and involuntary conversions*—(1) *General rule.* If farm land is disposed of and gain (determined without regard to section 1252) is not recognized in whole or in part under section 1031 (relating to like kind exchanges) or section 1033 (relating to involuntary conversions), then the amount of gain recognized as ordinary income by the transferor under section 1252(a)(1) shall not exceed the sum of—

(i) The excess (if any) of (*a*) the amount of gain recognized on such disposition (determined without regard to section 1252) over (ii) the amount (if any) of gain recognized as ordinary income under section 1251(c)(1), plus

(ii) The fair market value of property acquired which is not farm land and which is not taken into account under subdivision (i) of this subparagraph (that is, the fair market value of property other than farm land acquired which is qualifying property under section 1031 or 1033, as the case may be).

(2) *Examples.* The provisions of subparagraph (1) of this paragraph may be illustrated by the following examples:

Example (1). (i) Assume the same facts as in example (2)(ii) of paragraph (d)(3) of § 1.1251-4. Assume further that the aggregate of the amount of sections 175 and 182 deductions allowable is equal to the amount allowed. Under paragraph (a)(1) of § 1.1252-1, $18,000 would be recognized as ordinary income under section 1252(a)(1) (determined without regard to subparagraph (1) of this paragraph), computed as follows:

(1) Aggregate of deductions allowed under sections 175 and 182	$18,000
(2) Minus: Gain recognized as ordinary income under section 1251(c)(1)	$ 0
(3) Difference	$18,000
(4) Multiply: Applicable percentage for property disposed of within the fifth year after it was acquired	100%
(5) Amount in paragraph (a)(1)(i)(*a*) of § 1.1252-1	$18,000
(6) Gain realized (amount realized, $67,500, less adjusted basis, $48,000)	$19,500
(7) Minus: Amount in line (2)	0

Reg. § 1.1252-2(d)(1)

Rules for Determining Capital Gains and Losses

See p. 20,601 for regulations not amended to reflect law changes

(8) Amount in paragraph (a)(1)(i)(*b*) of § 1.1252-1	$19,500
(9) Lower of line (5) or line (8)	$18,000

(ii) Although no gain was recognized under section 1251(c)(1) and the stock purchased by A for $67,500 is farm recapture property for purposes of section 1251, it is not farm land for purposes of section 1252. Nevertheless, although no gain would be recognized under sections 1033(a)(3) and 1251(c)(1) (determined without regard to section 1252), the limitation under subparagraph (1) of this paragraph is $67,500 (that is, the fair market value of property other than farm land acquired which is qualifying property under section 1033). Since the amount of gain which would be recognized as ordinary income under section 1252(a)(1) (determined without regard to subparagraph (1) of this paragraph), $18,000 (as computed in subdivision (i) of this example), is lower than the amount of such limitation, $67,500, accordingly, only $18,000 is recognized as ordinary income under section 1252(a)(1). For determination of basis of the stock acquired, see subparagraph (5) of this paragraph.

Example (2). (i) Assume the same facts as in example (1) of this subparagraph, except that the cost of the stock was $62,500 (its fair market value). Thus, the amount of gain recognized on the disposition under section 1033(a)(3) (determined without regard to sections 1251 and 1252) is $5,000, that is, $67,500 minus $62,500. Assume further that $5,000 (the amount of gain recognized under section 1033(a)(3) (so determined)) was recognized as ordinary income under section 1251(c)(1). The amount of gain recognized as ordinary income under section 1252(a)(1) is $13,000, computed as follows:

(1)	Amount of gain under section 1252(a)(1) (determined without regard to subparagraph (1) of this paragraph):	
	(a) Aggregate of deductions allowed under sections 175 and 182	$18,000
	(b) Minus: Gain recognized as ordinary income under section 1251(c)(1)	5,000
	(c) Difference	$13,000
	(d) Multiply: Applicable percentage for property disposed of within the fifth year after it was acquired	100%
	(e) Amount in paragraph (a)(1)(i)(*a*) of § 1.1252-1	$13,000
	(f) Gain realized (amount realized, $67,500, less adjusted basis, $48,000)	$19,500
	(g) Minus: Amount in line (b)	5,000
	(h) Amount in paragraph (a)(1)(i)(*b*) of § 1.1252-1	$14,500
	(i) Lower of line (e) or (h)	$13,000
(2)	Limitation in subparagraph (1) of this paragraph:	
	(a) Gain recognized (determined without regard to section 1252)	$ 5,000
	(b) Minus: Gain recognized as ordinary income under section 1251(c)(1)	5,000
	(c) Difference	$ 0
	(d) Plus: The fair market value of property other than farm land acquired which is qualifying property under section 1033	62,500
	(e) Sum of lines (c) and (d)	$62,500
(3)	Lower of line (1)(i) or line (2)(e)	$13,000

(3) *Application to single disposition of farm land and property of different class.* (i) If upon a sale of farm land gain would be recognized under section 1252(a)(1), and if such land together with property of a different class or classes is disposed of in one transaction in which gain is not recognized in whole or in part under section 1031 or 1033 (without regard to section 1252(a)(1)), then rules consistent with the principles of paragraph (d)(6) of § 1.1250-3 (relating to gain from disposition of certain depreciable realty) shall apply for purposes of allocating the amount realized to each of the classes of property disposed of and for purposes of determining what property the amount realized for each class consists of.

(ii) For purposes of this subparagraph, the classes of property other than farm recapture property (as defined in section 1251(e) and paragraph (a)(1) of § 1.1251-3) are (*a*) section 1245 property, (*b*) section 1250 property, and (*c*) other property.

Reg. § 1.1252-2(d)(3)

53,610 Rules for Determining Capital Gains and Losses

See p. 20,601 for regulations not amended to reflect law changes

(iii) For purposes of this subparagraph, the classes of farm recapture property are (a) land, (b) section 1245 property, and (c) other property.

(4) *Treatment of farm land received in like kind exchange or involunary conversion.* The aggregate of the deductions allowed under sections 175 and 182 in respect of land acquired in a transaction described in subparagraph (1) of this paragraph shall include the aggregate of the deductions allowed under sections 175 and 182 in respect of the land transferred or converted (as the case may be) in such transaction minus the amount of gain taken into account under sections 1251(c) and 1252(a) with respect to the land transferred or converted. Upon a subsequent disposition of such land, the holding period shall include the holding period with respect to the land transferred or converted.

(5) *Basis adjustment.* In order to reflect gain recognized under section 1252(a)(1) if property is acquired in a transaction to which subparagraph (1) of this paragraph applies, its basis shall be determined under the rules of section 1031(d) or 1033(c).

(e) *Partnerships* [Reserved]

(f) *Treatment of farm land received by a transferee in a disposition by gift and certain tax-free transactions*—(1) *General rule.* If farm land is disposed of in a transaction which is either a gift to which paragraph (a)(1) of this section applies, or a completely tax-free transfer to which paragraph (c)(1) of this section applies, then for purposes of section 1252—

(i) The aggregate of the deductions allowed under section 175 and 182 in respect of the land in the hands of the transferee immediately after the disposition shall be an amount equal to the amount of such aggregate in the hands of the transferor immediately before the disposition, and

(ii) For purposes of applying section 1252 upon a subsequent disposition by the transferee (including a computation of the applicable percentage), the holding period of the transferee shall include the holding period of the transferor.

(2) *Certain partially tax-free transfers.* If farm land is disposed of in a transaction which either is in part a sale or exchange and in part a gift to which paragraph (a)(2) of this section applies, or is partially tax-free transfer to which paragraph (c)(1) of this section applies, then for purposes of section 1252 the amount determined under subparagraph (1)(i) of this paragraph shall be reduced by the amount of gain taken into account under sections 1251(c) and 1252(a) by the transferor upon the disposition. Upon a subsequent disposition by the transferee, the holding period for purposes of computing the amount under section 1252(a)(1)(A), with respect to the 175 and 182 deductions taken by the transferor, shall include the holding period of the transferor. With respect to the 175 and 182 deductions taken by the transferee, the holding period shall not include the holding period of the transferor.

(3) *Examples.* The provisions of subparagraphs (1) and (2) of this paragraph may be illustrated by the following examples:

Example (1). Assume the same facts as in example (1) of paragraph (a)(4) of this section. Therefore, on the date B receives the farm land in the gift transaction, under subparagraph (1) of this paragraph the aggregate of the deductions allowed under sections 175 and 182 in respect of the farm land in the hands of B is the amount in the hands of A, $24,000, and for purposes of applying section 1252 upon a subsequent disposition by B (including a computation of the applicable percentage) the holding period of B includes the holding period of A.

Example (2). Assume the same facts as in example (2) of paragraph (a)(4) of this section. Under subparagraph (2) of this paragraph, the aggregate of the sections 175 and 182 deductions which pass over to B for purposes of section 1252 is $14,000 ($24,000 deductions allowable under sections 175 and 182 minus $3,000 gain recognized under section 1251(c) in accordance with example (2) of paragraph (a)(4) of § 1.1251-4, minus $7,000 gain recognized under section 1252(a) in accordance with example (2) of paragraph (a)(4) of this section), B's holding period includes the holding period of A (*i.e.*, the period back to January 15, 1971) with respect to A's deductions.

(g) *Disposition of farm land not specifically covered.* If farm land is disposed of in a transaction not specifically covered under § 1.1252-1 and this section, then the principles of section 1245 shall apply. [Reg. § 1.1252-2.]

☐ [*T.D.* 7418, 5-6-76.]

[Reg. § 1.1254-0]

§ 1.1254-0. **Table of contents for section 1254 recapture rules.**—This section lists the major captions contained in §§ 1.1254-1 through 1.1254-6.

§ 1.1254-1. *Treatment of gain from disposition of natural resource recapture property.*

(a) In general.

(b) Definitions.

(1) Section 1254 costs.

(2) Natural resource recapture property.

(3) Disposition.

Reg. § 1.1254-0

Rules for Determining Capital Gains and Losses

(c) Disposition of a portion of natural resource recapture property.

(1) Disposition of a portion (other than an undivided interest) of natural resource recapture property.

(2) Disposition of an undivided interest.

(3) Alternative allocation rule.

(d) Installment method.

§ 1.1254-2. Exceptions and limitations.

(a) Exception for gifts and section 1041 transfers.

(1) General rule.

(2) Part gift transactions.

(b) Exception for transfers at death.

(c) Limitation for certain tax-free transactions.

(1) General rule.

(2) Special rule for dispositions to certain tax exempt organizations.

(3) Transfers described.

(4) Special rules for section 332 transfers.

(d) Limitation for like kind exchanges and involuntary conversions.

(1) General rule.

(2) Disposition and acquisition of both natural resource recapture property and other property.

§ 1.1254-3. Section 1254 costs immediately after certain acquisitions.

(a) Transactions in which basis is determined by reference to cost or fair market value of property transferred.

(1) Basis determined under section 1012.

(2) Basis determined under section 301(d), 334(a), or 358(a)(2).

(3) Basis determined solely under former section 334(b)(2) or former section 334(c).

(4) Basis determined by reason of the application of section 1014(a).

(b) Gifts and certain tax-free transactions.

(1) General rule.

(2) Transactions covered.

(c) Certain transfers at death.

(d) Property received in a like kind exchange or involuntary conversion.

(1) General rule.

(2) Allocation of section 1254 costs among multiple natural resource recapture property acquired.

(e) Property transferred in cases to which section 1071 or 1081(b) applies.

§ 1.1254-4. Special rules for S corporations and their shareholders.

(a) In general.

(b) Determination of gain treated as ordinary income under section 1254 upon a disposition of natural resource recapture property by an S corporation.

(1) General rule.

(2) Examples.

(c) Character of gain recognized by a shareholder upon a sale or exchange of S corporation stock.

(1) General rule.

(2) Exceptions.

(3) Examples.

(d) Section 1254 costs of a shareholder.

(e) Section 1254 costs of an acquiring shareholder after certain acquisitions.

(1) Basis determined under section 1012.

(2) Basis determined under section 1014(a).

(3) Basis determined under section 1014(b)(9).

(4) Gifts and section 1041 transfers.

(f) Special rules for a corporation that was formerly an S corporation or formerly a C corporation.

(1) Section 1254 costs of an S corporation that was formerly a C corporation.

(2) Examples.

(3) Section 1254 costs of a C corporation that was formerly an S corporation.

(g) Determination of a shareholder's section 1254 costs upon certain stock transactions

(1) Issuance of stock.

(2) Natural resource recapture property acquired in exchange for stock.

(3) Treatment of nonvested stock.

(4) Exception.

(5) Aggregate of S corporation shareholders' section 1254 costs with respect to natural resource recapture property held by the S corporation

(6) Examples.

§ 1.1254-5. Special rules for partnerships and their partners.

(a) In general.

(b) Determination of gain treated as ordinary income under section 1254 upon the disposition of natural resource recapture property by a partnership.

(1) General rule.

(2) Exception to partner level recapture in the case of abusive allocations.

Reg. § 1.1254-0

(3) Examples.

(c) Section 1254 costs of a partner.

(1) General rule.

(2) Section 1254 costs of a transferee partner after certain acquisitions.

(d) Property distributed to a partner.

(1) In general.

(2) Aggregate of partners' section 1254 costs with respect to natural resource recapture property held by a partnership.

§ 1.1254-6. Effective date of regulations.

[Reg. § 1.1254-0.]

☐ [T.D. 8586, 1-9-95. Amended by T.D. 8684, 10-9-96.]

[Reg. § 1.1254-1]

§ 1.1254-1. Treatment of gain from disposition of natural resource recapture property.—(a) *In general.* Upon any disposition of section 1254 property or any disposition after December 31, 1975 of oil, gas, or geothermal property, gain is treated as ordinary income in an amount equal to the lesser of the amount of the section 1254 costs (as defined in paragraph (b)(1) of this section) with respect to the property, or the amount, if any, by which the amount realized on the sale, exchange, or involuntary conversion, or the fair market value of the property on any other disposition, exceeds the adjusted basis of the property. However, any amount treated as ordinary income under the preceding sentence is not included in the taxpayer's *gross income from the property* for purposes of section 613. Generally, the lesser of the amounts described in this paragraph (a) is treated as ordinary income even though, in the absence of section 1254(a), no gain would be recognized upon the disposition under any other provision of the Internal Revenue Code. For the definition of the term *section 1254 costs,* see paragraph (b)(1) of this section. For the definition of the terms *section 1254 property, oil, gas,* or *geothermal property,* and *natural resource recapture property,* see paragraph (b)(2) of this section. For rules relating to the *disposition* of natural resource recapture property, see paragraphs (b)(3), (c), and (d) of this section. For exceptions and limitations to the application of section 1254(a), see § 1.1254-2.

(b) *Definitions*—(1) *Section 1254 costs*—(i) *Property placed in service after December 31, 1986.* With respect to any property placed in service by the taxpayer after December 31, 1986, the term *section 1254 costs* means—

(A) The aggregate amount of expenditures that have been deducted by the taxpayer or any person under section 263, 616, or 617 with respect to such property and that, but for the deduction, would have been included in the adjusted basis of the property or in the adjusted basis of certain depreciable property associated with the property; and

(B) The deductions for depletion under section 611 that reduced the adjusted basis of the property.

(ii) *Property placed in service before January 1, 1987.* With respect to any property placed in service by the taxpayer before January 1, 1987, the term *section 1254 costs* means—

(A) The aggregate amount of costs paid or incurred after December 31, 1975, with respect to such property, that have been deducted as intangible drilling and development costs under section 263(c) by the taxpayer or any other person (except that section 1254 costs do not include costs incurred with respect to geothermal wells commenced before October 1, 1978) and that, but for the deduction, would be reflected in the adjusted basis of the property or in the adjusted basis of certain depreciable property associated with the property; reduced by

(B) The amount (if any) by which the deduction for depletion allowed under section 611 that was computed either under section 612 or sections 613 and 613A, with respect to the property, would have been increased if the costs (paid or incurred after December 31, 1975) had been charged to capital account rather than deducted.

(iii) *Deductions under section 59 and section 291.* Amounts capitalized pursuant to an election under section 59(e) or pursuant to section 291(b) are treated as section 1254 costs in the year in which an amortization deduction is claimed under section 59(e)(1) or section 291(b)(2).

(iv) *Suspended deductions.* If a deduction of a section 1254 cost has been suspended as of the date of disposition of section 1254 property, the deduction is not treated as a section 1254 cost if it is included in basis for determining gain or loss on the disposition. On the other hand, if the deduction will eventually be claimed, it is a section 1254 cost as of the date of disposition. For example, a deduction suspended pursuant to the 65 percent of taxable income limitation of section 613A(d)(1) may either be included in basis upon disposition of the property or may be deducted in a year after the year of disposition. See § 1.613A-4(a)(1). If it is included in the basis then it is not a section 1254 cost, but if it is deductible in a later year it is a section 1254 cost as of the date of the disposition.

(v) *Previously recaptured amounts.* If an amount has been previously treated as ordinary income pursuant to section 1254, it is not a section 1254 cost.

(vi) *Nonproductive wells.* The aggregate amount of section 1254 costs paid or incurred on any property includes the amount of intangible drilling and development costs incurred on nonproductive wells, but only to the extent that the taxpayer recognizes income on the foreclosure of a nonrecourse debt the proceeds from which were used to finance the section 1254 costs with respect to the property. For this purpose, the term nonproductive well means a well that does not produce oil or gas in commercial quantities, including a well that is drilled for the purpose of ascertaining the existence, location, or extent of an oil or gas reservoir (e.g., a delineation well). The term *nonproductive well* does not include an injection well (other than an injection well drilled as part of a project that does not result in production in commercial quantities).

(vii) *Calculation of amount described in paragraph (b)(1)(ii)(B) of this section (hypothetical depletion offset)*—(A) *In general.* In calculating the amount described in paragraph (b)(1)(ii)(B) of this section, the taxpayer shall apply the following rules. The taxpayer may use the 65-percent-of-taxable-income limitation of section 613A(d)(1). If the taxpayer uses that limitation, the taxpayer is not required to recalculate the effect of such limitation with respect to any property not disposed of. That is, the taxpayer may assume that the hypothetical capitalization of intangible drilling and development costs with respect to any property disposed of does not affect the allowable depletion with respect to property retained by the taxpayer. Any intangible drilling and development costs that, if they had not been treated as expenses under section 263(c), would have properly been capitalized under §1.612-4(b)(2) (relating to items recoverable through depreciation under section 167 or cost recovery under section 168) are treated as costs described in §1.612-4(b)(1) (relating to items recoverable through depletion). The increase in depletion attributable to the capitalization of intangible drilling and development costs is computed by subtracting the amount of cost or percentage depletion actually claimed from the amount of cost or percentage depletion that would have been allowable if intangible drilling and development costs had been capitalized. If the remainder is zero or less than zero, the entire amount of intangible drilling and development costs attributable to the property is recapturable.

(B) *Example.* The following example illustrates the principles of paragraph (b)(1)(vii)(A).

Example. Hypothetical depletion offset. In 1976, A purchased undeveloped property for $10,000. During 1977, A incurred $200,000 of productive well intangible drilling and development costs with respect to the property. A deducted the intangible drilling and development costs as expenses under section 263(c). Estimated reserves of 150,000 barrels of recoverable oil were discovered in 1977 and production began in 1978. In 1978, A produced and sold 30,000 barrels of oil at $8 per barrel, resulting in $240,000 of gross income. A had no other oil or gas production in 1978. A claimed a percentage depletion deduction of $52,800 (i.e., 22% of $240,000 gross income from the property). If A had capitalized the intangible drilling and development costs, assume that $200,000 of the costs would have been allocated to the depletable property and none to depreciable property. A's cost depletion deduction if the intangible drilling and development costs had been capitalized would have been $42,000 (i.e., (($200,000 intangible drilling and development costs + $10,000 acquisition costs) x 30,000 barrels of production) / 150,000 barrels of estimated recoverable reserves). Since this amount is less than A's depletion deduction of $52,800 (percentage depletion), no reduction is made to the amount of intangible drilling and development costs ($200,000). On January 1, 1979, A sold the oil property to B for $360,000 and calculated section 1254 recapture without reference to the 65-percent-of-taxable-income limitation. A's gain on the sale is the entire $360,000, because A's basis in the property at the beginning of 1979 is zero (i.e., $10,000 cost less $52,800 depletion deduction for 1978). Since the section 1254 costs ($200,000) are less than A's gain on the sale, $200,000 is treated as ordinary income under section 1254(a). The remaining amount of A's gain ($160,000) is not subject to section 1254(a).

(2) *Natural resource recapture property*—(i) *In general.* The term *natural resource recapture property* means section 1254 property or oil, gas, or geothermal property as those terms are defined in this section.

(ii) *Section 1254 property.* The term *section 1254 property* means any property (within the meaning of section 614) that is placed in service by the taxpayer after December 31, 1986, if any expenditures described in paragraph (b)(1)(i)(A) of this section (relating to costs under section 263, 616, or 617) are properly chargeable to such property, or if the adjusted basis of such property includes adjustments for deductions for depletion under section 611.

(iii) *Oil, gas, or geothermal property.* The term *oil, gas, or geothermal property* means any

Reg. § 1.1254-1(b)(2)

property (within the meaning of section 614) that was placed in service by the taxpayer before January 1, 1987, if any expenditures described in paragraph (b)(1)(ii)(A) of this section are properly chargeable to such property.

(iv) *Property to which section 1254 costs are properly chargeable.*—(A) An expenditure is properly chargeable to property if—

(*1*) The property is an operating mineral interest with respect to which the expenditure has been deducted;

(*2*) The property is a nonoperating mineral interest (e.g., a net profits interest or an overriding royalty interest) burdening an operating mineral interest if the nonoperating mineral interest is carved out of an operating mineral interest described in paragraph (b)(2)(iv)(A)(*1*) of this section;

(*3*) The property is a nonoperating mineral interest retained by a lessor or sublessor if such lessor or sublessor held, prior to the lease or sublease, an operating mineral interest described in paragraph (b)(2)(iv)(A)(*1*) of this section; or

(*4*) The property is an operating or a nonoperating mineral interest held by a taxpayer if a party related to the taxpayer (within the meaning of section 267(b) or section 707(b)) held an operating mineral interest (described in paragraph (b)(2)(iv)(A)(*1*) of this section) in the same tract or parcel of land that terminated (in whole or in part) without being disposed of (e.g., a working interest which terminated after a specified period of time or a given amount of production), but only if there exists between the related parties an arrangement or plan to avoid recapture under section 1254. In such a case, the taxpayer's section 1254 costs with respect to the property include those of the related party.

(B) *Example.* The following example illustrates the provisions of paragraph (2)(iv)(A)(*4*) of this section:

Example. Arrangement or plan to avoid recapture. C, an individual, owns 100% of the stock of both X Co. and Y Co. On January 1, 1998, X Co. enters into a standard oil and gas lease. X Co. immediately assigns to Y Co. 1% of the working interest for one year, and 99% of the working interest thereafter. In 1998, X Co. and Y Co. expend $300 in intangible drilling and development costs developing the tract, of which $297 are deducted by X Co. under section 263(c). On January 1, 1999, Y Co. sells its 99% share of the working interest to an unrelated person. Based on all the facts and circumstances, the arrangement between X Co. and Y Co. is part of a plan or arrangement to avoid recapture under section 1254. Therefore, Y Co. must include in its section 1254 costs the $297 of intangible drilling and development costs deducted by X Co.

(v) *Property the basis of which includes adjustments for depletion deductions.* The adjusted basis of property includes adjustments for depletion under section 611 if—

(A) The basis of the property has been reduced by reason of depletion deductions; or

(B) The property has been carved out of or is a portion of property the basis of which has been reduced by reason of depletion deductions.

(vi) *Property held by a transferee.* Property held by a transferee is natural resource recapture property if the property was natural resource recapture property in the hands of the transferor and the transferee's basis in the property is determined with reference to the transferor's basis in the property (e.g., a gift) or is determined under section 732.

(vii) *Property held by a transferor.* Property held by a transferor of natural resource recapture property is natural resource recapture property if the transferor's basis in the property received is determined with reference to the transferor's basis in the property transferred by the transferor (e.g., a like kind exchange). For purposes of this paragraph (b)(2), property described in this paragraph (b)(2)(vii) is treated as placed in service at the time the property transferred by the transferor was placed in service by the transferor.

(3) *Disposition*—(i) *General rule.* The term *disposition* has the same meaning as in section 1245, relating to gain from dispositions of certain depreciable property.

(ii) *Exceptions.* The term *disposition* does not include—

(A) Any transaction that is merely a financing device, such as a mortgage or a production payment that is treated as a loan under section 636 and the regulations thereunder;

(B) Any abandonment (except that an abandonment is a disposition to the extent the taxpayer recognizes income on the foreclosure of a nonrecourse debt);

(C) Any creation of a lease or sublease of natural resource recapture property;

(D) Any termination or election of the status of an S corporation;

(E) Any unitization or pooling arrangement;

(F) Any expiration or reversion of an operating mineral interest that expires or reverts by its own terms, in whole or in part; or

Reg. § 1.1254-1(b)(3)

(G) Any conversion of an overriding royalty interest that, at the option of the grantor or successor in interest, converts to an operating mineral interest after a certain amount of production.

(iii) *Special rule for carrying arrangements.* In a carrying arrangement, liability for section 1254 costs attributable to the entire operating mineral interest held by the carrying party prior to reversion or conversion remains attributable to the reduced operating mineral interest retained by the carrying party after a portion of the operating mineral interest has reverted to the carried party or after the conversion of an overriding royalty interest that, at the option of the grantor or successor in interest, converts to an operating mineral interest after a certain amount of production.

(c) *Disposition of a portion of natural resource recapture property*—(1) *Disposition of a portion (other than an undivided interest) of natural resource recapture property*—(i) *Natural resource recapture property subject to the general rules of § 1.1254-1.* For purposes of section 1254(a)(1) and paragraph (a) of this section, except as provided in paragraphs (c)(1)(ii) and (3) of this section, in the case of the disposition of a portion (that is not an undivided interest) of natural resource recapture property, the entire amount of the section 1254 costs with respect to the natural resource recapture property is treated as allocable to that portion of the property to the extent of the amount of gain to which section 1254(a)(1) applies. If the amount of the gain to which section 1254(a)(1) applies is less than the amount of the section 1254 costs with respect to the natural resource recapture property, the balance of the section 1254 costs remaining after allocation to the portion of the property that was disposed of remains subject to recapture by the taxpayer under section 1254(a)(1) upon disposition of the remaining portion of the property. For example, assume that A owns an 80-acre tract of land with respect to which A has deducted intangible drilling and development costs under section 263(c). If A sells the north 40 acres, the entire amount of the section 1254 costs with respect to the 80-acre tract is treated as allocable to the 40-acre portion sold (to the extent of the amount of gain to which section 1254(a)(1) applies).

(ii) *Natural resource recapture property subject to the exceptions and limitations of § 1.1254-2.* For purposes of section 1254(a)(1) and paragraph (a) of this section, except as provided in paragraph (b)(3) of this section, in the case of the disposition of a portion (that is not an undivided interest) of natural resource recapture property to which section 1254(a)(1) does not apply by reason of the application of § 1.1254-2 (certain nonrecognition transactions), the following rule for allocation of costs applies. An amount of the section 1254 costs that bears the same ratio to the entire amount of such costs with respect to the entire natural resource recapture property as the value of the property transferred bears to the value of the entire natural resource recapture property is treated as allocable to the portion of the natural resource recapture property transferred. The balance of the section 1254 costs remaining after allocation to that portion of the transferred property remains subject to recapture by the taxpayer under section 1254(a)(1) upon disposition of the remaining portion of the property. For example, assume that A owns an 80-acre tract of land with respect to which A has deducted intangible drilling and development costs under section 263(c). If A gives away the north 40 acres, and if 60 percent of the value of the 80-acre tract were attributable to the north 40 acres given away, 60 percent of the section 1254 costs with respect to the 80-acre tract is allocable to the north 40 acres given away.

(2) *Disposition of an undivided interest*—(i) *Natural resource recapture property subject to the general rules of § 1.1254-1.* For purposes of section 1254(a)(1), except as provided in paragraphs (b)(2)(ii) and (b)(3) of this section, in the case of the disposition of an undivided interest in natural resource recapture property (or a portion thereof), a proportionate part of the section 1254 costs with respect to the natural resource recapture property is treated as allocable to the transferred undivided interest to the extent of the amount of gain to which section 1254(a)(1) applies. For example, assume that A owns an 80-acre tract of land with respect to which A has deducted intangible drilling and development costs under section 263(c). If A sells an undivided 40 percent interest in the 80-acre tract, 40 percent of the section 1254 costs with respect to the 80-acre tract is allocable to the transferred 40 percent interest in the 80-acre tract. However, if the amount of gain recognized on the sale of the 40 percent undivided interest were equal to only 35 percent of the amount of section 1254 costs attributable to the 80-acre tract, only 35 percent of the section 1254 costs would be treated as attributable to the undivided 40 percent interest. See paragraph (c)(3) of this section for an alternative allocation rule.

(ii) *Natural resource recapture property subject to the exceptions and limitations of § 1.1254-2.* For purposes of section 1254(a)(1) and paragraph (a) of this section, except as provided in paragraph (b)(3) of this section, in the case of a

Reg. § 1.1254-1(c)(2)

disposition of an undivided interest in natural resource recapture property (or a portion thereof) to which section 1254(a)(1) does not apply by reason of § 1.1254-2, a proportionate part of the section 1254 costs with respect to the natural resource recapture property is treated as allocable to the transferred undivided interest. See paragraph (c)(3) of this section for an alternative allocation rule.

(3) *Alternative allocation rule*—(i) *In general.* The rules for the allocation of costs set forth in section 1254(a)(2) and paragraphs (c)(1) and (2) of this section do not apply with respect to section 1254 costs that the taxpayer establishes to the satisfaction of the Commissioner do not relate to the transferred property. Except as provided in paragraphs (c)(3)(ii) and (iii) of this section, a taxpayer may satisfy this requirement only by receiving a private letter ruling from the Internal Revenue Service that the section 1254 costs do not relate to the transferred property.

(ii) *Portion of property.* Upon the transfer of a portion of a natural resource recapture property (other than an undivided interest) with respect to which section 1254 costs have been incurred, a taxpayer may treat section 1254 costs as not relating to the transferred portion if the transferred portion does not include any part of any deposit with respect to which the costs were incurred.

(iii) *Undivided interest.* Upon the transfer of an undivided interest in a natural resource recapture property with respect to which section 1254 costs have been incurred, a taxpayer may treat costs as not relating to the transferred interest if the undivided interest is an undivided interest in a portion of the natural resource recapture property, and the portion would be eligible for the alternative allocation rule under paragraph (c)(3)(ii) of this section.

(iv) *Substantiation.* If a taxpayer treats section 1254 costs incurred with respect to a natural resource recapture property as not relating to a transferred interest in a portion of the property, the taxpayer must indicate on his or her tax return that the costs do not relate to the transferred portion and maintain the records and supporting evidence that substantiate this position.

(d) *Installment method.* Gain from a disposition to which section 1254(a)(1) applies is reported on the installment method if that method otherwise applies under section 453 or 453A of the Internal Revenue Code and the regulations thereunder. The portion of each installment payment as reported that represents income (other than interest) is treated as gain to which section 1254(a)(1) applies until all of the gain (to which section 1254(a)(1) applies) has been reported, and the remaining portion (if any) of the income is then treated as gain to which section 1254(a)(1) does not apply. For treatment of amounts as interest on certain deferred payments, see sections 483, 1274, and the regulations thereunder. [Reg. § 1.1254-1.]

☐ [T.D. 8586, 1-9-95.]

[Reg. § 1.1254-2]

§ 1.1254-2. Exceptions and limitations.—(a) *Exception for gifts and section 1041 transfers*—(1) *General rule.* No gain is recognized under section 1254(a)(1) upon a disposition of natural resource recapture property by a gift or by a transfer in which no gain or loss is recognized pursuant to section 1041 (relating to transfers between spouses). For purposes of this paragraph (a), the term *gift* means, except to the extent that paragraph (a)(2) of this section applies, a transfer of natural resource recapture property that, in the hands of the transferee, has a basis determined under the provisions of sections 1015(a) or (d) (relating to basis of property acquired by gift). For rules concerning the potential reduction in the amount of the charitable contribution in the case of natural resource recapture property, see section 170(e) and § 1.170A-4. See § 1.1254-3(b)(1) for determination of potential recapture of section 1254 costs on property acquired by gift. See § 1.1254-1(c)(1)(ii) and (c)(2)(ii) for apportionment of section 1254 costs on a gift of a portion of natural resource recapture property.

(2) *Part gift transactions.* If a disposition of natural resource recapture property is in part a sale or exchange and in part a gift, the gain that is treated as ordinary income pursuant to section 1254(a)(1) is the lower of the section 1254 costs with respect to the property or the excess of the amount realized upon the disposition of the property over the adjusted basis of the property. In the case of a transfer subject to section 1011(b) (relating to bargain sales to charitable organizations), the adjusted basis for purposes of the preceding sentence is the adjusted basis for determining gain or loss under section 1011(b).

(b) *Exception for transfers at death.* Except as provided in section 691 (relating to income in respect of a decedent), no gain is recognized under section 1254(a)(1) upon a transfer at death. For purposes of this paragraph, the term *transfer at death* means a transfer of natural resource recapture property that, in the hands of the transferee, has a basis determined under the provisions of section 1014(a) (relating to basis of property acquired from a decedent) because of the death of the transferor. See § 1.1254-3(a)(4) and (c) for the determination of potential recapture of section

1254 costs on property acquired in a transfer at death.

(c) *Limitation for certain tax-free transactions*—(1) *General rule.* Upon a transfer of property described in paragraph (c)(3) of this section, the amount of gain treated as ordinary income by the transferor under section 1254(a)(1) may not exceed the amount of gain recognized to the transferor on the transfer (determined without regard to section 1254). In the case of a transfer of both natural resource recapture property and property that is not natural resource recapture property in one transaction, the amount realized from the disposition of the natural resource recapture property is deemed to be equal to the amount that bears the same ratio to the total amount realized as the fair market value of the natural resource recapture property bears to the aggregate fair market value of all the property transferred. The preceding sentence is applied solely for purposes of computing the portion of the total gain (determined without regard to section 1254) that may be recognized as ordinary income under section 1254(a)(1).

(2) *Special rule for dispositions to certain tax exempt organizations.* Paragraph (c)(1) of this section does not apply to a disposition of natural resource recapture property to an organization (other than a cooperative described in section 521) that is exempt from the tax imposed by chapter I of the Internal Revenue Code. The preceding sentence does not apply to a disposition of natural resource recapture property to an organization described in section 511(a)(2) or (b)(2) (relating to imposition of tax on unrelated business income of charitable, etc., organizations) if, immediately after the disposition, the organization uses the property in an unrelated trade or business as defined in section 513. If any property with respect to which gain is not recognized by reason of the exception of this paragraph (c)(2) ceases to be used in an unrelated trade or business of the organization acquiring the property, that organization is, for purposes of section 1254, treated as having disposed of the property on the date of the cessation.

(3) *Transfers described.* The transfers referred to in paragraph (c)(1) of this section are transfers of natural resource recapture property in which the basis of the natural resource recapture property in the hands of the transferee is determined by reference to its basis in the hands of the transferor by reason of the application of any of the following provisions:

(i) Section 332 (relating to certain liquidations of subsidiaries). See paragraph (c)(4) of this section.

(ii) Section 351 (relating to transfer to a corporation controlled by transferor).

(iii) Section 361 (relating to exchanges pursuant to certain corporate reorganizations).

(iv) Section 721 (relating to transfers to a partnership in exchange for a partnership interest).

(v) Section 731 (relating to distributions by a partnership to a partner). For purposes of this paragraph, the basis of natural resource recapture property distributed by a partnership to a partner is deemed to be determined by reference to the adjusted basis of such property to the partnership.

(4) *Special rules for section 332 transfers.* In the case of a distribution in complete liquidation of a subsidiary to which section 332 applies, the limitation provided in this paragraph (c) is confined to instances in which the basis of the natural resource recapture property in the hands of the transferee is determined, under section 334(b)(1), by reference to its basis in the hands of the transferor. Thus, for example, the limitation may apply in respect of a liquidating distribution of natural resource recapture property by a subsidiary corporation to the parent corporation, but does not apply in respect of a liquidating distribution of natural resource recapture property to a minority shareholder. This paragraph (c) does not apply to a liquidating distribution of natural resource recapture property by a subsidiary to its parent if the parent's basis for the property is determined under section 334(b)(2) (as in effect before enactment of the Tax Reform Act of 1986), by reference to its basis for the stock of the subsidiary. This paragraph (c) does not apply to a liquidating distribution under section 332 of natural resource recapture property by a subsidiary to its parent if gain is recognized and there is a corresponding increase in the parent's basis in the property (e.g., certain distributions to a tax-exempt or foreign corporation).

(d) *Limitation for like kind exchanges and involuntary conversions*—(1) *General rule.* If natural resource recapture property is disposed of and gain (determined without regard to section 1254) is not recognized in whole or in part under section 1031 (relating to like kind exchanges) or section 1033 (relating to involuntary conversions), the amount of gain taken into account by the transferor under section 1254(a)(1) may not exceed the sum of—

(i) The amount of gain recognized on the disposition (determined without regard to section 1254); plus

(ii) The fair market value of property acquired that is not natural resource recapture property (determined without regard to § 1.1254-1(b)(2)(vii)) and is not taken into account under paragraph (d)(1)(i) of this section (that is, qualifying property under section 1031 or 1033 that is not natural resource recapture property).

(2) *Disposition and acquisition of both natural resource recapture property and other property.* For purposes of this paragraph (d), if both natural resource recapture property and property that is not natural resource recapture property are acquired as the result of one disposition in which both natural resource recapture property and property that is not natural resource recapture property are disposed of—

(i) The total amount realized upon the disposition is allocated between the natural resource recapture property and the property that is not natural resource recapture property disposed of in proportion to their respective fair market values;

(ii) The amount realized upon the disposition of the natural resource recapture property is deemed to consist of so much of the fair market value of the natural resource recapture property acquired as is not in excess of the amount realized from the natural resource recapture property disposed of, and the remaining portion (if any) of the amount realized upon the disposition of such property is deemed to consist of so much of the fair market value of the property that is not natural resource recapture property acquired as is not in excess of the remaining portion; and

(iii) The amount realized upon the disposition of the property that is not natural resource recapture property is deemed to consist of so much of the fair market value of all the property acquired which was not taken into account under paragraph (d)(2)(ii) of this section. Except as provided in section 1060 and the regulations thereunder, if a buyer and seller have adverse interests as to such allocation of the amount realized, any arm's-length agreement between the buyer and seller is used to establish the allocation. In the absence of such an agreement, the allocation is made by taking into account the appropriate facts and circumstances. [Reg. § 1.1254-2.]

☐ [T.D. 8586, 1-9-95. Amended by T.D. 8684, 10-9-96.]

[Reg. § 1.1254-3]

§ 1.1254-3. Section 1254 costs immediately after certain acquisitions.—(a) *Transactions in which basis is determined by reference to cost or fair market value of property transferred*—(1) *Basis determined under section 1012.* If, on the date a person acquires natural resource recapture property, the person's basis for the property is determined solely by reference to its cost (within the meaning of section 1012), the amount of section 1254 costs with respect to the natural resource recapture property in the person's hands is zero on the acquisition date.

(2) *Basis determined under section 301(d), 334(a), or 358(a)(2).* If, on the date a person acquires natural resource recapture property, the person's basis for the property is determined solely by reason of the application of section 301(d) (relating to basis of property received in a corporate distribution), section 334(a) (relating to basis of property received in a liquidation in which gain or loss is recognized), or section 358(a)(2) (relating to basis of other property received in certain exchanges), the amount of the section 1254 costs with respect to the natural resource recapture property in the person's hands is zero on the acquisition date.

(3) *Basis determined solely under former section 334(b)(2) or former section 334(c).* If, on the date a person acquires natural resource recapture property, the person's basis for the property is determined solely under the provisions of section 334(b)(2) (prior to amendment of that section by the Tax Equity and Fiscal Responsibility Act of 1982) or (c) (prior to repeal of that section by the Tax Reform Act of 1986) (relating to basis of property received in certain corporate liquidations), the amount of section 1254 costs with respect to the natural resource recapture property in the person's hands is zero on the acquisition date.

(4) *Basis determined by reason of the application of section 1014(a).* If, on the date a person acquires natural resource recapture property from a decedent, the person's basis is determined, by reason of the application of section 1014(a), solely by reference to the fair market value of the property on the date of the decedent's death or on the applicable date provided in section 2032 (relating to alternate valuation date), the amount of section 1254 costs with respect to the natural resource recapture property in the person's hands is zero on the acquisition date. See paragraph (c) of this section for the treatment of certain transfers at death.

(b) *Gifts and certain tax-free transactions*—(1) *General rule.* If natural resource recapture property is transferred in a transaction described in paragraph (b)(2) of this section, the amount of section 1254 costs with respect to the natural resource recapture property in the hands of the transferee immediately after the disposition is an amount equal to—

(i) The amount of section 1254 costs with respect to the natural resource recapture property in the hands of the transferor immediately before the disposition (and in the case of an S corporation or partnership transferor, the section 1254 costs of the shareholders or partners with respect to the natural resource recapture property); minus

(ii) The amount of any gain taken into account as ordinary income under section 1254(a)(1) by the transferor upon the disposition (and in the case of an S corporation or partnership transferor, any such gain taken into account as ordinary income by the shareholders or partners).

(2) *Transactions covered.* The transactions to which paragraph (b)(1) of this section apply are—

(i) A disposition that is a gift or in part a sale or exchange and in part a gift;

(ii) A transaction described in section 1041(a); or

(iii) A disposition described in § 1.1254-2(c)(3) (relating to certain tax-free transactions).

(c) *Certain transfers at death.* If natural resource recapture property is acquired in a transfer at death, the amount of section 1254 costs with respect to the natural resource recapture property in the hands of the transferee immediately after the transfer includes the amount, if any, of the section 1254 costs deducted by the transferee before the decedent's death, to the extent that the basis of the natural resource recapture property (determined under section 1014(a)) is required to be reduced under the second sentence of section 1014(b)(9) (relating to adjustments to basis where the property is acquired from a decedent prior to death).

(d) *Property received in a like kind exchange or involuntary conversion*—(1) *General rule.* If natural resource recapture property is disposed of in a like kind exchange under section 1031 or involuntary conversion under section 1033, then immediately after the disposition the amount of section 1254 costs with respect to any natural resource recapture property acquired for the property transferred is an amount equal to—

(i) The amount of section 1254 costs with respect to the natural resource recapture property disposed of (including the section 1254 costs of the shareholders of an S corporation or of the partners of a partnership with respect to the natural resource recapture property); minus

(ii) The amount of any gain taken into account as ordinary income under section 1254(a)(1) by the transferor upon the disposition (and in the case of an S corporation or partnership transferor, any such gain taken into account as ordinary income by the shareholders or partners).

(2) *Allocation of section 1254 costs among multiple natural resource recapture properties acquired.* If more than one parcel of natural resource recapture property is acquired at the same time from the same person in a transaction referred to in paragraph (d)(1) of this section, the total amount of section 1254 costs with respect to the parcels is allocated to the parcels in proportion to their respective adjusted bases.

(e) *Property transferred in cases to which section 1071 or 1081(b) applies.* Rules similar to the rules of section 1245(b)(5) shall apply under section 1254. [Reg. § 1.1254-3.]

☐ [T.D. 8586, 1-9-95. Amended by T.D. 8684, 10-9-96.]

[Reg. § 1.1254-4]

§ 1.1254-4. **Special rules for S corporations and their shareholders.**—(a) *In general.* This section provides rules for applying the provisions of section 1254 to S corporations and their shareholders upon the disposition by an S corporation (and a corporation that was formerly an S corporation) of natural resource recapture property and upon the disposition by a shareholder of stock of an S corporation that holds natural resource recapture property.

(b) *Determination of gain treated as ordinary income under section 1254 upon a disposition of natural resource recapture property by an S corporation*—(1) *General rule.* Upon a disposition of natural resource recapture property by an S corporation, the amount of gain treated as ordinary income under section 1254 is determined at the shareholder level. Each shareholder must recognize as ordinary income under section 1254 the lesser of—

(i) The shareholder's section 1254 costs with respect to the property disposed of; or

(ii) The shareholder's share of the amount, if any, by which the amount realized on the sale, exchange, or involuntary conversion, or the fair market value of the property upon any other disposition (including a distribution), exceeds the adjusted basis of the property.

(2) *Examples.* The following examples illustrate the provisions of paragraph (b)(1) of this section:

Example 1. Disposition of natural resource recapture property other than oil and gas property. A and B are equal shareholders in X, an S corporation. On January 1, 1997, X acquires for $90,000 an undeveloped mineral property, its sole property. During 1997, X expends and deducts $100,000 in developing the property. On January

15, 1998, X sells the property for $250,000 when X's basis in the property is $90,000. Thus, X recognizes gain of $160,000 on the sale. A and B's share of the $160,000 gain recognized is $80,000 each. Each shareholder has $50,000 of section 1254 costs with respect to the property. Under these circumstances, A and B each are required to recognize $50,000 of the $80,000 of gain on the sale of the property as ordinary income under section 1254.

Example 2. Disposition of oil and gas property the adjusted basis of which is allocated to the shareholders under section 613A(c)(11). C and D are equal shareholders in Y, an S corporation. On January 1, 1997, Y acquires for $150,000 an undeveloped oil and gas property, its sole property. During 1997, Y expends in developing the property $40,000 in intangible drilling costs which it elects to expense under section 263(c). On January 15, 1998, Y sells the property for $200,000. C and D's share of the $200,000 amount realized on the sale is $100,000 each. C and D each have a basis of $75,000 in the property and $20,000 of section 1254 costs with respect to the property. Under these circumstances, C and D each are required to recognize $20,000 of the $25,000 gain on the sale of the property as ordinary income under section 1254.

(c) *Character of gain recognized by a shareholder upon a sale or exchange of S corporation stock*—(1) *General rule.* Except as provided in paragraph (c)(2) of this section, if an S corporation shareholder recognizes gain upon a sale or exchange of stock in the S corporation (determined without regard to section 1254), the gain is treated as ordinary income under section 1254 to the extent of the shareholder's section 1254 costs (with respect to the shares sold or exchanged).

(2) *Exceptions*—(i) *Gain not attributable to section 1254 costs*—(A) *General rule.* Paragraph (c)(1) of this section does not apply to any portion of the gain recognized on the sale or exchange of the stock that the taxpayer establishes is not attributable to section 1254 costs. The portion of the gain recognized that is not attributable to section 1254 costs is that portion of the gain recognized that exceeds the amount of ordinary income that the shareholder would have recognized under section 1254 (with respect to the shares sold or exchanged) if, immediately prior to the sale or exchange of the stock, the corporation had sold at fair market value all of the corporation's property the disposition of which would result in the recognition by the shareholder of ordinary income under section 1254.

(B) *Substantiation.* To establish that a portion of the gain recognized is not attributable to a shareholder's section 1254 costs so as to qualify for the exception contained in paragraph (c)(2)(i)(A) of this section, the shareholder must attach to the shareholder's tax return a statement detailing the shareholder's share of the fair market value and basis, and the shareholder's section 1254 costs, for each of the S corporation's natural resource recapture properties held immediately before the sale or exchange of stock.

(ii) *Transactions entered into as part of a plan to avoid recognition of ordinary income under section 1254.* In the case of a contribution of property prior to a sale or exchange of stock pursuant to a plan a principal purpose of which is to avoid recognition of ordinary income under section 1254, paragraph (c)(1) of this section does not apply. Instead, the amount recognized as ordinary income under section 1254 is the amount of ordinary income the selling or exchanging shareholder would have recognized under section 1254 (with respect to the shares sold or exchanged) had the S corporation sold its natural resource recapture property the disposition of which would have resulted in the recognition of ordinary income under section 1254. The amount recognized as ordinary income under the preceding sentence reduces the amount realized on the sale or exchange of the stock. This reduced amount realized is used in determining any gain or loss on the sale or exchange.

(3) *Examples.* The following examples illustrate the provisions of this paragraph (c):

Example 1. Application of general rule upon a sale of S corporation stock. C and D are equal shareholders in Y, an S corporation. As of January 1, 1997, Y holds two mining properties: Blackacre, with an adjusted basis of $5,000 and a fair market value of $35,000, and Whiteacre, with an adjusted basis of $20,000 and a fair market value of $15,000. Y also holds securities with a basis of $5,000 and a fair market value of $10,000. On January 1, 1997, D sells 50 percent of D's Y stock to E for $15,000. As of the date of the sale, D's adjusted basis in the Y stock sold is $7,500, and D has $18,000 of section 1254 costs with respect to Blackacre and $12,000 of section 1254 costs with respect to Whiteacre. Under this paragraph (c), the gain recognized by D upon the sale of Y stock is treated as ordinary income to the extent of D's section 1254 costs with respect to the stock sold, unless D establishes that a portion of such excess is not attributable to D's section 1254 costs. However, because D would recognize $7,500 in ordinary income under section 1254 with respect to the stock sold if Y sold Blackacre (the only asset the disposition of which would result in ordinary income to D under section 1254), the $7,500 of

Rules for Determining Capital Gains and Losses

gain recognized by D upon the sale of D's Y stock is attributable to D's section 1254 costs. Therefore, upon the sale of stock to E, D recognizes $7,500 of ordinary income under this paragraph (c).

Example 2. Sale of S corporation stock where gain is not entirely attributable to section 1254 costs. Assume the same facts as in Example 1, except that Blackacre has a fair market value of $25,000, and the securities have a fair market value of $20,000. Immediately prior to the sale of stock to E, if Y had sold Blackacre (its only asset the disposition of which would result in the recognition of ordinary income to D under section 1254), D would recognize $5,000 in ordinary income with respect to the stock sold under section 1254. D attaches a statement to D's tax return for 1997 detailing D's share of the fair market values and bases, and D's section 1254 costs with respect to Blackacre and Whiteacre. Therefore, upon the sale of stock to E, of the $7,500 gain recognized by D, $5,000 is ordinary income under this paragraph (c).

Example 3. Contribution of property prior to sale of S corporation stock as part of a plan to avoid recognition of ordinary income under section 1254. H owns all of the stock of Z, an S corporation. As of January 1, 1997, H has $3,000 of section 1254 costs with respect to property P, which is natural resource recapture property and Z's only asset. Property P has an adjusted basis of $5,000 and a fair market value of $8,000. H has a basis of $5,000 in Z stock, which has a fair market value of $8,000. On January 1, 1997, H contributes securities to Z which have a basis of $7,000 and a fair market value of $4,000. On April 15, 1997, H sells all of the Z stock to J for $12,000. On that date, H's adjusted basis in the Z stock is also $12,000. Based on all the facts and circumstances, the sale of stock is part of a plan (along with the contribution by H of the securities to Z) that has a principal purpose to avoid recognition of ordinary income under section 1254. Consequently, under paragraph (c)(2)(ii) of this section, H must recognize $3,000 as ordinary income under section 1254, the amount of ordinary income that H would recognize as ordinary income under section 1254 if property P were sold at fair market value. In addition, H reduces the amount realized on the sale of the stock ($12,000) by $3,000. As a result, H also recognizes a $3,000 capital loss on the sale of the stock ($9,000 amount realized less $12,000 adjusted basis).

(d) *Section 1254 costs of a shareholder.* An S corporation shareholder's section 1254 costs with respect to any natural resource recapture property held by the corporation include all of the shareholder's section 1254 costs with respect to the property in the hands of the S corporation. See § 1.1254-1(b)(1) for the definition of section 1254 costs.

(e) *Section 1254 costs of an acquiring shareholder after certain acquisitions*—(1) *Basis determined under section 1012.* If stock in an S corporation that holds natural resource recapture property is acquired and the acquiring shareholder's basis for the stock is determined solely by reference to its cost (within the meaning of section 1012), the amount of section 1254 costs with respect to the property held by the corporation in the acquiring shareholder's hands is zero on the acquisition date.

(2) *Basis determined under section 1014(a).* If stock in an S corporation that holds natural resource recapture property is acquired from a decedent and the acquiring shareholder's basis is determined, by reason of the application of section 1014(a), solely by reference to the fair market value of the stock on the date of the decedent's death or on the applicable date provided in section 2032 (relating to alternate valuation date), the amount of section 1254 costs with respect to the property held by the corporation in the acquiring shareholder's hands is zero on the acquisition date.

(3) *Basis determined under section 1014(b)(9).* If stock in an S corporation that holds natural resource recapture property is acquired before the death of the decedent, the amount of section 1254 costs with respect to the property held by the corporation in the acquiring shareholder's hands includes the amount, if any, of the section 1254 costs deducted by the acquiring shareholder before the decedent's death, to the extent that the basis of the stock (determined under section 1014(a)) is required to be reduced under section 1014(b)(9) (relating to adjustments to basis when the property is acquired before the death of the decedent).

(4) *Gifts and section 1041 transfers.* If stock is acquired in a transfer that is a gift, in a transfer that is a part sale or exchange and part gift, or in a transfer that is described in section 1041(a), the amount of section 1254 costs with respect to the property held by the corporation in the acquiring shareholder's hands immediately after the transfer is an amount equal to—

(i) The amount of section 1254 costs with respect to the property held by the corporation in the hands of the transferor immediately before the transfer; minus

(ii) The amount of any gain recognized as ordinary income under section 1254 by the transferor upon the transfer.

Reg. § 1.1254-4(e)(4)

(f) *Special rules for a corporation that was formerly an S corporation or formerly a C corporation*—(1) *Section 1254 costs of an S corporation that was formerly a C corporation.* In the case of a C corporation that holds natural resource recapture property and that elects to be an S corporation, each shareholder's section 1254 costs as of the beginning of the corporation's first taxable year as an S corporation include a pro rata share of the section 1254 costs of the corporation as of the close of the last taxable year that the corporation was a C corporation.

(2) *Examples.* The following examples illustrate the application of the provisions of paragraph (f)(1) of this section:

Example 1. *Sale of natural resource recapture property held by an S corporation that was formerly a C corporation*—(i) Y is a C corporation that elects to be an S corporation effective January 1, 1997. On that date, Y owns Oil Well, which is natural resource recapture property and a capital asset. Y has section 1254 costs of $20,000 as of the close of the last taxable year that it was a C corporation. On January 1, 1997, Oil Well has a value of $200,000 and a basis of $100,000. Thus, under section 1374, Y's net unrealized built-in gain is $100,000. Also on that date, Y's basis in Oil Well is allocated to A, Y's sole shareholder, under section 613A(c)(11) and the section 1254 costs are allocated to A under paragraph (f)(1) of this section. In addition, A has a basis in A's Y stock of $100,000.

(ii) On November 1, 1997, Y sells Oil Well for $250,000. During 1997, Y has taxable income greater than $100,000, and no other transactions or items treated as recognized built-in gain or loss. Under section 1374, Y has net recognized built-in gain of $100,000. Assuming a tax rate of 35 percent on capital gain, Y has a tax of $35,000 under section 1374. The tax of $35,000 is treated as a capital loss under section 1366(f)(2). A has a realized gain on the sale of $150,000 ($250,000 minus $100,000) of which $20,000 is recognized as ordinary income under section 1254, and $130,000 is recognized as capital gain. Consequently, A recognizes ordinary income of $20,000 and net capital gain of $95,000 ($130,000 minus $35,000) on the sale.

Example 2. *Sale of stock followed by sale of natural resource recapture property held by an S corporation that was formerly a C corporation*— (i) Assume the same facts as in *Example 1*(i). On November 1, 1997, A sells all of A's Y stock to P for $250,000. A has a realized gain on the sale of $150,000 ($250,000 minus $100,000) of which $20,000 is recognized as ordinary income under section 1254, and $130,000 is recognized as capital gain.

(ii) On November 2, 1997, Y sells Oil Well for $250,000. During 1997, Y has taxable income greater than $100,000, and no other transactions or items treated as recognized built-in gain or loss. Under section 1374, Y has net recognized built-in gain of $100,000. Assuming a tax rate of 35 percent on capital gain, Y has a tax of $35,000 under section 1374. The tax of $35,000 is treated as a capital loss under section 1366(f)(2). P has a realized gain on the sale of $150,000 ($250,000 minus $100,000), which is recognized as capital gain. Consequently, P recognizes net capital gain of $115,000 ($150,000 minus $35,000) on the sale.

(3) *Section 1254 costs of a C corporation that was formerly an S corporation.* In the case of an S corporation that becomes a C corporation, the C corporation's section 1254 costs with respect to any natural resource recapture property held by the corporation as of the beginning of the corporation's first taxable year as a C corporation include the sum of its shareholders' section 1254 costs with respect to the property as of the close of the last taxable year that the corporation was an S corporation. In the case of an S termination year as defined in section 1362(e)(4), the shareholders' section 1254 costs are determined as of the close of the S short year as defined in section 1362(e)(1)(A). See paragraph (g)(5) of this section for rules on determining the aggregate amount of the shareholders' section 1254 costs.

(g) *Determination of a shareholder's section 1254 costs upon certain stock transactions*—(1) *Issuance of stock.* Upon an issuance of stock (whether such stock is newly-issued or had been held as treasury stock) by an S corporation in a reorganization described in section 368 or otherwise—

(i) Each recipient of shares must be allocated a pro rata share (determined solely with respect to the shares issued in the transaction) of the aggregate of the S corporation shareholders' section 1254 costs with respect to natural resource recapture property held by the S corporation immediately before the issuance (as determined pursuant to paragraph (g)(5) of this section); and

(ii) Each pre-existing shareholder must reduce his or her section 1254 costs with respect to natural resource recapture property held by the S corporation immediately before the issuance by an amount equal to the pre-existing shareholder's section 1254 costs immediately before the issuance multiplied by the percentage of stock of the corporation issued in the transaction.

(2) *Natural resource recapture property acquired in exchange for stock.* If natural resource

Reg. § 1.1254-4(f)(2)

recapture property is transferred to an S corporation in exchange for stock of the S corporation (for example, in a section 351 transaction, or in a reorganization described in section 368), the S corporation must allocate to its shareholders a pro rata share of the S corporation's section 1254 costs with respect to the property immediately after the transaction (as determined under § 1.1254-3(b)(1)).

(3) *Treatment of nonvested stock.* Stock issued in connection with the performance of services that is substantially nonvested (within the meaning of § 1.83-3(b)) is treated as issued for purposes of this section at the first time it is treated as outstanding stock of the S corporation for purposes of section 1361.

(4) *Exception.* Paragraph (g)(1) of this section does not apply to stock issued in exchange for stock of the same S corporation (as for example, in a recapitalization described in section 368(a)(1)(E)).

(5) *Aggregate of S corporation shareholders' section 1254 costs with respect to natural resource recapture property held by the S corporation*—(i) *In general.* The aggregate of S corporation shareholders' section 1254 costs is equal to the sum of each shareholder's section 1254 costs. The S corporation must determine each shareholder's section 1254 costs under either paragraph (g)(5)(ii) (written data) or paragraph (g)(5)(iii) (assumptions) of this section. The S corporation may determine the section 1254 costs of some shareholders under paragraph (g)(5)(ii) of this section and of others under paragraph (g)(5)(iii) of this section.

(ii) *Written data.* An S corporation may determine a shareholder's section 1254 costs by using written data provided by a shareholder showing the shareholder's section 1254 costs with respect to natural resource recapture property held by the S corporation unless the S corporation knows or has reason to know that the written data is inaccurate. If an S corporation does not receive written data upon which it may rely, the S corporation must use the assumptions provided in paragraph (g)(5)(iii) of this section in determining a shareholder's section 1254 costs.

(iii) *Assumptions.* An S corporation that does not use written data pursuant to paragraph (g)(5)(ii) of this section to determine a shareholder's section 1254 costs must use the following assumptions to determine the shareholder's section 1254 costs—

(A) The shareholder deducted his or her share of the amount of deductions under sections 263(c), 616, and 617 in the first year in which the shareholder could claim a deduction for such amounts, unless in the case of expenditures under sections 263(c) or 616 the S corporation elected to capitalize such amounts;

(B) The shareholder was not subject to the following limitations with respect to the shareholder's depletion allowance under section 611, except to the extent a limitation applied at the corporate level: the taxable income limitation of section 613(a); the depletable quantity limitations of section 613A(c); or the limitations of sections 613A(d)(2), (3), and (4) (exclusion of retailers and refiners).

(6) *Examples.* The following examples illustrate the provisions of this paragraph (g):

Example 1. Transfer of natural resource recapture property to an S corporation in a section 351 transaction. As of January 1, 1997, A owns all the stock (20 shares) in X, an S corporation. X holds property that is not natural resource recapture property that has a fair market value of $2,000 and an adjusted basis of $2,000. On January 1, 1997, B transfers natural resource recapture property, Property P, to X in exchange for 80 shares of X stock in a transaction that qualifies under section 351. Property P has a fair market value of $8,000 and an adjusted basis of $5,000. Pursuant to section 351, B does not recognize gain on the transaction. Immediately prior to the transaction, B's section 1254 costs with respect to Property P equaled $6,000. Under § 1.1254-2(c)(1), B does not recognize any gain under section 1254 on the section 351 transaction and, under § 1.1254-3(b)(1), X's section 1254 costs with respect to Property P immediately after the contribution equal $6,000. Under paragraph (g)(2) of this section, each shareholder is allocated a pro rata share of X's section 1254 costs. The pro rata share of X's section 1254 costs that is allocated to A equals $1,200 (20 percent interest in X multiplied by X's $6,000 of section 1254 costs). The pro rata share of X's section 1254 costs that is allocated to B equals $4,800 (80 percent interest in X multiplied by X's $6,000 of section 1254 costs).

Example 2. Contribution of money in exchange for stock of an S corporation holding natural resource recapture property. As of January 1, 1997, A and B each own 50 percent of the stock (50 shares each) in X, an S corporation. X holds natural resource recapture property, Property P, which has a fair market value of $20,000 and an adjusted basis of $14,000. A's and B's section 1254 costs with respect to Property P are $4,000 and $1,500, respectively. On January 1, 1997, C contributes $20,000 to X in exchange for 100 shares of X's stock. Under paragraph (g)(1)(i) of this section, X must allocate to C a pro rata share of its shareholders' section 1254 costs. Using the

Reg. § 1.1254-4(g)(6)

assumptions set forth in paragraph (g)(5)(iii) of this section, X determines that A's section 1254 costs with respect to natural resource recapture property held by X equal $4,500. Using written data provided by B, X determines that B's section 1254 costs with respect to Property P equal $1,500. Thus, the aggregate of X's shareholders' section 1254 costs equals $6,000. C's pro rata share of the $6,000 of section 1254 costs equals $3,000 (C's 50 percent interest in X multiplied by $6,000). Under paragraph (g)(1)(ii) of this section, A's section 1254 costs are reduced by $2,000 (A's actual section 1254 costs ($4,000) multiplied by 50 percent). B's section 1254 costs are reduced by $750 (B's actual section 1254 costs ($1,500) multiplied by 50 percent).

Example 3. Merger involving an S corporation that holds natural resource recapture property. X, an S corporation with one shareholder, A, holds as its sole asset natural resource recapture property that has a fair market value of $120,000 and an adjusted basis of $40,000. A has section 1254 costs with respect to the property of $60,000. For valid business reasons, X merges into Y, an S corporation with one shareholder, B, in a reorganization described in section 368(a)(1)(A). Y holds property that is not natural resource recapture property that has a fair market value of $120,000 and basis of $120,000. Under paragraph (c) of this section, A does not recognize ordinary income under section 1254 upon the exchange of stock in the merger because A did not otherwise recognize gain on the merger. Under paragraph (g)(2) of this section, Y must allocate to A and B a pro rata share of its $60,000 of section 1254 costs. Thus, A and B are each allocated $30,000 of section 1254 costs (50 percent interest in X, each, multiplied by $60,000). [Reg. § 1.1254-4.]

☐ [T.D. 8586, 1-9-95. Amended by T.D. 8684, 10-9-96.]

[Reg. § 1.1254-5]

§ 1.1254-5. Special rules for partnerships and their partners.—(a) *In general.* This section provides rules for applying the provisions of section 1254 to partnerships and their partners upon the disposition of natural resource recapture property by the partnership and certain distributions of property by a partnership. See section 751 and the regulations thereunder for rules concerning the treatment of gain upon the transfer of a partnership interest.

(b) *Determination of gain treated as ordinary income under section 1254 upon the disposition of natural resource recapture property by a partnership*—(1) *General rule.* Upon a disposition of natural resource recapture property by a partnership, the amount treated as ordinary income under section 1254 is determined at the partner level. Each partner must recognize as ordinary income under section 1254 the lesser of—

(i) The partner's section 1254 costs with respect to the property disposed of; or

(ii) The partner's share of the amount, if any, by which the amount realized upon the sale, exchange, or involuntary conversion, or the fair market value of the property upon any other disposition, exceeds the adjusted basis of the property.

(2) *Exception to partner level recapture in the case of abusive allocations.* Paragraph (b)(1) of this section does not apply in determining the amount treated as ordinary income under section 1254 upon a disposition of section 1254 property by a partnership if the partnership has allocated the amount realized or gain recognized from the disposition with a principal purpose of avoiding the recognition of ordinary income under section 1254. In such case, the amount of gain on the disposition recaptured as ordinary income under section 1254 is determined at the partnership level.

(3) *Examples.* The provisions of paragraphs (a) and (b) of this section are illustrated by the following examples which assume that capital accounts are maintained in accordance with section 704(b) and the regulations thereunder:

Example 1. Partner level recapture—In general. A, B, and C, have equal interests in capital in Partnership ABC that was formed on January 1, 1985. The partnership acquired an undeveloped domestic oil property on January 1, 1985, for $120,000. The partnership allocated the property's basis to each partner in proportion to the partner's interest in partnership capital, so each partner was allocated $40,000 of basis. In 1985, the partnership incurred $60,000 of productive well intangible drilling and development costs with respect to the property. The partnership elected to deduct the intangible drilling and development costs as expenses under section 263(c). Each partner deducted $20,000 of the intangible drilling and development costs. Assume that depletion allowable under section 613A(c)(7)(D) for each partner for 1985 was $10,000. On January 1, 1986, the partnership sold the oil property to an unrelated third party for $210,000. Each partner's allocable share of the amount realized is $70,000. Each partner's basis in the oil property at the end of 1985 is $30,000 ($40,000 cost − $10,000 depletion deductions claimed). Each partner has a gain of $40,000 on the sale of the oil property ($70,000 amount realized − $30,000 adjusted basis in the oil property). Assume that

Reg. § 1.1254-5(a)

Rules for Determining Capital Gains and Losses

each partner's depletion allowance would not have been increased if the intangible drilling and development costs had been capitalized. Each partner's section 1254 costs with respect to the property are $20,000. Thus, A, B, and C each must treat $20,000 of gain recognized as ordinary income under section 1254(a).

Example 2. Special allocation of intangible drilling and development costs. K and L form a partnership on January 1, 1997, to acquire and develop a geothermal property as defined under section 613(e)(2). The partnership agreement provides that all intangible drilling and development costs will be allocated to partner K, and that all other items of income, gain, or loss will be allocated equally between the two partners. Assume these allocations have substantial economic effect under section 704(b) and the regulations thereunder. The partnership acquires a lease covering undeveloped acreage located in the United States for $50,000. In 1997, the partnership incurs $50,000 of intangible drilling and development costs that are allocated to partner K. The partnership also has $30,000 of depletion deductions, which are allocated equally between K and L. On January 1, 1998, the partnership sells the geothermal property to an unrelated third party for $160,000 and recognizes a gain of $140,000 ($160,000 amount realized less $20,000 adjusted basis ($50,000 unadjusted basis less $30,000 depletion deductions)). This gain is allocated equally between K and L. Because K's section 1254 costs are $65,000 and L's section 1254 costs are $15,000, K recognizes $65,000 as ordinary income under section 1254(a) and L recognizes $15,000 as ordinary income under section 1254(a). The remaining $5,000 of gain allocated to K and $55,000 of gain allocated to L is characterized without regard to section 1254.

Example 3. Section 59(e) election to capitalize intangible drilling and development costs. Partnership DK has 50 equal partners. On January 1, 1995, the partnership purchases an undeveloped oil and gas property for $100,000. The partnership allocates the property's basis equally among the partners, so each partner is allocated $2,000 of basis. In January 1995, the partnership incurs $240,000 of intangible drilling and development costs with respect to the property. The partnership elects to deduct the intangible drilling and development costs as expenses under section 263(c). Each partner is allocated $4,800 of intangible drilling and development costs. One of the partners, H, elects under section 59(e) to capitalize his $4,800 share of intangible drilling and development costs. Therefore, H is permitted to amortize his $4,800 share of intangible drilling and development costs over 60 months. H takes a $960 amortization deduction in 1995. Each of the remaining 49 partners deducts his $4,800 share of intangible drilling and development costs in 1995. Assume that depletion allowable for each partner under section 613A(c)(7)(D) for 1995 is $1,000. On December 31, 1995, the partnership sells the property for $300,000. Each partner is allocated $6,000 of amount realized. Each partner that deducted the intangible drilling and development costs has a basis in the oil property at the end of 1995 of $1,000 ($2,000 cost − $1,000 depletion deductions claimed). Each of these partners has a gain of $5,000 on the sale of the oil property ($6,000 amount realized − $1,000 adjusted basis in the property). The section 1254 costs of each partner that deducted intangible drilling and development costs are $5,800 ($4,800 intangible drilling and development costs deducted + $1,000 depletion deductions claimed). Because each partner's section 1254 costs ($5,800) exceed each partner's share of amount realized less each partner's adjusted basis ($5,000), each partner must treat his $5,000 gain recognized on the sale of the oil property as ordinary income under section 1254(a). Because H elected under section 59(e) to capitalize the $4,800 of intangible drilling and development costs and amortized only $960 of the costs in 1995, the $3,840 of unamortized intangible drilling and development costs are included in H's basis in the oil property. Therefore, at the end of 1995 H's basis in the oil property is $4,840 (($2,000 cost + $4,800 capitalized intangible drilling and development costs) − ($960 intangible drilling and development costs amortized + $1,000 depletion deduction claimed)). H's gain on the sale of the oil property is $1,160 ($6,000 amount realized − $4,840 adjusted basis). H's section 1254 costs are $1,960 ($960 intangible drilling and development costs amortized + $1,000 depletion deductions claimed). Because H's section 1254 costs ($1,960) exceed H's share of amount realized less H's adjusted basis ($1,160), H must treat the $1,160 of gain recognized as ordinary income under section 1254(a).

(c) *Section 1254 costs of a partner*—(1) *General rule.* A partner's section 1254 costs with respect to property held by a partnership include all of the partner's section 1254 costs with respect to the property in the hands of the partnership. In the case of property contributed to a partnership in a transaction described in section 721, a partner's section 1254 costs include all of the partner's section 1254 costs with respect to the property prior to contribution. Section 1.1254-1(b)(1)(iv), which provides rules concerning the treatment of suspended deductions, applies to amounts not deductible pursuant to section 704(d).

Reg. § 1.1254-5(c)(1)

(2) *Section 1254 costs of a transferee partner after certain acquisitions*—(i) *Basis determined under section 1012.* If a person acquires an interest in a partnership that holds natural resource recapture property (transferee partner) and the transferee partner's basis for the interest is determined by reference to its cost (within the meaning of section 1012), the amount of the transferee partner's section 1254 costs with respect to the property held by the partnership is zero on the acquisition date.

(ii) *Basis determined by reason of the application of section 1014(a).* If a transferee partner acquires an interest in a partnership that holds natural resource recapture property from a decedent and the transferee partner's basis is determined, by reason of the application of section 1014(a), solely by reference to the fair market value of the partnership interest on the date of the decedent's death or on the applicable date provided in section 2032 (relating to alternate valuation date), the amount of the transferee partner's section 1254 costs with respect to property held by the partnership is zero on the acquisition date.

(iii) *Basis determined by reason of the application of section 1014(b)(9).* If an interest in a partnership that holds natural resource recapture property is acquired before the death of the decedent, the amount of the transferee partner's section 1254 costs with respect to property held by the partnership shall include the amount, if any, of the section 1254 costs deducted by the transferee partner before the decedent's death, to the extent that the basis of the partner's interest (determined under section 1014(a)) is required to be reduced under section 1014(b)(9) (relating to adjustments to basis when the property is acquired before the death of the decedent).

(iv) *Gifts and section 1041 transfers.* If an interest in a partnership is transferred in a transfer that is a gift, a part sale or exchange and part gift, or a transfer that is described in section 1041(a), the amount of the transferee partner's section 1254 costs with respect to property held by the partnership immediately after the transfer is an amount equal to—

(A) The amount of the transferor partner's section 1254 costs with respect to the property immediately before the transfer; minus

(B) The amount of any gain recognized as ordinary income under section 1254 by the transferor partner upon the transfer.

(d) *Property distributed to a partner*—(1) *In general.* The section 1254 costs for any natural resource recapture property received by a partner in a distribution with respect to part or all of an interest in a partnership include—

(i) The aggregate of the partners' section 1254 costs with respect to the natural resource recapture property immediately prior to the distribution; reduced by

(ii) The amount of any gain taken into account as ordinary income under section 751 by the partnership or the partners (as constituted after the distribution) on the distribution of the natural resource recapture property.

(2) *Aggregate of partners' section 1254 costs with respect to natural resource recapture property held by a partnership*—(i) *In general.* The aggregate of partners' section 1254 costs is equal to the sum of each partner's section 1254 costs. The partnership must determine each partner's section 1254 costs under either paragraph (d)(2)(i)(A) (written data) or paragraph (d)(2)(i)(B) (assumptions) of this section. The partnership may determine the section 1254 costs of some of the partners under paragraph (d)(2)(i)(A) of this section and of others under paragraph (d)(2)(i)(B) of this section.

(A) *Written data.* A partnership may determine a partner's section 1254 costs by using written data provided by a partner showing the partner's section 1254 costs with respect to natural resource recapture property held by the partnership unless the partnership knows or has reason to know that the written data is inaccurate. If a partnership does not receive written data upon which it may rely, the partnership must use the assumptions provided in paragraph (d)(2)(i)(B) of this section in determining a partner's section 1254 costs.

(B) *Assumptions.* A partnership that does not use written data pursuant to paragraph (d)(2)(i)(A) of this section to determine a partner's section 1254 costs must use the following assumptions to determine the partner's section 1254 costs:

(*1*) The partner deducted his or her share of deductions under section 263(c), 616, or 617 for the first year in which the partner could claim a deduction for such amounts, unless in the case of expenditures under section 263(c) or 616, the partnership elected to capitalize such amounts;

(*2*) The partner was not subject to the following limitations with respect to the partner's depletion allowance under section 611, except to the extent a limitation applied at the partnership level: the taxable income limitation of section 613(a); the depletable quantity limitations of section 613A(c); or the limitations of section

Reg. § 1.1254-5(c)(2)

Rules for Determining Capital Gains and Losses

613A(d)(2), (3), and (4) (exclusion of retailers and refiners). [Reg. § 1.1254-5.]

☐ [T.D. 8586, 1-9-95.]

[Reg. § 1.1254-6]

§ 1.1254-6. Effective date of regulations.—Sections 1.1254-1 through 1.1254-3 and § 1.1254-5 are effective with respect to any disposition of natural resource recapture property occurring after March 13, 1995. The rule in § 1.1254-1(b)(2)(iv)(A)(2), relating to a nonoperating mineral interest carved out of an operating mineral interest with respect to which an expenditure has been deducted, is effective with respect to any disposition occurring after March 13, 1995, of property (within the meaning of section 614) that is placed in service by the taxpayer after December 31, 1986. Section 1.1254-4 applies to dispositions of natural resource recapture property by an S corporation (and a corporation that was formerly an S corporation) and dispositions of S corporation stock occurring on or after October 10, 1996. Sections 1.1254-2(d)(1)(ii) and 1.1254-3(b)(1)(i) and (ii) and (d)(1)(i) and (ii) are effective for dispositions of property occurring on or after October 10, 1996. [Reg. § 1.1254-6.]

☐ [T.D. 8586, 1-9-95. Amended by T.D. 8684, 10-9-96.]

[Reg. § 16A.1255-1]

§ 16A.1255-1. General rule for treatment of gain from disposition of section 126 property (Temporary).—(a) *Ordinary income*—(1) *General rule.* Except as otherwise provided in this section and § 16A.1255-2, if section 126 property is disposed of after September 30, 1979, then under section 1255(a)(1) there shall be recognized as ordinary income the lesser of—

(i) The "excludable portion" under section 126,

or

(ii)(A) The excess of the amount realized (in the case of a sale, exchange, or involuntary conversion), or the fair market value of the section 126 property (in the case of any other disposition), over the adjusted basis of the property, less

(B) The amount recognized as ordinary income under the other provisions of chapter 1, subchapter P, part IV of the Code.

(2) *Application of section.* Any gain treated as ordinary income under section 1255(a)(1) shall be recognized as ordinary income notwithstanding any other provision of subtitle A of the Code except that section 1255 does not apply to the extent the gain is recognized as ordinary income under the other provisions of subchapter P, part IV of the Code. For special rules with respect to the application of section 1255, see § 16A.1255-2. For the relation of section 1255 to other provisions, see paragraph (c) of this section.

(3) *Meaning of terms.* For purposes of section 1255 and these regulations—

(i) The term "section 126 property" means any property acquired, improved, or otherwise modified as a result of a payment listed in section 126(a) which has been certified by the Secretary of Agriculture as primarily for the purpose of conservation;

(ii) The term "excludable portion" is defined in § 16A.126-1(b)(5);

(iii) The term "disposition" has the same meaning as in § 1.1245-1(a)(3);

(iv) The term "date of receipt of the section 126 payment" means the last date the government made a payment for the improvements.

(4) *Applicable percentage.* If section 126 property is disposed of less than 10 years after the date of receipt of the last payment which has been certified by the Secretary of Agriculture as primarily for the purpose of conservation, the "applicable percentage" is 100 percent; if section 126 property is disposed of more than 10 years after that date, the applicable percentage is 100 percent reduced (but not below zero) by 10 percent for each year or part thereof in excess of 10 years such property was held after the date of the section 126 payment.

(5) *Portion of parcel.* The amount of gain to be recognized as ordinary income under section 1255(a)(1) shall be determined separately for each parcel of section 126 property in a manner consistent with the principles of § 1.1245-1(a)(4) and (5) relating to gain from disposition of certain depreciable property. If (i) only a portion of a parcel of section 126 property is disposed of in a transaction, or if two or more portions of a single parcel are disposed of in one transaction, and (ii) the aggregate of "excludable portions" with respect to any such portion cannot be established to the satisfaction of the Commissioner, then the aggregate of the "excludable portions" in respect of the entire parcel shall be allocated to each portion in proportion to the fair market value of each at the time of the disposition.

(b) *Instances of nonapplication*—(1) *In general.* Section 1255 does not apply if a taxpayer disposes of section 126 property more than 20 years after receipt of the last section 126 payment with respect to the property.

(2) *Losses.* Section 1255(a)(1) does not apply to losses. Thus, section 1255(a)(1) does not apply if a loss is realized upon a sale, exchange, or involuntary conversion of property, all of which is

Reg. § 16A.1255-1(b)(2)

section 126 property, nor does the section apply to a disposition of the property other than by way of sale, exchange, or involuntary conversion if at the time of the disposition the fair market value of the property is not greater than its adjusted basis.

(c) *Relation of section 1255 to other provisions*—(1) *General.* The provisions of section 1255 apply notwithstanding any other provisions of subtitle A of the Code except that they do not apply to the extent gain is recognized as ordinary income under the other provisions of subchapter P, part IV of the Code. Thus, unless an exception or limitation under § 16A.1255-2 applies, gain under section 1255(a)(1) is recognized notwithstanding any contrary nonrecognition provision or income characterizing provision. For example, since section 1255 overrides section 1231 (relating to property used in the trade or business), the gain recognized under section 1255 upon a disposition of section 126 property will be treated as ordinary income and only the remaining gain, if any, from the disposition may be considered as gain from the sale or exchange of property to which section 1231 applies. See example (1) of paragraph (d) of this section.

(2) *Nonrecognition sections overridden.* The nonrecognition of gain provisions of subtitle A of the Code which section 1255 overrides include, but are not limited to, sections 267(d), 311(a), 336, 337, and 512(b)(5). See § 16A.1255-2 for the extent to which section 1255(a)(1) overrides sections 332, 351, 361, 371(a), 374(a), 721, 731, 1031, and 1033.

(3) *Installment method.* Gain from a disposition to which section 1255(a)(1) applies may be reported under the installment method if such method is otherwise available under section 453 of the Code. In such a case, the portion of the installment payment that is gain is treated as follows: first as ordinary gain under other sections of chapter I, subchapter P, part IV of the Code until all that gain has been reported; next as ordinary gain to which section 1255 applies until all that gain is reported; and finally as gain under other sections of chapter I, subchapter D, part IV of the Code. For treatment of amounts as interest on certain deferred payments, see section 483.

(4) *Exempt income.* With regard to exempt income, the principles of § 1.1245-6(e) shall be applicable.

(5) *Treatment of gain not recognized under section 1255(a)(1).* For treatment of gain not recognized under this section, the principles of § 1.1245-6(f) shall be applicable.

(d) *Example.* The provisions of this section may be illustrated by the following example:

Example (1). Individual A uses the calendar year as his taxable year. On April 10, 1995, A sells for $75,000 section 126 property with an adjusted basis of $52,500 for a realized gain of $22,500. The excludable portion under section 126 was $18,000. A received the section 126 payment on January 5, 1990. No gain is recognized as ordinary gain under sections 1231 through 1254. Because the applicable percentage, 100 percent, of the aggregate of the section 126 improvements ($18,000), $18,000, is lower than the gain realized, $22,500, the amount of gain recognized as ordinary income under section 1255(a)(1) is $18,000. The remaining $4,500 of the gain may be treated as gain from the sale or exchange of property described in section 1231. [Temporary Reg. § 16A.1255-1.]

□ [T.D. 7778, 5-18-81.]

[Reg. § 16A.1255-2]

§ 16A.1255-2. **Special rules (Temporary).**—(a) *Exception for gifts*—(1) *General rule.* In general, no gain shall be recognized under section 1255(a)(1) upon a disposition of section 126 property by gift. For purposes of section 1255 and this paragraph, the term "gift" shall have the same meaning as in § 1.1245-4(a) and, with respect to the application of this paragraph, principles illustrated by the examples of § 1.1245-4(a)(2) shall apply.

(2) *Disposition in part a sale or exchange and in part a gift.* Where a disposition of section 126 property is in part a sale or exchange and in part a gift, the amount of gain which shall be recognized as ordinary income under section 1255(a)(1) shall be computed under § 16A.1255-1(a)(1), applied by treating the gain realized (for purposes of § 16A.1255-1(a)(1)(ii)), as the excess of the amount realized over the adjusted basis of the section 126 property.

(3) *Treatment of section 126 property in hands of transferee.* See paragraph (d) of this section for treatment of the transferee in the case of a disposition to which this paragraph applies.

(4) *Examples.* The provisions of this paragraph may be illustrated by the following examples:

Example (1). On March 2, 1986, A makes a gift to B of a parcel of land having an adjusted basis of $40,000 and fair market value of $65,000. On the date of that gift, the aggregate of excludable portions under section 126 was $24,000. The section 126 payments were all received on January 15, 1981. Upon making the gift, A recognizes no gain under section 1255(a)(1). See paragraph (a)(1) of this section. For treatment of the prop-

Rules for Determining Capital Gains and Losses

erty in the hands of B, see example (1) of paragraph (d)(3) of this section.

Example (2). (i) Assume the same facts as in example (1), except that A transfers the land to B for $50,000. Assume further that no gain is recognized as ordinary income under any other provision of chapter I, subchapter P, part IV of the Code. Thus, the gain realized is $10,000 (amount realized, $50,000, minus adjusted basis, $40,000), and A has made a gift of $15,000 (fair market value, $65,000, minus amount realized, $50,000).

(ii) Upon the transfer of the land to B, A recognizes $10,000 as ordinary income under section 1255(a)(1), computed under paragraph (a)(2) of this section as follows:

(1) Aggregate of excludable portions under section 126	$24,000
(2) Multiply: Applicable percentage for land disposed if within sixth year after section 126 payments were received	100%
(3) Amount in § 16A.1255-1(a)(1)(i)	$24,000
(4) Gain realized (see (i) of this example)	$10,000
(5) Amount in § 16A.1255-1(a)(1)(ii) applied in accordance with paragraph (a)(2) of this section	$10,000
(6) Lower of line (3) or line (5)	$10,000

Thus, the entire gain realized on the transfer, $10,000, is recognized as ordinary income. For treatment of the farm land in the hands of B, see example (2) of paragraph (d)(3) of this section.

(b) *Exception for transfer at death* —(1) *In general.* Except as provided in section 691 (relating to income in respect of a decedent), no gain shall be recognized under section 1255(a)(1) upon a transfer at death. For purposes of section 1255 and this paragraph, the term "transfer at death" shall have the same meaning as in § 1.1245-4(b) and, with respect to the application of this paragraph, principles illustrated by the examples of § 1.1245-4(b)(2) shall apply.

(2) *Treatment of section 126 property in hands of transferee.* If, as of the date a person acquires section 126 property from a decedent, the person's basis is determined by reason of the application of section 1014(a), solely by reference to the fair market value of the property on the date of the decedent's death, or on the applicable date provided in section 2032 (relating to alternative valuation date), then on that date the aggregate of excludable portions under section 126 in the hands of such transferee is zero.

(c) *Limitation for certain tax-free transactions*—(1) *Limitation on amount of gain.* Upon a transfer of section 126 property described in paragraph (c)(2) of this section, the amount of gain recognized as ordinary income under section 1255(a)(1) shall not exceed an amount equal to the excess (if any) or (i) the amount of gain recognized to the transferor on the transfer (determined without regard to section 1255) over (ii) the amount (if any) of gain recognized as ordinary income under the other provisions of chapter I, subchapter P, part IV of the Code. For purposes of paragraph (c)(1) of this section, the principles of § 1.1245-4(c)(1) shall apply. Thus, in the case of a transfer of section 126 property and other property in one transaction, the amount realized from the disposition of the section 126 property (as determined in a manner consistent with the principles of § 1.1245-1(a)(5)) shall consist of that portion of the fair market value of each property acquired which bears the same ratio to the fair market value of the acquired property as the amount realized from the disposition of the section 126 property bears to the total amount realized. The preceding sentence shall be applied solely for purposes of computing the portion of the total gain (determined without regard to section 1255) which is eligible to be recognized as ordinary income under section 1255(a)(1). The provisions of this paragraph do not apply to a disposition of property to an organization (other than a cooperative described in section 521) which is exempt from the tax imposed by chapter 1 of the Code.

(2) *Transfers covered.* The transfers referred to in paragraph (c)(1) of this section are transfers of section 126 property in which the basis of the property in the hands of the transferee is determined by reference to its basis in the hands of the transferor by reason of the application of any of the following provisions:

(i) Section 332 (relating to distributions in complete liquidation of an 80-percent-or-more controlled subsidiary corporation). For application of paragraph (c)(1) of this section to such a complete liquidation, the principles of § 1.1245-4(c)(3) shall apply. Thus, for example, the provisions of paragraph (c)(1) of this section do not apply to a liquidating distribution of section 126 property by an 80-percent-or-more controlled subsidiary to its parent if the parent's basis for the property is determined, under section

Reg. § 16A.1255-2(c)(2)

53,630 Rules for Determining Capital Gains and Losses

See p. 20,601 for regulations not amended to reflect law changes

334(b)(2), by reference to its basis for the stock of the subsidiary.

(ii) Section 351 (relating to transfer to a corporation controlled by the transferor).

(iii) Section 361 (relating to exchanges pursuant to certain corporate reorganizations).

(iv) Section 371(a) (relating to exchanges pursuant to certain receivership and bankruptcy proceedings).

(v) Section 374(a) (relating to exchanges pursuant to certain railroad reorganizations).

(vi) Section 721 (relating to transfers to a partnership in exchange for a partnership interest). See paragraph (e) of this section.

(vii) Section 731 (relating to distributions by a partnership to a partner). For special carry-over of basis rule, see paragraph (e) of this section.

(viii) Section 1031 (relating to like kind exchanges).

(ix) Section 1034 (relating to rollover of gain on the sale of a principal residence).

(3) *Treatment of section 126 property in the hands of transferee.* See paragraph (d) of this section for treatment of the transferee in the case of a disposition to which this paragraph applies.

(4) *Examples.* The provisions of this paragraph may be illustrated by the following examples:

Example (1). On January 4, 1986, A holds a parcel of property that is section 126 property having an adjusted basis of $15,000 and a fair market value of $40,000. On that date he transfers the parcel to corporation M in exchange for stock in the corporation worth $40,000 in a transaction qualifying under section 351. On the date of the transfer, the aggregate of excludable portions under section 126 with respect to the transferred property is $18,000 and all of such amount was received on March 25, 1981. With regard to section 1255, A would recognize no gain under section 351 upon the transfer and M's basis for the land would be determined under section 362(a) by reference to its basis in the hands of A. Thus, as a result of the disposition, no gain is recognized as ordinary income under section 1255 by A since the amount of gain recognized under that section is limited to the amount of gain which is recognized under section 351 (determined without regard to section 1255). See paragraph (c)(1) of this section. For treatment of the section 126 property in the hands of B, see paragraph (d)(1) of this section.

Example (2). Assume the same facts in example (1), except that A transferred the property to M for stock in the corporation worth $32,000 and $8,000 cash. The gain realized is $25,000 (amount realized, $40,000, minus adjusted basis, $15,000). Without regard to section 1255, A would recognize $8,000 of gain under section 351(b). Assume further that no gain is recognized as ordinary income under the other provisions of chapter 1, subchapter P, part IV of the Code. Therefore, since the applicable percentage, 100 percent of the aggregate excludable portions under section 126, $18,000, is lower than the gain realized, $25,000, the amount of gain to be recognized as ordinary income under section 1255(a)(1) would be $18,000 if the provisions of paragraph (c)(1) of this section do not apply. Since under section 351(b) gain in the amount of $8,000 would be recognized to the transferor without regard to section 1255, the limitation provided in paragraph (c)(1) of this section limits the gain taken into account by A under section 1255(a)(1) to $8,000.

Example (3). Assume the same facts as in example (2), except that $5,000 of gain is recognized as ordinary income under section 1251(c)(1). The amount of gain recognized as ordinary income under section 1255(a)(1) is $3,000 computed as follows:

(1) Amount of gain under section 1255(a)(1) (determined without regard to paragraph (c)(1) of this section):
    (a) Aggregate of excludable portions under section 126 .... $18,000
    (b) Multiply: Applicable percentage for property disposed of within the fifth year after section 126 payments were received 100%
    (c) Amount in § 16A.1255-1(a)(1)(i) $18,000

    (d) Gain realized (amount realized $40,000 less adjusted basis, $15,000) $25,000
    (e) Lower of line (c) or line (d)... $18,000

(2) Limitation in paragraph (c)(1) of this section:
    (a) Gain recognized (determined without regard to section 1255) .... $ 8,000
    (b) Minus: Gain recognized as ordinary income under section 1251(c)(1) .... $ 5,000

    (c) Difference.. $ 3,000
(3) Lower of line (1)(e) or line (2)(c) .... $ 3,000

Reg. § 16A.1255-2(c)(3)

Thus, the entire gain recognized under section 351(b) (determined without regard to sections 1251 and 1255), $8,000, is recognized as ordinary income since that amount is equal to the sum of the gain recognized as ordinary income under section 1251(c)(1), $5,000, and under section 1255(a)(1), $3,000.

(d) *Treatment of section 126 property received by a transferee in a disposition by gift and certain tax-free transactions*—(1) *General rule.* If section 126 property is disposed of in a transaction which is either a gift to which paragraph (a)(1) of this section applies, or a completely tax-free transfer to which paragraph (c)(1) of this section applies, then for purposes of section 1255—

(i) The aggregate of the excludable portions under section 126 in respect of the land in the hands of the transferee immediately after the disposition shall be an amount equal to the amount of such aggregate in the hands of the transferor immediately before the disposition, and

(ii) For purposes of applying section 1255 upon a subsequent disposition by the transferee (including a computation of the applicable percentage), the dates of receipt of section 126 payments shall not be affected by the dispositions.

(2) *Certain partially tax-free transfers.* If section 126 property is disposed of in a transaction which either is in part a sale or exchange and in part a gift to which paragraph (a)(2) of this section applies, or is a partially tax-free transfer to which paragraph (c)(1) of this section applies, then for purposes of section 1255 the amount determined under paragraph (d)(1) of this section shall be reduced by the amount of gain taken into account under section 1255 by the transferor upon the disposition. Upon a subsequent disposition by the transferee, the dates of receipt of section 126 payments remain the same in the hands of the transferee as they were in the hands of the transferor. With respect to the 175 and 182 deductions taken by the transferee, the holding period shall not include the holding period of the transferor.

(3) *Examples.* The provisions of this paragraph may be illustrated by the following examples:

Example (1). Assume the same facts as in example (1) of paragraph (a)(4) of this section. Therefore, on the date B receives the land in the gift transaction, under paragraph (d)(1) of this section the aggregate of excludable portions under section 126 in respect of the land in the hands of B is the amount in the hands of A, $24,000, and for purposes of applying section 1255 upon a subsequent disposition by B (including a computation of the applicable percentage) the date the section 126 payments were received is the same as it was when the property was in A's hands (January 15, 1981).

Example (2). Assume the same facts as in example (2) of paragraph (a)(4) of this section. Under paragraph (d)(2) of this section, the aggregate of excludable portions under section 126 which pass over to B for purposes of section 1255 is $14,000 ($24,000 excluded under section 126 minus $10,000 gain recognized under section 1255(d)(1) in accordance with example (2) of paragraph (a)(4) of this section). The date the section 126 payments were received is the same as when the property was in B's hands (January 15, 1981).

(e) *Disposition of section 126 property not specifically covered.* If section 126 property is disposed of in a transaction not specifically covered under § 16A.1255-1, and this section, then the principles of section 1245 shall apply. [Temporary Reg. § 16A.1255-2.]

☐ [T.D. 7778, 5-18-81.]

[Reg. § 1.1256(e)-1]

§ 1.1256(e)-1. Identification of hedging transactions.—(a) *Identification and recordkeeping requirements.* Under section 1256(e)(2)(C), a taxpayer that enters into a hedging transaction must identify the transaction as a hedging transaction before the close of the day on which the taxpayer enters into the transaction.

(b) *Requirements for identification.* The identification of a hedging transaction for purposes of section 1256(e)(2)(C) must satisfy the requirements of § 1.1221-2(e)(1). Solely for purposes of section 1256(f)(1), however, an identification that does not satisfy all of the requirements of § 1.1221-2(e)(1) is nevertheless treated as an identification under section 1256(e)(2)(C).

(c) *Consistency with § 1.1221-2.* Any identification for purposes of § 1.1221-2(e)(1) is also an identification for purposes of this section. If a taxpayer satisfies the requirements of paragraph (f)(1)(ii) of § 1.1221-2, the transaction is treated as if it were not identified as a hedging transaction for purposes of section 1256(e)(2)(C).

(d) *Effective date.* This section applies to transactions entered into on or after October 1, 1994. [Reg. § 1.1256(e)-1.]

☐ [T.D. 8555, 7-13-94.]

[Reg. § 1.1258-1]

§ 1.1258-1. Netting rule for certain conversion transactions.—(a) *Purpose.* The purpose of this section is to provide taxpayers with a method to net certain gains and losses from positions of the same conversion transaction before determining the amount of gain treated as ordinary income under section 1258(a).

Reg. § 1.1258-1(a)

(b) *Netting of gain and loss for identified transactions*—(1) *In general.* If a taxpayer disposes of or terminates all the positions of an identified netting transaction (as defined in paragraph (b)(2) of this section) within a 14-day period in a single taxable year, all gains and losses on those positions taken into account for federal tax purposes within that period (other than built-in losses as defined in paragraph (c) of this section) are netted solely for purposes of determining the amount of gain treated as ordinary income under section 1258(a). For purposes of the preceding sentence, a taxpayer is treated as disposing of any position that is treated as sold under any provision of the Code or regulations thereunder (for example, under section 1256(a)(1)).

(2) *Identified netting transaction.* For purposes of this section, an identified netting transaction is a conversion transaction (as defined in section 1258(c)) that the taxpayer identifies as an identified netting transaction on its books and records. Identification of each position of the conversion transaction must be made before the close of the day on which the position becomes part of the conversion transaction. No particular form of identification is necessary, but all the positions of a single conversion transaction must be identified as part of the same transaction and must be distinguished from all other positions.

(c) *Definition of built-in loss.* For purposes of this section, built-in loss means—

(1) Built-in loss as defined in section 1258(d)(3)(B); and

(2) If a taxpayer realizes gain or loss on any one position of a conversion transaction (for example, under section 1256), as of the date that gain or loss is realized, any unrecognized loss in any other position of the conversion transaction that is not disposed of, terminated, or treated as sold under any provision of the Code or regulations thereunder within 14 days of and within the same taxable year as the realization event.

(d) *Examples.* These examples illustrate this section:

Example 1. Identified netting transaction with simultaneous actual dispositions. (i) On December 1, 1995, *A* purchases 1,000 shares of *XYZ* stock for $100,000 and enters into a forward contract to sell 1,000 shares of *XYZ* stock on November 30, 1997, for $110,000. The *XYZ* stock is actively traded as defined in § 1.1092(d)-1(a) and is a capital asset in *A*'s hands. *A* maintains books and records on which, on December 1, 1995, it identifies the two positions as all the positions of a single conversion transaction. *A* owns no other *XYZ* stock. On December 1, 1996, when the applicable imputed income amount for the transaction is $7,000, *A* sells the 1,000 shares of *XYZ* stock for $95,000. On the same day, *A* terminates its forward contract with its counterparty, receiving $10,200. No dividends were received on the stock during the time it was part of the conversion transaction.

(ii) The *XYZ* stock and forward contract are positions of a conversion transaction. Under section 1258(c)(1), substantially all of *A*'s expected return from the overall transaction is attributable to the time value of the net investment in the transaction. Under section 1258(c)(2)(B), the transaction is an applicable straddle as defined in section 1258(d)(1).

(iii) *A* disposed of or terminated all the positions of the conversion transaction within 14 days and within the same taxable year as required by paragraph (b)(1) of this section. The transaction is an identified netting transaction because it meets the identification requirement of paragraph (b)(2) of this section. Solely for purposes of section 1258(a), the $5,000 loss realized ($100,000 basis less $95,000 amount realized) on the disposition of the *XYZ* stock is netted against the $10,200 gain recognized on the disposition of the forward contract. Thus, the net gain from the conversion transaction for purposes of section 1258(a) is $5,200 ($10,200 gain less $5,000 loss). Only the $5,200 net gain is recharacterized as ordinary income under section 1258(a) even though the applicable imputed income amount is $7,000. For federal tax purposes other than section 1258(a), *A* has recognized a $10,200 gain on the disposition of the forward contract ($5,200 of which is treated as ordinary income) and realized a separate $5,000 loss on the sale of the *XYZ* stock.

Example 2. Identified netting transaction with built-in loss. (i) The facts are the same as in *Example 1*, except that *A* had purchased the *XYZ* stock for $104,000 on May 15, 1995. The *XYZ* stock had a fair market value of $100,000 on December 1, 1995, the date it became part of a conversion transaction.

(ii) The results are the same as in *Example 1*, except that *A* has built-in loss (in addition to the $5,000 loss that arose economically during the period of the conversion transaction), as defined in section 1258(d)(3)(B), of $4,000 on the *XYZ* stock. That $4,000 built-in loss is not netted against the $10,200 gain on the forward contract for purposes of section 1258(a). Thus, the net gain from the conversion transaction for purposes of section 1258(a) is $5,200, the same as in *Example*

Reg. § 1.1258-1(b)(1)

1. The $4,000 built-in loss is recognized and has a character determined without regard to section 1258.

(e) *Effective date and transition rule*—(1) *In general.* These regulations are effective for conversion transactions that are outstanding on or after December 21, 1995.

(2) *Transition rule for identification requirements.* In the case of a conversion transaction entered into before February 20, 1996, paragraph (b)(2) of this section is treated as satisfied if the identification is made before the close of business on February 20, 1996. [Reg. § 1.1258-1.]

☐ [*T.D.* 8649, 12-20-95.]

Special Rules for Bonds and Other Debt Instruments
[Reg. § 1.1271-0]

§ 1.1271-0. **Original issue discount; effective date; table of contents.**—(a) *Effective date.* Except as otherwise provided, §§ 1.1271-1 through 1.1275-5 apply to debt instruments issued on or after April 4, 1994. Taxpayers, however, may rely on these sections (as contained in 26 CFR part 1 revised April 1, 1996) for debt instruments issued after December 21, 1992, and before April 4, 1994.

(b) *Table of contents.* This section lists captioned paragraphs contained in §§ 1.1271-1 through 1.1275-7T.

§ 1.1271-1. *Special rules applicable to amounts received on retirement, sale, or exchange of debt instruments.*

(a) Intention to call before maturity.

(1) In general.

(2) Exceptions.

(b) Short-term obligations.

(1) In general.

(2) Method of making elections.

(3) Counting conventions.

§ 1.1272-1. *Current inclusion of OID in income.*

(a) Overview.

(1) In general.

(2) Debt instruments not subject to OID inclusion rules.

(b) Accrual of OID.

(1) Constant yield method.

(2) Exceptions.

(3) Modifications.

(4) Special rules for determining the OID allocable to an accrual period.

(c) Yield and maturity of certain debt instruments subject to contingencies.

(1) Applicability.

(2) Payment schedule that is significantly more likely than not to occur.

(3) Mandatory sinking fund provision.

(4) Consistency rule. [Reserved]

(5) Treatment of certain options.

(6) Subsequent adjustments.

(7) Effective date.

(d) Certain debt instruments that provide for a fixed yield.

(e) Convertible debt instruments.

(f) Special rules to determine whether a debt instrument is a short-term obligation.

(1) Counting of either the issue date or maturity date.

(2) Coordination with paragraph (c) of this section for certain sections of the Internal Revenue Code.

(g) Basis adjustment.

(h) Debt instruments denominated in a currency other than the U.S. dollar.

(i) [Reserved]

(j) Examples.

§ 1.1272-2. *Treatment of debt instruments purchased at a premium.*

(a) In general.

(b) Definitions and special rules.

(1) Purchase.

(2) Premium.

(3) Acquisition premium.

(4) Acquisition premium fraction.

(5) Election to accrue discount on a constant yield basis.

(6) Special rules for determining basis.

(c) Examples.

§ 1.1272-3. *Election by a holder to treat all interest on a debt instrument as OID.*

(a) Election.

(b) Scope of election.

(1) In general.

(2) Exceptions, limitations, and special rules.

(c) Mechanics of the constant yield method.

(1) In general.

(2) Special rules to determine adjusted basis.

(d) Time and manner of making the election.

(e) Revocation of election.

(f) Effective date.

§ 1.1273-1. *Definition of OID.*

(a) In general.

53,634 Special Rules, Bonds & Other Debt Instruments

See p. 20,601 for regulations not amended to reflect law changes

(b) Stated redemption price at maturity.

(c) Qualified stated interest.

(1) Definition.

(2) Debt instruments subject to contingencies.

(3) Variable rate debt instrument.

(4) Stated interest in excess of qualified stated interest.

(5) Short-term obligations.

(d) *De minimis* OID.

(1) In general.

(2) *De minimis* amount.

(3) Installment obligations.

(4) Special rule for interest holidays, teaser rates, and other interest shortfalls.

(5) Treatment of *de minimis* OID by holders.

(e) Definitions.

(1) Installment obligation.

(2) Self-amortizing installment obligation.

(3) Weighted average maturity.

(f) Examples.

§ 1.1273-2. Determination of issue price and issue date.

(a) Debt instruments issued for money.

(1) Issue price.

(2) Issue date.

(b) Publicly traded debt instruments issued for property.

(1) Issue price.

(2) Issue date.

(c) Debt instruments issued for publicly traded property.

(1) Issue price.

(2) Issue date.

(d) Other debt instruments.

(1) Issue price.

(2) Issue date.

(e) Special rule for certain sales to bond houses, brokers, or similar persons.

(f) Traded on an established market (publicly traded).

(1) In general.

(2) Exchange listed property.

(3) Market traded property.

(4) Property appearing on a quotation medium.

(5) Readily quotable debt instruments.

(6) Effect of certain temporary restrictions on trading.

(7) Convertible debt instruments.

(g) Treatment of certain cash payments incident to lending transactions.

(1) Applicability.

(2) Payments from borrower to lender.

(3) Payments from lender to borrower.

(4) Payments between lender and third party.

(5) Examples.

(h) Investment units.

(1) In general.

(2) Consistent allocation by holders and issuer.

(i) [Reserved]

(j) Convertible debt instruments.

(k) Below-market loans subject to section 7872(b).

(l) [Reserved]

(m) Treatment of amounts representing pre-issuance accrued interest.

(1) Applicability.

(2) Exclusion of pre-issuance accrued interest from issue price.

(3) Example.

§ 1.1274-1. Debt instruments to which section 1274 applies.

(a) In general.

(b) Exceptions.

(1) Debt instrument with adequate stated interest and no OID.

(2) Exceptions under sections 1274(c)(1)(B), 1274(c)(3), 1274A(c), and 1275(b)(1).

(3) Other exceptions to section 1274.

(c) Examples.

§ 1.1274-2. Issue price of debt instruments to which section 1274 applies.

(a) In general.

(b) Issue price.

(1) Debt instruments that provide for adequate stated interest; stated principal amount.

(2) Debt instruments that do not provide for adequate stated interest; imputed principal amount.

(3) Debt instruments issued in a potentially abusive situation; fair market value.

(c) Determination of whether a debt instrument provides for adequate stated interest.

(1) In general.

(2) Determination of present value.

(d) Treatment of certain options.

(e) Mandatory sinking funds.

Reg. § 1.1271-0(b)

Special Rules, Bonds & Other Debt Instruments

See p. 20,601 for regulations not amended to reflect law changes

(f) Treatment of variable rate debt instruments.

(1) Stated interest at a qualified floating rate.

(2) Stated interest at a single objective rate.

(g) Treatment of contingent payment debt instruments.

(h) Examples.

(i) [Reserved]

(j) Special rules for tax-exempt obligations.

(1) Certain variable rate debt instruments.

(2) Contingent payment debt instruments.

(3) Effective date.

§ 1.1274-3. Potentially abusive situations defined.

(a) In general.

(b) Operating rules.

(1) Debt instrument exchanged for nonrecourse financing.

(2) Nonrecourse debt with substantial down payment.

(3) Clearly excessive interest.

(c) Other situations to be specified by Commissioner.

(d) Consistency rule.

§ 1.1274-4. Test rate.

(a) Determination of test rate of interest.

(1) In general.

(2) Test rate for certain debt instruments.

(b) Applicable Federal rate.

(c) Special rules to determine the term of a debt instrument for purposes of determining the applicable Federal rate.

(1) Installment obligations.

(2) Certain variable rate debt instruments.

(3) Counting of either the issue date or the maturity date.

(4) Certain debt instruments that provide for principal payments uncertain as to time.

(d) Foreign currency loans.

(e) Examples.

§ 1.1274-5. Assumptions.

(a) In general.

(b) Modifications of debt instruments.

(1) In general.

(2) Election to treat buyer as modifying the debt instrument.

(c) Wraparound indebtedness.

(d) Consideration attributable to assumed debt.

§ 1.1274A-1. Special rules for certain transactions where stated principal amount does not exceed $2,800,000.

(a) In general.

(b) Rules for both qualified and cash method debt instruments.

(1) Sale-leaseback transactions.

(2) Debt instruments calling for contingent payments.

(3) Aggregation of transactions.

(4) Inflation adjustment of dollar amounts.

(c) Rules for cash method debt instruments.

(1) Time and manner of making cash method election.

(2) Successors of electing parties.

(3) Modified debt instrument.

(4) Debt incurred or continued to purchase or carry a cash method debt instrument.

§ 1.1275-1. Definitions.

(a) Applicability.

(b) Adjusted issue price.

(1) In general.

(2) Adjusted issue price for subsequent holders.

(c) OID.

(d) Debt instrument.

(e) Tax-exempt obligations.

(f) Issue.

(1) Debt instruments issued on or after March 13, 2001.

(2) Debt instruments issued before March 13, 2001.

(3) Transition rule.

(4) Cross-references for reopening and aggregation rules.

(g) Debt instruments issued by a natural person.

(h) Publicly offered debt instrument.

(i) [Reserved]

(j) Life annuity exception under section 1275(a)(1)(B)(i).

(1) Purpose.

(2) General rule.

(3) Availability of a cash surrender option.

(4) Availability of a loan secured by the contract.

(5) Minimum payout provision.

(6) Maximum payout provision.

(7) Decreasing payout provision.

(8) Effective dates.

Reg. § 1.1271-0(b)

53,636   Special Rules, Bonds & Other Debt Instruments

See p. 20,601 for regulations not amended to reflect law changes

§ 1.1275-2. Special rules relating to debt instruments.

(a) Payment ordering rule.

(1) In general.

(2) Exceptions.

(b) Debt instruments distributed by corporations with respect to stock.

(1) Treatment of distribution.

(2) Issue date.

(c) Aggregation of debt instruments.

(1) General rule.

(2) Exception if separate issue price established.

(3) Special rule for debt instruments that provide for the issuance of additional debt instruments.

(4) Examples.

(d) Special rules for Treasury securities.

(1) Issue price and issue date.

(2) Reopenings of Treasury securities.

(e) Disclosure of certain information to holders.

(f) Treatment of pro rata prepayments.

(1) Treatment as retirement of separate debt instrument.

(2) Definition of pro rata prepayment.

(g) Anti-abuse rule.

(1) In general.

(2) Unreasonable result.

(3) Examples.

(4) Effective date.

(h) Remote and incidental contingencies.

(1) In general.

(2) Remote contingencies.

(3) Incidental contingencies.

(4) Aggregation rule.

(5) Consistency rule.

(6) Subsequent adjustments.

(7) Effective date.

(i) [Reserved]

(j) Treatment of certain modifications.

(k) Reopenings.

(1) In general.

(2) Definitions.

(3) Qualified reopening.

(4) Issuer's treatment of a qualified reopening.

(5) Effective date.

§ 1.1275-3. OID information reporting requirements.

(a) In general.

(b) Information required to be set forth on face of debt instruments that are not publicly offered.

(1) In general.

(2) Time for legending.

(3) Legend must survive reissuance upon transfer.

(4) Exceptions.

(c) Information required to be reported to Secretary upon issuance of publicly offered debt instruments.

(1) In general.

(2) Time for filing information return.

(3) Exceptions.

(d) Application to foreign issuers and U.S. issuers of foreign-targeted debt instruments.

(e) Penalties.

(f) Effective date.

§ 1.1275-4. Contingent payment debt instruments.

(a) Applicability.

(1) In general.

(2) Exceptions.

(3) Insolvency and default.

(4) Convertible debt instruments.

(5) Remote and incidental contingencies.

(b) Noncontingent bond method.

(1) Applicability.

(2) In general.

(3) Description of method.

(4) Comparable yield and projected payment schedule.

(5) Qualified stated interest.

(6) Adjustments.

(7) Adjusted issue price, adjusted basis, and retirement.

(8) Character on sale, exchange, or retirement.

(9) Operating rules.

(c) Method for debt instruments not subject to the noncontingent bond method.

(1) Applicability.

(2) Separation into components.

(3) Treatment of noncontingent payments.

(4) Treatment of contingent payments.

(5) Basis different from adjusted issue price.

(6) Treatment of a holder on sale, exchange, or retirement.

(7) Examples.

(d) Rules for tax-exempt obligations.

Reg. § 1.1271-0(b)

Special Rules, Bonds & Other Debt Instruments

See p. 20,601 for regulations not amended to reflect law changes

(1) In general.

(2) Certain tax-exempt obligations with interest-based or revenue-based payments

(3) All other tax-exempt obligations.

(4) Basis different from adjusted issue price.

(e) Amounts treated as interest under this section.

(f) Effective date.

§ 1.1275-5. Variable rate debt instruments.

(a) Applicability.

(1) In general.

(2) Principal payments.

(3) Stated interest.

(4) Current value.

(5) No contingent principal payments.

(6) Special rule for debt instruments issued for nonpublicly traded property.

(b) Qualified floating rate.

(1) In general.

(2) Certain rates based on a qualified floating rate.

(3) Restrictions on the stated rate of interest.

(c) Objective rate.

(1) Definition.

(2) Other objective rates to be specified by Commissioner.

(3) Qualified inverse floating rate.

(4) Significant front-loading or back-loading of interest.

(5) Tax-exempt obligations.

(d) Examples.

(e) Qualified stated interest and OID with respect to a variable rate debt instrument.

(1) In general.

(2) Variable rate debt instrument that provides for annual payments of interest at a single variable rate.

(3) All other variable rate debt instruments except for those that provide for a fixed rate.

(4) Variable rate debt instrument that provides for a single fixed rate.

(f) Special rule for certain reset bonds.

§ 1.1275-6. Integration of qualifying debt instruments.

(a) In general.

(b) Definitions.

(1) Qualifying debt instrument.

(2) Section 1.1275-6 hedge.

(3) Financial instrument.

(4) Synthetic debt instrument.

(c) Integrated transaction.

(1) Integration by taxpayer.

(2) Integration by Commissioner.

(d) Special rules for legging into and legging out of an integrated transaction.

(1) Legging into.

(2) Legging out.

(e) Identification requirements.

(f) Taxation of integrated transactions.

(1) General rule.

(2) Issue date.

(3) Term.

(4) Issue price.

(5) Adjusted issue price.

(6) Qualified stated interest.

(7) Stated redemption price at maturity.

(8) Source of interest income and allocation of expense.

(9) Effectively connected income.

(10) Not a short-term obligation.

(11) Special rules in the event of integration by the Commissioner.

(12) Retention of separate transaction rules for certain purposes.

(13) Coordination with consolidated return rules.

(g) Predecessors and successors.

(h) Examples.

(i) [Reserved]

(j) Effective date.

§ 1.1275-7. Inflation-indexed debt instruments.

(a) Overview.

(b) Applicability.

(1) In general.

(2) Exceptions.

(c) Definitions.

(1) Inflation-indexed debt instrument.

(2) Reference index.

(3) Qualified inflation index.

(4) Inflation-adjusted principal amount.

(5) Minimum guarantee payment.

(d) Coupon bond method.

(1) In general.

(2) Applicability.

(3) Qualified stated interest.

(4) Inflation adjustments.

(5) Example.

(e) Discount bond method.

(1) In general.

Reg. § 1.1271-0(b)

(2) No qualified stated interest.

(3) OID.

(4) Example.

(f) Special rules.

(1) Deflation adjustments.

(2) Adjusted basis.

(3) Subsequent holders.

(4) Minimum guarantee.

(5) Temporary unavailability of a qualified inflation index.

(g) Reopenings.

(h) Effective date.

[Reg. § 1.1271-0.]

☐ [T.D. 8517, 1-27-94. Amended by T.D. 8674, 6-11-96; T.D. 8709, 12-31-96; T.D. 8754, 1-7-98; T.D. 8838, 9-3-99; T.D. 8840, 11-3-99 and T.D. 8934, 1-11-2001.]

[Reg. § 1.1271-1]

§ 1.1271-1. Special rules applicable to amounts received on retirement, sale, or exchange of debt instruments.—(a) *Intention to call before maturity*—(1) *In general.* For purposes of section 1271(a)(2), all or a portion of gain realized on a sale or exchange of a debt instrument to which section 1271 applies is treated as interest income if there was an intention to call the debt instrument before maturity. An intention to call a debt instrument before maturity means a written or oral agreement or understanding not provided for in the debt instrument between the issuer and the original holder of the debt instrument that the issuer will redeem the debt instrument before maturity. In the case of debt instruments that are part of an issue, the agreement or understanding must be between the issuer and the original holders of a substantial amount of the debt instruments in the issue. An intention to call before maturity can exist even if the intention is conditional (e.g., the issuer's decision to call depends on the financial condition of the issuer on the potential call date) or is not legally binding. For purposes of this section, original holder means the first holder (other than an underwriter or dealer that purchased the debt instrument for resale in the ordinary course of its trade or business).

(2) *Exceptions.* In addition to the exceptions provided in sections 1271(a)(2)(B) and 1271(b), section 1271(a)(2) does not apply to—

(i) A debt instrument that is publicly offered (as defined in § 1.1275-1(h));

(ii) A debt instrument to which section 1272(a)(6) applies (relating to certain interests in or mortgages held by a REMIC, and certain other debt instruments with payments subject to acceleration); or

(iii) A debt instrument sold pursuant to a private placement memorandum that is distributed to more than ten offerees and that is subject to the sanctions of section 12(2) of the Securities Act of 1933 (15 U.S.C 77l) or the prohibitions of section 10(b) of the Securities Exchange Act of 1934 (15 U.S.C. 78j).

(b) *Short-term obligations*—(1) *In general.* Under sections 1271(a)(3) and (a)(4), all or a portion of the gain realized on the sale or exchange of a short-term government or nongovernment obligation is treated as interest income. Sections 1271(a)(3) and (a)(4), however, do not apply to any short-term obligation subject to section 1281. See § 1.1272-1(f) for rules to determine if an obligation is a short-term obligation.

(2) *Method of making elections.* Elections to accrue on a constant yield basis under sections 1271(a)(3)(E) and (a)(4)(D) are made on an obligation-by-obligation basis by reporting the transaction on the basis of daily compounding on the taxpayer's timely filed Federal income tax return for the year of the sale or exchange. These elections are irrevocable.

(3) *Counting conventions.* In computing the ratable share of acquisition discount under section 1271(a)(3) or OID under section 1271(a)(4), any reasonable counting convention may be used (e.g., 30 days per month/360 days per year). [Reg. § 1.1271-1.]

☐ [T.D. 8517, 1-27-94.]

[Reg. § 1.1272-1]

§ 1.1272-1. Current inclusion of OID in income.—(a) *Overview*—(1) *In general.* Under section 1272(a)(1), a holder of a debt instrument includes accrued OID in gross income (as interest), regardless of the holder's regular method of accounting. A holder includes qualified stated interest (as defined in § 1.1273-1(c)) in income under the holder's regular method of accounting. See §§ 1.446-2 and 1.451-1.

(2) *Debt instruments not subject to OID inclusion rules.* Sections 1272(a)(2) and 1272(c) list exceptions to the general inclusion rule of section 1272(a)(1). For purposes of section 1272(a)(2)(E) (relating to certain loans between natural persons), a loan does not include a stripped bond or stripped coupon within the meaning of section 1286(e), and the rule in section 1272(a)(2)(E)(iii), which treats a husband and wife as 1 person, does not apply to loans made between a husband and wife.

(b) *Accrual of OID*—(1) *Constant yield method.* Except as provided in paragraphs (b)(2) and (b)(3) of this section, the amount of OID includible in the income of a holder of a debt instrument for any taxable year is determined using the constant yield method as described under this paragraph (b)(1).

(i) *Step one: Determine the debt instrument's yield to maturity.* The yield to maturity or yield of a debt instrument is the discount rate that, when used in computing the present value of all principal and interest payments to be made under the debt instrument, produces an amount equal to the issue price of the debt instrument. The yield must be constant over the term of the debt instrument and, when expressed as a percentage, must be calculated to at least two decimal places. See paragraph (c) of this section for rules relating to the yield of certain debt instruments subject to contingencies.

(ii) *Step two: Determine the accrual periods.* An accrual period is an interval of time over which the accrual of OID is measured. Accrual periods may be of any length and may vary in length over the term of the debt instrument, provided that each accrual period is no longer than 1 year and each scheduled payment of principal or interest occurs either on the final day of an accrual period or on the first day of an accrual period. In general, the computation of OID is simplest if accrual periods correspond to the intervals between payment dates provided by the terms of the debt instrument. In computing the length of accrual periods, any reasonable counting convention may be used (e.g., 30 days per month/360 days per year).

(iii) *Step three: Determine the OID allocable to each accrual period.* Except as provided in paragraph (b)(4) of this section, the OID allocable to an accrual period equals the product of the adjusted issue price of the debt instrument (as defined in § 1.1275-1(b)) at the beginning of the accrual period and the yield of the debt instrument, less the amount of any qualified stated interest allocable to the accrual period. In performing this calculation, the yield must be stated appropriately taking into account the length of the particular accrual period. *Example 1* in paragraph (j) of this section provides a formula for converting a yield based upon an accrual period of one length to an equivalent yield based upon an accrual period of a different length.

(iv) *Step four: Determine the daily portions of OID.* The daily portions of OID are determined by allocating to each day in an accrual period the ratable portion of the OID allocable to the accrual period. The holder of the debt instrument includes in income the daily portions of OID for each day during the taxable year on which the holder held the debt instrument.

(2) *Exceptions.* Paragraph (b)(1) of this section does not apply to—

(i) A debt instrument to which section 1272(a)(6) applies (certain interests in or mortgages held by a REMIC, and certain other debt instruments with payments subject to acceleration);

(ii) A debt instrument that provides for contingent payments, other than a debt instrument described in paragraph (c) or (d) of this section or except as provided in § 1.1275-4; or

(iii) A variable rate debt instrument to which § 1.1275-5 applies, except as provided in § 1.1275-5.

(3) *Modifications.* The amount of OID includible in income by a holder under paragraph (b)(1) of this section is adjusted if—

(i) The holder purchased the debt instrument at a premium or an acquisition premium (within the meaning of § 1.1272-2); or

(ii) The holder made an election for the debt instrument under § 1.1272-3 to treat all interest as OID.

(4) *Special rules for determining the OID allocable to an accrual period.* The following rules apply to determine the OID allocable to an accrual period under paragraph (b)(1)(iii) of this section.

(i) *Unpaid qualified stated interest allocable to an accrual period.* In determining the OID allocable to an accrual period, if an interval between payments of qualified stated interest contains more than 1 accrual period—

(A) The amount of qualified stated interest payable at the end of the interval (including any qualified stated interest that is payable on the first day of the accrual period immediately following the interval) is allocated on a pro rata basis to each accrual period in the interval; and

(B) The adjusted issue price at the beginning of each accrual period in the interval must be increased by the amount of any qualified stated interest that has accrued prior to the first day of the accrual period but that is not payable until the end of the interval. See *Example 2* of paragraph (j) of this section for an example illustrating the rules in this paragraph (b)(4)(i).

(ii) *Final accrual period.* The OID allocable to the final accrual period is the difference between the amount payable at maturity (other than a payment of qualified stated interest) and the adjusted issue price at the beginning of the final accrual period.

Reg. § 1.1272-1(b)(4)

(iii) *Initial short accrual period.* If all accrual periods are of equal length, except for either an initial shorter accrual period or an initial and a final shorter accrual period, the amount of OID allocable to the initial accrual period may be computed using any reasonable method. See *Example 3* in paragraph (j) of this section.

(iv) *Payment on first day of an accrual period.* The adjusted issue price at the beginning of an accrual period is reduced by the amount of any payment (other than a payment of qualified stated interest) that is made on the first day of the accrual period.

(c) *Yield and maturity of certain debt instruments subject to contingencies*—(1) *Applicability.* This paragraph (c) provides rules to determine the yield and maturity of certain debt instruments that provide for an alternative payment schedule (or schedules) applicable upon the occurrence of a contingency (or contingencies). This paragraph (c) applies, however, only if the timing and amounts of the payments that comprise each payment schedule are known as of the issue date and the debt instrument is subject to paragraph (c)(2), (3), or (5) of this section. A debt instrument does not provide for an alternative payment schedule merely because there is a possibility of impairment of a payment (or payments) by insolvency, default, or similar circumstances. See § 1.1275-4 for the treatment of a debt instrument that provides for a contingency that is not described in this paragraph (c). See § 1.1273-1(c) to determine whether stated interest on a debt instrument subject to this paragraph (c) is qualified stated interest.

(2) *Payment schedule that is significantly more likely than not to occur.* If, based on all the facts and circumstances as of the issue date, a single payment schedule for a debt instrument, including the stated payment schedule, is significantly more likely than not to occur, the yield and maturity of the debt instrument are computed based on this payment schedule.

(3) *Mandatory sinking fund provision.* Notwithstanding paragraph (c)(2) of this section, if a debt instrument is subject to a mandatory sinking fund provision, the provision is ignored for purposes of computing the yield and maturity of the debt instrument if the use and terms of the provision meet reasonable commercial standards. For purposes of the preceding sentence, a mandatory sinking fund provision is a provision that meets the following requirements:

(i) The provision requires the issuer to redeem a certain amount of debt instruments in an issue prior to maturity.

(ii) The debt instruments actually redeemed are chosen by lot or purchased by the issuer either in the open market or pursuant to an offer made to all holders (with any proration determined by lot).

(iii) On the issue date, the specific debt instruments that will be redeemed on any date prior to maturity cannot be identified.

(4) *Consistency rule.* [Reserved]

(5) *Treatment of certain options.* Notwithstanding paragraphs (c)(2) and (3) of this section, the rules of this paragraph (c)(5) determine the yield and maturity of a debt instrument that provides the holder or issuer with an unconditional option or options, exercisable on one or more dates during the term of the debt instrument, that, if exercised, require payments to be made on the debt instrument under an alternative payment schedule or schedules (e.g., an option to extend or an option to call a debt instrument at a fixed premium). Under this paragraph (c)(5), an issuer is deemed to exercise or not exercise an option or combination of options in a manner that minimizes the yield on the debt instrument, and a holder is deemed to exercise or not exercise an option or combination of options in a manner that maximizes the yield on the debt instrument. If both the issuer and the holder have options, the rules of this paragraph (c)(5) are applied to the options in the order that they may be exercised. See paragraph (j) *Example 5* through *Example 8* of this section.

(6) *Subsequent adjustments.* If a contingency described in this paragraph (c) (including the exercise of an option described in paragraph (c)(5) of this section) actually occurs or does not occur, contrary to the assumption made pursuant to this paragraph (c) (a change in circumstances), then, solely for purposes of sections 1272 and 1273, the debt instrument is treated as retired and then reissued on the date of the change in circumstances for an amount equal to its adjusted issue price on that date. See paragraph (j) *Example 5* and *Example 7* of this section. If, however, the change in circumstances results in a substantially contemporaneous pro-rata prepayment as defined in § 1.1275-2(f)(2), the pro-rata prepayment is treated as a payment in retirement of a portion of the debt instrument, which may result in gain or loss to the holder. See paragraph (j) *Example 6* and *Example 8* of this section.

(7) *Effective date.* This paragraph (c) applies to debt instruments issued on or after August 13, 1996.

(d) *Certain debt instruments that provide for a fixed yield.* If a debt instrument provides for one or more contingent payments but all possible pay-

Reg. § 1.1272-1(c)(1)

ment schedules under the terms of the instrument result in the same fixed yield, the yield of the debt instrument is the fixed yield. For example, the yield of a debt instrument with principal payments that are fixed in total amount but that are uncertain as to time (such as a demand loan) is the stated interest rate if the issue price of the instrument is equal to the stated principal amount and interest is paid or compounded at a fixed rate over the entire term of the instrument. This paragraph (d) applies to debt instruments issued on or after August 13, 1996.

(e) *Convertible debt instruments.* For purposes of section 1272, an option is ignored if it is an option to convert a debt instrument into the stock of the issuer, into the stock or debt of a related party (within the meaning of section 267(b) or 707(b)(1)), or into cash or other property in an amount equal to the approximate value of such stock or debt.

(f) *Special rules to determine whether a debt instrument is a short-term obligation*—(1) *Counting of either the issue date or maturity date.* For purposes of determining whether a debt instrument is a short-term obligation (i.e., a debt instrument with a fixed maturity date that is not more than 1 year from the date of issue), the term of the debt instrument includes either the issue date or the maturity date, but not both dates.

(2) *Coordination with paragraph (c) of this section for certain sections of the Internal Revenue Code.* Notwithstanding paragraph (c) of this section, solely for purposes of determining whether a debt instrument is a short-term obligation under sections 871(g)(1)(B)(i), 881, 1271(a)(3), 1271(a)(4), 1272(a)(2)(C), and 1283(a)(1), the maturity date of a debt instrument is the last possible date that the instrument could be outstanding under the terms of the instrument. For purposes of the preceding sentence, the last possible date that the debt instrument could be outstanding is determined without regard to § 1.1275-2(h) (relating to payments subject to remote or incidental contingencies).

(g) *Basis adjustment.* The basis of a debt instrument in the hands of the holder is increased by the amount of OID included in the holder's gross income and decreased by the amount of any payment from the issuer to the holder under the debt instrument other than a payment of qualified stated interest. See, however, § 1.1275-2(f) for rules regarding basis adjustments on a pro rata prepayment.

(h) *Debt instruments denominated in a currency other than the U.S. dollar.* Section 1272 and this section apply to a debt instrument that provides for all payments denominated in, or determined by reference to, the functional currency of the taxpayer or qualified business unit of the taxpayer (even if that currency is other than the U.S. dollar). See § 1.988-2(b) to determine interest income or expense for debt instruments that provide for payments denominated in, or determined by reference to, a nonfunctional currency.

(i) [Reserved]

(j) *Examples.* The following examples illustrate the rules of this section. Each example assumes that all taxpayers use the calendar year as the taxable year. In addition, each example assumes a 30-day month, 360-day year, and that the initial accrual period begins on the issue date and the final accrual period ends on the day before the stated maturity date. Although, for purposes of simplicity, the yield as stated is rounded to two decimal places, the computations do not reflect any such rounding convention.

Example 1. Accrual of OID on zero coupon debt instrument; choice of accrual periods—(i) *Facts.* On July 1, 1994, A purchases at original issue, for $675,564.17, a debt instrument that matures on July 1, 1999, and provides for a single payment of $1,000,000 at maturity.

(ii) *Determination of yield.* Under paragraph (b)(1)(i) of this section, the yield of the debt instrument is 8 percent, compounded semiannually.

(iii) *Determination of accrual period.* Under paragraph (b)(1)(ii) of this section, accrual periods may be of any length, provided that each accrual period is no longer than 1 year and each scheduled payment of principal or interest occurs either on the first or final day of an accrual period. The yield to maturity to be used in computing OID accruals in any accrual period, however, must reflect the length of the accrual period chosen. A yield based on compounding b times per year is equivalent to a yield based on compounding c times per year as indicated by the following formula:

$$r = c\{(1 + i/b)^{b/c} - 1\}$$

In which:

i	=	The yield based on compounding b times per year expressed as a decimal
r	=	The equivalent yield based on compounding c times per year expressed as a decimal
b	=	The number of compounding periods in a year on which i is based (for example, 12, if i is based on monthly compounding)
c	=	The number of compounding periods in a year on which r is based

Reg. § 1.1272-1(j)

Special Rules, Bonds & Other Debt Instruments

(iv) *Determination of OID allocable to each accrual period.* Assume that A decides to compute OID on the debt instrument using semiannual accrual periods. Under paragraph (b)(1)(iii) of this section, the OID allocable to the first semiannual accrual period is $27,022.56: the product of the issue price ($675,564.17) and the yield properly adjusted for the length of the accrual period (8 percent/2), less qualified stated interest allocable to the accrual period ($0). The daily portion of OID for the first semiannual period is $150.13 ($27,022.56/180).

(v) *Determination of OID if monthly accrual periods are used.* Alternatively, assume that A decides to compute OID on the debt instrument using monthly accrual periods. Using the above formula, the yield on the debt instrument reflecting monthly compounding is 7.87 percent, compounded monthly $(12 \{ (1 + .08/2)^{2/12} - 1 \})$. Under paragraph (b)(1)(iii) of this section, the OID allocable to the first monthly accrual period is $4,430.48: the product of the issue price ($675,564.17) and the yield properly adjusted for the length of the accrual period (7.87 percent/12), less qualified stated interest allocable to the accrual period ($0). The daily portion of OID for the first monthly accrual period is $147.68 ($4,430.48/30).

Example 2. Accrual of OID on debt instrument with qualified stated interest—(i) *Facts.* On September 1, 1994, A purchases at original issue, for $90,000, B corporation's debt instrument that matures on September 1, 2004, and has a stated principal amount of $100,000, payable on that date. The debt instrument provides for semiannual payments of interest of $3,000, payable on September 1 and March 1 of each year, beginning on March 1, 1995.

(ii) *Determination of yield.* The debt instrument is a 10-year debt instrument with an issue price of $90,000 and a stated redemption price at maturity of $100,000. The semiannual payments of $3,000 are qualified stated interest payments. Under paragraph (b)(1)(i) of this section, the yield is 7.44 percent, compounded semiannually.

(iii) *Accrual of OID if semiannual accrual periods are used.* Assume that A decides to compute OID on the debt instrument using semiannual accrual periods. Under paragraph (b)(1)(iii) of this section, the OID allocable to the first semiannual accrual period equals the product of the issue price ($90,000) and the yield properly adjusted for the length of the accrual period (7.44 percent/2), less qualified stated interest allocable to the accrual period ($3,000). Therefore, the amount of OID for the first semiannual accrual period is $345.78 ($3,345.78 − $3,000).

(iv) *Adjustment for accrued but unpaid qualified stated interest if monthly accrual periods are used.* Assume, alternatively, that A decides to compute OID on the debt instrument using monthly accrual periods. The yield, compounded monthly, is 7.32 percent. Under paragraph (b)(1)(iii) of this section, the OID allocable to the first monthly accrual period is the product of the issue price ($90,000) and the yield properly adjusted for the length of the accrual period (7.32 percent/12), less qualified stated interest allocable to the accrual period. Under paragraph (b)(4)(i)(A) of this section, the qualified stated interest allocable to the first monthly accrual period is the pro rata amount of qualified stated interest allocable to the interval between payment dates ($3,000 × 1/6, or $500). Therefore, the amount of OID for the first monthly accrual period is $49.18 ($549.18 − $500). Under paragraph (b)(4)(i)(B) of this section, the adjusted issue price of the debt instrument for purposes of determining the amount of OID for the second monthly accrual period is $90,549.18 ($90,000 + $49.18 + $500). Although the adjusted issue price of the debt instrument for this purpose includes the amount of qualified stated interest allocable to the first monthly accrual period, A includes the qualified stated interest in income based on A's regular method of accounting (e.g., an accrual method or the cash receipts and disbursements method).

Example 3. Accrual of OID for debt instrument with initial short accrual period—(i) *Facts.* On May 1, 1994, G purchases, at original issue, for $80,000, H corporation's debt instrument maturing on July 1, 2004. The debt instrument provides for a single payment at maturity of $250,000. G computes its OID using 6-month accrual periods ending on January 1 and July 1 of each year and an initial short 2-month accrual period from May 1, 1994, through June 30, 1994.

(ii) *Determination of yield.* The yield on the debt instrument is 11.53 percent, compounded semiannually.

(iii) *Determination of OID allocable to initial short accrual period.* Under paragraph (b)(4)(iii) of this section, G may use any reasonable method to compute OID for the initial short accrual period. One reasonable method is to calculate the amount of OID pursuant to the following formula:

Reg. § 1.1272-1(j)

Special Rules, Bonds & Other Debt Instruments

See p. 20,601 for regulations not amended to reflect law changes

$$OID_{short} = IP \times (i/k) \times f$$

In which:

OID_{short}	=	The amount of OID allocable to the initial short accrual period
IP	=	The issue price of the debt instrument
i	=	The yield to maturity expressed as a decimal
k	=	The number of accrual periods in a year
f	=	A fraction whose numerator is the number of days in the initial short accrual period, and whose denominator is the number of days in a full accrual period

(iv) *Amount of OID for the initial short accrual period.* Under this method, the amount of OID for the initial short accrual period is $1,537 ($80,000 × (11.53 percent/2) × (60/180)).

(v) *Alternative method.* Another reasonable method is to calculate the amount of OID for the initial short accrual period using the yield based on bi-monthly compounding, computed pursuant to the formula set forth in *Example 1* of paragraph (j) of this section. Under this method, the amount of OID for the initial short accrual period is $1,508.38 ($80,000 × (11.31 percent/6)).

Example 4. Impermissible accrual of OID using a method other than constant yield method—(i) *Facts.* On July 1, 1994, B purchases at original issue, for $100,000, C corporation's debt instrument that matures on July 1, 1999, and has a stated principal amount of $100,000. The debt instrument provides for a single payment at maturity of $148,024.43. The yield of the debt instrument is 8 percent, compounded semiannually.

(ii) *Determination of yield.* Assume that C uses 6 monthly accrual periods to compute its OID for 1994. The yield must reflect monthly compounding (as determined using the formula described in *Example 1* of paragraph (j) of this section). As a result, the monthly yield of the debt instrument is 7.87 percent, divided by 12. C may not compute its monthly yield for the last 6 months in 1994 by dividing 8 percent by 12.

Example 5. Debt instrument subject to put option—(i) *Facts.* On January 1, 1995, G purchases at original issue, for $70,000, H corporation's debt instrument maturing on January 1, 2010, with a stated principal amount of $100,000, payable at maturity. The debt instrument provides for semiannual payments of interest of $4,000, payable on January 1 and July 1 of each year, beginning on July 1, 1995. The debt instrument gives G an unconditional right to put the bond back to H, exercisable on January 1, 2005, in return for $85,000 (exclusive of the $4,000 of stated interest payable on that date).

(ii) *Determination of yield and maturity.* Yield determined without regard to the put option is 12.47 percent compounded semiannually. Yield determined by assuming that the put option is exercised (i.e., by using January 1, 2005, as the maturity date and $85,000 as the stated principal amount payable on that date) is 12.56 percent, compounded semiannually. Thus, under paragraph (c)(5) of this section, it is assumed that G will exercise the put option, because exercise of the option would increase the yield of the debt instrument. Thus, for purposes of calculating OID, the debt instrument is assumed to be a 10-year debt instrument with an issue price of $70,000, a stated redemption price at maturity of $85,000, and a yield of 12.56 percent, compounded semiannually.

(iii) *Consequences if put option is, in fact, not exercised.* If the put option is in fact, not exercised, then, under paragraph (c)(6) of this section, the debt instrument is treated, solely for purposes of sections 1272 and 1273, as if it were reissued on January 1, 2005, for an amount equal to its adjusted issue price on that date, $85,000. The new debt instrument matures on January 1, 2010, with a stated principal amount of $100,000 payable on that date and provides for semiannual payments of interest of $4,000. The yield of the new debt instrument is 12.08 percent, compounded semiannually.

Example 6. Debt instrument subject to partial call option—(i) *Facts.* On January 1, 1995, H purchases at original issue, for $95,000, J corporation's debt instrument that matures on January 1, 2000, and has a stated principal amount of $100,000, payable on that date. The debt instrument provides for semiannual payments of interest of $4,000, payable on January 1 and July 1 of each year, beginning on July 1, 1995. On January 1, 1998, J has an unconditional right to call 50 percent of the principal amount of the debt instrument for $55,000 (exclusive of the $4,000 of stated interest payable on that date). If the call is exercised, the semiannual payments of interest made after the call date will be reduced to $2,000.

(ii) *Determination of yield and maturity.* Yield determined without regard to the call option is 9.27 percent, compounded semiannually. Yield determined by assuming J exercises its call option is 10.75 percent, compounded semiannually. Thus, under paragraph (c)(5) of this section, it is assumed that J will not exercise the call option because exercise of the option would increase the yield of the debt instrument. Thus, for purposes of

Reg. § 1.1272-1(j)

calculating OID, the debt instrument is assumed to be a 5-year debt instrument with a single principal payment at maturity of $100,000, and a yield of 9.27 percent, compounded semiannually.

(iii) *Consequences if the call option is, in fact, exercised.* If the call option is, in fact, exercised, then under paragraph (c)(6) of this section, the debt instrument is treated as if the issuer made a pro rata prepayment of $55,000 that is subject to § 1.1275-2(f). Consequently, under § 1.1275-2(f)(1), the instrument is treated as consisting of two debt instruments, one that is retired on the call date and one that remains outstanding after the call date. The adjusted issue price, adjusted basis in the hands of the holder, and accrued OID of the original debt instrument is allocated between the two instruments based on the portion of the original instrument treated as retired. Since each payment remaining to be made after the call date is reduced by one-half, one-half of the adjusted issue price, adjusted basis, and accrued OID is allocated to the debt instrument that is treated as retired. The adjusted issue price of the original debt instrument immediately prior to the call date is $97,725.12, which equals the issue price of the original debt instrument ($95,000) increased by the OID previously includible in gross income ($2,725.12). One-half of this adjusted issue price is allocated to the debt instrument treated as retired, and the other half is allocated to the debt instrument that is treated as remaining outstanding. Thus, the debt instrument treated as remaining outstanding has an adjusted issue price immediately after the call date of $97,725.12/2, or $48,862.56. The yield of this debt instrument continues to be 9.27 percent, compounded semiannually. In addition, the portion of H's adjusted basis allocated to the debt instrument treated as retired is $97,725.12/2 or $48,862.56. Accordingly, under section 1271, H realizes a gain on the deemed retirement equal to $6,137.44 ($55,000 − $48,862.56).

Example 7. Debt instrument issued at par that provides for payment of interest in kind—(i) *Facts.* On January 1, 1995, A purchases at original issue, for $100,000, X corporation's debt instrument maturing on January 1, 2000, at a stated principal amount of $100,000, payable on that date. The debt instrument provides for annual payments of interest of $6,000 on January 1 of each year, beginning on January 1, 1996. The debt instrument gives X the unconditional right to issue, in lieu of the first interest payment, a second debt instrument (PIK instrument) maturing on January 1, 2000, with a stated principal amount of $6,000. The PIK instrument, if issued, would provide for annual payments of interest of $360 on January 1 of each year, beginning on January 1, 1997.

(ii) *Aggregation of PIK instrument with original debt instrument.* Under § 1.1275-2(c)(3), the issuance of the PIK instrument is not considered a payment made on the original debt instrument, and the PIK instrument is aggregated with the original debt instrument. The issue date of the PIK instrument is the same as the original debt instrument.

(iii) *Determination of yield and maturity.* The right to issue the PIK instrument is treated as an option to defer the initial interest payment until maturity. Yield determined without regard to the option is 6 percent, compounded annually. Yield determined by assuming X exercises the option is 6 percent, compounded annually. Thus, under paragraph (c)(5) of this section, it is assumed that X will not exercise the option by issuing the PIK instrument because exercise of the option would not decrease the yield of the debt instrument. For purposes of calculating OID, the debt instrument is assumed to be a 5-year debt instrument with a single principal payment at maturity of $100,000 and ten semiannual interest payments of $6,000, beginning on January 1, 1996. As a result, the yield is 6 percent, compounded annually.

(iv) *Determination of OID.* Under the payment schedule that would result if the option was exercised, none of the interest on the debt instrument would be qualified stated interest. Accordingly, under § 1.1273-1(c)(2), no payments on the debt instrument are qualified stated interest payments. Thus, $6,000 of OID accrues during the first annual accrual period. If the PIK instrument is not issued, $6,000 of OID accrues during each annual accrual period.

(v) *Consequences if the PIK instrument is issued.* Under paragraph (c)(6) of this section, if X issues the PIK instrument on January 1, 1996, the issuance of the PIK instrument is not a payment on the debt instrument. Solely for purposes of sections 1272 and 1273, the debt instrument is deemed reissued on January 1, 1996, for an issue price of $106,000. The recomputed yield is 6 percent, compounded annually. The OID for the first annual accrual period after the deemed reissuance is $6,360. The adjusted issue price of the debt instrument at the beginning of the next annual accrual period is $106,000 ($106,000 + $6,360 − $6,360). The OID for each of the four remaining annual accrual periods is $6,360.

Example 8. Debt instrument issued at a discount that provides for payment of interest in kind—(i) *Facts.* On January 1, 1995, T purchases at original issue, for $75,500, U corporation's debt instrument maturing on January 1, 2000, at a stated principal amount of $100,000, payable on that date. The debt instrument provides for annual payments of interest of $4,000 on January 1 of each year, beginning on January 1, 1996. The debt instrument gives U the unconditional right to issue, in lieu of the first interest payment, a second debt instrument (PIK instrument) maturing on January 1, 2000, with a stated principal amount of $4,000. The PIK instrument, if issued, would provide for annual payments of interest of $160 on January 1 of each year, beginning on January 1, 1997.

(ii) *Aggregation of PIK instrument with original debt instrument.* Under § 1.1275-2(c)(3), the issuance of the PIK instrument is not considered a payment made on the original debt instrument, and the PIK instrument is aggregated with the original debt instrument. The issue date of the PIK instrument is the same as the original debt instrument.

(iii) *Determination of yield and maturity.* The right to issue the PIK instrument is treated as an option to defer the initial interest payment until maturity. Yield determined without regard to the option is 10.55 percent, compounded annually. Yield determined by assuming U exercises the option is 10.32 percent, compounded annually. Thus, under paragraph (c)(5) of this section, it is assumed that U will exercise the option by issuing the PIK instrument because exercise of the option would decrease the yield of the debt instrument. For purposes of calculating OID, the debt instrument is assumed to be a 5-year debt instrument with a single principal payment at maturity of $104,000 and four annual interest payments of $4,160, beginning on January 1, 1997. As a result, the yield is 10.32 percent, compounded annually.

(iv) *Consequences if the PIK instrument is not issued.* Assume that T chooses to compute OID accruals on the basis of an annual accrual period. On January 1, 1996, the adjusted issue price of the debt instrument, and T's adjusted basis in the instrument, is $83,295.15. Under paragraph (c)(6) of this section, if U actually makes the $4,000 interest payment on January 1, 1996, the debt instrument is treated as if U made a pro rata prepayment (within the meaning of § 1.1275-2(f)(2)) of $4,000, which reduces the amount of each payment remaining on the instrument by a factor of 4/104, or 1/26. Thus, under § 1.1275-2(f)(1) and section 1271, T realizes a gain of $796.34 ($4,000 − ($83,295.15/26)). The adjusted issue price of the debt instrument and T's adjusted basis immediately after the payment is $80,091.49 ($83,295.15 × 25/26) and the yield continues to be 10.32 percent, compounded annually.

Example 9. Debt instrument with stepped interest rate—(i) *Facts.* On July 1, 1994, G purchases at original issue, for $85,000, H corporation's debt instrument maturing on July 1, 2004. The debt instrument has a stated principal amount of $100,000, payable on the maturity date and provides for semiannual interest payments on January 1 and July 1 of each year, beginning on January 1, 1995. The amount of each payment is $2,000 for the first 5 years and $5,000 for the final 5 years.

(ii) *Determination of OID.* Assume that G computes its OID using 6-month accrual periods ending on January 1 and July 1 of each year. The yield of the debt instrument, determined under paragraph (b)(1)(i) of this section, is 8.65 percent, compounded semiannually. Interest is unconditionally payable at a fixed rate of at least 4 percent, compounded semiannually, for the entire term of the debt instrument. Consequently, under § 1.1273-1(c)(1), the semiannual payments are qualified stated interest payments to the extent of $2,000. The amount of OID for the first 6-month accrual period is $1,674.34 (the issue price of the debt instrument ($85,000) times the yield of the debt instrument for that accrual period (.0865/2) less the amount of any qualified stated interest allocable to that accrual period ($2,000).

Example 10. Debt instrument payable on demand that provides for interest at a constant rate—(i) *Facts.* On January 1, 1995, V purchases at original issue, for $100,000, W corporation's debt instrument. The debt instrument calls for interest to accrue at a rate of 9 percent, compounded annually. The debt instrument is redeemable at any time at the option of V for an amount equal to $100,000, plus accrued interest. V uses annual accrual periods to accrue OID on the debt instrument.

(ii) *Amount of OID.* Pursuant to paragraph (d) of this section, the yield of the debt instrument is 9 percent, compounded annually. If the debt instrument is not redeemed during 1995, the amount of OID allocable to the year is $9,000. [Reg. § 1.1272-1.]

☐ [T.D. 8517, 1-27-94. Amended by T.D. 8674, 6-11-96.]

[Reg. § 1.1272-2]

§ 1.1272-2. Treatment of debt instruments purchased at a premium.—(a) *In general.* Under section 1272(c)(1), if a holder purchases a debt instrument at a premium, the holder does not include any OID in gross income. Under section 1272(a)(7), if a holder purchases a debt instrument at an acquisition premium, the holder reduces the amount of OID includible in gross

53,646 Special Rules, Bonds & Other Debt Instruments
See p. 20,601 for regulations not amended to reflect law changes

income by the fraction determined under paragraph (b)(4) of this section.

(b) *Definitions and special rules*—(1) *Purchase.* For purposes of section 1272 and this section, purchase means any acquisition of a debt instrument, including the acquisition of a newly issued debt instrument in a debt-for-debt exchange or the acquisition of a debt instrument from a donor.

(2) *Premium.* A debt instrument is purchased at a premium if its adjusted basis, immediately after its purchase by the holder (including a purchase at original issue), exceeds the sum of all amounts payable on the instrument after the purchase date other than payments of qualified stated interest (as defined in § 1.1273-1(c)).

(3) *Acquisition premium.* A debt instrument is purchased at an acquisition premium if its adjusted basis, immediately after its purchase (including a purchase at original issue), is—

(i) Less than or equal to the sum of all amounts payable on the instrument after the purchase date other than payments of qualified stated interest (as defined in § 1.1273-1(c)); and

(ii) Greater than the instrument's adjusted issue price (as defined in § 1.1275-1(b)).

(4) *Acquisition premium fraction.* In applying section 1272(a)(7), the cost of a debt instrument is its adjusted basis immediately after its acquisition by the purchaser. Thus, the numerator of the fraction determined under section 1272(a)(7)(B) is the excess of the adjusted basis of the debt instrument immediately after its acquisition by the purchaser over the adjusted issue price of the debt instrument. The denominator of the fraction determined under section 1272(a)(7)(B) is the excess of the sum of all amounts payable on the debt instrument after the purchase date, other than payments of qualified stated interest, over the instrument's adjusted issue price.

(5) *Election to accrue discount on a constant yield basis.* Rather than applying the acquisition premium fraction, a holder of a debt instrument purchased at an acquisition premium may elect under § 1.1272-3 to compute OID accruals by treating the purchase as a purchase at original issuance and applying the mechanics of the constant yield method.

(6) *Special rules for determining basis*—(i) *Debt instruments acquired in exchange for other property.* For purposes of section 1272(a)(7), section 1272(c)(1), and this section, if a debt instrument is acquired in an exchange for other property (other than in a reorganization defined in section 368) and the basis of the debt instrument is determined, in whole or in part, by reference to the basis of the other property, the basis of

the debt instrument may not exceed its fair market value immediately after the exchange. For example, if a debt instrument is distributed by a partnership to a partner in a liquidating distribution and the partner's basis in the debt instrument would otherwise be determined under section 732, the partner's basis in the debt instrument may not exceed its fair market value for purposes of this section.

(ii) *Acquisition by gift.* For purposes of this section, a donee's adjusted basis in a debt instrument is the donee's basis for determining gain under section 1015(a).

(c) *Examples.* The following examples illustrate the rules of this section.

Example 1. Debt instrument purchased at an acquisition premium—(i) *Facts.* On July 1, 1994, A purchased at original issue, for $500, a debt instrument issued by Corporation X. The debt instrument matures on July 1, 1999, and calls for a single payment at maturity of $1,000. Under section 1273(a), the debt instrument has a stated redemption price at maturity of $1,000 and, thus, OID of $500. On July 1, 1996, when the debt instrument's adjusted issue price is $659.75, A sells the debt instrument to B for $750 in cash.

(ii) *Acquisition premium fraction.* Because the cost to B of the debt instrument is less than the amount payable on the debt instrument after the purchase date, but is greater than the debt instrument's adjusted issue price, B has paid an acquisition premium for the debt instrument. Accordingly, the daily portion of OID for any day that B holds the debt instrument is reduced by a fraction, the numerator of which is $90.25 (the excess of the cost of the debt instrument over its adjusted issue price) and the denominator of which is $340.25 (the excess of the sum of all payments after the purchase date over its adjusted issue price).

Example 2. Debt-for-debt exchange where holder is considered to purchase new debt instrument at a premium—(i) *Facts.* On January 1, 1995, H purchases at original issue, for $1,000, a debt instrument issued by Corporation X. On July 1, 1997, when H's adjusted basis in the debt instrument is $1,000, Corporation X issues a new debt instrument with a stated redemption price at maturity of $750 to H in exchange for the old debt instrument. Assume that the issue price of the new debt instrument is $600. Thus, under section 1273(a), the debt instrument has OID of $150. The exchange qualifies as a recapitalization under section 368(a)(1)(E), with the consequence that, under sections 354 and 358, H recognizes no loss on the exchange and has an adjusted basis in the new debt instrument of $1,000.

Reg. § 1.1272-2(b)(1)

(ii) *Application of section 1272(c)(1)*. Under paragraphs (b)(1) and (b)(2) of this section, H purchases the new debt instrument at a premium of $250. Accordingly, under section 1272(c)(1), H is not required to include OID in income with respect to the new debt instrument.

Example 3. Debt-for-debt exchange where holder is considered to purchase new debt instrument at an acquisition premium—(i) *Facts.* The facts are the same as in *Example 2* of paragraph (c) of this section, except that H purchases the old debt instrument from another holder on July 1, 1995, and on July 1, 1997, H's adjusted basis in the old debt instrument is $700. Under section 1273(a), the new debt instrument is issued with OID of $150.

(ii) *Application of section 1272(a)(7)*. Under paragraphs (b)(1) and (b)(3) of this section, H purchases the new debt instrument at an acquisition premium of $100. Accordingly, the daily portion of OID that is includible in H's income is reduced by the fraction determined under section 1272(a)(7).

Example 4. Treatment of acquisition premium for debt instrument acquired by gift—(i) *Facts.* On July 1, 1994, D receives as a gift a debt instrument with a stated redemption price at maturity of $1,000 and an adjusted issue price of $800. On that date, the fair market value of the debt instrument is $900 and the donor's adjusted basis in the debt instrument is $950.

(ii) *Application of section 1272(a)(7)*. Under paragraphs (b)(1), (b)(3), and (b)(6)(ii) of this section, D is considered to have purchased the debt instrument at an acquisition premium of $150. Accordingly, the daily portion of OID that is includible in D's income is reduced by the fraction determined under section 1272(a)(7). [Reg. § 1.1272-2.]

☐ [*T.D.* 8517, 1-27-94.]

[Reg. § 1.1272-3]

§ 1.1272-3. Election by a holder to treat all interest on a debt instrument as OID.—(a) *Election.* A holder of a debt instrument may elect to include in gross income all interest that accrues on the instrument by using the constant yield method described in paragraph (c) of his section. For purposes of this election, interest includes stated interest, acquisition discount, OID, de minimis OID, market discount, de minimis market discount, and unstated interest, as adjusted by any amortizable bond premium or acquisition premium.

(b) *Scope of election*—(1) *In general.* Except as provided in paragraph (b)(2) of this section, a holder may make the election for any debt instrument.

(2) *Exceptions, limitations, and special rules*—(i) *Debt instrument with amortizable bond premium (as determined under section 171)*.—(A) A holder may make the election for a debt instrument with amortizable bond premium only if the instrument qualifies as a bond under section 171(d).

(B) If a holder makes the election under this section for a debt instrument with amortizable bond premium, the holder is deemed to have made the election under section 171(c)(2) for the taxable year in which the instrument was acquired. If the holder has previously made the election under section 171(c)(2), the requirements of that election with respect to any debt instrument are satisfied by electing to amortize the bond premium under the rules provided by this section.

(ii) *Debt instrument with market discount.* (A) A holder may make the election under this section for a debt instrument with market discount only if the holder is eligible to make an election under section 1278(b).

(B) If a holder makes the election under this section for a debt instrument with market discount, the holder is deemed to have made both the election under section 1276(b)(2) for that instrument and the election under section 1278(b) for the taxable year in which the instrument was acquired. If the holder has previously made the election under section 1278(b), the requirements of that election with respect to any debt instrument are satisfied by electing to include the market discount in income in accordance with the rules provided by this section.

(iii) *Tax-exempt debt instrument.* A holder may not make the election for a tax-exempt obligation as defined in section 1275(a)(3).

(c) *Mechanics of the constant yield method*—(1) *In general.* For purposes of this section, the amount of interest that accrues during an accrual period is determined under rules similar to those under section 1272 (the constant yield method). In applying the constant yield method, however, a debt instrument subject to the election is treated as if—

(i) The instrument is issued for the holder's adjusted basis immediately after its acquisition by the holder;

(ii) The instrument is issued on the holder's acquisition date; and

(iii) None of the interest payments provided for in the instrument are qualified stated interest payments.

(2) *Special rules to determine adjusted basis.* For purposes of paragraph (c)(1)(i) of this section—

(i) If the debt instrument is acquired in an exchange for other property (other than in a reorganization defined in section 368) and the basis of the debt instrument is determined, in whole or in part, by reference to the basis of the other property, the adjusted basis of the debt instrument may not exceed its fair market value immediately after the exchange; and

(ii) If the debt instrument was acquired with amortizable bond premium (as determined under section 171), the adjusted basis of the debt instrument is reduced by an amount equal to the value attributable to any conversion feature.

(d) *Time and manner of making the election.* The election must be made for the taxable year in which the holder acquires the debt instrument. A holder makes the election by attaching to the holder's timely filed Federal income tax return a statement that the holder is making an election under this section and that identifies the debt instruments subject to the election. A holder may make the election for a class or group of debt instruments by attaching a statement describing the type or types of debt instruments being designated for the election.

(e) *Revocation of election.* The election may not be revoked unless approved by the Commissioner.

(f) *Effective date.* This section applies to debt instruments acquired on or after April 4, 1994. [Reg. § 1.1272-3.]

☐ [T.D. 8517, 1-27-94.]

[Reg. § 1.1273-1]

§ 1.1273-1. **Definition of OID.**—(a) *In general.* Section 1273(a)(1) defines OID as the excess of a debt instrument's stated redemption price at maturity over its issue price. Section 1.1273-2 defines issue price, and paragraph (b) of this section defines stated redemption price at maturity. Paragraph (d) of this section provides rules for de minimis amounts of OID. Although the total amount of OID for a debt instrument may be indeterminate, § 1.1272-1(d) provides a rule to determine OID accruals on certain debt instruments that provide for a fixed yield. See *Example 10* in § 1.1272-1(j).

(b) *Stated redemption price at maturity.* A debt instrument's stated redemption price at maturity is the sum of all payments provided by the debt instrument other than qualified stated interest payments. If the payment schedule of a debt instrument is determined under § 1.1272-1(c) (relating to certain debt instruments subject to contingencies), that payment schedule is used to determine the instrument's stated redemption price at maturity.

(c) *Qualified stated interest*—(1) *Definition*—(i) *In general.* Qualified stated interest is stated interest that is unconditionally payable in cash or in property (other than debt instruments of the issuer), or that will be constructively received under section 451, at least annually at a single fixed rate (within the meaning of paragraph (c)(1)(iii) of this section).

(ii) *Unconditionally payable.* Interest is unconditionally payable only if reasonable legal remedies exist to compel timely payment or the debt instrument otherwise provides terms and conditions that make the likelihood of late payment (other than a late payment that occurs within a reasonable grace period) or nonpayment a remote contingency (within the meaning of § 1.1275-2(h)). For purposes of the preceding sentence, remedies or other terms and conditions are not taken into account if the lending transaction does not reflect arm's length dealing and the holder does not intend to enforce the remedies or other terms and conditions. For purposes of determining whether interest is unconditionally payable, the possibility of nonpayment due to default, insolvency, or similar circumstances, or due to the exercise of a conversion option described in § 1.1272-1(e) is ignored. This paragraph (c)(1)(ii) applies to debt instruments issued on or after August 13, 1996.

(iii) *Single fixed rate*—(A) *In general.* Interest is payable at a single fixed rate only if the rate appropriately takes into account the length of the interval between payments. Thus, if the interval between payments varies during the term of the debt instrument, the value of the fixed rate on which a payment is based generally must be adjusted to reflect a compounding assumption that is consistent with the length of the interval preceding the payment. See *Example 1* in paragraph (f) of this section.

(B) *Special rule for certain first and final payment intervals.* Notwithstanding paragraph (c)(1)(iii)(A) of this section, if a debt instrument provides for payment intervals that are equal in length throughout the term of the instrument, except that the first or final payment interval differs in length from the other payment intervals, the first or final interest payment is considered to be made at a fixed rate if the value of the rate on which the payment is based is adjusted in any reasonable manner to take into account the length of the interval. See *Example 2* of paragraph (f) of this section. The rule in this paragraph (c)(1)(iii)(B) also applies if the lengths of both the first and final payment intervals differ from the length of the other payment intervals.

(2) *Debt instruments subject to contingencies.* The determination of whether a debt instrument described in § 1.1272-1(c) (a debt instrument providing for an alternative payment schedule (or schedules) upon the occurrence of one or more contingencies) provides for qualified stated interest is made by analyzing each alternative payment schedule (including the stated payment schedule) as if it were the debt instrument's sole payment schedule. Under this analysis, the debt instrument provides for qualified stated interest to the extent of the lowest fixed rate at which qualified stated interest would be payable under any payment schedule. See *Example 4* of paragraph (f) of this section.

(3) *Variable rate debt instrument.* In the case of a variable rate debt instrument, qualified stated interest is determined under § 1.1275-5(e).

(4) *Stated interest in excess of qualified stated interest.* To the extent that stated interest payable under a debt instrument exceeds qualified stated interest, the excess is included in the debt instrument's stated redemption price at maturity.

(5) *Short-term obligations.* In the case of a debt instrument with a term that is not more than 1 year from the date of issue, no payments of interest are treated as qualified stated interest payments.

(d) *De minimis OID*—(1) *In general.* If the amount of OID with respect to a debt instrument is less than the de minimis amount, the amount of OID is treated as zero, and all stated interest (including stated interest that would otherwise be characterized as OID) is treated as qualified stated interest.

(2) *De minimis amount.* The de minimis amount is an amount equal to 0.0025 multiplied by the product of the stated redemption price at maturity and the number of complete years to maturity from the issue date.

(3) *Installment obligations.* In the case of an installment obligation (as defined in paragraph (e)(1) of this section), paragraph (d)(2) of this section is applied by substituting for the number of complete years to maturity the weighted average maturity (as defined in paragraph (e)(3) of this section). Alternatively, in the case of a debt instrument that provides for payments of principal no more rapidly than self-amortizing installment obligation (as defined in paragraph (e)(2) of this section), the de minimis amount defined in paragraph (d)(2) of this section may be calculated by substituting 0.00167 for 0.0025.

(4) *Special rule for interest holidays, teaser rates, and other interest shortfalls*—(i) *In general.* This paragraph (d)(4) provides a special rule to determine whether a debt instrument with a teaser rate (or rates), an interest holiday, or any other interest shortfall has de minimis OID. This rule applies if—

(A) The amount of OID on the debt instrument is more than the de minimis amount as otherwise determined under paragraph (d) of this section; and

(B) All stated interest provided for in the debt instrument would be qualified stated interest under paragraph (c) of this section except that for 1 or more accrual periods the interest rate is below the rate applicable for the remainder of the instrument's term (e.g., if as a result of an interest holiday, none of the stated interest is qualified stated interest).

(ii) *Redetermination of OID for purposes of the de minimis test.* For purposes of determining whether a debt instrument described in paragraph (d)(4)(i) of this section has de minimis OID, the instrument's stated redemption price at maturity is treated as equal to the instrument's issue price plus the greater of the amount of foregone interest or the excess (if any) of the instrument's stated principal amount over its issue price. The amount of foregone interest is the amount of additional stated interest that would be required to be payable on the debt instrument during the period of the teaser rate, holiday, or shortfall so that all stated interest would be qualified stated interest under paragraph (c) of this section. See *Example 5* and *Example 6* of paragraph (f) of this section. In addition, for purposes of computing the de minimis amount of OID the weighted average maturity of the debt instrument is determined by treating all stated interest payments as qualified stated interest payments.

(5) *Treatment of de minimis OID by holders*—(i) *Allocation of de minimis OID to principal payments.* The holder of a debt instrument includes any de minimis OID (other than de minimis OID treated as qualified stated interest under paragraph (d)(1) of this section, such as de minimis OID attributable to a teaser rate or interest holiday) in income as stated principal payments are made. The amount includible in income with respect to each principal payment equals the product of the total amount of de minimis OID on the debt instrument and a fraction, the numerator of which is the amount of the principal payment made, and the denominator of which is the stated principal amount of the instrument.

(ii) *Character of de minimis OID*—(A) *De minimis OID treated as gain recognized on retire-*

Reg. § 1.1273-1(d)(5)

ment. Any amount of de minimis OID includible in income under this paragraph (d)(5) is treated as gain recognized on retirement of the debt instrument. See section 1271 to determine whether a retirement is treated as an exchange of the debt instrument.

(B) *Treatment of de minimis OID on sale or exchange.* Any gain attributable to de minimis OID that is recognized on the sale or exchange of a debt instrument is capital gain if the debt instrument is a capital asset in the hands of the seller.

(iii) *Treatment of subsequent holders.* If a subsequent holder purchases a debt instrument issued with de minimis OID at a premium (as defined in § 1.1272-2(b)(2)), the subsequent holder does not include the de minimis OID in income. Otherwise, a subsequent holder includes any discount in income under the market discount rules (sections 1276 through 1278) rather than under the rules of this paragraph (d)(5).

(iv) *Cross-reference.* See § 1.1272-3 for an election by a holder to treat de minimis OID as OID.

(e) *Definitions*—(1) *Installment obligation.* An installment obligation is a debt instrument that provides for the payment of any amount other than qualified stated interest before maturity.

(2) *Self-amortizing installment obligation.* A self-amortizing installment obligation is an obligation that provides for equal payments composed of principal and qualified stated interest that are unconditionally payable at least annually during the entire term of the debt instrument with no additional payment required at maturity.

(3) *Weighted average maturity.* The weighted average maturity of a debt instrument is the sum of the following amounts determined for each payment under the instrument (other than a payment of qualified stated interest)—

(i) The number of complete years from the issue date until the payment is made, multiplied by

(ii) A fraction, the numerator of which is the amount of the payment and the denominator of which is the debt instrument's stated redemption price at maturity.

(f) *Examples.* The following examples illustrate the rules of this section.

Example 1. Qualified stated interest—(i) *Facts.* On January 1, 1995, A purchases at original issue for $100,000, a debt instrument that matures on January 1, 1999, and has a stated principal amount of $100,000, payable at maturity. The debt instrument provides for interest payments of $8,000 on January 1, 1996, and January 1, 1997, and quarterly interest payments of $1,942.65, beginning on April 1, 1997.

(ii) *Amount of qualified stated interest.* The annual payments of $8,000 and the quarterly payments of $1,942.65 are payable at a single fixed rate because 8 percent, compounded annually, is equivalent to 7.77 percent, compounded quarterly. Consequently, all stated interest payments under the debt instrument are qualified stated interest payments.

Example 2. Qualified stated interest with short initial payment interval. On October 1, 1994, A purchases at original issue, for $100,000, a debt instrument that matures on January 1, 1998, and has a stated principal amount of $100,000, payable at maturity. The debt instrument provides for an interest payment of $2,000 on January 1, 1995, and interest payments of $8,000 on January 1, 1996, January 1, 1997, and January 1, 1998. Under paragraph (c)(1)(iii)(B) of this section, all stated interest payments on the debt instrument are computed at a single fixed rate and are qualified stated interest payments.

Example 3. Stated interest in excess of qualified stated interest—(i) *Facts.* On January 1, 1995, B purchases at original issue, for $100,000, C corporation's 5-year debt instrument. The debt instrument provides for a principal payment of $100,000, payable at maturity, and calls for annual interest payments of $10,000 for the first 3 years and annual interest payments of $10,600 for the last 2 years.

(ii) *Payments in excess of qualified stated interest.* All of the first three interest payments and $10,000 of each of the last two interest payments are qualified stated interest payments within the meaning of paragraph (c)(1) of this section. Under paragraph (c)(4) of this section, the remaining $600 of each of the last two interest payments is included in the stated redemption price at maturity, so that the stated redemption price at maturity is $101,200. Pursuant to paragraph (e)(3) of this section, the weighted average maturity of the debt instrument is 4.994 years [(4 years × $600/$101,200) + (5 years × $100,600/$101,200)]. The de minimis amount, or one-fourth of 1 percent of the stated redemption price at maturity multiplied by the weighted average maturity, is $1,263.50. Because the actual amount of discount, $1,200, is less than the de minimis amount, the instrument is treated as having no OID, and, under paragraph (d)(1) of this section, all of the interest payments are treated as qualified stated interest payments.

Example 4. Qualified stated interest on a debt instrument that is subject to an option—(i) *Facts.* On January 1, 1997, A issues, for $100,000, a

Reg. § 1.1273-1(e)(1)

10-year debt instrument that provides for a $100,000 principal payment at maturity and for annual interest payments of $10,000. Under the terms of the debt instrument, A has the option, exercisable on January 1, 2002, to lower the annual interest payments to $8,000. In addition, the debt instrument gives the holder an unconditional right to put the debt instrument back to A, exercisable on January 1, 2002, in return for $100,000.

(ii) *Amount of qualified stated interest.* Under paragraph (c)(2) of this section, the debt instrument provides for qualified stated interest to the extent of the lowest fixed rate at which qualified stated interest would be payable under any payment schedule. If the payment schedule determined by assuming that the issuer's option will be exercised and the put option will not be exercised were treated as the debt instrument's sole payment schedule, only $8,000 of each annual interest payment would be qualified stated interest. Under any other payment schedule, the debt instrument would provide for annual qualified stated interest payments of $10,000. Accordingly, only $8,000 of each annual interest payment is qualified stated interest. Any excess of each annual interest payment over $8,000 is included in the debt instrument's stated redemption price at maturity.

Example 5. De minimis OID; interest holiday—(i) *Facts.* On January 1, 1995, C purchases at original issue, for $97,561, a debt instrument that matures on January 1, 2007, and has a stated principal amount of $100,000, payable at maturity. The debt instrument provides for an initial interest holiday of 1 quarter and quarterly interest payments of $2,500 thereafter (beginning on July 1, 1995). The issue price of the debt instrument is $97,561. C chooses to accrue OID based on quarterly accrual periods.

(ii) *De minimis amount of OID.* But for the interest holiday, all stated interest on the debt instrument would be qualified stated interest. Under paragraph (d)(4) of this section, for purposes of determining whether the debt instrument has de minimis OID, the stated, redemption price at maturity of the instrument is $100,061 ($97,561 issue price) plus $2,500, (the greater of the amount of foregone interest ($2,500) and the amount equal to the excess of the instrument's stated principal amount over its issue price ($2,439)). Thus, the debt instrument is treated as having OID of $2,500 ($100,061 minus $97,561). Because this amount is less than the de minimis amount of $3,001.83 (0.0025 multiplied by $100,061 multiplied by 12 complete years to maturity), the debt instrument is treated as having

no OID, and all stated interest is treated as qualified stated interest.

Example 6. De minimis OID; teaser rate—(i) *Facts.* The facts are the same as in *Example 5* of this paragraph (f) except that C uses an initial semiannual accrual period rather than an initial quarterly accrual period.

(ii) *De minimis amount of OID.* The debt instrument provides for an initial teaser rate because the interest rate for the semiannual accrual period is less than the interest rate applicable to the subsequent quarterly accrual periods. But for the initial teaser rate, all stated interest on the debt instrument would be qualified stated interest. Under paragraph (d)(4) of this section, for purposes of determining whether the debt instrument has de minimis OID, the stated redemption price at maturity of the instrument is $100,123.50 ($97,561 (issue price) plus $2,562.50 (the greater of the amount of foregone interest ($2,562.50) and the amount equal to the excess of the instrument's stated principal amount over its issue price ($2,439)). Thus, the debt instrument is treated as having OID of $2,562.50 ($100,123.50 minus $97,561). Because this amount is less than the de minimis amount of $3,003.71 (0.0025 multiplied by $100,123.50 multiplied by 12 complete years to maturity), the debt instrument is treated as having no OID, and all stated interest is treated as qualified stated interest. [Reg. § 1.1273-1.]

☐ [T.D. 8517, 1-27-94. Amended by T.D. 8674, 6-11-96.]

[Reg. § 1.1273-2]

§ 1.1273-2. Determination of issue price and issue date.—(a) *Debt instruments issued for money*—(1) *Issue price.* If a substantial amount of the debt instruments in an issue is issued for money, the issue price of each debt instrument in the issue is the first price at which a substantial amount of the debt instruments is sold for money. Thus, if an issue consists of a single debt instrument that is issued for money, the issue price of the debt instrument is the amount paid for the instrument. For example, in the case of a debt instrument evidencing a loan to a natural person, the issue price of the instrument is the amount loaned. See § 1.1275-2(d) for rules regarding Treasury securities. For purposes of this paragraph (a), money includes functional currency and, in certain circumstances, nonfunctional currency. See § 1.988-2(b)(2) for circumstances when nonfunctional currency is treated as money rather than as property.

(2) *Issue date.* The issue date of an issue described in paragraph (a)(1) of this section is the

Reg. § 1.1273-2(a)(2)

first settlement date or closing date, whichever is applicable, on which a substantial amount of the debt instruments in the issue is sold for money.

(b) *Publicly traded debt instruments issued for property.*—(1) *Issue price.* If a substantial amount of the debt instruments in an issue is traded on an established market (within the meaning of paragraph (f) of this section) and the issue is not described in paragraph (a)(1) of this section, the issue price of each debt instrument in the issue is the fair market value of the debt instrument, determined as of the issue date (as defined in paragraph (b)(2) of this section).

(2) *Issue date.* The issue date of an issue described in paragraph (b)(1) of this section is the first date on which a substantial amount of the traded debt instruments in the issue is issued.

(c) *Debt instruments issued for publicly traded property*—(1) *Issue price.* If a substantial amount of the debt instrument in an issue is issued for property that is traded on an established market (within the meaning of paragraph (f) of this section) and the issue is not described in paragraph (a)(1) or (b)(1) of this section, the issue price of each debt instrument in the issue is the fair market value of the property, determined as of the issue date (as defined in paragraph (c)(2) of this section). For purposes of the preceding sentence, property means a debt instrument, stock, security, contract, commodity, or nonfunctional currency. But see § 1.988-2(b)(2) for circumstances when nonfunctional currency is treated as money rather than as property.

(2) *Issue date.* The issue date of an issue described in paragraph (c)(1) of this section is the first date on which a substantial amount of the debt instruments in the issue is issued for traded property.

(d) *Other debt instruments*—(1) *Issue price.* If an issue of debt instruments is not described in paragraph (a)(1), (b)(1), or (c)(1) of this section, the issue price of each debt instrument in the issue is determined as if the debt instrument were a separate issue. If the issue price of a debt instrument that is treated as a separate issue under the preceding sentence is not determined under paragraph (a)(1), (b)(1), or (c)(1) of this section, and if section 1274 applies to the debt instrument, the issue price of the instrument is determined under section 1274. Otherwise, the issue price of the debt instrument is its stated redemption price at maturity under section 1273(b)(4). See section 1274(c) and § 1.1274-1 to determine if section 1274 applies to a debt instrument.

(2) *Issue date.* The issue date of an issue described in paragraph (d)(1) of this section is the date on which the debt instrument is issued for money or in a sale or exchange.

(e) *Special rule for certain sales to bond houses, brokers, or similar persons.* For purposes of determining the issue price and issue date of a debt instrument under this section, sales to bond houses, brokers, or similar persons or organizations acting in the capacity of underwriters, placement agents, or wholesalers are ignored.

(f) *Traded on an established market (publicly traded)*—(1) *In general.* Property (including a debt instrument described in paragraph (b)(1) of this section) is traded on an established market for purposes of this section if, at any time during the 60-day period ending 30 days after the issue date, the property is described in paragraph (f)(2), (f)(3), (f)(4), or (f)(5) of this section.

(2) *Exchange listed property.* Property is described in this paragraph (f)(2) if it is listed on—

(i) A national securities exchange registered under section 6 of the Securities Exchange Act of 1934 (15 U.S.C. 78f);

(ii) An interdealer quotation system sponsored by a national securities association registered under section 15A of the Securities Exchange Act of 1934 (15 U.S.C. 78o-3); or

(iii) The International Stock Exchange of the United Kingdom and the Republic of Ireland, Limited, the Frankfurt Stock Exchange, the Tokyo Stock Exchange, or any other foreign exchange or board of trade that is designated by the Commissioner in the Internal Revenue Bulletin (see § 601.601(d)(2)(ii) of this chapter).

(3) *Market traded property.* Property is described in this paragraph (f)(3) if it is property of a kind that is traded either on a board of trade designated as a contract market by the Commodities Futures Trading Commission or on an interbank market.

(4) *Property appearing on a quotation medium.* Property is described in this paragraph (f)(4) if it appears on a system of general circulation (including a computer listing disseminated to subscribing brokers, dealers, or traders) that provides a reasonable basis to determine fair market value by disseminating either recent price quotations (including rates, yields, or other pricing information) of one or more identified brokers, dealers, or traders or actual prices (including rates, yields, or other pricing information) of recent sales transactions (a quotation medium). A quotation medium does not include a directory or listing of brokers, dealers, or traders for specific securities, such as yellow sheets, that provides neither price quotations nor actual prices of recent sales transactions.

Reg. § 1.1273-2(b)(1)

Special Rules, Bonds & Other Debt Instruments

(5) *Readily quotable debt instruments*—(i) *In general.* A debt instrument is described in this paragraph (f)(5) if price quotations are readily available from dealers, brokers, or traders.

(ii) *Safe harbors.* A debt instrument is not considered to be described in paragraph (f)(5)(i) of this section if—

(A) No other outstanding debt instrument of the issuer (or of any person who gurantees the debt instrument) is described in paragraph (f)(2), (f)(3), or (f)(4) of this section (other traded debt);

(B) The original stated principal amount of the issue that includes the debt instrument does not exceed $25 million;

(C) The conditions and covenants relating to the issuer's performance with respect to the debt instrument are materially less restrictive than the conditions and covenants included in all of the issuer's other traded debt (e.g., the debt instrument is subject to an economically significant subordination provision whereas the issuer's other traded debt is senior); or

(D) The maturity date of the debt instrument is more than 3 years after the latest maturity date of the issuer's other traded debt.

(6) *Effect of certain temporary restrictions on trading.* If there is any temporary restriction on trading a purpose of which is to avoid the characterization of the property as one that is traded on an established market for Federal income tax purposes, then the property is treated as traded on an established market. For purposes of the preceding sentence, a temporary restriction on trading need not be imposed by the issuer.

(7) *Convertible debt instruments.* A debt instrument is not treated as traded on an established market solely because the debt instrument is convertible into property that is so traded.

(g) *Treatment of certain cash payments incident to lending transactions*—(1) *Applicability.* The provisions of this paragraph (g) apply to cash payments made incident to private lending transactions (including seller financing).

(2) *Payments from borrower to lender*—(i) *Money lending transaction.* In a lending transaction to which section 1273(b)(2) applies, a payment from the borrower to the lender (other than a payment for property or for services provided by the lender, such as commitment fees or loan processing costs) reduces the issue price of the debt instrument evidencing the loan. However, solely for purposes of determining the tax consequences to the borrower, the issue price is not reduced if the payment is deductible under section 461(g)(2).

(ii) *Section 1274 transaction.* In a lending transaction to which section 1274 applies, a payment from the buyer-borrower to the seller-lender that is designated as interest or points reduces the stated principal amount of the debt instrument evidencing the loan, but is included in the purchase price of the property. If the payment is deductible under section 461(g)(2), however, the issuer price of the debt instrument (as otherwise determined under section 1274 and the rule in the preceding sentence) is increased by the amount of the payment to compute the buyer-borrower's interest deductions under section 163.

(3) *Payments from lender to borrower.* A payment from the lender to the borrower in a lending transaction is treated as an amount loaned.

(4) *Payments between lender and third party.* If, as part of a lending transaction, a party other than the borrower (the third party) makes a payment to the lender, that payment is treated in appropriate circumstances as made from the third party to the borrower followed by a payment in the same amount from the borrower to the lender and governed by the provisions of paragraph (g)(2) of this section. If, as part of a lending transaction, the lender makes a payment to a third party, that payment is treated in appropriate circumstances as an additional amount loaned to the borrower and then paid by the borrower to the third party. The character of the deemed payment between the borrower and the third party depends on the substance of the transaction.

(5) *Examples.* The following examples illustrate the rules of this paragraph (g).

Example 1. Payments from borrower to lender in a cash transaction—(i) *Facts.* A lends $100,000 to B for a term of 10 years. At the time the loan is made, B pays $4,000 in points to A. Assume that the points are not deductible by B under section 461(g)(2) and that the stated redemption price at maturity of the debt instrument is $100,000.

(ii) *Payment results in OID.* Under paragraph (g)(2)(i) of this section, the issue price of B's debt instrument evidencing the loan is $96,000. Because the amount of OID on the debt instrument ($4,000) is more than a de minimis amount of OID, A accounts for the OID under § 1.1272-1. B accounts for the OID under § 1.163-7.

Example 2. Payments from borrower to lender in a section 1274 transaction—(i) *Facts.* A sells property to B for $1,000,000 in a transaction that is not a potentially abusive situation (within the meaning of § 1.1274-3). In consideration for

Reg. § 1.1273-2(g)(5)

the property, B gives A $300,000 and issues a 5-year debt instrument that has a stated principal amount of $700,000, payable at maturity, and that calls for semiannual payments of interest at a rate of 8.5 percent. In addition to the cash downpayment, B pays A $14,000 designated as points on the loan. Assume that the points are not deductible under section 461(g)(2).

(ii) *Issue price.* Under paragraph (g)(2)(ii) of this section, the stated principal amount of B's debt instrument is $686,000 ($700,000 minus $14,000). Assuming a test rate of 9 percent, compounded semiannually, the imputed principal amount of B's debt instrument under § 1.1274-2(c)(1) is $686,153. Under § 1.1274-2(b)(1), the issue price of B's debt instrument is the stated principal amount of $686,000. Because the amount of OID on the debt instrument ($700,000 − $686,000, or $14,000) is more than a de minimis amount of OID, A accounts for the OID under § 1.1272-1 and B accounts for the OID under § 1.163-7. B's basis in the property purchased is $1,000,000 ($686,000 debt instrument plus $314,000 cash payments).

Example 3. Payments between lender and third party (seller-paid points)—(i) *Facts.* A sells real property to B for $500,000 in a transaction that is not a potentially abusive situation (within the meaning of § 1.1274-3). B makes a cash down payment of $100,000 and borrows $400,000 of the purchase price from a lender, L, repayable in annual installments over a term of 15 years calling for interest at a rate of 9 percent, compounded annually. As part of the transaction, A makes a payment of $8,000 to L to facilitate the loan to B.

(ii) *Payment results in a de minimis amount of OID.* Under the provisions of paragraphs (g)(2)(i) and (g)(4) of this section, B is treated as having made an $8,000 payment directly to L and a payment of only $492,000 to A for the property. Thus, B's basis in the property is $492,000. The payment to L reduces the issue price of B's debt instrument to $392,000, resulting in $8,000 of OID ($400,000 − $392,000). Because the amount of OID is de minimis under § 1.1273-1(d), L accounts for the de minimis OID under § 1.1273-1(d)(5). But see § 1.1272-3 (election to treat de minimis OID as OID). B accounts for the de minimis OID under § 1.163-7.

(h) *Investment units*—(1) *In general.* Under section 1273(c)(2), an investment unit is treated as if the investment unit were a debt instrument. The issue price of the investment unit is determined under paragraph (a)(1), (b)(1), or (c)(1) of this section, if applicable. The issue price of the investment unit is then allocated between the debt instrument and the property right (or rights) that comprise the unit based on their relative fair market values. If paragraphs (a)(1), (b)(1), and (c)(1) of this section are not applicable, however, the issue price of the debt instrument that is part of the investment unit is determined under section 1273(b)(4) or 1274, whichever is applicable.

(2) *Consistent allocation by holders and issuer.* The issuer's allocation of the issue price of the investment unit is binding on all holders of the investment unit. However, the issuer's determination is not binding on a holder that explicitly discloses that its allocation is different from the issuer's allocation. Unless otherwise provided by the Commissioner, the disclosure must be made on a statement attached to the holder's timely filed Federal income tax return for the taxable year that includes the acquisition date of the investment unit. See § 1.1275-2(e) for rules relating to the issuer's obligation to disclose certain information to holders.

(i) [Reserved]

(j) *Convertible debt instruments.* The issue price of a debt instrument includes any amount paid for an option to convert the instrument into stock (or another debt instrument) of either the issuer or a related party (within the meaning of section 267(b) or 707(b)(1)) or into cash or other property in an amount equal to the approximate value of such stock (or debt instrument).

(k) *Below-market loans subject to section 7872(b).* The issue price of a below-market loan subject to section 7872(b) (a term loan other than a gift loan) is the issue price determined under this section, reduced by the excess amount determined under section 7872(b)(1).

(l) [Reserved]

(m) *Treatment of amounts representing pre-issuance accrued interest*—(1) *Applicability.* Paragraph (m)(2) of this section provides an alternative to the general rule of this section for determining the issue price of a debt instrument if—

(i) A portion of the initial purchase price of the instrument is allocable to interest that has accrued prior to the issue date (pre-issuance accrued interest); and

(ii) The instrument provides for a payment of stated interest on the first payment date within 1 year of the issue date that equals or exceeds the amount of the pre-issuance accrued interest.

(2) *Exclusiion of pre-issuance accrued interest from issue price.* If a debt instrument meets the requirements of paragraph (m)(1) of this section, the instrument's issue price may be computed by subtracting from the issue price (as

Reg. § 1.1273-2(h)(1)

otherwise computed under this section) the amount of pre-issuance accrued interest. If the issue price of the debt instrument is computed in this manner, a portion of the stated interest payable on the first payment date must be treated as a return of the excluded pre-issuance accrued interest, rather than as an amount payable on the instrument.

(3) *Example.* The following example illustrates the rule of paragraph (m) of this section.

Example. (i) *Facts.* On January 15, 1995, A purchases at original issue, for $1,005, B corporation's debt instrument. The debt instrument provides for a payment of principal of $1,000 on January 1, 2005, and provides for semiannual interest payments of $60 on January 1 and July 1 of each year, beginning on July 1, 1995.

(ii) *Determination of pre-issuance accrued interest.* Under paragraphs (m)(1) and (m)(2) of this section, $5 of the $1,005 initial purchase price of the debt instrument is allocable to pre-issuance accrued interest. Accordingly, the debt instrument's issue price may be computed by subtracting the amount of pre-issuance accrued interest ($5) from the issue price otherwise computed under this section ($1,005), resulting in an issue price of $1,000. If the issue price is computed in this manner, $5 of the $60 payment made on July 1, 1995, must be treated as a repayment by B of the pre-issuance accrued interest. [Reg. § 1.1273-2.]

☐ [*T.D.* 8517, 1-27-94.]

[Reg. § 1.1274-1]

§ 1.1274-1. Debt instruments to which section 1274 applies.—(a) *In general.* Subject to the exceptions and limitations in paragraph (b) of this section, section 1274 and this section apply to any debt instrument issued in consideration for the sale or exchange of property. For purposes of section 1274, property includes debt instruments and investment units, but does not include money, services, or the right to use property. For the treatment of certain obligations given in exchange for services or the use of property, see sections 404 and 467. For purposes of this paragraph (a), money includes functional currency and, in certain circumstances, nonfunctional currency. See § 1.988-2(b)(2) for circumstances when nonfunctional currency is treated as money rather than as property.

(b) *Exceptions*—(1) *Debt instrument with adequate stated interest and no OID.* Section 1274 does not apply to a debt instrument if—

(i) All interest payable on the instrument is qualified stated interest;

(ii) The stated rate of interest is at least equal to the test rate of interest (as defined in § 1.1274-4);

(iii) The debt instrument is not issued in a potentially abusive situation (as defined in § 1.1274-3); and

(iv) No payment from the buyer-borrower to the seller-lender designated as points or interest is made at the time of issuance of the debt instrument.

(2) *Exceptions under sections 1274(c)(1)(B), 1274(c)(3), 1274A(c), and 1275(b)(1)*—(i) *In general.* Sections 1274(c)(1)(B), 1274(c)(3), 1274A(c), and 1275(b)(1) describe certain transactions to which section 1274 does not apply. This paragraph (b)(2) provides certain rules to be used in applying those exceptions.

(ii) *Special rules for certain exceptions under section 1274(c)(3)*—(A) *Determination of sales price for certain sales of farms.* For purposes of section 1274(c)(3)(A), the determination as to whether the sales price cannot exceed $1,000,000 is made without regard to any other exception to, or limitation on, the applicability of section 1274 (e.g., without regard to the special rules regarding sales of principal residences and land transfers between related persons). In addition, the sales price is determined without regard to section 1274 and without regard to any stated interest. The sales price includes the amount of any liability included in the amount realized from the sale or exchange. See § 1.1001-2.

(B) *Sales involving total payments of $250,000 or less.* Under section 1274(c)(3)(C), the determination of the amount of payments due under all debt instruments and the amount of other consideration to be received is made as of the date of the sale or exchange or, if earlier, the contract date. If the precise amount due under any debt instrument or the precise amount of any other consideration to be received cannot be determined as of that date, section 1274(c)(3)(C) applies only if it can be determined that the maximum of the aggregate amount of payments due under the debt instruments and other consideration to be received cannot exceed $250,000. For purposes of section 1274(c)(3)(C), if a liability is assumed or property is taken subject to a liability, the aggregate amount of payments due includes the outstanding principal balance or adjusted issue price (in the case of an obligation originally issued at a discount) of the obligation.

(C) *Coordination with section 1273 and § 1.1273-2.* In accordance with section 1274(c)(3)(D), section 1274 and this section do not apply if the issue price of a debt instrument issued in consideration for the sale or exchange of

Reg. § 1.1274-1(b)(2)

53,656 Special Rules, Bonds & Other Debt Instruments

See p. 20,601 for regulations not amended to reflect law changes

property is determined under paragraph (a)(1), (b)(1), or (c)(1) of § 1.1273-2.

(3) *Other exceptions to section 1274*—(i) *Holders of certain below-market instruments.* Section 1274 does not apply to any holder of a debt instrument that is issued in consideration for the sale or exchange of personal use property (within the meaning of section 1275(b)(3)) in the hands of the issuer and that evidences a below-market loan described in section 7872(c)(1).

(ii) *Transactions involving certain demand loans.* Section 1274 does not apply to any debt instrument that evidences a demand loan that is a below-market loan described in section 7872(c)(1).

(iii) *Certain transfers subject to section 1041.* Section 1274 does not apply to any debt instrument issued in consideration for a transfer of property subject to section 1041 (relating to transfers of property between spouses or incident to divorce).

(c) *Examples.* The following examples illustrate the rules of this section.

Example 1. Single stated rate paid semiannually. A debt instrument issued in consideration for the sale of nonpublicly traded property in a transaction that is not a potentially abusive situation calls for the payment of a principal amount of $1,000,000 at the end of a 10-year term and 20 semiannual interest payments of $60,000. Assume that the test rate of interest is 12 percent, compounded semiannually. The debt instrument is not subject to section 1274 because it provides for interest equal to the test rate and all interest payable on the instrument is qualified stated interest.

Example 2. Sale of farm for debt instrument with contingent interest—(i) *Facts.* On July 1, 1995, A, an individual, sells to B land used as a farm within the meaning of section 6420(c)(2). As partial consideration for the sale, B issues a debt instrument calling for a single $500,000 payment due in 10 years unless profits from the land in each of the 10 years preceding maturity of the debt instrument exceed a specified amount, in which case B is to make a payment of $1,200,000. The debt instrument does not provide for interest.

(ii) *Total payments may exceed $1,000,000.* Even though the total payments ultimately payable under the contract may be less than $1,000,000, at the time of the sale or exchange it cannot be determined that the sales price cannot exceed $1,000,000. Thus, the sale of the land used as a farm is not an excepted transaction described in section 1274(c)(3)(A).

Example 3. Sale between related parties subject to section 483(e)—(i) *Facts.* On July 1, 1995, A, an individual, sells land (not used as a farm within the meaning of section 6420(c)(2)) to A's child B for $650,000. In consideration for the sale, B issues a 10-year debt instrument to A that calls for a payment of $650,000. No other consideration is given. The debt instrument does not provide for interest.

(ii) *Treatment of debt instrument.* For purposes of section 483(e), the $650,000 debt instrument is treated as two separate debt instruments: a $500,000 debt instrument and a $150,000 debt instrument. The $500,000 debt instrument is subject to section 483(e), and accordingly is covered by the exception from section 1274 described in section 1274(c)(3)(F). Because the amount of the payments due as consideration for the sale exceeds $250,000, however, the $150,000 debt instrument is subject to section 1274.

[Reg. § 1.1274-1.]

☐ [T.D. 8517, 1-27-94.]

[Reg. § 1.1274-2]

§ 1.1274-2. Issue price of debt instruments to which section 1274 applies.—(a) *In general.* If section 1274 applies to a debt instrument, section 1274 and this section determine the issue price of the debt instrument. For rules relating to the determination of the amount and timing of OID to be included in income, see section 1272 and the regulations thereunder.

(b) *Issue price*—(1) *Debt instruments that provide for adequate stated interest; stated principal amount.* The issue price of a debt instrument that provides for adequate stated interest is the stated principal amount of the debt instrument. For purposes of section 1274, the stated principal amount of a debt instrument is the aggregate amount of all payments due under the debt instrument, excluding any amount of stated interest. Under § 1.1273-2(g)(2)(ii), however, the stated principal amount of a debt instrument is reduced by any payment from the buyer-borrower to the seller-lender that is designated as interest or points. See *Example 2* of § 1.1273-2(g)(5).

(2) *Debt instruments that do not provide for adequate stated interest; imputed principal amount.* The issue price of a debt instrument that does not provide for adequate stated interest is the imputed principal amount of the debt instrument.

(3) *Debt instruments issued in a potentially abusive situation; fair market value.* Notwithstanding paragraphs (b)(1) and (b)(2) of this section, in the case of a debt instrument issued in a potentially abusive situation (as defined in § 1.1274-3), the issue price of the debt instrument is the fair market value of the property received

Reg. § 1.1274-2(a)

Special Rules, Bonds & Other Debt Instruments

See p. 20,601 for regulations not amended to reflect law changes

in exchange for the debt instrument, reduced by the fair market value of any consideration other than the debt instrument issued in consideration for the sale or exchange.

(c) *Determination of whether a debt instrument provides for adequate stated interest*—(1) *In general.* A debt instrument provides for adequate stated interest if its stated principal amount is less than or equal to its imputed principal amount. Imputed principal amount means the sum of the present values, as of the issue date, of all payments, including payments of stated interest, due under the debt instrument (determined by using a discount rate equal to the test rate of interest as determined under § 1.1274-4). If a debt instrument has a single fixed rate of interest that is paid or compounded at least annually, and that rate is equal to or greater than the test rate, the debt instrument has adequate stated interest.

(2) *Determination of present value.* The present value of a payment is determined by discounting the payment from the date it becomes due to the date of the sale or exchange at the test rate of interest. To determine present value, a compounding period must be selected, and the test rate must be based on the same compounding period.

(d) *Treatment of certain options.* This paragraph (d) provides rules for determining the issue price of a debt instrument to which section 1274 applies (other than a debt instrument issued in a potentially abusive situation) that is subject to one or more options described in both paragraphs (c)(1) and (c)(5) of § 1.1272-1. Under this paragraph (d), an issuer will be deemed to exercise or not exercise an option or combination of options in a manner that minimizes the instrument's imputed principal amount, and a holder will be deemed to exercise or not exercise an option or combination of options in a manner that maximizes the instrument's imputed principal amount. If both the issuer and the holder have options, the rules of this paragraph (d) are applied to the options in the order that they may be exercised. Thus, the deemed exercise of one option may eliminate other options that are later in time. See § 1.1272-1(c)(5) to determine the debt instrument's yield and maturity for purposes of determining the accrual of OID with respect to the instrument.

(e) *Mandatory sinking funds.* In determining the issue price of a debt instrument to which section 1274 applies (other than a debt instrument issued in a potentially abusive situation) and that is subject to a mandatory sinking fund provision described in § 1.1272-1(c)(3), the mandatory sinking fund provision is ignored.

(f) *Treatment of variable rate debt instruments*—(1) *Stated interest at a qualified floating rate*—(i) *In general.* For purposes of paragraph (c) of this section, the imputed principal amount of a variable rate debt instrument (within the meaning of § 1.1275-5(a)) that provides for stated interest at a qualified floating rate (or rates) is determined by assuming that the instrument provides for a fixed rate of interest for each accrual period to which a qualified floating rate applies. For purposes of the preceding sentence, the assumed fixed rate in each accrual period is the greater of—

(A) The value of the applicable qualified floating rate as of the first date on which there is a binding written contract that substantially sets forth the terms under which the sale or exchange is ultimately consummated; or

(B) The value of the applicable qualified floating rate as of the date on which the sale or exchange occurs.

(ii) *Interest rate restrictions.* Notwithstanding paragraph (f)(1)(i) of this section, if, as a result of interest rate restrictions (such as an interest rate cap), the expected yield of the debt instrument taking the restrictions into account is signifcantly less than the expected yield of the debt instrument without regard to the restrictions, the interest payments on the debt instrument (other than any fixed interest payments) are treated as contingent payments. Reasonably symmetric interest rate caps and floors, or reasonably symmetric governors, that are fixed throughout the term of the debt instrument do not result in the debt instrument being subject to this rule.

(2) *Stated interest at a single objective rate.* For purposes of paragraph (c) of this section, the imputed principal amount of a variable rate debt instrument (within the meaning of § 1.1275-5(a)) that provides for stated interest at a single objective rate is determined by treating the interest payments as contingent payments.

(g) *Treatment of contingent payment debt instruments.* Notwithstanding paragraph (b) of this section, if a debt instrument subject to section 1274 provides for one or more contingent payments, the issue price of the debt instrument is the lesser of the instrument's noncontingent principal payments and the sum of the present values of the noncontingent payments (as determined under paragraph (c) of this section). However, if the debt instrument is issued in a potentially abusive situation, the issue price of the debt instrument is the fair market value of the noncontingent payments. For additional rules relating to a debt instrument that provides for one or more contingent payments, see § 1.1275-4. This para-

Reg. § 1.1274-2(g)

53,658 Special Rules, Bonds & Other Debt Instruments

See p. 20,601 for regulations not amended to reflect law changes

graph (g) applies to debt instruments issued on or after August 13, 1996.

(h) *Examples.* The following examples illustrate the rules of this section. Each example assumes a 30-day month, 360-day year. In addition, each example assumes that the debt instrument is not a qualified debt instrument (as defined in section 1274A(b)) and is not issued in a potentially abusive situation.

Example 1. Debt instrument without a fixed rate over its entire term—(i) *Facts.* On January 1, 1995, A sells nonpublicly traded property to B for a stated purchase price of $3,500,000. In consideration for the sale, B makes a down payment of $500,000 and issues a 10-year debt instrument with a stated principal amount of $3,000,000, payable at maturity. The debt instrument calls for no interest in the first 2 years and interest at a rate of 15 percent payable annually over the remaining 8 years of the debt instrument. The first interest payment of $450,000 is due on December 31, 1997, and the last interest payment is due on December 31, 2004, together with the $3,000,000 payment of principal. Assume that the test rate of interest applicable to the debt instrument is 10.5 percent, compounded annually.

(ii) *Applicability of section 1274.* Because the debt instrument does not provide for any interest during the first 2 years, none of the interest on the debt instrument is qualified stated interest. Therefore, the issue price of the debt instrument is determined under section 1274. See § 1.1274-1(b)(1). If the debt instrument has adequate stated interest, the issue price of the instrument is its stated principal amount. Otherwise, the issue price of the debt instrument is its imputed principal amount. The debt instrument has adequate stated interest only if the stated principal amount is less than or equal to the imputed principal amount.

(iii) *Determination of imputed principal amount.* To compute the imputed principal amount of the debt instrument, all payments due under the debt instrument are discounted back to the issue date at 10.5 percent, compounded annually, as follows:

(A) The present value of the $3,000,000 principal payment payable on December 31, 2004, is $1,105,346.59, determined as follows:

$$\$1,105,346.59 = \frac{\$3,000,000}{(1 + .105/1)^{10}}$$

(B) The present value of the eight interest payments of $450,000 as of January 1, 1997, is $2,357,634.55, determined as follows:

$$\$2,357,634.55 = \$450,000 \times \frac{1 - (1 + .105/1)^{-8}}{(.105/1)}$$

(C) The present value of this interim amount as of January 1, 1995, is $1,930,865.09, determined as follows:

$$\$1,930,865.09 = \frac{\$2,357,634.55}{(1 + .105/1)^2}$$

(iv) *Determination of issue price.* The debt instrument's imputed principal amount (that is, the present value of all payments due under the debt instrument) is $3,036,211.68 ($1,105,346.59 + $1,930,865.09). Because the stated principal amount ($3,000,000) is less than the imputed principal amount, the debt instrument provides for adequate stated interest. Therefore, the issue price of the debt instrument is its stated principal amount ($3,000,000).

Example 2. Debt instrument subject to issuer call option—(i) *Facts.* On January 1, 1995, in partial consideration for the sale of nonpublicly traded property, H corporation issues to G a 10-year debt instrument, maturing on January 1, 2005, with a stated principal amount of $10,000,000, payable on that date. The debt instrument provides for annual payments of interest of 8 percent for the first 5 years and 14 percent for the final 5 years, payable on January 1 of each year, beginning on January 1, 1996. In addition, the debt instrument provides H with the unconditional option to call (prepay) the debt instrument at the end of 5 years for its stated principal amount of $10,000,000. Assume that the Federal mid-term and long-term rates applicable to the sale based on annual compounding are 9 percent and 10 percent, respectively.

(ii) *Option presumed exercised.* Assuming exercise of the call option, the imputed principal amount as determined under paragraph (d) of this section is $9,611,034.87 (the present value of all of the payments due within a 5-year term discounted at a test rate of 9 percent, compounded annually). Assuming nonexercise of the call option, the imputed principal amount is $10,183,354.78 (the present value of all of the payments due within a 10-year term discounted at a test rate of 10 percent, compounded annually). For purposes of determining the imputed principal amount, the option is presumed exercised because the imputed principal amount, assuming exercise of the option, is less than the imputed principal amount, assuming the option is not exercised. Because the option is presumed exercised, the debt instrument fails to provide for adequate stated interest because the imputed

Reg. § 1.1274-2(h)

principal amount ($9,611,034.87) is less than the stated principal amount ($10,000,000). Thus, the issue price of the debt instrument is $9,611,034.87.

Example 3. Variable rate debt instrument with a single rate over its entire term—(i) *Facts.* On January 1, 1995, A sells B nonpublicly traded property. In partial consideration for the sale, B issues a debt instrument in the principal amount of $1,000,000, payable in 5 years. The debt instrument calls for interest payable monthly at a rate of 1 percentage point above the average prime lending rate of a major bank for the month preceding the month of the interest payment. Assume that the test rate of interest applicable to the debt instrument is 10.5 percent, compounded monthly. Assume also that 1 percentage point above the prime lending rate of the designated bank on the date of the sale is 12.5 percent, compounded monthly, which is greater than 1 percentage point above the prime lending rate of the designated bank on the first date on which there is a binding written contract that substantially sets forth the terms under which the sale is consummated.

(ii) *Debt instrument has adequate stated interest.* The debt instrument is a variable rate debt instrument (within the meaning of § 1.1275-5) that provides for stated interest at a qualified floating rate. Under paragraph (f)(1)(i) of this section, the debt instrument is treated as if it provided for a fixed rate of interest equal to 12.5 percent, compounded monthly. Because the test rate of interest is 10.5 percent, compounded monthly, the debt instrument provides for adequate stated interest.

Example 4. Debt instrument with a capped variable rate. On July 1, 1995, A sells nonpublicly traded property to B in return for a debt instrument with a stated principal amount of $10,000,000, payable on July 1, 2005. Interest is payble on July 1 of each year, beginning on July 1, 1996, at the Federal short-term rate for June of the same year. The debt instrument provides, however, that the interest rate cannot rise above 8.5 percent, compounded annually. Assume that, as of the date the test rate of interest for the debt instrument is determined, the Federal short-term rate is 8 percent, compounded annually. Assume further that, as a result of the interest rate cap of 8.5 percent, compounded annually, the expected yield of the debt instrument is significantly less than the expected yield of the debt instrument if it did not include the interest rate cap. Under paragraph (f)(1)(ii) of this section, the variable payments are treated as contingent payments for purposes of this section.

(i) [Reserved]

(j) *Special rules for tax-exempt obligations*—(1) *Certain variable rate debt instruments.* Notwithstanding paragraph (b) of this section, if a tax-exempt obligation (as defined in section 1275(a)(3)) is a variable rate debt instrument (within the meaning of § 1.1275-5) that pays interest at an objective rate and is subject to section 1274, the issue price of the obligation is the greater of the obligation's fair market value and its stated principal amount.

(2) *Contingent payment debt instruments.* Notwithstanding paragraphs (b) and (g) of this section, if a tax-exempt obligation (as defined in section 1275(a)(3)) is subject to section 1274 and § 1.1275-4, the issue price of the obligation is the fair market value of the obligation. However, in the case of a tax-exempt obligation that is subject to § 1.1275-4(d)(2) (an obligation that provides for interest-based or revenue-based payments), the issue price of the obligation is the greater of the obligation's fair market value and its stated principal amount.

(3) *Effective date.* This paragraph (j) applies to debt instruments issued on or after August 13, 1996. [Reg. § 1.1274-2.]

☐ [T.D. 8517, 1-27-94. Amended by T.D. 8674, 6-11-96.]

[Reg. § 1.1274-3]

§ 1.1274-3. Potentially abusive situations defined.—(a) *In general.* For purposes of section 1274, a potentially abusive situation means—

(1) A tax shelter (as defined in section 6662(d)(2)(C)(ii)); or

(2) Any other situation involving—

(i) A recent sales transaction;

(ii) Nonrecourse financing;

(iii) Financing with a term in excess of the useful life of the property; or

(iv) A debt instrument with clearly excessive interest.

(b) *Operating rules*—(1) *Debt instrument exchanged for nonrecourse financing.* Nonrecourse financing does not include an exchange of a nonrecourse debt instrument for an outstanding recourse or nonrecourse debt instrument.

(2) *Nonrecourse debt with substantial down payment.* Nonrecourse financing does not include a sale or exchange of a real property interest financed by a nonrecourse debt instrument if, in addition to the nonrecourse debt instrument, the purchaser makes a down payment in money that equals or exceeds 20 percent of the total stated purchase price of the real property interest. For purposes of the preceding sentence, a real prop-

Reg. § 1.1274-3(b)(2)

erty interest means any interest, other than an interest solely as a creditor, in real property.

(3) *Clearly excessive interest.* Interest on a debt instrument is clearly excessive if the interest, in light of the terms of the debt instrument and the creditworthiness of the borrower, is clearly greater than the arm's length amount of interest that would have been charged in a cash lending transaction between the same two parties.

(c) *Other situations to be specified by Commissioner.* The Commissioner may designate in the Internal Revenue Bulletin situations that, although described in paragraph (a)(2) of this section, will not be treated as potentially abusive because they do not have the effect of signficantly misstating basis or amount realized (see § 601.601(d)(2)(ii) of this chapter).

(d) *Consistency rule.* The issuer's determination that the debt instrument is or is not issued in a potentially abusive situation is binding on all holders of the debt instrument. However, the issuer's determination is not binding on a holder who explicitly discloses a position that is inconsistent with the issuer's determination. Unless otherwise prescribed by the Commissioner, the disclosure must be made on a statement attached to the holder's timely filed Federal income tax return for the taxable year that includes the acquisition date of the debt instrument. See § 1.1275-2(e) for rules relating to the issuer's obligation to disclose certain information to holders. [Reg. § 1.1274-3.]

☐ [T.D. 8517, 1-27-94.]

[Reg. § 1.1274-4]

§ 1.1274-4. Test rate.—(a) *Determination of test rate of interest*—(1) *In general*—(i) *Test rate is the 3-month rate.* Except as provided in paragraph (a)(2) of this section, the test rate of interest for a debt instrument issued in consideration for the sale or exchange of property is the 3-month rate.

(ii) *The 3-month rate.* Except as provided in paragraph (a)(1)(iii) of this section, the 3-month rate is the lower of—

(A) The lowest applicable Federal rate (based on the appropriate compounding period) in effect during the 3-month period ending with the first month in which there is a binding written contract that substantially sets forth the terms under which the sale or exchange is ultimately consummated; or

(B) The lowest applicable Federal rate (based on the appropriate compounding period) in effect during the 3-month period ending with the month in which the sale or exchange occurs.

(iii) *Special rule if there is no binding written contract.* If there is no binding written contract that substantially sets forth the terms under which the sale or exchange is ultimately consummated, the 3-month rate is the lowest applicable Federal rate (based on the appropriate compounding period) in effect during the 3-month period ending with the month in which the sale or exchange occurs.

(2) *Test rate for certain debt instruments—* (i) *Sale-leaseback transactions.* Under section 1274(e) (relating to certain sale-leaseback transactions), the test rate is 110 percent of the 3-month rate determined under paragraph (a)(1) of this section. For purposes of section 1274(e)(3), related party means a person related to the transferor within the meaning of section 267(b) or 707(b)(1).

(ii) *Qualified debt instrument.* Under section 1274A(a), the test rate for a qualified debt instrument is no greater than 9 percent, compounded semiannually, or an equivalent rate based on an appropriate compounding period.

(iii) *Alternative test rate for short-term obligations*—(A) *Requirements.* This paragraph (a)(2)(iii)(A) provides an alternative test rate under section 1274(d)(1)(D) for a debt instrument with a maturity of 1 year or less. This alternative test rate applies, however, only if the debt instrument provides for adequate stated interest using the alternative test rate, the issuer provides on the face of the debt instrument that the instrument qualifies as having adequate stated interest under section 1274(d)(1)(D), and the issuer and holder treat or agree to treat the instrument as having adequate stated interest.

(B) *Alternative test rate.* For purposes of paragraph (a)(2)(iii)(A), the alternative test rate is the market yield on U.S. Treasury bills with the same maturity date as the debt instrument. If the same maturity date is not available, the market yield on U.S. Treasury bills that mature in the same week or month as the debt instrument is used. The alternative test rate is determined as of the date on which there is a binding written contract that substantially sets forth the terms under which the sale or exchange is ultimately consummated or as of the date of the sale or exchange, whichever date results in a lower rate. If there is no binding written contract, however, the alternative test rate is determined as of the date of the sale or exchange.

(b) *Applicable Federal rate.* Except as otherwise provided in this section, the applicable Federal rate for a debt instrument is based on the term of the instrument (i.e., short-term, mid-term, or long-term). See section 1274(d)(1). The Inter-

Special Rules, Bonds & Other Debt Instruments

See p. 20,601 for regulations not amended to reflect law changes

nal Revenue Service publishes the applicable Federal rates for each month in the Internal Revenue Bulletin (see § 601.601(d)(2)(ii) of this chapter). The applicable Federal rates are based on the yield to maturity of outstanding marketable obligations of the United States of similar maturities during the one month period ending on the 14th day of the month preceding the month for which the rates are applicable.

(c) *Special rules to determine the term of a debt instrument for purposes of determining the applicable Federal rate*—(1) *Installment obligation.* If a debt instrument is an installment obligation (as defined in § 1.1273-1(e)(1)), the term of the instrument is the instrument's weighted average maturity (as defined in § 1.1273-1(e)(3)).

(2) *Certain variable rate debt instruments*—(i) *In general.* Except as otherwise provided in paragraph (c)(2)(ii) of this section, if a variable rate debt instrument (as defined in § 1.1275-5(a)) provides for stated interest at a qualified floating rate (or rates), the term of the instrument is determined by reference to the longest interval between interest adjustment dates, or, if the variable rate debt instrument provides for a fixed rate, the interval between the issue date and the last day on which the fixed rate applies, if this interval is longer.

(ii) *Restrictions on adjustments.* If, due to significant restrictions on variations in a qualified floating rate or the use of certain formulae pursuant to § 1.1275-5(b)(2) (e.g., 15 percent of 1-year LIBOR, plus 800 basis points), the rate in substance resembles a fixed rate, the applicable Federal rate is determined by reference to the term of the debt instrument.

(3) *Counting of either the issue date or the maturity date.* The term of a debt instrument includes either the issue date or the maturity date, but not both dates.

(4) *Certain debt instruments that provide for principal payments uncertain as to time.* If a debt instrument provides for principal payments that are fixed in total amount but uncertain as to time, the term of the instrument is determined by reference to the latest possible date on which a principal payment can be made or, in the case of an installment obligation, by reference to the longest weighted average maturity under any possible payment schedule.

(d) *Foreign currency loans.* If all of the payments of a debt instrument are denominated in, or determined by reference to, a currency other than the U.S. dollar, the applicable Federal rate for the debt instrument is a foreign currency rate of interest that is analogous to the applicable Federal rate described in this section. For this purpose, an analogous rate of interest is a rate based on yields (with the appropriate compounding period) of the highest grade of outstanding marketable obligations denominated in such currency (excluding any obligations that benefit from special tax exemptions or preferential tax rates not available to debt instruments generally) with due consideration given to the maturities of the obligations.

(e) *Examples.* The following examples illustrate the rules of this section.

Example 1. Variable rate debt instrument that limits the amount of increase and decrease in the rate—(i) *Facts.* On July 1, 1996, A sells nonpublicly traded property to B in return for a 5-year debt instrument that provides for interest to be paid on July 1 of each year, beginning on July 1, 1997, based on the prime rate of a local bank on that date. However, the interest rate cannot increase or decrease from one year to the next by more than .25 percentage points (25 basis points).

(ii) *Significant restriction.* The debt instrument is a variable rate debt instrument (as defined in § 1.1275-5) that provides for stated interest at a qualified floating rate. Assume that based on all the facts and circumstances, the restriction is a significant restriction on the variations in the rate of interest. Under paragraph (c)(2)(ii) of this section, the applicable Federal rate is determined by reference to the term of the debt instrument, and the applicable Federal rate is the Federal mid-term rate.

Example 2. Installment obligation—(i) *Facts.* On January 1, 1996, A sells nonpublicly traded property to B in exchange for a debt instrument that calls for a payment of $500,000 on January 1, 2001, and a payment of $1,000,000 on January 1, 2006. The debt instrument does not provide for any stated interest.

(ii) *Determination of term.* The debt instrument is an installment obligation. Under paragraph (c)(1) of this section, the term of the debt instrument is its weighted average maturity (as defined in § 1.1273-1(e)(3)). The debt instrument's weighted average maturity is 8.33 years, which is the sum of (A) the ratio of the first payment to total payments (500,000/1,500,000), multiplied by the number of complete years from the issue date until the payment is due (5 years), and (b) the ratio of the second payment to total payments (1,000,000/1,500,000), multiplied by the number of complete years from the issue date until the second payment is due (10 years).

(iii) *Applicable Federal rate.* Based on the calculation in paragraph (ii) of this example, the term of the debt instrument is treated as 8.33 years. Consequently, the applicable Federal rate is the Federal mid-term rate.

[Reg. § 1.1274-4.]

☐ [T.D. 8517, 1-27-94.]

Reg. § 1.1274-4(e)

[Reg. § 1.1274-5]

§ 1.1274-5. Assumptions.—(a) *In general.* Section 1274 does not apply to a debt instrument if the debt instrument is assumed, or property is taken subject to the debt instrument, in connection with a sale or exchange of property, unless the terms of the debt instrument, as part of the sale or exchange, are modified in a manner that would constitute an exchange under section 1001.

(b) *Modifications of debt instruments*—(1) *In general.* Except as provided in paragraph (b)(2) of this section, if a debt instrument is assumed, or property is taken subject to a debt instrument, in connection with a sale or exchange of property, the terms of the debt instrument are modified as part of the sale or exchange, and the modification triggers an exchange under section 1001, the modification is treated as a separate transaction taking place immediately before the sale or exchange and is attributed to the seller of the property. For purposes of this paragraph (b), a debt instrument is not considered to be modified as part of the sale or exchange unless the seller knew or had reason to know about the modification.

(2) *Election to treat buyer as modifying the debt instrument*—(i) *In general.* Rather than having the rules in paragraph (b)(1) of this section apply, the seller and buyer may jointly elect to treat the transaction as one in which the buyer first assumed the original (unmodified) debt instrument and then subsequently modified the debt instrument. For this purpose, the modification is treated as a separate transaction taking place immediately after the sale or exchange.

(ii) *Time and manner of making the election.* The buyer and seller make the election under paragraph (b)(2)(i) of this section by jointly signing a statement that includes the names, addresses, and taxpayer identification numbers of the seller and buyer, and a clear indication that the election is being made under paragraph (b)(2)(i) of this section. Both the buyer and the seller must sign this statement not later than the earlier of the last day (including extensions) for filing the Federal income tax return of the buyer or seller for the taxable year in which the sale or exchange of the property occurs. The buyer and seller should attach this signed statement (or a copy thereof) to their timely filed Federal income tax returns.

(c) *Wraparound indebtedness.* For purposes of paragraph (a) of this section, the issuance of wraparound indebtedness is not considered an assumption.

(d) *Consideration attributable to assumed debt.* If as part of the consideration for the sale or exchange of property, the buyer assumes, or takes the property subject to, an indebtedness that was issued with OID (including a debt instrument issued in a prior sale or exchange to which section 1274 applied), the portion of the buyer's basis in the property and the seller's amount realized attributable to the debt instrument equals the adjusted issue price of the debt instrument as of the date of the sale or exchange. [Reg. § 1.1274-5.]

☐ [T.D. 8517, 1-27-94.]

[Reg. § 1.1274A-1]

§ 1.1274A-1. Special rules for certain transactions where stated principal amount does not exceed $2,800,000.—(a) *In general.* Section 1274A allows the use of a lower test rate for purposes of sections 483 and 1274 in the case of a qualified debt instrument (as defined in section 1274A(b)) and, if elected by the borrower and the lender, the use of the cash receipts and disbursements method of accounting for interest on a cash method debt instrument (as defined in section 1274A(c)(2)). This section provides special rules for qualified debt instruments and cash method debt instruments.

(b) *Rules for both qualified and cash method debt instruments*—(1) *Sale-leaseback transactions.* A debt instrument issued in a sale-leaseback transaction (within the meaning of section 1274(e)) cannot be either a qualified debt instrument or a cash method debt instrument.

(2) *Debt instruments calling for contingent payments.* A debt instrument that provides for contingent payments cannot be a qualified debt instrument unless it can be determined at the time of the sale or exchange that the maximum stated principal amount due under the debt instrument cannot exceed the amount specified in section 1274A(b). Similarly, a debt instrument that provides for contingent payments cannot be a cash method debt instrument unless it can be determined at the time of the sale or exchange that the maximum stated principal amount due under the debt instrument cannot exceed the amount specified in section 1274A(c)(2)(A).

(3) *Aggregation of transactions*—(i) *General rule.* The aggregation rules of section 1274A(d)(1) are applied using a facts and circumstances test.

(ii) *Examples.* The following examples illustrate the application of section 1274A(d)(1) and paragraph (b)(3)(i) of this section.

Example 1. Aggregation of two sales to a single person. In two transactions evidenced by separate sales agreements, A sells undivided half interests in Blackacre to B. The sales are pursuant to a plan for the sale of a 100 percent interest in Blackacre to B. These sales or exchanges are part of a series of related transactions and, thus, are treated as a single sale for purposes of section 1274A.

Reg. § 1.1274-5(a)

Example 2. Aggregation of two purchases by unrelated individuals. Pursuant to a plan, unrelated individuals X and Y purchase undivided half interests in Blackacre from A and subsequently contribute these interests to a partnership in exchange for equal interests in the partnership. These purchases are treated as part of the same transaction and, thus, are treated as a single sale for purposes of section 1274A.

Example 3. Aggregation of sales made pursuant to a tender offer. Fifteen unrelated individuals own all of the stock of X Corporation. Y Corporation makes a tender offer to these 15 shareholders. The terms offered to each shareholder are identical. Shareholders holding a majority of the shares of X Corporation elect to tender their shares pursuant to Y Corporation's offer. These sales are part of the same transaction and, thus, are treated as a single sale for purposes of section 1274A.

Example 4. No aggregation for separate sales of similar property to unrelated persons. Pursuant to a newspaper advertisement, X Corporation offers for sale similar condominiums in a single building. The prices of the units vary due to a variety of factors, but the financing terms offered by X Corporation to all buyers are identical. The units are purchased by unrelated buyers who decided whether to purchase units in the building at the price and on the terms offered by X Corporation, without regard to the actions of other buyers. Because each buyer acts individually, the sales are not part of the same transaction or a series of related transactions and, thus, are treated as separate sales.

(4) *Inflation adjustment of dollar amounts.* Under section 1274A(d)(2), the dollar amounts specified in sections 1274A(b) and 1274A(c)(2)(A) are adjusted for inflation. The dollar amounts, adjusted for inflation, are published in the Internal Revenue Bulletin (see § 601.601(d)(2)(ii) of this chapter).

(c) *Rules for cash method debt instruments*—(1) *Time and manner of making cash method election.* The borrower and lender make the election described in section 1274A(c)(2)(D) by jointly signing a statement that includes the names, addresses, and taxpayer identification numbers of the borrower and lender, a clear indication that an election is being made under section 1274A(c)(2), and a declaration that debt instrument with respect to which the election is being made fulfills the requirements of a cash method debt instrument. Both the borrower and the lender must sign this statement not later than the earlier of the last day (including extensions) for filing the Federal income tax return of the borrower or lender for the taxable year in which the debt instrument is issued. The borrower and lender should attach this signed statement (or a copy thereof) to their timely filed Federal income tax returns.

(2) *Successors of electing parties.* Except as otherwise provided in this paragraph (c)(2), the cash method election under section 1274A(c) applies to any successor of the electing lender or borrower. Thus, for any period after the transfer of a cash method debt instrument, the successor takes into account the interest (including unstated interest) on the instrument under the cash receipts and disbursements method of accounting. Nevertheless, if the lender (or any successor thereof) transfers the cash method debt instrument to a taxpayer who uses an accrual method of accounting, section 1272 rather than section 1274A(c) applies to the successor of the lender with respect to the debt instrument for any period after the date of the transfer. The borrower (or any successor thereof), however, remains on the cash receipts and disbursements method of accounting with respect to the cash method debt instrument.

(3) *Modified debt instrument.* In the case of a debt instrument issued in a debt-for-debt exchange that qualifies as an exchange under section 1001, the debt instrument is eligible for the election to be a cash method debt instrument if the other prerequisites to making the election in section 1274A(c) are met. However, if a principal purpose of the modification is to defer interest income or deductions through the use of the election, then the debt instrument is not eligible for the election.

(4) *Debt incurred or continued to purchase or carry a cash method debt instrument.* If a debt instrument is incurred or continued to purchase or carry a cash method debt instrument, rules similar to those under section 1277 apply to determine the timing of the interest deductions for the debt instrument. For purposes of the preceding sentence, rules similar to those under section 265(a)(2) apply to determine whether a debt instrument is incurred or continued to purchase or carry a cash method debt instrument. [Reg. § 1.1274A-1.]

☐ [T.D. 8517, 1-27-94.]

[Reg. § 1.1275-1]

§ 1.1275-1. Definitions.—(a) *Applicability.* The definitions contained in this section apply for purposes of sections 163(e) and 1271 through 1275 and the regulations thereunder.

(b) *Adjusted issue price*—(1) *In general.* The adjusted issue price of a debt instrument at the beginning of the first accrual period is the issue price. Thereafter, the adjusted issue price of the debt instrument is the issue price of the debt instrument—

(i) Increased by the amount of OID previously includible in the gross income of any holder (determined without regard to section 1272(a)(7) and section 1272(c)(1)); and

(ii) Decreased by the amount of any payment previously made on the debt instrument other than a payment of qualified stated interest. See § 1.1275-2(f) for rules regarding adjustments to adjusted issue price on a pro rata prepayment.

(2) *Bond issuance premium.* If a debt instrument is issued with bond issuance premium (as defined in § 1.163-13(c)), for purposes of determining the issuer's adjusted issue price, the adjusted issue price determined under paragraph (b)(1) of this section is also decreased by the amount of bond issuance premium previously allocable under § 1.163-13(d)(3).

(3) *Adjusted issue price for subsequent holders.* for purposes of calculating OID accruals, acquisition premium, or market discount, a holder (other than a purchaser at original issuance) determines adjusted issue price in any manner consistent with the regulations under sections 1271 through 1275.

(c) *OID.* OID means original issue discount (as defined in section 1273(a) and § 1.1273-1).

(d) *Debt instrument.* Except as provided in section 1275(a)(1)(B) (relating to certain annuity contracts; see paragraph (j) of this section), debt instrument means any instrument or contractual arrangement that constitutes indebtedness under general principles of Federal income tax law (including, for example, a certificate of deposit or a loan). Nothing in the regulations under sections 163(e), 483, and 1271 through 1275, however, shall influence whether an instrument constitutes indebtedness for Federal income tax purposes.

(e) *Tax-exempt obligations.* For purposes of section 1275(a)(3)(B), exempt from tax means exempt from Federal income tax.

(f) *Issue*—(1) *Debt instruments issued on or after March 13, 2001.* Except as provided in paragraph (f)(3) of this section, two or more debt instruments are part of the same issue if the debt instruments—

(i) Have the same credit and payment terms;

(ii) Are issued either pursuant to a common plan or as part of a single transaction or a series of related transactions;

(iii) Are issued within a period of thirteen days beginning with the date on which the first debt instrument that would be part of the issue is issued to a person other than a bond house, broker, or similar person or organization acting in the capacity of an underwriter, placement agent, or wholesaler; and

(iv) Are issued on or after March 13, 2001.

(2) *Debt instruments issued before March 13, 2001.* Except as provided in paragraph (f)(3) of this section, two or more debt instruments are part of the same issue if the debt instruments—

(i) Have the same credit and payment terms;

(ii) Are sold reasonably close in time either pursuant to a common plan or as part of a single transaction or a series of related transactions; and

(iii) Are issued on or after April 4, 1994, and before March 13, 2001.

(3) *Transition rule.* If the issue date of any of the debt instruments that would be part of the same issue (determined as if each debt instrument were part of a separate issue) is on or after March 13, 2001, then the definition of the term *issue* in paragraph (f)(1) of this section applies rather than the definition in paragraph (f)(2) of this section to determine if the debt instruments are part of the same issue.

(4) *Cross-references for reopening and aggregation rules.* See § 1.1275-2(d) and (k) for rules that treat debt instruments issued in certain reopenings as part of an issue of original (outstanding) debt instruments. See § 1.1275-2(c) for rules that treat two or more debt instruments as a single debt instrument.

(g) *Debt instruments issued by a natural person.* If an entity is a primary obligor under a debt instrument, the debt instrument is considered to be issued by the entity and not by a natural person even if a natural person is a co-maker and is jointly liable for the debt instrument's repayment. A debt instrument issued by a partnership is considered to be issued by the partnership as an entity even if the partnership is composed entirely of natural persons.

(h) *Publicly offered debt instrument.* A debt instrument is publicly offered if it is part of an issue of debt instruments the initial offering of which—

(1) Is registered with the Securities and Exchange Commission; or

Reg. § 1.1275-1(a)

(2) Would be required to be registered under the Securities Act of 1933 (15 U.S.C. 77a et seq.) but for an exemption from registration—

(i) Under section 3 of the Securities Act of 1933 (relating to exempted securities);

(ii) Under any law (other than the Securities Act of 1933) because of the identity of the issuer or the nature of the security; or

(iii) Because the issue is intended for distribution to persons who are not United States persons.

(i) [Reserved]

(j) *Life annuity exception under section 1275(a)(1)(B)(i)*—(1) *Purpose.* Section 1275(a)(1)(B)(i) excepts an annuity contract from the definition of *debt instrument* if section 72 applies to the contract and the contract depends (in whole or in substantial part) on the life expectancy of one or more individuals. This paragraph (j) provides rules to ensure that an annuity contract qualifies for the exception in section 1275(a)(1)(B)(i) only in cases where the life contingency under the contract is real and significant.

(2) *General rule*—(i) *Rule.* For purposes of section 1275(a)(1)(B)(i), an annuity contract depends (in whole or in substantial part) on the life expectancy of one or more individuals only if—

(A) The contract provides for periodic distributions made not less frequently than annually for the life (or joint lives) of an individual (or a reasonable number of individuals); and

(B) The contract does not contain any terms or provisions that can significantly reduce the probability that total distributions under the contract will increase commensurately with the longevity of the annuitant (or annuitants).

(ii) *Terminology.* For purposes of this paragraph (j):

(A) *Contract.* The term *contract* includes all written or unwritten understandings among the parties as well as any person or persons acting in concert with one or more of the parties.

(B) *Annuitant.* The term *annuitant* refers to the individual (or reasonable number of individuals) referred to in paragraph (j)(2)(i)(A) of this section.

(C) *Terminating death.* The phrase *terminating death* refers to the annuitant death that can terminate periodic distributions under the contract. (See paragraph (j)(2)(i)(A) of this section.) For example, if a contract provides for periodic distributions until the later of the death of the last-surviving annuitant or the end of a term certain, the terminating death is the death of the last-surviving annuitant.

(iii) *Coordination with specific rules.* Paragraphs (j)(3) through (7) of this section describe certain terms and conditions that can significantly reduce the probability that total distributions under the contract will increase commensurately with the longevity of the annuitant (or annuitants). If a term or provision is not specifically described in paragraphs (j)(3) through (7) of this section, the annuity contract must be tested under the general rule of paragraph (j)(2)(i) of this section to determine whether it depends (in whole or in substantial part) on the life expectancy of one or more individuals.

(3) *Availability of a cash surrender option*—(i) *Impact on life contingency.* The availability of a cash surrender option can significantly reduce the probability that total distributions under the contract will increase commensurately with the longevity of the annuitant (or annuitants). Thus, the availability of any cash surrender option causes the contract to fail to be described in section 1275(a)(1)(B)(i). A cash surrender option is available if there is reason to believe that the issuer (or a person acting in concert with the issuer) will be willing to terminate or purchase all or a part of the annuity contract by making one or more payments of cash or property (other than an annuity contract described in this paragraph (j)).

(ii) *Examples.* The following examples illustrate the rules of this paragraph (j)(3):

Example 1. (i) *Facts.* On March 1, 1998, X issues a contract to A for cash. The contract provides that, effective on any date chosen by A (the annuity starting date), X will begin equal monthly distributions for A's life. The amount of each monthly distribution will be no less than an amount based on the contract's account value as of the annuity starting date, A's age on that date, and permanent purchase rate guarantees contained in the contract. The contract also provides that, at any time before the annuity starting date, A may surrender the contract to X for the account value less a surrender charge equal to a declining percentage of the account value. For this purpose, the initial account value is equal to the cash invested. Thereafter, the account value increases annually by at least a minimum guaranteed rate.

(ii) *Analysis.* The ability to obtain the account value less the surrender charge, if any, is a cash surrender option. This ability can significantly reduce the probability that total distributions under the contract will increase commensurately with A's longevity. Thus, the contract fails to be described in section 1275(a)(1)(B)(i).

Example 2. (i) *Facts.* On March 1, 1998, X issues a contract to B for cash. The contract

Reg. § 1.1275-1(j)(3)

provides that beginning on March 1, 1999, X will distribute to B a fixed amount of cash each month for B's life. Based on X's advertisements, marketing literature, or illustrations or on oral representations by X's sales personnel, there is reason to believe that an affiliate of X stands ready to purchase B's contract for its commuted value.

(ii) *Analysis.* Because there is reason to believe that an affiliate of X stands ready to purchase B's contract for its commuted value, a cash surrender option is available within the meaning of paragraph (j)(3)(i) of this section. This availability can significantly reduce the probability that total distributions under the contract will increase commensurately with B's longevity. Thus, the contract fails to be described in section 1275(a)(1)(B)(i).

(4) *Availability of a loan secured by the contract*—(i) Impact on life contingency. The availability of a loan secured by the contract can significantly reduce the probability that total distributions under the contract will increase commensurately with the longevity of the annuitant (or annuitants). Thus, the availability of any such loan causes the contract to fail to be described in section 1275(a)(1)(B)(i). A loan secured by the contract is available if there is reason to believe that the issuer (or a person acting in concert with the issuer) will be willing to make a loan that is directly or indirectly secured by the annuity contract.

(ii) *Example.* The following example illustrates the rules of this paragraph (j)(4):

Example. (i) *Facts.* On March 1, 1998, X issues a contract to C for $100,000. The contract provides that, effective on any date chosen by C (the annuity starting date), X will begin equal monthly distributions for C's life. The amount of each monthly distribution will be no less than an amount based on the contract's account value as of the annuity starting date, C's age on that date, and permanent purchase rate guarantees contained in the contract. From marketing literature circulated by Y, there is reason to believe that, at any time before the annuity starting date, C may pledge the contract to borrow up to $75,000 from Y. Y is acting in concert with X.

(ii) *Analysis.* Because there is reason to believe that Y, a person acting in concert with X, is willing to lend money against C's contract, a loan secured by the contract is available within the meaning of paragraph (j)(4)(i) of this section. This availability can significantly reduce the probability that total distributions under the contract will increase commensurately with C's longevity. Thus, the contract fails to be described in section 1275(a)(1)(B)(i).

(5) *Minimum payout provision*—(i) *Impact on life contingency.* The existence of a minimum payout provision can significantly reduce the probability that total distributions under the contract will increase commensurately with the longevity of the annuitant (or annuitants). Thus, the existence of any minimum payout provision causes the contract to fail to be described in section 1275(a)(1)(B)(i).

(ii) *Definition of minimum payout provision.* A minimum payout provision is a contractual provision (for example, an agreement to make distributions over a term certain) that provides for one or more distributions made—

(A) After the terminating death under the contract; or

(B) By reason of the death of any individual (including distributions triggered by or increased by terminal or chronic illness, as defined in section 101(g)(1)(A) and (B)).

(iii) *Exceptions for certain minimum payouts*—(A) *Recovery of consideration paid for the contract.* Notwithstanding paragraphs (j)(2)(i)(A) and (j)(5)(i) of this section, a contract does not fail to be described in section 1275(a)(1)(B)(i) merely because it provides that, after the terminating death, there will be one or more distributions that, in the aggregate, do not exceed the consideration paid for the contract less total distributions previously made under the contract.

(B) *Payout for one-half of life expectancy.* Notwithstanding paragraphs (j)(2)(i)(A) and (j)(5)(i) of this section, a contract does not fail to be described in section 1275(a)(1)(B)(i) merely because it provides that, if the terminating death occurs after the annuity starting date, distributions under the contract will continue to be made after the terminating death until a date that is no later than the halfway date. This exception does not apply unless the amounts distributed in each contract year will not exceed the amounts that would have been distributed in that year if the terminating death had not occurred until the expected date of the terminating death, determined under paragraph (j)(5)(iii)(C) of this section.

(C) *Definition of halfway date.* For purposes of this paragraph (j)(5)(iii), the halfway date is the date halfway between the annuity starting date and the expected date of the terminating death, determined as of the annuity starting date, with respect to all then-surviving annuitants. The expected date of the terminating death must be determined by reference to the applicable mortality table prescribed under section 417(e)(3)(A)(ii)(I).

Reg. § 1.1275-1(j)(4)

(iv) *Examples.* The following examples illustrate the rules of this paragraph (j)(5):

Example 1. (i) *Facts.* On March 1, 1998, X issues a contract to D for cash. The contract provides that, effective on any date D chooses (the annuity starting date), X will begin equal monthly distributions for the greater of D's life or 10 years, regardless of D's age as of the annuity starting date. The amount of each monthly distribution will be no less than an amount based on the contract's account value as of the annuity starting date, D's age on that date, and permanent purchase rate guarantees contained in the contract.

(ii) *Analysis.* A minimum payout provision exists because, if D dies within 10 years of the annuity starting date, one or more distributions will be made after D's death. The minimum payout provision does not qualify for the exception in paragraph (j)(5)(iii)(B) of this section because D may defer the annuity starting date until his remaining life expectancy is less than 20 years. If, on the annuity starting date, D's life expectancy is less than 20 years, the minimum payout period (10 years) will last beyond the halfway date. The minimum payout provision, therefore, can significantly reduce the probability that total distributions under the contract will increase commensurately with D's longevity. Thus, the contract fails to be described in section 1275(a)(1)(B)(i).

Example 2. (i) *Facts.* The facts are the same as in *Example 1* of this paragraph (j)(5)(iv) except that the monthly distributions will last for the greater of D's life or a term certain. D may choose the length of the term certain subject to the restriction that, on the annuity starting date, the term certain must not exceed one-half of D's life expectancy as of the annuity starting date. The contract also does not provide for any adjustment in the amount of distributions by reason of the death of D or any other individual, except for a refund of D's aggregate premium payments less the sum of all prior distributions under the contract.

(ii) *Analysis.* The minimum payout provision qualifies for the exception in paragraph (j)(5)(iii)(B) of this section because distributions under the minimum payout provision will not continue past the halfway date and the contract does not provide for any adjustments in the amount of distributions by reason of the death of D or any other individual, other than a guaranteed death benefit described in paragraph (j)(5)(iii)(A) of this section. Accordingly, the existence of this minimum payout provision does not prevent the contract from being described in section 1275(a)(1)(B)(i).

(6) *Maximum payout provision*—(i) *Impact on life contingency.* The existence of a maximum payout provision can significantly reduce the probability that total distributions under the contract will increase commensurately with the longevity of the annuitant (or annuitants). Thus, the existence of any maximum payout provision causes the contract to fail to be described in section 1275(a)(1)(B)(i).

(ii) *Definition of maximum payout provision.* A maximum payout provision is a contractual provision that provides that no distributions under the contract may be made after some date (the termination date), even if the terminating death has not yet occurred.

(iii) *Exception.* Notwithstanding paragraphs (j)(2)(i)(A) and (j)(6)(i) of this section, an annuity contract does not fail to be described in section 1275(a)(1)(B)(i) merely because the contract contains a maximum payout provision, provided that the period of time from the annuity starting date to the termination date is at least twice as long as the period of time from the annuity starting date to the expected date of the terminating death, determined as of the annuity starting date, with respect to all then-surviving annuitants. The expected date of the terminating death must be determined by reference to the applicable mortality table prescribed under section 417(e)(3)(A)(ii)(I).

(iv) *Example.* The following example illustrates the rules of this paragraph (j)(6):

Example. (i) *Facts.* On March 1, 1998, X issues a contract to E for cash. The contract provides that beginning on April 1, 1998, X will distribute to E a fixed amount of cash each month for E's life but that no distributions will be made after April 1, 2018. On April 1, 1998, E's life expectancy is 9 years.

(ii) *Analysis.* A maximum payout provision exists because if E survives beyond April 1, 2018, E will receive no further distributions under the contract. The period of time from the annuity starting date (April 1, 1998) to the termination date (April 1, 2018) is 20 years. Because this 20-year period is more than twice as long as E's life expectancy on April 1, 1998, the maximum payout provision qualifies for the exception in paragraph (j)(6)(iii) of this section. Accordingly, the existence of this maximum payout provision does not prevent the contract from being described in section 1275(a)(1)(B)(i).

(7) *Decreasing payout provision*—(i) *General rule.* If the amount of distributions during any contract year (other than the last year during

which distributions are made) may be less than the amount of distributions during the preceding year, this possibility can significantly reduce the probability that total distributions under the contract will increase commensurately with the longevity of the annuitant (or annuitants). Thus, the existence of this possibility causes the contract to fail to be described in section 1275(a)(1)(B)(i).

(ii) *Exception for certain variable distributions.* Notwithstanding paragraph (j)(7)(i) of this section, if an annuity contract provides that the amount of each distribution must increase and decrease in accordance with investment experience, cost of living indices, or similar fluctuating criteria, then the possibility that the amount of a distribution may decrease for this reason does not significantly reduce the probability that the distributions under the contract will increase commensurately with the longevity of the annuitant (or annuitants).

(iii) *Examples.* The following examples illustrate the rules of this paragraph (j)(7):

Example 1. (i) *Facts.* On March 1, 1998, X issues a contract to F for $100,000. The contract provides that beginning on March 1, 1999, X will make distributions to F each year until F's death. Prior to March 1, 2009, distributions are to be made at a rate of $12,000 per year. Beginning on March 1, 2009, distributions are to be made at a rate of $3,000 per year.

(ii) *Analysis.* If F is alive in 2009, the amount distributed in 2009 ($3,000) will be less than the amount distributed in 2008 ($12,000). The exception in paragraph (j)(7)(ii) of this section does not apply. The decrease in the amount of any distributions made on or after March 1, 2009, can significantly reduce the probability that total distributions under the contract will increase commensurately with F's longevity. Thus, the contract fails to be described in section 1275(a)(1)(B)(i).

Example 2. (i) *Facts.* On March 1, 1998, X issues a contract to G for cash. The contract provides that, effective on any date G chooses (the annuity starting date), X will begin monthly distributions to G for G's life. Prior to the annuity starting date, the account value of the contract reflects the investment return, including changes in the market value, of an identifiable pool of assets. When G chooses the annuity starting date, G must also choose whether the distributions are to be fixed or variable. If fixed, the amount of each monthly distribution will remain constant at an amount that is no less than an amount based on the contract's account value as of the annuity starting date, G's age on that date, and permanent purchase rate guarantees contained in the contract. If variable, the monthly distributions will fluctuate to reflect the investment return, including changes in the market value, of the pool of assets. The monthly distributions under the contract will not otherwise decline from year to year.

(ii) *Analysis.* Because the only possible year-to-year declines in annuity distributions are described in paragraph (j)(7)(ii) of this section, the possibility that the amount of distributions may decline from the previous year does not reduce the probability that total distributions under the contract will increase commensurately with G's longevity. Thus, the potential fluctuation in the annuity distributions does not cause the contract to fail to be described in section 1275(a)(1)(B)(i).

(8) *Effective dates*—(i) *In general.* Except as provided in paragraph (j)(8)(ii) and (iii) of this section, this paragraph (j) is applicable for interest accruals on or after February 9, 1998 on annuity contracts held on or after February 9, 1998.

(ii) *Grandfathered contracts.* This paragraph (j) does not apply to an annuity contract that was purchased before April 7, 1995. For purposes of this paragraph (j)(8), if any additional investment in such a contract is made on or after April 7, 1995, and the additional investment is not required to be made under a binding contractual obligation that was entered into before April 7, 1995, then the additional investment is treated as the purchase of a contract after April 7, 1995.

(iii) *Contracts consistent with the provisions of FI-33-94, published at 1995-1 C.B. 920.* See § 601.601(d)(2)(ii)(b) of this chapter. This paragraph (j) does not apply to a contract purchased on or after April 7, 1995, and before February 9, 1998, if all payments under the contract are periodic payments that are made at least annually for the life (or lives) of one or more individuals, do not increase at any time during the term of the contract, and are part of a series of distributions that begins within one year of the date of the initial investment in the contract. An annuity contract that is otherwise described in the preceding sentence does not fail to be described therein merely because it also provides for a payment (or payments) made by reason of the death of one or more individuals. [Reg. § 1.1275-1.]

☐ [T.D. 8517, 1-27-94. Amended by T.D. 8746, 12-30-97; T.D. 8754, 1-7-98 and T.D. 8934, 1-11-2001.]

[Reg. § 1.1275-2]

§ 1.1275-2. Special rules relating to debt instruments.—(a) *Payment ordering rule*—(1) *In general.* Except as provided in paragraph (a)(2) of this section, each payment under a debt instrument is treated first as a payment of OID to the extent of the OID that has accrued as of the date the payment is due and has not been allocated to prior payments, and second as a payment of principal. Thus, no portion of any payment is treated as prepaid interest.

(2) *Exceptions.* The rule in paragraph (a)(1) of this section does not apply to—

(i) A payment of qualified stated interest;

(ii) A payment of points deductible under section 461(g)(2), in the case of the issuer;

(iii) A pro rata prepayment described in paragraph (f)(2) of this section; or

(iv) A payment of additional interest or a similar charge provided with respect to amounts that are not paid when due.

(b) *Debt instruments distributed by corporations with respect to stock*—(1) *Treatment of distribution.* For purposes of determining the issue price of a debt instrument distributed by a corporation with respect to its stock, the instrument is treated as issued by the corporation for property. See section 1275(a)(4). Thus, under section 1273(b)(3), the issue price of a distributed debt instrument that is traded on an established market is its fair market value. The issue price of a distributed debt instrument that is not traded on an established market is determined under section 1274 or section 1273(b)(4).

(2) *Issue date.* The issue date of a debt instrument distributed by a corporation with respect to its stock is the date of the distribution.

(c) *Aggregation of debt instruments*—(1) *General rule.* Except as provided in paragraph (c)(2) of this section, debt instruments issued in connection with the same transaction or related transactions (determined based on all the facts and circumstances) are treated as a single debt instrument for purposes of sections 1271 through 1275 and the regulations thereunder. This rule ordinarily applies only to debt instruments of a single issuer that are issued to a single holder. The Commissioner may, however, aggregate debt instruments that are issued by more than one issuer or that are issued to more than one holder if the debt instruments are issued in an arrangement that is designed to avoid the aggregation rule (e.g., debt instruments issued by or to related parties or debt instruments originally issued to different holders with the understanding that the debt instruments will be transferred to a single holder).

(2) *Exception if separate issue price established.* Paragraph (c)(1) of this section does not apply to a debt instrument if—

(i) The debt instrument is part of an issue a substantial portion of which is traded on an established market within the meaning of § 1.1273-2(f); or

(ii) The debt instrument is part of an issue a substantial portion of which is issued for money (or for property traded on an established market within the meaning of § 1.1273-2(f)) to parties who are not related to the issuer or holder and who do not purchase other debt instruments of the same issuer in connection with the same transaction or related transactions.

(3) *Special rule for debt instruments that provide for the issuance of additional debt instruments.* If, under the terms of a debt instrument (the original debt instrument), the holder may receive one or more additional debt instruments of the issuer, the additional debt instrument or instruments are aggregated with the original debt instrument. Thus, the payments made pursuant to an additional debt instrument are treated as made on the original debt instrument, and the distribution by the issuer of the additional debt instrument is not considered to be a payment made on the original debt instrument. This paragraph (c)(3) applies regardless of whether the right to receive an additional debt instrument is fixed as of the issue date or is contingent upon subsequent events. See § 1.1272-1(c) for the treatment of certain rights to issue additional debt instruments in lieu of cash payments.

(4) *Examples.* The following examples illustrate the rules set forth in paragraphs (c)(1) and (c)(2) of this section.

Example 1. Exception for debt instruments issued separately to other purchasers. On January 1, 1995, Corporation M issues two series of bonds, Series A and Series B. The two series are sold for cash and have different terms. Although some holders purchase bonds from both series, a substantial portion of the bonds is issued to different holders. H purchases bonds from both series. Under the exception in paragraph (c)(2)(ii) of this section, the Series A and Series B bonds purchased by H are not aggregated.

Example 2. Tiered REMICs. Z forms a dual tier real estate mortgage investment conduit (REMIC). In the dual tier structure, Z forms REMIC A to acquire a pool of real estate mortgages and to issue a residual interest and several classes of regular interests. Contemporaneously, Z forms REMIC B to acquire as qualified mortgages all of the regular interests in REMIC A. REMIC B issues several classes of regular interests and a residual interest, and Z sells all of those interests to unrelated parties in a public offering. Under the general rule set out in paragraph (c)(1) of this section, all of the regular interests issued by REMIC A and held by REMIC B are treated as a single debt instrument for purposes of sections 1271 through 1275.

(d) *Special rules for Treasury securities*—(1) *Issue price and issue date.* The issue price of an issue of Treasury securities is the average price of the securities sold. The issue date of an issue of Treasury securities is the first settlement date on which a substantial amount of the securities in the issue is sold. For an issue of Treasury securities sold from November 1, 1998, to March 13, 2001, the issue price of the issue is the price of the securities sold at auction.

(2) *Reopenings of Treasury securities*—(i) *Treatment of additional Treasury securities.* Notwithstanding § 1.1275-1(f), additional Treasury securities issued in a qualified reopening are part of the same issue as the original Treasury securities. As a result, the additional Treasury securities have the same issue price, issue date, and (with respect to holders) the same adjusted issue price as the original Treasury securities. This paragraph (d)(2) applies to qualified reopenings that occur on or after March 25, 1992.

(ii) *Definitions*—(A) *Additional Treasury securities.* Additional Treasury securities are Treasury securities with terms that are in all respects identical to the terms of the original Treasury securities.

(B) *Original Treasury securities.* Original Treasury securities are securities comprising any issue of outstanding Treasury securities.

(C) *Qualified reopening—reopenings on or after March 13, 2001.* For a reopening of Treasury securities that occurs on or after March 13, 2001, a qualified reopening is a reopening that occurs not more than one year after the original Treasury securities were first issued to the public or, under paragraph (k)(3)(iii) of this section, a reopening in which the additional Treasury securities are issued with no more than a de minimis amount of OID.

(D) *Qualified reopening—reopenings before March 13, 2001.* For a reopening of Treasury securities that occurs before March 13, 2001, a qualified reopening is a reopening that occurs not more than one year after the original Treasury securities were first issued to the public. However, for a reopening of Treasury securities (other than Treasury Inflation-Indexed Securities) that occurred prior to November 5, 1999, a qualified reopening is a reopening of Treasury securities that satisfied the preceding sentence and that was intended to alleviate an acute, protracted shortage of the original Treasury securities.

(e) *Disclosure of certain information to holders.* Certain provisions of the regulations under section 163(e) and sections 1271 through 1275 provide that the issuer's determination of an item controls the holder's treatment of the item. In such a case, the issuer must provide the relevant information to the holder in a reasonable manner. For example, the issuer may provide the name or title and either the address or telephone number of a representative of the issuer who will make available to holders upon request the information required for holders to comply with these provisions of the regulations.

(f) *Treatment of pro rata prepayments.*—(1) *Treatment as retirement of separate debt instrument.* A pro rata prepayment is treated as a payment in retirement of a portion of a debt instrument, which may result in a gain or loss to the holder. Generally, the gain or loss is calculated by assuming that the original debt instrument consists of two instruments, one that is retired and one that remains outstanding. The adjusted issue price, holder's adjusted basis, and accrued but unpaid OID of the original debt instrument, determined immediately before the pro rata prepayment, are allocated between these two instruments based on the portion of the instrument that is treated as retired by the pro rata prepayment.

(2) *Definition of pro rata prepayment.* For purposes of paragraph (f)(1) of this section, a pro rata prepayment is a payment on a debt instrument made prior to maturity that—

(i) Is not made pursuant to the instrument's payment schedule (including a payment schedule determined under § 1.1272-1(c)); and

(ii) Results in a substantially pro rata reduction of each payment remaining to be paid on the instrument.

(g) *Anti-abuse rule*—(1) *In general.* If a principal purpose in structuring a debt instrument or engaging in a transaction is to achieve a result that is unreasonable in light of the purposes of section 163(e), sections 1271 through 1275, or any related section of the Code, the Commissioner can apply or depart from the regulations under the applicable sections as necessary or appropriate to achieve a reasonable result. For example, if this paragraph (g) applies to a debt instrument that provides for a contingent payment, the Commissioner can treat the contingency as if it were a separate position.

(2) *Unreasonable result.* Whether a result is unreasonable is determined based on all the facts

and circumstances. In making this determination, a significant fact is whether the treatment of the debt instrument is expected to have a substantial effect on the issuer's or a holder's U.S. tax liability. In the case of a contingent payment debt instrument, another significant fact is whether the result is obtainable without the application of § 1.1275-4 and any related provisions (e.g., if the debt instrument and the contingency were entered into separately). A result will not be considered unreasonable, however, in the absence of an expected substantial effect on the present value of a taxpayer's tax liability.

(3) *Examples.* The following examples illustrate the provisions of this paragraph (g):

Example 1. A issues a current-pay, increasing-rate note that provides for an early call option. Although the option is deemed exercised on the call date under § 1.1272-1(c)(5), the option is not expected to be exercised by A. In addition, a principal purpose of including the option in the terms of the note is to limit the amount of interest income includible by the holder in the period prior to the call date by virtue of the option rules in § 1.1272-1(c)(5). Moreover, the application of the option rules is expected to substantially reduce the present value of the holder's tax liability. Based on these facts, the application of § 1.1272-1(c)(5) produces an unreasonable result. Therefore, under this paragraph (g), the Commissioner can apply the regulations (in whole or in part) to the note without regard to § 1.1272-1(c)(5).

Example 2. C, a foreign corporation not subject to U.S. taxation, issues to a U.S. holder a debt instrument that provides for a contingent payment. The debt instrument is issued for cash and is subject to the noncontingent bond method in § 1.1275-4(b). Six months after issuance, C and the holder modify the debt instrument so that there is a deemed reissuance of the instrument under section 1001. The new debt instrument is subject to the rules of § 1.1275-4(c) rather than § 1.1275-4(b). The application of § 1.1275-4(c) is expected to substantially reduce the present value of the holder's tax liability as compared to the application of § 1.1275-4(b). In addition, a principal purpose of the modification is to substantially reduce the present value of the holder's tax liability through the application of § 1.1275-4(c). Based on these facts, the application of § 1.1275-4(c) produces an unreasonable result. Therefore, under this paragraph (g), the Commissioner can apply the noncontingent bond method to the modified debt instrument.

Example 3. D issues a convertible debt instrument rather than an economically equivalent investment unit consisting of a debt instrument and a warrant. The convertible debt instrument is issued at par and provides for annual payments of interest. D issues the convertible debt instrument rather than the investment unit so that the debt instrument would not have OID. See § 1.1273-2(j). In general, this is a reasonable result in light of the purposes of the applicable statutes. Therefore, the Commissioner generally will not use the authority under this paragraph (g) to depart from the application of § 1.1273-2(j) in this case.

(4) *Effective date.* This paragraph (g) applies to debt instruments issued on or after August 13, 1996.

(h) *Remote and incidental contingencies*—(1) *In general.* This paragraph (h) applies to a debt instrument if one or more payments on the instrument are subject to either a remote or incidental contingency. Whether a contingency is remote or incidental is determined as of the issue date of the debt instrument, including any date there is a deemed reissuance of the debt instrument under paragraph (h)(6)(ii) or (j) of this section or § 1.1272-1(c)(6). Except as otherwise provided, the treatment of the contingency under this paragraph (h) applies for all purposes of sections 163(e) (other than sections 163(e)(5)) and 1271 through 1275 and the regulations thereunder. For purposes of this paragraph (h), the possibility of impairment of a payment by insolvency, default, or similar circumstances is not a contingency.

(2) *Remote contingencies.* A contingency is remote if there is a remote likelihood either that the contingency will occur or that the contingency will not occur. If there is a remote likelihood that the contingency will occur, it is assumed that the contingency will not occur. If there is a remote likelihood that the contingency will not occur, it is assumed that the contingency will occur.

(3) *Incidental contingencies*—(i) *Contingency relating to amount.* A contingency relating to the amount of a payment is incidental if, under all reasonably expected market conditions, the potential amount of the payment is insignificant relative to the total expected amount of the remaining payments on the debt instrument. If a payment on a debt instrument is subject to an incidental contingency described in this paragraph (h)(3)(i), the payment is ignored until the payment is made. However, see paragraph (h)(6)(i)(B) of this section for the treatment of the debt instrument if a change in circumstances occurs prior to the date the payment is made.

(ii) *Contingency relating to time.* A contingency relating to the timing of a payment is incidental if, under all reasonably expected market conditions, the potential difference in the tim-

Reg. § 1.1275-2(h)(3)

ing of the payment (from the earliest date to the latest date) is insignificant. If a payment on a debt instrument is subject to an incidental contingency described in this paragraph (h)(3)(ii), the payment is treated as made on the earliest date that the payment could be made pursuant to the contingency. If the payment is not made on this date, a taxpayer makes appropriate adjustments to take into account the delay in payment. However, see paragraph (h)(6)(i)(C) of this section for the treatment of the debt instrument if the delay is not insignificant.

(4) *Aggregation rule.* For purposes of paragraph (h)(2) of this section, if a debt instrument provides for multiple contingencies each of which has a remote likelihood of occurring but, when all of the contingencies are considered together, there is a greater than remote likelihood that at least one of the contingencies will occur, none of the contingencies is treated as a remote contingency. For purposes of paragraph (h)(3)(i) of this section, if a debt instrument provides for multiple contingencies each of which is incidental but the potential total amount of all of the payments subject to the contingencies is not, under reasonably expected market conditions, insignificant relative to the total expected amount of the remaining payments on the debt instrument, none of the contingencies is treated as incidental.

(5) *Consistency rule.* For purposes of paragraphs (h)(2) and (3) of this section, the issuer's determination that a contingency is either remote or incidental is binding on all holders. However, the issuer's determination is not binding on a holder that explicitly discloses that its determination is different from the issuer's determination. Unless otherwise prescribed by the Commissioner, the disclosure must be made on a statement attached to the holder's timely filed federal income tax return for the taxable year that includes the acquisition date of the debt instrument. See § 1.1275-2(e) for rules relating to the issuer's obligation to disclose certain information to holders.

(6) *Subsequent adjustments*—(i) *Applicability.* This paragraph (h)(6) applies to a debt instrument when there is a change in circumstances. For purposes of the preceding sentence, there is a change in circumstances if—

(A) A remote contingency actually occurs or does not occur, contrary to the assumption made in paragraph (h)(2) of this section;

(B) A payment subject to an incidental contingency described in paragraph (h)(3)(i) of this section becomes fixed in an amount that is not insignificant relative to the total expected amount of the remaining payments on the debt instrument; or

(C) A payment subject to an incidental contingency described in paragraph (h)(3)(ii) of this section becomes fixed such that the difference between the assumed payment date and the due date of the payment is not insignificant.

(ii) *In general.* If a change in circumstances occurs, solely for purposes of sections 1272 and 1273, the debt instrument is treated as retired and then reissued on the date of the change in circumstances for an amount equal to the instrument's adjusted issue price on that date.

(iii) *Contingent payment debt instruments.* Notwithstanding paragraph (h)(6)(ii) of this section, in the case of a contingent payment debt instrument subject to § 1.1275-4, if a change in circumstances occurs, no retirement or reissuance is treated as occurring, but any payment that is fixed as a result of the change in circumstances is governed by the rules in § 1.1275-4 that apply when the amount of a contingent payment becomes fixed.

(7) *Effective date.* This paragraph (h) applies to debt instruments issued on or after August 13, 1996.

(i) [Reserved]

(j) *Treatment of certain modifications.* If the terms of a debt instrument are modified to defer one or more payments, and the modification does not cause an exchange under section 1001, then, solely for purposes of sections 1272 and 1273, the debt instrument is treated as retired and then reissued on the date of the modification for an amount equal to the instrument's adjusted issue price on that date. This paragraph (j) applies to debt instruments issued on or after August 13, 1996.

(k) *Reopenings*—(1) *In general.* Notwithstanding § 1.1275-1(f), additional debt instruments issued in a qualified reopening are part of the same issue as the original debt instruments. As a result, the additional debt instruments have the same issue date, the same issue price, and (with respect to holders) the same adjusted issue price as the original debt instruments.

(2) *Definitions*—(i) *Original debt instruments.* Original debt instruments are debt instruments comprising any single issue of outstanding debt instruments. For purposes of determining whether a particular reopening is a qualified reopening, debt instruments issued in prior qualified reopenings are treated as original debt instruments and debt instruments issued in the particular reopening are not so treated.

Reg. § 1.1275-2(h)(4)

(ii) *Additional debt instruments.* Additional debt instruments are debt instruments that, without the application of this paragraph (k)—

(A) Are part of a single issue of debt instruments;

(B) Are not part of the same issue as the original debt instruments; and

(C) Have terms that are in all respects identical to the terms of the original debt instruments as of the reopening date.

(iii) *Reopening date.* The reopening date is the issue date of the additional debt instruments (determined without the application of this paragraph (k)).

(iv) *Announcement date.* The announcement date is the later of seven days before the date on which the price of the additional debt instruments is established or the date on which the issuer's intent to reopen a security is publicly announced through one or more media, including an announcement reported on the standard electronic news services used by security broker-dealers (for example, Reuters, Telerate, or Bloomberg).

(3) *Qualified reopening*—(i) *Definition.* A qualified reopening is a reopening of original debt instruments that is described in paragraph (k)(3)(ii) or (iii) of this section. In addition, see paragraph (d)(2) of this section to determine if a reopening of Treasury securities is a qualified reopening.

(ii) *Reopening within six months.* A reopening is described in this paragraph (k)(3)(ii) if—

(A) The original debt instruments are publicly traded (within the meaning of § 1.1273-2(f));

(B) The reopening date of the additional debt instruments is not more than six months after the issue date of the original debt instruments; and

(C) On the date on which the price of the additional debt instruments is established (or, if earlier, the announcement date), the yield of the original debt instruments (based on their fair market value) is not more than 110 percent of the yield of the original debt instruments on their issue date (or, if the original debt instruments were issued with no more than a de minimis amount of OID, the coupon rate).

(iii) *Reopening with de minimis OID.* A reopening (including a reopening of Treasury securities) is described in this paragraph (k)(3)(iii) if—

(A) The original debt instruments are publicly traded (within the meaning of § 1.1273-2(f)); and

(B) The additional debt instruments are issued with no more than a de minimis amount of OID (determined without the application of this paragraph (k)).

(iv) *Exceptions.* This paragraph (k)(3) does not apply to a reopening of tax-exempt obligations (as defined in section 1275(a)(3)) or contingent payment debt instruments (within the meaning of § 1.1275-4).

(4) *Issuer's treatment of a qualified reopening.* See § 1.163-7(e) for the issuer's treatment of the debt instruments that are part of a qualified reopening.

(5) *Effective date.* This paragraph (k) applies to debt instruments that are part of a reopening where the reopening date is on or after March 13, 2001. [Reg. § 1.1275-2.]

□ [*T.D.* 8517, 1-27-94. Amended by *T.D.* 8674, 6-11-96; *T.D.* 8840, 11-3-99 *and T.D.* 8934, 1-11-2001.]

[Reg. § 1.1275-3]

§ 1.1275-3. OID information reporting requirements.—(a) *In general.* This section provides legending and information reporting requirements intended to facilitate the reporting of OID.

(b) *Information required to be set forth on face of debt instruments that are not publicly offered*—(1) *In general.* Except as provided in paragraph (b)(4) or paragraph (d) of this section, this paragraph (b) applies to any debt instrument that is not publicly offered (within the meaning of § 1.1275-1(h)), is issued in physical form, and has OID. The issuer of any such debt instrument must legend the instrument by stating on the face of the instrument that the debt instrument was issued with OID. In addition, the issuer must either—

(i) Set forth on the face of the debt instrument the issue price, the amount of OID, the issue date, the yield to maturity, and, in the case of a debt instrument subject to the rules of § 1.1275-4(b), the comparable yield and projected payment schedule; or

(ii) Provide the name or title and either the address or telephone number of a representative of the issuer who will, beginning no later than 10 days after the issue date, promptly make available to holders upon request the information described in paragraph (b)(1)(i) of this section.

(2) *Time for legending.* An issuer may satisfy the requirements of this paragraph (b) by legend-

ing the debt instrument when it is first issued in physical form. Legending is not required, however, before the first holder of the debt instrument disposes of the instrument.

(3) *Legend must survive reissuance upon transfer.* Any new security that is issued (for example, upon registration of transfer of ownership) must contain any required legend.

(4) *Exceptions.* Paragraph (b)(1) of this section does not apply to debt instruments described in section 1272(a)(2) (relating to debt instruments not subject to the periodic OID inclusion rules), debt instruments issued by natural persons (as defined in § 1.6049-4(f)(2)), REMIC regular interests or other debt instruments subject to section 1272(a)(6), or stripped bonds and coupons within the meaning of section 1286.

(c) *Information required to be reported to Secretary upon issuance of publicly offered debt instruments*—(1) *In general.* Except as provided in paragraph (c)(3) or paragraph (d) of this section, the information reporting requirements of this paragraph (c) apply to any debt instrument that is publicly offered and has original issue discount. The issuer of any such debt instrument must make an information return on the form prescribed by the Commissioner (Form 8281, as of September 2, 1992). The prescribed form must be filed with the Internal Revenue Service in the manner specified on the form. The taxpayer must use the prescribed form even if other information returns are filed using other methods (e.g., electronic media), unless the Commissioner announces otherwise in a revenue procedure.

(2) *Time for filing information return.* The prescribed form must be filed for each issue of publicly offered debt instruments within 30 days after the issue date of the issue.

(3) *Exceptions.* The rules of paragraph (c)(1) of this section do not apply to debt instruments described in section 1272(a)(2), debt instruments issued by natural persons (as defined in § 1.6049-4(f)(2)), certificates of deposit, REMIC regular interests or other debt instruments subject to section 1272(a)(6), or (unless otherwise required by the Commissioner pursuant to a revenue ruling or revenue procedure) stripped bonds and coupons (within the meaning of section 1286).

(d) *Application to foreign issuers and U.S. issuers of foreign-targeted debt instruments.* A foreign or domestic issuer is subject to the rules of this section with respect to an issue of debt instruments unless the issue is not offered for sale or resale in the United States in connection with its original issuance.

(e) *Penalties.* See section 6706 for rules relating to the penalty imposed for failure to meet the information reporting requirements imposed by this section.

(f) *Effective date.* Paragraphs (c), (d), and (e) of this section are effective for an issue of debt instruments issued after September 2, 1992. [Reg. § 1.1275-3.]

☐ [T.D. 8431, 9-2-92. *Amended by* T.D. 8517, 1-27-94 *and* T.D. 8674, 6-11-96.]

[Reg. § 1.1275-4]

§ 1.1275-4. **Contingent payment debt instruments.**—(a) *Applicability*—(1) *In general.* Except as provided in paragraph (a)(2) of this section, this section applies to any debt instrument that provides for one or more contingent payments. In general, paragraph (b) of this section applies to a contingent payment debt instrument that is issued for money or publicly traded property and paragraph (c) of this section applies to a contingent payment debt instrument that is issued for nonpublicly traded property. Paragraph (d) of this section provides special rules for tax-exempt obligations. See § 1.1275-6 for a taxpayer's treatment of a contingent payment debt instrument and a hedge.

(2) *Exceptions.* This section does not apply to—

(i) A debt instrument that has an issue price determined under section 1273(b)(4) (e.g., a debt instrument subject to section 483);

(ii) A variable rate debt instrument (as defined in § 1.1275-5);

(iii) A debt instrument subject to § 1.1272-1(c) (a debt instrument that provides for certain contingencies) or § 1.1272-1(d) (a debt instrument that provides for a fixed yield);

(iv) A debt instrument subject to section 988 (except as provided in section 988 and the regulations thereunder);

(v) A debt instrument to which section 1272(a)(6) applies (certain interests in or mortgages held by a REMIC, and certain other debt instruments with payments subject to acceleration);

(vi) A debt instrument (other than a tax-exempt obligation) described in section 1272(a)(2) (e.g., U.S. savings bonds, certain loans between natural persons, and short-term taxable obligations);

(vii) An inflation-indexed debt instrument (as defined in § 1.1275-7); or

(viii) A debt instrument issued pursuant to a plan or arrangement if—

(A) The plan or arrangement is created by a state statute;

Reg. § 1.1275-4(a)(1)

(B) A primary objective of the plan or arrangement is to enable the participants to pay for the costs of post-secondary education for themselves or their designated beneficiaries; and

(C) Contingent payments on the debt instrument are related to such objective.

(3) *Insolvency and default.* A payment is not contingent merely because of the possibility of impairment by insolvency, default, or similar circumstances.

(4) *Convertible debt instruments.* A debt instrument does not provide for contingent payments merely because it provides for an option to convert the debt instrument into the stock of the issuer, into the stock or debt of a related party (within the meaning of section 267(b) or 707(b)(1)), or into cash or other property in an amount equal to the approximate value of such stock or debt.

(5) *Remote and incidental contingencies.* A payment is not a contingent payment merely because of a contingency that, as of the issue date, is either remote or incidental. See § 1.1275-2(h) for the treatment of remote and incidental contingencies.

(b) *Noncontingent bond method*—(1) *Applicability.* The noncontingent bond method described in this paragraph (b) applies to a contingent payment debt instrument that has an issue price determined under § 1.1273-2 (e.g., a contingent payment debt instrument that is issued for money or publicly traded property).

(2) *In general.* Under the noncontingent bond method, interest on a debt instrument must be taken into account whether or not the amount of any payment is fixed or determinable in the taxable year. The amount of interest that is taken into account for each accrual period is determined by constructing a projected payment schedule for the debt instrument and applying rules similar to those for accruing OID on a noncontingent debt instrument. If the actual amount of a contingent payment is not equal to the projected amount, appropriate adjustments are made to reflect the difference.

(3) *Description of method.* The following steps describe how to compute the amount of income, deductions, gain, and loss under the noncontingent bond method:

(i) *Step one: Determine the comparable yield.* Determine the comparable yield for the debt instrument under the rules of paragraph (b)(4) of this section. The comparable yield is determined as of the debt instrument's issue date.

(ii) *Step two: Determine the projected payment schedule.* Determine the projected payment schedule for the debt instrument under the rules of paragraph (b)(4) of this section. The projected payment schedule is determined as of the issue date and remains fixed throughout the term of the debt instrument (except under paragraph (b)(9)(ii) of this section, which applies to a payment that is fixed more than 6 months before it is due).

(iii) *Step three: Determine the daily portions of interest.* Determine the daily portions of interest on the debt instrument for a taxable year as follows. The amount of interest that accrues in each accrual period is the product of the comparable yield of the debt instrument (properly adjusted for the length of the accrual period) and the debt instrument's adjusted issue price at the beginning of the accrual period. See paragraph (b)(7)(ii) of this section to determine the adjusted issue price of the debt instrument. The daily portions of interest are determined by allocating to each day in the accrual period the ratable portion of the interest that accrues in the accrual period. Except as modified by paragraph (b)(3)(iv) of this section, the daily portions of interest are includible in income by a holder for each day in the holder's taxable year on which the holder held the debt instrument and are deductible by the issuer for each day during the issuer's taxable year on which the issuer was primarily liable on the debt instrument.

(iv) *Step four: Adjust the amount of income or deductions for differences between projected and actual contingent payments.* Make appropriate adjustments to the amount of income or deductions attributable to the debt instrument in a taxable year for any differences between projected and actual contingent payments. See paragraph (b)(6) of this section to determine the amount of an adjustment and the treatment of the adjustment.

(4) *Comparable yield and projected payment schedule.* This paragraph (b)(4) provides rules for determining the comparable yield and projected payment schedule for a debt instrument. The comparable yield and projected payment schedule must be supported by contemporaneous documentation showing that both are reasonable, are based on reliable, complete, and accurate data, and are made in good faith.

(i) *Comparable yield*—(A) *In general.* Except as provided in paragraph (b)(4)(i)(B) of this section, the comparable yield for a debt instrument is the yield at which the issuer would issue a fixed rate debt instrument with terms and conditions similar to those of the contingent payment debt instrument (the comparable fixed rate debt instrument), including the level of subordination,

Reg. § 1.1275-4(b)(4)

term, timing of payments, and general market conditions. For example, if a § 1.1275-6 hedge (or the substantial equivalent) is available, the comparable yield is the yield on the synthetic fixed rate debt instrument that would result if the issuer entered into the § 1.1275-6 hedge. If a § 1.1275-6 hedge (or the substantial equivalent) is not available, but similar fixed rate debt instruments of the issuer trade at a price that reflects a spread above a benchmark rate, the comparable yield is the sum of the value of the benchmark rate on the issue date and the spread. In determining the comparable yield, no adjustments are made for the riskiness of the contingencies or the liquidity of the debt instrument. The comparable yield must be a reasonable yield for the issuer and must not be less than the applicable Federal rate (based on the overall maturity of the debt instrument).

(B) *Presumption for certain debt instruments.* This paragraph (b)(4)(i)(B) applies to a debt instrument if the instrument provides for one or more contingent payments not based on market information and the instrument is part of an issue that is marketed or sold in substantial part to persons for whom the inclusion of interest under this paragraph (b) is not expected to have a substantial effect on their U.S. tax liability. If this paragraph (b)(4)(i)(B) applies to a debt instrument, the instrument's comparable yield is presumed to be the applicable Federal rate (based on the overall maturity of the debt instrument). A taxpayer may overcome this presumption only with clear and convincing evidence that the comparable yield for the debt instrument should be a specific yield (determined using the principles in paragraph (b)(4)(i)(A) of this section) that is higher than the applicable Federal rate. The presumption may not be overcome with appraisals or other valuations of nonpublicly traded property. Evidence used to overcome the presumption must be specific to the issuer and must not be based on comparable issuers or general market conditions.

(ii) *Projected payment schedule.* The projected payment schedule for a debt instrument includes each noncontingent payment and an amount for each contingent payment determined as follows:

(A) *Market-based payments.* If a contingent payment is based on market information (a market-based payment), the amount of the projected payment is the forward price of the contingent payment. The forward price of a contingent payment is the amount one party would agree, as of the issue date, to pay an unrelated party for the right to the contingent payment on the settlement date (e.g., the date the contingent payment is made). For example, if the right to a contingent payment is substantially similar to an exchange-traded option, the forward price is the spot price of the option (the option premium) compounded at the applicable Federal rate from the issue date to the date the contingent payment is due.

(B) *Other payments.* If a contingent payment is not based on market information (a non-market-based payment), the amount of the projected payment is the expected value of the contingent payment as of the issue date.

(C) *Adjustments to the projected payment schedule.* The projected payment schedule must produce the comparable yield. If the projected payment schedule does not produce the comparable yield, the schedule must be adjusted consistent with the principles of this paragraph (b)(4) to produce the comparable yield. For example, the adjusted amounts of non-market-based payments must reasonably reflect the relative expected values of the payments and must not be set to accelerate or defer income or deductions. If the debt instrument contains both market-based and non-market-based payments, adjustments are generally made first to the non-market-based payments because more objective information is available for the market-based payments.

(iii) *Market information.* For purposes of this paragraph (b), market information is any information on which an objective rate can be based under § 1.1275-5(c)(1) or (2).

(iv) *Issuer/holder consistency.* The issuer's projected payment schedule is used to determine the holder's interest accruals and adjustments. The issuer must provide the projected payment schedule to the holder in a manner consistent with the issuer disclosure rules of § 1.1275-2(e). If the issuer does not create a projected payment schedule for a debt instrument or the issuer's projected payment schedule is unreasonable, the holder of the debt instrument must determine the comparable yield and projected payment schedule for the debt instrument under the rules of this paragraph (b)(4). A holder that determines its own projected payment schedule must explicitly disclose this fact and the reason why the holder set its own schedule (e.g., why the issuer's projected payment schedule is unreasonable). Unless otherwise prescribed by the Commissioner, the disclosure must be made on a statement attached to the holder's timely filed federal income tax return for the taxable year that includes the acquisition date of the debt instrument.

(v) *Issuer's determination respected*—(A) *In general.* If the issuer maintains the contemporaneous documentation required by this paragraph (b)(4), the issuer's determination of the

Special Rules, Bonds & Other Debt Instruments 53,677
See p. 20,601 for regulations not amended to reflect law changes

comparable yield and projected payment schedule will be respected unless either is unreasonable.

(B) *Unreasonable determination.* For purposes of paragraph (b)(4)(v)(A) of this section, a comparable yield or projected payment schedule generally will be considered unreasonable if it is set with a purpose to overstate, understate, accelerate, or defer interest accruals on the debt instrument. In a determination of whether a comparable yield or projected payment schedule is unreasonable, consideration will be given to whether the treatment of the debt instrument under this section is expected to have a substantial effect on the issuer's or holder's U.S. tax liability. For example, if a taxable issuer markets a debt instrument to a holder not subject to U.S. taxation, the comparable yield will be given close scrutiny and will not be respected unless contemporaneous documentation shows that the yield is not too high.

(C) *Exception.* Paragraph (b)(4)(v)(A) of this section does not apply to a debt instrument subject to paragraph (b)(4)(i)(B) of this section (concerning a yield presumption for certain debt instruments that provide for non-market-based payments).

(vi) *Examples.* The following examples illustrate the provisions of this paragraph (b)(4). In each example, assume that the instrument described is a debt instrument for federal income tax purposes. No inference is intended, however, as to whether the instrument is a debt instrument for federal income tax purposes.

Example 1. Market-based payment—(i) *Facts.* On December 31, 1996, X corporation issues for $1,000,000 a debt instrument that matures on December 31, 2006. The debt instrument provides for annual payments of interest, beginning in 1997, at the rate of 6 percent and for a payment at maturity equal to $1,000,000 plus the excess, if any, of the price of 10,000 shares of publicly traded stock in an unrelated corporation on the maturity date over $350,000, or less the excess, if any, of $350,000 over the price of 10,000 shares of the stock on the maturity date. On the issue date, the forward price to purchase 10,000 shares of the stock on December 31, 2006, is $350,000.

(ii) *Comparable yield.* Under paragraph (b)(4)(i) of this section, the debt instrument's comparable yield is the yield on the synthetic debt instrument that would result if X corporation entered into a § 1.1275-6 hedge. A § 1.1275-6 hedge in this case is a forward contract to purchase 10,000 shares of the stock on December 31, 2006. If X corporation entered into this hedge, the resulting synthetic debt instrument would yield 6 percent, compounded annually. Thus, the comparable yield on the debt instrument is 6 percent, compounded annually.

(iii) *Projected payment schedule.* Under paragraph (b)(4)(ii) of this section, the projected payment schedule for the debt instrument consists of 10 annual payments of $60,000 and a projected amount for the contingent payment at maturity. Because the right to the contingent payment is based on market information, the projected amount of the contingent payment is the forward price of the payment. The right to the contingent payment is substantially similar to a right to a payment of $1,000,000 combined with a cash-settled forward contract for the purchase of 10,000 shares of the stock for $350,000 on December 31, 2006. Because the forward price to purchase 10,000 shares of the stock on December 31, 2006, is $350,000, the amount to be received or paid under the forward contract is projected to be zero. As a result, the projected amount of the contingent payment at maturity is $1,000,000, consisting of the $1,000,000 base amount and no additional amount to be received or paid under the forward contract.

(A) Assume, alternatively, that on the issue date the forward price to purchase 10,000 shares of the stock on December 31, 2006, is $370,000. If X corporation entered into a § 1.1275-6 hedge (a forward contract to purchase the shares for $370,000), the resulting synthetic debt instrument would yield 6.15 percent, compounded annually. Thus, the comparable yield on the debt instrument is 6.15 percent, compounded annually. The projected payment schedule for the debt instrument consists of 10 annual payments of $60,000 and a projected amount for the contingent payment at maturity. The projected amount of the contingent payment is $1,020,000, consisting of the $1,000,000 base amount plus the excess $20,000 of the forward price of the stock over the purchase price of the stock under the forward contract.

(B) Assume, alternatively, that on the issue date the forward price to purchase 10,000 shares of the stock on December 31, 2006, is $330,000. If X corporation entered into a § 1.1275-6 hedge, the resulting synthetic debt instrument would yield 5.85 percent, compounded annually. Thus, the comparable yield on the debt instrument is 5.85 percent, compounded annually. The projected payment schedule for the debt instrument consists of 10 annual payments of $60,000 and a projected amount for the contingent payment at maturity. The projected amount of the contingent payment is $980,000, consisting of the $1,000,000 base amount minus the excess

Reg. § 1.1275-4(b)(4)

$20,000 of the purchase price of the stock under the forward contract over the forward price of the stock.

Example 2. Non-market-based payments—(i) Facts. On December 31, 1996, Y issues to Z for $1,000,000 a debt instrument that matures on December 31, 2000. The debt instrument has a stated principal amount of $1,000,000, payable at maturity, and provides for payments on December 31 of each year, beginning in 1997, of $20,000 plus 1 percent of Y's gross receipts, if any, for the year. On the issue date, Y has outstanding fixed rate debt instruments with maturities of 2 to 10 years that trade at a price that reflects an average of 100 basis points over Treasury bonds. These debt instruments have terms and conditions similar to those of the debt instrument. Assume that on December 31, 1996, 4-year Treasury bonds have a yield of 6.5 percent, compounded annually, and that no § 1.1275-6 hedge is available for the debt instrument. In addition, assume that the interest inclusions attributable to the debt instrument are expected to have a substantial effect on Z's U.S. tax liability.

(ii) Comparable yield. The comparable yield for the debt instrument is equal to the value of the benchmark rate (i.e., the yield on 4-year Treasury bonds) on the issue date plus the spread. Thus, the debt instrument's comparable yield is 7.5 percent, compounded annually.

(iii) Projected payment schedule. Y anticipates that it will have no gross receipts in 1997, but that it will have gross receipts in later years, and those gross receipts will grow each year for the next three years. Based on its business projections, Y believes that it is not unreasonable to expect that its gross receipts in 1999 and each year thereafter will grow by between 6 percent and 13 percent over the prior year. Thus, Y must take these expectations into account in establishing a projected payment schedule for the debt instrument that results in a yield of 7.5 percent, compounded annually. Accordingly, Y could reasonably set the following projected payment schedule for the debt instrument:

Date	Noncontingent payment	Contingent payment
12/31/1997	$ 20,000	$ 0
12/31/1998	20,000	70,000
12/31/1999	20,000	75,600
12/31/2000	1,020,000	83,850

(5) Qualified stated interest. No amounts payable on a debt instrument to which this paragraph (b) applies are qualified stated interest within the meaning of § 1.1273-1(c).

(6) Adjustments. This paragraph (b)(6) provides rules for the treatment of positive and negative adjustments under the noncontingent bond method. A taxpayer takes into account only those adjustments that occur during a taxable year while the debt instrument is held by the taxpayer or while the taxpayer is primarily liable on the debt instrument.

(i) Determination of positive and negative adjustments. If the amount of a contingent payment is more than the projected amount of the contingent payment, the difference is a positive adjustment on the date of the payment. If the amount of a contingent payment is less than the projected amount of the contingent payment, the difference is a negative adjustment on the date of the payment (or on the scheduled date of the payment if the amount of the payment is zero).

(ii) Treatment of net positive adjustments. The amount, if any, by which total positive adjustments on a debt instrument in a taxable year exceed the total negative adjustments on the debt instrument in the taxable year is a net positive adjustment. A net positive adjustment is treated as additional interest for the taxable year.

(iii) Treatment of net negative adjustments. The amount, if any, by which total negative adjustments on a debt instrument in a taxable year exceed the total positive adjustments on the debt instrument in the taxable year is a net negative adjustment. A taxpayer's net negative adjustment on a debt instrument for a taxable year is treated as follows:

(A) Reduction of interest accruals. A net negative adjustment first reduces interest for the taxable year that the taxpayer would otherwise account for on the debt instrument under paragraph (b)(3)(iii) of this section.

(B) Ordinary income or loss. If the net negative adjustment exceeds the interest for the taxable year that the taxpayer would otherwise account for on the debt instrument under paragraph (b)(3)(iii) of this section, the excess is treated as ordinary loss by a holder and ordinary income by an issuer. However, the amount treated as ordinary loss by a holder is limited to the amount by which the holder's total interest inclusions on the debt instrument exceed the total amount of the holder's net negative adjustments treated as ordinary loss on the debt instrument in prior taxable years. The amount treated as ordi-

Reg. § 1.1275-4(b)(5)

nary income by an issuer is limited to the amount by which the issuer's total interest deductions on the debt instrument exceed the total amount of the issuer's net negative adjustments treated as ordinary income on the debt instrument in prior taxable years.

(C) *Carryforward.* If the net negative adjustment exceeds the sum of the amounts treated by the taxpayer as a reduction of interest and as ordinary income or loss (as the case may be) on the debt instrument for the taxable year, the excess is a negative adjustment carryforward for the taxable year. In general, a taxpayer treats a negative adjustment carryforward for a taxable year as a negative adjustment on the debt instrument on the first day of the succeeding taxable year. However, if a holder of a debt instrument has a negative adjustment carryforward on the debt instrument in a taxable year in which the debt instrument is sold, exchanged, or retired, the negative adjustment carryforward reduces the holder's amount realized on the sale, exchange, or retirement. If an issuer of a debt instrument has a negative adjustment carryforward on the debt instrument for a taxable year in which the debt instrument is retired, the issuer takes the negative adjustment carryforward into account as ordinary income.

(D) *Treatment under section 67.* A net negative adjustment is not subject to section 67 (the 2-percent floor on miscellaneous itemized deductions).

(iv) *Cross-references.* If a holder has a basis in a debt instrument that is different from the debt instrument's adjusted issue price, the holder may have additional positive or negative adjustments under paragraph (b)(9)(i) of this section. If the amount of a contingent payment is fixed more than 6 months before the date it is due, the amount and timing of the adjustment are determined under paragraph (b)(9)(ii) of this section.

(7) *Adjusted issue price, adjusted basis, and retirement*—(i) *In general.* If a debt instrument is subject to the noncontingent bond method, this paragraph (b)(7) provides rules to determine the adjusted issue price of the debt instrument, the holder's basis in the debt instrument, and the treatment of any scheduled or unscheduled retirements. In general, because any difference between the actual amount of a contingent payment and the projected amount of the payment is taken into account as an adjustment to income or deduction, the projected payments are treated as the actual payments for purposes of making adjustments to issue price and basis and determining the amount of any contingent payment made on a scheduled retirement.

(ii) *Definition of adjusted issue price.* The adjusted issue price of a debt instrument is equal to the debt instrument's issue price, increased by the interest previously accrued on the debt instrument under paragraph (b)(3)(iii) of this section (determined without regard to any adjustments taken into account under paragraph (b)(3)(iv) of this section), and decreased by the amount of any noncontingent payment and the projected amount of any contingent payment previously made on the debt instrument. See paragraph (b)(9)(ii) of this section for special rules that apply when a contingent payment is fixed more than 6 months before it is due.

(iii) *Adjustments to basis.* A holder's basis in a debt instrument is increased by the interest previously accrued by the holder on the debt instrument under paragraph (b)(3)(iii) of this section (determined without regard to any adjustments taken into account under paragraph (b)(3)(iv) of this section), and decreased by the amount of any noncontingent payment and the projected amount of any contingent payment previously made on the debt instrument to the holder. See paragraph (b)(9)(i) of this section for special rules that apply when basis is different from adjusted issue price and paragraph (b)(9)(ii) of this section for special rules that apply when a contingent payment is fixed more than 6 months before it is due.

(iv) *Scheduled retirements.* For purposes of determining the amount realized by a holder and the repurchase price paid by the issuer on the scheduled retirement of a debt instrument, a holder is treated as receiving, and the issuer is treated as paying, the projected amount of any contingent payment due at maturity. If the amount paid or received is different from the projected amount, see paragraph (b)(6) of this section for the treatment of the difference by the taxpayer. Under paragraph (b)(6)(iii)(C) of this section, the amount realized by a holder on the retirement of a debt instrument is reduced by any negative adjustment carryforward determined in the taxable year of the retirement.

(v) *Unscheduled retirements.* An unscheduled retirement of debt instrument (or the receipt of a pro-rata prepayment that is treated as a retirement of a portion of a debt instrument under § 1.1275-2(f)) is treated as a repurchase of the debt instrument (or a pro-rata portion of the debt instrument) by the issuer from the holder for the amount paid by the issuer to the holder.

(vi) *Examples.* The following examples illustrate the following provisions of paragraphs (b)(6) and (7) of this section. In each example, assume that the instrument described is a debt

Reg. § 1.1275-4(b)(7)

instrument for federal income tax purposes. No inference is intended, however, as to whether the instrument is a debt instrument for federal income tax purposes.

Example 1. Treatment of positive and negative adjustments—(i) *Facts.* On December 31, 1996, Z, a calendar year taxpayer, purchases a debt instrument subject to this paragraph (b) at original issue for $1,000. The debt instrument's comparable yield is 10 percent, compounded annually, and the projected payment schedule provides for payments of $500 on December 31, 1997 (consisting of a noncontingent payment of $375 and a projected amount of $125) and $660 on December 31, 1998 (consisting of a noncontingent payment of $600 and a projected amount of $60). The debt instrument is a capital asset in the hands of Z.

(ii) *Adjustment in 1997.* Based on the projected payment schedule, Z's total daily portions of interest on the debt instrument are $100 for 1997 (issue price of $1,000 x 10 percent). Assume that the payment actually made on December 31, 1997, is $375, rather than the projected $500. Under paragraph (b)(6)(i) of this section, Z has a negative adjustment of $125 on December 31, 1997, attributable to the difference between the amount of the actual payment and the amount of the projected payment. Because Z has no positive adjustments for 1997, Z has a net negative adjustment of $125 on the debt instrument for 1997. This net negative adjustment reduces to zero the $100 total daily portions of interest Z would otherwise include in income in 1997. Accordingly, Z has no interest income on the debt instrument for 1997. Because Z had no interest inclusions on the debt instrument for prior taxable years, the remaining $25 of the net negative adjustment is a negative adjustment carryforward for 1997 that results in a negative adjustment of $25 on January 1, 1998.

(iii) *Adjustment to issue price and basis.* Z's total daily portions of interest on the debt instrument are $100 for 1997. The adjusted issue price of the debt instrument and Z's adjusted basis in the debt instrument are increased by this amount, despite the fact that Z does not include this amount in income because of the net negative adjustment for 1997. In addition, the adjusted issue price of the debt instrument and Z's adjusted basis in the debt instrument are decreased on December 31, 1997, by the projected amount of the payment on that date ($500). Thus, on January 1, 1998, Z's adjusted basis in the debt instrument and the adjusted issue price of the debt instrument are $600.

(iv) *Adjustments in 1998.* Based on the projected payment schedule, Z's total daily portions of interest are $60 for 1998 (adjusted issue price of $600 x 10 percent). Assume that the payment actually made on December 31, 1998, is $700, rather than the projected $660. Under paragraph (b)(6)(i) of this section, Z has a positive adjustment of $40 on December 31, 1998, attributable to the difference between the amount of the actual payment and the amount of the projected payment. Because Z also has a negative adjustment of $25 on January 1, 1998, Z has a net positive adjustment of $15 on the debt instrument for 1998 (the excess of the $40 positive adjustment over the $25 negative adjustment). As a result, Z has $75 of interest income on the debt instrument for 1998 (the $15 net positive adjustment plus the $60 total daily portions of interest that are taken into account by Z in that year).

(v) *Retirement.* Based on the projected payment schedule, Z's adjusted basis in the debt instrument immediately before the payment at maturity is $660 ($600 plus $60 total daily portions of interest for 1998). Even though Z receives $700 at maturity, for purposes of determining the amount realized by Z on retirement of the debt instrument, Z is treated as receiving the projected amount of the contingent payment on December 31, 1998. Therefore, Z is treated as receiving $660 on December 31, 1998. Because Z's adjusted basis in the debt instrument immediately before its retirement is $660, Z recognizes no gain or loss on the retirement.

Example 2. Negative adjustment carryforward for year of sale—(i) *Facts.* Assume the same facts as in *Example 1* of this paragraph (b)(7)(vi), except that Z sells the debt instrument on January 1, 1998, for $630.

(ii) *Gain on sale.* On the date the debt instrument is sold, Z's adjusted basis in the debt instrument is $600. Because Z has a negative adjustment of $25 on the debt instrument on January 1, 1998, and has no positive adjustments on the debt instrument in 1998, Z has a net negative adjustment for 1998 of $25. Because Z has not included in income any interest on the debt instrument, the entire $25 net negative adjustment is a negative adjustment carryforward for the taxable year of the sale. Under paragraph (b)(6)(iii)(C) of this section, the $25 negative adjustment carryforward reduces the amount realized by Z on the sale of the debt instrument from $630 to $605. Thus, Z has a gain on the sale of $5 ($605-$600). Under paragraph (b)(8)(i) of this section, the gain is treated as interest income.

Example 3. Negative adjustment carryforward for year of retirement—(i) *Facts.* Assume

Reg. § 1.1275-4(b)(7)

the same facts as in *Example 1* of this paragraph (b)(7)(vi), except that the payment actually made on December 31, 1998, is $615, rather than the projected $660.

(ii) *Adjustments in 1998.* Under paragraph (b)(6)(i) of this section, Z has a negative adjustment of $45 on December 31, 1998, attributable to the difference between the amount of the actual payment and the amount of the projected payment. In addition, Z has a negative adjustment of $25 on January 1, 1998. See *Example 1* (ii) of this paragraph (b)(7)(vi). Because Z has no positive adjustments in 1998, Z has a net negative adjustment of $70 for 1998. This net negative adjustment reduces to zero the $60 total daily portions of interest Z would otherwise include in income for 1998. Therefore, Z has no interest income on the debt instrument for 1998. Because Z had no interest inclusions on the debt instrument for 1997, the remaining $10 of the net negative adjustment is a negative adjustment carryforward for 1998 that reduces the amount realized by Z on retirement of the debt instrument.

(iii) *Loss on retirement.* Immediately before the payment at maturity, Z's adjusted basis in the debt instrument is $660. Under paragraph (b)(7)(iv) of this section, Z is treated as receiving the projected amount of the contingent payment, or $660, as the payment at maturity. Under paragraph (b)(6)(iii)(C) of this section, however, this amount is reduced by any negative adjustment carryforward determined for the taxable year of retirement to calculate the amount Z realizes on retirement of the debt instrument. Thus, Z has a loss of $10 on the retirement of the debt instrument, equal to the amount by which Z's adjusted basis in the debt instrument ($660) exceeds the amount Z realizes on the retirement of the debt instrument ($660 minus the $10 negative adjustment carryforward). Under paragraph (b)(8)(ii) of this section, the loss is a capital loss.

(8) *Character on sale, exchange, or retirement*—(i) *Gain.* Any gain recognized by a holder on the sale, exchange, or retirement of a debt instrument subject to this paragraph (b) is interest income.

(ii) *Loss.* Any loss recognized by a holder on the sale, exchange, or retirement of a debt instrument subject to this paragraph (b) is ordinary loss to the extent that the holder's total interest inclusions on the debt instrument exceed the total net negative adjustments on the debt instrument the holder took into account as ordinary loss. Any additional *loss is* treated as *loss* from the sale, exchange, or retirement of the debt instrument. However, any loss that would otherwise be ordinary under this paragraph (b)(8)(ii) and that is attributable to the holder's basis that could not be amortized under section 171(b)(4) is loss from the sale, exchange, or retirement of the debt instrument.

(iii) *Special rule if there are no remaining contingent payments on the debt instrument*—(A) *In general.* Notwithstanding paragraphs (b)(8)(i) and (ii) of this section, if, at the time of the sale, exchange, or retirement of the debt instrument, there are no remaining contingent payments due on the debt instrument under the projected payment schedule, any gain or loss recognized by the holder is gain or loss from the sale, exchange, or retirement of the debt instrument. See paragraph (b)(9)(ii) of this section to determine whether there are no remaining contingent payments on a debt instrument that provides for fixed but deferred contingent payments.

(B) *Exception for certain positive adjustments.* Notwithstanding paragraph (b)(8)(iii)(A) of this section, if a positive adjustment on a debt instrument is spread under paragraph (b)(9)(ii)(F) or (G) of this section, any gain recognized by the holder on the sale, exchange, or retirement of the instrument is treated as interest income to the extent of the positive adjustment that has not yet been accrued and included in income by the holder.

(iv) *Examples.* The following examples illustrate the provisions of this paragraph (b)(8). In each example, assume that the instrument described is a debt instrument for federal income tax purposes. No inference is intended, however, as to whether the instrument is a debt instrument for federal income tax purposes.

Example 1. Gain on sale—(i) *Facts.* On January 1, 1998, D, a calendar year taxpayer, sells a debt instrument that is subject to paragraph (b) of this section for $1,350. The projected payment schedule for the debt instrument provides for contingent payments after January 1, 1998. On January 1, 1998, D has an adjusted basis in the debt instrument of $1,200. In addition, D has a negative adjustment carryforward of $50 for 1997 that, under paragraph (b)(6)(iii)(C) of this section, results in a negative adjustment of $50 on January 1, 1998. D has no positive adjustments on the debt instrument on January 1, 1998.

(ii) *Character of gain.* Under paragraph (b)(6) of this section, the $50 negative adjustment on January 1, 1998, results in a negative adjustment carryforward for 1998, the taxable year of the sale of the debt instrument. Under paragraph (b)(6)(iii)(C) of this section, the negative adjustment carryforward reduces the amount realized by D on the sale of the debt instrument from $1,350 to $1,300. As a result, D realizes a $100 gain on the sale of the debt instrument, equal to the $1,300 amount realized minus D's $1,200 adjusted basis in the debt instrument. Under paragraph (b)(8)(i) of this section, the gain is interest income to D.

Example 2. Loss on sale—(i) *Facts.* On December 31, 1996, E, a calendar year taxpayer, purchases a debt instrument at original issue for $1,000. The debt instrument is a capital asset in the hands of E. The debt instrument provides for a single payment on December 31, 1998 (the maturity date of the instrument), of $1,000 plus an amount based on the increase, if any, in the price of a specified commodity over the term of the instrument. The comparable yield for the debt instrument is 9.54 percent, compounded annually, and the projected payment schedule provides for a payment of $1,200 on December 31, 1998. Based on the projected payment schedule, the total daily portions of interest are $95 for 1997 and $105 for 1998.

(ii) *Ordinary loss.* Assume that E sells the debt instrument for $1,050 on December 31, 1997. On that date, E has an adjusted basis in the debt instrument of $1,095 ($1,000 original basis, plus total daily portions of $95 for 1997). Therefore, E realizes a $45 loss on the sale of the debt instrument ($1,050 - $1,095). The loss is ordinary to the extent E's total interest inclusions on the debt instrument ($95) exceed the total net negative adjustments on the instrument that E took into account as an ordinary loss. Because E has not had any net negative adjustments on the debt instrument, the $45 loss is an ordinary loss.

(iii) *Capital loss.* Alternatively, assume that E sells the debt instrument for $990 on December 31, 1997. E realizes a $105 loss on the sale of the debt instrument ($990 - $1,095). The loss is ordinary to the extent E's total interest inclusions on the debt instrument ($95) exceed the total net negative adjustments on the instrument that E took into account as an ordinary loss. Because E has not had any net negative adjustments on the debt instrument, $95 of the $105 loss is an ordinary loss. The remaining $10 of the $105 loss is a capital loss.

(9) *Operating rules.* The rules of this paragraph (b)(9) apply to a debt instrument subject to the noncontingent bond method notwithstanding any other rule of this paragraph (b).

(i) *Basis different from adjusted issue price.* This paragraph (b)(9)(i) provides rules for a holder whose basis in a debt instrument is different from the adjusted issue price of the debt instrument (e.g., a subsequent holder that purchases the debt instrument for more or less than the instrument's adjusted issue price).

(A) *General rule.* The holder accrues interest under paragraph (b)(3)(iii) of this section and makes adjustments under paragraph (b)(3)(iv) of this section based on the projected payment schedule determined as of the issue date of the debt instrument. However, upon acquiring the debt instrument, the holder must reasonably allocate any difference between the adjusted issue price and the basis to daily portions of interest or projected payments over the remaining term of the debt instrument. Allocations are taken into account under paragraphs (b)(9)(i)(B) and (C) of this section.

(B) *Basis greater than adjusted issue price.* If the holder's basis in the debt instrument exceeds the debt instrument's adjusted issue price, the amount of the difference allocated to a daily portion of interest or to a projected payment is treated as a negative adjustment on the date the daily portion accrues or the payment is made. On the date of the adjustment, the holder's adjusted basis in the debt instrument is reduced by the amount the holder treats as a negative adjustment under this paragraph (b)(9)(i)(B). See paragraph (b)(9)(ii)(E) of this section for a special rule that applies when a contingent payment is fixed more than 6 months before it is due.

(C) *Basis less than adjusted issue price.* If the holder's basis in the debt instrument is less than the debt instrument's adjusted issue price, the amount of the difference allocated to a daily portion of interest or to a projected payment is treated as a positive adjustment on the date the daily portion accrues or the payment is made. On the date of the adjustment, the holder's adjusted basis in the debt instrument is increased by the amount the holder treats as a positive adjustment under this paragraph (b)(9)(i)(C). See paragraph (b)(9)(ii)(E) of this section for a special rule that applies when a contingent payment is fixed more than 6 months before it is due.

(D) *Premium and discount rules do not apply.* The rules for accruing premium and discount in sections 171, 1272(a)(7), 1276, and 1281 do not apply. Other rules of those sections, such as section 171(b)(4), continue to apply to the extent relevant.

(E) *Safe harbor for exchange listed debt instruments.* If the debt instrument is exchange listed property (within the meaning of § 1.1273-2(f)(2), it is reasonable for the holder to allocate any difference between the holder's basis and the adjusted issue price of the debt instrument pro-rata to daily portions of interest (as determined under paragraph (b)(3)(iii) of this section) over the remaining term of the debt instrument. A pro-rata allocation is not reasonable,

Reg. § 1.1275-4(b)(9)

however, to the extent the holder's yield on the debt instrument, determined after taking into account the amounts allocated under this paragraph (b)(9)(i)(E), is less than the applicable Federal rate for the instrument. For purposes of the preceding sentence, the applicable Federal rate for the debt instrument is determined as if the purchase date were the issue date and the remaining term of the instrument were the term of the instrument.

(F) *Examples.* The following examples illustrate the provisions of this paragraph (b)(9)(i). In each example, assume that the instrument described is a debt instrument for federal income tax purposes. No inference is intended, however, as to whether the instrument is a debt instrument for federal income tax purposes. In addition, assume that each instrument is not exchange listed property.

Example 1. Basis greater than adjusted issue price—(i) *Facts.* On July 1, 1998, Z purchases for $1,405 a debt instrument that matures on December 31, 1999, and promises to pay on the maturity date $1,000 plus the increase, if any, in the price of a specified amount of a commodity from the issue date to the maturity date. The debt instrument was originally issued on December 31, 1996, for an issue price of $1,000. The comparable yield for the debt instrument is 10.25 percent, compounded semiannually, and the projected payment schedule for the debt instrument (determined as of the issue date) provides for a single payment at maturity of $1,350. At the time of the purchase, the debt instrument has an adjusted issue price of $1,162, assuming semiannual accrual periods ending on December 31 and June 30 of each year. The increase in the value of the debt instrument over its adjusted issue price is due to an increase in the expected amount of the contingent payment and not to a decrease in market interest rates. The debt instrument is a capital asset in the hands of Z. Z is a calendar year taxpayer.

(ii) *Allocation of the difference between basis and adjusted issue price.* Z's basis in the debt instrument on July 1, 1998, is $1,405. Under paragraph (b)(9)(i)(A) of this section, Z allocates the $243 difference between basis ($1,405) and adjusted issue price ($1,162) to the contingent payment at maturity. Z's allocation of the difference between basis and adjusted issue price is reasonable because the increase in the value of the debt instrument over its adjusted issue price is due to an increase in the expected amount of the contingent payment.

(iii) *Treatment of debt instrument for 1998.* Based on the projected payment schedule, $60 of interest accrues on the debt instrument from July 1, 1998 to December 31, 1998 (the product of the debt instrument's adjusted issue price on July 1, 1998 ($1,162) and the comparable yield properly adjusted for the length of the accrual period (10.25 percent/2)). Z has no net negative or positive adjustments for 1998. Thus, Z includes in income $60 of total daily portions of interest for 1998. On December 31, 1998, Z's adjusted basis in the debt instrument is $1,465 ($1,405 original basis, plus total daily portions of $60 for 1998).

(iv) *Effect of allocation to contingent payment at maturity.* Assume that the payment actually made on December 31, 1999, is $1,400, rather than the projected $1,350. Thus, under paragraph (b)(6)(i) of this section, Z has a positive adjustment of $50 on December 31, 1999. In addition, under paragraph (b)(9)(i)(B) of this section, Z has a negative adjustment of $243 on December 31, 1999, which is attributable to the difference between Z's basis in the debt instrument on July 1, 1998, and the instrument's adjusted issue price on that date. As a result, Z has a net negative adjustment of $193 for 1999. This net negative adjustment reduces to zero the $128 total daily portions of interest Z would otherwise include in income in 1999. Accordingly, Z has no interest income on the debt instrument for 1999. Because Z had $60 of interest inclusions for 1998, $60 of the remaining $65 net negative adjustment is treated by Z as an ordinary loss for 1999. The remaining $5 of the net negative adjustment is a negative adjustment carryforward for 1999 that reduces the amount realized by Z on the retirement of the debt instrument from $1,350 to $1,345.

(v) *Loss at maturity.* On December 31, 1999, Z's basis in the debt instrument is $1,350 ($1,405 original basis, plus total daily portions of $60 for 1998 and $128 for 1999, minus the negative adjustment of $243). As a result, Z realizes a loss of $5 on the retirement of the debt instrument (the difference between the amount realized on the retirement ($1,345) and Z's adjusted basis in the debt instrument ($1,350)). Under paragraph (b)(8)(ii) of this section, the $5 loss is treated as loss from the retirement of the debt instrument. Consequently, Z realizes a total loss of $65 on the debt instrument for 1999 (a $60 ordinary loss and a $5 capital loss).

Example 2. Basis less than adjusted issue price—(i) *Facts.* On January 1, 1999, Y purchases for $910 a debt instrument that pays 7 percent interest semiannually on June 30 and December 31 of each year, and that promises to pay on December 31, 2001, $1,000 plus or minus

Reg. § 1.1275-4(b)(9)

$10 times the positive or negative difference, if any, between a specified amount and the value of an index on December 31, 2001. However, the payment on December 31, 2001, may not be less than $650. The debt instrument was originally issued on December 31, 1996, for an issue price of $1,000. The comparable yield for the debt instrument is 9.80 percent, compounded semiannually, and the projected payment schedule for the debt instrument (determined as of the issue date) provides for semiannual payments of $35 and a contingent payment at maturity of $1,175. On January 1, 1999, the debt instrument has an adjusted issue price of $1,060, assuming semiannual accrual periods ending on December 31 and June 30 of each year. Y is a calendar year taxpayer.

(ii) *Allocation of the difference between basis and adjusted issue price.* Y's basis in the debt instrument on January 1, 1999, is $910. Under paragraph (b)(9)(i)(A) of this section, Y must allocate the $150 difference between basis ($910) and adjusted issue price ($1,060) to daily portions of interest or to projected payments. These amounts will be positive adjustments taken into account at the time the daily portions accrue or the payments are made.

(A) Assume that, because of a decrease in the relevant index, the expected value of the payment at maturity has declined by about 9 percent. Based on forward prices on January 1, 1999, Y determines that approximately $105 of the difference between basis and adjusted issue price is allocable to the contingent payment. Y allocates the remaining $45 to daily portions of interest on a pro-rata basis (i.e., the amount allocated to an accrual period equals the product of $45 and a fraction, the numerator of which is the total daily portions for the accrual period and the denominator of which is the total daily portions remaining on the debt instrument on January 1, 1999). This allocation is reasonable.

(B) Assume alternatively that, based on yields of comparable debt instruments and its purchase price for the debt instrument, Y determines that an appropriate yield for the debt instrument is 13 percent, compounded semiannually. Based on this determination, Y allocates $55.75 of the difference between basis and adjusted issue price to daily portions of interest as follows: $15.19 to the daily portions of interest for the taxable year ending December 31, 1999; $18.40 to the daily portions of interest for the taxable year ending December 31, 2000; and $22.16 to the daily portions of interest for the taxable year ending December 31, 2001. Y allocates the remaining $94.25 to the contingent payment at maturity. This allocation is reasonable.

(ii) *Fixed but deferred contingent payments.* This paragraph (b)(9)(ii) provides rules that apply when the amount of a contingent payment becomes fixed before the payment is due. For purposes of paragraph (b) of this section, if a contingent payment becomes fixed within the 6-month period ending on the due date of the payment, the payment is treated as a contingent payment even after the payment is fixed. If a contingent payment becomes fixed more than 6 months before the payment is due, the following rules apply to the debt instrument.

(A) *Determining adjustments.* The amount of the adjustment attributable to the contingent payment is equal to the difference between the present value of the amount that is fixed and the present value of the projected amount of the contingent payment. The present value of each amount is determined by discounting the amount from the date the payment is due to the date the payment becomes fixed, using a discount rate equal to the comparable yield on the debt instrument. The adjustment is treated as a positive or negative adjustment, as appropriate, on the date the contingent payment becomes fixed. See paragraph (b)(9)(ii)(G) of this section to determine the timing of the adjustment if all remaining contingent payments on the debt instrument become fixed substantially contemporaneously.

(B) *Payment schedule.* The contingent payment is no longer treated as a contingent payment after the date the amount of the payment becomes fixed. On the date the contingent payment becomes fixed, the projected payment schedule for the debt instrument is modified prospectively to reflect the fixed amount of the payment. Therefore, no adjustment is made under paragraph (b)(3)(iv) of this section when the contingent payment is actually made.

(C) *Accrual period.* Notwithstanding the determination under § 1.1272-1(b)(1)(ii) of accrual periods for the debt instrument, an accrual period ends on the day the contingent payment becomes fixed, and a new accrual period begins on the day after the day the contingent payment becomes fixed.

(D) *Adjustments to basis and adjusted issue price.* The amount of any positive adjustment on a debt instrument determined under paragraph (b)(9)(ii)(A) of this section increases the adjusted issue price of the instrument and the holder's adjusted basis in the instrument. Similarly, the amount of any negative adjustment on a debt instrument determined under paragraph (b)(9)(ii)(A) of this section decreases the adjusted issue price of the instrument and the holder's adjusted basis in the instrument.

(E) *Basis different from adjusted issue price.* If a holder's basis in a debt instrument exceeds the debt instrument's adjusted issue price, the amount allocated to a projected payment under paragraph (b)(9)(i) of this section is treated as a negative adjustment on the date the payment becomes fixed. If a holder's basis in a debt instrument is less than the debt instrument's adjusted issue price, the amount allocated to a projected payment under paragraph (b)(9)(i) of this section is treated as a positive adjustment on the date the payment becomes fixed.

(F) *Special rule for certain contingent interest payments.* Notwithstanding paragraph (b)(9)(ii)(A) of this section, this paragraph (b)(9)(ii)(F) applies to contingent stated interest payments that are adjusted to compensate for contingencies regarding the reasonableness of the debt instrument's stated rate of interest. For example, this paragraph (b)(9)(ii)(F) applies to a debt instrument that provides for an increase in the stated rate of interest if the credit quality of the issuer or liquidity of the debt instrument deteriorates. Contingent stated interest payments of this type are recognized over the period to which they relate in a reasonable manner.

(G) *Special rule when all contingent payments become fixed.* Notwithstanding paragraph (b)(9)(ii)(A) of this section, if all the remaining contingent payments on a debt instrument become fixed substantially contemporaneously, any positive or negative adjustments on the instrument are taken into account in a reasonable manner over the period to which they relate. For purposes of the preceding sentence, a payment is treated as a fixed payment if all remaining contingencies with respect to the payment are remote or incidental (within the meaning of § 1.1275-2(h)).

(H) *Example.* The following example illustrates the provisions of this paragraph (b)(9)(ii). In this example, assume that the instrument described is a debt instrument for federal income tax purposes. No inference is intended, however, as to whether the instrument is a debt instrument for federal income tax purposes.

Example. Fixed but deferred payments—(i) *Facts.* On December 31, 1996, B, a calendar year taxpayer, purchases a debt instrument at original issue for $1,000. The debt instrument matures on December 31, 2002, and provides for a payment of $1,000 at maturity. In addition, on December 31, 1999, and December 31, 2002, the debt instrument provides for payments equal to the excess of the average daily value of an index for the 6-month period ending on September 30 of the preceding year over a specified amount. The debt instrument's comparable yield is 10 percent, compounded annually, and the instrument's projected payment schedule consists of a payment of $250 on December 31, 1999, and a payment of $1,439 on December 31, 2002. B uses annual accrual periods.

(ii) *Interest accrual for 1997.* Based on the projected payment schedule, B includes a total of $100 of daily portions of interest in income in 1997. B's adjusted basis in the debt instrument and the debt instrument's adjusted issue price on December 31, 1997, is $1,100.

(iii) *Interest accrual for 1998*—(A) *Adjustment.* Based on the projected payment schedule, B would include $110 of total daily portions of interest in income in 1998. However, assume that on September 30, 1998, the payment due on December 31, 1999, fixes at $300, rather than the projected $250. Thus, on September 30, 1998, B has an adjustment equal to the difference between the present value of the $300 fixed amount and the present value of the $250 projected amount of the contingent payment. The present values of the two payments are determined by discounting each payment from the date the payment is due (December 31, 1999) to the date the payment becomes fixed (September 30, 1998), using a discount rate equal to 10 percent, compounded annually. The present value of the fixed payment is $266.30 and the present value of the projected amount of the contingent payment is $221.91. Thus, on September 30, 1998, B has a positive adjustment of $44.39 ($266.30 - $221.91).

(B) *Effect of adjustment.* Under paragraph (b)(9)(ii)(C) of this section, B's accrual period ends on September 30, 1998. The daily portions of interest on the debt instrument for the period from January 1, 1998 to September 30, 1998 total $81.51. The adjusted issue price of the debt instrument and B's adjusted basis in the debt instrument are thus increased over this period by $125.90 (the sum of the daily portions of interest of $81.51 and the positive adjustment of $44.39 made at the end of the period) to $1,225.90. For purposes of all future accrual periods, including the new accrual period from October 1, 1998, to December 31, 1998, the debt instrument's projected payment schedule is modified to reflect a fixed payment of $300 on December 31, 1999. Based on the new adjusted issue price of the debt instrument and the new projected payment schedule, the yield on the debt instrument does not change.

(C) *Interest accrual for 1998.* Based on the modified projected payment schedule, $29.56

Reg. § 1.1275-4(b)(9)

of interest accrues during the accrual period that ends on December 31, 1998. Because B has no other adjustments during 1998, the $44.39 positive adjustment on September 30, 1998, results in a net positive adjustment for 1998, which is additional interest for that year. Thus, B includes $155.46 ($81.51 + $29.56 + $44.39) of interest in income in 1998. B's adjusted basis in the debt instrument and the debt instrument's adjusted issue price on December 31, 1998, is $1,255.46 ($1,225.90 from the end of the prior accrual period plus $29.56 total daily portions for the current accrual period).

(iii) *Timing contingencies.* This paragraph (b)(9)(iii) provides rules for debt instruments that have payments that are contingent as to time.

(A) *Treatment of certain options.* If a taxpayer has an unconditional option to put or call the debt instrument, to exchange the debt instrument for other property, or to extend the maturity date of the debt instrument, the projected payment schedule is determined by using the principles of § 1.1272-1(c)(5).

(B) *Other timing contingencies.* [Reserved]

(iv) *Cross-border transactions*—(A) *Allocation of deductions.* For purposes of § 1.861-8, the holder of a debt instrument shall treat any deduction or loss treated as an ordinary loss under paragraph (b)(6)(iii)(B) or (b)(8)(ii) of this section as a deduction that is definitely related to the class of gross income to which income from such debt instrument belongs. Accordingly, if a U.S. person holds a debt instrument issued by a related controlled foreign corporation and, pursuant to section 904(d)(3) and the regulations thereunder, any interest accrued by such U.S. person with respect to such debt instrument would be treated as foreign source general limitation income, any deductions relating to a net negative adjustment will reduce the U.S. person's foreign source general limitation income. The holder shall apply the general rules relating to allocation and apportionment of deductions to any other deduction or loss realized by the holder with respect to the debt instrument.

(B) *Investments in United States real property.* Notwithstanding paragraph (b)(8)(i) of this section, gain on the sale, exchange, or retirement of a debt instrument that is a United States real property interest is treated as gain for purposes of sections 897, 1445, and 6039C.

(v) *Coordination with subchapter M and related provisions.* For purposes of sections 852(c)(2) and 4982 and § 1.852-11, any positive adjustment, negative adjustment, income, or loss on a debt instrument that occurs after October 31 of a taxable year is treated in the same manner as foreign currency gain or loss that is attributable to a section 988 transaction.

(vi) *Coordination with section 1092.* A holder treats a negative adjustment and an issuer treats a positive adjustment as a loss with respect to a position in a straddle if the debt instrument is a position in a straddle and the contingency (or any portion of the contingency) to which the adjustment relates would be part of the straddle if entered into as a separate position.

(c) *Method for debt instruments not subject to the noncontingent bond method*—(1) *Applicability.* This paragraph (c) applies to a contingent payment debt instrument (other than a tax-exempt obligation) that has an issue price determined under § 1.1274-2. For example, this paragraph (c) generally applies to a contingent payment debt instrument that is issued for nonpublicly traded property.

(2) *Separation into components.* If paragraph (c) of this section applies to a debt instrument (the overall debt instrument), the noncontingent payments are subject to the rules in paragraph (c)(3) of this section, and the contingent payments are accounted for separately under the rules in paragraph (c)(4) of this section.

(3) *Treatment of noncontingent payments.* The noncontingent payments are treated as a separate debt instrument. The issue price of the separate debt instrument is the issue price of the overall debt instrument, determined under § 1.1274-2(g). No interest payments on the separate debt instrument are qualified stated interest payments (within the meaning of § 1.1273-1(c)) and the de minimis rules of section 1273(a)(3) and § 1.1273-1(d) do not apply to the separate debt instrument.

(4) *Treatment of contingent payments*—(i) *In general.* Except as provided in paragraph (c)(4)(iii) of this section, the portion of a contingent payment treated as interest under paragraph (c)(4)(ii) of this section is includible in gross income by the holder and deductible from gross income by the issuer in their respective taxable years in which the payment is made.

(ii) *Characterization of contingent payments as principal and interest*—(A) *General rule.* A contingent payment is treated as a payment of principal in an amount equal to the present value of the payment, determined by discounting the payment at the test rate from the date the payment is made to the issue date. The amount of the payment in excess of the amount treated as principal under the preceding sentence is treated as a payment of interest.

Reg. § 1.1275-4(c)(1)

(B) *Test rate.* The test rate used for purposes of paragraph (c)(4)(ii)(A) of this section is the rate that would be the test rate for the overall debt instrument under § 1.1274-4 if the term of the overall debt instrument began on the issue date of the overall debt instrument and ended on the date the contingent payment is made. However, in the case of a contingent payment that consists of a payment of stated principal accompanied by a payment of stated interest at a rate that exceeds the test rate determined under the preceding sentence, the test rate is the stated interest rate.

(iii) *Certain delayed contingent payments*—(A) *General rule.* Notwithstanding paragraph (c)(4)(ii) of this section, if a contingent payment becomes fixed more than 6 months before the payment is due, the issuer and holder are treated as if the issuer had issued a separate debt instrument on the date the payment becomes fixed, maturing on the date the payment is due. This separate debt instrument is treated as a debt instrument to which section 1274 applies. The stated principal amount of this separate debt instrument is the amount of the payment that becomes fixed. An amount equal to the issue price of this debt instrument is characterized as interest or principal under the rules of paragraph (c)(4)(ii) of this section and accounted for as if this amount had been paid by the issuer to the holder on the date that the amount of the payment becomes fixed. To determine the issue price of the separate debt instrument, the payment is discounted at the test rate from the maturity date of the separate debt instrument to the date that the amount of the payment becomes fixed.

(B) *Test rate.* The test rate used for purposes of paragraph (c)(4)(iii)(A) of this section is determined in the same manner as the test rate under paragraph (c)(4)(ii)(B) of this section is determined except that the date the contingent payment is due is used rather than the date the contingent payment is made.

(5) *Basis different from adjusted issue price.* This paragraph (c)(5) provides rules for a holder whose basis in a debt instrument is different from the instrument's adjusted issue price (e.g., a subsequent holder). This paragraph (c)(5), however, does not apply if the holder is reporting income under the installment method of section 453.

(i) *Allocation of basis.* The holder must allocate basis to the noncontingent component (i.e., the right to the noncontingent payments) and to any separate debt instruments described in paragraph (c)(4)(iii) of this section in an amount up to the total of the adjusted issue price of the noncontingent component and the adjusted issue prices of the separate debt instruments. The holder must allocate the remaining basis, if any, to the contingent component (i.e., the right to the contingent payments).

(ii) *Noncontingent component.* Any difference between the holder's basis in the noncontingent component and the adjusted issue price of the noncontingent component, and any difference between the holder's basis in a separate debt instrument and the adjusted issue price of the separate debt instrument, is taken into account under the rules for market discount, premium, and acquisition premium that apply to a noncontingent debt instrument.

(iii) *Contingent component.* Amounts received by the holder that are treated as principal payments under paragraph (c)(4)(ii) of this section reduce the holder's basis in the contingent component. If the holder's basis in the contingent component is reduced to zero, any additional principal payments on the contingent component are treated as gain from the sale or exchange of the debt instrument. Any basis remaining on the contingent component on the date the final contingent payment is made increases the holder's adjusted basis in the noncontingent component (or, if there are no remaining noncontingent payments, is treated as loss from the sale or exchange of the debt instrument).

(6) *Treatment of a holder on sale, exchange, or retirement.* This paragraph (c)(6) provides rules for the treatment of a holder on the sale, exchange, or retirement of a debt instrument subject to this paragraph (c). Under this paragraph (c)(6), the holder must allocate the amount received from the sale, exchange, or retirement of a debt instrument first to the noncontingent component and to any separate debt instruments described in paragraph (c)(4)(ii) of this section in an amount up to the total of the adjusted issue price of the noncontingent component and the adjusted issue prices of the separate debt instruments. The holder must allocate the remaining amount received, if any, to the contingent component.

(i) *Amount allocated to the noncontingent component.* The amount allocated to the noncontingent component and any separate debt instruments is treated as an amount realized from the sale, exchange, or retirement of the noncontingent component or separate debt instrument.

(ii) *Amount allocated to the contingent component.* The amount allocated to the contingent component is treated as a contingent payment that is made on the date of the sale, exchange, or retirement and is characterized as interest and principal under the rules of paragraph (c)(4)(ii) of this section.

Reg. § 1.1275-4(c)(6)

(7) *Examples.* The following examples illustrate the provisions of this paragraph (c). In each example, assume that the instrument described is a debt instrument for federal income tax purposes. No inference is intended, however, as to whether the instrument is a debt instrument for federal income tax purposes.

Example 1. Contingent interest Payments—(i) *Facts.* A owns Blackacre, unencumbered depreciable real estate. On January 1, 1997, A sells Blackacre to B. As consideration for the sale, B makes a downpayment of $1,000,000 and issues to A a debt instrument that matures on December 31, 2001. The debt instrument provides for a payment of principal at maturity of $5,000,000 and a contingent payment of interest on December 31 of each year equal to a fixed percentage of the gross rents B receives from Blackacre in that year. Assume that the debt instrument is not issued in a potentially abusive situation. Assume also that on January 1, 1997, the short-term applicable Federal rate is 5 percent, compounded annually, and the mid-term applicable Federal rate is 6 percent, compounded annually.

(ii) *Determination of issue price.* Under § 1.1274-2(g), the issue price of the debt instrument is $3,736,291, which is the present value, as of the issue date, of the $5,000,000 noncontingent payment due at maturity, calculated using a discount rate equal to the mid-term applicable Federal rate. Under § 1.1012-1(g)(1), B's basis in Blackacre on January 1, 1997, is $4,736,291 ($1,000,000 down payment plus the $3,736,291 issue price of the debt instrument).

(iii) *Noncontingent payment treated as separate debt instrument.* Under paragraph (c)(3) of this section, the right to the noncontingent payment of principal at maturity is treated as a separate debt instrument. The issue price of this separate debt instrument is $3,736,291 (the issue price of the overall debt instrument). The separate debt instrument has a stated redemption price at maturity of $5,000,000 and, therefore, OID of $1,263,709.

(iv) *Treatment of contingent payments.* Assume that the amount of contingent interest that is fixed and paid on December 31, 1997, is $200,000. Under paragraph (c)(4)(ii) of this section, this payment is treated as consisting of a payment of principal of $190,476, which is the present value of the payment, determined by discounting the payment at the test rate of 5 percent, compounded annually, from the date the payment is made to the issue date. The remainder of the $200,000 payment ($9,524) is treated as interest. The additional amount treated as principal gives B additional basis in Blackacre on December 31, 1997. The portion of the payment treated as interest is includible in gross income by A and deductible by B in their respective taxable years in which December 31, 1997 occurs. The remaining contingent payments on the debt instrument are accounted for similarly, using a test rate of 5 percent, compounded annually, for the contingent payments due on December 31, 1998, and December 31, 1999, and a test rate of 6 percent, compounded annually, for the contingent payments due on December 31, 2000, and December 31, 2001.

Example 2. Fixed but deferred payment—(i) *Facts.* The facts are the same as in paragraph (c)(7) *Example 1* of this section, except that the contingent payment of interest that is fixed on December 31, 1997, is not payable until December 31, 2001, the maturity date.

(ii) *Treatment of deferred contingent payment.* Assume that the amount of the payment that becomes fixed on December 31, 1997, is $200,000. Because this amount is not payable until December 31, 2001, under paragraph (c)(4)(iii) of this section, a separate debt instrument to which section 1274 applies is treated as issued by B on December 31, 1997 (the date the payment is fixed). The maturity date of this separate debt instrument is December 31, 2001 (the date on which the payment is due). The stated principal amount of this separate debt instrument is $200,000, the amount of the payment that becomes fixed. The imputed principal amount of the separate debt instrument is $158,419, which is the present value, as of December 31, 1997, of the $200,000 payment, computed using a discount rate equal to the test rate of the overall debt instrument (6 percent, compounded annually). An amount equal to the issue price of the separate debt instrument is treated as an amount paid on December 31, 1997, and characterized as interest and principal under the rules of paragraph (c)(4)(ii) of this section. The amount of the deemed payment characterized as principal is equal to $150,875, which is the present value, as of January 1, 1997 (the issue date of the overall debt instrument), of the deemed payment, computed using a discount rate of 5 percent, compounded annually. The amount of the deemed payment characterized as interest is $7,544 ($158,419 − $150,875), which is includible in gross income by A and deductible by B in their respective taxable years in which December 31, 1997 occurs.

(d) *Rules for tax-exempt obligations*—(1) *In general.* Except as modified by this paragraph (d), the noncontingent bond method described in paragraph (b) of this section applies to a tax-exempt obligation (as defined in section 1275(a)(3)) to which this section applies. Paragraph (d)(2) of this section applies to certain tax-exempt obligations that provide for interest-based payments or revenue-based payments and paragraph (d)(3) of this section applies to all other obligations. Paragraph (d)(4) of this section provides rules for a holder whose basis in a tax-exempt obligation is different from the adjusted issue price of the obligation.

(2) *Certain tax-exempt obligations with interest-based or revenue-based payments*—(i) *Applicability.* This paragraph (d)(2) applies to a tax-exempt obligation that provides for interest-based payments or revenue-based payments.

(ii) *Interest-based payments.* A tax-exempt obligation provides for interest-based payments if the obligation would otherwise qualify as a variable rate debt instrument under § 1.1275-5 except that—

(A) The obligation provides for more than one fixed rate;

(B) The obligation provides for one or more caps, floors, or governors (or similar restrictions) that are fixed as of the issue date;

(C) The interest on the obligation is not compounded or paid at least annually; or

(D) The obligation provides for interest at one or more rates equal to the product of a qualified floating rate and a fixed multiple greater than zero and less than .65, or at one or more rates equal to the product of a qualified floating rate and a fixed multiple greater than zero and less than .65, increased or decreased by a fixed rate.

(iii) *Revenue-based payments.* A tax-exempt obligation provides for revenue-based payments if the obligation—

(A) Is issued to refinance (including a series of refinancings) an obligation (in a series of refinancings, the original obligation), the proceeds of which were used to finance a project or enterprise; and

(B) Would otherwise qualify as a variable rate debt instrument under § 1.1275-5 except that it provides for stated interest payments at least annually based on a single fixed percentage of the revenue, value, change in value, or other similar measure of the performance of the refinanced project or enterprise.

(iv) *Modifications to the noncontingent bond method.* If a tax-exempt obligation is subject to this paragraph (d)(2), the following modifications to the noncontingent bond method described in paragraph (b) of this section apply to the obligation.

(A) *Daily portions and net positive adjustments.* The daily portions of interest determined under paragraph (b)(3)(iii) of this section and any net positive adjustment on the obligation are interest for purposes of section 103.

(B) *Net negative adjustments.* A net negative adjustment for a taxable year reduces the amount of tax-exempt interest the holder would otherwise account for on the obligation for the taxable year under paragraph (b)(3)(iii) of this section. If the net negative adjustment exceeds this amount, the excess is a nondeductible, noncapitalizable loss. If a regulated investment company (RIC) within the meaning of section 851 has a net negative adjustment in a taxable year that would be a nondeductible, noncapitalizable loss under the prior sentence, the RIC must use this loss to reduce its tax-exempt interest income on other tax-exempt obligations held during the taxable year.

(C) *Gains.* Any gain recognized on the sale, exchange, or retirement of the obligation is gain from the sale or exchange of the obligation.

(D) *Losses.* Any loss recognized on the sale, exchange, or retirement of the obligation is treated the same as a net negative adjustment under paragraph (d)(2)(iv)(B) of this section.

(E) *Special rule for losses and net negative adjustments.* Notwithstanding paragraphs (d)(2)(iv)(B) and (D) of this section, on the sale, exchange, or retirement of the obligation, the holder may claim a loss from the sale or exchange of the obligation to the extent the holder has not received in cash or property the sum of its original investment in the obligation and any amounts included in income under paragraph (d)(4)(ii) of this section.

(3) *All other tax-exempt obligations*—(i) *Applicability.* This paragraph (d)(3) applies to a tax-exempt obligation that is not subject to paragraph (d)(2) of this section.

(ii) *Modifications to the noncontingent bond method.* If a tax-exempt obligation is subject to this paragraph (d)(3), the following modifications to the noncontingent bond method described in paragraph (b) of this section apply to the obligation.

(A) *Modification to projected payment schedule.* The comparable yield for the obligation is the greater of the obligation's yield, determined without regard to the contingent payments, and the tax-exempt applicable Federal rate that applies to the obligation. The Internal Revenue Service publishes the tax-exempt applicable Federal rate for each month in the Internal Revenue Bulletin (see § 601.601(d)(2)(ii) of this chapter).

Reg. § 1.1275-4(d)(3)

(B) *Daily portions.* The daily portions of interest determined under paragraph (b)(3)(iii) of this section are interest for purposes of section 103.

(C) *Adjustments.* A net positive adjustment on the obligation is treated as gain to the holder from the sale or exchange of the obligation in the taxable year of the adjustment. A net negative adjustment on the obligation is treated as a loss to the holder from the sale or exchange of the obligation in the taxable year of the adjustment.

(D) *Gains and losses.* Any gain or loss recognized on the sale, exchange, or retirement of the obligation is gain or loss from the sale or exchange of the obligation.

(4) *Basis different from adjusted issue price.* This paragraph (d)(4) provides rules for a holder whose basis in a tax-exempt obligation is different from the adjusted issue price of the obligation. The rules of paragraph (b)(9)(i) of this section do not apply to tax-exempt obligations.

(i) *Basis greater than adjusted issue price.* If the holder's basis in the obligation exceeds the obligation's adjusted issue price, the holder, upon acquiring the obligation, must allocate this difference to daily portions of interest on a yield to maturity basis over the remaining term of the obligation. The amount allocated to a daily portion of interest is not deductible by the holder. However, the holder's basis in the obligation is reduced by the amount allocated to a daily portion of interest on the date the daily portion accrues.

(ii) *Basis less than adjusted issue price.* If the holder's basis in the obligation is less than the obligation's adjusted issue price, the holder, upon acquiring the obligation, must allocate this difference to daily portions of interest on a yield to maturity basis over the remaining term of the obligation. The amount allocated to a daily portion of interest is includible in income by the holder as ordinary income on the date the daily portion accrues. The holder's adjusted basis in the obligation is increased by the amount includible in income by the holder under this paragraph (d)(4)(ii) on the date the daily portion accrues.

(iii) *Premium and discount rules do not apply.* The rules for accruing premium and discount in sections 171, 1276, and 1288 do not apply. Other rules of those sections continue to apply to the extent relevant.

(e) *Amounts treated as interest under this section.* Amounts treated as interest under this section are treated as OID for all purposes of the Internal Revenue Code.

(f) *Effective date.* This section applies to debt instruments issued on or after August 13, 1996. [Reg. § 1.1275-4.]

☐ [T.D. 8674, 6-11-96. Amended by T.D. 8709, 12-31-96 and T.D. 8838, 9-3-99.]

[Reg. § 1.1275-5]

§ 1.1275-5. Variable rate debt instruments.—(a) *Applicability*—(1) *In general.* This section provides rules for variable rate debt instruments. Except as provided in paragraph (a)(6) of this section, a variable rate debt instrument is a debt instrument that meets the conditions described in paragraphs (a)(2), (3), (4), and (5) of this section. If a debt instrument that provides for a variable rate of interest does not qualify as a variable rate debt instrument, the debt instrument is a contingent payment debt instrument. See § 1.1275-4 for the treatment of a contingent payment debt instrument. See § 1.1275-6 for a taxpayer's treatment of a variable rate debt instrument and a hedge.

(2) *Principal payments.* The issue price of the debt instrument must not exceed the total noncontingent principal payments by more than an amount equal to the lesser of—

(i) .015 multiplied by the product of the total noncontingent principal payments and the number of complete years to maturity from the issue date (or, in the case of an installment obligation, the weighted average maturity as defined in § 1.1273-1(e)(3)); or

(ii) 15 percent of the total noncontingent principal payments.

(3) *Stated interest*—(i) *General rule.* The debt instrument must not provide for any stated interest other than stated interest (compounded or paid at least annually) at—

(A) One or more qualified floating rates;

(B) a single fixed rate and one or more qualified floating rates;

(C) A single objective rate; or

(D) A single fixed rate and a single objective rate that is a qualified inverse floating rate.

(ii) *Certain debt instruments bearing interest at a fixed rate for an initial period.* If interest on a debt instrument is stated at a fixed rate for an initial period of 1 year or less followed by a variable rate that is either a qualified floating rate or an objective rate for a subsequent period, and the value of the variable rate on the issue date is intended to approximate the fixed rate, the fixed rate and the variable rate together constitute a single qualified floating rate or objective rate. A fixed rate and a variable rate will be

Reg. § 1.1275-5(a)(1)

conclusively presumed to meet the requirements of the preceding sentence if the value of the variable rate on the issue date does not differ from the value of the fixed rate by more than .25 percentage points (25 basis points).

(4) *Current value.* The debt instrument must provide that a qualified floating rate or objective rate in effect at any time during the term of the instrument is set at a current value of that rate. A current value is the value of the rate on any day that is no earlier than 3 months prior to the first day on which that value is in effect and no later than 1 year following that first day.

(5) *No contingent principal payments.* Except as provided in paragraph (a)(2) of this section, the debt instrument must not provide for any principal payments that are contingent (within the meaning of § 1.1275-4(a)).

(6) *Special rule for debt instruments issued for nonpublicly traded property.* A debt instrument (other than a tax-exempt obligation) that would otherwise qualify as a variable rate debt instrument under this section is not a variable rate debt instrument if section 1274 applies to the instrument and any stated interest payments on the instrument are treated as contingent payments under § 1.1274-2. This paragraph (a)(6) applies to debt instruments issued on or after August 13, 1996.

(b) *Qualified floating rate*—(1) *In general.* A variable rate is a qualified floating rate if variations in the value of the rate can reasonably be expected to measure contemporaneous variations in the cost of newly borrowed funds in the currency in which the debt instrument is denominated. The rate may measure contemporaneous variations in borrowing costs for the issuer of the debt instrument or for issuers in general. Except as provided in paragraph (b)(2) of this section, a multiple of a qualified floating rate is not a qualified floating rate. If a debt instrument provides for two or more qualified floating rates that can reasonably be expected to have approximately the same values throughout the term of the instrument, the qualified floating rates together constitute a single qualified floating rate. Two or more qualified floating rates will be conclusively presumed to meet the requirements of the preceding sentence if the values of all rates on the issue date are within .25 percentage points (25 basis points) of each other.

(2) *Certain rates based on a qualified floating rate.* For a debt instrument issued on or after August 13, 1996, a variable rate is a qualified floating rate if it is equal to either—

(i) The product of a qualified floating rate described in paragraph (b)(1) of this section and a fixed multiple that is greater than .65 but not more than 1.35; or

(ii) The product of a qualified floating rate described in paragraph (b)(1) of this section and a fixed multiple that is greater than .65 but not more than 1.35, increased or decreased by a fixed rate.

(3) *Restrictions on the stated rate of interest.* A variable rate is not a qualified floating rate if it is subject to a restriction or restrictions on the maximum stated interest rate (cap), a restriction or restrictions on the minimum stated interest rate (floor), a restriction or restrictions on the amount of increase or decrease in the stated interest rate (governor), or other similar restrictions. Notwithstanding the preceding sentence, the following restrictions will not cause a variable rate to fail to be a qualified floating rate—

(i) A cap, floor, or governor that is fixed throughout the term of the debt instrument;

(ii) A cap or similar restriction that is not reasonably expected as of the issue date to cause the yield on the debt instrument to be significantly less than the expected yield determined without the cap;

(iii) A floor or similar restriction that is not reasonably expected as of the issue date to cause the yield on the debt instrument to be significantly more than the expected yield determined without the floor; or

(iv) A governor or similar restriction that is not reasonably expected as of the issue date to cause the yield on the debt instrument to be significantly more or significantly less than the expected yield determined without the governor.

(c) *Objective rate*—(1) *Definition*—(i) *In general.* For debt instruments issued on or after August 13, 1996, an objective rate is a rate (other than a qualified floating rate) that is determined using a single fixed formula and that is based on objective financial or economic information. For example, an objective rate generally includes a rate that is based on one or more qualified floating rates or on the yield of actively traded personal property (within the meaning of section 1092(d)(1)).

(ii) *Exception.* For purposes of paragraph (c)(1)(i) of this section, an objective rate does not include a rate based on information that is within the control of the issuer (or a related party within the meaning of section 267(b) or 707(b)(1)) or that is unique to the circumstances of the issuer (or a related party within the meaning of section 267(b) or 707(b)(1)), such as dividends, profits, or the value of the issuer's stock. However, a rate does not fail to be an objective rate merely be-

Reg. § 1.1275-5(c)(1)

cause it is based on the credit quality of the issuer.

(2) *Other objective rates to be specified by Commissioner.* The Commissioner may designate in the Internal Revenue Bulletin variable rates other than those described in paragraph (c)(1) of this section that will be treated as objective rates (see § 601.601(d)(2)(ii) of this chapter).

(3) *Qualified inverse floating rate.* An objective rate described in paragraph (c)(1) of this section is a qualified inverse floating rate if—

(i) The rate is equal to a fixed rate minus a qualified floating rate; and

(ii) The variations in the rate can reasonably be expected to inversely reflect contemporaneous variations in the qualified floating rate (disregarding any restrictions on the rate that are described in paragraphs (b)(3)(i), (b)(3)(ii), (b)(3)(iii), and (b)(3)(iv) of this section).

(4) *Significant front-loading or back-loading of interest.* Notwithstanding paragraph (c)(1) of this section, a variable rate of interest on a debt instrument is not an objective rate if it is reasonably expected that the average value of the rate during the first half of the instrument's term will be either significantly less than or significantly greater than average value of the rate during the final half of the instrument's term.

(5) *Tax-exempt obligations.* Notwithstanding paragraph (c)(1) of this section, in the case of a tax-exempt obligation (within the meaning of section 1275(a)(3)), a variable rate is an objective rate only if it is a qualified inverse floating rate or a qualified inflation rate. A rate is a qualified inflation rate if the rate measures contemporaneous changes in inflation based on a general inflation index.

(d) *Examples.* The following examples illustrate the rules of paragraphs (b) and (c) of this section. For purposes of these examples, assume that the debt instrument is not a tax-exempt obligation. In addition, unless otherwise provided, assume that the rate is not reasonably expected to result in a significant front-loading or back-loading of interest and that the rate is not based on objective financial or economic information that is within the control of the issuer (or a related party) or that is unique to the circumstances of the issuer (or a related party).

Example 1. Rate based on LIBOR. X issues a debt instrument that provides for annual payments of interest at a rate equal to the value of the 1-year London Interbank Offered Rate (LIBOR) at the end of each year. Variations in the value of 1-year LIBOR over the term of the debt instrument can reasonably be expected to measure contemporaneous variations in the cost of newly borrowed funds over that term. Accordingly, the rate is a qualified floating rate.

Example 2. Rate increased by a fixed amount. X issues a debt instrument that provides for annual payments of interest at a rate equal to 200 basis points (2 percent) plus the current value, at the end of each year, of the average yield on 1-year Treasury securities as published in Federal Reserve bulletins. Variations in the value of this interest rate can reasonably be expected to measure contemporaneous variations in the cost of newly borrowed funds. Accordingly, the rate is a qualified floating rate.

Example 3. Rate based on commercial paper rate. X issues a debt instrument that provides for a rate of interest that is periodically adjusted to equal the current interest rate of Bank's commercial paper. Variations in the value of this interest rate can reasonably be expected to measure contemporaneous variations in the cost of newly-borrowed funds. Accordingly, the rate is a qualified floating rate.

Example 4. Rate based on changes in the value of a commodity index. On January 1, 1997, X issues a debt instrument that provides for annual interest payments at the end of each year at a rate equal to the percentage increase, if any, in the value of an index for the year immediately preceding the payment. The index is based on the prices of several actively traded commodities. Variations in the value of this interest rate cannot reasonably be expected to measure contemporaneous variations in the cost of newly borrowed funds. Accordingly, the rate is not a qualified floating rate. However, because the rate is based on objective financial information using a single fixed formula, the rate is an objective rate.

Example 5. Rate based on a percentage of S&P 500 Index. On January 1, 1997, X issues a debt instrument that provides for annual interest payments at the end of each year based on a fixed percentage of the value of the S&P 500 Index. Variations in the value of this interest rate cannot reasonably be expected to measure contemporaneous variations in the cost of newly borrowed funds and, therefore, the rate is not a qualified floating rate. Although the rate is described in paragraph (c)(1)(i) of this section, the rate is not an objective rate because, based on historical data, it is reasonably expected that the average value of the rate during the first half of the instrument's term will be significantly less than the average value of the rate during the final half of the instrument's term.

Example 6. Rate based on issuer's profits. On January 1, 1997, Z issues a debt instrument that provides for annual interest payments equal to 1 percent of Z's gross profits earned during the year immediately preceding the payment. Variations in the value of this interest rate cannot reasonably be expected to measure contemporaneous variations in the cost of newly borrowed funds. Accordingly, the rate is not a qualified floating rate. In addition, because the rate is based on information that is unique to the issuer's circumstances, the rate is not an objective rate.

Example 7. Rate based on a multiple of an interest index. On January 1, 1997, Z issues a debt instrument with annual interest payments at a rate equal to two times the value of 1-year LIBOR as of the payment date. Because the rate is a multiple greater than 1.35 times a qualified floating rate, the rate is not a qualified floating rate. However, because the rate is based on objective financial information using a single fixed formula, the rate is an objective rate.

Example 8. Variable rate based on the cost of borrowed funds in a foreign currency. On January 1, 1997, Y issues a 5-year dollar denominated debt instrument that provides for annual interest payments at a rate equal to the value of 1-year French franc LIBOR as of the payment date. Variations in the value of French franc LIBOR do not measure contemporaneous changes in the cost of newly borrowed funds in dollars. As a result, the rate is not a qualified floating rate for an instrument denominated in dollars. However, because the rate is based on objective financial information using a single fixed formula, the rate is an objective rate.

Example 9. Qualified inverse floating rate. On January 1, 1997, X issues a debt instrument that provides for annual interest payments at the end of each year at a rate equal to 12 percent minus the value of 1-year LIBOR as of the payment date. On the issue date, the value of 1-year LIBOR is 6 percent. Because the rate can reasonably be expected to inversely reflect contemporaneous variations in 1-year LIBOR, it is a qualified inverse floating rate. However, if the value of 1-year LIBOR on the issue date were 11 percent rather than 6 percent, the rate would not be a qualified inverse floating rate because the rate could not reasonably be expected to inversely reflect contemporaneous variations in 1-year LIBOR.

Example 10. Rate based on an inflation index. On January 1, 1997, X issues a debt instrument that provides for annual interest payments at the end of each year at a rate equal to 400 basis points (4 percent) plus the annual percentage change in a general inflation index (e.g., the Consumer Price Index, U.S. City Average, All Items, for all Urban Consumers, seasonally unadjusted).

The rate, however, may not be less than zero. Variations in the value of this interest rate cannot reasonably be expected to measure contemporaneous variations in the cost of newly borrowed funds. Accordingly, the rate is not a qualified floating rate. However, because the rate is based on objective economic information using a single fixed formula, the rate is an objective rate.

(e) *Qualified stated interest and OID with respect to a variable rate debt instrument*—(1) *In general.* This paragraph (e) provides rules to determine the amount and accrual of OID and qualified stated interest on a variable rate debt instrument. In general, the rules convert the debt instrument into a fixed rate debt instrument and then apply the general OID rules to the debt instrument. The issue price of a variable rate debt instrument, however, is not determined under this paragraph (e). See § § 1.1273-2 and 1.1274-2 to determine the issue price of a variable rate debt instrument.

(2) *Variable rate debt instrument that provides for annual payments of interest at a single variable rate.* If a variable rate debt instrument provides for stated interest at a single qualified floating rate or objective rate and the interest is unconditionally payable in cash or in property (other than debt instruments of the issuer), or will be constructively received under section 451, at least annually, the following rules apply to the instrument:

(i) All stated interest with respect to the debt instrument is qualified stated interest.

(ii) The amount of qualified stated interest and the amount of OID, if any, that accrues during an accrual period is determined under the rules applicable to fixed rate debt instruments by assuming that the variable rate is a fixed rate equal to—

(A) In the case of a qualified floating rate or qualified inverse floating rate, the value, as of the issue date, of the qualified floating rate or qualified inverse floating rate; or

(B) In the case of an objective rate (other than a qualified inverse floating rate), a fixed rate that reflects the yield that is reasonably expected for the debt instrument.

(iii) The qualified stated interest allocable to an accrual period is increased (or decreased) if the interest actually paid during an accrual period exceeds (or is less than) the interest assumed to be paid during the accrual period under paragraph (e)(2)(ii) of this section.

(3) *All other variable rate debt instruments except for those that provide for a fixed rate.* If a variable rate debt instrument is not described in

Reg. § 1.1275-5(e)(3)

paragraph (e)(2) of this section and does not provide for interest payable at a fixed rate (other than an initial fixed rate described in paragraph (a)(3)(ii) of this section), the amount of interest and OID accruals for the instrument are determined under this paragraph (e)(3).

(i) *Step one: Determine the fixed rate substitute for each variable rate provided under the debt instrument*—(A) *Qualified floating rate.* The fixed rate substitute for each qualified floating rate provided for in the debt instrument is the value of each rate as of the issue date. If, however, a variable rate debt instrument provides for two or more qualified floating rates with different intervals between interest adjustment dates, the fixed rate substitutes for the rates must be based on intervals that are equal in length. For example, if a 4-year debt instrument provides for 24 monthly interest payments based on the value of the 30-day commercial paper rate on each payment date followed by 8 quarterly interest payments based on the value of quarterly LIBOR on each payment date, the fixed rate substitutes may be based on the values as of the issue date, of the 90-day commercial paper rate and quarterly LIBOR. Alternatively, the fixed rate substitutes may be based on the values, as of the issue date, of the 30-day commercial paper rate and monthly LIBOR.

(B) *Qualified inverse floating rate.* The fixed rate substitute for a qualified inverse floating rate is the value of the qualified inverse floating rate as of the issue date.

(C) *Objective rate.* The fixed rate substitute for an objective rate (other than a qualified inverse floating rate) is a fixed rate that reflects the yield that is reasonably expected for the debt instrument.

(ii) *Step two: Construct the equivalent fixed rate debt instrument.* The equivalent fixed rate debt instrument has terms that are identical to those provided under the variable rate debt instrument, except that the equivalent fixed rate debt instrument provides for the fixed rate substitutes (determined in paragraph (e)(3)(i) of this section) in lieu of the qualified floating rates or objective rate provided under the variable rate debt instrument.

(iii) *Step three: Determine the amount of qualified stated interest and OID with respect to the equivalent fixed rate debt instrument.* The amount of qualified stated interest and OID, if any, are determined for the equivalent fixed rate debt instrument under the rules applicable to fixed rate debt instruments and are taken into account as if the holder held the equivalent fixed rate debt instrument.

(iv) *Step four: Make appropriate adjustments for actual variable rates.* Qualified stated interest or OID allocable to an accrual period must be increased (or decreased) if the interest actually accrued or paid during an accrual period exceeds (or is less than) the interest assumed to be accrued or paid during the accrual period under the equivalent fixed rate debt instrument. This increase or decrease is an adjustment to qualified stated interest for the accrual period if the equivalent fixed rate debt instrument (as determined under paragraph (e)(3)(ii) of this section) provides for qualified stated interest and the increase or decrease is reflected in the amount actually paid during the accrual period. Otherwise, this increase or decrease is an adjustment to OID for the accrual period.

(v) *Examples.* The following examples illustrate the rules in paragraphs (e)(2) and (3) of this section.

Example 1. Equivalent fixed rate debt instrument—(i) *Facts.* X purchases at original issue a 6-year variable rate debt instrument that provides for semiannual payments of interest. For the first 3 years, the rate of interest is the value of 6-month LIBOR on the payment date. For the final 3 years, the rate is the value of the 6-month T-bill rate on the payment date. On the issue date, the value of 6-month LIBOR is 3 percent, compounded semiannually, and the 6-month T-bill rate is 2 percent, compounded semiannually.

(ii) *Determination of equivalent fixed rate debt instrument.* Under paragraph (e)(3)(i) of this section, the fixed rate substitute for 6-month LIBOR is 3 percent, compounded semiannually, and the fixed rate substitute for the 6-month T-bill rate is 2 percent, compounded semiannually. Under paragraph (e)(3)(ii) of this section, the equivalent fixed rate debt instrument is a 6-year debt instrument that provides for semiannual payments of interest at 3 percent, compounded semiannually, for the first 3 years followed by 2 percent, compounded semiannually, for the final 3 years.

Example 2. Equivalent fixed rate debt instrument with de minimis OID—(i) *Facts.* Y purchases at original issue, for $100,000, a 4-year variable rate debt instrument that has a stated principal amount of $100,000, payable at maturity. The debt instrument provides for monthly payments of interest at the end of each month. For the first year, the interest rate is the monthly commercial paper rate and for the last 3 years, the interest rate is the monthly commercial paper rate plus 100 basis points. On the issue date, the monthly commercial paper rate is 3 percent, compounded monthly.

Reg. § 1.1275-5(e)(3)

(ii) *Equivalent fixed rate debt instrument.* Under paragraph (e)(3)(ii) of this section, the equivalent fixed rate debt instrument for the variable rate debt instrument is a 4-year debt instrument that has an issue price and stated principal amount of $100,000. The equivalent fixed rate debt instrument provides for monthly payments of interest at 3 percent, compounded monthly, for the first year ($250 per month) and monthly payments of interest at 4 percent, compounded monthly, for the last 3 years ($333.33 per month).

(iii) *De minimis OID.* Under § 1.1273-1(a), because a portion (100 basis points) of each interest payment in the final 3 years is not a qualified stated interest payment, the equivalent fixed rate debt instrument has OID of $2,999.88 ($102,999.88 − $100,000) However, under § 1.1273-1(d)(4) (the *de minimis* rule relating to teaser rates and interest holidays), the stated redemption price at maturity of the equivalent fixed rate debt instrument is $100,999.96 ($100,000 (issue price) plus $999.96 (the greater of the amount of foregone interest ($999.96) and the amount equal to the excess of the instrument's stated principal amount over its issue price ($0)). Thus, the equivalent fixed rate debt instrument is treated as having OID of $999.96 ($100,999.96 − $100,000). Because this amount is less than the *de minimis* amount of $1,010 (0.0025 multiplied by $100,999.96 multiplied by 4 complete years to maturity), the equivalent fixed rate debt instrument has *de minimis* OID. Therefore, the variable rate debt instrument has zero OID and all stated interest payments are qualified stated interest payments.

Example 3. Adjustment to qualified stated interest for actual payment of interest—(i) *Facts.* On January 1, 1995, Z purchases at original issue, for $90,000, a variable rate debt instrument that matures on January 1, 1997, and has a stated principal amount of $100,000, payable at maturity. The debt instrument provides for annual payments of interest on January 1 of each year, beginning on January 1, 1996. The amount of interest payable is the value of annual LIBOR on the payment date. The value of annual LIBOR on January 1, 1995, and January 1, 1996, is 5 percent, compounded annually. The value of annual LIBOR on January 1, 1997, is 7 percent, compounded annually.

(ii) *Accrual of OID and qualified stated interest.* Under paragraph (e)(2) of this section, the variable rate debt instrument is treated as a 2-year debt instrument that has an issue price of $90,000, a stated principal amount of $100,000, and interest payments of $5,000 at the end of each year. The debt instrument has $10,000 of OID and the annual interest payments of $5,000 are qualified stated interest payments. Under § 1.1272-1, the debt instrument has a yield of 10.82 percent, compounded annually. The amount of OID allocable to the first annual accrual period (assuming Z uses annual accrual periods) is $4,743.25 (($90,000 × .1082) − $5,000), and the amount of OID allocable to the second annual accrual period is $5,256.75 ($100,000 − $94,743.25). Under paragraph (e)(2)(iii) of this section, the $2,000 difference between the $7,000 interest payment actually made at maturity and the $5,000 interest payment assumed to be made at maturity under the equivalent fixed rate debt instrument is treated as additional qualified stated interest for the period.

(4) *Variable rate debt instrument that provides for a single fixed rate*—(i) *General rule.* If a variable rate debt instrument provides for stated interest either at one or more qualified floating rates or at a qualified inverse floating rate and in addition provides for stated interest at a single fixed rate (other than an initial fixed rate described in paragraph (a)(3)(ii) of this section), the amount of interest and OID are determined using the method of paragraph (e)(3) of this section, as modified by this paragraph (e)(4). For purposes of paragraphs (e)(3)(i) through (e)(3)(iii) of this section, the variable rate debt instrument is treated as if it provided for a qualified floating rate (or a qualified inverse floating rate, if the debt instrument provides for a qualified inverse floating rate), rather than the fixed rate. The qualified floating rate (or qualified inverse floating rate) replacing the fixed rate must be such that the fair market value of the variable rate debt instrument as of the issue date would be approximately the same as the fair market value of an otherwise identical debt instrument that provides for the qualified floating rate (or qualified inverse floating rate) rather than the fixed rate.

(ii) *Example.* The following example illustrates the rule in paragraph (e)(4)(i) of this section.

Example. Variable rate debt instrument that provides for a single fixed rate—(i) *Facts.* On January 1, 1995, X purchases at original issue, for $100,000, a variable rate debt instrument that matures on January, 1, 2001, and that has a stated principal amount of $100,000. The debt instrument provides for payments of interest on January 1 of each year, beginning on January 1, 1996. For the first 4 years, the interest rate is 4 percent, compounded annually, and for the last 2 years the interest rate is the value of 1-year LIBOR, as of the payment date, plus 200 basis points. On January 1, 1995, the value of 1-year

Reg. § 1.1275-5(e)(4)

LIBOR is 2 percent, compounded annually. In addition, assume that on January 1, 1995, the variable, rate debt instrument has approximately the same fair market value as an otherwise identical debt instrument that provides for an interest rate equal to the value of 1-year LIBOR, as of the payment date, for the first 4 years.

(ii) *Equivalent fixed rate debt instrument.* Under paragraph (e)(4)(i) of this section, for purposes of paragraphs (e)(3)(i) through (e)(3)(iii) of this section, the variable rate debt instrument is treated as if it provided for an interest rate equal to the value of 1-year LIBOR, as of the payment date, for the first 4 years. Under paragraph (e)(3)(ii) of this section, the equivalent fixed rate debt instrument for the variable rate debt instrument is a 6-year debt instrument that has an issue price and stated principal amount of $100,000. The equivalent fixed rate debt instrument provides for interest payments of $2,000 for the first 4 years and $4,000 for the last 2 years.

(iii) *Accrual of OID and qualified stated interest.* Under § 1.1273-1, the equivalent fixed rate debt instrument has OID of $4,000 because a portion (200 basis points) of each interest payment in the last 2 years is not a qualified stated interest payment. The $4,000 of OID is allocable over the 6-year term of the debt instrument under § 1.1272-1. Under paragraph (e)(3)(iv) of this section, the difference between the $4,000 payment made in the first 4 years and the $2,000 payment assumed to be made on the equivalent fixed rate debt instrument in those years is an adjustment to qualified stated interest. In addition, any difference between the amount actually paid in each of the last 2 years and the $4,000 payment assumed to be made on the equivalent fixed rate debt instrument is an adjustment to qualified stated interest.

(f) *Special rule for certain reset bonds.* Notwithstanding paragraph (e) of this section, this paragraph (f) provides a special rule for a variable rate debt instrument that provides for stated interest at a fixed rate for an initial interval, and provides that on the date immediately following the end of the initial interval (the effective date) the stated interest rate will be a rate determined under a procedure (such as an auction procedure) so that the fair market value of the instrument on the effective date will be a fixed amount (the reset value). Solely for purposes of calculating the accrual of OID, the variable rate debt instrument is treated as—

(1) Maturing on the date immediately preceding the effective date for an amount equal to the reset value; and

(2) Reissued on the effective date for an amount equal to the reset value. [Reg. § 1.1275-5.]

☐ [T.D. 8517, 1-27-94. Amended by T.D. 8674, 6-11-96.]

[Reg. § 1.1275-6]

§ 1.1275-6. Integration of qualifying debt instruments.—(a) *In general.* This section generally provides for the integration of a qualifying debt instrument with a hedge or combination of hedges if the combined cash flows of the components are substantially equivalent to the cash flows on a fixed or variable rate debt instrument. The integrated transaction is generally subject to the rules of this section rather than the rules to which each component of the transaction would be subject on a separate basis. The purpose of this section is to permit a more appropriate determination of the character and timing of income, deductions, gains, or losses than would be permitted by separate treatment of the components. The rules of this section affect only the taxpayer who holds (or issues) the qualifying debt instrument and enters into the hedge.

(b) *Definitions*—(1) *Qualifying debt instrument.* A qualifying debt instrument is any debt instrument (including an integrated transaction as defined in paragraph (c) of this section) other than—

(i) A tax-exempt obligation as defined in section 1275(a)(3);

(ii) A debt instrument to which section 1272(a)(6) applies (certain interests in or mortgages held by a REMIC, and certain other debt instruments with payments subject to acceleration); or

(iii) A debt instrument that is subject to § 1.483-4 or § 1.1275-4(c) (certain contingent payment debt instruments issued for nonpublicly traded property).

(2) *Section 1.1275-6 hedge*—(i) *In general.* A § 1.1275-6 hedge is any financial instrument (as defined in paragraph (b)(3) of this section) if the combined cash flows of the financial instrument and the qualifying debt instrument permit the calculation of a yield to maturity (under the principles of section 1272), or the right to the combined cash flows would qualify under § 1.1275-5 as a variable rate debt instrument that pays interest at a qualified floating rate or rates (except for the requirement that the interest payments be stated as interest). A financial instrument is not a § 1.1275-6 hedge, however, if the resulting synthetic debt instrument does not have the same term as the remaining term of the qualifying debt

instrument. A financial instrument that hedges currency risk is not a § 1.1275-6 hedge.

(ii) *Limitations*—(A) A debt instrument issued by a taxpayer and a debt instrument held by the taxpayer cannot be part of the same integrated transaction.

(B) A debt instrument can be a § 1.1275-6 hedge only if it is issued substantially contemporaneously with, and has the same maturity (including rights to accelerate or delay payments) as, the qualifying debt instrument.

(3) *Financial instrument.* For purposes of this section, a financial instrument is a spot, forward, or futures contract, an option, a notional principal contract, a debt instrument, or a similar instrument, or combination or series of financial instruments. Stock is not a financial instrument for purposes of this section.

(4) *Synthetic debt instrument.* The synthetic debt instrument is the hypothetical debt instrument with the same cash flows as the combined cash flows of the qualifying debt instrument and the § 1.1275-6 hedge.

(c) *Integrated transaction*—(1) *Integration by taxpayer.* Except as otherwise provided in this section, a qualifying debt instrument and a § 1.1275-6 hedge are an integrated transaction if all of the following requirements are satisfied:

(i) The taxpayer satisfies the identification requirements of paragraph (e) of this section on or before the date the taxpayer enters into the § 1.1275-6 hedge.

(ii) None of the parties to the § 1.1275-6 hedge are related within the meaning of section 267(b) or 707(b)(1), or, if the parties are related, the party providing the hedge uses, for federal income tax purposes, a mark-to-market method of accounting for the hedge and all similar or related transactions.

(iii) Both the qualifying debt instrument and the § 1.1275-6 hedge are entered into by the same individual, partnership, trust, estate, or corporation (regardless of whether the corporation is a member of an affiliated group of corporations that files a consolidated return).

(iv) If the taxpayer is a foreign person engaged in a U.S. trade or business and the taxpayer issues or acquires a qualifying debt instrument, or enters into a § 1.1275-6 hedge, through the trade or business, all items of income and expense associated with the qualifying debt instrument and the § 1.1275-6 hedge (other than interest expense that is subject to § 1.882-5) would have been effectively connected with the U.S. trade or business throughout the term of the qualifying debt instrument had this section not applied.

(v) Neither the qualifying debt instrument, nor any other debt instrument that is part of the same issue as the qualifying debt instrument, nor the § 1.1275-6 hedge was, with respect to the taxpayer, part of an integrated transaction that was terminated or otherwise legged out of within the 30 days immediately preceding the date that would be the issue date of the synthetic debt instrument.

(vi) The qualifying debt instrument is issued or acquired by the taxpayer on or before the date of the first payment on the § 1.1275-6 hedge, whether made or received by the taxpayer (including a payment made to purchase the hedge). If the qualifying debt instrument is issued or acquired by the taxpayer after, but substantially contemporaneously with, the date of the first payment on the § 1.1275-6 hedge, the qualifying debt instrument is treated, solely for purposes of this paragraph (c)(1)(vi), as meeting the requirements of the preceding sentence.

(vii) Neither the § 1.1275-6 hedge nor the qualifying debt instrument was, with respect to the taxpayer, part of a straddle (as defined in section 1092(c)) prior to the issue date of the synthetic debt instrument.

(2) *Integration by Commissioner.* The Commissioner may treat a qualifying debt instrument and a financial instrument (whether entered into by the taxpayer or by a related party) as an integrated transaction if the combined cash flows on the qualifying debt instrument and financial instrument are substantially the same as the combined cash flows required for the financial instrument to be a § 1.1275-6 hedge. The Commissioner, however, may not integrate a transaction unless the qualifying debt instrument either is subject to § 1.1275-4 or is subject to § 1.1275-5 and pays interest at an objective rate. The circumstances under which the Commissioner may require integration include, but are not limited to, the following:

(i) A taxpayer fails to identify a qualifying debt instrument and the § 1.1275-6 hedge under paragraph (e) of this section.

(ii) A taxpayer issues or acquires a qualifying debt instrument and a related party (within the meaning of section 267(b) or 707(b)(1)) enters into the § 1.1275-6 hedge.

(iii) A taxpayer issues or acquires a qualifying debt instrument and enters into the § 1.1275-6 hedge with a related party (within the meaning of section 267(b) or 707(b)(1)).

Reg. § 1.1275-6(c)(2)

(iv) The taxpayer legs out of an integrated transaction and within 30 days enters into a new § 1.1275-6 hedge with respect to the same qualifying debt instrument or another debt instrument that is part of the same issue.

(d) *Special rules for legging into and legging out of an integrated transaction*—(1) *Legging into*—(i) *Definition.* Legging into an integrated transaction under this section means that a § 1.1275-6 hedge is entered into after the date the qualifying debt instrument is issued or acquired by the taxpayer, and the requirements of paragraph (c)(1) of this section are satisfied on the date the § 1.1275-6 hedge is entered into (the leg-in date).

(ii) *Treatment.* If a taxpayer legs into an integrated transaction, the taxpayer treats the qualifying debt instrument under the applicable rules for taking interest and OID into account up to the leg-in date, except that the day before the leg-in date is treated as the end of an accrual period. As of the leg-in date, the qualifying debt instrument is subject to the rules of paragraph (f) of this section.

(iii) *Anti-abuse rule.* If a taxpayer legs into an integrated transaction with a principal purpose of deferring or accelerating income or deductions on the qualifying debt instrument, the Commissioner may—

(A) Treat the qualifying debt instrument as sold for its fair market value on the leg-in date; or

(B) Refuse to allow the taxpayer to integrate the qualifying debt instrument and the § 1.1275-6 hedge.

(2) *Legging out*—(i) *Definition*—(A) *Legging out if the taxpayer has integrated.* If a taxpayer has integrated a qualifying debt instrument and a § 1.1275-6 hedge under paragraph (c)(1) of this section, legging out means that, prior to the maturity of the synthetic debt instrument, the § 1.1275-6 hedge ceases to meet the requirements for a § 1.1275-6 hedge, the taxpayer fails to meet any requirement of paragraph (c)(1) of this section, or the taxpayer disposes of or otherwise terminates all or a part of the qualifying debt instrument or § 1.1275-6 hedge. If the taxpayer fails to meet the requirements of paragraph (c)(1) of this section but meets the requirements of paragraph (c)(2) of this section, the Commissioner may treat the taxpayer as not legging out.

(B) *Legging out if the Commissioner has integrated.* If the Commissioner has integrated a qualifying debt instrument and a financial instrument under paragraph (c)(2) of this section, legging out means that, prior to the maturity of the synthetic debt instrument, the requirements for Commissioner integration under paragraph (c)(2) of this section are not met or the taxpayer fails to meet the requirements for taxpayer integration under paragraph (c)(1) of this section and the Commissioner agrees to allow the taxpayer to be treated as legging out.

(C) *Exception for certain nonrecognition transactions.* If, in a single nonrecognition transaction, a taxpayer disposes of, or ceases to be primarily liable on, the qualifying debt instrument and the § 1.1275-6 hedge, the taxpayer is not treated as legging out. Instead, the integrated transaction is treated under the rules governing the nonrecognition transaction. For example, if a holder of an integrated transaction is acquired in a reorganization under section 368(a)(1)(A), the holder is treated as disposing of the synthetic debt instrument in the reorganization rather than legging out. If the successor holder is not eligible for integrated treatment, the successor is treated as legging out.

(ii) *Operating rules.* If a taxpayer legs out (or is treated as legging out) of an integrated transaction, the following rules apply:

(A) The transaction is treated as an integrated transaction during the time the requirements of paragraph (c)(1) or (2) of this section, as appropriate, are satisfied.

(B) Immediately before the taxpayer legs out, the taxpayer is treated as selling or otherwise terminating the synthetic debt instrument for its fair market value and, except as provided in paragraph (d)(2)(ii)(D) of this section, any income, deduction, gain, or loss is realized and recognized at that time.

(C) If, immediately after the taxpayer legs out, the taxpayer holds or remains primarily liable on the qualifying debt instrument, adjustments are made to reflect any difference between the fair market value of the qualifying debt instrument and the adjusted issue price of the qualifying debt instrument. If, immediately after the taxpayer legs out, the taxpayer is a party to a § 1.1275-6 hedge, the § 1.1275-6 hedge is treated as entered into at its fair market value.

(D) If a taxpayer legs out of an integrated transaction by disposing of or otherwise terminating a § 1.1275-6 hedge within 30 days of legging into the integrated transaction, then any loss or deduction determined under paragraph (d)(2)(ii)(B) of this section is not allowed. Appropriate adjustments are made to the qualifying debt instrument for any disallowed loss. The adjustments are taken into account on a yield to maturity basis over the remaining term of the qualifying debt instrument.

(E) If a holder of a debt instrument subject to § 1.1275-4 legs into an integrated transaction with respect to the instrument and subsequently legs out of the integrated transaction, any gain recognized under paragraph (d)(2)(ii)(B) or (C) of this section is treated as interest income to the extent determined under the principles of § 1.1275-4(b)(8)(iii)(B) (rules for determining the character of gain on the sale of a debt instrument all of the payments on which have been fixed). If the synthetic debt instrument would qualify as a variable rate debt instrument, the equivalent fixed rate debt instrument determined under § 1.1275-5(e) is used for this purpose.

(e) *Identification requirements.* For each integrated transaction, a taxpayer must enter and retain as part of its books and records the following information—

(1) The date the qualifying debt instrument was issued or acquired (or is expected to be issued or acquired) by the taxpayer and the date the § 1.1275-6 hedge was entered into by the taxpayer;

(2) A description of the qualifying debt instrument and the § 1.1275-6 hedge; and

(3) A summary of the cash flows and accruals resulting from treating the qualifying debt instrument and the § 1.1275-6 hedge as an integrated transaction (i.e., the cash flows and accruals on the synthetic debt instrument).

(f) *Taxation of integrated transactions*—(1) *General rule.* An integrated transaction is generally treated as a single transaction by the taxpayer during the period that the transaction qualifies as an integrated transaction. Except as provided in paragraph (f)(12) of this section, while a qualifying debt instrument and a § 1.1275-6 hedge are part of an integrated transaction, neither the qualifying debt instrument nor the § 1.1275-6 hedge is subject to the rules that would apply on a separate basis to the debt instrument and the § 1.1275-6 hedge, including section 1092 or § 1.446-4. The rules that would govern the treatment of the synthetic debt instrument generally govern the treatment of the integrated transaction. For example, the integrated transaction may be subject to section 263(g) or, if the synthetic debt instrument would be part of a straddle, section 1092. Generally, the synthetic debt instrument is subject to sections 163(e) and 1271 through 1275, with terms as set forth in paragraphs (f)(2) through (13) of this section.

(2) *Issue date.* The issue date of the synthetic debt instrument is the first date on which the taxpayer entered into all of the components of the synthetic debt instrument.

(3) *Term.* The term of the synthetic debt instrument is the period beginning on the issue date of the synthetic debt instrument and ending on the maturity date of the qualifying debt instrument.

(4) *Issue price.* The issue price of the synthetic debt instrument is the adjusted issue price of the qualifying debt instrument on the issue date of the synthetic debt instrument. If, as a result of entering into the § 1.1275-6 hedge, the taxpayer pays or receives one or more payments that are substantially contemporaneous with the issue date of the synthetic debt instrument, the payments reduce or increase the issue price as appropriate.

(5) *Adjusted issue price.* In general, the adjusted issue price of the synthetic debt instrument is determined under the principles of § 1.1275-1(b).

(6) *Qualified stated interest.* No amounts payable on the synthetic debt instrument are qualified stated interest within the meaning of § 1.1273-1(c).

(7) *Stated redemption price at maturity*—(i) *Synthetic debt instruments that are borrowings.* In general, if the synthetic debt instrument is a borrowing, the instrument's stated redemption price at maturity is the sum of all amounts paid or to be paid on the qualifying debt instrument and the § 1.1275-6 hedge, reduced by any amounts received or to be received on the § 1.1275-6 hedge.

(ii) *Synthetic debt instruments that are held by the taxpayer.* In general, if the synthetic debt instrument is held by the taxpayer, the instrument's stated redemption price at maturity is the sum of all amounts received or to be received by the taxpayer on the qualifying debt instrument and the § 1.1275-6 hedge, reduced by any amounts paid or to be paid by the taxpayer on the § 1.1275-6 hedge.

(iii) *Certain amounts ignored.* For purposes of this paragraph (f)(7), if an amount paid or received on the § 1.1275-6 hedge is taken into account under paragraph (f)(4) of this section to determine the issue price of the synthetic debt instrument, the amount is not taken into account to determine the synthetic debt instrument's stated redemption price at maturity.

(8) *Source of interest income and allocation of expense.* The source of interest income from the synthetic debt instrument is determined by reference to the source of income of the qualifying debt instrument under sections 861(a)(1) and 862(a)(1). For purposes of section 904, the character of interest from the synthetic debt instrument is determined by reference to the character of the interest income from the qualifying debt instrument. Interest expense is allocated and appor-

Reg. § 1.1275-6(f)(8)

(9) *Effectively connected income.* If the requirements of paragraph (c)(1)(iv) of this section are satisfied, any interest income resulting from the synthetic debt instrument entered into by the foreign person is treated as effectively connected with a U.S. trade or business, and any interest expense resulting from the synthetic debt instrument entered into by the foreign person is allocated and apportioned under § 1.882-5.

(10) *Not a short-term obligation.* For purposes of section 1272(a)(2)(C), a synthetic debt instrument is not treated as a short-term obligation.

(11) *Special rules in the event of integration by the Commissioner.* If the Commissioner requires integration, appropriate adjustments are made to the treatment of the synthetic debt instrument, and, if necessary, the qualifying debt instrument and financial instrument. For example, the Commissioner may treat a financial instrument that is not a § 1.1275-6 hedge as a § 1.1275-6 hedge when applying the rules of this section. The issue date of the synthetic debt instrument is the date determined appropriate by the Commissioner to require integration.

(12) *Retention of separate transaction rules for certain purposes.* This paragraph (f)(12) provides for the retention of separate transaction rules for certain purposes. In addition, by publication in the Internal Revenue Bulletin (see § 601.601(d)(2)(ii) of this chapter), the Commissioner may require use of separate transaction rules for any aspect of an integrated transaction.

(i) *Foreign persons that enter into integrated transactions giving rise to U.S. source income not effectively connected with a U.S. trade or business.* If a foreign person enters into an integrated transaction that gives rise to U.S. source interest income (determined under the source rules for the synthetic debt instrument) not effectively connected with a U.S. trade or business of the foreign person, paragraph (f) of this section does not apply for purposes of sections 871(a), 881, 1441, 1442, and 6049. These sections of the Internal Revenue Code are applied to the qualifying debt instrument and the § 1.1275-6 hedge on a separate basis.

(ii) *Relationship between taxpayer and other persons.* Because the rules of this section affect only the taxpayer that enters into an integrated transaction (i.e., either the issuer or a particular holder of a qualifying debt instrument), any provisions of the Internal Revenue Code or regulations that govern the relationship between the taxpayer and any other person are applied on a separate basis. For example, taxpayers must comply with any reporting or disclosure requirements on any qualifying debt instrument as if it were not part of an integrated transaction. Thus, if required under § 1.1275-4(b)(4), an issuer of a contingent payment debt instrument subject to integrated treatment must provide the projected payment schedule to holders. Similarly, if a U.S. corporation enters into an integrated transaction that includes a notional principal contract, the source of any payment received by the counterparty on the notional principal contract is determined under § 1.863-7 as if the contract were not part of an integrated transaction, and, if received by a foreign person who is not engaged in a U.S. trade or business, the payment is non-U.S. source income that is not subject to U.S. withholding tax.

(13) *Coordination with consolidated return rules.* If a taxpayer enters into a § 1.1275-6 hedge with a member of the same consolidated group (the counterparty) and the § 1.1275-6 hedge is part of an integrated transaction for the taxpayer, the § 1.1275-6 hedge is not treated as an intercompany transaction for purposes of § 1.1502-13. If the taxpayer legs out of integrated treatment, the taxpayer and the counterparty are each treated as disposing of its position in the § 1.1275-6 hedge under the principles of paragraph (d)(2) of this section. If the § 1.1275-6 hedge remains in existence after the leg-out date, the § 1.1275-6 hedge is treated under the rules that would otherwise apply to the transaction (including § 1.1502-13 if the transaction is between members).

(g) *Predecessors and successors.* For purposes of this section, any reference to a taxpayer, holder, issuer, or person includes, where appropriate, a reference to a predecessor or successor. For purposes of the preceding sentence, a predecessor is a transferor of an asset or liability (including an integrated transaction) to a transferee (the successor) in a nonrecognition transaction. Appropriate adjustments, if necessary, are made in the application of this section to predecessors and successors.

(h) *Examples.* The following examples illustrate the provisions of this section. In each example, assume that the qualifying debt instrument is a debt instrument for federal income tax purposes. No inference is intended, however, as to whether the debt instrument is a debt instrument for federal income tax purposes.

Example 1. Issuer hedge—(i) *Facts.* On January 1, 1997, V, a domestic corporation, issues a 5-year debt instrument for $1,000. The debt instrument provides for annual payments of inter-

Reg. § 1.1275-6(f)(9)

est at a rate equal to the value of 1-year LIBOR and a principal payment of $1,000 at maturity. On the same day, V enters into a 5-year interest rate swap agreement with an unrelated party. Under the swap, V pays 6 percent and receives 1-year LIBOR on a notional principal amount of $1,000. The payments on the swap are fixed and made on the same days as the payments on the debt instrument. On January 1, 1997, V identifies the debt instrument and the swap as an integrated transaction in accordance with the requirements of paragraph (e) of this section.

(ii) *Eligibility for integration.* The debt instrument is a qualifying debt instrument. The swap is a § 1.1275-6 hedge because it is a financial instrument and a yield to maturity on the combined cash flows of the swap and the debt instrument can be calculated. V has met the identification requirements, and the other requirements of paragraph (c)(1) of this section are satisfied. Therefore, the transaction is an integrated transaction under this section.

(iii) *Treatment of the synthetic debt instrument.* The synthetic debt instrument is a 5-year debt instrument that has an issue price of $1,000 and provides for annual interest payments of $60 and a principal payment of $1,000 at maturity. Under paragraph (f)(6) of this section, no amounts payable on the synthetic debt instrument are qualified stated interest. Thus, under paragraph (f)(7)(i) of this section, the synthetic debt instrument has a stated redemption price at maturity of $1,300 (the sum of all amounts to be paid on the qualifying debt instrument and the swap, reduced by amounts to be received on the swap). The synthetic debt instrument, therefore, has $300 of OID.

Example 2. *Issuer hedge with an option*—(i) Facts. On December 31, 1996, W, a domestic corporation, issues for $1,000 a debt instrument that matures on December 31, 1999. The debt instrument has a stated principal amount of $1,000 payable at maturity. The debt instrument also provides for a payment at maturity equal to $10 times the increase, if any, in the value of a nationally known composite index of stocks from December 31, 1996, to the maturity date. On December 31, 1996, W purchases from an unrelated party an option that pays $10 times the increase, if any, in the stock index from December 31, 1996, to December 31, 1999. W pays $250 for the option. On December 31, 1996, W identifies the debt instrument and option as an integrated transaction in accordance with the requirements of paragraph (e) of this section.

(ii) *Eligibility for integration.* The debt instrument is a qualifying debt instrument. The option is a § 1.1275-6 hedge because it is a financial instrument and a yield to maturity on the combined cash flows of the option and the debt instrument can be calculated. W has met the identification requirements, and the other requirements of paragraph (c)(1) of this section are satisfied. Therefore, the transaction is an integrated transaction under this section.

(iii) *Treatment of the synthetic debt instrument.* Under paragraph (f)(4) of this section, the issue price of the synthetic debt instrument is equal to the issue price of the debt instrument ($1,000) reduced by the payment for the option ($250). As a result, the synthetic debt instrument is a 3-year debt instrument with an issue price of $750. Under paragraph (f)(7) of this section, the synthetic debt instrument has a stated redemption price at maturity of $1,000 (the $250 payment for the option is not taken into account). The synthetic debt instrument, therefore, has $250 of OID.

Example 3. *Hedge with prepaid swap*—(i) Facts. On January 1, 1997, H purchases for £1,000 a 5-year debt instrument that provides for semiannual payments based on 6-month pound LIBOR and a payment of the £1,000 principal at maturity. On the same day, H enters into a swap with an unrelated third party under which H receives semiannual payments, in pounds, of 10 percent, compounded semiannually, and makes semiannual payments, in pounds, of 6-month pound LIBOR on a notional principal amount of £1,000. Payments on the swap are fixed and made on the same dates as the payments on the debt instrument. H also makes a £162 prepayment on the swap. On January 1, 1997, H identifies the swap and the debt instrument as an integrated transaction in accordance with the requirements of paragraph (e) of this section.

(ii) *Eligibility for integration.* The debt instrument is a qualifying debt instrument. The swap is a § 1.1275-6 hedge because it is a financial instrument and a yield to maturity on the combined cash flows of the swap and the debt instrument can be calculated. Although the debt instrument is denominated in pounds, the swap hedges only interest rate risk, not currency risk. Therefore, the transaction is an integrated transaction under this section. See § 1.988-5(a) for the treatment of a debt instrument and a swap if the swap hedges currency risk.

(iii) *Treatment of the synthetic debt instrument.* Under paragraph (f)(4) of this section, the issue price of the synthetic debt instrument is equal to the issue price of the debt instrument (£1,000) increased by the prepayment on the swap (£162). As a result, the synthetic debt in-

Reg. § 1.1275-6(h)

strument is a 5-year debt instrument that has an issue price of £1,162 and provides for semiannual interest payments of £50 and a principal payment of £1,000 at maturity. Under paragraph (f)(6) of this section, no amounts payable on the synthetic debt instrument are qualified stated interest. Thus, under paragraph (f)(7)(ii) of this section, the synthetic debt instrument's stated redemption price at maturity is £1,500 (the sum of all amounts to be received on the qualifying debt instrument and the § 1.1275-6 hedge, reduced by all amounts to be paid on the § 1.1275-6 hedge other than the £162 prepayment for the swap). The synthetic debt instrument, therefore, has £338 of OID.

Example 4. Legging into an integrated transaction by a holder—(i) *Facts.* On December 31, 1996, X corporation purchases for $1,000,000 a debt instrument that matures on December 31, 2006. The debt instrument provides for annual payments of interest at the rate of 6 percent and for a payment at maturity equal to $1,000,000, increased by the excess, if any, of the price of 1,000 units of a commodity on December 31, 2006, over $350,000, and decreased by the excess, if any, of $350,000 over the price of 1,000 units of the commodity on that date. The projected amount of the payment at maturity determined under § 1.1275-4(b)(4) is $1,020,000. On December 31, 1999, X enters into a cash-settled forward contract with an unrelated party to sell 1,000 units of the commodity on December 31, 2006, for $450,000. On December 31, 1999, X also identifies the debt instrument and the forward contract as an integrated transaction in accordance with the requirements of paragraph (e) of this section.

(ii) *Eligibility for integration.* X meets the requirements for integration as of December 31, 1999. Therefore, X legged into an integrated transaction on that date. Prior to that date, X treats the debt instrument under the applicable rules of § 1.1275-4.

(iii) *Treatment of the synthetic debt instrument.* As of December 31, 1999, the debt instrument and the forward contract are treated as an integrated transaction. The issue price of the synthetic debt instrument is equal to the adjusted issue price of the qualifying debt instrument on the leg-in date, $1,004,804 (assuming one year accrual periods). The term of the synthetic debt instrument is from December 31, 1999, to December 31, 2006. The synthetic debt instrument provides for annual interest payments of $60,000 and a principal payment at maturity of $1,100,000 ($1,000,000 + $450,000 − $350,000). Under paragraph (f)(6) of this section, no amounts payable on the synthetic debt instrument are qualified stated interest. Thus, under paragraph (f)(7)(ii) of this section, the synthetic debt instrument's stated redemption price at maturity is $1,520,000 (the sum of all amounts to be received by X on the qualifying debt instrument and the § 1.1275-6 hedge, reduced by all amounts to be paid by X on the § 1.1275-6 hedge). The synthetic debt instrument, therefore, has $515,196 of OID.

Example 5. Abusive leg-in—(i) *Facts.* On January 1, 1997, Y corporation purchases for $1,000,000 a debt instrument that matures on December 31, 2001. The debt instrument provides for annual payments of interest at the rate of 6 percent, a payment on December 31, 1999, of the increase, if any, in the price of a commodity from January 1, 1997, to December 31, 1999, and a payment at maturity of $1,000,000 and the increase, if any, in the price of the commodity from December 31, 1999 to maturity. Because the debt instrument is a contingent payment debt instrument subject to § 1.1275-4, Y accrues interest based on the projected payment schedule.

(ii) *Leg-in.* By late 1999, the price of the commodity has substantially increased, and Y expects a positive adjustment on December 31, 1999. In late 1999, Y enters into an agreement to exchange the two commodity based payments on the debt instrument for two payments on the same dates of $100,000 each. Y identifies the transaction as an integrated transaction in accordance with the requirements of paragraph (e) of this section. Y disposes of the hedge in early 2000.

(iii) *Treatment.* The legging into an integrated transaction has the effect of deferring the positive adjustment from 1999 to 2000. Because Y legged into the integrated transaction with a principal purpose to defer the positive adjustment, the Commissioner may treat the debt instrument as sold for its fair market value on the leg-in date or refuse to allow integration.

Example 6. Integration of offsetting debt instruments—(i) *Facts.* On January 1, 1997, Z issues two 10-year debt instruments. The first, Issue 1, has an issue price of $1,000, pays interest annually at 6 percent, and, at maturity, pays $1,000, increased by $1 times the increase, if any, in the value of the S&P 100 Index over the term of the instrument and reduced by $1 times the decrease, if any, in the value of the S&P 100 Index over the term of the instrument. However, the amount paid at maturity may not be less than $500 or more than $1,500. The second, Issue 2, has an issue price of $1,000, pays interest annually at 8 percent, and, at maturity, pays $1,000, reduced by $1 times the increase, if any, in the value of the S&P 100 Index over the term of the instrument and increased by $1 times the de-

Reg. § 1.1275-6(h)

crease, if any, in the value of the S&P 100 Index over the term of the instrument. The amount paid at maturity may not be less than $500 or more than $1,500. On January 1, 1997, Z identifies Issue 1 as the qualifying debt instrument, Issue 2 as a § 1.1275-6 hedge, and otherwise meets the identification requirements of paragraph (e) of this section.

(ii) *Eligibility for integration.* Both Issue 1 and Issue 2 are qualifying debt instruments. Z has met the identification requirements by identifying Issue 1 as the qualifying debt instrument and Issue 2 as the § 1.1275-6 hedge. The other requirements of paragraph (c)(1) of this section are satisfied. Therefore, the transaction is an integrated transaction under this section.

(iii) *Treatment of the synthetic debt instrument.* The synthetic debt instrument has an issue price of $2,000, provides for a payment at maturity of $2,000, and, in addition, provides for annual payments of $140. Under paragraph (f)(6) of this section, no amounts payable on the synthetic debt instrument are qualified stated interest. Thus, under paragraph (f)(7)(i) of this section, the synthetic debt instrument's stated redemption price at maturity is $3,400 (the sum of all amounts to be paid on the qualifying debt instrument and the § 1.1275-6 hedge, reduced by amounts to be received on the § 1.1275-6 hedge other than the $1,000 payment received on the issue date). The synthetic debt instrument, therefore, has $1,400 of OID.

Example 7. Integrated transaction entered into by a foreign person—(i) *Facts.* X, a foreign person, enters into an integrated transaction by purchasing a qualifying debt instrument that pays U.S. source interest and entering into a notional principal contract with a U.S. corporation. Neither the income from the qualifying debt instrument nor the income from the notional principal contract is effectively connected with a U.S. trade or business. The notional principal contract is a § 1.1275-6 hedge.

(ii) *Treatment of integrated transaction.* Under paragraph (f)(8) of this section, X will receive U.S. source income from the integrated transaction. However, under paragraph (f)(12)(i) of this section, the qualifying debt instrument and the notional principal contract are treated as if they are not part of an integrated transaction for purposes of determining whether tax is due and must be withheld on income. Accordingly, because the § 1.1275-6 hedge would produce foreign source income under § 1.863-7 to X if it were not part of an integrated transaction, any income on the § 1.1275-6 hedge generally will not be subject to tax under sections 871(a) and 881, and the U.S. corporation that is the counterparty will not be required to withhold tax on payments under the § 1.1275-6 hedge under sections 1441 and 1442.

(i) [Reserved]

(j) *Effective date.* This section applies to a qualifying debt instrument issued on or after August 13, 1996. This section also applies to a qualifying debt instrument acquired by the taxpayer on or after August 13, 1996, if—

(1) The qualifying debt instrument is a fixed rate debt instrument or a variable rate debt instrument; or

(2) The qualifying debt instrument and the § 1.1275-6 hedge are acquired by the taxpayer substantially contemporaneously. [Reg. § 1.1275-6.]

☐ [T.D. 8674, 6-11-96.]

[Reg. § 1.1275-7]

§ 1.1275-7. Inflation-indexed debt instruments.—(a) *Overview.* This section provides rules for the federal income tax treatment of an inflation-indexed debt instrument. If a debt instrument is an inflation-indexed debt instrument, one of two methods will apply to the instrument: the coupon bond method (as described in paragraph (d) of this section) or the discount bond method (as described in paragraph (e) of this section). Both methods determine the amount of OID that is taken into account each year by a holder or an issuer of an inflation-indexed debt instrument.

(b) *Applicability*—(1) *In general.* Except as provided in paragraph (b)(2) of this section, this section applies to an inflation-indexed debt instrument as defined in paragraph (c)(1) of this section. For example, this section applies to Treasury Inflation-Indexed Securities.

(2) *Exceptions.* This section does not apply to an inflation-indexed debt instrument that is also—

(i) A debt instrument (other than a tax-exempt obligation) described in section 1272(a)(2) (for example, U.S. savings bonds, certain loans between natural persons, and short-term taxable obligations); or

(ii) A debt instrument subject to section 529 (certain debt instruments issued by qualified state tuition programs).

(c) *Definitions.* The following definitions apply for purposes of this section:

(1) *Inflation-indexed debt instrument.* An inflation-indexed debt instrument is a debt instrument that satisfies the following conditions:

(i) *Issued for cash.* The debt instrument is issued for U.S. dollars and all payments on the instrument are denominated in U.S. dollars.

Reg. § 1.1275-7(c)(1)

(ii) *Indexed for inflation and deflation.* Except for a minimum guarantee payment (as defined in paragraph (c)(5) of this section), each payment on the debt instrument is indexed for inflation and deflation. A payment is indexed for inflation and deflation if the amount of the payment is equal to—

(A) The amount that would be payable if there were no inflation or deflation over the term of the debt instrument, multiplied by

(B) A ratio, the numerator of which is the value of the reference index for the date of the payment and the denominator of which is the value of the reference index for the issue date.

(iii) *No other contingencies.* No payment on the debt instrument is subject to a contingency other than the inflation contingency or the contingencies described in this paragraph (c)(1)(iii). A debt instrument may provide for—

(A) A minimum guarantee payment as defined in paragraph (c)(5) of this section; or

(B) Payments under one or more alternate payment schedules if the payments under each payment schedule are indexed for inflation and deflation and a payment schedule for the debt instrument can be determined under § 1.1272-1(c). (For purposes of this section, the rules of § 1.1272-1(c) are applied to the debt instrument by assuming that no inflation or deflation will occur over the term of the instrument.)

(2) *Reference index.* The reference index is an index used to measure inflation and deflation over the term of a debt instrument. To qualify as a reference index, an index must satisfy the following conditions:

(i) The value of the index is reset once a month to a current value of a single qualified inflation index (as defined in paragraph (c)(3) of this section). For this purpose, a value of a qualified inflation index is current if the value has been updated and published within the preceding six month period.

(ii) The reset occurs on the same day of each month (the reset date).

(iii) The value of the index for any date between reset dates is determined through straight-line interpolation.

(3) *Qualified inflation index.* A qualified inflation index is a general price or wage index that is updated and published at least monthly by an agency of the United States Government (for example, the non-seasonally adjusted U.S. City Average All Items Consumer Price Index for All Urban Consumers (CPI-U), which is published by the Bureau of Labor Statistics of the Department of Labor).

(4) *Inflation-adjusted principal amount.* For any date, the inflation-adjusted principal amount of an inflation-indexed debt instrument is an amount equal to—

(i) The outstanding principal amount of the debt instrument (determined as if there were no inflation or deflation over the term of the instrument), multiplied by

(ii) A ratio, the numerator of which is the value of the reference index for the date and the denominator of which is the value of the reference index for the issue date.

(5) *Minimum guarantee payment.* In general, a minimum guarantee payment is an additional payment made at maturity on a debt instrument if the total amount of inflation-adjusted principal paid on the instrument is less than the instrument's stated principal amount. The amount of the additional payment must be no more than the excess, if any, of the debt instrument's stated principal amount over the total amount of inflation-adjusted principal paid on the instrument. An additional payment is not a minimum guarantee payment unless the qualified inflation index used to determine the reference index is either the CPI-U or an index designated for this purpose by the Commissioner in the Federal Register or the Internal Revenue Bulletin (see § 601.601(d)(2)(ii) of this chapter). See paragraph (f)(4) of this section for the treatment of a minimum guarantee payment.

(d) *Coupon bond method*—(1) *In general.* This paragraph (d) describes the method (coupon bond method) to be used to account for qualified stated interest and inflation adjustments (OID) on an inflation-indexed debt instrument described in paragraph (d)(2) of this section.

(2) *Applicability.* The coupon bond method applies to an inflation-indexed debt instrument that satisfies the following conditions:

(i) *Issued at par.* The debt instrument is issued at par. A debt instrument is issued at par if the difference between its issue price and principal amount for the issue date is less than the de minimis amount. For this purpose, the de minimis amount is determined using the principles of § 1.1273-1(d).

(ii) *All stated interest is qualified stated interest.* All stated interest on the debt instrument is qualified stated interest. For purposes of this paragraph (d), stated interest is qualified stated interest if the interest is unconditionally payable in cash, or is constructively received under section 451, at least annually at a single fixed rate. Stated interest is payable at a single fixed rate if the amount of each interest payment is determined by multiplying the inflation ad-

Reg. § 1.1275-7(c)(2)

justed principal amount for the payment date by the single fixed rate.

(3) *Qualified stated interest.* Under the coupon bond method, qualified stated interest is taken into account under the taxpayer's regular method of accounting. The amount of accrued but unpaid qualified stated interest as of any date is determined by using the principles of § 1.446-3(e)(2)(ii) (relating to notional principal contracts). For example, if the interval between interest payment dates spans two taxable years, a taxpayer using an accrual method of accounting determines the amount of accrued qualified stated interest for the first taxable year by reference to the inflation-adjusted principal amount at the end of the first taxable year.

(4) *Inflation adjustments*—(i) *Current accrual.* Under the coupon bond method, an inflation adjustment is taken into account for each taxable year in which the debt instrument is outstanding.

(ii) *Amount of inflation adjustment.* For any relevant period (such as the taxable year or the portion of the taxable year during which a taxpayer holds an inflation-indexed debt instrument), the amount of the inflation adjustment is equal to—

(A) The sum of the inflation-adjusted principal amount at the end of the period and the principal payments made during the period, minus

(B) The inflation-adjusted principal amount at the beginning of the period.

(iii) *Positive inflation adjustments.* A positive inflation adjustment is OID.

(iv) *Negative inflation adjustments.* A negative inflation adjustment is a deflation adjustment that is taken into account under the rules of paragraph (f)(1) of this section.

(5) *Example.* The following example illustrates the coupon bond method:

Example. (i) *Facts.* On October 15, 1997, X purchases at original issue, for $100,000, a debt instrument that is indexed for inflation and deflation. The debt instrument matures on October 15, 1999, has a stated principal amount of $100,000, and has a stated interest rate of 5 percent, compounded semiannually. The debt instrument provides that the principal amount is indexed to the CPI-U. Interest is payable on April 15 and October 15 of each year. The amount of each interest payment is determined by multiplying the inflation-adjusted principal amount for each interest payment date by the stated interest rate, adjusted for the length of the accrual period. The debt instrument provides for a single payment of the inflation-adjusted principal amount at maturity. In addition, the debt instrument provides for an additional payment at maturity equal to the excess, if any, of $100,000 over the inflation-adjusted principal amount at maturity. X uses the cash receipts and disbursements method of accounting and the calendar year as its taxable year.

(ii) *Indexing methodology.* The debt instrument provides that the inflation-adjusted principal amount for any day is determined by multiplying the principal amount of the instrument for the issue date by a ratio, the numerator of which is the value of the reference index for the day the inflation-adjusted principal amount is to be determined and the denominator of which is the value of the reference index for the issue date. The value of the reference index for the first day of a month is the value of the CPI-U for the third preceding month. The value of the reference index for any day other than the first day of a month is determined based on a straight-line interpolation between the value of the reference index for the first day of the month and the value of the reference index for the first day of the next month.

(iii) *Inflation-indexed debt instrument subject to the coupon bond method.* Under paragraph (c)(1) of this section, the debt instrument is an inflation-indexed debt instrument. Because there is no difference between the debt instrument's issue price ($100,000) and its principal amount for the issue date ($100,000) and because all stated interest is qualified stated interest, the coupon bond method applies to the instrument.

(iv) *Reference index values.* Assume the following table lists the relevant reference index values for 1997 through 1999:

Date	Reference index value
October 15, 1997	100
January 1, 1998	101
April 15, 1998	103
October 15, 1998	105
January 1, 1999	99

(v) *Treatment of X in 1997.* X does not receive any payments of interest on the debt instrument in 1997. Therefore, X has no qualified stated interest income for 1997. X, however, must take into account the inflation adjustment for 1997. The inflation-adjusted principal amount for January 1, 1998, is $101,000 ($100,000 x 101/100). Therefore, the inflation adjustment for 1997 is $1,000, the inflation-adjusted principal amount for January 1, 1998 ($101,000) minus the principal amount for the issue date ($100,000). X includes the $1,000 inflation adjustment in income as OID in 1997.

Reg. § 1.1275-7(d)(5)

(vi) *Treatment of X in 1998.* In 1998, X receives two payments of interest: On April 15, 1998, X receives a payment of $2,575 ($100,000 x 103/100 x .05/2), and on October 15, 1998, X receives a payment of $2,625 ($100,000 x 105/100 x .05/2). Therefore, X's qualified stated interest income for 1998 is $5,200 ($2,575 + $2,625). X also must take into account the inflation adjustment for 1998. The inflation-adjusted principal amount for January 1, 1999, is $99,000 ($100,000 x 99/100). Therefore, the inflation adjustment for 1998 is negative $2,000, the inflation-adjusted principal amount for January 1, 1999 ($99,000) minus the inflation-adjusted principal amount for January 1, 1998 ($101,000). Because the amount of the inflation adjustment is negative, it is a deflation adjustment. Under paragraph (f)(1)(i) of this section, X uses this $2,000 deflation adjustment to reduce the interest otherwise includible in income by X with respect to the debt instrument in 1998. Therefore, X includes $3,200 in income for 1998, the qualified stated interest income for 1998 ($5,200) minus the deflation adjustment ($2,000).

(e) *Discount bond method*—(1) *In general.* This paragraph (e) describes the method (discount bond method) to be used to account for OID on an inflation-indexed debt instrument that does not qualify for the coupon bond method.

(2) *No qualified stated interest.* Under the discount bond method, no interest on an inflation-indexed debt instrument is qualified stated interest.

(3) *OID.* Under the discount bond method, the amount of OID that accrues on an inflation-indexed debt instrument is determined as follows:

(i) *Step one: Determine the debt instrument's yield to maturity.* The yield of the debt instrument is determined under the rules of § 1.1272-1(b)(1)(i). In calculating the yield under those rules for purposes of this paragraph (e)(3)(i), the payment schedule of the debt instrument is determined as if there were no inflation or deflation over the term of the instrument.

(ii) *Step two: Determine the accrual periods.* The accrual periods are determined under the rules of § 1.1272-1(b)(1)(ii). However, no accrual period can be longer than 1 month.

(iii) *Step three: Determine the percentage change in the reference index during the accrual period.* The percentage change in the reference index during the accrual period is equal to—

(A) The ratio of the value of the reference index at the end of the period to the value of the reference index at the beginning of the period,

(B) Minus one.

(iv) *Step four: Determine the OID allocable to each accrual period.* The OID allocable to an accrual period (n) is determined by using the following formula:

$$OID_{(n)} = AIP_{(n)} \times [r + inf_{(n)} + (r \times inf_{(n)})]$$

in which,

r = yield of the debt instrument as determined under paragraph (e)(3)(i) of this section (adjusted for the length of the accrual period);

$inf_{(n)}$ = percentage change in the value of the reference index for period (n) as determined under paragraph (e)(3)(iii) of this section; and

$AIP_{(n)}$ = adjusted issue price at the beginning of period (n).

(v) *Step five: Determine the daily portions of OID.* The daily portions of OID are determined and taken into account under the rules of § 1.1272-1(b)(1)(iv). If the daily portions determined under this paragraph (e)(3)(v) are negative amounts, however, these amounts (deflation adjustments) are taken into account under the rules for deflation adjustments described in paragraph (f)(1) of this section.

(4) *Example.* The following example illustrates the discount bond method:

Example. (i) *Facts.* On November 15, 1997, X purchases at original issue, for $91,403, a zero-coupon debt instrument that is indexed for inflation and deflation. The principal amount of the debt instrument for the issue date is $100,000. The debt instrument provides for a single payment on November 15, 2000. The amount of the payment will be determined by multiplying $100,000 by a fraction, the numerator of which is the CPI-U for September 2000, and the denominator of which is the CPI-U for September 1997. The debt instrument also provides that in no event will the payment on November 15, 2000, be less than $100,000. X uses the cash receipts and disbursements method of accounting and the calendar year as its taxable year.

(ii) *Inflation-indexed debt instrument.* Under paragraph (c)(1) of this section, the instrument is an inflation-indexed debt instrument. The debt instrument's principal amount for the issue date ($100,000) exceeds its issue price ($91,403) by $8,597, which is more than the de minimis amount for the debt instrument ($750). Therefore, the coupon bond method does not apply to the debt instrument. As a result, the discount bond method applies to the debt instrument.

(iii) *Yield and accrual period.* Assume X chooses monthly accrual periods ending on the 15th day of each month. The yield of the debt instrument is determined as if there were no inflation or deflation over the term of the instrument.

Reg. § 1.1275-7(e)(1)

Therefore, based on the issue price of $91,403 and an assumed payment at maturity of $100,000, the yield of the debt instrument is 3 percent, compounded monthly.

(iv) *Percentage change in reference index.* Assume that the CPI-U for September 1997 is 160; for October 1997 is 161.2; and for November 1997 is 161.7. The value of the reference index for November 15, 1997, is 160, the value of the CPI-U for September 1997. Similarly, the value of the reference index for December 15, 1997, is 161.2, and for January 15, 1998, is 161.7. The percentage change in the reference index from November 15, 1997, to December 15, 1997, (inf_1) is 0.0075 (161.2/160 − 1); the percentage change in the reference index from December 15, 1997, to January 15, 1998, (inf_2) is 0.0031 (161.7/161.2 − 1).

(v) *Treatment of X in 1997.* For the accrual period ending on December 15, 1997, r is .0025 (.03/12), inf_1 is .0075, and the product of r and inf_1 is .00001875. Under paragraph (e)(3) of this section, the amount of OID allocable to the accrual period ending on December 15, 1997, is $916. This amount is determined by multiplying the issue price of the debt instrument ($91,403) by .01001875 (the sum of r, inf_1, and the product of r and inf_1). The adjusted issue price of the debt instrument on December 15, 1997, is $92,319 ($91,403 + $916). For the accrual period ending on January 15, 1998, r is .0025 (.03/12), inf_2 is .0031, and the product of r and inf_2 is .00000775. Under paragraph (e)(3) of this section, the amount of OID allocable to the accrual period ending on January 15, 1998, is $518. This amount is determined by multiplying the adjusted issue price of the debt instrument ($92,319) by .00560775 (the sum of r, inf_2, and the product of r and inf_2). Because the accrual period ending on January 15, 1998, spans two taxable years, only $259 of this amount ($518/30 days x 15 days) is allocable to 1997. Therefore, X includes $1,175 of OID in income for 1997 ($916 + $259).

(f) *Special rules.* The following rules apply to an inflation-indexed debt instrument:

(1) *Deflation adjustments*—(i) *Holder.* A deflation adjustment reduces the amount of interest otherwise includible in income by a holder with respect to the debt instrument for the taxable year. For purposes of this paragraph (f)(1)(i), interest includes OID, qualified stated interest, and market discount. If the amount of the deflation adjustment exceeds the interest otherwise includible in income by the holder with respect to the debt instrument for the taxable year, the excess is treated as an ordinary loss by the holder for the taxable year. However, the amount treated as an ordinary loss is limited to the amount by which the holder's total interest inclusions on the debt instrument in prior taxable years exceed the total amount treated by the holder as an ordinary loss on the debt instrument in prior taxable years. If the deflation adjustment exceeds the interest otherwise includible in income by the holder with respect to the debt instrument for the taxable year and the amount treated as an ordinary loss for the taxable year, this excess is carried forward to reduce the amount of interest otherwise includible in income by the holder with respect to the debt instrument for subsequent taxable years.

(ii) *Issuer.* A deflation adjustment reduces the interest otherwise deductible by the issuer with respect to the debt instrument for the taxable year. For purposes of this paragraph (f)(1)(ii), interest includes OID and qualified stated interest. If the amount of the deflation adjustment exceeds the interest otherwise deductible by the issuer with respect to the debt instrument for the taxable year, the excess is treated as ordinary income by the issuer for the taxable year. However, the amount treated as ordinary income is limited to the amount by which the issuer's total interest deductions on the debt instrument in prior taxable years exceed the total amount treated by the issuer as ordinary income on the debt instrument in prior taxable years. If the deflation adjustment exceeds the interest otherwise deductible by the issuer with respect to the debt instrument for the taxable year and the amount treated as ordinary income for the taxable year, this excess is carried forward to reduce the interest otherwise deductible by the issuer with respect to the debt instrument for subsequent taxable years. If there is any excess remaining upon the retirement of the debt instrument, the issuer takes the excess amount into account as ordinary income.

(2) *Adjusted basis.* A holder's adjusted basis in an inflation-indexed debt instrument is determined under § 1.1272-1(g). However, a holder's adjusted basis in the debt instrument is decreased by the amount of any deflation adjustment the holder takes into account to reduce the amount of interest otherwise includible in income or treats as an ordinary loss with respect to the instrument during the taxable year. The decrease occurs when the deflation adjustment is taken into account under paragraph (f)(1) of this section.

(3) *Subsequent holders.* A holder determines the amount of acquisition premium or market discount on an inflation-indexed debt instrument by reference to the adjusted issue price of the instrument on the date the holder acquires the instrument. A holder determines the amount of bond premium on an inflation-indexed debt in-

Reg. § 1.1275-7(f)(3)

strument by assuming that the amount payable at maturity on the instrument is equal to the instrument's inflation-adjusted principal amount for the day the holder acquires the instrument. Any premium or market discount is taken into account over the remaining term of the debt instrument as if there were no further inflation or deflation. See section 171 for additional rules relating to the amortization of bond premium and sections 1276 through 1278 for additional rules relating to market discount.

(4) *Minimum guarantee.* Under both the coupon bond method and the discount bond method, a minimum guarantee payment is ignored until the payment is made. If there is a minimum guarantee payment, the payment is treated as interest on the date it is paid.

(5) *Temporary unavailability of a qualified inflation index.* Notwithstanding any other rule of this section, an inflation-indexed debt instrument may provide for a substitute value of the qualified inflation index if and when the publication of the value of the qualified inflation index is temporarily delayed. The substitute value may be determined by the issuer under any reasonable method. For example, if the CPI-U is not reported for a particular month, the debt instrument may provide that a substitute value may be determined by increasing the last reported value by the average monthly percentage increase in the qualified inflation index over the preceding twelve months. The use of a substitute value does not result in a reissuance of the debt instrument.

(g) *Reopenings.* For rules concerning a reopening of Treasury Inflation-Indexed Securities, see paragraphs (d)(2) and (k)(3)(iii) of § 1.1275-2.

(h) *Effective date.* This section applies to an inflation-indexed debt instrument issued on or after January 6, 1997. [Reg. § 1.1275-7.]

☐ [T.D. 8709, 12-31-96. *Redesignated by T.D. 8838, 9-3-99. Amended by T.D. 8840, 11-3-99 and T.D. 8934, 1-11-2001.*]

[Reg. § 1.1286-1]

§ 1.1286-1. **Tax treatment of certain stripped bonds and stripped coupons.**—(a) *De minimis OID.* If the original issue discount determined under section 1286(a) with respect to the purchase of a stripped bond or stripped coupon is less than the amount computed under subparagraphs (A) and (B) of section 1273(a)(3) and the regulations thereunder, then the amount of original issue discount with respect to that purchase (other than any tax-exempt portion thereof, determined under section 1286(d)(2)) shall be considered to be zero. For purposes of this computation, the number of complete years to maturity is measured from the date the stripped bond or stripped coupon is purchased.

(b) *Treatment of certain stripped bonds as market discount bonds*—(1) *In general.* By publication in the Internal Revenue Bulletin (see § 601.601(d)(2)(ii)(*b*) of the Statement of Procedural Rules), the Internal Revenue Service may (subject to the limitation of paragraph (b)(2) of this section) provide that certain mortgage loans that are stripped bonds are to be treated as market discount bonds under section 1278. Thus, any purchaser of such a bond is to account for any discount on the bond as market discount rather than original issue discount.

(2) *Limitation.* This treatment may be provided for a stripped bond only if, immediately after the most recent disposition referred to in section 1286(b)—

(i) The amount of original issue discount with respect to the stripped bond is determined under paragraph (a) of this section (concerning *de minimis* OID); or

(ii) The annual stated rate of interest payable on the stripped bond is no more than 100 basis points lower than the annual stated rate of interest payable on the original bond from which it and any other stripped bond or bonds and any stripped coupon or coupons were stripped.

(c) *Effective date.* This section is effective on and after August 8, 1991. [Reg. § 1.1286-1.]

☐ [T.D. 8463, 12-28-92.]

[Reg. § 1.1286-2]

§ 1.1286-2. **Stripped inflation-indexed debt instruments.**—*Stripped inflation-indexed debt instruments.* If a Treasury Inflation-Indexed Security is stripped under the Department of the Treasury's Separate Trading of Registered Interest and Principal of Securities (STRIPS) program, the holders of the principal and coupon components must use the discount bond method (as described in § 1.1275-7(e)) to account for the original issue discount on the components. [Reg. § 1.1286-2.]

☐ [T.D. 8709, 12-31-96. *Redesignated and amended by T.D. 8838, 9-3-99.*]

[Reg. § 1.1287-1]

§ 1.1287-1. **Denial of capital gains treatment for gains on registration-required obligations not in registered form.**—(a) *In general.* Except as provided in paragraph (c) of this section, any gain on the sale or other disposition of a registration-required obligation held after December 31, 1982, that is not in registered form shall be treated as ordinary income unless the issuance of the obligation was subject to tax under section

4701. The term "registration-required obligation" has the meaning given to that term in section 163(f)(2), except that clause (iv) of subparagraph (A) thereof shall not apply. Therefore, although an obligation that is not in registered form is described in § 1.163-5(c)(1), the holder of such an obligation shall be required to treat the gain on the sale or other disposition of such obligation as ordinary income. The term "holder" means the person that would be denied a loss deduction under section 165(j)(1) or denied capital gain treatment under section 1287(a).

(b) *Registered form*—(1) *Obligations issued after September 21, 1984.* With respect to any obligation originally issued after September 21, 1984, the term "registered form" has the meaning given that term in section 103(j)(3) and the regulations thereunder. Therefore, an obligation that would otherwise be in registered form is not considered to be in registered form if it can be transferred at that time or at any time until its maturity by any means not described in § 5f.103-1(c). An obligation that, as of a particular time, is not considered to be in registered form because it can be transferred by any means not described in § 5f.103-1(c) is considered to be in registered form at all times during the period beginning with a later time and ending with the maturity of the obligation in which the obligation can be transferred only by a means described in § 5f.103-1(c).

(2) *Obligations issued after December 31, 1982 and on or before September 21, 1984.* With respect to any obligation originally issued after December 31, 1982 and on or before September 21, 1984 or an obligation originally issued after September 21, 1984 pursuant to the exercise of a warrant or the conversion of a convertible obligation, which warrant or obligation (including conversion privilege) was issued after December 31, 1982 and on or before September 21, 1984 that obligation will be considered to be in registered form if it satisfied § 5f.163-1 or the proposed regulations provided in § 1.163-5(c) and published in the Federal Register on September 2, 1983 (48 FR 39953).

(c) *Registration-required obligations not in registered form which are not subject to section 1287(c).* Notwithstanding the fact that an obligation is a registration-required obligation that is not in registered form, the holder will not be subject to section 1287(a) if the holder meets the conditions of § 1.165-12(c).

(d) *Effective date.* These regulations apply generally to obligations issued after January 20, 1987. However, a taxpayer may choose to apply the rules of § 1.1287-1 with respect to an obligation issued after December 31, 1982 and on or before January 20, 1987, which obligation is held after January 20, 1987. [Reg. § 1.1287-1.]

☐ [*T.D.* 8110, 12-16-86.]

Passive Foreign Investment Companies

[Reg. § 1.1291-0]

§ 1.1291-0. Treatment of shareholders of certain passive foreign investment companies; table of contents.—This section contains a listing of the headings for §§ 1.1291-9 and 1.1291-10.

§ *1.1291-9 Deemed dividend election.*

(a) Deemed dividend election.

(1) In general.

(2) Post-1986 earnings and profits defined.

(i) In general.

(ii) Pro rata share of post-1986 earnings and profits attributable to shareholder's stock.

(A) In general.

(B) Reduction for previously taxed amounts.

(b) Who may make the election.

(c) Time for making the election.

(d) Manner of making the election.

(1) In general.

(2) Attachment to Form 8621

(e) Qualification date.

(1) In general.

(2) Elections made after March 31, 1995, and before January 27, 1997.

(i) In general.

(ii) Exception.

(3) Examples.

(f) Adjustment to basis.

(g) Treatment of holding period.

(i) Election inapplicable to shareholder of former PFIC.

(1) [Reserved].

(2) Former PFIC.

(j) Definitions.

(1) Passive foreign investment company (PFIC).

(2) Types of PFICs.

(i) Qualified electing fund (QEF).

(ii) Pedigreed QEF.

(iii) Unpedigreed QEF.

(iv) Former PFIC.

(3) Shareholder.

(k) Effective date.

Reg. § 1.1291-0

Passive Foreign Investment Companies

See p. 20,601 for regulations not amended to reflect law changes

§ 1.1291-10 Deemed sale election.

(a) Deemed sale election.

(b) Who may make the election.

(c) Time for making the election.

(d) Manner of making the election.

(e) Qualification date.

(1) In general.

(2) Elections made after March 31, 1995, and before January 27, 1997.

(i) In general.

(ii) Exception.

(f) Adjustments to basis.

(1) In general.

(2) Adjustment to basis for section 1293 inclusion with respect to deemed sale election made after March 31, 1995, and before January 27, 1997.

(g) Treatment of holding period.

(h) Election inapplicable to shareholder of former PFIC.

(i) Effective date.

[Reg. § 1.1291-0.]

☐ [T.D. 8701, 12-26-96. Amended by T.D. 8750, 12-31-97.]

[Reg. § 1.1291-0T]

§ 1.1291-0T. [Reserved].

☐ [T.D. 8178, 2-26-88. Amended by T.D. 8404, 3-31-92; T.D. 8701, 12-26-96 and T.D. 8750, 12-31-97.]

[Reg. § 1.1291-1]

§ 1.1291-1. Taxation of U.S. persons that are shareholders of PFICs that are not pedigreed QEFs.—(a) through (d) [Reserved].

(e) *Exempt organization as shareholder*—(1) *In general*. If the shareholder of a PFIC is an organization exempt from tax under this chapter, section 1291 and these regulations apply to such shareholder only if a dividend from the PFIC would be taxable to the organization under subchapter F.

(2) *Effective date*. Paragraph (e)(1) of this section is applicable on and after April 1, 1992. [Reg. § 1.1291-1.]

☐ [T.D. 8750, 12-31-97. Redesignated by T.D. 8870, 2-4-2000.]

[Reg. § 1.1291-9]

§ 1.1291-9. Deemed dividend election.—(a) *Deemed dividend election*—(1) *In general*. This section provides rules for making the election under section 1291(d)(2)(B) (deemed dividend election). Under that section, a shareholder (as defined in paragraph (j)(3) of this section) of a PFIC that is an unpedigreed QEF may elect to include in income as a dividend the shareholder's pro rata share of the post-1986 earnings and profits of the PFIC attributable to the stock held on the qualification date (as defined in paragraph (e) of this section), provided the PFIC is a controlled foreign corporation (CFC) within the meaning of section 957(a) for the taxable year for which the shareholder elects under section 1295 to treat the PFIC as a QEF (section 1295 election). If the shareholder makes the deemed dividend election, the PFIC will become a pedigreed QEF with respect to the shareholder. The deemed dividend is taxed under section 1291 as an excess distribution received on the qualification date. The excess distribution determined under this paragraph (a) is allocated under section 1291(a)(1)(A) only to those days in the shareholder's holding period during which the foreign corporation qualified as a PFIC. For purposes of the preceding sentence, the holding period of the PFIC stock with respect to which the election is made ends on the day before the qualification date. For the definitions of PFIC, QEF, unpedigreed QEF, and pedigreed QEF, see paragraph (j)(1) and (2) of this section.

(2) *Post-1986 earnings and profits defined*—(i) *In general*. For purposes of this section, the term post-1986 earnings and profits means the undistributed earnings and profits, within the meaning of section 902(c)(1), as of the day before the qualification date, that were accumulated and not distributed in taxable years of the PFIC beginning after 1986 and during which it was a PFIC, but without regard to whether the earnings relate to a period during which the PFIC was a CFC.

(ii) *Pro rata share of post-1986 earnings and profits attributable to shareholder's stock*—(A) *In general*. A shareholder's pro rata share of the post-1986 earnings and profits of the PFIC attributable to the stock held by the shareholder on the qualification date is the amount of post-1986 earnings and profits of the PFIC accumulated during any portion of the shareholder's holding period ending at the close of the day before the qualification date and attributable, under the principles of section 1248 and the regulations under that section, to the PFIC stock held on the qualification date.

(B) *Reduction for previously taxed amounts*. A shareholder's pro rata share of the post-1986 earnings and profits of the PFIC does not include any amount that the shareholder demonstrates to the satisfaction of the Commissioner (in the manner provided in paragraph (d)(2) of this section) was, pursuant to another provision of

Reg. § 1.1291-0T

the law, previously included in the income of the shareholder, or of another U.S. person if the shareholder's holding period of the PFIC stock includes the period during which the stock was held by that other U.S. person.

(b) *Who may make the election.* A shareholder of an unpedigreed QEF that is a CFC for the taxable year of the PFIC for which the shareholder makes the section 1295 election may make the deemed dividend election provided the shareholder held stock of that PFIC on the qualification date. A shareholder is treated as holding stock of the PFIC on the qualification date if its holding period with respect to that stock under section 1223 includes the qualification date. A shareholder may make the deemed dividend election without regard to whether the shareholder is a United States shareholder within the meaning of section 951(b). A deemed dividend election may be made by a shareholder whose pro rata share of the post-1986 earnings and profits of the PFIC attributable to the PFIC stock held on the qualification date is zero.

(c) *Time for making the election.* The shareholder makes the deemed dividend election in the shareholder's return for the taxable year that includes the qualification date. If the shareholder and the PFIC have the same taxable year, the shareholder makes the deemed dividend election in either the original return for the taxable year for which the shareholder makes the section 1295 election, or in an amended return for that year. If the shareholder and the PFIC have different taxable years, the deemed dividend election must be made in an amended return for the taxable year that includes the qualification date. If the deemed dividend election is made in an amended return, the amended return must be filed by a date that is within three years of the due date, as extended under section 6081, of the original return for the taxable year that includes the qualification date.

(d) *Manner of making the election*—(1) *In general.* A shareholder makes the deemed dividend election by filing Form 8621 and the attachment to Form 8621 described in paragraph (d)(2) of this section with the return for the taxable year of the shareholder that includes the qualification date, reporting the deemed dividend as an excess distribution pursuant to section 1291(a)(1), and paying the tax and interest due on the excess distribution. A shareholder that makes the deemed dividend election after the due date of the return (determined without regard to extensions) for the taxable year that includes the qualification date must pay additional interest, pursuant to section 6601, on the amount of the underpayment of tax for that year.

(2) *Attachment to Form 8621.* The shareholder must attach a schedule to Form 8621 that demonstrates the calculation of the shareholder's pro rata share of the post-1986 earnings and profits of the PFIC that is treated as distributed to the shareholder on the qualification date pursuant to this section. If the shareholder is claiming an exclusion from its pro rata share of the post-1986 earnings and profits for an amount previously included in its income or the income of another U.S. person, the shareholder must include the following information:

(i) The name, address, and taxpayer identification number of each U.S. person that previously included an amount in income, the amount previously included in income by each such U.S. person, the provision of the law pursuant to which the amount was previously included in income, and the taxable year or years of inclusion of each amount; and

(ii) A description of the transaction pursuant to which the shareholder acquired, directly or indirectly, the stock of the PFIC from another U.S. person, and the provisions of law pursuant to which the shareholder's holding period includes the period the other U.S. person held the CFC stock.

(e) *Qualification date*—(1) *In general.* Except as otherwise provided in this paragraph (e), the qualification date is the first day of the PFIC's first taxable year as a QEF (first QEF year).

(2) *Elections made after March 31, 1995, and before January 27, 1997*—(i) *In general.* The qualification date for deemed dividend elections made after March 31, 1995, and before January 27, 1997, is the first day of the shareholder's election year. The shareholder's election year is the taxable year of the shareholder for which it made the section 1295 election.

(ii) *Exception.* A shareholder who made the deemed dividend election after May 1, 1992, and before January 27, 1997, may elect to change its qualification date to the first day of the first QEF year, provided the periods of limitations on assessment for the taxable year that includes that date and for the shareholder's election year have not expired. A shareholder changes the qualification date by filing amended returns, with revised Forms 8621 and the attachments described in paragraph (d)(2) of this section, for the shareholder's election year and the shareholder's taxable year that includes the first day of the first QEF year, and making all appropriate adjustments and payments.

(3) *Examples.* The rules of this paragraph (e) are illustrated by the following examples:

Example 1—(i) *Eligibility to make deemed dividend election.* A is a U.S. person who files its income tax return on a calendar year basis. On January 2, 1994, A purchased one percent of the stock of M, a PFIC with a taxable year ending November 30. M was both a CFC and a PFIC, but not a QEF, for all of its taxable years. On December 3, 1996, M made a distribution to its shareholders. A received $100, all of which A reported in its 1996 return as an excess distribution as provided in section 1291(a)(1). A decides to make the section 1295 election in A's 1997 taxable year to treat M as a QEF effective for M's taxable year beginning December 1, 1996. Because A did not make the section 1295 election in 1994, the first year in its holding period of M stock that M qualified as a PFIC, M would be an unpedigreed QEF and A would be subject to both sections 1291 and 1293. A, however, may elect under section 1291(d)(2) to purge the years M was not a QEF from A's holding period. If A makes the section 1291(d)(2) election, the December 3 distribution will not be taxable under section 1291(a). Because M is a CFC, even though A is not a U.S. shareholder within the meaning of section 951(b), A may make the deemed dividend election under section 1291(d)(2)(B).

(ii) *Making the election.* Under paragraph (e)(1) of this section, the qualification date, and therefore the date of the deemed dividend, is December 1, 1996. Accordingly, to make the deemed dividend election, A must file an amended return for 1996, and include the deemed dividend in income in that year. As a result, M will be a pedigreed QEF as of December 1, 1996, and the December 3, 1996, distribution will not be taxable as an excess distribution. Therefore, in its amended return, A may report the December 3, 1996, distribution consistent with section 1293 and the general rules applicable to corporate distributions.

Example 2. X, a U.S. person, owned a five percent interest in the stock of FC, a PFIC with a taxable year ending June 30. X never made the section 1295 election with respect to FC. X transferred her interest in FC to her granddaughter, Y, a U.S. person, on February 14, 1996. The transfer qualified as a gift for federal income tax purposes, and no gain was recognized on the transfer (see Regulation Project INTL-656-87, published in 1992-1 C.B. 1124; see § 601.601(d)(2)(ii)(*b*) of this chapter). As provided in section 1223(2), Y's holding period includes the period that X held the FC stock. Y decides to make the section 1295 election in her 1996 return to treat FC as a QEF for its taxable year beginning July 1, 1995. However, because Y's holding period includes the period that X held the FC stock, and FC was a PFIC but not a QEF during that period, FC will be an unpedigreed QEF with respect to Y unless Y makes a section 1291(d)(2) election. Although Y did not actually own the stock of FC on the qualification date (July 1, 1995), Y's holding period includes that date. Therefore, provided FC is a CFC for its taxable year beginning July 1, 1995, Y may make a section 1291(d)(2)(B) election to treat FC as a pedigreed QEF.

(f) *Adjustment to basis.* A shareholder that makes the deemed dividend election increases its adjusted basis of the stock of the PFIC owned directly by the shareholder by the amount of the deemed dividend. If the shareholder makes the deemed dividend election with respect to a PFIC of which it is an indirect shareholder, the shareholder's adjusted basis of the stock or other property owned directly by the shareholder, through which ownership of the PFIC is attributed to the shareholder, is increased by the amount of the deemed dividend. In addition, solely for purposes of determining the subsequent treatment under the Code and regulations of a shareholder of the stock of the PFIC, the adjusted basis of the direct owner of the stock of the PFIC is increased by the amount of the deemed dividend.

(g) *Treatment of holding period.* For purposes of applying sections 1291 through 1297 to the shareholder after the deemed dividend, the shareholder's holding period of the stock of the PFIC begins on the qualification date. For other purposes of the Code and regulations, this holding period rule does not apply.

(h) *Coordination with section 959(e).* For purposes of section 959(e), the entire deemed dividend is treated as included in gross income under section 1248(a).

(i) *Election inapplicable to shareholder of former PFIC*—(1) [Reserved].

(2) *Former PFIC.* A shareholder may not make the section 1295 and deemed dividend elections if the foreign corporation is a former PFIC (as defined in paragraph (j)(2)(iv) of this section) with respect to the shareholder. For the rules regarding the election by a shareholder of a former PFIC, see § 1.1297-3T.

(j) *Definitions*—(1) *Passive foreign investment company (PFIC).* A passive foreign investment company (PFIC) is a foreign corporation that satisfies either the income test of section 1296(a)(1) or the asset test of section 1296(a)(2). A corporation will not be treated as a PFIC with respect to a shareholder for those days included in the shareholder's holding period when the shareholder, or a person whose holding period of the stock is included in the shareholder's holding period, was not a United States person within the meaning of section 7701(a)(30).

(2) *Types of PFICs*—(i) *Qualified electing fund (QEF).* A PFIC is a qualified electing fund (QEF) with respect to a shareholder that has elected, under section 1295, to be taxed currently on its share of the PFIC's earnings and profits pursuant to section 1293.

(ii) *Pedigreed QEF.* A PFIC is a pedigreed QEF with respect to a shareholder if the PFIC has been a QEF with respect to the shareholder for all taxable years during which the corporation was a PFIC that are included wholly or partly in the shareholder's holding period of the PFIC stock.

(iii) *Unpedigreed QEF.* A PFIC is an unpedigreed QEF for a taxable year if—

(A) An election under section 1295 is in effect for that year;

(B) The PFIC has been a QEF with respect to the shareholder for at least one, but not all, of the taxable years during which the corporation was a PFIC that are included wholly or partly in the shareholder's holding period of the PFIC stock; and

(C) The shareholder has not made an election under section 1291(d)(2) and this section or § 1.1291-10 with respect to the PFIC to purge the nonQEF years from the shareholder's holding period.

(iv) *Former PFIC.* A foreign corporation is a former PFIC with respect to a shareholder if the corporation satisfies neither the income test of section 1296(a)(1) nor the asset test of section 1296(a)(2), but whose stock, held by that shareholder, is treated as stock of a PFIC, pursuant to section 1297(b)(1), because at any time during the shareholder's holding period of the stock the corporation was a PFIC that was not a QEF.

(3) *Shareholder.* A shareholder is a U.S. person that is a direct or indirect shareholder as defined in Regulation Project INTL-656-87 published in 1992-1 C.B. 1124; see § 601.601(d)(2)(ii)(*b*) of this chapter.

(k) *Effective date.* The rules of this section are applicable as of April 1, 1995. [Reg. § 1.1291-9.]

☐ [T.D. 8701, 12-26-96. Amended by T.D. 8750, 12-31-97.]

[Reg. § 1.1291-10]

§ 1.1291-10. **Deemed sale election.**—(a) *Deemed sale election.* This section provides rules for making the election under section 1291(d)(2)(A) (deemed sale election). Under that section, a shareholder (as defined in § 1.1291-9(j)(3)) of a PFIC that is an unpedigreed QEF may elect to recognize gain with respect to the stock of the unpedigreed QEF held on the qualification date (as defined in paragraph (e) of this section). If the shareholder makes the deemed sale election, the PFIC will become a pedigreed QEF with respect to the shareholder. A shareholder that makes the deemed sale election is treated as having sold, for its fair market value, the stock of the PFIC that the shareholder held on the qualification date. The gain recognized on the deemed sale is taxed under section 1291 as an excess distribution received on the qualification date. In the case of an election made by an indirect shareholder, the amount of gain to be recognized and taxed as an excess distribution is the amount of gain that the direct owner of the stock of the PFIC would have realized on an actual sale or other disposition of the stock of the PFIC indirectly owned by the shareholder. Any loss realized on the deemed sale is not recognized. For the definitions of PFIC, QEF, unpedigreed QEF, and pedigreed QEF, see § 1.1291-9(j)(1) and (2).

(b) *Who may make the election.* A shareholder of an unpedigreed QEF may make the deemed sale election provided the shareholder held stock of that PFIC on the qualification date. A shareholder is treated as holding stock of the PFIC on the qualification date if its holding period with respect to that stock under section 1223 includes the qualification date. A deemed sale election may be made by a shareholder that would realize a loss on the deemed sale.

(c) *Time for making the election.* The shareholder makes the deemed sale election in the shareholder's return for the taxable year that includes the qualification date. If the shareholder and the PFIC have the same taxable year, the shareholder makes the deemed sale election in either the original return for the taxable year for which the shareholder makes the section 1295 election, or in an amended return for that year. If the shareholder and the PFIC have different taxable years, the deemed sale election must be made in an amended return for the taxable year that includes the qualification date. If the deemed sale election is made in an amended return, the amended return must be filed by a date that is within three years of the due date, as extended under section 6081, of the original return for the taxable year that includes the qualification date.

(d) *Manner of making the election.* A shareholder makes the deemed sale election by filing Form 8621 with the return for the taxable year of the shareholder that includes the qualification date, reporting the gain as an excess distribution pursuant to section 1291(a), and paying the tax and interest due on the excess distribution. A shareholder that makes the deemed sale election

Reg. § 1.1291-10(d)

after the due date of the return (determined without regard to extensions) for the taxable year that includes the qualification date must pay additional interest, pursuant to section 6601, on the amount of the underpayment of tax for that year. A shareholder that realizes a loss on the deemed sale reports the loss on Form 8621, but does not recognize the loss.

(e) *Qualification date*—(1) *In general.* Except as otherwise provided in this paragraph (e), the qualification date is the first day of the PFIC's first taxable year as a QEF (first QEF year).

(2) *Elections made after March 31, 1995, and before January 27, 1997*—(i) *In general.* The qualification date for deemed sale elections made after March 31, 1995, and before January 27, 1997, is the first day of the shareholder's election year. The shareholder's election year is the taxable year of the shareholder for which it made the section 1295 election.

(ii) *Exception.* A shareholder who made the deemed sale election after May 1, 1992, and before January 27, 1997, may elect to change its qualification date to the first day of the first QEF year, provided the periods of limitations on assessment for the taxable year that includes that date and for the shareholder's election year have not expired. A shareholder changes the qualification date by filing amended returns, with revised Forms 8621, for the shareholder's election year and the shareholder's taxable year that includes the first day of the first QEF year, and making all appropriate adjustments and payments.

(f) *Adjustments to basis*—(1) *In general.* A shareholder that makes the deemed sale election increases its adjusted basis of the PFIC stock owned directly by the amount of gain recognized on the deemed sale. If the shareholder makes the deemed sale election with respect to a PFIC of which it is an indirect shareholder, the shareholder's adjusted basis of the stock or other property owned directly by the shareholder, through which ownership of the PFIC is attributed to the shareholder, is increased by the amount of gain recognized by the shareholder. In addition, solely for purposes of determining the subsequent treatment under the Code and regulations of a shareholder of the stock of the PFIC, the adjusted basis of the direct owner of the stock of the PFIC is increased by the amount of gain recognized on the deemed sale. A shareholder shall not adjust the basis of any stock with respect to which the shareholder realized a loss on the deemed sale.

(2) *Adjustment of basis for section 1293 inclusion with respect to deemed sale election made after March 31, 1995, and before January 27, 1997.* For purposes of determining the amount of gain recognized with respect to a deemed sale election made after March 31, 1995, and before January 27, 1997, by a shareholder that treats the first day of the shareholder's election year as the qualification date, the adjusted basis of the stock deemed sold includes the shareholder's section 1293(a) inclusion attributable to the period beginning with the first day of the PFIC's first QEF year and ending on the day before the qualification date.

(g) *Treatment of holding period.* For purposes of applying sections 1291 through 1297 to the shareholder after the deemed sale, the shareholder's holding period of the stock of the PFIC begins on the qualification date, without regard to whether the shareholder recognized gain on the deemed sale. For other purposes of the Code and regulations, this holding period rule does not apply.

(h) *Election inapplicable to shareholder of former PFIC.* A shareholder may not make the section 1295 and deemed sale elections if the foreign corporation is a former PFIC (as defined in § 1.1291-9(j)(2)(iv)) with respect to the shareholder. For the rules regarding the election by a shareholder of a former PFIC, see 1.1297-3T.

(i) *Effective date.* The rules of this section are applicable as of April 1, 1995. [Reg. § 1.1291-10.]

☐ [T.D. 8701, 12-26-96.]

[Reg. § 1.1293-0]

§ 1.1293-0. Table of contents.—This section contains a listing of the headings for § 1.1293-1.

§ 1.1293-1. Current inclusion of income of qualified electing funds.

(a) In general. [Reserved].

(1) Other rules. [Reserved].

(2) Net capital gain defined.

(i) In general.

(ii) Effective date.

(b) Other rules. [Reserved].

(c) Application of rules of inclusion with respect to stock held by a pass through entity.

(1) In general.

(2) QEF stock transferred to a pass through entity.

(i) Pass through entity makes a section 1295 election.

(ii) Pass through entity does not make a section 1295 election.

(3) Effective date.

[Reg. § 1.1293-0.]

☐ [T.D. 8750, 12-31-97. Amended by T.D. 8870, 2-4-2000 (*corrected 3-27-2000*).]

Passive Foreign Investment Companies

See p. 20,601 for regulations not amended to reflect law changes

[Reg. § 1.1293-1]

§ 1.1293-1. Current taxation of income from qualified electing funds.—(a) *In general.* [Reserved].

(1) *Other rules.* [Reserved].

(2) *Net capital gain defined*—(i) *In general.* This paragraph (a)(2) defines the term net capital gain for purposes of sections 1293 and 1295 and the regulations under those sections. The QEF, as defined in § 1.1291-9(j)(2)(i), in determining its net capital gain for a taxable year, may either—

(A) Calculate and report the amount of each category of long-term capital gain provided in section 1(h) that was recognized by the PFIC in the taxable year;

(B) Calculate and report the amount of net capital gain recognized by the PFIC in the taxable year, stating that that amount is subject to the highest capital gain rate of tax applicable to the shareholder; or

(C) Calculate its earnings and profits for the taxable year and report the entire amount as ordinary earnings.

(ii) *Effective date.* Paragraph (a)(2)(i) of this section is applicable to sales by QEFs during their taxable years ending on or after May 7, 1997.

(b) *Other rules.* [Reserved].

(c) *Application of rules of inclusion with respect to stock held by a pass through entity*—(1) *In general.* If a domestic pass through entity makes a section 1295 election, as provided in paragraph (d)(2) of this section, with respect to the PFIC shares that it owns, directly or indirectly, the domestic pass through entity takes into account its pro rata share of the ordinary earnings and net capital gain attributable to the QEF shares held by the pass through entity. A U.S. person that indirectly owns QEF shares through the domestic pass through entity accounts for its pro rata shares of ordinary earnings and net capital gain attributable to the QEF shares according to the general rules applicable to inclusions of income from the domestic pass through entity. For the definition of pass through entity, see § 1.1295-1(j).

(2) *QEF stock transferred to a pass through entity*—(i) *Pass through entity makes a section 1295 election.* If a shareholder transfers stock subject to a section 1295 election to a domestic pass through entity of which it is an interest holder and the pass through entity makes a section 1295 election with respect to that stock, as provided in § 1.1295-1(d)(2), the shareholder takes into account its pro rata shares of the ordinary earnings and net capital gain attributable to the QEF shares under the rules applicable to inclusions of income from the pass through entity.

(ii) *Pass through entity does not make a section 1295 election.* If the pass through entity does not make a section 1295 election with respect to the PFIC, the shares of which were transferred to the pass through entity subject to the 1295 election of the shareholder, the shareholder continues to be subject, in its capacity as an indirect shareholder, to the income inclusion rules of section 1293 and reporting rules required of shareholders of QEFs. Proper adjustments to reflect an inclusion in income under section 1293 by the indirect shareholder must be made, under the principles of § 1.1291-9(f), to the basis of the indirect shareholder's interest in the pass through entity.

(3) *Effective date.* Paragraph (c) of this section is applicable to taxable years of shareholders beginning after December 31, 1997. [Reg. § 1.1293-1.]

☐ [T.D. 8750, 12-31-97. Redesignated and amended by T.D. 8870, 2-4-2000.]

[Reg. § 1.1294-0]

§ 1.1294-0. Table of contents.—This section contains a listing of the headings for § 1.1294-1T.

§ 1.1294-1T. Election to extend the time for payment of tax on undistributed earnings of a qualified electing fund.

(a) Purpose and scope.

(b) Election to extend time for payment of tax.

(1) In general.

(2) Exception.

(3) Undistributed earnings.

(i) In general.

(ii) Effect of loan, pledge or guarantee.

(c) Time for making the election.

(1) In general.

(2) Exception.

(d) Manner of making the election.

(1) In general.

(2) Information to be included in the election.

(e) Termination of the extension.

(f) Undistributed PFIC earnings tax liability.

(g) Authority to require a bond.

(h) Annual reporting requirement.

[Reg. § 1.1294-0.]

☐ [T.D. 8750, 12-31-97.]

Passive Foreign Investment Companies

See p. 20,601 for regulations not amended to reflect law changes

[Reg. § 1.1294-1T]

§ 1.1294-1T. Election to extend the time for payment of tax on undistributed earnings of a qualified electing fund (Temporary).—(a) *Purpose and scope.* This section provides rules for making the annual election under section 1294. Under that section, a U.S. person that is a shareholder in a qualified electing fund (QEF) may elect to extend the time for payment of its tax liability which is attributable to its share of the undistributed earnings of the QEF. In general, a QEF is a passive foreign investment company (PFIC), as defined in section 1296, that makes the election under section 1295. Under section 1293, a U.S. person that owns, or is treated as owning, stock of a QEF at any time during the taxable year of the QEF shall include in gross income, as ordinary income, its pro rata share of the ordinary earnings of the QEF for the taxable year and, as long-term capital gain, its pro rata share of the net capital gain of the QEF for the taxable year. The shareholder's share of the earnings shall be included in the shareholder's taxable year in which or with which the taxable year of the QEF ends.

(b) *Election to extend time for payment*—(1) *In general.* A U.S. person that is a shareholder of a QEF on the last day of the QEF's taxable year may elect under section 1294 to extend the time for payment of that portion of its tax liability which is attributable to the inclusion in income pursuant to section 1293 of the shareholder's share of the QEF's undistributed earnings. The election under section 1294 may be made only with respect to undistributed earnings, and interest is imposed under section 6601 on the amount of the tax liability which is subject to the extension. This interest must be paid on the termination of the election.

(2) *Exception.* An election under this § 1.1294-1T cannot be made for a taxable year of the shareholder if any portion of the QEF's earnings is includible in the gross income of the shareholder for such year under either section 551 (relating to foreign personal holding companies) or section 951 (relating to controlled foreign corporations).

(3) *Undistributed earnings*—(i) *In general.* For purposes of this § 1.1294-1T the term "undistributed earnings" means the excess, if any, of the amount includible in gross income by reason of section 1293(a) for the shareholder's taxable year (the includible amount) over the sum of (A) the amount of any distribution to the shareholder during the QEF's taxable year and (B) the portion of the includible amount that is attributable to stock in the QEF that the shareholder transferred or otherwise disposed of before the end of the QEF's year. For purposes of this paragraph, a distribution will be treated as made from the most recently accumulated earnings and profits.

(ii) *Effect of a loan, pledge or guarantee.* A loan, pledge, or guarantee described in § 1.1294-1T(e)(2) or (4) will be treated as a distribution of earnings for purposes of paragraph (b)(3)(i)(A). If earnings are treated as distributed in a taxable year by reason of a loan, pledge or guarantee described in § 1.1294-1T(e)(2) or (4), but the amount of the deemed distribution resulting therefrom was less than the amount of the actual loan by the QEF (or the amount of the loan secured by the pledge or guarantee), earnings derived by the QEF in a subsequent taxable year will be treated as distributed in such subsequent year to the shareholder for purposes of paragraph (b)(3)(i)(A) by virtue of such loan, but only to the extent of the difference between the outstanding principal balance on the loan in such subsequent year and the prior years' deemed distributions resulting from the loan. For this purpose, the outstanding principal balance on a loan in a taxable year shall be treated as equal to the greatest amount of the outstanding balance at any time during such year.

Example (1). (i) *Facts.* FC is a PFIC that made the election under section 1295 to be a QEF for its taxable year beginning January 1, 1987. S owned 500 shares, or 50 percent, of FC throughout the first six months of 1987, but on June 30, 1987 sold 10 percent, or 50 shares, of the FC stock that it held. FC had $100,000x of ordinary earnings but no net capital gain in 1987. No part of FC's earnings is includible in S's income under either section 551 or 951. FC made no distributions to its shareholders in 1987. S's pro rata share of income is determined by attributing FC's income ratably to each day in FC's year. Accordingly, FC's daily earnings are $274x ($100,000x/365). S's share of the earnings of FC is $47,484x, determined as follows.

$$FC\text{'s daily earnings} \times \begin{array}{c}\text{number of days}\\ \text{percentage}\\ \text{held by } S\end{array} \times \begin{array}{c}\text{percentage of}\\ \text{ownership in}\\ FC.\end{array}$$

Accordingly, S's pro rata share of FC's earnings for the first six months of FC's year deemed earned while S held 50 percent of FC's stock is $24,797x ($274x × 181 days × 50%). S's pro rata share of FC's earnings for the remainder of FC's year deemed earned while S held 45 percent of FC's stock is $22,687x ($274x × 184 days × 45%). Therefore, S's total share of FC's earnings to be

Reg. § 1.1294-1T(a)

included in income under section 1293 is $47,484x ($24,797x + $22,687x).

(ii) *Election.* S intends to make the election under section 1294 to defer the payment of its tax liability that is attributable to the undistributed earnings of FC. The amount of current year undistributed earnings as defined in § 1.1294-1T(b)(3) with respect to which S can make the election is the excess of S's inclusion in gross income under section 1293(a) for the taxable year over the sum of (1) the cash and other property distributed to S during FC's tax year out of earnings included in income pursuant to section 1293(a), and (2) the earnings attributable to stock disposed of during FC's tax year. Because S sold 10 percent, or 50 shares, of the FC stock that it held during the first six months of the year, 10 percent of its share of the earnings for that part of the year, which is $2,480x ($24,797x × 10%), is attributable to the shares sold. S therefore cannot make the election under section 1294 to extend the time for payment of its tax liability on that amount. Accordingly, S can make the election under section 1294 with respect to its tax on $45,004x ($47,484x less $2,480x), which is its pro rata share of FC's earnings, reduced by the earnings attributable to the stock disposed of during the year.

Example (2). (i) *Facts.* The facts are the same as in Example (1) with the following exceptions. S did not sell any FC stock during 1987. Therefore, because S held 50 percent of the FC stock throughout 1987, S's pro rata share of FC's ordinary earnings was $50,000x, no part of which was includible in S's income under either section 551 or 951. There were no actual distributions of earnings to S in 1988. On December 31, 1987, S pledged the FC stock as security for a bank loan of $75,000x. The pledge is treated as a disposition of the FC stock and therefore a distribution of S's share of the undistributed earnings of FC up to the amount of the loan principal. S's entire share of the undistributed earnings of FC are deemed distributed as a result of the pledge of the FC stock. S therefore cannot make the election under section 1294 to extend the time for payment of its tax liability on its share of FC's earnings for 1987.

(ii) *Deemed distribution.* In 1988, FC has ordinary earnings of $100,000x but no net capital gain. S's pro rata share of FC's 1988 ordinary earnings was $50,000x. S's loan remained outstanding throughout 1988; the highest loan balance during 1988 was $74,000x. Of S's share of the ordinary earnings of FC of $50,000x, $24,000x is deemed distributed to S. This is the amount by which the highest loan balance for the year ($74,000x) exceeds the portion of the undistributed earnings of FC deemed distributed to S in 1987 by reason of the pledge ($50,000x). S may make the election under section 1294 to extend the time for payment of its tax liability on $26,000x, which is the amount by which S's includible amount for 1988 exceeds the amount deemed distributed to S during 1988.

(c) *Time for making the election*—(1) *In general.* An election under this § 1.1294-1T may be made for any taxable year in which a shareholder reports income pursuant to section 1293. Except as provided in paragraph (c)(2), the election shall be made by the due date, as extended, of the tax return for the shareholder's taxable year for which the election is made.

(2) *Exception.* An election under this section may be made within 60 days of receipt of notification from the QEF of the shareholder's pro rata share of the ordinary earnings and net capital gain if notification is received after the time for filing the election provided in paragraph (c)(1) (and requires the filing of an amended return to report income pursuant to section 1293). If the notification reports an increase in the shareholder's pro rata share of the earnings previously reported to the shareholder by the QEF, the shareholder may make the election under this paragraph (c)(2) only with respect to the amount of such increase.

(d) *Manner of making the election*—(1) *In general.* A shareholder shall make the election by (i) attaching to its return for the year of the election Form 8621 or a statement containing the information and representations required by this section and (ii) filing a copy of Form 8621 or the statement with the Internal Revenue Service Center, P.O. Box 21086, Philadelphia, Pennsylvania 19114.

(2) *Information to be included in the election statement.* If a statement is used in lieu of Form 8621, the statement should be identified, in a heading, as an election under section 1294 of the Code. The statement must include the following information and representations:

(i) The name, address, and taxpayer identification number of the electing shareholder and the taxable year of the shareholder for which the election is being made;

(ii) The name, address and taxpayer identification number of the QEF if provided to the shareholder;

(iii) A statement that the shareholder is making the election under section 1294 of the Code;

(iv) A schedule containing the following information:

Reg. § 1.1294-1T(d)(2)

(A) the ordinary earnings and net capital gain for the current year included in the shareholder's income under section 1293;

(B) the amount of cash and other property distributed by the QEF during its taxable year with respect to stock held directly or indirectly by the shareholder during that year, identifying the amount of such distributions that is paid out of current earnings and profits and the amount paid out of each prior year's earnings and profits; and

(C) the undistributed PFIC earnings tax liability (as defined in paragraph (f) of this section) for the taxable year, payment of which is being deferred by reason of the election under section 1294;

(v) The number of shares of stock held in the QEF during the QEF's taxable year which gave rise to the section 1293 inclusion and the number of such shares transferred, deemed transferred or otherwise disposed of by the electing shareholder before the end of the QEF's taxable year, and the date of transfer; and

(vi) The representations of the electing shareholder that—

(A) No part of the QEF's earnings for the taxable year is includible in the electing shareholder's gross income under either section 551 or 951 of the Code;

(B) The election is made only with respect to the shareholder's pro rata share of the undistributed earnings of the QEF; and

(C) The electing shareholder, upon termination of the election to extend the date for payment, shall pay the undistributed PFIC earnings tax liability attributable to those earnings to which the termination applies as well as interest on such tax liability pursuant to section 6601. Payment of this tax and interest must be made by the due date (determined without extensions) of the tax return for the taxable year in which the termination occurs.

(e) *Termination of the extension.* The election to extend the date for payment of tax will be terminated in whole or in part upon the occurrence of any of the following events:

(1) The QEF's distribution of earnings to which the section 1294 extensic pay tax is attributable; the extension will terminate only with respect to the tax attributable to the earnings that were distributed.

(2) The electing shareholder's transfer of stock in the QEF (or use thereof as security for a loan) with respect to which an election under this § 1.1294-1T was made. The election will be terminated with respect to the undistributed earnings attributable to the shares of the stock transferred. In the case of a pledge of the stock, the election will be terminated with respect to undistributed earnings equal to the amount of the loan for which the stock is pledged.

(3) Revocation of the QEF's election as a QEF or cessation of the QEF's status as a PFIC. A revocation of the QEF election or cessation of PFIC status will result in the complete termination of the extension.

(4) A loan of property by the QEF directly or indirectly to the electing shareholder or related person, or a pledge or guarantee by the QEF with respect to a loan made by another party to the electing shareholder or related person. The election will be terminated with respect to undistributed earnings in an amount equal to the amount of the loan, pledge, or guarantee.

(5) A determination by the District Director pursuant to section 1294(c)(3) that collection of the tax is in jeopardy. The amount of undistributed earnings with respect to which the extension is terminated under this paragraph (d)(5) will be left to the discretion of the District Director.

(f) *Undistributed PFIC earnings tax liability.* The electing shareholder's tax liability attributable to the ordinary earnings and net capital gain included in gross income under section 1293 shall be the excess of the tax imposed under chapter 1 of the Code for the taxable year over the tax that would be imposed for the taxable year without regard to the inclusion in income under section 1293 of the undistributed earnings as defined in paragraph (b)(3) of this section.

Example. The facts are the same as in § 1.1294-1T(b)(3), *Example (1),* with the following exceptions. S, a domestic corporation, did not dispose of any FC stock in 1987. Therefore, because S held 50 percent of the FC stock throughout 1987, S's pro rata share of FC's ordinary earnings was $50,000x. In addition to $50,000x of ordinary earnings from FC, S had $12,500x of domestic source income and $6,000x of expenses (other than interest expense) not definitely related to any gross income. These expenses are apportioned, pursuant to § 1.861-8(c)(2), on a pro rata basis between the domestic and foreign source income—$1,200x of expenses, or one-fifth, to domestic source income, and $4,800x of expenses, or four-fifths, to the section 1293 inclusion. FC paid foreign taxes of $25,000x in 1987. Accordingly, S is entitled to claim as an indirect foreign tax credit pursuant to section 1293(f) a proportionate amount of the foreign taxes paid by FC, which is $12,500x ($25,000x × $50,000x/$100,000x). S is taxed in the U.S. at the rate of 34

Reg. § 1.1294-1T(e)(1)

Passive Foreign Investment Companies

See p. 20,601 for regulations not amended to reflect law changes

percent. The amount for payment is determined as follows:

1987 Tax Liability (with section 1293 inclusion)

Source	U.S.	Foreign
Income	12,500x	0
Section 1293	0	50,000x
Expenses	−1,200x	−4,800x
Taxable income	11,300x	45,200x

Total taxable income	56,500x
U.S. income tax rate	×34%
Pre-credit U.S. tax	19,210x
Foreign tax credit	−12,500x
1987 Tax Liability	6,710x

1987 Tax Liability (without section 1293 inclusion)

Source	U.S.	Foreign
Income	12,500x	0
Expenses	−6,000x	
Taxable income	6,500x	
U.S. tax rate	×34%	
U.S. tax	2,210x	
Foreign tax credit	0	
Hypothetical 1987 Tax Liability	2,210x	

The amount of tax, payment of which S may defer pursuant to section 1294, is $4,500x ($6,710x less $2,210x).

(g) *Authority to require a bond.* Pursuant to the authority granted in section 6165 and in the manner provided therein, and subject to notification, the District Director may require the electing shareholder to furnish a bond to secure payment of the tax, the time for payment of which is extended under this section. If the electing shareholder does not furnish the bond within 60 days after receiving a request from the District Director, the election will be revoked.

(h) *Annual reporting requirement.* The electing shareholder must attach Form 8621 or a statement to its income tax return for each year during which an election under this section is outstanding. The statement must contain the following information: (1) the total amount of undistributed earnings as of the end of the taxable year to which the outstanding elections apply; (2) the total amount of the undistributed PFIC earnings tax liability and accrued interest charge as of the end of the year; (3) the total amount of distributions received during the taxable year; and (4) a description of the occurrence of any other termination event described in paragraph (e) of this section that occurred during the taxable year. The electing shareholder also shall file by the due date, as extended, for its return a copy of Form 8621 or the statement with the Philadelphia Service Center, P.O. Box 21086, Philadelphia, Pennsylvania 19114. [Temporary Reg. § 1.1294-1T.]

☐ [T.D. 8178, 2-26-88.]

[Reg. § 1.1295-0]

§ 1.1295-0. **Table of contents.**—This section contains a listing of the headings for §§ 1.1295-1 and 1.1295-3.

§ 1.1295-1 Qualified electing funds.

(a) In general. [Reserved].

(b) Application of section 1295 election. [Reserved].

(1) Election personal to shareholder. [Reserved].

(2) Election applicable to specific corporation only.

(i) In general. [Reserved].

(ii) Stock of QEF received in a nonrecognition transfer. [Reserved].

(iii) Exception for options.

(3) Application of general rules to stock held by a pass through entity.

(i) Stock subject to a section 1295 election transferred to a pass through entity.

(ii) Limitation on application of pass through entity's section 1295 election.

(iii) Effect of partnership termination on section 1295 election.

(iv) Characterization of stock held through a pass through entity.

(4) Application of general rules to a taxpayer filing a joint return under section 6013.

Reg. § 1.1295-0

53,720 Passive Foreign Investment Companies

See p. 20,601 for regulations not amended to reflect law changes

(c) Effect of section 1295 election.

(1) In general.

(2) Years to which section 1295 election applies.

   (i) In general.

   (ii) Effect of PFIC status on election.

   (iii) Effect on election of complete termination of a shareholder's interest in the PFIC.

   (iv) Effect on section 1295 election of transfer of stock to a domestic pass through entity.

   (v) Examples.

(d) Who may make a section 1295 election.

(1) General rule.

(2) Application of general rule to pass through entities.

   (i) Partnerships.

     (A) Domestic partnership.

     (B) Foreign partnership.

   (ii) S corporation.

   (iii) Trust or estate.

     (A) Domestic trust or estate.

        (*1*) Nongrantor trust or estate.

        (*2*) Grantor trust.

     (B) Foreign trust or estate.

        (*1*) Nongrantor trust or estate.

        (*2*) Grantor trust.

   (iv) Indirect ownership of the pass through entity or the PFIC.

(3) Indirect ownership of a PFIC through other PFICs.

(4) Member of consolidated return group as shareholder.

(5) Option holder.

(6) Exempt organization.

(e) Time for making a section 1295 election.

(1) General rule.

(2) Examples.

(f) Manner of making a section 1295 election and the annual election requirements of the shareholder.

(1) Manner of making the election.

(2) Annual election requirements.

   (i) In general.

   (ii) Retention of documents.

(g) Annual election requirements of the PFIC or intermediary.

(1) PFIC Annual Information Statement.

(2) Alternative documentation.

(3) Annual Intermediary Statement.

(4) Combined statements.

   (i) PFIC Annual Information Statement.

   (ii) Annual Intermediary Statement.

(h) Transition rules.

(i) Invalidation, termination or revocation of section 1295 election.

(1) Invalidation or termination of election at the discretion of the Commissioner.

   (i) In general.

   (ii) Deferral of section 1293 inclusion.

   (iii) When effective.

(2) Shareholder revocation.

   (i) In general.

   (ii) Time for and manner of requesting consent to revoke.

     (A) Time.

     (B) Manner of making request.

   (iii) When effective.

(3) Effect of invalidation, termination, or revocation.

(4) Election after invalidation, termination, or revocation.

(j) Definitions.

(k) Effective date.

§ 1.1295-3 Retroactive elections.

(a) In general.

(b) General rule.

(c) Protective Statement.

(1) In general.

(2) Reasonable belief statement.

(3) Who executes and files the Protective Statement.

(4) Waiver of the periods of limitations.

   (i) Time for and manner of extending periods of limitations.

     (A) In general.

     (B) Application of general rule to domestic partnerships.

        (*1*) In general.

        (*2*) Special rules.

           (*i*) Addition of partner to non-TEFRA partnership.

           (*ii*) Change in status from non-TEFRA partnership to TEFRA partnership.

     (C) Application of general rule to domestic nongrantor trusts and domestic estates.

     (D) Application of general rule to S corporations.

Reg. § 1.1295-0

(E) Effect on waiver of complete termination of a pass through entity or pass through entity's business.

(F) Application of general rule to foreign partnerships, foreign trusts, domestic or foreign grantor trusts, and foreign estates.

(ii) Terms of waiver.

(A) Scope of waiver.

(B) Period of waiver.

(5) Time for and manner of filing a Protective Statement.

(i) In general.

(ii) Special rule for taxable years ended before January 2, 1998.

(6) Applicability of the Protective Statement.

(i) In general.

(ii) Invalidity of the Protective Statement.

(7) Retention of Protective Statement and information demonstrating reasonable belief.

(d) Reasonable belief.

(1) In general.

(2) Knowledge of law required.

(e) Special rules for qualified shareholders.

(1) In general.

(2) Qualified shareholder.

(3) Exceptions.

(f) Special consent.

(1) In general.

(2) Reasonable reliance on a qualified tax professional.

(i) In general.

(ii) Shareholder deemed to have not reasonably relied on a qualified tax professional.

(3) Prejudice to the interests of the United States government.

(i) General rule.

(ii) Elimination of prejudice to the interests of the United States government.

(4) Procedural requirements.

(i) Filing instructions.

(ii) Affidavit from shareholder.

(iii) Affidavits from other persons.

(iv) Other information.

(v) Notification of Internal Revenue Service.

(vi) Who requests special consent under this paragraph (f) and who enters into a closing agreement.

(g) Time for and manner of making a retroactive election.

(1) Time for making a retroactive election.

(i) In general.

(ii) Transition rule.

(iii) Ownership not required at time retroactive election is made.

(2) Manner of making a retroactive election.

(3) Who makes the retroactive election.

(4) Other elections.

(i) Section 1291(d)(2) election.

(ii) Section 1294 election.

(h) Effective date.

[Reg. § 1.1295-0.]

☐ [T.D. 8750, 12-31-97. Amended by T.D. 8870, 2-4-2000.]

[Reg. § 1.1295-1]

§ 1.1295-1. Qualified electing funds.—(a) *In general.* [Reserved].

(b) *Application of section 1295 election.* [Reserved].

(1) *Election personal to shareholder.* [Reserved].

(2) *Election applicable to specific corporation only*—

(i) *In general.* [Reserved].

(ii) *Stock of QEF received in a nonrecognition transfer.* [Reserved].

(iii) *Exception for options.* A shareholder's section 1295 election does not apply to any option to buy stock of the PFIC.

(3) *Application of general rules to stock held by a pass through entity*—(i) *Stock subject to a section 1295 election transferred to a pass through entity.* A shareholder's section 1295 election will not apply to a domestic pass through entity to which the shareholder transfers stock subject to a section 1295 election, or to any other U.S. person that is an interest holder or beneficiary of the domestic pass through entity. However, as provided in paragraph (c)(2)(iv) of this section (relating to a transfer to a domestic pass through entity of stock subject to a section 1295 election), a shareholder that transfers stock subject to a section 1295 election to a pass through entity will continue to be subject to the section 1295 election with respect to the stock indirectly owned through the pass through entity and any other stock of that PFIC owned by the shareholder.

(ii) *Limitation on application of pass through entity's section 1295 election.* Except as provided in paragraph (c)(2)(iv) of this section, a section 1295 election made by a domestic pass through entity does not apply to other stock of the

Reg. § 1.1295-1(b)(3)

PFIC held directly or indirectly by the interest holder or beneficiary.

(iii) *Effect of partnership termination on section 1295 election.* Termination of a section 1295 election made by a domestic partnership by reason of the termination of the partnership under section 708(b) will not terminate the section 1295 election with respect to partners of the terminated partnership that are partners of the new partnership. Except as otherwise provided, the stock of the PFIC of which the new partners are indirect shareholders will be treated as stock of a QEF only if the new domestic partnership makes a section 1295 election with respect to that stock.

(iv) *Characterization of stock held through a pass through entity.* Stock of a PFIC held through a pass through entity will be treated as stock of a pedigreed QEF with respect to an interest holder or beneficiary only if—

(A) In the case of PFIC stock acquired (other than in a transaction in which gain is not recognized pursuant to regulations under section 1291(f) with respect to that stock) and held by a domestic pass through entity, the pass through entity makes the section 1295 election and the PFIC has been a QEF with respect to the pass through entity for all taxable years that are included wholly or partly in the pass through entity's holding period of the PFIC stock and during which the foreign corporation was a PFIC within the meaning of § 1.1291-9(j)(1); or

(B) In the case of PFIC stock transferred by an interest holder or beneficiary to a pass through entity in a transaction in which gain is not fully recognized (including pursuant to regulations under section 1291(f)), the pass through entity makes the section 1295 election with respect to the PFIC stock transferred for the taxable year in which the transfer was made. The PFIC stock transferred will be treated as stock of a pedigreed QEF by the pass through entity, however, only if that stock was treated as stock of a pedigreed QEF with respect to the interest holder or beneficiary at the time of the transfer, and the PFIC has been a QEF with respect to the pass through entity for all taxable years of the PFIC that are included wholly or partly in the pass through entity's holding period of the PFIC stock during which the foreign corporation was a PFIC within the meaning of § 1.1291-9(j).

(v) *Characterization of stock distributed by a partnership.* In the case of PFIC stock distributed by a partnership to a partner in a transaction in which gain is not fully recognized, the PFIC stock will be treated as stock of a pedigreed QEF by the partners only if that stock was treated as stock of a pedigreed QEF with respect to the partnership for all taxable years of the PFIC that are included wholly or partly in the partnership's holding period of the PFIC stock during which the foreign corporation was a PFIC within the meaning of § 1.1291-9(j), and the partner has a section 1295 election in effect with respect to the distributed PFIC stock for the partner's taxable year in which the distribution was made. If the partner does not have a section 1295 election in effect, the stock shall be treated as stock in a section 1291 fund. See paragraph (k) of this section for special applicability date of paragraph (b)(3)(v) of this section.

(4) *Application of general rules to a taxpayer filing a joint return under section 6013.* A section 1295 election made by a taxpayer in a joint return, within the meaning of section 6013, will be treated as also made by the spouse that joins in the filing of that return. See paragraph (k) of this section for special applicability date of paragraph (b)(4) of this section.

(c) *Effect of section 1295 election*—(1) *In general.* Except as otherwise provided in this paragraph (c), the effect of a shareholder's section 1295 election is to treat the foreign corporation as a QEF with respect to the shareholder for each taxable year of the foreign corporation ending with or within a taxable year of the shareholder for which the election is effective. A section 1295 election is effective for the shareholder's election year and all subsequent taxable years of the shareholder unless invalidated, terminated or revoked as provided in paragraph (i) of this section. The terms shareholder and shareholder's election year are defined in paragraph (j) of this section.

(2) *Years to which section 1295 election applies*—(i) *In general.* Except as otherwise provided in this paragraph (c), a foreign corporation with respect to which a section 1295 election is made will be treated as a QEF for its taxable year ending with or within the shareholder's election year and all subsequent taxable years of the foreign corporation that are included wholly or partly in the shareholder's holding period (or periods) of stock of the foreign corporation.

(ii) *Effect of PFIC status on election.* A foreign corporation will not be treated as a QEF for any taxable year of the foreign corporation that the foreign corporation is not a PFIC under section 1297(a) and is not treated as a PFIC under section 1298(b)(1). Therefore, a shareholder shall not be required to include pursuant to section 1293 the shareholder's pro rata share of ordinary earnings and net capital gain for such year and shall not be required to satisfy the section 1295 annual reporting requirement of paragraph (f)(2) of this section for such year. Cessation of a

Reg. § 1.1295-1(b)(4)

foreign corporation's status as a PFIC will not, however, terminate a section 1295 election. Thus, if the foreign corporation is a PFIC in any taxable year after a year in which it is not treated as a PFIC, the shareholder's original election under section 1295 continues to apply and the shareholder must take into account its pro rata share of ordinary earnings and net capital gain for such year and comply with the section 1295 annual reporting requirement.

(iii) *Effect on election of complete termination of a shareholder's interest in the PFIC.* Complete termination of a shareholder's direct and indirect interest in stock of a foreign corporation will not terminate a shareholder's section 1295 election with respect to the foreign corporation. Therefore, if a shareholder reacquires a direct or indirect interest in any stock of the foreign corporation, that stock is considered to be stock for which an election under section 1295 has been made and the shareholder is subject to the income inclusion and reporting rules required of a shareholder of a QEF.

(iv) *Effect on section 1295 election of transfer of stock to a domestic pass through entity.* The transfer of a shareholder's direct or indirect interest in stock of a foreign corporation to a domestic pass through entity (as defined in paragraph (j) of this section) will not terminate the shareholder's section 1295 election with respect to the foreign corporation, whether or not the pass through entity makes a section 1295 election. For the rules concerning the application of section 1293 to stock transferred to a domestic pass through entity, see § 1.1293-1(c).

(v) *Examples.* The following examples illustrate the rules of this paragraph (c)(2).

Example 1. In 1998, C, a U.S. person, purchased stock of FC, a foreign corporation that is a PFIC. Both FC and C are calendar year taxpayers. C made a timely section 1295 election to treat FC as a QEF in C's 1998 return, and FC was therefore a pedigreed QEF. C included its shares of FC's 1998 ordinary earnings and net capital gain in C's 1998 income and did not make a section 1294 election to defer the time for payment of tax on that income. In 1999, 2000, and 2001, FC did not satisfy either the income or asset test of section 1296(a), and therefore was neither a PFIC nor a QEF. C therefore did not have to include its pro rata shares of the ordinary earnings and net capital gain of FC pursuant to section 1293, or satisfy the section 1295 annual reporting requirements for any of those years. FC qualified as a PFIC again in 2002. Because C had made a section 1295 election in 1998, and the election had not been invalidated, terminated, or revoked, within the meaning of paragraph (i) of this section, C's section 1295 election remains in effect for 2002. C therefore is subject in 2002 to the income inclusion and reporting rules required of shareholders of QEFs.

Example 2. The facts are the same as in Example (1) except that FC did not lose PFIC status in any year and C sold all the FC stock in 1999 and repurchased stock of FC in 2002. Because C had made a section 1295 election in 1998 with respect to stock of FC, and the election had not been invalidated, terminated, or revoked, within the meaning of paragraph (i) of this section, C's section 1295 election remained in effect and therefore applies to the stock of FC purchased by C in 2002. C therefore is subject in 2002 to the income inclusion and reporting rules required of shareholders of QEFs.

Example 3. The facts are the same as in Example (2) except that C is a partner in domestic partnership P and C transferred its FC stock to P in 1999. Because C had made a section 1295 election in 1998 with respect to stock of FC, and the election had not been invalidated, terminated, or revoked, within the meaning of paragraph (i) of this section, C's section 1295 election remains in effect with respect to its indirect interest in the stock of FC. If P does not make the section 1295 election with respect to the FC stock, C will continue to be subject, in C's capacity as an indirect shareholder of FC, to the income inclusion and reporting rules required of shareholders of QEFs in 1999 and subsequent years for that portion of the FC stock C is treated as owning indirectly through the partnership. If P makes the section 1295 election, C will take into account its pro rata shares of the ordinary earnings and net capital gain of the FC under the rules applicable to inclusions of income from P.

(d) *Who may make a section 1295 election*—(1) *General rule.* Except as otherwise provided in this paragraph (d), any U.S. person that is a shareholder (as defined in paragraph (j) of this section) of a PFIC, including a shareholder that holds stock of a PFIC in bearer form, may make a section 1295 election with respect to that PFIC. The shareholder need not own directly or indirectly any stock of the PFIC at the time the shareholder makes the section 1295 election provided the shareholder is a shareholder of the PFIC during the taxable year of the PFIC that ends with or within the taxable year of the shareholder for which the section 1295 election is made. Except in the case of a shareholder that is an exempt organization that may not make a section 1295 election, as provided in paragraph (d)(6) of this section, in a chain of ownership only the first U.S.

person that is a shareholder of the PFIC may make the section 1295 election.

(2) *Application of general rule to pass through entities*—(i) *Partnerships*—(A) *Domestic partnership.* A domestic partnership that holds an interest in stock of a PFIC makes the section 1295 election with respect to that PFIC. The partnership election applies only to the stock of the PFIC held directly or indirectly by the partnership and not to any other stock held directly or indirectly by any partner. As provided in § 1.1293-1(c)(1), shareholders owning stock of a QEF by reason of an interest in the partnership take into account the section 1293 inclusions with respect to the QEF shares owned by the partnership under the rules applicable to inclusions of income from the partnership.

(B) *Foreign partnership.* A U.S. person that holds an interest in a foreign partnership that, in turn, holds an interest in stock of a PFIC makes the section 1295 election with respect to that PFIC. A partner's election applies to the stock of the PFIC owned directly or indirectly by the foreign partnership and to any other stock of the PFIC owned by that partner. A section 1295 election by a partner applies only to that partner.

(ii) *S corporation.* An S corporation that holds an interest in stock of a PFIC makes the section 1295 election with respect to that PFIC. The S corporation election applies only to the stock of the PFIC held directly or indirectly by the S corporation and not to any other stock held directly or indirectly by any S corporation shareholder. As provided in § 1.1293-1(c)(1), shareholders owning stock of a QEF by reason of an interest in the S corporation take into account the section 1293 inclusions with respect to the QEF shares under the rules applicable to inclusions of income from the S corporation.

(iii) *Trust or estate*—(A) *Domestic trust or estate*—(*1*) *Nongrantor trust or estate.* A domestic nongrantor trust or a domestic estate that holds an interest in stock of a PFIC makes the section 1295 election with respect to that PFIC. The trust or estate's election applies only to the stock of the PFIC held directly or indirectly by the trust or estate and not to any other stock held directly or indirectly by any beneficiary. As provided in § 1.1293-1(c)(1), shareholders owning stock of a QEF by reason of an interest in a domestic trust or estate take into account the section 1293 inclusions with respect to the QEF shares under the rules applicable to inclusions of income from the trust or estate.

(*2*) *Grantor trust.* A U.S. person that is treated under sections 671 through 678 as the owner of the portion of a domestic trust that owns an interest in stock of a PFIC makes the section 1295 election with respect to that PFIC. If that person ceases to be treated as the owner of the portion of the trust that owns an interest in the PFIC stock and is a beneficiary of the trust, that person's section 1295 election will continue to apply to the PFIC stock indirectly owned by that person under the rules of paragraph (c)(2)(iv) of this section as if the person had transferred its interest in the PFIC stock to the trust. However, the stock will be treated as stock of a PFIC that is not a QEF with respect to other beneficiaries of the trust, unless the trust makes the section 1295 election as provided in paragraph (d)(2)(iii)(A)(*1*) of this section.

(B) *Foreign trust or estate*—(*1*) *Nongrantor trust or estate.* A U.S. person that is a beneficiary of a foreign nongrantor trust or estate that holds an interest in stock of a PFIC makes the section 1295 election with respect to that PFIC. A beneficiary's section 1295 election applies to all the PFIC stock owned directly and indirectly by the trust or estate and to the other PFIC stock owned directly or indirectly by the beneficiary. A section 1295 election by a beneficiary applies only to that beneficiary.

(*2*) *Grantor trust.* A U.S. person that is treated under sections 671 through 679 as the owner of the portion of a foreign trust that owns an interest in stock of a PFIC stock makes the section 1295 election with respect to that PFIC. If that person ceases to be treated as the owner of the portion of the trust that owns an interest in the PFIC stock and is a beneficiary of the trust, that person's section 1295 election will continue to apply to the PFIC stock indirectly owned by that person under the rules of paragraph (c)(2)(iv) of this section. However, as provided in paragraph (d)(2)(iii)(B)(*1*) of this section, any other shareholder that is a beneficiary of the trust and that wishes to treat the PFIC as a QEF must make the section 1295 election.

(iv) *Indirect ownership of the pass through entity or the PFIC.* The rules of this paragraph (d)(2) apply whether or not the shareholder holds its interest in the pass through entity directly or indirectly and whether or not the pass through entity holds its interest in the PFIC directly or indirectly.

(3) *Indirect ownership of a PFIC through other PFICs* —(i) *In general.* An election under section 1295 shall apply only to the foreign corporation for which an election is made. Therefore, if a shareholder makes an election under section 1295 to treat a PFIC as a QEF, that election applies only to stock in that foreign corporation and not to the stock in any other corporation

Reg. § 1.1295-1(d)(2)

which the shareholder is treated as owning by virtue of its ownership of stock in the QEF.

(ii) *Example.* The following example illustrates the rules of paragraph (d)(3)(i) of this section:

Example. In 1988, T, a U.S. person, purchased stock of FC, a foreign corporation that is a PFIC. FC also owns the stock of SC, a foreign corporation that is a PFIC. T makes an election under section 1295 to treat FC as a QEF. T's section 1295 election applies only to the stock T owns in FC, and does not apply to the stock T indirectly owns in SC.

(4) *Member of consolidated return group as shareholder.* Pursuant to § 1.1502-77(a), the common parent of an affiliated group of corporations that join in filing a consolidated income tax return makes a section 1295 election for all members of the affiliated group. An election by a common parent will be effective for all members of the affiliated group with respect to interests in PFIC stock held at the time the election is made or at any time thereafter. A separate election must be made by the common parent for each PFIC of which a member of the affiliated group is a shareholder.

(5) *Option holder.* A holder of an option to acquire stock of a PFIC may not make a section 1295 election that will apply to the option or to the stock subject to the option.

(6) *Exempt organization.* A tax-exempt organization that is not taxable under section 1291, pursuant to § 1.1291-1(e), with respect to a PFIC may not make a section 1295 election with respect to that PFIC. In addition, such an exempt organization will not be subject to any section 1295 election made by a domestic pass through entity.

(e) *Time for making a section 1295 election*—(1) *In general.* Except as provided in § 1.1295-3, a shareholder making the section 1295 election must make the election on or before the due date, as extended under section 6081 (election due date), for filing the shareholder's income tax return for the first taxable year to which the election will apply. The section 1295 election must be made in the original return for that year, or in an amended return, provided the amended return is filed on or before the election due date.

(2) *Examples.* The following examples illustrate the rules of paragraph (e)(1) of this section:

Example 1. In 1998, C, a domestic corporation, purchased stock of FC, a foreign corporation that is a PFIC. Both C and FC are calendar year taxpayers. C wishes to make the section 1295 election for its taxable year ended December 31, 1998. The section 1295 election must be made on or before March 15, 1999, the due date of C's 1998 income tax return as provided by section 6072(b). On March 14, 1999, C files a request for a three-month extension of time to file its 1998 income tax return under section 6081(b). C's time to file its 1998 income tax return and to make the section 1295 election is thereby extended to June 15, 1999.

Example 2. The facts are the same as in *Example 1* except that on May 1, 1999, C filed its 1998 income tax return and failed to include the section 1295 election. C may file an amended income tax return for 1998 to make the section 1295 election provided the amended return is filed on or before the extended due date of June 15, 1999.

(f) *Manner of making a section 1295 election and the annual election requirements of the shareholder*—(1) *Manner of making the election.* A shareholder must make a section 1295 election by—

(i) Completing Form 8621 in the manner required by that form and this section for making the section 1295 election;

(ii) Attaching Form 8621 to its federal income tax return filed by the election due date for the shareholder's election year; and

(iii) Receiving and reflecting in Form 8621 the information provided in the PFIC Annual Information Statement described in paragraph (g)(1) of this section, the Annual Intermediary Statement described in paragraph (g)(3) of this section, or the applicable combined statement described in paragraph (g)(4) of this section, for the taxable year of the PFIC ending with or within the taxable year for which Form 8621 is being filed. If the PFIC Annual Information Statement contains a statement described in paragraph (g)(1)(ii)(C) of this section, the shareholder must attach a statement to Form 8621 that indicates that the shareholder rather than the PFIC calculated the PFIC's ordinary earnings and net capital gain.

(2) *Annual election requirements*—(i) *In general.* A shareholder that makes a section 1295 election with respect to a PFIC held directly or indirectly, for each taxable year to which the section 1295 election applies, must—

(A) Complete Form 8621 in the manner required by that form and this section;

(B) Attach Form 8621 to its federal income tax return filed by the due date of the return, as extended; and

(C) Receive and reflect in Form 8621 the PFIC Annual Information Statement described in paragraph (g)(1) of this section, the

Reg. § 1.1295-1(f)(2)

Annual Intermediary Statement described in paragraph (g)(3) of this section, or the applicable combined statement described in paragraph (g)(4) of this section, for the taxable year of the PFIC ending with or within the taxable year for which Form 8621 is being filed. If the PFIC Annual Information Statement contains a statement described in paragraph (g)(1)(ii)(C) of this section, the shareholder must attach a statement to its Form 8621 that the shareholder rather than the PFIC provided the calculations of the PFIC's ordinary earnings and net capital gain.

(ii) *Retention of documents.* For all taxable years subject to the section 1295 election, the shareholder must retain copies of all Forms 8621, with their attachments, and PFIC Annual Information Statements or Annual Intermediary Statements. Failure to produce those documents at the request of the Commissioner in connection with an examination may result in invalidation or termination of the shareholder's section 1295 election.

(3) *Effective date.* See paragraph (k) of this section for special applicability date of paragraph (f) of this section.

(g) *Annual election requirements of the PFIC or intermediary*—(1) *PFIC Annual Information Statement.* For each year of the PFIC ending in a taxable year of a shareholder to which the shareholder's section 1295 election applies, the PFIC must provide the shareholder with a PFIC Annual Information Statement. The PFIC Annual Information Statement is a statement of the PFIC, signed by the PFIC or an authorized representative of the PFIC, that contains the following information and representations—

(i) The first and last days of the taxable year of the PFIC to which the PFIC Annual Information Statement applies;

(ii) Either—

(A) The shareholder's pro rata shares of the ordinary earnings and net capital gain (as defined in § 1.1293-1(a)(2)) of the PFIC for the taxable year indicated in paragraph (g)(1)(i) of this section; or

(B) Sufficient information to enable the shareholder to calculate its pro rata shares of the PFIC's ordinary earnings and net capital gain, for that taxable year; or

(C) A statement that the foreign corporation has permitted the shareholder to examine the books of account, records, and other documents of the foreign corporation for the shareholder to calculate the amounts of the PFIC's ordinary earnings and the net capital gain according to federal income tax accounting principles and to calculate the shareholder's pro rata shares of the PFIC's ordinary earnings and net capital gain;

(iii) The amount of cash and the fair market value of other property distributed or deemed distributed to the shareholder during the taxable year of the PFIC to which the PFIC Annual Information Statement pertains; and

(iv) Either—

(A) A statement that the PFIC will permit the shareholder to inspect and copy the PFIC's permanent books of account, records, and such other documents as may be maintained by the PFIC to establish that the PFIC's ordinary earnings and net capital gain are computed in accordance with U.S. income tax principles, and to verify these amounts and the shareholder's pro rata shares thereof; or

(B) In lieu of the statement required in paragraph (g)(1)(iv)(A) of this section, a description of the alternative documentation requirements approved by the Commissioner, with a copy of the private letter ruling and the closing agreement entered into by the Commissioner and the PFIC pursuant to paragraph (g)(2) of this section.

(2) *Alternative documentation.* In rare and unusual circumstances, the Commissioner will consider alternative documentation requirements necessary to verify the ordinary earnings and net capital gain of a PFIC other than the documentation requirements described in paragraph (g)(1)(iv)(A) of this section. Alternative documentation requirements will be allowed only pursuant to a private letter ruling and a closing agreement entered into by the Commissioner and the PFIC describing an alternative method of verifying the PFIC's ordinary earnings and net capital gain. If the PFIC has not obtained a private letter ruling from the Commissioner approving an alternative method of verifying the PFIC's ordinary earnings and net capital gain by the time a shareholder is required to make a section 1295 election, the shareholder may not use an alternative method for that taxable year.

(3) *Annual Intermediary Statement.* In the case of a U.S. person that is an indirect shareholder of a PFIC that is owned through an intermediary, as defined in paragraph (j) of this section, an Annual Intermediary Statement issued by an intermediary containing the information described in paragraph (g)(1) of this section and reporting the indirect shareholder's pro rata share of the ordinary earnings and net capital gain of the QEF as described in paragraph (g)(1)(ii)(A) of this section, may be provided to the indirect shareholder in lieu of the PFIC Annual Informa-

Reg. § 1.1295-1(f)(3)

Passive Foreign Investment Companies 53,727
See p. 20,601 for regulations not amended to reflect law changes

tion Statement if the following conditions are satisfied—

(i) The intermediary receives a copy of the PFIC Annual Information Statement or the intermediary receives an annual intermediary statement from another intermediary which contains a statement that the other intermediary has received a copy of the PFIC Annual Information Statement and represents that the conditions of paragraphs (g)(3)(ii) and (g)(3)(iii) of this section are met;

(ii) The representations and information contained in the Annual Intermediary Statement reflect the representations and information contained in the PFIC Annual Information Statement; and

(iii) The PFIC Annual Information Statement issued to the intermediary contains either the representation set forth in paragraph (g)(1)(iv)(A) of this section, or, if alternative documentation requirements were approved by the Commissioner pursuant to paragraph (g)(2) of this section, a copy of the private letter ruling and closing agreement between the Commissioner and the PFIC, agreeing to an alternative method of verifying PFIC ordinary earnings and net capital gain as described in paragraph (g)(2) of this section;

(4) *Combined statements*—(i) *PFIC Annual Information Statement.* A PFIC that owns directly or indirectly any stock of one or more PFICs with respect to which a shareholder may make the section 1295 election may prepare a PFIC Annual Information Statement that combines with its own information and representations the information and representations of all the PFICs. The PFIC may use any format for a combined PFIC Annual Information Statement provided the required information and representations are separately stated and identified with the respective corporations.

(ii) *Annual Intermediary Statement.* An intermediary described in paragraph (g)(3) of this section that owns directly or indirectly stock of one or more PFICs with respect to which an indirect shareholder may make the section 1295 election may prepare an Annual Intermediary Statement that combines with its own information and representations the information and representations with respect to all the PFICs. The intermediary may use any format for a combined Annual Intermediary Statement provided the required information and representations are separately stated and identified with the intermediary and the respective corporations.

(5) *Effective date.* See paragraph (k) of this section for special applicability date of paragraph (g) of this section.

(h) *Transition rules.* Taxpayers may rely on Notice 88-125 (1988-2 C.B. 535) (see § 601.601(d)(2) of this chapter), for rules on making and maintaining elections for shareholder election years (as defined in paragraph (j) of this section) beginning after December 31, 1986, and before January 1, 1998. Elections made under Notice 88-125 must be maintained as provided in § 1.1295-1 for taxable years beginning after December 31, 1997. A section 1295 election made prior to February 2, 1998, that was intended to be effective for the taxable year of the PFIC that began during the shareholder's election year will be effective for that taxable year of the foreign corporation provided that it is clear from all the facts and circumstances that the shareholder intended the election to be effective for that taxable year of the foreign corporation.

(i) *Invalidation, termination, or revocation of section 1295 election*—(1) *Invalidation or termination of election at the discretion of the Commissioner*—(i) *In general.* The Commissioner, in the Commissioner's discretion, may invalidate or terminate a section 1295 election applicable to a shareholder if the shareholder, the PFIC, or any intermediary fails to satisfy the requirements for making a section 1295 election or the annual election requirements of this section to which the shareholder, PFIC, or intermediary is subject, including the requirement to provide, on request, copies of the books and records of the PFIC or other documentation substantiating the ordinary earnings and net capital gain of the PFIC.

(ii) *Deferral of section 1293 inclusion.* The Commissioner may invalidate any pass through entity section 1295 election with respect to an interest holder or beneficiary if the section 1293 inclusion with respect to that interest holder or beneficiary is not included in the gross income of either the pass through entity, an intermediate pass through entity, or the interest holder or beneficiary within two years of the end of the PFIC's taxable year due to nonconforming taxable years of the interest holder and the pass through entity or any intermediate pass through entity.

(iii) *When effective.* Termination of a shareholder's section 1295 election will be effective for the taxable year of the PFIC determined by the Commissioner in the Commissioner's discretion. An invalidation of a shareholder's section 1295 election will be effective for the first taxable year to which the section 1295 election applied, and the shareholder whose election is invalidated

Reg. § 1.1295-1(i)(1)

will be treated as if the section 1295 election was never made.

(2) *Shareholder revocation*—(i) *In general*. In the Commissioner's discretion, upon a finding of a substantial change in circumstances, the Commissioner may consent to a shareholder's request to revoke a section 1295 election. Request for revocation must be made by the shareholder that made the election and at the time and in the manner provided in paragraph (i)(2)(ii) of this section.

(ii) *Time for and manner of requesting consent to revoke*—(A) *Time.* The shareholder must request consent to revoke the section 1295 election no later than 12 calendar months after the discovery of the substantial change of circumstances that forms the basis for the shareholder's request to revoke the section 1295 election.

(B) *Manner of making request.* A shareholder requests consent to revoke a section 1295 election by filing a ruling request with the Office of the Associate Chief Counsel (International). The ruling request must satisfy the requirements, including payment of the user fee, for filing ruling requests with that office.

(iii) *When effective.* Unless otherwise determined by the Commissioner, revocation of a section 1295 election will be effective for the first taxable year of the PFIC beginning after the date the Commissioner consents to the revocation.

(3) *Effect of invalidation, termination, or revocation.* An invalidation, termination, or revocation of a section 1295 election—

(i) Terminates all section 1294 elections, as provided in § 1.1294-1T(e), and the undistributed PFIC earnings tax liability and interest thereon are due by the due date, without regard to extensions, for the return for the last taxable year of the shareholder to which the section 1295 election applies;

(ii) In the Commissioner's discretion, results in a deemed sale of the QEF stock on the last day of the PFIC's last taxable year as a QEF, in which gain, but not loss, will be recognized and with respect to which appropriate basis and holding period adjustments will be made; and

(iii) Subjects the shareholder to any other terms and conditions that the Commissioner determines are necessary to ensure the shareholder's compliance with sections 1291 through 1298 or any other provisions of the Code.

(4) *Election after invalidation, termination, or revocation.* Without the Commissioner's consent a shareholder whose section 1295 election was invalidated, terminated, or revoked under this paragraph (i) may not make the section 1295 election with respect to the PFIC before the sixth taxable year ending after the taxable year in which the invalidation, termination, or revocation became effective.

(j) *Definitions.* For purposes of this section—

Intermediary is a nominee or shareholder of record that holds stock on behalf of the shareholder or on behalf of another person in a chain of ownership between the shareholder and the PFIC, and any direct or indirect beneficial owner of PFIC stock (including a beneficial owner that is a pass through entity) in the chain of ownership between the shareholder and the PFIC.

Pass through entity is a partnership, S corporation, trust, or estate.

Shareholder has the same meaning as the term shareholder in § 1.1291-9(j)(3), except that for purposes of this section, a partnership and an S corporation also are treated as shareholders. Furthermore, unless otherwise provided, an interest holder of a pass through entity, which is treated as a shareholder of a PFIC, also will be treated as a shareholder of the PFIC.

Shareholder's election year is the taxable year of the shareholder for which it made the section 1295 election.

(k) *Effective dates.* Paragraphs (b)(2)(iii), (b)(3), (b)(4) and (c) through (j) of this section are applicable to taxable years of shareholders beginning after December 31, 1997. However, taxpayers may apply the rules under paragraphs (b)(4), (f) and (g) of this section to a taxable year beginning before January 1, 1998, provided the statute of limitations on the assessment of tax has not expired as of April 27, 1998 and, in the case of paragraph (b)(4) of this section, the taxpayers who filed the joint return have consistently applied the rules of that section to all taxable years following the year the election was made. Paragraph (b)(3)(v) of this section is applicable as of February 7, 2000, however a taxpayer may apply the rules to a taxable year prior to the applicable date provided the statute of limitations on the assessment of tax for that taxable year has not expired. [Reg. § 1.1295-1.]

☐ [T.D. 8750, 12-31-97. Redesignated and amended by T.D. 8870, 2-4-2000.]

[Reg. § 1.1295-3]

§ 1.1295-3. Retroactive elections.—(a) *In general.* This section prescribes the exclusive rules under which a shareholder, as defined in § 1.1295-1(j), may make a section 1295 election for a taxable year after the election due date, as defined in § 1.1295-1(e) (retroactive election). Therefore, a shareholder may not seek such relief under any other provision of the law, including

§ 301.9100 of this chapter. Paragraph (b) of this section describes the general rules for a shareholder to preserve the ability to make a retroactive election. These rules require that the shareholder possess reasonable belief as of the election due date that the foreign corporation was not a PFIC for its taxable year that ended in the shareholder's taxable year to which the election due date pertains, and that the shareholder file a Protective Statement to preserve its ability to make a retroactive election. Paragraph (c) of this section establishes the terms, conditions and other requirements with respect to a Protective Statement required to be filed under the general rules. Paragraph (d) of this section sets forth factors that establish a shareholder's reasonable belief that a foreign corporation was not a PFIC. Paragraph (e) of this section prescribes special rules for certain shareholders that are deemed to satisfy the reasonable belief requirement and therefore are not required to file a Protective Statement. Paragraph (f) of this section describes the limited circumstances under which the Commissioner may permit a shareholder that lacked the requisite reasonable belief or failed to satisfy the requirements of paragraph (b) or (e) of this section to make a retroactive election. Paragraph (g) of this section provides the time for and manner of making a retroactive election. Paragraph (h) of this section provides the effective date of this section.

(b) *General rule.* Except as provided in paragraphs (e) and (f) of this section, a shareholder may make a retroactive election for a taxable year of the shareholder (retroactive election year) only if the shareholder—

(1) Reasonably believed, within the meaning of paragraph (d) of this section, that as of the election due date, as defined in § 1.1295-1(e), the foreign corporation was not a PFIC for its taxable year that ended during the retroactive election year;

(2) Filed a Protective Statement with respect to the foreign corporation, applicable to the retroactive election year, in which the shareholder described the basis for its reasonable belief and extended, in the manner provided in paragraph (c)(4) of this section, the periods of limitations on the assessment of taxes determined under sections 1291 through 1298 with respect to the foreign corporation (PFIC related taxes) for all taxable years of the shareholder to which the Protective Statement applies; and

(3) Complied with the other terms and conditions of the Protective Statement.

(c) *Protective Statement*—(1) *In general.* A Protective Statement is a statement executed under penalties of perjury by the shareholder, or a person authorized to sign a federal income tax return on behalf of the shareholder, that preserves the shareholder's ability to make a retroactive election. To file a Protective Statement that applies to a taxable year of the shareholder, the shareholder must reasonably believe as of the election due date that the foreign corporation was not a PFIC for the foreign corporation's taxable year that ended during the retroactive election year. The Protective Statement must contain—

(i) The shareholder's reasonable belief statement, as described in paragraph (c)(2) of this section;

(ii) The shareholder's agreement extending the periods of limitations on the assessment of PFIC related taxes for all taxable years to which the Protective Statement applies, as provided in paragraph (c)(4) of this section; and

(iii) The following information and representations—

(A) The shareholder's name, address, taxpayer identification number, and the shareholder's first taxable year to which the Protective Statement applies;

(B) The foreign corporation's name, address, and taxpayer identification number, if any; and

(C) The highest percentage of shares of each class of stock of the foreign corporation held directly or indirectly by the shareholder during the shareholder's first taxable year to which the Protective Statement applies.

(2) *Reasonable belief statement.* The Protective Statement must contain a reasonable belief statement, as described in paragraph (c)(1) of this section. The reasonable belief statement is a description of the shareholder's basis for its reasonable belief that the foreign corporation was not a PFIC for its taxable year that ended with or within the shareholder's first taxable year to which the Protective Statement applies. If the Protective Statement applies to a taxable year or years described in paragraph (c)(5)(ii) of this section, the reasonable belief statement must describe the shareholder's basis for its reasonable belief that the foreign corporation was not a PFIC for the foreign corporation's taxable year or years that ended in such taxable year or years of the shareholder. The reasonable belief statement must discuss the application of the income and asset tests to the foreign corporation and the factors, including those stated in paragraph (d) of this section, that affect the results of those tests.

(3) *Who executes and files the Protective Statement.* The person that executes and files the

Reg. § 1.1295-3(c)(3)

Protective Statement is the person that makes the section 1295 election, as provided in § 1.1295-1(d).

(4) *Waiver of the periods of limitations*—(i) *Time for and manner of extending periods of limitations.*—(A) *In general.* A shareholder that files the Protective Statement with the Commissioner must extend the periods of limitations on the assessment of all PFIC related taxes for all of the shareholder's taxable years to which the Protective Statement applies, as provided in this paragraph (c)(4). The shareholder is required to execute the waiver on such form as the Commissioner may prescribe for purposes of this paragraph (c)(4). Until that form is published, the shareholder must execute a statement in which the shareholder agrees to extend the periods of limitations on the assessment of all PFIC related taxes for all the shareholder's taxable years to which the Protective Statement applies, as provided in this paragraph (c)(4), and agrees to the restrictions in paragraph (c)(4)(ii)(A) of this section. The shareholder or a person authorized to sign the shareholder's federal income tax return must sign the form or statement. A properly executed form or statement authorized by this paragraph (c)(4) will be deemed consented to and signed by a Service Center Director or the Assistant Commissioner (International) for purposes of § 301.6501(c)-1(d) of this chapter.

(B) *Application of general rule to domestic partnerships*—(*1*) *In general.* A domestic partnership that holds an interest in stock of a PFIC satisfies the waiver requirement of paragraph (c)(4) of this section pursuant to the rules of this paragraph (c)(4)(i)(B)(*1*). The partnership must file one or more waivers obtained or arranged under this paragraph (c)(4)(i)(B) as part of the Protective Statement, as provided in paragraph (c)(1) of this section. The partnership must either—

(*i*) Obtain from each partner the partner's waiver of the periods of limitations;

(*ii*) Obtain from each partner a duly executed power of attorney under § 601.501 of this chapter authorizing the partnership to extend that partner's periods of limitations, and execute a waiver on behalf of the partners; or

(*iii*) In the case of a domestic partnership governed by the unified audit and litigation procedures of sections 6221 through 6233 (TEFRA partnership), arrange for the tax matters partner (or any other person authorized to enter into an agreement to extend the periods of limitations), as provided in section 6229(b), to execute a waiver on behalf of all the partners.

(*2*) *Special rules*—(*i*) *Addition of partner to non-TEFRA partnership.* In the case of any individual who becomes a partner in a domestic partnership other than a TEFRA partnership (non-TEFRA partnership) in a taxable year subsequent to the year in which the partnership filed a Protective Statement, the partner and the partnership must comply with the rules applicable to non-TEFRA partnerships, as provided in paragraph (c)(4)(i)(B)(*1*) of this section, by the due date, as extended, for the federal income tax return of the partnership for the taxable year during which the individual became a partner. Failure to so comply will render the Protective Statement invalid with respect to the partnership and partners.

(*ii*) *Change in status from non-TEFRA partnership to TEFRA partnership.* If a partnership is a non-TEFRA partnership in one taxable year but becomes a TEFRA partnership in a subsequent taxable year, the partnership must file one or more waivers obtained or arranged under this paragraph (c)(4)(i)(B)(*2*)(*ii*), as part of the Protective Statement, as provided in paragraph (c)(1) of this section. The partnership must either obtain from any new partner the partner's waiver described in this paragraph (c)(4); obtain from the new partner a duly executed power of attorney under § 601.501 of this chapter authorizing the partnership to extend the partner's periods of limitations, and execute a waiver on behalf of the new partner; or arrange for the tax matters partner (or any other person authorized to enter into an agreement to extend the periods of limitations) to execute a waiver on behalf of all the partners. In each case, the partnership must attach any new waiver of a partner's periods of limitations, and a copy of the Protective Statement to its federal income tax return for that taxable year.

(C) *Application of general rule to domestic nongrantor trusts and domestic estates.* A domestic nongrantor trust or a domestic estate that holds an interest in stock of a PFIC satisfies the waiver requirement of this paragraph (c)(4) at the entity level. For this purpose, such entity must comply with rules similar to those applicable to non-TEFRA partnerships, as provided in paragraph (c)(4)(i)(B)(*1*) of this section.

(D) *Application of general rule to S corporations.* An S corporation that holds an interest in stock of a PFIC satisfies the waiver requirement of this paragraph (c)(4) at the S corporation level. For this purpose, the S corporation must comply with rules similar to those applicable to non-TEFRA partnerships, as provided in paragraph (c)(4)(i)(B)(*1*) of this section. However, in

Reg. § 1.1295-3(c)(4)

the case of an S corporation that was governed by the unified audit corporate proceedings of sections 6241 through 6245 for any taxable year to which a Protective Statement applies (former TEFRA S corporation), the tax matters person (or any other person authorized to enter into such an agreement), as was provided in sections 6241 through 6245, may execute a waiver described in this paragraph (c)(4) that applies to such taxable year; for any other taxable year, the former TEFRA S corporation must comply with rules similar to those applicable to non-TEFRA partnerships.

(E) *Effect on waiver of complete termination of a pass through entity or pass through entity's business.* The complete termination of a pass through entity described in paragraphs (c)(4)(i)(B) through (D) of this section, or a pass through entity's trade or business, will not terminate a waiver that applies to a partner, shareholder, or beneficiary.

(F) *Application of general rule to foreign partnerships, foreign trusts, domestic or foreign grantor trusts, and foreign estates.* A U.S. person that is a partner or beneficiary of a foreign partnership, foreign trust, or foreign estate that holds an interest in stock of a PFIC satisfies the waiver requirement of this paragraph (c)(4) at the partner or beneficiary level. A U.S. person that is treated under sections 671 through 679 as the owner of the portion of a domestic or foreign trust that owns an interest in PFIC stock also satisfies the waiver requirement at the owner level. A waiver by a partner or beneficiary applies only to that partner or beneficiary, and is not affected by a complete termination of the entity or the entity's trade or business.

(ii) *Terms of waiver*—(A) *Scope of waiver.* The waiver of the periods of limitations is limited to the assessment of PFIC related taxes. If the period of limitations for a taxable year affected by a retroactive election has expired with respect to the assessment of other non-PFIC related taxes, no adjustments, other than consequential changes, may be made by the Internal Revenue Service or by the shareholder to any other items of income, deduction, or credit for that year. If the period of limitations for refunds or credits for a taxable year affected by a retroactive election is open only by virtue of the assessment period extension and section 6511(c), no refund or credit is allowable on grounds other than adjustments to PFIC related taxes and consequential changes.

(B) *Period of waiver.* The extension of the periods of limitations on the assessment of PFIC related taxes will be effective for all of the shareholder's taxable years to which the Protective Statement applies. In addition, the waiver, to the extent it applies to the period of limitations for a particular year, will terminate with respect to that year no sooner than three years from the date on which the shareholder files an amended return, as provided in paragraph (g) of this section, for that year. For the suspension of the running of the period of limitations for the collection of taxes for which a shareholder has elected under section 1294 to extend the time for payment, as provided in paragraph (g)(3)(ii) of this section, see sections 6503(i) and 6229(h).

(5) *Time of and manner for filing a Protective Statement*—(i) *In general.* Except as provided in paragraph (c)(5)(ii) of this section, a Protective Statement must be attached to the shareholder's federal income tax return for the shareholder's first taxable year to which the Protective Statement will apply. The shareholder must file its return and the copy of the Protective Statement by the due date, as extended under section 6081, for the return.

(ii) *Special rule for taxable years ended before January 2, 1998.* A shareholder may file a Protective Statement that applies to the shareholder's taxable year or years that ended before January 2, 1998, provided the period of limitations on the assessment of taxes for any such year has not expired (open year). The shareholder must file the Protective Statement applicable to such open year or years, as provided in paragraph (c)(5)(i) of this section, by the due date, as extended, for the shareholder's return for the first taxable year ending after January 2, 1998.

(6) *Applicability of the Protective Statement*—(i) *In general.* Except as otherwise provided in this paragraph (c)(6), a Protective Statement applies to the shareholder's first taxable year for which the Protective Statement was filed and to each subsequent taxable year. The Protective Statement will not apply to any taxable year of the shareholder during which the shareholder does not own any stock of the foreign corporation or to any taxable year thereafter. Accordingly, if the shareholder has not made a retroactive election with respect to the previously owned stock by the time the shareholder reacquires stock of the foreign corporation, the shareholder must file another Protective Statement to preserve its right to make a retroactive election with respect to the later acquired stock. For the rule that provides that a section 1295 election made with respect to a foreign corporation applies to stock of that corporation acquired after a lapse in ownership, see § 1.1295-1(c)(2)(iii).

Reg. § 1.1295-3(c)(6)

(ii) *Invalidity of the Protective Statement.* A shareholder will be treated as if it never filed a Protective Statement if—

(A) The shareholder failed to make a retroactive election by the date prescribed for making the retroactive election in paragraph (g)(1) of this section; or

(B) The waiver of the periods of limitations terminates (by reason of a court decision or other determination) with respect to any taxable year before the expiration of three years from the date of filing of an amended return for that year pursuant to paragraph (g) of this section.

(7) *Retention of Protective Statement and information demonstrating reasonable belief.* A shareholder that files a Protective Statement must retain a copy of the Protective Statement and its attachments and must, for each taxable year of the shareholder to which the Protective Statement applies, retain information sufficient to demonstrate the shareholder's reasonable belief that the foreign corporation was not a PFIC for the taxable year of the foreign corporation ending during each such taxable year of the shareholder.

(d) *Reasonable belief*—(1) *In general.* A foreign corporation is a PFIC for a taxable year if the foreign corporation satisfies either the income or asset test of section 1297(a). To determine whether a shareholder had reasonable belief that the foreign corporation is not a PFIC under section 1297(a), the shareholder must consider all relevant facts and circumstances. Reasonable belief may be based on a variety of factors, including reasonable asset valuations as well as reasonable interpretations of the applicable provisions of the Code, regulations, and administrative guidance regarding the direct or indirect ownership of the income or assets of the foreign corporation, the proper character of that income or those assets, and similar issues. Reasonable belief may be based on reasonable predictions regarding income to be earned and assets to be owned in subsequent years where qualification of the foreign corporation as a PFIC for the current taxable year will depend on the qualification of the corporation as a PFIC in a subsequent year. Reasonable belief may be based on an analysis of generally available financial information of the foreign corporation. To determine whether a shareholder had reasonable belief that the foreign corporation was not a PFIC, the Commissioner may consider the size of the shareholder's interest in the foreign corporation.

(2) *Knowledge of law required.* Reasonable belief must be based on a good faith effort to apply the Code, regulations, and related administrative guidance. Any person's failure to know or apply these provisions will not form the basis of reasonable belief.

(e) *Special rules for qualified shareholders*—(1) *In general.* A shareholder that is a qualified shareholder, as defined in paragraph (e)(2) of this section, for a taxable year of the shareholder is not required to satisfy the reasonable belief requirement of paragraph (b)(1) of this section or file a Protective Statement to preserve its ability to make a retroactive election with respect to such taxable year. Accordingly, a qualified shareholder may make a retroactive election for any open taxable year in the shareholder's holding period. The retroactive election will be treated as made in the earliest taxable year of the shareholder during which the foreign corporation qualified as a PFIC (including a taxable year ending prior January 2, 1998) and the shareholder will be treated as a shareholder of a pedigreed QEF, as defined in § 1.1291-9(j)(2)(ii), provided the shareholder—

(i) Has been a qualified shareholder with respect to the foreign corporation for all taxable years of the shareholder included in the shareholder's holding period during which the foreign corporation was a PFIC, or in the case of taxable years ending before January 2, 1998, the shareholder satisfies the criteria of a qualified shareholder, for all such years; or

(ii) Has been a qualified shareholder, or in the case of taxable years ending before January 2, 1998, satisfies the criteria of a qualified shareholder, for all taxable years in its holding period before it filed a Protective Statement, which Protective Statement is applicable to all subsequent years, beginning with the first taxable year in which the shareholder is not a qualified shareholder.

(2) *Qualified shareholder.* A shareholder will be treated as a qualified shareholder for a taxable year if the shareholder did not file a Protective Statement applicable to an earlier taxable year included in the shareholder's holding period of the stock of the foreign corporation currently held and—

(i) At all times during the taxable year the shareholder owned, within the meaning of section 958, directly, indirectly, or constructively, less than two percent of the vote and value of each class of stock of the foreign corporation; and

(ii) With respect to the taxable year of the foreign corporation ending within the shareholder's taxable year, the foreign corporation or U.S. counsel for the foreign corporation indicated in a public filing, disclosure statement or other notice provided to U.S. persons that are shareholders of the foreign corporation (corporate filing) that the foreign corporation—

Reg. § 1.1295-3(c)(7)

(A) Reasonably believes that it is not or should not constitute a PFIC for the corporation's taxable year; or

(B) Is unable to conclude that it is not or should not be a PFIC (due to certain asset valuation or interpretation issues, or because PFIC status will depend on the income or assets of the foreign corporation in the corporation's subsequent taxable years) but reasonably believes that, more likely than not, it ultimately will not be a PFIC.

(3) *Exceptions.* Notwithstanding paragraph (e)(2)(ii) of this section, a shareholder will not be treated as a qualified shareholder for a taxable year of the shareholder if the shareholder knew or had reason to know that a corporate filing regarding the foreign corporation's PFIC status was inaccurate, or knew that the foreign corporation was a PFIC for the taxable year of the foreign corporation ending with or within such taxable year of the shareholder. For purposes of this paragraph, a shareholder will be treated as knowing that a foreign corporation was a PFIC if the principal activity of the foreign corporation, directly or indirectly, is owning or trading a diversified portfolio of stock, securities, or other financial contracts.

(f) *Special consent*—(1) *In general.* A shareholder that has not satisfied the requirements of paragraph (b) or (e) of this section may request the consent of the Commissioner to make a retroactive election for a taxable year of the shareholder provided the shareholder satisfies the requirements set forth in this paragraph (f). The Commissioner will grant relief under this paragraph (f) only if—

(i) The shareholder reasonably relied on a qualified tax professional, within the meaning of paragraph (f)(2) of this section;

(ii) Granting consent will not prejudice the interests of the United States government, as provided in paragraph (f)(3) of this section;

(iii) The shareholder requests consent under paragraph (f) of this section before a representative of the Internal Revenue Service raises upon audit the PFIC status of the corporation for any taxable year of the shareholder; and

(iv) The shareholder satisfies the procedural requirements set forth in paragraph (f)(4) of this section.

(2) *Reasonable reliance on a qualified tax professional*—(i) *In general.* Except as provided in paragraph (f)(2)(ii) of this section, a shareholder is deemed to have reasonably relied on a qualified tax professional only if the shareholder reasonably relied on a qualified tax professional (including a tax professional employed by the shareholder) who failed to identify the foreign corporation as a PFIC or failed to advise the shareholder of the consequences of making, or failing to make, the section 1295 election. A shareholder will not be considered to have reasonably relied on a qualified tax professional if the shareholder knew, or reasonably should have known, that the foreign corporation was a PFIC and of the availability of a section 1295 election, or knew or reasonably should have known that the qualified tax professional—

(A) Was not competent to render tax advice with respect to the ownership of shares of a foreign corporation; or

(B) Did not have access to all relevant facts and circumstances.

(ii) *Shareholder deemed to have not reasonably relied on a qualified tax professional.* For purposes of this paragraph (f)(2), a shareholder is deemed to have not reasonably relied on a qualified tax professional if the shareholder was informed by the qualified tax professional that the foreign corporation was a PFIC and of the availability of the section 1295 election and related tax consequences, but either chose not to make the section 1295 election or was unable to make a valid section 1295 election.

(3) *Prejudice to the interests of the United States government*—(i) *General rule.* Except as otherwise provided in paragraph (f)(3)(ii) of this section, the Commissioner will not grant consent under paragraph (f) of this section if doing so would prejudice the interests of the United States government. The interests of the United States government are prejudiced if granting relief would result in the shareholder having a lower tax liability, taking into account applicable interest charges, in the aggregate for all years affected by the retroactive election (other than by a de minimis amount) than the shareholder would have had if the shareholder had made the section 1295 election by the election due date. The time value of money is taken into account for purposes of this computation.

(ii) *Elimination of prejudice to the interests of the United States government.* Notwithstanding the general rule of paragraph (f)(3)(i) of this section, if granting relief would prejudice the interests of the United States government, the Commissioner may, in the Commissioner's sole discretion, grant consent to make the election provided the shareholder enters into a closing agreement with the Commissioner that requires the shareholder to pay an amount sufficient to eliminate any prejudice to the United States government as a consequence of the shareholder's

Reg. § 1.1295-3(f)(3)

inability to file amended returns for closed taxable years.

(4) *Procedural requirements*—(i) *Filing instructions.* A shareholder requests consent under paragraph (f) of this section to make a retroactive election by filing with the Office of the Associate Chief Counsel (International) a ruling request that includes the affidavits required by this paragraph (f)(4). The ruling request must satisfy the requirements, including payment of the user fee, for ruling requests filed with that office.

(ii) *Affidavit from shareholder.* The shareholder, or a person authorized to sign a federal income tax return on behalf of the shareholder, must submit a detailed affidavit describing the events that led to the failure to make a section 1295 election by the election due date, and to the discovery thereof. The shareholder's affidavit must describe the engagement and responsibilities of the qualified tax professional as well as the extent to which the shareholder relied on the tax professional. The shareholder must sign the affidavit under penalties of perjury. An individual who signs for an entity must have personal knowledge of the facts and circumstances at issue.

(iii) *Affidavits from other persons.* The shareholder must submit detailed affidavits from individuals having knowledge or information about the events that led to the failure to make a section 1295 election by the election due date, and to the discovery thereof. These individuals must include the qualified tax professional upon whose advice the shareholder relied, as well as any individual (including an employee of the shareholder) who made a substantial contribution to the return's preparation, and any accountant or attorney, knowledgeable in tax matters, who advised the shareholder with regard to its ownership of the stock of the foreign corporation. Each affidavit must describe the individual's engagement and responsibilities as well as the advice concerning the tax treatment of the foreign corporation that the individual provided to the shareholder. Each affidavit also must include the individual's name, address, and taxpayer identification number, and must be signed by the individual under penalties of perjury.

(iv) *Other information.* In connection with a request for consent under this paragraph (f), a shareholder must provide any additional information requested by the Commissioner.

(v) *Notification of Internal Revenue Service.* The shareholder must notify the branch of the Associate Chief Counsel (International) considering the request for relief under this paragraph (f) if, while the shareholder's request for consent is pending, the Internal Revenue Service begins an examination of the shareholder's return for the retroactive election year or for any subsequent taxable year during which the shareholder holds stock of the foreign corporation.

(vi) *Who requests special consent under this paragraph (f) and who enters into a closing agreement.* The person that requests consent under this paragraph (f) is the person that makes the section 1295 election, as provided in § 1.1295-1(d). If a shareholder is required to enter into a closing agreement with the Commissioner, as described in paragraph (f)(3)(ii) of this section, rules similar to those under paragraphs (c)(4)(i)(B) through (E) of this section apply for purposes of determining the person that enters into the closing agreement.

(g) *Time for and manner of making a retroactive election*—(1) *Time for making a retroactive election*—(i) *In general.* Except as otherwise provided in paragraph (g)(1)(ii) of this section, a shareholder must make a retroactive election, in the manner provided in paragraph (g)(2) of this section, on or before the due date, as extended, for the shareholder's return—

(A) In the case of a shareholder that makes a retroactive election pursuant to paragraph (b) or (e) of this section, for the taxable year in which the shareholder determines or reasonably should have determined that the foreign corporation was a PFIC; or

(B) In the case of a shareholder that obtains the consent of the Commissioner pursuant to paragraph (f) of this section, for the taxable year in which such consent is granted.

(ii) *Transition rule.* A shareholder that files a Protective Statement for a taxable year described in paragraph (c)(5)(ii) of this section may make a retroactive election by the due date, as extended, for the return for the first taxable year ended after January 2, 1998, even if the shareholder determined or should have determined that the foreign corporation was a PFIC for a year described in paragraph (c)(5)(ii) of this section at any time on or before January 2, 1998.

(iii) *Ownership not required at time retroactive election is made.* The shareholder need not own shares of the foreign corporation at the time the shareholder makes a retroactive election with respect to the foreign corporation.

(2) *Manner of making a retroactive election.* A shareholder that has satisfied the requirements of paragraph (b) or (e) of this section, or a shareholder that has been granted consent under paragraph (f) of this section, must make a retroactive election in the manner provided in Form 8621 for making a section 1295 election, and must attach Form 8621 to an amended return for the later of

Reg. § 1.1295-3(f)(4)

the retroactive election year or the earliest open taxable year of the shareholder. The shareholder also must file an amended return for each of its subsequent taxable years affected by the retroactive election. In each amended return the shareholder must redetermine its income tax liability for that year to take into account the assessment of PFIC related taxes. If the period of limitations for the assessment of taxes for a taxable year affected by the retroactive election has expired except to the extent the waiver of limitations, described in paragraph (c)(4) of this section, has extended such period, no adjustments, other than consequential changes, may be made to any other items of income, deduction, or credit in that year. In addition, the shareholder must pay all taxes and interest owing by reason of the PFIC and QEF status of the foreign corporation in those years (except to the extent a section 1294 election extends the time to pay the taxes and interest). A shareholder that filed a Protective Statement must attach to Form 8621 filed with each amended return a representation that the shareholder, until the taxable year in which it determined or reasonably should have determined that the foreign corporation was a PFIC, reasonably believed, within the meaning of paragraph (d) of this section, that the foreign corporation was not a PFIC in the taxable year for which the amended return is filed, and in all other taxable years to which the Protective Statement applies. A shareholder that entered into a closing agreement must comply with the terms of that agreement, as provided in paragraph (f)(3)(ii) of this section, to eliminate any prejudice to the United States government's interests, as described in paragraph (f)(3) of this section.

(3) *Who makes the retroactive election.* The person that makes the retroactive election is the person that makes the section 1295 election, as provided in § 1.1295-1(d). A partner, shareholder, or beneficiary for which a pass through entity, as described in paragraphs (c)(4)(i)(B) through (D) of this section, filed a Protective Statement may make a retroactive election, if the pass through entity completely terminates its business or otherwise ceases to exist.

(4) *Other elections*—(i) *Section 1291(d)(2) election.* If the foreign corporation for which the shareholder makes a retroactive election will be treated as an unpedigreed QEF, as defined in § 1.1291-9(j)(2)(iii), with respect to the shareholder, the shareholder may make an election under section 1291(d)(2) to purge its holding period of the years or parts of years before the effective date of the retroactive election. If the qualification date, within the meaning of § 1.1291-9(e) or 1.1291-10(e), falls in a taxable year for which the period of limitations has expired, the shareholder may treat the first day of the retroactive election year as the qualification date. The shareholder may make a section 1291(d)(2) election at the time that it makes the retroactive election, but no later than two years after the date that the amended return in which the retroactive election is made is filed. For the requirements for making a section 1291(d)(2) election, see §§ 1.1291-9 and 1.1291-10.

(ii) *Section 1294 election.* A shareholder may make an election under section 1294 to extend the time for payment of tax on the shareholder's pro rata shares of the ordinary earnings and net capital gain of the foreign corporation reported in the shareholder's amended return, and section 6621 interest attributable to such tax, but only to the extent the tax and interest are attributable to earnings that have not been distributed to the shareholder. The shareholder must make a section 1294 election for a taxable year at the time that it files its amended return for that year, as provided in paragraph (g)(1) of this section. For the requirements for making a section 1294 election, see § 1.1294-1T.

(h) *Effective date.* The rules of this section are effective as of January 2, 1998. [Reg. § 1.1295-3.]

☐ [T.D. 8750, 12-31-97. *Redesignated and amended by T.D. 8870, 2-4-2000.*]

[Reg. § 1.1296(e)-1]

§ 1.1296(e)-1. Definition of marketable stock.—(a) *General rule.* For purposes of section 1296, the term *marketable stock* means—

(1) Passive foreign investment company (PFIC) stock that is regularly traded, as defined in paragraph (b) of this section, on a qualified exchange or other market, as defined in paragraph (c) of this section;

(2) Stock in certain PFICs, as described in paragraph (d) of this section; and

(3) Options on stock that is described in paragraph (a)(1) or (2) of this section, to the extent provided in paragraph (e) of this section.

(b) *Regularly traded*—(1) *General rule.* For purposes of paragraph (a)(1) of this section, a class of stock that is traded on one or more qualified exchanges or other markets, as defined in paragraph (c) of this section, is regularly traded on such exchanges or markets for any calendar year during which such class of stock is traded, other than in de minimis quantities, on at least 15 days during each calendar quarter.

(2) *Anti-abuse rule.* Trades that have as one of their principal purposes the meeting of the trading requirement of paragraph (b)(1) of this section shall be disregarded. Further, a class of

stock shall not be treated as meeting the trading requirement of paragraph (b)(1) of this section if there is a pattern of trades conducted to meet the requirement of paragraph (b)(1) of this section.

(c) *Qualified exchange or other market*—(1) *General rule.* For purposes of paragraph (a)(1) of this section, the term *qualified exchange or other market* means, for any calendar year—

(i) A national securities exchange that is registered with the Securities and Exchange Commission or the national market system established pursuant to section 11A of the Securities Exchange Act of 1934 (15 U.S.C. 78f); or

(ii) A foreign securities exchange that is regulated or supervised by a governmental authority of the country in which the market is located and which has the following characteristics—

(A) The exchange has trading volume, listing, financial disclosure, surveillance, and other requirements designed to prevent fraudulent and manipulative acts and practices, to remove impediments to and perfect the mechanism of a free and open, fair and orderly, market, and to protect investors; and the laws of the country in which the exchange is located and the rules of the exchange ensure that such requirements are actually enforced; and

(B) The rules of the exchange effectively promote active trading of listed stocks.

(2) *Exchange with multiple tiers.* If an exchange in a foreign country has more than one tier or market level on which stock may be separately listed or traded, each such tier shall be treated as a separate exchange.

(d) *Stock in certain PFICs*—(1) *General rule.* Except as provided in paragraph (d)(2) of this section, a foreign corporation is a corporation described in section 1296(e)(1)(B), and paragraph (a)(2) of this section, if the foreign corporation offers for sale or has outstanding stock of which it is the issuer and which is redeemable at its net asset value and if the foreign corporation satisfies the following conditions with respect to the class of shares held by the electing taxpayer—

(i) At all times during the calendar year, the foreign corporation has more than one hundred shareholders with respect to the class, other than shareholders who are related under section 267(b);

(ii) At all times during the calendar year, the class of shares of the foreign corporation is readily available for purchase by the general public at its net asset value and the foreign corporation does not require a minimum initial investment of greater than $10,000 (U.S.);

(iii) At all times during the calendar year, quotations for the class of shares of the foreign corporation are determined and published no less frequently than on a weekly basis in a widely-available permanent medium not controlled by the issuer of the shares, such as a newspaper of general circulation or a trade publication;

(iv) No less frequently than annually, independent auditors prepare financial statements of the foreign corporation that include balance sheets (statements of assets, liabilities, and net assets) and statements of income and expenses, and those statements are made available to the public;

(v) The foreign corporation is supervised or regulated as an investment company by a foreign government or an agency or instrumentality thereof that has broad inspection and enforcement authority and effective oversight over investment companies;

(vi) At all times during the calendar year, the foreign corporation has no senior securities authorized or outstanding, including any debt other than in de minimis amounts;

(vii) Ninety percent or more of the gross income of the foreign corporation for its taxable year is passive income, as defined in section 1297(a)(1) and the regulations thereunder; and

(viii) The average percentage of assets held by the foreign corporation during its taxable year which produce passive income or which are held for the production of passive income, as defined in section 1297(a)(2) and the regulations thereunder, is at least 90 percent.

(2) *Anti-abuse rule.* If a foreign corporation undertakes any actions that have as one of their principal purposes the manipulation of the net asset value of a class of its shares, for the calendar year in which the manipulation occurs, the shares are not marketable stock for purposes of paragraph (d)(1) of this section.

(e) [Reserved]

(f) *Special rules for regulated investment companies (RICs)*—(1) *General rule.* In the case of any RIC that is offering for sale, or has outstanding, any stock of which it is the issuer and which is redeemable at net asset value, if the RIC owns directly or indirectly, as defined in sections 958(a)(1) and (2), stock in any passive foreign investment company, that stock will be treated as marketable stock owned by that RIC for purposes of section 1296. Except as provided in paragraph (f)(2) of this section, in the case of any other RIC that publishes net asset valuations at least annually, if the RIC owns directly or indirectly, as defined in sections 958(a)(1) and (2), stock in any

Reg. § 1.1296(e)-1(c)(1)

passive foreign investment company, that stock will be treated as marketable stock owned by that RIC for purposes of section 1296.

(2) [Reserved]

(g) *Effective date.* This section applies to shareholders whose taxable year ends on or after January 25, 2000 for stock in a foreign corporation whose taxable year ends with or within the shareholder's taxable year. In addition, shareholders may elect to apply these regulations to any taxable year beginning after December 31, 1997, for stock in a foreign corporation whose taxable year ends with or within the shareholder's taxable year. [Reg. § 1.1296(e)-1.]

☐ [*T.D.* 8867, 1-25-2000.]

[Reg. § 1.1297-0]

§ 1.1297-0. **Table of contents.**—This section contains a listing of the headings for § 1.1297-3T.

§ 1.1297-3T. Deemed sale election by a United States person that is a shareholder of a passive foreign investment company.

(a) In general.

(b) Time and manner for making the election.

(1) In general.

(2) Information to be included in the election.

(3) Adjustment to basis; treatment of holding period.

[Reg. § 1.1297-0.]

☐ [*T.D.* 8750, 12-31-97.]

[Reg. § 1.1297-3T]

§ 1.1297-3T. **Deemed sale election by a United States person that is a shareholder of a passive foreign investment company (Temporary).**—(a) *In general.* Except as indicated below, a shareholder of a foreign corporation that no longer qualifies as a passive foreign investment company (PFIC) shall be treated for tax purposes as holding stock in a PFIC and therefore continue to be subject to taxation under section 1291 unless the shareholder makes the election under section 1297(b)(1). This continuing PFIC taint shall not apply to stock in a PFIC for which an election under section 1295 to be a qualified electing fund (QEF) has been in effect throughout that portion of the shareholder's holding period during which the PFIC qualified as a PFIC. A U.S. person making the election under section 1297(b)(1) shall be treated as having sold its stock in the PFIC on the last day of the last taxable year of the foreign corporation during which it qualified as a PFIC (termination date). The shareholder thereafter shall not be treated as holding stock in a PFIC and shall not be subject to taxation under section 1291. The deemed sale is taxed as a disposition under section 1291. Pursuant to that section, the gain, if any, is considered earned pro rata over the shareholder's holding period in the stock and is taxed as ordinary income. The tax on the gain is based on the value of the tax deferral and includes an interest charge. Any loss realized in the deemed sale may not be recognized. This section provides rules for making the election under section 1297(b)(1). The election is available to a U.S. person that is a shareholder of a foreign corporation if—

(1) The foreign corporation was a PFIC at any time during the period the U.S. person held the stock;

(2) At any one time during the U.S. person's holding period, the foreign corporation qualified as a PFIC but was not a QEF; and

(3) The foreign corporation is no longer a PFIC within the meaning of section 1296.

(b) *Time and manner of making the election*— (1) *In general.* The shareholder shall make the election under this section and section 1297(b)(1) by filing an amended income tax return for its taxable year that includes the termination date within three years of the due date, as extended, for the shareholder's tax return for such taxable year. The shareholder must attach to the amended return either Form 8621 or a statement, prepared in accordance with paragraph (c)(2) of this section, reporting the gain on the deemed sale of the stock as required by section 1291(a)(2) (as if such deemed sale occurred under section 1291(d)(2)), and by paying the tax on the gain as required by section 1291 (including the payment of the deferred tax amount required under sections 1291(a)(1)(C) and 1291(c)). The electing shareholder also shall pay interest, pursuant to section 6601, on the underpayment of tax for the taxable year of termination. An electing shareholder that realizes a loss shall report the loss on Form 8621, but shall not recognize the loss.

(2) *Information to be included in the election.* If a statement is used, the statement should be identified, in a heading, as an election under section 1297(b)(1). The statement must include the following information and representations:

(i) The name, address and taxpayer identification number of the electing shareholder;

(ii) The name, address and taxpayer identification number, if any, of the PFIC;

(iii) A statement that the shareholder is making the election under section 1297(b)(1);

(iv) The period in the electing shareholder's holding period in the stock during which the foreign corporation was a PFIC, the period

Reg. § 1.1297-3T(b)(2)

during which it was a QEF (and whether the shareholder elected under section 1294 to defer payment of its tax liability attributable to any portion of such period), and the termination date;

(v) The manner in which the PFIC lost the characteristics of a PFIC;

(vi) A schedule listing the shares in the PFIC held by the electing shareholder on the termination, listing the date(s) each share or block of shares acquired, the number of shares acquired on each date listed, and the tax basis of each share;

(vii) The fair market value of the stock in the PFIC on the termination date; for this purpose, the fair market value of the stock shall be determined according to the rules of § 1.1295-1T(b)(9); and

(viii) A schedule showing the computation of the gain recognized on the deemed sale, and a calculation of the deferred tax amount, as defined in section 1291(c).

(3) *Adjustment to basis; treatment of holding period.* An electing shareholder that recognizes gain on the deemed sale of stock shall increase its adjusted basis in the stock by the amount of gain recognized. An electing shareholder shall not adjust the basis in stock with respect to which the shareholder realized a loss on the deemed sale. An electing shareholder shall thereafter treat its holding period in the stock, for purposes of sections 1291 through 1297, as beginning on the day following the termination date without regard to whether it recognized gain on the deemed sale; for section 1223 purposes, the holding period in the stock in the PFIC shall include the period prior to the deemed sale.

(c) *Application of deemed dividend election rules*—(1) *In general.* A shareholder of a former PFIC, within the meaning of § 1.1291-9(j)(2)(iv), that was a controlled foreign corporation, within the meaning of section 957(a) (CFC), during its last taxable year as a PFIC under section 1296(a), may apply the rules of section 1291(d)(2)(B) and § 1.1291-9 to an election under section 1297(b)(1) and this section made by the time and in the manner provided in paragraph (b) of this section.

(2) *Transition rule.* If the time for making an election under this section, as provided in paragraph (b) of this section, expired before January 2, 1998, a shareholder that applied rules similar to the rules of section 1291(d)(2)(A) and § 1.1291-10 to an election under this section made with respect to a corporation that was a CFC during its last taxable year as a PFIC under section 1296(a) may file an amended return for the taxable year that includes the termination date, as defined in paragraph (a) of this section, and apply the rules of section 1291(d)(2)(B) and § 1.1291-9 at any time before the expiration of the period of limitations for the assessment of taxes for that taxable year.

(3) *Effective date.* The rules of this paragraph are effective as of January 2, 1998. [Temporary Reg. § 1.1297-3T.]

☐ [T.D. 8178, 2-26-88. Amended by T.D. 8750, 12-31-97.]

READJUSTMENT OF TAX BETWEEN YEARS AND SPECIAL LIMITATIONS

Income Averaging

[Reg. § 1.1301-1]

§ 1.1301-1. **Averaging of farm income.**—(a) *Overview.* An individual engaged in a farming business may elect to compute current year (election year) income tax liability under section 1 by averaging, over the prior three-year period (base years), all or a portion of the individual's current year electible farm income as defined in paragraph (e) of this section. To average farm income, the individual—

(1) Designates all or a portion of his or her electible farm income for the election year as elected farm income; and

(2) Determines the election year section 1 tax by determining the sum of—

(i) The section 1 tax that would be imposed for the election year if taxable income for the year were reduced by elected farm income; plus

(ii) For each base year, the amount by which the section 1 tax would be increased if taxable income for the year were increased by one-third of elected farm income.

(b) *Individual engaged in a farming business*—(1) *In general. Farming business* has the same meaning as provided in section 263A(e)(4) and the regulations thereunder. An individual engaged in a farming business includes a sole proprietor of a farming business, a partner in a partnership engaged in a farming business, and a shareholder of an S corporation engaged in a farming business. Services performed as an employee are disregarded in determining whether an individual is engaged in a farming business for purposes of section 1301. An individual is not required to have been engaged in a farming business in any of the base years in order to make a farm income averaging election.

(2) *Certain landlords.* A landlord is engaged in a farming business for purposes of section 1301 with respect to rental income that is based on a share of production from a tenant's farming business and, with respect to amounts received on or after January 1, 2003, is determined under a written agreement entered into before the tenant begins significant activities on the land. A landlord is not engaged in a farming business for purposes of section 1301 with respect to either fixed rent or, with respect to amounts received on or after January 1, 2003, rental income based on a share of a tenant's production determined under an unwritten agreement or a written agreement entered into after the tenant begins significant activities on the land. Whether the landlord materially participates in the tenant's farming business is irrelevant for purposes of section 1301.

(c) *Making, changing, or revoking an election*—(1) *In general.* A farm income averaging election is made by filing Schedule J, "Farm Income Averaging," with an individual's Federal income tax return for the election year (including a late or amended return if the period of limitations on filing a claim for credit or refund has not expired).

(2) *Changing or revoking an election.* An individual may change the amount of the elected farm income in a previous election or revoke a previous election if the period of limitations on filing a claim for credit or refund has not expired for the election year.

(d) *Guidelines for calculation of section 1 tax*—(1) *Actual taxable income not affected.* Under paragraph (a)(2) of this section, a determination of the section 1 tax for the election year involves a computation of the section 1 tax that would be imposed if taxable income for the election year were reduced by elected farm income and taxable income for each of the base years were increased by one-third of elected farm income. The reduction and increases required for purposes of this computation do not affect the actual taxable income for either the election year or the base years. Thus, for each of those years, the actual taxable income is taxable income determined without regard to any hypothetical reduction or increase required for purposes of the computation under paragraph (a)(2) of this section. The following illustrates this principle:

(i) Any reduction or increase in taxable income required for purposes of the computation under paragraph (a)(2) of this section is disregarded in determining the taxable year in which a net operating loss carryover or net capital loss carryover is applied.

(ii) The net section 1231 gain or loss and the character of any section 1231 items for the election year is determined without regard to any reduction in taxable income required for purposes of the computation under paragraph (a)(2) of this section.

(iii) The section 68 overall limitation on itemized deductions for the election year is determined without regard to any reduction in taxable income required for purposes of the computation under paragraph (a)(2) of this section. Similarly, the section 68 limitation for a base year is not recomputed to take into account any allocation of elected farm income to the base year for such purposes.

(iv) If a base year had a partially used capital loss, the remaining capital loss may not be applied to reduce the elected farm income allocated to the year for purposes of the computation under paragraph (a)(2) of this section.

(v) If a base year had a partially used credit, the remaining credit may not be applied to reduce the section 1 tax attributable to the elected farm income allocated to the year for purposes of the computation under paragraph (a)(2) of this section.

(2) *Computation in base years*—(i) *In general.* As provided in paragraph (a)(2)(ii) of this section, the election year section 1 tax includes the amounts by which the section 1 tax for each base year would be increased if taxable income for the year were increased by one-third of elected farm income. For this purpose, all allowable deductions (including the full amount of any net operating loss carryover) are taken into account in determining the taxable income for the base year even if the deductions exceed gross income and the result is negative. If the result is negative, however, any amount that may provide a benefit in another taxable year is added back in determining base year taxable income. Amounts that may provide a benefit in another year include—

(A) The net operating loss (as defined in section 172(c)) for the base year;

(B) The net operating loss for any other year to the extent carried forward from the base year under section 172(b)(2); and

(C) The capital loss deduction allowed for the base year under section 1211(b)(1) or (2) to the extent such deduction does not reduce the capital loss carryover from the base year because it exceeds adjusted taxable income (as defined in section 1212(b)(2)(B)).

Reg. § 1.1301-1(d)(2)

(ii) *Example.* The rules of this paragraph (d)(2) are illustrated by the following example:

Example. In 2001, F and F's spouse on their joint return elect to average $24,000 of income attributable to a farming business. One-third of the elected farm income, $8,000, is added to the 1999 base year income. In 1999, F and F's spouse reported adjusted gross income of $7,300 and claimed a standard deduction of $7,200 and a deduction for personal exemptions of $8,250. Therefore, their 1999 base year taxable income is −$8,150 [$7,300 − ($7,200 + $8,250)]. After adding the elected farm income to the negative taxable income, their 1999 base year taxable income would be zero [$8,000 + (−$8,150) = −$150]. If F and F's spouse elected to income average in 2002, and made the adjustments described in paragraph (d)(3) of this section to account for the 2001 election, their 1999 base year taxable income for the 2002 election would be −$150.

(3) *Effect on subsequent elections*—(i) *In general.* The reduction and increases in taxable income assumed in computing the election year section 1 tax (within the meaning of paragraph (a)(2) of this section) for an election year are treated as having actually occurred for purposes of computing the election year section 1 tax for any subsequent election year. Thus, if a base year for a farm income averaging election is also an election year for another farm income averaging election, the increase in the section 1 tax for that base year is determined after reducing taxable income by the elected farm income from the earlier election year. Similarly, if a base year for a farm income averaging election is also a base year for another farm income averaging election, the increase in the section 1 tax for that base year is determined after increasing taxable income by elected farm income allocated to the year from the earlier election year.

(ii) *Example.* The rules of this paragraph (d)(3) are illustrated by the following example:

Example. (i) In each of years 1998, 1999, and 2000, T had taxable income of $20,000. In 2001, T had taxable income of $30,000 (prior to any farm income averaging election) and electible farm income of $10,000. T makes a farm income averaging election with respect to $9,000 of his electible farm income for 2001. Thus, for purposes of the computation under paragraph (a)(2) of this section, $3,000 of elected farm income is allocated to each of years 1998, 1999, and 2000. T's 2001 tax liability is the sum of—

(A) The section 1 tax on $21,000 (2001 taxable income minus elected farm income); plus

(B) For each of years 1998, 1999, and 2000, the section 1 tax on $23,000 minus the section 1 tax on $20,000 (the amount by which section 1 tax would be increased if one-third of elected farm income were allocated to such year).

(ii) In 2002, T has taxable income of $50,000 and electible farm income of $12,000. T makes a farm income averaging election with respect to all $12,000 of his electible farm income for 2002. Thus, for purposes of the computation under paragraph (a)(2) of this section, $4,000 of elected farm income is allocated to each of years 1990, 2000, and 2001. T's 2002 tax liability is the sum of—

(A) The section 1 tax on $38,000 (2002 taxable income minus elected farm income); plus

(B) For each of years 1999 and 2000, the section 1 tax on $27,000 minus the section 1 tax on $23,000 (the amount by which section 1 tax would be increased if one-third of elected farm income were allocated to such years after increasing taxable income for such years by the elected income allocated to such years from the 2001 election year); plus

(C) For year 2001, the section 1 tax on $25,000 minus the section 1 tax on $21,000 (the amount by which section 1 tax would be increased if one-third of elected farm income were allocated to such year after reducing taxable income for such year by the 2001 elected farm income).

(e) *Electible farm income*—(1) *Identification of items attributable to a farming business*—(i) *In general.* Farm income includes items of income, deduction, gain, and loss attributable to the individual's farming business. Farm losses include a net operating loss carryover or carryback, or a net capital loss carryover, to an election year that is attributable to a farming business. Income, gain, or loss from the sale of development rights, grazing rights, and other similar rights is not treated as attributable to a farming business. In general, farm income does not include compensation received by an employee. However, a shareholder of an S corporation engaged in a farming business may treat compensation received from the corporation that is attributable to the farming business as farm income.

(ii) *Gain or loss on sale or other disposition of property*—(A) *In general.* Gain or loss from the sale or other disposition of property that was regularly used in the individual's farming business for a substantial period of time is treated as attributable to a farming business. For this purpose, the term *property* does not include land, but does include structures affixed to land. Property that has always been used solely in the farming business by the individual is deemed to meet both

Reg. § 1.1301-1(d)(3)

the regularly used and substantial period tests. Whether property not used solely in the farming business was regularly used in the farming business for a substantial period of time depends on all of the facts and circumstances.

(B) *Cessation of a farming business.* If gain or loss described in paragraph (e)(1)(ii)(A) of this section is realized after cessation of a farming business, such gain or loss is treated as attributable to a farming business only if the property is sold within a reasonable time after cessation of the farming business. A sale or other disposition within one year of cessation of the farming business is presumed to be within a reasonable time. Whether a sale or other disposition that occurs more than one year after cessation of the farming business is within a reasonable time depends on all of the facts and circumstances.

(2) *Determination of amount that may be elected farm income*—(i) *Electible farm income.* The maximum amount of income that an individual may elect to average (electible farm income) is the sum of any farm income and gains minus any farm deductions or losses (including loss carryovers and carrybacks) that are allowed as a deduction in computing the individual's taxable income. However, electible farm income may not exceed taxable income. In addition, electible farm income from net capital gain attributable to a farming business cannot exceed total net capital gain. Subject to these limitations, an individual who has both ordinary and net capital gain farm income may elect to average any combination of such ordinary and net capital gain farm income.

(ii) *Examples.* The rules of paragraph (e)(2)(i) of this section are illustrated by the following examples:

Example 1. A has farm gross receipts of $200,000 and farm ordinary deductions of $50,000. A's taxable income is $150,000 ($200,000 − $50,000). A's electible farm income is $150,000, all of which is ordinary income.

Example 2. B has ordinary farm income of $200,000 and ordinary nonfarm losses of $50,000. B's taxable income is $150,000 ($200,000 − $50,000). B's electible farm income is $150,000, all of which is ordinary income.

Example 3. C has a farm capital gain of $50,000 and a nonfarm capital loss of $40,000. C also has ordinary farm income of $60,000. C has taxable income of $70,000 ($50,000 − $40,000 + $60,000). C's electible farm income is $70,000. C can elect to average up to $10,000 of farm capital gain and up to $60,000 of farm ordinary income.

Example 4. D has a nonfarm capital gain of $40,000 and a farm capital loss of $30,000. D also has ordinary farm income of $100,000. D has taxable income of $110,000 ($40,000 − $30,000 + $100,000). D's electible farm income is $70,000 ($100,000 ordinary farm income minus $30,000 farm capital loss), all of which is ordinary income.

Example 5. E has a nonfarm capital gain of $20,000 and a farm capital loss of $30,000. E also has ordinary farm income of $100,000. E has taxable income of $97,000 ($20,000 − $23,000 ($30,000 loss limited by section 1211(b)) + $100,000). E has a farm capital loss carryover of $7,000 ($30,000 − $23,000 allowed as a deduction). E's electible farm income is $77,000 ($100,000 ordinary farm income minus $23,000 farm capital loss), all of which is ordinary income.

(f) *Miscellaneous rules*—(1) *Short taxable year*—(i) *In general.* If a base year or an election year is a short taxable year, the rules of section 443 and the regulations thereunder apply for purposes of calculating the section 1 tax.

(ii) *Base year is a short taxable year.* If a base year is a short taxable year, elected farm income is allocated to such year for purposes of paragraph (a)(2) of this section after the taxable income for such year has been annualized.

(iii) *Election year is a short taxable year.* In applying paragraph (a)(2) of this section for purposes of determining tax computed on the annual basis (within the meaning of section 443(b)(1)) for an election year that is a short taxable year—

(A) The taxable income and the electible farm income for the year are annualized; and

(B) The taxpayer may designate all or any part of the annualized electible farm income as elected farm income.

(2) *Changes in filing status.* An individual is not prohibited from making a farm income averaging election solely because the individual's filing status is not the same in an election year and the base years. For example, an individual who files married filing jointly in the election year, but filed as single in one or more of the base years, may still elect to average farm income using the single filing status used in the base year.

(3) *Employment tax.* A farm income averaging election has no effect in determining the amount of wages for purposes of the Federal Insurance Contributions Act (FICA), the Federal Unemployment Tax Act (FUTA), and the Collection of Income Tax at Source on Wages (Federal income tax withholding), or the amount of net earnings from self-employment for purposes of the Self-Employment Contributions Act (SECA).

(4) *Alternative minimum tax.* A farm income averaging election does not apply in determining the section 55 alternative minimum tax for any

Reg. § 1.1301-1(f)(4)

Income Averaging

base year or the section 55(b) tentative minimum tax for the election year or any base year. The election does, however, apply in determining the regular tax under sections 53(c) and 55(c) for the election year.

(5) *Unearned income of minor child.* In an election year, if a minor child's investment income is taxable under section 1(g) and a parent makes a farm income averaging election, the tax rate used for purposes of applying section 1(g) is the rate determined after application of the election. In a base year, however, the tax on a minor child's investment income is not affected by a farm income averaging election.

(g) *Effective date.* The rules of this section apply to taxable years beginning after December 31, 2001, except with respect to the written agreement requirement of paragraph (b)(2) of this section. [Reg. § 1.1301-1.]

☐ [*T.D.* 8972, 1-7-2002.]

[Reg. § 5c.1305-1]

§ 5c.1305-1. Special income averaging rules for taxpayers otherwise required to compute tax in accordance with § 5c.1256-3 (Temporary).—(a) *In general.* If an eligible individual (as defined in section 1303 and the regulations thereunder) is described in the first sentence of § 5c.1256-3(a), chooses the benefits of income averaging and otherwise complies with the special rules under section 1304 and the regulations thereunder, and has averagable income (as defined in section 1302 and the regulations thereunder) in excess of $3,000, then the individual shall compute the tax under section 1301 as provided in this section. The computation under this section shall be in lieu of the computation under § 5c.1256-3.

(b) *Computation of tax.* The individual shall compute the tax under section 1301 as follows:

Step (1). Compute tax under section 1301 and the regulations thereunder on all taxable income, including gains or losses on regulated futures contracts subject to section 1256(a) and the regulations thereunder, using rates applicable to the taxpayer for the taxable year which includes June 23, 1981.

Step (2). Compute tax under section 1301 and the regulations thereunder on all taxable income, including gains or losses on regulated futures contracts subject to section 1256(a) and the regulations thereunder, using rates applicable to the taxpayer for taxable years beginning in 1982.

Step (3). Compute the percentage of adjusted gross income attributable to all sources except regulated futures contracts subject to section 1256(a) and the regulations thereunder.

Step (4). Compute the percentage of adjusted gross income attributable to regulated futures contracts subject to section 1256(a) and the regulations thereunder. Both the percentage in Step (3) and the percentage in Step (4) are to be rounded to the nearest percent. The sum of both percentages must equal 100 percent.

Step (5). Multiply the result of Step (1) with the result of Step (3).

Step (6). Multiply the result of Step (2) with the result of Step (4).

Step (7). Add the result of Step (5) and the result of Step (6). This is the tax for the individual under section 1301 for the taxable year which includes June 23, 1981.

(c) *Option to defer tax.* If an individual computes the tax under section 1301 as provided in paragraph (a) of this section, the individual may also opt to pay part or all of the deferrable tax under income averaging (as defined in paragraph (d) of this section) for the taxable year which includes June 23, 1981, in 2 or more, but not more than 5, equal installments in accordance with this section. Such individual may not opt to pay part or all of the deferrable tax in installments under § 5c.1256-3. An individual opting to defer payment must attach a statement to Form 6781 indicating the computation of deferrable tax under income averaging, the number of installments in which the individual opts to pay the deferrable tax under income averaging, and the amount of each such payment.

(d) *Deferrable tax under income averaging.* The deferrable tax under income averaging is the excess of—

(1) The tax for the taxable year which includes June 23, 1981, computed pursuant to paragraph (b) of this section, over

(2) The tax for the taxable year which includes June 23, 1981, computed pursuant to paragraph (b) of this section, except that pretransitional year gain or loss (as described in § 5c.1256-2(g)) is omitted for purposes of recomputing the percentage in Step (4). As computed under this subparagraph (2), the sum of the percentage in Step (3) and Step (4) will not equal 100 percent.

(e) *Rules of application.* The provisions of § 5c.1256-3(c), (f), (g), (h), (i), and (j) shall apply in computing the tax and in determining the deferrable tax under income averaging under this section.

(f) *Examples.* The application of this section may be illustrated by the following examples:

Example (1). Individual A is a single, calendar year taxpayer with no dependents.

Reg. § 5c.1305-1(a)

Mitigation of Effect of Limitations—Other Provisions

See p. 20,601 for regulations not amended to reflect law changes

A reported the following amounts for the following years on line 34 of Form 1040:

1977 —	$ 80,000
1978 —	$ 90,000
1979 —	$100,000
1980 —	$110,000

A reports the following amounts for the following lines on Form 1040 for 1981:

line 7 —	$120,000
line 12 —	$600,000
line 32b —	$ 19,000
line 33 —	$ 1,000

The amount on line 12 is computed as follows: $937,500 of gain is attributable to regulated futures contracts subject to section 1256(a). Of that total, 40 percent is short term capital gain ($375,000) and 60 percent is long term capital gain ($562,500). Of the long term capital gain, 40 percent is taxable ($225,000). Therefore, A reports $600,000 on line 12 ($375,000 + $225,000).

The result of Step (1) is $464,013.41. The result of Step (2) is $337,051.52. The result of Step (3) is 17 percent. The result of Step (4) is 83 percent. The result of Step (5) is $78,882.28. The result of Step (6) is $279,752.76. The result of Step (7) is $358,635.04. This is A's tax for 1981 under section 1301.

Example (2). The facts are the same as in Example (1), except that $703,125 of the $937,500 gain attributable to regulated futures contracts is pre-transitional year gain or loss (as described in § 5c.1256-2(g)). A's tax for 1981 under section 1301 is $358,635.04. A may opt to pay in installments a maximum of $221,004.68 of the tax due in 1981. If A opts to defer the maximum amount and pay in 5 equal installments, A must pay for 1981 a tax of $181,831.30. Each of the 4 succeeding installments is $44,200.94 plus interest computed in accordance with § 5c.1256-3(g)(3). [Temporary Reg. § 5c.1305-1.]

☐ [T.D. 7826, 8-27-82.]

Mitigation of Effect of Limitations—Other Provisions
[Reg. § 1.1311(a)-1]

§ 1.1311(a)-1. Introduction.—(a) Part II (section 1311 and following) subchapter Q, chapter 1 of the Code, provides certain rules for the correction of the effect of an erroneous treatment of an item in a taxable year which is closed by the statute of limitations or otherwise, in cases where, in connection with the ascertainment of the tax for another taxable year, it has been determined that there was an erroneous treatment of such item in the closed year.

(b) In most situations falling within this part the correction of the effect of the error on a closed year can be made only if either the Commissioner or the taxpayer has taken a position in another taxable year which is inconsistent with the erroneous treatment of the item in the closed year. If a refund or credit would result from the correction of the error in the closed year, then the Commissioner must be the one maintaining the inconsistent position. For example, if the taxpayer erroneously included an item of income on his return for an earlier year which is now closed and the Commissioner successfully requires it to be included in a later year, then the correction of the effect of the erroneous inclusion of that item in the closed year may be made since the Commissioner has maintained a position inconsistent with the treatment of such item in such closed year. On the other hand, if an additional assessment would result from the correction of the error in the closed year, then the taxpayer must be the one maintaining the inconsistent position. For example, if the taxpayer deducted an item in an earlier year which is now closed and he successfully contends that the item should be deducted in a later year, then the correction of the effect of the erroneous deduction of that item in the closed year may be made since the taxpayer has taken a position inconsistent with the treatment of such item in such earlier year.

(c) There are two special circumstances which fall within this part but which do not require that an inconsistent position be maintained. One of these circumstances relates to the inclusion of an item of income in the correct year and the other relates to the allowance of a deduction in the correct year. In the first situation, if the Commissioner takes the position by a deficiency notice or before the Tax Court that an item of income should be included in the gross income of a taxpayer for a particular year and it is ultimately determined that such item was not so includible, then such item can be included in the income of the proper year if that year was not closed at the time the Commissioner took his position. In the second situation, if the taxpayer claims that a deduction should be allowed for a particular year and it is ultimately determined that the deduction was not allowable in that year, then the taxpayer may take the deduction in the proper year if that year was not closed at the time the taxpayer first claimed a deduction. [Reg. § 1.1311(a)-1.]

☐ [T.D. 6162, 2-8-56.]

Reg. § 1.1311(a)-1(c)

53,744 Mitigation of Effect of Limitations—Other Provisions

See p. 20,601 for regulations not amended to reflect law changes

[Reg. § 1.1311(a)-2]

§ 1.1311(a)-2. Purpose and scope of section 1311.—(a) Section 1311 provides for the correction of the effect of certain errors under circumstances specified in section 1312 when one or more provisions of law, such as the statute of limitations, would otherwise prevent such correction. Section 1311 may be applied to correct the effect of certain errors if, on the date of a determination (as defined in section 1313(a) and the regulations thereunder), correction is prevented by the operation of any provision of law other than sections 1311 through 1315 and section 7122 (relating to compromises) and the corresponding provisions of prior revenue laws. Examples of provisions preventing such corrections are sections 6501, 6511, 6532, and 6901(c), (d) and (e), relating to periods of limitations; sections 6212(c) and 6512 relating to the effect of petition to the Tax Court of the United States on further deficiency letters and on credits or refunds; section 7121 relating to closing agreements; and sections 6401 and 6514 relating to payments, refunds, or credits after the period of limitations has expired. Section 1311 may also be applied to correct the effect of an error if, on the date of the determination, correction of the error is prevented by the operation of any rule of law, such as *res judicata* or *estoppel*.

(b) The determination (including a determination under section 1313(a)(4)) may be with respect to any of the taxes imposed by subtitle A of the Internal Revenue Code of 1954, by chapter 1 and subchapters A, B, D, and E of chapter 2 of the Internal Revenue Code of 1939, or by the corresponding provisions of any prior revenue act, or by more than one of such provisions. Section 1311 may be applied to correct the effect of the error only as to the tax or taxes with respect to which the error was made which correspond to the tax or taxes with respect to which the determination relates. Thus, if the determination relates to a tax imposed by chapter 1 of the Internal Revenue Code of 1954, the adjustment may be only with respect to the tax imposed by such chapter or by the corresponding provisions of prior law.

(c) Section 1311 is not applicable if, on the date of the determination, correction of the effect of the error is permissible without recourse to said section.

(d) If the tax liability for the year with respect to which the error was made has been compromised under section 7122 or the corresponding provisions of prior revenue laws, no adjustment may be made under section 1311 with respect to said year.

(e) No adjustment may be made under section 1311 for any taxable year beginning prior to January 1, 1932. See section 1314(d).

(f) Section 1311 applies only to a determination (as defined in section 1313(a) and § § 1.1313(a)-1 to 1.1313(a)-4, inclusive) made after November 14, 1954. Section 3801 of the Internal Revenue Code of 1939 and the regulations thereunder apply to determinations, as defined therein, made on or before November 14, 1954. See section 1315. [Reg. § 1.1311(a)-2.]

☐ [T.D. 6162, 2-8-56.]

[Reg. § 1.1311(b)-1]

§ 1.1311(b)-1. Maintenance of an inconsistent position.—(a) *In general.* Under the circumstances stated in § 1.1312-1, § 1.1312-2, paragraph (a) of § 1.1312-3, § 1.1312-5, § 1.1312-6, and § 1.1312-7, the maintenance of an inconsistent position is a condition necessary for adjustment. The requirement in such circumstances is that a position maintained with respect to the taxable year of the determination and which is adopted in the determination be inconsistent with the erroneous inclusion, exclusion, omission, allowance, disallowance, recognition, or nonrecognition, as the case may be, with respect to the taxable year of the error. That is, a position successfully maintained with respect to the taxable year of the determination must be inconsistent with the treatment accorded an item which was the subject of an error in the computation of the tax for the closed taxable year. Adjustments under the circumstances stated in paragraph (b) of § 1.1312-3 and in § 1.1312-4 are made without regard to the maintenance of an inconsistent position.

(b) *Adjustments resulting in refund or credit.* (1) An adjustment under any of the circumstances stated in § 1.1312-1, § 1.1312-5, § 1.1312-6, or § 1.1312-7 which would result in the allowance of a refund or credit is authorized only if (i) the Commissioner, in connection with a determination, has maintained a position which is inconsistent with the erroneous inclusion, omission, disallowance, recognition, or nonrecognition, as the case may be, in the year of the error, and (ii) such inconsistent position is adopted in the determination.

Example. A taxpayer who keeps his books on the cash method erroneously included as income on his return for 1954 an item of accrued interest. After the period of limitations on refunds for 1954 had expired, the district director, on behalf of the Commissioner, proposed an adjustment for the year 1955 on the ground that the item of interest was received in 1955 and, therefore, was properly

Reg. § 1.1311(a)-2(a)

Mitigation of Effect of Limitations—Other Provisions

See p. 20,601 for regulations not amended to reflect law changes

includible in gross income for that year. The taxpayer and the district director entered into an agreement which meets all of the requirements of § 1.1313(a)-4 and which determines that the interest item was includible in gross income for 1955. The Commissioner has maintained a position inconsistent with the inclusion of the interest item for 1954. As the determination (the agreement pursuant to § 1.1313(a)-4) adopted such inconsistent position, an adjustment is authorized for the year 1954.

(2) An adjustment under circumstances stated in § 1.1312-1, § 1.1312-5, § 1.1312-6, or § 1.1312-7 which would result in the allowance of a refund or credit is not authorized if the taxpayer with respect to whom the determination is made, and not the Commissioner, has maintained such inconsistent position.

Example. In the example in subparagraph (1) of this paragraph, assume that the Commissioner asserted a deficiency for 1955 based upon other items for that year but, in computing the net income upon which such deficiency was based, did not include the item of interest. The taxpayer appealed to the Tax Court and in his petition asserted that the interest item should be included in gross income for 1955. The Tax Court in 1960 included the item of interest in its redetermination of tax for the year 1955. In such case no adjustment would be authorized for 1954 as the taxpayer, and not the Commissioner, maintained a position inconsistent with the erroneous inclusion of the item of interest in the gross income of the taxpayer for that year.

(c) *Adjustments resulting in additional assessments.* (1) An adjustment under any of the circumstances stated in § 1.1312-2, paragraph (a) of § 1.1312-3, § 1.1312-5, § 1.1312-6, or § 1.1312-7, which would result in an additional assessment is authorized only if (i) the taxpayer with respect to whom the determination is made has, in connection therewith, maintained a position which is inconsistent with the erroneous exclusion, omission, allowance, recognition, or nonrecognition, as the case may be, in the year of the error, and (ii) such inconsistent position is adopted in the determination.

Example. A taxpayer in his return for 1950 claimed and was allowed a deduction for a loss arising from a casualty. After the taxpayer had filed his return for 1951 and after the period of limitations upon the assessment of a deficiency for 1950 had expired, it was discovered that the loss actually occurred in 1951. The taxpayer, therefore, filed a claim for refund for the year 1951 based upon the allowance of a deduction for the loss in that year, and the claim was allowed by the Commissioner in 1955. The taxpayer thus has maintained a position inconsistent with the allowance of the deduction for 1950 by filing a claim for refund for 1951 based upon the same deduction. As the determination (the allowance of the claim for refund) adopts such inconsistent position, an adjustment is authorized for the year 1950.

(2) An adjustment under the circumstances stated in § 1.1312-2, paragraph (a) of § 1.1312-3, § 1.1312-5, § 1.1312-6, or § 1.1312-7 which would result in an additional assessment is not authorized if the Commissioner, and not the taxpayer, has maintained such inconsistent position.

Example. In the example in subparagraph (1) of this paragraph, assume that the taxpayer did not file a claim for refund for 1951 but the Commissioner issued a notice of deficiency for 1951 based upon other items. The taxpayer filed a petition with the Tax Court of the United States and the Commissioner in his answer voluntarily proposed the allowance for 1951 of a deduction for the loss previously allowed for 1950. The Tax Court took the deduction into account in its redetermination in 1955 of the tax for the year 1951. In such case no adjustment would be authorized for the year 1950 as the Commissioner, and not the taxpayer, has maintained a position inconsistent with the allowance of a deduction for the loss in that year. [Reg. § 1.1311(b)-1.]

☐ [T.D. 6162, 2-8-56. Amended by T.D. 6617, 11-6-62.]

[Reg. § 1.1311(b)-2]

§ 1.1311(b)-2. **Correction not barred at time of erroneous action.**—(a) An adjustment under the circumstances stated in paragraph (b) of § 1.1312-3 (relating to the double exclusion of an item of gross income) which would result in an additional assessment, is authorized only if assessment of a deficiency against the taxpayer or related taxpayer for the taxable year in which the item is includible was not barred by any law or rule of law at the time the Commissioner first maintained, in a notice of deficiency sent pursuant to section 6212 (or section 272(a) of the Internal Revenue Code of 1939) or before the Tax Court of the United States, that the item described in paragraph (b) of § 1.1312-3 should be included in the gross income of the taxpayer in the taxable year to which the determination relates.

(b) An adjustment under the circumstances stated in § 1.1312-4 (relating to the double disallowance of a deduction or credit), which would result in the allowance of a credit or refund, is authorized only if a credit or refund to the tax-

53,746 Mitigation of Effect of Limitations—Other Provisions

payer or related taxpayer, attributable to such adjustment, was not barred by any law or rule of law when the taxpayer first maintained in writing before the Commissioner or the Tax Court that he was entitled to such deduction or credit for the taxable year to which the determination relates. The taxpayer will be considered to have first maintained in writing before the Commissioner or the Tax Court that he was entitled to such deduction or credit when he first formally asserts his right to such deduction or credit as, for example, in a return, in a claim for refund, or in a petition (or an amended petition) before the Tax Court.

(c) Under the circumstances of adjustment with respect to which the conditions stated in this section are applicable, the conditions stated in § 1.1311(b)-1 (maintenance of an inconsistent position) are not required. See paragraph (b) of § 1.1312-3 and § 1.1312-4 for examples of the application of this section. [Reg. § 1.1311(b)-2.]

☐ [T.D. 6162, 2-8-56.]

[Reg. § 1.1311(b)-3]

§ 1.1311(b)-3. **Existence of relationship in case of adjustment by way of deficiency assessment.**—(a) Except for cases described in paragraph (b) of § 1.1312-3, no adjustment by way of a deficiency assessment shall be made, with respect to a related taxpayer, unless the relationship existed both at some time during the taxable year with respect to which the error was made and at the time the taxpayer with respect to whom the determination is made first maintained the inconsistent position with respect to the taxable year to which the determination relates. In the case of an adjustment by way of a deficiency assessment under the circumstance described in paragraph (b) of § 1.1312-3 (where the maintenance of an inconsistent position is not required), the relationship need exist only at some time during the taxable year in which the error was made.

(b) If the inconsistent position is maintained in a return, claim for refund, or petition (or amended petition) to the Tax Court of the United States for the taxable year in respect to which the determination is made, the requisite relationship must exist on the date of filing such document. If the inconsistent position is maintained in more than one of such documents, the requisite date is the date of filing of the document in which it was first maintained. If the inconsistent position was not thus maintained, then the relationship must exist on the date of the determination as, for example, where at the instance of the taxpayer a deduction is allowed, the right to which was not asserted in a return, claim for refund, or petition to the Tax Court, and a determination is effected by means of a closing agreement or an agreement under section 1313(a)(4). [Reg. § 1.1311(b)-3.]

☐ [T.D. 6162, 2-8-56.]

[Reg. § 1.1312-1]

§ 1.1312-1. **Double inclusion of an item of gross income.**—(a) Paragraph (1) of section 1312 applies if the determination requires the inclusion in a taxpayer's gross income of an item which was erroneously included in the gross income of the same taxpayer for another taxable year or of a related taxpayer for the same or another taxable year.

(b) The application of paragraph (a) of this section may be illustrated by the following examples:

Example (1). A taxpayer who keeps his books on the cash method erroneously included in income on his return for 1947 an item of accrued rent. In 1952, after the period of limitation on refunds for 1947 had expired, the Commissioner discovered that the taxpayer received this rent in 1948 and asserted a deficiency for the year 1948 which is sustained by the Tax Court of the United States in 1955. An adjustment in favor of the taxpayer is authorized with respect to the year 1947. If the taxpayer had returned the rent for both 1947 and 1948 and by a determination was denied a refund claim for 1948 on account of the rent item, a similar adjustment is authorized.

Example (2). A husband assigned to his wife salary to be earned by him in the year 1952. The wife included such salary in her separate return for that year and the husband omitted it. The Commissioner asserted a deficiency against the wife for 1952 with respect to a different item; she contested that deficiency, and the Tax Court entered an order in her case which became final in 1955. The wife would therefore be barred by section 6512(a) from claiming a refund for 1952. Thereafter, the Commissioner asserted a deficiency against the husband on account of the omission of such salary from his return for 1952. In 1955 the husband and the Commissioner enter into a closing agreement for the year 1952 in which the salary is taxed to the husband. An adjustment is authorized with respect to the wife's tax for 1952. [Reg. § 1.1312-1.]

☐ [T.D. 6162, 2-8-56.]

[Reg. § 1.1312-2]

§ 1.1312-2. **Double allowance of a deduction or credit.**—(a) Paragraph (2) of section 1312 applies if the determination allows the taxpayer a deduction or credit which was erroneously allowed the same taxpayer for another taxable year or a

Reg. § 1.1311(b)-3(a)

related taxpayer for the same or another taxable year.

(b) The application of paragraph (a) of this section may be illustrated by the following examples:

Example (1). A taxpayer in his return for 1950 claimed and was allowed a deduction for destruction of timber by a forest fire. Subsequently, it was discovered that the forest fire occurred in 1951 rather than 1950. After the expiration of the period of limitations for the assessment of a deficiency for 1950, the taxpayer filed a claim for refund for 1951 based upon a deduction for the fire loss in that year. The Commissioner in 1955 allows the claim for refund. An adjustment is authorized with respect to the year 1950.

Example (2). The beneficiary of a testamentary trust in his return for 1949 claimed, and was allowed, a deduction for depreciation of the trust property. The Commissioner asserted a deficiency against the beneficiary for 1949 with respect to a different item and a final decision of the Tax Court of the United States was rendered in 1951, so that the Commissioner was thereafter barred by section 272(f) of the Internal Revenue Code of 1939 from asserting a further deficiency against the beneficiary for 1949. The trustee thereafter filed a timely refund claim contending that, under the terms of the will, the trust, and not the beneficiary, was entitled to the allowance for depreciation. The court in 1955 sustains the refund claim. An adjustment is authorized with respect to the beneficiary's tax for 1949. [Reg. § 1.1312-2.]

☐ [T.D. 6162, 2-8-56.]

[Reg. § 1.1312-3]

§ 1.1312-3. **Double exclusion of an item of gross income.**—(a) *Items included in income or with respect to which a tax was paid.* (1) Paragraph (3)(A) of section 1312 applies if the determination requires the exclusion, from a taxpayer's gross income, of an item included in a return filed by the taxpayer, or with respect to which tax was paid, and which was erroneously excluded or omitted from the gross income of the same taxpayer for another taxable year or of a related taxpayer for the same or another taxable year.

(2) The application of subparagraph (1) of this paragraph may be illustrated by the following examples:

Example (1). (i) A taxpayer received payments in 1951 under a contract for the performance of services and included the payments in his return for that year. After the expiration of the period of limitations for the assessment of a deficiency for 1950, the Commissioner issued a notice of deficiency to the taxpayer for the year 1951 based upon adjustments to other items, and the taxpayer filed a petition with the Tax Court of the United States and maintained in the proceeding before the Tax Court that he kept his books on the accrual basis and that the payments received in 1951 were on income that had accrued and was properly taxable in 1950. A final decision of the Tax Court was rendered in 1955 excluding the payments from 1951 income. An adjustment in favor of the Commissioner is authorized with respect to the year 1950, whether or not a tax had been paid on the income reported in the 1951 return.

(ii) Assume the same facts as in (i), except that the taxpayer had not included the payments in any return and had not paid a tax thereon. No adjustment would be authorized under section 1312(3)(A) with respect to the year 1950. If the taxpayer, however, had paid a deficiency asserted for 1951 based upon the inclusion of the payments in 1951 income and thereafter successfully sued for refund thereof, an adjustment would be authorized with respect to the year 1950. (See paragraph (b) of this section for circumstances under which correction is authorized with respect to items not included in income and on which a tax was not paid.)

Example (2). A father and son conducted a partnership business, each being entitled to one-half of the net profits. The father included the entire net income of the partnership in his return for 1948, and the son included no portion of this income in his return for that year. Shortly before the expiration of the period of limitations with respect to deficiency assessments and refund claims for both father and son for 1948, the father filed a claim for refund of that portion of his 1948 tax attributable to the half of the partnership income which should have been included in the son's return. The court sustains the claim for refund in 1955. An adjustment is authorized with respect to the son's tax for 1948.

(b) *Items not included in income and with respect to which the tax was not paid.* (1) Paragraph (3)(B) of section 1312 applies if the determination requires the exclusion from gross income of an item not included in a return filed by the taxpayer and with respect to which a tax was not paid, but which is includible in the gross income of the same taxpayer for another taxable year, or in the gross income of a related taxpayer for the same or another taxable year. This is one of the two circumstances in which the maintenance of an inconsistent position is not a requirement for an adjustment, but the requirements in paragraph (a) of § 1.1311(b)-2 must be fulfilled (correction not barred at time of erroneous action).

Reg. § 1.1312-3(b)

53,748 Mitigation of Effect of Limitations—Other Provisions

See p. 20,601 for regulations not amended to reflect law changes

(2) The application of subparagraph (1) of this paragraph may be illustrated by the following examples:

Example (1). The taxpayer, A, who computes his income by use of the accrual method of accounting, performed in 1949 services for which he received payments in 1949 and 1950. He did not include in his return for either 1949 or 1950 the payments which he received in 1950, and he paid no tax with respect to such payments. In 1952 the Commissioner sent a notice of deficiency to A with respect to the year 1949, contending that A should have included all of such payments in his return for that year. A contested the deficiency on the basis that in 1949 he had no accruable right to the payments which he received in 1950. In 1955 (after the expiration of the period of limitations for assessing deficiencies with respect to 1950), the Tax Court sustains A's position. The Commissioner may assess a deficiency for 1950, since a deficiency assessment for that year was not barred when he sent the notice of deficiency with respect to 1949.

Example (2). B and C were partners in 1950, each being entitled to one-half of the profits of the partnership business. During 1950, B received an item of income which he treated as partnership income so that his return for that year reflected only 50 percent of such item. C, however, included no part of such item in any return and paid no tax with respect thereto. In 1952, the Commissioner sent to C a notice of deficiency with respect to 1950, contending that his return for that year should have reflected 50 percent of such item. C contested the deficiency on the basis that such item was not partnership income. In 1955, after the expiration of the period of limitations for assessing deficiencies with respect to 1950, the Tax Court sustained C's position. The Commissioner may assess a deficiency against B with respect to 1950 requiring him to include the entire amount of such item in his income since assessment of the deficiency was not barred when the Commissioner sent the notice of deficiency with respect to such item to C. [Reg. § 1.1312-3.]

☐ [T.D. 6162, 2-8-56.]

[Reg. § 1.1312-4]

§ 1.1312-4. Double disallowance of a deduction or credit.—(a) Paragraph (4) of section 1312 applies if the determination disallows a deduction or credit which should have been, but was not, allowed to the same taxpayer for another taxable year or to a related taxpayer for the same or another taxable year. This is one of the two circumstances in which the maintenance of an inconsistent position is not a requirement for an adjustment but the requirements in paragraph (b) of § 1.1311(b)-2 must be fulfilled (correction not barred at time of erroneous action).

(b) The application of paragraph (a) of this section may be illustrated by the following examples:

Example (1). The taxpayer, A, who computes his income by use of the accrual method of accounting, deducted in his return for the taxable year 1951 an item of expense which he paid in such year. At the time A filed his return for 1951, the statute of limitations for 1950 had not expired. Subsequently, the Commissioner asserted a deficiency for 1951 based on the position that the liability for such expense should have been accrued for the taxable year 1950. In 1955, after the period of limitations on refunds for 1950 had expired, there was a determination by the Tax Court disallowing such deduction for the taxable year 1951. A is entitled to an adjustment for the taxable year 1950. However, if such liability should have been accrued for the taxable year 1946 instead of 1950, A would not be entitled to an adjustment, if a credit or refund with respect to 1946 was already barred when he deducted such expense for the taxable year 1951.

Example (2). The taxpayer, B, in his return for 1951 claimed a deduction for a charitable contribution. The Commissioner asserted a deficiency for such year contending that 50 percent of the deduction should be disallowed, since the contribution was made from community property 50 percent of which was attributable to B's spouse. The deficiency is sustained by the Tax Court in 1956, subsequent to the period of limitations within which B's spouse could claim a refund with respect to 1951. An adjustment is permitted to B's spouse, a related taxpayer, since a refund attributable to a deduction by her of such contribution was not barred when B claimed the deduction. [Reg. § 1.1312-4.]

☐ [T.D. 6162, 2-8-56.]

[Reg. § 1.1312-5]

§ 1.1312-5. Correlative deductions and inclusions for trusts or estates and legatees, beneficiaries, or heirs.—(a) Paragraph (5) of section 1312 applies to distributions by a trust or an estate to the beneficiaries, heirs, or legatees. If the determination relates to the amount of the deduction allowed by sections 651 and 661 or the inclusion in taxable income of the beneficiary required by sections 652 and 662 (including amounts falling within subpart D, of subchapter J, chapter 1 of the Code, relating to treatment of excess distributions by trusts), or if the determination relates to the additional deduction (or inclusion) specified in section 162(b) and (c) of the Internal Revenue

Reg. § 1.1312-4(a)

Mitigation of Effect of Limitations—Other Provisions

Code of 1939 (or the corresponding provisions of a prior revenue act), with respect to amounts paid, credited, or required to be distributed to the beneficiaries, heirs, and legatees, and such determination requires:

(1) The allowance to the estate or trust of the deduction when such amounts have been erroneously omitted or excluded from the income of the beneficiaries, heirs, or legatees; or

(2) The inclusion of such amounts in the income of the beneficiaries, heirs, or legatees when the deduction has been erroneously disallowed to or omitted by the estate or trust; or

(3) The disallowance to an estate or trust of the deduction when such amounts have been erroneously included in the income of the beneficiaries, heirs, or legatees; or

(4) The exclusion of such amounts from the income of the beneficiaries, heirs, or legatees when the deduction has been erroneously allowed to the estate or trust.

(b) The application of paragraph (a)(1) of this section may be illustrated by the following example:

Example. For the taxable year 1954, a trustee, directed by the trust instrument to accumulate the trust income, made no distribution to the beneficiary and returned the entire income as taxable to the trust. Accordingly the beneficiary did not include the trust income in his return for the year 1954. In 1957, a State court holds invalid the clause directing accumulation and determines that the income is required to be currently distributed. It also rules that certain extraordinary dividends which the trustee in good faith allocated to corpus in 1954 were properly allocable to income. In 1958, the trustee, relying upon the court decision, files a claim for refund of the tax paid on behalf of the trust for the year 1954 and thereafter files a suit in the District Court. The claim is sustained by the court (except as to the tax on the extraordinary dividends) in 1959 after the expiration of the period of limitations upon deficiency assessments against the beneficiary for the year 1954. An adjustment is authorized with respect to the beneficiary's tax for the year 1954. The treatment of the distribution to the beneficiary of the extraordinary dividends shall be determined under subpart D of subchapter J.

(c) The application of paragraph (a)(2) of this section may be illustrated by the following example:

Example. Assume the same facts as in the example in paragraph (b) of this section, except that, instead of the trustee's filing a refund claim, the Commissioner, relying upon the decision of the State court, asserts a deficiency against the beneficiary for 1954. The deficiency is sustained by final decision of the Tax Court of the United States in 1959, after the expiration of the period for filing claim for refund on behalf of the trust for 1954. An adjustment is authorized with respect to the trust for the year 1954.

(d) The application of paragraph (a)(3) of this section may be illustrated by the following example:

Example. A trustee claimed in the trust return for 1954 for amounts paid to the beneficiary a deduction to the extent of distributable net income. This amount was included by the beneficiary in gross income in his return for 1954. In computing distributable net income the trustee had included short and long-term capital gains. In 1958, the Commissioner asserts a deficiency against the trust on the ground that the capital gains were not includible in distributable net income, and that, therefore, the gains were taxable to the trust, not the beneficiary. The deficiency is sustained by a final decision of the Tax Court in 1960, after the expiration of the period for filing claims for refund by the beneficiary for 1954. An adjustment is authorized with respect to the beneficiary's tax for the year 1954, based on the exclusion from 1954 gross income of the capital gains previously considered distributed by the trust under section 662.

(e) The application of paragraph (a)(4) of this section may be illustrated by the following example:

Example. Assume the same facts as in the example in paragraph (d) of this section, except that, instead of the Commissioner's asserting a deficiency, the beneficiary filed a refund claim for 1954 on the same ground. The claim is sustained by the court in 1960 after the expiration of the period of limitations upon deficiency assessments against the trust for 1954. An adjustment is authorized with respect to the trust for the year 1954. [Reg. § 1.1312-5.]

☐ [T.D. 6162, 2-8-56.]

[Reg. § 1.1312-6]

§ 1.1312-6. Correlative deductions and credits for certain related corporations.—(a) Paragraph (6) of section 1312 applies if the determination allows or disallows a deduction (including a credit) to a corporation, and if a correlative deduction or credit has been erroneously allowed, omitted, or disallowed in respect of a related taxpayer described in section 1313(c)(7).

(b) The application of paragraph (a) of this section may be illustrated by the following examples:

53,750 Mitigation of Effect of Limitations—Other Provisions

See p. 20,601 for regulations not amended to reflect law changes

Example (1). X Corporation is a wholly-owned subsidiary of Y Corporation. In 1955, X Corporation paid $5,000 to Y Corporation and claimed an interest deduction for this amount in its return for 1955. Y Corporation included this amount in its gross income for 1955. In 1958, the Commissioner asserted a deficiency against X Corporation for 1955, contending that the deduction for interest paid should be disallowed on the ground that the payment was in reality the payment of a dividend to Y Corporation. X Corporation contested the deficiency, and ultimately in June 1959, a final decision of the Tax Court sustained the Commissioner. Since the amount of the payment is a dividend, Y Corporation should have been allowed for 1955 the corporate dividends-received deduction under section 243 with respect to such payment. However, the Tax Court's decision sustaining the deficiency against X Corporation occurred after the expiration of the period for filing claim for refund by Y Corporation for 1955. An adjustment is authorized with respect to Y Corporation for 1955.

Example (2). Assume the same facts as in example (1) except that, instead of the Commissioner asserting a deficiency against X Corporation for 1955, Y Corporation filed a claim for refund in 1958, alleging that the payment received in 1955 from X Corporation was in reality a dividend to which the corporate dividends-received deduction (section 243) applies. The Commissioner denied the claim, and ultimately in June 1959, the district court, in a final decision, sustained Y Corporation. Since the amount of the payment is a dividend, X Corporation should not have been allowed an interest deduction for the amount paid to Y Corporation. However, the district court's decision sustaining the claim for refund occurred after the expiration of the period of limitations for assessing a deficiency against X Corporation for the year 1955. An adjustment is authorized with respect to X Corporation's tax for 1955. [Reg. § 1.1312-6.]

☐ [T.D. 6617, 11-6-62.]

[Reg. § 1.1312-7]

§ 1.1312-7. Basis of property after erroneous treatment of a prior transaction.—(a) Paragraph (7) of section 1312 applies if the determination establishes the basis of property, and there occurred one of the following types of errors in respect of a prior transaction upon which such basis depends, or in respect of a prior transaction which was erroneously treated as affecting such basis:

(1) An erroneous inclusion in, or omission from, gross income, or

(2) An erroneous recognition or nonrecognition of gain or loss, or

(3) An erroneous deduction of an item properly chargeable to capital account or an erroneous charge to capital account of an item properly deductible.

(b) For this section to apply, the taxpayer with respect to whom the erroneous treatment occurred must be—

(1) The taxpayer with respect to whom the determination is made, or

(2) A taxpayer who acquired title to the property in the erroneously treated transaction and from whom, mediately or immediately, the taxpayer with respect to whom the determination is made derived title in such a manner that he will have a basis ascertained by reference to the basis in the hands of the taxpayer who acquired title to the property in the erroneously treated transaction, or

(3) A taxpayer who had title to the property at the time of the erroneously treated transaction and from whom, mediately or immediately, the taxpayer with respect to whom the determination is made derived title, if the basis of the property in the hands of the taxpayer with respect to whom the determination is made is determined under section 1015(a) (relating to the basis of property acquired by gift).

No adjustment is authorized with respect to the transferor of the property in a transaction upon which the basis of the property depends, when the determination is with respect to the original transferee or a subsequent transferee of such original transferee.

(c) The application of this section may be illustrated by the following examples:

Example (1). In 1949 taxpayer A transferred property which had cost him $5,000 to the X Corporation in exchange for an original issue of shares of its stock having a fair market value of $10,000. In his return for 1949 taxpayer A treated the exchange as one in which the gain or loss was not recognizable:

(i) In 1955 the X Corporation maintains that the gain should have been recognized in the exchange in 1949 and therefore the property it received had a $10,000 basis for depreciation. Its position is adopted in a closing agreement. No adjustment is authorized with respect to the tax of the X Corporation for 1949, as none of the three types of errors specified in paragraph (a) of this section occurred with respect to the X Corporation in the treatment of the exchange in 1949. Moreover, no adjustment is authorized with respect to taxpayer A, as he is not within any of the

Reg. § 1.1312-7(a)(1)

three classes of taxpayers described in paragraph (b) of this section.

(ii) In 1953 taxpayer A sells the stock which he received in 1949 and maintains that, as gain should have been recognized in the exchange in 1949 the basis for computing the profit on the sale is $10,000. His position is confirmed in a closing agreement executed in 1955. An adjustment is authorized with respect to his tax for the year 1949 as the basis for computing the gain on the sale depends upon the transaction in 1949, and in respect of that transaction there was an erroneous nonrecognition of gain to taxpayer A, the taxpayer with respect to whom the determination is made.

Example (2). In 1950 taxpayer A was the owner of 10 shares of the common stock of the Z Corporation which had a basis of $1,500. In that year he received as a dividend thereon 10 shares of the preferred stock of the same corporation having a fair market value of $1,000. On his books, entries were made reducing the basis of the common stock by allocating $500 of the basis to the preferred stock, and on his return for 1950 he did not include the dividend in gross income.

(i) In 1951 taxpayer A made a gift of the preferred stock of the Z Corporation to taxpayer B, an unrelated individual. Taxpayer B sold the stock in 1953 and on his return for that year he reported the sale and claimed a basis of $1,000, contending that the dividend of preferred stock was taxable to A in 1950 at its fair market value of $1,000. The basis of $1,000 is confirmed by a closing agreement executed in 1955. An adjustment is authorized with respect to taxpayer A's tax for 1950, as the closing agreement determines basis of property, and in a prior transaction upon which such basis depends there was an erroneous omission from gross income of taxpayer A, a taxpayer who acquired title to the property in the erroneously treated transaction and from whom, immediately, the taxpayer with respect to whom the determination is made derived title.

(ii) Assuming the same facts as in (i) except that the common stock instead of the preferred stock was the subject of the gift, and the basis claimed by taxpayer B and confirmed in the closing agreement was $1,500. An adjustment is authorized with respect to taxpayer A's tax for 1950, as the closing agreement determines the basis of property, and in a prior transaction which was erroneously treated as affecting such basis there was an erroneous omission from gross income of taxpayer A, a taxpayer who had title to the property at the time of the erroneously treated transaction, and from whom, immediately, taxpayer B, with respect to whom the determination is made, derived title. The basis of the property in taxpayer B's hands with respect to whom the determination is made is determined under section 1015(a) (relating to the basis of property acquired by gift).

Example (3). In 1950 taxpayer A sold property acquired at a cost of $5,000 to taxpayer B for $10,000. In his return for 1950 taxpayer A failed to include the profit on such sale. In 1953 taxpayer B sold the property for $12,000, and in his return for 1953 reported a gain of $2,000 upon the sale which is confirmed by a closing agreement executed in 1955. No adjustment is authorized with respect to the tax of taxpayer A for 1950, as he does not come within any of the three classes of taxpayers described in paragraph (b) of this section.

Example (4). In 1950 a taxpayer who owned 100 shares of stock in Corporation Y received $1,000 from the corporation which amount the taxpayer reported on his return for 1950 as a taxable dividend. In 1952 Corporation Y was completely liquidated and the taxpayer received in that year liquidating distributions totalling $8,000. In his return for 1952 the taxpayer reported the receipt of the $8,000 and computed his gain or loss upon the liquidation by using as a basis the amount which he paid for the stock. The Commissioner maintained that the distribution in 1950 was a distribution out of capital and that in computing the taxpayer's gain or loss upon the liquidation in 1952, the basis of the stock should be reduced by the $1,000. This position is adopted in a closing agreement executed in 1955 with respect to the year 1952. An adjustment is authorized with respect to the year 1950 as the basis for computing gain or loss in 1952 depends upon the transaction in 1950, and in respect of the 1950 transaction (upon which the basis of the property depends) there was an erroneous inclusion in gross income of the taxpayer with respect to whom the determination is made.

Example (5). In 1946 a taxpayer received 100 shares of stock of the X Corporation having a fair market value of $5,000, in exchange for shares of stock in the Y Corporation which he had acquired at a cost of $12,000. In his return for 1946 the taxpayer treated the exchange as one in which gain or loss was not recognizable. The taxpayer sold 50 shares of the X Corporation stock in 1947 and in his return for that year treated such shares as having a $6,000 basis. In 1952, the taxpayer sold the remaining 50 shares of stock of the X Corporation for $7,500 and reported $1,500 gain in his return for 1952. After the expiration of the period of limitations on deficiency assessments and on refund claims for 1946 and 1947, the

Reg. § 1.1312-7(c)

53,752 Mitigation of Effect of Limitations—Other Provisions
See p. 20,601 for regulations not amended to reflect law changes

Commissioner asserted a deficiency for 1952 on the ground that the loss realized on the exchange in 1946 was erroneously treated as nonrecognizable, and the basis for computing gain upon the sale in 1952 was $2,500, resulting in a gain of $5,000. The deficiency is sustained by the Tax Court in 1955. An adjustment is authorized with respect to the year 1946 as to the entire $7,000 loss realized on the exchange, as the Court's decision determines the basis of property, and in a prior transaction upon which such basis depends there was an erroneous nonrecognition of loss to the taxpayer with respect to whom the determination was made. No adjustment is authorized with respect to the year 1947 as the basis for computing gain upon the sale of the 50 shares in 1952 does not depend upon the transaction in 1947 but upon the transaction in 1946. [Reg. § 1.1312-7.]

☐ [T.D. 6162, 2-8-56. Amended by T.D. 6617, 11-6-62.]

[Reg. § 1.1312-8]

§ 1.1312-8. Law applicable in determination of error.—The question whether there was an erroneous inclusion, exclusion, omission, allowance, disallowance, recognition, or nonrecognition is determined under the provisions of the internal revenue laws applicable with respect to the year as to which the inclusion, exclusion, omission, allowance, disallowance, recognition, or nonrecognition, as the case may be, was made. The fact that the inclusion, exclusion, omission, allowance, disallowance, recognition, or nonrecognition, as the case may be, was in pursuance of an interpretation, either judicial or administrative, accorded such provisions of the internal revenue laws at the time of such action is not necessarily determinative of this question. For example, if a later judicial decision authoritatively alters such interpretation so that such action was contrary to such provisions of the internal revenue laws as later interpreted, the inclusion, exclusion, omission, allowance, disallowance, recognition, or nonrecognition, as the case may be, is erroneous within the meaning of section 1312. [Reg. § 1.1312-8.]

☐ [T.D. 6162, 2-8-56. Amended by T.D. 6617, 11-6-62.]

[Reg. § 1.1313(a)-1]

§ 1.1313(a)-1. Decision by Tax Court or other court as a determination.—(a) A determination may take the form of a decision by the Tax Court of the United States or a judgment, decree, or other order by any court of competent jurisdiction, which has become final.

(b) The date upon which a decision by the Tax Court becomes final is prescribed in section 7481.

(c) The date upon which a judgment of any other court becomes final must be determined upon the basis of the facts in the particular case. Ordinarily, a judgment of a United States district court becomes final upon the expiration of the time allowed for taking an appeal, if no such appeal is duly taken within such time; and a judgment of the United States Court of Claims becomes final upon the expiration of the time allowed for filing a petition for certiorari if no such petition is duly filed within such time. [Reg. § 1.1313(a)-1.]

☐ [T.D. 6162, 2-8-56.]

[Reg. § 1.1313(a)-2]

§ 1.1313(a)-2. Closing agreement as a determination.—A determination may take the form of a closing agreement authorized by section 7121. Such an agreement may relate to the total tax liability of the taxpayer for a particular taxable year or years or to one or more separate items affecting such liability. A closing agreement becomes final for the purpose of this section on the date of its approval by the Commissioner. [Reg. § 1.1313(a)-2.]

☐ [T.D. 6162, 2-8-56.]

[Reg. § 1.1313(a)-3]

§ 1.1313(a)-3. Final disposition of claim for refund as a determination.—(a) *In general.* A determination may take the form of a final disposition of a claim for refund. Such disposition may result in a determination with respect to two classes of items, i.e., items included by the taxpayer in a claim for refund and items applied by the Commissioner to offset the alleged overpayment. The time at which a disposition in respect of a particular item becomes final may depend not only upon what action is taken with respect to that item but also upon whether the claim for refund is allowed or disallowed.

(b) *Items with respect to which the taxpayer's claim is allowed.* (1) The disposition with respect to an item as to which the taxpayer's contention in the claim for refund is sustained becomes final on the date of allowance of the refund or credit if—

(i) The taxpayer's claim for refund is unqualifiedly allowed; or

(ii) The taxpayer's contention with respect to an item is sustained and with respect to other items is denied, so that the net result is an allowance of refund or credit; or

(iii) The taxpayer's contention with respect to an item is sustained, but the Commissioner applies other items to offset the amount of the alleged overpayment and the items so applied

Reg. § 1.1312-8

Mitigation of Effect of Limitations—Other Provisions

do not completely offset such amount but merely reduce it so that the net result is an allowance of refund or credit.

(2) If the taxpayer's contention in the claim for refund with respect to an item is sustained but the Commissioner applies other items to offset the amount of the alleged overpayment so that the net result is a disallowance of the claim for refund, the date of mailing, by registered mail, of the notice of disallowance (see section 6532) is the date of the final disposition as to the item with respect to which the taxpayer's contention is sustained.

(c) *Items with respect to which the taxpayer's claim is disallowed.* The disposition with respect to an item as to which the taxpayer's contention in the claim for refund is denied becomes final upon the expiration of the time allowed by section 6532 for instituting suit on the claim for refund, unless the suit is instituted prior to the expiration of such period, if—

(1) The taxpayer's claim for refund is unqualifiedly disallowed; or

(2) The taxpayer's contention with respect to an item is denied and with respect to other items is sustained so that the net result is an allowance of refund or credit; or

(3) The taxpayer's contention with respect to an item is sustained in part and denied in part. For example, assume that the taxpayer claimed a deductible loss of $10,000 and a consequent overpayment of $2,500 and the Commissioner concedes that a deductible loss was sustained, but only in the amount of $5,000. The disposition of the claim for refund with respect to the allowance of the $5,000 and the disallowance of the remaining $5,000 becomes final upon the expiration of the time for instituting suit on the claim for refund unless suit is instituted prior to the expiration of such period.

(d) *Items applied by the Commissioner in reduction of the refund or credit.* If the Commissioner applies an item in reduction of the overpayment alleged in the claim for refund, and the net result is an allowance of refund or credit, the disposition with respect to the item so applied by the Commissioner becomes final upon the expiration of the time allowed by section 6532 for instituting suit on the claim for refund, unless suit is instituted prior to the expiration of such period. If such application of the item results in the assertion of a deficiency, such action does not constitute a final disposition of a claim for refund within the meaning of § 1.1313(a)-3, but subsequent action taken with respect to such deficiency may result in a determination under §§ 1.1313(a)-1, 1.1313(a)-2, or 1.1313(a)-4.

(e) *Elimination of waiting period.* The necessity of waiting for the expiration of the 2-year period of limitations provided in section 6532 may be avoided in such cases as are described in paragraph (c) or (d) of this section by the use of a closing agreement (see § 1.1313(a)-2) or agreement under § 1.1313(a)-4 to effect a determination. [Reg. § 1.1313(a)-3.]

☐ [*T.D.* 6162, 2-8-56.]

[Reg. § 1.1313(a)-4]

§ 1.1313(a)-4. **Agreement pursuant to section 1313(a)(4) as a determination.**—(a) *In general.* (1) A determination may take the form of an agreement made pursuant to this section. This section is intended to provide an expeditious method for obtaining an adjustment under section 1311 and for offsetting deficiencies and refunds whenever possible. The provisions of part II (section 1311 and following), subchapter Q, chapter 1 of the Code, must be strictly complied with in any such agreement.

(2) An agreement made pursuant to this section will not, in itself, establish the tax liability for the open taxable year to which it relates, but it will state the amount of the tax, as then determined, for such open year. The tax may be the amount of tax shown on the return as filed by the taxpayer, but if any changes in the amount have been made, or if any are being made by documents executed concurrently with the execution of said agreement, such changes must be taken into account. For example, an agreement pursuant to this section may be executed concurrently with the execution of a waiver of restrictions on assessment and collection of a deficiency or acceptance of an overassessment with respect to the open taxable year, or concurrently with the execution and filing of a stipulation in a proceeding before the Tax Court of the United States, where an item which is to be the subject of an adjustment under section 1311 is disposed of by the stipulation and is not left for determination by the court.

(b) *Contents of agreement.* An agreement made pursuant to this section shall be so designated in the heading of the agreement, and it shall contain the following:

(1) A statement of the amount of the tax determined for the open taxable year to which the agreement relates, and if said liability is established or altered by a document executed concurrently with the execution of the agreement, a reference to said document.

(2) A concise statement of the material facts with respect to the item that was the subject of the error in the closed taxable year or years, and a statement of the manner in which such item was

53,754 Mitigation of Effect of Limitations—Other Provisions
See p. 20,601 for regulations not amended to reflect law changes

treated in computing the tax liability set forth pursuant to subparagraph (1) of this paragraph.

(3) A statement as to the amount of the adjustment ascertained pursuant to § 1.1314(a)-1 for the taxable year with respect to which the error was made and, where applicable, a statement as to the amount of the adjustment or adjustments ascertained pursuant to § 1.1314(a)-2 with respect to any other taxable year or years; and

(4) A waiver of restrictions on assessment and collection of any deficiencies set forth pursuant to subparagraph 3 of this paragraph.

(c) *Execution and effect of agreement.* An agreement made pursuant to this section shall be signed by the taxpayer with respect to whom the determination is made, or on the taxpayer's behalf by an agent or attorney acting pursuant to a power of attorney on file with the Internal Revenue Service. If an adjustment is to be made in a case of a related taxpayer, the agreement shall be signed also by the related taxpayer, or on the related taxpayer's behalf by an agent or attorney acting pursuant to a power of attorney on file with the Internal Revenue Service. It may be signed on behalf of the Commissioner by the district director, or such other person as is authorized by the Commissioner. When duly executed, such agreement will constitute the authority for an allowance of any refund or credit agreed to therein, and for the immediate assessment of any deficiency agreed to therein for the taxable year with respect to which the error was made, or any closed taxable year or years affected, or treated as affected, by a net operating loss deduction or capital loss carryover determined with reference to the taxable year with respect to which the error was made.

(d) *Finality of determination.* A determination made by an agreement pursuant to this section becomes final when the tax liability for the open taxable year to which the determination relates becomes final. During the period, if any, that a deficiency may be assessed or a refund or credit allowed with respect to such year, either the taxpayer or the Commissioner may properly pursue any of the procedures provided by law to secure a further modification of the tax liability for such year. For example, if the taxpayer subsequently files a claim for refund, or if the Commissioner subsequently issues a notice of deficiency with respect to such year, either may adopt a position with respect to the item that was the subject of the adjustment that is at variance with the manner in which said item was treated in the agreement. Any assessment, refund, or credit that is subsequently made with respect to the tax liability for such open taxable year, to the extent that it is based upon a revision in the treatment of the item that was the subject of the adjustment, shall constitute an alteration or revocation of the determination for the purpose of a redetermination of the adjustment pursuant to paragraph (d) of § 1.1314 (b)-1. [Reg. § 1.1313(a)-4.]

☐ [T.D. 6162, 2-8-56.]

[Reg. § 1.1313(c)-1]

§ 1.1313(c)-1. Related taxpayer.—An adjustment in the case of the taxpayer with respect to whom the error was made may be authorized under section 1311 although the determination is made with respect to a different taxpayer, provided that such taxpayers stand in one of the relationships specified in section 1313(c). The concept of "related taxpayer" has application to all of the circumstances of adjustment specified in § 1.1312-1 through § 1.1312-5 if the related taxpayer is one described in section 1313(c); it has application to the circumstances of adjustment specified in § 1.1312-6 only if the related taxpayer is one described in section 1313(c)(7); it does not apply in the circumstances specified in § 1.1312-7. If such relationship exists, it is not essential that the error involve a transaction made possible only by reason of the existence of the relationship. For example, if the error with respect to which an adjustment is sought under section 1311 grew out of an assignment of rents between taxpayer A and taxpayer B, who are partners, and the determination is with respect to taxpayer A, an adjustment with respect to taxpayer B may be permissible despite the fact that the assignment had nothing to do with the business of the partnership. The relationship need not exist throughout the entire taxable year with respect to which the error was made, but only at some time during that taxable year. For example, if a taxpayer on February 15 assigns to his fiancee the net rents of a building which the taxpayer owns, and the two are married before the end of a taxable year, an adjustment may be permissible if the determination relates to such rents despite the fact that they were not husband and wife at the time of the assignment. See § 1.1311(b)-3 for the requirement in certain cases that the relationship exist at the time an inconsistent postion is first maintained. [Reg. § 1.1313(c)-1.]

☐ [T.D. 6162, 2-8-56. *Amended by* T.D. 6617, 11-6-62.]

[Reg. § 1.1314(a)-1]

§ 1.1314(a)-1. Ascertainment of amount of adjustment in year of error.—(a) In computing the amount of the adjustment under sections 1311 to 1315, inclusive, there must first be ascertained the amount of the tax previously determined for the taxpayer as to whom the error was made for the taxable year with respect to which the error

Reg. § 1.1313(c)-1

Mitigation of Effect of Limitations—Other Provisions 53,755

See p. 20,601 for regulations not amended to reflect law changes

was made. The tax previously determined for any taxable year may be the amount of tax shown on the taxpayer's return, but if any changes in that amount have been made, they must be taken into account. In such cases, the tax previously determined will be the sum of the amount shown as the tax by the taxpayer upon his return and the amounts previously assessed (or collected without assessment) as deficiencies, reduced by the amount of any rebates made. The amount shown as the tax by the taxpayer upon his return and the amount of any rebates or deficiencies shall be determined in accordance with the provisions of section 6211 and the regulations thereunder.

(b)(1) The tax previously determined may consist of tax for any taxable year beginning after December 31, 1931, imposed by subtitle A of the Internal Revenue Code of 1954, by chapter 1 and subchapters A, B, D, and E of chapter 2 of the Internal Revenue Code of 1939, or by the corresponding provisions of prior internal revenue laws, or by any one or more of such provisions.

(2) After the tax previously determined has been ascertained, a recomputation must then be made under the laws applicable to said taxable year to ascertain the increase or decrease in tax, if any, resulting from the correction of the error. The difference between the tax previously determined and the tax as recomputed after correction of the error will be the amount of the adjustment.

(c) No change shall be made in the treatment given any item upon which the tax previously determined was based other than in the correction of the item or items with respect to which the error was made. However, due regard shall be given to the effect that such correction may have on the computation of gross income, taxable income, and other matters under chapter 1 of the Code. If the treatment of any item upon which the tax previously determined was based, or if the application of any provisions of the internal revenue laws with respect to such tax, depends upon the amount of income (e.g., charitable contributions, foreign tax credit, dividends received credit, medical expenses, and percentage depletion), readjustment in these particulars will be necessary as part of the recomputation in conformity with the change in the amount of the income which results from the correct treatment of the item or items in respect of which the error was made.

(d) Any interest or additions to the tax collected as a result of the error shall be taken into account in determining the amount of the adjustment.

(e) The application of this section may be illustrated by the following example:

Example. (1) For the taxable year 1949 a taxpayer with no dependents, who kept his books on the cash receipts and disbursements method, filed a joint return with his wife disclosing adjusted gross income of $42,000, deductions amounting to $12,000, and a net income of $30,000. Included among other items in the gross income were salary in the amount of $15,000 and rents accrued but not yet received in the amount of $5,000. During the taxable year he donated $10,000 to the American Red Cross and in his return claimed a deduction of $6,300 on account thereof, representing the maximum deduction allowable under the 15-percent limitation imposed by section 23(o) of the Internal Revenue Code of 1939 as applicable to the year 1949. In computing his net income he omitted interest income amounting to $6,000 and neglected to take a deduction for interest paid in the amount of $4,500. The return disclosed a tax liability of $7,788, which was assessed and paid. After the expiration of the period of limitations upon the assessment of a deficiency or the allowance of a refund for 1949, the Commissioner included the item of rental income amounting to $5,000 in the taxpayer's gross income for the year 1950 and asserted a deficiency for that year. As a result of a final decision of the Tax Court of the United States in 1955 sustaining the deficiency for 1950, an adjustment is authorized for the year 1949.

(2) The amount of the adjustment is computed as follows:

Tax previously determined for 1949	$ 7,788
Net income for 1949 upon which tax previously determined was based	$30,000
Less: Rents erroneously included	5,000
Balance	$25,000
Adjustment for contributions (add 15 percent of $5,000)	750
Net income as adjusted	$25,750
Tax as recomputed	$ 6,152
Tax previously determined	7,788
Difference	$ 1,636
Amount of adjustment to be refunded or credited	1,636

Reg. § 1.1314(a)-1(e)(2)

53,756 Mitigation of Effect of Limitations—Other Provisions

See p. 20,601 for regulations not amended to reflect law changes

(3) In accordance with the provisions of paragraph (c) of this section, the recomputation to determine the amount of the adjustment does not take into consideration the item of $6,000 representing interest received, which was omitted from gross income, or the item of $4,500 representing interest paid, for which no deduction was allowed. [Reg. § 1.1314(a)-1.]

☐ [T.D. 6162, 2-8-56.]

[Reg. § 1.1314(a)-2]

§ 1.1314(a)-2. Adjustment to other barred taxable years.—(a) An adjustment is authorized under section 1311 with respect to a taxable year or years other than the year of the error, but only if all of the following requirements are met:

(1) The tax liability for such other year or years must be affected, or must have been treated as affected, by a net operating loss deduction (as defined in section 172) or by a capital loss carryback or carryover (as defined in section 1212).

(2) The net operating loss deduction or capital loss carryback or carryover must be determined with reference to the taxable year with respect to which the error was made.

(3) On the date of the determination, the adjustment with respect to such other year or years must be prevented by some law or rule of law, other than sections 1311 through 1315 and section 7122 and the corresponding provisions of prior revenue laws.

(b) The amount of the adjustment for such other year or years shall be computed in a manner similar to that provided in § 1.1314(a)-1. The tax previously determined for such other year or years shall be ascertained. A recomputation must then be made to ascertain the increase or decrease in tax, if any, resulting solely from the correction of the net operating loss deduction or capital loss carryback or carryover. The difference between the tax previously determined and the tax as recomputed is the amount of the adjustment. In the recomputation, no consideration shall be given to items other than the following: (1) the items upon which the tax previously determined for such other year or years was based, and (2) the net operating loss deduction or capital loss carryback or carryover as corrected. In determining the correct net operating loss deduction or capital loss carryback or carryover, no changes shall be made in taxable income (net income in the case of taxable years subject to the provisions of the Internal Revenue Code of 1939 or prior revenue laws), net operating loss or capital loss, for any barred taxable year, except as provided in section 1314. Section 172 and the corresponding provisions of prior revenue laws, and the regulations promulgated thereunder, prescribe the methods of computing the net operating loss deduction. Section 1212 and the corresponding provisions of prior revenue laws, and the regulations promulgated thereunder, prescribe the methods of computing the capital loss carryback or carryover.

(c) A net operating loss deduction or a capital loss carryback or carryover determined with reference to the year of the error may affect, or may have been treated as affecting, a taxable year with respect to which an adjustment is not prevented by the operation of any law or rule of law. In such case, the appropriate adjustment shall be made with respect to such open taxable year. However, the redetermination of the tax for such open taxable year is not made pursuant to part II (section 1311 and following), subchapter Q, chapter 1 of the Code, and the adjustment for such open year and the method of computation are not limited by the provisions of said sections.

(d) The application of this section may be illustrated by the following example:

Example. The taxpayer is a corporation which makes its income tax returns on a calendar year basis. Its net income in 1949, computed without any net operating loss deduction was $10,000, but because of a net operating loss deduction in excess of that amount resulting from a carryback of a net operating loss claimed for 1950, it paid no income tax for 1949. On its return for 1950 it showed an excess of deductions over gross income of $14,000, and it paid no income tax for 1950. For the year 1951 its net income, computed without any net operating loss deduction, was $15,000, and a net operating loss deduction of $13,000 was allowed ($4,000 of which was attributable to the carryover from 1950 and $9,000 of which was attributable to the carryback of a net operating loss of $9,000 sustained in 1952). In 1957 the assessment of deficiencies or the allowance of refunds for all of said years are barred by the statute of limitations.

(i) A Tax Court decision entered in 1957 with respect to the taxable year 1953 constituted a determination under which an adjustment is authorized to the taxable year 1950, the year with respect to which the error was made. This adjustment increases income for said year by $15,000, so that instead of a net operating loss of $14,000, its corrected net income is $1,000 for 1950, and the tax computed on that income will be assessed as a deficiency for 1950. An adjustment is authorized under this section with respect to each of the years 1949 and 1951, as the tax liability for each year was treated as affected by a net operating loss deduction which was determined by a compu-

Reg. § 1.1314(a)-2(a)(1)

Mitigation of Effect of Limitations—Other Provisions 53,757
See p. 20,601 for regulations not amended to reflect law changes

tation in which reference was made to the year 1950. In the recomputation of the tax for 1949, the net operating loss carryback from 1950 will be eliminated, and in the recomputation of the tax for 1951 the net operating loss carryover from 1950 will be eliminated; for each of the years 1949 and 1951 there will be an adjustment which will be treated as a deficiency for said year.

(ii) Assuming the same facts except that the correction with respect to the year 1950 increases the net operating loss for said year from $14,000 to $20,000. As a result of this correction, there will be no change in the tax due for 1949 and 1950. However, the net operating loss deduction for 1951 is recomputed to be $19,000, the aggregate of the $10,000 carryover from 1950 and the $9,000 carryback from 1952 (the carryover from 1950 is the excess of the $20,000 net operating loss for 1950 over the $10,000 net income for 1949, such 1949 income being determined without any net operating loss deduction). As a result of the correction of the net operating loss deduction for 1951, the tax recomputation will show no tax due for said year, and the adjustment for 1951 will result in a refund or credit of the tax previously paid. Moreover, computations resulting from this adjustment will disclose a net operating loss carryover from 1952 to 1953 of $4,000, that is, the excess of the $9,000 net operating loss for 1952 over the $5,000 net income for 1951 (such net income for 1951 being computed as the $15,000 reduced by the carryover of $10,000 from 1950, the carryback from 1952 not being taken into account). A further adjustment is authorized under section 1311 with respect to any subsequent barred year in which the tax liability is affected by a carryover of the net operating loss from 1952, inasmuch as such carryover from 1952 has been determined by a computation in which reference was made to 1950, the taxable year of the error. [Reg. § 1.1314(a)-2.]

☐ [T.D. 6162, 2-8-56. Amended by T.D. 7301, 1-3-74.]

[Reg. § 1.1314(b)-1]

§ 1.1314(b)-1. Method of adjustment.—(a) If the amount of the adjustment ascertained pursuant to § 1.1314(a)-1 or § 1.1314(a)-2 represents an increase in tax, it is to be treated as if it were a deficiency determined by the Commissioner with respect to the taxpayer as to whom the error was made and for the taxable year or years with respect to which such adjustment was made. The amount of such adjustment is thus to be assessed and collected under the law and regulations applicable to the assessment and collection of deficiencies, subject, however, to the limitations imposed by § 1.1314(c)-1. Notice of deficiency, unless waived, must be issued with respect to such amount or amounts, and the taxpayer may contest the deficiency before the Tax Court of the United States or, if he chooses, may pay the deficiency and later file claim for refund. If the amount of the adjustment ascertained pursuant to § 1.1314(a)-1 or § 1.1314(a)-2 represents a decrease in tax, it is to be treated as if it were an overpayment claimed by the taxpayer with respect to whom the error was made for the taxable year or years with respect to which such adjustment was made. Such amount may be recovered under the law and regulations applicable to overpayments of tax, subject however, to the limitations imposed by § 1.1314(c)-1. The taxpayer must file a claim for refund thereof, unless the overpayment is refunded without such claim, and if the claim is denied or not acted upon by the Commissioner within the prescribed time, the taxpayer may then file suit for refund.

(b) For the purpose of the adjustments authorized by section 1311, the period of limitations upon the making of an assessment or upon refund or credit, as the case may be, for the taxable year of an adjustment shall be considered as if, on the date of the determination, one year remained before the expiration of such period. The Commissioner thus has one year from the date of the determination within which to mail a notice of deficiency in respect of the amount of the adjustment where such adjustment is treated as if it were a deficiency. The issuance of such notice of deficiency, in accordance with the law and regulations applicable to the assessment of deficiencies will suspend the running of the 1-year period of limitations provided in section 1314(b). In accordance with the applicable law and regulations governing the collection of deficiencies, the period of limitation for collection of the amount of the adjustment will commence to run from the date of assessment of such amount. (See section 6502 and corresponding provisions of prior revenue laws.) Similarly, the taxpayer has a period of one year from the date of the determination within which to file a claim for refund in respect of the amount of the adjustment where such adjustment is treated as if it were an overpayment. Where the amount of the adjustment is treated as if it were a deficiency and the taxpayer chooses to pay such deficiency and contest it by way of a claim for refund, the period of limitation upon filing a claim for refund will commence to run from the date of such payment. See section 6511 and corresponding provisions of prior revenue laws.

(c) The amount of an adjustment treated as if it were a deficiency or an overpayment, as the case

Reg. § 1.1314(b)-1(c)

53,758 Mitigation of Effect of Limitations—Other Provisions
See p. 20,601 for regulations not amended to reflect law changes

may be, will bear interest and be subject to additions to the tax to the extent provided by the internal revenue laws applicable to deficiencies and overpayments for the taxable year with respect to which the adjustment is made. In the case of an adjustment resulting from an increase or decrease in a net operating loss or net capital loss which is carried back to the year of adjustment, interest shall not be collected or paid for any period prior to the close of the taxable year in which the net operating loss or net capital loss arises.

(d) If, as a result of a determination provided for in § 1.1313(a)-4, an adjustment has been made by the assessment and collection of a deficiency or the refund or credit of an overpayment, and subsequently such determination is altered or revoked, the amount of the adjustment ascertained under § 1.1314(a)-1 and § 1.1314(a)-2 shall be redetermined on the basis of such alteration or revocation, and any overpayment or deficiency resulting from such redetermination shall be refunded or credited, or assessed and collected, as the case may be, as an adjustment under section 1311. For the circumstances under which such an agreement can be altered or revoked, see paragraph (d) of § 1.1313(a)-4. [Reg. § 1.1314(b)-1.]

☐ [T.D. 6162, 2-8-56. Amended by T.D. 7301, 1-3-74.]

[Reg. § 1.1314(c)-1]

§ 1.1314(c)-1. **Adjustment unaffected by other items.**—(a) The amount of any adjustment ascertained under § 1.1314(a)-1 or § 1.1314(a)-2 shall not be diminished by any credit or set-off based upon any item other than the one that was the subject of the adjustment.

(b) The application of this section may be illustrated by the following examples:

Example (1). In the example set forth in paragraph (e) of § 1.1314(a)-1, if, after the amount of the adjustment had been ascertained, the taxpayer filed a refund claim for the amount thereof, the Commissioner could not diminish the amount of that claim by offsetting against it the amount of tax which should have been paid with respect to the $6,000 interest item omitted from gross income for the year 1949; nor could the court, if suit were brought on such claim for refund, offset against the amount of the adjustment the amount of tax which should have been paid with respect to such interest. Similarly, the amount of the refund could not be increased by any amount attributable to the taxpayer's failure to deduct the $4,500 interest paid in the year 1949.

Example (2). Assume that a taxpayer included in his gross income for the year 1953 an item which should have been included in his gross income for the year 1952. After the expiration of the period of limitations upon the assessment of a deficiency or the allowance of a refund for 1952, the taxpayer filed a claim for refund for the year 1953 on the ground that such item was not properly includible in gross income for that year. The claim for refund was allowed by the Commissioner and as a result of such determination an adjustment was authorized under section 1311 with respect to the tax for 1952. If, in such case, the Commissioner issued a notice of deficiency for the amount of the adjustment and the taxpayer contested the deficiency before the Tax Court of the United States, the taxpayer could not in such proceeding claim an offset based upon his failure to take an allowable deduction for the year 1952; nor could the Tax Court in its decision offset against the amount of the adjustment any overpayment for the year 1952 resulting from the failure to take such deduction.

(c) If the Commissioner has refunded the amount of an adjustment under section 1311, the amount so refunded may not subsequently be recovered by the Commissioner in any suit for erroneous refund based upon any item other than the one that was the subject of the adjustment.

Example. In the example set forth in paragraph (e) of § 1.1314(a)-1, if the Commissioner had refunded the amount of the adjustment, no part of the amount so refunded could subsequently be recovered by the Commissioner by a suit for erroneous refund based on the ground that there was no overpayment for 1949, as the taxpayer had failed to include in gross income the $6,000 item of interest received in that year.

(d) If the Commissioner has assessed and collected the amount of an adjustment under section 1311, no part thereof may be recovered by the taxpayer in any suit for refund based upon any item other than the one that was the subject of the adjustment.

Example. In example (2) of paragraph (b) of this section, if the taxpayer had paid the amount of the adjustment, he could not subsequently recover any part of such payment in a suit for refund based upon the failure to take an allowable deduction for the year 1952.

(e) If the amount of the adjustment is considered an overpayment, it may be credited, under applicable law and regulations, together with any interest allowed thereon, against any liability in respect of an internal revenue tax on the part of the person who made such overpayment. Like-

Reg. § 1.1314(c)-1(a)

wise, if the amount of the adjustment is considered as a deficiency, any overpayment by the taxpayer of any internal revenue tax may be credited against the amount of such adjustment in accordance with the applicable law and regulations thereunder. (See section 6402 and the corresponding provisions of prior revenue laws.) Accordingly, it may be possible in one transaction between the Commissioner and the taxpayer to settle the taxpayer's tax liability for the year with respect to which the determination is made and to make the adjustment under section 1311 for the year with respect to which the error was made or for a year which is affected, or treated as affected, by a net operating loss deduction or a capital loss carryover from the year of the error. [Reg. § 1.1314(c)-1.]

☐ [T.D. 6162, 2-8-56.]

Claim of Right

[Reg. § 1.1341-1]

§ 1.1341-1. **Restoration of amounts received or accrued under claim of right.**—(a) *In general.* (1) If, during the taxable year, the taxpayer is entitled under other provisions of chapter 1 of the Internal Revenue Code of 1954 to a deduction of more than $3,000 because of the restoration to another of an item which was included in the taxpayer's gross income for a prior taxable year (or years) under a claim of right, the tax imposed by chapter 1 of the Internal Revenue Code of 1954 for the taxable year shall be the tax provided in paragraph (b) of this section.

(2) For the purpose of this section "income included under a claim of right" means an item included in gross income because it appeared from all the facts available in the year of inclusion that the taxpayer had an unrestricted right to such item, and "restoration to another" means a restoration resulting because it was established after the close of such prior taxable year (or years) that the taxpayer did not have an unrestricted right to such item (or portion thereof).

(3) For purposes of determining whether the amount of a deduction described in section 1341(a)(2) exceeds $3,000 for the taxable year, there shall be taken into account the aggregate of all such deductions with respect to each item of income (described in section 1341(a)(1)) of the same class.

(b) *Determination of tax.* (1) Under the circumstances described in paragraph (a) of this section, the tax imposed by chapter 1 of the Internal Revenue Code of 1954 for the taxable year shall be the lesser of—

(i) The tax for the taxable year computed under section 1341 (a)(4), that is, with the deduction taken into account, or

(ii) The tax for the taxable year computed under section 1341 (a)(5), that is, without taking such deduction into account, minus the decrease in tax (net of any increase in tax imposed by section 56, relating to the minimum tax for tax preferences) (under chapter 1 of the Internal Revenue Code of 1954, under chapter 1 (other than subchapter E) and subchapter E of chapter 2 of the Internal Revenue Code of 1939, or under the corresponding provisions of prior revenue laws) for the prior taxable year (or years) which would result solely from the exclusion from the gross income of all or that portion of the income included under a claim of right to which the deduction is attributable. For the purpose of this subdivision, the amount of the decrease in tax is not limited to the amount of the tax for the taxable year. See paragraph (i) of this section where the decrease in tax for the prior taxable year (or years) exceeds the tax for the taxable year.

(iii) For purposes of computing, under section 1341(a)(4) and subdivision (i) of this subparagraph, the tax for a taxable year beginning after December 31, 1961, if the deduction of the amount of the restoration results in a net operating loss for the taxable year of restoration, such net operating loss shall, pursuant to section 1341(b)(4)(A), be carried back to the same extent and in the same manner as is provided under section 172 (relating to the net operating loss deduction) and the regulations thereunder. If the aggregate decrease in tax for the taxable year (or years) to which such net operating loss is carried back is greater than the excess of—

(a) The amount of decrease in tax for a prior taxable year (or years) computed under section 1341(a)(5)(B), over

(b) The tax for the taxable year computed under section 1341(a)(5)(A),

the tax imposed for the taxable year under chapter 1 shall be the tax determined under section 1341(a)(4) and subdivision (i) of this subparagraph. If the tax imposed for the taxable year is determined under section 1341(a)(4) and subdivision (i) of this subparagraph, the decrease in tax for the taxable year (or years) to which the net operating loss is carried back shall be an overpayment of tax for the taxable year (or years) to which the net operating loss is carried back and shall be refunded or credited as an overpayment for such taxable year (or years). See section 6511(d)(2), relating to special period of limitation with respect to net operating loss carrybacks.

Reg. § 1.1341-1(b)

(2) Except as otherwise provided in section 1341(b)(4)(B) and paragraph (d)(1)(ii) and (4)(ii) of this section, if the taxpayer computes his tax for the taxable year under the provisions of section 1341(a)(5) and subparagraph (1)(ii) of this paragraph, the amount of the restoration shall not be taken into account in computing taxable income or loss for the taxable year, including the computation of any net operating loss carryback or carryover or any capital loss carryover. However, the amount of such restoration shall be taken into account in adjusting earnings and profits for the current taxable year.

(3) If the tax determined under subparagraph (1)(i) of this paragraph is the same as the tax determined under subparagraph (1)(ii) of this paragraph, the tax imposed for the taxable year under chapter 1 shall be the tax determined under subparagraph (1)(i) of this paragraph, and section 1341 and this section shall not otherwise apply.

(4) After it has been determined whether the tax imposed for a taxable year of restoration beginning after December 31, 1961, shall be computed under the provisions of section 1341(a)(4) or under the provisions of section 1341(a)(5), the net operating loss, if any, which remains after the application of section 1341(b)(4)(A) or the net operating loss or capital loss, if any, which remains after the application of section 1341(b)(4)(B) shall be taken into account in accordance with the following rules—

(i) If it is determined that section 1341(a)(4) and subparagraph (1)(i) of this paragraph apply, then that portion, if any, of the net operating loss for the taxable year which remains after the application of section 1341(b)(4)(A) and subparagraph (1)(iii) of this paragraph shall be taken into account under section 172 for taxable years subsequent to the taxable year of restoration to the same extent and in the same manner as a net operating loss sustained in such taxable year of restoration. Thus, if the net operating loss for the taxable year of restoration (computed with the deduction referred to in section 1341(a)(4)) exceeds the taxable income (computed with the modifications prescribed in section 172) for the taxable year (or years) to which it is carried back, such excess shall be available as a carryover to taxable years subsequent to the taxable year of restoration.

(ii) If it is determined that section 1341(a)(5) and subparagraph (1)(ii) of this paragraph apply, then that portion, if any, of a net operating loss or capital loss which remains after the application of section 1341(b)(4)(B) and paragraph (d)(4) of this section shall be taken into account under section 172 or section 1212, as the case may be, for taxable years subsequent to the taxable year of restoration to the same extent and in the same manner as a net operating loss or capital loss sustained in the prior taxable year (or years). For example, if the net operating loss for the prior taxable year (computed with the exclusion referred to in section 1341(a)(5)(B)) exceeds the taxable income (computed with the modifications prescribed in section 172) for prior taxable years to which such net operating loss is carried back or carried over (including for this purpose the taxable year of restoration), such excess shall be available as a carryover to taxable years subsequent to the taxable year of restoration in accordance with the rules prescribed in section 172 which are applicable to such prior taxable year (or years).

(c) *Application to deductions which are capital in nature.* Section 1341 and this section shall also apply to a deduction which is capital in nature otherwise allowable in the taxable year. If the deduction otherwise allowable is capital in nature, the determination of whether the taxpayer is entitled to the benefits of section 1341 and this section shall be made without regard to the net capital loss limitation imposed by section 1211. For example, if a taxpayer restores $4,000 in the taxable year and such amount is a long-term capital loss, the taxpayer will, nevertheless, be considered to have met the $3,000 deduction requirement for purposes of applying this section, although the full amount of the loss might not be allowable as a deduction for the taxable year. However, if the tax for the taxable year is computed with the deduction taken into account, the deduction allowable will be subject to the limitation on capital losses provided in section 1211, and the capital loss carryover provided in section 1212.

(d) *Determination of decrease in tax for prior taxable years*—(1) *Prior taxable years.* (i) Except as otherwise provided in subsection (ii) of this subparagraph, the prior taxable year (or years) referred to in paragraph (b) of this section is the year (or years) in which the item to which the deduction is attributable was included in gross income under a claim of right and, in addition, any other prior taxable year (or years) the tax for which will be affected by the exclusion from gross income in such prior taxable year (or years) of such income.

(ii) For purposes of applying section 1341(b)(4)(B) in computing the amount of the decrease referred to in paragraph (b)(1)(ii) of this section for any taxable year beginning after December 31, 1961, the term "prior taxable year (or years)" includes the taxable year of restoration.

Reg. § 1.1341-1(b)(2)

Under section 1341(b)(4)(B), for taxable years of restoration beginning after December 31, 1961, in any case where the exclusion referred to in section 1341(a)(5)(B) and paragraph (b)(1)(ii) of this section results in a net operating loss or capital loss for the prior taxable year (or years), such loss shall, for purposes of computing the decrease in tax for the prior taxable year (or years) under such section 1341(a)(5)(B) and such paragraph (b)(1)(ii) of this section, be carried back and carried over to the same extent and in the same manner as is provided under section 172 (relating to the net operating loss deduction) or section 1212 (relating to capital loss carryover), except that no carryover beyond the taxable year shall be taken into account. See subparagraph (4) of this paragraph for rules relating to the computation of the amount of decrease in tax.

(2) *Amount of exclusion from gross income in prior taxable years.* (i) The amount to be excluded from gross income for the prior taxable year (or years) in determining the decrease in tax under section 1341(a)(5)(B) and paragraph (b)(1)(ii) of this section shall be the amount restored in the taxable year, but shall not exceed the amount included in gross income in the prior taxable year (or years) under the claim of right to which the deduction for the restoration is attributable, and shall be adjusted as provided in subdivision (ii) of this subparagraph.

(ii) If the amount included in gross income for the prior taxable year (or years) under the claim of right in question was reduced in such year (or years) by a deduction allowed under section 1202 (or section 117(b) of the Internal Revenue Code of 1939 or corresponding provisions of prior revenue laws), then the amount determined under subdivision (i) of this subparagraph to be excluded from gross income for such year (or years) shall be reduced in the same proportion that the amount included in gross income under a claim of right was reduced.

(iii) The determination of the amount of the exclusion from gross income of the prior taxable year shall be made without regard to the capital loss limitation contained in section 1211 applicable in computing taxable income for the current taxable year. The amount of the exclusion from gross income in a prior taxable year (or years) shall not exceed the amount which would, but for the application of section 1211, be allowable as a deduction in the taxable year of restoration.

(iv) The rule provided in subdivision (iii) of this subparagraph may be illustrated as follows:

Example. For the taxable year 1952, and individual taxpayer had long-term capital gains of $50,000 and long-term capital losses of $10,000, a net long-term gain of $40,000. He also had other income of $5,000. In 1956, taxpayer restored the $50,000 of long-term gain. He had no capital gains or losses in 1956 but had other income of $5,000. If his tax liability for 1956, the taxable year of restoration, is computed by taking the deduction into account, the taxpayer would be entitled to a deduction under section 1211 of only $1,000 on account of the capital loss. However, if the taxpayer computes his tax under section 1341(a)(5) and paragraph (b)(1)(ii) of this section, it is necessary to determine the decrease in tax for 1952. In such a determination, $50,000 is to be excluded from gross income for that year, resulting in a net capital loss for that year of $10,000, and a capital loss deduction of $1,000 under section 117(d) of the Internal Revenue Code of 1939 (corresponding to section 1211 of the Internal Revenue Code of 1954) with carryover privileges. The difference between the tax previously determined and the tax as recomputed after such exclusion for the years affected will be the amount of the decrease.

(3) *Determination of amount of deduction attributable to prior taxable years.* (i) If the deduction otherwise allowable for the taxable year relates to income included in gross income under a claim of right in more than one prior taxable year and the amount attributable to each such prior taxable year cannot be readily identified, then the portion attributable to each such prior taxable year shall be that proportion of the deduction otherwise allowable for the taxable year which the amount of the income included under the claim of right in question for the prior taxable year bears to the total of all such income included under the claim of right for all such prior taxable years.

(ii) The rule provided in subdivision (i) of this subparagraph may be illustrated as follows:

Example. Under a claim of right, A included in his gross income over a period of three taxable years an aggregate of $9,000 for services to a certain employer, in amounts as follows: $2,000 for taxable year 1952, $4,000 for taxable year 1953, and $3,000 for taxable year 1954. In 1955 it is established that A must restore $6,750 of these amounts to his employer, and that A is entitled to a deduction of this amount in the taxable year 1955. The amount of the deduction attributable to each of the prior taxable years cannot be identified. Accordingly, the amount of the deduction attributable to each prior taxable year is:

Reg. § 1.1341-1(d)(3)

Claim of Right

See p. 20,601 for regulations not amended to reflect law changes

$$1952\text{---}\$6{,}750 \times \frac{\$2{,}000}{\$9{,}000} = \$1{,}500$$

$$1953\text{---}\$6{,}750 \times \frac{\$4{,}000}{\$9{,}000} = \$3{,}000$$

$$1954\text{---}\$6{,}750 \times \frac{\$3{,}000}{\$9{,}000} = \$2{,}250$$

(4) *Computation of amount of decrease in tax.* (i) In computing the amount of decrease in tax for a prior taxable year (or years) resulting from the exclusion from gross income of the income included under a claim of right, there must first be ascertained the amount of tax previously determined for the taxpayer for such prior taxable year (or years). The tax previously determined shall be the sum of the amounts shown by the taxpayer on his return or returns, plus any amounts which have been previously assessed (or collected without assessment) as deficiencies or which appropriately should be assessed or collected, reduced by the amount of any refunds or credits which have previously been made or which appropriately should be made. For taxable years beginning after December 31, 1961, if the provisions of section 1341(b)(4)(B) are applicable, the tax previously determined shall include the tax for the taxable year of restoration computed without taking the deduction for the amount of the restoration into account. After the tax previously determined has been ascertained, a recomputation must then be made to determine the decrease in tax, if any, resulting from the exclusion from gross income of all or that portion of the income included under a claim of right to which the deduction otherwise allowable in the taxable year is attributable.

(ii) No item other than the exclusion of the income previously included under a claim of right shall be considered in computing the amount of decrease in tax if reconsideration of such other item is prevented by the operation of any provision of the internal revenue laws or any other rule of law. However, if the amounts of other items in the return are dependent upon the amount of adjusted gross income, taxable income, or net income (such as charitable contributions, foreign tax credit, deductions for depletion, and net operating loss), appropriate adjustment shall be made as part of the computation of the decrease in tax. For the purpose of determining the decrease in tax for the prior taxable year (or years) which would result from the exclusion from gross income of the item included under a claim of right, the exclusion of such item shall be given effect not only in the prior taxable year in which it was included in gross income but in all other prior taxable years (including the taxable year of restoration if such year begins after December 31, 1961, and section 1341(b)(4)(B) applies, see subparagraph (1)(ii) of this paragraph) affected by the inclusion of the item (for example, prior taxable years affected by a net operating loss carryback or carryover or capital loss carryover).

(iii) The rules provided in this subparagraph may be illustrated as follows:

Example (1). For the taxable year 1954, a corporation had taxable income of $35,000, on which it paid a tax of $12,700. Included in gross income for the year was $20,000 received under a claim of rights as royalties. In 1957, the corporation is required to return $10,000 of the royalties. It otherwise has taxable income in 1957 of $5,000, so that without the application of section 1341 it has a net operating loss of $5,000 in that year. Facts also come to light in 1957 which entitle the corporation to an additional deduction of $5,000 for 1954. When a computation is made under paragraph (b)(1)(i) of this section, the corporation has no tax for the taxable year 1957. When a computation is made under paragraph (b)(1)(ii) of this section, the tax for 1957, without taking the restoration into account, is $1,500, based on a taxable income of $5,000. The decrease in tax for 1954 is computed as follows:

Tax shown on return for 1954	$12,700
Taxable income for 1954 upon which tax shown on return was based	$35,000
Less: Additional deduction (on account of which credit or refund could be made)	5,000
Total	$30,000
Tax on $30,000 (adjusted taxable income for 1954)	10,100
Tax on $30,000 (adjusted taxable income for 1954)	$10,100

Taxable income for 1954, as adjusted	$30,000	
Less exclusion of amount restored	10,000	
Taxable income for 1954 by applying paragraph (b)(1)(ii) of this section	$20,000	
Tax on $20,000		$ 6,000

Reg. § 1.1341-1(d)(4)

Claim of Right

See p. 20,601 for regulations not amended to reflect law changes

Decrease in tax for 1954 by applying paragraph (b)(1)(ii) of this section	$ 4,100
Tax for 1957 without taking the restoration into account	1,500
Amount by which decrease exceeds the tax for 1957 computed without taking restoration into account	$ 2,600

(The $2,600 is treated as having been paid on the last day prescribed by law for the payment of the tax for 1957 and is available as a refund. In addition the taxpayer has made an overpayment of $2,600 ($12,700 less $10,100) for 1954 because of the additional deduction of $5,000.)

Example (2). Assume the same facts as in example (1) except that, instead of the corporation being entitled to an additional deduction of $5,000 for 1954, it is determined that the corporation failed to include an item of $5,000 in gross income for that year. The decrease in tax for 1954 is computed as follows:

Tax shown on return for 1954		$12,700
Taxable income for 1954 upon which tax shown on return was based		$35,000
Plus: Additional income (on account of which deficiency assessment could be made)		5,000
Total		$40,000
Tax on $40,000 (adjusted taxable income for 1954)		$15,300
Tax on $40,000 (adjusted taxable income for 1954)		$15,300
Taxable income for 1954 as adjusted	$40,000	
Less: Exclusion of amount restored	10,000	
Taxable income for 1954 by applying paragraph (b)(1)(ii) of this section	30,000	
Tax on $30,000		10,100
Decrease in tax for 1954 by applying paragraph (b)(1)(ii) of this section		$ 5,200
Tax for 1957 without taking the restoration into account		1,500
Amount by which decrease exceeds the tax for 1957 computed without taking the restoration into account		$ 3,700

(The $3,700 is treated as having been paid on the last day prescribed by law for the payment of the tax for 1957 and is available as a refund. In addition the taxpayer has a deficiency of $2,600 ($15,300 less $12,700) for 1954 because of the additional income of $5,000.)

Example (3). For the taxable year 1954, a corporation had taxable income of $25,000, on which it paid a tax of $7,500. Included in gross income for the year was $10,000 received under a claim of right as commissions. In 1956, the corporation is required to return $5,000 of the commissions. The corporation has a net operating loss of $10,000 for 1956, excluding the deduction for the $5,000 restored. When a computation is made under either paragraph (b)(1)(i) or paragraph (b)(1)(ii) of this section, the corporation has no tax for the taxable year 1956. The decrease in tax for 1954 is computed as follows:

Tax shown on return for 1954		$ 7,500
Taxable income for 1954 upon which tax shown on return was based		$25,000
Less: Additional deduction (on account of net operating loss carryback from 1956)		10,000
Net income as adjusted		$15,000
Tax on $15,000 (adjusted taxable income for 1954)		4,500
Tax on $15,000 (adjusted taxable income for 1954)		$ 4,500
Taxable income for 1954, as adjusted	$15,000	
Less: Exclusion of amount restored	5,000	
Taxable income for 1954 by applying paragraph (b)(1)(ii) of this section	10,000	
Tax on $10,000		3,000
Decrease in tax for 1954 by applying paragraph (b)(1)(ii) of this section		$ 1,500
Tax for 1956 without taking the restoration into account		None
Amount by which decrease exceeds the tax for 1956 computed without taking the restoration into account		$ 1,500

(The $1,500 is treated as having been paid on the last day prescribed by law for the payment of the tax for 1956 and is available as a refund. In addition, the taxpayer has an overpayment of

Reg. § 1.1341-1(d)(4)

Claim of Right

See p. 20,601 for regulations not amended to reflect law changes

$3,000 ($7,500 less $4,500) for 1954 because of the net operating loss deduction of $10,000.)

Example (4). For the taxable year 1946 a married man with no dependents, who kept his books on the cash receipts and disbursements basis, filed a return (claiming two exemptions) disclosing adjusted gross income of $42,000, deductions amounting to $12,000, and a net income of $30,000. Gross income included among other items salary in the amount of $15,000 and rental income in the amount of $5,000. During the taxable year he donated $10,000 to the American Red Cross and in his return claimed a deduction of $6,300 on account thereof, representing the maximum deduction allowable under the 15-percent limitation imposed by section 23(o) of the Internal Revenue Code of 1939 for the year 1946. In computing his net income he omitted interest income amounting to $6,000 and neglected to take a deduction for interest paid in the amount of $4,500. The return disclosed a tax liability of $11,970, which was assessed and paid. In 1955, after the expiration of the period of limitations upon the assessment of a deficiency or the allowance of a refund for 1946, the taxpayer had to restore the $5,000 included in his gross income in 1946 as rental income. The amount of the decrease in tax for 1946 is $2,467.62, computed as follows:

Tax previously determined for 1946	$11,970.00
Net income for 1946 upon which tax previously determined was based	$30,000.00
Less: Rents included under claim of right	$ 5,000.00
Balance	25,000.00
Adjustment for contributions (add 15 percent of $5,000)	750.00
Net income as adjusted	25,750.00
Tax on $25,750	9,502.38
Amount of decrease in tax for 1946:	
Tax previously determined	$11,970.00
Tax as recomputed	9,502.38
Decrease in tax	$ 2,467.62

The recomputation to determine the amount of the decrease in tax for 1946 does not take into consideration the barred item of $6,000 representing interest received, which was omitted from gross income, or the barred item of $4,500 representing interest paid for which no deduction was allowed. See subdivision (ii) of this subparagraph.

Example (5). (a) *Facts.* For the taxable year 1959, a corporation reporting income on the calendar year basis had taxable income of $20,000 on which it paid a tax of $6,000. Included in gross income for such year was $100,000 received under a claim of right as royalties. For each of its taxable years 1956, 1957, 1958, 1960, 1961, and 1962, the corporation had taxable income of $10,000 on which it paid tax of $3,000 for each year. In 1963, the corporation returns the entire amount of $100,000 of the royalties. In such taxable year the corporation has taxable income of $25,000 (without taking the deduction of $100,000 into account), and has a net operating loss of $75,000 (taking the deduction of $100,000 into account). In determining whether section 1341(a)(4) or section 1341(a)(5) applies, the corporation will compute the lesser amount of tax referred to in section 1341(a) by applying the rules provided in section 1341(b)(4).

(b) *Tax under section 1341(a)(4) and (b)(4)(A).* The net operating loss of $75,000 for 1963 (taking into account the deduction of $100,000) is carried back to the three taxable years (1960, 1961, and 1962) in the manner provided under section 172. For purposes of this example it is assumed that no modifications under section 172 are necessary. Since the aggregate taxable income for such three taxable years is only $30,000 the entire taxable income for such years is eliminated by the carryback, and the corporation would be entitled to a refund of the tax for such years in the aggregate amount of $9,000. (In addition, the remaining $45,000 of the net operating loss for 1963 would be available as a carryover to taxable years after the taxable year (1963) to the extent and in the manner provided by section 172.)

(c) *Tax under section 1341(a)(5) and (b)(4)(B).* The tax for the taxable year (1963) on $25,000 of taxable income (computed without the deduction of $100,000) is $7,500. The exclusion of $100,000 from gross income for the taxable year 1959 (the year in which the item was included) results in a net operating loss of $80,000 for such year ($20,000 taxable income minus the $100,000 exclusion, no adjustments under section 172 being necessary), thus decreasing the tax for such year by the entire amount of $6,000 paid. The resulting net operating loss of $80,000 for 1959 is available as a carryback to 1956, 1957, and 1958, and

Reg. § 1.1341-1(d)(4)

as a carryover to 1960, 1961, 1962, and 1963. For purposes of this example it is assumed that no modifications under section 172 are necessary. Since the aggregate taxable income for such taxable years is $85,000, all except $5,000 of the 1963 taxable income is eliminated by such carryback and carryover. The tax on such remaining $5,000 of taxable income for 1963 is $1,500, thus decreasing the tax determined for such year by $6,000 ($7,500 minus $1,500). Under section 1341(a)(5) and (b)(4)(B), the decrease in tax for the prior taxable years exceeds the tax for the taxable year of restoration computed without the deduction of the amount of the restoration by $22,500, computed as follows:

Tax for taxable year 1963 (on taxable income of $25,000 without the deduction)			$ 7,500
Decrease in tax for prior taxable years:			
Due to exclusion (1959)		$6,000	
Due to net operating loss carryback:			
1956	$3,000		
1957	3,000		
1958	3,000	$9,000	
Due to net operating loss carryover:			
1961	3,000		
1962	3,000		
1963	6,000	15,000	30,000
Excess of the decrease in tax for the prior taxable years over the tax for taxable year 1963 ($30,000 less $7,500 tax for the taxable year)			$22,500

(d) *Application of section 1341(a)(4) or section 1341(a)(5).* Since the computation under section 1341(a)(4) and (b)(4)(A) results in an available refund of only $9,000 tax for the taxable years to which the net operating loss for 1963 is carried back, and since the computation under section 1341(a)(5) and (b)(4)(B) results in an overpayment of $22,500, it is determined that section 1341(a)(5) applies. Accordingly, the $22,500 is treated as having been paid on the last day prescribed by law for the payment of tax for 1963 and is available as a refund.

(e) *Method of accounting.* The provisions of section 1341 and this section shall be applicable in the case of a taxpayer on the cash receipts and disbursements method of accounting only to the taxable year in which the item of income included in a prior year (or years) under a claim of right is actually repaid. However, in the case of a taxpayer on the cash receipts and disbursements method of accounting who constructively received an item of income under a claim of right and included such item of income in gross income in a prior year (or years), the provisions of section 1341 and this section shall be applicable to the taxable year in which the taxpayer is required to relinquish his right to receive such item of income. Such provisions shall be applicable in the case of other taxpayers only to the taxable year which is the proper taxable year (under the method of accounting used by the taxpayer in computing taxable income) for taking into account the deduction resulting from the restoration of the item of income included in a prior year (or years) under a claim of right. For example, if the taxpayer is on an accrual method of accounting, the provisions of this section shall apply to the year in which the obligation properly accrues for the repayment of the item included under a claim of right.

(f) *Inventory items, stock in trade, and property held primarily for sale in the ordinary course of trade or business.* (1) Except for amounts specified in subparagraphs (2) and (3) of this paragraph, the provisions of section 1341 and this section do not apply to deductions attributable to items which were included in gross income by reason of the sale or other disposition of stock in trade of the taxpayer (or other property of a kind which would properly have been included in the inventory of the taxpayer if on hand at the close of the prior taxable year) or property held by the taxpayer primarily for sale to customers in the ordinary course of the taxpayer's trade or business. This section is, therefore, not applicable to sales returns and allowances and similar items.

(2)(i) In the case of taxable years beginning after December 31, 1957, the provisions of section 1341 and this section apply to deductions which arise out of refunds or repayments with respect to rates made by a regulated public utility, as defined in section 7701(a)(33) without regard to the limitation contained in the last two sentences thereof (for taxable years beginning before January 1, 1964, as defined in section 1503(c)(1) or (3) and paragraph (g) of § 1.1502-2A (as contained in the 26 C.F.R. edition revised as of April 1, 1996)), if such refunds or repayments are required to be made by the Government, political subdivision, agency, or instrumentality referred to in such section, or are required to be made by an order of a court, or are made in settlement of litigation or under threat or imminence of litigation. Thus,

Reg. § 1.1341-1(f)(2)

deductions attributable to refunds of charges for the sale of natural gas under rates approved temporarily by a proper governmental authority are, in the case of taxable years beginning after December 31, 1957, eligible for the benefits of section 1341 and this section, if such refunds are required by the governmental authority, or by an order of a court, or are made in settlement of litigation or under threat or imminence of litigation.

(ii) In the case of taxable years beginning before January 1, 1958, the provisions of section 1341 and this section apply to deductions which arise out of refunds or repayments (whether or not with respect to rates) made by a regulated public utility, as defined in section 7701(a)(33) without regard to the limitation contained in the last two sentences thereof (for taxable years beginning before January 1, 1964, as defined in section 1503(c)(1) or (3) and paragraph (g) of § 1.1502-2A), if such refunds or repayments are required to be made by the Government, political subdivision, agency, or instrumentality referred to in such section. Thus, in the case of taxable years beginning before January 1, 1958, deductions attributable to refunds or repayments may be eligible for the benefits of section 1341 and this section, even though such refunds or repayments are not with respect to rates. On the other hand, in the case of such taxable years, section 1341 and this section do not apply to any deduction which arises out of a refund or repayment (whether or not with respect to rates) which is required to be made by an order of a court, or which is made in settlement of litigation or under threat or imminence of litigation.

(3) The provisions of section 1341 and this section apply to a deduction which arises out of a payment or repayment made pursuant to a price redetermination provision in a subcontract—

(i) If such subcontract was entered into before January 1, 1958, between persons other than those bearing a relationship set forth in section 267(b);

(ii) If such subcontract is subject to statutory renegotiation; and

(iii) If section 1481 (relating to mitigation of effect of renegotiation of Government contracts) does not apply to such payment or repayment solely because such payment or repayment is not paid or repaid to the United States or any agency thereof.

Thus, a taxpayer who enters into a subcontract to furnish items to a prime contractor with the United States may, pursuant to a price redetermination provision in the subcontract, be required to refund an amount to the prime contractor or to another subcontractor. Since the refund would be made directly to the prime contractor or to another subcontractor, and not directly to the United States, the taxpayer would be unable to avail himself of the benefits of section 1481. However, the provisions of section 1341 and this section will apply in such a case, if the conditions set forth in subdivisions (i), (ii), and (iii) of this subparagraph are met. For provisions relating to the mitigation of the effect of a redetermination of price with respect to subcontracts entered into after December 31, 1957, when repayment is made to a party other than the United States or any agency thereof, see section 1482.

(g) *Bad debts.* The provisions of section 1341 and this section do not apply to deductions attributable to bad debts.

(h) *Legal fees and other expenses.* Section 1341 and this section do not apply to legal fees or other expenses incurred by a taxpayer in contesting the restoration of an item previously included in income. This rule may be illustrated by the following example:

Example. A sold his personal residence to B in a prior taxable year and realized a capital gain on the sale. C claimed that under an agreement with A he was entitled to a 5-percent share of the purchase price since he brought the parties together and was instrumental in closing the sale. A rejected C's demand and included the entire amount of the capital gain in gross income for the year of sale. C instituted action and in the taxable year judgment is rendered against A who pays C the amount involved. In addition, A pays legal fees in the taxable year which were incurred in the defense of the action. Section 1341 applies to the payment of the 5-percent share of the purchase price to C. However, the payment of the legal fees, whether or not otherwise deductible, does not constitute an item restored for purposes of section 1341 (a) and paragraph (a) of this section.

(i) *Refunds.* If the decrease in tax for the prior taxable year (or years) determined under section 1341(a)(5)(B) and paragraph (b)(1)(ii) of this section exceeds the tax imposed by chapter 1 of the Code for the taxable year computed without the deduction, and for taxable years beginning after December 31, 1961, if such excess is greater than the decrease in tax for the taxable year (or years) to which the net operating loss described in section 1341(b)(4)(A) and paragraph (b)(1)(iii) of this section is carried back, such excess shall be considered to be a payment of tax for the taxable year of restoration. Such payment is deemed to have been made on the last day prescribed by law for the payment of tax for the taxable year and

Reg. § 1.1341-1(f)(3)

shall be refunded or credited in the same manner as if it were an overpayment of tax for such taxable year. However, no interest shall be allowed or paid if such an excess results from the application of section 1341(a)(5)(B) in the case of a deduction described in paragraph (f)(3) of this section (relating to payments or repayments pursuant to price redetermination). If the tax for the taxable year of restoration is computed under section 1341(a)(4) and results in a decrease in tax for the taxable year (or years) to which a net operating loss described in section 1341(b)(4)(A) is carried back, see paragraph (b)(1)(iii) of this section. [Reg. § 1.1341-1.]

☐ [T.D. 6242, 7-19-57. Amended by T.D. 6617, 11-6-62; T.D. 6747, 7-20-64; T.D. 7244, 12-29-72; T.D. 7564, 9-11-78 and T.D. 8677, 6-26-96.]

S Corporations and Their Shareholders

[Reg. § 1.1361-0]

§ 1.1361-0. Table of contents.—This section lists captions contained in §§ 1.1361-1, 1.1361-2, 1.1361-3, 1.1361-4, 1.1361-5, and 1.1361-6.

§ 1.1361-1 S Corporation defined.
(a) In general.
(b) Small business corporation defined.
(1) In general.
(2) Estate in bankruptcy.
(3) Treatment of restricted stock.
(4) Treatment of deferred compensation plans.
(5) Treatment of straight debt.
(6) Effective date provisions.
(c) Domestic corporation.
(d) Ineligible corporation.
(1) General rule.
(2) Exceptions.
(e) Number of shareholders.
(1) General rule.
(2) Special rules relating to stock owned by husband and wife.
(f) Shareholder must be an individual or estate.
(g) No nonresident alien shareholder.
(1) General rule.
(2) Special rule for dual residents.
(h) Special rules relating to trusts.
(1) General rule.
(2) Foreign trust.
(3) Determination of shareholders.
(i) [Reserved]
(j) Qualified subchapter S trust.
(1) Definition.
(2) Special rules.
(3) Separate and independent shares of a trust.
(4) Qualified terminable interest property trust.
(5) Ceasing to meet the QSST requirements.
(6) Qualified subchapter S trust election.
(7) Treatment as shareholder.
(8) Coordination with grantor trust rules.
(9) Successive income beneficiary.
(10) Affirmative refusal to consent.
(11) Revocation of QSST election.
(k)(1) Examples.
(2) Effective date.
(l) Classes of stock.
(1) General rule.
(2) Determination of whether stock confers identical rights to distribution and liquidation proceeds.
(3) Stock taken into account.
(4) Other instruments, obligations, or arrangements treated as a second class of stock.
(5) Straight debt safe harbor.
(6) Inadvertent terminations.
(7) Effective date.

§ 1.1361-2 Definitions relating to S corporation subsidiaries.
(a) In general.
(b) Stock treated as held by S corporation.
(c) Straight debt safe harbor.
(d) Examples.

§ 1.1361-3 QSub election.
(a) Time and manner of making election.
(1) In general.
(2) Manner of making election.
(3) Time of making election.
(4) Effective date of election.
(5) Example.
(6) Extension of time for making a QSub election.
(b) Revocation of QSub election.
(1) Manner of revoking QSub election.
(2) Effective date of revocation.
(3) Revocation after termination.
(4) Revocation before QSub election effective.

§ 1.1361-4 Effect of QSub election.

Reg. § 1.1361-0

S Corporations and Their Shareholders

See p. 20,601 for regulations not amended to reflect law changes

(a) Separate existence ignored.
  (1) In general.
  (2) Liquidation of subsidiary.
    (i) In general.
    (ii) Examples
    (iii) Adoption of plan of liquidation.
    (iv) Example.
    (v) Stock ownership requirements of section 332.
  (3) Treatment of banks.
    (i) In general.
    (ii) Examples.
    (iii) Effective date.
  (4) Treatment of stock of QSub.
  (5) Transitional relief.
    (i) General rule.
    (ii) Examples.
(b) Timing of the liquidation.
  (1) In general.
  (2) Application to elections in tiered situations.
  (3) Acquisitions.
    (i) In general.
    (ii) Special rules for acquired S corporations.
  (4) Coordination with section 338 election.
(c) Carryover of disallowed losses and deductions.
(d) Examples.

§ 1.1361-5 Termination of QSub election.
(a) In general.
  (1) Effective date.
  (2) Information to be provided upon termination of QSub election by failure to qualify as a QSub.
  (3) QSub joins a consolidated group.
  (4) Examples.
(b) Effect of termination of QSub election.
  (1) Formation of new corporation.
    (i) In general.
    (ii) Termination for tiered QSubs.
  (2) Carryover of disallowed losses and deductions.
  (3) Examples.
(c) Election after QSub termination.
  (1) In general.
  (2) Exception.
  (3) Examples.
§ 1.1361-6 Effective date.

[Reg. § 1.1361-0.]

☐ [T.D. 8104, 9-25-86. *Amended by* T.D. 8419, 5-28-92; T.D. 8600, 7-20-95 *and* T.D. 8869, 1-20-2000.]

[Reg. § 1.1361-1]

§ 1.1361-1. S corporation defined.—(a) *In general.* For purposes of this title, with respect to any taxable year—(1) The term *S corporation* means a small business corporation (as defined in paragraph (b) of this section) for which an election under section 1362(a) is in effect for that taxable year.

(2) The term *C corporation* means a corporation that is not an S corporation for that taxable year.

(b) *Small business corporation defined*—(1) *In general.* For purposes of subchapter S, chapter 1 of the Code and the regulations thereunder, the term *small business corporation* means a domestic corporation that is not an ineligible corporation (as defined in section 1361(b)(2)) and that does not have—

(i) More than 75 shareholders (35 for taxable years beginning before January 1, 1997);

(ii) As a shareholder, a person (other than an estate and other than certain trusts described in section 1361(c)(2)) who is not an individual;

(iii) A nonresident alien as a shareholder; or

(iv) More than one class of stock.

(2) *Estate in bankruptcy.* The term *estate*, for purposes of this paragraph, includes the estate of an individual in a case under title 11 of the United States Code.

(3) *Treatment of restricted stock.* For purposes of subchapter S, stock that is issued in connection with the performance of services (within the meaning of § 1.83-3(f)) and that is substantially nonvested (within the meaning of § 1.83-3(b)) is not treated as outstanding stock of the corporation, and the holder of that stock is not treated as a shareholder solely by reason of holding the stock, unless the holder makes an election with respect to the stock under section 83(b). In the event of such an election, the stock is treated as outstanding stock of the corporation, and the holder of the stock is treated as a shareholder for purposes of subchapter S. See paragraphs (l)(1) and (3) of this section for rules for determining whether substantially nonvested stock with respect to which an election under section 83(b) has been made is treated as a second class of stock.

(4) *Treatment of deferred compensation plans.* For purposes of subchapter S, an instru-

Reg. § 1.1361-1(a)(1)

ment, obligation, or arrangement is not outstanding stock if it—

(i) Does not convey the right to vote;

(ii) Is an unfunded and unsecured promise to pay money or property in the future;

(iii) Is issued to an individual who is an employee in connection with the performance of services for the corporation or to an individual who is an independent contractor in connection with the performance of services for the corporation (and is not excessive by reference to the services performed); and

(iv) Is issued pursuant to a plan with respect to which the employee or independent contractor is not taxed currently on income.

A deferred compensation plan that has a current payment feature (*e.g.*, payment of dividend equivalent amounts that are taxed currently as compensation) is not for that reason excluded from this paragraph (b)(4).

(5) *Treatment of straight debt.* For purposes of subchapter S, an instrument or obligation that satisfies the definition of straight debt in paragraph (l)(5) of this section is not treated as outstanding stock.

(6) *Effective date provision.* Section 1.1361-1(b) generally applies to taxable years of a corporation beginning on or after May 28, 1992. However, a corporation and its shareholders may apply this § 1.1361-1(b) to prior taxable years. In addition, substantially nonvested stock issued on or before May 28, 1992, that has been treated as outstanding by the corporation is treated as outstanding for purposes of subchapter S, and the fact that it is substantially nonvested and no section 83(b) election has been made with respect to it will not cause the stock to be treated as a second class of stock.

(c) *Domestic corporation.* For purposes of paragraph (b) of this section, the term *domestic corporation* means a domestic corporation as defined in § 301.7701-5 of this chapter, and the term *corporation* includes an entity that is classified as an association taxable as a corporation under § 301.7701-2 of this chapter.

(d) *Ineligible corporation*—(1) *General rule.* Except as otherwise provided in this paragraph (d), the term *ineligible corporation* means a corporation that is—

(i) For taxable years beginning on or after January 1, 1997, a financial institution that uses the reserve method of accounting for bad debts described in section 585 (for taxable years beginning prior to January 1, 1997, a financial institution to which section 585 applies (or would apply but for section 585(c)) or to which section 593 applies);

(ii) An insurance company subject to tax under subchapter

(iii) A corporation to which an election under section 936 applies; or

(iv) A DISC or former DISC.

(2) *Exceptions.* See the special rules and exceptions provided in sections 6(c)(2), (3) and (4) of Pub. L. 97-354 that are applicable for certain casualty insurance companies and qualified oil corporations.

(e) *Number of shareholders*—(1) *General rule.* A corporation does not qualify as a small business corporation if it has more than 75 shareholders (35 for taxable years beginning prior to January 1, 1997). Ordinarily, the person who would have to include in gross income dividends distributed with respect to the stock of the corporation (if the corporation were a C corporation) is considered to be the shareholder of the corporation. For example, if stock (owned other than by a husband and wife) is owned by tenants in common or joint tenants, each tenant in common or joint tenant is generally considered to be a shareholder of the corporation. (For special rules relating to stock owned by husband and wife, see paragraph (e)(2) of this section; for special rules relating to restricted stock, see paragraphs (b)(3) and (6) of this section.) The person for whom stock of a corporation is held by a nominee, guardian, custodian, or an agent is considered to be the shareholder of the corporation for purposes of this paragraph (e) and paragraphs (f) and (g) of this section. For example, a partnership may be a nominee of S corporation stock for a person who qualifies as a shareholder of an S corporation. However, if the partnership is the beneficial owner of the stock, then the partnership is the shareholder, and the corporation does not qualify as a small business corporation. In addition, in the case of stock held for a minor under a uniform gifts to minors or similar statute, the minor and not the custodian is the shareholder. For purposes of this paragraph (e) and paragraphs (f) and (g) of this section, if stock is held by a decedent's estate, the estate (and not the beneficiaries of the estate) is considered to be the shareholder; however, if stock is held by a subpart E trust (which includes voting trusts), the deemed owner is considered to be the shareholder.

(2) *Special rules relating to stock owned by husband and wife.* For purposes of paragraph (e)(1) of this section, stock owned by a husband and wife (or by either or both of their estates) is treated as if owned by one shareholder, regardless of the form in which they own the stock. For

Reg. § 1.1361-1(e)(2)

example, if husband and wife are owners of a subpart E trust, they will be treated as one individual. Both husband and wife must be U.S. citizens or residents, and a decedent spouse's estate must not be a foreign estate as defined in section 7701(a)(31). The treatment described in this paragraph (e)(2) will cease upon dissolution of the marriage for any reason other than death.

(f) *Shareholder must be an individual or estate.* Except as otherwise provided in paragraph (e)(1) (relating to nominees and paragraph (h) (relating to certain trusts) of this section, a corporation in which any shareholder is a corporation, partnership, or trust does not qualify as a small business corporation.

(g) *Nonresident alien shareholder*—(1) *General rule.* (i) A corporation having a shareholder who is a nonresident alien as defined in section 7701(b)(1)(B) does not qualify as a small business corporation. If a U.S. shareholder's spouse is a nonresident alien who has a current ownership interest (as opposed, for example, to a survivorship interest) in the stock of the corporation by reason of any applicable law, such as a state community property law or a foreign country's law, the corporation does not qualify as a small business corporation from the time the nonresident alien spouse acquires the interest in the stock. If a corporation's S election is inadvertently terminated as a result of a nonresident alien spouse being considered a shareholder, the corporation may request relief under section 1362(f).

(ii) The following examples illustrate this paragraph (g)(1)(i):

Example 1. In 1990, W, a U.S. citizen, married H, a citizen of a foreign country. At all times H is a nonresident alien under section 7701(b)(1)(B). Under the foreign country's law, all property acquired by a husband and wife during the existence of the marriage is community property and owned jointly by the husband and wife. In 1996 while residing in the foreign country, W formed X, a U.S. corporation, and X simultaneously filed an election to be an S corporation. X issued all of its outstanding stock in W's name. Under the foreign country's law, X's stock became the community property of and jointly owned by H and W. Thus, X does not meet the definition of a small business corporation and therefore could not file a valid S election because H, a nonresident alien, has a current interest in the stock.

Example 2. Assume the same facts as *Example 1*, except that in 1991, W and H filed a section 6013(g) election allowing them to file a joint U.S. tax return and causing H to be treated as a U.S. resident for purposes of chapters 1, 5, and 24 of the Internal Revenue Code. The section 6013(g) election applies to the taxable year for which made and to all subsequent taxable years until terminated. Because H is treated as a U.S. resident under section 6013(g), X does meet the definition of a small business corporation. Thus, the election filed by X to be an S corporation is valid.

(2) *Special rule for dual residents.* [Reserved]

(h) *Special rules relating to trusts*—(1) *General rule.* In general, a trust is not a permitted small business corporation shareholder. However, except as provided in paragraph (h)(2) of this section, the following trusts are permitted shareholders:

(i) *Qualified Subpart E trust.* A trust all of which is treated (under subpart E, part I, subchapter J, chapter 1) as owned by an individual (whether or not the grantor) who is a citizen or resident of the United States (a qualified subpart E trust). This requirement applies only during the period that the trust holds S corporation stock.

(ii) *Subpart E trust ceasing to be a qualified subpart E trust after the death of deemed owner.* A trust which was a qualified subpart E trust immediately before the death of the deemed owner and which continues in existence after the death of the deemed owner, but only for the 60-day period beginning on the day of the deemed owner's death. However, if a trust is described in the preceding sentence and the entire corpus of the trust is includible in the gross estate of the deemed owner, the trust is a permitted shareholder for the 2-year period beginning on the day of the deemed owner's death. A trust is considered to continue in existence if the trust continues to hold the stock of the S corporation during the period of administration of the decedent's estate or if, after the period of administration, the trust continues to hold the stock pursuant to the terms of the will or the trust agreement. See § 1.641(b)-3 for rules concerning the termination of estates and trusts for federal income tax purposes. If the trust consists of community property, and the decedent's community property interest in the trust is includible in the decedent's gross estate under chapter 11 (section 2001 and following, relating to estate tax), then the entire corpus of the trust will be deemed includible in the decedent's gross estate. Further, for the purpose of determining whether the entire corpus of the trust is includible in the gross estate of the deemed owner, if the decedent's spouse was treated as an owner of a portion of the trust under subpart E immediately before the decedent's death, the surviving spouse's portion is disregarded.

(iii) *Electing Qualified subchapter S trusts.* A qualified subchapter S trust (QSST) that has a section 1361(d)(2) election in effect (an electing QSST). See paragraph (j) of this section for rules concerning QSSTs including the manner for making the section 1361(d)(2) election.

(iv) *Testamentary trusts.* A trust (other than a qualified subpart E trust or an electing QSST) to which S corporation stock is transferred pursuant to the terms of a will, but only for the 60-day period beginning on the day the stock is transferred to the trust.

(v) *Qualified Voting trusts.* A trust created primarily to exercise the voting power of S corporation stock transferred to it. To qualify as a voting trust for purposes of this section (a qualified voting trust), the beneficial owners must be treated as the owners of their respective portions of the trust under subpart E and the trust must have been created pursuant to a written trust agreement entered into by the shareholders, that—

(A) Delegates to one or more trustees the right to vote;

(B) Requires all distributions with respect to the stock of the corporation held by the trust to be paid to, or on behalf of, the beneficial owners of that stock;

(C) Requires title and possession of that stock to be delivered to those beneficial owners upon termination of the trust; and

(D) Terminates, under its terms or by state law, on or before a specific date or event.

(2) *Foreign trust.* For purposes of paragraph (h)(1) of this section, in any case where stock is held by a foreign trust as defined in section 7701(a)(31), the trust is considered to be the shareholder and is an ineligible shareholder. Thus, even if a foreign trust qualifies as a subpart E trust (e.g., a qualified voting trust), any corporation in which the trust holds stock does not qualify as a small business corporation.

(3) *Determination of shareholders*—(i) *General rule.* For purposes of paragraph (b) of this section (qualification as a small business corporation), and, except as provided in paragraph (h)(3)(ii) of this section, for purposes of sections 1366 (relating to the pass-through of items of income, loss, deduction, or credit), 1367 (relating to adjustments to basis of shareholder's stock), and 1368 (relating to distributions), the shareholder of S corporation stock held by a trust that is a permitted shareholder under paragraph (h)(1) of this section is determined as follows:

(A) If stock is held by a qualified subpart E trust, the deemed owner of the trust is treated as the shareholder.

(B) If stock is held by a trust defined in paragraph (h)(1)(ii) of this section, the estate of the deemed owner is generally treated as the shareholder as of the day of the deemed owner's death. However, if stock is held by such a trust in a community property state, the decedent's estate is the shareholder only of the portion of the trust included in the decedent's gross estate (and the surviving spouse continues to be the shareholder of the portion of the trust owned by that spouse under the applicable state's community property law). The estate ordinarily will cease to be treated as the shareholder upon the earlier of the transfer of the stock by the trust or the expiration of the 60-day period (or, if applicable, the 2-year period) beginning on the day of the deemed owner's death. If the trust qualifies and becomes an electing QSST, the beneficiary and not the estate is treated as the shareholder as of the effective date of the QSST election, and the rules provided in paragraph (j)(7) of this section apply.

(C) If stock is held by an electing QSST, see paragraph (j)(7) of this section for the rules on who is treated as the shareholder.

(D) If stock is transferred to a testamentary trust (other than a qualified subpart E trust or an electing QSST), the estate of the testator is treated as the shareholder until the earlier of the transfer of that stock by the trust or the expiration of the 60-day period beginning on the day that the stock is transferred to the trust.

(E) If stock is held by a qualified voting trust, each beneficial owner of the stock, as determined under subpart E, is treated as a shareholder with respect to the owner's proportionate share of the stock held by the trust.

(ii) *Exceptions.* Solely for purposes of section 1366, 1367, and 1368 the shareholder of S corporation stock held by a trust is determined as follows—

(A) If stock is held by a trust (as defined in paragraph (h)(1)(ii) of this section) that does not qualify as a QSST, the trust is treated as the shareholder. If the trust continues to own the stock after the expiration of the 60-day period (or, if applicable, the 2-year period), the corporation's S election will terminate unless the trust is otherwise a permitted shareholder. If the trust is a QSST described in section 1361(d) and the income beneficiary of the trust makes a timely QSST election, the beneficiary and not the trust is treated as the shareholder from the effective date of the QSST election; and

(B) If stock is transferred to a testamentary trust described in paragraph (h)(1)(iii) of this section (other than a qualified subpart E trust or a trust that has a QSST election in effect), the trust is treated as the shareholder. If the trust continues to own the stock after the expiration of the 60-day period, the corporation's S election will terminate unless the trust otherwise qualifies as a permitted shareholder.

(i) [Reserved]

(j) *Qualified subchapter S trust*—(1) *Definition.* A qualified subchapter S trust (QSST) is a trust (whether intervivos or testamentary), other than a foreign trust described in section 7701(a)(31), that satisfies the following requirements:

(i) All of the income (within the meaning of § 1.643(b)-1) of the trust is distributed (or is required to be distributed) currently to one individual who is a citizen or resident of the United States. For purposes of the preceding sentence, unless otherwise provided under local law (including pertinent provisions of the governing instrument that are effective under local law), income of the trust includes distributions to the trust from the S corporation for the taxable year in question, but does not include the trust's pro rata share of the S corporation's items of income, loss, deduction, or credit determined under section 1366. See §§ 1.651(a)-2(a) and 1.663(b)-1(a) for rules relating to the determination of whether all of the income of a trust is distributed (or is required to be distributed) currently. If under the terms of the trust income is not required to be distributed currently, the trustee may elect under section 663(b) to consider a distribution made in the first 65 days of a taxable year as made on the last day of the preceding taxable year. See section 663(b) and § 1.663(b)-2 for rules on the time and manner for making the election. The income distribution requirement must be satisfied for the taxable year of the trust or for that part of the trust's taxable year during which it holds S corporation stock.

(ii) The terms of the trust must require that—

(A) During the life of the current income beneficiary, there will be only one income beneficiary of the trust;

(B) Any corpus distributed during the life of the current income beneficiary may be distributed only to that income beneficiary;

(C) The current income beneficiary's income interest in the trust will terminate on the earlier of that income beneficiary's death or the termination of the trust; and

(D) Upon termination of the trust during the life of the current income beneficiary, the trust will distribute all of its assets to that income beneficiary.

(iii) The terms of the trust must satisfy the requirements of paragraph (j)(1)(ii) of this section from the date the QSST election is made or from the effective date of the QSST election, whichever is earlier, throughout the entire period that the current income beneficiary and any successor income beneficiary is the income beneficiary of the trust. If the terms of the trust do not preclude the possibility that any of the requirements stated in paragraph (j)(1)(ii) of this section will not be met, the trust will not qualify as a QSST. For example, if the terms of the trust are silent with respect to corpus distributions, and distributions of corpus to a person other than the current income beneficiary are permitted under local law during the life of the current income beneficiary, then the terms of the trust do not preclude the possibility that corpus may be distributed to a person other than the current income beneficiary and, therefore, the trust is not a QSST.

(2) *Special rules*—(i) If a husband and wife are income beneficiaries of the same trust, the husband and wife file a joint return, and each is a U.S. citizen or resident, the husband and wife are treated as one beneficiary for purposes of paragraph (j) of this section. If a husband and wife are treated by the preceding sentence as one beneficiary, any action required by this section to be taken by an income beneficiary requires joinder of both of them. For example, each spouse must sign the QSST election, continue to be a U.S. citizen or resident, and continue to file joint returns for the entire period that the QSST election is in effect.

(ii) (A) *Terms of the trust and applicable local law.* The determination of whether the terms of a trust meet all of the requirements under paragraph (j)(1)(ii) of this section depends upon the terms of the trust instrument and the applicable local law. For example, a trust whose governing instrument provides that A is the sole income beneficiary of the trust is, nevertheless, considered to have two income beneficiaries if, under the applicable local law, A and B are considered to be the income beneficiaries of the trust.

(B) *Legal obligation to support.* If under local law a distribution to the income beneficiary is in satisfaction of the grantor's legal obligation of support to that income beneficiary, the trust will not qualify as a QSST as of the date of distribution because, under section 677(b), if income is distributed, the grantor will be treated as the owner of the ordinary income portion of the trust or, if trust corpus is distributed, the grantor will be treated as a beneficiary under section 662. See § 1.677(b)-1 for rules on the treatment of trusts for support and § 1.662(a)-4 for rules concerning amounts used in discharge of a legal obligation.

Reg. § 1.1361-1(i)

(C) *Example.* The following example illustrates the rules of paragraph (j)(2)(ii)(B) of this section:

Example. F creates a trust for the benefit of F's minor child, G. Under the terms of the trust, all income is payable to G until the trust terminates on the earlier of G's attaining age 35 or G's death. Upon the termination of the trust, all corpus must be distributed to G or G's estate. The trust includes all of the provisions prescribed by section 1361(d)(3)(A) and paragraph (j)(1)(ii) of this section, but does not preclude the trustee from making income distributions to G that will be in satisfaction of F's legal obligation to support G. Under the applicable local law, distributions of trust income to G will satisfy F's legal obligation to support G. If the trustee distributes income to G in satisfaction of F's legal obligation to support G, the trust will not qualify as a QSST because F will be treated as the owner of the ordinary income portion of the trust. Further, the trust will not be a qualified subpart E trust because the trust will be subject to tax on the income allocable to corpus.

(iii) If, under the terms of the trust, a person (including the income beneficiary) has a special power to appoint, during the life of the income beneficiary, trust income or corpus to any person other than the current income beneficiary, the trust will not qualify as a QSST. However, if the power of appointment results in the grantor being treated as the owner of the entire trust under the rules of subpart E, the trust may be a permitted shareholder under section 1361(c)(2)(A)(i) and paragraph (h)(1)(i) of this section.

(iv) If the terms of a trust or local law do not preclude the current income beneficiary from transferring the beneficiary's interest in the trust or do not preclude a person other than the current income beneficiary named in the trust instrument from being treated as a beneficiary of the trust under § 1.643(c)-1, the trust will still qualify as a QSST. However, if the income beneficiary transfers or assigns the income interest or a portion of the income interest to another, the trust may no longer qualify as a QSST, depending on the facts and circumstances, because any transferee of the current income beneficiary's income interest and any person treated as a beneficiary under § 1.643(c)-1 will be treated as a current income beneficiary for purposes of paragraph (j)(1)(ii) of this section and the trust may no longer meet the QSST requirements.

(v) If the terms of the trust do not preclude a person other than the current income beneficiary named in the trust instrument from being awarded an interest in the trust by the order of a court, the trust will qualify as a QSST assuming the trust meets the requirements of paragraphs (j)(1)(i) and (ii) of this section. However, if as a result of such court order, the trust no longer meets the QSST requirements, the trust no longer qualifies as a QSST and the corporation's S election will terminate.

(vi) A trust may qualify as a QSST even though a person other than the current income beneficiary is treated under subpart E as the owner of a part or all of that portion of a trust which does not consist of the S corporation stock, provided the entire trust meets the QSST requirements stated in paragraphs (j)(1)(i) and (ii) of this section.

(3) *Separate and independent shares of a trust.* For purposes of sections 1361(c) and (d), a substantially separate and independent share of a trust, within the meaning of section 663(c) and the regulations thereunder, is treated as a separate trust. For a separate share which holds S corporation stock to qualify as a QSST, the terms of the trust applicable to that separate share must meet the QSST requirements stated in paragraphs (j)(1)(i) and (ii) of this section.

(4) *Qualified terminable interest property trust.* If property, including S corporation stock, or stock of a corporation that intends to make an S election, is transferred to a trust and an election is made to treat all or a portion of the transferred property as qualified terminable interest property (QTIP) under section 2056(b)(7), the income beneficiary may make the QSST election if the trust meets the requirements set out in paragraphs (j)(1)(i) and (ii) of this section. However, if property is transferred to a QTIP trust under section 2523(f), the income beneficiary may not make a QSST election even if the trust meets the requirements set forth in paragraph (j)(1)(ii) of this section because the grantor would be treated as the owner of the income portion of the trust under section 677. In addition, if property is transferred to a QTIP trust under section 2523(f), the trust does not qualify as a permitted shareholder under section 1361(c)(2)(A)(i) and paragraph (h)(1)(i) of this section (a qualified subpart E trust), unless under the terms of the QTIP trust, the grantor is treated as the owner of the entire trust under sections 671 to 677. If the grantor ceases to be the income beneficiary's spouse, the trust may qualify as a QSST if it otherwise satisfies the requirements under paragraphs (j)(1)(i) and (ii) of this section.

(5) *Ceasing to meet the QSST requirements.* If a QSST for which an election under section 1361(d)(2) has been made (as described in para-

Reg. § 1.1361-1(j)(5)

graph (j) (6) of this section) ceases to meet any of the requirements specified in paragraph (j)(1)(ii) of this section, the provisions of this paragraph (j) will cease to apply as of the first day on which that requirement ceases to be met. If such a trust ceases to meet the income distribution requirement specified in paragraph (j)(1)(i) of this section, but continues to meet all of the requirements in paragraph (j)(1)(ii) of this section, the provisions of this paragraph (j) will cease to apply as of the first day of the first taxable year beginning after the first taxable year for which the trust ceased to meet the income distribution requirement of paragraph (j)(1)(i) of this section. If a corporation's S election is inadvertently terminated as a result of a trust ceasing to meet the QSST requirements, the corporation may request relief under section 1362(f).

(6) *Qualified subchapter S trust election*—(i) *In general.* This paragraph (j)(6) applies to the election provided in section 1361(d)(2) (the QSST election) to treat a QSST (as defined in paragraph (j)(1) of this section) as a trust described in section 1361(c)(2)(A)(i), and thus a permitted shareholder. This election must be made separately with respect to each corporation whose stock is held by the trust. The QSST election does not itself constitute an election as to the status of the corporation; the corporation must make the election provided by section 1362(a) to be an S corporation. Until the effective date of a corporation's S election, the beneficiary is not treated as the owner of the stock of the corporation for purposes of section 678. Any action required by this paragraph (j) to be taken by a person who is under a legal disability by reason of age may be taken by that person's guardian or other legal representative, or if there be none, by that person's natural or adoptive parent.

(ii) *Filing the QSST election.* The current income beneficiary of the trust must make the election by signing and filing with the service center with which the corporation files its income tax return the applicable form or a statement that—

(A) Contains the name, address, and taxpayer identification number of the current income beneficiary, the trust, and the corporation;

(B) Identifies the election as an election made under section 1361(d)(2);

(C) Specifies the date on which the election is to become effective (not earlier than 15 days and two months before the date on which the election is filed);

(D) Specifies the date (or dates) on which the stock of the corporation was transferred to the trust; and

(E) Provides all information and representations necessary to show that:

(*1*) Under the terms of the trust and applicable local law—

(*i*) During the life of the current income beneficiary, there will be only one income beneficiary of the trust (if husband and wife are beneficiaries, that they will file joint returns and that both are U.S. residents or citizens);

(*ii*) Any corpus distributed during the life of the current income beneficiary may be distributed only to that beneficiary;

(*iii*) The current beneficiary's income interest in the trust will terminate on the earlier of the beneficiary's death or upon termination of the trust; and

(*iv*) Upon the termination of the trust during the life of such income beneficiary, the trust will distribute all its assets to such beneficiary.

(*2*) The trust is required to distribute all of its income currently, or that the trustee will distribute all of its income currently if not so required by the terms of the trust.

(*3*) No distribution of income or corpus by the trust will be in satisfaction of the grantor's legal obligation to support or maintain the income beneficiary.

(iii) *When to file the QSST election.* (A) If S corporation stock is transferred to a trust, the QSST election must be made within the 16-day-and-2-month period beginning on the day that the stock is transferred to the trust. If a C corporation has made an election under section 1362(a) to be an S corporation (S election) and, before that corporation's S election is in effect, stock of that corporation is transferred to a trust, the QSST election must be made within the 16-day-and-2-month period beginning on the day that the stock is transferred to the trust.

(B) If a trust holds C corporation stock and that C corporation makes an S election effective for the first day of the taxable year in which the S election is made, the QSST election must be made within the 16-day-and-2-month period beginning on the day that the S election is effective. If a trust holds C corporation stock and that C corporation makes an S election effective for the first day of the taxable year following the taxable year in which the S election is made, the QSST election must be made within the 16-day-and-2-month period beginning on the day that the S election is made. If a trust holds C corporation stock and that corporation makes an S election intending the S election to be effective for the first day of the taxable year in which the S election is

Reg. § 1.1361-1(j)(6)

made but, under § 1.1362-6(a)(2), such S election is subsequently treated as effective for the first day of the taxable year following the taxable year in which the S election is made, the fact that the QSST election states that the effective date of the QSST election is the first day of the taxable year in which the S election is made will not cause the QSST election to be ineffective for the first year in which the corporation's S election is effective.

(C) If a trust ceases to be a qualified subpart E trust but also satisfies the requirements of a QSST, the QSST election must be filed within the 16-day-and-2-month period beginning on the date on which the trust ceases to be a qualified subpart E trust. If the estate of the deemed owner of the trust is treated as the shareholder under paragraph (h) (3) (ii) of this section, the QSST election may be filed at any time but no later than the end of the 16-day-and-2-month period beginning on the date on which the estate of the deemed owner ceases to be treated as a shareholder.

(D) If a corporation's S election terminates because of a late QSST election, the corporation may request inadvertent termination relief under section 1362(f). See § 1.1362-4 for rules concerning inadvertent terminations.

(iv) *Protective QSST election when a person is an owner under subpart E.* If the grantor of a trust is treated as the owner under subpart E of all of the trust, or of a portion of the trust which consists of S corporation stock, and the current income beneficiary is not the grantor, the current income beneficiary may not make the QSST election, even if the trust meets the QSST requirements stated in paragraph (j)(1)(ii) of this section. See paragraph (j)(6)(iii)(C) of this section as to when the QSST election may be made. See also paragraph (j) (2) (vi) of this section. However, if the current income beneficiary (or beneficiaries who are husband and wife, if both spouses are U.S. citizens or residents and file a joint return) of a trust is treated under subpart E as owning all or a portion of the trust consisting of S corporation stock, the current income beneficiary (or beneficiaries who are husband and wife, if both spouses are U.S. citizens or residents and file a joint return) may make the QSST election. See *Example 8* of paragraph (k) (l) of this section.

(7) *Treatment as shareholder.* (i) The income beneficiary who makes the QSST election and is treated (for purposes of section 678(a)) as the owner of that portion of the trust that consists of S corporation stock is treated as the shareholder for purposes of sections 1361(b)(1), 1366, 1367, and 1368.

(ii) If, upon the death of an income beneficiary, the trust continues in existence, continues to hold S corporation stock but no longer satisfies the QSST requirements, and is not a qualified subpart E trust, then, solely for purposes of section 1361(b)(1), as of the date of the income beneficiary's death, the estate of that income beneficiary is treated as the shareholder of the S corporation with respect to which the income beneficiary made the QSST election. The estate ordinarily will cease to be treated as the shareholder for purposes of section 1361(b)(1) upon the earlier of the transfer of that stock by the trust or the expiration of the 60-day period beginning on the day of the income beneficiary's death. However, if the entire corpus of the trust is includible in the gross estate of that income beneficiary, the estate will cease to be treated as the shareholder for purposes of section 1361(b)(1) upon the earlier of the transfer of that stock by the trust or the expiration of the 2-year period beginning on the day of the income beneficiary's death. For the purpose of determining whether the entire trust corpus is includible in the gross estate of the income beneficiary, any community property interest in the trust held by the income beneficiary's spouse which arises by reason of applicable U.S. state law is disregarded. During the period that the estate is treated as the shareholder for purposes of section 1361(b)(1), the trust is treated as the shareholder for purposes of sections 1366, 1367, and 1368. If, after the 60-day period, or the 2-year period, if applicable, the trust continues to hold S corporation stock, the corporation's S election terminates. If the termination is inadvertent, the corporation may request relief under section 1362(f).

(8) *Coordination with grantor trust rules.* If a valid QSST election is made, the income beneficiary is treated as the owner, for purposes of section 678(a), of that portion of the trust that consists of the stock of the S corporation for which the QSST election was made. However, solely for purposes of applying the preceding sentence to a QSST, an income beneficiary who is a deemed section 678 owner only by reason of section 1361(d)(1) will not be treated as the owner of the S corporation stock in determining and attributing the federal income tax consequences of a disposition of the stock by the QSST. For example, if the disposition is a sale, the QSST election terminates as to the stock sold and any gain or loss recognized on the sale will be that of the trust, not the income beneficiary. Similarly, if a QSST distributes its S corporation stock to the income beneficiary, the QSST election terminates as to the distributed stock and the consequences of the distribution are determined by reference to the status of the trust

Reg. § 1.1361-1(j)(8)

apart from the income beneficiary's terminating ownership status under sections 678 and 1361(d)(1). The portions of the trust other than the portion consisting of S corporation stock are subject to subparts A through D of subchapter J of chapter 1, except as otherwise required by subpart E of the Internal Revenue Code.

(9) *Successive income beneficiary.* (i) If the income beneficiary of a QSST who made a QSST election dies, each successive income beneficiary of that trust is treated as consenting to the election unless a successive income beneficiary affirmatively refuses to consent to the election. For this purpose, the term *successive income beneficiary* includes a beneficiary of a trust whose interest is a separate share within the meaning of section 663(c), but does not include any beneficiary of a trust that is created upon the death of the income beneficiary of the QSST and which is a new trust under local law.

(ii) The application of this paragraph (j)(9) is illustrated by the following examples:

Example 1. Shares of stock in Corporation X, an S corporation, are held by Trust A, a QSST for which a QSST election was made. B is the sole income beneficiary of Trust A. On B's death, under the terms of Trust A, J and K become the current income beneficiaries of Trust A. J and K each hold a separate and independent share of Trust A within the meaning of section 663(c). J and K are successive income beneficiaries of Trust A, and they are treated as consenting to B's QSST election.

Example 2. Assume the same facts as in *Example 1,* except that on B's death, under the terms of Trust A and local law, Trust A terminates and the principal is to be divided equally and held in newly created Trust B and Trust C. The sole income beneficiaries of Trust B and Trust C are J and K, respectively. Because Trust A terminated, J and K are not successive income beneficiaries of Trust A. J and K must make QSST elections for their respective trusts to qualify as QSSTs, if they qualify. The result is the same whether or not the trustee of Trusts B and C is the same as the trustee of trust A.

(10) *Affirmative refusal to consent*—(i) *Required statement.* A successive income beneficiary of a QSST must make an affirmative refusal to consent by signing and filing with the service center where the corporation files its income tax return a statement that—

(A) Contains the name, address, and taxpayer identification number of the successive income beneficiary, the trust, and the corporation for which the election was made;

(B) Identifies the refusal as an affirmative refusal to consent under section 1361(d)(2); and

(C) Sets forth the date on which the successive income beneficiary became the income beneficiary.

(ii) *Filing date and effectiveness.* The affirmative refusal to consent must be filed within 15 days and 2 months after the date on which the successive income beneficiary becomes the income beneficiary. The affirmative refusal to consent will be effective as of the date on which the successive income beneficiary becomes the current income beneficiary.

(11) *Revocation of QSST election.* A QSST election may be revoked only with the consent of the Commissioner. The Commissioner will not grant a revocation when one of its purposes is the avoidance of federal income taxes or when the taxable year is closed. The application for consent to revoke the election must be submitted to the Internal Revenue Service in the form of a letter ruling request under the appropriate revenue procedure. The application must be signed by the current income beneficiary and must—

(i) Contain the name, address, and taxpayer identification number of the current income beneficiary, the trust, and the corporation with respect to which the QSST election was made;

(ii) Identify the election being revoked as an election made under section 1361(d)(2); and

(iii) Explain why the current income beneficiary seeks to revoke the QSST election and indicate that the beneficiary understands the consequences of the revocation.

(k)(1) *Examples.* The provisions of paragraphs (h) and (j) of this section are illustrated by the following examples in which it is assumed that all noncorporate persons are citizens or residents of the United States:

Example 1. (i) *Terms of the trust.* In 1996, A and A's spouse, B, created an intervivos trust and each funded the trust with separately owned stock of an S corporation. Under the terms of the trust, A and B designated themselves as the income beneficiaries and each, individually, retained the power to amend or revoke the trust with respect to the trust assets attributable to their respective trust contributions. Upon A's death, the trust is to be divided into two separate parts; one part attributable to the assets A contributed to the trust and one part attributable to B's contributions. Before the trust is divided, and during the administration of A's estate, all trust income is payable to B. The part of the trust attributable to B's contributions is to continue in trust under the

Reg. § 1.1361-1(j)(9)

terms of which B is designated as the sole income beneficiary and retains the power to amend or revoke the trust. The part attributable to A's contributions is to be divided into two separate trusts both of which have B as the sole income beneficiary for life. One trust, the *Credit Shelter Trust,* is to be funded with an amount that can pass free of estate tax by reason of A's available estate tax unified credit. The terms of the Credit Shelter Trust meet the requirements of section 1361(d)(3) as a QSST. The balance of the property passes to a Marital Trust, the terms of which satisfy the requirements of section 1361(d)(3) as a QSST and section 2056(b)(7) as QTIP. The appropriate fiduciary under § 20.2056(b)-7(b)(3) is directed to make an election under section 2056(b)(7).

(ii) *Results after deemed owner's death.* On February 3, 1997, A dies and the portion of the trust assets attributable to A's contributions including the S stock contributed by A, is includible in A's gross estate under sections 2036 and 2038. During the administration of A's estate, the trust holds the S corporation stock. Under section 1361(c)(2)(B)(ii), A's estate is treated as the shareholder of the S corporation stock that was included in A's gross estate for purposes of section 1361(b)(1); however, for purposes of sections 1366, 1367, and 1368, the trust is treated as the shareholder. B's part of the trust continues to be a qualified subpart E trust of which B is the owner under sections 676 and 677. B, therefore, continues to be treated as the shareholder of the S corporation stock in that portion of the trust. On May 13, 1997, during the continuing administration of A's estate, the trust is divided into separate trusts in accordance with the terms of the trust instrument. The S corporation stock that was included in A's gross estate is distributed to the Marital Trust and to the Credit Shelter Trust. A's estate will cease to be treated as the shareholder of the S corporation under section 1361(c)(2)(B)(ii) on May 13, 1997 (the date on which the S corporation stock was transferred to the trusts). B, as the income beneficiary of the Marital Trust and the Credit Shelter Trust, must make the QSST election for each trust by July 28, 1997 (the end of the 16-day-and-2-month period beginning on the date the estate ceases to be treated as a shareholder) to have the trusts become permitted shareholders of the S corporation.

Example 2. (i) *Qualified subpart E trust as shareholder.* In 1997, A, an individual established a trust and transferred to the trust A's shares of stock of Corporation M, an S corporation. A has the power to revoke the entire trust. The terms of the trust require that all income be paid to B and otherwise meet the requirements of a QSST under section 1361(d)(3). The trust will continue in existence after A's death. The trust is a qualified subpart E trust described in section 1361(c)(2)(A)(i) during A's life, and A (not the trust) is treated as the shareholder for purposes of sections 1361(b)(1), 1366, 1367, and 1368.

(ii) *Trust ceasing to be a qualified subpart E trust on deemed owner's death.* Assume the same facts as paragraph (i) of this *Example 2,* except that A dies without having exercised A's power to revoke. Upon A's death, the trust ceases to be a qualified subpart E trust described in section 1361(c)(2)(A)(i). A's estate (and not the trust) is treated as the shareholder for purposes of section 1361(b)(1). Because the entire corpus of the trust is includible in A's gross estate under section 2038, A's estate will cease to be treated as the shareholder for purposes of section 1361(b)(1) upon the earlier of the transfer of the Corporation M stock by the trust (other than to A's estate), the expiration of the 2-year period beginning on the day of A's death, or the effective date of a QSST election if the trust qualifies as a QSST. However, until that time, because the trust continues in existence after A's death and will receive any distributions with respect to the stock it holds, the trust is treated as the shareholder for purposes of sections 1366, 1367, and 1368. After the 2-year period, if no QSST election is made, the corporation ceases to be an S corporation, but the trust continues as the shareholder of a C corporation.

(iii) *Trust continuing to be a qualified subpart E trust on deemed owner's death.* Assume the same facts as paragraph (ii) of this *Example 2,* except that the terms of the trust also provide that if A does not exercise the power to revoke before A's death, B will have the sole power to withdraw all trust property at any time after A's death. The trust continues to qualify as a qualified subpart E trust after A's death because, upon A's death, B is deemed to be the owner of the entire trust under section 678. Because the trust does not cease to be a qualified subpart E trust upon A's death, B (and not A's estate) is treated as the shareholder for purposes of sections 1361(b)(1), 1366, 1367, and 1368. Since the trust qualifies as a QSST, B may make a protective QSST election under paragraph (j) (6) (iv) of this section.

Example 3. 60-*day rule under section* 1361(c)(2)(A)(ii) *and* (iii). F owns stock of Corporation P, an S corporation. In addition, F is the deemed owner of a qualified subpart E trust that holds stock in Corporation 0, an S corporation. F dies on July 1, 1996. The trust continues in existence after F's death but is no longer a qualified subpart E trust. The entire corpus of the trust is not includible in F's gross estate. On August 1, 1996, F's shares of stock in Corporation P are transferred to the trust pursuant to the terms of F's will. Because the stock of Corporation P was not held by the trust when F died, section 1361(c)(2)(A)(ii) does not apply with respect to that stock. Under section 1361(c)(2)(A)(iii), the last day on which F's estate could be treated as a permitted shareholder of Corporation P is September 29, 1996 (that is, the last day of the 60-day period that begins on the date of the transfer from the estate to the trust). With respect to the shares of stock in Corporation O held by the trust at the time of F's death, section 1361(c)(2)(A)(ii) applies and the last day on which F's estate could be treated as a permitted shareholder of Corporation O is August 29, 1996 (that is, the last day of the 60-day period that begins on the date of F's death).

Example 4. (i) *QSST when terms do not require current distribution of income.* Corporation Q, a calender year corporation, makes an election to be an S corporation effective for calendar year 1996. On July 1, 1996, G, a shareholder of Corporation Q, transfers G's shares of Corporation Q stock to a trust with H as its current income beneficiary. The terms of the trust otherwise satisfy the QSST requirements, but authorize the trustee in its discretion to accumulate or distribute the trust income. However, the trust, which uses the calendar year as its taxable year, initially satisfies the income distribution requirement because the trustee is currently distributing all of the income. On August 1, 1996, H makes a QSST election with respect to Corporation Q that is effective as of July 1, 1996. Accordingly, as of July 1, 1996, the trust is a QSST and H is treated as the shareholder for purposes of sections 1361(b)(1), 1366, 1367, and 1368.

(ii) *QSST when trust income is not distributed currently.* Assume the same facts as in paragraph (i) of this *Example 4*, except that, for the taxable year ending on December 31, 1997, the trustee accumulates some trust income. The trust ceases to be a QSST on January 1, 1998, because the trust failed to distribute all of its income for the taxable year ending December 31, 1997. Thus, Corporation Q ceases to be an S corporation as of January 1, 1998, because the trust is not a permitted shareholder.

(iii) *QSST when a person other than the current income beneficiary may receive trust corpus.* Assume the same facts as in paragraph (i) of this *Example 4*, except that H dies on November 1, 1996. Under the terms of the trust, after H's death, L is the income beneficiary of the trust and the trustee is authorized to distribute trust corpus to L as well as to J. The trust ceases to be a QSST as of November 1, 1996, because corpus distributions may be made to someone other than L, the current (successive) income beneficiary. Under section 1361(c)(2)(A)(ii), H's estate (and not the trust) is considered to be the shareholder for purposes of section 1361(b)(1) for the 60-day period beginning on November 1, 1996. However, because the trust continues in existence after H's death and will receive any distributions from the corporation, the trust (and not H's estate) is treated as the shareholder for purposes of sections 1366, 1367, and 1368, during that 60-day period. After the 60day period, the S election terminates and the trust continues as a shareholder of a C corporation. If the termination is inadvertent, Corporation Q may request relief under section 1362(f). However, the S election would not terminate if the trustee distributed all Corporation Q shares to L, J, or both before December 30, 1996, (the last day of the 60-day period) assuming that neither L nor J becomes the 36th shareholder of Corporation Q as a result of the distribution.

Example 5. QSST when current income beneficiary assigns the income interest to a person not named in the trust. On January 1, 1996, stock of Corporation R, a calendar year S corporation, is transferred to a trust that satisfies all of the requirements to be a QSST. Neither the terms of the trust nor local law preclude the current income beneficiary, K, from assigning K's income interest in the trust. K files a timely QSST election that is effective January 1, 1996. On July 1, 1996, K assigns the income interest in the trust to N. Under applicable state law, the trustee is bound as a result of the assignment to distribute the trust income to N. Thus, the QSST will cease to qualify as a QSST under section 1361(d)(3)(A)(iii) because N's interest will terminate on K's death (rather than on N's death). Accordingly, as of the date of the assignment, the trust ceases to be a QSST and Corporation R ceases to be an S corporation.

Example 6. QSST when terms fail to provide for distribution of trust assets upon termination during life of current income beneficiary. A contributes S corporation stock to a trust the terms of which provide for one income beneficiary, annual distributions of income, discretionary invasion of corpus only for the benefit of the income beneficiary, and termination of the trust only upon the death of the current income beneficiary. Since the trust can terminate only upon the death of the income beneficiary, the governing instrument fails to provide for any distribution of trust assets during the income beneficiary's life. The governing instrument's silence on this point does not

Reg. § 1.1361-1(k)

disqualify the trust under section 1361(d)(3)(A)(ii) or (iv).

Example 7. QSST when settlor of trust retains a reversion in the trust. On January 10, 1996, M transfers to a trust shares of stock in corporation X, an S corporation. D, who is 13 years old and not a lineal descendant of M, is the sole income beneficiary of the trust. On termination of the trust, the principal (including the X shares) is to revert to M. The trust instrument provides that the trust will terminate upon the earlier of D's death or D's 21st birthday. The terms of the trust satisfy all of the requirements to be a QSST except those of section 1361(d)(3)(A)(ii) (that corpus may be distributed during the current income beneficiary's life only to that beneficiary) and (iv) (that, upon termination of the trust during the life of the current income beneficiary, the corpus, must be distributed to that beneficiary). On February 10, 1996, M makes a gift of M's reversionary interest to D. Until M assigns M's reversion in the trust to D, M is deemed to own the entire trust under section 673(a) and the trust is a qualified subpart E trust. For purposes of section 1361(b)(1), 1366, 1367, and 1368, M is the shareholder of X. The trust ceases to be a qualified subpart E trust on February 10, 1996. Assuming that, by virtue of the assignment to D of M's reversionary interest, D (upon his 21st birthday) or D's estate (in the case of D's death before reaching age 21) is entitled under local law to receive the trust principal, the trust will be deemed as of February 10, 1996, to have satisfied the conditions of section 1361(d)(3)(A)(ii) and (iv) even though the terms of the trust do not explicitly so provide. D must make a QSST election by no later than April 25, 1996 (the end of the 16-day-and-2-month period that begins on February 10, 1996, the date on which the X stock is deemed transferred to the trust by M). See example (5) of § 1.1001-2(c) of the regulations.

Example 8. QSST when the income beneficiary has the power to withdraw corpus. On January 1, 1996, F transfers stock of an S corporation to an irrevocable trust whose income beneficiary is F's son, C. Under the terms of the trust, C is given the noncumulative power to withdraw from the corpus of the trust the greater of $5,000 or 5 percent of the value of the corpus on a yearly basis. The terms of the trust meet the QSST requirements. Assuming the trust distributions are not in satisfaction of F's legal obligation to support C, the trust qualifies as a QSST. C (or if C is a minor, C's legal representative) must make the QSST election no later than March 16, 1996 (the end of the 16-day-and-2-month period that begins on the date the stock is transferred to the trust).

Example 9. (i) *Filing the QSST election.* On January 1, 1996, stock of Corporation T, a calendar year C corporation, is transferred to a trust that satisfies all of the requirements to be a QSST. On January 31, 1996, Corporation T files an election to be an S corporation that is to be effective for its taxable year beginning on January 1, 1996. In order for the S election to be effective for the 1996 taxable year, the QSST election must be effective January 1, 1996, and must be filed within the period beginning on January 1, 1996, and ending March 16, 1996 (the 16-day-and-2-month period beginning on the first day of the first taxable year for which the election to be an S corporation is intended to be effective).

(ii) *QSST election when the S election is filed late.* Assume the same facts as in paragraph (i) of this *Example 9,* except that Corporation T's election to be an S corporation is filed on April 1, 1996 (after the 15th day of the 3rd month of the first taxable year for which it is to be effective but before the end of that taxable year). Because the election to be an S corporation is not timely filed for the 1996 taxable year, under section 1362(b)(3), the S election is treated as made for the taxable year beginning on January 1, 1997. The QSST election must be filed within the 16-day-and-2-month period beginning on April 1, 1996, the date the S election was made, and ending on June 16, 1996.

Example 10. (i) *Transfers to QTIP trust.* On June 1, 1996, A transferred S corporation stock to a trust for the benefit of A's spouse B, the terms of which satisfy the requirements of section 2523(f)(2) as qualified terminable interest property. Under the terms of the trust, B is the sole income beneficiary for life. In addition, corpus may be distributed to B, at the trustee's discretion, during B's lifetime. However, under section 677(a), A is treated as the owner of the trust. Accordingly, the trust is a permitted shareholder of the S corporation under section 1361(c)(2)(A)(i), and A is treated as the shareholder for purposes of sections 1361(b)(1), 1366, 1367, and 1368.

(ii) *Transfers to QTIP trust where husband and wife divorce.* Assume the same facts as in paragraph (i) of this *Example 10,* except that A and B divorce on May 2, 1997. Under section 682, A ceases to be treated as the owner of the trust under section 677(a) because A and B are no longer husband and wife. Under section 682, after the divorce, B is the income beneficiary of the trust and corpus of the trust may only be distributed to B. Accordingly, assuming the trust other-

Reg. § 1.1361-1(k)

wise meets the requirements of section 1361(d)(3), B must make the QSST election within 2 months and 15 days after the date of the divorce.

(iii) *Transfers to QTIP trust where no corpus distribution is permitted.* Assume the same facts as in paragraph (i) of this *Example 10,* except that the terms of the trust do not permit corpus to be distributed to B and require its retention by the trust for distribution to A and B's surviving children after the death of B. Under section 677, A is treated as the owner of the ordinary income portion of the trust, but the trust will be subject to tax on gross income allocable to corpus. Accordingly, the trust does not qualify as an eligible shareholder of the S corporation because it is neither a qualified subpart E trust nor a QSST.

(2) *Effective date*—(i) *In general.* Paragraph (a), and paragraphs (c) through (k) of this section apply to taxable years of a corporation beginning after July 21, 1995. For taxable years beginning on or before July 21, 1995, to which paragraph (a), and paragraphs (c) through (k) do not apply, see § 18.1361-1 of this chapter (as contained in the 26 CFR edition revised April 1, 1995).

(ii) *Exception.* If a QSST has sold or otherwise disposed of all or a portion of its S corporation stock in a tax year that is open for the QSST and the income beneficiary but on or before July 21, 1995, the QSST and the income beneficiary may both treat the transaction as if the beneficiary was the owner of the stock sold or disposed of, and thus recognize any gain or loss, or as if the QSST was the owner of the stock sold or disposed of as described in paragraph (j)(8) of this section. This exception applies only if the QSST and the income beneficiary take consistent reporting positions. The QSST and the income beneficiary must disclose by a statement on their respective returns (or amended returns), that they are taking consistent reporting positions.

(l) *Classes of stock*—(1) *General rule.* A corporation that has more than one class of stock does not qualify as a small business corporation. Except as provided in paragraph (l)(4) of this section (relating to instruments, obligations, or arrangements treated as a second class of stock), a corporation is treated as having only one class of stock if all outstanding shares of stock of the corporation confer identical rights to distribution and liquidation proceeds. Differences in voting rights among shares of stock of a corporation are disregarded in determining whether a corporation has more than one class of stock. Thus, if all shares of stock of an S corporation have identical rights to distribution and liquidation proceeds, the corporation may have voting and nonvoting common stock, a class of stock that may vote only on certain issues, irrevocable proxy agreements, or groups of shares that differ with respect to rights to elect members of the board of directors.

(2) *Determination of whether stock confers identical rights to distribution and liquidation proceeds*—(i) *In general.* The determination of whether all outstanding shares of stock confer identical rights to distribution and liquidation proceeds is made based on the corporate charter, articles of incorporation, bylaws, applicable state law, and binding agreements relating to distribution and liquidation proceeds (collectively, the governing provisions). A commercial contractual agreement, such as a lease, employment agreement, or loan agreement, is not a binding agreement relating to distribution and liquidation proceeds and thus is not a governing provision unless a principal purpose of the agreement is to circumvent the one class of stock requirement of section 1361(b)(1)(D) and this paragraph (l). Although a corporation is not treated as having more than one class of stock so long as the governing provisions provide for identical distribution and liquidation rights, any distributions (including actual, constructive, or deemed distributions) that differ in timing or amount are to be given appropriate tax effect in accordance with the facts and circumstances.

(ii) *State law requirements for payment and withholding of income tax.* State laws may require a corporation to pay or withhold state income taxes on behalf of some or all of the corporation's shareholders. Such laws are disregarded in determining whether all outstanding shares of stock of the corporation confer identical rights to distribution and liquidation proceeds, within the meaning of paragraph (l)(1) of this section, provided that, when the constructive distributions resulting from the payment or withholding of taxes by the corporation are taken into account, the outstanding shares confer identical rights to distribution and liquidation proceeds. A difference in timing between the constructive distributions and the actual distributions to the other shareholders does not cause the corporation to be treated as having more than one class of stock.

(iii) *Buy-sell and redemption agreements*—(A) *In general.* Buy-sell agreements among shareholders, agreements restricting the transferability of stock, and redemption agreements are disregarded in determining whether a corporation's outstanding shares of stock confer identical distribution and liquidation rights unless—

(*1*) A principal purpose of the agreement is to circumvent the one class of stock requirement of section 1361(b)(1)(D) and this paragraph (1), and

(2) The agreement establishes a purchase price that, at the time the agreement is entered into, is significantly in excess of or below the fair market value of the stock.

Agreements that provide for the purchase or redemption of stock at book value or at a price between fair market value and book value are not considered to establish a price that is significantly in excess of or below the fair market value of the stock and, thus, are disregarded in determining whether the outstanding shares of stock confer identical rights. For purposes of this paragraph (l)(2)(iii)(A), a good faith determination of fair market value will be respected unless it can be shown that the value was substantially in error and the determination of the value was not performed with reasonable diligence. Although an agreement may be disregarded in determining whether shares of stock confer identical distribution and liquidation rights, payments pursuant to the agreement may have income or transfer tax consequences.

(B) *Exception for certain agreements.* Bona fide agreements to redeem or purchase stock at the time of death, divorce, disability, or termination of employment are disregarded in determining whether a corporation's shares of stock confer identical rights. In addition, if stock that is substantially nonvested (within the meaning of § 1.83-3(b)) is treated as outstanding under these regulations, the forfeiture provisions that cause the stock to be substantially nonvested are disregarded. Furthermore, the Commissioner may provide by Revenue Ruling or other published guidance that other types of bona fide agreements to redeem or purchase stock are disregarded.

(C) *Safe harbors for determinations of book value.* A determination of book value will be respected if—

(1) The book value is determined in accordance with Generally Accepted Accounting Principles (including permitted optional adjustments); or

(2) The book value is used for any substantial nontax purpose.

(iv) *Distributions that take into account varying interests in stock during a taxable year.* A governing provision does not, within the meaning of paragraph (l)(2)(i) of this section, alter the rights to liquidation and distribution proceeds conferred by an S corporation's stock merely because the governing provision provides that, as a result of a change in stock ownership, distributions in a taxable year are to be made on the basis of the shareholders' varying interests in the S corporation's income in the current or immediately preceding taxable year. If distributions pursuant to the provision are not made within a reasonable time after the close of the taxable year in which the varying interests occur, the distributions may be recharacterized depending on the facts and circumstances, but will not result in a second class of stock.

(v) *Special rule for section 338(h)(10) elections.* If the shareholders of an S corporation sell their stock in a transaction for which an election is made under section 338(h)(10) and § 1.338(h)(10)-1, the receipt of varying amounts per share by the shareholders will not cause the S corporation to have more than one class of stock, provided that the varying amounts are determined in arm's length negotiations with the purchaser.

(vi) *Examples.* The application of paragraph (l)(2) of this section may be illustrated by the following examples. In each of the examples, the S corporation requirements of section 1361 are satisfied except as otherwise stated, the corporation has in effect an S election under section 1362, and the corporation has only the shareholders described.

Example 1. Determination of whether stock confers identical rights to distribution and liquidation proceeds. (i) The law of State A requires that permission be obtained from the State Commissioner of Corporations before stock may be issued by a corporation. The Commissioner grants permission to S, a corporation, to issue its stock subject to the restriction that any person who is issued stock in exchange for property, and not cash, must waive all rights to receive distributions until the shareholders who contributed cash for stock have received distributions in the amount of their cash contributions.

(ii) The condition imposed by the Commissioner pursuant to state law alters the rights to distribution and liquidation proceeds conferred by the outstanding stock of S so that those rights are not identical. Accordingly, under paragraph (l)(2)(i) of this section, S is treated as having more than one class of stock and does not qualify as a small business corporation.

Example 2. Distributions that differ in timing. (i) S, a corporation, has two equal shareholders, A and B. Under S's bylaws, A and B are entitled to equal distributions. S distributes $50,000 to A in the current year, but does not distribute $50,000 to B until one year later. The circumstances indicate that the difference in timing did not occur by reason of a binding agreement relating to distribution or liquidation proceeds.

Reg. § 1.1361-1(l)(2)

(ii) Under paragraph (l)(2)(i) of this section, the difference in timing of the distributions to A and B does not cause S to be treated as having more than one class of stock. However, section 7872 or other recharacterization principles may apply to determine the appropriate tax consequences.

Example 3. Treatment of excessive compensation. (i) S, a corporation, has two equal shareholders, C and D, who are each employed by S and have binding employment agreements with S. The compensation paid by S to C under C's employment agreement is reasonable. The compensation paid by S to D under D's employment agreement, however, is found to be excessive. The facts and circumstances do not reflect that a principal purpose of D's employment agreement is to circumvent the one class of stock requirement of section 1361(b)(1)(D) and this paragraph (l).

(ii) Under paragraph (l)(2)(i) of this section, the employment agreements are not governing provisions. Accordingly, S is not treated as having more than one class of stock by reason of the employment agreements, even though S is not allowed a deduction for the excessive compensation paid to D.

Example 4. Agreement to pay fringe benefits. (i) S, a corporation, is required under binding agreements to pay accident and health insurance premiums on behalf of certain of its employees who are also shareholders. Different premium amounts are paid by S for each employee-shareholder. The facts and circumstances do not reflect that a principal purpose of the agreements is to circumvent the one class of stock requirement of section 1361(b)(1)(D) and this paragraph (1).

(ii) Under paragraph (l)(2)(i) of this section, the agreements are not governing provisions. Accordingly, S is not treated as having more than one class of stock by reason of the agreements. In addition, S is not treated as having more than one class of stock by reason of the payment of fringe benefits.

Example 5. Below-market corporation-shareholder loan. (i) E is a shareholder of S, a corporation. S makes a below-market loan to E that is a corporation-shareholder loan to which section 7872 applies. Under section 7872, E is deemed to receive a distribution with respect to S stock by reason of the loan. The facts and circumstances do not reflect that a principal purpose of the loan is to circumvent the one class of stock requirement of section 1361(b)(1)(D) and this paragraph (1).

(ii) Under paragraph (1)(2)(i) of this section, the loan agreement is not a governing provision. Accordingly, S is not treated as having more than one class of stock by reason of the below-market loan to E.

Example 6. Agreement to adjust distributions for state tax burdens. (i) S, a corporation, executes a binding agreement with its shareholders to modify its normal distribution policy by making upward adjustments of its distributions to those shareholders who bear heavier state tax burdens. The adjustments are based on a formula that will give the shareholders equal after-tax distributions.

(ii) The binding agreement relates to distribution or liquidation proceeds. The agreement is thus a governing provision that alters the rights conferred by the outstanding stock of S to distribution proceeds so that those rights are not identical. Therefore, under paragraph (l)(2)(i) of this section, S is treated as having more than one class of stock.

Example 7. State law requirements for payment and withholding of income tax. (i) The law of State X requires corporations to pay state income taxes on behalf of nonresident shareholders. The law of State X does not require corporations to pay state income taxes on behalf of resident shareholders. S is incorporated in State X. S's resident shareholders have the right (for example, under the law of State X or pursuant to S's bylaws or a binding agreement) to distributions that take into account the payments S makes on behalf of its nonresident shareholders.

(ii) The payment by S of state income taxes on behalf of its nonresident shareholders are generally treated as constructive distributions to those shareholders. Because S's resident shareholders have the right to equal distributions, taking into account the constructive distributions to the nonresident shareholders, S's shares confer identical rights to distribution proceeds. Accordingly, under paragraph (l)(2)(ii) of this section, the state law requiring S to pay state income taxes on behalf of its nonresident shareholders is disregarded in determining whether S has more than one class of stock.

(iii) The same result would follow if the payments of state income taxes on behalf of nonresident shareholders are instead treated as advances to those shareholders and the governing provisions require the advances to be repaid or offset by reductions in distributions to those shareholders.

Example 8. Redemption agreements. (i) F, G, and H are shareholders of S, a corporation. F is also an employee of S. By agreement, S is to redeem F's shares on the termination of F's employment.

Reg. § 1.1361-1(l)(2)

S Corporations and Their Shareholders

(ii) On these facts, under paragraph (l)(2)(iii)(B) of this section, the agreement is disregarded in determining whether all outstanding shares of S's stock confer identical rights to distribution and liquidation proceeds.

Example 9. Analysis of redemption agreements. (i) J, K, and L are shareholders of S, a corporation. L is also an employee of S. L's shares were not issued to L in connection with the performance of services. By agreement, S is to redeem L's shares for an amount significantly below their fair market value on the termination of L's employment or if S's sales fall below certain levels.

(ii) Under paragraph (l)(2)(iii)(B) of this section, the portion of the agreement providing for redemption of L's stock on termination of employment is disregarded. Under paragraph (l)(2)(iii)(A), the portion of the agreement providing for redemption of L's stock if S's sales fall below certain levels is disregarded unless a principal purpose of that portion of the agreement is to circumvent the one class of stock requirement of section 1361(b)(1)(D) and this paragraph (l).

(3) *Stock taken into account.* Except as provided in paragraphs (b)(3), (4), and (5) of this section (relating to restricted stock, deferred compensation plans, and straight debt), in determining whether all outstanding shares of stock confer identical rights to distribution and liquidation proceeds, all outstanding shares of stock of a corporation are taken into account. For example, substantially nonvested stock with respect to which an election under section 83(b) has been made is taken into account in determining whether a corporation has a second class of stock, and such stock is not treated as a second class of stock if the stock confers rights to distribution and liquidation proceeds that are identical, within the meaning of paragraph (l)(1) of this section, to the rights conferred by the other outstanding shares of stock.

(4) *Other instruments, obligations, or arrangements treated as a second class of stock*—(i) *In general.* Instruments, obligations, or arrangements are not treated as a second class of stock for purposes of this paragraph (l) unless they are described in paragraphs (l)(4)(ii) or (iii) of this section. However, in no event are instruments, obligations, or arrangements described in paragraph (b)(4) of this section (relating to deferred compensation plans), paragraphs (l)(4)(iii)(B) and (C) of this section (relating to the exceptions and safe harbor for options), paragraph (l)(4)(ii)(B) of this section (relating to the safe harbors for certain short-term unwritten advances and proportionally-held debt), or paragraph (l)(5) of this section (relating to the safe harbor for straight debt), treated as a second class of stock for purposes of this paragraph (l).

(ii) *Instruments, obligations, or arrangements treated as equity under general principles*—(A) *In general.* Except as provided in paragraph (l)(4)(i) of this section, any instrument, obligation, or arrangement issued by a corporation (other than outstanding shares of stock described in paragraph (l)(3) of this section), regardless of whether designated as debt, is treated as a second class of stock of the corporation—

(*1*) If the instrument, obligation, or arrangement constitutes equity or otherwise results in the holder being treated as the owner of stock under general principles of Federal tax law; and

(*2*) A principal purpose of issuing or entering into the instrument, obligation, or arrangement is to circumvent the rights to distribution or liquidation proceeds conferred by the outstanding shares of stock or to circumvent the limitation on eligible shareholders contained in paragraph (b)(1) of this section.

(B) *Safe harbor for certain short-term unwritten advances and proportionately held obligations*—(*1*) *Short-term unwritten advances.* Unwritten advances from a shareholder that do not exceed $10,000 in the aggregate at any time during the taxable year of the corporation, are treated as debt by the parties, and are expected to be repaid within a reasonable time are not treated as a second class of stock for that taxable year, even if the advances are considered equity under general principles of Federal tax law. The failure of an unwritten advance to meet this safe harbor will not result in a second class of stock unless the advance is considered equity under paragraph (l)(4)(ii)(A)(*1*) of this section and a principal purpose of the advance is to circumvent the rights of the outstanding shares of stock or the limitation on eligible shareholders under paragraph (l)(4)(ii)(A)(*2*) of this section.

(*2*) *Proportionately-held obligations.* Obligations of the same class that are considered equity under general principles of Federal tax law, but are owned solely by the owners of, and in the same proportion as, the outstanding stock of the corporation, are not treated as a second class of stock. Furthermore, an obligation or obligations owned by the sole shareholder of a corporation are always held proportionately to the corporation's outstanding stock. The obligations that are considered equity that do not meet this safe harbor will not result in a second class of stock unless a principal purpose of the obligations is to circumvent the rights of the outstanding shares of stock

Reg. § 1.1361-1(l)(4)

or the limitation on eligible shareholders under paragraph (l)(4)(ii)(A)(*2*) of this section.

(iii) *Certain call options, warrants or similar instruments*—(A) *In general.* Except as otherwise provided in this paragraph (l)(4)(iii), a call option, warrant, or similar instrument (collectively, call option) issued by a corporation is treated as a second class of stock of the corporation if, taking into account all the facts and circumstances, the call option is substantially certain to be exercised (by the holder or a potential transferee) and has a strike price substantially below the fair market value of the underlying stock on the date that the call option is issued, transferred by a person who is an eligible shareholder under paragraph (b)(1) of this section to a person who is not an eligible shareholder under paragraph (b)(1) of this section, or materially modified. For purposes of this paragraph (l)(4)(iii), if an option is issued in connection with a loan and the time period in which the option can be exercised is extended in connection with (and consistent with) a modification of the terms of the loan, the extension of the time period in which the option may be exercised is not considered a material modification. In addition, a call option does not have a strike price substantially below fair market value if the price at the time of exercise cannot, pursuant to the terms of the instrument, be substantially below the fair market value of the underlying stock at the time of exercise.

(B) *Certain exceptions.* (*1*) A call option is not treated as a second class of stock for purposes of this paragraph (l) if it is issued to a person that is actively and regularly engaged in the business of lending and issued in connection with a commercially reasonable loan to the corporation. This paragraph (l)(4)(iii)(B)(*1*) continues to apply if the call option is transferred with the loan (or if a portion of the call option is transferred with a corresponding portion of the loan). However, if the call option is transferred without a corresponding portion of the loan, this paragraph (l)(4)(iii)(B)(*1*) ceases to apply. Upon that transfer, the call option is tested under paragraph (l)(4)(iii)(A) (notwithstanding anything in that paragraph to the contrary) if, but for this paragraph, the call option would have been treated as a second class of stock on the date it was issued.

(*2*) A call option that is issued to an individual who is either an employee or an independent contractor in connection with the performance of services for the corporation or a related corporation (and that is not excessive by reference to the services performed) is not treated as a second class of stock for purposes of this paragraph (l) if—

(*i*) The call option is nontransferable within the meaning of § 1.83-3(d); and

(*ii*) The call option does not have a readily ascertainable fair market value as defined in § 1.83-7(b) at the time the option is issued.

If the call option becomes transferable, this paragraph (l)(4)(iii)(B)(*2*) ceases to apply. Solely for purposes of this paragraph (l)(4)(iii)(B)(*2*), a corporation is related to the issuing corporation if more than 50 percent of the total voting power and total value of its stock is owned by the issuing corporation.

(*3*) The Commissioner may provide other exceptions by Revenue Ruling or other published guidance.

(C) *Safe harbor for certain options.* A call option is not treated as a second class of stock if, on the date the call option is issued, transferred by a person who is an eligible shareholder under paragraph (b)(1) of this section to a person who is not an eligible shareholder under paragraph (b)(1) of this section, or materially modified, the strike price of the call option is at least 90 percent of the fair market value of the underlying stock on that date. For purposes of this paragraph (l)(4)(iii)(C), a good faith determination of fair market value by the corporation will be respected unless it can be shown that the value was substantially in error and the determination of the value was not performed with reasonable diligence to obtain a fair value. Failure of an option to meet this safe harbor will not necessarily result in the option being treated as a second class of stock.

(iv) *Convertible debt.* A convertible debt instrument is considered a second class of stock if—

(A) It would be treated as a second class of stock under paragraph (l)(4)(ii) of this section (relating to instruments, obligations, or arrangements treated as equity under general principles); or

(B) It embodies rights equivalent to those of a call option that would be treated as a second class of stock under paragraph (l)(4)(iii) of this section (relating to certain call options, warrants, and similar instruments).

(v) *Examples.* The application of this paragraph (l)(4) may be illustrated by the following examples. In each of the examples, the S corporation requirements of section 1361 are satisfied except as otherwise stated, the corporation has in effect an S election under section 1362, and the corporation has only the shareholders described.

Reg. § 1.1361-1(l)(4)

Example 1. Transfer of call option by eligible shareholder to ineligible shareholder. (i) S, a corporation, has 10 shareholders. S issues call options to A, B, and C, individuals who are U.S. residents. A, B, and C are not shareholders, employees, or independent contractors of S. The options have a strike price of $40 and are issued on a date when the fair market value of S stock is also $40. A year later, P, a partnership, purchases A's option. On the date of transfer, the fair market value of S stock is $80.

(ii) On the date the call option is issued, its strike price is not substantially below the fair market value of the S stock. Under paragraph (l)(4)(iii)(A) of this section, whether a call option is a second class of stock must be redetermined if the call option is transferred by a person who is an eligible shareholder under paragraph (b)(1) of this section to a person who is not an eligible shareholder under paragraph (b)(1) of this section. In this case, A is an eligible shareholder of S under paragraph (b)(1) of this section, but P is not. Accordingly, the option is retested on the date it is transferred to D.

(iii) Because on the date the call option is transferred to P its strike price is 50% of the fair market value, the strike price is substantially below the fair market value of the S stock. Accordingly, the call option is treated as a second class of stock as of the date it is transferred to P if, at that time, it is determined that the option is substantially certain to be exercised. The determination of whether the option is substantially certain to be exercised is made on the basis of all the facts and circumstances.

Example 2. Call option issued in connection with the performance of services. (i) E is a bona fide employee of S, a corporation. S issues to E a call option in connection with E's performance of services. At the time the call option is issued, it is not transferable and does not have a readily ascertainable fair market value. However, the call option becomes transferable before it is exercised by E.

(ii) While the option is not transferable, under paragraph (l)(4)(iii)(B)(*2*) of this section, it is not treated as a second class of stock, regardless of its strike price. When the option becomes transferable, that paragraph ceases to apply, and the general rule of paragraph (l)(4)(iii)(A) of this section applies. Accordingly, if the option is materially modified or is transferred to a person who is not an eligible shareholder under paragraph (b)(1) of this section, and on the date of such modification or transfer, the option is substantially certain to be exercised and has a strike price substantially below the fair market value of the underlying stock, the option is treated as a second class of stock.

(iii) If E left S's employment before the option became transferable, the exception provided by paragraph (l)(4)(iii)(B)(*2*) would continue to apply until the option became transferable.

(5) *Straight debt safe harbor*—(i) *In general.* Notwithstanding paragraph (l)(4) of this section, straight debt is not treated as a second class of stock. For purposes of section 1361(c)(5) and this section, the term straight debt means a written unconditional obligation, regardless of whether embodied in a formal note, to pay a sum certain on demand, or on a specified due date, which—

(A) Does not provide for an interest rate or payment dates that are contingent on profits, the borrower's discretion, the payment of dividends with respect to common stock, or similar factors;

(B) Is not convertible (directly or indirectly) into stock or any other equity interest of the S corporation; and

(C) Is held by an individual (other than a nonresident alien), an estate, or a trust described in section 1361(c)(2).

(ii) *Subordination.* The fact that an obligation is subordinated to other debt of the corporation does not prevent the obligation from qualifying as straight debt.

(iii) *Modification or transfer.* An obligation that originally qualifies as straight debt ceases to so qualify if the obligation—

(A) Is materially modified so that it no longer satisfies the definition of straight debt; or

(B) Is transferred to a third party who is not an eligible shareholder under paragraph (b)(1) of this section.

(iv) *Treatment of straight debt for other purposes.* An obligation of an S corporation that satisfies the definition of straight debt in paragraph (l)(5)(i) of this section is not treated as a second class of stock even if it is considered equity under general principles of Federal tax law. Such an obligation is generally treated as debt and when so treated is subject to the applicable rules governing indebtedness for other purposes of the Code. Accordingly, interest paid or accrued with respect to a straight debt obligation is generally treated as interest by the corporation and the recipient and does not constitute a distribution to which section 1368 applies. However, if a straight debt obligation bears a rate of interest that is unreasonably high, an appropriate portion of the interest may be recharacterized and treated as a

Reg. § 1.1361-1(l)(5)

payment that is not interest. Such a recharacterization does not result in a second class of stock.

(v) *Treatment of C corporation debt upon conversion to S status.* If a C corporation has outstanding an obligation that satisfies the definition of straight debt in paragraph (l)(5)(i) of this section, but that is considered equity under general principles of Federal tax law, the obligation is not treated as a second class of stock for purposes of this section if the C corporation converts to S status. In addition, the conversion from C corporation status to S corporation status is not treated as an exchange of debt for stock with respect to such an instrument.

(6) *Inadvertent terminations.* See section 1362(f) and the regulations thereunder for rules relating to inadvertent terminations in cases where the one class of stock requirement has been inadvertently breached.

(7) *Effective date.* Section 1.1361-1(l) generally applies to taxable years of a corporation beginning on or after May 28, 1992. However, § 1.1361-1(l) does not apply to: an instrument, obligation, or arrangement issued or entered into before May 28, 1992, and not materially modified after that date; a buy-sell agreement, redemption agreement, or agreement restricting transferability entered into before May 28, 1992, and not materially modified after that date; or a call option or similar instrument issued before May 28, 1992, and not materially modified after that date. In addition, a corporation and its shareholders may apply this § 1.1361-1(l) to prior taxable years. [Reg. § 1.1361-1.]

☐ [*T.D.* 8419, 5-28-92. *Amended by T.D.* 8600, 7-20-95; *T.D.* 8869, 1-20-2000 *and T.D.* 8940, 2-12-2001.]

[Reg. § 1.1361-2]

§ 1.1361-2. **Definitions relating to S corporation subsidiaries.**—(a) *In general.* The term *qualified subchapter S subsidiary* (QSub) means any domestic corporation that is not an ineligible corporation (as defined in section 1361(b)(2) and the regulations thereunder), if—

(1) 100 percent of the stock of such corporation is held by an S corporation; and

(2) The S corporation properly elects to treat the subsidiary as a QSub under § 1.1361-3.

(b) *Stock treated as held by S corporation.* For purposes of satisfying the 100 percent stock ownership requirement in section 1361(b)(3)(B)(i) and paragraph (a)(1) of this section—

(1) Stock of a corporation is treated as held by an S corporation if the S corporation is the owner of that stock for Federal income tax purposes; and

(2) Any outstanding instruments, obligations, or arrangements of the corporation which would not be considered stock for purposes of section 1361(b)(1)(D) if the corporation were an S corporation are not treated as outstanding stock of the QSub.

(c) *Straight debt safe harbor.* Section 1.1361-1(1)(5)(iv) and (v) apply to an obligation of a corporation for which a QSub election is made if that obligation would satisfy the definition of straight debt in § 1.1361-1(1)(5) if issued by the S corporation.

(d) *Examples.* The following examples illustrate the application of this section:

Example 1. X, an S corporation, owns 100 percent of Y, a corporation for which a valid QSub election is in effect for the taxable year. Y owns 100 percent of Z, a corporation otherwise eligible for QSub status. X may elect to treat Z as a QSub under section 1361(b)(3)(B)(ii).

Example 2. Assume the same facts as in *Example 1*, except that Y is a business entity that is disregarded as an entity separate from its owner under § 301.7701-2(c)(2) of this chapter. X may elect to treat Z as a QSub.

Example 3. Assume the same facts as in *Example 1*, except that Y owns 50 percent of Z, and X owns the other 50 percent. X may elect to treat Z as a QSub.

Example 4. Assume the same facts as in *Example 1*, except that Y is a C corporation. Although Y is a domestic corporation that is otherwise eligible to be a QSub, no QSub election has been made for Y. Thus, X is not treated as holding the stock of Z. Consequently, X may not elect to treat Z as a QSub.

Example 5. Individuals A and B own 100 percent of the stock of corporation X, an S corporation, and, except for C's interest (described below), X owns 100 percent of corporation Y, a C corporation. Individual C holds an instrument issued by Y that is considered to be equity under general principles of tax law but would satisfy the definition of straight debt under § 1.1361-1(1)(5) if Y were an S corporation. In determining whether X owns 100 percent of Y for purposes of making the QSub election, the instrument held by C is not considered outstanding stock. In addition, under § 1.1361-1(1)(5)(v), the QSub election is not treated as an exchange of debt for stock with respect to such instrument, and § 1.1361-1(1)(5)(iv) applies to determine the tax treatment of payments on the instrument while Y's QSub election is in effect.

[Reg. § 1.1361-2.]

☐ [*T.D.* 8869, 1-20-2000.]

S Corporations and Their Shareholders

See p. 20,601 for regulations not amended to reflect law changes

[Reg. § 1.1361-3]

§ **1.1361-3. QSub election.**—(a) *Time and manner of making election*—(1) *In general.* The corporation for which the QSub election is made must meet all the requirements of section 1361(b)(3)(B) at the time the election is made and for all periods for which the election is to be effective.

(2) *Manner of making election.* Except as provided in section 1361(b)(3)(D) and § 1.1361-5(c) (five-year prohibition on reelection), an S corporation may elect to treat an eligible subsidiary as a QSub by filing a completed form to be prescribed by the IRS. The election form must be signed by a person authorized to sign the S corporation's return required to be filed under section 6037. Unless the election form provides otherwise, the election must be submitted to the service center where the subsidiary filed its most recent tax return (if applicable), and, if an S corporation forms a subsidiary and makes a valid QSub election (effective upon the date of the subsidiary's formation) for the subsidiary, the election should be submitted to the service center where the S corporation filed its most recent return.

(3) *Time of making election.* A QSub election may be made by the S corporation parent at any time during the taxable year.

(4) *Effective date of election.* A QSub election will be effective on the date specified on the election form or on the date the election form is filed if no date is specified. The effective date specified on the form cannot be more than two months and 15 days prior to the date of filing and cannot be more than 12 months after the date of filing. For this purpose, the definition of the term *month* found in § 1.1362-6(a)(2)(ii)(C) applies. If an election form specifies an effective date more than two months and 15 days prior to the date on which the election form is filed, it will be effective two months and 15 days prior to the date it is filed. If an election form specifies an effective date more than 12 months after the date on which the election is filed, it will be effective 12 months after the date it is filed.

(5) *Example.* The following example illustrates the application of paragraph (a)(4) of this section:

Example. X has been a calendar year S corporation engaged in a trade or business for several years. X acquires the stock of Y, a calendar year C corporation, on April 1, 2002. On August 10, 2002, X makes an election to treat Y as a QSub. Unless otherwise specified on the election form, the election will be effective as of August 10, 2002. If specified on the election form, the election may be effective on some other date that is not more than two months and 15 days prior to August 10, 2002, and not more than 12 months after August 10, 2002.

(6) *Extension of time for making a QSub election.* An extension of time to make a QSub election may be available under the procedures applicable under §§ 301.9100-1 and 301.9100-3 of this chapter.

(b) *Revocation of QSub election*—(1) *Manner of revoking QSub election.* An S corporation may revoke a QSub election under section 1361 by filing a statement with the service center where the S corporation's most recent tax return was properly filed. The revocation statement must include the names, addresses, and taxpayer identification numbers of both the parent S corporation and the QSub, if any. The statement must be signed by a person authorized to sign the S corporation's return required to be filed under section 6037.

(2) *Effective date of revocation.* The revocation of a QSub election is effective on the date specified on the revocation statement or on the date the revocation statement is filed if no date is specified. The effective date specified on the revocation statement cannot be more than two months and 15 days prior to the date on which the revocation statement is filed and cannot be more than 12 months after the date on which the revocation statement is filed. If a revocation statement specifies an effective date more than two months and 15 days prior to the date on which the statement is filed, it will be effective two months and 15 days prior to the date it is filed. If a revocation statement specifies an effective date more than 12 months after the date on which the statement is filed, it will be effective 12 months after the date it is filed.

(3) *Revocation after termination.* A revocation may not be made after the occurrence of an event that renders the subsidiary ineligible for QSub status under section 1361(b)(3)(B).

(4) *Revocation before QSub election effective.* For purposes of Section 1361(b)(3)(D) and § 1.1361-5(c) (five-year prohibition on re-election), a revocation effective on the first day the QSub election was to be effective will not be treated as a termination of a QSub election. [Reg. § 1.1361-3.]

☐ [T.D. 8869, 1-20-2000.]

[Reg. § 1.1361-4]

§ 1.1361-4. Effect of QSub election.—(a) *Separate existence ignored*—(1) *In general.* Except as otherwise provided in paragraph (a)(3) of this section, for Federal tax purposes—

(i) A corporation which is a QSub shall not be treated as a separate corporation; and

(ii) All assets, liabilities, and items of income, deduction, and credit of a QSub shall be treated as assets, liabilities, and items of income, deduction, and credit of the S corporation.

(2) *Liquidation of subsidiary*—(i) *In general.* If an S corporation makes a valid QSub election with respect to a subsidiary, the subsidiary is deemed to have liquidated into the S corporation. Except as provided in paragraph (a)(5) of this section, the tax treatment of the liquidation or of a larger transaction that includes the liquidation will be determined under the Internal Revenue Code and general principles of tax law, including the step transaction doctrine. Thus, for example, if an S corporation forms a subsidiary and makes a valid QSub election (effective upon the date of the subsidiary's formation) for the subsidiary, the transfer of assets to the subsidiary and the deemed liquidation are disregarded, and the corporation will be deemed to be a QSub from its inception.

(ii) *Examples.* The following examples illustrate the application of this paragraph (a)(2)(i) of this section:

Example 1. Corporation X acquires all of the outstanding stock of solvent corporation Y from an unrelated individual for cash and short-term notes. Thereafter, as part of the same plan, X immediately makes an S election and a QSub election for Y. Because X acquired all of the stock of Y in a qualified stock purchase within the meaning of section 338(d)(3), the liquidation described in paragraph (a)(2) of this section is respected as an independent step separate from the stock acquisition, and the tax consequences of the liquidation are determined under sections 332 and 337.

Example 2. Corporation X, pursuant to a plan, acquires all of the outstanding stock of corporation Y from the shareholders of Y solely in exchange for 10 percent of the voting stock of X. Prior to the transaction, Y and its shareholders are unrelated to X. Thereafter, as part of the same plan, X immediately makes an S election and a QSub election for Y. The transaction is a reorganization described in section 368(a)(1)(C), assuming the other conditions for reorganization treatment (e.g., continuity of business enterprise) are satisfied.

Example 3. After the expiration of the transition period provided in paragraph (a)(5)(i) of this section, individual A, pursuant to a plan, contributes all of the outstanding stock of Y to his wholly owned S corporation, X, and immediately causes X to make a QSub election for Y. The transaction is a reorganization under section 368(a)(1)(D), assuming the other conditions for reorganization treatment (e.g., continuity of business enterprise) are satisfied. If the sum of the amount of liabilities of Y treated as assumed by X exceeds the total of the adjusted basis of the property of Y, then section 357(c) applies and such excess is considered as gain from the sale or exchange of a capital asset or of property which is not a capital asset, as the case may be.

(iii) *Adoption of plan of liquidation.* For purposes of satisfying the requirement of adoption of a plan of liquidation under section 332, unless a formal plan of liquidation that contemplates the QSub election is adopted on an earlier date, the making of the QSub election is considered to be the adoption of a plan of liquidation immediately before the deemed liquidation described in paragraph (a)(2)(i) of this section.

(iv) *Example.* The following example illustrates the application of paragraph (a)(2)(iii) of this section:

Example. Corporation X owns 75 percent of a solvent corporation Y, and individual A owns the remaining 25 percent of Y. As part of a plan to make a QSub election for Y, X causes Y to redeem A's 25 percent interest on June 1 for cash and makes a QSub election for Y effective on June 3. The making of the QSub election is considered to be the adoption of a plan of liquidation immediately before the deemed liquidation. The deemed liquidation satisfies the requirements of section 332.

(v) *Stock ownership requirements of section 332.* The deemed exercise of an option under § 1.1504-4 and any instruments, obligations, or arrangements that are not considered stock under § 1.1361-2(b)(2) are disregarded in determining if the stock ownership requirements of section 332(b) are met with respect to the deemed liquidation provided in paragraph (a)(2)(i) of this section.

(3) *Treatment of banks*—(i) *In general.* If an S corporation is a bank, or if an S corporation makes a valid QSub election for a subsidiary that is a bank, any special rules applicable to banks under the Internal Revenue Code continue to apply separately to the bank parent or bank subsidiary as if the deemed liquidation of any QSub under paragraph (a)(2) of this section had not occurred (except as other published guidance may

apply section 265(b) and section 291(a)(3) and (e)(1)(B) not only to the bank parent or bank subsidiary but also to any QSub deemed to have liquidated under paragraph (a)(2) of this section). For any QSub that is a bank, however, all assets, liabilities, and items of income, deduction, and credit of the QSub, as determined in accordance with the special bank rules, are treated as assets, liabilities, and items of income, deduction, and credit of the S corporation. For purposes of this paragraph (a)(3)(i), the term *bank* has the same meaning as in section 581.

(ii) *Examples.* The following examples illustrate the application of this paragraph (a)(3):

Example 1. X, an S corporation, is a bank as defined in section 581. X owns 100 percent of Y and Z, corporations for which valid QSub elections are in effect. Y is a bank as defined in section 581, and Z is not a financial institution. Pursuant to paragraph (a)(3)(i) of this section, any special rules applicable to banks under the Internal Revenue Code continue to apply separately to X and Y and do not apply to Z. Thus, for example, section 265(b), which provides special rules for interest expense deductions of banks, applies separately to X and Y. That is, X and Y each must make a separate determination under section 265(b) of interest expense allocable to tax-exempt interest, and no deduction is allowed for that interest expense. Section 265(b) does not apply to Z except as published guidance may provide otherwise.

Example 2. X, an S corporation, is a bank holding company and thus is not a bank as defined in section 581. X owns 100 percent of Y, a corporation for which a valid QSub election is in effect. Y is a bank as defined in section 581. Pursuant to paragraph (a)(3)(i) of this section, any special rules applicable to banks under the Internal Revenue Code continue to apply to Y and do not apply to X. However, all of Y's assets, liabilities, and items of income, deduction, and credit, as determined in accordance with the special bank rules, are treated as those of X. Thus, for example, section 582(c), which provides special rules for sales and exchanges of debt by banks, applies only to sales and exchanges by Y. However, any gain or loss on such a transaction by Y that is considered ordinary income or ordinary loss pursuant to section 582(c) is treated as ordinary income or ordinary loss of X.

(iii) *Effective date.* This paragraph (a)(3) applies to taxable years beginning after December 31, 1996.

(4) *Treatment of stock of QSub.* Except for purposes of section 1361(b)(3)(B)(i) and § 1.1361-2(a)(1), the stock of a QSub shall be disregarded for all Federal tax purposes.

(5) *Transitional relief*—(i) *General rule.* If an S corporation and another corporation (the related corporation) are persons specified in section 267(b) prior to an acquisition by the S corporation of some or all of the stock of the related corporation followed by a QSub election for the related corporation, the step transaction doctrine will not apply to determine the tax consequences of the acquisition. This paragraph (a)(5) shall apply to QSub elections effective before January 1, 2001.

(ii) *Examples.* The following examples illustrate the application of this paragraph (a)(5):

Example 1. Individual A owns 100 percent of the stock of X, an S corporation. X owns 79 percent of the stock of Y, a solvent corporation, and A owns the remaining 21 percent. On May 4, 1998, A contributes its Y stock to X in exchange for X stock. X makes a QSub election with respect to Y effective immediately following the transfer. The liquidation described in paragraph (a)(2) of this section is respected as an independent step separate from the stock acquisition, and the tax consequences of the liquidation are determined under sections 332 and 337. The contribution by A of the Y stock qualifies under section 351, and no gain or loss is recognized by A, X, or Y.

Example 2. Individual A owns 100 percent of the stock of two solvent S corporations, X and Y. On May 4, 1998, A contributes the stock of Y to X. X makes a QSub election with respect to Y immediately following the transfer. The liquidation described in paragraph (a)(2) of this section is respected as an independent step separate from the stock acquisition, and the tax consequences of the liquidation are determined under sections 332 and 337. The contribution by A of the Y stock to X qualifies under section 351, and no gain or loss is recognized by A, X, or Y. Y is not treated as a C corporation for any period solely because of the transfer of its stock to X, an ineligible shareholder. Compare *Example 3* of § 1.1361-4(a)(2)(ii).

(b) *Timing of the liquidation*—(1) *In general.* Except as otherwise provided in paragraph (b)(3) or (4) of this section, the liquidation described in paragraph (a)(2) of this section occurs at the close of the day before the Qsub election is effective. Thus, for example, if a C corporation elects to be treated as an S corporation and makes a QSub election (effective the same date as the S election) with respect to a subsidiary, the liquidation occurs immediately before the S election becomes effective, while the S electing parent is still a C corporation.

(2) *Application to elections in tiered situations.* When QSub elections for a tiered group of

subsidiaries are effective on the same date, the S corporation may specify the order of the liquidations. If no order is specified, the liquidations that are deemed to occur as a result of the QSub elections will be treated as occurring first for the lowest tier entity and proceed successively upward until all of the liquidations under paragraph (a)(2) of this section have occurred. For example, S, an S corporation, owns 100 percent of C, the common parent of an affiliated group of corporations that includes X and Y. C owns all of the stock of X and X owns all of the stock of Y. S elects under § 1.1361-3 to treat C, X and Y as QSubs effective on the same date. If no order is specified for the elections, the following liquidations are deemed to occur as a result of the elections, with each successive liquidation occuring on the same day immediately after the preceding liquidation: Y is treated as liquidating into X, then X is treated as liquidating into C, and finally C is treated as liquidating into S.

(3) *Acquisitions*—(i) *In general.* If an S corporation does not own 100 percent of the stock of the subsidiary on the day before the QSub election is effective, the liquidation described in paragraph (a)(2) of this section occurs immediately after the time at which the S corporation first owns 100 percent of the stock.

(ii) *Special rules for acquired S corporations.* Except as provided in paragraph (b)(4) of this section, if a corporation (Y) for which an election under section 1362(a) was in effect is acquired, and a QSub election is made effective on the day Y is acquired, Y is deemed to liquidate into the S corporation at the beginning of the day the termination of its S election is effective. As a result, if corporation X acquires Y, an S corporation, and makes an S election for itself and a QSub election for Y effective on the day of acquisition, Y liquidates into X at the beginning of the day when X's S election is effective, and there is no period between the termination of Y's S election and the deemed liquidation of Y during which Y is a C corporation. Y's taxable year ends for all Federal income tax purposes at the close of the preceding day. Furthermore, if Y owns Z, a corporation for which a QSub election was in effect prior to the acquisition of Y by X, and X makes QSub elections for Y and Z, effective on the day of acquisition, the transfer of assets to Z and the deemed liquidation of Z are disregarded. See §§ 1.1361-4(a)(2) and 1.1361-5(b)(1)(i).

(4) *Coordination with section 338 election.* An S corporation that makes a qualified stock purchase of a target may make an election under section 338 with respect to the acquisition if it meets the requirements for the election, and may make a QSub election with respect to the target. If an S corporation makes an election under section 338 with respect to a subsidiary acquired in a qualified stock purchase, a QSub election made with respect to that subsidiary is not effective before the day after the acquisition date (within the meaning of section 338(h)(2)). If the QSub election is effective on the day after the acquisition date, the liquidation under paragraph (a)(2) of this section occurs immediately after the deemed asset purchase by the new target corporation under section 338. If an S corporation makes an election under section 338 (without a section 338(h)(10) election) with respect to a target, the target must file a final return as a C corporation reflecting the deemed sale. See § 1.338-10(a). If the target was an S corporation on the day before the acquisition date, the final return as a C corporation must reflect the activities of the target for the acquisition date, including the deemed sale. See § 1.338-10(a)(3).

(c) *Carryover of disallowed losses and deductions.* If an S corporation (S1) acquires the stock of another S corporation (S2), and S1 makes a QSub election with respect to S2 effective on the day of the acquisition, see § 1.1366-2(c)(1) for provisions relating to the carryover of losses and deductions with respect to a former shareholder of S2 that may be available to that shareholder as a shareholder of S1.

(d) *Examples.* The following examples illustrate the application of this section:

Example 1. X, an S corporation, owns 100 percent of the stock of Y, a C corporation. On June 2, 2002, X makes a valid QSub election for Y, effective June 2, 2002. Assume that, under general principles of tax law, including the step transaction doctrine, X's acquisition of the Y stock and the subsequent QSub election would not be treated as related. The liquidation described in paragraph (a)(2) of this section occurs at the close of the day on June 1, 2002, the day before the QSub election is effective, and the plan of liquidation is considered adopted on that date. Y's taxable year and separate existence for Federal tax purposes end at the close of June 1, 2002.

Example 2. X, a C corporation, owns 100 percent of the stock of Y, another C corporation. On December 31, 2002, X makes an election under section 1362 to be treated as an S corporation and a valid QSub election for Y, both effective January 1, 2003. Assume that, under general principles of tax law, including the step transaction doctrine, X's acquisition of the Y stock and the subsequent QSub election would not be treated as related. The liquidation described in paragraph (a)(2) of this section occurs at the close of December 31, 2002, the day before the QSub election is effective. The QSub election for Y is effective on the same day that X's S election is effective, and the deemed liquidation is treated as occurring before the S election is effective, when X is still a C corporation. Y's taxable year ends at the close of December 31, 2002. See § 1.381(b)-1.

Example 3. On June 1, 2002, X, an S corporation, acquires 100 percent of the stock of Y, an existing S corporation, for cash in a transaction meeting the requirements of a qualified stock purchase (QSP) under section 338. X immediately makes a QSub election for Y effective June 2, 2002, and also makes a joint election under section 338(h)(10) with the shareholder of Y. Under section 338(a) and § 1.338(h)(10)-1(d)(3), Y is treated as having sold all of its assets at the close of the acquisition date, June 1, 2002. Y is treated as a new corporation which purchased all of those assets as of the beginning of June 2, 2002, the day after the acquisition date. Section 338(a)(2). The QSub election is effective on June 2, 2002, and the liquidation under paragraph (a)(2) of this section occurs immediately after the deemed asset purchase by the new corporation.

Example 4. X, an S corporation, owns 100 percent of Y, a corporation for which a QSub election is in effect. On May 12, 2002, a date on which the QSub election is in effect, X issues Y a $10,000 note under state law that matures in ten years with a market rate of interest. Y is not treated as a separate corporation, and X's issuance of the note to Y on May 12, 2002, is disregarded for Federal tax purposes.

Example 5. X, an S corporation, owns 100 percent of the stock of Y, a C corporation. At a time when Y is indebted to X in an amount that exceeds the fair market value of Y's assets, X makes a QSub election effective on the date it is filed with respect to Y. The liquidation described in paragraph (a)(2) of this section does not qualify under sections 332 and 337 and, thus, Y recognizes gain or loss on the assets distributed, subject to the limitations of section 267.

[Reg. § 1.1361-4.]

☐ [T.D. 8869, 1-20-2000 (*corrected* 3-27-2000). Amended by T.D. 8940, 2-12-2001.]

[Reg. § 1.1361-5]

§ 1.1361-5. Termination of QSub election.— (a) *In general*—(1) *Effective date.* The termination of a QSub election is effective—

(i) On the effective date contained in the revocation statement if a QSub election is revoked under § 91.1361-3(b);

(ii) At the close of the last day of the parent's last taxable year as an S corporation if the parent's S election terminates under § 1.1362-2; or

(iii) At the close of the day on which an event (other than an event described in paragraph (a)(1)(ii) of this section) occurs that renders the subsidiary ineligible for QSub status under section 1361(b)(3)(B).

(2) *Information to be provided upon termination of QSub election by failure to qualify as a Qsub.* If a QSub election terminates because an event renders the subsidiary ineligible for QSub status, the S corporation must attach to its return for the taxable year in which the termination occurs a notification that a QSub election has terminated, the date of the termination, and the names, addresses, and employer identification numbers of both the parent corporation and the QSub.

(3) *QSub joins a consolidated group.* If a QSub election terminates because the S corporation becomes a member of a consolidated group (and no election under section 338(g) is made) the principles of § 1.1502-76(b)(1)(ii)(A)(2) (relating to a special rule for S corporations that join a consolidated group) apply to any QSub of the S corporation that also becomes a member of the consolidated group at the same time as the S corporation. See *Example 4* of paragraph (a)(4) of this section.

(4) *Examples.* The following examples illustrate the application of this paragraph (a):

Example 1. Termination because parent's S election terminates. X, an S corporation, owns 100 percent of Y. A QSub election is in effect with respect to Y for 2001. Effective on January 1, 2002, X revokes its S election. Because X is no longer an S corporation, Y no longer qualifies as a QSub at the close of December 31, 2001.

Example 2. Termination due to transfer of QSub stock. X, an S corporation, owns 100 percent of. Y. A QSub-election is in effect with respect to Y. On December 10, 2002, X sells one share of Y stock to A, an individual. Because X no longer owns 100 percent of the stock of Y, Y no longer qualifies as a QSub. Accordingly, the QSub election made with respect to Y terminates at the close of December 10, 2002.

Example 3. No termination on stock transfer between QSub and parent. X, an S corporation, owns 100 percent of the stock of Y, and Y owns 100 percent of the stock of Z. QSub elections are in effect with respect to both Y and Z. Y transfers all of its Z stock to X. Because X is treated as owning the stock of Z both before and after the transfer of stock solely for purposes of determining whether the requirements of section 1361(b)(3)(B)(i) and § 1.1361-2(a)(1) have been satisfied, the transfer of Z stock does not terminate Z's QSub election. Because the stock of Z is disregarded for all other Federal tax purposes, no gain is recognized under section 311.

Example 4. Termination due to acquisition of S parent by a consolidated group. X, an S corporation, owns 100 percent of Y, a corporation for which a QSub election is in effect. Z, the common parent of a consolidated group of corporations, acquires 80 percent of the stock of X on June 1, 2002. Z does not make an election under section 338(g) with respect to the purchase of X stock. X's S election terminates as of the close of the preceding day, May 31, 2002. Y's QSub election also terminates at the close of May 31, 2002. Under § 1.1502-76(b)(1)(ii)(A)(2) and paragraph (a)(3) of this section, X and Y become members of Z's consolidated group of corporations as of the beginning of the day June 1, 2002.

Example 5. Termination due to acquisition of QSub by a consolidated group. The facts are the same as in *Example 4*, except that Z acquires 80 percent of the stock of Y (instead of X) on June 1, 2002. In this case, Y's QSub election terminates as of the close of June 1, 2002, and, under § 1.1502-76(b)(1)(ii)(A)(1), Y becomes a member of the consolidated group at that time.

(b) *Effect of termination of QSub election*—(1) *Formation of new corporation*—(i) *In general.* If a QSub election terminates under paragraph (a) of this section, the former QSub is treated as a new corporation acquiring all of its assets (and assuming all of its liabilities) immediately before the termination from the S corporation parent in exchange for stock of the new corporation. The tax treatment of this transaction or of a larger transaction that includes this transaction will be determined under the Internal Revenue Code and general principles of tax law, including the step transaction doctrine. For purposes of determining the application of section 351 with respect to this transaction, instruments, obligations, or other arrangements that are not treated as stock of the QSub under § 1.1361-2(b) are disregarded in determining control for purposes of section 368(c) even if they are equity under general principles of tax law.

(ii) *Termination for tiered QSubs.* If QSub elections terminate for tiered QSubs on the same day, the formation of any higher tier subsidiary precedes the formation of its lower tier subsidiary. See *Example 6* in paragraph (b)(3) of this section.

(2) *Carryover of disallowed losses and deductions.* If a QSub terminates because the S corporation distributes the QSub stock to some or all of the S corporation's shareholders in a transaction to which section 368(a)(1)(D) applies by reason of section 355 (or so much of section 356 as relates to section 355), see § 1.1366-2(c)(2) for provisions relating to the carryover of disallowed losses and deductions that may be available.

(3) *Examples.* The following examples illustrate the application of this paragraph (b):

Example 1. X, an S corporation, owns 100 percent of the stock of Y, a corporation for which a QSub election is in effect. X sells 21 percent of the Y stock to Z, an unrelated corporation, for cash, thereby terminating the QSub election. Y is treated as a new corporation acquiring all of its assets (and assuming all of its liabilities) in exchange for Y stock immediately before the termination from the S corporation. The deemed exchange by X of assets for Y stock does not qualify under section 351 because X is not in control of Y within the meaning of section 368(c) immediately after the transfer as a result of the sale of stock to Z. Therefore, X must recognize gain, if any, on the assets transferred to Y in exchange for its stock. X's losses, if any, on the assets transferred are subject to the limitations of section 267.

Example 2. (i) X, an S corporation, owns 100 percent of the stock of Y, a corporation for which a QSub election is in effect. As part of a plan to sell a portion of Y, X causes Y to merge into T, a limited liability company wholly owned by X that is disregarded an as entity separate from its owner for Federal tax purposes. X then sells 21 percent of T to Z, an unrelated corporation, for cash. Following the sale, no entity classification election is made under § 301.7701-3(c) of this chapter to treat the limited liability company as an association for Federal tax purposes.

(ii) The merger of Y into T causes a termination of Y's QSub election. The new corporation (Newco) that is formed as a result of the termination is immediately merged into T, an entity that is disregarded for Federal tax purposes. Because, at the end of the series of transactions, the assets continue to be held by X for Federal tax purposes, under step transaction principles, the formation of Newco and the transfer of assets pursuant to the merger of Newco into T are disregarded. The sale of 21 percent of T is treated as a sale of a 21 percent undivided interest in each of T's assets. Immediately thereafter, X and Z are treated as contributing their respective interests in those assets to a partnership in exchange for ownership interests in the partnership.

(iii) Under section 1001, X recognizes gain or loss from the deemed sale of the 21 percent interest in each asset of the limited liability company to Z. Under section 721(a), no gain or loss is recognized by X and Z as a result of the deemed

Reg. § 1.1361-5(b)(1)

contribution of their respective interests in the assets to the partnership in exchange for ownership interests in the partnership.

Example 3. Assume the same facts as in *Example 1,* except that, instead of purchasing Y stock, Z contributes to Y an operating asset in exchange for 21 percent of the Y stock. Y is treated as a new corporation acquiring all of its assets (and assuming all of its liabilities) in exchange for Y stock immediately before the termination. Because X and Z are co-transferors that control the transferee immediately after the transfer, the transaction qualifies under section 351.

Example 4. X, an S corporation, owns 100 percent of the stock of Y, a corporation for which a QSub election is in effect. X distributes all of the Y stock pro rata to its shareholders, and the distribution terminates the QSub election. The transaction can qualify as a distribution to which sections 368(a)(1)(D) and 355 apply if the transaction otherwise satisfies the requirements of those sections.

Example 5. X, an S corporation, owns 100 percent of the stock of Y, a corporation for which a QSub election is in effect. X subsequently revokes the QSub election. Y is treated as a new corporation acquiring all of its assets (and assuming all of its liabilities) immediately before the revocation from its S corporation parent in a deemed exchange for Y stock. On a subsequent date, X sells 21 percent of the stock of Y to Z, an unrelated corporation, for cash. Assume that under general principles of tax law including the step transaction doctrine, the sale is not taken into account in determining whether X is in control of Y immediately after the deemed exchange of assets for stock. The deemed exchange by X of assets for Y stock and the deemed assumption by Y of its liabilities qualify under section 351 because, for purposes of that section, X is in control of Y within the meaning of section 368(c) immediately after the transfer.

Example 6. (i) X, an S corporation, owns 100 percent of the stock of Y, and X owns 100 percent of the stock of Z. Y and Z are corporations for which QSub elections are in effect. X subsequently revokes the QSub elections and the effective date specified on each revocation statement is June 26, 2002, a date that is less than 12 months after the date on which the revocation statements are filed.

(ii) Immediately before the QSub elections terminate, Y is treated as a new corporation acquiring all of its assets (and assuming all of its liabilities) directly from X in exchange for the stock of Y. Z is treated as a new corporation acquiring all of its assets (and assuming all of its liabilities) directly from Y in exchange for the stock of Z.

Example 7. (i) The facts are the same as in *Example 6,* except that, prior to June 26, 2002 (the effective date of the revocations), Y distributes the Z stock to X under state law.

(ii) Immediately before the QSub elections terminate, Y is treated as a new corporation acquiring all of its assets (and assuming all of its liabilities) directly from X in exchange for the stock of Y. Z is also treated as a new corporation acquiring all of its assets (and assuming all of its liabilities) directly from X in exchange for the stock of Z.

Example 8. Merger of parent into QSub. X, an S corporation, owns 100 percent of the stock of Y, a corporation for which a QSub election is in effect. X merges into Y under state law, causing the QSub election for Y to terminate, and Y survives the merger. The formation of the new corporation, Y, and the merger of X into Y can qualify as a reorganization described in section 368(a)(1)(F) if the transaction otherwise satisfies the requirements of that section.

Example 9. Transfer of 100 percent of QSub. X, an S corporation, owns 100 percent of the stock of Y, a corporation for which a QSub election is in effect. Z, an unrelated C corporation, acquires 100 percent of the stock of Y. The deemed formation of Y by X (as a consequence of the termination of Y's QSub election) is disregarded for Federal income tax purposes. The transaction is treated as a transfer of the assets of Y to Z, followed by Z's transfer of these assets to the capital of Y in exchange for Y stock. Furthermore, if Z is an S corporation and makes a QSub election for Y effective as of the acquisition, Z's transfer of the assets of Y in exchange for Y stock, followed by the immediate liquidation of Y as a consequence of the QSub election are disregarded for Federal income tax purposes.

(c) *Election after QSub termination*—(1) *In general.* Absent the Commissioner's consent, and except as provided in paragraph (c)(2) of this section, a corporation whose QSub election has terminated under paragraph (a) of this section (or a successor corporation as defined in paragraph (b) of this section) may not make an S election under section 1362 or have a QSub election under section 1361(b)(3)(B)(ii) made with respect to it for five taxable years (as described in section 1361(b)(3)(D)). The Commissioner may permit an S election by the corporation or a new QSub election with respect to the corporation before the five-year period expires. The corporation requesting consent to make the election has the burden of establishing that, under the relevant facts and circumstances, the Commissioner should consent to a new election.

(2) *Exception.* In the case of S and QSub elections effective after December 31, 1996, if a corporation's QSub election terminates, the corporation may, without requesting the Commissioner's consent, make an S election or have a QSub election made with respect to it before the expiration of the five-year period described in section 1361(b)(3)(D) and paragraph (c)(1) of this section, provided that—

(i) Immediately following the termination, the corporation (or its successor corporation) is otherwise eligible to make an S election or have a QSub election made for it; and

(ii) The relevant election is made effective immediately following the termination of the QSub election.

(3) *Examples.* The following examples illustrate the application of this paragraph (c):

Example 1. Termination upon distribution of QSub stock to shareholders of parent. X, an S corporation, owns Y, a QSub. X distributes all of its Y stock to X's shareholders. The distribution terminates the QSub election because Y no longer satisfies the requirements of a QSub. Assuming Y is otherwise eligible to be treated as an S corporation, Y's shareholders may elect to treat Y as an S corporation effective on the date of the stock distribution without requesting the Commissioner's consent.

Example 2. Sale of 100 percent of QSub stock. X, an S corporation, owns Y, a QSub. X sells 100 percent of the stock of Y to Z, an unrelated S corporation. Z may elect to treat Y as a QSub effective on the date of purchase without requesting the Commissioner's consent.

[Reg. § 1.1361-5.]

☐ [T.D. 8869, 1-20-2000.]

[Reg. § 1.1361-6]

§ 1.1361-6. **Effective date.**—Except as provided in §§ 1.1361-4(a)(3)(iii), 1.1361-4(a)(5)(i), and 1.1361-5(c)(2), the provisions of §§ 1.1361-2 through 1.1361-5 apply to taxable years beginning on or after January 20, 2000; however, taxpayers may elect to apply the regulations in whole, but not in part (aside from those sections with special dates of applicability), for taxable years beginning on or after January 1, 2000, provided all affected taxpayers apply the regulations in a consistent manner. To make this election, the corporation and all affected taxpayers must file a return or an amended return that is consistent with these rules for the taxable year for which the election is made. For purposes of this section, affected taxpayers means all taxpayers whose returns are affected by the election to apply the regulations. [Reg. § 1.1361-6.]

☐ [T.D. 8869, 1-20-2000.]

[Reg. § 18.0]

§ 18.0. **Effective date of temporary regulations under the Subchapter S Revision Act of 1982.**—The temporary regulations provided under §§ 18.1377-1, 18.1379-1, and 18.1379-2 are effective with respect to taxable years beginning after 1982, and the temporary regulations provided under § 18.1378-1 are effective with respect to elections made after October 19, 1982. [Temporary Reg. § 18.0.]

☐ [T.D. 7872, 1-21-83. *Amended by T.D.* 7976, 9-5-84 *and by T.D.* 8600, 7-20-95.]

[Reg. § 1.1362-0]

§ 1.1362-0. **Table of contents.**—This section lists the captions that appear in the regulations under section 1362.

§ 1.1362-1. Election to be an S corporation.

(a) In general.

(b) Years for which election is effective.

§ 1.1362-2. Termination of election.

(a) Termination by revocation.

(1) In general.

(2) When effective.

(i) In general.

(ii) Revocations specifying a prospective revocation date.

(3) Effect on taxable year of corporation.

(4) Rescission of a revocation.

(b) Termination by reason of corporation ceasing to be a small business corporation.

(1) In general.

(2) When effective.

(3) Effect on taxable year of corporation.

(c) Termination by reason of excess passive investment income.

(1) In general.

(2) When effective.

(3) Subchapter C earnings and profits.

(4) Gross receipts.

(i) In general.

(ii) Special rules for sales of capital assets, stock and securities.

(A) Sales of capital assets.

(B) Sales of stock or securities.

(*1*) In general.

Reg. § 1.1361-6

S Corporations and Their Shareholders

(2) Treatment of certain liquidations.
(3) Definition of stock or securities.
(4) General partner interests.
  (i) In general.
  (ii) Exception.
(iii) Other exclusions from gross receipts.
(5) Passive investment income.
  (i) In general.
  (ii) Definitions.
    (A) Royalties.
      (1) In general.
      (2) Royalties derived in the ordinary course of a trade or business.
      (3) Copyright, mineral, oil and gas, and active business computer software royalties.
    (B) Rents.
      (1) In general.
      (2) Rents derived in the active trade or business of renting property.
      (3) Produced film rents.
      (4) Income from leasing self-produced tangible property.
    (C) Dividends.
    (D) Interest.
      (1) In general.
      (2) Interest on obligations acquired in the ordinary course of a trade or business.
    (E) Annuities.
    (F) Gross receipts from the sale of stock or securities.
    (G) Identified income.
  (iii) Special rules.
    (A) Options or commodities dealers.
    (B) Treatment of certain lending, financing and other businesses.
      (1) In general.
      (2) Directly derived.
    (C) Payment to a patron of a cooperative.
(6) Examples.

§ 1.1362-3. Treatment of S termination year.
(a) In general.
(b) Allocations other than pro rata.
  (1) Elections under section 1362(e)(3).
  (2) Purchase of stock treated as an asset purchase.
  (3) 50 percent change in ownership during S termination year.
(c) Special rules.

(1) S corporation that is a partner in a partnership.
(2) Tax for the C short year.
(3) Each short year treated as taxable year.
(4) Year for carryover purposes.
(5) Due date for S short year return.
(6) Year in which income from S short year is includible.
(d) Examples.

§ 1.1362-4. Inadvertent terminations.
(a) In general.
(b) Inadvertent termination.
(c) Corporation's request for determination of an inadvertent termination.
(d) Adjustments.
(e) Corporation and shareholder consents.
(f) Status of corporation.

§ 1.1362-5. Election after termination.
(a) In general.
(b) Successor corporation.
(c) Automatic consent after certain terminations.

§ 1.1362-6. Elections and consents.
(a) Time and manner of making elections.
  (1) In general.
  (2) Election to be an S corporation.
    (i) Manner of making election.
    (ii) Time of making election.
      (A) In general.
      (B) Elections made during the first 2½ months treated as made for the following taxable year.
      (C) Definition of month and beginning of the taxable year.
    (iii) Examples.
  (3) Revocation of S election.
    (i) Manner of revoking election.
    (ii) Time of revoking election.
    (iii) Examples.
  (4) Rescission of a revocation.
    (i) Manner of rescinding a revocation.
    (ii) Time of rescinding a revocation.
  (5) Election not to apply pro rata allocation.
(b) Shareholders' consents.
  (1) Manner of consents in general.
  (2) Persons required to consent.
    (i) Community interest in stock.
    (ii) Minor.
    (iii) Estate.

Reg. § 1.1362-0

(iv) Trust.

(3) Special rules for consent of shareholder to election to be an S corporation.

(i) In general.

(ii) Examples.

(iii) Extension of time for filing consents to an election.

(A) In general.

(B) Required consents.

§ 1.1362-7. Effective date.

(a) In general.

(b) Special effective date for passive investment income provisions.

§ 1.1362-8. Dividends received from affiliated subsidiaries.

(a) In general.

(b) Determination of active or passive earnings and profits.

(1) In general.

(2) Lower tier subsidiaries.

(3) De minimis exception.

(4) Special rules for earnings and profits accumulated by a C corporation prior to 80 percent acquisition.

(5) Gross receipts safe harbor.

(c) Allocating distributions to active or passive earnings and profits.

(1) Distributions from current earnings and profits.

(2) Distributions from accumulated earnings and profits.

(3) Adjustments to active earnings and profits.

(4) Special rules for consolidated groups.

(d) Examples.

(e) Effective date.

[Reg. § 1.1362-0.]

☐ [T.D. 8449, 11-24-92. Amended by T.D. 8869, 1-20-2000]

[Reg. § 1.1362-1]

§ 1.1362-1. Election to be an S corporation.—(a) *In general.* Except as provided in § 1.1362-5, a small business corporation as defined in section 1361 may elect to be an S corporation under section 1362(a). An election may be made only with the consent of all of the shareholders of the corporation at the time of the election. See § 1.1362-6(a) for rules concerning the time and manner of making this election.

(b) *Years for which election is effective.* An election under section 1362(a) is effective for the entire taxable year of the corporation for which it is made and for all succeeding taxable years of the corporation, until the election is terminated. [Reg. § 1.1362-1.]

☐ [T.D. 8449, 11-24-92.]

[Reg. § 1.1362-2]

§ 1.1362-2. Termination of election.—(a) *Termination by revocation*—(1) *In general.* An election made under section 1362(a) is terminated if the corporation revokes the election for any taxable year of the corporation for which the election is effective, including the first taxable year. A revocation may be made only with the consent of shareholders who, at the time the revocation is made, hold more than one-half of the number of issued and outstanding shares of stock (including non-voting stock) of the corporation. See § 1.1362-6(a) for rules concerning the time and manner of revoking an election made under section 1362(a).

(2) *When effective*—(i) *In general.* Except as provided in paragraph (a)(2)(ii) of this section, a revocation made during the taxable year and before the 16th day of the third month of the taxable year is effective on the first day of the taxable year and a revocation made after the 15th day of the third month of the taxable year is effective for the following taxable year. If a corporation makes an election to be an S corporation that is to be effective beginning with the next taxable year and revokes its election on or before the first day of the next taxable year, the corporation is deemed to have revoked its election on the first day of the next taxable year.

(ii) *Revocations specifying a prospective revocation date.* If a corporation specifies a date for revocation and the date is expressed in terms of a stated day, month, and year that is on or after the date the revocation is filed, the revocation is effective on and after the date so specified.

(3) *Effect on taxable year of corporation.* In the case of a corporation that revokes its election to be an S corporation effective on the first day of the first taxable year for which its election is to be effective, any statement made with the election regarding a change in the corporation's taxable year has no effect.

(4) *Rescission of a revocation.* A corporation may rescind a revocation made under paragraph (a)(2) of this section at any time before the revocation becomes effective. A rescission may be made only with the consent of each person who consented to the revocation and by each person who became a shareholder of the corporation within the period beginning on the first day after the date the revocation was made and ending on

Reg. § 1.1362-1(a)

the date on which the rescission is made. See § 1.1362-6(a) for rules concerning the time and manner of rescinding a revocation.

(b) *Termination by reason of corporation ceasing to be a small business corporation*—(1) *In general.* If a corporation ceases to be a small business corporation, as defined in section 1361(b), at any time on or after the first day of the first taxable year for which its election under section 1362(a) is effective, the election terminates. In the event of a termination under this paragraph (b)(1), the corporation should attach to its return for the taxable year in which the termination occurs a notification that a termination has occurred and the date of the termination.

(2) *When effective.* If an election terminates because of a specific event that causes the corporation to fail to meet the definition of a small business corporation, the termination is effective as of the date on which the event occurs. If a corporation makes an election to be an S corporation that is effective beginning with the following taxable year and is not a small business corporation on the first day of that following taxable year, the election is treated as having terminated on that first day. If a corporation is a small business corporation on the first day of the taxable year for which its election is effective, its election does not terminate even if the corporation was not a small business corporation during all or part of the period beginning after the date the election was made and ending before the first day of the taxable year for which the election is effective.

(3) *Effect on taxable year of corporation.* In the case of a corporation that fails to meet the definition of a small business corporation on the first day of the first taxable year for which its election to be an S corporation is to be effective, any statement made with the election regarding a change in the corporation's taxable year has no effect.

(c) *Termination by reason of excess passive investment income*—(1) *In general.* A corporation's election under section 1362(a) terminates if the corporation has subchapter C earnings and profits at the close of each of three consecutive taxable years and, for each of those taxable years, has passive investment income in excess of 25 percent of gross receipts. See section 1375 for the tax imposed on excess passive investment income.

(2) *When effective.* A termination under this paragraph (c) is effective on the first day of the first taxable year beginning after the third consecutive year in which the S corporation had excess passive investment income.

(3) *Subchapter C earnings and profits.* For purposes of this paragraph (c), *subchapter C earnings and profits* of a corporation are the earnings and profits of any corporation, including the S corporation or an acquired or predecessor corporation, for any period with respect to which an election under section 1362(a) (or under section 1372 of prior law) was not in effect. The subchapter C earnings and profits of an S corporation are modified as required by section 1371(c).

(4) *Gross receipts*—(i) *In general.* For purposes of this paragraph (c), *gross receipts* generally means the total amount received or accrued under the method of accounting used by the corporation in computing its taxable income and is not reduced by returns and allowances, cost of goods sold, or deductions.

(ii) *Special rules for sales of capital assets, stock and securities*—(A) *Sales of capital assets.* For purposes of this paragraph (c), gross receipts from the sales or exchanges of capital assets (as defined in section 1221), other than stock and securities, are taken into account only to the extent of capital gain net income (as defined in section 1222).

(B) *Sales of stock or securities*—(*1*) *In general.* For purposes of this paragraph (c), gross receipts from the sales or exchanges of stock or securities are taken into account only to the extent of gains therefrom. In addition, for purposes of computing gross receipts from sales or exchanges of stock or securities, losses do not offset gains.

(*2*) *Treatment of certain liquidations.* Gross receipts from the sales or exchanges of stock or securities do not include amounts described in section 1362(d)(3)(D)(iv), relating to the treatment of certain liquidations. For purposes of section 1362(d)(3)(D)(iv), stock of the liquidating corporation owned by an S corporation shareholder is not treated as owned by the S corporation.

(*3*) *Definition of stock or securities.* For purposes of this paragraph (c), *stock or securities* includes shares or certificates of stock, stock rights or warrants, or an interest in any corporation (including any joint stock company, insurance company, association, or other organization classified as a corporation under section 7701); an interest as a limited partner in a partnership; certificates of interest or participation in any profit-sharing agreement, or in any oil, gas, or other mineral property, or lease; collateral trust certificates; voting trust certificates; bonds; debentures; certificates of indebtedness; notes; car trust certificates; bills of exchange; or obligations

Reg. § 1.1362-2(c)(4)

issued by or on behalf of a State, Territory, or political subdivision thereof.

(4) *General partner interests*—(*i*) *In general.* Except as provided in paragraph (c)(4)(ii)(B)(4)(*ii*) of this section, if an S corporation disposes of a general partner interest, the gain on the disposition is treated as gain from the sale of stock or securities to the extent of the amount the S corporation would have received as a distributive share of gain from the sale of stock or securities held by the partnership if all of the stock and securities held by the partnership had been sold by the partnership at fair market value at the time the S corporation disposes of the general partner interest. In applying this rule, the S corporation's distributive share of gain from the sale of stock or securities held by the partnership is not reduced to reflect any loss that would be recognized from the sale of stock or securities held by the partnership. In the case of tiered partnerships, the rules of this section apply by looking through each tier.

(*ii*) *Exception.* An S corporation that disposes of a general partner interest may treat the disposition, for purposes of this paragraph (c), in the same manner as the disposition of an interest as a limited partner.

(*iii*) *Other exclusions from gross receipts.* For purposes of this paragraph (c), gross receipts do not include—

(A) Amounts received in nontaxable sales or exchanges except to the extent that gain is recognized by the corporation on the sale or exchange; or

(B) Amounts received as a loan, as a repayment of a loan, as a contribution to capital, or on the issuance by the corporation of its own stock.

(5) *Passive investment income*—(i) *In general.* In general, *passive investment income* means gross receipts (as defined in paragraph (c)(4) of this section) derived from royalties, rents, dividends, interest, annuities, and gains from the sales or exchanges of stock or securities.

(ii) *Definitions.* For purposes of this paragraph (c)(5), the following definitions apply:

(A) *Royalties*—(*1*) *In general. Royalties* means all royalties, including mineral, oil, and gas royalties, and amounts received for the privilege of using patents, copyrights, secret processes and formulas, good will, trademarks, tradebrands, franchises, and other like property. The gross amount of royalties is not reduced by any part of the cost of the rights under which the royalties are received or by any amount allowable as a deduction in computing taxable income.

(*2*) *Royalties derived in the ordinary course of a trade or business. Royalties* does not include royalties derived in the ordinary course of a trade or business of franchising or licensing property. Royalties received by a corporation are derived in the ordinary course of a trade or business of franchising or licensing property only if, based on all the facts and circumstances, the corporation—

(*i*) Created the property; or

(*ii*) Performed significant services or incurred substantial costs with respect to the development or marketing of the property.

(*3*) *Copyright, mineral, oil and gas, and active business computer software royalties. Royalties* does not include copyright royalties, nor mineral, oil and gas royalties if the income from those royalties would not be treated as personal holding company income under sections 543(a)(3) and (a)(4) if the corporation were a C corporation; amounts received upon disposal of timber, coal, or domestic iron ore with respect to which the special rules of sections 631(b) and (c) apply; and active business computer software royalties as defined under section 543(d) (without regard to paragraph (d)(5) of section 543).

(B) *Rents*—(*1*) *In general. Rents* means amounts received for the use of, or right to use, property (whether real or personal) of the corporation.

(*2*) *Rents derived in the active trade or business of renting property. Rents* does not include rents derived in the active trade or business of renting property. Rents received by a corporation are derived in an active trade or business of renting property only if, based on all the facts and circumstances, the corporation provides significant services or incurs substantial costs in the rental business. Generally, significant services are not rendered and substantial costs are not incurred in connection with net leases. Whether significant services are performed or substantial costs are incurred in the rental business is determined based upon all the facts and circumstances including, but not limited to, the number of persons employed to provide the services and the types and amounts of costs and expenses incurred (other than depreciation).

(*3*) *Produced film rents. Rents* does not include produced film rents as defined under section 543(a)(5).

(*4*) *Income from leasing self-produced tangible property. Rents* does not include compensation, however designated, for the use of, or right to use, any real or tangible personal property developed, manufactured, or produced by the taxpayer, if during the taxable year the

Reg. § 1.1362-2(c)(5)

taxpayer is engaged in substantial development, manufacturing, or production of real or tangible personal property of the same type.

(C) *Dividends. Dividends* includes dividends as defined in section 316, amounts to be included in gross income under section 551 (relating to foreign personal holding company income taxed to U.S. shareholders), and consent dividends as provided in section 565. See paragraphs (c)(5)(iii)(B) and (C) of this section for special rules for the treatment of certain dividends and certain payments to a patron of a cooperative. See § 1.1362-8 for special rules regarding the treatment of dividends received by an S corporation from a C corporation in which the S corporation holds stock meeting the requirements of section 1504(a)(2).

(D) *Interest*—(*1*) *In general.* Interest means any amount received for the use of money (including tax-exempt interest and amounts treated as interest under section 483, 1272, 1274, or 7872). See paragraph (c)(5)(iii)(B) of this section for a special rule for the treatment of interest derived in certain businesses.

(*2*) *Interest on obligations acquired in the ordinary course of a trade or business.* Interest does not include interest on any obligation acquired from the sale of property described in section 1221(1) or the performance of services in the ordinary course of a trade or business of selling the property or performing the services.

(E) *Annuities. Annuities* means the entire amount received as an annuity under an annuity, endowment, or life insurance contract, if any part of the amount would be includible in gross income under section 72.

(F) *Gross receipts from the sale of stock or securities.* Gross receipts from the sales or exchanges of stock or securities, as described in paragraph (c)(4)(ii)(B) of this section, are passive investment income to the extent of gains therefrom. See paragraph (c)(5)(iii)(B) of this section for a special rule for the treatment of gains derived in certain businesses.

(G) *Identified income. Passive investment income* does not include income identified by the Commissioner by regulations, revenue ruling, or revenue procedure as income derived in the ordinary course of a trade or business for purposes of this section.

(iii) *Special rules.* For purposes of this paragraph (c)(5), the following special rules apply:

(A) *Options or commodities dealers.* In the case of an options dealer or commodities dealer, *passive investment income* does not include any gain or loss (in the normal course of the taxpayer's activity of dealing in or trading section 1256 contracts) from any section 1256 contract or property related to the contract. *Options dealer, commodities dealer,* and *section 1256 contract* have the same meaning as in section 1362(d)(3)(E)(ii).

(B) *Treatment of certain lending, financing and other businesses*—(*1*) *In general.* Passive investment income does not include gross receipts that are directly derived in the ordinary course of a trade or business of—

(*i*) Lending or financing;

(*ii*) Dealing in property;

(*iii*) Purchasing or discounting accounts receivable, notes, or installment obligations; or

(*iv*) Servicing mortgages.

(*2*) *Directly derived.* For purposes of this paragraph (c)(5)(iii)(B), gross receipts directly derived in the ordinary course of business includes gain (as well as interest income) with respect to loans originated in a lending business, or interest income (as well as gain) from debt obligations of a dealer in such obligations. However, interest earned from the investment of idle funds in short-term securities does not constitute gross receipts directly derived in the ordinary course of business. Similarly, a dealer's income or gain from an item of property is not directly derived in the ordinary course of its trade or business if the dealer held the property for investment at any time before the income or gain is recognized.

(C) *Payment to a patron of a cooperative.* Passive investment income does not include amounts included in the gross income of a patron of a cooperative (within the meaning of section 1381(a), without regard to paragraph (2)(A) or (C) of section 1381(a)) by reason of any payment or allocation to the patron based on patronage occurring in the case of a trade or business of the patron.

(6) *Examples.* The principles of paragraphs (c)(4) and (c)(5) of this section are illustrated by the following examples. Unless otherwise provided in an example, S is an S corporation with subchapter C earnings and profits, and S's gross receipts from operations are gross receipts not derived from royalties, rents, dividends, interest, annuities, or gains from the sales or exchanges of stock or securities. S is a calendar year taxpayer and its first taxable year as an S corporation is 1993.

Example 1. Sales of capital assets, stock and securities. (i) S uses an accrual method of accounting and sells:

Reg. § 1.1362-2(c)(6)

(1) a depreciable asset, held for more than 6 months, which is used in the corporation's business;

(2) a capital asset (other than stock or securities) for a gain;

(3) a capital asset (other than stock or securities) for a loss; and

(4) securities.

S receives payment for each asset partly in money and partly in the form of a note payable at a future time, and elects not to report the sales on the installment method.

(ii) The amount of money and the face amount (or issue price if different) of the note received for the business asset are considered gross receipts in the taxable year of sale and are not reduced by the adjusted basis of the property, costs of sale, or any other amount. With respect to the sales of the capital assets, gross receipts include the cash down payment and face amount (or issue price if different) of any notes, but only to the extent of S's capital gain net income. In the case of the sale of the securities, gross receipts include the cash down payment and face amount (or issue price if different) of the notes, but only to the extent of gain on the sale. In determining gross receipts from sales of securities, losses are not netted against gains.

Example 2. Long-term contract reported on percentage-of-completion method. S has a long-term contract as defined in § 1.451-3(b) with respect to which it reports income according to the percentage-of-completion method as described in § 1.451-3(c)(1). The portion of the gross contract price which corresponds to the percentage of the entire contract which has been completed during the taxable year is included in S's gross receipts for the year.

Example 3. Income reported on installment sale method. For its 1993 taxable year, S sells personal property on the installment plan and elects to report its taxable income from the sale of the property (other than property qualifying as a capital asset or stock or securities) on the installment method in accordance with section 453. The installment payment actually received in a given taxable year of S is included in gross receipts for the year.

Example 4. Partnership interests. In 1993, S and two of its shareholders contribute cash to form a general partnership, PRS. S receives a 50 percent interest in the capital and profits of PRS. S formed PRS to indirectly invest in marketable stocks and securities. The only assets of PRS are the stock and securities, and certain real and tangible personal property. In 1994, S needs cash in its business and sells its partnership interest at a gain rather than having PRS sell the marketable stock or securities that have appreciated. Under paragraph (c)(4)(ii)(B)(4) of this section, the gain on S's disposition of its interest in PRS is treated as gain from the sale or exchange of stock or securities to the extent of the amount the distributive share of gain S would have received from the sale of stock or securities held by PRS if PRS has sold all of its stock or securities at fair market value at the time S disposed of its interest in PRS.

Example 5. Royalties derived in ordinary course of trade or business. (i) In 1993, S has gross receipts of $75,000. Of this amount, $5,000 is from royalty payments with respect to Trademark A, $8,000 is from royalty payments with respect to Trademark B, and $62,000 is gross receipts from operations. S created Trademark A, but S did not create Trademark B or perform significant services or incur substantial costs with respect to the development or marketing of Trademark B.

(ii) Because S created Trademark A, the royalty payments with respect to Trademark A are derived in the ordinary course of S's business and are not included within the definition of *royalties* for purposes of determining S's passive investment income. However, the royalty payments with respect to Trademark B are included within the definition of *royalties* for purposes of determining S's passive investment income. See paragraph (c)(5)(ii)(A) of this section. S's passive investment income for the year is $8,000, and S's passive investment income percentage for the taxable year is 10.67% ($8,000/$75,000). This does not exceed 25 percent of S's gross receipts and consequently the three-year period described in section 1362(d)(3) does not begin to run.

Example 6. Dividends; gain on sale of stock derived in the ordinary course of trade or business. (i) In 1993, S receives dividends of $10,000 on stock of corporations P and O, recognizes a gain of $25,000 on sale of the P stock, and recognizes a loss of $12,000 on sale of the O stock. S held the P and O stock for investment, rather than for sale in the ordinary course of a trade or business. S has gross receipts from operations and from gain on the sale of stock in the ordinary course of its trade or business of $110,000.

(ii) S's gross receipts are calculated as follows:

Reg. § 1.1362-2(c)(6)

$110,000	Gross receipts from operations and from gain on the sale of stock in the ordinary course of a trade or business
10,000	Gross dividend receipts
25,000	Gain on sale of P stock (Loss on O stock not taken into account)
$145,000	Total gross receipts

(iii) S's passive investment income is determined as follows:

$10,000	Gross dividend receipts
25,000	Gain on sale of P stock (Loss on O stock not taken into account)
$35,000	Total passive investment income

(iv) S's passive investment income percentage for its first year as an S corporation is 24.1% ($35,000/$145,000). This does not exceed 25 percent of S's gross receipts and consequently the three-year period described in section 1362(d)(3) does not begin to run.

Example 7. Interest on accounts receivable; netting of gain on sale of real property investments. (i) In 1993, S receives $6,000 of interest on accounts receivable arising from S's sales of inventory property. S also receives dividends with respect to stock held for investment of $1,500. In addition, S sells two parcels of real property (Property J and Property K) that S had purchased and held for investment. S sells Property J, in which S has a basis of $5,000, for $10,000 (a gain of $5,000). S sells Property K, in which S has a basis of $12,000, for $9,000 (a loss of $3,000). S has gross receipts from operations of $90,000.

(ii) S's gross receipts are calculated as follows:

$90,000	Gross receipts from operations
6,000	Gross interest receipts
1,500	Gross dividend receipts
2,000	Net gain on sale of real property investments
$99,500	Total gross receipts

(iii) Under paragraph (c)(5)(ii)(D) of this section, S's gross interest receipts are not passive investment income. In addition, gain on the sale of real property ($2,000) is not passive investment income. S's passive investment income includes only the $1,500 of gross dividend receipts. Accordingly, S's passive investment income percentage for its first year as an S corporation is 1.51% ($1,500/$99,500). This does not exceed 25 percent of S's gross receipts and consequently the three-year period described in section 1362(d)(3) does not begin to run.

Example 8. Interest received in the ordinary course of a lending business. (i) In 1993, S has gross receipts of $100,000 from loans and investments made in the ordinary course of S's mortgage banking business. This includes, for example, mortgage servicing fees, interest earned on mortgages prior to sale of the mortgages, and gain on sale of mortgages. In addition, S receives, from the investment of idle funds in short-term securities, $15,000 of gross interest income and $5,000 of gain.

(ii) S's gross receipts are calculated as follows:

$100,000	Gross receipts from operations
15,000	Gross interest receipts
5,000	Gain on sale of securities
$120,000	Total gross receipts

(iii) S's passive investment income is determined as follows:

$15,000	Gross interest receipts
5,000	Gain on sale of securities
$20,000	Total passive investment income

(iv) S's passive investment income percentage for its first year as an S corporation is 16.67% ($20,000/$120,000). This does not exceed 25 percent of S's gross receipts and consequently the three-year period described in section 1362(d)(3) does not begin to run. [Reg. § 1.1362-2.]

☐ [*T.D.* 8449, 11-24-92. Amended by *T.D.* 8869, 1-20-2000]

Reg. § 1.1362-2(c)(6)

[Reg. § 1.1362-3]

§ 1.1362-3. Treatment of S termination year.—(a) *In general.* If an S election terminates under section 1362(d) on a date other than the first day of a taxable year of the corporation, the corporation's taxable year in which the termination occurs is an S termination year. The portion of the S termination year ending at the close of the day prior to the termination is treated as a short taxable year for which the corporation is an S corporation (the *S short year*). The portion of the S termination year beginning on the day the termination is effective is treated as a short taxable year for which the corporation is a C corporation (the *C short year*). Except as provided in paragraphs (b) and (c)(1) of this section, the corporation allocates income or loss for the entire year on a pro rata basis as described in section 1362(e)(2). To the extent that income or loss is not allocated on a pro rata basis under this section, items of income, gain, loss, deduction, and credit are assigned to each short taxable year on the basis of the corporation's normal method of accounting as determined under section 446. See, however, § 1.1502-76(b)(1)(ii)(A)(*2*) for special rules for an S election that terminates under section 1362(d) immediately before the S corporation becomes a member of a consolidated group (within the meaning of § 1.1502-1(h)).

(b) *Allocations other than pro rata*—(1) *Elections under section 1362(e)(3).* The pro rata allocation rules of section 1362(e)(2) do not apply if the corporation elects to allocate its S termination year income on the basis of its normal tax accounting method. This election may be made only with the consent of each person who is a shareholder in the corporation at any time during the S short year and of each person who is a shareholder in the corporation on the first day of the C short year. See § 1.1362-6(a) for rules concerning the time and manner of making this election.

(2) *Purchase of stock treated as an asset purchase.* The pro rata allocation rules of section 1362(e)(2) do not apply with respect to any item resulting from the application of section 338.

(3) *50 percent change in ownership during S termination year.* The pro rata allocation rules of section 1362(e)(2) do not apply if at any time during the S termination year, as a result of sales or exchanges of stock in the corporation during that year, there is a change in ownership of 50 percent or more of the issued and outstanding shares of stock of the corporation. If stock has already been sold or exchanged during the S termination year, subsequent sales or exchanges of that stock are not taken into account for purposes of this paragraph (b)(3).

(c) *Special rules*—(1) *S corporation that is a partner in a partnership.* For purposes of section 706(c) only, the termination of the election of an S corporation that is a partner in a partnership during any portion of the S short year under § 1.1362-2(a) or (b), is treated as a sale or exchange of the corporation's entire interest in the partnership on the last day of the S short year, if—

(i) The pro rata allocation rules do not apply to the corporation; and

(ii) Any taxable year of the partnership ends with or within the C short year.

(2) *Tax for the C short year.* The taxable income for the C short year is determined on an annualized basis as described in section 1362(e)(5).

(3) *Each short year treated as taxable year.* Except as otherwise provided in paragraph (c)(4) of this section, the S and C short years are treated as two separate years for purposes of all provisions of the Internal Revenue Code.

(4) *Year for carryover purposes.* The S and C short years are treated as one year for purposes of determining the number of taxable years to which any item may be carried back or forward by the corporation.

(5) *Due date for S short year return.* The date by which the return for the S short year must be filed is the same as the date by which the return for the C short year must be filed (including extensions).

(6) *Year in which income from S short year is includible.* A shareholder must include in taxable income the shareholder's pro rata share of the items described in section 1366(a) for the S short year for the taxable year with or within which the S termination year ends.

(d) *Examples.* The provisions of this section are illustrated by the following examples:

Example 1. S termination year not created. (i) On January 1, 1993, the first day of its taxable year, a subchapter C corporation had three eligible shareholders. During 1993, the corporation properly elected to be treated as an S corporation effective January 1, 1994, the first day of the succeeding taxable year. Subsequently, a transfer of some of the stock in the corporation was made to an ineligible shareholder. The ineligible shareholder still holds the stock on January 1, 1994.

(ii) The corporation fails to meet the definition of a small business corporation on January 1, 1994, and its election is treated as having terminated on that date. See § 1.1362-2(b)(2) for the termination rules. Because the corporation ceases to be a small business corporation on the first day of a taxable year, an S termination year is not

Reg. § 1.1362-3(a)

created. In addition, if the corporation in the future meets the definition of a small business corporation and desires to elect to be treated as an S corporation, the corporation is automatically granted consent to reelect before the expiration of the 5-year waiting period. See § 1.1362-5 for special rules concerning automatic consent to reelect.

Example 2. More than 50 percent change in ownership during S short year. A, an individual, owns all 100 outstanding shares of stock of S, a calendar year S corporation. On January 31, 1993, A sells 60 shares of S stock to B, an individual. On June 1, 1993, A sells 5 shares of S stock to PRS, a partnership. S ceases to be a small business corporation on June 1, 1993, and pursuant to section 1362(d)(2), its election terminates on that date. Because there was a more than 50 percent change in ownership of the issued and outstanding shares of S stock, S must assign the items of income, loss, deduction, or credit for the S termination year to the two short taxable years on the basis of S's normal method of accounting under the rules of paragraph (b)(3) of this section.

Example 3. More than 50 percent change in ownership during C short year. A, an individual, owns all 100 outstanding shares of stock of S, a calendar year S corporation. On June 1, 1993, A sells 5 shares of S stock to PRS, a partnership. S ceases to be a small business corporation on that date and pursuant to section 1362(d)(3), its election terminates on that date. On July 1, 1993, A sells 60 shares of S stock to B, an individual. Since there was a more than 50 percent change in ownership of the issued and outstanding shares of S stock during the S termination year, S must assign the items of income, loss, deduction, or credit for the S termination year to the two short taxable years on the basis of S's normal method of accounting under the rules of paragraph (b)(3) of this section.

Example 4. Stock acquired other than by sale or exchange. C and D are shareholders in S, a calendar year S corporation. Each owns 50 percent of the issued and outstanding shares of the corporation on December 31, 1993. On March 1, 1994, C makes a gift of his entire shareholder interest to T, a trust not permitted as a shareholder under section 1361(c)(2). S ceases to be a small business corporation on March 1, 1994, and pursuant to section 1362(d)(2), its S corporation election terminates effective on that date. As a result of the gift, T owns 50 percent of S's issued and outstanding stock. However, because T acquired the stock by gift from C rather than by sale or exchange, there has not been a more than 50 percent change in ownership by sale or exchange of S that would cause the rules of paragraph (b)(3) of this section to apply. [Reg. § 1.1362-3.]

☐ [T.D. 8449, 11-24-92. Amended by T.D. 8842, 11-9-99.]

[Reg. § 1.1362-4]

§ 1.1362-4. Inadvertent terminations.—(a) *In general.* A corporation is treated as continuing to be an S corporation during the period specified by the Commissioner if—

(1) The corporation made a valid election under section 1362(a) and the election terminated;

(2) The Commissioner determines that the termination was inadvertent;

(3) Steps were taken by the corporation to return to small business corporation status within a reasonable period after discovery of the terminating event; and

(4) The corporation and shareholders agree to adjustments that the Commissioner may require for the period.

(b) *Inadvertent termination.* For purposes of paragraph (a) of this section, the determination of whether a termination was inadvertent is made by the Commissioner. The corporation has the burden of establishing that under the relevant facts and circumstances the Commissioner should determine that the termination was inadvertent. The fact that the terminating event was not reasonably within the control of the corporation and was not part of a plan to terminate the election, or the fact that the event took place without the knowledge of the corporation, notwithstanding its due diligence to safeguard itself against such an event, tends to establish that the termination was inadvertent.

(c) *Corporation's request for determination of an inadvertent termination.* A corporation that believes its election was terminated inadvertently may request a determination of inadvertent termination from the Commissioner. The request is made in the form of a ruling request and should set forth all relevant facts pertaining to the event including, but not limited to, the facts described in paragraph (b) of this section, the date of the corporation's election under section 1362(a), a detailed explanation of the event causing termination, when and how the event was discovered, and the steps taken to return the corporation to small business corporation status.

(d) *Adjustments.* The Commissioner may require any adjustments that are appropriate. In general, the adjustments required should be consistent with the treatment of the corporation as an S corporation during the period specified by the Commissioner. In the case of a transfer of stock to an ineligible shareholder that causes an inadvertent termination under section 1362(f), the Commissioner may require the ineligible shareholder to be treated as a shareholder of an S corporation during the period the ineligible shareholder actually held stock in the corporation. Moreover, the Commissioner may require protective adjustments that prevent any loss of revenue due to a transfer of stock to an ineligible shareholder (*e.g.*, a transfer to a nonresident alien).

(e) *Corporation and shareholder consents.* The corporation and all persons who were shareholders of the corporation at any time during the period specified by the Commissioner must consent to any adjustments that the Commissioner may require. Each consent should be in the form of a statement agreeing to make the adjustments. The statement must be signed by the shareholder (in the case of shareholder consent) or a person authorized to sign the return required by section 6037 (in the case of corporate consent). See § 1.1362-6(b)(2) for persons required to sign consents. A shareholder's consent statement should include the name, address, and taxpayer identification numbers of the corporation and shareholder, the number of shares of stock owned by the shareholder, and the dates on which the shareholder owned any stock. The corporate consent statement should include the name, address, and taxpayer identification numbers of the corporation and each shareholder.

(f) *Status of corporation.* The status of the corporation after the terminating event and before the determination of inadvertence is determined by the Commissioner. Inadvertent termination relief may be granted retroactive for all years for which the terminating event was effective, in which case the corporation is treated as if its election had not terminated. Alternatively, relief may be granted only for the period in which the corporation again became eligible for subchapter S treatment, in which case the corporation is treated as a C corporation during the period for which the corporation was not eligible to be an S corporation. [Reg. § 1.1362-4.]

☐ [*T.D.* 8449, 11-24-92.]

[Reg. § 1.1362-5]

§ 1.1362-5. Election after termination.—(a) *In general.* Absent the Commissioner's consent, an S corporation whose election has terminated (or a successor corporation) may not make a new election under section 1362(a) for five taxable years as described in section 1362(g). However, the Commissioner may permit the corporation to make a new election before the 5-year period expires. The corporation has the burden of establishing that under the relevant facts and circumstances, the Commissioner should consent to a new election. The fact that more than 50 percent of the stock in the corporation is owned by persons who did not own any stock in the corporation on the date of the termination tends to establish that consent should be granted. In the absence of this fact, consent ordinarily is denied unless the corporation shows that the event causing termination was not reasonably within the control of the corporation or shareholders having a substantial interest in the corporation and was not part of a plan on the part of the corporation or of such shareholders to terminate the election.

(b) *Successor corporation.* A corporation is a *successor corporation* to a corporation whose election under section 1362 has been terminated if—

(1) 50 percent or more of the stock of the corporation (the new corporation) is owned, directly or indirectly, by the same persons who, on the date of the termination, owned 50 percent or more of the stock of the corporation whose election terminated (the old corporation); and

(2) Either the new corporation acquires a substantial portion of the assets of the old corporation, or a substantial portion of the assets of the new corporation were assets of the old corporation.

(c) *Automatic consent after certain terminations.* A corporation may, without requesting the Commissioner's consent, make a new election under section 1362(a) before the 5-year period described in section 1362(g) expires if the termination occurred because the corporation—

(1) Revoked its election effective on the first day of the first taxable year for which its election was to be effective (see § 1.1362-2(a)(2)); or

(2) Failed to meet the definition of a small business corporation on the first day of the first taxable year for which its election was to be effective (see § 1.1362-2(b)(2)). [Reg. § 1.1362-5.]

☐ [*T.D.* 8449, 11-24-92.]

[Reg. § 1.1362-6]

§ 1.1362-6. Elections and consents.—(a) *Time and manner of making elections*—(1) *In general.* An election statement made under this section must identify the election being made, set forth the name, address, and taxpayer identification number of the corporation, and be signed by a person authorized to sign the return required to be filed under section 6037.

(2) *Election to be an S corporation*—(i) *Manner of making election.* A small business corporation makes an election under section 1362(a) to be an S corporation by filing a completed Form 2553. The election form must be filed with the service center designated in the instructions applicable to Form 2553. The election is not valid unless all

Reg. § 1.1362-5(a)

shareholders of the corporation at the time of the election consent to the election in the manner provided in paragraph (b) of this section. However, once a valid election is made, new shareholders need not consent to that election.

(ii) *Time of making election*—(A) *In general.* The election described in paragraph (a)(2)(i) of this section may be made by a small business corporation at any time during the taxable year that immediately precedes the taxable year for which the election is to be effective, or during the taxable year for which the election is to be effective provided that the election is made before the 16th day of the third month of the year. If a corporation makes an election for a taxable year, and the election meets all the requirements of this section but is made during the period beginning after the 15th day of the third month of the taxable year, the election is treated as being made for the following taxable year provided that the corporation meets all the requirements of section 1361(b) at the time the election is made. For taxable years of 2½ months or less, an election made before the 16th day of the third month after the first day of the taxable year is treated as made during that year.

(B) *Elections made during the first 2½ months treated as made for the following taxable year.* A timely election made by a small business corporation during the taxable year for which it is intended to be effective is nonetheless treated as made for the following taxable year if—

(*1*) The corporation is not a small business corporation during the entire portion of the taxable year which occurs before the date the election is made; or

(*2*) Any person who held stock in the corporation at any time during the portion of the taxable year which occurs before the time the election is made, and who does not hold stock at the time the election is made, does not consent to the election.

(C) *Definition of month and beginning of the taxable year. Month* means a period commencing on the same numerical day of any calendar month as the day of the calendar month on which the taxable year began and ending with the close of the day preceding the numerically corresponding day of the succeeding calendar month or, if there is no corresponding day, with the close of the last day of the succeeding calendar month. In addition, the taxable year of a new corporation begins on the date that the corporation has shareholders, acquires assets, or begins doing business, whichever is the first to occur. The existence of incorporators does not necessarily begin the taxable year of a new corporation.

(iii) *Examples.* The provisions of this section are illustrated by the following examples:

Example 1. Effective election; no prior taxable year. A calendar year small business corporation begins its first taxable year on January 7, 1993. To be an S corporation beginning with its first taxable year, the corporation must make the election set forth in this section during the period that begins January 7, 1993, and ends before March 22, 1993. Because the corporation had no taxable year immediately preceding the taxable year for which the election is to be effective, an election made earlier than January 7, 1993, will not be valid.

Example 2. Effective election; taxable year less than 2½ months. A calendar year small business corporation begins its first taxable year on November 8, 1993. To be an S corporation beginning with its first taxable year, the corporation must make the election set forth in this section during the period that begins November 8, 1993, and ends before January 23, 1994.

Example 3. Election effective for the following taxable year; ineligible shareholder. On January 1, 1993, two individuals and a partnership own all of the stock of a calendar year subchapter C corporation. On January 31, 1993, the partnership dissolved and distributed its shares in the corporation to its five partners, all individuals. On February 28, 1993, the seven shareholders of the corporation consented to the corporation's election of subchapter S status. The corporation files a properly completed Form 2553 on March 2, 1993. The corporation is not eligible to be a subchapter S corporation for the 1993 taxable year because during the period of the taxable year prior to the election it had an ineligible shareholder. However, under paragraph (a)(2)(ii)(B) of this section, the election is treated as made for the corporation's 1994 taxable year.

(3) *Revocation of S election*—(i) *Manner of revoking election.* To revoke an election, the corporation files a statement that the corporation revokes the election made under section 1362(a). The statement must be filed with the service center where the election was properly filed. The revocation statement must include the number of shares of stock (including non-voting stock) issued and outstanding at the time the revocation is made. A revocation may be made only with the consent of shareholders who, at the time the revocation is made, hold more than one-half of the number of issued and outstanding shares of stock (including non-voting stock) of the corporation. Each shareholder who consents to the revocation must consent in the manner required under paragraph (b) of this section. In addition, each consent

Reg. § 1.1362-6(a)(3)

should indicate the number of issued and outstanding shares of stock (including non-voting stock) held by each shareholder at the time of the revocation.

(ii) *Time of revoking election.* For rules concerning when a revocation is effective, see § 1.1362-2(a)(2).

(iii) *Examples.* The principles of this paragraph (a)(3) are illustrated by the following examples:

Example 1. *Revocation; consent of shareholders owning more than one-half of issued and outstanding shares.* A calendar year S corporation has issued and outstanding 40,000 shares of class A voting common stock and 20,000 shares of class B non-voting common stock. The corporation wishes to revoke its election of subchapter S status. Shareholders owning 11,000 shares of class A stock sign revocation consents. Shareholders owning 20,000 shares of class B stock sign revocation consents. The corporation has obtained the required shareholder consent to revoke its subchapter S election because shareholders owning more than one-half of the total number of issued and outstanding shares of stock of the corporation consented to the revocation.

Example 2. *Effective prospective revocation.* In June 1993, a calendar year S corporation determines that it will revoke its subchapter S election effective August 1, 1993. To do so it must file its revocation statement with consents attached on or before August 1, 1993, and the statement must indicate that the revocation is intended to be effective August 1, 1993.

(4) *Rescission of a revocation*—(i) *Manner of rescinding a revocation.* To rescind a revocation, the corporation files a statement that the corporation rescinds the revocation made under section 1362(d)(1). The statement must be filed with the service center where the revocation was properly filed. A rescission may be made only with the consent (in the manner required under paragraph (b)(1) of this section) of each person who consented to the revocation and of each person who became a shareholder of the corporation within the period beginning on the first day after the date the revocation was made and ending on the date on which the rescission is made.

(ii) *Time of rescinding a revocation.* If the rescission statement is filed before the revocation becomes effective and is filed with proper service center, the rescission is effective on the date it is so filed.

(5) *Election not to apply pro rata allocation.* To elect not to apply the pro rata allocation rules to an S termination year, a corporation files a statement that it elects under section 1362(e)(3) not to apply the rules provided in section 1362(e)(2). In addition to meeting the requirements of paragraph (a)(1) of this section, the statement must set forth the cause of the termination and the date thereof. The statement must be filed with the corporation's return for the C short year. This election may be made only with the consent of all persons who are shareholders of the corporation at any time during the S short year and all persons who are shareholders of the corporation on the first day of the C short year (in the manner required under paragraph (b)(1) of this section).

(b) *Shareholders' consents*—(1) *Manner of consents in general.* A shareholder's consent required under paragraph (a) of this section must be in the form of a written statement that sets forth the name, address, and taxpayer identification number of the shareholder, the number of shares of stock owned by the shareholder, the date (or dates) on which the stock was acquired, the date on which the shareholder's taxable year ends, the name of the S corporation, the corporation's taxpayer identification number, and the election to which the shareholder consents. The statement must be signed by the shareholder under penalties of perjury. Except as provided in paragraph (b)(3)(iii) of this section, the election of the corporation is not valid if any required consent is not filed in accordance with the rules contained in this paragraph (b). The consent statement should be attached to the corporation's election statement.

(2) *Persons required to consent.* The following rules apply in determining persons required to consent:

(i) *Community interest in stock.* When stock of the corporation is owned by husband and wife as community property (or the income from the stock is community property), or is owned by tenants in common, joint tenants, or tenants by the entirety, each person having a community interest in the stock or income therefrom and each tenant in common, joint tenant and tenant by the entirety must consent to the election.

(ii) *Minor.* The consent of a minor must be made by the minor or by the legal representative of the minor (or by a natural or an adoptive parent of the minor if no legal representative has been appointed).

(iii) *Estate.* The consent of an estate must be made by an executor or administrator thereof, or by any other fiduciary appointed by testamentary instrument or appointed by the court having jurisdiction over the administration of the estate.

(iv) *Trust.* In the case of a trust described in section 1361(c)(2)(A) (including a trust treated

Reg. § 1.1362-6(a)(4)

under section 1361(d)(1)(A) as a trust described in section 1361(c)(2)(A)(i)), only the person treated as the shareholder for purposes of section 1361(b)(1) must consent to the election. When stock of the corporation is held by a trust, both husband and wife must consent to any election if the husband and wife have a community interest in the trust property. See paragraph (b)(2)(i) of this section for rules concerning community interests in S corporation stock.

(3) *Special rules for consent of shareholder to election to be an S corporation*—(i) *In general.* The consent of a shareholder to an election by a small business corporation under section 1362(a) may be made on Form 2553 or on a separate statement in the manner described in paragraph (b)(1) of this section. In addition, the separate statement must set forth the name, address, and taxpayer identification number of the corporation. A shareholder's consent is binding and may not be withdrawn after a valid election is made by the corporation. Each person who is a shareholder (including any person who is treated as a shareholder under section 1361(c)(2)(B)) at the time the election is made) must consent to the election. If the election is made before the 16th day of the third month of the taxable year and is intended to be effective for that year, each person who was a shareholder (including any person who was treated as a shareholder under section 1361(c)(2)(B)) at any time during the portion of that year which occurs before the time the election is made, and who is not a shareholder at the time the election is made, must also consent to the election. If the election is to be effective for the following taxable year, no consent need be filed by any shareholder who is not a shareholder on the date of the election. Any person who is considered to be a shareholder under applicable state law solely by virtue of his or her status as an incorporator is not treated as a shareholder for purposes of this paragraph (b)(3)(i).

(ii) *Examples.* The principles of this section are illustrated by the following examples:

Example 1. Effective election; shareholder consents. On January 1, 1993, the first day of its taxable year, a subchapter C corporation had 15 shareholders. On January 30, 1993, two of the C corporation's shareholders, *A* and *B,* both individuals, sold their shares in the corporation to *P, Q,* and *R,* all individuals. On March 1, 1993, the corporation filed its election to be an S corporation for the 1993 taxable year. The election will be effective (assuming the other requirements of section 1361(b) are met) provided that all of the shareholders as of March 1, 1993, as well as former shareholders *A* and *B,* consent to the election.

Example 2. Consent of new shareholder unnecessary. On January 1, 1993, three individuals own all of the stock of a calendar year subchapter C corporation. On April 15, 1993, the corporation, in accordance with paragraph (a)(2) of this section, files a properly completed Form 2553. The corporation anticipates that the election will be effective beginning January 1, 1994, the first day of the succeeding taxable year. On October 1, 1993, the three shareholders collectively sell 75% of their shares in the corporation to another individual. On January 1, 1994, the corporation's shareholders are the three original individuals and the new shareholder. Because the election was valid and binding when made, it is not necessary for the new shareholder to consent to the election. The corporation's subchapter S election is effective on January 1, 1994 (assuming the other requirements of section 1361(b) are met).

(iii) *Extension of time for filing consents to an election*—(A) *In general.* An election that is timely filed for any taxable year and that would be valid except for the failure of any shareholder to file a timely consent is not invalid if consents are filed as required under paragraph (b)(3)(iii)(B) of this section and it is shown to the satisfaction of the district director or director of the service center with which the corporation files its income tax return that—

(*1*) There was reasonable cause for the failure to file the consent;

(*2*) The request for the extension of time to file a consent is made within a reasonable time under the circumstances; and

(*3*) The interests of the Government will not be jeopardized by treating the election as valid.

(B) *Required consents.* Consents must be filed within the extended period of time as may be granted by the Internal Revenue Service, by all persons who—

(*1*) Were shareholders of the corporation at any time during the period beginning as of the date of the invalid election and ending on the date on which an extension of time is granted in accordance with this paragraph (b)(3)(iii); and

(*2*) Have not previously consented to the election. [Reg. § 1.1362-6.]

☐ [*T.D.* 8449, 11-24-92]

[Reg. § 1.1362-7]

§ **1.1362-7. Effective date.**—(a) *In general.* The provisions of §§ 1.1362-1 through 1.1362-6 apply to taxable years of corporations beginning after December 31, 1992. For taxable years to which these regulations do not apply, corporations and shareholders subject to the provisions of section 1362 must take reasonable return positions taking into consideration the statute; its legislative history; the provisions of §§ 18.1362-1 through 18.1362-5 (see 26 CFR part 18 as contained in the CFR edition revised as of April 1, 1992). In addition, following these regulations is a reasonable return position. See Notice 92-56, 1992-49 I.R.B. (see § 601.601(d)(2)(ii)(b) of this chapter), for additional guidance regarding reasonable return positions for years to which §§ 1.1362-1 through 1.1362-6 do not apply.

(b) *Special effective date for passive investment income provisions.* For taxable years of an S corporation and all affected shareholders that are not closed, the S corporation and all affected shareholders may elect to apply the provisions of § 1.1362-2(c)(5). To make the election, the corporation and all affected shareholders must file a return or an amended return that is consistent with these rules for the taxable year for which the election is made and each subsequent taxable year. For purposes of this section, *affected shareholders* means all shareholders who received distributive shares of S corporation items in the taxable year for which the election is made and all shareholders of the S corporation for all subsequent taxable years. However, the Commissioner may, in appropriate circumstances, permit taxpayers to make this election even if all affected shareholders cannot file consistent returns. [Reg. § 1.1362-7.]

☐ [T.D. 8449, 11-24-92.]

[Reg. § 1.1362-8]

§ 1.1362-8. **Dividends received from affiliated subsidiaries.**—(a) *In general.* For purposes of section 1362(d)(3), if an S corporation holds stock in a C corporation meeting the requirements of section 1504(a)(2), the term *passive investment income* does not include dividends from the C corporation to the extent those dividends are attributable to the earnings and profits of the C corporation derived from the active conduct of a trade or business (active earnings and profits). For purposes of applying section 1362(d)(3), earnings and profits of a C corporation are active earnings and profits to the extent that the earnings and profits are derived from activities that would not produce passive investment income (as defined in section 1362(d)(3)) if the C corporation were an S corporation.

(b) *Determination of active or passive earnings and profits*—(1) *In general.* An S corporation may use any reasonable method to determine the amount of dividends that are not treated as passive investment income under section 1362(d)(3)(E). Paragraph (b)(5) of this section describes a method of determining the amount of dividends that are not treated as passive investment income under section 1362(d)(3)(E) that is deemed to be reasonable under all circumstances.

(2) *Lower tier subsidiaries.* If a C corporation subsidiary (upper tier corporation) holds stock in another C corporation (lower tier subsidiary) meeting the requirements of section 1504(a)(2), the upper tier corporation's gross receipts attributable to a dividend from the lower tier subsidiary are considered to be derived from the active conduct of a trade or business to the extent the lower tier subsidiary's earnings and profits are attributable to the active conduct of a trade or business by the subsidiary under paragraph (b)(1), (3), (4), or (5) of this section. For purposes of this section, distributions by the lower tier subsidiary will be considered attributable to active earnings and profits according to the rule in paragraph (c) of this section. This paragraph (b)(2) does not apply to any member of a consolidated group (as defined in § 1.1502-1(h)).

(3) *De minimis exception.* If less than 10 percent of a C corporation's earnings and profits for a taxable year are derived from activities that would produce passive investment income if the C corporation were an S corporation, all earnings and profits produced by the corporation during that taxable year are considered active earnings and profits.

(4) *Special rules for earnings and profits accumulated by a C corporation prior to 80 percent acquisition.* A C corporation may treat all earnings and profits accumulated by the corporation in all taxable years ending before the S corporation held stock meeting the requirements of section 1504(a)(2) as active earnings and profits in the same proportion as the C corporation's active earnings and profits for the three taxable years ending prior to the time when the S corporation acquired 80 percent of the C corporation bears to the C corporation's total earnings and profits for those three taxable years.

(5) *Gross receipts safe harbor.* A corporation may treat its earnings and profits for a year as active earnings and profits in the same proportion as the corporation's gross receipts (as defined in § 1.1362-2(c)(4)) derived from activities that would not produce passive investment income (if the C corporation were an S corporation), including those that do not produce passive investment income under paragraphs (b)(2) through (b)(4) of this section, bear to the corporation's total gross receipts for the year in which the earnings and profits are produced.

(c) *Allocating distributions to active or passive earnings and profits*—(1) *Distributions from cur-*

rent earnings and profits. Dividends distributed by a C corporation from current earnings and profits are attributable to active earnings and profits in the same proportion as current active earnings and profits bear to total current earnings and profits of the C corporation.

(2) *Distributions from accumulated earnings and profits.* Dividends distributed by a C corporation out of accumulated earnings and profits for a taxable year are attributable to active earnings and profits in the same proportion as accumulated active earnings and profits for that taxable year bear to total accumulated earnings and profits for that taxable year immediately prior to the distribution.

(3) *Adjustments to active earnings and profits.* For purposes of applying paragraph (c)(1) or (2) of this section to a distribution, the active earnings and profits of a corporation shall be reduced by the amount of any prior distribution properly treated as attributable to active earnings and profits from the same taxable year.

(4) *Special rules for consolidated groups.* For purposes of applying section 1362(d)(3) and this section to dividends received by an S corporation from the common parent of a consolidated group (as defined in § 1.1502-1(h)), the following rules apply—

(i) The current earnings and profits, accumulated earnings and profits, and active earnings and profits of the common parent shall be determined under the principles of § 1.1502-33 (relating to earnings and profits of any member of a consolidated group owning stock of another member); and

(ii) The gross receipts of the common parent shall be the sum of the gross receipts of each member of the consolidated group (including the common parent), adjusted to eliminate gross receipts from intercompany transactions (as defined in § 1.1502-13(b)(1)(i)).

(d) *Examples.* The following examples illustrate the principles of this section:

Example 1. (i) X, an S corporation, owns 85 percent of the one class of stock of Y. On December 31, 2002, Y declares a dividend of $100 ($85 to X), which is equal to Y's current earnings and profits. In 2002, Y has total gross receipts of $1,000, $200 of which would be passive investment income if Y were an S corporation.

(ii) One-fifth ($200/$1,000) of Y's gross receipts for 2002 is attributable to activities that would produce passive investment income. Accordingly, one-fifth of the $100 of earnings and profits is passive, and $17 (1/5 of $85) of the dividend from Y to X is passive investment income.

Example 2. (i) The facts are the same as in Example 1, except that Y owns 90 percent of the stock of Z. Y and Z do not join in the filing of a consolidated return. In 2002, Z has gross receipts of $15,000, $12,000 of which are derived from activities that would produce passive investment income. On December 31, 2002, Z declares a dividend of $1,000 ($900 to Y) from current earnings and profits.

(ii) Four-fifths ($12,000/$15,000) of the dividend from Z to Y are attributable to passive earnings and profits. Accordingly, $720 (4/5 of $900) of the dividend from Z to Y is considered gross receipts from an activity that would produce passive investment income. The $900 dividend to Y gives Y a total of $1,900 ($1,000 + $900) in gross receipts, $920 ($200 + $720) of which is attributable to passive investment income-producing activities. Under these facts, $41 ($920/$1,900 of $85) of Y's distribution to X is passive investment income to X.

(e) *Effective date.* This section applies to dividends received in taxable years beginning on or after January 20, 2000; however, taxpayers may elect to apply the regulations in whole, but not in part, for taxable years beginning on or after January 1, 2000, provided all affected taxpayers apply the regulations in a consistent manner. To make this election, the corporation and all affected taxpayers must file a return or an amended return that is consistent with these rules for the taxable year for which the election is made. For purposes of this section, affected taxpayers means all taxpayers whose returns are affected by the election to apply the regulations. [Reg. § 1.1362-8.]

☐ [T.D. 8869, 1-20-2000 (corrected 3-27-2000).]

[Reg. § 1.1363-1]

§ 1.1363-1. Effect of election on corporation.—(a) *Exemption of corporation from income tax*—(1) *In general.* Except as provided in this paragraph (a), a small business corporation that makes a valid election under section 1362(a) is exempt from the taxes imposed by chapter 1 of the Internal Revenue Code with respect to taxable years of the corporation for which the election is in effect.

(2) *Corporate level taxes.* An S corporation is not exempt from the tax imposed by section 1374 (relating to the tax imposed on certain built-in gains), or section 1375 (relating to the tax on excess passive investment income). See also section 1363(d) (relating to the recapture of LIFO

benefits) for the rules regarding the payment by an S corporation of LIFO recapture amounts.

(b) *Computation of corporate taxable income.* The taxable income of an S corporation is computed as described in section 1363(b).

(c) *Elections of the S corporation*—(1) *In general.* Any elections (other than those described in paragraph (c)(2) of this section) affecting the computation of items derived from an S corporation are made by the corporation. For example, elections of methods of accounting, of computing depreciation, of treating soil and water conservation expenditures, and the option to deduct as expenses intangible drilling and development costs, are made by the corporation and not by the shareholders separately. All corporate elections are applicable to all shareholders.

(2) *Exceptions.* (i) Each shareholder's pro rata share of expenses described in section 617 paid or accrued by the S corporation is treated according to the shareholder's method of treating those expenses, notwithstanding the treatment of the expenses by the corporation.

(ii) Each shareholder may elect to amortize that shareholder's pro rata share of any qualified expenditure described in section 59(e) paid or accrued by the S corporation.

(iii) Each shareholder's pro rata share of taxes described in section 901 paid or accrued by the S corporation to foreign countries or possessions of the United States (according to its method of treating those taxes) is treated according to the shareholder's method of treating those taxes, and each shareholder may elect to use the total amount either as a credit against tax or as a deduction from income.

(d) *Effective date.* This section applies to taxable years of corporations beginning after December 31, 1992. For taxable years to which this section does not apply, corporations and shareholders subject to the provisions of section 1363 must take reasonable return positions taking into consideration the statute, its legislative history and these regulations. See Notice 92-56, 1992-49 I.R.B. (see § 601.601(d)(2)(ii)(b) of this chapter), for additional guidance regarding reasonable return positions for taxable years to which this section does not apply. [Reg. § 1.1363-1.]

☐ [T.D. 8449, 11-24-92.]

[Reg. § 1.1363-2]

§ 1.1363-2. Recapture of LIFO benefits.—(a) *In general.* A C corporation must include the LIFO recapture amount (as defined in section 1363(d)(3)) in its gross income—

(1) In its last taxable year as a C corporation if the corporation inventoried assets under the LIFO method for its last taxable year before its S corporation election becomes effective; or

(2) In the year of transfer by the C corporation to an S corporation of the LIFO inventory assets if paragraph (a)(1) of this section does not apply and the C corporation—

(i) Inventoried assets under the LIFO method during the taxable year of the transfer of those LIFO inventory assets; and

(ii) Transferred the LIFO inventory assets to the S corporation in a nonrecognition transaction (within the meaning of section 7701(a)(45)) in which the transferred assets constitute transferred basis property (within the meaning of section 7701(a)(43)).

(b) *Payment of tax.* Any increase in tax caused by including the LIFO recapture amount in the gross income of the C corporation is payable in four equal installments. The C corporation must pay the first installment of this payment by the due date of its return, determined without regard to extensions, for the last taxable year it operated as a C corporation if paragraph (a)(1) of this section applies, or for the taxable year of the transfer if paragraph (a)(2) of this section applies. The three succeeding installments must be paid—

(1) For a transaction described in paragraph (a)(1) of this section, by the corporation (that made the election under section 1362(a) to be an S corporation) on or before the due date for the corporation's returns (determined without regard to extensions) for the succeeding three taxable years; and

(2) For a transaction described in paragraph (a)(2) of this section, by the transferee S corporation on or before the due date for the transferee corporation's returns (determined without regard to extensions) for the succeeding three taxable years.

(c) *Basis adjustments.* Appropriate adjustments to the basis of inventory are to be made to reflect any amount included in income under this section.

(d) *Effective dates.* (1) The provisions of paragraph (a)(1) of this section apply to S elections made after December 17, 1987. For an exception, see section 10227(b)(2) of the Revenue Act of 1987.

(2) The provisions of paragraph (a)(2) of this section apply to transfers made after August 18, 1993. [Reg. § 1.1363-2.]

☐ [T.D. 8567, 10-6-94.]

Reg. § 1.1363-2(a)(1)

S Corporations and Their Shareholders

See p. 20,601 for regulations not amended to reflect law changes

[Reg. § 1.1366-0]

§ 1.1366-0. Table of contents.—The following table of contents is provided to facilitate the use of §§ 1.1366-1 through 1.1366-5:

§ 1.1366-1. Shareholder's share of items of an S corporation.

(a) Determination of shareholder's tax liability.

(1) In general.

(2) Separately stated items of income, loss, deduction, or credit.

(3) Nonseparately computed income or loss.

(4) Separate activities requirement.

(5) Aggregation of deductions or exclusions for purposes of limitations.

(b) Character of items constituting pro rata share.

(1) In general.

(2) Exception for contribution of noncapital gain property.

(3) Exception for contribution of capital loss property.

(c) Gross income of a shareholder.

(1) In general.

(2) Gross income for substantial omission of items.

(d) Shareholders holding stock subject to community property laws.

(e) Net operating loss deduction of shareholder of S corporation.

(f) Cross-reference.

§ 1.1366-2. Limitations on deduction of passthrough items of an S corporation to its shareholders.

(a) In general.

(1) Limitation on losses and deductions.

(2) Carryover of disallowance.

(3) Basis limitation amount.

(i) Stock portion.

(ii) Indebtedness portion.

(4) Limitation on losses and deductions allocated to each item.

(5) Nontransferability of losses and deductions.

(6) Basis of stock acquired by gift.

(b) Special rules for carryover of disallowed losses and deductions to post-termination transition period described in section 1377(b).

(1) In general.

(2) Limitation on losses and deductions.

(3) Limitation on losses and deductions allocated to each item.

(4) Adjustment to the basis of stock.

(c) Carryover of disallowed losses and deductions in the case of liquidations, reorganizations, and divisions.

(1) Liquidations and reorganizations.

(2) Corporate separations to which section 368(a)(1)(D) applies.

§ 1.1366-3. Treatment of family groups.

(a) In general.

(b) Examples.

§ 1.1366-4. Special rules limiting the passthrough of certain items of an S corporation to its shareholders.

(a) Passthrough inapplicable to section 34 credit.

(b) Reduction in passthrough for tax imposed on built-in gains.

(c) Reduction in passthrough for tax imposed on excess net passive income.

§ 1.1366-5. Effective date.

[Reg. § 1.1366-0.]

☐ [T.D. 8852, 12-21-99.]

[Reg. § 1.1366-1]

§ 1.1366-1. Shareholder's share of items of an S corporation.—(a) *Determination of shareholder's tax liability*—(1) *In general.* An S corporation must report, and a shareholder is required to take into account in the shareholder's return, the shareholder's pro rata share, whether or not distributed, of the S corporation's items of income, loss, deduction, or credit described in paragraphs (a)(2), (3), and (4) of this section. A shareholder's pro rata share is determined in accordance with the provisions of section 1377(a) and the regulations thereunder. The shareholder takes these items into account in determining the shareholder's taxable income and tax liability for the shareholder's taxable year with or within which the taxable year of the corporation ends. If the shareholder dies (or if the shareholder is an estate or trust and the estate or trust terminates) before the end of the taxable year of the corporation, the shareholder's pro rata share of these items is taken into account on the shareholder's final return. For the limitation on allowance of a shareholder's pro rata share of S corporation losses or deductions, see section 1366(d) and § 1.1366-2.

(2) *Separately stated items of income, loss, deduction, or credit.* Each shareholder must take into account separately the shareholder's pro rata share of any item of income (including tax-exempt income), loss, deduction, or credit of the S corporation that if separately taken into account by any shareholder could affect the shareholder's tax lia-

Reg. § 1.1366-1(a)(2)

bility for that taxable year differently than if the shareholder did not take the item into account separately. The separately stated items of the S corporation include, but are not limited to, the following items—

(i) The corporation's combined net amount of gains and losses from sales or exchanges of capital assets grouped by applicable holding periods, by applicable rate of tax under section 1(h), and by any other classification that may be relevant in determining the shareholder's tax liability;

(ii) The corporation's combined net amount of gains and losses from sales or exchanges of property described in section 1231 (relating to property used in the trade or business and involuntary conversions), grouped by applicable holding periods, by applicable rate of tax under section 1(h), and by any other classification that may be relevant in determining the shareholder's tax liability;

(iii) Charitable contributions, grouped by the percentage limitations of section 170(b), paid by the corporation within the taxable year of the corporation;

(iv) The taxes described in section 901 that have been paid (or accrued) by the corporation to foreign countries or to possessions of the United States;

(v) Each of the corporation's separate items involved in the determination of credits against tax allowable under part IV of subchapter A (section 21 and following) of the Internal Revenue Code, except for any credit allowed under section 34 (relating to certain uses of gasoline and special fuels);

(vi) Each of the corporation's separate items of gains and losses from wagering transactions (section 165(d)); soil and water conservation expenditures (section 175); deduction under an election to expense certain depreciable business expenses (section 179); medical, dental, etc., expenses (section 213); the additional itemized deductions for individuals provided in part VII of subchapter B (section 212 and following) of the Internal Revenue Code; and any other itemized deductions for which the limitations on itemized deductions under sections 67 or 68 applies;

(vii) Any of the corporation's items of portfolio income or loss, and expenses related thereto, as defined in the regulations under section 469;

(viii) The corporation's tax-exempt income. For purposes of subchapter S, tax-exempt income is income that is permanently excludible from gross income in all circumstances in which the applicable provision of the Internal Revenue Code applies. For example, income that is excludible from gross income under section 101 (certain death benefits) or section 103 (interest on state and local bonds) is tax-exempt income, while income that is excludible from gross income under section 108 (income from discharge of indebtedness) or section 109 (improvements by lessee on lessor's property) is not tax-exempt income;

(ix) The corporation's adjustments described in sections 56 and 58, and items of tax preference described in section 57; and

(x) Any item identified in guidance (including forms and instructions) issued by the Commissioner as an item required to be separately stated under this paragraph (a)(2).

(3) *Nonseparately computed income or loss.* Each shareholder must take into account separately the shareholder's pro rata share of the nonseparately computed income or loss of the S corporation. For this purpose, nonseparately computed income or loss means the corporation's gross income less the deductions allowed to the corporation under chapter 1 of the Internal Revenue Code, determined by excluding any item requiring separate computation under paragraph (a)(2) of this section.

(4) *Separate activities requirement.* An S corporation must report, and each shareholder must take into account in the shareholder's return, the shareholder's pro rata share of an S corporation's items of income, loss, deduction, or credit described in paragraphs (a)(2) and (3) of this section for each of the corporation's activities as defined in section 469 and the regulations thereunder.

(5) *Aggregation of deductions or exclusions for purposes of limitations*—(i) *In general.* A shareholder aggregates the shareholder's separate deductions or exclusions with the shareholder's pro rata share of the S corporation's separately stated deductions or exclusions in determining the amount of any deduction or exclusion allowable to the shareholder under subtitle A of the Internal Revenue Code as to which a limitation is imposed.

(ii) *Example.* The provisions of paragraph (a)(5)(i) of this section are illustrated by the following example:

Example. In 1999, Corporation M, a calendar year S corporation, purchases and places in service section 179 property costing $10,000. Corporation M elects to expense the entire cost of the property. Shareholder A owns 50 percent of the stock of Corporation M. Shareholder A's pro rata share of this item after Corporation M applies the section 179(b) limitations is $5,000. Because the aggregate amount of Shareholder A's pro rata share and separately acquired section 179 expense may not exceed $19,000 (the aggregate maximum

Reg. § 1.1366-1(a)(3)

cost that may be taken into account under section 179(a) for the applicable taxable year), Shareholder A may elect to expense up to $14,000 of separately acquired section 179 property that is purchased and placed in service in 1999, subject to the limitations of section 179(b).

(b) *Character of items constituting pro rata share*—(1) *In general.* Except as provided in paragraph (b)(2) or (3) of this section, the character of any item of income, loss, deduction, or credit described in section 1366(a)(1)(A) or (B) and paragraph (a) of this section is determined for the S corporation and retains that character in the hands of the shareholder. For example, if an S corporation has capital gain on the sale or exchange of a capital asset, a shareholder's pro rata share of that gain will also be characterized as a capital gain regardless of whether the shareholder is otherwise a dealer in that type of property. Similarly, if an S corporation engages in an activity that is not for profit (as defined in section 183), a shareholder's pro rata share of the S corporation's deductions will be characterized as not for profit. Also, if an S corporation makes a charitable contribution to an organization qualifying under section 170(b)(1)(A), a shareholder's pro rata share of the S corporation's charitable contribution will be characterized as made to an organization qualifying under section 170 (b)(1)(A).

(2) *Exception for contribution of noncapital gain property.* If an S corporation is formed or availed of by any shareholder or group of shareholders for a principal purpose of selling or exchanging contributed property that in the hands of the shareholder or shareholders would not have produced capital gain if sold or exchanged by the shareholder or shareholders, then the gain on the sale or exchange of the property recognized by the corporation is not treated as a capital gain.

(3) *Exception for contribution of capital loss property.* If an S corporation is formed or availed of by any shareholder or group of shareholders for a principal purpose of selling or exchanging contributed property that in the hands of the shareholder or shareholders would have produced capital loss if sold or exchanged by the shareholder or shareholders, then the loss on the sale or exchange of the property recognized by the corporation is treated as a capital loss to the extent that, immediately before the contribution, the adjusted basis of the property in the hands of the shareholder or shareholders exceeded the fair market value of the property.

(c) *Gross income of a shareholder*—(1) *In general.* Where it is necessary to determine the amount or character of the gross income of a shareholder, the shareholder's gross income includes the shareholder's pro rata share of the gross income of the S corporation. The shareholder's pro rata share of the gross income of the S corporation is the amount of gross income of the corporation used in deriving the shareholder's pro rata share of S corporation taxable income or loss (including items described in section 1366(a)(1)(A) or (B) and paragraph (a) of this section). For example, a shareholder is required to include the shareholder's pro rata share of S corporation gross income in computing the shareholder's gross income for the purposes of determining the necessity of filing a return (section 6012(a)) and the shareholder's gross income derived from farming (sections 175 and 6654(i)).

(2) *Gross income for substantial omission of items*—(i) *In general.* For purposes of determining the applicability of the 6-year period of limitation on assessment and collection provided in section 6501(e) (relating to omission of more than 25 percent of gross income), a shareholder's gross income includes the shareholder's pro rata share of S corporation gross income (as described in section 6501(e)(1)(A)(i)). In this respect, the amount of S corporation gross income used in deriving the shareholder's pro rata share of any item of S corporation income, loss, deduction, or credit (as included or disclosed in the shareholder's return) is considered as an amount of gross income stated in the shareholder's return for purposes of section 6501(e).

(ii) *Example.* The following example illustrates the provisions of paragraph (c)(2)(i) of this section:

Example. Shareholder A, an individual, owns 25 percent of the stock of Corporation N, an S corporation that has $10,000 gross income and $2,000 taxable income. A reports only $300 as A's pro rata share of N's taxable income. A should have reported $500 as A's pro rata share of taxable income, derived from A's pro rata share, $2,500, of N's gross income. Because A's return included only $300 without a disclosure meeting the requirements of section 6501(e)(1)(A)(ii) describing the difference of $200, A is regarded as having reported on the return only $1,500 ($300/$500 of $2,500) as gross income from N.

(d) *Shareholders holding stock subject to community property laws.* If a shareholder holds S corporation stock that is community property, then the shareholder's pro rata share of any item or items listed in paragraphs (a)(2), (3), and (4) of this section with respect to that stock is reported by the husband and wife in accordance with community property rules.

(e) *Net operating loss deduction of shareholder of S corporation.* For purposes of determining a

Reg. § 1.1366-1(e)

net operating loss deduction under section 172, a shareholder of an S corporation must take into account the shareholder's pro rata share of items of income, loss, deduction, or credit of the corporation. See section 1366(b) and paragraph (b) of this section for rules on determining the character of the items. In determining under section 172(d)(4) the nonbusiness deductions allowable to a shareholder of an S corporation (arising from both corporation sources and any other sources), the shareholder separately takes into account the shareholder's pro rata share of the deductions of the corporation that are not attributable to a trade or business and combines this amount with the shareholder's nonbusiness deductions from any other sources. The shareholder also separately takes into account the shareholder's pro rata share of the gross income of the corporation not derived from a trade or business and combines this amount with the shareholder's nonbusiness income from all other sources. See section 172 and the regulations thereunder.

(f) *Cross-reference.* For rules relating to the consistent tax treatment of subchapter S items, see section 6037(c). [Reg. § 1.1366-1.]

☐ [*T.D.* 8852, 12-21-99.]

[Reg. § 1.1366-2]

§ 1.1366-2. Limitations on deduction of pass-through items of an S corporation to its shareholders.—(a) *In general*—(1) *Limitation on losses and deductions.* The aggregate amount of losses and deductions taken into account by a shareholder under § 1.1366-1(a)(2), (3), and (4) for any taxable year of an S corporation cannot exceed the sum of—

(i) The adjusted basis of the shareholder's stock in the corporation (as determined under paragraph (a)(3)(i) of this section); and

(ii) The adjusted basis of any indebtedness of the corporation to the shareholder (as determined under paragraph (a)(3)(ii) of this section).

(2) *Carryover of disallowance.* A shareholder's aggregate amount of losses and deductions for a taxable year in excess of the sum of the adjusted basis of the shareholder's stock in an S corporation and of any indebtedness of the S corporation to the shareholder is not allowed for the taxable year. However, any disallowed loss or deduction retains its character and is treated as incurred by the corporation in the corporation's first succeeding taxable year, and subsequent taxable years, with respect to the shareholder. For rules on determining the adjusted bases of stock of an S corporation and indebtedness of the corporation to the shareholder, see paragraphs (a)(3)(i) and (ii) of this section.

(3) *Basis limitation amount*—(i) *Stock portion.* A shareholder generally determines the adjusted basis of stock for purposes of paragraphs (a)(1)(i) and (2) of this section (limiting losses and deductions) by taking into account only increases in basis under section 1367(a)(1) for the taxable year and decreases in basis under section 1367(a)(2)(A), (D) and (E) (relating to distributions, noncapital, nondeductible expenses, and certain oil and gas depletion deductions) for the taxable year. In so determining this loss limitation amount, the shareholder disregards decreases in basis under section 1367(a)(2)(B) and (C) (for losses and deductions, including losses and deductions previously disallowed) for the taxable year., However, if the shareholder has in effect for the taxable year an election under § 1.1367-1(g) to decrease basis by items of loss and deduction prior to decreasing basis by noncapital, nondeductible expenses and certain oil and gas depletion deductions, the shareholder also disregards decreases in basis under section 1367(a)(2)(D) and (E). This basis limitation amount for stock is determined at the time prescribed under § 1.1367-1(d)(1) for adjustments to the basis of stock.

(ii) *Indebtedness portion.* A shareholder determines the shareholder's adjusted basis in indebtedness of the corporation for purposes of paragraphs (a)(1)(ii) and (2) of this section (limiting losses and deductions) without regard to any adjustment under section 1367(b)(2)(A) for the taxable year. This basis limitation amount for indebtedness is determined at the time prescribed under § 1.1367-2(d)(1) for adjustments to the basis of indebtedness.

(4) *Limitation on losses and deductions allocated to each item.* If a shareholder's pro rata share of the aggregate amount of losses and deductions specified in § 1.1366-1(a)(2), (3), and (4) exceeds the sum of the adjusted basis of the shareholder's stock in the corporation (determined in accordance with paragraph (a)(3)(i) of this section) and the adjusted basis of any indebtedness of the corporation to the shareholder (determined in accordance with paragraph (a)(3)(ii) of this section), then the limitation on losses and deductions under section 1366(d)(1) must be allocated among the shareholder's pro rata share of each loss or deduction. The amount of the limitation allocated to any loss or deduction is an amount that bears the same ratio to the amount of the limitation as the loss or deduction bears to the total of the losses and deductions. For this purpose, the total of losses and deductions for the taxable year is the sum of the shareholder's pro rata share of losses and deductions for the taxable year, and the losses and deductions disallowed and carried forward from prior years pursuant to section 1366(d)(2).

(5) *Nontransferability of losses and deductions.* Any loss or deduction disallowed under paragraph (a)(1) of this section is personal to the shareholder and cannot in any manner be transferred to another person. If a shareholder transfers some but not all of the shareholder's stock in the corporation, the amount of any disallowed loss or deduction under this section is not reduced and the transferee does not acquire any portion of the disallowed loss or deduction. If a shareholder transfers all of the shareholder's stock in the corporation, any disallowed loss or deduction is permanently disallowed.

(6) *Basis of stock acquired by gift.* For purposes of section 1366(d)(1)(A) and paragraphs (a)(1)(i) and (2) of this section, the basis of stock in a corporation acquired by gift is the basis of the stock that is used for purposes of determining loss under section 1015(a).

(b) *Special rules for carryover of disallowed losses and deductions to post-termination transition period described in section 1377(b)*—(1) *In general.* If, for the last taxable year of a corporation for which it was an S corporation, a loss or deduction was disallowed to a shareholder by reason of the limitation in paragraph (a) of this section, the loss or deduction is treated under section 1366(d)(3) as incurred by that shareholder on the last day of any post-termination transition period (within the meaning of section 1377(b)).

(2) *Limitation on losses and deductions.* The aggregate amount of losses and deductions taken into account by a shareholder under paragraph (b)(1) of this section cannot exceed the adjusted basis of the shareholder's stock in the corporation determined at the close of the last day of the post-termination transition period. For this purpose, the adjusted basis of a shareholder's stock in the corporation is determined at the close of the last day of the post-termination transition period without regard to any reduction required under paragraph (b)(4) of this section. If a shareholder disposes of a share of stock prior to the close of the last day of the post-termination transition period, the adjusted basis of that share is its basis as of the close of the day of disposition. Any losses and deductions in excess of a shareholder's adjusted stock basis are permanently disallowed. For purposes of section 1366(d)(3)(B) and this paragraph (b)(2), the basis of stock in a corporation acquired by gift is the basis of the stock that is used for purposes of determining loss under section 1015(a).

(3) *Limitation on losses and deductions allocated to each item.* If the aggregate amount of losses and deductions treated as incurred by the shareholder under paragraph (b)(1) of this section exceeds the adjusted basis of the shareholder's stock determined under paragraph (b)(2) of this section, the limitation on losses and deductions under section 1366(d)(3)(B) must be allocated among each loss or deduction. The amount of the limitation allocated to each loss or deduction is an amount that bears the same ratio to the amount of the limitation as the amount of each loss or deduction bears to the total of all the losses and deductions.

(4) *Adjustment to the basis of stock.* The shareholder's basis in the stock of the corporation is reduced by the amount allowed as a deduction by reason of this paragraph (b). For rules regarding adjustments to the basis of a shareholder's stock in an S corporation, see § 1.1367-1.

(c) *Carryover of disallowed losses and deductions in the case of liquidations, reorganizations, and divisions*—(1) *Liquidations and reorganizations.* If a corporation acquires the assets of an S corporation in a transaction to which section 381(a) applies, any loss or deduction disallowed under paragraph (a) of this section with respect to a shareholder of the distributor or transferor S corporation is available to that shareholder as a shareholder of the acquiring corporation. Thus, where the acquiring corporation is an S corporation, a loss or deduction of a shareholder of the distributor or transferor S corporation disallowed prior to or during the taxable year of the transaction is treated as incurred by the acquiring S corporation with respect to that shareholder if the shareholder is a shareholder of the acquiring S corporation after the transaction. Where the acquiring corporation is a C corporation, a post-termination transition period arises the day after the last day that an S corporation was in existence and the rules provided in paragraph (b) of this section apply with respect to any shareholder of the acquired S corporation that is also a shareholder of the acquiring C corporation after the transaction. See the special rules under section 1377 for the availability of the post-termination transition period if the acquiring corporation is a C corporation.

(2) *Corporate separations to which section 368(a)(1)(D) applies.* If an S corporation transfers a portion of its assets constituting an active trade or business to another corporation in a transaction to which section 368(a)(1)(D) applies, and immediately thereafter the stock and securities of the controlled corporation are distributed in a distribution or exchange to which section 355 (or so much of section 356 as relates to section 355) applies, any loss or deduction disallowed under paragraph (a) of this section with respect to a shareholder of the distributing S corporation im-

Reg. § 1.1366-2(c)(2)

mediately before the transaction is allocated between the distributing corporation and the controlled corporation with respect to the shareholder. Such allocation shall be made according to any reasonable method, including a method based on the relative fair market value of the shareholder's stock in the distributing and controlled corporations immediately after the distribution, a method based on the relative adjusted basis of the assets in the distributing and controlled corporations immediately after the distribution, or, in the case of losses and deductions clearly attributable to either the distributing or controlled corporation, any method that allocates such losses and deductions accordingly. [Reg. § 1.1366-2.]

☐ [T.D. 8247, 4-4-89. Amended by T.D. 8852, 12-21-99.]

[Reg. § 1.1366-3]

§ 1.1366-3. Treatment of family groups.—(a) *In general.* Under section 1366(e), if an individual, who is a member of the family of one or more shareholders of an S corporation, renders services for, or furnishes capital to, the corporation without receiving reasonable compensation, the Commissioner shall prescribe adjustments to those items taken into account by the individual and the shareholders as may be necessary to reflect the value of the services rendered or capital furnished. For these purposes, in determining the reasonable value for services rendered, or capital furnished, to the corporation, consideration will be given to all the facts and circumstances, including the amount that ordinarily would be paid in order to obtain comparable services or capital from a person (other than a member of the family) who is not a shareholder in the corporation. In addition, for purposes of section 1366(e), if a member of the family of one or more shareholders of the S corporation holds an interest in a passthrough entity (e.g., a partnership, S corporation, trust, or estate), that performs services for, or furnishes capital to, the S corporation without receiving reasonable compensation, the Commissioner shall prescribe adjustments to the passthrough entity and the corporation as may be necessary to reflect the value of the services rendered or capital furnished. For purposes of section 1366(e), the term *family* of any shareholder includes only the shareholder's spouse, ancestors, lineal descendants, and any trust for the primary benefit of any of these persons.

(b) *Examples.* The provisions of this section may be illustrated by the following examples:

Example 1. The stock of an S corporation is owned 50 percent by F and 50 percent by T, the minor son of F. For the taxable year, the corporation has items of taxable income equal to $70,000. Compensation of $10,000 is paid by the corporation to F for services rendered during the taxable year, and no compensation is paid to T, who rendered no services. Based on all the relevant facts and circumstances, reasonable compensation for the services rendered by F would be $30,000. In the discretion of the Internal Revenue Service, up to an additional $20,000 of the $70,000 of the corporation's taxable income, for tax purposes, may be allocated to F as compensation for services rendered. If the Internal Revenue Service allocates $20,000 of the corporation's taxable income to F as compensation for services, taxable income of the corporation would be reduced by $20,000 to $50,000, of which F and T each would be allocated $25,000. F would have $30,000 of total compensation paid by the corporation for services rendered.

Example 2. The stock of an S corporation is owned by A and B. For the taxable year, the corporation has paid compensation to a partnership that rendered services to the corporation during the taxable year. The spouse of A is a partner in that partnership. Consequently, if based on all the relevant facts and circumstances the partnership did not receive reasonable compensation for the services rendered to the corporation, the Internal Revenue Service, in its discretion, may make adjustments to those items taken into account by the partnership and the corporation as may be necessary to reflect the value of the services rendered.

[Reg. § 1.1366-3.]

☐ [T.D. 8852, 12-21-99.]

[Reg. § 1.1366-4]

§ 1.1366-4. Special rules limiting the passthrough of certain items of an S corporation to its shareholders.—(a) *Passthrough inapplicable to section 34 credit.* Section 1.1366-1(a) does not apply to any credit allowable under section 34 (relating to certain uses of gasoline and special fuels).

(b) *Reduction in passthrough for tax imposed on built-in gains.* For purposes of § 1.1366-1(a), if for any taxable year of the S corporation a tax is imposed on the corporation under section 1374, the amount of the tax imposed is treated as a loss sustained by the S corporation during the taxable year. The character of the deemed loss is determined by allocating the loss proportionately among the net recognized built-in gains giving rise to the tax and attributing the character of each net recognized built-in gain to the allocable portion of the loss.

(c) *Reduction in passthrough for tax imposed on excess net passive income.* For purposes of

Reg. § 1.1366-3(a)

§ 1.1366-1(a), if for any taxable year of the S corporation a tax is imposed on the corporation under section 1375, each item of passive investment income shall be reduced by an amount that bears the same ratio to the amount of the tax as the net amount of the item bears to the total net passive investment income for that taxable year. [Reg. § 1.1366-4.]

☐ [T.D. 8852, 12-21-99 (corrected 3-8-2000).]

[Reg. § 1.1366-5]

§ **1.1366-5. Effective date.**—Sections 1.1366-1 through 1.1366-4 apply to taxable years of an S corporation beginning on or after August 18, 1998. [Reg. § 1.1366-5.]

☐ [T.D. 8852, 12-21-99.]

[Reg. § 1.1367-0]

§ **1.1367-0. Table of contents.**—The following table of contents is provided to facilitate the use of §§ 1.1367-1 through 1.1367-3.

§ *1.1367-1. Adjustments to basis of shareholder's stock in an S corporation.*

(a) In general.

(1) Adjustments under section 1367.

(2) Applicability of other Internal Revenue Code provisions.

(b) Increase in basis of stock.

(1) In general.

(2) Amount of increase in basis of individual shares.

(c) Decrease in basis of stock.

(1) In general.

(2) Noncapital, nondeductible expenses.

(3) Amount of decrease in basis of individual shares.

(d) Time at which adjustments to basis of stock are effective.

(1) In general.

(2) Adjustment for nontaxable item.

(3) Effect of election under section 1377(a)(2) or § 1.1368-1(g)(2).

(e) Ordering rules for taxable years beginning before January 1, 1997.

(f) Ordering rules for taxable years beginning on or after August 18, 1998.

(g) Elective ordering rule.

(h) Examples.

(i) [Reserved]

(j) Adjustments for items of income in respect of a decedent.

§ *1.1367-2. Adjustments to basis of indebtedness to shareholder.*

(a) In general.

(b) Reduction in basis of indebtedness.

(1) General rule.

(2) Termination of shareholder's interest in corporation during taxable year.

(3) Multiple indebtedness.

(c) Restoration of basis.

(1) General rule.

(2) Multiple indebtedness.

(d) Time at which adjustments to basis of indebtedness are effective.

(1) In general.

(2) Effect of election under section 1377(a)(2) or § 1.1368-1(g)(2).

(e) Examples.

§ *1.1367-3. Effective date and transition rule.* [Reg. § 1.1367-0.]

☐ [T.D. 8508, 12-30-93. Amended by T.D. 8852, 12-21-99.]

[Reg. § 1.1367-1]

§ **1.1367-1. Adjustments to basis of shareholder's stock in an S corporation.**—(a) *In general*—(1) *Adjustments under section 1367.* This section provides rules relating to adjustments required by section 1367 to the basis of a shareholder's stock in an S corporation. Paragraph (b) of this section provides rules concerning increases in the basis of a shareholder's stock, and paragraph (c) of this section provides rules concerning decreases in the basis of a shareholder's stock.

(2) *Applicability of other Internal Revenue Code provisions.* In addition to the adjustments required by section 1367 and this section, the basis of stock is determined or adjusted under other applicable provisions of the Internal Revenue Code.

(b) *Increase in basis of stock*—(1) *In general.* Except as provided in § 1.1367-2(c) (relating to restoration of basis of indebtedness to the shareholder), the basis of a shareholder's stock in an S corporation is increased by the sum of the items described in section 1367(a)(1). The increase in basis described in section 1367(a)(1)(C) for the excess of the deduction for depletion over the basis of the property subject to depletion does not include the depletion deduction attributable to oil or gas property. See section 613(A)(c)(11).

(2) *Amount of increase in basis of individual shares.* The basis of a shareholder's share of stock is increased by an amount equal to the shareholder's pro rata portion of the items described in section 1367(a)(1) that is attributable to that share, determined on a per share, per day basis in accordance with section 1377(a).

Reg. § 1.1367-1(b)(2)

(c) *Decrease in basis of stock*—(1) *In general.* The basis of a shareholder's stock in an S corporation is decreased (but not below zero) by the sum of the items described in section 1367(a)(2).

(2) *Noncapital, nondeductible expenses.* For purposes of section 1367(a)(2)(D), expenses of the corporation not deductible in computing its taxable income and not properly chargeable to a capital account (*noncapital, nondeductible expenses*) are only those items for which no loss or deduction is allowable and do not include items the deduction for which is deferred to a later taxable year. Examples of noncapital, nondeductible expenses include (but are not limited to) the following: illegal bribes, kickbacks, and other payments not deductible under section 162(c); fines and penalties not deductible under section 162(f); expenses and interest relating to tax-exempt income under section 265; losses for which the deduction is disallowed under section 267(a)(1); the portion of meals and entertainment expenses disallowed under section 274; and the two-thirds portion of treble damages paid for violating antitrust laws not deductible under section 162.

(3) *Amount of decrease in basis of individual shares.* The basis of a shareholder's share of stock is decreased by an amount equal to the shareholder's pro rata portion of the passthrough items and distributions described in section 1367(a)(2) attributable to that share, determined on a per share, per day basis in accordance with section 1377(a). If the amount attributable to a share exceeds its basis, the excess is applied to reduce (but not below zero) the remaining bases of all other shares of stock in the corporation owned by the shareholder in proportion to the remaining basis of each of those shares.

(d) *Time at which adjustments to basis of stock are effective*—(1) *In general.* The adjustments described in section 1367(a) to the basis of a shareholder's stock are determined as of the close of the corporation's taxable year, and the adjustments generally are effective as of that date. However, if a shareholder disposes of stock during the corporation's taxable year, the adjustments with respect to that stock are effective immediately prior to the disposition.

(2) *Adjustment for nontaxable item.* An adjustment for a nontaxable item is determined for the taxable year in which the item would have been includible or deductible under the corporation's method of accounting for federal income tax purposes if the item had been subject to federal income taxation.

(3) *Effect of election under section 1377(a)(2) or § 1.1368-1(g)(2).* If an election under section 1377(a)(2) (to terminate the year in the case of the termination of a shareholder's interest) or under § 1.1368-1(g)(2) (to terminate the year in the case of a qualifying disposition) is made with respect to the taxable year of a corporation, this paragraph (d) applies as if the taxable year consisted of separate taxable years, the first of which ends at the close of the day on which either the shareholder's interest is terminated or a qualifying disposition occurs, whichever the case may be.

(e) *Ordering rules for taxable years beginning before January 1, 1997.* For any taxable year of a corporation beginning before January 1, 1997, except as provided in paragraph (g) of this section, the adjustments required by section 1367(a) are made in the following order—

(1) Any increase in basis attributable to the income items described in section 1367(a)(1)(A) and (B) and the excess of the deductions for depletion described in section 1367(a)(1)(C);

(2) Any decrease in basis attributable to noncapital, nondeductible expenses described in section 1367(a)(2)(D) and the oil and gas depletion deduction described in section 1367(a)(2)(E);

(3) Any decrease in basis attributable to items of loss or deduction described in section 1367(a)(2)(B) and (C); and

(4) Any decrease in basis attributable to a distribution by the corporation described in section 1367(a)(2)(A).

(f) *Ordering rules for taxable years beginning on or after August 18, 1998.* For any taxable year of a corporation beginning on or after August 18, 1998, except as provided in paragraph (g) of this section, the adjustments required by section 1367(a) are made in the following order—

(1) Any increase in basis attributable to the income items described in section 1367(a)(1)(A) and (B), and the excess of the deductions for depletion described in section 1367(a)(1)(C);

(2) Any decrease in basis attributable to a distribution by the corporation described in section 1367(a)(2)(A);

(3) Any decrease in basis attributable to noncapital, nondeductible expenses described in section 1367(a)(2)(D), and the oil and gas depletion deduction described in section 1367(a)(2)(E); and

(4) Any decrease in basis attributable to items of loss or deduction described in section 1367(a)(2)(B) and (C).

(g) *Elective ordering rule.* A shareholder may elect to decrease basis under paragraph (e)(3) or (f)(4) of this section, whichever applies, prior to decreasing basis under paragraph (e)(2) or (f)(3) of this section, whichever applies. If a shareholder makes this election, any amount described in par-

Reg. § 1.1367-1(c)(1)

S Corporations and Their Shareholders

See p. 20,601 for regulations not amended to reflect law changes

agraph (e)(2) or (f)(3) of this section, whichever applies, that is in excess of the shareholder's basis in stock and indebtedness is treated, solely for purposes of this section, as an amount described in paragraph (e)(2) or (f)(3) of this section, whichever applies, in the succeeding taxable year. A shareholder makes the election under this paragraph by attaching a statement to the shareholder's timely filed original or amended return that states that the shareholder agrees to the carryover rule of the preceding sentence. Once a shareholder makes an election under this paragraph with respect to an S corporation, the shareholder must continue to use the rules of this paragraph for that S corporation in future taxable years unless the shareholder receives the permission of the Commissioner.

(h) *Examples.* The following examples illustrate the principles of § 1.1367-1. In each example, the corporation is a calendar year S corporation:

Example 1. Adjustments to basis of stock for taxable years beginning before January 1, 1997. (i) On December 31, 1994, A owns a block of 50 shares of stock with an adjusted basis per share of $6 in Corporation S. On December 31, 1994, A purchases for $400 an additional block of 50 shares of stock with an adjusted basis of $8 per share. Thus, A holds 100 shares of stock for each day of the 1995 taxable year. For S's 1995 taxable year, A's pro rata share of the amount of the items described in section 1367(a)(1)(A) (relating to increases in basis of stock) is $300, and A's pro rata share of the amount of the items described in section 1367(a)(2)(B) and (D) (relating to decreases in basis of stock) is $500. S makes a distribution to A in the amount of $100 during 1995.

(ii) Pursuant to the ordering rules of paragraph (e) of this section, A increases the basis of each share of stock by $3 ($300 ÷ 100 shares) and decreases the basis of each share of stock by $5 ($500 ÷ 100 shares). Then A reduces the basis of each share by $1 ($100 ÷ 100 shares) for the distribution. Thus, on January 1, 1996, A has a basis of $3 per share in his original block of 50 shares ($6 + $3 − $5 − $1) and a basis of $5 per share in the second block of 50 shares ($8 + $3 − $5 − $1).

Example 2. Adjustments to basis of stock for taxable years beginning on or after August 18, 1998. (i) On December 31, 2001, A owns a block of 50 shares of stock with an adjusted basis per share of $6 in Corporation S. On December 31, 2001, A purchases for $400 an additional block of 50 shares of stock with an adjusted basis of $8 per share. Thus, A holds 100 shares of stock for each day of the 2002 taxable year. For S's 2002 taxable year, A's pro rata share of the amount of items described in section 1367(a)(1)(A) (relating to increases in basis of stock) is $300, A's pro rata share of the amount of the items described in section 1367(a)(2)(B) (relating to decreases in basis of stock attributable to items of loss and deduction) is $300, and A's pro rata share of the amount of the items described in section 1367(a)(2)(D) (relating to decreases in basis of stock attributable to noncapital, nondeductible expenses) is $200. S makes a distribution to A in the amount of $100 during 2002.

(ii) Pursuant to the ordering rules of paragraph (f) of this section, A first increases the basis of each share of stock by $3 ($300/100 shares) and then decreases the basis of each share by $1 ($100/100 shares) for the distribution. A next decreases the basis of each share by $2 ($200/100 shares) for the noncapital, nondeductible expenses and then decreases the basis of each share by $3 ($300/100 shares) for the items of loss. Thus, on January 1, 2003, A has a basis of $3 per share in the original block of 50 shares ($6 + $3 − $1 − $2 − $3) and a basis of $5 per share in the second block of 100 shares ($8 + $3 − $1 − $2 − $3).

Example 3. Adjustments attributable to basis of individual shares of stock. (i) On December 31, 1993, B owns one share of S corporation's 10 outstanding shares of stock. The basis of B's share is $30. On July 2, 1994, B purchases from another shareholder two shares for $25 each. During 1994, S corporation has no income or deductions but incurs a loss of $365. Under section 1377(a)(1)(A) and paragraph (c)(3) of this section, the amount of the loss assigned to each day of S's taxable year is $1.00 ($365/365 days). For each day, $.10 is allocated to each outstanding share ($1.00 amount of loss assigned to each day/10 shares).

(ii) B owned one share for 365 days and, therefore, reduces the basis of that share by the amount of loss attributable to it, *i.e.*, $36.50 ($.10 × 365 days). B owned two shares for 182 days and, therefore, reduces the basis of each of those shares by the amount of the loss attributable to each, *i.e.*, $18.20 ($.10 × 182 days).

(iii) The bases of the shares are decreased as follows:

Share	Original Basis	Decrease	Adjusted Basis	Excess Basis Reduction
No. 1	$30.00	$36.50	$ 0	$6.50
No. 2	25.00	18.20	6.80	0
No. 3	25.00	18.20	6.80	0
Total remaining basis			13.60	

Reg. § 1.1367-1(h)

(iv) Because the decrease in basis attributable to share No. 1 exceeds the basis of share No. 1 by $6.50 ($36.50 − $30.00), the excess is applied to reduce the bases of shares No. 2 and No. 3 in proportion to their remaining bases. Therefore, the bases of share No. 2 and share No. 3 are each decreased by an additional $3.25 ($6.50 × $6.80/$13.60). After this decrease, Share No. 1 has a basis of zero, Share No. 2 has a basis of $3.55, and Share No. 3 has a basis of $3.55.

Example 4. Effects of section 1377(a)(2) election and distribution on basis of stock for taxable years beginning before January 1, 1997. (i) On January 1, 1994, individuals B and C each own 50 of the 100 shares of issued and outstanding stock of Corporation S. B's adjusted basis in each share of stock is $120, and C's is $80. On June 30, 1994, S distributes $6,000 to B and $6,000 to C. On June 30, 1994, B sells all of her S stock for $10,000 to D. S elects under section 1377(a)(2) to treat its 1994 taxable year as consisting of two taxable years, the first of which ends at the close of June 30, the date on which B terminates her interest in S.

(ii) For the period January 1, 1994, through June 30, 1994, S has nonseparately computed income of $6,000 and a separately stated deduction item of $4,000. Therefore, on June 30, 1994, B and C, pursuant to the ordering rules of paragraph (e) of this section, increase the basis of each share by $60 ($6,000/100 shares) and decrease the basis of each share by $40 ($4,000/100 shares). Then B and C reduce the basis of each share by $120 ($12,000/100 shares) for the distribution.

(iii) The basis of B's stock is reduced from $120 to $20 per share ($120 + $60 − $40 − $120). The basis of C's stock is reduced from $80 to $0 per share ($80 + $60 − $40 − $120). See section 1368 and § 1.1368-1(c) and (d) for rules relating to the tax treatment of the distributions.

(iv) Pursuant to paragraph (d)(3) of this section, the net reduction in the basis of B's shares of the S stock required by section 1367 and this section is effective immediately prior to B's sale of her stock. Thus, B's basis for determining gain or loss on the sale of the S stock is $20 per share, and B has a gain on the sale of $180 ($200 − $20) per share.

Example 5. Effects of section 1377(a)(2) election and distribution on basis of stock for taxable years beginning on or after August 18, 1998. (i) The facts are the same as in *Example 4*, except that all of the events occur in 2001 rather than in 1994 and except as follows: On June 30, 2001, B sells 25 shares of her stock for $5,000 to D and 25 shares back to Corporation S for $5,000. Under section 1377(a)(2)(B) and § 1.1377-1(b)(2), B, C, and D are affected shareholders because B has transferred shares to Corporations S and D. Pursuant to section 1377(a)(2)(A) and § 1.1377-1(b)(1), B, C, and D, the affected shareholders, and Corporation S agree to treat the taxable year 2001 as if it consisted of two separate taxable years for all affected shareholders for the purposes set forth in § 1.1377-1(b)(3)(i).

(ii) On June 30, 2001, B and C, pursuant to the ordering rules of paragraph (f)(1) of this section, increase the basis of each share by $60 ($6,000/100 shares) for the nonseparately computed income. Then B and C reduce the basis of each share by $120 ($12,000/100 shares) for the distribution. Finally, B and C decrease the basis of each share by $40 ($4,000/100 shares) for the separately stated deduction item.

(iii) The basis of the stock of B is reduced from $120 to $20 per share ($120 + $60 − $120 − $40). Prior to accounting for the separately stated deduction item, the basis of the stock of C is reduced from $80 to $20 ($80 + $60 − $120). Finally, because the period from January 1 through June 30, 2001 is treated under § 1.1377-1(b)(3)(i) as a separate taxable year for purposes of making adjustments to the basis of stock, under section 1366(d) and § 1.1366-2(a)(2), C may deduct only $20 per share of the remaining $40 of the separately stated deduction item, and the basis of the stock of C is reduced from $20 per share to $0 per share. Under section 1366 and § 1.1366-2(a)(2), C's remaining separately stated deduction item of $20 per share is treated as having been incurred in the first succeeding taxable year of Corporation S, which, for this purpose, begins on July 1, 2001.

(i) [Reserved]

(j) *Adjustments for items of income in respect of a decedent.* The basis determined under section 1014 of any stock in an S corporation is reduced by the portion of the value of the stock that is attributable to items constituting income in respect of a decedent. For the determination of items realized by an S corporation constituting income in respect of a decedent, see sections 1367(b)(4)(A) and 691 and applicable regulations thereunder. For the determination of the allowance of a deduction for the amount of estate tax attributable to income in respect of a decedent, see section 691(c) and applicable regulations thereunder. [Reg. § 1.1367-1.]

☐ [T.D. 8508, 12-30-93. Amended by T.D. 8852, 12-21-99 (corrected 3-8-2000).]

Reg. § 1.1367-1(i)

S Corporations and Their Shareholders

See p. 20,601 for regulations not amended to reflect law changes

[Reg. § 1.1367-2]

§ 1.1367-2. Adjustments to basis of indebtedness to shareholder.—(a) *In general.* This section provides rules relating to adjustments required by subchapter S to the basis of indebtedness of an S corporation to a shareholder. For purposes of this section, shareholder advances not evidenced by separate written instruments and repayments on the advances (*open account debt*) are treated as a single indebtedness. The basis of indebtedness of the S corporation to a shareholder is reduced as provided in paragraph (b) of this section and restored as provided in paragraph (c) of this section.

(b) *Reduction in basis of indebtedness*—(1) *General rule.* If, after making the adjustments required by section 1367(a)(1) for any taxable year of the S corporation, the amounts specified in section 1367(a)(2)(B), (C), (D), and (E) (relating to losses, deductions, noncapital, nondeductible expenses, and certain oil and gas depletion deductions) exceed the basis of a shareholder's stock in the corporation, the excess is applied to reduce (but not below zero) the basis of any indebtedness of the S corporation to the shareholder held by the shareholder at the close of the corporation's taxable year. Any such indebtedness that has been satisfied by the corporation, or disposed of or forgiven by the shareholder, during the taxable year, is not held by the shareholder at the close of that year and is not subject to basis reduction.

(2) *Termination of shareholder's interest in corporation during taxable year.* If a shareholder terminates his or her interest in the corporation during the taxable year, the rules of this paragraph (b) are applied with respect to any indebtedness of the S corporation held by the shareholder immediately prior to the termination of the shareholder's interest in the corporation.

(3) *Multiple indebtedness.* If a shareholder holds more than one indebtedness at the close of the corporation's taxable year or, if applicable, immediately prior to the termination of the shareholder's interest in the corporation, the reduction in basis is applied to each indebtedness in the same proportion that the basis of each indebtedness bears to the aggregate bases of the indebtedness to the shareholder.

(c) *Restoration of basis*—(1) *General rule.* If, for any taxable year of an S corporation beginning after December 31, 1982, there has been a reduction in the basis of an indebtedness of the S corporation to a shareholder under section 1367(b)(2)(A), any *net increase* in any subsequent taxable year of the corporation is applied to restore that reduction. For purposes of this section, *net increase* with respect to a shareholder means the amount by which the shareholder's pro rata share of the items described in section 1367(a)(1) (relating to income items and excess deduction for depletion) exceed the items described in section 1367(a)(2) (relating to losses, deductions, noncapital, nondeductible expenses, certain oil and gas depletion deductions, and certain distributions) for the taxable year. These restoration rules apply only to indebtedness held by a shareholder as of the beginning of the taxable year in which the net increase arises. The reduction in basis of indebtedness must be restored before any net increase is applied to restore the basis of a shareholder's stock in an S corporation. In no event may the shareholder's basis of indebtedness be restored above the adjusted basis of the indebtedness under section 1016(a), excluding any adjustments under section 1016(a)(17) for prior taxable years, determined as of the beginning of the taxable year in which the net increase arises.

(2) *Multiple indebtedness.* If a shareholder holds more than one indebtedness as of the beginning of a corporation's taxable year, any net increase is applied first to restore the reduction of basis in any indebtedness repaid (in whole or in part) in that taxable year to the extent necessary to offset any gain that would otherwise be realized on the repayment. Any remaining net increase is applied to restore each outstanding indebtedness in proportion to the amount that the basis of each outstanding indebtedness has been reduced under section 1367(b)(2)(A) and paragraph (b) of this section and not restored under section 1367(b)(2)(B) and this paragraph (c).

(d) *Time at which adjustments to basis of indebtedness are effective*—(1) *In general.* The amounts of the adjustments to basis of indebtedness provided in section 1367(b)(2) and this section are determined as of the close of the corporation's taxable year, and the adjustments are generally effective as of the close of the corporation's taxable year. However, if the shareholder is not a shareholder in the corporation at that time, these adjustments are effective immediately before the shareholder terminates his or her interest in the corporation. If a debt is disposed of or repaid in whole or in part before the close of the taxable year, the basis of that indebtedness is restored under paragraph (c) of this section, effective immediately before the disposition or the first repayment on the debt during the taxable year.

(2) *Effect of election under section 1377(a)(2) or § 1.1368-1(g)(2).* If an election is made under section 1377(a)(2) (to terminate the year in the case of the termination of a shareholder's interest) or under § 1.1368-1(g)(2) (to terminate the year in the case of a qualifying

Reg. § 1.1367-2(d)(2)

disposition), this paragraph (d) applies as if the taxable year consisted of separate taxable years, the first of which ends at the close of the day on which the shareholder either terminates his or her interest in the corporation or disposes of a substantial amount of stock, whichever the case may be.

(e) *Examples.* The following examples illustrate the principles of § 1.1367-2. In each example, the corporation is a calendar year S corporation. The lending transactions described in the examples do not result in foregone interest (within the meaning of section 7872(e)(2)), original issue discount (within the meaning of section 1273), or total unstated interest (within the meaning of section 483(b)).

Example 1. Reduction in basis of indebtedness. (i) A has been the sole shareholder in Corporation S since 1992. In 1993, A loans S $1,000 (Debt No. 1), which is evidenced by a ten-year promissory note in the face amount of $1,000. In 1996, A loans S $5,000 (Debt No. 2), which is evidenced by a demand promissory note. On December 31, 1996, the basis of A's stock is zero; the basis of Debt No. 1 has been reduced under paragraph (b) of this section to $0; and the basis of Debt No. 2 has been reduced to $1,000. On January 1, 1997, A loans S $4,000 (Debt No. 3), which is evidenced by a demand promissory note. For S's 1997 taxable year, the sum of the amounts specified in section 1367(a)(1) (in this case, nonseparately computed income and the excess deduction for depletion) is $6,000, and the sum of the amounts specified in section 1367(a)(2)(B), (D) and (E) (in this case, items of separately stated deductions and losses, noncapital, nondeductible expenses, and certain oil and gas depletion deductions—there is no nonseparately computed loss) is $10,000. Corporation S makes no payments to A on any of the loans during 1997.

(ii) The $4,000 excess of loss and deduction items is applied to reduce the basis of each indebtedness in proportion to the basis of that indebtedness over the aggregate bases of the indebtedness to the shareholder (determined immediately before any adjustment under section 1367(b)(2)(A) and paragraph (b) of this section is effective for the taxable year). Thus, the basis of Debt No. 2 is reduced in an amount equal to $800 ($4,000 (excess) × $1,000 (basis of Debt No. 2)/ $5,000 (total basis of all debt)). Similarly, the basis in Debt No. 3 is reduced in an amount equal to $3,200 ($4,000 × $4,000/$5,000). Accordingly, on December 31, 1997, A's basis in his stock is zero and his bases in the three debts are as follows:

Debt	1/1/96 Basis	12/31/96 Reduction	1/1/97 Basis	12/31/97 Reduction	1/1/98 Basis
No. 1	$1,000	$1,000	$ 0	$ 0	$ 0
No. 2	5,000	4,000	1,000	800	200
No. 3			4,000	3,200	800

Example 2. Restoration of basis of indebtedness. (i) The facts are the same as in *Example 1.* On July 1, 1998, S completely repays Debt No. 3, and, for S's 1998 taxable year, the net increase (within the meaning of paragraph (c) of this section) with respect to A equals $4,500.

(ii) The net increase is applied first to restore the bases in the debts held on January 1, 1998, before any of the net increase is applied to increase A's basis in his shares of S stock. The net increase is applied to restore first the reduction of basis in indebtedness repaid in 1998. Any remaining net increase is applied to restore the bases of the outstanding debts in proportion to the amount that each of these outstanding debts have been reduced previously under paragraph (b) of this section and have not been restored. As of December 31, 1998, the total reduction in A's debts held on January 1, 1998 equals $9,000. Thus, the basis of Debt No. 3 is restored by $3,200 (the amount of the previous reduction) to $4,000. A's basis in Debt No. 3 is treated as restored immediately before that debt is repaid. Accordingly, A does not realize any gain on the repayment. The remaining net increase of $1,300 ($4,500 − $3,200) is applied to restore the bases of Debt No. 1 and Debt No. 2. As of December 31, 1998, the total reduction in these outstanding debts is $5,800 ($9,000 − $3,200). The basis of Debt No. 1 is restored in an amount equal to $224 ($1,300 × $1,000/$5,800). Similarly, the basis in Debt No. 2 is restored in an amount equal to $1,076 ($1,300 × $4,800/$5,800). On December 31, 1998, A's basis in his S stock is zero and his bases in the two remaining debts are as follows:

Original Basis	Amount Reduced	1/1/98 Basis	Amount Restored	12/31/98 Basis
$1,000	$1,000	$ 0	$ 224	$ 224
5,000	4,800	200	1,076	1,276

Example 3. Full restoration of basis in indebtedness when debt is repaid in part during the taxable year. (i) C has been a shareholder in Corporation S since 1992. In 1997, C loans S

Reg. § 1.1367-2(e)

$1,000. S issues its note to C in the amount of $1,000, of which $950 is payable on March 1, 1998, and $50 is payable on March 1, 1999. On December 31, 1997, C's basis in all her shares of S stock is zero and her basis in the note has been reduced under paragraph (b) of this section to $900. For 1998, the net increase (within the meaning of paragraph (c) of this section) with respect to C is $300.

(ii) Because C's basis of indebtedness was reduced in a prior taxable year under § 1.1367-2(b), the net increase for 1998 is applied to restore this reduction. The restored basis cannot exceed the adjusted basis of the debt as of the beginning of the first day of 1998, excluding prior adjustments under section 1367, or $1,000. Therefore, $100 of the $300 net increase is applied to restore the basis of the debt from $900 to $1,000 effective immediately before the repayment on March 1, 1998. The remaining net increase of $200 increases C's basis in her stock.

Example 4. Determination of net increase—distribution in excess of increase in basis. (i) D has been the sole shareholder in Corporation S since 1990. On January 1, 1996, D loans S $10,000 in return for a note from S in the amount of $10,000 of which $5,000 is payable on each of January 1, 2000, and January 1, 2001. On December 31, 1997, the basis of D's shares of S stock is zero, and his basis in the note has been reduced under paragraph (b) of this section to $8,000. During 1998, the sum of the items under section 1367(a)(1) (relating to increases in basis of stock) with respect to D equals $10,000 (in this case, nonseparately computed income), and the sum of the items under section 1367(a)(2)(B), (C), (D), and (E) (relating to decreases in basis of stock) with respect to D equals $0. During 1998, S also makes distributions to D totaling $11,000. This distribution is an item that reduces basis of stock under section 1367(a)(2)(A) and must be taken into account for purposes of determining whether there is a net increase for the taxable year. Thus, for 1998, there is no net increase with respect to D because the amount of the items provided in section 1367(a)(1) do not exceed the amount of the items provided in section 1367(a)(2).

(ii) Because there is no net increase with respect to D for 1998, none of the 1997 reduction in D's basis in the indebtedness is restored. The $10,000 increase in basis under section 1367(a)(1) is applied to increase D's basis in his S stock. Under section 1367(a)(2)(A), the $11,000 distribution with respect to D's stock reduces D's basis in his shares of S stock to $0. See section 1368 and § 1.1368-1(c) and (d) for the tax treatment of the $1,000 distribution in excess of D's basis.

Example 5. Distributions less than increase in basis. (i) The facts are the same as in *Example 4*, except that in 1998 S makes distributions to D totaling $8,000. On these facts, for 1998, there is a net increase with respect to D of $2,000 (the amount by which the items provided in section 1367(a)(1) exceed the amount of the items provided in section 1367(a)(2)).

(ii) Because there is a net increase of $2,000 with respect to D for 1998, $2,000 of the $10,000 increase in basis under section 1367(a)(1) is first applied to restore D's basis in the indebtedness to $10,000 ($8,000 + $2,000). Accordingly, on December 31, 1998, D has a basis in his shares of S stock of $0 ($0 + $8,000 (increase in basis remaining after restoring basis in indebtedness) − $8,000 (distribution)) and a basis in the note of $10,000. [Reg. § 1.1367-2.]

☐ [*T.D.* 8508, 12-30-93.]

[Reg. § 1.1367-3]

§ 1.1367-3. Effective date and transition rule.—Except for § 1.1367-1(f), (h) *Example 2* and *Example 5*, and (j), §§ 1.1367-1 and 1.1367-2 apply to taxable years of the corporation beginning on or after January 1, 1994. Section 1.1367-1(f), (h) *Example 2* and *Example 5*, and (j) apply only to taxable years of the corporation beginning on or after August 18, 1998. For taxable years beginning before January 1, 1994, and taxable years beginning on or after January 1, 1997, and before August 18, 1998, the basis of a shareholder's stock must be determined in a reasonable manner, taking into account the statute and legislative history. Except for § 1.1367-1(f), (h) *Example 2* and *Example 5*, and (j), return positions consistent with §§ 1.1367-1 and 1.1367-2 are reasonable for taxable years beginning before January 1, 1994. Return positions consistent with § 1.1367-1(f), (h) *Example 2* and *Example 5*, and (j) are reasonable for taxable years beginning on or after January 1, 1997, and before August 18, 1998. [Reg. § 1.1367-3.]

☐ [*T.D.* 8508, 12-30-93. Amended by *T.D.* 8852, 12-21-99.]

[Reg. § 1.1368-0]

§ 1.1368-0. Table of contents.—The following table of contents is provided to facilitate the use of §§ 1.1368-1 through 1.1368-4.

§ 1.1368-1. Distributions by S corporations.

(a) In general.

(b) Date distribution made.

(c) S corporation with no earnings and profits.

(d) S corporation with earnings and profits.

(1) General treatment of distribution.

S Corporations and Their Shareholders

(2) Previously taxed income.

(e) Certain adjustments taken into account.

(1) Taxable years beginning before January 1, 1997.

(2) Taxable years beginning on or after August 18, 1998.

(f) Elections relating to source of distributions.

(1) In general.

(2) Election to distribute earnings and profits first.

(i) In general.

(ii) Previously taxed income.

(iii) Corporation with subchapter C and subchapter S earnings and profits.

(3) Election to make a deemed dividend.

(4) Election to forego previously taxed income.

(5) Time and manner of making elections.

(i) For earnings and profits.

(ii) For previously taxed income and deemed dividends.

(iii) Corporate statement regarding elections.

(iv) Irrevocable elections.

(g) Special rule.

(1) Election to terminate year under § 1.1368-1(g)(2).

(2) Election in case of a qualifying disposition

(i) In general.

(ii) Effect of the election.

(iii) Time and manner of making election.

(iv) Coordination with election under section 1377(a)(2).

§ 1.1368-2. Accumulated adjustments account (AAA).

(a) Accumulated adjustments account.

(1) In general.

(2) Increases to the AAA.

(3) Decreases to the AAA.

(i) In general.

(ii) Extent of allowable reduction.

(iii) Decrease to the AAA for distributions.

(4) Ordering rules for the AAA for taxable years beginning before January 1, 1997.

(5) Ordering rules for the AAA for taxable years beginning on or after August 18, 1998.

(b) Distributions in excess of the AAA.

(1) In general.

(2) Amount of the AAA allocated to each distribution.

(c) Distribution of money and loss property.

(1) In general.

(2) Allocating the AAA to loss property.

(d) Adjustment in the case of redemptions, liquidations, reorganizations, and divisions.

(1) Redemptions.

(i) General rule.

(ii) Special rule for years in which a corporation makes both ordinary and redemption distributions.

(iii) Adjustments to earnings and profits.

(2) Liquidations and reorganizations.

(3) Corporate separations to which section 368(a)(1)(D) applies.

(e) Election to terminate year under section 1377(a)(2) or § 1.1368-1(g)(2).

§ 1.1368-3. Examples.

§ 1.1368-4. Effective date and transition rule.

[Reg. § 1.1368-0.]

☐ [T.D. 8508, 12-30-93. Amended by T.D. 8696, 12-20-96; T.D. 8852, 12-21-99 and T.D. 8869, 1-20-2000.]

[Reg. § 1.1368-1]

§ 1.1368-1. Distributions by S corporations.—(a) *In general.* This section provides rules for distributions made by an S corporation with respect to its stock which, but for section 1368(a) and this section, would be subject to section 301(c) and other rules of the Internal Revenue Code that characterize a distribution as a dividend.

(b) *Date distribution made.* For purposes of section 1368, a distribution is taken into account on the date the corporation makes the distribution, regardless of when the distribution is treated as received by the shareholder.

(c) *S corporation with no earnings and profits.* A distribution made by an S corporation that has no accumulated earnings and profits as of the end of the taxable year of the S corporation in which the distribution is made is treated in the manner provided in section 1368(b).

(d) *S corporation with earnings and profits*—(1) *General treatment of distribution.* Except as provided in paragraph (d)(2) of this section, a distribution made with respect to its stock by an S corporation that has accumulated earnings and profits as of the end of the taxable year of the S corporation in which the distribution is made is treated in the manner provided in section 1368(c). See section 316 and § 1.316-2 for provisions relat-

Reg. § 1.1368-1(a)

S Corporations and Their Shareholders

See p. 20,601 for regulations not amended to reflect law changes

ing to the allocation of earnings and profits among distributions.

(2) *Previously taxed income.* This paragraph (d)(2) applies to distributions by a corporation that has both accumulated earnings and profits and previously taxed income (within the meaning of section 1375(d)(2), as in effect prior to its amendment by the Subchapter S Revision Act of 1982, and the regulations thereunder) with respect to one or more shareholders. In the case of such a distribution, that portion remaining after the application of section 1368(c)(1) (relating to distributions from the accumulated adjustments account (AAA) as defined in § 1.1368-2(a)) is treated in the manner provided in section 1368(b) (relating to S corporations without earnings and profits) to the extent that portion is a distribution of money and does not exceed the shareholder's net share immediately before the distribution of the corporation's previously taxed income. The AAA and the earnings and profits of the corporation are not decreased by that portion of the distribution. Any distribution remaining after the application of this paragraph (d)(2) is treated in the manner provided in section 1368(c)(2) and (3).

(e) *Certain adjustments taken into account*—(1) *Taxable years beginning before January 1, 1997.* For any taxable year of the corporation beginning before January 1, 1997, paragraphs (c) and (d) of this section are applied only after taking into account—

(i) The adjustments to the basis of the shares of a shareholder's stock described in section 1367 (without regard to section 1367(a)(2)(A) (relating to decreases attributable to distributions not includible in income)) for the S corporation's taxable year; and

(ii) The adjustments to the AAA required by section 1368(e)(1)(A) (but without regard to the adjustments for distributions under § 1.1368-2(a)(3)(iii)) for the S corporation's taxable year.

(2) *Taxable years beginning on or after August 18, 1998.* For any taxable year of the corporation beginning on or after August 18, 1998, paragraphs (c) and (d) of this section are applied only after taking into account—

(i) The adjustments to the basis of the shares of a shareholder's stock described in section 1367(a)(1) (relating to increases in basis of stock) for the S corporation's taxable year; and

(ii) The adjustments to the AAA required by section 1368(e)(1)(A) (but without regard to the adjustments for distributions under § 1.1368-2(a)(3)(iii)) for the S corporation's taxable year. Any net negative adjustment (as defined in section 1368(e)(1)(C)(ii)) for the taxable year shall not be taken into account.

(f) *Elections relating to source of distributions*—(1) *In general.* An S corporation may modify the application of paragraphs (c) and (d) of this section by electing (pursuant to paragraph (f)(5) of this section)—

(i) To distribute earnings and profits first as described in paragraph (f)(2) of this section;

(ii) To make a deemed dividend as described in paragraph (f)(3) of this section; or

(iii) To forego previously taxed income as described in paragraph (f)(4) of this section.

(2) *Election to distribute earnings and profits first*—(i) *In general.* An S corporation with accumulated earnings and profits may elect under this paragraph (f)(2) for any taxable year to distribute earnings and profits first as provided in section 1368(e)(3). Except as provided in paragraph (f)(2)(ii) of this section, distributions made by an S corporation making this election are treated as made first from earnings and profits under section 1368(c)(2) and second from the AAA under section 1368(c)(1). Any remaining portion of the distribution is treated in the manner provided in section 1368(b). This election is effective for all distributions made during the year for which the election is made.

(ii) *Previously taxed income.* If a corporation to which paragraph (d)(2) of this section (relating to corporations with previously taxed income) applies makes the election provided in this paragraph (f)(2) for the taxable year, and does not make the election to forego previously taxed income under paragraph (f)(4) of this section, distributions by the S corporation during the taxable year are treated as made first, from previously taxed income under paragraph (d)(2) of this section; second, from earnings and profits under section 1368(c)(2); and third, from the AAA under section 1368(c)(1). Any portion of a distribution remaining after the previously taxed income, earnings and profits, and the AAA are exhausted is treated in the manner provided in section 1368(b).

(iii) *Corporation with subchapter C and subchapter S earnings and profits.* If an S corporation that makes the election provided in this paragraph (f)(2) has both subchapter C earnings and profits (as defined in section 1362(d)(3)(B)) and subchapter S earnings and profits in a taxable year of the corporation in which the distribution is made, the distribution is treated as made first from subchapter C earnings and profits, and second from subchapter S earnings and profits. *Subchapter S earnings and profits* are earnings and profits accumulated in a taxable year beginning

Reg. § 1.1368-1(f)(2)

before January 1, 1983 (or in the case of a qualified casualty insurance electing small business corporation or a qualified oil corporation, earnings and profits accumulated in any taxable year), for which an election under subchapter S of chapter 1 of the Internal Revenue Code was in effect.

(3) *Election to make a deemed dividend.* An S corporation may elect under this paragraph (f)(3) to distribute all or part of its subchapter C earnings and profits through a deemed dividend. If an S corporation makes the election provided in this paragraph (f)(3), the S corporation will be considered to have made the election provided in paragraph (f)(2) of this section (relating to the election to distribute earnings and profits first). The amount of the deemed dividend may not exceed the subchapter C earnings and profits of the corporation on the last day of the taxable year, reduced by any actual distributions of subchapter C earnings and profits made during the taxable year. The amount of the deemed dividend is considered, for all purposes of the Internal Revenue Code, as if it were distributed in money to the shareholders in proportion to their stock ownership, received by the shareholders, and immediately contributed by the shareholders to the corporation, all on the last day of the corporation's taxable year.

(4) *Election to forego previously taxed income.* An S corporation may elect to forego distributions of previously taxed income. If such an election is made, paragraph (d)(2) of this section (relating to corporations with previously taxed income) does not apply to any distribution made during the taxable year. Thus, distributions by a corporation that makes the election to forego previously taxed income for a taxable year under this paragraph (f)(4) and does not make the election to distribute earnings and profits first under paragraph (f)(2) of this section are treated in the manner provided in section 1368(c) (relating to distributions by corporations with earnings and profits). Distributions by a corporation that makes both the election to distribute earnings and profits first under paragraph (f)(2) of this section and the election to forego previously taxed income under this paragraph (f)(4), are treated in the manner provided in paragraph (f)(2)(i) of this section.

(5) *Time and manner of making elections*—(i) *For earnings and profits.* If an election is made under paragraph (f)(2) of this section to distribute earnings and profits first, see section 1368(e)(3) regarding the consent required by shareholders.

(ii) *For previously taxed income and deemed dividends.* If an election is made to forego previously taxed income under paragraph (f)(4) of this section or to make a deemed dividend under paragraph (f)(3) of this section, consent by each "affected shareholder," as defined in section 1368(e)(3)(B), is required.

(iii) *Corporate statement regarding elections.* A corporation makes an election for a taxable year under this paragraph (f) by attaching a statement to a timely filed original or amended return required to be filed under section 6037 for that taxable year. In the statement, the corporation must identify the election it is making under § 1.1368-1(f) and must state that each shareholder consents to the election. An officer of the corporation must sign under penalties of perjury the statement on behalf of the corporation. A statement of election to make a deemed dividend under this paragraph must include the amount of the deemed dividend that is distributed to each shareholder.

(iv) *Irrevocable elections.* The elections under this paragraph (f) are irrevocable and are effective only for the taxable year for which they are made. In applying the preceding sentence to elections under this paragraph (f), an election to terminate the taxable year under section 1377(a)(2) or § 1.1368-1(g)(2) is disregarded.

(g) *Special rule*—(1) *Election to terminate year under § 1.1368-1(g)(2).* If an election is made under paragraph (g)(2) of this section to terminate the year when there is a qualifying disposition, this section applies as if the taxable year consisted of separate taxable years, the first of which ends at the close of the day on which there is a qualifying disposition of stock.

(2) *Election in case of a qualifying disposition*—(i) *In general.* In the case of a qualifying disposition, a corporation may elect under this paragraph (g)(2)(i) to treat the year as if it consisted of separate taxable years, the first of which ends at the close of the day on which the qualifying disposition occurs. A *qualifying disposition* is—

(A) A disposition by a shareholder of 20 percent or more of the outstanding stock of the corporation in one or more transactions during any thirty-day period during the corporation's taxable year;

(B) A redemption treated as an exchange under section 302(a) or section 303(a) of 20 percent or more of the outstanding stock of the corporation from a shareholder in one or more transactions during any thirty-day period during the corporation's taxable year; or

(C) An issuance of an amount of stock equal to or greater than 25 percent of the previously outstanding stock to one or more new share-

Reg. § 1.1368-1(f)(3)

holders during any thirty-day period during the corporation's taxable year.

(ii) *Effect of the election.* A corporation making an election under paragraph (g)(2)(i) of this section must treat the taxable year as separate taxable years for purposes of allocating items of income and loss; making adjustments to the AAA, earnings and profits, and basis; and determining the tax effect of distributions under section 1368(b) and (c). An election made under paragraph (g)(2)(i) of this section may be made upon the occurrence of any qualifying disposition. Dispositions of stock that are taken into account as part of a qualifying disposition are not taken into account in determining whether a subsequent qualifying disposition has been made.

(iii) *Time and manner of making election.* A corporation makes an election under paragraph (g)(2)(i) of this section for a taxable year by attaching a statement to a timely filed original or amended return required to be filed under section 6037 for a taxable year (without regard to the election under paragraph (g)(2)(i) of this section). In the statement, the corporation must state that it is electing for the taxable year under § 1.1368-1(g)(2)(i) to treat the taxable year as if it consisted of separate taxable years. The corporation also must set forth facts in the statement relating to the qualifying disposition (e.g., sale, gift, stock issuance, or redemption), and state that each shareholder who held stock in the corporation during the taxable year (without regard to the election under paragraph (g)(2)(i) of this section) consents to this election. An officer of the corporation must sign under penalties of perjury the statement on behalf of the corporation. For purposes of this election, a shareholder of the corporation for the taxable year is a shareholder as described in section 1362(a)(2). A single election statement may be filed for all elections made under paragraph (g)(2)(i) of this section for the taxable year. An election made under paragraph (g)(2)(i) of this section is irrevocable.

(iv) *Coordination with election under section 1377(a)(2).* If the event resulting in a qualifying disposition also results in a termination of a shareholder's entire interest as described in § 1.1377-1(b)(4), the election under this paragraph (g)(2) cannot be made. Rather, the election under section 1377(a)(2) and § 1.1377-1(b) may be made. See § 1.1377-1(b) (concerning the election under section 1377(a)(2)). [Reg. § 1.1368-1.]

☐ [T.D. 8508, 12-30-93. *Amended by* T.D. 8696, 12-20-96 *and* T.D. 8852, 12-21-99.]

[Reg. § 1.1368-2]

§ 1.1368-2. **Accumulated adjustments account (AAA).**—(a) *Accumulated adjustments account*—(1) *In general.* The accumulated adjustments account is an account of the S corporation and is not apportioned among shareholders. The AAA is relevant for all taxable years beginning on or after January 1, 1983, for which the corporation is an S corporation. On the first day of the first year for which the corporation is an S corporation, the balance of the AAA is zero. The AAA is increased in the manner provided in paragraph (a)(2) of this section and is decreased in the manner provided in paragraph (a)(3) of this section. For the adjustments to the AAA in the case of redemptions, liquidations, reorganizations, and corporate separations, see paragraph (d) of this section.

(2) *Increases to the AAA.* The AAA is increased for the taxable year of the corporation by the sum of the following items with respect to the corporation for the taxable year:

(i) The items of income described in section 1366(a)(1)(A) other than income that is exempt from tax;

(ii) Any nonseparately computed income determined under section 1366(a)(1)(B); and

(iii) The excess of the deductions for depletion over the basis of property subject to depletion unless the property is an oil or gas property the basis of which has been allocated to shareholders under section 613A(c)(11).

(3) *Decreases to the AAA*—(i) *In general.* The AAA is decreased for the taxable year of the corporation by the sum of the following items with respect to the corporation for the taxable year—

(A) The items of loss or deduction described in section 1366(a)(1)(A);

(B) Any nonseparately computed loss determined under section 1366(a)(1)(B);

(C) Any expense of the corporation not deductible in computing its taxable income and not properly chargeable to a capital account, other than—

(*1*) Federal taxes attributable to any taxable year in which the corporation was a C corporation; and

(*2*) Expenses related to income that is exempt from tax; and

(D) The sum of the shareholders' deductions for depletion for any oil or gas property held by the corporation described in section 1367(a)(2)(E).

(ii) *Extent of allowable reduction.* The AAA may be decreased under paragraph (a)(3)(i) of this section below zero. The AAA is decreased by noncapital, nondeductible expenses under paragraph (a)(3)(i)(C) of this section even though a portion of the noncapital, nondeductible expenses is not taken into account by a shareholder under § 1.1367-1(g) (relating to the elective ordering rule). The AAA is also decreased by the entire amount of any loss or deduction even though a portion of the loss or deduction is not taken into account by a shareholder under section 1366(d)(1) or is otherwise not currently deductible under the Internal Revenue Code. However, in any subsequent taxable year in which the loss, deduction, or noncapital, nondeductible expense is treated as incurred by the corporation with respect to the shareholder under section 1366(d)(2) or § 1.1367-1(g) (or in which the loss or deduction is otherwise allowed to the shareholder), no further adjustment is made to the AAA.

(iii) *Decrease to the AAA for distributions.* The AAA is decreased (but not below zero) by any portion of a distribution to which section 1368(b) or (c)(1) applies.

(4) *Ordering rules for the AAA for taxable years beginning before January 1, 1997.* For any taxable year beginning before January 1, 1997, the adjustments to the AAA are made in the following order—

(i) The AAA is increased under paragraph (a)(2) of this section before it is decreased under paragraph (a)(3) of this section for the taxable year;

(ii) The AAA is decreased under paragraph (a)(3)(i) of this section before it is decreased under paragraph (a)(3)(iii) of this section;

(iii) The AAA is decreased (but not below zero) by any portion of an ordinary distribution to which section 1368(b) or (c)(1) applies; and

(iv) The AAA is adjusted (whether negative or positive) for redemption distributions under paragraph (d)(1) of this section.

(5) *Ordering rules for the AAA for taxable years beginning on or after August 18, 1998.* For any taxable year of the S corporation beginning on or after August 18, 1998, the adjustments to the AAA are made in the following order—

(i) The AAA is increased under paragraph (a)(2) of this section before it is decreased under paragraph (a)(3)(i) of this section for the taxable year;

(ii) The AAA is decreased under paragraph (a)(3)(i) of this section (without taking into account any net negative adjustment (as defined in section 1368(e)(1)(C)(ii)) before it is decreased under paragraph (a)(3)(iii) of this section;

(iii) The AAA is decreased (but not below zero) by any portion of an ordinary distribution to which section 1368(b) or (c)(1) applies;

(iv) The AAA is decreased by any net negative adjustment (as defined in section 1368(e)(1)(C)(ii)); and

(v) The AAA is adjusted (whether negative or positive) for redemption distributions under paragraph (d)(1) of this section.

(b) *Distributions in excess of the AAA*—(1) *In general.* A portion of the AAA (determined under paragraph (b)(2) of this section) is allocated to each of the distributions made for the taxable year if—

(i) An S corporation makes more than one distribution of property with respect to its stock during the taxable year of the corporation (including an S short year as defined under section 1362(e)(1)(A));

(ii) The AAA has a positive balance at the close of the year; and

(iii) The sum of the distributions made during the corporation's taxable year exceeds the balance of the AAA at the close of the year.

(2) *Amount of the AAA allocated to each distribution.* The amount of the AAA allocated to each distribution is determined by multiplying the balance of the AAA at the close of the current taxable year by a fraction, the numerator of which is the amount of the distribution and the denominator of which is the amount of all distributions made during the taxable year. For purposes of this paragraph (b)(2), the term *all distributions made during the taxable year* does not include any distribution treated as from earnings and profits or previously taxed income pursuant to an election made under section 1368(e)(3) and § 1.1368-1(f)(2). See paragraph (d)(1) of this section for rules relating to the adjustments to the AAA for redemptions and distributions in the year of a redemption.

(c) *Distribution of money and loss property*—(1) *In general.* The amount of the AAA allocated to a distribution under this section must be further allocated (under paragraph (c)(2) of this section) if the distribution—

(i) Consists of property the adjusted basis of which exceeds its fair market value on the date of the distribution and money;

(ii) Is a distribution to which § 1.1368-1(d)(1) applies; and

(iii) Exceeds the amount of the corporation's AAA properly allocable to that distribution.

(2) *Allocating the AAA to loss property.* The amount of the AAA allocated to the property other than money is equal to the amount of the

Reg. § 1.1368-2(a)(4)

AAA allocated to the distribution multiplied by a fraction, the numerator of which is the fair market value of the property other than money on the date of distribution and the denominator of which is the amount of the distribution. The amount of the AAA allocated to the money is equal to the amount of the AAA allocated to the distribution reduced by the amount of the AAA allocated to the property other than money.

(d) *Adjustment in the case of redemptions, liquidations, reorganizations, and divisions*—(1) *Redemptions*—(i) *General Rule.* In the case of a redemption distribution by an S corporation that is treated as an exchange under section 302(a) or section 303(a) (a *redemption distribution*), the AAA of the corporation is adjusted in an amount equal to the ratable share of the corporation's AAA (whether negative or positive) attributable to the redeemed stock as of the date of the redemption.

(ii) *Special rule for years in which a corporation makes both ordinary and redemption distributions.* In any year in which a corporation makes one or more distributions to which section 1368(a) applies (*ordinary distributions*) and makes one or more redemption distributions, the AAA of the corporation is adjusted first for any ordinary distributions and then for any redemption distributions.

(iii) *Adjustments to earnings and profits.* Earnings and profits are adjusted under section 312 independently of any adjustments made to the AAA.

(2) *Liquidations and reorganizations.* An S corporation acquiring the assets of another S corporation in a transaction to which section 381(a) applies will succeed to and merge its AAA (whether positive or negative) with the AAA (whether positive or negative) of the distributor or transferor S corporation as of the close of the date of distribution or transfer. Thus, the AAA of the acquiring corporation after the transaction is the sum of the AAAs of the corporations prior to the transaction.

(3) *Corporate separations to which section 368(a)(1)(D) applies.* If an S corporation with accumulated earnings and profits transfers a part of its assets constituting an active trade or business to another corporation in a transaction to which section 368(a)(1)(D) applies, and immediately thereafter the stock and securities of the controlled corporation are distributed in a distribution or exchange to which section 355 (or so much of section 356 as relates to section 355) applies, the AAA of the distributing corporation immediately before the transaction is allocated between the distributing corporation and the controlled corporation in a manner similar to the manner in which the earnings and profits of the distributing corporation are allocated under section 312(h). See § 1.312-10(a).

(e) *Election to terminate year under section 1377(a)(2) or § 1.1368-1(g)(2).* If an election is made under section 1377(a)(2) (to terminate the year in the case of termination of a shareholder's interest) or § 1.1368-1(g)(2) (to terminate the year in the case of a qualifying disposition), this section applies as if the taxable year consisted of separate taxable years, the first of which ends at the close of the day on which the shareholder terminated his or her interest in the corporation or makes a substantial disposition of stock, whichever the case may be. [Reg. § 1.1368-2.]

☐ [T.D. 8508, 12-30-93. Amended by T.D. 8852, 12-21-99 and T.D. 8869, 1-20-2000.]

[Reg. § 1.1368-3]

§ 1.1368-3. Examples.—The principles of §§ 1.1368-1 and 1.1368-2 are illustrated by the examples below. In each example Corporation S is a calendar year corporation:

Example 1. Distributions by S corporations without C corporation earnings and profits for taxable years beginning before January 1, 1997. (i) Corporation S, an S corporation, has no earnings and profits as of January 1, 1996, the first day of its 1996 taxable year. S's sole shareholder, A, holds 10 shares of S stock with a basis of $1 per share as of that date. On March 1, 1996, S makes a distribution of $38 to A. For S's 1996 taxable year, A's pro rata share of the amount of the items described in section 1367(a)(1) (relating to increases in basis of stock) is $50 and A's pro rata share of the amount of the items described in section 1367(a)(2)(B) through (D) (relating to decreases in basis of stock for items other than distributions) is $26.

(ii) Under section 1368(d)(1) and § 1.1368-1(e)(1), the adjustments to the bases of A's stock in S described in section 1367 are made before the distribution rules of section 1368 are applied. Thus, A's basis per share in the stock is $3.40 ($1 + [($50 − $26) / 10 shares]) before taking into account the distribution. Under section 1367(a)(2)(A), the basis of A's stock is decreased by distributions to A that are not includible in A's income. Under § 1.1367-1(c)(3), the amount of the distribution that is attributable to each share of A's stock is $3.80 ($38 distribution / 10 shares). However, A only has a basis of $3.40 in each share, and basis may not be reduced below zero. Therefore, the basis of each share of his stock is reduced by $3.40 to zero, and the remaining $4.00 of the distribution ([$3.80 −

$3.40] \times 10$ shares) is treated as gain from the sale or exchange of property. As of January 1, 1997, A has a basis of $0 in his shares of S stock.

Example 2. Distributions by S corporations without earnings and profits for taxable years beginning on or after August 18, 1998. (i) Corporation S, an S corporation, has no earnings and profits as of January 1, 2001, the first day of its 2001 taxable year. S's sole shareholder, A, holds 10 shares of S stock with a basis of $1 per share as of that date. On March 1, 2001, S makes a distribution of $38 to A. The balance in Corporation S's AAA is $100. For S's 2001 taxable year, A's pro rata share of the amount of the items described in section 1367(a)(1) (relating to increases in basis of stock) is $50. A's pro rata share of the amount of the items described in sections 1367(a)(2)(B) through (D) (relating to decreases in basis of stock for items other than distributions) is $26, $20 of which is attributable to items described in section 1367(a)(2)(B) and (C) and $6 of which is attributable to items described in section 1367(a)(2)(D) (relating to decreases in basis attributable to noncapital, nondeductible expenses).

(ii) Under section 1368(d)(1) and § 1.1368-1(e)(1) and (2), the adjustments to the basis of A's stock in S described in sections 1367(a)(1) are made before the distribution rules of section 1368 are applied. Thus, A's basis per share in the stock is $6.00 ($1 + [$50/10]) before taking into account the distribution. Under section 1367(a)(2)(A), the basis of A's stock is decreased by distributions to A that are not includible in A's income. Under § 1.1367-1(c)(3), the amount of the distribution that is attributable to each share of A's stock is $3.80 ($38 distribution/10 shares). Thus, A's basis per share in the stock is $2.20 ($6.00 − $3.80), after taking into account the distribution. Under section 1367(a)(2)(D), the basis of each share of A's stock in S after taking into account the distribution, $2.20, is decreased by $.60 ($6 noncapital, nondeductible expenses/10). Thus, A's basis per share after taking into account the nondeductible, noncapital expenses is $1.60. Under section 1367(a)(2)(B) and (C), A's basis per share is further decreased by $2 ($20 items described in section 1367(a)(2)(B) and (C) /10 shares). However, basis may not be reduced below zero. Therefore, the basis of each share of A's stock is reduced to zero. As of January 1, 2002, A has a basis of $0 in his shares of S stock. Pursuant to section 1366(d)(2), the $.40 of loss in excess of A's basis in each of his shares of S stock is treated as incurred by the corporation in the succeeding taxable year with respect to A.

Example 3. Distributions by S corporations with C corporation earnings and profits for taxable years beginning before January 1, 1997. (i) Corporation S properly elects to be an S corporation beginning January 1, 1997, and as of that date has accumulated earnings and profits of $30. B, an individual and sole shareholder of Corporation S, has 10 shares of S stock with a basis of $12 per share. In addition, B lends $30 to S evidenced by a demand note.

(ii) During 1997, S has a nonseparately computed loss of $150. S makes no distributions to B during 1997. Under section 1366(d)(1), B is allowed a loss equal to $150, the amount equal to the sum of B's bases in his shares of stock and his basis in the debt. Under section 1367, the loss reduces B's adjusted basis in his stock and debt to $0. Under § 1.1368-2(a)(3), S's AAA as of December 31, 1997, has a deficit of $150 as a result of S's loss for the year.

(iii) For 1998, S has $220 of separately stated income and distributes $110 to B. The balance in the AAA (negative $150 from 1997) is increased by $220 for S's income for the year and decreased to $0 for the portion of the distribution that is treated as being from the AAA ($70). Under § 1.1367-2(c), B's net increase is $150, determined by reducing the $220 of income by the $70 of the distribution not includible in income by B. Thus, B's basis in the debt is fully restored to $30, and B's basis in S stock (before accounting for the distribution) is increased from zero to $19 per share ([$220 − $30 applied to the debt]/10). Thirty dollars of the distribution is considered a dividend to the extent of S's $30 of earnings and profits, and the remaining $10 of the distribution reduces B's basis in the S stock. Thus, B's basis in the S stock as of December 31, 1998, is $11 per share ($19 − [$70 AAA distribution/10] − [10 distribution treated as a reduction in basis/10]). The balance in the AAA is $0, S's earnings and profits are $0, and B's basis in the loan is $30.

Example 4. Distributions by S corporations with earnings and profits and no net negative adjustment for taxable years beginning on or after August 18, 1998. (i) Corporation S, an S corporation, has accumulated earnings and profits of $1,000 and a balance in the AAA of $2,000 on January 1, 2001. S's sole shareholder B holds 100 shares of stock with a basis of $20 per share as of January 1, 2001. On April 1, 2001, S makes a distribution of $1,500 to B. B's pro rata share of the income earned by S during 2001 is $2,000 and B's pro rata share of S's losses is $1,500. For the taxable year ending December 31, 2001, S does not have a net negative adjustment as defined in section 1368(e)(1)(C). S does not make the elec-

Reg. § 1.1368-3

tion under section 1368(e)(3) and § 1.1368-1(f)(2) to distribute its earnings and profits before its AAA.

(ii) The AAA is increased from $2,000 to $4,000 for the $2,000 of income earned during the 2001 taxable year. The AAA is decreased from $4,000 to $2,500 for the $1,500 of losses. The AAA is decreased from $2,500 to $1,000 for the portion of the distribution ($1,500) to B that does not exceed the AAA.

(iii) As of December 31, 2001, B's basis in his stock is $10 ($20 + $20 ($2,000 income/100 shares) − $15 ($1,500 distribution/100 shares) − $15 ($1,500 loss/100 shares).

Example 5. Distributions by S corporations with earnings and profits and net negative adjustment for taxable years beginning on or after August 18, 1998. (i) Corporation S, an S corporation, has accumulated earnings and profits of $1,000 and a balance in the AAA of $2,000 on January 1, 2001. S's sole shareholder B holds 100 shares of stock with a basis of $20 per share as of January 1, 2001. On April 1, 2001, S makes a distribution of $2,000 to B. B's pro rata share of the income earned by S during 2001 is $2,000 and B's pro rata share of S's losses is $3,500. For the taxable year ending December 31, 2001, S has a net negative adjustment as defined in section 1368(e)(1)(C). S does not make the election under section 1368(e)(3) and § 1.1368-1(f)(2) to distribute its earnings and profits before its AAA.

(ii) The AAA is increased from $2,000 to $4,000 for the $2,000 of income earned during the 2001 taxable year. Because under section 1368(e)(1)(C)(ii) and § 1.1368-2(a)(ii), the net negative adjustment is not taken into account, the AAA is decreased from $4,000 to $2,000 for the portion of the losses ($2,000) that does not exceed the income earned during the 2001 taxable year. The AAA is reduced from $2,000 to zero for the portion of the distribution to B ($2,000) that does not exceed the AAA. The AAA is decreased from zero to a negative $1,500 for the portion of the $3,500 of loss that exceeds the $2,000 of income earned during the 2001 taxable year.

(iii) Under § 1.1367-1(c)(1), the basis of a shareholder's share in an S corporation stock may not be reduced below zero. Accordingly, as of December 31, 2001, B's basis per share in his stock is zero ($20 + $20 income − $20 distribution − $35 loss). Pursuant to section 1366(d)(2), the $15 of loss in excess of B's basis in each of his shares of S stock is treated as incurred by the corporation in the succeeding taxable year with respect to B.

Example 6. Election in case of disposition of substantial amount of stock. (i) Corporation S, an S corporation, has earnings and profits of $3,000 and a balance in the AAA of $1,000 on January 1, 1997. C, an individual and the sole shareholder of Corporation S, has 100 shares of S stock with a basis of $10 per share. On July 3, 1997, C sells 50 shares of his S stock to D, an individual, for $250. For 1997, S has taxable income of $1,000, of which $500 was earned on or before July 3, 1997, and $500 earned after July 3, 1997. During its 1997 taxable year, S distributes $1,000 to C on February 1 and $1,000 to each of C and D on August 1. S does not make the election under section 1368(e)(3) and § 1.1368-1(f)(2) to distribute its earnings and profits before its AAA. S makes the election under § 1.1368-1(g)(2) to treat its taxable year as if it consisted of separate taxable years, the first of which ends at the close of July 3, 1997, the date of the qualifying disposition.

(ii) Under section § 1.1368-1(g)(2), for the period ending on July 3, 1997, S's AAA is $500 ($1,000 (AAA as of January 1, 1997) + $500 (income earned from January 1, 1997 through July 3, 1997) − $1,000 (distribution made on February 1, 1997)). C's bases in his shares of stock is decreased to $5 per share ($10 (original basis) + $5 (increase per share for income) − $10 (decrease per share for distribution)).

(iii) The AAA is adjusted at the end of the taxable year for the period July 4 through December 31, 1997. It is increased from $500 (AAA as of the close of July 3, 1997) to $1,000 for the income earned during this period and is decreased by $1,000, the portion of the distribution ($2,000 in total) made to C and D on August 1 that does not exceed the AAA. The $1,000 portion of the distribution that remains after the AAA is reduced to zero is attributable to earnings and profits. Therefore C and D each have a dividend of $500, which does not affect their basis or S's AAA. The earnings and profits account is reduced from $3,000 to $2,000.

(iv) As of December 31, 1997, C and D have bases in their shares of stock of zero ($5 (basis as of July 4) + $5 ($500 income/100 shares) − $10 ($1,000 distribution/100 shares)). C and D each will report $500 as dividend income, which does not affect their basis or S's AAA.

Example 7. Election to distribute earnings and profits first. (i) Corporation S has been a calendar year C corporation since 1975. For 1982, S elects for the first time to be taxed under subchapter S, and during 1982 has $60 of earnings and profits. As of December 31, 1995, S has an AAA of $10 and earnings and profits of $160, consisting of $100 of subchapter C earnings and profits and $60 of subchapter S earnings and profits. For 1996, S has $200 of taxable income and the AAA

Reg. § 1.1368-3

is increased to $210 (before taking distributions into account). During 1996, S distributes $240 to its shareholders. With its 1996 tax return, S properly elects under section 1368(e)(3) and § 1.1368-1(f)(2) to distribute its earnings and profits before its AAA.

(ii) Because S elected to distribute its earnings and profits before its AAA, the first $100 of the distribution is characterized as a distribution from subchapter C earnings and profits; the next $60 of the distribution is characterized as a distribution from subchapter S earnings and profits. Because $160 of the distribution is from earnings and profits, the shareholders of S have a $160 dividend. The remaining $80 of the distribution is a distribution from S's AAA and is treated by the shareholders as a return of capital or gain from the sale or exchange of property, as appropriate, under § 1.1368-1(d)(1). S's AAA, as of December 31, 1996, equals $130 ($210 − $80).

Example 8. Distributions in excess of the AAA. (i) On January 1, 1995, Corporation S has $40 of earnings and profits and a balance in the AAA of $100. S has two shareholders, E and F, each of whom own 50 shares of S's stock. For 1995, S has taxable income of $50, which increases the AAA to $150 as of December 31, 1995 (before taking into account distributions made during 1995). On February 1, 1995, S distributes $60 to each shareholder. On September 1, 1995, S distributes $30 to each shareholder. S does not make the election under section 1368(e)(3) and § 1.1368-1(f)(2) to distribute its earnings and profits before its AAA.

(ii) The sum of the distributions exceed S's AAA. Therefore, under § 1.1368-2(b), a portion of S's $150 balance in the AAA as of December 31, 1995, is allocated to each of the February 1 and September 1 distributions based on the respective sizes of the distributions. Accordingly, S must allocate $100 ($150 (AAA) × ($120 (February 1 distribution) / $180 (the sum of the distributions))) of the AAA to the February 1 distribution, and $50 ($150 × ($60 / $180)) to the September 1 distribution. The portions of the distributions to which the AAA is allocated are treated by the shareholder as a return of capital or gain from the sale or exchange of property, as appropriate. The remainder of the two distributions is treated as a dividend to the extent that it does not exceed S's earnings and profits. E and F must each report $10 of dividend income for the February 1 distribution. For the September 1 distribution, E and F must each report $5 of dividend income.

Example 9. Ordinary and redemption distributions in the same taxable year. (i) On January 1, 1995, Corporation S, an S corporation, has $20 of earnings and profits and a balance in the AAA of $10. S has two shareholders, G and H, each of whom owns 50 shares of S's stock. For 1995, S has taxable income of $16, which increases the AAA to $26 as of December 31, 1995 (before taking into account distributions made during 1995). On February 1, 1995, S distributes $10 to each shareholder. On December 31, 1995, S redeems for $13 all of shareholder G's stock in a redemption that is treated as a sale or exchange under section 302(a).

(ii) The sum of the ordinary distributions does not exceed S's AAA. Therefore, S must reduce the $26 balance in the AAA by $20 for the February 1 ordinary distribution. The portions of the distribution by which the AAA is reduced are treated by the shareholders as a return of capital or gain from the sale or exchange of property. S must adjust the remaining AAA, $6, in an amount equal to the ratable share of the remaining AAA attributable to the redeemed stock, or $3 (50% × $6).

(iii) S also must adjust the earnings and profits of $20 in an amount equal to the ratable share of the earnings and profits attributable to the redeemed stock. Therefore, S adjusts the earnings and profits by $10 (50% × $20), the ratable share of the earnings and profits attributable to the redeemed stock.

[Reg. § 1.1368-3.]

☐ [T.D. 8508, 12-30-93. Amended by T.D. 8852, 12-21-99.]

[Reg. § 1.1368-4]

§ 1.1368-4. Effective date and transition rule.—Except for § § 1.1368-1(e)(2), 1.1368-2(a)(5), and 1.1368-3 *Example 2, Example 4,* and *Example 5,* § § 1.1368-1, 1.1368-2, and 1.1368-3 apply to taxable years of the corporation beginning on or after January 1, 1994. Section 1.1368-1(e)(2), § 1.1368-2(a)(5), and § 1.1368-3 *Example 2, Example 4,* and *Example 5* apply only to taxable years of the corporation beginning on or after August 18, 1998. For taxable years beginning before January 1, 1994, and taxable years beginning on or after January 1, 1997, and before August 18, 1998, the treatment of distributions by an S corporation to its shareholders must be determined in a reasonable manner, taking into account the statute and legislative history. Except with regard to the deemed dividend rule under § 1.1368-1(f)(3), § 1.1368-1(e)(2), § 1.1368-2(a)(5), and § 1.1368-3 *Example 2, Example 4,* and *Example 5,* return positions consistent with § § 1.1368-1, 1.1368-2, and 1.1368-3 are reasonable for taxable years beginning before January 1, 1994. Return positions consistent with § § 1.1368-1(e)(2), 1.1368-2(a)(5), and 1.1368-3 *Example 2, Example 4,* and *Example 5* are rea-

S Corporations and Their Shareholders

See p. 20,601 for regulations not amended to reflect law changes

sonable for taxable years beginning on or after January 1, 1997, and before August 18, 1998. [Reg. § 1.1368-4].

☐ [T.D. 8508, 12-30-93. Amended by T.D. 8852, 12-21-99.]

[Reg. § 18.1371-1]

§ 18.1371-1. Election to treat distributions as dividends during certain post-termination transition periods (Temporary).—A corporation may make an election under section 1371(e) (as amended by section 721(o) of the Act) to treat all distributions of money made during the post-termination transition period described in section 1377(b)(1)(A) as coming out of the corporation's earnings and profits (after earnings and profits have been eliminated, the distributions are applied against and reduce the adjusted basis of the stock). The election may be made only with the consent of each shareholder to whom the corporation makes a distribution (whether or not it is a cash distribution) during such post-termination transition period. Any such election shall be made by the corporation by attaching to its income tax return for the C year in which such post-termination transition period ends a statement which clearly indicates that the corporation elects to have section 1371(e)(1) not apply to all distributions made during such post-termination transition period. The election shall not be effective unless such statement is signed by a person authorized to sign the return required to be filed under section 6012 and by each shareholder required to consent to the election. [Temporary Reg. § 18.1371-1.]

☐ [T.D. 7976, 9-5-84.]

[Reg. § 1.1374-0]

§ 1.1374-0. Table of contents.—This section lists the major paragraph headings for §§ 1.1374-1 through 1.1374-10.

§ 1.1374-1. General rules and definitions.
 (a) Computation of tax.
 (b) Anti-trafficking rules.
 (c) Section 1374 attributes.
 (d) Recognition period.
 (e) Predecessor corporation.
§ 1.1374-2. Net recognized built-in gain.
 (a) In general.
 (b) Allocation rule.
 (c) Recognized built-in gain carryover.
 (d) Accounting methods.
 (e) Example.
§ 1.1374-3. Net unrealized built-in gain.
 (a) In general.
 (b) Example.
§ 1.1374-4. Recognized built-in gain or loss.
 (a) Sales and exchanges.
  (1) In general.
  (2) Oil and gas property.
  (3) Examples.
 (b) Accrual method rule.
  (1) Income items.
  (2) Deduction items.
  (3) Examples.
 (c) Section 267(a)(2) and 404(a)(5) deductions.
  (1) Section 267(a)(2).
  (2) Section 404(a)(5).
  (3) Examples.
 (d) Section 481(a) adjustments.
  (1) In general.
  (2) Examples.
 (e) Section 995(b)(2) deemed distributions.
 (f) Discharge of indebtedness and bad debts.
 (g) Completion of contract.
 (h) Installment method.
  (1) In general.
  (2) Limitation on amount subject to tax.
  (3) Rollover rule.
  (4) Use of losses and section 1374 attributes.
  (5) Examples.
 (i) Partnership interests.
  (1) In general.
  (2) Limitations.
   (i) Partnership RBIG.
   (ii) Partnership RBIL.
  (3) Disposition of partnership interest.
  (4) RBIG and RBIL limitations.
   (i) Sale of partnership interest.
   (ii) Amounts of limitations.
  (5) Small interest exception.
   (i) In general.
   (ii) Contributed assets.
   (iii) Anti-abuse rule.
  (6) Section 704(c) gain or loss.
  (7) Disposition of distributed partnership asset.
  (8) Examples.
§ 1.1374-5. Loss carryforwards.
 (a) In general.
 (b) Example.
§ 1.1374-6. Credits and credit carryforwards.
 (a) In general.

Reg. § 1.1374-0

S Corporations and Their Shareholders

See p. 20,601 for regulations not amended to reflect law changes

(b) Limitations.
(c) Examples.

§ 1.1374-7. Inventory.
(a) Valuation.
(b) Identity of dispositions.

§ 1.1374-8. Section 1374(d)(8) transactions.
(a) In general.
(b) Separate determination of tax.
(c) Taxable income limitation.
(d) Examples.

§ 1.1374-9. Anti-stuffing rule.

§ 1.1374-10. Effective date and additional rules.
(a) In general.
(b) Additional rules.
(1) Certain transfers to partnerships.
(2) Certain inventory dispositions.
(3) Certain contributions of built-in loss assets.
(4) Certain installment sales.
(i) In general.
(ii) Examples.

[Reg. § 1.1374-0.]

☐ [T.D. 8579, 12-23-94.]

[Reg. § 1.1374-1]

§ 1.1374-1. General rules and definitions.—(a) *Computation of tax.* The tax imposed on the income of an S corporation by section 1374(a) for any taxable year during the recognition period is computed as follows—

(1) Step One: Determine the net recognized built-in gain of the corporation for the taxable year under section 1374(d)(2) and § 1.1374-2;

(2) Step Two: Reduce the net recognized built-in gain (but not below zero) by any net operating loss and capital loss carryforward allowed under section 1374(b)(2) and § 1.1374-5;

(3) Step Three: Compute a tentative tax by applying the rate of tax determined under section 1374(b)(1) for the taxable year to the amount determined under paragraph (a)(2) of this section;

(4) Step Four: Compute the final tax by reducing the tentative tax (but not below zero) by any credit allowed under section 1374(b)(3) and § 1.1374-6.

(b) *Anti-trafficking rules.* If section 382, 383, or 384 would have applied to limit the use of a corporation's recognized built-in loss or section 1374 attributes at the beginning of the first day of the recognition period if the corporation had remained a C corporation, these sections apply to limit their use in determining the S corporation's pre-limitation amount, taxable income limitation, net unrealized built-in gain limitation, deductions against net recognized built-in gain, and credits against the section 1374 tax.

(c) *Section 1374 attributes.* Section 1374 attributes are the loss carryforwards allowed under section 1374(b)(2) as a deduction against net recognized built-in gain and the credit and credit carryforwards allowed under section 1374(b)(3) as a credit against the section 1374 tax.

(d) *Recognition period.* The recognition period is the 10-year (120-month) period beginning on the first day the corporation is an S corporation or the day an S corporation acquires assets in a section 1374(d)(8) transaction. For example, if the first day of the recognition period is July 14, 1996, the last day of the recognition period is July 13, 2006. If the recognition period for certain assets ends during an S corporation's taxable year (for example, because the corporation was on a fiscal year as a C corporation and changed to a calendar year as an S corporation or because an S corporation acquired assets in a section 1374(d)(8) transaction during a taxable year), the S corporation must determine its pre-limitation amount (as defined in § 1.1374-2(a)(1)) for the year as if the corporation's books were closed at the end of the recognition period.

(e) *Predecessor corporation.* For purposes of section 1374(c)(1), if the basis of an asset of the S corporation is determined (in whole or in part) by reference to the basis of the asset (or any other property) in the hands of another corporation, the other corporation is a predecessor corporation of the S corporation. [Reg. § 1.1374-1.]

☐ [T.D. 8579, 12-23-94.]

[Reg. § 1.1374-1A]

§ 1.1374-1A. Tax imposed on certain capital gains.—(a) *General rule.* Except as otherwise provided in paragraph (c) of this section, if for a taxable year beginning after 1982 of an S corporation—

(1) The net capital gain of such corporation exceeds $25,000, and

(2) The net capital gain of such corporation exceeds 50 percent of its taxable income (as defined in paragraph (d) of this section) for such year, and

(3) The taxable income of such corporation (as defined in paragraph (d) of this section) for such year exceeds $25,000,

section 1374 imposes a tax (computed under paragraph (b) of this section) on the income of such corporation. The tax is imposed on the S corporation and not on the shareholders.

Reg. § 1.1374-1(a)(1)

(b) *Amount of tax.* The amount of tax shall be the lower of—

(1) An amount equal to the tax, determined as provided in section 1201(a)(2), on the amount by which the net capital gain of the corporation for the taxable year exceeds $25,000, or

(2) An amount equal to the tax which would be imposed by section 11 on the taxable income of the corporation (as defined in paragraph (d) of this section) for the taxable year were it not an S corporation.

No credit shall be allowable under Part IV of Subchapter A of Chapter 1 of the Internal Revenue Code of 1954 (other than under section 34) against the tax imposed by section 1374(a) and this section. See section 1375(c)(2) and § 1.1375-1(c)(2) for a special rule that reduces the amount of the net capital gain of the corporation for purposes of this paragraph (b) in cases where a net capital gain is taxed as excess net passive income under section 1375. See section 1374(c)(3) and paragraph (c)(1)(ii) of this section for a special rule that limits the amount of tax on property with a substituted basis in certain cases.

(c) *Exceptions to taxation*—(1) *New corporations and corporations with election in effect for 3 immediately preceding years*—(i) *In general.* If an S corporation would be subject to the tax imposed by section 1374 for a taxable year pursuant to paragraph (a) of this section, the corporation shall, nevertheless, not be subject to such tax for such year, if:

(A) The election under section 1362(a) which is in effect with respect to such corporation for such year has been in effect for the corporation's three immediately preceding taxable years, or

(B) An election under section 1362(a) has been in effect with respect to such corporation for each of its taxable years for which it has been in existence, unless there is a net capital gain for the taxable year which is attributable to property with a substituted basis within the meaning of paragraph (c)(1)(iii) of this section.

(ii) *Amount of tax on net capital gain attributable to property with a substituted basis.* If for a taxable year of an S corporation either paragraph (c)(1)(i)(A) or (B) of this section is satisfied, but the S corporation has a net capital gain for such taxable year which is attributable to property with a substituted basis (within the meaning of paragraph (c)(1)(iii) of this section), then paragraph (a) of this section shall apply for the taxable year, but the amount of tax determined under paragraph (b) of this section shall not exceed a tax, determined as provided in section 1201(a), on the net capital gain attributable to property with a substituted basis.

(iii) *Property with substituted basis.* For purposes of this section, the term "property with a substituted basis" means:

(A) Property acquired by a corporation ("the acquiring corporation") during the period beginning 36 months before the first day of the acquiring corporation's taxable year and ending on the last day of such year;

(B) The basis of such property in the hands of the acquiring corporation is determined in whole or in part by reference to the basis of any property in the hands of another corporation; and

(C) Such other corporation was not an S corporation throughout the period beginning the later of:

(*1*) 36 months before the first day of the acquiring corporation's taxable year, or

(*2*) The time such other corporation came into existence, and ending on the date such other corporation transferred the property, the basis of which is used to determine, in whole or in part, the basis of the property in the hands of the acquiring corporation. An S corporation and any predecessor corporation shall not be treated as one corporation for purposes of this paragraph (c)(1).

(vi) *Existence of a corporation.* For purposes of this section, a corporation shall not be considered to be in existence for any month which precedes the first month in which such corporation has shareholders or acquires assets or begins business, whichever is first to occur.

(v) *References to prior law included.* For purposes of this paragraph (c), the term "S corporation" shall include an electing small business corporation under prior subchapter S law, and the term "election under section 1362(a)" shall include an election under section 1372 of prior subchapter S law.

(vi) *Examples.* The provisions of this paragraph may be illustrated by the following examples:

Example (1). M Corporation was organized and began business in 1977. M subsequently made an election under section 1362(a) which was effective for its 1984 taxable year. If such election does not terminate under section 1362 for its taxable years 1984, 1985, and 1986, M is not subject to the tax imposed by section 1374 for its taxable year 1987, or for any subsequent year for which such election remains in effect, unless it has, for any such year, an excess of net long-term capital gain over net short-term capital loss attributable to property with a substituted basis. If there is such an excess for any such year, and the

Reg. § 1.1374-1A(c)(1)

requirements of paragraph (a) of this section are met, M will be subject to the tax for such year. If there is no such excess for any year after 1986, M will not be subject to the tax for any such year even though the requirements of paragraph (a) of this section are met.

Example (2). N corporation was organized in 1983, and was an S corporation for its first taxable year. N is not subject to the tax imposed by section 1374 for 1983, or for any subsequent year for which its original election under section 1362(a) has not terminated under section 1362(d), unless, for any such year, it has an excess of net long-term capital gain over net short-term capital loss attributable to property with a substituted basis and the requirements of paragraph (a) of this section are met.

(2) *Treatment of certain gains of options and commodities dealers*—(i) *Exclusion of certain capital gains.* For purposes of this section, the net capital gain of any options dealer or commodities dealer shall be determined by not taking into account any gain or loss (in the normal course of the taxpayer's activity of dealing in or trading section 1256 contracts) from any section 1256 contract or property related to such a contract.

(ii) *Definitions.* For purposes of this paragraph (c)(2)—

(A) *Options dealer.* The term "options dealer" has the meaning given to such term by section 1256(g)(8).

(B) *Commodities dealer.* The term "commodities dealer" means a person who is actively engaged in trading section 1256 contracts and is registered with a domestic board of trade which is designated as a contract market by the Commodities Futures Trading Commission.

(C) *Section 1256 contracts.* The term "section 1256 contracts" has the meaning given to such term by section 1256(b).

(iii) *Effective dates*—(A) *In general.* Except as otherwise provided in this paragraph (c)(2)(iii), this paragraph (c)(2) shall apply to positions established after July 18, 1984, in taxable years ending after such date.

(B) *Special rule for options on regulated futures contracts.* In the case of any option with respect to a regulated futures contract (within the meaning of section 1256), this paragraph (c)(2) shall apply to positions established after October 31, 1983, in taxable years ending after such date.

(C) *Elections with respect to property held on or before July 18, 1984.* See §§ 1.1256(h)-1T and 1.1256(h)-2T for rules concerning an election to have this paragraph (c)(2) apply to certain property held on or before July 18, 1984.

(d) *Determination of taxable income*—(1) *General rule.* For purposes of this section, taxable income of the corporation shall be determined under section 63(a) as if the corporation were a C corporation rather than an S corporation, except that the following deductions shall not apply in the computation—

(i) The deduction allowed by section 172 (relating to net operating loss deduction), and

(ii) The deductions allowed by Part VIII of Subchapter B (other than the deduction allowed by section 248, relating to organization expenditures).

For any taxable year in which a tax under this section is imposed on an S corporation, the S corporation shall attach a Form 1120 completed in accordance with this paragraph (d) and the instructions to Form 1120S to its tax return filed for such taxable year.

(2) *Special rule for net capital gains taxed as excess net passive income under section 1375.* See section 1375(c)(2) and § 1.1375-1(c)(2) for a special rule that reduces the taxable income of the corporation for purposes of section 1374(b)(2) and § 1.1374-1(b)(2) in cases where a net capital gain is taxed as excess net passive income under section 1375.

(e) *Reduction in pass-thru for tax imposed on capital gain.* See section 1366(f)(2) for a special rule reducing the S corporation's long-term capital gains and the corporation's gain from sales or exchanges of property described in section 1231 for purposes of section 1366(a) by an amount of tax imposed under section 1374 and this section.

(f) *Examples.* The following examples illustrate the principles of this section and assume that a tax will not be imposed under section 1375:

Example (1). Corporation M is an S corporation for its taxable year beginning January 1, 1983. For 1983, M has an excess of net long-term capital gain over net short-term capital loss in the amount of $30,000. However, its taxable income for the year is only $20,000 as a result of other deductions in excess of other income. Thus, although the excess of the net long-term capital gain over the net short-term capital loss exceeds $25,000 and also exceeds 50 percent of taxable income, M is not subject to the tax imposed by section 1374 for 1983 because its taxable income does not exceed $25,000.

Example (2). Corporation N is an S corporation for its 1983 taxable year. For 1983, N has an excess of net long-term capital gain over net short-term capital loss in the amount of $30,000, and

Reg. § 1.1374-1A(c)(2)

taxable income of $65,000. Thus, although N's net capital gain ($30,000) exceeds $25,000, it does not exceed 50 percent of the corporation's taxable income for the year (50 percent of $65,000, or $32,500), and therefore N is not subject to the tax imposed by section 1374 for such year.

Example (3). Assume that Corporation O, an S corporation, is subject to the tax imposed by section 1374 for its taxable year 1983. For 1983, O has an excess of net long-term capital gain over net short-term capital loss in the amount of $73,000, and taxable income within the meaning of section 1374, which includes capital gains and losses, of $100,000. The amount of tax computed under paragraph (b)(1) of this section is 28 percent of $48,000 ($73,000 − $25,000), or $13,440. Since this is lower than the amount computed under paragraph (b)(2) of this section, which is $25,750 ($3,750 + $4,500 + $7,500 + $10,000), $13,440 is the amount of tax imposed by section 1374.

Example (4). Assume that in example (3) the taxable income of O for 1983 is $35,000. This results from an excess of deductions over income with respect to items which were not included in determining the excess of the net long-term capital gain over the net short-term capital loss. In such case, the amount of tax, computed under paragraph (b)(2) of this section, is $5,550. Since this is lower than the amount computed under paragraph (b)(1) of this section, $5,550 is the amount of tax imposed by section 1374.

Example (5). Corporation P, an S corporation, for its taxable year 1983 has an excess of net long-term capital gain over net short-term capital loss in the amount of $65,000 and has taxable income of $80,000. P's election under section 1362 has been in effect for its three immediately preceding taxable years, but P, nevertheless, is subject to the tax imposed by section 1374 for 1983 since it has an excess of net long-term capital gain over net short-term capital loss (in the amount of $20,000) attributable to property with a substituted basis. The tax computed under paragraph (b)(1) of this section, $11,200 (28 percent of $40,000 ($65,000 − $25,000)), is less than the tax computed under paragraph (b)(2) of this section, $17,750. However, under the limitation provided in paragraph (c) of this section which is applicable in this factual situation, the tax imposed by section 1374 for 1983 may not exceed $5,600 (28 percent of $20,000, the excess of net long-term capital gain over net short-term capital loss attributable to property with substituted basis). [Reg. § 1.1374-1A.]

☐ [T.D. 8104, 9-25-86. Amended by T.D. 8419, 5-28-92. Redesignated by T.D. 8579, 12-23-94.]

[Reg. § 1.1374-2]

§ 1.1374-2. Net recognized built-in gain.—(a) *In general.* An S corporation's net recognized built-in gain for any taxable year is the least of—

(1) Its taxable income determined by using all rules applying to C corporations and considering only its recognized built-in gain, recognized built-in loss, and recognized built-in gain carryover (pre-limitation amount);

(2) Its taxable income determined by using all rules applying to C corporations as modified by section 1375(b)(1)(B) (taxable income limitation); and

(3) The amount by which its net unrealized built-in gain exceeds its net recognized built-in gain for all prior taxable years (net unrealized built-in gain limitation).

(b) *Allocation rule.* If an S corporation's pre-limitation amount for any taxable year exceeds its net recognized built-in gain for that year, the S corporation's net recognized built-in gain consists of a ratable portion of each item of income, gain, loss, and deduction included in the pre-limitation amount.

(c) *Recognized built-in gain carryover.* If an S corporation's net recognized built-in gain for any taxable year is equal to its taxable income limitation, the amount by which its pre-limitation amount exceeds its taxable income limitation is a recognized built-in gain carryover included in its pre-limitation amount for the succeeding taxable year. The recognized built-in gain carryover consists of that portion of each item of income, gain, loss, and deduction not included in the S corporation's net recognized built-in gain for the year the carryover arose, as determined under paragraph (b) of this section.

(d) *Accounting methods.* In determining its taxable income for pre-limitation amount and taxable income limitation purposes, a corporation must use the accounting method(s) it uses for tax purposes as an S corporation.

(e) *Example.* The rules of this section are illustrated by the following example.

Example. Net recognized built-in gain. X is a calendar year C corporation that elects to become an S corporation on January 1, 1996. X has a net unrealized built-in gain of $50,000 and no net operating loss or capital loss carryforwards. In 1996, X has a pre-limitation amount of $20,000, consisting of ordinary income of $15,000 and capital gain of $5,000, a taxable income limitation of $9,600, and a net unrealized built-in gain limitation of $50,000. Therefore, X's net recognized built-in gain for 1996 is $9,600, because that is the least of the three amounts described in paragraph (a) of this section. Under paragraph (b) of this section, X's net recognized built-in gain consists of recognized built-in ordinary income of $7,200 [$15,000 × ($9,600/$20,000) = $7,200] and recognized built-in capital gain of $2,400 [$5,000 × ($9,600/$20,000) = $2,400]. Under paragraph (c) of this section, X has a recognized built-in gain carryover to 1997 of $10,400 ($20,000 − $9,600 = $10,400), consisting of $7,800 ($15,000 − $7,200 = $7,800) of recognized built-in ordinary income and $2,600 ($5,000 − $2,400 = $2,600) of recognized built-in capital gain.

[Reg. § 1.1374-2.]

[T.D. 8579, 12-23-94.]

[Reg. § 1.1374-3]

§ 1.1374-3. Net unrealized built-in gain.—(a) *In general.* An S corporation's net unrealized built-in gain is the total of the following—

(1) The amount that would be the amount realized if, at the beginning of the first day of the recognition period, the corporation had remained a C corporation and had sold all its assets at fair market value to an unrelated party that assumed all its liabilities; decreased by

(2) Any liability of the corporation that would be included in the amount realized on the sale referred to in paragraph (a)(1) of this section, but only if the corporation would be allowed a deduction on payment of the liability; decreased by

(3) The aggregate adjusted bases of the corporation's assets at the time of the sale referred to in paragraph (a)(1) of this section; increased or decreased by

(4) The corporation's section 481 adjustments that would be taken into account on the sale referred to in paragraph (a)(1) of this section; and increased by

(5) Any recognized built-in loss that would not be allowed as a deduction under section 382, 383, or 384 on the sale referred to in paragraph (a)(1) of this section.

(b) *Example.* The rules of this section are illustrated by the following example.

Example. Net unrealized built-in gain. (i) (a) X, a calendar year C corporation using the cash method, elects to become an S corporation on January 1, 1996. On December 31, 1995, X has assets and liabilities as follows:

Assets	FMV	Basis
Factory	$ 500,000	$900,000
Accounts Receivable	300,000	0
Goodwill	250,000	0
Total	$1,050,000	$900,000

Liabilities	Amount
Mortgage	$ 200,000
Accounts Payable	100,000
Total	$ 300,000

(b) Further, X must include a total of $60,000 in taxable income in 1996, 1997, and 1998 under section 481(a).

(ii) If, on December 31, 1995, X sold all its assets to a third party that assumed all its liabilities, X's amount realized would be $1,050,000 ($750,000 cash received + $300,000 liabilities assumed = $1,050,000). Thus, X's net unrealized built-in gain is determined as follows:

Amount realized	$1,050,000
Deduction allowed	(100,000)
Basis of X's assets	(900,000)
Section 481 adjustments	60,000
Net unrealized built-in gain	$110,000

(3) *Examples.* The rules of this paragraph (a) are illustrated by the following examples.

Example 1. Production and sale of oil. X is a C corporation that purchased a working interest in an oil and gas property for $100,000 on July 1, 1993. X elects to become an S corporation effective January 1, 1996. On that date, the working interest has a fair market value of $250,000 and an adjusted basis of $50,000, but no oil has as yet been extracted. In 1996, X begins production of the working interest, sells oil that it has produced to a refinery for $75,000, and includes that amount in gross income. Under paragraph (a)(1) of this section, the $75,000 is not recognized built-in gain because as of the beginning of the recognition period X held only a working interest in the

[Reg. § 1.1374-3.]

[☐ [T.D.8579, 12-23-94.]

[Reg. § 1.1374-4]

§ 1.1374-4. **Recognized built-in gain or loss.**—(a) *Sales and exchanges*—(1) *In general.* Section 1374(d)(3) or 1374(d)(4) applies to any gain or loss recognized during the recognition period in a transaction treated as a sale or exchange for federal income tax purposes.

(2) *Oil and gas property.* For purposes of paragraph (a)(1) of this section, an S corporation's adjusted basis in oil and gas property equals the sum of the shareholders' adjusted bases in the property as determined in section 613A(c)(11)(B).

oil and gas property (since the oil had not yet been extracted from the ground), and not the oil itself.

Example 2. Sale of oil and gas property. Y is a C corporation that elects to become an S corporation effective January 1, 1996. Y has two shareholders, A and B. A and B each own 50 percent of Y's stock. In addition, Y owns a royalty interest in an oil and gas property with a fair market value of $300,000 and an adjusted basis of $200,000. Under section 613A(c)(11)(B), Y's $200,000 adjusted basis in the royalty interest is allocated $100,000 to A and $100,000 to B. During 1996, A and B take depletion deductions with respect to the royalty interest of $10,000 and $15,000, respectively. As of January 1, 1997, A and B have a basis in the royalty interest of $90,000 and $85,000, respectively. On January 1, 1997, Y sells the royalty interest for $250,000. Under paragraph (a)(1) of this section, Y has gain recognized and recognized built-in gain of $75,000 ($250,000 − ($90,000 + $85,000) = $75,000) on the sale.

(b) *Accrual method rule*—(1) *Income items.* Except as otherwise provided in this section, any item of income properly taken into account during the recognition period is recognized built-in gain if the item would have been properly included in gross income before the beginning of the recognition period by an accrual method taxpayer (disregarding any method of accounting for which an election by the taxpayer must be made unless the taxpayer actually used the method when it was a C corporation).

(2) *Deduction items.* Except as otherwise provided in this section, any item of deduction properly taken into account during the recognition period is recognized built-in loss if the item would have been properly allowed as a deduction against gross income before the beginning of the recognition period to an accrual method taxpayer (disregarding any method of accounting for which an election by the taxpayer must be made unless the taxpayer actually used the method when it was a C corporation). In determining whether an item would have been properly allowed as a deduction against gross income by an accrual method taxpayer for purposes of this paragraph, section 461(h)(2)(C) and § 1.461-4(g) (relating to liabilities for tort, worker's compensation, breach of contract, violation of law, rebates, refunds, awards, prizes, jackpots, insurance contracts, warranty contracts, service contracts, taxes, and other liabilities) do not apply.

(3) *Examples.* The rules of this paragraph (b) are illustrated by the following examples.

Example 1. Accounts receivable. X is a C corporation using the cash method that elects to become an S corporation effective January 1, 1996. On January 1, 1996, X has $50,000 of accounts receivable for services rendered before that date. On that date, the accounts receivable have a fair market value of $40,000 and an adjusted basis of $0. In 1996, X collects $50,000 on the accounts receivable and includes that amount in gross income. Under paragraph (b)(1) of this section, the $50,000 included in gross income in 1996 is recognized built-in gain because it would have been included in gross income before the beginning of the recognition period if X had been an accrual method taxpayer. However, if X instead disposes of the accounts receivable for $45,000 on July 1, 1996, in a transaction treated as a sale or exchange for federal income tax purposes, X would have recognized built-in gain of $40,000 on the disposition.

Example 2. Contingent liability. Y is a C corporation using the cash method that elects to become an S corporation effective January 1, 1996. In 1995, a lawsuit was filed against Y claiming $1,000,000 in damages. In 1996, Y loses the lawsuit, pays a $500,000 judgment, and properly claims a deduction for that amount. Under paragraph (b)(2) of this section, the $500,000 deduction allowed in 1996 is not recognized built-in loss because it would not have been allowed as a deduction against gross income before the beginning of the recognition period if Y had been an accrual method taxpayer (even disregarding section 461(h)(2)(C) and § 1.461-4(g)).

Example 3. Deferred payment liabilities. X is a C corporation using the cash method that elects to become an S corporation on January 1, 1996. In 1995, X lost a lawsuit and became obligated to pay $150,000 in damages. Under section 461(h)(2)(C), this amount is not allowed as a deduction until X makes payment. In 1996, X makes payment and properly claims a deduction for the amount of the payment. Under paragraph (b)(2) of this section, the $150,000 deduction allowed in 1996 is recognized built-in loss because it would have been allowed as a deduction against gross income before the beginning of the recognition period if X had been an accrual method taxpayer (disregarding section 461(h)(2)(C) and § 1.461-4(g)).

Example 4. Deferred prepayment income. Y is a C corporation using an accrual method that elects to become an S corporation effective January 1, 1996. In 1995, Y received $2,500 for services to be rendered in 1996, and properly elected to include the $2,500 in gross income in 1996 under Rev. Proc. 71-21, 1971-2 C.B. 549 (see

Reg. § 1.1374-4(b)(3)

§ 601.601(d)(2)(ii)(b) of this chapter). Under paragraph (b)(1) of this section, the $2,500 included in gross income in 1996 is not recognized built-in gain because it would not have been included in gross income before the beginning of the recognition period by an accrual method taxpayer using the method that Y actually used before the beginning of the recognition period.

Example 5. Change in method. X is a C corporation using an accrual method that elects to become an S corporation effective January 1, 1996. In 1995, X received $5,000 for services to be rendered in 1996, and properly included the $5,000 in gross income. In 1996, X properly elects to include the $5,000 in gross income in 1996 under Rev. Proc. 71-21, 1971-2 C.B. 549 (see § 601.601(d)(2)(ii)(b) of this chapter). As a result of the change in method of accounting, X has a $5,000 negative section 481(a) adjustment. Under paragraph (b)(1) of this section, the $5,000 included in gross income in 1996 is recognized built-in gain because it would have been included in gross income before the beginning of the recognition period by an accrual method taxpayer using the method that X actually used before the beginning of the recognition period. In addition, the $5,000 negative section 481(a) adjustment is recognized built-in loss because it relates to an item (the $5,000 X received for services in 1995) attributable to periods before the beginning of the recognition period under the principles for determining recognized built-in gain or loss in this section. See paragraph (d) of this section for rules regarding section 481(a) adjustments.

(c) *Section 267(a)(2) and 404(a)(5) deductions*—(1) *Section 267(a)(2).* Notwithstanding paragraph (b)(2) of this section, any amount properly deducted in the recognition period under section 267(a)(2), relating to payments to related parties, is recognized built-in loss to the extent—

(i) All events have occurred that establish the fact of the liability to pay the amount, and the exact amount of the liability can be determined, as of the beginning of the recognition period; and

(ii) The amount is paid—

(A) In the first two and one-half months of the recognition period; or

(B) To a related party owning, under the attribution rules of section 267, less than 5 percent, by voting power and value, of the corporation's stock, both as of the beginning of the recognition period and when the amount is paid.

(2) *Section 404(a)(5).* Notwithstanding paragraph (b)(2) of this section, any amount properly deducted in the recognition period under section 404(a)(5), relating to payments for deferred compensation, is recognized built-in loss to the extent—

(i) All events have occurred that establish the fact of the liability to pay the amount, and the exact amount of the liability can be determined, as of the beginning of the recognition period; and

(ii) The amount is not paid to a related party to which section 267(a)(2) applies.

(3) *Examples.* The rules of this paragraph (c) are illustrated by the following examples.

Example 1. Fixed annuity. X is a C corporation that elects to become an S corporation effective January 1, 1996. On December 31, 1995, A is age 60, has provided services to X as an employee for 20 years, and is a vested participant in X's unfunded nonqualified retirement plan. Under the plan, A receives $1,000 per month upon retirement until death. The plan provides no additional benefits. A retires on December 31, 1997, after working for X for 22 years. A at no time is a shareholder of X. X's deductions under section 404(a)(5) in the recognition period on paying A the $1,000 per month are recognized built-in loss because all events have occurred that establish the fact of the liability to pay the amount, and the exact amount of the liability can be determined, as of the beginning of the recognition period.

Example 2. Increase in annuity for working beyond 20 years. The facts are the same as *Example 1,* except that under the plan A receives $1,000 per month, plus $100 per month for each year A works for X beyond 20 years, upon retirement until death. X's deductions on paying A the $1,000 per month are recognized built-in loss. However, X's deductions on paying A the $200 per month for the two years A worked for X beyond 20 years are not recognized built-in loss because all events have not occurred that establish the fact of the liability to pay the amount, and the exact amount of the liability cannot be determined, as of the beginning of the recognition period.

Example 3. Cost of living adjustment. The facts are the same as *Example 1,* except that under the plan A receives $1,000 per month, plus annual cost of living adjustments, upon retirement until death. X's deductions under section 404(a)(5) on paying A the $1,000 per month are recognized built-in loss. However, X's deductions under section 404(a)(5) on paying A the annual cost of living adjustment are not recognized built-in loss because all events have not occurred that establish the fact of the liability to pay the amount, and the exact amount of the liability

Reg. § 1.1374-4(c)(1)

cannot be determined, as of the beginning of the recognition period.

(d) *Section 481(a) adjustments*—(1) *In general.* Any section 481(a) adjustment taken into account in the recognition period is recognized built-in gain or loss to the extent the adjustment relates to items attributable to periods before the beginning of the recognition period under the principles for determining recognized built-in gain or loss in this section. The principles for determining recognized built-in gain or loss in this section include, for example, the accrual method rule under paragraph (b) of this section.

(2) *Examples.* The rules of this paragraph (d) are illustrated by the following examples.

Example 1. Omitted item attributable to pre-recognition period. X is a C corporation that elects to become an S corporation effective January 1, 1996. X improperly capitalizes repair costs and recovers the costs through depreciation of the related assets. In 1999, X properly changes to deducting repair costs as they are incurred. Under section 481(a), the basis of the related assets are reduced by an amount equal to the excess of the repair costs incurred before the year of change over the repair costs recovered through depreciation before the year of change. In addition, X has a negative section 481(a) adjustment equal to the basis reduction. Under paragraph (d)(1) of this section, the portion of X's negative section 481(a) adjustment relating to the repair costs incurred before the recognition period is recognized built-in loss because those repair costs are items attributable to periods before the beginning of the recognition period under the principles for determining recognized built-in gain or loss in this section.

Example 2. Duplicated item attributable to pre-recognition period. Y is a C corporation that elects to become an S corporation effective January 1, 1996. Y improperly uses an accrual method without regard to the economic performance rules of section 461(h) to account for worker's compensation claims. As a result, Y takes deductions when claims are filed. In 1999, Y properly changes to an accrual method with regard to the economic performance rules under section 461(h)(2)(C) for worker's compensation claims. As a result, Y takes deductions when claims are paid. The positive section 481(a) adjustment resulting from the change is equal to the amount of claims filed, but unpaid, before the year of change. Under paragraph (b)(2) of this section, the deduction allowed in the recognition period for claims filed, but unpaid, before the recognition period is recognized built-in loss because a deduction was allowed for those claims before the recognition period under an accrual method without regard to section 461(h)(2)(C). Under paragraph (d)(1) of this section, the portion of Y's positive section 481(a) adjustment relating to claims filed, but unpaid, before the recognition period is recognized built-in gain because those claims are items attributable to periods before the beginning of the recognition period under the principles for determining recognized built-in gain or loss in this section.

(e) *Section 995(b)(2) deemed distributions.* Any item of income properly taken into account during the recognition period under section 995(b)(2) is recognized built-in gain if the item results from a DISC termination or disqualification occurring before the beginning of the recognition period.

(f) *Discharge of indebtedness and bad debts.* Any item of income or deduction properly taken into account during the first year of the recognition period as discharge of indebtedness income under section 61(a)(12) or as a bad debt deduction under section 166 is recognized built-in gain or loss if the item arises from a debt owed by or to an S corporation at the beginning of the recognition period.

(g) *Completion of contract.* Any item of income properly taken into account during the recognition period under the completed contract method (as described in § 1.451-3(d)) where the corporation began performance of the contract before the beginning of the recognition period is recognized built-in gain if the item would have been included in gross income before the beginning of the recognition period under the percentage of completion method (as described in § 1.451-3(c)). Any similar item of deduction is recognized built-in loss if the item would have been allowed as a deduction against gross income before the beginning of the recognition period under the percentage of completion method.

(h) *Installment method*—(1) *In general.* If a corporation sells an asset before or during the recognition period and reports the income from the sale using the installment method under section 453 during or after the recognition period, that income is subject to tax under section 1374.

(2) *Limitation on amount subject to tax.* For purposes of paragraph (h)(1) of this section, the taxable income limitation under § 1.1374-2(a)(2) is equal to the amount by which the S corporation's net recognized built-in gain would have been increased from the year of the sale to the earlier of the year the income is reported under the installment method or the last year of the recognition period, assuming all income from the sale had been reported in the year of the sale and all provisions of section 1374 applied. For purposes of the preceding sentence, if the corporation

Reg. § 1.1374-4(h)(2)

sells the asset before the recognition period, the income from the sale that is not reported before the recognition period is treated as having been reported in the first year of the recognition period.

(3) *Rollover rule.* If the limitation in paragraph (h)(2) of this section applies, the excess of the amount reported under the installment method over the amount subject to tax under the limitation is treated as if it were reported in the succeeding taxable year(s), but only for succeeding taxable year(s) in the recognition period. The amount reported in the succeeding taxable year(s) under the preceding sentence is reduced to the extent that the amount not subject to tax under the limitation in paragraph (h)(2) of this section was not subject to tax because the S corporation had an excess of recognized built-in loss over recognized built-in gain in the taxable year of the sale and succeeding taxable year(s) in the recognition period.

(4) *Use of losses and section 1374 attributes.* If income is reported under the installment method by an S corporation for a taxable year after the recognition period and the income is subject to tax under paragraph (h)(1) of this section, the S corporation's section 1374 attributes may be used to the extent their use is allowed under all applicable provisions of the Code in determining the section 1374 tax. However, the S corporation's loss recognized for a taxable year after the recognition period that would have been recognized built-in loss if it had been recognized in the recognition period may not be used in determining the section 1374 tax.

(5) *Examples.* The rules of this paragraph (h) are illustrated by the following examples.

Example 1. Rollover rule. X is a C corporation that elects to become an S corporation effective January 1, 1996. On that date, X sells Blackacre with a basis of $0 and a value of $100,000 in exchange for a $100,000 note bearing a market rate of interest payable on January 1, 2001. X does not make the election under section 453(d) and, therefore, reports the $100,000 gain using the installment method under section 453. In the year 2001, X has income of $100,000 on collecting the note, unexpired C year attributes of $0, recognized built-in loss of $0, current losses of $100,000, and taxable income of $0. If X had reported the $100,000 gain in 1996, X's net recognized built-in gain from 1996 through 2001 would have been $75,000 greater than otherwise. Under paragraph (h) of this section, X has $75,000 net recognized built-in gain subject to tax under section 1374. X also must treat the $25,000 excess of the amount reported, $100,000, over the amount subject to tax, $75,000, as income reported under the installment method in the succeeding taxable year(s) in the recognition period, except to the extent X establishes that the $25,000 was not subject to tax under section 1374 in the year 2001 because X had an excess of recognized built-in loss over recognized built-in gain in the taxable year of the sale and succeeding taxable year(s) in the recognition period.

Example 2. Use of losses. Y is a C corporation that elects to become an S corporation effective January 1, 1996. On that date, Y sells Whiteacre with a basis of $0 and a value of $250,000 in exchange for a $250,000 note bearing a market rate of interest payable on January 1, 2006. Y does not make the election under section 453(d) and, therefore, reports the $250,000 gain using the installment method under section 453. In the year 2006, Y has income of $250,000 on collecting the note, unexpired C year attributes of $0, loss of $100,000 that would have been recognized built-in loss if it had been recognized in the recognition period, current losses of $150,000, and taxable income of $0. If Y had reported the $250,000 gain in 1996, X's net recognized built-in gain from 1996 through 2005 (that is, during the recognition period) would have been $225,000 greater than otherwise. Under paragraph (h) of this section, X has $225,000 net recognized built-in gain subject to tax under section 1374.

Example 3. Use of section 1374 attribute. Z is a C corporation that elects to become an S corporation effective January 1, 1996. On that date, Z sells Greenacre with a basis of $0 and a value of $500,000 in exchange for a $500,000 note bearing a market rate of interest payable on January 1, 2011. Z does not make the election under section 453(d) and, therefore, reports the $500,000 gain using the installment method under section 453. In the year 2011, Z has income of $500,000 on collecting the note, loss of $0 that would have been recognized built-in loss if it had been recognized in the recognition period, current losses of $0, taxable income of $500,000, and a minimum tax credit of $60,000 arising in 1995. None of Z's minimum tax credit is limited under sections 53(c) or 383. If Z had reported the $500,000 gain in 1996, Z's net recognized built-in gain from 1996 through 2005 (that is, during the recognition period) would have been $350,000 greater than otherwise. Under paragraph (h) of this section, Z has $350,000 net recognized built-in gain subject to tax under section 1374, a tentative section 1374 tax of $122,500 ($350,000 × .35 = $122,500), and a section 1374 tax after using its minimum tax credit arising in 1995 of $62,250 ($122,500 − $60,000 = $62,250).

Reg. § 1.1374-4(h)(3)

(i) *Partnership interests*—(1) *In general.* If an S corporation owns a partnership interest at the beginning of the recognition period or transfers property to a partnership in a transaction to which section 1374(d)(6) applies during the recognition period, the S corporation determines the effect on net recognized built-in gain from its distributive share of partnership items as follows—

(i) Step One: Apply the rules of section 1374(d) to the S corporation's distributive share of partnership items of income, gain, loss, or deduction included in income or allowed as a deduction under the rules of subchapter K to determine the extent to which it would have been treated as recognized built-in gain or loss if the partnership items had originated in and been taken into account directly by the S corporation (partnership 1374 items);

(ii) Step Two: Determine the S corporation's net recognized built-in gain without partnership 1374 items;

(iii) Step Three: Determine the S corporation's net recognized built-in gain with partnership 1374 items; and

(iv) Step Four: If the amount computed under Step Three (paragraph (i)(1)(iii) of this section) exceeds the amount computed under Step Two (paragraph (i)(1)(ii) of this section), the excess (as limited by paragraph (i)(2)(i) of this section) is the S corporation's partnership RBIG, and the S corporation's net recognized built-in gain is the sum of the amount computed under Step Two (paragraph (i)(1)(ii) of this section) plus the partnership RBIG. If the amount computed under Step Two (paragraph (i)(1)(ii) of this section) exceeds the amount computed under Step Three (paragraph (i)(1)(iii) of this section), the excess (as limited by paragraph (i)(2)(ii) of this section) is the S corporation's partnership RBIL, and the S corporation's net recognized built-in gain is the remainder of the amount computed under Step Two (paragraph (i)(1)(ii) of this section) after subtracting the partnership RBIL.

(2) *Limitations*—(i) *Partnership RBIG.* An S corporation's partnership RBIG for any taxable year may not exceed the excess (if any) of the S corporation's RBIG limitation over its partnership RBIG for prior taxable years. The preceding sentence does not apply if a corporation forms or avails of a partnership with a principal purpose of avoiding the tax imposed under section 1374.

(ii) *Partnership RBIL.* An S corporation's partnership RBIL for any taxable year may not exceed the excess (if any) of the S corporation's RBIL limitation over its partnership RBIL for prior taxable years.

(3) *Disposition of partnership interest.* If an S corporation disposes of its partnership interest, the amount that may be treated as recognized built-in gain may not exceed the excess (if any) of the S corporation's RBIG limitation over its partnership RBIG during the recognition period. Similarly, the amount that may be treated as recognized built-in loss may not exceed the excess (if any) of the S corporation's RBIL limitation over its partnership RBIL during the recognition period.

(4) *RBIG and RBIL limitations*—(i) *Sale of partnership interest.* An S corporation's RBIG or RBIL limitation is the total of the following—

(A) The amount that would be the amount realized if, at the beginning of the first day of the recognition period, the corporation had remained a C corporation and had sold its partnership interest (and any assets the corporation contributed to the partnership during the recognition period) at fair market value to an unrelated party; decreased by

(B) The corporation's adjusted basis in the partnership interest (and any assets the corporation contributed to the partnership during the recognition period) at the time of the sale referred to in paragraph (i)(4)(i)(A) of this section; and increased or decreased by

(C) The corporation's allocable share of the partnership's section 481(a) adjustments at the time of the sale referred to in paragraph (i)(4)(i)(A) of this section.

(ii) *Amounts of limitations.* If the result in paragraph (i)(4)(i) of this section is a positive amount, the S corporation has a RBIG limitation equal to that amount and a RBIL limitation of $0, but if the result in paragraph (i)(4)(i) of this section is a negative amount, the S corporation has a RBIL limitation equal to that amount and a RBIG limitation of $0.

(5) *Small interest exception*—(i) *In general.* Paragraph (i)(1) of this section does not apply to a taxable year in the recognition period if the S corporation's partnership interest represents less than 10 percent of the partnership's capital and profits at all times during the taxable year and prior taxable years in the recognition period, and the fair market value of the S corporation's partnership interest as of the beginning of the recognition period is less than $100,000.

(ii) *Contributed assets.* For purposes of paragraph (i)(5)(i) of this section, if the S corporation contributes any assets to the partnership during the recognition period and the S corporation held the assets as of the beginning of the recognition period, the fair market value of the S corporation's partnership interest as of the begin-

Reg. § 1.1374-4(i)(5)

ning of the recognition period is determined as if the assets were contributed to the partnership before the beginning of the recognition period (using the fair market value of each contributed asset as of the beginning of the recognition period). The contribution does not affect whether paragraph (i)(5)(i) of this section applies for taxable years in the recognition period before the taxable year in which the contribution was made.

(iii) *Anti-abuse rule.* Paragraph (i)(5)(i) of this section does not apply if a corporation forms or avails of a partnership with a principal purpose of avoiding the tax imposed under section 1374.

(6) *Section 704(c) gain or loss.* Solely for purposes of section 1374, an S corporation's section 704(c) gain or loss amount with respect to any asset is not reduced during the recognition period, except for amounts treated as recognized built-in gain or loss with respect to that asset under this paragraph.

(7) *Disposition of distributed partnership asset.* If on the first day of the recognition period an S corporation holds an interest in a partnership that holds an asset and during the recognition period the partnership distributes the asset to the S corporation that thereafter disposes of the asset, the asset is treated as having been held by the S corporation on the first day of the recognition period and as having the fair market value and adjusted basis in the hands of the S corporation that it had in the hands of the partnership on that day.

(8) *Examples.* The rules of this paragraph (i) are illustrated by the following examples.

Example 1. Pre-conversion partnership interest. X is a C corporation that elects to become an S corporation on January 1, 1996. On that date, X owns a 50 percent interest in partnership P and P owns (among other assets) Blackacre with a basis of $25,000 and a value of $45,000. In 1996, P buys Whiteacre for $50,000. In 1999, P sells Blackacre for $55,000 and recognizes a gain of $30,000 of which $15,000 is included in X's distributive share. P also sells Whiteacre in 1999 for $42,000 and recognizes a loss of $8,000 of which $4,000 is included in X's distributive share. Under this paragraph and section 1374(d)(3), X's $15,000 gain is presumed to be recognized built-in gain and thus treated as a partnership 1374 item, but this presumption is rebutted if X establishes that P's gain would have been only $20,000 ($45,000 − $25,000 = $20,000) if Blackacre had been sold on the first day of the recognition period. In such a case, only X's distributive share of the $20,000 built-in gain, $10,000, would be treated as a partnership 1374 item. Under this paragraph and section 1374(d)(4), X's $4,000 loss is not treated as a partnership 1374 item because P did not hold Whiteacre on the first day of the recognition period.

Example 2. Post-conversion contribution. Y is a C corporation that elects to become an S corporation on January 1, 1996. On that date, Y owns (among other assets) Blackacre with a basis of $100,000 and a value of $200,000. On January 1, 1998, when Blackacre has a basis of $100,000 and a value of $200,000, Y contributes Blackacre to partnership P for a 50 percent interest in P. On January 1, 2000, P sells Blackacre for $300,000 and recognizes a gain of $200,000 on the sale ($300,000 − $100,000 = $200,000). P is allocated $100,000 of the gain under section 704(c), and another $50,000 of the gain for its fifty percent share of the remainder, for a total of $150,000. Under this paragraph and section 1374(d)(3), if Y establishes that P's gain would have been only $100,000 ($200,000 − $100,000 = $100,000) if Blackacre had been sold on the first day of the recognition period, Y would treat only $100,000 as a partnership 1374 item.

Example 3. RBIG limitation of $100,000 or $50,000. X is a C corporation that elects to become an S corporation on January 1, 1996. On that date, X owns a 50 percent interest in partnership P with a RBIG limitation of $100,000 and a RBIL limitation of $0. P owns (among other assets) Blackacre with a basis of $50,000 and a value of $200,000. In 1996, P sells Blackacre for $200,000 and recognizes a gain of $150,000 of which $75,000 is included in X's distributive share and treated as a partnership 1374 item. X's net recognized built-in gain for 1996 computed without partnership 1374 items is $35,000 and with partnership 1374 items is $110,000. Thus, X has a partnership RBIG of $75,000 except as limited under paragraph (i)(2)(i) of this section. Because X's RBIG limitation is $100,000, X's partnership RBIG of $75,000 is not limited and X's net recognized built-in gain for the year is $110,000 ($35,000 + $75,000 = $110,000). However, if X had a RBIG limitation of $50,000 instead of $100,000, X's partnership RBIG would be limited to $50,000 under paragraph (i)(2)(i) of this section and X's net recognized built-in gain would be $85,000 ($35,000 + $50,000 = $85,000).

Example 4. RBIL limitation of $60,000 or $40,000. Y is a C corporation that elects to become an S corporation on January 1, 1996. On that date, Y owns a 50 percent interest in partnership P with a RBIG limitation of $0 and a RBIL limitation of $60,000. P owns (among other assets) Blackacre with a basis of $225,000 and a value of $125,000. In 1996, P sells Blackacre for $125,000 and recognizes a loss of $100,000 of which $50,000 is included in Y's distributive share and treated as a partnership 1374 item. Y's net recognized built-in gain for 1996 computed without partnership 1374 items is $75,000 and with partnership 1374 items is $25,000. Thus, Y has a partnership RBIL of $50,000 for the year except as limited under paragraph (i)(2)(ii) of this section. Because Y's RBIL limitation is $60,000, Y's partnership RBIL for the year is not limited and Y's net recognized built-in gain for the year is $25,000 ($75,000 − $50,000 = $25,000). However, if Y had a RBIL limitation of $40,000 instead of $60,000, Y's partnership RBIL would be limited to $40,000 under paragraph (i)(2)(ii) of this section and Y's net recognized built-in gain for the year would be $35,000 ($75,000 − $40,000 = $35,000).

Example 5. RBIG limitation of $0. (i) X is a C corporation that elects to become an S corporation on January 1, 1996. X owns a 50 percent interest in partnership P with a RBIG limitation of $0 and a RBIL limitation of $25,000.

(a) In 1996, P's partnership 1374 items are—

(1) Ordinary income of $25,000; and

(2) Capital gain of $75,000.

(b) X itself has—

(1) Recognized built-in ordinary income of $40,000; and

(2) Recognized built-in capital loss of $90,000.

(ii) X's net recognized built-in gain for 1996 computed without partnership 1374 items is $40,000 and with partnership 1374 items is $65,000 ($40,000 + $25,000 = $65,000). Thus, X's partnership RBIG is $25,000 for the year except as limited under paragraph (i)(2)(i) of this section. Because X's RBIG limitation is $0, X's partnership RBIG of $25,000 is limited to $0 and X's net recognized built-in gain for the year is $40,000.

Example 6. RBIL limitation of $0. (i) Y is a C corporation that elects to become an S corporation on January 1, 1996. Y owns a 50 percent interest in partnership P with a RBIG limitation of $60,000 and a RBIL limitation of $0.

(a) In 1996, P's partnership 1374 items are—

(1) Ordinary income of $25,000; and

(2) Capital loss of $90,000.

(b) Y itself has—

(1) recognized built-in ordinary income of $40,000; and

(2) recognized built-in capital gain of $75,000.

(ii) Y's net recognized built-in gain for 1996 computed without partnership 1374 items is $115,000 ($40,000 + $75,000 = $115,000) and with partnership 1374 items is $65,000 ($40,000 + $25,000 = $65,000). Thus, Y's partnership RBIL is $50,000 for the year except as limited under paragraph (i)(2)(ii) of this section. Because Y's RBIL limitation is $0, Y's partnership RBIL of $50,000 is limited to $0 and Y's net recognized built-in gain is $115,000.

Example 7. Disposition of partnership interest. X is a C corporation that elects to become an S corporation on January 1, 1996. On that date, X owns a 50 percent interest in partnership P with a RBIG limitation of $200,000 and a RBIL limitation of $0. P owns (among other assets) Blackacre with a basis of $20,000 and a value of $140,000. In 1996, P sells Blackacre for $140,000 and recognizes a gain of $120,000 of which $60,000 is included in X's distributive share and treated as a partnership 1374 item. X's net recognized built-in gain for 1996 computed without partnership 1374 items is $95,000 and with partnership 1374 items is $155,000. Thus, X has a partnership RBIG of $60,000. In 1999, X sells its entire interest in P for $350,000 and recognizes a gain of $250,000. Under paragraph (i)(3) of this section, X's recognized built-in gain on the sale is limited by its RBIG limitation to $140,000 ($200,000 − $60,000 = $140,000).

Example 8. Section 704(c) case. Y is a C corporation that elects to become an S corporation on January 1, 1996. On that date, Y contributes Asset 1, 5-year property with a value of $40,000 and a basis of $0, and an unrelated party contributes $40,000 in cash, each for a 50 percent interest in partnership P. The partnership adopts the traditional method under § 1.704-3(b). If P sold Asset 1 for $40,000 immediately after it was contributed by Y, P's $40,000 gain would be allocated to Y under section 704(c). Instead, Asset 1 is sold by P in 1999 for $36,000 and P recognizes gain of $36,000 ($36,000 − $0 = $36,000) on the sale. However, because book depreciation of $8,000 per year has been taken on Asset 1 in 1996, 1997, and 1998, Y is allocated only $16,000 of P's $36,000 gain ($40,000 − (3 × $8,000) = ($16,000 − $0) = $16,000) under section 704(c). The remaining $20,000 of P's $36,000 gain ($36,000 − $16,000 = $20,000) is allocated 50 percent to each partner under section 704(b). Thus, a total of $26,000 ($16,000 + $10,000 = $26,000) of P's $36,000 gain is allocated to Y. However, under paragraph (i)(6) of this section, Y treats $36,000 as a partnership 1374 item on P's sale of Asset 1.

Reg. § 1.1374-4(i)(8)

Example 9. Disposition of distributed partnership asset. X is a C corporation that elects to become an S corporation on January 1, 1996. On that date, X owns a fifty percent interest in partnership P and P owns (among other assets) Blackacre with a basis of $20,000 and a value of $40,000. On January 1, 1998, P distributes Blackacre to X, when Blackacre has a basis of $20,000 and a value of $50,000. Under section 732(a)(1), X has a transferred basis of $20,000 in Blackacre. On January 1, 1999, X sells Blackacre for $60,000 and recognizes a gain of $40,000. Under paragraph (i)(7) of this section and section 1374(d)(3), X has recognized built-in gain from the sale of $20,000, the amount of built-in gain in Blackacre on the first day of the recognition period. [Reg. § 1.1374-4.]

☐ [T.D. 8579, 12-23-94.]

[Reg. § 1.1374-5]

§ 1.1374-5. Loss carryforwards.—(a) *In general.* The loss carryforwards allowed as deductions against net recognized built-in gain under section 1374(b)(2) are allowed only to the extent their use is allowed under the rules applying to C corporations. Any other loss carryforwards, such as charitable contribution carryforwards under section 170(d)(2), are not allowed as deductions against net recognized built-in gain.

(b) *Example.* The rules of this section are illustrated by the following example.

Example. Section 382 limitation. X is a C corporation that has an ownership change under section 382(g)(1) on January 1, 1994. On that date, X has a fair market value of $500,000, NOL carryforwards of $400,000, and a net unrealized built-in gain under section 382(h)(3)(A) of $0. Assume X's section 382 limitation under section 382(b)(1) is $40,000. X elects to become an S corporation on January 1, 1998. On that date, X has NOL carryforwards of $240,000 (having used $160,000 of its pre-change net operating losses in its 4 preceding taxable years) and a section 1374 net unrealized built-in gain of $250,000. In 1998, X has net recognized built-in gain of $100,000. X may use $40,000 of its NOL carryforwards as a deduction against its $100,000 net recognized built-in gain, because X's section 382 limitation is $40,000. [Reg. § 1.1374-5.]

☐ [T.D. 8579, 12-23-94.]

[Reg. § 1.1374-6]

§ 1.1374-6. Credits and credit carryforwards.—(a) *In general.* The credits and credit carryforwards allowed as credits against the section 1374 tax under section 1374(b)(3) are allowed only to the extent their use is allowed under the rules applying to C corporations. Any other credits or credit carryforwards, such as foreign tax credits under section 901, are not allowed as credits against the section 1374 tax.

(b) *Limitations.* The amount of business credit carryforwards and minimum tax credit allowed against the section 1374 tax are subject to the limitations described in section 38(c) and section 53(c), respectively, as modified by this paragraph. The tentative tax determined under paragraph (a)(3) of § 1.1374-1 is treated as the regular tax liability described in sections 38(c)(1) and 53(c)(1), and as the net income tax and net regular tax liability described in section 38(c)(1). The tentative minimum tax described in section 55(b) is determined using the rate of tax applicable to corporations and without regard to any alternative minimum tax foreign tax credit described in that section and by treating the net recognized built-in gain determined under § 1.1374-2, modified to take into account the adjustments of sections 56 and 58 applicable to corporations and the preferences of section 57, as the alternative minimum taxable income described in section 55(b)(2).

(c) *Examples.* The rules of this section are illustrated by the following examples.

Example 1. Business credit carryforward. X is a C corporation that elects to become an S corporation effective January 1, 1996. On that date, X has a $500,000 business credit carryforward from a C year and Asset #1 with a fair market value of $400,000, a basis for regular tax purposes of $95,000, and a basis for alternative minimum tax purposes of $150,000. In 1996, X has net recognized built-in gain of $305,000 from selling Asset #1 for $400,000. Thus, X's tentative tax under paragraph (a)(3) of § 1.1374-1 and regular tax liability under paragraph (b) of this section is $106,750 ($400,000 − $95,000 = $305,000 × .35 = $106,750, assuming a 35 percent tax rate). Also, X's tentative minimum tax determined under paragraph (b) of this section is $47,000 [$400,000 − $150,000 = $250,000 − $15,000 ($40,000 corporate exemption amount − $25,000 phase-out = $15,000) = $235,000 × .20 = $47,000, assuming a 20 percent tax rate]. Thus, the business credit limitation under section 38(c) is $59,750 [$106,750 − $47,000 (the greater of $47,000 or $20,438 (.25 × $81,750 ($106,750 − $25,000 = $81,750))) = $59,750]. As a result, X's section 1374 tax is $47,000 ($106,750 − $59,750 = $47,000) for 1996 and X has $440,250 ($500,000 − $59,750 = $440,250) of business credit carryforwards for succeeding taxable years.

Example 2. Minimum tax credit. Y is a C corporation that elects to become an S corporation effective January 1, 1996. On that date, Asset #1 has a fair market value of $5,000,000, a basis for regular tax purposes of $4,000,000, and a basis for alternative minimum tax purposes of $4,750,000. Y also has a minimum tax credit of $310,000 from 1995. Y has no other assets, no net operating or capital loss carryforwards, and no business credit carryforwards. In 1996, Y's only transaction is the sale of Asset #1 for $5,000,000. Therefore, Y has net recognized built-in gain in 1996 of $1,000,000 ($5,000,000 − $4,000,000 = $1,000,000) and a tentative tax under paragraph (a)(3) of § 1.1374-1 of $350,000 ($1,000,000 × .35 = $350,000, assuming a 35 percent tax rate). Also, Y's tentative minimum tax determined under paragraph (b) of this section is $47,000 [$5,000,000 − $4,750,000 = $250,000 − $15,000 ($40,000 corporate exemption amount − $25,000 phase-out = $15,000) = $235,000 × .20 = $47,000, assuming a 20 percent tax rate]. Thus, Y may use its minimum tax credit in the amount of $303,000 ($350,000 − $47,000 = $303,000) to offset its section 1374 tentative tax. As a result, Y's section 1374 tax is $47,000 ($350,000 − $303,000 = $47,000) in 1996 and Y has a minimum tax credit attributable to years for which Y was a C corporation of $7,000 ($310,000 − $303,000 = $7,000). [Reg. § 1.1374-6.]

☐ [T.D. 8579, 12-23-94.]

[Reg. § 1.1374-7]

§ 1.1374-7. Inventory.—(a) *Valuation.* The fair market value of the inventory of an S corporation on the first day of the recognition period equals the amount that a willing buyer would pay a willing seller for the inventory in a purchase of all the S corporation's assets by a buyer that expects to continue to operate the S corporation's business. For purposes of the preceding sentence, the buyer and seller are presumed not to be under any compulsion to buy or sell and to have reasonable knowledge of all relevant facts.

(b) *Identity of dispositions.* The inventory method used by an S corporation for tax purposes must be used to identify whether the inventory it disposes of during the recognition period is inventory it held on the first day of that period. Thus, a corporation using the LIFO method does not dispose of inventory it held on the first day of the recognition period unless the carrying value of its inventory for a taxable year during that period is less than the carrying value of its inventory on the first day of the recognition period (determined using the LIFO method as described in section 472). However, if a corporation changes its method of accounting for inventory (for example, from the FIFO method to the LIFO method or from the LIFO method to the FIFO method) with a principal purpose of avoiding the tax imposed under section 1374, it must use its former method to identify its dispositions of inventory. [Reg. § 1.1374-7.]

☐ [T.D. 8579, 12-23-94.]

[Reg. § 1.1374-8]

§ 1.1374-8. Section 1374(d)(8) transactions.—(a) *In general.* If any S corporation acquires any asset in a transaction in which the S corporation's basis in the asset is determined (in whole or in part) by reference to a C corporation's basis in the assets (or any other property) (a section 1374(d)(8) transaction), section 1374 applies to the net recognized built-in gain attributable to the assets acquired in any section 1374(d)(8) transaction.

(b) *Separate determination of tax.* For purposes of the tax imposed under section 1374(d)(8), a separate determination of tax is made with respect to the assets the S corporation acquires in one section 1374(d)(8) transaction from the assets the S corporation acquires in another section 1374(d)(8) transaction and from the assets the corporation held when it became an S corporation. Thus, an S corporation's section 1374 attributes when it became an S corporation may only be used to reduce the section 1374 tax imposed on dispositions of assets the S corporation held at that time. Similarly, an S corporation's section 1374 attributes acquired in a section 1374(d)(8) transaction may only be used to reduce a section 1374 tax imposed on dispositions of assets the S corporation acquired in the same transaction. If an S corporation makes QSub elections under section 1361(b)(3) for a tiered group of subsidiaries effective on the same day, see § 1.1361-4(b)(2).

(c) *Taxable income limitation.* For purposes of paragraph (a) of this section, an S corporation's taxable income limitation under § 1.1374-2(a)(2) for any taxable year is allocated between or among each of the S corporation's separate determinations of net recognized built-in gain for that year (determined without regard to the taxable income limitation) based on the ratio of each of those determinations to the sum of all of those determinations.

(d) *Examples.* The rules of this section are illustrated by the following examples.

Example 1. Separate determination of tax. (i) X is a C corporation that elected to become an S corporation effective January 1, 1986 (before section 1374 was amended in the Tax Reform Act of 1986). X has a net operating loss carryforward of $20,000 arising in 1985 when X was a C corporation. On January 1, 1996, Y (an unrelated C corporation) merges into X in a transaction to which section 368(a)(1)(A) applies. Y has no loss

Reg. § 1.1374-8(d)

carryforwards, credits, or credit carryforwards. The assets X acquired from Y are subject to tax under section 1374 and have a net unrealized built-in gain of $150,000.

(ii) In 1996, X has a pre-limitation amount of $50,000 on dispositions of assets acquired from Y and a taxable income limitation of $100,000 (because only one group of assets is subject to section 1374, there is no allocation of the taxable income limitation). As a result, X has a net recognized built-in gain on those assets of $50,000. X's $20,000 net operating loss carryforward may not be used as a deduction against its $50,000 net recognized built-in gain on the assets X acquired from Y. Therefore, X has a section 1374 tax of $17,500 ($50,000 × .35 = $17,500, assuming a 35 percent tax rate) for its 1996 taxable year.

Example 2. Allocation of taxable income limitation. (i) Y is a C corporation that elects to become an S corporation effective January 1, 1996. The assets Y holds when it becomes an S corporation have a net unrealized built-in gain of $5,000. Y has no loss carryforwards, credits, or credit carryforwards. On January 1, 1997, Z (an unrelated C corporation) merges into Y in a transaction to which section 368(a)(1)(A) applies. Z has no loss carryforwards, credits, or credit carryforwards. The assets Y acquired from Z are subject to tax under section 1374 and have a net unrealized built-in gain of $80,000.

(ii) In 1997, Y has a pre-limitation amount on the assets it held when it became an S corporation of $15,000, a pre-limitation amount on the assets Y acquired from Z of $15,000, and a taxable income limitation of $10,000. However, because the assets Y held on becoming an S corporation have a net unrealized built-in gain of $5,000, its net recognized built-in gain on those assets is limited to $5,000 before taking into account the taxable income limitation. Y's taxable income limitation of $10,000 is allocated between the assets Y held on becoming an S corporation and the assets Y acquired from Z for purposes of determining the net recognized built-in gain from each pool of assets. Thus, Y's net recognized built-in gain on the assets Y held on becoming an S corporation is $2,500 [$10,000 × ($5,000/$20,000) = $2,500]. Y's net recognized built-in gain on the assets Y acquired from Z is $7,500 [$10,000 × ($15,000/$20,000) = $7,500]. Therefore, Y has a section 1374 tax of $3,500 [($2,500 + $7,500) × .35 = $3,500, assuming a 35 percent tax rate] for its 1997 taxable year.

[Reg. § 1.1374-8.]

☐ [T.D. 8579, 12-23-94. Amended by T.D. 8869, 1-20-2000]

Reg. § 1.1374-9

[Reg. § 1.1374-9]

§ 1.1374-9. Anti-stuffing rule.—If a corporation acquires an asset before or during the recognition period with a principal purpose of avoiding the tax imposed under section 1374, the asset and any loss, deduction, loss carryforward, credit, or credit carryforward attributable to the asset is disregarded in determining the S corporation's pre-limitation amount, taxable income limitation, net unrealized built-in gain limitation, deductions against net recognized built-in gain, and credits against the section 1374 tax. [Reg. § 1.1374-9.]

☐ [T.D. 8579, 12-23-94.]

[Reg. § 1.1374-10]

§ 1.1374-10. Effective date and additional rules.—(a) In general. Sections 1.1374-1 through 1.1374-9 apply for taxable years ending on or after December 27, 1994, but only in cases where the S corporation's return for the taxable year is filed pursuant to an S election or a section 1374(d)(8) transaction occurring on or after December 27, 1994.

(b) Additional rules. This paragraph (b) provides rules applicable to certain S corporations, assets, or transactions to which §§ 1.1374-1 through 1.1374-9 do not apply.

(1) Certain transfers to partnerships. If a corporation transfers an asset to a partnership in a transaction to which section 721(a) applies and the transfer is made in contemplation of an S election or during the recognition period, section 1374 applies on a disposition of the asset by the partnership as if the S corporation had disposed of the asset itself. This paragraph (b)(1) applies as of the effective date of section 1374, unless the recognition period with respect to the contributed asset is pursuant to an S election or a section 1374(d)(8) transaction occurring on or after December 27, 1994.

(2) Certain inventory dispositions. For purposes of section 1374(d)(2)(A), the inventory method used by the taxpayer for tax purposes (FIFO, LIFO, etc.) must be used to identify whether goods disposed of following conversion to S corporation status were held by the corporation at the time of conversion. Thus, for example, a corporation using the LIFO inventory method will not be subject to the built-in gain tax with respect to sales of inventory except to the extent that a LIFO layer existing prior to the beginning of the first taxable year as an S corporation is invaded after the beginning of that year. This paragraph (b)(2) applies as of the effective date of section 1374, unless the recognition period with respect to the inventory is pursuant to an S election or a

section 1374(d)(8) transaction occurring on or after December 27, 1994.

(3) *Certain contributions of built-in loss assets.* If a built-in loss asset (that is, an asset with an adjusted tax basis in excess of its fair market value) is contributed to a corporation within 2 years before the earlier of the beginning of its first taxable year as an S corporation, or the filing of its S election, the loss inherent in the asset will not reduce net unrealized built-in gain, as defined in section 1374(d)(1), unless the taxpayer demonstrates a clear and substantial relationship between the contributed property and the conduct of the corporation's current or future business enterprises. This paragraph (b)(3) applies as of the effective date of section 1374, unless the recognition period with respect to the contributed asset is pursuant to an S election or a section 1374(d)(8) transaction occurring on or after December 27, 1994.

(4) *Certain installment sales*—(i) *In general.* If a taxpayer sells an asset either prior to or during the recognition period and recognizes income either during or after the recognition period from the sale under the installment method, the income will, when recognized, be taxed under section 1374 to the extent it would have been so taxed in prior taxable years if the selling corporation had made the election under section 453(d) not to report the income under the installment method. For purposes of determining the extent to which the income would have been subject to tax if the section 453(d) election had not been made, the taxable income limitation of section 1374(d)(2)(A)(ii) and the built-in gain carryover rule of section 1374(d)(2)(B) will be taken into account. This paragraph (b)(4) applies for installment sales occurring on or after March 26, 1990, and before December 27, 1994.

(ii) *Examples.* The rules of this paragraph (b)(4) are illustrated by the following examples.

Example 1. In year 1 of the recognition period under section 1374, a corporation realizes a gain of $100,000 on the sale of an asset with built-in gain. The corporation is to receive full payment for the asset in year 11. Because the corporation does not make an election under section 453(d), all $100,000 of the gain from the sale is reported under the installment method in year 11. If the corporation had made an election under section 453(d) with respect to the sale, the gain would have been recognized in year 1 and, taking into account the corporation's income and gains from other sources, application of the taxable income limitation of section 1374(d)(2)(A)(ii) and the built-in gain carryover rule of section 1374(d)(2)(B) would have resulted in $40,000 of the gain being subject to tax during the recognition period under section 1374. Therefore, $40,000 of the gain recognized in year 11 is subject to tax under section 1374.

Example 2. In year 1 of the recognition period under section 1374, a corporation realizes a gain of $100,000 on the sale of an asset with built-in gain. The corporation is to receive full payment for the asset in year 6. Because the corporation does not make an election under section 453(d), all $100,000 of the gain from the sale is reported under the installment method in year 6. If the corporation had made an election under section 453(d) with respect to the sale, the gain would have been recognized in year 1 and, taking into account the corporation's income and gains from other sources, application of the taxable income limitation of section 1374(d)(2)(A)(ii) and the built-in gain carryover rule of section 1374(d)(2)(B) would have resulted in all of the gain being subjected to tax under section 1374 in years 1 through 5. Therefore, notwithstanding that the taxable income limitation of section 1374(d)(2)(A)(ii) might otherwise limit the taxation of the gain recognized in year 6, the entire $100,000 of gain will be subject to tax under section 1374 when it is recognized in year 6.

[Reg. § 1.1374-10.]

☐ [T.D. 8579, 12-23-94.]

[Reg. § 1.1375-1]

§ 1.1375-1. **Tax imposed when passive investment income of corporation having subchapter C earnings and profits exceeds 25 percent of gross receipts.**—(a) *General rule.* For taxable years beginning after 1981, section 1375(a) imposes a tax on the income of certain S corporations that have passive investment income. In the case of a taxable year beginning during 1982, an electing small business corporation may elect to have the rules under this section not apply. See the regulations under section 1362 for rules on the election. For purposes of this section, the term "S corporation" shall include an electing small business corporation under prior law. This tax shall apply to an S corporation for a taxable year if the S corporation has—

(1) Subchapter C earnings and profits at the close of such taxable year, and

(2) Gross receipts more than 25 percent of which are passive investment income.

If the S corporation has no subchapter C earnings and profits at the close of the taxable year (because, for example, such earnings and profits were distributed in accordance with section 1368), the tax shall not be imposed even though the S corporation has passive investment income for the

Reg. § 1.1375-1(a)(2)

taxable year. If the tax is imposed, the tax shall be computed by multiplying the excess net passive income (as defined in paragraph (b) of this section) by the highest rate of tax specified in section 11(b).

(b) *Definitions*—(1) *Excess net passive income*—(i) *In general.* The term "excess net passive income" is defined in section 1375(b)(1), and can be expressed by the following formula:

$$ENPI = NPI \times \frac{PII - (.25 \times GR)}{PII}$$

Where:
ENPI = excess net passive income
NPI = net passive income
PII = passive investment income
GR = total gross receipts

(ii) *Limitation.* The amount of the excess net passive income for any taxable year shall not exceed the corporation's taxable income for the taxable year (determined in accordance with section 1374(d) and § 1.1374-1(d)).

(2) *Net passive income.* The term "net passive income" means—

(i) Passive investment income, reduced by

(ii) The deductions allowable under chapter 1 of the Internal Revenue Code of 1954 which are directly connected (within the meaning of (b)(3) of this section) with the production of such income (other than deductions allowable under section 172 and part VIII of subchapter B).

(3) *Directly connected*— (i) *In general.* For purposes of paragraph (b)(2)(ii) of this section to be directly connected with the production of income, an item of deduction must have proximate and primary relationship to the income. Expenses, depreciation, and similar items attributable solely to such income qualify for deduction.

(ii) *Allocation of deduction.* If an item of deduction is attributable (within the meaning of paragraph (b)(3)(i) of this section) in part to passive investment income and in part to income other than passive investment income, the deduction shall be allocated between the two types of items on a reasonable basis. The portion of any deduction so allocated to passive investment income shall be treated as proximately and primarily related to such income.

(4) *Other definitions.* The terms "subchapter C earnings and profits," "passive investment income," and "gross receipts" shall have the same meaning given these terms in section 1362(d)(3) and the regulations thereunder.

(c) *Special rules*—(1) *Disallowance of credits.* No credit is allowed under part IV of subchapter A of chapter 1 of the Code (other than section 34) against the tax imposed by section 1375(a) and this section.

(2) *Coordination with section 1374.* If any gain—

(i) Is taken into account in determining passive income for purposes of this section, and

(ii) Is taken into account under section 1374, the amount of such gain taken into account under section 1374(b) and § 1.1374-1(b)(1) and (2) in determining the amount of tax shall be reduced by the portion of the excess net passive income for the taxable year which is attributable (on a pro rata basis) to such gain. For purposes of the preceding sentence, the portion of excess net passive income for the taxable year which is attributable to such capital gain is equal to the amount determined by multiplying the excess net passive income by the following fraction:

$$NCG = \frac{E}{NPI}$$

Where:
NCG = net capital gain
NPI = net passive income
E = Expense attributable to net capital gain

(d) *Waiver of tax in certain cases*—(1) *In general.* If an S corporation establishes to the satisfaction of the Commissioner that—

(i) It determined in good faith that it had no subchapter C earnings and profits at the close of the taxable year, and

(ii) During a reasonable period of time after it was determined that it did have subchapter C earnings and profits at the close of such taxable year such earnings and profits were distributed,

the Commissioner may waive the tax imposed by section 1375 for such taxable year. The S corporation has the burden of establishing that under the relevant facts and circumstances the Commissioner should waive the tax. For example, if an S corporation establishes that in good faith and using due diligence it determined that it had no subchapter C earnings and profits at the close of a taxable year, but it was later determined on audit that it did have subchapter C earnings and profits at the close of such taxable year, and if the corporation establishes that it distributed such earnings and profits within a reasonable time after the audit, it may be appropriate for the Commissioner to waive the tax on passive income for such taxable year.

(2) *Corporation's request for a waiver.* A request for waiver of the tax imposed by section 1375 shall be made in writing to the district director request and shall contain all relevant

Reg. § 1.1375-1(b)(1)

S Corporations and Their Shareholders

See p. 20,601 for regulations not amended to reflect law changes

facts to establish that the requirements of paragraph (d)(1) of this section are met. Such request shall contain a description of how and on what date the S corporation in good faith and using due diligence determined that it had no subchapter C earnings and profits at the close of the taxable year, a description of how and on what date it was determined that the S corporation had subshapter C earnings and profits at the close of the year and a description (including dates) of any steps taken to distribute such earnings and profits. If the earnings and profits have not yet been distributed, the request shall contain a timetable for distribution and an explanation of why such timetable is reasonable. On the date the waiver is to become effective, all subchapter C earnings and profits must have been distributed.

(e) *Reduction in pass-thru for tax imposed on excess net passive income.* See section 1366(f)(3) for a special rule reducing each item of the corporation's passive investment income for purposes of section 1366(a) if a tax is imposed on the corporation under section 1375.

(f) *Examples.* The following examples illustrate the principles of this section:

Example (1). Assume Corporation M, an S corporation, has for its taxable year total gross receipts of $200,000, passive investment income of $100,000, $60,000 of which is interest income, and expenses directly connected with the production of such interest income in the amount of $10,000. Assume also that at the end of the taxable year Corporation M has subchapter C earnings and profits. Since more than 25 percent of Corporation M's total gross receipts are passive investment income, and since Corporation M has subchapter C earnings and profits at the end of the taxable year, Corporation M will be subject to the tax imposed by section 1375. The amount of excess net passive investment income is $45,000 ($90,000 × ($50,000/$100,000)). Assume that the other $40,000 of passive investment income is attributable to net capital gain and that there are no expenses directly connected with such gain. Under these facts, $20,000 of the excess net passive income is attributable to the net capital gain ($45,000 × ($40,000/$90,000)). Accordingly, the amount of gain taken into account under section 1374(b)(1) and the taxable income of Corporation M under section 1374(b)(2) shall be reduced by $20,000.

Example (2). Assume an S corporation with subchapter C earnings and profits has tax-exempt income of $400, its only passive income, gross receipts of $1,000 and taxable income of $250 and there are no expenses associated with the tax-exempt income. The corporation's excess net passive income for the taxable year would total $150 (400 × ((400 − 250)/400)). This amount is subject to the tax imposed by section 1375, notwithstanding that such amount is otherwise tax-exempt income. [Reg. § 1.1375-1.]

☐ [T.D. 8104, 9-25-86. Amended by T.D. 8419, 5-28-92.]

[Reg. § 1.1377-0]

§ 1.1377-0. **Table of contents.**—The following table of contents is provided to facilitate the use of § § 1.1377-1 through 1.1377-3:

§ 1.1377-1 *Pro rata share.*

  (a) Computation of pro rata shares.

    (1) In general.

    (2) Special rules.

      (i) Days on which stock has not been issued.

      (ii) Determining shareholder for day of stock disposition.

  (b) Election to terminate year.

    (1) In general.

    (2) Affected shareholders.

    (3) Effect of the terminating election.

      (i) In general.

      (ii) Due date of S corporation return.

      (iii) Taxable year of inclusion by shareholder.

      (iv) S Corporation that is a partner in a partnership.

    (4) Determination of whether an S shareholder's entire interest has terminated.

    (5) Time and manner of making a terminating election.

      (i) In general.

      (ii) Affected shareholders required to consent.

      (iii) More than one terminating election.

  (c) Examples.

§ 1.1377-2 *Post-termination transition period.*

  (a) In general.

  (b) Special rules for post-termination transition period.

  (c) Determination defined.

  (d) Date a determination becomes effective.

    (1) Determination under section 1313(a).

    (2) Written agreement.

    (3) Implied agreement.

§ 1.1377-3 *Effective date.*

[Reg. § 1.1377-0.]

☐ [T.D. 8696, 12-20-96.]

[Reg. § 1.1377-1]

§ 1.1377-1. Pro rata share.—(a) *Computation of pro rata shares*—(1) *In general.* For purposes of subchapter S of chapter 1 of the Internal Revenue Code and this section, each shareholder's pro rata share of any S corporation item described in section 1366(a) for any taxable year is the sum of the amounts determined with respect to the shareholder by assigning an equal portion of the item to each day of the S corporation's taxable year, and then dividing that portion pro rata among the shares outstanding on that day. See paragraph (b) of this section for rules pertaining to the computation of each shareholder's pro rata share when an election is made under section 1377(a)(2) to treat the taxable year of an S corporation as if it consisted of two taxable years in the case of a termination of a shareholder's entire interest in the corporation.

(2) *Special rules*—(i) *Days on which stock has not been issued.* Solely for purposes of determining a shareholder's pro rata share of an item for a taxable year under section 1377(a) and this section, the beneficial owners of the corporation are treated as the shareholders of the corporation for any day on which the corporation has not issued any stock.

(ii) *Determining shareholder for day of stock disposition.* A shareholder who disposes of stock in an S corporation is treated as the shareholder for the day of the disposition. A shareholder who dies is treated as the shareholder for the day of the shareholder's death.

(b) *Election to terminate year*—(1) *In general.* If a shareholder's entire interest in an S corporation is terminated during the S corporation's taxable year and the corporation and all affected shareholders agree, the S corporation may elect under section 1377(a)(2) and this paragraph (b) (terminating election) to apply paragraph (a) of this section to the affected shareholders as if the corporation's taxable year consisted of two separate taxable years, the first of which ends at the close of the day on which the shareholder's entire interest in the S corporation is terminated. If the event resulting in the termination of the shareholder's entire interest also constitutes a qualifying disposition as described in § 1.1368-1(g)(2)(i), the election under § 1.1368-1(g)(2) cannot be made. An S corporation may not make a terminating election if the cessation of a shareholder's interest occurs in a transaction that results in a termination under section 1362(d)(2) of the corporation's election to be an S corporation. (See section 1362(e)(3) for an election to have items assigned to each short taxable year under normal tax accounting rules in the case of a termination of a corporation's election to be an S corporation.) A terminating election is irrevocable and is effective only for the terminating event for which it is made.

(2) *Affected shareholders.* For purposes of the terminating election under section 1377(a)(2) and paragraph (b) of this section, the term *affected shareholders* means the shareholder whose interest is terminated and all shareholders to whom such shareholder has transferred shares during the taxable year. If such shareholder has transferred shares to the corporation, the term *affected shareholders* includes all persons who are shareholders during the taxable year.

(3) *Effect of the terminating election*—(i) *In general.* An S corporation that makes a terminating election for a taxable year must treat the taxable year as separate taxable years for all affected shareholders for purposes of allocating items of income (including tax-exempt income), loss, deduction, and credit; making adjustments to the accumulated adjustments account, earnings and profits, and basis; and determining the tax effect of a distribution. An S corporation that makes a terminating election must assign items of income (including tax-exempt income), loss, deduction, and credit to each deemed separate taxable year using its normal method of accounting as determined under section 446(a).

(ii) *Due date of S corporation return.* A terminating election does not affect the due date of the S corporation's return required to be filed under section 6037(a) for a taxable year (determined without regard to a terminating election).

(iii) *Taxable year of inclusion by shareholder.* A terminating election does not affect the taxable year in which an affected shareholder must take into account the affected shareholder's pro rata share of the S corporation's items of income, loss, deduction, and credit.

(iv) *S corporation that is a partner in a partnership.* A terminating election by an S corporation that is a partner in a partnership is treated as a sale or exchange of the corporation's entire interest in the partnership for purposes of section 706(c) (relating to closing the partnership taxable year), if the taxable year of the partnership ends after the shareholder's interest is terminated and within the taxable year of the S corporation (determined without regard to any terminating election) for which the terminating election is made.

(4) *Determination of whether an S shareholder's entire interest has terminated.* For purposes of the terminating election under section 1377(a)(2) and paragraph (b) of this section, a shareholder's entire interest in an S corporation is terminated on the occurrence of any event

Reg. § 1.1377-1(a)(1)

through which a shareholder's entire stock ownership in the S corporation ceases, including a sale, exchange, or other disposition of all of the stock held by the shareholder; a gift under section 102(a) of all the shareholder's stock; a spousal transfer under section 1041(a) of all the shareholder's stock; a redemption, as defined in section 317(b), of all the shareholder's stock, regardless of the tax treatment of the redemption under section 302; and the death of the shareholder. A shareholder's entire interest in an S corporation is not terminated if the shareholder retains ownership of any stock (including an interest treated as stock under § 1.1361-1(1)) that would result in the shareholder continuing to be considered a shareholder of the corporation for purposes of section 1362(a)(2). Thus, in determining whether a shareholder's entire interest in an S corporation has been terminated, any interest held by the shareholder as a creditor, employee, director, or in any other non-shareholder capacity is disregarded.

(5) *Time and manner of making a terminating election*—(i) *In general.* An S corporation makes a terminating election by attaching a statement to its timely filed original or amended return required to be filed under section 6037(a) (that is, a Form 1120S) for the taxable year during which a shareholder's entire interest is terminated. A single election statement may be filed by the S corporation for all terminating elections for the taxable year. The election statement must include—

(A) A declaration by the S corporation that it is electing under section 1377(a)(2) and this paragraph to treat the taxable year as if it consisted of two separate taxable years;

(B) Information setting forth when and how the shareholder's entire interest was terminated (for example, a sale or gift);

(C) The signature on behalf of the S corporation of an authorized officer of the corporation under penalties of perjury; and

(D) A statement by the corporation that the corporation and each affected shareholder consent to the S corporation making the terminating election.

(ii) *Affected shareholders required to consent.* For purposes of paragraph (b)(5)(i)(D) of this section, a shareholder of the S corporation for the taxable year is a shareholder as described in section 1362(a)(2). For example, the person who under § 1.1362-6(b)(2) must consent to a corporation's S election in certain special cases is the person who must consent to the terminating election. In addition, an executor or administrator of the estate of a deceased affected shareholder may consent to the terminating election on behalf of the deceased affected shareholder.

(iii) *More than one terminating election.* A shareholder whose entire interest in an S corporation is terminated in an event for which a terminating election was made is not required to consent to a terminating election made with respect to a subsequent termination within the same taxable year unless the shareholder is an affected shareholder with respect to the subsequent termination.

(c) *Examples.* The following examples illustrate the provisions of this section:

Example 1. Shareholder's pro rata share in the case of a partial disposition of stock. (i) On January 6, 1997, X incorporates as a calendar year corporation, issues 100 shares of common stock to each of A and B, and files an election to be an S corporation for its 1997 taxable year. On July 24, 1997, B sells 50 shares of X stock to C. Thus, in 1997, A owned 50 percent of the outstanding shares of X on each day of X's 1997 taxable year, B owned 50 percent on each day from January 6, 1997, to July 24, 1997 (200 days), and 25 percent from July 25, 1997, to December 31, 1997 (160 days), and C owned 25 percent from July 25, 1997, to December 31, 1997 (160 days).

(ii) Because B's entire interest in X is not terminated when B sells 50 shares to C on July 24, 1997, X cannot make a terminating election under section 1377(a)(2) and paragraph (b) of this section for B's sale of 50 shares to C. Although B's sale of 50 shares to C is a qualifying disposition under § 1.1368-1(g)(2)(i), X does not make an election to terminate its taxable year under § 1.1368-1(g)(2). During its 1997 taxable year, X has nonseparately computed income of $720,000.

(iii) For each day in X's 1997 taxable year, A's daily pro rata share of X's nonseparately computed income is $1,000 ($720,000/360 days × 50%). Thus, A's pro rata share of X's nonseparately computed income for 1997 is $360,000 ($1,000 × 360 days). B's daily pro rata share of X's nonseparately computed income is $1,000 ($720,000/360 × 50%) for the first 200 days of X's 1997 taxable year, and $500 ($720,000/360 × 25%) for the following 160 days in 1997. Thus, B's pro rata share of X's nonseparately computed income for 1997 is $280,000 (($1,000 × 200 days) + ($500 × 160 days)). C's daily pro rata share of X's nonseparately computed income is $500 ($720,000/360 × 25%) for 160 days in 1997. Thus, C's pro rata share of X's nonseparately computed income for 1997 is $80,000 ($500 × 160 days).

Example 2. Shareholder's pro rata share when an S corporation makes a terminating election under section 1377(a)(2). (i) On January 6, 1997, X incorporates as a calendar year corporation, issues 100 shares of common stock to each of A and B, and files an election to be an S corporation for its 1997 taxable year. On July 24, 1997, B sells B's entire 100 shares of X stock to C. With the consent of B and C, X makes an election under section 1377(a)(2) and paragraph (b) of this section for the termination of B's entire interest arising from B's sale of 100 shares to C. As a result of the election, the pro rata shares of B and C are determined as if X's taxable year consisted of two separate taxable years, the first of which ends on July 24, 1997, the date B's entire interest in X terminates. Because A is not an affected shareholder as defined by section 1377(a)(2)(B) and paragraph (b)(2) of this section, the treatment as separate taxable years does not apply to A.

(ii) During its 1997 taxable year, X has nonseparately computed income of $720,000. Under X's normal method of accounting, $200,000 of the $720,000 of nonseparately computed income is allocable to the period of January 6, 1997, through July 24, 1997 (the first deemed taxable year), and the remaining $520,000 is allocable to the period of July 25, 1997, through December 31, 1997 (the second deemed taxable year).

(iii) B's pro rata share of the $200,000 of nonseparately computed income for the first deemed taxable year is determined by assigning the $200,000 of nonseparately computed income to each day of the first deemed taxable year ($200,000/200 days = $1,000 per day). Because B held 50% of X's authorized and issued shares on each day of the first deemed taxable year, B's daily pro rata share for each day of the first deemed taxable year is $500 ($1,000 per day × 50%). Thus, B's pro rata share of the $200,000 of nonseparately computed income for the first deemed taxable year is $100,000 ($500 per day × 200 days). B must report this amount for B's taxable year with or within which X's full taxable year ends (December 31, 1997).

(iv) C's pro rata share of the $520,000 of nonseparately computed income for the second deemed taxable year is determined by assigning the $520,000 of nonseparately computed income to each day of the second deemed taxable year ($520,000/160 days = $3,250 per day). Because C held 50% of X's authorized and issued shares on each day of the second deemed taxable year, C's daily pro rata shares for each day of the second deemed taxable year is $1,625 ($3,250 per day × 50%). Therefore, C's pro rata share of the $520,000 of nonseparately computed income is $260,000 ($1,625 per day × 160 days). C must

report this amount for C's taxable year with or within which X's full taxable year ends (December 31, 1997).

[Reg. § 1.1377-1.]

☐ [*T.D.* 8696, 12-20-96.]

[Reg. § 1.1377-2]

§ 1.1377-2. Post-termination transition period.—(a) *In general.* For purposes of subchapter S of chapter 1 of the Internal Revenue Code (Code) and this section, the term *post-termination transition period* means—

(1) The period beginning on the day after the last day of the corporation's last taxable year as an S corporation and ending on the later of—

(i) The day which is 1 year after such last day; or

(ii) The due date for filing the return for the last taxable year as an S corporation (including extensions);

(2) The 120-day period beginning on the date of any determination pursuant to an audit of the taxpayer which follows the termination of the corporation's election and which adjusts a subchapter S item of income, loss, or deduction of the corporation arising during the S period (as defined in section 1368(e)(2)); and

(3) The 120-day period beginning on the date of a determination that the corporation's election under section 1362(a) had terminated for a previous taxable year.

(b) *Special rules for post-termination transition period.* Pursuant to section 1377(b)(1) and paragraph (a)(1) of this section, a post-termination transition period arises the day after the last day that an S corporation was in existence if a C corporation acquires the assets of the S corporation in a transaction to which section 381(a)(2) applies. However, if an S corporation acquires the assets of another S corporation in a transaction to which section 381(a)(2) applies, a post-termination transition period does not arise. (See § 1.1368-2(d)(2) for the treatment of the acquisition of the assets of an S corporation by another S corporation in a transaction to which section 381(a)(2) applies.) The special treatment under section 1371(e)(1) of distributions of money by a corporation with respect to its stock during the post-termination transition period is available only to those shareholders who were shareholders in the S corporation at the time of the termination.

(c) *Determination defined.* For purposes of section 1377(b)(1) and paragraph (a) of this section, the term *determination* means—

S Corporations and Their Shareholders

See p. 20,601 for regulations not amended to reflect law changes

(1) A determination as defined in section 1313(a);

(2) A written agreement between the corporation and the Commissioner (including a statement acknowledging that the corporation's election to be an S corporation terminated under section 1362(d)) that the corporation failed to qualify as an S corporation;

(3) For a corporation subject to the audit and assessment provisions of subchapter C of chapter 63 of subtitle A of the Code, the expiration of the period specified in section 6226 for filing a petition for readjustment of a final S corporation administrative adjustment finding that the corporation failed to qualify as an S corporation, provided that no petition was timely filed before the expiration of the period; and

(4) For a corporation not subject to the audit and assessment provisions of subchapter C of chapter 63 of subtitle A of the Code, the expiration of the period for filing a petition under section 6213 for the shareholder's taxable year for which the Commissioner has made a finding that the corporation failed to qualify as an S corporation, provided that no petition was timely filed before the expiration of the period.

(d) *Date a determination becomes effective*— (1) *Determination under section 1313(a).* A determination under paragraph (c)(1) of this section becomes effective on the date prescribed in section 1313 and the regulations thereunder.

(2) *Written agreement.* A determination under paragraph (c)(2) of this section becomes effective when it is signed by the district director having jurisdiction over the corporation (or by another Service official to whom authority to sign the agreement is delegated) and by an officer of the corporation authorized to sign on its behalf. Neither the request for a written agreement nor the terms of the written agreement suspend the running of any statute of limitations.

(3) *Implied agreement.* A determination under paragraph (c)(3) or (4) of this section becomes effective on the day after the date of expiration of the period specified under section 6226 or 6213, respectively. [Reg. § 1.1377-2.]

☐ [T.D. 8696, 12-20-96.]

[Reg. § 1.1377-3]

§ 1.1377-3. Effective date.—Sections 1.1377-1 and 1.1377-2 apply to taxable years of an S corporation beginning after December 31, 1996. [Reg. § 1.1377-3.]

☐ [T.D. 8696, 12-20-96.]

[Reg. § 18.1378-1]

§ 18.1378-1. Taxable year of S corporation (Temporary).—(a) *In general.* No corporation may make an election to be an S corporation for any taxable year unless the taxable year is a permitted year. In addition, an S corporation shall not change its taxable year to any taxable year other than a permitted year. A permitted year is a taxable year ending on December 31 or is any other taxable year for which the corporation establishes a business purpose (within the meaning of § 1.442-1(b)(1)) to the satisfaction of the Commissioner.

(b) *Corporations qualifying for automatic change of taxable year to a taxable year ending December 31 and corporations adopting a taxable year ending December 31*—(1) *Qualification for automatic change.* Notwithstanding section 442 (relating to change of taxable year) and the regulations thereunder, a corporation may automatically change its taxable year to a taxable year ending on December 31 to comply with the permitted year requirement if all of its principal shareholders have taxable years ending on December 31, or if all of its principal shareholders concurrently change to such taxable year. A shareholder may not change his or her taxable year without securing prior approval from the Commissioner. See section 442 and the regulations thereunder. For purposes of this paragraph, a principal shareholder is a shareholder having 5% or more of the issued and outstanding stock of the corporation. See paragraph (d) of this section in the case where a corporation does not qualify under this subparagraph for an automatic change of its taxable year to a taxable year ending on December 31.

(2) *Effect of filing an election*—(i) *General rule.* The filing of an election to be an S corporation by a corporation that has, prior to making the election, adopted a taxable year ending other than on December 31, and that qualifies under paragraph (b)(1) of this section for an automatic change of its taxable year to a taxable year ending on December 31, shall constitute such automatic change for the first taxable year for which the election is effective. The filing of an election to be an S corporation by a corporation that has not, prior to making the election, adopted a taxable year shall constitute the adoption of a taxable year (or, if the corporation qualifies under paragraph (b)(1) of this section for the automatic change, the change to a taxable year) ending on December 31 for the first taxable year for which the election is effective. Where the taxable year has been changed pursuant to this subdivision and paragraph (b)(1) of this section, the first taxable

Reg. § 18.1378-1(b)(2)

year for which the election shall be effective shall commence on the first day of the first taxable year for which the election would have been effective if the taxable year had not been changed and shall end on December 31 of that taxable year. See § 1.1362-6(b)(2)(ii) of this chapter for the time within which to make an election to be an S corporation.

(ii) *Request to retain (or adopt) a taxable year ending other than December 31.* A request to retain (or adopt) a taxable year ending other than on December 31 by a corporation subject to subdivision (i) of this subparagraph shall (except as provided in subparagraph (3)(ii) of this paragraph and in paragraph (c) of this section) be made on Form 2553 when the election to be an S corporation is filed. See § 1.1362-6(b)(2)(i) of this chapter for the manner of making an election to be an S corporation. If such corporation receives permission to retain (or adopt) a taxable year ending other than on December 31, the election shall be effective and the provisions of subdivision (i) of this subparagraph shall be inapplicable. Denial of the request shall render the election ineffective unless—

(A) The request is accompanied by another request in which the corporation states that, in the event the request to retain (or adopt) a taxable year ending other than on December 31 is denied, it chooses to be governed by the provisions of subdivision (i) of this subparagraph, or

(B) The Commissioner waives the requirement to file the additional request described in subdivision (ii)(A) of this subparagraph and permits the corporation to be governed by the provisions of subdivision (i) of this subparagraph.

(c) [Reserved.]

(d) *Elections by corporations not qualifying for automatic change.* An election to be an S corporation made after October 19, 1982, by a corporation that has a taxable year ending other than on December 31, and that does not qualify under paragraph (b)(1) of this section for an automatic change of its taxable year to a taxable year ending on December 31, shall be ineffective unless the corporation has first secured a permitted year. At the request of a corporation wishing to secure a permitted year, the Commissioner shall make a determination that—

(1) The corporation's taxable year is a permitted year, or

(2) The corporation may, under § 1.442-1(b)(1), change its taxable year to a taxable year ending on December 31, or

(3) The corporation may, under § 1.442-1(b)(1), change its taxable year to a taxable year ending other than on December 31, which taxable year shall be a permitted year. [Temporary Reg. § 18.1378-1.]

☐ [*T.D. 7872, 1-21-83. Amended by T.D. 8123, 2-4-87 and by T.D. 8600, 7-20-95.*]

[Reg. § 18.1379-1]

§ 18.1379-1. **Transitional rules on enactment (Temporary).**—(a) *Prior elections.* Any election that was made under section 1372(a) (as in effect before the enactment of the Subchapter S Revision Act of 1982), and that is still in effect as of the first day of a taxable year beginning in 1983, shall be treated as being an election made under section 1362(a). In addition, any election that was made under section 1371(g)(2) (as in effect before the enactment of that Act), and that is still in effect as of the first day of a taxable year beginning in 1983, shall be treated as being an election made under section 1362(d)(2) [1361(d)(2)].

(b) *Prior terminations.* For purposes of section 1362(g), any termination under section 1372(e) (as in effect before the enactment of the Subchapter S Revision Act of 1982) shall not be taken into account.

(c) *Time and manner of making an election under section 6(c)(3)(B) of the Subchapter S Revision Act of 1982.* In the case of a qualified oil corporation (as defined in section 6(c)(3)(B) of the Subchapter S Revision Act of 1982), the corporation may elect under that section of the Act to have the amendments made by the Act not apply and to have subchapter S (as in effect on July 1, 1982), chapter 1 of the Internal Revenue Code of 1954 apply. The election shall be made by the corporation by filing a statement that—

(1) Contains the name, address, and taxpayer identification number of the corporation and of each shareholder,

(2) Identifies the election as an election under section 6(c)(3)(B) of the Subchapter S Revision Act of 1982, and

(3) Provides all information necessary in the judgment of the district director to show that the corporation meets the requirements (other than the requirement of making this election) of a qualified oil corporation.

The statement shall be signed by any person authorized to sign the return required to be filed under section 6037 and by each person who is or was a shareholder in the corporation at any time during the taxable year beginning in 1983 and shall be filed with the return for that taxable year. [Temporary Reg. § 18.1379-1.]

☐ [*T.D. 7872, 1-21-83.*]

Reg. § 18.1379-1(a)

Cooperatives

[Reg. § 18.1379-2]

§ 18.1379-2. **Special rules for all elections, consents, and refusals (Temporary).**—(a) *Additional information required.* If later regulations issued under the section of the Code or of the Subchapter S Revision Act of 1982 under which the election, consent, or refusal was made require the furnishing of information in addition to that which was furnished with the statement of election, consent, or refusal as provided by Part 18 of this Title, and if an office of the Internal Revenue Service requests the taxpayer to provide the additional information, the taxpayer shall furnish the additional information in a statement filed with that office of the Internal Revenue Service within 60 days after the date on which the request is made. This statement shall also—

(1) Contain the name, address, and taxpayer identification number of each party identified in connection with the election, consent, or refusal,

(2) Identify the election, consent, or refusal by reference to the section of the Code or Act under which the election, consent, or refusal was made, and

(3) Specify the scope of the election, consent, or refusal.

If the additional information is not provided within 60 days after the date on which the request is made, the election, consent, or refusal may, at the discretion of the Commissioner, be held invalid.

(b) *State law incorporator.* For purposes of any election, consent, or refusal provided in Part 18 of this Title, any person who is considered to be a shareholder for state law purposes solely by virtue of his or her status as an incorporator shall not be treated as a shareholder. [Temporary Reg. § 18.1379-2.]

☐ [T.D. 7872, 1-21-83.]

COOPERATIVES AND THEIR PATRONS

Cooperatives

[Reg. § 1.1381-1]

§ 1.1381-1. **Organizations to which part applies.**—(a) *In general.* Except as provided in paragraph (b) of this section, part I, subchapter T, chapter 1 of the Code, applies to any corporation operating on a cooperative basis and allocating amounts to patrons on the basis of the business done with or for such patrons.

(b) *Exceptions.* Part I of such subchapter T does not apply to—

(1) Any organization which is exempt from income taxes under chapter 1 of the Code (other than an exempt farmers' cooperative described in section 521);

(2) Any organization which is subject to the provisions of part II (section 591 and following), subchapter H, chapter 1 of the Code (relating to mutual savings banks, etc.);

(3) Any organization which is subject to the provisions of subchapter L (section 801 and following), chapter 1 of the Code (relating to insurance companies); or

(4) Any organization which is engaged in generating, transmitting, or otherwise furnishing electric energy, or which provides telephone service, to persons in rural areas. The terms "rural areas" and "telephone service" shall have the meaning assigned to them in section 5 of the Rural Electrification Act of 1936, as amended (7 U.S.C. 924). [Reg. § 1.1381-1.]

☐ [T.D. 6643, 4-1-63.]

[Reg. § 1.1381-2]

§ 1.1381-2. **Tax on certain farmers' cooperatives.**—(a) *In general.* (1) For taxable years beginning after December 31, 1962, farmers', fruit growers', or like associations, organized and operated in compliance with the requirements of section 521 and § 1.521-1, shall be subject to the taxes imposed by section 11 or section 1201. Although such associations are subject to both normal tax and surtax, as in the case of corporations generally, certain special deductions are provided for them in section 1382(c) and § 1.1382-3. For the purpose of any law which refers to organizations exempt from income taxes such an association shall, however, be considered as an organization exempt under section 501. Thus, the provisions of section 243, providing a credit for dividends received from a domestic corporation subject to taxation, are not applicable to dividends received from a cooperative association organized and operated in compliance with the requirements of section 521 and § 1.521-1. The provisions of section 1501, relating to consolidated returns, are likewise not applicable.

(2) Rules governing the manner in which amounts paid as patronage dividends are allowable as deductions in computing the taxable income of such an association are set forth in section 1382(b) and § 1.1382-2. For the tax treatment, as to patrons, of amounts received during the taxable year as patronage dividends, see section 1385 and the regulations thereunder.

Reg. § 1.1381-2(a)(2)

(b) *Cross references.* For tax treatment of exempt cooperative associations for taxable years beginning before January 1, 1963, or for taxable years beginning after December 31, 1962, with respect to payments attributable to patronage occurring during taxable years beginning before January 1, 1963, see section 522 and the regulations thereunder. For requirements of annual returns by such associations, see sections 6012 and 6072(d) and paragraph (f) of § 1.6012-2. [Reg. § 1.1381-2.]

☐ [*T.D.* 6643, 4-1-63.]

[Reg. § 1.1382-1]

§ 1.1382-1. **Taxable income of cooperatives; gross income.**—(a) *Introduction.* Section 1382(b) provides that the amount of certain patronage dividends (and amounts paid in redemption of nonqualified written notices of allocation) shall not be taken into account by a cooperative organization in determining its taxable income. Such section also provides that, for purposes of the Internal Revenue Code, an amount not taken into account is to be treated in the same manner as an item of gross income and as a deduction therefrom. Therefore, such an amount is treated as a deduction for purposes of applying the Internal Revenue Code and the regulations thereunder and, for simplicity, is referred to as a deduction in the regulations under such Code. However, this should not be regarded as a determination of the character of the amount for other purposes.

(b) *Computation of gross income.* Any cooperative organization to which part I, subchapter T, chapter 1 of the Code, applies shall not, for any purpose under the Code, exclude from its gross income (as a reduction in gross receipts, an increase in cost of goods sold, or otherwise) the amount of any allocation or distribution to a patron out of the net earnings of such organization with respect to patronage occurring during a taxable year beginning after December 31, 1962. See, however, section 1382(b) and § 1.1382-2 for deductions for certain amounts paid to patrons out of net earnings. [Reg. § 1.1382-1.]

☐ [*T.D.* 6643, 4-1-63.]

[Reg. § 1.1382-2]

§ 1.1382-2. **Taxable income of cooperatives; treatment of patronage dividends.**—(a) *In general.* (1) In determining the taxable income of any cooperative organization to which part I, subchapter T, chapter 1 of the Code, applies, there shall be allowed as deductions from gross income, in addition to the other deductions allowable under chapter 1 of the Code, the deductions with respect to patronage dividends provided in section 1382(b) and paragraphs (b) and (c) of this section.

(2) For the definition of terms used in this section see section 1388 and § 1.1388-1; to determine the payment period for a taxable year, see section 1382(d) and § 1.1382-4.

(b) *Deduction for patronage dividends*—(1) *In general.* In the case of a taxable year beginning after December 31, 1962, there is allowed as a deduction from the gross income of any cooperative organization to which part I of subchapter T applies, amounts paid to patrons during the payment period for the taxable year as patronage dividends with respect to patronage occurring during such taxable year, but only to the extent that such amounts are paid in money, qualified written notices of allocation, or other property (other than nonqualified written notices of allocation). See section 1382(e) and (f) and §§ 1.1382-5 and 1.1382-6 for special rules relating to the time when patronage is deemed to occur where products are marketed under a pooling arrangement or where earnings are includible in the gross income of the cooperative organization for a taxable year after the year in which the patronage occurred. For purposes of this paragraph, a written notice of allocation is considered paid when it is issued to the patron. A patronage dividend shall be treated as paid in money during the payment period for the taxable year to the extent it is paid by a qualified check which is issued during the payment period for such taxable year and endorsed and cashed on or before the ninetieth day after the close of such payment period. In determining the amount paid which is allowable as a deduction under this paragraph, property (other than written notices of allocation) shall be taken into account at its fair market value when paid, and a qualified written notice of allocation shall be taken into account at its stated dollar amount.

(2) *Special rule for certain taxable years.* No deduction is allowed under this section for amounts paid during taxable years beginning before January 1, 1963, or for amounts paid during taxable years beginning after December 31, 1962, with respect to patronage occurring during taxable years beginning before January 1, 1963. With respect to such amounts, the Internal Revenue Code of 1954 (including section 522 and the regulations thereunder) shall be applicable without regard to subchapter T.

(c) *Deduction for amounts paid in redemption of certain nonqualified written notices of allocation.* In the case of a taxable year beginning after December 31, 1962, there is allowed as a deduction from the gross income of a cooperative organization to which part I of subchapter T applies, amounts paid by such organization during the payment period for such taxable year in redemp-

Reg. § 1.1382-1(a)

tion of a nonqualified written notice of allocation which was previously paid as a patronage dividend during the payment period for the taxable year during which the patronage occurred, but only to the extent such amounts (1) are paid in money or other property (other than written notices of allocation) and (2) do not exceed the stated dollar amount of such written notice of allocation. No deduction shall be allowed under this paragraph, however, for amounts paid in redemption of nonqualified written notices of allocation which were paid with respect to patronage occurring during a taxable year beginning before January 1, 1963. For purposes of this paragraph, if an amount is paid within the payment period for two or more taxable years, it will be allowable as a deduction only for the earliest of such taxable years. Thus, if a cooperative which reports its income on a calendar year basis pays an amount in redemption of a nonqualified written notice of allocation on January 15, 1966, it will be allowed a deduction for such amount only for its 1965 taxable year. In determining the amount paid which is allowable as a deduction under this paragraph, property (other than written notices of allocation) shall be taken into account at its fair market value when paid. Amounts paid in redemption of a nonqualified written notice of allocation in excess of its stated dollar amount shall be treated under the applicable provisions of the Code. For example, if such excess is in the nature of interest, its deductibility will be governed by section 163 and the regulations thereunder. [Reg. § 1.1382-2.]

☐ [T.D. 6643, 4-1-63.]

[Reg. § 1.1382-3]

§ 1.1382-3. **Taxable income of cooperatives; special deductions for exempt farmers' cooperatives.**—(a) *In general.* (1) Section 1382(c) provides that in determining the taxable income of a farmers', fruit growers', or like association, described in section 1381(a)(1) and organized and operated in compliance with the requirements of section 521 and § 1.521-1, there shall be allowed as deductions from the gross income of such organization, in addition to the other deductions allowable under chapter 1 of the Code (including the deductions allowed by section 1382(b)) the special deductions provided in section 1382(c) and paragraphs (b), (c), and (d) of this section.

(2) For the definition of terms used in this section, see section 1388 and § 1.1388-1; to determine the payment period for a taxable year, see section 1382(d) and § 1.1382-4.

(b) *Deduction for dividends paid on capital stock.* In the case of a taxable year beginning after December 31, 1962, there is allowed as a deduction from the gross income of a cooperative association operated in compliance with the requirements of section 521 and § 1.521-1, amounts paid as dividends during the taxable year on the capital stock of such cooperative association. For the purpose of the preceding sentence, the term "capital stock" includes common stock (whether voting or nonvoting), preferred stock, or any other form of capital represented by capital retain certificates, revolving fund certificates, letters of advice, or other evidence of a proprietary interest in a cooperative association. Such deduction is applicable only to the taxable year in which the dividends are actually or constructively paid to the holder of capital stock or other proprietary interest of the cooperative association. If a dividend is paid by check and the check bearing a date within the taxable year is deposited in the mail, in a cover properly stamped and addressed to the shareholder at his last known address, at such time that in the ordinary handling of the mails the check would be received by such holder within the taxable year, a presumption arises that the dividend was paid to such holder in such year. The determination of whether a dividend has been paid to such holder by the corporation during its taxable year is in no way dependent upon the method of accounting regularly employed by the corporation in keeping its books. For further rules as to the determination of the right to a deduction for dividends paid, under certain specific circumstances, see section 561 and the regulations thereunder.

(c) *Deduction for amounts allocated from income not derived from patronage*—(1) *In general.* In the case of a taxable year beginning after December 31, 1962, there is allowed as a deduction from the gross income of a cooperative association operated in compliance with the requirements of section 521 and § 1.521-1, amounts paid to patrons, during the payment period for the taxable year, on a patronage basis with respect to its income derived during such taxable year either from business done with or for the United States or any of its agencies or from sources other than patronage, but only to the extent such amounts are paid in money, qualified written notices of allocation, or other property (other than nonqualified written notices of allocation). For purposes of this subparagraph a written notice of allocation is considered paid when it is issued to the patron. An amount shall be treated as paid in money during the payment period for the taxable year to the extent it is paid by a qualified check which is issued during the payment period for such taxable year and endorsed and cashed on or before the ninetieth day after the close of such payment period. In determining

Reg. § 1.1382-3(c)(1)

the amount paid which is allowable as a deduction under this paragraph, property (other than written notices of allocation) shall be taken into account at its fair market value when paid, and a qualified written notice of allocation shall be taken into account at its stated dollar amount.

(2) *Definition.* As used in this paragraph, the term "income derived from sources other than patronage" means incidental income derived from sources not directly related to the marketing, purchasing, or service activities of the cooperative association. For example, income derived from the lease of premises, from investment in securities, or from the sale or exchange of capital assets, constitutes income derived from sources other than patronage.

(3) *Basis of distribution.* In order that the deduction for amounts paid with respect to income derived from business done with or for the United States or any of its agencies or from sources other than patronage may be applicable, it is necessary that the amount sought to be deducted be paid on a patronage basis in proportion, insofar as is practicable, to the amount of business done by or for patrons during the period to which such income is attributable. For example, if capital gains are realized from the sale or exchange of capital assets acquired and disposed of during the taxable year, income realized from such gains must be paid to patrons of such year in proportion to the amount of business done by such patrons during the taxable year. Similarly, if capital gains are realized by the association from the sale or exchange of capital assets held for a period extending into more than one taxable year income realized from such gains must be paid, insofar as is practicable, to the persons who were patrons during the taxable years in which the asset was owned by the association in proportion to the amount of business done by such patrons during such taxable years.

(4) *Special rules for certain taxable years.* No deduction is allowable under this paragraph for amounts paid during taxable years beginning before January 1, 1963, or for amounts paid during taxable years beginning after December 31, 1962, with respect to income derived during taxable years beginning before January 1, 1963. With respect to such amounts, the Internal Revenue Code of 1954 (including section 522 and the regulations thereunder) shall be applicable without regard to subchapter T.

(d) *Deduction for amounts paid in redemption of certain nonqualified written notices of allocation.* In the case of a taxable year beginning after December 31, 1962, there is allowed as a deduction from the gross income of a cooperative association operated in compliance with the requirements of section 521 and §1.521-1, amounts paid by such association during the payment period for such taxable year in redemption of certain nonqualified written notices of allocation, but only to the extent such amounts (1) are paid in money or other property (other than written notices of allocation) and (2) do not exceed the stated dollar amount of such nonqualified written notices of allocation. The nonqualified written notices of allocation referred to in the preceding sentence are those which were previously paid to patrons on a patronage basis with respect to earnings derived either from business done with or for the United States or any of its agencies or from sources other than patronage, provided that such nonqualified written notices of allocation were paid during the payment period for the taxable year during which such earnings were derived. No deduction shall be allowed under this paragraph, however, for amounts paid in redemption of nonqualified written notices of allocation which were paid with respect to earnings derived during a taxable year beginning before January 1, 1963. For purposes of this paragraph, if an amount is paid within the payment period for two or more taxable years, it will be allowable as a deduction only for the earliest of such taxable years. In determining the amount paid which is allowable as a deduction under this paragraph, property (other than written notices of allocation) shall be taken into account at its fair market value when paid. Amounts paid in redemption of a nonqualified written notice of allocation in excess of its stated dollar amount shall be treated under the applicable provisions of the Code. [Reg. § 1.1382-3.]

☐ [*T.D.* 6643, 4-1-63.]

[Reg. § 1.1382-4]

§ 1.1382-4. **Taxable income of cooperatives; payment period for each taxable year.**—The payment period for a taxable year is the period beginning with the first day of such taxable year and ending with the fifteenth day of the ninth month following the close of such year. [Reg. § 1.1382-4.]

☐ [*T.D.* 6643, 4-1-63.]

[Reg. § 1.1382-5]

§ 1.1382-5. **Taxable income of cooperatives; products marketed under pooling arrangements.**—For purposes of section 1382(b) and § 1.1382-2, in the case of a pooling arrangement for the marketing of products the patronage under such pool shall be treated as occurring during the taxable year in which the pool closes. The determination of when a pool is closed will be made on

Reg. § 1.1382-4

the basis of the facts and circumstances in each case, but generally the practices and operations of the cooperative organization shall control. This section may be illustrated by the following example:

Example. Farmer A delivers to the X Cooperative 100 bushels of wheat on August 15, 1963, at which time he receives a "per bushel" advance. (Both farmer A and the X Cooperative file returns on a calendar year basis.) On October 15, 1963 farmer A receives an additional "per bushel" payment. The pool sells some of its wheat in 1963 and the remainder in January of 1964. The pool is closed on February 15, 1964. For purposes of section 1382(b), A's patronage is considered as occurring in 1964. [Reg. § 1.1382-5.]

☐ [*T.D.* 6643, 4-1-63.]

[Reg. § 1.1382-6]

§ 1.1382-6. **Taxable income of cooperatives; treatment of earnings received after patronage occurred.**—If earnings derived from business done with or for patrons are includible in the gross income of the cooperative organization for a taxable year after the taxable year during which the patronage occurred, then, for purposes of determining whether the cooperative is allowed a deduction under section 1382(b) and § 1.1382-2, the patronage to which these earnings relate shall be considered to have occurred during the taxable year for which such earnings are includible in the cooperative's gross income. Thus, if the cooperative organization pays these earnings out as patronage dividends during the payment period for the taxable year for which the earnings are includible in its gross income, it will be allowed a deduction for such payments under section 1382(b)(1) and paragraph (b) of § 1.1382-2, to the extent they are paid in money, qualified written notices of allocation, or other property (other than written notices of allocation). [Reg. § 1.1382-6.]

☐ [*T.D.* 6643, 4-1-63.]

[Reg. § 1.1382-7]

§ 1.1382-7. **Special rules applicable to cooperative associations exempt from tax before January 1, 1952.**—(a) *Basis of property.* The adjustments to the cost or other basis provided in sections 1011 and 1016 and the regulations thereunder, are applicable for the entire period since the acquisition of the property. Thus, proper adjustment to basis must be made under section 1016 for depreciation, obsolescence, amortization, and depletion for all taxable years beginning prior to January 1, 1952, although the cooperative association was exempt from tax under section 521 or corresponding provisions of prior law for such years. However, no adjustment for percentage or discovery depletion is to be made for any year during which the association was exempt from tax. If a cooperative association has made a proper election in accordance with section 1020 and the regulations prescribed thereunder with respect to a taxable year beginning before 1952 in which the association was not exempt from tax, the adjustment to basis for depreciation for such years shall be limited in accordance with the provisions of section 1016(a)(2).

(b) *Amortization of bond premium.* In the case of tax exempt and partially taxable bonds purchased at a premium and subject to amortization under section 171, proper adjustment to basis must be made to reflect amortization with respect to such premium from the date of acquisition of the bond. (For principles governing the method of computation, see the example in paragraph (b) of § 1.1016-9, relating to mutual savings banks, building and loan associations, and cooperative banks.) The basis of a fully taxable bond purchased at a premium shall be adjusted from the date of the election to amortize such premium in accordance with the provisions of section 171 except that no adjustment shall be allowable for such portion of the premium attributable to the period prior to the election.

(c) *Amortization of mortgage premium.* In the case of a mortgage acquired at a premium where the principal of such mortgage is payable in installments, adjustments to the basis for the premium must be made for all taxable years (whether or not the association was exempt from tax under section 521 during such years) in which installment payments are received. Such adjustments may be made on an individual mortgage basis or on a composite basis by reference to the average period of payments of the mortgage loans of such association. For the purpose of this adjustment, the term "premium" includes the excess of the acquisition value of the mortgage over its maturity value. The acquisition value of the mortgage is the cost including buying commissions, attorneys' fees, or brokerage fees, but such value does not include amounts paid for accrued interest. [Reg. § 1.1382-7.]

☐ [*T.D.* 6643, 4-1-63.]

[Reg. § 1.1383-1]

§ 1.1383-1. **Computation of tax where cooperative redeems nonqualified written notices of allocation.**—(a) *General rule.* (1) If, during the taxable year, a cooperative organization is entitled to a deduction under section 1382(b)(2) or (c)(2)(B) for amounts paid in redemption of nonqualified written notices of allocation, the tax imposed for the taxable year by chapter 1 of the Code shall be the lesser of—

Reg. § 1.1383-1(a)

(i) The tax for the taxable year computed under section 1383(a)(1), that is, with such deduction taken into account, or

(ii) The tax for the taxable year computed under section 1383(a)(2), that is, without taking such deduction into account, minus the decrease in tax (under chapter 1 of the Code) for any prior taxable year (or years) which would result solely from treating all such nonqualified written notices of allocation redeemed during the taxable year as qualified written notices of allocation when paid. For the purpose of this subdivision, the amount of the decrease in tax is not limited to the amount of the tax for the taxable year. See paragraph (c) of this section for rules relating to a refund of tax where the decrease in tax for the prior taxable year (or years) exceeds the tax for the taxable year.

(2) If the cooperative organization computes its tax for the taxable year under the provisions of section 1383(a)(2) and subparagraph (1)(ii) of this paragraph, then no deduction under section 1382(b)(2) or (c)(2)(B) shall be taken into account in computing taxable income or loss for the taxable year, including the computation of any net operating loss carryback or carryover. However, the amount of the deduction shall be taken into account in adjusting earnings and profits for the taxable year.

(3) If the tax determined under subparagraph (1)(i) of this paragraph is the same as the tax determined under subparagraph (1)(ii) of this paragraph, the tax imposed for the taxable year under chapter 1 of the Code shall be the tax determined under subparagraph (1)(i) of this paragraph, and section 1383 and this section shall not otherwise apply. The tax imposed for the taxable year shall be the tax determined under subparagraph (1)(ii) of this paragraph in any case when a credit or refund would be allowable for the taxable year under section 1383(b)(1).

(b) *Determination of decrease in tax for prior taxable years*—(1) *Prior taxable years.* The prior taxable year (or years) referred to in paragraph (a) of this section is the year (or years) within the payment period for which the nonqualified written notices of allocation were paid and, in addition, any other prior taxable year (or years) which is affected by the adjustment to income by reason of treating such nonqualified written notices of allocation as qualified written notices of allocation when paid.

(2) *Adjustment to income in prior taxable years.* The deduction for the prior taxable year (or years) in determining the decrease in tax under section 1383(a)(2)(B) and paragraph (a)(1)(ii) of this section shall be the amount paid in redemption of the nonqualified written notices of allocation which, without regard to section 1383, is allowable as a deduction under section 1382(b)(2) or (c)(2)(B) for the current taxable year.

(3) *Computation of decrease in tax for prior taxable years.* In computing the amount of decrease in tax for a prior taxable year (or years) resulting under this section, there must first be ascertained the amount of tax previously determined for the taxpayer for such prior taxable year (or years). The tax previously determined shall be the sum of the amounts shown as such tax by the taxpayer on his return or returns, plus any amounts which have been previously assessed (or collected without assessment) as deficiencies, reduced by the amount of any rebates which have previously been made. The amount shown as the tax by the taxpayer on his return and the amount of any rebates or deficiencies shall be determined in accordance with the provisions of section 6211 and the regulations thereunder. After the tax previously determined has been ascertained, a recomputation must then be made to determine the decrease in tax, if any, resulting under this section. In determining the decrease in tax for the prior taxable year (or years), appropriate adjustment shall be made to any item which is dependent upon the amount of gross income or taxable income (such as charitable contributions, net operating losses, the foreign tax credit, and the dividends received credit).

(c) *Refunds.* If the decrease in tax for the prior taxable year (or years) determined under section 1383(a)(2)(B) and paragraph (a)(1)(ii) of this section exceeds the tax imposed by chapter 1 of the Code for the taxable year computed without the deduction under section 1382(b) or (c)(2)(B), the excess shall be considered to be a payment of tax for the taxable year of the deduction. Such payment is deemed to have been made on the last day prescribed by law for the payment of tax for the taxable year and shall be refunded or credited in the same manner as if it were an overpayment of tax for such taxable year. See section 6151 and the regulations thereunder, for rules relating to time and place for paying tax shown on returns.

(d) *Example.* The application of section 1383 may be illustrated by the following example:

Example. The X Cooperative (which reports its income on a calendar year basis) pays patronage dividends of $100,000 in nonqualified written notices of allocation on February 1, 1964, with respect to patronage occurring in 1963. Since the patronage dividends of $100,000 were paid in nonqualified written notices of allocation the X Cooperative is not allowed a deduction for that amount for 1963. On December 1, 1966, the X

Reg. § 1.1383-1(a)(2)

Cooperative redeems these nonqualified written notices of allocation for $50,000. Under section 1382(b)(2), a deduction of $50,000 is allowable in computing its taxable income for 1966. However, the X Cooperative has a loss for 1966 determined without regard to this deduction. The X Cooperative, therefore, makes the computation under the alternative method provided in section 1383(a)(2). Under this alternative method, it will claim a credit or refund (as an overpayment of tax for 1966) of the decrease in tax for 1963 and for such other years prior to 1966 as are affected which results from recomputing its tax for 1963 (and such other years affected) as if patronage dividends of $50,000 had been paid on February 1, 1964, in qualified written notices of allocation. In addition, under this alternative the X Cooperative cannot use the $50,000 as a deduction for 1966 so as to increase its net operating loss for such year for purposes of computing a net operating loss carryback or carryover. If the X Cooperative also redeems on December 1, 1966, nonqualified written notices of allocation which were paid as patronage dividends on February 1, 1965, with respect to patronage occurring in 1964, it will claim a credit or refund (as an overpayment of tax for 1966) of the decrease in tax for 1964 and for such other years prior to 1966 as are affected. It shall not, however, apply one method for computing the tax with respect to the redemptions in 1966 of the nonqualified written notices of allocation paid in 1964 and the other method with respect to the redemption in 1966 of the nonqualified written notices of allocation paid in 1965. [Reg. § 1.1383-1.]

☐ [*T.D.* 6643, 4-1-63.]

Tax Treatment of Patronage Dividends, Etc.
[Reg. § 1.1385-1]

§ 1.1385-1. **Amounts includible in patron's gross income.**—(a) *General rules.* Section 1385(a) requires every person to include in gross income the following amounts received by him during the taxable year, to the extent paid by the organization in money, a qualified written notice of allocation, or other property (other than a nonqualified written notice of allocation):

(1) The amount of any patronage dividend received from an organization subject to the provisions of part I, subchapter T, chapter 1 of the Code, unless such amount is excludable from gross income under the provisions of section 1385(b) and paragraph (c) of this section, and

(2) The amount of any distribution received from a farmers', fruit growers', or like association, organized and operated in compliance with the requirements of section 521 and § 1.521-1, which is paid on a patronage basis with respect to earnings derived by such association either from business done with or for the United States or any of its agencies or from sources other than patronage.

The amounts described in subparagraphs (1) and (2) of this paragraph are includible in gross income for the taxable year in which they are received even though the cooperative organization was allowed a deduction for such amounts for its preceding taxable year because they were paid during the payment period for such preceding taxable year. Similarly, such amounts are includible in gross income even though the cooperative organization is not permitted any deduction for such amounts under the provisions of section 1382 because such amounts were not paid within the time prescribed by such section.

(b) *Treatment of certain nonqualified written notices of allocation.* (1) Except as provided in paragraph (c) of this section, any gain on the redemption, sale, or other disposition of a nonqualified written notice of allocation described in subparagraph (2) of this paragraph shall, to the extent that the stated dollar amount of such written notice of allocation exceeds its basis, be considered as gain from the sale or exchange of property which is not a capital asset, whether such gain is realized by the patron who received the nonqualified written notice of allocation initially or by any subsequent holder. Any amount realized on the redemption, sale, or other disposition of such a nonqualified written notice of allocation in excess of its stated dollar amount will be treated under the applicable provisions of the Code. For example, amounts received in redemption of a nonqualified written notice of allocation which are in excess of the stated dollar amount of such written notice of allocation and which, in effect, constitute interest shall be treated by the recipient as interest.

(2) The nonqualified written notices of allocation to which subparagraph (1) of this paragraph applies are the following:

(i) A nonqualified written notice of allocation which was paid as a patronage dividend (within the meaning of section 1388(a) and paragraph (a) of § 1.1388-1), by a cooperative organization subject to the provisions of part I of subchapter T, and

(ii) A nonqualified written notice of allocation which was paid by a farmers', fruit growers', or like association, organized and operated in compliance with the requirements of section 521 and § 1.521-1, to patrons on a patronage basis with

Reg. § 1.1385-1(b)(2)

respect to earnings derived either from business done with or for the United States or any of its agencies or from sources other than patronage.

(3) The basis of any nonqualified written notice of allocation described in subparagraph (2) of this paragraph, in the hands of the patron to whom such written notice of allocation was initially paid shall be zero, and the basis of such a written notice of allocation which was acquired from a decedent shall be its basis in the hands of the decedent.

(4) The application of this paragraph may be illustrated by the following example:

Example. A, a farmer, receives a patronage dividend from the X Cooperative, in the form of a nonqualified written notice of allocation, which is attributable to the sale of his crop to that cooperative organization. The stated dollar amount of the nonqualified written notice of allocation is $100. The basis of the written notice of allocation in the hands of A is zero and he must report any amount up to $100 received by him on its redemption, sale, or other disposition, as ordinary income. If A gives the written notice of allocation to his son B, B takes A's (the donor's) basis which is zero, and any gain up to $100 which B later realizes on its redemption, sale, or other disposition is ordinary income. Similarly, if A dies before realizing any gain on the nonqualified written notice of allocation, B, his legatee, has a zero basis for such written notice of allocation and any gain up to $100 which he then realizes on its redemption, sale, or other disposition is also ordinary income. Such gain is income in respect of a decedent within the meaning of section 691(a) and § 1.691(a)-1.

(c) *Treatment of patronage dividends received with respect to certain property*—(1) *Exclusions from gross income.* Except as provided in subparagraph (2) of this paragraph, gross income shall not include—

(i) Any amount of a patronage dividend described in paragraph (a)(1) of this section which is received with respect to the purchase of supplies, equipment, or services, which were not used in the trade or business and the cost of which was not deductible under section 212, or which is received with respect to the marketing or purchasing of a capital asset (as defined in section 1221) or property used in the trade or business of a character which is subject to the allowance for depreciation provided in section 167; and

(ii) Any amount (to the extent treated as ordinary income under paragraph (b) of this section) received on the redemption, sale, or other disposition of a nonqualified written notice of allocation which was received as a patronage dividend with respect to the purchase of supplies, equipment, or services, which were not used in the trade or business and the cost of which was not deductible under section 212, or which was received as a patronage dividend with respect to the marketing or purchasing of a capital asset (as defined in section 1221) or property used in the trade or business of a character which is subject to the allowance for depreciation provided in section 167.

(2) *Special rules.* (i) If an amount described in subparagraph (1) of this paragraph relates to the purchase of a capital asset (as defined in section 1221), or property used in the trade or business of a character which is subject to the allowance for depreciation provided in section 167, and the person receiving such amount owned such asset or property at any time during the taxable year in which such amount is received, then such amount shall be taken into account as an adjustment to the basis of such property or asset as of the first day of the taxable year in which such amount is received. To the extent that such amount exceeds the adjusted basis of such property it shall be taken into account as ordinary income.

(ii) If an amount described in subparagraph (1) of this paragraph relates to the marketing or purchasing of a capital asset (as defined in section 1221), or property used in the trade or business of a character which is subject to the allowance for depreciation provided in section 167, and the person receiving such amount did not own the asset or property at any time during the taxable year in which such amount is received, then such amount shall be included in gross income as ordinary income except that—

(*a*) If such amount relates to a capital asset (as defined in section 1221) which was held by the recipient for more than 1 year (6 months for taxable years beginning before 1977; 9 months for taxable years beginning in 1977) and with respect to which a loss was or would have been deductible under section 165, such amount shall be taken into account as gain from the sale or exchange of a capital asset held for more than 1 year (6 months for taxable years beginning before 1977; 9 months for taxable years beginning in 1977);

(*b*) If such amount relates to a capital asset (as defined in section 1221) with respect to which a loss was not or would not have been deductible under section 165, such amount shall not be taken into account.

(iii) If an amount described in subparagraph (1) of this paragraph relates to the marketing of a capital asset (as defined in section 1221)

Reg. § 1.1385-1(b)(3)

Tax Treatment of Patronage Dividends, Etc.

See p. 20,601 for regulations not amended to reflect law changes

or property used in the trade or business of a character which is subject to the allowance for depreciation provided in section 167, and such amount is received by the patron in the same taxable year during which he marketed the asset to which it relates, such amount shall be treated as an additional amount received on the sale or other disposition of such asset.

(iv) If a person receiving a patronage dividend or an amount on the redemption, sale, or other disposition of a nonqualified written notice of allocation which was received as a patronage dividend is unable to determine the item to which it relates, he shall include such patronage dividend or such amount in gross income as ordinary income in the manner and to the extent provided in paragraph (a) or (b) of this section, whichever is applicable.

(3) The application of this paragraph may be illustrated by the following examples:

Example (1). On July 1, 1964, P, a patron of a cooperative association, purchases an implement for use in his farming business from such association for $2,900. The implement has an estimated useful life of three years and has an estimated salvage value of $200 which P chooses to take into account in the computation of depreciation. P files his income tax returns on a calendar year basis. For 1964 P claims depreciation of $450 with respect to the implement pursuant to his use of the straight-line method at the rate of $900 per year. On July 1, 1965, the cooperative association pays a patronage dividend to P of $300 in cash with respect to his purchase of the farm implement. P will adjust the basis of the implement and will compute his depreciation deduction for 1965 (and subsequent taxable years) as follows:

Cost of farm implement, July 1, 1964		$2,900
Less:		
Salvage value	$200	
Depreciation for 1964 (6 mos.)	450	
Adjustment as of Jan. 1, 1965 for cash patronage dividend	300	950
Basis for depreciation for the remaining 2½ years of estimated life		1,950
Depreciation deduction for 1965 ($1,950 divided by the 2½ years of remaining life)		780

Example (2). Assume the same facts as in example (1), except that on July 1, 1965, the cooperative association paid a patronage dividend to P with respect to his purchase of the implement in the form of a nonqualified written notice of allocation having a stated dollar amount of $300. Since such written notice of allocation was not qualified, no amount of the patronage dividend was taken into account by P as an adjustment to the basis of the implement, or in computing his depreciation deduction, for the year 1965. In 1968, P receives $300 cash from the association in full redemption of the written notice of allocation. Prior to 1968, he had recovered through depreciation $2,700 of the cost of the implement, leaving an adjusted basis of $200 (the salvage value). For the year 1968, the redemption proceeds of $300 are applied against the adjusted basis of $200, reducing the basis of the implement to zero, and the balance of the redemption proceeds, $100, is includible as ordinary income in P's gross income for the calendar year 1968. If the patronage dividend paid to P on July 1, 1965, had been in the form of $60 cash (20 percent of $300) and a qualified written notice of allocation with a stated dollar amount of $240, then the tax treatment of such patronage dividend would be that illustrated in example (1).

Example (3). Assume the same facts as in example (2), except that the nonqualified written notice of allocation is redeemed in cash on July 1, 1966. The full $300 received on redemption will reduce the adjusted basis of the implement as of January 1, 1966, and the depreciation allowances for 1966 and 1967 are computed as follows:

Cost of farm implement, July 1, 1964		$2,900
Less:		
Salvage value	$200	
Depreciation for 1964 (6 mos.)	450	
Depreciation for 1965	900	
Adjustment as of Jan. 1, 1966 for proceeds of the redemption	300	
		1,850
Basis for depreciation on Jan. 1, 1966		1,050

Reg. § 1.1385-1(c)(3)

If P uses the implement in his business until fully depreciated, he would be entitled to the following depreciation allowances with respect to such implement:

For 1966	$700
For 1967	350
	$1,050
Balance to be depreciated	0

Example (4). Assume the same facts as in example (3), except that P sells the implement in 1965. The entire $300 received in 1966 in redemption of the nonqualified written notice of allocation is includible as ordinary income in P's gross income for the year 1966.

(d) *Determination of amount received.* In determining the amount received for purposes of this section—

(1) Property (other than written notices of allocation) shall be taken into account at its fair market value when received;

(2) A qualified written notice of allocation shall be taken into account at its stated dollar amount; and

(3) The amount of a qualified check shall be considered an amount received in money during the taxable year in which such check is received if the check is endorsed and cashed on or before the ninetieth day after the close of the payment period for the taxable year of the cooperative organization in which the patronage to which such amount relates occurred.

(e) *Effective date.* This section shall not apply to any distribution or allocation received from a cooperative organization, or to any gain or loss on the redemption, sale, or other disposition of any allocation received from such an organization, if such distribution or allocation was received with respect to patronage occurring in a taxable year of the organization beginning before January 1, 1963. See § 1.61-5 for the tax treatment by patrons of such distributions or allocations. [Reg. § 1.1385-1.]

☐ [T.D. 6643, 4-1-63. Amended by T.D. 7728, 10-31-80.]

Definitions; Special Rules

[Reg. § 1.1388-1]

§ 1.1388-1. **Definitions and special rules.**—(a) *Patronage dividend*—(1) *In general.* The term "patronage dividend" means an amount paid to a patron by a cooperative organization subject to the provisions of Part I, subchapter T, chapter 1 of the Code, which is paid—

(i) On the basis of quantity or value of business done with or for such patron,

(ii) Under a valid enforceable written obligation of such organization to the patron to pay such amount, which obligation existed before the cooperative organization received the amount so paid, and

(iii) Which is determined by reference to the net earnings of the cooperative organization from business done with or for its patrons.

For the purpose of subdivision (ii) of this subparagraph, amounts paid by a cooperative organization are paid under a valid enforceable written obligation if such payments are required by State law or are paid pursuant to provisions of the bylaws, articles of incorporation, or other written contract, whereby the organization is obligated to make such payment. The term "net earnings", for purposes of subdivision (iii) of this subparagraph includes the excess of amounts retained (or assessed) by the organization to cover expenses or other items. For purposes of such subdivision (iii), net earnings shall not be reduced by any taxes imposed by subtitle A of the Code, but shall be reduced by dividends paid on capital stock or other proprietary capital interests.

(2) *Exceptions.* The term "patronage dividend" does not include the following:

(i) An amount paid to a patron by a cooperative organization to the extent that such amount is paid out of earnings not derived from business done with or for patrons.

(ii) An amount paid to a patron by a cooperative organization to the extent that such amount is paid out of earnings from business done with or for other patrons to whom no amounts are paid, or to whom smaller amounts are paid, with respect to substantially identical transactions. Thus, if a cooperative organization does not pay any patronage dividends to nonmembers, any portion of the amounts paid to members which is out of net earnings from patronage with nonmembers, and which would have been paid to the nonmembers if all patrons were treated alike, is not a patronage dividend.

(iii) An amount paid to a patron by a cooperative organization to the extent that such amount is paid in redemption of capital stock, or in redemption or satisfaction of certificates of indebtedness, revolving fund certificates, retain certificates, letters of advice, or other similar doc-

Reg. § 1.1388-1(a)(1)

Definitions; Special Rules

uments, even if such documents were originally paid as patronage dividends.

(iv) An amount paid to a patron by a cooperative organization to the extent that such amount is fixed without reference to the net earnings of the cooperative organization from business done with or for its patrons.

(3) *Examples.* The application of subparagraphs (1) and (2) of this paragraph may be illustrated by the following examples:

Example (1). (i) Cooperative A, a marketing association operating on a pooling basis, receives the products of patron W on January 5, 1964. On the same day cooperative A advances to W 45 cents per unit for the products so delivered and allocates to him a "retain certificate" having a face value calculated at the rate of 5 cents per unit. During the operation of the pool, and before substantially all the products in the pool are disposed of, cooperative A advances to W an additional 40 cents per unit, the amount being determined by reference to the market price of the products sold and the anticipated price of the unsold products. At the close of the pool on November 10, 1964, cooperative A determines the excess of its receipts over the sum of its expenses and its previous advances to patrons, and allocates to W an additional 3 cents per unit and shares of the capital stock of A having an aggregate stated dollar amount calculated at the rate of 2 cents per unit. Under the provisions of section 1382(e), W's patronage is deemed to occur in 1964, the year in which the pool is closed.

(ii) The patronage dividend paid to W during 1964 amounts to 5 cents per unit, consisting of the aggregate of the following per-unit allocations: The amount of the cash distribution (3 cents), and the stated dollar amount of the capital stock of A (2 cents), which are fixed with reference to the net earnings of A. The amount of the two distributions in cash (85 cents) and the face amount of the "retain certificate" (5 cents), which are fixed without reference to the net earnings of A, do not constitute patronage dividends.

Example (2). Cooperative B, a marketing association operating on a pooling basis, receives the products of patron X on March 5, 1964. On the same day cooperative B pays to X $1.00 per unit for such products, this amount being determined by reference to the market price of the product when received, and issues to him a participation certificate having no face value but which entitles X on the close of the pool to the proceeds derived from the sale of his products less the previous payment of $1.00 and the expenses and other charges attributable to such products. On March 5, 1967, cooperative B, having sold the products in the pool, having deducted the previous payments for such products, and having determined the expenses and other charges of the pool pays to X, in cash, 10 cents per unit pursuant to the participation certificate. Under the provisions of section 1382(e), X's patronage is deemed to occur in 1967, the year in which the pool is closed. The payment made to X during 1967, amounting to 10 cents per unit, is a patronage dividend. Neither the payment to X in 1964 of $1.00 nor the issuance to him of the participation certificate in that year constitutes a patronage dividend.

Example (3). Cooperative C, a purchasing association, obtains supplies for patron Y on May 1, 1964, and receives in return therefor $100. On February 1, 1965, cooperative C, having determined the excess of its receipts over its costs and expenses, pays to Y a cash distribution of $1.00 and a revolving fund certificate with a stated dollar amount of $1.00. The amount of patronage dividend paid to Y in 1965 is $2.00, the aggregate of the cash distribution ($1.00) and the stated dollar amount of the revolving fund certificate ($1.00).

Example (4). Cooperative D, a service association, sells the products of members on a fee basis. It receives the products of patron Z under an agreement not to pool his products with those of other members, to sell his products, and to deliver to him the proceeds of the sale. Patron Z makes payments to cooperative D during 1964 aggregating $75 for service rendered him by cooperative D during that year. On May 15, 1965, cooperative D, having determined the excess of its receipts over its costs and expenses, pays to Z a cash distribution of $2.00. Such amount is a patronage dividend paid by cooperative D during 1965.

(b) *Written notice of allocation.* The term "written notice of allocation" means any capital stock, revolving fund certificate, retain certificate, certificate of indebtedness, letter of advice, or other written notice, which discloses to the patron the stated dollar amount allocated to him on the books of the cooperative organization, and the portion thereof, if any, which constitutes a patronage dividend. Thus, a mere credit to the account of a patron on the books of the organization without disclosure to the patron, is not a written notice of allocation. A written notice of allocation may disclose to the patron the amount of the allocation which constitutes a patronage dividend either as a dollar amount or as a percentage of the stated dollar amount of the written notice of allocation.

(c) *Qualified written notice of allocation*—(1) *In general.* The term "qualified written notice of allocation" means a written notice of allocation—

(i) Which meets the requirements of subparagraph (2) or (3) of this paragraph, and

Reg. § 1.1388-1(c)(1)

(ii) Which is paid as part of a patronage dividend, or as part of a payment by a cooperative association organized and operated in compliance with the provisions of section 521 and § 1.521-1 to patrons on a patronage basis with respect to earnings derived from business done with or for the United States or any of its agencies or from sources other than patronage, that also includes a payment in money or by qualified check equal to at least 20 percent of such patronage dividend or such payment.

In determining, for purposes of subdivision (ii) of this subparagraph, whether 20 percent of a patronage dividend or a payment with respect to nonpatronage earnings is paid in money or by qualified check, any portion of such dividend or payment which is paid in nonqualified written notices of allocation may be disregarded. Thus, if a cooperative pays a patronage dividend of $100 in the form of a nonqualified written notice of allocation with a stated dollar amount of $50, a written notice of allocation with a stated dollar amount of $40, and money in the amount of $10, the written notice of allocation with a stated dollar amount of $40 will constitute a qualified written notice of allocation if it meets the requirements of subparagraph (2) or (3) of this paragraph. A "payment in money", as that term is used in subdivision (ii) of this subparagraph, includes a payment by a check drawn on a bank but does not include a credit against amounts owed by the patron to the cooperative organization, a credit against the purchase price of a share of stock or of a membership in such organization, nor does it include a payment by means of a document redeemable by such organization for money.

(2) *Written notice of allocation redeemable in cash.* The term "qualified written notice of allocation" includes a written notice of allocation which meets the requirement of subparagraph (1)(ii) of this paragraph and which may be redeemed in cash at its stated dollar amount at any time within a period beginning on the date such written notice of allocation is paid and ending not earlier than 90 days from such date, but only if the distributee receives written notice of the right of redemption at the time he receives such written notice of allocation. The written notice of the right of redemption referred to in the preceding sentence shall be given separately to each patron. Thus, a written notice of the right of redemption which is published in a newspaper or posted at the cooperative's place of business would not be sufficient to qualify a written notice of allocation which is otherwise described in this subparagraph.

(3) *Consent of patron.* The term "qualified written notice of allocation" also includes a written notice of allocation which meets the requirement of subparagraph (1)(ii) of this paragraph and which the distributee has consented, in a manner provided in this subparagraph, to take into account at its stated dollar amount as provided in section 1385 and § 1.1385-1.

(i) *Consent in writing.* A distributee may consent to take the stated dollar amount of written notices of allocation into account under section 1385 by signing and furnishing a written consent to the cooperative organization. No special form is required for the written consent so long as the document on which it is made clearly discloses the terms of the consent. Thus, the written consent may be made on a signed invoice, sales slip, delivery ticket, marketing agreement, or other document, on which appears the appropriate consent. Unless the written consent specifically provides to the contrary, it shall be effective with respect to all patronage occurring during the taxable year of the cooperative organization in which such consent is received by such organization and, unless revoked under section 1388(c)(3)(B), for all subsequent taxable years. Section 1388(c)(3)(B)(i) provides that a written consent may be revoked by the patron at any time. Thus, any written consent which is, by its terms, irrevocable is not a consent that would qualify a written notice of allocation. A revocation, to be effective, must be in writing, signed by the patron, and furnished to the cooperative organization. Such a revocation shall be effective only with respect to patronage occurring after the close of the taxable year of the cooperative organization during which the revocation is filed with it. In the case of a pooling arrangement described in section 1382(e) and § 1.1382-5, a written consent which is made at any time before the close of the taxable year of the cooperative organization during which the pool closes shall be effective with respect to all patronage under that pool. In addition, any subsequent revocation of such consent by the patron will not be effective for that pool or any other pool with respect to which he has been a patron before such revocation.

(ii) *Consent by membership.* (a) A distributee may consent to take the stated dollar amount of written notices of allocation into account under section 1385 by obtaining or retaining membership in the cooperative organization after such organization has adopted a valid bylaw providing that membership in such cooperative organization constitutes such consent, but such consent shall take effect only after the distributee has received a written notification of the adoption of the bylaw provision and a copy of such bylaw. The bylaw must have been adopted by the cooperative organization after October 16, 1962, and must contain

Reg. § 1.1388-1(c)(2)

a clear statement that membership in the cooperative organization constitutes the prescribed consent. The written notification from the cooperative organization must inform the patron that this bylaw has been adopted and of its significance. The notification and copy of the bylaw shall be given separately to each member (or prospective member); thus, a written notice and copy of the bylaw which are published in a newspaper or posted at the cooperative's place of business are not sufficient to qualify a written notice of allocation under this subdivision. A member (or prospective member) is presumed to have received the notification and copy of the bylaw if they were sent to his last known address by ordinary mail. A prospective member must receive the notification and copy of the bylaw before he becomes a member of the organization in order to have his membership in the organization constitute consent. A consent made in the manner described in this subdivision shall be effective only with respect to patronage occurring after the patron has received a copy of the bylaw and the prerequisite notice and while he is a member of the organization. Thus, any such consent shall not be effective with respect to any patronage occurring after the patron ceases to be a member of the cooperative organization or after the bylaw provision is repealed by such organization. In the case of a pooling arrangement described in section 1382(e) and § 1.1382-5, a consent made under this subdivision will be effective only with respect to the patron's actual patronage occurring after he receives the notification and copy of the bylaw and while he is a member of the cooperative organization. Thus such a consent shall not be effective with respect to any patronage under a pool after the patron ceases to be a member of the cooperative organization or after the bylaw provision is repealed by the organization.

(*b*) The following is an example of a bylaw provision which would meet the requirements prescribed in (*a*) of this subdivision.

Example. Each person who hereafter applies for and is accepted to membership in this cooperative and each member of this cooperative on the effective date of this bylaw who continues as a member after such date shall, by such act alone, consent that the amount of any distributions with respect to his patronage occurring after ...., which are made in written notices of allocation (as defined in 26 U.S.C. 1388) and which are received by him from the cooperative, will be taken into account by him at their stated dollar amounts in the manner provided in 26 U.S.C. 1385(a) in the taxable year in which such written notices of allocation are received by him.

(*c*) For purposes of this subdivision the term "member" means a person who is entitled to participate in the management of the cooperative organization.

(iii) *Consent by qualified check.* (*a*) A distributee may consent to take the stated dollar amount of a written notice of allocation into account under section 1385 by endorsing and cashing a qualified check which is paid as a part of the same patronage dividend or payment described in subparagraph (1)(ii) of this paragraph of which the written notice of allocation is also a part. In order to constitute an effective consent under this subdivision, however, the qualified check must be endorsed and cashed by the payee on or before the ninetieth day after the close of the payment period for the taxable year of the cooperative organization with respect to which the patronage dividend or payment is paid (or on or before such earlier day as may be prescribed by the cooperative organization). The endorsing and cashing of a qualified check shall be considered a consent only with respect to written notices of allocation which are part of the same patronage dividend or payment as the qualified check and for which a consent under subdivision (i) or (ii) of this subparagraph is not in effect. A qualified check is presumed to be endorsed and cashed within the 90-day period if the earliest bank endorsement which appears thereon bears a date no later than 3 days after the end of such 90-day period (excluding Saturdays, Sundays, and legal holidays).

(*b*) The term "qualified check" means a check, or other instrument redeemable in money, which is paid as a part of a patronage dividend or payment described in subparagraph (1)(ii) of this paragraph, on which there is clearly imprinted a statement that the endorsement and cashing of the check or other instrument constitutes the consent of the payee to take into account, as provided in the Federal income tax laws, the stated dollar amount of any written notices of allocation which are paid as a part of the patronage dividend or payment of which such check or other instrument is also a part. A qualified check need not be in the form of an ordinary check which is payable through the banking system. It may, for example, be in the form of an instrument which is redeemable in money by the cooperative organization. The term "qualified check" does not include a check or other instrument paid as part of a patronage dividend or payment with respect to which a consent under subdivision (i) or (ii) of this subparagraph is in effect. In addition, the term "qualified check" does not include a check or other instrument which is paid as part of a patronage dividend or payment, if such patronage dividend or payment does not also include a writ-

Reg. § 1.1388-1(c)(3)

ten notice of allocation (other than a written notice of allocation that may be redeemed in cash at its stated dollar amount which meets the requirements of section 1388(c)(1)(A) and subparagraph (2) of this paragraph). Thus, a check which is paid as part of a patronage dividend is not a qualified check (even though it has the required statement imprinted on it) if the remaining portion of such patronage dividend is paid in cash or if the only written notices of allocation included in the payment are qualified under section 1388(c)(1)(A) and subparagraph (2) of this paragraph (relating to certain written notices of allocation which are redeemable by the patron within a period of at least 90 days).

(c) The provisions of this subdivision may be illustrated by the following example:

Example. (1) The A Cooperative is a cooperative organization filing its income tax returns on a calendar year basis. None of its patrons have consented in the manner prescribed in section 1388(c)(2)(A) or (B). On August 1, 1964, the A Cooperative pays patronage dividends to its patrons with respect to their 1963 patronage, and the payment to each such patron is partly by a qualified check and partly in the form of a written notice of allocation which is not redeemable for cash. Each patron who endorses and cashes his qualified check on or before December 14, 1964 (the ninetieth day following the close of the 1963 payment period) shall be considered to have consented with respect to the accompanying written notice of allocation and the amount of such check is treated as a patronage dividend paid in money on August 1, 1964.

(2) As to any patron who has not endorsed and cashed his qualified check by December 14, 1964, there is no consent and both the written notice of allocation and the qualified check constitute nonqualified written notices of allocation within the meaning of section 1388(d) and paragraph (d) of this section. If such a patron then cashes his check on January 2, 1965, he shall treat the amount received as an amount received on January 2, 1965, in redemption of a nonqualified written notice of allocation. Likewise, the cooperative shall treat the amount of the check as an amount paid on January 2, 1965, in redemption of a nonqualified written notice of allocation.

(d) *Nonqualified written notice of allocation.* The term "nonqualified written notice of allocation" means a written notice of allocation which is not a qualified written notice of allocation described in section 1388(c) and paragraph (c) of this section, or a qualified check which is not cashed on or before the ninetieth day after the close of the payment period for the taxable year of the cooperative organization for which the payment of which it is a part is paid.

(e) *Patron.* The term "patron" includes any person with whom or for whom the cooperative association does business on a cooperative basis, whether a member or a non-member of the cooperative association, and whether an individual, a trust, estate, partnership, company, corporation, or cooperative association. [Reg. § 1.1388-1.]

☐ [T.D. 6643, 4-1-63.]

[Reg. § 1.1394-0]

§ 1.1394-0. **Table of contents.**—This section lists the major paragraph headings contained in § 1.1394-1.

§ 1.1394-1. *Enterprise zone facility bonds.*

(a) Scope.

(b) Period of compliance.

(1) In general.

(2) Compliance after an issue is retired

(3) Deemed compliance,

(c) Special rules for requirements of sections 1397B and 1397C.

(1) Start of compliance period.

(2) Compliance period for certain prohibited activities.

(3) Minimum compliance period.

(4) Initial testing date.

(d) Testing on an average basis.

(e) Resident employee requirements.

(1) Determination of employee status.

(2) Employee treated as zone resident.

(3) Resident employee percentage.

(f) Application to pooled financing bond and loan recycling programs.

(g) Limitation on amount of bonds.

(1) Determination of outstanding amount.

(2) Pooled financing bond programs.

(h) Original use requirement for purposes of qualified zone property.

(i) Land.

(j) Principal user.

(1) In general.

(2) Rental of real property.

(3) Pooled financing bond program.

(k) Treatment as separately incorporated business.

(l) Substantially all.

(m) Application of sections 142 and 146 through 150.

(1) In general.

Definitions; Special Rules

See p. 20,601 for regulations not amended to reflect law changes

(2) Maturity limitation.

(3) Volume cap.

(4) Remedial actions.

(n) Continuing compliance and change of use penalties.

(1) In general.

(2) Coordination with deemed compliance provisions.

(3) Application to pooled financing bond and loan recycling programs.

(4) Section 150(b)(4) inapplicable.

(o) Refunding bonds.

(1) In general.

(2) Maturity limitation.

(p) Examples.

(q) Effective dates.

(1) In general.

(2) Elective retroactive application in whole.

[Reg. § 1.1394-0.]

☐ [T.D. 8673, 5-30-96.]

[Reg. § 1.1394-1]

§ 1.1394-1. **Enterprise zone facility bonds.**—(a) *Scope.* This section contains rules relating to tax-exempt bonds under section 1394 (enterprise zone facility bonds) to provide enterprise zone facilities in both empowerment zones and enterprise communities (zones). See sections 1394, 1397B, and 1397C for other rules and definitions.

(b) *Period of compliance*—(1) *In general.* Except as provided in paragraphs (b)(2) and (c) of this section, the requirements under sections 1394(a) and (b) applicable to enterprise zone facility bonds must be complied with throughout the greater of the following—

(i) The remainder of the period during which the zone designation is in effect under section 1391 (zone designation period); and

(ii) The period that ends on the weighted average maturity date of the enterprise zone facility bonds.

(2) *Compliance after an issue is retired.* Except as provided in paragraph (c)(3) of this section, the requirements applicable to enterprise zone facility bonds do not apply to an issue after the date on which no enterprise zone facility bonds of the issue are outstanding.

(3) *Deemed compliance*—(i) *General rule.* An issue is deemed to comply with the requirements of sections 1394(a) and (b) if—

(A) The issuer and the principal user in good faith attempt to meet the requirements of sections 1394(a) and (b) throughout the period of compliance required under this section; and

(B) Any failure to meet these requirements is corrected within a one-year period after the failure is first discovered.

(ii) *Exception.* The provisions of paragraph (b)(3)(i) of this section do not apply to the requirements of section 1397B(d)(5)(A) (relating to certain prohibited business activities).

(iii) *Good faith.* In order to satisfy the good faith requirement of paragraph (b)(3)(i)(A) of this section, the principal user must at least annually demonstrate to the issuer the principal user's monitoring of compliance with the requirements of sections 1394(a) and (b).

(c) *Special rules for requirements of sections 1397B and 1397C*—(1) *Start of compliance period.* Except as provided in paragraph (c)(2) of this section, the requirements of sections 1397B (relating to qualification as an enterprise zone business) and 1397C (relating to satisfaction of the rules for qualified zone property) do not apply prior to the *initial testing date* (as defined in paragraph (c)(4) of this section) if—

(i) The issuer and the principal user reasonably expect on the issue date of the enterprise zone facility bonds that those requirements will be met by the principal user on or before the initial testing date; and

(ii) The issuer and the principal user exercise due diligence to meet those requirements prior to the initial testing date.

(2) *Compliance period for certain prohibited activities.* The requirements of section 1397B(d)(5)(A) (relating to certain prohibited business activities) must be complied with throughout the term of the enterprise zone facility bonds.

(3) *Minimum compliance period.* The requirements of sections 1397B(b) or (c) and 1397C must be satisfied for a continuous period of at least three years after the initial testing date, notwithstanding that—

(i) The period of compliance required under paragraph (b)(1) of this section expires before the end of the three-year period; or

(ii) The enterprise zone facility bonds are retired before the end of the three-year period.

(4) *Initial testing date*—(i) *In general.* Except as otherwise provided in paragraph (c)(4)(ii) of this section, the initial testing date is the date that is 18 months after the later of the issue date of the enterprise zone facility bonds or the date on which the financed property is placed in service; provided, however, it is not later than—

(A) Three years after the issue date; or

(B) Five years after the issue date, if the issue finances a construction project for which both the issuer and a licensed architect or engineer certify on or before the issue date of the enterprise zone facility bonds that more than three years after the issue date is necessary to complete construction of the project.

(ii) *Alternative initial testing date.* If the issuer identifies as the initial testing date a date after the issue date of the enterprise zone facility bonds and prior to the initial testing date that would have been determined under paragraph (c)(4)(i) of this section, that earlier date is treated as the initial testing date.

(d) *Testing on an average basis.* Compliance with each of the requirements of section 1397B(b) or (c) is tested each taxable year. Compliance with any of the requirements may be tested on an average basis, taking into account up to four immediately preceding taxable years plus the current taxable year. The earliest taxable year that may be taken into account for purposes of the preceding sentence is the taxable year that includes the initial testing date. A taxable year is disregarded if the part of the taxable year that falls in a required compliance period does not exceed 90 days.

(e) *Resident employee requirements*—(1) *Determination of employee status.* For purposes of the requirement of section 1397B(b)(6) or (c)(5) that at least 35 percent of the employees are residents of the zone, the issuer and the principal user may rely on a certification, signed under penalties of perjury by the employee, provided—

(i) The certification provides to the principal user the address of the employee's principal residence;

(ii) The employee is required by the certification to notify the principal user of a change of the employee's principal residence; and

(iii) Neither the issuer nor the principal user has actual knowledge that the principal residence set forth in the certification is not the employee's principal residence.

(2) *Employee treated as zone resident.* If an issue fails to comply with the requirement of section 1397B(b)(6) or (c)(5) because an employee who initially resided in the zone moves out of the zone, that employee is treated as still residing in the zone if—

(i) That employee was a bona fide resident of the zone at the time of the certification described in paragraph (e)(1) of this section;

(ii) That employee continues to perform services for the principal user in an enterprise zone business and substantially all of those services are performed in the zone; and

(iii) A resident of the zone meeting the requirements of section 1397B(b)(5) or (c)(4) is hired by the principal user for the next available comparable (or lesser) position.

(3) *Resident employee percentage.* For purposes of meeting the requirement of section 1397B(b)(6) or (c)(5) that at least 35 percent of the employees of an enterprise zone business are residents of a zone, paragraphs (e)(3)(i) and (ii) of this section apply.

(i) The term *employee* includes a self-employed individual within the meaning of section 401(c)(1).

(ii) The resident employee percentage is determined on any reasonable basis consistently applied throughout the period of compliance required under this section. The per-employee fraction (as defined in paragraph (e)(3)(ii)(A) of this section) or the employee actual work hour fraction (as defined in paragraph (e)(3)(ii)(B) of this section) are both reasonable methods.

(A) The term *per-employee fraction* means the fraction, the numerator of which is, during the taxable year, the number of employees who work at least 15 hours a week for the principal user, who reside in the zone, and who are employed for at least 90 days, and the denominator of which is, during the same taxable year, the aggregate number of all employees who work at least 15 hours a week for the principal user and who are employed for at least 90 days.

(B) The term *employee actual work hour fraction* means the fraction, the numerator of which is the aggregate total actual hours of work for the principal user of employees who reside in the zone during a taxable year, and the denominator of which is the aggregate total actual hours of work for the principal user of all employees during the same taxable year.

(f) *Application to pooled financing bond and loan recycling programs.* In the case of a pooled financing bond program described in paragraph (g)(2) of this section or a loan recycling program described in paragraph (m)(2)(ii) of this section, the requirements of paragraphs (b) through (e) of this section apply on a loan-by-loan basis. See also paragraphs (g)(2) (relating to limitation on amount of bonds), (m)(2) (relating to maturity limitations), (m)(3) (relating to volume cap), and (m)(4) (relating to remedial actions) of this section.

(g) *Limitation on amount of bonds*—(1) *Determination of outstanding amount.* Whether an issue satisfies the requirements of section 1394(c) (relating to the $3 million and $20 million aggregate limitations on the amount of outstanding enterprise zone facility bonds) is determined as of

Reg. § 1.1394-1(d)

the issue date of that issue, based on the issue price of that issue and the adjusted issue price of outstanding enterprise zone facility bonds. Amounts of outstanding enterprise zone facility bonds allocable to any entity are determined under rules contained in section 144(a)(10)(C) and the underlying regulations. Thus, the definition of *principal user* for purposes of section 1394(c) is different from the definition of *principal user* for purposes of paragraph (j) of this section.

(2) *Pooled financing bond programs*—(i) *In general.* The limitations of section 1394(c) for an issue for a pooled financing bond program are determined with regard to the amount of the actual loans to enterprise zone businesses rather than the amount lent to *intermediary lenders* as defined in paragraph (g)(2)(ii) of this section. This paragraph (g)(2) applies only to the extent the proceeds of those enterprise zone facility bonds are loaned to one or more enterprise zone businesses within 42 months of the issue date of the enterprise zone facility bonds or are used to redeem enterprise zone facility bonds of the issue within that 42-month period.

(ii) *Pooled financing bond program defined.* For purposes of this section, a *pooled financing bond program* is a program in which the issuer of enterprise zone facility bonds, in order to provide loans to enterprise zone businesses, lends the proceeds of the enterprise zone facility bonds to a bank or similar intermediary (intermediary lender) which must then relend the proceeds to two or more enterprise zone businesses.

(h) *Original use requirement for purposes of qualified zone property.* In general, for purposes of section 1397C(a)(1)(B), the term *original use* means the first use to which the property is put within the zone. For purposes of section 1394, if property is vacant for at least a one-year period including the date of zone designation, use prior to that period is disregarded for purposes of determining original use. For this purpose, de minimis incidental uses of property, such as renting the side of a building for a billboard, are disregarded.

(i) *Land.* The determination of whether land is functionally related and subordinate to qualified zone property is made in a manner consistent with the rules for exempt facilities under section 142.

(j) *Principal user*—(1) *In general.* Except as provided in paragraph (j)(2) of this section, the term *principal user* means the owner of financed property.

(2) *Rental of real property*—(i) *A lessee as the principal user.* If an owner of real property financed with enterprise zone facility bonds is not an enterprise zone business within the meaning of section 1397B, but the rental of the property is a qualified business within the meaning of section 1397B(d)(2), the term *principal user* for purposes of sections 1394(b) and (e) means the lessee or lessees.

(ii) *Allocation of enterprise zone facility bonds.* If a lessee is the principal user of real property under paragraph (j)(2)(i) of this section, then proceeds of enterprise zone facility bonds may be allocated to expenditures for real property only to the extent of the property allocable to the lessee's leased space, including expenditures for common areas.

(3) *Pooled financing bond program.* An intermediary lender in a pooled financing bond program described in paragraph (g)(2) of this section is not treated as the principal user.

(k) *Treatment as separately incorporated business.* For purposes of section 1394(b)(3)(B), a trade or business may be treated as separately incorporated if allocations of income and activities attributable to the business conducted within the zone are made using a reasonable allocation method and if that trade or business has evidence of those allocations sufficient to establish compliance with the requirements of paragraphs (b) through (f) of this section. Whether an allocation method is reasonable will depend upon the facts and circumstances. An allocation method will not be considered to be reasonable unless the allocation method is applied consistently by the trade or business and is consistent with the purposes of section 1394.

(l) *Substantially all.* For purposes of sections 1397B and 1397C(a), the term *substantially all* means 85 percent.

(m) *Application of sections 142 and 146 through 150*—(1) *In general.* Except as provided in this paragraph (m), enterprise zone facility bonds are treated as exempt facility bonds that are described in section 142(a), and all regulations generally applicable to exempt facility bonds apply to enterprise zone facility bonds. For this purpose, enterprise zone businesses are treated as meeting the public use requirement. Sections 147(c)(1)(A) (relating to limitations on financing the acquisition of land), 147(d) (relating to financing the acquisition of existing property), and 142(b)(2) (relating to limitations on financing office space) do not apply to enterprise zone facility bonds. See also paragraph (n)(4) of this section.

(2) *Maturity limitation*—(i) *Requirements.* An issue of enterprise zone facility bonds, the proceeds of which are to be used as part of a loan recycling program, satisfies the requirements of section 147(b) if—

Reg. § 1.1394-1(m)(2)

(A) Each loan satisfies the requirements of section 147(b) (determined by treating each separate loan as a separate issue); and

(B) The term of the issue does not exceed 30 years.

(ii) *Loan recycling program defined.* A *loan recycling program* is a program in which—

(A) The issuer reasonably expects as of the issue date of the enterprise zone facility bonds that loan repayments from principal users will be used to make additional loans during the zone designation period;

(B) Repayments of principal on loans (including prepayments) received during the zone designation period are used within six months of the date of receipt either to make new loans to enterprise zone businesses or to redeem enterprise zone facility bonds that are part of the issue; and

(C) Repayments of principal on loans (including prepayments) received after the zone designation period are used to redeem enterprise zone facility bonds that are part of the issue within six months of the date of receipt.

(3) *Volume cap.* For purposes of applying section 146(f)(5)(A) (relating to elective carryforward of unused volume limitation), issuing enterprise zone facility bonds is a carryforward purpose.

(4) *Remedial actions.* In the case of a pooled financing bond program described in paragraph (g)(2) of this section or a loan recycling program described in paragraph (m)(2)(ii) of this section, if a loan fails to meet the requirements of paragraphs (b) through (f) of this section, within six months of noncompliance (after taking into account the deemed compliance provisions of paragraph (b)(3) of this section, if applicable), an amount equal to the outstanding loan principal must be prepaid and the issuer must—

(i) Reloan the amount of the prepayment; or

(ii) Use the prepayment to redeem an amount of outstanding enterprise zone facility bonds equal to the outstanding principal amount of the loan that no longer meets those requirements.

(n) *Continuing compliance and change of use penalties*—(1) *In general.* The penalty provisions of section 1394(e) apply throughout the period of compliance required under paragraph (b) (1) of this section.

(2) *Coordination with deemed compliance provisions.* Section 1394(e)(2) does not apply during any period during which the issue is deemed to comply with the requirements of section 1394 under the deemed compliance provisions of paragraph (b)(3) of this section.

(3) *Application to pooled financing bond and loan recycling programs.* In the case of a pooled financing bond program described in paragraph (g)(2) of this section or a loan recycling program described in paragraph (m)(2)(ii) of this section, section 1394(e) applies on a loan-by-loan basis.

(4) *Section 150(b)(4) inapplicable.* Section 150(b)(4) does not apply to enterprise zone facility bonds.

(o) *Refunding bonds*—(1) *In general.* An issue of bonds issued after the zone designation period to refund enterprise zone facility bonds (other than in an advance refunding) are treated as enterprise zone facility bonds if the refunding issue and the prior issue, if treated as a single combined issue, would meet all of the requirements for enterprise zone facility bonds, except the requirements in section 1394(c). For example, the compliance period described in paragraph(b)(1) of this section is calculated taking into account any extension of the weighted average maturity of the refunding issue compared to the remaining weighted average maturity of the prior issue. The proceeds of the refunding issue are allocated to the same expenditures and purpose investments as the prior issue.

(2) *Maturity limitation.* The maturity limitation of section 147(b) is applied to a refunding issue by taking into account the issuer's reasonable expectations about the economic life of the financed property as of the issue date of the prior issue and the actual weighted average maturity of the combined refunding issue and prior issue.

(p) *Examples.* The following examples illustrate paragraphs (a) through (o) of this section:

Example 1. Averaging of enterprise zone business requirements. City C issues enterprise zone facility bonds, the proceeds of which are loaned by C to Corporation B to finance the acquisition of equipment for its existing business located in a zone. On the issue date of the enterprise zone facility bonds, B meets all of the requirements of section 1397B(b), except that only 25% of B's employees reside in the zone. C and B reasonably expect on the issue date to meet all requirements of section 1397B(b) by the date that 18 months after the equipment is placed in service (the initial testing date). In each of the first, second, and third taxable years after the initial testing date, 35% 40% and 45%, respectively, of B's employees are zone residents. In the fourth year after the testing date, only 25% of B's employees are zone residents. B continues to meet the 35% resident employee requirement, because the average of zone resident employees for those four taxable years is approximately 36%. The percentage of zone residents employed by B before the initial testing date is not included in determining whether B continues to comply with the 35% resident employee requirement.

Example 2. Measurement of resident employee percentage. Authority D issues enterprise zone facility bonds, the proceeds of which are loaned to Sole Proprietor F to establish an accounting business in a zone. In the first year after the initial testing date, the staff working for F includes F, who works 40 hours per week and does not live in the zone, one employee who resides in the zone and works 40 hours per week, one employee who does not reside in the zone and works 20 hours per week, and one employee who does not reside in the zone and works 10 hours per week. F meets the 35% resident employee test by calculating the percentage on the basis of employee actual work hours as described in paragraph (e)(3)(ii)(B) of this section. If F uses the per-employee basis as described in paragraph (e)(3)(ii)(A) of this section to determine if the resident employee test is met, the percentage of employees who are zone residents on a per-employee basis is only 33% because F must exclude from the numerator and the denominator the employee who works only 10 hours per week. If F calculates the resident employee test as a percentage of employee actual work hours as described in paragraph (e)(3)(ii)(B) of this section in the first year, F must calculate the resident employee test as a percentage of employee actual work hours each year.

Example 3. Active conduct of business within the zone. State G issues enterprise zone facility bonds and loans the proceeds to Corporation H to finance the acquisition of equipment for H's mail order clothing business, which is located in a zone. H purchases the supplies for its clothing business from suppliers located both within and outside of the zone and expects that orders will be received both from customers who will reside or work within the zone and from others outside the zone. All orders are received and filled at, and are shipped from, H's clothing business located in the zone. H meets the requirement that at least 80% of its gross income is derived from the active conduct of business within the zone.

Example 4. Enterprise zone business definition. City J issues enterprise zone facility bonds, the proceeds of which are loaned to Partnership K to finance the acquisition of equipment for its printing operation located in the zone. All orders are taken and completed, and all billing and accounting activities are performed, at the print shop located in the zone. K, on occasion, uses its equipment (including its trucks) and employees to deliver large print jobs to customers who reside outside -of the zone. So long as K is able to establish that its trucks are used in the zone at least 85% of the time and its employees perform at least 85% of services for K in the zone, K meets the requirements of sections 1397B(b)(3) and (5).

Example 5. Treatment as a separately incorporated business. The facts are the same as in *Example 4* except that six years after the issue date of the enterprise zone facility bonds, K determines to expand its operations to a second location outside of the boundaries of the zone. Although the expansion would result in the failure of K to meet the tests of 1397B(b), K, using a reasonable allocation method, allocates income and activities to its operations within the zone and has evidence of these allocations sufficient to establish compliance with the requirements of paragraphs (b) through (f) of this section. The bonds will not fail to be enterprise zone facility bonds merely because of the expansion.

Example 6. Treatment of pooled financing bond programs. Authority L issues bonds in the aggregate principal amount of $5,000,000 and loans the proceeds to Bank M pursuant to a loans-to-lenders program. M does not meet the definition of enterprise zone business contained in section 1397B. Prior to the issue date of the bonds, L held a public hearing regarding issuance of the bonds for the loans-to-lenders program, describing the projects of identified borrowers to be financed initially with $4,000,000 of the proceeds of the bonds. The applicable elected representative of L approved issuance of the bonds subsequent to the public hearing. The loan agreement between L and N provides that the other proceeds of the bonds will be held by M and loaned to borrowers that qualify as enterprise zone businesses, following a public hearing and approval by the applicable elected representative of L of each loan by M to an enterprise zone business. None of the loans will be in principal amounts in excess of $3,000,000. The loans by M will otherwise meet the requirements of section 1394. The bonds will be enterprise zone facility bonds.

Example 7. Original use requirement for purposes of qualified zone property. City N issues enterprise zone facility bonds, the proceeds of which are loaned to Corporation P to finance the acquisition of equipment. P uses the proceeds after the zone designation date to purchase used equipment located outside of the zone and places the equipment in service at its location in the zone. Substantially all of the use of the equipment is in the zone and is in the active conduct of a qualified business by P. The equipment is treated as qualified enterprise zone property under sec-

Reg. § 1.1394-1(p)

tion 1397C because P makes the first use of the property within the zone after the zone designation date.

Example 8. Principal user. State R issues enterprise zone facility bonds and loans the proceeds to Partnership S to finance the construction of a small shopping center to be located in a zone. S is in the business of commercial real estate. S is not an enterprise zone business, but has secured one anchor lessee, Corporation T, for the shopping center. T would qualify as an enterprise zone business. S will derive 60% of its gross rental income of the shopping center from T. S does not anticipate that the remaining rental income will come from enterprise zone businesses. T will occupy 60% of the total rentable space in the shopping center. S can use enterprise zone facility bond proceeds to finance the portion of the costs of the shopping center allocable to T (60%) because T is treated as the principal user of the enterprise zone facility bond proceeds.

Example 9. Remedial actions. State W issues pooled financing enterprise zone facility bonds, the proceeds of which will be loaned to several enterprise zone businesses in the two enterprise communities and one empowerment zone in W. Proceeds of the pooled financing bonds are loaned to Corporation X, an enterprise zone business, for a term of 10 years. Six years after the date of the loan, X expands its operations beyond the empowerment zone and is no longer able to meet the requirements of section 1394. X does not reasonably expect to be able to cure the noncompliance. The loan documents provide that X must prepay its loan in the event of noncompliance. W does not expect to be able to reloan the prepayment by X within six months of noncompliance. X's noncompliance will not affect the qualification of the pooled financing bonds as enterprise zone facility bonds if W uses the proceeds from the loan prepayment to redeem outstanding enterprise zone facility bonds within six months of noncompliance in an amount comparable to the outstanding amount of the loan immediately prior to prepayment. X will be denied an interest expense deduction for the interest accruing from the first day of the taxable year in which the noncompliance began.

(q) *Effective dates*—(1) *In general.* Except as otherwise provided in this section, the provisions of this section apply to all issues issued after July 30, 1996, and subject to section 1394.

(2) *Elective retroactive application in whole.* An issuer may apply the provisions of this section in whole, but not in part, to any issue that is outstanding on July 30, 1996, and is subject to section 1394. [Reg. § 1.1394-1.]

☐ [T.D. 8673, 5-30-96.]

Empowerment Zone Employment Credit
[Reg. § 1.1396-1]

§ 1.1396-1. **Qualified zone employees.**—(a) *In general.* A qualified zone employee of an employer is an employee who satisfies the location-of-services requirement and the abode requirement with respect to the same empowerment zone and is not otherwise excluded by section 1396(d).

(1) *Location-of-services requirement.* The location-of-services requirement is satisfied if substantially all of the services performed by the employee for the employer are performed in the empowerment zone in a trade or business of the employer.

(2) *Abode requirement.* The abode requirement is satisfied if the employee's principal place of abode while performing those services is in the empowerment zone.

(b) *Period for applying location-of-services requirement.* In applying the location-of-services requirement, an employer may use either the pay period method described in paragraph (b)(1) of this section or the calendar year method described in paragraph (b)(2) of this section. For each taxable year of an employer, the employer must either use the pay period method with respect to all of its employees or use the calendar year method with respect to all of its employees. The employer may change the method applied to all of its employees from one taxable year to the next.

(1) *Pay period method*—(i) *Relevant period.* Under the pay period method, the relevant period for applying the location-of-services requirement is each pay period in which an employee provides services to the employer during the calendar year with respect to which the credit is being claimed (i.e., the calendar year that ends with or within the relevant taxable year). If an employer has one pay period for certain employees and a different pay period for other employees (*e.g.*, a weekly pay period for hourly wage employees and a bi-weekly pay period for salaried employees), the pay period actually applicable to a particular employee is the relevant pay period for that employee under this method.

(ii) *Application of method.* Under this method, an employee does not satisfy the location-of-services requirement during a pay period unless substantially all of the services performed by the employee for the employer during that pay period are performed within the empowerment zone in a trade or business of the employer.

(2) *Calendar year method*—(i) *Relevant Period.* Under the calendar year method, the relevant period for an employee is the entire calendar year with respect to which the credit is being claimed. However, for any employee who is employed by the employer for less than the entire calendar year, the relevant period is the portion of that calendar year during which the employee is employed by the employer.

(ii) *Application of method.* Under this method, an employee does not satisfy the location-of-services requirement during any part of a calendar year unless substantially all of the services performed by the employee for the employer during that calendar year (or, if the employee is employed by the employer for less than the entire calendar year, the portion of that calendar year during which the employee is employed by the employer) are performed within the empowerment zone in a trade or business of the employer.

(3) *Examples.* This paragraph (b) may be illustrated by the following examples. In each example, the following assumptions apply. The employees satisfy the abode requirement at all relevant times and all services performed by the employees for their employer are performed in a trade or business of the employer. The employees are not precluded from being qualified zone employees by section 1396(d)(2) (certain employees ineligible). No portion of the employees' wages is precluded from being qualified zone wages by section 1396(c)(2) (only first $15,000 of wages taken into account) or section 1396(c)(3) (coordination with targeted jobs credit and work opportunity credit). The examples are as follows:

Example 1. (i) Employer X has a weekly pay period for all its employees. Employee A works for X throughout 1997. During each of the first 20 weekly pay periods in 1997, substantially all of A's work for X is performed within the empowerment zone in which A resides. A also works in the zone at various times during the rest of the year, but there is no other pay period in which substantially all of A's work for X is performed within the empowerment zone. Employer X uses the pay period method.

(ii) For each of the first 20 pay periods of 1997, A is a qualified zone employee, all of A's wages from X are qualified zone wages, and X may claim the empowerment zone employment credit with respect to those wages. X cannot claim the credit with respect to any of A's wages for the rest of 1997.

Example 2. (i) Employer Y has a weekly pay period for its factory workers and a bi-weekly pay period for its office workers. Employee B works for Y in various factories and Employee C works for Y in various offices. Employer Y uses the pay period method.

(ii) Y must use B's weekly pay periods to determine the periods (if any) in which B is a qualified zone employee. Y may claim the empowerment zone employment credit with respect to B's wages only for the weekly pay periods for which B is a qualified zone employee, because those are B's only wages that are qualified zone wages. Y must use C's bi-weekly pay periods to determine the periods (if any) in which C is a qualified zone employee. Y may claim the credit with respect to C's wages only for the bi-weekly pay periods for which C is a qualified zone employee, because those are C's only wages that are qualified zone wages.

Example 3. (i) Employees D and E work for Employer Z throughout 1997. Although some of D's work for Z in 1997 is performed outside the empowerment zone in which D resides, substantially all of it is performed within that empowerment zone. E's work for Z is performed within the empowerment zone in which E resides for several weeks of 1997 but outside the zone for the rest of the year so that, viewed on an annual basis, E's work is not substantially all performed within the empowerment zone. Employer Z uses the calendar year method.

(ii) D is a qualified zone employee for the entire year, all of D's 1997 wages from Z are qualified zone wages, and Z may claim the empowerment zone employment credit with respect to all of those wages, including the portion attributable to work outside the zone. Under the calendar year method, E is not a qualified zone employee for any part of 1997, none of E's 1997 wages are qualified zone wages, and Z cannot claim any empowerment zone employment credit with respect to E's wages for 1997. Z cannot use the calendar year method for D and the pay period method for E because Z must use the same method for all employees. For 1998, however, Z can switch to the pay period method for E if Z also switches to the pay period method for D and all of Z's other employees.

(c) *Effective date.* This section applies with respect to wages paid or incurred on or after December 21, 1994. [Reg. § 1.1396-1.]

☐ [T.D. 8747, 12-29-97.]

[Reg. § 1.1397E-1]

§ 1.1397E-1. **Qualified zone academy bonds.**—(a) *Overview.* In general, a qualified zone academy bond is a taxable bond issued by a state or local government the proceeds of which are used to improve certain eligible public schools. An eligible taxpayer that holds a qualified zone academy bond generally is allowed annual federal income tax credits in lieu of periodic interest payments. These credits compensate the eligible taxpayer for lending money to the issuer and function as payments of interest on the bond. Accordingly, this section generally treats the allowance of a credit as if it were a payment of interest on the bond. In addition, this section provides rules to determine the credit rate, the present value of qualified contributions from private entities, and the maximum term of a qualified zone academy bond.

(b) *Credit rate.* The Secretary shall determine monthly (or more often as deemed necessary by the Secretary) the credit rate the Secretary estimates will generally permit the issuance of a qualified zone academy bond without discount and without interest cost to the issuer. The manner for ascertaining the credit rate for a qualified zone academy bond as determined by the Secretary shall be set forth in procedures, notices, forms, or instructions prescribed by the Commissioner.

(c) *Private business contribution requirement*—(1) *Reasonable discount rate.* To determine the present value (as of the issue date) of qualified contributions from private entities under section 1397E(d)(2), the issuer must use a reasonable discount rate. The credit rate determined under paragraph (b) of this section is a reasonable discount rate.

(2) *Definition of private entities.* For purposes of section 1397E(d)(2)(A), the term *private entities* includes any person (as defined in section 7701(a)) other than the United States, a State or local government, or any agency or instrumentality thereof or related party with respect thereto. To determine whether a person is related to the United States or a State or local government under this paragraph (c)(2), rules similar to those for determining whether a person is a related party under § 1.150-1(b) shall apply (treating the United States as a governmental unit for purposes of § 1.150-1(b)).

(3) *Qualified contribution.* For purposes of section 1397E(d)(2)(A), the term *qualified contribution* means any contribution (of a type and quality acceptable to the eligible local education agency) of any property or service described in section 1397E(d)(2)(B)(i), (ii), (iii), (iv) or (v). In addition, cash received with respect to a qualified zone academy from a private entity (other than cash received indirectly from a person that is not a private entity as part of a plan to avoid the requirements of section 1397E) constitutes a qualified contribution if it is to be used to purchase any property or service described in section 1397E(d)(2)(B)(i), (ii), (iii), (iv) or (v). Services of employees of the eligible local education agency do not constitute qualified contributions.

(d) *Maximum term.* The maximum term for a qualified zone academy bond is determined under section 1397E(d)(3) by using a discount rate equal to 110 percent of the long-term adjusted AFR, compounded semi-annually, for the month in which the bond is issued. The Internal Revenue Service publishes this figure each month in a revenue ruling that is published in the Internal Revenue Bulletin. See § 601.601(d)(2)(ii)(b) of this Chapter.

(e) *Tax credit*—(1) *Eligible taxpayer.* An eligible taxpayer (within the meaning of section 1397E(d)(6)) that holds a qualified zone academy bond on a credit allowance date is allowed a tax credit against the federal income tax imposed on the taxpayer for the taxable year that includes the credit allowance date. The amount of the credit is equal to the product of the credit rate and the outstanding principal amount of the bond on the credit allowance date. The credit is subject to a limitation based on the eligible taxpayer's income tax liability. See section 1397E(c).

(2) *Ineligible taxpayer.* A taxpayer that is not an eligible taxpayer is not allowed a credit.

(f) *Treatment of the allowance of the credit as a payment of interest*—(1) *General rule.* The holder of a qualified zone academy bond must treat the bond as if it pays qualified stated interest (within the meaning of § 1.1273-1(c)) on each credit allowance date. The amount of the deemed payment of interest on each credit allowance date is equal to the product of the credit rate and the outstanding principal amount of the bond on that date. Thus, for example, if the holder uses an accrual method of accounting, the holder must accrue as interest income the amount of the credit over the one-year accrual period that ends on the credit allowance date.

(2) *Adjustment if the holder cannot use the credit to offset a tax liability.* If a holder holds a qualified zone academy bond on the credit allowance date but cannot use all or a portion of the credit to reduce its income tax liability (for example, because the holder is not an eligible taxpayer or because the limitation in section 1397E(c) applies), the holder is allowed a deduction for the taxable year that includes the credit allowance date (or, at the option of the holder, the next succeeding taxable year). The amount of the deduction is equal to the amount of the unused credit deemed paid on the credit allowance date.

(g) *Not a tax-exempt obligation.* A qualified zone academy bond is not an obligation the inter-

Reg. § 1.1397E-1(b)

est on which is excluded from gross income under section 103(a).

(h) *Reimbursement.* An expenditure for a qualified purpose may be reimbursed with proceeds of a qualified zone academy bond. For this purpose, rules similar to those in § 1.150-2 shall apply.

(i) *State or local government*—(1) *In general.* For purposes of section 1397E(d)(1)(B), the term *State or local government* means a State or political subdivision as defined for purposes of section 103(c).

(2) *On behalf of issuer.* A qualified zone academy bond may be issued on behalf of a State or local government under rules similar to those for determining whether a bond issued on behalf of a State or political subdivision constitutes an obligation of that State or political subdivision for purposes of section 103.

(j) *Cross-references.* See section 171 and the regulations thereunder for rules relating to amortizable bond premium. See § 1.61-7(d) for the seller's treatment of a bond sold between interest payment dates (credit allowance dates) and § 1.61-7(c) for the buyer's treatment of a bond purchased between interest payment dates (credit allowance dates).

(k) *Effective dates.* Except as provided in this paragraph (k), this section applies to bonds sold on or after September 26, 2000. Each of paragraphs (c) and (i) of this section may be applied by issuers to bonds that are sold before September 26, 2000. [Reg. § 1.1397E-1.]

☐ [*T.D.* 8903, 9-25-2000.]

TITLE 11 CASES

[Reg. § 1.1398-1]

§ 1.1398-1. **Treatment of passive activity losses and passive activity credits in individuals' title 11 cases.**—(a) *Scope.* This section applies to cases under chapter 7 or chapter 11 of title 11 of the United States Code, but only if the debtor is an individual.

(b) *Definitions and rules of general application.* For purposes of this section—

(1) *Passive activity* and *former passive activity* have the meanings given in section 469(c) and (f)(3);

(2) The unused passive activity loss (determined as of the first day of a taxable year) is the passive activity loss (as defined in section 469(d)(1)) that is disallowed under section 469 for the previous taxable year; and

(3) The unused passive activity credit (determined as of the first day of a taxable year) is the passive activity credit (as defined in section 469(d)(2)) that is disallowed under section 469 for the previous taxable year.

(c) *Estate succeeds to losses and credits upon commencement of case.* The bankruptcy estate (estate) succeeds to and takes into account, beginning with its first taxable year, the debtor's unused passive activity loss and unused passive activity credit (determined as of the first day of the debtor's taxable year in which the case commences).

(d) *Transfers from estate to debtor*— (1) *Transfer not treated as taxable event.* If, before the termination of the estate, the estate transfers an interest in a passive activity or former passive activity to the debtor (other than by sale or exchange), the transfer is not treated as a disposition for purposes of any provision of the Internal Revenue Code assigning tax consequences to a disposition. The transfers to which this rule applies include transfers from the estate to the debtor of property that is exempt under section 522 of title 11 of the United States Code and abandonments of estate property to the debtor under section 554(a) of such title.

(2) *Treatment of passive activity loss and credit.* If, before the termination of the estate, the estate transfers an interest in a passive activity or former passive activity to the debtor (other than by sale or exchange)—

(i) The estate must allocate to the transferred interest, in accordance with § 1.469-1(f)(4), part or all of the estate's unused passive activity loss and unused passive activity credit (determined as of the first day of the estate's taxable year in which the transfer occurs); and

(ii) The debtor succeeds to and takes into account, beginning with the debtor's taxable year in which the transfer occurs, the unused passive activity loss and unused passive activity credit (or part thereof) allocated to the transferred interest.

(e) *Debtor succeeds to loss and credit of the estate upon its termination.* Upon termination of the estate, the debtor succeeds to and takes into account, beginning with the debtor's taxable year in which the termination occurs, the passive activity loss and passive activity credit disallowed under section 469 for the estate's last taxable year.

(f) *Effective date*— (1) *Cases commencing on or after November 9, 1992.* This section applies to cases commencing on or after November 9, 1992.

(2) *Cases commencing before November 9. 1992*—(i) *Election required.* This section applies to a case commencing before November 9, 1992, and terminating on or after that date if the debtor and the estate jointly elect its application in the manner prescribed in paragraph (f)(2)(v) of this section (the election). The caption "ELECTION PURSUANT TO § 1.1398-1" must be placed prominently on the first page of each of the debtor's returns that is affected by the election (other than returns for taxable years that begin after the termination of the estate) and on the first page of each of the estate's returns that is affected by the election. In the case of returns that are amended under paragraph (f)(2)(iii) of this section, this requirement is satisfied by placing the caption on the amended return.

(ii) *Scope of election.* This election applies to the passive and former passive activities and unused passive activity losses and passive activity credits of the taxpayers making the election.

(iii) *Amendment of previously filed returns.* The debtor and the estate making the election must amend all returns (except to the extent they are for a year that is a closed year within the meaning of paragraph (f)(2)(iv)(D) of this section) they filed before the date of the election to the extent necessary to provide that no claim of a deduction or credit is inconsistent with the succession under this section to unused losses and credits. The Commissioner may revoke or limit the effect of the election if either the debtor or the estate fails to satisfy the requirement of this paragraph (f)(2)(iii).

(iv) *Rules relating to closed years*—(A) *Estate succeeds to debtor's passive activity loss and credit as of the commencement date.* If, by reason of an election under this paragraph (f), this section applies to a case that was commenced in a closed year, the estate, nevertheless, succeeds to and takes into account the unused passive activity loss and unused passive activity credit of the debtor (determined as of the first day of the debtor's taxable year in which the case commenced).

(B) *No reduction of unused passive activity loss and credit for passive activity loss and credit not claimed for a closed year.* In determining a taxpayer's carryover of a passive activity loss or credit to its taxable year following a closed year, a deduction or credit that the taxpayer failed to claim in the closed year, if attributable to an unused passive activity loss or credit to which the taxpayer succeeded under this section, is treated as a deduction or credit that was disallowed under section 469.

(C) *Passive activity loss and credit to which taxpayer succeeds reflects deductions of prior holder in a closed year.* A loss or credit to which a taxpayer would otherwise succeed under this section is reduced to the extent the loss or credit was allowed to its prior holder for a closed year.

(D) *Closed year.* For purposes of this paragraph (f)(2)(iv), a taxable year is closed to the extent the assessment of a deficiency or refund of an overpayment is prevented, on the date of the election and at all times thereafter, by any law or rule of law.

(v) *Manner of making election*— (A) *Chapter 7 cases.* In a case under chapter 7 of title 11 of the United States Code, the election is made by obtaining the written consent of the bankruptcy trustee and filing a copy of the written consent with the returns (or amended returns) of the debtor and the estate for their first taxable years ending after November 9, 1992.

(B) *Chapter 11 cases.* In a case under chapter 11 of title 11 of the United States Code, the election is made by incorporating the election into a bankruptcy plan that is confirmed by the bankruptcy court or into an order of such court and filing the pertinent portion of the plan or order with the returns (or amended returns) of the debtor and the estate for their first taxable years ending after November 9, 1992.

(vi) *Election is binding and irrevocable.* Except as provided in paragraph (f)(2)(iii) of this section, the election, once made, is binding on both the debtor and the estate and is irrevocable. [Reg. § 1.1398-1.]

□ [*T.D.* 8537, 5-12-94.]

[Reg. § 1.1398-2]

§ 1.1398-2. **Treatment of section 465 losses in individuals' title 11 cases.**—(a) *Scope.* This section applies to cases under chapter 7 or chapter 11 of title 11 of the United States Code, but only if the debtor is an individual.

(b) *Definition and rules of general application.* For purposes of this section—

(1) *Section 465 activity* means an activity to which section 465 applies; and

(2) For each section 465 activity, the unused section 465 loss from the activity (determined as of the first day of a taxable year) is the loss (as defined in section 465(d)) that is not allowed under section 465(a)(1) for the previous taxable year.

(c) *Estate succeeds to losses upon commencement of case.* The bankruptcy estate (the estate) succeeds to and takes into account, beginning with its first taxable year, the debtor's unused section 465 losses (determined as of the first day of the debtor's taxable year in which the case commences).

(d) *Transfers from estate to debtor*—(1) *Transfer not treated as taxable event.* If, before the termination of the estate, the estate transfers an interest in a section 465 activity to the debtor (other than by sale or exchange), the transfer is not treated as a disposition for purposes of any provision of the Internal Revenue Code assigning tax consequences to a disposition. The transfers to which this rule applies include transfers from the estate to the debtor of property that is exempt under section 522 of title 11 of the United States Code and abandonments of estate property to the debtor under section 554(a) of such title.

(2) *Treatment of section 465 losses.* If, before the termination of the estate, the estate transfers an interest in a section 465 activity to the debtor (other than by sale or exchange) the debtor succeeds to and takes into account, beginning with the debtor's taxable year in which the transfer occurs, the transferred interest's share of the estate's unused section 465 loss from the activity (determined as of the first day of the estate's taxable year in which the transfer occurs). For this purpose, the transferred interest's share of such loss is the amount, if any, by which such loss would be reduced if the transfer had occurred as of the close of the preceding taxable year of the estate and been treated as a disposition on which gain or loss is recognized.

(e) *Debtor succeeds to losses of the estate upon its termination.* Upon termination of the estate, the debtor succeeds to and takes into account, beginning with the debtor's taxable year in which the termination occurs, the losses not allowed under section 465 for the estate's last taxable year.

(f) *Effective date*—(1) *Cases commencing on or after November 9, 1992.* This section applies to cases commencing on or after November 9, 1992.

(2) *Cases commencing before November 9, 1992*—(i) *Election required.* This section applies to a case commencing before November 9, 1992, and terminating on or after that date if the debtor and the estate jointly elect its application in the manner prescribed in paragraph (f)(2)(v) of this section (the election). The caption "ELECTION PURSUANT TO § 1.1398-2" must be placed prominently on the first page of each of the debtor's returns that is affected by the election (other than returns for taxable years that begin after the termination of the estate) and on the first page of each of the estate's returns that is affected by the election. In the case of returns that are amended under paragraph (f)(2)(iii) of this section, this requirement is satisfied by placing the caption on the amended return.

(ii) *Scope of election.* This election applies to the section 465 activities and unused losses from section 465 activities of the taxpayers making the election.

(iii) *Amendment of previously filed returns.* The debtor and the estate making the election must amend all returns (except to the extent they are for a year that is a closed year within the meaning of paragraph (f)(2)(iv)(D) of this section) they filed before the date of the election to the extent necessary to provide that no claim of a deduction is inconsistent with the succession under this section to unused losses from section 465 activities. The Commissioner may revoke or limit the effect of the election if either the debtor or the estate fails to satisfy the requirement of this paragraph (f)(2)(iii).

(iv) *Rules relating to closed years*—(A) *Estate succeeds to debtor's section 465 loss as of the commencement date.* If, by reason of an election under this paragraph (f), this section applies to a case that was commenced in a closed year, the estate, nevertheless, succeeds to and takes into account the section 465 losses of the debtor (determined as of the first day of the debtor's taxable year in which the case commenced).

(B) *No reduction of unused section 465 loss for loss not claimed for a closed year.* In determining a taxpayer's carryover of an unused section 465 loss to its taxable year following a closed year, a deduction that the taxpayer failed to claim in the closed year, if attributable to an unused section 465 loss to which the taxpayer succeeds under this section, is treated as a deduction that was not allowed under section 465.

(C) *Loss to which taxpayer succeeds reflects deductions of prior holder in a closed year.* A loss to which a taxpayer would otherwise succeed under this section is reduced to the extent the loss was allowed to its prior holder for a closed year.

(D) *Closed year.* For purposes of this paragraph (f)(2)(iv), a taxable year is closed to the extent the assessment of a deficiency or refund of an overpayment is prevented, on the date of the election and at all times thereafter, by any law or rule of law.

(v) *Manner of making election*—(A) *Chapter 7 cases.* In a case under chapter 7 of title 11 of the United States Code, the election is made by obtaining the written consent of the bankruptcy trustee and filing a copy of the written consent with the returns (or amended returns) of the debtor and the estate for their first taxable years ending after November 9, 1992.

Reg. § 1.1398-2(f)(2)

(B) *Chapter 11 cases.* In a case under chapter 11 of title 11 of the United States Code, the election is made by incorporating the election into a bankruptcy plan that is confirmed by the bankruptcy court or into an order of such court and filing the pertinent portion of the plan or order with the returns (or amended returns) of the debtor and the estate for their first taxable years ending after November 9, 1992.

(vi) *Election is binding and irrevocable.* Except as provided in paragraph (f)(2)(iii) of this section, the election, once made, is binding on both the debtor and the estate and is irrevocable. [Reg. § 1.1398-2.]

☐ [*T.D.* 8537, 5-12-94.]

[The next page is 56,501.]

Tax on Self-Employment Income

[Reg. § 1.1401-1]

§ 1.1401-1. Tax on self-employment income.—(a) There is imposed, in addition to other taxes, a tax upon the self-employment income of every individual at the rates prescribed in section 1401(a) (old-age, survivors, and disability insurance) and (b) (hospital insurance). (See subparagraphs (1) and (2) of paragraph (b) of this section.) This tax shall be levied, assessed, and collected as part of the income tax imposed by subtitle A of the Code and, except as otherwise expressly provided, will be included with the tax imposed by section 1 or 3 in computing any deficiency or overpayment and in computing the interest and additions to any deficiency, overpayment, or tax. Since the tax on self-employment income is part of the income tax, it is subject to the jurisdiction of the Tax Court of the United States to the same extent and in the same manner as the other taxes under subtitle A of the Code. Furthermore, with respect to taxable years beginning after December 31, 1966, this tax must be taken into account in computing any estimate of the taxes required to be declared under section 6015.

(b) The rates of tax on self-employment income are as follows:

(1) For old-age, survivors, and disability insurance:

Taxable Year	Percent
Beginning before January 1, 1957	3
Beginning after December 31, 1956 and before January 1, 1959	3.375
Beginning after December 31, 1958 and before January 1, 1960	3.75
Beginning after December 31, 1959 and before January 1, 1962	4.5
Beginning after December 31, 1961 and before January 1, 1963	4.7
Beginning after December 31, 1962 and before January 1, 1966	5.4
Beginning after December 31, 1965 and before January 1, 1967	5.8
Beginning after December 31, 1966 and before January 1, 1968	5.9
Beginning after December 31, 1967 and before January 1, 1969	5.8
Beginning after December 31, 1968 and before January 1, 1971	6.3
Beginning after December 31, 1970 and before January 1, 1973	6.9
Beginning after December 31, 1972	7.0

(2) For hospital insurance:

Taxable Year	Percent
Beginning after December 31, 1965 and before January 1, 1967	0.35
Beginning after December 31, 1966 and before January 1, 1968	.50
Beginning after December 31, 1967 and before January 1, 1973	.60
Beginning after December 31, 1972 and before January 1, 1974	1.0
Beginning after December 31, 1973 and before January 1, 1978	.90
Beginning after December 31, 1977 and before January 1, 1981	1.10
Beginning after December 31, 1980 and before January 1, 1986	1.35
Beginning after December 31, 1985	1.50

(c) In general, self-employment income consists of the net earnings derived by an individual (other than a nonresident alien) from a trade or business carried on by him as sole proprietor or by a partnership of which he is a member, including the net earnings of certain employees as set forth in § 1.1402(c)-3, and of crew leaders, as defined in section 3121(o) (see such section and the regulations thereunder in Part 31 of this chapter (Employment Tax Regulations)). See, however, the exclusions, exceptions, and limitations set forth in §§ 1.1402(a)-1 through 1.1402(h)-1. [Reg. § 1.1401-1.]

☐ [T.D. 6196, 8-13-56. Amended by T.D. 6691, 12-2-63, T.D. 6993, 1-17-69 and T.D. 7333, 12-19-74.]

[Reg. § 1.1402(a)-1]

§ 1.1402(a)-1. Definition of net earnings from self-employment.—(a) Subject to the special rules set forth in §§ 1.1402(a)-3 to 1.1402(a)-17, inclusive, and to the exclusions set forth in §§ 1.1402(c)-2 to 1.1402(c)-7, inclusive, the term "net earnings from self-employment" means—

(1) The gross income derived by an individual from any trade or business carried on by such individual, less the deductions allowed by chapter 1 of the Code which are attributable to such trade or business, plus

(2) His distributive share (whether or not distributed), as determined under section 704, of the income (or minus the loss), described in section 702(a)(9) and as computed under section 703, from any trade or business carried on by any partnership of which he is a member.

(b) Gross income derived by an individual from a trade or business includes payments received by him from a partnership of which he is a member for services rendered to the partnership or for the use of capital by the partnership, to the extent the payments are determined without regard to the income of the partnership. However, such payments received from a partnership not engaged in a trade or business within the meaning of section 1402(c) and § 1.1402(c)-1 do not constitute gross

Reg. § 1.1402(a)-1(b)

income derived by an individual from a trade or business. See section 707(c) and the regulations thereunder, relating to guaranteed payments to a member of a partnership for services or the use of capital. See also section 706(a) and the regulations thereunder, relating to the taxable year of the partner in which such guaranteed payments are to be included in computing taxable income.

(c) Gross income derived by an individual from a trade or business includes gross income received (in the case of an individual reporting income on the cash receipts and disbursements method) or accrued (in the case of an individual reporting income on the accrual method) in the taxable year from a trade or business even though such income may be attributable in whole or in part to services rendered or other acts performed in a prior taxable year as to which the individual was not subject to the tax on self-employment income. [Reg. § 1.1402(a)-1.]

☐ [T.D. 6196, 8-13-56. Amended by T.D. 6691, 12-2-63, and T.D. 7333, 12-19-74.]

[Reg. § 1.1402(a)-2]

§ 1.1402(a)-2. **Computation of net earnings from self-employment.**—(a) *General rule.* In general, the gross income and deductions of an individual attributable to a trade or business (including a trade or business conducted by an employee referred to in paragraphs (b), (c), (d), or (e) of § 1.1402(c)-3, for the purpose of ascertaining his net earnings from self-employment, are to be determined by reference to the provisions of law and regulations applicable with respect to the taxes imposed by sections 1 and 3. Thus, if an individual uses the accrual method of accounting in computing taxable income from a trade or business for the purpose of the tax imposed by section 1 or 3, he must use the same method in determining net earnings from self-employment. Likewise, if a taxpayer engaged in a trade or business of selling property on the installment plan elects, under the provisions of section 453, to use the installment method in computing income for purposes of the tax under section 1 or 3, he must use the same method in determining net earnings from self-employment. Income which is excludable from gross income under any provision of subtitle A of the Internal Revenue Code is not taken into account in determining net earnings from self-employment except as otherwise provided in § 1.1402(a)-9, relating to certain residents of Puerto Rico, in § 1.1402(a)-11, relating to ministers or members of religious orders, and in § 1.1402(a)-12, relating to the term "possession of the United States" as used for purposes of the tax on self-employment income. Thus, in the case of a citizen of the United States conducting, in a foreign country, a trade or business in which both personal services and capital are material income-producing factors, any part of the income therefrom which is excluded from gross income as earned income under the provisions of section 911 and the regulations thereunder is not taken into account in determining net earnings from self-employment.

(b) *Trade or business carried on.* The trade or business must be carried on by the individual, either personally or through agents or employees. Accordingly, income derived from a trade or business carried on by an estate or trust is not included in determining the net earnings from self-employment of the individual beneficiaries of such estate or trust.

(c) *Aggregate net earnings.* Where an individual is engaged in more than one trade or business within the meaning of section 1402(c) and § 1.1402(c)-1, his net earnings from self-employment consist of the aggregate of the net income and losses (computed subject to the special rules provided in § § 1.1402(a)-1 to 1.1402(a)-17, inclusive) of all such trades or businesses carried on by him. Thus, a loss sustained in one trade or business carried on by an individual will operate to offset the income derived by him from another trade or business.

(d) *Partnerships.* The net earnings from self-employment of an individual include, in addition to the earnings from a trade or business carried on by him, his distributive share of the income or loss, described in section 702(a)(9), from any trade or business carried on by each partnership of which he is a member. An individual's distributive share of such income or loss of a partnership shall be determined as provided in section 704, subject to the special rules set forth in section 1402(a) and in § § 1.1402(a)-1 to 1.1402(a)-17, inclusive, and to the exclusions provided in section 1402(c) and § § 1.1402(c)-2 to 1.1402(c)-7, inclusive. For provisions relating to the computation of the taxable income of a partnership, see section 703.

(e) *Different taxable years.* If the taxable year of a partner differs from that of the partnership, the partner shall include, in computing net earnings from self-employment, his distributive share of the income or loss, described in section 702(a)(9), of the partnership for its taxable year ending with or within the taxable year of the partner. For the special rule in case of the termination of a partner's taxable year as result of death, see § § 1.1402(f) and 1.1402(f)-1.

(f) *Meaning of partnerships.* For the purpose of determining net earnings from self-employment, a partnership is one which is recognized as such for income tax purposes. For income tax purposes, the term "partnership" includes not only a partnership as known at common law, but, also, a syndicate, group, pool, joint venture, or other unincorporated organization which carries on any trade or business, financial operation, or venture, and which is not, within the meaning of the Code, a trust, estate, or a corporation. An organization described in the preceding sentence shall be treated as a partnership for purposes of the tax on self-employment income even though such organization has elected, pursuant to section 1361 and the regulations thereunder, to be taxed as a domestic corporation.

(g) *Nature of partnership interest.* The net earnings from self-employment of a partner include his distributive share of the income or loss, described in section 702(a)(9), of the partnership of which he is a member, irrespective of the nature of his membership. Thus, in determining his net earnings from self-employment, a limited or inactive partner includes his distributive share of such partnership income or loss. In the case of a partner who is a member of a partnership with respect to which an election has been made pursuant to section 1361 and the regulations thereunder to be taxed as a domestic corporation, net earnings from self-employment include his distributive share of the income or loss, described in section 702(a)(9), from the trade or business carried on by the partnership computed without regard to the fact that the partnership has elected to be taxed as a domestic corporation.

(h) *Proprietorship taxed as domestic corporation.* A proprietor of an unincorporated business enterprise with respect to which an election has been made pursuant to section 1361 and the regulations thereunder to be taxed as a domestic corporation shall compute his net earnings from self-employment without regard to the fact that such election has been made. [Reg. § 1.1402(a)-2.]

☐ [*T.D.* 6691, 12-2-63. Amended by *T.D.* 7333, 12-19-74.]

[Reg. § 1.1402(a)-3]

§ 1.1402(a)-3. **Special rules for computing net earnings from self-employment.**—For the purpose of computing net earnings from self-employment, the gross income derived by an individual from a trade or business carried on by him, the allowable deductions attributable to such trade or business, and the individual's distributive share of the income or loss, described in section 702(a)(9), from any trade or business carried on by a partnership of which he is a member shall be computed in accordance with the special rules set forth in §§ 1.1402(a)-4 to 1.1402(a)-17, inclusive. [Reg. § 1.1402(a)-3.]

☐ [*T.D.* 6691, 12-2-63. Amended by *T.D.* 7710, 7-28-80.]

[Reg. § 1.1402(a)-4]

§ 1.1402(a)-4. **Rentals from real estate.**—(a) *In general.* Rentals from real estate and from personal property leased with the real estate (including such rentals paid in crop shares), and the deductions attributable thereto, unless such rentals are received by an individual in the course of a trade or business as a real-estate dealer, are excluded. Whether or not an individual is engaged in the trade or business of a real-estate dealer is determined by the application of the principles followed in respect of the taxes imposed by sections 1 and 3. In general, an individual who is engaged in the business of selling real estate to customers with a view to the gains and profits that may be derived from such sales is a real-estate dealer. On the other hand, an individual who merely holds real estate for investment or speculation and receives rentals therefrom is not considered a real-estate dealer. Where a real-estate dealer holds real estate for investment or speculation in addition to real estate held for sale to customers in the ordinary course of his trade or business as a real-estate dealer, only the rentals from the real estate held for sale to customers in the ordinary course of his trade or business as a real-estate dealer, and the deductions attributable thereto, are included in determining net earnings from self-employment; the rentals from the real estate held for investment or speculation, and the deductions attributable thereto, are excluded. Rentals paid in crop shares include income derived by an owner or lessee of land under an agreement entered into with another person pursuant to which such other person undertakes to produce a crop or livestock on such land and pursuant to which (1) the crop or livestock, or the proceeds thereof, are to be divided between such owner or lessee and such other person, and (2) the share of the owner or lessee depends on the amount of the crop or livestock produced. See, however, paragraph (b) of this section.

(b) *Special rule for "includible farm rental income"*—(1) *In general.* Notwithstanding the rules set forth in paragraph (a) of this section, there shall be included in determining net earnings from self-employment for taxable years ending after 1955 any income derived by an owner or tenant of land, if the following requirements are met with respect to such income:

(i) The income is derived under an arrangement between the owner or tenant of land and another person which provides that such other person shall produce agricultural or horticultural commodities on such land, and that there

Reg. § 1.1402(a)-4(b)(1)

shall be material participation by the owner or tenant in the production or the management of the production of such agricultural or horticultural commodities; and

(ii) There is material participation by the owner or tenant with respect to any such agricultural or horticultural commodity.

Income so derived shall be referred to in this section as "includible farm rental income".

(2) *Requirement that income be derived under an arrangement.* In order for rental income received by an owner or tenant of land to be treated as includible farm rental income, such income must be derived pursuant to a sharefarming or other rental arrangement which contemplates material participation by the owner or tenant in the production or management of production of agricultural or horticultural commodities.

(3) *Nature of arrangement.* (i) The arrangement between the owner or tenant and the person referred to in subparagraph (1) of this paragraph may be either oral or written. The arrangement must impose upon such other person the obligation to produce one or more agricultural or horticultural commodities (including livestock, bees, poultry, and fur-bearing animals and wildlife) on the land of the owner or tenant. In addition, it must be within the contemplation of the parties that the owner or tenant will participate in the production or the management of the production of the agricultural or horticultural commodities required to be produced by the other person under such arrangement to an extent which is material with respect either to the production or to the management of production of such commodities or is material with respect to the production and management of production when the total required participation in connection with both is considered.

(ii) The term "production", wherever used in this paragraph, refers to the physical work performed and the expenses incurred in producing a commodity. It includes such activities as the actual work of planting, cultivating, and harvesting crops, and the furnishing of machinery, implements, seed, and livestock. An arrangement will be treated as contemplating that the owner or tenant will materially participate in the "production" of the commodities required to be produced by the other person under the arrangement if under the arrangement it is understood that the owner or tenant is to engage to a material degree in the physical work related to the production of such commodities. The mere undertaking to furnish machinery, implements, and livestock and to incur expenses is not, in and of itself, sufficient.

Such factors may be significant, however, in cases where the degree of physical work intended of the owner or tenant is not material. For example, if under the arrangement it is understood that the owner or tenant is to engage periodically in physical work to a degree which is not material in and of itself and, in addition, to furnish a substantial portion of the machinery, implements, and livestock to be used in the production of the commodities or to furnish or advance funds or assume financial responsibility for a substantial part of the expense involved in the production of the commodities, the arrangement will be treated as contemplating material participation of the owner or tenant in the production of such commodities.

(iii) The term "management of the production", wherever used in this paragraph, refers to services performed in making managerial decisions relating to the production, such as when to plant, cultivate, dust, spray, or harvest the crop, and includes advising and consulting, making inspections, and making decisions as to matters such as rotation of crops, the type of crops to be grown, the type of livestock to be raised, and the type of machinery and implements to be furnished. An arrangement will be treated as contemplating that the owner or tenant is to participate materially in the "management of the production" of the commodities required to be produced by the other person under the arrangement if the owner or tenant is to engage to a material degree in the management decisions related to the production of such commodities. The services which are considered of particular importance in making such management decisions are those services performed in making inspections of the production activities and in advising and consulting with such person as to the production of the commodities. Thus, if under the arrangement it is understood that the owner or tenant is to advise or consult periodically with the other person as to the production of the commodities required to be produced by such person under the arrangement and to inspect periodically the production activities on the land, a strong inference will be drawn that the arrangement contemplates participation by the owner or tenant in the management of the production of such commodities. The mere undertaking to select the crops or livestock to be produced or the type of machinery and implements to be furnished or to make decisions as to the rotation of crops generally is not, in and of itself, sufficient. Such factors may be significant, however, in making the over-all determination of whether the arrangement contemplates that the owner or tenant is to materially participate in the management of the production of the commodities. Thus, if in addition to the under-

Reg. § 1.1402(a)-4(b)(2)

standing that the owner or tenant is to advise or consult periodically with the other person as to the production of the commodities and inspect periodically the production activities on the land, it is also understood that the owner is to select the type of crops and livestock to be produced and the type of machinery and implements to be furnished and to make decisions as to the rotation of crops, the arrangement will be treated as contemplating material participation of the owner or tenant in the management of production of such commodities.

(4) *Actual participation.* In order for the rental income received by the owner or tenant of land to be treated as includible farm rental income, not only must it be derived pursuant to the arrangement described in subparagraph (1) of this paragraph, but also the owner or tenant must actually participate to a material degree in the production or in the management of the production of any of the commodities required to be produced under the arrangement, or he must actually participate in both the production and the management of the production to an extent that his participation in the one when combined with his participation in the other will be considered participation to a material degree. If the owner or tenant shows that he periodically advises or consults with the other person, who under the arrangement produces the agricultural or horticultural commodities, as to the production of any of these commodities and also shows that he periodically inspects the production activities on the land, he will have presented strong evidence of the existence of the degree of participation contemplated by section 1402(a)(1). If, in addition to the foregoing, the owner or tenant shows that he furnishes a substantial portion of the machinery, implements, and livestock used in the production of the commodities or that he furnishes or advances funds, or assumes financial responsibility, for a substantial part of the expense involved in the production of the commodities, he will have established the existence of the degree of participation contemplated by section 1402(a)(1) and this paragraph.

(5) *Employees or agents.* An agreement entered into by an employee or agent of an owner or tenant and another person is considered to be an arrangement entered into by the owner or tenant for purposes of satisfying the requirement set forth in paragraph (b)(2) that the income must be derived under an arrangement between the owner or tenant and another person. For purposes of determining whether the arrangement satisfies the requirement set forth in paragraph (b)(3) that the parties contemplate that the owner or tenant will materially participate in the production or management of production of a commodity, services which will be performed by an employee or agent of the owner or tenant are not considered to be services which the arrangement contemplates will be performed by the owner or tenant. Services actually performed by such employee or agent are not considered services performed by the owner or tenant in determining the extent to which the owner or tenant has participated in the production or management of production of a commodity. For taxable years beginning before January 1, 1974, contemplated or actual services of an agent or an employee of the owner or tenant are deemed to be contemplated or actual services of the owner or tenant under paragraphs (b)(3) and (b)(4) of this section.

(6) *Examples.* Application of the rules prescribed in this paragraph may be illustrated by the following examples:

Example (1). After the death of her husband, Mrs. A rents her farm, together with its machinery and equipment, to B for one-half of the proceeds from the commodities produced on such farm by B. It is agreed that B will live in the tenant house on the farm and be responsible for the over-all operation of the farm, such as planting, cultivating, and harvesting the field crops, caring for the orchard and harvesting the fruit and caring for the livestock and poultry. It also is agreed that Mrs. A will continue to live in the farm residence and help B operate the farm. Under the agreement it is contemplated that Mrs. A will regularly operate and clean the cream separator and feed the poultry flock and collect the eggs. When possible she will assist B in such work as spraying the fruit trees, penning livestock, culling the poultry, and controlling weeds. She will also assist in preparing the meals when B engages seasonal workers. The agreement between Mrs. A and B clearly provides that she will materially participate in the over-all production operations to be conducted on her farm by B. In actual practice, Mrs. A performs such regular and intermittent services. The regularly performed services are material to the production of an agricultural commodity, and the intermittent services performed are material to the production operations to which they relate. The furnishing of a substantial portion of the farm machinery and equipment also adds support to a conclusion that Mrs. A has materially participated. Accordingly, the rental income Mrs. A receives from her farm should be included in net earnings from self-employment.

Example (2). D agrees to produce a crop on C's cotton farm under an arrangement providing that C and D will each receive one-half of the proceeds from such production. C agrees to fur-

Reg. § 1.1402(a)-4(b)(6)

nish all the necessary equipment, and it is understood that he is to advise D when to plant the cotton and when it needs to be chopped, plowed, sprayed, and picked. It is also understood that during the growing season C is to inspect the crop every few days to determine whether D is properly taking care of the crop. Under the arrangement, D is required to furnish all labor needed to grow and harvest the crop. C, in fact, renders such advice, makes such inspections, and furnishes such equipment. C's contemplated participation in management decisions is considered material with respect to the management of the cotton production operation. C's actual participation pursuant to the arrangement is also considered to be material with respect to the management of the production of cotton. Accordingly, the income C receives from his cotton farm is to be included in computing his net earnings from self-employment.

Example (3). E owns a grain farm and turns its operation over to his son, F. By the oral rental arrangement between E and F, the latter agrees to produce crops of grain on the farm, and E agrees that he will be available for consultation and advice and will inspect and help to harvest the crops. E furnishes most of the equipment, including a tractor, a combine, plows, wagons, drills, and harrows: he continues to live on the farm and does some of the work such as repairing barns and farm machinery, going to town for supplies, cutting weeds, etc.; he regularly inspects the crops during the growing season; and he helps F to harvest the crops. Although the final decisions are made by F, he frequently consults with his father regarding the production of the crops. An evaluation of all of E's actual activities indicates that they are sufficiently substantial and regular to support a conclusion that he is materially participating in the crop production operations and the management thereof. If it can be shown that the degree of E's actual participation was contemplated by the arrangement, E's income from the grain farm will be included in computing net earnings from self-employment.

Example (4). G owns a fully-equipped farm which he rents to H under an arrangement which contemplates that G shall materially participate in the management of the production of crops raised on the farm pursuant to the arrangement. G lives in town about 5 miles from the farm. About twice a month he visits the farm and looks over the buildings and equipment. G may occasionally, in an emergency, discuss with H some phase of a crop production activity. In effect, H has complete charge of the management of farming operations regardless of the understanding between him and G. Although G pays one-half of the cost of the seed and fertilizer and is charged for the cost of materials purchased by H to make all necessary repairs, G's activities do not constitute material participation in the crop production activities. Accordingly, G's income from the crops is not included in computing net earnings from self-employment.

Example (5). I owned a farm several miles from the town in which he lived. He rented the farm to J under an arrangement which contemplated I's material participation in the management of production of wheat. I furnished one-half of the seed and fertilizer and all the farm equipment and livestock. He employed K to perform all the services in advising, consulting, and inspecting contemplated by the arrangement. I is not materially participating in the management of production of wheat by J. The work done by I's employee, K, is not attributable to I in determining the extent of I's participation. I's rental income from the arrangement is, therefore, not to be included in computing his net earnings from self-employment. For taxable years beginning before January 1, 1974, however, I's rental income would be includible in those earnings.

Example (6). L, a calendar-year taxpayer, appointed M as his agent to rent his fully equipped farm for 1974. M entered into a rental arrangement with N under which M was to direct the planting of crops, inspect them weekly during the growing season, and consult with N on any problems that might arise in connection with irrigation, etc., while N furnished all the labor needed to grow and harvest the crops. M did in fact fulfill its responsibilities under the arrangement. Although the arrangement entered into by M and N is considered to have been made by L, M's services are not attributable to L, and L's furnishing of a fully equipped farm is insufficient by itself to constitute material participation in the production of the crops. Accordingly, L's rental income from the arrangement is not included in his net earnings from self-employment for that year. For taxable years beginning before January 1, 1974, however, L's rental income would be includible in those earnings.

(c) *Rentals from living quarters*—(1) *No services rendered for occupants.* Payments for the use or occupancy of entire private residences or living quarters in duplex or multiple-housing units are generally rentals from real estate. Except in the case of real-estate dealers, such payments are excluded in determining net earnings from self-employment even though such payments are in part attributable to personal property furnished under the lease.

Reg. § 1.1402(a)-4(c)(1)

(2) *Services rendered for occupants.* Payments for the use or occupancy of rooms or other space where services are also rendered to the occupant, such as for the use or occupancy of rooms or other quarters in hotels, boarding houses, or apartment houses furnishing hotel services, or in tourist camps or tourist homes, or payments for the use or occupancy of space in parking lots, warehouses, or storage garages, do not constitute rentals from real estate; consequently, such payments are included in determining net earnings from self-employment. Generally, services are considered rendered to the occupant if they are primarily for his convenience and are other than those usually or customarily rendered in connection with the rental of rooms or other space for occupancy only. The supplying of maid service, for example, constitutes such service; whereas the furnishing of heat and light, the cleaning of public entrances, exits, stairways and lobbies, the collection of trash, and so forth, are not considered as services rendered to the occupant.

(3) *Example.* The application of this paragraph may be illustrated by the following example:

Example. A, an individual, owns a building containing four apartments. During the taxable year, he receives $1,400 from apartments numbered 1 and 2, which are rented without services rendered to the occupants, and $3,600 from apartments numbered 3 and 4, which are rented with services rendered to the occupants. His fixed expenses for the four apartments aggregate $1,200 during the taxable year. In addition, he has $500 of expenses attributable to the services rendered to the occupants of apartments 3 and 4. In determining his net earnings from self-employment, A includes the $3,600 received from apartments 3 and 4, and the expenses of $1,100 ($500 plus one-half of $1,200) attributable thereto. The rentals and expenses attributable to apartments 1 and 2 are excluded. Therefore, A has $2,500 of net earnings from self-employment for the taxable year from the building.

(d) *Treatment of business income which includes rentals from real estate.* Except in the case of a real-estate dealer, where an individual or a partnership is engaged in a trade or business the income of which is classifiable in part as rentals from real estate, only that portion of such income which is not classifiable as rentals from real estate, and the expenses attributable to such portion, are included in determining net earnings from self-employment. [Reg. § 1.1402(a)-4.]

☐ [T.D. 6691, 12-2-63. Amended by T.D. 7710, 7-28-80.]

[Reg. § 1.1402(a)-5]

§ 1.1402(a)-5. Dividends and interest.—(a) All dividends on shares of stock are excluded unless they are received by an individual in the course of his trade or business as a dealer in stocks or securities.

(b) Interest on any bond, debenture, note, or certificate, or other evidence of indebtedness, issued with interest coupons or in registered form by any corporation (including one issued by a government or political subdivision thereof) is excluded unless such interest is received in the course of a trade or business as a dealer in stocks or securities. However, interest with respect to which a credit against tax is allowable as provided in section 35, that is, interest on certain obligations of the United States and its instrumentalities, is not included in net earnings from self-employment even though received in the course of a trade or business as a dealer in stocks or securities. Only interest on bonds, debentures, notes, or certificates, or other evidence of indebtedness, issued with interest coupons or in registered form by a corporation, is excluded in the case of all persons other than dealers in stocks or securities; other interest received in the course of any trade or business (such as interest received by a pawnbroker on his loans or interest received by a merchant on his accounts or notes receivable) is not excluded.

(c) Dividends and interest of the character excludable under paragraphs (a) and (b) of this section received by an individual on stocks or securities held for speculation or investment are excluded whether or not the individual is a dealer in stocks or securities.

(d) A dealer in stocks or securities is a merchant of stocks or securities with an established place of business, regularly engaged in the business of purchasing stocks or securities and reselling them to customers; that is, he is one who as a merchant buys stocks or securities and sells them to customers with a view to the gains and profits that may be derived therefrom. Persons who buy and sell or hold stocks or securities for investment or speculation, irrespective of whether such buying or selling constitutes the carrying on of a trade or business, are not dealers in stocks or securities. [Reg. § 1.1402(a)-5.]

☐ [T.D. 6691, 12-2-63.]

[Reg. § 1.1402(a)-6]

§ 1.1402(a)-6. Gain or loss from disposition of property.—(a) There is excluded any gain or loss: (1) Which is considered as gain or loss from the sale or exchange of a capital asset; (2) from the cutting of timber or the disposal of timber, coal, or iron ore, even though held primarily for sale to customers, if section 631 is applicable to such gain or loss; and (3) from the sale, exchange, involuntary conversion, or other disposition of property if such property is neither (i) stock in trade or other property of a kind which would properly be includible in inventory if on hand at the close of the taxable year, nor (ii) property held primarily for sale to customers in the ordinary course of a trade or business. For the purpose of the special rule in subparagraph (3) of this paragraph, it is immaterial whether a gain or loss is treated as a capital gain or loss or as an ordinary gain or loss for purposes other than determining net earnings from self-employment. For instance, where the character of a loss is governed by the provisions of section 1231, such loss is excluded in determining net earnings from self-employment even though such loss is treated under section 1231 as an ordinary loss. For the purposes of this special rule, the term "involuntary conversion" means a compulsory or involuntary conversion of property into other property or money as a result of its destruction in whole or in part, theft or seizure, or an exercise of the power of requisition or condemnation or the threat or imminence thereof; and the term "other disposition" includes the destruction or loss, in whole or in part, of property by fire, storm, shipwreck, or other casualty, or by theft, even though there is no conversion of such property into other property or money.

(b) The application of this section may be illustrated by the following example:

Example. During the taxable year 1954, A, who owns a grocery store, realized a net profit of $1,500 from the sale of groceries and a gain of $350 from the sale of a refrigerator case. During the same year, he sustained a loss of $2,000 as a result of damage by fire to the store building. In computing taxable income, all of these items are taken into account. In determining net earnings from self-employment, however, only the $1,500 of profit derived from the sale of groceries is included. The $350 gain and the $2,000 loss are excluded. [Reg. § 1.1402(a)-6.]

☐ [T.D. 6691, 12-2-63. Amended by T.D. 6841, 7-26-65.]

[Reg. § 1.1402(a)-7]

§ 1.1402(a)-7. **Net operating loss deduction.**—The deduction provided by section 172, relating to net operating losses sustained in years other than the taxable year, is excluded. [Reg. § 1.1402(a)-7.]

☐ [T.D. 6691, 12-2-63.]

[Reg. § 1.1402(a)-8]

§ 1.1402(a)-8. **Community income.**—(a) *In case of an individual.* If any of the income derived by an individual from a trade or business (other than a trade or business carried on by a partnership) is community income under community property laws applicable to such income, all of the gross income, and the deductions attributable to such income, shall be treated as the gross income and deductions of the husband unless the wife exercises substantially all of the management and control of such trade or business, in which case all of such gross income and deductions shall be treated as the gross income and deductions of the wife. For the purpose of this special rule, the term "management and control" means management and control in fact, not the management and control imputed to the husband under the community property laws. For example, a wife who operates a beauty parlor without any appreciable collaboration on the part of her husband will be considered as having substantially all of the management and control of such business despite the provision of any community property law vesting in the husband the right of management and control of community property; and the income and deductions attributable to the operation of such beauty parlor will be considered the income and deductions of the wife.

(b) *In case of a partnership.* Even though a portion of a partner's distributive share of the income or loss, described in section 702(a)(9), from a trade or business carried on by a partnership is community income or loss under the community property laws applicable to such share, all of such distributive share shall be included in computing the net earnings from self-employment of such partner; no part of such share shall be taken into account in computing the net earnings from self-employment of the spouse of such partner. In any case in which both spouses are members of the same partnership, the distributive share of the income or loss of each spouse is included in computing the net earnings from self-employment of that spouse. [Reg. § 1.1402(a)-8.]

☐ [T.D. 6691, 12-2-63.]

[Reg. § 1.1402(a)-9]

§ 1.1402(a)-9. **Puerto Rico.**—(a) *Residents.* A resident of Puerto Rico, whether or not a bona fide resident thereof during the entire taxable year, and whether or not an alien, a citizen of the United States, or a citizen of Puerto Rico, shall compute his net earnings from self-employment in the same manner as would a citizen of the United States residing in the United States. See paragraph (d) of § 1.1402(b)-1 for regulations relating to nonresident aliens. For the purposes of the tax on self-employment income, the gross income of such a resident of Puerto Rico also includes income from Puerto Rican sources. Thus, under this special rule, income from Puerto Rican sources will be included in determining net earnings from self-employment of a resident of Puerto Rico engaged in the active conduct of a trade or business in Puerto Rico despite the fact that, under section 933, such income may not be taken into account for purposes of the tax under section 1 or 3.

(b) *Nonresidents.* A citizen of Puerto Rico who is also a citizen of the United States and who is not a resident of Puerto Rico will compute his net earnings from self-employment in the same manner and subject to the same provisions of law and regulations as other citizens of the United States. [Reg. § 1.1402(a)-9.]

☐ [*T.D.* 6691, 12-2-63.]

[Reg. § 1.1402(a)-10]

§ 1.1402(a)-10. **Personal exemption deduction.**—The deduction provided by section 151, relating to personal exemptions, is excluded. [Reg. § 1.1402(a)-10.]

☐ [*T.D.* 6691, 12-2-63.]

[Reg. § 1.1402(a)-11]

§ 1.1402(a)-11. **Ministers and members of religious orders.**—(a) *In general.* For each taxable year ending after 1954 in which a minister or member of a religious order is engaged in a trade or business, within the meaning of section 1402(c) and § 1.1402(c)-5, with respect to service performed in the exercise of his ministry or in the exercise of duties required by such order, net earnings from self-employment from such trade or business include the gross income derived during the taxable year from any such service, less the deductions attributable to such gross income. For each taxable year ending on or after December 31, 1957, such minister or member of a religious order shall compute his net earnings from self-employment derived from the performance of such service without regard to the exclusions from gross income provided by section 107 (relating to rental value of parsonages) and section 119 (relating to meals and lodging furnished for the convenience of the employer). Thus, a minister who is subject to self-employment tax with respect to his services as a minister will include in the computation of his net earnings from self-employment for a taxable year ending on or after December 31, 1957, the rental value of a home furnished to him as remuneration for services performed in the exercise of his ministry or the rental allowance paid to him as remuneration for such services irrespective of whether such rental value or rental allowance is excluded from gross income by section 107. Similarly, the value of any meals or lodging furnished to a minister or to a member of a religious order in connection with service performed in the exercise of his ministry or as a member of such order will be included in the computation of his net earnings from self-employment for a taxable year ending on or after December 31, 1957, notwithstanding the exclusion of such value from gross income by section 119.

(b) *In employ of American employer.* If a minister or member of a religious order engaged in a trade or business described in section 1402(c) and § 1.1402(c)-5 is a citizen of the United States and performs service, in his capacity as a minister or member of a religious order, as an employee of an American employer, as defined in section 3121(h) and the regulations thereunder in Part 31 of this chapter (Employment Tax Regulations), his net earnings from self-employment derived from such service shall be computed as provided in paragraph (a) of this section but without regard to the exclusions from gross income provided in section 911, relating to earned income from sources without the United States, and section 931, relating to income from sources within possessions of the United States. Thus, even though all the income of the minister or member for service of the character to which this paragraph is applicable was derived from sources without the United States, or from sources within possessions of the United States, and therefore may be excluded from gross income, such income is included in computing net earnings from self-employment.

(c) *Minister in a foreign country whose congregation is composed predominantly of citizens of the United States*—(1) *Taxable years ending after 1956.* For any taxable year ending after 1956, a minister of a church, who is engaged in a trade or business within the meaning of section 1402(c) and § 1.1402(c)-5, is a citizen of the United States, is performing service in the exercise of his ministry in a foreign country, and has a congregation composed predominantly of United States citizens, shall compute his net earnings from self-employment derived from his services as a minister for such taxable year without regard to the exclusion from gross income provided in section 911, relating to earned income from sources without the United States. For taxable years ending on or after December 31, 1957, such minister shall also disregard sections 107 and 119 in the computation of his net earnings from self-employment. (See paragraph (a) of this section.) For purposes of section 1402(a)(8) and this paragraph a "congregation composed predominantly of citizens of the United States" means a congregation the majority of which throughout the greater portion of

Reg. § 1.1402(a)-11(c)

its minister's taxable year were United States citizens.

(2) *Election for taxable years ending after 1954 and before 1957.* (i) A minister described in subparagraph (1) of this paragraph who, for a taxable year ending after 1954 and before 1957, had income from service described in such subparagraph which would have been included in computing net earnings from self-employment if such income had been derived in a taxable year ending after 1956 by an individual who had filed a waiver certificate under section 1402(e), may elect to have section 1402(a)(8) and subparagraph (1) of this paragraph apply to his income from such service for his taxable years ending after 1954 and before 1957. If such minister filed a waiver certificate prior to August 1, 1956, in accordance with § 1.1402(e)(1)-1, or he files such a waiver certificate on or before the due date of his return (including any extensions thereof) for his last taxable year ending before 1957, he must make such election on or before the due date of his return (including any extensions thereof) for such taxable year or before April 16, 1957, whichever is the later. If the waiver certificate is not so filed, the minister must make his election on or before the due date of the return (including any extensions thereof) for his first taxable year ending after 1956. Notwithstanding the expiration of the period prescribed by section 1402(e)(2) for filing such waiver, the minister may file a waiver certificate at the time he makes the election. In no event shall an election be valid unless the minister files prior to or at the time of the election a waiver certificate in accordance with § 1.1402(e)(1)-1.

(ii) The election shall be made by filing with the district director of internal revenue with whom the waiver certificate, Form 2031, is filed a written statement indicating that, by reason of the Social Security Amendments of 1956, the minister desires to have the Federal old-age, survivors, and disability insurance system established by title II of the Social Security Act extended to his services performed in a foreign country as a minister of a congregation composed predominantly of United States citizens beginning with the first taxable year ending after 1954 and prior to 1957 for which he had income from such services. The statement shall be dated and signed by the minister and shall clearly state that it is an election for retroactive self-employment tax coverage under the Self-Employment Contributions Act of 1954. In addition, the statement shall include the following information:

(*a*) The name and address of the minister.

(*b*) His social security account number, if he has one.

(*c*) That he is a duly ordained, commissioned, or licensed minister of a church.

(*d*) That he is a citizen of the United States.

(*e*) That he is performing services in the exercise of his ministry in a foreign country.

(*f*) That his congregation is composed predominantly of citizens of the United States.

(*g*)(*1*) That he has filed a waiver certificate and, if so, where and under what circumstances the certificate was filed and the taxable year for which it is effective; or (*2*) That he is filing a waiver certificate with his election for retroactive coverage and, if so, the taxable year for which it is effective.

(*h*) That he has or has not filed income tax returns for his taxable years ending after 1954 and before 1957. If he has filed such returns, he shall state the years for which they were filed and indicate the district director of internal revenue with whom they were filed.

(iii) Notwithstanding section 1402(e)(3), a waiver certificate filed pursuant to § 1.1402(e)(1)-1 by a minister making an election under this paragraph shall be effective (regardless of when such certificate is filed) for such minister's first taxable year ending after 1954 in which he had income from service described in subparagraph (1) of this paragraph or for the taxable year of the minister prescribed by section 1402(e)(3), if such taxable year is earlier, and for all succeeding taxable years.

(iv) No interest or penalty shall be assessed or collected for failure to file a return within the time prescribed by law if such failure arises solely by reason of an election made by a minister pursuant to this paragraph or for any underpayment of self-employment income tax arising solely by reason of such election, for the period ending with the date such minister makes an election pursuant to this paragraph.

(d) *Treatment of certain remuneration paid in 1955 and 1956 as wages.* For treatment of remuneration paid to an individual for service described in section 3121(b)(8)(A) which was erroneously treated by the organization employing him as employment within the meaning of chapter 21 of the Internal Revenue Code, see § 1.1402(e)(4)-1. [Reg. § 1.1402(a)-11.]

☐ [T.D. 6691, 12-2-63.]

[Reg. § 1.1402(a)-12]

§ 1.1402(a)-12. **Possession of the United States.**—For purposes of the tax on self-employment income, the term "possession of the United States", as used in section 931 (relating to income from sources within possessions of the United States) and section 932 (relating to citizens of possessions of the United States) shall be deemed not to include the Virgin Islands, Guam, or American Samoa. The provisions of section 1402(a)(9) and of this section insofar as they involve nonapplication of sections 931 and 932 to Guam or American Samoa, shall apply only in the case of taxable years beginning after 1960. For definition of the term "United States" and for other geographical definitions relating to the continental shelf see section 638 and § 1.638-1. [Reg. § 1.1402(a)-12.]

☐ [*T.D.* 6691, 12-2-63. *Amended by T.D.* 7277, 5-14-73.]

[Reg. § 1.1402(a)-13]

§ 1.1402(a)-13. **Income from agricultural activity.**—(a) *Agricultural trade or business.* (1) An agricultural trade or business is one in which, if the trade or business were carried on exclusively by employees, the major portion of the services would constitute agricultural labor as defined in section 3121(g) and the regulations thereunder in Part 31 of this chapter (Employment Tax Regulations). In case the services are in part agricultural and in part nonagricultural, the time devoted to the performance of each type of service is the test to be used to determine whether the major portion of the services would constitute agricultural labor. If more than half of the time spent in performing all the services is spent in performing services which would constitute agricultural labor under section 3121(g), the trade or business is agricultural. If only half, or less, of the time spent in performing all the services is spent in performing services which would constitute agricultural labor under section 3121(g), the trade or business is not agricultural. In every case the time spent in performing the services will be computed by adding the time spent in the trade or business during the taxable year by every individual (including the individual carrying on such trade or business and the members of his family) in performing such services. The operation of this special rule is not affected by section 3121(c), relating to the included-excluded rule for determining employment.

(2) The rules prescribed in subparagraph (1) of this paragraph have no application where the nonagricultural services are performed in connection with an enterprise which constitutes a trade or business separate and distinct from the trade or business conducted as an agricultural enterprise. Thus, the operation of a roadside automobile service station on farm premises constitutes a trade or business separate and distinct from the agricultural enterprise, and the gross income derived from such service station, less the deductions attributable thereto, is to be taken into account in determining net earnings from self-employment.

(b) *Farm operator's income for taxable years ending before 1955.* Income derived in a taxable year ending before 1955 from any agricultural trade or business (see paragraph (a) of this section), and all deductions attributable to such income, are excluded in computing net earnings from self-employment.

(c) *Farm operator's income for taxable years ending after 1954.* Income derived in a taxable year ending after 1954 from an agricultural trade or business (see paragraph (a) of this section) is includible in computing net earnings from self-employment. Income derived from an agricultural trade or business includes income derived by an individual under an agreement entered into by such individual with another person pursuant to which such individual undertakes to produce agricultural or horticultural commodities (including livestock, bees, poultry, and fur-bearing animals and wildlife) on land owned or leased by such other person and pursuant to which the agricultural or horticultural commodities produced by such individual, or the proceeds therefrom, are to be divided between such individual and such other person, and the amount of such individual's share depends on the amount of the agricultural or horticultural commodities produced. However, except as provided in paragraph (d) of this section, relating to arrangements involving material participation, the income derived under such an agreement by the owner or lessee of the land is not includible in computing net earnings from self-employment. See § 1.1402(a)-4. For options relating to the computation of net earnings from self-employment, see §§ 1.1402(a)-14 and 1.1402(a)-15.

(d) *Includible farm rental income for taxable years ending after 1955.* For taxable years ending after 1955, income derived from an agricultural trade or business (see paragraph (a) of this section) includes also income derived by the owner or tenant of land under an arrangement between such owner or tenant and another person, if such arrangement provides that such other person shall produce agricultural or horticultural commodities (including livestock, bees, poultry, and fur-bearing animals and wildlife) on such land, and that there shall be material participation by the owner or tenant in the production or the management of the production of such agricultural or horticultural commodities, and if there is material participation by the owner or tenant with respect to any such agricultural or horticultural commodity. See paragraph (b) of § 1.1402(a)-4. For options relating to the computation of net earnings from self-employment, see § § 1.1402(a)-14 and 1.1402(a)-15.

(e) *Income from service performed after 1956 as a crew leader.* Income derived by a crew leader (see section 3121(o) and the regulations thereunder in Part 31 of this chapter (Employment Tax Regulations)) from service performed after 1956 in furnishing individuals to perform agricultural labor for another person and from service performed after 1956 in agricultural labor as a member of the crew is considered to be income derived from a trade or business for purposes of § 1.1402(c)-1. Whether such trade or business is an agricultural trade or business shall be determined by applying the rules set forth in this section. [Reg. § 1.1402(a)-13.]

☐ [*T.D.* 6691, 12-2-63.]

[Reg. § 1.1402(a)-14]

§ 1.1402(a)-14. Options available to farmers in computing net earnings from self-employment for taxable years ending after 1954 and before December 31, 1956.—[This regulation is now obsolete.—CCH.]

[Reg. § 1.1402(a)-15]

§ 1.1402(a)-15. Options available to farmers in computing net earnings from self-employment for taxable years ending on or after December 31, 1956.—(a) *Computation of net earnings.* In the case of any trade or business which is carried on by an individual or by a partnership and in which, if such trade or business were carried on exclusively by employees, the major portion of the services would constitute agricultural labor as defined in section 3121(g) (see paragraph (a) of § 1.1402(a)-13), net earnings from self-employment may, for a taxable year ending on or after December 31, 1956, at the option of the taxpayer, be computed as follows:

(1) *In case of an individual*—(i) *Gross income of less than specified amount.* If the gross income, computed as provided in paragraph (b) of this section, from such trade or business is $2,400 or less ($1,800 or less for a taxable year ending on or after December 31, 1956, and beginning before January 1, 1966), the taxpayer may, at his option, treat as net earnings from self-employment from such trade or business an amount equal to 66⅔ percent of such gross income. If the taxpayer so elects, the amount equal to 66⅔ percent of such gross income shall be used in computing his self-employment income in lieu of his actual net earnings from such trade or business, if any.

(ii) *Gross income in excess of specified amount.* If the gross income, computed as provided in paragraph (b) of this section, from such trade or business is more than $2,400 ($1,800 for a taxable year ending on or after December 31, 1956, and beginning before January 1, 1966), and the net earnings from self-employment from such trade or business (computed without regard to this section) are less than $1,600 ($1,200 for a taxable year ending on or after December 31, 1956, and beginning before January 1, 1966), the taxpayer may, at his option, treat $1,600 ($1,200 for a taxable year ending on or after December 31, 1956, and beginning before January 1, 1966) as net earnings from self-employment. If the taxpayer so elects, $1,600 ($1,200 for a taxable year ending on or after December 31, 1956, and beginning before January 1, 1966) shall be used in computing his self-employment income in lieu of his actual net earnings from such trade or business, if any. However, if the taxpayer's actual net earnings from such trade or business, as computed in accordance with the applicable provisions of § § 1.1402(a)-1 to 1.1402(a)-13, inclusive, are $1,600 or more ($1,200 or more for a taxable year ending on or after December 31, 1956, and beginning before January 1, 1966) such actual net earnings shall be used in computing his self-employment income.

(2) *In case of a member of a partnership*—(i) *Distributive share of gross income of less than specified amount.* If a taxpayer's distributive share of the gross income of a partnership (as such gross income is computed under the provisions of paragraph (b) of this section) derived from such trade or business (after such gross income has been reduced by the sum of all payments to which section 707(c) applies) is $2,400 or less ($1,800 or less for a taxable year ending on or after December 31, 1956, and beginning before January 1, 1966), the taxpayer may, at his option, treat as his distributive share of income described in section 702(a)(9) derived from such trade or business an amount equal to 66⅔ percent of his distributive share of such gross income (after such gross income has been reduced by the sum of all payments to which section 707(c) applies). If the taxpayer so elects, the amount equal to 66⅔ percent of his distributive share of such gross income shall be used by him in the computation of his net earnings from self-employment in lieu of the actual amount of his distributive share of income described in section 702(a)(9) from such trade or business, if any.

(ii) *Distributive share of gross income in excess of specified amount.* If a taxpayer's distributive share of the gross income of a partnership (as such gross income is computed under the pro-

Reg. § 1.1402(a)-14

visions of paragraph (b) of this section) derived from such trade or business (after such gross income has been reduced by the sum of all payments to which section 707(c) applies) is more than $2,400 ($1,800 for a taxable year ending on or after December 31, 1956, and beginning before January 1, 1966) and the actual amount of his distributive share (whether or not distributed) of income described in section 702(a)(9) derived from such trade or business (computed without regard to this section) is less than $1,600 ($1,200 for a taxable year ending on or after December 31, 1956, and beginning before January 1, 1966), the taxpayer may, at his option, treat $1,600 ($1,200 for a taxable year ending on or after December 31, 1956, and beginning before January 1, 1966) as his distributive share of income described in section 702(a)(9) derived from such trade or business. If the taxpayer so elects, $1,600 ($1,200 for a taxable year ending on or after December 31, 1956, and beginning before January 1, 1966) shall be used by him in the computation of his net earnings from self-employment in lieu of the actual amount of his distributive share of income described in section 702(a)(9) from such trade or business, if any. However, if the actual amount of the taxpayer's distributive share of income described in section 702(a)(9) from such trade or business, as computed in accordance with the applicable provisions of §§ 1.1402(a)-1 to 1.1402(a)-13, inclusive, is $1,600 or more ($1,200 or more for a taxable year ending on or after December 31, 1956, and beginning before January 1, 1966), such actual amount of the taxpayer's distributive share shall be used in computing his net earnings from self-employment.

(iii) *Cross reference.* For a special rule in the case of certain deceased partners, see paragraph (c) of § 1.1402(f)-1.

(b) *Computation of gross income.* For purposes of this section gross income has the following meanings:

(1) In the case of any such trade or business in which the income is computed under a cash receipts and disbursements method, the gross receipts from such trade or business reduced by the cost or other basis of property which was purchased and sold in carrying on such trade or business (see paragraphs (a) and (c), other than paragraph (a)(5), of § 1.61-4), adjusted (after such reduction) in accordance with the applicable provisions of §§ 1.1402(a)-3 to 1.1402(a)-13, inclusive.

(2) In the case of any such trade or business in which the income is computed under an accrual method (see paragraphs (b) and (c), other than paragraph (b)(5), of § 1.61-4), the gross income from such trade or business, adjusted in accordance with the applicable provisions of §§ 1.1402(a)-3 to 1.1402(a)-13, inclusive.

(c) *Two or more agricultural activities.* If an individual (including a member of a partnership) derives gross income (as defined in paragraph (b) of this section) from more than one agricultural trade or business, such gross income (including his distributive share of the gross income of any partnership derived from any such trade or business) shall be deemed to have been derived from one trade or business. Thus, such an individual shall aggregate his gross income derived from each agricultural trade or business carried on by him (which includes, under paragraph (b) of § 1.1402(a)-1, any guaranteed payment, within the meaning of section 707(c), received by him from a farm partnership of which he is a member) and his distributive share of partnership gross income (after such gross income has been reduced by any guaranteed payment within the meaning of section 707(c)) derived from each farm partnership of which he is a member. Such gross income is the amount to be considered for purposes of the optional method provided in this section for computing net earnings from self-employment. If the aggregate gross income of an individual includes income derived from an agricultural trade or business carried on by him and a distributive share of partnership income derived from an agricultural trade or business carried on by a partnership of which he is a member, such aggregate gross income shall be treated as income derived from a single trade or business carried on by him, and such individual shall apply the optional method applicable to individuals set forth in paragraph (a)(1) of this section for purposes of computing his net earnings from self-employment.

(d) *Examples.* The application of this section may be illustrated by the following examples:

Example (1). F is engaged in the business of farming and computes his income under the cash receipts and disbursements method. He files his income tax returns on the basis of the calendar year. During the year 1966, F's gross income from the business of farming (computed in accordance with paragraph (b)(1) of this section) is $2,325. His actual net earnings from self-employment derived from such business are $1,250. As his net earnings from self-employment, F may report $1,250 or, by the optional computation method, he may report $1,550 (66 2/3 percent of $2,325).

Example (2). G is engaged in the business of farming and computes his income under the accrual method. His income tax returns are filed on the calendar year basis. For the year 1966, G's gross income from the operation of his farm (com-

Reg. § 1.1402(a)-15(d)

puted in accordance with paragraph (b)(2) of this section) is $2,800. He has actual net earnings from self-employment derived from such farm in the amount of $1,250. As his net earnings from self-employment derived from his farm, G may report his actual net earnings of $1,250, or by the optional method he may report $1,600. If G's actual net earnings from self-employment from his farming activities for 1966 were in an amount of $1,600 or more, he would be required to report such amount in computing his self-employment income.

Example (3). M, who files his income tax returns on a calendar year basis, is one of the three partners of the XYZ Company, a partnership, engaged in the business of farming. The taxable year of the partnership is the calendar year, and its income is computed under the cash receipts and disbursements method. For M's services in connection with the planting, cultivating, and harvesting of the crops during the year 1966 the partnership agrees to pay him $500, the full amount of which is determined without regard to the income of the partnership and constitutes a guaranteed payment within the meaning of section 707(c). This guaranteed payment to M is the only such payment made during such year. The gross income derived from the business for the year 1966 computed in accordance with paragraph (b)(1) of this section and after being reduced by the guaranteed payment of $500 made to M, is $3,000. One-third of the $3,000 ($1,000), is M's distributive share of such gross income. Under paragraph (c) of this section, the guaranteed payment ($500) received by M and his distributive share of the partnership gross income ($1,000) are deemed to have been derived from one trade or business, and such amounts must be aggregated for purposes of the optional method of computing net earnings from self-employment. Since M's combined gross income from his two agricultural businesses ($1,000 and $500) is not more than $2,400 and since such income is deemed to be derived from one trade or business, M's net earnings from self-employment derived from such farming business may, at his option, be deemed to be $1,000 (66⅔ percent of $1,500).

Example (4). A is one of the two partners of the AB partnership which is engaged in the business of farming. The taxable year of the partnership is the calendar year and its income is computed under the accrual method. A files his income tax returns on the calendar year basis. The partnership agreement provides for an equal sharing in the profits and losses of the partnership by the two partners. A is an experienced farmer and for his services as manager of the partnership's farm activities during the year 1966 he receives $6,000 which amount constitutes a guaranteed payment within the meaning of section 707(c). The gross income of the partnership derived from such business for the year 1966, computed in accordance with paragraph (b)(2) of this section and after being reduced by the guaranteed payment made to A, is $9,600. A's distributive share of such gross income is $4,800 and his distributive share of income described in section 702(a)(9) derived from the partnership's business is $1,900. Under paragraph (c) of this section, the guaranteed payment received by A and his distributive share of the partnership gross income are deemed to have been derived from one trade or business, and such amounts must be aggregated for purposes of the optional method of computing his net earnings from self-employment. Since the aggregate of A's guaranteed payment ($6,000) and his distributive share of partnership gross income ($4,800) is more than $2,400 and since the aggregate of A's guaranteed payment ($6,000) and his distributive share ($1,900) of partnership income described in section 702(a)(9) is not less than $1,600, the optional method of computing net earnings from self-employment is not available to A.

Example (5). F is a member of the EFG partnership which is engaged in the business of farming. F files his income tax returns on the calendar year basis. The taxable year of the partnership is the calendar year, and its income is computed under a cash receipts and disbursements method. Under the partnership agreement the partners are to share equally the profits or losses of the business. The gross income derived from the partnership business for the year 1966, computed in accordance with paragraph (b)(1) of this section is $7,500. F's share of such gross income is $2,500. Due to drought and an epidemic among the livestock, the partnership sustains a net loss of $7,800 for the year 1966 of which loss F's share is $2,600. Since F's distributive share of gross income derived from such business is in excess of $2,400 and since F does not receive income described in section 702(a)(9) of $1,600 or more from such business, he may, at his option, be deemed to have received $1,600 as his distributive share of income described in section 702(a)(9) from such business. [Reg. § 1.1402(a)-15.]

☐ [T.D. 6691, 12-2-63. Amended by T.D. 6993, 1-17-69.]

[Reg. § 1.1402(a)-16]

§ 1.1402(a)-16. **Exercise of option.**—A taxpayer shall, for each taxable year with respect to which he is eligible to use the optional method described in § 1.1402(a)-14 or § 1.1402(a)-15, make a determination as to whether his net earnings from self-employment are to be computed in accordance with such method. If the taxpayer elects the optional method for a taxable year, he shall signify such election by computing net earnings from self-employment under the optional method as set forth in Schedule F (Form 1040) of the income tax return filed by the taxpayer for such taxable year. If the optional method is not elected at the time of the filing of the return for a taxable year with respect to which the taxpayer is eligible to elect such optional method, such method may be elected on an amended return (or on such other form as may be prescribed for such use) filed within the period prescribed by section 6501 and the regulations thereunder for the assessment of the tax for such taxable year. If the optional method is elected on a return for a taxable year, the taxpayer may revoke such election by filing an amended return (or such other form as may be prescribed for such use) for the taxable year within the period prescribed by section 6501 and the regulations thereunder for the assessment of the tax for such taxable year. If the taxpayer is deceased or unable to make an election, the person designated in section 6012(b) and the regulations thereunder may, within the period prescribed in this section elect the optional method for any taxable year with respect to which the taxpayer is eligible to use the optional method and revoke an election previously made by or for the taxpayer. [Reg. § 1.1402(a)-16.]

☐ [*T.D.* 6691, 12-2-63.]

[Reg. § 1.1402(a)-17]

§ **1.1402(a)-17. Retirement payments to retired partners.**—(a) *In general*—There shall be excluded, in computing net earnings from self-employment for taxable years ending on or after December 31, 1967, certain payments made on a periodic basis by a partnership, pursuant to a written plan of the partnership, to a retired partner on account of his retirement. The exclusion applies only if the payments are made pursuant to a plan which meets the requirements prescribed in paragraph (b) of this section, and, in addition, the conditions set forth in paragraph (c) of this section are met.

(b) *Retirement plan of partnership*—(1) To meet the requirements of section 1402(a)(10), the written plan of the partnership must set forth the terms and conditions of the program or system established by the partnership for the purpose of making payments to retired partners on account of their retirement. To qualify as payments on account of retirement, the payments must constitute bona fide retirement income. Thus, payments of benefits not customarily included in a pension or retirement plan such as layoff benefits are not payments on account of retirement. Eligibility for retirement generally is established on the basis of age, physical condition, or a combination of age or physical condition and years of service. Generally, retirement benefits are measured by, and based on, such factors as years of service and compensation received. In determining whether the plan of the partnership provides for payments on account of retirement, factors, formulas, etc., reflected in public, and in broad based private, pension or retirement plans in prescribing eligibility requirements and in computing benefits may be taken into account.

(2) The plan of the partnership must provide for payments on account of retirement—

(i) To partners generally or to a class or classes of partners,

(ii) On a periodic basis, and

(iii) Which continue at least until the partner's death.

For purposes of subdivision (i) of this subparagraph, a class of partners may, in an appropriate case, contain only one member. Payments are made on a periodic basis if made at regularly recurring intervals (usually monthly) not exceeding one year.

(c) *Conditions relating to exclusion*—(1) *In general*—A payment made pursuant to a written plan of a partnership which meets the requirements of paragraph (b) of this section shall be excluded, in computing net earnings from self-employment, only if—

(i) The retired partner to whom the payment is made rendered no service with respect to any trade or business carried on by the partnership (or its successors) during the taxable year of the partnership (or its successors), which ends within or with the taxable year of the retired partner and in which the payment was received by him;

(ii) No obligation (whether certain in amount or contingent on a subsequent event) exists (as of the close of the partnership's taxable year referred to in subdivision (i) of this subparagraph) from the other partners to the retired partner except with respect to retirement payments under the plan or rights such as benefits payable on account of sickness, accident, hospitalization, medical expenses, or death; and

(iii) The retired partner's share (if any) of the capital of the partnership has been paid to him in full before the close of the partnership's taxable year referred to in subdivision (i) of this subparagraph.

By application of the conditions set forth in this subparagraph, either all payments on account of retirement received by a retired partner during

Tax on Self-Employment Income

See p. 20,601 for regulations not amended to reflect law changes

the taxable year of the partnership ending within or with his taxable year are excluded or none of the payments are excluded. Subdivision (ii) of this subparagraph has application only to obligations from other partners in their capacity as partners as distinguished from an obligation which arose and exists from a transaction unrelated to the partnership or to a trade or business carried on by the partnership. The effect of the conditions set forth in subdivisions (ii) and (iii) of this subparagraph is that the exclusion may apply with respect to payments received by a retired partner during the taxable year of the partnership ending within or with his taxable year only if at the close of the partnership's taxable year the retired partner had no financial interest in the partnership except for the right to retirement payments.

(2) *Examples*—The application of subparagraph (1) of this paragraph may be illustrated by the following examples. Each example assumes that the partnership plan pursuant to which the payments are made meets the requirements of paragraph (b) of this section.

Example (1). A, who files his income tax returns on a calendar year basis, is a partner in the ABC partnership. The taxable year of the partnership is the period July 1 to June 30, inclusive. A retired from the partnership on January 1, 1973, and receives monthly payments on account of his retirement. As of June 30, 1973, no obligation existed from the other partners to A (except with respect to retirement payments under the plan) and A's share of the capital of the partnership had been paid to him in full. The monthly retirement payments received by A from the partnership in his taxable year ending on December 31, 1973, are not excluded from net earnings from self-employment since A rendered service to the partnership during a portion of the partnership's taxable year (July 1, 1972, through June 30, 1973) which ends within A's taxable year ending on December 31, 1973.

Example (2). D, a partner in the DEF partnership, retired from the partnership as of the close of December 31, 1972. The taxable year of both D and the partnership is the calendar year. During the partnership's taxable year ending December 31, 1973, D rendered no service with respect to any trade or business carried on by the partnership. On or before December 31, 1973, all obligations (other than with respect to retirement payments under the plan) from the other partners to D have been liquidated, and D's share of the capital of the partnership has been paid to him. Retirement payments received by D pursuant to the partnership's plan in his taxable year ending December 31, 1973, are excluded in determining his net earnings from self-employment (if any) for that taxable year.

Example (3). Assume the same facts as in example (2) except that as of the close of December 31, 1973, D has a right to a fixed percentage of any amounts collected by the partnership after that date which are attributable to services rendered by him prior to his retirement for clients of the partnership. The monthly payments received by D in his taxable year ending December 31, 1973, are not excluded from net earnings from self-employment since as of the close of the partnership's taxable year which ends with D's taxable year, an obligation (other than an obligation with respect to retirement payments) exists from the other partners to D. [Reg. § 1.1402(a)-17.]

☐ [T.D. 7333, 12-19-74.]

[Reg. § 1.1402(b)-1]

§ 1.1402(b)-1. Self-employment income.—(a) *In general.* Except for the exclusions in paragraphs (b) and (c) of this section and the exception in paragraph (d) of this section, the term "self-employment income" means the net earnings from self-employment derived by an individual during a taxable year.

(b) *Maximum self-employment income*—(1) *General rule.* Subject to the special rules described in subparagraph (2) of this paragraph, the maximum self-employment income of an individual for a taxable year (whether a period of 12 months or less) is—

(i) For any taxable year beginning in a calendar year after 1974, an amount equal to the contribution and benefit base (as determined under section 230 of the Social Security Act) which is effective for such calendar year; and

(ii) For any taxable year—

Ending before 1955	$ 3,600
Ending after 1954 and before 1959	4,200
Ending after 1958 and before 1966	4,800
Ending after 1965 and before 1968	6,600
Ending after 1967 and beginning before 1972	7,800
Beginning after 1971 and before 1973	9,000
Beginning after 1972 and before 1974	10,800
Beginning after 1973 and before 1975	13,200

(2) *Special rules.* (i) If an individual is paid wages as defined in subparagraph (3) of this paragraph in a taxable year, the maximum self-employment income for such taxable year is computed as provided in subdivision (ii) or (iii) of this subparagraph.

(ii) If an individual is paid wages as defined in subparagraph (3)(i) or (ii) of this paragraph in a taxable year, the maximum self-employment income of such individual for such taxable year is the excess of the amounts indi-

Reg. § 1.1402(b)-1(a)

cated in subparagraph (1) of this paragraph over the amount of the wages, as defined in subparagraph (3)(i) and (ii) of this paragraph, paid to him during the taxable year. For example, if for his taxable year beginning in 1974, an individual has $15,000 of net earnings from self-employment and during such taxable year is paid $1,000 of wages as defined in section 3121(a) (see subparagraph (3)(i) of this paragraph), he has $12,200 ($13,200 − $1,000) of self-employment income for the taxable year.

(iii) For taxable years ending on or after December 31, 1968, wages, as defined in subparagraph (3)(iii) of this paragraph, are taken into account in determining the maximum self-employment income of an individual for purposes of the tax imposed under section 1401(b) (hospital insurance), but not for purposes of the tax imposed under section 1401(a) (old-age, survivors, and disability insurance). If an individual is paid wages as defined in subparagraph (3)(iii) of this paragraph in a taxable year, his maximum self-employment income for such taxable year for purposes of the tax imposed under section 1401(a) is computed under subparagraph (1) of this paragraph or subdivision (ii) of this subparagraph (whichever is applicable), and his maximum self-employment income for such taxable year for purposes of the tax imposed under section 1401(b) is the excess of his section 1401(a) maximum self-employment income over the amount of wages, as defined in subparagraph (3)(iii) of this paragraph, paid to him during the taxable year. For purposes of this subdivision, wages as defined in subparagraph (3)(iii) of this paragraph are deemed paid to an individual in the period with respect to which the payment is made, that is, the period in which the compensation was earned or deemed earned within the meaning of section 3231(e). For an explanation of the term "compensation" and for provisions relating to when compensation is earned, see the regulations under section 3231(e) in Part 31 of this chapter (Employment Tax Regulations). The application of the rules set forth in this subdivision may be illustrated by the following example:

Example. M, a calendar-year taxpayer, has $15,000 of net earnings from self-employment for 1974 and during the taxable year is paid $1,000 of wages as defined in section 3121(a) (see subparagraph (3)(i) of this paragraph) and $1,600 of compensation subject to tax under section 3201 (see subparagraph (3)(iii) of this paragraph). Of the $1,600 of taxable compensation, $1,200 represents compensation for services rendered in 1974 and the balance ($400) represents compensation which pursuant to the provisions of section 3231(e) is earned or deemed earned in 1973. M's maximum self-employment income for 1974 for purposes of the tax imposed under section 1401(a), computed as provided in subdivision (ii) of this subparagraph, is $12,200 ($13,200 − $1,000), and for purposes of the tax imposed under section 1401(b) is $11,000 ($12,200 − $1,200). However, M may recompute his maximum self-employment income for 1973 for purposes of the tax imposed under section 1401(b) by taking into account the $400 of compensation which is deemed paid in 1973.

(3) *Meaning of term "wages".* For the purpose of the computation described in subparagraph (2) of this paragraph, the term "wages" includes:

(i) Wages as defined in section 3121(a);

(ii) Such remuneration paid to an employee for services covered by—

(*a*) An agreement entered into pursuant to section 218 of the Social Security Act (42 U.S.C. 418), which section provides for extension of the Federal old-age, survivors and disability insurance system to State and local government employees under voluntary agreements between the States and the Secretary of Health, Education, and Welfare (Federal Security Administrator before April 11, 1953), or

(*b*) An agreement entered into pursuant to the provisions of section 3121(1), relating to coverage of citizens of the United States who are employees of foreign subsidiaries of domestic corporations,

as would be wages under section 3121(a) if such services constituted employment under section 3121(b). For an explanation of the term "wages", see the regulations under section 3121(a) in Part 31 of this chapter (Employment Tax Regulations); and

(iii) Compensation, as defined in section 3231(e), which is subject to the employee tax imposed by section 3201 or the employee representative tax imposed by section 3211.

(c) *Minimum net earnings from self-employment.* Self-employment income does not include the net earnings from self-employment of an individual when the amount of such earnings for the taxable year is less than $400. Thus, an individual having only $300 of net earnings from self-employment for the taxable year would not have any self-employment income. However, an individual having net earnings from self-employment of $400 or more for the taxable year may, by application of paragraph (b)(2) of this section, have less than $400 of self-employment income for purposes of the tax imposed under section 1401(a) and the tax imposed under section 1401(b) or may have self-

Reg. § 1.1402(b)-1(c)

employment income of $400 or more for purposes of the tax imposed under section 1401(a) and of less than $400 for purposes of the tax imposed under section 1401(b). This could occur in a case in which the amount of the individual's net earnings from self-employment is $400 or more for a taxable year and the amount of such net earnings from self-employment plus the amount of wages, as defined in paragraph (b)(3) of this section, paid to him during the taxable year exceed the maximum self-employment income, as set forth in paragraph (b)(1) of this section, for the taxable year. However, the result occurs only if such maximum self-employment income exceeds the amount of such wages. The application of this paragraph may be illustrated by the following example:

Example. For 1974 M, a calendar-year taxpayer, has net earnings from self-employment of $2,000 and wages (as defined in paragraph (b)(3)(i) and (ii) of this section) of $12,500. Since M's net earnings from self-employment plus his wages exceed the maximum self-employment income for 1974 ($13,200), his self-employment income for 1974 is $700 ($13,200 − $12,500). If M also had wages, as defined in paragraph (b)(3)(iii) of this section, of $200, his self-employment income would be $700 for purposes of the tax imposed under section 1401(a) and $500 ($13,200 − $12,700 ($12,500 + $200)) for purposes of the tax imposed under section 1401(b).

For provisions relating to when wages as defined in paragraph (b)(3)(iii) of this section are treated as paid, see paragraph (b)(2)(iii) of this section.

(d) *Nonresident aliens.* A nonresident alien individual never has self-employment income. While a nonresident alien individual who derives income from a trade or business carried on within the United States, Puerto Rico, the Virgin Islands, Guam, or American Samoa (whether by agents or employees, or by a partnership of which he is a member) may be subject to the applicable income tax provisions on such income, such nonresident alien individual will not be subject to the tax on self-employment income, since any net earnings which he may have from self-employment do not constitute self-employment income. For the purpose of the tax on self-employment income, an individual who is not a citizen of the United States but who is a resident of the Commonwealth of Puerto Rico, the Virgin Islands, or, for taxable years beginning after 1960, of Guam or American Samoa is not considered to be a nonresident alien individual. [Reg. § 1.1402(b)-1.]

☐ [T.D. 6196, 8-13-56. Amended by T.D. 6691, 12-2-63, T.D. 6993, 1-17-69 and T.D. 7333, 12-19-74.]

[Reg. § 1.1402(c)-1]

§ 1.1402(c)-1. **Trade or business.**—In order for an individual to have net earnings from self-employment, he must carry on a trade or business, either as an individual or as a member of a partnership. Except for the exclusions discussed in §§ 1.1402(c)-2 to 1.1402(c)-7, inclusive, the term "trade or business", for the purpose of the tax on self-employment income, shall have the same meaning as when used in section 162. An individual engaged in one of the excluded activities specified in such sections of the regulations may also be engaged in carrying on activities which constitute a trade or business for purposes of the tax on self-employment income. Whether or not he is also engaged in carrying on a trade or business will be dependent upon all of the facts and circumstances in the particular case. An individual who is a crew leader, as defined in section 3121(o) (see such section and the regulations thereunder in Part 31 of this chapter (Employment Tax Regulations)), is considered to be engaged in carrying on a trade or business with respect to services performed by him after 1956 in furnishing individuals to perform agricultural labor for another person or services performed by him after 1956 as a member of the crew. [Reg. § 1.1402(c)-1.]

☐ [T.D. 6196, 8-13-56. Amended by T.D. 6691, 12-2-63 and T.D. 6978, 10-29-68.]

[Reg. § 1.1402(c)-2]

§ 1.1402(c)-2. **Public office.**—(a) *In general*—(1) *General rule.* Except as otherwise provided in subparagraph (2) of this paragraph, the performance of the functions of a public office does not constitute a trade or business.

(2) *Fee basis public officials*—(i) *In general.* If an individual receives fees after 1967 for the performance of the functions of a public office of a State or a political subdivision thereof for which he is compensated solely on a fee basis, and if the service performed in such office is eligible for (but is not made the subject of) an agreement between the State and the Secretary of Health, Education, and Welfare pursuant to section 218 of the Social Security Act to extend social security coverage thereto, the service for which such fees are received constitutes a trade or business within the meaning of section 1402(c) and § 1.1402(c)-1. If an individual performs service for a State or a political subdivision thereof in any period in more than one position, each position is treated separately for purposes of the preceding sentence. See also paragraph (f) of § 1.1402(c)-3 relating to the performance of service by an individual as an employee of a State or a political subdivision

thereof in a position compensated solely on a fee basis.

(ii) *Election with respect to fees received in 1968.* (A) Any individual who in 1968 receives fees for service performed by him with respect to the functions of a public office of a State or a political subdivision thereof in any period in which the functions are performed in a position compensated solely on a fee basis may elect, if the performance of the service for which such fees are received constitutes a trade or business pursuant to the provisions of subdivision (i) of this subparagraph, to have such performance of service treated as excluded from the term "trade or business" for the purpose of the tax on self-employment income, pursuant to the provisions of section 122(c)(2) of the Social Security Amendments of 1967 (as quoted in § 1.1402(c)). Such election shall not be limited to service to which the fees received in 1968 are attributable but must also be applicable to service (if any) in subsequent years which, except for the election, would constitute a trade or business pursuant to the provisions of subdivision (i) of this subparagraph. An election made pursuant to the provisions of this subparagraph is irrevocable.

(B) The election referred to in subdivision (ii)(A) of this subparagraph shall be made by filing a certificate of election of exemption (Form 4415) on or before the due date of the income tax return (see section 6072), including any extension thereof (see section 6081), for the taxable year of the individual making the election which begins in 1968. The certificate of election of exemption shall be filed with an internal revenue office in accordance with the instructions on the certificate.

(b) *Meaning of public office.* The term "public office" includes any elective or appointive office of the United States or any possession thereof, of the District of Columbia, of a State or its political subdivisions, or of a wholly-owned instrumentality of any one or more of the foregoing. For example, the President, the Vice President, a governor, a mayor, the Secretary of State, a member of Congress, a State representative, a county commissioner, a judge, a justice of the peace, a county or city attorney, a marshal, a sheriff, a constable, a registrar of deeds, or a notary public performs the functions of a public office. (However, the service of a notary public could not be made the subject of a section 218 agreement under the Social Security Act because notaries are not "employees" within the meaning of that section. Accordingly, such service does not constitute a trade or business.) [Reg. § 1.1402(c)-2.]

☐ [T.D. 6691, 12-2-63. Amended by T.D. 7333, 12-19-74 and T.D. 7372, 7-23-75.]

[Reg. § 1.1402(c)-3]

§ 1.1402(c)-3. Employees.—(a) *General rule.* Generally, the performance of service by an individual as an employee, as defined in the Federal Insurance Contributions Act (chapter 21 of the Internal Revenue Code) does not constitute a trade or business within the meaning of section 1402(c) and § 1.1402(c)-1. However, in six cases set forth in paragraphs (b) to (g), inclusive, of this section, the performance of service by an individual is considered to constitute a trade or business within the meaning of section 1402(c) and § 1.1402(c)-1. (As to when an individual is an employee, see section 3121(d) and (o) and section 3506 and the regulations under those sections in part 31 of this chapter (Employment Tax Regulations).)

(b) *Newspaper vendors.* Service performed by an individual who has attained the age of 18 constitutes a trade or business for purposes of the tax on self-employment income within the meaning of section 1402(c) and § 1.1402(c)-1 if performed in, and at the time of, the sale of newspapers or magazines to ultimate consumers, under an arrangement under which the newspapers or magazines are to be sold by him at a fixed price, his compensation being based on the retention of the excess of such price over the amount at which the newspapers or magazines are charged to him, whether or not he is guaranteed a minimum amount of compensation for such service, or is entitled to be credited with the unsold newspapers or magazines turned back.

(c) *Sharecroppers.* Service performed by an individual under an arrangement with the owner or tenant of land pursuant to which—

(1) Such individual undertakes to produce agricultural or horticultural commodities (including livestock, bees, poultry, and furbearing animals and wildlife) on such land,

(2) The agricultural or horticultural commodities produced by such individual, or the proceeds therefrom, are to be divided between such individual and such owner or tenant, and

(3) The amount of such individual's share depends on the amount of the agricultural or horticultural commodities produced,

constitutes a trade or business within the meaning of section 1402(c) and § 1.1402(c)-1.

(d) *Employees of foreign government, instrumentality wholly owned by foreign government, or international organization.* Service performed in the United States, as defined in section 3121(e)(2) (see such section and the regulations

Reg. § 1.1402(c)-3(d)

thereunder in Part 31 of this chapter (Employment Tax Regulations)), by an individual who is a citizen of the United States constitutes a trade or business within the meaning of section 1402(c) and § 1.1402(c)-1 if such service is excepted from employment, for purposes of the Federal Insurance Contributions Act (chapter 21 of the Code), by—

(1) Section 3121(b)(11), relating to service in the employ of a foreign government (for regulations under section 3121(b)(11), see § 31.3121(b)(11)-1 of this chapter);

(2) Section 3121(b)(12), relating to service in the employ of an instrumentality wholly owned by a foreign government (for regulations under section 3121(b)(12), see § 31.3121(b)(12)-1 of this chapter); or

(3) Section 3121(b)(15), relating to service in the employ of an international organization (for regulations under section 3121(b)(15), see § 31.3121(b)(15)-1 of this chapter).

This paragraph is applicable to service performed in any taxable year ending on or after December 31, 1960, except that it does not apply to service performed before 1961 in Guam or American Samoa.

(e) *Ministers and members of religious orders*— (1) *Taxable years ending before 1968.* Service described in section 1402(c)(4) performed by an individual during taxable years ending before 1968 for which a certificate filed pursuant to section 1402(e) is in effect constitutes a trade or business within the meaning of section 1402(c) and § 1.1402(c)-1. See also § 1.1402(c)-5.

(2) *Taxable years ending after 1967.* Service described in section 1402(c)(4) performed by an individual during taxable years ending after 1967 constitutes a trade or business within the meaning of section 1402(c) and § 1.1402(c)-1 unless an exemption under section 1402(e) (see §§ 1.1402(e)-1A through 1.1402(e)-4A) is efffective with respect to such individual for the taxable year during which the service is performed. See also § 1.1402(c)-5.

(f) *State and local government employees compensated on fee basis*—(1) *In general.* (i) Section 1402(c)(2)(E) and this paragraph are applicable only with respect to fees received by an individual after 1967 for services performed by him as an employee of a State or a political subdivision thereof in a position compensated solely on a fee basis. If an individual performs service for a State or a political subdivision thereof in more than one position, each position is treated separately for purposes of determining whether the service performed in such position is performed by an employee and whether compensation for service performed in the position is solely on a fee basis.

(ii) If an individual receives fees after 1967 for service performed by him as an employee of a State or a political subdivision thereof in a position compensated solely on a fee basis, the service for which such fees are received constitutes a trade or business within the meaning of section 1402(c) and § 1.1402(c)-1 except that if service performed in such position is covered under an agreement entered into by the State and the Secretary of Health, Education, and Welfare pursuant to section 218 of the Social Security Act at the time a fee is received, the service to which such fee relates does not constitute a trade or business. See also paragraph (a) of § 1.1402(c)-2, relating, in part, to the performance of the functions of a public office of a State or a political subdivision thereof by an individual.

(2) *Election with respect to fees received in 1968*—(i) Any individual who in 1968 receives fees for service as an employee of a State or a political subdivision thereof in a position compensated solely on a fee basis may elect, if the performance of the service for which such fees are received constitutes a trade or business pursuant to the provisions of subparagraph (1) of this paragraph, to have such performance of service treated as excluded from the term "trade or business" for the purpose of the tax on self-employment income, pursuant to the provisions of section 122(c)(2) of the Social Security Amendments of 1967 (as quoted in § 1.1402(c)). Such election shall not be limited to service to which the fees received in 1968 are attributable but must also be applicable to service (if any) in subsequent years which, except for the election, would constitute a trade or business pursuant to the provisions of subparagraph (1) of this paragraph. An election made pursuant to the provisions of this subparagraph is irrevocable.

(ii) The election referred to in subdivision (i) of this subparagraph shall be made by filing a certificate of election of exemption (Form 4415) on or before the due date of the income tax return (see section 6072), including any extension thereof (see section 6081), for the taxable year of the individual making the election which begins in 1968. The certificate of election of exemption shall be filed with an internal revenue office in accordance with the instructions on the certificate.

(g) *Individuals engaged in fishing.* For taxable years ending after December 31, 1954, service performed by an individual on a boat engaged in catching fish or other forms of aquatic animal life (hereinafter "fish") constitutes a trade or business

Reg. § 1.1402(c)-3(d)(1)

within the meaning of section 1402(c) and § 1.1402(c)-1 if the service is excepted from the definition of employment by section 3121(b)(20) and § 31.3121(b)(20)-1(a). However, the preceding sentence does not apply to services performed after December 31, 1954, and before October 4, 1976, on a boat engaged in catching fish if the owner or operator of the boat treated the individual as an employee in the manner described in § 31.3121(b)(20)-1(b). [Reg. § 1.1402(c)-3.]

☐ [T.D. 6691, 12-2-63. Amended by T.D. 6978, 10-29-68, T.D. 7333, 12-19-74, T.D. 7691, 4-8-80 and T.D. 7716, 8-26-80.]

[Reg. § 1.1402(c)-4]

§ 1.1402(c)-4. **Individuals under Railroad Retirement System.**—The performance of service by an individual as an employee or employee representative as defined in section 3231(b) and (c), respectively (see §§ 31.3231(b)-1 and 31.3231(c)-1 of Part 31 of this chapter (Employment Tax Regulations)), that is, an individual covered under the railroad retirement system, does not constitute a trade or business. [Reg. § 1.1402(c)-4.]

☐ [T.D. 6691, 12-2-63.]

[Reg. § 1.1402(c)-5]

§ 1.1402(c)-5. **Ministers and members of religious orders.**—(a) *In general*—(1) *Taxable years ending before 1968.* For taxable years ending before 1955, a duly ordained, commissioned, or licensed minister of a church or a member of a religious order is not engaged in carrying on a trade or business with respect to service performed by him in the exercise of his ministry or in the exercise of duties required by such order. However, for taxable years ending after 1954 and before 1968, any individual who is a duly ordained, commissioned, or licensed minister of a church or a member of a religious order (other than a member of a religious order who has taken a vow of poverty as a member of such order) may elect, as provided in § 1.1402(e)(1)-1, to have the Federal old-age, survivors, and disability insurance system established by title II of the Social Security Act extended to service performed by him in his capacity as such a minister or member. If such a minister or a member of a religious order makes an election pursuant to § 1.1402(e)(1)-1 he is, with respect to service performed by him in such capacity, engaged in carrying on a trade or business for each taxable year to which the election is effective. An election by a minister or member of a religious order has no application to service performed by such minister or member which is not in the exercise of his ministry or in the exercise of duties required by such order.

(2) *Taxable years ending after 1967.* For any taxable year ending after 1967, a duly ordained, commissioned, or licensed minister of a church or a member of a religious order (other than a member of a religious order who has taken a vow of poverty as a member of such order) is engaged in carrying on a trade or business with respect to service performed by him in the exercise of his ministry or in the exercise of duties required by such order unless an exemption under section 1402(e) (see §§ 1.1402(e)-1A through 1.1402(e)-4A) is effective with respect to such individual for the taxable year during which the service is performed. An exemption which is effective with respect to a minister or a member of a religious order has no application to service performed by such minister or member which is not in the exercise of his ministry or in the exercise of duties required by such order.

(b) *Service by a minister in the exercise of his ministry.* (1)(i) A certificate of election filed by a duly ordained, commissioned, or licensed minister of a church under the provisions of § 1.1402(e)(1)-1 has application only to service performed by him in the exercise of his ministry.

(ii) An exemption under section 1402(e) (see §§ 1.1402(e)-1A through 1.1402(e)-4A) which is effective with respect to a duly ordained, commissioned, or licensed minister of a church has application only to service performed by him in the exercise of his ministry.

(2) Except as provided in paragraph (c)(3) of this section, service performed by a minister in the exercise of his ministry includes the ministration of sacerdotal functions and the conduct of religious worship, and the control, conduct, and maintenance of religious organizations (including the religious boards, societies, and other integral agencies of such organizations), under the authority of a religious body constituting a church or church denomination. The following rules are applicable in determining whether services performed by a minister are performed in the exercise of his ministry:

(i) Whether service performed by a minister constitutes the conduct of religious worship or the ministration of sacerdotal functions depends on the tenets and practices of the particular religious body constituting his church or church denomination.

(ii) Service performed by a minister in the control, conduct, and maintenance of a religious organization relates to directing, managing, or promoting the activities of such organization. Any religious organization is deemed to be under the authority of a religious body constituting a church or church denomination if it is organized and

Reg. § 1.1402(c)-5(b)(2)

dedicated to carrying out the tenets and principles of a faith in accordance with either the requirements or sanctions governing the creation of institutions of the faith. The term "religious organization" has the same meaning and application as is given to the term for income tax purposes.

(iii) If a minister is performing service in the conduct of religious worship or the ministration of sacerdotal functions, such service is in the exercise of his ministry whether or not it is performed for a religious organization. The application of this rule may be illustrated by the following example:

Example. M, a duly ordained minister, is engaged to perform service as chaplain at N University. M devotes his entire time to performing his duties as chaplain which include the conduct of religious worship, offering spiritual counsel to the university students, and teaching a class in religion. M is performing service in the exercise of his ministry.

(iv) If a minister is performing service for an organization which is operated as an integral agency of a religious organization under the authority of a religious body constituting a church or church denomination, all service performed by the minister in the conduct of religious worship, in the ministration of sacerdotal functions, or in the control, conduct, and maintenance of such organization (see subparagraph (2)(ii) of this paragraph) is in the exercise of his ministry. The application of this rule may be illustrated by the following example:

Example. M, a duly ordained minister, is engaged by the N Religious Board to serve as director of one of its departments. He performs no other service. The N Religious Board is an integral agency of O, a religious organization operating under the authority of a religious body constituting a church denomination. M is performing service in the exercise of his ministry.

(v) If a minister, pursuant to an assignment or designation by a religious body constituting his church, performs service for an organization which is neither a religious organization nor operated as an integral agency of a religious organization, all service performed by him, even though such service may not involve the conduct of religious worship or the ministration of sacerdotal functions, is in the exercise of his ministry. The application of this rule may be illustrated by the following example:

Example. M, a duly ordained minister, is assigned by X, the religious body constituting his church, to perform advisory service to Y Company in connection with the publication of a book dealing with the history of M's church denomination. Y is neither a religious organization nor operated as an integral agency of a religious organization. M performs no other service for X or Y. M is performing service in the exercise of his ministry.

(c) *Service by a minister not in the exercise of his ministry.* (1)(i) A certificate filed by a duly ordained, commissioned, or licensed minister of a church under the provisions of § 1.1402(e)(1)-1 has no application to service performed by him which is not in the exercise of his ministry.

(ii) An exemption under section 1402(e) (see §§ 1.1402(e)-1A through 1.1402(e)-4A) which is effective with respect to a duly ordained, commissioned, or licensed minister of a church has no application to service performed by him which is not in the exercise of his ministry.

(2) If a minister is performing service for an organization which is neither a religious organization nor operated as an integral agency of a religious organization and the service is not performed pursuant to an assignment or designation by his ecclesiastical superiors, then only the service performed by him in the conduct of religious worship or the ministration of sacerdotal functions is in the exercise of his ministry. See, however, subparagraph (3) of this paragraph. The application of the rule in this subparagraph may be illustrated by the following example:

Example. M, a duly ordained minister, is engaged by N University to teach history and mathematics. He performs no other service for N although from time to time he performs marriages and conducts funerals for relatives and friends. N University is neither a religious organization nor operated as an integral agency of a religious organization. M is not performing the service for N pursuant to an assignment or designation by his ecclesiastical superiors. The service performed by M for N University is not in the exercise of his ministry. However, service performed by M in performing marriages and conducting funerals is in the exercise of his ministry.

(3) Service performed by a duly ordained, commissioned, or licensed minister of a church as an employee of the United States, or a State, Territory, or possession of the United States, or the District of Columbia, or a foreign government, or a political subdivision of any of the foregoing, is not considered to be in the exercise of his ministry for purposes of the tax on self-employment income, even though such service may involve the ministration of sacerdotal functions or the conduct of religious worship. Thus, for example, service performed by an individual as a chaplain in the Armed Forces of the United States is consid-

Reg. § 1.1402(c)-5(c)(2)

ered to be performed by a commissioned officer in his capacity as such, and not by a minister in the exercise of his ministry. Similarly, service performed by an employee of a State as a chaplain in a State prison is considered to be performed by a civil servant of the State and not by a minister in the exercise of his ministry.

(d) *Service in the exercise of duties required by a religious order*—(1) *Certificate of election.* A certificate of election filed by a member of a religious order (other than a member of a religious order who has taken a vow of poverty as a member of such order) under the provisions of § 1.1402(e)(1)-1 has application to all duties required of him by such order.

(2) *Exemption.* An exemption under section 1402(e) (see §§ 1.1402(e)-1A through 1.1402(e)-4A) which is effective with respect to a member of a religious order (other than a member of a religious order who has taken a vow of poverty as a member of such order) has application only to the duties required of him by such order.

(3) *Service.* For purposes of subparagraphs (1) and (2) of this paragraph, the nature or extent of the duties required of the member by the order is immaterial so long as it is a service which he is directed or required to perform by his ecclesiastical superiors. [Reg. § 1.1402(c)-5.]

☐ [*T.D.* 6691, 12-2-63. *Amended by T.D.* 6978, 10-29-68.]

[Reg. § 1.1402(c)-6]

§ 1.1402(c)-6. **Members of certain professions.**—(a) *Periods of exclusion*—(1) *Taxable years ending before 1955.* For taxable years ending before 1955, an individual is not engaged in carrying on a trade or business with respect to the performance of service in the exercise of his profession as a physician, lawyer, dentist, osteopath, veterinarian, chiropractor, naturopath, optometrist, Christian Science practitioner, architect, certified public accountant, accountant registered or licensed as an accountant under State or municipal law, full-time practicing public accountant, funeral director, or professional engineer.

(2) *Taxable years ending in 1955.* Except as provided in paragraph (b) of this section, for a taxable year ending in 1955 an individual is not engaged in carrying on a trade or business with respect to the performance of service in the exercise of his profession as a physician, lawyer, dentist, osteopath, veterinarian, chiropractor, naturopath, optometrist, or Christian Science practitioner.

(3) *Taxable years ending after 1955*—(i) *Doctors of medicine.* For taxable years ending after 1955 and before December 31, 1965, an individual is not engaged in carrying on a trade or business with respect to the performance of service in the exercise of his profession as a doctor of medicine. For taxable years ending after December 30, 1965, an individual is engaged in carrying on a trade or business with respect to the performance of service in the exercise of his profession as a doctor of medicine.

(ii) *Christian Science practitioners.* Except as provided in paragraph (b)(1), of this section, for taxable years ending after 1955 and before 1968, an individual is not engaged in carrying on a trade or business with respect to the performance of service in the exercise of his profession as a Christian Science practitioner. For provisions relating to the performance of service in taxable years ending after 1967 by an individual in the exercise of his profession as a Christian Science practitioner, see paragraph (b)(2) of this section.

(b) *Christian Science practitioner*—(1) *Certain taxable years ending before 1968; election.* For taxable years ending after 1954 and before 1968, a Christian Science practitioner may elect, as provided in § 1.1402(e)(1)-1, to have the Federal old-age, survivors, and disability insurance system established by title II of the Social Security Act extended to service performed by him in the exercise of his profession as a Christian Science practitioner. If an election is made pursuant to § 1.1402(e)(1)-1, the Christian Science practitioner is, with respect to the performance of service in the exercise of such profession, engaged in carrying on a trade or business for each taxable year for which the election is effective. An election by a Christian Science practitioner has no application to service performed by him which is not in the exercise of his profession as a Christian Science practitioner.

(2) *Taxable years ending after 1967; exemption.* For a taxable year ending after 1967, a Christian Science practitioner is, with respect to the performance of service in the exercise of his profession as a Christian Science practitioner, engaged in carrying on a trade or business unless an exemption under section 1402(e) (see §§ 1.1402(e)-1A through 1.1402(e)-4A) if effective with respect to him for the taxable year during which the service is performed. An exemption which is effective with respect to a Christian Science practitioner has no application to service performed by him which is not in the exercise of his profession as a Christian Science practitioner.

(c) *Meaning of terms.* The designations in this section are to be given their commonly accepted meanings. For taxable years ending after 1955, an individual who is a doctor of osteopathy, and who is not a doctor of medicine within the commonly accepted meaning of that term, is deemed, for purposes of this section, not to be engaged in carrying on a trade or business in the exercise of the profession of doctor of medicine.

(d) *Legal requirements.* The exclusions specified in paragraph (a) of this section apply only if the individuals meet the legal requirements, if any, for practicing their professions in the place where they perform the service.

(e) *Partnerships.* In the case of a partnership engaged in the practice of any of the designated excluded professions, the partnership shall not be considered as carrying on a trade or business for the purpose of the tax on self-employment income, and none of the distributive shares of the income or loss, described in section 702(a)(9), of such partnership shall be included in computing net earnings from self-employment of any member of the partnership. On the other hand, where a partnership is engaged in a trade or business not within any of the designated excluded professions, each partner must include his distributive share of the income or loss, described in section 702(a)(9), of such partnership in computing his net earnings from self-employment, irrespective of whether such partner is engaged in the practice of one or more of such professions and contributes his professional services to the partnership. [Reg. § 1.1402(c)-6.]

☐ [T.D. 6691, 12-2-63. Amended by T.D. 6978, 10-29-68.]

[Reg. § 1.1402(c)-7]

§ 1.1402(c)-7. **Members of religious groups opposed to insurance.**—The performance of service by an individual—

(a) Who is a member of a recognized religious sect or division thereof, and

(b) Who is an adherent of established tenets or teachings of such sect or division by reason of which he is conscientiously opposed to acceptance of the benefits of any private or public insurance which makes payments in the event of death, disability, old age, or retirement or makes payments toward the cost of, or provides services for, medical care (including the benefits of any insurance system established by the Social Security Act),

during any taxable year for which he is granted a tax exemption, pursuant to section 1402(h), does not constitute a trade or business within the meaning of section 1402(c) and § 1.1402(c)-1. See also §§ 1.1402(h) and 1.1402(h)-1. [Reg. § 1.1402(c)-7.]

☐ [T.D. 6993, 1-17-69.]

Reg. § 1.1402(c)-7(a)

[Reg. § 1.1402(d)-1]

§ 1.1402(d)-1. **Employee and wages.**—For the purpose of the tax on self-employment income, the term "employee" and the term "wages" shall have the same meaning as when used in the Federal Insurance Contributions Act. For an explanation of these terms, see Subpart B of Part 31 of this chapter (Employment Tax Regulations). [Reg. § 1.1402(d)-1.]

☐ [T.D. 6196, 8-13-56. Amended by T.D. 6691, 12-2-63.]

[Reg. § 1.1402(e)-1A]

§ 1.1402(e)-1A. **Application of regulations under section 1402(e).**—The regulations in §§ 1.1402(e)-2A through 1.1402(e)-4A relate to section 1402(e) as amended by section 115(b)(2) of the Social Security Amendments of 1967 (81 Stat. 839) and apply to taxable years ending after 1967. Section 1.1402(e)-5A reflects changes made by section 1704(a) of the Tax Reform Act of 1986 (100 Stat. 2085, 2779) and applies to applications for exemption under section 1402(e) filed after December 31, 1986. For regulations under section 1402(e) (as in effect prior to amendment by the Social Security Amendments of 1967) applicable to taxable years ending before 1968, see §§ 1.1402(e)(1)-1 through 1.1402(e)(6)-1. [Reg. § 1.1402(e)-1A.]

☐ [T.D. 6978, 10-29-68. Amended by T.D. 8221, 8-30-88.]

[Reg. § 1.1402(e)-2A]

§ 1.1402(e)-2A. **Ministers, members of religious orders and Christian Science practitioners; application for exemption from self-employment tax.**—(a) *In general*—(1) Subject to the limitations set forth in subparagraphs (2) and (3) of this paragraph, any individual who is (i) a duly ordained, commissioned, or licensed minister of a church or a member of a religious order (other than a member of a religious order who has taken a vow of poverty as a member of such order) or (ii) a Christian Science practitioner may request an exemption from the tax on self-employment income (see §§ 1.1401 and 1.1401-1) with respect to services performed by him in his capacity as a minister or member, or as a Christian Science practitioner, as the case may be. Such a request shall be made by filing an application for exemption on Form 4361 in the manner provided in paragraph (b) of this section and within the time specified in § 1.1402(e)-3A. For provisions relating to the taxable year or years for which an exemption from the tax on self-employment income with respect to service performed by a minister or member or a Christian Science practitioner in his capacity as such is effective, see

§ 1.1402(e)-4A. For additional provisions applicable to services performed by individuals referred to in this subparagraph, see paragraph (e) of § 1.1402(c)-3 and § 1.1402(c)-5 relating to ministers and members of religious orders, and paragraphs (a)(3)(ii) and (b) of § 1.1402(c)-6 relating to Christian Science practitioners.

(2) The application for exemption shall contain, or there shall be filed with such application, a statement to the effect that the individual making application for exemption is conscientiously opposed to, or because of religious principles is opposed to, the acceptance (with respect to services performed by him in his capacity as a minister, member, or Christian Science practitioner) of any public insurance which makes payments in the event of death, disability, old age, or retirement or makes payments toward the cost of, or provides services for, medical care (including the benefits of any insurance system established by the Social Security Act). Thus, ministers, members of religious orders, and Christian Science practitioners requesting exemption from social security coverage must meet either of two alternative tests: (1) A religious principles test which refers to the institutional principles and discipline of the particular religious denomination to which he belongs, or (2) a conscientious opposition test which refers to the opposition because of religious considerations of individual ministers, members of religious orders, and Christian Science practitioners (rather than opposition based upon the general conscience of any such individual or individuals). The term "public insurance," as used in section 1402(e) and this paragraph, refers to governmental, as distinguished from private, insurance and does not include insurance carried with a commercial insurance carrier. To be eligible to file an application for exemption on Form 4361, a minister, member, or Christian Science practitioners need not be opposed to the acceptance of all public insurance making payments of this specified type; he must, however, be opposed on religious grounds to the acceptance of any such payment which, in whole or in part, is based on, or measured by earnings from, services performed by him in his capacity as a minister or member (see § 1.1402(c)-5) or in his capacity as a Christian Science practitioner (see paragraph (b)(2) of § 1.1402(c)-6). For example, a minister performing service in the exercise of his ministry may be eligible to file an application for exemption on Form 4361 even though he is not opposed to the acceptance of benefits under the Social Security Act with respect to service performed by him which is not in the exercise of his ministry.

(3) An exemption from the tax imposed on self-employment income with respect to service performed by a minister, member, or Christian Science practitioner in his capacity as such may not be granted to a minister, member, or practitioner who (in accordance with the provisions of section 1402(e) as in effect prior to amendment by section 115(b)(2) of the Social Security Amendments of 1967 (81 Stat. 839)) filed a valid waiver certificate on Form 2031 electing to have the Federal old-age, survivors, and disability insurance system established by title II of the Social Security Act extended to service performed by him in the exercise of his ministry or in the exercise of duties required by the order of which he is a member, or in the exercise of his profession as a Christian Science practitioner. For provisions relating to waiver certificates on Form 2031, see §§ 1.1402(e)(1)-1 through 1.1402(e)(6)-1.

(b) *Application for exemption.* An application for exemption on Form 4361 shall be filed in triplicate with the internal revenue officer or the internal revenue office, as the case may be, designated in the instructions relating to the application for exemption. The application for exemption must be filed within the time prescribed in § 1.1402(e)-3A. If the last original Federal income tax return of an individual to whom paragraph (a) of this section applies which was filed before the expiration of such time limitation for filing an application for exemption shows no liability for tax on self-employment income, such return will be treated as an application for exemption, provided that before February 28, 1975 such individual also files a properly executed Form 4361.

(c) *Approval of application for exemption.* The filing of an application for exemption on Form 4361 by a minister, a member of a religious order, or a Christian Science practitioner does not constitute an exemption from the tax on self-employment income with respect to services performed by him in his capacity as a minister, member, or practitioner. The exemption is granted only if the application is approved by an appropriate internal revenue officer. See § 1.1402(e)-4A relating to the period for which an exemption is effective. [Reg. § 1.1402(e)-2A.]

☐ [T.D. 7333, 12-19-74.]

[Reg. § 1.1402(e)-3A]

§ 1.1402(e)-3A. Time limitation for filing application for exemption.—(a) *General rule.* (1) Any individual referred to in paragraph (a) of § 1.1402(e)-2A who desires an exemption from the tax on self-employment income with respect to service performed by him in his capacity as a minister or member of a religious order or as a Christian Science practitioner must file the application for exemption (Form 4361) prescribed by

§ 1.1402(e)-2A on or before whichever of the following dates is later:

(i) The due date of the income tax return (see section 6072), including any extension thereof (see section 6081), for his second taxable year ending after 1967, or

(ii) The due date of the income tax return, including any extension thereof, for his second taxable year beginning after 1953 for which he has net earnings from self-employment of $400 or more, any part of which—

(a) In the case of a duly ordained, commissioned, or licensed minister of a church, consists of remuneration for service performed in the exercise of his ministry,

(b) In the case of a member of a religious order who has not taken a vow of poverty as a member of such order, consists of remuneration for service performed in the exercise of duties required by such order, or

(c) In the case of a Christian Science practitioner, consists of remuneration for service performed in the exercise of his profession as a Christian Science practitioner.

See paragraph (c) of this section for provisions relating to the computation of net earnings from self-employment.

(2) If a minister, a member of a religious order, or a Christian Science practitioner derives gross income in a taxable year both from service performed in such capacity and from the conduct of another trade or business, and the deductions allowed by chapter 1 of the Internal Revenue Code which are attributable to the gross income derived from service performed in such capacity equal or exceed the gross income derived from service performed in such capacity, no part of the net earnings from self-employment (computed as prescribed in paragraph (c) of this section) for the taxable year shall be considered as derived from service performed in such capacity.

(3) The application of the rules set forth in subparagraphs (1) and (2) of this paragraph may be illustrated by the following examples:

Example (1). M, who makes his income tax returns on a calendar year basis, was ordained as a minister in January 1960. During each of two or more taxable years ending before 1968 M has net earnings from self-employment in excess of $400, some part of which is from service performed in the exercise of his ministry. M has not filed an effective waiver certificate on Form 2031 (see paragraph (a)(3) of § 1.1402(e)-2A). If M desires an exemption from the tax on self-employment income with respect to service performed in the exercise of his ministry, he must file an application for exemption on or before the due date of his income tax return for 1969 (his second taxable year ending after 1967), or any extension thereof.

Example (2). M, who makes his income tax returns on a calendar year basis, was ordained as a minister in January 1966. M has net earnings of $350 for the taxable year 1966 and has net earnings in excess of $400 for each of his taxable years 1967 and 1968 (some part or all of which is derived from service performed in the exercise of his ministry). M has not filed an effective waiver certificate on Form 2031 (see paragraph (a)(3) of § 1.1402(e)-2A). If M desires an exemption from the tax on self-employment income with respect to service performed in the exercise of his ministry, he must file an application for exemption on or before the due date of his income tax return for 1969 (his second taxable year ending after 1967), or any extension thereof.

Example (3). Assume the same facts as in example (2) except that M has net earnings in excess of $400 for each of his taxable years 1967 and 1969 (but less than $400 in 1968). The application for exemption must be filed on or before the due date of his income tax return for 1969, or any extension thereof.

Example (4). M was ordained as a minister in May 1973. During each of the taxable years 1973 and 1975, M, who makes his income tax returns on a calendar year basis, derives net earnings in excess of $400 from his activities as a minister. M has net earnings of $350 for the taxable year 1974, $200 of which is derived from service performed by him in the exercise of his ministry. If M desires an exemption from the tax on self-employment income with respect to service performed in the exercise of his ministry, he must file an application for exemption on or before the due date of his income tax return for 1975, or any extension thereof.

Example (5). M, who was ordained a minister in January 1973, is employed as a toolmaker by the XYZ Corporation for the taxable years 1973 and 1974 and also engages in activities as a minister on weekends. M makes his income tax returns on the basis of a calendar year. During each of the taxable years 1973 and 1974 M receives wages of $14,000 from the XYZ Corporation and derives net earnings of $400 from his activities as a minister. If M desires an exemption from the tax on self-employment income with respect to service performed in the exercise of his ministry, he must file an application for exemption on or before the due date of his income tax return for 1974, or any extension thereof. It should be noted that although by reason of section 1402(b)(1)(G) and (H) no part of the $400 represents "self-employment

Reg. § 1.1402(e)-3A(a)(2)

Tax on Self-Employment Income 56,527

See p. 20,601 for regulations not amended to reflect law changes

income," nevertheless the entire $400 constitutes "net earnings from self-employment" for purposes of fulfilling the requirements of section 1402(e)(2).

Example (6). M, who files his income tax returns on a calendar year basis, was ordained as a minister in March 1973. During 1973 he receives $410 for service performed in the exercise of his ministry. In addition to his ministerial services, M is engaged during the year 1973 in a mercantile venture from which he derives net earnings from self-employment in the amount of $4,000. The expenses incurred by him in connection with his ministerial services during 1973 and which are allowable deductions under chapter 1 of the Internal Revenue Code amount to $410. During 1974 and 1975, M has net earnings from self-employment in amounts of $4,600 and $4,800, respectively, and some part of each of these amounts is from the exercise of his ministry. The deductions allowed in each of the years 1974 and 1975 by chapter 1 which are attributable to the gross income derived by M from the exercise of his ministry in each of such years, respectively, do not equal or exceed such gross income in such year. If M desires an exemption from the tax on self-employment income with respect to service performed in the exercise of his ministry, he must file an application for exemption on or before the due date of his income tax return for 1975, or an extension thereof.

(b) *Effect of death*—The right of an individual to file an application for exemption shall cease upon his death. Thus, the surviving spouse, administrator, or executor of a decedent shall not be permitted to file an application for exemption for such decedent.

(c) *Computation of net earnings*—(1) *Taxable years ending before 1968*—For purposes of this section net earnings from self-employment for taxable years ending before 1968 shall be determined without regard to the fact that, without an election under section 1402(e) (as in effect prior to amendment by section 115(b)(2) of the Social Security Amendments of 1967, see § 1.1402(e)-1A), the performance of services by a duly ordained, commissioned, or licensed minister of a church in the exercise of his ministry, or by a member of a religious order in the exercise of duties required by such order, or the performance of service by an individual in the exercise of his profession as a Christian Science practitioner, does not constitute a trade or business for purposes of the tax on self-employment income.

(2) *Taxable years ending after 1967.* For purposes of this section and § 1.1402(e)-4A net earnings from self-employment for taxable years ending after 1967 shall be determined without regard to section 1402(c)(4) and (5). See § 1.1402(c)-3(e)(2) and § 1.1402(c)-5 relating to ministers and members of religious orders, and paragraphs (a)(3)(ii) and (b) of § 1.1402(c)-6 relating to Christian Science practitioners. [Reg. § 1.1402(e)-3A.]

☐ [T.D. 7333, 12-19-74.]

[Reg. § 1.1402(e)-4A]

§ 1.1402(e)-4A. **Period for which exemption is effective.**—(a) *In general.* If an application for exemption on Form 4361—

(1) Is filed by a minister, a member of a religious order, or a Christian Science practitioner eligible to file such an application (see particularly paragraph (a)(2) and (3) of § 1.1402(e)-2A), and

(2) Is approved (see paragraph (c) of § 1.1402(e)-2A),

the exemption from the tax on self-employment income shall be effective for the first taxable year ending after 1967 for which such minister, member, or practitioner has net earnings from self-employment of $400 or more any part of which was derived from the performance of service in his capacity as a minister, member, or practitioner, and for all succeeding taxable years. See, however, paragraphs (b)(1)(ii) and (d)(2) of § 1.1402(c)-5 relating to ministers and members of religious orders and paragraph (b)(2) of § 1.1402(c)-6 relating to Christian Science practitioners.

(b) *Exemption irrevocable.* An exemption granted to a minister, a member of a religious order, or a Christian Science practitioner pursuant to the provisions of section 1402(e) is irrevocable. [Reg. § 1.1402(e)-4A.]

☐ [T.D. 7333, 12-19-74.]

[Reg. § 1.1402(e)-5A]

§ 1.1402(e)-5A. **Applications for exemption from self-employment taxes filed after December 31, 1986, by ministers, certain members of religious orders, and Christian Science practitioners.**—(a) *In general.* (1) Except as provided in paragraph (a)(2) of this section, this section applies to any individual who is a duly ordained, commissioned, or licensed minister of a church, member of a religious order (other than a member of a religious order who has taken a vow of poverty as a member of such order), or a Christian Science practitioner who files an application after December 31, 1986, for exemption from the tax on self-employment income (see section 1401 and § 1.1401-1) with respect to services performed by him or her in his or her capacity as a minister, member, or practitioner pursuant to

Reg. § 1.1402(e)-5A

§§ 1.1402(e)-2A through 1.1402(e)-4A. This section does not apply to applications for exemption under section 1402(e) that are filed before January 1, 1987.

(2) *Application of this section to Christian Science practitioners.* Paragraph (b) of this section does not apply to Christian Science practitioners. Thus, Christian Science practitioners filing applications for exemption from self-employment taxes under section 1402(e) should follow the procedures set forth in §§ 1.1402(e)-2A through 1.1402(e)-4A, and are not required to include the statement described in paragraph (b)(1)(ii) of this section. However, see paragraph (c) of this section for verification procedures with respect to applications for exemption from self-employment taxes filed after December 31, 1986, by Christian Science practitioners.

(b) *Church or order must be informed*—(1) *In general.* Any individual, other than a Christian Science practitioner, who files an application for exemption from the tax on self-employment income under section 1402(e) after December 31, 1986:

(i) Shall file such application in accordance with the procedures set forth in §§ 1.1402(e)-2A through 1.1402(e)-4A, and

(ii) Shall include with such application a statement to the effect that the individual making application for exemption has informed the ordaining, commissioning, or licensing body of the church or order that he or she is opposed to the acceptance (for services performed as a minister or member of a religious order not under a vow of poverty) of any public insurance that makes payments in the event of death, disability, old age, or retirement, or that makes payments toward the cost of, or provides services for, medical care (including the benefits of any insurance system established by the Social Security Act).

(2) *Statement to be filed with Form.* If the form provided by the Service for applying for exemption under 1402(e) does not contain the statement set forth in paragraph (b)(1)(ii) of this section, any individual required to include this statement with his or her application under this paragraph (b) shall file such statement with the individual's application at the time and place prescribed for filing such application under §§ 1.1402(e)-2A and 1.1402(e)-3A. The statement shall contain the information set forth in paragraph (b)(1)(ii) of this section and shall be signed by such individual under penalties of perjury.

(c) *Verification of Application*—(1) *In general.* The Service will approve an application for an exemption filed by an individual to whom this section applies only after verifying that the individual applying for the exemption is aware of the grounds on which the individual may receive an exemption under section 1402(e) (see § 1.1402(e)-2A) and that the individual seeks exemption on such grounds in accordance with the procedures set forth in paragraph (c)(2) of this section.

(2) *Verification procedure.* Upon receipt of an application for exemption from self-employment taxes under section 1402(e) and this section, the Service will mail to the applicant a statement that describes the grounds on which an individual may receive an exemption under section 1402(e). The individual filing the application shall certify that he or she has read the statement and that he or she seeks exemption from self-employment taxes on the grounds listed in the statement. The certification shall be made by signing a copy of the statement under penalties of perjury and mailing the signed copy to the Service Center from which the statement was issued not later than 90 days after the date on which the statement was mailed to the individual. If the signed copy of the statement is not mailed to the Service Center within 90 days of the date on which the statement was mailed to the individual, that individual's exemption will not be effective until the date that the signed copy of the statement is received at the Service Center. [Reg. § 1.1402(e)-5A.]

☐ [*T.D.* 8821, 8-30-88.]

[Reg. § 1.1402(f)-1]

§ 1.1402(f)-1. **Computation of partner's net earnings from self-employment for taxable years ending as result of his death.**—(a) *Taxable years ending after August 28, 1958*—(1) *In general.* The rules for the computation of a partner's net earnings from self-employment are set forth in paragraphs (d) to (g), inclusive, of § 1.1402(a)-2. In addition to the net earnings from self-employment computed under such rules for the last taxable year of a deceased partner, if a partner's taxable year ends after August 28, 1958, solely because of death, and on a day other than the last day of the partnership's taxable year, the deceased partner's net earnings from self-employment for such year shall also include so much of the deceased partner's distributive share of partnership ordinary income or loss (see subparagraph (3) of this paragraph) for the taxable year of the partnership in which his death occurs as is attributable to an interest in the partnership prior to the month following the month of his death.

(2) *Computation.* (i) The deceased partner's distributive share of partnership ordinary income or loss for the partnership taxable year in which he died shall be determined by applying the rules

contained in paragraphs (d) to (g), inclusive, of § 1.1402(a)-2, except that paragraph (e) shall not apply.

(ii) The portion of such distributive share to be included under this section in the deceased partner's net earnings from self-employment for his last taxable year shall be determined by treating the ordinary income or loss constituting such distributive share as having been realized or sustained ratably over the period of the partnership taxable year during which the deceased partner had an interest in the partnership and during which his estate, or any other person succeeding by reason of his death to rights with respect to his partnership interest, held such interest in the partnership or held a right with respect to such interest. The amount to be included under this section in the deceased partner's net earnings from self-employment for his last taxable year will, therefore, be determined by multiplying the deceased partner's distributive share of partnership ordinary income or loss for the partnership taxable year in which he died, as determined under subdivision (i) of this subparagraph, by a fraction, the denominator of which is the number of calendar months in the partnership taxable year over which the ordinary income or loss constituting the deceased partner's distributive share of partnership income or loss for such year is treated as having been realized or sustained under the preceding sentence and the numerator of which is the number of calendar months in such partnership taxable year that precede the month following the month of his death.

(3) *Definition of "deceased partner's distributive share."* For the purpose of this section, the term "deceased partner's distributive share" includes the distributive share of his estate or of any other person succeeding, by reason of his death, to rights with respect to his partnership interest. It does not include any share attributable to a partnership interest which was not held by the deceased partner at the time of his death. Thus, if a deceased partner's estate should acquire an interest in a partnership additional to the interest to which it succeeded upon the death of the deceased partner, the amount of the distributive share attributable to such additional interest acquired by the estate would not be included in computing the "deceased partner's distributive share" of the partnership's ordinary income or loss for the partnership taxable year.

(4) *Examples.* The application of this paragraph may be illustrated by the following examples:

Example (1). B, an individual who files his income tax returns on the calendar year basis, is a member of the ABC partnership, the taxable year of which ends on June 30. B dies on October 17, 1958, and his estate succeeds to his partnership interest and continues as a partner in its own right under local law until June 30, 1959. B's distributive share of the partnership's ordinary income, as determined under paragraphs (d) to (g), inclusive, of § 1.1402(a)-2, for the taxable year of the partnership ended June 30, 1958 is $2,400. His distributive share, including the share of his estate, of such partnership's ordinary income, as determined under paragraphs (d) to (g), inclusive, of § 1.1402(a)-2 (with the exception of paragraph (e)), for the taxable year of the partnership ended June 30, 1959 is $4,500. The portion of such $4,500 attributable to an interest in the partnership prior to the month following the month in which he died is $4,500 × 4/12 (4 being the number of months in the partnership taxable year in which B died which precede the month following the month of his death and 12 being the number of months in such partnership taxable year in which B and his estate had an interest in the partnership) or $1,500. The amount to be included in the deceased partner's net earnings from self-employment for his last taxable year is $3,900 ($2,400 plus $1,500).

Example (2). If in the preceding example B's estate is entitled to only $1,000, the amount of B's distributive share of partnership ordinary income for the period July 1, 1958 through October 17, 1958, such $1,000 is considered to have been realized ratably over the period preceding B's death and will be included in B's net earnings from self-employment for his last taxable year.

Example (3). X, who reports his income on a calendar year basis, is a member of a partnership which also reports its income on a calendar year basis. X dies on June 30, 1959, and his estate succeeds to his partnership interest and continues as a partner in its own right under local law. On September 15, 1959, X's estate sells the partnership interest to which it succeeded on the death of X. X's distributive share of partnership income for 1959 is $5,500. $600 of such amount is X's share of the gain from the sale of a capital asset which occurs on May 1, 1959, and $400 of such amount is the estate's share of the gain from the sale of a capital asset which occurs on July 15, 1959. The remainder of such amount is income from services rendered. X's distributive share of partnership ordinary income for 1959, as determined under paragraphs (d) to (g), inclusive, of § 1.1402(a)-2 (with the exception of paragraph (e)), is $4,500 ($5,500 minus $1,000). The portion of such share attributable to an interest in the partnership prior to the month following the month of his death is $4,500 × 6/8.5 (6 being the

Reg. § 1.1402(f)-1(a)(4)

Tax on Self-Employment Income

See p. 20,601 for regulations not amended to reflect law changes

number of months in the partnership taxable year in which X died as precede the month following the month of his death and 8.5 being the number of months in such partnership taxable year in which X and his estate had an interest in the partnership) or $3,176.47.

(b) *Options available to farmers*—(1) *Special rule.* In determining whether the optional method available to a member of a farm partnership in computing his net earnings from self-employment may be applied, and in applying such method, it is necessary to determine the partner's distributive share of partnership gross income and the partner's distributive share of income described in section 702(a)(9). See section 1402(a) and § 1.1402(a)-15. If section 1402(f) and this section apply, or may be made applicable under section 403(b)(2) of the Social Security Amendments of 1958 and paragraph (c) of this section, for the last taxable year of a deceased partner, such partner's distributive share of income described in section 702(a)(9) for his last taxable year shall be determined by including therein any amount which is included under section 1402(f) and this section in his net earnings from self-employment for such taxable year. Such a partner's distributive share of partnership gross income for his last taxable year shall be determined by including therein so much of the deceased partner's distributive share (see paragraph (a)(3) of this section) of partnership gross income, as defined in section 1402(a) and paragraph (b) of § 1.1402(a)-15, for the partnership taxable year in which he died as is attributable to an interest in the partnership prior to the month following the month of his death. Such allocation shall be made in the same manner as is prescribed in paragraph (a)(2) of this section for determining the portion of a deceased partner's distributive share of partnership ordinary income or loss to be included under section 1402(f) and this section in his net earnings from self-employment for his last taxable year.

(2) *Examples.* The principles set forth in this paragraph may be illustrated by the following examples:

Example (1). X, an individual who files his income tax returns on a calendar year basis, is a member of the XYZ farm partnership, the taxable year of which ends on March 31. X dies on May 31, 1967, and his estate succeeds to his partnership interest and continues as a partner in its own right under local law until March 31, 1968. X's distributive share of the partnership's ordinary income, determined under paragraphs (d) to (g), inclusive, of § 1.1402(a)-2, for the taxable year of the partnership ended March 31, 1967, is $1,600. His distributive share, including the share of his estate, of such partnership's ordinary loss as determined under paragraphs (d) to (g), inclusive, of § 1.1402(a)-2 (with the exception of paragraph (e)), for the taxable year of the partnership ended March 31, 1968, is $1,200. The portion of such $1,200 attributable to an interest in the partnership prior to the month following the month in which he died is $1,200 × 2/12 (2 being the number of months in the partnership taxable year in which X died which precede the month following the month of his death and 12 being the number of months in such partnership taxable year in which X and his estate had an interest in the partnership) or $200. X is also a member of the ABX farm partnership, the taxable year of which ends on May 31. His distributive share of the partnership loss described in section 702(a)(9) for the partnership taxable year ending May 31, 1967, is $300. Section 1402(f) and this section do not apply with respect to such $300 since X's last taxable year ends, as a result of his death, with the taxable year of the ABX partnership. Under this paragraph the $200 loss must be included in determining X's distributive share of XYZ partnership income described in section 702(a)(9) for the purpose of applying the optional method available to farmers for computing net earnings from self-employment. Further, the resulting $1,400 of income must be aggregated, pursuant to paragraph (c) of § 1.1402(a)-15, with the $300 loss, X's distributive share of ABX partnership loss described in section 702(a)(9), for purposes of applying such option. The representative of X's estate may exercise the option described in paragraph (a)(2)(ii) of § 1.1402(a)-15, provided the portion of X's distributive share of XYZ partnership gross income for the taxable year ended March 31, 1968, attributable to an interest in the partnership prior to the month following the month in which he died (the allocation being made in the manner prescribed for allocating his $1,200 distributive share of XYZ partnership loss for such year), when aggregated with his distributive share of XYZ partnership gross income for the partnership taxable year ended March 31, 1967, and with his distributive share of ABX partnership gross income for the partnership taxable year ended May 31, 1967, results in X having more than $2,400 of gross income from the trade or business of farming. If such aggregate amount of gross income is not more than $2,400, the option described in paragraph (a)(2)(i) of § 1.1402(a)-15, is available.

Example (2). A, a sole proprietor engaged in the business of farming, files his income tax returns on a calendar year basis. A is also a member of a partnership engaged in an agricultural activity. The partnership files its returns on the basis

Reg. § 1.1402(f)-1(b)(1)

of a fiscal year ending March 31. A dies June 29, 1967. A's gross income from farming as a sole proprietor for the 6-month period comprising his taxable year which ends because of death is $1,600 and his actual net earnings from self-employment based thereon are $400. As of March 31, 1967, A's distributive share of the gross income of the farm partnership is $2,200 and his distributive share of income described in section 702(a)(9) based thereon is $1,000. The amount of A's distributive share of the partnership's ordinary income for its taxable year ended March 31, 1968, which may be included in his net earnings from self-employment under section 1402(f) and paragraph (a) of this section is $300. The amount of the deceased partner's distributive share of partnership gross income attributable to an interest in the partnership prior to the month following the month of his death as is determined, pursuant to subparagraph (1) of this paragraph, under paragraph (a) of this section is $2,000. An aggregation of the above figures produces a gross income from farming of $5,800 and actual net earnings from self-employment of $1,700. Under these circumstances none of the options provided by section 1402(a) may be used. If the actual net earnings from self-employment had been less than $1,600, the option described in paragraph (a)(2)(ii) of § 1.1402(a)-15 would have been available.

(c) *Taxable years ending after 1955 and on or before August 28, 1958*—(1) *Requirement of election.* If a partner's taxable year ended, as a result of his death, after 1955 and on or before August 28, 1958, the rules set forth in paragraph (a) of this section may be made applicable in computing the deceased partner's net earnings from self-employment for his last taxable year provided that—

(i) Before January 1, 1960, there is filed, by the person designated in section 6012(b)(1) and paragraph (b)(1) of § 1.6012-3, a return (or amended return) of the tax imposed by chapter 2 for the taxable year ending as a result of death, and

(ii) Such return, if filed solely for the purpose of reporting net earnings from self-employment resulting from the enactment of section 1402(f), is accompanied by the amount of tax attributable to such net earnings.

(2) *Administrative rule of special application.* Notwithstanding the provisions of sections 6601, 6651, and 6653 (see such sections and the regulations thereunder) no interest or penalty shall be assessed or collected on the amount of any self-employment tax due solely by reason of the operation of section 1402(f) in the case of an individual who died after 1955 and before August 29, 1958. [Reg. § 1.1402(f)-1.]

☐ [*T.D. 6691, 12-2-63. Amended by T.D. 6993, 1-17-69.*]

[Reg. § 1.1402(g)-1]

§ 1.1402(g)-1. **Treatment of certain remuneration erroneously reported as net earnings from self-employment.**—(a) *General rule.* If an amount is erroneously paid as self-employment tax, for any taxable year ending after 1954 and before 1962, with respect to remuneration for service (other than service described in section 3121(b)(8)(A)) performed in the employ of an organization described in section 501(c)(3) and exempt from income tax under section 501(a), and if such remuneration is reported as self-employment income on a return filed on or before the due date prescribed for filing such return (including any extension thereof), the individual who paid such amount (or a fiduciary acting for such individual or his estate, or his survivor (within the meaning of section 205(c)(1)(C) of the Social Security Act)), may request that such remuneration be deemed to constitute net earnings from self-employment. If such request is filed during the period September 14, 1960, to April 16, 1962, inclusive, and on or after the date on which the organization which paid such remuneration to such individual for services performed in its employ has filed, pursuant to section 3121(k), a certificate waiving exemption from taxes under the Federal Insurance Contributions Act, and if no credit or refund of any portion of the amount erroneously paid for such taxable year as self-employment tax (other than a credit or refund which would be allowable if such tax were applicable with respect to such remuneration) has been obtained before the date on which such request is filed or, if obtained, the amount credited or refunded (including any interest under section 6611) is repaid on or before such date, then, for purposes of the Self-Employment Contributions Act of 1954 and the Federal Insurance Contributions Act, any amount of such remuneration which is paid to such individual before the calendar quarter in which such request is filed (or before the succeeding quarter if such certificate first becomes effective with respect to services performed by such individual in such succeeding quarter) and with respect to which no tax (other than an amount erroneously paid as tax) has been paid under the Federal Insurance Contributions Act, shall be deemed to constitute net earnings from self-employment and not remuneration for employment. If the certificate filed by such organization pursuant to section 3121(k) is not effective with respect to services performed by such individual on or before the first day of the calendar quarter in which the request is filed, then, for purposes of section 3121(b)(8)(B)(ii) and (iii), such individual shall be deemed to have become an employee of such organization (or to have become a member of a group, described in section 3121(k)(1)(E), of employees of such organization) on the first day of the succeeding quarter.

(b) *Request for validation.* (1) No particular form is prescribed for making a request under paragraph (a) of this section. The request should be in writing, should be signed and dated by the person making the request, and should indicate clearly that it is a request that, pursuant to section 1402(g) of the Code, remuneration for service described in section 3121(b)(8) (other than service described in section 3121(b)(8)(A)) erroneously reported as self-employment income for one or more specified years be deemed to constitute net earnings from self-employment and not remuneration for employment. In addition, the following information shall be shown in connection with the request:

(i) The name, address, and social security account number of the individual with respect to whose remuneration the request is made.

(ii) The taxable year or years (ending after 1954 and before 1962) to which the request relates.

(iii) A statement that the remuneration was erroneously reported as self-employment income on the individual's return for each year specified and that the return was filed on or before its due date (including any extension thereof).

(iv) Location of the office of the district director with whom each return was filed.

(v) A statement that no portion of the amount erroneously paid by the individual as self-employment tax with respect to the remuneration has been credited or refunded (other than a credit or refund which would have been allowable if the tax had been applicable with respect to the remuneration); or, if a credit or refund of any portion of such amount has been obtained, a statement identifying the credit or refund and showing how and when the amount credited or refunded, together with any interest received in connection therewith, was repaid.

(vi) The name and address of the organization which paid the remuneration to the individual.

(vii) The date on which the organization filed a waiver certificate on Form SS-15, and the location of the office of the district director with whom it was filed.

(viii) The date on which the certificate became effective with respect to services performed by the individual.

(ix) If the request is made by a person other than the individual to whom the remuneration was paid, the name and address of that person and evidence which shows the authority of such person to make the request.

(2) The request should be filed with the district director of internal revenue with whom the latest of the returns specified in the request pursuant to subparagraph (1)(iii) of this paragraph was filed.

(c) *Cross references.* For regulations relating to section 3121(b)(8) and (k), see §§ 31.3121(b)(8)-2 and 31.3121(k)-1 of Subpart B of Part 31 of this chapter (Employment Tax Regulations). For regulations relating to exemption from income tax of an organization described in section 501(c)(3), see § 1.501(c)(3)-1. [Reg. § 1.1402(g)-1.]

☐ [*T.D.* 6691, 12-2-63.]

[Reg. § 1.1402(h)-1]

§ 1.1402(h)-1. **Members of certain religious groups opposed to insurance.**—(a) *In general.* An individual—

(1) Who is a member of a recognized religious sect or division thereof and

(2) Who is an adherent of established tenets or teachings of such sect or division and by reason thereof is conscientiously opposed to acceptance of the benefits of any private or public insurance which makes payments in the event of death, disability, old age, or retirement or makes payments toward the cost of, or provides services for, medical care (including the benefits of any insurance system established by the Social Security Act), may file an application for exemption from the tax under section 1401. The form of insurance to which section 1402(h) and this section refer does not include liability insurance of a kind that provides only for the protection of other persons, or property of other persons, who may be injured or damaged by or on property belonging to, or by an action of, an individual who otherwise meets the requirements of this section. An application for exemption under section 1402(h) and this section shall be made in the manner provided in paragraph (b) of this section and within the time specified in paragraph (c) of this section. For provisions relating to the filing of an application for exemption by a fiduciary or survivor, see paragraph (d) of this section.

(b) *Application for exemption.* The application for exemption shall be filed on Form 4029 in duplicate with the internal revenue official or office designated on the form. The filing of a return by a member of a religious group opposed to insurance showing no self-employment income or self-employment tax shall not be construed as an application for exemption referred to in paragraph (a) of this section.

(c) *Time limitation for filing application for exemption*—(1) *Taxable years ending before December 31, 1967.* A member of a religious group opposed to insurance within the meaning of paragraph (a) of this section—

(i) Who has self-employment income (determined without regard to subsections (c)(6) and (h) of section 1402 and this section) for one or more taxable years ending before December 31, 1967, and

(ii) Who desires to be exempt from the payment of the self-employment tax under section 1401,

must file the application for exemption on or before December 31, 1968.

(2) *Taxable year ending on or after December 31, 1967*—(i) *General rule.* Except as provided in subdivision (ii) of this subparagraph, a member of a religious group opposed to insurance within the meaning of paragraph (a) of this section—

(*a*) Who has no self-employment income (determined without regard to subsections (c)(6) and (h) of section 1402 and this section) for any taxable year ending before December 31, 1967, and

(*b*) Who desires to be exempt from the payment of the self-employment tax under section 1401 for any taxable year ending on or after December 31, 1967,

must file the application for exemption on or before the due date of the income tax return (see section 6072), including any extension thereof (see section 6081), for the first taxable year ending on or after December 31, 1967, for which he has self-employment income (determined without regard to subsections (c)(6) and (h) of section 1402 and this section).

(ii) *Exception to general rule.* If an individual to whom subdivision (i) of this subparagraph applies—

(*a*) Is notified in writing by a district director of internal revenue or the Director of International Operations that he has not filed the application for exemption on or before the date specified in such subdivision (i), and

(*b*) Files the application for exemption on or before the last day of the third calendar month following the calendar month in which he is so notified,

such application shall be considered a timely filed application for exemption.

(d) *Application by fiduciary or survivor.* If an individual who was a member of a religious group opposed to insurance dies before the expiration of the time prescribed in section 1402(h)(2) and paragraph (c) of this section during which an application could have been filed by him, an application for exemption with respect to such deceased individual may be filed by a fiduciary acting for such individual's estate or by such individual's survivor within the meaning of section 205(c)(1)(C) of the Social Security Act. An application for exemption with respect to a deceased individual executed by a fiduciary or survivor may be approved only if it could have been approved if the individual were not deceased and had filed the application on the date the application was filed by the fiduciary or executor.

(e) *Approval of application for exemption*—(1) *In general.* The filing of an application for exemption on Form 4029 by a member of a religious group opposed to insurance does not constitute an exemption from the payment of the tax on self-employment income. An individual who files such an application is exempt from the payment of the tax only if the application is approved by the official with whom the application is required to be filed (see paragraph (b) of this section).

(2) *Conditions relating to approval or disapproval of application.* An application for exemption on Form 4029 will not be approved unless the Secretary of Health, Education, and Welfare finds with respect to the religious sect or division thereof of which the individual filing the application is a member—

(i) That the sect or division thereof has the established tenets or teachings by reason of which the individual applicant is conscientiously opposed to the benefits of insurance of the type referred to in section 1402(h) (see paragraph (a) of this section),

(ii) That it is the practice, and has been for a period of time which the Secretary of Health, Education, and Welfare deems to be substantial, for members of such sect or division thereof to make provisions for their dependent members which, in the judgment of such Secretary, is reasonable in view of the general level of living of the members of the sect or division thereof; and

(iii) That the sect or division thereof has been in existence continuously since December 31, 1950.

In addition, an application for exemption on Form 4029 will not be approved if any benefit or other payment under title II or title XVIII of the Social Security Act became payable (or, but for section

Reg. § 1.1402(h)-1(e)(2)

203, relating to reduction of insurance benefits, or 222(b), relating to reduction of insurance benefits on account of refusal to accept rehabilitation services, of the Social Security Act would have been payable) at or before the time of the filing of the application for exemption. Any determination required to be made pursuant to the preceding sentence will be made by the Secretary of Health, Education, and Welfare.

(f) *Period for which exemption is effective*—(1) *General rule.* An application for exemption shall be in effect (if approved as provided in paragraph (e) of this section) for all taxable years beginning after December 31, 1950 except as otherwise provided in subparagraph (2) of this paragraph.

(2) *Exceptions.* An application for exemption referred to in subparagraph (1) of this paragraph shall not be effective for any taxable year which—

(i) Begins (*a*) before the taxable year in which the individual filing the application first met the requirements of subparagraphs (1) and (2) of paragraph (a) of this section, or (*b*) before the time as of which the Secretary of Health, Education, and Welfare finds that the sect or division thereof of which the individual is a member met the requirements of subparagraphs (C) and (D) of section 1402(h)(1) (see subdivisions (i) and (ii) of paragraph (e)(2) of this section), or

(ii) Ends (*a*) after the time at which the individual filing the application ceases to meet the requirements of subparagraphs (1) and (2) of paragraph (a) of this section, or (*b*) after the time as of which the Secretary of Health, Education, and Welfare finds that the sect or division thereof of which the individual is a member ceases to meet the requirements of subparagraphs (C) and (D) of section 1402(h)(1) (see subdivisions (i) and (ii) of paragraph (e)(2) of this section).

(g) *Refund or credit.* An application for exemption on Form 4029 filed on or before December 31, 1968 (if approved as provided in paragraph (e) of this section), shall constitute a claim for refund or credit of any tax on self-employment income under section 1401 (or under section 480 of the Internal Revenue Code of 1939) paid or incurred in respect of any taxable year beginning after December 31, 1950, and ending before December 31, 1967, for which an exemption is granted. Refund or credit of any tax referred to in the preceding sentence may be made, pursuant to the provisions of section 501(c) of the Social Security Amendments of 1967 (81 Stat. 933), notwithstanding that the refund or credit would otherwise be prevented by operation of any law or rule of law. No interest shall be allowed or paid in respect of any refund or credit made or allowed in connection with a claim for refund or credit made on Form 4029. [Reg. § 1.1402(h)-1.]

☐ [T.D. 6993, 1-17-69.]

[Reg. § 1.1403-1]

§ 1.1403-1. Cross references.—For provisions relating to the requirement for filing returns with respect to net earnings from self-employment, see § 1.6017-1. For provisions relating to declarations of estimated tax on self-employment income, see §§ 1.6015(a)-1 to 1.6015(j)-1, inclusive. For other administrative provisions relating to the tax on self-employment income, see the applicable sections of the regulations in this part (§ 1.6001-1 et seq.) and the applicable sections of the regulations in Part 301 of this chapter (Regulations on Procedure and Administration). [Reg. § 1.1403-1.]

☐ [T.D. 6196, 8-13-56. Amended by T.D. 7427, 8-9-76.]

Withholding of Tax on Nonresident Aliens and Foreign Corporations

NONRESIDENT ALIENS AND FOREIGN CORPORATIONS

[Reg. § 1.1441-0]

§ 1.1441-0. Outline of regulation provisions for section 1441.—This section lists captions contained in §§ 1.1441-1 through 1.1441-9.

§ 1.1441-1 Requirement for the deduction and withholding of tax on payments to foreign persons.

(a) Purpose and scope.

(b) General rules of withholding.

(1) Requirement to withhold on payments to foreign persons.

(2) Determination of payee and payee's status.

(i) In general.

(ii) Payments to a U.S. agent of a foreign person.

(iii) Payments to wholly-owned entities.

(A) Foreign-owned domestic entity.

(B) Foreign entity.

(iv) Payments to a U.S. branch of certain foreign banks or foreign insurance companies

Nonresident Aliens and Foreign Corporations 56,535

See p. 20,601 for regulations not amended to reflect law changes

(A) U.S. branch treated as a U.S. person in certain cases.

(B) Consequences to the withholding agent.

(C) Consequences to the U.S. branch.

(D) Definition of payment to a U.S. branch.

(E) Payments to other U.S. branches.

(v) Payments to a foreign intermediary.

(A) Payments treated as made to persons for whom the intermediary collects the payment.

(B) Payments treated as made to foreign intermediary.

(vi) Other payees.

(vii) Rules for reliably associating a payment with a withholding certificate or other appropriate documentation.

(A) Generally.

(B) Special rules applicable to a withholding certificate from a nonqualified intermediary or flow-through entity.

(C) Special rules applicable to a withholding certificate provided by a qualified intermediary that does not assume primary withholding responsibility.

(D) Special rules applicable to a withholding certificate provided by a qualified intermediary that assumes primary withholding responsibility under chapter 3 of the Internal Revenue Code.

(E) Special rules applicable to a withholding certificate provided by a qualified intermediary that assumes primary Form 1099 reporting and backup withholding responsibility but not primary withholding under chapter 3.

(F) Special rules applicable to a withholding certificate provided by a qualified intermediary that assumes primary withholding responsibility under chapter 3 and primary Form 1099 reporting and backup withholding responsibility and a withholding certificate provided by a withholding foreign partnership.

(3) Presumptions regarding payee's status in the absence of documentation.

(i) General rules.

(ii) Presumptions of classification as individual, corporation, partnership, etc.

(A) In general.

(B) No documentation provided.

(C) Documentary evidence furnished for offshore account.

(iii) Presumption of U.S. or foreign status.

(A) Payments to exempt recipients.

(B) Scholarships and grants.

(C) Pensions, annuities, etc.

(D) Certain payments to offshore accounts.

(iv) Grace period.

(v) Special rules applicable to payments to foreign intermediaries.

(A) Reliance on claim of status as foreign intermediary.

(B) Beneficial owner documentation or allocation information is lacking or unreliable.

(C) Information regarding allocation of payment is lacking or unreliable.

(D) Certification that the foreign intermediary has furnished documentation for all of the persons to whom the intermediary certificate relates is lacking or unreliable.

(vi) U.S. branches.

(vii) Joint payees.

(A) In general.

(B) Special rule for offshore accounts.

(viii) Rebuttal of presumptions.

(ix) Effect of reliance on presumptions and of actual knowledge or reason to know otherwise.

(A) General rule.

(B) Actual knowledge or reason to know that amount of withholding is greater than is required under the presumptions or that reporting of the payment is required.

(x) Examples.

(4) List of exemptions from, or reduced rates of, withholding under chapter 3 of the Code.

(5) Establishing foreign status under applicable provisions of chapter 61 of the Code.

(6) Rules of withholding for payments by a foreign intermediary or certain U.S. branches.

(i) In general.

(ii) Example.

(7) Liability for failure to obtain documentation timely or to act in accordance with applicable presumptions.

(i) General rule.

(ii) Proof that tax liability has been satisfied.

(iii) Liability for interest and penalties.

(iv) Special effective date.

(v) Examples.

(8) Adjustments, refunds, or credits of overwithheld amounts.

(9) Payments to joint owners.

Reg. § 1.1441-0

Nonresident Aliens and Foreign Corporations

See p. 20,601 for regulations not amended to reflect law changes

(c) Definitions.
 (1) Withholding.
 (2) Foreign and U.S. person.
 (3) Individual.
  (i) Alien individual.
  (ii) Nonresident alien individual.
 (4) Certain foreign corporations.
 (5) Financial institution and foreign financial institution.
 (6) Beneficial owner.
  (i) General rule.
  (ii) Special rules.
   (A) General rule.
   (B) Foreign partnerships.
   (C) Foreign simple trusts and foreign grantor trusts.
   (D) Other foreign trusts and foreign estates.
 (7) Withholding agent.
 (8) Person
 (9) Source of income.
 (10) Chapter 3 of the Code.
 (11) Reduced rate.
 (12) Payee.
 (13) Intermediary.
 (14) Nonqualified intermediary.
 (15) Qualified intermediary.
 (16) Withholding certificate.
 (17) Documentary evidence; other appropriate documentation.
 (18) Documentation.
 (19) Payor.
 (20) Exempt recipient.
 (21) Non-exempt recipient.
 (22) Reportable amounts.
 (23) Flow-through entity.
 (24) Foreign simple trust.
 (25) Foreign complex trust.
 (26) Foreign grantor trust.
 (27) Partnership.
 (28) Nonwithholding foreign partnership.
 (29) Withholding foreign partnership.
(d) Beneficial owner's or payee's claim of U.S. status.
 (1) In general.
 (2) Payments for which a Form W-9 is otherwise required.
 (3) Payments for which a Form W-9 is not otherwise required.

 (4) When a payment to an intermediary or flow-through entity may be treated as made to a U.S. payee.
(e) Beneficial owner's claim of foreign status.
 (1) Withholding agent's reliance.
  (i) In general.
  (ii) Payments that a withholding agent may treat as made to a foreign person that is a beneficial owner.
   (A) General rule.
   (B) Additional requirements.
 (2) Beneficial owner withholding certificate.
  (i) In general.
  (ii) Requirements for validity of certificate.
 (3) Intermediary, flow-through, or U.S. branch withholding certificate.
  (i) In general.
  (ii) Intermediary withholding certificate from a qualified intermediary.
  (iii) Intermediary withholding certificate from a nonqualified intermediary.
  (iv) Withholding statement provided by nonqualified Intermediary.
   (A) In general.
   (B) General requirements.
   (C) Content of withholding statement.
   (D) Alternative procedures.
   (E) Notice procedures.
  (v) Withholding certificate from certain U.S. branches.
  (vi) Reportable amounts.
 (4) Applicable rules.
  (i) Who may sign the certificate.
  (ii) Period of validity.
   (A) Three-year period.
   (B) Indefinite validity period.
   (C) Withholding certificate for effectively connected income.
   (D) Change in circumstances.
  (iii) Retention of withholding certificate.
  (iv) Electronic transmission of information.
   (A) In general.
   (B) Requirements.
   (C) Special requirements for transmission of Forms W-8 by an intermediary. [Reserved]
  (v) Electronic confirmation of taxpayer identifying number on withholding certificate.
  (vi) Acceptable substitute form.

Reg. § 1.1441-0

Nonresident Aliens and Foreign Corporations

See p. 20,601 for regulations not amended to reflect law changes

(vii) Requirement of taxpayer identifying number.

(viii) Reliance rules.

(A) Classification.

(B) Status of payee as an intermediary or as a person acting for its own account.

(ix) Certificates to be furnished for each account unless exception applies.

(A) Coordinated account information system in effect.

(B) Family of mutual funds.

(C) Special rule for brokers.

(5) Qualified intermediaries.

(i) General rule.

(ii) Definition of qualified intermediary.

(iii) Withholding agreement.

(A) In general.

(B) Terms of the withholding agreement.

(iv) Assignment of primary withholding responsibility.

(v) Withholding statement.

(A) General rule.

(B) Content of withholding statement.

(C) Withholding rate pools.

(f) Effective date.

(1) In general.

(2) Transition rules.

(i) Special rules for existing documentation.

(ii) Lack of documentation for past years.

§ 1.1441-2 Amounts subject to withholding.

(a) In general.

(b) Fixed or determinable annual or periodical income.

(1) In general.

(i) Definition.

(ii) Manner of payment.

(iii) Determinability of amount.

(2) Exceptions.

(3) Original issue discount.

(i) Amount subject to tax.

(ii) Amounts subject to withholding.

(4) Securities lending transactions and equivalent transactions.

(c) Other income subject to withholding.

(d) Exceptions to withholding where no money or property is paid or lack of knowledge.

(1) General rule.

(2) Cancellation of debt.

(3) Satisfaction of liability following underwithholding by withholding agent.

(e) Payment.

(1) General rule.

(2) Income allocated under section 482.

(3) Blocked income.

(4) Special rules for dividends.

(5) Certain interest accrued by a foreign corporation.

(6) Payments other than in U.S. dollars.

(f) Effective date.

§ 1.1441-3 Determination of amounts to be withheld.

(a) Withholding on gross amount.

(b) Withholding on payments on certain obligations.

(1) Withholding at time of payment of interest.

(2) No withholding between interest payment dates.

(i) In general.

(ii) Anti-abuse rule.

(c) Corporate distributions.

(1) General rule.

(2) Exception to withholding on distributions.

(i) In general.

(ii) Reasonable estimate of accumulated and current earnings and profits on the date of payment.

(A) General rule.

(B) Procedures in case of underwithholding.

(C) Reliance by intermediary on reasonable estimate.

(D) Example.

(3) Special rules in the case of distributions from a regulated investment company.

(i) General rule

(ii) Reliance by intermediary on reasonable estimate.

(4) Coordination with withholding under section 1445.

(i) In general.

(A) Withholding under section 1441.

(B) Withholding under both sections 1441 and 1445.

(C) Coordination with REIT withholding.

(ii) Intermediary reliance rule.

Reg. § 1.1441-0

56,538 Nonresident Aliens and Foreign Corporations

See p. 20,601 for regulations not amended to reflect law changes

(d) Withholding on payments that include an undetermined amount of income.

(1) In general.

(2) Withholding on certain gains.

(e) Payments other than in U.S. dollars.

(1) In general.

(2) Payments in foreign currency.

(f) Tax liability of beneficial owner satisfied by withholding agent.

(1) General rule.

(2) Example.

(g) Conduit financing arrangements

(h) Effective date.

§ 1.1441-4 Exemptions from withholding for certain effectively connected income and other amounts.

(a) Certain income connected with a U.S. trade or business.

(1) In general.

(2) Withholding agent's reliance on a claim of effectively connected income.

(i) In general.

(ii) Special rules for U.S. branches of foreign persons.

(A) U.S. branches of certain foreign banks or foreign insurance companies.

(B) Other U.S. branches.

(3) Income on notional principal contracts.

(i) General rule.

(ii) Exception for certain payments.

(b) Compensation for personal services of an individual.

(1) Exemption from withholding.

(2) Manner of obtaining withholding exemption under tax treaty.

(i) In general.

(ii) Withholding certificate claiming withholding exemption.

(iii) Review by withholding agent.

(iv) Acceptance by withholding agent.

(v) Copies of Form 8233.

(3) Withholding agreements.

(4) Final payments exemption.

(i) General rule.

(ii) Final payment of compensation for personal services.

(iii) Manner of applying for final payment exemption.

(iv) Letter to withholding agent.

(5) Requirement of return.

(6) Personal exemption.

(i) In general.

(ii) Multiple exemptions.

(iii) Special rule where both certain scholarship and compensation income are received.

(c) Special rules for scholarship and fellowship income.

(1) In general.

(2) Alternate withholding election.

(d) Annuities received under qualified plans.

(e) Per diem of certain alien trainees.

(f) Failure to receive withholding certificates timely or to act in accordance with applicable presumptions.

(g) Effective date.

(1) General rule.

(2) Transition rules.

§ 1.1441-5 Withholding on payments to partnerships, trusts, and estates.

(a) In general.

(b) Rules applicable to U.S. partnerships, trusts, and estates.

(1) Payments to U.S. partnerships, trusts, and estates.

(2) Withholding by U.S. payees.

(i) U.S. partnerships.

(A) In general.

(B) Effectively connected income of partners.

(ii) U.S. simple trusts.

(iii) U.S. complex trusts and U.S. estates.

(iv) U.S. grantor trusts

(v) Subsequent distribution

(c) Foreign partnerships.

(1) Determination of payee.

(i) Payments treated as made to partners.

(ii) Payments treated as made to the partnership.

(iii) Rules for reliably associating a payment with documentation.

(iv) Examples.

(2) Withholding foreign partnerships.

(i) Reliance on claim of withholding foreign partnership status.

(ii) Withholding agreement.

(iii) Withholding responsibility.

(iv) Withholding certificate from a withholding foreign partnership.

(3) Nonwithholding foreign partnerships.

Reg. § 1.1441-0

Nonresident Aliens and Foreign Corporations 56,539

See p. 20,601 for regulations not amended to reflect law changes

(i) Reliance on claim of foreign partnership status.

(ii) Reliance on claim of reduced withholding by a partnership for its partners.

(iii) Withholding certificate from a nonwithholding foreign partnership.

(iv) Withholding statement provided by nonwithholding foreign partnership.

(v) Withholding and reporting by a foreign partnership.

(d) Presumption rules.

(1) In general.

(2) Determination of partnership's status as domestic or foreign in the absence of documentation.

(3) Determination of partners' status in the absence of certain documentation.

(4) Determination by a withholding foreign partnership of the status of its partners.

(e) Foreign trusts and estates.

(1) In general.

(2) Payments to foreign complex trusts and estates.

(3) Payees of payments to foreign simple trusts and foreign grantor trusts.

(i) Payments for which beneficiaries and owners are payees.

(ii) Payments for which trust is payee.

(4) Reliance on claim of foreign complex trust or foreign estate status.

(5) Foreign simple trust and foreign grantor trust.

(i) Reliance on claim of foreign simple trust or foreign grantor trust status.

(ii) Reliance on claim of reduced withholding by a foreign simple trust or foreign grantor trust for its beneficiaries or owners.

(iii) Withholding certificate from foreign simple trust or foreign grantor trust.

(iv) Withholding statement provided by a foreign simple trust or foreign grantor trust.

(v) Withholding foreign trusts.

(6) Presumption rules

(i) In general

(ii) Determination of status as U.S. or foreign trust or estate in the absence of documentation.

(iii) Determination of beneficiary or owner's status in the absence of certain documentation.

(f) Failure to receive withholding certificate timely or to act in accordance with applicable presumptions.

(g) Effective date.

(1) General rule.

(2) Transition rules.

§ 1.1441-6 Claim of reduced withholding under an income tax treaty.

(a) In general.

(b) Reliance on claim of reduced withholding under an income tax treaty.

(1) In general.

(2) Payment to fiscally transparent entity.

(i) In general.

(ii) Certification by qualified intermediary.

(iii) Dual treatment.

(iv) Examples.

(3) Certified TIN.

(4) Claim of benefits under an income tax treaty by a U.S. person.

(c) Exemption from requirement to furnish a taxpayer identifying number and special documentary evidence rules for certain income.

(1) In general.

(2) Income to which special rules apply.

(3) Certificate of residence.

(4) Documentary evidence establishing residence in the treaty country.

(i) Individuals.

(ii) Persons other than individuals.

(5) Statements regarding entitlement to treaty benefits.

(i) Statement regarding conditions under a limitation on benefits provision.

(ii) Statement regarding whether the taxpayer derives the income.

(d) Joint owners.

(e) Competent authority.

(f) Failure to receive withholding certificate timely.

(g) Effective date.

(1) General rule.

(2) Transition rules.

§ 1.1441-7 General provisions relating to withholding agents.

(a) Withholding agent defined.

(1) In general.

(2) Examples.

(b) Standards of knowledge.

Reg. § 1.1441-0

56,540 Nonresident Aliens and Foreign Corporations

See p. 20,601 for regulations not amended to reflect law changes

(1) In general.

(2) Reason to know.

(3) Financial institutions—limits on reason to know.

(4) Rules applicable to withholding certificates.

(i) In general.

(ii) Examples.

(5) Withholding certificate—establishment of foreign status.

(6) Withholding certificate—claim of reduced rate of withholding under treaty.

(7) Documentary evidence.

(8) Documentary evidence—establishment of foreign status.

(9) Documentary evidence—claim of reduced rate of withholding under treaty.

(10) Limits on reason to know—indirect account holders.

(11) Additional guidance.

(c) Authorized agent.

(1) In general.

(2) Authorized foreign agent.

(3) Notification.

(4) Liability of U.S. withholding agent.

(5) Filing of returns.

(d) United States obligations.

(e) Assumed obligations.

(f) Conduit financing arrangements.

(g) Effective date.

§ 1.1441-8 Exemption from withholding for payments to foreign governments, international organizations, foreign central banks of issue, and the Bank for International Settlements.

(a) Foreign governments.

(b) Reliance on claim of exemption by foreign government.

(c) Income of a foreign central bank of issue or the Bank for International Settlements.

(1) Certain interest income.

(2) Bankers' acceptances.

(d) Exemption for payments to international organizations.

(e) Failure to receive withholding certificate timely and other applicable procedures.

(f) Effective date.

(1) In general.

(2) Transition rules.

§ 1.1441-9 Exemption from withholding on exempt income of a foreign tax-exempt organization, including foreign private foundations.

(a) Exemption from withholding for exempt income.

(b) Reliance on foreign organization's claim of exemption from withholding.

(1) General rule.

(2) Withholding certificate.

(3) Presumptions in the absence of documentation.

(4) Reason to know.

(c) Failure to receive withholding certificate timely and other applicable procedures.

(d) Effective date.

(1) In general.

(2) Transition rules.

[Reg. § 1.1441-0.]

☐ [T.D. 8734, 10-6-97 (T.D. 8804 delayed the effective date of T.D. 8734 from January 1, 1999, to January 1, 2000; T.D. 8856 further delayed the effective date of T.D. 8734 until January 1, 2001). Amended by T.D. 8881, 5-15-2000.]

[Reg. § 1.1441-1]

§ 1.1441-1. Requirement for the deduction and withholding of tax on payments to foreign persons.—(a) *Purpose and scope.* This section, §§ 1.1441-2 through 1.1441-9, and 1.1443-1 provide rules for withholding under sections 1441, 1442, and 1443 when a payment is made to a foreign person. This section provides definitions of terms used in chapter 3 of the Internal Revenue Code (Code) and regulations thereunder. It prescribes procedures to determine whether an amount must be withheld under chapter 3 of the Code and documentation that a withholding agent may rely upon to determine the status of a payee or a beneficial owner as a U.S. person or as a foreign person and other relevant characteristics of the payee that may affect a withholding agent's obligation to withhold under chapter 3 of the Code and the regulations thereunder. Special procedures regarding payments to foreign persons that act as intermediaries are also provided. Section 1.1441-2 defines the income subject to withholding under section 1441, 1442, and 1443 and the regulations under these sections. Section 1.1441-3 provides rules regarding the amount subject to withholding. Section 1.1441-4 provides exemptions from withholding for, among other things, certain income effectively connected with the conduct of a trade or business in the United States, including certain compensation for the personal services of an individual. Section 1.1441-5 provides rules for withholding on payments made to flow-through entities and other similar arrangements. Section 1.1441-6 provides rules for claiming a reduced rate of withholding

Reg. § 1.1441-1(a)

Nonresident Aliens and Foreign Corporations

under an income tax treaty. Section 1.1441-7 defines the term *withholding agent* and provides due diligence rules governing a withholding agent's obligation to withhold. Section 1.1441-8 provides rules for relying on claims of exemption from withholding for payments to a foreign government, an international organization, a foreign central bank of issue, or the Bank for International Settlements. Sections 1.1441-9 and 1.1443-1 provide rules for relying on claims of exemption from withholding for payments to foreign tax exempt organizations and foreign private foundations.

(b) *General rules of withholding*—(1) *Requirement to withhold on payments to foreign persons.* A withholding agent must withhold 30-percent of any payment of an amount subject to withholding made to a payee that is a foreign person unless it can reliably associate the payment with documentation upon which it can rely to treat the payment as made to a payee that is a U.S. person or as made to a beneficial owner that is a foreign person entitled to a reduced rate of withholding. However, a withholding agent making a payment to a foreign person need not withhold where the foreign person assumes responsibility for withholding on the payment under chapter 3 of the Code and the regulations thereunder as a qualified intermediary (see paragraph (e)(5) of this section), as a U.S. branch of a foreign person (see paragraph (b)(2)(iv) of this section), as a withholding foreign partnership (see § 1.1441-5(c)(2)(i)), or as an authorized foreign agent (see § 1.1441-7(c)(1)). This section (dealing with general rules of withholding and claims of foreign or U.S. status by a payee or a beneficial owner), and §§ 1.1441-4, 1.1441-5, 1.1441-6, 1.1441-8, 1.1441-9, and 1.1443-1 provide rules for determining whether documentation is required as a condition for reducing the rate of withholding on a payment to a foreign beneficial owner or to a U.S. payee and if so, the nature of the documentation upon which a withholding agent may rely in order to reduce such rate. Paragraph (b)(2) of this section prescribes the rules for determining who the payee is, the extent to which a payment is treated as made to a foreign payee, and reliable association of a payment with documentation. Paragraph (b)(3) of this section describes the applicable presumptions for determining the payee's status as U.S. or foreign and the payee's other characteristics (i.e., as an owner or intermediary, as an individual, partnership, corporation, etc.). Paragraph (b)(4) of this section lists the types of payments for which the 30-percent withholding rate may be reduced. Because the treatment of a payee as a U.S. or a foreign person also has consequences for purposes of making an information return under the provisions of chapter 61 of the Code and for withholding under other provisions of the Code, such as sections 3402, 3405 or 3406, paragraph (b)(5) of this section lists applicable provisions outside chapter 3 of the Code that require certain payees to establish their foreign status (e.g., in order to be exempt from information reporting). Paragraph (b)(6) of this section describes the withholding obligations of a foreign person making a payment that it has received in its capacity as an intermediary. Paragraph (b)(7) of this section describes the liability of a withholding agent that fails to withhold at the required 30-percent rate in the absence of documentation. Paragraph (b)(8) of this section deals with adjustments and refunds in the case of overwithholding. Paragraph (b)(9) of this section deals with determining the status of the payee when the payment is jointly owned. See paragraph (c)(6) of this section for a definition of beneficial owner. See § 1.1441-7(a) for a definition of withholding agent. See § 1.1441-2(a) for the determination of an amount subject to withholding. See § 1.1441-2(e) for the definition of a payment and when it is considered made. Except as otherwise provided, the provisions of this section apply only for purposes of determining a withholding agent's obligation to withhold under chapter 3 of the Code and the regulations thereunder.

(2) *Determination of payee and payee's status*—(i) *In general.* Except as otherwise provided in this paragraph (b)(2) and § 1.1441-5(c)(1) and (e)(3), a payee is the person to whom a payment is made, regardless of whether such person is the beneficial owner of the amount (as defined in paragraph (c)(6) of this section). A foreign payee is a payee who is a foreign person. A U.S. payee is a payee who is a U.S. person. Generally, the determination by a withholding agent of the U.S. or foreign status of a payee and of its other relevant characteristics (e.g., as a beneficial owner or intermediary, or as an individual, corporation, or flow-through entity) is made on the basis of a withholding certificate that is a Form W-8 or a Form 8233 (indicating foreign status of the payee or beneficial owner) or a Form W-9 (indicating U.S. status of the payee). The provisions of this paragraph (b)(2), paragraph (b)(3) of this section, and § 1.1441-5(c), (d), and (e) dealing with determinations of payee and applicable presumptions in the absence of documentation, apply only to payments of amounts subject to withholding under chapter 3 of the Code (within the meaning of § 1.1441-2(a)). Similar payee and presumption provisions are set forth under § 1.6049-5(d) for payments of amounts that are not subject to withholding under chapter 3 of the Code (or the regulations thereunder) but that may

Reg. § 1.1441-1(b)(2)

be reportable under provisions of chapter 61 of the Code (and the regulations thereunder). See paragraph (d) of this section for documentation upon which the withholding agent may rely in order to treat the payee or beneficial owner as a U.S. person. See paragraph (e) of this section for documentation upon which the withholding agent may rely in order to treat the payee or beneficial owner as a foreign person. For applicable presumptions of status in the absence of documentation, see paragraph (b)(3) of this section and § 1.1441-5(d). For definitions of a foreign person and U.S. person, see paragraph (c)(2) of this section.

(ii) *Payments to a U.S. agent of a foreign person.* A withholding agent making a payment to a U.S. person (other than to a U.S. branch that is treated as a U.S. person pursuant to paragraph (b)(2)(iv) of this section) and who has actual knowledge that the U.S. person receives the payment as an agent of a foreign person must treat the payment as made to the foreign person. However, the withholding agent may treat the payment as made to the U.S. person if the U.S. person is a financial institution and the withholding agent has no reason to believe that the financial institution will not comply with its obligation to withhold. See paragraph (c)(5) of this section for the definition of a financial institution.

(iii) *Payments to wholly-owned entities*—(A) *Foreign-owned domestic entity.* A payment to a wholly-owned domestic entity that is disregarded for federal tax purposes under § 301.7701-2(c)(2) of this chapter as an entity separate from its owner and whose single owner is a foreign person shall be treated as a payment to the owner of the entity, subject to the provisions of paragraph (b)(2)(iv) of this section. For purposes of this paragraph (b)(2)(iii)(A), a domestic entity means a person that would be treated as a U.S. person if it had an election in effect under § 301.7701-3(c)(1)(i) of this chapter to be treated as a corporation. For example, a limited liability company, A, organized under the laws of the State of Delaware, opens an account at a U.S. bank. Upon opening of the account, the bank requests A to furnish a Form W-9 as required under section 6049(a) and the regulations under that section. A does not have an election in effect under § 301.7701-3(c)(1)(i) of this chapter and, therefore, is not treated as an organization taxable as a corporation, including for purposes of the exempt recipient provisions in § 1.6049-4(c)(1). If A has a single owner and the owner is a foreign person (as defined in paragraph (c)(2) of this section), then A may not furnish a Form W-9 because it may not represent that it is a U.S. person for purposes of the provisions of chapters 3 and 61 of the Code, and section 3406. Therefore, A must furnish a Form W-8 with the name, address, and taxpayer identifying number (TIN) (if required) of the foreign person who is the single owner in the same manner as if the account were opened directly by the foreign single owner. See §§ 1.894-1T(d) and 1.1441-6(b)(2) for special rules where the entity's owner is claiming a reduced rate of withholding under an income tax treaty.

(B) *Foreign entity.* A payment to a wholly-owned foreign entity that is disregarded under § 301.7701-2(c)(2) of this chapter as an entity separate from its owner shall be treated as a payment to the single owner of the entity, subject to the provisions of paragraph (b)(2)(iv) of this section if the foreign entity has a U.S. branch in the United States. For purposes of this paragraph (b)(2)(iii)(B), a foreign entity means a person that would be treated as a foreign person if it had an election in effect under § 301.7701-3(c)(1)(i) of this chapter to be treated as a corporation. See §§ 1.894-1T(d) and 1.1441-6(b)(2) for special rules where the foreign entity or its owner is claiming a reduced rate of withholding under an income tax treaty. Thus, for example, if the foreign entity's single owner is a U.S. person, the payment shall be treated as a payment to a U.S. person. Therefore, based on the saving clause in U.S. income tax treaties, such an entity may not claim benefits under an income tax treaty even if the entity is organized in a country with which the United States has an income tax treaty in effect and treats the entity as a non-fiscally transparent entity. See § 1.894-1T(d)(6), *Example 10.* Unless it has actual knowledge or reason to know that the foreign entity to whom the payment is made is disregarded under § 301.7701-2(c)(2) of this chapter, a withholding agent may treat a foreign entity as an entity separate from its owner unless it can reliably associate the payment with a withholding certificate from the entity's owner.

(iv) *Payments to a U.S. branch of certain foreign banks or foreign insurance companies*—(A) *U.S. branch treated as a U.S. person in certain cases.* A payment to a U.S. branch of a foreign person is a payment to a foreign person. However, a U.S. branch described in this paragraph (b)(2)(iv)(A) and a withholding agent (including another U.S. branch described in this paragraph (b)(2)(iv)(A)) may agree to treat the branch as a U.S. person for purposes of withholding on specified payments to the U.S. branch. Notwithstanding the preceding sentence, a withholding agent making a payment to a U.S. branch treated as a U.S. person under this paragraph (b)(2)(iv)(A) shall not treat the branch as a U.S. person for purposes of reporting the payment made to the branch. Therefore, a payment to such U.S. branch shall be reported on Form 1042-S under § 1.1461-1(c). Further, a U.S. branch that is treated as a U.S. person under this paragraph (b)(2)(iv)(A) shall not be treated as a U.S. person for purposes of the withholding certificate it may provide to a withholding agent. Therefore, the U.S. branch must furnish a U.S. branch withholding certificate on Form W-8 as provided in paragraph (e)(3)(v) of this section and not a Form W-9. An agreement to treat a U.S. branch as a U.S. person must be evidenced by a U.S. branch withholding certificate described in paragraph (e)(3)(v) of this section furnished by the U.S. branch to the withholding agent. A U.S. branch described in this paragraph (b)(2)(iv)(A) is any U.S. branch of a foreign bank subject to regulatory supervision by the Federal Reserve Board or a U.S. branch of a foreign insurance company required to file an annual statement on a form approved by the National Association of Insurance Commissioners with the Insurance Department of a State, a Territory, or the District of Columbia. The Internal Revenue Service (IRS) may approve a list of U.S. branches that may qualify for treatment as a U.S. person under this paragraph (b)(2)(iv)(A) (see § 601.601(d)(2) of this chapter). See § 1.6049-5(c)(5)(vi) for the treatment of U.S. branches as U.S. payors if they make a payment that is subject to reporting under chapter 61 of the Internal Revenue Code. Also see § 1.6049-5(d)(1)(ii) for the treatment of U.S. branches as foreign payees under chapter 61 of the Internal Revenue Code.

(B) *Consequences to the withholding agent.* Any person that is otherwise a withholding agent regarding a payment to a U.S. branch described in paragraph (b)(2)(iv)(A) of this section shall treat the payment in one of the following ways—

(*1*) As a payment to a U.S. person, in which case the withholding agent is not responsible for withholding on such payment to the extent it can reliably associate the payment with a withholding certificate described in paragraph (e)(3)(v) of this section that has been furnished by the U.S. branch under its agreement with the withholding agent to be treated as U.S. person;

(*2*) As a payment directly to the persons whose names are on withholding certificates or other appropriate documentation forwarded by the U.S. branch to the withholding agent when no agreement is in effect to treat the U.S. branch as a U.S. person for such payment, to the extent the withholding agent can reliably associate the payment with such certificates or documentation; or

(*3*) As a payment to a foreign person of income that is effectively connected with the conduct of a trade or business in the United States if the withholding agent cannot reliably associate the payment with a withholding certificate from the U.S. branch or any other certificate or other appropriate documentation from another person. See § 1.1441-4(a)(2)(ii).

(C) *Consequences to the U.S. branch* A U.S. branch that is treated as a U.S. person under paragraph (b)(2)(iv)(A) of this section shall be treated as a separate person solely for purposes of section 1441(a) and all other provisions of chapter 3 of the Internal Revenue Code and the regulations thereunder (other than for purposes of reporting the payment to the U.S. branch under § 1.1461-1(c) or for purposes of the documentation such a branch must furnish under paragraph (e)(3)(v) of this section) for any payment that it receives as such. Thus, the U.S. branch shall be responsible for withholding on the payment in accordance with the provisions under chapter 3 of the Internal Revenue Code and the regulations thereunder and other applicable withholding provisions of the Internal Revenue Code. For this purpose, it shall obtain and retain documentation from payees or beneficial owners of the payments that it receives as a U.S. person in the same manner as if it were a separate entity. For example, if a U.S. branch receives a payment on behalf of its home office and the home office is a qualified intermediary, the U.S. branch must obtain a qualified intermediary withholding certificate described in paragraph (e)(3)(ii) of this section from its home office. In addition, a U.S. branch that has not provided documentation to the withholding agent for a payment that is, in fact, not effectively connected income is a withholding agent with respect to that payment. See paragraph (b)(6) of this section and § 1.1441-4(a)(2)(ii).

(D) *Definition of payment to a U.S. branch.* A payment is treated as a payment to a U.S. branch of a foreign bank or foreign insurance company if the payment is credited to an account maintained in the United States in the name of a U.S. branch of the foreign person, or the payment is made to an address in the United States where the U.S. branch is located and the name of the U.S. branch appears on documents (in written or electronic form) associated with the payment (e.g., the check mailed or a letter addressed to the branch).

(E) *Payments to other U.S. branches.* Similar withholding procedures may apply to payments to U.S. branches that are not described in paragraph (b)(2)(iv)(A) of this section to the extent permitted by the district director or the Assistant Commissioner (International). Any such branch must establish that its situation is analogous to that of a U.S. branch described in paragraph (b)(2)(iv)(A) of this section regarding its registration with, and regulation by, a U.S. governmental institution, the type and amounts of assets it is required to, or actually maintains in the United States, and the personnel who carry out the activities of the branch in the United States. In the alternative, the branch must establish that the withholding and reporting requirements under chapter 3 of the Code and the regulations thereunder impose an undue administrative burden and that the collection of the tax imposed by section 871(a) or 881(a) on the foreign person (or its members in the case of a foreign partnership) will not be jeopardized by the exemption from withholding. Generally, an undue administrative burden will be found to exist in a case where the person entitled to the income, such as a foreign insurance company, receives from the withholding agent income on securities issued by a single corporation, some of which is, and some of which is not, effectively connected with conduct of a trade or business within the United States and the criteria for determining the effective connection are unduly difficult to apply because of the circumstances under which such securities are held. No exemption from withholding shall be granted under this paragraph (b)(2)(iv)(E) unless the person entitled to the income complies with such other requirements as may be imposed by the district director or the Assistant Commissioner (International) and unless the district director or the Assistant Commissioner (International) is satisfied that the collection of the tax on the income involved will not be jeopardized by the exemption from withholding. The IRS may prescribe such procedures as are necessary to make these determinations (see § 601.601(d)(2) of this chapter).

(v) *Payments to a foreign intermediary*— (A) *Payments treated as made to persons for whom the intermediary collects the payment.* Except as otherwise provided in paragraph (b)(2)(v)(B) of this section, the payee of a payment to a person that the withholding agent may treat as a foreign intermediary in accordance with the provisions of paragraph (b)(3)(ii)(C) or (b)(3)(v)(A) of this section is the person or persons for whom the intermediary collects the payment. Thus, for example, the payee of a payment that the withholding agent can reliably associate with a withholding certificate from a qualified intermediary (defined in paragraph (e)(5)(ii) of this section) that does not assume primary withholding responsibility or a payment to a nonqualified intermediary are the persons for whom the qualified intermediary or nonqualified intermediary acts and not to the intermediary itself. See paragraph (b)(3)(v) of this section for presumptions that apply if the payment cannot be reliably associated with valid documentation. For similar rules for payments to flow-through entities, see § 1.1441-5(c)(1) and (e)(3).

(B) *Payments treated as made to foreign intermediary.* The payee of a payment to a person that the withholding agent may treat as a qualified intermediary is the qualified intermediary to the extent that the qualified intermediary assumes primary withholding responsibility under paragraph (e)(5)(iv) of this section for the payment. For example if a qualified intermediary assumes primary withholding responsibility under chapter 3 of the Internal Revenue Code but does not assume primary reporting or withholding responsibility under chapter 61 or section 3406 of the Internal Revenue Code and therefore provides Forms W-9 for U.S. non-exempt recipients, the qualified intermediary is the payee except to the extent the payment is reliably associated with a Form W-9 from a U.S. non-exempt recipient.

(vi) *Other payees.* A payment to a person described in § 1.6049-4(c)(1)(ii) that the withholding agent would treat as a payment to a foreign person without obtaining documentation for purposes of information reporting under section 6049 (if the payment were interest) is treated as a payment to a foreign payee for purposes of chapter 3 of the Code and the regulations thereunder (or to a foreign beneficial owner to the extent provided in paragraph (e)(1)(ii)(A)(6) or (7) of this section). Further, payments that the withholding agent can reliably associate with documentary evidence described in § 1.6049-5(c)(1) relating to the payee is treated as a payment to a foreign payee. A payment that the withholding agent may treat as a payment to an authorized foreign agent (as defined in § 1.1441-7(c)(2)) is treated as a payment to the agent and not to the persons for whom the agent collects the payment. See § 1.1441-5(b)(1) and (c)(1) for payee determinations for payments to partnerships. See § 1.1441-5(e) for payee determinations for payments to foreign trusts or foreign estates.

(vii) *Rules for reliably associating a payment with a withholding certificate or other appropriate documentation*—(A) *Generally.* The presumption rules of paragraph (b)(3) of this section and §§ 1.1441-5(d) and (e)(6) and 1.6049-5(d) apply to any payment, or portion of a payment, that a withholding agent cannot reliably associate with valid documentation. Generally, a withholding agent can reliably associate a payment with valid documentation if, prior to the payment, it holds valid documentation (either directly or through an agent), it can reliably determine how much of the payment relates to the valid documentation, and it has no actual knowledge or reason to know that any of the information, certifications, or statements in, or associated with, the documentation are incorrect. Special rules apply for payments made to intermediaries, flow-through entities, and certain U.S. branches. See paragraph (b)(2)(vii)(B) through (F) of this section. The documentation referred to in this paragraph (b)(2)(vii) is documentation described in paragraphs (c)(16) and (17) of this section upon which a withholding agent may rely to treat the payment as a payment made to a payee or beneficial owner, and to ascertain the characteristics of the payee or beneficial owner that are relevant to withholding or reporting under chapter 3 of the Internal Revenue Code and the regulations thereunder. For purposes of this paragraph (b)(2)(vii), documentation also includes the agreement that the withholding agent has in effect with an authorized foreign agent in accordance with § 1.1441-7(c)(2)(i). A withholding agent that is not required to obtain documentation with respect to a payment is considered to lack documentation for purposes of this paragraph (b)(2)(vii). For example, a withholding agent paying U.S. source interest to a person that is an exempt recipient, as defined in § 1.6049-4(c)(1)(ii), is not required to obtain documentation from that person in order to determine whether an amount paid to that person is reportable under an applicable information reporting provision under chapter 61 of the Internal Revenue Code. The withholding agent must, however, treat the payment as made to an undocumented person for purposes of chapter 3 of the Internal Revenue Code. Therefore, the presumption rules of paragraph (b)(3)(iii) of this section apply to determine whether the person is presumed to be a U.S. person (in which case, no withholding is required under this section), or whether the person is presumed to be a foreign person (in which case 30-percent withholding is required under this section). See paragraph (b)(3)(v) of this section for special reliance rules in the case of a payment to a foreign intermediary and § 1.1441-5(d) and (e)(6) for special reliance rules in the case of a payment to a flow-through entity.

(B) *Special rules applicable to a withholding certificate from a nonqualified intermediary or flow-through entity*—(*1*) In the case of a payment made to a nonqualified intermediary, a flow-through entity (as defined in paragraph (c)(23) of this section), and a U.S. branch described in paragraph (b)(2)(iv) of this section (other than a branch that is treated as a U.S. person), a withholding agent can reliably associate the payment with valid documentation only to the extent that, prior to the payment, the withholding agent can allocate the payment to a valid nonqualified intermediary, flow-through, or U.S. branch withholding certificate; the withholding agent can reliably determine how much of the payment relates to valid documentation provided by a payee as determined under paragraph (c)(12) of this section (i.e., a person that is not itself an intermediary, flow-through entity, or U.S. branch); and the withholding agent has sufficient information to report the payment on Form 1042-S or Form 1099, if reporting is required. See paragraph (e)(3)(iii) of this section for the requirements of a nonqualified intermediary withholding certificate, paragraph (e)(3)(v) of this section for the requirements of a U.S. branch certificate, and §§ 1.1441-5(c)(3)(iii) and (e)(5)(iii) for the requirements of a flow-through withholding certificate. Thus, a payment cannot be reliably associated with valid documentation provided by a payee to the extent such documentation is lacking or unreliable, or to the extent that information required to allocate and report all or a portion of the payment to each payee is lacking or unreliable. If a withholding certificate attached to an intermediary, U.S. branch, or flow-through withholding certificate is another intermediary, U.S. branch, or flow-through withholding certificate, the rules of this paragraph (b)(2)(vii)(B) apply by treating the share of the payment allocable to the other intermediary, U.S. branch, or flow-through entity as if the payment were made directly to such other entity. See paragraph (e)(3)(iv)(D) of this section for rules permitting information allocating a payment to documentation to be received after the payment is made.

(*2*) The rules of paragraph (b)(2)(vii)(B)(*1*) of this section are illustrated by the following examples:

Example 1. WH, a withholding agent, makes a payment of U.S. source interest to NQI, an intermediary that is a nonqualified intermediary. NQI provides a valid intermediary withholding certificate under paragraph (e)(3)(iii) of this section. NQI does not, however, provide valid documentation from the persons on whose behalf it receives the interest payment, and, therefore, the interest payment cannot be reliably associated with valid documentation provided by a payee. WH must apply the presumption rules of paragraph (b)(3)(v) of this section to the payment.

Reg. § 1.1441-1(b)(2)

Nonresident Aliens and Foreign Corporations

Example 2. The facts are the same as in *Example 1*, except that NQI does attach valid beneficial owner withholding certificates (as defined in paragraph (e)(2)(i) of this section) from A, B, C, and D establishing their status as foreign persons. NQI does not, however, provide WH with any information allocating the payment among A, B, C, and D and, therefore, WH cannot determine the portion of the payment that relates to each beneficial owner withholding certificate. The interest payment cannot be reliably associated with valid documentation from a payee and WH must apply the presumption rules of paragraph (b)(3)(v) of this section to the payment. See, however, paragraph (e)(3)(iv)(D) of this section providing special rules permitting allocation information to be received after a payment is made.

Example 3. The facts are the same as in *Example 2*, except that NQI does provide allocation information associated with its intermediary withholding certificate indicating that 25 percent of the interest payment is allocable to A and 25 percent to B. NQI does not provide any allocation information regarding the remaining 50 percent of the payment. WH may treat 25 percent of the payment as made to A and 25 percent as made to B. The remaining 50 percent of the payment cannot be reliably associated with valid documentation from a payee, however, since NQI did not provide information allocating the payment. Thus, the remaining 50 percent of the payment is subject to the presumption rules of paragraph (b)(3)(v) of this section.

Example 4. WH makes a payment of U.S. source interest to NQI1, an intermediary that is not a qualified intermediary. NQI1 provides WH with a valid nonqualified intermediary withholding certificate as well a valid beneficial owner withholding certificates from A and B and a valid nonqualified intermediary withholding certificate from NQI2. NQI2 has provided valid beneficial owner documentation from C sufficient to establish C's status as a foreign person. Based on information provided by NQI1, WH can allocate 20 percent of the interest payment to A, and 20 percent to B. Based on information that NQI2 provided NQI1 and that NQI1 provides to WH, WH can allocate 60 percent of the payment to NQI 2, but can only allocate one half of that payment (30 percent) to C. Therefore, WH cannot reliably associate 30 percent of the payment made to NQI2 with valid documentation and must apply the presumption rules of paragraph (b)(3)(v) of this section to that portion of the payment.

(C) *Special rules applicable to a withholding certificate provided by a qualified intermediary that does not assume primary withholding responsibility*—(*1*) If a payment is made to a qualified intermediary that does not assume primary withholding responsibility under chapter 3 of the Internal Revenue Code or primary Form 1099 reporting and backup withholding responsibility under chapter 61 and section 3406 of the Internal Revenue Code for the payment, a withholding agent can reliably associate the payment with valid documentation only to the extent that, prior to the payment, the withholding agent has received a valid qualified intermediary withholding certificate and the withholding agent can reliably determine the portion of the payment that relates to a withholding rate pool, as defined in paragraph (e)(5)(v)(C) of this section. In the case of a withholding rate pool attributable to a U.S. non-exempt recipient, a payment cannot be reliably associated with valid documentation unless, prior to the payment, the qualified intermediary has provided the U.S. person's Form W-9 (or, in the absence of the form, the name, address, and TIN, if available, of the U.S. person) and sufficient information for the withholding agent to report the payment on Form 1099. See paragraph (e)(5)(v)(C)(*2*) of this section for special rules regarding allocation of payments among U.S. non-exempt recipients.

(*2*) The rules of this paragraph (b)(2)(vii)(C) are illustrated by the following examples:

Example 1. WH, a withholding agent, makes a payment of U.S. source dividends to QI. QI provides WH with a valid qualified intermediary withholding certificate on which it indicates that it does not assume primary withholding responsibility under chapter 3 of the Internal Revenue Code or primary Form 1099 reporting and backup withholding responsibility under chapter 61 and section 3406 of the Internal Revenue Code. QI does not provide any information allocating the dividend to withholding rate pools. WH cannot reliably associate the payment with valid payee documentation and therefore must apply the presumption rules of paragraph (b)(3)(v) of this section.

Example 2. WH makes a payment of U.S. source dividends to QI. QI has 5 customers: A, B, C, D, and E. QI has obtained documentation from A and B establishing their entitlement to a 15 percent rate of tax on U.S. source dividends under an income tax treaty. C is a U.S. person that is an exempt recipient as defined in paragraph (c)(20) of this section. D and E are U.S. non-exempt recipients who have provided Forms W-9 to QI. A, B, C, D, and E are each entitled to 20 percent of the dividend payment. QI provides

Reg. § 1.1441-1(b)(2)

WH with a valid qualified intermediary withholding certificate as described in paragraph (e)(2)(ii) of this section with which it associates the Forms W-9 from D and E. QI associates the following allocation information with its qualified intermediary withholding certificate: 40 percent of the payment is allocable to the 15 percent withholding rate pool, and 20 percent is allocable to each of D and E. QI does not provide any allocation information regarding the remaining 20 percent of the payment. WH cannot reliably associate 20 percent of the payment with valid documentation and, therefore, must apply the presumption rules of paragraph (b)(3)(v) of this section to that portion of the payment. The 20 percent of the payment allocable to the 15 percent withholding rate pool, and the portion of the payments allocable to D and E are payments that can be reliably associated with documentation.

(D) *Special rules applicable to a withholding certificate provided by a qualified intermediary that assumes primary withholding responsibility under chapter 3 of the Internal Revenue Code*—(*1*) In the case of a payment made to a qualified intermediary that assumes primary withholding responsibility under chapter 3 of the Internal Revenue Code with respect to that payment (but does not assume primary Form 1099 reporting and backup withholding responsibility under chapter 61 and section 3406 of the Internal Revenue Code), a withholding agent can reliably associate the payment with valid documentation only to the extent that, prior to the payment, the withholding agent has received a valid qualified intermediary withholding certificate and the withholding agent can reliably determine the portion of the payment that relates to the withholding rate pool for which the qualified intermediary assumes primary withholding responsibility under chapter 3 of the Internal Revenue Code and the portion of the payment attributable to withholding rate pools for each U.S. non-exempt recipient for whom the qualified intermediary has provided a Form W-9 (or, in absence of the form, the name, address, and TIN, if available, of the U.S. non-exempt recipient). See paragraph (e)(5)(v)(C)(*2*) of this section for alternative allocation procedures for payments made to U.S. persons that are not exempt recipients.

(*2*) *Examples.* The following examples illustrate the rules of paragraph (b)(2)(vii)(D)(*1*) of this section:

Example 1. WH makes a payment of U.S. source interest to QI, a qualified intermediary. QI provides WH with a withholding certificate that indicates that QI will assume primary withholding responsibility under chapter 3 of the Internal Revenue Code with respect to the payment. In addition, QI attaches a Form W-9 from A, a U.S. nonexempt recipient, as defined in paragraph (c)(21) of this section, and provides the name, address, and TIN of B, a U.S. person that is also a non-exempt recipient but who has not provided a Form W-9. QI associates a withholding statement with its qualified intermediary withholding certificate indicating that 10 percent of the payment is attributable to A, and 10 percent to B, and that QI will assume primary withholding responsibility with respect to the remaining 80 percent of the payment. WH can reliably associate the entire payment with valid documentation. Although under the presumption rule of paragraph (b)(3)(v) of this section, an undocumented person receiving U.S. source interest is generally presumed to be a foreign person, WH has actual knowledge that B is a U.S. non-exempt recipient and therefore must report the payment on Form 1099 and backup withhold on the interest payment under section 3406.

Example 2. The facts are the same as in *Example 1*, except that no Forms W-9 or other information have been provided for the 20 percent of the payment that is allocable to A and B. Thus, QI has accepted withholding responsibility for 80 percent of the payment, but has provided no information for the remaining 20 percent. In this case, 20 percent of the payment cannot be reliably associated with valid documentation, and WH must apply the presumption rule of paragraph (b)(3)(v) of this section.

(E) *Special rules applicable to a withholding certificate provided by a qualified intermediary that assumes primary Form 1099 reporting and backup withholding responsibility but not primary withholding under chapter 3*—(*1*) If a payment is made to a qualified intermediary that assumes primary Form 1099 reporting and backup withholding responsibility for the payment (but does not assume primary withholding responsibility under chapter 3 of the Internal Revenue Code), a withholding agent can reliably associate the payment with valid documentation only to the extent that, prior to the payment, the withholding agent has received a valid qualified intermediary withholding certificate and the withholding agent can reliably determine the portion of the payment that relates to a withholding rate pool or pools provided as part of the qualified intermediary's withholding statement and the portion of the payment for which the qualified intermediary assumes primary Form 1099 reporting and backup withholding responsibility.

Reg. § 1.1441-1(b)(2)

(2) The following example illustrates the rules of paragraph (b)(2)((vii)(D)(1) of this section:

Example. WH makes a payment of U.S. source dividends to QI, a qualified intermediary. QI has provided WH with a valid qualified intermediary withholding certificate. QI states on its withholding statement accompanying the certificate that it assumes primary Form 1099 reporting and backup withholding responsibility but does not assume primary withholding responsibility under chapter 3 of the Internal Revenue Code. QI represents that 15 percent of the dividend is subject to a 30 percent rate of withholding, 75 percent of the dividend is subject to a 15 percent rate of withholding, and that QI assumed primary Form 1099 reporting and backup withholding for the remaining 10 percent of the payment. The entire payment can be reliably associated with valid documentation.

(F) *Special rules applicable to a withholding certificate provided by a qualified intermediary that assumes primary withholding responsibility under chapter 3 and primary Form 1099 reporting and backup withholding responsibility and a withholding certificate provided by a withholding foreign partnership.* If a payment is made to a qualified intermediary that assumes both primary withholding responsibility under chapter 3 of the Internal Revenue Code and primary Form 1099 reporting and backup withholding responsibility under chapter 61 and section 3406 of the Internal Revenue Code for the payment, a withholding agent can reliably associate a payment with valid documentation provided that it receives a valid qualified intermediary withholding certificate as described in paragraph (e)(3)(ii) of this section. In the case of a payment made to a withholding foreign partnership, the withholding agent can reliably associate the payment with valid documentation to the extent it can associate the payment with a valid withholding certificate described in § 1.1441-5(c)(2)(iv).

(3) *Presumptions regarding payee's status in the absence of documentation*—(i) *General rules.* A withholding agent that cannot, prior to the payment, reliably associate (within the meaning of paragraph (b)(2)(vii) of this section) a payment of an amount subject to withholding (as described in § 1.1441-2(a)) with valid documentation may rely on the presumptions of this paragraph (b)(3) to determine the status of the payee as a U.S. or a foreign person and the payee's other relevant characteristics (e.g., as an owner or intermediary, as an individual, trust, partnership, or corporation). The determination of withholding and reporting requirements applicable to payments to a person presumed to be a foreign person is governed only by the provisions of chapter 3 of the Code and the regulations thereunder. For the determination of withholding and reporting requirements applicable to payments to a person presumed to be a U.S. person, see chapter 61 of the Code, sections 3402, 3405, or 3406, and the regulations under these provisions. A presumption that a payee is a foreign payee is not a presumption that the payee is a foreign beneficial owner. Therefore, the provisions of this paragraph (b)(3) have no effect for purposes of reducing the withholding rate if associating the payment with documentation of foreign beneficial ownership is required as a condition for such rate reduction. See paragraph (b)(3)(ix) of this section for consequences to a withholding agent that fails to withhold in accordance with the presumptions set forth in this paragraph (b)(3) or if the withholding agent has actual knowledge or reason to know of facts that are contrary to the presumptions set forth in this paragraph (b)(3). See paragraph (b)(2)(vii) of this section for rules regarding the extent which a withholding agent can reliably associate a payment with documentation.

(ii) *Presumptions of classification as individual, corporation, partnership, etc.*—(A) *In general.* A withholding agent that cannot reliably associate a payment with a valid withholding certificate or that has received valid documentary evidence under §§ 1.1441-1(e)(1)(ii)(2) and 1.6049-5(c)(1) or (4) but cannot determine a payee's classification from the documentary evidence must apply the rules of this paragraph (b)(3)(ii) to determine the payee's classification as an individual, trust, estate, corporation, or partnership. The fact that a payee is presumed to have a certain status under the provisions of this paragraph (b)(3)(ii) does not mean that it is excused from furnishing documentation if documentation is otherwise required to obtain a reduced rate of withholding under this section. For example, if, for purposes of this paragraph (b)(3)(ii), a payee is presumed to be a tax-exempt organization based on § 1.6049-4(c)(1)(ii)(B), the withholding agent cannot rely on this presumption to reduce the rate of withholding on payments to such person (if such person is also presumed to be a foreign person under paragraph (b)(3)(iii)(A) of this section) because a reduction in the rate of withholding for payments to a foreign tax-exempt organization generally requires that a valid Form W-8 described in § 1.1441-9(b)(2) be furnished to the withholding agent.

(B) *No documentation provided.* If the withholding agent cannot reliably associate a payment with a valid withholding certificate or valid documentary evidence, it must presume that the

Reg. § 1.1441-1(b)(3)

payee is an individual, a trust, or an estate, if the payee appears to be such person (e.g., based on the payee's name or other indications). In the absence of reliable indications that the payee is an individual, trust, or an estate, the withholding agent must presume that the payee is a corporation or one of the persons enumerated under § 1.6049-4(c)(1)(ii)(B) through (Q) if it can be so treated under § 1.6049-4(c)(1)(ii)(A)(*1*) or any one of the paragraphs under § 1.6049-4(c)(1)(ii)(B) through (Q) without the need to furnish documentation. If the withholding agent cannot treat a payee as a person described in § 1.6049-4(c)(1)(ii)(A)(*1*) through (Q), then the payee shall be presumed to be a partnership. If such a partnership is presumed to be foreign, it is not the beneficial owner of the income paid to it. See paragraph (c)(6) of this section. If such a partnership is presumed to be domestic, it is a U.S. non-exempt recipient for purposes of chapter 61 of the Internal Revenue Code.

(C) *Documentary evidence furnished for offshore account.* If the withholding agent receives valid documentary evidence, as described in § 1.6049-5(c)(1) or (4), with respect to an offshore account from an entity but the documentary evidence does not establish the entity's classification as a corporation, trust, estate, or partnership, the withholding agent may presume (in the absence of actual knowledge otherwise) that the entity is the type of person enumerated under § 1.6049-4(c)(1)(ii)(B) through (Q) if it can be so treated under any one of those paragraphs without the need to furnish documentation. If the withholding agent cannot treat a payee as a person described in § 1.6049-4(c)(1)(ii)(B) through (Q), then the payee shall be presumed to be a corporation unless the withholding agent knows, or has reason to know, that the entity is not classified as a corporation for U.S. tax purposes. If a payee is, or is presumed to be, a corporation under this paragraph (b)(3)(ii)(C) and a foreign person under paragraph (b)(3)(iii) of this section, a withholding agent shall not treat the payee as the beneficial owner of income if the withholding agent knows, or has reason to know, that the payee is not the beneficial owner of the income. For this purpose, a withholding agent shall have reason to know that the payee is not a beneficial owner if the documentary evidence indicates that the payee is a bank, broker, intermediary, custodian, or other agent, or is treated under § 1.6049-4(c)(1)(ii)(B) through (Q) as such a person. A withholding agent may, however, treat such a person as a beneficial owner if the foreign person provides a statement, in writing and signed by a person with authority to sign the statement, that is attached to the documentary evidence stating it is the beneficial owner of the income.

(iii) *Presumption of U.S. or foreign status.* A payment that the withholding agent cannot reliably associate with documentation is presumed to be made to a U.S. person, except as otherwise provided in this paragraph (b)(3)(iii), in paragraphs (b)(3)(iv) and (v) of this section, or in § 1.1441-5(d) or (e).

(A) *Payments to exempt recipients.* If a withholding agent cannot reliably associate a payment with documentation from the payee and the payee is an exempt recipient (as determined under the provisions of § 1.6049-4(c)(1)(ii) in the case of interest, or under similar provisions under chapter 61 of the Code applicable to the type of payment involved, but not including a payee that the withholding agent may treat as a foreign intermediary in accordance with paragraph (b)(3)(v) of this section), the payee is presumed to be a foreign person and not a U.S. person—

(*1*) If the withholding agent has actual knowledge of the payee's employer identification number and that number begins with the two digits "98";

(*2*) If the withholding agent's communications with the payee are mailed to an address in a foreign country;

(*3*) If the name of the payee indicates that the entity is the type of entity that is on the per se list of foreign corporations contained in § 301.7701-2(b)(8)(i) of this chapter; or

(*4*) If the payment is made outside the United States (as defined in § 1.6049-5(e)).

(B) *Scholarships and grants.* A payment representing taxable scholarship or fellowship grant income that does not represent compensation for services (but is not excluded from tax under section 117) and that a withholding agent cannot reliably associate with documentation is presumed to be made to a foreign person if the withholding agent has a record that the payee has a U.S. visa that is not an immigrant visa. See section 871(c) and § 1.1441-4(c) for applicable tax rate and withholding rules.

(C) *Pensions, annuities, etc.* A payment from a trust described in section 401(a), an annuity plan described in section 403(a), a payment with respect to any annuity, custodial account, or retirement income account described in section 403(b), or a payment from an individual retirement account or individual retirement annuity described in section 408 that a withholding agent cannot reliably associate with documentation is presumed to be made to a U.S. person only if the withholding agent has a record of a Social Secu-

Reg. § 1.1441-1(b)(3)

rity number for the payee and relies on a mailing address described in the following sentence. A mailing address is an address used for purposes of information reporting or otherwise communicating with the payee that is an address in the United States or in a foreign country with which the United States has an income tax treaty in effect and the treaty provides that the payee, if an individual resident in that country, would be entitled to an exemption from U.S. tax on amounts described in this paragraph (b)(3)(iii)(C). Any payment described in this paragraph (b)(3)(iii)(C) that is not presumed to be made to a U.S. person is presumed to be made to a foreign person. A withholding agent making a payment to a person presumed to be a foreign person may not reduce the 30-percent amount of withholding required on such payment unless it receives a withholding certificate described in paragraph (e)(2)(i) of this section furnished by the beneficial owner. For reduction in the 30-percent rate, see §§ 1.1441-4(e) or 1.1441-6(b).

(D) *Certain payments to offshore accounts.* A payment is presumed made to a foreign payee if the payment is made outside the United States (as defined in § 1.6049-5(e)) to an offshore account (as defined in § 1.6049-5(c)(1)) and the withholding agent does not have actual knowledge that the payee is a U.S. person. See § 1.6049-5(d)(2) and (3) for exceptions to this rule.

(iv) *Grace period.* A withholding agent may choose to apply the provisions of § 1.6049-5(d)(2)(ii) regarding a 90-day grace period for purposes of this paragraph (b)(3) (by applying the term *withholding agent* instead of the term *payor*) to amounts described in § 1.1441-6(c)(2) and to amounts covered by a Form 8233 described in § 1.1441-4(b)(2)(ii). Thus, for these amounts, a withholding agent may choose to treat an account holder as a foreign person and withhold under chapter 3 of the Internal Revenue Code (and the regulations thereunder) while awaiting documentation. For purposes of determining the rate of withholding under this section, the withholding agent must withhold at the unreduced 30-percent rate at the time that the amounts are credited to an account. However, a withholding agent who can reliably associate the payment with a withholding certificate that is otherwise valid within the meaning of the applicable provisions except for the fact that it is transmitted by facsimile may rely on that facsimile form for purposes of withholding at the claimed reduced rate. For reporting of amounts credited both before and after the grace period, see § 1.1461-1(c)(4)(i)(A). The following adjustments shall be made at the expiration of the grace period:

(A) If, at the end of the grace period, the documentation is not furnished in the manner required under this section and the account holder is presumed to be a U.S. nonexempt recipient, then backup withholding applies to amounts credited to the account after the expiration of the grace period only. Amounts credited to the account during the grace period shall be treated as owned by a foreign payee and adjustments must be made to correct any underwithholding on such amounts in the manner described in § 1.1461-2.

(B) If, at the end of the grace period, the documentation is not furnished in the manner required under this section, or if documentation is furnished that does not support the claimed rate reduction, and the account holder is presumed to be a foreign person then adjustments must be made to correct any underwithholding on amounts credited to the account during the grace period, based on the adjustment procedures described in § 1.1461-2.

(v) *Special rules applicable to payments to foreign intermediaries*—(A) *Reliance on claim of status as foreign intermediary.* The presumption rules of paragraph (b)(3)(v)(B) of this section apply to a payment made to an intermediary (whether the intermediary is a qualified or nonqualified intermediary) that has provided a valid withholding certificate under paragraph (e)(3)(ii) or (iii) of this section (or has provided documentary evidence described in paragraph (b)(3)(ii)(C) of this section that indicates it is a bank, broker, custodian, intermediary, or other agent) to the extent the withholding agent cannot treat the payment as being reliably associated with valid documentation under the rules of paragraph (b)(2)(vii) of this section. For this purpose, a U.S. person's foreign branch that is a qualified intermediary defined in paragraph (e)(5)(ii) of this section shall be treated as a foreign intermediary. A payee that the withholding agent may not reliably treat as a foreign intermediary under this paragraph (b)(3)(v)(A) is presumed to be a payee other than an intermediary whose classification as an individual, corporation, partnership, etc., must be determined in accordance with paragraph (b)(3)(ii) of this section to the extent relevant. In addition, such payee is presumed to be a U.S. or a foreign payee based upon the presumptions described in paragraph (b)(3)(iii) of this section. The provisions of paragraph (b)(3)(v)(B) of this section are not relevant to a withholding agent that can reliably associate a payment with a withholding certificate from a person representing to be a qualified intermediary to the extent the qualified

Reg. § 1.1441-1(b)(3)

Nonresident Aliens and Foreign Corporations

intermediary has assumed primary withholding responsibility in accordance with paragraph (e)(5)(iv) of this section.

(B) *Beneficial owner documentation or allocation information is lacking or unreliable.* Any portion of a payment that the withholding agent may treat as made to a foreign intermediary (whether a nonqualified or a qualified intermediary) but that the withholding agent cannot treat as reliably associated with valid documentation under the rules of paragraph (b)(2)(vii) of this section is presumed made to an unknown, undocumented foreign payee. As a result, a withholding agent must deduct and withhold 30 percent from any payment of an amount subject to withholding. If a withholding certificate attached to an intermediary certificate is another intermediary withholding certificate or a flow-through withholding certificate, the rules of this paragraph (b)(3)(v)(B) (or § 1.1441-5(d)(3) or (e)(6)(iii)) apply by treating the share of the payment allocable to the other intermediary or flow-through entity as if it were made directly to the other intermediary or flow-through entity. Any payment of an amount subject to withholding that is presumed made to an undocumented foreign person must be reported on Form 1042-S. See § 1.1461-1(c). See § 1.6049-5(d) for payments that are not subject to withholding.

(vi) *U.S. branches.* The rules of paragraph (b)(3)(v)(B) of this section shall apply to payments to a U.S. branch described in paragraph (b)(2)(iv)(A) of this section that has provided a withholding certificate as described in paragraph (e)(3)(v) of this section on which it has not agreed to be treated as a U.S. person.

(vii) *Joint payees*—(A) *In general.* Except as provided in paragraph (b)(3)(vii)(B) of this section, if a withholding agent makes a payment to joint payees and cannot reliably associate a payment with valid documentation from all payees, the payment is presumed made to an unidentified U.S. person. However, if one of the joint payees provides a Form W-9 furnished in accordance with the procedures described in §§ 31.3406(d)-1 through 31.3406(d)-5 of this chapter, the payment shall be treated as made to that payee. See § 31.3406(h)-2 of this chapter for rules to determine the relevant payee if more than one Form W-9 is provided. For purposes of applying this paragraph (b)(3), the grace period rules in paragraph (b)(3)(iv) of this section shall apply only if each payee meets the conditions described in paragraph (b)(3)(iv) of this section.

(B) *Special rule for offshore accounts.* If a withholding agent makes a payment to joint payees and cannot reliably associate a payment with valid documentation from all payees, the payment is presumed made to an unknown foreign payee if the payment is made outside the United States (as defined in § 1.6049-5(e)) to an offshore account (as defined in § 1.6049-5(c)(1)).

(viii) *Rebuttal of presumptions.* A payee or beneficial owner may rebut the presumptions described in this paragraph (b)(3) by providing reliable documentation to the withholding agent or, if applicable, to the IRS.

(ix) *Effect of reliance on presumptions and of actual knowledge or reason to know otherwise*—(A) *General rule.* Except as otherwise provided in paragraph (b)(3)(ix)(B) of this section, a withholding agent that withholds on a payment under section 3402, 3405 or 3406 in accordance with the presumptions set forth in this paragraph (b)(3) shall not be liable for withholding under this section even it is later established that the beneficial owner of the payment is, in fact, a foreign person. Similarly, a withholding agent that withholds on a payment under this section in accordance with the presumptions set forth in this paragraph (b)(3) shall not be liable for withholding under section 3402 or 3405 or for backup withholding under section 3406 even if it is later established that the payee or beneficial owner is, in fact, a U.S. person. A withholding agent that, instead of relying on the presumptions described in this paragraph (b)(3), relies on its own actual knowledge to withhold a lesser amount, not withhold, or not report a payment, even though reporting of the payment or withholding a greater amount would be required if the withholding agent relied on the presumptions described in this paragraph (b)(3) shall be liable for tax, interest, and penalties to the extent provided under section 1461 and the regulations under that section. See paragraph (b)(7) of this section for provisions regarding such liability if the withholding agent fails to withhold in accordance with the presumptions described in this paragraph (b)(3).

(B) *Actual knowledge or reason to know that amount of withholding is greater than is required under the presumptions or that reporting of the payment is required.* Notwithstanding the provisions of paragraph (b)(3)(ix)(A) of this section, a withholding agent may not rely on the presumptions described in this paragraph (b)(3) to the extent it has actual knowledge or reason to know that the status or characteristics of the payee or of the beneficial owner are other than what is presumed under this paragraph (b)(3) and, if based on such knowledge or reason to know, it should withhold (under this section or another withholding provision of the Code) an amount greater than would be the case if it relied

Reg. § 1.1441-1(b)(3)

on the presumptions described in this paragraph (b)(3) or it should report (under this section or under another provision of the Code) an amount that would not otherwise be reportable if it relied on the presumptions described in this paragraph (b)(3). In such a case, the withholding agent must rely on its actual knowledge or reason to know rather than on the presumptions set forth in this paragraph (b)(3). Failure to do so and, as a result, failure to withhold the higher amount or to report the payment, shall result in liability for tax, interest, and penalties to the extent provided under sections 1461 and 1463 and the regulations under those sections.

(x) *Examples.* The provisions of this paragraph (b)(3) are illustrated by the following examples:

Example 1. A withholding agent, W, makes a payment of U.S. source dividends to person X, Inc. at an address outside the United States. W cannot reliably associate the payment to X with documentation. Under §§ 1.6042-3(b)(1)(vii) and 1.6049-4(c)(1)(ii)(A)(*1*), W may treat X as a corporation. Thus, under the presumptions described in paragraph (b)(3)(iii) of this section, W must presume that X is a foreign person (because the payment is made outside the United States). However, W knows that X is a U.S. person who is an exempt recipient. W may not rely on its actual knowledge to not withhold under this section. If W's knowledge is, in fact, incorrect, W would be liable for tax, interest, and, if applicable, penalties, under section 1461. W would be permitted to reduce or eliminate its liability for the tax by establishing, in accordance with paragraph (b)(7) of this section, that the tax is not due or has been satisfied. If W's actual knowledge is, in fact, correct, W may nevertheless be liable for tax, interest, or penalties under section 1461 for the amount that W should have withheld based upon the presumptions. W would be permitted to reduce or eliminate its liability for the tax by establishing, in accordance with paragraph (b)(7) of this section, that its actual knowledge was, in fact, correct and that no tax or a lesser amount of tax was due.

Example 2. A withholding agent, W, makes a payment of U.S. source dividends to Y who does not qualify as an exempt recipient under §§ 1.6042-3(b)(1)(vii) and 1.6049-4(c)(1)(ii). W cannot reliably associate the payment to Y with documentation. Under the presumptions described in paragraph (b)(3)(iii) of this section, W must presume that Y is a U.S. person who is not an exempt recipient for purposes of section 6042. However, W knows that Y is a foreign person. W may not rely on its actual knowledge to withhold under this section rather than backup withhold under section 3406. If W's knowledge is, in fact, incorrect, W would be liable for tax, interest, and, if applicable, penalties, under section 3403. If W's actual knowledge is, in fact, correct, W may nevertheless be liable for tax, interest, or penalties under section 3403 for the amount that W should have withheld based upon the presumptions. Paragraph (b)(7) of this section does not apply to provide relief from liability under section 3403.

Example 3. A withholding agent, W, makes a payment of U.S. source dividends to X, Inc. W cannot reliably associate the payment to X, Inc. with documentation. X, Inc. presents none of the indicia of foreign status described in paragraph (b)(3)(iii)(A) of this section, but W has actual knowledge that X, Inc. is a foreign corporation. W may treat X, Inc. as an exempt recipient under § 1.6042-3(b)(1)(vii). Because there are no indicia of foreign status, W would, absent actual knowledge or reason to know otherwise, be permitted to treat X, Inc. as a domestic corporation in accordance with the presumptions of paragraph (b)(3)(iii) of this section. However, under paragraph (b)(3)(ix)(B) of this section, W may not rely on the presumption of U.S. status since reliance on its actual knowledge requires that it withhold an amount greater than would be the case under the presumptions.

Example 4. A withholding agent, W, is a plan administrator who makes pension payments to person X with a mailing address in a foreign country with which the United States has an income tax treaty in effect. Under that treaty, the type of pension income paid to X is taxable solely in the country of residence. The plan administrator has a record of X's U.S. social security number. W has no actual knowledge or reason to know that X is a foreign person. W may rely on the presumption of paragraph (b)(3)(iii)(C) of this section in order to treat X as a U.S. person. Therefore, any withholding and reporting requirements for the payment are governed by the provisions of section 3405 and the regulations under that section.

(4) *List of exemptions from, or reduced rates of, withholding under chapter 3 of the Code.* A withholding agent that has determined that the payee is a foreign person for purposes of paragraph (b)(1) of this section must determine whether the payee is entitled to a reduced rate of withholding under section 1441, 1442, or 1443. This paragraph (b)(4) identifies items for which a reduction in the rate of withholding may apply and whether the rate reduction is conditioned upon documentation being furnished to the with-

Nonresident Aliens and Foreign Corporations 56,553

See p. 20,601 for regulations not amended to reflect law changes

holding agent. Documentation required under this paragraph (b)(4) is documentation that a withholding agent must be able to associate with a payment upon which it can rely to treat the payment as made to a foreign person that is the beneficial owner of the payment in accordance with paragraph (e)(1)(ii) of this section. This paragraph (b)(4) also cross-references other sections of the Code and applicable regulations in which some of these exceptions, exemptions, or reductions are further explained. See, for example, paragraph (b)(4)(viii) of this section, dealing with effectively connected income, that cross-references § 1.1441-4(a); see paragraph (b)(4)(xv) of this section, dealing with exemptions from, or reductions of, withholding under an income tax treaty, that cross-references § 1.1441-6. This paragraph (b)(4) is not an exclusive list of items to which a reduction of the rate of withholding may apply and, thus, does not preclude an exemption from, or reduction in, the rate of withholding that may otherwise be allowed under the regulations under the provisions of chapter 3 of the Code for a particular item of income identified in this paragraph (b)(4).

(i) Portfolio interest described in section 871(h) or 881(c) and substitute interest payments described in § 1.871-7(b)(2) or 1.881-2(b)(2) are exempt from withholding under section 1441(a). See § 1.871-14 for regulations regarding portfolio interest and section 1441(c)(9) for exemption from withholding. Documentation establishing foreign status is required for interest on an obligation in registered form to qualify as portfolio interest. See section 871(h)(2)(B)(ii) and § 1.871-14(c)(1)(ii)(C). For special documentation rules regarding foreign-targeted registered obligations described in § 1.871-14(e)(2), see § 1.871-14(e)(3) and (4) and, in particular, § 1.871-14(e)(4)(i)(A) and (ii)(A) regarding the time when the withholding agent must receive the documentation. The documentation furnished for purposes of qualifying interest as portfolio interest serves as the basis for the withholding exemption for purposes of this section and for purposes of establishing foreign status for purposes of section 6049. See § 1.6049-5(b)(8). Documentation establishing foreign status is not required for qualifying interest on an obligation in bearer form described in § 1.871-14(b)(1) as portfolio interest. However, in certain cases, documentation for portfolio interest on a bearer obligation may have to be furnished in order to establish foreign status for purposes of the information reporting provisions of section 6049 and backup withholding under section 3406. See § 1.6049-5(b)(7).

(ii) Bank deposit interest and similar types of deposit interest (including original issue discount) described in section 871(i)(2)(A) or 881(d) that are from sources within the United States are exempt from withholding under section 1441(a). See section 1441(c)(10). Documentation establishing foreign status is not required for purposes of this withholding exemption but may have to be furnished for purposes of the information reporting provisions of section 6049 and backup withholding under section 3406. See § 1.6049-5(d)(3)(iii) for exceptions to the foreign payee and exempt recipient rules regarding this type of income. See also § 1.6049-5(b)(11) for applicable documentation exemptions for certain bank deposit interest paid on obligations in bearer form.

(iii) Bank deposit interest (including original issue discount) described in section 861(a)(1)(B) is exempt from withholding under sections 1441(a) as income that is not from U.S. sources. Documentation establishing foreign status is not required for purposes of this withholding exemption but may have to be furnished for purposes of the information reporting provisions of section 6049 and backup withholding under section 3406. Reporting requirements for payments of such interest are governed by section 6049 and the regulations under that section. See § 1.6049-5(b)(12) and alternative documentation rules under § 1.6049-5(c)(1).

(iv) Interest or original issue discount from sources within the United States on certain short-term obligations described in section 871(g)(1)(B) or 881(a)(3) is exempt from withholding under sections 1441(a). Documentation establishing foreign status is not required for purposes of this withholding exemption but may have to be furnished for purposes of the information reporting provisions of section 6049 and backup withholding under section 3406. See § 1.6049-5(b)(12) for applicable documentation for establishing foreign status and § 1.6049-5(d)(3)(iii) for exceptions to the foreign payee and exempt recipient rules regarding this type of income. See also § 1.6049-5(b)(10) for applicable documentation exemptions for certain obligations in bearer form.

(v) Income from sources without the United States is exempt from withholding under sections 1441(a). Documentation establishing foreign status is not required for purposes of this withholding exemption but may have to be furnished for purposes of the information reporting provisions of section 6049 or other applicable provisions of chapter 61 of the Code and backup withholding under section 3406. See, for example, § 1.6049-5(b)(6) and (12) and alternative documentation rules under § 1.6049-5(c). See also paragraph (b)(5) of this section for cross references to

Reg. § 1.1441-1(b)(4)

other applicable provisions of the regulations under chapter 61 of the Code.

(vi) Distributions from certain domestic corporations described in section 871(i)(2)(B) or 881(d) are exempt from withholding under section 1441(a). See section 1441(c)(10). Documentation establishing foreign status is not required for purposes of this withholding exemption but may have to be furnished for purposes of the information reporting provisions of section 6042 and backup withholding under section 3406. See § 1.6042-3(b)(1)(iii) through (vi).

(vii) Dividends paid by certain foreign corporations that are treated as income from sources within the United States by reason of section 861(a)(2)(B) are exempt from withholding under section 884(e)(3) to the extent that the distributions are paid out of earnings and profits in any taxable year that the corporation was subject to branch profits tax for that year. Documentation establishing foreign status is not required for purposes of this withholding exemption but may have to be furnished for purposes of the information reporting provisions of section 6042 and backup withholding under section 3406. See § 1.6042-3(b)(1)(iii) through (vii).

(viii) Certain income that is effectively connected with the conduct of a U.S. trade or business is exempt from withholding under section 1441(a). See section 1441(c)(1). Documentation establishing foreign status and status of the income as effectively connected must be furnished for purposes of this withholding exemption to the extent required under the provisions of § 1.1441-4(a). Documentation furnished for this purpose also serves as documentation establishing foreign status for purposes of applicable information reporting provisions under chapter 61 of the Code and for backup withholding under section 3406. See, for example, § 1.6041-4(a)(1).

(ix) Certain income with respect to compensation for personal services of an individual that are performed in the United States is exempt from withholding under section 1441(a). See section 1441(c)(4) and § 1.1441-4(b). However, such income may be subject to withholding as wages under section 3402. Documentation establishing foreign status must be furnished for purposes of any withholding exemption or reduction to the extent required under § 1.1441-4(b) or 31.3401(a)(6)-1(e) and (f) of this chapter. Documentation furnished for this purpose also serves as documentation establishing foreign status for purposes of information reporting under section 6041. See § 1.6041-4(a)(1).

(x) Amounts described in section 871(f) that are received as annuities from certain qualified plans are exempt from withholding under section 1441(a). See section 1441(c)(7). Documentation establishing foreign status must be furnished for purposes of the withholding exemption as required under § 1.1441-4(d). Documentation furnished for this purpose also serves as documentation establishing foreign status for purposes of information reporting under section 6041. See § 1.6041-4(a)(1).

(xi) Payments to a foreign government (including a foreign central bank of issue) that are excludable from gross income under section 892(a) are exempt from withholding under section 1442. See § 1.1441-8(b). Documentation establishing status as a foreign government is required for purposes of this withholding exemption. Payments to a foreign government are exempt from information reporting under chapter 61 of the Code (see § 1.6049-4(c)(1)(ii)(F)).

(xii) Payments of certain interest income to a foreign central bank of issue or the Bank for International Settlements that are exempt from tax under section 895 are exempt from withholding under section 1442. Documentation establishing eligibility for such exemption is required to the extent provided in § 1.1441-8(c)(1). Payments to a foreign central bank of issue or to the Bank for International Settlements are exempt from information reporting under chapter 61 of the Code (see § 1.6049-4(c)(1)(ii)(H) and (M)).

(xiii) Amounts derived by a foreign central bank of issue from bankers' acceptances described in section 871(i)(2)(C) or 881(d) are exempt from tax and, therefore, from withholding. See section 1441(c)(10). Documentation establishing foreign status is not required for purposes of this withholding exemption if the name of the payee and other facts surrounding the payment reasonably indicate that the beneficial owner of the payment is a foreign central bank of issue as defined in § 1.861-2(b)(4). See § 1.1441-8(c)(2) for withholding procedures. See also § § 1.6049-4(c)(1)(ii)(H) and 1.6041-3(q)(8) for a similar exemption from information reporting.

(xiv) Payments to an international organization from investments in the United States of stocks, bonds, or other domestic securities or from interest on deposits in banks in the United States of funds belonging to such international organization are exempt from tax under section 892(b) and, thus, from withholding. Documentation establishing status as an international organization is not required if the name of the payee and other facts surrounding the payment reasonably indicate that the beneficial owner of the payment is an international organization within the meaning of section 7701(a)(18). See § 1.1441-8(d). Pay-

Reg. § 1.1441-1(b)(4)

ments to an international organization are exempt from information reporting under chapter 61 of the Code (see § 1.6049-4(c)(1)(ii)(G)).

(xv) Amounts may be exempt from, or subject to a reduced rate of, withholding under an income tax treaty. Documentation establishing eligibility for benefits under an income tax treaty is required for this purpose as provided under §§ 1.1441-6. Documentation furnished for this purpose also serves as documentation establishing foreign status for purposes of applicable information reporting provisions under chapter 61 of the Code and for backup withholding under section 3406. See, for example, § 1.6041-4(a)(1).

(xvi) Amounts of scholarships and grants paid to certain exchange or training program participants that do not represent compensation for services but are not excluded from tax under section 117 are subject to a reduced rate of withholding of 14-percent under section 1441(b). Documentation establishing foreign status is required for purposes of this reduction in rate as provided under § 1.1441-4(c). This income is not subject to information reporting under chapter 61 of the Code nor to backup withholding under section 3406. The compensatory portion of a scholarship or grant is reportable as wage income. See § 1.6041-3(o).

(xvii) Amounts paid to a foreign organization described in section 501(c) are exempt from withholding under section 1441 to the extent that the amounts are not income includible under section 512 in computing the organization's unrelated business taxable income and are not subject to the tax imposed by section 4948(a). Documentation establishing status as a tax-exempt organization is required for purposes of this exemption to the extent provided in § 1.1441-9. Amounts includible under section 512 in computing the organization's unrelated business taxable income are subject to withholding to the extent provided in section 1443(a) and § 1.1443-1(a). Gross investment income (as defined in section 4940(c)(2)) of a private foundation is subject to withholding at a 4-percent rate to the extent provided in section 1443(b) and § 1.1443-1(b). Payments to a tax-exempt organization are exempt from information reporting under chapter 61 of the Code and the regulations thereunder (see § 1.6049-4(c)(1)(ii)(B)(*1*)).

(xviii) Per diem amounts for subsistence paid by the U.S. government to a nonresident alien individual who is engaged in any program of training in the United States under the Mutual Security Act of 1954 are exempt from withholding under section 1441(a). See section 1441(c)(6). Documentation of foreign status is not required under § 1.1441-4(e) for purposes of establishing eligibility for this exemption. See § 1.6041-3(p).

(xix) Interest with respect to tax-free covenant bonds issued prior to 1934 is subject to special withholding procedures set forth in § 1.1461-1 in effect prior to January 1, 2001 (see § 1.1461-1 as contained in 26 CFR part 1, revised April 1, 1999).

(xx) Income from certain gambling winnings of a nonresident alien individual is exempt from tax under section 871(j) and from withholding under section 1441(a). See section 1441(c)(11). Documentation establishing foreign status is not required for purposes of this exemption but may have to be furnished for purposes of the information reporting provisions of section 6041 and backup withholding under section 3406. See §§ 1.6041-1 and 1.6041-4(a)(1).

(xxi) Any payments not otherwise mentioned in this paragraph (b)(4) shall be subject to withholding at the rate of 30-percent if it is an amount subject to withholding (as defined in § 1.1441-2(a)) unless and to the extent the IRS may otherwise prescribe in published guidance (see § 601.601(d)(2) of this chapter) or unless otherwise provided in regulations under chapter 3 of the Code.

(5) *Establishing foreign status under applicable provisions of chapter 61 of the Code.* This paragraph (b)(5) identifies relevant provisions of the regulations under chapter 61 of the Code that exempt payments from information reporting, and therefore, from backup withholding under section 3406, based on the payee's status as a foreign person. Many of these exemptions require that the payee's foreign status be established in order for the exemption to apply. The regulations under applicable provisions of chapter 61 of the Code generally provide that the documentation described in this section may be relied upon for purposes of determining foreign status.

(i) Payments to a foreign person that are governed by section 6041 (dealing with certain trade or business income) are exempt from information reporting under § 1.6041-4(a).

(ii) Payments to a foreign person that are governed by section 6041A (dealing with remuneration for services and certain sales) are exempt from information reporting under § 1.6041A-1(d)(3).

(iii) Payments to a foreign person that are governed by section 6042 (dealing with dividends) are exempt from information reporting under § 1.6042-3(b)(1)(iii) through (vi).

(iv) Payments to a foreign person that are governed by section 6044 (dealing with patronage dividends) are exempt from information reporting under § 1.6044-3(c)(1).

(v) Payments to a foreign person that are governed by section 6045 (dealing with broker proceeds) are exempt from information reporting under § 1.6045-1(g).

(vi) Payments to a foreign person that are governed by section 6049 (dealing with interest) to a foreign person are exempt from information reporting under § 1.6049-5(b)(6) through (15).

(vii) Payments to a foreign person that are governed by section 6050N (dealing with royalties) are exempt from information reporting under § 1.6050N-1(c).

(viii) Payments to a foreign person that are governed by section 6050P (dealing with income from cancellation of debt) are exempt from information reporting under section 6050P or the regulations under that section except to the extent provided in Notice 96-61 (1996-2 C.B. 227); see also § 601.601(b)(2) of this chapter.

(6) *Rules of withholding for payments by a foreign intermediary or certain U.S. branches*—(i) *In general.* A foreign intermediary described in paragraph (e)(3)(i) of this section or a U.S. branch described in paragraph (b)(2)(iv) of this section that receives an amount subject to withholding (as defined in § 1.1441-2(a)) shall be required to withhold (if another withholding agent has not withheld the full amount required) and report such payment under chapter 3 of the Internal Revenue Code and the regulations thereunder except as otherwise provided in this paragraph (b)(6). A nonqualified intermediary or U.S. branch described in paragraph (b)(2)(iv) of this section (other than a branch that is treated as a U.S. person) shall not be required to withhold or report if it has provided a valid nonqualified intermediary withholding certificate or a U.S. branch withholding certificate, it has provided all of the information required by paragraph (e)(3)(iv) of this section (withholding statement), and it does not know, and has no reason to know, that another withholding agent failed to withhold the correct amount or failed to report the payment correctly under § 1.1461-1(c). A qualified intermediary's obligations to withhold and report shall be determined in accordance with its qualified intermediary withholding agreement.

(ii) *Examples.* The following examples illustrate the rules of paragraph (b)(6)(i) of this section:

Example 1. FB, a foreign bank, acts an intermediary for five different persons, A, B, C, D, and E, each of whom owns U.S. securities that generate U.S. source dividends. The dividends are paid by USWA, a U.S. withholding agent. FB furnished USWA with a nonqualified intermediary withholding certificate, described in paragraph (e)(3)(iii) of this section, to which it attached the withholding certificates of each of A, B, C, D, and E. The withholding certificates from A and B claim a 15 percent reduced rate of withholding under an income tax treaty. C, D, and E claim no reduced rate of withholding. FB provides a withholding statement that meets all of the requirements of paragraph (e)(3)(iv) of this section, including information allocating 20 percent of each dividend payment to each of A, B, C, D, and E. FB does not have actual knowledge or reason to know that USWA did not withhold the correct amounts or report the dividends on Forms 1042-S to each of A, B, C, D, and E. FB is not required to withhold or to report the dividends to A, B, C, D, and E.

Example 2. The facts are the same as in *Example 1,* except that FB did not provide any information for USWA to determine how much of the dividend payments were made to A, B, C, D, and E. Because USWA could not reliably associate the dividend payments with documentation under paragraph (b)(2)(vii) of this section, USWA applied the presumption rules of paragraph (b)(3)(v) of this section and withheld 30 percent from all dividend payments. In addition, USWA filed a single Form 1042-S reporting the payment to an unknown foreign payee. FB is deemed to know that USWA did not report the payment to A, B, C, D, and E because it did not provide all of the information required on a withholding statement under paragraph (e)(3)(iv) of this section (i.e., allocation information). Although FB is not required to withhold on the payment because the full 30 percent withholding was imposed by USWA, it is required to report the payments on Forms 1042-S to A, B, C, D, and E. FB's intentional failure to do so will subject it to intentional disregard penalties under sections 6721 and 6722.

(7) *Liability for failure to obtain documentation timely or to act in accordance with applicable presumptions*—(i) *General rule.* A withholding agent that cannot reliably associate a payment with documentation on the date of payment and that does not withhold under this section, or withholds at less than the 30-percent rate prescribed under section 1441(a) and paragraph (b)(1) of this section, is liable under section 1461 for the tax required to be withheld under chapter 3 of the Code and the regulations thereunder, without the benefit of a reduced rate unless—

(A) The withholding agent has appropriately relied on the presumptions described in paragraph (b)(3) of this section (including the grace period described in paragraph (b)(3)(iv) of this

Reg. § 1.1441-1(b)(6)

section) in order to treat the payee as a U.S. person or, if applicable, on the presumptions described in § 1.1441-4(a)(2)(ii) or (3)(i) to treat the payment as effectively connected income; or

(B) The withholding agent can demonstrate to the satisfaction of the district director or the Assistant Commissioner (International) that the proper amount of tax, if any, was in fact paid to the IRS; or

(C) No documentation is required under section 1441 or this section in order for a reduced rate of withholding to apply.

(ii) *Proof that tax liability has been satisfied.* Proof of payment of tax may be established for purposes of paragraph (b)(7)(i)(B) of this section on the basis of a Form 4669 (or such other form as the IRS may prescribe in published guidance (see § 601.601(d)(2) of this chapter)), establishing the amount of tax, if any, actually paid by or for the beneficial owner on the income. Proof that a reduced rate of withholding was, in fact, appropriate under the provisions of chapter 3 of the Code and the regulations thereunder may also be established after the date of payment by the withholding agent on the basis of a valid withholding certificate or other appropriate documentation furnished after that date. However, in the case of a withholding certificate or other appropriate documentation received after the date of payment (or after the grace period specified in paragraph (b)(3)(iv) of this section), the district director or the Assistant Commissioner (International) may require additional proof if it is determined that the delays in obtaining the withholding certificate affect its reliability.

(iii) *Liability for interest and penalties.* A withholding agent that has failed to withhold other than based on appropriate reliance on the presumptions described in paragraph (b)(3) of this section or in § 1.1441-4(a)(2)(ii) or (3)(i) is not relieved from liability for interest under section 6601. Such liability exists even if there is no underlying tax liability due. The interest on the amount that should have been withheld shall be imposed as prescribed under section 6601 beginning on the last date for paying the tax due under section 1461 (which, under section 6601, is the due date for filing the withholding agent's return of tax). The interest shall stop accruing on the earlier of the date that the required withholding certificate or other documentation is provided to the withholding agent and to the extent of the amount of tax that is determined not to be due based on documentation provided, or the date, and to the extent, that the unpaid tax liability under section 871, 881 or under section 1461 is satisfied. Further, in the event that a tax liability is assessed against the beneficial owner under section 871, 881, or 882 and interest under section 6601(a) is assessed against, and collected from, the beneficial owner, the interest charge imposed on the withholding agent shall be abated to that extent so as to avoid the imposition of a double interest charge. However, the withholding agent is not relieved of any applicable penalties. See section 1464.

(iv) *Special effective date.* See paragraph (f)(2)(ii) of this section for the special effective date applicable to this paragraph (b)(7).

(v) *Examples.* The provisions of paragraph (b)(7) of this section are illustrated by the following examples:

Example 1. On June 15, 2001, a withholding agent pays U.S. source interest on an obligation in registered form (issued after July 18, 1984) to a foreign corporation that it cannot reliably associate with a Form W-8 or other appropriate documentation upon which to rely to treat the beneficial owner as a foreign person. The withholding agent does not withhold from the payment. On September 30, 2003, the withholding agent receives from the foreign corporation a valid Form W-8 described in paragraph (e)(2)(ii) of this section. Thus, the interest qualifies as portfolio interest retroactively to June 15, 2001 (the date of payment). See § 1.871-14(c)(3). The foreign corporation does not file a U.S. federal income tax return and does not pay the tax owed. The withholding agent is not liable under section 1461 for the 30-percent tax on the interest income because the receipt of the Form W-8 exempts the interest from tax for purposes of sections 881(a) and 1461. The withholding agent, however, is liable for interest on the amount of withholding that should have been deducted from the payment on June 15, 2001 and deposited. Under paragraph (b)(7)(iii) of this section, the period during which interest may be assessed against the withholding agent runs from March 15, 2002 (the due date for the Form 1042 relating to the payment) until September 30, 2003 (i.e., the date that appropriate documentation is furnished to the withholding agent).

Example 2. On June 15, 2001, a withholding agent pays U.S. source dividends to a foreign corporation that it cannot reliably associate with a Form W-8 or other appropriate documentation upon which to rely to treat the beneficial owner as a foreign person. The withholding agent does not withhold from the payment. On September 30, 2003, the withholding agent receives from the foreign corporation a valid Form W-8 described in paragraph (e)(2)(ii) of this section claiming a reduced 15-percent rate of withholding under a U.S.

Reg. § 1.1441-1(b)(7)

income tax treaty. The dividend qualifies for the reduced treaty rate retroactively to June 15, 2001, (the date of payment). The foreign corporation does not file a U.S. federal income tax return and does not pay the tax owed. Under section 1461, the withholding agent is liable only for a 15-percent tax on the dividend income because the receipt of the Form W-8 allows the tax rate to be reduced for purposes of sections 881(a) and 1461 from 30-percent to 15-percent. The withholding agent, however, is liable for interest on the full 30-percent amount that should have been deducted and withheld from the payment on June 15, 2001, and deposited, over a period running from March 15, 2002, (the due date for the Form 1042 relating to the payment) until September 30, 2003, (the date that the appropriate documentation is furnished to the withholding agent supporting a reduction in rate under a tax treaty). Additional interest may be assessed relating to the outstanding 15-percent tax liability (i.e., the portion of the 30-percent total tax liability that is not reduced under the treaty). Such additional interest runs from March 15, 2002, until such date as that 15-percent tax liability is satisfied by the withholding agent or the taxpayer (subject to abatement in order to avoid a double interest charge).

(8) *Adjustments, refunds, or credits of overwithheld amounts.* If the amount withheld under section 1441, 1442, or 1443 is greater than the tax due by the withholding agent or the taxpayer, adjustments may be made in accordance with the procedures described in § 1.1461-2(a). Alternatively, refunds or credits may be claimed in accordance with the procedures described in § 1.1464-1, relating to refunds or credits claimed by the beneficial owner, or § 1.6414-1, relating to refunds or credits claimed by the withholding agent. If an amount was withheld under section 3406 or is subsequently determined to have been paid to a foreign person, see paragraph (b)(3)(vii) of this section and § 31.6413(a)-3(a)(1) of this chapter.

(9) *Payments to joint owners.* A payment to joint owners that requires documentation in order to reduce the rate of withholding under chapter 3 of the Code and the regulations thereunder does not qualify for such reduced rate unless the withholding agent can reliably associate the payment with documentation from each owner. Notwithstanding the preceding sentence, a payment to joint owners qualifies as a payment exempt from withholding under this section if any one of the owners provides a certificate of U.S. status on a Form W-9 in accordance with paragraph (d)(2) or (3) of this section or the withholding agent can associate the payment with an intermediary or flow-through withholding certificate upon which it can rely to treat the payment as made to a U.S. payee under paragraph (d)(4) of this section. See § 31.3406(h)-2(a)(3)(i)(B) of this chapter.

(c) *Definitions*—(1) *Withholding.* The term *withholding* means the deduction and withholding of tax at the applicable rate from the payment.

(2) *Foreign and U.S. person.* The term *foreign person* means a nonresident alien individual, a foreign corporation, a foreign partnership, a foreign trust, a foreign estate, and any other person that is not a U.S. person described in the next sentence. Solely for purposes of the regulations under chapter 3 of the Internal Revenue Code, the term *foreign person* also means, with respect to a payment by a withholding agent, a foreign branch of a U.S. person that furnishes an intermediary withholding certificate described in paragraph (e)(3)(ii) of this section. Such a branch continues to be a U.S. payor for purposes of chapter 61 of the Internal Revenue Code. See § 1.6049-5(c)(4). A U.S. person is a person described in section 7701(a)(30), the U.S. government (including an agency or instrumentality thereof), a State (including an agency or instrumentality thereof), or the District of Columbia (including an agency or instrumentality thereof).

(3) *Individual*—(i) *Alien individual.* The term *alien individual* means an individual who is not a citizen or a national of the United States. See § 1.1-1(c).

(ii) *Nonresident alien individual.* The term *nonresident alien individual* means a person described in section 7701(b)(1)(B), an alien individual who is a resident of a foreign country under the residence article of an income tax treaty and § 301.7701(b)-7(a)(1) of this chapter, or an alien individual who is a resident of Puerto Rico, Guam, the Commonwealth of Northern Mariana Islands, the U.S. Virgin Islands, or American Samoa as determined under § 301.7701(b)-1(d) of this chapter. An alien individual who has made an election under section 6013(g) or (h) to be treated as a resident of the United States is nevertheless treated as a nonresident alien individual for purposes of withholding under chapter 3 of the Code and the regulations thereunder.

(4) *Certain foreign corporations.* For purposes of this section, a corporation created or organized in Guam, the Commonwealth of Northern Mariana Islands, the U.S. Virgin Islands, and American Samoa, is not treated as a foreign corporation if the requirements of sections 881(b)(1)(A), (B), and (C) are met for such corporation. Further, a payment made to a foreign government or an international organization shall be treated as a payment made to a foreign corpo-

Reg. § 1.1441-1(b)(8)

ration for purposes of withholding under chapter 3 of the Code and the regulations thereunder.

(5) *Financial institution and foreign financial institution.* For purposes of the regulations under chapter 3 of the Code, the term *financial institution* means a person described in § 1.165-12(c)(1)(iv) (not including a person providing pension or other similar benefits or a regulated investment company or other mutual fund, unless otherwise indicated) and the term *foreign financial institution* means a financial institution that is a foreign person, as defined in paragraph (c)(2) of this section.

(6) *Beneficial owner*—(i) *General rule.* This paragraph (c)(6) defines the term *beneficial owner* for payments of income other than a payment for which a reduced rate of withholding is claimed under an income tax treaty. The term *beneficial owner* means the person who is the owner of the income for tax purposes and who beneficially owns that income. A person shall be treated as the owner of the income to the extent that it is required under U.S. tax principles to include the amount paid in gross income under section 61 (determined without regard to an exclusion or exemption from gross income under the Internal Revenue Code). Beneficial ownership of income is determined under the provisions of section 7701(l) and the regulations under that section and any other applicable general U.S. tax principles, including principles governing the determination of whether a transaction is a conduit transaction. Thus, a person receiving income in a capacity as a nominee, agent, or custodian for another person is not the beneficial owner of the income. In the case of a scholarship, the student receiving the scholarship is the beneficial owner of that scholarship. In the case of a payment of an amount that is not income, the beneficial owner determination shall be made under this paragraph (c)(6) as if the amount were income.

(ii) *Special rules*—(A) *General rule.* The beneficial owners of income paid to an entity described in this paragraph (c)(6)(ii) are those persons described in paragraphs (c)(6)(ii)(B) through (D) of this section.

(B) *Foreign partnerships.* The beneficial owners of income paid to a foreign partnership (whether a nonwithholding or a withholding foreign partnership) are the partners in the partnership, unless they themselves are not the beneficial owners of the income under this paragraph (c)(6). For example, a partnership (first tier) that is a partner in another partnership (second tier) is not the beneficial owner of income paid to the second tier partnership since the first tier partnership is not the owner of the income under U.S. tax principles. Rather, the partners of the first tier partnership are the beneficial owners (to the extent they are not themselves persons that are not beneficial owners under this paragraph (c)(6)). See § 1.1441-5(b) for applicable withholding procedures for payments to a domestic partnership. See also § 1.1441-5(c)(3)(ii) for applicable withholding procedures for payments to a foreign partnership where one of the partners (at any level in the chain of tiers) is a domestic partnership.

(C) *Foreign simple trusts and foreign grantor trusts.* The beneficial owners of income paid to a foreign simple trust, as described in paragraph (c)(23) of this section, are the beneficiaries of the trust, unless they themselves are not the beneficial owners of the income under this paragraph (c)(6). The beneficial owners of income paid to a foreign grantor trust, as described in paragraph (c)(26) of this section, are the persons treated as the owners of the trust, unless they themselves are not the beneficial owners of the income under this paragraph (c)(6).

(D) *Other foreign trusts and foreign estates.* The beneficial owner of income paid to a foreign complex trust as defined in paragraph (c)(25) of this section or to a foreign estate is the foreign complex trust or estate itself.

(7) *Withholding agent.* For a definition of the term *withholding agent* and applicable rules, see § 1.1441-7.

(8) *Person.* For purposes of the regulations under chapter 3 of the Code, the term *person* shall mean a person described in section 7701(a)(1) and the regulations under that section and a U.S. branch to the extent treated as a U.S. person under paragraph (b)(2)(iv) of this section. For purposes of the regulations under chapter 3 of the Code, the term *person* does not include a wholly-owned entity that is disregarded for federal tax purposes under § 301.7701-2(c)(2) of this chapter as an entity separate from its owner. See paragraph (b)(2)(iii) of this section for procedures applicable to payments to such entities.

(9) *Source of income.* The source of income is determined under the provisions of part I (section 861 and following), subchapter N, chapter 1 of the Code and the regulations under those provisions.

(10) *Chapter 3 of the Code.* For purposes of the regulations under sections 1441, 1442, and 1443, any reference to chapter 3 of the Code shall not include references to sections 1445 and 1446, unless the context indicates otherwise.

(11) *Reduced rate.* For purposes of regulations under chapter 3 of the Code, and other withholding provisions of the Code, the term *reduced rate,* when used in regulations under chap-

Reg. § 1.1441-1(c)(11)

ter 3 of the Code, shall include an exemption from tax.

(12) *Payee.* For purposes of chapter 3 of the Internal Revenue Code, the term *payee* of a payment is determined under paragraph (b)(2) of this section, § 1.1441-5(c)(1) (relating to partnerships), and § 1.1441-5(e)(2) and (3) (relating to trusts and estates) and includes foreign persons, U.S. exempt recipients, and U.S. non-exempt recipients. A nonqualified intermediary and a qualified intermediary (to the extent it does not assume primary withholding responsibility) are not payees if they are acting as intermediaries and not the beneficial owner of income. In addition, a flow-through entity is not a payee unless the income is (or is deemed to be) effectively connected with the conduct of a trade or business in the United States. See § 1.6049-5(d)(1) for rules to determine the payee for purposes of chapter 61 of the Internal Revenue Code. See §§ 1.1441-1(b)(3), 1.1441-5(d), and (e)(6) and 1.6049-5(d)(3) for presumption rules that apply if a payee's identity cannot be determined on the basis of valid documentation.

(13) *Intermediary.* An *intermediary* means, with respect to a payment that it receives, a person that, for that payment, acts as a custodian, broker, nominee, or otherwise as an agent for another person, regardless of whether such other person is the beneficial owner of the amount paid, a flow-through entity, or another intermediary.

(14) *Nonqualified intermediary.* A *nonqualified intermediary* means any intermediary that is not a U.S. person and not a qualified intermediary, as defined in paragraph (e)(5)(ii) of this section, or a qualified intermediary that is not acting in its capacity as a qualified intermediary with respect to a payment. For example, to the extent an entity that is a qualified intermediary provides another withholding agent with a foreign beneficial owner withholding certificate as defined in paragraph (e)(2)(i) of this section, the entity is not acting in its capacity as a qualified intermediary. Notwithstanding the preceding sentence, a qualified intermediary is acting as a qualified intermediary to the extent it provides another withholding agent with Forms W-9, or other information regarding U.S. non-exempt recipients pursuant to its qualified intermediary agreement with the IRS.

(15) *Qualified intermediary.* The term *qualified intermediary* is defined in paragraph (e)(5)(ii) of this section.

(16) *Withholding certificate.* The term *withholding certificate* means a Form W-8 described in paragraph (e)(2)(i) of this section (relating to foreign beneficial owners), paragraph (e)(3)(i) of this section (relating to foreign intermediaries), § 1.1441-5(c)(2)(iv), (c)(3)(iii), and (e)(3)(iv) (relating to flow-through entities), a Form 8233 described in § 1.1441-4(b)(2), a Form W-9 as described in paragraph (d) of this section, a statement described in § 1.871-14(c)(2)(v) (relating to portfolio interest), or any other certificates that under the Internal Revenue Code or regulations certifies or establishes the status of a payee or beneficial owner as a U.S. or a foreign person.

(17) *Documentary evidence: other appropriate documentation.* The terms *documentary evidence* or *other appropriate documentation* refer to documents other than a withholding certificate that may be provided for payments made outside the United States to offshore accounts or any other evidence that under the Internal Revenue Code or regulations certifies or establishes the status of a payee or beneficial owner as a U.S. or foreign person. See §§ 1.1441-6(b)(2), (c)(3) and (4) (relating to treaty benefits), and 1.6049-5(c)(1) and (4) (relating to chapter 61 reporting). Also see § 1.1441-4(a)(3)(ii) regarding documentary evidence for notional principal contracts.

(18) *Documentation.* The term *documentation* refers to both withholding certificates, as defined in paragraph (c)(16) of this section, and documentary evidence or other appropriate documentation, as defined in paragraph (c)(17) of this section.

(19) *Payor.* The term *payor* is defined in § 31.3406(a)-2 of this chapter and § 1.6049-4(a)(2) and generally includes a withholding agent, as defined in § 1.1441-7(a). The term also includes any person that makes a payment to an intermediary, flow-through entity, or U.S. branch that is not treated as a U.S. person to the extent the intermediary, flow-through, or U.S. branch provides a Form W-9 or other appropriate information relating to a payee so that the payment can be reported under chapter 61 of the Internal Revenue Code and, if required, subject to backup withholding under section 3406. This latter rule does not preclude the intermediary, flow-through entity, or U.S. branch from also being a payor.

(20) *Exempt recipient.* The term *exempt recipient* means a person that is exempt from reporting under chapter 61 of the Internal Revenue Code and backup withholding under section 3406 and that is described in §§ 1.6041-3(q), 1.6045-2(b)(2)(i), and 1.6049-4(c)(1)(ii), and § 5f.6045-1(c)(3)(i)(B) of this chapter. Exempt recipients are not exempt from withholding under chapter 3 of the Internal Revenue Code unless

they are U.S. persons or foreign persons entitled to an exemption from withholding under chapter 3.

(21) *Non-exempt recipient.* A *non-exempt recipient* is any person that is not an exempt recipient under paragraph (c)(20) of this section.

(22) *Reportable amounts.* Reportable amounts are defined in paragraph (e)(3)(vi) of this section.

(23) *Flow-through entity.* A *flow-through entity* means any entity that is described in this paragraph (c)(23) and that may provide documentation on behalf of others to a withholding agent. The entities described in this paragraph are a foreign partnership (other than a withholding foreign partnership), a foreign simple trust (other than a withholding foreign trust) that is described in paragraph (c)(24) of this section, a foreign grantor trust (other than a withholding foreign trust) that is described in paragraph (c)(25) of this section, or, for any payments for which a reduced rate of withholding under an income tax treaty is claimed, any entity to the extent the entity is considered to be fiscally transparent under section 894 with respect to the payment by an interest holder's jurisdiction.

(24) *Foreign simple trust.* A *foreign simple trust* is a foreign trust that is described in section 651(a).

(25) *Foreign complex trust.* A *foreign complex trust* is a foreign trust other than a trust described in section 651(a) or sections 671 through 679.

(26) *Foreign grantor trust.* A *foreign grantor trust* is a foreign trust but only to the extent all or a portion of the income of the trust is treated as owned by the grantor or another person under sections 671 through 679.

(27) *Partnership.* The term *partnership* means any entity treated as a partnership under § 301.7701-2 or -3 of this chapter.

(28) *Nonwithholding foreign partnership.* A *nonwithholding foreign partnership* is a foreign partnership that is not a withholding foreign partnership, as defined in § 1.1441-5(c)(2)(i).

(29) *Withholding foreign partnership.* A withholding foreign partnership is defined in § 1.1441-5(c)(2)(i).

(d) *Beneficial owner's or payee's claim of U.S. status*—(1) *In general.* Under paragraph (b)(1) of this section, a withholding agent is not required to withhold under chapter 3 of the Code on payments to a U.S. payee, to a person presumed to be a U.S. payee in accordance with the provisions of paragraph (b)(3) of this section, or to a person that the withholding agent may treat as a U.S. beneficial owner of the payment. Absent actual knowledge or reason to know otherwise, a withholding agent may rely on the provisions of this paragraph (d) in order to determine whether to treat a payee or beneficial owner as a U.S. person.

(2) *Payments for which a Form W-9 is otherwise required.* A withholding agent may treat as a U.S. payee any person who is required to furnish a Form W-9 and who furnishes it in accordance with the procedures described in §§ 31.3406(d)-1 through 31.3406(d)-5 of this chapter (including the requirement that the payee furnish its taxpayer identifying number (TIN)) if the withholding agent meets all the requirements described in § 31.3406(h)-3(e) of this chapter regarding reliance by a payor on a Form W-9. Providing a Form W-9 or valid substitute form shall serve as a statement that the person whose name is on the form is a U.S. person. Therefore, a foreign person, including a U.S. branch treated as a U.S. person under paragraph (b)(2)(iv) of this section, shall not provide a Form W-9. A U.S. branch of a foreign person may establish its status as a foreign person exempt from reporting under chapter 61 and backup withholding under section 3406 by providing a withholding certificate on Form W-8.

(3) *Payments for which a Form W-9 is not otherwise required.* In the case of a payee who is not required to furnish a Form W-9 under section 3406 (e.g., a person exempt from reporting under chapter 61 of the Internal Revenue Code), the withholding agent may treat the payee as a U.S. payee if the payee provides the withholding agent with a Form W-9 or a substitute form described in § 31.3406(h)-3(c)(2) of this chapter (relating to forms for exempt recipients) that contains the payee's name, address, and TIN. The form must be signed under penalties of perjury by the payee if so required by the form or by § 31.3406(h)-3 of this chapter. Providing a Form W-9 or valid substitute form shall serve as a statement that the person whose name is on the certificate is a U.S. person. A Form W-9 or valid substitute form shall not be provided by a foreign person, including any U.S. branch of a foreign person whether or not the branch is treated as a U.S. person under paragraph (b)(2)(iv) of this section. See paragraph (e)(3)(v) of this section for withholding certificates provided by U.S. branches described in paragraph (b)(2)(iv) of this section. The procedures described in § 31.3406(h)-2(a) of this chapter shall apply to payments to joint payees. A withholding agent that receives a Form W-9 to satisfy this paragraph (d)(3) must retain the form in accordance with the provisions of § 31.3406(h)-3(g) of this chapter, if applicable, or of paragraph (e)(4)(iii) of this section (relating to the retention of withholding certificates) if § 31.3406(h)-3(g) of this chapter does not apply. The rules of this

Reg. § 1.1441-1(d)(3)

paragraph (d)(3) are only intended to provide a method by which a withholding agent may determine that a payee is a U.S. person and do not otherwise impose a requirement that documentation be furnished by a person who is otherwise treated as an exempt recipient for purposes of the applicable information reporting provisions under chapter 61 of the Internal Revenue Code (e.g., § 1.6049-4(c)(1)(ii) for payments of interest).

(4) *When a payment to an intermediary or flow-through entity may be treated as made to a U.S. payee.* A withholding agent that makes a payment to an intermediary (whether a qualified intermediary or nonqualified intermediary), a flow-through entity, or a U.S. branch described in paragraph (b)(2)(iv) of this section may treat the payment as made to a U.S. payee to the extent that, prior to the payment, the withholding agent can reliably associate the payment with a Form W-9 described in paragraph (d)(2) or (3) of this section attached to a valid intermediary, flow-through, or U.S. branch withholding certificate described in paragraph (e)(3)(i) of this section or to the extent the withholding agent can reliably associate the payment with a Form W-8 described in paragraph (e)(3)(v) of this section that evidences an agreement to treat a U.S. branch described in paragraph (b)(2)(iv) of this section as a U.S. person. In addition, a withholding agent may treat the payment as made to a U.S. payee only if it complies with the electronic confirmation procedures described in paragraph (e)(4)(v) of this section, if required, and it has not been notified by the IRS that any of the information on the withholding certificate or other documentation is incorrect or unreliable. In the case of a Form W-9 that is required to be furnished for a reportable payment that may be subject to backup withholding, the withholding agent may be notified in accordance with section 3406(a)(1)(B) and the regulations under that section. See applicable procedures under section 3406(a)(1)(B) and the regulations under that section for payors who have been notified with regard to such a Form W-9. Withholding agents who have been notified in relation to other Forms W-9, including under section 6724(b) pursuant to section 6721, may rely on the withholding certificate or other documentation only to the extent provided under procedures as prescribed by the IRS (see § 601.601(d)(2) of this chapter).

(e) *Beneficial owner's claim of foreign status—* (1) *Withholding agent's reliance*—(i) *In general.* Absent actual knowledge or reason to know otherwise, a withholding agent may treat a payment as made to a foreign beneficial owner in accordance with the provisions of paragraph (e)(1)(ii) of this section. See paragraph (e)(4)(viii) of this section for applicable reliance rules. See paragraph (b)(4) of this section for a description of payments for which a claim of foreign status is relevant for purposes of claiming a reduced rate of withholding for purposes of section 1441, 1442, or 1443. See paragraph (b)(5) of this section for a list of payments for which a claim of foreign status is relevant for other purposes, such as claiming an exemption from information reporting under chapter 61 of the Code.

(ii) *Payments that a withholding agent may treat as made to a foreign person that is a beneficial owner*—(A) *General rule.* The withholding agent may treat a payment as made to a foreign person that is a beneficial owner if it complies with the requirements described in paragraph (e)(1)(ii)(B) of this section and, then, only to the extent—

(*1*) That the withholding agent can reliably associate the payment with a beneficial owner withholding certificate described in paragraph (e)(2) of this section furnished by the person whose name is on the certificate or attached to a valid foreign intermediary, flow-through, or U.S. branch withholding certificate;

(*2*) That the payment is made outside the United States (within the meaning of § 1.6049-5(e)) to an offshore account (within the meaning of § 1.6049-5(c)(1)) and the withholding agent can reliably associate the payment with documentary evidence described in §§ 1.1441-6(c)(3) or (4), or 1.6049-5(c)(1) relating to the beneficial owner;

(*3*) That the withholding agent can reliably associate the payment with a valid qualified intermediary withholding certificate, as described in paragraph (e)(3)(ii) of this section, and the qualified intermediary has provided sufficient information for the withholding agent to allocate the payment to a withholding rate pool other than a withholding rate pool or pools established for U.S. non-exempt recipients;

(*4*) That the withholding agent can reliably associate the payment with a withholding certificate described in § 1.1441-5(c)(3)(iii) or (e)(5)(iii) from a flow-through entity claiming the income is effectively connected income;

(*5*) That the withholding agent identifies the payee as a U.S. branch described in paragraph (b)(2)(iv) of this section, the payment to which it treats as effectively connected income in accordance with § 1.1441-4(a)(2)(ii) or (3);

(*6*) That the withholding agent identifies the payee as an international organization (or any wholly-owned agency or instrumentality thereof) as defined in section 7701(a)(18) that has

Reg. § 1.1441-1(d)(4)

been designated as such by executive order (pursuant to 22 U.S.C. 288 through 288(f)); or

(7) That the withholding agent pays interest from bankers' acceptances and identifies the payee as a foreign central bank of issue (as defined in § 1.861-2(b)(4)).

(B) *Additional requirements.* In order for a payment described in paragraph (e)(1)(ii)(A) of this section to be treated as made to a foreign beneficial owner, the withholding agent must hold the documentation (if required) prior to the payment, comply with the electronic confirmation procedures described in paragraph (e)(4)(v) of this section (if required), and must not have been notified by the IRS that any of the information on the withholding certificate or other documentation is incorrect or unreliable. If the withholding agent has been so notified, it may rely on the withholding certificate or other documentation only to the extent provided under procedures prescribed by the IRS (see § 601.601(d)(2) of this chapter). See paragraph (b)(2)(vii) of this section for rules regarding reliable association of a payment with a withholding certificate or other appropriate documentation.

(2) *Beneficial owner withholding certificate*—(i) *In general.* A beneficial owner withholding certificate is a statement by which the beneficial owner of the payment represents that it is a foreign person and, if applicable, claims a reduced rate of withholding under section 1441. A separate withholding certificate must be submitted to each withholding agent. If the beneficial owner receives more than one type of payment from a single withholding agent, the beneficial owner may have to submit more than one withholding certificate to the single withholding agent for the different types of payments as may be required by the applicable forms and instructions, or as the withholding agent may require (such as to facilitate the withholding agent's compliance with its obligations to determine withholding under this section or the reporting of the amounts under § 1.1461-1(b) and (c)). For example, if a beneficial owner claims that some but not all of the income it receives is effectively connected with the conduct of a trade or business in the United States, it may be required to submit two separate withholding certificates, one for income that is not effectively connected and one for income that is so connected. See § 1.1441-6(b)(2) for special rules for determining who must furnish a beneficial owner withholding certificate when a benefit is claimed under an income tax treaty. See paragraph (e)(4)(ix) of this section for reliance rules in the case of certificates held by another person or at a different branch location of the same person.

(ii) *Requirements for validity of certificate.* A beneficial owner withholding certificate is valid only if it is provided on a Form W-8, or a Form 8233 in the case of personal services income described in § 1.1441-4(b) or certain scholarship or grant amounts described in § 1.1441-4(c) (or a substitute form described in paragraph (e)(4)(vi) of this section, or such other form as the IRS may prescribe). A Form W-8 is valid only if its validity period has not expired, it is signed under penalties of perjury by the beneficial owner, and it contains all of the information required on the form. The required information is the beneficial owner's name, permanent residence address, and TIN (if required), the country under the laws of which the beneficial owner is created, incorporated, or governed (if a person other than an individual), the classification of the entity, and such other information as may be required by the regulations under section 1441 or by the form or accompanying instructions in addition to, or in lieu of, the information described in this paragraph (e)(2)(ii). A person's permanent residence address is an address in the country where the person claims to be a resident for purposes of that country's income tax. In the case of a certificate furnished in order to claim a reduced rate of withholding under an income tax treaty, the residence must be determined in the manner prescribed under the applicable treaty. See § 1.1441-6(b). The address of a financial institution with which the beneficial owner maintains an account, a post office box, or an address used solely for mailing purposes is not a residence address for this purpose. If the beneficial owner is an individual who does not have a tax residence in any country, the permanent residence address is the place at which the beneficial owner normally resides. If the beneficial owner is not an individual and does not have a tax residence in any country, then the permanent residence address is the place at which the person maintains its principal office. See paragraph (e)(4)(vii) of this section for circumstances in which a TIN is required on a beneficial owner withholding certificate. See paragraph (f)(2)(i) of this section for continued validity of certificates during a transition period.

(3) *Intermediary, flow-through, or U.S. branch withholding certificate*—(i) *In general.* An intermediary withholding certificate is a Form W-8 by which a payee represents that it is a foreign person and that it is an intermediary (whether a qualified or nonqualified intermediary) with respect to a payment and not the beneficial owner. See paragraphs (e)(3)(ii) and (iii) of this section. A flow-through withholding certifi-

Reg. § 1.1441-1(e)(3)

cate is a Form W-8 used by a flow-through entity as defined in paragraph (c)(23) of this section. See § 1.1441-5(c)(3)(iii) (a nonwithholding foreign partnership), § 1.1441-5(e)(5)(iii) (a foreign simple trust or foreign grantor trust) or § 1.1441-6(b)(2) (foreign entity presenting claims on behalf of its interest holders for a reduced rate of withholding under an income tax treaty). A U.S. branch certificate is a Form W-8 furnished under paragraph (e)(3)(v) of this section by a U.S. branch described in paragraph (b)(2)(iv) of this section. See paragraph (e)(4)(viii) of this section for applicable reliance rules.

(ii) *Intermediary withholding certificate from a qualified intermediary.* A qualified intermediary shall provide a qualified intermediary withholding certificate for reportable amounts received by the qualified intermediary. See paragraph (e)(3)(vi) of this section for the definition of reportable amount. A qualified intermediary-withholding certificate is valid only if it is furnished on a Form W-8, an acceptable substitute form, or such other form as the IRS may prescribe, it is signed under penalties of perjury by a person with authority to sign for the qualified intermediary, its validity has not expired, and it contains the following information, statement, and certifications—

(A) The name, permanent residence address (as described in paragraph (e)(2)(ii) of this section), qualified intermediary employer identification number (QI-EIN), and the country under the laws of which the intermediary is created, incorporated, or governed. A qualified intermediary that does not act in its capacity as a qualified intermediary must not use its QI-EIN. Rather the intermediary should provide a nonqualified intermediary withholding certificate, if it is acting as an intermediary, and should use the taxpayer identification number, if any, that it uses for all other purposes;

(B) A certification that, with respect to accounts it identifies on its withholding statement (as described in paragraph (e)(5)(v) of this section), the qualified intermediary is not acting for its own account but is acting as a qualified intermediary;

(C) A certification that the qualified intermediary has provided, or will provide, a withholding statement as required by paragraph (e)(5)(v) of this section; and

(D) Any other information, certifications, or statements as may be required by the form or accompanying instructions in addition to, or in lieu of, the information and certifications described in this paragraph (e)(3)(ii) or paragraph (e)(3)(v) of this section. See paragraph (e)(5)(v) of this section for the requirements of a withholding statement associated with the qualified intermediary withholding certificate.

(iii) *Intermediary withholding certificate from a nonqualified intermediary.* A nonqualified intermediary shall provide a nonqualified intermediary withholding certificate for reportable amounts received by the nonqualified intermediary. See paragraph (e)(3)(vi) of this section for the definition of reportable amount. A nonqualified intermediary withholding certificate is valid only to the extent it is furnished on a Form W-8, an acceptable substitute form, or such other form as the IRS may prescribe, it is signed under penalties of perjury by a person authorized to sign for the nonqualified intermediary, it contains the information, statements, and certifications described in this paragraph (e)(3)(iii) and paragraph (e)(3)(iv) of this section, its validity has not expired, and the withholding certificates and other appropriate documentation for all persons to whom the certificate relates are associated with the certificate. Withholding certificates and other appropriate documentation consist of beneficial owner withholding certificates described in paragraph (e)(2)(i) of this section, intermediary and flow-through withholding certificates described in paragraph (e)(3)(i) of this section, withholding foreign partnership certificates described in § 1.1441-5(c)(2)(iv), documentary evidence described in §§ 1.1441-6(c)(3) or (4) and 1.6049-5(c)(1), and any other documentation or certificates applicable under other provisions of the Internal Revenue Code or regulations that certify or establish the status of the payee or beneficial owner as a U.S. or a foreign person. If a nonqualified intermediary is acting on behalf of another nonqualified intermediary or a flow-through entity, then the nonqualified intermediary must associate with its own withholding certificate the other nonqualified intermediary withholding certificate or the flow-through withholding certificate and separately identify all of the withholding certificates and other appropriate documentation that are associated with the withholding certificate of the other nonqualified intermediary or flow-through entity. Nothing in this paragraph (e)(3)(iii) shall require an intermediary to furnish original documentation. Copies of certificates or documentary evidence may be transmitted to the U.S. withholding agent, in which case the nonqualified intermediary must retain the original documentation for the same time period that the copy is required to be retained by the withholding agent under paragraph (e)(4)(iii) of this section and must provide it to the withholding agent upon request. For purposes of this paragraph (e)(3)(iii), a valid intermediary with-

Reg. § 1.1441-1(e)(3)

holding certificate also includes a statement described in § 1.871-14(c)(2)(v) furnished for interest to qualify as portfolio interest for purposes of sections 871(h) and 881(c). The information and certifications required on a Form W-8 described in this paragraph (e)(3)(iii) are as follows—

(A) The name and permanent resident address (as described in paragraph (e)(2)(ii) of this section) of the nonqualified intermediary, and the country under the laws of which the nonqualified intermediary is created, incorporated, or governed;

(B) A certification that the nonqualified intermediary is not acting for its own account;

(C) If the nonqualified intermediary withholding certificate is used to transmit withholding certificates or other appropriate documentation for more than one person on whose behalf the nonqualified intermediary is acting, a withholding statement associated with the Form W-8 that provides all the information required by paragraph (e)(3)(iv) of this section; and

(D) Any other information, certifications, or statements as may be required by the form or accompanying instructions in addition to, or in lieu of, the information, certifications, and statements described in this paragraph (e)(3)(iii) or paragraph (e)(5)(iv) of this section.

(iv) *Withholding statement provided by nonqualified intermediary*—(A) *In general.* A nonqualified intermediary shall provide a withholding statement required by this paragraph (e)(3)(iv) to the extent the nonqualified intermediary is required to furnish, or does furnish, documentation for payees on whose behalf it receives reportable amounts (as defined in paragraph (e)(3)(vi) of this section) or to the extent it otherwise provides the documentation of such payees to a withholding agent. A nonqualified intermediary is not required to disclose information regarding persons for whom it collects reportable amounts unless it has actual knowledge that any such person is a U.S. non-exempt recipient as defined in paragraph (c)(21) of this section. Information regarding U.S. non-exempt recipients required under this paragraph (e)(3)(iv) must be provided irrespective of any requirement under foreign law that prohibits the disclosure of the identity of an account holder of a nonqualified intermediary or financial information relating to such account holder. Although a nonqualified intermediary is not required to provide documentation and other information required by this paragraph (e)(3)(iv) for persons other than U.S. non-exempt recipients, a withholding agent that does not receive documentation and such information must apply the presumption rules of paragraph (b) of this section, §§ 1.1441-5(d) and (e)(6) and 1.6049-5(d) or the withholding agent shall be liable for tax, interest, and penalties. A withholding agent must apply the presumption rules even if it is not required under chapter 61 of the Internal Revenue Code to obtain documentation to treat a payee as an exempt recipient and even though it has actual knowledge that the payee is a U.S. person. For example, if a nonqualified intermediary fails to provide a withholding agent with a Form W-9 for an account holder that is a U.S. exempt recipient, the withholding agent must presume (even if it has actual knowledge that the account holder is a U.S. exempt recipient), that the account holder is an undocumented foreign person with respect to amounts subject to withholding. See paragraph (b)(3)(v) of this section for applicable presumptions. Therefore, the withholding agent must withhold 30 percent from the payment even though if a Form W-9 had been provided, no withholding or reporting on the payment attributable to a U.S. exempt recipient would apply. Further, a nonqualified intermediary that fails to provide the documentation and the information under this paragraph (e)(3)(iv) for another withholding agent to report the payments on Forms 1042-S and Forms 1099 is not relieved of its responsibility to file information returns. See paragraph (b)(6) of this section. Therefore, unless the nonqualified intermediary itself files such returns and provides copies to the payees, it shall be liable for penalties under sections 6721 (failure to file information returns), and 6722 (failure to furnish payee statements), including the penalties under those sections for intentional failure to file information returns. In addition, failure to provide either the documentation or the information required by this paragraph (e)(3)(iv) results in a payment not being reliably associated with valid documentation. Therefore, the beneficial owners of the payment are not entitled to reduced rates of withholding and if the full amount required to be held under the presumption rules is not withheld by the withholding agent, the nonqualified intermediary must withhold the difference between the amount withheld by the withholding agent and the amount required to be withheld. Failure to withhold shall result in the nonqualified intermediary being liable for tax under section 1461, interest, and penalties, including penalties under section 6656 (failure to deposit) and section 6672 (failure to collect and pay over tax).

(B) *General requirements.* A withholding statement must be provided prior to the payment of a reportable amount and must contain the information specified in paragraph (e)(3)(iv)(C) of this section. The statement must be updated as often as required to keep the information in the withholding statement correct prior to each subsequent payment. The withholding statement forms an integral part of the withholding certificate provided under paragraph (e)(3)(iii) of this section, and the penalties of perjury statement provided on the withholding certificate shall apply to the withholding statement. The withholding statement may be provided in any manner the nonqualified intermediary and the withholding agent mutually agree, including electronically. If the withholding statement is provided electronically, there must be sufficient safeguards to ensure that the information received by the withholding agent is the information sent by the nonqualified intermediary and all occasions of user access that result in the submission or modification of the withholding statement information must be recorded. In addition, an electronic system must be capable of providing a hard copy of all withholding statements provided by the nonqualified intermediary. A withholding agent will be liable for tax, interest, and penalties in accordance with paragraph (b)(7) of this section to the extent it does not follow the presumption rules of paragraph (b)(3) of this section or §§ 1.1441-5(d) and (e)(6), and 1.6049-5(d) for any payment of a reportable amount, or portion thereof, for which it does not have a valid withholding statement prior to making a payment.

(C) *Content of withholding statement.* The withholding statement provided by a nonqualified intermediary must contain the information required by this paragraph (e)(3)(iv)(C).

(*1*) The withholding statement must contain the name, address, TIN (if any) and the type of documentation (documentary evidence, Form W-9, or type of Form W-8) for every person from whom documentation has been received by the nonqualified intermediary and provided to the withholding agent and whether that person is a U.S. exempt recipient, a U.S. non-exempt recipient, or a foreign person. See paragraphs (c)(2), (20), and (21) of this section for the definitions of foreign person, U.S. exempt recipient, and U.S. non-exempt recipient. In the case of a foreign person, the statement must indicate whether the foreign person is a beneficial owner or an intermediary, flow-through entity, or U.S. branch described in paragraph (b)(2)(iv) of this section and include the type of recipient, based on recipient codes used for filing Forms 1042-S, if the foreign person is a recipient as defined in § 1.1461-1 (c)(1)(ii).

(*2*) The withholding statement must allocate each payment, by income type, to every payee (including U.S. exempt recipients) for whom documentation has been provided. Any payment that cannot be reliably associated with valid documentation from a payee shall be treated as made to an unknown payee in accordance with the presumption rules of paragraph (b) of this section and §§ 1.1441-5(d) and (e)(6) and 1.6049-5(d). For this purpose, a type of income is determined by the types of income required to be reported on Forms 1042-S or 1099, as appropriate. Notwithstanding the preceding sentence, deposit interest (including original issue discount) described in section 871(i)(2)(A) or 881(d) and interest or original issue discount on short-term obligations as described in section 871(g)(1)(B) or 881(e) is only required to be allocated to the extent it is required to be reported on Form 1099 or Form 1042-S. See § 1.6049-8 (regarding reporting of bank deposit interest to certain foreign persons). If a payee receives income through another nonqualified intermediary, flow-through entity, or U.S. branch described in paragraph (e)(2)(iv) of this section (other than a U.S. branch treated as a U.S. person), the withholding statement must also state, with respect to the payee, the name, address, and TIN, if known, of the other nonqualified intermediary or U.S. branch from which the payee directly receives the payment or the flow-through entity in which the payee has a direct ownership interest. If another nonqualified intermediary, flow-through entity, or U.S. branch fails to allocate a payment, the name of the nonqualified intermediary, flow-through entity, or U.S. branch that failed to allocate the payment shall be provided with respect to such payment.

(*3*) If a payee is identified as a foreign person, the nonqualified intermediary must specify the rate of withholding to which the payee is subject, the payee's country of residence and, if a reduced rate of withholding is claimed, the basis for that reduced rate (e.g., treaty benefit, portfolio interest, exempt under section 501(c)(3), 892, or 895). The allocation statement must also include the taxpayer identification numbers of those foreign persons for whom such a number is required under paragraph (e)(4)(vii) of this section or § 1.1441-6(b)(1) (regarding claims for treaty benefits). In the case of a claim of treaty benefits, the nonqualified intermediary's withholding statement must also state whether the limitation on benefits and section 894 statements required by § 1.1441-6(c)(5) have been provided, if required, in the beneficial owner's Form W-8 or associated with such owner's documentary evidence.

(*4*) The withholding statement must also contain any other information the withholding agent reasonably requests in order to fulfill its

Reg. § 1.1441-1(e)(3)

obligations under chapter 3, chapter 61 of the Internal Revenue Code, and section 3406.

(D) *Alternative procedures*—(*1*) *In general.* Under the alternative procedures of this paragraph (e)(3)(iv)(D), a nonqualified intermediary may provide information allocating a payment of a reportable amount to each payee (including U.S. exempt recipients) otherwise required under paragraph (e)(3)(iv)(B)(*2*) of this section after a payment is made. To use the alternative procedure of this paragraph (e)(3)(iv)(D), the nonqualified intermediary must inform the withholding agent on a statement associated with its nonqualified intermediary withholding certificate that it is using the procedure under this paragraph (e)(3)(iv)(D) and the withholding agent must agree to the procedure. If the requirements of the alternative procedure are met, a withholding agent, including the nonqualified intermediary using the procedures, can treat the payment as reliably associated with documentation and, therefore, the presumption rules of paragraph (b)(3) of this section and §§ 1.1441-5(d) and (e)(6) and 1.6049-5(d) do not apply even though information allocating the payment to each payee has not been received prior to the payment. See paragraph (e)(3)(iv)(D)(*7*) of this section, however, for a nonqualified intermediary's liability for tax and penalties if the requirements of this paragraph (e)(3)(iv)(D) are not met. These alternative procedures shall not be used for payments that are allocable to U.S. non-exempt recipients. Therefore, a nonqualified intermediary is required to provide a withholding agent with information allocating payments of reportable amounts to U.S. non-exempt recipients prior to the payment being made by the withholding agent.

(*2*) *Withholding rate pools.* In place of the information required in paragraph (e)(3)(iv)(C)(*2*) of this section allocating payments to each payee, the nonqualified intermediary must provide a withholding agent with withholding rate pool information prior to the payment of a reportable amount. The withholding statement must contain all other information required by paragraph (e)(3)(iv)(C) of this section. Further, each payee listed in the withholding statement must be assigned to an identified withholding rate pool. To the extent a nonqualified intermediary is required to, or does provide, documentation, the alternative procedures do not relieve the nonqualified intermediary from the requirement to provide documentation prior to the payment being made. Therefore, withholding certificates or other appropriate documentation and all information required by paragraph (e)(3)(iv)(C) of this section (other than allocation information) must be provided to a withholding agent before any new payee receives a reportable amount. In addition, the withholding statement must be updated by assigning a new payee to a withholding rate pool prior to the payment of a reportable amount. A withholding rate pool is a payment of a single type of income, determined in accordance with the categories of income used to file Form 1042-S, that is subject to a single rate of withholding. A withholding rate pool may be established by any reasonable method to which the nonqualified intermediary and a withholding agent agree (e.g., by establishing a separate account for a single withholding rate pool, or by dividing a payment made to a single account into portions allocable to each withholding rate pool). The nonqualified intermediary shall determine withholding rate pools based on valid documentation or, to the extent a payment cannot be reliably associated with valid documentation, the presumption rules of paragraph (b)(3) of this section and §§ 1.1441-5(d) and (e)(6) and 1.6049-5(d).

(*3*) *Allocation information.* The nonqualified intermediary must provide the withholding agent with sufficient information to allocate the income in each withholding rate pool to each payee (including U.S. exempt recipients) within the pool no later than January 31 of the year following the year of payment. Any payments that are not allocated to payees for whom documentation has been provided shall be allocated to an undocumented payee in accordance with the presumption rules of paragraph (b)(3) of this section and §§ 1.1441-5(d) and (e)(6) and 1.6049-5(d). Notwithstanding the preceding sentence, deposit interest (including original issue discount) described in section 871(i)(2)(A) or 881(d) and interest or original issue discount on short-term obligations as described in section 871(g)(1)(B) or 881(e) is not required to be allocated to a U.S. exempt recipient or a foreign payee, except as required under § 1.6049-8 (regarding reporting of deposit interest paid to certain foreign persons).

(*4*) *Failure to provide allocation information.* If a nonqualified intermediary fails to provide allocation information, if required, by January 31 for any withholding rate pool, a withholding agent shall not apply the alternative procedures of this paragraph (e)(3)(iv)(D) to any payments of reportable amounts paid after January 31 in the taxable year following the calendar year for which allocation information was not given and any subsequent taxable year. Further, the alternative procedures shall be unavailable for any other withholding rate pool even though allocation information was given for that other pool. Therefore, the withholding agent must withhold on a payment of a reportable amount in accordance with the presumption rules of paragraph (b)(3) of this section, and §§ 1.1441-5(d) and (e)(6) and 1.6049-5(d), unless the nonqualified intermediary provides all of the information, including information sufficient to allocate the payment to each specific payee, required by paragraph (e)(3)(iv)(A) through (C) of this section prior to the payment. A nonqualified intermediary must allocate at least 90 percent of the income required to be allocated for each withholding rate pool or the nonqualified intermediary will be treated as having failed to provide allocation information for purposes of this paragraph (e)(3)(iv)(D). See paragraph (e)(3)(iv)(D)(7) of this section for liability for tax and penalties if a nonqualified intermediary fails to provide allocation information in whole or in part.

(5) *Cure provision.* A nonqualified intermediary may cure any failure to provide allocation information by providing the required allocation information to the withholding agent no later than February 14 following the calendar year of payment. If the withholding agent receives the allocation information by that date, it may apply the adjustment procedures of § 1.1461-2 to any excess withholding for payments made on or after February 1 and on or before February 14. Any nonqualified intermediary that fails to cure by February 14, may request the ability to use the alternative procedures of this paragraph (e)(3)(iv)(D) by submitting a request, in writing, to the Assistant Commissioner (International). The request must state the reason that the nonqualified intermediary did not comply with the alternative procedures of this paragraph (e)(3)(iv)(D) and steps that the nonqualified intermediary has taken, or will take, to ensure that no failures occur in the future. If the Assistant Commissioner (International) determines that the alternative procedures of this paragraph (e)(3)(iv)(D) may apply, a determination to that effect will be issued by the IRS to the nonqualified intermediary.

(6) *Form 1042-S reporting in case of allocation failure.* If a nonqualified intermediary fails to provide allocation information by February 14 following the year of payment for a withholding rate pool, the withholding agent must file Forms 1042-S for payments made to each payee in that pool (other than U.S. exempt recipients) in the prior calendar year by pro rating the payment to each payee (including U.S. exempt recipients) listed in the withholding statement for that withholding rate pool. If the nonqualified intermediary fails to allocate 10 percent or less of an amount required to be allocated for a withholding rate pool, a withholding agent shall report the unallocated amount as paid to a single unknown payee in accordance with the presumption rules of paragraph (b) of this section and §§ 1.1441-5(d) and (e)(6) and 1.6049-5(d). The portion of the payment that can be allocated to specific recipients, as defined in § 1.1461-1(c)(1)(ii), shall be reported to each recipient in accordance with the rules of § 1.1461-1(c).

(7) *Liability for tax, interest, and penalties.* If a nonqualified intermediary fails to provide allocation information by February 14 following the year of payment for all or a portion of the payments made to any withholding rate pool, the withholding agent from whom the nonqualified intermediary received payments of reportable amounts shall not be liable for any tax, interest, or penalties, due solely to the errors or omissions of the nonqualified intermediary. See § 1.1441-7(b)(2) through (10) for the due diligence requirements of a withholding agent. Because failure by the nonqualified intermediary to provide allocation information results in a payment not being reliably associated with valid documentation, the beneficial owners for whom the nonqualified intermediary acts are not entitled to a reduced rate of withholding. Therefore, the nonqualified intermediary, as a withholding agent, shall be liable for any tax not withheld by the withholding agent in accordance with the presumption rules, interest on the under withheld tax if the nonqualified intermediary fails to pay the tax timely, and any applicable penalties, including the penalties under sections 6656 (failure to deposit), 6721 (failure to file information returns) and 6722 (failure to file payee statements). Failure to provide allocation information for more than 10 percent of the payments made to a particular withholding rate pool will be presumed to be an intentional failure within the meaning of sections 6721(e) and 6722(c). The nonqualified intermediary may rebut the presumption.

(8) *Applicability to flow-through entities and certain U.S. branches.* See paragraph (e)(3)(v) of this section and § 1.1441-5(c)(3)(iv) and (e)(5)(iv) for the applicability of this paragraph (e)(3)(iv) to U.S. branches described in paragraph (b)(2)(iv) of this section (other than U.S. branches treated as U.S. persons) and flow-through entities.

(E) *Notice procedures.* The IRS may notify a withholding agent that the alternative procedures of paragraph (e)(3)(iv)(D) of this section are not applicable to a specified nonqualified intermediary, a U.S. branch described in paragraph (b)(2)(iv) of this section, or a flow-through entity. If a withholding agent receives such a notice, it must commence withholding in accordance with the presumption rules of paragraph (b)(3) of this section and §§ 1.1441-5(d) and (e)(6) and 1.6049-5(d) unless the nonqualified intermediary, U.S. branch, or flow-through entity complies with the procedures in paragraphs (e)(3)(iv)(A) through (C) of this section. In addition, the IRS may notify a withholding agent, in appropriate circumstances, that it must apply the presumption rules of paragraph (b)(3) of this section and §§ 1.1441-5(d) and (e)(6) and 1.6049-5(d) to payments made to a nonqualified intermediary, a U.S. branch, or a flow-through entity even if the nonqualified intermediary, U.S. branch or flow-through entity provides allocation information prior to the payment. A withholding agent that receives a notice under this paragraph (e)(3)(iv)(E) must commence withholding in accordance with the presumption rules within 30 days of the date of the notice. The IRS may withdraw its prohibition against using the alternative procedures of paragraph (e)(3)(iv)(D) of this section, or its requirement to follow the presumption rules, if the nonqualified intermediary, U.S. branch, or flow-through entity can demonstrate to the satisfaction of the Assistant Commissioner (International) or his delegate that it is capable of complying with the rules under chapter 3 of the Internal Revenue Code and any other conditions required by the Assistant Commissioner (International).

(v) *Withholding certificate from certain U.S. branches.* A U.S. branch certificate is a withholding certificate provided by a U.S. branch described in paragraph (b)(2)(iv) of this section that is not the beneficial owner of the income. The withholding certificate is provided with respect to reportable amounts and must state that such amounts are not effectively connected with the conduct of a trade or business in the United States. The withholding certificate must either transmit the appropriate documentation for the persons for whom the branch receives the payment (i.e., as an intermediary) or be provided as evidence of its agreement with the withholding agent to be treated as a U.S. person with respect to any payment associated with the certificate. A U.S. branch withholding certificate is valid only if it is furnished on a Form W-8, an acceptable substitute form, or such other form as the IRS may prescribe, it is signed under penalties of perjury by a person authorized to sign for the branch, its validity has not expired, and it contains the information, statements, and certifications described in this paragraph (e)(3)(v). If the certificate is furnished to transmit withholding certificates and other documentation, it must contain the information, certifications, and statements described in paragraphs (e)(3)(v)(A) through (C) of this section and in paragraphs (e)(3)(iii) and (iv) (alternative procedures) of this section, applying the term *U.S. branch* instead of the term *nonqualified intermediary.* If the certificate is furnished pursuant to an agreement to treat the U.S. branch as a U.S. person, the information and certifications required on the withholding certificate are limited to the following—

(A) The name of the person of which the branch is a part and the address of the branch in the United States;

(B) A certification that the payments associated with the certificate are not effectively connected with the conduct of its trade or business in the United States; and

(C) Any other information, certifications, or statements as may be required by the form or accompanying instructions in addition to, or in lieu of, the information and certification described in this paragraph (e)(3)(v).

(vi) *Reportable amounts.* For purposes of chapter 3 of the Internal Revenue Code, a nonqualified intermediary, qualified intermediary, flow-through entity, and U.S. branch described in paragraph (b)(2)(iv) of this section (other than a U.S. branch that agrees to be treated as a U.S. person) must provide a withholding certificate and associated documentation and other information with respect to reportable amounts. For purposes of the regulations under chapter 3 of the Internal Revenue Code, the term reportable amount means an amount subject to withholding within the meaning of § 1.1441-2(a), bank deposit interest (including original issue discount) and similar types of deposit interest described in section 871(i)(2)(A) or 881(d) that are from sources within the United States, and any amount of interest or original issue discount from sources within the United States on the redemption of certain short-term obligations described in section 871(g)(1)(B) or 881(e). Reportable amounts shall not include amounts received on the sale or exchange (other than a redemption) of an obligation described in section 871(g)(1)(B) or 881(e) that is effected at an office outside the United States. See § 1.6045-1(g)(3) to determine whether a sale is effected at an office outside the United States. Reportable amounts also do not include payments with respect to deposits with banks and other financial institutions that remain on deposit for a period of two weeks or less, to amounts of original issue discount arising from a sale and repurchase transaction that is completed within a period of two weeks or less, or to amounts described in § 1.6049-5(b)(7), (10) or (11) (relating to certain obligations issued in bearer form). While short-term OID and bank deposit interest are not subject to withholding under chapter 3 of the Internal Revenue Code, such amounts may be subject to information reporting under section 6049 if paid to a U.S. person who is not an exempt recipient described in § 1.6049-4(c)(1)(ii) and to backup withholding under section 3406 in the absence of documentation. See § 1.6049-5(d)(3)(iii) for applicable procedures when such amounts are paid to a foreign intermediary.

(4) *Applicable rules.* The provisions in this paragraph (e)(4) describe procedures applicable to withholding certificates on Form W-8 or Form 8233 (or a substitute form) or documentary evidence furnished to establish foreign status. These provisions do not apply to Forms W-9 (or their substitutes). For corresponding provisions regrading Form W-9 (or a substitute form), see section 3406 and the regulations under that section.

(i) *Who may sign the certificate.* A withholding certificate (or other acceptable substitute) may be signed by any person authorized to sign a declaration under penalties of perjury on behalf of the person whose name is on the certificate as provided in section 6061 and the regulations under that section (relating to who may sign generally for an individual, estate, or trust, which includes certain agents who may sign returns and other documents), section 6062 and the regulations under that section (relating to who may sign corporate returns), and section 6063 and the regulations under that section (relating to who may sign partnership returns).

(ii) *Period of validity*—(A) *Three-year period.* A withholding certificate described in paragraph (e)(2)(i) of this section, or a certificate described in § 1.871-14(c)(2)(v) (furnished to qualify interest as portfolio interest for purposes of sections 871(h) and 881(c)), shall remain valid until the earlier of the last day of the third calendar year following the year in which the withholding certificate is signed or the day that a change in circumstances occurs that makes any information on the certificate incorrect. For example, a withholding certificate signed on September 30, 2001, remains valid through December 31, 2004, unless circumstances change that make the information on the form no longer correct. Documentary evidence described in §§ 1.1441-6(c)(3) or (4) or 1.6049-5(c)(1) shall remain valid until the earlier of the last day of the third calendar year following the year in which the documentary evidence is provided to the withholding agent or the day that a change in circumstances occurs that makes any information on the documentary evidence incorrect.

(B) *Indefinite validity period.* Notwithstanding paragraph (e)(4)(ii)(A) of this section, the following certificates or parts of certificates shall remain valid until the status of the person whose name is on the certificate is changed in a way relevant to the certificate or circumstances change that make the information on the certificate no longer correct:

(1) A withholding certificate described in paragraph (e)(2)(ii) of this section that is furnished with a TIN, provided that the withholding agent reports at least one payment annually to the beneficial owner under § 1.1461-1(c) or the TIN furnished on the certificate is reported to the IRS under the procedures described in § 1.1461-1(d). For example, assume a withholding agent receives a Form W-8 in 2001 from a beneficial owner with respect to an account that contains bonds, the interest on which must be reported on Form 1042-S under § 1.1461-1(c). The Form W-8 contains a valid TIN and the withholding agent reports on Forms 1042-S interest to the beneficial owner for 2001 through 2005. In 2005, the beneficial owner sells some of the bonds. For purposes of the exemption from Form 1099 reporting under § 1.6045-1(g), the withholding agent may consider the Form W-8 as valid, even though the payment of the sales proceeds is not reportable on Form 1042-S under § 1.1461-1(c) and even though the Form W-8 was provided more than three years previously.

(2) certificate described in paragraph (e)(3)(ii) of this section (a qualified intermediary withholding certificate) but not including the withholding certificates, documentary evidence, statements or other information associated with the certificate.

(3) A certificate described in paragraph (e)(3)(iii) of this section (a nonqualified intermediary certificate), but not including the withholding certificates, documentary evidence, statements or other information associated with the certificate.

(4) A certificate described in paragraph (e)(3)(v) of this section (a U.S. branch withholding certificate), but not including the withholding certificates, documentary evidence, statements or other information associated with the certificate.

(5) A certificate described in § 1.1441-5(c)(2)(iv) (dealing with a certificate from a person representing to be a withholding foreign partnership).

(6) A certificate described in § 1.1441-5(c)(3)(iii) (a withholding certificate from a nonwithholding foreign partnership) but not including the withholding certificates, documentary evidence, statements or other information required to be associated with the certificate.

Reg. § 1.1441-1(e)(4)

(7) A certificate furnished by a person representing to be an integral part of a foreign government (within the meaning of § 1.892-2T(a)(2)) in accordance with § 1.1441-8(b), or by a person representing to be a foreign central bank of issue (within the meaning of § 1.861-2(b)(4)) or the Bank for International Settlements in accordance with § 1.1441-8(c)(1).

(8) A withholding certificate described in § 1.1441-5(e)(5)(iii) provided by a foreign simple trust or a foreign grantor trust to transmit documentation of beneficiaries or owners, but not including the withholding certificates, documentary evidence, statements or other information associated with the certificate.

(C) *Withholding certificate for effectively connected income.* Notwithstanding paragraph (e)(4)(ii)(B)(*1*) of this section, the period of validity of a withholding certificate furnished to a withholding agent to claim a reduced rate of withholding for income that is effectively connected with the conduct of a trade or business within the United States shall be limited to the three-year period described in paragraph (e)(4)(ii)(A) of this section.

(D) *Change in circumstances.* If a change in circumstances makes any information on a certificate or other documentation incorrect, then the person whose name is on the certificate or other documentation must inform the withholding agent within 30 days of the change and furnish a new certificate or new documentation. A certificate or documentation becomes invalid from the date that the withholding agent holding the certificate or documentation knows or has reason to know that circumstances affecting the correctness of the certificate or documentation have changed. However, a withholding agent may choose to apply the provisions of paragraph (b)(3)(iv) of this section regarding the 90-day grace period as of that date while awaiting a new certificate or documentation or while seeking information regarding changes, or suspected changes, in the person's circumstances. If an intermediary (including a U.S. branch described in paragraph (b)(2)(iv)(A) of this section that passes through certificates to a withholding agent) or a flow-through entity becomes aware that a certificate or other appropriate documentation it has furnished to the person from whom it collects the payment is no longer valid because of a change in the circumstances of the person who issued the certificate or furnished the other appropriate documentation, then the intermediary or flow-through entity must notify the person from whom it collects the payment of the change of circumstances. It must also obtain a new withholding certificate or new appropriate documentation to replace the existing certificate or documentation whose validity has expired due to the change in circumstances. If a beneficial owner withholding certificate is used to claim foreign status only (and not, also, residence in a particular foreign country for purposes of an income tax treaty), a change of address is a change in circumstances for purposes of this paragraph (e)(4)(ii)(D) only if it changes to an address in the United States. Further, a change of address within the same foreign country is not a change in circumstances for purposes of this paragraph (e)(4)(ii)(D). A change in the circumstances affecting the withholding information provided to the withholding agent in accordance with the provisions in paragraph (e)(3)(iv) or (5)(v) of this section or in § 1.1441-5(c)(3)(iv) shall terminate the validity of the withholding certificate with respect to the information that is no longer reliable unless the information is updated. A withholding agent may rely on a certificate without having to inquire into possible changes of circumstances that may affect the validity of the statement, unless it knows or has reason to know that circumstances have changed. A withholding agent may require a new certificate at any time prior to a payment, even though the withholding agent has no actual knowledge or reason to know that any information stated on the certificate has changed.

(iii) *Retention of withholding certificate.* A withholding agent must retain each withholding certificate and other documentation for as long as it may be relevant to the determination of the withholding agent's tax liability under section 1461 and § 1.1461-1.

(iv) *Electronic transmission of information*—(A) *In general.* A withholding agent may establish a system for a beneficial owner or payee to electronically furnish a Form W-8, an acceptable substitute Form W-8, or such other form as the Internal Revenue Service may prescribe. The system must meet the requirements described in paragraph (e)(4)(iv)(B) of this section. A withholding agent may accept Forms W-8 that are furnished electronically on or after January 1, 2000, provided the requirements of paragraph (e)(4)(iv)(B) of this section are met.

(B) *Requirements*—(*1*) *In general.* The electronic system must ensure that the information received is the information sent, and must document all occasions of user access that result in the submission renewal, or modification of a Form W-8. In addition, the design and operation of the electronic system, including access procedures, must make it reasonably certain that the

Reg. § 1.1441-1(e)(4)

person accessing the system and furnishing Form W-8 is the person named in the Form.

(2) *Same information as paper Form W-8.* The electronic transmission must provide the withholding agent or payor with exactly the same information as the paper Form W-8.

(3) *Perjury statement and signature requirements.* The electronic transmission must contain an electronic signature by the person whose name is on the Form W-8 and the signature must be under penalties of perjury in the manner described in this paragraph (e)(4)(iv)(B)(3).

(i) *Perjury statement.* The perjury statement must contain the language that appears on the paper Form W-8. The electronic system must inform the person whose name is on the Form W-8 that the person must make the declaration contained in the perjury statement and that the declaration is made by signing the Form W-8. The instructions and the language of the perjury statement must immediately follow the person's certifying statements and immediately precede the person's electronic signature.

(ii) *Electronic signature.* The act of the electronic signature must be effected by the person whose name is on the electronic Form W-8. The signature must also authenticate and verify the submission. For this purpose, the terms *authenticate* and *verify* have the same meanings as they do when applied to a written signature on a paper Form W-8. An electronic signature can be in any form that satisfies the foregoing requirements. The electronic signature must be the final entry in the person's Form W-8 submission.

(4) *Requests for electronic Form W-8 data.* Upon request by the Internal Revenue Service during an examination, the withholding agent must supply a hard copy of the electronic Form W-8 and a statement that, to the best of the withholding agent's knowledge, the electronic Form W-8 was filed by the person whose name is on the form. The hard copy of the electronic Form W-8 must provide exactly the same information as, but need not be identical to, the paper Form W-8.

(C) *Special requirements for transmission of Forms W-8 by an intermediary.* [Reserved]

(v) *Electronic confirmation of taxpayer identifying number on withholding certificate.* The Commissioner may prescribe procedures in a revenue procedure (see § 601.601(d)(2) of this chapter) or other appropriate guidance to require a withholding agent to confirm electronically with the IRS information concerning any TIN stated on a withholding certificate.

(vi) *Acceptable substitute form.* A withholding agent may substitute its own form instead of an official Form W-8 or 8233 (or such other official form as the IRS may prescribe). Such a substitute for an official form will be acceptable if it contains provisions that are substantially similar to those of the official form, it contains the same certifications relevant to the transactions as are contained on the official form and these certifications are clearly set forth, and the substitute form includes a signature-under-penalties-of-perjury statement identical to the one stated on the official form. The substitute form is acceptable even if it does not contain all of the provisions contained on the official form, so long as it contains those provisions that are relevant to the transaction for which it is furnished. For example, a withholding agent that pays no income for which treaty benefits are claimed may develop a substitute form that is identical to the official form, except that it does not include information regarding claim of benefits under an income tax treaty. A withholding agent who uses a substitute form must furnish instructions relevant to the substitute form only to the extent and in the manner specified in the instructions to the official form. A withholding agent may refuse to accept a certificate from a payee or beneficial owner (including the official Form W-8 or 8233) if the certificate is not provided on the acceptable substitute form provided by the withholding agent. However, a withholding agent may refuse to accept a certificate provided by a payee or beneficial owner only if the withholding agent furnishes the payee or beneficial owner with an acceptable substitute form immediately upon receipt of an unacceptable form or within 5 business days of receipt of an unacceptable form from the payee or beneficial owner. In that case, the substitute form is acceptable only if it contains a notice that the withholding agent has refused to accept the form submitted by the payee or beneficial owner and that the payee or beneficial owner must submit the acceptable form provided by the withholding agent in order for the payee or beneficial owner to be treated as having furnished the required withholding certificate.

(vii) *Requirement of taxpayer identifying number.* A TIN must be stated on a withholding certificate when required by this paragraph (e)(4)(vii). A TIN is required to be stated on—

(A) A withholding certificate on which a beneficial owner is claiming the benefit of a reduced rate under an income tax treaty (other than for amounts described in § 1.1441-6(c)(2);

(B) A withholding certificate on which a beneficial owner is claiming exemption from with-

Reg. § 1.1441-1(e)(4)

holding because income is effectively connected with a U.S. trade or business;

(C) A withholding certificate on which a beneficial owner is claiming exemption from withholding under section 871(f) for certain annuities received under qualified plans;

(D) A withholding certificate on which a beneficial owner is claiming an exemption based solely on a foreign organization's claim of tax exempt status under section 501(c) or private foundation status (however, a TIN is not required from a foreign private foundation that is subject to the 4-percent tax under section 4948(a) on income if that income would be exempt from withholding but for section 4948(a) (e.g., portfolio interest));

(E) A withholding certificate from a person representing to be a qualified intermediary described in paragraph (e)(5)(ii) of this section;

(F) A withholding certificate from a person representing to be a withholding foreign partnership described in § 1.1441-5(c)(2)(i));

(G) A withholding certificate from a person representing to be a foreign grantor trust with 5 or fewer grantors;

(H) A withholding certificate provided by a foreign organization that is described in section 501(c);

(I) A withholding certificate from a person representing to be a U.S. branch described in paragraph (b)(2)(iv) of this section.

(viii) *Reliance rules.* A withholding agent may rely on the information and certifications stated on withholding certificates or other documentation without having to inquire into the truthfulness of this information or certification, unless it has actual knowledge or reason to know that the same is untrue. In the case of amounts described in § 1.1441-6(c)(2), a withholding agent described in § 1.1441-7(b)(2)(ii) has reason to know that the information or certifications on a certificate are untrue only to the extent provided in § 1.1441-7(b)(2)(ii). See § 1.1441-6(b)(1) for reliance on representations regarding eligibility for a reduced rate under an income tax treaty. Paragraphs (e)(4)(viii)(A) and (B) of this section provide examples of such reliance.

(A) *Classification.* A withholding agent may rely on the claim of entity classification indicated on the withholding certificate that it receives from or for the beneficial owner, unless it has actual knowledge or reason to know that the classification claimed is incorrect. A withholding agent may not rely on a person's claim of classification other than as a corporation if the name of the corporation indicates that the person is a per se corporation described in § 301.7701-2(b)(8)(i) of this chapter unless the certificate contains a statement that the person is a grandfathered per se corporation described in § 301.7701-2(b)(8) of this chapter and that its grandfathered status has not been terminated. In the absence of reliable representation or information regarding the classification of the payee or beneficial owner, see § 1.1441-1(b)(3)(ii) for applicable presumptions.

(B) *Status of payee as an intermediary or as a person acting for its own account.* A withholding agent may rely on the type of certificate furnished as indicative of the payee's status as an intermediary or as an owner, unless the withholding agent has actual knowledge or reason to know otherwise. For example, a withholding agent that receives a beneficial owner withholding certificate from a foreign financial institution may treat the institution as the beneficial owner, unless it has information in its records that would indicate otherwise or the certificate contains information that is not consistent with beneficial owner status (e.g., sub-account numbers or names). If the financial institution also acts as an intermediary, the withholding agent may request that the institution furnish two certificates, i.e., a beneficial owner certificate described in paragraph (e)(2)(i) of this section for the amounts that it receives as a beneficial owner, and an intermediary withholding certificate described in paragraph (e)(3)(i) of this section for the amounts that it receives as an intermediary. In the absence of reliable representation or information regarding the status of the payee as an owner or as an intermediary, see paragraph (b)(3)(v)(A) for applicable presumptions.

(ix) *Certificates to be furnished for each account unless exception applies.* Unless otherwise provided in this paragraph (e)(4)(ix), a withholding agent that is a financial institution with which a customer may open an account shall obtain withholding certificates or other appropriate documentation on an account-by-account basis.

(A) *Coordinated account information system in effect.* A withholding agent may rely on the withholding certificate or other appropriate documentation furnished by a customer for a pre-existing account under any one or more of the circumstances described in this paragraph (e)(4)(ix)(A).

(*1*) A withholding agent may rely on documentation furnished by a customer for another account if all such accounts are held at the same branch location.

(*2*) A withholding agent may rely on documentation furnished by a customer for an

Reg. § 1.1441-1(e)(4)

account held at another branch location of the same withholding agent or at a branch location of a person related to the withholding agent if the withholding agent and the related person are part of a universal account system that uses a customer identifier that can be used to retrieve systematically all other accounts of the customer. See § 31.3406(c)-1(c)(3)(ii) and (iii)(C) of this chapter for an identical procedure for purposes of backup withholding. For purposes of this paragraph (e)(4)(ix)(A), a withholding agent is related to another person if it is related within the meaning of section 267(b) or 707(b).

(*3*) A withholding agent may rely on documentation furnished by a customer for an account held at another branch location of the same withholding agent or at a branch location of a person related to the withholding agent if the withholding agent and the related person are part of an information system other than a universal account system and the information system is described in this paragraph (e)(4)(ix)(A)(*3*). The system must allow the withholding agent to easily access data regarding the nature of the documentation, the information contained in the documentation, and its validity status, and must allow the withholding agent to easily transmit data into the system regarding any facts of which it becomes aware that may affect the reliability of the documentation. The withholding agent must be able to establish how and when it has accessed the data regarding the documentation and, if applicable, how and when it has transmitted data regarding any facts of which it became aware that may affect the reliability of the documentation. In addition, the withholding agent or the related party must be able to establish that any data it has transmitted to the information system has been processed and appropriate due diligence has been exercised regarding the validity of the documentation.

(*4*) A withholding agent may rely on documentation furnished by a beneficial owner or payee to an agent of the withholding agent. The agent may retain the documentation as part of an information system maintained for a single or multiple withholding agents provided that the system permits any withholding agent that uses the system to easily access data regarding the nature of the documentation, the information contained in the documentation, and its validity, and must allow the withholding agent to easily transmit data into the system regarding any facts of which it becomes aware that may affect the reliability of the documentation. The withholding agent must be able to establish how and when it has accessed the data regarding the documentation and, if applicable, how and when it has transmitted data regarding any facts of which it became aware that may affect the reliability of the documentation. In addition, the withholding agent must be able to establish that any data it has transmitted to the information system has been processed and appropriate due diligence has been exercised regarding the validity of the documentation.

(B) *Family of mutual funds.* An interest in a mutual fund that has a common investment advisor or common principal underwriter with other mutual funds (within the same family of funds) may, in the discretion of the mutual fund, be represented by one single withholding certificate where shares are acquired or owned in any of the funds. See § 31.3406(h)-3(a)(2) of this chapter for an identical procedures for purposes of backup withholding.

(C) *Special rule for brokers*—(*1*) *In general.* A withholding agent may rely on the certification of a broker that the broker holds a valid beneficial owner withholding certificate described in paragraph (e)(2)(i) of this section or other appropriate documentation for that beneficial owner with respect to any readily tradable instrument, as defined in § 31.3406(h)-1(d) of this chapter, if the broker is a United States person (including a U.S. branch treated as a U.S. person under paragraph (b)(2)(iv) of this section) that is acting as the agent of a beneficial owner and the U.S. broker has been provided a valid Form W-8 or other appropriate documentation. The certification must be in writing or in electronic form and contain all of the information required of a non-qualified intermediary under paragraphs (e)(3)(iv)(B) and (C) of this section. If a U.S. broker chooses to use this paragraph (e)(4)(ix)(C), that U.S. broker will be solely responsible for applying the rules of § 1.1441-7(b) to the withholding certificates or other appropriate documentation. For purposes of this paragraph (c)(4)(ix)(C), the term broker means a person treated as a broker under § 1.6045-1(a).

(*2*) The following example illustrates the rules of this paragraph (e)(4)(ix)(C):

Example. SCO is a U.S. securities clearing organization that provides clearing services for correspondent broker, CB, a U.S. corporation. Pursuant to a fully disclosed clearing agreement, CB fully discloses the identity of each of its customers to SCO. Part of SCO's clearing duties include the crediting of income and gross proceeds of readily tradeable instruments (as defined in § 31.3406(h)-1(d)) to each customer's account. For each disclosed customer that is a foreign beneficial owner, CB provides SCO with information required under paragraphs

Reg. § 1.1441-1(e)(4)

(e)(3)(iv)(B) and (C) of this section that is necessary to apply the correct rate of withholding and to file Forms 1042-S. SCO may use the representations and beneficial owner information provided by CB to determine the proper amount of withholding and to file Forms 1042-S. CB is responsible for determining the validity of the withholding certificates or other appropriate documentation under § 1.1441-1(b).

(5) *Qualified intermediaries*—(i) *General rule.* A qualified intermediary, as defined in paragraph (e)(5)(ii) of this section, may furnish a qualified intermediary withholding certificate to a withholding agent. The withholding certificate provides certifications on behalf of other persons for the purpose of claiming and verifying reduced rates of withholding under section 1441 or 1442 and for the purpose of reporting and withholding under other provisions of the Internal Revenue Code, such as the provisions under chapter 61 and section 3406 (and the regulations under those provisions). Furnishing such a certificate is in lieu of transmitting to a withholding agent withholding certificates or other appropriate documentation for the persons for whom the qualified intermediary receives the payment, including interest holders in a qualified intermediary that is fiscally transparent under the regulations under section 894. Although the qualified intermediary is required to obtain withholding certificates or other appropriate documentation from beneficial owners, payees, or interest holders pursuant to its agreement with the IRS, it is generally not required to attach such documentation to the intermediary withholding certificate. Notwithstanding the preceding sentence a qualified intermediary must provide a withholding agent with the Forms W-9, or disclose the names, addresses, and taxpayer identifying numbers, if known, of those U.S. non-exempt recipients for whom the qualified intermediary receives reportable amounts (within the meaning of paragraph (e)(3)(vi) of this section) to the extent required in the qualified intermediary's agreement with the IRS. A person may claim qualified intermediary status before an agreement is executed with the IRS if it has applied for such status and the IRS authorizes such status on an interim basis under such procedures as the IRS may prescribe.

(ii) *Definition of qualified intermediary.* With respect to a payment to a foreign person, the term *qualified intermediary* means a person that is a party to a withholding agreement with the IRS and such person is—

(A) A foreign financial institution or a foreign clearing organization (as defined in § 1.163-5(c)(2)(i)(D)(8), without regard to the requirement that the organization hold obligations for members), other than a U.S. branch or U.S. office of such institution or organization;

(B) A foreign branch or office of a U.S. financial institution or a foreign branch or office of a U.S. clearing organization (as defined in § 1.163-5(c)(2)(i)(D)(8), without regard to the requirement that the organization hold obligations for members);

(C) A foreign corporation for purposes of presenting claims of benefits under an income tax treaty on behalf of its shareholders; or

(D) Any other person acceptable to the IRS.

(iii) *Withholding agreement*—(A) *In general.* The IRS may, upon request, enter into a withholding agreement with a foreign person described in paragraph (e)(5)(ii) of this section pursuant to such procedures as the IRS may prescribe in published guidance (see § 601.601(d)(2) of this chapter). Under the withholding agreement, a qualified intermediary shall generally be subject to the applicable withholding and reporting provisions applicable to withholding agents and payors under chapters 3 and 61 of the Internal Revenue Code, section 3406, the regulations under those provisions, and other withholding provisions of the Internal Revenue Code, except to the extent provided under the agreement.

(B) *Terms of the withholding agreement.* Generally, the agreement shall specify the type of certifications and documentation upon which the qualified intermediary may rely to ascertain the classification (e.g., corporation or partnership) and status (i.e., U.S. or foreign) of beneficial owners and payees who receive payments collected by the qualified intermediary and, if necessary, entitlement to the benefits of a reduced rate under an income tax treaty. The agreement shall specify if, and to what extent, the qualified intermediary may assume primary withholding responsibility in accordance with paragraph (e)(5)(iv) of this section. It shall also specify the extent to which applicable return filing and information reporting requirements are modified so that, in appropriate cases, the qualified intermediary may report payments to the IRS on an aggregated basis, without having to disclose the identity of beneficial owners and payees. However, the qualified intermediary may be required to provide to the IRS the name and address of those foreign customers who benefit from a reduced rate under an income tax treaty pursuant to the qualified intermediary arrangement for purposes of verifying entitlement to such benefits, particularly under an applicable limitation on benefits provision. Under the agreement, a qualified intermediary may agree to act as an acceptance agent to perform the duties described in § 301.6109-1(d)(3)(iv)(A) of this chapter. The agreement may specify the manner in which applicable procedures for adjustments for underwithholding and overwithholding, including refund procedures, apply in the context of a qualified intermediary arrangement and the extent to which applicable procedures may be modified. In particular, a qualified intermediary agreement may allow a qualified intermediary to claim refunds of overwithheld amounts. If relevant, the agreement shall specify the manner in which the qualified intermediary may deal with payments to other intermediaries and flow-through entities. In addition, the agreement shall specify the manner in which the IRS will verify compliance with the agreement. In appropriate cases, the IRS may agree to rely on audits performed by an intermediary's approved auditor. In such a case, the IRS's audit may be limited to the audit of the auditor's records (including work papers of the auditor and reports prepared by the auditor indicating the methodology employed to verify the entity's compliance with the agreement). For this purpose, the agreement shall specify the auditor or class of auditors that are approved. Generally, an auditor will not be approved if the auditor is not subject to laws, regulations, or rules that impose sanctions for failure to exercise its independence and to perform the audit competently. The agreement may include provisions for the assessment and collection of tax in the event that failure to comply with the terms of the agreement results in the failure by the withholding agent or the qualified intermediary to withhold and deposit the required amount of tax. Further, the agreement may specify the procedures by which deposits of amounts withheld are to be deposited, if different from the deposit procedures under the Internal Revenue Code and applicable regulations. To determine whether to enter a qualified intermediary withholding agreement and the terms of any particular withholding agreement, the IRS will consider appropriate factors including whether or not the foreign person agrees to assume primary withholding responsibility, the type of local know-your-customer laws and practices to which it is subject, the extent and nature of supervisory and regulatory control exercised under the laws of the foreign country over the foreign person, the volume of investments in U.S. securities (determined in dollar amounts and number of account holders), the financial condition of the foreign person, and whether the qualified intermediary is a resident of a country with which the United States has an income tax treaty.

(iv) *Assignment of primary withholding responsibility.* Any person who meets the definition of a withholding agent under § 1.1441-7(a) (whether a U.S. person or a foreign person) is required to withhold and deposit any amount withheld under § 1.1461-1(a) and to make the returns prescribed by § 1.1461-1(b) and (c). If permitted by its qualified intermediary agreement, a qualified intermediary agreement may, however, inform a withholding agent from which it receives a payment that it will assume the primary obligation to withhold, deposit, and report amounts under chapter 3 of the Internal Revenue Code and/or under chapter 61 of the Internal Revenue Code and section 3406. If a withholding agent makes a payment of an amount subject to withholding, as defined in § 1.1441-2(a), or a reportable payment, as defined in section 3406(b), to a qualified intermediary that represents to the withholding agent that it has assumed primary withholding responsibility for the payment, the withholding agent is not required to withhold on the payment. The withholding agent is not required to determine that the qualified intermediary agreement actually permits the qualified intermediary to assume primary withholding responsibility. A qualified intermediary that assumes primary withholding responsibility under chapter 3 of the Internal Revenue Code or primary reporting and backup withholding responsibility under chapter 61 and section 3406 is not required to assume primary withholding responsibility for all accounts it has with a withholding agent but must assume primary withholding responsibility for all payments made to any one account that it has with the withholding agent. A qualified intermediary may agree with the withholding agent to assume primary withholding responsibility under chapter 3 and section 3406, only if expressly permitted to do so under its agreement with the IRS.

(v) *Withholding statement*—(A) *In general.* A qualified intermediary must provide each withholding agent from which it receives reportable amounts, as defined in paragraph (e)(3)(vi) of this section, as a qualified intermediary with a written statement (the withholding statement) containing the information specified in paragraph (e)(5)(v)(B) of this section. A withholding statement is not required, however, if all of the information a withholding agent needs to fulfill its withholding and reporting requirements is contained in the withholding certificate. The qualified intermediary agreement may require, in appropriate circumstances, the qualified intermediary to include information in its withholding statement relating to payments other than payments of reportable amounts. The withholding

Reg. § 1.1441-1(e)(5)

statement forms an integral part of the qualified intermediary's qualified intermediary withholding certificate and the penalties of perjury statement provided on the withholding certificate shall apply to the withholding statement as well. The withholding statement may be provided in any manner, and in any form, to which qualified intermediary and the withholding agent mutually agree, including electronically. If the withholding statement is provided electronically, there must be sufficient safeguards to ensure that the information received by the withholding agent is the information sent by qualified intermediary and must also document all occasions of user access that result in the submission or modification of withholding statement information. In addition, the electronic system must be capable of providing a hard copy of all withholding statements provided by the qualified intermediary. The withholding statement shall be updated as often as necessary for the withholding agent to meet its reporting and withholding obligations under chapters 3 and 61 of the Internal Revenue Code and section 3406. A withholding agent will be liable for tax, interest, and penalties in accordance with paragraph (b)(7) of this section to the extent it does not follow the presumption rules of paragraph (b)(3) of this section, §§ 1.1441-5(d) and (e)(6), and 1.6049-5(d) for any payment, or portion thereof, for which it does not have a valid withholding statement prior to making a payment.

(B) *Content of withholding statement.* The withholding statement must contain sufficient information for a withholding agent to apply the correct rate of withholding on payments from the accounts identified on the statement and to properly report such payments on Forms 1042-S and Forms 1099, as applicable. The withholding statement must—

(*1*) Designate those accounts for which the qualified intermediary acts as a qualified intermediary;

(*2*) Designate those accounts for which qualified intermediary assumes primary withholding responsibility under chapter 3 of the Internal Revenue Code and/or primary reporting and backup withholding responsibility under chapter 61 and section 3406; and

(*3*) Provide information regarding withholding rate pools, as described in paragraph (e)(5)(v)(C) of this section.

(C) *Withholding rate pools*—(*1*) *In general.* Except to the extent it has assumed both primary withholding responsibility under chapter 3 of the Internal Revenue Code and primary reporting and backup withholding responsibility under chapter 61 and section 3406 with respect to a payment, a qualified intermediary shall provide as part of its withholding statement the withholding rate pool information that is required for the withholding agent to meet its withholding and reporting obligations under chapters 3 and 61 of the Internal Revenue Code and section 3406. A withholding rate pool is a payment of a single type of income, determined in accordance with the categories of income reported on Form 1042-S or Form 1099, as applicable, that is subject to a single rate of withholding. A withholding rate pool may be established by any reasonable method on which the qualified intermediary and a withholding agent agree (e.g., by establishing a separate account for a single withholding rate pool, or by dividing a payment made to a single account into portions allocable to each withholding rate pool). To the extent a qualified intermediary does not assume primary reporting and backup withholding responsibility under chapter 61 and section 3406, a qualified intermediary's withholding statement must establish a separate withholding rate pool for each U.S. non-exempt recipient account holder that the qualified intermediary has disclosed to the withholding agent unless the qualified intermediary uses the alternative procedures in paragraph (e)(5)(v)(C)(*2*) of this section. A qualified intermediary shall determine withholding rate pools based on valid documentation that it obtains under its withholding agreement with the IRS, or if a payment cannot be reliably associated with valid documentation, under the applicable presumption rules. If a qualified intermediary has an account holder that is another intermediary (whether a qualified intermediary or a non-qualified intermediary) or a flow-through entity, the qualified intermediary may combine the account holder information provided by the intermediary or flow-through entity with the qualified intermediary's direct account holder information to determine the qualified intermediary's withholding rate pools.

(*2*) *Alternative procedure for U.S. non-exempt recipients.* If permitted under its agreement with the IRS, a qualified intermediary may, by mutual agreement with a withholding agent, establish a single zero withholding rate pool that includes U.S. non-exempt recipient account holders for whom the qualified intermediary has provided Forms W-9 prior to the withholding agent paying any reportable payments, as defined in the qualified intermediary agreement, and a separate withholding rate pool (subject to 31-percent withholding) that includes only U.S. non-exempt recipient account holders for whom a qualified intermediary has not provided Forms W-9 prior to the withholding agent paying any

Reg. § 1.1441-1(e)(5)

reportable payments. If a qualified intermediary chooses the alternative procedure of this paragraph (e)(5)(v)(C)(2), the qualified intermediary must provide the information required by its qualified intermediary agreement to the withholding agent no later than January 15 of the year following the year in which the payments are paid. Failure to provide such information will result in the application of penalties to the qualified intermediary under sections 6721 and 6722, as well as any other applicable penalties, and may result in the termination of the qualified intermediary's withholding agreement with the IRS. A withholding agent shall not be liable for tax, interest, or penalties for failure to backup withhold or report information under chapter 61 of the Internal Revenue Code due solely to the errors or omissions of the qualified intermediary. If a qualified intermediary fails to provide the allocation information required by this paragraph (e)(5)(v)(C)(2), with respect to U.S. non-exempt recipients, the withholding agent shall report the unallocated amount paid from the withholding rate pool to an unknown recipient, or otherwise in accordance with the appropriate Form 1099 and the instructions accompanying the form.

(f) *Effective date*—(1) *In general.* This section applies to payments made after December 31, 2000.

(2) *Transition rules*—(i) *Special rules for existing documentation.* For purposes of paragraphs (d)(3) and (e)(2)(i) of this section, the validity of a withholding certificate (namely, Form W-8, 8233, 1001, 4224, or 1078 , or a statement described in § 1.1441-5 in effect prior to January 1, 2001 (see § 1.1441-5 as contained in 26 CFR part 1, revised April 1, 1999)) that was valid on January 1, 1998 under the regulations in effect prior to January 1, 2001 (see 26 CFR parts 1 and 35a, revised April 1, 1999) and expired, or will expire, at any time during 1998, is extended until December 31, 1998. The validity of a withholding certificate that is valid on or after January 1, 1999, remains valid until its validity expires under the regulations in effect prior to January 1, 2001 (see 26 CFR parts 1 and 35a, revised April 1, 1999) but in no event will such withholding certificate remain valid after December 31, 2000. The rule in this paragraph (f)(2)(i), however, does not apply to extend the validity period of a withholding certificate that expires solely by reason of changes in the circumstances of the person whose name is on the certificate. Notwithstanding the first three sentences of this paragraph (f)(2)(i), a withholding agent may choose to not take advantage of the transition rule in this paragraph (f)(2)(i) with respect to one or more withholding certificates valid under the regulations in effect prior to January 1, 2001 (see 26 CFR parts 1 and 35a, revised April 1, 1999) and, therefore, to require withholding certificates conforming to the requirements described in this section (new withholding certificates). For purposes of this section, a new withholding certificate is deemed to satisfy the documentation requirement under the regulations in effect prior to January 1, 2001 (see 26 CFR parts 1 and 35a, revised April 1, 1999). Further, a new withholding certificate remains valid for the period specified in paragraph (e)(4)(ii) of this section, regardless of when the certificate is obtained.

(ii) *Lack of documentation for past years.* A taxpayer may elect to apply the provisions of paragraphs (b)(7)(i)(B), (ii), and (iii) of this section, dealing with liability for failure to obtain documentation timely, to all of its open tax years, including tax years that are currently under examination by the IRS. The election is made by simply taking action under those provisions in the same manner as the taxpayer would take action for payments made after December 31, 2000. [Reg. § 1.1441-1.]

□ [*T.D.* 6187, 7-5-56. *Amended by T.D.* 6592, 2-27-62, T.D. 6908, 12-30-66, T.D. 7157, 12-29-71, T.D. 7385, 10-28-75; T.D. 7670, 1-30-80; T.D. 8734, 10-6-97; T.D. 8804, 12-30-98; T.D. 8856, 12-29-99 (*corrected* 3-27-2000) *and* T.D. 8881, 5-15-2000 (*corrected* 4-5-2001).]

[Reg. § 1.1441-2]

§ 1.1441-2. Amounts subject to withholding.—(a) *In general.* For purposes of the regulations under chapter 3 of the Internal Revenue Code, the term *amounts subject to withholding* means amounts from sources within the United States that constitute either fixed or determinable annual or periodical income described in paragraph (b) of this section or other amounts subject to withholding described in paragraph (c) of this section. For purposes of this paragraph (a), an amount shall be treated as being from sources within the United States if the source of the amount cannot be determined at the time of payment. See § 1.1441-3(d)(1) for determining the amount to be withheld from a payment in the absence of information at the time of payment regarding the source of the amount. Amounts subject to withholding include amounts that are not fixed or determinable annual or periodical income and upon which withholding is specifically required under a provision of this section or another section of the regulations under chapter 3 of the Internal Revenue Code (such as corporate distributions upon which withholding is required under § 1.1441-3(c)(1) that do not constitute dividend

Reg. § 1.1441-2(a)

income). Amounts subject to withholding do not include—

(1) Amounts described in § 1.1441-1(b)(4)(i) to the extent they involve interest on obligations in bearer form or on foreign-targeted registered obligations (but, in the case of a foreign-targeted registered obligation, only to the extent of those amounts paid to a registered owner that is a financial institution within the meaning of section 871(h)(5)(B) or a member of a clearing organization which member is the beneficial owner of the obligation);

(2) Amounts described in § 1.1441-1(b)(4)(ii) (dealing with bank deposit interest and similar types of interest (including original issue discount) described in section 871(i)(2)(A) or 881(d));

(3) Amounts described in § 1.1441-1(b)(4)(iv) (dealing with interest or original issue discount on certain short-term obligations described in section 871(g)(1)(B) or 881(e));

(4) Amounts described in § 1.1441-1(b)(4)(xx) (dealing with income from certain gambling winnings exempt from tax under section 871(j));

(5) Amounts paid as part of the purchase price of an obligation sold or exchanged between interest payment dates, unless the sale or exchange is part of a plan the principal purpose of which is to avoid tax and the withholding agent has actual knowledge or reason to know of such plan;

(6) Original issue discount paid as part of the purchase price of an obligation sold or exchanged in a transaction other than a redemption of such obligation, unless the purchase is part of a plan the principal purpose of which is to avoid tax and the withholding agent has actual knowledge or reason to know of such plan; and

(7) Insurance premiums paid with respect to a contract that is subject to the section 4371 excise tax.

(b) *Fixed or determinable annual or periodical income*—(1) *In general*—(i) *Definition.* For purposes of chapter 3 of the Internal Revenue Code and the regulations thereunder, fixed or determinable annual or periodical income includes all income included in gross income under section 61 (including original issue discount) except for the items specified in paragraph (b)(2) of this section. Items of income that are excluded from gross income under a provision of law without regard to the U.S. or foreign status of the owner of the income, such as interest excluded from gross income under section 103(a) or qualified scholarship income under section 117, shall not be treated as fixed or determinable annual or periodical income under chapter 3 of the Internal Revenue Code. Income excluded from gross income under section 892 (income of foreign governments) or section 115 (income of a U.S. possession) is fixed or determinable annual or periodical income since the exclusion from gross income under those sections is dependent on the foreign status of the owner of the income. See § 1.306-3(h) for treating income from the disposition of section 306 stock as fixed or determinable annual or periodical income.

(ii) *Manner of payment.* The term *fixed or determinable annual or periodical* is merely descriptive of the character of a class of income. If an item of income falls within the class of income contemplated in the statute and described in paragraph (a) of this section, it is immaterial whether payment of that item is made in a series of payments or in a single lump sum. Further, the income need not be paid annually if it is paid periodically; that is to say, from time to time, whether or not at regular intervals. The fact that a payment is not made annually or periodically does not, however, prevent it from being fixed or determinable annual or periodical income (e.g., a lump sum payment). In addition, the fact that the length of time during which the payments are to be made may be increased or diminished in accordance with someone's will or with the happening of an event does not disqualify the payment as determinable or periodical. For this purpose, the share of the fixed or determinable annual or periodical income of an estate or trust from sources within the United States which is required to be distributed currently, or which has been paid or credited during the taxable year, to a nonresident alien beneficiary of such estate or trust constitutes fixed or determinable annual or periodical income.

(iii) *Determinability of amount.* An item of income is fixed when it is to be paid in amounts definitely pre-determined. An item of income is determinable if the amount to be paid is not known but there is a basis of calculation by which the amount may be ascertained at a later time. For example, interest is determinable even if it is contingent in that its amount cannot be determined at the time of payment of an amount with respect to a loan because the calculation of the interest portion of the payment is contingent upon factors that are not fixed at the time of the payment. For purposes of this section, an amount of income does not have to be determined at the time that the payment is made in order to be determinable. An amount of income described in paragraph (a) of this section which the withholding agent knows is part of a payment it makes but which it cannot calculate exactly at the time of payment, is nevertheless determinable if the determination of the exact amount depends upon events expected to occur at a future date. In contrast, a payment which may be income in the future based upon events that are not anticipated at the time the payment is made is not determinable. For example, loan proceeds may become income to the borrower when and to the extent the loan is canceled without repayment. While the cancellation of the debt is income to the borrower when it occurs, it is not determinable at the time the loan proceeds are disbursed to the borrower if the lack of repayment leading to the cancellation of part or all of the debt was not anticipated at the time of disbursement. The fact that the source of an item of income cannot be determined at the time that the payment is made does not render a payment not determinable. See § 1.1441-3(d)(1) for determining the amount to be withheld from a payment in the absence of information at the time of payment regarding the source of the amount.

(2) *Exceptions.* For purposes of chapter 3 of the Code and the regulations thereunder, the items of income described in this paragraph (b)(2) are not fixed or determinable annual or periodical income—

(i) Gains derived from the sale of property (including market discount and option premiums), except for gains described in paragraph (b)(3) or (c) of this section; and

(ii) Any other income that the Internal Revenue Service (IRS) may determine, in published guidance (see § 601.601(d)(2) of this chapter), is not fixed or determinable annual or periodical income.

(3) *Original issue discount*—(i) *Amount subject to tax.* An amount representing original issue discount is fixed or determinable annual or periodical income that is subject to tax under sections 871(a)(1)(C) and 881(a)(3) to the extent provided in those sections and this paragraph (b)(3) if not otherwise excluded under paragraph (a) of this section. An amount of original issue discount is subject to tax with respect to a foreign beneficial owner of an obligation carrying original issue discount upon a sale or exchange of the obligation or when a payment is made on such obligation. The amount taxable is the amount of original issue discount that accrued while the foreign person held the obligation up to the time that the obligation is sold or exchanged or that a payment is made on the obligation, reduced by any amount of original issue discount that was taken into account prior to that time (due to a payment made on the obligation). In the case of a payment made on the obligation, the tax due on the amount of original issue discount may not exceed the amount of the payment reduced by the tax imposed on any portion of the payment that is qualified stated interest.

(ii) *Amounts subject to withholding.* A withholding agent must withhold on the taxable amount of original issue discount paid on the redemption of an original issue discount obligation unless an exception to withholding applies (e.g., portfolio interest or treaty exception). In addition, withholding is required on the taxable amount of original issue discount upon the sale or exchange of an original issue discount obligation, other than in a redemption, to the extent the withholding agent has actual knowledge or reason to know that the sale or exchange is part of a plan the principal purpose of which is to avoid tax. If a withholding agent cannot determine the taxable amount of original issue discount on the redemption of an original issue discount obligation (or on the sale or exchange of such an obligation if the principal purpose of the sale is to avoid tax), then it must withhold on the entire amount of original issue discount accrued from the date of issue until the date of redemption (or the date the obligation is sold or exchanged) determined on the basis of the most recently published "List of Original Issue Discount Instruments" (IRS Publication 1212, available from the IRS Forms Distribution Center) or similar list published by the IRS as if the beneficial owner of the obligation had held the obligation since its original issue.

(iii) *Exceptions to withholding.* To the extent that this paragraph (b)(3) applies to require withholding by a person other than an issuer of an original issue discount obligation, or the issuer's agent, it shall apply only to obligations issued after December 31, 2000.

(4) *Securities lending transactions and equivalent transactions.* See § § 1.871-7(b)(2) and 1.881-2(b)(2) regarding the character of substitute payments as fixed and determinable annual or periodical income. Such amounts constitute income subject to withholding to the extent they are from sources within the United States, as determined under section § § 1.861-2(a)(7) and 1.861-3(a)(6). See § § 1.6042-3(a)(2) and 1.6049-5(a)(5) for reporting requirements applicable to substitute dividend and interest payments, respectively.

(c) *Other income subject to withholding.* Withholding is also required on the following items of income—

(1) Gains described in sections 631(b) or (c), relating to treatment of gain on disposal of timber, coal, or domestic iron ore with a retained economic interest; and

Reg. § 1.1441-2(b)(2)

(2) Gains subject to the 30-percent tax under section 871(a)(1)(D) or 881(a)(4), relating to contingent payments received from the sale or exchange of patents, copyrights, and similar intangible property.

(d) *Exceptions to withholding where no money or property is paid or lack of knowledge*—(1) *General rule.* A withholding agent who is not related to the recipient or beneficial owner has an obligation to withhold under section 1441 only to the extent that, at any time between the date that the obligation to withhold would arise (but for the provisions of this paragraph (d)) and the due date for the filing of return on Form 1042 (including extensions) for the year in which the payment occurs, it has control over, or custody of money or property owned by the recipient or beneficial owner from which to withhold an amount and has knowledge of the facts that give rise to the payment. The exemption from the obligation to withhold under this paragraph (d) shall not apply, however, to distributions with respect to stock or if the lack of control or custody of money or property from which to withhold is part of a prearranged plan known to the withholding agent to avoid withholding under section 1441, 1442, or 1443. For purposes of this paragraph (d), a withholding agent is related to the recipient or beneficial owner if it is related within the meaning of section 482. Any exemption from withholding pursuant to this paragraph (d) applies without a requirement that documentation be furnished to the withholding agent. However, documentation may have to be furnished for purposes of the information reporting provisions under chapter 61 of the Code and backup withholding under section 3406. The exemption from withholding under this paragraph (d) is not a determination that the amounts are not fixed or determinable annual or periodical income, nor does it constitute an exemption from reporting the amount under § 1.1461-1(b) and (c).

(2) *Cancellation of debt.* A lender of funds who forgives any portion of the loan is deemed to have made a payment of income to the borrower under § 1.61-12 at the time the event of forgiveness occurs. However, based on the rules of paragraph (d)(1) of this section, the lender shall have no obligation to withhold on such amount to the extent that it does not have custody or control over money or property of the borrower at any time between the time that the loan is forgiven and the due date (including extensions) of the Form 1042 for the year in which the payment is deemed to occur. A payment received by the lender from the borrower in partial settlement of the debt obligation does not, for this purpose, constitute an amount of money or property belonging to the borrower from which the withholding tax liability can be satisfied.

(3) *Satisfaction of liability following underwithholding by withholding agent.* A withholding agent who, after failing to withhold the proper amount from a payment, satisfies the underwithheld amount out of its own funds may cause the beneficial owner to realize income to the extent of such satisfaction or may be considered to have advanced funds to the beneficial owner. Such determination depends upon the contractual arrangements governing the satisfaction of such tax liability (e.g., arrangements in which the withholding agent agrees to pay the amount due under section 1441 for the beneficial owner) or applicable laws governing the transaction. If the satisfaction of the tax liability is considered to constitute an advance of funds by the withholding agent to the beneficial owner and the withholding agent fails to collect the amount from the beneficial owner, a cancellation of indebtedness may result, giving rise to income to the beneficial owner under § 1.61-12. While such income is annual or periodical fixed or determinable, the withholding agent shall have no liability to withhold on such income to the extent the conditions set forth in paragraphs (d)(1) and (2) of this section are satisfied with respect to this income. Contrast the rules of this paragraph (d)(3) with the rules in § 1.1441-3(f)(1) dealing with a situation in which the satisfaction of the beneficial owner's tax liability itself constitutes additional income to the beneficial owner. See, also, § 1.1441-3(c)(2)(ii)(B) for a special rule regarding underwithholding on corporate distributions due to underestimating an amount of earnings and profits.

(e) *Payment*—(1) *General rule.* A payment is considered made to a person if that person realizes income whether or not such income results from an actual transfer of cash or other property. For example, realization of income from cancellation of debt results in a deemed payment. A payment is considered made when the amount would be includible in the income of the beneficial owner under the U.S. tax principles governing the cash basis method of accounting. A payment is considered made whether it is made directly to the beneficial owner or to another person for the benefit of the beneficial owner (e.g., to the agent of the beneficial owner). Thus, a payment of income is considered made to a beneficial owner if it is paid in complete or partial satisfaction of the beneficial owner's debt to a creditor. In the event of a conflict between the rules of this paragraph (e)(1) governing whether a payment has occurred and its timing and the rules of § 31.3406(a)-4 of this chapter, the rules in § 31.3406(a)-4 of this chapter shall apply to the extent that the application of

Reg. § 1.1441-2(e)(1)

section 3406 is relevant to the transaction at issue.

(2) *Income allocated under section 482.* A payment is considered made to the extent income subject to withholding is allocated under section 482. Further, income arising as a result of a secondary adjustment made in conjunction with a reallocation of income under section 482 from a foreign person to a related U.S. person is considered paid to a foreign person unless the taxpayer to whom the income is reallocated has entered into a repatriation agreement with the IRS and the agreement eliminates the liability for withholding under this section. For purposes of determining the liability for withholding, the payment of income is deemed to have occurred on the last day of the taxable year in which the transactions that give rise to the allocation of income and the secondary adjustments, if any, took place.

(3) *Blocked income.* Income is not considered paid if it is blocked under executive authority, such as the President's exercise of emergency power under the Trading with the Enemy Act (50 U.S.C. App. 5), or the International Emergency Economic Powers Act (50 U.S.C. 1701 et seq).. However, on the date that the blocking restrictions are removed, the income that was blocked is considered constructively received by the beneficial owner (and therefore paid for purposes of this section) and subject to withholding under § 1.1441-1. Any exemption from withholding pursuant to this paragraph (e)(3) applies without a requirement that documentation be furnished to the withholding agent. However, documentation may have to be furnished for purposes of the information reporting provisions under chapter 61 of the Code and backup withholding under section 3406. The exemption from withholding granted by this paragraph (e)(3) is not a determination that the amounts are not fixed or determinable annual or periodical income.

(4) *Special rules for dividends.* For purposes of sections 1441 and 6042, in the case of stock for which the record date is earlier than the payment date, dividends are considered paid on the payment date. In the case of a corporate reorganization, if a beneficial owner is required to exchange stock held in a former corporation for stock in a new corporation before dividends that are to be paid with respect to the stock in the new corporation will be paid on such stock, the dividend is considered paid on the date that the payee or beneficial owner actually exchanges the stock and receives the dividend. See § 31.3406(a)-4(a)(2) of this chapter.

(5) *Certain interest accrued by a foreign corporation.* For purposes of sections 1441 and 6049, a foreign corporation shall be treated as having made a payment of interest as of the last day of the taxable year if it has made an election under § 1.884-4(c)(1) to treat accrued interest as if it were paid in that taxable year.

(6) *Payments other than in U.S. dollars.* For purposes of section 1441, a payment includes amounts paid in a medium other than U.S. dollars. See § 1.1441-3(e) for rules regarding the amount subject to withholding in the case of such payments.

(f) *Effective date.* This section applies to payments made after December 31, 2000. [Reg. § 1.1441-2.]

☐ [T.D. 6187, 7-5-56. Amended by T.D. 6464, 5-11-60, T.D. 6592, 2-27-62, T.D. 6841, 7-26-65, T.D. 6873, 1-24-66, T.D. 6908, 12-30-66; T.D. 7977, 9-19-84; T.D. 8734, 10-6-97; T.D. 8804, 12-30-98; T.D. 8856, 12-29-99 and T.D. 8881, 5-15-2000.]

[Reg. § 1.1441-3]

§ 1.1441-3. Determination of amounts to be withheld.—(a) *Withholding on gross amount.* Except as otherwise provided in regulations under section 1441, the amount subject to withholding under § 1.1441-1 is the gross amount of income subject to withholding that is paid to a foreign person. The gross amount of income subject to withholding may not be reduced by any deductions, except to the extent that one or more personal exemptions are allowed as provided under § 1.1441-4(b)(6).

(b) *Withholding on payments on certain obligations*—(1) *Withholding at time of payment of interest.* When making a payment on an interest-bearing obligation, a withholding agent must withhold under § 1.1441-1 upon the gross amount of stated interest payable on the interest payment date, regardless of whether the payment constitutes a return of capital or the payment of income within the meaning of section 61. To the extent an amount was withheld on an amount of capital rather than interest, see the rules for adjustments, refunds, or credits under § 1.1441-1(b)(8).

(2) *No withholding between interest payment dates*—(i) *In general.* A withholding agent is not required to withhold under § 1.1441-1 upon interest accrued on the date of a sale or exchange of a debt obligation when that sale occurs between two interest payment dates (even though the amount is treated as interest under § 1.61-7(c) or (d) and is subject to tax under section 871 or 881). See § 1.6045-1(c) for reporting requirements by brokers with respect to sale proceeds. See § 1.61-7(c) regarding the character of payments received by the acquirer of an obligation subse-

Reg. § 1.1441-3(a)

quent to such acquisition (that is, as a return of capital or interest accrued after the acquisition). Any exemption from withholding pursuant to this paragraph (b)(2)(i) applies without a requirement that documentation be furnished to the withholding agent. However, documentation may have to be furnished for purposes of the information reporting provisions under section 6045 or 6049 and backup withholding under section 3406. The exemption from withholding granted by this paragraph (b)(2) is not a determination that the accrued interest is not fixed or determinable annual or periodical income under section 871 (a) or 881(a).

(ii) *Anti-abuse rule.* The exemption in paragraph (b)(2)(i) of this section does not apply if the sale of securities is part of a plan the principal purpose of which is to avoid tax by selling and repurchasing securities and the withholding agent has actual knowledge or reason to know of such plan.

(c) *Corporate distributions*—(1) *General rule.* A corporation making a distribution with respect to its stock or any intermediary (described in § 1.1441-1(c)(13)) making a payment of such a distribution is required to withhold under section 1441, 1442, or 1443 on the entire amount of the distribution, unless it elects to reduce the amount of withholding under the provisions of this paragraph (c). Any exceptions from withholding provided by this paragraph (c) apply without any requirement to furnish documentation to the withholding agent. However, documentation may have to be furnished for purposes of the information reporting provisions under section 6042 or 6045 and backup withholding under section 3406. See § 1.1461-1(c) to determine whether amounts excepted from withholding under this section are considered amounts that are subject to reporting.

(2) *Exception to withholding on distributions*—(i) *In general.* An election described in paragraph (c)(1) of this section is made by actually reducing the amount of withholding at the time that the payment is made. An intermediary that makes a payment of a distribution is not required to reduce the withholding based on the distributing corporation's estimates under this paragraph (c)(2), even if the distributing corporation itself elects to reduce the withholding on payments of distributions that it itself makes to foreign persons. Conversely, an intermediary may elect to reduce the amount of withholding with respect to the payment of a distribution even if the distributing corporation does not so elect for the payments of distributions that it itself makes of distributions to foreign persons. The amounts with respect to which a distributing corporation or intermediary may elect to reduce the withholding are as follows:

(A) A distributing corporation or intermediary may elect to not withhold on a distribution to the extent it represents a nontaxable distribution payable in stock or stock rights.

(B) A distributing corporation or intermediary may elect to not withhold on a distribution to the extent it represents a distribution in part or full payment in exchange for stock.

(C) A distributing corporation or intermediary may elect to not withhold on a distribution (actual or deemed) to the extent it is not paid out of accumulated earnings and profits or current earnings and profits, based on a reasonable estimate determined under paragraph (c)(2)(ii) of this section.

(D) A regulated investment company or intermediary may elect to not withhold on a distribution representing a capital gain dividend (as defined in section 852(b)(3)(C)) or an exempt interest dividend (as defined in section 852(b)(5)(A)) based on the applicable procedures described under paragraph (c)(3) of this section.

(E) A U.S. Real Property Holding Corporation (defined in section 897(c)(2)) or a real estate investment trust (defined in section 856) or intermediary may elect to not withhold on a distribution to the extent it is subject to withholding under section 1445 and the regulations under that section. See paragraph (c)(4) of this section for applicable procedures.

(ii) *Reasonable estimate of accumulated and current earnings and profits on the date of payment*—(A) *General rule.* A reasonable estimate for purposes of paragraph (c)(2)(i)(C) of this section is a determination made by the distributing corporation at a time reasonably close to the date of payment of the extent to which the distribution will constitute a dividend, as defined in section 316. The determination is based upon the anticipated amount of accumulated earnings and profits and current earnings and profits for the taxable year in which the distribution is made, the distributions made prior to the distribution for which the estimate is made and all other relevant facts and circumstances. A reasonable estimate may be made based on the procedures described in § 31.3406(b)(2)-4(c)(2) of this chapter.

(B) *Procedures in case of underwithholding.* A distributing corporation or intermediary that is a withholding agent with respect to a distribution and that determines at the end of the taxable year in which the distribution is made that it underwithheld under section 1441 on the distribution shall be liable for the amount underwithheld as a withholding agent under section

Reg. § 1.1441-3(c)(2)

1461. However, for purposes of this section and § 1.1461-1, any amount underwithheld paid by a distributing corporation, its paying agent, or an intermediary shall not be treated as income subject to additional withholding even if that amount is treated as additional income to the shareholders unless the additional amount is income to the shareholder as a result of a contractual arrangement between the parties regarding the satisfaction of the shareholder's tax liabilities. In addition, no penalties shall be imposed for failure to withhold and deposit the tax if—

(*1*) The distributing corporation made a reasonable estimate as provided in paragraph (c)(2)(ii)(A) of this section; and

(*2*) Either—

(*i*) The corporation or intermediary pays over the underwithheld amount on or before the due date for filing a Form 1042 for the calendar year in which the distribution is made, pursuant to § 1.1461-2(b); or

(*ii*) The corporation or intermediary is not a calendar year taxpayer and it files an amended return on Form 1042X (or such other form as the Commissioner may prescribe) for the calendar year in which the distribution is made and pays the underwithheld amount and interest within 60 days after the close of the taxable year in which the distribution is made.

(C) *Reliance by intermediary on reasonable estimate.* For purposes of determining whether the payment of a corporate distribution is a dividend, a withholding agent that is not the distributing corporation may, absent actual knowledge or reason to know otherwise, rely on representations made by the distributing corporation regarding the reasonable estimate of the anticipated accumulated and current earnings and profits made in accordance with paragraph (c)(2)(ii)(A) of this section. Failure by the withholding agent to withhold the required amount due to a failure by the distributing corporation to reasonably estimate the portion of the distribution treated as a dividend or to properly communicate the information to the withholding agent shall be imputed to the distributing corporation. In such a case, the Internal Revenue Service (IRS) may collect from the distributing corporation any underwithheld amount and subject the distributing corporation to applicable interest and penalties as a withholding agent.

(D) *Example.* The rules of this paragraph (c)(2) are illustrated by the following example:

Example. (i) *Facts.* Corporation X, a publicly traded corporation with both U.S. and foreign shareholders and a calendar year taxpayer, has an accumulated deficit in earnings and profits at the close of 2000. In 2001, Corporation X generates $1 million of current earnings and profits each month and makes an $18 million distribution, resulting in a $12 million dividend. Corporation X plans to make an additional $18 million distribution on October 1, 2002. Approximately one month before that date, Corporation X's management receives an internal report from its legal and accounting department concerning Corporation X's estimated current earnings and profits. The report states that Corporation X should generate only $5.1 million of current earnings and profits by the close of the third quarter due to costs relating to substantial organizational and product changes, but these changes will enable Corporation X to generate $1.3 million of earnings and profits monthly for the last quarter of the 2002 fiscal year. Thus, the total amount of current and earnings and profits for 2002 is estimated to be $9 million.

(ii) *Analysis.* Based on the facts in paragraph (i) of this *Example*, including the fact that earnings and profits estimate was made within a reasonable time before the distribution, Corporation X can rely on the estimate under paragraph (c)(2)(ii)(A) of this section. Therefore, Corporation X may treat $9 million of the $18 million of the October 1, 2002, distribution to foreign shareholders as a non-dividend distribution.

(3) *Special rules in the case of distributions from a regulated investment company*—(i) *General rule.* If the amount of any distributions designated as being subject to section 852(b)(3)(C) or (5)(A) exceeds the amount that may be designated under those sections for the taxable year, then no penalties will be asserted for any resulting underwithholding if the designations were based on a reasonable estimate (made pursuant to the same procedures as are described in paragraph (c)(2)(ii)(A) of this section) and the adjustments to the amount withheld are made within the time period described in paragraph (c)(2)(ii)(B) of this section. Any adjustment to the amount of tax due and paid to the IRS by the withholding agent as a result of underwithholding shall not be treated as a distribution for purposes of section 562(c) and the regulations thereunder. Any amount of U.S. tax that a foreign shareholder is treated as having paid on the undistributed capital gain of a regulated investment company under section 852(b)(3)(D) may be claimed by the foreign shareholder as a credit or refund under § 1.1464-1.

(ii) *Reliance by intermediary on reasonable estimate.* For purposes of determining whether a payment is a distribution designated as subject to section 852(b)(3)(C) or (5)(A), a withholding agent that is not the distributing regulated investment company may, absent actual knowledge or reason to know otherwise, rely on the designations that the distributing company represents have been made in accordance with paragraph (c)(3)(i) of this section. Failure by the withholding agent to withhold the required amount due to a failure by the regulated investment company to reasonably estimate the required amounts or to properly communicate the relevant information to the withholding agent shall be imputed to the distributing company. In such a case, the IRS may collect from the distributing company any underwithheld amount and subject the company to applicable interest and penalties as a withholding agent.

(4) *Coordination with withholding under section 1445*—(i) *In general.* A distribution from a U.S. Real Property Holding Corporation (USRPHC) (or from a corporation that was a USRPHC at any time during the five-year period ending on the date of distribution) with respect to stock that is a U.S. real property interest under section 897(c) or from a Real Estate Investment Trust (REIT) with respect to its stock is subject to the withholding provisions under section 1441 (or section 1442 or 1443) and section 1445. A USRPHC making a distribution shall be treated as satisfying its withholding obligations under both sections if it withholds in accordance with one of the procedures described in either paragraph (c)(4)(i)(A) or (B) of this section. A USRPHC must apply the same withholding procedure to all the distributions made during the taxable year. However, the USRPHC may change the applicable withholding procedure from year to year. For rules regarding distributions by REITs, see paragraph (c)(4)(i)(C) of this section.

(A) *Withholding under section 1441.* The USRPHC may choose to withhold on a distribution only under section 1441 (or 1442 or 1443) and not under section 1445. In such a case, the USRPHC must withhold under section 1441 (or 1442 or 1443) on the full amount of the distribution, whether or not any portion of the distribution represents a return of basis or capital gain. If a reduced tax rate under an income tax treaty applies to the distribution by the USRPHC, then the applicable rate of withholding on the distribution shall be no less than 10-percent, unless the applicable treaty specifies an applicable lower rate for distributions from a USRPHC, in which case the lower rate may apply.

(B) *Withholding under both sections 1441 and 1445.* As an alternative to the procedure described in paragraph (c)(4)(i)(A) of this section, a USRPHC may choose to withhold under both sections 1441 (or 1442 or 1443) and 1445 under the procedures set forth in this paragraph (c)(4)(i)(B). The USRPHC must make a reasonable estimate of the portion of the distribution that is a dividend under paragraph (c)(2)(ii)(A) of this section, and must—

(*1*) Withhold under section 1441 (or 1442 or 1443) on the portion of the distribution that is estimated to be a dividend under paragraph (c)(2)(ii)(A) of this section; and

(*2*) Withhold under section 1445(e)(3) and § 1.1445-5(e) on the remainder of the distribution or on such smaller portion based on a withholding certificate obtained in accordance with § 1.1445-5(e)(2)(iv).

(C) *Coordination with REIT withholding.* Withholding is required under section 1441 (or 1442 or 1443) on the portion of a distribution from a REIT that is not designated as a capital gain dividend, a return of basis, or a distribution in excess of a shareholder's adjusted basis in the stock of the REIT that is treated as a capital gain under section 301(c)(3). A distribution in excess of a shareholder's adjusted basis in the stock of the REIT is, however, subject to withholding under section 1445, unless the interest in the REIT is not a U.S. real property interest (e.g., an interest in a domestically controlled REIT under section 897(h)(2)). In addition, withholding is required under section 1445 on the portion of the distribution designated by a REIT as a capital gain dividend. See § 1.1445-8.

(ii) *Intermediary reliance rule.* A withholding agent that is not the distributing USRPHC must withhold under paragraph (c)(4)(i) of this section, but may, absent actual knowledge or reason to know otherwise, rely on representations made by the USRPHC regarding the determinations required under paragraph (c)(4)(i) of this section. Failure by the withholding agent to withhold the required amount due to a failure by the distributing USRPHC to make these determinations in a reasonable manner or to properly communicate the determinations to the withholding agent shall be imputed to the distributing USRPHC. In such a case, the IRS may collect from the distributing USRPHC any underwithheld amount and subject the distributing USRPHC to applicable interest and penalties as a withholding agent.

(d) *Withholding on payments that include an undetermined amount of income*—(1) *In general.* Where the withholding agent makes a payment and does not know at the time of payment the amount that is subject to withholding because the determination of the source of the income or the calculation of the amount of income subject to tax depends upon facts that are not known at the time of payment, then the withholding agent must withhold an amount under § 1.1441-1 based on the entire amount paid that is necessary to assure that the tax withheld is not less than 30 percent (or other applicable percentage) of the amount that will subsequently be determined to be from sources within the United States or to be income subject to tax. The amount so withheld shall not exceed 30 percent of the amount paid. In the alternative, the withholding agent may make a reasonable estimate of the amount from U.S. sources or of the taxable amount and set aside a corresponding portion of the amount due under the transaction and hold such portion in escrow until the amount from U.S. sources or the taxable amount can be determined, at which point withholding becomes due under § 1.1441-1. See § 1.1441-1(b)(8) regarding adjustments in the case of overwithholding. The provisions of this paragraph (d)(1) shall not apply to the extent that other provisions of the regulations under chapter 3 of the Internal Revenue Code (Code) specify the amount to be withheld, if any, when the withholding agent lacks knowledge at the time of payment (e.g., lack of reliable knowledge regarding the status of the payee or beneficial owner, addressed in § 1.1441-1(b)(3), or lack of knowledge regarding the amount of original issue discount under § 1.1441-2(b)(3)).

(2) *Withholding on certain gains.* Absent actual knowledge or reason to know otherwise, a withholding agent may rely on a claim regarding the amount of gain described in § 1.1441-2(c) if the beneficial owner withholding certificate, or other appropriate withholding certificate, states the beneficial owner's basis in the property giving rise to the gain. In the absence of a reliable representation on a withholding certificate, the withholding agent must withhold an amount under § 1.1441-1 that is necessary to assure that the tax withheld is not less than 30 percent (or other applicable percentage) of the recognized gain. For this purpose, the recognized gain is determined without regard to any deduction allowed by the Code from the gains. The amount so withheld shall not exceed 30 percent of the amount payable by reason of the transaction giving rise to the recognized gain. See § 1.1441-1(b)(8) regarding adjustments in the case of overwithholding.

(e) *Payments other than in U.S. dollars*—(1) *In general.* The amount of a payment made in a medium other than U.S. dollars is measured by the fair market value of the property or services provided in lieu of U.S. dollars. The withholding agent may liquidate the property prior to payment in order to withhold the required amount of tax under section 1441 or obtain payment of the tax from an alternative source. However, the obligation to withhold under section 1441 is not deferred even if no alternative source can be located. Thus, for purposes of withholding under chapter 3 of the Code, the provisions of § 31.3406(h)-2(b)(2)(ii) of this chapter (relating to backup withholding from another source) shall not apply. If the withholding agent satisfies the tax liability related to such payments, the rules of paragraph (f) of this section apply.

(2) *Payments in foreign currency.* If the amount subject to withholding tax is paid in a currency other than the U.S. dollar, the amount of withholding under section 1441 shall be determined by applying the applicable rate of withholding to the foreign currency amount and converting the amount withheld into U.S. dollars on the date of payment at the spot rate (as defined in § 1.988-1(d)(1)) in effect on that date. A withholding agent making regular or frequent payments in foreign currency may use a month-end spot rate or a monthly average spot rate. A spot rate convention must be used consistently for all non-dollar amounts withheld and from year to year. Such convention cannot be changed without the consent of the Commissioner. The U.S. dollar amount so determined shall be treated by the beneficial owner as the amount of tax paid on the income for purposes of determining the final U.S. tax liability and, if applicable, claiming a refund or credit of tax.

(f) *Tax liability of beneficial owner satisfied by withholding agent*—(1) *General rule.* In the event that the satisfaction of a tax liability of a beneficial owner by a withholding agent constitutes income to the beneficial owner and such income is of a type that is subject to withholding, the amount of the payment deemed made by the withholding agent for purposes of this paragraph (f) shall be determined under the gross-up formula provided in this paragraph (f)(1). Whether the payment of the tax by the withholding agent constitutes a satisfaction of the beneficial owner's tax liability and whether, as such, it constitutes additional income to the beneficial owner, must be determined under all the facts and circumstances surrounding the transaction, including any agreements between the parties and applicable law. The formula described in this paragraph (f)(1) is as follows:

$$\text{Payment} = \frac{\text{Gross payment without withholding}}{1 - (\text{tax rate})}$$

(2) *Example.* The following example illustrates the provisions of this paragraph (f):

Example. College X awards a qualified scholarship within the meaning of section 117(b) to foreign student, FS, who is in the United States on an F visa. FS is a resident of a country that does not have an income tax treaty with the United States. The scholarship is $20,000 to be applied to tuition, mandatory fees and books, plus benefits in kind consisting of room and board and round-trip air transportation. College X agrees to pay any U.S. income tax owed by FS with respect to the scholarship. The fair market value of the room and board measured by the amount College X charges non-scholarship students is $6,000. The cost of the roundtrip air transportation is $2,600. Therefore, the total fair market value of the scholarship received by FS is $28,600. However, the amount taxable is limited to the fair market value of the benefits in kind ($8,600) because the portion of the scholarship amount for tuition, fees, and books is not included in gross income under section 117. The applicable rate of withholding is 14 percent under section 1441(b). Therefore, under the gross-up formula, College X is deemed to make a payment of $10,000 ($8,600 divided by (1-.14). The U.S. tax that must be deducted and withheld from the payment under section 1441(b) is $1,400 (.14 x $10,000). College X reports scholarship income of $30,000 and $1,400 of U.S. tax withheld on Forms 1042 and 1042-S.

(g) *Conduit financing arrangements*—(1) *Duty to withhold.* A financed entity or other person required to withhold tax under section 1441 with respect to a financing arrangement that is a conduit financing arrangement within the meaning of § 1.881-3(a)(2)(iv) shall be required to withhold under section 1441 as if the district director had determined, pursuant to § 1.881-3(a)(3), that all conduit entities that are parties to the conduit financing arrangement should be disregarded. The amount of tax required to be withheld shall be determined under § 1.881-3(d). The withholding agent may withhold tax at a reduced rate if the financing entity establishes that it is entitled to the benefit of a treaty that provides a reduced rate of tax on a payment of the type deemed to have been paid to the financing entity. Section 1.881-3(a)(3)(ii)(E) shall not apply for purposes of determining whether any person is required to deduct and withhold tax pursuant to this paragraph (g), or whether any party to a financing arrangement is liable for failure to withhold or entitled to a refund of tax under sections 1441 or 1461 to 1464 (except to the extent the amount withheld exceeds the tax liability determined under § 1.881-3(d)). See § 1.1441-7(f) relating to withholding tax liability of the withholding agent in conduit financing arrangements subject to § 1.881-3.

(2) *Effective date.* This paragraph (g) is effective for payments made by financed entities on or after September 11, 1995. This paragraph shall not apply to interest payments covered by section 127(g)(3) of the Tax Reform Act of 1984, and to interest payments with respect to other debt obligations issued prior to October 15, 1984 (whether or not such debt was issued by a Netherlands Antilles corporation).

(h) *Effective date.* Except as otherwise provided in paragraph (g) of this section, this section applies to payments made after December 31, 2000. [Reg. § 1.1441-3.]

☐ [*T.D.* 6187, 7-5-56. *Amended by T.D.* 6592, 2-27-62; *T.D.* 6636, 2-25-63; *T.D.* 6669, 8-26-63; *T.D.* 6777, 12-15-64; *T.D.* 6908, 12-30-66; *T.D.* 7378, 9-29-75; *T.D.* 7977, 9-19-84; *T.D.* 8611, 8-10-95; *T.D.* 8734, 10-6-97; *T.D.* 8804, 12-30-98; *T.D.* 8856, 12-29-99 *and T.D.* 8881, 5-15-2000.]

[Reg. § 1.1441-4]

§ 1.1441-4. **Exemptions from withholding for certain effectively connected income and other amounts.**—(a) *Certain income connected with a U.S. trade or business*—(1) *In general.* No withholding is required under section 1441 on income otherwise subject to withholding if the income is (or is deemed to be) effectively connected with the conduct of a trade or business within the United States and is includible in the beneficial owner's gross income for the taxable year. For purposes of this paragraph (a), an amount is not deemed to be includible in gross income if the amount is (or is deemed to be) effectively connected with the conduct of a trade or business within the United States and the beneficial owner claims an exemption from tax under an income tax treaty because the income is not attributable to a permanent establishment in the United States. To claim a reduced rate of withholding because the income is not attributable to a permanent establishment, see § 1.1441-6(b)(1). This paragraph (a) does not apply to income of a foreign corporation to which section 543(a)(7) applies for the taxable year or to compensation for personal services performed by an individual. See paragraph (b) of this section for compensation for personal services performed by an individual.

(2) *Withholding agent's reliance on a claim of effectively connected income*—(i) *In general.* Absent actual knowledge or reason to know otherwise, a withholding agent may rely on a claim of exemption based upon paragraph (a)(1) of this section if, prior to the payment to the foreign person, the withholding agent can reliably associate the payment with a Form W-8 upon which it can rely to treat the payment as made to a foreign beneficial owner in accordance with § 1.1441-1(e)(1)(ii). For purposes of this paragraph (a), a withholding certificate is valid only

if, in addition to other applicable requirements, it includes the taxpayer identifying number of the person whose name is on the Form W-8 and represents, under penalties of perjury, that the amounts for which the certificate is furnished are effectively connected with the conduct of a trade or business in the United States and is includable in the beneficial owner's gross income for the taxable year. In the absence of a reliable claim that the income is effectively connected with the conduct of a trade or business in the United States, the income is presumed not to be effectively connected, except as otherwise provided in paragraph (a)(2)(ii) or (3) of this section. See § 1.1441-1(e)(4)(ii)(C) for the period of validity applicable to a certificate provided under this section and § 1.1441-1(e)(4)(ii)(D) for changes in circumstances arising during the taxable year indicating that the income to which the certificate relates is not, or is no longer expected to be, effectively connected with the conduct of a trade or business within the United States. A withholding certificate shall be effective only for the item or items of income specified therein. The provisions of § 1.1441-1(b)(3)(iv) dealing with a 90-day grace period shall apply for purposes of this section.

(ii) *Special rules for U.S. branches of foreign persons*—(A) *U.S. branches of certain foreign banks or foreign insurance companies.* A payment to a U.S. branch described in § 1.1441-1(b)(2)(iv)(A) is presumed to be effectively connected with the conduct of a trade or business in the United States without the need to furnish a certificate, unless the U.S. branch provides a U.S. branch withholding certificate described in § 1.1441-1(e)(3)(v) that represents otherwise. If no certificate is furnished but the income is not, in fact, effectively connected income, then the branch must withhold whether the payment is collected on behalf of other persons or on behalf of another branch of the same entity. See § 1.1441-1(b)(2)(iv) and (6) for general rules applicable to payments to U.S. branches of foreign persons.

(B) *Other U.S. branches.* See § 1.1441-1(b)(2)(iv)(E) for similar procedures for other U.S. branches to the extent provided in a determination letter from the district director or the Assistant Commissioner (International).

(3) *Income on notional principal contracts*—(i) *General rule.* A withholding agent that pays amounts attributable to a notional principal contract described in § 1.863-7(a) or 1.988-2(e) shall have no obligation to withhold on the amounts paid under the terms of the notional principal contract regardless of whether a withholding certificate is provided. However, a withholding agent must file returns under § 1.1461-1(b) and (c) reporting the income that it must treat as effectively connected with the conduct of a trade or business in the United States under the provisions of this paragraph (a)(3). Except as otherwise provided in paragraph (a)(3)(ii) of this section, a withholding agent must treat the income as effectively connected with the conduct of a U.S. trade or business if the income is paid to, or to the account of, a qualified business unit of a foreign person located in the United States or, if the payment is paid to, or to the account of, a qualified business unit of a foreign person located outside the United States, the withholding agent knows, or has reason to know, the payment is effectively connected with the conduct of a trade or business within the United States. Income on a notional principal contract does not include the amount characterized as interest under the provisions of § 1.446-3(g)(4).

(ii) *Exception for certain payments.* A payment shall not be treated as effectively connected with the conduct of a trade or business within the United States for purposes of paragraph (a)(3)(i) of this section even if no withholding certificate is furnished if the payee provides a representation in a master agreement that governs the transactions in notional principal contracts between the parties (for example an International Swaps and Derivatives Association (ISDA) Agreement, including the Schedule thereto) or in the confirmation on the particular notional principal contract transaction that the payee is a U.S. person or a non-U.S. branch of a foreign person.

(b) *Compensation for personal services of an individual*—(1) *Exemption from withholding.* Withholding is not required under § 1.1441-1 from salaries, wages, remuneration, or any other compensation for personal services of a nonresident alien individual if such compensation is effectively connected with the conduct of a trade or business within the United States and—

(i) Such compensation is subject to withholding under section 3402 (relating to withholding on wages) and the regulations under that section;

(ii) Such compensation would be subject to withholding under section 3402 but for the provisions of section 3401(a) (not including section 3401(a)(6)) and the regulations under that section. This paragraph (b)(1)(ii) does not apply to payments to a nonresident alien individual from any trust described in section 401(a), any annuity plan described in section 403(a), any annuity, custodial account, or retirement income account

Reg. § 1.1441-4(a)(3)

described in section 403(b), or an individual retirement account or individual retirement annuity described in section 408. Instead, these payments are subject to withholding under this section to the extent they are exempted from the definition of wages under section 3401(a)(12) or to the extent they are from an annuity, custodial account, or retirement income account described in section 403(b), or an individual retirement account or individual retirement annuity described in section 408. Thus, for example, payments to a nonresident alien individual from a trust described in section 401 (a) are subject to withholding under section 1441 and not under section 3405 or section 3406;

(iii) Such compensation is for services performed by a nonresident alien individual who is a resident of Canada or Mexico and who enters and leaves the United States at frequent intervals;

(iv) Such compensation is, or will be, exempt from the income tax imposed by chapter 1 of the Code by reason of a provision of the Internal Revenue Code or a tax treaty to which the United States is a party;

(v) Such compensation is paid after January 3, 1979 as a commission or rebate paid by a ship supplier to a nonresident alien individual, who is employed by a nonresident alien individual, foreign partnership, or foreign corporation in the operation of a ship or ships of foreign registry, for placing orders for supplies to be used in the operation of such ship or ships with the supplier. See section 162(c) and the regulations thereunder for denial of deductions for illegal bribes, kickbacks, and other payments; or

(vi) Compensation that is exempt from withholding under section 3402 by reason of section 3402(e), provided that the employee and his employer enter into an agreement under section 3402(p) to provide for the withholding of income tax upon payments of amounts described in § 31.3401(a)-3(b)(1) of this chapter. An employee who desires to enter into such an agreement should furnish his employer with Form W-4 (withholding exemption certificate) (or such other form as the Internal Revenue Service (IRS) may prescribe). See section 3402(f) and the regulations thereunder and § 31.3402(p)-1 of this chapter.

(2) *Manner of obtaining withholding exemption under tax treaty*—(i) *In general.* In order to obtain the exemption from withholding by reason of a tax treaty, provided by paragraph (b)(1)(iv) of this section, a nonresident alien individual must submit a withholding certificate (described in paragraph (b)(2)(ii) of this section) to each withholding agent from whom amounts are to be received. A separate withholding certificate must be filed for each taxable year of the alien individual. If the withholding agent is satisfied that an exemption from withholding is warranted (see paragraph (b)(2)(iii) of this section), the withholding certificate shall be accepted in the manner set forth in paragraph (b)(2)(iv) of this section. The exemption from withholding becomes effective for payments made at least ten days after a copy of the accepted withholding certificate is forwarded to the Assistant Commissioner (International). The withholding agent may rely on an accepted withholding certificate only if the IRS has not objected to the certificate. For purposes of this paragraph (b)(2)(i), the IRS will be considered to have not objected to the certificate if it has not notified the withholding agent within a 10-day period beginning from the date that the withholding certificate is forwarded to the IRS pursuant to paragraph (b)(2)(v) of this section. After expiration of the 10-day period, the withholding agent may rely on the withholding certificate retroactive to the date of the first payment covered by the certificate. The fact that the IRS does not object to the withholding certificate within the 10-day period provided in this paragraph (b)(2)(i) shall not preclude the IRS from examining the withholding agent at a later date in light of facts that the withholding agent knew or had reason to know regarding the payment and eligibility for a reduced rate and that were not disclosed to the IRS as part of the 10-day review process.

(ii) *Withholding certificate claiming withholding exemption.* The statement claiming an exemption from withholding shall be made on Form 8233 (or an acceptable substitute or such other form as the IRS may prescribe). Form 8233 shall be dated, signed by the beneficial owner under penalties of perjury, and contain the following information—

(A) The individual's name, permanent residence address, taxpayer identifying number (or a copy of a completed Form W-7 or SS-5 showing that a number has been applied for), and the U.S. visa number, if any;

(B) The individual's current immigration status and visa type;

(C) The individual's original date of entry into the United States;

(D) The country that issued the individual's passport and the number of such passport, or the individual's permanent address if a citizen of Canada or Mexico;

(E) The taxable year, for which the statement is to apply the compensation to which it relates, and the amount (or estimated amount if exact amount not known) of such compensation;

Reg. § 1.1441-4(b)(2)

(F) A statement that the individual is not a citizen or resident of the United States;

(G) The number of personal exemptions claimed by the individual;

(H) A statement as to whether the compensation to be paid to him or her during the taxable year is or will be exempt from income tax and the reason why the compensation is exempt;

(I) If the compensation is exempt from withholding by reason of an income tax treaty to which the United States is a party, the tax treaty and provision under which the exemption from withholding is claimed and the country of which the individual is a resident;

(J) Sufficient facts to justify the claim in exemption from withholding; and

(K) Any other information as may be required by the form or accompanying instructions in addition to, or in lieu of, the information described in this paragraph (b)(2)(ii).

(iii) *Review by withholding agent.* The exemption from withholding provided by paragraph (b)(1)(iv) of this section shall not apply unless the withholding agent accepts (in the manner provided in paragraph (b)(2)(iv) of this section) the statement on Form 8233 supplied by the nonresident alien individual. Before accepting the statement the withholding agent must examine the statement. If the withholding agent knows or has reason to know that any of the facts or assertions on Form 8233 may be false or that the eligibility of the individual's compensation for the exemption cannot be readily determined, the withholding agent may not accept the statement on Form 8233 and is required to withhold under this section. If the withholding agent accepts the statement and subsequently finds that any of the facts or assertions contained on Form 8233 may be false or that the eligibility of the individual's compensation for the exemption can no longer be readily determined, then the withholding agent shall promptly so notify the Assistant Commissioner (International) by letter, and the withholding agent is not relieved of liability to withhold on any amounts still to be paid. If the withholding agent is notified by the Assistant Commissioner (International) that the eligibility of the individual's compensation for the exemption is in doubt or that such compensation is not eligible for the exemption, the withholding agent is required to withhold under this section. The rules of this paragraph are illustrated by the following examples.

Example 1. C, a nonresident alien individual, submits Form 8233 to W, a withholding agent. The statement on Form 8233 does not include all the information required by paragraph (b)(2)(ii) of this section. Therefore, W has reason to know that he or she cannot readily determine whether C's compensation for personal services is eligible for an exemption from withholding and, therefore, W must withhold.

Example 2. D, a nonresident alien, is performing services for W, a withholding agent. W has accepted a statement on Form 8233 submitted by D, according to the provisions of this section. W receives notice from the Internal Revenue Service that the eligibility of D's compensation for a withholding exemption is in doubt. Therefore, W has reason to know that the eligibility of the compensation for a withholding exemption cannot be readily determined, as of the date W receives the notification, and W must withhold tax under section 1441 on amounts paid after receipt of the notification.

Example 3. E, a nonresident alien individual, submits Form 8233 to W, a withholding agent for whom E is to perform personal services. The statement contains all the information requested on Form 8233. E claims an exemption from withholding based on a personal exemption amount computed on the number of days E will perform personal services for W in the United States. If W does not know or have reason to know that any statement on the Form 8233 is false or that the eligibility of E's compensation for the withholding exemption cannot be readily determined, W can accept the statement on Form 8233 and exempt from withholding the appropriate amount of E's income.

(iv) *Acceptance by withholding agent.* If after the review described in paragraph (b)(2)(iii) of this section the withholding agent is satisfied that an exemption from withholding is warranted, the withholding agent may accept the statement by making a certification, verified by a declaration that it is made under the penalties of perjury, on Form 8233. The certification shall be—

(A) That the withholding agent has examined the statement,

(B) That the withholding agent is satisfied that an exemption from withholding is warranted, and

(C) That the withholding agent does not know or have reason to know that the individual's compensation is not entitled to the exemption or that the eligibility of the individual's compensation for the exemption cannot be readily determined.

(v) *Copies of Form 8233.* The withholding agent shall forward one copy of each Form 8233 that is accepted under paragraph (b)(2)(iv) of this section to the Assistant Commissioner (International), within five days of such acceptance. The

Reg. § 1.1441-4(b)(2)

withholding agent shall retain a copy of Form 8233.

(3) *Withholding agreements.* Compensation for personal services of a nonresident alien individual who is engaged during the taxable year in the conduct of a trade or business within the United States may be wholly or partially exempted from the withholding required by § 1.1441-1 if an agreement is reached between the Assistant Commissioner (International) and the alien individual with respect to the amount of withholding required. Such agreement shall be available in the circumstances and in the manner set forth by the Internal Revenue Service, and shall be effective for payments covered by the agreement that are made after the agreement is executed by all parties. The alien individual must agree to timely file an income tax return for the current taxable year.

(4) *Final payment exemption*—(i) *General rule.* Compensation for independent personal services of a nonresident alien individual who is engaged during the taxable year in the conduct of a trade or business within the United States may be wholly or partially exempted from the withholding required by § 1.1441-1 from the final payment of compensation for independent personal services. This exemption does not apply to wages. This exemption from withholding is available only once during an alien individual's taxable year and is obtained by the alien individual presenting to the withholding agent a letter in duplicate from a district director stating the amount of compensation subject to the exemption and the amount that would otherwise be withheld from such final payment under section 1441 that shall be paid to the alien individual due to the exemption. The alien individual shall attach a copy of the letter to his or her income tax return for the taxable year for which the exemption is effective.

(ii) *Final payment of compensation for personal services.* For purposes of this paragraph, final payment of compensation for personal services means the last payment of compensation, other than wages, for personal services rendered within the United States that the individual expects to receive from any withholding agent during the taxable year.

(iii) *Manner of applying for final payment exemption.* In order to obtain the final payment exemption provided by paragraph (b)(4)(i) of this section, the nonresident alien individual (or his or her agent) must file the forms and provide the information required by the district director. Ordinary and necessary business expenses may be taken into account if substantiated to the satisfaction of the district director. The alien individual must submit a statement, signed by him or her and verified by a declaration that it is made under the penalties of perjury, that all the information provided is true and that to his or her knowledge no relevant information has been omitted. The information required to be submitted includes, but is not limited to—

(A) A statement by each withholding agent from whom amounts of gross income effectively connected with the conduct of a trade or business within the United States have been received by the alien individual during the taxable year, of the amount of such income paid and the amount of tax withheld, signed and verified by a declaration that it is made under penalties of perjury;

(B) A statement by the withholding agent from whom the final payment of compensation for personal services will be received, of the amount of such final payment and the amount which would be withheld under § 1.1441-1 if a final payment exemption under paragraph (b)(4)(i) of this section is not granted, signed and verified by a declaration that it is made under penalties of perjury;

(C) A statement by the individual that he or she does not intend to receive any other amounts of gross income effectively connected with the conduct of a trade or business within the United States during the current taxable year;

(D) The amount of tax which has been withheld (or paid) under any other provision of the Code or regulations with respect to any income effectively connected with the conduct of a trade or business within the United States during the current taxable year;

(E) The amount of any outstanding tax liabilities (and interest and penalties relating thereto) from the current taxable year or prior taxable periods; and

(F) The provision of any income tax treaty under which a partial or complete exemption from withholding may be claimed, the country of the individual's residence, and a statement of sufficient facts to justify an exemption pursuant to such treaty.

(iv) *Letter to withholding agent.* If the district director is satisfied that the information provided under paragraph (b)(4)(iii) of this section is sufficient, the district director will, after coordination with the Director of the Foreign Operations District, ascertain the amount of the alien individual's tentative income tax for the taxable year with respect to gross income that is effectively connected with the conduct of a trade or business within the United States. After the tentative tax has been ascertained, the district

Reg. § 1.1441-4(b)(4)

director will provide the alien individual with a letter to the withholding agent stating the amount of the final payment of compensation for personal services that is exempt from withholding, and the amount that would otherwise be withheld under section 1441 that shall be paid to the alien individual due to the exemption. The amount of compensation for personal services exempt from withholding under this paragraph (b)(4) shall not exceed $5,000.

Example 1. On July 15, 1983, B, a nonresident alien individual, appears before a district director with the information required by paragraph (b)(4)(iii) of this section. B has received personal service income in 1983 from which $3,000 has been withheld under section 1441. On August 1, 1983, B will receive $5,000 in personal service income from W. B does not intend to receive any other income subject to U.S. tax during 1983. Taking into account B's substantiated deductible business expenses, the district director computes the tentative tax liability on B's income effectively connected with the conduct of a trade or business in the United States during 1983 (including the $5,000 payment to be made on August 1, 1983) to be $3,300. B does not owe U.S. tax for any other taxable periods. The amount of B's final payment exemption is determined as follows:

(1) The amount of total withholding is $4,500 ($3,000 previously withheld plus $1,500, 30% of the $5,000 final payment);

(2) The amount of tentative excess withholding is $1,200 (total withholding of $4,500 minus B's tentative tax liability of $3,300); and

(3) To allow B to receive $1,200 of the amount which would otherwise have been withheld from the final payment, the district director allows a withholding exemption for $4,000 of B's final payment. W must withhold $300 from the final payment.

Example 2. The facts are the same as in Example 1 except B will receive a final payment of compensation on August 1, 1983, in the amount of $10,000 and B's tentative tax liability is $3,900. The amount of B's final payment exemption is determined as follows:

(1) The amount of total withholding is $6,000 ($3,000 previously withheld plus $3,000, 30% of the $10,000 final payment);

(2) The amount of tentative excess withholding is $2,100 (total withholding of $6,000 minus B's tentative tax liability of $3,900); and

(3) To allow B to receive $2,100 of the amount which would otherwise be withheld from the final payment, $7,000 of the final payment would have to be exempt from withholding; however, as no more than $5,000 of the final payment can be exempt from withholding under this paragraph (b)(4), the district director allows a withholding exemption for $5,000 of B's final payment. B must file a claim for refund at the end of the taxable year to obtain a refund of $600. W must withhold $1,500 from the final payment.

(5) *Requirement of return.* The tentative tax determined by the district director under paragraph (b)(4)(iv) of this section or by the Director of the Foreign Operations District under the withholding agreement procedure of paragraph (b)(3) of this section shall not constitute a final determination of the income tax liability of the nonresident alien individual, nor shall such determination constitute a tax return of the nonresident alien individual for any taxable period. An alien individual who applies for or obtains an exemption from withholding under the procedures of paragraphs (b)(2), (3), or (4) of this section is not relieved of the obligation to file a return of income under section 6012.

(6) *Personal exemption*—(i) *In general.* To determine the tax to be withheld at source under § 1.1441-1 from remuneration paid for personal services performed within the United States by a nonresident alien individual and from scholarship and fellowship income described in paragraph (c) of this section, a withholding agent may take into account one personal exemption pursuant to sections 873(b)(3) and 151 regardless of whether the income is effectively connected. For purposes of withholding under section 1441 on remuneration for personal services, the exemption must be prorated upon a daily basis for the period during which the personal services are performed within the United States by the nonresident alien individual by dividing by 365 the number of days in the period during which the individual is present in the United States for the purpose of performing the services and multiplying the result by the amount of the personal exemption in effect for the taxable year. See § 31.3402(f)(6)-1 of this chapter.

(ii) *Multiple exemptions.* More than one personal exemption may be claimed in the case of a resident of a contiguous country or a national of the United States under section 873(b)(3). In addition, residents of a country with which the United States has an income tax treaty in effect may be eligible to claim more than one personal exemption if the treaty so provides. Claims for more than one personal exemption shall be made on the withholding certificate furnished to the withholding agent. The exemption must be prorated on a daily basis in the same manner as described in paragraph (b)(6)(i) of this section.

Reg. § 1.1441-4(b)(5)

(iii) *Special rule where both certain scholarship and compensation income are received.* The fact that both non-compensatory scholarship income and compensation income (including compensatory scholarship income) are received during the taxable year does not entitle the taxpayer to claim more than one personal exemption amount (or more than the additional amounts permitted under paragraph (b)(6)(ii) of this section). Thus, if a nonresident alien student receives non-compensatory taxable scholarship income from one withholding agent and compensation income from another withholding agent, no more than the total personal exemption amount permitted under the Internal Revenue Code or under an income tax treaty may be taken into account by both withholding agents. For this purpose, the withholding agent may rely on a representation from the beneficial owner that the exemption amount claimed does not exceed the amount permissible under this section.

(c) *Special rules for scholarship and fellowship income*—(1) *In general.* Under section 871(c), certain amounts paid as a scholarship or fellowship for study, training, or research in the United States to a nonresident alien individual temporarily present in the United States as a nonimmigrant under section 101(a)(15)(F), (J), (M), or (Q) of the Immigration and Nationality Act are treated as income effectively connected with the conduct of a trade or business within the United States. The amounts described in the preceding sentence are those amounts that do not represent compensation for services. Such amounts (as described in the second sentence of section 1441(b)) are subject to withholding under section 1441, but at the lower rate of 14 percent. That rate may be reduced under the provisions of an income tax treaty. Claims of a reduced rate under an income tax treaty shall be made under the procedures described in § 1.1441-6(b)(1). Therefore, claims for reduction in withholding under an income tax treaty on amounts described in this paragraph (c)(1) may not be made on a Form 8233. However, if the payee is receiving both compensation for personal services (including compensatory scholarship income) and non-compensatory scholarship income described in this paragraph (c)(1) from the same withholding agent, claims for reduction of withholding on both types of income may be made on Form 8233.

(2) *Alternate withholding election.* A withholding agent may elect to withhold on the amounts described in paragraph (c)(1) of this section at the rates applicable under section 3402, as if the income were wages. Such election shall be made by obtaining a Form W-4 (or an acceptable substitute or such other form as the IRS may prescribe) from the beneficial owner. The fact that the withholding agent asks the beneficial owner to furnish a Form W-4 for such fellowship or scholarship income or to take such income into account in preparing such Form W-4 shall serve as notice to the beneficial owner that the income is being treated as wages for purposes of withholding tax under section 1441.

(d) *Annuities received under qualified plans.* Withholding is not required under section § 1.1441-1 in the case of any amount received as an annuity if the amount is exempt from tax under section 871(f) and the regulations under that section. The withholding agent may exempt the payment from withholding if, prior to payment, it can reliably associate the payment with documentation upon which it can rely to treat the payment as made to a beneficial owner in accordance with § 1.1441-1(e)(1)(ii). A beneficial owner withholding certificate furnished for purposes of claiming the benefits of the exemption under this paragraph (d) is valid only if, in addition to other applicable requirements, it contains a taxpayer identifying number.

(e) *Per diem of certain alien trainees.* Withholding is not required under section 1441(a) and § 1.1441-1 on per diem amounts paid for subsistence by the United States Government (directly or by contract) to any nonresident alien individual who is engaged in any program of training in the United States under the Mutual Security Act of 1954, as amended (22 U.S.C. chapter 24). This rule shall apply even though such amounts are subject to tax under section 871. Any exemption from withholding pursuant to this paragraph (e) applies without a requirement that documentation be furnished to the withholding agent. However, documentation may have to be furnished for purposes of the information reporting provisions under section 6041 and backup withholding under section 3406. The exemption from withholding granted by this paragraph (e) is not a determination that the amounts are not fixed or determinable annual or periodical income.

(f) *Failure to receive withholding certificates timely or to act in accordance with applicable presumptions.* See applicable procedures described in § 1.1441-1(b)(7) in the event the withholding agent does not hold an appropriate withholding certificate or other appropriate documentation at the time of payment or does not act in accordance with applicable presumptions described in paragraph (a)(2)(i), (2)(ii), or (3) of this section.

(g) *Effective date*—(1) *General rule.* This section applies to payments made after December 31, 2000.

Reg. § 1.1441-4(g)(1)

(2) *Transition rules.* The validity of a Form 4224 or 8233 that was valid on January 1, 1998, under the regulations in effect prior to January 1, 2001 (see 26 CFR part 1, revised April 1, 1999) and expired, or will expire, at any time during 1998, is extended until December 31, 1998. The validity of a Form 4224 or 8233 that is valid on or after January 1, 1999, remains valid until its validity expires under the regulations in effect prior to January 1, 2001 (see 26 CFR part 1, revised April 1, 1999) but in no event will such form remain valid after December 31, 2000. The rule in this paragraph (g)(2), however, does not apply to extend the validity period of a Form 4224 or 8223 that expires solely by reason of changes in the circumstances of the person whose name is on the certificate. Notwithstanding the first three sentences of this paragraph (g)(2), a withholding agent may choose to not take advantage of the transition rule in this paragraph (g)(2) with respect to one or more withholding certificates valid under the regulations in effect prior to January 1, 2001 (see 26 CFR part 1, revised April 1, 1999) and, therefore, to require withholding certificates conforming to the requirements described in this section (new withholding certificates). For purposes of this section, a new withholding certificate is deemed to satisfy the documentation requirement under the regulations in effect prior to January 1, 2001 (see 26 CFR part 1, revised April 1, 1999). Further, a new withholding certificate remains valid for the period specified in § 1.1441-1(e)(4)(ii), regardless of when the certificate is obtained. [Reg. § 1.1441-4.]

☐ [T.D. 6187, 7-5-56. Amended by T.D. 6229, 4-22-57; T.D. 6592, 2-27-62; T.D. 6908, 12-30-66; T.D. 6922, 6-16-67; T.D. 7378, 9-29-75; T.D. 7582, 1-2-79; T.D. 7777, 5-18-81; T.D. 7842, 11-2-82; T.D. 7977, 9-19-84; T.D. 8015, 3-25-85; T.D. 8288, 2-2-90; T.D. 8734, 10-6-97; T.D. 8804, 12-30-98; T.D. 8856, 12-29-99 and T.D. 8881, 5-15-2000.]

[Reg. § 1.1441-5]

§ 1.1441-5. **Withholding on payments to partnerships, trusts, and estates.**—(a) *In general.* This section describes the rules that apply to payments made to partnerships, trusts, and estates. Paragraph (b) of this section prescribes the rules that apply to a withholding agent making a payment to a U.S. partnership, trust, or estate. It also prescribes the obligations of a U.S. partnership, trust, or estate that makes a payment to a foreign partner, beneficiary, or owner. Paragraph (c) of this section prescribes rules that apply to a withholding agent that makes a payment to a foreign partnership. Paragraph (d) of this section provides presumption rules that apply to payments made to foreign partnerships. Paragraph (e) of this section prescribes rules, including presumption rules, that apply to a withholding agent that makes a payment to a foreign trust or foreign estate.

(b) *Rules applicable to U.S. partnerships, trusts, and estates*—(1) *Payments to U.S. partnerships, trusts, and estates.* No withholding is required under section 1.1441-1(b)(1) on a payment of an amount subject to withholding (as defined in § 1.1441-2(a)) that a withholding agent may treat as made to a U.S. payee. Therefore, if a withholding agent can reliably associate (within the meaning of § 1.1441-2(b)(vii)) a Form W-9 provided in accordance with § 1.1441-1(d)(2) or (4) by a U.S. partnership, U.S. trust, or a U.S. estate the withholding agent may treat the payment as made to a U.S. payee and the payment is not subject to withholding under section 1441 even though the partnership, trust, or estate may have foreign partners, beneficiaries, or owners. A withholding agent is also not required to withhold under section 1441 on a payment it makes to an entity presumed to be a U.S. payee under paragraphs (d)(2) and (e)(6)(ii) of this section.

(2) *Withholding by U.S. payees*—(i) *U.S. partnerships*—(A) *In general.* A U.S. partnership is required to withhold under § 1.1441-1 as a withholding agent on an amount subject to withholding (as defined in § 1.1441-2(a)) that is includible in the gross income of a partner that is a foreign person. Subject to paragraph (b)(2)(v) of this section, a U.S. partnership shall withhold when any distributions that include amounts subject to withholding (including guaranteed payments made by a U.S. partnership) are made. To the extent a foreign partner's distributive share of income subject to withholding has not actually been distributed to the foreign partner, the U.S. partnership must withhold on the foreign partner's distributive share of the income on the earlier of the date that the statement required under section 6031(b) is mailed or otherwise provided to the partner or the due date for furnishing the statement.

(B) *Effectively connected income of partners.* Withholding on items of income that are effectively connected income in the hands of the partners who are foreign persons is governed by section 1446 and not by this section. In such a case, partners in a domestic partnership are not required to furnish a withholding certificate in order to claim an exemption from withholding under section 1441(c)(1) and § 1.1441-4.

(ii) *U.S. simple trusts.* A U.S. trust that is described in section 651(a) (a U.S. simple trust) is required to withhold under chapter 3 of the Internal Revenue Code as a withholding agent on the distributable net income includible in the gross income of a foreign beneficiary to the extent the distributable net income is an amount subject to withholding (as defined in § 1.1441-2(a)). A U.S. simple trust shall withhold when a distribution is made to a foreign beneficiary. The U.S. trust may make a reasonable estimate of the portion of the distribution that constitutes distributable net income consisting of an amount subject to withholding and apply the appropriate rate of withholding to the estimated amount. If, at the end of the taxable year in which the distribution is made, the U.S. simple trust determines that it underwithheld under section 1441 or 1442, the trust shall be liable as a withholding agent for the amount under withheld under section 1461. No penalties shall be imposed for failure to withhold and deposit the tax if the U.S. simple trust's estimate was reasonable and the trust pays the underwithheld amount on or before the due date of Form 1042 under section 1461. Any payment of underwithheld amounts by the U.S. simple trust shall not be treated as income subject to additional withholding even if that amount is treated as additional income to the foreign beneficiary, unless the additional amount is income to the foreign beneficiary as a result of a contractual arrangement between the parties regarding the satisfaction of the foreign beneficiary's tax liability. To the extent a U.S. simple trust is required to, but does not, distribute such income to a foreign beneficiary, the U.S. trust must withhold on the foreign beneficiary's allocable share at the time the income is required (without extension) to be reported on Form 1042-S under § 1.1461-1(c).

(iii) *U.S. complex trusts and U.S. estates.* A U.S. trust that is not a trust described in section 651(a) (a U.S. complex trust) is required to withhold under chapter 3 of the Internal Revenue Code as a withholding agent on the distributable net income includible in the gross income of a foreign beneficiary to the extent the distributable net income consists of an amount subject to withholding (as defined in § 1.1441-2(a)) that is, or is required to be, distributed currently. The U.S. complex trust shall withhold when a distribution is made to a foreign beneficiary. The trust may use the same procedures regarding an estimate of the amount subject to withholding as a U.S. simple trust under paragraph (b)(2)(ii) of this section. To the extent an amount subject to withholding is required to be, but is not actually distributed, the U.S. complex trust must withhold on the foreign beneficiary's allocable share at the time the income is required to be reported on Form 1042-S under § 1.1461-1(c), without extension. A U.S. estate is required to withhold under chapter 3 of the Internal Revenue Code on the distributable net income includible in the gross income of a foreign beneficiary to the extent the distributable net income consists of an amount subject to withholding (as defined in § 1.1441-2(a)) that is actually distributed. A U.S. estate may also use the reasonable estimate procedures of paragraph (b)(2)(ii) of this section. However, those procedures apply to an estate that has a taxable year other than a calendar year only if the estate files an amended return on Form 1042 for the calendar year in which the distribution was made and pays the underwithheld tax and interest within 60 days after the close of the taxable year in which the distribution was made.

(iv) *U.S. grantor trusts.* A U.S. trust that is described in section 671 through 679 (a U.S. grantor trust) must withhold on any income includible in the gross income of a foreign person that is treated as an owner of the grantor trust to the extent the amount includible consists of an amount that is subject to withholding (as described in § 1.1441-2(a)). The withholding must occur at the time the income is received by, or credited to, the trust.

(v) *Subsequent distribution.* If a U.S. partnership or U.S. trust withholds on a foreign partner, beneficiary, or owner's share of an amount subject to withholding before the amount is actually distributed to the partner, beneficiary, or owner, withholding is not required when the amount is subsequently distributed.

(c) *Foreign partnerships*—(1) *Determination of payee*—(i) *Payments treated as made to partners.* Except as otherwise provided in paragraph (c)(1)(ii) of this section, the payees of a payment to a person that the withholding agent may treat as a nonwithholding foreign partnership under paragraph (c)(3)(i) or (d)(2) of this section are the partners (looking through partners that are foreign intermediaries or flow-through entities) as follows—

(A) If the withholding agent can reliably associate a partner's distributive share of the payment with a valid Form W-9 provided under § 1.1441-1 (d), the partner is a U.S. payee;

(B) If the withholding agent can reliably associate a partner's distributive share of the payment with a valid Form W-8, or other appropriate documentation, provided under § 1.1441-1 (e)(1)(ii), the partner is a payee that is a foreign beneficial owner;

(C) If the withholding agent can reliably associate a partner's distributive share of the payment with a qualified intermediary withholding certificate under § 1.1441-1(e)(3)(ii), a nonquali-

Reg. § 1.1441-5(c)(1)

fied intermediary withholding certificate under § 1.1441-1(e)(3)(iii), or a U.S. branch certificate under § 1.1441-1(e)(3)(v), then the rules of § 1.1441-1(b)(2)(v) shall apply to determine who the payee is in the same manner as if the partner's distributive share of the payment had been paid directly to such intermediary or U.S. branch;

(D) If the withholding agent can reliably associate the partner's distributive share with a withholding foreign partnership certificate under paragraph (c)(2)(iv) of this section or a nonwithholding foreign partnership certificate under paragraph (c)(3)(iii) of this section, then the rules of this paragraph (c)(1)(i) or paragraph (c)(1)(ii) of this section shall apply to determine whether the payment is treated as made to the partners of the higher-tier partnership under this paragraph (c)(1)(i) or to the higher-tier partnership itself (under the rules of paragraph (c)(1)(ii) of this section) in the same manner as if the partner's distributive share of the payment had been paid directly to the higher-tier foreign partnership;

(E) If the withholding agent can reliably associate the partner's distributive share with a withholding certificate described in paragraph (e) of this section regarding a foreign trust or estate, then the rules of paragraph (e) of this section shall apply to determine who the payees are; and

(F) If the withholding agent cannot reliably associate the partner's distributive share with a withholding certificate or other appropriate documentation, the partners are considered to be the payees and the presumptions described in paragraph (d)(3) of this section shall apply to determine their classification and status.

(ii) *Payments treated as made to the partnership.* A payment to a person that the withholding agent may treat as a foreign partnership is treated as a payment to the foreign partnership and not to its partners only if—

(A) The withholding agent can reliably associate the payment with a withholding certificate described in paragraph (c)(2)(iv) of this section (withholding certificate of a withholding foreign partnership);

(B) The withholding agent can reliably associate the payment with a withholding certificate described in paragraph (c)(3)(iii) of this section (nonwithholding foreign partnership) certifying that the payment is income that is effectively connected with the conduct of a trade or business in the United States; or

(C) The withholding agent can treat the income as effectively connected income under the presumption rules of § 1.1441-4(a)(2)(ii) or (3)(i).

(iii) *Rules for reliably associating a payment with documentation.* For rules regarding the reliable association of a payment with documentation, see § 1.1441-1(b)(2)(vii). In the absence of documentation, see §§ 1.1441-1(b)(3) and 1.6049-5(d) and paragraphs (d) and (e)(6) of this section for applicable presumptions.

(iv) *Examples.* The rules of paragraphs (c)(1)(i) and (ii) of this section are illustrated by the following examples:

Example 1. FP is a nonwithholding foreign partnership organized in Country X. FP has two partners, FC, a foreign corporation, and USP, a U.S. partnership. USWH, a U.S. withholding agent, makes a payment of U.S. source interest to FP. FP has provided USWH with a valid nonwithholding foreign partnership certificate, as described in paragraph (c)(3)(iii) of this section, with which it associates a beneficial owner withholding certificate from FC and a Form W-9 from USP together with the withholding statement required by paragraph (c)(3)(iv) of this section. USWH can reliably associate the payment of interest with the withholding certificates from FC and USP. Under paragraph (c)(1)(i) of this section, the payees of the interest payment are FC and USP.

Example 2. The facts are the same as in Example 1, except that FP1, a nonwithholding foreign partnership, is a partner in FP rather than USP. FP1 has two partners, A and B, both foreign persons. FP provides USWH with a valid nonwithholding foreign partnership certificate, as described in paragraph (c)(3)(iii) of this section, with which it associates a beneficial owner withholding certificate from FC and a nonwithholding foreign partnership certificate from FP1. In addition, foreign beneficial owner withholding certificates from A and B are associated with the nonwithholding foreign partnership withholding certificate from FP1. FP also provides the withholding statement required by paragraph (c)(3)(iv) of this section. USWH can reliably associate the interest payment with the withholding certificates provided by FC, A, and B. Therefore, under paragraph (c)(1)(i) of this section, the payees of the interest payment are FC, A, and B.

Example 3. USWH makes a payment of U.S. source dividends to WFP, a withholding foreign partnership. WFP has two partners, FC1 and FC2, both foreign corporations. USWH can reliably associate the payment with a valid withholding foreign partnership withholding certificate from WFP. Therefore, under paragraph(c)(1)(ii)(A) of this section, WFP is the payee of the dividends.

Reg. § 1.1441-5(c)(1)

Example 4. USWH makes a payment of U.S. source royalties to FP, a foreign partnership. USWH can reliably associate the royalties with a valid withholding certificate from FP on which FP certifies that the income is effectively connected with the conduct of a trade or business in the United States. Therefore, under paragraph (c)(1)(ii)(B) of this section, FP is the payee of the royalties.

(2) *Withholding foreign partnerships*—(i) *Reliance on claim of withholding foreign partnership status.* A withholding foreign partnership is a foreign partnership that has entered into an agreement with the Internal Revenue Service (IRS), as described in paragraph (c)(2)(ii) of this section, with respect to distributions and guaranteed payments it makes to its partners. A withholding agent that can reliably associate a payment with a certificate described in paragraph (c)(2)(iv) of this section may treat the person to whom it makes the payment as a withholding foreign partnership for purposes of withholding under chapter 3 of the Internal Revenue Code, information reporting under chapter 61 of the Internal Revenue Code, backup withholding under section 3406, and withholding under other provisions of the Internal Revenue Code. Furnishing such a certificate is in lieu of transmitting to a withholding agent withholding certificates or other appropriate documentation for its partners. Although the withholding foreign partnership generally will be required to obtain withholding certificates or other appropriate documentation from its partners pursuant to its agreement with the IRS, it will generally not be required to attach such documentation to its withholding foreign partnership withholding certificate. A foreign partnership may act as a qualified intermediary under § 1.1441-1(e)(5) with respect to payments it makes to persons other than its partners. In addition, the IRS may permit a foreign partnership to act as a qualified intermediary under § 1.1441-1(e)(5)(ii)(D) with respect to its partners in appropriate circumstances.

(ii) *Withholding agreement.* The IRS may, upon request, enter into a withholding agreement with a foreign partnership pursuant to such procedures as the IRS may prescribe in published guidance (see § 601.601(d)(2) of this chapter). Under the withholding agreement, a foreign partnership shall generally be subject to the applicable withholding and reporting provisions applicable to withholding agents and payors under chapters 3 and 61 of the Internal Revenue Code, section 3406, the regulations under those provisions, and other withholding provisions of the Internal Revenue Code, except to the extent provided under the agreement. Under the agreement, a foreign partnership may agree to act as an acceptance agent to perform the duties described in § 301.6109-1(d)(3)(iv)(A) of this chapter. The agreement may specify the manner in which applicable procedures for adjustments for underwithholding and overwithholding, including refund procedures, apply to the withholding foreign partnership and its partners and the extent to which applicable procedures may be modified. In particular, a withholding agreement may allow a withholding foreign partnership to claim refunds of overwithheld amounts on behalf of its customers. In addition, the agreement must specify the manner in which the IRS will audit the foreign partnership's books and records in order to verify the partnership's compliance with its agreement. A withholding foreign partnership must file a return on Form 1042 and information returns on Form 1042-S. The withholding foreign partnership agreement may also require a withholding foreign partnership to file a partnership return under section 6031(a) and partner statements under 6031(b).

(iii) *Withholding responsibility.* A withholding foreign partnership must assume primary withholding responsibility under chapter 3 of the Internal Revenue Code. It is not required to provide information to the withholding agent regarding each partner's distributive share of the payment. The withholding foreign partnership will be responsible for reporting the payments under § 1.1461-1(c) and chapter 61 of the Internal Revenue Code. A withholding agent making a payment to a withholding foreign partnership is not required to withhold any amount under chapter 3 of the Internal Revenue Code on a payment to the withholding foreign partnership, unless it has actual knowledge or reason to know that the foreign partnership is not a withholding foreign partnership. The withholding foreign partnership shall withhold the payments under the same procedures and at the same time as prescribed for withholding by a U.S. partnership under paragraph (b)(2) of this section, except that, for purposes of determining the partner's status, the provisions of paragraph (d)(4) of this section shall apply.

(iv) *Withholding certificate from a withholding foreign partnership.* The rules of § 1.1441-1(e)(4) shall apply to withholding certificates described in this paragraph (c)(2)(iv). A withholding certificate furnished by a withholding foreign partnership is valid with regard to any partner on whose behalf the certificate is furnished only if it is furnished on a Form W-8, an acceptable substitute form, or such other form as the IRS may prescribe, it is signed under penalties of perjury by a partner with authority to sign

Reg. § 1.1441-5(c)(2)

for the partnership, its validity has not expired, and it contains the information, statement, and certifications described in this paragraph (c)(2)(iv) as follows—

(A) The name, permanent residence address (as described in § 1.1441-1(e)(2)(ii)), and the employer identification number of the partnership, and the country under the laws of which the partnership is created or governed;

(B) A certification that the partnership is a withholding foreign partnership within the meaning of paragraph (c)(2)(i) of this section; and

(C) Any other information, certifications or statements as may be required by the withholding foreign partnership agreement with the IRS or the form or accompanying instructions in addition to, or in lieu of, the information, statements, and certifications described in this paragraph (c)(2)(iv).

(3) *Nonwithholding foreign partnerships*—(i) *Reliance on claim of foreign partnership status.* A withholding agent may treat a person as a nonwithholding foreign partnership if it receives from that person a nonwithholding foreign partnership withholding certificate as described in paragraph (c)(3)(iii) of this section. A withholding agent that does not receive a nonwithholding foreign partnership withholding certificate, or does not receive a valid withholding certificate, from an entity it knows, or has reason to know, is a foreign partnership, must apply the presumption rules of §§ 1.1441-1(b)(3) and 1.6049-5(d) and paragraphs (d) and (e)(6) of this section. In addition, to the extent a withholding agent cannot, prior to a payment, reliably associate the payment with valid documentation from a payee that is associated with the nonwithholding foreign partnership withholding certificate or has insufficient information to report the payment on Form 1042-S or Form 1099, to the extent reporting is required, must also apply the presumption rules. See § 1.1441-1(b)(2)(vii)(A) and (B) for rules regarding reliable association. See paragraph (c)(3)(iv) of this section and § 1.1441-1(e)(3)(iv) for alternative procedures permitting allocation information to be received after a payment is made.

(ii) *Reliance on claim of reduced withholding by a partnership for its partners.* This paragraph (c)(3)(ii) describes the manner in which a withholding agent may rely on a claim of reduced withholding when making a payment to a nonwithholding foreign partnership. To the extent that a withholding agent treats a payment to a nonwithholding foreign partnership as a payment to the nonwithholding foreign partnership's partners (whether direct or indirect) in accordance with paragraph (c)(1)(i) of this section, it may rely on a claim for reduced withholding by the partner if, prior to the payment, the withholding agent can reliably associate the payment (within the meaning of § 1.1441-1(b)(2)(vii)) with a valid withholding certificate or other appropriate documentation from the partner that establishes entitlement to a reduced rate of withholding. A withholding certificate or other appropriate documentation that establishes entitlement to a reduced rate of withholding is a beneficial owner withholding certificate described in § 1.1441-1(e)(2)(i), documentary evidence described in § 1.1441-6(c)(3) or (4) or 1.6049-5(c)(1) (for a partner claiming to be a foreign person and a beneficial owner, determined under the provisions of § 1.1441-1(c)(6)), a Form W-9 described in § 1.1441-1(d) (for a partner claiming to be a U.S. payee), or a withholding foreign partnership withholding certificate described in paragraph (c)(2)(iv) of this section. Unless a nonwithholding foreign partnership withholding certificate is provided for income claimed to be effectively connected with the conduct of a trade or business in the United States, a claim must be presented for each portion of the payment that represents an item of income includible in the distributive share of a partner as required under paragraph (c)(3)(iii)(C) of this section. When making a claim for several partners, the partnership may present a single nonwithholding foreign partnership withholding certificate to which the partners' certificates or other appropriate documentation are associated. Where the nonwithholding foreign partnership withholding certificate is provided for income claimed to be effectively connected with the conduct of a trade or business in the United States under paragraph (c)(3)(iii)(D) of this section, the claim may be presented without having to identify any partner's distributive share of the payment.

(iii) *Withholding certificate from a nonwithholding foreign partnership.* A nonwithholding foreign partnership shall provide a nonwithholding foreign partnership withholding certificate with respect to reportable amounts received by the nonwithholding foreign partnership. A nonwithholding foreign partnership withholding certificate is valid only to the extent it is furnished on a Form W-8 (or an acceptable substitute form or such other form as the IRS may prescribe), it is signed under penalties of perjury by a partner with authority to sign for the partnership, its validity has not expired, and it contains the information, statements, and certifications described in this paragraph (c)(3)(iii) and paragraph (c)(3)(iv) of this section, and the withholding certificates and other appro-

Reg. § 1.1441-5(c)(3)

priate documentation for all the persons to whom the certificate relates are associated with the certificate. The rules of § 1.1441-1(e)(4) shall apply to withholding certificates described in this paragraph (c)(3)(iii). No withholding certificates or other appropriate documentation from persons who derive income through a partnership (whether or not U.S. exempt recipients) are required to be associated with the nonwithholding foreign partnership withholding certificate if the certificate is furnished solely for income claimed to be effectively connected with the conduct of a trade or business in the United States. Withholding certificates and other appropriate documentation that may be associated with the nonwithholding foreign partnership withholding certificate consist of beneficial owner withholding certificates under § 1.1441-1(e)(2)(i), intermediary withholding certificates under § 1.1441-1(e)(3)(i), withholding foreign partnership withholding certificates under paragraph (c)(2)(iv) of this section, nonwithholding foreign partnership withholding certificates under this paragraph (c)(3)(iii), withholding certificates from foreign trusts or estates under paragraph (e) of this section, documentary evidence described in § 1.1441-6(c)(3) or (4) or documentary evidence described in § 1.6049-5(c)(1), and any other documentation or certificates applicable under other provisions of the Internal Revenue Code or regulations that certify or establish the status of the payee or beneficial owner as a U.S. or a foreign person. Nothing in this paragraph (c)(3)(iii) shall require a nonwithholding foreign partnership to furnish original documentation. Copies of certificates or documentary evidence may be transmitted to the U.S. withholding agent, in which case the nonwithholding foreign partnership must retain the original documentation for the same time period that the copy is required to be retained by the withholding agent under § 1.1441-1(e)(4)(iii) and must provide it to the withholding agent upon request. The information, statement, and certifications required on the withholding certificate are as follows—

(A) The name, permanent residence address (as described in § 1.1441-1(e)(2)(ii)), and the employer identification number of the partnership, if any, and the country under the laws of which the partnership is created or governed;

(B) A certification that the person whose name is on the certificate is a foreign partnership;

(C) A withholding statement associated with the nonwithholding foreign partnership withholding certificate that provides all of the information required by paragraph (c)(3)(iv) of this section and § 1.1441-1(e)(3)(iv). No withholding statement is required, however, for a nonwithholding foreign partnership withholding certificate furnished for income claimed to be effectively connected with the conduct of a trade or business in the United States;

(D) A certification that the income is effectively connected with the conduct of a trade or business in the United States, if applicable; and

(E) Any other information, certifications, or statements required by the form or accompanying instructions in addition to, or in lieu of, the information and certifications described in this paragraph (c)(3)(iii).

(iv) *Withholding statement provided by nonwithholding foreign partnership.* The provisions of § 1.1441-1(e)(3)(iv) (regarding a withholding statement) shall apply to a nonwithholding foreign partnership by substituting the term nonwithholding foreign partnership for the term nonqualified intermediary.

(v) *Withholding and reporting by a foreign partnership.* A nonwithholding foreign partnership described in this paragraph (c)(3) that receives an amount subject to withholding (as defined in § 1.1441-2(a)) shall be required to withhold and report such payment under chapter 3 of the Internal Revenue Code and the regulations thereunder except as otherwise provided in this paragraph (c)(3)(v). A nonwithholding foreign partnership shall not be required to withhold and report if it has provided a valid nonwithholding foreign partnership withholding certificate, it has provided all of the information required by paragraph (c)(3)(iv) of this section (withholding statement), and it does not know, and has no reason to know, that another withholding agent failed to withhold the correct amount or failed to report the payment correctly under § 1.1461-1(c). A withholding foreign partnership's obligations to withhold and report shall be determined in accordance with its withholding foreign partnership agreement.

(d) *Presumption rules*—(1) *In general.* This paragraph (d) contains the applicable presumptions for a withholding agent (including a partnership) to determine the classification and status of a partnership and its partners in the absence of documentation. The provisions of § 1.1441-1(b)(3)(iv) (regarding the 90-day grace period) and § 1.1441-1(b)(3)(vii) through (ix) shall apply for purposes of this paragraph (d).

(2) *Determination of partnership status as U.S. or foreign in the absence of documentation.* In the absence of a valid representation of U.S. partnership status in accordance with paragraph (b)(1) of this section or of foreign partnership status in accordance with paragraph (c)(2)(i) or

Reg. § 1.1441-5(d)(2)

(3)(i) of this section, the withholding agent shall determine the classification of the payee under the presumptions set forth in § 1.1441-1(b)(3)(ii). If the withholding agent treats the payee as a partnership under § 1.1441-1(b)(3)(ii), the withholding agent shall presume the partnership to be a U.S. partnership unless there are indicia of foreign status. If there are indicia of foreign status, the withholding agent may presume the partnership to be foreign. Indicia of foreign status exist only if the withholding agent has actual knowledge of the payee's employer identification number and that number begins with the two digits "98," the withholding agent's communications with the payee are mailed to an address in a foreign country, or the payment is made outside the United States (as defined in § 1.6049-5(e)). For rules regarding reliable association with a withholding certificate from a domestic or a foreign partnership, see § 1.1441-1(b)(2)(vii).

(3) *Determination of partners' status in the absence of certain documentation.* If a nonwithholding foreign partnership has provided a nonwithholding foreign partnership withholding certificate under paragraph (c)(3)(iii) of this section that would be valid except that the withholding agent cannot reliably associate all or a portion of the payment with valid documentation from a partner of the partnership, then the withholding agent may apply the presumption rule of this paragraph (d)(3) with respect to all or a portion of the payment for which documentation has not been received. See § 1.1441-1(b)(2)(vii)(A) and (B) for rules regarding reliable association. The presumption rule of this paragraph (d)(3) also applies to a person that is presumed to be a foreign partnership under the rule of paragraph (d)(2) of this section. Any portion of a payment that the withholding agent cannot treat as reliably associated with valid documentation from a partner may be presumed made to a foreign payee. As a result, any payment of an amount subject to withholding is subject to withholding at a rate of 30 percent. Any payment that is presumed to be made to an undocumented foreign payee must be reported on Form 1042-S. See § 1.1461-1(c).

(4) *Determination by a withholding foreign partnership of the status of its partners.* A withholding foreign partnership shall determine whether the partners or some other persons are the payees of the partners' distributive shares of any payment made by a withholding foreign partnership by applying the rules of § 1.1441-1(b)(2), paragraph (c)(1) of this section (in the case of a partner that is a foreign partnership), and paragraph (e)(3) of this section (in the case of a partner that is a foreign estate or a foreign trust). Further, the provisions of paragraph (d)(3) of this section shall apply to determine the status of partners and the applicable withholding rates to the extent that, at the time the foreign partnership is required to withhold on a payment, it cannot reliably associate the amount with documentation for any one or more of its partners.

(e) *Foreign trusts and estates*—(1) *In general.* This paragraph (e) provides rules applicable to payments of amounts subject to withholding (as defined in § 1.1441-2(a)) that a withholding agent may treat as made to any foreign trust or a foreign estate. For rules relating to payments to a U.S. trust or a U.S. estate, see paragraph (b) of this section. For the definitions of foreign simple trust, foreign complex trust, and foreign grantor trust, see § 1.1441-1(c)(24), (25), and (26).

(2) *Payments to foreign complex trusts and foreign estates.* Under § 1.1441-1(c)(6)(ii)(D), a foreign complex trust or foreign estate is generally considered to be the beneficial owner of income paid to the foreign complex trust or foreign estate. See paragraph (e)(4) of this section for rules describing when a withholding agent may treat a payment as made to a foreign complex trust or a foreign estate.

(3) *Payees of payments to foreign simple trusts and foreign grantor trusts*—(i) *Payments for which beneficiaries and owners are payees.* For purposes of the regulations under chapters 3 and 61 of the Internal Revenue Code and section 3406, a foreign simple trust is not a beneficial owner or a payee of a payment. Also, a foreign grantor trust (or a portion of a trust that is a foreign grantor trust) is not considered a beneficial owner or a payee of a payment. Except as otherwise provided in paragraph (e)(3)(ii) of this section, the payees of a payment made to a person that the withholding agent may treat as a foreign simple trust or a foreign grantor trust (or a portion of a trust that is a foreign grantor trust) are determined under the rules of this paragraph (e)(3)(i). The payees shall be treated as the beneficial owners if they may be so treated under § 1.1441-1(c)(6)(ii)(C) and they provide documentation supporting their status as the beneficial owners. The payees of a payment to a foreign simple trust or foreign grantor trust are determined as follows—

(A) If the withholding agent can reliably associate a payment with a valid Form W-9 provided under § 1.1441-1(d) from a beneficiary or owner of the foreign trust, then the beneficiary or owner is a U.S. payee;

(B) If the withholding agent can reliably associate a payment with a valid Form W-8, or other appropriate documentation, provided under § 1.1441-1(e)(1)(ii) from a beneficiary or owner of

Reg. § 1.1441-5(d)(3)

the foreign trust, then the beneficiary or owner is a payee that is a foreign beneficial owner;

(C) If the withholding agent can reliably associate a payment with a qualified intermediary withholding certificate under § 1.1441-1(e)(3)(ii), a nonqualified intermediary withholding certificate under § 1.1441-1(e)(3)(ii), or a U.S. branch withholding certificate under § 1.1441-1(e)(3)(v), then the rules of § 1.1441-1(b)(2)(v) shall apply to determine the payee in the same manner as if the payment had been paid directly to such intermediary or U.S. branch;

(D) If the withholding agent can reliably associate a payment with a withholding foreign partnership withholding certificate under paragraph (c)(2)(iv) of this section or a nonwithholding foreign partnership withholding certificate under paragraph (c)(3)(iii) of this section, then the rules of paragraph (c)(1)(i) or (ii) of this section shall apply to determine the payee;

(E) If the withholding agent can reliably associate the payment with a foreign simple trust withholding certificate or a foreign grantor trust withholding certificate (both described in paragraph (e)(5)(iii) of this section) from a second or higher-tier foreign simple trust or foreign grantor trust, then the rules of this paragraph (e)(3)(i) or paragraph (e)(3)(ii) of this section shall apply to determine whether the payment is treated as made to a beneficiary or owner of the higher-tier trust or to the trust itself in the same manner as if the payment had been made directly to the higher-tier trust; and

(F) If the withholding agent cannot reliably associate a payment with a withholding certificate or other appropriate documentation, the payees shall be determined by applying the presumptions described in paragraph (e)(6) of this section.

(ii) *Payments for which trust is payee.* A payment to a person that the withholding agent may treat as made to a foreign trust under paragraph (e)(5)(iii) of this section is treated as a payment to the trust, and not to a beneficiary of the trust, only if—

(A) The withholding agent can reliably associate the payment with a foreign complex trust withholding certificate under paragraph (e)(4) of this section;

(B) The withholding agent can reliably associate the payment with a foreign simple trust withholding certificate under paragraph (e)(5)(iii) of this section certifying that the payment is income that is treated as effectively connected with the conduct of a trade or business in the United States; or

(C) The withholding agent can treat the income as effectively connected income under the presumption rules of § 1.1441-4(a)(3)(i).

(4) *Reliance on claim of foreign complex trust or foreign estate status.* A withholding agent may treat a payment as made to a foreign complex trust or a foreign estate if the withholding agent can reliably associate the payment with a beneficial owner withholding certificate described in § 1.1441-1(e)(2)(i) or other documentary evidence under § 1.1441-6(c)(3) or (4) (regarding a claim for treaty benefits) or § 1.6049-5(c)(1) (regarding documentary evidence to establish foreign status for purposes of chapter 61 of the Internal Revenue Code) that establishes the foreign complex trust or foreign estate's status as a beneficial owner. See paragraph (e)(6) of this section for presumption rules if documentation is lacking.

(5) *Foreign simple trust and foreign grantor trust*—(i) *Reliance on claim of foreign simple trust or foreign grantor trust status.* A withholding agent may treat a person as a foreign simple trust or foreign grantor trust if it receives from that person a foreign simple trust or foreign grantor trust withholding certificate as described in paragraph (e)(5)(iii) of this section. A withholding agent must apply the presumption rules of §§ 1.1441-1(b)(3) and 1.6049-5(d) and paragraphs (d) and (e)(6) of this section to the extent it cannot, prior to the payment, reliably associate a payment (within the meaning of § 1.1441-1(b)(2)(vii)) with a valid foreign simple trust or foreign grantor trust withholding certificate, it cannot reliably determine how much of the payment relates to valid documentation provided by a payee (e.g., a person that is not itself a nonqualified intermediary, flow-through entity, or U.S. branch) associated with the foreign simple trust or foreign grantor trust withholding certificate, or it does not have sufficient information to report the payment on Form 1042-S or Form 1099, if reporting is required. See § 1.1441-1(b)(2)(vii)(A) and (B).

(ii) *Reliance on claim of reduced withholding by a foreign simple trust or foreign grantor trust for its beneficiaries or owners.* This paragraph (e)(5)(ii) describes the manner in which a withholding agent may rely on a claim of reduced withholding when making a payment to a foreign simple trust or foreign grantor trust. To the extent that a withholding agent treats a payment to a foreign simple trust or foreign grantor trust as a payment to payees other than the trust in accordance with paragraph (e)(3)(i) of this section, it may rely on a claim for reduced withholding by a beneficiary or owner if, prior to the payment, the withholding agent can reliably associate the pay-

Reg. § 1.1441-5(e)(5)

ment (within the meaning of § 1.1441-1(b)(2)(vii)) with a valid withholding certificate or other appropriate documentation from a payee or beneficial owner that establishes entitlement to a reduced rate of withholding. A withholding certificate or other appropriate documentation that establishes entitlement to a reduced rate of withholding is a beneficial owner withholding certificate described in § 1.1441-1(e)(2)(i) or documentary evidence described in § 1.1441-6(c)(3) or (4) or in § 1.6049-5(c)(1) (for a beneficiary or owner claiming to be a foreign person and a beneficial owner, determined under the provisions of § 1.1441-1(c)(6)), a Form W-9 described in § 1.1441-1(d) (for a beneficiary or owner claiming to be a U.S. payee), or a withholding foreign partnership withholding certificate described in paragraph (c)(2)(iv) of this section. Unless a foreign simple trust or foreign grantor trust withholding certificate is provided for income treated as income effectively connected with the conduct of a trade or business in the United States, a claim must be presented for each payee's portion of the payment. When making a claim for several payees, the trust may present a single foreign simple trust or foreign grantor trust withholding certificate with which the payees' certificates or other appropriate documentation are associated. Where the foreign simple trust or foreign grantor trust withholding certificate is provided for income that is treated as effectively connected with the conduct of a trade or business in the United States under paragraph (e)(5)(iii)(D) of this section, the claim may be presented without having to identify any beneficiary's or grantor's distributive share of the payment.

(iii) *Withholding certificate from foreign simple trust or foreign grantor trust.* A withholding certificate furnished by a foreign simple trust or a foreign grantor trust that is not a withholding foreign trust (within the meaning of paragraph (e)(5)(v) of this section) is valid only if it is furnished on a Form W-8, an acceptable substitute form, or such other form as the IRS may prescribe, it is signed under penalties of perjury by a trustee, its validity has not expired, it contains the information, statements, and certifications required by this paragraph (e)(5)(iii) and § 1.1441-1(e)(3)(iv), and the withholding certificates or other appropriate documentation for all of the payees (as determined under paragraph (e)(3)(i) of this section) to whom the certificate relates are associated with the foreign simple trust or foreign grantor trust withholding certificate. The rules of § 1.1441-1(e)(4) shall apply to withholding certificates described in this paragraph (e)(5)(iii). No withholding certificates or other appropriate documentation from persons who derive income through a foreign simple trust or a foreign grantor trust (whether or not U.S. exempt recipients) are required to be associated with the foreign simple trust or foreign grantor trust withholding certificate if the certificate is furnished solely for income that is treated as effectively connected with the conduct of a trade or business in the United States. Withholding certificates and other appropriate documentation (as determined under paragraph (e)(3)(i) of this section) that may be associated with a foreign simple trust or foreign grantor trust withholding certificate consist of beneficial owner withholding certificates under § 1.1441-1(e)(2)(i), intermediary withholding certificates under § 1.1441-1(e)(3)(i), withholding foreign partnership withholding certificates under paragraph (c)(2)(iv) of this section, nonwithholding foreign partnership withholding certificates under paragraph (c)(3)(iii) of this section, withholding certificates from foreign trusts or estates under paragraph (e)(4) or (5)(iii) of this section, documentary evidence described in §§ 1.1441-6(c)(3) or (4), or 1.6049-5(c)(1), and any other documentation or certificates applicable under other provisions of the Internal Revenue Code or regulations that certify or establish the status of the payee or beneficial owner as a U.S. or a foreign person. Nothing in this paragraph (e)(5)(iii) shall require a foreign simple trust or foreign grantor trust to provide original documentation. Copies of certificates or documentary evidence may be passed up to the U.S. withholding agent, in which case the foreign simple trust or foreign grantor trust must retain the original documentation for the same time period that the copy is required to be retained by the withholding agent under § 1.1441-1(e)(4)(iii) and must provide it to the withholding agent upon request. The information, statement, and certifications required on a foreign simple trust or foreign grantor trust withholding certificate are as follows—

(A) The name, permanent residence address (as described in § 1.1441-1(e)(2)(ii)), and the employer identification number, if required, of the trust and the country under the laws of which the trust is created;

(B) A certification that the person whose name is on the certificate is a foreign simple trust or a foreign grantor trust;

(C) A withholding statement associated with the foreign simple trust or foreign grantor trust withholding certificate that provides all of the information required by paragraph (e)(5)(iv) of this section. No withholding statement is required, however, for a foreign simple trust withholding certificate furnished for income that is

Reg. § 1.1441-5(e)(5)

treated as effectively connected with the conduct of a trade or business in the United States;

(D) A certification on a foreign simple trust withholding certificate that the income is treated as effectively connected with the conduct of a trade or business in the United States, if applicable; and

(E) Any other information, certifications, or statements required by the form or accompanying instructions in addition to, or in lieu of, the information, certifications, and statements described in this paragraph (e)(5)(iii);

(iv) *Withholding statement provided by a foreign simple trust or foreign grantor trust.* The provisions of § 1.1441-1(e)(3)(iv) (regarding a withholding statement) shall apply to a foreign simple trust or foreign grantor trust by substituting the term foreign simple trust or foreign grantor trust for the term nonqualified intermediary.

(v) *Withholding foreign trusts.* The IRS may enter an agreement with a foreign trust to treat the trust or estate as a withholding foreign trust. Such an agreement shall generally follow the same principles as an agreement with a withholding foreign partnership under paragraph (c)(2)(ii) of this section. A withholding agent may treat a payment to a withholding foreign trust in the same manner the withholding agent would treat a payment to a withholding foreign partnership. The IRS may also enter an agreement to treat a trust as a qualified intermediary in appropriate circumstances. See § 1.1441-1(e)(5)(ii)(D).

(6) *Presumption rules*—(i) *In general.* This paragraph (e)(6) contains the applicable presumptions for a withholding agent (including a trust or estate) to determine the classification and status of a trust or estate and its beneficiaries or owners in the absence of valid documentation. The provisions of § 1.1441-1(b)(3)(iv) (regarding the 90-day grace period) and § 1.1441-1(b)(3)(vii) through (ix) shall apply for purposes of this paragraph (e)(6).

(ii) *Determination of status as U.S. or foreign trust or estate in the absence of documentation.* In the absence of valid documentation that establishes the U.S. status of a trust or estate under paragraph (b)(1) of this section and of documentation that establishes the foreign status of a trust or estate under paragraph (e)(4) or (5)(iii) of this section, the withholding agent shall determine the classification of the payee based upon the presumptions set forth in § 1.1441-1(b)(3)(ii). If, based upon those presumptions, the withholding agent classifies the payee as a trust or estate, the trust or estate shall be presumed to be a U.S. trust or U.S. estate unless there are indicia of foreign status, in which case the trust or estate shall be presumed to be foreign. Indicia of foreign status exists if the withholding agent has actual knowledge of the payee's employer identification number and that number begins with the two digits "98," the withholding agent's communications with the payee are mailed to an address in a foreign country, or the payment is made outside the United States (as defined in § 1.6049-5(e)). If an undocumented payee is presumed to be a foreign trust it shall be presumed to be a foreign complex trust. If a withholding agent has documentary evidence that establishes that an entity is a foreign trust, but the withholding agent cannot determine whether the foreign trust is a complex trust, a simple trust, or foreign grantor trust, the withholding agent may presume that the trust is a foreign complex trust.

(iii) *Determination of beneficiary or owner's status in the absence of certain documentation.* If a foreign simple trust or foreign grantor trust has provided a foreign simple trust or foreign grantor trust withholding certificate under paragraph (e)(5)(iii) of this section but the payment to such trust cannot be reliably associated with valid documentation from a specific beneficiary or owner of the trust, then any portion of a payment that a withholding agent cannot treat as reliably associated with valid documentation from a beneficiary or owner may be presumed made to a foreign payee. As a result, any payment of an amount subject to withholding is subject to withholding at a rate of 30 percent. Any such payment that is presumed to be made to an undocumented foreign person must be reported on Form 1042-S. See § 1.1461-1(c).

(f) *Failure to receive withholding certificate timely or to act in accordance with applicable presumptions.* See applicable procedures described in § 1.1441-1(b)(7) in the event the withholding agent does not hold an appropriate withholding certificate or other appropriate documentation at the time of payment or fails to rely on the presumptions set forth in § 1.1441-1(b)(3) or in paragraph (d) or (e) of this section.

(g) *Effective date*—(1) *General rule.* This section applies to payments made after December 31, 2000.

(2) *Transition rules.* The validity of a withholding certificate that was valid on January 1, 1998, under the regulations in effect prior to January 1, 2001 (see 26 CFR parts 1 and 35a, revised April 1, 1999) and expired, or will expire, at any time during 1998, is extended until December 31, 1998. The validity of a withholding certificate that is valid on or after January 1, 1999, remains valid until its validity expires under the regula-

Reg. § 1.1441-5(g)(2)

tions in effect prior to January 1, 2001 (see 26 CFR parts 1 and 35a, revised April 1, 1999) but in no event will such a withholding certificate remain valid after December 31, 2000. The rule in this paragraph (g)(2), however, does not apply to extend the validity period of a withholding certificate that expires solely by reason of changes in the circumstances of the person whose name is on the certificate. Notwithstanding the first three sentences of this paragraph (g)(2), a withholding agent may choose to not take advantage of the transition rule in this paragraph (g)(2) with respect to one or more withholding certificates valid under the regulations in effect prior to January 1, 2001 (see 26 CFR parts 1 and 35a, revised April 1, 1999) and, therefore, to require withholding certificates conforming to the requirements described in this section (new withholding certificates). For purposes of this section, a new withholding certificate is deemed to satisfy the documentation requirement under the regulations in effect prior to January 1, 2001 (see 26 CFR parts 1 and 35a, revised April 1, 1999). Further, a new withholding certificate remains valid for the period specified in § 1.1441-1(e)(4)(ii), regardless of when the certificate is obtained. [Reg. § 1.1441-5.]

☐ [*T.D.* 6187, 7-5-56. Amended by *T.D.* 6238, 6-10-57; *T.D.* 6908, 12-30-66; *T.D.* 7277, 5-14-73; *T.D.* 7842, 11-2-82; *T.D.* 7977, 9-19-84; *T.D.* 8160, 9-8-87; *T.D.* 8411, 4-24-92; *T.D.* 8734, 10-6-97; *T.D.* 8804, 12-30-98; *T.D.* 8856, 12-29-99 and *T.D.* 8881, 5-15-2000 (*corrected* 4-5-2001).]

[Reg. § 1.1441-6]

§ 1.1441-6. Claim of reduced withholding under an income tax treay.—(a) *In general.* The rate of withholding on a payment of income subject to withholding may be reduced to the extent provided under an income tax treaty in effect between the United States and a foreign country. Most benefits under income tax treaties are to foreign persons who reside in the treaty country. In some cases, benefits are available under an income tax treaty to U.S. citizens or U.S. residents or to residents of a third country. See paragraph (b)(5) of this section for claims of benefits by U.S. persons. If the requirements of this section are met, the amount withheld from the payment may be reduced at source to account for the treaty benefit. See also § 1.1441-4(b)(2) for rules regarding claims of reduced rate of withholding under an income tax treaty in the case of compensation from personal services.

(b) *Reliance on claim of reduced withholding under an income tax treaty*—(1) *In general.* The withholding imposed under section 1441, 1442, or 1443 on any payment to a foreign person is eligible for reduction under the terms of an income tax treaty only to the extent that such payment is treated as derived by a resident of an applicable treaty jurisdiction, such resident is a beneficial owner, and all other requirements for benefits under the treaty are satisfied. See section 894 and the regulations thereunder to determine whether a resident of a treaty country derives the income. Absent actual knowledge or reason to know otherwise, a withholding agent may rely on a claim that a beneficial owner is entitled to a reduced rate of withholding based upon an income tax treaty if, prior to the payment, the withholding agent can reliably associate the payment with a beneficial owner withholding certificate, described in § 1.1441-1(e)(2), that contains the information necessary to support the claim, or, in the case of a payment of income described in paragraph (c)(2) of this section made outside the United States with respect to an offshore account, documentary evidence described in paragraphs (c)(3), (4) and (5) of this section. See §§ 1.6049-5(e) for the definition of payments made outside the United States and 1.6049-5(c)(1) for the definition of offshore account. For purposes of this paragraph (b)(1), a beneficial owner withholding certificate described in § 1.1441-1(e)(2)(i) contains information necessary to support the claim for a treaty benefit only if it includes the beneficial owner's taxpayer identifying number (except as otherwise provided in paragraph (c)(1) of this section) and the representations that the beneficial owner derives the income under section 894 and the regulations thereunder, if required, and meets the limitation on benefits provisions of the treaty, if any. The withholding certificate must also contain any other representations required by this section and any other information, certifications, or statements as may be required by the form or accompanying instructions in addition to, or in place of, the information and certifications described in this section. Absent actual knowledge or reason to know that the claims are incorrect (and subject to the standards of knowledge in § 1.1441-7(b)), a withholding agent may rely on the claims made on a withholding certificate or on documentary evidence. A withholding agent may also rely on the information contained in a withholding statement provided under §§ 1.1441-1(e)(3)(iv) and 1.1441-5(c)(3)(iv) and (e)(5)(iv) to determine whether the appropriate statements regarding section 894 and limitation on benefits have been provided in connection with documentary evidence. If the beneficial owner is a person related to the withholding agent within the meaning of section 482, the withholding certificate must also contain a representation that the beneficial owner will file the statement required under

Reg. § 1.1441-6(a)

§ 301.6114-1(d) of this chapter (if applicable). The requirement to file an information statement under section 6114 for income subject to withholding applies only to amounts received during the calendar year that, in the aggregate, exceed $500,000. See § 301.6114-1(d) of this chapter. The Internal Revenue Service (IRS) may apply the provisions of § 1.1441-1(e)(1)(ii)(B) to notify the withholding agent that the certificate cannot be relied upon to grant benefits under an income tax treaty. See § 1.1441-1(e)(4)(viii) regarding reliance on a withholding certificate by a withholding agent. The provisions of § 1.1441-1(b)(3)(iv) dealing with a 90-day grace period shall apply for purposes of this section.

(2) *Payment to fiscally transparent entity*— (i) *In general.* If the person claiming a reduced rate of withholding under an income tax treaty is the interest holder of an entity that is considered to be fiscally transparent (as defined in the regulations under section 894) by the interest holder's jurisdiction with respect to an item of income, then, with respect to such income derived by that person through the entity, the entity shall be treated as a flow-through entity and may provide a flow-through withholding certificate with which the withholding certificate or other documentary evidence of the interest holder that supports the claim for treaty benefits is associated. For purposes of the preceding sentence, interest holders do not include any direct or indirect interest holders that are themselves treated as fiscally transparent entities with respect to that income by the interest holder's jurisdiction. See § 1.1441-1(c)(23) and (e)(3)(i) for the definition of flow-through entity and flow-through withholding certificate. The entity may provide a beneficial owner withholding certificate, or beneficial owner documentation, with respect to any remaining portion of the income to the extent the entity is receiving income and is not treated as fiscally transparent by its own jurisdiction. Further, the entity may claim a reduced rate of withholding with respect to the portion of a payment for which it is not treated as fiscally transparent if it meets all the requirements to make such a claim and, in the case of treaty benefits, it provides the documentation required by paragraph (b)(1) of this section. If dual claims, as described in paragraph (b)(2)(iii) of this section, are made, multiple withholding certificates may have to be furnished. Multiple withholding certificates may also have to be furnished if the entity receives income for which a reduction of withholding is claimed under a provision of the Internal Revenue Code (e.g., portfolio interest) and income for which a reduction of withholding is claimed under an income tax treaty.

(ii) *Certification by qualified intermediary.* Notwithstanding paragraph (b)(2)(i) of this section, a foreign entity that is fiscally transparent, as defined in the regulations under section 894, that is also a qualified intermediary for purposes of claiming a reduced rate of withholding under an income tax treaty for its interest holders (who are deriving the income paid to the entity as residents of an applicable treaty jurisdiction) may furnish a single qualified intermediary withholding certificate, as described in § 1.1441-1(e)(3)(ii), for amounts for which it claims a reduced rate of withholding under an income tax treaty on behalf of its interest holders.

(iii) *Dual treatment.* Under paragraph (b)(2)(i) of this section, a withholding agent may make a payment to a foreign entity that is simultaneously claiming to be the beneficial owner of a portion of the income (whether or not it is also claiming a reduced rate of tax on its own behalf) and a reduced rate on behalf of persons in their capacity as interest holders in the entity with respect to the same, or a different, portion of the income. If the same portion of a payment may be reliably associated with both the entity's claim and an interest holder's claim, the withholding agent may choose to reject both claims and request new documentation and information allocating the payment among the beneficial owners of the payment or the withholding agent may choose which claim to apply. If the entity and the interest holder's claims are reliably associated with separate portions of the payment, the withholding agent may, at its option, accept such dual claims based on withholding certificates or other appropriate documentation furnished by the entity and its interest holders with respect to their respective shares of the payment even though this will result in the withholding agent treating the entity differently with respect to different portions of the same payment. Alternatively, the withholding agent may choose to apply only the claim made by the entity, provided the entity may be treated as a beneficial owner of the income. If the withholding agent does not accept claims for a reduced rate of withholding presented by any one or more of the interest holders, or by the entity, any interest holder or the entity may subsequently claim a refund or credit of any amount so withheld to the extent the interest holder's or entity's share of such withholding exceeds the amount of tax due.

(iv) *Examples.* The following examples illustrate the rules of this paragraph (b)(2):

Example 1. (i) *Facts.* Entity E is a business organization formed under the laws of country Y. Country Y has an income tax treaty with the United States. The treaty contains a limitation on benefits provision. E receives U.S. source royalties from withholding agent W and claims a reduced rate of withholding under the U.S.-Y tax treaty on its own behalf (rather than on behalf of its interest holders). E furnishes a beneficial owner withholding certificate described in paragraph (b)(1) of this section that represents that E is a resident of country Y (within the meaning of the U.S.-Y tax treaty), is the beneficial owner of the income, derives the income under section 894 and the regulations thereunder, and is not precluded from claiming benefits by the treaty's limitation on benefits provision.

(ii) *Analysis.* Absent actual knowledge or reason to know otherwise, W may rely on the representations made by E to apply a reduced rate of withholding.

Example 2. (i) *Facts.* The facts are the same as under *Example 1,* except that one of E's interest holders, H, is an entity organized in country Z. The U.S.-Z tax treaty reduces the rate on royalties to zero whereas the rate on royalties under the U.S.-Y tax treaty applicable to E is 5 percent. H is not fiscally transparent under country Z's tax law with respect to such income. H furnishes a beneficial owner withholding certificate to E that represents that H derives, within the meaning of section 894 and the regulations thereunder, its share of the royalty income paid to E as a resident of country Z, is the beneficial owner of the royalty income, and is not precluded from claiming treaty benefits by virtue of the limitation on benefits provision in the U.S.-Z treaty. E furnishes to W a flow-through withholding certificate described in § 1.1441-1(e)(3)(i) to which it attaches H's beneficial owner withholding certificate and a withholding statement for the portion of the payment that H claims as its distributive share of the royalty income. E also furnishes to W a beneficial owner withholding certificate for itself for the portion of the payment that H does not claim as its distributive share.

(ii) *Analysis.* Absent actual knowledge or reason to know otherwise, W may rely on the documentation furnished by E to treat the royalty payment to a single foreign entity (E) as derived by different residents of tax treaty countries as a result of the claims presented under different treaties. W may, at its option, grant dual treatment, that is, a reduced rate of zero percent under the U.S.-Z treaty on the portion of the royalty payment that H claims to derive as a resident of country Z and a reduced rate of 5 percent under the U.S.-Y treaty for the balance. However, under paragraph (b)(2)(iii) of this section, W may, at its option, treat E as the only relevant person deriving the royalty and grant benefits under the U.S.-Y treaty only.

Example 3. (i) *Facts.* E is a business organization formed under the laws of country X. Country X has an income tax treaty with the United States. E has two interest holders, H1, organized in country Y, and H2, organized in country Z. E receives from W, a U.S. withholding agent, U.S. source royalties and interest that is eligible for the portfolio interest exception under sections 871(h) and 881(c), provided W receives the appropriate beneficial owner statement required under section 871(h)(5). E is classified as a corporation under U.S. tax law principles. Country X, E's country of organization, treats E as an entity that is not fiscally transparent with respect to items of income under the regulations under section 894. Under the U.S.-X income tax treaty, royalties are subject to 5 percent rate of withholding. Country Y, H1's country of organization, treats E as fiscally transparent with respect to items of income under section 894 and H1 as not fiscally transparent with respect to items of income. Under the country Y-U.S. income tax treaty, royalties are exempt from U.S. tax. Country Z, H2's country of organization, treats E as not fiscally transparent under section 894 with respect to items of income. E provides W with a flow-through beneficial owner withholding certificate with which it associates a beneficial owner withholding certificate from H1. H1's withholding certificate states that H1 is a resident of country Y, derives the royalty income under section 894, meets the applicable limitations on benefits provisions of the U.S.-Y treaty, and is the beneficial owner of the income. The withholding statement attached to E's flow-through withholding certificate allocates one-half of the royalty payment to H1. E also provides W with a beneficial owner withholding certificate for the interest income and the remaining one-half of the royalty income. The withholding certificate states that E is a resident of country X, derives the royalty income under section 894, meets the limitation on benefits provisions of the U.S.-X treaty, and is the beneficial owner of the income.

(ii) *Analysis.* Absent actual knowledge or reason to know that the claims are incorrect, W may treat one-half of the royalty derived by E as subject to a 5 percent withholding rate and one-half of the royalty as derived by H1 and subject to no withholding. Further, it may treat all of the interest as being paid to E and as qualifying for the portfolio interest exception. W can, at its option, treat the entire royalty as paid to E and subject it to withholding at a 5 percent rate of withholding. In that case, H1 would be entitled to

Reg. § 1.1441-6(b)(2)

claim a refund with respect to its one-half of the royalty.

(3) *Certified TIN.* The IRS may issue guidance requiring a foreign person claiming treaty benefits and for whom a TIN is required to establish with the IRS, at the time the TIN is requested or after the TIN is issued, that the person is a resident in a treaty country and meets other conditions (such as limitation on benefits provisions) of the treaty. See § 601.601(d)(2) of this chapter.

(4) *Claim of benefits under an income tax treaty by a U.S. person.* In certain cases, a U.S. person may claim the benefit of an income tax treaty. For example, under certain treaties, a U.S. citizen residing in the treaty country may claim a reduced rate of U.S. tax on certain amounts representing a pension or an annuity from U.S. sources. Claims of treaty benefits by a U.S. person may be made by furnishing a Form W-9 to the withholding agent or such other form as the IRS may prescribe in published guidance (see § 601.601(d)(2) of this chapter).

(c) *Exemption from requirement to furnish a taxpayer identifying number and special documentary evidence rules for certain income*—(1) *General rule.* In the case of income described in paragraph (c)(2) of this section, a withholding agent may rely on a beneficial owner withholding certificate described in paragraph (b)(1) of this section without regard to the requirement that the withholding certificate include the beneficial owner's taxpayer identifying number. In the case of payments of income described in paragraph (c)(2) of this section made outside the United States (as defined in § 1.6049-5(e)) with respect to an offshore account (as defined in § 1.6049-5(c)(1)), a withholding agent may, as an alternative to a withholding certificate described in paragraph (b)(1) of this section, rely on a certificate of residence described in paragraph (c)(3) of this section or documentary evidence described in paragraph (c)(4) of this section, relating to the beneficial owner, that the withholding agent has reviewed and maintains in its records in accordance with § 1.1441-1(e)(4)(iii). In the case of a payment to a person other than an individual, the certificate of residence or documentary evidence must be accompanied by the statements described in paragraphs (c)(5)(i) and (ii) of this section regarding limitation on benefits and whether the amount paid is derived by such person or by one of its interest holders. The withholding agent maintains the reviewed documents by retaining either the documents viewed or a photocopy thereof and noting in its records the date on which, and by whom, the documents were received and reviewed. This paragraph (c)(1) shall not apply to amounts that are exempt from withholding based on a claim that the income is effectively connected with the conduct of a trade or business in the United States.

(2) *Income to which special rules apply.* The income to which paragraph (c)(1) of this section applies is dividends and interest from stocks and debt obligations that are actively traded, dividends from any redeemable security issued by an investment company registered under the Investment Company Act of 1940 (15 U.S.C. 80a-1), dividends, interest, or royalties from units of beneficial interest in a unit investment trust that are (or were upon issuance) publicly offered and are registered with the Securities and Exchange Commission under the Securities Act of 1933 (15 U.S.C. 77a) and amounts paid with respect to loans of securities described in this paragraph (c)(2). For purposes of this paragraph (c)(2), a stock or debt obligation is actively traded if it is actively traded within the meaning of section 1092(d) and § 1.1092(d)-1 when documentation is provided.

(3) *Certificate of residence.* A certificate of residence referred to in paragraph (c)(1) of this section is a certification issued by an appropriate tax official of the treaty country of which the taxpayer claims to be a resident that the taxpayer has filed its most recent income tax return as a resident of that country (within the meaning of the applicable tax treaty). The certificate of residence must have been issued by such official within three years prior to its being presented to the withholding agent, or such other period as the IRS may prescribe in published guidance (see § 601.601(d)(2) of this chapter). See § 1.1441-1(e)(4)(ii)(A) for the period during which a withholding agent may rely on a certificate of residence. The competent authorities may agree to a different procedure for certifying residence, in which case such procedure shall govern for payments made to a person claiming to be a resident of the country with which such an agreement is in effect.

(4) *Documentary evidence establishing residence in the treaty country*—(i) *Individuals.* For an individual, the documentary evidence referred to in paragraph (c)(1) of this section is any documentation that includes the individuals name, address, and photograph, is an official document issued by an authorized governmental body (i.e., a government or agency thereof, or a municipality), and has been issued no more than three years prior to presentation to the withholding agent. A document older than three years may be relied upon as proof of residence only if it is accompa-

Reg. § 1.1441-6(c)(4)

nied by additional evidence of the person's residence in the treaty country (e.g., a bank statement, utility bills, or medical bills). Documentary evidence must be in the form of original documents or certified copies thereof.

(ii) *Persons other than individuals.* For a person other than an individual, the documentary evidence referred to in paragraph (c)(1) of this section is any documentation that includes the name of the entity and the address of its principal office in the treaty country, and is an official document issued by an authorized governmental body (e.g., a government or agency thereof, or a municipality).

(5) *Statements regarding entitlement to treaty benefits*—(i) Statement regarding conditions under a limitation on benefits provision. In addition to the documentary evidence described in (c)(4)(ii) of this section, a taxpayer that is not an individual must provide a statement that it meets one or more of the conditions set forth in the limitation on benefits article (if any, or in a similar provision) contained in the applicable tax treaty.

(ii) *Statement regarding whether the taxpayer derives the income.* A taxpayer that is not an individual must also provide, in addition to the documentary evidence and the statement described in paragraph (c)(5)(i) of this section, a statement that any income for which it intends to claim benefits under an applicable income tax treaty is income that will properly be treated as derived by itself as a resident of the applicable treaty jurisdiction within the meaning of section 894 and the regulations thereunder. This requirement does not apply if the taxpayer furnishes a certificate of residence that certifies that fact.

(d) *Joint owners.* In the case of a payment to joint owners, each owner must furnish a withholding certificate or, if applicable, documentary evidence or a certificate of residence. The applicable rate of withholding on a payment of income to joint owners shall be the highest applicable rate.

(e) *Competent authority.* The procedures described in this section may be modified to the extent the U.S. competent authority may agree with the competent authority of a country with which the United States has an income tax treaty in effect.

(f) *Failure to receive withholding certificate timely.* See applicable procedures described in § 1.1441-1(b)(7) in the event the withholding agent does not hold an appropriate withholding certificate or other appropriate documentation at the time of payment.

(g) *Effective date*—(1) *General rule.* This section applies to payments made after December 31, 2000.

(2) *Transition rules.* For purposes of this section, the validity of a Form 1001 or 8233 that was valid on January 1, 1998, under the regulations in effect prior to January 1, 2001 (see 26 CFR parts 1 and 35a, revised April 1, 1999) and expired, or will expire, at any time during 1998, is extended until December 31, 1998. The validity of a Form 1001 or 8233 that is valid on or after January 1, 1999, remains valid until its validity expires under the regulations in effect prior to January 1, 2001 (see 26 CFR parts 1 and 35a, revised April 1, 1999) but in no event will such a form remain valid after December 31, 2000. The rule in this paragraph (g)(2), however, does not apply to extend the validity period of a Form 1001 or 8233 that expires solely by reason of changes in the circumstances of the person whose name is on the certificate or in interpretation of the law under the regulations under § 1.894-1T(d). Notwithstanding the first three sentences of this paragraph (g)(2), a withholding agent may choose to not take advantage of the transition rule in this paragraph (g)(2) with respect to one or more withholding certificates valid under the regulations in effect prior to January 1, 2001 (see 26 CFR parts 1 and 35a, revised April 1, 1999) and, therefore, to require withholding certificates conforming to the requirements described in this section (new withholding certificates). For purposes of this section, a new withholding certificate is deemed to satisfy the documentation requirement under the regulations in effect prior to January 1, 2001 (see 26 CFR parts 1 and 35a, revised April 1, 1999). Further, a new withholding certificate remains valid for the period specified in § 1.1441-1(e)(4)(ii), regardless of when the certificate is obtained. [Reg. § 1.1441-6.]

☐ [T.D. 7157, 12-29-71. Amended by T.D. 7842, 11-2-82; T.D. 7977, 9-19-84; T.D. 8734, 10-6-97; T.D. 8804, 12-30-98; T.D. 8856, 12-29-99 (*corrected* 3-27-2000) *and T.D.* 8881, 5-15-2000.]

[Reg. § 1.1441-7]

§ 1.1441-7. **General provisions relating to withholding agents.**—(a) *Withholding agent defined*—(1) *In general.* For purposes of chapter 3 of the Internal Revenue Code and the regulations under such chapter, the term *withholding agent* means any person, U.S. or foreign, that has the control, receipt, custody, disposal, or payment of an item of income of a foreign person subject to withholding, including (but not limited to) a foreign intermediary described in § 1.1441-1(e)(3)(i), a foreign partnership, or a U.S. branch described in § 1.1441-1(b)(2)(iv)(A) or (E). See

§§ 1.1441-1(b)(2) and (3) and 1.1441-5(c), (d), and (e), for rules to determine whether a payment is considered made to a foreign person. Any person who meets the definition of a withholding agent is required to deposit any tax withheld under § 1.1461-1(a) and to make the returns prescribed by § 1.1461-1(b) and (c), except as otherwise may be required by a qualified intermediary withholding agreement, a withholding foreign partnership agreement, or a withholding foreign trust agreement. When several persons qualify as withholding agents with respect to a single payment, only one tax is required to be withheld and deposited. See § 1.1461-1. A person who, as a nominee described in § 1.6031(c)-1T, has furnished to a partnership all of the information required to be furnished under § 1.6031(c)-1T(a) shall not be treated as a withholding agent if it has notified the partnership that it is treating the provision of information to the partnership as a discharge of its obligations as a withholding agent.

(2) *Examples.* The following examples illustrate the rules of paragraph (a)(1) of this section:

Example 1. USB is a broker organized in the United States. USB pays U.S. source dividends and interest, which are amounts subject to withholding under § 1.1441-2(a), to FC, a foreign corporation that has an investment account with USB. USB is a withholding agent as defined in paragraph (a)(1) of this section.

Example 2. USB is a bank organized in the United States. FB is a bank organized in country X. X has an omnibus account with USB through which FB invests in debt and equity instruments that pay amounts subject to withholding as defined in § 1.1441-2(a). FB is a nonqualified intermediary, as defined in § 1.1441-1(c)(14). Both USB and FB are withholding agents as defined in paragraph (a)(1) of this section.

Example 3. The facts are the same as in *Example 2,* except that FB is a qualified intermediary. Both USB and FB are withholding agents as defined in paragraph (a)(1) of this section.

Example 4. FB is a bank organized in country X. FB has a branch in the United States. FB's branch has customers that are foreign persons who receive amounts subject to withholding, as defined in § 1.1441-2(a). FB is a withholding agent under paragraph (a)(1) of this section and is required to withhold and report payments of amounts subject to withholding in accordance with chapter 3 of the Internal Revenue Code.

Example 5. X is a foreign corporation. X pays dividends to shareholders who are foreign persons. Under section 861(a)(2)(B), a portion of the dividends are from sources within the United States and constitute amounts subject to withholding within the meaning of § 1.1441-2(a). The dividends are not subject to tax under section 884(a). See 884(e)(3). X is a withholding agent under paragraph (a)(1) of this section.

(b) *Standards of knowledge*—(1) *In general.* A withholding agent must withhold at the full 30-percent rate under section 1441, 1442, or 1443(a) or at the full 4-percent rate under section 1443(b) if it has actual knowledge or reason to know that a claim of U.S. status or of a reduced rate of withholding under section 1441, 1442, or 1443 is unreliable or incorrect. A withholding agent shall be liable for tax, interest, and penalties to the extent provided under sections 1461 and 1463 and the regulations under those sections if it fails to withhold the correct amount despite its actual knowledge or reason to know the amount required to be withheld. For purposes of the regulations under sections 1441, 1442, and 1443, a withholding agent may rely on information or certifications contained in, or associated with, a withholding certificate or other documentation furnished by or for a beneficial owner or payee unless the withholding agent has actual knowledge or reason to know that the information or certifications are incorrect or unreliable and, if based on such knowledge or reason to know, it should withhold (under chapter 3 of the Code or another withholding provision of the Code) an amount greater than would be the case if it relied on the information or certifications, or it should report (under chapter 3 of the Code or under another provision of the Code) an amount that would not otherwise be reportable if it relied on the information or certifications. See § 1.1441-1(e)(4)(viii) for applicable reliance rules. A withholding agent that has received notification by the Internal Revenue Service (IRS) that a claim of U.S. status or of a reduced rate is incorrect has actual knowledge beginning on the date that is 30 calendar days after the date the notice is received. A withholding agent that fails to act in accordance with the presumptions set forth in §§ 1.1441-1(b)(3), 1.1441-4(a), 1.1441-5(d) and (e), or 1.1441-9(b)(3) may also be liable for tax, interest, and penalties. See § 1.1441-1(b)(3)(ix) and (7).

(2) *Reason to know.* A withholding agent shall be considered to have reason to know if its knowledge of relevant facts or of statements contained in the withholding certificates or other documentation is such that a reasonably prudent person in the position of the withholding agent would question the claims made.

(3) *Financial institutions—limits on reason to know.* For purposes of this paragraph (b)(3) and paragraphs (b)(4) through (b)(10) of this sec-

Reg. § 1.1441-7(b)(3)

tion, the terms *withholding certificate, documentary evidence,* and *documentation* are defined in § 1.1441-1(c)(16), (17) and (18). Except as otherwise provided in paragraphs (b)(4) through (b)(9) of this section, a withholding agent that is a financial institution (including a regulated investment company) that has a direct account relationship with a beneficial owner (a direct account holder) has a reason to know, with respect to amounts described in § 1.1441-6(c)(2), that documentation provided by the direct account holder is unreliable or incorrect only if one or more of the circumstances described in paragraphs (b)(4) through (b)(9) of this section exist. If a direct account holder has provided documentation that is unreliable or incorrect under the rules of paragraph (b)(4) through (b)(9) of this section, the withholding agent may require new documentation. Alternatively, the withholding agent may rely on the documentation originally provided if the rules of paragraphs (b)(4) through (b)(9) of this section permit such reliance based on additional statements and documentation. Paragraph (b)(10) of this section provides limits on reason to know for financial institutions that receive beneficial owner documentation from persons (indirect account holders) that have an account relationship with, or an ownership interest in, a direct account holder. For rules regarding reliance on Form W-9, see § 31.3406(g)-3(e)(2) of this chapter.

(4) *Rules applicable to withholding certificates*—(i) *In general.* A withholding agent has reason to know that a beneficial owner withholding certificate provided by a direct account holder in connection with a payment of an amount described in § 1.1441-6(c)(2) is unreliable or incorrect if the withholding certificate is incomplete with respect to any item on the certificate that is relevant to the claims made by the direct account holder, the withholding certificate contains any information that is inconsistent with the direct account holder's claim, the withholding agent has other account information that is inconsistent with the direct account holder's claim, or the withholding certificate lacks information necessary to establish entitlement to a reduced rate of withholding. For purposes of establishing a direct account holder's status as a foreign person or resident of a treaty country a withholding certificate shall be considered unreliable or inconsistent with an account holder's claims only if it is not reliable under the rules of paragraphs (b)(5) and (6) of this section. A withholding agent that relies on an agent to review and maintain a withholding certificate is considered to know or have reason to know the facts within the knowledge of the agent.

(ii) *Examples.* The rules of paragraph (b)(4) of this section are illustrated by the following examples:

Example 1. F, a foreign person that has a direct account relationship with USB, a bank that is a U.S. person, provides USB with a beneficial owner withholding certificate for the purpose of claiming a reduced rate of withholding on U.S. source dividends. F resides in a treaty country that has a limitation on benefits provision in its income tax treaty with the United States. The withholding certificate, however, does not contain a statement regarding limitations on benefits or deriving the income under section 894 as required by § 1.1441-6(b)(1). USB cannot rely on the withholding certificate to grant a reduced rate of withholding because it is incomplete with respect to the claim made by F.

Example 2. F, a foreign person that has a direct account relationship with USB, a broker that is a U.S. person, provides USB with a withholding certificate for the purpose of claiming the portfolio interest exception under section 881(c), which applies to foreign corporations. F indicates on its withholding certificate, however, that it is a partnership. USB may not treat F as a beneficial owner of the interest for purposes of the portfolio interest exception because F has indicated on its withholding certificate that it is a foreign partnership, and therefore under § 1.1441-1(c)(6)(ii) it is not the beneficial owner of the interest payment.

(5) *Withholding certificate—establishment of foreign status.* A withholding agent has reason to know that a beneficial owner withholding certificate (as defined in § 1.1441-1(e)(2)) provided by a direct account holder in connection with a payment of an amount described in § 1.1441-6(c)(2) is unreliable or incorrect for purposes of establishing the account holder's status as a foreign person if the certificate is described in paragraph (b)(5)(i) or (ii) of this section.

(i) A withholding certificate is unreliable or incorrect if the withholding certificate has a permanent residence address (as defined in § 1.1441-1(e)(2)(ii)) in the United States, the withholding certificate has a mailing address in the United States, the withholding agent has a residence or mailing address as part of its account information that is an address in the United States, or the direct account holder notifies the withholding agent of a new residence or mailing address in the United States (whether or not provided on a withholding certificate). A withholding agent may, however, rely on the beneficial owner withholding certificate as establishing the account holder's foreign status if it may do so under the

Reg. § 1.1441-7(b)(4)

provisions of paragraph (b)(5)(i)(A) or (B) of this section.

(A) A withholding agent may treat a direct account holder as a foreign person if the beneficial owner withholding certificate has been provided by an individual and—

(1) The withholding agent has in its possession or obtains documentary evidence (which does not contain a U.S. address) that has been provided within the past three years, was valid at the time it was provided, the documentary evidence supports the claim of foreign status, and the direct account holder provides the withholding agent with a reasonable explanation, in writing, supporting the account holder's foreign status; or

(2) The account is maintained at an office of the withholding agent outside the United States and the withholding agent is required to report annually a payment to the direct account holder on a tax information statement that is filed with the tax authority of the country in which the office is located and that country has an income tax treaty in effect with the United States.

(B) A withholding agent may treat an account holder as a foreign person if the beneficial owner withholding certificate has been provided by an entity that the withholding agent does not know, or does not have reason to know, is a flow-through entity and—

(1) The withholding agent has in its possession, or obtains, documentation that substantiates that the entity is actually organized or created under the laws of a foreign country; or

(2) The account is maintained at an office of the withholding agent outside the United States and the withholding agent is required to report annually a payment to the direct account holder on a tax information statement that is filed with the tax authority of the country in which the office is located and that country has an income tax treaty in effect with the United States.

(ii) A beneficial owner withholding certificate is unreliable or incorrect if it is provided with respect to an offshore account (as defined in § 1.6049-5(c)(1)) and the direct account holder has standing instructions directing the withholding agent to pay amounts from its account to an address or an account maintained in the United States. The withholding agent may treat the direct account holder as a foreign person, however, if the direct account holder provides a reasonable explanation in writing that supports its foreign status.

(6) *Withholding certificate—claim of reduced rate of withholding under treaty.* A withholding agent has reason to know that a withholding certificate (other than Form W-9) provided by a direct account holder in connection with a payment of an amount described in § 1.1441-6(c)(2) is unreliable or incorrect for purposes of establishing that the direct account holder is a resident of a country with which the United States has an income tax treaty if it is described in paragraphs (b)(6)(i) through (iii) of this section.

(i) A beneficial owner withholding certificate is unreliable or incorrect if the permanent residence address on the beneficial owner withholding certificate is not in the country whose treaty is invoked, or the direct account holder notifies the withholding agent of a new permanent residence address that is not in the treaty country. A withholding agent may, however, treat a direct account holder as entitled to a reduced rate of withholding under an income tax treaty if the direct account holder provides a reasonable explanation for the permanent residence address outside the treaty country (e.g., the address is the address of a branch of the beneficial owner located outside the treaty country in which the entity is a resident) or the withholding agent has in its possession, or obtains, documentary evidence that establishes residency in a treaty country.

(ii) A beneficial owner withholding certificate is unreliable or incorrect if the permanent residence address on the withholding certificate is in the applicable treaty country but the withholding certificate contains a mailing address outside the treaty country or the withholding agent has a mailing address as part of its account information that is outside the treaty country. A mailing address that is a P.O. Box, in-care-of address, or address at a financial institution (if the financial institution is not a beneficial owner) shall not preclude a withholding agent from treating the direct account holder as a resident of a treaty country if such address is in the treaty country. If a withholding agent has a mailing address (whether or not contained on the withholding certificate) outside the applicable treaty country, the withholding agent may nevertheless treat a direct account holder as a resident of an applicable treaty country if—

(A) The withholding agent has in its possession, or obtains, additional documentation supporting the direct account holder's claim of residence in the applicable treaty country (and the additional documentation does not contain an address outside the treaty country);

(B) The withholding agent has in its possession, or obtains, documentation that establishes that the direct account holder is an entity

Reg. § 1.1441-7(b)(6)

organized in a treaty country (or an entity managed and controlled in a treaty country, if the applicable treaty so requires);

(C) The withholding agent knows that the address outside the applicable treaty country (other than a P.O. box, or in-care-of address) is a branch of a bank or insurance company that is a resident of the applicable treaty country; or

(D) The withholding agent obtains a written statement from the direct account holder that reasonably establishes entitlement to treaty benefits.

(iii) A beneficial owner withholding certificate is unreliable or incorrect to establish entitlement to a reduced rate of withholding under an income tax treaty if the direct account holder has standing instructions for the withholding agent to pay amounts from its account to an address or an account outside the treaty country unless the direct account holder provides a reasonable explanation, in writing, establishing the direct account holder's residence in the applicable treaty country.

(7) *Documentary evidence.* A withholding agent shall not treat documentary evidence provided by a direct account holder as valid if the documentary evidence does not reasonably establish the identity of the person presenting the documentary evidence. For example, documentary evidence is not valid if it is provided in person by a direct account holder that is a natural person and the photograph or signature on the documentary evidence, if any, does not match the appearance or signature of the person presenting the document. A withholding agent shall not rely on documentary evidence to reduce the rate of withholding that would otherwise apply under the presumption rules of §§ 1.1441-1(b)(3), 1.1441-5(d) and (e)(6), and 1.6049-5(d) if the documentary evidence contains information that is inconsistent with the direct account holder's claim of a reduced rate of withholding, the withholding agent has other account information that is inconsistent with the direct account holder's claim, or the documentary evidence lacks information necessary to establish entitlement to a reduced rate of withholding. For example, if a direct account holder provides documentary evidence to claim treaty benefits and the documentary evidence establishes the direct account holder's status as a foreign person and a resident of a treaty country, but the account holder fails to provide the treaty statements required by § 1.1441-6(c)(5), the documentary evidence does not establish the direct account holder's entitlement to a reduced rate of withholding. For purposes of establishing a direct account holder's status as a foreign person or resident of a country with which the United States has an income tax treaty with respect to income described in § 1.1441-6(c)(2), documentary evidence shall be considered unreliable or incorrect only if it is not reliable under the rules of paragraph (b)(8) and (9) of this section.

(8) *Documentary evidence—establishment of foreign status.* A withholding agent has reason to know that documentary evidence provided in connection with a payment of an amount described in § 1.1441-6(c)(2) is unreliable or incorrect for purposes of establishing the direct account holder's status as a foreign person if the documentary evidence is described in paragraphs (b)(8)(i), (ii), (iii) or (iv) of this section.

(i) A withholding agent shall not treat documentary evidence provided by an account holder after December 31, 2000, as valid for purposes of establishing the direct account holder's foreign status if the only mailing or residence address that is available to the withholding agent is an address at a financial institution (unless the financial institution is a beneficial owner of the income), an in-care-of address, or a P.O. box. In this case, the withholding agent must obtain additional documentation that is sufficient to establish the direct account holder's status as a foreign person. A withholding agent shall not treat documentary evidence provided by an account holder before January 1, 2001, as valid for purposes of establishing a direct account holder's status as a foreign person if it has actual knowledge that the direct account holder is a U.S. person or if it has a mailing or residence address for the direct account holder in the United States. If a withholding agent has an address for the direct account holder in the United States, the withholding agent may nevertheless treat the direct account holder as a foreign person if it can so treat the direct account holder under the rules of paragraph (b)(8)(ii) of this section.

(ii) Documentary evidence is unreliable or incorrect to establish a direct account holder's status as a foreign person if the withholding agent has a mailing or residence address (whether or not on the documentation) for the direct account holder in the United States or if the direct account holder notifies the withholding agent of a new address in the United States. A withholding agent may, however, rely on documentary evidence as establishing the direct account holder's foreign status if it may do so under the provisions of paragraph (b)(8)(ii)(A) or (B) of this section.

(A) A withholding agent may treat a direct account holder that is an individual as a foreign person even if it has a mailing or residence

Reg. § 1.1441-7(b)(7)

address for the direct account holder in the United States if the withholding agent—

(1) Has in its possession or obtains additional documentary evidence (which does not contain a U.S. address) supporting the claim of foreign status and a reasonable explanation in writing supporting the account holder's foreign status;

(2) Has in its possession or obtains a valid beneficial owner withholding certificate on Form W-8 and the Form W-8 contains a permanent residence address outside the United States and a mailing address outside the United States (or if a mailing address is inside the United States the direct account holder provides a reasonable explanation in writing supporting the direct account holder's foreign status); or

(3) The account is maintained at an office of the withholding agent outside the United States and the withholding agent is required to report annually a payment to the direct account holder on a tax information statement that is filed with the tax authority of the country in which the office is located and that country has an income tax treaty in effect with the United States.

(B) A withholding agent may treat a direct account holder that is an entity (other than a flow-through entity) as a foreign person even if it has a mailing or residence address for the direct account holder in the United States if the withholding agent—

(1) Has in its possession, or obtains, documentation that substantiates that the entity is actually organized or created under the laws of a foreign country;

(2) Obtains a valid beneficial owner withholding certificate on Form W-8 and the Form W-8 contains a permanent residence address outside the United States and a mailing address outside the United States (or if a mailing address is inside the United States the direct account holder provides additional documentary evidence sufficient to establish the direct account holder's foreign status); or

(3) The account is maintained at an office of the withholding agent outside the United States and the withholding agent is required to report annually a payment to the direct account holder on a tax information statement that is filed with the tax authority of the country in which the office is located and that country has an income tax treaty in effect with the United States.

(iii) Documentary evidence is unreliable or incorrect if the direct account holder has standing instructions directing the withholding agent to pay amounts from its account to an address or an account maintained in the United States. The withholding agent may treat the direct account holder as a foreign person, however, if the account holder provides a reasonable explanation in writing that supports its foreign status.

(9) *Documentary evidence—claim of reduced rate of withholding under treaty.* A withholding agent has reason to know that documentary evidence provided in connection with a payment of an amount described in § 1.1441-6(c)(2) is unreliable or incorrect for purposes of establishing that a direct account holder is a resident of a country with which the United States has an income tax treaty if it is described in paragraph (b)(9)(i) or (ii) of this section.

(i) Documentary evidence is unreliable or incorrect if the withholding agent has a mailing or residence address for the direct account holder (whether or not on the documentary evidence) that is outside the applicable treaty country, or the only address that the withholding agent has (whether in or outside of the applicable treaty country) is a P.O. box, an in-care-of address, or the address of a financial institution (if the financial institution is not the beneficial owner). If a withholding agent has a mailing or residence address for the direct account holder outside the applicable treaty country, the withholding agent may nevertheless treat a direct account holder as a resident of an applicable treaty country if the withholding agent—

(A) Has in its possession, or obtains, additional documentary evidence supporting the direct account holder's claim of residence in the applicable treaty country (and the documentary evidence does not contain an address outside the applicable treaty country, a P.O. box, an in-care-of address, or the address of a financial institution);

(B) Has in its possession, or obtains, documentary evidence that establishes the direct account holder is an entity organized in a treaty country (or an entity managed and controlled in a treaty country, if the applicable treaty so requires); or

(C) Obtains a valid beneficial owner withholding certificate on Form W-8 that contains a permanent residence address and a mailing address in the applicable treaty country.

(ii) Documentary evidence is unreliable or incorrect if the direct account holder has standing instructions directing the withholding agent to pay amounts from its account to an address or an account maintained outside the treaty country unless the direct account holder provides a reasonable explanation, in writing, establishing the di-

Reg. § 1.1441-7(b)(9)

rect account holder's residence in the applicable treaty country.

(10) *Limits on reason to know—indirect account holders.* A financial institution that receives documentation from a payee through a nonqualified intermediary, a flow-through entity, or a U.S. branch described in § 1.1441-1(b)(2)(iv) (other than a U.S. branch that is treated as a U.S. person) with respect to a payment of an amount described in § 1.1441-6(c)(2) has reason to know that the documentation is unreliable or incorrect if a reasonably prudent person in the position of a withholding agent would question the claims made. This standard requires, but is not limited to, a withholding agent's compliance with the rules of paragraphs (b)(10)(i) through (iii).

(i) The withholding agent must review the withholding statement described in § 1.1441-1(e)(3)(iv) and may not rely on information in the statement to the extent the information does not support the claims made for any payee. For this purpose, a withholding agent may not treat a payee as a foreign person if an address in the United States is provided for such payee and may not treat a person as a resident of a country with which the United States has an income tax treaty if the address for that person is outside the applicable treaty country. Notwithstanding a U.S. address or an address outside a treaty country, the withholding agent may treat a payee as a foreign person or a foreign person as a resident of a treaty country if a reasonable explanation is provided, in writing, by the nonqualified intermediary, flow-through entity, or U.S. branch supporting the payee's foreign status or the foreign person's residency in a treaty country.

(ii) The withholding agent must review each withholding certificate in accordance with the requirements of paragraphs (b)(5) and (6) of this section and verify that the information on the withholding certificate is consistent with the information on the withholding statement required under § 1.1441-1(e)(3)(iv). If there is a discrepancy between the withholding certificate and the withholding statement, the withholding agent may choose to rely on the withholding certificate, if valid, and instruct the nonqualified intermediary, flow-through entity, or U.S. branch to correct the withholding statement or apply the presumption rules of §§ 1.1441-1(b), 1.1441-5(d) and (e)(6), and 1.6049-5(d) to the payment allocable to the payee who provided the withholding certificate. A withholding agent that receives a withholding certificate before December 31,2001, is not required to review the information on withholding certificates or determine if it is consistent with the information on the withholding statement until December 31, 2001. A withholding agent may withhold and report in accordance with a withholding statement until December 31, 2001, unless it has actually performed the verification procedures required by this paragraph (b)(10)(ii) and determined that the withholding statement is inaccurate with respect to a particular payee.

(iii) The withholding agent must review the documentary evidence provided by the nonqualified intermediary, flow-through entity, or U.S. branch to determine that there is no obvious indication that the payee is a U.S. non-exempt recipient or that the documentary evidence does not establish the identity of the person who provided the documentation (e.g., the documentary evidence does not appear to be an identification document).

(11) *Additional guidance.* The IRS may prescribe other circumstances for which a withholding certificate or documentary evidence is unreliable or incorrect in addition to the circumstances described in paragraph (b) of this section to establish an account holder's status as a foreign person or a beneficial owner entitled to a reduced rate of withholding in published guidance (see § 601.601(d)(2) of this chapter).

(c) *Authorized agent*—(1) *In general.* The acts of an agent of a withholding agent (including the receipt of withholding certificates, the payment of amounts of income subject to withholding, and the deposit of tax withheld) are imputed to the withholding agent on whose behalf it is acting. However, if the agent is a foreign person, a withholding agent that is a U.S. person may treat the acts of the foreign agent as its own for purposes of determining whether it has complied with the provisions of this section, but only if the agent is an authorized foreign agent, as defined in paragraph (c)(2) of this section. An authorized foreign agent cannot apply the provisions of this paragraph (c) to appoint another person its authorized foreign agent with respect to the payments it receives from the withholding agent.

(2) *Authorized foreign agent.* An agent is an authorized foreign agent only if—

(i) There is a written agreement between the withholding agent and the foreign person acting as agent;

(ii) The notification procedures described in paragraph (c)(3) of this section have been complied with;

(iii) Books and records and relevant personnel of the foreign agent are available (on a continuous basis, including after termination of the relationship) for examination by the IRS in order to evaluate the withholding agent's compli-

Reg. § 1.1441-7(b)(10)

Nonresident Aliens and Foreign Corporations

See p. 20,601 for regulations not amended to reflect law changes

ance with the provisions of chapters 3 and 61 of the Code, section 3406, and the regulations under those provisions; and

(iv) The U.S. withholding agent remains fully liable for the acts of its agent and does not assert any of the defenses that may otherwise be available, including under common law principles of agency in order to avoid tax liability under the Internal Revenue Code.

(3) *Notification.* A withholding agent that appoints an authorized agent to act on its behalf for purposes of § 1.871-14(c)(2), the withholding provisions of chapter 3 of the Code, section 3406 or other withholding provisions of the Internal Revenue Code, or the reporting provisions of chapter 61 of the Code, is required to file notice of such appointment with the Office of the Assistant Commissioner (International). Such notice shall be filed before the first payment for which the authorized agent acts as such. Such notice shall acknowledge the withholding agent liability as provided in paragraph (c)(2)(iv) of this section.

(4) *Liability of U.S. withholding agent.* An authorized foreign agent is subject to the same withholding and reporting obligations that apply to any withholding agent under the provisions of chapter 3 of the Code and the regulations thereunder. In particular, an authorized foreign agent does not benefit from the special procedures or exceptions that may apply to a qualified intermediary. A withholding agent acting through an authorized foreign agent is liable for any failure of the agent, such as failure to withhold an amount or make payment of tax, in the same manner and to the same extent as if the agent's failure had been the failure of the U.S. withholding agent. For this purpose, the foreign agent's actual knowledge or reason to know shall be imputed to the U.S. withholding agent. The U.S. withholding agent's liability shall exist irrespective of the fact that the authorized foreign agent is also a withholding agent and is itself separately liable for failure to comply with the provisions of the regulations under section 1441, 1442, or 1443. However, the same tax, interest, or penalties shall not be collected more than once.

(5) *Filing of returns.* See § 1.1461-1(b)(2)(iii) and (c)(4)(iii) regarding returns required to be made where a U.S. withholding agent acts through an authorized foreign agent.

(d) *United States obligations.* If the United States is a withholding agent for an item of interest, including original issue discount, on obligations of the United States or of any agency or instrumentality thereof, the withholding obligation of the United States is assumed and discharged by—

(1) The Commissioner of the Public Debt, for interest paid by checks issued through the Bureau of the Public Debt;

(2) The Treasurer of the United States, for interest paid by him or her, whether by check or otherwise;

(3) Each Federal Reserve Bank, for interest paid by it, whether by check or otherwise; or

(4) Such other person as may be designated by the IRS.

(e) *Assumed obligations.* If, in connection with the sale of a corporation's property, payment on the bonds or other obligations of the corporation is assumed by a person, then that person shall be a withholding agent to the extent amounts subject to withholding are paid to a foreign person. Thus, the person shall withhold such amounts under § 1.1441-1 as would be required to be withheld by the seller or corporation had no such sale or assumption been made.

(f) *Conduit financing arrangements*—(1) *Liability of withholding agent.* Subject to paragraph (f)(2) of this section, any person that is required to deduct and withhold tax under § 1.1441-3(g) is made liable for that tax by section 1461. A person that is required to deduct and withhold tax but fails to do so is liable for the payment of the tax and any applicable penalties and interest.

(2) *Exception for withholding agents that do not know of conduit financing arrangement*—(i) *In general.* A withholding agent will not be liable under paragraph (f)(1) of this section for failing to deduct and withhold with respect to a conduit financing arrangement unless the person knows or has reason to know that the financing arrangement is a conduit financing arrangement. This standard shall be satisfied if the withholding agent knows or has reason to know of facts sufficient to establish that the financing arrangement is a conduit financing arrangement, including facts sufficient to establish that the participation of the intermediate entity in the financing arrangement is pursuant to a tax avoidance plan. A withholding agent that knows only of the financing transactions that comprise the financing arrangement will not be considered to know or have reason to know of facts sufficient to establish that the financing arrangement is a conduit financing arrangement.

(ii) *Examples.* The following examples illustrate the operation of paragraph (d)(2) of this section.

Example 1. (i) DS is a U.S. subsidiary of FP, a corporation organized in Country N, a country that does not have an income tax treaty with the United States. FS is a special purpose subsidi-

Reg. § 1.1441-7(f)(2)

ary of FP that is incorporated in Country T, a country that has an income tax treaty with the United States that prohibits the imposition of withholding tax on payments of interest. FS is capitalized with $10,000,000 in debt from BK, a Country N bank, and $1,000,000 in capital from FS.

(ii) On May 1, 1995, C, a U.S. person, purchases an automobile from DS in return for an installment note. On July 1, 1995, DS sells a number of installment notes, including C's, to FS in exchange for $10,000,000. DS continues to service the installment notes for FS and C is not notified of the sale of its obligation and continues to make payments to DS. But for the withholding tax on payments of interest by DS to BK, DS would have borrowed directly from BK, pledging the installment notes as collateral.

(iii) The C installment note is a financing transaction, whether held by DS or by FS, and the FS note held by BK also is a financing transaction. After FS purchases the installment note, and during the time the installment note is held by FS, the transactions constitute a financing arrangement, within the meaning of § 1.881-3(a)(2)(i). BK is the financing entity, FS is the intermediate entity, and C is the financed entity. Because the participation of FS in the financing arrangement reduces the tax imposed by section 881 and because there was a tax avoidance plan, FS is a conduit entity.

(iv) Because C does not know or have reason to know of the tax avoidance plan (and by extension that the financing arrangement is a conduit financing arrangement), C is not required to withhold tax under section 1441. However, DS, who knows that FS's participation in the financing arrangement is pursuant to a tax avoidance plan and is a withholding agent for purposes of section 1441, is not relieved of its withholding responsibilities.

Example 2. Assume the same facts as in Example 1, except that C receives a new payment booklet on which DS is described as "agent". Although C may deduce that its installment note has been sold, without more C has no reason to know of the existence of a financing arrangement. Accordingly, C is not liable for failure to withhold, although DS still is not relieved of its withholding responsibilities.

Example 3. (i) DC is a U.S. corporation that is in the process of negotiating a loan of $10,000,000 from BK1, a bank located in Country N, a country that does not have an income tax treaty with the United States. Before the loan agreement is signed, DC's tax lawyers point out that interest on the loan would not be subject to withholding tax if the loan were made by BK2, a subsidiary of BK1 that is incorporated in Country T, a country that has an income tax treaty with the United States that prohibits the imposition of withholding tax on payments of interest. BK1 makes a loan to BK2 to enable BK2 to make the loan to DC. Without the loan from BK1 to BK2, BK2 would not have been able to make the loan to DC.

(ii) The loan from BK1 to BK2 and the loan from BK2 to DC are both financing transactions and together constitute a financing arrangement within the meaning of § 1.881-3(a)(2)(i). BK1 is the financing entity, BK2 is the intermediate entity, and DC is the financed entity. Because the participation of BK2 in the financing arrangement reduces the tax imposed by section 881 and because there is a tax avoidance plan, BK2 is a conduit entity.

(iii) Because DC is a party to the tax avoidance plan (and accordingly knows of its existence), DC must withhold tax under section 1441. If DC does not withhold tax on its payment of interest, BK2, a party to the plan and a withholding agent for purposes of section 1441, must withhold tax as required by section 1441.

Example 4. (i) DC is a U.S. corporation that has a long-standing banking relationship with BK2, a U.S. subsidiary of BK1, a bank incorporated in Country N, a country that does not have an income tax treaty with the United States. DC has borrowed amounts of as much as $75,000,000 from BK2 in the past. On January 1, 1995, DC asks to borrow $50,000,000 from BK2. BK2 does not have the funds available to make a loan of that size. BK2 considers asking BK1 to enter into a loan with DC but rejects this possibility because of the additional withholding tax that would be incurred. Accordingly, BK2 borrows the necessary amount from BK1 with the intention of on-lending to DC. BK1 does not make the loan directly to DC because of the withholding tax that would apply to payments of interest from DC to BK1. DC does not negotiate with BK1 and has no reason to know that BK1 was the source of the loan.

(ii) The loan from BK2 to DC and the loan from BK1 to BK2 are both financing transactions and together constitute a financing arrangement within the meaning of § 1.881-3(a)(2)(i). BK1 is the financing entity, BK2 is the intermediate entity, and DC is the financed entity. The participation of BK2 in the financing arrangement reduces the tax imposed by section 881. Because the participation of BK2 in the financing arrangement reduces the tax imposed by section 881 and

Reg. § 1.1441-7(f)(2)

because there was a tax avoidance plan, BK2 is a conduit entity.

(iii) Because DC does not know or have reason to know of the tax avoidance plan (and by extension that the financing arrangement is a conduit financing arrangement), DC is not required to withhold tax under section 1441. However, BK2, who is also a withholding agent under section 1441 and who knows that the financing arrangement is a conduit financing arrangement, is not relieved of its withholding responsibilities.

(3) *Effective date.* This paragraph (f) is effective for payments made by financed entities on or after September 11, 1995. This paragraph shall not apply to interest payments covered by section 127(g)(3) of the Tax Reform Act of 1984, and to interest payments with respect to other debt obligations issued prior to October 15, 1984 (whether or not such debt was issued by a Netherlands Antilles corporation).

(g) *Effective date.* Except as otherwise provided in paragraph (f)(3) of this section, this section applies to payments made after December 31, 2000. [Reg. § 1.1441-7.]

□ [T.D. 7977, 9-19-84. Amended by T.D. 8611, 8-10-95; T.D. 8734, 10-6-97; T.D. 8804, 12-30-98; T.D. 8856, 12-29-99 and T.D. 8881, 5-15-2000 (*corrected* 4-5-2001).]

[Reg. § 1.1441-8]

§ 1.1441-8. Exemption from withholding for payments to foreign governments, international organizations, foreign central banks of issue, and the Bank for International Settlements.—(a) *Foreign governments.* Under section 892, certain specific types of income received by foreign governments are excluded from gross income and are exempt from taxation, unless derived from the conduct of a commercial activity or received from or by a controlled commercial entity. Accordingly, withholding is not required under § 1.1441-1 with regard to any item of income which is exempt from taxation under section 892.

(b) *Reliance on claim of exemption by foreign government.* Absent actual knowledge or reason to know otherwise, the withholding agent may rely upon a claim of exemption made by the foreign government if, prior to the payment, the withholding agent can reliably associate the payment with documentation upon which it can rely to treat the payment as made to a beneficial owner in accordance with § 1.1441-1(e)(1)(ii). A Form W-8 furnished by a foreign government for purposes of claiming an exemption under this paragraph (b) is valid only if, in addition to other applicable requirements, it certifies that the income is, or will be, exempt from taxation under section 892 and the regulations under that section and whether the person whose name is on the certificate is an integral part of a foreign government (as defined in § 1.892-2T(a)(2)) or a controlled entity (as defined in § 1.892-2T(a)(3)).

(c) *Income of a foreign central bank of issue or the Bank for International Settlements*—(1) *Certain interest income.* Section 895 provides for the exclusion from gross income of certain income derived by a foreign central bank of issue, or by the Bank for International Settlements, from obligations of the United States or of any agency or instrumentality thereof or from interest on deposits with persons carrying on the banking business if the bank is the owner of the obligations or deposits and does not hold the obligations or deposits for, or use them in connection with, the conduct of a commercial banking function or other commercial activity by such bank. See § 1.895-1. Absent actual knowledge or reason to know that a foreign central bank of issue, or the Bank for International Settlements, is operating outside the scope of the exclusion granted by section 895 and the regulations under that section, the withholding agent may rely on a claim of exemption if, prior to the payment, the withholding agent can reliably associate the payment with documentation upon which it can rely to treat the foreign central bank of issue or the Bank for International Settlements as the beneficial owner of the payment in accordance with § 1.1441-1(e)(1)(ii). A Form W-8 furnished by a foreign central bank of issue or the Bank for International Settlements for purposes of claiming an exemption under this paragraph (c)(1) is valid only if, in addition to other applicable requirements, it certifies that the person whose name is on the certificate is a foreign central bank of issue, or the Bank for International Settlements, and that the bank does not, and will not, hold the obligations or the bank deposits covered by the Form W-8 for, or use them in connection with, the conduct of a commercial banking function or other commercial activity.

(2) *Bankers' acceptances.* Interest derived by a foreign central bank of issue from bankers' acceptances is exempt from tax under sections 871(i)(2)(C) and 881(d) and § 1.861-2(b)(4). With respect to bankers' acceptances, a withholding agent may treat a payee as a foreign central bank of issue without requiring a withholding certificate if the name of the payee and other facts surrounding the payment reasonably indicate that the payee or beneficial owner is a foreign central bank of issue, as defined in § 1.861-2(b)(4).

(d) *Exemption for payments to international organizations.* A payment to an international organization (within the meaning of section 7701(a)(18)) is exempt from withholding on any payment. A withholding agent may treat a payee as an international organization without requiring a withholding certificate if the name of the payee is one that is designated as an international organization by executive order (pursuant to 22 U.S.C. 288 through 288(f)) and other facts surrounding the transaction reasonably indicate that the international organization is the beneficial owner of the payment.

(e) *Failure to receive withholding certificate timely and other applicable procedures.* See applicable procedures described in § 1.1441-1(b)(7) in the event the withholding agent does not hold a valid withholding certificate described in paragraph (b) or (c)(1) of this section or other appropriate documentation at the time of payment. Further, the provisions of § 1.1441-1(e)(4) shall apply to withholding certificates and other documents related thereto furnished under the provisions of this section.

(f) *Effective date*—(1) *In general.* This section applies to payments made after December 31, 2000.

(2) *Transition rules.* For purposes of this section, the validity of a Form 8709 that was valid on January 1, 1998, under the regulations in effect prior to January 1, 2001 (see 26 CFR part 1, revised April 1, 1999) and expired, or will expire, at any time during 1998, is extended until December 31, 1998. The validity of a Form 8709 that is valid on or after January 1, 1999, remains valid until its validity expires under the regulations in effect prior to January 1, 2001 (see 26 CFR part 1, revised April 1, 1999) but in no event shall such a form remain valid after December 31, 2000. The rule in this paragraph (f)(2), however, does not apply to extend the validity period of a Form 8709 that expires solely by reason of changes in the circumstances of the person whose name is on the certificate. Notwithstanding the first three sentences of this paragraph (f)(2), a withholding agent may choose to not take advantage of the transition rule in this paragraph (f)(2) with respect to one or more withholding certificates valid under the regulations in effect prior to January 1, 2001 (see 26 CFR part 1, revised April 1, 1999) and, therefore, to require withholding certificates conforming to the requirements described in this section (new withholding certificates). For purposes of this section, a new withholding certificate is deemed to satisfy the documentation requirement under the regulations in effect prior to January 1, 2001 (see 26 CFR part 1, revised April 1,

1999). Further, a new withholding certificate remains valid for the period specified in § 1.1441-1(e)(4)(ii), regardless of when the certificate is obtained. [Reg. § 1.1441-8.]

☐ [T.D. 8211, 6-24-88. *Redesignated and amended by T.D. 8734, 10-6-97 and amended by T.D. 8804, 12-30-98 and T.D. 8856, 12-29-99.*]

[Reg. § 1.1441-9]

§ 1.1441-9. Exemption from withholding on exempt income of a foreign tax-exempt organization, including foreign private foundations.—(a) *Exemption from withholding for exempt income.* No withholding is required under section 1441(a) or 1442, and the regulations under those sections, on amounts paid to a foreign organization that is described in section 501(c) to the extent that the amounts are not income includible under section 512 in computing the organization's unrelated business taxable income. See, however, § 1.1443-1 for withholding on payments of unrelated business income to foreign tax-exempt organizations and on payments subject to tax under section 4948. For a foreign organization to claim an exemption from withholding under section 1441(a) or 1442 based on its status as an organization described in section 501(c), it must furnish the withholding agent with a withholding certificate described in paragraph (b)(2) of this section. A foreign organization described in section 501(c) may choose to claim a reduced rate of withholding under the procedures described in other sections of the regulations under section 1441 and not under this section. In particular, if an organization chooses to claim benefits under an income tax treaty, the withholding procedures applicable to claims of such a reduced rate are governed solely by the provisions of § 1.1441-6 and not of this section.

(b) *Reliance on foreign organization's claim of exemption from withholding*—(1) *General rule.* A withholding agent may rely on a claim of exemption under this section only if, prior to the payment, the withholding agent can reliably associate the payment with a valid withholding certificate described in paragraph (b)(2) of this section.

(2) *Withholding certificate.* A withholding certificate under this paragraph (b)(2) is valid only if it is a Form W-8 and if, in addition to other applicable requirements, the Form W-8 includes the taxpayer identifying number of the organization whose name is on the certificate, and it certifies that the Internal Revenue Service (IRS) has issued a favorable determination letter (and the date thereof) that is currently in effect, what portion, if any, of the amounts paid constitute income includible under section 512 in computing the organization's unrelated business taxable in-

Reg. § 1.1441-9(a)

come, and, if the organization is described in section 501(c)(3), whether it is a private foundation described in section 509. Notwithstanding the preceding sentence, if the organization cannot certify that it has been issued a favorable determination letter that is still in effect, its withholding certificate is nevertheless valid under this paragraph (b)(2) if the organization attaches to the withholding certificate an opinion that is acceptable to the withholding agent from a U.S. counsel (or any other person as the IRS may prescribe in published guidance (see § 601.601(d)(2) of this chapter)) concluding that the organization is described in section 501(c). If the determination letter or opinion of counsel to which the withholding certificate refers concludes that the organization is described in section 501(c)(3), and the certificate further certifies that the organization is not a private foundation described in section 509, an affidavit of the organization setting forth sufficient facts concerning the operations and support of the organization for the Internal Revenue Service (IRS) to determine that such organization would be likely to qualify as an organization described in section 509(a)(1), (2), (3), or (4) must be attached to the withholding certificate. An organization that provides an opinion of U.S. counsel or an affidavit may provide the same opinion or affidavit to more than one withholding agent provided that the opinion is acceptable to each withholding agent who receives it in conjunction with a withholding certificate. Any such opinion of counsel or affidavit must be renewed whenever there is a change in facts or circumstances that are relevant to determine the organization's status under section 501(c) or, if relevant, that the organization is or is not a private foundation described in section 509.

(3) *Presumptions in the absence of documentation.* Notwithstanding paragraph (b)(1) of this section, if the organization's certification with respect to whether amounts paid constitute income includible under section 512 in computing the organization's unrelated business taxable income is not reliable or is lacking but all other certifications are reliable, the withholding agent may rely on the certificate but the amounts paid are presumed to be income includible under section 512 in computing the organization's unrelated business taxable income. If the certification regarding private foundation status is not reliable, the withholding agent may rely on the certificate but the amounts paid are presumed to be paid to a foreign beneficial owner that is a private foundation.

(4) *Reason to know.* Reliance by a withholding agent on the information and certifications stated on a withholding certificate is subject to the agent's actual knowledge or reason to know that such information or certification is incorrect as provided in § 1.1441-7(b). For example, a withholding agent must cease to treat a foreign organization's claim for exemption from withholding based on the organization's tax-exempt status as valid beginning on the earlier of the date on which such agent knows that the IRS has given notice to such foreign organization that it is not an organization described in section 501(c) or the date on which the IRS gives notice to the public that such foreign organization is not an organization described in section 501(c). Similarly, a withholding agent may no longer rely on a certification that an amount is not subject to tax under section 4948 beginning on the earlier of the date on which such agent knows that the IRS has given notice to such foreign organization that it is subject to tax under section 4948 or the date on which the IRS gives notice that such foreign organization is a private foundation within the meaning of section 509(a).

(c) *Failure to receive withholding certificate timely and other applicable procedures.* See applicable procedures described in § 1.1441-1(b)(7) in the event the withholding agent does not hold a valid withholding certificate or other appropriate documentation at the time of payment. Further, the provisions of § 1.1441-1(e)(4) shall apply to withholding certificates and other documents related thereto furnished under the provisions of this section.

(d) *Effective date*—(1) *In general.* This section applies to payments made after December 31, 2000.

(2) *Transition rules.* For purposes of this section, the validity of a Form W-8, 1001, or 4224 or a statement that was valid on January 1, 1998, under the regulations in effect prior to January 1, 2001 (see 26 CFR parts 1 and 35a, revised April 1, 1999) and expired, or will expire, at any time during 1998, is extended until December 31, 1998. The validity of a Form W-8, 1001, or 4224 or a statement that is valid on or after January 1, 1999 remains valid until its validity expires under the regulations in effect prior to January 1, 2001 (see 26 CFR parts 1 and 35a, revised April 1, 1999) but in no event shall such form or statement remain valid after December 31, 2000. The rule in this paragraph (d)(2), however, does not apply to extend the validity period of a Form W-8, 1001, or 4224 or a statement that expires solely by reason of changes in the circumstances of the person whose name is on the certificate. Notwithstanding the first three sentences of this paragraph (d)(2), a withholding agent may choose to not take advantage of the transition rule in this paragraph (d)(2) with respect to one or more withholding certificates valid under the regula-

Reg. § 1.1441-9(d)(2)

tions in effect prior to January 1, 2001 (see 26 CFR parts 1 and 35a, revised April 1, 1999) and, therefore, to require withholding certificates conforming to the requirements described in this section (new withholding certificates). For purposes of this section, a new withholding certificate is deemed to satisfy the documentation requirement under the regulations in effect prior to January 1, 2001 (see 26 CFR parts 1 and 35a, revised April 1, 1999). Further, a new withholding certificate remains valid for the period specified in § 1.1441-1(e)(4)(ii), regardless of when the certificate is obtained. [Reg. § 1.1441-9.]

☐ [T.D. 8734, 10-6-97. Amended by T.D. 8804, 12-30-98; T.D. 8856, 12-29-99 and T.D. 8881, 5-15-2000.]

[Reg. § 1.1441-10]

§ 1.1441-10. Withholding agents with respect to fast-pay arrangements.—(a) *In general.* A corporation that issues fast-pay stock in a fast-pay arrangement described in § 1.7701(l)-3(b)(1) is a withholding agent with respect to payments made on the fast-pay stock and payments deemed made under the recharacterization rules of § 1.7701(l)-3. Except as provided in this paragraph (a) or in paragraph (b) of this section, the withholding tax rules under section 1441 and section 1442 apply with respect to a fast-pay arrangement described in § 1.7701(l)-3(c)(1)(i) in accordance with the recharacterization rules provided in § 1.7701(l)-3(c). In all cases, notwithstanding paragraph (b) of this section, if at any time the withholding agent knows or has reason to know that the Commissioner has exercised the discretion under either § 1.7701(l)-3(c)(1)(ii) to apply the recharacterization rules of § 1.7701(l)-3(c), or § 1.7701(l)-3(d) to depart from the recharacterization rules of § 1.7701(l)-3(c) for a taxpayer, the withholding agent must withhold on payments made (or deemed made) to that taxpayer in accordance with the characterization of the fast-pay arrangement imposed by the Commissioner under § 1.7701(l)-3.

(b) *Exception.* If at any time the withholding agent knows or has reason to know that any taxpayer entered into a fast-pay arrangement with a principal purpose of applying the recharacterization rules of § 1.7701(l)-3(c) to avoid tax under section 871(a) or section 881, then for each payment made or deemed made to such taxpayer under the arrangement, the withholding agent must withhold, under section 1441 or section 1442, the higher of—

(1) The amount of withholding that would apply to such payment determined under the form of the arrangement; or

(2) The amount of withholding that would apply to deemed payments determined under the recharacterization rules of § 1.7701(l)-3(c).

(c) *Liability.* Any person required to deduct and withhold tax under this section is made liable for that tax by section 1461, and is also liable for applicable penalties and interest for failing to comply with section 1461.

(d) *Examples.* The following examples illustrate the rules of this section:

Example 1. REIT W issues shares of fast-pay stock to foreign individual A, a resident of Country C. United States source dividends paid to residents of C are subject to a 30 percent withholding tax. W issues all shares of benefited stock to foreign individuals who are residents of Country D. D's income tax convention with the United States reduces the United States withholding tax on dividends to 15 percent. Under § 1.7701(l)-3(c), the dividends paid by W to A are deemed to be paid by W to the benefited shareholders. W has reason to know that A entered into the fast-pay arrangement with a principal purpose of using the recharacterization rules of § 1.7701(l)-3(c) to reduce United States withholding tax. W must withhold at the 30 percent rate because the amount of withholding that applies to the payments determined under the form of the arrangement is higher than the amount of withholding that applies to the payments determined under § 1.7701(l)-3(c).

Example 2. The facts are the same as in *Example 1* of this paragraph (d) except that W does not know, or have reason to know, that A entered into the arrangement with a principal purpose of using the recharacterization rules of § 1.7701(l)-3(c) to reduce United States withholding tax. Further, the Commissioner has not exercised the discretion under § 1.7701(l)-3(d) to depart from the recharacterization rules of § 1.7701(l)-3(c). Accordingly, W must withhold tax at a 15 percent rate on the dividends deemed paid to the benefited shareholders.

(e) *Effective date.* This section applies to payments made (or deemed made) on or after January 6, 1999. [Reg. § 1.1441-10.]

☐ [T.D. 8853, 1-7-2000.]

[Reg. § 1.1442-1]

§ 1.1442-1. Withholding of tax on foreign corporations.—For regulations concerning the withholding of tax at source under section 1442 in the case of foreign corporations, foreign governments, international organizations, foreign tax-exempt corporations, or foreign private foundations, see §§ 1.1441-1 through 1.1441-9. [Reg. § 1.1442-1.]

Reg. § 1.1441-10(a)

☐ [T.D. 6187, 7-5-56. Amended by T.D. 6908, 12-30-66 and T.D. 8734, 10-6-97 (T.D. 8804 delayed the effective date of T.D. 8734 from January 1, 1999, to January 1, 2000; T.D. 8856 further delayed the effective date of T.D. 8734 until January 1, 2001).]

[Reg. § 1.1442-2]

§ 1.1442-2. Exemption under a tax treaty.—For regulations providing for a claim of reduced withholding tax under section 1442 by certain foreign corporations pursuant to the provisions of an income tax treaty, see § 1.1441-6. [Reg. § 1.1442-2.]

☐ [T.D. 6908, 12-30-66. Amended by T.D. 8734, 10-6-97 (T.D. 8804 delayed the effective date of T.D. 8734 from January 1, 1999, to January 1, 2000; T.D. 8856 further delayed the effective date of T.D. 8734 until January 1, 2001).]

[Reg. § 1.1442-3]

§ 1.1442-3. Tax exempt income of a foreign tax-exempt corporation.—For regulations providing for a claim of exemption for income exempt from tax under section 501(a) of a foreign tax-exempt corporation, see § 1.1441-9. See § 1.1443-1 for withholding rules applicable to foreign private foundations and to the unrelated business income of foreign tax-exempt organizations. [Reg. § 1.1442-3.]

☐ [T.D. 8734, 10-6-97 (T.D. 8804 delayed the effective date of T.D. 8734 from January 1, 1999, to January 1, 2000; T.D. 8856 further delayed the effective date of T.D. 8734 until January 1, 2001).]

[Reg. § 1.1443-1]

§ 1.1443-1. Foreign tax-exempt organizations.—(a) *Income includible under section 512 in computing unrelated business taxable income.* In the case of a foreign organization that is described in section 501(c), amounts paid to the organization includible under section 512 in computing the organization's unrelated business taxable income are subject to withholding under §§ 1.1441-1, 1.1441-4, and 1.1441-6 in the same manner as payments of the same amounts to any foreign person that is not a tax-exempt organization. Therefore, a foreign organization receiving amounts includible under section 512 in computing the organization's unrelated business taxable income may claim an exemption from withholding or a reduced rate of withholding with respect to that income in the same manner as a foreign person that is not a tax-exempt organization. See § 1.1441-9(b)(3) for presumption that amounts are includible under section 512 in computing the organization's unrelated business taxable income in the absence of a reliable certification.

(b) *Income subject to tax under section 4948*—(1) *In general.* The gross investment income (as defined in section 4940(c)(2)) of a foreign private foundation is subject to withholding under section 1443(b) at the rate of 4 percent to the extent that the income is from sources within the United States and is subject to the tax imposed by section 4948(a) and the regulations under that section. Withholding under this paragraph (b) is required irrespective of the fact that the income may be effectively connected with the conduct of a trade or business in the United States by the foreign organization. See § 1.1441-9(b)(3) for applicable presumptions that amounts are subject to tax under section 4948. The withholding imposed under this paragraph (b)(1) does not obviate a private foundation's obligation to file any return required by law with respect to such organization, such as the form that the foundation is required to file under section 6033 for the taxable year.

(2) *Reliance on a foreign organization's claim of foreign private foundation status.* For reliance by a withholding agent on a foreign organization's claim of foreign private foundation status, see § 1.1441-9(b) and (c).

(3) *Applicable procedures.* A withholding agent withholding the 4-percent amount pursuant to paragraph (b)(1) of this section shall treat such withholding as withholding under section 1441(a) or 1442(a) for all purposes, including reporting of the payment on a Form 1042 and a Form 1042-S pursuant to § 1.1461-1(b) and (c). Similarly, the foreign private foundation shall treat the 4-percent withholding as withholding under section 1441(a) or 1442(a), including for purposes of claims for refunds and credits.

(4) *Claim of benefits under an income tax treaty.* The withholding procedures applicable to claims of a reduced rate under an income tax treaty are governed solely by the provisions of § 1.1441-6 and not by this section.

(c) *Effective date*—(1) *In general.* This section applies to payments made after December 31, 2000.

(2) *Transition rules.* For purposes of this section, the validity of an affidavit or opinion of counsel described in § 1.1443-1(b)(4)(i) in effect prior to January 1, 2001 (see § 1.1443-1(b)(4)(i) as contained in 26 CFR part 1, revised April 1, 1999) is extended until December 31, 2000. However, a withholding agent may chose to not take advantage of the transition rule in this paragraph (c)(2) with respect to one or more withholding certificates valid under the regulations in effect prior to January 1, 2001 (see CFR part 1, revised

Reg. § 1.1443-1(c)(2)

April 1, 1999) and, therefore, to require withholding certificates conforming to the requirements described in this section (new withholding certificates). For purposes of this section, a new withholding certificate is deemed to satisfy the documentation requirement under the regulations in effect prior to January 1, 2001 (see 26 CFR part 1, revised April 1, 1999). Further, a new withholding certificate remains valid for the period specified in § 1.1441-1(e)(4)(ii), regardless of when the certificate is obtained. [Reg. § 1.1443-1.]

☐ [T.D. 6187, 7-5-56. Amended by T.D. 6908, 12-30-66 and T.D. 7229, 12-20-72; T.D. 7247, 12-29-72; T.D. 8734, 10-6-97; T.D. 8804, 12-30-98 and T.D. 8856, 12-29-99.]

[Reg. § 1.1445-1]

§ 1.1445-1. Withholding on dispositions of U.S. real property interests by foreign persons: In general.—(a) *Purpose and scope of regulations.* These regulations set forth rules relating to the withholding requirements of section 1445. In general, section 1445(a) provides that any person who acquires a U.S. real property interest from a foreign person must withhold a tax of 10 percent from the amount realized by the transferor foreign person (or a lesser amount established by agreement with the Internal Revenue Service). Section 1445(e) provides special rules requiring withholding on distributions and certain other transactions by corporations, partnerships, trusts, and estates. This § 1.1445-1 provides general rules concerning the withholding requirement of section 1445(a), as well as definitions applicable under both sections 1445(a) and 1445(e). Section 1.1445-2 provides for various situations in which withholding is not required under section 1445(a). Section 1.1445-3 provides for adjustments to the amount required to be withheld by transferees under section 1445(a). Section 1.1445-4 prescribes the duties of agents in transactions subject to withholding under either section 1445(a) or 1445(e). Section 1.1445-5 provides rules concerning the withholding required under section 1445(e), while § 1.1445-6 provides for adjustments to the amount required to be withheld under section 1445(e). Finally, § 1.1445-7 provides rules concerning the treatment of a foreign corporation that has made an election under section 897(i) to be treated as a domestic corporation.

(b) *Duty to withhold*—(1) *In general.* Transferees of U.S. real property interests are required to deduct and withhold a tax equal to 10 percent of the amount realized by the transferor, if the transferor is a foreign person and the disposition takes place on or after January 1, 1985. Neither the transferee's duty to withhold nor the amount required to be withheld is affected by the amount of cash to be paid by the transferee. Amounts withheld must be reported and paid over in accordance with the requirements of paragraph (c) of this section. Failures to withhold and pay over are subject to the liabilities set forth in paragraph (e) of this section. If two or more persons are joint transferees of a U.S. real property interest, each such person is subject to the obligation to withhold. That obligation is fulfilled with respect to each such person if any one of them withholds and pays over the required amount in accordance with the rules of this section. If the amount realized (as defined in paragraph (g)(5) of this section) by the transferor is zero, then no withholding is required. For example, if a real property interest is transferred as a gift (i.e., the recipient does not assume any liabilities or furnish any other consideration to the transferor) then no withholding is required. Withholding is not required with respect to dispositions that take place before January 1, 1985, even if the first payment of consideration is made after December 31, 1984.

(2) *U.S. real property interest owned jointly by foreign and non-foreign transferors.* The amount subject to withholding under paragraph (b)(1) of this section with respect to the transfer of a U.S. real property interest owned by one or more foreign persons (as defined in § 1.897-1(k)) and one or more non-foreign persons shall be determined by allocating the amount realized from the transfer between (or among) such transferors based upon the capital contribution of each transferor with respect to the property and by aggregating the amounts allocated to any foreign person (or persons). For this purpose, a husband and wife will each be deemed to have contributed 50 percent of the aggregate capital contributed by such husband and wife. See § 1.1445-1(f)(3)(iv) with respect to the crediting of the amount withheld between or among joint foreign transferors.

(3) *Options to acquire a U.S. real property interest.—*

(i) *No withholding on grant of option.* No withholding is required under section 1445 with respect to any amount realized by the grantor on the grant of an option to acquire a U.S. real property interest.

(ii) *No withholding upon lapse of option.* No withholding is required under section 1445 with respect to any amount realized by the grantor upon the lapse of an option to acquire a U.S. real property interest.

(iii) *Withholding required upon the sale or exchange of option.* A transferee of an option to acquire a U.S. real property interest must deduct

Reg. § 1.1445-1(a)

and withhold a tax equal to 10 percent of the amount realized by the transferor upon the disposition. This § 1.1445-1(b)(3)(iii) does not apply to require withholding upon the initial grant of an option.

(iv) *Withholding required on exercise of option.* If the holder exercises an option to purchase a U.S. real property interest, the amount paid for the option shall be considered an amount realized by the grantor/transferor upon the transfer of the property with respect to which the option was granted, and shall thus be subject to withholding on the day that such underlying property is transferred. The preceding sentence applies regardless of whether or not the terms of the option specifically provide that the option price is applied to the purchase price.

(4) *Exceptions and modifications.* The duty to withhold under section 1445(a) is subject to the exceptions and modifications contained in §§ 1.1445-2 and 1.1445-3. Generally, § 1.1445-2 provides rules for determining that withholding is not required because either the transferor is not a foreign person or the interest transferred is not a U.S. real property interest. In addition, § 1.1445-2 provides exceptions to the withholding requirement, including a rule that exempts from withholding any person who acquires a U.S. real property interest for use as a residence for a contract price of $300,000 or less. If withholding is required under section 1445(a), § 1.1445-3 allows the amount withheld to be modified pursuant to a withholding certificate issued by the Internal Revenue Service. If a transferee cannot withhold the full amount required because the first payment of consideration for the transfer does not involve sufficient cash (or other liquid assets convertible into cash, such as foreign currency), then a withholding certificate must be obtained pursuant to § 1.1445-3.

(c) *Reporting and paying over of withheld amounts*—(1) *In general.* A transferee must report and pay over any tax withheld by the 20th day after the date of the transfer. Forms 8288 and 8288-A are used for this purpose, and must be filed with the Internal Revenue Service Center, Philadelphia, PA 19255. Pursuant to section 7502 and regulations thereunder, the timely mailing of Forms 8288 and 8288-A will be treated as their timely filing. Form 8288-A will be stamped by the IRS to show receipt, and a stamped copy will be mailed by the IRS to the transferor (at the address reported on the form) for the transferor's use. See §§ 1.1445-1(f) and 1.1445-3(f).

(2) *Pending application for withholding certificate*—(i) *In general.*

(A) *Delayed reporting and payment with respect to application submitted by transferee.* If an application for a withholding certificate with respect to a transfer of a U.S. real property interest is submitted to the Internal Revenue Service by the transferee on the day of or at any time prior to the transfer, the transferee must withhold 10 percent of the amount realized as required by paragraph (b) of this section. However, the amount withheld, or a lesser amount as determined by the Service, need not be reported and paid over to the Service until the 20th day following the Service's final determination with respect to the application for a withholding certificate. For this purpose, the Service's final determination occurs on the day when the withholding certificate is mailed to the transferee by the Service or when a notification denying the request for a withholding certificate is mailed to the transferee by the Service. An application is submitted to the Service on the day it is actually received by the Service at the address provided in § 1.1445-1(g)(10) or, under the rules of section 7502, on the day it is mailed to the Service at the address provided in § 1.1445-1(g)(10).

(B) *Delayed reporting and payment with respect to application submitted by transferor.* If an application for a withholding certificate with respect to a transfer of a U.S. real property interest is submitted to the Internal Revenue Service by the transferor on the day of or any time prior to the transfer, such transferor must provide notice to the transferee prior to the transfer. No particular form is required but the notice must set forth the name, address, and taxpayer identification number, if any, of the transferor, a brief description of the property which is the subject of the application, and the date the application was submitted to the Service. The transferee must withhold 10 percent of the amount realized as required in paragraph (b) of this section but need not report or pay over to the Service such amount (or a lesser amount as determined by the Service) until the 20th day following the Service's final determination with respect to the application. The Service will send a copy of the withholding certificate or copy of the notification denying the request for a withholding certificate to the transferee. For this purpose, the Service's final determination will be deemed to occur on the day when the copy of the withholding certificate or the copy of the notification denying the request for a withholding certificate is mailed by the Service to the transferee (or transferees). An application is submitted to the Service on the day it is actually received by the Service at the address provided in § 1.1445-1(g)(10) or, under the rules of § 7502, on the day it is mailed to the

Service at the address provided in §1.1445-1(g)(10).

(ii) *Anti-abuse rule*—(A) *In general.* A transferee that in reliance upon the rules of this paragraph (c)(2) fails to report and pay over amounts withheld by the 20th day following the date of the transfer, shall be subject to the payment of interest and penalties if the relevant application for a withholding certificate (or an amendment to the application for a withholding certificate) was submitted for a principal purpose of delaying the transferee's payment to the IRS of the amount withheld. Interest and penalties shall be assessed on the amount that is ultimately paid over (or collected pursuant to the agreement) with respect to the period between the 20th day after the date of the transfer and the date on which payment is made (or collected).

(B) *Presumption.* A principal purpose of delaying payment of the amount withheld shall be presumed if—

(*1*) The transferee applies for a withholding certificate pursuant to §1.1445-3(c) based on a determination of the transferor's maximum tax liability, and

(*2*) Such liability is ultimately determined to be equal to 90 percent or more of the amount that was otherwise required to be withheld and paid over.

However, the presumption created by the previous sentence may be rebutted by evidence establishing that delaying payment of the amount withheld was not a principal purpose of the transaction.

(d) *Contents of Forms 8288 and 8288-A*—(1) *Transactions subject to section 1445(a).* Any person that is required to file Forms 8288 and 8288-A pursuant to section 1445(a) and the rules of this section must set forth thereon the following information:

(i) The name, identifying number (if any), and home address (in the case of an individual) or office address (in the case of any entity) of the transferee(s) filing the return;

(ii) The name, identifying number (if any), and home address (in the case of an individual) or office address (in the case of any entity) of the transferor(s);

(iii) A brief description of the U.S. real property interest transferred, including its location and the nature of any substantial improvements in the case of real property, and the class or type and amount of interests transferred in the case of interests in a corporation that constitute U.S. real property interests;

(iv) The date of the transfer;

(v) The amount realized by the transferor, as defined in paragraph (g)(5) of this section;

(vi) The amount withheld by the transferee and whether withholding is at the statutory or reduced rate; and

(vii) Such other information as the Commissioner may require.

For purposes of paragraph (d)(1)(i) and (ii), mailing addresses may be provided in addition to, but not in lieu of, home addresses or office addresses.

(2) *Transactions subject to section 1445(e).* Any person that is required to file Forms 8288 and 8288-A pursuant to the rules of §1.1445-5 must set forth thereon the following information:

(i) The name, identifying number (if any), and office address of the entity or fiduciary filing the return;

(ii) The amount withheld by the entity or fiduciary;

(iii) The date of the transfer;

(iv) In the case of a transaction subject to withholding pursuant to section 1445(e)(1) and §1.1445-5(c):

(A) A brief description of the U.S. real property interest transferred, as described in paragraph (d)(1)(iii) of this section;

(B) The name, identifying number (if any), and home address (in the case of an individual) or office address (in the case of an entity) of each holder of an interest in the entity that is a foreign person; and

(C) Each such interest-holder's pro rata share of the amount withheld;

(v) In the case of a distribution subject to withholding pursuant to section 1445(e)(2) and §1.1445-5(d):

(A) A brief description of the U.S. real property interest transferred, as described in paragraph (d)(1)(iii) of this section; and

(B) The amount of gain recognized upon the distribution by the corporation.

(vi) In the case of a distribution subject to withholding pursuant to section 1445(e)(3) and §1.1445-5(e):

(A) A brief description of the property distributed by the corporation;

(B) The name, identifying number (if any), and home address (in the case of an individual) or office address (in the case of an entity) of each holder of an interest in the entity that is a foreign person;

(C) The amount realized upon the distribution by each such foreign interest holder; and

Reg. § 1.1445-1(d)(1)

(D) Each foreign interest-holder's pro rata share of the amount withheld; and

(vii) Such other information as the Commissioner may require.

(e) *Liability of transferee upon failure to withhold*—(1) *In general.* Every person required to deduct and withhold tax under section 1445 is made liable for that tax by section 1461. Therefore, a person that is required to deduct and withhold tax but fails to do so may be held liable for the payment of the tax and any applicable penalties and interest.

(2) *Transferor's liability not otherwise satisfied*—(i) *Tax and penalties.* Except as provided in paragraph (e)(3) of this section, if a transferee is required to deduct and withhold tax under section 1445 but fails to do so, then the tax shall be assessed against and collected from that transferee. Such person may also be subject to any of the civil and criminal penalties that apply. Corporate officers or other responsible persons may be subject to a civil penalty under section 6672 equal to the amount that should have been withheld and paid over.

(ii) *Interest.* If a transferee is required to deduct and withhold tax under section 1445 but fails to do so, then such transferee shall be liable for the payment of interest pursuant to section 6601 and the regulations thereunder. Interest shall be payable with respect to the period between—

(A) The last date on which the tax imposed under section 1445 was required to be paid over by the transferee, and

(B) The date on which such tax is actually paid. Interest shall be payable with respect to the entire amount that is required to be deducted and withheld. However, if the Service issues a withholding certificate providing for withholding of a reduced amount, then, for the period after the issuance of the certificate, interest shall be payable with respect to that reduced amount.

(3) *Transferor's liability otherwise satisfied*—(i) *Tax and penalties.* If a transferee is required to deduct and withhold tax under section 1445 but fails to do so, and the transferor's tax liability with respect to the transfer was satisfied (or was established to be zero) by—

(A) The transferor's filing of an income tax return (and payment of any tax due) with respect to the transfer, or

(B) The issuance of a withholding certificate by the Internal Revenue Service establishing that the transferor's maximum tax liability is zero,

then the tax required to be withheld under section 1445 shall not be collected from the transferee. Such transferee's liability for tax, and the requirement that such person file Forms 8288 and 8288-A, shall be deemed to have been satisfied as of the date on which the transferor's income tax return was filed or the withholding certificate was issued. No penalty shall be imposed on or collected from such person for failure to return or pay the tax, unless such failure was fraudulent and for the purpose of evading payment. A transferee that seeks to avoid liability for tax and penalties pursuant to the rule of paragraph (e)(3)(i) must provide sufficient information for the Service to determine whether the transferor's tax liability was satisfied (or was established to be zero).

(ii) *Interest.* If a transferee is required to deduct and withhold tax under section 1445 but fails to do so, then such person shall be liable for the payment of interest under section 6601 and regulations thereunder. Such transferee's liability for the payment of interest shall not be excused by reason of the deemed satisfaction, pursuant to subdivision (i) of this paragraph (e)(3), of the transferee's liability under section 1445, because the deemed satisfaction of that liability is the equivalent of the late payment of a liability, on which interest must be paid. Interest shall be payable with respect to the period between—

(A) The last date on which the tax imposed under section 1445 was required to be paid over, and

(B) The date (established from information supplied to the Service by the transferee) on which any tax due is paid with respect to the transferor's relevant income tax return, or the date the withholding certificate is issued establishing that the transferor's maximum tax liability is zero.

Interest shall be payable with respect to the entire amount that is required to be deducted and withheld. However, if the Service issues a withholding certificate providing for withholding of a reduced amount, then for the period after the issuance of the certificate interest shall be payable with respect to that reduced amount.

(4) *Coordination with entity withholding rules.* For purposes of section 1445(e) and §§ 1.1445-5, 1.1445-6, 1.1445-7, and 1.1445-8T, the rules of this paragraph (e) shall be applied by—

(i) Substituting the words "person required to withhold" for the word "transferee" each place it appears in this paragraph (e), and

Reg. § 1.1445-1(e)(4)

(ii) Substituting the words "person subject to withholding" for the word "transferor" each place it appears in this paragraph (e).

(f) *Effect of withholding on transferor*—(1) *In general.* The withholding of tax under section 1445(a) does not excuse a foreign person that disposes of a U.S. real property interest from filing a U.S. tax return with respect to the income arising from the disposition. Form 1040NR, 1041, or 1120F, as appropriate, must be filed, and any tax due must be paid, by the filing deadline generally applicable to such person. (The return may be filed by such later date as is provided in an extension granted by the Internal Revenue Service.) Any tax withheld under section 1445(a) shall be credited against the amount of income tax as computed in such return.

(2) *Manner of obtaining credit or refund.* A stamped copy of Form 8288-A will be provided to the transferor by the Service (under paragraph (c) of this section), and must be attached to the transferor's return, to establish the amount withheld that is available as a credit. If the amount withheld under section 1445(a) constitutes less than the full amount of the transferor's U.S. tax liability for that taxable year, then a payment of estimated tax may be required to be made pursuant to section 6154 or 6654 prior to the filing of the income tax return for that year. Alternatively, if the amount withheld under section 1445(a) exceeds the transferor's maximum tax liability with respect to the disposition (as determined by the IRS), then the transferor may seek an early refund of the excess pursuant to § 1.1445-3T(g), or a normal refund upon filing of a tax return.

(3) *Special rules*—(i) *Failure to receive Form 8288-A.* If a stamped copy of Form 8288-A has not been provided to the transferor by the Service, the transferor may establish the amount of tax withheld by the transferee by attaching to its return substantial evidence (*e.g.*, closing documents) of such amount. Such a transferor must attach to its return a statement which supplies all of the information required by § 1.1445-1(d) (except such information that was not obtained after a diligent effort).

(ii) *U.S. persons subjected to withholding.* If a transferee withholds tax under section 1445(a) with respect to a person who is not a foreign person, such person may credit the amount of any tax withheld against his income tax liability in accordance with the provisions of this § 1.1445-1(f) or apply for an early refund under § 1.1445-3(g).

(iii) *Refund in case of installment sale.* A transferor that takes gain into account in accordance with the provisions of section 453 shall not be entitled to a refund of the amount withheld, unless a withholding certificate providing for such a refund is obtained from the Internal Revenue Service pursuant to the provisions of § 1.1445-3.

(iv) *Joint foreign transferors.* If two or more foreign persons jointly transfer a U.S. real property interest, each transferor shall be credited with such portion of the amount withheld as such transferors mutually agree. Such transferors must request that the transferee reflect the agreed-upon crediting of the amount withheld on the Forms 8288-A filed by the transferee. If the foreign transferors fail to request that the transferee reflect the agreed-upon crediting of the amount withheld by the 10th day after the date of transfer, the transferee must credit the amount withheld equally between (or among) the foreign transferors. In such case, the transferee is indemnified pursuant to section 1461 against any claim by a transferor objecting to the resulting division of credits. For rules regarding the amount realized allocated to joint foreign and non-foreign transferors, see § 1.1445-1(b)(2).

(g) *Definitions*—(1) *In general.* Unless otherwise specified, the definitions of terms provided in § 1.897-1 shall apply for purposes of this section and §§ 1.1445-2 through 1.1445-7. For purposes of section 1445 and the regulations thereunder, definitions of other relevant terms are provided in this paragraph (g). In addition, the term "residence" is defined in § 1.1445-2(d)(1), the terms "transferor's agent" and "transferee's agent" are defined in § 1.1445-4(f), and the term "relevant taxpayer" is defined in § 1.1445-6(a)(2).

(2) *Transfer.* The term "transfer" means any transaction that would constitute a disposition for any purpose of the Internal Revenue Code and regulations thereunder. For purposes of §§ 1.1445-5 and 1.1445-6, the term includes distributions to shareholders of a corporation, partners of a partnership, and beneficiaries of a trust or estate.

(3) *Transferor.* The term "transferor" means any person, foreign or domestic, that disposes of a U.S. real property interest by sale, exchange, gift or any other transfer. The term "U.S. real property interest" is defined in § 1.897-1(c).

(4) *Transferee.* The term "transferee" means any person, foreign or domestic, that acquires a U.S. real property interest by purchase, exchange, gift, or any other transfer.

(5) *Amount realized.* The amount realized by the transferor for the transfer of a U.S. real property interest is the sum of:

(i) The cash paid, or to be paid,

Reg. § 1.1445-1(f)(1)

(ii) The fair market value of other property transferred, or to be transferred, and

(iii) The outstanding amount of any liability assumed by the transferee or to which the U.S. real property interest is subject immediately before and after the transfer. The term "cash paid or to be paid" does not include stated or unstated interest or original issue discount (as determined under the rules of sections 1271 through 1275).

(6) *Contract price.* The contract price of a U.S. real property interest is the sum that is agreed to by the transferee and transferor as the total amount of consideration to be paid for the property. That amount will generally be equal to the amount realized by the transferor, as defined in paragraph (b)(5) of this section.

(7) *Fair market value.* The fair market value of property means the price at which the property would change hands between an unrelated willing buyer and willing seller, neither being under any compulsion to buy or to sell and both having reasonable knowledge of all relevant facts.

(8) *Date of transfer.* The date of transfer of a U.S. real property interest is the first date on which consideration is paid (or a liability assumed) by the transferee. However, for purposes of section 1445(e)(2), (3), and (4) and § 1.1445-5(c)(1)(iii) and 1.1445-5(c)(3) only, the date of transfer is the date of the distribution that gives rise to the obligation to withhold. For purposes of this paragraph (g)(8), the payment of consideration does not include the payment, prior to the passage of legal or equitable title (other than pursuant to an initial contract for purchase), of earnest money, a good-faith deposit, or any similar sum that is primarily intended to bind the transferee or transferor to the entering or performance of a contract. Such a payment will not constitute a payment of consideration solely because it may ultimately be applied against the amount owed to the transferor by the transferee. Such a payment is presumed to be earnest money, a good faith deposit, or a similar sum if it is subject to forfeiture in the event of a failure to enter into a contract or a breach of contract. However, a payment that is not forfeitable may nevertheless be found to constitute earnest money, a good faith deposit, or a similar sum.

(9) *Identifying number.* Pursuant to § 1.897-1(p), an individual's identifying number is the social security number (or the identification numbers assigned by the Internal Revenue Service). The identifying number of any other person is its United States employer identification number.

(10) *Address of the Assistant Commissioner International.* Any written communication directed to the Assistant Commissioner (International) is to be addressed as follows: Director, Philadelphia Service Center; 11601 Roosevelt Blvd.; Philadelphia, PA 19255; ATTN: Drop Point 543X. [Reg. § 1.1445-1.]

☐ [T.D. 8113, 12-18-86. *Amended by T.D.* 8647, 12-20-95.]

[Reg. § 1.1445-2]

§ 1.1445-2. **Situations in which withholding is not required under section 1445(a).**—(a) *Purpose and scope of section.* This section provides rules concerning various situations in which withholding is not required under section 1445(a). In general, a transferee has a duty to withhold under section 1445(a) only if both of the following are true:

(1) The transferor is a foreign person; and

(2) The transferee is acquiring a U.S. real property interest.

Thus, paragraphs (b) and (c) of this section provide rules under which a transferee of property can ascertain that he has no duty to withhold because one or the other of the two key elements is missing. Under paragraph (b), a transferee may determine that no withholding is required because the transferor is not a foreign person. Under paragraph (c), a transferee may determine that no withholding is required because the property acquired is not a U.S. real property interest. Finally, paragraph (d) of this section provides rules concerning exceptions to the withholding requirement.

(b) *Transferor not a foreign person*—(1) *In general.* No withholding is required under section 1445 if the transferor of a U.S. real property interest is not a foreign person. Therefore, paragraph (b)(2) of this section provides rules pursuant to which the transferor can provide a certification of non-foreign status to inform the transferee that withholding is not required. A transferee that obtains such a certification must retain that document for five years, as provided in paragraph (b)(3) of this section. Except to the extent provided in paragraph (b)(4) of this section, the obtaining of this certification excuses the transferee from any liability otherwise imposed by section 1445 and § 1.1445-1(e). However, section 1445 and the rules of this section do not impose any obligation upon a transferee to obtain a certification from the transferor; thus, a transferee may instead rely upon other means to ascertain the non-foreign status of the transferor. If, however, the transferee relies upon other means and the transferor was, in fact, a foreign person, then the transferee is subject to the liability imposed by section 1445 and § 1.1445-1(e).

Reg. § 1.1445-2(b)(1)

A transferee is in no event required to rely upon other means to ascertain the non-foreign status of the transferor and may demand a certification of non-foreign status. If the certification is not provided, the transferee may withhold tax under section 1445 and will be considered, for purposes of sections 1461 through 1463, to have been required to withhold such tax.

(2) *Transferor's certification of non-foreign status*—(i) *In general*. A transferee of a U.S. real property interest is not required to withhold under section 1445(a) if, prior to or at the time of the transfer, the transferor furnishes to the transferee a certification that—

(A) States that the transferor is not a foreign person,

(B) Sets forth the transferor's name, identifying number and home address (in the case of an individual) or office address (in the case of an entity), and

(C) Is signed under penalties of perjury.

In general, a foreign person is a nonresident alien individual, foreign corporation, foreign partnership, foreign trust, or foreign estate, but not a resident alien individual. In this regard, see § 1.897-1(k). However, a foreign corporation that has made a valid election under section 897(i) is generally not treated as a foreign person for purposes of section 1445. In this regard, see § 1.1445-7. Pursuant to § 1.897-1(p), an individual's identifying number is the individual's Social Security number and any other person's identifying number is its U.S. employer identification number. A certification pursuant to this paragraph (b) must be verified as true and signed under penalties of perjury by a responsible officer in the case of a corporation, by a general partner in the case of a partnership, and by a trustee, executor, or equivalent fiduciary in the case of a trust or estate. No particular form is needed for a certification pursuant to this paragraph (b), nor is any particular language required, so long as the document meets the requirements of this paragraph (b)(2)(i). Samples of acceptable certifications are provided in paragraph (b)(2)(iii) of this section.

(ii) *Foreign corporation that has made election under section 897(i)*. A foreign corporation that has made a valid election under section 897(i) to be treated as a domestic corporation for purposes of section 897 may provide a certification of non-foreign status pursuant to this paragraph (b)(2). However, an electing foreign corporation must attach to such certification a copy of the acknowledgment of the election provided to the corporation by the Internal Revenue Service pursuant to § 1.897-3(d)(4). An acknowledgement is valid for this purpose only if it states that the information required by § 1.897-3 has been determined to be complete.

(iii) *Sample certifications*—(A) *Individual transferor*. "Section 1445 of the Internal Revenue Code provides that a transferee (buyer) of a U.S. real property interest must withhold tax if the transferor (seller) is a foreign person. To inform the transferee (buyer) that withholding of tax is not required upon my disposition of a U.S. real property interest, I, [*name of transferor*], hereby certify the following:

1. I am not a nonresident alien for purposes of U.S. income taxation;

2. My U.S. taxpayer identifying number (Social Security number) is ―――――; and

3. My home address is

―――――――――――――――――――
―――――――――――――――――――

I understand that this certification may be disclosed to the Internal Revenue Service by the transferee and that any false statement I have made here could be punished by fine, imprisonment, or both.

Under penalties of perjury I declare that I have examined this certification and to the best of my knowledge and belief it is true, correct, and complete.

[Signature and Date]"

(B) *Entity transferor*. "Section 1445 of the Internal Revenue Code provides that a transferee of a U.S. real property interest must withhold tax if the transferor is a foreign person. To inform the transferee that withholding of tax is not required upon the disposition of a U.S. real property interest by [*name of transferor*], the undersigned hereby certifies the following on behalf of [*name of transferor*]:

1. [*Name of transferor*] is not a foreign corporation, foreign partnership, foreign trust, or foreign estate (as those terms are defined in the Internal Revenue Code and Income Tax Regulations);

2. [*Name of transferor*]'s U.S. employer identification number is ―――――, and

3. [*Name of transferor*]'s office address is

―――――――――――――――――――

[*Name of transferor*] understands that this certification may be disclosed to the Internal Revenue Service by transferee and that any false statement contained herein could be punished by fine, imprisonment, or both.

Under penalties of perjury I declare that I have examined this certification and to the best of my knowledge and belief it is true, correct and complete, and I further declare that I have authority

Reg. § 1.1445-2(b)(2)

to sign this document on behalf of [*name of transferor*].

[Signature and date]

[Title]"

(3) *Transferee must retain certification.* If a transferee obtains a transferor's certification pursuant to the rules of this paragraph (b), then the transferee must retain that certification until the end of the fifth taxable year following the taxable year in which the transfer takes place. The transferee must retain the certification, and make it available to the Internal Revenue Service when requested in accordance with the requirements of section 6001 and regulations thereunder.

(4) *Reliance upon certification not permitted*—(i) *In general.* A transferee may not rely upon a transferor's certification pursuant to this paragraph (b) under the circumstances set forth in either subdivision (ii) or (iii) of this paragraph (b)(4). In either of those circumstances, a transferee's withholding obligation shall apply as if a certification had never been obtained, and the transferee is fully liable pursuant to section 1445 and § 1445-1(e) for any failure to withhold.

(ii) *Failure to attach IRS acknowledgment of election.* A transferee that knows that the transferor is a foreign corporation may not rely upon a certification of non-foreign status provided by the corporation on the basis of election under section 897(i), unless there is attached to the certification a copy of the acknowledgment by the Internal Revenue Service of the corporation's election, as required by paragraph (b)(2)(ii) of this section.

(iii) *Knowledge of falsity.* A transferee is not entitled to rely upon a transferor's certification if prior to or at the time of the transfer the transferee either—

(A) Has actual knowledge that the transferor's certification is false; or

(B) Receives a notice that the certification is false from a transferor's or transferee's agent, pursuant to § 1.1445-4.

(iv) *Belated notice of false certification.* If after the date of the transfer a transferee receives a notice that a certification is false, then that transferee is entitled to rely upon the certification only with respect to consideration that was paid prior to receipt of the notice. Such a transferee is required to withhold a full 10 percent of the amount realized from the consideration that remains to be paid to the transferor if possible. Thus, if 10 percent or more of the amount realized remains to be paid to the transferor then the transferee is required to withhold and pay over the full 10 percent. The transferee must do so by withholding and paying over the entire amount of each successive payment of consideration to the transferor until the full 10 percent of the amount realized has been withheld and paid over. Amounts so withheld must be reported and paid over by the 20th day following the date on which each such payment of consideration is made. A transferee that is subject to the rules of this paragraph (b)(4)(iv) may not obtain a withholding certificate pursuant to § 1.1445-3, but must instead withhold and pay over the amounts required by this paragraph.

(c) *Transferred property not a U.S. real property interest*—(1) *In general.* No withholding is required under section 1445 if the transferee acquires only property that is not a U.S. real property interest. As defined in section 897(c) and § 1.897-1(c), a U.S. real property interest includes certain interests in U.S. corporations, as well as direct interests in real property and certain associated personal property. This paragraph (c) provides rules pursuant to which a person acquiring an interest in a U.S. corporation may determine that withholding is not required because that interest is not a U.S. real property interest. To determine whether an interest in tangible property constitutes a U.S. real property interest the acquisition of which would be subject to withholding, see § 1.897-1(b) and (c).

(2) *Interests in publicly traded entities.* No withholding is required under section 1445(a) upon the acquisition of an interest in a domestic corporation if any class of stock of the corporation is regularly traded on an established securities market. This exemption shall apply if the disposition is incident to an initial public offering of stock pursuant to a registration statement filed with the Securities and Exchange Commission. Similarly, no withholding is required under section 1445(a) upon the acquisition of an interest in a publicly traded partnership or trust. However, the rule of this paragraph (c)(2) shall not apply to the acquisition, from a single transferor (or related transferors as defined in § 1.897-1(i)) in a single transaction (or related transactions), of an interest described in § 1.897-1(c)(2)(iii)(B) (relating to substantial amounts of non-publicly traded interests in publicly traded corporations) or to similar interests in publicly traded partnerships or trusts. The person making an acquisition described in the preceding sentence must otherwise determine whether withholding is required, pursuant to section 1445 and the regulations thereunder. Transactions shall be deemed to be related if they are undertaken within 90 days of one another or if it can otherwise be shown that they were undertaken in pursuance of a prearranged plan.

Reg. § 1.1445-2(c)(2)

(3) *Transferee receives statement that interest in corporation is not a U.S. real property interest*—(i) *In general.* No withholding is required under section 1445(a) upon the acquisition of an interest in a domestic corporation, if the transferor provides the transferee with a copy of a statement, issued by the corporation pursuant to § 1.897-2(h), certifying that the interest is not a U.S. real property interest. In general, a corporation may issue such a statement only if the corporation was not a U.S. real property holding corporation at any time during the previous five years (or the period in which the interest was held by its present holder, if shorter) or if interests in the corporation ceased to be United States real property interests under section 897(c)(1)(B). (A corporation may not provide such a statement based on its determination that the interest in question is an interest solely as a creditor.) See § 1.897-2(f) and (h). The corporation may provide such a statement directly to the transferee at the transferor's request. The transferor must request such a statement prior to the transfer, and shall, to the extent possible, specify the anticipated date of the transfer. A corporation's statement may be relied upon for purposes of this paragraph (c)(3) only if the statement is dated not more than 30 days prior to the date of the transfer. A transferee may also rely upon a corporation's statement that is voluntarily provided by the corporation in response to a request from the transferee, if that statement otherwise complies with the requirements of this paragraph (c)(3) and § 1.897-2(h).

(ii) *Reliance on statement not permitted.* A transferee is not entitled to rely upon a statement that a corporation is not a U.S. real property holding corporation if, prior to or at the time of the transfer, the transferee either—

(A) Has actual knowledge that the statement is false, or

(B) Receives a notice that the statement is false from a transferor's or transferee's agent, pursuant to § 1.1445-4.

Such a transferee's withholding obligations shall apply as if a statement had never been given, and such a transferee may be held fully liable pursuant to § 1.1445-1(e) for any failure to withhold.

(iii) *Belated notice of false statement.* If after the date of the transfer, a transferee receives notice that a statement provided under § 1.1445-2(c)(3)(i) (that an interest in a corporation is not a U.S. real property interest) is false, then such transferee may rely on the statement only with respect to consideration that was paid prior to the receipt of the notice. Such a transferee is required to withhold a full 10 percent of the amount realized from the consideration that remains to be paid to the transferor, if possible. Thus, if 10 percent or more of the amount realized remains to be paid to the transferor, then the transferee is required to withhold any pay over the full 10 percent. The transferee must do so by withholding and paying over the entire amount of each successive payment of consideration to the transferor, until the full 10 percent of the amount realized has been withheld and paid over. Amounts so withheld must be reported and paid over by the 20th day following the date on which each such payment of consideration is made. A transferee that is subject to the rules of this paragraph 1.1445-2(c)(3)(iii) may not obtain a withholding certificate pursuant to § 1.1445-3, but must instead withhold and pay over the amounts required by this paragraph.

(d) *Exceptions to requirement of withholding*— (1) *Purchase of residence for $300,000 or less.* No withholding is required under section 1445(a) if one or more individual transferees acquire a U.S. real property interest for use as a residence and the amount realized on the transaction is $300,000 or less. For purposes of this section, a U.S. real property interest is acquired for use as a residence if on the date of the transfer the transferee (or transferees) has definite plans to reside at the property for at least 50 percent of the number of days that the property is used by any person during each of the first two 12-month periods following the date of the transfer. The number of days that the property will be vacant is not taken into account in determining the number of days such property is used by any person. A transferee shall be considered to reside at a property on any day on which a member of the transferee's family, as defined in section 267(c)(4), resides at the property. No form or other document need be filed with the Internal Revenue Service to establish a transferee's entitlement to rely upon the exception provided by this paragraph (d)(1). A transferee who fails to withhold in reliance upon this exception, but who does not in fact reside at the property for the minimum number of days set forth above, shall be liable for the failure to withhold (if the transferor was a foreign person and did not pay the full U.S. tax due on any gain recognized upon the transfer). However, if the transferee establishes that the failure to reside the minimum number of days was caused by a change in circumstances that could not reasonably have been anticipated at the time of the transfer, then the transferee shall not be liable for the failure to withhold. The exception provided by paragraph (d)(1) does not apply in any case where the transferee is other than an individual even if the property is acquired for or on behalf of an individual who will use the property as a resi-

Reg. § 1.1445-2(c)(3)

dence. However, this exception applies regardless of the organizational structure of the transferor (i.e., regardless of whether the transferor is an individual, partnership, trust, corporation, etc.)

(2) *Coordination with nonrecognition provisions*—(i) *In general.* A transferee shall not be required to withhold under section 1445(a) with respect to the transfer of a U.S. real property interest if—

(A) The transferor notifies the transferee, in the manner described in paragraph (d)(2)(iii) of this section, that by reason of the operation of a nonrecognition provision of the Internal Revenue Code or the provisions of any United States treaty the transferor is not required to recognize any gain or loss with respect to the transfer; and

(B) By the 20th day after the date of the transfer the transferee provides a copy of the transferor's notice to the Assistant Commissioner (International), at the address provided in § 1.1445-1(g)(10), together with a cover letter setting forth the name, identifying number (if any), and home address (in the case of an individual) or office address (in the case of an entity) of the transferee providing the notice to the Service.

The rule of this paragraph (d)(2)(i) is subject to the exceptions set forth in paragraph (d)(2)(ii). For purposes of this paragraph (d)(2) a nonrecognition provision is any provision of the Internal Revenue Code for not recognizing gain or loss.

(ii) *Exceptions.* A transferee may not rely upon the rule of paragraph (d)(2)(i) of this section, and must therefore withhold under section 1445(a) with respect to the transfer of a U.S. real property interest, if either:

(A) The transferor qualifies for nonrecognition treatment with respect to part, but not all, of the gain realized by the transferor upon the transfer; or

(B) The transferee knows or has reason to know that the transferor is not entitled to the nonrecognition treatment claimed by the transferor.

In either of the above circumstances the transferee or transferor may request a withholding certificate from the Internal Revenue Service pursuant to the rules of § 1.1445-3.

(iii) [Removed by T.D. 8198 effective after August 3, 1988.]

(iv) [Removed by T.D. 8198 effective after June 6, 1988.]

(3) *Special procedural rules applicable to foreclosures*—(i) *Amount to be withheld*—(A) *Foreclosures.* A transferee that acquires a U.S. real property interest pursuant to a repossession or foreclosure on such property under a mortgage, security agreement, deed of trust or other instrument securing a debt must withhold tax under section 1445(a) equal to 10 percent of the amount realized on such sale. Such amount must be reported and paid over to the Service under the general rules of § 1.1445-1. However, if the transferee complies with the notice requirements of § 1.1445-2(d)(3)(ii) and (iii), such transferee may report and pay over to the Service on or before the 20th day following the final determination by a court or trustee with jurisdiction over the foreclosure action, the lesser of:

(*1*) the amount otherwise required to be withheld under section 1445(a), or

(*2*) the "alternative amount" as defined in the succeeding sentence.

The alternative amount is the entire amount, if any, determined by a court or trustee with jurisdiction over the matter, that accrues to the debtor/transferor out of the amount realized from the foreclosure sale. The amount of any mortgage, lien, or other security agreement secured by the property, that is terminated, assumed by another person, or otherwise extinguished (as to the debtor/transferor) shall not be treated as an amount that accrues to the debtor/transferor for purposes of this § 1.1445-2(d)(3)(i)(A). If the alternative amount is zero, no withholding is required. Any difference between the amount withheld at the time of the foreclosure sale and the amount to be reported and paid over to the Service must be transferred to the court or trustee with jurisdiction over the foreclosure action. Amounts withheld, if any, are to be reported and paid over to the Service by using Forms 8288 and 8288-A in conformity with § 1.1445-1(d).

(B) *Deeds in lieu of foreclosures.* A transferee of a U.S. real property interest pursuant to a deed in lieu of foreclosure must withhold tax equal to 10 percent of the amount realized by the debtor/transferor on the transfer. However, no withholding is required if:

(*1*) The transferee is the only person with a security interest in the property,

(*2*) No cash or other property (other than incidental fees incurred with respect to the transfer) is paid, directly or indirectly, to any person with respect to the transfer, and

(*3*) The notice requirements of § 1.1445-2(d)(3) are satisfied.

The amount withheld, if any, must be reported and paid over to the Service not later than the 20th day following the date of transfer. In a case where withholding would otherwise be required, a

Reg. § 1.1445-2(d)(3)

withholding certificate may be requested in accordance with § 1.1445-3.

(ii) *Notice to the court or trustee in a foreclosure action*—(A) *Notice on day of purchase.* A transferee in a foreclosure sale that chooses to use the special rules applicable to foreclosures must provide notice to the court or trustee with jurisdiction over the foreclosure action on the day the property is transferred with respect to such transferee's withholding obligation. No particular form is necessary but the notice must set forth the transferee's name, home address in the case of an individual, office address in the case of an entity, a brief description of the property, the date of the transfer, the amount realized on the sale of the foreclosed property and the amount withheld under section 1445(a).

(B) *Notice whether amount withheld or alternative amount is reported and paid over the Service.* A purchaser/transferee in a foreclosure that chooses to use the special rules applicable to foreclosures must provide notice to the court or trustee with jurisdiction over the foreclosure action regarding whether the amount withheld or the alternative amount will be (or has been) reported and paid over to the Service. The notice should set forth all the information required by the preceding paragraph (d)(3)(ii)(A), the amount withheld or alternative amount that will be (or has been) reported and paid over to the Service, and the amount that will be (or has been) paid over to the court or trustee.

(iii) *Notice to the Service*—(A) *General rule.* A transferee that in reliance upon the rules of this paragraph (d)(3) withholds an alternative amount (or does not withhold because the alternative amount is zero) must, on or before the 20th day following the final determination by a court or trustee in a foreclosure action or on or before the 20th day following the date of the transfer with respect to a transfer pursuant to a deed in lieu of foreclosure, provide notice thereof to the Assistant Commissioner (International) at the address provided in § 1.1445-1(g)(10). (The filing of such a notice shall not relieve a creditor of any obligation it may have to file a notice pursuant to section 6050J and the regulations thereunder.) No particular form is required but the following information must be set forth in paragraphs labelled to correspond with the numbers set forth below.

(*1*) A statement that the notice constitutes a notice of foreclosure action or transfer pursuant to a deed in lieu of foreclosure under § 1.1445-2(d)(3).

(*2*) The name, identifying number (if any) and home address (in the case of an individual) or office address (in the case of an entity) of the purchaser/transferee.

(*3*) The name, identifying number (if any), and home address (in the case of an individual) or office address (in the case of an entity) of the debtor/transferor.

(*4*) In a foreclosure action, the date of the final determination by a court or trustee regarding the distribution of the amount realized from the foreclosure sale. In a transfer pursuant to a deed in lieu of foreclosure, the date the property is transferred to the purchaser/transferee.

(*5*) A brief description of the property.

(*6*) The amount realized from the foreclosure sale or with respect to the transfer pursuant to a deed in lieu of foreclosure.

(*7*) The alternative amount.

(B) *Special rule for lenders required to file Form 1099-A where the alternative amount is zero.* A person required under section 6050J to file Form 1099-A does not have to comply with the notice requirement of § 1.1445-2(d)(3)(iii)(A) if the alternative amount is zero. In such case, the filing of the Form 1099-A will be deemed to satisfy the notice requirement of § 1.1445-2(d)(3)(iii)(A).

(iv) *Requirements not applicable.* A transferee is not required to withhold tax or provide notice pursuant to the rules of this paragraph (d)(3) if no substantive withholding liability applies to the transfer of the property by the debtor/transferor. For example, if the debtor/transferor provides the transferee with a certification of non-foreign status pursuant to paragraph (b) of this section, then no substantive withholding liability would exist with respect to the acquisition of the property from the debtor transferor. In such a case, no withholding of tax or notice to the Internal Revenue Service is required of the transferee with respect to the repossession or foreclosure.

(v) *Anti-abuse rule.* If a U.S. real property interest is transferred in foreclosure or pursuant to a deed in lieu of foreclosure for a principal purpose of avoiding the requirements of section 1445(a), then the provisions of this paragraph (d)(3) shall not apply to the transfer and the transferee shall be fully liable for any failure to withhold with respect to the transfer. A principal purpose to avoid section 1445(a) will be presumed (subject to rebuttal on the basis of all relevant facts and circumstances) if:

Reg. § 1.1445-2(d)(3)

(A) The transferee acquires property in which it, or a related party, has a security interest;

(B) The security interest did not arise in connection with the debtor/transferor's or a related party's or predecessor in interest's acquisition, improvement, or maintenance of the property; and

(C) The total amount of all debts secured by the property exceeds 90 percent of the fair market value of the property.

(4) *Installment payments.* A transferee of a U.S. real property interest is not required to withhold under section 1445 when making installment payments on an obligation arising out of a disposition that took place before January 1, 1985. With respect to dispositions that take place after December 31, 1984, the transferee shall be required to satisfy its entire withholding obligation within the time specified in § 1.1445-1(c) regardless of the amount actually paid by the transferee. Thereafter, no withholding is required upon further installment payments on an obligation arising out of the transfer. A transferee that is unable to satisfy its entire withholding obligation within the time specified in § 1.1445-1(c) may request a withholding certificate pursuant to § 1.1445-3.

(5) *Acquisitions by governmental bodies.* No withholding of tax is required under section 1445 with respect to any acquisition of property by the United States, a state or possession of the United States, a political subdivision thereof, or the District of Columbia.

(6) [Reserved.]

(7) *Withholding certificate obtained by transferee or transferor.* No withholding is required under section 1445(a) if the transferee is provided with a withholding certificate that so specifies. Either the transferor or the transferee may seek a withholding certificate from the Internal Revenue Service, pursuant to the provisions of § 1.1445-3.

(8) *Amount realized by transferor is zero.* If the amount realized by the transferor on a transfer of a U.S. real property interest is zero, no withholding is required. [Reg. § 1.1445-2.]

☐ [*T.D.* 8113, 12-18-86. *Amended by T.D.* 8198, 5-4-88.]

[Reg. § 1.1445-3]

§ 1.1445-3. **Adjustments to amount required to be withheld pursuant to withholding certificate.**—(a) *In general.* Withholding under section 1445(a) may be reduced or eliminated pursuant to a withholding certificate issued by the Internal Revenue Service in accordance with the rules of this section. A withholding certificate may be issued by the Service in cases where reduced withholding is appropriate (see paragraph (c) of this section), where the transferor is exempt from U.S. tax (see paragraph (d) of this section), or where an agreement for the payment of tax is entered into with the Service (see paragraph (e) of this section). A withholding certificate that is obtained prior to a transfer notifies the transferee that no withholding is required. A withholding certificate that is obtained after a transfer has been made may authorize a normal refund or an early refund pursuant to paragraph (g) of this section. Either a transferee or transferor may apply for a withholding certificate. The Internal Revenue Service will act upon an application for a withholding certificate not later than the 90th day after it is received. Solely for this purpose (i.e., determining the day upon which the 90-day period commences), an application is received by the Service on the date that all information necessary for the Service to make a determination is provided by the applicant. (For rules regarding whether an application for a withholding certificate has been timely submitted, see § 1.1445-1(c)(2).) The Service may deny a request for a withholding certificate where, after due notice, an applicant fails to provide information necessary for the Service to make a determination. The Service will act upon an application for an early refund not later than the 90th day after it is received. An application for an early refund must either (1) include a copy of a withholding certificate issued by the Service with respect to the transaction, or (2) be combined with an application for a withholding certificate. Where an application for an early refund is combined with an application for a withholding certificate, the Service will act upon both applications not later than the 90th day after receipt. In the case of an application for a certificate based on nonconforming security under paragraph (e)(3)(v) of this section, and in unusually complicated cases, the Service may be unable to provide a final withholding certificate by the 90th day. In such a case the Service will notify the applicant, by the 45th day after receipt of the application, that additional processing time will be necessary. The Service's notice may request additional information or explanation concerning particular aspects of the application, and will provide a target date for final action (contingent upon the applicant's timely submission of any requested information). A withholding certificate issued pursuant to the provisions of this section serves to fulfill the requirements of section 1445(b)(4) concerning qualifying statements, section 1445(c)(1) concerning the transferor's maximum tax liability, or section 1445(c)(2) concerning the Secretary's authority to prescribe reduced withholding.

Reg. § 1.1445-3(a)

(b) *Applications for withholding certificates*—(1) *In general.* An application for a withholding certificate must be submitted to the Assistant Commissioner (International), at the address provided in § 1.1445-1(g)(10). An application for a withholding certificate must be signed by a responsible officer in the case of a corporation, by a general partner in the case of a partnership, by a trustee, executor, or equivalent fiduciary in the case of a trust or estate, and in the case of an individual by the individual himself. A duly authorized agent may sign the application but the application must contain a valid power of attorney authorizing the agent to sign the application on behalf of the applicant. The person signing the application must verify under penalties of perjury that all representations made in connection with the application are true, correct, and complete to his knowledge and belief. No particular form is required for an application, but the application must set forth the information described in paragraphs (b)(2), (3), and (4) of this section.

(2) *Parties to the transaction.* The application must set forth the name, address, and identifying number (if any) of the person submitting the application (specifying whether that person is the transferee or transferor), and the name, address, and identifying number (if any) of other parties to the transaction (specifying whether each such party is a transferee or transferor). The applicant must determine if an identifying number exists for each party concerned and if none exists for a particular party the application must so state. The address provided in the case of an individual must be that individual's home address, and the address provided in the case of an entity must be that entity's office address. A mailing address may be provided in addition to, but not in lieu of, a home address or office address.

(3) *Real property interest to be transferred.* The application must set forth information concerning the U.S. real property interest with respect to which the withholding certificate is sought, including the type of interest, the contract price, and, in the case of an interest in real property, its location and general description, or in the case of an interest in a U.S. real property holding corporation, the class or type and amount of the interest.

(4) *Basis for certificate*—(i) *Reduced withholding.* If a withholding certificate is sought on the basis of a claim that reduced withholding is appropriate, the application must include:

(A) A calculation of the maximum tax that may be imposed on the disposition in accordance with paragraph (c)(2) of this section. Such calculation must be accompanied by a copy of the relevant contract and depreciation schedules or other evidence that confirms the contract price and adjusted basis of the property. If no depreciation schedules are provided, the application must state the nature of the use of the property and why depreciation was not allowable. Evidence that supports any claimed adjustment to the maximum tax on the disposition must also be provided;

(B) A calculation of the transferor's unsatisfied withholding liability, or evidence supporting the claim that no such liability exists, in accordance with paragraph (c)(3) of this section; and

(C) In the case of a request for a special reduction of withholding pursuant to paragraph (c)(4) of this section, a statement of law and facts in support of the request.

(ii) *Exemption.* If a withholding certificate is sought on the basis of the transferor's exemption from U.S. tax, the application must set forth a brief statement of the law and facts that support the claimed exemption. In this regard, see paragraph (d) of this section.

(iii) *Agreement.* If a withholding certificate is sought on the basis of an agreement for the payment of tax, the application must include a signed copy of the agreement proposed by the applicant and a copy of the security instrument (if any) proposed by the applicant. In this regard, see paragraph (e) of this section.

(c) *Adjustment of amount required to be withheld*—(1) *In general.* The Internal Revenue Service may issue a withholding certificate that excuses withholding or that permits the transferee to withhold an adjusted amount reflecting the transferor's maximum tax liability. The transferor's maximum tax liability is the sum of—

(i) The maximum amount which could be imposed as tax under section 871 or 882 upon the transferor's disposition of the subject real property interest, as determined under paragraph (c)(2) of this section, and

(ii) The transferor's unsatisfied withholding liability with respect to the subject real property interest, as determined under paragraph (c)(3) of this section.

In addition, the Internal Revenue Service may issue a withholding certificate that permits the transferee to withhold a reduced amount if the Service determines pursuant to paragraph (c)(4) of this section that reduced withholding will not jeopardize the collection of tax.

(2) *Maximum tax imposed on disposition.* The first element of the transferor's maximum tax

Reg. § 1.1445-3(b)(1)

liability is the maximum amount which the transferor could be required to pay as tax upon the disposition of the subject real property interest. In the case of an individual transferor that amount will generally be the contract price of the property minus its adjusted basis, multiplied by the maximum individual income tax rate applicable to long-term capital gain. In the case of a corporate transferor, that amount will generally be the contract price of the property minus its adjusted basis, multiplied by the maximum corporate income tax rate applicable to long-term capital gain. However, that amount must be adjusted to take into account the following:

(i) Any reduction of tax to which the transferor is entitled under the provisions of a U.S. income tax treaty;

(ii) The effect of any nonrecognition provision that is applicable to the transaction;

(iii) Any losses realized and recognized upon the previous disposition of U.S. real property interests during the taxable year;

(iv) Any amount that is required to be treated as ordinary income; and

(v) Any other factor that may increase or reduce the tax upon the disposition.

(3) *Transferor's unsatisfied withholding liability*—(i) *In general.* The second element of the transferor's maximum tax liability is the transferor's unsatisfied withholding liability. That liability is the amount of any tax that the transferor was required to but did not withhold and pay over under section 1445 upon the acquisition of the subject U.S. real property interest or a predecessor interest. The transferor's unsatisfied withholding liability is included in the calculation of maximum tax liability so that such prior withholding liability can be satisfied by the transferee's withholding upon the current transfer. Alternatively, the transferor's unsatisfied withholding liability may be disregarded for purposes of calculating the maximum tax liability, if either—

(A) Such prior withholding liability is fully satisfied by a payment that is made with the application submitted pursuant to this section; or

(B) An agreement is entered into for the payment of that liability pursuant to the rules of paragraph (e) of this section. Because section 1445 only requires withholding after December 31, 1984, no transferor's unsatisfied withholding liability can exist unless the transferor acquired the subject or predecessor real property interest after that date. For purposes of this paragraph (c), a predecessor interest is one that was exchanged for the subject U.S. real property interest in a transaction in which the transferor was not required to recognize the full amount of the gain or loss realized upon the transfer.

(ii) *Evidence that no unsatisfied withholding liability exists.* For purposes of paragraph (b)(4)(i)(B) of this section (concerning information that must be submitted with an application for a withholding certificate), evidence that the transferor has no unsatisfied withholding liability includes any one of the following documents:

(A) Evidence that the transferor acquired the subject or predecessor real property interest prior to January 1, 1985;

(B) A copy of the Form 8288 that was filed by the transferor, and proof of payment of the amount shown due thereon, with respect to the transferor's acquisition of the subject or predecessor real property interest;

(C) A copy of a withholding certificate with respect to the transferor's acquisition of the subject or predecessor real property interest, plus a copy of Form 8288 and proof of payment with respect to any withholding required under that certificate;

(D) A copy of the non-foreign certification furnished by the person from whom the subject or predecessor U.S. real property interest was acquired, executed at the time of that acquisition;

(E) Evidence that the transferor purchased the subject or predecessor real property for $300,000 or less, and a statement, signed by the transferor under penalties of perjury, that the transferor purchased the property for use as a residence within the meaning of § 1.1445-2(d)(1);

(F) Evidence that the person from whom the transferor acquired the subject or predecessor U.S. real property interest fully paid any tax imposed on that transaction pursuant to section 897;

(G) A copy of a notice of nonrecognition treatment provided to the transferor pursuant to § 1.1445-2(d)(2) by the person from whom the transferor acquired the subject or predecessor U.S. real property interest; and

(H) A statement, signed by the transferor under penalties of perjury, setting forth the facts and circumstances that supported the transferor's conclusion that no withholding was required under section 1445(a) with respect to the transferor's acquisition of the subject or predecessor real property interest.

(4) *Special reduction of amount required to be withheld.* The Internal Revenue Service may, in its discretion, issue a withholding certificate that permits the transferee to withhold a reduced amount based upon a determination that reduced

Reg. § 1.1445-3(c)(4)

withholding will not jeopardize the collection of tax. A transferor that requests a withholding certificate pursuant to this paragraph (c)(4) is required pursuant to paragraph (b)(4)(i)(C) of this section to submit a statement of law and facts in support of the request. That statement must explain why the transferor is unable to enter into an agreement for the payment of tax pursuant to paragraph (e) of this section.

(d) *Transferor's exemption from U.S. tax*—(1) *In general.* The Internal Revenue Service will issue a withholding certificate that excuses all withholding by a transferee if it is established that:

(i) The transferor's gain from the disposition of the subject U.S. real property interest will be exempt from U.S. tax, and

(ii) The transferor has no unsatisfied withholding liability.

For the available exemptions, see paragraph (d)(2) of this section. The transferor's unsatisfied withholding liability shall be determined in accordance with the provisions of paragraph (c)(3) of this section. A transferor that is entitled to a reduction of (rather than an exemption from) U.S. tax may obtain a withholding certificate to that effect pursuant to the provisions of paragraph (c) of this section.

(2) *Available exemptions.* A transferor's gain from the disposition of a U.S. real property interest may be exempt from U.S. tax because either:

(i) The transferor is an integral part or controlled entity of a foreign government and the disposition of the subject property is not a commercial activity, as determined pursuant to section 892 and the regulations thereunder; or

(ii) The transferor is entitled to the benefits of an income tax treaty that provides for such an exemption (subject to the limitations imposed by section 1125(c) of Pub. L. 96-499, which, in general, overrides such benefits as of January 1, 1985).

(e) *Agreement for the payment of tax*—(1) *In general.* The Internal Revenue Service will issue a withholding certificate that excuses withholding or that permits a transferee to withhold a reduced amount, if either the transferee or the transferor enters into an agreement for the payment of tax pursuant to the provisions of this paragraph (e). An agreement for the payment of tax is a contract between the Service and any other person that consists of two necessary elements. Those elements are—

(i) A contract between the Service and the other person, setting forth in detail the rights and obligations of each; and

(ii) A security instrument or other form of security acceptable to the Director, Foreign Operations District.

(2) *Contents of agreement*—(i) *In general.* An agreement for the payment of tax must cover an amount described in subdivision (ii) or (iii) of this paragraph (e)(2). The agreement may either provide adequate security for the payment of the chosen amount in accordance with paragraph (e)(3) of this section, or provide for the payment of that amount through a combination of security and withholding of tax by the transferee.

(ii) *Tax that would otherwise be withheld.* An agreement for the payment of tax may cover the amount of tax that would otherwise be required to be withheld pursuant to section 1445(a). In addition to the amount computed pursuant to section 1445(a), the applicant must agree to pay interest upon that amount, at the rate established under section 6621, with respect to the period between the date on which the tax imposed by section 1445(a) would otherwise be due (*i.e.*, the 20th day after the date of transfer) and the date on which the transferor's payment of tax with respect to the disposition will be due under the agreement. The amount of interest agreed upon must be paid by the applicant regardless of whether or not the Service is required to draw upon any security provided pursuant to the agreement. The interest may be paid either with the return or by the Service drawing upon the security.

(iii) *Maximum tax liability.* An agreement for the payment of tax may cover the transferor's maximum tax liability, determined in accordance with paragraph (c) of this section. The agreement must also provide for the payment of an additional amount equal to 25 percent of the amount determined under paragraph (c) of this section. This additional amount secures the interest and penalties that would accrue between the date of a failure to file a return and pay tax with respect to the disposition, and the date on which the Service collects upon that liability pursuant to the agreement. Such additional amount will only be collected if the Service finds it necessary to draw upon any security provided due to the transferor's failure to file a return and pay tax with respect to the relevant disposition.

(3) *Major types of security*—(i) *In general.* The following are the major types of security acceptable to the Service. Further details with respect to the terms and conditions of each type may be specified by Revenue Procedure.

(ii) *Bond with surety or guarantor.* The Service may accept as security with respect to a transferor's tax liability a bond that is executed

Reg. § 1.1445-3(d)(1)

with a satisfactory surety or guarantor. Only the following persons may act as surety or guarantor for this purpose:

(A) A surety company holding a certificate of authority from the Secretary as an acceptable surety on Federal bonds, as listed in Treasury Department Circular No. 570, published annually in the Federal Register on the first working day of July;

(B) A person that is engaged within or without the United States in the conduct of a banking, financing, or similar business under the principles of § 1.864-4(c)(5) and that is subject to U.S. or foreign local or national regulation of such business, if that person is otherwise acceptable to the Service; and

(C) A person that is engaged within or without the United States in the conduct of an insurance business that is subject to U.S. or foreign local or national regulation, if that person is otherwise acceptable to the Service.

(iii) *Bond with collateral.* The Service may accept as security with respect to a transferor's tax liability a bond that is secured by acceptable collateral. All collateral must be deposited with a responsible financial institution acting as escrow agent or, in the Service's discretion, with the Service. Only the following types of collateral are acceptable:

(A) Bonds, notes, or other public debt obligations of the United States, in accordance with the rules of 31 CFR Part 225; and

(B) A certified cashier's, or treasurer's check, drawn on an entity acceptable to the Service that is engaged within or without the United States in the conduct of a banking, financing, or similar business under the principles of § 1.864-4(c)(5) and that is subject to U.S. or foreign local or national regulation of such business.

(iv) *Letter of credit.* The Service may accept as security with respect to a transferor's tax liability an irrevocable letter of credit. The Service may accept a letter of credit issued by an entity acceptable to the Service that is engaged within or without the United States in the conduct of a banking, financing or similar business under the principles of § 1.884-4(c)(5) and that is subject to U.S. or foreign local or national regulation of such business. However, the Director will accept a letter of credit from an entity that is not engaged in trade or business in the United States only if such letter may be drawn on an advising bank within the United States.

(v) *Guarantees and other nonconforming security*—(A) *Guarantee.* The Service may in its discretion accept as security with respect to a transferor's tax liability the applicant's guarantee that it will pay such liability. The Service will in general accept such a guarantee only from a corporation, foreign or domestic, any class of stock of which is regularly traded on an established securities market on the date of the transfer.

(B) *Other forms of security.* The Service may in unusual circumstances and at its discretion accept any form of security that it finds to be adequate. An application for a withholding certificate that proposes a form of security that does not conform with any of the preferred types set forth in paragraph (e)(3)(ii) through (iv) of this section or any relevant Revenue Procedure must include:

(*1*) A detailed statement of the facts and circumstances supporting the use of the proposed form of security, and

(*2*) A memorandum of law concerning the validity and enforceability of the proposed form of security.

(4) *Terms of security instrument.* Any security instrument that is furnished pursuant to this section must provide that—

(i) The amount of each deposit of estimated tax that will be required with respect to the gain realized on the subject disposition may be collected by levy upon the security as of the date following the date on which each such deposit is due (unless such deposit is timely made);

(ii) The entire amount of the liability may be collected by levy upon the security at any time during the nine months following the date on which the payment of tax with respect to the subject disposition is due, subject to release of the security upon the full payment of the tax and any interest and penalties due. If the transferor requests an extension of time to file a return with respect to the disposition, then the Director may require that the term of the security instrument be extended until the date that is nine months after the filing deadline as extended.

(f) *Amendments to application for withholding certificate*—(1) *In general.* An applicant for a withholding certificate may amend an otherwise complete application by submitting an amending statement to the Assistant Commissioner (International), at the address provided in § 1.1445-1(g)(10). The amending statement shall provide the information required by § 1.1445-3(f)(3) and must be signed and accompanied by a penalties of perjury statement in accordance with § 1.1445-3(b)(1).

(2) *Extension of time for the Service to process requests for withholding certificates*—(i) *In general.* If an amending statement is submitted, the time in which the Internal Revenue Service

Reg. § 1.1445-3(f)(2)

must act upon the amended application shall be extended by 30 days.

(ii) *Substantial amendments.* If an amending statement is submitted and the Service finds that the statement substantially amends the facts of the underlying application or substantially alters the terms of the withholding certificate as requested in the initial application, the time within which the Service must act upon the amended application shall be extended by 60 days. The applicant shall be so notified.

(iii) *Amending statement received after the requested withholding certificate has been signed by the Assistant Commissioner (International).* If an amending statement is received after the withholding certificate, drafted in response to the underlying application, has been signed by the Assistant Commissioner (International) or his delegate and prior to the day such certificate is mailed to the applicant, the time in which the Service must act upon the amended application shall be extended by 90 days. The applicant will be so notified.

(3) *Information required to be submitted.* No particular form is required for an amending statement but the statement must provide the following information:

(i) *Identification of applicant.* The amending statement must set forth the name, address and identifying number (if any) of the person submitting the amending statement (specifying whether that person is the transferee or transferor).

(ii) *Date of underlying application.* The amending statement must set forth the date of the underlying application for a withholding certificate.

(iii) *Real property interest to be (or that has been) transferred.* The amending statement must set forth a brief description of the real property interest with respect to which the underlying application for a withholding certificate was submitted.

(iv) *Amending information.* The amending statement must fully set forth the basis for the amendment including any modification of the facts supporting the application for a withholding certificate and any change sought in the terms of the withholding certificate.

(g) *Early refund of overwithheld amounts.* If a transferor receives a withholding certificate pursuant to this section, and an amount greater than that specified in the certificate was withheld by the transferee, then pursuant to the rules of this paragraph (g) the transferor may apply for a refund (without interest) of the excess amount prior to the date on which the transferor's tax return is due (without extensions). (Any interest payable on refunds issued after the filing of a tax return shall be determined in accordance with the provisions of section 6611 and regulations thereunder.) An application for an early refund must be addressed to the Assistant Commissioner (International), at the address provided in § 1.1445-1(g)(10). No particular form is required for the application, but the following information must be set forth in separate paragraphs numbered to correspond with the number given below:

(1) Name, address, and identifying number (if any) of the transferor seeking the refund;

(2) Amount required to be withheld pursuant to the withholding certificate issued by Internal Revenue Service;

(3) Amount withheld by the transferee (attach a copy of Form 8288-A stamped by IRS pursuant to § 1.1445-1(c));

(4) Amount to be refunded to the transferor. An application for an early refund cannot be processed unless the required copy of Form 8288-A (or substantial evidence of the amount withheld in the case of a failure to receive Form 8288-A as provided in § 1.1445-1(f)(3)) is attached to the application. If an application for a withholding certificate based upon the transferor's maximum tax liability is submitted after the transfer takes place, then that application may be combined with an application for an early refund. The Service will act upon a claim for refund within the time limits set forth in paragraph (a) of this section. [Reg. § 1.1445-3.]

☐ [T.D. 8113, 12-18-86.]

[Reg. § 1.1445-4]

§ 1.1445-4. Liability of agents.—(a) *Duty to provide notice of false certification or statement to transferee.* A transferee's or transferor's agent must provide notice to the transferee if either—

(1) The transferee is furnished with a non-U.S. real property interest statement pursuant to § 1.1445-2(c)(3) and the agent knows that the statement is false; or

(2) The transferee is furnished with a non-foreign certification pursuant to § 1.1445-2(b)(2) and either (i) the agent knows that the certification is false, or (ii) the agent represents a transferor that is a foreign corporation.

An agent that represents a transferor that is a foreign corporation is not required to provide notice to the transferee if the foreign corporation provided a nonforeign certification to the transferee prior to such agent's employment and the agent does not know that the corporation did so.

Reg. § 1.1445-4(a)(1)

(b) *Duty to provide notice of false certification or statement to entity or fiduciary.* A transferee's or transferor's agent must provide notice to an entity or fiduciary that plans to carry out a transaction described in section 1445(e)(1), (2), (3), or (4) if either—

(1) The entity or fiduciary is furnished with a non-U.S. real property interest statement pursuant to § 1.1445-5(b)(4)(iii) and the agent knows that such statement is false; or

(2) The entity or fiduciary is furnished with a non-foreign certification pursuant to § 1.1445-5(b)(3)(ii) and either (i) the agent knows that such certification is false, or (ii) the agent represents a foreign corporation that made such a certification.

(c) *Procedural requirements*—(1) *Notice to transferee, entity, or fiduciary.* An agent who is required by this section to provide notice must do so in writing as soon as possible after learning of the false certification or statement, but not later than the date of the transfer (prior to the transferee's payment of consideration). If an agent first learns of a false certification or statement after the date of the transfer, notice must be given by the third day following that discovery. The notice must state that the certification or statement is false and may not be relied upon. The notice must also explain the possible consequences to the recipient of a failure to withhold. The notice need not disclose the information on which the agent's statement is based. The following is an example of an acceptable notice: "This is to notify you that you may be required to withhold tax in connection with *(describe transaction).* You have been provided with a certification of nonforeign status (or a non-U.S. real property interest statement) in connection with that transaction. I have learned that that document is false. Therefore, you may not rely upon it as a basis for failing to withhold under section 1445 of the Internal Revenue Code. Section 1445 provides that any person who acquires a U.S. real property interest from a foreign person must withhold a tax equal to 10 percent of the total purchase price. (The term "U.S. real property interest" includes real property, stock in U.S. corporations whose assets are primarily real property, and some personal property associated with realty.) Any person who is required to withhold but fails to do so can be held liable for the tax. Thus, if you do not withhold the 10 percent tax from the total that you pay on this transaction, you could be required to pay the tax yourself, if what you are acquiring is a U.S. real property interest and the transferor is a foreign person. Tax that is withheld must be promptly paid over to the IRS using Form 8288. For further information see sections 897 and 1445 of the Internal Revenue Code and the related regulations."

(2) *Notice to be filed with IRS.* An agent who is required by paragraph (a) or (b) of this section to provide notice to a transferee, entity, or fiduciary must furnish a copy of that notice to the Internal Revenue Service by the date on which the notice is required to be given to the transferee, entity, or fiduciary. The copy of the notice must be delivered to the Assistant Commissioner (International) at the address provided in § 1.1445-1(g)(10), and must be accompanied by a cover letter stating that the copy is being filed pursuant to the requirements of this § 1.1445-4(c)(2).

(d) *Effect on recipient.* A transferee, entity, or fiduciary that receives a notice pursuant to this section prior to the date of the transfer from any agent of the transferor or transferee may not rely upon the subject certification or statement for purposes of excusing withholding pursuant to § 1.1445-2 or § 1.1445-5. Therefore, the recipient of a notice may be held liable for any failure to deduct and withhold tax under section 1445 as if such certification or statement had never been given. For special rules concerning the effect of the receipt of a notice after the date of the transfer, see §§ 1.1445-2(b)(4)(iv) and 1.1445-5(c), (d) and (e).

(e) *Failure to provide notice.* Any agent who is required to provide notice but who fails to do so in the manner required by paragraph (a) or (b) of this section shall be held liable for the tax that the recipient of the notice would have been required to withhold under section 1445 if such notice had been given. However, an agent's liability under this paragraph (e) is limited to the amount of compensation that that agent derives from the transaction. In addition, an agent who assists in the preparation of, or fails to disclose knowledge of, a false certification or statement may be liable for civil or criminal penalties.

(f) *Definition of transferor's or transferee's agent*—(1) *In general.* For purposes of this section, the terms "transferor's agent" and "transferee's agent" mean any person who represents the transferor or transferee (respectively)—

(i) In any negotiation with another person (or another person's agent) relating to the transaction; or

(ii) In settling the transaction.

(2) *Transactions subject to section 1445(e).* In the case of transactions subject to section 1445(e), the following definitions apply.

(i) The term "transferor's agent" means any person that represents or advises an entity or

Reg. § 1.1445-4(f)(2)

fiduciary with respect to the planning, arrangement, or consummation by the entity of a transaction described in section 1445(e)(1), (2), (3), or (4).

(ii) The term "transferee's agent" means any person that represents or advises the holder of an interest in an entity with respect to the planning, arrangement or consummation by the entity of a transaction described in section 1445(e)(1), (2), (3), or (4).

(3) *Exclusion of settlement officers and clerical personnel.* For purposes of this section, a person shall not be treated as a transferor's agent or transferee's agent with respect to any transaction solely because such person performs one or more of the following activities:

(i) The receipt and disbursement of any portion of the consideration for the transaction;

(ii) The recording of any document in connection with the transaction; or

(iii) Typing, copying, and other clerical tasks;

(iv) The obtaining of title insurance reports and reports concerning the condition of the real property that is the subject of the transaction; or

(v) The transmission or delivery of documents between the parties.

(4) *Exclusion for governing body of a condominium association and the board of directors of a cooperative housing corporation.* The members of a board, committee or other governing body of a condominium association and the board of directors and officers of a cooperative housing corporation will not be deemed agents of the transferor or transferee if such individuals function exclusively in their capacity as representatives of such association or corporation with respect to the transaction. In addition, the managing agent of a cooperative housing corporation or condominium association will not be deemed to be an agent of the transferee or transferor if such person functions exclusively in its capacity as a managing agent. If a person's activities include advising the transferee or transferor with respect to the transfer, this exclusion shall not apply. [Reg. § 1.1445-4.]

☐ [T.D. 8113, 12-18-86.]

[Reg. § 1.1445-5]

§ 1.1445-5. Special rules concerning distributions and other transactions by corporations, partnerships, trusts, and estates.—(a) *Purpose and scope.* This section provides special rules concerning the withholding that is required under section 1445(e) upon distributions and other transactions involving domestic or foreign corporations, partnerships, trusts, and estates. Paragraph (b) of this section provides rules that apply generally to the various withholding requirements set forth in this section. Under section 1445(e)(1) and paragraph (c) of this section, a domestic partnership or the fiduciary of a domestic trust or estate is required to withhold tax upon the entity's disposition of a U.S. real property interest if any foreign persons are partners or beneficiaries of the entity. Paragraph (d) provides rules concerning the requirement of section 1445(e)(2) that a foreign corporation withhold tax upon its distribution of a U.S. real property interest to its interest-holders. Finally, under section 1445(e)(3) and paragraph (e) of this section a domestic U.S. real property holding corporation is required to withhold tax upon certain distributions to interest-holders that are foreign persons. Paragraphs (f) and (g) of this section are reserved to provide rules concerning transactions involving interests in partnerships, trusts, and estates that will be subject to withholding pursuant to section 1445(e)(4) and (5).

(b) *Rules of general application*—(1) *Double withholding not required.* If tax is required to be withheld with respect to a transfer of property in accordance with the rules of this section, then no additional tax is required to be withheld by the transferee of the property with respect to that transfer pursuant to the general rules of section 1445(a) and § 1.1445-1. For rules coordinating the withholding under section 1441 (or section 1442 or 1443) and under section 1445 on distributions from a corporation, see § 1.1441-3(b)(4). If a transfer of a U.S. real property interest described in section 1445(e) is exempt from withholding under the rules of this section, then no withholding is required under the general rules of section 1445(a) and § 1.1445-1.

(2) *Coordination with nonrecognition provisions*—(i) *In general.* Withholding shall not be required under the rules of this section with respect to a transfer described in section 1445(e) of a U.S. real property interest if—

(A) By reason of the operation of a nonrecognition provision of the Internal Revenue Code or the provisions of any treaty of the United States no gain or loss is required to be recognized by the foreign person with respect to which withholding would otherwise be required; and

(B) The entity or fiduciary that is otherwise required to withhold complies with the notice requirements of paragraph (b)(2)(ii) of this section. The entity or fiduciary must determine whether gain or loss is required to be recognized pursuant to the rules of section 897 and the appli-

Reg. § 1.1445-5(a)

cable nonrecognition provisions of the Internal Revenue Code. An entity or fiduciary may obtain a withholding certificate from the Internal Revenue Service that confirms the applicability of a nonrecognition provision, but is not required to do so. For purposes of this paragraph (b)(2), a nonrecognition provision is any provision of the Internal Revenue Code for not recognizing gain or loss. If nonrecognition treatment is available only with respect to part of the gain realized on a transfer, the exemption from withholding provided by this paragraph (b)(2) shall not apply. In such cases a withholding certificate may be sought pursuant to the provisions of § 1.1445-6.

(ii) *Notice of nonrecognition transfer.* An entity or fiduciary that fails to withhold tax with respect to a transfer in reliance upon the rules of this paragraph (b)(2) must by the 20th day after the date of the transfer deliver a notice thereof to the Assistant Commissioner, (International), at the address provided in § 1.1445-1(g)(10). No particular form is required for a notice of transfer, but the following information must be set forth in paragraphs labelled to correspond with the letter set forth below:

(A) A statement that the document submitted constitutes a notice of a nonrecognition transfer pursuant to the requirements of § 1.1445-5(b)(2)(ii);

(B) The name, office address, and identifying number (if any) of the entity of fiduciary submitting the notice;

(C) The name, identifying number (if any), and home address (in the case of an individual) or office address (in the case of an entity) of each foreign person with respect to which withholding would otherwise be required;

(D) A brief description of the transfer; and

(E) A brief statement of the law and facts supporting the claim that recognition of gain or loss is not required with respect to the transfer.

(3) *Interest-holder not a foreign person*—(i) *In general.* Pursuant to the provisions of paragraphs (c) and (e) of this section, an entity or fiduciary is required to withhold with respect to certain transfers of property if a holder of an interest in the entity is a foreign person. For purposes of determining whether a holder of an interest is a foreign person, an entity or fiduciary may rely upon a certification of non-foreign status provided by that person in accordance with paragraph (b)(3)(ii) of this section. Except to the extent provided in paragraph (b)(3)(iii) of this section, such a certification excuses the entity or fiduciary from any liability otherwise imposed pursuant to section 1445(e) and regulations thereunder. However, no obligation is imposed upon an entity or fiduciary to obtain certifications from interest-holders; an entity or fiduciary may instead rely upon other means to ascertain the non-foreign status of an interest-holder. If the entity or fiduciary does rely upon other means but the interest-holder proves, in fact, to be a foreign person, then the entity or fiduciary is subject to any liability imposed pursuant to section 1445 and regulations thereunder. An entity or fiduciary is not required to rely upon other means to ascertain the non-foreign status of an interest-holder and may demand a certification of non-foreign status. If the certification is not provided, the entity or fiduciary may withhold tax under section 1445 and will be considered, for purposes of sections 1461 through 1463, to have been required to withhold such tax.

(ii) *Interest-holder's certification of non-foreign status*—(A) *In general.* For purposes of this section, an entity or fiduciary may treat any holder of an interest in the entity as a U.S. person if that interest-holder furnishes to the entity or fiduciary a certification stating that the interest-holder is not a foreign person, in accordance with the provisions of paragraph (b)(3)(ii)(B) of this section. In general, a foreign person is a nonresident alien individual, foreign corporation, foreign partnership, foreign trust, or foreign estate, but not a resident alien individual. In this regard, see § 1.897-1(k).

(B) *Procedural rules.* An interest-holder's certification of non-foreign status must—

(*1*) State that the interest-holder is not a foreign person;

(*2*) Set forth the interest-holder's name, identifying number, home address (in the case of an individual) or office address (in the case of an entity), and place of incorporation (in the case of a corporation); and

(*3*) Be signed under penalties of perjury.

Pursuant to § 1.897-1(p), an individual's identifying number is the individual's Social Security number and any other person's identifying number is its U.S. employer identification number. The certification must be signed by a responsible officer in the case of a corporation, by a general partner in the case of a partnership, and by a trustee, executor, or equivalent fiduciary in the case of a trust or estate. No particular form is needed for a certification pursuant to this paragraph (b)(3)(ii)(B), nor is any particular language required, so long as the document meets the requirements of this paragraph. Samples of acceptable certifications are provided in paragraph (b)(3)(ii)(D) of this section. An entity may rely

Reg. § 1.1445-5(b)(3)

upon a certification pursuant to this paragraph (b)(3)(ii)(B) for a period of two calendar years following the close of the calendar year in which the certification was given. If an interest holder becomes a foreign person within the period described in the preceding sentence, the interest holder must notify the entity prior to any further dispositions or distributions and upon receipt of such notice (or any other notification of the foreign status of the interest holder) the entity may no longer rely upon the prior certification. An entity that obtains and relies upon a certification must retain that certification with its books and records for a period of three calendar years following the close of the last calendar year in which the entity relied upon the certification.

(C) *Foreign corporation that has made an election under section 897(i).* A foreign corporation that has made a valid election under section 897(i) to be treated as a domestic corporation for purposes of section 897 may provide a certification of non-foreign status pursuant to this paragraph (b)(3)(ii). However, an electing foreign corporation must attach to such certification a copy of the acknowledgment of the election provided to the corporation by the Internal Revenue Service pursuant to § 1.897-3(d)(4).

An acknowledgment is valid for this purpose only if it states that the information required by § 1.897-3 has been determined to be complete.

(D) *Sample certifications—(1) Individual interest-holder.* "Under section 1445(e) of the Internal Revenue Code, a corporation, partnership, trust or estate must withhold tax with respect to certain transfers of property if a holder of an interest in the entity is a foreign person. To inform [*name of entity*] that no withholding is required with respect to my interest in it, I, [*name of interest-holder*], hereby certify the following:

1. I am not a nonresident alien for purposes of U.S. income taxation;

2. My U.S. taxpayer identifying number (Social Security number) is ———; and

3. My home address is

———————————————————
———————————————————

I agree to inform [name of entity] promptly if I become a nonresident alien at any time during the three years immediately following the date of this notice.

I understand that this certification may be disclosed to the Internal Revenue Service by [*name of entity*] and that any false statement I have made here could be punished by fine, imprisonment, or both.

Under penalties of perjury I declare that I have examined this certification and to the best of my knowledge and belief it is true, correct, and complete.

[*Signature and date*]"

(2) *Entity interest-holder.* "Under section 1445(e) of the Internal Revenue Code, a corporation, partnership, trust, or estate must withhold tax with respect to certain transfers of property if a holder of an interest in the entity is a foreign person. To inform [*name of entity*] that no withholding is required with respect to [*name of interest-holder*]'s interest in it, the undersigned hereby certifies the following on behalf of [*name of interest-holder*]:

1. [*Name of interest-holder*] is not a foreign corporation, foreign partnership, foreign trust, or foreign estate (as those terms are defined in the Internal Revenue Code and Income Tax Regulations);

2. [*Name of interest-holder*]'s U.S. employer identification number is ———; and

3. [*Name of interest-holder*]'s office address is

———————————————————

and place of incorporation (if applicable) is

———————————————————

[Name of interest holder] agrees to inform [name of entity] if it becomes a foreign person at any time during the three year period immediately following the date of this notice.

[*Name of interest-holder*] understands that this certification may be disclosed to the Internal Revenue Service by [*name of entity*] and that any false statement contained herein could be punished by fine, imprisonment, or both.

Under penalties of perjury I declare that I have examined this certification and to the best of my knowledge and belief it is true, correct, and complete, and I further declare that I have authority to sign this document on behalf of [*name of interest-holder*].

[*Signature and date*]

[*Title*]"

(iii) *Reliance upon certification not permitted.* An entity or fiduciary may not rely upon an interest-holder's certification of non-foreign status if, prior to or at the time of the transfer with respect to which withholding would be required, the entity or fiduciary either—

(A) Has actual knowledge that the certification is false;

(B) Has received a notice that the certification is false from a transferor's or transferee's agent, pursuant to § 1.1445-4; or

Reg. § 1.1445-5(b)(3)

(C) Has received from a corporation that it knows to be a foreign corporation a certification that does not have attached to it a copy of the IRS acknowledgment of the corporation's election under section 897(i), as required by paragraph (b)(3)(ii)(C) of this section.

Such an entity's or fiduciary's withholding obligations shall apply as if a statement had never been given, and such an entity or fiduciary may be held fully liable pursuant to § 1.1445-1(e) for any failure to withhold. For special rules concerning an entity's belated receipt of a notice concerning a false certification, see paragraphs (c)(2)(ii) and (e)(2)(iii) of this section.

(4) *Property transferred not a U.S. real property interest*—(i) *In general.* Pursuant to the provisions of paragraphs (c) and (d) of this section, an entity or fiduciary is required to withhold with respect to certain transfers of property, if the property transferred is a U.S. real property interest. (In addition, taxable distributions of U.S. real property interests by domestic or foreign partnerships, trusts, and estates will be subject to withholding pursuant to section 1445(e)(4) and paragraph (f) of this section after publication of a Treasury decision under sections 897(e)(2) and (g).) As defined in section 897(c) and § 1.897-1(c), a U.S. real property interest includes certain interests in U.S. corporations, as well as direct interests in real property and certain associated personal property. This paragraph (b)(4) provides rules pursuant to which an entity (or fiduciary thereof) that transfers an interest in a U.S. corporation may determine that withholding is not required because the interest transferred is not a U.S. real property interest. To determine whether an interest in tangible property constitutes a U.S. real property interest the transfer of which would be subject to withholding, see § 1.897-1(b) and (c).

(ii) *Interests in publicly traded entities.* Withholding is not required under paragraph (c) or (d) of this section upon an entity's transfer of an interest in a domestic corporation if any class of stock of the corporation is regularly traded on an established securities market. This exemption shall apply to a disposition incident to an initial public offering of stock pursuant to a registration statement filed with the Securities and Exchange Commission. Similarly, no withholding is required under paragraph (c) or (d) of this section upon an entity's transfer of an interest in a publicly traded partnership or trust. However, the rule of this paragraph (b)(4)(ii) shall not apply to the transfer, to a single transferee (or related transferees as defined in § 1.897-1(i)) in a single transaction (or related transactions), of an interest described in § 1.897-1(c)(2)(iii)(B) (relating to substantial amounts of non-publicly traded interests in publicly traded corporations) or of similar interests in publicly traded partnerships or trusts. The entity making a transfer described in the preceding sentence must otherwise determine whether withholding is required, pursuant to section 1445(e) and the regulations thereunder. Transactions shall be deemed to be related if they are undertaken within 90 days of one another or if if can otherwise be shown that they were undertaken in pursuance of a prearranged plan.

(iii) *Corporation's statement that interest is not a U.S. real property interest*—(A) *In general.* No withholding is required under paragraph (c) or (d) of this section upon an entity's transfer of an interest in a domestic corporation if, prior to the transfer, the entity or fiduciary obtains a statement, issued by the corporation pursuant to § 1.897-2(h), certifying that the interest is not a U.S. real property interest. In general, a corporation may issue such a statement only if the corporation was not a U.S. real property holding corporation at any time during the previous five years (or the period in which the interest was held by its present holder, if shorter) or if interests in the corporation ceased to be United States real property interests under section 897(c)(1)(B). (A corporation may not provide such a statement based on its determination that the interest in question is an interest solely as a creditor.) See § 1.897-2(f) and (h). A corporation's statement may be relied upon for purposes of this paragraph (b)(4)(iii) only if the statement is dated not more than 30 days prior to the date of the transfer.

(B) *Reliance on statement not permitted.* An entity or fiduciary is not entitled to rely upon a statement that an interest in a corporation is not a U.S. real property interest if, prior to or at the time of the transfer, the entity or fiduciary either—

(*1*) Has actual knowledge that the statement is false, or

(*2*) Receives a notice that the statement is false from a transferor's or transferee's agent, pursuant to § 1.1445-4.

Such an entity's or fiduciary's withholding obligations shall apply as if a statement had never been given, and such an entity or fiduciary may be held fully liable pursuant to § 1.1445-1(e) for any failure to withhold. For special rules concerning an entity's belated receipt of a notice concerning a false statement, see paragraphs (c)(2)(iii) and (d)(2)(i) of this section.

(5) *Reporting and paying over of withheld amounts*—(i) *In general.* An entity or fiduciary must report and pay over to the Internal Revenue Service any tax withheld pursuant to section

Reg. § 1.1445-5(b)(5)

1445(e) and this section by the 20th day after the date of the transfer (as defined in § 1.1445-1(g)(8)). Forms 8288 and 8288-A are used for this purpose and must be filed with the Internal Revenue Service Center, Philadelphia, PA 19255. The contents of Forms 8288 and 8288-A are described in § 1.1445-1(d). Pursuant to section 7502 and regulations thereunder, the timely mailing of Forms 8288 and 8288-A by U.S. mail will be treated as their timely filing. Form 8288-A will be stamped by the Internal Revenue Service to show receipt, and a stamped copy will be mailed by the Service to the interest-holder, at the address shown on the form, for the interest-holder's use. See paragraph (b)(7) of this section.

If an application for a withholding certificate with respect to a transfer of a U.S. real property interest was submitted to the Internal Revenue Service on the day of or at any time prior to the transfer, the entity or fiduciary must withhold the amount required under section 1445(e) and the rules of this section. However, the amount withheld, or a lesser amount as determined by the Service, need not be reported and paid over to the Service until the 20th day following the Service's final determination. For this purpose, the Service's final determination occurs on the day when the withholding certificate is mailed to the applicant by the Service or when notification denying the request for a withholding certificate is mailed to the applicant by the Service. An application is submitted to the Service on the day it is actualy received by the Service at the address provided in § 1.1445-1(g)(10) or, under the rules of section 7502, on the day it is mailed to the Service at the address provided in § 1.1445-1(g)(10), concerning the issuance of withholding certificates see § 1.1445-6.

(ii) *Anti-abuse rule.* An entity or fiduciary that in reliance upon the rules of this paragraph (b)(5)(ii) fails to report and pay over amounts withheld by the 20th day following the date of the transfer, shall be subject to the payment of interest and penalties if the relevant application for a withholding certificate (or an amendment of the application for a withholding certificate) was submitted for a principle purpose of delaying the payment to the IRS of the amount withheld. Interest and penalties shall be assessed on the amount that is ultimately paid over with respect to the period between the 20th day after the date of the transfer and the date on which payment is made.

(6) *Liability upon failure to withhold.* For rules regarding liability upon failure to withhold under section 1445(e) and this § 1.1445-5, see § 1.1445-1(e).

(7) *Effect of withholding by entity or fiduciary upon interest holder.* The withholding of tax under section 1445(e) does not excuse a foreign person that is subject to U.S. tax by reason of the operation of section 897 from filing a U.S. tax return. Thus, Form 1040NR, 1041, or 1120F as appropriate must be filed and any tax due must be paid by the filing date otherwise applicable to such person (or any extension therof). The tax withheld with respect to the foreign person under section 1445(e) (as shown on Form 8288-A) shall be credited against the amount of income tax as computed in such return, but only if the stamped copy of Form 8288-A provided to the entity or fiduciary (under paragraph (b)(5) of this section) is attached to the return or substantial evidence of the amount of tax withheld is attached to the return in accordance with the succeeding sentence. If a stamped copy of Form 8288-A has not been provided to the interest-holder by the Service, the interest-holder may establish the amount of tax withheld by the entity or fiduciary by attaching to its return substantial evidence of such amount. Such an interest-holder must attach to its return a statement which supplies all of the information required by § 1.1445-1(d)(2) (except such information that was not obtained by a diligent effort). If the amount withheld under section 1445(e) constitutes less than the full amount of the foreign person's U.S. tax liability for that taxable year, then a payment of estimated tax may be required to be made pursuant to section 6154 or 6654 prior to the filing of the income tax return for that year. Alternatively, if the amount withheld under section 1445(e) exceeds the foreign person's maximum tax liability with respect to the transaction (as *reflected* in a withholding certificate issued by the Internal Revenue Service pursuant to § 1.1445-6), then the foreign person may seek an early refund of the excess pursuant to § 1.1445-6(g). A foreign person that takes gain into account in accordance with the provisions of section 453 shall not be entitled to a refund of the amount withheld unless a withholding certificate providing for such a refund is obtained pursuant to § 1.1445-6.

If an entity or fiduciary withholds tax under section 1445(e) with respect to a beneficial owner of an interest who is not a foreign person, such beneficial owner may credit the amount of any tax withheld against his income tax liability in accordance with the provisions of this § 1.1445-5(b)(7) or apply for an early refund under § 1.1445-6(g).

(8) *Effective dates*—(i) *Partnership, trust, and estate dispositions of U.S. real property interests.* The provisions of section 1445(e)(1) and paragraph (c) of this section, requiring withholding

Reg. § 1.1445-5(b)(6)

upon certain dispositions of U.S. real property interests by domestic partnerships, trusts and estates, shall apply to any disposition on or after January 1, 1985.

(ii) *Certain distributions by foreign corporations.* The provisions of section 1445(e)(2) and paragraph (d) of this section requiring withholding upon distributions of U.S. real property interest by foreign corporations, shall apply to distributions made on or after January 1, 1985.

(iii) *Distributions by certain domestic corporations to foreign shareholders.* The provisions of section 1445(e)(3) and paragraph (e) of this section, requiring withholding upon distributions by U.S. real property holding corporations to foreign shareholders, shall apply to distributions made on or after January 1, 1985.

(iv) *Taxable distributions by domestic or foreign partnerships, trusts, and estates.* The provisions of section 1445(e)(4), requiring withholding upon certain taxable distributions by domestic or foreign partnerships, trusts, and estates, shall apply to distributions made on or after the effective date of a Treasury decision under section 897(e)(2)(B)(ii) and (g).

(v) [Removed]

(vi) *Tiered partnerships.* No withholding is required upon the disposition of a U.S. real property interest by a partnership which is directly owned, in whole or in part, by another domestic partnership (but only to the extent that the amount realized is attributable to the partnership interest of that other partnership) until the effective date of a Treasury Decision published under section 1445(e) providing rules governing this matter.

(c) *Dispositions of U.S. real property interests by domestic partnerships, trusts, and estates.*—(1) *Withholding required*—(i) *In general.* If a domestic partnership, trust, or estate disposes of a U.S. real property interest and any partner, beneficiary, or owner of the entity is a foreign person, then the partnership or the trustee, executor, or equivalent fiduciary of the trust or estate must withhold tax with respect to each such foreign person in accordance with the provisions of subdivision (ii), (iii), or (iv) of this paragraph (c)(1) (as applicable). The withholding obligation imposed by this paragraph (c) applies to the fiduciary of a trust even if the grantor of the trust or another person is treated as the owner of the trust or any portion thereof for purposes of the Internal Revenue Code. Thus, the withholding obligation imposed by this paragraph (c) applies to the trustee of a land trust or similar arrangement, even if such a trustee is not ordinarily treated under the applicable provisions of local law as a true fiduciary.

(ii) *Disposition by partnership.* A partnership must withhold a tax equal to 35 percent (or the highest rate specified in section 1445(e)(1)) of each foreign partner's distributive share of the gain realized by the partnership upon the disposition of each U.S. real property interest. Such distributive share of the gain must be determined pursuant to the principles of section 704 and the regulations thereunder. For the rules applicable to partnerships, interests in which are regularly traded on an established securities market, see § 1.1445-8.

(iii) *Disposition by trust or estate*—(A) *In general.* A trustee, fiduciary, executor or equivalent fiduciary (hereafter collectively referred to as the fiduciary) of a trust or estate having one or more foreign beneficiaries must withhold tax in accordance with the rules of this § 1.1445-5(c)(1)(iii). Such a fiduciary must establish a U.S. real property interest account and must enter in such account all gains and losses realized during the taxable year of the trust or estate from dispositions of U.S. real property interests. The fiduciary must withhold 35 percent (or the highest rate specified in section 1445(e)(1)) of any distribution to a foreign beneficiary that is attributable to the balance in the U.S. real property interest account on the day of the distribution. A distribution from a trust or estate to a beneficiary (domestic or foreign) shall, solely for purposes of section 1445(e)(1), be deemed to be attributable first to any balance in the U.S. real property interest account and then to other amounts. However, a distribution that occurs prior to the transfer of a U.S. real property interest in a taxable year or at any other time when the amount contained in the U.S. real property interest account is zero, is not subject to withholding under this § 1.1445-5(c)(1)(iii). The U.S. real property interest account is reduced by the amount distributed to all beneficiaries (domestic and foreign) attributable to such account during the taxable year of the trust or estate. Any ending balance of the U.S. real property interest account not distributed by the close of the taxable year of the trust or estate is cancelled and is not carried over (or carried back) to any other year. Thus, the beginning balance of such account in any taxable year of the trust or estate is always zero. For rules applicable to grantor trusts see § 1.1445-5(c)(1)(iv). For rules applicable to trusts, interests in which are regularly traded on an established securities market and real estate investment trusts, see § 1.1445-8.

Reg. § 1.1445-5(c)

(B) *Example.* The following example illustrates the rules of paragraph (c)(1)(iii)(A) of this section.

On January 1, 1994, A establishes a domestic trust (which has as its taxable year, the calendar year) for the benefit of B, a nonresident alien, and C, a U.S. citizen. The trust is not a trust subject to sections 671 through 679. Under the terms of the trust, the trustee, T, is given discretion to distribute income and corpus of the trust to provide for the reasonable needs of B and C. During the trust's 1994 tax year, T disposes of three parcels of vacant land located in the United States. The following chart illustrates the computation of the amount subject to withholding under section 1445 with respect to distributions made by T to B and C during 1994.

Date	Parcel sold	Gains or (loss) realized	Distributions to C	Distributions to B (before withholding)	Section 1445 withholding (35% rate)	U.S. real property interest account
1/01/94						–0–
3/01/94	Parcel 1	140,000				140,000
3/05/94			5,000	10,000	3,500	125,000
3/15/94			10,000	5,000	1,750	110,000
5/01/94	Parcel 2	300,000				410,000
5/15/94	Parcel 3	(50,000)				360,000
12/01/94			170,000	170,000	59,500	20,000
1/01/95						–0–

(iv) *Disposition by grantor trust.* The trustee or equivalent fiduciary of a trust that is subject to the provisions of subpart E of part I of subchapter J (sections 671 through 679) must withhold a tax equal to 35 percent (or the highest rate specified in section 1445(e)(1)) of the gain realized from each disposition of a U.S. real property interest to the extent such gain is allocable to a portion of the trust treated as owned by a foreign person under subpart E of part I of subchapter J.

(2) *Withholding not required under paragraph (c)*—(i) [Removed]

(ii) *Interest-holder not a foreign person*—(A) *In general.* A domestic partnership, trust, or estate that disposes of a U.S. real property interest shall not be required to withhold with respect to any partner or beneficiary that it determines, pursuant to the rules of paragraph (b)(3) of this section, not to be a foreign person.

(B) *Belated notice of false certification.* If after the date of the transfer a partnership or fiduciary learns that a partner's or beneficiary's certification of non-foreign status is false, then that partnership or fiduciary shall be required to withhold, with respect to the foreign partner or beneficiary that gave the false certification, the lesser of—

(*1*) The amount otherwise required to be withheld under the rules of this paragraph (c), or

(*2*) An amount equal to that partner's or beneficiary's remaining interests in the income or assets of the partnership, trust, or estate.

Amounts so withheld must be reported and paid over by the 60th day following the date on which the partnership or fiduciary learns that the certification is false. For rules concerning the notifications of false certifications that may be required to be given to partnerships and fiduciaries, see § 1.1445-4(b).

(iii) *Property disposed of not a U.S. real property interest*—(A) *In general.* No withholding is required under this paragraph (c) if a domestic partnership, trust, or estate that disposes of property determines pursuant to the rules of paragraph (b)(4) of this section that the property disposed of is not a U.S. real property interest.

(B) *Belated notice of false statement.* If after the date of the transfer a partnership or fiduciary learns that a corporation's statement (that an interest in the corporation is not a U.S. real property interest) is false, then that partnership or fiduciary shall be required to withhold, with respect to each foreign partner or beneficiary, the lesser of—

(*1*) The amount otherwise required to be withheld under the rules of this paragraph (c), or

(*2*) An amount equal to that partner's or beneficiary's remaining interests in the income or assets of the partnership, trust, or estate.

Amounts so withheld must be reported and paid over by the 60th day following the date on which the partnership or fiduciary learns that the statement is false. For rules concerning the notifications of false statements that may be required to be given to partnerships or fiduciaries, see § 1.1445-4(b).

(iv) *Withholding certificate.* No withholding is required under this paragraph (c) with respect to the transfer of a U.S. real property

Reg. § 1.1445-5(c)(2)

interest if the Internal Revenue Service issues a withholding certificate that so provides. For rules concerning the issuance of withholding certificates, see § 1.1445-6.

(v) *Nonrecognition transactions.* For special rules concerning transactions entitled to nonrecognition of gain or loss, see paragraph (b)(2) of this section.

(3) *Large partnerships or trusts*—(i) *In general.* If a partnership or trust has more than 100 partners or beneficiaries, then the partnership or fiduciary of the trust may elect to withhold in accordance with the provisions of this § 1.1445-5(c)(3) in lieu of withholding in the manner required by § 1.1445-5(c)(1). However, the rules of this § 1.1445-5(c)(3) shall not apply to any partnership or trust interests in which are regularly traded on an established securities market except as described in § 1.1445-8(c)(1). The rules of this § 1.1445-5(c)(3) shall not apply to any real estate investment trust. See § 1.1445-8.

(ii) *Amount to be withheld.* A partnership or trust electing to withhold under this § 1.1445-5(c)(3) shall withhold from each distribution to a foreign person an amount equal to 35 percent (or the highest rate specified in section 1445(e)(1)) of the amount attributable to section 1445(e)(1) transfers.

(iii) *Amounts attributable to section 1445(e)(1) transfers.* A distribution is attributable to section 1445(e)(1) transfers to the extent of the partner's or beneficiary's proportionate share of the current balance of the entity's section 1445(e)(1) account. A distribution from a partnership or trust that has made an election under this § 1.1445-5(c)(3) shall be deemed first to be attributable to a section 1445(e)(1) transfer to the extent of the balance in the section 1445(e)(1) account. An entity's section 1445(e)(1) account shall be equal to—

(A) The total amount of net gain realized by the entity upon all transfers of U.S. real property interests carried out by the entity after the date of its election under this § 1.1445-5(c)(3); minus

(B) The total amount of all distributions by the entity to domestic and foreign distributees from such account.

(iv) *Special rules for entities that make recurring sales of growing crops and timber.* An entity that makes an election under § 1.1445-5(c)(3) and that makes recurring sales of growing crops and timber may further elect to determine the amount subject to withholding under the rules of this § 1.1445-5(c)(3)(iv). Such an entity must withhold from each distribution to a foreign partner or beneficiary an amount equal to 10 percent of such partner's or beneficiary's proportionate share of the current balance of the entity's gross section 1445(e)(1) account. An entity's gross section 1445(e)(1) account equals—

(A) The total amount realized by the entity upon all transfers of U.S. real property interests carried out by the entity after the date of its election under this § 1.1445-5(c)(3)(iv); minus

(B) The total amount of all distributions to domestic and foreign distributees from such account.

An entity that elects to compute the amount subject to withholding under this § 1.1445-5(c)(3)(iv), shall make such election in accordance with § 1.1445-5(c)(3)(vi) and shall be subject to the provisions otherwise applicable under § 1.1445-5(c)(3).

(v) *Procedural rules.* An election under paragraph (c)(3) may be made by filing a notice thereof with the Assistant Commissioner (International), at the address provided in § 1.1445-1(g)(10). The notice must be submitted by a general partner (in the case of a partnership) or the trustee or equivalent fiduciary (in the case of a trust). The notice must set forth the name, office address, and identifying number of the partnership or fiduciary making the election, and, in the case of a partnership, must include the name, office address, and identifying number of the general partner submitting the election. An election under this paragraph (c)(3) may be revoked only with the consent of the Internal Revenue Service. Consent of the Service may be requested by filing an application to revoke the election with the Assistant Commissioner (International) at the address stated above. This application must include all information provided to the Service with the election notice and must provide an explanation of the reasons for revoking the election. The application to revoke an election must also specify the amount remaining to be distributed in the section 1445(e)(1) account or the gross section 1445(e)(1) account. An entity that ceases to qualify under section 1.1445-5(c)(3) because such entity does not have more than 100 partners or beneficiaries may revoke its election only with the consent of the Internal Revenue Service.

(d) *Distributions of U.S. real property interests by foreign corporations*—(1) *In general.* A foreign corporation that distributes a U.S. real property interest must deduct and withhold a tax equal to 35 percent (or the rate specified in section 1445(e)(2)) of the amount of gain recognized by the corporation on the distribution. The amount of gain required to be recognized by the corpora-

Reg. § 1.1445-5(d)(1)

tion must be detemined pursuant to the rules of section 897 and any other applicable section. For special rules concerning the applicability of a nonrecognition provision to a distribution, see paragraph (b)(2) of this section. The withholding liability imposed by this paragraph (d) applies to the same taxpayer that owes the related substantive income tax liability pursuant to the operation of section 897. Only one such liability will be assessed and collected from a foreign corporation, but separate penalties for failures to comply with the two requirements will be asserted.

(2) *Withholding not required*—(i) *Property distributed not a U.S. real property interest*—(A) *In general.* No withholding is required under this paragraph (d) if a foreign corporation that distributes property determines pursuant to the rules of paragraph (b)(3) of this section that the property distributed is not a U.S. real property interest.

(B) *Belated notice of false statement.* If after the date of a distribution described in paragraph (d)(1) of this section a foreign corporation learns that another corporation's statement (that an interest in that other corporation is not a U.S. real property interest) is false, then the foreign corporation may not rely upon that statement for any purpose. Such a foreign corporation's withholding obligations under this paragaph (d) shall apply as if a statement had never been given, and such a corporation may be held fully liable pursuant to § 1.1445-5(b)(5) for any failure to withhold. Amounts withheld pursuant to the rule of this paragraph (d)(2)(i)(B) must be reported and paid over by the 60th day following the date on which the foreign corporation learns that the statement is false. No penalties or interest will be assessed for failures to withhold prior to that date. For rules concerning the notifications of false statements that may be required to be given to foreign corporations, see § 1.1445-4(b).

(ii) *Withholding certificate.* No withholding is required under this paragraph (d) with respect to a foreign corporation's distribution of a U.S. real property interest if the distributing corporation obtains a withholding certificate from the Internal Revenue Service that so provides. For rules concerning the issuance of withholding certificates, see § 1.1445-6.

(e) *Distributions to foreign persons by U.S. real property holding corporations*—(1) *In general.* A domestic corporation that distributes any property to a foreign person that holds an interest in the corporation must deduct and withhold a tax equal to 10 percent of the fair market value of the property distributed to the foreign person, if—

(i) The foreign person's interest in the corporation constitutes a U.S. real property interest under the provisions of section 897 and regulations thereunder; and

(ii) The property is distributed either—

(A) In redemption of stock under section 302; or

(B) In liquidation of the corporation pursuant to the provisions of Part II of Subchapter C (sections 331 through 341). For the treatment of a domestic corporation's transfer of a U.S. real property interest to a foreign interestholder in a distribution to which section 301 applies, see sections 897(f), 1441, and 1442.

(2) *Withholding not required*—(i) *Foreign person's interest not a U.S. real property interest.* Withholding is required under this paragraph (e) only with respect to distributions to foreign persons holding interests in the corporation that constitute U.S. real property interests. In general, a foreign person's interest in a domestic corporation constitutes a U.S. real property interest if the corporation was a U.S. real property holding corporation at any time during the shorter of (A) the period in which the foreign person held the interest or (B) the previous five years (but not earlier than June 19, 1980). See section 897(c) and §§ 1.897-1(c) and 1.897-2(b) and (h). However, an interest in such a corporation ceases to be a U.S. real property interest after all of the U.S. real property interests held by the corporation itself are disposed of in transactions on which gain or loss is recognized. See section 897(c)(1)(B) and § 1.897-2(f)(2). Thus, if a U.S. real property holding corporation in the process of liquidation does not elect section 337 nonrecognition treatment upon its sale of all U.S. real property interests held by the corporation, and recognizes gain or loss upon such sales, interests in that corporation cease to be U.S. real property interests. Therefore, no withholding would be required with respect to that corporation's subsequent liquidating distribution to a foreign shareholder of property other than a U.S. real property interest.

(ii) *Nonrecognition transactions.* For special rules concerning the applicability of a nonrecognition provision to a distribution described in paragraph (e)(1) of this section, see paragraph (b)(2) of this section.

(iii) *Interest-holder not a foreign person*—(A) *In general.* A domestic corporation shall not be required to withhold under this paragraph (e) with respect to a distribution of property to any distributee that it determines, pursuant to the rules of paragraph (b)(3) of this section, not to be a foreign person.

(B) *Belated notice of false certification.* If after the date of a distribution described in paragraph (e)(1) of this section a domestic corporation learns that an interest-holder's certification of non-foreign status is false, then the corporation may rely upon that certification only if the person providing the false certification holds (or held) less than 10 percent of the value of the outstanding stock of the corporation. With respect to less than 10 percent interest-holders, no withholding is required under this paragraph (e) upon receipt of a belated notice of false certification. With respect to 10 percent or greater interest-holders, the corporation's withholding obligations under this paragraph (e) shall apply as if a certification had never been given, and such a corporation may be held fully liable pursuant to § 1.1445-5(b)(6) for any failure to withhold as of the date specified in this § 1.1445-5(e)(2)(iii)(B). Amounts withheld pursuant to the rule of this paragraph (e)(2)(iii)(B) must be reported and paid over by the 60th day following the date on which the corporation learns that the certification is false. No penalties or interest for failures to withhold will be assessed prior to that date. For rules concerning the notifications of false certifications that may be required to be given to U.S. real property holding corporations, see § 1.1445-4(b).

(iv) *Withholding certificate.* No withholding, or reduced withholding, is required under this paragraph (e) with respect to a domestic corporation's distribution of property if the distributing corporation obtains a withholding certificate from the Internal Revenue Service that so provides. For rules concerning the issuance of withholding certificates, see § 1.1445-6.

(f) *Taxable distributions by domestic or foreign partnerships, trusts, or estates.* [Reserved]

(g) *Dispositions of interests in partnerships, trusts, and estates.* [Reserved]

[Reg. § 1.1445-5.]

☐ [*T.D.* 8113, 12-18-86. *Amended by T.D.* 8198, 5-4-88; *T.D.* 8321, 12-6-90; *T.D.* 8647, 12-20-95 *and T.D.* 8734, 10-6-97 (T.D. 8804 delayed the effective date of T.D. 8734 from January 1, 1999, to January 1, 2000; T.D. 8856 further delayed the effective date of T.D. 8734 until January 1, 2001).]

[Reg. § 1.1445-6]

§ 1.1445-6. **Adjustments pursuant to withholding certificate of amount required to be withheld under section 1445(e).**—(a) *Withholding certificate for purposes of section 1445(e)*—(1) *In general.* Pursuant to the provisions of § 1.1445-5(c)(2)(iv), (d)(2)(ii), and (e)(2)(iv), withholding under section 1445(e) may be reduced or eliminated pursuant to a withholding certificate issued by the Internal Revenue Service in accordance with the rules of this § 1.1445-6. A withholding certificate may be issued in cases where adjusted withholding is appropriate (e.g., because of the applicability of a nonrecognition provision—see paragraph (c) of this section), where the relevant taxpayers are exempt from U.S. tax (see paragraph (d) of this section), or where an agreement for the payment of tax is entered into with the Service (see paragraph (e) of this section). A withholding certificate that is obtained prior to a transfer allows the entity or fiduciary to withhold a reduced amount or excuses withholding entirely. A withholding certificate that is obtained after a transfer has been made may authorize a normal refund or an early refund pursuant to paragraph (g) of this section.

The Internal Revenue Service will act upon an application for a withholding certificate not later than the 90th day after it is received. (The Service may deny a request for a withholding certificate where, after due notice, an applicant fails to provide the information necessary to make a determination.) Solely for this purpose (i.e., determining the day upon which the 90 day period commences), an application is received by the Service on the date when all information necessary for the Service to make a determination is provided by the applicant. (For rules regarding whether an application has been timely submitted, see § 1.1445-5(b)(5).) The Internal Revenue Service will act upon an application for an early refund not later than the 90th day after it is received. An application for an early refund must either (i) include a copy of a withholding certificate issued by the Service with respect to the transaction, or (ii) be combined with an application for a withholding certificate. Where an application for an early refund is combined with an application for a withholding certificate, the Service will act upon both applications not later than the 90th day after receipt. Either an entity, a fiduciary, or a relevant taxpayer (as defined in paragraph (a)(2) of this section) may apply for a withholding certificate. An entity or fiduciary may apply for a withholding certificate with respect to all or less than all relevant taxpayers. For special rules concerning the issuance of a withholding certificate to a foreign corporation that has made an election under section 897(i), see § 1.1445-7(d).

(2) *Relevant taxpayer.* For purposes of this section, the term "relevant taxpayer" means any foreign person that will bear substantive income tax liability by reason of the operation of section 897 with respect to a transaction upon which withholding is required under section 1445(e).

(b) *Applications for withholding certificates*— (1) *In general.* An application for a withholding

Reg. § 1.1445-6(b)(1)

certificate pursuant to this § 1.1445-6 must be submitted in the manner provided in § 1.1445-3(b). However, in lieu of the information required to be submitted pursuant to § 1.1445-3(b)(4), the applicant must provide the information required by paragraph (b)(2) of this section. In addition, the information required by paragraph (b)(3) of this section must be submitted with the application.

(2) *Basis for certificate*—(i) *Adjusted withholding.* If a withholding certificate is sought on the basis of a claim that adjusted withholding is appropriate, the application must include a calculation, in accordance with paragraph (c) of this section, of the maximum tax that may be imposed on each relevant taxpayer with respect to which adjusted withholding is sought. The application must also include all evidence necessary to substantiate the claimed calculation, such as records of adjustments to basis or appraisals of fair market value.

(ii) *Exemption.* If a withholding certificate is sought on the basis of a relevant taxpayer's exemption from U.S. tax, the application must set forth a brief statement of the law and facts that support the claimed exemption. See paragraph (d) of this section.

(iii) *Agreement.* If a withholding certificate is sought on the basis of an agreement for the payment of tax, the application must include a copy of the agreement proposed by the applicant and a copy of the security instrument (if any) proposed by the applicant. In this regard, see paragraph (e) of this section.

(3) *Relevant taxpayers.* An application for withholding certificate pursuant to this section must set forth the name, identifying number (if any) and home address (in the case of an individual) or office address (in the case of an entity) of each relevant taxpayer with respect to which adjusted withholding is sought.

(c) *Adjustment of amount required to be withheld.* The Internal Revenue Service may issue a withholding certificate that excuses withholding, or that permits an entity or fiduciary to withhold an adjusted amount reflecting the relevant taxpayers' maximum tax liability. A relevant taxpayer's maximum tax liability is the maximum amount which that taxpayer could be required to pay as tax by reason of the transaction upon which withholding is required. In the case of an individual taxpayer that amount will generally be the gain realized by the individual, multiplied by the maximum individual income tax rate applicable to long term capital gain. In the case of a corporate taxpayer, that amount will generally be the gain realized by the corporation, multiplied by the maximum corporate income tax rate applicable to long term capital gain. However, that amount must be adjusted to take into account the following:

(1) Any reduction of tax to which the relevant taxpayer is entitled under the provisions of a U.S. income tax treaty;

(2) The effect of any nonrecognition provision that is applicable to the transaction;

(3) Any losses previously realized and recognized by the relevant taxpayer during the taxable year by reason of the operation of section 897;

(4) Any amount realized upon the subject transfer by the relevant taxpayer that is required to be treated as ordinary income under any provision of the Code; and

(5) Any other factor that may increase or reduce the tax upon the transaction.

(d) *Relevant taxpayer's exemption from U.S. tax*—(1) *In general.* The Internal Revenue Service will issue a withholding certificate that excuses withholding by an entity or fiduciary if it is established that a relevant taxpayer's income from the transaction will be exempt from U.S. tax. For the available exemptions, see paragraph (d)(2) of this section. If a relevant taxpayer is entitled to a reduction of (rather than an exemption from) U.S. tax, then the entity or fiduciary may obtain a withholding certificate to that effect pursuant to the provisions of paragraph (c) of this section.

(2) *Available exemptions.* A relevant taxpayer's income from a transaction with respect to which withholding is required under section 1445(e) may be exempt from U.S. tax because either:

(i) The relevant taxpayer is an integral part or controlled entity of a foreign government and the subject income is exempt from U.S. tax pursuant to section 892 and the regulations thereunder; or

(ii) The relevant taxpayer is entitled to the benefits of an income tax treaty that provides for such an exemption (subject to the limitations imposed by section 1125(c) of Pub. L. 96-499, which, in general, overrides such benefits as of January 1, 1985).

(e) *Agreement for the payment of tax*—(1) *In general.* The Internal Revenue Service will issue a withholding certificate that excuses withholding or that permits an entity or fiduciary to withhold a reduced amount, if the entity, fiduciary, or a relevant taxpayer enters into an agreement for the payment of tax pursuant to the provisions of this paragraph (e). An agreement for the payment of tax is a contract between the Service and the

Reg. § 1.1445-6(b)(2)

entity, fiduciary, or relevant taxpayer that consists of two necessary elements. Those elements are—

(i) A contract between the Service and the other person, setting forth in detail the rights and obligations of each; and

(ii) A security instrument or other form of security acceptable to the Assistant Commissioner (International).

(2) *Contents of agreement*—(i) *In general.* An agreement for the payment of tax must cover an amount described in subdivision (ii) or (iii) of this paragraph (e)(2). The agreement may either provide adequate security for the payment of the chosen amount with respect to the relevant taxpayer in accordance with paragraph (e)(3) of this section, or provide for the payment of that amount through a combination of security and withholding of tax by the entity or fiduciary.

(ii) *Tax that would otherwise be withheld.* An agreement for the payment of tax may cover the amount of tax that would otherwise be required to be withheld with respect to the relevant taxpayer pursuant to section 1445(e). In addition to the amount computed pursuant to section 1445(e), the applicant must agree to pay interest upon that amount, at the rate established under section 6621, with respect to the period between the date on which withholding tax under section 1445(e) would otherwise be due and the date on which the relevant taxpayer's payment of tax with respect to the disposition will be due. The amount of interest agreed upon must be paid by the applicant regardless of whether or not the Service is required to draw upon any security provided pursuant to the agreement. The interest may be paid either with the return or by the Service drawing upon the security.

(iii) *Maximum tax liability.* An agreement for the payment of tax may cover the relevant taxpayer's maximum tax liability, determined in accordance with paragraph (c) of this section. The agreement must also provide for the payment of an additional amount equal to 25 percent of the amount determined under paragraph (c) of this section. This additional amount secures the interest and penalties that would accrue between the date of the relevant taxpayer's failure to file a return and pay tax with respect to the disposition, and the date on which the Service collects upon that liability pursuant to the agreement.

(iv) *Allocation of payment.* An agreement for the payment of tax pursuant to this section must set forth an allocation of the payment provided for by the agreement among the relevant taxpayers with respect to which the withholding certificate is sought. In the case of an agreement that covers an amount described in subdivision (ii) of this paragraph (e)(2), such allocation must be based upon the amount that would otherwise be required to be withheld with respect to each relevant taxpayer. In the case of an agreement that covers an amount described in subdivision (iii) of this paragraph (e)(2), such allocation must be based upon each relevant taxpayer's maximum tax liability.

(3) *Major types of security.* The major types of security that are acceptable to the Internal Revenue Service for purposes of this section are described in § 1.1445-3(e)(3).

(4) *Terms of security instrument.* Any security instrument that is furnished pursuant to this section must contain the terms described in § 1.1445-3(e)(4).

(f) *Amendments to application for withholding certificates*—(1) *In general.* An applicant for a withholding certificate may amend an otherwise complete application by submitting an amending statement to the Assistant Commissioner (International) at the address provided in § 1.1445-1(g)(10). The amending statement shall provide the information required by § 1.1445-6(f)(3) and must be signed and accompanied by a penalties of perjury statement in accordance with § 1.1445-6(b).

(2) *Extension of time for the Service to process requests for withholding certificates*—(i) *In general.* If an amending statement is submitted, the time in which the Internal Revenue Service must act upon the amended application shall be extended by 30 days.

(ii) *Substantial amendments.* If an amending statement is submitted and the Service finds that the statement substantially amends to the facts of the underlying application or substantially alters the terms of the withholding certificate as requested in the initial application, the time within which the Service must act upon the amended application shall be extended by 60 days. The applicant shall be so notified.

(iii) *Amending statement received after the requested withholding certificate has been signed by the Assistant Commissioner (International).* If an amending statement is received after the withholding certificate, drafted in response to the underlying application, has been signed by the Assistant Commissioner (International) or his delegate and prior to the day such certificate is mailed to the applicant, the time in which the Service must act upon the amended application shall be extended by 90 days.

(3) *Information required to be submitted.* No particular form is required for an amending state-

Reg. § 1.1445-6(f)(3)

ment but the statement must provide the following information:

(i) *Identification of applicant.* The amending statement must set forth the name, address, and identifying number (if any) of the person submitting the amending statement.

(ii) *Date of application.* The amending statement must set forth the date of the underlying application for a withholding certificate.

(iii) *Real property interest to be (or that has been) transferred.* The amending statement must set forth a brief description of the real property interest with respect to which the underlying application for a withholding certificate was submitted.

(iv) *Amending information.* The amending statement must fully set forth the basis for the amendment including any modification of the facts supporting the application for a withholding certificate and any change sought in the terms of the withholding certificate.

(g) *Early refund of overwithheld amounts.* If the Internal Revenue Service issues a withholding certificate pursuant to this section, and an amount greater than that specified in the certificate was withheld by the entity or fiduciary, then pursuant to the rules of this paragraph (g) a relevant taxpayer may apply for an early refund of a proportionate share of the excess amount (without interest) prior to the date on which the relevant taxpayer's return is due (without extensions). An application for an early refund must be addressed to the Assistant Commissioner (International), at the address provided in § 1.1445-1(g)(10). No particular form is required for the application, but the following information must be set forth in separate paragraphs numbered to correspond with the numbers given below:

(1) Name, address, and identifying number (if any) of the relevant taxpayer seeking the refund;

(2) Amount required to be withheld pursuant to withholding certificate;

(3) Amount withheld by entity or fiduciary (attach a copy of Form 8288-A stamped by IRS pursuant to § 1.1445-5(b)(4) or provide substantial evidence of the amount withheld in the case of a failure to receive Form 8288-A, as provided in § 1.1445-5(b)(7));

(4) Amount to be refunded to the relevant taxpayer.

An application for an early refund cannot be processed unless the required copy of Form 8288-A or substantial evidence of the amount withheld in the case of a failure to receive Form 8288-A (as provided in § 1.1445-5(b)(7)) is attached to the application. If an application for a withholding certificate is submitted after the transfer takes place, then that application may be combined with an application for an early refund. The Service will act upon a claim for refund within the time limits set forth in § 1.1445-6(a)(1). [Reg. § 1.1445-6.]

☐ [*T.D.* 8113, 12-18-86.]

[Reg. § 1.1445-7]

§ 1.1445-7. Treatment of foreign corporation that has made an election under section 897(i) to be treated as a domestic corporation.—(a) *In general.* Pursuant to section 897(i) a foreign corporation may elect to be treated as a domestic corporation for purposes of sections 897 and 6039C. A foreign corporation that has made such an election shall also be treated as a domestic corporation for purposes of the withholding required under section 1445, in accordance with the provisions of this section.

(b) *Withholding under section 1445(a)*—(1) *Dispositions by corporation.* A foreign corporation that has made an election under section 897(i) may provide a transferee with a certification of non-foreign status in connection with the corporation's disposition of a U.S. real property interest. However, in accordance with the provisions of §§ 1.1445-2(b)(2)(ii) and 1.1445-5(b)(3)(ii)(C), such an electing foreign corporation must attach to such certification a copy of the acknowledgment of the election provided to the corporation by the Internal Revenue Service pursuant to § 1.897-3(d)(4) which states that the information required by § 1.897-3 has been determined to be complete.

(2) *Dispositions of interests in corporation.* Dispositions of interests in electing foreign corporations shall be subject to the withholding requirements of section 1445(a) and the rules of §§ 1.1445-1 through 1.1445-4. Therefore, if a foreign person disposes of an interest in such a corporation, and that interest is a U.S. real property interest under the provisions of section 897 and regulations thereunder, then the transferee is required to withhold under section 1445(a).

(c) *Withholding under section 1445(e).* Because a foreign corporation that has made an election under section 897(i) is treated as a domestic corporation for purposes of determining withholding obligations under section 1445, such a corporation is not subject to the requirement of section 1445(e)(2) that a foreign corporation withhold at the corporate capital gain rate from the gain recognized upon the distribution of a U.S. real property interest. Such a corporation is subject to

Reg. § 1.1445-7(a)

the provisions of section 1445(e)(3). Thus, if interests in an electing corporation constitute U.S. real property interests, then the corporation is required to withhold with respect to the non-dividend distribution of any property to an interest-holder that is a foreign person. See § 1.1445-5(e). Dividend distributions (distributions that are described in section 301) shall be treated as provided in sections 897(f), 1441 and 1442. In addition, if interests in an electing foreign corporation do not constitute U.S. real property interests, then distributions by such corporation shall be treated as provided in sections 897(f) (if applicable), 1441 and 1442. Approved by the Office of Management and Budget under control number 545-0902. [Reg. § 1.1445-7.]

☐ [T.D. 8113, 12-18-86.]

[Reg. § 1.1445-8]

§ 1.1445-8. **Special rules regarding publicly traded partnerships, publicly traded trusts and real estate investment trusts (REITS).**—(a) *Entities to which this section applies.* The rules of this section apply to—

(1) Any partnership or trust, interests in which are regularly traded on an established securities market (regardless of the number of its partners or beneficiaries), and

(2) Any REIT (regardless of the form of its organization).

For purposes of paragraph (a)(1) of this section, the rules of section 1445(e)(1) and this section shall not apply to a publicly traded partnership (as defined in section 7704) which is treated as a corporation under section 7704(a), or to those entities that are classified as "associations" and taxed as corporations. See § 301.7701-2.

(b) *Obligation to withhold*—(1) *In general.* An entity described in paragraph (a) of this section is not required to withhold under the provisions of § 1.1445-5(c), which states the withholding requirements of domestic partnerships, trusts and estates upon the disposition of U.S. real property interests. Except as otherwise provided in this paragraph (b), an entity described in paragraph (a) of this section shall be liable to withhold tax upon the distribution of any amount attributable to the disposition of a U.S. real property interest, with respect to each holder of an interest in the entity that is a foreign person. The amount to be withheld is described in paragraph (c) of this section.

(2) *Publicly traded partnerships.* Publicly traded partnerships which comply with the withholding procedures under section 1446 will be deemed to have satisfied their withholding obligations under this paragraph (b).

(3) *Special rule for certain distributions to nominees.* In the case of a person that—

(i) Is a nominee (as defined in paragraph (d) of this section),

(ii) Receives a distribution attributable to the disposition of a U.S. real property interest directly from an entity described in paragraph (a) of this section or indirectly from such entity through a nominee,

(iii) Receives the distribution for payment to any foreign person, or the account of any foreign person, and

(iv) Receives a qualified notice pursuant to paragraph (f) of this section,

then the obligation to withhold in accordance with the general rules of section 1445(e)(1) and this paragraph (b) shall be imposed solely on that person to the extent of the amount specified by the qualified notice. A person obligated to withhold by reason of this paragraph (b)(3) is referred to as a withholding agent.

(4) *Person designated to act for withholding agent.* The rules stated in § 1.1441-7(b)(1) and (2) regarding a person designated to act for a withholding agent shall apply for purposes of this section.

(5) *Effect of withholding exemption granted under § 1.1441-4(f).* A letter issued by a district director under the provisions of § 1.1441-4(f), which exempts a person from withholding under section 1441 or section 1442, shall also exempt that person from withholding under this paragraph (b), if—

(i) The letter identifies another person as the withholding agent for purposes of section 1441 or 1442, and

(ii) Such other person enters into a written agreement, with the district director who issued the letter, to be the withholding agent for purposes of this paragraph (b).

The exemption granted, and the corresponding withholding obligation imposed, by this paragraph (b)(5) shall apply with respect to the first distribution made after execution of the agreement described in the preceding sentence and shall continue to apply to all distributions made during the period in which the exemption granted under § 1.1441-4(f) is in effect.

(6) *Payment other than in money.* The rule stated in § 1.1441-7(c) regarding payment other than in money shall apply for purposes of this section.

(c) *Amount to be withheld*—(1) *Distribution from a publicly traded partnership or publicly traded trust.* The amount to be withheld under this section with respect to a distribution by a

Reg. § 1.1445-8(c)(1)

publicly traded partnership or publicly traded trust shall be computed in the manner described in § 1.1445-5(c)(3)(ii) and (iii), subject to the rules of this section.

(2) *REITs*—(i) *In general.* The amount to be withheld with respect to a distribution by a REIT, under this section shall be equal to 35 percent (or the highest rate specified in section 1445(e)(1)) of the amount described in paragraph (c)(2)(ii) of this section.

(ii) *Amount subject to withholding—* (A) *In general.* Except as otherwise provided in paragraph (c)(2)(ii)(C) of this section, the amount subject to withholding is the amount of any distribution, determined with respect to each share or certificate of beneficial interest, designated by a REIT as a capital gain dividend, multiplied by the number of shares or certificates of beneficial interest owned by the foreign person. Solely for purposes of this paragraph, the largest amount of any distribution occurring after March 7, 1991 that could be designated as a capital gain dividend under section 857(b)(3)(C) shall be deemed to have been designated by a REIT as a capital gain dividend regardless of the amount actually designated.

(B) *Distribution attributable to net short-term capital gain from the disposition of a U.S. real property interest.* [Reserved]

(C) *Designation of prior distribution as capital gain dividend.* If a REIT makes an actual designation of a prior distribution, in whole or in part, as a capital gain dividend, such prior distribution shall not be subject to withholding under this section. Rather, a REIT must characterize and treat as a capital gain dividend distribution (solely for purposes of section 1445(e)(1)) each distribution, determined with respect to each share or certificate of beneficial interest, made on the day of, or any time subsequent to, such designation as a capital gain dividend until such characterized amounts equal the amount of the prior distribution designated as a capital gain dividend. The provisions of this paragraph shall not be applicable in any taxable year in which the REIT adopts a formal or informal resolution or plan of complete liquidation.

(iii) *Example.* The following example illustrates the rules of paragraph (c)(2)(ii)(C) of this section.

In the first quarter of 1988, XYZ REIT makes a dividend distribution of $2X. In the second quarter of 1988, XYZ sells real property, recognizing a long term capital gain of $15X, and makes a dividend distribution of $5X. In the third quarter of 1988, XYZ makes a distribution of $3X. In the fourth quarter of 1988, XYZ sells real property recognizing a long term capital loss of $2X. Within 30 days after the close of the taxable year, XYZ designates a capital gain dividend for the year of $13X. It subsequently makes a fourth quarter distribution of $7X. Since XYZ has made an actual designation of prior distributions during the taxable year as capital gain dividends, withholding on those prior distributions will not be required. However, the REIT must characterize, solely for purposes of § 1445(e)(1), a total amount of $13X of dividend distributions as capital gain dividends. Therefore, the fourth quarter dividend distribution of $7X must be characterized as a capital gain dividend subject to withholding under this section. In addition, XYZ will be required to characterize an additional $6X of subsequent dividend distributions as capital gain dividends.

(d) *Definition of nominee.* For purposes of this section, the term "nominee" means a domestic person that holds an interest in an entity described in paragraph (a) of this section on behalf of another domestic or foreign person.

(e) *Determination of non-foreign status by withholding agent.* A withholding agent may rely on a certificate of non-foreign status pursuant to § 1.1445-2(b) or on the statements and address provided to it on Form W-9 or a form that is substantially similar to such form, to determine whether an interest holder is a domestic person. Reliance on these documents will excuse the withholding agent from liability imposed under section 1445(e)(1) in the absence of actual knowledge that the interest holder is a foreign person. A withholding agent may also employ other means to determine the status of an interest holder, but, if the agent relies on such other means and the interest holder proves, in fact, to be a foreign person, then the withholding agent is subject to any liability imposed pursuant to section 1445 and the regulations thereunder for failure to withhold.

(f) *Qualified notice.* A qualified notice for purposes of paragraph (b)(3)(iv) of this section is a notice given by a partnership, trust or REIT regarding a distribution that is attributable to the disposition of a U.S. real property interest in accordance with the notice requirements with respect to dividends described in 17 C.F.R. 240.10b-17(b)(1) or (3) issued pursuant to the Securities Exchange Act of 1934, 15 U.S.C. § 78a *et seq.* In the case of a REIT, a qualified notice is only a notice of a distribution, all or any portion of which the REIT actually designates, or characterizes in accordance with paragraph (c)(2)(ii)(C) of this section, as a capital gain dividend in accordance with 17 C.F.R. 240.10b-17(b)(1) or (3), with respect to each share or certificate of beneficial interest. A deemed designation under paragraph (c)(2)(ii)(A) of this section may not be the subject of a qualified notice under this paragraph (f). A person described in paragraph (b)(3) of this section shall be treated as receiving a qualified notice at the time such notice is published in accordance with 17 C.F.R. 240.10b-17(b)(1) or (3).

(g) *Reporting and paying over withheld amounts.* With respect to an amount withheld under this section, a withholding agent is not required to conform to the requirements of § 1.1445-5(b)(5) but is required to report and pay over to the Internal Revenue Service any amount required to be withheld pursuant to the rules and procedures of section 1461, the regulations thereunder and § 1.6302-2. Forms 1042 and 1042S are to be used for this purpose.

(h) *Early refund procedure not available.* The early refund procedure set forth in § 1.1445-6(g) shall not apply to amounts withheld under the rules of this section. For adjustment of over-withheld amounts, see § 1.1461-4.

(i) *Liability upon failure to withhold.* For rules regarding liability upon failure to withhold under § 1445(e) and this section, see § 1.1445-1(e). [Reg. § 1.1445-8.]

☐ [T.D. 8321, 12-6-90. Amended by T.D. 8647, 12-20-95.]

[Reg. § 1.1445-9T]

§ 1.1445-9T. Special rule for section 1034 nonrecognition (Temporary).—(a) *Purpose and scope.* This section provides a temporary regulation that, if and when adopted as a final regulation, will add a new paragraph (d)(2)(iii) to § 1.1445-2. Paragraph (b) of this section would then appear as paragraph (d)(2)(iii) of § 1.1445-2.

(b) No particular form is required for a transferor's notice to a transferee that the transferor is not required to recognize gain or loss with respect to a transfer. The notice must be verified as true and signed under penalties of perjury by a responsible officer in the case of a corporation, by a general partner in the case of a partnership, and by a trustee or equivalent fiduciary in the case of a trust or estate. The following information must be set forth in paragraphs labeled to correspond with the designation set forth below:

(1) A statement that the document submitted constitutes a notice of a nonrecognition transfer pursuant to the requirements of § 1.1445-2(d)(2);

(2) The name, identifying number (if any), and home address (in the case of an individual) or office address (in the case of an entity) of the transferor submitting the notice;

(3) A statement that the transferor is not required to recognize any gain or loss with respect to the transfer;

(4) A brief description of the transfer;

(5) A brief summary of the law and facts supporting the claim that recognition of gain or loss is not required with respect to the transfer; and

(6) If the transferor claims nonrecognition on the sale or exchange of a principal residence under section 1034(a) and another principal residence in the United States has not been purchased as of the date of sale of the principal residence, either (i) a copy of an executed binding contract for purchase by the transferor of a further principal residence in the United States with a purchase price exceeding the adjusted sales price of the old principal residence or (ii) an affidavit by the transferor signed under penalties of perjury stating that the transferor intends to complete purchase of another principal residence within the United States with a purchase price exceeding the adjusted sales price of the old principal residence by April 15 of the year following the taxable year of the sale of the principal residence, and that the transferor is expected to continue to be employed or stationed in the United States for a period of two years from the sale of the principal residence. If the transferor's adjusted sales price of the old principal residence exceeds the transferor's cost of purchasing another principal residence in the United States, withholding shall be required at the rate of ten percent on the portion of the gross amount realized on the sale or exchange of the principal residence equal to such excess.

(c) *Effective Date.* The rules of this section are effective with respect to sale of a principal residence after August 3, 1988. [Temporary Reg. § 1.1445-9T.]

☐ [T.D. 8198, 5-4-88.]

[Reg. § 1.1445-10T]

§ 1.1445-10T. Special rule for foreign governments (Temporary).—(a) This section provides a temporary regulation that, if and when adopted as a final regulation, will add a new paragraph (d)(6) to § 1.1445-2. Paragraph (b) of this section would then appear as paragraph (d)(6) of § 1.1445-2.

(b) *Foreign government*—(1) *As transferor.* A foreign government is subject to U.S. taxation under section 897 on the disposition of a U.S. real property interest except to the extent specifically otherwise provided in the regulations issued under section 892. A foreign government that disposes of a U.S. real property interest that is not subject to taxation as specifically provided by the regulations under section 892 may present a notice of nonrecognition treatment pursuant to paragraph (d)(2) of this section that specifically cites the provision of such regulation, and thereby avoids withholding by the transferee of the property. A foreign government that disposes of a U.S. real property interest or the transferee of the property may obtain a withholding certificate from the Internal Revenue Service that confirms the applicability of section 892, but neither is required to do so. Rules concerning the issuance of withholding certificates are provided in § 1.1445-3.

(2) *As transferee.* A foreign government or international organization that acquires a U.S. real property interest is fully subject to section 1445 and the regulations thereunder. Therefore, such an entity is required to withhold tax upon the acquisition of a U.S. real property interest from a foreign person.

(c) *Effective date.* The rules of this section shall be effective for transfers, exchanges, distributions and other dispositions occurring on or after June 6, 1988. [Temporary Reg. § 1.1445-10T.]

☐ [T.D. 8198, 5-4-88.]

[Reg. § 1.1445-11T]

§ 1.1445-11T. **Special rules requiring withholding under § 1.1445-5 (Temporary).**—(a) *Purpose and scope.* This section provides temporary regulations that, if and when adopted as a final regulation, will add certain new paragraphs within § 1.1445-5(b) and (c). The paragraphs of this section would then appear as set forth below. Paragraph (b) of this section would then appear as paragraph (b)(8)(v) of § 1.1445-5. Paragraph (c) of this section would then appear as paragraph (c)(2)(i) of § 1.1445-5. Paragraph (d) of this section would then appear as paragraph (g) of § 1.1445-5.

(b) *Disposition of interests in partnerships, trusts, and estates.* The provisions of section 1445(e)(5), requiring withholding upon certain dispositions of interests in partnerships, trusts, and estates, that own directly or indirectly a U.S. real property interest shall apply to dispositions on or after the effective date of a later Treasury decision under section 897(g) of the Code except in the case of dispositions of interests in partnerships in which fifty percent of the value of the gross assets consist of U.S. real property interests and ninety percent or more of the value of the gross assets consist of U.S. real property interests plus any cash or cash equivalents. The provisions of section 1445(e)(5), shall apply, however, to dispositions after June 6, 1988, of interests in partnerships in which fifty percent or more of the value of the gross assets consist of U.S. real property interests, and ninety percent or more of the value of the gross assets consist of U.S. real property interests plus any cash or cash equivalents. See paragraph (d) of this section.

(c) *Transactions covered elsewhere.* No withholding is required under this paragraph (c) with respect to the distribution of a U.S. real property interest by a partnership, trust, or estate. Such distributions shall be subject to withholding under section 1445(e)(4) and paragraph (f) of this § 1.1445-5 on the effective date of a later Treasury decision published under section 897(g) of the Code. No withholding is required at this time for distributions described in the preceding sentence. See paragraph (b)(8)(iv) of this § 1.1445-5. No withholding is required under this paragraph with respect to the disposition of an interest in a trust, estate, or partnership except in the case of a partnership in which fifty percent or more of the value of the gross assets consist of U.S. real property interests, and ninety percent or more of the value of the gross assets consist of U.S. real property interests plus any cash or cash equivalents. See paragraph (b)(8)(v) of § 1.1445-5. Withholding shall be required as provided in section 1445(e)(5) and paragraph (g) of this section with respect to the disposition after June 6, 1988, of an interest in a partnership in which fifty percent or more of the value of the gross assets consist of U.S. real property interests, and ninety percent or more of the value of the gross assets consist of U.S. real property interests plus any cash or cash equivalents.

(d) *Dispositions of interests in partnerships, trusts, and estates*—(1) *Withholding required on disposition of certain partnership interests.* Withholding is required under section 1445(e)(5) and this paragraph with respect to the disposition by a foreign partner of an interest in a domestic or foreign partnership in which fifty percent or more of the value of the gross assets consist of U.S. real property interests, and ninety percent or more of the value of the gross assets consist of U.S. real property interests plus any cash or cash equivalents. For purposes of this paragraph cash equivalents means any asset readily convertible into cash (whether or not denominated in U.S. dollars), including, but not limited to, bank accounts, certificates of deposit, money market accounts, commercial paper, U.S. and foreign treasury obligations and bonds, corporate obligations and bonds, precious metals or commodities, and publicly traded instruments. The taxpayer on filing an income tax return for the year of the disposition may demonstrate the extent to which the gain on the disposition of the interest is not

Application of Withholding Provisions

See p. 20,601 for regulations not amended to reflect law changes

attributable to U.S. real property interests. A taxpayer is also permitted by § 1.1445-3 to apply for a withholding certificate in instances where reduced withholding is appropriate.

(2) *Withholding not required*—(i) *Transferee receives statement that interest in partnership is not described in paragraph (d)(1)*. No withholding is required under paragraph (d)(1) of this section upon the disposition of a partnership interest otherwise described in that paragraph if the transferee is provided a statement, issued by the partnership and signed by a general partner under penalties of perjury no earlier than 30 days before the transfer, certifying that fifty percent or more of the value of the gross assets does not consist of U.S. real property interests, or that ninety percent or more of the value of the gross assets of the partnership does not consist of U.S. real property interests plus cash or cash equivalents.

(ii) *Reliance on statement not permitted.* A transferee is not entitled to rely upon a statement described in paragraph (d)(2)(i) of this section if, prior to or at the time of the transfer, the transferee either—

(A) Has actual knowledge that the statement is false, or

(B) Receives a notice, pursuant to § 1.1445-4.

Such a transferee's withholding obligations shall apply as if the statement had never been given, and such a transferee may be held fully liable pursuant to § 1.1445-1(e) for any failure to withhold.

(iii) *Belated notice of false statement.* If, after the date of the transfer, a transferee receives notice that a statement provided under paragraph (d)(2)(i) of this section is false, then such transferee may rely on the statement only with respect to consideration that was paid prior to the receipt of the notice. Such a transferee is required to withhold a full 10 percent of the amount realized from the consideration that remains to be paid to the transferor. Thus, if 10 percent or more of the amount realized remains to be paid to the transferor, then the transferee is required to withhold and pay over the full 10 percent. The transferee must do so by withholding and paying over the entire amount of each successive payment of consideration to the transferor, until the full 10 percent of the amount realized has been withheld and paid over. Amounts so withheld must be reported and paid over by the 20th day following the date on which each such payment of consideration is made. A transferee that is subject to the rules of this § 1.1445-10T(d)(2)(iii) may not obtain a withholding certificate pursuant to § 1.1445-3, but must instead withhold and pay over the amounts required by this paragraph.

(e) *Effective date.* The rules of this section are effective for transactions after June 6, 1988. [Temporary Reg. § 1.1445-11T.]

☐ [*T.D.* 8198, 5-4-88.]

Application of Withholding Provisions

[Reg. § 1.1461-1]

§ 1.1461-1. Payment and returns of tax withheld.—(a) *Payment of withheld tax*—(1) *Deposits of tax.* Every withholding agent who withholds tax pursuant to chapter 3 of the Internal Revenue Code (Code) and the regulations under such chapter shall deposit such amount of tax with an authorized financial institution as provided in § 1.6302-2(a). If for any reason the total amount of tax required to be returned for any calendar year pursuant to paragraph (b) of this section has not been deposited pursuant to § 1.6302-2, the withholding agent shall pay the balance of tax due for such year at such place as the Internal Revenue Service (IRS) shall specify. The tax shall be paid when filing the return required under paragraph (b)(1) of this section for such year, unless the IRS specifies otherwise.

(2) *Penalties for failure to pay tax.* For penalties and additions to the tax for failure to timely pay the tax required to be withheld under chapter 3 of the Code, see sections 6656, 6672, and 7202 and the regulations under those sections.

(b) *Income tax return*—(1) *General rule.* A withholding agent shall make an income tax return on Form 1042 (or such other form as the IRS may prescribe) for income paid during the preceding calendar year that the withholding agent is required to report on an information return on Form 1042-S (or such other form as the IRS may prescribe) under paragraph (c)(1) of this section. See section 6011 and § 1.6011-1(c). The withholding agent must file the return on or before March 15 of the calendar year following the year in which the income was paid. The return must show the aggregate amount of income paid and tax withheld required to be reported on all the Forms 1042-S for the preceding calendar year by the withholding agent, in addition to such information as is required by the form and accompanying instructions. Withholding certificates or other statements or information provided to a withholding agent are not required to be attached to the

Reg. § 1.1461-1(b)(1)

return. A return must be filed under this paragraph (b)(1) even though no tax was required to be withheld during the preceding calendar year. The withholding agent must retain a copy of Form 1042 for the applicable statute of limitations on assessments and collection with respect to the amounts required to be reported on the Form 1042. See section 6501 and the regulations thereunder for the applicable statute of limitations. Adjustments to the total amount of tax withheld, as described in § 1.1461-2, shall be stated on the return as prescribed by the form and accompanying instructions.

(2) *Amended returns.* An amended return may be filed on a Form 1042 or such other form as the IRS may prescribe. An amended return must include such information as the form or accompanying instructions shall require, including, with respect to any information that has changed from the time of the filing of the return, the information that was shown on the original return and the corrected information.

(c) *Information returns*—(1) *Filing requirement*—(i) *In general.* A withholding agent (other than an individual who is not acting in the course of a trade or business with respect to a payment) must make an information return on Form 1042-S (or such other form as the IRS may prescribe) to report the amounts subject to reporting, as defined in paragraph (c)(2) of this section, that were paid during the preceding calendar year. Notwithstanding the preceding sentence, any person that withholds or is required to withhold an amount under sections 1441, 1442, or 1443 must file a Form 1042-S for the payment withheld upon whether or not that person is engaged in a trade or business and whether or not the payment is an amount subject to reporting. A Form 1042-S shall be prepared for each recipient of an amount subject to reporting. The Form 1042-S shall be prepared in such manner as the form and accompanying instructions prescribe. One copy of the Form 1042-S shall be filed with the IRS on or before March 15 of the calendar year following the year in which the amount subject to reporting was paid. It shall be filed with a transmittal form as provided in the instructions to the Form 1042-S and to the transmittal form. Withholding certificates, documentary evidence, or other statements or documentation provided to a withholding agent are not required to be attached to the form. Another copy of the Form 1042-S must be furnished to the recipient for whom the form is prepared (or any other person, as required under this paragraph (c) or the instructions to the form) on or before March 15 of the calendar year following the year in which the amount subject to reporting was paid. The withholding agent must retain a copy of each Form 1042-S for the statute of limitations on assessment and collection applicable to the Form 1042 to which the Form 1042-S relates.

(ii) *Recipient*—(A) *Defined.* For purposes of this section, the term *recipient* means—

(*1*) A beneficial owner as defined in § 1.1441-1(c)(6), including a foreign estate or a foreign complex trust, as defined in § 1.1441-1(c)(25);

(*2*) A qualified intermediary as defined in § 1.1441-1(e)(5)(ii);

(*3*) A withholding foreign partnership as defined in § 1.1441-5(c)(2) or a withholding foreign trust under § 1.1441-5(e)(5)(v);

(*4*) An authorized foreign agent as defined in § 1.1441-7(c);

(*5*) A U.S. branch that is treated as a U.S. person under § 1.1441-1(b)(2)(iv)(A);

(*6*) A nonwithholding foreign partnership or a foreign simple trust as defined in § 1.1441-1(c)(24), but only to the extent the income is (or is treated as) effectively connected with the conduct of a trade or business in the United States by such entity;

(*7*) A payee, as defined in § 1.1441-1(b)(2) that is presumed to be a foreign person under the presumption rules of § 1.1441-1(b)(3); 1.1441-5(d) or (e)(6), or 1.6049-5(d); and

(*8*) Any other person as required on Form 1042-S or the instructions to the form.

(B) *Persons that are not recipients.* A recipient does not include—

(*1*) A nonqualified intermediary;

(*2*) A payment to a wholly-owned entity that is disregarded under § 301.7701-2(c)(2) of this chapter as an entity separate from its owner;

(*3*) A flow-through entity, as defined in § 1.1441-1(c)(23) (to the extent it is receiving amounts subject to reporting other than income effectively connected with the conduct of a trade or business in the United States); and

(*4*) A U.S. branch described in § 1.1441-1(b)(2)(iv) that is not treated as a U.S. person under that section.

(2) *Amounts subject to reporting*—(i) *In general.* Subject to the exceptions described in paragraph (c)(2)(ii) of this section, amounts subject to reporting on Form 1042-S are amounts paid to a foreign payee (including persons presumed to be foreign) that are amounts subject to withholding as defined in § 1.1441-2(a). Amounts subject to reporting include amounts subject to withholding even if no amount is deducted and withheld from

Application of Withholding Provisions

See p. 20,601 for regulations not amended to reflect law changes

the payment because of a treaty or Internal Revenue Code exception to taxation or because an amount withheld was reimbursed to the payee under the adjustment procedures of § 1.1461-2. In addition, amounts subject to reporting include any amounts paid to a foreign payee on which a withholding agent withheld an amount (either under chapter 3 of the Internal Revenue Code or section 3406) whether or not the amount is subject to withholding. Amounts subject to reporting include, but are not limited to, the following items—

(A) The entire amount of a corporate distribution (whether actual or deemed) irrespective of any estimate of the portion of the distribution that represents a taxable dividend;

(B) Interest, including the portion of a notional principal contract payment that is characterized as interest. Interest shall also be reported on Form 1042-S if it is bank deposit interest paid to nonresident alien individuals as required under § 1.6049-8;

(C) Rents;

(D) Royalties;

(E) Compensation for dependent and independent personal services performed in the United States;

(F) Annuities;

(G) Pension distributions and other deferred income;

(H) Gambling winnings that are not exempt from tax under section 871(j);

(I) Income from the cancellation of indebtedness unless the withholding agent is unrelated to the debtor and does not have knowledge of the facts that give rise to the payment (see § 1.1441-2(d));

(J) Amounts that are (or are presumed to be) effectively connected with the conduct of a trade or business in the United States (including deposit interest as defined in sections 871(i)(2)(A) and 881(d)) even if no withholding certificate is required to be furnished by the payee or beneficial owner. In the case of amounts paid on a notional principal contract described in § 1.1441-4(a)(3) that are presumed to be effectively connected with the conduct of a trade or business in the United States, the amount required to be reported is limited to the amount of cash paid from the notional principal contract;

(K) Scholarship, fellowship, or grant income and compensation for personal services that is not excludible from gross income under section 117 (whether or not the taxable scholarship, fellowship, grant income, or compensation for personal services is exempt from tax under an income tax treaty) paid to foreign students, trainees, teachers, or researchers;

(L) Amounts paid to foreign governments, international organizations, or the Bank for International Settlements, whether or not documentation must be provided; and

(M) Original issue discount paid on the redemption of an OID obligation. The amount to be reported is the amount of OID includible in the gross income of the holder of the obligation, if known, or, if not known, the total amount of original issue discount determined as if the holder held the obligation from its original issuance. A withholding agent may determine the total amount of OID by using the most recently published "List of Original Issue Discount Instruments," (Publication 1212, available from the IRS Forms Distribution Centers).

(ii) *Exceptions to reporting.* The amounts listed in this paragraph (c)(2)(ii) are not required to be reported on Form 1042-S—

(A) Interest (including original issue discount) that is deposit interest under sections 871(i)(2)(A) and 881(d) and that is not effectively connected with the conduct of a trade or business in the United States, unless reporting is required under § 1.6049-8 (regarding payments to certain foreign residents) or is interest that is effectively connected with the conduct of a trade or business in the United States;

(B) Interest or original issue discount on certain short-term obligations, described in section 871(g)(1)(B) or 881(a)(3);

(C) Interest paid on obligations sold between interest payment dates and the portion of the purchase price of an OID obligation that is sold or exchanged in a transaction other than a redemption, unless the sale or exchange is part of a plan, the principal purpose of which is to avoid tax and the withholding agent has actual knowledge or reason to know of such plan (see § 1.1441-2(a)(5) and (6));

(D) Any item required to be reported on a Form W-2, including an item required to be shown on Form W-2 solely by reason of § 1.6041-2 (relating to return of information for payments to employees) or § 1.6052-1 (relating to information regarding payment of wages in the form of group-term life insurance);

(E) Any item required to be reported on Form 1099, and such other forms as are prescribed pursuant to the information reporting provisions of sections 6041 through 6050P and the regulations under those sections;

(F) Amounts paid on a notional principal contract described in § 1.1441-4(a)(3)(i) that

Reg. § 1.1461-1(c)(2)

are not effectively connected with the conduct of a trade or business in the United States (or not treated as effectively connected pursuant to § 1.1441-4(a)(3)(ii));

(G) Amounts required to be reported on Form 8288 (U.S. Withholding Tax Return for Dispositions by Foreign Persons of U.S. Real Property Interests) or Form 8804 (Annual Return for Partnership Withholding Tax (section 1446)). A withholding agent that must report a distribution partly on a Form 8288 or 8804 and partly on a Form 1042-S may elect to report the entire amount on a Form 8288 or 8804;

(H) Interest (including original issue discount) paid with respect to foreign-targeted registered obligations described in § 1.871-14(e)(2) to the extent the documentation requirements described in § 1.871-14(e)(3) and (4) are required to be satisfied (taking into account the provisions of § 1.871-14(e)(4)(ii), if applicable;

(I) Interest on a foreign targeted bearer obligation (see §§ 1.1441-1(b)(4)(i) and 1.1441-2(a));

(J) Gain described in section 301(c)(3); and

(K) Amounts described in § 1.1441-1(b)(4)(xviii) (dealing with certain amounts paid by the U.S. government).

(3) *Required information.* The information required to be furnished under this paragraph (c)(3) shall be based upon the information provided by or on behalf of the recipient of an amount subject to reporting (as corrected and supplemented based on the withholding agent's actual knowledge) or the presumption rules of §§ 1.1441-1(b)(3), 1.1441-4(a); 1.1441-5(d) and (e); 1.1441-9(b)(3) or 1.6049-5(d). The Form 1042-S must include the following information, if applicable—

(i) The name, address, and taxpayer identifying number of the withholding agent;

(ii) A description of each category of income paid based on the income codes provided on the form (e.g., interest, dividends, royalties, etc.) and the aggregate amount in each category expressed in U.S. dollars;

(iii) The rate of withholding applied or the basis for exempting the payment from withholding (based on exemption codes provided on the form);

(iv) The name and address of the recipient;

(v) The name and address of any nonqualified intermediary, flow-through entity, or U.S. branch as described in § 1.1441-1(b)(2)(iv) (other than a branch that is treated as a U.S. person) to which the payment was made;

(vi) The taxpayer identifying number of the recipient if required under § 1.1441-1(e)(4)(vii) or if actually known to the withholding agent making the return;

(vii) The taxpayer identifying number of a nonqualified intermediary or flow-through entity (to the extent it is not a recipient) or other flow-through entity to the extent it is known to the withholding agent;

(viii) The country (based on the country codes provided on the form) of the recipient and of any nonqualified intermediary or flow-through entity the name of which appears on the form; and

(ix) Such information as the form or the instructions may require in addition to, or in lieu of, information required under this paragraph (c)(3).

(4) *Method of reporting*—(i) *Payments by U.S. withholding agents to recipients.* A withholding agent that is a U.S. person (other than a foreign branch of a U.S. person that is a qualified intermediary as defined in § 1.1441-1(e)(5)(ii)) and that makes payments of amounts subject to reporting on Form 1042-S must file a separate Form 1042-S for each recipient who receives such amount. For purposes of this paragraph (c)(4), a U.S. person includes a U.S. branch described in § 1.1441-1(e)(2)(iv)(A) or (E) that agrees to be treated as a U.S. person. Except as may otherwise be required on Form 1042-S or the instructions to the form, only payments for which the income code, exemption code, withholding rate and recipient code are the same may be reported on a single Form 1042-S. See paragraph (c)(4)(ii) of this section for reporting of payments made to a person that is not a recipient.

(A) *Payments to beneficial owners.* If a U.S. withholding agent makes a payment directly to a beneficial owner it must complete Form 1042-S treating the beneficial owner as the recipient. Under the grace period rule of § 1.1441-1(b)(3)(iv), a U.S. withholding agent may, under certain circumstances, treat a payee as a foreign person while the withholding agent awaits a valid withholding certificate. A U.S. withholding agent who relies on the grace period rule to treat a payee as a foreign person must file a Form 1042-S to report all payments on Form 1042-S during the period that person was presumed to be foreign even if that person is later determined to be a U.S. person based on appropriate documentation or is presumed to be a U.S. person after the grace period ends. In the case of joint owners, a withholding agent may provide a single Form 1042-S made out to the owner whose status the U.S. withholding agent relied upon to

Reg. § 1.1461-1(c)(3)

Application of Withholding Provisions

determine the applicable rate of withholding. If, however, any one of the owners requests its own Form 1042-S, the withholding agent must furnish a Form 1042-S to the person who requests it. If more than one Form 1042-S is issued for a single payment, the aggregate amount paid and tax withheld that is reported on all Forms 1042-S cannot exceed the total amounts paid to joint owners and the tax withheld thereon.

(B) *Payments to a qualified intermediary, a withholding foreign partnership, or a withholding foreign trust.* A U.S. withholding agent that makes payments to a qualified intermediary (whether or not the qualified intermediary assumes primary withholding responsibility), a withholding foreign partnership, or a withholding foreign trust shall complete Forms 1042-S treating the qualified intermediary or withholding foreign partnership as the recipient. The U.S. withholding agent must complete a separate Form 1042-S for each withholding rate pool. A withholding rate pool is a payment of a single type of income (determined by the income codes on Form 1042-S) that is subject to a single rate of withholding. A qualified intermediary that does not assume primary withholding responsibility on all payments it receives provides information regarding the proportions of income subject to a particular withholding rate to the withholding agent on a withholding statement associated with a qualified intermediary withholding certificate. A qualified intermediary may provide a U.S. withholding agent with information regarding withholding rate pools for U.S. non-exempt recipients (as defined under § 1.1441-1(c)(21)). Amounts paid with respect to such withholding rate pools must be reported on Form 1099 completed for each U.S. non-exempt recipient to the extent they are subject to Form 1099 reporting. These amounts must not be reported on Form 1042-S. In addition, the qualified intermediary may provide the U.S. withholding agent information regarding withholding rate pools for U.S. persons that are exempt recipients as defined under § 1.1441-1(c)(20). If such information is provided, a U.S. withholding agent should not report such withholding rate pools on Form 1042-S.

(C) *Amounts paid to U.S. branches treated as U.S. persons.* A U.S. withholding agent making a payment to a U.S. branch of a foreign person described in § 1.1441-1(b)(2)(iv) shall complete Form 1042-S as follows—

(1) If the branch has provided the U.S. withholding agent with a withholding certificate that evidences its agreement with the withholding agent to be treated as a U.S. person, the U.S. withholding agent files Forms 1042-S treating the U.S. branch as the recipient;

(2) If the branch has provided the U.S. withholding agent with a withholding certificate that transmits information regarding beneficial owners, qualified intermediaries, withholding foreign partnerships, or other recipients, the U.S. withholding agent must complete a separate Form 1042-S for each recipient whose documentation is associated with the U.S. branch's withholding certificate; or

(3) If the U.S. withholding agent cannot reliably associate a payment with a valid withholding certificate from the U.S. branch, it shall treat the U.S. branch as the recipient and report the income as effectively connected with the conduct of a trade or business in the United States.

(D) *Amounts paid to an authorized foreign agent.* If a U.S. withholding agent makes a payment to an authorized foreign agent, the withholding agent files Forms 1042-S treating the authorized foreign agent as the recipient, provided that the authorized foreign agent reports the payments on Forms 1042-S to each recipient to which it makes payments. If the authorized foreign agent fails to report the amounts paid on Forms 1042-S for each recipient to which the payment is made, the U.S. withholding agent remains responsible for such reporting.

(E) *Dual claims.* A U.S. withholding agent may make a payment to a foreign entity that is simultaneously claiming a reduced rate of tax on its own behalf for a portion of the payment and a reduced rate on behalf of persons in their capacity as interest holders in that entity on the remaining portion. See § 1.1441-6(b)(2)(iii). If the claims are consistent and the withholding agent accepts the multiple claims, the withholding agent must file a separate Form 1042-S for those payments for which the entity is treated as the beneficial owner and Forms 1042-S for each of the interest holder in the entity for which the interest holder is treated as the recipient. For those payments for which the interest holder in an entity is treated as the recipient, the U.S. withholding agent shall prepare the Form 1042-S in the same manner as a payment made to a nonqualified intermediary or flow-through entity as set forth in paragraph (c)(4)(ii) of this section. If the claims are consistent but the withholding agent has not chosen to accept the multiple claims, or if the claims are inconsistent, the withholding agent must file a separate Form 1042-S for the person or persons it has chosen to treat as the recipients.

(ii) *Payments made by U.S. withholding agents to persons that are not recipients*—(A)

Reg. § 1.1461-1(c)(4)

Amounts paid to a nonqualified intermediary, a flow-through entity, and certain U.S. branches. If a U.S. withholding agent makes a payment to a nonqualified intermediary, a flow-through entity, or a U.S. branch described in § 1.1441-1(b)(2)(iv) (other than a branch that agrees to be treated as a U.S. person), it must complete a separate Form 1042-S for each recipient to the extent the withholding agent can reliably associate a payment with valid documentation (within the meaning of § 1.1441-1(b)(2)(vii)) from the recipient which is associated with the withholding certificate provided by the nonqualified intermediary, flow-through entity, or U.S. branch. If a payment is made through tiers of nonqualified intermediaries or flow-through entities, the withholding agent must nevertheless complete Form 1042-S for the recipients to the extent it can reliably associate the payment with documentation from the recipients. A withholding agent that is completing a Form 1042-S for a recipient that receives a payment through a nonqualified intermediary, a flow-through entity, or a U.S. branch must include on the Form 1042-S the name of the nonqualified intermediary or flow-through entity from which the recipient directly receives the payment. If a U.S. withholding agent cannot reliably associate the payment, or any portion of the payment, with valid documentation from a recipient either because no such documentation has been provided or because the nonqualified intermediary, flow-through entity, or U.S. branch has failed to provide sufficient allocation information so that the withholding agent can associate the payment, or any portion thereof, with valid documentation, then the withholding agent must report the payments as made to an unknown recipient in accordance with the appropriate presumption rules for that payment. Thus, if under the presumption rules the payment is presumed to be made to a foreign person, the withholding agent must generally withhold 30 percent of the payment and report the payment on Form 1042-S made out to an unknown recipient and shall also include the name of the nonqualified intermediary or flow-through entity that received the payment on behalf of the unknown recipient. If, however, the recipient is presumed to be a U.S. non-exempt recipient (as defined in § 1.1441-1(c)(21)), the withholding agent must withhold on the payment as required under section 3406 and report the payment as made to an unknown recipient on the appropriate Form 1099 as required under chapter 61 of the Internal Revenue Code.

(B) *Disregarded entities.* If a U.S. withholding agent makes a payment to a disregarded entity but receives a valid withholding certificate or other documentary evidence from a foreign person that is the single owner of a disregarded entity, the withholding agent must file a Form 1042-S treating the foreign single owner as the recipient. The taxpayer identifying number on the Form 1042-S, if required, must be the foreign single owner's TIN.

(iii) *Reporting by qualified intermediaries, withholding foreign partnerships, and withholding foreign trusts.* A qualified intermediary, a withholding foreign partnership, and a withholding foreign trust shall report payments on Form 1042-S as provided in their agreements with the IRS and the instructions to the form.

(iv) *Reporting by a nonqualified intermediary, flow-through entity, and certain U.S. branches.* A nonqualified intermediary, flow-through entity, or U.S. branch described in § 1.1441-1(e)(2)(iv) (other than a U.S. branch that is treated as a U.S. person) is a withholding agent and must file Forms 1042-S for amounts paid to recipients in the same manner as a U.S. withholding agent. A Form 1042-S will not be required, however, if another withholding agent has reported the same amount to the same recipient for which the nonqualified intermediary, flow-through entity, or U.S. branch would be required to file a return and the entire amount that should be withheld from such payment has been withheld. A nonqualified intermediary, flow-through entity, or U.S. branch must report payments made to recipients to the extent it has failed to provide the appropriate documentation to another withholding agent together with the information required for that withholding agent to reliably associate the payment with the recipient documentation or to the extent it knows, or has reason to know, that less than the required amount has been withheld. A nonqualified intermediary or flow-through entity that is required to report a payment on Form 1042-S must follow the same rules as apply to a U.S. withholding agent under paragraph (c)(4)(i) and (ii) of this section.

(v) *Pro rata reporting for allocation failures.* If a nonqualified intermediary, flow-through entity, or U.S. branch described in § 1.1441-1(b)(2)(iv) (other than a branch treated as a U.S. person) that uses the alternative procedures of § 1.1441-1(e)(3)(iv)(D) fails to provide information sufficient to allocate the amount subject to reporting paid to a withholding rate pool to the payees identified for that pool, then the withholding agent shall report the payment in accordance with the rule provided in § 1.1441-1(e)(3)(iv)(D)(6).

(vi) *Other withholding agents.* Any person that is a withholding agent not described in paragraph (c)(4)(i), (iii), or (iv) of this section (e.g., a

Reg. § 1.1461-1(c)(4)

foreign person that is not a qualified intermediary, flow-through entity, or U.S. branch) shall file Form 1042-S in the same manner as a U.S. withholding agent and in accordance with the instructions to the form.

(5) *Magnetic media reporting.* A withholding agent that makes 250 or more Form 1042-S information returns for a taxable year must file Form 1042-S returns on magnetic media. See § 301.6011-2 of this chapter for requirements applicable to a withholding agent that files Forms 1042-S with the IRS on magnetic media and publications of the IRS relating to magnetic media filing.

(d) *Report of taxpayer identifying numbers.* When so required under procedures that the IRS may prescribe in published guidance (see § 601.601(d)(2) of this chapter), a withholding agent must attach to the Form 1042 a list of all the taxpayer identifying numbers (and corresponding names) that have been furnished to the withholding agent and upon which the withholding agent has relied to grant a reduced rate of withholding and that are not otherwise required to be reported on a Form 1042-S under the provisions of this section.

(e) *Indemnification of withholding agent.* A withholding agent is indemnified against the claims and demands of any person for the amount of any tax it deducts and withholds in accordance with the provisions of chapter 3 of the Code and the regulations under that chapter. A withholding agent that withholds based on a reasonable belief that such withholding is required under chapter 3 of the Code and the regulations under that chapter is treated for purposes of section 1461 and this paragraph (e) as having withheld tax in accordance with the provisions of chapter 3 of the Code and the regulations under that chapter. In addition, a withholding agent is indemnified against the claims and demands of any person for the amount of any payments made in accordance with the grace period provisions set forth in § 1.1441-1(b)(3)(iv). This paragraph (e) does not apply to relieve a withholding agent from tax liability under chapter 3 of the Code or the regulations under that chapter.

(f) *Amounts paid not constituting gross income.* Any amount withheld in accordance with § 1.1441-3 shall be reported and paid in accordance with this section, even though the amount paid to the beneficial owner may not constitute gross income in whole or in part. For this purpose, a reference in this section and § 1.1461-2 to an amount shall, where appropriate, be deemed to refer to the amount subject to withholding under § 1.1441-3.

(g) *Extensions of time to file Forms 1042 and 1042-S.* The IRS may grant an extension of time in which to file a Form 1042 or a Form 1042-S. Form 2758, Application for Extension of Time to File Certain Excise, Income, Information, and Other Returns (or such other form as the IRS may prescribe), must be used to request an extension of time for a Form 1042. Form 8809, Request for Extension of Time to File Information Returns (or such other form as the IRS may prescribe) must be used to request an extension of time for a Form 1042-S. The request must contain a statement of the reasons for requesting the extension and such other information as the forms or instructions may require. It must be mailed or delivered not later than March 15 of the year following the end of the calendar year for which the return will be filed.

(h) *Penalties.* For penalties and additions to the tax for failure to file returns or furnish statements in accordance with this section, see sections 6651, 6662, 6663, 6721, 6722, 6723, 6724(c), 7201, 7203, and the regulations under those sections.

(i) *Effective date.* This section shall apply to returns required for payments made after December 31, 2000. [Reg. § 1.1461-1.]

☐ [T.D. 6187, 7-5-56. Amended by T.D. 6213, 11-20-56; T.D. 6908, 12-30-66; T.D. 7157, 12-29-71; T.D. 7977, 9-19-84; T.D. 8734, 10-6-97; T.D. 8804, 12-30-98; T.D. 8856, 12-29-99; 8881, 5-15-2000 (corrected 4-5-2001) and T.D. 8952, 6-25-2001.]

[Reg. § 1.1461-2]

§ 1.1461-2. **Adjustments for overwithholding or underwithholding of tax.**—(a) *Adjustments of overwithheld tax*—(1) *In general.* A withholding agent that has overwithheld under chapter 3 of the Internal Revenue Code (Code) and made a deposit of the tax as provided in § 1.6302-2(a) may adjust the overwithheld amount either pursuant to the reimbursement procedure described in paragraph (a)(2) of this section or pursuant to the set-off procedure described in paragraph (a)(3) of this section. Adjustments under this paragraph (a) may only be made within the time prescribed under paragraph (a)(2) or (3) of this section. After such time, a refund of the amount overwithheld can only be claimed by the beneficial owner with the Internal Revenue Service (IRS) pursuant to the procedures described in chapter 65 of the Code. For purposes of this section, the term overwithholding means any amount actually withheld (determined before application of the adjustment procedures under this section) from an item of income pursuant to chapter 3 of the Code or the regulations thereunder in excess of the actual tax liability due, regardless of

Reg. § 1.1461-2(a)(1)

whether such overwithholding was in error or appeared correct at the time it occurred.

(2) *Reimbursement of tax—*(i) *General rule.* Under the reimbursement procedure, the withholding agent repays the beneficial owner or payee for the amount overwithheld. In such a case, the withholding agent may reimburse itself by reducing, by the amount of tax actually repaid to the beneficial owner or payee, the amount of any deposit of tax made by the withholding agent under § 1.6302-2(a)(1)(iii) for any subsequent payment period occurring before the end of the calendar year following the calendar year of overwithholding. Any such reduction that occurs for a payment period in the calendar year following the calendar year of overwithholding shall be allowed only if—

(A) The withholding agent states, on a timely filed (not including extensions) Form 1042-S for the calendar year of overwithholding, the amount of tax withheld and the amount of any actual repayment; and

(B) The withholding agent states on a timely filed (not including extensions) Form 1042 for the calendar year of overwithholding, that the filing of the Form 1042 constitutes a claim for credit in accordance with § 1.6414-1.

(ii) *Record maintenance.* If the beneficial owner is repaid an amount of withholding tax under the provisions of this paragraph (a)(2), the withholding agent shall keep as part of its records a receipt showing the date and amount of repayment and the withholding agent must provide a copy of such receipt to the beneficial owner. For this purpose, a canceled check or an entry in a statement is sufficient provided that the check or statement contains a specific notation that it is a refund of tax overwithheld.

(3) *Set-offs.* Under the set-off procedure, the withholding agent may repay the beneficial owner or payee by applying the amount overwithheld against any amount which otherwise would be required under chapter 3 of the Code or the regulations thereunder to be withheld from income paid by the withholding agent to such person before the earlier of the due date (without regard to extensions) for filing the Form 1042-S for the calendar year of overwithholding or the date that the Form 1042-S is actually filed with the IRS. For purposes of making a return on Form 1042 or 1042-S (or an amended form) for the calendar year of overwithholding and for purposes of making a deposit of the amount withheld, the reduced amount shall be considered the amount required to be withheld from such income under chapter 3 of the Code and the regulations thereunder.

(4) *Examples.* The principles of this paragraph (a) are illustrated by the following examples:

Example 1. (i) N is a nonresident alien individual who is a resident of the United Kingdom. In December 2001, a domestic corporation C pays a dividend of $100 to N, at which time C withholds $30 and remits the balance of $70 to N. On February 10, 2002, prior to the time that C files its Form 1042, N furnishes a valid Form W-8 described in § 1.1441-1(e)(2)(i) upon which C may rely to reduce the rate of withholding to 15 percent under the provisions of the U.S.-U.K. tax treaty. Consequently, N advises C that its tax liability is only $15 and not $30 and requests reimbursement of $15. Although C has already deposited the $30 that was withheld, as required by § 1.6302-2(a)(1)(iv), C repays N in the amount of $15.

(ii) During 2001, C makes no other payments upon which tax is required to be withheld under chapter 3 of the Code; accordingly, its return on Form 1042 for such year, which is filed on March 15, 2002, shows total tax withheld of $30, an adjusted total tax withheld of $15, and $30 previously paid for such year. Pursuant to § 1.6414-1(b), C claims a credit for the overpayment of $15 shown on the Form 1042 for 2001. Accordingly, it is permitted to reduce by $15 any deposit required by § 1.6302-2 to be made of tax withheld during the calendar year 2002. The Form 1042-S required to be filed by C with respect to the dividend of $100 paid to N in 2001 is required to show tax withheld of $30 and tax released of $15.

Example 2. The facts are the same as in Example 1. In addition, during 2002, C makes payments to N upon which it is required to withhold $200 under chapter 3 of the Code, all of which is withheld in June 2002. Pursuant to § 1.6302-2(a)(1)(iii), C deposits the amount of $185 on July 15, 2002 ($200 less the $15 for which credit is claimed on the Form 1042 for 2001). On March 15, 2003, C Corporation files its return on Form 1042 for calendar year 2002, which shows total tax withheld of $200, $185 previously deposited by C, and $15 allowable credit.

Example 3. The facts are the same as in Example 1. Under § 1.6032-2(a)(1)(ii), C is required to deposit on a quarter-monthly basis the tax withheld under chapter 3 of the Code. C withholds tax of $100 between February 8 and February 15, 2002, and deposits $75 [($100 x 90 percent) less $15] of the withheld tax within 3 banking days after February 15, 2002, and by depositing $10 [($100 − $15) less $75] within 3 banking days after March 15, 2002.

Reg. § 1.1461-2(a)(2)

(b) *Withholding of additional tax when underwithholding occurs.* A withholding agent may withhold from future payments made to a beneficial owner the tax that should have been withheld from previous payments to such beneficial owner. In the alternative, the withholding agent may satisfy the tax from property that it holds in custody for the beneficial owner or property over which it has control. Such additional withholding or satisfaction of the tax owed may only be made before the date that the Form 1042 is required to be filed (not including extensions) for the calendar year in which the underwithholding occurred. See § 1.6302-2 for making deposits of tax or § 1.1461-1(a) for making payment of the balance due for a calendar year.

(c) *Definition.* For purposes of this section, the term *payment period* means the period for which the withholding agent is required by § 1.6302-2(a)(1) to make a deposit of tax withheld under chapter 3 of the Code.

(d) *Effective date.* This section applies to payments made after December 31, 2000. [Reg. § 1.1461-2.]

☐ [*T.D. 6187, 7-5-56. Amended by T.D. 6213, 11-20-56; T.D. 6922, 6-16-67; T.D. 7157, 12-29-71; T.D. 7284, 8-2-73; T.D. 7977, 9-19-84; T.D. 8734, 10-6-97; T.D. 8804, 12-30-98 and T.D. 8856, 12-29-99.*]

[Reg. § 1.1462-1]

§ 1.1462-1. **Withheld tax as credit to recipient of income.**—(a) *Creditable tax.* The entire amount of the income from which the tax is required to be withheld (including amounts calculated under the gross-up formula in § 1.1441-3(f)(1)) shall be included in gross income in the return required to be made by the beneficial owner of the income, without deduction for the amount required to be or actually withheld, but the amount of tax actually withheld shall be allowed as a credit against the total income tax computed in the beneficial owner's return.

(b) *Amounts paid to persons who are not the beneficial owner.* Amounts withheld at source under chapter 3 of the Internal Revenue Code (Code) on payments to a fiduciary, partnership, or intermediary is deemed to have been paid by the taxpayer ultimately liable for the tax upon such income. Thus, for example, if a beneficiary of a trust is subject to the taxes imposed by section 1, 2, 3, or 11 upon any portion of the income received from a foreign trust, the part of any amount withheld at source which is properly allocable to the income so taxed to such beneficiary shall be credited against the amount of the income tax computed upon the beneficiary's return, and any excess shall be refunded. Further, if a partnership withholds an amount under chapter 3 of the Code with respect to the distributive share of a partner that is a partnership or with respect to the distributive share of partners in an upper tier partnership, such amount is deemed to have been withheld by the upper tier partnership.

(c) *Effective date.* This section applies to payments made after December 31, 2000. [Reg. § 1.1462-1.]

☐ [*T.D. 6187, 7-5-56. Amended by T.D. 7977, 9-19-84; T.D. 8734, 10-6-97; T.D. 8804, 12-30-98 and T.D. 8856, 12-29-99.*]

[Reg. § 1.1463-1]

§ 1.1463-1. **Tax paid by recipient of income.**—(a) *Tax paid.* If the tax required to be withheld under chapter 3 of the Internal Revenue Code is paid by the beneficial owner of the income or by the withholding agent, it shall not be re-collected from the other, regardless of the original liability therefor. However, this section does not relieve the person that did not withhold tax from liability for interest or any penalties or additions to tax otherwise applicable. See § 1.1441-7(b) for additional applicable rules.

(b) *Effective date.* This section applies to failures to withhold occurring after December 31, 2000. [Reg. § 1.1463-1.]

☐ [*T.D. 6187, 7-5-56. Amended by T.D. 8734, 10-6-97; T.D. 8804, 12-30-98 and T.D. 8856, 12-29-99.*]

[Reg. § 1.1464-1]

§ 1.1464-1. **Refunds or credits.**—(a) *In general.* The refund or credit under chapter 65 of the Code of an overpayment of tax which has actually been withheld at the source under chapter 3 of the Code shall be made to the taxpayer from whose income the amount of such tax was in fact withheld. To the extent that the overpayment under chapter 3 was not in fact withheld at the source, but was paid, by the withholding agent the refund or credit under chapter 65 of the overpayment shall be made to the withholding agent. Thus, where a debtor corporation assumes liability pursuant to its tax-free covenant for the tax required to be withheld under chapter 3 upon interest and pays the tax in behalf of its bondholder, and it can be shown that the bondholder is not in fact liable for any tax, the overpayment of tax shall be credited or refunded to the withholding agent in accordance with chapter 65 since the tax was not actually deducted and withheld from the interest paid to the bondholder. In further illustration, where a withholding agent who is required by chapter 3 to withhold $300 tax from rents paid to a nonresident alien individual mistakenly withholds $320 and mistakenly pays $350 as internal revenue tax, the amount of $30 shall be credited or refunded to the withholding agent in accordance with chapter 65 and the amount of $20 shall be credited or refunded in accordance with such chapter to the person from whose income such amount has been withheld.

(b) *Tax repaid to payee.* For purposes of this section and § 1.6414-1, any amount of tax withheld under chapter 3 of the Code, which, pursuant to paragraph (a)(1) of § 1.1461-2, is repaid by the withholding agent to the person from whose income such amount was erroneously withheld shall be considered as tax which, within the meaning of sections 1464 and 6414, was not actually withheld by the withholding agent. [Reg. § 1.1464-1.]

☐ [*T.D. 6187, 7-5-56. Amended by T.D. 6922, 6-16-67 and T.D. 8804, 12-30-98.*]

[Reg. § 1.1491-1]

§ 1.1491-1. **Imposition of tax.**—Section 1491 imposes an excise tax upon transfers of stock or securities by a citizen or resident of the United States, or by a domestic corporation or partnership, or by a trust which is not a foreign trust, to a foreign corporation as paid-in surplus or as a contribution to capital, or to a foreign trust, or to a foreign partnership. The tax is in an amount equal to 27½ percent of the excess of (a) the value of the stock or securities so transferred over (b) its adjusted basis, as provided in section 1011, for determining gain in the hands of the transferor. [Reg. § 1.1491-1.]

☐ [*T.D. 6127, 3-17-55.*]

[Reg. § 1.1492-1]

§ 1.1492-1. **Nontaxable transfers.**—(a) The tax imposed by section 1491 does not apply:

(1) If the transferee is an organization (other than an organization described in section 401(a)) exempt from income tax under the provisions of sections 501 to 504, inclusive; or

(2) If before the transfer it has been established to the satisfaction of the Commissioner that the transfer is not in pursuance of a plan having as one of its principal purposes the avoidance of Federal income taxes.

(b) Whether a transfer of stock or securities is in pursuance of a plan having as one of its principal purposes the avoidance of Federal income taxes is a question to be determined from the facts and circumstances of each particular case. In any such case where a transferor desires to establish that the transfer is not in pursuance of such a plan, a statement of the facts relating to the plan under which the transfer is to be made or was made, together with a copy of the plan if in writing, shall be forwarded to the Commissioner of Internal Revenue, Washington 25, D.C., for a ruling. This statement shall contain, or be verified by, a written declaration that it is made under the penalties of perjury. A letter notifying the transferor of the Commissioner's determination will be mailed to the transferor. [Reg. § 1.1492-1.]

☐ [*T.D. 6127, 3-17-55.*]

[Reg. § 1.1494-1]

§ 1.1494-1. **Returns; payment and collection of tax.**—(a) *Returns and payment.* Every person making a transfer described in section 1491 shall make a return to the district director on the day on which the transfer is made and, unless the transfer is nontaxable under section 1492, pay the tax due on such transfer. This return, which shall contain, or be verified by, a written declaration that it is made under the penalties of perjury, shall be made on Form 926 and shall be filed with the district director to whom the transferor's return of income is required to be made. The return shall set forth in detail the following information:

(1) Name and address of transferor, and place of organization or creation, if a corporation, partnership, or trust.

(2) Name and address of transferee, place of organization or creation, and whether the transferee is a foreign corporation, a foreign trust, or a foreign partnership. If the transferee is a foreign trust or a foreign partnership, the name and address of the fiduciary and each beneficiary, in the case of a trust, or of each partner, in the case of a partnership, must be shown.

(3) Description and amount of stock or securities transferred, the date of transfer, and a complete statement showing all the facts relating to the transfer, accompanied by a copy of the plan under which the transfer was made.

(4) The fair market value of the stock or securities transferred as of the date of transfer, and the adjusted basis provided in section 1011 for determining gain in the hands of the transferor.

(5) Whether the transfer was made in pursuance of a plan submitted to and approved by the Commissioner as not having as one of its principal purposes the avoidance of Federal income taxes. If the plan has been so approved, a copy of the Commissioner's letter approving the plan shall accompany the return.

(6) Such other information as may be required by the return form.

(b) *Certificate.* (1) If the transferee of the stock or securities, the transfer of which is reported in the return, is a foreign organization meeting the tests of exemption from income tax provided in part I (section 501 and following), subchapter F, chapter 1 of the Code, and the transferor on that account claims that no liability for tax is imposed by section 1491, such transferor must file with Form 926 a certificate establishing the exemption of the transferee under such part I. This certificate, which shall contain, or be verified by, a written declaration that it is made under the penalties of perjury, shall contain complete information showing the character of the transferee, the purpose for which it was organized, its actual activities, the source of its income and the disposition of such income, whether or not any of its income is credited to surplus or may inure to the benefit of any private shareholder or individual, and in general all facts relating to its operations which affect its right to exemption. To such certificate shall be attached a copy of the charter or articles of incorporation, the by-laws of the organization, and the latest financial statement showing the assets, liabilities, receipts, and disbursements of the organization.

(2) If the transferee is a foreign organization which has been held to be exempt from income tax under such part I (or corresponding provisions of prior law), a copy of the Commissioner's letter so holding shall be filed with Form 926 in lieu of the above certificate and attachments.

(c) *Assessment and collection.* The determination, assessment, and collection of the tax and the examination of returns and claims filed pursuant to chapter 5 of the Code will be made under such procedure as may be prescribed from time to time by the Commissioner. [Reg. § 1.1494-1.]

☐ [*T.D.* 6127, 3-17-55.]

[Reg. § 1.1494-2]

§ 1.1494-2. **Effective date.**—Chapter 5 (section 1491 and following) of the Internal Revenue Code of 1954 and the regulations prescribed thereunder apply with respect to transfers occurring after December 31, 1954. (See section 7851(a)(1)(B).) Chapter 7 (section 1250 and following) of the Internal Revenue Code of 1939 and the regulations applicable thereto apply with respect to transfers occurring prior to January 1, 1955. [Reg. § 1.1494-2.]

☐ [*T.D.* 6127, 3-17-55.]

Consolidated Returns

RETURNS AND PAYMENT OF TAX

[Reg. § 1.1502-0]

§ 1.1502-0. **Effective dates.**—(a) The regulations under section 1502 are applicable to taxable years beginning after December 31, 1965, except as otherwise provided therein.

(b) The provisions of §§ 1.1502-0A through 1.1502-3A, 1.1502-10A through 1.1502-19A, and 1.1502-30A through 1.1502-51A (as contained in the 26 CFR part 1 edition revised April 1, 1996) are applicable to taxable years beginning before January 1, 1966. [Reg. § 1.1502-0.]

☐ [*T.D.* 6894, 9-7-66. Amended by *T.D.* 8677, 6-26-96.]

→ *Caution: Reg. § 1.1502-1(a) below, prior to amendment by T.D. 8560, is effective before January 1, 1995.*←

[Reg. § 1.1502-1]

§ 1.1502-1. **Definitions.**—(a) *Group.* The term "group" means an affiliated group of corporations as defined in section 1504. See § 1.1502-75 (d) as to when a group remains in existence.

→ *Caution: Reg. § 1.1502-1(a) below, as amended by T.D. 8560, is effective on January 1, 1995.*←

(a) *Group.* The term "group" means an affiliated group of corporations as defined in section 1504. See § 1.1502-75 (d) as to when a group remains in existence. Except as the context otherwise requires, references to a group are references to a consolidated group (as defined in paragraph (h) of this section).

(b) *Member.* The term *member* means a corporation (including the common parent) that is included in the group, or as the context may require, a corporation that is included in a subgroup.

(c) *Subsidiary.* The term "subsidiary" means a corporation other than the common parent which is a member of such group.

(d) *Consolidated return year.* The term "consolidated return year" means a taxable year for which a consolidated return is filed or required to be filed by such group.

Reg. § 1.1502-1(d)

(e) *Separate return year.* The term "separate return year" means a taxable year of a corporation for which it files a separate return or for which it joins in the filing of a consolidated return by another group.

(f) *Separate return limitation year*—(1) *In general.* Except as provided in paragraphs (f)(2) and (3) of this section, the term *separate return limitation year* (or *SRLY*) means any separate return year of a member or of a predecessor of a member.

(2) *Exceptions.* The term *separate return limitation year* (or *SRLY*) does not include:

(i) A separate return year of the corporation which is the common parent for the consolidated return year to which the tax attribute is to be carried (except as provided in § 1.1502-75(d)(2)(ii) and subparagraph (3) of this paragraph),

(ii) A separate return year of any corporation which was a member of the group for each day of such year, or

(iii) A separate return year of a predecessor of any member if such predecessor was a member of the group for each day of such year, provided that an election under section 1562(a) (relating to the privilege to elect multiple surtax exemptions) was never effective (or is no longer effective as a result of a termination of such election) for such year. An election under section 1562(a) which is effective for a taxable year beginning in 1963 and ending in 1964 shall be disregarded.

(3) *Reverse acquisitions.* In the event of an acquisition to which § 1.1502-75(d)(3) applies, all taxable years of the first corporation and of each of its subsidiaries ending on or before the date of the acquisition shall be treated as separate return limitation years, and the separate return years (if any) of the second corporation and each of its subsidiaries shall not be treated as separate return limitation years (unless they were so treated immediately before the acquisition). For example, if corporation P merges into corporation T, and the persons who were stockholders of P immediately before the merger, as a result of owning the stock of P, own more than 50 percent of the fair market value of the outstanding stock of T, then a loss incurred before the merger by T (even though it is the common parent), or by a subsidiary of T, is treated as having been incurred in a separate return limitation year. Conversely, a loss incurred before the merger by P, or by a subsidiary of P in a separate return year during all of which such subsidiary was a member of the group of which P was the common parent and for which section 1562 was not effective, is treated as having been incurred in a year which is not a separate return limitation year.

(4) *Predecessor and successors.* The term *predecessor* means a transferor or distributor of assets to a member (the successor) in a transaction—

(i) To which section 381(a) applies; or

(ii) That occurs on or after January 1, 1997, in which the successor's basis for the assets is determined, directly or indirectly, in whole or in part, by reference to the basis of the assets of the transferor or distributor, but in the case of a transaction that occurs before June 25, 1999, only if the amount by which basis differs from value, in the aggregate, is material. For a transaction that occurs before June 25, 1999, only one member may be considered a predecessor to or a successor of one other member.

(g) *Consolidated return change of ownership*—(1) *In general.* A consolidated return change of ownership occurs during any taxable year (referred to in this subparagraph as the "year of change") of the corporation which is the common parent for the taxable year to which the tax attribute is to be carried, if, at the end of the year of change—

(i) Any one or more of the persons described in section 382(a) (2) own a percentage of the fair market value of the outstanding stock of such corporation which is more than 50 percentage points greater than such person or persons owned at—

(*a*) The beginning of such taxable year, or

(*b*) The beginning of the preceding taxable year, and

(ii) The increase in percentage points at the end of such year is attributable to—

(*a*) A purchase (within the meaning of section 382(a)(4)) by such person or persons of such stock, the stock of another corporation owning stock in such corporation, or an interest in a partnership or trust owning stock in such corporation, or

(*b*) A decrease in the amount of such stock outstanding or the amount of stock outstanding of another corporation owning stock in such corporation, except a decrease resulting from a redemption to pay death taxes to which section 303 applies.

For purposes of subdivision (i)(*a*) and (*b*) of this subparagraph, the beginning of the taxable years specified therein shall be the beginning of such taxable years or October 1, 1965, whichever occurs later.

Reg. § 1.1502-1(e)

(2) *Operating rules.* For purposes of this paragraph—

(i) The term "stock" means all shares except nonvoting stock which is limited and preferred as to dividends, and

(ii) Section 318 (relating to constructive ownership of stock) shall apply in determining the ownership of stock, except that section 318(a)(2)(C) and (3)(C) shall be applied without regard to the 50-percent limitation contained therein.

(3) *Old members.* The term "old members" of a group means—

(i) Those corporations which were members of such group immediately preceding the first day of the taxable year in which the consolidated return change of ownership occurs, or

(ii) If the group was not in existence prior to the taxable year in which the consolidated return change of ownership occurs, the corporation which is the common parent for the taxable year to which the tax attribute is to be carried.

(4) *Reverse acquisitions.* If there has been a consolidated return change of ownership of a corporation under subparagraph (1) of this paragraph and the stock or assets of such corporation are subsequently acquired by another corporation in an acquisition to which § 1.1502-7(d)(3) applies so that the group of which the former corporation is the common parent is treated as continuing in existence, then the "old members", as defined in subparagraph (3) of this paragraph, of such group immediately before the acquisition shall continue to be treated as "old members" immediately after the acquisition. For example, assume that corporations P and S comprise group PS, and PS undergoes a consolidated return change of ownership. Subsequently, the stock of P, the common parent, is acquired by corporation T, the common parent of group TU, in an acquisition to which section 368(a)(1)(B) and § 1.1502-75(d)(3) apply. The PS group is treated as continuing in existence with T as the common parent. P and S continue to be treated as old members, as defined in subparagraph (3) of this paragraph.

(h) *Consolidated group.* The term "consolidated group" means a group filing (or required to file) consolidated returns for the tax year.

(i) [Reserved]

(j) *Affiliated.* Corporations are affiliated if they are members of a group with each other. [Reg. § 1.1502-1.]

□ [T.D. 6894, 9-7-66. *Amended by* T.D. 7246, 12-29-72; T.D. 8319, 11-19-90; T.D. 8560, 8-12-94; T.D. 8677, 6-26-96 *and* T.D. 8823, 6-25-99.]

[Reg. § 1.1502-2]

§ 1.1502-2. Computation of tax liability.— The tax liability of a group for a consolidated return year shall be determined by adding together—

(a) The tax imposed by section 11 on the consolidated taxable income for such year (see § 1.1502-11 for the computation of consolidated taxable income);

(b) The tax imposed by section 541 on the consolidated undistributed personal holding company income;

(c) If paragraph (b) of this section does not apply, the aggregate of the taxes imposed by section 541 on the separate undistributed personal holding company income of the members of the group which are personal holding companies;

(d) If paragraph (b) of this section does not apply, the tax imposed by section 531 on the consolidated accumulated taxable income (see § 1.1502-43);

(e) The tax imposed by section 594(a) in lieu of the taxes imposed by section 11 or 1201 on the taxable income of a life insurance department of the common parent of a group which is a mutual savings bank;

(f) The tax imposed by section 802(a) on consolidated life insurance company taxable income;

(g) The tax imposed by section 831(a) on the consolidated insurance company taxable income of the members which are subject to such tax;

(h) The tax imposed by section 1201, instead of the taxes computed under paragraphs (a) and (g) of this section, computed by reference to the net capital gain of the group (see § 1.1502-22) (or, for consolidated return years to which § 1.1502-22 does not apply, computed by reference to the excess of the consolidated net long-term capital gain over the consolidated net short-term capital loss (see § 1.1502-41A for the determination of the consolidated net long-term capital gain and the consolidated net short-term capital loss));

(i) [Reserved]

(j) The tax imposed by section 1333 on war loss recoveries; and

by allowing as a credit against such taxes the investment credit under section 38 (see § 1.1502-3) and the foreign tax credit under section 33 (see § 1.1502-4). For purposes of this section, the surtax exemption of the group for a consolidated return year is $25,000, or if a lesser amount is allowed under section 1561, such lesser amount. See § 1.1561-2(a)(2). For increase in tax due to the application of section 47, see § 1.1502-3(f). For amount of tax surcharge, see section 51 and § 1.1502-7. [Reg. § 1.1502-2.]

Reg. § 1.1502-2(j)

[[T.D. 6894, 9-7-66. Amended by T.D. 7093, 3-12-71; T.D. 7937, 1-26-84; T.D. 8677, 6-26-96 and T.D. 8823, 6-25-99.]

[Reg. § 1.1502-3]

§ 1.1502-3. Consolidated tax credits.—(a) *Determination of amount of consolidated credit*—(1) *In general.* The credit allowed by section 38 for a consolidated return year of a group shall be equal to the consolidated credit earned. The consolidated credit earned is equal to the aggregate of the credit earned (as determined under subparagraph (2) of this paragraph) by all members of the group for the consolidated return year.

(2) *Determination of credit earned.* The credit earned of a member of the group is an amount equal to 7 percent of such member's qualified investment (determined under section 46(c)). For purposes of computing a member's qualified investment, the basis of property shall not include any gain or loss realized with respect to such property by another member in an inter company transaction (as defined in § 1.1502-13(b)), whether or not such gain or loss is deferred. Thus, if section 38 property acquired in an intercompany transaction has a basis of $100 to the purchasing member, and if the selling member has a $20 gain with respect to such property, the basis of such property for purposes of computing the purchaser's qualified investment is only $80. Such $80 basis shall also be used for purposes of applying section 47 to such property. See paragraph (f) of this section.

(3) *Consolidated limitation based on amount of tax.* (i) Notwithstanding the amount of the consolidated credit earned for the taxable year, the consolidated credit allowed by section 38 to the group for the consolidated return year is limited to—

(*a*) So much of the consolidated liability for tax as does not exceed $25,000, plus

(*b*) For taxable years ending on or before March 9, 1967, 25 percent of the consolidated liability for tax in excess of $25,000, or

(*c*) For taxable years ending after March 9, 1967, 50 percent of the consolidated liability for tax in excess of $25,000.

The $25,000 amount referred to in the preceding sentence shall be reduced by any part of such $25,000 amount apportioned under § 1.46-1 to component members of the controlled group (as defined in section 46(a)(5)) which do not join in the filing of the consolidated return. For further rules for computing the limitation based on amount of tax with respect to the suspension period (as defined in section 48(j)), see section 46(a)(2). The amount determined under this subparagraph is referred to in this section as the "consolidated limitation based on amount of tax."

(ii) If an organization to which section 593 applies or a cooperative organization described in section 1381(a) joins in the filing of the consolidated return, the $25,000 amount referred to in subdivision (i) of this subparagraph (reduced as provided in such subdivision) shall be apportioned equally among the members of the group filing the consolidated return. The amount so apportioned equally to any such organization shall then be decreased in accordance with the provisions of section 46(d). Finally, the sum of all such equal portions (as decreased under section 46(d)) of each member of the group shall be substituted for the $25,000 amount referred to in subdivision (i) of this subparagraph.

(4) *Consolidated liability for tax.* For purposes of subparagraph (3) of this paragraph, the consolidated liability for tax shall be the income tax imposed for the taxable year upon the group by chapter 1 of the Code, reduced by the consolidated foreign tax credit allowable under § 1.1502-4. The tax imposed by section 56 (relating to minimum tax for tax preferences), section 531 (relating to accumulated earnings tax), section 541 (relating to personal holding company tax), and any additional tax imposed by section 1351(d)(1) (relating to recoveries of foreign expropriation losses), shall not be considered tax imposed by chapter 1 of the Code. In addition, any increase in tax resulting from the application of section 47 (relating to certain dispositions, etc., of section 38 property) shall not be treated as tax imposed by chapter 1 for purposes of computing the consolidated liability for tax.

(b) *Carryback and carryover of unused credits*—(1) *Allowance of unused credit as consolidated carryback or carryover.* A group shall be allowed to add to the amount allowable as a credit under paragraph (a)(1) of this section for any consolidated return year an amount equal to the aggregate of the consolidated investment credit carryovers and carrybacks to such year. The consolidated investment credit carryovers and carrybacks to the taxable year shall consist of any consolidated unused credits of the group, plus any unused credits of members of the group arising in separate return years of such members, which may be carried over or back to the taxable year under the principles of section 46(b). However, such consolidated carryovers and carrybacks shall not include any consolidated unused credits apportioned to a corporation for a separate return year pursuant to paragraph (c) of § 1.1502-79 and shall be subject to the limitations contained in paragraphs (c) and (e) of this section. A consolidated unused credit for any consolidated return year is the excess of the consolidated credit earned over the consolidated limitation based on amount of tax for such year.

(2) *Absorption rules.* For purposes of determining the amount, if any, of an unused credit (whether consolidated or separate) which can be carried to a taxable year (consolidated or separate), the amount of such unused credit which is absorbed in a prior consolidated return year under section 46(b) shall be determined by—

(i) Applying all unused credits which can be carried to such prior year in the order of the taxable years in which such unused credits arose, beginning with the taxable year which ends earliest, and

(ii) Applying all such unused credits which can be carried to such prior year from taxable years ending on the same date on a pro rata basis.

(3) *Example.* The provisions of paragraphs (a) and (b) of this section may be illustrated by the following example:

Example. (i) Corporation P is incorporated on January 1, 1966. On that same day P incorporates corporation S, a wholly owned subsidiary. P and S file consolidated returns for calendar years 1966 and 1967. P's and S's credit earned, the consolidated credit earned, and the consolidated limitation based on amount of tax for 1966 and 1967 are as follows:

	Credit earned	Consolidated credit earned	Consolidated limitation based on amount of tax
1966:			
P	$60,000		
S	$30,000	$90,000	$100,000
1967:			
P	$40,000		
S	$25,000	$65,000	$50,000

(ii) P's and S's credit earned for 1966 are aggregated, and the group's consolidated credit earned, $90,000, is allowable in full to the group as a credit under section 38 for 1966 since such amount is less than the consolidated limitation based on amount of tax for 1966, $100,000.

(iii) Since the consolidated limitation based on amount of tax for 1967 is $50,000, only $50,000 of the $65,000 consolidated credit earned for such year is allowable to the group under section 38 as a credit for 1967. The consolidated unused credit for 1967 of $15,000 ($65,000 less $50,000) is a consolidated investment credit carryback and carryover to the years prescribed in section 46(b). In this case the consolidated unused credit is a consolidated investment credit carryback to 1966 (since P and S were not in existence in 1964 and 1965) and a consolidated investment credit carryover to 1968 and subsequent years. The portion of the consolidated unused credit for 1967 which is allowable as a credit for 1966 is $10,000. This amount shall be added to the amount allowable as a credit to the group for 1966. The balance of the consolidated unused credit for 1967 to be carried to 1968 is $5,000. These amounts are computed as follows:

Consolidated carryback to 1966		$15,000
1966 consolidated limitation based on tax		$100,000
Less: Consolidated credit earned for 1966	$90,000	
Consolidated unused credits attributable to years preceding 1967	0	$ 90,000
Limit on amount of 1967 consolidated unused credit which may be added as a credit for 1966		$10,000
Balance of 1967 consolidated unused credit to be carried to 1968		$ 5,000

(c) *Limitation on investment credit carryovers and carrybacks from separate return limitation years applicable for consolidated return years for which the due date of the return is on or before March 13, 1998*—(1) *General rule.* In the case of an unused credit of a member of the group arising in a separate return limitation year (as defined in § 1.1502-1(f)) of such member (and in a separate return limitation year of any predecessor of such member), the amount which may be included under paragraph (b) of this section (computed without regard to the limitation contained in paragraph (e) of this section) shall not exceed the amount determined under paragraph (c)(2) of this section.

(2) *Computation of limitation.* The amount referred to in paragraph (c)(1) of this section with

respect to a member of the group is the excess, if any, of—

(i) The limitation based on amount of tax of the group, minus such limitation recomputed by excluding the items of income, deduction, and foreign tax credit of such member; over

(ii) The sum of the investment credit earned by such member for such consolidated return year, and the unused credits attributable to such member which may be carried to such consolidated return year arising in unused credit years ending prior to the particular separate return limitation year.

(3) *Special effective date.* This paragraph (c) applies to consolidated return years for which the due date of the income tax return (without extensions) is on or before March 13, 1998. See paragraph (d) of this section for the rule that limits the group's use of a section 38 credit carryover or carryback from a SRLY for a consolidated return year for which the due date of the income tax return (without extensions) is after March 13, 1998. See also paragraph (d)(4) of this section for an optional effective date rule (generally making the rules of this paragraph (c) inapplicable to a consolidated return year beginning after December 31, 1996, if the due date of the income tax return (without extensions) for such year is on or before March 13, 1998).

(4) *Examples.* The provisions of this paragraph (c) may be illustrated by the following examples:

Example 1. (i) Assume the same facts as in the example contained in paragraph (b)(3) of this section, except that all the stock of corporation T, also a calendar year taxpayer, is acquired by P on January 1, 1968, and that P, S, and T file a consolidated return for 1968. In 1966, T had an unused credit of $10,000 which has not been absorbed and is available as an investment credit carryover to 1968. Such carryover is from a separate return limitation year. P's and S's credit earned for 1968 is $10,000 each, and T's credit earned is $8,000; the consolidated credit earned is therefore $28,000. The group's consolidated limitation based on amount of tax for 1968 is $50,000. Such limitation recomputed by excluding the items of income, deduction, and foreign tax credit of T is $30,000. Thus, the amount determined under paragraph (c)(2)(i) of this section is $20,000 ($50,000 minus $30,000). Accordingly, the limitation on the carryover of T's unused credit is $12,000, the excess of $20,000 over $8,000 (the sum of T's credit earned for the taxable year and any carryovers from prior unused credit years (none in this case)). Therefore T's $10,000 unused credit from 1966 may be carried over to the consolidated return year without limitation.

(ii) The group's consolidated credit earned for 1968, $28,000, is allowable in full as a credit under section 38 since such amount is less than the consolidated limitation based on amount of tax, $50,000.

(iii) The group's consolidated investment credit carryover to 1968 is $15,000, consisting of the consolidated unused credits of the group ($5,000) plus T's separate return year unused credit ($10,000). The entire $15,000 consolidated carryover shall be added to the amount allowable to the group as a credit under section 38 for 1968, since such amount is less than $22,000 (the excess of the consolidated limitation based on tax, $50,000, over the sum of the consolidated credit earned for 1968, $28,000, and unused credits arising in prior unused credit years, zero).

Example 2. Assume the same facts as in *Example 1,* except that the amount determined under paragraph (c)(2)(i) of this section is $12,000. Therefore, the limitation on the carryover of T's unused credit is $4,000. Accordingly, the consolidated investment credit carryover is only $9,000 since the amount of T's separate return year unused credit which may be added to the group's $5,000 consolidated unused credit is $4,000. These amounts are computed as follows:

T's carryover to 1968		$10,000
Consolidated limitation based on amount of tax minus recomputed limitation		$12,000
Less: T's credit earned for 1968	$8,000	
Unused credits attributable to T arising in unused credit years preceding 1966	0	$ 8,000
Limit on amount of 1966 unused credit of T which may be added to consolidated investment credit carryover		$ 4,000
Balance of 1966 unused credit of T to be carried to 1969 (subject to the limitation contained in paragraph (c) of this section)		$ 6,000

(d) *Limitation on tax credit carryovers and carrybacks from separate return limitation years applicable for consolidated return years for which the due date of the return is after March 13, 1998*—(1) *General rule.* The aggregate of a member's unused section 38 credits arising in SRLYs

Reg. § 1.1502-3(c)(3)

that are included in the consolidated section 38 credits for all consolidated return years of the group may not exceed—

(i) The aggregate for all consolidated return years of the member's contributions to the consolidated section 38(c) limitation for each consolidated return year; reduced by

(ii) The aggregate of the member's section 38 credits arising and absorbed in all consolidated return years (whether or not absorbed by the member).

(2) *Computational rules*—(i) *Member's contribution to the consolidated section 38(c) limitation.* If the consolidated section 38(c) limitation for a consolidated return year is determined by reference to the consolidated tentative minimum tax (see section 38(c)(1)(A)), then a member's contribution to the consolidated section 38(c) limitation for such year equals the member's share of the consolidated net income tax minus the member's share of the consolidated tentative minimum tax. If the consolidated section 38(c) limitation for a consolidated return year is determined by reference to the consolidated net regular tax liability (see section 38(c)(1)(B)), then a member's contribution to the consolidated section 38(c) limitation for such year equals the member's share of the consolidated net income tax minus 25 percent of the quantity which is equal to so much of the member's share of the consolidated net regular tax liability less its portion of the $25,000 amount specified in section 38(c)(1)(B). The group computes the member's shares by applying to the respective consolidated amounts the principles of section 1552 and the percentage method under § 1.1502-33(d)(3), assuming a 100% allocation of any decreased tax liability. The group must make proper adjustments so that taxes and credits not taken into account in computing the limitation under section 38(c) are not taken into account in computing the member's share of the consolidated net income tax, etc. (See, for example, the taxes described in section 26(b) that are disregarded in computing regular tax liability.) Also, the group may apportion all or a part of the $25,000 amount (or lesser amount if reduced by section 38(c)(3)) for any year to one or more members.

(ii) *Years included in computation.* For purposes of computing the limitation under this paragraph (d), the consolidated return years of the group include only those years, including the year to which a credit is carried, that the member has been continuously included in the group's consolidated return, but exclude—

(A) For carryovers, any years ending after the year to which the credit is carried; and

(B) For carrybacks, any years ending after the year in which the credit arose.

(iii) *Subgroups and successors.* The SRLY subgroup principles under § 1.1502-21(c)(2) apply for purposes of this paragraph (d). The predecessor and successor principles under § 1.1502-21(f) also apply for purposes of this paragraph (d).

(iv) *Overlap with section 383.* The principles under § 1.1502-21(g) apply for purposes of this paragraph (d). For example, an overlap of paragraph (d) of this section and the application of section 383 with respect to a credit carryover occurs if a corporation becomes a member of a consolidated group (the SRLY event) within six months of the change date of an ownership change giving rise to a section 383 credit limitation with respect to that carryover (the section 383 event), with the result that the limitation of this paragraph (d) does not apply. See §§ 1.1502-21(g)(2)(ii)(A) and 1.383-1; see also § 1.1502-21(g)(4) (subgroup rules).

(3) *Effective date*—(i) *In general.* This paragraph (d) generally applies to consolidated return years for which the due date of the income tax return (without extensions) is after March 13, 1998.

(A) *Contribution years.* Except as provided in paragraph (d)(4)(ii) of this section, a group does not take into account a consolidated taxable year for which the due date of the income tax return (without extensions) is on or before March 13, 1998, in determining a member's (or subgroup's) contributions to the consolidated section 38(c) limitation under this paragraph (d).

(B) *Special subgroup rule.* In the event that the principles of § 1.1502-21(g)(1) do not apply to a particular credit carryover in the current group, then solely for purposes of applying paragraph (d) of this section to determine the limitation with respect to that carryover and with respect to which the SRLY register (the aggregate of the member's or subgroup's contribution to consolidated section 38(c) limitation reduced by the aggregate of the member's or subgroup's section 38 credits arising and absorbed in all consolidated return years) began in a taxable year for which the due date of the return is on or before May 25, 2000, the principles of § 1.1502-21(c)(2) shall be applied without regard to the phrase "or for a carryover that was subject to the overlap rule described in paragraph (g) of this section or § 1.1502-15(g) with respect to another group (the former group)."

(ii) *Overlap rule.* Paragraph (d)(2)(iv) of this section (relating to overlap with section 383) applies to taxable years for which the due date (without extensions) of the consolidated return is

Reg. § 1.1502-3(d)(3)

after May 25, 2000. For purposes of this section, only an ownership change to which section 383, as amended by the Tax Reform Act of 1986 (100 Stat. 2085), applies and which results in a section 383 credit limitation shall constitute a section 383 event.

(4) *Optional effective date of January 1, 1997.*—(i) For consolidated taxable years beginning on or after January 1, 1997, for which the due date of the income tax return (without extensions) is on or before March 13, 1998, in lieu of paragraphs (c) and (e)(3) of this section (relating to the general business credit), § 1.1502-4(f)(3) and (g)(3) (relating to the foreign tax credit), the next to last sentence of § 1.1502-9A(a)(2), § 1.1502-9A(b)(1)(v) (relating to overall foreign losses), and § 1.1502-55(h)(4)(iii) (relating to the alternative minimum tax credit), a consolidated group may apply the corresponding provisions as they appear in 1998-1 C.B. 655 through 661 (see § 601.601(d)(2) of this chapter) (treating references in such corresponding provisions to § § 1.1502-9(b)(1)(ii), (iii), and (iv) as references to § § 1.1502-9A(b)(1)(ii), (iii), and (iv)). Also, in the case of a consolidated return change of ownership that occurs on or after January 1, 1997, in a taxable year for which the due date of the income tax return (without extensions) is on or before March 13, 1998, a consolidated group may choose not to apply paragraph (e) of this section and § 1.1502-4(g) to taxable years ending after December 31, 1996. A consolidated group making the choices described in the two preceding sentences generally must apply all such corresponding provisions (including not applying paragraph (e) of this section and § 1.1502-4(g)) for all relevant years. However, a consolidated group making the election provided in § 1.1502-9A(b)(1)(vi) (electing not to apply § 1.1502-9A(b)(1)(v) to years beginning before January 1, 1998) may nevertheless choose to apply all such corresponding provisions referred to in this paragraph (d)(4)(i) other than the provision corresponding to § 1.1502-9A(b)(1)(v) for all relevant years.

(ii) If a consolidated group chooses to apply the corresponding provisions referred to in paragraph (d)(4)(i) of this section, the consolidated group shall not take into account a consolidated taxable year beginning before January 1, 1997, in determining a member's (or subgroup's) contributions to the consolidated section 38(c) limitation under this paragraph (d).

(5) *Example.* The following example illustrates the provisions of this paragraph (d):

Example. (i) Individual A owns all of the stock of P and T. P is the common parent of the P group. P acquires all the stock of T at the beginning of Year 2. T carries over an unused section 38 general business credit from Year 1 of $100,000. The table in paragraph (i) of this *Example* shows the group's net consolidated income tax, consolidated tentative minimum tax, and consolidated net regular tax liabilities, and T's share of such taxes computed under the principles of section 1552 and the percentage method under § 1.1502-33(d)(3), assuming a 100% allocation of any decreased tax liability, for Year 2. (The effects of the lower section 11 brackets are ignored, there are no other tax credits affecting a group amount or member's share, and $1,000s are omitted.)

Year 2

	Group	P's share of col. 1	T's share of col. 1
1. consolidated taxable income	$2,000	$1,200	$800
2. consolidated net regular tax	$ 700	$ 420	$280
3. consolidated alternative minimum taxable income	$4,000	$3,200	$800
4. consolidated tentative minimum tax	$ 800	$ 640	$160
5. consolidated net income tax	$ 800	$ 520	$280
6. greater of line 4 or 25% of (line 2 minus $25,000) *for the group*	$ 800		
7. consolidated § 38(c) limitation (line 5 minus line 6)	$ 0		

(ii) T's Year 1 is a SRLY with respect to the P group. See § 1.1502-1(f)(2)(ii). T did not undergo an ownership change giving rise to a section 383 credit limitation within 6 months of joining the P group. Thus, T's $100,000 general business credit arising in Year 1 is subject to a SRLY limitation in the P group. The amount of T's unused section 38 credits from Year 1 that are included in the consolidated section 38 credits for Year 2 may not exceed T's contribution to the consolidated section 38(c) limitation. For Year 2, the group determines the consolidated section 38(c) limitation by reference to consolidated tentative minimum tax for Year 2. Therefore, T's contribution to the consolidated section 38(c) limitation for Year 2 equals its share of consolidated net income tax minus its share of consolidated tentative minimum tax. T's contribution is $280,000 minus $160,000, or $120,000. However, because the group has a consolidated section 38

Reg. § 1.1502-3(d)(4)

limitation of zero, it may not include any of T's unused section 38 credits in the consolidated section 38 credits for Year 2.

(iii) The following table shows similar information for the group for Year 3:

Year 3

	Group	P's share of col. 1	T's share of col. 1
1. consolidated taxable income	$1,200	$1,500	$(300)
2. consolidated net regular tax	$ 420	$ 525	$(105)
3. consolidated alternative minimum taxable income	$1,500	$1,700	$(200)
4. consolidated tentative minimum tax	$ 300	$ 340	$ (40)
5. consolidated net income tax	$ 420	$ 525	$(105)
6. greater of line 4 or 25% of (line 2 minus $25,000) *for the group*	$ 300		
7. consolidated § 38(c) limitation (line 5 minus line 6)	$ 120		

(iv) The amount of T's unused section 38 credits from Year 1 that are included in the consolidated section 38 credits for Year 3 may not exceed T's aggregate contribution to the consolidated section 38(c) limitation for Years 2 and 3. For Year 3, the group determines the consolidated section 38(c) limitation by reference to the consolidated tentative minimum tax for Year 3. Therefore, T's contribution to the consolidated section 38(c) limitation for Year 3 equals its share of consolidated net income tax minus its share of consolidated tentative minimum tax. Applying the principles of section 1552 and § 1.1502-33(d) (taking into account, for example, that T's positive earnings and profits adjustment under § 1.1502-33(d) reflects its losses actually absorbed by the group), T's contribution is $(105,000) minus $(40,000), or $(65,000). T's aggregate contribution to the consolidated section 38(c) limitation for Years 2 and 3 is $120,000 + $(65,000), or $55,000. The group may include $55,000 of T's Year 1 unused section 38 credits in its consolidated section 38 tax credit in Year 3.

(e) *Limitation on investment credit carryovers where there has been a consolidated return change of ownership*—(1) *General rule.* If a consolidated return change of ownership (as defined in paragraph (g) of § 1.1502-1) occurs during the taxable year or an earlier taxable year, the amount which may be included under paragraph (b) of this section in the consolidated investment credit carryovers to the taxable year with respect to the aggregate unused credits attributable to old members of the group (as defined in paragraph (g)(3) of § 1.1502-1) arising in taxable years (consolidated or separate) ending on the same day and before the taxable year in which the consolidated return change of ownership occurred shall not exceed the amount determined under subparagraph (2) of this paragraph.

(2) *Computation of limitation.* The amount referred to in subparagraph (1) of this paragraph shall be the excess of the consolidated limitation based on the amount of tax for the taxable year, recomputed by including only the items of income, deduction, and foreign tax credit of the old members, over the sum of—

(i) The aggregate investment credits earned by the old members for the taxable year, and

(ii) The aggregate unused investment credits attributable to the old members which may be carried to the taxable year arising in unused credit years ending prior to the particular unused credit year or years.

(3) *Special effective date.* This paragraph (e) applies only to a consolidated return change of ownership that occurred during a consolidated return year for which the due date of the income tax return (without extensions) is on or before March 13, 1998. See paragraph (d)(4) of this section for an optional effective date rule (generally making the rules of this paragraph (e) also inapplicable if the consolidated return change of ownership occurred on or after January 1, 1997, and during a consolidated return year for which the due date of the income tax return (without extensions) is on or before March 13, 1998).

(f) *Early dispositions, etc., of section 38 property*—(1) *Dispositions of section 38 property during and after consolidated return year.* If property is subject to section 47(a)(1) or (2) with respect to a member during a consolidated return year, any increase in tax shall be added to the tax liability of the group under § 1.1502-2 (regardless of whether the property was placed in service in a consolidated or separate return year). Also, if property is subject to section 47(a)(1) or (2) with respect to a corporation during a taxable year for which such corporation files on a separate return basis, any increase in tax shall be added to the tax liability of such corporation (regardless of whether such property was placed in service in a consolidated or separate return year).

(2) *Exception for transfer to another member.* (i) Except as provided in subdivisions (ii) and

Reg. § 1.1502-3(f)(2)

(iii) of this subparagraph, a transfer of section 38 property from one member of the group to another member of such group during a consolidated return year shall not be treated as a disposition or cessation within the meaning of section 47(a)(1). If such section 38 property is disposed of, or otherwise ceases to be section 38 property or becomes public utility property with respect to the transferee, before the close of the estimated useful life which was taken into account in computing qualified investment, then section 47(a)(1) or (2) shall apply to the transferee with respect to such property (determined by taking into account the period of use, qualified investment, other dispositions, etc., of the transferor). Any increase in tax due to the application of section 47(a)(1) or (2) shall be added to the tax liability of such transferee (or the tax liability of a group, if the transferee joins in the filing of a consolidated return).

(ii) Except as provided in subdivision (iii) of this subparagraph, if section 38 property is disposed of during a consolidated return year by one member of the group to another member of such group which is an organization to which section 593 applies or a cooperative organization described in section 1381(a), the tax under chapter 1 of the Code for such consolidated return year shall be increased by an amount equal to the aggregate decrease in the credits allowed under section 38 for all prior taxable years which would result solely from treating such property, for purposes of determining qualified investment, as placed in service by such organization to which section 593 applies or such cooperative organization described in section 1381(a), as the case may be, but with due regard to the use of the property before such transfer.

(iii) Section 47(a)(1) shall apply to a transfer of section 38 property by a corporation during a consolidated return year if such corporation is liquidated in a transaction to which section 334(b)(2) applies.

(3) *Examples.* The provisions of this paragraph may be illustrated by the following examples:

Example (1). P, S, and T file a consolidated return for calendar year 1967. In such year S places in service section 38 property having an estimated useful life of more than 8 years. In 1968, P, S, and T file a consolidated return, and in such year S sells such property to T. Such sale will not cause section 47(a)(1) to apply.

Example (2). Assume the same facts as in example (1), except that P, S, and T filed separate returns for 1967. The sale from S to T will not cause section 47(a)(1) to apply.

Example (3). Assume the same facts as in example (1), except that P, S, and T continue to file consolidated returns through 1971 and in such year T disposes of the property to individual A. Section 47(a)(1) will apply to the group and any increase in tax shall be added to the tax liability of the group. For the purposes of determining the actual period of use by T, such period shall include S's period of use.

Example (4). Assume the same facts as in example (3), except that T files a separate return in 1971. Again, the actual periods of use by S and T will be combined in applying section 47. If the disposition results in an increase in tax under section 47(a)(1), such additional tax shall be added to the separate tax liability of T.

Example (5). Assume the same facts as in example (1), except that in 1969, P sells all the stock of T to a third party. Such sale will not cause section 47(a)(1) to apply.

[Reg. § 1.1502-3.]

☐ [T.D. 6894, 9-7-66. Amended by T.D. 7246, 12-29-72; T.D. 8597, 7-12-95; T.D. 8751, 1-9-98; T.D. 8766, 3-13-98 and T.D. 8884, 5-24-2000 (corrected 8-7-2000).]

[Reg. § 1.1502-4]

§ 1.1502-4. **Consolidated foreign tax credit.**—(a) *In general.* The credit under section 901 for taxes paid or accrued to any foreign country or possession of the United States shall be allowed to the group only if the common parent corporation chooses to use such credit in the computation of the tax liability of the group for the consolidated return year. If this choice is made, no deduction may be taken on the consolidated return for such taxes paid or accrued by any member of the group. See section 275(a)(4).

(b) *Limitation effective under section 904(a) for the group*—(1) *Common parent's limitation effective for group.* The determination of whether the overall limitation or the per-country limitation applies for a consolidated return year shall be made by reference to the limitation effective with respect to the common parent corporation for such year. If the limitation effective with respect to a member for its immediately preceding separate return year differs from the limitation effective with respect to the common parent corporation for the consolidated return year, then such member shall, if the overall limitation is effective with respect to the common parent, be deemed to have made an election to use such overall limitation, or, if the per-country limitation is effective with respect to the common parent, be deemed to have revoked its election to use the overall limitation. Consent of the Secretary or his

Reg. § 1.1502-4(a)

delegate (if otherwise required) is hereby given to such member for such election or revocation. Any such election or revocation shall apply only prospectively beginning with such consolidated return year.

(2) *Limitation effective for subsequent years.* The limitation effective with respect to a member for the last year for which it joins in the filing of a consolidated return with a group shall remain in effect for a subsequent separate return year and may be changed by such corporation for such subsequent year only in accordance with the provisions of section 904(b) (and this paragraph if it joins in the filing of a consolidated return with another group). Any retroactive change in the limitation by the common parent corporation for such member's last consolidated return year shall change the election effective with respect to such member for such last period. Thus, if the common parent (P) elects the overall limitation with respect to calendar year 1966, such election would be effective with respect to its subsidiary S for 1966. If S leaves the group at the beginning of calendar year 1967, such election shall be effective for 1967 with respect to S (unless S revokes such election for 1967 or a subsequent year in accordance with section 904(b), or this paragraph if it joins in the filing of a consolidated return with another group). However, if P retroactively changes back to the per-country limitation with respect to 1966, such limitation would be effective with respect to S for 1966 and subsequent years (unless S elects the overall limitation for any such subsequent year).

(c) *Computation of consolidated foreign tax credit.* The foreign tax credit for the consolidated return year shall be determined on a consolidated basis under the principles of sections 901 through 905 and section 960. For example, if the per-country limitation applies to the consolidated return year, taxes paid or accrued for such year (including those deemed paid or accrued under sections 902 and 960(a) and paragraph (e) of this section) to each foreign country or possession by the members of the group shall be aggregated. If the overall limitation applies, taxes paid or accrued for such year (including those deemed paid or accrued) to all foreign countries and possessions by members of the group shall be aggregated. If the overall limitation applies and a member of the group qualifies as a Western Hemisphere trade corporation, see section 1503(b).

(d) *Computation of limitation on credit.* For purposes of computing the group's applicable limitation under section 904(a), the following rules shall apply:

(1) *Computation of taxable income from foreign sources.* The numerator of the applicable limiting fraction under section 904(a) shall be an amount (not in excess of the amount determined under subparagraph (2) of this paragraph) equal to the aggregate of the separate taxable incomes of the members from sources within each foreign country or possession of the United States (if the per-country limitation is applicable), or from sources without the United States (if the overall limitation is applicable), determined under § 1.1502-12, adjusted for the following items taken into account in the computation of consolidated taxable income:

(i) The portion of the consolidated net operating loss deduction, the consolidated charitable contributions deduction, the consolidated dividends received deduction, and the consolidated section 922 deduction, attributable to such foreign source income;

(ii) Any such foreign source capital gain net income (net capital gain for taxable years beginning before January 1, 1977) (determined without regard to any net capital loss carryover or carryback);

(iii) Any such foreign source net capital loss and section 1231 net loss, reduced by the portion of the consolidated net capital loss attributable to such foreign source loss; and

(iv) The portion of any consolidated net capital loss carryover or carryback attributable to such foreign source income which is absorbed in the taxable year.

(2) *Computation of entire taxable income.* The denominator of the applicable limiting fraction under section 904(a) (that is, the entire taxable income of the group) shall be the consolidated taxable income of the group computed in accordance with § 1.1502-11.

(3) *Computation of tax against which credit is taken.* The tax against which the limiting fraction under section 904(a) is applied shall be the consolidated tax liability of the group determined under § 1.1502-2, but without regard to paragraphs (b), (c), (d), and (j) thereof, and without regard to any credit against such liability.

(e) *Carryover and carryback of unused foreign tax*—(1) *Allowance of unused foreign tax as consolidated carryover or carryback.* The aggregate of the consolidated unused foreign tax carryovers and carrybacks to the taxable year, to the extent absorbed for such year under the principles of section 904(d), shall be deemed to be paid or accrued to a foreign country or possession for such year. The consolidated unused foreign tax carryovers and carrybacks to the taxable year shall consist of any consolidated unused foreign tax,

Reg. § 1.1502-4(e)(1)

plus any unused foreign tax of members for separate return years of such members, which may be carried over or back to the taxable year under the principles of section 904(d) and (e). However, such consolidated carryovers and carrybacks shall not include any consolidated unused foreign taxes apportioned to a corporation for a separate return year pursuant to § 1.1502-79(d) and shall be subject to the limitations contained in paragraphs (f) and (g) of this section. A consolidated unused foreign tax is the excess of the foreign taxes paid or accrued by the group (or deemed paid or accrued by the group, other than by reason of section 904(d)) over the applicable limitation for the consolidated return year.

(2) *Absorption rules.* For purposes of determining the amount, if any, of an unused foreign tax (consolidated or separate) which can be carried to a taxable year (consolidated or separate), the amount of such unused tax which is absorbed in a prior consolidated return year under section 904(d) shall be determined by—

(i) Applying all unused foreign taxes which can be carried to such prior year in the order of the taxable years in which such unused taxes arose, beginning with the taxable year which ends earliest, and

(ii) Applying all such unused taxes which can be carried to such prior year from taxable years ending on the same date on a pro rata basis.

(f) *Limitation on unused foreign tax carryover or carryback from separate return limitation years*—(1) *General rule.* In the case of an unused foreign tax of a member of the group arising in a separate return limitation year (as defined in paragraph (f) of § 1.1502-1) of such member, the amount which may be included under paragraph (e) of this section (computed without regard to the limitation contained in paragraph (g) of this section) shall not exceed the amount determined under subparagraph (2) of this paragraph.

(2) *Computation of limitation.* The amount referred to in subparagraph (1) of this paragraph with respect to a member of the group is the excess, if any, of—

(i) The section 904(a) limitation of the group, minus such limitation recomputed by excluding the items of income and deduction of such member, over

(ii) The sum of (*a*) the foreign taxes paid (or deemed paid, other than be reason of section 904(d)) by such member for the consolidated return year, and (*b*) the unused foreign tax attributable to such member which may be carried to such consolidated return year arising in taxable years ending prior to the particular separate return limitation year.

(3) *Limitation on unused foreign tax credit carryover or carryback from separate return limitation years.* Paragraphs (f)(1) and (2) of this section do not apply for consolidated return years for which the due date of the income tax return (without extensions) is after March 13, 1998. For consolidated return years for which the due date of the income tax return (without extensions) is after March 13, 1998, a group shall include an unused foreign tax of a member arising in a SRLY without regard to the contribution of the member to consolidated tax liability for the consolidated return year. See also § 1.1502-3(d)(4) for an optional effective date rule (generally making the rules of paragraphs (f)(1) and (2) of this section also inapplicable to a consolidated return year beginning on or after January 1, 1997, if the due date of the income tax return (without extensions) for such year is on or before March 13, 1998).

(g) *Limitation on unused foreign tax carryover where there has been a consolidated return change of ownership*—(1) *General rule.* If a consolidated return change of ownership (as defined in paragraph (g) of § 1.1502-1) occurs during the taxable year or an earlier taxable year, the amount which may be included under paragraph (e) of this section in the consolidated unused foreign tax carryovers to the taxable year with respect to the aggregate unused credits attributable to the old members of the group (as defined in paragraph (g)(3) of § 1.1502-1) arising in taxable years (consolidated or separate) ending on the same day and before the taxable year in which the consolidated return change of ownership occurred shall not exceed the amount determined under subparagraph (2) of this paragraph.

(2) *Computation of limitation.* The amount referred to in subparagraph (1) of this paragraph shall be the excess of the section 904(a) limitation of the group for the taxable year, recomputed by including only the items of income and deduction of the old members of the group, over the sum of—

(i) The aggregate foreign taxes paid (or deemed paid, other than by reason of section 904(d)) by the old members for the taxable year, and

(ii) The aggregate unused foreign tax attributable to the old members which can be carried to the taxable year arising in taxable years ending prior to the particular unused foreign tax year or years.

(3) *Special effective date for CRCO limitation.* Paragraphs (g)(1) and (2) of this section apply only to a consolidated return change of ownership that occurred during a consolidated return year for which the due date of the income

Reg. § 1.1502-4(e)(2)

tax return (without extensions) is on or before March 13, 1998. See also § 1.1502-3(d)(4) for an optional effective date rule (generally making the rules of paragraph (g)(1) and (2) of this section also inapplicable if the consolidated return change of ownership occurred on or after January 1, 1997, and during a consolidated return year for which the due date of the income tax return (without extensions) is on or before March 13, 1998).

(h) *Amount of credit with respect to interest income.* If any member of the group has interest income described in section 904(f)(2) (for a year for which it filed on a consolidated or separate basis), the group's foreign tax credit with respect to such interest shall be computed separately in accordance with the principles of section 904(f) and this section.

(i) [Reserved]

(j) *Examples.* The provisions of this section may be illustrated by the following examples:

Example (1). Domestic corporation P is incorporated on January 1, 1966. On that same day it also incorporates domestic corporations S and T, wholly owned subsidiaries. P, S, and T file consolidated returns for 1966 and 1967 on the basis of a calendar year. T engages in business solely in country A. S transacts business solely in countries A and B. P does business solely in the United States. During 1966 T sold an item of inventory to P at a profit of $2,000. Under § 1.1502-13 (as contained in the 26 CFR part 1 edition revised as of April 1, 1995) such profit is deferred and none of the circumstances of restoration contained in paragraph (d), (e), or (f) of § 1.1502-13 have occurred as of the close of 1966. The taxable income for 1966 from foreign and United States sources, and the foreign taxes paid on such foreign income are as follows:

Corporation	U.S. Taxable income	Country A Taxable income	Country A Foreign tax paid	Country B Taxable income	Country B Foreign tax paid	Total Taxable income
P	$40,000	.....	.....	.....	.....	$40,000
T	.....	$20,000	$12,000	.....	.....	20,000
S	.....	10,000	6,000	$10,000	$3,000	20,000
						$80,000

Such taxable income was computed by taking into account the rules provided in § 1.1502-12. Thus, the $2,000 deferred profit is not included in T's taxable income for 1966 (but will be included for the taxable year for which one of the events specified in paragraph (d), (e), or (f) of § 1.1502-13 occurs). The consolidated taxable income of the group (computed in accordance with § 1.1502-11 is $80,000. The consolidated tax liability against which the credit may be taken (computed in accordance with paragraph (d)(3) of this section) is $31,900.

(i) Assuming P chooses to use the foreign taxes paid as a credit and the group is subject to the per-country limitation, the group may take as a credit against the consolidated tax liability $11,962.50 of the amount paid to country A, plus the $3,000 paid to country B. Such amounts are computed as follows: The aggregate taxes paid to country A of $18,000 is limited to $11,962.50 ($31,900 times $30,000/$80,000). The unused foreign tax with respect to country A is $6,037.50 ($18,000 less $11,962.50), and is a consolidated unused foreign tax which shall be carried to the years prescribed by section 904(d). A credit of $3,000 is available with respect to the taxes paid to country B since such amount is less than the limitation of $3,987.50 ($31,900 times $10,000/$80,000).

(ii) Assuming the overall limitation is in effect for the taxable year, the group may take $15,950 as a credit, computed as follows: The aggregate taxes paid to all foreign countries of $21,000 is limited to $15,950 ($31,900 times $40,000/$80,000). The unused foreign tax is $5,050 ($21,000 less $15,950), and is a consolidated unused foreign tax which shall be carried to the years prescribed by section 904(d).

Example (2). Assume the same facts as in example (1), except that T has a $10,000 long-term capital gain (derived from a sale to a nonmember in country A) and P has a $10,000 long-term capital loss (derived from a sale to a nonmember in the United States). Notwithstanding that the consolidated net capital gain (capital gain net income for taxable years beginning after December 31, 1976) of the group is zero, T's capital gain shall be reflected in full in the computation of taxable income from foreign sources.

Example (3). Assume the same facts as in example (1), except that the group had a consolidated section 172 deduction of $8,000 which is attributable to a net operating loss sustained by T. The $8,000 consolidated net operating loss deduction is offset against T's income from country

Reg. § 1.1502-4(j)

A, thus reducing T's taxable income from country A to $12,000. [Reg. § 1.1502-4.]

☐ [T.D. 6894, 9-7-66. Amended by T.D. 7637, 8-6-79; T.D. 7728, 10-31-80; T.D. 8597, 7-12-95; T.D. 8751, 1-9-98; T.D. 8766, 3-13-98 and T.D. 8884, 5-24-2000.]

[Reg. § 1.1502-5]

§ 1.1502-5. Estimated tax.—(a) *General rule*—(1) *Consolidated estimated tax.* If a group files a consolidated return for two consecutive taxable years, it must make payments of estimated tax on a consolidated basis for each subsequent taxable year, until such time as separate returns are properly filed. Until such time, the group is treated as a single corporation for purposes of section 6154 (relating to payment of estimated tax by corporations). If separate returns are filed by the members for a taxable year, the amount of any estimated tax payments made with respect to a consolidated payment of estimated tax for such year shall be credited against the separate tax liabilities of the members in any manner designated by the common parent which is satisfactory to the Commissioner. The consolidated payments of estimated tax shall be deposited with the authorized financial institution with which the common parent deposits its estimated tax payments. A statement should be attached to the payment setting forth the name, address, employer identification number, and internal revenue service center of each member.

(2) *First two consolidated return years.* For the first 2 years for which a group files a consolidated return, it may make payments of estimated tax on either a consolidated or separate basis. If a consolidated return is filed for such year, the amount of any estimated tax payments made for such year by any member shall be credited against the tax liability of the group.

(3) *Effective date.* This section applies to taxable years for which the due date (without extensions) for filing returns is after August 6, 1979. For prior taxable years see 26 CFR § 1.1502-5. (Revised as of April 1, 1978).

(b) *Addition to tax for failure to pay estimated tax under section 6655*—(1) *Consolidated return filed.* For the first two taxable years for which a group files a consolidated return, the group may compute the amount of the penalty (if any) under section 6655 on a consolidated basis or separate member basis, regardless of the method of payment. Thereafter, for a taxable year for which the group files a consolidated return, the group must compute the penalty on a consolidated basis.

(2) *Computation of penalty on consolidated basis.* (i) This paragraph (b)(2) gives the rules for computing the penalty under section 6655 on a consolidated basis.

(ii) The tax and facts shown on the return for the preceding taxable year referred to in section 6655(d)(1) and (2) are, if a consolidated return was filed for that preceding year, such items shown on the consolidated return for that preceding year or, if one was not filed for that preceding year, the aggregate taxes and the facts shown on the separate returns of the common parent and any other corporation that was a member of the same affiliated group as the common parent for that preceding year.

(iii) If estimated tax was not paid on a consolidated basis, then the amount of the group's payments of estimated tax for the taxable year is the aggregate of the payments made by all members for the year.

(iv) Section 6655(d)(1) applies only if the common parent's consolidated return, or each member's separate return, for the preceding taxable year (as the case may be) was a taxable year of 12 months.

(3) *Computation of penalty on separate member basis.* To compute any penalty under section 6655 on a separate member basis, for purposes of section 6655(b)(1), the "tax shown on the return for the taxable year" is the portion of the tax shown on the consolidated return allocable to the member under paragraph (b)(5) of this section. If the member was included in the consolidated return filed by the group for the preceding taxable year then—

(i) For purposes of section 6655(d)(1), the "tax shown on the return" for any member shall be the portion of the tax shown on the consolidated return for the preceding year allocable to the member under paragraph (b)(5) of this section.

(ii) For purposes of section 6655(d)(2), the "facts shown on the return" shall be the facts shown on the consolidated return for the preceding year and the tax computed under that section shall be allocated under the rules of paragraph (b)(5) of this section.

(4) *Consolidated payments if separate returns filed.* If the group does not file a consolidated return for the taxable year, but makes payments of estimated tax on a consolidated basis, for purposes of section 6655(b)(2), the "amount, if any of the installment paid" by any member is an amount apportioned to the member in a manner designated by the common parent that is satisfactory to the Commissioner. If the member was included in the consolidated return filed by the group for the preceding taxable year, the amount of a member's penalty under section

Reg. § 1.1502-5(a)(1)

6655 is computed on the separate member basis described in paragraph (b)(3)(i) and (ii) of this section.

(5) *Rules for allocation of consolidated tax liability.* For purposes of subparagraphs (1) and (2) of this paragraph, the tax shown on a consolidated return shall be allocated to the members of the group under the method which the group has elected pursuant to section 1552 and § 1.1502-33(d)(2).

(c) *Examples.* The provisions of this section may be illustrated by the following examples:

Example (1). Corporations P and S-1 file a consolidated return for the first time for calendar year 1978. P and S-1 also file consolidated returns for 1979 and 1980. For 1978 and 1979, P and S-1 may make payments of estimated tax on either a separate or consolidated basis. For 1980, however, the group must pay its estimated tax on a consolidated basis. In determining whether P and S-1 come within the exception provided in section 6655(d)(1) for 1980, the "tax shown on the return" is the tax shown on the consolidated return for 1979.

Example (2). Assume the same facts as in example (1). Assume further that corporation S-2 is a member of the group during 1979, and joins in the filing of the consolidated return for such year, but ceases to be a member of the group on September 15, 1980. In determining whether the group (which no longer includes S-2) comes within the exception provided in section 6655(d)(1) for 1980, the "tax shown on the return" is the tax shown on the consolidated return for 1979.

Example (3). Assume the same facts as in example (1). Assume further that corporation S-2 becomes a member of the group on July 1, 1980, and joins in the filing of the consolidated return for 1980. In determining whether the group (which now includes S-2) comes within the exception provided in section 6655(d)(1) for 1980, the "tax shown on the return" is the tax shown on the consolidated return for 1979. Any tax of S-2 for any separate return year is not included as a part of the "tax shown on the return" for purposes of applying section 6655(d)(1).

Example (4). Corporations X and Y filed consolidated returns for the calendar years 1977 and 1978 and separate returns for 1979. In determining whether X or Y comes within the exception provided in section 6655(d)(1) for 1979, the "tax shown on the return" is the amount of tax shown on the consolidated return for 1978 allocable to X and to Y in accordance with paragraph (b)(5) of this section.

(d) *Cross reference.* For provisions relating to quick refunds of corporate estimated tax payments, see § 1.1502-78, and § 1.6425-1 through § 1.6425-3, of this chapter. [Reg. § 1.1502-5.]

☐ [*T.D.* 6894, 9-7-66. Amended by *T.D.* 7059, 9-16-70; *T.D.* 7637, 8-6-79 *and T.D.* 8952, 6-25-2001.]

[Reg. § 1.1502-6]

§ 1.1502-6. **Liability for tax.**—(a) *Several liability of members of group.* Except as provided in paragraph (b) of this section, the common parent corporation and each subsidiary which was a member of the group during any part of the consolidated return year shall be severally liable for the tax for such year computed in accordance with the regulations under section 1502 prescribed on or before the due date (not including extensions of time) for the filing of the consolidated return for such year.

(b) *Liability of subsidiary after withdrawal.* If a subsidiary has ceased to be a member of the group and if such cessation resulted from a bona fide sale or exchange of its stock for fair value and occurred prior to the date upon which any deficiency is assessed, the district director may, if he believes that the assessment or collection of the balance of the deficiency will not be jeopardized, make assessment and collection of such deficiency from such former subsidiary in an amount not exceeding the portion of such deficiency which the district director may determine to be allocable to it. If the district director makes assessment and collection of any part of a deficiency from such former subsidiary, then for purposes of any credit or refund of the amount collected from such former subsidiary the agency of the common parent under the provisions of § 1.1502-77 shall not apply.

(c) *Effect of intercompany agreements.* No agreement entered into by one or more members of the group with any other member of such group or with any other person shall in any case have the effect of reducing the liability prescribed under this section. [Reg. § 1.1502-6.]

☐ [*T.D.* 6894, 9-7-66.]

[Reg. § 1.1502-9]

§ 1.1502-9. **Consolidated overall foreign losses and separate limitation losses.**—(a) *In general.* This section provides rules for applying section 904(f) (including its definitions and nomenclature) to a group and its members. Generally, section 904(f) concerns rules relating to overall foreign losses (OFLs) and separate limitation losses (SLLs) and the consequences of such losses. As provided in section 904(f)(5), losses are computed separately in each category of income described in section 904(d)(1) (basket). Paragraph

(b) of this section defines terms and provides computational and accounting rules, including rules regarding recapture. Paragraph (c) of this section provides rules that apply to OFLs and SLLs when a member becomes or ceases to be a member of a group. Paragraph (d) of this section provides a predecessor and successor rule. Paragraph (e) of this section provides effective dates.

(b) *Consolidated application of section 904(f).* A group applies section 904(f) for a consolidated return year in accordance with that section, subject to the following rules:

(1) *Computation of CSLI or CSLL and consolidated U.S. source income or loss.* The group computes its consolidated separate limitation income (CSLI) or consolidated separate limitation loss (CSLL) for each basket under the principles of § 1.1502-11 by aggregating each member's foreign-source taxable income or loss in such basket computed under the principles of § 1.1502-12, and taking into account the foreign portion of the consolidated items described in § 1.1502-11(a)(2) through (8) for such basket. The group computes its consolidated U.S.-source taxable income or loss under similar principles.

(2) *Netting CSLLs, CSLIs, and consolidated U.S. source taxable income or loss.* The group applies section 904(f)(5) to determine the extent to which a CSLL for a basket reduces CSLI for another basket or consolidated U.S.-source taxable income.

(3) *CSLL and COFL accounts.* To the extent provided in section 904(f), the amount by which a CSLL for a basket (the loss basket) reduces CSLI for another basket (the income basket) shall result in the creation of (or addition to) a CSLL account for the loss basket with respect to the income basket. Likewise, the amount by which a CSLL for a loss basket reduces consolidated U.S.-source income will create (or add to) a consolidated overall foreign loss account (a COFL account).

(4) *Recapture of COFL and CSLL accounts.* In the case of a COFL account for a loss basket, section 904(f)(1) and (3) recharacterizes some or all of the foreign-source income in the loss basket as U.S.-source income. In the case of a CSLL account for a loss basket with respect to an income basket, section 904(f)(5)(C) and (F) recharacterizes some or all of the foreign-source income in the loss basket as foreign-source income in the income basket. The COFL account or CSLL account is reduced to the extent amounts are recharacterized with respect to such account.

(5) *Intercompany transactions*—(i) *Nonapplication of section 904(f) disposition rules.* Neither section 904(f)(3) (in the case of a COFL account) nor (5)(F) (in the case of a CSLL account) applies at the time of a disposition that is an intercompany transaction to which § 1.1502-13 applies. Instead, section 904(f)(3) and (5)(F) applies only at such time and only to the extent that the group is required under § 1.1502-13 (without regard to section 904(f)(3) and (5)(F)) to take into account any intercompany items resulting from the disposition, based on the COFL or CSLL account existing at the end of the consolidated return year during which the group takes the intercompany items into account.

(ii) *Example.* Paragraph (b)(5)(i) of this section is illustrated by the following examples. The identity of the parties and the basic assumptions set forth in § 1.1502-13(c)(7)(i) apply to the examples. Except as otherwise stated, assume further that the consolidated group recognizes no foreign-source income other than as a result of the transactions described. The examples are as follows:

Example 1. (i) On June 10, Year 1, S transfers nondepreciable property with a basis of $100 and a fair market value of $250 to B in a transaction to which section 351 applies. The property was predominantly used without the United States in a trade or business, within the meaning of section 904(f)(3). B continues to use the property without the United States. The group has a COFL account in the relevant loss basket of $120 as of December 31, Year 1.

(ii) Because the contribution from S to B is an intercompany transaction, section 904(f)(3) does not apply to result in any gain recognition in Year 1. See paragraph (b)(5)(i) of this section.

(iii) On January 10, Year 4, B ceases to be a member of the group. Because S did not recognize gain in Year 1 under section 351, no gain is taken into account in Year 4 under § 1.1502-13(d). Thus, no portion of the group's COFL account is recaptured in Year 4. For rules requiring apportionment of a portion of the COFL account to B, see paragraph (c)(2) of this section.

Example 2. (i) The facts are the same as in paragraph (i) of *Example 1.* On January 10, Year 4, B sells the property to X for $300. As of December 31, Year 4, the group's COFL account is $40. (The COFL account was reduced between Year 1 and Year 4 due to unrelated foreign-source income taken into account by the group.)

(ii) B takes into account gain of $200 in Year 4. The $40 COFL account in Year 4 recharacterizes $40 of the gain as U.S. source. See section 904(f)(3).

Example 3. (i) On June 10, Year 1, S sells nondepreciable property with a basis of $100 and a fair market value of $250 to B for $250 cash. The property was predominantly used without the

Reg. § 1.1502-9(b)(1)

United States in a trade or business, within the meaning of section 904(f)(3). The group has a COFL account in the relevant loss basket of $120 as of December 31, Year 1. B predominately uses the property in a trade or business without the United States.

(ii) Because the sale is an intercompany transaction, section 904(f)(3) does not require the group to take into account any gain in Year 1. Thus, under paragraph (b)(5)(i) of this section, the COFL account is not reduced in Year 1.

(iii) On January 10, Year 4, B sells the property to X for $300. As of December 31, Year 4, the group's COFL account is $60. (The COFL account was reduced between Year 1 and Year 4 due to unrelated foreign-source income taken into account by the group.)

(iv) In Year 4, S's $150 intercompany gain and B's $50 corresponding gain are taken into account to produce the same effect on consolidated taxable income as if S and B were divisions of a single corporation. See § 1.1502-13(c). All of B's $50 corresponding gain is recharacterized under section 904(f)(3). If S and B were divisions of a single corporation and the intercompany sale were a transfer between the divisions, B would succeed to S's $100 basis in the property and would have $200 of gain ($60 of which would be recharacterized under section 904(f)(3)), instead of a $50 gain. Consequently, S's $150 intercompany gain and B's $50 corresponding gain are taken into account, and $10 of S's gain is recharacterized under section 904(f)(3) as U.S. source to reflect the $10 difference between B's $50 recharacterized gain and the $60 recomputed gain that would have been recharacterized.

(c) *Becoming or ceasing to be a member of a group*—(1) *Adding separate accounts on becoming a member.* At the time that a corporation becomes a member of a group (a new member), the group adds to the balance of its COFL or CSLL account the balance of the new member's corresponding OFL account or SLL account. A new member's OFL account corresponds to a COFL account if the account is for the same loss basket. A new member's SLL account corresponds to a CSLL account if the account is for the same loss basket and with respect to the same income basket. If the group does not have a COFL or CSLL account corresponding to the new member's account, it creates a COFL or CSLL account with a balance equal to the balance of the member's account.

(2) *Apportionment of consolidated account to departing member*—(i) *In general.* A group apportions to a member that ceases to be a member (a departing member) a portion of each COFL and CSLL account as of the end of the year during which the member ceases to be a member and after the group makes the additions or reductions to such account required under paragraphs (b)(3), (b)(4) and (c)(1) of this section (other than an addition under paragraph (c)(1) of this section attributable to a member becoming a member after the departing member ceases to be a member). The group computes such portion under paragraph (c)(2)(ii) of this section, as limited by paragraph (c)(2)(iii) of this section. The departing member carries such portion to its first separate return year after it ceases to be a member. Also, the group reduces each account by such portion and carries such reduced amount to its first consolidated return year beginning after the year in which the member ceases to be a member. If two or more members cease to be members in the same year, the group computes the portion allocable to each such member (and reduces its accounts by such portion) in the order that the members cease to be members.

(ii) *Departing member's portion of group's account.* A departing member's portion of a group's COFL or CSLL account for a loss basket is computed based upon the member's share of the group's assets that generate income subject to recapture at the time that the member ceases to be a member. Under the characterization principles of §§ 1.861-9T(g)(3) and 1.861-12T, the group identifies the assets of the departing member and the remaining members that generate foreign-source income (foreign assets) in each basket. The assets are characterized based upon the income that the assets are reasonably expected to generate after the member ceases to be a member. The member's portion of a group's COFL or CSLL account for a loss basket is the group's COFL or CSLL account, respectively, multiplied by a fraction, the numerator of which is the value of the member's foreign assets for the loss basket and the denominator of which is the value of the foreign assets of the group (including the departing member) for the loss basket. The value of the foreign assets is determined under the asset valuation rules of § 1.861-9T(g)(1) and (2) using either tax book value or fair market value under the method chosen by the group for purposes of interest apportionment as provided in § 1.861-9T(g)(1)(ii). For purposes of this paragraph (c)(2)(ii), § 1.861-9T(g)(2)(iv) (assets in intercompany transactions) shall apply, but § 1.861-9T(g)(2)(iii) (adjustments for directly allocated interest) shall not apply. If the group uses the tax book value method, the member's portions of COFL and CSLL accounts are limited by paragraph (c)(2)(iii) of this section. In addition, for purposes of this paragraph (c)(2)(ii), the tax book value of

Reg. § 1.1502-9(c)(2)

assets transferred in intercompany transactions shall be determined without regard to previously deferred gain or loss that is taken into account by the group as a result of the transaction in which the member ceases to be a member. The assets should be valued at the time the member ceases to be a member, but values on other dates may be used unless this creates substantial distortions. For example, if a member ceases to be a member in the middle of the group's consolidated return year, an average of the values of assets at the beginning and end of the year (as provided in § 1.861-9T(g)(2)) may be used or, if a member ceases to be a member in the early part of the group's consolidated return year, values at the beginning of the year may be used, unless this creates substantial distortions.

(iii) *Limitation on member's portion for groups using tax book value method.* If a group uses the tax book value method of valuing assets for purposes of paragraph (c)(2)(ii) of this section and the aggregate of a member's portions of COFL and CSLL accounts for a loss basket (with respect to one or more income baskets) determined under paragraph (c)(2)(ii) of this section exceeds 150 percent of the actual fair market value of the member's foreign assets in the loss basket, the member's portion of the COFL or CSLL accounts for the loss basket shall be reduced (proportionately, in the case of multiple accounts) by such excess. This rule does not apply if the departing member and all other members that cease to be members as part of the same transaction own all (or substantially all) the foreign assets in the loss basket.

(iv) *Determination of values of foreign assets binding on departing member.* The group's determination of the value of the member's and the group's foreign assets for a loss basket is binding on the member, unless the Commissioner concludes that the determination is not appropriate. The common parent of the group must attach a statement to the return for the taxable year that the departing member ceases to be a member of the group that sets forth the name and taxpayer identification number of the departing member, the amount of each COFL or CSLL for each loss basket that is apportioned to the departing member under this paragraph (c)(2), the method used to determine the value of the member's and the group's foreign assets in each such loss basket, and the value of the member's and the group's foreign assets in each such loss basket. The common parent must also furnish a copy of the statement to the departing member.

(v) *Anti-abuse rule.* If a corporation becomes a member and ceases to be a member, and a principal purpose of the corporation becoming and ceasing to be a member is to transfer the corporation's OFL account or SLL account to the group or to transfer the group's COFL or CSLL account to the corporation, appropriate adjustments will be made to eliminate the benefit of such a transfer of accounts. Similarly, if any member acquires assets or disposes of assets (including a transfer of assets between members of the group and the departing member) with a principal purpose of affecting the apportionment of accounts under paragraph (c)(2)(i) of this section, appropriate adjustments will be made to eliminate the benefit of such acquisition or disposition.

(vi) *Examples.* The following examples illustrate this paragraph (c):

Example 1. (i) On November 6, Year 1, S, a member of the P group, a consolidated group with a calendar consolidated return year, ceases to be a member of the group. On December 31, Year 1, the P group has a $40 COFL account for the general limitation basket, a $20 CSLL account for the general limitation basket (i.e., the loss basket) with respect to the passive basket (i.e., the income basket), and a $10 CSLL account for the shipping income basket (i.e., the loss basket) with respect to the passive basket (i.e., the income basket). No member of the group has foreign-source income or loss in Year 1. The group apportions its interest expense according to the tax book value method.

(ii) On November 6, Year 1, the group identifies S's assets and its own assets (including S's assets) expected to produce foreign general limitation income. Use of end-of-the-year values will not create substantial distortions in determining the relative values of S's and the group's relevant assets on November 6, Year 1. The group determines that S's relevant assets have a tax book value of $2,000 and a fair market value of $2,200. Also, the group's relevant assets (including S's assets) have a tax book value of $8,000. On November 6, Year 1, S has no assets expected to produce foreign shipping income.

(iii) Under paragraph (c)(2)(ii) of this section, S takes a $10 COFL account for the general limitation basket ($40 × $2000/$8000) and a $5 CSLL account for the general limitation basket with respect to the passive basket ($20 × $2000/$8000). S does not take any portion of the shipping income basket CSLL account. The limitation described in paragraph (c)(2)(iii) of this section does not apply because the aggregate of the COFL and CSLL accounts for the general limitation basket that are apportioned to S ($15) is less than 150 percent of the actual fair market

Reg. § 1.1502-9(c)(2)

value of S's general limitation foreign assets ($2,200 × 150%).

Example 2. (i) Assume the same facts as in Example 1, except that the fair market value of S's general limitation foreign assets is $4 as of November 6, Year 1.

(ii) Under paragraph (c)(2)(iii) of this section, S's COFL and CSLL accounts for the general limitation basket must be reduced by $9, which is the excess of $15 (the aggregate amount of the accounts apportioned under paragraph (c)(2)(ii) of this section) over $6 (150 percent of the $4 actual fair market value of S's general limitation foreign assets). S thus takes a $4 COFL account for the general limitation basket ($10 − ($9 × $10/$15)) and a $2 CSLL account for the general limitation basket with respect to the passive basket ($5 − ($9 × $5/$15)).

(d) *Predecessor and successor.* A reference to a member includes, as the context may require, a reference to a predecessor or successor of the member. See § 1.1502-1(f).

(e) *Effective dates.* This section applies to consolidated return years for which the due date of the income tax return (without extensions) is after August 11, 1999. However, paragraph (b)(5) of this section (intercompany transactions) is not applicable for intercompany transactions that occur before January 28, 1999. A group applies the principles of § 1.1502-9A(e) to a disposition which is an intercompany transaction to which § 1.1502-13 applies and that occurs before January 28, 1999. Also, paragraph (c)(2) of this section (apportionment of consolidated account to departing member) is not applicable for members ceasing to be members of a group before January 28, 1999. A group applies the principles of § 1.1502-9A (rather than paragraph (c)(2) of this section) to determine the amount of a consolidated account that is apportioned to a member that ceases to be a member of the group before January 28, 1999 (and reduces its consolidated account by such apportioned amount) before applying paragraph (c)(2) of this section to members that cease to be members on or after January 28, 1999. [Reg. § 1.1502-9.]

☐ [T.D. 8833, 8-10-99.]

[Reg. § 1.1502-9A]

§ 1.1502-9A. **Application of overall foreign loss recapture rules to corporations filing consolidated returns due on or before August 11, 1999.**—(a) *Scope*—(1) *Effective date.* This section applies only to consolidated return years for which the due date of the income tax return (without extensions) is on or before August 11, 1999.

(2) *In general.* An affiliated group of corporations filing a consolidated return sustains an overall foreign loss (a consolidated overall foreign loss) in any taxable year in which its gross income from sources without the United States subject to a separate limitation (as defined in § 1.904(f)-1(c)(2)) is exceeded by the sum of the deductions properly allocated and apportioned thereto. However, for taxable years prior to 1983, affiliated groups may have determined their overall foreign losses for income subject to the passive interest limitation, DISC dividend limitation, and general limitation on a combined basis in accordance with the rules in § 1.904(f)-1(c)(1). The rules contained in §§ 1.904(f)-1 through 1.904(f)-6 are applicable to affiliated groups filing consolidated returns. This section provides special rules for applying those sections to such groups. Paragraph (b) provides rules for additions and subtractions of a portion of overall foreign losses to and from consolidated overall foreign loss accounts. Paragraph (c) requires that separate notional overall foreign loss accounts be kept for each member of the group that contributes to a consolidated overall foreign loss account and provides for allocation of a portion of the group's overall foreign loss account to a member when the member leaves the group prior to recapture of the entire amount of the loss account. These rules are similar to the rules provided in § 1.1502-21(b)(2) (or § 1.1502-79A, as appropriate) concerning the apportionment of consolidated net operating losses to a member who leaves the group. However, the rules differ somewhat because the absorption rule of § 1.1502-21(b)(1) (or § 1.1502-79A, as appropriate) is applied year-by-year, consistently with the sequence rules of section 172(b), and recapture of overall foreign losses is based on overall foreign loss accounts that may consist of losses in more than one year. Paragraph (d) provides rules for recapture of amounts in consolidated overall foreign loss accounts. Paragraph (e) provides special rules pertaining to section 904(f)(3) dispositions between members of a group. Paragraphs (b), (c), and (e) also contain special rules that apply to overall foreign losses that arise in separate return limitation years; the principles therein also apply to overall foreign losses when there has been a consolidated return change of ownership (as defined in § 1.1502-1(g)). See § 1.1502-9T(b)(1)(v) for the rule that ends the separate return limitation year limitation for consolidated return years for which the due date of the income tax return (without extensions) is after March 13, 1998, and § 1.1502-9T(b)(1)(vi) for an election to continue the separate return limitation year limitation for consolidated return years beginning before January 1, 1998. See also

Reg. § 1.1502-9A(a)(2)

§ 1.1502-3(d)(4) for an optional effective date rule (generally making the rules of paragraphs (b)(1)(iii) and (iv) of this section inapplicable for a consolidated return year beginning after December 31, 1996, if the due date of the income tax return (without extensions) for such year is on or before March 13, 1998).

(b) *Consolidated overall foreign loss accounts.* Any group that sustains an overall foreign loss (or acquires a member with a balance in an overall foreign loss account) must establish a consolidated overall foreign loss account for such loss, and amounts shall be added to and subtracted from such account as provided in §§ 1.904(f)-1 through 1.904(f)-6 and this section.

(1) *Additions to the consolidated overall foreign loss accounts.*—(i) *Consolidated overall foreign losses.* Any consolidated overall foreign loss shall be added to the applicable consolidated overall foreign loss account for such separate limitation, to the extent that the overall foreign loss has reduced United States source income, in accordance with the rules of §§ 1.904(f)-1 and 1.904(f)-3.

(ii) *Overall foreign losses from separate return years.* If a corporation joins in the filing of a consolidated return in a taxable year in which such corporation has a balance in an overall foreign loss account from a prior separate return year that is not a separate return limitation year, such balance shall be added to the applicable consolidated overall foreign loss account in such year and treated as a consolidated overall foreign loss incurred in the previous year (and shall therefore be subject to recapture, in accordance with paragraph (d) of this section, beginning in the same year in which it is added to the consolidated overall foreign loss account).

(iii) *Overall foreign losses from separate return limitation years.* If a corporation joins in the filing of a consolidated return in a taxable year in which such corporation has a balance in an overall foreign loss account from a prior separate return limitation year, such balance shall be added to the applicable consolidated overall foreign loss account in such consolidated return year to the extent of the lesser of the balance in the overall foreign loss account from the separate return limitation year or 50 percent (or such larger percentage as the taxpayer may elect) of the difference between the consolidated foreign source taxable income subject to the same separate limitation (computed in accordance with §§ 1.904(f)-2(b) and 1.1502-4(d)(1)) minus such consolidated foreign source taxable income recomputed by excluding the items of income and deduction of such corporation (but not less than zero). The amount added to a consolidated overall foreign loss account in any taxable year under this paragraph (b)(1)(iii) shall be treated as a consolidated overall foreign loss in the previous year (and shall therefore be subject to recapture, in accordance with paragraph (d) of this section, beginning in the same year in which it is added to the consolidated overall foreign loss account).

(iv) *Overall foreign losses that are part of a net operating loss or net capital loss carried over from a separate return limitation year.* Overall foreign losses that are part of a net operating loss or net capital loss carryover from a separate return limitation year of a member that is absorbed in a consolidated return year shall be treated as though they were added to an overall foreign loss account in a separate return limitation year of such member and will be subject to the limitation on recapture of SRLY losses contained in paragraph (b)(1)(iii) of this section. See paragraph (c)(2) of this section for rules regarding the addition of such losses to the applicable overall foreign loss account of such member.

(v) *Special effective date for SRLY limitation.* Except as provided in paragraph (b)(1)(vi) of this section, paragraphs (b)(1)(iii) and (iv) of this section apply only to consolidated return years for which the due date of the income tax return (without extensions) is on or before March 13, 1998. For consolidated return years for which the due date of the income tax return (without extensions) is after March 13, 1998, the rules of paragraph (b)(1)(ii) of this section shall apply to overall foreign losses from separate return years that are separate return limitation years. For purposes of applying paragraph (b)(1)(ii) of this section in such years, the group treats a member with a balance in an overall foreign loss account from a separate return limitation year on the first day of the first consolidated return year for which the due date of the income tax return (without extensions) is after March 13, 1998, as a corporation joining the group on such first day. An overall foreign loss that is part of a net operating loss or net capital loss carryover from a separate return limitation year of a member that is absorbed in a consolidated return year for which the due date of the income tax return (without extensions) is after March 13, 1998, shall be added to the appropriate consolidated overall foreign loss account in the year that it is absorbed. For consolidated return years for which the due date of the income tax return (without extensions) is after March 13, 1998, similar principles apply to overall foreign losses when there has been a consolidated return change of ownership (regardless of when the change of ownership occurred). See also § 1.1502-3(d)(4) for an optional effective date rule

Reg. § 1.1502-9A(b)(1)

(generally making this paragraph (b)(1)(v) applicable to a consolidated return year beginning after December 31, 1996, if the due date of the income tax return (without extensions) for such year is on or before March 13, 1998).

(vi) *Election to defer application of special effective date.* A consolidated group may elect not to apply paragraph (b)(1)(v) of this section to consolidated return years beginning before January 1, 1998. To make this election, a consolidated group must write "Election Pursuant to Notice 98-40" across the top of page 1 of an original or amended tax return for each consolidated return year subject to the election. For the first consolidated return year to which the overall foreign loss provisions of paragraph (b)(1)(v) of this section apply (i.e., the first year beginning on or after January 1, 1998), such consolidated group must write "Notice 98-40 Election in Effect in Prior Years" across the top of page 1 of the consolidated tax return for that year. For purposes of applying paragraph (b)(1)(ii) of this section with respect to such year, any member with a balance in an overall foreign loss account from a separate return limitation year on the first day of such year shall be treated as joining the group on such first day.

(2) *Reductions of the consolidated overall foreign loss accounts*—(i) *Amounts allocated to members leaving the group.* When a member leaves the group, each applicable consolidated overall foreign loss account shall be reduced by the amount allocated from such account to such member in accordance with paragraph (c)(3)(i) of this section.

(ii) *Amounts recaptured.* A consolidated overall foreign loss account shall be reduced by the amount of any overall foreign loss under the same separate limitation that is recaptured from consolidated income in accordance with § 1.904(f)-2.

(c) *Allocation of overall foreign losses among members of an affiliated group*—(1) *Notional overall foreign loss accounts.* Separate notional overall foreign loss accounts shall be established for each member of a group that contributes to a consolidated overall foreign loss account. Additions to and reductions of such notional accounts shall be made when additions or reductions are made to consolidated overall foreign loss accounts in accordance with paragraph (b) of this section and § 1.904(f)-1.

(i) *Additions to notional accounts*—(A) *Consolidated overall foreign losses.* When a consolidated overall foreign loss is added to a consolidated overall foreign loss account, each member shall add its pro rata share of the amount of such loss to the member's notional overall foreign loss account. A member's pro rata share of a consolidated overall foreign loss for any taxable year is determined by multiplying the consolidated loss by a fraction. The numerator of this fraction is the amount by which the member's separate gross income for the taxable year from sources without the United States subject to the applicable separate limitation is exceeded by the sum of the deductions properly allocated and apportioned thereto (including such member's share of any consolidated net operating loss deduction and consolidated net capital loss carryovers and carrybacks to the taxable year), for each member with such deductions in excess of such income. The denominator of this fraction is the sum of the numerators of this fraction for all such members of the group.

(B) *Overall foreign losses from separate return years and separate return limitation years.* When an amount from a member's overall foreign loss account from a separate return year or separate return limitation year is added to a consolidated overall foreign loss account in accordance with paragraph (b)(1)(ii) or (iii) of this section, such amount shall also be added to that member's notional overall foreign loss account for such separate limitation.

(ii) *Reductions of notional accounts.* When a consolidated overall foreign loss account is reduced by recapture, in accordance with paragraph (b)(2)(ii) of this section, each member of the group shall reduce its notional overall foreign loss account for that separate limitation by its pro rata share of the amount by which the consolidated overall foreign loss account is reduced. A member's pro rata share of the amount by which a consolidated overall foreign loss account is reduced is determined by multiplying the amount recaptured by a fraction, the numerator of which is the amount in such member's notional account under such separate limitation, and the denominator of which is the amount in the consolidated overall foreign loss account under such separate limitation before reduction for the amount recaptured for that taxable year.

(2) *Overall foreign losses that are part of a net operating loss or net capital loss from a separate return limitation year.* An overall foreign loss that is part of a net operating loss or net capital loss carryover from a separate return limitation year of a member that is absorbed in a consolidated return year shall be treated as an overall foreign loss of such member (rather than the group) and shall be added to such member's separate overall foreign loss account to the extent it reduces United States source income, in accordance with § 1.904(f)-1(d)(5). Such overall foreign

Reg. § 1.1502-9A(c)(2)

losses shall be added to the appropriate consolidated overall foreign loss account in later years in accordance with paragraph (b)(1)(iii) of this section.

(3) *Allocation of a portion of overall foreign loss accounts to a member leaving the group*—(i) *Consolidated overall foreign losses.* When a corporation ceases to be a member of an affiliated group filing consolidated returns, a portion of the balance in each applicable consolidated overall foreign loss account shall be allocated to such corporation. The amount allocated to such corporation shall be equal to the amount, if any, in such member's notional overall foreign loss account under the same separate limitation.

(ii) *Overall foreign losses from separate return limitation years.* When a corporation ceases to be a member of an affiliated group filing consolidated returns, it shall take with it the remaining portion of each separate overall foreign loss account for overall foreign losses from separate return limitation years (including amounts added to such accounts under paragraph (c)(2) of this section).

(d) *Recapture of consolidated overall foreign losses.* The amount in any consolidated overall foreign loss account shall be recaptured under §§ 1.904(f)-1 through 1.904(f)-6 by recharacterizing consolidated foreign source taxable income subject to the separate limitation under which the loss arose as United States source taxable income. For purposes of recapture, consolidated foreign source taxable income subject to the separate limitation under which the loss arose shall be determined in accordance with §§ 1.904(f)-2 and 1.1502-4. Amounts in a member's excess loss account that are included in income under § 1.1502-19 shall be subject to recapture to the extent that they are included in consolidated foreign source taxable income subject to the separate limitation under which the loss arose.

(e) *Dispositions of property between members of the same affiliated group during a consolidated return year*—(1) *In general.* Except as provided in paragraph (2) with respect to overall foreign losses of a selling member from a separate return limitation year, the rules of § 1.1502-13 with respect to intercompany transactions will apply to dispositions of property to which section 904(f)(3)(A) applies.

(2) *Recapture of overall foreign loss from a separate return limitation year.* Paragraph (1) will not apply and gain will be recognized to the extent that the selling member has a balance in its overall foreign loss account from a separate return limitation year unless the selling member adds the entire amount of its overall foreign loss account from separate return limitation years to the applicable consolidated overall foreign loss account and treats such amount as an overall foreign loss incurred in the previous year. Such loss shall be subject to recapture, in accordance with paragraph (d) of § 1.1502-9, beginning in the same year in which it is added to the consolidated overall foreign loss account.

(f) *Illustrations.* The provisions of this section are illustrated by the following examples. All foreign source income or loss in these examples is subject to the general limitation.

Example (1). A, B, and C are the members of an affiliated group of corporations (as defined in section 1504), and all use the calendar year as their taxable year. For 1983, A, B, and C file a consolidated return. ABC has United States source income of $1,000 and foreign source losses (overall foreign loss) of $400. In accordance with paragraph (b)(1)(i) of this section, ABC adds $400 to its consolidated overall foreign loss account at the end of 1983. For 1983, the separate foreign source taxable income (or loss) of A is $400, of B is ($200), and of C is ($600). Under paragraph (c)(1) of this section, B and C must establish separate notional overall foreign loss accounts. Under paragraph (c)(1)(i)(A) of this section, the amount added to each notional account is the pro rata share of the consolidated overall foreign loss of each member contributing to such loss. The pro rata share is determined by multiplying the consolidated loss by the member's proportionate share of the total foreign source losses of all members having such losses. B's foreign source loss is $200 and C's foreign source loss is $600, totaling $800. B must add $400 × 200/800, or $100, to its notional overall foreign loss account. C must add $400 × 600/800, or $300, to its notional overall foreign loss account.

Example (2). The facts are the same as in example (1). In 1984, ABC has consolidated foreign source taxable income of $200. Under paragraph (d) of this section and § 1.904(f)-2, ABC is required to recapture $100 of the amount in its consolidated overall foreign loss account, which reduces that account by $100 under paragraph (b)(2)(ii) of this section. In accordance with paragraph (c)(1)(ii) of this section, B reduces its notional account by $100 × 100/400, or $25, and C reduces its notional account by $100 × 300/400, or $75. At the end of 1984 ABC has $300 in its consolidated overall foreign loss account, B has $75 in its notional account, and C has $225 in its notional account.

Example (3). D and E are members of an affiliated group and file separate returns using the calendar year as their taxable year for 1980. In

Reg. § 1.1502-9A(c)(3)

1980, D has an overall foreign loss of $200, which it adds to its overall foreign loss account, and E has no overall foreign losses. For 1981, D and E file a consolidated return, and DE must establish a consolidated overall foreign loss account, to which D's overall foreign loss from 1980 is added under paragraph (b)(1)(ii) of this section. D also adds the same amount $200 to its notional account under paragraph (c)(1)(i)(B) of this section. In 1981, DE has consolidated foreign source taxable income of $300. Since the amount added to the consolidated overall foreign loss account in 1981 is treated as a consolidated overall foreign loss from 1980, DE must recapture $150 in 1981 under paragraph (d) of this section and § 1.904(f)-2. DE's consolidated overall foreign loss account is reduced by $150 under paragraph (b)(2)(ii) of this section, and D's notional account is reduced by $150 under paragraph (c)(1)(ii) of this section, leaving balances of $50 in each of those accounts at the end of 1981.

Example (4). F and G are not members of an affiliated group in 1980, and G has an overall foreign loss of $200, which it adds to its overall foreign loss account. F has no overall foreign loss. On January 1, 1981, F acquires G, and FG files a consolidated return for the calendar year 1981. In 1981, F has no foreign source taxable income or loss, and G has $100 of foreign source taxable income. FG's consolidated foreign source taxable income, $100, minus such income without G's items of income and deduction, $0, is $100. Therefore 50% of that amount, $50, of G's overall foreign loss from its 1980 separate return limitation year is added to FG's consolidated overall foreign loss account under paragraph (b)(1)(iii) of this section, and the same amount is added to G's notional account under paragraph (c)(1)(i)(B) of this section. In accordance with paragraph (d) of this section and § 1.904(f)-2, FG must recapture the $50 balance in its consolidated overall foreign loss account in 1981 because the amount added from G's separate return limitation year is treated as a 1980 consolidated overall foreign loss. At the end of 1981, FG has a balance of $0 in its consolidated overall foreign loss account, G has $0 in its notional account, and G also has $150 remaining from its 1980 overall foreign loss that has not yet been added to the consolidated overall foreign loss account.

On January 1, 1982, F sells G and G leaves the affiliated group. Under paragraph (c)(3)(i) of this section, G takes with it the balance in its overall foreign loss account from 1980 (its prior separate return limitation year) that has not been added to the consolidated account. G has $150 of overall foreign loss in its overall foreign loss account. Because the amount in the consolidated overall foreign loss account is zero, no amount from that account is allocated to G.

Example (5). (i) In 1982 corporation H has United States source income of $300 and foreign source losses of $500, resulting in a net operating loss of $200 and a balance in H's overall foreign loss account at the end of 1982 of $300.

(ii) On January 1, 1983, H is acquired by J, and for the calendar year 1983 JH files a consolidated return. JH has consolidated taxable income of $700 in 1983, including a consolidated net operating loss deduction of $100. This net operating loss deduction is $100 of H's $200 net operating loss from 1982 (a separate return limitation year), which is limited by § 1.1502-21A(c). For 1983, H has separate taxable income of $100, comprised of $100 of United States source taxable income and zero foreign source taxable income, and J has separate taxable income of $700, comprised of $700 of United States source taxable income and zero foreign source taxable income. Under paragraph (c)(2) of this section, H adds $100 to its separate overall foreign loss account, since that amount of its net operating loss has reduced United States source income. H has $400 in its separate overall foreign loss account at the end of 1983, none of which has been added to a consolidated overall foreign loss account.

(iii) In 1984, H has separate taxable income of $400, comprised of $100 of United States source taxable income and $300 of foreign source taxable income. J has separate taxable income of $900, comprised of $700 of United States source taxable income and $200 of foreign source taxable income. JH has consolidated taxable income of $1200, which includes $100 of consolidated net operating loss deduction from H's 1982 net operating loss. Since this net operating loss deduction is allocated to foreign source income, it does not reduce United States source income and will not be added to an overall foreign loss account. Under paragraph (b)(1)(iii) of this section, $100 from H's overall foreign loss is added to the consolidated overall foreign loss account computed as follows:

Consolidated foreign source taxable income	$400
Consolidated foreign source taxable income recomputed by excluding H's foreign source income and deductions	−200
	$200
× 50%	$100

Amount from H's separate return limitation year overall foreign loss account added to the consolidated overall foreign loss account

This amount is subject to recapture beginning in the same taxable year, as it is treated as a consolidated overall foreign loss incurred in a previous year. Therefore, under paragraph (d) of this section and § 1.904(f)-2, JH also recaptures this $100, reducing the consolidated overall foreign loss account to $0. H has $300 remaining in its separate overall foreign loss account at the end of 1984.

(iv) In 1985, H has separate taxable income of $400, comprised of $100 of United States source taxable income and $300 of foreign source taxable income. J has separate taxable income of $300 comprised of $600 of United States source taxable income and $300 of foreign source losses. JH has consolidated taxable income of $700, all of which is United States source. Under paragraph (b)(1)(iii) of this section, an additional $150 from H's separate overall foreign loss is added to the consolidated overall foreign loss account, computed as follows:

Consolidated foreign source taxable income	$ 0
Consolidated foreign source taxable income recomputed by excluding H's foreign source income and deductions	– (300)
	$ 300
× 50%	$ 150
Amount from H's separate return limitation year overall foreign loss account added to the consolidated overall foreign loss account	$ 150

Thus, an additional $150 of H's separate overall foreign loss is added to the consolidated overall foreign loss account, and, under paragraph (c)(1)(i)(B) of this section, the same amount is added to J's notional account. While this amount is subject to recapture beginning in the same taxable year, JH has no consolidated foreign source taxable income in 1985, so no overall foreign loss is recaptured. H has a remaining balance of $150 in its separate return limitation year overall foreign loss account and HJ has $150 in its consolidated overall foreign loss account.

Example (6). A, B, and C are members of an affiliated group of corporations (as defined in section 1504), and all use the calendar year as their taxable year. For 1986, A, B, and C file a consolidated return. A has an overall foreign loss account which arose in a separate return limitation year. The amount in the overall foreign loss account is $2,000. A makes a disposition of all its assets to B on January 1, 1986. The gain on the transfer is $1,500, all of which would be recognized under section 904(f)(3). However, if A adds the total amount of its overall foreign loss from separate return limitation years to ABC's consolidated overall foreign loss account, no gain will be recognized on the transfer until the intercompany gain is taken into account under § 1.1502-13. In the interim, any foreign source gain of the purchasing member (or any other member of the consolidated group) may be used to recapture on a consolidated basis the amount in ABC's consolidated overall foreign loss account. [Reg. § 1.1502-9A.]

☐ [T.D. 8153, 8-21-87. *Amended by T.D.* 8597, 7-12-95; *T.D.* 8677, 6-26-96; *T.D.* 8751, 1-9-98; *T.D.* 8766, 3-13-98; *T.D.* 8800, 12-28-98 *and T.D.* 8823, 6-25-99. *Redesignated and amended by T.D.* 8833, 8-10-99. *Amended by T.D.* 8884, 5-24-2000.]

[Reg. § 1.1502-11]

§ 1.1502-11. **Consolidated taxable income.**—
(a) *In general.* The consolidated taxable income for a consolidated return year shall be determined by taking into account—

(1) The separate taxable income of each member of the group (see § 1.1502-12 for the computation of separate taxable income);

(2) Any consolidated net operating loss deduction (see § 1.1502-21 (or 1.1502-21A, as appropriate) for the computation of the consolidated net operating loss deduction);

(3) Any consolidated capital gain net income (net capital gain for taxable years beginning before January 1, 1977) (see § 1.1502-22 (or 1.1502-22A, as appropriate) for the computation of the consolidated capital gain net income (net capital gain for taxable years beginning before January 1, 1977));

(4) Any consolidated section 1231 net loss (see § 1.1502-23 (or 1.1502-23A, as appropriate) for the computation of the consolidated section 1231 net loss);

(5) Any consolidated charitable contributions deduction (see § 1.1502-24 for the computation of the consolidated charitable contributions deduction);

(6) Any consolidated section 922 deduction (see § 1.1502-25 for the computation of the consolidated section 922 deduction);

(7) Any consolidated dividends received deduction (see § 1.1502-26 for the computation of the consolidated dividends received deduction); and

(8) Any consolidated section 247 deduction (see § 1.1502-27 for the computation of the consolidated section 247 deduction).

(b) *Elimination of circular stock basis adjustments*—(1) *In general.* If one member (P) disposes of the stock of another member (S), this paragraph (b) limits the use of S's deductions and losses in the year of disposition and the carryback of items to prior years. The purpose of the limitation is to prevent P's income or gain from the disposition of S's stock from increasing the absorption of S's deductions and losses, because the increased absorption would reduce P's basis (or increase its excess loss account) in S's stock under § 1.1502-32 and, in turn, increase P's income or gain. See paragraph (b)(3) of this section for the application of these principles to P's deduction or loss from the disposition of S's stock, and paragraph (b)(4) of this section for the application of these principles to multiple stock dispositions. See § 1.1502-19(c) for the definition of disposition.

(2) *Limitation on deductions and losses*—(i) *Determination of amount of limitation.* If P disposes of one or more shares of S's stock, the extent to which S's deductions and losses for the tax year of the disposition (and its deductions and losses carried over from prior years) may offset income and gain is subject to limitation. The amount of S's deductions and losses that may offset income and gain is determined by tentatively computing taxable income (or loss) for the year of disposition (and any prior years to which the deductions or losses may be carried) without taking into account P's income and gain from the disposition.

(ii) *Application of limitation.* S's deductions and losses offset income and gain only to the extent of the amount determined under paragraph (b)(2)(i) of this section. To the extent S's deductions and losses in the year of disposition cannot offset income or gain because of the limitation under this paragraph (b), the items are carried to other years under the applicable provisions of the Internal Revenue Code and regulations as if they were the only items incurred by S in the year of disposition. For example, to the extent S incurs an operating loss in the year of disposition that is limited, the loss is treated as a separate net operating loss attributable to S arising in that year. The tentative computation does not affect the manner in which S's unlimited deductions and losses are absorbed or the manner in which deductions and losses of other members are absorbed. (If the amount of S's unlimited deductions and losses actually absorbed is less than the amount absorbed in the tentative computation, P's stock basis adjustments under § 1.1502-32 reflect only the amounts actually absorbed.)

(iii) *Examples.* For purposes of the examples in this paragraph (b), unless otherwise stated, P owns all of the only class of S's stock for the entire year, S owns no stock of lower-tier members, the tax year of all persons is the calendar year, all persons use the accrual method of accounting, the facts set forth the only corporate activity, all transactions are between unrelated persons, and tax liabilities are disregarded. The principles of this paragraph (b)(2) are illustrated by the following examples.

Example 1. Limitation on losses with respect to stock gain. (a) P has a $500 basis in S's stock. For Year 1, P has ordinary income of $30 (determined without taking P's gain or loss from the disposition of S's stock into account) and S has an $80 ordinary loss. P sells S's stock for $520 at the close of Year 1.

(b) To determine the amount of the limitation on S's loss under paragraph (b)(2)(i) of this section, and the effect under § 1.1502-32(b) of the absorption of S's loss on P's basis in S's stock, P's gain or loss from the disposition of S's stock is not taken into account. The group is tentatively treated as having a consolidated net operating loss of $50 (P's $30 of income minus S's $80 loss). Thus, $50 of S's loss is limited under this paragraph (b).

(c) Because $30 of S's loss is absorbed in the determination of consolidated taxable income under paragraph (b)(2)(ii) of this section, P's basis in S's stock is reduced under § 1.1502-32(b) from $500 to $470 immediately before the disposition. Consequently, P recognizes a $50 gain from the sale of S's stock and the group has consolidated taxable income of $50 for Year 1 (P's $30 of ordinary income and $50 gain from the sale of S's stock, less the $30 of S's loss). In addition, S's limited loss of $50 is treated as a separate net operating loss attributable to S and, because S ceases to be a member, the loss is apportioned to S under § 1.1502-21 (or § 1.1502-79A, as appropriate) and carried to its first separate return year.

Reg. § 1.1502-11(b)(2)

Example 2. Carrybacks and carryovers. (a) For Year 1, the P group has consolidated taxable income of $30, and a consolidated net capital loss of $100 ($50 attributable to P and $50 to S). At the beginning of Year 2, P has a $300 basis in S's stock. For Year 2, P has ordinary income of $30, and a $20 capital gain (determined without taking the $100 consolidated net capital loss carryover or P's gain or loss from the disposition of S's stock into account), and S has a $100 ordinary loss. P sells S's stock for $280 at the close of Year 2.

(b) To determine the amount of the limitation under paragraph (b)(2)(i) of this section on S's losses, and the effect of the absorption of S's losses on P's basis in S's stock under § 1.1502-32(b), P's gain or loss from the disposition of S's stock is not taken into account. For Year 2, the P group is tentatively treated as having a $70 consolidated net operating loss (S's $100 ordinary loss, less P's $30 of ordinary income). The P group is also treated as having no consolidated net capital gain in Year 2, because P's $20 capital gain is reduced by $20 of the consolidated net capital loss carryover from Year 1 under section 1212(a) (the absorption of which is attributed equally to P and S). In addition, of the $70 consolidated net operating loss, $30 is carried back to Year 1 and offsets P's ordinary income in that year, and $40 is carried forward. Consequently, $40 of S's operating loss from Year 2, and $40 of the consolidated net capital loss carryover from Year 1 attributable to S, are limited under this paragraph (b).

(c) Under paragraph (b)(2)(ii) of this section, the limitation under this paragraph (b) does not affect the absorption of any deductions and losses attributable to P, $60 of S's operating loss from Year 2, and $10 of the consolidated net capital loss from Year 1 attributable to S. Consequently, P's basis in S's stock is reduced under § 1.1502-32(b) by $70, from $300 to $230, and P recognizes a $50 gain from the sale of S's stock in Year 2. Thus, the P group is treated as having a $20 unlimited net operating loss that is carried back to Year 1:

Ordinary income:	
P	$ 30
S (excluding the $40 limited loss)	(60)
Sub Total	$(30)
Consolidated net capital gain:	
P ($20 + $50 from S stock − $50 from Year 1)	$ 20
S (−$10 from Year 1)	(10)
Sub Total	$ 10
Consolidated taxable income	$(20)

(d) Under paragraph (b)(2)(ii) of this section, S's $40 ordinary loss from Year 2 that is limited under this paragraph (b) is treated as a separate net operating loss arising in Year 2. Similarly, $40 of the consolidated net capital loss from Year 1 attributable to S is treated as a separate net capital loss carried over from Year 1. Because S ceases to be a member, the $40 net operating loss from Year 2 and the $40 consolidated net capital loss from Year 1 are allocated to S under §§ 1.1502-21 and 1.1502-22, respectively (or § 1.1502-79A, as appropriate) and are carried to S's first separate return year.

Example 3. Allocation of basis adjustments. (a) For Year 1, the P group has consolidated taxable income of $100. At the beginning of Year 2, P has a $40 basis in each of the 10 shares of S's stock. For Year 2, P has an $80 ordinary loss (determined without taking into account P's gain or loss from the disposition of S's stock) and S has an $80 ordinary loss. P sells 2 shares of S's stock for $85 each at the close of Year 2.

(b) Under paragraph (b)(2)(i) of this section, the amount of the limitation on S's loss is determined by tentatively treating the P group as having a $160 consolidated net operating loss for Year 2. Of this amount, $100 is carried back under section 172 and absorbed in Year 1 ($50 attributable to S and $50 attributable to P). Consequently, $30 of S's loss is limited under this paragraph (b).

(c) Under paragraph (b)(2)(ii) of this section, the limitation under this paragraph (b) does not affect the absorption of P's $80 ordinary loss or $50 of S's ordinary loss. Consequently, P's basis in each share of S's stock is reduced from $40 to $35 under § 1.1502-32(b), and P recognizes a $100 gain from the sale of the 2 shares. Thus, the P group is treated as having a $30 unlimited net operating loss:

Reg. § 1.1502-11(b)(2)

Ordinary loss:
P .... $ (80)
S (excluding the $30 limited loss) .... (50)

Sub Total .... $(130)

Consolidated net capital gain:
P .... $ 100
S 0

Sub Total .... $ 100
Unlimited consolidated net operating loss .... $ (30)

(d) A portion of the $130 of unlimited operating losses for Year 2 is fully absorbed in that year, and a portion is carried back to Year 1. Thus, $61.50 of P's $80 loss ($100 multiplied by $80/$130) and $38.50 of S's $50 unlimited loss ($100 multiplied by $50/$130) are absorbed in Year 2. P's remaining $18.50 of loss and S's remaining $11.50 of loss are not subject to limitation and are carried back and absorbed in Year 1.

(e) Under paragraph (b)(2)(ii) of this section, S's $30 of loss limited under this paragraph (b) is treated as a separate net operating loss.

(3) *Loss dispositions*—(i) *General rule.* The principles of paragraph (b)(2) of this section apply to the extent necessary to carry out the purposes of paragraph (b)(1) of this section if P recognizes a deduction or loss from the disposition of S's stock.

(ii) *Example.* The principles of this paragraph (b)(3) are illustrated by the following example.

Example. (a) P has a $400 basis in S's stock. For Year 1, P has a capital gain of $100 (determined without taking P's gain or loss from the disposition of S's stock into account) and S has both a $60 capital loss and a $200 ordinary loss. P sells S's stock for $140 at the close of Year 1.

(b) Under paragraph (b)(3) of this section, the amount of S's ordinary and capital losses that may offset income and gain is determined by tentatively computing the group's consolidated net operating loss and consolidated net capital loss without taking into account P's loss from the disposition of S's stock. The limitation is necessary to prevent P's loss from the disposition of S's stock from affecting the absorption of S's losses and thereby the adjustments to P's basis in S's stock under § 1.1502-32(b) (which would, in turn, affect P's loss).

(c) Under the principles of paragraph (b)(2)(i) of this section, the amount of the limitation on S's loss is determined by tentatively treating the P group as having a $40 consolidated net capital gain and a $200 ordinary loss, which results in a $160 consolidated net operating loss for Year 1, all of which is attributable to S. Thus, $160 of S's ordinary loss is limited under this paragraph (b). See also § 1.1502-20 for rules applicable to losses from the sale of stock of subsidiaries.

(4) *Multiple dispositions*—(i) *Stock of a member.* To the extent income, gain, deduction, or loss from a prior disposition of S's stock is deferred under any rule of law, the limitation under paragraph (b)(2) of this section is determined by treating the year the deferred amount is taken into account as the year of the disposition.

(ii) *Stock of different members.* If S is a higher-tier corporation with respect to another member (T), and all of T's items of income, gain, deduction, and loss (including the absorption of T's deduction or loss) would be fully reflected in P's basis in S's stock under § 1.1502-32, the limitation under paragraph (b)(2)(i) of this section with respect to T's deductions and losses is determined without taking into account any income, gain, deduction, or loss from the disposition of the stock of S or T (or of the stock of members owned in the chain connecting S and T). However, this paragraph (b) does not otherwise limit the absorption of one member's deduction or loss with respect to the disposition of another member's stock.

(iii) *Examples.* The principles of this paragraph (b)(4) are illustrated by the following examples.

Example 1. Chain of subsidiaries. (a) P owns all of S's stock with a $500 basis, and S owns all of T's stock with a $500 basis. For Year 1, P has ordinary income of $30, S has no income or loss, and T has an $80 ordinary loss. P sells S's stock for $520 at the close of Year 1.

(b) Under paragraph (b)(4) of this section, to determine the amount of the limitation under paragraph (b) of this section on T's loss, and the effect of the absorption of T's loss on P's basis in S's stock under § 1.1502-32(b), P's gain or loss from the disposition of S's stock is not taken into account. The group is tentatively treated as having a consolidated net operating loss of $50 (P's $30 of income minus T's $80 loss). Because only $30 of T's loss offsets income or gain, P's basis in S's stock is reduced under § 1.1502-32(b) from $500 to $470 immediately before the disposition

Reg. § 1.1502-11(b)(4)

of S's stock. Thus, P takes into account a $50 gain from the sale of S's stock.

(c) The facts are the same as in paragraph (a) of this *Example 1*, except that S has a $10 excess loss account in T's stock (rather than a $500 basis). Under paragraph (b)(4) of this section, neither P's gain or loss from the disposition of S's stock nor S's gain or loss from the disposition of T's stock (under § 1.1502-19) are taken into account for purposes of the tentative computations and the effect of any absorption under § 1.1502-32(b) on P's basis in S's stock and S's excess loss account in T's stock. The group is tentatively treated as having a consolidated net operating loss of $50 (P's $30 of income minus T's $80 loss), and only $30 of T's loss may offset the group's income or gain. Under § 1.1502-32(b), the absorption of $30 of T's loss increases S's excess loss account in T's stock to $40 and, under § 1.1502-19, the excess loss account is taken into account. Moreover, under § 1.1502-32(b), P's basis in S's stock is increased immediately before the sale by $10 (S's $40 gain under § 1.1502-19(b) minus T's $30 loss absorbed and tiered up under § 1.1502-32(b)), from $500 to $510. Thus, P takes into account a $10 gain from the sale of S's stock, and S takes into account a $40 gain from its excess loss account in T's stock.

Example 2. Brother-sister subsidiaries. (a) P owns all of the stock of S1 and S2, each with a $50 basis. For Year 1, the group has a $100 consolidated net operating loss ($50 of which is attributable to S1, and $50 to S2) determined without taking gain or loss from the disposition of member stock into account. At the close of Year 1, P sells the stock of S1 and S2 for $100 each.

(b) Paragraph (b)(4) of this section does not limit the loss of S1 or S2 with respect to the disposition of stock of the other. Consequently, each subsidiary's loss may offset P's gain from the disposition of the stock of the other subsidiary. Because this absorption results in a $50 reduction in P's basis in the stock of each subsidiary under § 1.1502-32(b), P's aggregate gain from the stock dispositions is increased from $100 to $200, $100 of which is offset by the losses of the subsidiaries.

(5) *Effective date.* This paragraph (b) applies to stock dispositions occurring in consolidated return years beginning on or after January 1, 1995. For prior years, see § 1.1502-11(b) as contained in the 26 CFR part 1 edition revised as of April 1, 1994.

(c) *Disallowance of loss attributable to pre-1966 distributions.* No loss shall be allowed upon the sale or other disposition of stock, bonds, or other obligations of a member or former member to the extent that such loss is attributable to a distribution made in an affiliated year beginning before January 1, 1966, out of earnings and profits accumulated before the distributing corporation became a member. [Reg. § 1.1502-11.]

☐ [T.D. 6894, 9-7-66. Amended by T.D. 7246, 12-29-72; T.D. 7728, 10-31-80; T.D. 8560, 8-12-94; T.D. 8677, 6-26-96 and T.D. 8823, 6-25-99.]

[Reg. § 1.1502-12]

§ 1.1502-12. **Separate taxable income.**—The separate taxable income of a member (including a case in which deductions exceed gross income) is computed in accordance with the provisions of the Code covering the determination of taxable income of separate corporations, subject to the following modifications:

(a) Transactions between members and transactions with respect to stock, bonds, or other obligations of members shall be reflected according to the provisions of § 1.1502-13;

(b) Any deduction which is disallowed under §§ 1.1502-15A or 1.1502-15 shall be taken into account as provided in those sections;

(c) The limitation on deductions provided in section 615(c) or section 617(h) shall be taken into account as provided in § 1.1502-16;

(d) The method of accounting under which such computation is made and the adjustments to be made because of any change in method of accounting shall be determined under § 1.1502-17;

(e) Inventory adjustments shall be made as provided in § 1.1502-18;

(f) Any amount included in income under § 1.1502-19 shall be taken into account;

(g) In the computation of the deduction under section 167, property shall not lose its character as new property as a result of a transfer from one member to another member during a consolidated return year if—

(1) The transfer occurs on or before January 4, 1973, or

(2) The transfer occurs after January 4, 1973, and the transfer is an intercompany transaction as defined in § 1.1502-13 or the basis of the property in the hands of the transferee is determined (in whole or in part) by reference to its basis in the hands of the transferor;

(h) No net operating loss deduction shall be taken into account;

(i) [Reserved]

(j) No capital gains or losses shall be taken into account;

(k) No gains and losses subject to section 1231 shall be taken into account;

Reg. § 1.1502-12(a)

(l) No deduction under section 170 with respect to charitable contributions shall be taken into account;

(m) No deduction under section 922 (relating to the deduction for Western Hemisphere trade corporations) shall be taken into account;

(n) No deductions under section 243(a)(1), 244(a), 245, or 247 (relating to deductions with respect to dividends received and dividends paid) shall be taken into account;

(o) Basis shall be determined under §§ 1.1502-31 and 1.1502-32, and earnings and profits shall be determined under § 1.1502-33; and

(p) The limitation on deductions provided in section 613A shall be taken into account for each member's oil and gas properties as provided in § 1.1502-44.

(q) A thrift institution's deduction under section 593(b)(2) (relating to the addition to the reserve for bad debts of a thrift institution under the percentage of taxable income method) shall be determined under § 1.1502-42.

The term "separate taxable income" shall include a case in which the determination under this section results in an excess of deductions over gross income.

(r) For rules relating to loss disallowance or basis reduction on the disposition or deconsolidation of stock of a subsidiary, see §§ 1.337(d)-1, 1.337(d)-2 and 1.1502-20. [Reg. § 1.1502-12.]

☐ [T.D. 6894, 9-7-66. Amended by T.D. 7192, 6-29-72; T.D. 7246, 12-29-72; T.D. 7725, 9-30-80; T.D. 7876, 3-14-83; T.D. 8294, 3-9-90; T.D. 8319, 11-19-90; T.D. 8364, 9-13-91; T.D. 8597, 7-12-95; T.D. 8677, 6-26-96 and T.D. 8823, 6-25-99.]

→ *Caution: Prior law may apply to certain transactions, see Reg. § 1.1502-13(l)(1), below. For Reg. § 1.1502-13 prior to revision by T.D. 8597, see Caution Note and text following this version of Reg. § 1.1502-13.*←

[Reg. § 1.1502-13]

§ 1.1502-13. **Intercompany transactions.**—(a) *In general*—(1) *Purpose.* This section provides rules for taking into account items of income, gain, deduction, and loss of members from intercompany transactions. The purpose of this section is to provide rules to clearly reflect the taxable income (and tax liability) of the group as a whole by preventing intercompany transactions from creating, accelerating, avoiding, or deferring consolidated taxable income (or consolidated tax liability).

(2) *Separate entity and single entity treatment.* Under this section, the selling member (S) and the buying member (B) are treated as separate entities for some purposes but as divisions of a single corporation for other purposes. The *amount* and *location* of S's intercompany items and B's corresponding items are determined on a separate entity basis (separate entity treatment). For example, S determines its gain or loss from a sale of property to B on a separate entity basis, and B has a cost basis in the property. The *timing,* and the *character, source,* and other *attributes* of the intercompany items and corresponding items, although initially determined on a separate entity basis, are redetermined under this section to produce the effect of transactions between divisions of a single corporation (single entity treatment). For example, if S sells land to B at a gain and B sells the land to a nonmember, S does not take its gain into account until B's sale to the nonmember.

(3) *Timing rules as a method of accounting*—(i) *In general.* The timing rules of this section are a method of accounting for intercompany transactions, to be applied by each member in addition to the member's other methods of accounting. See § 1.1502-17. To the extent the timing rules of this section are inconsistent with a member's otherwise applicable methods of accounting, the timing rules of this section control. For example, if S sells property to B in exchange for B's note, the timing rules of this section apply instead of the installment sale rules of section 453. S's or B's application of the timing rules of this section to an intercompany transaction clearly reflects income only if the effect of that transaction as a whole (including, for example, related costs and expenses) on consolidated taxable income is clearly reflected.

(ii) *Automatic consent for joining and departing members*—(A) *Consent granted.* Section 446(e) consent is granted under this section to the extent a change in method of accounting is necessary solely by reason of the timing rules of this section—

(*1*) For each member, with respect to its intercompany transactions, in the first consolidated return year which follows a separate return year and in which the member engages in an intercompany transaction; and

(*2*) For each former member, with respect to its transactions with members that would otherwise be intercompany transactions if the former member were still a member, in the

Reg. § 1.1502-13(a)(3)

→ **Caution: Prior law may apply to certain transactions, see Reg. § 1.1502-13(l)(1), below. For Reg. § 1.1502-13 prior to revision by T.D. 8597, see Caution Note and text following this version of Reg. § 1.1502-13.**←

first separate return year in which the former member engages in such a transaction.

(B) *Cut-off basis.* Any change in method of accounting described in paragraph (a)(3)(ii)(A) of this section is to be effected on a cut-off basis for transactions entered into on or after the first day of the year for which consent is granted under paragraph (a)(3)(ii)(A) of this section.

(4) *Other law.* The rules of this section apply in addition to other applicable law (including nonstatutory authorities). For example, this section applies in addition to sections 267(f) (additional rules for certain losses), 269 (acquisitions to evade or avoid income tax), and 482 (allocations among commonly controlled taxpayers). Thus, an item taken into account under this section can be deferred, disallowed, or eliminated under other applicable law, for example, section 1091 (losses from wash sales).

(5) *References.* References in other sections to this section include, as appropriate, references to prior law. For effective dates and prior law see paragraph (l) of this section.

(6) *Overview*—(i) *In general.* The principal rules of this section that implement single entity treatment are the matching rule and the acceleration rule of paragraphs (c) and (d) of this section. Under the matching rule, S and B are generally treated as divisions of a single corporation for purposes of taking into account their items from intercompany transactions. The acceleration rule provides additional rules for taking the items into account if the effect of treating S and B as divisions cannot be achieved (for example, if S or B becomes a nonmember). Paragraph (b) of this section provides definitions. Paragraph (e) of this section provides simplifying rules for certain transactions. Paragraphs (f) and (g) of this section provide additional rules for stock and obligations of members. Paragraphs (h) and (j) of this section provide anti-avoidance rules and miscellaneous operating rules.

(ii) *Table of examples.* Set forth below is a table of the examples contained in this section.

Matching rule. (§ 1.1502-13(c)(7)(ii))
    Example 1. Intercompany sale of land.
    Example 2. Dealer activities.
    Example 3. Intercompany section 351 transfer.
    Example 4. Depreciable property.
    Example 5. Intercompany sale followed by installment sale.
    Example 6. Intercompany sale of installment obligation.
    Example 7. Performance of services.
    Example 8. Rental of property.
    Example 9. Intercompany sale of a partnership interest.
    Example 10. Net operating losses subject to section 382 or the SRLY rules.
    Example 11. Section 475.
    Example 12. Section 1092.
    Example 13. Manufacturer incentive payments.
    Example 14. Source of income under section 863.
    Example 15. Section 1248.

Acceleration rule. (§ 1.1502-13(d)(3))
    Example 1. Becoming a nonmember—timing.
    Example 2. Becoming a nonmember—attributes.
    Example 3. Selling member's disposition of installment note.
    Example 4. Cancellation of debt and attribute reduction under section 108(b).
    Example 5. Section 481.

Simplifying rules—inventory. (§ 1.1502-13(e)(1)(v))
    Example 1. Increment averaging method.
    Example 2. Increment valuation method.
    Example 3. Other reasonable inventory methods.

Stock of members. (§ 1.1502-13(f)(7))
    Example 1. Dividend exclusion and property distribution.
    Example 2. Excess loss accounts.
    Example 3. Intercompany reorganization.
    Example 4. Stock redemptions and distributions.
    Example 5. Intercompany stock sale followed by section 332 liquidation.
    Example 6. Intercompany stock sale followed by section 355 distribution.

Reg. § 1.1502-13(a)(4)

Consolidated Returns

→ **Caution:** *Prior law may apply to certain transactions, see Reg. § 1.1502-13(l)(1), below. For Reg. § 1.1502-13 prior to revision by T.D. 8597, see Caution Note and text following this version of Reg. § 1.1502-13.*←

Obligations of members. (§ 1.1502-13(g)(5))
    Example 1. Interest on intercompany debt.
    Example 2. Intercompany debt becomes nonintercompany debt.
    Example 3. Loss or bad debt deduction with respect to intercompany debt.
    Example 4. Nonintercompany debt becomes intercompany debt.
    Example 5. Notional principal contracts.

Anti-avoidance rules. (§ 1.1502-13(h)(2))
    Example 1. Sale of a partnership interest.
    Example 2. Transitory status as an intercompany obligation.
    Example 3. Corporate mixing bowl.
    Example 4. Partnership mixing bowl.
    Example 5. Sale and leaseback.

Miscellaneous operating rules. (§ 1.1502-13(j)(9))
    Example 1. Intercompany sale followed by section 351 transfer to member.
    Example 2. Intercompany sale of member stock followed by recapitalization.
    Example 3. Back-to-back intercompany transactions—matching.
    Example 4. Back-to-back intercompany transactions—acceleration.
    Example 5. Successor group.
    Example 6. Liquidation—80% distributee.
    Example 7. Liquidation—no 80% distributee.

(b) *Definitions.* For purposes of this section—

(1) *Intercompany transactions*—(i) *In general.* An intercompany transaction is a transaction between corporations that are members of the same consolidated group immediately after the transaction. S is the member transferring property or providing services, and B is the member receiving the property or services. Intercompany transactions include—

    (A) S's sale of property (or other transfer, such as an exchange or contribution) to B, whether or not gain or loss is recognized;

    (B) S's performance of services for B, and B's payment or accrual of its expenditure for S's performance;

    (C) S's licensing of technology, rental of property, or loan of money to B, and B's payment or accrual of its expenditure; and

    (D) S's distribution to B with respect to S stock.

(ii) *Time of transaction.* If a transaction occurs in part while S and B are members and in part while they are not members, the transaction is treated as occurring when performance by either S or B takes place, or when payment for performance would be taken into account under the rules of this section if it were an intercompany transaction, whichever is earliest. Appropriate adjustments must be made in such cases by, for example, dividing the transaction into two separate transactions reflecting the extent to which S or B has performed.

(iii) *Separate transactions.* Except as otherwise provided in this section, each transaction is analyzed separately. For example, if S simultaneously sells two properties to B, one at a gain and the other at a loss, each property is treated as sold in a separate transaction. Thus, the gain and loss cannot be offset or netted against each other for purposes of this section. Similarly, each payment or accrual of interest on a loan is a separate transaction. In addition, an accrual of premium is treated as a separate transaction, or as an offset to interest that is not a separate transaction, to the extent required under separate entity treatment. If two members exchange property, each member is S with respect to the property it transfers and B with respect to the property it receives. If two members enter into a notional principal contract, each payment under the contract is a separate transaction and the member making the payment is B with respect to that payment and the member receiving the payment is S. See paragraph (j)(4) of this section for rules aggregating certain transactions.

(2) *Intercompany items*—(i) *In general.* S's income, gain, deduction, and loss from an intercompany transaction are its intercompany items. For example, S's gain from the sale of property to B is intercompany gain. An item is an intercompany item whether it is directly or indirectly from an intercompany transaction.

(ii) *Related costs or expenses.* S's costs or expenses related to an intercompany transaction are included in determining its intercompany items. For example, if S sells inventory to B, S's direct and indirect costs properly includible under section 263A are included in determining its intercompany income. similarly, related costs or expenses that are not capitalized under S's separate entity method of accounting are included in deter-

Reg. § 1.1502-13(b)(2)

→ **Caution:** *Prior law may apply to certain transactions, see Reg. § 1.1502-13(l)(1), below. For Reg. § 1.1502-13 prior to revision by T.D. 8597, see Caution Note and text following this version of Reg. § 1.1502-13.*←

mining its intercompany items. For example, deductions for employee wages, in addition to other related costs, are included in determining S's intercompany items from performing services for B, and depreciation deductions are included in determining S's intercompany items from renting property to B.

(iii) *Amounts not yet recognized or incurred.* S's intercompany items include amounts from an intercompany transaction that are not yet taken into account under its separate entity method of accounting. For example, if S is a cash method taxpayer, S's intercompany income might be taken into account under this section even if the cash is not yet received. Similarly, an amount reflected in basis (or an amount equivalent to basis) under S's separate entity method of accounting that is a substitute for income, gain, deduction or loss from an intercompany transaction is an intercompany item.

(3) *Corresponding items*—(i) *In general.* B's income, gain, deduction, and loss from an intercompany transaction, or from property acquired in an intercompany transaction, are its corresponding items. For example, if B pays rent to S, B's deduction for the rent is a corresponding deduction. If B buys property from S and sells it to a nonmember, B's gain or loss from the sale to the nonmember is a corresponding gain or loss; alternatively, if B recovers the cost of the property through depreciation, B's depreciation deductions are corresponding deductions. An item is a corresponding item whether it is directly or indirectly from an intercompany transaction (or from property acquired in an intercompany transaction).

(ii) *Disallowed or eliminated amounts.* B's corresponding items include amounts that are permanently disallowed or permanently eliminated, whether directly or indirectly. Thus, corresponding items include amounts disallowed under section 265 (expenses relating to tax-exempt income), and amounts not recognized under section 311(a) (nonrecognition of loss on distributions), section 332 (nonrecognition on liquidating distributions), or section 355(c) (certain distributions of stock of a subsidiary). On the other hand, an amount is not permanently disallowed or permanently eliminated (and therefore is not a corresponding item) to the extent it is not recognized in a transaction in which B receives a successor asset within the meaning of paragraph (j)(1) of this section. For example, B's corresponding items do not include amounts not recognized from a transaction with a nonmember to which section 1031 applies or from another transaction in which B receives exchanged basis property.

(4) *Recomputed corresponding items.* The recomputed corresponding item is the corresponding item that B would take into account if S and B were divisions of a single corporation and the intercompany transaction were between those divisions. For example, if S sells property with a $70 basis to B for $100, and B later sells the property to a nonmember for $90, B's corresponding item is its $10 loss, and the recomputed corresponding item is $20 of gain (determined by comparing the $90 sales price with the $70 basis the property would have if S and B were divisions of a single corporation). Although neither S nor B actually takes the recomputed corresponding item into account, it is computed as if B did take it into account (based on reasonable and consistently applied assumptions, including any provision of the Internal Revenue Code or regulations that would affect its timing or attributes).

(5) *Treatment as a separate entity.* Treatment as a separate entity means treatment without application of the rules of this section, but with the application of the other consolidated return regulations. For example, if S sells the stock of another member to B, S's gain or loss on a separate entity basis is determined with the application of § 1.1502-80(b) (non-applicability of section 304), but without redetermination under paragraph (c) or (d) of this section.

(6) *Attributes.* The attributes of an intercompany item or corresponding item are all of the item's characteristics, except *amount, location,* and *timing,* necessary to determine the item's effect on taxable income (and tax liability). For example, attributes include character, source, treatment as excluded from gross income or as a noncapital, nondeductible amount, and treatment as built-in gain or loss under section 382(h) or 384. In contrast, the characteristics of property, such as a member's holding period, or the fact that property is included in inventory, are not attributes of an item, but these characteristics might affect the determination of the attributes of items from the property.

(c) *Matching rule.* For each consolidated return year, B's corresponding items and S's intercompany items are taken into account under the following rules:

(1) *Attributes and holding periods*—(i) *Attributes.* The separate entity attributes of S's in-

Reg. § 1.1502-13(b)(3)

→ **Caution:** *Prior law may apply to certain transactions, see Reg. § 1.1502-13(l)(1), below. For Reg. § 1.1502-13 prior to revision by T.D. 8597, see Caution Note and text following this version of Reg. § 1.1502-13.*←

tercompany items and B's corresponding items are redetermined to the extent necessary to produce the same effect on consolidated taxable income (and consolidated tax liability) as if S and B were divisions of a single corporation, and the intercompany transaction were a transaction between divisions. Thus, the activities of both S and B might affect the attributes of both intercompany items and corresponding items. For example, if S holds property for sale to unrelated customers in the ordinary course of its trade or business, S sells the property to B at a gain and B sells the property to an unrelated person at a further gain, S's intercompany gain and B's corresponding gain might be ordinary because of S's activities with respect to the property. Similar principles apply if S performs services, rents property, or engages in any other intercompany transaction.

(ii) *Holding periods.* The holding period of property transferred in an intercompany transaction is the aggregate of the holding periods of S and B. However, if the basis of the property is determined by reference to the basis of other property, the property's holding period is determined by reference to the holding period of the other property. For example, if S distributes stock to B in a transaction to which section 355 applies, B's holding period in the distributed stock is determined by reference to B's holding period in the stock of S.

(2) *Timing*—(i) *B's items.* B takes its corresponding items into account under its accounting method, but the redetermination of the attributes of a corresponding item might affect its timing. For example, if B's sale of property acquired from S is treated as a dealer disposition because of S's activities, section 453(b) prevents any corresponding income of B from being taken into account under the installment method.

(ii) *S's items.* S takes its intercompany item into account to reflect the difference for the year between B's corresponding item taken into account and the recomputed corresponding item.

(3) *Divisions of a single corporation.* As divisions of a single corporation, S and B are treated as engaging in their actual transaction and owning any actual property involved in the transaction (rather than treating the transaction as not occurring). For example, S's sale of land held for investment to B for cash is not disregarded, but is treated as an exchange of land for cash between divisions (and B therefore succeeds to S's basis in the property). Similarly, S's issuance of its own stock to B in exchange for property is not disregarded, B is treated as owning the stock it receives in the exchange, and section 1032 does not apply to B on its subsequent sale of the S stock. Although treated as divisions, S and B nevertheless are treated as:

(i) Operating separate trades or businesses. See, e.g., § 1.446-1(d) (accounting methods for a taxpayer engaged in more than one business).

(ii) Having any special status that they have under the Internal Revenue Code or regulations. For example, a bank defined in section 581, a domestic building and loan association defined in section 7701(a)(19), and an insurance company to which section 801 or 831 applies are treated as divisions having separate special status. On the other hand, the fact that a member holds property for sale to customers in the ordinary course of its trade or business is not a special status.

(4) *Conflict or allocation of attributes.* This paragraph (c)(4) provides special rules for redetermining and allocating attributes under paragraph (c)(1)(i) of this section.

(i) *Offsetting amounts*—(A) *In general.* To the extent B's corresponding item offsets S's intercompany item in amount, the attributes of B's corresponding item, determined based on both S's and B's activities, control the attributes of S's offsetting intercompany item. For example, if S sells depreciable property to B at a gain and B depreciates the property, the attributes of B's depreciation deduction (ordinary deduction) control the attributes of S's offsetting intercompany gain. Accordingly, S's gain is ordinary.

(B) *B controls unreasonable.* To the extent the results under paragraph (c)(4)(i)(A) are inconsistent with treating S and B as divisions of a single corporation, the attributes of the offsetting items must be redetermined in a manner consistent with treating S and B as divisions of a single corporation. To the extent, however, that B's corresponding item on a separate entity basis is excluded from gross income, is a noncapital, nondeductible amount, or is otherwise permanently disallowed or eliminated, the attributes of B's corresponding item always control the attributes of S's offsetting intercompany item.

(ii) *Allocation.* To the extent S's intercompany item and B's corresponding item do not offset in amount, the attributes redetermined under paragraph (c)(1)(i) of this section must be allocated to S's intercompany item and B's corresponding item by using a method that is reasona-

Reg. § 1.1502-13(c)(4)

→ **Caution:** *Prior law may apply to certain transactions, see Reg. § 1.1502-13(l)(1), below. For Reg. § 1.1502-13 prior to revision by T.D. 8597, see Caution Note and text following this version of Reg. § 1.1502-13.* ←

ble in light of all the facts and circumstances, including the purposes of this section and any other rule affected by the attributes of S's intercompany item and B's corresponding item. A method of allocation or redetermination is unreasonable if it is not used consistently by all members of the group from year to year.

(5) *Special status.* Notwithstanding the general rule of paragraph (c)(1)(i) of this section, to the extent an item's attributes determined under this section are permitted or not permitted to a member under the Internal Revenue Code or regulations by reason of the member's special status, the attributes required under the Internal Revenue Code or regulations apply to that member's items (but not the other member). For example, if S is a bank to which section 582(c) applies, and sells debt securities at a gain to B, a nonbank, the character of S's intercompany gain is ordinary as required under section 582(c), but the character of B's corresponding item as capital or ordinary is determined under paragraph (c)(1)(i) of this section without the application of section 582(c). For other special status issues, see, for example, sections 595(b) (foreclosure on property securing loans), 818(b) (life insurance company treatment of capital gains and losses), and 1503(c) (limitation on absorption of certain losses).

(6) *Treatment of intercompany items if corresponding items are excluded or nondeductible—* (i) *In general.* Under paragraph (c)(1)(i) of this section, S's intercompany item might be redetermined to be excluded from gross income or treated as a noncapital, nondeductible amount. For example, S's intercompany loss from the sale of property to B is treated as a noncapital, nondeductible amount if B distributes the property to a nonmember shareholder at no further gain or loss (because, if S and B were divisions of a single corporation, the loss would not have been recognized under section 311(a)). Paragraph (c)(6)(ii) of this section, however, provides limitations on the application of this rule to intercompany income or gain. See also §§ 1.1502-32 and 1.1502-33 (adjustments to S's stock basis and earnings and profits to reflect amounts so treated).

(ii) *Limitation on treatment of intercompany items as excluded from gross income.* Notwithstanding the general rule of paragraph (c)(1)(i) of this section, S's intercompany income or gain is redetermined to be excluded from gross income only to the extent one of the following applies:

(A) *Disallowed amounts.* B's corresponding item is a deduction or loss and, in the taxable year the item is taken into account under this section, it is permanently and explicitly disallowed under another provision of the Internal Revenue Code or regulations. For example, deductions that are disallowed under section 265 are permanently and explicitly disallowed. An amount is not permanently and explicitly disallowed, for example, to the extent that—

(*1*) The Internal Revenue Code or regulations provide that the amount is not recognized (for example, a loss that is realized but not recognized under section 332 or section 355(c) is not permanently and explicitly disallowed, notwithstanding that it is a corresponding item within the meaning of paragraph (b)(3)(ii) of this section (certain disallowed or eliminated amounts));

(*2*) A related amount might be taken into account by B with respect to successor property, such as under section 280B (demolition costs recoverable as capitalized amounts);

(*3*) A related amount might be taken into account by another taxpayer, such as under section 267(d) (disallowed loss under section 267(a) might result in nonrecognition of gain for a related person);

(*4*) A related amount might be taken into account as a deduction or loss, including as a carryforward to a later year, under any provision of the Internal Revenue Code or regulations (whether or not the carryforward expires in a later year); or

(*5*) The amount is reflected in the computation of any credit against (or other reduction of) Federal income tax (whether allowed for the taxable year or carried forward to a later year).

(B) *Section 311.* The corresponding item is a loss that is realized, but not recognized under section 311(a) on a distribution to a nonmember (even though the loss is not a permanently and explicitly disallowed amount within the meaning of paragraph (c)(6)(ii)(A) of this section).

(C) *Other amounts.* The Commissioner determines that treating S's intercompany item as excluded from gross income is consistent with the purposes of this section and other applicable provisions of the Internal Revenue Code and regulations.

(7) *Examples*—(i) *In general.* For purposes of the examples in this section, unless otherwise

Consolidated Returns

→ *Caution: Prior law may apply to certain transactions, see Reg. § 1.1502-13(l)(1), below. For Reg. § 1.1502-13 prior to revision by T.D. 8597, see Caution Note and text following this version of Reg. § 1.1502-13.*←

stated, P is the common parent of the P consolidated group, P owns all of the only class of stock of subsidiaries S and B, X is a person unrelated to any member of the P group, the taxable year of all persons is the calendar year, all persons use the accrual method of accounting, tax liabilities are disregarded, the facts set forth the only corporate activity, no member has any special status, and the transaction is not otherwise subject to recharacterization. If a member acts as both a selling member and a buying member (e.g., with respect to different aspects of a single transaction, or with respect to related transactions), the member is referred to as M, M1, or M2 (rather than as S or B).

(ii) *Matching rule.* The matching rule of this paragraph (c) is illustrated by the following examples.

Example 1. Intercompany sale of land followed by sale to a nonmember. (a) *Facts.* S holds land for investment with a basis of $70. S has held the land for more than one year. On January 1 of Year 1, S sells the land to B for $100. B also holds the land for investment. On July 1 of Year 3, B sells the land to X for $110.

(b) *Definitions.* Under paragraph (b)(1) of this section, S's sale of the land to B is an intercompany transaction, S is the selling member, and B is the buying member. Under paragraphs (b)(2) and (3) of this section, S's $30 gain from the sale to B is its intercompany item, and B's $10 gain from the sale to X is its corresponding item.

(c) *Attributes.* Under the matching rule of paragraph (c) of this section, S's $30 intercompany gain and B's $10 corresponding gain are taken into account to produce the same effect on consolidated taxable income (and consolidated tax liability) as if S and B were divisions of a single corporation. In addition, the holding periods of S and B for the land are aggregated. Thus, the group's entire $40 of gain is long-term capital gain. Because both S's intercompany item and B's corresponding item on a separate entity basis are long-term capital gain, the attributes are not redetermined under paragraph (c)(1)(i) of this section.

(d) *Timing.* For each consolidated return year, S takes its intercompany item into account under the matching rule to reflect the difference for the year between B's corresponding item taken into account and the recomputed corresponding item. If S and B were divisions of a single corporation and the intercompany sale were a transfer between the divisions, B would succeed to S's $70 basis in the land and would have a $40 gain from the sale to X in Year 3, instead of a $10 gain. Consequently, S takes no gain into account in Years 1 and 2, and takes the entire $30 gain into account in Year 3, to reflect the $30 difference in that year between the $10 gain B takes into account and the $40 recomputed gain (the recomputed corresponding item). Under §§ 1.1502-32 and 1.1502-33, P's basis in its S stock and the earnings and profits of S and P do not reflect S's $30 gain until the gain is taken into account in Year 3. (Under paragraph (a)(3) of this section, the results would be the same if S sold the land to B in an installment sale to which section 453 would otherwise apply, because S must take its intercompany gain into account under this section.)

(e) *Intercompany loss followed by sale to a nonmember at a gain.* The facts are the same as in paragraph (a) of this *Example* 1, except that S's basis in the land is $130 (rather than $70). The attributes and timing of S's intercompany loss and B's corresponding gain are determined under the matching rule in the manner provided in paragraphs (c) and (d) of this *Example* 1. If S and B were divisions of a single corporation and the intercompany sale were a transfer between the divisions, B would succeed to S's $130 basis in the land and would have a $20 loss from the sale to X instead of a $10 gain. Thus, S takes its entire $30 loss into account in Year 3 to reflect the $30 difference between B's $10 gain taken into account and the $20 recomputed loss. (The results are the same under section 267(f).) S's $30 loss is long-term capital loss, and B's $10 gain is long-term capital gain.

(f) *Intercompany gain followed by sale to a nonmember at a loss.* The facts are the same as in paragraph (a) of this *Example* 1 except that B sells the land to X for $90 (rather than $110). The attributes and timing of S's intercompany gain and B's corresponding loss are determined under the matching rule. If S and B were divisions of a single corporation and the intercompany sale were a transfer between the divisions, B would succeed to S's $70 basis in the land and would have a $20 gain from the sale to X instead of a $10 loss. Thus, S takes its entire $30 gain into account in Year 3 to reflect the $30 difference between B's $10 loss taken into account and the $20 recomputed gain. S's $30 gain is long-term capital gain, and B's $10 loss is long-term capital loss.

Reg. § 1.1502-13(c)(7)

→ **Caution:** *Prior law may apply to certain transactions, see Reg. § 1.1502-13(l)(1), below. For Reg. § 1.1502-13 prior to revision by T.D. 8597, see Caution Note and text following this version of Reg. § 1.1502-13.*←

(g) *Intercompany gain followed by distribution to a nonmember at a loss.* The facts are the same as in paragraph (a) of this *Example 1*, except that B distributes the land to X, a minority shareholder of B, and at the time of the distribution the land has a fair market value of $90. The attributes and timing of S's intercompany gain and B's corresponding loss are determined under the matching rule. Under section 311(a), B does not recognize its $10 loss on the distribution to X. If S and B were divisions of a single corporation and the intercompany sale were a transfer between divisions, B would succeed to S's $70 basis in the land and would have a $20 gain from the distribution to X instead of an unrecognized $10 loss. Under paragraph (b)(3)(ii) of this section, B's loss that is not recognized under section 311(a) is a corresponding item. Thus, S takes its $30 gain into account under the matching rule in Year 3 to reflect the difference between B's $10 corresponding unrecognized loss and the $20 recomputed gain. B's $10 corresponding loss offsets $10 of S's intercompany gain and, under paragraph (c)(4)(i) of this section, the attributes of B's corresponding item control the attributes of S's intercompany item. Paragraph (c)(6) of this section does not prevent the redetermination of S's intercompany item as excluded from gross income. (See paragraph (c)(6)(ii)(B) of this section). Thus, $10 of S's $30 gain is redetermined to be excluded from gross income.

(h) *Intercompany sale followed by section 1031 exchange with nonmember.* The facts are the same as in paragraph (a) of this *Example 1*, except, that, instead of selling the land to X, B exchanges the land for land owned by X in a transaction to which section 1031 applies. There is no difference in Year 3 between B's $0 corresponding item taken into account and the $0 recomputed corresponding item. Thus, none of S's intercompany gain is taken into account under the matching rule as a result of the section 1031 exchange. Instead, B's gain is preserved in the land received from X and, under the successor asset rule of paragraph (j)(1) of this section, S's intercompany gain is taken into account by reference to the replacement property. (If B takes gain into account as a result of boot received in the exchange, S's intercompany gain is taken into account under the matching rule to the extent the boot causes a difference between B's gain taken into account and the recomputed gain.)

(j) *Intercompany sale followed by section 351 transfer to nonmember.* The facts are the same as in paragraph (a) of this *Example 1*, except that, instead of selling the land to X, B transfers the land to X in a transaction to which section 351(a) applies and X remains a nonmember. There is no difference in Year 3 between B's $0 corresponding item taken into account and the $0 recomputed corresponding item. Thus, none of S's intercompany gain is taken into account under the matching rule as a result of the section 351(a) transfer. However, S's entire gain is taken into account in Year 3 under the acceleration rule of paragraph (d) of this section (because X, a nonmember, reflects B's $100 cost basis in the land under section 362).

Example 2. Dealer activities. (a) *Facts.* S holds land for investment with a basis of $70. On January 1 of Year 1, S sells the land to B for $100. B develops the land as residential real estate, and sells developed lots to customers during Year 3 for an aggregate amount of $110.

(b) *Attributes.* S and B are treated under the matching rule as divisions of a single corporation for purposes of determining the attributes of S's intercompany item and B's corresponding item. Thus, although S held the land for investment, whether the gain is treated as from the sale of property described in section 1221(1) is based on the activities of both S and B. If, based on both's S's and B's activities, the land is described in section 1221(1), both S's gain and B's gain are ordinary income.

Example 3. Intercompany section 351 transfer. (a) *Facts.* S holds land with a $70 basis and a $100 fair market value for sale to customers in the ordinary course of business. On January 1 of Year 1, S transfers the land to B in exchange for all of the stock of B in a transaction to which section 351 applies. S has no gain or loss under section 351(a), and its basis in the B stock is $70 under section 358. Under section 362, B's basis in the land is $70. B holds the land for investment. On July 1 of Year 3, B sells the land to X for $100. Assume that if S and B were divisions of a single corporation, B's gain from the sale would be ordinary income because of S's activities.

(b) *Timing and attributes.* Under paragraph (b)(1) of this section, S's transfer to B is an intercompany transaction. Under paragraph (c)(3) of this section, S is treated as transferring the land in exchange for B's stock even though, as divisions, S could not own stock of B. S has no intercompany item, but B's $30 gain from its sale of the land to X is a corresponding item because the land was acquired in an intercompany trans-

Reg. § 1.1502-13(c)(7)

→ *Caution: Prior law may apply to certain transactions, see Reg. § 1.1502-13(l)(1), below. For Reg. § 1.1502-13 prior to revision by T.D. 8597, see Caution Note and text following this version of Reg. § 1.1502-13.*←

action. B's $30 gain is ordinary income that is taken into account under B's method of accounting.

(c) *Intercompany section 351 transfer with boot* The facts are the same as in paragraph (a) of this *Example 3*, except, that S receives $10 cash in addition to the B stock in the transfer. S recognizes $10 of gain under section 351(b), and its basis in the B stock is $70 under section 358. Under section 362, B's basis in the land is $80. S takes its $10 intercompany gain into account in Year 3 to reflect the $10 difference between B's $20 corresponding gain taken into account and the $30 recomputed gain. Both S's $10 gain and B's $20 gain are ordinary income.

(d) *Partial disposition.* The facts are the same as in paragraph (c) of this *Example 3*, except B sells a only a one-half, undivided interest in the land to X for $50. The timing and attributes are determined in the manner provided in paragraph (b) of this *Example 3*, except that S takes only $5 of its gain into account in Year 3 to reflect the $5 difference between B's $10 gain taken into account and the $15 recomputed gain.

Example 4. Depreciable property. (a) *Facts.* On January 1 of Year 1, S buys 10-year recovery property for $100 and depreciates it under the straight-line method. On January 1 of Year 3, S sells the property to B for $130. Under section 168(i)(7), B is treated as S for purposes of section 168 to the extent B's $130 basis does not exceed S's adjusted basis at the time of the sale. B's additional basis is treated as new 10-year recovery property for which B elects the straight-line method of recovery. (To simplify the example, the half-year convention is disregarded.)

(b) *Depreciation through Year 3; intercompany gain.* S claims $10 of depreciation for each of Years 1 and 2 and has an $80 basis at the time of the sale to B. Thus, S has a $50 intercompany gain from its sale to B. For Year 3, B has $10 of depreciation with respect to $80 of its basis (the portion of its $130 basis not exceeding S's adjusted basis). In addition, B has $5 of depreciation with respect to the $50 of its additional basis that exceeds S's adjusted basis.

(c) *Timing.* S's $50 gain is taken into account to reflect the difference for each consolidated return year between B's depreciation taken into account with respect to the property and the recomputed depreciation. For Year 3, B takes $15 of depreciation into account. If the intercompany transaction were a transfer between divisions of a single corporation, B would succeed to S's adjusted basis in the property and take into account only $10 of depreciation for Year 3. Thus, S takes $5 of gain into account in Year 3. In each subsequent year that B takes into account $15 of depreciation with respect to the property, S takes into account $5 of gain.

(d) *Attributes.* Under paragraph (c)(1)(i) of this section, the attributes of S's gain and B's depreciation must be redetermined to the extent necessary to produce the same effect on consolidated taxable income as if the intercompany transaction were between divisions of a single corporation (the group must have a net depreciation deduction of $10). In each year, $5 of B's corresponding depreciation deduction offsets S's $5 intercompany gain taken into account and, under paragraph (c)(4)(i) of this section, the attributes of B's corresponding item control the attributes of S's intercompany item. Accordingly, S's intercompany gain that is taken into account as a result of B's depreciation deduction is ordinary income.

(e) *Sale of property to a nonmember.* The facts are the same as in paragraph (a) of this *Example 4*, except that B sells the property to X on January 1 of Year 5 for $110. As set forth in paragraphs (c) and (d) of this *Example 4*, B has $15 of depreciation with respect to the property in each of Years 3 and 4, causing S to take $5 of intercompany gain into account in each year as ordinary income. The $40 balance of S's intercompany gain is taken into account in Year 5 as a result of B's sale to X, to reflect the $40 difference between B's $10 gain taken into account and the $50 of recomputed gain ($110 of sale proceeds minus the $60 basis B would have if the intercompany sale were a transfer between divisions of a single corporation). Treating S and B as divisions of a single corporation, $40 of the gain is section 1245 gain and $10 is section 1231 gain. On a separate entity basis, S would have more than $10 treated as section 1231 gain, and B would have no amount treated as section 1231 gain. Under paragraph (c)(4)(ii) of this section, all $10 of the section 1231 gain is allocated to S. S's remaining $30 of gain, and all of B's $10 gain, is treated as section 1245 gain.

Example 5. Intercompany sale followed by installment sale. (a) *Facts.* S holds land for investment with a basis of $70x. On January 1 of Year 1, S sells the land to B for $100x. B also holds the land for investment. On July 1 of Year 3, B sells the land to X in exchange for X's $110x note. The

Reg. § 1.1502-13(c)(7)

→ *Caution: Prior law may apply to certain transactions, see Reg. § 1.1502-13(l)(1), below. For Reg. § 1.1502-13 prior to revision by T.D. 8597, see Caution Note and text following this version of Reg. § 1.1502-13.* ←

note bears a market rate of interest in excess of the applicable Federal rate, and provides for principal payments of $55x in Year 4 and $55x in Year 5. The interest charge under section 453A(c) applies to X's note.

(b) *Timing and attributes.* S takes its $30x gain into account to reflect the difference in each consolidated return year between B's gain taken into account for the year and the recomputed gain. Under section 453, B takes into account $5x of gain in Year 4 and $5x of gain in Year 5. Thus, S takes into account $15x of gain in Year 4 and $15x of gain in Year 5 to reflect the $15x difference in each of those years between B's $5x gain taken into account and the $20x recomputed gain. Both S's $30x gain and B's $10x gain are subject to the section 453A(c) interest charge beginning in Year 3.

(c) *Election out under section 453(d).* If, under the facts in paragraph (a) of this *Example 5,* the P group wishes to elect not to apply section 453 with respect to S's gain, an election under section 453(d) must be made for Year 3 with respect to B's gain. This election will cause B's $10x gain to be taken into account in Year 3. Under the matching rule, this will result in S's $30x gain being taken into account in Year 3. (An election by the P group solely with respect to S's gain has no effect because the gain from S's sale to B is taken into account under the matching rule, and therefore must reflect the difference between B's gain taken into account and the recomputed gain.)

(d) *Sale to a nonmember at a loss, but overall gain.* The facts are the same as in paragraph (a) of this *Example 5,* except that B sells the land to X in exchange for X's $90x note (rather than $110x note). If S and B were divisions of a single corporation, B would succeed to S's basis in the land, and the sale to X would be eligible for installment reporting under section 453, because it resulted in an overall gain. However, because only gains may be reported on the installment method, B's $10x corresponding loss is taken into account in, Year 3. Under paragraph (b)(4) of this section the recomputed corresponding item is $20x gain that would be taken into account under the installment method, $0 in Year 3 and $10x in each of Years 4 and 5. Thus, in Year 3 S takes $10x of gain into account to reflect the difference between B's $10x loss taken into account and the $0 recomputed gain for Year 3. Under paragraph (c)(4)(i) of this section, B's $10x corresponding loss offsets $10x of S's intercompany gain, and B's attributes control. S takes $10x of gain into into account in each of Years 4 and 5 to reflect the difference in those years between B's $0 gain taken into account and the $10x recomputed gain that would be taken into account under the installment method. only the $20x of S's gain taken into account in Years 4 and 5 is subject to the interest charge under section 453A(c) beginning in Year 3. (If P elects under section 453(d) for Year 3 not to apply section 453 with respect to the gain, all of S's $30x gain will be taken into account in Year 3 to reflect the difference between B's $10x loss taken into account and the $20x recomputed gain.)

(e) *Intercompany loss, installment gain.* The facts are the same as in paragraph (a) of this *Example 5,* except that S has a $130x (rather than $70x) basis in the land. Under paragraph (c)(1)(i) of this section, the separate entity attributes of S's and B's items from the intercompany transaction must be redetermined to produce the same effect on consolidated taxable income (and tax liability) as if the transaction had been a transfer between divisions. If S and B were divisions of a single corporation, B would succeed to S's basis in the land and the group would have $20x loss from the sale to X, installment reporting would be unavailable, and the interest charge under section 453A(c) would not apply. Accordingly, B's gain from the transaction is not eligible for installment treatment under section 453. B takes its $10x gain into account in Year 3, and S takes its $30x of loss into account in Year 3 to reflect the difference between B's $10x gain and the $20x recomputed loss.

(f) *Recapture income.* The facts are the same as in paragraph (a) of this *Example 5,* except that S bought depreciable property (rather than land) for $100x, claimed depreciation deductions, and reduced the property's basis to $70x before Year 1. (To simplify the example, B's depreciation is disregarded.) If the intercompany sale of property had been a transfer between divisions of a single corporation, $30x of the $40x gain from the sale to X would be section 1245 gain (which is ineligible for installment reporting) and $10x would be section 1231 gain (which is eligible for installment reporting). On a separate entity basis, S would have $30x of section 1245 gain and B would have $10x of section 1231 gain. Accordingly, the attributes are not redetermined under paragraph (c)(1)(i) of this section. All of B's $10x gain is eligible for installment reporting and is taken into account $5x each in Years 4 and 5 (and

Reg. § 1.1502-13(c)(7)

→ **Caution: Prior law may apply to certain transactions, see Reg. § 1.1502-13(l)(1), below. For Reg. § 1.1502-13 prior to revision by T.D. 8597, see Caution Note and text following this version of Reg. § 1.1502-13.**←

is subject to the interest charge under section 453A(c). S's $30x gain is taken into account in Year 3 to reflect the difference between B's $0 gain taken into account and the $30x of recomputed gain. (If S had bought the depreciable property for $110X and its recomputed basis under section 1245 had been $110x (rather than $100x), B's $10x gain and S's $30x gain would both be recapture income ineligible for installment reporting.)

Example 6. Intercompany sale of installment obligation. (a) *Facts.* S holds land for investment with a basis of $70x. On January 1 of Year 1, S sells the land to X in exchange for X's $100x note, and S reports its gain on the installment method under section 453. X's note bears interest at a market rate of interest in excess of the applicable Federal rate, and provides for principal payments of $50x in Year 5 and $50x in Year 6. Section 453A applies to X's note. On July 1 of Year 3, S sells X's note to B for $100x, resulting in $30x gain from S's prior sale of the land to X under section 453B(a).

(b) *Timing and attributes.* S's sale of X's note to B is an intercompany transaction, and S's $30x gain is intercompany gain. S takes $15x of the gain into account in each of Years 5 and 6 to reflect the $15x difference in each year between B's $0 gain taken into account and the $15x recomputed gain. S's gain continues to be treated as its gain from the sale to X, and the deferred tax liability remains subject to the interest charge under section 453A(c).

(c) *Worthlessness.* The facts are the same as in paragraph (a) of this *Example 6,* except that X's note becomes worthless on December 1 of Year 3 and B has a $100x short-term capital loss under section 165(g) on a separate entity basis. Under paragraph (c)(1)(i) of this section, B's holding period for X's note is aggregated with S's holding period. Thus, B's loss is a long-term capital loss. S takes its $30x gain into account in Year 3 to reflect the $30x difference between B's $100x loss taken into account and the $70x recomputed loss. Under paragraph (c)(1)(i) of this section, S's gain is long-term capital gain.

(d) *Pledge.* The facts are the same as in paragraph (a) of this *Example 6,* except, that, on December 1 of Year 3, B borrows $100x from an unrelated bank and secures the indebtedness with X's note. X's note remains subject to section 453A(d) following the sale to B. Under section 453A(d), B's $100x of proceeds from the secured indebtedness is treated as an amount received on December 1 of Year 3 by B on X's note. Thus, S takes its entire $30x gain into account in Year 3.

Example 7. Performance of services. (a) *Facts.* S is a driller of water wells. B operates a ranch in a remote location, and B's taxable income from the ranch is not subject to section 447. B's ranch requires water to maintain its cattle. During Year 1, S drills an artesian well on B's ranch in exchange for $100 from B, and S incurs $80 of expenses (e.g., for employees and equipment). B capitalizes its $100 cost for the well under section 263, and takes into account $10 of cost recovery deductions in each of Years 2 through 11. Under its separate entity method of accounting, S would take its income and expenses into account in Year 1. If S and B were divisions of a single corporation, the costs incurred in drilling the well would be capitalized.

(b) *Definitions.* Under paragraph (b)(1) of this section, the service transaction is an intercompany transaction, S is the selling member, and B is the buying member. Under paragraph (b)(2)(ii) of this section, S's $100 of income and $80 of related expenses are both included in determining its intercompany income of $20.

(c) *Timing and attributes.* S's $20 of intercompany income is taken into account under the matching rule to reflect the $20 difference between B's corresponding items taken into account (based on its $100 cost basis in the well) and the recomputed corresponding items (based on the $80 basis that B would have if S and B were divisions of a single corporation and B's basis were determined by reference to S's $80 of expenses). In Year 1, S takes into account $80 of its income and the $80 of expenses. In each of Years 2 through 11, S takes $2 of its $20 intercompany income into account to reflect the annual $2 difference between B's $10 of cost recovery deductions taken into account and the $8 of recomputed cost recovery deductions. S's $100 income and $80 expenses, and B's cost recovery deductions, are ordinary items (because S's and B's items would be ordinary on a separate entity basis, the attributes are not redetermined under paragraph (c)(1)(i) of this section). If S's offsetting $80 of income and expense would not be taken into account in the same year under its separate entity method of accounting, they nevertheless must be taken into account under this section in a manner that clearly reflects consolidated taxable income. See paragraph (a)(3)(i) of this section.

(d) *Sale of capitalized services.* The facts are the same as in paragraph (a) of this *Example*

Reg. § 1.1502-13(c)(7)

→ *Caution: Prior law may apply to certain transactions, see Reg. § 1.1502-13(l)(1), below. For Reg. § 1.1502-13 prior to revision by T.D. 8597, see Caution Note and text following this version of Reg. § 1.1502-13.*←

7, except that B sells the ranch before Year 11 and recognizes gain attributable to the well. To the extent of S's income taken into account as a result of B's cost recovery deductions, as well as S's offsetting $80 of income and expense, the timing and attributes are determined in the manner provided in paragraph (c) of this *Example 7*. The attributes of the remainder of S's $20 of income and B's gain from the sale are redetermined to produce the same effect on consolidated taxable income as if S and B were divisions of a single corporation. Accordingly, S's remaining intercompany income is treated as recapture income or section 1231 gain, even though it is from S's performance of services.

Example 8. Rental of property. B operates a ranch that requires grazing land for its cattle. S owns undeveloped land adjoining B's ranch. On January 1 of Year 1, S leases grazing rights to B for Year 1. B's $100 rent expense is deductible for Year 1 under its separate entity accounting method. Under paragraph (b)(1) of this section, the rental transaction is an intercompany transaction, S is the selling member, and B is the buying member. S takes its $100 of income into account in Year 1 to reflect the $100 difference between B's rental deduction taken into account and the $0 recomputed rental deduction. S's income and B's deduction are ordinary items (because S's intercompany item and B's corresponding item would both be ordinary on a separate entity basis, the attributes are not redetermined under paragraph (c)(1)(i) of this section).

Example 9. Intercompany sale of a partnership interest. (a) *Facts.* S owns a 20% interest in the capital and profits of a general partnership. The partnership holds land for investment with a basis equal to its value, and operates depreciable assets which have value in excess of basis. S's basis in its partnership interest equals its share of the adjusted basis of the partnership's land and depreciable assets. The partnership has an election under section 754 in effect. On January 1 of Year 1, S sells its partnership interest to B at a gain. During Years 1 through 10, the partnership depreciates the operating assets, and B's depreciation deductions from the partnership reflect the increase in the basis of the depreciable assets under section 743(b).

(b) *Timing and attributes.* S's gain is taken into account during Years 1 though 10 to reflect the difference in each year between B's depreciation deductions from the partnership taken into account and the recomputed depreciation deductions from the partnership. Under paragraphs (c)(1)(i) and (c)(4)(i) of this section, S's gain taken into account is ordinary income. (The acceleration rule does not apply to S's gain as a result of the section 743(b) adjustment, because the adjustment is solely with respect to B and therefore no nonmember reflects any part of the intercompany transaction.)

(c) *Partnership sale of assets.* The facts are the same as in paragraph (a) of this *Example 9*, and the partnership sells some of its depreciable assets to X at a gain on December 31 of Year 4. In addition to the intercompany gain taken into account as a result of the partnership's depreciation, S takes intercompany gain into account in Year 4 to reflect the difference between B's partnership items taken into account from the sale (which reflect the basis increase under section 743(b)) and the recomputed partnership items. The attributes of S's additional gain are redetermined to produce the same effect on consolidated taxable income as if S and B were divisions of a single corporation (recapture income or section 1231 gain).

(d) *B's sale of partnership interest.* The facts are the same as in paragraph (a) of this *Example 9*, and on December 31 of Year 4, B sells its partnership interest to X at no gain or loss. In addition to the intercompany gain taken into account as a result of the partnership's depreciation, the remaining balance of S's intercompany gain is taken into account in Year 4 to reflect the difference between B's $0 gain taken into account from the sale of the partnership interest and the recomputed gain The character of S's remaining intercompany item and B's corresponding item are determined on a separate entity basis under section 751, and then redetermined to the extent necessary to produce the same effect as treating the intercompany transaction as occurring between divisions of a single corporation.

(e) *No section 754 election.* The facts are the same as in paragraph (d) of this *Example 9*, except that the partnership does not have a section 754 election in effect, and B recognizes a capital loss from its sale of the partnership interest to X on December 31 of Year 4. Because there is no difference between B's depreciation deductions from the partnership taken into account and the recomputed depreciation deductions, S does not take any of its gain into account during Years 1 through 4 as a result of B's partnership's items. Instead, S's entire intercompany gain is taken

Reg. § 1.1502-13(c)(7)

Consolidated Returns

See p. 20,601 for regulations not amended to reflect law changes

→ *Caution: Prior law may apply to certain transactions, see Reg. § 1.1502-13(l)(1), below. For Reg. § 1.1502-13 prior to revision by T.D. 8597, see Caution Note and text following this version of Reg. § 1.1502-13.*←

into account in Year 4 to reflect the difference between B's loss taken into account from the sale to X and the recomputed gain or loss.

Example 10. Net operating losses subject to section 382 or the SRLY rules. (a) *Facts.* On January 1 of Year 1, P buys all of S's stock. S has net operating loss carryovers from prior years. P's acquisition results in an ownership change under section 382 with respect to S's loss carryovers, and S has a net unrealized built-in gain (within the meaning of section 382(h)(3)). S owns nondepreciable property with a $70 basis and $100 value. On July 1 of Year 3, S sells the property to B for $100, and its $30 gain is recognized built-in gain (within the meaning of section 382(h)(2)) on a separate entity basis. On December 1 of Year 5, B sells the property to X for $90.

(b) *Timing and attributes.* S's $30 gain is taken into account in Year 5 to reflect the $30 difference between B's $10 loss taken into account and the recomputed $20 gain. S and B are treated as divisions of a single corporation for purposes of applying section 382 in connection with the intercompany transaction. Under a single entity analysis, the single corporation has losses subject to limitation under section 382, and this limitation may be increased under section 382(h) if the single corporation has recognized built-in gain with respect to those losses. B's $10 corresponding loss offsets $10 of S's intercompany gain, and thus, under paragraph (c)(4)(i) of this section, $10 of S's intercompany gain is redetermined not to be recognized built-in gain. S's remaining $20 intercompany gain continues to be treated as recognized built-in gain.

(c) *B's recognized built-in gain.* The facts are the same as in paragraph (a) of this *Example 10,* except that the property declines in value after S becomes a member of the P group, S sells the property to B for its $70 basis, and B sells the property to X for $90 during Year 5. Treating S and B as divisions of a single corporation, S's sale to B does not cause the property to cease to be built-in gain property. Thus, B's $20 gain from its sale to X is recognized built-in gain that increases the section 382 limitation applicable to S's losses.

(d) *SRLY limitation.* The facts are the same as in paragraph (a) of this *Example 10,* except that P's acquisition of S is not subject to the overlap rule of § 1.1502-21(g), and S's net operating loss carryovers are subject to the separate return limitation year (SRLY) rules. See § 1.1502-21(c). The application of the SRLY rules depends on S's status as a separate corporation having losses from separate return limitation years. Under paragraph (c)(5), the attribute of S's intercompany item as it relates to S's SRLY limitation is not redetermined, because the SRLY limitation depends on S's special status. Accordingly, S's $30 intercompany gain is included in determining its SRLY limitation for Year 5.

Example 11. Section 475. (a) *Facts.* S, a dealer in securities within the meaning of section 475(c), owns a security with a basis of $70. The security is held for sale to customers and is not identified under section 475(b) as within an exception to marking to market. On July 1 of Year 1, S sells the security to B for $100. B is not a dealer and holds the security for investment. On December 31 of Year 1, the fair market value of the security is $100. On July 1 of Year 2, B sells the security to X for $110.

(b) *Attributes.* Under section 475, a dealer in securities can treat a security as within an exception to marking to market under section 475(b) only if it timely identifies the security as so described. Under the matching rule, attributes must be redetermined by treating S and B as divisions of a single corporation. As a result of S's activities, the single corporation is treated as a dealer with respect to securities, and B must continue to mark to market the security acquired from S. Thus, B's corresponding items and the recomputed corresponding items are determined by continuing to treat the security as not within an exception to marking to market. Under section 475(d)(3), it is possible for the character of S's intercompany items to differ from the character of B's corresponding items.

(c) *Timing and character.* S has a $30 gain when it disposes of the security by selling it to B. This gain is intercompany gain that is taken into account in Year 1 to reflect the $30 difference between B's $0 gain taken into account from marking the security to market under section 475 and the recomputed $30 gain that would be taken into account. The character of S's gain and B's gain are redetermined as if the security were transferred between divisions. Accordingly, S's gain is ordinary income under section 475(d)(3)(A)(i), but under section 475(d)(3)(B)(ii) B's $10 gain from its sale to X is capital gain that is taken into account in Year 2.

(d) *Nondealer to dealer.* The facts are the same as in paragraph (a) of this *Example 11,* except that S is not a dealer and holds the security for investment with a $70 basis, B is a dealer to which section 475 applies and, immediately after

Reg. § 1.1502-13(c)(7)

→ *Caution: Prior law may apply to certain transactions, see Reg. § 1.1502-13(l)(1), below. For Reg. § 1.1502-13 prior to revision by T.D. 8597, see Caution Note and text following this version of Reg. § 1.1502-13.*←

acquiring the security from S for $100, B holds the security for sale to customers in the ordinary course of its trade or business. Because S is not a dealer and held the security for investment, the security is treated as properly identified as held for investment under section 475(b)(1) until it is sold to B. Under section 475(b)(3), the security thereafter ceases to be described in section 475(b)(1) because B holds the security for sale to customers. The mark-to-market requirement applies only to changes in the value of the security after B's acquisition. B's mark-to-market gain taken into account and the recomputed mark-to-market gain are both determined based on changes from the $100 value of the security at the time of B's acquisition. There is no difference between B's $0 mark-to-market gain taken into account in Year 1 and the $0 recomputed mark-to-market gain. Therefore, none of S's gain is taken into account in Year 1 as a result of B's marking the security to market in Year 1. In Year 2, B has a $10 gain when it disposes of the security by selling it to X, but would have had a $40 gain if S and B were divisions of a single corporation. Thus, S takes its $30 gain into account in Year 2 under the matching rule. Under section 475(d)(3), S's gain is capital gain even though B's subsequent gain or loss from marking to market or disposing of the security is ordinary gain or loss. If B disposes of the security at a $10 loss in Year 2, S's gain taken into account in Year 2 is still capital because on a single entity basis section 475(d)(3) would provide for $30 of capital gain and $10 of ordinary loss. Because the attributes are not redetermined under paragraph (c)(1)(i) of this section, paragraph (c)(4)(i) of this section does not apply. Furthermore, if B held the security for investment, and so identified the security under section 475(b)(1), the security would continue to be excepted from marking to market.

Example 12. Section 1092. (a) *Facts.* On July 1 of Year 1, S enters into offsetting long and short positions with respect to actively traded personal property. The positions are not section 1256 contracts, and they are the only positions taken into account for purposes of applying section 1092. On August 1 of Year 1, S sells the long position to B at an $11 loss, and there is $11 of unrealized gain in the offsetting short position. On December 1 of Year 1, B sells the long position to X at no gain or loss. On December 31 of Year 1, there is still $11 of unrealized gain in the short position. On February 1 of Year 2, S closes the short position at an $11 gain.

(b) *Timing and attributes.* If the sale from S to B were a transfer between divisions of a single corporation, the $11 loss on the sale to X would have been deferred under section 1092(a)(1)(A). Accordingly, there is no difference in Year 1 between B's corresponding item of $0 and the recomputed corresponding item of $0. S takes its $11 loss into account in Year 2 to reflect the difference between B's corresponding item of $0 taken into account in Year 2 and the recomputed loss of $11 that would have been taken into account in Year 2 under section 1092(a)(1)(B) if S and B had been divisions of a single corporation. (The results are the same under section 267(f).)

Example 13. Manufacturer incentive payments. (a) *Facts.* B is a manufacturer that sells its products to independent dealers for resale. S is a credit company that offers financing, including financing to customers of the dealers. S also purchases the product from the dealers for lease to customers of the dealers. During Year 1, B initiates a program of incentive payments to the dealers' customers. Under B's program, S buys a product from an independent dealer for $100 and leases it to a nonmember. S pays $90 to the dealer for the product, and assigns to the dealer its $10 incentive payment from B. Under their separate entity accounting methods, B would deduct the $10 incentive payment in Year 1 and S would take a $90 basis in the product. Assume that if S and B were divisions of a single corporation, the $10 payment would not be deductible and the basis of the property would be $100.

(b) *Timing and attributes.* Under paragraph (b)(1) of this section, the incentive payment transaction is an intercompany transaction. Under paragraph (b)(2)(iii) of this section, S has a $10 intercompany item not yet taken into account under its separate entity method of accounting. Under the matching rule, S takes its intercompany item into account to reflect the difference between B's corresponding item taken into account and the recomputed corresponding item. In Year 1 there is a $10 difference between B's $10 deduction taken into account and the $0 recomputed deduction. Accordingly, under the matching rule S must take the $10 incentive payment into account as intercompany income in Year 1. S's $10 of income and B's $10 deduction are ordinary items. S's basis in the product is $100 rather than the $90 it would be under S's separate entity method of accounting. S's additional $10 of basis in the product is recovered based on subse-

Reg. § 1.1502-13(c)(7)

Consolidated Returns

See p. 20,601 for regulations not amended to reflect law changes

→ *Caution: Prior law may apply to certain transactions, see Reg. § 1.1502-13(l)(1), below. For Reg. § 1.1502-13 prior to revision by T.D. 8597, see Caution Note and text following this version of Reg. § 1.1502-13.*←

quent events (e.g., S's cost recovery deductions or its sale of the product).

Example 14. Source of income under section 863. (a) *Intercompany sale with no independent factory price.* S manufactures inventory in the United States, and recognizes $75 of income on sales to B in Year 1. B distributes the inventory in Country Y and recognizes $25 of income on sales to X, also in Year 1. Title passes from S to B, and from B to X, in Country Y. There is no independent factory price (as defined in regulations under section 863) for the sale from S to B. Under the matching rule, S's $75 intercompany income and B's $25 corresponding income are taken into account in Year 1. In determining the source of income, S and B are treated as divisions of a single corporation, and section 863 applies as if $100 of income were recognized from producing in the United States and selling in Country Y. Assume that applying the section 863 regulations on a single entity basis, $50 is treated as foreign source income and $50 as U.S. source income. Assume further that on a separate entity basis, S would have $37.50 of foreign source income and $37.50 of U.S. source income, and that all of B's $25 of income would be foreign source income. Thus, on a separate entity basis, S and B would have $62.50 of combined foreign source income and $37.50 of U.S. source income. Accordingly, under single entity treatment, $12.50 that would be treated as foreign source income on a separate entity basis is redetermined to be U.S. source income. Under paragraph (c)(1)(i) of this section, attributes are redetermined only to the extent of the $12.50 necessary to achieve the same effect as a single entity determination. Under paragraph (c)(4)(ii) of this section, the redetermined attribute must be allocated between S and B using a reasonable method. For example, it may be reasonable to recharacterize only S's foreign source income as U.S. source income because only S would have any U.S. source income on a separate entity basis. However, it may also be reasonable to allocate the redetermined attribute between S and B in proportion to their separate entity amounts of foreign source income (in a 3:2 ratio, so that $7.50 of S's foreign source income is redetermined to be U.S. source and $5 of B's foreign source income is redetermined to be U.S. source), provided the same method is applied to all similar transactions within the group.

(b) *Intercompany sale with independent factory price.* The facts are the same as in paragraph (a) of this *Example 14*, except that an independent factory price exists for the sale by S to B such that $70 of S's $75 of income is attributable to the production function. Assume that on a single entity basis, $70 is treated as U.S. source income (because of the existence of the independent factory price) and $30 is treated as foreign source income. Assume that on a separate entity basis, $70 of S's income would be treated as U.S. source, $5 of S's income would be treated as foreign source income, and all of B's $25 income would be treated as foreign source income. Because the results are the same on a single entity basis and a separate entity basis, the attributes are not redetermined under paragraph (c)(1)(i) of this section.

(c) *Sale of property reflecting intercompany services or intangibles.* S earns $10 of income performing services in the United States for B. B capitalizes S's fees into the basis of property that it manufactures in the United States and sells to an unrelated person in Year 1 at a $90 profit, with title passing in Country Y. Under the matching rule, S's $10 income and B's $90 income are taken into account in Year 1. In determining the source of income, S and B are treated as divisions of a single corporation, and section 863 applies as if $100 were earned from manufacturing in the United States and selling in Country Y. Assume that on a single entity basis $50 is treated as foreign source income and $50 is treated as U.S. source income. Assume that on a separate entity basis, S would have $10 of U.S. source income, and B would have $45 of foreign source income and $45 of U.S. source income. Accordingly, under single entity treatment, $5 of income that would be treated as U.S. source income on a separate entity basis is redetermined to be foreign source income. Under paragraph (c)(1)(i) of this section, attributes are redetermined only to the extent of the $5 necessary to achieve the same effect as a single entity determination. Under paragraph (c)(4)(ii) of this section, the redetermined attribute must be allocated between S and B using a reasonable method. (If instead of performing services, S licensed an intangible to B and earned $10 that would be treated as U.S. source income on a separate entity basis, the results would be the same.)

Example 15. Section 1248. (a) *Facts.* On January 1 of Year 1, S forms FT, a wholly owned foreign subsidiary, with a $10 contribution. During Years 1 through 3, FT has earnings and profits of $40. None of the earnings and profits is taxed as subpart F income under section 951, and

Reg. § 1.1502-13(c)(7)

→ *Caution: Prior law may apply to certain transactions, see Reg.
§ 1.1502-13(l)(1), below. For Reg. § 1.1502-13 prior to revision by T.D. 8597, see Caution Note and text following this version of Reg. § 1.1502-13.*←

FT distributes no dividends to S during this period. On January 1 of Year 4, S sells its FT stock to B for $50. While B owns FT, FT has a deficit in earnings and profits of $10. On July 1 of Year 6, B sells its FT stock for $70 to X, an unrelated foreign corporation.

(b) *Timing.* S's $40 of intercompany gain is taken into account in Year 6 to reflect the difference between B's $20 of gain taken into account and the $60 recomputed gain.

(c) *Attributes.* Under the matching rule, the attributes of S's intercompany gain and B's corresponding gain are redetermined to have the same effect on consolidated taxable income (and consolidated tax liability) as if S and B were divisions of a single corporation. On a single entity basis, there is $60 of gain and the portion which is characterized as a dividend under section 1248 is determined on the basis of FT's $30 of earnings and profits at the time of the sale of FT to X (the sum of FT's $40 of earnings and profits while held by S and FT's $10 deficit in earnings and profits while held by B). Therefore, $30 of the $60 gain is treated as a dividend under section 1248. The remaining $30 is treated as capital gain. On a separate entity basis, all of S's $40 gain would be treated as a dividend under section 1248 and all of B's $20 gain would be treated as capital gain. Thus, as a result of the single entity determination, $10 that would be treated as a dividend under section 1248 on a separate entity basis is redetermined to be capital gain. Under paragraph (c)(4)(ii) of this section, this redetermined attribute must be allocated between S's intercompany item and B's corresponding item by using a reasonable method. On a separate entity basis, only S would have any amount treated as a dividend under section 1248 available for redetermination. Accordingly, $10 of S's income is redetermined to be not subject to section 1248, with the result that $30 of S's intercompany gain is treated as a dividend and the remaining $10 is treated as capital gain. All of B's corresponding gain is treated as capital gain, as it would be on a separate entity basis.

(d) *B has loss.* The facts are the same as in paragraph (a) of this *Example 15,* except that FT has no earnings and profits or deficit in earnings and profits while B owns FT, and B sells the FT stock to X for $40. On a single entity basis, there is $30 of gain, and section 1248 is applied on the basis of FT's $40 earnings and profits at the time of the sale of FT to X. Under section 1248, the amount treated as a dividend is limited to $30 (the amount of the gain). On a separate entity basis, S's entire $40 gain would be treated as a dividend under section 1248, and B's $10 loss would be a capital loss. B's $10 corresponding loss offsets $10 of S's intercompany gain and, under paragraph (c)(4)(i) of this section, the attributes of B's corresponding item control. Accordingly, $10 of S's gain must be redetermined to be capital gain. B's $10 loss remains a capital loss. (If, however, S sold FT to B at a loss and B sold FT to X at a gain, it may be unreasonable for the attributes of B's corresponding gain to control S's offsetting intercompany loss. If B's attributes were to control, for example, the group could possibly claim a larger foreign tax credit than would be available if S and B were divisions of a single corporation.)

(d) *Acceleration rule.* S's intercompany items and B's corresponding items are taken into account under this paragraph (d) to the extent they cannot be taken into account to produce the effect of treating S and B as divisions of a single corporation. For this purpose, the following rules apply:

(1) *S's items*—(i) *Timing.* S takes its intercompany items into account to the extent they cannot be taken into account to produce the effect of treating S and B as divisions of a single corporation. The items are taken into account immediately before it first becomes impossible to achieve this effect. For this purpose, the effect cannot be achieved—

(A) To the extent an intercompany item or corresponding item will not be taken into account in determining the group's consolidated taxable income (or consolidated tax liability) under the matching rule (for example, if S or B becomes a nonmember, or if S's intercompany item is no longer reflected in the difference between B's basis (or an amount equivalent to basis) in property and the basis (or equivalent amount) the property would have if S and B were divisions of a single corporation); or

(B) To the extent a nonmember reflects, directly or indirectly, any aspect of the intercompany transaction (e.g., if B's cost basis in property purchased from S is reflected by a nonmember under section 362 following a section 351 transaction).

(ii) *Attributes.* The attributes of S's intercompany items taken into account under this paragraph (d)(1) are determined as follows:

(A) *Sale, exchange, or distribution.* If the item is from an intercompany sale, exchange,

Consolidated Returns

→ *Caution: Prior law may apply to certain transactions, see Reg. § 1.1502-13(l)(1), below. For Reg. § 1.1502-13 prior to revision by T.D. 8597, see Caution Note and text following this version of Reg. § 1.1502-13.*←

or distribution of property, its attributes are determined under the principles of the matching rule as if B sold the property, at the time the item is taken into account under paragraph (d)(1)(i) of this section, for a cash payment equal to B's adjusted basis in the property (i.e., at no net gain or loss), to the following person:

(*1*) *Property leaves the group.* If the property is owned by a nonmember immediately after S's item is taken into account, B is treated as selling the property to that nonmember. If the nonmember is related for purposes of any provision of the Internal Revenue Code or regulations to any party to the intercompany transaction (or any related transaction) or to the common parent, the nonmember is treated as related to B for purposes of that provision. For example, if the nonmember is related to P within the meaning of section 1239(b), the deemed sale is treated as being described in section 1239(a). See paragraph (j)(6) of this section, under which property is not treated as being owned by a nonmember if it is owned by the common parent after the common parent becomes the only remaining member.

(*2*) *Property does not leave the group.* If the property is not owned by a nonmember immediately after S's item is taken into account, B is treated as selling the property to an affiliated corporation that is not a member of the group.

(B) *Other transactions.* If the item is from an intercompany transaction other than a sale, exchange, or distribution of property (e.g., income from S's services capitalized by B), its attributes are determined on a separate entity basis.

(2) *B's items*—(i) *Attributes.* The attributes of B's corresponding items continue to be redetermined under the principles of the matching rule, with the following adjustments:

(A) If S and B continue to join with each other in the filing of consolidated returns, the attributes of B's corresponding items (and any applicable holding periods) are determined by continuing to treat S and B as divisions of a single corporation.

(B) Once S and B no longer join with each other in the filing of consolidated returns, the attributes of B's corresponding items are determined as if the S division (but not the B division) were transferred by the single corporation to an unrelated person. Thus, S's activities (and any applicable holding period) before the intercompany transaction continue to affect the attributes of the corresponding items (and any applicable holding period).

(ii) *Timing.* If paragraph (d)(1) of this section applies to S, B nevertheless continues to take its corresponding items into account under its accounting method. However, the redetermination of the attributes of a corresponding item under this paragraph (d)(2) might affect its timing.

(3) *Examples.* The acceleration rule of this paragraph (d) is illustrated by the following examples.

Example 1. Becoming a nonmember—timing. (a) *Facts.* S owns land with a basis of $70. On January 1 of Year 1, S sells the land to B for $100. On July 1 of Year 3, P sells 60% of S's stock to X for $60 and, as a result, S becomes a nonmember.

(b) *Matching rule.* Under the matching rule, none of S's $30 gain is taken into account in Years 1 through 3 because there is no difference between B's $0 gain or loss taken into account and the recomputed gain or loss.

(c) *Acceleration of S's intercompany items.* Under the acceleration rule of paragraph (d) of this section, S's $30 gain is taken into account in computing consolidated taxable income (and consolidated tax liability) immediately before the effect of treating S and B as divisions of a single corporation cannot be produced. Because the effect cannot be produced once S becomes a nonmember, S takes its $30 gain into account in Year 3 immediately before becoming a nonmember. S's gain is reflected under § 1.1502-32 in P's basis in the S stock immediately before P's sale of the stock. Under § 1.1502-32, P's basis in the S stock is increased by $30, and therefore P's gain is reduced (or loss is increased) by $18 (60% of $30). See also §§ 1.1502-33 and 1.1502-76(b). (The results would be the same if S sold the land to B in an installment sale to which section 453 would otherwise apply, because S must take its intercompany gain into account under this section.)

(d) *B's corresponding items.* Notwithstanding the acceleration of S's gain, B continues to take its corresponding items into account under its accounting method. Thus, B's items from the land are taken into account based on subsequent events (e.g., its sale of the land).

(e) *Sale of B's stock.* The facts are the same as in paragraph (a) of this *Example 1*, except that P sells 60% of B's stock (rather than S stock) to X for $60 and, as a result, B becomes a nonmember.

Reg. § 1.1502-13(d)(3)

56,712 **Consolidated Returns**

See p. 20,601 for regulations not amended to reflect law changes

→ *Caution: Prior law may apply to certain transactions, see Reg. § 1.1502-13(l)(1), below. For Reg. § 1.1502-13 prior to revision by T.D. 8597, see Caution Note and text following this version of Reg. § 1.1502-13.*←

Because the effect of treating S and B as divisions of a single corporation cannot be produced once B becomes a nonmember, S takes its $30 gain into account under the acceleration rule immediately before B becomes a nonmember. (The results would be the same if S sold the land to B in an installment sale to which section 453 would otherwise apply, because S must take its intercompany gain into account under this section.)

(f) *Discontinue filing consolidated returns.* The facts are the same as in paragraph (a) of this *Example 1*, except that the P group receives permission under § 1.1502-75(c) to discontinue filing consolidated returns beginning in Year 3. Under the acceleration rule, S takes its $30 gain into account on December 31 of Year 2.

(g) *No subgroups.* The facts are the same as in paragraph (a) of this *Example 1*, except that P simultaneously sells all of the stock of both S and B to X (rather than 60% of S's stock), and S and B become members of the X consolidated group. Because the effect of treating S and B as divisions of a single corporation in the P group cannot be produced once S and B become nonmembers, S takes its $30 gain into account under the acceleration rule immediately before S and B become nonmembers. (Paragraph (j)(5) of this section does not apply to treat the X consolidated group as succeeding to the P group because the X group acquired only the stock of S and B.) However, so long as S and B continue to join with each other in the filing of consolidated returns, B continues to treat S and B as divisions of a single corporation for purposes of determining the attributes of B's corresponding items from the land.

Example 2. Becoming a nonmember—attributes. (a) *Facts.* S holds land for investment with a basis of $70. On January 1 of Year 1, S sells the land to B for $100. B holds the land for sale to customers in the ordinary course of business, and expends substantial resources over a two-year period subdividing, developing, and marketing the land. On July 1 of Year 3, before B has sold any of the land, P sells 60% of S's stock to X for $60 and, as a result, S becomes a nonmember.

(b) *Attributes.* Under the acceleration rule, the attributes of S's gain are redetermined under the principles of the matching rule as if B sold the land to an affiliated corporation that is not a member of the group for a cash payment equal to B's adjusted basis in the land (because the land continues to be held within the group). Thus, whether S's gain is capital gain or ordinary income depends on the activities of both S and B. Because S and B no longer join with each other in the filing of consolidated returns, the attributes of B's corresponding items (e.g., from its subsequent sale of the land) are redetermined under the principles of the matching rule as if the S division (but not the B division) were transferred by the single corporation to an unrelated person at the time of P's sale of the S stock. Thus, B continues to take into account the activities of S with respect to the land before the intercompany transaction.

(c) *Depreciable property.* The facts are the same as in paragraph (a) of this *Example 2*, except that the property sold by S to B is depreciable property. Section 1239 applies to treat all of S's gain as ordinary income because it is taken into account as a result of B's deemed sale of the property to a affiliated corporation that is not a member of the group (a related person within the meaning of section 1239(b)).

Example 3. Selling member's disposition of installment note. (a) *Facts.* S owns land with a basis of $70. On January 1 of Year 1, S sells the land to B in exchange for B's $110 note. The note bears a market rate of interest in excess of the applicable Federal rate, and provides for principal payments of $55 in Year 4 and $55 in Year 5. On July 1 of Year 3, S sells B's note to X for $110.

(b) *Timing.* S's intercompany gain is taken into account under this section, and not under the rules of section 453. Consequently, S's sale of B's note does not result in its intercompany gain from the land being taken into account (e.g., under section 453B). The sale does not prevent S's intercompany items and B's corresponding items from being taken into account in determining the group's consolidated taxable income under the matching rule, and X does not reflect any aspect of the intercompany transaction (X has its own cost basis in the note). S will take the intercompany gain into account under the matching rule or acceleration rule based on subsequent events (e.g., B's sale of the land). See also paragraph (g) of this section for additional rules applicable to B's note as an intercompany obligation.

Example 4. Cancellation of debt and attribute reduction under section 108(b). (a) *Facts.* S holds land for investment with a basis of $0. On January 1 of Year 1, S sells the land to B for $100. B also holds the land for investment. During Year 3, B is insolvent and B's nonmember creditors discharge $60 of B's indebtedness. Because of insolvency, B's $60 discharge is excluded from B's gross income under section 108(a), and B reduces

Reg. § 1.1502-13(d)(3)

Consolidated Returns

See p. 20,601 for regulations not amended to reflect law changes

→ *Caution: Prior law may apply to certain transactions, see Reg. § 1.1502-13(l)(1), below. For Reg. § 1.1502-13 prior to revision by T.D. 8597, see Caution Note and text following this version of Reg. § 1.1502-13.*←

the basis of the land by $60 under sections 108(b) and 1017.

(b) *Acceleration rule.* As a result of B's basis reduction under section 1017, $60 of S's intercompany gain will not be taken into account under the matching rule (because there is only a $40 difference between B's $40 basis in the land and the $0 basis the land would have if S and B were divisions of a single corporation). Accordingly, S takes $60 of its gain into account under the acceleration rule in Year 3. S's gain is long-term capital gain, determined under paragraph (d)(1)(ii) of this section as if B sold the land to an affiliated corporation that is not a member of the group for $100 immediately before the basis reduction.

(c) *Purchase price adjustment.* Assume instead that S sells the land to B in exchange for B's $100 purchase money note, B remains solvent, and S subsequently agrees to discharge $60 of the note as a purchase price adjustment to which section 108(e)(5) applies. Under applicable principles of tax law, $60 of S's gain and $60 of B's basis in the land are eliminated and never taken into account. Similarly, the note is not treated as satisfied and reissued under paragraph (g) of this section.

Example 5. Section 481. (a) *Facts.* S operates several trades or businesses, including a manufacturing business. S receives permission to change its method of accounting for valuing inventory for its manufacturing business. S increases the basis of its ending inventory by $100, and the related $100 positive section 481(a) adjustment is to be taken into account ratably over six taxable years, beginning in Year 1. During Year 3, S sells all of the assets used in its manufacturing business to B at a gain. Immediately after the transfer, B does not use the same inventory valuation method as S. On a separate entity basis, S's sale results in an acceleration of the balance of the section 481(a) adjustment to Year 3.

(b) *Timing and attributes.* Under paragraph (b)(2) of this section, the balance of S's section 481(a) adjustment accelerated to Year 3 is intercompany income. However, S's $100 basis increase before the intercompany transaction eliminates the related difference for this amount between B's corresponding items taken into account and the recomputed corresponding items in subsequent periods. Because the accelerated section 481(a) adjustment will not be taken into account in determining the group's consolidated taxable income (and consolidated tax liability) under the matching rule, the balance of S's section 481 adjustment is taken into account under the acceleration rule as ordinary income at the time of the intercompany transaction. (If S's sale had not resulted in accelerating S's section 481(a) adjustment on a separate entity basis, S would have no intercompany income to be taken into account under this section.)

(e) *Simplifying rules*—(1) *Dollar-value LIFO inventory methods*—(i) *In general.* This paragraph (e)(1) applies if either S or B uses a dollar-value LIFO inventory method to account for intercompany transactions. Rather than applying the matching rule separately to each intercompany inventory transaction, this paragraph (e)(1) provides methods to apply an aggregate approach that is based on dollar-value LIFO inventory accounting. Any method selected under this paragraph (e)(1) must be applied consistently.

(ii) *B uses dollar-value LIFO*—(A) *In general.* If B uses a dollar-value LIFO inventory method to account for its intercompany inventory purchases, and includes all of its inventory costs incurred for a year in its cost of goods sold for the year (that is, B has no inventory increment for the year), S takes into account all of its intercompany inventory items for the year. If B does not include all of its inventory costs incurred for the year in its cost of goods sold for the year (that is, B has an inventory increment for the year), S does not take all of its intercompany inventory income or loss into account. The amount not taken into account is determined under either the increment averaging method of paragraph (e)(1)(ii)(B) of this section or the increment valuation method of paragraph (e)(1)(ii)(C) of this section. Separate computations are made for each pool of B that receives intercompany purchases from S, and S's amount not taken into account is layered based on B's LIFO inventory layers.

(B) *Increment averaging method.* Under this paragraph (e)(1)(ii)(B), the amount not taken into account is the amount of S's intercompany inventory income or loss multiplied by the ratio of the LIFO value of B's current-year costs of its layer of increment to B's total inventory costs incurred for the year under its LIFO inventory method. If B includes more than its inventory costs incurred during any subsequent year in its cost of goods sold (a decrement), S takes into account the intercompany inventory income or loss layers in the same manner and proportion as B takes into account its inventory decrements.

(C) *Increment valuation method.* Under this paragraph (e)(1)(ii)(C), the amount not taken

Reg. § 1.1502-13(e)(1)

Consolidated Returns

→ *Caution: Prior law may apply to certain transactions, see Reg. § 1.1502-13(l)(1), below. For Reg. § 1.1502-13 prior to revision by T.D. 8597, see Caution Note and text following this version of Reg. § 1.1502-13.* ←

into account is the amount of S's intercompany inventory income or loss for the appropriate period multiplied by the ratio of the LIFO value of B's current-year costs of its layer of increment to B's total inventory costs incurred in the appropriate period under its LIFO inventory method. The principles of paragraph (e)(1)(ii)(B) of this section otherwise apply. The appropriate period is the period of B's year used to determine its current-year costs.

(iii) *S uses dollar-value LIFO.* If S uses a dollar-Value LIFO inventory method to account for its intercompany inventory sales, S may use any reasonable method of allocating its LIFO inventory costs to intercompany transactions. LIFO inventory costs include costs of prior layers if a decrement occurs. For example, a reasonable allocation of the most recent costs incurred during the consolidated return year can be used to compute S's intercompany inventory income or loss for the year if S has an inventory increment and uses the earliest acquisitions costs method, but S must apportion costs from the most recent appropriate layers of increment if an inventory decrement occurs for the year.

(iv) *Other reasonable methods.* S or B may use a method not specifically provided in this paragraph (e)(1) that is expected to reasonably take into account intercompany items and corresponding items from intercompany inventory transactions. However, if the method used results, for any year, in a cumulative amount of intercompany inventory items not taken into account by S that significantly exceeds the cumulative amount that would not be taken into account under paragraph (e)(1)(ii) or (iii) of this section, S must take into account for that year the amount necessary to eliminate the excess. The method is thereafter applied with appropriate adjustments to reflect the amount taken into account.

(v) *Examples.* The inventory rules of this paragraph (e)(1) are illustrated by the following examples.

Example 1. Increment averaging method. (a) *Facts.* Both S and B use a double-extension, dollar-value LIFO inventory method, and both value inventory increments using the earliest acquisitions cost valuation method. During Year 2, S sells 25 units of product Q to B on January 15 at $10/unit. S sells another 25 units on April 15, on July 15, and on September 15, at $12/unit. S's earliest cost of product Q is $7.50/unit and S's most recent cost of product Q is $8.00/unit. Both S and B have an inventory increment for the year. B's total inventory costs incurred during Year 2 are $6,000 and the LIFO value of B's Year 2 layer of increment is $600.

(b) *Intercompany inventory income.* Under paragraph (e)(1)(iii) of this section, S must use a reasonable method of allocating its LIFO inventory costs to intercompany transactions. Because S has an inventory increment for Year 2 and uses the earliest acquisitions cost method, a reasonable method of determining its intercompany cost of goods sold for product Q is to use its most recent costs. Thus, its intercompany cost of goods sold is $800 ($8.00 most recent cost, multiplied by 100 units sold to B), and its intercompany inventory income is $350 ($1,150 sales proceeds from B minus $800 cost).

(c) *Timing.* (i) Under the increment averaging method of paragraph (e)(1)(ii)(B) of this section, $35 of S's $350 of intercompany inventory income is not taken into account in Year 2, computed as follows:

$$\frac{\text{LIFO value of B's Year 2 layer of increment}}{\text{B's total inventory costs for Year 2}} = \frac{\$600}{\$6,000} = 10\%$$

10% × S's $350 intercompany inventory income = $35

(ii) Thus, $315 of S's intercompany inventory income is taken into account in Year 2 ($350 of total intercompany inventory income minus $35 not taken into account).

(d) *S incurs a decrement.* The facts are the same as in paragraph (a) of this *Example 1,* except that in Year 2, S incurs a decrement equal to 50% of its Year 1 layer. Under paragraph (e)(1)(iii) of this section, S must reasonably allocate the LIFO cost of the decrement to the cost of goods sold to B to determine S's intercompany inventory income.

(e) *B incurs a decrement.* The facts are the same as in paragraph (a) of this *Example 1,* except that B incurs a decrement in Year 2. S must take into account the entire $350 of Year 2 intercompany inventory income because all 100 units of product Q are deemed sold by B in Year 2.

Example 2. Increment valuation method. (a) The facts are the same as in Example 1. In addition, B's use of the earliest acquisition's cost method of valuing its increments-results in B valuing its year-end inventory using costs incurred

Reg. § 1.1502-13(e)(1)

→ **Caution:** *Prior law may apply to certain transactions, see Reg. § 1.1502-13(l)(1), below. For Reg. § 1.1502-13 prior to revision by T.D. 8597, see Caution Note and text following this version of Reg. § 1.1502-13.*←

from January through March. B's costs incurred during the year are: $1,428 in the period January through March; $1,498 in the period April through June; $1,524 in the period July through September; and $1,550 in the period October through December. S's intercompany inventory income for these periods is: $50 in the period January through March ((25 × $10) − (25 × $8)); $100 in the period April through June ((25 × $12) − (25 × $8)); $100 in the period July through September ((25 × $12) − (25 × $8)); and $100 in the period October through December ((25 × $12) − (25 × $8)).

(b) *Timing.* (i) Under the increment valuation method of paragraph (e)(1)(ii)(C) of this section, $21 of S's $350 of intercompany inventory income is not taken into account in Year 2, computed as follows:

$$\frac{\text{LIFO value of B's Year 2 layer of increment}}{\text{B's total inventory costs from January through March of Year 2}} = \frac{\$600}{\$1,428} = 42\%$$

42% × S's $50 intercompany inventory income for the period from January through March = $21

(ii) Thus, $329 of S's intercompany inventory income is taken into account in Year 2 ($350 of total intercompany inventory income minus $21 not taken into account).

(c) *B incurs a subsequent decrement.* The facts are the same as in paragraph (a) of this *Example 2.* In addition, assume that in Year 3, B experiences a decrement in its pool that receives intercompany purchases from S. B's decrement equals 20% of the base-year costs for its Year 2 layer. The fact that B has incurred a decrement means that all of its inventory costs incurred for Year 3 are included in cost of goods sold. As a result, S takes into account its entire amount of intercompany inventory income from its Year 3 sales. In addition, S takes into account $4.20 of its Year 2 layer of intercompany inventory income not already taken into account (20% of $21).

Example 3. Other reasonable inventory methods. (a) *Facts.* Both S and B use a dollar-value LIFO inventory method for their inventory transactions. During Year 1, S sells inventory to B and to X. Under paragraph (e)(1)(iv) of this section, to compute its intercompany inventory income and the amount of this income not taken into account, S computes its intercompany inventory income using the transfer price of the inventory items less a FIFO cost for the goods, takes into account these items based on a FIFO cost flow assumption for B's corresponding items, and the LIFO methods used by S and B are ignored for these computations. These computations are comparable to the methods used by S and B for financial reporting purposes, and the book methods and results are used for tax purposes. S adjusts the amount of intercompany inventory items not taken into account as required by section 263A.

(b) *Reasonable method.* The method used by S is a reasonable method under paragraph (e)(1)(iv) of this section if the cumulative amount of intercompany inventory items not taken into account by S is not significantly greater than the cumulative amount that would not be taken into account under the methods specifically described in paragraph (e)(1) of this section. If, for any year, the method results in a cumulative amount of intercompany inventory items not taken into account by S that significantly exceeds the cumulative amount that would not be taken into account under the methods specifically provided, S must take into account for that year the amount necessary to eliminate the excess. The method is thereafter applied with appropriate adjustments to reflect the amount taken into account (e.g., to prevent the amount from being taken into account more than once).

(2) *Reserve accounting*—(i) *Banks and thrifts.* Except as provided in paragraph (g)(3)(iv) of this section (deferral of items from an intercompany obligation), a member's addition to, or reduction of, a reserve for bad debts that is maintained under section 585 or 593 is taken into account on a separate entity basis. For example, if S makes a loan to a nonmember and subsequently sells the loan to B, any deduction for an addition to a bad debt reserve under section 585 and any recapture income (or reduced bad debt deductions) are taken into account on a separate entity basis rather than as intercompany items or corresponding items taken into account under this section. Any gain or loss of S from its sale of the loan to B is taken into account under this section, however, to the extent it is not attributable to recapture of the reserve.

(ii) *Insurance companies*—(A) *Direct insurance.* If a member provides insurance to another member in an intercompany transaction, the transaction is taken into account by both members on a separate entity basis. For example, if one member provides life insurance coverage for

Reg. § 1.1502-13(e)(2)

→ *Caution: Prior law may apply to certain transactions, see Reg. § 1.1502-13(l)(1), below. For Reg. § 1.1502-13 prior to revision by T.D. 8597, see Caution Note and text following this version of Reg. § 1.1502-13.*←

another member with respect to its employees, the premiums, reserve increases and decreases, and death benefit payments are determined and taken into account by both members on a separate entity basis rather than taken into account under this section as intercompany items and corresponding items.

(B) *Reinsurance*—(*1*) *In general.* Paragraph (e)(2)(ii)(A) of this section does not apply to a reinsurance transaction that is an intercompany transaction. For example, if a member assumes all or a portion of the risk on an insurance contract written by another member, the amounts transferred as reinsurance premiums, expense allowances, benefit reimbursements, reimbursed policyholder dividends, experience rating adjustments, and other similar items are taken into account under the matching rule and the acceleration rule. For purposes of this section, the assuming company is treated as B and the ceding company is treated as S.

(*2*) *Reserves determined on a separate entity basis.* For purposes of determining the amount of a member's increase or decrease in reserves, the amount of any reserve item listed in section 807(c) or 832(b)(5) resulting from a reinsurance transaction that is an intercompany transaction is determined on a separate entity basis. But see section 845, under which the Commissioner may allocate between or among the members any items, recharacterize any such items, or make any other adjustments necessary to reflect the proper source and character of the separate taxable income of a member.

(3) *Consent to treat intercompany transactions on a separate entity basis*—(i) *General rule.* The common parent may request consent to take into account on a separate entity basis items from intercompany transactions other than intercompany transactions with respect to stock or obligations of members. Consent may be granted for all items, or for items from a class or classes of transactions. The consent is effective only if granted in writing by the Internal Revenue Service. Unless revoked with the written consent of the Internal Revenue Service, the separate entity treatment applies to all affected intercompany transactions in the consolidated return year for which consent is granted and in all subsequent consolidated return years. Consent under this paragraph (e) (3) does not apply for purposes of taking into account losses and deductions deferred under section 267(f).

(ii) *Time and manner for requesting consent.* The request for consent described in paragraph (e)(3)(i) of this section must be made in the form of a ruling request. The request must be signed by the common parent, include any information required by the Internal Revenue Service, and be filed on or before the due date of the consolidated return (not including extensions of time) for the first consolidated return year to which the consent is to apply. The Internal Revenue Service may impose terms and conditions for granting consent. A copy of the consent must be attached to the group's consolidated returns (or amended returns) as required by the terms of the consent.

(iii) *Effect of consent on methods of accounting.* A consent for separate entity accounting under this paragraph (e)(3), and a revocation of that consent, may require changes in members' methods of accounting for intercompany transactions. Because the consent, or a revocation of the consent, is effective for all intercompany transactions occurring in the consolidated return year for which the consent or revocation is first effective, any change in method is effected on a cut-off basis. Section 446(e) consent is granted for any changes in methods of accounting for intercompany transactions that are necessary solely to conform a member's methods to a binding consent with respect to the group under this paragraph (e) (3) or the revocation of that consent, provided the changes are made in the first consolidated return year for which the consent or revocation under this paragraph (e)(3) is effective. Therefore, section 446(e) consent must be separately requested under applicable administrative procedures if a member has failed to conform its practices to the separate entity accounting provided under this paragraph (e)(3) or the revocation of that treatment in the first consolidated return year for which the consent to use separate entity accounting or revocation of that consent is effective.

(iv) *Consent to treat intercompany transactions on a separate entity basis under prior law.* A group that has received consent that is in effect as of the first day of the first consolidated return year beginning on or after July 12, 1995 to treat certain intercompany transactions as provided in § 1.1502-13(c)(3) of the regulations (as contained in the 26 CFR part 1 edition revised as of April 1, 1995) will be considered to have obtained the consent of the Commissioner to take items from intercompany transactions into account on a separate entity basis as provided in paragraph (e) (3)

Reg. § 1.1502-13(e)(3)

Consolidated Returns

See p. 20,601 for regulations not amended to reflect law changes

→ *Caution: Prior law may apply to certain transactions, see Reg. § 1.1502-13(l)(1), below. For Reg. § 1.1502-13 prior to revision by T.D. 8597, see Caution Note and text following this version of Reg. § 1.1502-13.* ←

(i) of this section. This treatment is applicable only to the items, class or classes of transactions for which consent was granted under prior law.

(f) *Stock of members*—(1) *In general.* In addition to the general rules of this section, the rules of this paragraph (f) apply to stock of members.

(2) *Intercompany distributions to which section 301 applies*—(i) *In general.* This paragraph (f)(2) provides rules for intercompany transactions to which section 301 applies (intercompany distributions). For purposes of determining whether a distribution is an intercompany distribution, it is treated as occurring under the principles of the entitlement rule of paragraph (f)(2)(iv) of this section. A distribution is not an intercompany distribution to the extent it is deducted by the distributing member. See, for example, section 1382(c)(1).

(ii) *Distributee member.* An intercompany distribution is not included in the gross income of the distributee member (B). However, this exclusion applies to a distribution only to the extent there is a corresponding negative adjustment reflected under § 1.1502-32 in B's basis in the stock of the distributing member (S). For example, no amount is included in B's gross income under section 301(c)(3) from a distribution in excess of the basis of the stock of a subsidiary that results in an excess loss account under § 1.1502-32(a) which is treated as negative basis under § 1.1502-19. B's dividend received deduction under section 243(a)(3) is determined without regard to any intercompany distributions under this paragraph (f)(2) to the extent they are not included in gross income. See § 1.1502-26(b) (applicability of the dividends received deduction to distributions not excluded from gross income, such as a distribution from the common parent to a subsidiary owning stock of the common parent).

(iii) *Distributing member.* The principles of section 311(b) apply to S's loss, as well as gain, from an intercompany distribution of property. Thus, S's loss is taken into account under the matching rule if the property is subsequently sold to a nonmember. However, section 311(a) continues to apply to distributions to nonmembers (for example, loss is not recognized).

(iv) *Entitlement rule*—(A) *In general.* For all Federal income tax purposes, an intercompany distribution is treated as taken into account when the shareholding member becomes entitled to it (generally on the record date). For example, if B becomes entitled to a cash distribution before it is made, the distribution is treated as made when B becomes entitled to it. For this purpose, B is treated as entitled to a distribution no later than the time the distribution is taken into account under the Internal Revenue Code (e.g., under section 305(c)). To the extent a distribution is not made, appropriate adjustments must be made as of the date it was taken into account.

(B) *Nonmember shareholders.* If nonmembers own stock of the distributing corporation at the time the distribution is treated as occurring under this paragraph (f)(2)(iv), appropriate adjustments must be made to prevent the acceleration of the distribution to members from affecting distributions to nonmembers.

(3) *Boot in an intercompany reorganization*—(i) *Scope.* This paragraph (f)(3) provides additional rules for an intercompany transaction in which the receipt of money or other property (nonqualifying property) results in the application of section 356. For example, the distribution of stock of a lower-tier member to a higher tier member in an intercompany transaction to which section 355 would apply but for the receipt of nonqualifying property is a transaction to which this paragraph (f)(3) applies. This paragraph (f)(3) does not apply if a party to the transaction becomes a member or nonmember as part of the same plan or arrangement. For example, if S merges into a nonmember in a transaction described in section 368(a)(1)(A), this paragraph (f)(3) does not apply.

(ii) *Treatment.* Nonqualifying property received as part of a transaction described in this paragraph (f) (3) is treated as received by the member shareholder in a separate transaction. See, for example, sections 302 and 311 (rather than sections 356 and 361). The nonqualifying property is treated as taken into account immediately after the transaction if section 354 would apply but for the fact that nonqualifying property is received. It is treated as taken into account immediately before the transaction if section 355 would apply but for the fact that nonqualifying property is received. The treatment under this paragraph (f) (3)(ii) applies for all Federal income tax purposes.

(4) *Acquisition by issuer of its own stock.* If a member acquires its own stock, or an option to buy or sell its own stock, in an intercompany transaction, the member's basis in that stock or option is treated as eliminated for all purposes. Accordingly, S's intercompany items from the stock or options of B are taken into account under

Reg. § 1.1502-13(f)(4)

→ *Caution: Prior law may apply to certain transactions, see Reg. § 1.1502-13(l)(1), below. For Reg. § 1.1502-13 prior to revision by T.D. 8597, see Caution Note and text following this version of Reg. § 1.1502-13.*←

this section if B acquires the stock or options in an intercompany transaction (unless, for example, B acquires the stock in exchange for successor property within the meaning of paragraph (j)(1) (1) of this section in a nonrecognition transaction). For example, if B redeems its stock from S in a transaction to which section 302(a) applies, S's gain from the transaction is taken into account immediately under the acceleration rule.

(5) *Certain liquidations and distributions*— (i) *Netting allowed.* S's intercompany item from a transfer to B of the stock of another corporation (T) is taken into account under this section in certain circumstances even though the T stock is never held by a nonmember after the intercompany transaction. For example, if S sells all of T's stock to B at a gain, and T subsequently liquidates into B in a separate transaction to which section 332 applies, S's gain is taken into account under the matching rule. Under paragraph (c)(6)(ii) of this section, S's intercompany gain taken into account as a result of a liquidation under section 332 or a comparable nonrecognition transaction is not redetermined to be excluded from gross income. Under this paragraph (f)(5)(i), if S has both intercompany income or gain and intercompany deduction or loss attributable to stock of the same corporation having the same material terms, only the income or gain in excess of the deduction or loss is subject to paragraph (c)(6)(ii) of this section. This paragraph (f)(5)(i) applies only to a transaction in which B's basis in its T stock is permanently eliminated in a liquidation under section 332 or any comparable nonrecognition transaction, including—

(A) A merger of B into T under section 368(a);

(B) A distribution by B of its T stock in a transaction described in section 355; or

(C) A deemed liquidation of T resulting from an election under section 338(h)(10).

(ii) *Elective relief*—(A) *In general.* If an election is made pursuant to this paragraph (f)(5)(ii), certain transactions are recharacterized to prevent S's items from being taken into account or to provide offsets to those items. This paragraph (f) (5) (ii) applies only if T is a member throughout the period beginning with S's transfer and ending with the completion of the nonrecognition transaction.

(B) *Section 332*—(*1*) *In general.* If section 332 applies to T's liquidation into B, and B transfers T's assets to a new member (new T) in a transaction not otherwise pursuant to the same plan or arrangement as the liquidation, the transfer is nevertheless treated for all Federal income tax purposes as pursuant to the same plan or arrangement as the liquidation. For example, if T liquidates into B, but B forms new T by transferring substantially all of T's former assets to new T, S's intercompany gain or loss generally is not taken into account solely as a result of the liquidation if the liquidation and transfer would qualify as a reorganization described in section 368(a). (Under paragraph (j)(1) of this section, B's stock in new T would be a successor asset to B's stock in T, and S's gain would be taken into account based on the new T stock.)

(*2*) *Time limitation and adjustments.* The transfer of an asset to new T not otherwise pursuant to the same plan or arrangement as the liquidation is treated under this paragraph (f) (5) (ii) (B) as pursuant to the same plan or arrangement only if B transfers it to new T pursuant to a written plan, a copy of which is attached to a timely filed original return (including extensions) for the year of T's liquidation, and the transfer is completed within 12 months of the filing of that return. Appropriate adjustments are made to reflect any events occurring before the formation of new T and to reflect any assets not transferred to new T as part of the same plan or arrangement. For example, if B retains an asset in the reorganization, the asset is treated under paragraph (f)(3) of this section as acquired by new T but distributed to B immediately after the reorganization.

(*3*) *Downstream merger, etc.* The principles of this paragraph (f)(5)(ii)(B) apply, with appropriate adjustments, if B's basis in the T stock is eliminated in a transaction similar to a section 332 liquidation, such as a transaction described in section 368 in which B merges into T. For example, if S and B are subsidiaries, and S sells all of T's stock to B at a gain followed by B's merger into T in a separate transaction described in section 368(a), S's gain is not taken into account solely as a result of the merger if T (as successor to B) forms new T with substantially all of T's former assets.

(C) *Section 338(h)(10)*—(*1*) *In general.* This paragraph (f)(5)(ii)(C) applies to a deemed liquidation of T under section 332 as the result of an election under section 338(h)(10). This paragraph (f)(5)(ii)(C) does not apply if paragraph (f)(5)(ii)(B) of this section is applied to the deemed liquidation. Under this paragraph, B is treated with respect to each share of its T stock as

Reg. § 1.1502-13(f)(5)

Consolidated Returns

See p. 20,601 for regulations not amended to reflect law changes

→ *Caution: Prior law may apply to certain transactions, see Reg. § 1.1502-13(l)(1), below. For Reg. § 1.1502-13 prior to revision by T.D. 8597, see Caution Note and text following this version of Reg. § 1.1502-13.* ←

recognizing as a corresponding item any loss or deduction it would recognize (determined after adjusting stock basis under § 1.1502-32) if section 331 applied to the deemed liquidation. For all other Federal income tax purposes, the deemed liquidation remains subject to section 332.

(2) *Limitation on amount of loss.* The amount of B's loss or deduction under this paragraph (f)(5)(ii)(C) is limited as follows—

(*i*) The aggregate amount of loss recognized with respect to T stock cannot exceed the amount of S's intercompany income or gain that is in excess of S's intercompany deduction or loss with respect to shares of T stock having the same material terms as the shares giving rise to S's intercompany income or gain; and

(*ii*) The aggregate amount of loss recognized under this paragraph (f)(5)(ii)(C) from T's deemed liquidation cannot exceed the net amount of deduction or loss (if any) that would be taken into account from the deemed liquidation if section 331 applied with respect to all T shares.

(3) *Asset sale, etc.* The principles of this paragraph (f)(5)(ii)(C) apply, with appropriate adjustments, if T transfers all of its assets to a nonmember and completely liquidates in a transaction comparable to the section 338(h)(10) transaction described in paragraph (f)(5)(ii)(C)(1) of this section. For example, if S sells all of T's stock to B at a gain followed by T's merger into a nonmember in exchange for a cash payment to B in a transaction treated for Federal income tax purposes as T's sale of its assets to the nonmember and complete liquidation, the merger is ordinarily treated as a comparable transaction.

(D) *Section 355.* If B distributes the T stock in an intercompany transaction to which section 355 applies (including an intercompany transaction to which 355 applies because of the application of paragraph (f)(3) of this section), the redetermination of the basis of the T stock under section 358 could cause S's gain or loss to be taken into account under this section. This paragraph (f)(5)(ii)(D) applies to treat B's distribution as subject to section 301 and 311 (as modified by this paragraph (f)), rather than section 355. The election will prevent S's gain or loss from being taken into account immediately to the extent matching remains possible, but B's gain or loss from the distribution will also be taken into account under this section.

(E) *Election.* An election to apply this paragraph (f)(5)(ii) is made in a separate statement entitled "[Insert Name and Employer Identification Number of Common Parent] HEREBY ELECTS THE APPLICATION OF § 1.1502-13(f)(5)(ii)." The election must include a description of S's intercompany transaction and T's liquidation (or other transaction). It must specify which provision of § 1.1502-13(f)(5)(ii) applies and how it alters the otherwise applicable results under this section (including, for example, the amount of S's intercompany items and the amount deferred or offset as a result of this § 1.1502-13(f)(5)(ii)). A separate election must be made for each application of this paragraph (f)(5)(ii). The election must be signed by the common parent and filed with the group's income tax return for the year of T's liquidation (or other transaction). The Commissioner may impose reasonable terms and conditions to the application of this paragraph (f)(5)(ii) that are consistent with the purposes of this section.

(6) *Stock of common parent.* In addition to the general rules of this section, this paragraph (f)(6) applies to parent stock (P stock) and positions in P stock held or entered into by another member. For this purpose, P stock is any stock of the common parent held (directly or indirectly) by another member or any stock of a member (the issuer) that was the common parent if the stock was held (directly or indirectly) by another member while the issuer was the common parent.

(i) *Loss stock*—(A) *Recognized loss.* Any loss recognized, directly or indirectly, by a member with respect to P stock is permanently disallowed and does not reduce earnings and profits. See § 1.1502-32(b)(3)(iii)(A) for a corresponding reduction in the basis of the member's stock.

(B) *Other cases.* If a member, M, owns P stock, the stock is subsequently owned by a nonmember, and, immediately before the stock is owned by the nonmember, M's basis in the share exceeds its fair market value, then, to the extent paragraph (f)(6)(i)(A) of this section does not apply, M's basis in the share is reduced to the share's fair market value immediately before the share is held by the nonmember. For example, if M owns shares of P stock with a $100x basis and M becomes a nonmember at a time when the P shares have a value of $60x, M's basis in the P shares is reduced to $60x immediately before M becomes a nonmember. Similarly, if M contributes the P stock to a nonmember in a transaction subject to section 351, M's basis in the shares is reduced to $60x immediately before the contribu-

Reg. § 1.1502-13(f)(6)

→ *Caution: Prior law may apply to certain transactions, see Reg. § 1.1502-13(l)(1), below. For Reg. § 1.1502-13 prior to revision by T.D. 8597, see Caution Note and text following this version of Reg. § 1.1502-13.* ←

tion. See § 1.1502-32(b)(3)(iii)(B) for a corresponding reduction in the basis of M's stock.

(C) *Waiver of built-in loss on P stock*— (*1*) *In general.* If a nonmember that owns P stock with a basis in excess of its fair market value becomes a member of the P consolidated group in a qualifying cost basis transaction, the group may make an irrevocable election to reduce the basis of the P stock to its fair market value immediately before the nonmember becomes a member of the P group. If the nonmember was a member of another consolidated group immediately before becoming a member of the P group, the reduction in basis is treated as occurring immediately after it ceases to be a member of the prior group. A qualifying cost basis transaction is the purchase (i.e., a transaction in which basis is determined under section 1012) by members of the P consolidated group (while they are members) in a 12-month period of an amount of the nonmember's stock satisfying the requirements of section 1504(a)(2).

(*2*) *Election.* The election described in this paragraph (6)(i)(C) must be made in a separate statement entitled "ELECTION TO REDUCE BASIS OF P STOCK UNDER § 1.1502-13(f)(6)." The statement must be filed with the P consolidated group's return for the year in which the nonmember becomes a member, and it must be signed by both P and the nonmember. The statement must identify the fair market value of, and the amount of the basis reduction in, the P stock.

(ii) *Gain stock.* If a member, M, would otherwise recognize gain on a qualified disposition of P stock, then immediately before the qualified disposition, M is treated as purchasing the P stock from P for fair market value with cash contributed to M by P (or, if necessary, through any intermediate members). A disposition is a qualified disposition only if—

(A) The member acquires the P stock directly from the common parent (P) through a contribution to capital or a transaction qualifying under section 351(a) (or, if necessary, through a series of such transactions involving only members);

(B) Pursuant to a plan, the member transfers the stock immediately to a nonmember that is not related, within the meaning of section 267(b) or 707(b), to any member of the group;

(C) No nonmember receives a substituted basis in the stock within the meaning of section 7701(a)(42);

(D) The P stock is not exchanged for P stock;

(E) P neither becomes nor ceases to be the common parent as part of, or in contemplation of, the disposition or plan; and

(F) M is neither a nonmember that becomes a member nor a member that becomes a nonmember as part of, or in contemplation of, the disposition or plan.

(iii) *Mark-to-market of P stock.* Paragraphs (f)(6)(i) and (ii) of this section shall not apply to any gain or loss from a share of P stock held by a member, M, if—

(A) M regularly trades in P stock (of the same class) with customers in the ordinary course of its business as a dealer;

(B) The gain or loss on the share is taken into account by M pursuant to section 475(a);

(C) M's basis in the share is not adjusted by reference to the basis of any other property or by reference to income, gain, deduction, or loss from other property; and

(D) Neither M nor any other member of the group has structured or engaged in any transaction while a member (or in anticipation of becoming a member), during the taxable year or in any year within the preceding five taxable years that is open for assessment under section 6501, with a principal purpose of avoiding gain or creating loss on P stock subject to section 475(a).

(iv) *Options, warrants, and other positions*—(A) *In general.* This paragraph (f)(6) applies with appropriate adjustments to positions in P stock to the extent that P's gain or loss from an equivalent position would not be recognized under section 1032. Thus, if M purchases an option to buy or sell P stock and sells the option at a loss, the loss is permanently disallowed under paragraph (f)(6)(i)(A) of this section. Similarly, if M is the grantor of such an option and becomes a nonmember, then the principles of paragraph (f)(6)(i)(B) of this section apply to the extent that M would recognize loss from cash settlement of the option at its fair market value immediately before M becomes a nonmember, and proper adjustments must be made in the amount of any gain or loss subsequently realized from the position by M. If P grants M an option to acquire P stock in a transaction meeting the requirements of paragraph (f)(6)(ii) of this section, M is treated

Reg. § 1.1502-13(f)(6)

Consolidated Returns

See p. 20,601 for regulations not amended to reflect law changes

→ *Caution: Prior law may apply to certain transactions, see Reg. § 1.1502-13(l)(1), below. For Reg. § 1.1502-13 prior to revision by T.D. 8597, see Caution Note and text following this version of Reg. § 1.1502-13.*←

as having purchased the option from P for fair market value with cash contributed to M by P.

(B) *Mark-to-market of positions in P stock.* For purposes of paragraph (f)(6)(iii) of this section, gain or loss with respect to a position taken into account under section 1256(a) is treated as taken into account under section 475(a) to the extent that the gain or loss would be taken into account under the principles of section 475.

(v) *Effective date.* This paragraph (f)(6) applies to gain or loss taken into account on or after July 12, 1995, and to transactions occurring on or after July 12, 1995. However, paragraph (f)(6)(ii) of this section and the last sentence of paragraph (f)(6)(iv)(A) of this section do not apply to dispositions of P stock or options occurring on or after May 16, 2000. For example, if S sells P stock to B at a loss prior to July 12, 1995, and B sells the P stock to a nonmember after July 12, 1995, S's loss is disallowed because it is taken into account after July 12, 1995. If a taxpayer takes a gain or loss into account or engages in a transaction on or after July 12, 1995, during a tax year ending prior to December 31, 1995, the taxpayer may treat the gain or loss or the transaction under the rules of § 1.1502-13T(f)(6) (published in 1995-32 I.R.B. 47), instead of under the rules of this paragraph (f)(6).

(7) *Examples.* The application of this section to intercompany transactions with respect to stock of members is illustrated by the following examples.

Example 1. Dividend exclusion and property distribution. (a) *Facts.* S owns land with a $70 basis and $100 value. On January 1 of Year 1, P's basis in S's stock is $100. During Year 1, S declares and makes a dividend distribution of the land to P. Under section 311(b), S has a $30 gain. Under section 301(d), P's basis in the land is $100. On July 1 of Year 3, P sells the land to X for $110.

(b) *Dividend elimination and stock basis adjustments.* Under paragraph (b)(1) of this section, S's distribution to P is an intercompany distribution. Under paragraph (f)(2)(ii) of this section, P's $100 of dividend income is not included in gross income. Under § 1.1502-32, P's basis in S's stock is reduced from $100 to $0 in Year 1.

(c) *Matching rule and stock basis adjustments.* Under the matching rule (treating P as the buying member and S as the selling member), S takes its $30 gain into account in Year 3 to reflect the $30 difference between P's $10 gain taken into account and the $40 recomputed gain. Under § 1.1502-32, P's basis in S's stock is increased from $0 to $30 in Year 3.

(d) *Loss property.* The facts are the same as in paragraph (a) of this *Example* except, that S has a $130 (rather than $70) basis in the land. Under paragraph (f)(2)(iii) of this section, the principles of section 311(b) apply to S's loss from the intercompany distribution. Thus, S has a $30 loss that is taken into account under the matching rule in Year 3 to reflect the $30 difference between P's $10 gain taken into account and the $20 recomputed loss. (The results are the same under section 267(f).) Under § 1.1502-32, P's basis in S's stock is reduced from $100 to $0 in Year 1, and from $0 to a $30 excess loss account in Year 3. (If P had distributed the land to its shareholders, rather than selling the land to X, P would take its $10 gain under section 311(b) into account, and S would take its $30 loss into account under the matching rule with $10 offset by P's gain and $20 recharacterized as a noncapital, nondeductible amount.)

(e) *Entitlement rule.* The facts are the same as in paragraph (a) of this *Example 1,* except that, after P becomes entitled to the distribution but before the distribution is made, S issues additional stock to the public and becomes a nonmember. Under paragraph (f)(2)(i) of this section, the determination of whether a distribution is an intercompany distribution is made under the entitlement rule of paragraph (f)(2)(iv) of this section. Treating S's distribution as made when P becomes entitled to it results in the distribution being an intercompany distribution. Under paragraph (f)(2)(ii) of this section, the distribution is not included in P's gross income. S's $30 gain from the distribution is intercompany gain that is taken into account under the acceleration rule immediately before S becomes a nonmember. Thus, there is a net $70 decrease in P's basis in its S stock under § 1.1502-32 ($100 decrease for the distribution and a $30 increase for S's $30 gain). See also § 1.1502-20(b) (additional stock basis reductions applicable to certain deconsolidations). Under paragraph (f)(2)(iv) of this section, P does not take the distribution into account again under separate return rules when received, and P is not entitled to a dividends received deduction.

Example 2. Excess loss accounts. (a) *Facts.* S owns all of T's only class of stock with a $10 basis and $100 value. S has substantial earnings and profits, and T has $10 of earnings and profits. On January 1 of Year 1, S declares and distributes a

Reg. § 1.1502-13(f)(7)

→ Caution: Prior law may apply to certain transactions, see Reg. § 1.1502-13(l)(1), below. For Reg. § 1.1502-13 prior to revision by T.D. 8597, see Caution Note and text following this version of Reg. § 1.1502-13. ←

dividend of all of the T stock to P. Under section 311(b), S has a $90 gain. Under section 301(d), P's basis in the T stock is $100. During Year 3, T borrows $90 and declares and makes a $90 distribution to P to which section 301 applies, and P's basis in the T stock is reduced under § 1.1502-32 from $100 to $10. During Year 6, T has $5 of earnings that increase P's basis in the T stock under § 1.1502-32 from $10 to $15. On December 1 of Year 9, T issues additional stock to X and, as a result, T becomes a nonmember.

(b) *Dividend exclusion.* Under paragraph (f)(2)(ii) of this section, P's $100 of dividend income from S's distribution of the T stock, and its $10 of dividend income from T's $90 distribution, are not included in gross income.

(c) *Matching and acceleration rules.* Under § 1.1502-19(b)(1), when T becomes a nonmember P must include in income the amount of its excess loss account (if any) in T stock. P has no excess loss account in the T stock. Therefore P's corresponding item from the deconsolidation of T is $0. Treating S and P as divisions of a single corporation, the T stock would continue to have a $10 basis after the distribution, and the adjustments under § 1.1502-32 for T's $90 distribution and $5 of earnings would result in a $75 excess loss account. Thus, the recomputed corresponding item from the deconsolidation is $75. Under the matching rule, S takes $75 of its $90 gain into account in Year 9 as a result of T becoming a nonmember, to reflect the difference between P's $0 gain taken into account and the $75 recomputed gain. S's remaining $15 of gain is taken into account under the matching and acceleration rules based on subsequent events (for example, under the matching rule if P subsequently sells its T stock, or under the acceleration rule if S becomes a nonmember).

(d) *Reverse sequence.* The facts are the same as in paragraph (a) of this *Example 2,* except that T borrows $90 and makes its $90 distribution to S before S distributes T's stock to P. Under paragraph (f)(2)(ii) of this section, T's $90 distribution to S ($10 of which is a dividend) is not included in S's gross income. The corresponding negative adjustment under § 1.1502-32 reduces S's basis in the T stock from $10 to an $80 excess loss account. Under section 311(b), S has a $90 gain from the distribution of T stock to P. Under section 301(d) P's initial basis in the T stock is $10 (the stock's fair market value), and the basis increases to $15 under § 1.1502-32 as a result of T's earnings in Year 6. The timing and attributes of S's gain are determined in the manner provided in paragraph (c) of this *Example 2.* Thus, $75 of S's gain is taken into account under the matching rule in Year 9 as a result of T becoming a nonmember, and the remaining $15 is taken into account under the matching and acceleration rules based on subsequent events.

(e) *Partial stock sale.* The facts are the same as in paragraph (a) of this *Example 2,* except that P sells 10% of T's stock to X on December 1 of Year 9 for $1.50 (rather than T's issuing additional stock and becoming a nonmember). Under the matching rule, S takes $9 of its gain into account to reflect the difference between P's $0 gain taken into account ($1.50 sale proceeds minus $1.50 basis) and the $9 recomputed gain ($1.50 sale proceeds plus $7.50 excess loss account).

(f) *Loss, rather than cash distribution.* The facts are the same as in paragraph (a) of this *Example 2,* except that T retains the loan proceeds and incurs a $90 loss in Year 3 that is absorbed by the group. The timing and attributes of S's gain are determined in the same manner provided in paragraph (c) of this *Example 2.* Under § 1.1502-32, the loss in Year 3 reduces P's basis in the T stock from $100 to $10, and T's $5 of earnings in Year 6 increase the basis to $15. Thus, $75 of S's gain is taken into account under the matching rule in Year 9 as a result of T becoming a nonmember, and the remaining $15 is taken into account under the matching and acceleration rules based on subsequent events. (The timing and attributes of S's gain would be determined in the same manner provided in paragraph (d) of this *Example 2* if T incurred the $90 loss before S's distribution of the T stock to P.)

(g) *Stock sale, rather than stock distribution.* The facts are the same as in paragraph (a) of this *Example* except, that S sells the T stock to P for $100 (rather than distributing the stock). The timing and attributes of S's gain are determined in the same manner provided in paragraph (c) of this *Example 2.* Thus, $75 of S's gain is taken into account under the matching rule in Year 9 as a result of T becoming a nonmember, and the remaining $15 is taken into account under the matching and acceleration rules based on subsequent events.

Example 3. Intercompany reorganization. (a) *Facts.* P forms S and B by contributing $200 to the capital of each. During Years 1 through 4, S and B each earn $50, and under § 1.1502-32 P adjusts its basis in the stock of each to $250. (See § 1.1502-33 for adjustments to earnings and prof-

Reg. § 1.1502-13(f)(7)

→ *Caution: Prior law may apply to certain transactions, see Reg. § 1.1502-13(l)(1), below. For Reg. § 1.1502-13 prior to revision by T.D. 8597, see Caution Note and text following this version of Reg. § 1.1502-13.*←

its.) On January 1 of Year 5, the fair market value of S's assets and its stock is $500, and S merges into B in a tax-free reorganization. Pursuant to the plan of reorganization, P receives B stock with a fair market value of $350 and $150 of cash.

(b) *Treatment as a section 301 distribution.* The merger of S into B is a transaction to which paragraph (f)(3) of this section applies. P is treated as receiving additional B stock with a fair market value of $500 and, under section 358, a basis of $250. Immediately after the merger, $150 of the stock received is treated as redeemed, and the redemption is treated under section 302(d) as a distribution to which section 301 applies. Because the $150 distribution is treated as not received as part of the merger, section 356 does not apply and no basis adjustments are required under section 358(a)(1)(A) and (B). Because B is treated under section 381(c)(2) as receiving S's earnings and profits and the redemption is treated as occurring after the merger, $100 of the distribution is treated as a dividend under section 301 and P's basis in the B stock is reduced correspondingly under § 1.1502-32. The remaining $50 of the distribution reduces P's basis in the B stock. Section 301(c)(2) and § 1.1502-32. Under paragraph (f)(2)(ii) of this section, P's $100 of dividend income is not included in gross income. Under § 1.302-2(c), proper adjustments are made to P's basis in its B stock to reflect its basis in the B stock redeemed, with the result that P's basis in the B stock is reduced by the entire $150 distribution.

(c) *Depreciated property.* The facts are the same as in paragraph (a) of this *Example 3*, except that property of S with a $200 basis and $150 fair market value is distributed to p (rather than cash of B). As in paragraph (b) of this *Example 3*, P is treated as receiving additional B stock in the merger and a $150 distribution to which section 301 applies immediately after the merger. Under paragraph (f)(2)(iii) of this section, the principles of section 311(b) apply to B's $50 loss and the loss is taken into account under the matching and acceleration rules based on subsequent events (e.g., under the matching rule if P subsequently sells the property, or under the acceleration rule if B becomes a nonmember). The results are the same under section 267(f).

(d) *Divisive transaction.* Assume instead that, pursuant to a plan, S distributes the stock of a lower-tier subsidiary in a spin-off transaction to which section 355 applies together with $150 of cash. The distribution of stock is a transaction to which paragraph (f)(3) of this section applies. P is treated as receiving the $150 of cash immediately before the section 355 distribution, as a distribution to which section 301 applies. Section 356(b) does not apply and no basis adjustments are required under section 358(a)(1)(A) and (B). Because the $150 distribution is treated as made before the section 355 distribution, the distribution reduces P's basis in the S stock under § 1.1502-32, and the basis allocated under section 358(c) between the S stock and the lower-tier subsidiary stock received reflects this basis reduction.

Example 4. Stock redemptions and distributions. (a) *Facts.* Before becoming a member of the P group, S owns P stock with a $30 basis. on January 1 of Year 1, P buys all of S's stock. On July 1 of Year 3, P redeems the P stock held by S for $100 in a transaction to which section 302(a) applies.

(b) *Gain under section 302.* Under paragraph (f)(4) of this section, P's basis in the P stock acquired from S is treated as eliminated. As a result of this elimination, S's intercompany item will never be taken into account under the matching rule because P's basis in the stock does not reflect S's intercompany item. Therefore, S's $70 gain is taken into account under the acceleration rule in Year 3. The attributes of S's item are determined under paragraph (d)(1)(ii) of this section by applying the matching rule as if p had sold the stock to an affiliated corporation that is not a member of the group at no gain or loss. Although P's corresponding item from a sale of its stock would have been excluded from gross income under section 1032, paragraph (c)(6)(ii) of this section prevents S's gain from being treated as excluded from gross income; instead S's gain is capital gain.

(c) *Gain under section 311.* The facts are the same as in paragraph (a) of this *Example except*, except that S distributes the P stock to P in a transaction to which section 301 applies (rather than the stock being redeemed), and S has a $70 gain under section 311(b). The timing and attributes of S's gain are determined in the manner provided in paragraph (b) of this *Example 4*.

(d) *Loss stock.* The facts are the same as in paragraph (a) of this *Example 4*, except that S has a $130 (rather than $30) basis in the P stock and has a $30 loss under section 302(a). The limitation under paragraph (c)(6)(ii) of this section does not apply to intercompany losses. Thus,

Reg. § 1.1502-13(f)(7)

56,724   **Consolidated Returns**

See p. 20,601 for regulations not amended to reflect law changes

→ *Caution: Prior law may apply to certain transactions, see Reg. § 1.1502-13(l)(1), below. For Reg. § 1.1502-13 prior to revision by T.D. 8597, see Caution Note and text following this version of Reg. § 1.1502-13.*←

S's loss is taken into account in Year 3 as a noncapital, nondeductible amount.

Example 5. Intercompany stock sale followed by section 332 liquidation. (a) *Facts.* S owns all of the stock of T, with a $70 basis and $100 value, and T's assets have a $10 basis and $100 value. On January 1 of Year 1, S sells all of T's stock to B for $100. On July 1 of Year 3, when T's assets are still worth $100, T distributes all of its assets to B in an unrelated complete liquidation to which section 332 applies.

(b) *Timing and attributes.* Under paragraph (b)(3)(ii) of this section, B's unrecognized gain or loss under section 332 is a corresponding item for purposes of applying the matching rule. In Year 3 when T liquidates, B has $0 of unrecognized gain or loss under section 332 because B has a $100 basis in the T stock and receives a $100 distribution with respect to its T stock. Treating S and B as divisions of a single corporation, the recomputed corresponding item would have been $30 of unrecognized gain under section because B would have succeeded to S's $70 basis in the T stock. Thus, under the matching rule, S's $30 intercompany gain is taken into account in Year 3 as a result of T's liquidation. Under paragraph (c)(1)(i) of this section, the attributes of S's gain and B's corresponding item are redetermined as if S and B were divisions of a single corporation. Although S's gain ordinarily would be redetermined to be treated as excluded from gross income to reflect the nonrecognition of B's gain under section 332, S's gain remains capital gain because B's unrecognized gain under section 332 is not permanently and explicitly disallowed under the Code. See paragraph (c)(6)(ii) of this section. However, relief may be elected under paragraph (f)(5)(ii) of this section.

(c) *Intercompany sale at a loss.* The facts are the same as in paragraph (a) of this *Example 5*, except that S has a $130 (rather than $70) basis in the T stock. The limitation under paragraph (c)(6)(ii) of this section does not apply to intercompany losses. Thus, S's intercompany loss is taken into account in Year 3 as a noncapital, nondeductible amount. However, relief may be elected under paragraph (f)(5)(ii) of this section.

Example 6. Intercompany stock sale followed by section 355 distribution. (a) *Facts.* S owns all of the stock of T with a $70 basis and $100 value. On January 1 of Year 1, S sells all of T's stock to M for $100. on June 1I of Year 6, M distributes all of its T stock to its nonmember shareholders in a transaction to which section 355 applies. At the time of the distribution, M has a basis in T stock of $100 and T has a value of $150.

(b) *Timing and attributes.* Under paragraph (b)(3)(ii) of this section, M's $50 gain not recognized on the distribution under section 355 is a corresponding item. Treating S and M as divisions of a single corporation, the recomputed corresponding item would be $80 of unrecognized gain under section 355 because M would have succeeded to S's $70 basis in the T stock. Thus, under the matching rule, S's $30 intercompany gain is taken into account in Year 6 as a result of the distribution. Under paragraph (c)(1)(i) of this section, the attributes of S's intercompany item and M's corresponding item are redetermined to produce the same effect on consolidated taxable income as if S and M were divisions of a single corporation. Although S's gain ordinarily would be redetermined to be treated as excluded from gross income to reflect the nonrecognition of M's gain under section 355(c), S's gain remains capital gain because M's unrecognized gain under section 355(c) is not permanently and explicitly disallowed under the Code. See paragraph (c)(6)(ii) of this section. Because M's distribution of the T stock is not an intercompany transaction, relief is not available under paragraph (f)(5)(ii) of this section.

(c) *Section 355 distribution within the group.* The facts are the same as under paragraph (a) of this *Example 6*, except that M distributes the T stock to B (another member of the group), and B takes a $75 basis in the T stock under section 358. Under paragraph (j)(2) of this section, B is a successor to M for purposes of taking S's intercompany gain into account, and therefore both M and B might have corresponding items with respect to S's intercompany gain. To the extent it is possible, matching with respect to B's corresponding items produces the result most consistent with treating S, M, and B as divisions of a single corporation. See paragraphs (j)(3) and (j)(4) of this section. However, because there is only $5 difference between B's $75 basis in the T stock and the $70 basis the stock would have if S, M, and B were divisions of a single corporation, only $5 can be taken into account under the matching rule with respect to B's corresponding items. (This $5 is taken into account with respect to B's corresponding items based on subsequent events.) The remaining $25 of S's $30 intercompany gain is taken into account in Year 6 under the matching rule with respect to M's corresponding item from its distribution of the T stock. The attributes of

Reg. § 1.1502-13(f)(7)

Consolidated Returns

See p. 20,601 for regulations not amended to reflect law changes

→ *Caution: Prior law may apply to certain transactions, see Reg. § 1.1502-13(l)(1), below. For Reg. § 1.1502-13 prior to revision by T.D. 8597, see Caution Note and text following this version of Reg. § 1.1502-13.*←

S's remaining $25 of gain are determined in the same manner as in paragraph (b) of this *Example 6.*

(d) *Relief elected.* The facts are the same as in paragraph (c) of this *Example 6* except that P elects relief pursuant to paragraph (f)(5)(ii)(D) of this section. As a result of the election, M's distribution of the T stock is treated as subject to sections 301 and 311 instead of section 355. Accordingly, M recognizes $50 of intercompany gain from the distribution, B takes a basis in the stock equal to its fair market value of $150, and S and M take their intercompany gains into account with respect to B's corresponding items based on subsequent events. (None of S's gain is taken into account in Year 6 as a result of M's distribution of the T stock.)

(g) *Obligations of members*—(1) *In general.* In addition to the general rules of this section, the rules of this paragraph (g) apply to intercompany obligations.

(2) *Definitions.* For purposes of this section—

(i) *Obligation of a member.* An obligation of a member is—

(A) Any obligation of the member constituting indebtedness under general principles of Federal income tax law (for example, under nonstatutory authorities, or under section 108, section 163, section 171, or section 1275), but not an executory obligation to purchase or provide goods or services; and

(B) Any security of the member described in section 475(c)(2)(D) or (E), and any comparable security with respect to commodities, but not if the security is a position with respect to the member's stock. See paragraphs (f)(4) and (6) of this section and § 1.1502-13T(f)(6) for special rules applicable to positions with respect to a member's stock.

(ii) *Intercompany obligations.* An intercompany obligation is an obligation between members, but only for the period during which both parties are members.

(3) *Deemed satisfaction and reissuance of intercompany obligations*—(i) *Application*—(A) *In general.* If a member realizes an amount (other than zero) of income, gain, deduction, or loss, directly or indirectly, from the assignment or extinguishment of all or part of its remaining rights or obligations under an intercompany obligation, the intercompany obligation is treated for all Federal income tax purposes as satisfied under paragraph (g)(3)(ii) of this section and, if it remains outstanding, reissued under paragraph (g)(3)(iii) of this section. Similar principles apply under this paragraph (g)(3) if a member realizes any such amount, directly or indirectly, from a comparable transaction (for example, a marking-to-market of an obligation or a bad debt deduction), or if an intercompany obligation becomes an obligation that is not an intercompany obligation.

(B) *Exceptions.* This paragraph (g)(3) does not apply to an obligation if any of the following applies:

(*1*) The obligation became an intercompany obligation by reason of an event described in § 1.108-2(e) (exceptions to the application of section 108(e)(4)).

(*2*) The amount realized is from reserve accounting under section 585 or section 593 (see paragraph (g)(3)(iv) of this section for special rules).

(*3*) The amount realized is from the conversion of an obligation into stock of the obligor.

(*4*) Treating the obligation as satisfied and reissued will not have a significant effect on any person's Federal income tax liability for any year. For this purpose, obligations issued in connection with the same transaction or related transactions are treated as a single obligation. However, this paragraph (g)(3)(i)(B)(4) does not apply to any obligation if the aggregate effect of this treatment for all obligations in a year would be significant.

(ii) *Satisfaction*—(A) *General rule.* If a creditor member sells intercompany debt for cash, the debt is treated as satisfied by the debtor immediately before the sale for the amount of the cash. For other transactions, similar principles apply to treat the intercompany debt as satisfied immediately before the transaction. Thus, if the debt is transferred for property, it is treated as satisfied for an amount consistent with the amount for which the debt is deemed reissued under paragraph (g)(3)(iii) of this section, and the basis of the property is also adjusted to reflect that amount. If this paragraph (g)(3) applies because the debtor or creditor becomes a nonmember, the obligation is treated as satisfied for cash in an amount equal to its fair market value immediately before the debtor or creditor becomes a nonmember. Similar principles apply to intercompany obligations other than debt.

Reg. § 1.1502-13(g)(3)

Consolidated Returns

See p. 20,601 for regulations not amended to reflect law changes

→ *Caution: Prior law may apply to certain transactions, see Reg. § 1.1502-13(l)(1), below. For Reg. § 1.1502-13 prior to revision by T.D. 8597, see Caution Note and text following this version of Reg. § 1.1502-13.←*

(B) *Timing and attributes.* For purposes of applying the matching rule and the acceleration rule—

(*1*) Paragraph (c)(6)(ii) of this section (limitation on treatment of intercompany income or gain as excluded from gross income) does not apply to prevent any intercompany income or gain from being excluded from gross income; and

(*2*) Any gain or loss from an intercompany obligation is not subject to section 108(a), section 354 or section 1091.

(iii) *Reissuance.* If a creditor member sells intercompany debt for cash, the debt is treated as a new debt (with a new holding period) issued by the debtor immediately after the sale for the amount of cash. For other transactions, if the intercompany debt remains outstanding, similar principles apply to treat the debt as reissued immediately after the transaction. Thus, if the debt is transferred for property, it is treated as new debt issued for the property. See, for example, section 1273(b)(3) or section 1274. If this paragraph (g)(3) applies because the debtor or creditor becomes a nonmember, the debt is treated as new debt issued for an amount of cash equal to its fair market value immediately after the debtor or creditor becomes a nonmember. Similar principles apply to intercompany obligations other than debt.

(iv) *Bad debt reserve.* A member's deduction under section 585 or section 593 for an addition to its reserve for bad debts with respect to an intercompany obligation is not taken into account, and is not treated as realized under this paragraph (g)(3) until the intercompany obligation becomes an obligation that is not an intercompany obligation, or, if earlier, the redemption or cancellation of the intercompany obligation.

(4) *Deemed satisfaction and reissuance of obligations becoming intercompany obligations*—(i) *Application*—(A) *In general.* This paragraph (g)(4) applies if an obligation that is not an intercompany obligation becomes an intercompany obligation.

(B) *Exceptions.* This paragraph (g)(4) does not apply to an obligation if—

(*1*) The obligation becomes an intercompany obligation by reason of an event described in § 1.108-2(e) (exceptions to the application of section 108(e)(4)); or

(*2*) Treating the obligation as satisfied and reissued will not have a significant effect on any person's Federal income tax liability for any year. For this purpose, obligations issued in connection with the same transaction or related transactions are treated as a single obligation. However, this paragraph (g)(4)(i)(B)(2) does not apply to any obligation if the aggregate effect of this treatment for all obligations in a year would be significant.

(ii) *Intercompany debt.* If this paragraph (g)(4) applies to an intercompany debt—

(A) Section 108(e)(4) does not apply;

(B) The debt is treated for all Federal income tax purposes, immediately after it becomes an intercompany debt, as satisfied and a new debt issued to the holder (with a new holding period) in an amount determined under the principles of § 1.108-2(f);

(C) The attributes of all items taken into account from the satisfaction are determined on a separate entity basis, rather than by treating S and B as divisions of a single corporation;

(D) Any intercompany gain or loss taken into account is treated as not subject to section 354 or section 1091; and

(E) Solely for purposes of § 1.1502-32(b)(4) and the effect of any election under that provision, any loss taken into account under this paragraph (g)(4) by a corporation that becomes a member as a result of the transaction in which the obligation becomes an intercompany obligation is treated as a loss carryover from a separate return limitation year.

(iii) *Other intercompany obligations.* If this paragraph (g)(4) applies to an intercompany obligation other than debt, the principles of paragraph (g)(4)(ii) of this section apply to treat the intercompany obligation as satisfied and reissued for an amount of cash equal to its fair market value immediately after the obligation becomes an intercompany obligation.

(5) *Examples.* The application of this section to obligations of members is illustrated by the following examples.

Example 1. Interest on intercompany debt. (a) *Facts.* On January 1 of Year 1, B borrows $100 from S in return for B's note providing for $10 of interest annually at the end of each year, and repayment of $100 at the end of Year 5. B fully performs its obligations. Under their separate entity methods of accounting, B accrues a $10 interest deduction annually under section 163, and S

Reg. § 1.1502-13(g)(4)

Consolidated Returns

→ *Caution: Prior law may apply to certain transactions, see Reg. § 1.1502-13(l)(1), below. For Reg. § 1.1502-13 prior to revision by T.D. 8597, see Caution Note and text following this version of Reg. § 1.1502-13.*←

accrues $10 of interest income annually under section 61(a)(4).

(b) *Matching rule.* Under paragraph (b)(1) of this section, the accrual of interest on B's note is an intercompany transaction. Under the matching rule, S takes its $10 of income into account in each of Years 1 through 5 to reflect the $10 difference between B's $10 of interest expense taken into account and the $0 recomputed expense. S's income and B's deduction are ordinary items. (Because S's intercompany item and B's corresponding item would both be ordinary on a separate entity basis, the attributes are not redetermined under paragraph (c)(1)(i) of this section.)

(c) *Original issue discount.* The facts are the same as in paragraph (a) of this *Example 1,* except that B borrows $90 (rather than $100) from S in return for B's note providing for $10 of interest annually and repayment of $100 at the end of Year 5. The principles described in paragraph (b) of this *Example 1* for stated interest also apply to the $10 of original issue discount. Thus, as B takes into account its corresponding expense under section 163(e), S takes into account its intercompany income. S's income and B's deduction are ordinary items.

(d) *Tax-exempt income.* The facts are the same as in paragraph (a) of this *Example 1,* except that B's borrowing from S is allocable under section 265 to B's purchase of state and local bonds to which section 103 applies. The timing of S's income is the same as in paragraph (b) of this *Example 1.* Under paragraph (c)(4)(i) of this section, the attributes of B's corresponding item of disallowed interest expense control the attributes of S's offsetting intercompany interest income. Paragraph (c)(6)(ii) of this section does not prevent the redetermination of S's intercompany item as excluded from gross income, because section 265 permanently and explicitly disallows B's corresponding deduction. Accordingly, S's intercompany income is treated as excluded from gross income.

Example 2. Intercompany debt becomes nonintercompany debt. (a) *Facts.* On January 1 of Year 1, B borrows $100 from S in return for B's note providing for $10 of interest annually at the end of each year, and repayment of $100 at the end of Year 20. As of January 1 of Year 3, B has paid the interest accruing under the note and S sells B's note to X for $70, reflecting a change in the value of the note as a result of increases in prevailing market interest rates. B is never insolvent within the meaning of section 108(d)(3).

(b) *Deemed satisfaction.* Under paragraph (g)(3) of this section, B's note is treated as satisfied for $70 immediately before S's sale to X. As a result of the deemed satisfaction of the obligation for less than its adjusted issue price, B takes into account $30 of discharge of indebtedness income under section 61(a)(12). On a separate entity basis, S's $30 loss would be a capital loss under section 1271(a)(1). Under the matching rule, however, the attributes of S's intercompany item and B's corresponding item must be redetermined to produce the same effect as if the transaction had occurred between divisions of a single corporation. B's corresponding item completely offsets S's intercompany item in amount. Accordingly, under paragraph (c)(4)(i) of this section, the attributes of B's $30 of discharge of indebtedness income control the attributes of S's loss. Thus, S's loss is treated as ordinary loss.

(c) *Deemed reissuance.* Under paragraph (g)(3) of this section, B is also treated as reissuing, directly to X, a new note with a $70 issue price and a $100 stated redemption price at maturity. The new note is not an intercompany obligation, it has a $70 issue price and $100 stated redemption price at maturity, and the $30 of original issue discount will be taken into account by B and X under sections 163(e) and 1272.

(d) *Creditor deconsolidation.* The facts are the same as in paragraph (a) of this *Example 2,* except that P sells S's stock to X (rather than S's selling the note of B). Under paragraph (g)(3) of this section, the note is treated as satisfied by B for its $70 fair market value immediately before S becomes a nonmember, and B is treated as reissuing a new note to S immediately after S becomes a nonmember. The results for S's $30 of loss and B's discharge of indebtedness income are the same as in paragraph(b) of this *Example 2.* The new note is not an intercompany obligation, it has a $70 issue price and $100 stated redemption price at maturity, and the $30 of original issue discount will be taken into account by B and S under sections 163(e) and 1272.

(e) *Debtor deconsolidation.* The facts are the same as in paragraph (a) of this *Example 2,* except that P sells B's stock to X (rather than S's selling the note of B). The results are the same as in paragraph (d) of this *Example 2.*

(f) *Appreciated note.* The facts are the same as in paragraph (a) of this *Example 2,* except that

Reg. § 1.1502-13(g)(5)

→ *Caution: Prior law may apply to certain transactions, see Reg. § 1.1502-13(l)(1), below. For Reg. § 1.1502-13 prior to revision by T.D. 8597, see Caution Note and text following this version of Reg. § 1.1502-13.*←

S sells B's note to X for $130 (rather than $70), reflecting a decline in prevailing market interest rates. Under paragraph (g)(3) of this section, B's note is treated as satisfied for $130 immediately before S's sale of the note to X. Under § 1.163-7(c), B takes into account $30 of repurchase premium. On a separate entity basis, S's $30 gain would be a capital gain under section 1271(a)(1), and B's $30 premium deduction would be an ordinary deduction. Under the matching rule, however, the attributes of S's intercompany item and B's corresponding item must be redetermined to produce the same effect as if the transaction had occurred between divisions of a single corporation. Under paragraph (c)(4)(i) of this section, the attributes of B's corresponding premium deduction control the attributes of S's intercompany gain. Accordingly, S's gain is treated as ordinary income. B is also treated as reissuing a new note directly to X which is not an intercompany obligation. The new note has a $130 issue price and a $100 stated redemption price at maturity. Under § 1.61-12(c), B's $30 premium income under the new note is taken into account over the life of the new note.

Example 3. Loss or bad debt deduction with respect to intercompany debt. (a) *Facts.* On January 1 of Year 1, B borrows $100 from S in return for B's note providing for $10 of interest annually at the end of each year, and repayment of $100 at the end of Year 5. In Year 3, S sells B's note to P for $60. B is never insolvent within the meaning of section 108(d)(3). Assume B's note is not a security within the meaning of section 165(g)(2).

(b) *Deemed satisfaction and reissuance.* Under paragraph (g)(3) of this section, B is treated as satisfying its note for $60 immediately before the sale, and reissuing a new note directly to P with a $60 issue price and a $100 stated redemption price at maturity. On a separate entity basis, S's $40 loss would be a capital loss, and B's $40 income would be ordinary income. Under the matching rule, however, the attributes of S's intercompany item and B's corresponding item must be redetermined to produce the same effect as if the transaction had occurred between divisions of a single corporation. Under paragraph (c)(4)(i) of this section, the attributes of B's corresponding discharge of indebtedness income control the attributes of S's intercompany loss. Accordingly, S's loss is treated as ordinary loss.

(c) *Partial bad debt deduction.* The facts are the same as in paragraph (a) of this *Example 3*, except that S claims a $40 partial bad debt deduction under section 166(a)(2) (rather than selling the note to P). The results are the same as in paragraph (b) of this *Example 3*. B's note is treated as satisfied and reissued with a $60 issue price. S's $40 intercompany deduction and B's $40 corresponding income are both ordinary.

(d) *Insolvent debtor.* The facts are the same as in paragraph (a) of this *Example 3*, except that B is insolvent within the meaning of section 108(d)(3) at the time that S sells the note to P. On a separate entity basis, S's $40 loss would be capital, B's $40 income would be excluded from gross income under section 108(a), and B would reduce attributes under section 108(b) or section 1017. However, under paragraph (g)(3)(ii)(B) of this section, section 108(a) does not apply to B's income to characterize it as excluded from gross income. Accordingly, the attributes of S's intercompany loss and B's corresponding income are redetermined in the same manner as in paragraph (b) of this *Example 3*.

Example 4. Nonintercompany debt becomes intercompany debt. (a) *Facts.* On January 1 of Year 1, B borrows $100 from X in return for B's note providing for $10 of interest annually at the end of each year, and repayment of $100 at the end of Year 5. As of January 1 of Year 3, B has fully performed its obligations, but the note's fair market value is $70. On January 1 of Year 3, P buys all of X's stock. B is solvent within the meaning of section 108(d)(3).

(b) *Deemed satisfied and reissuance.* Under paragraph (g)(4) of this section, B is treated as satisfying its indebtedness for $70 (determined under the principles of § 1.108-2(f)(2)) immediately after X becomes a member. Both X's $30 capital loss under section 1271(a)(1) and B's $30 of discharge of indebtedness income under section 61(a)(12) are taken into account in determining consolidated taxable income for Year 3. Under paragraph (g)(4)(ii)(C) of this section, the attributes of items resulting from the satisfaction are determined on a separate entity basis. But see section 382 and § 1.1502-15 (as appropriate). B is also treated as reissuing a new note. The new note is an intercompany obligation, it has a $70 issue price and $100 stated redemption price at maturity, and the $30 of original issue discount will be taken into account by B and X in the same manner as provided in paragraph (c) of *Example 1* of this paragraph (g)(5).

(c) *Election to file consolidated returns.* Assume instead that B borrows $100 from S during Year 1, but the P group does not file consolidated

Reg. § 1.1502-13(g)(5)

→ **Caution: Prior law may apply to certain transactions, see Reg. § 1.1502-13(l)(1), below. For Reg. § 1.1502-13 prior to revision by T.D. 8597, see Caution Note and text following this version of Reg. § 1.1502-13.**←

returns until Year 3. Under paragraph (g)(4) of this section, B's indebtedness is treated as satisfied and a new note reissued immediately after the debt becomes intercompany debt. The satisfaction and reissuance are deemed to occur on January 1 of Year 3, for the fair market value of the note (determined under the principles of § 1.108-2(f)(2)) at that time.

Example 5. Notional principal contracts. (a) *Facts.* On April 1 of Year 1, M1 enters into a contract with counterparty M2 under which, for a term of five years, M1 is obligated to make a payment to M2 each April 1, beginning in Year 2, in an amount equal to the London Interbank Offered Rate (LIBOR), as determined on the immediately preceding April 1, multiplied by a $1,000 notional principal amount. M2 is obligated to make a payment to M1 each April 1, beginning in Year 2, in an amount equal to 8% multiplied by the same notional principal amount. LIBOR is 7.80% on April 1 of Year 1. On April 1 of Year 2, M2 owes $2 to M1.

(b) *Matching rule.* Under § 1.446-3(d), the net income (or net deduction) from a notional principal contract for a taxable year is included in (or deducted from) gross income. Under § 1.446-3(e), the ratable daily portion of M2's obligation to M1 as of December 31 of Year 1 is $1.50 ($2 multiplied by 275/365). Under the matching rule, M1's net income for Year 1 of $1.50 is taken into account to reflect the difference between M2's net deduction of $1.50 taken into account and the $0 recomputed net deduction. Similarly, the $.50 balance of the $2 of net periodic payments made on April 1 of Year 2 is taken into account for Year 2 in M1's and M2's net income and net deduction from the contract. In addition, the attributes of M1's intercompany income and M2's corresponding deduction are redetermined to produce the same effect as if the transaction had occurred between divisions of a single corporation. Under paragraph (c)(4)(i) of this section, the attributes of M2's corresponding deduction control the attributes of M1's intercompany income. (Although M1 is the selling member with respect to the payment on April 1 of Year 2, it might be the buying member in a subsequent period if it owes the net payment.)

(c) *Dealer.* The facts are the same as in paragraph (a) of this *Example 5*, except that M2 is a dealer in securities, and the contract with M1 is not inventory in the hands of M2. Under section 475, M2 must mark its securities to market at year-end. Assume that under section 475, M2's loss from marking to market the contract with M1 is $100. Under paragraph (g)(3) of this section, M2 is treated as making a $100 payment to M1 to terminate the contract immediately before section 475 is applied. M1's $100 of income from the termination payment is taken into account under the matching rule to reflect M2's deduction under § 1.446-3(h). The attributes of M1's intercompany income and M2's corresponding deduction are redetermined to produce the same effect as if the transaction had occurred between divisions of a single corporation. Under paragraph (c)(4)(i) of this section, the attributes of M2's corresponding deduction control the attributes of M1's intercompany income. Accordingly, M1's income is treated as ordinary income. Paragraph (g)(3) of this section also provides that, immediately after section 475 would apply, a new contract is treated as reissued with an upfront payment of $100. Under § 1.446-3(f), the deemed $100 up front payment by M1 to M2 is taken into account over the term of the new contract in a manner reflecting the economic substance of the contract (for example, allocating the payment in accordance with the forward rates of a series of cash-settled forward contracts that reflect the specified index and the $1,000 notional principal amount). (The timing of taking items into account is the same if M1, rather than M2, is the dealer subject to the mark-to-market requirement of section 475 at year-end. However in this case, because the attributes of the corresponding deduction control the attributes of the intercompany income, M1's income from the deemed termination payment might be ordinary or capital.)

(h) *Anti-avoidance rules*—(1) *In general.* If a transaction is engaged in or structured with a principal purpose to avoid the purposes of this section (including, for example, by avoiding treatment as an intercompany transaction), adjustments must be made to carry out the purposes of this section.

(2) *Examples.* The anti-avoidance rules of this paragraph (h) are illustrated by the following examples. The examples set forth below do not address common law doctrines or other authorities that might apply to recast a transaction or to otherwise affect the tax treatment of a transaction. Thus, in addition to adjustments under this paragraph (h), the Commissioner can, for example, apply the rules of section 269 or § 1.701-2 to disallow a deduction or to recast a transaction.

Example 1. Sale of a partnership interest. (a) *Facts.* S owns land with a $10 basis and $100

Reg. § 1.1502-13(h)(2)

→ *Caution: Prior law may apply to certain transactions, see Reg. § 1.1502-13(l)(1), below. For Reg. § 1.1502-13 prior to revision by T.D. 8597, see Caution Note and text following this version of Reg. § 1.1502-13.* ←

value. B has net operating losses from separate return limitation years (SRLYs) subject to limitation under § 1.1502-21(c). Pursuant to a plan to absorb the losses without limitation by the SRLY rules, S transfers the land to an unrelated, calendar-year partnership in exchange for a 10% interest in the capital and profits of the partnership in a transaction to which section 721 applies. The partnership does not have a section 754 election in effect. S later sells its partnership interest to B for $100. In the following year, the partnership sells the land to X for $100. Because the partnership does not have a section 754 election in effect, its $10 basis in the land does not reflect B's $100 basis in the partnership interest. Under section 704(c), the partnership's $90 built-in gain is allocated to B, and B's basis in the partnership interest increases to $190 under section 705. In a later year, B sells the partnership interest to a nonmember for $100.

(b) *Adjustments*. Under § 1.1502-21(c), the partnership's $90 built-in gain allocated to B ordinarily increases the amount of B's SRLY limitation, and B's $90 loss from its sale of the partnership interest ordinarily is not subject to limitation under the SRLY rules. Because the contribution of property to the partnership and the sale of the partnership interest were part of a plan a principal purpose of which was to achieve a reduction in consolidated tax liability by creating offsetting gain and loss for B while deferring S's intercompany gain, B's allocable share of the partnership's gain from its sale of the land is treated under paragraph (h)(1) of this section as not increasing the amount of B's SRLY limitation.

Example 2. Transitory status as an intercompany obligation. (a) *Facts.* P historically has owned 70% of X's stock and the remaining 30% is owned by unrelated shareholders. On January 1 of Year 1, S borrows $100 from X in return for S's note requiring $10 of interest annually at the end of each year, and repayment of $100 at the end of Year 20. As of January 1 of Year 3, the P group has substantial net operating loss carryovers, and the fair market value of S's note falls to $70 due to an increase in prevailing market interest rates. X is not permitted under section 166(a)(2) to take into account a $30 loss with respect to the note. Pursuant to a plan to permit X to take into account its $30 loss without disposing of the note, P acquires an additional 10% of X's stock, causing X to become a member, and P subsequently resells the 10% interest. X's $30 loss with respect to the note is a net unrealized built-in loss within the meaning of § 1.1502-15.

(b) *Adjustments.* Under paragraph (g)(4) of this section, X ordinarily would take into account its $30 loss as a result of the note becoming an intercompany obligation, and S would take into account $30 of discharge of indebtedness income. Under § 1.1502-22, X's loss is not combined with items of the other members and the loss would be carried to X's separate return years as a result of X becoming a nonmember. However, the transitory status of S's indebtedness to X as an intercompany obligation is structured with a principal purpose to accelerate the recognition of X's loss. Thus, S's note is treated under paragraph (h)(1) of this section as not becoming an intercompany obligation.

Example 3. Corporate mixing bowl. (a) *Facts.* M1 and M2 are subsidiaries of P. M1 operates a manufacturing business on land it leases from M2. The land is the only asset held by M2. P intends to dispose of the M1 business, including the land owned by M2; P's basis in the M1 stock is equal to the stock's fair market value. M2's land has a value of $20 and a basis of $0 and P has a $0 basis in the stock of M2. In Year 1, with a principal purpose of avoiding gain from the sale of the land (by transferring the land to M1 with a carry-over basis without affecting P's basis in the stock of M1 or M2), M1 and M2 form corporation T; M1 contributes cash in exchange for 80% of the T stock and M2 contributes the land in exchange for 20% of the stock. In Year 3, T liquidates, distributing $20 cash to M2 and the land (plus $60 cash) to M1. Under § 1.1502-34, section 332 applies to both M1 and M2. Under section 337, T recognizes no gain or loss from its liquidating distribution of the land to M1. T has neither gain nor loss on its distribution of cash to M2. In Year 4, P sells all of the stock of M1 to X and liquidates M2.

(b) *Adjustments.* A principal purpose for the formation and liquidation of T was to avoid gain from the sale of M2's land. Thus, under paragraph (h)(1) of this section, M2 must take $20 of gain into account when the stock of M1 is sold to X.

Example 4. Partnership mixing bowl. (a) *Facts.* M1 owns a self-created intangible asset with a $0 basis and a fair market value of $100. M2 owns land with a basis of $100 and a fair market value of $100. In Year 1, with a principal purpose of creating basis in the intangible asset (which would be eligible for amortization under section 197), M1 and M2 form partnership PRS;

Reg. § 1.1502-13(h)(2)

Consolidated Returns

See p. 20,601 for regulations not amended to reflect law changes

→ *Caution: Prior law may apply to certain transactions, see Reg. § 1.1502-13(l)(1), below. For Reg. § 1.1502-13 prior to revision by T.D. 8597, see Caution Note and text following this version of Reg. § 1.1502-13.*←

M1 contributes the intangible asset and M2 contributes the land. X, an unrelated person, contributes cash to PRS in exchange for a substantial interest in the partnership. PRS uses the contributed assets in legitimate business activities. Five years and six months later, PRS liquidates, distributing the land to M1, the intangible to M2, and cash to X. The group reports no gain under sections 707(a)(2)(B) and 737(a) and claims that M2'S basis in the intangible asset is $100 under section 732 and that the asset is eligible for amortization under section 197.

(b) *Adjustments.* A principal purpose of the formation and liquidation of PRS was to create additional amortization without an offsetting increase in consolidated taxable income by avoiding treatment as an intercompany transaction. Thus, under paragraph (h)(1) of this section, appropriate adjustments must be made.

Example 5. Sale and leaseback. (a) *Facts.* S operates a factory with a $70 basis and $100 value, and has loss carryovers from SRLYS. Pursuant to a plan to take into account the $30 unrealized gain while continuing to operate the factory, S sells the factory to X for $100 and leases it back on a long-term basis. In the transaction, a substantial interest in the factory is transferred to X. The sale and leaseback are not recharacterized under general principles of Federal income tax law. As a result of S's sale to X, the $30 gain is taken into account and increases S's SRLY limitation.

(b) *No adjustments.* Although S's sale was pursuant to a plan to accelerate the $30 gain, it is not subject to adjustment under paragraph (h)(1) of this section. The sale is not treated as engaged in or structured with a principal purpose to avoid the purposes of this section.

(i) [Reserved]

(j) *Miscellaneous operating rules.* For purposes of this section—

(1) *Successor assets.* Any reference to an asset includes, as the context may require, a reference to any other asset the basis of which is determined, directly or indirectly, in whole or in part, by reference to the basis of the first asset.

(2) *Successor persons*—(i) *In general.* Any reference to a person includes, as the context may require, a reference to a predecessor or successor. For this purpose, a predecessor is a transferor of assets to a transferee (the successor) in a transaction—

(A) To which section 381(a) applies;

(B) In which substantially all of the assets of the transferor are transferred to members in a complete liquidation;

(C) In which the successor's basis in assets is determined (directly or indirectly, in whole or in part) by reference to the basis of the transferor, but the transferee is a successor only with respect to the assets the basis of which is so determined; or

(D) Which is an intercompany transaction, but only with respect to assets that are being accounted for by the transferor in a prior intercompany transaction.

(ii) *Intercompany items.* If the assets of a predecessor are acquired by a successor member, the successor succeeds to, and takes into account (under the rules of this section), the predecessor's intercompany items. If two or more successor members acquire assets of the predecessor, the successors take into account the predecessor's intercompany items in a manner that is consistently applied and reasonably carries out the purposes of this section and applicable provisions of law.

(3) *Multiple triggers.* If more than one corresponding item can cause an intercompany item to be taken into account under the matching rule, the intercompany item is taken into account in connection with the corresponding item most consistent with the treatment of members as divisions of a single corporation. For example, if S sells a truck to B, its intercompany gain from the sale is not taken into account by reference to B's depreciation if the depreciation is capitalized under section 263A as part of B's cost for a building; instead, S's gain relating to the capitalized depreciation is taken into account when the building is sold or as it is depreciated. Similarly, if B purchases appreciated land from S and transfers the land to a lower-tier member in exchange for stock, thereby duplicating the basis of the land in the basis of the stock, items with respect to both the stock and the land can cause S's intercompany gain to be taken into account; if the lower-tier member becomes a nonmember as a result of the sale of its stock, the attributes of S's intercompany gain are determined with respect to the land rather than the stock.

(4) *Multiple or successive intercompany transactions.* If a member's intercompany item or corresponding item affects the accounting for more than one intercompany transaction, appropriate adjustments are made to treat all of the intercompany transactions as transactions be-

Reg. § 1.1502-13(j)(4)

→ *Caution: Prior law may apply to certain transactions, see Reg. § 1.1502-13(l)(1), below. For Reg. § 1.1502-13 prior to revision by T.D. 8597, see Caution Note and text following this version of Reg. § 1.1502-13.*←

tween divisions of a single corporation. For example, if S sells property to M, and M sells the property to B, then S, M, and B are treated as divisions of a single corporation for purposes of applying the rules of this section. Similar principles apply with respect to intercompany transactions that are part of the same plan or arrangement. For example, if S sells separate properties to different members as part of the same plan or arrangement, all of the participating members are treated as divisions of a single corporation for purposes of determining the attributes (which might also affect timing) of the intercompany items and corresponding items from each of the properties.

(5) *Acquisition of group*—(i) *Scope.* This paragraph (j)(5) applies only if a consolidated group (the terminating group) ceases to exist as a result of—

(A) The acquisition by a member of another consolidated group of either the assets of the common parent of the terminating group in a reorganization described in section 381(a)(2), or the stock of the common parent of the terminating group; or

(B) The application of the principles of § 1.1502-75(d)(2) or (d)(3).

(ii) *Application.* If the terminating group ceases to exist under circumstances described in paragraph (j)(5)(i) of this section, the surviving group is treated as the terminating group for purposes of applying this section to the intercompany transactions of the terminating group. For example, intercompany items and corresponding items from intercompany transactions between members of the terminating group are taken into account under the rules of this section by the surviving group. This treatment does not apply, however, to members of the terminating group that are not members of the surviving group immediately after the terminating group ceases to exist (for example, under section 1504(a)(3) relating to reconsolidation, or section 1504(c) relating to includible insurance companies).

(6) *Former common parent treated as continuation of group.* If a group terminates because the common parent is the only remaining member, the common parent succeeds to the treatment of the terminating group for purposes of applying this section so long as it neither becomes a member of an affiliated group filing separate returns nor becomes a corporation described in section 1504(b). For example, if the only subsidiary of the group liquidates into the common parent in a complete liquidation to which section 332 applies, or the common parent merges into the subsidiary and the subsidiary is treated as the common parent's successor under paragraph (j)(2)(i) of this section, the taxable income of the surviving corporation is treated as the group's consolidated taxable income in which the intercompany and corresponding items must be included. See § 1.267(f)-1 for additional rules applicable to intercompany losses or deductions.

(7) *Becoming a nonmember.* For purposes of this section, a member is treated as becoming a nonmember if it has a separate return year (including another group's consolidated return year). A member is not treated as having a separate return year if its items are treated as taken into account in computing the group's consolidated taxable income under paragraph (j)(5) or (6) of this section.

(8) *Recordkeeping.* Intercompany and corresponding items must be reflected on permanent records (including work papers). See also section 6001, requiring records to be maintained. The group must be able to identify from these permanent records the amount, location, timing, and attributes of the items, so as to permit the application of the rules of this section for each year.

(9) *Examples.* The operating rules of this paragraph (j) are illustrated generally throughout this section, and by the following examples.

Example 1. Intercompany sale followed by section 351 transfer to member. (a) *Facts.* S holds land for investment with a basis of $70. On January 1 of Year 1, S sells the land to M for $100. M also holds the land for investment. On July 1 of Year 3, M transfers the land to B in exchange for all of B's stock in a transaction to which section 351 applies. Under section 358, M's basis in the B stock is $100. B holds the land for sale to customers in the ordinary course of business and, under section 362(b), B's basis in the land is $100. On December 1 of Year 5, M sells 20% of the B stock to X for $22. In an unrelated transaction on July 1 of Year 8, B sells 20% of the land for $22.

(b) *Definitions.* Under paragraph (b)(1) of this section, S's sale of the land to M and M's transfer of the land to B are both intercompany transactions. S is the selling member and M is the buying member in the first intercompany transaction, and M is the selling member and B is the buying member in the second intercompany transaction. M has no intercompany items under para-

Reg. § 1.1502-13(j)(5)

→ *Caution: Prior law may apply to certain transactions, see Reg. § 1.1502-13(l)(1), below. For Reg. § 1.1502-13 prior to revision by T.D. 8597, see Caution Note and text following this version of Reg. § 1.1502-13.*←

graph (b)(2) of this section. Because B acquired the land in an intercompany transaction, B's items from the land are corresponding items to be taken into account under this section. Under the successor asset rule of paragraph (j)(1) of this section, references to the land include references to M's B stock. Under the successor person rule of paragraph (j)(2) of this section, references to M include references to B with respect to the land.

(c) *Timing and attributes resulting from the stock sale.* Under paragraph (c)(3) of this section, M is treated as owning and selling B's stock for purposes of the matching rule even though, as divisions, M could not own and sell stock in B. Under paragraph (j)(3) of this section, both M's B stock and B's land can cause S's intercompany gain to be taken into account under the matching rule. Thus, S takes $6 of its gain into account in Year 5 to reflect the $6 difference between M's $2 gain taken into account from its sale of B stock and the $8 recomputed gain. Under paragraph (j)(4) of this section, the attributes of this gain are determined by treating S, M, and B as divisions of a single corporation. Under paragraph (c)(1) of this section, S's $6 gain and M's $2 gain are treated as long-term capital gain. The gain would be capital on a separate entity basis (assuming that section 341 does not apply), and this treatment is not inconsistent with treating S, M, and B as divisions of a single corporation because the stock sale and subsequent land sale are unrelated transactions and B remains a member following the sale.

(d) *Timing and attributes resulting from the land sale.* Under paragraph (j)(3) of this section, S takes $6 of its gain into account in Year 8 under the matching rule to reflect the $6 difference between B's $2 gain taken into account from its sale of an interest in the land and the $8 recomputed gain. Under paragraph (j)(4) of this section, the attributes of this gain are determined by treating S, M, and B as divisions of a single corporation and taking into account the activities of S, M, and B with respect to the land. Thus, both S's gain and B's gain might be ordinary income as a result of B's activities. (If B subsequently sells the balance of the land, S's gain taken into account is limited to its remaining $18 of intercompany gain.)

(e) *Sale of successor stock resulting in deconsolidation.* The facts are the same as in paragraph (a) of this *Example 1*, except that M sells 60% of the B stock to X for $66 on December 1 of Year 5 and B becomes a nonmember. Under the matching rule, M's sale of B stock results in $18 of S's gain being taken into account (to reflect the difference between M's $6 gain taken into account and the $24 recomputed gain). Under the acceleration rule, however, the entire $30 gain is taken into account (to reflect B becoming a nonmember, because its basis in the land reflects M's $100 cost basis from the prior intercompany transaction). Under paragraph (j)(4) of this section, the attributes of S's gain are determined by treating S, M, and B as divisions of a single corporation. Because M's cost basis in the land will be reflected by B as a nonmember, all of S's gain is treated as from the land (rather than a portion being from B's stock), and B's activities with respect to the land might therefore result in S's gain being ordinary income.

Example 2. Intercompany sale of member stock followed by recapitalization. (a) *Facts.* Before becoming a member of the P group, S owns P stock with a basis of $70. On January 1 of Year 1, P buys all of S's stock. On July 1 of Year 3, S sells the P stock to M for $100. On December 1 of Year 5, P acquires M's original P stock in exchange for new P stock in a recapitalization described in section 368(a)(1)(E).

(b) *Timing and attributes.* Although P's basis in the stock acquired from M is eliminated under paragraph (f)(4) of this section, the new P stock received by M is exchanged basis property (within the meaning of section 7701(a)(44)) having a basis under section 358 equal to M's basis in the original P stock. Under the successor asset rule of paragraph (j)(1) of this section, references to M's original P stock include references to M's new P stock. Because it is still possible to take S's intercompany item into account under the matching rule with respect to the successor asset, S's gain is not taken into account under the acceleration rule as a result of the basis elimination under paragraph (f)(4) of this section. Instead, the gain is taken into account based on subsequent events with respect to M's new P stock (for example, a subsequent distribution or redemption of the new stock).

Example 3. Back-to-back intercompany transactions—matching. (a) *Facts.* S holds land for investment with a basis of $70. On January 1 of Year 1, S sells the land to M for $90. M also holds the land for investment. On July 1 of Year 3, M sells the land for $100 to B, and B holds the land for sale to customers in the ordinary course of business. During Year 5, B sells all of the land to customers for $105.

Reg. § 1.1502-13(j)(9)

→ *Caution: Prior law may apply to certain transactions, see Reg. § 1.1502-13(l)(1), below. For Reg. § 1.1502-13 prior to revision by T.D. 8597, see Caution Note and text following this version of Reg. § 1.1502-13.* ←

(b) *Timing.* Under paragraph (b)(1) of this section, S's sale of the land to M and M's sale of the land to B are both intercompany transactions. S is the selling member and M is the buying member in the first intercompany transaction, and M is the selling member and B is the buying member in the second intercompany transaction. Under paragraph (j)(4) of this section, S, M and B are treated as divisions of a single corporation for purposes of determining the timing of their items from the intercompany transactions. See also paragraph (j)(2) of this section (B is treated as a successor to M for purposes of taking S's intercompany gain into account). Thus, S's $20 gain and M's $10 gain are both taken into account in Year 5 to reflect the difference between B's $5 gain taken into account with respect to the land and the $35 recomputed gain (the gain that B would have taken into account if the intercompany sales had been transfers between divisions of a single corporation, and B succeeded to S's $70 basis).

(c) *Attributes.* Under paragraphs (j)(4) of this section, the attributes of the intercompany items and corresponding items of S, M, and B are also determined by treating S, M, and B as divisions of a single corporation. For example, the attributes of S's and M's intercompany items are determined by taking B's activities into account.

Example 4. Back-to-back intercompany transactions—acceleration. (a) *Facts.* During Year 1, S performs services for M in exchange for $10 from M. S incurs $8 of employee expenses. M capitalizes the $10 cost of S's services under section 263 as part of M's cost to acquire real property from X. Under its separate entity method of accounting, S would take its income and expenses into account in Year 1. M holds the real property for investment and, on July 1 of Year 5, M sells it to B at a gain. B also holds the real property for investment. On December 1 of Year 8, while B still owns the real property, P sells all of M's stock to X and M becomes a nonmember.

(b) *M's items.* M takes its gain into account immediately before it becomes a nonmember. Because the real property stays in the group, the acceleration rule redetermines the attributes of M's gain under the principles of the matching rule as if B sold the real property to an affiliated corporation that is not a member of the group for a cash payment equal to B's adjusted basis in the real property, and S, M, and B were divisions of a single corporation. Thus, M's gain is capital gain.

(c) *S's items.* Under paragraph (b)(2)(ii) of this section, S includes the $8 of expenses in determining its $2 intercompany income. In Year 1, S takes into account $8 of income and $8 of expenses. Under paragraph (j)(4) of this section, appropriate adjustments must be made to treat both S's performance of services for M and M's sale to B as occurring between divisions of a single corporation. Thus, S's $2 of intercompany income is not taken into account as a result of M becoming a nonmember, but instead will be taken into account based on subsequent events (e.g., under the matching rule based on B's sale of the real property to a nonmember, or under the acceleration rule based on P's sale of the stock of S or B to a nonmember). See the successor person rules of paragraph (j)(2) of this section (B is treated as a successor to M for purposes of taking S's intercompany income into account).

(d) *Sale of S's stock.* The facts are the same as in paragraph (a) of this *Example 4*, except that P sells all of S's stock (rather than M's stock) and S becomes a nonmember on July 1 of Year 5. S's remaining $2 of intercompany income is taken into account immediately before S becomes a nonmember. Because S's intercompany income is not from an intercompany sale, exchange, or distribution of property, the attributes of the intercompany income are determined on a separate entity basis. Thus, S's $2 of intercompany income is ordinary income. M does not take any of its intercompany gain into account as a result of S becoming a nonmember.

(e) *Intercompany income followed by intercompany loss.* The facts are the same as in paragraph (a) of this *Example 4*, except that M sells the real property to B at a $1 loss (rather than a gain). M takes its $1 loss into account under the acceleration rule immediately before M becomes a nonmember. But see § 1.267(f)-1 (which might further defer M's loss if M and B remain in a controlled group relationship after M becomes a nonmember). Under paragraph (j)(4) of this section appropriate adjustments must be made to treat the group as if both intercompany transactions occurred between divisions of a single corporation. Accordingly, P's sale of M stock also results in S taking into account $1 of intercompany income as capital gain to offset M's $1 of corresponding capital loss. The remaining $1 of S's intercompany income is taken into account based on subsequent events.

Example 5. Successor group. (a) *Facts.* On January 1 of Year 1, B borrows $100 from S in return for B's note providing for $10 of interest annually at the end of each year, and repayment

Reg. § 1.1502-13(j)(9)

→ **Caution:** *Prior law may apply to certain transactions, see Reg. § 1.1502-13(l)(1), below. For Reg. § 1.1502-13 prior to revision by T.D. 8597, see Caution Note and text following this version of Reg. § 1.1502-13.*←

of $100 at the end of Year 20. As of January 1 of Year 3, B has paid the interest accruing under the note. On that date, X acquires all of P's stock and the former P group members become members of the X consolidated group.

(b) *Successor.* Under paragraph (j)(5) of this section; although B's note ceases to be an intercompany obligation of the P group, the note is not treated as satisfied and reissued under paragraph (g) of this section as a result of X's acquisition of P stock. Instead, the X consolidated group succeeds to the treatment of the P group for purposes of paragraph (g) of this section, and B's note is treated as an intercompany obligation of the X consolidated group.

(c) *No subgroups.* The facts are the same as in paragraph (a) of this *Example 5*, except that X simultaneously acquires the stock of S and B from P (rather than X acquiring all of P's stock). Paragraph (j)(5) of this section does not apply to X's acquisitions. Unless an exception described in paragraph (g)(3)(i)(B) applies, B's note is treated as satisfied immediately before S and B become nonmembers, and reissued immediately after they become members of the X consolidated group. The amount at which the note is satisfied and reissued under paragraph (g)(3) of this section is based on the fair market value of the note at the time of P's sales to X. Paragraph (g)(4) of this section does not apply to the reissued B note in the X consolidated group, because the new note is always an intercompany obligation of the X consolidated group.

Example 6. Liquidation—80% distributee. (a) *Facts.* X has had preferred stock described in section 1504(a)(4) outstanding for several years. On January 1 of Year 1, S buys all of X's common stock for $60, and B buys all of X's preferred stock for $40. X's assets have a $0 basis and $100 value. On July 1 of Year 3, X distributes all of its assets to S and B in a complete liquidation. Under § 1.1502-34, section 332 applies to both S and B. Under section 337, X has no gain or loss from its liquidating distribution to S. Under sections 336 and 337(c), X has a $40 gain from its liquidating distribution to B. B has a $40 basis under section 334(a) in the assets received from X, and S has a $0 basis under section 334(b) in the assets received from X.

(b) *Intercompany items from the liquidation.* Under the matching rule, X's $40 gain from its liquidating distribution to B is not taken into account under this section as a result of the liquidation (and therefore is not yet reflected under §§ 1.1502-32 and 1.1502-33). Under the successor person rule of paragraph (j)(2)(i) of this section, S and B are both successors to X. Under section 337(c), X recognizes gain or loss only with respect to the assets distributed to B. Under paragraph (j)(2)(ii) of this section, to be consistent with the purposes of this section, S succeeds to X's $40 intercompany gain. The gain will be taken into account by S under the matching and acceleration rules of this section based on subsequent events. (The allocation of the intercompany gain to S does not govern the allocation of any other attributes.)

Example 7. Liquidation—no 80% distributee. (a) *Facts.* X has only common stock outstanding. On January 1 of Year 1, S buys 60% of X's stock for $60, and B buys 40% of X's stock for $40. X's assets have a $0 basis and $100 value. On July 1 of Year 3, X distributes all of its assets to S and B in a complete liquidation. Under § 1.1502-34, section 332 applies to both S and B. Under sections 336 and 337(c), X has a $100 gain from its liquidating distributions to S and B. Under section 334(b), S has a $60 basis in the assets received from X and B has a $40 basis in the assets received from X.

(b) *Intercompany items from the liquidation.* Under the matching rule, X's $100 intercompany gain from its liquidating distributions to S and B is not taken into account under this section as a result of the liquidation (and therefore is not yet reflected under §§ 1.1502-32 and 1.1502-33). Under the successor person rule of paragraph (j)(2)(i) of this section, S and B are both successors to X. Under paragraph (j)(2)(ii) of this section, to be consistent with the purposes of this section, S succeeds to X's $40 intercompany gain with respect to the assets distributed to B, and B succeeds to X's $60 intercompany gain with respect to the assets distributed to S. The gain will be taken into account by S and B under the matching and acceleration rules of this section based on subsequent events. (The allocation of the intercompany gain does not govern the allocation of any other attributes.)

(k) *Cross references*—(1) *Section 108.* See § 1.108-3 for the treatment of intercompany deductions and losses as subject to attribute reduction under section 108(b).

(2) *Section 263A(f).* See section 263A(f) and § 1.263A9(g)(5) for special rules regarding interest from intercompany transactions.

(3) *Section 267(f).* See section 267(f) and § 1.267(f)-1 for special rules applicable to certain

→ *Caution: Prior law may apply to certain transactions, see Reg. § 1.1502-13(l)(1), below. For Reg. § 1.1502-13 prior to revision by T.D. 8597, see Caution Note and text following this version of Reg. § 1.1502-13.* ←

losses and deductions from transactions between members of a controlled group.

(4) *Section 460.* See § 1.460-4(j) for special rules regarding the application of section 460 to intercompany transactions.

(5) *Section 469.* See § 1.469-1(h) for special rules regarding the application of section 469 to intercompany transactions.

(6) *§ 1.1502-80.* See § 1.1502-80 for the non-application of certain Internal Revenue Code rules.

(l) *Effective dates*—(1) *In general.* This section applies with respect to transactions occurring in years beginning on or after July 12, 1995. If both this section and prior law apply to a transaction, or neither applies, with the result that items may be duplicated, omitted, or eliminated in determining taxable income (or tax liability), or items may be treated inconsistently, prior law (and not this section) applies to the transaction. For example, S's and B's items from S's sale of property to B which occurs in a consolidated return year beginning before July 12, 1995, are taken into account under prior law, even though B may dispose of the property in a consolidated return year beginning on or after July 12, 1995. Similarly, an intercompany distribution to which a shareholder becomes entitled in a consolidated return year beginning before July 12, 1995, but which is distributed in a consolidated return year beginning on or after that date is taken into account under prior law (generally when distributed), because this section generally takes dividends into account when the shareholder becomes entitled to them but this section does not apply at that time. If application of prior law to S's deferred gain or loss from a deferred intercompany transaction (as defined under prior law) occurring in a consolidated return year beginning prior to July 12, 1995, would be affected by an intercompany transaction (as defined under this section) occurring in a consolidated return year beginning on or after July 12, 1995, S's deferred gain or loss continues to be taken into account as provided under prior law, and the items from the subsequent intercompany transaction are taken into account under this section. Appropriate adjustments must be made to prevent items from being duplicated, omitted, or eliminated in determining taxable income as a result of the application of both this section and prior law to the successive transactions, and to ensure the proper application of prior law.

(2) *Avoidance transactions.* This paragraph (1)(2) applies if a transaction is engaged in or structured on or after April 8, 1994, with a principal purpose to avoid the rules of this section (and instead to apply prior law). If this paragraph (1)(2) applies, appropriate adjustments must be made in years beginning on or after July 12, 1995, to prevent the avoidance, duplication, omission, or elimination of any item (or tax liability), or any other inconsistency with the rules of this section. For example, if S is a dealer in real property and sells land to B on March 16, 1995 with a principal purpose of converting any future appreciation in the land to capital gain, B's gain from the sale of the land on May 11, 1997 might be characterized as ordinary income under this paragraph (1)(2).

(3) *Election for certain stock elimination transactions*—(i) *In general.* A group may elect pursuant to this paragraph (1)(3) to apply this section (including the elections available under paragraph (f)(5)(ii) of this section) to stock elimination transactions to which prior law would otherwise apply. If an election is made, this section, and not prior law, applies to determine the timing and attributes of S's and B's gain or loss from stock with respect to all stock elimination transactions.

(ii) *Stock elimination transactions.* For purposes of this paragraph (1)(3), a stock elimination transaction is a transaction in which stock transferred from S to B—

(A) Is cancelled or redeemed on or after July 12, 1995;

(B) Is treated as cancelled in a liquidation pursuant to an election under section 338(h)(10) with respect to a qualified stock purchase with an acquisition date on or after July 12, 1995;

(C) Is distributed on or after July 12, 1995; or

(D) Is exchanged on or after July 12, 1995 for stock of a member (determined immediately after the exchange) in a transaction that would cause S's gain or loss from the transfer to be taken into account under prior law.

(iii) *Time and manner of making election.* An election under this paragraph (1)(3) is made by attaching to a timely filed original return (including extensions) for the consolidated return year including July 12, 1995 a statement entitled "[Insert Name and Employer Identification Number of Common Parent] HEREBY ELECTS THE APPLICATION OF § 1.1502-13(1)(3)." See

Reg. § 1.1502-13(k)(4)

Consolidated Returns

See p. 20,601 for regulations not amended to reflect law changes

→ *Caution: Prior law may apply to certain transactions, see Reg. § 1.1502-13(l)(1), below. For Reg. § 1.1502-13 prior to revision by T.D. 8597, see Caution Note and text following this version of Reg. § 1.1502-13.*←

paragraph (f)(5)(ii)(E) of this section for the manner of electing the relief provisions of paragraph (f)(5)(ii) of this section.

(4) *Prior law.* For transactions occurring in S's years beginning before July 12, 1995, see the applicable regulations issued under section 1502. See §§ 1.1502-13, 1.1502-13T, 1.1502-14, 1.1502-14T, 1.1502-31, and 1.1502-32 (as contained in the 26 CFR part 1 edition revised as of April 1, 1995).

(5) *Consent to adopt method of accounting.* For intercompany transactions occurring in a consolidated group's first taxable year beginning on or after July 12, 1995, the Commissioner's consent under section 446(e) is hereby granted for any changes in methods of accounting that are necessary solely by reason of the timing rules of this section. Changes in method of accounting for these transactions are to be effected on a cut-off basis. [Reg. § 1.1502-13.]

☐ [*T.D.* 6894, 9-7-66. Amended by *T.D.* 7246, 12-29-72; *T.D.* 8131, 3-24-87; *T.D.* 8196, 4-14-88; *T.D.* 8295, 3-9-90; *T.D.* 8478, 3-9-93; *T.D.* 8482, 8-6-93; *T.D.* 8560, 8-12-94; *T.D.* 8584, 12-28-94; *T.D.* 8597, 7-12-95; *T.D.* 8660, 3-13-96; *T.D.* 8677, 6-26-96; *T.D.* 8823, 6-25-99 and *T.D.* 8883, 5-11-2000.]

→ *Caution: Prior law Reg. § 1.1502-13, below, before revision by T.D. 8597, may apply to certain transactions after July 12, 1995. See Reg. § 1.1502-13(l)(1) above.*←

[Reg. § 1.1502-13]

§ 1.1502-13. [Prior Law, see caution note.—CCH.] **Intercompany transactions.**—(a) *Definitions.* For purposes of §§ 1.1502-1 through 1.1502-80—

(1) *"Intercompany transaction."* (i) Except as provided in subdivision (ii) of this subparagraph, the term "intercompany transaction" means a transaction during a consolidated return year between corporations which are members of the same group immediately after such transaction. Thus, for example, an intercompany transaction would include a sale of property by one member of a group (hereinafter referred to as the "selling member") to another member of the same group ("purchasing member"), the performance of services by one member of a group ("selling member") for another member of the same group ("purchasing member"), or the payment of interest by one member of a group ("purchasing member") to another member of the same group ("selling member"), during a consolidated return year.

(ii) The term "intercompany transaction" does not include a distribution by one member of a group to another member of the same group with respect to the distributing member's stock, or a contribution to capital on which no gain is realized. Thus, for example, dividend distributions, redemptions, and liquidations are not intercompany transactions. The term also does not include sales and other dispositions of, and bad debts with respect to, obligations of other members of the group. See § 1.1502-14, relating to amounts received with respect to stock, bonds, or other obligations of a member of the group.

(2) *"Deferred intercompany transaction".* The term "deferred intercompany transaction" means—

(i) The sale or exchange of property,

(ii) The performance of services in a case where the amount of the expenditure for such services is capitalized (for example, a builder's fee, architect's fee, or other similar cost which is included in the basis of property), or

(iii) Any other expenditure in a case where the amount of the expenditure is capitalized (for example, prepaid rent, or interest which is included in the basis of property),

in an intercompany transaction.

(b) *Treatment of intercompany transactions other than deferred intercompany transactions—* (1) *General rule.* Gain or loss on intercompany transactions (other than deferred intercompany transactions) shall not be deferred or eliminated. Thus, for example, if, during a consolidated return year, a purchasing member makes an interest payment on an indebtedness to a selling member in an intercompany transaction, the purchasing member shall take the deduction for interest into account and the selling member shall take the interest income into account.

(2) *Special rule.* If, in an intercompany transaction (other than a deferred intercompany transaction), one member would otherwise properly take an item of income or a deduction into account for a consolidated return year earlier than the year (whether consolidated or separate) for

Reg. § 1.1502-13(b)(2)

56,738 **Consolidated Returns**

See p. 20,601 for regulations not amended to reflect law changes

→ *Caution: Prior law Reg. § 1.1502-13, below, before revision by T.D. 8597, may apply to certain transactions after July 12, 1995. See Reg. § 1.1502-13(l)(1) above.*←

which another member of the group can properly take into account the corresponding item of income or deduction, then both the item of income and the deduction shall be taken into account for the later year (whether consolidated or separate). On the other hand, if one member properly takes an item of income or a deduction into account for a separate return year earlier than the consolidated return year for which the other member can properly take into account the corresponding item of income or deduction, then such other member shall take the corresponding deduction or item of income into account for such later consolidated return year.

(c) *Deferral of gain or loss on deferred intercompany transactions*—(1) *General rule.*—(i) To the extent gain or loss on a deferred intercompany transaction is recognized under the Code for a consolidated return year, such gain or loss shall be deferred by the selling member (hereinafter referred to as "deferred gain or loss"). See, however, paragraph (c)(2) of this section for determining the amount of deferred gain or loss on a deferred intercompany transaction that involves interest capitalized under section 263A(f).

(ii) The following rules apply with respect to the deferral of gain or loss on deferred intercompany transactions:

(a) The selling member may not report gain on the installment method under section 453;

(b) A selling member shall take into account the gain or loss on a deferred intercompany transaction in accordance with the provisions of paragraphs (d), (e), or (f) of this section, notwithstanding that such selling member, under its method of accounting, would not otherwise recognize such gain or loss until a later taxable year. Thus, for example, a selling member must take into account its gain on a deferred intercompany transaction for the first taxable year for which the purchasing member is allowed a deduction for depreciation with respect to the property involved, even though the selling member, under its method of accounting, would not otherwise recognize such gain until a later taxable year.

(iii) See paragraphs (d), (e), (f), (l), (m), (n), and (o) of this section, relating to the time and manner of restoring deferred gain or loss.

(2) *Determination of amount of deferred gain or loss.* In determining the amount of deferred gain or loss, the cost of property, services, or any other expenditure shall include both direct costs and indirect costs which are properly includible in the cost of goods sold or cost of the services or other expenditure. See the regulations under section 263A for costs properly includible in cost of goods sold. Additionally, see section 263A(f) and the regulations thereunder to determine the amount of deferred gain or loss on a deferred intercompany transaction that involves interest capitalized under section 263A(f).

(3) *Election not to defer.* A group may elect with the consent of the Commissioner not to defer gain or loss on any deferred intercompany transactions with respect to all property or any class or classes of property. Applications for such consent must be filed with the Commissioner of Internal Revenue, Washington, D.C. 20224, on or before the due date of the consolidated return (not including extensions of time) for the taxable year to which the election is to apply. An election under this subparagraph shall, unless revoked with the consent of the Commissioner, apply to all members of the group for the consolidated return year for which made and all subsequent consolidated return years ending prior to the first year for which such group does not file a consolidated return.

(4) *Character and source of deferred gain or loss.* (i) Except as provided in subdivision (ii) of this subparagraph, the character and source of deferred gain or loss on a deferred intercompany transaction shall be determined at the time of the deferred intercompany transaction as if such transaction had not occurred during a consolidated return year.

(ii) Deferred gain or loss taken into account by the selling member under paragraph (d)(1) of this section, or (as a result of abandonment) under paragraph (f) of this section, shall be treated as ordinary income or loss.

(5) *Accounting for deferred gain or loss.* The amount of deferred gain or loss shall be reflected on permanent records (including work papers). From such permanent records the group must be able to identify the character and source of the deferred gain or loss to the selling member, and must be able to apply the restoration rules of paragraphs (d), (e), and (f) of this section.

(6) *Inheritance of deferred gain or loss.* If the assets of a selling member are acquired by one or more other members in an acquisition to which section 381(a) applies, the member acquiring the greatest portion of the assets (measured by fair market value) of the selling member shall be subject to the provisions of paragraphs (d), (e), and

Reg. § 1.1502-13(c)(1)

Consolidated Returns

See p. 20,601 for regulations not amended to reflect law changes

→ *Caution: Prior law Reg. § 1.1502-13, below, before revision by T.D. 8597, may apply to certain transactions after July 12, 1995. See Reg. § 1.1502-13(l)(1) above.*←

(f) of this section with respect to the entire remaining balance of the deferred gain or loss. If two or more members acquire the same portion (which is greater than that acquired by any other members), the common parent shall select which such member shall be subject to the provisions of paragraphs (d), (e), and (f) of this section. For purposes of this section, a member which inherits the balance of the deferred gain or loss under this subparagraph shall be treated as the selling member.

(7) *Basis.* The basis of property acquired by a purchasing member in a deferred intercompany transaction is determined as if separate returns were filed. For example, if S owns property with an adjusted basis of $80 and sells it to P for $100 in a deferred intercompany transaction, P's basis in the property is $100 even though S defers its $20 gain on the sale under this paragraph (c).

(8) *Cross reference to temporary regulations.* For rules relating to inheritance of deferred gain or loss in the case of acquisitions in taxable years for which the due date (without extensions) of the income tax return is after April 14, 1988, see § 1.1502-13T(c).

(d) *Restoration of deferred gain or loss for property subject to depreciation, amortization, or depletion*—(1) *General rule.* (i) If property (including a capitalized expenditure for services, or any other capitalized expenditure) acquired in a deferred intercompany transaction is, in the hands of any member of the group, subject to depreciation, amortization, or depletion, then, for each taxable year (whether consolidated or separate) for which a depreciation, amortization, or depletion deduction is allowed to any member of the group with respect to such property, a portion (as determined under subdivision (ii) of this subparagraph) of the deferred gain or loss attributable to such property shall be taken into account by the selling member.

(ii) The portion of the deferred gain or loss attributable to any property which shall be taken into account by the selling member shall be an amount equal to—

(*a*) The amount of gain or loss deferred by the selling member at the time of the deferred intercompany transaction (and if a member has transferred the property to another member of the group, the remaining balance at the time of such transfer), multiplied by

(*b*) A fraction, the numerator of which is the amount of the depreciation, amortization, or depletion deduction with respect to such property allowed to any member of the group for the year (whether consolidated or separate), and the denominator of which is the depreciable basis (*i.e.*, basis reduced by salvage value required to be taken into account, if any) of such property in the hands of such member immediately after such property was transferred to such member.

(2) *Multiple asset accounts.* In the case of property contained in a multiple asset account (or in single asset accounts for which an average rate is used), for purposes of subparagraph (1)(ii)(*b*) of this paragraph the depreciation deduction allowed for a particular taxable year shall be determined by reference to the rate and method of depreciation applied to such multiple asset account (or average rate and method of depreciation applied to such single asset accounts). Thus, if property with an estimated useful life of 3 years is placed in a multiple asset account which is depreciated on the straight-line method at a rate of 20 percent, the depreciation deduction allowed for each taxable year shall be assumed to be 20 percent of the basis of such property (reduced by the salvage value taken into account).

(3) *Reduction of deferred gain or loss.* The deferred gain or loss shall be reduced by the amount taken into account by the selling member under subparagraph (1) of this paragraph. If the deferred gain includes any ordinary income, the reduction shall first be applied against the ordinary income. Thus, for example, if the selling member has deferred gain of $100, of which $70 is capital gain and $30 is ordinary income, the first $30 taken into account by the selling member under subparagraph (1) of this paragraph shall be applied against the ordinary income, and any additional amounts so taken into account shall be applied against the capital gain.

(e) *Restoration of deferred gain or loss for installment obligations and sales*—(1) *Installment obligations.* If an installment obligation (within the meaning of section 453(d)) is transferred in a deferred intercompany transaction, then on each date on which the obligation is satisfied the selling member shall take into account an amount equal to the deferred gain or loss on such transfer, multiplied by a fraction, the numerator of which is the portion of such obligation satisfied on such date, and the denominator of which is the aggregate unpaid installments immediately after the deferred intercompany transaction.

(2) *Installment sales.* If—

Reg. § 1.1502-13(e)(2)

56,740   **Consolidated Returns**

See p. 20,601 for regulations not amended to reflect law changes

→ *Caution: Prior law Reg. § 1.1502-13, below, before revision by T.D. 8597, may apply to certain transactions after July 12, 1995. See Reg. § 1.1502-13(l)(1) above.*←

(i) Property acquired in a deferred intercompany transaction is disposed of outside the group, and

(ii) The purchasing member-vendor reports its income on the installment method under section 453, then on each date on which the purchasing member-vendor receives an installment payment the selling member shall take into account an amount equal to the deferred gain or loss attributable to such property (after taking into account any prior reductions under paragraph (d)(3) of this section) multiplied by a fraction, the numerator of which is the installment payment received and the denominator of which is the total contract price. If the deferred gain includes any ordinary income, the ordinary income shall be taken into account first.

(3) *Reduction of deferred gain or loss.* The deferred gain or loss shall be reduced by the amount taken into account by the selling member under subparagraph (1) or (2) of this paragraph. If the deferred gain includes any ordinary income, the reduction shall first be applied against the ordinary income.

(f) *Restoration of deferred gain or loss on dispositions, etc.*—(1) *General rule.* The remaining balance (after taking into account any prior reductions under paragraphs (d)(3) and (e)(3) of this section) of the deferred gain or loss attributable to property, services, or other expenditure shall be taken into account by the selling member as of the earliest of the following dates:

(i) The date on which such property is disposed of outside the group (including abandoned) other than in a transaction described in paragraph (e)(2) of this section (but not including a normal retirement, as defined in paragraph (b) of § 1.167(a)-8, from an average-life multiple asset account or from a single asset account for which an average rate is used). If such property is of a kind which would properly be included in the inventory of a member if on hand at the close of its taxable year, such member shall determine whether or not such item of property has been disposed of outside the group by reference to its method of inventory identification (*e.g.*, first-in, first-out, last-in, first-out, or specific identification);

(ii) In the case of a transaction described in paragraph (e)(2) of this section, the date on which the installment debt is written off, satisfied, discharged, or disposed of outside the group or the property sold is repossessed (except as provided in section 1038), whichever occurs earliest;

(iii) Immediately preceding the time when either the selling member or the member which owns the property ceases to be a member of the group;

(iv) In the case of property which is stock in trade or other property of a kind which would be properly included in inventory of the member which owns the property if on hand at the close of such member's taxable year, or held primarily for sale to customers in the ordinary course of such member's trade or business, the first day of the first separate return year of the selling member or the member which owns the property;

(v) In the case of an obligation (other than an obligation of a member of the group), the date on which such obligation is satisfied or becomes worthless;

(vi) In the case of stock, the date on which such stock is redeemed (whether or not it is cancelled, retired, or held as treasury stock) or becomes worthless; or

(vii) If consolidated returns are filed by the group for fewer than three consecutive taxable years immediately preceding a separate return year of the common parent, the first day of such separate return year; or

(viii) In the case of inventory, the date on which its value is written down to market (if the lower-of-cost-or-market method is used by the purchaser), but only to the extent of such writedown.

(2) *Exceptions.* (i) Subparagraph (1) of this paragraph shall not apply solely because of a termination of the group (hereinafter referred to as the "terminating group") resulting from—

(a) The acquisition by a nonmember corporation of (*1*) the assets of the common parent in a reorganization described in subparagraph (A), (C), or (D) (but only if the requirements of subparagraphs (A) and (B) of section 354(b)(1) are met) of section 368(a)(1), or (*2*) stock of the common parent, or

(b) The acquisition (in a transaction to which § 1.1502-75(d)(3) applies) by a member of (*1*) the assets of a nonmember corporation in a reorganization referred to in subdivision (*a*), or (*2*) stock of a nonmember corporation,

if all the members of the terminating group (other than such common parent if its assets are acquired) immediately before the acquisition are members immediately after the acquisition of an-

Reg. § 1.1502-13(e)(3)

→ **Caution:** *Prior law Reg. § 1.1502-13, below, before revision by T.D. 8597, may apply to certain transactions after July 12, 1995. See Reg. § 1.1502-13(l)(1) above.*←

other group (hereinafter referred to as the "succeeding group") which files a consolidated return for the first taxable year ending after the date of acquisition. The members of the succeeding group shall succeed to any deferred gain or loss of members of the terminating group and to the status of such members as selling or purchasing members. This subdivision shall not apply with respect to acquisitions occurring before August 25, 1971, except that in the case of an acquisition occurring after April 16, 1968, and before August 25, 1971, this subdivision shall apply if the terminating group and the succeeding group elect to apply § 1.1502-18(c)(4) (notwithstanding the last sentence thereof) with respect to such acquisition. The election shall be made in a joint statement filed by the terminating and succeeding groups on or before March 5, 1973, with the Internal Revenue Service Center or Centers with which the terminating and succeeding groups filed their consolidated returns for the taxable year which includes the date of the acquisition. Such election shall be irrevocable.

(ii) Subparagraph (1)(iii) of this paragraph shall not apply in a case where—

(*a*) The selling member or the member which owns the property, as the case may be, ceases to be a member of the group by reason of an acquisition to which section 381(a) applies, and the acquiring corporation is a member, or

(*b*) The group is terminated, and immediately after such termination the corporation which was the common parent (or a corporation which was a member of the affiliated group and has succeeded to and become the owner of substantially all of the assets of such former parent) owns the property involved and is the selling member or is treated as the selling member under paragraph (c)(6) of this section.

Paragraphs (d) and (e) of this section and this paragraph shall apply to such selling member. Thus, for example, subparagraph (1)(iii) of this paragraph does not apply in a case where corporation P, the common parent of a group consisting of P and corporations S and T, sells an asset to S in a deferred intercompany transaction, and subsequently all of the assets of S are distributed to P in complete liquidation of S. Moreover, if, after the liquidation of S, P sold T, subparagraph (1)(iii) of this paragraph would not apply even though P ceased to be a member of the group.

(iii) See § 1.1502-13T(f) for a modification of an exception to paragraph (f)(1)(iii) of this section.

(3) *Certain divestitures.* If, pursuant to a final judgment or a final order of a court or an agency of the Federal or a state government, any member or members are required to divest themselves of control of any other member and, as a result, any member ceases to be a member, the Commissioner may enter into a closing agreement under section 7121 with the group. Such closing agreement may provide that any deferred gain or loss which would otherwise be taken into account under subparagraph (1)(iii) of this paragraph shall instead be taken into account over an appropriate period of time related to the period of time within which the deferred income would have been taken into account had the divestiture not taken place, but not in excess of 10 years. Ordinarily, application for such closing agreement will not be granted where such divestiture is occasioned by the acquisition after August 31, 1966, of control of a corporation or of assets. In no event will any such application be granted unless the group establishes to the satisfaction of the Commissioner that the collection of the tax liability attributable to any deferred gain will not be jeopardized by the delay.

(g) *Holding period.* In determining the period for which a purchasing member has held property acquired in a deferred intercompany transaction, the period such property was held by the selling member shall not be included.

(h) *Examples.* This section may be illustrated by the following examples:

Example (1). (i) Corporations P and S file consolidated returns on a calendar year basis. On January 10, 1966, S sells land, which it has used in its trade or business, to P for $100,000. Immediately before the sale the basis of the land in S's hands is $60,000. P holds the land primarily for sale to customers in the ordinary course of its trade or business. On July 12, 1967, P sells the land to A, an individual.

(ii) The sale by S to P is a deferred intercompany transaction; S defers its $40,000 gain on the land ($100,000 less $60,000), which is gain from the sale of property described in section 1231. As of July 12, 1967, S takes the $40,000 deferred gain into account since on such date the property is disposed of outside the group. Such $40,000 gain is taken into account in determining the consoli-

56,742 Consolidated Returns

See p. 20,601 for regulations not amended to reflect law changes

→ *Caution: Prior law Reg. § 1.1502-13, below, before revision by T.D. 8597, may apply to certain transactions after July 12, 1995. See Reg. § 1.1502-13(l)(1) above.*←

dated section 1231 net gain or loss for 1967 under § 1.1502-23.

Example (2). Corporations P and S file consolidated returns on a calendar year basis. On August 1, 1966, P transfers property with a fair market value of $100,000 and an adjusted basis in its hands of $85,000 to S in exchange for stock and $10,000 cash. Under section 351(b), only $10,000 of the $15,000 gain is recognized by P. The transfer is a deferred intercompany transaction; P defers the $10,000 gain recognized under section 351(b).

Example (3). Corporations P and S file consolidated returns on a calendar year basis and report income on the cash basis. On July 1, 1966, S pays P $1,000 interest on a loan made in 1961. The payment of interest is an intercompany transaction other than a deferred intercompany transaction; S does not defer or eliminate the $1,000 deduction for interest, and P does not defer or eliminate the $1,000 item of interest income. Thus, consolidated taxable income for 1966 reflects interest income of $1,000 and a corresponding deduction for interest of $1,000.

Example (4). (i) Corporations P, S, and T file consolidated returns on a calendar year basis. On January 1, 1966, S, which is in the business of manufacturing machinery, sells a machine to P for $1,000. The cost of the machine is $800. P uses the machine in its trade or business and depreciates it on the straight-line method over an estimated useful life of 10 years. Salvage value of $200 is taken into account. Thus, its annual depreciation deduction with respect to the machine is $80 ($800 ($1,000 less $200 salvage) divided by 10). On January 1, 1969, P sells the machine to A, an individual.

(ii) The sale by S to P is a deferred intercompany transaction; S defers its $200 gain on the machine ($1,000 less $800), which is characterized as ordinary income. For each of the 3 taxable years (1966, 1967, and 1968) prior to the sale to A, S takes into account $20 of its deferred gain, computed as follows:

$$\$200 \text{ deferred gain} \times \frac{\$80 \text{ depreciation deduction}}{\$800 \text{ basis to P subject to depreciation}}$$

Such $20 gain retains its character as ordinary income.

(iii) As of January 1, 1969, S takes the $140 remaining balance of the deferred gain ($200 less $60) into account since on such date the machine is disposed of outside the group. Such $140 gain retains its character as ordinary income.

Example (5). (i) The facts are the same as in example (4) except that beginning with 1968 P and S file separate returns.

(ii) Assuming that P, S, and T filed a consolidated return for 1965, the result is the same as in example (4). Thus, for each of the years 1966, 1967, and 1968 S takes into account $20 of its deferred gain and as of January 1, 1969, S takes the remaining $140 ($200 less $60) into account.

(iii) Assuming that P, S, and T filed separate returns for 1965, as of January 1, 1968, S takes the $160 remaining balance of the deferred gain ($200 less $40) into account since P filed a separate return for 1968 and the group had filed consolidated returns for only 2 consecutive years preceding 1968.

Example (6). (i) The facts are the same as in example (4) except that on January 1, 1969, P sells the machine to T for $660 in a transaction in which gain is recognized. T uses the machine in its trade or business and depreciates it on the straight-line method over an estimated useful life of 10 years. No salvage value is taken into account. Thus, T's annual depreciation deduction with respect to the machine is $66 ($660 divided by 10).

(ii) The sale by S to P is a deferred intercompany transaction; S defers its $200 gain on the machine ($1,000 less $800), which is characterized as ordinary income. For each of the 3 years (1966, 1967, and 1968) prior to the sale to T, S takes into account $20 of its deferred gain.

(iii) The sale by P to T is also a deferred intercompany transaction; P defers its $100 loss on the machine (adjusted basis of $760 ($1,000 less $240 total depreciation) less $660).

(iv) For 1969 S takes into account $14 of its deferred gain, computed as follows:

$$\$140 \text{ remaining balance of deferred gain} \times \frac{\$66 \text{ depreciation deduction}}{\$660 \text{ basis to T subject to depreciation}}$$

Reg. § 1.1502-13(h)

Consolidated Returns

See p. 20,601 for regulations not amended to reflect law changes

→ **Caution: Prior law Reg. § 1.1502-13, below, before revision by T.D. 8597, may apply to certain transactions after July 12, 1995. See Reg. § 1.1502-13(l)(1) above.** ←

(v) For 1969 P takes into account $10 of its deferred loss, computed as follows:

$$\$100 \text{ deferred loss} \times \frac{\$66 \text{ depreciation deduction}}{\$660 \text{ basis to T subject to depreciation}}$$

Example (7). (i) Corporations P and S file consolidated returns on a calendar year basis. On May 2, 1966, S sells a machine with an adjusted basis of $50 to P for $100 in a transaction in which gain is recognized. S used the machine in its trade or business. For purposes of depreciation, P places the machine, which has an estimated useful life of 3 years, in an average life multiple asset account which is depreciated on the straight-line method at a rate of 20 percent. Under P's consistent depreciation practice it takes a full year's depreciation on all purchases made in the first half of its taxable year.

(ii) The sale by S to P is a deferred intercompany transaction; S defers its $50 gain on the machine ($100 less $50). For each of the taxable years 1966, 1967, 1968, 1969, and 1970 S takes into account $10 of its deferred gain, computed as follows:

$$\$50 \text{ deferred gain} \times \frac{\$20 \text{ depreciation deduction}}{\$100 \text{ basis to P subject to depreciation}}$$

Such $10 is characterized as gain from the sale or exchange of property which is neither a capital asset nor property described in section 1231, notwithstanding the character of the $50 gain determined at the time of the sale.

Example (8). The facts are the same as in example (7) and in addition during 1969 the machine is disposed of outside the group. Such disposal is treated as a normal retirement (as defined in paragraph (b) of § 1.167(a)-8). The result is the same as in example (7). Thus, S takes into account $10 for each of the years 1966, 1967, 1968, 1969, and 1970 even though the property was disposed of in 1969.

Example (9). (i) The facts are the same as in example (7) except that the multiple asset account is depreciated over a 5-year average useful life on the double declining balance method.

(ii) For 1966 S takes into account $20 of its deferred gain, computed as follows:

$$\$50 \text{ deferred gain} \times \frac{\$40 \,(\$100 \times 40\%) \text{ depreciation deduction}}{\$100 \text{ basis to P subject to depreciation}}$$

For 1967 S takes into account $12 of its deferred gain, computed as follows:

$$\$50 \text{ deferred gain} \times \frac{\$24 \,(\$60 \,(\$100 \text{ less } \$40) \times 40\%) \text{ depreciation deduction}}{\$100 \text{ basis to P subject to depreciation}}$$

Example (10). (i) P Corporation and S Corporation, its wholly-owned subsidiary, file consolidated returns on a calendar year basis. On January 10, 1966, S sells land, with a basis of $60,000, to P for $100,000. As of the close of business on June 10, 1969, P sells 25 percent of the outstanding stock of S to A, an individual.

(ii) The sale by S to P is a deferred intercompany transaction; S defers its $40,000 gain on the land ($100,000 less $60,000). As of June 10, 1969, S takes the $40,000 gain into account for 1969 since it ceases to be a member of the group as of the close of business on such date.

Example (11). (i) Corporations P and S file consolidated returns on a calendar year basis. On January 15, 1966, P sells an obligation payable in installments, with a basis of $48 in its hands, to S for $60. At the time of the sale the debtor owes 3 annual installments of $20 payable each year on July 1. Such installments are paid timely.

(ii) The sale by P to S is a deferred intercompany transaction; P defers its $12 gain on the obligation ($60 less $48).

(iii) For each of the years 1966, 1967, and 1968 P takes into account $4 of its deferred gain, computed as follows:

Reg. § 1.1502-13(h)

Consolidated Returns

See p. 20,601 for regulations not amended to reflect law changes

→ *Caution: Prior law Reg. § 1.1502-13, below, before revision by T.D. 8597, may apply to certain transactions after July 12, 1995. See Reg. § 1.1502-13(l)(1) above.*←

$$\$12 \text{ deferred gain} \times \frac{\$20 \text{ portion satisfied}}{\$60 \text{ aggregate unpaid portions}}$$

Example (12). (i) Corporations P and S file consolidated returns on a calendar year basis. On January 2, 1966, S, a manufacturer, sells a machine to P, a distributor, for $2,000. The machine cost S $1,200. On February 1, 1966, P sells the machine to A, an individual for $2,200 and, under section 453, reports its income thereon on the installment plan. A makes monthly payments of $110 starting with March 1966.

(ii) The sale by S to P is a deferred intercompany transaction; S defers its $800 gain ($2,000 less $1,200).

(iii) For 1966 S takes into account $400 of its deferred gain, computed as follows:

$$\$800 \text{ deferred gain} \times \frac{\$1,000 \text{ installment payments received}}{\$2,200 \text{ total contract price}}$$

Example (13). Corporations P and S file consolidated returns on a calendar year basis for 1966 and 1967. S reports income on the accrual method while P reports income on the cash method. On December 31, 1966, S would properly accrue interest of $1,000 which is payable to P. On February 1, 1967, S pays P the $1,000. Both the deduction and the item of income are taken into account for 1967, the later year. Thus, S takes the $1,000 interest deduction into account for 1967, which is the year P also takes the $1,000 item of interest income into account. Consolidated taxable income for 1967 reflects both interest income of $1,000 and a corresponding deduction for interest of $1,000.

Example (14). The facts are the same as in example (13) except that for 1967 S and P file separate returns. The result is the same as in example (13).

Example (15). (i) The facts are the same as in example (13) except that for 1966 P and S file separate returns.

(ii) For 1966 S takes into account the $1,000 deduction for interest; for 1967 P takes into account the $1,000 item of interest income.

Example (16). Corporations P and S file consolidated returns on a calendar year basis. On January 10, 1968, P sells an issue of its $100 par value bonds. S purchases a bond from P for $110. S does not elect under section 171 to amortize the $10 premium. P may not take the $10 premium into account as income until it redeems the bond since S cannot properly take a deduction for the $10 premium until the bond is redeemed.

Example (17). (i) Corporations P, S, and M file consolidated returns on a calendar year basis. On November 20, 1962, S sold land, with a basis of $60,000, to P for $100,000. Under paragraph (b)(1) of § 1.1502-31A the $40,000 gain was eliminated. Thus, S did not take into account such $40,000 gain for 1962 and P's basis in the land is only $60,000. On February 10, 1966, P sells the land to A, an individual, for $104,000.

(ii) P takes the entire $44,000 gain ($104,000 less $60,000) on the land into account for 1966 since the deferral and basis rules provided in paragraph (c) of this section were not effective with respect to the sale of such land.

(iii) If, on February 10, 1966, P had sold the land to M for $104,000, P would defer its $44,000 gain on the land since the sale by P to M would be a deferred intercompany transaction.

Example (18). (i) Corporations P and S file separate returns on a calendar year basis for 1966 and file consolidated returns on a calendar year basis beginning with 1967. On January 2, 1966, S, a dealer in machinery, sells a machine to P for $2,000 and, under section 453, reports the income thereon on the installment plan. The machine cost S $1,200. P makes monthly payments of $100 starting with January 1966.

(ii) The sale by S to P is not an intercompany transaction since the sale did not occur during a consolidated return year. Therefore, S takes into account the gross profit on each of the 20 monthly payments under section 453.

(i) [Reserved]

(j) *Regulated public utilities.* Subject to the provisions of section 7121, the Commissioner may enter into a closing agreement which, notwithstanding the provisions of §§ 1.1502-13 and 1.1502-33, determines the consequences of deferred intercompany transactions or of any matters relating to or affected by such transactions, provided that—

(1) The purchasing members are domestic regulated public utilities as defined in section 7701(a)(4) and (33),

Reg. § 1.1502-13(i)

Consolidated Returns

See p. 20,601 for regulations not amended to reflect law changes

→ *Caution: Prior law Reg. § 1.1502-13, below, before revision by T.D. 8597, may apply to certain transactions after July 12, 1995. See Reg. § 1.1502-13(l)(1) above.*←

(2) In the taxable year immediately preceding the first taxable year for which this section is effective there was in effect among the members an arrangement relating to intercompany transactions which had a significant effect upon regulated rates of the public utility members of the group, and the accounting of the public utility members under the arrangement was accepted or approved by a regulatory agency having jurisdiction over the accounts of such members, and

(3) The Commissioner is satisfied that the terms of such closing agreement will not for any taxable year result in a reduction of the tax liability of the group (including former members) or of the shareholders of any members (or former members).

A request for such an agreement must be made on or before November 15, 1966.

(k) [Reserved]

(l) *Restoration of deferred gain before disposition outside group*—(1) *In general.* For purposes of § 1.1502-13, gain (or loss) deferred with respect to property sold or exchanged in an intercompany transaction shall be taken into account for any taxable year (whether consolidated or separate) in an amount equal to any increase (or decrease) in a deduction or basis recovery for the taxable year that is attributable to an increase (or decrease) in the basis of the property (or to the basis of any other property the basis of which is determined, directly or indirectly, in whole or in part, by reference to the basis of such property) resulting from the sale or exchange. For purposes of the preceding sentence, basis shall not be treated as recovered by reason of a subsequent deferred intercompany transaction or distribution described in § 1.1502-14(a) or (b).

(2) *Examples.* The application of this paragraph (l) is illustrated by the following examples.

Example (1). (i) Corporations P and S file consolidated returns on a calendar year basis. P owns a 40% interest in the capital and profits of XYZ, a partnership. P has a basis of $20 in its partnership interest. XYZ owns a single depreciable asset. P's share of the basis of the asset is $20 and its share of the value of the asset is $60. In 1989, P sells its partnership interest to S for $60 and recognizes a gain of $40, all of which is deferred under § 1.1502-13(c). S's basis in the XYZ interest is increased to $60. Because XYZ has made an election under section 754, the basis of the asset with respect to S is increased, under section 743, to $60 by reference to S's basis in the XYZ interest.

(ii) If P had not transferred its partnership interest to S, its allocable share of depreciation with respect to the asset would have been $5 for 1990. As a result of the basis adjustment under section 743 resulting from the sale of the XYZ interest to S, S's depreciation with respect to the asset for 1990 is $15 ($10 of which is attributable to the basis adjustment). P is therefore required to take into account $10 of deferred gain under this paragraph (l).

(iii) In 1991, XYZ sells the asset and S's share of the amount realized with respect to the sale is $65. Without regard to depreciation for 1991, if P had not transferred its XYZ interest to S, its basis recovery on the sale of the asset would have been $15. As a result of the basis adjustment under section 743 resulting from the sale of the XYZ interest to S, S's share of the basis of the asset at the time it is sold is $45 ($60 minus $15). Accordingly, there has been a $30 increase in basis recovery in 1991 as a result of the sale of the XYZ interest to S and, under this paragraph (l), P must therefore take into account the remaining $30 of deferred gain at the time of the sale.

Example (2). (i) Corporations P and S file consolidated returns on a calendar year basis. S purchases and places in service on August 1, 1989, construction equipment costing $1,000,000. S elects to use the straight-line method over the equipment's recovery period (5 years) and appropriately applies the half-year convention to compute its depreciation deduction for the equipment. Thus, S's depreciation deduction for the equipment for 1989 is $100,000 (1/2 of 20% of $1,000,000). In 1990, S sells the equipment to P and recognizes a gain of $500,000, all of which is deferred under § 1.1502-13(c). P does not dispose of the equipment before 1996.

(ii) Under section 168(i)(7), P must use the same depreciation method that S used over S's remaining recovery period for so much of the adjusted basis of the equipment in P's hands as does not exceed the adjusted basis of the equipment in S's hands immediately before the sale (the "carryover portion"). Therefore, P's depreciation deduction that is attributable to the carryover portion is the same in each year as S's deduction would have been if S had not sold the equipment to P. The amount of the deferred gain attributable to the equipment that S must take into account in any year (that is, the amount of the increased depreciation deduction to the group)

→ **Caution:** *Prior law Reg. § 1.1502-13, below, before revision by T.D. 8597, may apply to certain transactions after July 12, 1995. See Reg. § 1.1502-13(l)(1) above.*←

is the amount of the depreciation deduction attributable to the portion of P's basis which exceeds the carryover portion (the "excess portion"). P appropriately depreciates the excess portion ($500,000) under the 200-percent declining balance method over a 5-year recovery period, applying a half-year convention. Thus, the amount of deferred gain that S is required to take into account, which equals the amount of depreciation claimed by P on the excess portion, is $100,000 for 1990, $160,000 for 1991, $96,000 for 1992, $57,600 for 1993, $57,600 for 1994, and $28,800 for 1995.

(3) *Effective date.* This paragraph (l) applies to intercompany transactions in taxable years for which the due date (without extensions) of the income tax return is after March 14, 1990.

(m) *Restoration of deferred gain on disposition outside group*—(1) *In general.* Except as provided in paragraph (m)(2) of this section, for purposes of § 1.1502-13, if property sold or exchanged in an intercompany transaction (or property the basis of which is determined, directly or indirectly, in whole or in part, by reference to the basis of such property) is disposed of outside the group, any remaining deferred gain (and any associated tax consequences) shall be taken into account as if the selling member had disposed of the property at the same time and in the same manner as the property is disposed of outside the group. Notwithstanding the previous sentence, the source and character of the gain to the selling member and the status of the selling member for tax purposes (*e.g.,* as a dealer or non-dealer in the property sold) shall be determined as of the time of the intercompany transaction. Any event requiring the restoration of gain pursuant to § 1.1502-13(e) or § 1.1502-13(f), as modified by paragraph (f) of this section, is treated as a disposition outside the group.

(2) *Exception.* Paragraph (m)(1) of this section does not apply, and § 1.1502-13(e) and § 1.1502-13(f), as modified by paragraph (f) of this section, apply, to the extent that gain or loss is not recognized in a transaction in which property, which was sold or exchanged in an intercompany transaction, (or property the basis of which is determined, directly or indirectly, in whole or in part, by reference to such property) is disposed of outside the group. However, to the extent gain or loss is recognized in such transaction, paragraph (m)(1) of this section applies.

(3) *Examples.* The application of this paragraph (m) is illustrated by the following examples.

Example (1). (i) Corporations P and S file consolidated returns on a calendar year basis. P regularly sells real property in the ordinary course of business. In 1990. P sells nondepreciable real property with a basis of $7,000 to S for $10,000 and P recognizes $3,000 of gain, all of which is deferred under § 1.1502-13(c).

(ii) In 1991, S, which does not regularly sell real property in the ordinary course of business, sells the real property to X, an unrelated third party, for a $12,000 obligation, bearing interest at the applicable federal rate and payable in two equal annual installments of $6,000 in 1992 and 1993. If, instead of selling the property to S in 1990, P had sold it to X, P would not have been eligible, under section 453(b), to use the installment method of reporting with respect to its $3,000 gain because it was a dealer in real property in 1990. When S sells the real property to X in 1991, P must therefore take into account its entire $3,000 of deferred gain.

Example (2). (i) Corporations P and S file consolidated returns on a calendar year basis. S owns depreciable property described in section 1245 that it purchased for $10 million. At the end of 1989, when S's basis in the property has been reduced to $7 million as a result of depreciation deductions, S sells the property to P for $20 million and recognizes $13 million of gain, $3 million of which is subject to recapture under section 1245. All of the gain is deferred under § 1.1502-13(c).

(ii) At the end of 1990, P sells the property to X, an unrelated third party, for a $25 million obligation, bearing interest at the applicable federal rate and payable in two equal annual installments of $12.5 million in 1991 and 1992. Without regard to depreciation in 1990, P realizes $5 million of gain, which it reports on the installment method under section 453. If, instead of selling the property to P, S had sold it to X in an installment sale, S would have been required to report under section 453(i) the $3 million of recapture income. When P sells the property to X, S must therefore take into account $3 million of deferred gain that is subject to recapture under section 1245.

(iii) Under § 1.1502-13(e)(2), S takes into account the $10 million of deferred gain not subject to recapture as P receives the installment payments. Thus, P recognizes $2.5 million of gain under section 453, and S takes into account $5 million of its deferred gain, in each of 1991 and 1992. Section 453A requires interest to be paid on

Reg. § 1.1502-13(l)(3)

Consolidated Returns

See p. 20,601 for regulations not amended to reflect law changes

→ *Caution: Prior law Reg. § 1.1502-13, below, before revision by T.D. 8597, may apply to certain transactions after July 12, 1995. See Reg. § 1.1502-13(l)(1) above.*←

a group's tax liability deferred by reason of section 453 if the installment obligations of the group (and related persons) outstanding at the close of the group's taxable year exceed an aggregate face amount of $5 million. Because the aggregate face amount of the group's installment obligations, $25 million, exceeds $5 million, the deferred tax liabilities of both P and S must be taken into account in determining the interest charge under section 453A beginning with the taxable year in which P's sale occurs.

Example (3). (i) Corporations P, S and T file consolidated returns on a calendar year basis. S holds nondepreciable property A and T holds nondepreciable property B. Properties A and B each have a basis of $1,000 and a fair market value of $10,000. In 1989, T sells property B to P for $10,000. T recognizes $9,000 of gain in 1989 on its sale of property B to P, all of which is deferred under § 1.1502-13(c). P's basis in property B is $10,000.

(ii) In 1991, P and S exchange property A and property B in an exchange that qualifies for nonrecognition of gain or loss under section 1031 with respect to both P and S. P does not recognize gain or loss on the exchange, and P's basis in property A is $10,000.

(iii) In 1993, in a transaction to which sections 1031(f) and (g) do not apply, P sells property A to X, an unrelated third party, for $10,000. P realizes no gain on the sale of property A to X. T is required to take into account the $9,000 of deferred gain with respect to property B in 1993, because property A (the basis of which is determined by reference to the basis of property B) was disposed of outside the group.

(4) *Effective date*—(i) *In general.* Except as provided in paragraph (m)(4)(ii) of this section, this paragraph (m) applies to dispositions (as described in this paragraph) of property in taxable years for which the due date (without extensions) of the income tax return is after March 14, 1990.

(ii) *Exception.* Notwithstanding paragraph (m)(4)(i) of this section, this paragraph (m) does not apply to deferred gain taken into account on a disposition of property before March 9, 1990, if the gain was deferred in an intercompany transaction—

(A) after December 31, 1988, provided that, at the time of the intercompany transaction, there was no plan or intention to dispose of the property outside the group and the taxpayer files a separate statement with the taxpayer's return for the taxable year in which such property is disposed of disclosing—

(*1*) a description of the transferred property and the dates of the intercompany transaction and the disposition,

(*2*) the name and employer identification number (E.I.N.) of the member disposing of the property and the amount realized and gain realized by such member on the disposition, and

(*3*) the amount realized and gain realized by the selling member on the intercompany transaction with respect to the property and the name and E.I.N. of the selling member; or

(B) before January 1, 1989.

(n) *Exception to deferral rules*—(1) *In general.* Section 1.1502-13(c) shall not apply to defer gain or loss with respect to a sale or exchange in an intercompany transaction of property to the extent the gain (or loss) is attributable to any income and expense (i) accounted for (or required to be accounted for) by the selling member in accordance with the percentage of completion method and (ii) arising from any activity performed by the selling member for the benefit of, or by reason of, a long term contract between a member and a person not a member that is accounted for by such member, in whole or part, under the percentage of completion method.

(2) *Example.* This paragraph (n) is illustrated by the following example.

Example. (i) Corporations P and S file consolidated returns on a calendar year basis. In 1990, P enters into a contract with X, a person not a member of the group, for the manufacture and sale of 5 airplanes for a total contract price of $500 million. The contract is a long term contract within the meaning of section 460(f) and P is required to account for income and expense attributable to the contract under the percentage of completion method. By reason of the contract, S manufactures and sells engines for the airplanes to P for a total price of $50 million. S begins to manufacture the engines in 1991 and delivers them in 1992. In 1991, S incurs $20 million out of total estimated costs of $40 million, and, in 1992, S incurs an additional $20 million of costs to complete manufacture of the engines. S accounts for income and expense attributable to the production of the engines pursuant to the percentage of completion method.

(ii) S's sale of the engines to P is a deferred intercompany transaction. However, § 1.1502-13(c) does not apply to defer gain attrib-

Reg. § 1.1502-13(n)(2)

Consolidated Returns

See p. 20,601 for regulations not amended to reflect law changes

→ *Caution: Prior law Reg. § 1.1502-13, below, before revision by T.D. 8597, may apply to certain transactions after July 12, 1995. See Reg. § 1.1502-13(l)(1) above.* ←

utable to the income and expense accounted for by S under the percentage of completion method. Under the percentage of completion method, S takes into account $20 million in costs and $25 million in income in each of 1991 and 1992.

(3) *Effective date.* This paragraph (n) applies to intercompany transactions in taxable years for which the due date (without extensions) of the income tax return is after March 14, 1990 that are attributable to long term contracts entered into by a member after June 20, 1988.

(o) *Additional restoration of gain deferred on the sale of stock of a member*—(1) *Restoration rule.* For purposes of this section, deferred gain with respect to an acquisition of stock of a subsidiary in an intercompany transaction shall be taken into account—

(i) Upon a disposition (as defined in § 1.1502-19(c)(1)(ii) or (iii)) of the stock of the subsidiary in an amount equal to the amount that would have created or increased the excess loss account if the adjustment to basis (or excess loss account) of the stock of the subsidiary resulting from the acquisition had not occurred; or

(ii) Following a disposition (as defined in § 1.1502-19(c)(1)(ii) or (iii)) of the stock of the subsidiary, to the extent distributions with respect to the stock to which a member becomes entitled (*e.g.,* as of the record date) no later than 24 months after the disposition would exceed the basis of the stock if the adjustment to the basis of the stock resulting from the acquisition had not occurred.

(2) *Example.* This paragraph (o) may be illustrated by the following example:

Example. (i) Corporations P, S1, S2, and S3 file consolidated returns on a calendar year basis. P owns all of the outstanding stock of S1 and S2. S1 owns all 100 shares of the outstanding stock of S3. The S3 shares have an adjusted basis of $1,000 and value of $10,000. S1 sells all 100 shares of the S3 stock to S2 for $10,000 and recognizes $9,000 of gain. The gain is deferred under § 1.1502-13(c). S2 takes a $10,000 basis in the S3 stock.

(ii) S3 borrows $5,000 in 1992 and distributes the $5,000 to S2 in the same year. S3 has no current earnings and profits, and the distribution reduces S2's basis in the S3 stock from $10,000 to $5,000.

(iii) In 1993, S3 has no current earnings and profits. At the end of 1993, S3 issues 100 shares of stock to X, an unrelated third party. As a result, S2 no longer owns 80 percent or more of the S3 stock and S3 ceases to be a member of the group. S3's ceasing to be a member of the group is a disposition of the S3 stock under § 1.1502-19. If the basis of the S3 stock had not been adjusted as a result of the sale of the S3 stock by S1 to S2, the $5,000 distribution would have resulted in a $4,000 excess loss account with respect to the S3 stock. Accordingly, S1 is required to take into account $4,000 of the deferred gain (the amount that would have been in the excess loss account but for the adjustment to the basis of the S3 stock resulting from its sale).

(iv) In 1994, S2 sells its 100 shares of S3 stock to X for $6,000. S2 recognizes gain of $1,000 on the sale. Further, under § 1.1502-13(f)(1)(i), because the S3 stock is disposed of outside the group, S1 must take into account the remaining $5,000 of deferred gain on the S3 stock.

(3) *Effective date.* This paragraph (o) applies to acquisitions of stock of a subsidiary in an intercompany transaction occurring on or after July 24, 1991. [Reg. § 1.1502-13.]

☐ [Removed by T.D. 8597, 7-12-95.]

→ *Caution: Prior law may apply to certain transactions, see Reg. § 1.1502-13T(f)(6)(iv), below. For Reg. § 1.1502-13T prior to revision by T.D. 8598, see Caution Note and text following this version of Reg. § 1.1502-13T.* ←

[Reg. § 1.1502-13T]

§ 1.1502-13T. **Intercompany transactions (Temporary).**—(a) through (f)(5) [Reserved] For further guidance, see 1.1502-13.

(f)(6) *Stock of common parent.* In addition to the general rules of this section, this paragraph (f)(6) applies to parent stock (P stock) and positions in parent stock held by another member. For this purpose, P stock is any stock of the common parent held by another member or any stock of a member (the issuer) that was the common parent if the stock was held by another member while the issuer was the common parent.

(i) *Loss stock*—(A) *Recognized loss.* Any loss recognized, directly or indirectly, by a member with respect to P stock is permanently disallowed and does not reduce earnings and profits. See § 1.1502-32(b)(3)(iii)(A) for a corresponding reduction in the basis of the member's stock.

Reg. § 1.1502-13T(a)

Consolidated Returns

See p. 20,601 for regulations not amended to reflect law changes

→ *Caution: Prior law may apply to certain transactions, see Reg. § 1.1502-13T(f)(6)(iv), below. For Reg. § 1.1502-13T prior to revision by T.D. 8598, see Caution Note and text following this version of Reg. § 1.1502-13T.* ←

(B) *Other cases.* If a member, M, owns P stock, the stock is subsequently owned by a nonmember, and immediately before the stock is owned by the nonmember, M's basis in the share exceeds its fair market value, then to the extent paragraph (f)(6)(i)(A) of this section does not apply, M's basis in the share is reduced to the share's fair market value immediately before the share is held by the nonmember. For example, if M owns shares of P stock with a $100x basis and M becomes a nonmember at a time when the P shares have a value of $60x, M's basis in the P shares is reduced to $60x immediately before M becomes a nonmember. Similarly, if M contributes the P stock to a nonmember in a transaction subject to section 351, M's basis in the shares is reduced to $60x immediately before the contribution. See § 1.1502-32(b)(3)(iii)(B) for a corresponding reduction in the basis of M's stock.

(ii) *Gain stock.* If a member, M, would otherwise recognize gain on a qualified disposition of P stock, then immediately before the qualified disposition, M is treated as purchasing the P stock from P for fair market value with cash contributed to M by P (or, if necessary, through any intermediate members). A disposition is a qualified disposition only if—

(A) The member acquires the P stock directly from the common parent (P) through a contribution to capital or a transaction qualifying under section 351(a) (or, if necessary, through a series of such transactions involving only members);

(B) Pursuant to a plan, the member transfers the stock immediately to a nonmember that is not related, within the meaning of section 267(b) or 707(b), to any member of the group;

(C) No nonmember receives a substituted basis in the stock within the meaning of section 7701(a)(42);

(D) The P stock is not exchanged for P stock;

(E) P neither becomes nor ceases to be the common parent as part of, or in contemplation of, the plan or disposition; and

(F) M neither becomes nor ceases to be a member as part of, or in contemplation of, the plan or disposition.

(iii) *Options, warrants and other rights.* Paragraph (f)(6)(i) of this section applies to options, warrants, forward contracts, or other positions with respect to P stock (including, for example, cash-settled positions). For example, if S purchases (from any party) a warrant on P stock and the warrant lapses, any loss recognized by S is permanently disallowed. Similarly, if S purchases a warrant on P stock and S becomes a nonmember at a time when the value of the warrant is less than S's basis in the warrant, S's basis in the warrant is reduced to its fair market value immediately before S becomes a nonmember.

(iv) *Effective date.* This paragraph (f)(6) applies to transactions on or after July 12, 1995 (notwithstanding whether the intercompany transaction, if any, occurred prior to that date). [Temporary Reg. § 1.1502-13T.]

☐ [T.D. 8598, 7-12-95.]

→ *Caution: Prior law Reg. § 1.1502-13T, below, was removed by T.D. 8597 and is generally effective for transactions prior to July 12, 1995 (see above for current regulations).* ←

[Reg. § 1.1502-13T]

§ 1.1502-13T. [Prior Law, see caution note.—CCH.] **Temporary regulations for certain intercompany transactions.**—(a)-(b) [Reserved.]

(c) *Deferral of gain or loss on intercompany transactions*—(1) *Inheritance of deferred gain or loss.* If the assets of the selling member are acquired by one or more other members in an acquisition to which section 381(a) applies, or pursuant to a distribution in a complete liquidation not described in section 332(b), the member acquiring the greatest portion of the assets (measured by fair market value) of the selling member shall be subject to the provisions of § 1.1502-13(d), (e), and (f) with respect to the entire remaining balance of the deferred gain or loss. If two or more members acquire the same portion (which is greater than that acquired by any other members), the common parent shall select which such member shall be subject to the provisions of § 1.1502-13(d),(e) and (f). For purposes of this section and § 1.1502-13, a member which inherits the balance of the deferred gain or loss under this subparagraph (1) shall be treated as the selling member.

(2) *Effective, date.* Paragraph (c)(1) of this section applies, and § 1.1502-13(c)6) does not apply, to acquisitions of assets by one or more members from another member in taxable years for

Reg. § 1.1502-13T(c)(2)

56,750 Consolidated Returns

See p. 20,601 for regulations not amended to reflect law changes

→ **Caution: Prior law Reg. § 1.1502-13T, below, was removed by T.D. 8597 and is generally effective for transactions prior to July 12, 1995 (see above for current regulations).**←

which the due date (without extensions) of the income tax return is after April 14, 1988.

(d)-(e) [Reserved.]

(f) *Restoration of deferred gain or loss on dispositions, etc.*—(1) *Exception to general rule of § 1.1502-13(f)(1)(iii).* Section 1.1502-13(f)(1)(iii) shall not apply in a case where the selling member or the member which owns the property, as the case may be, ceases to be a member of the group by reason of an acquisition to which section 381(a) applies, or pursuant to a distribution in a complete liquidation not described in section 332(b), and the acquiring corporation is a member.

(2) *Effective date.* Paragraph (f)(1) of this section applies, and § 1.1502-13(f)(2)(ii)(a) does not apply, when the selling member or the member which owns the property ceases to be a member of the group in a taxable year for which the due date (without extensions) of the income tax return is after April 14, 1988.

(g)-(j) [Reserved.]

(k) *Priority of sections 267(f).* For application of section 267(f) when a consolidated return is filed, see § 1.267(f)-2T.

(l) through (o) [Reserved.] For further guidance see § 1.1502-13(l) through (o).

(p) *References.* A reference in this part to § 1.1502-13 is treated as including a reference to this section. [Reg. § 1.1502-13T.]

☐ [Removed by T.D. 8597, 7-12-95.]

→ **Caution: Prior law Reg. § 1.1502-14, below, was removed by T.D. 8597 and is generally effective for transactions prior to July 12, 1995.**←

[Reg. § 1.1502-14]

§ 1.1502-14. [Prior Law, see caution note.—CCH.] **Stock, bonds, and other obligations of members.**—(a) *Intercompany distributions with respect to stock*—(1) *Dividends.* A dividend distributed by one member to another member during a consolidated return year shall be eliminated. For purposes of this paragraph, the term "dividend" means a distribution which is described in section 301(c)(1) other than a distribution described in section 243(c)(1).

(2) *Nondividend distributions.* No gain is recognized to the distributee on a distribution with respect to stock, from one member to another member during a consolidated return year, which is described in section 301(c)(2) or (3). See §§ 1.1502-19 and 1.1502-32 for adjustments to stock basis (including negative adjustments in excess of basis).

(3) *Amount distributed.* For purposes of this paragraph, the amount of any distribution of property other than money shall be determined under section 301(b)(1)(B)(ii).

(4) *Basis of property distributed in kind.* The basis of property received in a distribution to which section 301 applies is determined under section 301(d)(2)(B).

(5) *Entitlement rule*—(i) *In general.* This paragraph (a)(5)(i) applies for consolidated return years beginning on or after January 1, 1995. For all Federal income tax purposes, a distribution to which this paragraph (a) applies is treated as taken into account when the shareholding member becomes entitled to it (generally on the record date). For example, if the distributee member becomes entitled to a cash distribution before it is made, the distribution is treated as made when the distributee member becomes entitled to it. For this purpose, stock is treated as entitled to a distribution no later than the time the distribution is taken into account under the Code (e.g., under section 305). Appropriate adjustments must be made, as of the date the distribution was taken into account, if a distribution is not made.

(ii) *Minority shareholders.* If nonmembers own stock of the distributing corporation at the time the distribution is treated as occurring under paragraph (a)(5)(i) of this section, appropriate adjustments must be made to prevent acceleration of the members' portion of the distribution from affecting the earnings and profits consequences of distributions to nonmembers.

(iii) *Prior period distributions.* For rules relating to distributions before paragraph (a)(5)(i) of this section applies, see §§ 1.1502-14(a) (intercompany distributions generally) and 1.1502-32(k) (distributions declared before, but paid after, a stock disposition) as contained in the 26 CFR part 1 edition revised as of April 1, 1994.

(6) *Example.* This paragraph may be illustrated by the following example:

Example. Assume that corporation P and its wholly owned subsidiary, corporation S, are members of a group filing consolidated returns on a calendar year basis. On December 31, 1966, S distributed to P with respect to its stock $5,000

Reg. § 1.1502-14(a)(1)

→ **Caution:** *Prior law Reg. § 1.1502-14, below, was removed by T.D. 8597 and is generally effective for transactions prior to July 12, 1995.*←

cash and land with an adjusted basis to S of $6,000 and a fair market value of $5,000. No part of the distribution constituted a dividend. On December 31, 1966, P had an adjusted basis of $3,000 in the stock of S. The amount distributed is $11,000; $3,000 of that amount is applied against and reduces the adjusted basis of the stock to zero, and the remaining $8,000 is treated as P's excess loss account for its stock in S. No gain is recognized by P. Pursuant to § 1.1502-31(b)(1) P's basis in the land is $6,000.

(b) *Intercompany distributions in cancellation or redemption of all or part of the stock of the distributing corporation*—(1) *General rule.* Except as provided in subparagraph (2) of this paragraph and in § 1.1502-19, no gain or loss shall be recognized on the receipt, during a consolidated return year, by one member of property (including cash) distributed in cancellation or redemption of all or a part of the stock of another member. For purposes of this paragraph, a distribution is in cancellation or redemption of all or a part of stock only if—

(i) It is in complete liquidation of the distributing corporation,

(ii) It is in partial liquidation of the distributing corporation within the meaning of section 346, and such corporation remains a member of the group immediately after the distribution, or

(iii) It is a distribution in redemption of the stock of the distributing corporation to which section 302(a) applies. and such corporation remains a member of the group immediately after the distribution.

(2) *Gain or loss recognized.* In the case of a distribution (other than a distribution to which section 332 applies) described in subparagraph (1) of this paragraph, the following rules shall apply—

(i) Gain shall be recognized to the extent that any cash distributed exceeds the sum of—

(a) The adjusted basis (determined after taking into account any adjustment under § 1.1502-32) of the stock of the distributing corporation held by the distributee which was cancelled or redeemed, plus

(b) Any liabilities assumed by the distributee (or to which the property received is subject).

(ii) If the property distributed consists only of cash, loss shall be recognized to the extent that the sum of—

(a) The adjusted basis (determined after taking into account any adjustment under § 1.1502-32) of the stock of the distributing corporation held by the distributee which was cancelled or redeemed, plus

(b) Any liabilities assumed by the distributee, exceeds the amount of cash distributed.

(iii) If the distribution is not in complete liquidation of the distributing corporation, any gain or loss recognized shall be deferred.

(3) *Restoration of gain or loss.* Gain or loss deferred under subparagraph (2) of this paragraph shall be taken into account immediately before the occurrence of the earliest of the following events:

(i) When the distributee corporation ceases to be a member, or

(ii) When the stock of the distributing corporation (or any successor member in an acquisition to which section 381(a) applies) is considered to be disposed of by any member under § 1.1502-19(c)(1)(ii)(B) or (iii).

(4) *Basis after liquidation or distribution.* The basis of property acquired in a transaction to which this paragraph (b) applies is determined as follows:

(i) *Section 332.* The basis of property acquired in a liquidation to which section 332 applies is determined as if separate returns were filed.

(ii) *Other liquidations and distributions.* This paragraph (b)(4)(ii) determines the aggregate basis of all property acquired in a distribution in cancellation or redemption of stock to which paragraph (b)(1) of this section applies, other than a liquidation to which section 332 applies. Once the amount of aggregate basis is determined, it is allocated among the assets received (except cash) in proportion to the fair market values of the assets on the date received. The aggregate amount of basis equals—

(A) The adjusted basis of the stock exchanged therefor (determined after taking into account the adjustments under § 1.1502-32); increased by

(B) The amount of any liabilities of the distributing corporation assumed by the distributee or to which the property acquired is subject; reduced by

(C) The amount of cash received in the distribution.

(c) *Treatment of distributing corporation*—(1) *Deferral in other than complete liquidations.* Ex-

Reg. § 1.1502-14(c)(1)

Consolidated Returns

See p. 20,601 for regulations not amended to reflect law changes

→ *Caution: Prior law Reg. § 1.1502-14, below, was removed by T.D. 8597 and is generally effective for transactions prior to July 12, 1995.*←

cept as provided in subparagraph (2) of this paragraph, to the extent gain or loss is recognized to the distributing corporation on a distribution described in paragraph (a) or (b) of this section (including any amount which is treated as gain under section 311, 336, 341(f)(2), 453(d), 1245(a)(1), 1250(a)(1) or 1254(a)(1)), such gain or loss shall be deferred by the distributing corporation. Such deferred gain or loss shall be taken into account by the distributing corporation at the time and in the manner specified in paragraphs (d), (e), and (f) of § 1.1502-13, as if such distributing corporation were a "selling member" and the distributee were a "purchasing member".

(2) *Complete liquidations.* Gain or loss shall be taken into account by the distributing corporation on a complete liquidation, in the same manner and to the same extent as if separate returns were filed.

(3) *Cross-reference to temporary regulations.* For distributions in taxable years for which the due date (without extensions) of the income tax return is after April 14, 1988 or after March 14, 1990, see § 1.1502-14T.

(d) *Gains and losses on obligations of members—* (1) *Deferral of gain or loss.* To the extent gain or loss is recognized under the Code to a member during a consolidated return year because of a sale or other disposition (other than a redemption or cancellation) of an obligation of another member (referred to in this paragraph as the "debtor member"), whether or not such obligation is evidenced by a security, such gain or loss shall be deferred. For purposes of this paragraph, a deduction because of the worthlessness of, or a deduction for a reasonable addition to a reserve for bad debts with respect to, an obligation described in this subparagraph shall be considered a loss from the disposition of such obligation.

(2) *Restoration of gain or loss where obligation leaves group.* If an obligation described in subparagraph (1) of this paragraph is sold or disposed of to a nonmember (or if the member holding the obligation becomes a nonmember), each member with deferred gain or loss with respect to such obligation under subparagraph (1) of this paragraph shall, except as provided in subparagraph (3) of this paragraph, take such gain or loss into account ratably over the remaining term of the obligation.

(3) *Restoration of gain or loss on other events.* Each member's gain or loss deferred with respect to an obligation under subparagraph (1) which has not been taken into account under subparagraph (2) of this paragraph shall be taken into account immediately before the occurrence of the earliest of the following events:

(i) When such member ceases to be a member,

(ii) When the stock of the debtor member (or any successor in an acquisition to which section 381(a) applies) is considered to be disposed of by any member under § 1.1502-19(c)(1)(ii)(B) or (iii), or

(iii) When the obligation is redeemed or cancelled.

(4) *Exception for obligations acquired in tax-free exchanges.*—(i) If—

(a) A member received an obligation of another member in exchange for property,

(b) The basis of the obligation was determined in whole or in part by reference to the basis of the property exchanged, and

(c) The obligation has never been held by a nonmember,

then any gain or loss of any member on redemption or cancellation of such obligation shall be deferred, and subparagraph (3) of this paragraph shall not apply.

(ii) Gain or loss deferred by a member under subdivision (i) of this subparagraph, and under subparagraph (1) of this paragraph with respect to an obligation to which this subparagraph applies, shall be taken into account immediately before the occurrence of the earliest of the following events:

(a) When such member ceases to be a member, or

(b) When the stock of the debtor member is considered to be disposed of by any member under § 1.1502-19(c)(1)(ii)(B) or (iii).

(iii) This subparagraph may be illustrated by the following example:

Example. Corporation P forms a subsidiary, S, in a transaction to which section 351 applies and receives as a result of such transaction, in addition to stock, a security with a face value of $100 and a basis of $50. If the security is redeemed for $100, the $50 gain on redemption is deferred and is not taken into account until P ceases to be a member or the stock of S is treated as disposed of under this subparagraph.

(5) *Premium and discount.* For treatment of premium and discount with respect to obligations described in this subparagraph, see § 1.1502-13(b) and example 16 of § 1.1502-13(h).

Reg. § 1.1502-14(c)(2)

Consolidated Returns

See p. 20,601 for regulations not amended to reflect law changes

→ *Caution: Prior law Reg. § 1.1502-14, below, was removed by T.D. 8597 and is generally effective for transactions prior to July 12, 1995.*←

(e) *Character and inheritance of deferred items*—(1) *Character.* The character of gain or loss deferred under paragraph (b)(2), (d)(1), or (d)(4) of this section shall be determined at the time of the transaction as if such transaction had not occurred during a consolidated return year.

(2) *Inheritance.* Paragraphs (b)(3)(i), (d)(3)(i), and (d)(4)(ii)(a) of this section shall not apply if a member with deferred gain or loss ceases to be a member because its assets are acquired by one or more members in an acquisition to which section 381(a) applies. The member acquiring the greatest portion of the assets (measured by fair market value) of such member shall be subject to the appropriate restoration provisions of paragraphs (b) and (d) of this section.

(f) *Acquisition of group.* Paragraphs (b)(3), (c), and (d)(2), (3) and (4)(ii) of this section shall not apply solely because of a termination of the group (hereinafter referred to as the "terminating group") resulting from—

(1) The acquisition by a nonmember corporation of (i) the assets of the common parent in a reorganization described in subparagraph (A), (C), or (D) (but only if the requirements of subparagraphs (A) and (B) of section 354(b)(1) are met) of section 368(a)(1), or (ii) stock of the common parent, or

(2) The acquisition (in a transaction to which § 1.1502-75(d)(3) applies) by a member of (i) the assets of a nonmember corporation in a reorganization referred to in subparagraph (1) of this paragraph, or (ii) stock of a nonmember corporation,

if all the members of the terminating group (other than such common parent if its assets are acquired) immediately before the acquisition are members immediately after the acquisition of another group (hereinafter referred to as the "succeeding group") which files a consolidated return for the first taxable year ending after the date of acquisition. The members of the succeeding group shall succeed to any deferred gain or loss of members of the terminating group and to the status of such members as distributing or distributee corporations. This paragraph shall not apply with respect to acquisitions occurring before August 25, 1971.

(g) *Additional restoration of gain deferred on distributions of stock of a member*—(1) *In general.* For purposes of this section and § 1.1502-13, gain deferred with respect to a distribution of stock of a subsidiary from one member to another member shall be taken into account—

(i) Upon a disposition (as defined in § 1.1502-19(c)(1)(ii) or (iii) of the stock of the subsidiary in an amount equal to the amount that would have created or increased the excess loss account if the adjustment to the basis (or the excess loss account) of the stock of the subsidiary resulting from the distribution had not occurred; or

(ii) Following a disposition (as defined in § 1.1502-19(c)(1)(ii) or (iii) of stock of the subsidiary, to the extent distributions with respect to the stock to which a member becomes entitled (e.g., as of the record date) no later than 24 months after the disposition would exceed the basis of the stock if the adjustment to the basis of the stock resulting from the distribution had not occurred.

(2) *Examples.* This paragraph (g) is illustrated by the following examples.

Example 1. (i) Corporations P, S, and T file consolidated returns on a calendar year basis. P owns all 100 shares of the outstanding stock of S. S owns all 200 shares of the outstanding stock of T. The T shares have an adjusted basis of $1,000 and a value of $10,000. S distributes all of its T stock to P. As a result of the distribution, S recognizes $9,000 of gain under section 311(b) and the gain is deferred under § 1.1502-14T(a). P receives a $10,000 basis in the T stock.

(ii) T borrows $9,000 in 1989 and distributes the $9,000 to P in the same year. T has no current earnings and profits, and the distribution reduces P's basis in the T stock from $10,000 to $1,000. In 1990, T has $1,000 of earnings and profits which are not distributed. At the end of 1990, T issues 100 shares of stock to X, an unrelated third party. As a result P no longer owns 80 percent or more of the stock of T and T ceases to be a member of the group. T's ceasing to be a member of the group constitutes a disposition of the T stock under § 1.1502-19. If the basis of the T stock had not been adjusted as a result of S's distribution of the T stock to P, the $9,000 distribution to P would have resulted in a $7,000 excess loss account with respect to the T stock. Accordingly, S is required to take into account $7,000 of deferred gain (the amount that would have been in the excess loss account but for the adjustment to the basis of the T stock resulting from its distribution).

(iii) At the end of 1991, P sells its 200 shares of T stock to Y for $2,000. P recognizes no gain or loss on the sale. Under § 1.1502-13(f)(1)(i), because the T stock is disposed of outside the group, S must take into account the remaining $2,000 of deferred gain on the T stock.

Reg. § 1.1502-14(g)(2)

→ **Caution: Prior law Reg. § 1.1502-14, below, was removed by T.D. 8597 and is generally effective for transactions prior to July 12, 1995.** ←

Example 2. The facts are the same as in Example 1 except that T borrows and distributes the $9,000 to S before S distributes the T stock to P. The results are the same as in *Example 1* because P would have had an excess loss account of $7,000 with respect to the T stock at the time T ceased to be a member of the P group but for the adjustment to the excess loss account resulting from S's distribution of the T stock to P.

(3) *Effective dates*—(i) *General rule.* Except as provided in paragraph (g)(3)(ii) of this section, this paragraph (g) applies to dispositions (as defined in this paragraph (g)) of stock of a subsidiary in taxable years for which the due date (without extensions) of the income tax return is after March 14, 1990.

(ii) *Exceptions.* Notwithstanding paragraph (g)(3)(i) of this section—

(A) This paragraph (g) does not apply to gain deferred with respect to a distribution of stock of a subsidiary from one member to another member before January 1, 1989, if the disposition (as defined in this paragraph (g)) of the stock of the subsidiary occurs before March 9, 1990.

(B) In computing its consolidated taxable income with respect to post-disposition distributions to which a member becomes entitled (*e.g.,* as of the record date) before March 9, 1993, a group may apply § 1.1502-14T(c)(1)(ii) (as contained in 26 CFR part 1 edition revised as of April 1, 1992). [Reg. § 1.1502-14.]

☐ [*Removed by T.D. 8597, 7-12-95.*]

→ **Caution: Reg. § 1.1502-14T, below, was removed by T.D. 8597 and is generally effective for transactions prior to July 12, 1995.** ←

[Reg. § 1.1502-14T]

§ 1.1502-14T. [Prior Law, see caution note.—CCH.] **Treatment of distributing corporation (temporary).**—(a) *Deferral of gain or loss.* To the extent gain or loss is recognized to the distributing corporation on a distribution described in § 1.1502-14(a) or (b) (including any amount which is treated as gain under sections 311, 336, 341(f)(2), 453B, 1245(a)(1) or 1250(a)(1)), such gain or loss shall be deferred by the distributing corporation. Such deferred gain or loss shall be taken into account at the time and in the manner specified in § 1.1502-13(d), (e), and (f), and § 1.1502-13(l) and (m), as if such distributing corporation were a "selling member," the distributee were a "purchasing member" and the distribution described in § 1.1502-14 were a "deferred intercompany transaction."

(b) *Effective, date.* Paragraph (a) of this section applies, and § 1.1502-14(c) does not apply, to distributions described in § 1.1502-14(a) or (b) that occur in taxable years for which the due date (without extensions) of the income tax return is after April 14, 1988.

(c) [Reserved] For further guidance see § 1.1502-14(g).

(d) *References.* A reference in this part to § 1.1502-14 is treated as including a reference to this section. [Reg. § 1.1502-14T.]

☐ [*Removed by T.D. 8597, 7-12-95.*]

→ **Caution: Reg. § 1.1502-15, below, is generally effective for built-in losses recognized in tax years for which the consolidated return due date is after June 25, 1999.** ←

[Reg. § 1.1502-15]

§ 1.1502-15. **SRLY limitation on built-in losses.**—(a) *SRLY limitation.* Except as provided in paragraph (f) of this section (relating to built-in losses of the common parent) and paragraph (g) of this section (relating to an overlap with section 382), built-in losses are subject to the SRLY limitation under §§ 1.1502-21(c) and 1.1502-22(c) (including applicable subgroup principles). Built-in losses are treated as deductions or losses in the year recognized, except for the purpose of determining the amount of, and the extent to which the built-in loss is limited by, the SRLY limitation for the year in which it is recognized. Solely for such purpose, a built-in loss is treated as a hypothetical net operating loss carryover or net capital loss carryover arising in a SRLY, instead of as a deduction or loss in the year recognized. To the extent that a built-in loss is allowed as a deduction under this section in the year it is recognized, it offsets any consolidated taxable income for the year before any loss carryovers or carrybacks are allowed as a deduction. To the extent not so allowed, it is treated as a separate net operating loss or net capital loss carryover or carryback arising in the year of recognition and, under

Reg. § 1.1502-14T(a)

Consolidated Returns

See p. 20,601 for regulations not amended to reflect law changes

→ *Caution: Reg. § 1.1502-15, below, is generally effective for built-in losses recognized in tax years for which the consolidated return due date is after June 25, 1999.*←

§ 1.1502-21(c) or 1.1502-22(c), the year of recognition is treated as a SRLY.

(b) *Built-in losses*—(1) *Defined.* If a corporation has a net unrealized built-in loss under section 382(h)(3) (as modified by this section) on the day it becomes a member of the group (whether or not the group is a consolidated group), its deductions and losses are built-in losses under this section to the extent they are treated as recognized built-in losses under section 382(h)(2)(B) (as modified by this section). This paragraph (b) generally applies separately with respect to each member, but see paragraph (c) of this section for circumstances in which it is applied on a subgroup basis.

(2) *Operating rules.* Solely for purposes of applying paragraph (b)(1) of this section, the principles of § 1.1502-94(c) apply with appropriate adjustments, including the following:

(i) *Stock acquisition.* A corporation is treated as having an ownership change under section 382(g) on the day the corporation becomes a member of a group, and no other events (e.g., a subsequent ownership change under section 382(g) while it is a member) are treated as causing an ownership change.

(ii) *Asset acquisition.* In the case of an asset acquisition by a group, the assets and liabilities acquired directly from the same transferor (whether corporate or non-corporate, foreign or domestic) pursuant to the same plan are treated as the assets and liabilities of a corporation that becomes a member of the group (and has an ownership change) on the date of the acquisition.

(iii) *Recognized built-in gain or loss.* A loss that is included in the determination of net unrealized built-in gain or loss and that is recognized but disallowed or deferred (e.g., under § 1.1502-20 or section 267) is not treated as a built-in loss unless and until the loss would be allowed during the recognition period without regard to the application of this section. Section 382(h)(1)(B)(ii) does not apply to the extent it limits the amount of recognized built-in loss that may be treated as a pre-change loss to the amount of the net unrealized built-in loss.

(c) *Built-in losses of subgroups*—(1) *In general.* In the case of a subgroup, the principles of paragraph (b) of this section apply to the subgroup, and not separately to its members. Thus, the net unrealized built-in loss and recognized built-in loss for purposes of paragraph (b) of this section are based on the aggregate amounts for each member of the subgroup.

(2) *Members of subgroups.* A subgroup is composed of those members that have been continuously affiliated with each other for the 60 consecutive month period ending immediately before they become members of the group in which the loss is recognized. A member remains a member of the subgroup until it ceases to be affiliated with the loss member. For this purpose, the principles of § 1.1502-21(c)(2)(iv) through (vi) apply with appropriate adjustments.

(3) *Coordination of 60 month affiliation requirement with the overlap rule.* If one or more corporations become members of a group and are included in the determination of a net unrealized built-in loss that is subject to the overlap rule described in paragraph (g)(1) of this section, then for purposes of paragraph (c)(2) of this section, such corporations that become members of the group are treated as having been affiliated for 60 consecutive months with the common parent of the group and are also treated as having been affiliated with any other members who have been affiliated or are treated as having been affiliated with the common parent at such time. The corporations are treated as having been affiliated with such other members for the same period of time that those members have been affiliated or are treated as having been affiliated with the common parent. If two or more corporations become members of the group at the same time, but this paragraph (c)(3) does not apply to every such corporation, then immediately after the corporations become members of the group, and solely for purposes of paragraph (c)(2) of this section, the corporations to which this paragraph (c)(3) applies are treated as having not been previously affiliated with the corporations to which this paragraph (c)(3) does not apply. If the common parent has become the common parent of an existing group within the previous five year period in a transaction described in § 1.1502-75(d)(2)(ii) or (3), the principles of §§ 1.1502-91(g)(6) and 1.1502-96(a)(2)(iii) shall apply.

(4) *Built-in amounts.* Solely for purposes of determining whether the subgroup has a net unrealized built-in loss or whether it has a recognized built-in loss, the principles of § 1.1502-91(g) and (h) apply with appropriate adjustments.

(d) *Examples.* For purposes of the examples in this section, unless otherwise stated, all groups file consolidated returns, all corporations have calendar taxable years, the facts set forth the only

Reg. § 1.1502-15(d)

Consolidated Returns

See p. 20,601 for regulations not amended to reflect law changes

→ *Caution: Reg. § 1.1502-15, below, is generally effective for built-in losses recognized in tax years for which the consolidated return due date is after June 25, 1999.*←

corporate activity, value means fair market value and the adjusted basis of each asset equals its value, all transactions are with unrelated persons, and the application of any limitation or threshold under section 382 is disregarded. The principles of this section are illustrated by the following examples:

Example 1. Determination of recognized built-in loss. (i) Individual A owns all of the stock of P and T. T has two depreciable assets. Asset 1 has an unrealized loss of $55 (basis $75, value $20), and asset 2 has an unrealized gain of $20 (basis $30, value $50). P acquires all the stock of T from Individual A during Year 1, and T becomes a member of the P group. P's acquisition of T is not an ownership change as defined by section 382(g). Paragraph (g) of this section does not apply because there is not an overlap of the application of the rules contained in paragraph (a) of this section and section 382.

(ii) Under paragraph (b)(2)(i) of this section, and solely for purposes of applying paragraph (b)(1) of this section, T is treated as having an ownership change under section 382(g) on becoming a member of the P group. Under paragraph (b)(1) of this section, none of T's $55 of unrealized loss is treated as a built-in loss unless T has a net unrealized built-in loss under section 382(h)(3) on becoming a member of the P group.

(iii) Under section 382(h)(3)(A), T has a $35 net unrealized built-in loss on becoming a member of the P group (($55) + $20 = ($35)). Assume that this amount exceeds the threshold requirement in section 382(h)(3)(B). Under section 382(h)(2)(B), the entire amount of T's $55 unrealized loss is treated as a built-in loss to the extent it is recognized during the 5-year recognition period described in section 382(h)(7). Under paragraph (b)(2)(iii) of this section, the restriction under section 382(h)(1)(B)(ii), which limits the amount of recognized built-in loss that is treated as pre-change loss to the amount of the net unrealized built-in loss, is inapplicable for this purpose. Consequently, the entire $55 of unrealized loss (not just the $35 net unrealized loss) is treated under paragraph (b)(1) of this section as a built-in loss to the extent it is recognized within 5 years of T's becoming a member of the P group. Under paragraph (a) of this section, a built-in loss is subject to the SRLY limitation under § 1.1502-21(c)(1).

(iv) Under paragraph (b)(2)(ii) of this section, the built-in loss would similarly be subject to a SRLY limitation under § 1.1502-21(c)(1) if T transferred all of its assets and liabilities to a subsidiary of the P group in a single transaction described in section 351. To the extent the built-in loss is recognized within 5 years of T's transfer, all of the items contributed by the acquiring subsidiary to consolidated taxable income (and not just the items attributable to the assets and liabilities transferred by T) are included for purposes of determining the SRLY limitation under § 1.1502-21(c)(1).

Example 2. Actual application of section 382 not relevant. (i) Individual A owns all of the stock of P, and Individual B owns all of the stock of T. T has two depreciable assets. Asset 1 has an unrealized loss of $25 (basis $75, value $50), and asset 2 has an unrealized gain of $20 (basis $30, value $50). P buys 55 percent of the stock of T in January of Year 1, resulting in an ownership change of T under section 382(g). During March of Year 2, P buys the 45 percent balance of the T stock, and T becomes a member of the P group.

(ii) Although T has an ownership change for purposes of section 382 in Year 1 and not Year 2, T's joining the P group in Year 2 is treated as an ownership change under section 382(g) solely for purposes of this section. Consequently, for purposes of this section, whether T has a net unrealized built-in loss under section 382(h)(3) is determined as if the day T joined the P group were a change date.

Example 3. Determination of a recognized built-in loss of a subgroup. (i) Individual A owns all of the stock of P, S, and M. P and M are each the common parent of a consolidated group. During Year 1, P acquires all of the stock of S from Individual A, and S becomes a member of the P group. P's acquisition of S is not an ownership change as defined by section 382(g). At the beginning of Year 7, M acquires all of the stock of P from Individual A, and P and S become members of the M group. M's acquisitions of P and S are also not ownership changes as defined by section 382(g). At the time of M's acquisition of the P stock, P has (disregarding the stock of S) a $10 net unrealized built-in gain (two depreciable assets, asset 1 with a basis of $35 and a value of $55, and asset 2 with a basis of $55 and a value of $45), and S has a $75 net unrealized built-in loss (two depreciable assets, asset 3 with a basis of $95 and a value of $10, and asset 4 with a basis of $10 and a value of $20).

(ii) Under paragraph (c) of this section, P and S compose a subgroup on becoming members of the M group because P and S were continuously affili-

Reg. § 1.1502-15(d)

Consolidated Returns

See p. 20,601 for regulations not amended to reflect law changes

→ **Caution:** *Reg. § 1.1502-15, below, is generally effective for built-in losses recognized in tax years for which the consolidated return due date is after June 25, 1999.*←

ated for the 60 month period ending immediately before they became members of the M group. Consequently, paragraph (b) of this section does not apply to P and S separately. Instead, their separately computed unrealized gains and losses are aggregated for purposes of determining whether, and the extent to which, any unrealized loss is treated as built-in loss under this section and is subject to the SRLY limitation under § 1.1502-21(c).

(iii) Under paragraph (c) of this section, the P subgroup has a net unrealized built-in loss on the day P and S become members of the M group, determined by treating the day they become members as a change date. The net unrealized built-in loss is the aggregate of P's net unrealized built-in gain of $10 and S's net unrealized built-in loss of $75, or an aggregate net unrealized built-in loss of $65. (The stock of S owned by P is disregarded for purposes of determining the net unrealized built-in loss. However, any loss allowed on the sale of the stock within the recognition period is taken into account in determining recognized loss.) Assume that the $65 net unrealized built-in loss exceeds the threshold requirement under section 382(h)(3)(B).

(iv) Under paragraphs (b)(1), (b)(2)(iii), and (c) of this section, a loss recognized during the 5-year recognition period on an asset of P or S held on the day that P and S became members of the M group is a built-in loss except to the extent the group establishes that such loss exceeds the amount by which the adjusted basis of such asset on the day the member became a member exceeded the fair market value of such asset on that same day. If P sells asset 2 for $45 in Year 7 and recognizes a $10 loss, the entire $10 loss is treated as a built-in loss under paragraphs (b)(2)(iii) and (c) of this section. If S sells asset 3 for $10 in Year 7 and recognizes an $85 loss, the entire $85 loss is treated as a built-in loss under paragraphs (b)(2)(iii) and (c) of this section (not just the $55 balance of the P subgroup's $65 net unrealized built-in loss).

(v) The determination of whether P and S constitute a SRLY subgroup for purposes of loss carryovers and carrybacks, and the extent to which built-in losses are not allowed under the SRLY limitation, is made under § 1.1502-21(c).

Example 4. Computation of SRLY limitation. (i) Individual A owns all of the stock of P, the common parent of a consolidated group. During Year 1, Individual A forms T by contributing $300 and T sustains a $100 net operating loss. During Year 2, T's assets decline in value to $100. At the beginning of Year 3, P acquires all the stock of T from Individual A, and T becomes a member of the P group with a net unrealized built-in loss of $100. P's acquisition of T is not an ownership change as defined by section 382(g). Assume that $100 exceeds the threshold requirements of section 382(h)(3)(B). During Year 3, T recognizes its unrealized built-in loss as a $100 ordinary loss. The members of the P group contribute the following net income to the consolidated taxable income of the P group (disregarding T's recognized built-in loss and any consolidated net operating loss deduction under § 1.1502-21) for Years 3 and 4:

	Year 3	Year 4	Total
P group (without T)	$100	$100	$200
T	$60	$40	$100
CTI	$160	$140	$300

(ii) Under paragraph (b) of this section, T's $100 ordinary loss in Year 3 (not taken into account in the consolidated taxable income computations above) is a built-in loss. Under paragraph (a) of this section, the built-in loss is treated as a net operating loss carryover for purposes of determining the SRLY limitation under § 1.1502-21(c).

(iii) For Year 3, § 1.1502-21(c) limits T's $100 built-in loss and $100 net operating loss carryover from Year 1 to the aggregate of the P group's consolidated taxable income through Year 3, determined by reference to only T's items. For this purpose, consolidated taxable income is determined without regard to any consolidated net operating loss deductions under § 1.1502-21(a).

(iv) The P group's consolidated taxable income through Year 3 is $60 when determined by reference to only T's items. Under § 1.1502-21(c), the SRLY limitation for Year 3 is therefore $60.

(v) Under paragraph (a) of this section, the $100 built-in loss is treated as a current deduction for all purposes other than determination of the SRLY limitation under § 1.1502-21(c). Consequently, a deduction for the built-in loss is allowed in Year 3 before T's loss carryover from Year 1 is

Reg. § 1.1502-15(d)

→ *Caution: Reg. § 1.1502-15, below, is generally effective for built-in losses recognized in tax years for which the consolidated return due date is after June 25, 1999.*←

allowed, but only to the extent of the $60 SRLY limitation. None of T's Year 1 loss carryover is allowed because the built-in loss ($100) exceeds the SRLY limitation for Year 3.

(vi) The $40 balance of the built-in loss that is not allowed in Year 3 because of the SRLY limitation is treated as a $40 net operating loss arising in Year 3 that is carried to other years in accordance with the rules of § 1.1502-21(b). The $40 net operating loss is treated under paragraph (a) of this section and § 1.1502-21(c)(1)(ii) as a loss carryover or carryback from Year 3 that arises in a SRLY, and is subject to the rules of § 1.1502-21 (including § 1.1502-21(c)) rather than this section. See also § 1.1502-21(c)(1)(iii) *Example 4*.

(vii) The facts are the same as in paragraphs (i) through (vi) of this *Example 4*, except that T has an additional built-in loss when it joins the P group which is recognized in Year 4. For purposes of determining the SRLY limitation for this additional loss in Year 4 (or any subsequent year), the $60 of built-in loss allowed as a deduction in Year 3 is treated under paragraph (a) of this section as a deduction in Year 3 that reduces the P group's consolidated taxable income when determined by reference to only T's items.

Example 5. Built-in loss exceeding consolidated taxable income in the year recognized. (i) Individual A owns all of the stock of P and T. During Year 1, P acquires all the stock of T from Individual A, and T becomes a member of the P group. P's acquisition of T was not an ownership change as defined by section 382(g). At the time of acquisition, T has a noncapital asset with an unrealized loss of $45 (basis $100, value $55), which exceeds the threshold requirements of section 382(h)(3)(B). During Year 2, T sells its asset for $55 and recognizes the unrealized built-in loss. The P group has $10 of consolidated taxable income in Year 2, computed by disregarding T's recognition of the $45 built-in loss and the consolidated net operating loss deduction, while the consolidated taxable income would be $25 if determined by reference to only T's items (other than the $45 loss).

(ii) T's $45 loss is recognized in Year 2 and, under paragraph (b) of this section, constitutes a built-in loss. Under paragraph (a) of this section and § 1.1502-21(c)(1)(ii), the loss is treated as a net operating loss carryover to Year 2 for purposes of applying the SRLY limitation under § 1.1502-21(c).

(iii) For Year 2, T's SRLY limitation is the aggregate of the P group's consolidated taxable income through Year 2 determined by reference to only T's items. For this purpose, consolidated taxable income is determined by disregarding any built-in loss that is treated as a net operating loss carryover, and any consolidated net operating loss deductions under § 1.1502-21(a). Consolidated taxable income so determined is $25.

(iv) Under § 1.1502-21(c), $25 of the $45 built-in loss could be deducted in Year 2. Because the P group has only $10 of consolidated taxable income (determined without regard to the $45), the $25 loss creates a consolidated net operating loss of $15. This loss is carried back or forward under the rules of § 1.1502-21(b) and absorbed under the rules of § 1.1502-21(a). This loss is not treated as arising in a SRLY (see § 1.1502-21(c)(1)(ii)) and therefore is not subject to the SRLY limitation under § 1.1502-21(c) in any consolidated return year of the group to which it is carried. The remaining $20 is treated as a loss carryover arising in a SRLY and is subject to the limitation of § 1.1502-21(c) in the year to which it is carried.

(e) *Predecessors and successors.* For purposes of this section, any reference to a corporation or member includes, as the context may require, a reference to a successor or predecessor, as defined in § 1.1502-1(f)(4).

(f) *Built-in losses recognized by common parent of group*—(1) *General rule.* Paragraph (a) of this section does not apply to any loss recognized by the group on an asset held by the common parent on the date the group is formed. Following an acquisition described in § 1.1502-75(d)(2) or (3), references to the common parent are to the corporation that was the common parent immediately before the acquisition.

(2) *Anti-avoidance rule.* If a corporation that becomes a common parent of a group acquires assets with a net unrealized built-in loss in excess of the threshold requirement of section 382(h)(3)(B) (and thereby increases its net unrealized built-in loss or decreases its net unrealized built-in gain) prior to, and in anticipation of, the formation of the group, paragraph (f)(1) of this section does not apply.

(g) *Overlap with section 382*—(1) *General rule.* The limitations provided in §§ 1.1502-21(c) and 1.1502-22(c) do not apply to recognized built-in losses or to loss carryovers or carrybacks attributable to recognized built-in losses when the appli-

Reg. § 1.1502-15(e)

→ **Caution: Reg. § 1.1502-15, below, is generally effective for built-in losses recognized in tax years for which the consolidated return due date is after June 25, 1999.**←

cation of paragraph (a) of this section results in an overlap with the application of section 382.

(2) *Definitions*—(i) *Generally.* For purposes of this paragraph (g), the definitions and nomenclature contained in section 382, the regulations thereunder, and §§ 1.1502-90 through 1.1502-99 apply.

(ii) *Overlap*—(A) An overlap of the application of paragraph (a) of this section and the application of section 382 with respect to built-in losses occurs if a corporation becomes a member of a consolidated group (the SRLY event) within six months of the change date of an ownership change giving rise to a section 382(a) limitation that would apply with respect to the corporation's recognized built-in losses (the section 382 event). Except as provided in paragraph (g)(3) of this section, application of the overlap rule does not require that the size and composition of the corporation's net unrealized built-in loss is the same on the date of the section 382 event and the SRLY event.

(B) For special rules in the event that there is a SRLY subgroup and/or a loss subgroup as defined in § 1.1502-91(d)(2) with respect to built-in losses, see paragraph (g)(4) of this section.

(3) *Operating rules*—(i) *Section 382 event before SRLY event.* If a SRLY event occurs on the same date as a section 382 event or within the six month period beginning on the date of the section 382 event, paragraph (g)(1) of this section applies beginning with the tax year that includes the SRLY event. Paragraph (g)(1) of this section does not apply, however, if a corporation that would otherwise be subject to the overlap rule acquires assets from a person other than a member of the group with a net unrealized built-in loss in excess of the threshold requirement of section 382(h)(3)(B) (and thereby increases its net unrealized built-in loss) after the section 382 event, and before the SRLY event.

(ii) *SRLY event before section 382 event.* If a section 382 event occurs within the period beginning the day after the SRLY event and ending six months after the SRLY event, paragraph (g)(1) of this section applies starting with the first tax year that begins after the section 382 event. However, paragraph (g)(1) of this section does not apply at any time if a corporation that otherwise would be subject to paragraph (g)(1) of this section transfers assets with an unrealized built-in loss to another member of the group after the SRLY event, but before the section 382 event, unless the corporation recognizes the built-in loss upon the transfer.

(4) *Subgroup rules.* In general, in the case of built-in losses for which there is a SRLY subgroup and the corporations joining the group at the time of the SRLY event also constitute a loss subgroup (as defined in § 1.1502-91(d)(2)), the principles of this paragraph (g) apply to the SRLY subgroup, and not separately to its members. However, paragraph (g)(1) of this section applies with respect to built-in losses only if—

(i) All members of the SRLY subgroup with respect to those built-in losses are also included in a loss subgroup (as defined in § 1.1502-91(d)(2)); and

(ii) All members of a loss subgroup (as defined in § 1.1502-91(d)(2)) are also members of a SRLY subgroup with respect to those built-in losses.

(5) *Asset acquisitions.* Notwithstanding the application of this paragraph (g), paragraph (a) of this section applies to asset acquisitions by the corporation that occurs after the latter of the SRLY event and the section 382 event. See, paragraph (b)(2)(ii) of this section.

(6) *Examples.* The principles of this paragraph (g) are illustrated by the following examples:

Example 1. Determination of subgroup. (i) Individual A owns all of the stock of P, P1, and S. In Year 1, P acquires all of the stock of P1, and they file a consolidated return. In Year 3, P acquires all of the stock of S, and S joins the P group. Individual B, unrelated to Individual A, owns all of the stock of M and K, each the common parent of a consolidated group. Individual C, unrelated to either Individual A or Individual B, owns all of the stock of T.

(ii) At the beginning of Year 7, M acquires all of the stock of P from Individual A, and, as a result, P, P1, and S become members of the M group. At the time of M's acquisition of the P stock, P has a $15 net unrealized built-in loss (disregarding the stock of P1), P1 has a net unrealized built-in gain of $10, and S has a net unrealized built-in gain of $5.

(iii) During Year 8, M acquires all of the stock of T, and T joins the M group. At the time of M's acquisition of the T stock, T had an unrealized built-in loss of $15. At the beginning of Year 9, K acquires all of the stock of M from Individual B, and the members of the M consolidated group including P, P1, S, and T become members of the

Reg. § 1.1502-15(g)(6)

→ **Caution: Reg. § 1.1502-15, below, is generally effective for built-in losses recognized in tax years for which the consolidated return due date is after June 25, 1999.** ←

K group. At the time of K's acquisition of the M stock, M has (disregarding the stock of P and T) a $15 net unrealized built-in loss, P has a $20 net unrealized built-in loss (disregarding the stock of P1), P1 has a net unrealized built-in gain of $5, S has a net unrealized built-in loss of $35, and T has a $15 net unrealized built-in loss.

(iv) M's acquisition of P in Year 7 results in P, P1, and S becoming members of the M group (the SRLY event). Under paragraph (c) of this section, P and P1 compose a SRLY built-in loss subgroup because they have been affiliated for the 60 consecutive month period immediately preceding joining the M group. S is not a member of the subgroup because on becoming a member of the M group it had not been continuously affiliated with P and P1 for the 60 month period ending immediately before it became a member of the M group. Consequently, § 1.1502-15 applies to S separately from the P and P1 subgroup.

(v) Assuming that the $5 net unrealized built-in loss of the P/P1 subgroup exceeds the threshold requirement under section 382(h)(3)(B), M's acquisition of P resulted in an ownership change of P and P1 within the meaning of section 382(g) that subjects P and P1 to a limitation under section 382(a) (the section 382 event). Because, with respect to P and P1, the SRLY event and the change date of the section 382 event occur on the same date and because the loss subgroup and SRLY subgroup are coextensive, there is an overlap of the application of the SRLY rules and the application of section 382.

(vi) S was not a loss corporation because it did not have a net operating loss carryover, or a net unrealized built-in loss, and therefore, M's acquisition of P did not result in an ownership change of S within the meaning of section 382(g). S, therefore is not subject to the overlap rule of paragraph (g) of this section.

(vii) M's acquisition of T resulted in T becoming a member of the M group (the SRLY event). Assuming that T's $15 net unrealized built-in loss exceeds the threshold requirement under section 382(h)(3)(B), M's acquisition of T also resulted in an ownership change of T within the meaning of section 382(g) that subjects T to a limitation under section 382(a) (the section 382 event). Because, with respect to T, the SRLY event and the change date of the section 382 event occur on the same date, there is an overlap of the application of the SRLY rules and the application of section 382 within the meaning of paragraph (g) of this section.

(viii) K's acquisition of M results in the members of the M consolidated group, including T, P, P1, and S, becoming members of the K group (the SRLY event). Because T, P, and P1 were each included in the determination of a net unrealized built-in loss that was subject to the overlap rule described in paragraph (g)(1) of this section when they each became members of the M group, they are deemed under paragraph (c)(3) of this section to have been continuously affiliated with M for the 60 month period ending immediately before becoming a member of the M group, notwithstanding their actual affiliation history. As a result, M, T, P, and P1 compose a SRLY built-in loss subgroup under paragraph (c)(2) of this section. K's acquisition of M is not subject to paragraph (g) of this section because it does not result in a section 382 event.

(ix) S, however, is not a member of the subgroup under paragraph (c)(2) of this section. Because S was not included in the determination of a net unrealized built-in loss that was subject to the overlap rule described in paragraph (g)(1) of this section when it joined the M group, S is treated as becoming an affiliate of M on the date it joined the M group. Furthermore, under paragraph (c)(3) of this section, S is deemed to have begun its affiliation with P and P1 on the date it joined the M group. Consequently, § 1.1502-15 applies to S separately to the extent its built-in loss is recognized within the recognition period.

Example 2. Post-overlap acquisition of assets. (i) Individual A owns all of the stock of P, the common parent of a consolidated group. B, an individual unrelated to Individual A, owns all of the stock of T. T has two depreciable assets. Asset 1 has an unrealized built-in loss of $25 (basis $75, value $50), and asset 2 has an unrealized built-in gain of $20 (basis $30, value $50). During Year 3, P buys all of the stock of T from Individual B. On January 1, Year 4, P contributes $80 cash and Individual A contributes asset 3, a depreciable asset, with a net unrealized built-in loss of $45 (basis $65, value $20), in exchange for T stock in a transaction that is described in section 351.

(ii) P's acquisition of T results in T becoming a member of the P group (the SRLY event) and also results in an ownership change of T, within the meaning of section 382(g), that gives rise to a limitation under section 382(a) (the section 382 event).

(iii) Because the SRLY event and the change date of the section 382 event occur on the same date, there is an overlap of the application of the

Reg. § 1.1502-15(g)(6)

→ *Caution: Reg. § 1.1502-15, below, is generally effective for built-in losses recognized in tax years for which the consolidated return due date is after June 25, 1999.*←

SRLY rules and the application of section 382. Consequently, under paragraph (g) of this section, the limitation under paragraph (a) of this section does not apply to T's net unrealized built-in loss when it joined the P group.

(iv) Individual A's Year 4 contribution of a depreciable asset occurred after T was a member of the P group. Assuming that the amount of the net unrealized built-in loss exceeds the threshold requirement of section 382(h)(3)(B), the sale of asset 3 within the recognition period is subject to the SRLY limitation of paragraphs (a) and (b)(2)(ii) of this section.

Example 3. Overlap rule. (i) Individual A owns all of the stock of P, the common parent of a consolidated group. B, an individual unrelated to Individual A, owns all of the stock of T. T has two depreciable assets. Asset 1 has an unrealized loss of $55 (basis $75, value $20), and asset 2 has an unrealized gain of $30 (basis $30, value $60). On February 28 of Year 2, P purchases 55% of T from Individual B. On June 30, of Year 2, P purchases an additional 35% of T from Individual B.

(ii) The February 28 purchase of 55% of T is a section 382 event because it results in an ownership change of T that gives rise to a section 382(a) limitation. The June 30 purchase of 35% of T results in T becoming a member of the P group and is therefore a SRLY event.

(iii) Because the SRLY event occurred within six months of the change date of the section 382 event, there is an overlap of the application of the SRLY rules and the application of section 382, and paragraph (a) of this section does not apply. Therefore, the SRLY limitation does not apply to any of the $55 loss in asset 1 recognized by T after T joined the P group. See § 1.1502-94 for rules relating to the application of section 382 with respect to T's $25 unrealized built-in loss.

Example 4. Overlap rule-Fluctuation in value. (i) The facts are the same as in *Example 3*, except that by June 30, of Year 2, asset 1 had declined in value by a further $10. Thus asset 1 had an unrealized loss of $65 (basis $75, value $10), and asset 2 had an unrealized gain of $30 (basis $30, value $60).

(ii) Because paragraph (a) of this section does not apply, the further decrease in asset 1's value is disregarded. Consequently, the results are the same as in *Example 3*.

(h) *Effective date*—(1) *In general.* This section generally applies to built-in losses recognized in taxable years for which the due date (without extensions) of the consolidated return is after June 25, 1999. However—

(i) In the event that paragraphs (f)(1) and (g)(1) of this section do not apply to a particular built-in loss in the current group, then solely for purposes of applying paragraph (a) of this section to determine a limitation with respect to that built-in loss and with respect to which the SRLY register (consolidated taxable income determined by reference to only the member's (or subgroup's) items of income, gain, deduction or loss) began in a taxable year for which the due date of the return was on or before June 25, 1999, paragraph (c)(3) of this section shall not apply; and

(ii) For purposes of paragraph (g) of this section, only an ownership change to which section 382(a) as amended by the Tax Reform Act of 1986 applies shall constitute a section 382 event.

(2) *Prior periods.* For certain taxable years ending on or before June 25, 1999, see § 1.1502-15T in effect prior to June 25, 1999, as contained in 26 CFR part 1 revised April 1, 1999, as applicable. [Reg. § 1.1502-15.]

☐ [*T.D.* 8823, 6-25-99 (*corrected* 7-30-99).]

[Reg. § 1.1502-15A]

§ 1.1502-15A. Limitations on the allowance of built-in deductions for consolidated return years beginning before January 1, 1997.—(a) *Limitation on built-in deductions*—(1) *General rule.* Built-in deductions (as defined in subparagraph (2) of this paragraph) for a taxable year shall be subject to the limitation of § 1.1502-21A(c) (determined without regard to such deductions and without regard to net operating loss carryovers to such year) and the limitation of § 1.1502-22A(c) (determined without regard to such deductions and without regard to captial loss carryovers to such year). If as a result of applying such limitations, built-in deductions are not allowable in such consolidated return year, such deductions shall be treated as a net operating loss or net capital loss (as the case may be) sustained in such year and shall be carried to those taxable years (consolidated or separate) to which a consolidated net operating loss or a consolidated net capital loss could be carried under §§ 1.1502-21A, 1.1502-22A, and 1.1502-79A (or §§ 1.1502-21T and 1.1502-22T, as appropriate), except that such losses shall be treated as losses subject to the limitations contained in § 1.1502-21T(c) or § 1.1502-22T(c) (or §§ 1.1502-21A(c) or 1.1502-22A(c), as appropriate), as the case may be. Thus, for example, if member X sells a capital asset during a consolidated return year at a $1,000 loss and such loss is treated as a built-in deduction, then such loss shall be subject to the limitation contained in § 1.1502-22(c), which, in general, would allow such loss to be offset only against X's own net capital gain. Assuming X had no capital gain net income (net capital gain for taxable years beginning before January 1, 1977) reflected in such year (after taking into account its capital losses, other than capital loss carryovers and the built-in deduction), such $1,000 loss shall be treated as a net capital loss and shall be carried over for 5 years under § 1.1502-22, subject to the limitation contained in § 1.1502-22(c) for consolidated return years.

(2) *Built-in deductions.* (i) For purposes of this paragraph, the term "built-in deductions" for a consolidated return year means those deductions or losses of a corporation which are recognized in such year, or which are recognized in a separate return year and carried over in the form of a net operating or net capital loss to such year, but which are economically accrued in a separate return limitation year (as defined in § 1.1502-1(f)). Such term does not include deductions or losses incurred in rehabilitating such corporation. Thus, for example, assume P is the common parent of a group filing consolidated returns on the basis of a calendar year and that P purchases all of the stock of S on December 31, 1966. Assume further that on December 31, 1966, S owns a capital asset with an adjusted basis of $100 and a fair market value of $50. If the group files a consolidated return for 1967, and S sells the asset for $30, $50 of the $70 loss is treated as a built-in deduction, since it was economically accrued in a separate return limitation year. If S sells the asset for $80 instead of $30, the $20 loss is treated as a built-in deduction. On the other hand, if such asset is a depreciable asset and is not sold by S, depreciation deductions attributable to the $50 difference between basis and fair market value are treated as built-in deductions.

(ii) In determining, for purposes of subdivision (i) of this subparagraph, whether a deduction or loss with respect to any asset is economically accrued in a separate return limitation year, the term "predecessor" as used in § 1.1502-1(f)(1) shall include any transferor of such asset if the basis of the asset in the hands of the transferee is determined (in whole or in part) by reference to its basis in the hands of such transferor.

(3) *Transitional rule.* If the assets which produced the built-in deductions were acquired (either directly or by acquiring a new member) by the group on or before January 4, 1973, and the separate return limitation year in which such deductions were economically accrued ended before such date, then at the option of the taxpayer, the provisions of this paragraph before amendment by T.D. 7246 shall apply, and, in addition, if such assets were acquired on or before April 17, 1968, and the separate return limitation year in which the built-in deductions were economically accrued ended on or before such date, then at the option of the taxpayer, the provisions of § 1.1502-31A(b)(9) (as contained in the 26 C.F.R. edition revised as of April 1, 1996) shall apply in lieu of this paragraph.

(4) *Exceptions.* (i) Subparagraphs (1), (2), and (3) of this paragraph shall not limit built-in deductions in a taxable year with respect to assets acquired (either directly or by acquiring a new member) by the group if—

(a) The group acquired the assets more than 10 years before the first day of such taxable year, or

(b) Immediately before the group acquired the assets, the aggregate of the adjusted basis of all assets (other than cash, marketable securities, and goodwill) acquired from the transferor or owned by the new member did not exceed the fair market value of all such assets by more than 15 percent.

(ii) For purposes of subdivision (i)*(b)* of this subparagraph, a security is not a marketable security if immediately before the group acquired the assets—

(a) The fair market value of the security is less than 95 percent of its adjusted basis, or

(b) The transferor or new member had held the security for at least 24 months, or

(c) The security is stock in a corporation at least 50 percent of the fair market value of the outstanding stock of which is owned by the transferor or new member.

(b) *Effective date.* This section applies to any consolidated return years to which § 1.1502-21T does not apply. See § 1.1502-21T(g) for effective dates of that section. [Reg. § 1.1502-15A.]

☐ [*T.D. 6894, 9-7-66 and T.D. 6909, 12-29-66. Amended by T.D. 7246, 12-29-72 and T.D. 7728, 10-31-80. Redesignated as Reg. § 1.1502-15A and amended by T.D. 8677, 6-26-96.*]

Reg. § 1.1502-15A(a)(2)

→ **Caution: Reg. § 1.1502-15T, below, was removed by T.D. 8823 and is generally effective for certain tax years ending on or before June 25, 1999.** ←

[Reg. § 1.1502-15T]

§ 1.1502-15T. SRLY limitation on built-in losses (temporary).—(a) *SRLY limitation.* Built-in losses are subject to the SRLY limitation under §§ 1.1502-21T(c) and 1.1502-22T(c) (including applicable subgroup principles). Built-in losses are treated as deductions or losses in the year recognized, except for the purpose of determining the amount of, and the extent to which the built-in loss is limited by, the SRLY limitation for the year in which it is recognized. Solely for such purpose, a built-in loss is treated as a hypothetical net operating loss carryover or net capital loss carryover arising in a SRLY, instead of as a deduction or loss in the year recognized. To the extent that a built-in loss is allowed as a deduction under this section in the year it is recognized, it offsets any consolidated taxable income for the year before any loss carryovers or carrybacks are allowed as a deduction. To the extent not so allowed, it is treated as a separate net operating loss or net capital loss carryover or carryback arising in the year of recognition and, under § 1.1502-21T(c) or § 1.1502-22T(c), the year of recognition is treated as a SRLY.

(b) *Built-in losses*—(1) *Defined.* If a corporation has a net unrealized built-in loss under section 382(h)(3) (as modified by this section) on the day it becomes a member of the group (whether or not the group is a consolidated group), its deductions and losses are built-in losses under this section to the extent they are treated as recognized built-in losses under section 382(h)(2)(B) (as modified by this section). This paragraph (b) generally applies separately with respect to each member, but see paragraph (c) of this section for circumstances in which it is applied on a subgroup basis.

(2) *Operating rules.* Solely for purposes of applying paragraph (b)(1) of this section, the principles of § 1.1502-94T(c) apply with appropriate adjustments, including the following:

(i) *Ownership change.* A corporation is treated as having an ownership change under section 382(g) on the day the corporation becomes a member of a group, and no other events (e.g., a subsequent ownership change under section 382(g) while it is a member) are treated as causing an ownership change. In the case of an asset acquisition by a group, the assets and liabilities acquired directly from the same transferor pursuant to the same plan are treated as the assets and liabilities of a corporation that becomes a member of the group (and has an ownership change) on the date of the acquisition.

(ii) *Recognized built-in gain or loss.* A loss that is included in the determination of net unrealized built-in gain or loss and that is recognized but disallowed or deferred (e.g., under § 1.1502-20 or section 267) is not treated as a built-in loss unless and until the loss would be allowed during the recognition period without regard to the application of this section. Section 382(h)(1)(B)(ii) does not apply to the extent it limits the amount of recognized built-in loss that may be treated as a pre-change loss to the amount of the net unrealized built-in loss.

(c) *Built-in losses of subgroups*—(1) *In general.* In the case of a subgroup, the principles of paragraph (b) of this section apply to the subgroup, and not separately to its members. Thus, the net unrealized built-in loss and recognized built-in loss for purposes of paragraph (b) of this section are based on the aggregate amounts for each member of the subgroup.

(2) *Members of subgroups.* A subgroup is composed of those members that have been continuously affiliated with each other for the 60 consecutive month period ending immediately before they become members of the group in which the loss is recognized. A member remains a member of the subgroup until it ceases to be affiliated with the loss member. For this purpose, the principles of § 1.1502-21T(c)(2)(iv) through (vi) apply with appropriate adjustments.

(3) *Built-in amounts.* Solely for purposes of determining whether the subgroup has a net unrealized built-in loss or whether it has a recognized built-in loss, the principles of §§ 1.1502-91T(g) and (h) apply with appropriate adjustments.

(d) *Examples.* For purposes of the examples in this section, unless otherwise stated, all groups file consolidated returns, all corporations have calendar taxable years, the facts set forth the only corporate activity, value means fair market value and the adjusted basis of each asset equals its value, all transactions are with unrelated persons, and the application of any limitation or threshold under section 382 is disregarded. The principles of this section are illustrated by the following examples:

Example 1. Determination of recognized built-in loss. (a) P buys all the stock of T during Year 1 for $100, and T becomes a member of the P group. T has three depreciable assets. Asset 1 has an unrealized loss of $20 (basis $45, value $25), asset

Reg. § 1.1502-15T(d)

→ *Caution: Reg. § 1.1502-15T, below, was removed by T.D. 8823 and is generally effective for certain tax years ending on or before June 25, 1999.* ←

2 has an unrealized loss of $25 (basis $50, value $25), and asset 3 has an unrealized gain of $25 (basis $25, value $50).

(b) Under paragraph (b)(2)(i) of this section, T is treated as having an ownership change under section 382(g) on becoming a member of the P group. This treatment does not depend on whether P's acquisition of the T stock actually constitutes an ownership change under section 382(g), or whether T is subject to any limitation under section 382. Under paragraph (b)(1) of this section, none of T's $45 of unrealized loss is treated as a built-in loss unless T has a net unrealized built-in loss under section 382(h)(3) on becoming a member of the P group.

(c) Under section 382(h)(3)(A), T has a $20 net unrealized built-in loss on becoming a member of the P group (($20) + ($25) + $25 = ($20)). Assume that this amount exceeds the threshold requirement in section 382(h)(3)(B). Under section 382(h)(2)(B), the entire amount of T's $45 unrealized loss is treated as a built-in loss to the extent it is recognized during the 5-year recognition period described in section 382(h)(7). Under paragraph (b)(2)(ii) of this section, the restriction under section 382(h)(1)(B)(ii), which limits the amount of recognized built-in loss that is treated as pre-change loss to the amount of the net unrealized built-in loss, is inapplicable for this purpose. Consequently, the entire $45 of unrealized loss (not just the $20 net unrealized loss) is treated under paragraph (b)(1) of this section as a built-in loss to the extent it is recognized within 5 years of T's becoming a member of the P group. Under paragraph (a) of this section, a built-in loss is subject to the SRLY limitation under § 1.1502-21T(c)(1).

(d) Under paragraph (b)(2)(i) of this section, the results would be the same if T transferred all of its assets and liabilities to a subsidiary of the P group in a single transaction described in section 351.

Example 2. Actual application of section 382 not relevant. (a) The facts are the same as in *Example 1*, except that P buys 55 percent of the stock of T during Year 1, resulting in an ownership change of T under section 382(g). During Year 2, P buys the 45 percent balance of the T stock, and T becomes a member of the P group.

(b) Although T has an ownership change for purposes of section 382 in Year 1 and not Year 2, T's joining the P group in Year 2 is treated as an ownership change under section 382(g) for purposes of this section. Consequently, for purposes of this section, whether T has a net unrealized built-in loss under section 382(h)(3) is determined as if the day T joined the P group were a change date. Thus, the results are the same as in *Example 1*.

Example 3. Determination of a recognized built-in loss of a subgroup. (a) During Year 1, P buys all of the stock of S for $100, and S becomes a member of the P group. M is the common parent of another group. At the beginning of Year 7, M acquires all of the stock of P, and P and S become members of the M group. At the time of M's acquisition of the P stock, P has (disregarding the stock of S) a $10 net unrealized built-in gain (two depreciable assets, asset 1 with a basis of $35 and a value of $55, and asset 2 with a basis of $55 and a value of $45), and S has a $75 net unrealized built-in loss (two depreciable assets, asset 3 with a basis of $95 and a value of $10, and asset 4 with a basis of $10 and a value of $20).

(b) Under paragraph (c) of this section, P and S compose a subgroup on becoming members of the M group because P and S were continuously affiliated for the 60 month period ending immediately before they became members of the M group. Consequently, paragraph (b) of this section does not apply to P and S separately. Instead, their separately computed unrealized gains and losses are aggregated for purposes of determining whether and the extent to which any unrealized loss is treated as built-in loss under this section and is subject to the SRLY limitation under § 1.1502-21T(c).

(c) Under paragraph (c) of this section, the P subgroup has a net unrealized built-in loss on the day P and S become members of the M group determined by treating the day they become members as a change date. The net unrealized built-in loss is the aggregate of P's net unrealized built-in gain of $10 and S's net unrealized built-in loss of $75, or an aggregate net unrealized built-in loss of $65. (The stock of S owned by P is disregarded for purposes of determining the net unrealized built-in loss. However, any loss allowed on the sale of the stock within the recognition period is taken into account in determining recognized built-in loss.) Assume that the $65 net unrealized built-in loss exceeds the threshold requirement under section 382(h)(3)(B).

(d) Under paragraphs (b)(1), (b)(2)(ii), and (c) of this section, a loss recognized during the 5-year recognition period on an asset of P or S held on the day that P and S became members of the M group is a built-in loss except to the extent the group establishes that such loss exceeds the amount by which the adjusted basis of such asset on the day

Reg. § 1.1502-15T(d)

→ **Caution: Reg. § 1.1502-15T, below, was removed by T.D. 8823 and is generally effective for certain tax years ending on or before June 25, 1999.**←

the member became a member exceeded the fair market value of such asset on that same day. If P sells asset 2 for $45 in Year 7 and recognizes a $10 loss, the entire $10 loss is treated as a built-in loss under paragraphs (b)(2)(ii) and (c) of this section. If S sells asset 3 for $10 in Year 7 and recognizes an $85 loss, the entire $85 loss is treated as a built-in loss under paragraphs (b)(2)(ii) and (c) of this section (not just the $55 balance of the P subgroup's $65 net unrealized built-in loss).

(e) The determination of whether P and S constitute a SRLY subgroup for purposes of loss carryovers and carrybacks, and the extent to which built-in losses are not allowed under the SRLY limitation, is made under § 1.1502-21T(c).

Example 4. Computation of SRLY limitation. (a) During Year 1, individual A forms T by contributing $300 and T sustains a $100 net operating loss. During Year 2, T's assets decline in value to $100. At the beginning of Year 3, P buys all the stock of T for $100, and T becomes a member of the P group with a net unrealized built-in loss of $100. Assume that $100 exceeds the threshold requirements of section 382(h)(3)(B). During Year 3, T recognizes its unrealized built-in loss as a $100 ordinary loss. The members of the P group contribute the following net income to the consolidated taxable income of the P group (disregarding T's recognized built-in loss and any consolidated net operating loss deduction under § 1.1502-21T) for Years 3 and 4:

	Year 3	Year 4	Total
P group (without T)	$ 100	$ 100	$ 200
T	60	40	100
CTI	$ 160	$ 140	$ 300

(b) Under paragraph (b) of this section, T's $100 ordinary loss in Year 3 (not taken into account in the consolidated taxable income computations above) is a built-in loss. Under paragraph (a) of this section, the built-in loss is treated as a net operating loss carryover for purposes of determining the SRLY limitation under § 1.1502-21T(c).

(c) For Year 3, § 1.1502-21T(c) limits T's $100 built-in loss and $100 net operating loss carryover from Year 1 to the aggregate of the P group's consolidated taxable income through Year 3 determined by reference to only T's items. For this purpose, consolidated taxable income is determined without regard to any consolidated net operating loss deductions under § 1.1502-21T(a).

(d) The P group's consolidated taxable income through Year 3 is $60 when determined by reference to only T's items. Under § 1.1502-21T(c), the SRLY limitation for Year 3 is therefore $60.

(e) Under paragraph (a) of this section, the $100 built-in loss is treated as a current deduction for all purposes other than determination of the SRLY limitation under § 1.1502-21T(c). Consequently, a deduction for the built-in loss is allowed in Year 3 before T's loss carryover from Year 1 is allowed, but only to the extent of the $60 SRLY limitation. None of T's Year 1 loss carryover is allowed because the built-in loss ($100) exceeds the SRLY limitation for Year 3.

(f) The $40 balance of the built-in loss that is not allowed in Year 3 because of the SRLY limitation is treated as a $40 net operating loss arising in Year 3 that is carried to other years in accordance with the rules of § 1.1502-21T(b). The $40 net operating loss is treated under paragraph (a) of this section and § 1.1502-21T(c)(1)(ii) as a loss carryover or carryback from Year 3 that arises in a SRLY, and is subject to the rules of § 1.1502-21T (including § 1.1502-21T(c)) rather than this section.

(g) The facts are the same as in paragraphs (a) through (f) of this *Example 4*, except that T also recognizes additional built-in losses in Year 4. For purposes of determining the SRLY limitation for these additional losses in Year 4 (or any subsequent year), the $60 of built-in loss allowed as a deduction in Year 3 is treated under paragraph (a) of this section as a deduction in Year 3 that reduces the P group's consolidated taxable income when determined by reference to only T's items.

Example 5. Built-in loss exceeding consolidated taxable income in the year recognized. (a) P buys all the stock of T during Year 1, and T becomes a member of the P group. At the time of acquisition, T has a depreciable asset with an unrealized loss of $45 (basis $100, value $55), which exceeds the threshold requirements of section 382(h)(3)(B). During Year 2, T sells its asset for $55 and recognizes the unrealized built-in loss. The P group has $10 of consolidated taxable income in Year 2, computed by disregarding T's recognition of the $45 built-in loss and the consolidated net operating loss deduction, while the consolidated

Reg. § 1.1502-15T(d)

Consolidated Returns

See p. 20,601 for regulations not amended to reflect law changes

→ *Caution: Reg. § 1.1502-15T, below, was removed by T.D. 8823 and is generally effective for certain tax years ending on or before June 25, 1999.* ←

taxable income would be $25 if determined by reference to only T's items (other than the $45 loss).

(b) T's $45 loss is recognized in Year 2 and, under paragraph (b) of this section, constitutes a built-in loss. Under paragraph (a) of this section and § 1.1502-21T(c)(1)(ii), the loss is treated as a net operating loss carryover to Year 2 for purposes of applying the SRLY limitation under § 1.1502-21T(c).

(c) For Year 2, T's SRLY limitation is the aggregate of the P group's consolidated taxable income through Year 2 determined by reference to only T's items. For this purpose, consolidated taxable income is determined by disregarding any built-in loss that is treated as a net operating loss carryover, and any consolidated net operating loss deductions under § 1.1502-21T(a). Consolidated taxable income so determined is $25.

(d) Under § 1.1502-21T(c), $25 of the $45 built-in loss could be deducted in Year 2. Because the P group has only $10 of consolidated taxable income (determined without regard to the $45), the $25 loss creates a consolidated net operating loss of $15. This loss is carried back or over under the rules of § 1.1502-21T(b) and absorbed under the rules of § 1.1502-21T(a). This loss is not treated as arising in a SRLY (see § 1.1502-21T(c)(1)(ii)) and therefore is not subject to the SRLY limitation under § 1.1502-21T(c) in any consolidated return year of the group to which it is carried. The remaining $20 is treated as a loss carryover arising in a SRLY and is subject to the limitation of § 1.1502-21T(c) in the year to which it is carried.

(e) *Predecessors and successors.* For purposes of this section, any reference to a corporation or member includes, as the context may require, a reference to a successor or predecessor, as defined in § 1.1502-1(f)(4).

(f) *Effective date*—(1) *In general.* This section applies to built-in losses recognized in consolidated return years beginning on or after January 1, 1997.

(2) *Application to prior periods.* See § 1.1502-21T(g)(3) for rules generally permitting a group to apply the rules of this section to consolidated return years ending on or after January 29, 1991, and beginning before January 1, 1997. A group must treat all corporations that were affiliated on January 1, 1987, and continuously thereafter as having met the 60 consecutive month requirement of paragraph (c)(2) of this section on any day before January 1, 1992, on which the determination of net unrealized built-in gain or loss of a subgroup is made. [Temporary Reg. § 1.1502-15T.]

☐ [T.D. 8677, 6-26-96. Removed by T.D. 8823, 6-25-99.]

[Reg. § 1.1502-16]

§ 1.1502-16. **Mine exploration expenditures.**—(a) *Section 617*—(1) *In general.* If the aggregate amount of the expenditures to which section 617(a) applies, paid or incurred with respect to mines or deposits located outside the United States (as defined in section 638 and the regulations thereunder), does not exceed—

(i) $400,000 minus

(ii) all amounts deducted or deferred during the taxable year and all preceding taxable years under section 617 or section 615 of the Internal Revenue Code of 1954 and section 23(ff) of the Internal Revenue Code of 1939 by corporations which are members of the group during the taxable year (and individuals or corporations which have transferred any mineral property to any such member within the meaning of section 617(g)(2)(B)) for taxable years ending after December 31, 1950 and prior to the taxable year,

then the deduction under section 617 with respect to such foreign expenditures and paragraph (c) of § 1.1502-12 for each member shall be no greater than an allocable portion of such amount hereinafter referred to as the "consolidated foreign exploration limitation." Such allocable portion shall be determined under subparagraph (2) of this paragraph. If the amount of such expenditures exceeds the consolidated foreign exploration limitation, no deduction shall be allowed with respect to such excess.

(2) *Allocable portion of limitation.* A member's allocable portion of the consolidated foreign exploration limitation for a consolidated return year shall be—

(i) The amount allocated by the common parent pursuant to an allocation plan adopted by the consolidated group, but in no event shall a member be allocated more than the amount it could have deducted had it filed a separate return. Such allocation plan must include a statement which also contains the total foreign exploration expenditures of each member which could have been deducted under section 617 if the member had filed a separate return. Such plan must be attached to a consolidated return filed on or before the due date of such return (including extensions of time), and may not be changed after such date, or

Reg. § 1.1502-16(a)(1)

(ii) If no plan is filed in accordance with subdivision (i) of this subparagraph, then the portion of the consolidated foreign exploration limitation allocable to each member incurring such expenditures is an amount equal to such limitation multiplied by a fraction, the numerator of which is the amount of foreign exploration expenditures which could have been deducted under section 617 by such member had it filed a separate return and the denominator of which is the aggregate of such amounts for all members of the group.

(b) *Section 615*—(1) *In general.* If the aggregate amount of the expenditures, to which section 615(a) applies, which are paid or incurred by the members of the group during any consolidated return year exceeds the lesser of—

(i) $100,000, or

(ii) $400,000 minus all such expenditures deducted (or deferred) by corporations which are members of the group during the taxable year (and individuals or corporations which have transferred any mineral property to any such member within the meaning of section 615(c)(2)(B)) for taxable years ending after December 31, 1950, and prior to the taxable year,

then the deduction (or amount deferrable) under section 615 and paragraph (c) of § 1.1502-12 for each member shall be no greater than an allocable portion of such lesser amount, hereinafter referred to as the "consolidated exploration limitation". Such allocable portion shall be determined under subparagraph (2) of this paragraph.

(2) *Allocable portion of limitation.* A member's allocable portion of the consolidated exploration limitation for a consolidated return year shall be—

(i) The amount allocated by the common parent pursuant to an allocation plan adopted by the consolidated group, but in no event shall a member be allocated more than the amount it could have deducted (or deferred) had it filed a separate return. Such allocation plan must include a statement which also contains the total exploration expenditures of each member for the taxable year, and the expenditures of each member which could have been deducted (or deferred) under section 615 if the member had filed a separate return. Such plan must be attached to a consolidated return filed on or before the due date of such return (including extensions of time), and may not be changed after such date, or

(ii) If no plan is filed in accordance with subdivision (i) of this subparagraph, then the portion of the consolidated exploration limitation allocable to each member incurring such expenditures is an amount equal to such limitation multiplied by a fraction, the numerator of which is the amount which could have been deducted (or deferred) under section 615 by such member had it filed a separate return and the denominator of which is the aggregate of such amounts for all members of the group.

(c) *Examples.* The provisions of this section may be illustrated by the following examples:

Example (1). Corporation X and its wholly-owned subsidiaries, corporations Y and Z, file a consolidated return for the calendar year 1971. None of the corporations have incurred exploration expenditures described in section 617 in previous years. During 1971, X incurred foreign exploration expenditures of $30,000, Y of $20,000 and Z of $40,000. The amount of foreign exploration expenditures deductible under section 617 for purposes of computing separate taxable income under § 1.1502-12 will be the amount actually expended by each corporation.

Example (2). Assume the same facts as in example (1) except that prior to 1971, X, Y, and Z had deducted (or deferred) under section 615 and 617 a total of $300,000 of exploration expenditures. During 1971, with respect to deposits located outside the United States X incurred exploration expenditures of $25,000, Y of $75,000 and Z of $125,000. The consolidated exploration limitation under paragraph (a) of this section with respect to the foreign deposits (there is no limitation with respect to the domestic expenditures) is $100,000. X may allocate the $100,000 in any manner among the three members, except that X may not be allocated more than $25,000 nor Y more than $75,000, the amount actually expended by X and Y and which they could have deducted had they each filed a separate return. If the allocation is not made in accordance with paragraph (a)(2)(i) of this section, the $100,000 limitation will be allocated under paragraph (a)(2)(ii) of this section as follows:

Corporation	Expenditure	Fraction	Limitation	Allocable portion
X	$25,000	$\dfrac{25,000}{200,000}$ × $100,000 =	$12,500
Y	$75,000	$\dfrac{75,000}{200,000}$ × $100,000 =	$37,500
Z	$125,000	$\dfrac{100,000}{200,000}$ × $100,000 =	$50,000

Reg. § 1.1502-16(c)

The denominator of $200,000 was calculated as follows:

X = $ 25,000
Y = $ 75,000
Z = $100,000 (maximum amount allowed if filed separately)
Total $200,000

Example (3). Assume the same facts as in example (2) and that on January 1, 1971, X acquired all of the stock of corporation T which prior to its taxable year beginning January 1, 1971, had previously deducted (or deferred) $310,000 of exploration expenditures. Assume further that in 1971 X incurred $25,000 of foreign exploration expenditures, Y $50,000, T $50,000 and Z none. A consolidated return is filed for 1971. None of the expenditures may be deducted under section 617 since the consolidated exploration limitation is zero. The limitation is zero since the aggregate amount of previously deducted (or deferred) exploration expenditures by the members of the group exceeds $400,000. (The total of such expenditures is $410,000, of which $310,000 is attributable to T and, assuming the allocation of the limitation in example (2) is made under paragraph (a)(2)(ii) of this section, $12,500 is attributable to X, $37,500 to Y, and $50,000 to Z.)

Example (4). Assume the same facts as in example (3) except that on December 31, 1971, X sold all of the stock in Z to an unrelated party. The consolidated exploration limitation for 1972 will be $40,000, computed by subtracting from $400,000 the aggregate amount of previously deducted (or deferred) exploration expenditures incurred by the members of the group prior to 1972. (The total of such expenditures is $360,000, of which $12,500 is attributable to X, $37,500 to Y and $310,000 to T.) Amounts previously deducted (or deferred) by Z are not taken into account since it was not a member of the group at any time during 1972. Amounts previously deducted (or deferred) by Z shall be taken into account by it for subsequent separate return years. [Reg. § 1.1502-16.]

☐ [T.D. 6894, 9-7-66. Amended by T.D. 7192, 6-29-72.]

[Reg. § 1.1502-17]

§ 1.1502-17. Methods of accounting.—(a) *General rule.* The method of accounting to be used by each member of the group shall be determined in accordance with the provisions of section 446 as if such member filed a separate return. For treatment of depreciable property after a transfer within the group, see paragraph (g) of § 1.1502-12.

(b) *Adjustments required if method of accounting changes*—(1) *General rule.* If a member of a group changes its method of accounting for a consolidated return year, the terms and conditions prescribed by the Commissioner under section 446(e), including section 481(a) where applicable, shall apply to the member. If the requirements of section 481(b) are met because applicable adjustments under section 481(a) are substantial, the increase in tax for any prior year shall be computed upon the basis of a consolidated return or a separate return, whichever was filed for such prior year.

(2) *Changes in method of accounting for intercompany transactions.* If a member changes its method of accounting for intercompany transactions for a consolidated return year, the change in method generally will be effected on a cut-off basis.

(c) *Anti-avoidance rules*—(1) *General rule.* If one member (B) directly or indirectly acquires an activity of another member (S), or undertakes S's activity, with the principal purpose to avail the group of an accounting method that would be unavailable (or would be unavailable without securing consent from the Commissioner) if S and B were treated as divisions of a single corporation, B must use the accounting method for the acquired or undertaken activity determined under paragraph (c)(2) of this section or must secure consent from the Commissioner under applicable administrative procedures to use a different method.

(2) *Treatment as divisions of a single corporation.* B must use the method of accounting that would be required if B acquired the activity from S in a transaction to which section 381 applied. Thus, the principles of section 381(c)(4) and (c)(5) apply to resolve any conflicts between the accounting methods of S and B, and the acquired or undertaken activity is treated as having the accounting method used by S. Appropriate adjustments are made to treat all acquisitions or undertakings that are part of the same plan or arrangement as a single acquisition or undertaking.

(d) *Examples.* The provisions of this section are illustrated by the following examples:

Example 1. Separate return treatment generally. X and its wholly owned subsidiary Y filed separate returns for their calendar years ending December 31, 1965. During calendar year 1965, X employed an accrual method of accounting, established a reserve for bad debts, and elected under section 171 to amortize bond premiums with respect to its fully taxable bonds. During calendar year 1965, Y employed the cash receipts and disbursements method, used the specific charge-off method with respect to its bad debts, and did not elect to amortize bond premiums under section 171 with respect to its bonds. X and Y filed a consolidated return for 1966. For 1966 X and Y must continue to compute income under their respective methods of accounting (unless a change in method under section 446 is made).

Example 2. Adopting methods. Corporation P is a member of a consolidated group. P provides consulting services to customers under various agreements. For one type of customer, P's agreements require payment only when the contract is completed (payment-on-completion contracts). P uses an overall accrual method of accounting. Accordingly, P takes its income from consulting contracts into account when earned, received, or due, whichever is earlier. With the principal purpose to avoid seeking the consent of the Commissioner to change its method of accounting for the payment-on-completion contracts to the cash method, P forms corporation S, and S begins to render services to those customers subject to the payment-on-completion contracts. P continues to render services to those customers not subject to these contracts.

(b) Under paragraph (c) of this section, S must account for the consulting income under the payment-on-completion contracts on an accrual method rather than adopting the cash method contemplated by P.

Example 3. Changing inventory sub-method. (a) Corporation P is a member of a consolidated group. P operates a manufacturing business that uses dollar-value LIFO, and has built up a substantial LIFO reserve. P has historically manufactured all its inventory and has used one natural business unit pool. P begins purchasing goods identical to its own finished goods from a foreign supplier, and is concerned that it must establish a separate resale pool under § 1.472-8(c). P anticipates that it will begin to purchase, rather than manufacture, a substantial portion of its inventory, resulting in a recapture of most of its LIFO reserve because of decrements in its manufacturing pool. With the principal purpose to avoid the decrements, P forms corporation S in Year 1. S operates as a distributor to nonmembers, and P sells all of its existing inventories to S. S adopts LIFO, and elects dollar-value LIFO with one resale pool. Thereafter, P continues to manufacture and purchase inventory, and to sell it to S for resale to nonmembers. P's intercompany gain from sales to S is taken into account under § 1.1502-13. S maintains its Year 1 base dollar value of inventory so that P will not be required to take its intercompany items (which include the effects of the LIFO reserve recapture) into account.

(b) Under paragraph (c) of this section, S must maintain two pools (manufacturing and resale) to the same extent that P would be required to maintain those pools under § 1.472-8 if it had not formed S.

(e) *Effective dates.* Paragraph (b) of this section applies to changes in method of accounting effective for years beginning on or after July 12, 1995. For changes in method of accounting effective for years beginning before that date, see § 1.1502-17 (as contained in the 26 CFR part 1 edition revised as of April 1, 1995). Paragraphs (c) and (d) apply with respect to acquisitions occurring or activities undertaken in years beginning on or after July 12, 1995. [Reg. § 1.1502-17.]

☐ [T.D. 6894, 9-7-66. *Amended by T.D.* 8597, 7-12-95.]

[Reg. § 1.1502-18]

§ 1.1502-18. **Inventory adjustments.**—(a) *Definition of intercompany profit amount.* For purposes of this section, the term "intercompany profit amount" for a taxable year means an amount equal to the profits of a corporation (other than those profits which such corporation has elected not to defer pursuant to § 1.1502-13(c)(3) or which have been taken into account pursuant to § 1.1502-13(f)(1)(viii)) arising in transactions with other members of the group with respect to goods which are, at the close of such corporation's taxable year, included in the inventories of any member of the group. See § 1.1502-13(c)(2) with respect to the determination of profits. See the last sentence of § 1.1502-13(f)(1)(i) for rules for determining which goods are considered to be disposed of outside the group and therefore not included in inventories of members.

(b) *Addition of initial inventory amount to taxable income.* If a corporation—

(1) Is a member of a group filing a consolidated return for the taxable year,

(2) Was a member of such group for its immediately preceding taxable year, and

(3) Filed a separate return for such preceding year,

then the intercompany profit amount of such corporation for such separate return year (hereinafter referred to as the "initial inventory amount") shall be added to the income of such corporation for the consolidated return year (or years) in which the goods to which the initial inventory amount is attributable are disposed of outside the group or such corporation becomes a nonmember. Such amount shall be treated as gain from the sale

Reg. § 1.1502-18(b)(3)

or exchange of property which is neither a capital asset nor property described in section 1231.

(c) *Recovery of initial inventory amount* —(1) *Unrecovered inventory amount.* The term "unrecovered inventory amount" for any consolidated return year means the lesser of—

(i) The intercompany profit amount for such year, or

(ii) The initial inventory amount.

However, if a corporation ceases to be a member of the group during a consolidated return year, its unrecovered inventory amount for such year shall be considered to be zero.

(2) *Recovery during consolidated return years.* (i) To the extent that the unrecovered inventory amount of a corporation for a consolidated return year is less than such amount for its immediately preceding year, such decrease shall be treated for such year by such corporation as a loss from the sale or exchange of property which is neither a capital asset nor property described in section 1231.

(ii) To the extent that the unrecovered inventory amount for a consolidated return year exceeds such amount for the preceding year, such increase shall be treated as gain from the sale or exchange of property which is neither a capital asset nor property described in section 1231.

(3) *Recovery during first separate return year.* For the first separate return year of a member following a consolidated return year, the unrecovered inventory amount for such consolidated return year (minus any part of the initial inventory amount which has not been added to income pursuant to paragraph (b) of this section) shall be treated as a loss from the sale or exchange of property which is neither a capital asset nor property described in section 1231.

(4) *Acquisition of group.* For purposes of this section, a member of a group shall not become a nonmember or be considered as filing a separate return solely because of a termination of the group (hereinafter referred to as the "terminating group") resulting from—

(i) The acquisition by a nonmember corporation of (a) the assets of the common parent in a reorganization described in subparagraph (A), (C), or (D) (but only if the requirements of subparagraphs (A) and (B) of section 354(b)(1) are met) of section 368(a)(1), or (b) stock of the common parent, or

(ii) The acquisition (in a transaction to which § 1.1502-75(d)(3) applies) by a member of (a) the assets of a nonmember corporation in a reorganization referred to in subdivision (i) of this subparagraph, or (b) stock of a nonmember corporation,

if all the members of the terminating group (other than such common parent if its assets are acquired) immediately before the acquisition are members immediately after the acquisition of another group (hereinafter referred to as the "succeeding group") which files a consolidated return for the first taxable year ending after the date of acquisition. The members of the succeeding group shall succeed to any initial inventory amount and to any unrecovered inventory amount of members of the terminating group. This subparagraph shall not apply with respect to acquisitions occurring before August 25, 1971.

(d) *Examples.* The provisions of paragraphs (a), (b), and (c) of this section may be illustrated by the following examples:

Example (1). Corporations P, S, and T report income on the basis of a calendar year. Such corporations file separate returns for 1965. P manufactures widgets which it sells to both S and T, who act as distributors. The inventories of S and T at the close of 1965 are comprised of widgets which they purchased from P and with respect to which P derived profits of $5,000 and $8,000, respectively. P, S, and T file a consolidated return for 1966. During 1966, P sells widgets to S and T with respect to which it derives profits of $7,000 and $10,000, respectively. The inventories of S and T as of December 31, 1966, are comprised of widgets on which P derived net profits of $4,000 and $8,000, respectively. P's initial inventory amount is $13,000, P's intercompany profit amount for 1965 (such $13,000 amount is the profits of P with respect to goods sold to S and T and included in their inventories at the close of 1965). Assuming that S and T identify their goods on a first-in, first-out basis, the entire opening inventory amount of $13,000 is added to P's income for 1966 as gain from the sale or exchange of property which is neither a capital asset nor property described in section 1231, since the goods to which the initial inventory amount is attributable were disposed of in 1966 outside the group. However, since P's unrecovered inventory amount for 1966, $12,000 (the intercompany profit amount for the year, which is less than the initial inventory amount), is less than the unrecovered inventory amount for 1965, $13,000, this decrease of $1,000 is treated by P for 1966 as a loss from the sale or exchange of property which is neither a capital asset nor property described in section 1231.

Example (2). Assume the same facts as in example (1) and that at the close of 1967, a consolidated return year, the inventories of S and T are comprised of widgets on which P derived profits of $5,000 and $3,000, respectively. Since P's unrecovered inventory amount for 1967, $8,000, is less than $12,000, the unrecovered inventory amount for 1966, this decrease of $4,000 is treated by P for 1967 as a loss from the sale or exchange of property which is neither a capital asset nor property described in section 1231.

Example (3). Assume the same facts as in examples (1) and (2) and that in 1968, a consolidated return year, P's intercompany profit amount is $11,000. P will report $3,000 (the excess of $11,000, P's unrecovered inventory amount for 1968, over $8,000, P's unrecovered inventory amount for 1967) for 1968 as a gain from the sale or exchange of property which is neither a capital asset nor property described in section 1231.

Example (4). Assume the same facts as in examples (1), (2), and (3) and that in 1969 P, S, and T file separate returns. P will report $11,000 (its unrecovered inventory amount for 1968, $11,000, minus the portion of the initial inventory amount which has not been added to income during 1966, 1967, and 1968, zero) as a loss from the sale or exchange of property which is neither a capital asset nor property described in section 1231.

Example (5). Corporations P and S file a consolidated return for the first time for the calendar year 1966. P manufactures machines and sells them to S, which sells them to users throughout the country. At the close of 1965, S has on hand 20 machines which it purchased from P and with respect to which P derived profits of $3,500. During 1966, P sells 6 machines to S on which it derives profits of $1,300, and S sells 5 machines which it had on hand at the beginning of the year (S specifically identifies the machines which it sells) and on which P had derived profits of $900. P's initial inventory amount is $3,500, of which $900 is added to P's income in 1966 as gain from the sale or exchange of property which is neither a capital asset nor property described in section 1231, since such $900 amount is attributable to goods disposed of in 1966 outside the group, which goods were included in S's inventory at the close of 1965. If P and S continue to file consolidated returns, the remaining $2,600 of the initial inventory amount will be added to P's income as the machines on which such profits were derived are disposed of outside the group.

Example (6). Assume that in example (5) S had elected to inventory its goods under section 472 (relating to last-in, first-out inventories). None of P's initial inventory amount of $3,500 would be added to P's income in 1966, since none of the goods to which such amount is attributable would be considered to be disposed of during such year under the last-in, first-out method of identifying inventories.

(e) *Section 381 transfer.* If a member of the group is a transferor or distributor of assets to another member of the group within the meaning of section 381(a), then the acquiring corporation shall be treated as succeeding to the initial inventory amount of the transferor or distributor corporation to the extent that as of the date of distribution or transfer such amount has not yet been added to income. Such amount shall then be added to the acquiring corporation's income under the provisions of paragraph (b) of this section. For purposes of applying paragraph (c) of this section—

(1) The initial inventory amount of the transferor or distributor corporation shall be added to such amount of the acquiring corporation as of the close of the acquiring corporation's taxable year in which the date of distribution or transfer occurs, and

(2) The unrecovered inventory amount of the transferor or distributor corporation for its taxable year preceding the taxable year of the group in which the date of distribution or transfer occurs shall be added to such amount of the acquiring corporation.

(f) *Transitional rules for years before 1966*—(1) *In general.* If—

(i) A group filed a consolidated return for the taxable year immediately preceding the first taxable year to which this section applies,

(ii) Any member of such group made an opening adjustment to its inventory pursuant to paragraph (b) of § 1.1502-39A (as contained in the 26 C.F.R. edition revised as of April 1, 1996), and

(iii) Paragraph (c) of § 1.1502-39A (as contained in the 26 C.F.R. edition revised as of April 1, 1996) has not been applicable for any taxable year subsequent to the taxable year for which such adjustment was made,

then subparagraphs (2) and (3) of this paragraph shall apply.

(2) *Closing adjustment to inventory.* (i) For the first consolidated return year to which this section applies, the increase in inventory prescribed in paragraph (c) of § 1.1502-39A (as contained in the 26 C.F.R. edition revised as of April

Reg. § 1.1502-18(f)(2)

1, 1996) shall be made as if such year were a separate return year.

(ii) For the first separate return year of a member to which this section applies, the adjustment to inventory (whether an increase or a decrease) prescribed in paragraph (c) of § 1.1502-39A (as contained in the 26 C.F.R. edition revised as of April 1, 1996), minus any adjustment already made pursuant to subdivision (i) of this subparagraph, shall be made to the inventory of such member.

(3) *Addition and recovery of initial inventory amount.* Each selling member shall treat as an initial inventory amount its share of the net amount by which the inventories of all members are increased pursuant to subparagraph (2)(i) of this paragraph for the first taxable year to which this section applies. A member's share shall be such net amount multiplied by a fraction, the numerator of which is its initial inventory amount (computed under paragraph (b) as if such taxable year were its first consolidated return year), and the denominator of which is the sum of such initial inventory amounts of all members. Such initial inventory amount shall be added to the income of such selling member and shall be recovered at the time and in the manner prescribed in paragraphs (b) and (c) of this section.

(4) *Example.* The provisions of this paragraph may be illustrated by the following example:

Example. (i) Corporations P, S, and T file consolidated returns for calendar 1966, having filed consolidated returns continuously since 1962. P is a wholesale distributor of groceries selling to chains of supermarkets, including those owned by S and T. The opening inventories of S and T for 1962 were reduced by $40,000 and $80,000, respectively, pursuant to paragraph (b) of § 1.1502-39A (as contained in the 26 C.F.R. edition revised as of April 1, 1996). At the close of 1965, S and T have on hand in their inventories goods on which P derived profits of $80,000 and $90,000, respectively. The inventories of S and T at the close of 1966 include goods which they purchased from P during the year on which P derived profits of $85,000 and $105,000, respectively.

(ii) The opening inventories of S and T for 1966, the first year to which this section applies, are increased by $40,000 and $80,000, respectively, pursuant to the provisions of subparagraph (2)(i) of this paragraph. P will take into account (as provided in paragraphs (b) and (c) of this section) an initial inventory amount of $120,000 as of the beginning of 1966, the net amount by which the inventories of S and T were increased in such year. Since the increases in the inventories of S and T are the maximum allowable under paragraph (c) of § 1.1502-39A (as contained in the 26 C.F.R. edition revised as of April 1, 1996) (*i.e.,* the amount by which such inventories were originally decreased), no further adjustments will be made pursuant to subparagraph (2)(ii) of this paragraph to such inventories in the event that separate returns are subsequently filed.

(5) *Election not to eliminate.* If a group filed a consolidated return for the taxable year immediately preceding the first taxable year to which this section applies, and for such preceding year the members of the group did not eliminate gain or loss on intercompany inventory transactions pursuant to the adoption under § 1.1502-31A(b)(1) (as contained in the 26 C.F.R. edition revised as of April 1, 1996) of a consistent accounting practice taking into account such gain or loss, then for purposes of this section each member shall be treated as if it had filed a separate return for such immediately preceding year.

(g) *Transitional rules for years beginning on or after July 12, 1995.* Paragraphs (a) through (f) of this section do not apply for taxable years beginning on or after July 12, 1995. Any remaining unrecovered inventory amount of a member under paragraph (c) of this section is recovered in the first taxable year beginning on or after July 12, 1995, under the principles of paragraph (c)(3) of this section by treating the first taxable year as the first separate return year of the member. The unrecovered inventory amount can be recovered only to the extent it was previously included in taxable income. The principles of this section apply, with appropriate adjustments, to comparable amounts under paragraph (f) of this section. [Reg. § 1.1502-18.]

☐ [T.D. 6894, 9-7-66. Amended by T.D. 7246, 12-29-72; T.D. 8597, 7-12-95 and T.D. 8677, 6-26-96.]

→ Caution: Reg. § 1.1502-19, below, prior to amendment by T.D. 8560, is effective before January 1, 1995. ←

[Reg. § 1.1502-19]

§ 1.1502-19. Excess losses.—(a) *Recognition of income*—(1) *In general.* Immediately before the disposition (as defined in paragraph (b) of this section) of stock of a subsidiary, there shall be included in the income of each member disposing of such stock that member's excess loss account

Reg. § 1.1502-19(a)(1)

Consolidated Returns 56,773

See p. 20,601 for regulations not amended to reflect law changes

→ **Caution: Reg. § 1.1502-19, below, prior to amendment by T.D. 8560, is effective before January 1, 1995.**←

(determined under §§ 1.1502-14 and 1.1502-32) with respect to the stock disposed of.

(2) *Character of income.* (i) *In general.* Except to the extent otherwise provided in this subparagraph, the amount included in income under subparagraph (1) of this paragraph shall be treated as gain from the sale of stock (that is, capital gain or ordinary income, as the case may be).

(ii) *Insolvency.* If, at the time of the disposition of stock of a subsidiary, the subsidiary is insolvent, then the amount included in income under subparagraph (1) of this paragraph, minus all amounts which increased the excess loss account under § 1.1502-14(a)(2) for any consolidated return year, shall be treated as ordinary income to the extent of such insolvency. For purposes of the preceding sentence, a subsidiary is insolvent to the extent that the sum of—

(a) All its liabilities,

(b) All its liabilities which were discharged during consolidated return years to the extent such discharge would have resulted in "cancellation of indebtedness income" but for the insolvency of such subsidiary, and

(c) The amount to which all stock of such subsidiary, which is limited and preferred as to dividends is entitled in liquidation, exceeds the fair market value of such subsidiary's assets. This subdivision shall not apply to the extent that the taxpayer establishes to the satisfaction of the Commissioner that the ordinary income portion of the excess loss account is attributable to losses of the subsidiary which reduced long-term capital gains of the group (without regard to section 1201).

(3) *Cancellation or redemption.* If stock of a subsidiary is considered to be disposed of under paragraph (b)(1)(ii) of this section other than in complete liquidation of such subsidiary, any amount which would otherwise be included in the income of the disposing member under subparagraph (1) of this paragraph shall be deferred and taken into account at the time provided in § 1.1502-14(b)(3).

(4) *Prior law.* To the extent the excess loss account is attributable to an adjustment under § 1.1502-32(f)(1) which was not subsequently reduced under § 1.1502-32(e)(2) or (3), it shall be taken into account in the same manner as it would have been taken into account under regulations effective for taxable years beginning before January 1, 1966. For example, assume that P is the common parent of a group which filed a consolidated return for 1965. During such taxable year a member of the group, corporation S, sustained a loss of $100, all of which was availed of in the consolidated return for 1965. P organized S on January 1, 1965, with a contribution to capital of $80 and a $10 loan. The group files a consolidated return for 1966. Under § 1.1502-32(f)(1), P's basis for the stock in S as of January 1, 1966 is reduced to zero, and P has an excess loss account with respect to such stock of $20. No part of the reduction for losses availed of is applied to reduce the basis of the $10 obligation. During 1966, S has earnings and profits of $5, and under § 1.1502-32(e)(2) P's excess loss account for its stock of S is reduced to $15. On December 31, 1966, P sells the stock of S for $5. P realizes a $5 gain on such sale. In addition, the excess loss account of $15 is applied to reduce the basis of S's obligation to zero, and the balance is otherwise taken into account in the same manner and to the same extent as it would have been taken into account under the regulations applicable to 1965. If, on December 31, 1966, P had sold S's obligation instead of its stock, the excess loss account would be applied to reduce the basis of the obligation to zero, and P would then have an excess loss account of $5 with respect to the stock of S.

(5) *Foreign expropriation losses.* If there is a disposition of stock of a subsidiary, subparagraph (1) of this paragraph shall not apply to the excess loss account with respect to such stock to the extent such excess loss account is attributable to a foreign expropriation loss occurring in a taxable year beginning before January 1, 1966, which is absorbed as part of a consolidated net capital or net operating loss carryover in a taxable year ending before January 1, 1971, and the regulations applicable to taxable years beginning before January 1, 1966, shall apply to such disposition.

(6) *Election to reduce basis of other investment.*—(i) *In general.* If there is a disposition (as defined in paragraph (b) of this section) after August 25, 1971, of stock of a subsidiary, all or any part of the excess loss account with respect to such stock may be applied to reduce the basis of any other stock or obligations of the subsidiary (whether or not evidenced by a security) held by the disposing member immediately before the disposition. Only the excess loss account which remains after such application shall be included in income under this paragraph. If subparagraph (4) of this paragraph applies to part of the excess loss account, such part must be applied to reduce the basis of stock or obligations under this subparagraph before the other part may be so applied.

Reg. § 1.1502-19(a)(6)

→ *Caution: Reg. § 1.1502-19, below, prior to amendment by T.D. 8560, is effective before January 1, 1995.* ←

(ii) *Limitation.* The basis of stock may not be reduced pursuant to an election under § 1.1502-19(a)(6)(i) to the extent the reduction has the effect of netting gain or loss in a manner that would not be permitted under § 1.1502-20(a)(4) and 1.1502-20(b)(4).

(b) *Disposition*—(1) *Disposition of particular share.* Except as otherwise provided in paragraphs (d) and (e) of this section, a member shall be considered for purposes of this section as having disposed of a share of stock in a subsidiary—

(i) On the day such share is transferred to any person, or

(ii) On the day such member receives a distribution in cancellation or redemption of such stock (as defined in § 1.1502-14(b)(1)).

(2) *Disposition of all shares.* Except as otherwise provided in paragraphs (d) and (e) of this section, a member shall be considered for purposes of this section as having disposed of all of its shares of stock in a subsidiary—

(i) On the day such subsidiary ceases to be a member,

(ii) On the day such member ceases to be a member,

(iii) On the last day of each taxable year of such subsidiary in which any of its stock is wholly worthless (within the meaning of section 165(g)), or in which an indebtedness of the subsidiary is discharged if such discharge would have resulted in "cancellation of indebtedness income" but for the insolvency of the subsidiary,

(iv) On the last day of each taxable year of the subsidiary for which the Commissioner is satisfied that 10 percent or less of the face amount of any obligation for which the subsidiary is personally liable (primarily or secondarily) is recoverable at maturity by its creditors,

(v) On the day on which a member transfers an obligation for which the subsidiary is personally liable (primarily or secondarily) to any nonmember for an amount which is 25 percent or less of the face amount of such obligation, or

(vi) On the last day of the taxable year preceding the first taxable year for which the group does not file a consolidated return.

(c) *Effect of chain of ownership*—(1) *Multiple dispositions.* If the stock of more than one subsidiary is disposed of in the same transaction, paragraph (a) of this section shall be applied in the order of the tiers, from the lowest to the highest.

(2) *Examples.* The provisions of this paragraph may be illustrated by the following examples:

Example (1). (a) Assume that corporations P, S, T, and U first file a consolidated return for the taxable year beginning January 1, 1966. On that date, P owns all the stock of S with an adjusted basis of $15, S owns all the stock of T with an adjusted basis of $5, and T owns all the stock of U with an adjusted basis of $10. For the year 1966, the group has consolidated taxable income but U has a deficit in earnings and profits of $20. Under § 1.1502-32(b)(2), T reduces its basis with respect to the stock of U to zero and has an excess loss account of $10, S reduces its basis in T's stock to zero and has an excess loss account of $15, and P decreases its basis in S's stock to zero and has an excess loss account of $5.

(b) In 1967 the stock of U becomes worthless. T is considered as having disposed of such stock under paragraph (b) of this section and realizes income of $10. If the group has elected to adjust earnings and profits currently, T will have earnings and profits of $10 resulting from the disposition of the stock of U (see § 1.1502-33(c)(4)(ii)(*b*)); if the group has not so elected, T will have a deficit in earnings and profits of $10 resulting from the disposition (see § 1.1502-33(c)(4)(i)(*b*)). However, for purposes of the adjustment under § 1.1502-32(b) to the basis of stock owned by higher-tier members, T's earnings and profits on the disposition are $10 regardless of whether the group adjusts earnings and profits currently (see § 1.1502-32(d)(1)(i)). S's excess loss account with respect to T's stock will be reduced to $5 (see § 1.1502-32(b)(1)(i)). P's excess loss account with respect to S's stock will be reduced to zero and its basis for S's stock will be increased to $5 (see § 1.1502-32(b)(1)(i) or (iii)).

Example (2). Assume the same facts as in example (1) except that the stock of T, rather than the stock of U, becomes worthless and thereFDfore S is considered as having disposed of its stock in T under paragraph (b) of this section and T is considered as having disposed of its stock in U. Since U is the lowest tier subsidiary, this section is applied first with respect to the excess loss account relating to the stock of U with the same result as in example (1). This section is then also applied with respect to the stock of T. Thus, in addition to the result in example (1), S will realize income of $5, and P's basis for S's stock will be increased by $5 to $10.

Example (3). Corporation P is the common parent of an affiliated group which filed a consoli-

Reg. § 1.1502-19(b)(1)

Consolidated Returns

See p. 20,601 for regulations not amended to reflect law changes

→ *Caution: Reg. § 1.1502-19, below, prior to amendment by T.D. 8560, is effective before January 1, 1995.* ←

dated return for 1966. Corporations S1 and S2 are wholly owned subsidiaries of P organized on January 1, 1966. Corporation T was also organized on January 1, 1966, its stock being owned 75 percent by S2 and 25 percent by S1. P originally invested $300 in ths stock of S1 and $200 in the stock of S2; S1 and S2 originally invested $50 and $150, respectively, in the stock of T. For the year 1966, there were the following undistributed earnings and profits or deficits, computed without regard to § 1.1502-33(c)(4):

S1	$ 50
S2	0
T	(400)

There were no consolidated net losses. Under § 1.1502-32(e) the basis and excess loss accounts would be as follows:

	S1 in T	S2 in T	P in S1	P in S2
Original basis	$50	$150	$300	$200
Deficit of T	(100)	(300)	(100)	(300)
Undistributed earnings and profits of S1	....	....	50	....
Basis or (excess loss account)	($50)	($150)	$250	($100)

Assume that the group does not file a consolidated return for 1967. As of December 31, 1966, the following adjustments would be made:

	S1 in T	S2 in T	P in S1	P in S2
Basis or (excess loss account)	($50)	($150)	$250	($100)
Income to S1	50	....	....	....
Adjustment under § 1.1502-32(b)(1)	...	....	50	....
Income to S2	...	150	....	....
Adjustment under § 1.1502-32(b)(1)	...	....	....	150
Basis of stock	0	0	$300	$50

(d) *Transfers of stock of subsidiary within the group.*—(1) *In general.* A transfer of stock of a subsidiary from one member to another member in a consolidated return year shall not be treated as a disposition for purposes of paragraph (b) of this section if the basis of such stock in the hands of the transferee is determined by reference to the basis of such stock in the hands of the transferor. In such case, the transferee member shall succeed to the transferor member's excess loss account with respect to the transferred stock. See example (5) of paragraph (f) of this section.

(2) *Contributions to capital.* If the transferor in a transfer described in subparagraph (1) of this paragraph owns or receives stock in the transferee, the transferor's excess loss account for the transferred stock shall also be immediately applied to reduce the basis, if any, of the stock which the transferor owns or receives in the transferee. The excess, if any, over such basis shall be the transferor's excess loss account with respect to the stock owned or received. See example (5) of paragraph (f) of this section.

(e) *Nontaxable liquidations and reorganizations to which the subsidiary is a party.* If, in a consolidated return year, a member is the transferor or distributor corporation and another member is the acquiring corporation in a transaction to which section 381(a) applies, members owning stock in the transferor or distributor corporation shall not, by reason of such transaction (or by reason of an exchange under section 354 pursuant to such transaction), be considered for purposes of paragraph (b) of this section as having disposed of such stock. If the transaction is a distribution in liquidation to which section 334(b)(1) applies, the excess loss account in the stock of the distributor corporation shall be eliminated. If the transaction involves an exchange to which section 354 applies, the excess loss account in the stock of the transferor corporation surrendered in exchange shall be applied to reduce the basis (or to increase the excess loss account) of the stock received in the exchange or previously owned. If, immediately before a transfer described in section 381(a), the transferor corporation owned stock of the acquiring corporation, the excess loss account in such stock shall be eliminated. For example, assume that corporation P owns all of the stock of corporation S with an excess loss account of $20, and that S owns all the stock of T with an excess loss account of $30. If S is merged into corporation U (another member) in a transaction described in section 368(a)(1)(A), P will apply the $20 excess

Reg. § 1.1502-19(e)

Consolidated Returns

See p. 20,601 for regulations not amended to reflect law changes

→ **Caution:** *Reg. § 1.1502-19, below, prior to amendment by T.D. 8560, is effective before January 1, 1995.*←

loss account against and reduce the basis (or increase the excess loss account) of any stock of U which P owns or receives pursuant to the merger. However, if S is merged into T, the $30 excess loss account in the T stock is eliminated (and is not included in income), and the $20 excess loss account in the S stock becomes a $20 excess loss account in the T stock in the hands of P.

(f) *Examples.* This section may be illustrated by the following examples:

Example (1). Corporation P is the common parent of an affiliated group which files consolidated returns for 1966 through 1970. Included in the group for all such years are corporations S1 and S2 which are wholly owned by P, corporation T which is owned 40 percent by P, and 60 percent by S2, and corporation U which is wholly owned by T. S1, S2, T, and U were each organized on January 1, 1966, with the following investments being made in their stock.

P in S1	$50
P in S2	150
P in T	40
S2 in T	60
T in U	50

During the period 1966-1970, S1, S2, T, and U made no distributions and had the following earnings and profits or deficits computed without regard to § 1.1502-33(c)(4):

S1	($70)
S2	60
T	(120)
U	(80)

There were no consolidated net losses in 1966-1970. Under § 1.1502-32(e) the basis and excess loss accounts for the stock of S1, S2, T, and U would be as follows:

	T in U	P in T	S2 in T	P in S2	P in S1
Original basis	$50	$40	$60	$150	$50
Undistributed earnings and profits or (deficits)					
of U	(80)	(32)	(48)	(48)	...
of T	...	(48)	(72)	(72)	...
of S2	...	...	...	60	...
of S1	...	...	...	...	(70)
Basis or (excess loss account)	($30)	($40)	($60)	$90	($20)

On January 1, 1971, P sells its stock to S1 to an unrelated person for $10. The group files a consolidated return for 1971. P must include in its income for 1971 the $20 in its excess loss account for S1 and the $10 gain from the sale of the stock of S1.

Example (2). Assume the same facts as in example (1) except that P does not sell its stock in S1, but on January 1, 1971, P sells its stock in S2 to an unrelated person for $170. Since S2, T, and U have ceased to be members of the group, the following adjustments must be made:

	T in U	P in T	S2 in T	P in S2
Basis or (excess loss account)	($30)	($40)	($60)	$90
T's excess loss account in U (see paragraph (c) of this section)	30	12	18	18
		($28)	($42)	$108
S2's excess loss account in T (see paragraph (c) of this section)	...	...	42	42
				$150
P's excess loss account in T	...	28	...	...
Basis or (excess loss account)	0	0	0	$150

For the year 1971, P, S2, and T would include in their incomes $28, $42, and $30, respectively. In addition, P would have a gain of $20 from the sale of the stock of S2, zero bases for its stock in T and S1, and a $20 excess account for its stock in S1.

Example (3). Assume the same facts as in example (2), except that a consolidated return is not filed for 1971. As of December 31, 1970, P, S2, and T would include in their incomes $28, $42, and $30, respectively (see example (2)), and P would have a $150 basis for its stock in S2 and zero bases for its stock in T and S1. In addition, P would include in its income $20 with respect to its excess loss account in S1. In 1971, P would have a gain of $20 from the sale of its stock in S2.

Example (4). Assume the same facts as in example (1), except that P does not sell its stock in S1, but on January 1, 1971, T redeems for $30

Reg. § 1.1502-19(f)

Consolidated Returns

See p. 20,601 for regulations not amended to reflect law changes

→ *Caution: Reg. § 1.1502-19, below, prior to amendment by T.D. 8560, is effective before January 1, 1995.*←

cash, in a transaction qualifying under section 346, one half of its stock held by P. P has income in 1971 of $20, but such income is deferred; P's excess loss account for its remaining stock in T is reduced to $20. In addition, P recognizes a gain of $30 on the redemption of the stock of T, which gain is deferred.

Example (5). Assume the same facts as in example (1), except that instead of selling its stock in S1 to an unrelated person, P transfers its stock in S1 to T in exchange for stock in T in a transaction to which section 351 applies. P's excess loss account of $20 for the stock in S1 which was transferred to T increases P's excess loss account for its stock in T from $40 to $60. In addition, T has a zero basis and an excess loss account of $20 for the stock it acquired in S1.

Example (6). Assume the same facts as in example (1), except that P does not sell its stock in S1, but on January 1, 1971, S2 is liquidated into P in a liquidation to which section 334(b)(1) applies. No income is realized by S2 by reason of its distribution to P of its stock in T. S2's excess loss account of $60 for its stock in T is added to, and is merged with, P's excess loss account for its stock in T. Thus, P has an excess loss account of $100 for all its stock in T.

Example (7). Assume the same facts as in example (6), except that S1, rather than S2, is liquidated into P in a liquidation which section 334(b)(1) applies. P's excess loss account for its stock in S1 is eliminated.

(g) *Acquisition of group*—(1) *In general.* Paragraph (b) of this section shall not apply solely because of a termination of the group (hereinafter referred to as the "terminating group") resulting from—

(i) The acquisition by a nonmember corporation of (a) the assets of the common parent in a reorganization described in subparagraph (A), (C), or (D) (but only if the requirements of subparagraphs (A) and (B) of section 354(b)(1) are met) of section 368(a)(1), or (b) stock of the common parent, or

(ii) The acquisition, in a transaction to which § 1.1502-75(d)(3) applies, by a member of (a) the assets of a nonmember corporation in a reorganization referred to in subdivision (i) of this subparagraph, or (b) stock of a nonmember corporation,

if all the members of the terminating group (other than such common parent if its assets are acquired) immediately before the acquisition are members immediately after the acquisition of another group (hereinafter referred to as the "succeeding group") which files a consolidated return for the first taxable year ending after the date of acquisition. The members of the succeeding group shall succeed to any excess loss accounts with respect to stock of members of the terminating group as of the date of acquisition. This paragraph shall not apply with respect to acquisitions occurring before August 25, 1971.

(2) *Adjustments*—(i) *In general.* If any stock of a member of the succeeding group is disposed of under this section, a higher tier limitation member (as defined in subdivision (ii) of this subparagraph) owning stock in the disposing member shall, in making the adjustment under § 1.1502-32(b) with respect to stock of such disposing member, take into account the increase in earnings and profits attributable to inclusion of the excess loss account in the income of such member only to the extent that the amount of such excess loss account exceeds the amount of any excess loss account with respect to the stock disposed of at the time of the acquisition. If there are intervening members between the member disposing of stock under this section and a higher tier limitation member, and if a member owning stock in the disposing member is not a higher tier limitation member, then solely for the purpose of the adjustment under § 1.1502-32(b) by the higher tier limitation member with respect to stock of a subsidiary, the adjustments under § 1.1502-32(b) for such intervening members shall be computed as if members owning stock in the disposing member were higher tier limitation members.

(ii) *Limitation member.* A higher tier member of the succeeding group is a "higher tier limitation member" unless such member (a) was a member immediately before the acquisition of the same group as the member with respect to the stock of which the excess loss account existed, or (b) acquired the assets of the common parent of such group in a reorganization described in subparagraph (1) of this paragraph.

(3) *Examples.* The provisions of this paragraph may be illustrated by the following examples:

Example (1). (a) Assume there are two affiliated groups, one comprising P, S, and T, and the other comprising X and Y, both of which file consolidated returns for the calendar year 1971. P owns all the stock of S with an adjusted basis of $100, and S owns all the stock of T with an adjusted basis of zero and an excess loss account of $30. X owns all the stock of Y with an adjusted

Reg. § 1.1502-19(g)(3)

→ **Caution: Reg. § 1.1502-19, below, prior to amendment by T.D. 8560, is effective before January 1, 1995.**←

basis of $200. On January 1, 1972, Y acquires all the assets of P in exchange for 20 percent of the stock of X in a reorganization to which section 368(a)(1)(C) applies. As a result of the acquisition of the assets of P by Y, the P-S-T group terminates. X, Y, S, and T file a consolidated return for the first taxable year ending after the date of the acquisition.

(b) Paragraph (b) of this section does not apply, merely because of the termination of the P group, to include in S's income its excess loss account with respect to the stock of T.

(c) If T has a deficit in earnings and profits of $10 for 1972, S would increase its excess loss account with respect to the stock of T to $40, Y would decrease the basis of its S stock (which is a carryover of P's basis) to $90, and X would decrease the basis of its Y stock to $190.

(d) Assume that the stock of T becomes worthless in 1973. S would include $40 in income. For purposes of the adjustments under § 1.1502-32(b), S would have earnings and profits of $40 resulting from the disposition of the stock of T (amount realized, $40, minus the adjusted basis of zero determined by taking into account the adjustments under § 1.1502-32(e)). If S had no other earnings and profits for the year, Y (which is not a higher tier limitation member) would adjust its basis for the stock of S under § 1.1502-32(b)(1)(i) by the full amount of S's earnings and profits, thus increasing the basis of the S stock to $130. The adjustment by Y with respect to the stock of S would ordinarily be reflected under § 1.1502-32(b)(1)(i) or (iii) in the adjustment by X with respect to the stock of Y. However, X is a higher tier limitation member, and, solely for the purpose of determining the adjustment by X with respect to the stock of Y, the adjustment by Y with respect to the stock of S must be recomputed by including only $10 (i.e., the amount by which S's excess loss account in the stock of T, $40, exceeds the excess loss account with respect to such stock at the time of the acquisition, $30) in the adjustment under § 1.1502-32(b)(1)(i). Thus, if there were no other adjustments under § 1.1502-32(b) with respect to the stock of S and Y, X would make a positive adjustment under § 1.1502-32(b)(1)(i) or (iii) and (e)(2) of $10 with respect to the stock of Y, increasing the basis of such stock to $200. The basis of stock of S held by Y is not affected by the recomputation.

Example (2). Assume the same facts as in example (1) except that the shareholders of P receive more than 50 percent of the stock of X so that the transaction is a reverse acquisition under § 1.1502-75(d)(3) with the X-Y group terminating and the P-S-T group surviving. The adjustments and limitations apply as in example (1).

Example (3). Assume the same facts as in example (1) except that subsequent to the acquisition T has earnings and profits of $100 in 1972 (thus eliminating the excess loss account with respect to the stock of T and increasing the basis of such stock to $70) and a deficit in earnings and profits of $110 in 1973, thereby decreasing the basis with respect to such stock to zero and creating an excess loss account of $40 which is included in S's income in 1973. The adjustments and limitations apply as in example (1).

→ **Caution: Reg. § 1.1502-19, below, as amended by T.D. 8560, is effective on January 1, 1995.**←

§ 1.1502-19. **Excess loss accounts.**—(a) *In general*—(1) *Purpose.* This section provides rules for a member (P) to include in income its excess loss account in the stock of another member (S). The purpose of the excess loss account is to recapture in consolidated taxable income P's negative adjustments with respect to S's stock (e.g., under § 1.1502-32 from S's deductions, losses, and distributions), to the extent the negative adjustments exceed P's basis in the stock.

(2) *Excess loss accounts*—(i) *In general.* P's basis in S's stock is adjusted under the consolidated return regulations and other rules of law. Negative adjustments may exceed P's basis in S's stock. The resulting negative amount is P's excess loss account in S's stock. For example:

(A) Once P's negative adjustments under § 1.1502-32 exceed its basis in S's stock, the excess is P's excess loss account in the S stock. If P has further adjustments, they first increase or decrease the excess loss account.

(B) If P forms S by transferring property subject to liabilities in excess of basis, § 1.1502-80(d) provides for the nonapplicability of section 357(c) and the resulting negative basis under section 358 is P's excess loss account in the S stock.

(ii) *Treatment as negative basis.* P's excess loss account is treated for all Federal income tax purposes as basis that is a negative amount, and a

Reg. § 1.1502-19(a)(1)

Consolidated Returns

→ **Caution:** Reg. § 1.1502-19, below, as amended by T.D. 8560, is effective on January 1, 1995. ←

reference to P's basis in S's stock includes a reference to P's excess loss account.

(3) *Application of other rules of law.* The rules of this section are in addition to other rules of law. See, e.g., §§ 1.1502-32 (investment adjustment rules establishisng and adjusting excess loss accounts) and 1.1502-80(d) (nonapplicability of section 357(c)). The provisions of this section and other rules of law must not be applied to recapture the same amount more than once. For purposes of this section, the definitions in § 1.1502-32 apply.

(b) *Excess loss account taken into account as income or gain*—(1) *General rule.* If P is treated under this section as disposing of a share of S's stock, P takes into account its excess loss account in the share as income or gain from the disposition. Except as provided in paragraph (b)(4) of this section, the disposition is treated as a sale or exchange for purposes of determining the character of the income or gain.

(2) *Nonrecognition or deferral*—(i) *In general.* P's income or gain under paragraph (b)(1) of this section is subject to any nonrecognition or deferral rules applicable to the disposition. For example, if S liquidates and the exchange of P's stock in S is subject to section 332, or P transfers all of its assets (including S's stock) to S in a reorganization to which section 361(a) applies, P's income or gain from the excess loss account is not recognized under these rules.

(ii) *Nonrecognition or deferral inapplicable.* If P's income or gain under paragraph (b)(1) of this section is from a disposition described in paragraph (c)(1)(ii) or (iii) of this section (relating to deconsolidations and worthlessness), the income or gain is taken into account notwithstanding any nonrecognition or deferral rules (even if the disposition is also described in paragraph (c)(1)(i) of this section). For example, if P transfers S's stock to a nonmember in a transaction to which section 351 applies, P's income or gain from the excess loss account is taken into account.

(3) *Tiering up in chains.* If the stock of more than one subsidiary is disposed of in the same transaction, the income or gain under this section is taken into account in the order of the tiers, from the lowest to the highest.

(4) *Insolvency*—(i) *In general.* Gain under this section is treated as ordinary income to the extent of the amount by which S is insolvent (within the meaning of section 108(d)(3)) immediately before the disposition. For this purpose S's liabilities include any amount to which preferred stock would be entitled if S were liquidated immediately before the disposition, and any former liabilities that were discharged to the extent the discharge was treated as tax-exempt income under § 1.1502-32(b)(3)(ii)(C) (special rule for discharges).

(ii) *Reduction for amount of distributions.* The amount treated as ordinary income under this paragraph (b)(4) is reduced to the extent it exceeds the amount of P's excess loss account redetermined without taking into account S's distributions to P to which § 1.1502-32(b)(2)(iv) applies.

(c) *Disposition of stock.* For purposes of this section:

(1) *In general.* P is treated as disposing of a share of S's stock.

(i) *Transfer, cancellation, etc.* At the time—

(A) P transfers or otherwise ceases to own the share for Federal income tax purposes, even if no gain or loss is taken into account; or

(B) P takes into account gain or loss (in whole or in part) with respect to the share.

(ii) *Deconsolidation.* At the time—

(A) P becomes a nonmember, or a nonmember determines its basis in the share (or any other asset) by reference to P's basis in the share, directly or indirectly, in whole or in part (e.g., under section 362); or

(B) S becomes a nonmember, or P's basis in the share is reflected, directly or indirectly, in whole or in part, in the basis of any asset other than member stock (e.g., under section 1071).

(iii) *Worthlessness.* At the time—

(A) Substantially all of S's assets are treated as disposed of, abandoned, or destroyed for Federal income tax purposes (e.g., under section 165(a) or § 1.1502-80(c), or, if S's asset is stock of a lower-tier member, the stock is treated as disposed of under this paragraph (c)). An asset of S is not considered to be disposed of or abandoned to the extent the disposition is in complete liquidation of S or is in exchange for consideration (other than relief from indebtedness);

(B) An indebtedness of S is discharged, if any part of the amount discharged is not included in gross income and is not treated as tax-exempt income under § 1.1502-32(b)(3)(ii)(C); or

(C) A member takes into account a deduction or loss for the uncollectibility of an indebtedness of S, and the deduction or loss is not matched in the same tax year by S's taking into account a corresponding amount of income or gain

Reg. § 1.1502-19(c)(1)

→ *Caution: Reg. § 1.1502-19, below, as amended by T.D. 8560, is effective on January 1, 1995.*←

from the indebtedness in determining consolidated taxable income.

(2) *Becoming a nonmember.* A member is treated as becoming a nonmember if it has a separate return year (including another group's consolidated return year). For example, S may become a nonmember if it issues additional stock to nonmembers, but S does not become a nonmember as a result of its complete liquidation. A disposition under paragraph (c)(1)(ii) of this section must be taken into account in the consolidated return of the group. For example, if a group ceases under § 1.1502-75(c) to file a consolidated return as of the close of its consolidated return year, the disposition under paragraph (c)(1)(ii) of this section is treated as occurring immediately before the close of the year. If S becomes a nonmember because P sells S's stock to a nonmember, P's sale is a disposition under both paragraphs (c)(1)(i) and (ii) of this section. If a group terminates under § 1.1502-75(d) because the common parent is the only remaining member, the common parent is not treated as having a deconsolidation event under paragraph (c)(1)(ii) of this section.

(3) *Exception for acquisition of group*—(i) *Application.* This paragraph (c)(3) applies only if a consolidated group (the terminating group) ceases to exist as a result of—

(A) The acquisition by a member of another consolidated group of either the assets of the common parent of the terminating group in a reorganization described in section 381(a)(2), or the stock of the common parent of the terminating group; or

(B) The application of the principles of § 1.1502-75(d)(2) or (d)(3).

(ii) *General rule.* Paragraph (c)(1)(ii) of this section does not apply solely by reason of the termination of a group in a transaction to which this paragraph (c)(3) applies, if there is a surviving group that is, immediately thereafter, a consolidated group. Instead, the surviving group is treated as the terminating group for purposes of applying this section to the terminating group. This treatment does not apply, however, to members of the terminating group that are not members of the surviving group immediately after the terminating group ceases to exist (e.g., under section 1504(a)(3) relating to reconsolidation, or section 1504(c) relating to includible insurance companies).

(d) *Special allocation of basis adjustments or determinations.* If a member has an excess loss account in shares of a class of S's stock at the time of a basis adjustment or determination under the Internal Revenue Code with respect to other shares of the same class of S's stock owned by the member, the adjustment or determination is allocated first to equalize and eliminate that member's excess loss account. For example, if P owns 50 shares of S's only class of stock with a $100 basis and 50 shares with a $100 excess loss account, and P contributes $200 to S without receiving additional shares, the contribution first eliminates P's excess loss account, then increases P's basis in each share by $1. (If P transfers the $200 in exchange for an additional 100 shares of S's stock in a transaction to which section 351 applies, P's excess loss account is first eliminated, and P's basis in the additional shares is $100.) See § 1.1502-32(c) for similar allocations of investment adjustments to prevent or eliminate excess loss accounts.

(e) *Anti-avoidance rule.* If any person acts with a principal purpose contrary to the purposes of this section, to avoid the effect of the rules of this section or apply the rules of this section to avoid the effect of any other provision of the consolidated return regulations, adjustments must be made as necessary to carry out the purposes of this section.

(f) *Predecessors and successors.* For purposes of this section, any reference to a corporation (or to a share of the corporation's stock) includes a reference to a successor or predecessor (or to a share of stock of a predecessor or successor), as the context may require.

(g) *Examples.* For purposes of the examples in this section, unless otherwise stated, P owns all 100 shares of the only class of S's stock and S owns all 100 shares of the only class of T's stock, the stock is owned for the entire year, T owns no stock of lower-tier members, the tax year of all persons is the calendar year, all persons use the accrual method of accounting, the facts set forth the only corporate activity, all transactions are between unrelated persons, and tax liabilities are disregarded. The principles of this section are illustrated by the following examples.

Example 1. Taxable disposition of stock. (a) *Facts.* P has a $150 basis in S's stock, and S has a $100 basis in T's stock. For Year 1, P has $500 of ordinary income, S has no income or loss, and T has a $200 ordinary loss. S sells T's stock to a nonmember for $60 at the close of Year 1.

(b) *Analysis.* Under paragraph (c) of this section, the sale is a disposition of T's stock at the

Reg. § 1.1502-19(c)(2)

→ *Caution: Reg. § 1.1502-19, below, as amended by T.D. 8560, is effective on January 1, 1995.*←

close of Year 1 (the day of the sale). Under § 1.1502-32(b), T's loss results in S having a $100 excess loss account in T's stock immediately before the sale. Under paragraph (b)(1) of this section, S takes into account the $100 excess loss account as an additional $100 of gain from the sale. Consequently, S takes into account a $160 gain from the sale in determining the group's consolidated taxable income. Under § 1.1502-32(b), T's $200 loss and S's $160 gain result in a net $40 decrease in P's basis in S's stock as of the close of Year 1, from $150 to $110.

(c) *Intercompany sale followed by sale to nonmember.* The facts are the same as in paragraph (a) of this *Example 1*, except that S sells T's stock to P for $60 at the close of Year 1, and P sells T's stock to a nonmember at a gain at the beginning of Year 5. Under paragraph (c) of this section, S's sale is treated as a disposition of T's stock at the close of Year 1 (the day of the sale). Under § 1.1502-13 and paragraph (b)(2) of this section, S's $160 gain from the sale is deferred and taken into account in Year 5 as a result of P's sale of the T stock. Under § 1.1502-32(b), the absorption of T's $200 loss in Year 1 results in P having a $50 excess loss account in S's stock at the close of Year 1. In Year 5, S's $160 gain taken into account eliminates P's excess loss account in S's stock and increases P's basis in the stock to $110.

(d) *Intercompany distribution followed by sale to a nonmember.* The facts are the same as in paragraph (a) of this *Example 1*, except that the value of the T stock is $60 and S declares and distributes a dividend of all of the T stock to P at the close of Year 1, and P sells the T stock to a nonmember at a gain at the beginning of Year 5. Under paragraph (c) of this section, S's distribution is treated as a disposition of T's stock at the close of Year 1 (the day of the distribution). S's $100 excess loss account in T's stock is treated as additional gain under section 311(b) from the distribution. Under section 301(d), P's basis in the T stock is $60. Under § 1.1502-13, and paragraph (b)(2) of this section, S's $160 gain from the distribution is deferred and taken into account in Year 5 as a result of P's sale of the T stock. Under § 1.1502-32(b), T's $200 loss and S's $60 distribution result in P having a $110 excess loss account in S's stock at the close of Year 1. In Year 5, S's $160 gain taken into account eliminates P's excess loss account in S's stock and increases P's basis in the stock to $50.

Example 2. Basis determinations under the Internal Revenue Code in intercompany reorganizations. (a) *Facts.* P owns all of the stock of S and T.

P has a $150 basis in S's stock and a $100 excess loss account in T's stock. P transfers T's stock to S without receiving additional S stock, in a transaction to which section 351 applies.

(b) *Analysis.* Under paragraph (c) of this section, P's transfer is treated as a disposition of T's stock. Under section 351 and paragraph (b)(2) of this section, P does not recognize gain from the disposition. Under section 358 and paragraph (a)(2)(ii) of this section, P's $100 excess loss account in T's stock decreases P's $150 basis in S's stock to $50. In addition, S takes a $100 excess loss account in T's stock under section 362. (If P had received additional S stock, paragraph (d) of this section would not apply to shift basis from P's original S stock because the basis of the original stock is not adjusted or determined as a result of the contribution; but paragraph (d) would apply to shift basis if P had transferred S's stock to T in exchange for additional T stock, because the basis of the additional T stock would be determined when P has an excess loss account in its original T stock.)

(c) *Intercompany merger.* The facts are the same as in paragraph (a) of this *Example 2*, except that T merges into S in a reorganization described in section 368(a)(1)(A) (and in section 368(a)(1)(D)), and P receives no additional S stock in the reorganization. Under section 354 and paragraph (b)(2) of this section, P does not recognize gain. Under section 358 and paragraph (a)(2)(ii) of this section, P's $100 excess loss account in T's stock decreases P's $150 basis in the S stock to $50. (Similarly, if S merges into T and P does not receive additional T stock, P's $150 basis in S's stock eliminates P's excess loss account in T's stock, and increases P's basis in T's stock to $50.)

(d) *Liquidation of only subsidiary.* Assume instead that P and S are the only members of the P group, P has a $100 excess loss account in S's stock, and S liquidates in a transaction to which section 332 applies. Under paragraph (c)(2) of this section, the liquidation is not a deconsolidation event under paragraph (c)(1)(ii) of this section merely because P is the only remaining member. Under section 332 and paragraph (b)(2) of this section, P does not recognize gain. Under section 334(b), P succeeds to S's basis in the assets it receives from S in the liquidation. (P would also not recognize gain if P transferred all of its assets (including S's stock) to S in a reorganization to which section 361(a) applied, because S would be a successor to P under paragraph (f) of this section.)

Reg. § 1.1502-19(g)

→ *Caution: Reg. § 1.1502-19, below, as amended by T.D. 8560, is effective on January 1, 1995.*←

Example 3. Section 355 distribution of stock with an excess loss account. (a) *Facts.* P has a $30 excess loss account in S's stock, and S has a $90 excess loss account in T's stock. S distributes the T stock to P in a transaction to which section 355 applies, and neither P nor S recognizes any gain or loss. At the time of the distribution, the T stock represents 33% of the value of the S stock. Following the distribution, P's basis in the S stock is allocated under § 1.358-2 in proportion to the fair market values of the S stock and the T stock.

(b) *Analysis.* Under paragraph (c) of this section, S's distribution of the T stock is treated as a disposition. Under section 355(c) and paragraph (b)(2) of this section, S does not recognize any gain from the distribution. Under section 358, S's excess loss account in the T stock is eliminated, and P's $30 excess loss account in the S stock is treated as basis allocated between the S stock and the T stock based on their relative values. Consequently, P has a $20 excess loss account in the S stock and a $10 excess loss account in the T stock. (If P had a $30 basis rather than a $30 excess loss account in the S stock, S would not recognize gain, its excess loss account in the T stock would be eliminated, and P's basis in the stock of S and T would be $20 and $10, respectively.)

(c) *Section 355 distribution to nonmember.* The facts are the same as in paragraph (a) of this *Example 3*, except that P also distributes the T stock to its shareholders in a transaction to which section 355 applies. Under paragraph (c) of this section, P's distribution is treated as a disposition of T's stock. Under paragraph (b)(2) of this section, because P's disposition is described in paragraph (c)(1)(ii) of this section, P's $10 excess loss account in the T stock must be taken into account at the time of the distribution, notwithstanding the nonrecognition rules of section 355(c).

Example 4. Deconsolidation of a member. (a) *Facts.* P has a $50 excess loss account in S's stock, and S has a $100 excess loss account in T's stock. T issues additional stock to a nonmember and, as a consequence, T becomes a nonmember.

(b) *Analysis.* Under paragraph (c)(2) of this section, S is treated as disposing of each of its shares of T's stock immediately before T becomes a nonmember. Under paragraph (b)(1) of this section, S takes into account its $100 excess loss account as gain from the sale or exchange of T's stock. Under § 1.1502-32(b) of this section, S's $100 gain eliminates P's excess loss account in S's stock and increases P's basis in S's stock to $50.

(c) *Deconsolidation of a higher-tier member.* The facts are the same as in paragraph (a) of this *Example 4*, except that S (rather than T) issues the stock and, as a consequence, both S and T become nonmembers. Under paragraph (c)(2) of this section, P is treated as disposing of S's stock and S is treated as disposing of T's stock immediately before S and T become nonmembers. Under § 1.1502-32(b) and paragraph (b)(3) of this section, because S and T become nonmembers in the same transaction and T is the lower-tier member, S is first treated under paragraph (b)(1) of this section as taking into account its $100 excess loss account as gain from the sale or exchange of T's stock. Under § 1.1502-32(b), S's $100 gain eliminates P's excess loss account in S's stock and increases P's basis in S's stock to $50 immediately before S becomes a nonmember. Thus, only S's $100 gain is taken into account in the determination of the group's consolidated taxable income.

(d) *Intercompany gain and deconsolidation.* The facts are the same as in paragraph (c) of this *Example 4*, except that T has $30 of gain that is deferred under § 1.1502-13 and taken into account in determining consolidated taxable income immediately before T becomes a nonmember. Under § 1.1502-32(b), T's $30 gain decreases S's excess loss account in T's stock from $100 to $70 immediately before S is treated as disposing of T's stock. Under paragraph (b)(1) of this section, S is treated as taking into account its $70 excess loss account as gain from the disposition of T's stock. Under § 1.1502-32(b), S's $70 gain from the excess loss account and T's $30 deferred gain that is taken into account eliminate P's $50 excess loss account in S's stock and increase P's basis in S's stock to $50 immediately before S becomes a nonmember.

Example 5. Worthlessness. (a) *Facts.* P forms S with a $150 contribution, and S borrows $150. For Year 1, S has a $50 ordinary loss that is carried over as part of the group's consolidated net operating loss. For Year 2, P has $160 of ordinary income, and S has a $160 ordinary loss. Under § 1.1502-32(b), S's loss results in P having a $10 excess loss account in S's stock. During Year 3, the value of S's assets (without taking S's liabilities into account) continues to decline and S's stock becomes worthless within the meaning of section 165(g) (without taking into account § 1.1502-80(c)). For Year 4, S has $10 of ordinary income.

(b) *Analysis.* Under paragraph (c)(1)(iii)(A) of this section, P is not treated as disposing of S's stock in Year 3 solely because S's stock becomes

Reg. § 1.1502-19(g)

→ *Caution: Reg. § 1.1502-19, below, as amended by T.D. 8560, is effective on January 1, 1995.*←

worthless within the meaning of section 165(g) (taking S's liabilities into account). In addition, because S's stock is not treated as worthless, section 382(g)(4)(D) does not prevent the Year 1 consolidated net operating loss carryover from offsetting S's $10 of income in Year 4.

(c) *Discharge of indebtedness.* The facts are the same as in paragraph (a) of this *Example 5*, except that, instead of S's stock becoming worthless within the meaning of section 165(g), S's creditor discharges $40 of S's indebtedness during Year 3, S is insolvent by more than $40 before the discharge, the discharge is excluded from the P group's gross income under section 108(a), and $40 of the $50 consolidated net operating loss carryover attributable to S is eliminated under section 108(b). Under § 1.1502-32(b)(3)(ii)(C), S's $40 of discharge income is treated as tax-exempt income because there is a corresponding decrease under § 1.1502-32(b)(3)(iii) for elimination of the loss carryover. Under paragraph (c)(1)(iii)(B) of this section, P is treated as disposing of S's stock if the amount discharged is not included in gross income and is not treated as tax-exempt income under § 1.1502-32(b)(3)(ii)(C). Because the discharge is treated as tax-exempt income, P is not treated as disposing of S's stock by reason of the discharge.

Example 6. Avoiding worthlessness. (a) *Facts.* P forms S with a $100 contribution and S borrows $150. For Years 1 through 5, S has a $210 ordinary loss that is absorbed by the group. Under § 1.1502-32(b), S's loss results in P having a $110 excess loss account in S's stock. S defaults on the indebtedness, but the creditor does not discharge the debt (or initiate collection procedures). At the beginning of Year 6, S ceases any substantial operations with respect to the assets, but maintains their ownership with a principal purpose to avoid P's taking into account its excess loss account in S's stock.

(b) *Analysis.* Under paragraph (c)(1)(iii)(A) of this section, P's excess loss account on each of its shares of S's stock ordinarily is taken into account at the time substantially all of S's assets are treated as disposed of, abandoned, or destroyed for Federal income tax purposes. Under paragraph (e) of this section, however, S's assets are not taken into account at the beginning of Year 6 for purposes of applying paragraph (c)(1)(iii)(A) of this section. Consequently, S is treated as worthless at the beginning of Year 6, and P's $110 excess loss account is taken into account.

(h) *Effective date*—(1) *Application.* This section applies with respect to determinations of the basis of (including an excess loss account in) the stock of a member in consolidated return years beginning on or after January 1, 1995. If this section applies, basis (and excess loss accounts) must be determined or redetermined as if this section were in effect for all years (including, for example, the consolidated return years of another consolidated group to the extent adjustments during those consolidated return years are still reflected). Any such determination or redetermination does not, however, affect any prior period.

(2) *Dispositions of stock before effective date*—(i) *In general.* If P was treated as disposing of stock of S in a tax year beginning before January 1, 1995 (including, for example, a deemed disposition because S was worthless) under the rules of this section then in effect, the amount of P's income, gain, deduction, or loss, and the stock basis reflected in that amount, are not redetermined under paragraph (h)(1) of this section. See paragraph (h)(3) of this section for the applicable rules.

(ii) *Intercompany amounts.* For purposes of this paragraph (h)(2), a disposition does not include a transaction to which § 1.1502-13, § 1.1502-13T, § 1.1502-14, or § 1.1502-14T applies. Instead, the transaction is deemed to occur as the income, gain, deduction, or loss (if any) is taken into account.

(3) *Prior law.* For prior determinations, see prior regulations under section 1502 as in effect with respect to the determination. See, e.g., § 1.1502-19 as contained in the 26 CFR part 1 edition revised as of April 1, 1994. [Reg. § 1.1502-19.]

☐ [T.D. 6909, 12-29-66. Amended by T.D. 7246, 12-29-72; T.D. 8364, 9-13-91 and T.D. 8560, 8-12-94.]

[Reg. § 1.1502-20]

§ 1.1502-20. **Loss disallowance.**—(a) *Loss disallowance*—(1) *General rule.* No deduction is allowed for any loss recognized by a member with respect to the disposition of stock of a subsidiary. See also §§ § 1.1502-11(c) (stock losses attributable to certain pre-1966 distributions) and 1.1502-80(c) (deferring the treatment of stock of members as worthless under section 165(g)).

(2) *Disposition.* "Disposition" means any event in which gain or loss is recognized, in whole or in part.

(3) *Coordination with loss deferral and other disallowance rules*—(i) *In general.* Loss with re-

spect to the stock of a subsidiary may be deferred or disallowed under other applicable provisions of the Code and regulations, including section 267(f). Paragraph (a)(1) of this section does not apply to loss that is disallowed under any other provision. If loss is deferred under any other provision, paragraph (a)(1) of this section applies when the loss is taken into account. However, if an overriding event described in paragraph (a)(3)(ii) of this section occurs before the deferred loss is taken into account, paragraph (a)(1) of this section applies to the loss immediately before the event occurs even though the loss may not be taken into account until a later time. Any loss not disallowed under paragraph (a)(1) of this section is subject to disallowance or deferral under other applicable provisions of the Code and regulations.

(ii) *Overriding events.* For purposes of paragraph (a)(3)(i) of this section, the following are overriding events:

(A) The stock ceases to be owned by a member of the consolidated group.

(B) The stock is canceled or redeemed (regardless of whether it is retired or held as treasury stock).

(C) The stock is treated as disposed of under § 1.1502-19(c)(1)(ii)(B) or (c)(1)(iii).

(4) *Netting.* Paragraph (a)(1) of this section does not apply to loss with respect to the disposition of stock of a subsidiary, to the extent that, as a consequence of the same plan or arrangement, gain is taken into account by members with respect to stock of the same subsidiary having the same material terms. If the gain to which this paragraph (a)(4) applies is less than the amount of the loss with respect to the disposition of the subsidiary's stock, the gain is applied to offset loss with respect to each share disposed of as a consequence of the same plan or arrangement in proportion to the amount of the loss deduction that would have been disallowed under paragraph (a)(1) of this section with respect to such share before the application of this paragraph (a)(4). If the same item of gain could be taken into account more than once in limiting the application of paragraphs (a)(1) and (b)(1) of this section, the item is taken into account only once.

(5) *Examples.* For purposes of the examples in this section, unless otherwise stated, all corporations have only one class of stock outstanding, all groups file consolidated returns on a calendar-year basis, the facts set forth the only corporate activity, all transactions are between unrelated persons, and tax liabilities are disregarded. The basis of each asset is the same for determining earnings and profits adjustments and taxable income. References to the investment adjustment system are references to the rules of §§ 1.1502-19, 1.1502-32 and 1.1502-33. The principles of this paragraph (a) are illustrated by the following examples.

Example 1. Loss attributable to recognized built-in gain. P buys all the stock of T for $100, and T becomes a member of the P group. T has an asset with a basis of $0 and a value of $100. T sells the asset for $100. Under the investment adjustment system, P's basis in the T stock increases to $200. Five years later, P sells all the T stock for $100 and recognizes a loss of $100. Under paragraph (a)(1) of this section, no deduction is allowed to P for the $100 loss.

Example 2. Effect of post-acquisition appreciation. P buys all the stock of T for $100, and T becomes a member of the P group. T has an asset with a basis of $0 and a value of $100. T sells the asset for $100. Under the investment adjustment system, P's basis in the T stock increases to $200. T reinvests the proceeds of the sale in an asset that appreciates in value to $180. Five years after the sale, P sells all the stock of T for $180 and recognizes a $20 loss. Under paragraph (a)(1) of this section, no deduction is allowed to P for the $20 loss.

Example 3. Disallowance of duplicated loss. P forms S with a contribution of $100 in exchange for all of the S stock, and S becomes a member of the P group. S has an operating loss of $60. The group is unable to use the loss, and the loss becomes a consolidated net operating loss carryover attributable to S. Five years later, P sells the stock of S for $40, recognizing a $60 loss. Under paragraph (a)(1) of this section, P's $60 loss on the sale of the S stock is disallowed. (See paragraph (g) of this section for the elective reattribution of S's $60 net operating loss to P in connection with the sale.)

Example 4. Deemed asset sale election. (i) P forms S with a contribution of $100 in exchange for all of the S stock, and S becomes a member of the P group. S buys an asset for $100, and the value of the asset declines to $40. P sells all the S stock to P1 for $40. Under paragraph (a)(1) of this section, P's $60 loss on the sale of the S stock is disallowed.

(ii) If P and P1 instead elect deemed asset sale treatment under section 338(h)(10), S is treated as selling all of its assets, and no loss is recognized by P on its sale of the S stock. As a result of the recharacterization of the stock sale as an asset sale, the $60 loss in the asset is recognized. Under section 338(h)(10), S's $60 loss is included in the consolidated return of the P group, and S is treated as liquidating into P under section 332 following the deemed asset sale. Para-

Reg. § 1.1502-20(a)(4)

graph (a)(1) of this section does not apply to S's $60 loss.

Example 5. Gain and loss recognized with respect to stock as a consequence of the same plan or arrangement. P, the common parent of a group, owns 50 shares of the stock of T with an aggregate basis of $50, and S, a wholly owned subsidiary of P, owns the remaining 50 shares of T's stock with an aggregate basis of $100. All of the stock has the same terms. P and S sell all the T stock to the public for $140 pursuant to a single public offering. P therefore recognizes a gain of $20 and S recognizes a loss of $30. For purposes of paragraph (a)(4) of this section, the gain and loss recognized by P and S is considered to be a consequence of the same plan or arrangement. Accordingly, the amount of S's $30 loss disallowed under paragraph (a)(1) of this section is limited to $10 (the $30 reduced by P's $20 gain).

Example 6. Deferred loss and recognized gain. (i) P is the common parent of a consolidated group, S is a wholly owned subsidiary of P, and T is a recently purchased, wholly owned subsidiary of S. S has a $100 basis in the T stock, and T has an asset with a basis of $40 and a value of $100. T sells the asset for $100, recognizing a $60 gain. Under the investment adjustment system, S's basis in the T stock increases from $100 to $160. S sells its T stock to P for $100 in an intercompany transaction, recognizing a $60 intercompany loss that is deferred under section 267(f) and § 1.1502-13. P subsequently sells all the stock of T for $100 to X, a member of the same controlled group (as defined in section 267(f)) as P but not a member of the P consolidated group.

(ii) Under paragraph (a)(3)(i) of this section, the application of paragraph (a)(1) of this section to S's $60 intercompany loss on the sale of its T stock to P is deferred, because S's intercompany loss is deferred under section 267(f) and § 1.1502-13. P's sale of the T stock to X ordinarily would result in S's intercompany loss being taken into account under the matching rule of § 1.1502-13(c). The deferred loss is not taken into account under § 1.267(f)-1, however, because P's sale to X (a member of the same controlled group as P) is a second intercompany transaction for purposes of section 267(f). Nevertheless, paragraph (a)(3)(ii) of this section provides that paragraph (a)(1) of this section applies to the intercompany loss as a result of P's sale to X because the T stock ceases to be owned by a member of the P consolidated group. Thus, the loss is disallowed under paragraph (a)(1) of this section immediately before P's sale and is therefore never taken into account under section 267(f).

(iii) The facts are the same as in (i) of this *Example,* except that S is liquidated after its sale of the T stock to P, but before P's sale of the T stock to X, and P sells the T stock to X for $110. Under §§ 1.1502-13(j) and 1.267(f)-1(b), P succeeds to S's intercompany loss as a result of S's liquidation. Thus, paragraph (a)(3)(i) of this section continues to defer the application of paragraph (a)(1) of this section until P's sale to X. Under paragraph (a)(4) of this section, the amount of S's $60 intercompany loss disallowed under paragraph (a)(1) of this section is limited to $50 because P's $10 gain on the disposition of the T stock is taken into account as a consequence of the same plan or arrangement.

(iv) The facts are the same as in (i) of this *Example,* except that P sells the T stock to A, a person related to P within the meaning of section 267(b)(2). Although S's intercompany loss is ordinarily taken into account under the matching rule of § 1.1502-13(c) as a result of P's sale, § 1.267(f)-1(c)(2)(ii) provides that none of the intercompany loss is taken into account because A is a nonmember that is related to P under section 267(b). Under paragraph (a)(3)(i) of this section, paragraph (a)(1) of this section does not apply to loss that is disallowed under any other provision. Because § 1.267(f)-1(c)(2)(ii) and section 267(d) provide that the benefit of the intercompany loss is retained by A if the property is later disposed of at a gain, the intercompany loss is not disallowed for purposes of paragraph (a)(3)(i) of this section. Thus, the intercompany loss is disallowed under paragraph (a)(1) of this section immediately before P's sale and is therefore never taken into account under section 267(d).

(b) *Basis reduction on deconsolidation*—(1) *General rule.* If a member's basis in a share of stock of a subsidiary exceeds its value immediately before a deconsolidation of the share, the basis of the share is reduced at that time to an amount equal to its value. If both a disposition and a deconsolidation occur with respect to a share in the same transaction, paragraph (a) of this section applies and, to the extent necessary to effectuate the purposes of this section, this paragraph (b) applies following the application of paragraph (a) of this section.

(2) *Deconsolidation.* "Deconsolidation" means any event that causes a share of stock of a subsidiary that remains outstanding to be no longer owned by a member of any consolidated group of which the subsidiary is also a member.

(3) *Value.* "Value" means fair market value.

(4) *Netting.* Paragraph (b)(1) of this section does not apply to reduce the basis of stock of a subsidiary, to the extent that, as a consequence of

Reg. § 1.1502-20(b)(4)

the same plan or arrangement as that giving rise to the deconsolidation, gain is taken into account by members with respect to stock of the same subsidiary having the same material terms. If the gain to which this paragraph (b)(4) applies is less than the amount of basis reduction with respect to shares of the subsidiary's stock, the gain is applied to offset basis reduction with respect to each share deconsolidated as a consequence of the same plan or arrangement in proportion to the amount of the reduction that would have been required under paragraph (b)(1) of this section with respect to such share before the application of this paragraph (b)(4).

(5) *Loss within 2 years after basis reduction*—(i) *In general.* If a share is deconsolidated and a direct or indirect disposition of the share occurs within 2 years after the date of the deconsolidation, a separate statement entitled "Statement Pursuant to Section 1.1502-20(b)(5)" must be filed with the taxpayer's return for the year of disposition. If the taxpayer fails to file the statement as required, no deduction is allowed for any loss recognized with respect to the disposition. A disposition after the 2-year period described in this paragraph (b)(5) that is pursuant to an agreement, option, or other arrangement entered into within the 2-year period is treated as a disposition within the 2-year period for purposes of this section.

(ii) *Contents of statement.* The statement required under paragraph (b)(5)(i) of this section must contain—

(A) The name and employer identification number (E.I.N.) of the subsidiary.

(B) The amount of prior basis reduction (if any) with respect to the stock of the subsidiary under paragraph (b)(1) of this section.

(C) The basis of the stock of the subsidiary immediately before the disposition.

(D) The amount realized on the disposition.

(E) The amount of the loss recognized on the disposition.

(6) *Examples.* The principles of this paragraph (b) are illustrated by the following examples.

Example 1. Simultaneous application of loss disallowance rule and basis reduction rule to stock of the same subsidiary. (i) P buys all the stock of T for $100, and T becomes a member of the P group. T has an asset with a basis of $0 and a value of $100. T sells the asset for $100. Under the investment adjustment system, P's basis in the T stock increases to $200. Five years later, P sells 60 shares of T stock for $60 and recognizes a $60 loss on the sale. The sale causes a deconsolidation of the remaining 40 shares of T stock held by P.

(ii) P's $60 loss on the sale of T stock is disallowed under paragraph (a)(1) of this section. Under paragraph (b)(1) of this section, P must reduce the basis of the 40 shares of T stock it continues to own from $80 to $40, the value of the shares immediately before the deconsolidation.

(iii) Although P's disposition of the 60 shares also causes a deconsolidation of these shares, paragraph (b)(1) of this section provides that, if both paragraph (a) and paragraph (b) of this section apply to a share in the same transaction, paragraph (a) of this section applies first and this paragraph (b) applies only to the extent necessary to effectuate the purposes of this section. Under paragraph (a)(1) of this section, P's $60 loss on the sale of the 60 shares is disallowed. Under the facts of this example, it is not necessary to also apply this paragraph (b) to the 60 shares in order to effectuate the purposes of this section.

Example 2. Deconsolidation of subsidiary stock on contribution to a partnership. (i) P buys all the stock of T for $100, and T becomes a member of the P group. T has an asset with a basis of $0 and a value of $100. T sells the asset for $100. Under the investment adjustment system, P's basis in the T stock increases to $200. Five years later, P transfers all the stock of T to partnership M in exchange for a partnership interest in M, in a transaction to which section 721 applies.

(ii) At the time of the exchange, P's basis in the T stock is $200 and the T stock's value is $100. Under paragraph (b) of this section, the transfer to M causes a deconsolidation of the T stock, and P must reduce its basis in the T stock, immediately before the transfer to M, from $200 to the stock's $100 value at the time of the transfer. As a result, P has a basis of $100 in its interest in M, and M has a basis of $100 in the stock of T.

Example 3. Simultaneous application of loss disallowance and basis reduction to stock of different subsidiaries. (i) P owns all the stock of S, which in turn owns all the stock of S1, and S and S1 are members of the P group. P's basis in the S stock is $100 and S's basis in the S1 stock is $100. S1 buys all the stock of T for $100, and T becomes a member of the P group. T has an asset with a basis of $0 and a value of $100. T sells the asset for $100. Under the investment adjustment system, S1's basis in the T stock, S's basis in the S1 stock, and P's basis in the S stock each increase from $100 to $200. S then sells all the S1 stock for $100 and recognizes a loss of $100.

Reg. § 1.1502-20(b)(5)

(ii) Under paragraph (a)(1) of this section, S's $100 loss on the sale of the S1 stock is disallowed.

(iii) If S1 and T are not members of a consolidated group immediately after the sale of the stock of S1, the T stock is deconsolidated and, under paragraph (b)(1) of this section, S1 must reduce the basis of the T stock to its $100 value immediately before the sale.

(iv) If S1 and T are members of a consolidated group immediately after the sale of the S1 stock, the T stock is not deconsolidated, and no reduction is required under paragraph (b)(1) of this section.

Example 4. Extending the time period for dispositions. (i) In Year 1, P, the common parent of a group, buys all 100 shares of the stock of T for $100. T's only asset has a basis of $0 and a value of $100. T sells the asset for $100. Under the investment adjustment system, P's basis in the T stock increases from $100 to $200. At the beginning of Year 5, P causes T to issue 30 additional shares of stock to the public for $30. This issuance causes a deconsolidation of the T stock owned by P, and paragraph (b)(1) of this section requires P to reduce its basis in the T stock from $200 to $100.

(ii) Within 2 years after the date of the basis reduction, P agrees to sell all of its T stock for $90 at the end of Year 7. Under paragraph (b)(5) of this section, P's disposition of the T stock at the end of Year 7 is treated as occurring within the 2-year period following the basis reduction, because the disposition is pursuant to an agreement reached within 2 years after the basis reduction. Accordingly, P's $10 loss may not be deducted unless P files the statement required under paragraph (b)(5) of this section. This result is reached whether or not the agreement is in writing. P's disposition would also have been treated as occurring within the 2-year period if the disposition were pursuant to an option issued within the period.

Example 5. Deferred loss and subsequent basis reduction. (i) P is the common parent of a consolidated group, S is a wholly owned subsidiary of P, and T is a recently purchased, wholly owned subsidiary of S. S has a $100 basis in the T stock, and T has an asset with a basis of $40 and a value of $100. T sells the asset for $100, recognizing $60 of gain. Under the investment adjustment system, S's basis in the T stock increases from $100 to $160. S sells its T stock to P for $100 in an intercompany transaction, recognizing a $60 intercompany loss that is deferred under section 267(f) and § 1.1502-13. T issues 30 additional shares of stock to the public for $30 which causes a deconsolidation of the T stock owned by P.

(ii) Under paragraph (a)(3)(i) of this section, the application of paragraph (a)(1) of this section to S's intercompany loss on the sale of its T stock to P is deferred because S's loss is deferred under section 267(f) and § 1.1502-13. Because the fair market value of the T stock owned by P is $100 immediately before the deconsolidation and P has a $100 basis in the stock at that time, no basis reduction is required under paragraph (b)(1) of this section.

(iii) T's issuance of additional shares to the public results in S's intercompany loss being taken into account under the acceleration rule of § 1.1502-13(d) because there is no difference between P's $100 basis in the T stock and the $100 basis the T stock would have had if P and S had been divisions of a single corporation. S's loss taken into account is disallowed under paragraph (a)(1) of this section.

Example 6. Gain and basis reduction with respect to the same plan or arrangement. (i) P, the common parent of a group, owns 50 shares of T stock with an aggregate basis of $50, and S, a wholly owned subsidiary of P, owns the remaining 50 shares of T stock with an aggregate basis of $100. All of the stock has the same terms. P sells all of its T stock to the public for $70 and recognizes a $20 gain. The sale causes a deconsolidation of S's 50 shares of T stock.

(ii) Under paragraph (b)(1) of this section, S must reduce the basis of its 50 shares of T stock from $100 to $70, the value of the shares immediately before the deconsolidation. However, under paragraph (b)(4) of this section, because P's $20 gain is recognized as a consequence of the same plan or arrangement as that giving rise to the deconsolidation, S's basis reduction is eliminated to the extent of $20. Thus, S must reduce the basis of its T stock from $100 to $90.

Example 7. Netting allocated between loss disallowance and basis reduction. (i) P is the common parent of a group and S is its wholly owned subsidiary. P and S each own 50 shares of T stock and each has an aggregate basis of $50. All of the stock has the same terms. S recently purchased its T stock from S1, a lower tier subsidiary, in an intercompany transaction in which S1 recognized a $30 intercompany gain that was deferred under § 1.1502-13. T has an asset with a basis of $0 and a value of $100. T sells the asset for $100, recognizing $100 of gain. Under the investment adjustment system, P and S each increase the basis of their T stock to $100. S sells all of its T stock to the public for $50 and recognizes a $50 loss. The sale causes a deconsolidation of P's T stock.

Reg. § 1.1502-20(b)(6)

(ii) S's $50 loss on the sale of T stock is disallowed under paragraph (a)(1) of this section. Under paragraph (b)(1) of this section, P must reduce its $100 basis in the T stock to the $50 value immediately before the deconsolidation.

(iii) Under the matching rule of § 1.1502-13, S's sale of its T stock results in S1's $30 intercompany gain being taken into account. Under paragraphs (a)(4) and (b)(4) of this section, the gain may be taken into account by P and S in limiting the application of paragraphs (a)(1) and (b)(1) of this section, but it may be taken into account only once. Under paragraph (a)(4) of this section, S may apply the gain to decrease the amount of loss disallowed under paragraph (a)(1) of this section from $50 to $20. None of the gain remains to decrease the $50 of P's basis reduction under paragraph (b)(1) of this section. (P may instead apply the gain to decrease the basis reduction under paragraph (b)(1) of this section instead of S decreasing its disallowed loss, but if the T stock is sold within 2 years, the statement described in paragraph (b)(5) of this section must be filed if a deduction is to be allowed for any loss recognized on the disposition.)

(c) *Allowable loss*—(1) *General rule.* The amount of loss disallowed under paragraph (a)(1) of this section and the amount of basis reduction under paragraph (b)(1) of this section with respect to a share of stock shall not exceed the sum of the following amounts—

(i) *Extraordinary gain dispositions.* The amount of income or gain (or its equivalent), net of directly related expenses, that is allocated to the share from extraordinary gain dispositions.

(ii) *Positive investment adjustments.* The amount of the positive adjustment (if any) with respect to the share under § 1.1502-32 for each consolidated return year, but only to the extent the amount exceeds the amount described in paragraph (c)(1)(i) of this section for the year.

(iii) *Duplicated loss.* The amount of duplicated loss with respect to the share.

(2) *Operating rules.* For purposes of applying paragraph (c)(1) of this section—

(i) *Extraordinary gain dispositions.* An "extraordinary gain disposition" is—

(A) An actual or deemed disposition of—

(*1*) A capital asset as defined in section 1221 (determined without the application of any other rules of law).

(*2*) Property used in a trade or business as defined in section 1231(b) (determined without the application of any holding period requirement).

(*3*) An asset described in section 1221(1), (3), (4), or (5), if substantially all the assets in such category from the same trade or business are disposed of in one transaction (or series of related transactions).

(*4*) Assets disposed of in an applicable asset acquisition under section 1060(c).

(B) A positive section 481(a) adjustment.

(C) A discharge of indebtedness.

(D) Any other event (or item) identified in guidance published in the Internal Revenue Bulletin.

An extraordinary gain disposition is taken into account under paragraph (c)(1)(i) of this section only if it occurs on or after November 19, 1990. For this purpose, federal income taxes may be directly related to extraordinary gain dispositions only to the extent of the excess (if any) of the group's income tax liability actually imposed under subtitle A of the Internal Revenue Code for the taxable year of the extraordinary gain dispositions over the group's income tax liability for the taxable year redetermined by not taking into account the extraordinary gain dispositions. For this purpose, the group's income tax liability actually imposed and its redetermined income tax liability are determined without taking into account the foreign tax credit under section 27(a) of the Code.

(ii) *Positive investment adjustments.* For purposes of paragraph (c)(1)(ii) of this section, a positive adjustment under § 1.1502-32 is the sum of the amounts under § 1.1502-32(b)(2)(i) through (iii) for the consolidated return year (the adjustment determined without taking distributions into account). However, amounts included in any loss carryover are taken into account in the year they arise rather than the year absorbed.

(iii) *Applicable amounts.* Amounts are described in paragraphs (c)(1)(i) and (ii) of this section only to the extent they are reflected in the basis of the share, directly or indirectly, immediately before the disposition or deconsolidation. For this purpose, an amount is reflected in the basis of a share if the share's basis would have been different without the amount. However, amounts included in any loss carryover are taken into account in the year they arise rather than the year absorbed.

(iv) *Related party rule.* The amounts described in paragraphs (c)(1)(i) and (ii) of this section are not reduced or eliminated by reason of an acquisition of the share from a person related within the meaning of section 267(b) or section 707(b)(1), substituting "10 percent" for "50 percent" each place that it appears, even if the share

Reg. § 1.1502-20(c)(1)

is not transferred basis property as defined in section 7701(a)(43).

(v) *Pre-September 13, 1991 positive investment adjustments*—(A) *In general.* The amount determined under paragraph (c)(1)(ii) of this section is limited for tax years of the subsidiary ending on or before September 13, 1991. The amount may not exceed the net increase, if any, in the basis of the share from—

(*1*) The date the share was first acquired by a member (whether or not a member at that time); to

(*2*) The end of the last taxable year ending on or before September 13, 1991 (or, if earlier, the date of the disposition or deconsolidation). If the share is transferred basis property (within the meaning of section 7701(a)(43) from a prior consolidated group, the date under paragraph (c)(2)(v)(A)(*1*) of this section is the date the share was first acquired by a member of the prior group. For purposes of this paragraph (c)(2)(v)(A), an increase in an excess loss account is treated as a decrease in stock basis and a decrease in an excess loss account is treated as an increase in stock basis.

(B) *Cessation of netting.* If a lower amount would result under paragraph (c)(1)(ii) of this section by determining the amount under this paragraph (c)(2)(v) as of the end of an earlier taxable year ending after December 31, 1986—

(*1*) The amount under this paragraph (c)(2)(v) is determined as of the earlier year end; and

(*2*) The amount determined under paragraph (c)(1)(ii) of this section is not limited for tax years of the subsidiary ending after the earlier year end.

(vi) *Duplicated loss.* "Duplicated loss" is determined immediately after a disposition or deconsolidation, and equals the excess (if any) of—

(A) The sum of—

(*1*) The aggregate adjusted basis of the assets of the subsidiary other than any stock and securities that the subsidiary owns in another subsidiary, and

(*2*) Any losses attributable to the subsidiary and carried to the subsidiary's first taxable year following the disposition or deconsolidation, and

(*3*) Any deferred deductions (such as deductions deferred under section 469) of the subsidiary, over

(B) The sum of—

(*1*) The value of the subsidiary's stock, and

(*2*) Any liabilities of the subsidiary, and

(*3*) Any other relevant items.

The amounts determined under this paragraph (c)(2)(vi) with respect to a subsidiary include its allocable share of corresponding amounts with respect to all lower tier subsidiaries. If 80 percent or more in value of the stock of a subsidiary is acquired by purchase in a single transaction (or in a series of related transactions during any 12-month period), the value of the subsidiary's stock may not exceed the purchase price of the stock divided by the percentage of the stock (by value) so purchased. For this purpose, stock is acquired by purchase if the transferee is not related to the transferor within the meaning of sections 267(b) and 707(b)(1), substituting "10 percent" for "50 percent" each place that it appears, and the transferee's basis in the stock is determined wholly by reference to the consideration paid for such stock.

(vii) *Disallowance amounts applied only once.* The amounts described in paragraph (c)(1) of this section are not applied more than once to disallow a loss, reduce basis, or reattribute loss under this section.

(3) *Statement of allowed loss.* Paragraph (c)(1) of this section applies only if the separate statement required under this paragraph (c)(3) is filed with the taxpayer's return for the year of the disposition or deconsolidation. The statement must be entitled "ALLOWED LOSS UNDER SECTION 1.1502-20(c)" and must contain—

(i) The name and employer identification number (E.I.N.) of the subsidiary.

(ii) The basis of the stock of the subsidiary immediately before the disposition or deconsolidation.

(iii) The amount realized on the disposition and the amount of fair market value on the deconsolidation.

(iv) The amount of the deduction not disallowed under paragraph (a)(1) of this section by reason of this paragraph (c) and the amount of basis not reduced under paragraph (b)(1) of this section by reason of this paragraph (c).

(v) The amount of loss disallowed under paragraph (a)(1) of this section and the amount of basis reduced under paragraph (b)(1) of this section.

(4) *Examples.* For purposes of the examples in this paragraph, unless otherwise stated, the group files the statement required under paragraph (c)(3) of this section. The principles of this

paragraph (c) are illustrated by the following examples.

Example 1. Allowable loss attributable to lost built-in gain. (i) Individual A forms T. P buys all the stock of T from A for $100, and T becomes a member of the P group. T has a capital asset with a basis of $0 and a value of $100. The value of the asset declines, and T sells the asset for $40. Under the investment adjustment system, P's basis in the T stock increases to $140. P then sells all the stock of T for $40 and recognizes a loss of $100.

(ii) The amount of the $100 loss disallowed under paragraph (a)(1) of this section may not exceed the amount determined under paragraph (c)(1) of this section. Under paragraphs (c)(2)(i) and (iii) of this section, T's $40 gain is from an extraordinary gain disposition and the amount is reflected in the basis of the T stock under § 1.1502-32 immediately before the disposition. Thus, the gain is described in paragraph (c)(1)(i) of this section. Because this amount is the only amount described in paragraph (c)(1) of this section, the amount of P's $100 loss that is disallowed under paragraph (a)(1) of this section is limited to $40. (No amount is described in paragraph (c)(1)(ii) of this section because the amount of T's positive investment adjustments does not exceed the amount included under paragraph (c)(1)(i) of this section.)

(iii) The results would be the same if the asset, instead of being owned by T, is owned by a partnership in which T is a partner and T is allocated the $40 of gain under section 704(b). Under paragraphs (c)(2)(i) and (iii) of this section, T's $40 gain is from an extraordinary gain disposition, and the gain is reflected in the basis of the T stock under § 1.1502-32 immediately before the disposition.

Example 2. Extraordinary gain dispositions. (i) Individual A forms T. P buys all the stock of T from A for $100 in Year 1, and T becomes a member of the P group. T owns a capital asset, asset 1, with a basis of $0 and a value of $100. T sells asset 1 for $100 in Year 1 and invests the proceeds in a trade or business asset, asset 2. For Year 2, asset 2 produces $30 of gross operating income and $20 of cost recovery deductions. On December 31 of Year 2, asset 2 has an $80 adjusted basis and T disposes of asset 2 for $85; however, because T incurs $20 of expenses directly related to the sale of asset 2, the disposition produces a $15 loss that is taken into account in the determination of taxable income or loss under § 1.1502-32(b)(2)(i) (the loss offsets T's $10 of operating income for Year 2, as well as $5 of operating income of P in that year). Under the investment adjustment system, P's basis in the T stock increases by $95, to $195, because T has $110 of income and a $15 loss. P sells the T stock for $95 in Year 5 and recognizes a $100 loss.

(ii) Under paragraphs (c)(2)(i) and (iii) of this section, the $100 gain from the disposition of asset 1 is from an extraordinary gain disposition and is reflected in the basis of the T stock. Thus, the gain is described in paragraph (c)(1)(i) of this section. The sale of asset 2 is not taken into account under paragraph (c)(1)(i) of this section because, net of directly related expenses, T does not have income or gain from the sale. (No amount is described under paragraph (c)(1)(ii) of this section because T's positive investment adjustments are taken into account under paragraph (c)(1)(i) of this section.) Because the $100 amount described under paragraph (c)(1)(i) of this section equals P's $100 loss from the disposition of the T stock, all of the loss is disallowed.

Example 3. Positive investment adjustments. (i) Individual A forms T. S, a member of the P group, buys all the stock of T from A for $100, and T becomes a member of the P group. T has an asset with a basis of $0 and a value of $100. The asset earns $100 of operating income in Year 1 and declines in value to $0. T invests the operating income in another asset that produces a $25 operating loss for Year 2. Under the investment adjustment system, S's basis in the T stock increases to $200 at the end of Year 1, and decreases to $175 at the end of Year 2. S sells all the stock of T for $75 in Year 5 and recognizes a loss of $100.

(ii) Under paragraph (c)(1)(ii) of this section, the $100 of income from Year 1 is a positive investment adjustment. The amount is not reduced by the $25 operating loss for Year 2. Because the $100 amount described under paragraph (c)(1)(ii) of this section equals S's $100 loss from the disposition of the T stock, all of the loss is disallowed.

Example 4. Treatment of net operating income as attributable to built-in gain. (i) Individual A forms T. P buys all the stock of T from A for $100, and T becomes a member of the P group. T has a capital asset with a basis of $0 and a value of $100. The asset declines in value to $40. The asset earns $100 of operating income unrelated to its $60 decline in value. Under the investment adjustment system, P's basis in the T stock increases to $200. P then sells all the stock of T for $140 (the asset worth $40 and $100 cash) and recognizes a loss of $60.

(ii) The $100 adjustment to the basis of the T stock is an amount described in paragraph (c)(1)(ii) of this section. Because this amount exceeds the amount of loss otherwise disallowed

Reg. § 1.1502-20(c)(4)

under paragraph (a)(1) of this section, P's entire $60 loss from the disposition of T stock is disallowed.

Example 5. Carryover basis transactions—amounts attributable to separate return years. (i) Individual A forms T. S purchases all the stock of T from A for $100, and T becomes a member of the S group. T has a capital asset with a basis of $0 and a value of $100. T sells the asset for $100. Under the investment adjustment system, S's basis in the T stock increases to $200. P buys all of the stock of S for $100, and both S and T become members of the P group. S then sells the T stock for $100 and recognizes a loss of $100.

(ii) Under paragraph (c)(2)(iii) of this section, the $100 adjustment to S's basis in the T stock while a member of the S group is an amount described in paragraph (c)(1)(i) of this section with respect to the P group because it continues to be reflected in the basis of the T stock immediately before the stock is disposed of. Because this amount equals the loss otherwise disallowed under paragraph (a)(1) of this section, S's $100 loss from the disposition of T stock is disallowed.

Example 6. Cost basis for subsidiary stock. (i) In Year 1, individual A forms T. T's assets appreciate in value from $0 to $100, and T recognizes $100 of gain in an extraordinary gain disposition. T reinvests the sale proceeds in assets that appreciate in value to $150. In Year 3, A sells all of the T stock to P for $150, and T becomes a member of the P group. While a member of the P group, T's assets decline in value to $130 and P sells the T stock in Year 7 for $130 and recognizes a $20 loss.

(ii) Although T has a $100 gain from extraordinary gain dispositions, the gain is not reflected in P's basis in the T stock within the meaning of paragraph (c)(2)(iii) of this section. P's basis reflects the stock's value at the time of P's purchase, and is determined without regard to whether T recognized the gain before the purchase. Thus, no part of T's gain is described in paragraph (c)(1) of this section, and no part of the $20 loss is disallowed under paragraph (a) of this section. (For rules that apply if A and P are related persons, see paragraph (c)(2)(iv) of this section.)

Example 7. Adjustments to stock basis under applicable rules of law. (i) Individual A forms T, and T's assets subsequently appreciate. T borrows $100 on a nonrecourse basis secured by the appreciated assets. P buys all of the stock of T from A for $150. After becoming a member of the P group, T has a $100 operating loss that is absorbed in the determination of consolidated taxable income and P's basis in the T stock is reduced to $50 under § 1.1502-32. Because T's assets have declined in value, T's creditors discharge $60 of T's indebtedness. The $60 discharge is not included in T's gross income under section 108(a), but no attributes are reduced under section 108(b).

(ii) Under paragraph (c)(2)(i) of this section, the discharge of indebtedness is an extraordinary gain disposition. Under § 1.1502-32(b)(3)(ii), however, the $60 discharge of indebtedness is not treated as tax-exempt income that increases P's basis in the T stock. Consequently, under paragraph (c)(2)(iii) of this section, T's discharge of indebtedness income is not reflected in P's basis in the T stock. Thus, there is no amount under paragraph (c)(1) of this section.

(iii) The facts are the same as in paragraph (i) of this *Example,* except that $60 of T's operating loss is not absorbed and is included in a consolidated net operating loss that is carried over under §§ 1.1502-21A or 1.1502-21, and the $60 is eliminated from the carryover under section 108(b) as a result of T's discharge of indebtedness. The absorption of $40 of T's loss reduces P's basis in the T stock from $150 to $110. The $60 discharge of indebtedness is treated as tax-exempt income that increases P's basis in the T stock, and the $60 attribute reduction is treated as a noncapital, nondeductible expense that reduces P's basis in the T stock. Thus, P's basis in T's stock remains $110 following the discharge and attribute reduction. Because P's basis is $110, rather than $50, the discharge of indebtedness income is reflected in P's basis for purposes of paragraph (c)(2)(iii) of this section. Thus, the amount under paragraph (c)(1)(i) of this section is $60.

Example 8. Duplicated loss. (i) Individual A forms T with a contribution of $100 in exchange for all of the T stock. Individual B forms T1 with a contribution of land that has a $90 basis and $100 value. T buys all the stock of T1 from B for $100. P buys all the stock of T from A for $100, and both T and T1 become members of the P group. The value of T1's land declines to $40. P sells all of the T stock for $40 and recognizes a loss of $60.

(ii) Under paragraph (c)(1)(iii) of this section, P's amount of duplicated loss is $50. This is computed under paragraph (c)(2)(vi) of this section immediately after the disposition as the excess of—

(A) The $90 aggregate adjusted basis of the assets of T and T1 (other than stock and securities of T1 owned by T), over

(B) The $40 fair market value of the T stock (determined under paragraph (c)(2)(vi) of this section). Because this amount is the only amount

Reg. § 1.1502-20(c)(4)

described in paragraph (c)(1) of this section, the amount of P's $60 loss disallowed under paragraph (a)(1) of this section is limited to $50.

(iii) The result would be the same if the value of T1's property did not decline and T1 instead had an operating loss of $60 (attributable to borrowed funds) which the P group was unable to use. In that case, the $50 excess of the sum of—

(A) The $90 aggregate adjusted basis of the assets of T and T1 (other than stock and securities of members of the P group), plus the $60 net operating loss attributable to T1 and carried to its first taxable year following the disposition, over

(B) The sum of the $40 fair market value of the T stock, plus the $60 of T1 liabilities, is an amount described in paragraph (c)(2)(vi) of this section. (See paragraph (g) of this section for the elective reattribution of T1's $60 net operating loss to P in connection with the sale.)

Example 9. Intercompany stock sales.

(i) P is the common parent of a consolidated group, S is a wholly owned subsidiary of P, and T is a wholly owned recently purchased subsidiary of S. S has a $100 basis in the T stock, and T has a capital asset with a basis of $0 and a value of $100. T's asset declines in value to $60. Before T has any positive investment adjustments or extraordinary gain dispositions, S sells its T stock to P for $60. T's asset reappreciates and is sold for $100, and T recognizes $100 of gain. Under the investment adjustment system, P's basis in the T stock increases to $160. P then sells all of the T stock for $100 and recognizes a loss of $60.

(ii) S's sale of the T stock to P is an intercompany transaction. Thus, S's $40 loss is deferred under section 267(f) and § 1.1502-13. Under paragraph (a)(3) of this section, the application of paragraph (a)(1) of this section to S's $40 loss is deferred until the loss is taken into account. Under the matching rule of § 1.1502-13(c), the loss is taken into account to reflect the difference for each year between P's corresponding items taken into account and P's recomputed corresponding items (the corresponding items that P would take into account for the year if S and P were divisions of a single corporation). If S and P were divisions of a single corporation and the intercompany sale were a transfer between the divisions, P would succeed to S's $100 basis and would have a $200 basis in the T stock at the time it sells the T stock ($100 of initial basis plus $100 under the investment adjustment system). S's $40 loss is taken into account at the time of P's sale of the T stock to reflect the $40 difference between the $60 loss P takes into account and P's recomputed $100 loss.

(iii) Under the matching rule of § 1.1502-13(c), the attributes of S's $40 loss and P's $60 loss are redetermined to produce the same effect on consolidated taxable income (and consolidated tax liability) as if S and P were divisions of a single corporation. Under § 1.1502-13(b)(6), attributes of the losses include whether they are disallowed under this section. Because the amount described in paragraph (c)(1) of this section is $100, both S's $40 loss and P's $60 loss are disallowed.

(d) *Successors*—(1) *General rule.* This section applies, to the extent necessary to effectuate the purposes of this section, to any property the basis of which is determined, directly or indirectly, in whole or in part, by reference to the basis of a subsidiary's stock.

(2) *Examples.* The principles of this paragraph (d) are illustrated by the following examples.

Example 1. Status of successor as member. (i) P, the common parent of a group, buys all the stock of T for $100. T's only asset has a basis of $0 and a value of $100. T sells the asset for $100, and buys another asset for $100. Under the investment adjustment system, P's basis in the T stock increases to $200, and the earnings and profits of P increase by $100. P later transfers all the stock of T to an unrelated consolidated group in exchange for 10 percent of the stock of X, the common parent of that group, in a transaction described in section 368(a)(1)(B). At the time of the exchange, the value of the X stock received by P is $80.

(ii) Under section 358, P has a basis of $200 in the X stock it receives in exchange for T. Under section 362, X has a $200 basis in the T stock.

(iii) Neither paragraph (a)(1) nor (b)(1) of this section applies to the stock of T on P's transfer of the stock to the X group, because no gain or loss is recognized on the transfer, and the transfer is not a deconsolidation of the stock of T under paragraph (b)(2) of this section.

(iv) The X stock owned by P after the reorganization is a successor interest to the T stock because P's basis in the X stock is determined by reference to P's basis in the T stock. The purposes of this section require that the reorganization exchange be treated as a deconsolidation event with respect to P's interest in the X stock. Because X is not a member of the P group, a failure to reduce the basis of the X stock owned by P to its fair market value would permit the P group to recognize and deduct the loss attributable to the T stock. However, because T is a member of the X group, a reduction in the basis of the T stock is not necessary to prevent the X group from recog-

Reg. § 1.1502-20(d)(1)

nizing and deducting the loss arising in the P group. The transfer of T stock to X therefore constitutes a deconsolidation of the X stock but not the T stock. Therefore, P must reduce its basis in the X stock from $200 to its $80 value at that time. However, X's basis in the T stock remains $200.

Example 2. Continued application after deconsolidation. (i) P, the common parent of a group, buys all the stock of T for $100. T's only asset has a basis of $0 and a value of $100. T sells the asset for $100, and buys another asset for $100. Under the investment adjustment system, P's basis in the T stock increases to $200. P later transfers all the stock of T to partnership M in exchange for a partnership interest in M, in a transaction to which section 721 applies. The value of the T stock immediately before the transfer to M is $100. Less than 2 years later, P sells its interest in M for $80.

(ii) Under paragraph (b)(1) of this section, because the stock of T is deconsolidated on the transfer to M, immediately before the transfer to M, P reduces its basis in the T stock to the stock's $100 value immediately before the transfer. As a result, P has a basis of $100 in its interest in M, and M has a basis of $100 in the T stock.

(iii) When P sells its interest in M for $80, it recognizes a $20 loss. Because the basis of P's interest in M is determined by reference to P's basis in the T stock, and the reporting requirements could otherwise be circumvented, P's partnership interest in M is a successor interest to the T stock. Under paragraph (b)(5) of this section, P is required to file a statement with its return for the year of its disposition of its interest in M in order to deduct its loss. If P does not file the required statement described in paragraph (b)(5) of this section, P's loss on the disposition of its interest in M is disallowed.

(e) *Anti-avoidance rules*—(1) *General rule.* The rules of § 1.1502-20 must be applied in a manner that is consistent with and reasonably carries out their purposes. If a taxpayer acts with a view to avoid the effect of the rules of this section, adjustments must be made as necessary to carry out their purposes.

(2) *Anti-stuffing rule*—(i) *Application.* This paragraph (e)(2) applies if—

(A) A transfer of any asset (including stock and securities) on or after March 9, 1990 is followed within 2 years by a direct or indirect disposition or a deconsolidation of stock, and

(B) The transfer is with a view to avoiding, directly or indirectly, in whole or in part—

(1) The disallowance of loss on the disposition or the basis reduction on the deconsolidation of stock of a subsidiary, or

(2) The recognition of unrealized gain following the transfer.

A disposition or deconsolidation after the 2-year period described in this paragraph (e)(2)(i) that is pursuant to an agreement, option, or other arrangement entered into within the 2-year period is treated as a disposition or deconsolidation within the 2-year period for purposes of this section.

(ii) *Basis reduction.* If this paragraph (e)(2) applies, the basis of the stock is reduced, immediately before the disposition or deconsolidation, to cause the disallowance of loss, the reduction of basis, or the recognition of gain, otherwise avoided by reason of the transfer.

(3) *Examples.* The principles of this paragraph (e) are illustrated by the following examples.

Example 1. Shifting of value. (i) P buys all the stock of T for $100, and T becomes a member of the P group. T has an asset with a basis of $0 and a value of $100. With the view described in paragraph (e)(1) of this section, P transfers land with a value of $100 and a basis of $100 to T in exchange for preferred stock with a $200 redemption price and liquidation preference. The $100 redemption premium (the excess of the $200 redemption price over the $100 issue price) ultimately increases the value of the preferred stock from $100 to $200 (and decreases the value of the common stock). T sells the built-in gain asset for $100, and P's aggregate basis in S's common and preferred stock increases to $300. In addition, as a result of a cumulative redetermination under § 1.1502-32(c)(4), P's basis in the T preferred stock increases from $100 to $200 and P's basis in the common stock remains $100. P subsequently sells the common stock at a loss.

(ii) Under section 305, the redemption premium is treated as a distribution of property to which section 301 and § 1.1502-13(f)(2) apply. Under §§ 1.1502-13 and 1.1502-32, P's aggregate basis in the preferred and common stock is unaffected by the deemed distributions.

(iii) P's loss on the sale of the common stock is disallowed under paragraph (e)(1) of this section. This disallowance prevents the preferred stock from shifting value and stock basis adjustments from the common stock to avoid the disallowance of loss under this section.

Example 2. Basic stuffing case. (i) In Year 1, P buys all the stock of T for $100, and T becomes a member of the P group. T has an asset with a

Reg. § 1.1502-20(e)(3)

basis of $0 and a value of $100. T sells the asset for $100. Under the investment adjustment system, P's basis in the T stock increases from $100 to $200. In Year 5, P transfers to T an asset with a basis of $0 and a value of $100 in a transaction to which section 351 applies, with the view described in paragraph (e)(2)(i) of this section. In Year 6, P sells all the stock of T for $200.

(ii) Under paragraph (e)(2)(ii) of this section, P must reduce the basis in its T stock by $100 immediately before the sale. This basis reduction causes a $100 gain to be recognized on the sale.

(iii) The $100 basis reduction also would be required if the T stock is deconsolidated in Year 6 instead of being sold. P must reduce the basis in its T stock by $100 immediately before the deconsolidation.

(iv) The $100 basis reduction also would be required if the P stock were acquired at the beginning of Year 6 by the M consolidated group, even though the asset transfer took place outside the M group. Paragraph (e)(2)(i) of this section requires only that the transferor have the view at the time of the transfer.

Example 3. Stacking rules. (i) In Year 1, P buys all the stock of T for $100, and T becomes a member of the P group. T has an asset with a basis of $0 and a value of $100. T sells the asset for $100. Under the investment adjustment system, P's basis in the T stock increases from $100 to $200. In Year 5, when the value of the T stock remains $100, P transfers to T an asset with a basis of $0 and a value of $100 in a transaction to which section 351 applies, with the view described in paragraph (e)(2)(i) of this section. Thereafter, the value of the contributed asset declines to $10. In Year 6, P sells all the T stock for $110 and recognizes a $90 loss.

(ii) Because the transferred asset declined in value by $90, the transfer enabled P to avoid the disallowance of loss on the sale of T only to the extent of $10. Under paragraph (e)(2)(ii) of this section, P must reduce the basis in its T stock immediately before the sale to cause recognition of gain in an amount equal to the loss disallowance otherwise avoided by reason of the transfer. The amount of this basis reduction is $100, causing a $10 gain to be recognized on the sale.

(iii) The facts are the same as in (i) of this *Example,* except that the transferred asset does not decline in value and that T reinvests the $100 in proceeds from the asset sale in another asset that appreciates in value to $190. In Year 6, P sells T for $290. Because the new asset appreciated in value by $90, the transfer enabled P to avoid the disallowance of loss on the sale of T only to the extent of $10. Under paragraph (e)(2)(ii) of this section, P must reduce the basis in its T stock immediately before the sale to cause recognition of gain in an amount equal to the loss disallowance otherwise avoided by reason of the transfer. The amount of this basis reduction is $10, causing a $100 gain to be recognized on the sale.

Example 4. Contribution of built-in loss asset. (i) In Year 1, P forms S with a contribution of $100 in exchange for all of S's stock, and S becomes a member of the P group. S buys an asset for $100, and the asset appreciates in value to $200. P then buys all the stock of T for $100, and T becomes a member of the P group. T has an asset with a basis of $0 and a value of $100. T sells the asset for $100, and under the investment adjustment system P's basis in the T stock increases from $100 to $200. In Year 5, when the value of the T stock remains $100, P transfers the T stock to S in a transaction to which section 351 applies, with the view described in paragraph (e)(2)(i) of this section. The transfer causes P's basis in the S stock to increase from $100 to $300 and the value of S to increase from $200 to $300. In Year 6, P sells the S stock for $300.

(ii) Under paragraph (e)(2)(ii) of this section, P must reduce the basis in its S stock immediately before the sale to cause recognition of gain in an amount equal to the gain recognition otherwise avoided by reason of the transfer. The amount of this basis reduction is $100, causing a $100 gain to be recognized on the sale.

Example 5. Absence of view. (i) In Year 1, P buys all the stock of T for $100, and T becomes a member of the P group. T has 2 historic assets, asset 1 with a basis of $40 and value of $90, and asset 2 with a basis of $60 and value of $10. In Year 2, T sells asset 1 for $90. Under the investment adjustment system, P's basis in the T stock increases from $100 to $150. Asset 2 is not essential to the operation of T's business, and T distributes asset 2 to P in Year 5 with a view to having the group retain its $50 loss inherent in the asset. Under § 1.1502-13(f)(2), and the application of the principles of this rule in section 267(f), T has a $50 intercompany loss that is deferred. Under § 1.1502-32(b)(3)(iv), the distribution reduces P's basis in the T stock by $10 to $140 in Year 5. In Year 6, P sells all the T stock for $90. Under the acceleration rule of § 1.1502-13(d), and the application of the principles of this rule in section 267(f), T's intercompany loss is ordinarily taken into account immediately before P's sale of the T stock. Assuming that the loss is absorbed by the group, P's basis in T's stock would be reduced from $140 to $90 under §1.1502-32(b)(3)(i), and there would be no gain or loss from the stock disposition. (Alternatively, if the loss is not ab-

Reg. § 1.1502-20(e)(3)

sorbed and the loss is reattributed to P under paragraph (g) of this section, the reattribution would reduce P's basis in T's stock from $140 to $90.)

(ii) A $50 loss is reflected both in T's basis in asset 2 and in P's basis in the T stock. Because the distribution results in the loss with respect to asset 2 being taken into account before the corresponding loss reflected in the T stock, and asset 2 is an historic asset of T, the distribution is not with the view described in paragraph (e)(2) of this section.

Example 6. Extending the time period for dispositions. (i) In Year 1, P buys all the stock of T for $100, and T becomes a member of the P group. T has an asset with a basis of $0 and a value of $100. T sells the asset for $100. Under the investment adjustment system, P's basis in the T stock increases from $100 to $200. At the beginning of Year 5, P transfers to T an asset with a basis of $0 and a value of $100 in a transaction to which section 351 applies, with the view described in paragraph (e)(2)(i) of this section. Within 2 years, P agrees to sell all the stock of T for $200 at the end of Year 7.

(ii) Under paragraph (e)(2)(i) of this section, P's disposition of the T stock at the end of Year 7 is treated as occurring within the 2-year period following P's transfer of the asset to T, because the disposition is pursuant to an agreement reached within 2 years after the transfer. Accordingly, under paragraph (e)(2)(ii) of this section, P must reduce the basis in its T stock by $100 immediately before the sale. This result is reached whether or not the agreement is in writing. P's disposition would also have been treated as occurring within the 2-year period if the disposition were pursuant to an option issued within the period.

(f) *No tiering up of certain adjustments*—(1) *General rule.* If the basis of stock of a subsidiary (S) owned by a [sic] another member (P) is reduced under this section on the deconsolidation of the S stock, no corresponding adjustment is made under § 1.1502-32 to the basis of the stock of P if there is a disposition or deconsolidation of the P stock in the same transaction. If there is a disposition or deconsolidation in the same transaction of less than all the stock of P, appropriate adjustments must be made under § 1.1502-32 with respect to P (and any higher-tier members).

(2) *Example.* The principles of this paragraph (f) are illustrated by the following example.

Example. (i) P, the common parent of a group, owns all the stock of S, S owns all the stock of S1, and S1 owns all the stock of S2. P's basis in the S stock is $100, S's basis in the S1 stock is $100, and S1's basis in the S2 stock is $100. In Year 1, S2 buys all the stock of T for $100. T has an asset with a basis of $0 and a value of $100. In Year 2, T sells the asset for $100. Under the investment adjustment system, the basis of each subsidiary's stock increases from $100 to $200. In Year 6, S sells all the stock of S1 for $100 to A, an individual, and recognizes a loss of $100. S1, S2, and T are not members of a consolidated group immediately after the sale because the new S1 group does not file a consolidated return for its first tax year.

(ii) Under paragraph (a)(1) of this section, no deduction is allowed to S for its loss from the sale of the S1 stock. Under § 1.1502-32(b)(3)(iii), S's disallowed loss is treated as a noncapital, nondeductible expense for Year 6 that reduces P's basis in the S stock. (Under § 1.1502-33, S's earnings and profits for Year 6 are reduced by the amount of S's disallowed loss for earnings and profits purposes and, under § 1.1502-33(b), this reduction is reflected in P's earnings and profits.)

(iii) Under paragraphs (b)(1) and (f)(1) of this section, because the stock of T and S2 are deconsolidated as a result of S's sale of the S1 stock, the basis of their stock must be reduced immediately before the sale from $200 to $100 (the value immediately before the deconsolidation). Under § 1.1502-32(b)(3)(iii), the basis reductions are treated as noncapital, nondeductible expenses for Year 6. Under paragraph (f)(2) of this section, however, because the S2 stock is deconsolidated in the same transaction, the basis reduction to the T stock does not tier up under § 1.1502-32(a)(3). Similarly, because the S1 stock is disposed of in the same transaction, the basis reduction to the S2 stock also does not tier up. (Comparable treatment applies for purposes of earnings and profits under § 1.1502-33.)

(g) *Reattribution of subsidiary's losses to common parent*—(1) *Reattribution rule.* If a member disposes of stock of a subsidiary and the member's loss would be disallowed under paragraph (a)(1) of this section, the common parent may make an irrevocable election to reattribute to itself any portion of the net operating loss carryovers and net capital loss carryovers attributable to the subsidiary (and any lower tier subsidiary) without regard to the order in which they were incurred. The amount reattributed may not exceed the amount of loss that would be disallowed if no election is made under this paragraph (g). For this purpose, the amount of loss that would be disallowed is determined by applying paragraph (c)(1) of this section (without taking into account the requirement under paragraph (c)(3) of this section that a statement be filed) and by not taking

Reg. § 1.1502-20(g)(1)

the reattribution into account. The amount of loss that would be disallowed and the losses that may be reattributed are determined immediately after the disposition, but the reattribution is deemed to be made immediately before the disposition. The common parent succeeds to the reattributed losses as if the losses were succeeded to in a transaction described in section 381(a). Any owner shift of the subsidiary (including any deemed owner shift resulting from section 382(g)(4)(D) or 382(l)(3)) in connection with the disposition is not taken into account under section 382 with respect to the reattributed losses. See § 1.1502-96(d) for rules relating to section 382 and the reattribution of losses under this paragraph (g).

(2) *Insolvency limitation.* If the subsidiary whose losses are to be reattributed, or any higher tier subsidiary, is insolvent within the meaning of section 108(d)(3) at the time of the disposition, losses of the subsidiary may be reattributed only to the extent they exceed the sum of the separate insolvencies of any subsidiaries (taking into account only the subsidiary and its higher tier subsidiaries) that are insolvent. For purposes of determining insolvency, liabilities owed to higher tier members are not taken into account, and stock of a subsidiary that is limited and preferred as to dividends and that is not owned by higher tier members is treated as a liability to the extent of the amount of preferred distributions to which the stock would be entitled if the subsidiary were liquidated on the date of the disposition.

(3) *Examples.* The principles of this paragraph (g) are illustrated by the following examples.

Example 1. Basic reattribution case. (i) P, the common parent of a group, forms S with a $100 contribution. For Year 1, S has a $60 operating loss that is not absorbed and is included in the group's consolidated net operating loss that is carried over under §§ 1.1502-21A or 1.1502-21. Under § 1.1502-32(b)(3)(i), P's basis in the S stock is not reduced to reflect S's loss because the loss is not absorbed. Under § 1.1502-33(b), S's deficit in earnings and profits is reflected in P's earnings and profits even though the loss is not absorbed for tax purposes. During Year 2, S's remaining assets appreciate in value and P sells the S stock for $55. But for an election to reattribute losses under paragraph (g) of this section, P would have a $45 loss from the sale that would be disallowed.

(ii) P elects under paragraph (g)(1) of this section to reattribute to itself $45 of S's losses (the maximum amount permitted). As a result, $45 of the $60 net operating loss carryover attributable to S is reattributed to P. This reattributed loss may be included in the net operating loss carryover to subsequent consolidated return years of the P group. P succeeds to these losses as if the losses were succeeded to in a transaction described in section 381(a) and they retain their character as ordinary losses. The remaining $15 of net operating loss carryover attributable to S is carried over to the first separate return year of S.

(iii) Under § 1.1502-32(b)(3)(iii), the reattribution of $45 of loss is a noncapital, nondeductible expense that reduces P's basis in the S stock from $100 to $55 immediately before the disposition. Consequently, P does not recognize any gain or loss from the disposition.

(iv) Assume that $20 of S's losses arose in Year 1 and $40 in Year 2, and that P elects to reattribute all $40 from Year 2 and $5 from Year 1. P succeeds to these losses as if the losses were succeeded to in a transaction described in section 381(a), and the losses retain their character as ordinary losses arising in Years 1 and 2. The losses continue to be subject to any limitations originally applicable to S, but P succeeds to them and may absorb the losses independently of S. (For example, P's use of the Year 2 losses does not depend on S's use of the Year 1 losses that were not reattributed to P.)

Example 2. Lower tier subsidiary. (i) P, the common parent of a group, forms S with a $100 contribution. S then forms T with a $40 contribution and T borrows $60. For Year 1, S has a $30 operating loss and T has a $55 operating loss. The losses are not absorbed and are included in the group's consolidated net operating loss that is carried over under § 1.1502-21A or 1.1502-21. Under § 1.1502-32(b)(3)(i), P's basis in the S stock, and S's basis in the T stock, are not reduced to reflect the S and T losses because the group is unable to absorb the losses. (Under § 1.1502-33(b), the deficits in earnings and profits of S and T are tiered up for earnings and profits purposes even though not absorbed for tax purposes.) During Year 2, P sells the S stock for $30 ($100 invested, minus S's $30 loss and $40 unrealized loss from its investment in the T stock). But for an election to reattribute losses under paragraph (g) of this section, P would have a $70 loss from the sale, which would be disallowed.

(ii) S's $30 portion of the net operating loss carryover may be reattributed to P under paragraph (g)(1) of this section. Because T is insolvent by $15, paragraph (g)(2) of this section provides that only $40 of its $55 portion of the net operating loss carryover may be reattributed to P under paragraph (g)(1) of this section. There is no limitation, however, on which $40 of T's $55 loss may be reattributed.

Reg. § 1.1502-20(g)(2)

(iii) P elects under paragraph (g)(1) of this section to reattribute to itself $40 of T's losses (the maximum amount permitted). P does not elect, however, to reattribute to itself any of S's losses. As a result, $40 of the $85 net operating loss carryover is reattributed to P. This reattributed loss may be included in the net operating loss carryover to subsequent consolidated return years of the P group. Of the $45 remaining net operating loss carryover, the $15 attributable to T and $30 attributable to S are carried over to their first separate return years.

(iv) Under § 1.1502-32(b)(3)(iii), the reattribution of loss is a noncapital, nondeductible expense that reduces P's basis in the S stock to $60 immediately before the disposition. Consequently, P recognizes only a $30 loss from the disposition of its S stock ($30 sale proceeds and $60 basis), and this loss is disallowed.

Example 3. Separate return limitation year losses. (i) P, the common parent of a group, buys the stock of S for $100. S has a net operating loss carryover of $40 from a separate return limitation year, and assets with a value and basis of $100. The assets of S decline in value by $40, and P sells all the stock of S for $60. But for an election to reattribute losses under this paragraph (g), P would have a $40 loss on the sale of S that would be disallowed.

(ii) S's $40 loss carryover from a separate return limitation year may be reattributed to P under paragraph (g)(1) of this section.

(iii) P elects under paragraph (g)(1) of this section to reattribute to itself S's $40 loss (the maximum amount permitted). Following the reattribution, the loss is included in the net operating loss carryover to subsequent consolidated return years of the P group.

(iv) Under § 1.1502-32(b)(3)(iii), the reattribution of loss is a noncapital, nondeductible expense that reduces P's basis in the S stock to $60 immediately before the disposition. Consequently, P recognizes no gain or loss from the disposition of its S stock. For P's treatment of the $40 reattributed loss, see § 1.1502-1(f).

(4) *Time and manner of making the election*—(i) *In general.* The election described in paragraph (g)(1) of this section must be made in a separate statement entitled "THIS IS AN ELECTION UNDER SECTION 1.1502-20(g)(1) TO REATTRIBUTE LOSSES OF [insert names and employer identification numbers (E.I.N.) of each subsidiary whose losses are reattributed] TO [insert name and employer identification number of common parent]." The statement must include the following information—

(A) For each subsidiary, the amount of each net operating loss and net capital loss, and the year in which each arose, that is reattributed to the common parent;

(B) If a subsidiary ceases to be a member, the name and employer identification number of the person acquiring the subsidiary's stock; and

(C) If the common parent is reattributing to itself all or any part of a section 382 limitation pursuant to § 1.1502-96(d)(5), the information required by paragraph (g)(4)(ii) of this section.

The statement must be signed by the common parent, and by each subsidiary with respect to which loss is reattributed under this paragraph (g) that does not remain a member of the common parent's group immediately following the disposition. The statement must be filed with the group's income tax return for the tax year of the disposition and a copy of the statement must be retained by the subsidiary. If the acquirer is a subsidiary in a consolidated group, the name and employer identification number of the common parent of the group must be included in the statement, and a copy of the statement must also be delivered to the common parent.

(ii) *Reattribution of section 382 limitation.* The information required by this paragraph (g)(4)(ii) is a separate list for each subsidiary (or a separate list for two or more subsidiaries that are members of a loss subgroup whose pre-change subgroup losses are being reattributed) with respect to which an apportionment of a separate section 382 limitation or subgroup section 382 limitation is being made, setting forth—

(A) the name and E.I.N. of the subsidiary (or subsidiaries that were members of a loss subgroup);

(B) A statement entitled "THIS IS AN ELECTION UNDER § 1.1502-96(d)(5) TO APPORTION ALL OR PART OF [insert A SEPARATE or A SUBGROUP or BOTH A SEPARATE AND A SUBGROUP] SECTION 382 LIMITATION TO [insert name and E.I.N. of the common parent]";

(C) The date of the ownership change giving rise to the separate section 382 limitation or subgroup section 382 limitation that is being apportioned;

(D) The amount of the separate (or subgroup) section 382 limitation for the taxable year in which the reattribution occurs (determined without reference to any apportionment under this section or § 1.1502-95(c));

Reg. § 1.1502-20(g)(4)

(E) The amount of each net operating loss carryover or capital loss carryover, and the year in which it arose, of the subsidiary (or subsidiaries) that is subject to the separate section 382 limitation or subgroup section 382 limitation that is being apportioned to the common parent, and the amount of the value element and adjustment element of that limitation that is apportioned to the common parent.

(iii) *Filing of subsidiary's copy of statement.* The subsidiary whose losses are reattributed (or the common parent of any consolidated group that acquires the subsidiary or lower tier subsidiary) must attach its copy of the statement described in paragraph (g)(5)(i) of this section to its income return for the first tax year ending after the due date, including extensions, of the return in which the election required by paragraph (g)(5)(i) of this section is to be filed.

(h) *Effective dates*—(1) *General rule.* Except as otherwise provided in this paragraph (h), this section applies with respect to dispositions and deconsolidations on or after February 1, 1991. For this purpose, dispositions deferred under § 1.1502-13 are deemed to occur at the time the deferred gain or loss is taken into account unless the stock was deconsolidated before February 1, 1991. If stock of a subsidiary became worthless during a taxable year including February 1, 1991, the disposition with respect to the stock is treated as occurring on the date the stock became worthless.

(2) *Election to accelerate effective date*—(i) *In general.* A group may make an irrevocable election to apply this section to all its members, instead of § 1.337(d)-2, with respect to all dispositions and deconsolidations on or after November 19, 1990.

(ii) *Time and manner of making the election—in general.* The election described in paragraph (h)(2)(i) of this section must be made in a separate statement entitled "This is an election under section 1.1502-20(h)(2) to accelerate the application of § 1.1502-20 to the consolidated group of which [insert name and employer identification number of common parent] is the common parent." The statement must be signed by the common parent and filed with the group's income tax return for the tax year of the first disposition or deconsolidation to which the election applies. If the separate statement required under this paragraph (h)(2)(ii) is to be filed with a return the due date (including extensions) of which is before April 16, 1991, the statement may be filed with an amended return for the year of the disposition or deconsolidation. Any other filings required under this § 1.1502-20, such as the statement required under § 1.1502-20(c)(3), which ordinarily cannot be made with an amended return, must be made at such time and in such manner as permitted by the Commissioner.

(3) *Binding contract rule.* For purposes of this paragraph (h), if a disposition or deconsolidation is pursuant to a binding written contract entered into before March 9, 1990, and in continuous effect until the disposition or deconsolidation, the date the contract became binding is treated as the date of the disposition or deconsolidation.

(4) *Application of § 1.1502-20T to certain transactions*—(i) *In general.* If a group files the certification described in paragraph (h)(4)(ii) of this section, it may apply § 1.1502-20T (as contained in the CFR edition revised as of April 1, 1990), to all of its members with respect to all dispositions and deconsolidations by the certifying group to which § 1.1502-20T otherwise applied by its terms occurring—

(A) On or after March 9, 1990 (but only if not pursuant to a binding contract described in § 1.337(d)-1T(e)(2) (as contained in the CFR edition revised as of April 1, 1990) that was entered into before March 9, 1990); and

(B) Before November 19, 1990 (or thereafter, if pursuant to a binding contract described in § 1.1502-20T(g)(3) that was entered into on or after March 9, 1990 and before November 19, 1990).

The certification under this paragraph (h)(4)(i) with respect to the application of § 1.1502-20T to any transaction described in this paragraph (h)(4)(i) may not be withdrawn and, if the certification is filed, § 1.1502-20T must be applied to all such transactions on all returns (including amended returns) on which such transactions are included.

(ii) *Time and manner of filing certification.* The certification described in paragraph (h)(4)(i) of this section must be made in a separate statement entitled "[insert name and employer identification number of common parent] hereby certifies under section 1.1502-20(h)(4) that the group of which it is the common parent is applying § 1.1502-20T to all transactions to which that section otherwise applied by its terms." The statement must be signed by the common parent and filed with the group's income tax return for the taxable year of the first disposition or deconsolidation to which the certification applies. If the separate statement required under this paragraph (h)(4) is to be filed with a return the due date (including extensions) of which is before November 16, 1991, the statement may be filed with an amended return for the year of the disposition

Reg. § 1.1502-20(h)(1)

or deconsolidation that is filed within 180 days after September 13, 1991. Any other filings required under § 1.1502-20T, such as the statement required under § 1.1502-20T(f)(5), may be made with the amended return, regardless of whether § 1.1502-20T permits such filing by amended return.

(5) *Cross reference.* For transitional loss limitation rules, see §§ 1.337(d)-1 and 1.337(d)-2. [Reg. § 1.1502-20.]

☐ [T.D. 8364, 9-13-91. Amended by T.D. 8560, 8-12-94; T.D. 8597, 7-12-95; T.D. 8677, 6-26-96; T.D. 8823, 6-25-99 and T.D. 8824, 6-25-99.]

→ *Caution: Reg. § 1.1502-21, below, is generally effective for tax years for which the consolidated return due date is after June 25, 1999.*←

[Reg. § 1.1502-21]

§ 1.1502-21. **Net operating losses.**—(a) *Consolidated net operating loss deduction.* The consolidated net operating loss deduction (or CNOL deduction) for any consolidated return year is the aggregate of the net operating loss carryovers and carrybacks to the year. The net operating loss carryovers and carrybacks consist of—

(1) Any CNOLs (as defined in paragraph (e) of this section) of the consolidated group; and

(2) Any net operating losses of the members arising in separate return years.

(b) *Net operating loss carryovers and carrybacks to consolidated return and separate return years.* Net operating losses of members arising during a consolidated return year are taken into account in determining the group's CNOL under paragraph (e) of this section for that year. Losses taken into account in determining the CNOL may be carried to other taxable years (whether consolidated or separate) only under this paragraph (b).

(1) *Carryovers and carrybacks generally.* The net operating loss carryovers and carrybacks to a taxable year are determined under the principles of section 172 and this section. Thus, losses permitted to be absorbed in a consolidated return year generally are absorbed in the order of the taxable years in which they arose, and losses carried from taxable years ending on the same date, and which are available to offset consolidated taxable income for the year, generally are absorbed on a pro rata basis. Additional rules provided under the Internal Revenue Code or regulations also apply. See, e.g., section 382(1)(2)(B) (if losses are carried from the same taxable year, losses subject to limitation under section 382 are absorbed before losses that are not subject to limitation under section 382). See *Example 2* of paragraph (c)(1)(iii) of this section for an illustration of pro rata absorption of losses subject to a SRLY limitation.

(2) *Carryovers and carrybacks of CNOLs to separate return years*—(i) *In general.* If any CNOL that is attributable to a member may be carried to a separate return year of the member, the amount of the CNOL that is attributable to the member is apportioned to the member (apportioned loss) and carried to the separate return year. If carried back to a separate return year, the apportioned loss may not be carried back to an equivalent, or earlier, consolidated return year of the group; if carried over to a separate return year, the apportioned loss may not be carried over to an equivalent, or later, consolidated return year of the group. For rules permitting the reattribution of losses of a subsidiary to the common parent when loss is disallowed on the disposition of subsidiary stock, see § 1.1502-20(g).

(ii) *Special rules*—(A) *Year of departure from group.* If a corporation ceases to be a member during a consolidated return year, net operating loss carryovers attributable to the corporation are first carried to the consolidated return year, and only the amount so attributable that is not absorbed by the group in that year is carried to the corporation's first separate return year. For rules concerning a member departing a subgroup, see paragraph (c)(2)(vii) of this section.

(B) *Offspring rule.* In the case of a member that has been a member continuously since its organization (determined without regard to whether the member is a successor to any other corporation), the CNOL attributable to the member is included in the carrybacks to consolidated return years before the member's existence. If the group did not file a consolidated return for a carryback year, the loss may be carried back to a separate return year of the common parent under paragraph (b)(2)(i) of this section, but only if the common parent was not a member of a different consolidated group or of an affiliated group filing separate returns for the year to which the loss is carried or any subsequent year in the carryback period. Following an acquisition described in § 1.1502-75(d)(2) or (3), references to the common parent are to the corporation that was the common parent immediately before the acquisition.

(iii) *Equivalent years.* Taxable years are equivalent if they bear the same numerical relationship to the consolidated return year in which a CNOL arises, counting forward or backward from the year of the loss. For example, in the case of a member's third taxable year (which was a

Reg. § 1.1502-21(b)(2)

Consolidated Returns

See p. 20,601 for regulations not amended to reflect law changes

→ *Caution: Reg. § 1.1502-21, below, is generally effective for tax years for which the consolidated return due date is after June 25, 1999.* ←

separate return year) that preceded the consolidated return year in which the loss arose, the equivalent year is the third consolidated return year preceding the consolidated return year in which the loss arose. See paragraph (b)(3)(iii) of this section for certain short taxable years that are disregarded in making this determination.

(iv) *Amount of CNOL attributable to a member.* The amount of a CNOL that is attributable to a member is determined by a fraction the numerator of which is the separate net operating loss of the member for the year of the loss and the denominator of which is the sum of the separate net operating losses for that year of all members having such losses. For this purpose, the separate net operating loss of a member is determined by computing the CNOL by reference to only the member's items of income, gain, deduction, and loss, including the member's losses and deductions actually absorbed by the group in the taxable year (whether or not absorbed by the member).

(v) *Examples.* For purposes of the examples in this section, unless otherwise stated, all groups file consolidated returns, all corporations have calendar taxable years, the facts set forth the only corporate activity, value means fair market value and the adjusted basis of each asset equals its value, all transactions are with unrelated persons, and the application of any limitation or threshold under section 382 is disregarded. The principles of this paragraph (b)(2) are illustrated by the following examples:

Example 1. Offspring rule. (i) During Year 1, Individual A forms P and T, and they each file a separate return. P forms S on March 15 of Year 2, and P and S file a consolidated return. P acquires all the stock of T from Individual A at the beginning of Year 3, and T becomes a member of the P group. P's acquisition of T is not an ownership change within the meaning of section 382. P, S, and T sustain a $1,100 CNOL in Year 3 and, under paragraph (b)(2)(iv) of this section, the loss is attributable $200 to P, $300 to S, and $600 to T.

(ii) Of the $1,100 CNOL in Year 3, the $500 amount of the CNOL that is attributable to P and S ($200 + $300) may be carried to P's separate return in Year 1. Even though S was not in existence in Year 1, the $300 amount of the CNOL attributable to S may be carried back to P's separate return in Year 1 because S (unlike T) has been a member of the P group since its organization and P is a qualified parent under paragraph (b)(2)(ii)(B) of this section. To the extent not absorbed in that year, the loss may then be carried to the P group's return in Year 2. The $600 amount of the CNOL attributable to T is a net operating loss carryback to T's separate return in Year 1, and if not absorbed in Year 1, then to Year 2.

Example 2. Departing members. (i) The facts are the same as in *Example 1*. In addition, on June 15 of Year 4, P sells all the stock of T. The P group's consolidated return for Year 4 includes the income of T through June 15. T files a separate return for the period from June 16 through December 31.

(ii) $600 of the Year 3 CNOL attributable to T is apportioned to T and is carried back to its separate return in Year 1. To the extent the $600 is not absorbed in T's separate return in Year 1 or Year 2, it is carried to the consolidated return in Year 4 before being carried to T's separate return in Year 4. Any portion of the loss not absorbed in T's Year 1 or Year 2 or in the P group's Year 4 is then carried to T's separate return in Year 4.

Example 3. Offspring rule following acquisition. (i) Individual A owns all of the stock of P, the common parent of a consolidated group. In Year 1, B, an individual unrelated to Individual A, forms T. P acquires all of the stock of T at the beginning of Year 3, and T becomes a member of the P group. The P group has $200 of consolidated taxable income in Year 2, and $300 of consolidated taxable income in Year 3 (computed without regard to the CNOL deduction). At the beginning of Year 4, T forms a subsidiary, Y, in a transaction described in section 351. The P group has a $300 consolidated net operating loss in Year 4, and under paragraph (b)(2)(iv) of this section, the loss is attributable entirely to Y.

(ii) Even though Y was not in existence in Year 2, $300, the amount of the consolidated net operating loss attributable to Y, may be carried back to the P group's Year 2 consolidated return under paragraph (b)(2)(ii)(B) of this section because Y has been a member of the P group since its organization. To the extent not absorbed in that year, the loss may then be carried to the P group's consolidated return in Year 3.

(3) *Special rules*—(i) *Election to relinquish carryback.* A group may make an irrevocable election under section 172(b)(3) to relinquish the entire carryback period with respect to a CNOL for any consolidated return year. Except as provided in paragraph (b)(3)(ii)(B) of this section, the election may not be made separately for any member (whether or not it remains a member), and must be made in a separate statement entitled "THIS

Reg. § 1.1502-21(b)(3)

Consolidated Returns

See p. 20,601 for regulations not amended to reflect law changes

→ *Caution: Reg. § 1.1502-21, below, is generally effective for tax years for which the consolidated return due date is after June 25, 1999.*←

IS AN ELECTION UNDER SECTION 1.1502-21(b)(3)(i) TO WAIVE THE ENTIRE CARRYBACK PERIOD PURSUANT TO SECTION 172(b)(3) FOR THE [insert consolidated return year] CNOLs OF THE CONSOLIDATED GROUP OF WHICH [insert name and employer identification number of common parent] IS THE COMMON PARENT." The statement must be signed by the common parent and filed with the group's income tax return for the consolidated return year in which the loss arises.

(ii) *Special elections*—(A) *Groups that include insolvent financial institutions.* For rules applicable to relinquishing the entire carryback period with respect to losses attributable to insolvent financial institutions, see § 301.6402-7 of this chapter.

(B) *Acquisition of member from another consolidated group.* If one or more members of a consolidated group becomes a member of another consolidated group, the acquiring group may make an irrevocable election to relinquish, with respect to all consolidated net operating losses attributable to the member, the portion of the carryback period for which the corporation was a member of another group, provided that any other corporation joining the acquiring group that was affiliated with the member immediately before it joined the acquiring group is also included in the waiver. This election is not a yearly election and applies to all losses that would otherwise be subject to a carryback to a former group under section 172. The election must be made in a separate statement entitled "THIS IS AN ELECTION UNDER SECTION 1.1502-21(b)(3)(ii)(B) TO WAIVE THE PRE- [insert first taxable year for which the member (or members) was not a member of another group] CARRYBACK PERIOD FOR THE CNOLs attributable to [insert names and employer identification number of members]." The statement must be filed with the acquiring consolidated group's original income tax return for the year the corporation (or corporations) became a member, and it must be signed by the common parent and each of the members to which it applies.

(iii) *Short years in connection with transactions to which section 381(a) applies.* If a member distributes or transfers assets to a corporation that is a member immediately after the distribution or transfer in a transaction to which section 381(a) applies, the transaction does not cause the distributor or transferor to have a short year within the consolidated return year of the group in which the transaction occurred that is counted as a separate year for purposes of determining the years to which a net operating loss may be carried.

(iv) *Special status losses.* [Reserved]

(c) *Limitations on net operating loss carryovers and carrybacks from separate return limitation years*—(1) *SRLY limitation*—(i) *General rule.* Except as provided in paragraph (g) of this section (relating to an overlap with section 382), the aggregate of the net operating loss carryovers and carrybacks of a member arising (or treated as arising) in SRLYs that are included in the CNOL deductions for all consolidated return years of the group under paragraph (a) of this section may not exceed the aggregate consolidated taxable income for all consolidated return years of the group determined by reference to only the member's items of income, gain, deduction, and loss. For this purpose—

(A) Consolidated taxable income is computed without regard to CNOL deductions;

(B) Consolidated taxable income takes into account the member's losses and deductions (including capital losses) actually absorbed by the group in consolidated return years (whether or not absorbed by the member);

(C) In computing consolidated taxable income, the consolidated return years of the group include only those years, including the year to which the loss is carried, that the member has been continuously included in the group's consolidated return but exclude—

(*1*) For carryovers, any years ending after the year to which the loss is carried; and

(*2*) For carrybacks, any years ending after the year in which the loss arose; and

(D) The treatment under § 1.1502-15 of a built-in loss as a hypothetical net operating loss carryover in the year recognized is solely for purposes of determining the limitation under this paragraph (c) with respect to the loss in that year and not for any other purpose. Thus, for purposes of determining consolidated taxable income for any other losses, a built-in loss allowed under this section in the year it arises is taken into account.

(ii) *Losses treated as arising in SRLYs.* If a net operating loss carryover or carryback did not arise in a SRLY but is attributable to a built-in loss (as defined under § 1.1502-15), the carryover or carryback is treated for purposes of this paragraph (c) as arising in a SRLY if the built-in loss was not allowed, after application of the SRLY limitation, in the year it arose. For an

Reg. § 1.1502-21(c)

→ *Caution: Reg. § 1.1502-21, below, is generally effective for tax years for which the consolidated return due date is after June 25, 1999.*←

illustration, see § 1.1502-15(d), *Example 5*. But see § 1.1502-15(g)(1).

(iii) *Examples.* The principles of this paragraph (c)(1) are illustrated by the following examples:

Example 1. Determination of SRLY limitation. (i) Individual A owns P. In Year 1, Individual A forms T, and T sustains a $100 net operating loss that is carried forward. P acquires all the stock of T at the beginning of Year 2, and T becomes a member of the P group. The P group has $300 of consolidated taxable income in Year 2 (computed without regard to the CNOL deduction). Such consolidated taxable income would be $70 if determined by reference to only T's items.

(ii) T's $100 net operating loss carryover from Year 1 arose in a SRLY. See § 1.1502-1(f)(2)(iii). P's acquisition of T was not an ownership change as defined by section 382(g). Thus, the $100 net operating loss carryover is subject to the SRLY limitation in paragraph (c)(1) of this section. The SRLY limitation for Year 2 is consolidated taxable income determined by reference to only T's items, or $70. Thus, $70 of the loss is included under paragraph (a) of this section in the P group's CNOL deduction for Year 2.

(iii) The facts are the same as in paragraph (i) of this *Example 1*, except that such consolidated taxable income (computed without regard to the CNOL deduction and by reference to only T's items) for Year 2 is a loss (a CNOL) of $370. Because the SRLY limitation may not exceed the consolidated taxable income determined by reference to only T's items, and such items aggregate to a CNOL, T's $100 net operating loss carryover from Year 1 is not allowed under the SRLY limitation in Year 2. Moreover, if consolidated taxable income (computed without regard to the CNOL deduction and by reference to only T's items) did not exceed $370 in Year 3, the carryover would still be restricted under paragraph (c) of this section in Year 3, because the aggregate consolidated taxable income for all consolidated return years of the group computed by reference to only T's items would not be a positive amount.

Example 2. Net operating loss carryovers. (i) In Year 1, Individual A forms P, and P sustains a $40 net operating loss that is carried forward. P has no income in Year 2. Individual A also owns T which sustains a net operating loss of $50 in Year 2 that is carried forward. P acquires the stock of T from Individual A during Year 3, but T is not a member of the P group for each day of the year. P and T file separate returns and sustain net operating losses of $120 and $60, respectively, for Year 3. The P group files consolidated returns beginning in Year 4. During Year 4, the P group has $160 of consolidated taxable income (computed without regard to the CNOL deduction). Such consolidated taxable income would be $70 if determined by reference to only T's items. These results are summarized as follows:

	Separate Year 1	Separate Year 2	Separate/ Affiliated Year 3	Consolidated Year 4
P	$(40)	$ 0	$(120)	$ 90
T	0	(50)	(60)	70
CTI				160

(ii) P's Year 1, Year 2, and Year 3 are not SRLYs with respect to the P group. See § 1.1502-1(f)(2)(i). Thus, P's $40 net operating loss arising in Year 1 and $120 net operating loss arising in Year 3 are not subject to the SRLY limitation under paragraph (c) of this section. Under the principles of section 172, paragraph (b) of this section requires that the loss arising in Year 1 be the first loss absorbed by the P group in Year 4. Absorption of this loss leaves $120 of the group's consolidated taxable income available for offset by other loss carryovers.

(iii) T's Year 2 and Year 3 are SRLYs with respect to the P group. See § 1.1502-1(f)(2)(ii). P's acquisition of T was not an ownership change as defined by section 382(g). Thus, T's $50 net operating loss arising in Year 2 and $60 net operating loss arising in Year 3 are subject to the SRLY limitation. Under paragraph (c)(1) of this section, the SRLY limitation for Year 4 is $70, and under paragraph (b) of this section, T's $50 loss from Year 2 must be included under paragraph (a) of this section in the P group's CNOL deduction for Year 4. The absorption of this loss leaves $70 of the group's consolidated taxable income available for offset by other loss carryovers.

(iv) P and T each carry over net operating losses to Year 4 from a taxable year ending on the same date (Year 3). The losses carried over from Year 3 total $180. Under paragraph (b) of this

Reg. § 1.1502-21(c)

Consolidated Returns

See p. 20,601 for regulations not amended to reflect law changes

→ **Caution: Reg. § 1.1502-21, below, is generally effective for tax years for which the consolidated return due date is after June 25, 1999.** ←

section, the losses carried over from Year 3 are absorbed on a pro rata basis, even though one arises in a SRLY and the other does not. However, the group cannot absorb more than $20 of T's $60 net operating loss arising in Year 3 because its $70 SRLY limitation for Year 4 is reduced by T's $50 Year 2 SRLY loss already included in the CNOL deduction for Year 4. Thus, the absorption of Year 3 losses is as follows:

Amount of P's Year 3 losses absorbed = $120 ÷ ($120 + $20) × $70 = $60.

Amount of T's Year 3 losses absorbed = $20 ÷ ($120 + $20) × $70 = $10.

(v) The absorption of $10 of T's Year 3 loss further reduces T's SRLY limitation to $10 ($70 of initial SRLY limitation, reduced by the $60 net operating loss already included in the CNOL deductions for Year 4 under paragraph (a) of this section).

(vi) P carries its remaining $60 Year 3 net operating loss and T carries its remaining $50 Year 3 net operating loss over to Year 5. Assume that, in Year 5, the P group has $90 of consolidated taxable income (computed without regard to the CNOL deduction). The group's CTI determined by reference to only T's items is a CNOL of $4. For Year 5, the CNOL deduction is $66, which includes $60 of P's Year 3 loss and $6 of T's Year 3 loss (the aggregate consolidated taxable income for Years 4 and 5 determined by reference to T's items, or $66, reduced by T's SRLY losses actually absorbed by the group in Year 4, or $60).

Example 3. Net operating loss carrybacks. (i) P owns all of the stock of S and T. The members of the P group contribute the following to the consolidated taxable income of the P group for Years 1, 2, and 3:

	Year 1	Year 2	Year 3	Total
P	$100	$60	$80	$240
S	20	20	30	70
T	30	10	(50)	(10)
CTI	150	90	60	300

(ii) P sells all of the stock of T to Individual A at the beginning of Year 4. For its Year 4 separate return year, T has a net operating loss of $30.

(iii) T's Year 4 is a SRLY with respect to the P group. See § 1.1502-1(f)(1). T's $30 net operating loss carryback to the P group from Year 4 is not allowed under paragraph (c) of this section to be included in the CNOL deduction under paragraph (a) of this section for Year 1, 2, or 3, because the P group's consolidated taxable income would not be a positive amount if determined by reference to only T's items for all consolidated return years through Year 4 (without regard to the $30 net operating loss). The $30 loss is carried forward to T's Year 5 and succeeding taxable years as provided under the Internal Revenue Code.

Example 4. Computation of SRLY limitation for built-in losses treated as net operating loss carryovers. (i) Individual A owns P. In Year 1, Individual A forms T by contributing $300 and T sustains a $100 net operating loss. During Year 2, T's assets decline in value by $100. At the beginning of Year 3, P acquires all the stock of T from Individual A, and T becomes a member of the P group in a transaction that does not result in an ownership change under section 382(g). At the time of the acquisition, T has a $100 net unrealized built-in loss, which exceeds the threshold requirements of section 382(h)(3)(B). During Year 3, T recognizes its unrealized loss as a $100 ordinary loss. The members of the P group contribute the following to the consolidated taxable income of the P group for Years 3 and 4 (computed without regard to T's recognition of its unrealized loss and any CNOL deduction under this section):

	Year 3	Year 4	Total
P group (without T)	$100	$100	$200
T	$60	$40	$100
CTI	$160	$140	$300

(ii) Under § 1.1502-15(a), T's $100 of ordinary loss in Year 3 constitutes a built-in loss that is subject to the SRLY limitation under paragraph (c) of this section. The amount of the limitation is determined by treating the deduction as a net operating loss carryover from a SRLY. The built-in loss is therefore subject to a $60 SRLY limitation for Year 3. The built-in loss is treated as a net operating loss carryover solely for purposes of determining the extent to which the loss

Reg. § 1.1502-21(c)

56,804   **Consolidated Returns**

See p. 20,601 for regulations not amended to reflect law changes

→ *Caution: Reg. § 1.1502-21, below, is generally effective for tax years for which the consolidated return due date is after June 25, 1999.*←

is not allowed by reason of the SRLY limitation, and for all other purposes the loss remains a loss arising in Year 3. Consequently, under paragraph (b) of this section, the $60 allowed under the SRLY limitation is absorbed by the P group before T's $100 net operating loss carryover from Year 1 is allowed.

(iii) Under § 1.1502-15(a), the $40 balance of the built-in loss that is not allowed in Year 3 because of the SRLY limitation is treated as a $40 net operating loss arising in Year 3 that is subject to the SRLY limitation because, under paragraph (c)(1)(ii) of this section, Year 3 is treated as a SRLY, and is carried to other years in accordance with the rules of paragraph (b) of this section. The SRLY limitation for Year 4 is the P group's consolidated taxable income for Year 3 and Year 4 determined by reference to only T's items and without regard to the group's CNOL deductions ($60 + $40), reduced by T's loss actually absorbed by the group in Year 3 ($60). The SRLY limitation for Year 4 is $40.

(iv) Under paragraph (c) of this section and the principles of section 172(b), $40 of T's $100 net operating loss carryover from Year 1 is included in the CNOL deduction under paragraph (a) of this section in Year 4.

Example 5. Dual SRLY registers and accounting for SRLY losses actually absorbed. (i) In Year 1, T sustains a $100 net operating loss and a $50 net capital loss. At the beginning of Year 2, T becomes a member of the P group in a transaction that does not result in an ownership change under section 382(g). Both of T's carryovers from Year 1 are subject to SRLY limits under this paragraph (c) and § 1.1502-22(c). The members of the P group contribute the following to the consolidated taxable income for Years 2 and 3 (computed without regard to T's CNOL deduction under this section or net capital loss carryover under § 1.1502-22):

	P	T
Year 1 (SRLY)		
Ordinary		(100)
Capital		(50)
Year 2		
Ordinary	30	60
Capital	0	(20)
Year 3		
Ordinary	10	40
Capital	0	30

(ii) For Year 2, the group computes separate SRLY limits for each of T's SRLY carryovers from Year 1. The group determines its ability to use its capital loss carryover before it determines its ability to use its ordinary loss carryover. Under section 1212, because the group has no Year 2 capital gain, it cannot absorb any capital losses in Year 2. T's Year 1 net capital loss and the group's Year 2 consolidated net capital loss (all of which is attributable to T) are carried over to Year 3.

(iii) Under this section, the aggregate amount of T's $100 net operating loss carryover from Year 1 that may be included in the CNOL deduction of the group for Year 2 may not exceed $60—the amount of the consolidated taxable income computed by reference only to T's items, including losses and deductions to the extent actually absorbed (i.e., $60 of T's ordinary income for Year 2). Thus, the group may include $60 of T's ordinary loss carryover from Year 1 in its Year 2 CNOL deduction. T carries over its remaining $40 of its Year 1 loss to Year 3.

(iv) For Year 3, the group again computes separate SRLY limits for each of T's SRLY carryovers from Year 1. The group has consolidated net capital gain (without taking into account a net capital loss carryover deduction) of $30. Under § 1.1502-22(c), the aggregate amount of T's $50 capital loss carryover from Year 1 that may be included in computing the group's consolidated net capital gain for all years of the group (here Years 2 and 3) may not exceed $30 (the aggregate consolidated net capital gain computed by reference only to T's items, including losses and deductions actually absorbed (i.e., $30 of capital gain in Year 3)). Thus, the group may include $30 of T's Year 1 capital loss carryover in its computation of consolidated net capital gain for Year 3, which offsets the group's capital gains for Year 3. T carries over its remaining $20 of its Year 1 loss to

Reg. § 1.1502-21(c)

→ **Caution: Reg. § 1.1502-21, below, is generally effective for tax years for which the consolidated return due date is after June 25, 1999.** ←

Year 4. The group carries over the Year 2 consolidated net capital loss to Year 4.

(v) Under this section, the aggregate amount of T's net operating loss carryover from Year 1 that may be included in the CNOL deduction of the group for Years 2 and 3 may not exceed $100, which is the amount of the aggregate consolidated taxable income for Years 2 and 3 determined by reference only to T's items, including losses and deductions actually absorbed (i.e., $60 of ordinary income in Year 2 plus $40 of ordinary income, $30 of capital gain, and $30 of SRLY capital losses actually absorbed in Year 3). The group included $60 of T's ordinary loss carryover in its Year 2 CNOL deduction. It may include the remaining $40 of the carryover in its Year 3 CNOL deduction.

(2) *SRLY subgroup limitation.* In the case of a net operating loss carryover or carryback for which there is a SRLY subgroup, the principles of paragraph (c)(1) of this section apply to the SRLY subgroup, and not separately to its members. Thus, the contribution to consolidated taxable income and the net operating loss carryovers and carrybacks arising (or treated as arising) in SRLYs that are included in the CNOL deductions for all consolidated return years of the group under paragraph (a) of this section are based on the aggregate amounts of income, gain, deduction, and loss of the members of the SRLY subgroup for the relevant consolidated return years (as provided in paragraph (c)(1)(i)(C) of this section). For an illustration of aggregate amounts during the relevant consolidated return years following the year in which a member of a SRLY subgroup ceases to be a member of the group, see paragraph (c)(2)(viii) *Example 4* of this section. A SRLY subgroup may exist only for a carryover or carryback arising in a year that is not a SRLY (and is not treated as a SRLY under paragraph (c)(1)(ii) of this section) with respect to another group (the former group), whether or not the group is a consolidated group, or for a carryover that was subject to the overlap rule described in paragraph (g) of this section or § 1.1502-15(g) with respect to another group (the former group). A separate SRLY subgroup is determined for each such carryover or carryback. A consolidated group may include more than one SRLY subgroup and a member may be a member of more than one SRLY subgroup. Solely for purposes of determining the members of a SRLY subgroup with respect to a loss:

(i) *Carryovers.* In the case of a carryover, the SRLY subgroup is composed of the member carrying over the loss (the loss member) and each other member that was a member of the former group that becomes a member of the group at the same time as the loss member. A member remains a member of the SRLY subgroup until it ceases to be affiliated with the loss member. The aggregate determination described in paragraph (c)(1) of this section and this paragraph (c)(2) includes the amounts of income, gain, deduction, and loss of each member of the SRLY subgroup for the consolidated return years during which it remains a member of the SRLY subgroup. For an illustration of the aggregate determination of a SRLY subgroup, see paragraph (c)(2)(viii) *Example 2* of this section.

(ii) *Carrybacks.* In the case of a carryback, the SRLY subgroup is composed of the member carrying back the loss (the loss member) and each other member of the group from which the loss is carried back that has been continuously affiliated with the loss member from the year to which the loss is carried through the year in which the loss arises.

(iii) *Built-in losses.* In the case of a built-in loss, the SRLY subgroup is composed of the member recognizing the loss (the loss member) and each other member that was part of the subgroup with respect to the loss determined under § 1.1502-15(c)(2) immediately before the members became members of the group. The principles of paragraphs (c)(2)(i) and (ii) of this section apply to determine the SRLY subgroup for the built-in loss that is, under paragraph (c)(1)(ii) of this section, treated as arising in a SRLY with respect to the group in which the loss is recognized. For this purpose and as the context requires, a reference in paragraphs (c)(2)(i) and (ii) of this section to a group or former group is a reference to the subgroup determined under § 1.1502-15(c)(2).

(iv) *Principal purpose of avoiding or increasing a SRLY limitation.* The members composing a SRLY subgroup are not treated as a SRLY subgroup if any of them is formed, acquired, or availed of with a principal purpose of avoiding the application of, or increasing any limitation under, this paragraph (c). Any member excluded from a SRLY subgroup, if excluded with a principal purpose of so avoiding or increasing any SRLY limitation, is treated as included in the SRLY subgroup.

(v) *Coordination with other limitations.* This paragraph (c) (2) does not allow a net operating loss to offset income to the extent inconsistent with other limitations or restrictions on the use of

Reg. § 1.1502-21(c)(2)

→ Caution: Reg. § 1.1502-21, below, is generally effective for tax years for which the consolidated return due date is after June 25, 1999.←

losses, such as a limitation based on the nature or activities of members. For example, any dual consolidated loss may not reduce the taxable income to an extent greater than that allowed under section 1503(d) and § 1.1503-2. See also § 1.1502-47(q) (relating to preemption of rules for life-nonlife groups).

(vi) *Anti-duplication.* If the same item of income or deduction could be taken into account more than once in determining a limitation under this paragraph (c), or in a manner inconsistent with any other provision of the Internal Revenue Code or regulations incorporating this paragraph (c), the item of income or deduction is taken into account only once and in such manner that losses are absorbed in accordance with the ordering rules in paragraph (b) of this section and the underlying purposes of this section.

(vii) *Corporations that leave a SRLY subgroup.* If a loss member ceases to be affiliated with a SRLY subgroup, the amount of the member's remaining SRLY loss from a specific year is determined by multiplying the aggregate of the unabsorbed net operating loss carryovers of the SRLY subgroup from that year by a fraction, the numerator of which is the net operating loss carryover for that year that the member leaving the subgroup had when it became a member of the group, and the denominator of which is the aggregate of the net operating loss carryovers of the members of the SRLY subgroup for that year when they joined the group. The unabsorbed net operating loss carryovers of the SRLY subgroup are those carryovers that have not been absorbed by the group as of the end of the taxable year in which the loss member leaves the group.

(viii) *Examples.* The principles of this paragraph (c)(2) are illustrated by the following examples:

Example 1. Members of SRLY subgroups. (i) Individual A owns all of the stock of P, S, T, and M. P and M are each the common parent of a consolidated group. During Year 1, P sustains a $50 net operating loss. At the beginning of Year 2, P acquires all the stock of S at a time when the aggregate basis of S's assets exceeds their aggregate value by $70 and S becomes a member of the P group. At the beginning of Year 3, P acquires all the stock of T, T has a $60 net operating loss carryover at the time of the acquisition, and T becomes a member of the P group. During Year 4, S forms S1 and T forms T1, each by contributing assets with built-in gains which are, in the aggregate, material. S1 and T1 become members of the P group. During Year 7, M acquires all of the stock of P, and the members of the P group become members of the M group for the balance of Year 7. The $50 and $60 loss carryovers of P and T are carried to Year 7 of the M group, and the value and basis of S's assets did not change after it became a member of the former P group. None of the transactions described above resulted in an ownership change under section 382(g).

(ii) Under paragraph (c)(2) of this section, a separate SRLY subgroup is determined for each loss carryover and built-in loss. In the P group, P's $50 loss carryover is not treated as arising in a SRLY. See § 1.1502-1(f). Consequently, the carryover is not subject to limitation under paragraph (c) of this section in the P group.

(iii) In the M group, P's $50 loss carryover is treated as arising in a SRLY and is subject to the limitation under paragraph (c) of this section. A SRLY subgroup with respect to that loss is composed of members which were members of the P group, the group as to which the loss was not a SRLY. The SRLY subgroup is composed of P, the member carrying over the loss, and each other member of the P group that became a member of the M group at the same time as P. A member of the SRLY subgroup remains a member until it ceases to be affiliated with P. For Year 7, the SRLY subgroup is composed of P, S, T, S1, and T1.

(iv) In the P group, S's $70 unrealized loss, if recognized within the 5-year recognition period after S becomes a member of the P group, is subject to limitation under paragraph (c) of this section. See § 1.1502-15 and paragraph (c)(1)(ii) of this section. Because S was not continuously affiliated with P, T, or T1 for 60 consecutive months prior to joining the P group, these corporations cannot be included in a SRLY subgroup with respect to S's unrealized loss in the P group. See paragraph (c)(2)(iii) of this section. As a successor to S, S1 is included in a subgroup with S in the P group, and because 100 percent of S1's stock is owned directly by corporations that were members of the SRLY subgroup when the members of the SRLY subgroup became members of the P group, its net positive income is not excluded from the consolidated taxable income of the P group that may be offset by the built-in loss. See paragraph (f) of this section.

(v) In the M group, S's $70 unrealized loss, if recognized within the 5-year recognition period after S becomes a member of the M group, is subject to limitation under paragraph (c) of this section. Prior to becoming a member of the M group, S had been continuously affiliated with P

Reg. § 1.1502-21(c)(2)

→ **Caution: Reg. § 1.1502-21, below, is generally effective for tax years for which the consolidated return due date is after June 25, 1999.** ←

(but not T or T1) for 60 consecutive months and S1 is a successor that has remained continuously affiliated with S. Those members had a net unrealized built-in loss immediately before they became members of the group under § 1.1502-15(c). Consequently, in Year 7, S, S1, and P compose a subgroup in the M group with respect to S's unrealized loss. Because S1 was a member of the SRLY subgroup when it became a member of the M group and also because 100 percent of S1's stock is owned directly by corporations that were members of the SRLY subgroup when the members of the SRLY subgroup became members of the M group its net positive income is not excluded from the consolidated taxable income of the M group that may be offset by the recognized built-in loss. See paragraph (f) of this section.

(vi) In the P group, T's $60 loss carryover arose in a SRLY and is subject to limitation under paragraph (c) of this section. P, S, and S1 were not members of the group in which T's loss arose and T's loss carryover was not subject to the overlap rule described in paragraph (g) of this section with respect to the P group (the former group). Thus, P, S, and S1 are not members of a SRLY subgroup with respect to the T carryover in the P group. See paragraph (c)(2)(i) of this section. As a successor to T, T1 is included in a SRLY subgroup with T in the P group; and, because 100 percent of T1's stock is owned directly by corporations that were members of the SRLY subgroup when the members of the SRLY subgroup became members of the P group, its net positive income is not excluded from the consolidated taxable income of the P group that may be offset by the carryover. See paragraph (f) of this section.

(vii) In the M group, T's $60 loss carryover arose in a SRLY and is subject to limitation under paragraph (c) of this section. T and T1 remain the only members of a SRLY subgroup with respect to the carryover. Because T1 was a member of the SRLY subgroup when it became a member of the M group and also because 100 percent of T1's stock is owned directly by corporations that were members of the SRLY subgroup when the members of the SRLY subgroup became members of the M group, its net positive income is not excluded from the consolidated taxable income of the M group that may be offset by the carryover. See paragraph (f) of this section.

Example 2. Computation of SRLY subgroup limitation. (i) Individual A owns all of the stock of S, T, P, and M. P and M are each the common parent of a consolidated group. In Year 2, P acquires all the stock of S and T from Individual A, and S and T become members of the P group. For Year 3, the P group has a $45 CNOL, which is attributable to P, and which P carries forward. M is the common parent of another group. At the beginning of Year 4, M acquires all of the stock of P and the former members of the P group become members of the M group. None of the transactions described above resulted in an ownership change under section 382(g).

(ii) P's year to which the loss is attributable, Year 3, is a SRLY with respect to the M group. See § 1.1502-1(f)(1). However, P, S, and T compose a SRLY subgroup with respect to the Year 3 loss under paragraph (c)(2)(i) of this section because Year 3 is not a SRLY (and is not treated as a SRLY) with respect to the P group. P's loss is carried over to the M group's Year 4 and is therefore subject to the SRLY subgroup limitation in paragraph (c)(2) of this section.

(iii) In Year 4, the M group has $10 of consolidated taxable income (computed without regard to the CNOL deduction for Year 4). Such consolidated taxable income would be $45 if determined by reference to only the items of P, S, and T, the members included in the SRLY subgroup with respect to P's loss carryover. Therefore, the SRLY subgroup limitation under paragraph (c)(2) of this section for P's net operating loss carryover from Year 3 is $45. Because the M group has only $10 of consolidated taxable income in Year 4, however, only $10 of P's net operating loss carryover is included in the CNOL deduction under paragraph (a) of this section in Year 4.

(iv) In Year 5, the M group has $100 of consolidated taxable income (computed without regard to the CNOL deduction for Year 5). Neither P, S, nor T has any items of income, gain, deduction, or loss in Year 5. Although the members of the SRLY subgroup do not contribute to the $100 of consolidated taxable income in Year 5, the SRLY subgroup limitation for Year 5 is $35 (the sum of SRLY subgroup consolidated taxable income of $45 in Year 4 and $0 in Year 5, less the $10 net operating loss carryover actually absorbed by the M group in Year 4). Therefore, $35 of P's net operating loss carryover is included in the CNOL deduction under paragraph (a) of this section in Year 5.

Example 3. Inclusion in more than one SRLY subgroup. (i) Individual A owns all of the stock of S, T, P, and M. S, P, and M are each the common parent of a consolidated group. At the beginning of Year 1, S acquires all the stock of T from Individual A, and T becomes a member of

Reg. § 1.1502-21(c)(2)

→ **Caution: Reg. § 1.1502-21, below, is generally effective for tax years for which the consolidated return due date is after June 25, 1999.** ←

the S group. For Year 1, the S group has a CNOL of $10, all of which is attributable to S and is carried over to Year 2. At the beginning of Year 2, P acquires all the stock of S, and S and T become members of the P group. For Year 2, the P group has a CNOL of $35, all of which is attributable to P and is carried over to Year 3. At the beginning of Year 3, M acquires all of the stock of P and the former members of the P group become members of the M group. None of the transactions described above resulted in an ownership change under section 382(g).

(ii) P's and S's net operating losses arising in SRLYs with respect to the M group are subject to limitation under paragraph (c) of this section. P, S, and T compose a SRLY subgroup for purposes of determining the limitation for P's $35 net operating loss carryover arising in Year 2 because, under paragraph (c)(2)(i) of this section, Year 2 is not a SRLY with respect to the P group. Similarly, S and T compose a SRLY subgroup for purposes of determining the limitation for S's $10 net operating loss carryover arising in Year 1 because Year 1 is not a SRLY with respect to the S group.

(iii) S and T are members of both the SRLY subgroup with respect to P's losses and the SRLY subgroup with respect to S's losses. Under paragraph (c)(2) of this section, S's and T's items cannot be included in the determination of the SRLY subgroup limitation for both SRLY subgroups for the same consolidated return year; paragraph (c)(2)(vi) of this section requires the M group to consider the items of S and T only once so that the losses are absorbed in the order of the taxable years in which they were sustained. Because S's loss was incurred in Year 1, while P's loss was incurred in Year 2, the items will be added in the determination of the consolidated taxable income of the S and T SRLY subgroup to enable S's loss to be absorbed first. The taxable income of the P, S, and T SRLY subgroup is then computed by including the consolidated taxable income for the S and T SRLY subgroup less the amount of any net operating loss carryover of S that is absorbed after applying this section to the S subgroup for the year.

Example 4. Corporation ceases to be affiliated with a SRLY subgroup. (i) Individual A owns all of the stock of P and M. P and S are members of the P group and the P group has a CNOL of $30 in Year 1, all of which is attributable to P and carried over to Year 2. At the beginning of Year 2, M acquires all of the stock of P, and P and S become members of the M group.

P and S compose a SRLY subgroup with respect to P's net operating loss carryover. For Year 2, consolidated taxable income of the M group determined by reference to only the items of P (and without regard to the CNOL deduction for Year 2) is $40. However, such consolidated taxable income of the M group determined by reference to the items of both P and S is a loss of $20. Thus, the SRLY subgroup limitation under paragraph (c)(2) of this section prevents the M group from including any of P's net operating loss carryover in the CNOL deduction under paragraph (a) of this section in Year 2, and P carries the Year 1 loss to Year 3.

(ii) At the end of Year 2, P sells all of the S stock and S ceases to be a member of the M group and the P subgroup. For Year 3, consolidated taxable income of the M group is $50 (determined without regard to the CNOL deduction for Year 3), and such consolidated taxable income would be $10 if determined by reference to only items of P. However, the limitation under paragraph (c) of this section for Year 3 for P's net operating loss carryover still prevents the M group from including any of P's loss in the CNOL deduction under paragraph (a) of this section. The limitation results from the inclusion of S's items for Year 2 in the determination of the SRLY subgroup limitation for Year 3 even though S ceased to be a member of the M group (and the P subgroup) at the end of Year 2. Thus, the M group's consolidated taxable income determined by reference to only the SRLY subgroup members' items for all consolidated return years of the group through Year 3 (determined without regard to the CNOL deduction) is not a positive amount.

(ix) *Application to other than loss carryovers.* Paragraph (g) of this section and the phrase "or for a carryover that was subject to the overlap rule described in paragraph (g) of this section or § 1.1502-15(g) with respect to another group (the former group)" in this paragraph (c)(2) apply only to carryovers of net operating losses, net capital losses, and for taxable years for which the due date (without extensions) of the consolidated return is after May 25, 2000, to carryovers of credits described in section 383(a)(2). Accordingly, as the context may require, if another regulation references this section and such other regulation does not concern a carryover of net operating losses, net capital losses, or for taxable years for which the due date (without extensions) of the consolidated return is after May 25, 2000, carryovers of credits described in section

Reg. § 1.1502-21(c)(2)

Consolidated Returns

See p. 20,601 for regulations not amended to reflect law changes

→ *Caution: Reg. § 1.1502-21, below, is generally effective for tax years for which the consolidated return due date is after June 25, 1999.*←

383(a)(2), then such reference does not include a reference to such paragraph or phrase.

(d) *Coordination with consolidated return change of ownership limitation and transactions subject to old section 382*—(1) *Consolidated return changes of ownership.* If a consolidated return change of ownership occurred before January 1, 1997, the principles of § 1.1502-21A(d) apply to determine the amount of the aggregate of the net operating losses attributable to old members of the group that may be included in the consolidated net operating loss deduction under paragraph (a) of this section. For this purpose, § 1.1502-1(g) is applied by treating that date as the end of the year of change.

(2) *Old section 382.* The principles of § 1.1502-21A(e) apply to disallow or reduce the amount of a net operating loss carryover of a member as a result of a transaction subject to old section 382.

(e) *Consolidated net operating loss.* Any excess of deductions over gross income, as determined under § 1.1502-11(a) (without regard to any consolidated net operating loss deduction), is also referred to as the consolidated net operating loss (or CNOL).

(f) *Predecessors and successors*—(1) *In general.* For purposes of this section, any reference to a corporation, member, common parent, or subsidiary, includes, as the context may require, a reference to a successor or predecessor, as defined in § 1.1502-1(f)(4).

(2) *Limitation on SRLY subgroups*—(i) *General rule.* Except as provided in paragraph (f)(2)(ii) of this section, if a successor's items of income and again exceed the successor's items of deduction and loss (net positive income), then the net positive income attributable to the successor is excluded from the computation of the consolidated taxable income of a SRLY subgroup.

(ii) *Exceptions.* A successor's net positive income is not excluded from the consolidated taxable income of a SRLY subgroup if—

(A) The successor acquires substantially all the assets and liabilities of its predecessor and the predecessor ceases to exist;

(B) The successor was a member of the SRLY subgroup when the SRLY subgroup members became members of the group;

(C) 100 percent of the stock of the successor is owned directly by corporations that were members of the SRLY subgroup when the SRLY subgroup members became members of the group; or

(D) The Commissioner so determines.

(g) *Overlap with section 382*—(1) *General rule.* The limitation provided in paragraph (c) of this section does not apply to net operating loss carryovers (other than a hypothetical carryover described in paragraph (c)(1)(i)(D) of this section and a carryover described in paragraph (c)(1)(ii) of this section) when the application of paragraph (c) of this section results in an overlap with the application of section 382. For a similar rule applying in the case of net operating loss carryovers described in paragraphs (c)(1)(i)(D) and (c)(1)(ii) of this section, see § 1.1502-15(g).

(2) *Definitions*—(i) *Generally.* For purposes of this paragraph (g), the definitions and nomenclature contained in section 382, the regulations thereunder, and §§ 1.1502-90 through 1.1502-99 apply.

(ii) *Overlap.* (A) An overlap of the application of paragraph (c) of this section and the application of section 382 with respect to a net operating loss carryover occurs if a corporation becomes a member of a consolidated group (the SRLY event) within six months of the change date of an ownership change giving rise to a section 382(a) limitation with respect to that carryover (the section 382 event).

(B) If an overlap described in paragraph (g)(2)(ii)(A) of this section occurs with respect to net operating loss carryovers of a corporation whose SRLY event occurs within the six month period beginning on the date of a section 382 event, then an overlap is treated as also occurring with respect to that corporation's net operating loss carryover that arises within the period beginning with the section 382 event and ending with the SRLY event.

(C) For special rules in the event that there is a SRLY subgroup and/or a loss subgroup as defined in § 1.1502-91(d)(1) with respect to a carryover, see paragraph (g)(4) of this section.

(3) *Operating rules*—(i) *Section 382 event before SRLY event.* If a SRLY event occurs on the same date as a section 382 event or within the six month period beginning on the date of the section 382 event, paragraph (g)(1) of this section applies beginning with the tax year that includes the SRLY event.

(ii) *SRLY event before section 382 event.* If a section 382 event occurs within the period beginning the day after the SRLY event and ending six months after the SRLY event, paragraph (g)(1) of this section applies starting with

Reg. § 1.1502-21(g)(3)

→ *Caution: Reg. § 1.1502-21, below, is generally effective for tax years for which the consolidated return due date is after June 25, 1999.* ←

the first tax year that begins after the section 382 event.

(4) *Subgroup rules.* In general, in the case of a net operating loss carryover for which there is a SRLY subgroup and a loss subgroup (as defined in § 1.1502-91(d)(1)), the principles of this paragraph (g) apply to the SRLY subgroup, and not separately to its members. However, paragraph (g)(1) of this section applies—

(i) With respect to a carryover described in paragraph (g)(2)(ii)(A) of this section only if—

(A) All members of the SRLY subgroup with respect to that carryover are also included in a loss subgroup with respect to that carryover; and

(B) All members of a loss subgroup with respect to that carryover are also members of a SRLY subgroup with respect to that carryover; and

(ii) With respect to a carryover described in paragraph (g)(2)(ii)(B) of this section only if all members of the SRLY subgroup for that carryover are also members of a SRLY subgroup that has net operating loss carryovers described in paragraph (g)(2)(ii)(A) of this section that are subject to the overlap rule of paragraph (g)(1) of this section.

(5) *Examples.* The principles of this paragraph (g) are illustrated by the following examples:

Example 1. Overlap—Simultaneous Acquisition. (i) Individual A owns all of the stock of P, which in turn owns all of the stock of S. P and S file a consolidated return. In Year 2, B, an individual unrelated to Individual A, forms T which incurs a $100 net operating loss for that year. At the beginning of Year 3, S acquires T.

(ii) S's acquisition of T results in T becoming a member of the P group (the SRLY event) and also results in an ownership change of T, within the meaning of section 382(g), that gives rise to a limitation under section 382(a) (the section 382 event) with respect to the T carryover.

(iii) Because the SRLY event and the change date of the section 382 event occur on the same date, there is an overlap of the application of the SRLY rules and the application of section 382.

(iv) Consequently, under this paragraph (g), in Year 3 the SRLY limitation does not apply to the Year 2 $100 net operating loss.

Example 2. Overlap—Section 382 event before SRLY event. (i) Individual A owns all of the stock of P, which in turn owns all of the stock of S. P and S file a consolidated return. In Year 1, B, an individual unrelated to Individual A, forms T which incurs a $100 net operating loss for that year. On February 28 of Year 2, S purchases 55% of T from Individual B. On June 30, of Year 2, S purchases an additional 35% of T from Individual B.

(ii) The February 28 purchase of 55% of T is a section 382 event because it results in an ownership change of T, under section 382(g), that gives rise to a section 382(a) limitation with respect to the T carryover. The June 30 purchase of 35% of T results in T becoming a member of the P group and is therefore a SRLY event.

(iii) Because the SRLY event occurred within six months of the change date of the section 382 event, there is an overlap of the application of the SRLY rules and the application of section 382.

(iv) Consequently, under paragraph (g) of this section, in Year 2 the SRLY limitation does not apply to the Year 1 $100 net operating loss.

Example 3. No overlap—Section 382 event before SRLY event. (i) The facts are the same as in *Example 2* except that Individual B does not sell the additional 35% of T to S until September 30, Year 2.

(ii) The February 28 purchase of 55% of T is a section 382 event because it results in an ownership change of T, under section 382(g), that gives rise to a section 382(a) limitation with respect to the T carryover. The September 30 purchase of 35% of T results in T becoming a member of the P group and is therefore a SRLY event.

(iii) Because the SRLY event did not occur within six months of the change date of the section 382 event, there is no overlap of the application of the SRLY rules and the application of section 382. Consequently, the Year 1 net operating loss is subject to a SRLY limitation and a section 382 limitation.

Example 4. Overlap—SRLY event before section 382 event. (i) P and S file a consolidated return. S has owned 40% of T for 6 years. For Year 6, T has a net operating loss of $500 that is carried forward. On March 31, Year 7, S acquires an additional 40% of T, and on August 31, Year 7, S acquires the remaining 20% of T.

(ii) The March 31 purchase of 40% of T results in T becoming a member of the P group and is therefore a SRLY event. The August 31 purchase of 20% of T is a section 382 event because it results in an ownership change of T, under section 382(g), that gives rise to a section 382(a) limitation with respect to the T carryover.

Reg. § 1.1502-21(g)(4)

→ **Caution: Reg. § 1.1502-21, below, is generally effective for tax years for which the consolidated return due date is after June 25, 1999.** ←

(iii) Because the SRLY event occurred within six months of the change date of the section 382 event, there is an overlap of the application of the SRLY rules and the application of section 382 within the meaning of this paragraph (g).

(iv) Under this paragraph (g), the SRLY rules of paragraph (c) of this section will apply to the Year 7 tax year. Beginning in Year 8 (the year after the section 382 event), any unabsorbed portion of the Year 6 net operating loss will not be subject to a SRLY limitation.

Example 5. Overlap—Coextensive subgroups. (i) Individual A owns all of the stock of S, which in turn owns all of the stock of T. S and T file a consolidated return beginning in Year 1. B, an individual unrelated to Individual A, owns all of the stock of P, the common parent of a consolidated group. In Year 2, the S group has a $200 consolidated net operating loss which is carried forward, of which $100 is attributable to S, and $100 is attributable to T. At the beginning of Year 3, the P group acquires all of the stock of S from Individual A.

(ii) P's acquisition of S results in S and T becoming members of the P group (the SRLY event). With respect to the Year 2 net operating loss carryover, S and T compose a SRLY subgroup under paragraph (c)(2) of this section.

(iii) S and T also compose a loss subgroup under § 1.1502-91(d)(1) with respect to the Year 2 net operating loss carryover. P's acquisition also results in an ownership change of S, the subgroup parent, within the meaning of section 382(g), that gives rise to a limitation under section 382(a) (the section 382 event) with respect to the Year 2 carryover.

(iv) Because the SRLY event and the change date of the section 382 event occur on the same date, there is an overlap of the application of the SRLY rules and the application of section 382 within the meaning of paragraph (g) of this section. Because the SRLY subgroup and the loss subgroup are coextensive, under paragraph (g) of this section, the SRLY limitation does not apply to the Year 2 $200 net operating loss.

Example 6. No Overlap—Different subgroups. (i) Individual B owns all of the stock of P, the common parent of a consolidated group. P owns all of the stock of S and all of the stock of T. Individual A owns all of the stock of X, the common parent of another consolidated group. In Year 1, the P group has a $200 consolidated net operating loss, of which $100 is attributable to S and $100 is attributable to T. At the beginning of

Year 3, the X group acquires all of the stock of S and T from P and does not make an election under § 1.1502-91(d)(4) (concerning an election to treat the loss subgroup parent requirement as having been satisfied).

(ii) X's acquisition of S and T results in S and T becoming members of the X group (the SRLY event). With respect to the Year 1 net operating loss, S and T compose a SRLY subgrop under paragraph (c)(2) of this section.

(iii) S and T do not bear (and are not treated as bearing) a section 1504(a)(1) relationship. Therefore S and T do not qualify as a loss subgroup under § 1.1502-91(d)(1). X's acquisition of S and T results in separate ownership changes of S and T, that give rise to separate limitations under section 382(a) (the section 382 events) with respect to each of S and T's Year 1 net operating loss carryovers. See § 1.1502-94.

(iv) The SRLY event and the change dates of the section 382 events occur on the same date. However, paragraph (g)(1) of this section does not apply because the SRLY subgroup (composed of S and T) is not coextensive with a loss subgroup with respect to the Year 1 carryovers. Consequently, the Year 1 net operating loss is subject to both a SRLY subgroup limitation and also separate section 382 limitations for each of S and T.

Example 7. No Overlap—Different subgroups. (i) Individual A owns all of the stock of T and all of the stock of S, the common parent of a consolidated group. B, an individual unrelated to Individual A, owns all of the stock of P, the common parent of another consolidated group. In Year 1, T has a net operating loss of $100 that is carried forward. At the end of Year 2, S acquires all of the stock of T from Individual A. In Year 3, the S group sustains a $200 consolidated net operating loss that is carried forward. In Year 8, the P group acquires all of the stock of S from Individual A.

(ii) S's acquisition of T in Year 1 results in T becoming a member of the S group. The acquisition, however, did not result in an ownership change under section 382(g). As a result, T's Year 1 net operating loss is subject to SRLY within the S group. At the end of Year 7, § 1.1502-96(a) treats T's Year 1 net operating loss as not having arisen in a SRLY with respect to the S group. Section 1.1502-96(a), however, applies only for purposes of §§ 1.1502-91 through 1.1502-96 and § 1.1502-98 but not for purposes of this section. See § 1.1502-96(a)(5).

Reg. § 1.1502-21(g)(5)

→ *Caution: Reg. § 1.1502-21, below, is generally effective for tax years for which the consolidated return due date is after June 25, 1999.*←

(iii) P's acquisition of S in Year 8 results in S and T becoming members of the P group (the SRLY event). With respect to the Year 1 net operating loss, S and T do not compose a SRLY subgroup under paragraph (c)(2) of this section.

(iv) S and T compose a loss subgroup under § 1.1502-91(d)(1) with respect to the Year 1 net operating loss carryover. P's acquisition of S results in an ownership change of the loss subgroup, within the meaning of section 382(g), that gives rise to a subgroup limitation under section 382(a) (the section 382 event) with respect to that carryover.

(v) The SRLY event and the change date of the section 382 event occur on the same date. However, under paragraph (g)(4) of this section, because the SRLY subgroup and the loss subgroup are not coextensive, T's Year 1 net operating loss carryover is subject to a SRLY limitation.

(vi) With respect to the Year 3 net operating loss carryover, S and T compose both a SRLY subgroup and a loss subgroup under §1.1502-91(d)(1). Thus, paragraph (g)(1) of this section applies and the S group's Year 3 net operating loss carryover is not subject to a SRLY limitation.

Example 8. SRLY after overlap. (i) Individual A owns all of the stock of R and M, each the common parent of a consolidated group. B, an individual unrelated to Individual A, owns all of the stock of D. In Year 1, D incurs a $100 net operating loss that is carried forward. At the beginning of Year 3, R acquires all of the stock of D. In Year 5, M acquires all of the stock of R in a transaction that did not result in an ownership change of R.

(ii) R's Year 3 acquisition of D results in D becoming a member of the R group (the SRLY event) and also results in an ownership change of D, that gives rise to a limitation under section 382(a) (the section 382 event) with respect to D's net operating loss carryover.

(iii) Because the SRLY event and the change date of the section 382 event occur on the same date, there is an overlap of the application of paragraph (c) of this section and section 382 with respect to D's net operating loss. Consequently, under this paragraph (g), D's Year 1 $100 net operating loss is not subject to a SRLY limitation in the R group.

(iv) M's Year 5 acquisition of R results in R and D becoming members of the M group (the SRLY event), but does not result in an ownership change of R or D that gives rise to a limitation under section 382(a). Because there is no section 382 event, the application of the SRLY rules and section 382 do not overlap. Consequently, D's Year 1 $100 net operating loss is subject to a SRLY limitation in the M group.

(v) Because D's Year 1 net operating loss carryover was subject to the overlap rule of paragraph (g) of this section when it joined the R group, under § 1.1502-21(c)(2) the SRLY subgroup with respect to that carryover includes all of the members of the R group that joined the M group at the same time as D.

Example 9. Overlap—Interim losses. (i) Individual A owns all of the stock of P and S, each the common parent of a consolidated group. S owns all of the stock of T, its only subsidiary. B, an individual unrelated to Individual A, owns all of the stock of M, the common parent of a consolidated group. In Year 1, the S group has a $100 consolidated net operating loss. On January 1 of Year 2, P acquires all of the stock of S from Individual A. On December 31 of Year 2, M acquires 51% of the stock of P from Individual A. On May 31 of Year 3, M acquires the remaining 49% of the stock of P from Individual A. The P group, for the Year 3 period prior to June 1 had a $50 consolidated net operating loss, and under paragraph (b)(2)(iv) of this section, the loss is attributable entirely to S. Other than the losses described above, the P group does not have any other consolidated net operating losses.

(ii) In the P group, S's $100 loss carryover is treated as arising in a SRLY and is subject to the limitation under paragraph (c) of this section. A SRLY subgroup with respect to that loss is composed of S and T, the members which were members of the S group as to which the loss was not a SRLY.

(iii) M's December 31 purchase of 51% of P is a section 382 event because it results in an ownership change of the S loss subgroup that gives rise to a section 382(a) limitation (the section 382 event) with respect to the Year 1 net operating loss carryover. The purchase, however, does not result in an ownership change of P because it is not a loss corporation under section 382(k)(1). M's May 31 purchase of 49% of P results in P, S, and T becoming members of the M group and is therefore a SRLY event.

(iv) With respect to the Year 1 net operating loss, S and T compose a SRLY subgroup under paragraph (c)(2) of this section and a loss subgroup under § 1.1502-91(d)(1). The loss subgroup does not include P because the only loss at the

Reg. § 1.1502-21(g)(5)

Consolidated Returns

See p. 20,601 for regulations not amended to reflect law changes

→ *Caution: Reg. § 1.1502-21, below, is generally effective for tax years for which the consolidated return due date is after June 25, 1999.* ←

time of the section 382 event was subject to SRLY with respect to the P group. See § 1.1502-91(d)(1).

(v) Because the SRLY event occurred within six months of the change date of the section 382 event and the SRLY subgroup and loss subgroup are coextensive with respect to the Year 1 net operating loss carryover, there is an overlap of the application of the SRLY rules and the application of section 382 within the meaning of paragraph (g) of this section. Thus, the SRLY limitation does not apply to that carryover.

(vi) The Year 3 net operating loss, which arose between the section 382 event and the SRLY event, is a net operating loss described in paragraph (g)(2)(ii)(B) of this section because it is the net operating loss of a corporation whose SRLY event occurs within the six month period beginning on the date of a section 382 event.

(vii) With respect to the Year 3 net operating loss, P, S, and T compose a SRLY subgroup under paragraph (c)(2) of this section. Because P, a member of the SRLY subgroup for the Year 3 carryover, is not also a member of a SRLY subgroup that has net operating loss carryovers described in paragraph (g)(2)(ii)(A) of this section (the Year 1 net operating loss), the Year 3 carryover is subject to a SRLY limitation in the M group. See paragraph (g)(4)(ii) of this section.

(h) *Effective date*—(1) *In general.* This section generally applies to taxable years for which the due date (without extensions) of the consolidated return is after June 25, 1999. However—

(i) In the event that paragraph (g)(1) of this section does not apply to a particular net operating loss carryover in the current group, then solely for purposes of applying paragraph (c) of this section to determine a limitation with respect to that carryover and with respect to which the SRLY register (consolidated taxable income determined by reference to only the member's or subgroup's items of income, gain, deduction or loss) began in a taxable year for which the due date of the return was on or before June 25, 1999, paragraph (c)(2) of this section shall be applied without regard to the phrase "or for a carryover that was subject to the overlap rule described in paragraph (g) of this section or § 1.1502-15(g) with respect to another group (the former group)"; and

(ii) For purposes of paragraph (g) of this section, only an ownership change to which section 382(a), as amended by the Tax Reform Act of 1986, applies shall constitute a section 382 event.

(2) *SRLY limitation.* Except in the case of those members (including members of a SRLY subgroup) described in paragraph (h)(3) of this section, a group does not take into account a consolidated taxable year beginning before January 1, 1997, in determining the aggregate of the consolidated taxable income under paragraph (c)(1) of this section (including for purposes of § 1.1502-15 and § 1.1502-22(c)) for the members (or SRLY subgroups).

(3) *Prior retroactive election.* A consolidated group that applied the rules of § 1.1502-21T(g)(3) in effect prior to June 25, 1999, as contained in 26 CFR part 1 revised April 1, 1999, to all consolidated return years ending on or after January 29, 1991, and beginning before January 1, 1997, does not take into account a consolidated taxable year beginning before January 29, 1991, in determining the aggregate of the consolidated taxable income under paragraph (c)(1) of this section (including for purposes of § 1.1502-15 and § 1.1502-22(c)) for the members (or SRLY subgroups).

(4) *Offspring rule.* Paragraph (b)(2)(ii)(B) of this section applies to net operating losses arising in taxable years ending on or after June 25, 1999.

(5) *Waiver of carrybacks.* Paragraph (b)(3)(ii)(B) of this section (relating to the waiver of carrybacks for acquired members) applies to acquisitions occurring after June 25, 1999.

(6) *Prior periods.* For certain taxable years ending on or before June 25, 1999, see § 1.1502-21T in effect prior to June 25, 1999, as contained in 26 CFR part 1 revised April 1, 1999, as applicable. [Reg. § 1.1502-21.]

☐ [T.D. 8823, 6-25-99 (*corrected* 7-30-99). Amended by T.D. 8884, 5-24-2000.]

[Reg. § 1.1502-21A]

§ 1.1502-21A. **Consolidated net operating loss deduction generally applicable for consolidated return years beginning before January 1, 1997.**—(a) *In general.* The consolidated net operating loss deduction shall be an amount equal to the aggregate of the consolidated net operating loss carryovers and carrybacks to the taxable year (as determined under paragraph (b) of this section).

(b) *Consolidated net operating loss carryovers and carrybacks*—(1) *In general.* The consolidated net operating loss carryovers and carrybacks to the taxable year shall consist of any consolidated net operating losses (as determined under paragraph (f) of this section) of the group, plus any net

Reg. § 1.1502-21A(b)(1)

operating losses sustained by members of the group in separate return years, which may be carried over or back to the taxable year under the principles of section 172(b). However, such consolidated carryovers and carrybacks shall not include any consolidated net operating loss apportioned to a corporation for a separate return year pursuant to § 1.1502-79A, and shall be subject to the limitations contained in paragraphs (c), (d), and (e) of this section and to the limitation contained in § 1.1502-15A (or § 1.1502-11(c), as appropriate).

(2) *Rules for applying section 172(b)(1)* —(i) *Regulated transportation corporations.* For purposes of applying section 172(b)(1)(C) (relating to net operating losses sustained by regulated transportation corporations), in the case of a consolidated net operating loss sustained in a taxable year for which a member of the group was a regulated transportation corporation (as defined in section 172(j)(1)), the portion, if any, of such consolidated net operating loss which is attributable to such corporation (as determined under this paragraph) shall be a carryover to the sixth taxable year following the loss year only if such corporation is a regulated transportation corporation for such sixth year, and shall be a carryover to the seventh taxable year following the loss year only if such corporation is a regulated transportation corporation for both such sixth and seventh years.

(ii) *Trade expansion losses.* In the case of a carryback of a consolidated net operating loss from a taxable year for which a member of the group has been issued a certification under section 317 of the Trade Expansion Act of 1962 and with respect to which the requirements of section 172(b)(3)(A) have been met, section 172(b)(1)(A)(ii) shall apply only to the portion of such consolidated net operating loss attributable to such member.

(iii) *Foreign expropriation losses.* An election under section 172(b)(3)(C) (relating to 10-year carryover of portion of net operating loss attributable to a foreign expropriation loss) may be made for a consolidated return year only if the sum of the foreign expropriation losses (as defined in section 172(k)) of the members of the group for such year equals or exceeds 50 percent of the consolidated net operating loss for such year. If such election is made, the amount which may be carried over under section 172(b)(1)(D) is the smaller of (*a*) the sum of such foreign expropriation losses, or (*b*) the consolidated net operating loss.

(3) *Absorption rules.* For purposes of determining the amount, if any, of a net operating loss (whether consolidated or separate) which can be carried to a taxable year (consolidated or separate), the amount of such net operating loss which is absorbed in a prior consolidated return year under section 172(b)(2) shall be determined by—

(i) Applying all net operating losses which can be carried to such prior year in the order of the taxable years in which such losses were sustained, beginning with the taxable year which ends earliest, and

(ii) Applying all such losses which can be carried to such prior year from taxable years ending on the same date on a pro rata basis, except that any portion of a net operating loss attributable to a foreign expropriation loss to which section 172(b)(1)(D) applies shall be applied last.

(c) *Limitation on net operating loss carryovers and carrybacks from separate return limitation years*—(1) *General rule.* In the case of a net operating loss of a member of the group arising in a separate return limitation year (as defined in paragraph (f) of § 1.1502-1) of such member (and in a separate return limitation year of any predecessor of such member), the amount which may be included under paragraph (b) of this section (computed without regard to the limitation contained in paragraph (d) of this section) in the consolidated net operating loss carryovers and carrybacks to a consolidated return year of the group shall not exceed the amount determined under subparagraph (2) of this paragraph.

(2) *Computation of limitation.* The amount referred to in subparagraph (1) of this paragraph with respect to a member of the group is the excess, if any, of—

(i) Consolidated taxable income (computed without regard to the consolidated net operating loss deduction), minus such consolidated taxable income recomputed by excluding the items of income and deduction of such member, over

(ii) The net operating losses attributable to such member which may be carried to the consolidated return year arising in taxable years ending prior to the particular separate return limitation year.

(3) *Examples.* The provisions of this paragraph and paragraphs (a) and (b) of this section may be illustrated by the following examples:

Example (1). (i) Corporation P formed corporations S and T on January 1, 1965. P, S, and T filed separate returns for the calendar year 1965, a year for which an election under section 1562 was effective. T's return for that year reflected a net operating loss of $10,000. The group filed a consolidated return for 1966 reflecting consolidated taxable income of $30,000 (computed without regard to the consolidated net operating loss deduction). Among the transactions occuring during 1966 were the following:

(a) P sold goods to T deriving deferred profits of $7,000 on such sales, $2,000 of which was restored to consolidated taxable income on the sale of such goods to outsiders;

(b) T sold a machine to S deriving a deferred profit of $5,000, $1,000 of which was restored to consolidated taxable income as a result of S's depreciation deductions;

(c) T distributed a $3,000 dividend to P; and

(d) In addition to the transactions described above, T had other taxable income of $6,000.

(ii) The carryover of T's 1965 net operating loss to 1966 is subject to the limitation contained in this paragraph, since 1965 was a separate return limitation year (an election under section 1562 was effective for such year). Thus, only $7,000 of T's $10,000 net operating loss is a consolidated net operating loss carryover to 1966, since such carryover is limited to consolidated taxable income (computed without regard to the consolidated net operating loss deduction), $30,000, minus such consolidated taxable income recomputed by excluding the items of income and deduction of T, $23,000 (i.e., consolidated taxable income computed without regard to the $1,000 restoration of T's deferred gain and T's $6,000 of other income). In making such recomputation, no change is made in the effect on consolidated taxable income of P's sale to T, or of the dividend from T to P.

Example (2). (i) Corporation P was formed on January 1, 1966. P filed separate returns for the calendar years 1966 and 1967 reflecting net operating losses of $4,000 and $12,000, respectively. P purchased corporation S on March 15, 1967. S was formed on February 1, 1966, and filed a separate return for the taxable year ending January 31, 1967. S also filed a short period return for the period from February 1 to December 31, 1967, and joined with P in filing a consolidated return for 1968. S sustained net operating losses of $5,000 and $6,000 for its taxable years ending January 31, 1967 and December 31, 1967, respectively. An election under section 1562 was not effective for P and S during the period involved. Consolidated taxable income for 1968 (computed without regard to the consolidated net operating loss deduction) was $16,000; such consolidated taxable income recomputed by disregarding the items of income and deduction of S was $9,000.

(ii) In order of time, the following losses are absorbed in 1968:

(a) P's $4,000 net operating loss for the calendar year 1966 (such loss is not subject to the limitation contained in this paragraph since P is the common parent corporation for 1968);

(b) S's $5,000 net operating loss for the year ended January 31, 1967. Such loss is subject to the limitation contained in this paragraph, since S was not a member of the group on each day of such year. However, such loss can be carried over and absorbed in full since such limitation is $7,000 (consolidated taxable income computed without regard to the consolidated net operating loss deduction, $16,000, minus such consolidated taxable income recomputed, $9,000); and

(c) $6,000 of P's net operating loss and $1,000 of S's net operating loss for the taxable years ending December 31, 1967. This is determined by applying the losses from such year which can be carried to 1968 (P's $12,000 loss and $2,000 of S's $6,000 loss, since such $6,000 loss is limited under this paragraph) on a pro rata basis against the amount of such losses which can be absorbed in that year, $7,000 (consolidated taxable income of $16,000 less the $9,000 of losses absorbed from prior years). The carryover of S's loss to 1968 is subject to the limitation contained in that paragraph, since S was not a member of the group on each day of its taxable year ending December 31, 1967. Such loss is limited to $2,000, the excess of $7,000 (as determined under (ii)(b)) over $5,000 (S's carryover from the year ended January 31, 1967). If a consolidated return is filed in 1969, the consolidated net operating loss carryovers will consist of P's unabsorbed loss of $6,000 ($12,000 minus $6,000) from 1967 and, subject to the limitation contained in this paragraph, S's unabsorbed loss of $5,000 ($6,000 minus $1,000) from its year ended December 31, 1967.

(d) *Limitations on carryovers where there has been a consolidated return change of ownership*—(1) *General rule.* If a consolidated return change of ownership (as defined in paragraph (g) of § 1.1502-1) occurs during the taxable year or an earlier taxable year, the amount which may be included under paragraph (b) of this section in the consolidated net operating loss carryovers to the taxable year with respect to the aggregate of the net operating losses attributable to old member of the group (as defined in paragraph (g)(3) of § 1.1502-1) arising in taxable years (consolidated or separate) ending on the same day and before the taxable year in which the consolidated return change of ownership occurred shall not exceed the amount determined under subparagraph (2) of this paragraph.

Reg. § 1.1502-21A(d)

(2) *Computation of limitation.* The amount referred to in subparagraph (1) of this paragraph shall be the excess of—

(i) The consolidated taxable income for the taxable year (determined without regard to the consolidated net operating loss deduction) recomputed by including only the items of income and deduction of the old members of the group, over

(ii) The sum of the net operating losses attributable to the old members of the group which may be carried to the taxable year arising in taxable years ending prior to the particular loss year or years.

(3) *Example.* The provisions of this paragraph may be illustrated by the following example:

Example. (i) Corporation P is formed on January 1, 1967 and on the same day it forms corporation S. P and S file a consolidated return for the calendar year 1967, reflecting a consolidated net operating loss of $500,000. On January 1, 1968, individual X purchases all of the outstanding stock of P. X subsequently contributes $1,000,000 to P and P purchases the stock of corporation T. P, S, and T file a consolidated return for 1968 reflecting consolidated taxable income of $600,000 (computed without regard to the consolidated net operating loss deduction). Such consolidated taxable income recomputed by including only the items of income and deduction of P and S is $350,000.

(ii) Since a consolidated return change of ownership took place in 1968 (there was more than a 50 percent change of ownership of P), the amount of the consolidated net operating loss from 1967 which can be carried over to 1968 is limited to $350,000, the excess of $350,000 (consolidated taxable income recomputed by including only the items of income and deduction of the old members of the group, P and S) over zero (the amount of the consolidated net operating loss carryovers attributable to the old members of the group arising in taxable years ending before 1967).

(4) *Cross-reference.* See § 1.1502-21T(d)(1) for the rule that applies the principles of this paragraph (d) in consolidated return years beginning on or after January 1, 1997, with respect to a consolidated return change of ownership occurring before January 1, 1997.

(e) *Limitations on net operating loss carryovers under section 382*—(1) *Section 382(a).* (i) If at the end of a taxable year (consolidated or separate) there has been an increase in ownership of the stock of the common parent of a group (within the meaning of section 382(a)(1)(A) and (B)), and any member of the group has not continued to carry on a trade or business substantially the same as that conducted before any such increase (within the meaning of section 382(a)(1)(C)), then the portion of any consolidated net operating loss sustained in prior taxable years attributable to such member (as determined under this paragraph) shall not be allowed as a carryover to such taxable year or to any subsequent taxable year.

(ii) If the provisions of section 382(a) disallow the deduction of a net operating loss carryover from a separate return year of a member of the group to a subsequent taxable year, no amount shall be included under paragraph (b) of this section as a consolidated net operating loss carryover to such a subsequent consolidated return year with respect to such separate return year of such member.

(iii) The provisions of this subparagraph may be illustrated by the following example:

Example. P, S, and T file a consolidated return for the calendar year 1969, reflecting a consolidated net operating loss attributable in part to each member. P owns 80 percent of S's stock and S owns 80 percent of T's stock. On January 1, 1970, A purchases 50 percent of P's stock. During 1970 T's business is discontinued. Since there has been a 50 percentage point increase in ownership of P, the common parent of the group, and since T has not continued to carry on the same trade or business after such increase, the portion of the 1969 consolidated net operating loss attributable to T shall not be included in any net operating loss deduction for 1970 or for any subsequent taxable years, whether consolidated or separate.

(2) *Section 382(b).* If a net operating loss carryover from a separate return year of a predecessor of a member of the group to the taxable year is reduced under the provisions of section 382(b), the amount included under paragraph (b) of this section with respect to such predecessor shall be so reduced.

(3) *Effective date.* This paragraph (e) disallows or reduces the net operating loss carryovers of a member as a result of a transaction to which old section 382 (as defined in § 1.382-2T(f)(21)) applies. See § 1.1502-21T(d)(2) for the rule that applies the principles of this paragraph (e) in consolidated return years beginning on or after January 1, 1997, with respect to such a transaction.

(f) *Consolidated net operating loss.* The consolidated net operating loss shall be determined by taking into account the following:

(1) The separate taxable income (as determined under § 1.1502-12) of each member of the

group, computed without regard to any deduction under section 242;

(2) Any consolidated capital gain net income (net capital gain for taxable years beginning before January 1, 1977);

(3) Any consolidated section 1231 net loss;

(4) Any consolidated charitable contributions deduction;

(5) Any consolidated dividends received deduction (determined under § 1.1502-26 without regard to paragraph (a)(2) of that section); and

(6) Any consolidated section 247 deduction (determined under § 1.1502-27 without regard to paragraph (a)(1)(ii) of that section).

(g) *Groups that include insolvent financial institutions.* For rules applicable to relinquishing the entire carryback period with respect to losses attributable to insolvent financial institutions, see § 301.6402-7 of this chapter.

(h) *Effective date.* Except as provided in § 1.1502-21T(d)(1), (d)(2), and (g)(3), this section applies to consolidated return years beginning before January 1, 1997. [Reg. § 1.1502-21A.]

☐ [T.D. 6894, 9-7-66. Amended by T.D. 7728, 10-31-80; T.D. 8387, 12-30-91 and T.D. 8446, 11-5-92. Redesignated as Reg. § 1.1502-21A and amended by T.D. 8677, 6-26-96.]

→ Caution: Reg. § 1.1502-21T, below, was removed by T.D. 8823 and is generally effective for certain tax years ending on or before June 25, 1999. ←

[Reg. § 1.1502-21T]

§ 1.1502-21T. Net operating losses (temporary).—(a) *Consolidated net operating loss deduction.* The consolidated net operating loss deduction (or CNOL deduction) for any consolidated return year is the aggregate of the net operating loss carryovers and carrybacks to the year. The net operating loss carryovers and carrybacks consist of—

(1) Any CNOLs (as defined in paragraph (e) of this section) of the consolidated group; and

(2) Any net operating losses of the members arising in separate return years.

(b) *Net operating loss carryovers and carrybacks to consolidated return and separate return years.* Net operating losses of members arising during a consolidated return year are taken into account in determining the group's CNOL under paragraph (e) of this section for that year. Losses taken into account in determining the CNOL may be carried to other taxable years (whether consolidated or separate) only under this paragraph (b).

(1) *Carryovers and carrybacks generally.* The net operating loss carryovers and carrybacks to a taxable year are determined under the principles of section 172 and this section. Thus, losses permitted to be absorbed in a consolidated return year generally are absorbed in the order of the taxable years in which they arose, and losses carried from taxable years ending on the same date, and which are available to offset consolidated taxable income for the year, generally are absorbed on a pro rata basis. See *Example 2* of paragraph (c)(1)(iii) of this section for an illustration of pro rata absorption of losses subject to a SRLY limitation. Additional rules provided under the Code or regulations also apply. See, e.g., section 382(l)(2)(B).

(2) *Carryovers and carrybacks of CNOLs to separate return years*—(i) *In general.* If any CNOL that is attributable to a member may be carried to a separate return year of the member, the amount of the CNOL that is attributable to the member is apportioned to the member (apportioned loss) and carried to the separate return year. If carried back to a separate return year, the apportioned loss may not be carried back to an equivalent, or earlier, consolidated return year of the group; if carried over to a separate return year, the apportioned loss may not be carried over to an equivalent, or later, consolidated return year of the group. For rules permitting the reattribution of losses of a subsidiary to the common parent when loss is disallowed on the disposition of subsidiary stock, see § 1.1502-20(g).

(ii) *Special rules*—(A) *Year of departure from group.* If a corporation ceases to be a member during a consolidated return year, net operating loss carryovers attributable to the corporation are first carried to the consolidated return year, and only the amount so attributable that is not absorbed by the group in that year is carried to the corporation's first separate return year.

(B) *Offspring rule.* In the case of a member that has been a member continuously since its organization, the CNOL attributable to the member is included in the carrybacks to consolidated return years before the member's existence. See paragraph (f) of this section for applications to predecessors and successors. If the group did not file a consolidated return for a carryback year, the loss may be carried back to a separate return year of the common parent under paragraph (b)(2)(i) of this section, but only if the common parent was not a member of a different consolidated group or of an affiliated group filing separate returns for the year to which the loss is carried or any subsequent year in the carryback period. Following an

→ *Caution: Reg. § 1.1502-21T, below, was removed by T.D. 8823 and is generally effective for certain tax years ending on or before June 25, 1999.*←

acquisition described in § 1.1502-75(d)(2) or (3), references to the common parent are to the corporation that was the common parent immediately before the acquisition.

(iii) *Equivalent years.* Taxable years are equivalent if they bear the same numerical relationship to the consolidated return year in which a CNOL arises, counting forward or backward from the year of the loss. For example, in the case of a member's third taxable year (which was a separate return year) that preceded the consolidated return year in which the loss arose, the equivalent year is the third consolidated return year preceding the consolidated return year in which the loss arose. See paragraph (b)(3)(iii) of this section for certain short taxable years that are disregarded in making this determination.

(iv) *Amount of CNOL attributable to a member.* The amount of a CNOL that is attributable to a member is determined by a fraction the numerator of which is the separate net operating loss of the member for the year of the loss and the denominator of which is the sum of the separate net operating losses for that year of all members having such losses. For this purpose, the separate net operating loss of a member is determined by computing the CNOL by reference to only the member's items of income, gain, deduction, and loss, including the member's losses and deductions actually absorbed by the group in the taxable year (whether or not absorbed by the member).

(v) *Examples.* For purposes of the examples in this section, unless otherwise stated, all groups file consolidated returns, all corporations have calendar taxable years, the facts set forth the only corporate activity, value means fair market value and the adjusted basis of each asset equals its value, all transactions are with unrelated persons, and the application of any limitation or threshold under section 382 is disregarded. The principles of this paragraph (b)(2) are illustrated by the following examples:

Example 1. Offspring rule. (a) P is formed at the beginning of Year 1 and files a separate return. P forms S on March 15 of Year 2, and P and S file a consolidated return. P purchases all the stock of T at the beginning of Year 3, and T becomes a member of the P group. T was formed in Year 2 and filed a separate return for that year. P, S, and T sustain a $1,100 CNOL in Year 3 and, under paragraph (b)(2)(iv) of this section, the loss is attributable $200 to P, $300 to S, and $600 to T.

(b) Of the $1,100 CNOL in Year 3, the $500 amount of the CNOL that is attributable to P and S ($200 + $300) may be carried to P's separate return in Year 1. Even though S was not in existence in Year 1, the $300 amount of the CNOL attributable to S may be carried back to P's separate return in Year 1 because S (unlike T) has been a member of the P group since its organization and P is a qualified parent under paragraph (b)(2)(ii)(B) of this section. To the extent not absorbed in that year, the loss may then be carried to the P group's return in Year 2. The $600 amount of the CNOL attributable to T is a net operating loss carryback to T's separate return in Year 2.

Example 2. Departing members. (a) The facts are the same as in *Example 1.* In addition, on June 15 of Year 4, P sells all the stock of T. The P group's consolidated return for Year 4 includes the income of T through June 15. T files a separate return for the period from June 16 through December 31.

(b) $600 of the Year 3 CNOL attributable to T is apportioned to T and is carried back to its separate return in Year 2. To the extent the $600 is not absorbed in T's separate return in Year 2, it is carried to the consolidated return in Year 4 before being carried to T's separate return in Year 4. Any portion of the loss not absorbed in T's Year 2 or in the P group's Year 4 is then carried to T's separate return in Year 4.

(3) *Special rules*—(i) *Election to relinquish carryback.* A group may make an irrevocable election under section 172(b)(3) to relinquish the entire carryback period with respect to a CNOL for any consolidated return year. The election may not be made separately for any member (whether or not it remains a member), and must be made in a separate statement entitled "THIS IS AN ELECTION UNDER SECTION 1.1502-21T(b)(3)(i) TO WAIVE THE ENTIRE CARRYBACK PERIOD PURSUANT TO SECTION 172(b)(3) FOR THE [insert consolidated return year] CNOLs OF THE CONSOLIDATED GROUP OF WHICH [insert name and employer identification number of common parent] IS THE COMMON PARENT." The statement must be signed by the common parent and filed with the group's income tax return for the consolidated return year in which the loss arises.

(ii) *Special election for groups that include insolvent financial institutions.* For rules applicable to relinquishing the entire carryback period with respect to losses attributable to insolvent

Reg. § 1.1502-21T(b)(3)

Consolidated Returns

See p. 20,601 for regulations not amended to reflect law changes

→ *Caution: Reg. § 1.1502-21T, below, was removed by T.D. 8823 and is generally effective for certain tax years ending on or before June 25, 1999.*←

financial institutions, see § 301.6402-7 of this chapter.

(iii) *Short years in connection with transactions to which section 381(a) applies.* If a member distributes or transfers assets to a corporation that is a member immediately after the distribution or transfer in a transaction to which section 381(a) applies, the transaction does not cause the distributor or transferor to have a short year within the consolidated return year of the group in which the transaction occurred that is counted as a separate year for purposes of determining the years to which a net operating loss may be carried.

(iv) *Special status losses.* [Reserved]

(c) *Limitations on net operating loss carryovers and carrybacks from separate return limitation years*—(1) *SRLY limitation*—(i) *General rule.* The aggregate of the net operating loss carryovers and carrybacks of a member arising (or treated as arising) in SRLYs that are included in the CNOL deductions for all consolidated return years of the group under paragraph (a) of this section may not exceed the aggregate consolidated taxable income for all consolidated return years of the group determined by reference to only the member's items of income, gain, deduction, and loss. For this purpose—

(A) Consolidated taxable income is computed without regard to CNOL deductions;

(B) Consolidated taxable income takes into account the member's losses and deductions (including capital losses) actually absorbed by the group in consolidated return years (whether or not absorbed by the member);

(C) In computing consolidated taxable income, the consolidated return years of the group include only those years, including the year to which the loss is carried, that the member has been continuously included in the group's consolidated return, but exclude:

(*1*) For carryovers, any years ending after the year to which the loss is carried; and

(*2*) For carrybacks, any years ending after the year in which the loss arose; and

(D) The treatment under § 1.1502-15T of a built-in loss as a hypothetical net operating loss carryover in the year recognized is solely for purposes of determining the limitation under this paragraph (c) with respect to the loss in that year and not for any other purpose. Thus, for purposes of determining consolidated taxable income for any other losses, a built-in loss allowed under this section in the year it arises is taken into account.

(ii) *Losses treated as arising in SRLYs.* If a net operating loss carryover or carryback did not arise in a SRLY but is attributable to a built-in loss (as defined under § 1.1502-15T), the carryover or carryback is treated for purposes of this paragraph (c) as arising in a SRLY if the built-in loss was not allowed, after application of the SRLY limitation, in the year it arose. For an illustration, see § 1.1502-15T(d), *Example 5.*

(iii) *Examples.* The principles of this paragraph (c)(1) are illustrated by the following examples:

Example 1. Determination of SRLY limitation. (a) In Year 1, individual A forms T and T sustains a $100 net operating loss that is carried forward. P buys all the stock of T at the beginning of Year 2, and T becomes a member of the P group. The P group has $300 of consolidated taxable income in Year 2 (computed without regard to the CNOL deduction). Such consolidated taxable income would be $70 if determined by reference to only T's items.

(b) T's $100 net operating loss carryover from Year 1 arose in a SRLY. See § 1.1502-1(f)(2)(iii). Thus, the $100 net operating loss carryover is subject to the SRLY limitation in paragraph (c)(1) of this section. The SRLY limitation for Year 2 is consolidated taxable income determined by reference to only T's items, or $70. Thus, $70 of the loss is included under paragraph (a) of this section in the P group's CNOL deduction for Year 2.

(c) The facts are the same as in paragraph (a) of this *Example 1*, except that such consolidated taxable income (computed without regard to the CNOL deduction and by reference to only T's items) is a loss (a CNOL) of $370. Because the SRLY limitation may not exceed the consolidated taxable income determined by reference to only T's items, and such items aggregate to a CNOL, T's $100 net operating loss carryover from Year 1 is not allowed under the SRLY limitation in Year 2. Moreover, if consolidated taxable income (computed without regard to the CNOL deduction and by reference to only T's items) did not exceed $370 in Year 3, the carryover would still be restricted under § 1.1502-21T(c) in Year 3, because the aggregate consolidated taxable income for all consolidated return years of the group computed by reference to only T's items would not be a positive amount.

Example 2. Net operating loss carryovers. (a) In Year 1, individual A forms P and P sustains a $40 net operating loss that is carried forward. P has no income in Year 2. Unrelated corporation T

Reg. § 1.1502-21T(c)

56,820   Consolidated Returns

See p. 20,601 for regulations not amended to reflect law changes

→ *Caution: Reg. § 1.1502-21T, below, was removed by T.D. 8823 and is generally effective for certain tax years ending on or before June 25, 1999.*←

sustains a net operating loss of $50 in Year 2 that is carried forward. P buys the stock of T during Year 3, but T is not a member of the P group for each day of the year. P and T file separate returns and sustain net operating losses of $120 and $60, respectively, for Year 3. The P group files consolidated returns beginning in Year 4. During Year 4, the P group has $160 of consolidated taxable income (computed without regard to the CNOL deduction). Such consolidated taxable income would be $70 if determined by reference to only T's items. These results are summarized as follows:

	Separate Year 1	Separate Year 2	Separate/ Affiliated Year 3	Consolidated Year 4
P	$(40)	$ 0	$(120)	$ 90
T	0	(50)	(60)	70
CTI				$ 160.

(b) P's Year 1, Year 2, and Year 3 are not SRLYs with respect to the P group. See § 1.1502-1(f)(2)(i). Thus, P's $40 net operating loss arising in Year 1 and $120 net operating loss arising in Year 3 are not subject to the SRLY limitation under paragraph (c) of this section. Under the principles of section 172, paragraph (b) of this section requires that the loss arising in Year 1 be the first loss absorbed by the P group in Year 4. Absorption of this loss leaves $120 of the group's consolidated taxable income available for offset by other loss carryovers.

(c) T's Year 2 and Year 3 are SRLYs with respect to the P group. See § 1.1502-1(f)(2)(ii). Thus, T's $50 net operating loss arising in Year 2 and $60 net operating loss arising in Year 3 are subject to the SRLY limitation. Under paragraph (c)(1) of this section, the SRLY limitation for Year 4 is $70, and under paragraph (b) of this section, T's $50 loss from Year 2 must be included under paragraph (a) of this section in the P group's CNOL deduction for Year 4. The absorption of this loss leaves $70 of the group's consolidated taxable income available for offset by other loss carryovers.

(d) P and T each carry over net operating losses to Year 4 from a taxable year ending on the same date (Year 3). The losses carried over from Year 3 total $180. Under paragraph (b) of this section, the losses carried over from Year 3 are absorbed on a pro rata basis, even though one arises in a SRLY and the other does not. However, the group cannot absorb more than $20 of T's $60 net operating loss arising in Year 3 because its $70 SRLY limitation for Year 4 is reduced by T's $50 Year 2 SRLY loss already included in the CNOL deduction for Year 4. Thus, the absorption of Year 3 losses is as follows:

Amount of P's Year 3 losses absorbed = $120/($120 + $20) × $70 = $60

Amount of T's Year 3 losses absorbed = $20/($120 + $20) × $70 = $10.

(e) The absorption of $10 of T's Year 3 loss further reduces T's SRLY limitation to $10 ($70 of initial SRLY limitation, reduced by the $60 net operating loss already included in the CNOL deductions for Year 4 under paragraph (a) of this section).

(f) P carries its remaining $60 Year 3 net operating loss and T carries its remaining $50 Year 3 net operating loss over to Year 5. Assume that, in Year 5, the P group has $90 of consolidated taxable income (computed without regard to the CNOL deduction). The group's CTI determined by reference to only T's items is a CNOL of $4. For Year 5, the CNOL deduction includes $60 of P's Year 3 loss but only $6 of T's Year 3 loss (the aggregate consolidated taxable income for Years 4 and 5 determined by reference to T's items, or $66, reduced by T's SRLY losses actually absorbed by the group in Year 4, or $60).

Example 3. Net operating loss carrybacks. (a)(1) P owns all of the stock of S and T. The members of the P group contribute the following to the consolidated taxable income of the P group for Years 1, 2, and 3:

	Year 1	Year 2	Year 3	Total
P	$ 100	$ 60	$ 80	$ 240
S	20	20	30	70
T	30	10	(50)	(10)
CTI	$ 150	$ 90	$ 60	$ 300.

(2) P sells all of the stock of T to individual A at the beginning of Year 4. For its Year 4 separate return year, T has a net operating loss of $30.

Reg. § 1.1502-21T(c)

Consolidated Returns

See p. 20,601 for regulations not amended to reflect law changes

→ **Caution: Reg. § 1.1502-21T, below, was removed by T.D. 8823 and is generally effective for certain tax years ending on or before June 25, 1999.** ←

(b) T's Year 4 is a SRLY with respect to the P group. See § 1.1502-1(f)(1). T's $30 net operating loss carryback to the P group from Year 4 is not allowed under § 1.1502-21T(c) to be included in the CNOL deduction under paragraph (a) of this section for Year 1, 2, or 3, because the P group's consolidated taxable income would not be a positive amount if determined by reference to only T's items for all consolidated return years through Year 4 (without regard to the $30 net operating loss). However, the $30 loss is carried forward to T's Year 5 and succeeding taxable years as provided under the Code.

Example 4. Computation of SRLY limitation for built-in losses treated as net operating loss carryovers. (a) In Year 1, individual A forms T by contributing $300 and T sustains a $100 net operating loss. During Year 2, T's assets decline in value by $100. At the beginning of Year 3, P buys all the stock of T for $100, and T becomes a member of the P group. At the time of the acquisition, T has a $100 net unrealized built-in loss, which exceeds the threshold requirements of section 382(h)(3)(B). During Year 3, T recognizes its unrealized loss as a $100 ordinary loss. The members of the P group contribute the following to the consolidated taxable income of the P group for Years 3 and 4 (computed without regard to T's recognition of its unrealized loss and any CNOL deduction under § 1.1502-21T):

	Year 3	Year 4	Total
P group (without T)	$ 100	$ 100	$ 200
T	60	40	100
CTI	$ 160	$ 140	$ 300

(b) Under § 1.1502-15T(a), T's $100 of ordinary loss in Year 3 constitutes a built-in loss that is subject to the SRLY limitation under § 1.1502-21T(c). The amount of the limitation is determined by treating the deduction as a net operating loss carryover from a SRLY. The built-in loss is therefore subject to a $60 SRLY limitation for Year 3. The built-in loss is treated as a net operating loss carryover solely for purposes of determining the extent to which the loss is not allowed by reason of the SRLY limitation, and for all other purposes the loss remains a loss arising in Year 3. Consequently, under paragraph (b) of this section, the $60 allowed under the SRLY limitation is absorbed by the P group before T's $100 net operating loss carryover from Year 1 is allowed.

(c) Under § 1.1502-15T(a), the $40 balance of the built-in loss that is not allowed in Year 3 because of the SRLY limitation is treated as a $40 net operating loss arising in Year 3 that is subject to the SRLY limitation because, under § 1.1502-21T(c)(1)(ii), Year 3 is treated as a SRLY, and is carried to other years in accordance with the rules of paragraph (b) of this section. The SRLY limitation for Year 4 is the P group's consolidated taxable income for Year 3 and Year 4 determined by reference to only T's items and without regard to the group's CNOL deductions ($60 + $40), reduced by T's loss actually absorbed by the group in Year 3 ($60). The SRLY limitation for Year 4 is $40.

(d) Under paragraph (c) of this section and the principles of section 172(b), $40 of T's $100 net operating loss carryover from Year 1 is included in the CNOL deduction under paragraph (a) of this section in Year 4.

Example 5. Dual SRLY registers and accounting for SRLY losses actually absorbed. (i) In Year 1, T sustains a $100 net operating loss and a $50 net capital loss. At the beginning of Year 2, T becomes a member of the P group. Both of T's carryovers from Year 1 are subject to SRLY limits under this paragraph (c) and § 1.1502-22T(c). The members of the P group contribute the following to the consolidated taxable income for Years 2 and 3 (computed without regard to T's CNOL deduction under § 1.1502-21T or net capital loss carryover under § 1.1502-22T):

Year 1 (SRLY)

	P	T
ordinary		(100)
capital		(50)

Year 2

	P	T
ordinary	30	60
capital	0	(20)

Year 3

	P	T
ordinary	10	40
capital	0	30

(ii) For Year 2, the group computes separate SRLY limits for each of T's SRLY carryovers from Year 1. Under normal Internal Revenue Code rules, it determines its ability to use its capital loss carryover before it determines its ability to use its ordinary loss carryover. Under section 1211, because the group has no Year 2 capital gain, it cannot absorb any capital losses in

Reg. § 1.1502-21T(c)

Consolidated Returns

See p. 20,601 for regulations not amended to reflect law changes

→ *Caution: Reg. § 1.1502-21T, below, was removed by T.D. 8823 and is generally effective for certain tax years ending on or before June 25, 1999.*←

Year 2. T's Year 1 net capital loss and the group's Year 2 consolidated net capital loss (all of which is attributable to T) are carried over to Year 3.

(iii) Under this section, the aggregate amount of T's $100 NOL carryover from Year 1 that may be included in the CNOL deduction of the group for Year 2 may not exceed $60—the amount of the consolidated taxable income computed by reference only to T's items, including losses and deductions to the extent actually absorbed (i.e., $60 of ordinary income for Year 2). Thus, the group may include $60 of T's ordinary loss carryover from Year 1 in its Year 2 CNOL deduction. T carries over its remaining $40 of its Year 1 loss to Year 3.

(iv) For Year 3, the group again computes separate SRLY limits for each of T's SRLY carryovers from Year 1. The group has consolidated net capital gain (without taking into account a net capital loss carryover deduction) of $30. Under § 1.1502-22T(c), the aggregate amount of T's $50 capital loss carryover from Year 1 that may be included in computing the groups consolidated net capital gain for all years of the group (here Years 2 and 3) may not exceed $30 (the aggregate consolidated net capital gain computed by reference only to T's items, including losses and deductions actually absorbed (i.e., $30 of capital gain in Year 3)). Thus, the group may include $30 of T's Year 1 capital loss carryover in its computation of consolidated net capital gain for Year 3, which offsets the group's capital gains for Year 3. T carries over its remaining $20 of its Year 1 loss to Year 4. The group carries over the Year 2 consolidated net capital loss to Year 4.

(v) Under this section, the aggregate amount of T's NOL carryover from Year 1 that may be included in the CNOL deduction of the group for Years 2 and 3 may not exceed $100, which is the amount of the aggregate consolidated taxable income for Years 2 and 3 determined by reference only to T's items, including losses and deductions actually absorbed (i.e., $60 of ordinary income in Year 2 plus $40 of ordinary income, $30 of capital gain, and $30 of SRLY capital losses actually absorbed in Year 3). The group included $60 of T's ordinary loss carryover in its Year 2 CNOL deduction. It may include the remaining $40 of the carryover in its Year 3 CNOL deduction.

(2) *SRLY subgroup limitation.* In the case of a net operating loss carryover or carryback for which there is a SRLY subgroup, the principles of paragraph (c)(1) of this section apply to the SRLY subgroup, and not separately to its members. Thus, the contribution to consolidated taxable income and the net operating loss carryovers and carrybacks arising (or treated as arising) in SRLYs that are included in the CNOL deductions for all consolidated return years of the group under paragraph (a) of this section are based on the aggregate amounts of income, gain, deduction, and loss of the members of the SRLY subgroup for the relevant consolidated return years (as provided in paragraph (c)(1)(i)(C) of this section). For an illustration of aggregate amounts during the relevant consolidated return years following the year in which a member of a SRLY subgroup ceases to be a member of the group, see paragraph (c)(2)(vii) *Example 4* of this section. A SRLY subgroup may exist only for a carryover or carryback arising in a year that is not a SRLY (and is not treated as a SRLY under paragraph (c)(1)(ii) of this section) with respect to another group (the former group), whether or not the group is a consolidated group. A separate SRLY subgroup is determined for each such carryover or carryback. A consolidated group may include more than one SRLY subgroup and a member may be a member of more than one SRLY subgroup. Solely for purposes of determining the members of a SRLY subgroup with respect to a loss:

(i) *Carryovers.* In the case of a carryover, the SRLY subgroup is composed of the member carrying over the loss (the loss member) and each other member that was a member of the former group that becomes a member of the group at the same time as the loss member. A member remains a member of the SRLY subgroup until it ceases to be affiliated with the loss member. The aggregate determination described in paragraph (c)(1) of this section and this paragraph (c)(2) includes the amounts of income, gain, deduction, and loss of each member of the SRLY subgroup for the consolidated return years during which it remains a member of the SRLY subgroup. For an illustration of the aggregate determination of a SRLY subgroup, see paragraph (c)(2)(vii) *Example 2* of this section.

(ii) *Carrybacks.* In the case of a carryback, the SRLY subgroup is composed of the member carrying back the loss (the loss member) and each other member of the group from which the loss is carried back that has been continuously affiliated with the loss member from the year to which the loss is carried through the year in which the loss arises.

(iii) *Built-in losses.* In the case of a built-in loss, the SRLY subgroup is composed of the mem-

Reg. § 1.1502-21T(c)(2)

Consolidated Returns

See p. 20,601 for regulations not amended to reflect law changes

→ **Caution:** *Reg. § 1.1502-21T, below, was removed by T.D. 8823 and is generally effective for certain tax years ending on or before June 25, 1999.* ←

ber recognizing the loss (the loss member) and each other member that was part of the subgroup with respect to the loss determined under § 1.1502-15T(c)(2) immediately before the members became members of the group. The principles of paragraphs (c)(2)(i) and (ii) of this section apply to determine the SRLY subgroup for the built-in loss that is, under paragraph (c)(1)(ii) of this section, treated as arising in a SRLY with respect to the group in which the loss is recognized. For this purpose and as the context requires, a reference in those paragraphs to a group or former group is a reference to the subgroup determined under § 1.1502-15T(c)(2).

(iv) *Principal purpose of avoiding or increasing a SRLY limitation.* The members composing a SRLY subgroup are not treated as a SRLY subgroup if any of them is formed, acquired, or availed of with a principal purpose of avoiding the application of, or increasing any limitation under, this paragraph (c). Any member excluded from a SRLY subgroup, if excluded with a principal purpose of so avoiding or increasing any SRLY limitation, is treated as included in the SRLY subgroup.

(v) *Coordination with other limitations.* This paragraph (c)(2) does not allow a net operating loss to offset income to the extent inconsistent with other limitations or restrictions on the use of losses, such as a limitation based on the nature or activities of members. For example, any dual consolidated loss may not reduce the taxable income to an extent greater than that allowed under section 1503(d) and § 1.1503-2. See also § 1.1502-47(q) (relating to preemption of rules for life-nonlife groups).

(vi) *Anti-duplication.* If the same item of income or deduction could be taken into account more than once in determining a limitation under this paragraph (c), or in a manner inconsistent with any other provision of the Code or regulations incorporating this paragraph (c), the item of income or deduction is taken into account only once and in such manner that losses are absorbed in accordance with the ordering rules in paragraph (b) of this section and the underlying purposes of this section.

(vii) *Examples.* The principles of this paragraph (c)(2) are illustrated by the following examples:

Example 1. Members of SRLY subgroups. (a) During Year 1, P sustains a $50 net operating loss. At the beginning of Year 2, P buys all the stock of S at a time when the aggregate basis of S's assets exceeds their aggregate value by $70 (as determined under § 1.1502-15T). At the beginning of Year 3, P buys all the stock of T, T has a $60 net operating loss carryover at the time of the acquisition, and T becomes a member of the P group. During Year 4, S forms S1 and T forms T1, each by contributing assets with built-in gains which are, in the aggregate, material. S1 and T1 become members of the P group. M is the common parent of another group. During Year 7, M acquires all of the stock of P, and the members of the P group become members of the M group for the balance of Year 7. The $50 and $60 loss carryovers of P and T are carried to Year 7 of the M group, and the value and basis of S's assets did not change after it became a member of the former P group.

(b) Under paragraph (c)(2) of this section, a separate SRLY subgroup is determined for each loss carryover and built-in loss. In the P group, P's $50 loss carryover is not treated as arising in a SRLY. See § 1.1502-1(f). Consequently, the carryover is not subject to limitation under paragraph (c) of this section in the P group.

(c) In the M group, P's $50 loss carryover is treated as arising in a SRLY and is subject to the limitation under paragraph (c) of this section. A SRLY subgroup with respect to that loss is composed of members which were members of the P group, the group as to which the loss was not a SRLY. The SRLY subgroup is composed of P, the member carrying over the loss, and each other member of the P group that became a member of the M group at the same time as P. A member of the SRLY subgroup remains a member until it ceases to be affiliated with P. For Year 7, the SRLY subgroup is composed of P, S, T, S1, and T1.

(d) In the P group, S's $70 unrealized loss, if recognized within the 5-year recognition period after S becomes a member of the P group, is subject to limitation under paragraph (c) of this section. See § 1.1502-15T and paragraph (c)(1)(ii) of this section. Because S was not continuously affiliated with P, T, or T1 for 60 consecutive months prior to joining the P group, these corporations cannot be included in a SRLY subgroup with respect to S's unrealized loss in the P group. See paragraph (c)(2)(iii) of this section. As a successor to S, S1 is included in a subgroup with S in the P group. Because S did not cease to exist, however, S1's contribution to consolidated taxable income may not be used to increase the consolidated taxable income of the P group that may be offset by the built-in loss. See paragraph (f) of this section.

Reg. § 1.1502-21T(c)(2)

→ *Caution: Reg. § 1.1502-21T, below, was removed by T.D. 8823 and is generally effective for certain tax years ending on or before June 25, 1999.*←

(e) In the M group, S's $70 unrealized loss, if recognized within the 5-year recognition period after S becomes a member of the M group, is subject to limitation under paragraph (c) of this section. Prior to becoming a member of the M group, S had been continuously affiliated with P (but not T or T1) for 60 consecutive months and S1 is a successor that has remained continuously affiliated with S. Those members had a net unrealized built-in loss immediately before they became members of the group under § 1.1502-15T(c). Consequently, in Year 7, S, S1, and P compose a subgroup in the M group with respect to S's unrealized loss. S1's contribution to consolidated taxable income may not be used to increase the consolidated taxable income of the M group that may be offset by the recognized built-in loss. See paragraph (f) of this section.

(f) In the P group, T's $60 loss carryover arose in a SRLY and is subject to limitation under paragraph (c) of this section. P, S, and S1 were not members of the group in which T's loss arose and cannot be members of a SRLY subgroup with respect to the carryover in the P group. See paragraph (c)(2)(i) of this section. As a successor to T, T1 is included in a SRLY subgroup with T in the P group; however, because T did not cease to exist, T1's contribution to consolidated taxable income may not be used to increase the consolidated taxable income of the P group that may be offset by the carryover. See paragraph (f) of this section.

(g) In the M group, T's $60 loss carryover arose in a SRLY and is subject to limitation under paragraph (c) of this section. T and T1 remain the only members of a SRLY subgroup with respect to the carryover, but T1's contribution to consolidated taxable income may not be used to increase consolidated taxable income of the M group that may be offset by the carryover. See paragraph (f) of this section.

Example 2. Computation of SRLY subgroup limitation. (a) Individual A forms S. Individual B forms T. In Year 2, P buys all the stock of S and T from A and B, and S and T become members of the P group. For Year 3, the P group has a $45 CNOL, which is attributable to P, and which P carries forward. M is the common parent of another group. At the beginning of Year 4, M acquires all of the stock of P and the former members of the P group become members of the M group.

(b) P's year to which the loss is attributable, Year 3, is a SRLY with respect to the M group. See § 1.1502-1(f)(1). However, P, S, and T compose a SRLY subgroup with respect to the Year 3 loss under paragraph (c)(2)(i) of this section because Year 3 is not a SRLY (and is not treated as a SRLY) with respect to the P group. P's loss is carried over to the M group's Year 4 and is therefore subject to the SRLY subgroup limitation in paragraph (c)(2) of this section.

(c) In Year 4, the M group has $10 of consolidated taxable income (computed without regard to the CNOL deduction for Year 4). However, such consolidated taxable income would be $45 if determined by reference to only the items of P, S, and T, the members included in the SRLY subgroup with respect to P's loss carryover. Therefore, the SRLY subgroup limitation under paragraph (c)(2) of this section for P's net operating loss carryover from Year 3 is $45. Because the M group has only $10 of consolidated taxable income in Year 4, however, only $10 of P's net operating loss carryover is included in the CNOL deduction under paragraph (a) of this section in Year 4.

(d) In Year 5, the M group has $100 of consolidated taxable income (computed without regard to the CNOL deduction for Year 5). Neither P, S, nor T has any items of income, gain, deduction, or loss in Year 5. Although the members of the SRLY subgroup do not contribute to the $100 of consolidated taxable income in Year 5, the SRLY subgroup limitation for Year 5 is $35 (the sum of SRLY subgroup consolidated taxable income of $45 in Year 4 and $0 in Year 5, less the $10 net operating loss carryover actually absorbed by the M group in Year 4). Therefore, $35 of P's net operating loss carryover is included in the CNOL deduction under paragraph (a) of this section in Year 5.

Example 3. Inclusion in more than one SRLY subgroup. (a) At the beginning of Year 1, S buys all the stock of T, and T becomes a member of the S group. For Year 1, the S group has a CNOL of $10, all of which is attributable to S and is carried over to Year 2. At the beginning of Year 2, P buys all the stock of S, and S and T become members of the P group. For Year 2, the P group has a CNOL of $35, all of which is attributable to P and is carried over to Year 3. At the beginning of Year 3, M acquires all of the stock of P and the former members of the P group become members of the M group.

(b) P's and S's net operating losses arising in SRLYs with respect to the M group are subject to limitation under paragraph (c) of this section. P, S, and T compose a SRLY subgroup for purposes of determining the limitation for P's $35 net

Reg. § 1.1502-21T(c)(2)

→ **Caution: Reg. § 1.1502-21T, below, was removed by T.D. 8823 and is generally effective for certain tax years ending on or before June 25, 1999.**←

operating loss carryover arising in Year 2 because, under paragraph (c)(2)(i) of this section, Year 2 is not a SRLY with respect to the P group. Similarly, S and T compose a SRLY subgroup for purposes of determining the limitation for S's $10 net operating loss carryover arising in Year 1 because Year 1 is not a SRLY with respect to the S group.

(c) S and T are members of both the SRLY subgroup with respect to P's losses and the SRLY subgroup with respect to S's losses. Under paragraph (c)(2) of this section, S's and T's items cannot be included in the determination of the SRLY subgroup limitation for both SRLY subgroups for the same consolidated return year; paragraph (c)(2)(vi) of this section requires the M group to consider the items of S and T only once so that the losses are absorbed in the order of the taxable years in which they were sustained. Because S's loss was incurred in Year 1, while P's loss was incurred in Year 2, the items will be added in the determination of the consolidated taxable income of the S and T SRLY subgroup to enable S's loss to be absorbed first. The taxable income of the P, S, and T SRLY subgroup is then computed by including the consolidated taxable income for the S and T SRLY subgroup less the amount of any net operating loss carryover of S that is absorbed after applying this section to the S subgroup for the year.

Example 4. Corporation ceases to be affiliated with a SRLY subgroup. (a) P and S are members of the P group and the P group has a CNOL of $30 in Year 1, all of which is attributable to P and carried over to Year 2. At the beginning of Year 2, M acquires all of the stock of P, and P and S become members of the M group. P and S compose a SRLY subgroup with respect to P's net operating loss carryover. For Year 2, consolidated taxable income of the M group determined by reference to only the items of P (and without regard to the CNOL deduction for Year 2) is $40. However, such consolidated taxable income of the M group determined by reference to the items of both P and S is a loss of $20. Thus, the SRLY subgroup limitation under paragraph (c)(2) of this section prevents the M group from including any of P's net operating loss carryover in the CNOL deduction under paragraph (a) of this section in Year 2, and P carries the loss to Year 3.

(b) At the end of Year 2, P sells all of the S stock and S ceases to be a member of the M group and, in turn, ceases to be affiliated with the P subgroup. For Year 3, consolidated taxable income of the M group is $50 (determined without regard to the CNOL deduction for Year 3), and such consolidated taxable income would be $10 if determined by reference to only items of P. However, the limitation under paragraph (c) of this section for Year 3 for P's net operating loss carryover still prevents the M group from including any of P's loss in the CNOL deduction under paragraph (a) of this section. The limitation results from the inclusion of S's items for Year 2 in the determination of the SRLY subgroup limitation for Year 3 even though S ceased to be a member of the M group (and the P subgroup) at the end of Year 2. Thus, the M group's consolidated taxable income determined by reference to only the SRLY subgroup members' items for all consolidated return years of the group through Year 3 (determined without regard to the CNOL deduction) is not a positive amount.

(d) *Coordination with consolidated return change of ownership limitation and transactions subject to old section 382*—(1) *Consolidated return changes of ownership.* If a consolidated return change of ownership occurred before January 1, 1997, the principles of § 1.1502-21A(d) apply to determine the amount of the aggregate of the net operating losses attributable to old members of the group that may be included in the consolidated net operating loss deduction under paragraph (a) of this section. For this purpose, § 1.1502-1(g) is applied by treating that date as the end of the year of change.

(2) *Old section 382.* The principles of § 1.1502-21A(e) apply to disallow or reduce the amount of a net operating loss carryover of a member as a result of a transaction subject to old section 382.

(e) *Consolidated net operating loss.* Any excess of deductions over gross income, as determined under § 1.1502-11(a) (without regard to any consolidated net operating loss deduction), is also referred to as the consolidated net operating loss (or CNOL).

(f) *Predecessors and successors*—(1) *In general.* For purposes of this section, any reference to a corporation, member, common parent, or subsidiary, includes, as the context may require, a reference to a successor or predecessor, as defined in § 1.1502-1(f)(4).

(2) *Limitation on SRLY subgroups.* Except as the Commissioner may otherwise determine, any increase in the consolidated taxable income of a SRLY subgroup that is attributable to a successor is disregarded unless the successor acquires

Reg. § 1.1502-21T(f)(2)

→ *Caution: Reg. § 1.1502-21T, below, was removed by T.D. 8823 and is generally effective for certain tax years ending on or before June 25, 1999.*←

substantially all the assets and liabilities of its predecessor and the predecessor ceases to exist.

(g) *Effective date*—(1) *In general.* This section generally applies to consolidated return years beginning on or after January 1, 1997.

(2) *SRLY limitation.* Except in the case of those members (including members of a SRLY subgroup) described in paragraph (g)(3)(iii) of this section, a group does not take into account a consolidated taxable year beginning before January 1, 1997, in determining the aggregate of the consolidated taxable income under paragraph (c)(1) of this section (including for purposes of § 1.1502-15T and § 1.1502-22T(c)) for the members (or SRLY subgroups).

(3) *Application to prior periods.* A consolidated group may apply the rules of this section to all consolidated return years ending on or after January 29, 1991, and beginning before January 1, 1997, provided that—

(i) The group's tax liability as shown on an original or an amended return is consistent with the application of the rules of this section (other than this paragraph (g)) and § § 1.1502-15T, 1.1502-22T, 1.1502-23T, 1.1502-91T through 1.1502-96T, and 1.1502-98T for each such year for which the statute of limitations does not preclude the filing of an amended return on January 1, 1997;

(ii) Each section described in paragraph (g)(3)(i) of this section and § 1.1502-1(f)(4)(ii) is applied by substituting "taxable years ending on or after January 29, 1991" for "taxable years beginning on or after January 1, 1997" (and "before January 29, 1991" for "before January 1, 1997" in the case of consolidated return changes of ownership) as the context requires.

(iii) The rules of paragraph (c) of this section and § § 1.1502-15T and 1.1502-22T(c) are applied only with respect to the losses and deductions of those corporations that became members of the group (including members of a subgroup), and to acquisitions occurring, on or after January 29, 1991, (and only with respect to such losses and deductions);

(iv) The rules of § § 1.1502-15A, 1.1502-21A(c) and 1.1502-22A(c) are applied with respect to the losses and deductions of those corporations that became members of the group, and to acquisitions occurring, before January 29, 1991; and

(v) Appropriate adjustments are made in the earliest subsequent open year to reflect any inconsistency in a year for which the statute of limitations precludes the filing of an amended return on January 1, 1997.

(4) *Waiver of carrybacks.* Paragraph (b)(3)(i) of this section (relating to the waiver of carrybacks) applies to net operating losses arising in a consolidated return year for which the due date of the income tax return (without regard to extensions) is on or after August 26, 1996. [Temporary Reg. § 1.1502-21T.]

☐ [T.D. 8677, 6-26-96. Amended by T.D. 8751, 1-9-98. Removed by T.D. 8823, 6-25-99.]

→ *Caution: Reg. § 1.1502-22, below, is generally effective for tax years for which the consolidated return due date is after June 25, 1999.*←

[Reg. § 1.1502-22]

§ 1.1502-22. **Consolidated capital gain and loss.**—(a) *Capital gain.* The determinations under section 1222, including capital gain net income, net long-term capital gain, and net capital gain, with respect to members during consolidated return years are not made separately. Instead, consolidated amounts are determined for the group as a whole. The consolidated capital gain net income for any consolidated return year is determined by reference to—

(1) The aggregate gains and losses of members from sales or exchanges of capital assets for the year (other than gains and losses to which section 1231 applies);

(2) The consolidated net section 1231 gain for the year (determined under § 1.1502-23); and

(3) The net capital loss carryovers or carrybacks to the year.

(b) *Net capital loss carryovers and carrybacks*—(1) *In general.* The determinations under section 1222, including net capital loss and net short-term capital loss, with respect to members during consolidated return years are not made separately. Instead, consolidated amounts are determined for the group as a whole. Losses included in the consolidated net capital loss may be carried to consolidated return years, and, after apportionment, may be carried to separate return years. The net capital loss carryovers and carrybacks consist of—

(i) Any consolidated net capital losses of the group; and

(ii) Any net capital losses of the members arising in separate return years.

Reg. § 1.1502-22(a)(1)

Consolidated Returns

See p. 20,601 for regulations not amended to reflect law changes

→ *Caution: Reg. § 1.1502-22, below, is generally effective for tax years for which the consolidated return due date is after June 25, 1999.*←

(2) *Carryovers and carrybacks generally.* The net capital loss carryovers and carrybacks to a taxable year are determined under the principles of section 1212 and this section. Thus, losses permitted to be absorbed in a consolidated return year generally are absorbed in the order of the taxable years in which they were sustained, and losses carried from taxable years ending on the same date, and which are available to offset consolidated capital gain net income, generally are absorbed on a pro rata basis. Additional rules provided under the Internal Revenue Code or regulations also apply, as well as the SRLY limitation under paragraph (c) of this section. See, e.g., section 382(1)(2)(B).

(3) *Carryovers and carrybacks of consolidated net capital losses to separate return years.* If any consolidated net capital loss that is attributable to a member may be carried to a separate return year under the principles of § 1.1502-21(b)(2), the amount of the consolidated net capital loss that is attributable to the member is apportioned and carried to the separate return year (apportioned loss).

(4) *Special rules*—(i) *Short years in connection with transactions to which section 381(a) applies.* If a member distributes or transfers assets to a corporation that is a member immediately after the distribution or transfer in a transaction to which section 381(a) applies, the transaction does not cause the distributor or transferor to have a short year within the consolidated return year of the group in which the transaction occurred that is counted as a separate year for purposes of determining the years to which a net capital loss may be carried.

(ii) *Special status losses.* [Reserved]

(c) *Limitations on net capital loss carryovers and carrybacks from separate return limitation years.* The aggregate of the net capital losses of a member arising (or treated as arising) in SRLYs that are included in the determination of consolidated capital gain net income for all consolidated return years of the group under paragraph (a) of this section may not exceed the aggregate of the consolidated capital gain net income for all consolidated return years of the group determined by reference to only the member's items of gain and loss from capital assets as defined in section 1221 and trade or business assets defined in section 1231(b), including the member's losses actually absorbed by the group in the taxable year (whether or not absorbed by the member). The principles of § 1.1502-21(c) (including the SRLY subgroup principles under § 1.1502-21(c)(2)) apply with appropriate adjustments for purposes of applying this paragraph (c).

(d) *Coordination with respect to consolidated return change of ownership limitation occurring in consolidated return years beginning before January 1, 1997.* If a consolidated return change of ownership occurred before January 1, 1997, the principles of § 1.1502-22A(d) apply to determine the amount of the aggregate of the net capital loss attributable to old members of the group (as those terms are defined in § 1.1502-1(g)), that may be included in the net capital loss carryover under paragraph (b) of this section. For this purpose, § 1.1502-1(g) is applied by treating that date as the end of the year of change.

(e) *Consolidated net capital loss.* Any excess of losses over gains, as determined under paragraph (a) of this section (without regard to any carryovers or carrybacks), is also referred to as the consolidated net capital loss.

(f) *Predecessors and successors.* For purposes of this section, the principles of § 1.1502-21(f) apply with appropriate adjustments.

(g) *Overlap with section 383*—(1) *General rule.* The limitation provided in paragraph (c) of this section does not apply to net capital loss carryovers ((other than a hypothetical carryover like those described in § 1.1502-21(c)(1)(i)(D) and a carryover like those described in § 1.1502-21(c)(1)(ii)) when the application of paragraph (c) of this section results in an overlap with the application of section 383. For a similar rule applying in the case of net capital loss carryovers like those described in §§ 1.1502-21(c)(1)(i)(D) and (c)(1)(ii), see § 1.1502-15(g).

(2) *Definitions*—(i) *Generally.* For purposes of this paragraph (g), the definitions and nomenclature contained in sections 382 and 383, the regulations thereunder, and §§ 1.1502-90 through 1.1502-99 apply.

(ii) *Overlap.* (A) An overlap of the application of paragraph (c) of this section and the application of section 383 with respect to a net capital loss carryover occurs if a corporation becomes a member of the consolidated group (the SRLY event) within six months of the change date of an ownership change giving rise to a section 382 limitation with respect to that carryover (the section 383 event).

(B) If an overlap described in paragraph (g)(2)(ii)(A) of this section occurs with respect to net capital loss carryovers of a corporation whose SRLY event occurs within the six month period

Reg. § 1.1502-22(g)(2)

Consolidated Returns

See p. 20,601 for regulations not amended to reflect law changes

→ *Caution: Reg. § 1.1502-22, below, is generally effective for tax years for which the consolidated return due date is after June 25, 1999.*←

beginning on the date of a section 383 event, then an overlap is treated as also occurring with respect to that corporation's net capital loss carryover that arises within the period beginning with the section 383 event and ending with the SRLY event.

(C) For special rules in the event that there is a SRLY subgroup and/or a loss subgroup as defined in § 1.1502-91(d)(1) with respect to a carryover, see paragraph (g)(4) of this section.

(3) *Operating rules*—(i) *Section 383 event before SRLY event.* If a SRLY event occurs on the same date as a section 383 event or within the six month period beginning on the date of the section 383 event, paragraph (g)(1) of this section applies beginning with the tax year that includes the SRLY event.

(ii) *SRLY event before section 383 event.* If a section 383 event occurs within the period beginning the day after the SRLY event and ending six months after the SRLY event, paragraph (g)(1) of this section applies starting with the first tax year that begins after the section 383 event.

(4) *Subgroup rules.* In general, in the case of a net capital loss carryover for which there is a SRLY subgroup and a loss subgroup (as defined in § 1.1502-91(d)(1)), the principles of this paragraph (g) apply to the SRLY subgroup, and not separately to its members. However, paragraph (g)(1) of this section applies—

(i) With respect to a carryover described in paragraph (g)(2)(ii)(A) of this section only if—

(A) All members of the SRLY subgroup with respect to that carryover are also included in a loss subgroup with respect to that carryover; and

(B) All members of a loss subgroup with respect to that carryover are also members of a SRLY subgroup with respect to that carryover; and

(ii) With respect to a carryover described in paragraph (g)(2)(ii)(B) of this section only if all members of the SRLY subgroup for that carryover are also members of a SRLY subgroup that has net capital loss carryovers described in paragraph (g)(2)(ii)(A) of this section that are subject to the overlap rule of paragraph (g)(1) of this section.

(h) *Effective date*—(1) *In general.* This section generally applies to taxable years for which the due date (without extensions) of the consolidated return is after June 25, 1999. However—

(i) In the event that paragraph (g)(1) of this section does not apply to a particular net capital loss carryover in the current group, then solely for purposes of applying paragraph (c) of this section to determine a limitation with respect to that carryover and with respect to which the SRLY register (consolidated taxable income determined by reference to only the member's or subgroup's items of income, gain, deduction or loss) began in a taxable year for which the due date of the return was on or before June 25, 1999, the principles of § 1.1502-21(c)(2) shall be applied without regard to the phrase "or for a carryover that was subject to the overlap rule described in paragraph (g) of this section or § 1.1502-15(g) with respect to another group (the former group)"; and

(ii) For purposes of paragraph (g) of this section, only an ownership change to which section 383, as amended by the Tax Reform Act of 1986, applies and which results in a section 382 limitation shall constitute a section 383 event.

(2) *Prior periods.* For certain taxable years ending on or before June 25, 1999, see § 1.1502-22T in effect prior to June 25, 1999, as contained in 26 CFR part 1 revised April 1, 1999, as applicable. [Reg. § 1.1502-22.]

☐ [*T.D.* 8823, 6-25-99.]

[Reg. § 1.1502-22A]

§ 1.1502-22A. Consolidated net capital gain or loss generally applicable for consolidated return years beginning before January 1, 1997.—(a) *Computation*—(1) *Consolidated capital gain net income.* The consolidated capital gain net income (net capital gain for taxable years beginning before January 1, 1977) for the taxable year shall be determined by taking into account—

(i) The aggregate of the capital gains and losses (determined without regard to gains or losses to which section 1231 applies or net capital loss carryovers or carrybacks) of the members of the group for the consolidated return year;

(ii) The consolidated section 1231 net gain for such year (computed in accordance with §§ 1.1502-23A or 1.1502-23T), and

(iii) The consolidated net capital loss carryovers or carrybacks to such year (as determined under paragraph (b) of this section).

(2) *Consolidated net capital loss.* The consolidated net capital loss shall be determined under subparagraph (1) of this paragraph but without regard to subdivision (iii) thereof.

Reg. § 1.1502-22A(a)(1)

(3) *Special rules.* For purposes of this section, capital gains and losses on intercompany transactions and transactions with respect to stock, bonds, and other obligations of a member of the group shall be reflected as provided in §§ 1.1502-13 and 1.1502-19, and capital losses shall be limited as provided in §§ 1.1502-15A and 1.1502-11(c).

(4) [Reserved]

(5) *Example.* The provisions of this paragraph may be illustrated by the following example:

Example. (i) Corporations P, S, and T file consolidated returns on a calendar year basis for 1966 and 1967. The members had the following transactions involving capital assets during 1967: P sold an asset with a $10,000 basis to S for $17,000 and none of the circumstances of restoration described in § 1.1502-13 occurred by the end of the consolidated return year; S sold an asset to individual A for $7,000 which S had purchased during 1966 from P for $10,000, and with respect to which P had deferred a gain of $2,000; T sold an asset with a basis of $10,000 to individual B for $25,000. The group has a consolidated net capital loss carryover to the taxable year of $10,000.

(ii) The consolidated net capital gain of the group is $4,000, determined as follows: P's net capital gain of $2,000, representing the deferred gain on the sale to S during the taxable year 1966, restored into income during taxable year 1967 (the $7,000 gain on P's deferred intercompany transaction is not taken into account for the current year), plus T's net capital gain of $15,000, minus S's net capital loss of $3,000 and the consolidated net capital loss carryover of $10,000.

(b) *Consolidated net capital loss carryovers and carrybacks*—(1) *In general.* The consolidated net capital loss carryovers and carrybacks to the taxable year shall consist of any consolidated net capital losses of the group, plus any net capital losses of members of the group arising in separate return years of such members, which may be carried over or back to the taxable year under the principles of section 1212(a). However, such consolidated carryovers and carrybacks shall not include any consolidated net capital loss apportioned to a corporation for a separate return year pursuant to § 1.1502-79A(b) (or § 1.1502-22T(b), as appropriate) and shall be subject to the limitations contained in paragraphs (c) and (d) of this section. For purposes of section 1212(a)(1), the portion of any consolidated net capital loss for any taxable year attributable to a foreign expropriation capital loss is the amount of the foreign expropriation capital losses of all the members for such year (but not in excess of the consolidated net capital loss for such year).

(2) *Absorption rules.* For purposes of determining the amount, if any, of a net capital loss (whether consolidated or separate) which can be carried to a taxable year (consolidated or separate), the amount of such net capital loss which is absorbed in a prior consolidated return year under section 1212(a)(1) shall be determined by—

(i) Applying all net capital losses which can be carried to such prior year in the order of the taxable years in which such losses were sustained, beginning with the taxable year which ends earliest, and

(ii) Applying all such losses which can be carried to such prior year from taxable years ending on the same date on a pro rata basis, except that any portion of a net capital loss attributable to a foreign expropriation capital loss to which section 1212(a)(1)(B) applies shall be applied last.

(c) *Limitation on net capital loss carryovers and carrybacks from separate return limitation years*—(1) *General rule.* In the case of a net capital loss of a member of the group arising in a separate return limitation year (as defined in paragraph (f) of § 1.1502-1) of such member (and in a separate return limitation year of any predecessor of such member), the amount that may be included under paragraph (b) of this section (computed without regard to the limitation contained in paragraph (d) of this section) shall not exceed the amount determined under subparagraph (2) of this paragraph.

(2) *Computation of limitation.* The amount referred to in subparagraph (1) of this paragraph with respect to a member of the group is the excess, if any, of—

(i) The consolidated capital gain net income (net capital gain for taxable years beginning before January 1, 1977) for the taxable year (computed without regard to any net capital loss carryovers or carrybacks), minus such consolidated capital gain net income (net capital gain for taxable years beginning before January 1, 1977) for the taxable year recomputed by excluding the capital gains and losses and the gains and losses to which section 1231 applies of such member, over

(ii) The net capital losses attributable to such member which can be carried to the taxable year arising in taxable years ending prior to the particular separate return limitation year.

(d) *Limitation on capital loss carryovers where there has been a consolidated return change of ownership*—(1) *General rule.* If a consolidated return change of ownership (as defined in para-

Reg. § 1.1502-22A(d)

graph (g) of § 1.1502-1) occurs during the taxable year or an earlier taxable year, the amount which may be included under paragraph (b) of this section in the consolidated net capital loss carryovers to the taxable year with respect to the aggregate of the net capital losses attributable to old members of the group (as defined in paragraph (g)(3) of § 1.1502-1) arising in taxable years (consolidated or separate) ending on the same day and before the taxable year in which the consolidated return change of ownership occurred shall not exceed the amount determined under subparagraph (2) of this paragraph.

(2) *Computation of limitation.* The amount referred to in subparagraph (1) of this paragraph shall be the excess of—

(i) The consolidated capital gain net income (net capital gain for taxable years beginning before January 1, 1977) (determined without regard to any net capital loss carryovers for the taxable year) recomputed by including only capital gains and losses and gains and losses to which section 1231 applies of the old members of the group, over

(ii) The aggregate net capital losses attributable to the old members of the group which may be carried to the taxable year arising in taxable years ending prior to the particular loss year or years.

(3) *Cross-reference.* See § 1.1502-22T(d) for the rule that applies the principles of this paragraph (d) in consolidated return years beginning on or after January 1, 1997, with respect to a consolidated return change of ownership occurring before January 1, 1997.

(e) *Effective date.* This section applies to any consolidated return years to which § 1.1502-21T(g) does not apply. See § 1.1502-21T(g) for effective dates of that section. [Reg. § 1.1502-22A.]

☐ [T.D. 6894, 9-7-66. Amended by T.D. 7637, 8-6-79; T.D. 7728, 10-31-80 and T.D. 8597, 7-12-95. Redesignated as Reg. § 1.1502-22A and amended by T.D. 8677, 6-26-96.]

→ *Caution: Reg. § 1.1502-22T, below, was removed by T.D. 8823 and is generally effective for certain tax years ending on or before June 25, 1999.* ←

[Reg. § 1.1502-22T]

§ 1.1502-22T. Consolidated capital gain and loss (temporary).—(a) *Capital gain.* The determinations under section 1222, including capital gain net income, net long-term capital gain, and net capital gain, with respect to members during consolidated return years are not made separately. Instead, consolidated amounts are determined for the group as a whole. The consolidated capital gain net income for any consolidated return year is determined by reference to—

(1) The aggregate gains and losses of members from sales or exchanges of capital assets for the year (other than gains and losses to which section 1231 applies);

(2) The consolidated net section 1231 gain for the year (determined under § 1.1502-23T); and

(3) The net capital loss carryovers or carrybacks to the year.

(b) *Net capital loss carryovers and carrybacks*—(1) *In general.* The determinations under section 1222, including net capital loss and net short-term capital loss, with respect to members during consolidated return years are not made separately. Instead, consolidated amounts are determined for the group as a whole. Losses included in the consolidated net capital loss may be carried to consolidated return years, and, after apportionment, may be carried to separate return years. The net capital loss carryovers and carrybacks consist of—

(i) Any consolidated net capital losses of the group; and

(ii) Any net capital losses of the members arising in separate return years.

(2) *Carryovers and carrybacks generally.* The net capital loss carryovers and carrybacks to a taxable year are determined under the principles of section 1212 and this section. Thus, losses permitted to be absorbed in a consolidated return year generally are absorbed in the order of the taxable years in which they were sustained, and losses carried from taxable years ending on the same date, and which are available to offset consolidated capital gain net income, generally are absorbed on a pro rata basis. Additional rules provided under the Code or regulations also apply, as well as the SRLY limitation under paragraph (c) of this section. See, e.g., section 382(l)(2)(B).

(3) *Carryovers and carrybacks of consolidated net capital losses to separate return years.* If any consolidated net capital loss that is attributable to a member may be carried to a separate return year under the principles of § 1.1502-21T(b)(2), the amount of the consolidated net capital loss that is attributable to the member is apportioned and carried to the separate return year (apportioned loss).

Reg. § 1.1502-22T(a)(1)

Consolidated Returns

→ **Caution: Reg. § 1.1502-22T, below, was removed by T.D. 8823 and is generally effective for certain tax years ending on or before June 25, 1999.**←

(4) *Special rules*—(i) *Short years in connection with transactions to which section 381(a) applies.* If a member distributes or transfers assets to a corporation that is a member immediately after the distribution or transfer in a transaction to which section 381(a) applies, the transaction does not cause the distributor or transferor to have a short year within the consolidated return year of the group in which the transaction occurred that is counted as a separate year for purposes of determining the years to which a net capital loss may be carried.

(ii) *Special status losses.* [Reserved]

(c) *Limitations on net capital loss carryovers and carrybacks from separate return limitation years.* The aggregate of the net capital losses of a member arising (or treated as arising) in SRLYs that are included in the determination of consolidated capital gain net income for all consolidated return years of the group under paragraph (a) of this section may not exceed the aggregate of the consolidated capital gain net income for all consolidated return years of the group determined by reference to only the member's items of gain and loss from capital assets as defined in section 1221 and trade or business assets defined in section 1231(b), including the member's losses actually absorbed by the group in the taxable year (whether or not absorbed by the member). The principles of § 1.1502-21T(c)(including the SRLY subgroup principles under § 1.1502-21T(c)(2)) apply with appropriate adjustments for purposes of applying this paragraph (c).

(d) *Coordination with respect to consolidated return change of ownership limitation occurring in consolidated return years beginning before January 1, 1997.* If a consolidated return change of ownership occurred before January 1, 1997, the principles of § 1.1502-22A(d) apply to determine the amount of the aggregate of the net capital loss attributable to old members of the group (as those terms are defined in § 1.1502-1(g)), that may be included in the net capital loss carryover under paragraph (b) of this section. For this purpose, § 1.1502-1(g) is applied by treating that date as the end of the year of change.

(e) *Consolidated net capital loss.* Any excess of losses over gains, as determined under paragraph (a) of this section (without regard to any carryovers or carrybacks), is also referred to as the consolidated net capital loss.

(f) *Predecessors and successors.* For purposes of this section, the principles of § 1.1502-21T(f) apply with appropriate adjustments.

(g) *Effective date*—(1) *In general.* This section applies to consolidated return years beginning on or after January 1, 1997.

(2) *Application to prior periods.* See § 1.1502-21T(g)(3) for rules generally permitting a group to apply the rules of this section to consolidated return years ending on or after January 29, 1991, and beginning before January 1, 1997. [Temporary Reg. § 1.1502-22T.]

☐ [*T.D. 8677, 6-26-96. Removed by T.D. 8823, 6-25-99.*]

→ **Caution: Reg. § 1.1502-23, below, is generally effective for tax years for which the consolidated return due date is after June 25, 1999.**←

[Reg. § 1.1502-23]

§ 1.1502-23. **Consolidated net section 1231 gain or loss.**—(a) *In general.* Net section 1231 gains and losses of members arising during consolidated return years are not determined separately. Instead, the consolidated net section 1231 gain or loss is determined under this section for the group as a whole.

(b) *Example.* The following example illustrates the provisions of this section:

Example. Use of SRLY registers with net gains and net losses under section 1231. (i) In Year 1, T sustains a $20 net capital loss. At the beginning of Year 2, T becomes a member of the P group. T's capital loss carryover from Year 1 is subject to SRLY limits under § 1.1502-22(c). The members of the P group contribute the following to the consolidated taxable income for Year 2 (computed without regard to T's net capital loss carryover under § 1.1502-22):

	P	T
Year 1 (SRLY)		
Ordinary		
Capital		(20)
Year 2		
Ordinary	10	20
Capital	70	0
§ 1231	(60)	30

Reg. § 1.1502-23(b)

Consolidated Returns

See p. 20,601 for regulations not amended to reflect law changes

→ *Caution: Reg. § 1.1502-23, below, is generally effective for tax years for which the consolidated return due date is after June 25, 1999.*←

(ii) Under section 1231, if the section 1231 losses for any taxable year exceed the section 1231 gains for such taxable year, such gains and losses are treated as ordinary gains or losses. Because the P group's section 1231 losses, $(60), exceed the section 1231 gains, $30, the P group's net loss is treated as an ordinary loss. T's net section 1231 gain has the same character as the P group's consolidated net section 1231 loss, so T's $30 of section 1231 income is treated as ordinary income for purposes of applying § 1.1502-22(c). Under § 1.1502-22(c), the group's consolidated net capital gain determined by reference only to T's items is $0. None of T's capital loss carryover from Year 1 may be taken into account in Year 2.

(c) *Recapture of ordinary loss.* [Reserved]

(d) *Effective date*—(1) *In general.* This section applies to gains and losses arising in the determination of consolidated net section 1231 gain or loss for taxable years for which the due date (without extensions) of the consolidated return is after June 25, 1999.

(2) *Application to prior periods.* See § 1.1502-21(h)(3) for rules applicable to groups that applied the rules of this section to consolidated return years ending on or after January 29, 1991, and beginning before January 1, 1997. [Reg. § 1.1502-23.]

☐ [*T.D. 8823, 6-25-99 (corrected 7-30-99).*]

[Reg. § 1.1502-23A]

§ 1.1502-23A. Consolidated net section 1231 gain or loss generally applicable for consolidated return years beginning before January 1, 1997.—(a) The consolidated section 1231 net gain or loss for the taxable year shall be determined by taking into account the aggregate of the gains and losses to which section 1231 applies of the members of the group for the consolidated return year. Section 1231 gains and losses on intercompany transactions shall be reflected as provided in § 1.1502-13. Section 1231 losses that are "built-in deductions" shall be subject to the limitations of §§ 1.1502-21A(c) and 1.1502-22A(c), as provided in § 1.1502-15A(a) (or §§ (1.1502-21T(c) in effect prior to June 25, 1999, as contained in 26 CFR part 1 revised April 1, 1999 and 1.1502-22T(c) in effect prior to June 25, 1999, as contained in 26 CFR part 1 revised April 1, 1999, as provided in 1.1502-15T(a) in effect prior to June 25, 1999, as contained in 26 CFR part 1 revised April 1, 1999) or (1.1502-21(c) and 1.1502-22(c), as provided in 1.1502-15(a), as applicable), as appropriate).

(b) *Effective date.* This section applies to any consolidated return years to which § 1.1502-21(h) or 1.1502-21T(g) in effect prior to June 25, 1999, as contained in 26 CFR part 1 revised April 1, 1999, as applicable does not apply. See § 1.1502-21(h) or 1.1502-21T(g) in effect prior to June 25, 1999, as contained in 26 CFR part 1 revised April 1, 1999, as applicable for effective dates of these sections. [Reg. § 1.1502-23A.]

☐ [*T.D. 6894, 9-7-66. Amended by T.D. 7246, 12-29-72. Redesignated and amended by T.D. 8677, 6-26-96. Amended by T.D. 8823, 6-25-99.*]

→ *Caution: Reg. § 1.1502-23T, below, was removed by T.D. 8823 and is generally effective for certain tax years ending on or before June 25, 1999.*←

[Reg. § 1.1502-23T]

§ 1.1502-23T. Consolidated net section 1231 gain or loss (temporary).—(a) *In general.* Net section 1231 gains and losses of members arising during consolidated return years are not determined separately. Instead, the consolidated net section 1231 gain or loss is determined under this section for the group as a whole.

(b) *Example.* The following example illustrates the provisions of this section:

Example. Use of SRLY registers with net gains and net losses under section 1231. (i) In Year 1, T sustains a $20 net capital loss. At the beginning of Year 2, T becomes a member of the P group. T's capital loss carryover from Year 1 is subject to SRLY limits under § 1.1502-22T(c). The members of the P group contribute the following to the consolidated taxable income for Year 2 (computed without regard to T's net capital loss carryover under § 1.1502-22T):

Year 1 (SRLY)

	P	T
ordinary		
capital		(20)

Year 2

	P	T
ordinary	10	20
capital	70	0
§ 1231	(60)	30

→ *Caution: Reg. § 1.1502-23T, below, was removed by T.D. 8823 and is generally effective for certain tax years ending on or before June 25, 1999.* ←

(ii) Under section 1231, if the section 1231 losses for any taxable year exceed the section 1231 gains for such taxable year, such gains and losses are treated as ordinary gains or losses. Because the P group's section 1231 losses, $(60), exceed the section 1231 gains, $30, the P group's net loss is treated as an ordinary loss. T's net section 1231 gain has the same character as the P group's consolidated net section 1231 loss, so T's $30 of section 1231 income is treated as ordinary income for purposes of applying § 1.1502-22T(c). Under § 1.1502-22T(c), the group's consolidated net capital gain determined by reference only to T's items is $0. None of T's capital loss carryover from Year 1 may be taken into account in Year 2.

(c) *Recapture of ordinary loss.* [Reserved]

(d) *Effective date*—(1) *In general.* This section applies to gains and losses arising in the determination of consolidated net section 1231 gain or loss for taxable years beginning on or after January 1, 1997.

(2) *Application to prior periods.* See § 1.1502-21T(g)(3) for rules generally permitting a group to apply the rules of this section to consolidated return years ending on or after January 29, 1991, and beginning before January 1, 1997. [Temporary Reg. § 1.1502-23T.]

☐ [T.D. 8677, 6-26-96. *Amended by* T.D. 8751, 1-9-98. Removed by T.D. 8823, 6-25-99.]

[Reg. § 1.1502-24]

§ 1.1502-24. Consolidated charitable contributions deductions.—(a) *Determination of amount of consolidated charitable contributions deduction.* The deduction allowed by section 170 for the taxable year shall be the lesser of—

(1) The aggregate deductions of the members of the group allowable under section 170 (determined without regard to section 170(b)(2)), plus the consolidated charitable contribution carryovers to such year, or

(2) Five percent of the adjusted consolidated taxable income as determined under paragraph (c) of this section.

(b) *Carryover of excess charitable contributions.* The consolidated charitable contribution carryovers to any consolidated return year shall consist of any excess consolidated charitable contributions of the group, plus any excess charitable contributions of members of the group arising in separate return years of such members, which may be carried over to the taxable year under the principles of section 170(b)(2) and (3). However, such consolidated carryovers shall not include any excess charitable contributions apportioned to a corporation for a separate return year pursuant to paragraph (e) of § 1.1502-79.

(c) *Adjusted consolidated taxable income.* For purposes of this section, the adjusted consolidated taxable income of the group for any consolidated return year shall be the consolidated taxable income computed without regard to this section, section 242, section 243(a)(2) and (3), §§ 1.1502-25, 1.1502-26, and 1.1502-27, and without regard to any consolidated net operating or net capital loss carrybacks to such year. [Reg. § 1.1502-24.]

☐ [T.D. 6894, 9-7-66. *Amended by* T.D. 7637, 8-6-79.]

[Reg. § 1.1502-26]

§ 1.1502-26. Consolidated dividends received deduction.—(a) *In general.*—(1) The consolidated dividends received deduction for the taxable year shall be the lesser of—

(i) The aggregate of the deduction of the members of the group allowable under sections 243(a)(1), 244(a) and 245 (computed without regard to the limitation provided in section 246(b)), or

(ii) 85 percent of the consolidated taxable income computed without regard to the consolidated net operating loss deduction, consolidated section 247 deduction, the consolidated dividends received deduction, and any consolidated net capital loss carryback to the taxable year.

Subdivision (ii) of this subparagraph shall not apply for any consolidated return year for which there is a consolidated net operating loss. (See §§ 1.1502-21(e) or 1.1502-21A(f), as appropriate for the definition of a consolidated net operating loss.)

(2) If any member computes a deduction under section 593(b)(2) for a taxable year beginning after July 11, 1969, and ending before August 30, 1975, the deduction otherwise computed under this section shall be reduced by an amount determined by multiplying the deduction (determined without regard to this sentence and without regard to dividends received by the common parent if such parent does not use the percentage of income method provided by section 593(b)(2)) by the applicable percentage of the member with the highest applicable percentage (determined under subparagraphs (A) and (B) of section 593(b)(2)).

Consolidated Returns

See p. 20,601 for regulations not amended to reflect law changes

(3) For taxable years ending on or after August 30, 1975, the deduction otherwise computed under this section shall be reduced by the sum of the amounts determined under paragraph (a)(4) of this section for each member that is a thrift institution that computes a deduction under section 593(b)(2).

(4) For each thrift institution, the amount determined under this subparagraph is the product of—

(i) The portion of the deduction determined with regard to the sum of the dividends received by (A) the thrift institution, and (B) any member in which that thrift institution owns, directly and with the application of paragraph (a)(5) of this section, 5 percent or more of the stock on any day during the consolidated return year, and

(ii) The thrift institution's applicable percentage determined under subparagraphs (A) and (B) of section 593(b)(2).

For purposes of this subparagraph, dividends allocated to a thrift institution under § 1.596-1(c) shall be considered received by the thrift institution.

(5) For purposes of paragraph (a)(4)(i) of this section, a member owning stock of another member (the "second member") shall be considered as owning its proportionate share of any stock of a member owned by the second member. Stock considered as being owned by reason of the preceding sentence shall, for purposes of applying that sentence, be treated as actually owned. The proportionate share of stock in a member owned by another member is the proportion which the value of the stock so owned bears to the value of all the outstanding stock in the member. For purposes of this paragraph the term "stock" includes nonvoting stock which is limited and preferred as to dividends.

(6) For purposes of paragraph (a)(4)(i) of this section, if two or more thrift institutions that are both members of the group each owns 5 percent or more of the same member's stock, the member's stock will be considered to be owned only by the thrift institution with the highest applicable percentage.

(b) *Intercompany dividends.* The deduction determined under paragraph (a) of this section is determined without taking into account intercompany dividends to the extent that, under § 1.1502-13(f)(2), they are not included in gross income. See § 1.1502-13 for additional rules relating to intercompany dividends.

(c) *Examples.* The provisions of this section may be illustrated by the following examples:

Example (1). Corporations P, S, and S-1 filed a consolidated return for the calendar year 1966 showing consolidated taxable income of $100,000 (determined without regard to the consolidated net operating loss deduction, consolidated dividends received deduction, and the consolidated section 247 deduction). Such corporations received dividends during such year from nonmember domestic corporations as follows:

Corporation	Dividends
P	$ 6,000
S	10,000
S-1	34,000
Total	$50,000

The dividends received deduction allowable to each member under section 243(a)(1) (computed without regard to the limitation in section 246(b)) is as follows: P has $5,100 (85 percent of $6,000), S has $8,500 (85 percent of $10,000), and S-1 has $28,900 (85 percent of $34,000), or a total of $42,500. Since $42,500 is less than $85,000 (85 percent of $100,000), the consolidated dividends received deduction is $42,500.

Example (2). Assume the same facts as in example (1) except that consolidated taxable income (computed without regard to the consolidated net operating loss deduction, consolidated dividends received deduction, and the consolidated section 247 deduction) was $40,000. The aggregate of the dividends received deductions, $42,500, computed without regard to section 246(b), results in a consolidated net operating loss of $2,500. See section 172(d)(6). Therefore, paragraph (a)(2) of this section does not apply and the consolidated dividends received deduction is $42,500. [Reg. § 1.1502-26.]

☐ [T.D. 6894, 9-7-66. Amended by T.D. 7246, 12-29-72; T.D. 7631, 7-10-79; T.D. 8597, 7-12-95; T.D. 8677, 6-26-96 and T.D. 8823, 6-25-99.]

[Reg. § 1.1502-27]

§ 1.1502-27. Consolidated section 247 deduction.—(a) *Amount of deduction.* The consolidated section 247 deduction for the taxable year shall be an amount computed as follows:

(1) First, determine the amount which is the lesser of—

(i) The aggregate of the dividends paid (within the meaning of section 247(a)) during such year by members of the group which are public utilities (within the meaning of section 247(b)(1)) on preferred stock (within the meaning of section 247(b)(2)), other than dividends paid to other members of the group, or

(ii) The aggregate of the taxable income (or loss) (as determined under paragraph (b) of

Reg. § 1.1502-27(a)(1)

this section) of each such member which is a public utility.

(2) Then, multiply the amount determined under subparagraph (1) of this paragraph by the fraction specified in section 247(a)(2).

(b) *Computation of taxable income.* For purposes of paragraph (a)(1)(ii) of this section, the taxable income (or loss) of a member of the group described in paragraph (a)(1)(i) shall be determined under § 1.1502-12, adjusted for the following items taken into account in the computation of consolidated taxable income:

(1) The portion of the consolidated net operating loss deduction, the consolidated charitable contributions deduction, and the consolidated dividends received deduction, attributable to such member;

(2) Such member's capital gain net income (net capital gain for taxable years beginning before January 1, 1977) (determined without regard to any net capital loss carryover or carryback attributable to such member);

(3) Such member's net capital loss and section 1231 net loss, reduced by the portion of the consolidated net capital loss attributable to such member; and

(4) The portion of any consolidated net capital loss carryover or carryback attributable to such member which is absorbed in the taxable year. [Reg. § 1.1502-27.]

☐ [T.D. 6894, 9-7-66. Amended by T.D. 7637, 8-6-79 and T.D. 7728, 10-31-80.]

[Reg. § 1.1502-30]

§ 1.1502-30. Stock basis after certain triangular reorganizations.—(a) *Scope.* This section provides rules for determining the basis of the stock of an acquiring corporation as a result of a triangular reorganization. The definitions and nomenclature contained in § 1.358-6 apply to this section.

(b) *General rules*—(1) *Forward triangular merger. triangular C reorganization, or triangular B reorganization.* P adjusts its basis in the stock of S as a result of a forward triangular merger, triangular C reorganization, or triangular B reorganization under § 1.358-6(c) and (d), except that § 1.358-6(c)(1)(ii) and (d)(2) do not apply. Instead, P adjusts such basis by taking into account the full amount of—

(i) T liabilities assumed by S or the amount of liabilities to which the T assets acquired by S are subject, and

(ii) The fair market value of any consideration not provided by P pursuant to the plan of reorganization.

(2) *Reverse triangular merger.* If P adjusts its basis in the T stock acquired as a result of a reverse triangular merger under § 1.358-6(c)(2)(i) and (d), § 1.358-6(c)(1)(ii) and (d)(2) do not apply. Instead, P adjusts such basis by taking into account the full amount of—

(i) T liabilities deemed assumed by S or the amount of liabilities to which the T assets deemed acquired by S are subject, and

(ii) The fair market value of any consideration not provided by P pursuant to the plan of reorganization.

(3) *Excess loss accounts.* Negative adjustments under this section may exceed P's basis in its S or T stock. The resulting negative amount is P's excess loss account in its S or T stock. See § 1.1502-19 for rules treating excess loss accounts as negative basis, and treating references to stock basis as including references to excess loss accounts.

(4) *Application of other rules of law.* The rules for this section are in addition to other rules of law. See § 1.1502-80(d) for the non-application of section 357(c) to P.

(5) *Examples.* The rules of this paragraph (b) are illustrated by the following examples. For purposes of these examples, P, S, and T are domestic corporations, P and S file consolidated returns P owns all of the only class of S stock, the P stock exchanged in the transaction satisfies the requirements of the applicable triangular reorganization provisions, the facts set forth the only corporate activity, and tax liabilities are disregarded.

Example 1. Liabilities. (a) *Facts.* T has assets with an aggregate basis of $60 and fair market value of $100. T's assets are subject to $70 of liabilities. Pursuant to a plan, P forms S with $5 of cash (which S retains), and T merges into S. In the merger, the T shareholders receive P stock worth $30 in exchange for their T stock. The transaction is a reorganization to which sections 368(a)(1)(A) and (a)(2)(D) apply.

(b) *Basis adjustment.* Under § 1.358-6, P adjusts its $5 basis in the S stock as if P had acquired the T assets with a carryover basis under section 362 and transferred these assets to S in a transaction in which P determines its basis in the S stock under section 358. Under the rules of this section, the limitation described in § 1.358-6(c)(1)(ii) does not apply. Thus, P adjusts its basis in the S stock by −$10 (the aggregate adjusted basis of T's assets decreased by the amount of liabilities to which the T assets are subject). Consequently, as a result of the reorganization, P has an excess loss account of $5 in its S stock.

Reg. § 1.1502-30(b)(5)

Example 2. Consideration not provided by P. (a) *Facts.* T has assets with an aggregate basis of $10 and fair market value of $100 and no liabilities. S is an operating company with substantial assets that has been in existence for several years. P has a $5 basis in its S stock. Pursuant to a plan, T merges into S and the T shareholders receive $70 of P stock provided by P pursuant to the plan of reorganization and $30 of cash provided by S in exchange for their T stock. The transaction is a reorganization to which sections 368(a)(1)(A) and (a)(2)(D) apply.

(b) *Basis adjustment.* Under § 1.358-6, P adjusts its $5 basis in the S stock as if P had acquired the T assets with a carryover basis under section 362 and transferred these assets to S in a transaction in which P determines its basis in the S stock under section 358. Under the rules of this section, the limitation described in § 1.358-6(d)(2) does not apply. Thus, P adjusts its basis in the S stock by −$20 (the aggregate adjusted basis of T's assets decreased by the fair market value of the consideration provided by S). As a result of the reorganization, P has an excess loss account of $15 in its S stock.

(c) *Appreciated asset.* The facts are the same as in paragraph (a) of this *Example 2*, except that in the reorganization S provides an asset with a $20 adjusted basis and $30 fair market value instead of $30 cash. The basis is adjusted in the same manner as in paragraph (b) of this *Example 2*. In addition, because S recognizes a $10 gain from the asset under section 1001, P's basis in its S stock is increased under § 1.1502-32(b) by S's $10 gain. Consequently, as a result of the reorganization P has an excess loss account of $5 in its S stock. (The results would be the same if the appreciated asset provided by S was P stock with respect to which S recognized gain. See § 1.1032-2(c)).

Example 3. Reverse triangular merger. (a) *Facts.* T has assets with an aggregate basis of $60 and fair market value of $100. T's assets are subject to $70 of liabilities. P owns all of the only class of S stock. P has a $5 basis in its S stock. Pursuant to a plan, S merges into T with T surviving. In the merger, the T shareholders exchange their T stock for $2 cash from P and $28 worth of P stock provided by P pursuant to the plan. The transaction is a reorganization to which sections 368(a)(1)(A) and (a)(2)(E) apply.

(b) *Basis adjustment.* Under § 1.358-6, P's basis in the T stock acquired equals its $5 basis in its S stock immediately before the transaction adjusted by the $60 basis in the T assets deemed transferred, and the $70 of liabilities to which the T assets are subject. Under the rules of this section, the limitation described in § 1.358-6(c)(1)(ii) does not apply. Consequently, P has an excess loss account of $5 in its T stock as a result of the transaction.

(c) *Effective date.* This section applies to reorganizations occurring on or after December 21, 1995. [Reg. § 1.1502-30.]

☐ [T.D. 8648, 12-20-95.]

[Reg. § 1.1502-31]

§ 1.1502-31. Stock basis after a group structure change.—(a) *In general*—(1) *Overview.* If one corporation (P) succeeds another corporation (T) under the principles of § 1.1502-75(d)(2) or (3) as the common parent of a consolidated group in a group structure change, the basis of members in the stock of the former common parent (or the stock of a successor) is adjusted or determined under this section. See § 1.1502-33(f)(1) for the definition of group structure change. For example, if P owns all of the stock of another corporation (S), and T merges into S in a group structure change that is a reorganization described in section 368(a)(2)(D) in which P becomes the common parent of the T group, P's basis in S's stock must be adjusted to reflect the change in S's assets and liabilities. The rules of this section coordinate with the earnings and profits adjustments required under § 1.1502-33(f)(1), generally conforming the results of transactions in which the T group continues under § 1.1502-75 with P as the common parent. By preserving in P the relationship between T's earnings and profits and asset basis, these adjustments limit possible distortions under section 1502 (e.g., in the deconsolidation rules for earnings and profits under § 1.1502-33(e), and the continued filing requirements of § 1.1502-75(a)). This section applies whether or not T continues to exist after the group structure change.

(2) *Application of other rules of law.* The rules of this section are in addition to other rules of law. The provisions of this section and other rules of law must not have the effect of duplicating an amount in P's basis in S's stock.

(b) *General rules.* Except as otherwise provided in this section—

(1) *Asset acquisitions.* If a corporation acquires the former common parent's assets (and any liabilities assumed or to which the assets are subject) in a group structure change, the basis of members in the stock of the acquiring corporation is adjusted immediately after the group structure change to reflect the acquiring corporation's allocable share of the former common parent's net asset basis as determined under paragraph (c) of this section. For example, if S acquires all of T's

Reg. § 1.1502-31(a)(1)

assets in a group structure change that is a reorganization described in section 368(a)(2)(D), P's basis in S's stock is adjusted to reflect T's net asset basis. If P owned some of T's stock before the group structure change, the results would be the same because P's basis in the T stock is not taken into account in determining P's basis in S's stock. If T's net asset basis is a negative amount, it reduces P's basis in S's stock and, if the reduction exceeds P's basis in S's stock, the excess is P's excess loss account in S's stock. See § 1.1502-19 for rules treating P's excess loss account as negative basis, and treating a reference to P's basis in S's stock as including an excess loss account.

(2) *Stock acquisitions.* If a corporation acquires stock of the former common parent in a group structure change, the basis of the members in the former common parent's stock immediately after the group structure change (including any stock of the former common parent owned before the group structure change) is redetermined in accordance with the results for an asset acquisition described in paragraph (b)(1) of this section. For example, if all of T's stock is contributed to P in a group structure change to which section 351 applies, P's basis in T's stock is T's net asset basis, rather than the amount determined under section 362. Similarly, if S merges into T in a group structure change described in section 368(a)(2)(E), P's basis in T's stock is the basis that P would have in S's stock under paragraph (b)(1) of this section if T had merged into S in a group structure change described in section 368(a)(2)(D).

(c) *Net asset basis.* The former common parent's net asset basis is the basis it would have in the stock of a newly formed subsidiary, if—

(1) The former common parent transferred its assets (and any liabilities assumed or to which the assets are subject) to the subsidiary in a transaction to which section 351 applies;

(2) The former common parent and the subsidiary were members of the same consolidated group (see § 1.1502-80(d) for the non-application of section 357(c) to the transfer); and

(3) The asset basis taken into account is each asset's basis immediately after the group structure change (e.g., taking into account any income or gain recognized in the group structure change and reflected in the asset's basis).

(d) *Additional adjustments.* In addition to the adjustments in paragraph (b) of this section, the following adjustments are made:

(1) *Consideration not provided by P.* The basis is reduced to reflect the fair market value of any consideration not provided by the member. For example, if S acquires T's assets in a group structure change described in section 368(a)(2)(D), and S provides an appreciated asset (e.g., stock of P) as partial consideration in the transaction, P's basis in S's stock is reduced by the fair market value of the asset.

(2) *Allocable share*—(i) *Asset acquisitions.* If a corporation receives less than all of the former common parent's assets and liabilities in the group structure change, the former common parent's net asset basis taken into account under paragraph (b)(1) of this section is adjusted accordingly.

(ii) *Stock acquisitions.* If a corporation owns less than all of the former common parent's stock immediately after a group structure change described in paragraph (b)(2) of this section, the percentage of the former common parent's net asset basis taken into account equals the percentage (by fair market value) of the former common parent's stock owned immediately after the group structure change. For example, if P owns less than all of the former common parent's stock immediately after the group structure change, only an allocable part of the basis determined under this section is reflected in the shares owned by P (and the amount allocable to shares owned by nonmembers has no effect on the basis of their shares).

(3) *Allocation among shares of stock.* The basis determined under this section is allocated among shares under the principles of section 358. For example, if P owns multiple classes of the former common parent's stock immediately after the group structure change, only an allocable part of the basis determined under this section is reflected in the basis of each share. See § 1.1502-19(d), for special allocations with respect to excess loss accounts.

(4) *Higher-tier members.* To the extent that the former common parent is owned by members other than the new common parent, the basis of members in the stock of all subsidiaries owning, directly or indirectly, in whole or in part, an interest in the former common parent's assets or liabilities is adjusted in accordance with the principles of this section. The adjustments are applied in the order of the tiers, from the lowest to the highest.

(e) *Waiver of loss carryovers of former common parent*—(1) *General rule.* An irrevocable election may be made to treat all or any portion of a loss carryover attributable to the common parent as expiring for all Federal income tax purposes immediately before the group structure change. Thus, if the loss carryover is treated as expiring under the election, it will not result in a negative adjustment to the basis of P's stock under § 1.1502-32(b).

Reg. § 1.1502-31(e)(1)

(2) *Election.* The election described in this paragraph (e) must be made in a separate statement entitled "ELECTION TO TREAT LOSS CARRYOVER AS EXPIRING UNDER § 1.1502-31(e)." The statement must be filed with the consolidated group's return for the year that includes the group structure change, and it must be signed by the former and the new common parent. The statement must identify the amount of each loss carryover deemed to expire (or the amount of each loss carryover deemed not to expire, with any balance of any loss carryovers being deemed to expire).

(f) *Predecessors and successors.* For purposes of this section, any reference to a corporation includes a reference to a successor or predecessor as the context may require. See § 1.1502-32(f) for definitions of predecessor and successor.

(g) *Examples.* For purposes of the examples in this section, unless otherwise stated, all corporations have only one class of stock outstanding, the tax year of all persons is the calendar year, all persons use the accrual method of accounting, the facts set forth the only corporate activity, all transactions are between unrelated persons, and tax liabilities are disregarded. The principles of this section are illustrated by the following examples.

Example 1. Forward triangular merger. (a) *Facts.* P is the common parent of one group and T is the common parent of another. T has assets with an aggregate basis of $60 and fair market value of $100 and no liabilities. T's shareholders have an aggregate basis of $50 in T's stock. In Year 1, pursuant to a plan, P forms S and T merges into S with the T shareholders receiving $100 of P stock in exchange for their T stock. The transaction is a reorganization described in section 368(a)(2)(D). The transaction is also a reverse acquisition under § 1.1502-75(d)(3) because the T shareholders, as a result of owning T's stock, own more than 50% of the value of P's stock immediately after the transaction. Thus, the transaction is a group structure change under § 1.1502-33(f)(1), and P's earnings and profits are adjusted to reflect T's earnings and profits immediately before T ceases to be the common parent of the T group.

(b) *Analysis.* Under paragraph (b)(1) of this section, P's basis in S's stock is adjusted to reflect T's net asset basis. Under paragraph (c) of this section, T's net asset basis is $60, the basis T would have in the stock of a subsidiary under section 358 if T had transferred all of its assets and liabilities to the subsidiary in a transaction to which section 351 applies. Thus, P has a $60 basis in S's stock.

(c) *Pre-existing S.* The facts are the same as in paragraph (a) of this *Example 1*, except that P has owned the stock of S for several years and P has a $50 basis in the S stock before the merger with T. Under paragraph (b)(1) of this section, P's $50 basis in S's stock is adjusted to reflect T's net asset basis. Thus, P's basis in S's stock is $110 ($50 plus $60).

(d) *Excess loss account included in former common parent's net asset basis.* The facts are the same as in paragraph (a) of this *Example 1*, except that T has two assets, an operating asset with an $80 basis and $90 fair market value, and stock of a subsidiary with a $20 excess loss account and $10 fair market value. Under paragraph (c) of this section, T's net asset basis is $60 ($80 minus $20). See sections 351 and 358, and § 1.1502-19. Consequently, P has a $60 basis in S's stock. Under section 362 and § 1.1502-19, S has an $80 basis in the operating asset and a $20 excess loss account in the stock of the subsidiary.

(e) *Liabilities in excess of basis.* The facts are the same as in paragraph (a) of this *Example 1*, except that T's assets have a fair market value of $170 (and $60 basis) and are subject to $70 of liabilities. Under paragraph (c) of this section, T's net asset basis is ($10) ($60 minus $70). See sections 351 and 358, and §§ 1.1502-19 and 1.1502-80(d). Thus, P has a $10 excess loss account in S's stock. Under section 362, S has a $60 basis in its assets (which are subject to $70 of liabilities). (Under paragraph (a)(2) of this section, because the liabilities are taken into account in determining net asset basis under paragraph (c) of this section, the liabilities are not also taken into account as consideration not provided by P under paragraph (d)(1) of this section.)

(f) *Consideration provided by S.* The facts are the same as in paragraph (a) of this *Example 1*, except that P forms S with a $100 contribution at the beginning of Year 1, and during Year 6, pursuant to a plan, S purchases $100 of P stock and T merges into S with the T shareholders receiving P stock in exchange for their T stock. Under paragraph (b)(1) of this section, P's $100 basis in S's stock is increased by $60 to reflect T's net asset basis. Under paragraph (d)(1) of this section, P's basis in S's stock is decreased by $100 (the fair market value of the P stock) because the P stock purchased by S and used in the transaction is consideration not provided by P.

(g) *Appreciated asset provided by S.* The facts are the same as in paragraph (a) of this *Example 1*, except that P has owned the stock of S for several years, and the shareholders of T receive $60 of P stock and an asset of S with a $30 adjusted basis and $40 fair market value. S recog-

Reg. § 1.1502-31(e)(2)

nizes a $10 gain from the asset under section 1001. Under paragraph (b)(1) of this section, P's basis in S's stock is increased by $60 to reflect T's net asset basis. Under paragraph (d)(1) of this section, P's basis in S's stock is decreased by $40 (the fair market value of the asset provided by S). In addition, P's basis in S's stock is increased under § 1.1502-32(b) by S's $10 gain.

(h) *Depreciated asset provided by S.* The facts are the same as in paragraph (a) of this *Example 1*, except that P has owned the stock of S for several years, and the shareholders of T receive $60 of P stock and an asset of S with a $50 adjusted basis and $40 fair market value. S recognizes a $10 loss from the asset under section 1001. Under paragraph (b)(1) of this section, P's basis in S's stock is increased by $60 to reflect T's net asset basis. Under paragraph (d)(1) of this section, P's basis in S's stock is decreased by $40 (the fair market value of the asset provided by S). In addition, S's $10 loss is taken into account under § 1.1502-32(b) in determining P's basis adjustments under that section.

Example 2. Stock acquisition. (a) *Facts.* P is the common parent of one group and T is the common parent of another. T has assets with an aggregate basis of $60 and fair market value of $100 and no liabilities. T's shareholders have an aggregate basis of $50 in T's stock. Pursuant to a plan, P forms S and S acquires all of T's stock in exchange for P stock in a transaction described in section 368(a)(1)(B). The transaction is also a reverse acquisition under § 1.1502-75(d)(3). Thus, the transaction is a group structure change under § 1.1502-33(f)(1), and the earnings and profits of P and S are adjusted to reflect T's earnings and profits immediately before T ceases to be the common parent of the T group.

(b) *Analysis.* Under paragraph (d)(4) of this section, although S is not the new common parent of the T group, adjustments must be made to S's basis in T's stock in accordance with the principles of this section. Although S's basis in T's stock would ordinarily be determined under section 362 by reference to the basis of T's shareholders in T's stock immediately before the group structure change, under the principles of paragraph (b)(2) of this section, S's basis in T's stock is determined by reference to T's net asset basis. Thus, S's basis in T's stock is $60.

(c) *Higher-tier adjustments.* Under paragraph (d)(4) of this section, P's basis in S's stock is adjusted to $60 (to be consistent with the adjustment to S's basis in T's stock).

(d) *Cross ownership.* The facts are the same as in paragraph (a) of this *Example 2*, except that S has owned 10% of T's stock for several years, and, pursuant to the plan, S acquires the remaining 90% of T's stock in exchange for P stock. The results are the same as in paragraphs (b) and (c) of this *Example 2*, because S's basis in the initial 10% of T's stock is redetermined under this section.

(e) *Allocable share.* The facts are the same as in paragraph (a) of this *Example 2*, except that P owns only 90% of S's stock immediately after the group structure change. S's basis in T's stock is the same as in paragraph (b) of this *Example 2*. Under paragraph (d)(2) of this section, P's basis in its S stock is adjusted to $54 (90% of S's $60 adjustment).

Example 3. Taxable stock acquisition. (a) *Facts.* P is the common parent of one group and T is the common parent of another. T has assets with an aggregate basis of $60 and fair market value of $100 and no liabilities. T's shareholders have an aggregate basis of $50 in T's stock. Pursuant to a plan, P acquires all of T's stock in exchange for $70 of P's stock and $30 in a transaction that is a group structure change under § 1.1502-33(f)(1). P's acquisition of T's stock is a taxable transaction. (Because of P's use of cash, the acquisition is not a transaction described in section 368(a)(1)(B).)

(b) *Analysis.* Under paragraph (b)(2) of this section, P's basis in T's stock is adjusted to reflect T's net asset basis. Thus, although P's basis in T's stock would ordinarily be a cost basis of $100, P's basis in T's stock under this section is $60.

(h) *Effective date*—(1) *General rule.* This section applies to group structure changes occurring in consolidated return years beginning on or after January 1, 1995.

(2) *Prior law.* For prior years, see prior regulations under section 1502 as in effect with respect to the transaction. See, e.g., § 1.1502-31T as contained in the 26 CFR part 1 edition revised as of April 1, 1994. [Reg. § 1.1502-31.]

☐ [T.D. 6909, 12-29-66. Amended by T.D. 7246, 12-29-72; T.D. 8226, 9-7-88 and T.D. 8560, 8-12-94.]

[Reg. § 1.1502-32]

§ 1.1502-32. **Investment adjustments.**—(a) *In general*—(1) *Purpose.* This section provides rules for adjusting the basis of the stock of a subsidiary (S) owned by another member (P). These rules modify the determination of P's basis in S's stock under applicable rules of law by adjusting P's basis to reflect S's distributions and S's items of income, gain, deduction, and loss taken into account for the period that S is a member of the consolidated group. The purpose of the adjustments is to treat P and S as a single entity so that consolidated taxable income reflects the group's income. For example, if P forms S with a $100 contribution, and S takes into account $10 of income, P's $100 basis in S's stock under section 358 is increased by $10 under this section to prevent S's income from being taken into account a second time on P's disposition of S's stock. Comparable adjustments are made for tax-exempt income and noncapital, nondeductible expenses that S takes into account, to preserve their treatment under the Internal Revenue Code.

(2) *Application of other rules of law.* The rules of this section are in addition to other rules of law. See, e.g., section 358 (basis determinations for distributees), section 1016 (adjustments to basis), § 1.1502-11(b) (limitations on the use of losses), § 1.1502-19 (treatment of excess loss accounts), § 1.1502-20 (additional rules relating to stock loss), and § 1.1502-31 (basis after a group structure change). P's basis in S's stock must not be adjusted under this section and other rules of law in a manner that has the effect of duplicating an adjustment. See also paragraph (h)(5) of this section for basis reductions applicable to certain former subsidiaries.

(3) *Overview*—(i) *In general.* The amount of the stock basis adjustments and their timing are determined under paragraph (b) of this section. Under paragraph (c) of this section, the amount of the adjustment is allocated among the shares of S's stock. Paragraphs (d) through (g) of this section provide definitions, an anti-avoidance rule, successor rules, and recordkeeping requirements.

(ii) *Excess loss account.* Negative adjustments under this section may exceed P's basis in S's stock. The resulting negative amount is P's excess loss account in S's stock. See § 1.1502-19 for rules treating excess loss accounts as negative basis, and treating references to stock basis as including references to excess loss accounts.

(iii) *Tiering up of adjustments.* The adjustments to S's stock under this section are taken into account in determining adjustments to higher-tier stock. The adjustments are applied in the order of the tiers, from the lowest to the highest. For example, if P is also a subsidiary, P's adjustment to S's stock is taken into account in determining the adjustments to stock of P owned by other members.

(b) *Stock basis adjustments*—(1) *Timing of adjustments*—(i) *In general.* Adjustments under this section are made as of the close of each consolidated return year, and as of any other time (an interim adjustment) if a determination at that time is necessary to determine a tax liability of any person. For example, adjustments are made as of P's sale of S's stock in order to measure P's gain or loss from the sale, and if P's interest in S's stock is not uniform throughout the year (e.g., because P disposes of a portion of its S stock, or S issues additional shares to another person), the adjustments under this section are made by taking into account the varying interests. An interim adjustment may be necessary even if tax liability is not affected until a later time. For example, if P sells only 50% of S's stock and S becomes a nonmember, adjustments must be made for the retained stock as of the disposition (whether or not P has an excess loss account in that stock). Similarly, if S liquidates during a consolidated return year, adjustments must be made as of the liquidation (even if the liquidation is tax free under section 332).

(ii) *Allocation of items.* If § 1.1502-76(b) applies to S for purposes of an adjustment before the close of the group's consolidated return year, the amount of the adjustment is determined under that section. If § 1.1502-76(b) does not apply to the interim adjustment, the adjustment is determined under the principles of § 1.1502-76(b), consistently applied, and ratable allocation under the principles of § 1.1502-76(b)(2)(ii) or (iii) may be used without filing an election under § 1.1502-76(b)(2). The principles would apply, for example, if P becomes a nonmember but S remains a member.

(2) *Amount of adjustments.* P's basis in S's stock is increased by positive adjustments and decreased by negative adjustments under this paragraph (b)(2). The amount of the adjustment, determined as of the time of the adjustment, is the net amount of S's—

(i) Taxable income or loss;

(ii) Tax-exempt income;

(iii) Noncapital, nondeductible expenses; and

(iv) Distributions with respect to S's stock.

(3) *Operating rules.* For purposes of determining P's adjustments to the basis of S's stock under paragraph (b)(2) of this section—

(i) *Taxable income or loss.* S's taxable income or loss is consolidated taxable income (or loss) determined by including only S's items of income, gain, deduction, and loss taken into account in determining consolidated taxable income (or loss), treating S's deductions and losses as taken into account to the extent they are absorbed by S or any other member. For this purpose:

(A) To the extent that S's deduction or loss is absorbed in the year it arises or is carried forward and absorbed in a subsequent year (e.g., under section 172, 465, or 1212), the deduction or loss is taken into account under paragraph (b)(2) of this section in the year in which it is absorbed.

(B) To the extent that S's deduction or loss is carried back and absorbed in a prior year (whether consolidated or separate), the deduction or loss is taken into account under paragraph (b)(2) of this section in the year in which it arises and not in the year in which it is absorbed.

(ii) *Tax-exempt income*—(A) *In general.* S's tax-exempt income is its income and gain which is taken into account but permanently excluded from its gross income under applicable law, and which increases, directly or indirectly, the basis of its assets (or an equivalent amount). For example, S's dividend income to which § 1.1502-13(f)(2)(ii) applies, and its interest excluded from gross income under section 103, are treated as tax-exempt income. However, S's income not recognized under section 1031 is not treated as tax-exempt income because the corresponding basis adjustments under section 1031(d) prevent S's nonrecognition from being permanent. Similarly, S's tax-exempt income does not include gain not recognized under section 332 from the liquidation of a lower-tier subsidiary, or not recognized under section 118 or section 351 from a transfer of assets to S.

(B) *Equivalent deductions.* To the extent that S's taxable income or gain is permanently offset by a deduction or loss that does not reduce, directly or indirectly, the basis of S's assets (or an equivalent amount), the income or gain is treated as tax-exempt income and is taken into account under paragraph (b)(3)(ii)(A) of this section. In addition, the income and the offsetting item are taken into account under paragraph (b)(3)(i) of this section. For example, if S receives a $100 dividend with respect to which a $70 dividends received deduction is allowed under section 243, $70 of the dividend is treated as tax-exempt income. Accordingly, P's basis in S's stock increases by $100 because the $100 dividend and $70 deduction are taken into account under paragraph (b)(3)(i) of this section (resulting in $30 of the increase), and $70 of the dividend is also taken into account under paragraph (b)(3)(ii)(A) of this section as tax-exempt income (resulting in $70 of the increase). (See paragraph (b)(3)(iii) of this section if there is a corresponding negative adjustment under section 1059.) Similarly, income from mineral properties is treated as tax-exempt income to the extent it is offset by deductions for depletion in excess of the basis of the property.

(C) *Discharge of indebtedness income*— (1) *In general.* Discharge of indebtedness income of S that is excluded from gross income under section 108 is treated as tax-exempt income only to the extent the discharge is applied to reduce tax attributes (e.g., under section 108 or 1017). Discharge of S's indebtedness is treated as applied to reduce tax attributes only to the extent the attribute reduction is taken into account as a reduction under paragraph (b)(3)(iii) of this section.

(2) *Expired loss carryovers.* If the amount of the discharge exceeds the amount of the attribute reduction, the excess is nevertheless treated as applied to reduce tax attributes to the extent a loss carryover expired without tax benefit, the expiration was taken into account as a noncapital, nondeductible expense under paragraph (b)(3)(iii) of this section, and the loss carryover would have been reduced had it not expired.

(D) *Basis shifts.* An increase in the basis of S's assets (or an equivalent as described in paragraph (b)(3)(iv)(B) of this section) is treated as tax-exempt income to the extent that the increase is not otherwise taken into account in determining stock basis, it corresponds to a negative adjustment that is taken into account by the group under this paragraph (b) (or incurred by the common parent), and it has the effect (viewing the group in the aggregate) of a permanent recovery of the reduction. For example, S's basis increase under section 50(c)(2) is treated as tax-exempt income to the extent the preceding basis reduction under section 50(c)(1) is reflected in the basis of a member's stock. On the other hand, if S increases the basis of an asset as the result of an accounting method change, and the related positive section 481(a) adjustment is taken into account over time, the basis increase is not treated as tax-exempt income.

(iii) *Noncapital, nondeductible expenses*— (A) *In general.* S's noncapital, nondeductible expenses are its deductions and losses that are taken into account but permanently disallowed or eliminated under applicable law in determining its taxable income or loss, and that decrease, directly or indirectly, the basis of its assets (or an equivalent amount). For example, S's Federal taxes described in section 275 and loss not recognized under section 311(a) are noncapital, nondeductible expenses. Similarly, if a loss carryover (e.g., under section 172 or 1212) attributable to S expires or is reduced under section 108(b), it becomes a noncapital, nondeductible expense at the close of the last tax year to which it may be carried. However, if S sells and repurchases a security subject to section 1091, the disallowed loss is not a noncapital, nondeductible expense because the corresponding basis adjustments under section 1091(d) prevent the disallowance from being permanent.

Reg. § 1.1502-32(b)(3)

(B) *Nondeductible basis recovery.* Any other decrease in the basis of S's assets (or an equivalent as described in paragraph (b)(3)(iv)(B) of this section) may be a noncapital, nondeductible expense to the extent that the decrease is not otherwise taken into account in determining stock basis and is permanently eliminated for purposes of determining S's taxable income or loss. Whether a decrease is so treated is determined by taking into account both the purposes of the Code or regulatory provision resulting in the decrease and the purposes of this section. For example, S's noncapital, nondeductible expenses include any basis reduction under section 50(c)(1), section 1017, section 1059, § 1.1502-20(b), or § 1.1502-20(g). Also included as a noncapital, nondeductible expense is the amount of any gross-up for taxes paid by another taxpayer that S is treated as having paid (e.g., income included under section 78, or the portion of an undistributed capital gain dividend that is treated as tax deemed to have been paid by a shareholder under section 852(b)(3)(D)(ii), whether or not any corresponding amount is claimed as a tax credit). In contrast, a decrease generally is not a noncapital, nondeductible expense if it results because S redeems stock in a transaction to which section 302(a) applies, S receives assets in a liquidation to which section 332 applies and its basis in the assets is less than its basis in the stock canceled, or S distributes the stock of a subsidiary in a distribution to which section 355 applies.

(iv) *Special rules for tax-exempt income and noncapital, nondeductible expenses.* For purposes of paragraphs (b)(3)(ii) and (iii) of this section:

(A) *Treatment as permanent.* An amount is permanently excluded from gross income, or permanently disallowed or eliminated, if it is so treated by S even though another person may take a corresponding amount into account. For example, if S sells property to a nonmember at a loss that is disallowed under section 267(a), S's loss is a noncapital, nondeductible expense even though under section 267(d) the nonmember may treat a corresponding amount of gain as not recognized. (If the nonmember is a subsidiary in another consolidated group, its gain not recognized under section 267(d) is tax-exempt income under paragraph (b)(3)(ii)(A) of this section.)

(B) *Amounts equivalent to basis and adjustments to basis.* Amounts equivalent to basis include the amount of money, the amount of a loss carryover, and the amount of an adjustment to gain or loss under section 475(a) for securities described in section 475(a)(2). An equivalent to a basis increase includes a decrease in an excess loss account, and an equivalent to a basis decrease includes the denial of basis for taxable income.

(C) *Timing.* An amount is taken into account in the year in which it would be taken into account under paragraph (b)(3)(i) of this section if it were subject to Federal income taxation.

(D) *Tax sharing agreements.* Taxes are taken into account by applying the principles of section 1552 and the percentage method under § 1.1502-33(d)(3) (and by assuming a 100% allocation of any decreased tax liability). The treatment of amounts allocated under this paragraph (b)(3)(iv)(D) is analogous to the treatment of allocations under § 1.1552-1(b)(2). For example, if one member owes a payment to a second member, the first member is treated as indebted to the second member. The right to receive payment is treated as a positive adjustment under paragraph (b)(3)(ii) of this section, and the obligation to make payment is treated as a negative adjustment under paragraph (b)(3)(iii) of this section. If the obligation is not paid, the amount not paid generally is treated as a distribution, contribution, or both, depending on the relationship between the members.

(v) *Distributions.* Distributions taken into account under paragraph (b)(2) of this section are distributions with respect to S's stock to which section 301 applies and all other distributions treated as dividends (e.g., under section 356(a)(2)). See § 1.1502-13(f)(2)(iv) for taking into account distributions to which section 301 applies (but not other distributions treated as dividends) under the entitlement rule.

(4) *Waiver of loss carryovers from separate return limitation years*—(i) *General rule.* If S has a loss carryover from a separate return limitation year when it becomes a member of a consolidated group, the group may make an irrevocable election to treat all or any portion of the loss carryover as expiring for all Federal income tax purposes immediately before S becomes a member of the consolidated group (deemed expiration). If S was a member of another group immediately before it became a member of the consolidated group, the expiration is also treated as occurring immediately after it ceases to be a member of the prior group.

(ii) *Stock basis adjustments from a waiver*—(A) *Qualifying transactions.* If S becomes a member of the consolidated group in a qualifying cost basis transaction and an election under this paragraph (b)(4) is made, the noncapital, nondeductible expense resulting from the deemed expiration does not result in a corresponding stock basis adjustment for any member under this sec-

Reg. § 1.1502-32(b)(4)

tion. A qualifying cost basis transaction is the purchase (i.e., a transaction in which basis is determined under section 1012) by members of the acquiring consolidated group (while they are members) in a 12-month period of an amount of S's stock satisfying the requirements of section 1504(a)(2).

(B) *Nonqualifying transactions.* If S becomes a member of the consolidated group other than in a qualifying cost basis transaction and an election under this paragraph (b)(4) is made, the basis of its stock that is owned by members immediately after it becomes a member is subject to reduction under the principles of this section to reflect the deemed expiration. The reduction occurs immediately before S becomes a member, but after it ceases to be a member of any prior group, and it therefore does not result in a corresponding stock basis adjustment for any higher-tier member of the transferring or acquiring consolidated group. Any basis reduction under this paragraph (b)(4)(ii)(B) is taken into account in making determinations of basis under the Code with respect to S's stock (e.g., a determination under section 362 because the stock is acquired in a transaction described in section 368(a)(1)(B)), but it does not result in corresponding stock basis adjustments under this section for any higher-tier member. If the basis reduction exceeds the basis of S's stock, the excess is treated as an excess loss account to which the members owning S's stock succeed.

(C) *Higher-tier corporations.* If S becomes a member of the consolidated group as a result, in whole or in part, of a higher-tier corporation becoming a member (whether or not in a qualifying cost basis transaction), additional adjustments are required. The highest-tier corporation (T) whose becoming a member resulted in S becoming a member, and T's chain of lower-tier corporations that includes S, are subject to the adjustment. The deemed expiration of S's loss carryover that results in a negative adjustment for the first higher-tier corporation is treated as an expiring loss carryover of that higher-tier corporation for purposes of applying paragraph (b)(4)(ii)(B) of this section to that corporation. For example, if P purchases all of the stock of T, T owns all of the stock of T1, T1 owns all of the stock of S, S becomes a member as a result of T becoming a member, and the election under this paragraph (b)(4) is made, the basis of the S stock is reduced and the reduction tiers up to T1, T1 treats the negative adjustment to its basis in S's stock as an expiring loss carryover of T1, and T then adjusts its basis in T1's stock. In addition, if T becomes a member of the acquiring group in a transaction other than a qualifying cost basis transaction, the amount that tiers up to T also reduces the basis of its stock under paragraph (b)(4)(ii)(B) of this section (but the amount does not tier up to higher-tier members).

(iii) *Net asset basis limitation.* Basis reduced under this paragraph (b)(4) is restored before S becomes a member (and before the basis of S's stock is taken into account in determining basis under the Code) to the extent necessary to conform a share's basis to its allocable portion of net asset basis. In the case of higher-tier corporations under paragraph (b)(4)(ii)(C) of this section, the restoration does not tier up but is instead applied separately to each higher-tier corporation. For purposes of determining each corporation's net asset basis (including the basis of stock in lower-tier corporations), the restoration is applied in the order of tiers, from the lowest to the highest. For purposes of the restoration:

(A) A member's net asset basis is the positive or negative difference between the adjusted basis of its assets (and the amount of any of its loss carryovers that are not deemed to expire) and its liabilities. Appropriate adjustments must be made, for example, to disregard liabilities that subsequently will give rise to deductions (e.g., liabilities to which section 461(h) applies).

(B) Within a class of stock, each share has the same allocable portion of net asset basis. If there is more than one class of common stock, the net asset basis is allocated to each class by taking into account the terms of each class and all other facts and circumstances relating to the overall economic arrangement.

(iv) *Election.* The election described in this paragraph (b)(4) must be made in a separate statement entitled "ELECTION TO TREAT LOSS CARRYOVER AS EXPIRING UNDER § 1.1502-32(b)(4)." The statement must be filed with the consolidated group's return for the year S becomes a member, and it must be signed by the common parent and S. A separate statement must be made for each member whose loss carryover is deemed to expire. The statement must identify the amount of each loss carryover deemed to expire (or the amount of each loss carryover deemed not to expire, with any balance of any loss carryovers being deemed to expire), the basis of any stock reduced as a result of the deemed expiration, and the computation of the basis reduction.

(5) *Examples*—(i) *In general.* For purposes of the examples in this section, unless otherwise stated, P owns all of the only class of S's stock, the stock is owned for the entire year, S owns no stock of lower-tier members, the tax year of all persons is the calendar year, all persons use the accrual method of accounting, the facts set forth the only corporate activity, preferred stock is described in

Reg. § 1.1502-32(b)(5)

section 1504(a)(4), all transactions are between unrelated persons, and tax liabilities are disregarded.

(ii) *Stock basis adjustments.* The principles of this paragraph (b) are illustrated by the following examples.

Example 1. Taxable income. (a) *Current taxable income.* For Year 1, the P group has $100 of taxable income when determined by including only S's items of income, gain, deduction, and loss taken into account. Under paragraph (b)(1) of this section, P's basis in S's stock is adjusted under this section as of the close of Year 1. Under paragraph (b)(2) of this section, P's basis in S's stock is increased by the amount of the P group's taxable income determined by including only S's items taken into account. Thus, P's basis in S's stock is increased by $100 as of the close of Year 1.

(b) *Intercompany gain that is not taken into account.* The facts are the same as in paragraph (a) of this *Example 1*, except that S also sells property to another member at a $25 gain in Year 1, the gain is deferred under § 1.1502-13 and taken into account in Year 3, and P sells 10% of S's stock to nonmembers in Year 2. Under paragraph (b)(3)(i) of this section, S's deferred gain is not additional taxable income for Year 1 or 2 because it is not taken into account in determining the P group's consolidated taxable income for either of those years. The deferred gain is not tax-exempt income under paragraph (b)(3)(ii) of this section because it is not permanently excluded from S's gross income. The deferred gain does not result in a basis adjustment until Year 3, when it is taken into account in determining the P group's consolidated taxable income. Consequently, P's basis in the S shares sold is not increased to reflect S's gain from the intercompany sale of the property. In Year 3, the deferred gain is taken into account, but the amount allocable to the shares sold by P does not increase their basis because these shares are held by nonmembers.

(c) *Intercompany gain taken into account.* The facts are the same as in paragraph (b) of this *Example 1*, except that P sells all of S's stock in Year 2 (rather than only 10%). Under § 1.1502-13, S takes the $25 gain into account immediately before S becomes a nonmember. Thus, P's basis in S's stock is increased to reflect S's gain from the intercompany sale of the property.

Example 2. Tax loss. (a) *Current absorption.* For Year 2, the P group has a $50 consolidated net operating loss when determined by taking into account only S's items of income, gain, deduction, and loss. S's loss is absorbed by the P group in Year 2, offsetting P's income for that year. Under paragraph (b)(3)(i)(A) of this section, because S's loss is absorbed in the year it arises, P has a $50 negative adjustment with respect to S's stock. Under paragraph (b)(2) of this section, P reduces its basis in S's stock by $50. Under paragraph (a)(3)(ii) of this section, if the decrease exceeds P's basis in S's stock, the excess is P's excess loss account in S's stock.

(b) *Interim determination from stock sale.* The facts are the same as in paragraph (a) of this *Example 2*, except that S's Year 2 loss arises in the first half of the calendar year, P sells 50% of S's stock on July 1 of Year 2, and P's income for Year 2 does not arise until after the sale of S's stock. P's income for Year 2 (exclusive of the sale of S's stock) is offset by S's loss, even though the income arises after the stock sale, and no loss remains to be apportioned to S. See §§ 1.1502-11 and 1.1502-21(b). Under paragraph (b)(3)(i)(A) of this section, because S's $50 loss is absorbed in the year it arises, it reduces P's basis in the S shares sold by $25 immediately before the stock sale. Because S becomes a nonmember, the loss also reduces P's basis in the retained S shares by $25 immediately before S becomes a nonmember. See also § 1.1502-20(b) (possible stock basis reduction on the deconsolidation of S).

(c) *Loss carryback.* The facts are the same as in paragraph (a) of this *Example 2*, except that P has no income or loss for Year 2, S's $50 loss is carried back and absorbed by the P group in Year 1 (offsetting the income of P or S), and the P group receives a $17 tax refund in Year 2 that is paid to S. Under paragraph (b)(3)(i)(B) of this section, because the $50 loss is carried back and absorbed in Year 1, it is treated as a tax loss for Year 2 (the year in which it arises). Under paragraph (b)(3)(ii) of this section, the refund is treated as tax-exempt income of S. Under paragraph (b)(3)(iv)(C) of this section, the tax-exempt income is taken into account in Year 2 because that is the year it would be taken into account under S's method of accounting if it were subject to Federal income taxation. Thus, under paragraph (b)(2) of this section, P reduces its basis in S's stock by $33 as of the close of Year 2 (the $50 tax loss, less the $17 tax refund).

(d) *Loss carryforward.* The facts are the same as in paragraph (a) of this *Example 2*, except that P has no income or loss for Year 2, and S's loss is carried forward and absorbed by the P group in Year 3 (offsetting the income of P or S). Under paragraph (b)(3)(i)(A) of this section, the loss is not treated as a tax loss under paragraph (b)(2) of this section until Year 3.

Example 3. Tax-exempt income and noncapital, nondeductible expenses. (a) *Facts.* For Year 1, the P group has $500 of consolidated taxable income. However, the P group has a $100 consolidated net operating loss when determined by including only S's items of income, gain, deduction, and loss taken into account. Also for Year 1, S has $80 of interest income that is permanently excluded from gross income under section 103, and S incurs $60 of related expense for which a deduction is permanently disallowed under section 265.

(b) *Analysis.* Under paragraph (b)(3)(i)(A) of this section, S has a $100 tax loss for Year 1. Under paragraph (b)(3)(ii)(A) of this section, S has $80 of tax-exempt income. Under paragraph (b)(3)(iii)(A) of this section, S has $60 of noncapital, nondeductible expense. Under paragraph (b)(3)(iv)(C) of this section, the tax-exempt income and noncapital, nondeductible expense are taken into account in Year 1 because that is the year they would be taken into account under S's method of accounting if they were subject to Federal income taxation. Thus, under paragraph (b) of this section, P reduces its basis in S's stock as of the close of Year 1 by an $80 net amount (the $100 tax loss, less $80 of tax-exempt income, plus $60 of noncapital, nondeductible expenses).

Example 4. Discharge of indebtedness. (a) *Facts.* P forms S on January 1 of Year 1 and S borrows $200. During Year 1, S's assets decline in value and the P group has a $100 consolidated net operating loss when determined by including only S's items of income, gain, deduction, and loss taken into account. None of the loss is absorbed by the group in Year 1, and S is discharged from $100 of indebtedness at the close of Year 1. Under section 108(a), S's $100 of discharge of indebtedness income is excluded from gross income because of insolvency. Under section 108(b), S's $100 net operating loss is reduced to zero at the close of Year 1.

(b) *Analysis.* Under paragraph (b)(3)(iii)(B) of this section, the reduction of the net operating loss is treated as a noncapital, nondeductible expense in Year 1 because the net operating loss is permanently disallowed by section 108(b). Under paragraph (b)(3)(ii)(C) of this section, all $100 of S's discharge of indebtedness income is treated as tax-exempt income in Year 1 because the discharge results in a $100 reduction to S's net operating loss. Consequently, the loss and the cancellation of the indebtedness result in no net adjustment to P's basis in S's stock under paragraph (b) of this section. (If the basis of assets were reduced under section 1017, rather than S's loss, the reduction would not occur until the beginning of Year 2 and the discharge would not be treated as tax-exempt income until that time.)

(c) *Insufficient attributes.* The facts are the same as in paragraph (a) of this *Example 4*, except that $70 of S's net operating loss is absorbed in Year 1, offsetting P's income for that year, and the indebtedness is discharged at the beginning of Year 2. Under paragraph (b) of this section, the $70 of S's loss absorbed in Year 1 reduces P's basis in S's stock by $70 as of the close of Year 1. Under section 108(a), S's discharge of indebtedness income in Year 2 is excluded from the P group's gross income because of insolvency. Under section 108(b), the remaining $30 of S's net operating loss carryover from Year 1 is reduced to zero at the close of Year 2. No other attributes are reduced. Under paragraph (b)(3)(iii)(B) of this section, the elimination of the remaining $30 net operating loss by section 108(b) is treated as a noncapital, nondeductible expense. Under paragraph (b)(3)(ii)(C) of this section, only $30 of the discharge is treated as tax-exempt income because only that amount is applied to reduce tax attributes. See also § 1.1502-19(c)(1)(iii) (taking into account any excess loss account of P in S's stock). The remaining $70 of discharge income excluded under section 108(a) has no effect on P's basis in S's stock.

(d) *Purchase price adjustment.* Assume instead that S buys land in Year 1 in exchange for S's $100 purchase money note (bearing interest at a market rate of interest in excess of the applicable Federal rate, and providing for a principal payment at the end of Year 10), and the seller agrees with S in Year 4 to discharge $60 of the note as a purchase price adjustment to which section 108(e)(5) applies. S has no discharge of indebtedness income that is treated as tax-exempt income under paragraph (b)(3)(ii) of this section. In addition, the $60 purchase price adjustment is not a noncapital, nondeductible expense under paragraph (b)(3)(iii) of this section. A purchase price adjustment is not equivalent to a discharge of indebtedness that is offset by a deduction or loss. Consequently, the purchase price adjustment results in no net adjustment to P's basis in S's stock under paragraph (b) of this section.

Example 5. Distributions. (a) *Amounts declared and distributed.* For Year 1, the P group has $120 of consolidated taxable income when determined by including only S's items of income, gain, deduction, and loss taken into account. S declares and makes a $10 dividend distribution to P at the close of Year 1. Under paragraph (b) of this section, P increases its basis in S's stock as of

Reg. § 1.1502-32(b)(5)

the close of Year 1 by a $110 net amount ($120 of taxable income, less a $10 distribution).

(b) *Distributions in later years.* The facts are the same as in paragraph (a) of this *Example 5*, except that S does not declare and distribute the $10 until Year 2. Under paragraph (b) of this section, P increases its basis in S's stock by $120 as of the close of Year 1, and decreases its basis by $10 as of the close of Year 2. (If P were also a subsidiary, the basis of its stock would also be increased in Year 1 to reflect P's $120 adjustment to basis of S's stock; the basis of P's stock would not be changed as a result of S's distribution in Year 2, because P's $10 of tax-exempt dividend income under paragraph (b)(3)(ii) of this section would be offset by the $10 negative adjustment to P's basis in S's stock for the distribution.)

(c) *Amounts declared but not distributed.* The facts are the same as in paragraph (a) of this *Example 5*, except that, during December of Year 1, S declares (and P becomes entitled to) another $70 dividend distribution with respect to its stock, but P does not receive the distribution until after it sells all of S's stock at the close of Year 1. Under § 1.1502-13(f)(2)(iv), S is treated as making a $70 distribution to P at the time P becomes entitled to the distribution. (If S is distributing an appreciated asset, its gain under section 311 is also taken into account under paragraph (b)(3)(i) of this section at the time P becomes entitled to the distribution.) Consequently, under paragraph (b) of this section, P increases its basis in S's stock as of the close of Year 1 by only a $40 net amount ($120 of taxable income, less two distributions totalling $80). Any further adjustments after S ceases to be a member and the $70 distribution is made would be duplicative, because the stock basis has already been adjusted for the distribution. Accordingly, the distribution will not result in further adjustments or gain, even if the distribution is a payment to which section 301(c)(2) or (3) applies.

Example 6. Reorganization with boot. (a) *Facts.* P owns all of the stock of S and T. On January 1 of Year 1, P has a $100 basis in the S stock and a $60 basis in the T stock. S and T have no items of income, gain, deduction, or loss for Year 1. S and T each have substantial earnings and profits. At the close of Year 1, T merges into S in a reorganization described in section 368(a)(1)(A) (and in section 368(a)(1)(D)). P receives no additional S stock, but does receive $10 which is treated as a dividend under section 356(a)(2).

(b) *Analysis.* Under section 358, P's basis in the S stock is increased by its basis in the T stock. Under § 1.1502-13(f)(3) the money received is treated as being taken into account immediately after the transaction. Thus, the $10 is treated as a dividend distribution under section 301 and under paragraph (b)(3)(v) of this section, the $10 is a distribution to which paragraph (b)(2)(iv) of this section applies. Accordingly, P's basis in the S stock is $160 immediately after the merger, which is then decreased by the $10 distribution taken into account immediately after the transaction, resulting in a basis of $150.

Example 7. Tiering up of basis adjustments. P owns all of S's stock, and S owns all of T's stock. For Year 1, the P group has $100 of consolidated taxable income when determined by including only T's items of income, gain, deduction, and loss taken into account, and $50 of consolidated taxable income when determined by including only S's items taken into account. S increases its basis in T's stock by $100 under paragraph (b) of this section. Under paragraph (a)(3) of this section, this $100 basis adjustment is taken into account in determining P's adjustments to its basis in S's stock. Thus, P increases its basis in S's stock by $150 under paragraph (b) of this section.

Example 8. Allocation of items. (a) *Acquisition in mid-year.* P is the common parent of a consolidated group, and S is an unaffiliated corporation filing separate returns on a calendar-year basis. P acquires all of S's stock and S becomes a member of the P group on July 1 of Year 1. For the entire calendar Year 1, S has $100 of ordinary income and under § 1.1502-76(b) $60 is allocated to the period from January 1 to June 30 and $40 to the period from July 1 to December 31. Under paragraph (b) of this section, P increases its basis in S's stock by $40.

(b) *Sale in mid-year.* The facts are the same as in paragraph (a) of this *Example 8*, except that S is a member of the P group at the beginning of Year 1 but ceases to be a member on June 30 as a result of P's sale of S's stock. Under paragraph (b) of this section, P increases its basis in S's stock by $60 immediately before the stock sale. (P's basis increase would be the same if S became a nonmember because S issued additional shares to nonmembers.)

(c) *Absorption of loss carryovers.* Assume instead that S is a member of the P group at the beginning of Year 1 but ceases to be a member on June 30 as a result of P's sale of S's stock, and a $100 consolidated net operating loss attributable to S is carried over by the P group to Year 1. The consolidated net operating loss may be apportioned to S for its first separate return year only to the extent not absorbed by the P group during Year 1. Under paragraph (b)(3)(i) of this section,

Reg. § 1.1502-32(b)(5)

if the loss is absorbed by the P group in Year 1, whether the offsetting income arises before or after P's sale of S's stock, the absorption of the loss carryover is included in the determination of S's taxable income or loss for Year 1. Thus, P's basis in S's stock is adjusted under paragraph (b) of this section to reflect any absorption of the loss by the P group.

Example 9. Gross-ups. (a) *Facts.* P owns all of the stock of S, and S owns all of the stock of T, a newly formed controlled foreign corporation that is not a passive foreign investment company. In Year 1, T has $100 of subpart F income and pays $34 of foreign income tax, leaving T with $66 of earnings and profits. The P group has $100 of consolidated taxable income when determined by taking into account only S's items (the inclusion under section 951(a), taking into account the section 78 gross-up). As a result of the section 951(a) inclusion, S increases its basis in T's stock by $66 under section 961(a).

(b) *Analysis.* Under paragraph (b)(3)(i) of this section, S has $100 of taxable income. Under paragraph (b)(3)(iii)(B) of this section, the $34 gross-up for taxes paid by T that S is treated as having paid is a noncapital, nondeductible expense (whether or not any corresponding amount is claimed by the P group as a tax credit). Thus, P increases it basis in S's stock under paragraph (b) of this section by the net adjustment of $66.

(c) *Subsequent distribution.* The facts are the same as in paragraph (a) of this *Example 9,* except that T distributes its $66 of earnings and profits in Year 2. The $66 distribution received by S is excluded from S's income under section 959(a) because the distribution represents earnings and profits attributable to amounts that were included in S's income under section 951(a) for Year 1. In addition, S's basis in T's stock is decreased by $66 under section 961(b). The excluded distribution is not tax-exempt income under paragraph (b)(3)(ii) of this section because of the corresponding reduction to S's basis in T's stock. Consequently, P's basis in S's stock is not adjusted under paragraph (b) of this section for Year 2.

Example 10. Recapture of tax-exempt items. (a) *Facts.* S is a life insurance company. For Year 1, the P group has $200 of consolidated taxable income, determined by including only S's items of income, gain, deduction, and loss taken into account (including a $300 small company deduction under section 806). In addition, S has $100 of tax-exempt interest income, $60 of which is S's *company share.* The remaining $40 of tax-exempt income is the *policyholders' share* that reduces S's deduction for increase in reserves.

(b) *Tax-exempt items generally.* Under paragraph (b)(3)(i) of this section, S has $200 of taxable income for Year 1. Also for Year 1, S has $100 of tax-exempt income under paragraph (b)(3)(ii)(A) of this section, and another $300 is treated as tax-exempt income under paragraph (b)(3)(ii)(B) of this section because of the deduction under section 806. Under paragraph (b)(3)(iii) of this section, S has $40 of noncapital, nondeductible expenses for Year 1 because S's deduction under section 807 for its increase in reserves has been permanently reduced by the $40 policyholders' share of the tax-exempt interest income. Thus, P increases its basis in S's stock by $560 under paragraph (b) of this section.

(c) *Recapture.* Assume instead that S is a property and casualty company and, for Year 1, S accrues $100 of estimated salvage recoverable under section 832. Of this amount, $87 (87% of $100) is excluded from gross income because of the "fresh start" provisions of Sec. 11305(c) of P.L. 101-508 (the Omnibus Budget Reconciliation Act of 1990). Thus, S has $87 of tax-exempt income under paragraph (b)(3)(ii)(A) of this section that increases P's basis in S's stock for Year 1. (S also has $13 of taxable income over the period of inclusion under section 481.) In Year 5, S determines that the $100 salvage recoverable was overestimated by $30 and deducts $30 for the reduction of the salvage recoverable. However, S has $26.10 (87% of $30) of taxable income in Year 5 due to the partial recapture of its fresh start. Because S has no basis corresponding to this income, S is treated under paragraph (b)(3)(iii)(B) of this section as having a $26.10 noncapital, nondeductible expense in Year 5. This treatment is necessary to reflect the elimination of the erroneous fresh start in S's stock basis and causes a decreases in P's basis in S's stock by $30 for Year 5 (a $3.90 taxable loss and a $26.10 special adjustment).

(c) *Allocation of adjustments among shares of stock*—(1) *In general.* The portion of the adjustment under paragraph (b) of this section that is described in paragraph (b)(2)(iv) of this section (negative adjustments for distributions) is allocated to the shares of S's stock to which the distribution relates. The remainder of the adjustment, described in paragraphs (b)(2)(i) through (iii) of this section (adjustments for taxable income or loss, tax-exempt income, and noncapital, nondeductible expenses), is allocated among the shares of S's stock as provided in paragraphs (c)(2) through (4) of this section. If the remainder of the adjustment is positive, it is allocated first to any preferred stock to the extent provided in paragraph (c)(3) of this section, and then to the common stock as provided in paragraph (c)(2) of

Reg. § 1.1502-32(c)(1)

this section. If the remainder of the adjustment is negative, it is allocated only to common stock as provided in paragraph (c)(2) of this section. An adjustment under this section allocated to a share for the period the share is owned by a nonmember has no effect on the basis of the share. See paragraph (c)(4) of this section for the reallocation of adjustments, and paragraph (d) of this section for definitions. See § 1.1502-19(d) for special allocations of basis determined or adjusted under the Code with respect to excess loss accounts.

(2) *Common stock*—(i) *Allocation within a class.* The portion of the adjustment described in paragraphs (b)(2)(i) through (iii) of this section (the adjustment determined without taking distributions into account) that is allocable to a class of common stock is generally allocated equally to each share within the class. However, if a member has an excess loss account in shares of a class of common stock at the time of a positive adjustment, the portion of the adjustment allocable to the member with respect to the class is allocated first to equalize and eliminate that member's excess loss accounts and then to increase equally its basis in the shares of that class. Similarly, any negative adjustment is allocated first to reduce the member's positive basis in shares of the class before creating or increasing its excess loss account. Distributions and any adjustments or determinations under the Internal Revenue Code (e.g., under section 358, including any modifications under § 1.1502-19(d)) are taken into account before the allocation is made under this paragraph (c)(2)(i).

(ii) *Allocation among classes*—(A) *General rule.* If S has more than one class of common stock, the extent to which the adjustment described in paragraphs (b)(2)(i) through (iii) of this section (the adjustment determined without taking distributions into account) is allocated to each class is determined, based on consistently applied assumptions, by taking into account the terms of each class and all other facts and circumstances relating to the overall economic arrangement. The allocation generally must reflect the manner in which the classes participate in the economic benefit or burden (if any) corresponding to the items of income, gain, deduction, or loss allocated. In determining participation, any differences in voting rights are not taken into account, and the following factors are among those to be considered—

(*1*) The interest of each share in economic profits and losses (if different from the interest in taxable income);

(*2*) The interest of each share in cash flow and other non-liquidating distributions; and

(*3*) The interest of each share in distributions in liquidation.

(B) *Distributions and Code adjustments.* Distributions and any adjustments or determinations under the Internal Revenue Code are taken into account before the allocation is made under this paragraph (c)(2)(ii).

(3) *Preferred stock.* If the adjustment under paragraphs (b)(2)(i) through (iii) of this section (the adjustment determined without taking distributions into account) is positive, it is allocated to preferred stock to the extent required (when aggregated with prior allocations to the preferred stock during the period that S is a member of the consolidated group) to reflect distributions described in section 301 (and all other distributions treated as dividends) to which the preferred stock becomes entitled, and arrearages arising, during the period that S is a member of the consolidated group. For this purpose, the preferred stock is treated as entitled to a distribution no later than the time the distribution is taken into account under the Internal Revenue Code (e.g., under section 305). If the amount of distributions and arrearages exceeds the positive amount (when aggregated with prior allocations), the positive amount is first allocated among classes of preferred stock to reflect their relative priorities, and the amount allocated to each class is then allocated pro rata within the class. An allocation to a share with respect to arrearages and distributions for the period the share is owned by a nonmember is not reflected in the basis of the share under paragraph (b) of this section. However, if P and S cease to be members of one consolidated group and remain affiliated as members of another consolidated group, P's ownership of S's stock during consolidated return years of the prior group is treated for this purpose as ownership by a member to the extent that the the adjustments during the prior consolidated return years are still reflected in the basis of the preferred stock.

(4) *Cumulative redetermination*—(i) *General rule.* A member's basis in each share of S's preferred and common stock must be redetermined whenever necessary to determine the tax liability of any person. See paragraph (b)(1) of this section. The redetermination is made by reallocating S's net adjustment described in paragraphs (b)(2)(i) through (iii) of this section (the adjustment determined without taking distributions into account) for each consolidated return year (or other applicable period) of the group by taking into account all of the facts and circumstances affecting allocations under this paragraph (c) as of the redetermination date with respect to all of S's shares. For this purpose:

Reg. § 1.1502-32(c)(2)

(A) Amounts may be reallocated from one class of S's stock to another class, but not from one share of a class to another share of the same class.

(B) If there is a change in the equity structure of S (e.g., as the result of S's issuance, redemption, or recapitalization of shares), a cumulative redetermination is made for the period before the change. If a reallocation is required by another redetermination after a change, amounts arising after the change are reallocated before amounts arising before the change.

(C) If S becomes a nonmember as a result of a change in its equity structure, any reallocation is made only among the shares of S's stock immediately before the change. For example, if S issues stock to a nonmember creditor in exchange for its debt, and the exchange results in S becoming a nonmember, any reallocation is only among the shares of S's stock immediately before the exchange.

(D) Any reallocation is treated for all purposes after it is made (including subsequent redeterminations) as the original allocation of an amount under this paragraph (c), but the reallocation does not affect any prior period.

(ii) *Prior use of allocations.* An amount may not be reallocated under paragraph (c)(4)(i) of this section to the extent that the amount has been used before the reallocation. For this purpose, an amount has been used to the extent it has been taken into account, directly or indirectly, by any member in determining income, gain, deduction, or loss, or in determining the basis of any property that is not subject to this section (e.g., stock of a corporation that has become a nonmember). For example, if P sells a share of S stock, an amount previously allocated to the share cannot be reallocated to another share of S stock, but an amount allocated to another share of S stock can still be reallocated to the sold share because the reallocated amount has not been taken into account; however, any adjustment reallocated to the sold share may effectively be eliminated, because the reallocation was not in effect when the share was previously sold and P's gain or loss from the sale is not redetermined. If, however, P sells the share of S stock to another member, the amount is not used until P's gain or loss is taken into account under § 1.1502-13.

(5) *Examples.* The principles of this paragraph (c) are illustrated by the following examples.

Example 1. Ownership of less than all the stock. (a) *Facts.* P owns 80% of S's only class of stock with an $800 basis. For Year 1, S has $100 of taxable income.

(b) *Analysis.* Under paragraph (c)(1) of this section, the $100 positive adjustment under paragraph (b) of this section for S's taxable income is allocated among the shares of S's stock, including shares owned by nonmembers. Under paragraph (c)(2)(i) of this section, the adjustment is allocated equally to each share of S's stock. Thus, P increases its basis in S's stock under paragraph (b) of this section as of the close of Year 1 by $80. (The basis of the 20% of S's stock owned by nonmembers is not adjusted under this section.)

(c) *Varying interest.* The facts are the same as in paragraph (a) of this *Example 1*, except that P buys the remaining 20% of S's stock at the close of business on June 30 of Year 1 for $208. Under paragraph (b)(1) of this section and the principles of § 1.1502-76(b), S's $100 of taxable income is allocable $40 to the period from January 1 to June 30 and $60 to the period from July 1 to December 31. Thus, for the period ending June 30, P is treated as having a $32 adjustment with respect to the S stock that P has owned since January 1 (80% of $40) and, under paragraph (c)(2)(i) of this section, the adjustment is allocated equally among those shares. For the period ending December 31, P is treated as having a $60 adjustment (100% of $60) that is also allocated equally among P's shares of S's stock owned after June 30. P's basis in the shares owned as of the beginning of the year therefore increases by $80 (the sum of 80% of $40 and 80% of $60), from $800 to $880, and P's basis in the shares purchased on June 30 increases by $12 (20% of $60), from $208 to $220. Thus, P's aggregate basis in S's stock as of the end of Year 1 is $1,100.

(d) *Tax liability.* The facts are the same as in paragraph (a) of this *Example 1*, except that P pays S's $34 share of the group's consolidated tax liability resulting from S's taxable income, and S does not reimburse P. S's $100 of taxable income results in a positive adjustment under paragraph (b)(3)(i) of this section, and S's $34 of tax liability results in a negative adjustment under paragraph (b)(3)(iv)(D) of this section and the principles of section 1552. Because S does not make any payment in recognition of the additional tax liability, by analogy to the treatment under § 1.1552-1(b)(2), S is treated as having made a $34 payment that is described in paragraph (b)(3)(iii) of this section (noncapital, nondeductible expenses) and as having received an equal amount from P as a capital contribution. Thus, P increases its basis in its S stock by $52.80 (80% of the $100 of taxable income, less 80% of the $34 tax payment). In addition, P increases its basis in S's stock by $34 under the Internal Revenue Code and paragraph (a)(2) of this section to reflect the capital contribution. In the aggregate, P increases

Reg. § 1.1502-32(c)(5)

its basis in S's stock by $86.80. (If, as in paragraph (c) of this *Example 1*, P buys the remaining 20% of S's stock at the close of business on June 30, P increases its basis in S's stock by another $7.90 for the additional 20% interest in S's income after June 30 ($60 multiplied by 20%, less 20% of the $20.40 tax payment on $60); the $34 capital contribution by P is reflected in all of its S shares (not just the original 80%), and P's aggregate basis adjustment under this section is $94.70 ($86.80 plus $7.90).)

Example 2. Preferred stock. (a) *Facts.* P owns all of S's common stock with an $800 basis, and nonmembers own all of S's preferred stock. The preferred stock was issued for $200, has a $20 annual, cumulative preference as to dividends, and has an initial liquidation preference of $200. For Year 1, S has $50 of taxable income and no distributions are declared or made.

(b) *Analysis of arrearages.* Under paragraphs (c)(1) and (3) of this section, $20 of the $50 positive adjustment under paragraph (b) of this section is allocated first to the preferred stock to reflect the dividend arrearage arising in Year 1. The remaining $30 of the positive adjustment is allocated to the common stock, increasing P's basis from $800 to $830 as of the close of Year 1. (The basis of the preferred stock owned by nonmembers is not adjusted under this section.)

(c) *Current distribution.* The facts are the same as in paragraph (a) of this *Example 2*, except that S declares and makes a $20 distribution with respect to the preferred stock during Year 1 in satisfaction of its preference. The results are the same as in paragraph (b) of this *Example 2*.

(d) *Varying interest.* The facts are the same as in paragraph (a) of this *Example 2*, except that S has no income or loss for Years 1 and 2, P purchases all of S's preferred stock at the beginning of Year 3 for $240, and S has $70 of taxable income for Year 3. Under paragraph (c)(3) of this section, $60 of the $70 positive adjustment under paragraph (b) of this section is allocated to the preferred stock to reflect the dividends arrearages for Years 1 through 3, but only the $20 for Year 3 is reflected in the basis of the preferred stock under paragraph (b) of this section. (The remaining $40 is not reflected because the preferred stock was owned by nonmembers during Years 1 and 2.) Thus, P increases its basis in S's preferred stock from $240 to $260, and its basis in S's common stock from $800 to $810, as of the close of Year 3. (If P had acquired all of S's preferred stock in a transaction to which section 351 applies, and P's initial basis in S's preferred stock was $200 under section 362, P's basis in S's preferred stock would increase from $200 to $220.)

(e) *Varying interest with current distributions.* The facts are the same as in paragraph (d) of this *Example 2*, except that S declares and makes a $20 distribution with respect to the preferred stock in each of Years 1 and 2 in satisfaction of its preference, and P purchases all of S's preferred stock at the beginning of Year 3 for $200. Under paragraph (c)(3) of this section, $40 of the $70 positive adjustment under paragraph (b) of this section is allocated to the preferred stock to reflect the distributions in Years 1 and 2, and $20 of the $70 is allocated to the preferred stock to reflect the arrearage for Year 3. However, as in paragraph (d) of this *Example 2*, only the $20 attributable to Year 3 is reflected in the basis of the preferred stock under paragraph (b) of this section. Thus, P increases its basis in S's preferred stock from $200 to $220, and P increases its basis in S's common stock from $800 to $810.

Example 3. Cumulative redetermination. (a) *Facts.* P owns all of S's common and preferred stock. The preferred stock has a $100 annual, cumulative preference as to dividends. For Year 1, S has $200 of taxable income, the first $100 of which is allocated to the preferred stock and the remaining $100 of which is allocated to the common stock. For Year 2, S has no adjustment under paragraph (b) of this section, and P sells all of S's common stock at the close of Year 2.

(b) *Analysis.* Under paragraph (c)(4) of this section, P's basis in S's common stock must be redetermined as of the sale of the stock. The redetermination is made by reallocating the $200 positive adjustment under paragraph (b) of this section for Year 1 by taking into account all of the facts and circumstances affecting allocations as of the sale. Thus, the $200 positive adjustment for Year 1 is reallocated entirely to the preferred stock to reflect the dividend arrearages for Years 1 and 2. The reallocation away from the common stock reflects the fact that, because of the additional amount of arrearage in Year 2, the common stock is not entitled to any part of the $200 of taxable income from Year 1. Thus, the common stock has no positive or negative adjustment, and the preferred stock has a $200 positive adjustment. These reallocations are treated as the original allocations for Years 1 and 2. (The results for the common stock would be the same if the common and preferred stock were not owned by the same member, or the preferred stock were owned by nonmembers.)

(c) *Preferred stock issued after adjustment arises.* The facts are the same as in paragraph (a) of this *Example 3*, except that S does not issue its preferred stock until the beginning of Year 2, S has no further adjustment under paragraph (b) of this section for Years 2 and 3, and P sells S's common stock at the close of Year 3. Under paragraphs (c)(1) and (2) of this section, the $200 positive adjustment for Year 1 is initially allocated entirely to the common stock. Under paragraph (c)(4) of this section, the $200 adjustment is reallocated to the preferred stock to reflect the arrearages for Years 2 and 3. Thus, the common stock has no positive or negative adjustment.

(d) *Common stock issued after adjustment arises.* The facts are the same as in paragraph (a) of this *Example 3*, except that S has no preferred stock, S issues additional common stock of the same class at the beginning of Year 2, S has no further adjustment under paragraph (b) of this section in Years 2 and 3, and P sells its S common stock at the close of Year 3. Under paragraphs (c)(1) and (2) of this section, the $200 positive adjustment for Year 1 is initially allocated entirely to the original common stock. Under paragraph (c)(4)(i)(A) of this section, the $200 adjustment is not reallocated among the original common stock and the additional stock. Unlike the preferred stock in paragraph (c) of this *Example 3*, the additional common stock is of the same class as the original stock, and there is no reallocation between shares of the same class.

(e) *Positive and negative adjustments.* The facts are the same as in paragraph (a) of this *Example 3*, except that S has a $200 loss for Year 2 that results in a negative adjustment to the common stock before any redetermination. For purposes of the basis redetermination under paragraph (c)(4) of this section, the Year 1 and 2 adjustments under paragraph (b) of this section are not netted. Thus, as in paragraph (b) of this *Example 3*, the redetermination is made by reallocating the $200 positive adjustment for Year 1 entirely to the preferred stock. The $200 negative adjustment for Year 2 is allocated entirely to the common stock. Consequently, the preferred stock has a $200 positive cumulative adjustment, and the common stock has a $200 negative cumulative adjustment. (The results would be the same if there were no other adjustments described in paragraph (b) of this section, P sells S's common stock at the close of Year 3 rather than Year 2, and an additional $100 arrearage arises in Year 3; only adjustments under paragraph (b) of this section may be reallocated, and there is no additional adjustment for Year 3.)

(f) *Current distributions.* The facts are the same as in paragraph (a) of this *Example 3*, except that, during Year 1, S declares and makes a distribution to P of $100 as a dividend on the preferred stock and $100 as a dividend on the common stock. The taxable income and distributions result in no Year 1 adjustment under paragraph (b) of this section for either the common or preferred stock. However, as in paragraph (b) of this *Example 3*, the redetermination under paragraph (c)(4) of this section is made by reallocating a $200 positive adjustment for Year 1 (S's net adjustment described in paragraph (b) of this section, determined without taking distributions into account) to the preferred stock. Consequently, the preferred stock has a $100 positive cumulative adjustment ($200 of taxable income, less a $100 distribution with respect to the preferred stock) and the common stock has a $100 negative cumulative adjustment (for the distribution).

(g) *Convertible preferred stock.* The facts are the same as in paragraph (a) of this *Example 3*, except that the preferred stock is convertible into common stock that is identical to the common stock already outstanding, the holders of the preferred stock convert the stock at the close of Year 2, and no stock is sold until the close of Year 5. Under paragraph (c)(4) of this section, the $200 positive adjustment for Year 1 is reallocated entirely to the preferred stock immediately before the conversion. The newly issued common stock is treated as a second class of S common stock, and adjustments under paragraph (b) of this section are allocated between the original and the new common stock under paragraph (c)(2)(ii) of this section. Although the preferred stock is converted to common stock, the $200 adjustment to the preferred stock is not subsequently reallocated between the original and the new common stock. Because the original and the new stock are equivalent, adjustments under paragraph (b) of this section for subsequent periods are allocated equally to each share.

(h) *Prior use of allocations.* The facts are the same as in paragraph (a) of this *Example 3*, except that P sells 10% of S's common stock at the close of Year 1, and the remaining 90% at the close of Year 2. P's basis in the common stock sold in Year 1 reflects $10 of the adjustment allocated to the common stock for Year 1. Under paragraph (c)(4)(ii) of this section, because $10 of the Year 1 adjustment was used in determining P's gain or loss, only $90 is reallocated to the preferred stock, and $10 remains allocated to the common stock sold.

(i) *Lower-tier members.* The facts are the same as in paragraph (a) of this *Example 3*, except that P owns only S's common stock, and P is also a subsidiary. If there is a redetermination under paragraph (c)(4) of this section by a member owning P's stock, a redetermination with respect to S's stock must be made first, and the effect of that redetermination on P's adjustments is taken into account under paragraph (b) of this section. However, as in paragraph (h) of this *Example 3*, to the extent an amount of the initial adjustments with respect to S's common stock have already been tiered up and used by a member owning P's stock, that amount remains with S's common stock (and the higher-tier member using the adjustment with respect to P's stock), and may not be reallocated to S's preferred stock.

Example 4. Allocation to preferred stock between groups. (a) *Facts.* P owns all of S's only class of stock, and S owns all of T's common and preferred stock. The preferred stock has a $100 annual, cumulative preference as to dividends. For Year 1, T has $200 of taxable income, the first $100 of which is allocated to the preferred stock and the remaining $100 of which is allocated to the common stock, and S has no adjustments other than the amounts tiered up from T. S and T have no adjustments under paragraph (b) of this section for Years 2 and 3. X, the common parent of another consolidated group, purchases all of S's stock at the close of Year 3, and S and T become members of the X group. For Year 4, T has $200 of taxable income, and S has no adjustments other than the amounts tiered up from T.

(b) *Analysis for Years 1 through 3.* Under paragraph (c)(4) of this section, the allocation of S's adjustments under paragraph (b) of this section (determined without taking distributions into account) must be redetermined as of the time P sells S's stock. As a result of this redetermination, T's common stock has no positive or negative adjustment and the preferred stock has a $200 positive adjustment.

(c) *Analysis for Year 4.* Under paragraph (c)(3) of this section, the allocation of T's $200 positive adjustment in Year 4 to T's preferred stock with respect to arrearages is made by taking into account the consolidated return years of both the P group and the X group. Thus, the allocation of the $200 positive adjustment for Year 4 to T's preferred stock is not treated as an allocation for a period for which the preferred stock is owned by a nonmember. Thus, the $200 adjustment is reflected in S's basis in T's preferred stock under paragraph (b) of this section.

(d) *Definitions.* For purposes of this section—

(1) *Class.* The shares of a member having the same material terms (without taking into account voting rights) are treated as a single class of stock.

(2) *Preferred stock.* Preferred stock is stock that is limited and preferred as to dividends and has a liquidation preference. A class of stock that is not described in section 1504(a)(4), however, is not treated as preferred stock for purposes of paragraph (c) of this section if members own less than 80% of each class of common stock (determined without taking this paragraph (d)(2) into account).

(3) *Common stock.* Common stock is stock that is not preferred stock.

(4) *Becoming a nonmember.* A member is treated as becoming a nonmember if it has a separate return year (including another group's consolidated return year). For example, S may become a nonmember if it issues additional stock to nonmembers, but S does not become a nonmember as a result of its complete liquidation.

(e) *Anti-avoidance rule*—(1) *General rule.* If any person acts with a principal purpose contrary to the purposes of this section, to avoid the effect of the rules of this section or apply the rules of this section to avoid the effect of any other provision of the consolidated return regulations, adjustments must be made as necessary to carry out the purposes of this section.

(2) *Examples.* The principles of this paragraph (e) are illustrated by the following examples.

Example 1. Preferred stock treated as common stock. (a) *Facts.* S has 100 shares of common stock and 100 shares of preferred stock described in section 1504(a)(4). P owns 80 shares of S's common stock and all of S's preferred stock. The shareholders expect that S will have negative adjustments under paragraph (b) of this section for Years 1 and 2 (all of which will be allocable to S's common stock), the negative adjustments will have no significant effect on the value of S's stock, and S will have offsetting positive adjustments thereafter. When the preferred stock was issued, P intended to cause S to recapitalize the preferred stock into additional common stock at the end of Year 2 in a transaction described in section 368(a)(1)(E). P's temporary ownership of the preferred stock is with a principal purpose to limit P's basis reductions under paragraph (b) of this section to 80% of the anticipated negative adjustments. The recapitalization is intended to cause significantly more than 80% of the anticipated positive adjustments to increase P's basis in S's stock because of P's increased ownership of S's common stock immediately after the recapitalization.

(b) *Analysis.* S has established a transitory capital structure with a principal purpose to enhance P's basis in S's stock under this section. Under paragraph (e)(1) of this section, all of S's common and preferred stock is treated as a single class of common stock in Years 1 and 2 for purposes of this section. Thus, S's items are allocated under the principles of paragraph (c)(2)(ii) of this section, and P decreases its basis in both the common and preferred stock accordingly.

Example 2. Contribution of appreciated property. (a) *Facts.* P owns all of the stock of S and T, and S and T each own 50% of the stock of U. P's S stock has a $150 basis and $200 value, and P's T stock has a $200 basis and $200 value. With a principal purpose to eliminate P's gain from an anticipated sale of S's stock, T contributes to U an asset with a $100 value and $0 basis, and S contributes $100 cash. U sells T's asset and recognizes a $100 gain that results in a $100 positive adjustment under paragraph (b) of this section.

(b) *Analysis.* Under paragraph (c)(2) of this section, U's adjustment ordinarily would be allocated equally to each share of U's stock. If so allocated, P's basis in S's stock would increase from $150 to $200 and P would recognize no gain from the sale of S's stock for $200. Under paragraph (e)(1) of this section, however, because T transferred an appreciated asset to U with a principal purpose to shift a portion of the stock basis increase from P's stock in T to P's stock in S, the allocation of the $100 positive adjustment under paragraph (c) of this section between the shares of U's stock must take into account the contribution. Consequently, all $100 of the positive adjustment is allocated to the U stock owned by T, rather than $50 to the U stock owned by S and $50 to the U stock owned by T. P's basis in S's stock remains $150, and its basis in T's stock increases to $300. Thus, P recognizes a $50 gain from its sale of S's stock for $200.

Example 3. Reorganizations. (a) *Facts.* P forms S with an $800 contribution, $200 of which is in exchange for S's preferred stock described in section 1504(a)(4) and the balance of which is for S's common stock. For Years 1 through 3, S has a total of $160 of ordinary income, $60 of which is distributed with respect to the preferred stock in satisfaction of its $20 annual preference as to dividends. Under this section, P's basis in S's preferred stock is unchanged, and its basis in S's common stock is increased from $600 to $700. To reduce its gain from an anticipated sale of S's preferred stock, P forms T at the close of Year 3 with a contribution of all of S's stock in exchange for corresponding common and preferred stock of T in a transaction to which section 351 applies. At the time of the contribution, the fair market value of the common stock is $700 and the fair market value of the preferred stock is $300 (due to a decrease in prevailing market interest rates). P subsequently sells T's preferred stock for $300.

(b) *Analysis.* Under section 358(b), P ordinarily has a $630 basis in T's common stock (70% of the $900 aggregate stock basis) and a $270 basis in T's preferred stock (30% of the $900 aggregate stock basis). However, because P transferred S's stock to T with a principal purpose to shift the allocation of basis adjustments under this section, adjustments are made under paragraph (e)(1) of this section to preserve the allocation under this section. Thus, P has a $700 basis in T's common stock and a $200 basis in T's preferred stock. Consequently, P recognizes a $100 gain from the sale of T's preferred stock.

Example 4. Post-deconsolidation basis adjustments. (a) *Facts.* For Year 1, the P group has $40 of taxable income when determined by including only S's items of income, gain, deduction, and loss taken into account, and P increases its basis in S's stock by $40 under paragraph (b) of this section. P anticipates that S will have a $40 ordinary loss for Year 2 that will be carried back and offset S's income in Year 1 and result in a $40 reduction to P's basis in S's stock for Year 2 under paragraph (b) of this section. With a principal purpose to avoid the reduction, P causes S to issue voting preferred stock that results in S becoming a nonmember at the beginning of Year 2. (Section 1.1502-20(b) does not reduce P's basis in the S stock as a result of S's deconsolidation.) As anticipated, S has a $40 loss for Year 2, which is carried back to Year 1 and offsets S's income from Year 1.

(b) *Analysis.* Under paragraph (e)(1) of this section, because P caused S to become a nonmember with a principal purpose to absorb S's loss but avoid the corresponding negative adjustment under this section, and P bears a substantial portion of the loss because of its continued ownership of S common stock, the basis of P's common stock in S is decreased by $40 for Year 2. (If P has less than a $40 basis in the retained S stock, P must recognize income for Year 2 to the extent of the excess.) Section 1504(a)(3) limits the ability of S to subsequently rejoin the P group's consolidated return.

(c) *Carryback to pre-consolidation year.* The facts are the same as in paragraph (a) of this *Example 4*, except that P anticipates that S's loss will be carried back and absorbed in a separate return year of S before Year 1 (rather than to the P group's consolidated return for Year 1). Although P causes S to become a nonmember with a principal purpose to avoid the negative adjustment under this section, and P bears a substantial portion of the loss because of its continued ownership of S common stock, both S's income and loss are taken into account under the separate return rules. Consequently, no one has acted with a prin-

Reg. § 1.1502-32(e)(2)

cipal purpose contrary to the purposes of this section, and no adjustments are necessary to carry out the purposes of this section.

Example 5. Pre-consolidation basis adjustments. (a) *Facts.* P forms S with a $100 contribution, and S becomes a member of the P affiliated group which does not file consolidated returns. For Years 1 through 3, S earns $300. P anticipates that it will elect under section 1501 for the P group to begin filing consolidated returns in Year 5. In anticipation of filing consolidated returns, and to avoid the negative stock basis adjustment that would result under paragraph (b) of this section from distributing S's earnings after Year 5, P causes S to distribute $300 during Year 4 as a qualifying dividend within the meaning of section 243(b). There is no plan or intention to recontribute the funds to S after the distribution.

(b) *Analysis.* Although S's distribution of $300 is with a principal purpose to avoid a corresponding negative adjustment under this section, the $300 was both earned and distributed entirely under the separate return rules. Consequently, P and S have not acted with a principal purpose contrary to the purposes of this section, and no adjustments are necessary to carry out the purposes of this section.

(f) *Predecessors and successors.* For purposes of this section, any reference to a corporation or to a share of stock includes a reference to a successor or predecessor as the context may require. A corporation is a successor if the basis of its assets is determined, directly or indirectly, in whole or in part, by reference to the basis of another corporation (the predecessor). For example, if T merges into S, S is treated, as the context may require, as a successor to T and as becoming a member of the group. A share is a successor if its basis is determined, directly or indirectly, in whole or in part, by reference to the basis of another share (the predecessor).

(g) *Recordkeeping.* Adjustments under this section must be reflected annually on permanent records (including work papers). See also section 6001, requiring records to be maintained. The group must be able to identify from these permanent records the amount and allocation of adjustments, including the nature of any tax-exempt income and noncapital, nondeductible expenses, so as to permit the application of the rules of this section for each year.

(h) *Effective date*—(1) *General rule.* This section applies with respect to determinations of the basis of the stock of a subsidiary (e.g., for determining gain or loss from a disposition of stock) in consolidated return years beginning on or after January 1, 1995. If this section applies, basis must be determined or redetermined as if this section were in effect for all years (including, for example, the consolidated return years of another consolidated group to the extent adjustments from those years are still reflected). For example, if the portion of a consolidated net operating loss carryover attributable to S expired in 1990 and is treated as a noncapital, nondeductible expense under paragraph (b) of this section, it is taken into account in tax years beginning on or after January 1, 1995 as a negative adjustment for 1990. Any such determination or redetermination does not, however, affect any prior period. Thus, the negative adjustment for S's noncapital, nondeductible expense is not taken into account for tax years beginning before January 1, 1995.

(2) *Dispositions of stock before effective date*—(i) *In general.* If P disposes of stock of S in a consolidated return year beginning before January 1, 1995, the amount of P's income, gain, deduction, or loss, and the basis reflected in that amount, are not redetermined under this section. See § 1.1502-19 as contained in the 26 CFR part 1 edition revised as of April 1, 1994 for the definition of disposition, and paragraph (h)(5) of this section for the rules applicable to such dispositions.

(ii) *Lower-tier members.* Although P disposes of S's stock in a tax year beginning before January 1, 1995, S's determinations or adjustments with respect to the stock of a lower-tier member with which it continues to file a consolidated return are redetermined in accordance with the rules of this section (even if they were previously taken into account by P and reflected in income, gain, deduction, or loss from the disposition of S's stock). For example, assume that P owns all of S's stock, S owns all of T's stock, and T owns all of U's stock. If S sells 80% of T's stock in a tax year beginning before January 1, 1995 (the effective date), the amount of S's income, gain, deduction, or loss from the sale, and the stock basis adjustments reflected in that amount, are not redetermined if P sells S's stock after the effective date. If S sells the remaining 20% of T's stock after the effective date, S's stock basis adjustments with respect to that T stock are also not redetermined because T became a nonmember before the effective date. However, if T and U continue to file a consolidated return with each other and T sells U's stock after the effective date, T's stock basis adjustments with respect to U's stock are redetermined (even though some of those adjustments may have been taken into account by S in its prior sale of T's stock before the effective date).

Reg. § 1.1502-32(f)

(iii) *Deferred amounts.* For purposes of this paragraph (h)(2), a disposition does not include a transaction to which § 1.1502-13, § 1.1502-13T, § 1.1502-14, or § 1.1502-14T applies. Instead, the transaction is deemed to occur as the income, gain, deduction, or loss (if any) is taken into account.

(3) *Distributions*—(i) *Deemed dividend elections.* If there is a deemed distribution and recontribution pursuant to § 1.1502-32(f)(2) as contained in the 26 CFR part 1 edition revised as of April 1, 1994 in a consolidated return year beginning before January 1, 1995, the deemed distribution and recontribution under the election are treated as an actual distribution by S and recontribution by P as provided under the election.

(ii) *Affiliated earnings and profits.* This section does not apply to reduce the basis in S's stock as a result of a distribution of earnings and profits accumulated in separate return years, if the distribution is made in a consolidated return year beginning before January 1, 1995, and the distribution does not cause a negative adjustment under the investment adjustment rules in effect at the time of the distribution. See paragraph (h)(5) of this section for the rules in effect with respect to the distribution.

(4) *Expiring loss carryovers.* If S became a member of a consolidated group in a consolidated return year beginning before January 1, 1995, and S had a loss carryover from a separate return limitation year at that time, the group does not treat any expiration of the loss carryover (even if in a tax year beginning on or after January 1, 1995) as a noncapital, nondeductible expense resulting in a negative adjustment under this section. If S becomes a member of a consolidated group in a consolidated return year beginning on or after January 1, 1995, and S has a loss carryover from a separate return limitation year at that time, adjustments with respect to the expiration are determined under this section.

(5) *Prior law*—(i) *In general.* For prior determinations, see prior regulations under section 1502 as in effect with respect to the determination. See, e.g., §§ 1.1502-32 and 1.1502-32T as contained in the 26 CFR part 1 edition revised as of April 1, 1994.

(ii) *Continuing basis reductions for certain deconsolidated subsidiaries.* If a subsidiary ceases to be a member of a group in a consolidated return year beginning before January 1, 1995, and its basis was subject to reduction under § 1.1502-32T or § 1.1502-32(g) as contained in the 26 CFR part 1 edition revised as of April 1, 1994, its basis remains subject to reduction under those principles. For example, if S ceased to be a member in 1990, and P's basis in any retained S stock was subject to a basis reduction account, the basis remains subject to reduction. Similarly, if an election could be made to apply § 1.1502-32T instead of § 1.1502-32(g), the election remains available. However, §§ 1.1502-32T and 1.1502-32(g) do not apply as a result of a subsidiary ceasing to be a member in tax years beginning on or after January 1, 1995. [Reg. § 1.1502-32.]

☐ [T.D. 6909, 12-29-66. Amended by T.D. 7246, 12-29-72; T.D. 7637, 8-6-79; T.D. 7655, 11-28-79; T.D. 7947, 3-5-84; T.D. 8188, 3-14-88; T.D. 8245, 3-14-89; T.D. 8294, 3-9-90; T.D. 8319, 11-19-90; T.D. 8364, 9-13-91; T.D. 8401, 3-13-92; T.D. 8560, 8-12-94; T.D. 8677, 6-26-96 and T.D. 8823, 6-25-99.]

[Reg. § 1.1502-33]

§ 1.1502-33. **Earnings and profits.**—(a) *In general*—(1) *Purpose.* This section provides rules for adjusting the earnings and profits of a subsidiary (S) and any member (P) owning S's stock. These rules modify the determination of P's earnings and profits under applicable rules of law, including section 312, by adjusting P's earnings and profits to reflect S's earnings and profits for the period that S is a member of the consolidated group. The purpose for modifying the determination of earnings and profits is to treat P and S as a single entity by reflecting the earnings and profits of lower-tier members in the earnings and profits of higher-tier members and consolidating the group's earnings and profits in the common parent. References in this section to earnings and profits include deficits in earnings and profits.

(2) *Application of other rules of law.* The rules of this section are in addition to other rules of law. For example, the allowance for depreciation is determined in accordance with section 312(k). P's earnings and profits must not be adjusted under this section and other rules of law in a manner that has the effect of duplicating an adjustment. For example, if S's earnings and profits are reflected in P's earnings and profits under paragraph (b) of this section, and S transfers its assets to P in a liquidation to which section 332 applies, S's earnings and profits that P succeeds to under section 381 must be adjusted to prevent duplication.

(b) *Tiering up earnings and profits*—(1) *General rule.* P's earnings and profits are adjusted under this section to reflect changes in S's earnings and profits in accordance with the applicable principles of § 1.1502-32, consistently applied, and an adjustment to P's earnings and profits for a tax year under this paragraph (b)(1) is treated as earnings and profits of P for the tax year in which the adjustment arises. Under these principles, for example, the adjustments are made as of the close of each consolidated return year, and as of any other time if a determination at that time is necessary to determine the earnings and profits of any person. Similarly, S's earnings and profits are allocated under the principles of § 1.1502-32(c), and the adjustments are applied in the order of the tiers, from the lowest to the highest. However, modifications to the principles include:

(i) The amount of P's adjustment is determined by reference to S's earnings and profits, rather than S's taxable and tax-exempt items (and therefore, for example, the deferral of a negative adjustment for S's unabsorbed losses does not apply).

(ii) The tax sharing rules under paragraph (d) of this section apply rather than those of § 1.1502-32(b)(3)(iv)(D).

(2) *Affiliated earnings and profits.* The reduction in S's earnings and profits under section 312 from a distribution of earnings and profits accumulated in separate return years of S that are not separate return limitation years does not tier up to P's earnings and profits. Thus, the increase in P's earnings and profits under section 312 from receipt of the distribution is not offset by a corresponding reduction.

(3) *Examples*—(i) *In general.* For purposes of the examples in this section, unless otherwise stated, P owns all of the only class of S's stock, the stock is owned for the entire year, S owns no stock of lower-tier members, the tax year of all persons is the calendar year, all persons use the accrual method of accounting, the facts set forth the only corporate activity, preferred stock is described in section 1504(a)(4), all transactions are between unrelated persons, and tax liabilities are disregarded.

(ii) *Tiering up earnings and profits.* The principles of this paragraph (b) are illustrated by the following examples.

Example 1. Tier-up and distribution of earnings and profits. (a) *Facts.* P forms S in Year 1 with a $100 contribution. S has $100 of earnings and profits for Year 1 and no earnings and profits for Year 2. During Year 2, S declares and distributes a $50 dividend to P.

(b) *Analysis.* Under paragraph (b)(1) of this section, S's $100 of earnings and profits for Year 1 increases P's earnings and profits for Year 1. P has no additional earnings and profits for Year 2 as a result of the $50 distribution in Year 2, because there is a $50 increase in P's earnings and profits as a result of the receipt of the dividend and a corresponding $50 decrease in S's earnings and profits under section 312(a) that is reflected in P's earnings and profits under paragraph (b)(1) of this section.

(c) *Distribution of current earnings and profits.* The facts are the same as in paragraph (a) of this *Example 1*, except that S distributes the $50 dividend at the end of Year 1 rather than during Year 2. Under paragraph (b)(1) of this section, P's earnings and profits are increased by $100 (S's $50 of undistributed earnings and profits, plus P's receipt of the $50 distribution). Thus, S's earnings and profits increase by $50 and P's earnings and profits increase by $100.

(d) *Affiliated earnings and profits.* The facts are the same as in paragraph (a) of this *Example 1*, except that P and S do not begin filing consolidated returns until Year 2. Because P and S file separate returns for Year 1, P's basis in S's stock remains $100 under § 1.1502-32 and this section, S has $100 of earnings and profits, and none of S's earnings and profits is reflected in P's earnings and profits under paragraph (b) of this section. S's distribution in Year 2 ordinarily would reduce S's earnings and profits but not increase P's earnings and profits. (P's $50 of earnings and profits from the dividend would be offset by S's $50 reduction in earnings and profits that tiers up under paragraph (b) of this section.) However, under paragraph (b)(2) of this section, the negative adjustment for S's distribution to P does not apply. Thus, S's distribution reduces its earnings and profits by $50 but increases P's earnings and profits by $50. (If S's earnings and profits had been accumulated in a separate return limitation year, paragraph (b)(2) of this section would not apply and the distribution would reduce S's earnings and profits but not increase P's earnings and profits.)

(e) *Earnings and profits deficit.* Assume instead that after P forms S in Year 1 with a $100 contribution, S borrows additional funds and has a $150 deficit in earnings and profits for Year 1. The corresponding loss for tax purposes is not absorbed in Year 1, and is included in the group's consolidated net operating loss carried forward to Year 2. Under paragraph (b)(1) of this section, however, S's $150 deficit in earnings and profits decreases P's earnings and profits for Year 1 by $150. (Absorption of the loss in a later tax year has no effect on the earnings and profits of P and S.)

Example 2. Section 355 distribution. (a) *Facts.* P owns all of S's stock and S owns all of T's stock. For Year 1, T has $100 of earnings and profits. Under paragraph (b)(1) of this section, the earnings and profits of T tier up to S and to P. S and P have no other earnings and profits for

Reg. § 1.1502-33(b)(2)

Consolidated Returns

Year 1. S distributes T's stock to P at the end of Year 1 in a distribution to which section 355 applies.

(b) *Analysis.* Because S's distribution of T's stock is a distribution to which section 355 applies, the applicable principles of § 1.1502-32(b)(2)(iv) do not require P's earnings and profits to be adjusted by reason of the distribution. In addition, although S's earnings and profits may be reduced under section 312(h) as a result of the distribution, the applicable principles of § 1.1502-32(b)(3)(iii) do not require P's earnings and profits to be adjusted to reflect this reduction in S's earnings and profits.

Example 3. Allocating earnings and profits among shares. P owns 80% of S's stock throughout Year 1. For Year 1, S has $100 of earnings and profits. Under paragraph (b)(1) of this section, $80 of S's earnings and profits is allocated to P based on P's ownership of S's stock. Accordingly, $80 of S's earnings and profits for Year 1 is reflected in P's earnings and profits for Year 1.

(c) *Special rules.* For purposes of this section—

(1) *Stock of members.* For purposes of determining P's earnings and profits from the disposition of S's stock, P's basis in S's stock is adjusted to reflect S's earnings and profits determined under paragraph (b) of this section, rather than under § 1.1502-32. For example, P's basis in S's stock is increased by positive earnings and profits and decreased by deficits in earnings and profits. Similarly, P's basis in S's stock is not reduced for distributions to which paragraph (b)(2) of this section applies (affiliated earnings and profits). P may have an excess loss account in S's stock for earnings and profits purposes (whether or not there is an excess loss account under § 1.1502-32), and the excess loss account is determined, adjusted, and taken into account in accordance with the principles of §§ 1.1502-19 and 1.1502-32.

(2) *Intercompany transactions.* Intercompany items and corresponding items are not reflected in earnings and profits before they are taken into account under § 1.1502-13. See § 1.1502-13 for the applicable rules and definitions.

(3) *Example.* The principles of this paragraph (c) are illustrated by the following example.

Example. Adjustments to stock basis. (a) *Facts.* P forms S in Year 1 with a $100 contribution. For Year 1, S has $75 of taxable income and $100 of earnings and profits. For Year 2, S has no taxable income or earnings and profits, and S declares and distributes a $50 dividend to P. P sells all of S's stock for $150 at the end of Year 2.

(b) *Analysis.* Under paragraph (c)(1) of this section, P's basis in S's stock for earnings and profits purposes immediately before the sale is $150 (the $100 initial basis, plus S's $100 of earnings and profits for Year 1, minus the $50 distribution of earnings and profits in Year 2). Thus, P recognizes no gain or loss from the sale of S's stock for earnings and profits purposes.

(c) *Earnings and profits deficit.* Assume instead that S has a $100 tax loss and earnings and profits deficit for Year 1. The tax loss is not absorbed in Year 1 and is included in the group's consolidated net operating loss carried forward to Year 2. Under paragraph (b) of this section, S's $100 deficit in earnings and profits decreases P's earnings and profits for Year 1. Under paragraph (c) of this section, P decreases its basis in S's stock for purposes of determining earnings and profits from $100 to $0. (If S had borrowed an additional $50 that it also lost in Year 1, P would have decreased its earnings and profits for Year 1 by the additional $50, and P would have had a $50 excess loss account in S's stock for earnings and profits purposes, which would be taken into account in determining P's earnings and profits from its sale of S's stock.)

(d) *Affiliated earnings and profits.* Assume instead that P and S do not begin filing consolidated returns until Year 2. Under paragraph (b) of this section, the negative adjustment under § 1.1502-32(b) for distributions does not apply to S's distribution of earnings and profits accumulated in a separate return year that is a not separate return limitation year. Thus, P's basis in S's stock for earnings and profits purposes remains $100, and P has $50 of earnings and profits from the sale of S's stock.

(d) *Federal income tax liability*—(1) *In general*—(i) *Extension of tax allocations.* Section 1552 allocates the tax liability of a consolidated group among its members for purposes of determining the amounts by which their earnings and profits are reduced for taxes. Section 1552 does not reflect the absorption by one member of another member's tax attributes (e.g., losses, deductions and credits). For example, if P's $100 of income is offset by S's $100 of deductions, consolidated tax liability is $0 and no amount is allocated under section 1552. However, the group may elect under this paragraph (d) to allocate additional amounts to reflect the absorption by one member of the tax attributes of another member. Permissible methods are set forth in paragraphs (d)(2) through (4) of this section, and election procedures are provided in paragraph (d)(5) of this section. Allocations under this paragraph (d) must be reflected annually on perma-

Reg. § 1.1502-33(d)(1)

nent records (including work papers). Any computations of separate return tax liability are subject to the principles of section 1561.

(ii) *Effect of extended tax allocations.* The amounts allocated under this paragraph (d) are treated as allocations of tax liability for purposes of § 1.1552-1(b)(2). For example, if P's taxable income is offset by S's loss, and tax liability is allocated under the percentage method of paragraph (d)(3) of this section, P's earnings and profits are reduced as if its income were subject to tax, P is treated as liable to S for the amount of the tax, and corresponding adjustments are made to S's earnings and profits. If the liability of one member to another is not paid, the amount not paid generally is treated as a distribution, contribution, or both, depending on the relationship between the members.

(2) *Wait-and-see method.* The wait-and-see method under this paragraph (d)(2) is derived from Securities and Exchange Commission procedures. In the year that a member's tax attribute is absorbed, the group's consolidated tax liability is allocated in accordance with the group's method under section 1552. When, in effect, the member with the tax attribute could have absorbed the attribute on a separate return basis in a later year, a portion of the group's consolidated tax liability for the later year that is otherwise allocated to members under section 1552 is reallocated. The reallocation takes into account all consolidated return years to which this paragraph (d) applies (the computation period), and is determined by comparing the tax allocated to a member during the computation period with the member's tax liability determined as if it had filed separate returns during the computation period.

(i) *Cap on allocation under section 1552.* A member's allocation under section 1552 for a tax year may not exceed the excess, if any, of—

(A) The total of the tax liabilities of the member for the computation period (including the current year), determined as if the member had filed separate returns; over

(B) The total amount allocated to the member under section 1552 and this paragraph (d) for the computation period (except the current year).

(ii) *Reallocation of capped amounts.* To the extent that the amount allocated to a member under section 1552 exceeds the limitation under paragraph (d)(2)(i) of this section, the excess is allocated among the remaining members in proportion to (but not to exceed the amount of) each member's excess, if any, of—

(A) The total of the tax liabilities of the member for the computation period (including the current year), determined as if the member had filed separate returns; over

(B) The total amount allocated to the member under section 1552 and this paragraph (d) for the computation period (including for the current year only the amount allocated under section 1552).

(iii) *Reallocation of excess capped amounts.* If the reductions under paragraph (d)(2)(i) of this section exceed the amounts allocable under paragraph (d)(2)(ii) of this section, the excess is allocated among the members in accordance with the group's method under section 1552 without taking this paragraph (d)(2) into account.

(3) *Percentage method.* The percentage method under this paragraph (d)(3) allocates tax liability based on the absorption of tax attributes, without taking into account the ability of any member to subsequently absorb its own tax attributes. The allocation under this method is in addition to the allocation under section 1552.

(i) *Decreased earnings and profits.* A member's allocation under section 1552 for any year is increased, thereby decreasing its earnings and profits, by a fixed percentage (not to exceed 100%) of the excess, if any, of—

(A) The member's separate return tax liability for the consolidated return year as determined under § 1.1552-1(a)(2)(ii); over

(B) The amount allocated to the member under section 1552.

(ii) *Increased earnings and profits.* An amount equal to the total decrease in earnings and profits under paragraph (d)(3)(i) of this section (including amounts allocated as a result of a carryback) increases the earnings and profits of the members whose attributes are absorbed, and is allocated among them in a manner that reasonably reflects the absorption of the tax attributes.

(4) *Additional methods.* The absorption by one member of the tax attributes of another member may be reflected under any other method approved in writing by the Commissioner.

(5) *Election of allocation method*—(i) *In general.* Tax liability may be allocated under this paragraph (d) only if an election is filed with the group's first return. The election must—

(A) Be made in a separate statement entitled "ELECTION TO ALLOCATE TAX LIABILITY UNDER § 1.1502-33(d)";

(B) State the allocation method elected under § 1.1502-33(d) and under section 1552;

Reg. § 1.1502-33(d)(2)

(C) If the percentage method is elected, state the percentage (not to exceed 100%) to be used; and

(D) If a method is permitted under paragraph (d)(4) of this section, attach evidence of approval of the method by the Commissioner.

(ii) *Consent*—(A) *Electing or changing methods.* An election for a later year, or an election to change methods, may be made only with the written consent of the Commissioner.

(B) *Prior law elections.* An election in effect for the last tax year beginning before January 1, 1995, remains in effect under this section. However, a group may elect to conform its earnings and profits computations to the method described in § 1.1502-32(b)(3)(iv)(D) (the percentage method, using a 100% allocation), whether or not it has previously made an election for earnings and profits purposes. If a conforming election is made, the group must make all adjustments necessary to prevent amounts from being duplicated or omitted. The conforming election is made by attaching a statement entitled "ELECTION TO CONFORM TAX ALLOCATIONS UNDER §§ 1.1502-32 and 1.1502-33(d)" to the consolidated group's return for its first tax year beginning on or after January 1, 1995. The statement must be signed by the common parent, and must specify whether the method is conformed only for years beginning on or after January 1, 1995 or as if the method were in effect for all prior years. The statement must also describe the adjustments made by reason of the change (e.g., to reflect prior use of earnings and profits).

(6) *Examples.* The principles of this paragraph (d) are illustrated by the following examples.

Example 1. Wait-and-see method. (a) *Facts.* P owns all of the stock of S1 and S2. The P group uses the wait-and-see method of allocation under paragraph (d)(2) of this section in conjunction with § 1.1552-1(a)(1). For Year 1, each member's taxable income, both for purposes of § 1.1552-1(a)(1) and redetermined as if the member had filed separate returns, is as follows: P $0, S1 $2,000, and S2 ($1,000). Thus, the P group's consolidated tax liability for Year 1 is $340 (assuming a 34% tax rate).

(b) *Analysis.* Under § 1.1552-1(a)(1)(i), the tax liability of the P group is allocated among the members in accordance with the portion of the consolidated taxable income attributable to each member having taxable income. Thus, all of the P group's $340 consolidated tax liability is allocated to S1. As a result, S1 decreases its earnings and profits under section 1552 by $340 (even if S1 does not pay the tax liability). No further allocations are made under paragraph (d)(2) of this section because S2 cannot yet absorb its loss on a separate return basis.

(c) *Payment of tax liability.* If S1 pays the $340 tax liability, there is no further effect on the income, earnings and profits, or stock basis of any member. If P pays the $340 tax liability (and the payment is not a loan from P to S1), P is treated as making a $340 contribution to the capital of S1; if S2 pays the $340 tax liability (and the payment is not a loan from S2 to S1), S2 is treated as making a $340 distribution to P with respect to its stock, and P is treated as making a $340 contribution to the capital of S1. See § 1.1552-1(b)(2).

(d) *Year 2.* For Year 2, each member's taxable income, under § 1.1552-1(a)(1)(ii) and redetermined as if the member had filed separate returns, without taking into account any carryover from Year 1, is as follows: P $0, S1 $1,000, and S2 $3,000. Thus, the P group's consolidated tax liability for Year 2 is $1,360 (assuming a 34% tax rate). Of this amount, section 1552 would allocate $340 to S1 and $1,020 to S2. However, under paragraph (d)(2)(i) of this section, no more than $680 may be allocated to S2. This is because S2 would have had an aggregate tax liability of $680 if it had filed separate returns for Years 1 and 2 (a $0 tax liability for Year 1, and a $680 tax liability for Year 2, taking into account a $1,000 net operating loss carryover from Year 1). Under paragraph (d)(2)(ii) of this section, the entire excess of $340 which would otherwise be allocated to S2 under § 1.1552-1(a)(1) is allocated to S1. This is because S1 would have had an additional $340 of aggregate tax liability if it had filed separate returns for Years 1 and 2 (a $680 tax liability for Year 1, and a $340 tax liability for Year 2, not taking into account S2's $1,000 net operating loss for Year 1). The effect of the allocation of $680 to S1 and $680 to S2 is determined under § 1.1552-1(b)(2).

Example 2. Percentage method. (a) *Facts.* The facts are the same as in *Example 1*, but the P group uses the percentage method of allocation under paragraph (d)(3) of this section, with a percentage of 100%. In addition, the taxable incomes and losses of the members are the same if computed as provided in § 1.1552-1(a)(2)(ii).

(b) *Analysis.* Under § 1.1552-1(a)(2)(ii), $340 of tax liability is allocated to S1 for Year 1. Under paragraph (d)(3)(i) of this section, S1 is allocated another $340 of tax liability because S1 would have had a $680 tax liability if it had filed separate returns but only $340 is allocated to S1 under section 1552. Thus, S1's earnings and profits are decreased by the $680 total. Under paragraph

Reg. § 1.1502-33(d)(6)

(d)(3)(ii) of this section, S2's earnings and profits are increased by $340 because the additional $340 allocated to S1 under paragraph (d)(3)(i) of this section is attributable to the absorption of S2's losses.

(c) *Payment of tax liability.* If S1 pays the $340 tax liability of the P group and pays $340 to S2, the Year 1 tax liability results in no further adjustments to the income, earnings and profits, or basis of any member's stock. If S1 pays the $340 tax liability of the P group and pays the other $340 to P instead of S2 because, for example, of an agreement among the members, S2 is treated as distributing $340 to P with respect to its stock in the year that S1 makes the payment to P. See § 1.1552-1(b)(2).

(d) *Year 2.* For Year 2, $340 is allocated to S1 and $1,020 is allocated to S2 under section 1552. No additional amounts are allocated under paragraph (d)(3) of this section.

(e) *Deconsolidations*—(1) *In general.* Immediately before it becomes a nonmember, S's earnings and profits are eliminated to the extent they were taken into account by any member under this section. If S's earnings and profits are eliminated under this paragraph (e)(1), no corresponding adjustment is made to the earnings and profits of P (or any other member) under paragraph (b) of this section or to any basis in a member's stock under paragraph (c) of this section. For this purpose, S is treated as becoming a nonmember on the first day of its first separate return year (including another group's consolidated return year).

(2) *Acquisition of group*—(i) *Application.* This paragraph (e)(2) applies only if a consolidated group (the terminating group) ceases to exist as a result of—

(A) The acquisition by a member of another consolidated group of either the assets of the common parent of the terminating group in a reorganization described in section 381(a)(2), or the stock of the common parent of the terminating group; or

(B) The application of the principles of § 1.1502-75(d)(2) or (d)(3).

(ii) *General rule.* Paragraph (e)(1) of this section does not apply solely by reason of the termination of a group because it is acquired, if there is a surviving group that is, immediately thereafter, a consolidated group. Instead, the surviving group is treated as the terminating group for purposes of applying this paragraph (e) to the terminating group. This treatment does not apply, however, to members of the terminating group that are not members of the surviving consolidated group immediately after the terminating group ceases to exist (e.g., under section 1504(a)(3) relating to reconsolidation, or section 1504(c) relating to includible insurance companies).

(3) *Certain corporate separations and reorganizations.* The adjustments under paragraph (e)(1) of this section must be modified to the extent necessary to effectuate the principles of section 312(h). Thus, P's earnings and profits rather than S's earnings and profits may be eliminated immediately before S becomes a nonmember. P's earnings and profits are eliminated to the extent that its earnings and profits reflect S's earnings and profits after applying section 312(h) immediately after S becomes a nonmember (determined without taking this paragraph (e) into account).

(4) *Special uses of earnings and profits.* Paragraph (e)(1) of this section does not apply for purposes of determining—

(i) The extent to which a distribution is charged to reserve accounts under section 593(e);

(ii) The extent to which a distribution is taxable to the recipient under sections 805(a)(4) and 832; and

(iii) Any other special use identified in guidance published in the Internal Revenue Bulletin.

(5) *Example.* The principles of this paragraph (e) are illustrated by the following example.

Example. (a) *Facts.* Individuals A and B own all of P's stock, and P owns all of the stock of S and T, each with a $500 basis. For Year 1, S has $100 of earnings and profits and T has $50 of earnings and profits. Under paragraph (b)(1) of this section, the earnings and profits of S and T tier up to P, and P has $150 of earnings and profits for Year 1. P sells all of S's stock for $600 at the close of Year 1.

(b) *Analysis.* Under paragraph (e)(1) of this section, S's $100 of earnings and profits is eliminated immediately before S becomes a nonmember because the earnings and profits are taken into account under paragraph (b) of this section in P's earnings and profits. However, no corresponding adjustment is made to P's earnings and profits or to P's basis in S's stock for purposes of earnings and profits. P's earnings and profits for Year 1 remain $150 following the sale of S's stock.

(c) *Forward merger.* The facts are the same as in paragraph (a) of this *Example*, except that, rather than P selling S's stock, S merges into a nonmember in a transaction described in section 368(a)(2)(D). Under paragraph (h) of this section, the nonmember is treated as a successor to S. Thus, as in paragraph (b) of this *Example*, S's

Reg. § 1.1502-33(e)(1)

$100 of earnings and profits is eliminated immediately before S ceases to be a member.

(d) *Acquisition of entire group.* The facts are the same as in paragraph (a) of this *Example*, except that X, the common parent of another consolidated group, purchases all of P's stock at the close of Year 1, and P sells S's stock during Year 3. Under paragraph (e)(2) of this section, the earnings and profits of S and T are not eliminated as a result of X purchasing P's stock. However, S's earnings and profits from consolidated return years of both the P group and the X group are eliminated immediately before S becomes a nonmember of the X group.

(e) *Earnings and profits deficit.* The facts are the same as in paragraph (d) of this *Example*, except that S has a $550 deficit in earnings and profits for Year 1. The effect of paragraph (e)(1) of this section is the same. Under paragraph (c)(1) of this section, P would have an excess loss account in S's stock for earnings and profits purposes under the principles of §§ 1.1502-19 and 1.1502-32, and, under the principles of § 1.1502-19(c)(2), the excess loss account is not taken into account as a result of X's purchase of P's stock. Under paragraph (e)(2) of this section, S's deficit is not eliminated under paragraph (e)(1) of this section immediately before X's purchase of P's stock. However, S's earnings and profits (or deficit) is eliminated immediately before S becomes a nonmember of the X group.

(f) *Section 355 distribution.* The facts are the same as in paragraph (a) of this *Example*, except that, rather than selling S's stock, P distributes S's stock to A at the close of Year 1 in a distribution to which section 355 applies. Under paragraph (e)(3) of this section, P's earnings and profits may be reduced under section 312(h) as a result of the distribution. To the extent that P's earnings and profits are reduced, S's earnings and profits are not eliminated under paragraph (e)(1) of this section.

(f) *Changes in the structure of the group*—(1) *Changes in the common parent*—(i) *General rule.* If P succeeds another corporation under the principles of § 1.1502-75(d)(2) or (3) as the common parent of a consolidated group (a group structure change), the earnings and profits of P are adjusted immediately after P becomes the new common parent to reflect the earnings and profits of the former common parent immediately before the former common parent ceases to be the common parent. The adjustment is made as if P succeeds to the earnings and profits of the former common parent in a transaction described in section 381(a). See § 1.1502-31 for the basis of the stock of members following a group structure change.

(ii) *Minority shareholders.* If the former common parent's stock is not wholly owned by members of the consolidated group immediately after the former common parent ceases to be the common parent, appropriate adjustments must be made to reflect in the new common parent only an allocable part of the former common parent's earnings and profits.

(iii) *Higher-tier members.* To the extent that earnings and profits are adjusted under this paragraph (f)(1), and the former common parent is owned by members other than P, the earnings and profits of the intermediate subsidiaries must be adjusted in accordance with the principles of this section.

(iv) *Example.* The principles of this paragraph (f)(1) are illustrated by the following example.

Example. (a) *Facts.* X is the common parent of a consolidated group with $100 of earnings and profits, and P is the common parent of another consolidated group with $20 of earnings and profits. P acquires all of X's stock at the close of Year 1 in exchange for 70% of P's stock. The exchange is a reverse acquisition under § 1.1502-75(d)(3), and the X group is treated as remaining in existence with P as its new common parent.

(b) *Adjustments for X group earnings and profits.* Under paragraph (f)(1) of this section, P's earnings and profits are adjusted immediately after P becomes the new common parent, to reflect X's $100 of earnings and profits immediately before X ceases to be the common parent. The adjustment is made as if P succeeds to X's earnings and profits in a transaction described in section 381(a). Thus, immediately after the acquisition, P has $120 of accumulated earnings and profits and X continues to have $100 of accumulated earnings and profits.

(c) *Adjustments for P group earnings and profits.* Although the P group terminates on P's acquisition of X's stock, under paragraph (e)(2) of this section, no adjustments are made to the earnings and profits of any subsidiaries in the terminating P group.

(d) *Acquisition of separate return corporation.* The facts are the same as in paragraph (a) of this *Example*, except that, immediately before the acquisition of its stock by P, X is not affiliated with any other corporation. The exchange is a reverse acquisition under § 1.1502-75(d)(3), and P is treated as the common parent of the X group. Consequently, the results are the same as in paragraphs (b) and (c) of this *Example*.

(2) *Change in the location of subsidiaries.* If the location of a member within a group changes,

Reg. § 1.1502-33(f)(2)

appropriate adjustments must be made to the earnings and profits of the members to prevent the earnings and profits from being eliminated. For example, if P transfers all of S's stock to another member in a transaction to which section 351 and § 1.1502-13 apply, the transferee's earnings and profits are adjusted immediately after the transfer to reflect S's earnings and profits immediately before the transfer from consolidated return years. On the other hand, if the transferee purchases S's stock from P, the transferee's earnings and profits are not adjusted.

(g) *Anti-avoidance rule.* If any person acts with a principal purpose contrary to the purposes of this section, to avoid the effect of the rules of this section or apply the rules of this section to avoid the effect of any other provision of the consolidated return regulations, adjustments must be made as necessary to carry out the purposes of this section.

(h) *Predecessors and successors.* For purposes of this section, any reference to a corporation or to a share includes a reference to a successor or predecessor as the context may require. A corporation is a successor if its earnings and profits are determined, directly or indirectly, in whole or in part, by reference to the earnings and profits of another corporation (the predecessor). A share is a successor if its basis is determined, directly or indirectly, in whole or in part, by reference to the basis of another share (the predecessor).

(i) [Reserved]

(j) *Effective date*—(1) *General rule.* This section applies with respect to determinations of the earnings and profits of a member (e.g., for purposes of a characterizing a distribution to which section 301 applies) in consolidated return years beginning on or after January 1, 1995. If this section applies, earnings and profits must be determined or redetermined as if this section were in effect for all years (including, for example, the consolidated return years of another consolidated group to the extent the earnings and profits from those years are still reflected). For example, if a distribution by P to a nonmember shareholder in 1990 was a dividend because of an unabsorbed loss carryover attributable to S, P's earnings and profits in tax years beginning after January 1, 1995 are redetermined by taking into account a negative adjustment in the tax year S's loss arose and in 1990 for P's distribution, and any subsequent absorption of the loss has no effect on earnings and profits. Any such determination or redetermination does not, however, affect any prior period. Thus, the shareholder's treatment in 1990 of the distribution as a dividend (and the effect of the distribution on stock basis) is not redetermined under this section.

(2) *Dispositions of stock before effective date*—(i) *In general.* If P disposes of stock of S in a consolidated return year beginning before January 1, 1995, the amount of P's earnings and profits with respect to S are not redetermined under paragraph (j)(1) of this section. See § 1.1502-19 as contained in the 26 CFR part 1 edition revised as of April 1, 1994 for the definition of disposition, and paragraph (j)(5) of this section for the rules applicable to such dispositions.

(ii) *Lower-tier members.* Although P disposes of S's stock in a tax year beginning before January 1, 1995, S's determinations or adjustments with respect to lower-tier members with which it continues to file a consolidated return are redetermined in accordance with the rules of this section (even if S's earnings and profits were previously taken into account by P). For example, assume that P owns all of S's stock, S owns all of T's stock, and T owns all of U's stock. If S sells 80% of T's stock in a tax year beginning before January 1, 1995 (the effective date), the amount of S's earnings and profits from the sale, and the adjustments to stock basis for earnings and profits purposes that are reflected in that amount, are not redetermined if P sells S's stock after the effective date. If S sells the remaining 20% of T's stock after the effective date, S's stock basis adjustments with respect to that T stock are also not redetermined because T became a nonmember before the effective date. However, if T and U continue to file a consolidated return with each other, paragraph (e)(1) of this section did not apply, and T sells U's stock after the effective date, T's earnings and profits with respect to U are redetermined (even though some of the earnings and profits may have been taken into account by S in its prior sale of T's stock before the effective date).

(iii) *Deferred amounts.* For purposes of this paragraph (j)(2), a disposition does not include a transaction to which § 1.1502-13, § 1.1502-13T, § 1.1502-14, or § 1.1502-14T applies. Instead, the transaction is deemed to occur as the earnings and profits (if any) are taken into account.

(3) *Deconsolidations and group structure changes*—(i) *In general.* Paragraphs (e) and (f) of this section apply with respect to deconsolidations and group structure changes occurring in consolidated return years beginning on or after January 1, 1995.

(ii) *Prior period group structure changes.* If there was a group structure change in a consolidated return year beginning before January 1,

Reg. § 1.1502-33(g)

1995, and earnings and profits were not determined under § 1.1502-33T(a) as contained in the 26 CFR part 1 edition revised as of April 1, 1994, a distribution in a tax year ending after September 7, 1988, of earnings and profits that are not reflected in the earnings and profits of the distributee member, but would have been so reflected if § 1.1502-33T(a) as contained in the 26 CFR part 1 edition revised as of April 1, 1994 had applied, the negative adjustment under paragraph (b) of this section for distributions does not apply (and there is therefore no offset to the increase in the earnings and profits of the distributee).

(4) *Deemed dividend elections.* If there is a deemed distribution and recontribution pursuant to § 1.1502-32(f)(2) as contained in the 26 CFR part 1 edition revised as of April 1, 1994 in a consolidated return year beginning before January 1, 1995, the deemed distribution and recontribution under the election are treated as an actual distribution by S and recontribution by P as provided under the election.

(5) *Prior law.* For prior determinations, see prior regulations under section 1502 as in effect with respect to the determination. See, e.g., §§ 1.1502-33 and 1.1502-33T as contained in the 26 CFR part 1 edition revised as of April 1, 1994. [Reg. § 1.1502-33.]

☐ [*T.D. 6909, 12-29-66. Amended by T.D. 6943, 1-15-68; T.D. 6962, 7-2-68; T.D. 7246, 12-29-72; T.D. 8226, 9-7-88; T.D. 8294, 3-9-90; T.D. 8319, 11-19-90; T.D. 8364, 9-13-91; T.D. 8560, 8-12-94 and T.D. 8597, 7-12-95.*]

[Reg. § 1.1502-34]

§ 1.1502-34. **Special aggregate stock ownership rules.**—For purposes of §§ 1.1502-1 through 1.1502-80, in determining the stock ownership of a member of the group in another corporation (the "issuing corporation") for purposes of determining the application of section 165(g)(3)(A), 332(b)(1), 333(b), 351(a), 732(f), or 904(f), in a consolidated return year, there shall be included stock owned by all other members of the group in the issuing corporation. Thus, assume that members A, B, and C each own 33⅓ percent of the stock issued by D. In such case, A, B, and C shall each be treated as meeting the 80-percent stock ownership requirement for purposes of section 332, and no member can elect to have section 333 apply. Furthermore, the special rule for minority shareholders in section 337(d) cannot apply with respect to amounts received by A, B, or C in liquidation of D. [Reg. § 1.1502-34.]

☐ [*T.D. 6894, 9-7-66. Amended by T.D. 8949, 6-18-2001.*]

[Reg. § 1.1502-41A]

§ 1.1502-41A. **Determination of consolidated net long-term capital gain and consolidated net short-term capital loss generally applicable for consolidated return years beginning before January 1, 1997.**—(a) *Consolidated net long-term capital gain.* The consolidated net long-term capital gain shall be determined by taking into account (1) those gains and losses to which § 1.1502-22A(a) applies which are treated as long term under section 1222, and (2) the consolidated section 1231 net gain (computed in accordance with § 1.1502-23A).

(b) *Consolidated net short term capital loss.* The consolidated net short term capital loss shall be determined by taking into account (1) those gains and losses to which § 1.1502-22A(a) applies which are treated as short term under section 1222, and (2) the consolidated net capital loss carryovers and carrybacks to the taxable year (as determined under § 1.1502-22A(b)).

(c) *Effective date.* This section applies to any consolidated return years to which § 1.1502-21(h) or 1.1502-21T(g) in effect prior to June 25, 1999, as contained in 26 CFR part 1 revised April 1, 1999, as applicable does not apply. See § 1.1502-21(h) or 1.1502-21T(g) in effect prior to June 25, 1999, as contained in 26 CFR part 1 revised April 1, 1999, as applicable for effective dates of these sections. [Reg. § 1.1502-41A.]

☐ [*T.D. 6984, 9-7-66. Amended by T.D. 7637, 8-6-79; T.D. 8677, 6-26-96 and T.D. 8823, 6-25-99.*]

[Reg. § 1.1502-42]

§ 1.1502-42. **Mutual savings banks, etc.**—(a) *In general.* This section applies to mutual savings banks and other institutions described in section 593(a).

(b) *Total deposits.* In computing for purposes of section 593(b)(1)(B)(ii) total deposits or withdrawable accounts at the close of the taxable year, the total deposits or withdrawable accounts of other members shall be excluded.

(c) *Taxable income; taxable years for which the due date (without extensions) for filing returns is before March 15, 1983.* For taxable years for which the due date (without extensions) for filing returns is before March 15, 1983, a member's taxable income for purposes of section 593(b)(2) is determined under § 1.1502-27(b) (computed without regard to any deduction under section 593(b)(2)). In addition, for taxable years beginning after July 11, 1969, taxable income as computed under the preceding sentence is subject to the adjustments provided in section 593(b)(2)(E). See § 1.593-6A(b)(5).

Reg. § 1.1502-42(c)

(d) *Taxable income; taxable years for which the due date (without extensions) for filing returns is after March 14, 1983*—(1) *In general.* For a taxable year for which the due date (without extensions) for filing returns is after March 14, 1983, a thrift's taxable income for purposes of section 593(b)(2) is its tentative taxable income (as defined in paragraph (e)(1) of this section).

(2) *Definitions.* For purposes of this section—

(i) A "thrift" is a member described in section 593(a).

(ii) A "nonthrift" is a member that is not a thrift.

(e) *Tentative taxable income (or loss)*—(1) *Thrift.* For purposes of this section, a thrift's tentative taxable income (or loss) is its separate taxable income (determined under § 1.1502-12 without paragraph (q) thereof and without any deduction under section 593(b)), subject to the following adjustments in the following order:

(i) the adjustments described in paragraph (e)(3) of this section;

(ii) the adjustments described in section 593(b)(2)(E) for those thrifts with separate taxable income greater than zero (determined after the adjustments under paragraph (e)(3) of this section); and

(iii) the adjustments described in paragraph (f) of this section.

(2) *Nonthrift.* For purposes of this section, a nonthrift's tentative taxable income (or loss) is its separate taxable income (determined under § 1.1502-12), adjusted for the portion of the consolidated net operating loss deduction attributable to the member, the portion of the consolidated net capital loss carryover or carryback attributable to the member, and further adjusted as described in paragraph (e)(3) of this section.

(3) *Adjustments for all members.* For each member, the following adjustments taken into account in the computation of consolidated taxable income are included in determining its tentative taxable income (or loss) in order to adjust separate taxable income of the member to take into account certain consolidated items:

(i) The portions of the consolidated charitable contributions deduction and the consolidated dividends received deduction attributable to the member.

(ii) The member's capital gain net income, determined without any net capital loss carryover or carryback attributable to the member.

(iii) The member's net capital loss and section 1231 net loss, reduced by the portion of the consolidated net capital loss attributable to the member.

(f) *Adjustments for thrifts*—(1) *Reductions.* A thrift's separate taxable income (as adjusted under paragraph (e)(3) of this section) is reduced (but not below zero) by losses of thrifts and to the extent attributable to functionally related activities, losses of a nonthrift. Certain operating rules for determining the amount of the reductions are provided in paragraph (f)(4) of this section. The reductions are made in the following amounts in the following order:

(i) The thrift's allocable share (as determined under paragraph (h)(2) of this section) of another thrift's tentative taxable loss. That tentative taxable loss is determined by including a deduction under section 593(b) (other than paragraph (2) thereof) for the year in which the loss arises.

(ii) The thrift's allocable share (as determined under paragraph (h)(3) of this section) of the portion of the consolidated net operating loss deduction attributable to it or another thrift. That consolidated net operating loss deduction is determined by including a deduction under section 593(b) (other than paragraph (2) thereof) for the year in which the loss arose. The portion of a consolidated net operating loss deduction attributable to another thrift is computed by excluding losses arising in taxable years for which the due date (without extensions) for filing returns is before March 15, 1983.

(iii) The thrift's allocable share (as determined under paragraph (h)(4) of this section) of the loss attributable to functionally related activities of a nonthrift (as determined under paragraph (g) of this section). For a rule netting that share against certain income attributable to functionally related activities of that nonthrift, see paragraph (f)(4)(iv) of this section.

(iv) The thrift's allocable share (as determined under paragraph (h)(3) of this section) of the portion of the consolidated net operating loss deduction attributable to functionally related activities of a nonthrift (as determined under paragraph (h)(5) of this section). That consolidated net operating loss deduction is determined by excluding losses arising in taxable years for which the due date (without extensions) for filing returns is before March 15, 1983. For a rule netting that share against certain income attributable to functionally related activities of that nonthrift, see paragraph (f)(4)(iv) of this section.

(2) *Increases.* (i) A thrift's separate taxable income (as adjusted under paragraphs (e)(3) and (f)(1) of this section) is increased in a subsequent consolidated return year to restore reductions

Reg. § 1.1502-42(d)(2)

made in a prior consolidated return year to a thrift's separate taxable income by reason of losses of a nonthrift. This increase is the amount of the thrift's allocable share (as determined under paragraph (h)(6) of this section) of the income attributable to functionally related activities of a nonthrift in a consolidated return year and is made only in that year. This increase is made only if both the thrift and the nonthrift were members of the group in the consolidated return years in which both the reduction and increase are made.

(ii) This subdivision (ii) limits the increases to a thrift's separate taxable income to assure that income of a particular nonthrift is used to restore reductions of a thrift only to the extent that such nonthrift's losses reduced the thrift's income. Therefore, as of the end of a consolidated return year, the cumulative increases to a thrift's tentative taxable income (by reason of income attributable to functionally related activities of a nonthrift) may not exceed the cumulative reductions to the thrift's separate taxable income made (by reason of the nonthrift's functionally related activities) under paragraph (f)(1)(iii) and (iv) of this section in the current and all prior consolidated return years during which both the thrift institution and the nonthrift institution were members of the group.

(iii) For a netting rule, see paragraph (f)(4)(iv) of this section.

(3) *Special rule.* (i) If a carryback to a thrift's separate taxable income diminishes the reduction to a thrift's separate taxable income for a prior consolidated return year otherwise required by paragraph (f)(1)(iii) or (iv) of this section, then any increase to a thrift's separate taxable income under paragraph (f)(2) of this section for an intervening consolidated return year must be recomputed to take into account the effect of such carryback. Thus, if a net operating loss attributable to a thrift is carried back and completely offsets the thrift's separate taxable income (before the reductions under paragraph (f)(1)(iii) or (iv) of this section), any increase to the thrift's separate taxable income under paragraph (f)(2) of this section (attributable to a reduction in the year to which the loss is carried) for an intervening consolidated return year will be eliminated. The recomputation required by this subparagraph (3) must be reflected on an amended return for the intervening consolidated return year for which the increase was previously reported. See example (2) in paragraph (j) of this section.

(ii) If a deficiency for an intervening consolidated return year results from the application of paragraph (f)(3)(i) of this section with respect to an item to which section 6501(h) applies, the deficiency may be assessed at any time within the period described in section 6501(h).

(iii) For purposes of chapter 67 of the Code (relating to interest), the last date prescribed for payment of any tax owed as a result of the application of paragraph (f)(3)(i) of this section is deemed to be the last day of the taxable year for which the item carried back arose.

(4) *Operating rules.* For purposes of paragraphs (d)-(j) of this section—

(i) The portion of a consolidated net operating loss deduction attributable to a member is determined as follows:

(A) First, determine under § 1.1502-21(b) (or § 1.1502-79A(a)(3), as appropriate) the portion of each consolidated net operating loss attributable to the member for the particular year in which the loss arose.

(B) Second, apply the anti-double-counting rule in paragraph (h)(3)(iii) of this section so as not to take the same loss into account twice.

(C) Finally, apply the loss absorption limit in paragraph (f)(4)(iii) of this section to the total amount of the consolidated net operating loss deduction from a particular loss year.

(ii) Capital loss carryovers and carrybacks shall be taken into account in a manner consistent with the principles of paragraphs (d)-(j) of this section.

(iii) This subdivision (iii) prescribes a loss absorption limit. The total amount of the consolidated net operating loss deduction from a given year (loss year) taken into account as reductions under paragraph (f)(1) of this section for another year (absorption year) shall not exceed the amount of the consolidated net operating loss deduction attributable to the loss year absorbed in computing consolidated taxable income for the absorption year. For this purpose, consolidated taxable income for the absorption year shall include a deduction under section 593(b) (other than paragraph (2) thereof) for each thrift member.

(iv) This subdivision (iv) prescribes a rule for netting in certain cases income attributable to functionally related activities of a nonthrift in a consolidated return year ("income year") against losses attributable to functionally related activities of that nonthrift which arise in a consolidated return year ("loss year"). That nonthrift's income is netted against the portion of that nonthrift's loss which would otherwise be applied in a consolidated return year ("reduction year") under para-

Reg. § 1.1502-42(f)(4)

graph (f)(1)(iii) or (iv) of this section to reduce a thrift's tentative taxable income, but—

(A) only if the income year is not later than the loss year and the reduction year, and

(B) only to the extent the income had not previously been taken into account under paragraph (f)(2) of this section or this subdivision (iv) as of the close of the later of the loss year and the reduction year.

(g) *Income (or loss) attributable to functionally related activities of a nonthrift*—(1) *In general.* For purposes of this section, the income (or loss) attributable to functionally related activities of a nonthrift is the income (or loss) of the nonthrift

(i) attributable to the provision of assets or the rendition of services to a thrift (such as the leasing of office space or providing computer or financial services), or

(ii) derived from the assets described in section 7701(a)(19)(C)(iii)-(x), but only if such assets comprise 5 percent or more of the gross assets of the nonthrift.

(2) *Amount of income (or loss).* The amount of income (or loss) from such activities is the excess of (i) gross income from such activities over (ii) the deductions of the nonthrift allocable and apportionable to that gross income under the principles of § 1.861-8. The loss attributable to functionally related activities of a nonthrift is the excess (if any) of such deductions over such gross income. That loss, however, may not exceed the amount of the tentative taxable loss of that nonthrift (determined by excluding losses arising in taxable years for which the due date (without extensions) for filing returns is before March 15, 1983).

(h) *Allocation of income and losses*—(1) *In general.* Paragraph (h)(2)-(5) of this section provides rules for allocating different losses among thrifts that have tentative taxable income greater than zero. Generally, these allocations are made in the order listed in paragraph (f)(1) of this section and are based upon the relative tentative taxable income of the thrifts to which the particular loss is allocated. For purposes of each allocation under a subdivision of such paragraph (f)(1), the tentative taxable income of the thrifts used in making this allocation is reduced by the thrift's allocable share of losses allocated to the thrift under a prior subdivision of such paragraph (f)(1). Accordingly, for purposes of this paragraph (h), tentative taxable income is determined without regard to paragraph (f) of this section, except as otherwise provided. Paragraph (h)(6) of this section provides rules for allocating income attributable to functionally related activities of a nonthrift based upon the relative reductions to thrift income made on account of that nonthrift.

(2) *Allocation of tentative taxable loss of other thrifts.* For purposes of paragraph (f)(1)(i) of this section, a thrift's allocable share of another thrift's tentative taxable loss is the loss multiplied by a fraction. The numerator of the fraction is the tentative taxable income (if greater than zero) of the thrift, and the denominator is the aggregate of such tentative taxable income of each thrift.

(3) *Allocation of portions of a consolidated net operating loss deduction.* (i) For purposes of paragraph (f)(1)(ii) of this section, a first thrift's allocable share of the portion of the consolidated net operating loss deduction attributable to another thrift is determined under paragraph (h)(2) of this section as if that portion were a tentative taxable loss of that other thrift and by computing tentative taxable income under such paragraph (h)(2) by taking into account paragraph (f)(1)(i) of this section. A thrift's allocable share of the portion of the consolidated net operating loss deduction attributable to that thrift is equal to that entire portion.

(ii) For purposes of paragraph (f)(1)(iv) of this section, a thrift's allocable share of the portion of a consolidated net operating loss deduction attributable to functionally related activities of a nonthrift (determined under paragraph (h)(5) of this section) is determined under paragraph (h)(4) of this section as if that portion were a loss attributable to functionally related activities of the nonthrift and by computing tentative taxable income under such paragraph (h)(4) by taking into account paragraph (f)(1)(i), (ii), and (iii) of this section.

(iii) This subdivision (iii) prevents the "double-counting" of losses. The reduction to the tentative taxable income of a thrift is diminished to the extent the loss that gave rise to the reduction has previously been taken into account in reducing a thrift's tentative taxable income. Thus, any loss taken into account as a reduction to a thrift's separate taxable income under any subdivision of paragraph (f)(1) of this section shall be reduced (but not below zero) to the extent taken into account—

(A) in a prior consolidated return year under any subdivision of such paragraph (f)(1) or

(B) in the current consolidated return year under a previous subdivision of such paragraph (f)(1).

(4) *Allocation of loss attributable to functionally related activities of a nonthrift.* For purposes of paragraph (f)(1)(iii) of this section, a thrift's allocable share of a loss attributable to functionally related activities of a nonthrift is determined

Reg. § 1.1502-42(g)(1)

by multiplying the loss by a fraction. The numerator of the fraction is the tentative taxable income (if greater than zero) of the thrift (taking into account paragraph (f)(1)(i) and (ii) of this section) and the denominator is the aggregate of such tentative taxable income (so determined) of each thrift.

(5) *Portion of the consolidated net operating loss deduction attributable to functionally related activities of a particular nonthrift.* The portion of the consolidated net operating loss deduction attributable to functionally related activities of a particular nonthrift is the lesser of the following two amounts:

(i) The portion of the consolidated net operating loss deduction attributable to that nonthrift.

(ii) The aggregate of the losses attributable to functionally related activities of that nonthrift for the taxable years in which the consolidated net operating loss deduction arose.

(6) *Allocation of income attributable to functionally related activities of a nonthrift.* For purposes of paragraph (f)(2) of this section, a thrift institution's allocable share of the income attributable to functionally related activities of a nonthrift is determined by multiplying that income by a fraction. The numerator of the fraction is the amount of the cumulative reductions referred to in paragraph (f)(2)(ii) of this section (minus the cumulative increases under paragraph (f)(2) of this section) made on account of that nonthrift for the thrift and the denominator is the sum of such cumulative reductions (minus such cumulative increases) made on account of that nonthrift for all thrifts.

(7) *Proper accounting.* The provisions of section 482 apply in determining a thrift institution's tentative taxable income, and in determining the gross income and deductions attributable to functionally related activities. For example, an expense such as the salary of an individual who performs services for both a thrift and a nonthrift must be allocated in a manner that fairly reflects the value of the services rendered to each.

(i) [Reserved]

(j) *Examples.* The provisions of this section may be illustrated by the following examples. In each example the letter "T" for a member denotes a thrift and the letters "NT" denote a nonthrift. Also, in each example, a thrift loss includes a bad debt deduction under section 593(b) (other than paragraph (2) thereof) for such year and a thrift with income would have such a bad debt deduction of zero.

Example (1). (a) In 1983, corporations T1, T2, NT1, and NT2 are formed. These corporations constitute an affiliated group that files a consolidated return on the basis of a calendar year. For 1983, 1984, and 1985, the tentative taxable income (or loss) of each member (before the application of paragraph (f) of this section) is as follows:

	1983	1984	1985
NT1	$ (60)	$(140)	$ 15
T1	1,000	500	750
NT2	(90)	(220)	150
T2	(300)	400	250

In 1983, NT1, in addition to its other business activities, acted as a collection agency for T1. Deductions attributable to those collection activities exceeded gross income attributable to those activities by $70. NT1's other activities generated a $10 gain. In 1984 and 1985, NT1 acted as a collection agency for T1 as its sole activity.

(b) The tentative taxable incomes of T1 and T2 for 1983 (determined under paragraph (e) of this section) as of the close of that year are adjusted by paragraph (f) of this section as follows:

(i) T1's tentative taxable income:
T1's tentative taxable income (before the application of paragraph (f) of this section) $1,000
Less:
T2's tentative taxable loss $300
NT1's functionally related loss (limited by NT1's overall loss) 60   360
T1's tentative taxable income for 1983 640

(ii) T2's tentative taxable income for 1983 is zero.

(c) The tentative taxable incomes of T1 and T2 for 1984 (determined under paragraph (e) of this section as of the close of that year) are adjusted by paragraph (f) of this section as follows:

(i) T1's tentative taxable income:
T1's tentative taxable income (before the application of paragraph (f) of this section) $500
Less:
T1's allocable portion of NT1's functionally related loss (140 × 500/(500 + 400)) 78
T1's tentative taxable income for 1984 . 422

(ii) T2's tentative taxable income:
T2's tentative taxable income (before the application of paragraph (f) of this section 400
Less:

Reg. § 1.1502-42(j)

56,868 Consolidated Returns

See p. 20,601 for regulations not amended to reflect law changes

T2's allocable portion of NT1's functionally related loss (140 × 400/(500 + 400)) 62
T2's tentative taxable income for 1984 . $338

(d) For 1985, the amount under paragraph (f)(2) of this section for both T1 and T2 is $15 (NT1's tentative taxable income from functionally related activities for 1985). For 1983 and 1984, T1's tentative taxable income was reduced by a total of $138 (i.e., $60 + $78) due to NT1's losses from functionally related activities. For 1984, T2's tentative taxable income was reduced by $62 due to those losses. Accordingly, under paragraph (f)(2) of this section, T1's tentative taxable income for 1983 is increased by $10 (i.e., $15 × $138/($138 + $62)) and T2's tentative taxable income is increased by $5 (i.e., $15 × $62/($138 + $62)).

Example (2). (a) In 1983, corporations T, NT1, and NT2 are formed. These corporations constitute an affiliated group. NT2 provides computer services to T as its sole activity. For the calendar years of 1983, 1984, and 1985, the group files a consolidated return. The tentative taxable income of each member (before the application of paragraph (f) of this section) is as follows:

	1983	1984	1985
T	$100	$ 0	$(200)
NT1	200	0	100
NT2	(20)	20	0

(b) Under paragraph (f)(1) of this section, T's tentative taxable income for 1983 (determined at the close of that year) is reduced to $80 (i.e., $100 less NT2's $20 loss). For 1984, under paragraph (f)(2) of this section, T's tentative taxable income is increased by $20. For 1985, the consolidated net operating loss of $100 (all of which is attributable to T) is carried back to 1983. That $100 carryback is not limited by paragraph (f)(4)(iii) of this section, since consolidated taxable income for 1983 available for absorption after a bad debt deduction of $0 under section 593(b) (other than paragraph (2) thereof) for that year is $280. Accordingly, under paragraph (f)(1)(ii) of this section, T's tentative taxable income is reduced by the full $100, which is taken into account before the previous reduction of T's tentative taxable income under paragraph (f)(1)(iii) of this section. In addition, under paragraph (f)(3)(i) of this section, the group must file an amended return for 1984 to eliminate the increase to T's bad debt deduction for 1984 by reason of the consolidated net operating loss carryback to 1983.

Example (3). (a) T and NT are formed in 1983 and are the only members of an affiliated group filing a consolidated return on a calendar year basis. NT provided computer services to T as its sole activity. For 1983, 1984, and 1985, the tentative taxable income of T and NT (before the application of paragraph (f) of this section) is as follows:

	1983	1984	1985
T	$100	$ 0	$ 0
NT	0	40	(40)

(b) At the close of 1983, T's tentative taxable income is $100. For 1985, however, the group has a consolidated net operating loss of $40, all of which is attributable to NT's functionally related activities and which is carried back to 1983. However, T's tentative taxable income for 1983 is not reduced under paragraph (f)(1)(iv) of this section, since, under paragraph (f)(4)(iv) of this section, NT's 1984 income attributable to functionally related activities of $40 is netted against that $40 carryback.

Example (4). (a) In 1983, corporations T1, T2, NT1, and NT2 are formed. For calendar years 1983, 1984, and 1985, the affiliated group consisting of T1, T2, NT1, and NT2 filed a consolidated return. NT1 provided computer services to T1 as its sole activity. The tentative taxable income of each member (before the application of paragraph (f) of this section) is as follows:

	1983	1984	1985
T1	($ 50)	$100	$ 30
T2	(50)	(80)	(25)
NT1	(50)	(40)	(99)
NT2	120	30	100

(b) For 1983, the group has a consolidated net operating loss of $30, apportioned $10 each to T1, T2, and NT1 under § 1.1502-79A(a)(3). For 1984, the only thrift with tentative taxable income greater than zero (before applying paragraph (f) of this section) is T1. That tentative taxable income of $100 is first reduced to $20 by T2's $80 1984 loss under paragraph (f)(1)(i) of this section. Next, T1's remaining tentative taxable income of $20 is reduced to $10 by the portions attributable to T1 and T2 of the 1983 consolidated net operating loss carryover to 1984 under paragraph (f)(1)(ii) of this section. The sum of those portions is limited to $10 (i.e., $5 each) by paragraph (f)(4)(iii) of this section because 1984 consolidated taxable income available for absorption after a bad debt deduction under section 593(b) (other than paragraph (2) thereof) for each thrift member for that year is $10. For that reason, paragraph (f)(4)(iii) of this section also prevents any further portion of that carryover from being taken into account in 1984 as a reduction under paragraph (f)(1) of this section. T1's remaining tentative taxable income of $10 is reduced to zero, under paragraph (f)(1)(iii) of this section, by NT1's 1984 tentative taxable loss.

Reg. § 1.1502-42(j)

(c) For 1985, the only thrift with tentative taxable income greater than zero (before applying paragraph (f) of this section) is T1. T1's tentative taxable income for 1985 of $30 is reduced to $5 by T2's 1985 loss of $25 under paragraph (f)(1)(i) of this section. Next, the portions attributable to T1 and T2 of the consolidated net operating loss carryover from 1983 to 1985 for purposes of paragraph (f)(1)(ii) of this section must be determined. That determination is made without applying the rules for loss absorption in computing consolidated taxable income under § 1.1502-21A(b)(3). Those portions are instead determined in 3 steps under paragraph (f)(4)(i) of this section. The first of those steps is to determine each of T1's and T2's attributable portions of the 1983 consolidated net operating loss which under § 1.1502-79A(a)(3) is $10 or $20 for both thrifts. The second of those steps is to apply the anti-double counting rule under paragraph (h)(3)(iii) of this section to reduce that $20 amount by the $10 total of the two $5 portions attributable to T1 and T2 of the consolidated net operating loss carryover from 1983 to 1984 taken into account as reductions to T1's tentative taxable income for 1984 under paragraph (f)(1)(ii) of this section. That leaves a $10 total amount available to be taken into account as reductions to T1's remaining tentative taxable income of $5 for 1985 under paragraph (f)(1)(ii) of this section. Under the third of those steps that $10 amount, however, is limited, under the loss absorption limit of paragraph (f)(4)(iii) of this section, to the $6 of the 1983 consolidated net operating loss carryover to 1985 which is absorbed in computing consolidated taxable income for 1985 since 1985 consolidated taxable income available for absorption after a bad debt deduction under section 593(b) (other than paragraph (2) thereof) for that year is $6 (*i.e.*, $30 + $100 − $99 − $25). Because separate taxable income cannot be reduced below zero under paragraph (f)(1) of this section, T1's remaining tentative taxable income of $5 if thus reduced to zero by the portions attributable to T1 and T2, respectively, of the consolidated net operating loss carryover from 1983 to 1985 under paragraph (f)(1)(ii) of this section. [Reg. § 1.1502-42.]

☐ [T.D. 7246, 12-29-72. Amended by T.D. 7637, 8-6-79; T.D. 7815, 3-12-82; T.D. 7876, 3-14-83; T.D. 8677, 6-26-96 *and* T.D. 8823, 6-25-99.]

[Reg. § 1.1502-43]

§ 1.1502-43. **Consolidated accumulated earnings tax.**—(a) *Group subject to tax*—(1) *General rule.* For a group filing a consolidated return for the taxable year, the accumulated earnings tax under section 531 is imposed on consolidated accumulated taxable income (as defined in paragraph (b) of this section). This tax applies to any group that is formed or availed of to avoid or prevent the imposition of the individual income tax on the shareholders of either any of its members or any other corporation by permitting earnings and profits to accumulate instead of dividing or distributing them. Section 531 and this section do not apply to a group that is treated as a "personal holding company" under section 542(a)(1) as a result of the application of section 542(b)(1). Special rules are provided in this section for other groups which include one or more personal holding companies.

(2) *Evidence of purpose to avoid income tax.* (i) Under section 533(a), the fact that the group's earnings and profits are permitted to accumulate beyond the reasonable needs of its business is determinative of the purpose to avoid the income tax with respect to shareholders, unless the group by the preponderance of the evidence proves to the contrary.

(ii) The fact that a group is a mere holding or investment group is prima facie evidence of the group's purpose to avoid the income tax with respect to shareholders. The activities of a member which is a personal holding company are not taken into account in determining if the group is a mere holding or investment group.

(3) *Earnings and profits.* For purposes of this paragraph (a) and paragraph (d) of this section, the following rules apply:

(i) If no member of the group is a personal holding company, the group's earnings and profits are the aggregate of the earnings and profits (or deficit) of each corporation that is a member at the close of the taxable year, determined in accordance with § 1.1502-33.

(ii) Earnings and profits resulting from the application of § 1.1502-33(b) are not taken into account.

(iii) Earnings and profits resulting from the disposition of a member's stock are determined without regard to the stock basis adjustments under §§ 1.1502-32 and 1.1502-33(c)(1).

(4) *Reasonable needs of the business.* The reasonable needs of the group's business include the reasonable needs of the business of any corporation (other than a personal holding company) that is a member at the close of the taxable year. Thus, the earnings and profits of one member may be accumulated with respect to the reasonable business needs of another member. If under § 1.537-3(b) the business of a nonmember corporation is considered the business of a member, then the earnings and profits of any member may be

accumulated with respect to such nonmember's reasonable business needs.

(5) *Burden of proof.* The notification described in section 534(b) and the statement described in section 534(c) are made to or by the common parent corporation in accordance with § 1.1502-77.

(b) *Consolidated accumulated taxable income*—(1) *In general.* "Consolidated accumulated taxable income" is the group's consolidated taxable income determined under § 1.1502-11 adjusted in the manner provided in paragraph (b)(2) of this section, minus the sum of—

(i) The consolidated dividends paid deduction determined under paragraph (c) of this section and

(ii) The consolidated accumulated earnings credit determined under paragraph (d) of this section.

(2) *Adjustments to consolidated taxable income.* For purposes of paragraph (b)(1) of this section, consolidated taxable income is adjusted as follows:

(i) Under section 535(b)(1), the deduction for taxes is the excess of—

(A) The consolidated liability for tax determined without § 1.1502-2(b) through (d) and without the foreign tax credit provided by section 33, over

(B) The consolidated foreign tax credit determined pursuant to § 1.1502-4.

Foreign taxes deductible under § 1.535-2(a)(2) are also allowed as a deduction under section 535(b)(1).

(ii) The consolidated charitable contributions deduction under § 1.1502-24 does not apply. Under section 535(b)(2), there shall be allowed the aggregate charitable contributions of the members allowable under section 170, determined without section 170(b)(2) and (d)(2).

(iii) Under section 535(b)(3), the deductions provided in §§ 1.1502-26 and 1.1502-27 are not allowed.

(iv) Under section 535(b)(4), the consolidated net operating loss deduction described in §§ 1.1502-21(a) or 1.1502-21A(a), as appropriate is not allowed.

(v) Under section 535(b)(5), there is allowed as a deduction the consolidated net capital loss, determined under §§ 1.1502-22(a) or 1.1502A(a), as appropriate.

(vi) Under section 535(b)(6), there is allowed as a deduction an amount equal to (A) the excess of the consolidated net long-term capital gain (determined under §§ 1.1502-22(a) or 1.1502-41A, as appropriate) over the consolidated net short-term capital loss (determined under §§ 1.1502-22(a) or 1.1502-41A, as appropriate), minus (B) the taxes attributable to this excess. This consolidated net short-term capital loss is determined without the consolidated net capital loss carryovers or carrybacks to the taxable year.

(vii) Under section 535(b)(7), the consolidated net capital loss carryovers and carrybacks are not allowed. See §§ 1.1502-22(b) or 1.1502-22A(b), as appropriate.

(viii) Sections 1.1502-15A (Limitations on built-in deductions not subject to § 1.1502-15) and 1.1502-15 do not apply.

(3) *Personal holding company a member.* If a member is a personal holding company for the taxable year—

(i) [Reserved].

(ii) In applying paragraph (b)(2)(i) of this section, consolidated liability for tax (as determined under that paragraph (b)(2)(i)) is reduced by the portion thereof allocable to that member under section 1552(a)(1), (2), (3), or (4) (or § 1.1502-33(d)), whichever is applicable. The consolidated foreign tax credit is computed by excluding the taxable income and any foreign taxes paid or accrued by that member, and foreign taxes deductible under § 1.535-2(a)(2) do not include foreign taxes attributable to that member.

(c) *Consolidated dividends paid deduction*—(1) *General rule.* For purposes of this section, the consolidated dividends paid deduction is the aggregate of the members' deductions under section 561(a)(1) and (2). This deduction is determined by excluding deductions for dividends paid to other members.

(2) *Exception for certain personal holding companies*—[Reserved].

(3) *Dividends paid defined.* For purposes of this paragraph (c), "dividends paid" and "dividend (or portion thereof) paid" include amounts treated as dividends paid during the taxable year under sections 562(b)(1), 563, and 565 (relating respectively to liquidating distributions, dividends paid after year end, and consent dividends).

(4) *Examples.* This paragraph (c) can be illustrated by the following examples:

Example (1). Corporations P and S constitute an affiliated group which files a consolidated return on a calendar year basis for 1984 and 1985. P owns all of S's stock and two individuals own all of P's stock. Neither member of the group is a personal holding company for 1984. Assume that on December 15, 1984, S pays a dividend (as defined in section 316(a)) of $2,000 to P, and P pays a dividend (as so defined) of $3,000 on January 15,

Reg. § 1.1502-43(a)(5)

1985 to its individual shareholders. All dividends are paid in cash and are pro rata with no preference as to any shares or class of stock. For purposes of this paragraph (c), the consolidated dividends paid deduction for 1984 is $3,000, i.e., the dividend paid on January 15, 1985, by P to its nonmember shareholders. See section 563(a). The $2,000 dividend paid by S to P is not taken into account in computing the consolidated dividends paid deduction.

Example (2) —[Reserved].

(d) *Consolidated accumulated earnings credit* —[Reserved]. [Reg. § 1.1502-43.]

☐ [T.D. 7937, 1-26-84. Amended by T.D. 8560, 8-12-94; T.D. 8677, 6-26-96 and T.D. 8823, 6-25-99.]

[Reg. § 1.1502-44]

§ 1.1502-44. Percentage depletion for independent producers and royalty owners.—(a) *In general.* The sum of the percentage depletion deductions for the taxable year for all oil or gas property owned by all members, plus any carryovers under section 613A(d)(1) or paragraph (d) of this section from a prior taxable year, may not exceed 65 percent of the group's adjusted consolidated taxable income (under paragraph (b) of this section) for the consolidated return year.

(b) *Adjusted consolidated taxable income.* For purposes of this section, adjusted consolidated taxable income is an amount (not less than zero) equal to the group's consolidated taxable income determined without—

(1) Any depletion with respect to an oil or gas property (other than a gas property with respect to which the depletion allowance for all production is determined pursuant to section 613A(b)) for which percentage depletion would exceed cost depletion in the absence of the depletable quantity limitations contained in section 613A(c)(1) and (6) and the consolidated taxable income limitation contained in paragraph (a) of this section,

(2) Any consolidated net operating loss carryback to the consolidated return year under §§ 1.1502-21 or 1.1502-21A (as appropriate), and

(3) Any consolidated net capital loss carryback to the consolidated return year under §§ 1.1502-22 or 1.1502-22A (as appropriate).

(c) *Allocation to oil and gas properties.* The maximum amount allowable as a deduction under section 613A(c), after the application of paragraph (a) of this section, is allocated to properties held by members in accordance with the regulations under section 613A(d). Those regulations provide for an initial allocation and possible reallocation of the maximum allowable percentage depletion deduction among oil and gas properties. Thus, if, after the initial allocation, cost depletion exceeds the percentage depletion that would be allowable for a particular oil or gas property, cost depletion must be used for that property and the maximum amount of percentage depletion allowable as a deduction for the group is reallocated among only the remaining properties held by all members.

(d) *Carryover for disallowed amounts.* (1) If any amount is disallowed as a deduction for the taxable year by reason of section 613A(d)(1) or paragraph (a) of this section, the disallowed amount for each oil or gas property is treated as an amount allowed as a deduction under section 613A(c), for the following taxable year for the member that owned the property, in accordance with the regulations under section 613A and paragraphs (a) and (d)(2) of this section.

(2) Any amount that was disallowed as a deduction in a separate return limitation year of a member may be carried to a consolidated return year only to the extent that 65 percent of the excess determined under paragraph (d)(3) of this section exceeds the sum of the otherwise allowable percentage depletion deductions for the member's oil and gas properties for the year.

(3) The excess determined in this subparagraph (3) for a member is the excess, if any, of adjusted consolidated taxable income for the year under paragraph (b) of this section over that income recomputed by excluding the items of income and deductions of the member.

(e) *Effective date.* This section applies to taxable years for which the due date (without extensions) for filing returns is after September 30, 1980. [Reg. § 1.1502-44.]

☐ [T.D. 7725, 9-30-80. Amended by T.D. 8677, 6-26-96 and T.D. 8823, 6-25-99.]

[Reg. § 5.1502-45]

§ 5.1502-45. Limitation on losses to amount at risk (Temporary).—(a) *In general*—(1) *Scope.* This section applies to a loss of any subsidiary if the common parent's stock meets the stock ownership requirement described in section 465(a)(1)(C).

(2) *Limitation on use of losses.* Except as provided in paragraph (a)(4) of this section, a loss from an activity of a subsidiary during a consolidated return year is includible in the computation of consolidated taxable income (or consolidated net operating loss) and consolidated capital gain net income (or consolidated net capital loss) only to the extent the loss does not exceed the amount that the parent is at risk in the activity at the close of that subsidiary's taxable year. In addi-

tion, the sum of a subsidiary's losses from all its activities is includible only to the extent that the parent is at risk in the subsidiary at the close of that year. Any excess may not be taken into account for the consolidated return year but will be treated as a deduction allocable to that activity of the subsidiary in the first succeeding taxable year.

(3) *Amount parent is at risk in subsidiary's activity.* The amount the parent is at risk in an activity of a subsidiary is the lesser of (i) the amount the parent is at risk in the subsidiary or (ii) the amount the subsidiary is at risk in the activity. These amounts are determined under paragraph (b) of this section and the principles of section 465. See section 465 and the regulations thereunder and the examples in paragraph (e) of this section.

(4) *Excluded activities.* The limitation on the use of losses in paragraph (a)(2) of this section does not apply to a loss attributable to an activity described in section 465 (c)(3)(D).

(5) *Substance over form.* Any transaction or arrangement between members (or between a member and a person that is not a member) which does not cause the parent to be economically at risk in an activity of a subsidiary will be treated in accordance with the substance of the transaction or arrangement notwithstanding any other provision of this section.

(b) *Rules for determining amount at risk* —(1) *Excluded amounts.* The amount a parent is at risk in an activity of a subsidiary at the close of the subsidiary's taxable year does not include any amount which would not be taken into account under section 465 were the subsidiary not a separate corporation. Thus, for example, if the amount a parent is at risk in the activity of a subsidiary is attributable to nonrecourse financing, the amount at risk is not more than the fair market value of the property (other than the subsidiary's stock or debt or assets) pledged as security.

(2) *Guarantees.* If a parent guarantees a loan by a person other than a member to a subsidiary, the loan increases the amount the parent is at risk in the activity of the subsidiary.

(c) *Application of section 465.* This section applies in a manner consistent with the provisions of section 465. Thus, for example, the recapture of losses provided in section 465(e) applies if the amount the parent is at risk in the activity of a subsidiary is reduced below zero.

(d) *Other consolidated return provisions unaffected.* This section limits only the extent to which losses of a subsidiary may be used in a consolidated return year. This section does not apply for other purposes, such as § 1.1502-32 and § 1.1502-19, relating to investment in stock of a subsidiary and excess loss accounts, respectively. Thus, a loss which reduces a subsidiary's earnings and profits in a consolidated return year, but is disallowed as a deduction for the year by reason of this section, may nonetheless result in a negative adjustment to the basis of an owning member's stock in the subsidiary or create (or increase) an excess loss account.

(e) *Examples.* The provisions of this section may be illustrated by the examples in this paragraph (e). In each example, the stock ownership requirement of section 465(a)(1)(C) is met for the stock of the parent (P), and each affiliated group files a consolidated return on a calendar year basis and comprises only the members described.

Example (1). In 1979, P forms S with a contribution of $200 in exchange for all of S's stock. During the year, S borrows $400 from a commercial lender and P guarantees $100 of the loan. S uses $500 of its funds to acquire a motion picture film. S incurs a loss of $120 for the year with respect to the film. At the close of 1979, the amount P is at risk in S's activity is $300. If S has no gain or loss in 1980, and there are no contributions from or distributions to P, at the close of 1980 P's amount at risk in S's activity will be $180.

Example (2). P forms S-1 with a capital contribution of $1 on January 1, 1980. On February 1, 1980, S-1 borrows $100 with full recourse and contributes all $101 to its newly formed subsidiary S-2. S-2 uses the proceeds to explore for natural oil and gas resources. S-2 incurs neither gain nor loss from its explorations during the taxable year. As of December 31, 1980, P is at risk in the exploration activity of S-2 only to the extent of $1.

(f) *Effective date.* This section applies to consolidated return years ending on or after December 31, 1979. [Temporary Reg. § 5.1502-45.]

☐ [T.D. 7685, 3-12-80.]

[Reg. § 1.1502-47]

§ 1.1502-47. **Consolidated returns by life-nonlife groups.**—(a) *Scope.*—(1) *In general.* Under section 1504(b)(2), insurance companies that are taxed under section 802 or 821 (relating respectively to life insurance companies and to certain mutual insurance companies) are not treated as includible corporations for purposes of determining under section 1504(a) the existence of an affiliated group and the composition of its membership. Section 1504(c)(2) provides an election whereby certain life insurance companies and mutual insurance companies may be treated as includible corporations, and thus members, of a group composed of other includible corporations.

This section provides regulations for the making of this election and for the determination of an electing group's composition and its consolidated tax liability.

(2) *General method of consolidation.*—(i) *Subgroup method.* The regulations adopt a subgroup method to determine consolidated taxable income. One subgroup is the group's nonlife companies (including those taxable under section 821). The other subgroup is the group's life insurance companies. Initially, the nonlife subgroup computes nonlife consolidated taxable income and the life subgroup computes consolidated partial life insurance company taxable income. A subgroup's income may in effect be reduced by a loss of the other subgroup. The life subgroup losses consist of consolidated loss from operations and life consolidated net capital loss. The nonlife subgroup losses consist of nonlife consolidated net operating loss and nonlife consolidated net capital loss. Consolidated taxable income is therefore defined in pertinent part as the sum of nonlife consolidated taxable income and consolidated partial life insurance company taxable income reduced by life subgroup losses or nonlife subgroup losses.

(ii) *Subgroup loss.* A subgroup loss does not actually affect the computation of nonlife consolidated taxable income or consolidated partial life insurance company taxable income. It merely constitutes a bottom-line adjustment in reaching consolidated taxable income. Furthermore, one subgroup's loss must first be carried back against income of the same subgroup before it may be used as a setoff against the second subgroup income in the taxable year the loss arose. (See section 1503(c)(1)). The carryback of the losses from one subgroup may not be used to offset income of the other subgroup in the year to which the loss is to be carried. This carryback of the first subgroup's loss may "bump" the second subgroup's loss that in effect previously reduced the income of the first subgroup. The second subgroup's loss that is bumped in appropriate cases may in effect reduce a succeeding year's income of the second or first subgroup. This approach gives the group the tax savings of the use of losses but the bumping rule assures that insofar as possible life deductions will be matched against life income and nonlife deductions against nonlife income.

(iii) *Carryover of subgroup loss.* A subgroup's loss may be used in a succeeding year, but in any particular succeeding year the loss must be used to reduce the income of the same subgroup before it may be used as a setoff against the other subgroup's income.

(3) *Authority.* This section is prescribed under the authority of sections 1502, 1503(c), 1504(c)(2), and 7805(b).

(4) *Other provisions.* The provisions of §§ 1.1502-1 through 1.1502-80 apply unless this section provides otherwise. Further, unless otherwise indicated in this section, a term used in this section has the same meaning as in sections 801-844.

(b) *Effective date.* This section is effective for taxable years for which the due date (without extensions) for filing returns is after March 14, 1983.

(c) *Cross references.* The following table provides cross references for some of the definitions and operating rules that are relevant in making the election and determining the group's composition and its tax liability:

Item and Paragraph
—General definitions (d)
—Eligible corporation (Five-year rules) (d)(12)
—Election (e)
—Consolidated taxable income (g)
—Nonlife consolidated taxable income (h)
—Consolidated partial life insurance company taxable income (j)
—Nonlife subgroup losses (m)
—Life subgroup losses (n)
—Alternative tax (o)

(d) *Definitions.* For purposes of this section—

(1) *Life insurance company.* The term "life company" means a life insurance company as defined in section 801. Section 801 applies to each company separately.

(2) *Mutual insurance company.* The term "mutual company" means a mutual insurance company taxable under section 821(a)(1).

(3) *Life insurance company taxable income.* The term "life insurance company taxable income" is referred to as LICTI. The terms "TII", "GO", and "LO" refer, respectively, to taxable investment income (section 804), gain from operations (section 809), and loss from operations (section 812). The term "consolidated partial LICTI" refers to consolidated LICTI without section 802(b)(3).

(4) *Group.* The term "group" means an affiliated group of corporations (as defined in section 1504(a)). Unless otherwise indicated in this section, a group's composition is determined without section 1504(b)(2).

(5) *Member.* The term "member" means a corporation (including the common parent) that is an includible corporation in the group. A life company or mutual company is tentatively treated as a member for any taxable year for purposes of

Reg. § 1.1502-47(d)(5)

determining if it is an eligible corporation under paragraph (d)(12) of this section and therefore if it is an includible corporation under section 1504(c)(2). If such a company is eligible and includible (under section 1504(c)(2)), it will actually be treated as a member of the group.

(6) *Life member.* A life member is a member of the group that is a life company.

(7) *Nonlife member.* A nonlife member is a member of the group that is not a life company.

(8) *Life subgroup.* A life subgroup is composed of those members that are life members. If the group has only one life member, it constitutes a life subgroup.

(9) *Nonlife subgroup.* A nonlife subgroup is composed of those members that are nonlife members. If the group has only one nonlife member, it constitutes a nonlife subgroup.

(10) *Separate return year.* The term "separate return year" means a taxable year of a corporation for which it files a separate return or for which it joins in the filing of a consolidated return by another group. For purposes of this subparagraph (10), the term "group" is defined with regard to section 1504(b)(2) for years in which an election under section 1504(c)(2) is not in effect. Thus, a separate return year includes a taxable year for which that election is not in effect.

(11) *Separate return limitation year.* Section 1.1502-1(f)(2) provides exceptions to the definition of the term "separate return limitation year". For purposes of applying those exceptions to this section, for taxable years ending after December 31, 1980, the term "group" is defined without regard to section 1504(b)(2) and the definition in this subparagraph (11) applies separately to the nonlife subgroup in determining nonlife consolidated taxable income under paragraph (h) of this section and to the life subgroup in determining consolidated partial LICTI under paragraph (j) of this section. Paragraph (m)(3)(ix) of this section defines the term "separate return limitation year" for purposes of determining whether the losses of one subgroup may be used against the income of the other subgroup.

(12) *Eligible corporations*—(i) *In general.* A corporation is an eligible corporation for a taxable year of a group only if, throughout every day of the base period the corporation—

(A) Was in existence and a member of the group determined without the exclusions in section 1504(b)(2) (see paragraphs (d)(12)(iii)-(vi) of this section),

(B) Was engaged in the active conduct of a trade or business ("active business"),

(C) Did not experience a change in tax character (see paragraph (d)(12)(vii) of this section), and

(D) Did not undergo disproportionate asset acquisitions (see paragraph (d)(12)(viii) of this section).

(ii) *Base period.* The base period consists of the common parent's five taxable years immediately preceding the group's taxable year for which the consolidated return and the determination of eligibility are made. Eligibility is determined for each consolidated return year beginning with the first year for which the election under section 1504(c)(2) is effective.

(iii) *In existence.* Except as provided in paragraph (d)(12)(v) and (vi) of this section, a corporation organized after the base period begins is not eligible even though it is a member of the group immediately after its organization. For purposes of this subdivision (iii), a corporation that was a party to a reorganization described in section 368(a)(1)(F) shall be treated as the same entity both before and after the reorganization.

(iv) *Membership period.* Except as provided in paragraph (d)(12)(v) and (vi) of this section, a corporation must have been a member of the group throughout the base period to be eligible. Thus, an ineligible corporation includes one whose stock was acquired from outside the group at any time during the base period or one which was a member of a different group (whether by application of reverse acquisition rules in § 1.1502-75(d)(3) or otherwise) at any time during the base period. For purposes of this subdivision (iv), the common parent of a group is treated as constituting a group (and hence is a member) during any period when it was not a member of an affiliated group within the meaning of section 1504(a) (applied without section 1504(b)(2)).

(v) *Tacking rule.* The period during which an "old" corporation is in existence and a member of the group engaged in active business is included in (or "tacks" onto) the period for the "new" corporation if the following five conditions listed in this subdivision (v) are met. For purposes of this subparagraph (12), a "new" corporation is a corporation (whether or not newly organized) during the period its eligibility depends upon the tacking rule. The five conditions are as follows:

(A) The first condition is that, at any time, 80 percent or more of the new corporation's assets it acquired (other than in the ordinary course of its trade or business) where acquired from the old corporation in one or more transactions described in section 351(a) or 381(a). This asset test is applied by using the fair market values of assets on the date they were acquired

Reg. § 1.1502-47(d)(6)

and without regard to liabilities. Assets acquired in the ordinary course of business will be excluded from total assets only if they were acquired after the new corporation became a member of the group (determined without section 1504(b)(2)). In addition, assets that the old corporation acquired from outside the group in transactions not conducted in the ordinary course of its trade or business are not included in the 80 percent (but are included in total assets) if the old corporation acquired those assets within five calendar years before the date of their transfer to the new corporation.

(B) The second condition is that at the end of the taxable year during which the first condition is first met, the old corporation and the new corporation must both have the same tax character. For purposes of this paragraph (d)(12), a corporation's tax character is the section under which it would be taxed (*i.e.*, sections 11, 802, 821, or 831) if it filed a separate return. If the old corporation is not in existence (or adopts a plan of complete liquidation) at the end of that taxable year, this subdivision (v)(B) will apply to the old corporation's taxable year immediately preceding the beginning of the taxable year during which the first condition is first met.

(C) The third condition is that, if the old and new corporation are life insurance companies, the transfer (or transfers) is not reasonably expected (at the time of the transfer) to result in the separation of profitable activities from loss activities.

(D) The fourth condition is that, at the end of the taxable year during which the first condition is first met, the new corporation does not undergo a disproportionate asset acquisition under paragraph (d)(12)(viii) of this section.

(E) The fifth condition is that, if there is more than one old corporation, the first three conditions apply to all of the corporations. Thus, the second condition (tax character) must be met by all of the old corporations transferring assets taken into account in meeting the test in paragraph (d)(12)(v)(A) of this section.

(vi) *Old group remaining in existence.* If the common parent of a group (or a new common parent) became the common parent in a transaction described in § 1.1502-75(d)(2) or (3) where a group remained in existence, then paragraph (d)(12)(ii)-(iv) of this section apply by treating that common parent as if it were also the previous common parent of the group that remains in existence. If this subdivision (vi) applies to a transaction, the tacking rule in paragraph (d)(12)(v) of this section does not apply to the transaction.

(vii) *Change in tax character.* A corporation must not experience during the base period a change in tax character (as defined in paragraph (d)(12)(v)(B) of this section) if the change is attributable to an acquisition of assets from outside the group in transactions not conducted in the ordinary course of its trade or business. However, if a new corporation relies on the tacking rules in paragraph (d)(12)(v) of this section, this subdivision (vii) shall apply during the base period and the current consolidated return year and even if the change in tax character is attributable to an asset acquisition from within the group.

(viii) *Disproportionate asset acquisition.* To be eligible, a corporation must not undergo during the base period disproportionate asset acquisitions which are attributable to an acquisition (or a series of acquisitions) of assets from outside the group in transactions not conducted in the ordinary course of its trade or business (special acquisition). Whether special acquisitions are disproportionate is determined at the end of each base period. Whether an acquisition results in a disproportionate asset acquisition depends on all of the facts and circumstances including the following factors and rules:

(A) One factor is the portion of the insurance reserves (*i.e.*, total reserves in section 801(c)) of the acquiring company at the end of the base period which is attributable to special acquisitions.

(B) A second factor is the portion of the fair market value of the assets (without reduction for liabilities) of the acquiring company at the end of the base period that is attributable to special acquisitions.

(C) A third factor is the portion of the premiums generated during the last taxable year of the base period which are attributable to special acquisitions.

(D) A corporation will not experience a disproportionate asset acquisition unless 75 percent of one factor (whether or not listed in this subdivision (viii)) is attributable to special acquisitions.

(E) Money or other property contributed to a corporation by a shareholder that is not a member of the group (without section 1504(b)(2)) is not a special acquisition.

(F) If a new corporation relies on the tacking rules in paragraph (d)(12)(v) of this section, this subdivision (viii) applies to that corporation during a consolidated return year. Thus, if at any time during a consolidated return year, a new corporation undergoes a disproportionate asset acquisition, the corporation becomes ineligible at that time.

Reg. § 1.1502-47(d)(12)

(13) *Ineligible corporation.* A corporation that is not an eligible corporation is ineligible. If a life company or mutual company is ineligible, it is not treated under section 1504(c)(2) as an includible corporation. Losses of a nonlife member arising in years when it is ineligible may not be used under section 1503(c)(2) and paragraph (m) of this section to set off the income of a life member. If a life or mutual company is ineligible and is the common parent of the group (without section 1504(b)(2)), the election under section 1504(c)(2) may not be made.

(14) *Illustrations.* The following examples illustrate this paragraph (d). In each example, L indicates a life company, another letter indicates a non-life company, and each corporation uses the calendar year as its taxable year.

Example (1). P has owned all of the stock of S since 1913. On January 1, 1980, P purchased all of the stock of L_1 which owns all of the stock of L_2 and S_2. L_1 and L_2 are treated as members for purposes of determining if they are eligible for 1982. However, for 1982, L_1, L_2, and S_2 are ineligible because none of them has been a member of the group for P's five taxable years preceding 1982. For 1982, L_1 and L_2 may elect to file a consolidated return because they constitute an affiliated group under section 1504(c)(1), and P and S may file a consolidated return.

Example (2). Since 1974, P has been a mutual insurance company owning all the stock of L_1. In 1980, P transfers assets to S_1, a new stock casualty company subject to taxation under section 831(a). For 1982, only P and L_1 are eligible corporations. The tacking rule in paragraph (d)(12)(v) of this section does not apply in 1982 because the old corporation (P) and the new corporation (S_1) do not have the same tax character. The result would be the same if P were a life company.

Example (3). Since 1974, L has owned all the stock of L_1 which has owned all the stock of S_1, a stock casualty company. L_1 writes some accident and health insurance business. In 1980, L_1 transfers this business, and S_1 transfers some of its business, to a new stock casualty company, S_2, in a transaction described in section 351(a). The property transferred to S_2 by L_1 had a fair market value of $50 million. The property transferred by S_1 had a fair market value of $40 million. S_2 is ineligible for 1982 because the tacking rule in paragraph (d)(12)(v) of this section does not apply. The old corporations (L_1 and S_1) and the new corporation (S_2) do not all have the same tax character. See subparagraph (d)(12)(v)(B) and (E) of this section. The result would be the same if L_1 transferred other property (*e.g.,* stock and securities) with the same value, rather than accident and health insurance contracts, to S_2.

Example (4). Since 1974, P has owned all the stock of S and L_1. L_1 is a large life company engaged in active business since 1974. On January 1, 1982, L_1 transfers in a section 351(a) transaction assets (not acquired from outside the group) to a new life company, L_2. For 1982, L_2 is eligible because under paragraph (d)(12)(v) of this section, L_2 is considered to have been in existence and a member of the group engaged in the active business since 1974 which is the period L_1, the old corporation, was in existence and a member of the group so engaged.

Example (5). The facts are the same as in example (4). Assume that the fair market value of the assets L_1 transferred to L_2 was $10 million on January 1, 1982 and that L_2 acquired no other assets prior to June 30, 1983. Assume further that on January 1, 1983, L_1 acquires (other than in the ordinary course of its trade or business) assets having a fair market value of $40 million from L_3, an unrelated life company. On June 30, 1983, L_1 transfers those assets to L_2. L_2 becomes ineligible on June 30, 1983. Since by fair market values, 80 percent (*i.e.,* 40/50) of L_2's assets are attributable to special acquisitions, L_2 has undergone a disproportionate asset acquisition at that time. See paragraph (d)(12)(viii)(B), (D), and (F) of this section.

Example (6). The facts are the same as in example (5) except that L_1 transfers assets (other than life insurance contracts) having a fair market value of $40 million to L_2 and L_2 purchases the assets of L_3 on June 30, 1983. The result of the 1983 acquisition is the same as in example (5).

Example (7). The facts are the same as in example (5) except the acquired assets acquired by L_2 in 1983 from L_1 have a fair market value of $20 million. In 1983, L_2 had $1 million of premiums on its pre-existing contracts but premiums generated by the acquired business for the entire year would have been $2 million. L_2 is eligible in 1983 because it did not experience a disproportionate asset acquisition on June 30, 1983.

Example (8). Since 1974, L, a State A corporation, has owned all of the stock of L_1 and S_1. On January 1, 1982, L merges into L_3, a smaller State B corporation, which owns the stock of S_2. The transaction is a reverse acquisition described in § 1.1502-75(d)(3) and the group of which L was the common parent remains in existence. Under paragraph (d)(12)(vi) of this section, L_3 is eligible for 1982. However, S_2 is ineligible in 1982 under paragraph (d)(12)(iv) of this section.

Example (9). The facts are the same as in example (8) except that L acquires the stock of

L_3. L_3 and S_2 are both ineligible for 1982. On January 1, 1983, the fair market value of L_3's assets are $5 million (without liabilities) and on that date L transfers assets (not acquired from outside the group) having a fair market value of $95 million (without liabilities) to L_3. L and L_3 are life companies at the end of 1983. L_3 is eligible in 1983 under the tacking rule in paragraph (d)(12)(v) of this section. S_2 is ineligible in that year. The result would be the same if L_3 was not a life company prior to January 1, 1983. See paragraph (d)(12)(v)(B) of this section.

Example (10). Since 1974, P has owned all of the stock of S_1 and L_1. On January 1, 1982, L_1 incorporates L_2 and transfers cash and securities to L_2. L_2 begins writing a new line of specialty life insurance products and it qualifies as a life company for calendar year 1982. L_2 generates a loss from operations (section 812) attributable to its writing of new business. For 1982, L_2 is ineligible under paragraph (d)(12)(v)(C) of this section.

Example (11). The facts are the same as in example (10) except that L_1 transfers to L_2 a block of insurance contracts that generated losses for L_1 and continued to generate losses for L_2, producing a loss from operations. L_2 is ineligible in 1982 under paragraph (d)(12)(v)(C) of this section.

Example (12). Since 1974, X, a foreign corporation, has owned all the stock of S_2 and S_1, and S_1 has owned all of the stock of L_1. On January 1, 1982, X incorporates a new U.S. company P, and transfers the stock of S_1 and S_2 to P. Assume that under § 1.1502-75(d)(3) (relating to reverse acquisitions), the S_1-L_1 affiliated group remains in existence. Under paragraph (d)(12)(vi) of this section, P, S_1, and L_1 are eligible but S_2 is ineligible. The result would be the same if X were an individual.

Example (13). The facts are the same as in example (12) except that X owns all of the stock of S_1, L_1, and S_2. In addition, on January 1, 1982, X transfers the stock of S_1 and S_2 to L_1. L_1 is eligible in 1982 under paragraph (d)(12)(iv) of this section. L_1 would still be eligible even if it owned a subsidiary during the base period but sold the subsidiary prior to January 1, 1982. S_1 and S_2 are ineligible in 1982.

Example (14). Since 1974, S_1 has owned all of the stock of L_1. S_2, an unrelated company, has owned all of the stock of L_2 and S_3 for 10 years. S_1 and S_2 are active stock casualty companies and not holding companies. On January 1, 1982, S_1 and S_2 merge into a new casualty company, S, in a transaction described in § 1.1502-75(d)(3) so that the group of which S_1 was the common parent remains in existence. S and L_1 are eligible in 1982 under paragraph (d)(12)(vi) of this section. L_2 and S_3 are ineligible.

Example (15). The facts are the same as in example (14) except that S_2 (the first corporation in § 1.1502-75(d)(3)) acquires the stock of S_1 in exchange for the stock of S_2. The result is that only S_2, S_1 and L_1 are eligible in 1982.

Example (16). Since 1974, S had owned all of the stock of L_1. L_1 is a large life company. On January 1, 1982, L_1 incorporates L_2 and transfers $40 million in cash and securities to L_3 in a transaction described in section 351(a). On March 1, 1982, L_3 purchases the assets of L_2, an unrelated life company. The purchased assets have a fair market value (without liabilities) of $30 million on March 1, 1982. L_2 is ineligible for 1982 because the tacking rule in paragraph (d)(12)(v) of this section does not apply. L_3 experienced a disproportionate asset acquisition in 1982. See paragraph (d)(12)(v)(D) of this section.

(e) *Election*—(1) *In general.* The election under section 1504(c)(2) may not be made if the group's common parent is an ineligible life company or an ineligible mutual company. The election under section 1504(c)(2) may only be made by the common parent of the group (as defined in section 1504(c)(2) without the exclusions in section 1504(b)(2)). For example, assume that P owns all of the stock of L_1, an eligible life company, which owns the stock of S_1. Assume further that P also owns the stock of L_2, an ineligible life member, which (for more than five years) has owned the stock of a nonlife company, S_2. Only P may make the election and, if it does so, P, L_1, and S_1 may file a consolidated return under this section. L_2 may not make the election under section 1504(c)(2) and may not file a consolidated return with S_2.

(2) *How election is made*—(i) *General rule.* The election under section 1504(c)(2) is generally made by the group's common parent in the same manner (and it has the same effect) as the election to file a consolidated return is made under § 1.1502-75(a) and (b) for a group which did not file a consolidated return for the immediately preceding taxable year. The procedure for making the election under section 1504(c)(2) is the same whether or not a consolidated return was filed by the life members or the nonlife members for the immediately preceding taxable year.

(ii) *Special rule.* Notwithstanding the general rule, however, if the nonlife members in the group filed a consolidated return for the immediately preceding taxable year and had executed and filed a Form 1122 that is effective for the preceding year, then such members will be treated as if they filed a Form 1122 when they join in the

Reg. § 1.1502-47(e)(2)

filing of a consolidated return under section 1504(c)(2) and they will be deemed to consent to the regulations under this section. However, an affiliation schedule (Form 851) must be filed by the group and the life members must execute a Form 1122 in the manner prescribed in § 1.1502-75(h)(2).

(3) *Irrevocability.* Except as provided in § 1.1502-75(c) and paragraph (e)(4) of this section, the election under section 1504(c)(2) is irrevocable.

(4) *Permission to discontinue*—(i) *General rule.* A "section 1504(c)(2) group" with a common parent that has made the election to file a consolidated return under section 1504(c)(2) in a previous taxable year is granted permission to elect (under § 1.1502-75(c)(2)(ii)) to discontinue filing such a consolidated return for that group's first taxable year for which the regulations under this section are effective. This election to discontinue shall be exercised in the time and manner prescribed in § 1.1502-75(c)(3), except that the group's common parent shall exercise this election to discontinue (and the other members of the section 1504(c)(2) group must comply with this election) by filing appropriate returns. For purposes of this paragraph (e)(4), an appropriate return is either a separate return or a consolidated return that is filed by newly exercising the privilege under § 1.1502-75(a)(1).

(ii) *Types of groups.* (A) A "section 1504(c)(2) group" is an affiliated group which files or filed a consolidated return pursuant to an election under section 1504(c)(2).

(B) A "limited group" is an affiliated group (determined without section 1504(c)(2)) having at least one member which was a member of a section 1504(c)(2) group on the date that the section 1504(c)(2) group elected to discontinue under paragraph (e)(4)(i) of this section.

(iii) *Effect on restoration rules.* If a group ceases to file a consolidated return or terminates or if a member leaves the group, certain items of income, gain, or loss on transactions between members are taken into account under §§ 1.1502-13, 1.1502-18, and 1.1502-19 ("restoration rules"). For purposes of applying these restoration rules solely by reason of an election under paragraph (e)(4)(i) or (e)(4)(v)(A) of this section to discontinue filing consolidated returns as a section 1504(c)(2) group, the following rules apply:

(A) The section 1504(c)(2) group shall not be considered to terminate and no member of that group shall be treated as ceasing to be a member.

(B) Members of that section 1504(c)(2) group that are included in the consolidated return of a limited group for the first taxable year for which the discontinuance is effective shall be considered to be filing a consolidated return as a continuation of the section 1504(c)(2) group. However, a corporation that is not a member of a particular limited group for that taxable year is considered to have a separate return year (and, for purposes of § 1.1502-19(c), not to be a member of a group filing a consolidated return) with respect to that limited group's members.

(C) Section 1.1502-13 shall be applied without regard to paragraph (f)(1)(vii).

(iv) *Illustrations.* The following examples illustrate paragraph (e)(4)(i)-(iii) of this section. In these examples, L indicates a life company and another letter indicates a nonlife company. All corporations use the calendar year as the taxable year. For all taxable years involved, P owns all the stock of L_1 and of S, L_1 owns all the stock of L_2, L_2 owns all the stock of L_3, and S owns all the stock of L_4. For 1981, P makes the life-nonlife election of section 1504(c)(2) and L_4 is an eligible corporation. For 1982, P makes the election to discontinue filing consolidated returns under section 1504(c)(2) in accordance with the permission granted in this paragraph (e)(4).

Example (1). L_1, L_2, and L_3 were eligible members. For 1982, P and S may either file separate returns or may file, as a limited group, a consolidated return. Similarly, L_1, L_2, and L_3 may either file separate returns or may file a consolidated return as a limited group under section 1504(c)(1). L_4 must file a separate return.

Example (2). For 1981, L_1 was an ineligible member and L_1, L_2, and L_3 filed a consolidated return under section 1504(c)(1). For 1982, L_1, L_2, and L_3 must continue filing a consolidated return under section 1504(c)(1).

Example (3). For 1981, L_1 was an eligible member and L_2 and L_3 were ineligible members. For 1982, L_1, L_2, and L_3 either must each file a separate return or must file a consolidated return as a limited group under section 1504(c)(1) having L_1 as the common parent.

Example (4). The facts are the same as in example (3). Assume further that for 1981, L_2 and L_3 file a consolidated return. During 1981, intercompany transactions (see § 1.1502-13) occur in the life-nonlife group between P and L_1, between P and S, and between S and L_4 and occur in the ineligible life subgroup between L_2 and L_3. For 1982, the restoration rules of § 1.1502-13, as modified by paragraph (e)(4)(iii)(B) of this section, will be applicable as indicated in the following table:

Consolidated Returns

See p. 20,601 for regulations not amended to reflect law changes

Intercompany transactions between:	§ 1.1502-13
P and L$_1$	Yes
P and S, if they file:	
Separate returns	Yes
A consolidated return	No
S and L$_4$	Yes
L$_2$ and L$_3$, if L$_1$, L$_2$, and L$_3$ file:	
Separate returns	Yes
A consolidated return	No

(v) *Additional rules.* (A) If a group with a taxable year ending in the month of December, 1982, had made the election under section 1504(c)(2) for a taxable year ending prior to December 1, 1982, and if that group meets the conditions of subdivision (vi) of this paragraph (e)(4), then the common parent may elect to discontinue filing a consolidated return for its taxable year ending in the month of December, 1982 (and other members of the section 1504(c)(2) group must comply with this election) by filing appropriate returns (see paragraph (e)(4)(i) of this section) before September 16, 1983.

(B) If a group made the election under section 1504(c)(2) for its taxable year ending in the month of December, 1982, and if that group meets the conditions of subdivision (vi) of this paragraph (e)(4), then the common parent may elect to withdraw the section 1504(c)(2) election (and all other members of the group determined without section 1504(b)(2) comply with the election) by filing before September 16, 1983, any returns for the appropriate taxable years that would have been filed had the section 1504(c)(2) election never been made.

(vi) A group referred to at subdivision (v)(A) or (B) of this paragraph (e)(4) meets the conditions of this subdivision (vi) if it—

(A) filed before March 16, 1983, a return for its taxable year ending in the month of December, 1982, and

(B) had not been granted an extension of time beyond March 15, 1983, for the filing of that return.

(vii) *Interest.* For purposes of section 6601(a), interest runs from the original due date (without extensions) for the filing of such returns as are filed pursuant to an election (to discontinue or withdraw as the case may be) under this paragraph (e)(4).

(5) *Consent to regulations.* If a group does not discontinue filing a consolidated return under paragraph (e)(4) of this section but continues to file a consolidated return for the group's first taxable year for which the regulations under this section are first effective, the members of the group will be deemed to have consented to the regulations under this section.

(6) *Cross reference.* If an election is made under section 1504(c)(2), see § 1.1502-75(e) and (f) for rules that apply for not including (or including) a member or a nonmember in the consolidated return.

(f) *Effect of election.* If the common parent makes the election under section 1504(c)(2), the following rules apply:

(1) *Termination of group.* A mere election under section 1504(c)(2) will not cause the creation of a new group or the termination of an affiliated group that files a consolidated return in the immediately preceding taxable year.

(2) *Effect of eligibility.* If a life member is eligible after an election under section 1504(c)(2), it may not be included as a member of an affiliated group as defined in section 1504(c)(1).

(3) *Eligible and ineligible life companies.* If any life company was a member of an affiliated group of life companies (as defined in section 1504(c)(1)) but is ineligible for a taxable year for which the election under section 1504(c)(2) is effective, that year is not a separate return year merely by reason of the election under section 1504(c)(2) in applying §§ 1.1502-13, 1.1502-18, and 1.1502-19 to transactions occurring in prior consolidated return years of that affiliated group. In addition, if more than one ineligible life member of the group (as defined in section 1504(c)(1)) joined in the filing of a consolidated return in the taxable year immediately preceding the year for which the election under section 1504(c)(2) is effective and, solely as a result of the election, one of the ineligible life members becomes the common parent of such a group (section 1504(c)(1)), the group must continue to file a consolidated return. For example, assume that L$_1$ owns all of the stock of S$_1$ and all of the stock of L$_2$. L$_2$ owns the stock of L$_3$. L$_1$, L$_2$, and L$_3$ are life companies and S$_1$ is a nonlife company. Assume further that in 1981, L$_1$, L$_2$, and L$_3$ file a consolidated return but L$_1$ makes the election under section 1504(c)(2) for 1982 and L$_2$ and L$_3$ are ineligible. L$_2$ and L$_3$ must continue to file a consolidated return in 1982. Moreover, L$_2$ could elect in 1982 to file a consolidated return (section 1504(c)(1)) with L$_3$ even if they did not file a consolidated return in 1981 with L$_1$.

(4) *Inclusion of life company.* If a life company is ineligible in the consolidated return year for which the election is effective, it will be treated as an includible corporation for the common parent's first taxable year in which the company becomes eligible.

(5) *Dividends received deduction.* Section 243(b)(5) defines the term affiliated group for purposes of the election to deduct 100 percent of

Reg. § 1.1502-47(f)(5)

the qualifying dividends received by a member from another member of the group. Section 246(b)(6) limits certain multiple tax benefits and the deduction itself. Section 243(b)(5) and (6) do not apply to the mutual companies and life companies that are eligible corporations. See section 1504(c)(2)(B)(i). Thus, the common parent of the group may elect to deduct 100 percent of the qualifying dividends received from an ineligible life company.

(6) *Controlled group.* Sections 1563(a)(4), (b)(2)(D), and (b)(3)(C) (insofar as it applies to corporations described in section 1563(b)(2)(D)) do not apply to any eligible or ineligible life company that is a member of the group for a taxable year during which the election is effective. See paragraph (d)(4) of this section for the definition of group.

(7) *Consolidated tax.* The tax liability of a group for a consolidated return year (before application of credits against that tax) is computed on a consolidated basis by adding together the following taxes:

(i) The tax imposed under section 11 on consolidated taxable income (as determined under paragraph (g) of this section). The taxes imposed under sections 802(a), 821(a), and 831(a) will each be treated as a tax imposed under section 11.

(ii) The tax imposed by section 1201 on consolidated net capital gain (as determined under paragraph (o) of this section) in lieu of the tax imposed under paragraph (f)(7)(i) of this section on that gain.

(iii) Any taxes described in § 1.1502-2 (other than by paragraphs (a), (f), and (h) thereof).

(g) *Consolidated taxable income.* The consolidated taxable income is the sum of the following three amounts:

(1) *Nonlife consolidated taxable income.* The nonlife consolidated taxable income (as defined in paragraph (h) of this section) of the nonlife subgroup, as set off by the life subgroup losses as provided in paragraph (n) of this section. The amount in this paragraph (g)(1) may not be less than zero.

(2) *Consolidated partial LICTI.* The consolidated partial LICTI (as defined in paragraph (j) of this section) of the life subgroup, as set off by the nonlife subgroup losses as provided in paragraph (m) of this section. The amount in this paragraph (g)(2) may not be less than zero.

(3) *Surplus accounts.* The sum of the amounts subtracted under section 815 from the policyholders' surplus accounts of the life members.

(h) *Nonlife consolidated taxable income.*—(1) *In general.* Nonlife consolidated taxable income is the consolidated taxable income of the nonlife subgroup, computed under § 1.1502-11 as modified by this paragraph (h). For this purpose, separate taxable income of a member includes separate mutual insurance company taxable income (as defined in section 821(b)) and insurance company taxable income (as defined in section 832).

(2) *Nonlife consolidated net operating loss deduction.*—(i) *In general.* In applying §§ 1.1502-21 or 1.1502-21A (as appropriate), the rules in this subparagraph (2) apply in determining for the nonlife subgroup the nonlife net operating loss and the portion of the nonlife net operating loss carryovers and carrybacks to the taxable year.

(ii) *Nonlife CNOL.* The nonlife consolidated net operating loss is determined under §§ 1.1502-21(A)(f) or 1.1502-21(e) (as appropriate) by treating the nonlife subgroup as the group.

(iii) *Carryback.* The nonlife consolidated net operating loss for the nonlife subgroup is carried back under §§ 1.1502-21A or 1.1502-21 (as appropriate) to the appropriate years (whether consolidated or separate) before the loss may be used as a nonlife subgroup loss under paragraphs (g)(2) and (m) of this section to set off consolidated partial LICTI in the year the loss arose. The election under section 172(b)(3)(C) to relinquish the entire carryback period for the net operating loss of the nonlife subgroup may be made by the common parent of the group. Furthermore, the election may be made even though the election under section 812(b)(3) and paragraph (l)(3)(iii) of this section is not made.

(iv) *Subgroup rule.* In determining the portion of the nonlife consolidated net operating loss that is absorbed when the loss is carried back to a consolidated return year beginning after December 31, 1981, §§ 1.1502-21A or 1.1502-21 (as appropriate) is applied by treating the nonlife subgroup as the group. Therefore, the absorption is determined without taking into account any life subgroup losses that were previously reported on a consolidated return as setting off nonlife consolidated taxable income for the year to which the nonlife loss is carried back.

(v) *Carryover.* The portion of the nonlife consolidated net operating loss that is not absorbed in a prior year as a carryback, or as a nonlife subgroup loss that set off consolidated partial LICTI for the year the loss arose, constitutes a nonlife carryover under this subparagraph (2) to reduce nonlife consolidated taxable income before that portion may constitute a nonlife sub-

Reg. § 1.1502-47(f)(6)

group loss that sets off consolidated partial LICTI for a particular year.

(vi) *Transitional rules.* The nonlife consolidated net operating loss deduction is subject to a transitional rule limitation in paragraph (h)(3) of this section.

(vii) *Example.* The following example illustrates this paragraph (h)(2). In the example, L indicates a life company, another letter indicates a nonlife company, and each corporation uses the calendar year as its taxable year.

Example. P owns all of the stock of S and L_1. L_1 owns all of the stock of L_2. For 1982, the group first files a consolidated return for which the election under section 1504(c)(2) is effective. P and S filed consolidated returns for 1979 through 1981. In 1982, the P-S group sustains a nonlife consolidated net operating loss. The loss is carried back to the consolidated return years 1979, 1980, and 1981 of P and S by using the principles of §§ 1.1502-21A and 1.1502-79A and, because the election in 1982 under section 1504(c)(2) does not result under paragraph (f)(1) of this section in the creation of a new group or the termination of the P-S nonlife group, the loss is absorbed on the consolidated return in those years without regard to whether the loss in 1982 is attributable to P or S and without regard to their contribution to consolidated taxable income in 1979, 1980, or 1981. The portion of the loss not absorbed in 1979, 1980, and 1981 may serve as a nonlife subgroup loss in 1982 that may set off the consolidated partial LICTI of L_1 and L_2 under paragraphs (g)(2) and (m) of this section.

(3) *Transitional rule.*—(i) *In general.* The portion of the nonlife consolidated net operating loss deduction in a consolidated return year beginning after December 31, 1980 (referred to as "post-1980 year") attributable to net operating losses sustained in separate return years ending before January 1, 1981 (referred to as "pre-1981 year"), is subject to the rules and limitations in this subparagraph (3).

(ii) *Separate nonlife groups.* To determine the limitation, first, identify for the post-1980 year one or more separate affiliated groups of nonlife companies (as defined in section 1504 without section 1504(c)(2)). For this purpose, a single nonlife company may constitute a separate affiliated group if (A) it is not otherwise a member of a separate group or (B) it has a net operating loss sustained in the pre-1981 year that may be carried over and that year is a separate return limitation year (determined under § 1.1502-1(f) without paragraph (d)(11) of this section).

(iii) *Carryover.* Second, identify the pre-1981 year net operating losses that may be carried over and that are attributable to each separate affiliated group of nonlife companies. The separate return limitation year rules in §§ 1.1502-21A(c) or 1.1502-21(c) (as appropriate) do not apply to any of these carryovers.

(iv) *Limitation.* Third, treat the last taxable year ending before January 1, 1981, as if in that year there was a consolidated return change of ownership of each such separate affiliated group of nonlife companies and apply the consolidated return change of ownership limitation in § 1.1502-21A(d) to the losses of each group by treating the members of each separate group as old members.

(v) *Examples.* The following examples illustrate this paragraph (h)(3). In the examples L indicates a life company, another letter indicates a nonlife company, and each corporation uses the calendar year as its taxable year.

Example (1). Throughout all of 1982, P owns all of the stock of S and L_1 and L_1 owns all of the stock of L_2 which in turn owns all of the stock of S_1. Thus, for 1982, there are two nonlife subgroups under this subparagraph (3), P-S and S_1. For 1981, P and S did not file a consolidated return and for 1980 P has a net operating loss of $200,000. Assume that P had no income in 1981. For 1982, the group makes an election under section 1504(c)(2) to file a consolidated return and all corporations are eligible corporations. The consolidated taxable income for the nonlife subgroup for 1982 (determined without the consolidated net operating loss deduction) recomputed by including only items of income and deduction of P and S is $120,000. If $120,000 is the § 1.1502-21A(d)(2) amount for P and S, then the amount of P's net operating loss for 1980 that may be carried over to P and S for 1982 cannot exceed $120,000.

Example (2). (a) P owns all of the stock of S_1. On January 1, 1979, P purchased all of the stock of L_1 which owns all of the stock of L_2 and S_2. Prior to 1984, all of the corporations filed separate returns. For 1984, the group makes an election under section 1504(c)(2) to file a consolidated return.

(b) 1981, 1982, and 1983 are not treated under paragraph (d)(11) of this section as separate return limitation years of the P_1, S_1, and S_2 nonlife subgroup. However, P and S_1 will be treated as old members under paragraph (h)(3)(iv) of this section and under § 1.1502-21A(d) with respect to their losses in 1979 and 1980 (whether a consolidated return was filed or separate returns were filed) so that the portion of nonlife consolidated taxable income attributable to S_2 may not absorb the losses of P or

Reg. § 1.1502-47(h)(3)

S_1. The rules that apply to the P-S_1 nonlife subgroup for 1979 and 1980 apply in an identical way to S_2 by treating S_2 as a subgroup separate from the P-S_1 nonlife subgroup. See section 1507(c)(2)(A) of the Tax Reform Act of 1976.

(c) Similarly, L_1 and L_2 are treated as old members under paragraphs (l)(3) and (h)(3)(iv) of this section for losses arising in 1979 and 1980. However, since the L_1—L_2 subgroup is also the life subgroup under paragraph (d)(8) of this section, the limitation in paragraph (h)(3)(iv) of this section does not affect the computation of consolidated partial LICTI for the life subgroup.

(4) *Nonlife consolidated capital gain net income or loss.*—(i) *In general.* In applying §§ 1.1502-22 or 1.1502-22A (as appropriate), the rules in this subparagraph (4) apply in determining for the nonlife subgroup the nonlife consolidated capital gain net income or loss and the portion of the nonlife net capital loss carryovers and carrybacks to the taxable year. In particular, the nonlife consolidated capital gain net income and nonlife consolidated net capital loss are determined under the principles of §§ 1.1502-22 or 1.1502-22A(a) (as appropriate) by treating the nonlife subgroup as the group.

(ii) *Additional principles.* In applying §§ 1.1502-22A or 1.1502-22 to nonlife consolidated net capital loss carryovers and carrybacks, the principles set forth in paragraph (h)(2)(iii) through (v) for applying §§ 1.1502-21 or 1.1502-21A (as appropriate) to nonlife consolidated net operating loss carryovers and carrybacks shall also apply. Further, the portion of nonlife consolidated net capital loss carryovers attributable to losses sustained in taxable years ending before January 1, 1981, is subject to the limitations in paragraph (h)(3) of this section applied by substituting "net capital loss" for the term "net operating loss" and "§ 1.1502-22A(d)" for "§ 1.1502-21A(d)".

(iii) *Special rules.* The nonlife consolidated net capital loss is reduced, for purposes of determining the carryovers and carrybacks under §§ 1.1502-22A(b)(1) or 1.1502-22(b) by the lesser of—

(A) The aggregate of the additional capital loss deductions allowed under section 822(c)(6) or section 832(c)(5), or

(B) The nonlife consolidated taxable income computed without capital gains and losses.

(i) [Reserved]

(j) *Consolidated partial LICTI.* [Reserved]

(k) *Consolidated TII.*—(1) *General rule.* [Reserved]

(2) *Separate TII.* [Reserved]

(3) *Company's share of investment yield.* [Reserved]

(4) *Life consolidated capital gain net income.* [Reserved]

(5) *Life consolidated net capital loss carryovers and carrybacks.* The life consolidated net capital loss carryovers and carrybacks for the life subgroup are determined by applying the principles of §§ 1.1502-22 or 1.1502-22A (as appropriate) as modified by the following rules in this subparagraph (5):

(i) Life consolidated net capital loss is first carried back (or apportioned to the life members for separate return years) to be absorbed by life consolidated capital gain net income without regard to any nonlife subgroup capital losses and before the life consolidated net capital loss may serve as a life subgroup capital loss that sets off nonlife consolidated capital gain net income in the year the life consolidated net capital loss arose.

(ii) If a life consolidated net capital loss is not carried back or is not a life subgroup loss that sets off nonlife consolidated capital gain net income in the year the life consolidated net capital loss arose, then it is carried over to the particular year under this paragraph (k)(5) first against life consolidated capital gain net income before it may serve as a life subgroup capital loss that sets off nonlife consolidated capital gain net income in that particular year.

(iii) *Section 818(f).* Capital losses may not be deducted more than once and capital gain will not be included more than once. See section 818(e) and also section 818(f).

(iv) Capital loss carryovers are subject to the transitional rule in paragraph (k)(6) of this section.

(6) *Transitional rule.* The portion of the life consolidated capital loss carryovers attributable to the net capital losses of the life members sustained in separate return years ending before January 1, 1981, is subject to the same limitations as the capital losses of nonlife members in paragraph (h)(4)(iii) of this section by applying the principles of paragraph (h)(3) of this section to each separate affiliated group of life companies.

(l) *Consolidated GO or LO.*—(1) *General rule.* [Reserved]

(2) *Separate GO.* [Reserved]

(3) *Consolidated operations loss deduction.*—(i) *General rule.* The consolidated operations loss deduction is an amount equal to the consolidated operations loss carryovers and carrybacks to the taxable year. The provisions of §§ 1.1502-21 or 1.1502-21A (as appropriate) and section 812 ap-

ply to the extent not inconsistent with this paragraph (l)(3).

(ii) *Consolidated offset.* For purposes of applying section 812(b) and (d), the term "consolidated offset" means the increase in the consolidated operations loss deduction which reduces consolidated partial LICTI to zero. For setoff of consolidated LO against nonlife consolidated taxable income, see paragraph (n)(2) of this section.

(iii) *Carrybacks.* A consolidated LO is first carried back to be absorbed by GO of a life member under section 809(d)(4) or consolidated partial LICTI (as the case may be under section 818(f)(2)) for prior consolidated return years (or apportioned to the life members for prior separate return years) without regard to any nonlife subgroup losses that were set off against consolidated partial LICTI and before the consolidated LO may serve as a life subgroup loss to be set off against nonlife consolidated taxable income in the year the consolidated LO arose. The election to relinquish the entire carryback period for the consolidated LO of the life subgroup may be made by the common parent of the group. See section 812(b)(3). Furthermore, the election may be made even though the election under section 172(b)(3)(C) and paragraph (h)(2)(iii) of this section is not made.

(iv) *Carryovers.* If a consolidated LO is not carried back or is not applied as a life subgroup loss that set off nonlife consolidated taxable income in the year the consolidated LO arose, then it is carried over to a particular year under this paragraph (l)(3) first against the GO of a life member under section 809(d)(4) or consolidated partial LICTI (as the case may be under section 818(f)(2)) before it may serve as a life subgroup loss that may be set off against nonlife consolidated taxable income for that particular year.

(v) *Transitional rule.* The portion of a consolidated operations loss deduction that is attributable to LOs sustained in separate return years ending before January 1, 1981, is subject to the same rules and limitations that the nonlife consolidated net operating loss deduction is subject to in paragraph (h)(3) of this section as applied by identifying separate affiliated groups of life companies.

(4) *Life consolidated capital gain net income or loss.* Life consolidated capital gain net income or loss is determined in the same manner as under paragraph (k)(4) of this section. However, a life member's company share is determined under section 809(a) and (b)(3).

(m) *Consolidated partial LICTI setoff by nonlife subgroup losses.*—(1) *In general.* The nonlife subgroup losses consist of the nonlife consolidated net operating loss and the nonlife consolidated net capital loss. Under paragraph (g)(2) of this section, consolidated partial LICTI is set off by the amounts of these two consolidated losses specified in paragraph (m)(2) of this section. The setoff is subject to the rules and limitations in paragraph (m)(3) of this section.

(2) *Amount of setoff.*—(i) *Current year.* Consolidated partial LICTI for the current taxable year is set off by the portion of the nonlife consolidated net operating loss and nonlife consolidated net capital loss arising in that year that cannot be carried back under paragraph (h) of this section to prior taxable years (whether consolidated or separate return years) of the nonlife subgroup.

(ii) *Carryovers.* The portion of the offsettable nonlife consolidated net operating loss or nonlife consolidated net capital loss that has not been used as a nonlife subgroup loss setoff against consolidated partial LICTI in the year it arose may be carried over to succeeding taxable years under the principles of §§ 1.1502-21 or 1.1502-21A (as appropriate) (relating to net operating loss deduction) or §§ 1.1502-22 or 1.1502-22A (as appropriate) (relating to net capital loss carryovers). However, in any particular succeeding year, the losses will be used under paragraph (h) of this section in computing nonlife consolidated taxable income before being used in that year as a nonlife subgroup loss that sets off consolidated partial LICTI.

(3) *Nonlife subgroup loss rules and limitations.* The nonlife subgroup losses are subject to the following operating rules and limitations:

(i) *Separate return years.* The carryovers in paragraph (m)(2)(ii) of this section may include net operating losses and net capital losses of the nonlife members arising in separate return years ending after December 31, 1980, that may be carried over to a succeeding year under the principles (including limitations) of §§ 1.1502-21 and 1.1502-22 (or §§ 1.1502-21A and 1.1502-22A, as appropriate). But see subdivision (ix) of this paragraph (m)(3).

(ii) *Capital loss.* Nonlife consolidated net capital loss sets off consolidated partial LICTI only to the extent of life consolidated capital gain net income (as determined under paragraph (l)(4) of this section) and this setoff applies before any nonlife consolidated net operating loss sets off consolidated partial LICTI.

(iii) *Capital gain.* Life consolidated capital gain net income is zero in any taxable year in which the life subgroup has a consolidated LO and, in any taxable year, it may not exceed consolidated partial LICTI.

Reg. § 1.1502-47(m)(3)

(iv) *Ordering rule.* Consolidated partial LICTI for a consolidated return year is set off by nonlife subgroup losses for that year before being set off (under paragraph (m)(2)(ii) of this section) by a carryover of a nonlife subgroup loss to that year.

(v) *Setoff at bottom line.* The setoff of nonlife subgroup losses against consolidated partial LICTI does not affect life member deductions that depend in whole or in part on GO or TII. Thus, the setoff does not affect the amount of consolidated partial LICTI (as determined under paragraph (j) of this section) for any taxable year but it merely constitutes an adjustment in arriving at the group's consolidated taxable income under paragraph (g) of this section.

(vi) *Ineligible nonlife member.* (A) The offsetable nonlife consolidated net operating loss that arises in any consolidated return year (that may be set off against consolidated partial LICTI in the current taxable year or in a succeeding taxable year) is the amount computed under paragraph (h)(2)(ii) of this section reduced by the ineligible NOL. For purposes of this subparagraph (3), the "ineligible NOL" is in the year the loss arose the amount of the separate net operating loss (determined under §§ 1.1502-21(b)) of any nonlife member that is ineligible in that year (and not the portion of the nonlife consolidated net operating loss attributable under §§ 1.1502-21(b) to such a member). (B) The carryovers of offsetable nonlife net operating losses under paragraph (m)(2)(ii) of this section do not include an ineligible NOL arising in a consolidated return year or a loss attributable to an ineligible member arising in a separate return year. See section 1503(c)(2). (C) For absorption within the nonlife subgroup of an ineligible NOL arising in a consolidated return year or a loss of an ineligible member arising in a separate return year which is not a separate return limitation year under paragraph (m)(3)(ix) of this section, see paragraph (m)(3)(vii) of this section.

(vii) *Absorption of ineligible NOL.* (A) If all or a portion of a nonlife member's ineligible NOL (determined under paragraph (m)(3)(vi)(A) of this section) may be carried back or carried over under paragraph (h)(2) of this section to a particular consolidated return year of the nonlife subgroup (absorption year), then notwithstanding § 1.1502-21A(b)(3)(ii) or 1.1502-21(b), the amount carried to the absorption year will be absorbed by that member's contribution (to the extent thereof) to nonlife consolidated taxable income for that year.

(B) For purposes of (A) of this subdivision (vii), a member's contribution to nonlife consolidated taxable income for an absorption year is the amount of such income (computed without the portion of the nonlife consolidated net operating loss deduction attributable to taxable years subsequent to the year the loss arose), minus such consolidated taxable income recomputed by excluding both that member's items of income and deductions for the absorption year. The deductions of the member include the prior application of this paragraph (m)(3)(vii) to the absorption of the nonlife consolidated net operating loss deduction for losses arising in taxable years prior to the particular loss year.

(viii) *Election to relinquish carryback.* The offsetable nonlife consolidated net operating loss does not include the amount that could be carried back under paragraph (h)(2) of this section but for the common parent's election under section 172(b)(3)(C) to relinquish the carryback. See section 1503(c)(1).

(ix) *Separate return limitation year.* The offsetable nonlife consolidated net operating and capital loss carryovers do not include any losses attributable to a nonlife member that were sustained (A) in a separate return limitation year (determined without section 1504(b)(2)) of that member (or a predecessor), or (B) in a separate return year ending after December 31, 1980, in which an election was in effect under neither section 1504(c)(2) nor section 243(b)(2). For purposes of this paragraph (m), a separate return limitation year includes a taxable year ending before January 1, 1981. See section 1507(c)(2)(A) of the Tax Reform Act of 1976 and §§ 1.1502-15 and 1.1502-15A (including applicable exceptions thereto).

(x) *Percentage limitation.* The offsetable nonlife consolidated net operating losses that may be set off against consolidated partial LICTI in a particular year may not exceed a percentage limitation. This limitation is the applicable percentage in section 1503(c)(1) of the lesser of two amounts. The first amount is the sum of the offsetable nonlife consolidated net operating losses under paragraph (m)(2) of this section that may serve in the particular year (determined without this limitation) as a setoff against consolidated partial LICTI. The second amount is consolidated partial LICTI (as defined in paragraph (j) of this section) in the particular year reduced by any nonlife consolidated net capital loss that sets off consolidated partial LICTI in that year.

(xi) *Further limitation.* Any offsetable nonlife consolidated net operating loss remaining after applying the percentage limitation that is carried over to a succeeding taxable year may not be set off against the consolidated partial LICTI

Reg. § 1.1502-47(m)(3)

attributable to a life member that was not an eligible life member in the year the loss arose. See section 1503(c)(2).

(xii) *Restoration rule.* The carryback of a consolidated LO or life consolidated net capital loss under paragraph (l) of this section that reduces consolidated partial LICTI (or life consolidated capital gain net income) for a prior year may reduce the amount of nonlife subgroup losses that would offset consolidated partial LICTI in that prior year. Thus, that amount may be carried over under paragraph (h)(2) or (4) of this section from that prior year in determining nonlife consolidated taxable income in a succeeding year or serve as offsetable nonlife subgroup losses in a succeeding year.

(4) *Acquired groups.* [Reserved]

(5) *Illustrations.* The following examples illustrate this paragraph (m). In the examples, L indicates a life company, another letter indicates a nonlife company, and each corporation uses the calendar year as its taxable year.

Example (1). P owns all of the stock of L and S. S owns all of the stock of I, a nonlife member that is an ineligible corporation for 1982 under paragraph (d)(13) of this section. For 1982, the group elects under section 1504(c)(2) to file a consolidated return. For 1982, assume that any nonlife consolidated net operating loss may not be carried back to a prior taxable year. Other facts are summarized in the following table:

	Separate taxable income (loss)
P	$100
S	(100)
I	(100)
Nonlife consolidated net operating loss	(100)

Under paragraph (m)(3)(vi) of this section, P's separate income is considered to absorb the loss of S, an eligible member, first and the offsetable nonlife consolidated net operating loss is zero, *i.e.,* the consolidated net operating loss ($100) reduced by I's loss ($100). The consolidated net operating loss ($100) may be carried over, but since it is entirely attributable to I (an ineligible member) its use is subject to the restrictions in paragraph (m)(3)(vi) of this section. The result would be the same if the group contained two additional members, S_1, an eligible member, and I_1, an ineligible member, where S_1 had a loss of ($100) and I_1 had income of $100.

Example (2). The facts are the same as in example (1) except that for 1982 S's separate net operating loss is $200. Assume further that L's consolidated partial LICTI is $200. Under paragraph (m)(3)(vi) of this section, the offsetable nonlife consolidated net operating loss is $100, *i.e.,* the nonlife consolidated net operating loss computed under paragraph (h)(2)(ii) of this section ($200), reduced by the separate net operating loss of I ($100). The offsetable nonlife consolidated net operating loss that may be set off against consolidated partial LICTI in 1982 is $30, *i.e.,* 30 percent of the lesser of the offsetable $100 or consolidated partial LICTI of $200. See paragraph (m)(3)(x) of this section. The nonlife subgroup may carry $170 to 1983 under paragraph (h)(2) of this section against nonlife consolidated taxable income, *i.e.,* consolidated net operating loss ($200) less amount used in 1982 ($30). Under paragraph (m)(2)(ii) of this section, the offsetable nonlife consolidated net operating loss that may be carried to 1983 is $70, *i.e.,* $100 minus $30. The facts and results are summarized in the table below:

	(Dollars omitted)			
	Facts (a)	Offsetable (b)	Limit (c)	Unused loss (d)
1. P	100	......	....	....
2. S	(200)	(100)	....	(70)
3. I	(100)	......	....	(100)
4. Nonlife subgroup	(200)	(100)	(100)	(170)
5. L	200	......	200	....
6. 30% of lower line 4(c) or 5(c)	....	......	30	....
7. Unused offsetable loss	....	......	....	(70)

Accordingly, under paragraph (g) of this section (assuming no amount is withdrawn from L's surplus accounts), consolidated taxable income is $170, *i.e.,* line 5(a) minus line 6(c).

Example (3). The facts are the same as in example (2) with the following additions for 1983. The nonlife subgroup has nonlife consolidated taxable income of $50 (all of which is attributable to I) before the nonlife consolidated net operating loss deduction under paragraph (h)(2) of this section. Consolidated partial LICTI is $100. Under paragraph (h)(2) of this section, $50 of the nonlife consolidated net operating loss carryover ($170) is used in 1983 and, under paragraph (m)(3)(vi) and (vii) of this section, the portion used in 1982 is attributable to I, the ineligible nonlife member. Accordingly, the offsetable nonlife consolidated

Reg. § 1.1502-47(m)(5)

net operating loss from 1982 under paragraph (m)(3)(ii) of this section is $70, i.e., the unused loss from 1982. The offsetable nonlife consolidated net operating loss in 1983 is $24.50, i.e., 35 percent of the lesser of the offsetable loss of $70 or consolidated partial LICTI of $100. Accordingly, under paragraph (g) of this section (assuming no amount is withdrawn from L's surplus accounts), consolidated taxable income is $75.50, i.e., consolidated partial LICTI of $100 minus the offsetable loss of $24.50.

Example (4). P owns all of the stock of S and L. For 1982, all corporations are eligible corporations, and the group elects under section 1504(c)(2) to file a consolidated return, the nonlife consolidated net operating loss is $100, and the nonlife consolidated net capital loss is $50. Assume that the losses may not be carried back and the capital losses are not attributable to built-in deductions under paragraph (m)(3)(ix) of this section or under § 1.1502-15A. Other facts and the results are set forth in the following table:

	P-S	L
1. Nonlife consolidated net operating loss	($100)	...
2. Nonlife consolidated capital loss	(50)	...
3. Consolidated partial LICTI	....	$100
4. Life consolidated capital gain net income included in line 3	....	50
5. Offsetable:		
(a) 30% of lower of line (1) or line (3) - (4)	(15)	...
(b) Line 2	(50)	...
(c) Total	(65)	...
6. Unused losses available to be carried over:		
(a) From line 1 (line 1 minus line 5(a))	(85)	...
(b) From line 2 (line 2 minus line 5(b))	0	...

Accordingly, under paragraph (g) of this section consolidated taxable income is $35, i.e., line 3 minus line 5(c).

Example (5). The facts are the same as in example (4). Assume further that for 1983 L has an LO that is carried back to 1982 and the LO is large enough to reduce consolidated partial LICTI for 1982 to zero as determined before any setoff for nonlife losses. Under paragraph (m)(3)(xii) of this section, the nonlife consolidated net operating loss of $15 and the nonlife consolidated net capital loss of $50 that were set off in 1982 respectively against consolidated partial LICTI and life consolidated capital gain net income are restored. These restored amounts may constitute part of the nonlife consolidated net operating loss carryover to 1983 under paragraph (h)(2) of this section or part of the nonlife net capital loss carryover to 1983 under paragraph (h)(4) of this section.

Example (6). The facts are the same as in example (5) except that L's LO for 1983 as carried back reduces consolidated partial LICTI in 1982 from $100 to $25. Since consolidated partial LICTI of $100 in 1982 (before the carryback) included life consolidated capital gain net income of $50, under paragraph (m)(3)(iii) of this section, the life consolidated capital gain net income is $25, i.e., $50 but not more than $25. Therefore, under paragraph (m)(3)(ii) of this section, the offsetable nonlife capital loss in 1982 is $25 and, under paragraph (m)(3)(xii) of this section, $25 of the $50 nonlife consolidated net capital loss in 1982 may be carried under paragraph (h)(4) of this section to 1983. No nonlife consolidated net operating loss is used as a setoff against consolidated partial LICTI in 1982 under paragraph (m)(3)(xii) of this section by reason of the carryback of the consolidated LO from 1983 to 1982.

(n) *Nonlife consolidated taxable income set off by life subgroup losses.*—(1) *In general.* The life subgroup losses consist of the consolidated LO and the life consolidated net capital loss (as determined under paragraph (l)(4) of this section). Under paragraph (g)(1) of this section, nonlife consolidated taxable income is set off by the amounts of these two consolidated losses specified in paragraph (n)(2) of this section.

(2) *Amount of setoff.* The portion of the consolidated LO or life consolidated net capital loss that may be set off against nonlife consolidated taxable income (determined under paragraph (h) of this section) is determined by applying the rules prescribed in paragraph (m)(2) and (3) of this section in the following manner:

(i) Substitute the term "life" for "nonlife", and vice versa.

(ii) Substitute the term "nonlife consolidated taxable income" for "consolidated partial LICTI", and vice versa.

(iii) Substitute the term "consolidated LO" for "non-life consolidated net operating loss", "paragraph (l)" or "paragraph (j)" for "paragraph (h)", and "section 812(b)(3)" for "section 172(b)(3)(C)".

(iv) Paragraphs (m)(3)(vi), (vii), (x), and (xi) of this section do not apply to a consolidated LO.

(v) Capital losses may not be deducted more than once. See section 818(e) and also the requirements in section 818(f).

(vi) The setoff of life subgroup losses against nonlife consolidated taxable income does

Reg. § 1.1502-47(n)(1)

not affect nonlife member deductions that depend in whole or in part on taxable income.

(3) *Illustrations.* The following examples illustrate this paragraph (n). In the examples, L indicates a life company, another letter indicates a nonlife company, and each corporation uses the calendar year as its taxable year.

Example (1). P, S, L_1 and L_2 constitute a group that elects under section 1504(c)(2) to file a consolidated return for 1982. In 1982, the nonlife subgroup consolidated taxable income is $100 and there is $20 of nonlife consolidated net capital loss that cannot be carried back under paragraph (h) of this section to taxable years (whether consolidated or separate) preceding 1982. The nonlife subgroup has no carryover from years prior to 1982. Consolidated LO is $150 which under paragraph (l) of this section includes life consolidated capital gain net income of $25. The $150 LO is carried back under paragraph (l)(3) of this section to taxable years (whether consolidated or separate) preceding 1982 before it may offset in 1982 nonlife consolidated taxable income. Since life consolidated capital gain net income is zero for 1982, the nonlife capital loss offset is zero.

Example (2). The facts are the same as in example (1). Assume further that no part of the $150 consolidated LO for 1982 can be used by L_1 and L_2 in years prior to 1982. For 1982, $100 of consolidated LO sets off the $100 nonlife consolidated taxable income. The life subgroup carries under paragraph (l)(3) of this section to 1983 $50 of the consolidated LO ($150 minus $100). See paragraph (l)(3)(ii) of this section. The $50 carryover will be used in 1983 against life subgroup income before it may be used in 1983 to setoff nonlife consolidated taxable income.

Example (3). (a) The facts are the same as in example (1), except that for 1982 the nonlife consolidated taxable income is $150 and includes nonlife consolidated capital gain net income of $50, consolidated partial LICTI is $200, and a life consolidated net capital loss is $50. Assume that the $50 life consolidated net capital loss sets off the $50 nonlife consolidated capital gain net income. Consolidated taxable income under paragraph (g) of this section is $300, *i.e.*, nonlife consolidated taxable income ($150) minus the setoff of the life consolidated net capital loss ($50), plus consolidated partial LICTI ($200).

(b) Assume that for 1983 the nonlife consolidated net operating loss is $150. Under paragraph (h)(2) of this section, the loss may be carried back to 1982 against nonlife consolidated taxable income. If P, the common parent, does not elect to relinquish the carryback under section 172(b)(3)(C), the entire $150 must be carried back reducing 1982 nonlife consolidated taxable income to zero and nonlife consolidated capital gain net income to zero. Under paragraph (m)(3)(xii) of this section, the setoff in 1982 of the nonlife consolidated capital gain net income ($50) by the life consolidated net capital loss ($50) is restored. Accordingly, the 1982 life consolidated net capital loss may be carried over by the life subgroup to 1983. Under paragraph (g) of this section, after the carryback consolidated taxable income for 1982 is $200, *i.e.*, nonlife consolidated taxable income ($0) plus consolidated partial LICTI ($200).

Example (4). The facts are the same as in example (3), except that P elects under section 172(b)(3)(C) to relinquish the carryback of $150 arising in 1983. The setoff in part (a) of example (3) is not restored. However, the offsetable nonlife consolidated net operating loss for 1983 (or that may be carried forward from 1983) is zero. See paragraph (m)(3)(viii) of this section. Nevertheless, the $150 nonlife consolidated net operating loss may be carried forward to be used by the nonlife group.

Example (5). P owns all of the stock of S_1 and of L_1. On January 1, 1978, L_1 purchases all of the stock of L_2. For 1982, the group elects under section 1504(c)(2) to file a consolidated return. For 1982, L_1 is an eligible corporation under paragraph (d)(12) of this section but L_2 is ineligible. Thus, L_1 but not L_2 is a member for 1982. In 1982, L_2 sustains an LO that cannot be carried back. For 1982, L_2 is treated under paragraph (f)(6) of this section as a member of a controlled group of corporations under section 1563 with P, S, and L_1. For 1983, L_2 is eligible and is included on the group's consolidated return. L_2's LO for 1982 that may be carried to 1983 is not treated under paragraph (d)(11) of this section as having been sustained in a separate return limitation year for purposes of computing consolidated partial LICTI of the L_1-L_2 life subgroup for 1983. Furthermore, the portion of L_2's LO not used under paragraph (l)(3) of this section against life subgroup income in 1983 may be included in offsetable consolidated operations loss under paragraph (n)(2) and (m)(3)(i) of this section that reduces in 1983 nonlife consolidated taxable income because L_2's loss in 1982 was not sustained in a separate return limitation year under paragraph (n)(2) and (m)(3)(ix)(A) of this section or in a separate return year (1982) when an election was in effect neither under section 1504(c)(2) nor section 243(b)(2).

(o) *Alternative tax.*—(1) *In general.* For purposes of the alternative tax under paragraph (f)(7)(ii) of this section, consolidated net capital gain is the sum of the following two amounts:

(i) The nonlife consolidated net capital gain reduced by any setoff of a life consolidated net capital loss.

(ii) The life consolidated net capital gain reduced by any setoff of a nonlife consolidated net capital loss.

(2) *Net capital gain.* For purposes of this paragraph (o)—

(i) Nonlife consolidated net capital gain is computed under §§ 1.1502-41A or 1.1502-22T (as appropriate) except that it may not exceed nonlife consolidated taxable income (computed under paragraph (h) of this section).

(ii) Life consolidated net capital gain is computed under §§ 1.1502-41A or 1.502-22T (as appropriate), applied in a manner consistent with paragraph (l)(4) of this section, except that it may not exceed consolidated partial LICTI (as determined under paragraph (j) of this section).

(iii) *Setoffs.* Setoffs are determined under paragraph (m) or (n) of this section (as the case may be).

(p) *Transitional rule for credit carryovers.* For limitations on credits arising in taxable years ending before January 1, 1981, that may be carried over to taxable years beginning on or after that date, section 1507(c)(2)(A) of the Tax Reform Act of 1976 and the principles in paragraph (h)(3) of this section (relating to limitations on loss carryovers) apply.

(q) *Preemption.* The rules in this section preempt any inconsistent rules in other sections (§ 1.1502-1 through 1.1502-80) of the consolidated return regulations. For example, the rules in paragraph (m)(3)(vi) apply notwithstanding §§ 1.1502-21A(b)(3) and 1.1502-79A(a)(3) (or § 1.1502-21, as appropriate).

(r) *Other consolidation principles.* The fact that this section treats the life and nonlife members as separate groups in computing, respectively, consolidated partial LICTI (or LO) and nonlife consolidated taxable income (or loss) does not affect the usual rules in §§ 1.1502-0—1.1502-80 unless this section provides otherwise. Thus, the usual rules in § 1.1502-13 (relating to intercompany transactions) apply to both the life and nonlife members by treating them as members of one affiliated group.

(s) *Filing requirements.* Nonlife consolidated taxable income or loss under paragraph (h) of this section shall be determined on a separate Form 1120 or 1120M and consolidated partial LICTI under paragraph (j) of this section shall be determined on a separate Form 1120L. The consolidated return shall be made on a separate Form 1120, 1120M, or 1120L by the common parent (if the group includes a life company), which shows the setoffs under paragraphs (g), (m), and (n) of this section and clearly indicates by notation on the face of the return that it is a life-nonlife consolidated return (if the group includes a life company). See also § 1.1502-75(j), relating to statements and schedules for subsidiaries. [Reg. § 1.1502-47.]

☐ [*T.D. 7877, 3-14-83. Amended by T.D. 7912, 9-1-83; T.D. 8560, 8-12-94; T.D. 8597, 7-12-95; T.D. 8677, 6-26-96 and T.D. 8823, 6-25-99.*]

[Reg. § 1.1502-55]

§ 1.1502-55. **Computation of alternative minimum tax of consolidated groups.**—(a) through (h)(3) [Reserved].

(h)(4) *Separate return year minimum tax credit.*

(i) and (ii) [Reserved].

(iii)(A) *Limitation on portion of separate return year minimum tax credit arising in separate return limitation years.* The aggregate of a member's minimum tax credits arising in SRLYs that are included in the consolidated minimum tax credits for all consolidated return years of the group may not exceed—

(*1*) The aggregate for all consolidated return years of the member's contributions to the consolidated section 53(c) limitation for each consolidated return year; reduced by

(*2*) The aggregate of the member's minimum tax credits arising and absorbed in all consolidated return years (whether or not absorbed by the member).

(B) *Computational rules*—(*1*) *Member's contribution to the consolidated section 53(c) limitation.* Except as provided in the special rule of paragraph (h)(4)(iii)(B)(*2*) of this section, a member's contribution to the consolidated section 53(c) limitation for a consolidated return year equals the member's share of the consolidated net regular tax liability minus its share of consolidated tentative minimum tax. The group computes the member's shares by applying to the respective consolidated amounts the principles of section 1552 and the percentage method under § 1.1502-33(d)(3), assuming a 100% allocation of any decreased tax liability. The group makes proper adjustments so that taxes and credits not taken into account in computing the limitation under section 53(c) are not taken into account in computing the member's share of the consolidated net regular tax, etc. (See, for example, the taxes described in section 26(b) that are disregarded in computing regular tax liability.)

Reg. § 1.1502-55(a)

(2) *Adjustment for year in which alternative minimum tax is paid.* For a consolidated return year for which consolidated tentative minimum tax is greater than consolidated regular tax liability, the group reduces the member's share of the consolidated tentative minimum tax by the member's share of the consolidated alternative minimum tax for the year. The group determines the member's share of consolidated alternative minimum tax for a year using the same method it uses to determine the member's share of the consolidated minimum tax credits for the year.

(3) *Years included in computation.* For purposes of computing the limitation under this paragraph (h)(4)(iii), the consolidated return years of the group include only those years, including the year to which a credit is carried, that the member has been continuously included in the group's consolidated return, but exclude any years after the year to which the credit is carried.

(4) *Subgroup principles.* The SRLY subgroup principles under § 1.1502-21(c)(2) apply for purposes of this paragraph (h)(4)(iii). The predecessor and successor principles under § 1.1502-21(f) also apply for purposes of this paragraph (h)(4)(iii).

(5) *Overlap with section 383.* The principles under § 1.1502-21(g) apply for purposes of this paragraph (h)(4)(iii). For example, an overlap of this paragraph (h)(4)(iii) and the application of section 383 with respect to a credit carryover occurs if a corporation becomes a member of a consolidated group (the SRLY event) within six months of the change date of an ownership change giving rise to a section 383 credit limitation with respect to that carryover (the section 383 event), with the result that the limitation of this paragraph (h)(4)(iii) does not apply. See §§ 1.1502-21(g)(2)(ii)(A) and 1.383-1; see also § 1.1502-21(g)(4) (subgroup rules).

(C) *Effective date—(1) In general.* This paragraph (h)(4)(iii) generally applies to consolidated return years for which the due date of the income tax return (without extensions) is after March 13, 1998. See § 1.1502-3(d)(4) for an optional effective date rule (generally making this paragraph (h)(4)(iii) also applicable to a consolidated return year beginning on or after January 1, 1997, if the due date of the income tax return (without extensions) was on or before March 13, 1998).

(i) *Contribution years.* In general, a group does not take into account a consolidated taxable year for which the due date of the income tax return (without extensions) is on or before March 13, 1998, in determining a member's (or subgroup's) contributions to the consolidated section 53(c) limitation under this paragraph (h)(4)(iii). However, if a consolidated group chooses to apply the optional effective date rule, the consolidated group shall not take into account a consolidated taxable year beginning before January 1, 1997 in determining a member's (or subgroup's) contributions to the consolidated section 53(c) limitation under this paragraph (h)(4)(iii).

(ii) *Special subgroup rule.* In the event that the principles of § 1.1502-21(g)(1) do not apply to a particular credit carryover in the current group, then solely for purposes of applying this paragraph (h)(4)(iii) to determine the limitation with respect to that carryover and with respect to which the SRLY register (the aggregate of the member's or subgroup's contribution to consolidated section 53(c) limitation reduced by the aggregate of the member's or subgroup's minimum tax credits arising and absorbed in all consolidated return years) began in a taxable year for which the due date of the return is on or before May 25, 2000, the principles of § 1.1502-21(c)(2) shall be applied without regard to the phrase "or for a carryover that was subject to the overlap rule described in paragraph (g) of this section or § 1.1502-15(g) with respect to another group (the former group)."

(2) *Overlap rule.* Paragraph (h)(4)(iii)(B)(5) of this section (relating to overlap with section 383) applies to taxable years for which the due date (without extensions) of the consolidated return is after May 25, 2000. For purposes of paragraph (h)(4)(iii)(B)(5) of this section, only an ownership change to which section 383, as amended by the Tax Reform Act of 1986 (100 Stat. 2095), applies and which results, in a section 383 credit limitation shall constitute a section 383 event. The optional effective date rule of § 1.1502-3(d)(4) (generally making this paragraph (h)(4)(iii) also applicable to a consolidated return year beginning on or after January 1, 1997, if the due date of the income tax return (without extensions) was on or before March 13, 1998) does not apply with respect to paragraph (h)(4)(iii)(B)(5) of this section (relating to the overlap rule). [Reg. § 1.1502-55.]

☐ [*T.D.* 8884, 5-24-2000.]

[Reg. § 1.1502-75]

§ 1.1502-75. **Filing of consolidated returns.**—(a) *Privilege of filing consolidated returns*—(1) *Exercise of privilege for first consolidated return year.* A group which did not file a consolidated return for the immediately preceding taxable year may file a consolidated return in lieu of separate returns for the taxable year, provided that each corporation which has been a member during any part of the taxable

Reg. § 1.1502-75(a)(1)

year for which the consolidated return is to be filed consents (in the manner provided in paragraph (b) of this section) to the regulations under section 1502. If a group wishes to exercise its privilege of filing a consolidated return, such consolidated return must be filed not later than the last day prescribed by law (including extensions of time) for the filing of the common parent's return. Such consolidated return may not be withdrawn after such last day (but the group may change the basis of its return at any time prior to such last day).

(2) *Continued filing requirement.* A group which filed (or was required to file) a consolidated return for the immediately preceding taxable year is required to file a consolidated return for the taxable year unless it has an election to discontinue filing consolidated returns under paragraph (c) of this section.

(b) *How consent for first consolidated year exercised*—(1) *General rule.* The consent of a corporation referred to in paragraph (a)(1) of this section shall be made by such corporation joining in the making of the consolidated return for such year. A corporation shall be deemed to have joined in the making of such return for such year if it files a Form 1122 in the manner specified in paragraph (h)(2) of this section.

(2) *Consent under facts and circumstances.* If a member of the group fails to file Form 1122, the Commissioner may under the facts and circumstances determine that such member has joined in the making of a consolidated return by such group. The following circumstances, among others, will be taken into account in making this determination:

(i) Whether or not the income and deductions of the member were included in the consolidated return;

(ii) Whether or not a separate return was filed by the member for that taxable year; and

(iii) Whether or not the member was included in the affiliations schedule, Form 851.

If the Commissioner determines that the member has joined in the making of the consolidated return, such member shall be treated as if it had filed a Form 1122 for such year for purposes of paragraph (h)(2) of this section.

(3) *Failure to consent due to mistake.* If any member has failed to join in the making of a consolidated return under either subparagraph (1) or (2) of this paragraph, then the tax liability of each member of the group shall be determined on the basis of separate returns unless the common parent corporation establishes to the satisfaction of the Commissioner that the failure of such member to join in the making of the consolidated return was due to a mistake of law or fact, or to inadvertence. In such case, such member shall be treated as if it had filed a Form 1122 for such year for purposes of paragraph (h)(2) of this section, and thus joined in the making of the consolidated return for such year.

(c) *Election to discontinue filing consolidated returns*—(1) *Good cause*—(i) *In general.* Notwithstanding that a consolidated return is required for a taxable year, the Commissioner, upon application by the common parent, may for good cause shown grant permission to a group to discontinue filing consolidated returns. Any such application shall be made to the Commissioner of Internal Revenue, Washington, D.C. 20224, and shall be made not later than the 90th day before the due date for the filing of the consolidated return (including extensions of time). In addition, if an amendment of the Code, or other law affecting the computation of tax liability, is enacted and the enactment is effective for a taxable year ending before or within 90 days after the date of enactment, then application for such a taxable year may be made not later than the 180th day after the date of enactment, and if the application is approved the permission to discontinue filing consolidated returns will apply to such taxable year notwithstanding that a consolidated return has already been filed for such year.

(ii) *Substantial adverse change in law affecting tax liability.* Ordinarily, the Commissioner will grant a group permission to discontinue filing consolidated returns if the net result of all amendments to the Code or regulations with effective dates commencing within the taxable year has a substantial adverse effect on the consolidated tax liability of the group for such year relative to what the aggregate tax liability would be if the members of the group filed separate returns for such year. Thus, for example, assume P and S filed a consolidated return for the calendar year 1966 and that the provisions of the Code have been amended by a bill which was enacted by Congress in 1966, but which is first effective for taxable years beginning on or after January 1, 1967. Assume further that P makes a timely application to discontinue filing consolidated returns. In order to determine whether the amendments have a substantial adverse effect on the consolidated tax liability for 1967, relative to what the aggregate tax liability would be if the members of the group filed separate returns for 1967, the difference between the tax liability of the group computed on a consolidated basis and taking into account the changes in the law effective for 1967 and the aggregate tax liability of the members of the group computed as if each such

Reg. § 1.1502-75(a)(2)

member filed separate returns for such year (also taking into account such changes) shall be compared with the difference between the tax liability of such group for 1967 computed on a consolidated basis without regard to the changes in the law effective in such year and the aggregate tax liability of the members of the group computed as if separate returns had been filed by such members for such year without regard to the changes in the law effective in such year.

(iii) *Other factors.* In addition, the Commissioner will take into account other factors in determining whether good cause exists for granting permission to discontinue filing consolidated returns beginning with the taxable year, including—

(*a*) Changes in law or circumstances, including changes which do not affect Federal income tax liability,

(*b*) Changes in law which are first effective in the taxable year and which result in a substantial reduction in the consolidated net operating loss (or consolidated unused investment credit) for such year relative to what the aggregate net operating losses (or investment credits) would be if the members of the group filed separate returns for such year, and

(*c*) Changes in the Code or regulations which are effective prior to the taxable year but which first have a substantial adverse effect on the filing of a consolidated return relative to the filing of separate returns by members of the group in such year.

(2) *Discretion of Commissioner to grant blanket permission*—(i) *Permission to all groups.* The Commissioner, in his discretion, may grant all groups permission to discontinue filing consolidated returns if any provision of the Code or regulations has been amended and such amendment is of the type which could have a substantial adverse effect on the filing of consolidated returns by substantially all groups, relative to the filing of separate returns. Ordinarily, the permission to discontinue shall apply with respect to the taxable year of each group which includes the effective date of such an amendment.

(ii) *Permission to a class of groups.* The Commissioner, in his discretion, may grant a particular class of groups permission to discontinue filing consolidated returns if any provision of the Code or regulations has been amended and such amendment is of the type which could have a substantial adverse effect on the filing of consolidated returns by substantially all such groups relative to the filing of separate returns. Ordinarily, the permission to discontinue shall apply with respect to the taxable year of each group within the class which includes the effective date of such an amendment.

(3) *Time and manner for exercising election.* If, under subparagraph (1) or (2) of this paragraph, a group has an election to discontinue filing consolidated returns for any taxable year and such group wishes to exercise such election, then the common parent must file a separate return for such year on or before the last day prescribed by law (including extensions of time) for the filing of the consolidated return for such year. See section 6081 (relating to extensions of time for filing returns).

(d) *When a group remains in existence*—(1) *General rule.* A group remains in existence for a tax year if the common parent remains as the common parent and at least one subsidiary that was affiliated with it at the end of the prior year remains affiliated with it at the beginning of the year, whether or not one or more corporations have ceased to be subsidiaries at any time after the group was formed. Thus, for example, assume that individual A forms corporation P. P acquires 100 percent of the stock of corporation S on January 1, 1965, and P and S file a consolidated return for the calendar year 1965. On May 1, 1966, P acquires 100 percent of the stock of S-1, and on July 1, 1966, P sells the stock of S. The group (consisting originally of P and S) remains in existence in 1966 since P has remained as the common parent and at least one subsidiary (now S-1) remains affiliated with it.

(2) *Common parent no longer in existence*—(i) *Mere change in identity.* For purposes of this paragraph, the common parent corporation shall remain as the common parent irrespective of a mere change in identity, form, or place of organization of such common parent corporation (see section 368(a)(1)(F)).

(ii) *Transfer of assets to subsidiary.* The group shall be considered as remaining in existence notwithstanding that the common parent is no longer in existence if the members of the affiliated group succeed to and become the owners of substantially all of the assets of such former parent and there remains one or more chains of includible corporations connected through stock ownership with a common parent corporation which is an includible corporation and which was a member of the group prior to the date such former parent ceases to exist. For purposes of applying paragraph (f)(2)(i) of § 1.1502-1 to separate return years ending on or before the date on which the former parent ceases to exist, such former parent, and not the new common parent, shall be considered to be the corporation described in such paragraph.

Reg. § 1.1502-75(d)(2)

(iii) *Taxable years.* If a transfer of assets described in subdivision (ii) of this subparagraph is an acquisition to which section 381(a) applies and if the group files a consolidated return for the taxable year in which the acquisition occurs, then for purposes of section 381—

(a) The former common parent shall not close its taxable year merely because of the acquisition, and all taxable years of such former parent ending on or before the date of acquisition shall be treated as taxable years of the acquiring corporation, and

(b) The corporation acquiring the assets shall close its taxable year as of the date of acquisition, and all taxable years of such corporation ending on or before the date of acquisition shall be treated as taxable years of the transferor corporation.

(iv) *Exception.* With respect to acquisitions occurring before January 1, 1971, subdivision (iii) of this subparagraph shall not apply if the group, in its income tax return, treats the taxable year of the former common parent as having closed as of the date of acquisition.

(3) *Reverse acquisitions*—(i) *In general.* If a corporation (hereinafter referred to as the "first corporation") or any member of a group of which the first corporation is the common parent acquires after October 1, 1965—

(a) Stock of another corporation (hereinafter referred to as the second corporation), and as a result the second corporation becomes (or would become but for the application of this subparagraph) a member of a group of which the first corporation is the common parent, or

(b) Substantially all the assets of the second corporation,

in exchange (in whole or in part) for stock of the first corporation, and the stockholders (immediately before the acquisition) of the second corporation, as a result of owning stock of the second corporation, own (immediately after the acquisition) more than 50 percent of the fair market value of the outstanding stock of the first corporation, then any group of which the first corporation was the common parent immediately before the acquisition shall cease to exist as of the date of acquisition, and any group of which the second corporation was the common parent immediately before the acquisition shall be treated as remaining in existence (with the first corporation becoming the common parent of the group). Thus, assume that corporations P and S comprised groups PS (P being the common parent), that P was merged into corporation T (the common parent of a group composed of T and corporation U), and that the shareholders of P immediately before the merger, as a result of owning stock in P, own 90 percent of the fair market value of T's stock immediately after the merger. The group of which P was the common parent is treated as continuing in existence with T and U being added as members of the group, and T taking the place of P as the common parent.

For purposes of determining under (a) of this subdivision whether the second corporation becomes (or would become) a member of the group of which the first corporation is the common parent, and for purposes of determining whether the former stockholders of the second corporation own more than 50 percent of the outstanding stock of the first corporation, there shall be taken into account any acquisitions or redemptions of the stock of either corporation which are pursuant to a plan of acquisition described in (a) or (b) of this subdivision.

(ii) *Prior ownership of stock.* For purposes of subdivision (i) of this subparagraph, if the first corporation, and any members of a group of which the first corporation is the common parent, have continuously owned for a period of at least five years ending on the date of the acquisition an aggregate of at least 25 percent of the fair market value of the outstanding stock of the second corporation, then the first corporation (and any subsidiary which owns stock of the second corporation immediately before the acquisition) shall, as a result of owning such stock, be treated as owning (immediately after the acquisition) a percentage of the fair market value of the first corporation's outstanding stock which bears the same ratio to (a) the percentage of the fair market value of all the stock of the second corporation owned immediately before the acquisition by the first corporation and its subsidiaries as (b) the fair market value of the total outstanding stock of the second corporation immediately before the acquisition bears to (c) the sum of (1) the fair market value, immediately before the acquisition, of the total outstanding stock of the first corporation, and (2) the fair market value, immediately before the acquisition, of the total outstanding stock of the second corporation (other than any such stock owned by the first corporation and any of its subsidiaries). For example, assume that corporation P owns stock in corporation T having a fair market value of $100,000, that P acquires the remaining stock of T from individuals in exchange for stock of P, that immediately before the acquisition the total outstanding stock of T had a fair market value of $150,000, and that immediately before the acquisition the total outstanding stock of P had a fair market value of $200,000. Assuming P owned at least 25 percent of the fair market value of T's stock for five years, then for purposes

Reg. § 1.1502-75(d)(3)

of this subparagraph, P is treated as owning (immediately after the acquisition) 40 percent of the fair market value of its own outstanding stock, determined as follows:

$$\frac{\$150,000}{\$200,000 + \$50,000} \times 66\tfrac{2}{3}\% = 40\%$$

Thus, if the former individual stockholders of T own, immediately after the acquisition more than 10 percent of the fair market value of the outstanding stock of P as a result of owning stock of T, the group of which T was the common parent is treated as continuing in existence with P as the common parent, and the group of which P was the common parent before the acquisition ceases to exist.

(iii) *Election.* The provisions of subdivision (ii) of this subparagraph shall not apply to any acquisition occurring in a taxable year ending after October 7, 1969, unless the first corporation elects to have such subdivision apply. The election shall be made by means of a statement, signed by any officer who is duly authorized to act on behalf of the first corporation, stating that the corporation elects to have the provisions of § 1.1502-75(d)(3)(ii) apply and identifying the acquisition to which such provisions will apply. The statement shall be filed, on or before the due date (including extensions of time) of the return for the group's first consolidated return year ending after the date of the acquisition, with the internal revenue officer with whom such return is required to be filed.

(iv) *Transfer of assets to subsidiary.* This subparagraph shall not apply to a transaction to which subparagraph (2)(ii) of this paragraph applies.

(v) *Taxable years.* If, in a transaction described in subdivision (i) of this subparagraph, the first corporation files a consolidated return for the first taxable year ending after the date of acquisition, then—

(*a*) The first corporation, and each corporation which, immediately before the acquisition, is a member of the group of which the first corporation is the common parent, shall close its taxable year as of the date of acquisition, and each such corporation shall, immediately after the acquisition, change to the taxable year of the second corporation, and

(*b*) If the acquisition is a transaction described in section 381(a)(2), then for purposes of section 381—

(*1*) All taxable years ending on or before the date of acquisition, of the first corporation and each corporation which, immediately before the acquisition, is a member of the group of which the first corporation is the common parent, shall be treated as taxable years of the transfer corporation, and

(*2*) The second corporation shall not close its taxable year merely because of such acquisition, and all taxable years ending on or before the date of acquisition, of the second corporation and each corporation which, immediately before the acquisition, is a member of any group of which the second corporation is the common parent, shall be treated as taxable years of the acquiring corporation.

(vi) *Exception.* With respect to acquisitions occurring before April 17, 1968, subdivision (v) of this subparagraph shall not apply if the parties to the transaction, in their income tax returns, treat subdivision (i) as not affecting the closing of taxable years or the operation of section 381.

(4) [Reserved.]

(5) *Coordination with section 833*—(i) *Election to continue old group.* If, solely by reason of the enactment of section 833 (relating to certain Blue Cross or Blue Shield organizations and certain other health insurers), an organization to which section 833 applies (a "section 833 organization") became the new common parent of an old group on January 1, 1987, the old group may elect to continue in existence with that section 833 organization as its new common parent, provided all the old groups having the same section 833 organization as their new common parent elect to continue in existence. To revoke this election, see paragraph (d)(5)(x) of this section. To file as a new group, see paragraph (d)(5)(v) of this section.

(ii) *Old group.* For purposes of this paragraph (d)(5), an old group is a group which, for its last taxable year ending in 1986, either filed a consolidated return or was eligible to (but did not) file a consolidated return.

(iii) *Manner of electing to continue*—(A) *Deemed election.* If all the members of all the old groups having the same section 833 organization as their new common parent are included for the first taxable year beginning after December 31, 1986, on the same consolidated (or amended consolidated) return and a Form 1122 was not filed, the old groups are deemed to have elected under paragraph (d)(5)(i) of this section to continue in existence.

(B) *Delayed election.* If a deemed election to continue in existence was not made under paragraph (d)(5)(iii)(A) of this section, all the members of all the old groups having the same section 833 organization as their new common parent may make a delayed election under para-

Reg. § 1.1502-75(d)(5)

graph (d)(5)(i) of this section to continue in existence by

(1) filing an appropriate consolidated (or amended consolidated) return or returns for each taxable year beginning after December 31, 1986, (notwithstanding § 1.1502-75(a)(1)) on or before January 3, 1991 and

(2) on the top of any such return prominently affixing a statement containing the following declaration: "THIS RETURN" (or, if applicable, "AMENDED RETURN") "REFLECTS A DELAYED ELECTION TO CONTINUE UNDER § 1.1502-75T(d)(5)(iii)(B)". A delayed election to continue in existence automatically revokes a deemed election to file as a new group which was made under paragraph (d)(5)(vi) of this section.

(iv) *Effects of election to continue in existence.* If an old group or groups elect to continue in existence under paragraph (d)(5)(i) of this section, the following rules apply:

(A) *Taxable years.* Each member that filed returns other than on a calendar year basis shall close its taxable year on December 31, 1986, and change to a calendar year beginning on January 1, 1987. See section 843 and § 1.1502-76(a)(1).

(B) *Carryovers from separate return limitation years.* For purposes of applying the separate return limitation year rules to carryovers from taxable years beginning before 1987 to taxable years beginning after 1986, the following rules apply:

(1) Any taxable year beginning before 1987 of a corporation that was not a member of an old group (including a section 833 organization) will be treated as a separate return limitation year;

(2) Any taxable year beginning before 1987 of a corporation that was a member of an old group that, without regard to this section and the enactment of section 833, was a separate return limitation year will continue to be treated as a separate return limitation year;

(3) Any taxable year beginning before 1987 of a member of an old group (other than a separate return limitation year described in paragraph (d)(5)(iv)(B)(2) of this section) will not be treated as a separate return limitation year with respect to any corporation that was a member of such group for each day of that taxable year; and

(4) Any taxable year beginning before 1987 of a member of an old group will be treated as a separate return limitation year with respect to any corporation that was not a member of such group for each day of that taxable year (*e.g.*, a corporation that was not a member of an old group, including a section 833 organization, or a corporation that was a member of another old group).

(C) *Five-year rules for life-nonlife groups.* Any life-nonlife election under section 1504(c)(2) in effect for an old group remains in effect. Any old group which was eligible to make a life-nonlife election will remain eligible to make the election. For purposes of section 1503(c), a nonlife member is treated as ineligible under § 1.1502-47(d)(13) with respect to a life member, unless both were members of the same affiliated group (determined without regard to the exclusions in section 1504(b)(1) and (2)) for five taxable years immediately preceding the taxable year in which the loss arose. See paragraph (d)(5)(ix) of this section for a tacking rule.

(v) *Election to file as a new group.* If, solely by reason of the enactment of section 833, a section 833 organization became the new common parent of an old group on January 1, 1987, the application of the five-year prohibition on reconsolidation in section 1504(a)(3)(A) to the old group is waived and the old group together with the new section 833 organization common parent may elect to file as a new group provided that all includible corporations elect to file a consolidated (or amended consolidated) return as a new group for the first taxable year beginning after December 31, 1986. To revoke this election, see paragraph (d)(5)(x) of this section.

(vi) *Manner of electing to file as a new group*—(A) *Deemed election.* The old group or groups and the section 833 organization are deemed to have elected under paragraph (d)(5)(v) of this section to file as a new group by filing, for the first taxable year beginning after December 31, 1986, a Form 1122 and a consolidated (or amended consolidated) tax return.

(B) *Delayed election.* If a deemed election to file as a new group was not made pursuant to paragraph (d)(5)(vi)(A) of this section, the old group or groups and the section 833 organization may make a delayed election under paragraph (d)(5)(v) of this section to file as a new group by

(1) filing an appropriate consolidated (or amended consolidated) return or returns for each taxable year beginning after December 31, 1986, (notwithstanding § 1.1502-75(a)(1)) on or before January 3, 1991 and

(2) on the top of any such return prominently affixing a statement containing the following declaration: "THIS RETURN" (or, if applicable, "AMENDED RETURN") "REFLECTS A DELAYED ELECTION TO FILE AS A NEW GROUP UNDER § 1.1502-75T(d)(5)(vi)(B)". A delayed election to

Reg. § 1.1502-75(d)(5)

file as a new group automatically revokes any deemed election to continue in existence which was made under paragraph (d)(5)(iii) of this section.

(vii) *Effects of election to file as a new group.* If an old group or groups elect to file as a new group under paragraph (d)(5)(v) of this section, the following rules apply:

(A) *Termination.* Each old group is treated as if it terminated on January 1, 1987, and the termination is not treated as resulting from the acquisition by a nonmember of all of the stock of the common parent.

(B) *Taxable years.* Each member that filed returns other than on a calendar year basis shall close its taxable year on December 31, 1986, and change to a calendar year beginning on January 1, 1987. See section 843 and § 1.1502-76(a)(1).

(C) *Separate return limitation year and life-nonlife groups.* For purposes of § 1.1502-1(f), sections 1503(c) and 1504(c), and § 1.1502-47, the group is treated as coming into existence as a new group on January 1, 1987. Thus, for example, paragraphs (d)(5)(iv)(B) and (C) of this section do not apply.

(viii) *Earnings and profits.* All distributions after January 1, 1987 by a corporation, whether or not such corporation was a member of an old group, to an existing Blue Cross or Blue Shield organization (as defined in section 833(c)(2)) out of earnings and profits accumulated before 1987 are deemed made out of earnings and profits accumulated in pre-affiliation years. See § 1.1502-32(h)(5).

(ix) *Five-year tacking rules for certain life-nonlife groups.* For purposes of applying § 1.1502-47(d)(5) and (12) to any taxable year ending after 1986 to a corporation, whether or not the corporation was a member of an old group, (A) the determination of whether the corporation was in existence and a member or tentatively treated as a member of a group, for taxable years ending before 1987, is made without regard to the exclusions under section 1504(b)(1) and (2) of any section 833 organization or life insurance company (as the case may be) and (B) a section 833 organization is not treated as having a change in tax character solely by reason of the loss of its tax-exempt status due to the enactment of section 833. This paragraph (d)(5)(ix) does not apply if an election to file as a new group under paragraph (d)(5)(v) of this section is made.

(x) *Time to revoke elections made before September 5, 1990.* An election by an old group to continue in existence or to file as a new group that was made (or deemed made) before September 5, 1990 may be revoked by filing an appropriate return (or returns) on or before January 3, 1991. For purposes of this paragraph (d)(5)(x), appropriate returns include separate returns filed by each member of the group or consolidated returns filed in accordance with a delayed election either under paragraph (d)(5)(iii)(B) or (vi)(B) of this section.

(xi) *Examples.* The following examples illustrate this paragraph (d)(5). In these examples, each corporation uses the calendar year as its taxable year.

Example 1. B is a section 833 organization. For several years, B has owned all of the outstanding stock of X, Y, and Z. X has owned all the outstanding stock of X_1, throughout X_1's existence and Y has owned all of the outstanding stock of Y_1 throughout Y_1's existence. For 1986, X and X_1 filed a consolidated federal income tax return but Y and Y_1 filed separate returns. Under paragraph (d)(5)(ii) of this section, X and X_1 and Y and Y_1 each constitute an old group because they either filed a consolidated return or were eligible to file a consolidated return for 1986. The X and Y groups may elect under paragraph (d)(5)(i) of this section to continue in existence. If they elect to continue, under paragraph (d)(5)(iv)(B) of this section, the separate return limitation year rules apply as follows: any taxable year of B or Z beginning before 1987 is treated as a separate return limitation year with respect to each other and to all other members of the group; any taxable year of X or X_1 beginning before 1987 is treated as a separate return limitation year with respect to B, Z, Y and Y_1, but not with respect to each other; and any taxable year of Y or Y_1 beginning before 1987 is treated as a separate return limitation year with respect to B, Z, X and X_1, but not with respect to each other.

Example 2. The facts are the same as in Example 1 except that B is owned by C, another section 833 organization. If the X and Y groups elect to continue, the results are the same as in Example 1, except that, under paragraph (d)(5)(iv)(B)(*1*) of this section, for purposes of applying the separate return limitation year rules, any taxable year of C beginning before 1987 is also treated as a separate return limitation year with respect to all other members of the group.

Example 3. The facts are the same as in Example 1 except that Y purchased Y_1 on January 1, 1985. If the X and Y groups elect to continue, the results are the same as in Example 1, except that, under paragraph (d)(5)(iv)(B)(*2*) of this section, for purposes of applying the separate return limitation year rules, any taxable year of Y_1 beginning before 1985 is treated as a separate return limitation year with respect to Y as

Reg. § 1.1502-75(d)(5)

well as with respect to all other members of the group.

Example 4. B, a section 833 organization, has owned all the stock of X since November 1984. X has owned all the stock of L, a life insurance company, throughout L's existence. In 1986, X and L properly filed a life-nonlife consolidated return. Under paragraph (d)(5)(i) of this section, the X group elects to continue in existence. Under paragraph (d)(5)(iv)(C) of this section, the life-nonlife election will remain in effect. However, losses of B which arise before 1990 cannot be used to offset the income of L. See section 1503(c)(2) and § 1.1502-47(d)(13) and paragraph (d)(5)(iv)(C) of this section. Under paragraph (d)(5)(iv)(B) of this section, the separate return limitation year rules apply as follows: any taxable year of B beginning before 1987 is treated as a separate return limitation year with respect to all other members of the group; and any taxable year of X or L beginning before 1987 is treated as a separate return limitation year with respect to B, but not with respect to each other.

Example 5. The facts are the same as [in] Example 4 except that, on January 1, 1984, B formed L_1, a life insurance company. Under paragraph (d)(5)(ix) of this section and section 1504(c), the first year L_1 is eligible to join in B's life-nonlife election is 1989.

Example 6. The facts are the same as in Example 4 except that B and the X group elect under paragraph (d)(5)(v) of this section to file as a new group. The X group will be considered to have terminated under § 1.1502-75(d)(1) on December 31, 1986. X and L are each separately subject to the separate return limitation year rules of § 1.1502-1(f). The first year L and L_1 are eligible to join the new group in a life-nonlife election is 1992 (five years after the new group is formed). See section 1504(c)(2) and paragraphs (d)(5)(vii)(C) and (ix) of this section.

(e) *Failure to include subsidiary.* If a consolidated return is required for the taxable year under the provisions of paragraph (a)(2) of this section, the tax liability of all members of the group for such year shall be computed on a consolidated basis even though—

(1) Separate returns are filed by one or more members of the group, or

(2) There has been a failure to include in the consolidated return the income of any member of the group.

If subparagraph (1) of this paragraph applies, the amounts assessed or paid upon the basis of separate returns shall be considered as having been assessed or paid upon the basis of a consolidated return.

(f) *Inclusion of one or more corporations not members of the group*—(1) *Method of determining tax liability.* If a consolidated return includes the income of a corporation which was not a member of the group at any time during the consolidated return year, the tax liability of such corporation will be determined upon the basis of a separate return (or a consolidated return of another group, if paragraph (a)(2) or (b)(3) of this section applies), and the consolidated return will be considered as including only the income of the corporations which were members of the group during that taxable year. If a consolidated return includes the income of two or more corporations which were not members of the group but which constitute another group, the tax liability of such corporations will be computed in the same manner as if separate returns had been made by such corporations unless the Commissioner upon application approves the making of a consolidated return for the other group or unless under paragraph (a)(2) of this section a consolidated return is required for the other group.

(2) *Allocation of tax liability.* In any case in which amounts have been assessed and paid upon the basis of a consolidated return and the tax liability of one or more of the corporations included in the consolidated return is to be computed in the manner described in subparagraph (1) of this paragraph, the amounts so paid shall be allocated between the group composed of the corporations properly included in the consolidated return and each of the corporations the tax liability of which is to be computed on a separate basis (or on the basis of a consolidated return of another group) in such manner as the corporations which were included in the consolidated return may, subject to the approval of the Commissioner, agree upon or in the absence of an agreement upon the method used in allocating the tax liability of the members of the group under the provisions of section 1552(a).

(g) *Computing periods of limitation*—(1) *Income incorrectly included in consolidated return.* If—

(i) A consolidated return is filed by a group for the taxable year, and

(ii) The tax liability of a corporation whose income is included in such return must be computed on the basis of a separate return (or on the basis of a consolidated return with another group),

then for the purpose of computing any period of limitation with respect to such separate return (or such other consolidated return), the filing of such consolidated return by the group shall be considered as the making of a return by such corporation.

Reg. § 1.1502-75(e)(1)

(2) *Income incorrectly included in separate returns.* If a consolidated return is required for the taxable year under the provisions of paragraph (a)(2) of this section, the filing of separate returns by the members of the group for such year shall not be considered as the making of a return for the purpose of computing any period of limitation with respect to such consolidated return unless there is attached to each such separate return a statement setting forth—

(i) The most recent taxable year of the member for which its income was included in a consolidated return, and

(ii) The reasons for the group's belief that a consolidated return is not required for the taxable year.

(h) *Method of filing return and forms*—(1) *Consolidated return made by common parent corporation.* The consolidated return shall be made on Form 1120 for the group by the common parent corporation. The consolidated return, with Form 851 (affiliations schedule) attached, shall be filed with the district director with whom the common parent would have filed a separate return.

(2) *Filing of Form 1122 for first year.* If, under the provisions of paragraph (a)(1) of this section, a group wishes to exercise its privilege of filing a consolidated return, then a Form 1122 must be executed by each subsidiary and must be attached to the consolidated return for such year. Form 1122 shall not be required for a taxable year if a consolidated return was filed (or was required to be filed) by the group for the immediately preceding taxable year.

(3) *Persons qualified to execute returns and forms.* Each return or form required to be made or prepared by a corporation must be executed by the person authorized under section 6062 to execute returns of separate corporations.

(i) [Reserved]

(j) *Statements and schedules for subsidiaries.* The statement of gross income and deductions and the schedules required by the instructions on the return shall be prepared and filed in columnar form so that the details of the items of gross income, deductions, and credits for each member may be readily audited. Such statements and schedules shall include in columnar form a reconciliation of surplus for each corporation, and a reconciliation of consolidated surplus. Consolidated balance sheets as of the beginning and close of the taxable year of the group, taken from the books of the members, shall accompany the consolidated return and shall be prepared in a form similar to that required for reconciliation of surplus.

(k) *Cross-reference.* See § 1.338(h)(10)-1(d)(7) for special rules regarding filing consolidated returns when a section 338(h)(10) election is made for a target acquired from a selling consolidated group. [Reg. § 1.1502-75.]

☐ [*T.D. 6894,* 9-7-66. Amended by *T.D. 7016,* 10-6-69; *T.D. 7024,* 2-9-70; *T.D. 7244,* 12-29-72; *T.D. 7246,* 12-29-72; *T.D. 8438,* 9-24-92; *T.D. 8515,* 1-12-94; *T.D. 8560,* 8-12-94; *T.D. 8858,* 1-5-2000 *and T.D. 8940,* 2-12-2001.]

[Reg. § 1.1502-76]

§ 1.1502-76. **Taxable year of members of group.**—(a) *Taxable year of members of group*— (1) *Change to parent's taxable year.* The consolidated return of a group must be filed on the basis of the common parent's taxable year, and each subsidiary must adopt the common parent's annual accounting period for the first consolidated return year for which the subsidiary's income is includible in the consolidated return. If any member is on a 52-53-week taxable year, the rule of the preceding sentence shall, with the advance consent of the Commissioner, be deemed satisfied if the taxable years of all members of the group end within the same 7-day period. Any request for such consent shall be filed with the Commissioner of Internal Revenue, Washington, D.C. 20224, not later than the thirtieth day before the due date (not including extensions of time) for the filing of the consolidated return.

(2) *Includible insurance company as member of group.* If an includible insurance company required by section 843 to file its return on the basis of a calendar year is a member of the group and if the common parent of such group files its return on the basis of a fiscal year, then the first consolidated return which includes the income of such insurance company may be filed on the basis of the common parent's fiscal year, provided, however, that if such insurance company is a member of the group on the last day of the common parent's taxable year, all members other than such insurance company change to a calendar year or to a 52-53 week taxable year ending within a 7-day period which includes December 31, effective immediately after the close of the common parent's taxable year. If any member changes to a 52-53 week taxable year, the advance consent of the Commissioner shall be obtained in accordance with subparagraph (1) of this paragraph.

(b) *Items included in the consolidated return*— (1) *General rules*—(i) *In general.* A consolidated return must include the common parent's items of income, gain, deduction, loss, and credit for the entire consolidated return year, and each subsidiary's items for the portion of the year for which it is a member. If the consolidated return includes the items of a corporation for only a portion of its tax year determined without taking this section into account, items for the portion of the year not included in the consolidated return must be included in a separate return (including the consolidated return of another group). The rules of this paragraph (b) must be applied to prevent the duplication or elimination of the corporation's items.

(ii) *The day a corporation becomes or ceases to be a member*—(A) *End of the day rule.*—(*1*) *In general.* If a corporation (S), other than one described in paragraph (b)(1)(ii)(A)(*2*) of this section, becomes or ceases to be a member during a consolidated return year, it becomes or ceases to be a member at the end of the day on which its status as a member changes, and its tax year ends for all Federal income tax purposes at the end of that day. Appropriate adjustments must be made if another provision of the Internal Revenue Code or the regulations thereunder contemplates the event occurring before or after S's change in status. For example, S's items restored under § 1.1502-13 immediately before it becomes a nonmember are taken into account in determining the basis of S's stock under § 1.1502-32. On the other hand, if a section 338(g) election is made in connection with S becoming a member, the deemed asset sale under that section takes place before S becomes a member. See § 1.338-10(a)(5) (deemed sale excluded from purchasing corporation's consolidated return.)

(*2*) *Special rule for former S corporations.* If S becomes a member in a transaction other than in a qualified stock purchase for which an election under section 338(g) is made, and immediately before becoming a member an election under section 1362(a) was in effect, then S will become a member at the beginning of the day the termination of its S corporation election is effective. S's tax year ends for all Federal income tax purposes at the end of the preceding day. This paragraph (b)(1)(ii)(A)(*2*) applies to transactions occurring after November 10, 1999.

(B) *Next day rule.* If, on the day of S's change in status as a member, a transaction occurs that is properly allocable to the portion of S's day after the event resulting in the change, S and all persons related to S under section 267(b) immediately after the event must treat the transaction for all Federal income tax purposes as occurring at the beginning of the following day. A determination as to whether a transaction is properly allocable to the portion of S's day after the event will be respected if it is reasonable and consistently applied by all affected persons. In determining whether an allocation is reasonable, the following factors are among those to be considered—

(*1*) Whether income, gain, deduction, loss, and credit are allocated inconsistently (e.g., to maximize a seller's stock basis adjustments under § 1.1502-32);

(*2*) If the item is from a transaction with respect to S stock, whether it reflects ownership of the stock before or after the event (e.g., if a member transfers encumbered land to nonmember S in exchange for additional S stock in a transaction to which section 351 applies and the exchange results in S becoming a member of the consolidated group, the applicability of section 357(c) to the exchange must be determined under § 1.1502-80(d) by treating the exchange as occurring after the event; on the other hand, if S is a member but has a minority shareholder and becomes a nonmember as a result of its redemption of stock with appreciated property, S's gain under section 311 is treated as from a transaction occurring before the event);

(*3*) Whether the allocation is inconsistent with other requirements under the Internal Revenue Code (e.g., if a section 338(g) election is made in connection with a group's acquisition of S, the deemed asset sale must take place before S becomes a member and S's gain or loss with respect to its assets must be taken into account by S as a nonmember) (but see § 1.338-1(d)); and

(*4*) Whether other facts exist, such as a prearranged transaction or multiples changes in S's status, indicating that the transaction is not properly allocable to the portion of S's day after the event resulting in S's change.

(C) *Successor corporations.* For purposes of this paragraph (b)(1)(ii), any reference to a corporation includes a reference to a successor or predecessor as the context may require. A corporation is a successor if the basis of its assets is determined, directly or indirectly, in whole or in part, by reference to the basis of the assets of another corporation (the predecessor). For example, if a member forms S, S is treated as a member from the beginning of its existence.

(iii) *Group structure changes.* If the common parent ceases to be the common parent but the group remains in existence, adjustments must be made in accordance with the principles of § 1.1502-75(d)(2) and (3).

(2) *Determination of items included in separate and consolidated returns*—(i) *In general.* The returns for the years that end and begin with S becoming (or ceasing to be) a member are separate tax years for all Federal income tax purposes. The returns are subject to the rules of the Internal Revenue Code applicable to short periods, as if S

Reg. § 1.1502-76(b)(2)

ceased to exist on becoming a member (or first existed on becoming a nonmember). For example, cost recovery deductions under section 168 must be allocated for short periods. On the other hand, annualization under section 443 is not required of S solely because it has a short year as a result of becoming a member. (Similarly, section 443 applies with respect to a consolidated return only to the extent that the group's return is for a short period and section 443 applies without taking this paragraph (b) into account.)

(ii) *Ratable allocation of a year's items*—(A) *Application.* Although the periods ending and beginning with S's change in status are different tax years, items (other than extraordinary items) may be ratably allocated between the periods if—

(*1*) S is not required to change its annual accounting period or its method of accounting as a result of its change in status (e.g., because its stock is sold between consolidated groups that have the same annual accounting periods); and

(*2*) An irrevocable ratable allocation election is made under paragraph (b)(2)(ii)(D) of this section.

(B) *General rule*—(*1*) *Allocation within original year.* Under a ratable allocation election, paragraph (b)(2) of this section applies by allocating to each day of S's original year (S's tax year determined without taking this section into account) an equal portion of S's items taken into account in the original year, except that extraordinary items must be allocated to the day that they are taken into account. All persons affected by the election must take into account S's extraordinary items and the ratable allocation of S's remaining items in a manner consistent with the election.

(*2*) *Items to be allocated.* Under ratable allocation, the items to be allocated and their timing, location, character, and source are generally determined by treating the original year as a single tax year, and the items are not subject to the rules of the Internal Revenue Code applicable to short periods (unless the original year is a short period). However, the years ending and beginning with S's change in status are treated as different tax years (and as short periods) with respect to any item carried to or from these years (e.g., a net operating loss carried under section 172) and with respect to the application of section 481.

(*3*) *Multiple applications.* If this paragraph (b) applies more than once with respect to an original year, adjustments must be made in accordance with the principles of this paragraph (b). For example, if S becomes a member of two different consolidated groups during the same original year and ratable allocation is elected with respect to both groups, ratable allocation is generally determined for both groups by treating the original year as a single tax year; however, if ratable allocation is elected only with respect to the first group, the ratable allocation is determined by treating the original year as a short period that does not include the period that S is a member of the second group. Ratable allocation is not a method of accounting, and ratable allocation with respect to one application of this paragraph (b) to S does not require ratable allocation to be subsequently applied with respect to S.

(C) *Extraordinary items.* An extraordinary item is—

(*1*) Any item from the disposition or abandonment of a capital asset as defined in section 1221 (determined without the application of any other rules of law);

(*2*) Any item from the disposition or abandonment of property used in a trade or business as defined in section 1231(b) (determined without the application of any holding period requirement);

(*3*) Any item from the disposition or abandonment of an asset described in section 1221(1), (3), (4), or (5), if substantially all the assets in the same category from the same trade or business are disposed of or abandoned in one transaction (or series of related transactions);

(*4*) Any item from assets disposed of in an applicable asset acquisition under section 1060(c);

(*5*) Any item carried to or from any portion of the original year (e.g., a net operating loss carried under section 172), and any section 481(a) adjustment;

(*6*) The effects of any change in accounting method initiated by the filing of the appropriate form after S's change in status;

(*7*) Any item from the discharge or retirement of indebtedness (e.g., cancellation of indebtedness income or a deduction for retirement at a premium);

(*8*) Any item from the settlement of a tort or similar third-party liability;

(*9*) Any compensation-related deduction in connection with S's change in status (including, for example, deductions from bonus, severance, and option cancellation payments made in connection with S's change in status);

(*10*) Any dividend income from a nonmember that S controls within the meaning of section 304 at the time the dividend is taken into account;

Reg. § 1.1502-76(b)(2)

(*11*) Any deemed income inclusion from a foreign corporation, or any deferred tax amount on an excess distribution from a passive foreign investment company under section 1291;

(*12*) Any interest expense allocable under section 172(h) to a corporate equity reduction transaction causing this paragraph (b) to apply;

(*13*) Any credit, to the extent it arises from activities or items that are not ratably allocated (e.g., the rehabilitation credit under section 47, which is based on placement in service); and

(*14*) Any item which, in the opinion of the Commissioner, would, if ratably allocated, result in a substantial distortion of income in any consolidated return or separate return in which the item is included.

(D) *Election.* The election to ratably allocate items under this paragraph (b)(2)(ii) must be made in a separate statement entitled "THIS IS AN ELECTION UNDER § 1.1502-76(b)(2)(ii) TO RATABLY ALLOCATE THE YEAR'S ITEMS OF [insert name and employer identification number of the member]." The statement must be signed by the member and by the common parent of each affected group, and must be filed with the returns including the items for the years ending and beginning with S's change in status. If two or more members of the same consolidated group, as a consequence of the same plan or arrangement, cease to be members of that group and remain affiliated as members of another consolidated group, an election under this paragraph (b)(2)(ii)(D) may be made only if it is made by each such member. The statement must provide all of the following:

(*1*) Identify the extraordinary items, their amounts, and the separate or consolidated returns in which they are included.

(*2*) Identify the aggregate amount to be ratably allocated, and the portion of the amount included in the separate and consolidated returns.

(*3*) Include the name and employer identification number of the common parent (if any) of each group that must take the items into account.

(iii) *Ratable allocation of a month's items.* If ratable allocation under paragraph (b)(2)(ii) of this section is not elected (e.g., because S is required to change its annual accounting period), this paragraph (b)(2)(iii) may be applied to ratably allocate only S's items taken into account in the month of its change in status, but only if the allocation is consistently applied by all affected persons. The ratable allocation is made by applying the principles of paragraph (b)(2)(ii) of this section under any reasonable method. For example, S may close its books both at the end of the preceding month and at the end of the month of the change, and allocate only its items (other than extraordinary items) from the month of the change. See paragraph (b)(1)(ii)(B) of this section for factors to be considered in determining whether the method is reasonable.

(iv) *Taxes.* To the extent properly taken into account during the member's tax year (determined without the application of this paragraph (b)), Federal, state, local, and foreign taxes are allocated under paragraph (b)(2) of this section on the basis of the items or activities to which the taxes relate. Thus, income tax is allocated based on the inclusion of the income (determined under the principles of this paragraph (b)) to which the tax relates. For example, if a calendar-year domestic corporation has $100 of foreign source dividend income (determined in accordance with United States tax accounting principles but without taking this paragraph (b) into account) that is passive income for purposes of section 904, and $60 of the income is allocated under this paragraph (b) to the period of the calendar year after it becomes a member of a consolidated group, then 60% of the corporation's deemed paid foreign tax credit associated with its dividend income for the calendar year is taken into account in computing the group's passive basket consolidated foreign tax credit. Similarly, property taxes relate to the ownership of property and are allocated over the period that the property is owned. This paragraph (b)(2)(iv) applies without regard to any determination or allocation by another taxing jurisdiction.

(v) *Acquisition of S corporation.* If a corporation is acquired in a transaction to which paragraph (b)(1)(ii)(A)(*2*) of this section applies, then paragraphs (b)(2)(ii) and (iii) of this section do not apply and items of income, gain, loss, deduction, and credit are assigned to each short taxable year on the basis of the corporation's normal method of accounting as determined under section 446. This paragraph (b)(2)(v) applies to transactions occurring after November 10, 1999.

(vi) *Passthrough entities*—(A) *In general.* If S is a partner in a partnership or an owner of a similar interest with respect to which items of the entity are taken into account by S, S is treated, solely for purposes of determining the year to which the entity's items are allocated under paragraph (b)(2) of this section, as selling or exchanging its entire interest in the entity immediately before S's change in status.

Reg. § 1.1502-76(b)(2)

(B) *Treatment as a conduit.* For purposes of this paragraph (b)(2), if a member (together with other members) would be treated under section 318(a)(2) as owning an aggregate of at least 50% of any stock owned by the pass-through entity, the method that is used to determine the inclusion of the entity's items in the consolidated or separate return must be the same method that is used to determine the inclusion of the member's items in the consolidated or separate return.

(C) *Exception for certain foreign entities.* This paragraph (b)(2)(v) does not apply to any foreign corporation generating the deemed inclusion of income, or to any passive foreign investment company generating a deferred tax amount on an excess distribution under section 1291.

(3) *Anti-avoidance rule.* If any person acts with a principal purpose contrary to the purposes of this paragraph (b), to substantially reduce the Federal income tax liability of any person, adjustments must be made as necessary to carry out the purposes of this section.

(4) *Determination of due date for separate return.* Paragraph (c) of this section contains rules for the filing of the separate return referred to in this paragraph (b). In applying paragraph (c) of this section, the due date for the filing of S's separate return shall also be determined without regard to the ending of the tax year under paragraph (b)(1)(ii) of this section or the deemed cessation of its existence under paragraph (b)(2)(i) of this section.

(5) *Examples.* For purposes of the examples in this paragraph (b), unless otherwise stated, P and X are common parents of calendar-year consolidated groups, P owns all of the only class of T's stock, T owns no stock of lower-tier members, all persons use the accrual method of accounting, the facts set forth the only corporate activity, all transactions are between unrelated persons, tax liabilities are disregarded, and any election required under paragraph (b)(2) of this section is properly made. The principles of this paragraph (b) are illustrated by the following examples.

Example 1. Items allocated between consolidated and separate returns. (a) *Facts.* P and S are the only members of the P group. P sells all of S's stock to individual A on June 30, and therefore S becomes a nonmember on July 1 of Year 2.

(b) *Analysis.* Under paragraph (b)(1) of this section, the P group's consolidated return for Year 2 includes P's income for the entire tax year and S's income for the period from January 1 to June 30, and S must file a separate return for the period from July 1 to December 31.

(c) *Acquisition of another subsidiary before end of tax year.* The facts are the same as in paragraph (a) of this *Example 1,* except that on July 31 P acquires all the stock of T (which filed a separate return for its year ending on November 30 of Year 1) and T therefore becomes a member on August 1 of Year 2. Under § 1.1502-75(d) and paragraph (b)(1) of this section, the P group's consolidated return for Year 2 includes P's income for the entire year, S's income from January 1 to June 30, and T's income from August 1 to December 31. S must file a separate return that includes its income from July 1 to December 31, and T must file a separate return that includes its income from December 1 of Year 1 to July 31 of Year 2. (If P had acquired T after December 31, the P group that included S is a different group from the P group that includes T, and, for example, the P group that includes T must make a separate election under section 1501 and § 1.1502-75 if consolidated returns are to be filed.)

Example 2. Group structure change. (a) *Facts.* P owns all of the stock of S and T. Shortly after the beginning of Year 1, P merges into T in a reorganization described in section 368(a)(1)(A) (and in section 368(a)(1)(D)), and P's shareholders receive T's stock in exchange for all of P's stock. The P group is treated under § 1.1502-75(d)(2)(ii) as remaining in existence with T as its common parent.

(b) *Analysis.* Under paragraph (b)(1) of this section, the P group's return must include the common parent's items for the entire consolidated return year and, if the common parent ceases to be the common parent but the group remains in existence, appropriate adjustments must be made. Consequently, although P did not exist for all of Year 1, P's items for the portion of Year 1 ending with the merger are treated as the items of the common parent that must be included in the P group's return for Year 1.

(c) *Reverse acquisition.* Assume instead that X acquires all of P's assets in exchange for more than 50% of X's stock in a reorganization described in section 368(a)(1)(D). The reorganization constitutes a reverse acquisition under § 1.1502-75(d)(3), with the X group terminating and the P group surviving with X as its common parent. Consequently, P's items for the portion of Year 1 ending with the acquisition are treated as the items of the common parent that must be included in the P group's return for Year 1, and X's items are treated for purposes of paragraph (b)(1) of this section as the items of a subsidiary included in the P group's return for the portion of Year 1 for which X is a member.

Reg. § 1.1502-76(b)(5)

Example 3. Ratable allocation. (a) *Facts.* P sells all of T's stock to X, and T becomes a nonmember on July 1 of Year 1. T engages in the production and sale of merchandise throughout Year 1 and is required to use inventories. The sale is treated as causing T's tax year to end on June 30, and the periods beginning and ending with the sale are treated as two tax years for Federal income tax purposes.

(b) *Analysis.* If ratable allocation under paragraph (b)(2)(ii) of this section is not elected, T must perform an inventory valuation as of the acquisition and also as of the end of Year 1. If ratable allocation is elected, T must perform an inventory valuation only as of the close of Year 1, and T's income from inventory is ratably allocated, along with T's other items that are not extraordinary items, between the P and X consolidated returns.

(c) *Merger into nonmember.* Assume instead that T merges into a wholly owned subsidiary of X in a reorganization described in section 368(a)(2)(D), and P receives 10% of X's stock in exchange for all of T's stock. Under paragraph (b)(2)(ii)(B) of this section, because T's tax year ends on June 30 under section 381(b)(1), T's original year determined without taking paragraph (b) of this section into account also ends on June 30. Consequently, a ratable allocation under paragraph (b)(2)(ii) of this section is the same as an allocation based on closing the books.

Example 4. Net operating loss. P sells all of T's stock to X, T becomes a nonmember on June 30 of Year 1, and ratable allocation under paragraph (b)(2)(ii) of this section is elected. Under ratable allocation, the X group has a $100 consolidated net operating loss for Year 1, all of which is attributable to T. However, because of extraordinary items, T has $100 of income for the portion of Year 1 that T is a member of the P group. Under paragraph (b)(2)(ii)(B)(*2*) of this section, T's loss may be carried back from the X group to the portion of Year 1 that T was a member of the P group. See also section 172 and § 1.1502-21(b). Under paragraph (b)(2)(ii)(C)(*5*) of this section, any item carried to or from any portion of the original year is an extraordinary item, and the loss therefore is not taken into account again in determining the ratable allocation under paragraph (b)(2)(ii) of this section.

Example 5. Employee benefit plans. (a) *Facts.* P sells all of T's stock to X, and T becomes a nonmember on June 30 of Year 1. On March 15 of Year 2, T contributes $100 to its retirement plan, which is a qualified plan under section 401(a). T is not required to make quarterly contributions to the plan for Year 1 under section 412(m). The contribution is made on account of T's taxable period beginning on July 1 of Year 1, and is deemed in accordance with section 404(a)(6) to have been made on the last day of T's taxable period beginning on July 1 of Year 1. Ratable allocation under paragraph (b)(2)(ii) of this section is not elected.

(b) *Analysis.* Under paragraph (b) of this section, the sale is treated as causing T's tax year to end on June 30, and the period beginning on July 1 is treated as a separate annual accounting period for all Federal income tax purposes. T's income from January 1 to June 30 is included in the P group's Year 1 return, and T's income from July 1 to December 31 is included in the X group's Year 1 return. Thus, the $100 contribution is deductible by T for the period of Year 1 that it is a member of the X group, subject to the applicable limitations of section 404, if a contribution on the last day of that period would otherwise be deductible.

(c) The facts are the same as in paragraph (a) of this *Example 5*, except that, in accordance with section 404(a)(6), $40 of the $100 contribution is made on account of T's taxable period beginning on January 1 of Year 1 and is deemed to be made on the last day of T's taxable period beginning on January 1 of Year 1. The remaining $60 is made on account of T's taxable period beginning on July 1 of Year 1 and is deemed to be made on the last day of T's taxable period beginning on July 1 of Year 1. As in paragraph (b) of this *Example 5,* under paragraph (b) of this section, the sale is treated as causing T's tax year to end on June 30, and the period beginning on July 1 is treated as a separate annual accounting period for all Federal income tax purposes. The $40 portion of the contribution is deductible by T for the period of Year 1 that it is a member of the P group, subject to the applicable limitations of section 404 and provided that a $40 contribution on the last day of that period would otherwise be deductible for that period, and the $60 portion is deductible by T for the period of Year 1 that it is a member of the X group, subject to the same conditions.

(d) *Ratable allocation.* The facts are the same as in paragraph (a) of this *Example 5,* except that P, T, and X elect ratable allocation under paragraph (b)(2)(ii) of this section and T's deduction for the retirement plan contribution is not an extraordinary item. T's deduction may be ratably allocated, subject to the applicable limitations of section 404, and is allowable only if a contribution on the last day of Year 1 otherwise would be deductible for any period in the year. (The results would be the same if S were an

Reg. § 1.1502-76(b)(5)

unaffiliated corporation when acquired by X, and the due date of its last separate return (including extensions) were before the pension contribution was made on March 15 of Year 2.)

Example 6. Allocation of partnership items. (a) *Facts.* P sells all of T's stock to X, and T becomes a nonmember on June 30 of Year 1. T has a 10% interest in the capital and profits of a calendar-year partnership.

(b) *Analysis.* Under paragraph (b)(2)(vi)(A) of this section, T is treated, solely for purposes of determining T's tax year in which the partnership's items are included, as selling or exchanging its entire interest in the partnership as of P's sale of T's stock. Thus, the deemed disposition is not taken into account under section 708, it does not result in gain or loss being recognized by T, and T's holding period is unaffected. However, under section 706(a), in determining T's income, T is required to include its distributive share of partnership items for the partnership's year ending within or with T's tax year. Under section 706(c)(2), the partnership's tax year is treated as closing with respect to T for this purpose as of P's sale of T's stock. The allocation of T's distributive share of partnership items must be made under § 1.706-1(c)(2)(ii).

(c) *Controlled partnership.* The facts are the same as in paragraph (a) of this *Example 6,* except that T has a 75% interest in the capital and profits of the partnership. Under paragraph (b)(2)(vi)(B) of this section, T's distributive share of the partnership items is treated as T's items for purposes of paragraph (b)(2) of this section. Thus, if ratable allocation under paragraph (b)(2)(ii) of this section is not elected, T's distributive share of the partnership's items must be determined under § 1.706-1(c)(2)(ii) by an interim closing of the partnership's books. Similarly, if ratable allocation is elected for T's items that are not extraordinary items, T's distributive share of the partnership's nonextraordinary items must also be ratably allocated under § 1.706-1(c)(2)(ii).

Example 7. Acquisition of S corporation. (a) *Facts.* Z is a small business corporation for which an election under section 1362(a) was in effect at all times since Year 1. At all times, Z had only 100 shares of stock outstanding, all of which were owned by individual A. On July 1 of Year 3, P acquired all of the Z stock. P does not make an election under section 338(g) with respect to its purchase of the Z stock.

(b) *Analysis.* As a result of P's acquisition of the Z stock, Z's election under section 1362(a) terminates. See sections 1361(b)(1)(B) and 1362(d)(2). Z is required to join in the filing of the P consolidated return. See § 1.1502-75. Z's tax year ends for all Federal income tax purposes on June 30 of Year 3. If no extension of time is sought, Z must file a separate return for the period from January 1 through June 30 of Year 3 on or before March 15 of Year 4. See paragraph (b)(4) of this section. Z will become a member of the P consolidated group as of July 1 of Year 3. See paragraph (b)(1)(ii)(A)(2) of this section. P group's Year 3 consolidated return will include Z's items from July 1 to December 31 of Year 3.

(6) *Effective date*—(i) *General rule.* Except as provided in paragraphs (b)(1)(ii)(A)(2) and (b)(2)(v) of this section, this paragraph (b) applies to corporations becoming or ceasing to be members of consolidated groups on or after January 1, 1995.

(ii) *Prior law.* For prior transactions, see prior regulations under section 1502 as in effect with respect to the transaction. See, e.g., § 1.1502-76(b) and (d) as contained in the 26 CFR part 1 edition revised as of April 1, 1994. However, § 1.1502-76(b)(5) and (6) as contained in the 26 CFR part 1 edition revised as of April 1, 1994 do not apply with respect to corporations becoming or ceasing to be members of consolidated groups on or after January 1, 1995. If both this paragraph (b) and prior law may apply to determine the inclusion of any amount in a return, appropriate adjustments must be made to prevent the omission or duplication of the amount.

(c) *Time for making separate returns for periods not included in consolidated return*—(1) *Consolidated return filed by due date for separate return.* If the group has filed a consolidated return on or before the due date for the filing of a subsidiary's separate return (including extensions of time and determined without regard to any change of its taxable year required under paragraph (a) of this section), then the separate return for any portion of the subsidiary's taxable year for which its income is not included in the consolidated return of the group must be filed no later than the due date of such consolidated return (including extensions of time).

(2) *Consolidated return not filed by due date for separate return.* If the group has not filed a consolidated return on or before the due date for the filing of a subsidiary corporation's separate return (including extensions of time and determined without regard to any change of its taxable year required under paragraph (a) of this section), then on or before such due date such subsidiary shall file a separate return either for the portion of its taxable year for which its income would not be included in a consolidated return if such a return were filed, or for its complete taxable year. However, if a separate return is filed for such

Reg. § 1.1502-76(c)(2)

portion of its taxable year and the group subsequently does not file a consolidated return, such subsidiary corporation shall file a substituted return for its complete taxable year not later than the due date (including extensions of time) prescribed for the filing of the common parent's return. On the other hand, if the return is filed for the subsidiary's complete taxable year and the group later files a consolidated return, such subsidiary must file an amended return not later than the due date (including extensions of time) for the filing of the consolidated return of the group. Such amended return shall be for that portion of such subsidiary's taxable year which is not included in the consolidated return. If, under this subparagraph, a substituted return must be filed, then the return previously filed shall not be considered a return within the meaning of section 6011. If, under this subparagraph, a substituted or amended return must be filed, then, for purposes of sections 6513(a) and 6601(a), the last date prescribed for payment of tax shall be the due date (not including extensions of time) for the filing of the subsidiary's separate return (determined without regard to this subparagraph and without regard to any change of its taxable year required under paragraph (a) of this section).

(3) *Examples.* The provisions of this paragraph may be illustrated by the following examples:

Example (1). Corporation P, which filed a separate return for the calendar year 1966, acquires all of the stock of corporation S as of the close of December 31, 1966. Corporation S reports its income on the basis of a fiscal year ending March 31. On June 15, 1967, the due date for the filing of a separate return by S (assuming no extensions of time), a consolidated return has not been filed for the group (P and S). On such date S may either file a return for the period April 1, 1966, through December 31, 1966, or it may file a return for the complete fiscal year ending March 31, 1967. If S files a return for the short period ending December 31, 1966, and if the group elects not to file a consolidated return for the calendar year 1967, S, on or before March 15, 1968 (the due date of P's return, assuming no extensions of time) must file a substituted return for the complete fiscal year ending March 31, 1967, in lieu of the return previously filed for the short period. Interest is computed from June 15, 1967. If, however, S files a return for the complete fiscal year ending March 31, 1967, and the group elects to file a consolidated return for the calendar year 1967, then S must file an amended return covering the period from April 1, 1966, through December 31, 1966, in lieu of the return previously filed for the complete fiscal year. Interest is computed from June 15, 1967.

Example (2). Assume the same facts as in example (1) except that corporation P acquires all of the stock of corporation S at the close of September 30, 1967, and that P files a consolidated return for the group for 1967 on March 15, 1968 (not having obtained any extensions of time). Since a consolidated return has been filed on or before the due date (June 15, 1968) for the filing of the separate return for the taxable year ending March 31, 1968, the return of S for the short taxable year beginning April 1, 1967, and ending September 30, 1967, should be filed no later than March 15, 1968.

[Reg. § 1.1502-76.]

☐ [T.D. 6894, 9-7-66. Amended by T.D. 7244, 12-29-72; T.D. 7246, 12-29-72; T.D. 8560, 8-12-94; T.D. 8842, 11-9-99; T.D. 8858, 1-5-2000 and T.D. 8940, 2-12-2001.]

[Reg. § 1.1502-77]

§ 1.1502-77. **Common parent agent for subsidiaries.**—(a) *Scope of agency of common parent corporation.* The common parent, for all purposes other than the making of the consent required by paragraph (a)(1) of § 1.1502-75, the making of an election under section 936(e), the making of an election to be treated as a DISC under § 1.992-2 and a change of the annual accounting period pursuant to paragraph (b)(3)(ii) of § 1.991-1, shall be the sole agent for each subsidiary in the group, duly authorized to act in its own name in all matters relating to the tax liability for the consolidated return year. Except as provided in the preceding sentence, no subsidiary shall have authority to act for or to represent itself in any such matter. For example, any election available to a subsidiary corporation in the computation of its separate taxable income must be made by the common parent, as must any change in an election previously made by the subsidiary corporation; all correspondence will be carried on directly with the common parent; the common parent shall file for all extensions of time including extensions of time for payment of tax under section 6164; notices of deficiencies will be mailed only to the common parent, and the mailing to the common parent shall be considered as a mailing to each subsidiary in the group; notice and demand for payment of taxes will be given only to the common parent and such notice and demand will be considered as a notice and demand to each subsidiary; the common parent will file petitions and conduct proceedings before the Tax Court of the United States, and any such petition shall be considered as also having been filed by each such subsidiary. The common parent will file claims for

Reg. § 1.1502-77(a)

refund or credit, and any refund will be made directly to and in the name of the common parent and will discharge any liability of the Government in respect thereof to any such subsidiary; and the common parent in its name will give waivers, give bonds, and execute closing agreements, offers in compromise, and all other documents, and any waiver or bond so given, or agreement, offer in compromise, or any other document so executed, shall be considered as having also been given or executed by each such subsidiary. Notwithstanding the provisions of this paragraph, any notice of deficiency, in respect of the tax for a consolidated return year, will name each corporation which was a member of the group during any part of such period (but a failure to include the name of any such member will not affect the validity of the notice of deficiency as to the other members); any notice and demand for payment will name each corporation which was a member of the group during any part of such period (but a failure to include the name of any such member will not affect the validity of the notice and demand as to the other members); and any levy, any notice of a lien, or any other proceeding to collect the amount of any assessment, after the assessment has been made, will name the corporation from which such collection is to be made. The provisions of this paragraph shall apply whether or not a consolidated return is made for any subsequent year, and whether or not one or more subsidiaries have become or have ceased to be members of the group at any time. Notwithstanding the provisions of this paragraph, the district director may, upon notifying the common parent, deal directly with any member of the group in respect of its liability, in which event such member shall have full authority to act for itself.

(b) *Notification of deficiency to corporation which has ceased to be a member of the group.* If a subsidiary has ceased to be a member of the group and if such subsidiary files written notice of such cessation with the district director with whom the consolidated return is filed, then such district director upon request of such subsidiary will furnish it with a copy of any notice of deficiency in respect of the tax for a consolidated return year for which it was a member and a copy of any notice and demand for payment of such deficiency. The filing of such written notification and request by a corporation shall not have the effect of limiting the scope of the agency of the common parent provided for in paragraph (a) of this section and a failure by such district director to comply with such written request shall not have the effect of limiting the tax liability of such corporation provided for in § 1.1502-6.

(c) *Effect of waiver given by common parent.* Unless the district director agrees to the contrary, an agreement entered into by the common parent extending the time within which an assessment may be made or levy or proceeding in court begun in respect of the tax for a consolidated return year shall be applicable—

(1) To each corporation which was a member of the group during any part of such taxable year, and

(2) To each corporation the income of which was included in the consolidated return for such taxable year, notwithstanding that the tax liability of any such corporation is subsequently computed on the basis of a separate return under the provisions of § 1.1502-75.

(d) *Effect of dissolution of common parent corporation.* If the common parent corporation contemplates dissolution, or is about to be dissolved, or if for any other reason its existence is about to terminate, it shall forthwith notify the district director with whom the consolidated return is filed of such fact and designate, subject to the approval of such district director, another member to act as agent in its place to the same extent and subject to the same conditions and limitations as are applicable to the common parent. If the notice thus required is not given by the common parent, or the designation is not approved by the district director, the remaining members may, subject to the approval of such district director, designate another member to act as such agent, and notice of such designation shall be given to such district director. Until a notice in writing designating a new agent has been approved by such district director, any notice of deficiency or other communication mailed to the common parent shall be considered as having been properly mailed to the agent of the group; or, if such district director has reason to believe that the existence of the common parent has terminated, he may, if he deems it advisable, deal directly with any member in respect of its liability.

(e) *Cross-references*—(1) *Alternative agents.* For rules relating to alternative agents of the group, see § 1.1502-77.

(2) *Groups that include insolvent financial institutions.* For further rules applicable to groups that include insolvent financial institutions, see § 301.6402-7 of this chapter. [Reg. § 1.1502-77.]

☐ [*T.D. 6894, 9-7-66. Amended by T.D. 7323, 9-24-74; T.D. 7673, 2-7-80; T.D. 8226, 9-7-88; T.D. 8387, 12-30-91 and T.D. 8446, 11-5-92.*]

[Reg. § 1.1502-77T]

§ 1.1502-77T. **Alternative agents of the group (temporary).**—(a) *General rules*—(1)

Scope. This section applies if the corporation that is the common parent of the group ceases to be the common parent, whether or not the group remains in existence under § 1.1502-75(d).

(2) *Notice of deficiency.* A notice of deficiency mailed to any one or more corporations referred to in paragraph (a)(4) of this section is deemed for purposes of § 1.1502-77 to be mailed to the agent of the group. If the group has designated an agent that has been approved by the district director under § 1.1502-77(d), a notice of deficiency shall be mailed to that designated agent in addition to any other corporation referred to in paragraph (a)(4) of this section. However, failure by the district director to mail a notice of deficiency to that designated agent shall not invalidate the notice of deficiency mailed to any other corporation referred to in paragraph (a)(4) of this section.

(3) *Waiver of statute of limitations.* A waiver of the statute of limitations with respect to the group given by any one or more corporations referred to in paragraph (a)(4) of this section is deemed to be given by the agent of the group.

(4) *Alternative agents.* The corporations referred to in paragraph (a)(2) and (3) of this section are—

(i) The common parent of the group for all or any part of the year to which the notice or waiver applies,

(ii) A successor to the former common parent in a transaction to which section 381(a) applies,

(iii) The agent designated by the group under § 1.1502-77(d), or

(iv) If the group remains in existence under § 1.1502-75(d)(2) or (3), the common parent of the group at the time the notice is mailed or the waiver given.

(b) *Effective date.* Paragraph (a) of this section applies to statutory notices and waivers of the statute of limitations for taxable years for which the due date (without extensions) of the consolidated return is after September 7, 1988. [Temporary Reg. § 1.1502-77T.]

☐ [T.D. 8226, 9-7-88.]

[Reg. § 1.1502-78]

§ 1.1502-78. **Tentative carryback adjustments.**—(a) *General rule.* If a group has a consolidated net operating loss, a consolidated net capital loss, or a consolidated unused investment credit for any taxable year, then any application under section 6411 for a tentative carryback adjustment of the taxes for a consolidated return year or years preceding such year shall be made by the common parent corporation to the extent such loss or unused investment credit is not apportioned to a corporation for a separate return year pursuant to §§ 1.1502-21(b), 1.1502-22(b), or 1.1502-79(c) (or §§ 1.1502-79A(a), 1.1502-79A(b), or 1.1502-79(c), as appropriate). In the case of the portion of a consolidated net operating loss or consolidated net capital loss or consolidated unused investment credit to which the preceding sentence does not apply, and in the case of a net capital or net operating loss or unused investment credit arising in a separate return year which may be carried back to a consolidated return year, the corporation or corporations to which any such loss or credit is attributable shall make any application under section 6411.

(b) *Special rules*—(1) *Payment of refund.* Any refund allowable under an application referred to in paragraph (a) of this section shall be made directly to and in the name of the corporation filing the application, except that in all cases where a loss is deducted from the consolidated taxable income or a credit is allowed in computing the consolidated tax liability for a consolidated return year, any refund shall be made directly to and in the name of the common parent corporation. The payment of any such refund shall discharge any liability of the Government with respect to such refund.

(2) *Several liability.* If a group filed a consolidated return for a taxable year for which there was an adjustment by reason of an application under section 6411, and if a deficiency is assessed against such group under section 6213(b)(2), then each member of such group shall be severally liable for such deficiency including any interest or penalty assessed in connection with such deficiency.

(3) *Groups that include insolvent financial institutions.* For further rules applicable to groups that include insolvent financial institutions, see § 301.6402-7 of this chapter.

(c) *Examples.* The provisions of paragraphs (a) and (b) of this section may be illustrated by the following examples:

Example (1). Corporations P, S, and S-1 filed a consolidated return for the calendar year 1966. P, S, and S-1 also filed a consolidated return for the calendar year 1969. The group incurred a consolidated net operating loss in 1969 attributable to S-1 which may be carried back to 1966 as a consolidated net operating loss carryback. If a tentative carryback adjustment is desired, P, the common parent, must file an application under section 6411 and any refund will be made to P.

Reg. § 1.1502-78(a)

Example (2). Assume the same facts as in example (1) except that P, S, and S-1 filed separate returns for the calendar year 1969, even though they were members of the same group for such year. S-1 incurred a net operating loss in 1969 which may be carried back to 1966. If a tentative carryback adjustment is desired, S-1 must file an application under section 6411 and any refund from such application will be made to P.

Example (3). Corporations X, Y, and Z filed a consolidated return for the calendar year 1966. Z ceased to be a member of the group in 1967. Z filed a separate return for 1968 while X and Y filed a consolidated return for such year. The group incurred a consolidated net operating loss in 1968 attributable to Y, which may be carried back to 1966. Z also incurred a net operating loss for 1968 which may be carried back to 1966. If a tentative carryback adjustment is claimed with respect to the consolidated net operating loss, X, the common parent, must file an application under section 6411. If a tentative carryback adjustment is desired with respect to Z's loss, Z must file an application. Any refunds attributable to either application will be made to X. If an assessment is made under section 6213(b)(2) to recover an excessive tentative allowance made with respect to calendar year 1966, X, Y, and Z are severally liable for such assessment.

Example (4). Corporations L and M filed a consolidated return for the calendar year 1966. Corporation N filed a separate return for such year. Later, N became a member of the group and filed a consolidated return with the group for the calendar year 1968. The group incurred a consolidated net operating loss in 1968 attributable to N which may be carried back to N's separate return for 1966. If a tentative carryback adjustment is desired, N must file an application under section 6411 and any refund will be made directly to N.

(d) *Adjustments of overpayments of estimated income tax.* If a group paid its estimated income tax on a consolidated basis, then any application under section 6425 for an adjustment of overpayment of estimated income tax shall be made by the common parent corporation. If the members of a group paid estimated income taxes on a separate basis, then any application under section 6425 shall be made by the member of the group which claims an overpayment on a separate basis. Any refund allowable under an application under section 6425 shall be made directly to and in the name of the corporation filing the application.

(e) *Time for filing application*—(1) *General rule.* The provisions of section 6411(a) apply to the filing of an application for a tentative carryback adjustment by a consolidated group.

(2) *Special rule for new members*—(i) *New member.* A new member is a corporation that, in the preceding taxable year, did not qualify as a member, as defined in § 1.1502-1(b), of the consolidated group that it now joins.

(ii) *End of taxable year.* Solely for the purpose of complying with the twelve-month requirement for making an application for a tentative carryback adjustment under section 6411(a), the separate return year of a qualified new member shall be treated as ending on the same date as the end of the current taxable year of the consolidated group that the qualified new member joins.

(iii) *Qualified new member.* A new member of a consolidated group qualifies for purposes of the provisions of this paragraph (e)(2) if, immediately prior to becoming a new member, either—

(A) It was the common parent of a consolidated group; or

(B) It was not required to join in the filing of a consolidated return.

(iv) *Examples.* The provisions of this paragraph (e)(2) may be illustrated by the following examples:

Example 1. Individual A owns 100 percent of the stock of X, a corporation that is not a member of a consolidated group and files separate tax returns on a calendar year basis. On January 31 of year 1, X becomes a member of the Y consolidated group, which also files returns on a calendar year basis. X is a qualified new member as defined in paragraph (e)(2)(iii)(B) of this section because, immediately prior to becoming a new member of the Y consolidated group, X was not required to join in the filing of a consolidated return. As a result of its becoming a new member of Group Y, X's separate return for the short taxable year (January 1 of year 1 through January 31 of year 1) is due September 15 of year 2 (with extensions). See § 1.1502-76(c). Group Y's consolidated return is also due September 15 of year 2 (with extensions). See '1.1502-76(c). Solely for the purpose of complying with the twelve-month requirement for making an application for a tentative carryback adjustment under section 6411(a), X's taxable year for the separate return year is treated as ending on December 31 of year 1. X's application for a tentative carryback adjustment is therefore due on or before December 31 of year 2.

Example 2. Assume the same facts as in Example 1 except that immediately prior to becoming a new member of Group Y, X was a member of the Z consolidated group. Because X was required to join in the filing of the consolidated return for Group Z, X is not a qualified new member as defined in paragraph (e)(2)(iii) of this

Reg. § 1.1502-78(e)(2)

section. X's items for the one-month period will be included in the consolidated return for Group Z. Group Z's application for a tentative carryback adjustment, if any, continues to be due within 12 months of the end of its taxable year, which is not affected by X's change in status as a new member of Group Y.

(v) *Effective date.* The provisions of this paragraph (e)(2) apply for applications by new members of consolidated groups for tentative carryback adjustments resulting from net operating losses, net capital losses, or unused business credits arising in separate return years of new members that begin on or after January 1, 2001. [Reg. § 1.1502-78.]

☐ [T.D. 6894, 9-7-66. Amended by T.D. 7059, 7-16-70; T.D. 7246, 12-29-72; T.D. 8387, 12-30-91; T.D. 8446, 11-5-92; T.D. 8677, 6-26-96; T.D. 8823, 6-25-99 and T.D. 8950, 6-21-2001.]

[Reg. § 1.1502-79]

§ 1.1502-79. **Separate return years.**—(a) *Carryover and carryback of consolidated net operating losses to separate return years.* For losses arising in consolidated return years beginning before January 1, 1997, see § 1.1502-79A(a). For later years, see § 1.1502-21(b).

(b) *Carryover and carryback of consolidated net capital loss to separate return years.* For losses arising in consolidated return years beginning before January 1, 1997, see § 1.1502-79A(b). For later years, see § 1.1502-22(b).

(c) *Carryover and carryback of consolidated unused investment credit to separate return years*—(1) *In general.* If a consolidated unused investment credit can be carried under the principles of section 46(b) and paragraph (b) of § 1.1502-3 to a separate return year of a corporation (or could have been so carried if such corporation were in existence) which was a member of the group in the year in which such unused credit arose, then the portion of such consolidated unused credit attributable to such corporation (as determined under subparagraph (2) of this paragraph) shall be apportioned to such corporation (and any successor to such corporation in a transaction to which section 381(a) applies) under the principles of § 1.1502-21(b) (or §§ 1.1502-79A(a)(1) and (2), as appropriate) and shall be an investment credit carryover or carryback to such separate return year.

(2) *Portion of consolidated unused investment credit attributable to a member*—(i) *Investment credit carryback.* In the case of a consolidated unused credit which is an investment credit carryback, the portion of such consolidated unused credit attributable to a member of the group is an amount equal to such consolidated unused credit multiplied by a fraction, the numerator of which is the credit earned of such member for the consolidated unused credit year, and the denominator of which is the consolidated credit earned for such unused credit year.

(ii) *Investment credit carryover.* In the case of a consolidated unused credit which is an investment credit carryover, the portion of such consolidated unused credit attributable to a member of the group is an amount equal to such consolidated unused credit multiplied by a fraction, the numerator of which is the credit earned with respect to any section 38 property placed in service in the consolidated unused credit year and owned by such member (whether or not placed in service by such member) at the close of the last day as of which the taxable income of such member is included in a consolidated return filed by the group, and the denominator of which is the consolidated credit earned for such unused credit year.

(d) *Carryover and carryback of consolidated unused foreign tax*—(1) *In general.* If a consolidated unused foreign tax can be carried under the principles of section 904(d) and paragraph (e) of § 1.1502-4 to a separate return year of a corporation (or could have been so carried if such corporation were in existence) which was a member of the group in the year in which such unused foreign tax arose, then the portion of such consolidated unused foreign tax attributable to such corporation (as determined under subparagraph (2) of this paragraph) shall be apportioned to such corporation (and any successor to such corporation in a transaction to which section 381(a) applies) under the principles of § 1.1502-21(b) (or §§ 1.1502-79A(a)(1) and (2), as appropriate) and shall be deemed paid or accrued in such separate return year to the extent provided in section 904(d).

(2) *Portion of consolidated unused foreign tax attributable to a member.* The portion of a consolidated unused foreign tax for any year attributable to a member of a group is an amount equal to such consolidated unused foreign tax multiplied by a fraction, the numerator of which is the foreign taxes paid or accrued for such year (including those taxes deemed paid or accrued, other than by reason of section 904(d)) to each foreign country or possession (or to all foreign countries or possessions if the overall limitation is effective) by such member, and the denominator of which is the aggregate of all such taxes paid or accrued for such year (including those taxes deemed paid or accrued, other than by reason of section 904(d)) to each such foreign country or possession (or to all

foreign countries or possessions if the overall limitation is effective) by all the members of the group.

(e) *Carryover of consolidated excess charitable contributions to separate return years*—(1) *In general.* If the consolidated excess charitable contributions for any taxable year can be carried under the principles of section 170(b)(2) and paragraph (b) of § 1.1502-24 to a separate return year of a corporation (or could have been so carried if such corporation were in existence) which was a member of the group in the year in which such excess contributions arose, then the portion of such consolidated excess charitable contributions attributable to such corporation (as determined under subparagraph (2) of this paragraph) shall be apportioned to such corporation (and any successor to such corporation in a transaction to which section 381(a) applies) under the principles of § 1.1502-21(b) (or §§ 1.1502-79A(a)(1) and (2), as appropriate) and shall be a charitable contribution carryover to such separate return year.

(2) *Portion of consolidated excess charitable contributions attributable to a member.* The portion of the consolidated excess charitable contributions attributable to a member of a group is an amount equal to such consolidated excess contributions multiplied by a fraction, the numerator of which is the charitable contributions paid by such member for the taxable year, and the denominator of which is the aggregate of all such charitable contributions paid for such year by all the members of the group. [Reg. § 1.1502-27.]

☐ [*T.D. 6894, 9-7-66. Amended by T.D. 7637, 8-6-79; T.D. 7728, 10-31-80; T.D. 8294, 3-9-90; T.D. 8319, 11-19-90; T.D. 8364, 9-13-91; T.D. 8597, 7-12-95; T.D. 8677, 6-26-96 and T.D. 8823, 6-25-99.*]

[Reg. § 1.1502-79A]

§ 1.1502-79A. **Separate return years generally applicable for consolidated return years beginning before January 1, 1997.**—(a) *Carryover and carryback of consolidated net operating losses to separate return years.*—(1) *In general.*—(i) If a consolidated net operating loss can be carried under the principles of section 172(b) and paragraph (b) of § 1.1502-21A to a separate return year of a corporation (or could have been so carried if such corporation were in existence) which was a member in the year in which such loss arose, then the portion of such consolidated net operating loss attributable to such corporation (as determined under subparagraph (3) of this paragraph) shall be apportioned to such corporation (and any successor to such corporation in a transaction to which section 381(a) applies) and shall be a net operating loss carryover or carryback to such separate return year; accordingly, such portion shall not be included in the consolidated net operating loss carryovers or carrybacks to the equivalent consolidated return year. Thus, for example, if a member filed a separate return for the third year preceding a consolidated return year in which a consolidated net operating loss was sustained and if any portion of such loss is apportioned to such member for such separate return year, such portion may not be carried back by the group to its third year preceding such consolidated return year.

(ii) If a corporation ceases to be a member during a consolidated return year, any consolidated net operating loss carryover from a prior taxable year must first be carried to such consolidated return year, notwithstanding that all or a portion of the consolidated net operating loss giving rise to the carryover is attributable to the corporation which ceases to be a member. To the extent not absorbed in such consolidated return year, the portion of the consolidated net operating loss attributable to the corporation ceasing to be a member shall then be carried to such corporation's first separate return year.

(iii) For rules permitting the reattribution of losses of a subsidiary to the common parent in the case of loss disallowance or basis reduction on the disposition or deconsolidation of stock of the subsidiary, see § 1.1502-20.

(2) *Nonapportionment to certain members not in existence.* Notwithstanding subparagraph (1) of this paragraph, the portion of a consolidated net operating loss attributable to a member shall not be apportioned to a prior separate return year for which such member was not in existence and shall be included in the consolidated net operating loss carrybacks to the equivalent consolidated return year of the group (or, if such equivalent year is a separate return year, then to such separate return year), provided that such member was a member of the group immediately after its organization.

(3) *Portion of consolidated net operating loss attributable to a member.* The portion of a consolidated net operating loss attributable to a member of a group is an amount equal to the consolidated net operating loss multiplied by a fraction, the numerator of which is the separate net operating loss of such corporation, and the denominator of which is the sum of the separate net operating losses of all members of the group in such year having such losses. For purposes of this subparagraph, the separate net operating loss of a member of the group shall be determined under § 1.1502-12 (except that no deduction shall be allowed under section 242), adjusted for the fol-

56,910 Consolidated Returns

See p. 20,601 for regulations not amended to reflect law changes

lowing items taken into account in the computation of the consolidated net operating loss:

(i) The portion of the consolidated dividends received deduction, the consolidated charitable contributions deductions, and the consolidated section 247 deduction, attributable to such member;

(ii) Such member's capital gain net income (net capital gain for taxable years beginning before January 1, 1977) (determined without regard to any net capital loss carryover attributable to such member);

(iii) Such member's net capital loss and section 1231 net loss, reduced by the portion of the consolidated net capital loss attributable to such member (as determined under paragraph (b)(2) of this section); and

(iv) The portion of any consolidated net capital loss carryover attributable to such member which is absorbed in the taxable year.

(4) *Examples.* The provisions of this paragraph may be illustrated by the following examples:

Example (1). (i) Corporation P was formed on January 1, 1966. P filed a separate return for the calendar year 1966. On March 15, 1967, P formed corporation S. P and S filed a consolidated return for 1967. On January 1, 1968, P purchased all the stock of corporation T, which had been formed in 1967 and had filed a separate return for its taxable year ending December 31, 1967.

(ii) P, S, and T join in the filing of a consolidated return for 1968, which return reflects a consolidated net operating loss of $11,000. $2,000 of such consolidated net operating loss is attributable to P, $3,000 to S, and $6,000 to T. Such apportionment of the consolidated net operating loss was made on the basis of the separate net operating losses of each member as determined under subparagraph (3) of this paragraph.

(iii) $5,000 of the 1968 consolidated net operating loss can be carried back to P's separate return for 1966. Such amount is the portion of the consolidated net operating loss attributable to P and S. Even though S was not in existence in 1966, the portion attributable to S can be carried back to P's separate return year, since S (unlike T) was a member of the group immediately after its organization. The 1968 consolidated net operating loss can be carried back against the group's income in 1967 except to the extent (*i.e.*, $6,000) that it is apportioned to T for its 1967 separate return year and to the extent that it was absorbed in P's 1966 separate return year. The portion of the 1968 consolidated net operating loss attributable to T ($6,000) is a net operating loss carryback to its 1967 separate return.

Example (2). (i) Assume the same facts as in example (1). Assume further that on June 15, 1969, P sells all the stock of T to an outsider, that P and S file a consolidated return for 1969 (which includes the income of T for the period January 1 through June 15), and that T files a separate return for the period June 16 through December 31, 1969.

(ii) The 1968 consolidated net operating loss, to the extent not absorbed in prior years, must first be carried to the consolidated return year 1969. Any portion of the $6,000 amount attributable to T which is not absorbed in T's 1967 separate return year or in the 1969 consolidated return year shall then be carried to T's separate return year ending December 31, 1969.

(b) *Carryover and carryback of consolidated net capital loss to separate return years*—(1) *In general.* If a consolidated net capital loss can be carried under the principles of section 1212(a) and paragraph (b) of § 1.1502-22A to a separate return year of a corporation (or could have been so carried if such corporation were in existence) which was a member of the group in the year in which such consolidated net capital loss arose, then the portion of such consolidated net capital loss attributable to such corporation (as determined under subparagraph (2) of this paragraph) shall be apportioned to such corporation (and any successor to such corporation in a transaction to which section 381(a) applies) under the principles of paragraph (a)(1), (2), and (3) of this section and shall be a net capital loss carryback or carryover to such separate return year.

(2) *Portion of consolidated net capital loss attributable to a member.* The portion of a consolidated net capital loss attributable to a member of a group is an amount equal to such consolidated net capital loss multiplied by a fraction, the numerator of which is the net capital loss of such member, and the denominator of which is the sum of the net capital losses of those members of the group having net capital losses. For purposes of this subparagraph, the net capital loss of a member of the group shall be determined by taking into account the following:

(i) Such member's capital gain net income (net capital gain for taxable years beginning before January 1, 1977) or loss (determined without regard to any net capital loss carryover or carryback); and

(ii) Such member's section 1231 net loss, reduced by the portion of the consolidated section 1231 net loss attributable to such member.

(a)[(c) through (e). [Reserved]

Reg. § 1.1502-79A(a)(4)

(f) *Effective date.* Paragraphs (a) and (b) of this section apply to losses arising in consolidated return years to which § 1.1502-21T(g) does not apply for this purpose net operating loss deductions, carryovers, and carrybacks arise in the year from which they are carried. See § 1.1502-21T(g) for effective dates of that section. [Reg. § 1.1502-79A.]

☐ [T.D. 8677, 6-26-96.]

[Reg. § 1.1502-80]

§ 1.1502-80. Applicability of other provisions of law.—(a) *In general.* The Internal Revenue Code, or other law, shall be applicable to the group to the extent the regulations do not exclude its application. Thus, for example, in a transaction to which section 381(a) applies, the acquiring corporation will succeed to the tax attributes described in section 381(c). Furthermore, sections 269 and 482 apply for any consolidated year. Section 304 applies except as provided in paragraph (b) of this section.

(b) *Non-applicability of section 304.* Section 304 does not apply to any acquisition of stock of a corporation in an intercompany transaction or to any intercompany item from such transaction occurring on or after July 24, 1991.

(c) *Deferral of section 165.* For consolidated return years beginning on or after January 1, 1995, stock of a member is not treated as worthless under section 165 before the stock is treated as disposed of under the principles of § 1.1502-19(c)(1)(iii). See §§ 1.1502-11(c) and 1.1502-20 for additional rules relating to stock loss.

(d) *Non-applicability of section 357(c)*—(1) *In general.* Section 357(c) does not apply to any transaction to which § 1.1502-13, § 1.1502-13T, § 1.1502-14, or § 1.1502-14T applies, if it occurs in a consolidated return year beginning on or after January 1, 1995. For example, P, S, and T are members of a consolidated group, P owns all of the stock of S and T with bases of $30 and $20, respectively, S has a $30 basis in its assets and $40 of liabilities, and S merges into T in a transaction described in section 368(a)(1)(A) (and in section 368(a)(1)(D)); section 357(c) does not apply to the merger, P's basis in T's stock increases to $50 ($30 plus $20), and T succeeds to S's $30 basis in the assets transferred subject to the $40 liability. Similarly, if S instead transferred its assets and liabilities to a newly formed subsidiary in a transaction to which section 351 applies, section 357(c) does not apply and S's basis in the subsidiary's stock is a $10 excess loss account. This paragraph (d) does not apply to a transaction if the transferor or transferee becomes a nonmember as part of the same plan or arrangement. The transferor (or transferee) is treated as becoming a nonmember once it is no longer a member of a consolidated group that includes the transferee (or transferor). For purposes of this paragraph (d), any reference to a transferor or transferee includes, as the context may require, a reference to a successor or predecessor.

(2) *Prior period transactions.* If, in a tax year beginning before January 1, 1995, a member's stock with an excess loss account is transferred in a transaction to which § 1.1502-13, § 1.1502-13T, § 1.1502-14, or § 1.1502-14T applies, paragraph (d)(1) of this section applies to the stock transfer to the extent that the income, gain, deduction, or loss (if any) is not taken into account in a tax year beginning before January 1, 1995. For example, if P, S, and T, are members of a consolidated group, T's stock has a excess loss account, and P transfers the T stock to S in 1993 in a transaction to which section 351 and § 1.1502-13 apply, section 357(c) applies to the transfer only to the extent P's gain is taken into account in tax years beginning before January 1, 1995.

(e) *Non-applicability of section 163(e)(5).* Section 163(e)(5) does not apply to any intercompany obligation (within the meaning of § 1.1502-13(g)) issued in a consolidated return year beginning on or after July 12, 1995.

(f) *Non-applicability of section 1031.* Section 1031 does not apply to any intercompany transaction occurring in consolidated return years beginning on or after July 12, 1995. [Reg. § 1.1502-80.]

☐ [T.D. 6894, 9-7-66. Amended by T.D. 8402, 3-13-92; T.D. 8560, 8-12-94; T.D. 8597, 7-12-95 and T.D. 8677, 6-26-96.]

[Reg. § 1.1502-81T]

§ 1.1502-81T. Alaska Native Corporations (Temporary).—(a) *General Rule.* The application of section 60(b)(5) of the Tax Reform Act of 1984 and section 1804(e)(4) of the Tax Reform Act of 1986 (relating to Native Corporations established under the Alaska Native Claims Settlement Act (43 U.S.C. 1601 et seq.)) is limited to the use on a consolidated return of losses and credits of a Native Corporation, and of a corporation all of whose stock is owned directly by a Native Corporation, during any taxable year (beginning after the effective date of such sections and before 1992), or any part thereof, against the income and tax liability of a corporation affiliated with the Native Corporation. Thus, no other tax saving, tax benefit, or tax loss is intended to result from the application of section 60(b)(5) of the Tax Reform Act of 1984 and section 1804(e)(4) of the Tax Reform Act of 1986 to any person (whether or

Reg. § 1.1502-81T(a)

not such person is a member of an affiliated group of which a Native Corporation is the common parent). In particular, except as approved by the Secretary, no positive adjustment under § 1.1502-32(b) will be made with respect to the basis of stock of a corporation that is affiliated with a Native Corporation through application of section 60(b)(5) of the Tax Reform Act of 1984 and section 1804(e)(4) of the Tax Reform Act of 1986.

(b) *Effective dates.* This section applies to taxable years beginning after December 31, 1984. [Temporary Reg. § 1.1502-81T.]

☐ [*T.D.* 8130, 3-13-87. *Amended by T.D.* 8560, 8-12-94.]

[Reg. § 1.1502-90]

§ 1.1502-90. **Table of contents.**—The following list contains the major headings in §§ 1.1502-91 through 1.1502-99:

§ 1.1502-91 Application of section 382 with respect to a consolidated group.

(a) Determination and effect of an ownership change.

(1) In general.

(2) Special rule for post-change year that includes the change date.

(3) Cross-reference.

(b) Definitions and nomenclature.

(c) Loss group.

(1) Defined.

(2) Coordination with rule that ends separate tracking.

(3) Example.

(d) Loss subgroup.

(1) Net operating loss carryovers.

(2) Net unrealized built-in loss.

(3) Loss subgroup parent.

(4) Election to treat loss subgroup parent requirement as satisfied.

(5) Principal purpose of avoiding a limitation.

(6) Special rules.

(7) Examples.

(e) Pre-change consolidated attribute.

(1) Defined.

(2) Example.

(f) Pre-change subgroup attribute.

(1) Defined.

(2) Example.

(g) Net unrealized built-in gain and loss.

(1) In general.

(2) Members included.

(i) Consolidated group with a net operating loss.

(ii) Determination whether a consolidated group has a net unrealized built-in loss.

(iii) Loss subgroup with net operating loss carryovers.

(iv) Determination whether subgroup has a net unrealized built-in loss.

(v) Separate determination of section 382 limitation for recognized built-in losses and net operating losses.

(3) Coordination with rule that ends separate tracking.

(4) Acquisitions of built-in gain or loss assets.

(5) Indirect ownership.

(6) Common parent not common parent for five years.

(h) Recognized built-in gain or loss.

(1) In general. [Reserved]

(2) Disposition of stock or an intercompany obligation of a member.

(3) Intercompany transactions.

(4) Exchanged basis property.

(i) [Reserved]

(j) Predecessor and successor corporations.

§ 1.1502-92 Ownership change of a loss group or a loss subgroup.

(a) Scope.

(b) Determination of an ownership change.

(1) Parent change method.

(i) Loss group.

(ii) Loss subgroup.

(iii) Special rule if election regarding section 1504(a)(1) relationship is made.

(2) Examples.

(3) Special adjustments.

(i) Common parent succeeded by a new common parent.

(ii) Newly created loss subgroup parent.

(iii) Examples.

(4) End of separate tracking of certain losses.

(c) Supplemental rules for determining ownership change.

(1) Scope.

(2) Cause for applying supplemental rule.

(3) Operating rules.

(4) Supplemental ownership change rules.

(i) Additional testing dates for the common parent (or loss subgroup parent).

(ii) Treatment of subsidiary stock as stock of the common parent (or loss subgroup parent).

(iii) Different testing periods.

(iv) Disaffiliation of a subsidiary.

(v) Subsidiary stock acquired first.

(vi) Anti-duplication rule.

(5) Examples.

(d) Testing period following ownership change under this section.

(e) Information statements.

(1) Common parent of a loss group.

(2) Abbreviated statement with respect to loss subgroups.

§ 1.1502-93 *Consolidated section 382 limitation (or subgroup section 382 limitation).*

(a) Determination of the consolidated section 382 limitation (or subgroup section 382 limitation).

(1) In general.

(2) Coordination with apportionment rule.

(b) Value of the loss group (or loss subgroup).

(1) Stock value immediately before ownership change.

(2) Adjustment to value.

(i) In general.

(ii) Anti-duplication.

(3) Examples.

(c) Recognized built-in gain of a loss group or loss subgroup.

(1) In general.

(2) Adjustments.

(d) Continuity of business.

(1) In general.

(2) Example.

(e) Limitations of losses under other rules.

§ 1.1502-94 *Coordination with section 382 and the regulations thereunder when a corporation becomes a member of a consolidated group.*

(a) Scope.

(1) In general.

(2) Successor corporation as new loss member.

(3) Coordination in the case of a loss subgroup.

(4) End of separate tracking of certain losses.

(5) Cross-reference.

(b) Application of section 382 to a new loss member.

(1) In general.

(2) Adjustment to value.

(3) Pre-change separate attribute defined.

(4) Examples.

(c) Built-in gains and losses.

(d) Information statements.

§ 1.1502-95 *Rules on ceasing to be a member of a consolidated group (or loss subgroup).*

(a) In general.

(1) Consolidated group.

(2) Election by common parent.

(3) Coordination with §§ 1.1502-91 through 1.1502-93.

(b) Separate application of section 382 when a member leaves a consolidated group.

(1) In general.

(2) Effect of a prior ownership change of the group.

(3) Application in the case of a loss subgroup.

(4) Examples.

(c) Apportionment of a consolidated section 382 limitation.

(1) In general.

(2) Amount which may be apportioned.

(i) Consolidated section 382 limitation.

(ii) Net unrealized built-in gain.

(3) Effect of apportionment on the consolidated group.

(i) Consolidated section 382 limitation.

(ii) Net unrealized built-in gain.

(4) Effect on corporations to which an apportionment is made.

(i) Consolidated section 382 limitation.

(ii) Net unrealized built-in gain.

(5) Deemed apportionment when loss group terminates.

(6) Appropriate adjustments when former member leaves during the year.

(7) Examples.

(d) Rules pertaining to ceasing to be a member of a loss subgroup.

(1) In general.

(2) Exceptions.

(3) Examples.

(e) Allocation of net unrealized built-in loss.

(1) In general.

(2) Amount of allocation.

(i) In general.

(ii) Transferred basis property and deferred gain or loss.

(iii) Assets for which gain or loss has been recognized.

Reg. § 1.1502-90

(iv) Exchanged basis property.

(v) Two or more members depart during the same year.

(vi) Anti-abuse rule.

(3) Effect of the allocation on the consolidated group.

(4) Effect on corporations to which the allocation is made.

(5) Subgroup principles.

(6) Apportionment of consolidated section 382 limitation (or subgroup section 382 limitation).

(i) In general.

(ii) Special rule for former members that become members of the same consolidated group.

(7) Examples.

(8) Reporting requirement.

(f) Filing the election to apportion the section 382 limitation and net unrealized built-in gain.

(1) Form of the election to apportion.

(2) Signing of the election.

(3) Filing of the election.

(4) Revocation of election.

§ 1.1502-96 Miscellaneous rules.

(a) End of separate tracking of losses.

(1) Application.

(2) Effect of end of separate tracking.

(i) Net operating loss carryovers.

(ii) Net unrealized built-in losses.

(iii) Common parent not common parent for five years.

(3) Continuing effect of end of separate tracking.

(i) In general.

(ii) Example.

(4) Special rule for testing period.

(5) Limits on effects of end of separate tracking.

(b) Ownership change of subsidiary.

(1) Ownership change of a subsidiary because of options or plan or arrangement.

(2) Effect of the ownership change.

(i) In general.

(ii) Pre-change losses.

(3) Coordination with §§ 1.1502-91, 1.1502-92, and 1.1502-94.

(4) Example.

(c) Continuing effect of an ownership change.

(d) Losses reattributed under § 1.1502-20(g).

(1) In general.

(2) Deemed section 381(a) transaction.

(3) Rules relating to owner shifts.

(i) In general.

(ii) Examples.

(4) Rules relating to the section 382 limitation.

(i) Reattributed loss is a pre-change separate attribute of a new loss member.

(ii) Reattributed loss is a pre-change subgroup attribute.

(iii) Potential application of section 382(l)(1).

(iv) Duplication or omission of value.

(v) Special rule for continuity of business requirement.

(5) Election to reattribute section 382 limitation.

(i) Effect of election.

(ii) Examples.

(e) Time and manner of making election under § 1.1502-91(d)(4).

(1) In general.

(2) Election statement.

§ 1.1502-97 Special rules under section 382 for members under the jurisdiction of a court in a title 11 or similar case. [Reserved].

§ 1.1502-98 Coordination with section 383.

§ 1.1502-99 Effective dates.

(a) Effective date.

(b) Special rules.

(1) Election to treat subgroup parent requirement as satisfied.

(2) Principal purpose of avoiding a limitation.

(3) Ceasing to be a member of a loss subgroup.

(i) Ownership change of a loss subgroup.

(ii) Expiration of 5-year period.

(4) Reattribution of net operating loss carryovers under § 1.1502-20(g).

(5) Election to apportion net unrealized built-in gain.

(c) Testing period may include a period beginning before June 25, 1999.

(1) In general.

(2) Transition rule for net unrealized built-in losses.

[Reg. § 1.1502-90.]

☐ [T.D. 8824, 6-25-99.]

Reg. § 1.1502-90

Consolidated Returns

[Reg. § 1.1502-90A]

§ 1.1502-90A. Table of contents.—The following list contains the major headings in §§ 1.1502-91A through 1.1502-99A:

§ 1.1502-91A Application of section 382 with respect to a consolidated group generally applicable for testing dates before June 25, 1999.

(a) Determination and effect of an ownership change.

(1) In general.

(2) Special rule for post-change year that includes the change date.

(3) Cross reference.

(b) Definitions and nomenclature.

(c) Loss group.

(1) Defined.

(2) Coordination with rule that ends separate tracking.

(3) Example.

(d) Loss subgroup.

(1) Net operating loss carryovers.

(2) Net unrealized built-in loss.

(3) Loss subgroup parent.

(4) Principal purpose of avoiding a limitation.

(5) Special rules.

(6) Examples.

(e) Pre-change consolidated attribute.

(1) Defined.

(2) Example.

(f) Pre-change subgroup attribute.

(1) Defined.

(2) Example.

(g) Net unrealized built-in gain and loss.

(1) In general.

(2) Members included.

(i) Consolidated group.

(ii) Loss subgroup.

(3) Acquisitions of built-in gain or loss assets.

(4) Indirect ownership.

(h) Recognized built-in gain or loss.

(1) In general. [Reserved]

(2) Disposition of stock or an intercompany obligation of a member.

(3) Deferred gain or loss.

(4) Exchanged basis property.

(i) [Reserved]

(j) Predecessor and successor corporations.

§ 1.1502-92A Ownership change of a loss group or a loss subgroup generally applicable for testing dates before June 25, 1999.

(a) Scope.

(b) Determination of an ownership change.

(1) Parent change method.

(i) Loss group.

(ii) Loss subgroup.

(2) Examples.

(3) Special adjustments.

(i) Common parent succeeded by a new common parent.

(ii) Newly created loss subgroup parent.

(iii) Examples.

(4) End of separate tracking of certain losses.

(c) Supplemental rules for determining ownership change.

(1) Scope.

(2) Cause for applying supplemental rule.

(3) Operating rules.

(4) Supplemental ownership change rules.

(i) Additional testing dates for the common parent (or loss subgroup parent).

(ii) Treatment of subsidiary stock as stock of the common parent (or loss subgroup parent).

(iii) 5-percent shareholder of the common parent (or loss subgroup parent).

(5) Examples.

(d) Testing period following ownership change under this section.

(e) Information statements.

(1) Common parent of a loss group.

(2) Abbreviated statement with respect to loss subgroups.

§ 1.1502-93A Consolidated section 382 limitation (or subgroup section 382 limitation) generally applicable for testing dates before June 25, 1999.

(a) Determination of the consolidated section 382 limitation (or subgroup section 382 limitation).

(1) In general.

(2) Coordination with apportionment rule.

(b) Value of the loss group (or loss subgroup).

(1) Stock value immediately before ownership change.

(2) Adjustment to value.

(3) Examples.

(c) Recognized built-in gain of a loss group or loss subgroup.

(d) Continuity of business.

(1) In general.

Reg. § 1.1502-90A

56,916 **Consolidated Returns**

See p. 20,601 for regulations not amended to reflect law changes

(2) Example.

(e) Limitations of losses under other rules.

§ 1.1502-94A *Coordination with section 382 and the regulations thereunder when a corporation becomes a member of a consolidated group generally applicable for corporations becoming members of a group before June 25, 1999.*

(a) Scope.

(1) In general.

(2) Successor corporation as new loss member.

(3) Coordination in the case of a loss subgroup.

(4) End of separate tracking of certain losses.

(5) Cross-reference.

(b) Application of section 382 to a new loss member.

(1) In general.

(2) Adjustment to value.

(3) Pre-change separate attribute defined.

(4) Examples.

(c) Built-in gains and losses.

(d) Information statements.

§ 1.1502-95A *Rules on ceasing to be a member of a consolidated group (or loss subgroup) generally applicable for corporations ceasing to be members before June 25, 1999.*

(a) In general.

(1) Consolidated group.

(2) Election by common parent.

(3) Coordination with §§ 1.1502-91T through 1.1502-93T.

(b) Separate application of section 382 when a member leaves a consolidated group.

(1) In general.

(2) Effect of a prior ownership change of the group.

(3) Application in the case of a loss subgroup.

(4) Examples.

(c) Apportionment of a consolidated section 382 limitation.

(1) In general.

(2) Amount of apportionment.

(3) Effect of apportionment on the consolidated section 382 limitation.

(4) Effect on corporations to which the consolidated section 382 limitation is apportioned.

(5) Deemed apportionment when loss group terminates.

(6) Appropriate adjustments when former member leaves during the year.

(7) Examples.

(d) Rules pertaining to ceasing to be a member of a loss subgroup.

(1) In general.

(2) Examples.

(e) Filing the election to apportion.

(1) Form of the election to apportion.

(2) Signing of the election.

(3) Filing of the election.

(4) Revocation of election.

§ 1.1502-96A *Miscellaneous rules generally applicable for testing dates before June 25, 1999.*

(a) End of separate tracking of losses.

(1) Application.

(2) Effect of end of separate tracking.

(3) Continuing effect of end of separate tracking.

(4) Special rule for testing period.

(5) Limits on effects of end of separate tracking.

(b) Ownership change of subsidiary.

(1) Ownership change of a subsidiary because of options or plan or arrangement.

(2) Effect of the ownership change.

(i) In general.

(ii) Pre-change losses.

(3) Coordination with §§ 1.1502-91T, 1.1502-92T, and 1.1502-94T.

(4) Example.

(c) Continuing effect of an ownership change.

§ 1.1502-97A *Special rules under section 382 for members under the jurisdiction of a court in a title 11 or similar case.* [Reserved]

§ 1.1502-98A *Coordination with section 383 generally applicable for testing dates (or members joining or leaving a group) before June 25, 1999.*

§ 1.1502-99A *Effective dates.*

(a) Effective date.

(1) In general.

(2) Anti-duplication rules for recognized built-in gain.

(b) Testing period may include a period beginning before January 1, 1997.

(c) Transition rules.

(1) Methods permitted.

(i) In general.

(ii) Adjustments to offset excess limitation.

(iii) Coordination with effective date.

(2) Permitted methods.

(d) Amended returns.

Reg. § 1.1502-90A

(e) Section 383.

[Reg. § 1.1502-90A.]

☐ [T.D. 8678, 6-26-96. Amended and redesignated by T.D. 8824, 6-25-99.]

[Reg. § 1.1502-91]

§ 1.1502-91. Application of section 382 with respect to a consolidated group.—(a) *Determination and effect of an ownership change*—(1) *In general.* This section and §§ 1.1502-92 and 1.1502-93 set forth the rules for determining an ownership change under section 382 for members of consolidated groups and the section 382 limitations with respect to attributes described in paragraphs (e) and (f) of this section. These rules generally provide that an ownership change and the section 382 limitation are determined with respect to these attributes for the group (or loss subgroup) on a single entity basis and not for its members separately. Following an ownership change of a loss group (or a loss subgroup) under § 1.1502-92, the amount of consolidated taxable income for any post-change year which may be offset by pre-change consolidated attributes (or pre-change subgroup attributes) shall not exceed the consolidated section 382 limitation (or subgroup section 382 limitation) for such year as determined under § 1.1502-93.

(2) *Special rule for post-change year that includes the change date.* If the post-change year includes the change date, section 382(b)(3)(A) is applied so that the consolidated section 382 limitation (or subgroup section 382 limitation) does not apply to the portion of consolidated taxable income that is allocable to the period in the year on or before the change date. See generally § 1.382-6 (relating to the allocation of income and loss). The allocation of consolidated taxable income for the post-change year that includes the change date must be made before taking into account any consolidated net operating loss deduction (as defined in § 1.1502-21(a)).

(3) *Cross-reference.* See §§ 1.1502-94 and 1.1502-95 for rules that apply section 382 to a corporation that becomes or ceases to be a member of a group or loss subgroup.

(b) *Definitions and nomenclature.* For purposes of this section and §§ 1.1502-92 through 1.1502-99, unless otherwise stated:

(1) The definitions and nomenclature contained in section 382 and the regulations thereunder (including the nomenclature and assumptions relating to the examples in § 1.382-2T(b)) and this section and §§ 1.1502-92 through 1.1502-99 apply.

(2) In all examples, all groups file consolidated returns, all corporations file their income tax returns on a calendar year basis, the only 5-percent shareholder of a corporation is a public group, the facts set forth the only owner shifts during the testing period, no election is made under paragraph (d)(4) of this section, and each asset of a corporation has a value equal to its adjusted basis.

(3) As the context requires, references to §§ 1.1502-91 through 1.1502-96 include references to corresponding provisions of §§ 1.1502-91A through 1.1502-96A. For example, a reference to an ownership change under § 1.1502-92 in § 1.1502-95(b) can include a reference to an ownership change under § 1.1502-92A.

(c) *Loss group*—(1) *Defined.* A loss group is a consolidated group that—

(i) Is entitled to use a net operating loss carryover to the taxable year that did not arise (and is not treated under § 1.1502-21(c) as arising) in a SRLY;

(ii) Has a consolidated net operating loss for the taxable year in which a testing date of the common parent occurs (determined by treating the common parent as a loss corporation); or

(iii) Has a net unrealized built-in loss (determined under paragraph (g) of this section by treating the date on which the determination is made as though it were a change date).

(2) *Coordination with rule that ends separate tracking.* A consolidated group may be a loss group because a member's losses that arose in (or are treated as arising in) a SRLY are treated as described in paragraph (c)(1)(i) of this section. See § 1.1502-96(a).

(3) *Example.* The following example illustrates the principles of this paragraph (c):

Example. Loss group. (i) L and L1 file separate returns and each has a net operating loss carryover arising in Year 1 that is carried over to Year 2. A owns 40 shares and L owns 60 shares of the 100 outstanding shares of L1 stock. At the close of Year 1, L buys the 40 shares of L1 stock from A. For Year 2, L and L1 file a consolidated return. The following is a graphic illustration of these facts:

Reg. § 1.1502-91(c)(3)

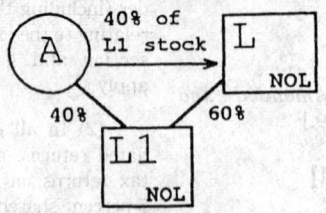

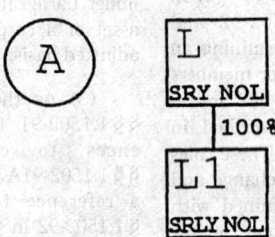

(ii) L and L1 become a loss group at the beginning of Year 2 because the group is entitled to use the Year 1 net operating loss carryover of L, the common parent, which did not arise (and is not treated under § 1.1502-21(c) as arising) in a SRLY. See § 1.1502-94 for rules relating to the application of section 382 with respect to L1's net operating loss carryover from Year 1 which did arise in a SRLY.

(d) *Loss subgroup*—(1) *Net operating loss carryovers.* Two or more corporations that become members of a consolidated group (the current group) compose a loss subgroup if—

(i) They were affiliated with each other in another group (the former group), whether or not the group was a consolidated group;

(ii) They bear the relationship described in section 1504(a)(1) to each other through a loss subgroup parent immediately after they become members of the current group (or are deemed to bear that relationship as a result of an election described in paragraph (d)(4) of this section); and

(iii) At least one of the members carries over a net operating loss that did not arise (and is not treated under § 1.1502-21(c) as arising) in a SRLY with respect to the former group.

(2) *Net unrealized built-in loss.* Two or more corporations that become members of a consolidated group compose a loss subgroup if they—

(i) Have been continuously affiliated with each other for the 5 consecutive year period ending immediately before they become members of the group;

(ii) Bear the relationship described in section 1504(a)(1) to each other through a loss subgroup parent immediately after they become members of the current group (or are deemed to bear that relationship as a result of an election described in paragraph (d)(4) of this section); and

(iii) Have a net unrealized built-in loss (determined under paragraph (g) of this section on the day they become members of the group by treating that day as though it were a change date).

(3) *Loss subgroup parent.* A loss subgroup parent is the corporation that bears the same relationship to the other members of the loss subgroup as a common parent bears to the members of a group.

(4) *Election to treat loss subgroup parent requirement as satisfied*—(i) *In general.* Solely for purposes of paragraphs (d)(1)(i) and (2)(ii) of this section, two or more corporations that become members of a consolidated group at the same time and that were affiliated with each other immediately before becoming members of the group are deemed to bear a section 1504(a)(1) relationship to each other immediately after they become members of the group if the common parent of that group makes an election under this paragraph (d)(4) with respect to those members. See § 1.1502-96(e) for the time and manner of making the election.

(ii) *Members included.* An election under this paragraph (d)(4) includes all corporations that become members of the current group at the same time and that were affiliated with each other immediately before they become members of the current group.

Reg. § 1.1502-91(d)(1)

(iii) *Each member included treated as loss subgroup parent.* If the members to which this election applies are a loss subgroup described in paragraph (d)(1) or (2) of this section, then each member is treated as a loss subgroup parent. See § 1.1502-92(b)(1)(iii) for special rules relating to an ownership change of a loss subgroup if the election under this paragraph (d)(4) is made.

(5) *Principal purpose of avoiding a limitation.* The corporations described in paragraphs (d)(1) or (2) of this section do not compose a loss subgroup if any one of them is formed, acquired, or availed of with a principal purpose of avoiding the application of, or increasing any limitation under, section 382. Instead, § 1.1502-94 applies with respect to the attributes of each such corporation. Any member excluded from a loss subgroup, if excluded with a principal purpose of so avoiding or increasing any section 382 limitation, is treated as included in the loss subgroup. This paragraph (d)(5) does not apply solely because, in connection with becoming members of the group, the members of a group (or loss subgroup) are rearranged (or, in the case of the preceding sentence, are not rearranged) to bear a relationship to the other members described in section 1504(a)(1).

(6) *Special rules.* See § 1.1502-95(d) for rules concerning when a corporation ceases to be a member of a loss subgroup, and for certain exceptions that may apply if a member does not continue to satisfy the loss subgroup parent requirement within the current group. See also § 1.1502-96(a) for a special rule regarding the end of separate tracking of SRLY losses of a member that has an ownership change or that has been a member of a group for at least 5 consecutive years.

(7) *Examples.* The following examples illustrate the principles of this paragraph (d):

Example 1. Loss subgroup. (i) P owns all the L stock and L owns all the L1 stock. The P group has a consolidated net operating loss arising in Year 1 that is carried to Year 2. On May 2, Year 2, P sells all the stock of L to A, and L and L1 thereafter file consolidated returns. A portion of the Year 1 consolidated net operating loss is apportioned under § 1.1502-21(b) to each of L and L1, which they carry over to Year 2. The following is a graphic illustration of these facts:

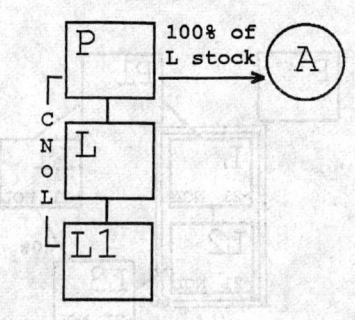

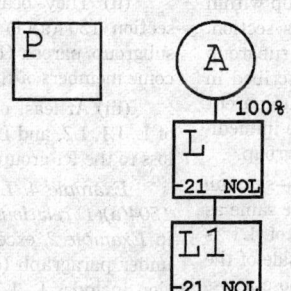

(ii) (a) L and L1 compose a loss subgroup within the meaning of paragraph (d)(1) of this section because—

(A) They were affiliated with each other in the P group (the former group);

Reg. § 1.1502-91(d)(7)

(B) They bear a relationship described in section 1504(a)(1) to each other through a loss subgroup parent (L) immediately after they became members of the L group; and

(C) At least one of the members (here, both L and L1) carries over a net operating loss to the L group (the current group) that did not arise in a SRLY with respect to the P group.

(b) Under paragraph (d)(3) of this section, L is the loss subgroup parent of the L loss subgroup.

Example 2. Loss subgroup—section 1504(a)(1) relationship. (i) P owns all the stock of L and L1. L owns all the stock of L2. L1 and L2 own 40 percent and 60 percent of the stock of L3, respectively. The P group has a consolidated net operating loss arising in Year 1 that is carried over to Year 2. On May 22, Year 2, P sells all the stock of L and L1 to P1, the common parent of another consolidated group. The Year 1 consolidated net operating loss is apportioned under § 1.1502-21(b), and each of L, L2, L2, and L3 carries over a portion of such loss to the first consolidated return year of the P1 group ending after the acquisition. The following is a graphic illustration of these facts:

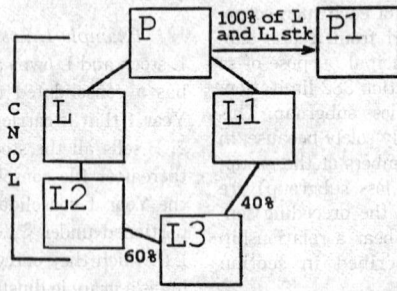

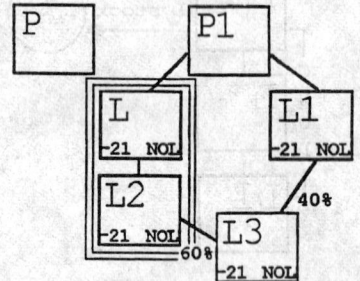

(ii) L and L2 compose a loss subgroup within the meaning of paragraph (d)(1) of this section. Neither L1 nor L3 is included in a loss subgroup because neither bears a relationship described in section 1504(a)(1) through a loss subgroup parent to any other member of the former group immediately after becoming members of the P1 group.

Example 3. Loss subgroup—section 1504(a)(1) relationship. The facts are the same as in *Example 2*, except that the stock of L1 is transferred to L in connection with the sale of the L stock to P1. L, L1, L2, and L3 compose a loss subgroup within the meaning of paragraph (d)(1) of this section because—

(i) They were affiliated with each other in the P group (the former group);

(ii) They bear a relationship described in section 1504(a)(1) to each other through a loss subgroup parent (L) immediately after they become members of the P1 group; and

(iii) At least one of the members (here, each of L, L1, L2, and L3) carries over a net operating loss to the P1 group (the current group).

Example 4. Loss subgroup—elective section 1504(a)(1) relationship. The facts are the same as in *Example 2*, except that P1 makes the election under paragraph (d)(4) of this section. The election includes L, L1, L2, and L3 (even though L and L2 would compose a loss subgroup without regard to the election) because they become members of the current group (the P1 group) at the same time and were affiliated with each other in

Reg. § 1.1502-91(d)(7)

the P group immediately before they became members of the P1 group. As a result of the election, L, L1, L2, and L3 are treated as satisfying the requirement that they bear the relationship described in section 1504(a)(1) to each other through a loss subgroup parent immediately after they become members of the P1 group. L, L1, L2, and L3 compose a loss subgroup within the meaning of paragraph (d)(1) of this section.

(e) *Pre-change consolidated attribute*—(1) *Defined.* A pre-change consolidated attribute of a loss group is—

(i) Any loss described in paragraph (c)(1)(i) or (ii) of this section (relating to the definition of loss group) that is allocable to the period ending on or before the change date; and

(ii) Any recognized built-in loss of the loss group.

(2) *Example.* The following example illustrates the principle of this paragraph (e):

Example. Pre-change consolidated attribute. (i) The L group has a consolidated net operating loss arising in Year 1 that is carried over to Year 2. The L loss group has an ownership change at the beginning of Year 2.

(ii) The net operating loss carryover of the L loss group from Year 1 is a pre-change consolidated attribute because the L group was entitled to use the loss in Year 2 and therefore the loss was described in paragraph (c)(1)(i) of this section. Under paragraph (a)(2)(i) of this section, the amount of consolidated taxable income of the L group for Year 2 that may be offset by this loss carryover may not exceed the consolidated section 382 limitation of the L group for that year. See § 1.1502-93 for rules relating to the computation of the consolidated section 382 limitation.

(f) *Pre-change subgroup attribute*—(1) *Defined.* A pre-change subgroup attribute of a loss subgroup is—

(i) Any net operating loss carryover described in paragraph (d)(1)(iii) of this section (relating to the definition of loss subgroup); and

(ii) Any recognized built-in loss of the loss subgroup.

(2) *Example.* The following example illustrates the principle of this paragraph (f):

Pre-change subgroup attribute. (i) P is the common parent of a consolidated group. P owns all the stock of L, and L owns all the stock of L1. L2 is not a member of an affiliated group, and has a net operating loss arising in Year 1 that is carried over to Year 2. On December 11, Year 2, L1 acquires all the stock of L2, causing an ownership change of L2. During Year 2, the P group has a consolidated net operating loss that is carried over to Year 3. On November 2, Year 3, M acquires all the L stock from P. M, L, L1, and L2 thereafter file consolidated returns. All of the P group Year 2 consolidated net operating loss is apportioned under § 1.1502-21(b) to L and L2, which they carry over to the M group.

(ii)(a) L, L1, and L2 compose a loss subgroup because—

(1) They were affiliated with each other in the P group (the former group);

(2) They bear a relationship described in section 1504(a)(1) to each other through a loss subgroup parent (L) immediately after they became members of the L group; and

(3) At least one of the members (here, both L and L2) carries over a net operating loss to the M group (the current group) that is described in paragraph (d)(1)(iii) of this section.

(b) For this purpose, L2's loss from Year 1 that was a SRLY loss with respect to the P group (the former group) is described in paragraph (d)(1)(iii) of this section because L2 had an ownership change on becoming a member of the P group (see § 1.1502-96(a)) on December 11, Year 2. Starting on December 12, Year 2, the P group no longer separately tracked owner shifts of the stock of L1 with respect to the Year 1 loss. M's acquisition results in an ownership change of L, and therefore the L loss subgroup under § 1.1502-92(a)(2). See § 1.1502-93 for rules governing the computation of the subgroup section 382 limitation.

(iii) In the M group, L2's Year 1 loss continues to be subject to a section 382 limitation resulting from the ownership change that occurred on December 11, Year 2. See § 1.1502-96(c).

(g) *Net unrealized built-in gain and loss*—(1) *In general.* The determination whether a consolidated group (or loss subgroup) has a net unrealized built-in gain or loss under section 382(h)(3) is based on the aggregate amount of the separately computed net unrealized built-in gains or losses of each member that is included in the group (or loss subgroup) under paragraph (g)(2) of this section, including items of built-in income and deduction described in section 382(h)(6). Thus, for example, amounts deferred under section 267, or under § 1.1502-13 (other than amounts deferred with respect to the stock of a member (or an intercompany obligation) included in the group (or loss subgroup) under paragraph (g)(2) of this section) are built-in items. The threshold requirement under section 382(h)(3)(B) applies on an aggregate basis and not on a member-by-member basis. The separately computed amount of a member included in a group or loss subgroup does not include any unrealized built-in gain or loss on

Reg. § 1.1502-91(g)(1)

stock (including stock described in section 1504(a)(4) and § 1.382-2T(f)(18)(ii) and (iii)) of another member included in the group or loss subgroup (or an intercompany obligation). However, a member of a group or loss subgroup includes in its separately computed amount the unrealized built-in gain or loss on stock (but not on an intercompany obligation) of another member not included in the group or loss subgroup. If a member is not included in the determination whether a group (or subgroup) has a net unrealized built-in loss under paragraph (g)(2)(ii) or (iv) of this section, that member is not included in the loss group or loss subgroup. See § 1.1502-94(c) (relating to built-in gain or loss of a new loss member) and § 1.1502-96(a) (relating to the end of separate tracking of certain losses).

(2) *Members included*—(i) *Consolidated group with a net operating loss*. The members included in the determination whether a consolidated group described in paragraph (c)(1)(i) or (ii) of this section (relating to loss groups with net operating losses) has a net unrealized built-in gain are all members of the consolidated group on the day that the determination is made.

(ii) *Determination whether a consolidated group has a net unrealized built-in loss*. The members included in the determination whether a consolidated group is a loss group described in paragraph (c)(1)(iii) of this section are—

(A) The common parent and all other members that have been affiliated with the common parent for the 5 consecutive year period ending on the day that the determination is made;

(B) Any other member that has a net unrealized built-in loss determined under paragraph (g)(1) of this section on the date that the determination is made, and that is neither a new loss member described in § 1.1502-94(a)(1)(ii) nor a member of a loss subgroup described in paragraph (d)(2) of this section;

(C) Any new loss member described in § 1.1502-94(a)(1)(ii) that has a net unrealized built-in gain determined under paragraph (g)(1) of this section on the day that the determination is made; and

(D) The members of a loss subgroup described in paragraph (d)(2) of this section if the members of the subgroup have, in the aggregate, a net unrealized built-in gain on the day that the determination is made.

(iii) *Loss subgroup with net operating loss carryovers*. The members included in the determination whether a loss subgroup described in paragraph (d)(1) of this section (relating to loss subgroups with net operating loss carryovers) has a net unrealized built-in gain are all members of the loss subgroup on the day that the determination is made.

(iv) *Determination whether subgroup has a net unrealized built-in loss*. The members included in the determination whether a subgroup has a net unrealized built-in loss are those members described in paragraphs (d)(2)(i) and (ii) of this section.

(v) *Separate determination of section 382 limitation for recognized built-in losses and net operating losses*. In determining whether a loss group described in paragraph (c)(1)(i) or (ii) of this section (relating to loss groups that have net operating loss carryovers) has a net unrealized built-in gain which, if recognized, increases the consolidated section 382 limitation, the group includes, under paragraph (g)(2)(i) of this section, all of its members on the day the determination is made. Under paragraph (g)(2)(ii) of this section, however, for purposes of determining whether a group has a net unrealized built-in loss described in paragraph (c)(1)(iii) of this section, not all members of the consolidated group may be included. Thus, a consolidated group may have recognized built-in gains that increase the amount of consolidated taxable income that may be offset by its pre-change net operating loss carryovers that did not arise (and are not treated as arising) in a SRLY, and also may have recognized built-in losses the absorption of which is limited. Similar results may obtain for loss subgroups under paragraphs (g)(2)(iii) and (iv) of this section. See § 1.1502-93(c)(2) for rules prohibiting the use of recognized built-in gains to increase the amount of consolidated taxable income that can be offset by recognized built-in losses.

(3) *Coordination with rule that ends separate tracking*. See § 1.1502-96(a) for special rules relating to members (or loss subgroups) that have an ownership change within six months before, on, or after becoming a member of the group.

(4) *Acquisitions of built-in gain or loss assets*. A member of a consolidated group (or loss subgroup) may not, in determining its separately computed net unrealized built-in gain or loss, include any gain or loss with respect to assets acquired with a principal purpose to affect the amount of its net unrealized built-in gain or loss. A group (or loss subgroup) may not, in determining its net unrealized built-in gain or loss, include any gain or loss of a member acquired with a principal purpose to affect the amount of its net unrealized built-in gain or loss.

(5) *Indirect ownership*. A member's separately computed net unrealized built-in gain or loss is adjusted to the extent necessary to prevent any duplication of unrealized gain or loss attribu-

Reg. § 1.1502-91(g)(2)

table to the member's indirect ownership interest in another member through a nonmember if the member has a 5-percent or greater ownership interest in the nonmember.

(6) *Common parent not common parent for five years.* If the common parent has become the common parent of an existing group within the previous 5 year period in a transaction described in § 1.1502-75(d)(2)(ii) or (3), appropriate adjustments must be made in applying paragraph (g)(2)(ii)(A) of this section so that corporations that have not been members of the group for five years are not included. In such a case, references to the common parent in paragraph (g)(2)(ii)(A) of this section are to the former common parent. Thus, members of the group remaining in existence (including the new common parent) that have not been affiliated with the former common parent (or that have not been members of that group) for the five consecutive year period ending on the day that the determination is made are not included under paragraph (g)(2)(ii)(A) of this section. See, however, § 1.1502-96(a)(2) for special rules relating to members (or loss subgroups) that have an ownership change within six months before, on, or after the time that the member becomes a member of the group.

(h) *Recognized built-in gain or loss*—(1) *In general.* [Reserved].

(2) *Disposition of stock or an intercompany obligation of a member.* Gain or loss recognized by a member on the disposition of stock (including stock described in section 1504(a)(4) and § 1.382-2T(f)(18)(ii) and (iii)) of another member is treated as a recognized gain or loss for purposes of section 382(h)(2) (unless disallowed under § 1.1502-20 or otherwise), even though gain or loss on such stock was not included in the determination of a net unrealized built-in gain or loss under paragraph (g)(1) of this section. Gain or loss recognized by a member with respect to an intercompany obligation is treated as recognized gain or loss only to the extent (if any) the transaction gives rise to aggregate income or loss within the consolidated group.

(3) *Intercompany transactions.* Gain or loss that is deferred under provisions such as section 267 and § 1.1502-13 is treated as recognized built-in gain or loss only to the extent taken into account by the group during the recognition period. See also § 1.1502-13(c)(7) *Example 10.*

(4) *Exchanged basis property.* If the adjusted basis of any asset is determined, directly or indirectly, in whole or in part, by reference to the adjusted basis of another asset held by the member a: the beginning of the recognition period, the asset is treated, with appropriate adjustments, as held by the member at the beginning of the recognition period.

(i) [Reserved]

(j) *Predecessor and successor corporations.* A reference in this section and §§ 1.1502-92 through 1.1502-99 to a corporation, member, common parent, loss subgroup parent, or subsidiary includes, as the context may require, a reference to a predecessor or successor corporation as defined in § 1.1502-1(f)(4). For example, the determination whether a successor satisfies the continuous affiliation requirement of paragraph (d)(2)(i) or (g)(2)(ii) of this section is made by reference to its predecessor. [Reg. § 1.1502-91.]

☐ [T.D. 8824, 6-25-99.]

[Reg. § 1.1502-91A]

§ 1.1502-91A. **Application of section 382 with respect to a consolidated group generally applicable for testing dates before June 25, 1999.**—(a) *Determination and effect of an ownership change*—(1) *In general.* This section and §§ 1.1502-92A and 1.1502-93A set forth the rules for determining an ownership change under section 382 for members of consolidated groups and the section 382 limitations with respect to attributes described in paragraphs (e) and (f) of this section. These rules generally provide that an ownership change and the section 382 limitation are determined with respect to these attributes for the group (or loss subgroup) on a single entity basis and not for its members separately. Following an ownership change of a loss group (or a loss subgroup) under § 1.1502-92A, the amount of consolidated taxable income for any post-change year which may be offset by pre-change consolidated attributes (or pre-change subgroup attributes) shall not exceed the consolidated section 382 limitation (or subgroup section 382 limitation) for such year as determined under § 1.1502-93A.

(2) *Special rule for post-change year that includes the change date.* If the post-change year includes the change date, section 382(b)(3)(A) is applied so that the consolidated section 382 limitation (or subgroup section 382 limitation) does not apply to the portion of consolidated taxable income that is allocable to the period in the year on or before the change date. See generally § 1.382-6 (relating to the allocation of income and loss). The allocation of consolidated taxable income for the post-change year that includes the change date must be made before taking into account any consolidated net operating loss deduction (as defined in § 1.1502-21(a) or 1.1502-21T(a) in effect prior to June 25, 1999, as contained in 26 CFR part 1 revised April 1, 1999, as applicable).

Reg. § 1.1502-91A(a)(2)

(3) *Cross reference.* See §§ 1.1502-94A and 1.1502-95A for rules that apply section 382 to a corporation that becomes or ceases to be a member of a group or loss subgroup.

(b) *Definitions and nomenclature.* For purposes of this section and §§ 1.1502-92A through 1.1502-99A, unless otherwise stated:

(1) The definitions and nomenclature contained in section 382 and the regulations thereunder (including the nomenclature and assumptions relating to the examples in § 1.382-2T(b)) and this section and §§ 1.1502-92A through 1.1502-99A apply; and

(2) In all examples, all groups file consolidated returns, all corporations file their income tax returns on a calendar year basis, the only 5-percent shareholder of a corporation is a public group, the facts set forth the only owner shifts during the testing period, and each asset of a corporation has a value equal to its adjusted basis.

(c) *Loss group*—(1) *Defined.* A loss group is a consolidated group that:

(i) Is entitled to use a net operating loss carryover to the taxable year that did not arise (and is not treated under § 1.1502-21T(c) as arising) in a SRLY;

(ii) Has a consolidated net operating loss for the taxable year in which a testing date of the common parent occurs (determined by treating the common parent as a loss corporation); or

(iii) Has a net unrealized built-in loss (determined under paragraph (g) of this section by treating the date on which the determination is made as though it were a change date).

(2) *Coordination with rule that ends separate tracking.* A consolidated group may be a loss group because a member's losses that arose in (or are treated as arising in) a SRLY are treated as described in paragraph (c)(1)(i) of this section. See § 1.1502-96A(a).

(3) *Example.* The following example illustrates the principles of this paragraph (c).

Example. Loss group. (a) L and L1 file separate returns and each has a net operating loss carryover arising in Year 1 that is carried over to Year 2. A owns 40 shares and L owns 60 shares of the 100 outstanding shares of L1 stock. At the close of Year 1, L buys the 40 shares of L1 stock from A. For Year 2, L and L1 file a consolidated return. The following is a graphic illustration of these facts:

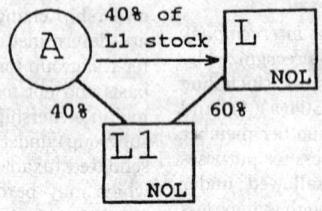

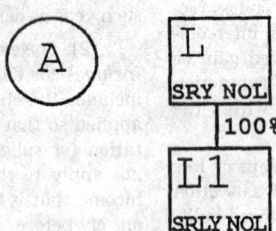

(b) L and L1 become a loss group at the beginning of Year 2 because the group is entitled to use the Year 1 net operating loss carryover of L, the common parent, which did not arise (and is not treated under § 1.1502-21(c) or 1.1502-21T(c) in effect prior to June 25, 1999, as contained in 26 CFR part 1 revised April 1, 1999, as applicable as arising) in a SRLY. See § 1.1502-94A for rules relating to the application of section 382 with respect to L1's net operating loss carryover from Year 1 which did arise in a SRLY.

(d) *Loss subgroup*—(1) *Net operating loss carryovers.* Two or more corporations that become members of a consolidated group (the current group) compose a loss subgroup if:

Reg. § 1.1502-91A(a)(3)

(i) They were affiliated with each other in another group (the former group), whether or not the group was a consolidated group;

(ii) They bear the relationship described in section 1504(a)(1) to each other through a loss subgroup parent immediately after they become members of the current group; and

(iii) At least one of the members carries over a net operating loss that did not arise (and is not treated under § 1.1502-21(c) or 1.1502-21T(c) in effect prior to June 25, 1999, as contained in 26 CFR part 1 revised April 1, 1999, as applicable as arising) in a SRLY with respect to the former group.

(2) *Net unrealized built-in loss.* Two or more corporations that become members of a consolidated group compose a loss subgroup if they:

(i) Have been continuously affiliated with each other for the 5 consecutive year period ending immediately before they become members of the group;

(ii) Bear the relationship described in section 1504(a)(1) to each other through a loss subgroup parent immediately after they become members of the current group; and

(iii) Have a net unrealized built-in loss (determined under paragraph (g) of this section on the day they become members of the group by treating that day as though it were a change date).

(3) *Loss subgroup parent.* A loss subgroup parent is the corporation that bears the same relationship to the other members of the loss subgroup as a common parent bears to the members of a group.

(4) *Principal purpose of avoiding a limitation.* The corporations described in paragraph (d)(1) or (2) of this section do not compose a loss subgroup if any one of them is formed, acquired, or availed of with a principal purpose of avoiding the application of, or increasing any limitation under, section 382. Instead, § 1.1502-94A applies with respect to the attributes of each such corporation. This paragraph (d)(4) does not apply solely because, in connection with becoming members of the group, the members of a group (or loss subgroup) are rearranged to bear a relationship to the other members described in section 1504(a)(1).

(5) *Special rules.* See § 1.1502-95A(d) for rules concerning when a corporation ceases to be a member of a loss subgroup. See also § 1.1502-96A(a) for a special rule regarding the end of separate tracking of SRLY losses of a member that has an ownership change or that has been a member of a group for at least 5 consecutive years.

(6) *Examples.* The following examples illustrate the principles of this paragraph (d).

Example 1. Loss subgroup. (a) P owns all the L stock and L owns all the L1 stock. The P group has a consolidated net operating loss arising in Year 1 that is carried to Year 2. On May 2, Year 2, P sells all the stock of L to A, and L and L1 thereafter file consolidated returns. A portion of the Year 1 consolidated net operating loss is apportioned under § 1.1502-21(b) or 1.1502-21T(b) in effect prior to June 25, 1999, as contained in 26 CFR part 1 revised April 1, 1999, as applicable to each of L and L1, which they carry over to Year 2. The following is a graphic illustration of these facts:

Reg. § 1.1502-91A(d)(6)

Consolidated Returns

See p. 20,601 for regulations not amended to reflect law changes

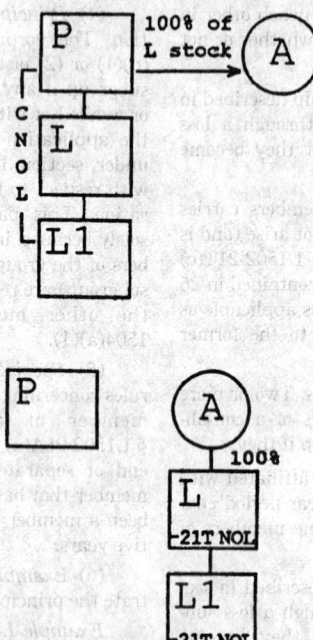

(b) (1) L and L1 compose a loss subgroup within the meaning of paragraph (d)(1) of this section because—

(i) They were affiliated with each other in the P group (the former group);

(ii) They bear a relationship described in section 1504(a)(1) to each other through a loss subgroup parent (L) immediately after they became members of the L group; and

(iii) At least one of the members (here, both L and L1) carries over a net operating loss to the L group (the current group) that did not arise in a SRLY with respect to the P group.

(2) Under paragraph (d)(3) of this section, L is the loss subgroup parent of the L loss subgroup.

Example 2. Loss subgroup—section 1504(a)(1) relationship. (a) P owns all the stock of L and L1. L owns all the stock of L2. L1 and L2 own 40 percent and 60 percent of the stock of L3, respectively. The P group has a consolidated net operating loss arising in Year 1 that is carried over to Year 2. On May 22, Year 2, P sells all the stock of L and L1 to P1, the common parent of another consolidated group. The Year 1 consolidated net operating loss is apportioned under § 1.1502-21(b) or 1.1502-21T(b) in effect prior to June 25, 1999, as contained in 26 CFR part 1 revised April 1, 1999, as applicable, and each of L, L1, L2, and L3 carries over a portion of such loss to the first consolidated return year of the P1 group ending after the acquisition. The following is a graphic illustration of these facts:

Reg. § 1.1502-91A(d)(6)

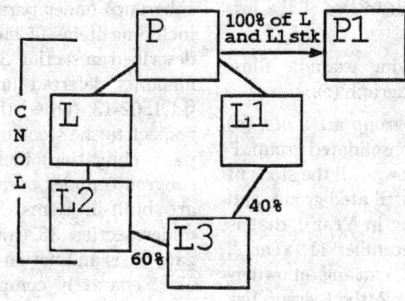

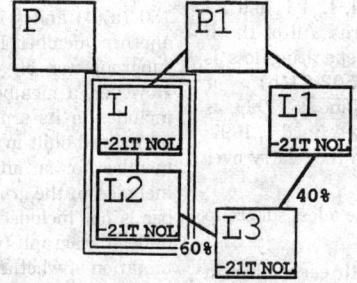

(b) L and L2 compose a loss subgroup within the meaning of paragraph (d)(1) of this section. Neither L1 nor L3 is included in a loss subgroup because neither bears a relationship described in section 1504(a)(1) through a loss subgroup parent to any other member of the former group immediately after becoming members of the P1 group.

Example 3. Loss subgroup—section 1504(a)(1) relationship. The facts are the same as in *Example 2*, except that the stock of L1 is transferred to L in connection with the sale of the L stock to P1. L, L1, L2, and L3 compose a loss subgroup within the meaning of paragraph (d)(1) of this section because—

(1) They were affiliated with each other in the P group (the former group);

(2) They bear a relationship described in section 1504(a)(1) to each other through a loss subgroup parent (L) immediately after they become members of the P1 group; and

(3) At least one of the members (here, each of L, L1, L2, and L3) carries over to the P1 group (the current group) a net operating loss that did not arise in a SRLY with respect to the P group (the former group).

(e) *Pre-change consolidated attribute*—(1) *Defined.* A pre-change consolidated attribute of a loss group is—

(i) Any loss described in paragraph (c)(1)(i) or (ii) of this section (relating to the definition of loss group) that is allocable to the period ending on or before the change date; and

(ii) Any recognized built-in loss of the loss group.

(2) *Example.* The following example illustrates the principle of this paragraph (e).

Example. Pre-change consolidated attribute. (a) The L group has a consolidated net operating loss arising in Year 1 that is carried over to Year 2. The L loss group has an ownership change at the beginning of Year 2.

(b) The net operating loss carryover of the L loss group from Year 1 is a pre-change consolidated attribute because the L group was entitled to use the loss in Year 2, the loss did not arise in a SRLY with respect to the L group, and therefore the loss was described in paragraph (c)(1)(i) of this section. Under paragraph (a) of this section, the amount of consolidated taxable income of the L group for Year 2 that may be offset by this loss carryover may not exceed the consolidated section 382 limitation of the L group for that year. See § 1.1502-93A for rules relating to the computation of the consolidated section 382 limitation.

(f) *Pre-change subgroup attribute*—(1) *Defined.* A pre-change subgroup attribute of a loss subgroup is—

(i) Any net operating loss carryover described in paragraph (d)(1)(iii) of this section (relating to the definition of loss subgroup); and

(ii) Any recognized built-in loss of the loss subgroup.

(2) *Example.* The following example illustrates the principle of this paragraph (f).

Example. Pre-change subgroup attribute. (a) P is the common parent of a consolidated group. P owns all the stock of L, and L owns all the stock of L1. L2 is not a member of an affiliated group, and has a net operating loss arising in Year 1 that is carried over to Year 2. On December 11, Year 2, L1 acquires all the stock of L2, causing an ownership change of L2. During Year 2, the P group has a consolidated net operating loss that is carried over to Year 3. On November 2, Year 3, M acquires all the L stock from P. M, L, L1, and L2 thereafter file consolidated returns. All of the P group Year 2 consolidated net operating loss is apportioned under § 1.1502-21(b) or 1.1502-21T(b) in effect prior to June 25, 1999, as contained in 26 CFR part 1 revised April 1, 1999, as applicable to L and L2, which they carry over to the M group.

(b)(1) L, L1, and L2 compose a loss subgroup because—

(i) They were affiliated with each other in the P group (the former group);

(ii) They bore a relationship described in section 1504(a)(1) to each other through a loss subgroup parent (L) immediately after they became members of the L group; and

(iii) At least one of the members (here, both L and L2) carries over a net operating loss to the M group (the current group) that is described in paragraph (d)(1)(iii) of this section.

(2) For this purpose, L2's loss from Year 1 that was a SRLY loss with respect to the P group (the former group) is treated as described in paragraph (d)(1)(iii) of this section because of the application of the principles of § 1.1502-96A(a). See paragraph (d)(5) of this section. M's acquisition results in an ownership change of L, and therefore the L loss subgroup under § 1.1502-92A(a)(2). See § 1.1502-93A for rules governing the computation of the subgroup section 382 limitation.

(c) In the M group, L2's Year 1 loss continues to be subject to a section 382 limitation resulting from the ownership change that occurred on December 11, Year 2. See § 1.1502-96A(c).

(g) *Net unrealized built-in gain and loss*—(1) *In general.* The determination whether a consolidated group (or loss subgroup) has a net unrealized built-in gain or loss under section 382(h)(3) is based on the aggregate amount of the separately computed net unrealized built-in gains or losses of each member that is included in the group (or loss subgroup) under paragraph (g)(2) of this section, including items of built-in income and deduction described in section 382(h)(6). Thus, for example, amounts deferred under section 267, or under § 1.1502-13 (other than amounts deferred with respect to the stock of a member (or an intercompany obligation) included in the group (or loss subgroup) under paragraph (g)(2) of this section) are built-in items. The threshold requirement under section 382(h)(3)(B) applies on an aggregate basis and not on a member-by-member basis. The separately computed amount of a member included in a group or loss subgroup does not include any unrealized built-in gain or loss on stock (including stock described in section 1504(a)(4) and § 1.382-2T(f)(18)(ii) and (iii)) of another member included in the group or loss subgroup (or on an intercompany obligation). However, a member of a group or loss subgroup includes in its separately computed amount the unrealized built-in gain or loss on stock of another member (or on an intercompany obligation) not included in the group or loss subgroup. If a member is not included in a group (or loss subgroup) under paragraph (g)(2) of this section, the determination of whether the member has a net unrealized built-in gain or loss under section 382(h)(3) is made on a separate entity basis. See § 1.1502-94A(c) (relating to built-in gain or loss of a new loss member) and § 1.1502-96A(a) (relating to the end of separate tracking of certain losses).

(2) *Members included*—(i) *Consolidated group.* The members included in the determination whether a consolidated group has a net unrealized built-in gain or loss are all members of the group on the day that the determination is made other than—

(A) A new loss member with a net unrealized built-in loss described in § 1.1502-94A(a)(1)(ii); and

(B) Members included in a loss subgroup described in § 1.1502-91A(d)(2).

(ii) *Loss subgroup.* The members included in the determination whether a loss subgroup has a net unrealized built-in gain or loss are those members described in paragraphs (d)(2)(i) and (ii) of this section.

(3) *Acquisitions of built-in gain or loss assets.* A member of a consolidated group (or loss subgroup) may not, in determining its separately computed net unrealized built-in gain or loss, include any gain or loss with respect to assets acquired with a principal purpose to affect the amount of its net unrealized built-in gain or loss. A group (or loss subgroup) may not, in determining its net unrealized built-in gain or loss, include any gain or loss of a member acquired with a

principal purpose to affect the amount of its net unrealized built-in gain or loss.

(4) *Indirect ownership.* A member's separately computed net unrealized built-in gain or loss is adjusted to the extent necessary to prevent any duplication of unrealized gain or loss attributable to the member's indirect ownership interest in another member through a nonmember if the member has a 5-percent or greater ownership interest in the nonmember.

(h) *Recognized built-in gain or loss*—(1) *In general.* [Reserved]

(2) *Disposition of stock or an intercompany obligation of a member.* Gain or loss recognized by a member on the disposition of stock (including stock described in section 1504(a)(4) and § 1.382-2T(f)(18)(ii) and (iii)) of another member (or an intercompany obligation disposed of before June 25, 1999) is treated as a recognized built-in gain or loss under section 382(h)(2) (unless disallowed under § 1.1502-20 or otherwise), even though gain or loss on such stock or obligation was not included in the determination of a net unrealized built-in gain or loss under paragraph (g)(1) of this section.

(3) *Deferred gain or loss.* Gain or loss that is deferred under provisions such as section 267 and § 1.1502-13 is treated as recognized built-in gain or loss only to the extent taken into account by the group during the recognition period.

(4) *Exchanged basis property.* If the adjusted basis of any asset is determined, directly or indirectly, in whole or in part, by reference to the adjusted basis of another asset held by the member at the beginning of the recognition period, the asset is treated, with appropriate adjustments, as held by the member at the beginning of the recognition period.

(i) [Reserved]

(j) *Predecessor and successor corporations.* A reference in this section and §§ 1.1502-92A through 1.1502-99A to a corporation, member, common parent, loss subgroup parent, or subsidiary includes, as the context may require, a reference to a predecessor or successor corporation. For example, the determination whether a successor satisfies the continuous affiliation requirement of paragraph (d)(2)(i) of this section is made by reference to its predecessor. [Reg. § 1.1502-91A.]

☐ [T.D. 8678, 6-26-96. Amended by T.D. 8823, 6-25-99 and amended and redesignated by T.D. 8824, 6-25-99.]

[Reg. § 1.1502-92]

§ 1.1502-92. **Ownership change of a loss group or a loss subgroup.**—(a) *Scope.* This section provides rules for determining if there is an ownership change for purposes of section 382 with respect to a loss group or a loss subgroup. See § 1.1502-94 for special rules for determining if there is an ownership change with respect to a new loss member and § 1.1502-96(b) for special rules for determining if there is an ownership change of a subsidiary.

(b) *Determination of an ownership change*—(1) *Parent change method*—(i) *Loss group.* A loss group has an ownership change if the loss group's common parent has an ownership change under section 382 and the regulations thereunder. Solely for purposes of determining whether the common parent has an ownership change—

(A) The losses described in § 1.1502-91(c) are treated as net operating losses (or a net unrealized built-in loss) of the common parent; and

(B) The common parent determines the earliest day that its testing period can begin by reference to only the attributes that make the group a loss group under § 1.1502-91(c).

(ii) *Loss subgroup.* A loss subgroup has an ownership change if the loss subgroup parent has an ownership change under section 382 and the regulations thereunder. The principles of § 1.1502-95(b) (relating to ceasing to be a member of a consolidated group) apply in determining whether the loss subgroup parent has an ownership change. Solely for purposes of determining whether the loss subgroup parent has an ownership change—

(A) The losses described in § 1.1502-91(d) are treated as net operating losses (or a net unrealized built-in loss) of the loss subgroup parent;

(B) The day that the members of the loss subgroup become members of the group (or a loss subgroup) is treated as a testing date within the meaning of § 1.382-2(a)(4); and

(C) The loss subgroup parent determines the earliest day that its testing period can begin under § 1.382-2T(d)(3) by reference to only the attributes that make the members a loss subgroup under § 1.1502-91(d).

(iii) *Special rule if election regarding section 1504(a)(1) relationship is made*—(A) *Ownership change of deemed loss subgroup parent is an ownership change of loss subgroup.* If the common parent makes an election under § 1.1502-91(d)(4), each of the members in the loss subgroup is treated as the loss subgroup parent for purposes of determining whether the loss subgroup has an ownership change under section 382 and the regulations thereunder on or after the day the members become members of the group.

Reg. § 1.1502-92(b)(1)

(B) *Exception.* Paragraph (b)(1)(iii)(A) of this section does not apply to cause an ownership change of a loss subgroup if a deemed loss subgroup parent has an ownership change upon (or after) ceasing to be a member of the current group.

(2) *Examples.* The following examples illustrate the principles of this paragraph (b):

Example 1. Loss group—ownership change of the common parent. (i) A owns all the L stock. L owns 80 percent and B owns 20 percent of the L1 stock. For Year 1, the L group has a consolidated net operating loss that resulted from the operations of L1 and that is carried over to Year 2. The value of the L stock is $1000. The total value of the L1 stock is $600 and the value of the L1 stock held by B is $120. The L group is a loss group under § 1.1502-91(c)(1) because it is entitled to use its net operating loss carryover from Year 1. On August 15, Year 2, A sells 51 percent of the L stock to C. The following is a graphic illustration of these facts:

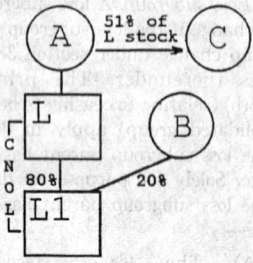

(ii) Under paragraph (b)(1)(i) of this section, section 382 and the regulations thereunder are applied to L to determine whether it (and therefore the L loss group) has an ownership change with respect to its net operating loss carryover from Year 1 attributable to L1 on August 15, Year 2. The sale of the L stock to C causes an ownership change of L under § 1.382-2T and of the L loss group under paragraph (b)(1)(i) of this section. The amount of consolidated taxable income of the L loss group for any post-change taxable year that may be offset by its pre-change consolidated attributes (that is, the net operating loss carryover from Year 1 attributable to L1) may not exceed the consolidated section 382 limitation for the L loss group for the taxable year.

Example 2. Loss group—owner shifts of subsidiaries disregarded. (i) The facts are the same as in *Example 1*, except that on August 15, Year 2, A sells only 49 percent of the L stock to C and, on December 12, Year 3, in an unrelated transaction, B sells the 20 percent of the L1 stock to D. A's sale of the L stock to C does not cause an ownership change of L under § 1.382-2T nor of the L loss group under paragraph (b)(1)(i) of this section. The following is a graphic illustration of these facts:

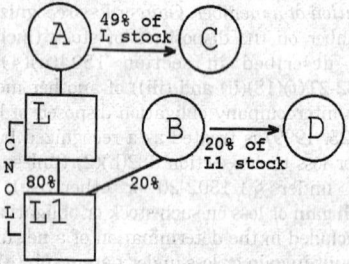

(ii) B's subsequent sale of L1 stock is not taken into account for purposes of determining whether the L loss group has an ownership change under paragraph (b)(1)(i) of this section, and, accordingly, there is no ownership change of the L loss group. See paragraph (c) of this section, however, for a supplemental ownership change method that would apply to cause an ownership change if the purchases by C and D were pursuant to a plan or arrangement and certain other conditions are satisfied.

Example 3. Loss subgroup—ownership change of loss subgroup parent controls. (i) P owns all the L stock. L owns 80 percent and A owns 20 percent of the L1 stock. The P group has a consolidated net operating loss arising in Year 1 that is carried over to Year 2. On September 9, Year 2, P sells 51 percent of the L stock to B, and L1 is apportioned a portion of the Year 1 consolidated net operating loss under § 1.1502-21(b), which it carries over to its next taxable year. L and L1 file a consolidated return for their first taxable year ending after the sale to B. The following is a graphic illustration of these facts:

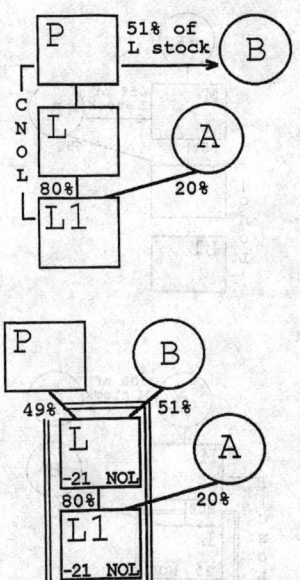

(ii) Under § 1.1502-91(d)(1), L and L1 compose a loss subgroup on September 9, Year 2, the day that they become members of the L group. Under paragraph (b)(1)(ii) of this section, section 382 and the regulations thereunder are applied to L to determine whether it (and therefore the L loss subgroup) has an ownership change with respect to the portion of the Year 1 consolidated net operating loss that is apportioned to L1 on September 9, Year 2. L has an ownership change resulting from P's sale of 51 percent of the L stock to A. Therefore, the L loss subgroup has an ownership change with respect to that loss.

Example 4. Loss group and loss subgroup— contemporaneous ownership changes. (i) A owns all the stock of corporation M, M owns 35 percent and B owns 65 percent of the L stock, and L owns all the L1 stock. The L group has a consolidated net operating loss arising in Year 1 that is carried over to Year 2. On May 19, Year 2, B sells 45 percent of the L stock to M for cash. M, L, and L1 thereafter file consolidated returns. L and L1 are each apportioned a portion of the Year 1 consolidated net operating loss, which they carry over to the M group's Year 2 and Year 3 consolidated return years. The M group has a consolidated net operating loss arising in Year 2 that is carried over to Year 3. On June 9, Year 3, A sells 70 percent of the M stock to C. The following is a graphic illustration of these facts:

Reg. § 1.1502-92(b)(2)

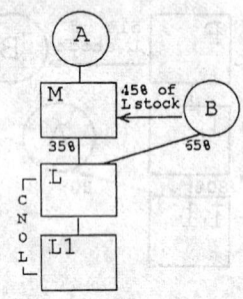

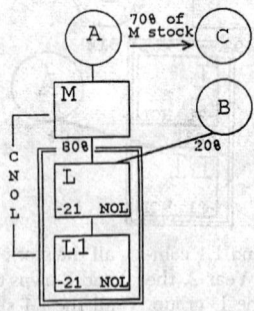

(ii) Under § 1.1502-91(d)(1), L and L1 compose a loss subgroup on May 19, Year 2, the day they become members of the M group. Under paragraph (b)(1)(ii) of this section, section 382 and the regulations thereunder are applied to L to determine whether L (and therefore the L loss subgroup) has an ownership change with respect to the loss carryovers from Year 1 on May 19, Year 2, a testing date because of B's sale of L stock to M. The sale of L stock to M results in only a 45 percentage point increase in A's ownership of L stock. Thus, there is no ownership change of L (or the L loss subgroup) with respect to those loss carryovers under paragraph (b)(1)(ii) of this section on that day.

(iii) June 9, Year 3, is also a testing date with respect to the L loss subgroup because of A's sale of M stock to C. The sale results in a 56 percentage point increase in C's ownership of L stock, and L has an ownership change. Therefore, the L loss subgroup has an ownership change on that day with respect to the loss carryovers from Year 1.

(iv) Paragraph (b)(1)(i) of this section requires that section 382 and the regulations thereunder be applied to M to determine whether M (and therefore the M loss group) has an ownership change with respect to the net operating loss carryover from Year 2 on June 9, Year 3, a testing date because of A's sale of M stock to C. The sale results in a 70 percentage point increase in C's ownership of M stock, and M has an ownership change. Therefore, the M loss group has an ownership change on that day with respect to that loss carryover.

Example 5—Deemed subgroup parent. (i) P owns all the stock of L and L1 and 80 percent of the stock of T. A owns the remaining 20 percent of the stock of T. L1 owns all the stock of L2. P1, which owns 60 percent of the stock of P, acquires, at the beginning of Year 2, the T, L, and L1 stock owned by P, and T, L, L1, and L2 become members of the P1 group. The P group has a consolidated net operating loss arising in Year 1 that is carried over to Year 2. L, L1, and L2 are each apportioned a portion of the Year 1 consolidated net operating loss under § 1.1502-21(b), which they carry over to the P1 group's Year 2 and Year 3 consolidated return years. P1 makes the election described in § 1.1502-91(d)(4) to treat T, L, L1 and L2 as meeting the section 1504(a)(1) requirement of § 1.1502-91(d)(1)(ii). As a result of the election, T, L, L1 and L2 compose a loss subgroup and T, L, L1, and L2 are each treated as the loss subgroup parent for purposes of this paragraph (b). Because of P1's indirect ownership of T, L, L1, and L2 prior to Pi's acquisition of the T, L, and L1 stock, P1's acquisition does not cause an ownership change of the loss subgroup.

(ii) On February 2, Year 3, L1 sells all of the stock of L2 to B. Although L2 is treated as a loss subgroup parent, the determination whether the

Reg. § 1.1502-92(b)(2)

loss subgroup comprised of T, L, and L1 has an ownership change under this paragraph (b) is made without regard to the sale of L2 because L2's ownership change occurred upon ceasing to be a member of the P1 group. See § 1.1502-95(b) to determine the application of section 382 to L2 when L2 ceases to be a member of the P1 group and the T, L, L1 and L2 loss subgroup.

(iii) On March 26, Year 3, A sells her 20 percent minority stock interest in T to C. C's purchase, together with the 32 percentage point owner shift effected by P1's acquisition of the T stock at the beginning of Year 2, causes an ownership change of T, and therefore of the loss subgroup comprised of T, L, and L1.

(3) *Special adjustments*—(i) *Common parent succeeded by a new common parent.* For purposes of determining if a loss group has an ownership change, if the common parent of a loss group is succeeded or acquired by a new common parent and the loss group remains in existence, the new common parent is treated as a continuation of the former common parent with appropriate adjustments to take into account shifts in ownership of the former common parent during the testing period (including shifts that occur incident to the common parent's becoming the former common parent). A new common parent may be a continuation of the former common parent even if, under § 1.1502-91(g)(2)(ii), the new common parent is not included in determining whether the group has a net unrealized built-in loss.

(ii) *Newly created loss subgroup parent.* For purposes of determining if a loss subgroup has an ownership change, if the member that is the loss subgroup parent has not been the loss subgroup parent for at least 3 years as of a testing date, appropriate adjustments must be made to take into account owner shifts of members of the loss subgroup so that the structure of the loss subgroup does not have the effect of avoiding an ownership change under section 382. (See paragraph (b)(3)(iii), *Example 3* of this section.)

(iii) *Examples.* The following examples illustrate the principles of this paragraph (b)(3):

Example 1. New common parent acquires old common parent. (i) A, who owns all the L stock, sells 30 percent of the L stock to B on August 26, Year 1. L owns all the L1 stock. The L group has a consolidated net operating loss arising in Year 1 that is carried over to Year 3. On July 16, Year 2, A and B transfer their L stock to a newly created holding company, HC, in exchange for 70 percent and 30 percent, respectively, of the HC stock. HC, L, and L1 thereafter file consolidated returns. Under the principles of § 1.1502-75(d), the L loss group is treated as remaining in existence, with HC taking the place of L as the new common parent of the loss group. The following is a graphic illustration of these facts:

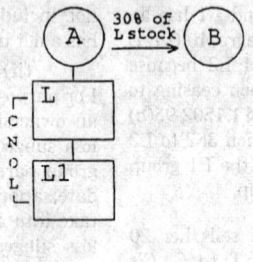

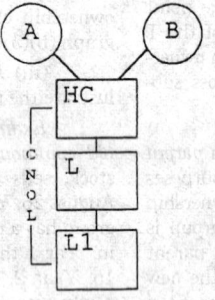

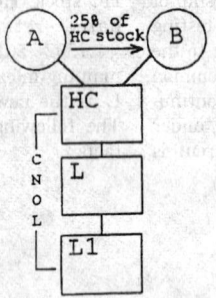

(ii) On November 11, Year 3, A sells 25 percent of the HC stock to B. For purposes of determining if the L loss group has an ownership change under paragraph (b)(1)(i) of this section on November 11, Year 3, HC is treated as a continuation of L under paragraph (b)(4)(i) of this section because it acquired L and became the common parent without terminating the L loss group. Accordingly, HC's testing period commences on January 1, Year 1, the first day of the taxable year of the L loss group in which the consolidated net operating loss that is carried over to Year 3 arose (see § 1.382-2T(d)(3)(i)). Immediately after the close of November 11, Year 3, B's percentage ownership interest in the common parent of the loss group (HC) has increased by 55 percentage points over its lowest percentage ownership during the testing period (zero percent).

Accordingly, HC and the L loss group have an ownership change on that day.

Example 2. New common parent in case in which common parent ceases to exist. (i) A, B, and C each own one-third of the L stock. L owns all the L1 stock. The L group has a consolidated net operating loss arising in Year 2 that is carried over to Year 3. On November 22, Year 3, L is merged into P, a corporation owned by D, and L1 thereafter files consolidated returns with P. A, B, and C, as a result of owning stock of L, own 90 percent of P's stock after the merger. D owns the remaining 10 percent of P's stock. The merger of L into P qualifies as a reverse acquisition of the L group under § 1.1502-75(d)(3)(i), and the L loss group is treated as remaining in existence, with P taking the place of L as the new common parent of the L group. The following is a graphic illustration of these facts:

Reg. § 1.1502-92(b)(3)

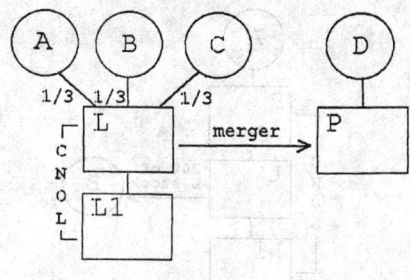

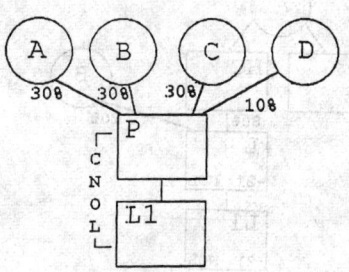

(ii) For purposes of determining if the L loss group has an ownership change on November 22, Year 3, the day of the merger, P is treated as a continuation of L so that the testing period for P begins on January 1, Year 2, the first day of the taxable year of the L loss group in which the consolidated net operating loss that is carried over to Year 3 arose. Immediately after the close of November 22, Year 3, D is the only 5-percent shareholder that has increased his ownership interest in P during the testing period (from zero to 10 percentage points).

(iii) The facts are the same as in paragraph (i) of this *Example 2*, except that A has held 23 1/3 shares (23 1/3 percent) of L's stock for five years, and A purchased an additional 10 shares of L stock from E two years before the merger. Immediately after the close of the day of the merger (a testing date), A's ownership interest in P, the common parent of the L loss group, has increased by 6 2/3 percentage points over A's lowest percentage ownership during the testing period (23 1/3 percent to 30 percent).

(iv) The facts are the same as in (i) of this *Example 2*, except that P has a net operating loss arising in Year 1 that is carried to the first consolidated return year ending after the day of the merger. Solely for purposes of determining whether the L loss group has an ownership change under paragraph (b)(1)(i) of this section, the testing period for P commences on January 1, Year 2. P does not determine the earliest day for its testing period by reference to its net operating loss carryover from Year 1, which §§ 1.1502-1(f)(3) and 1.1502-75(d)(3)(i) treat as arising in a SRLY. See § 1.1502-94 to determine the application of section 382 with respect to P's net operating loss carryover.

Example 3. Newly acquired loss subgroup parent. (i) P owns all the L stock and L owns all the L1 stock. The P group has a consolidated net operating loss arising in Year 1 that is carried over to Year 3. On January 19, Year 2, L issues a 20 percent stock interest to B. On February 5, Year 3, P contributes its L stock to a newly formed subsidiary, HC, in exchange for all the HC stock, and distributes the HC stock to its sole shareholder A. HC, L, and L1 thereafter file consolidated returns. A portion of the P group's Year 1 consolidated net operating loss is apportioned to L and L1 under § 1.1502-21(b) and is carried over to the HC group's year ending after February 5, Year 3. HC, L, and L1 compose a loss subgroup within the meaning of § 1.1502-91(d) with respect to the net operating loss carryovers from Year 1. The following is a graphic illustration of these facts:

Reg. § 1.1502-92(b)(3)

56,936   Consolidated Returns

See p. 20,601 for regulations not amended to reflect law changes

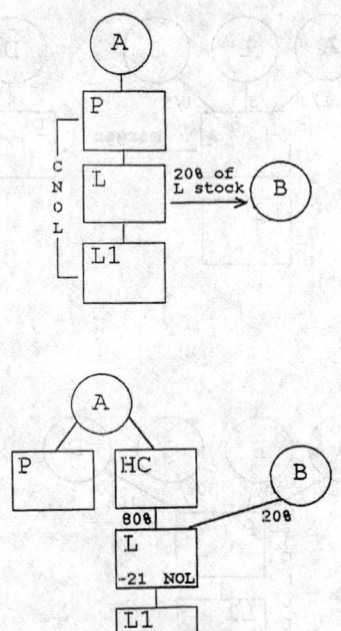

(ii) February 5, Year 3, is a testing date for HC as the loss subgroup parent with respect to the net operating loss carryovers of L and L1 from Year 1. See paragraph (b)(1)(ii)(B) of this section. For purposes of determining whether HC has an ownership change on the testing date, appropriate adjustments must be made with respect to the changes in the percentage ownership of the stock of HC because HC was not the loss subgroup parent for at least 3 years prior to the day on which it became a member of the HC loss subgroup (a testing date). The appropriate adjustments include adjustments so that HC succeeds to the owner shifts of other members of the former group. Thus, HC succeeds to the owner shift of L that resulted from the sale of the 20 percent interest to B in determining whether the HC loss subgroup has an ownership change on February 5, Year 3, and on any subsequent testing date that includes January 19, Year 2.

(4) *End of separate tracking of certain losses.* If § 1.1502-96(a) (relating to the end of separate tracking of attributes) applies to a loss subgroup, then, while one or more members that were included in the loss subgroup remain members of the consolidated group, there is an ownership change with respect to their attributes described in § 1.1502-96(a)(2) only if the consolidated group is a loss group and has an ownership change under paragraph (b)(1)(i) of this section (or such a member has an ownership change under § 1.1502-96(b)

(relating to ownership changes of subsidiaries)). If, however, the loss subgroup has had an ownership change before § 1.1502-96(a) applies, see § 1.1502-96(c) for the continuing application of the subgroup's section 382 limitation with respect to its pre-change subgroup attributes.

(c) *Supplemental rules for determining ownership change*—(1) *Scope.* This paragraph (c) contains a supplemental rule for determining whether there is an ownership change of a loss group (or loss subgroup). It applies in addition to, and not instead of, the rules of paragraph (b) of this section. Thus, for example, if the common parent of the loss group has an ownership change under paragraph (b) of this section, the loss group has an ownership change even if, by applying this paragraph (c), the common parent would not have an ownership change. This paragraph (c) does not apply in determining an ownership change of a loss subgroup for which an election under § 1.1502-91(d)(4) is made.

(2) *Cause for applying supplemental rule.* This paragraph (c) applies to a loss group (or loss subgroup) if—

(i) Any 5-percent shareholder of the common parent (or loss subgroup parent) increases its percentage ownership interest in the stock of both—

(A) A subsidiary of the loss group (or loss subgroup) other than by a direct or indirect

Reg. § 1.1502-92(b)(4)

acquisition of stock of the common parent (or loss subgroup parent); and

(B) The common parent (or loss subgroup parent);

(ii) Those increases occur within a 3 year period ending on any day of a consolidated return year or, if shorter, the period beginning on the first day following the most recent ownership change of the loss group (or loss subgroup); and

(iii) Either—

(A) The common parent (or loss subgroup parent) has actual knowledge of the increase in the 5-percent shareholder's ownership interest in the stock of the subsidiary (or has actual knowledge of the plan or arrangement described in paragraph (c)(3)(i) of this section) before the date that the group's income tax return is filed for the taxable year that includes the date of that increase; or

(B) At any time during the period described in paragraph (c)(2)(ii) of this section, the 5-percent shareholder of the common parent is also a 5-percent shareholder of the subsidiary (determined without regard to paragraph (c)(3)(i) of this section) whose percentage increase in the ownership of the stock of the subsidiary would be taken into account in determining if the subsidiary has an ownership change (determined as if the subsidiary was a loss corporation and applying the principles of § 1.382-2T(k), including the principles relating to duty to inquire).

(3) *Operating rules.* Solely for purposes of this paragraph (c)—

(i) A 5-percent shareholder of the common parent (or loss subgroup, parent) is treated as increasing its ownership interest in the stock of a subsidiary to the extent, if any, that another person or persons increases its percentage ownership interest in the stock of a subsidiary pursuant to a plan or arrangement under which the 5-percent shareholder increases its percentage ownership interest in the common parent (or loss subgroup parent);

(ii) The rules in section 382(l)(3) and §§ 1.382-2T(h) and 1.382-4(d) (relating to constructive ownership) apply with respect to the stock of the subsidiary by treating such stock as stock of a loss corporation; and

(iii) In the case of a loss subgroup, a subsidiary includes any member of the loss subgroup other than the loss subgroup parent. (A loss subgroup parent is, however, a subsidiary of the loss group of which it is a member.)

(4) *Supplemental ownership change rules.* The determination whether the common parent (or loss subgroup parent) has an ownership change is made by applying paragraph (b)(1) of this section as modified by the following additional rules:

(i) *Additional testing dates for the common parent (or loss subgroup parent).* A testing date for the common parent (or loss subgroup parent) also includes—

(A) Each day on which there is an increase in the percentage ownership of stock of a subsidiary as described in paragraph (c)(2) of this section; and

(B) The first day of the first consolidated return year for which the group is a loss group (or the members compose a loss subgroup).

(ii) *Treatment of subsidiary stock as stock of the common parent (or loss subgroup parent).* The common parent (or loss subgroup parent) is treated as though it had issued to the person acquiring (or deemed to acquire) the subsidiary stock an amount of its own stock (by value) that equals the value of the subsidiary stock represented by the percentage increase in that person's ownership of the subsidiary (determined on a separate entity basis). Similar principles apply if the increase in percentage ownership interest is effected by a redemption or similar transaction.

(iii) *Different testing periods.* Stock treated as issued under paragraph (c)(4)(ii) of this section on a testing date is not treated as so issued for purposes of applying the ownership change rules of this paragraph (c) and paragraph (b) (1) of this section in a testing period that does not include that testing date.

(iv) *Disaffiliation of a subsidiary.* If a deemed issuance of stock under paragraph (c)(4)(ii) of this section would not cause the loss group (or loss subgroup) to have an ownership change before the day (if any) on which the subsidiary ceases to be a member of the loss group (or subgroup), then paragraph (c)(4) of this section shall not apply.

(v) *Subsidiary stock acquired first.* If an increase of subsidiary stock described in paragraph (c)(2)(i)(A) of this section occurs before the date that the 5-percent shareholder increases its percentage ownership interest in the stock of the common parent (or loss subgroup parent), then the deemed issuance of stock is treated as occurring on that later date, but in an amount equal to the value of the subsidiary stock on the date it was acquired.

(vi) *Anti-duplication rule.* If two or more 5-percent shareholders are treated as increasing their percentage ownership interests pursuant to the same plan or arrangement described in paragraph (c)(3)(i) of this section, appropriate adjust-

Reg. § 1.1502-92(c)(4)

ments must be made so that the amount of stock treated as issued is not taken into account more than once.

(5) *Examples.* The following examples illustrate the principles of this paragraph (c):

Example 1. Stock of the common parent under supplemental rules. (i) A owns all the L stock. L is not a member of an affiliated group and has a net operating loss carryover arising in Year 1 that is carried over to Year 6. On September 20, Year 6, L transfers all of its assets and liabilities to a newly created subsidiary, S, in exchange for S stock. L and S thereafter file consolidated returns. On November 23, Year 6, B contributes cash to L in exchange for a 45 percent ownership interest in L and contributes cash to S for a 20 percent ownership interest in S.

(ii) During the 3 year period ending on November 23, Year 6, B is a 5% shareholder of L and of S that increases its ownership interest in L and S during that period. Under paragraph (c)(4)(ii) of this section, the determination whether L (the common parent of a loss group) has an ownership change on November 23, Year 6 (or, subject to paragraph (c)(4)(iv) of this section, on any testing date in the testing period which includes November 23, Year 6), is made by applying paragraph (b)(1)(i) of this section and by treating the value of B's 20 percent ownership interest in S as if it were L stock issued to B. Because B is a 5% shareholder of both L and S during the 3 year period ending on November 23, Year 6, and B's increase in its percentage ownership in the stock of S would be taken into account in determining if S (if it were a loss corporation) had an ownership change, it is not relevant whether L has actual knowledge of B's acquisition of S stock.

Example 2. Plan or arrangement—public offering of subsidiary stock. (i) A owns all the stock of L and L owns all the stock of L1. The L group has a consolidated net operating loss arising in Year 1 that resulted from the operations of L1 and that is carried over to Year 2. On October 7, Year 2, A sells 49 percent of the L stock to B. As part of a plan that includes the sale of L stock, A causes a public offering of L1 stock on November 6, Year 2. L has actual knowledge of the plan. The following is a graphic illustration of these facts:

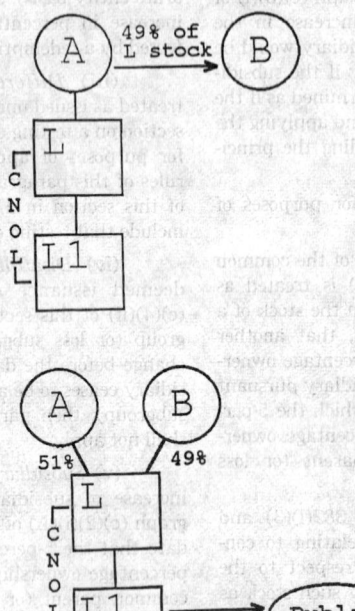

(ii) A's sale of the L stock to B does not cause an ownership change of the L loss group on October 7, Year 2, under the rules of § 1.382-2T and paragraph (b)(1)(i) of this section.

(iii) Because the issuance of L1 stock to the public occurs as part of the same plan as B's acquisition of L stock, and L has knowledge of the plan, paragraph (c)(4) of this section applies to determine whether the L loss group has an ownership change on November 6, Year 2 (or, subject to paragraph (c)(4)(iv) of this section, on any testing date for which the testing period includes November 6, Year 2).

(d) *Testing period following ownership change under this section.* If a loss group (or a loss subgroup) has had an ownership change under this section, the testing period for determining a subsequent ownership change with respect to pre-change consolidated attributes (or pre-change subgroup attributes) begins no earlier than the first day following the loss group's (or loss subgroup's) most recent change date.

(e) *Information statements*—(1) *Common parent of a loss group.* The common parent of a loss group must file the information statement required by § 1.382-2T(a)(2)(ii) for a consolidated return year because of any owner shift, equity structure shift, or other transaction described in § 1.382-2T(a)(2)(i)—

(i) With respect to the common parent and with respect to any subsidiary stock subject to paragraph (c) of this section; and

(ii) With respect to an ownership change described in § 1.1502-96(b) (relating to ownership changes of subsidiaries).

(2) *Abbreviated statement with respect to loss subgroups.* The common parent of a consolidated group that has a loss subgroup during a consolidated return year must file the information statement required by § 1.382-2T(a)(2)(ii) because of any owner shift, equity structure shift, or other transaction described in § 1.382-2T(a)(2)(i) with respect to the loss subgroup parent and with respect to any subsidiary stock subject to paragraph (c) of this section. Instead of filing a separate statement for each loss subgroup parent, the common parent (which is treated as a loss corporation) may file the single statement described in paragraph (e)(1) of this section. In addition to the information concerning stock ownership of the common parent, the single statement must identify each loss subgroup parent and state which loss subgroups, if any, have had ownership changes during the consolidated return year. The loss subgroup parent is, however, still required to maintain the records necessary to determine if the loss subgroup has an ownership change. This paragraph (e)(2) applies with respect to the attributes of a loss subgroup until, under § 1.1502-96(a), the attributes are no longer treated as described in § 1.1502-91(d) (relating to the definition of loss subgroup). After that time, the information statement described in paragraph (e)(1) of this section must be filed with respect to those attributes. [Reg. § 1.1502-92.]

☐ [*T.D. 8824, 6-25-99.*]

[Reg. § 1.1502-92A]

§ 1.1502-92A. Ownership change of a loss group or a loss subgroup generally applicable for testing dates before June 25, 1999.—(a) *Scope.* This section provides rules for determining if there is an ownership change for purposes of section 382 with respect to a loss group or a loss subgroup. See § 1.1502-94A for special rules for determining if there is an ownership change with respect to a new loss member and § 1.1502-96A(b) for special rules for determining if there is an ownership change of a subsidiary.

(b) *Determination of an ownership change*—(1) *Parent change method*—(i) *Loss group.* A loss group has an ownership change if the loss group's common parent has an ownership change under section 382 and the regulations thereunder. Solely for purposes of determining whether the common parent has an ownership change—

(A) The losses described in § 1.1502-91A(c) are treated as net operating losses (or a net unrealized built-in loss) of the common parent; and

(B) The common parent determines the earliest day that its testing period can begin by reference to only the attributes that make the group a loss group under § 1.1502-91A(c).

(ii) *Loss subgroup.* A loss subgroup has an ownership change if the loss subgroup parent has an ownership change under section 382 and the regulations thereunder. The principles of § 1.1502-95A(b) (relating to ceasing to be a member of a consolidated group) apply in determining whether the loss subgroup parent has an ownership change. Solely for purposes of determining whether the loss subgroup parent has an ownership change—

(A) The losses described in § 1.1502-91A(d) are treated as net operating losses (or a net unrealized built-in loss) of the loss subgroup parent;

(B) The day that the members of the loss subgroup become members of the group (or a loss subgroup) is treated as a testing date within the meaning of § 1.382-2(a)(4); and

(C) The loss subgroup parent determines the earliest day that its testing period can begin under § 1.382-2T(d)(3) by reference to only the attributes that make the members a loss subgroup under § 1.1502-91A(d).

(2) *Examples.* The following examples illustrate the principles of this paragraph (b).

Example 1. Loss group—ownership change of the common parent. (a) A owns all the L stock. L owns 80 percent and B owns 20 percent of the L1 stock. For Year 1, the L group has a consolidated net operating loss that resulted from the operations of L1 and that is carried over to Year 2. The value of the L stock is $1000. The total value of the L1 stock is $600 and the value of the L1 stock held by B is $120. The L group is a loss group under § 1.1502-91A(c)(1) because it is entitled to use its net operating loss carryover from Year 1. On August 15, Year 2, A sells 51 percent of the L stock to C. The following is a graphic illustration of these facts:

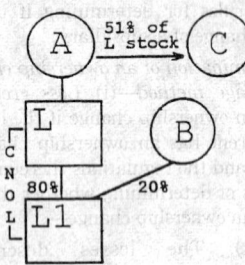

(b) Under paragraph (b)(1)(i) of this section, section 382 and the regulations thereunder are applied to L to determine whether it (and therefore the L loss group) has an ownership change with respect to its net operating loss carryover from Year 1 attributable to L1 on August 15, Year 2. The sale of the L stock to C causes an ownership change of L under § 1.382-2T and of the L loss group under paragraph (b)(1)(i) of this section. The amount of consolidated taxable income of the L loss group for any post-change taxable year that may be offset by its pre-change consolidated attributes (that is, the net operating loss carryover from Year 1 attributable to L1) may not exceed the consolidated section 382 limitation for the L loss group for the taxable year.

Example 2. Loss group—owner shifts of subsidiaries disregarded. (a) The facts are the same as in *Example 1*, except that on August 15, Year 2, A sells only 49 percent of the L stock to C and, on December 12, Year 3, in an unrelated transaction, B sells the 20 percent of the L1 stock to D. A's sale of the L stock to C does not cause an ownership change of L under § 1.382-2T nor of the L loss group under paragraph (b)(1)(i) of this section. The following is a graphic illustration of these facts:

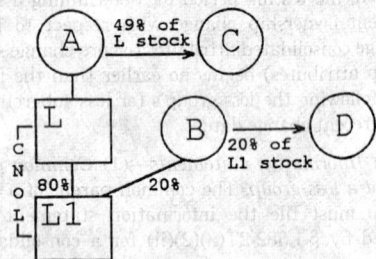

(b) B's subsequent sale of L1 stock is not taken into account for purposes of determining whether the L loss group has an ownership change under paragraph (b)(1)(i) of this section, and, accordingly, there is no ownership change of the L loss group. See paragraph (c) of this section, however, for a supplemental ownership change method that would apply to cause an ownership change if the purchases by C and D were pursuant to a plan or arrangement.

Example 3. Loss subgroup—ownership change of loss subgroup parent controls. (a) P owns all the L stock. L owns 80 percent and A owns 20 percent of the L1 stock. The P group has a consolidated net operating loss arising in Year 1 that is carried over to Year 2. On September 9, Year 2, P sells 51 percent of the L stock to B, and L1 is apportioned a portion of the Year 1 consolidated net operating loss under § 1.1502-21(b) or 1.1502-21T(b) in effect prior to June 25, 1999, as contained in 26 CFR part 1 revised April 1, 1999, as applicable, which it carries over to its next taxable year. L and L1 file a consolidated return for their first taxable year ending after the sale to B. The following is a graphic illustration of these facts:

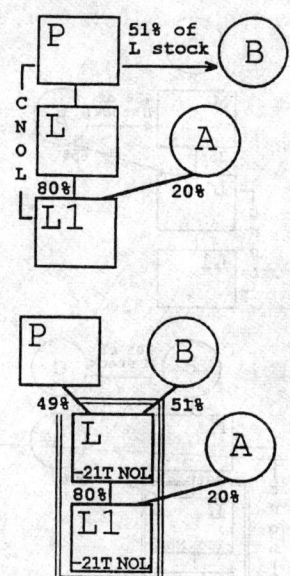

(b) Under § 1.1502-91A(d)(1), L and L1 compose a loss subgroup on September 9, Year 2, the day that they become members of the L group. Under paragraph (b)(1)(ii) of this section, section 382 and the regulations thereunder are applied to L to determine whether it (and therefore the L loss subgroup) has an ownership change with respect to the portion of the Year 1 consolidated net operating loss that is apportioned to L1 on September 9, Year 2. L has an ownership change resulting from P's sale of 51 percent of the L stock to A. Therefore, the L loss subgroup has an ownership change with respect to that loss.

Example 4. Loss group and loss subgroup—contemporaneous ownership changes. (a) A owns all the stock of corporation M, M owns 35 percent and B owns 65 percent of the L stock, and L owns all the L1 stock. The L group has a consolidated net operating loss arising in Year 1 that is carried over to Year 2. On May 19, Year 2, B sells 45 percent of the L stock to M for cash. M, L, and L1 thereafter file consolidated returns. L and L1 are each apportioned a portion of the Year 1 consolidated net operating loss, which they carry over to the M group's Year 2 and Year 3 consolidated return years. The M group has a consolidated net operating loss arising in Year 2 that is carried over to Year 3. On June 9, Year 3, A sells 70 percent of the M stock to C. The following is a graphic illustration of these facts:

Reg. § 1.1502-92A(b)(2)

Consolidated Returns

See p. 20,601 for regulations not amended to reflect law changes

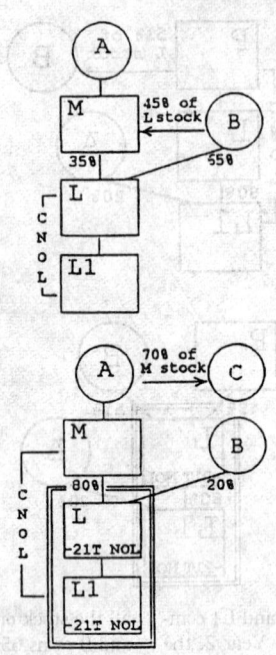

(b) Under § 1.1502-91A(d)(1), L and L1 compose a loss subgroup on May 19, Year 2, the day they become members of the M group. Under paragraph (b)(1)(ii) of this section, section 382 and the regulations thereunder are applied to L to determine whether L (and therefore the L loss subgroup) has an ownership change with respect to the loss carryovers from Year 1 on May 19, Year 2, a testing date because of B's sale of L stock to M. The sale of L stock to M results in only a 45 percentage point increase in A's ownership of L stock. Thus, there is no ownership change of L (or the L loss subgroup) with respect to those loss carryovers under paragraph (b)(1)(ii) of this section on that day.

(c) June 9, Year 3, is also a testing date with respect to the L loss subgroup because of A's sale of M stock to C. The sale results in a 56 percentage point increase in C's ownership of L stock, and L has an ownership change. Therefore, the L loss subgroup has an ownership change on that day with respect to the loss carryovers from Year 1.

(d) Paragraph (b)(1)(i) of this section requires that section 382 and the regulations thereunder be applied to M to determine whether M (and therefore the M loss group) has an ownership change with respect to the net operating loss carryover from Year 2 on June 9, Year 3, a testing date because of A's sale of M stock to C. The sale results in a 70 percentage point increase in C's ownership of M stock, and M has an ownership change. Therefore, the M loss group has an ownership change on that day with respect to that loss carryover.

(3) *Special adjustments*—(i) *Common parent succeeded by a new common parent.* For purposes of determining if a loss group has an ownership change, if the common parent of a loss group is succeeded or acquired by a new common parent and the loss group remains in existence, the new common parent is treated as a continuation of the former common parent with appropriate adjustments to take into account shifts in ownership of the former common parent during the testing period (including shifts that occur incident to the common parent's becoming the former common parent).

(ii) *Newly created loss subgroup parent.* For purposes of determining if a loss subgroup has an ownership change, if the member that is the loss subgroup parent has not been the loss subgroup parent for at least 3 years as of a testing date, appropriate adjustments must be made to take into account owner shifts of members of the loss subgroup so that the structure of the loss subgroup does not have the effect of avoiding an ownership change under section 382. (See paragraph (b)(3)(iii) *Example 3* of this section.)

(iii) *Examples.* The following examples illustrate the principles of this paragraph (b)(3).

Reg. § 1.1502-92A(b)(3)

Consolidated Returns

Example 1. New common parent acquires old common parent. (a) A, who owns all the L stock, sells 30 percent of the L stock to B on August 26, Year 1. L owns all the L1 stock. The L group has a consolidated net operating loss arising in Year 1 that is carried over to Year 3. On July 16, Year 2, A and B transfer their L stock to a newly created holding company, HC, in exchange for 70 percent and 30 percent, respectively, of the HC stock. HC, L, and L1 thereafter file consolidated returns. Under the principles of § 1.1502-75(d), the L loss group is treated as remaining in existence, with HC taking the place of L as the new common parent of the loss group. The following is a graphic illustration of these facts:

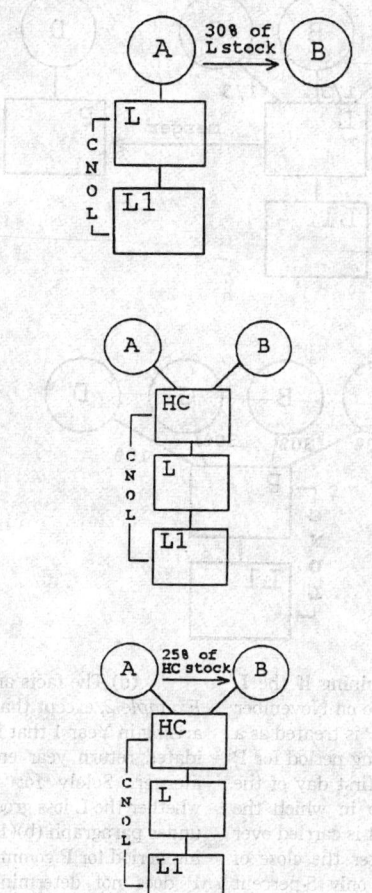

(b) On November 11, Year 3, A sells 25 percent of the HC stock to B. For purposes of determining if the L loss group has an ownership change under paragraph (b)(1)(i) of this section on November 11, Year 3, HC is treated as a continuation of L under paragraph (b)(3)(i) of this section because it acquired L and became the common parent without terminating the L loss group. Accordingly, HC's testing period commences on January 1, Year 1, the first day of the taxable year of the L loss group in which the consolidated net operating loss that is carried over to Year 3 arose (see § 1.382-2T(d)(3)(i)). Immediately after the close of November 11, Year 3, B's percentage ownership interest in the common parent of the loss group (HC) has increased by 55 percentage points over its lowest percentage ownership during the testing period (zero percent). Accordingly, HC and the L loss group have an ownership change on that day.

Example 2. New common parent in case in which common parent ceases to exist. (a) A, B, and C each own one-third of the L stock. L owns all the L1 stock. The L group has a consolidated

Reg. § 1.1502-92A(b)(3)

net operating loss arising in Year 2 that is carried over to Year 3. On November 22, Year 3, L is merged into P, a corporation owned by D, and L1 thereafter files consolidated returns with P. A, B, and C, as a result of owning stock of L, own 90 percent of P's stock after the merger. D owns the remaining 10 percent of P's stock. The merger of L into P qualifies as a reverse acquisition of the L group under § 1.1502-75(d)(3)(i), and the L loss group is treated as remaining in existence, with P taking the place of L as the new common parent of the L group. The following is a graphic illustration of these facts:

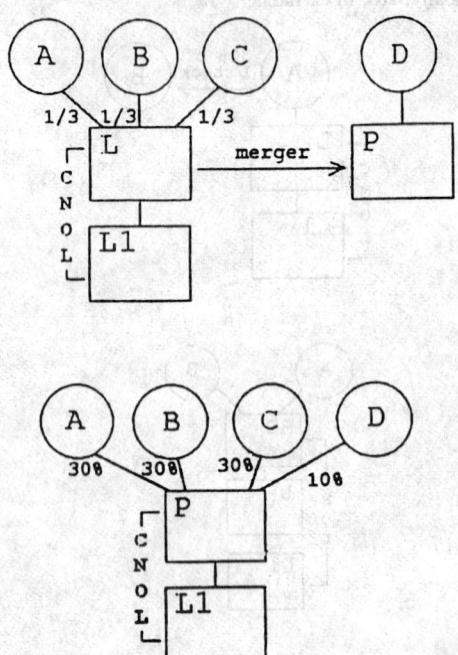

Reg. § 1.1502-92A(b)(3)

(b) For purposes of determining if the L loss group has an ownership change on November 22, Year 3, the day of the merger, P is treated as a continuation of L so that the testing period for P begins on January 1, Year 2, the first day of the taxable year of the L loss group in which the consolidated net operating loss that is carried over to Year 3 arose. Immediately after the close of November 22, Year 3, D is the only 5-percent shareholder that has increased his ownership interest in P during the testing period (from zero to 10 percentage points).

(c) The facts are the same as in paragraph (a) of this *Example 2*, except that A has held 23 1/3 shares (23 1/3 percent) of L's stock for five years, and A purchased an additional 10 shares of L stock from E two years before the merger. Immediately after the close of the day of the merger (a testing date), A's ownership interest in P, the common parent of the L loss group, has increased by 6 2/3 percentage points over her lowest percentage ownership during the testing period (23 1/3 percent to 30 percent).

(d) The facts are the same as in (a) of this *Example 2*, except that P has a net operating loss arising in Year 1 that is carried to the first consolidated return year ending after the day of the merger. Solely for purposes of determining whether the L loss group has an ownership change under paragraph (b)(1)(i) of this section, the testing period for P commences on January 1, Year 2. P does not determine the earliest day for its testing period by reference to its net operating loss carryover from Year 1, which § § 1502-1(f)(3) and 1.1502-75(d)(3)(i) treat as arising in a SRLY. See § 1.1502-94A to determine the application of section 382 with respect to P's net operating loss carryover.

Example 3. Newly acquired loss subgroup parent. (a) P owns all the L stock and L owns all the L1 stock. The P group has a consolidated net operating loss arising in Year 1 that is carried over to Year 3. On January 19, Year 2, L issues a 20 percent stock interest to B. On February 5, Year 3, P contributes its L stock to a newly formed subsidiary, HC, in exchange for all the HC stock, and distributes the HC stock to its sole shareholder A. HC, L, and L1 thereafter file consolidated returns. A portion of the P group's Year 1 consolidated net operating loss is apportioned to L and L1 under § 1.1502-21T(b) and is carried over to the HC group's year ending after February 5, Year 3. HC, L, and L1 compose a loss subgroup within the meaning of § 1.1502-91A(d) with respect to the net operating loss carryovers from Year 1. The following is a graphic illustration of these facts:

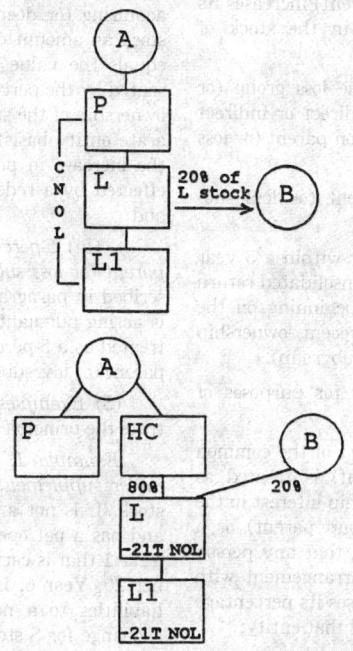

(b) February 5, Year 3, is a testing date for HC as the loss subgroup parent with respect to the net operating loss carryovers of L and L1 from Year 1. See paragraph (b)(1)(ii)(B) of this section. For purposes of determining whether HC has an ownership change on the testing date, appropriate adjustments must be made with respect to the changes in the percentage ownership of the stock of HC because HC was not the loss subgroup parent for at least 3 years prior to the day on which it became a member of the HC loss subgroup (a testing date). The appropriate adjustments include adjustments so that HC succeeds to the owner shifts of other members of the former group. Thus, HC succeeds to the owner shift of L that resulted from the sale of the 20 percent interest to B in determining whether the HC loss subgroup has an ownership change on February 5, Year 3, and on any subsequent testing date that includes January 19, Year 2.

(4) *End of separate tracking of certain losses.* If § 1.1502-96A(a) (relating to the end of separate tracking of attributes) applies to a loss subgroup, then, while one or more members that were included in the loss subgroup remain members of the consolidated group, there is an ownership change with respect to their attributes described in § 1.1502-96A(a)(2) only if the consolidated group is a loss group and has an ownership change under paragraph (b)(1)(i) of this section (or such a member has an ownership change under § 1.1502-96A(b) (relating to ownership changes of subsidiaries)). If, however, the loss subgroup has had an ownership change before § 1.1502-96A(a) applies, see § 1.1502-96A(c) for the continuing application of the subgroup's section 382 limitation with respect to its pre-change subgroup attributes.

(c) *Supplemental rules for determining ownership change* —(1) *Scope.* This paragraph (c) contains a supplemental rule for determining whether there is an ownership change of a loss group (or loss subgroup). It applies in addition to, and not instead of, the rules of paragraph (b) of this section. Thus, for example, if the common parent of the loss group has an ownership change under paragraph (b) of this section, the loss group has an ownership change even if, by applying this

Reg. § 1.1502-92A(c)(1)

paragraph (c), the common parent would not have an ownership change.

(2) *Cause for applying supplemental rule.* This paragraph (c) applies to a loss group (or loss subgroup) if—

(i) Any 5-percent shareholder of the common parent (or loss subgroup parent) increases its percentage ownership interest in the stock of both—

(A) A subsidiary of the loss group (or loss subgroup) other than by a direct or indirect acquisition of stock of the common parent (or loss subgroup parent); and

(B) The common parent (or loss subgroup parent); and

(ii) Those increases occur within a 3 year period ending on any day of a consolidated return year or, if shorter, the period beginning on the first day following the most recent ownership change of the loss group (or loss subgroup).

(3) *Operating rules.* Solely for purposes of this paragraph (c)—

(i) A 5-percent shareholder of the common parent (or loss subgroup parent) is treated as increasing its percentage ownership interest in the common parent (or loss subgroup parent) or a subsidiary to the extent, if any, that any person acting pursuant to a plan or arrangement with the 5-percent shareholder increases its percentage ownership interest in the stock of that entity;

(ii) The rules in section 382(l)(3) and §§ 1.382-2T(h) and 1.382-4(d) (relating to constructive ownership) apply with respect to the stock of the subsidiary by treating such stock as stock of a loss corporation; and

(iii) In the case of a loss subgroup, a subsidiary includes any member of the loss subgroup other than the loss subgroup parent. (The loss subgroup parent is, however, a subsidiary of the loss group of which it is a member.)

(4) *Supplemental ownership change rules.* The determination whether the common parent (or loss subgroup parent) has an ownership change is made by applying paragraph (b)(1) of this section as modified by the following additional rules—

(i) *Additional testing dates for the common parent (or loss subgroup parent).* A testing date for the common parent (or loss subgroup parent) also includes—

(A) Each day on which there is an increase in the percentage ownership of stock of a subsidiary as described in paragraph (c)(2) of this section; and

(B) The first day of the first consolidated return year for which the group is a loss group (or the members compose a loss subgroup);

(ii) *Treatment of subsidiary stock as stock of the common parent (or loss subgroup parent).* The common parent (or loss subgroup parent) is treated as though it had issued to the person acquiring (or deemed to acquire) the subsidiary stock an amount of its own stock (by value) that equals the value of the subsidiary stock represented by the percentage increase in that person's ownership of the subsidiary (determined on a separate entity basis). A similar principle applies if the increase in percentage ownership interest is effected by a redemption or similar transaction; and

(iii) *5-percent shareholder of the common parent (or loss subgroup parent).* Any person described in paragraph (c)(3)(i) of this section who is acting pursuant to the plan or arrangement is treated as a 5-percent shareholder of the common parent (or loss subgroup parent).

(5) *Examples.* The following examples illustrate the principles of this paragraph (c).

Example 1. Stock of the common parent under supplemental rules. (a) A owns all the L stock. L is not a member of an affiliated group and has a net operating loss carryover arising in Year 1 that is carried over to Year 6. On September 20, Year 6, L transfers all of its assets and liabilities to a newly created subsidiary, S, in exchange for S stock. L and S thereafter file consolidated returns. On November 23, Year 6, B contributes cash to L in exchange for a 45 percent ownership interest in L and contributes cash to S for a 20 percent ownership interest in S.

(b) B is a 5-percent shareholder of L who increases his percentage ownership interest in L and S during the 3 year period ending on November 23, Year 6. Under paragraph (c)(4)(ii) of this section, the determination whether L (the common parent of a loss group) has an ownership change on November 23, Year 6 (or on any testing date in the testing period which includes November 23, Year 6), is made by applying paragraph (b)(1)(i) of this section and by treating the value of B's 20 percent ownership interest in S as if it were L stock issued to B.

Example 2. Plan or arrangement—public offering of subsidiary stock. (a) A owns all the stock of L and L owns all the stock of L1. The L group has a consolidated net operating loss arising in Year 1 that resulted from the operations of L1 and that is carried over to Year 2. As part of a plan, A sells 49 percent of the L stock to B on October 7, Year 2, and L1 issues new stock representing a 20 percent ownership interest in L1 to

Reg. § 1.1502-92A(c)(2)

the public on November 6, Year 2. The following is a graphic illustration of these facts:

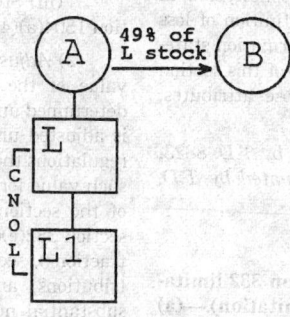

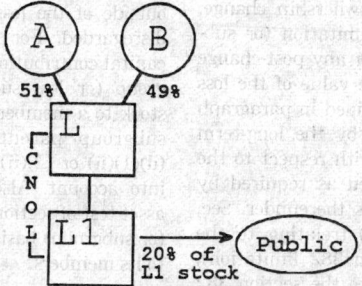

(b) A's sale of the L stock to B does not cause an ownership change of the L loss group on October 7, Year 2, under the rules of § 1.382-2T and paragraph (b)(1)(i) of this section.

(c) Because the issuance of L1 stock to the public occurs in connection with B's acquisition of L stock pursuant to a plan, paragraph (c)(4) of this section applies to determine whether the L loss group has an ownership change on November 6, Year 2 (or on any testing date for which the testing period includes November 6, Year 2).

(d) *Testing period following ownership change under this section.* If a loss group (or a loss subgroup) has had an ownership change under this section, the testing period for determining a subsequent ownership change with respect to pre-change consolidated attributes (or pre-change subgroup attributes) begins no earlier than the first day following the loss group's (or loss subgroup's) most recent change date.

(e) *Information statements*—(1) *Common parent of a loss group.* The common parent of a loss group must file the information statement required by § 1.382-2T(a)(2)(ii) for a consolidated return year because of any owner shift, equity structure shift, or the issuance or transfer of an option—

(i) With respect to the common parent and with respect to any subsidiary stock subject to paragraph (c) of this section; and

(ii) With respect to an ownership change described in § 1.1502-96A(b) (relating to ownership changes of subsidiaries).

(2) *Abbreviated statement with respect to loss subgroups.* The common parent of a consolidated group that has a loss subgroup during a consolidated return year must file the information statement required by § 1.382-2T(a)(2)(ii) because of any owner shift, equity structure shift, or issuance or transfer of an option with respect to the loss subgroup parent and with respect to any subsidiary stock subject to paragraph (c) of this section. Instead of filing a separate statement for each loss subgroup parent, the common parent (which is treated as a loss corporation) may file the single statement described in paragraph (e)(1) of this section. In addition to the information concerning stock ownership of the common parent, the single statement must identify each loss subgroup parent and state which loss subgroups, if any, have had ownership changes during the consolidated return year. The loss subgroup parent is, however, still required to maintain the records necessary to determine if the loss subgroup has an ownership change. This paragraph

Reg. § 1.1502-92A(e)(2)

(e)(2) applies with respect to the attributes of a loss subgroup until, under § 1.1502-96A(a), the attributes are no longer treated as described in § 1.1502-91A(d) (relating to the definition of loss subgroup). After that time, the information statement described in paragraph (e)(1) of this section must be filed with respect to those attributes. [Reg. § 1.1502-92A.]

☐ [T.D. 8678, 6-26-96. Amended by T.D. 8823, 6-25-99 *and amended and redesignated by T.D. 8824, 6-25-99.*]

[Reg. § 1.1502-93]

§ 1.1502-93. Consolidated section 382 limitation (or subgroup section 382 limitation).—(a) *Determination of the consolidated section 382 limitation (or subgroup section 382 limitation*— (1) *In general.* Following an ownership change, the consolidated section 382 limitation (or subgroup section 382 limitation) for any post-change year is an amount equal to the value of the loss group (or loss subgroup), as defined in paragraph (b) of this section, multiplied by the long-term tax-exempt rate that applies with respect to the ownership change, and adjusted as required by section 382 and the regulations thereunder. See, for example, section 382(b)(2) (relating to the carryforward of unused section 382 limitation), section 382(b)(3)(B) (relating to the section 382 limitation for the post-change year that includes the change date), section 382(h) (relating to recognized built-in gains and section 338 gains), and section 382(m)(2) (relating to short taxable years). For special rules relating to the recognized built-in gains of a loss group (or loss subgroup), see paragraph (c)(2) of this section.

(2) *Coordination with apportionment rule.* For special rules relating to apportionment of a consolidated section 382 limitation (or a subgroup section 382 limitation) or net unrealized built-in gain when one or more corporations cease to be members of a loss group (or a loss subgroup) and to aggregation of amounts so apportioned, see § 1.1502-95(c).

(b) *Value of the loss group (or loss subgroup)*— (1) *Stock value immediately before ownership change.* Subject to any adjustment under paragraph (b)(2) of this section, the value of the loss group (or loss subgroup) is the value, immediately before the ownership change, of the stock of each member, other than stock that is owned directly or indirectly by another member. For this purpose—

(i) Ownership is determined under § 1.382-2T;

(ii) A member is considered to indirectly own stock of another member through a nonmember only if the member has a 5-percent or greater ownership interest in the nonmember; and

(iii) Stock includes stock described in section 1504(a)(4) and § 1.382-2T(f)(18)(ii) and (iii).

(2) *Adjustment to value*—(i) *In general.* The value of the loss group (or loss subgroup), as determined under paragraph (b)(1) of this section, is adjusted under any rule in section 382 or the regulations thereunder requiring an adjustment to such value for purposes of computing the amount of the section 382 limitation. See, for example, section 382(e)(2) (redemptions and corporate contractions), section 382(l)(1) (certain capital contributions) and section 382(l)(4) (ownership of substantial nonbusiness assets). For purposes of section 382(e)(2), redemptions and corporate contractions that do not effect a transfer of value outside of the loss group (or loss subgroup) are disregarded. For purposes of section 382(l)(1), capital contributions between members of the loss group (or loss subgroup) (or a contribution of stock to a member made solely to satisfy the loss subgroup parent requirement of paragraph (d)(1)(ii) or (2)(ii) of this section), are not taken into account. Also, the substantial nonbusiness asset test of section 382(l)(4) is applied on a group (or subgroup) basis, and is not applied separately to its members.

(ii) *Anti-duplication.* Appropriate adjustments must be made to the extent necessary to prevent any duplication of the value of the stock of a member, even though corporations that do not file consolidated returns may not be required to make such an adjustment. In making these adjustments, the group (or loss subgroup) may apply the principles of § 1.382-8 (relating to controlled groups of corporations) in determining the value of a loss group (or loss subgroup) even if that section would not apply if separate returns were filed. Also, the principles of § 1.382-5(d) (relating to successive ownership changes and absorption of a section 382 limitation) may apply to adjust the consolidated section 382 limitation (or subgroup section 382 limitation) of a loss group (or loss subgroup) to avoid a duplication of value if there are simultaneous (rather than successive) ownership changes.

(3) *Examples.* The following examples illustrate the principles of this paragraph (b):

Example 1. Basic case. (i) L, L1, and L2 compose a loss group. L has outstanding common stock, the value of which is $100. L1 has outstanding common stock and preferred stock that is described in section 1504(a)(4). L owns 90 percent of the L1 common stock, and A owns the remaining 10 percent of the L1 common stock plus all the preferred stock. The value of the L1 common

Reg. § 1.1502-93(a)(2)

stock is $40, and the value of the L1 preferred stock is $30. L2 has outstanding common stock, 50 percent of which is owned by L and 50 percent by L1. The L group has an ownership change. The following is a graphic illustration of these facts:

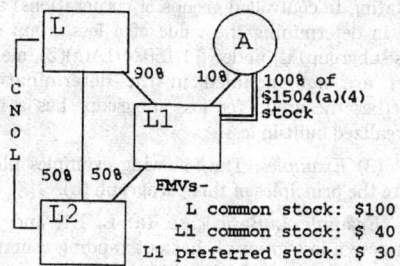

(ii) Under paragraph (b)(1) of this section, the L group does not include the value of the stock of any member that is owned directly or indirectly by another member in computing its consolidated section 382 limitation. Accordingly, the value of the stock of the loss group is $134, the sum of the value of—

(a) The common stock of L ($100);

(b) The 10 percent of the L1 common stock ($4) owned by A; and

(c) The L1 preferred stock ($30) owned by A.

Example 2—Indirect ownership. (i) L and L1 compose a consolidated group. L's stock has a value of $100. L owns 80 shares (worth $80) and corporation M owns 20 shares (worth $20) of the L1 stock. L also owns 79 percent of the stock of corporation M. The L group has an ownership change. The following is a graphic illustration of these facts:

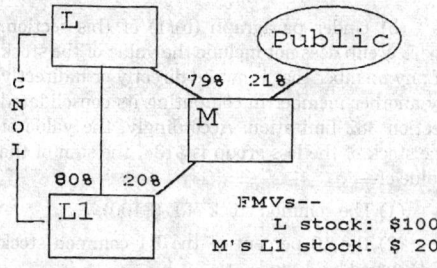

(ii) Under paragraph (b)(1) of this section, because of L's more than 5 percent ownership interest in M, a nonmember, L is considered to indirectly own 15.8 shares of the L1 stock held by M (79%×20 shares). The value of the L loss group is $104.20, the sum of the values of—

(a) The L stock ($100); and

(b) The L1 stock not owned directly or indirectly by L (21%×$20, or $4.20).

(c) *Recognized built-in gain of a loss group or loss subgroup*—(1) *In general.* If a loss group (or loss subgroup) has a net unrealized built-in gain, any recognized built-in gain of the loss group (or loss subgroup) is taken into account under section 382(h) in determining the consolidated section 382 limitation (or subgroup section 382 limitation).

(2) *Adjustments.* Appropriate adjustments must be made so that any recognized built-in gain of a member that increases more than one section 382 limitation (whether consolidated, subgroup, or separate) does not effect a duplication in the amount of consolidated taxable income that can be offset by pre-change net operating losses. For example, a consolidated section 382 limitation that is increased by recognized built-in gains is reduced to the extent that pre-change net operating losses of a loss subgroup absorb additional consolidated taxable income because the same recognized built-in gains caused an increase in that loss subgroup's section 382 limitation. In addition, recognized built-in gain may not increase the amount of consolidated taxable income that can be offset by recognized built-in losses.

(d) *Continuity of business*—(1) *In general.* A loss group (or a loss subgroup) is treated as a single entity for purposes of determining whether it satisfies the continuity of business enterprise requirement of section 382(c)(1).

(2) *Example.* The following example illustrates the principle of this paragraph (d):

Example. Continuity of business enterprise. L owns all the stock of two subsidiaries, L1 and L2. The L group has an ownership change. It has pre-change consolidated attributes attributable to L2. Each of the members has historically conducted a separate line of business. Each line of business is approximately equal in value. One year after the ownership change, L discontinues its separate business and the business of L2. The separate business of L1 is continued for the remainder of the 2 year period following the ownership change. The continuity of business enterprise requirement of section 382(c)(1) is met even though the separate businesses of L and L2 are discontinued.

(e) *Limitations of losses under other rules.* If a section 382 limitation for a post-change year exceeds the consolidated taxable income that may be offset by pre-change attributes for any reason, including the application of the limitation of § 1.1502-21(c), the amount of the excess is carried forward under section 382(b)(2) (relating to the carryforward of unused section 382 limitation). [Reg. § 1.1502-93.]

☐ [T.D. 8824, 6-25-99.]

Reg. § 1.1502-93(e)

[Reg. § 1.1502-93A]

§ 1.1502-93A. Consolidated section 382 limitation (or subgroup section 382 limitation) generally applicable for testing dates before June 25, 1999.—(a) *Determination of the consolidated section 382 limitation (or subgroup section 382 limitation)*—(1) *In general.* Following an ownership change, the consolidated section 382 limitation (or subgroup section 382 limitation) for any post-change year is an amount equal to the value of the loss group (or loss subgroup), as defined in paragraph (b) of this section, multiplied by the long-term tax-exempt rate that applies with respect to the ownership change, and adjusted as required by section 382 and the regulations thereunder. See, for example, section 382(b)(2) (relating to the carryforward of unused section 382 limitation), section 382(b)(3)(B) (relating to the section 382 limitation for the post-change year that includes the change date), section 382(m)(2) (relating to short taxable years), and section 382(h) (relating to recognized built-in gains and section 338 gains).

(2) *Coordination with apportionment rule.* For special rules relating to apportionment of a consolidated section 382 limitation (or a subgroup section 382 limitation) when one or more corporations cease to be members of a loss group (or a loss subgroup) and to aggregation of amounts so apportioned, see § 1.1502-95A(c).

(b) *Value of the loss group (or loss subgroup)*—(1) *Stock value immediately before ownership change.* Subject to any adjustment under paragraph (b)(2) of this section, the value of the loss group (or loss subgroup) is the value, immediately before the ownership change, of the stock of each member, other than stock that is owned directly or indirectly by another member. For this purpose—

(i) Ownership is determined under § 1.382-2T;

(ii) A member is considered to indirectly own stock of another member through a nonmember only if the member has a 5-percent or greater ownership interest in the nonmember; and

(iii) Stock includes stock described in section 1504(a)(4) and § 1.382-2T(f)(18)(ii) and (iii).

(2) *Adjustment to value.* The value of the loss group (or loss subgroup), as determined under paragraph (b)(1) of this section, is adjusted under any rule in section 382 or the regulations thereunder requiring an adjustment to such value for purposes of computing the amount of the section 382 limitation. See, for example, section 382(e)(2) (redemptions and corporate contractions), section 382(l)(1) (certain capital contributions) and section 382(l)(4) (ownership of substantial nonbusiness assets). The value of the loss group (or loss subgroup) determined under this paragraph (b) is also adjusted to the extent necessary to prevent any duplication of the value of the stock of a member. For example, the principles of § 1.382-8 (relating to controlled groups of corporations) apply in determining the value of a loss group (or loss subgroup) if, under § 1.1502-91A(g)(2), members are not included in the determination whether the group (or loss subgroup) has a net unrealized built-in loss.

(3) *Examples.* The following examples illustrate the principles of this paragraph (b).

Example 1. Basic case. (a) L, L1, and L2 compose a loss group. L has outstanding common stock, the value of which is $100. L1 has outstanding common stock and preferred stock that is described in section 1504(a)(4). L owns 90 percent of the L1 common stock, and A owns the remaining 10 percent of the L1 common stock plus all the preferred stock. The value of the L1 common stock is $40, and the value of the L1 preferred stock is $30. L2 has outstanding common stock, 50 percent of which is owned by L and 50 percent by L1. The L group has an ownership change. The following is a graphic illustration of these facts:

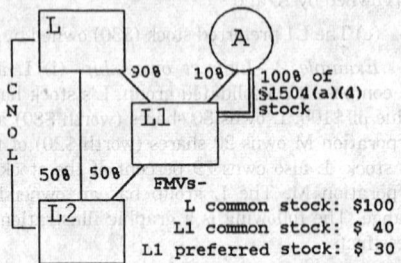

(b) Under paragraph (b)(1) of this section, the L group does not include the value of the stock of any member that is owned directly or indirectly by another member in computing its consolidated section 382 limitation. Accordingly, the value of the stock of the loss group is $134, the sum of the value of—

(1) The common stock of L ($100);

(2) the 10 percent of the L1 common stock ($4) owned by A; and

(3) The L1 preferred stock ($30) owned by A.

Example 2. Indirect ownership. (a) L and L1 compose a consolidated group. L's stock has a value of $100. L owns 80 shares (worth $80) and corporation M owns 20 shares (worth $20) of the L1 stock. L also owns 79 percent of the stock of corporation M. The L group has an ownership change. The following is a graphic illustration of these facts:

Consolidated Returns

See p. 20,601 for regulations not amended to reflect law changes

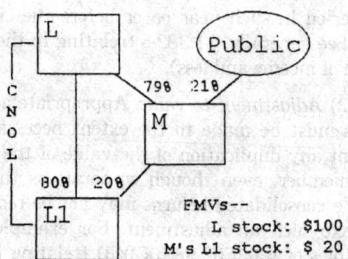

FMVs--
L stock: $100
M's L1 stock: $ 20

(b) Under paragraph (b)(1) of this section, because of L's more than 5 percent ownership interest in M, a nonmember, L is considered to indirectly own 15.8 shares of the L1 stock held by M (79% x 20 shares). The value of the L loss group is $104.20, the sum of the values of—

(1) The L stock ($100); and

(2) The L1 stock not owned directly or indirectly by L (21% x $20, or $4.20).

(c) *Recognized built-in gain of a loss group or loss subgroup.* If a loss group (or loss subgroup) has a net unrealized built-in gain, any recognized built-in gain of the loss group (or loss subgroup) is taken into account under section 382(h) in determining the consolidated section 382 limitation (or subgroup section 382 limitation). See § 1.1502-99A(a)(2) for a special rule relating to the application of § 1.502-93(c)(2) to consolidated return years for which the due date of the return is after June 25, 1999.

(d) *Continuity of business*—(1) *In general.* A loss group (or a loss subgroup) is treated as a single entity for purposes of determining whether it satisfies the continuity of business enterprise requirement of section 382(c)(1).

(2) *Example.* The following example illustrates the principle of this paragraph (d).

Example. Continuity of business enterprise. L owns all the stock of two subsidiaries, L1 and L2. The L group has an ownership change. It has pre-change consolidated attributes attributable to L2. Each of the members has historically conducted a separate line of business. Each line of business is approximately equal in value. One year after the ownership change, L discontinues its separate business and the business of L2. The separate business of L1 is continued for the remainder of the 2 year period following the ownership change. The continuity of business enterprise requirement of section 382(c)(1) is met even though the separate businesses of L and L2 are discontinued.

(e) *Limitations of losses under other rules.* If a section 382 limitation for a post-change year exceeds the consolidated taxable income that may be offset by pre-change attributes for any reason,

including the application of the limitation of § 1.1502-21(c) or 1.1502-21T(c) in effect prior to June 25, 1999, as contained in 26 CFR part 1 revised April 1, 1999, as applicable, the amount of the excess is carried forward under section 382(b)(2) (relating to the carryforward of unused section 382 limitation). [Reg. § 1.1502-93A.]

☐ [*T.D. 8678, 6-26-96. Amended by T.D. 8823, 6-25-99 and amended and redesignated by T.D. 8824, 6-25-99.*]

[Reg. § 1.1502-94]

§ 1.1502-94. **Coordination with section 382 and the regulations thereunder when a corporation becomes a member of a consolidated group.**—(a) *Scope*—(1) *In general.* This section applies section 382 and the regulations thereunder to a corporation that is a new loss member of a consolidated group. A corporation is a new loss member if it—

(i) Carries over a net operating loss that arose (or is treated under § 1.1502-21(c) as arising) in a SRLY with respect to the current group, and that is not described in § 1.1502-91(d)(1); or

(ii) Has a net unrealized built-in loss (determined under paragraph (c) of this section immediately before it becomes a member of the current group by treating that day as a change date) that is not taken into account under § 1.1502-91(d)(2) in determining whether two or more corporations compose a loss subgroup.

(2) *Successor corporation as new loss member.* A new loss member also includes any successor to a corporation that has a net operating loss carryover arising in a SRLY and that is treated as remaining in existence under § 1.382-2(a)(1)(ii) following a transaction described in section 381(a).

(3) *Coordination in the case of a loss subgroup.* For rules regarding the determination of whether there is an ownership change of a loss subgroup with respect to a net operating loss or a net unrealized built-in loss described in § 1.1502-91(d) (relating to the definition of loss subgroup) and the computation of a subgroup section 382 limitation following such an ownership change, see §§ 1.1502-92 and 1.1502-93.

(4) *End of separate tracking of certain losses.* If § 1.1502-96(a) (relating to the end of separate tracking of attributes) applies to a new loss member, then, while that member remains a member of the consolidated group, there is an ownership change with respect to its attributes described in § 1.1502-96(a)(2) only if the consolidated group is a loss group and has an ownership change under § 1.1502-92(b)(1)(i) (or that member has an ownership change under § 1.1502-96(b) (relating to

Reg. § 1.1502-94(a)(4)

ownership changes of subsidiaries)). If, however, the new loss member has had an ownership change before § 1.1502-96(a) applies, see § 1.1502-96(c) for the continuing application of the section 382 limitation with respect to the member's pre-change losses.

(5) *Cross-reference.* See section 382(a) and § 1.1502-96(c) for the continuing effect of an ownership change after a corporation becomes or ceases to be a member.

(b) *Application of section 382 to a new loss member*—(1) *In general.* Section 382 and the regulations thereunder apply to a new loss member to determine, on a separate entity basis, whether and to what extent a section 382 limitation applies to limit the amount of consolidated taxable income that may be offset by the new loss member's pre-change separate attributes. For example, if an ownership change with respect to the new loss member occurs under section 382 and the regulations thereunder, the amount of consolidated taxable income for any post-change year that may be offset by the new loss member's pre-change separate attributes shall not exceed the section 382 limitation as determined separately under section 382(b) with respect to that member for such year. If the post-change year includes the change date, section 382(b)(3)(A) is applied so that the section 382 limitation of the new loss member does not apply to the portion of the taxable income for such year that is allocable to the period in such year on or before the change date. See generally § 1.382-6 (relating to the allocation of income and loss).

(2) *Adjustment to value.* Appropriate adjustments must be made to the extent necessary to prevent any duplication of the value of the stock of a member, even though corporations that do not file consolidated returns may not be required to make such an adjustment. For example, the principles of § 1.1502-93(b)(2)(ii) (relating to adjustments to value) apply in determining the value of a new loss member.

(3) *Pre-change separate attribute defined.* A pre-change separate attribute of a new loss member is—

(i) Any net operating loss carryover of the new loss member described in paragraph (a)(1) of this section; and

(ii) Any recognized built-in loss of the new loss member.

(4) *Examples.* The following examples illustrate the principles of this paragraph (b):

Example 1. Basic case. (i) A and P each own 50 percent of the L stock. On December 19, Year 6, P purchases 30 percent of the L stock from A for cash. L has net operating losses arising in Year 1 and Year 2 that it carries over to Year 6 and Year 7. The following is a graphic illustration of these facts:

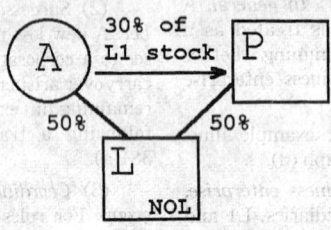

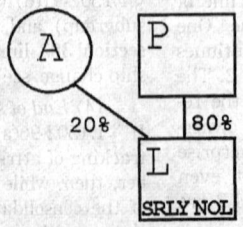

(ii) L is a new loss member because it has net operating loss carryovers that arose in a SRLY with respect to the P group and L is not a member of a loss subgroup under § 1.1502-91(d). Under section 382 and the regulations thereunder, L is a loss corporation on December 19, Year 6, that day is a testing date for L, and the testing period for L commences on December 20, Year 3.

Reg. § 1.1502-94(a)(5)

(iii) P's purchase of L stock does not cause an ownership change of L on December 19, Year 6, with respect to the net operating loss carryovers from Year 1 and Year 2 under section 382 and § 1.382-2T. The use of the loss carryovers, however, is subject to limitation under § 1.1502-21(c).

Example 2. Multiple new loss members. (i) The facts are the same as in *Example 1*, and, on December 31, Year 6, L purchases all the stock of L1 from B for cash. L1 has a net operating loss of $40 arising in Year 3 that it carries over to Year 7. The following is a graphic illustration of these facts:

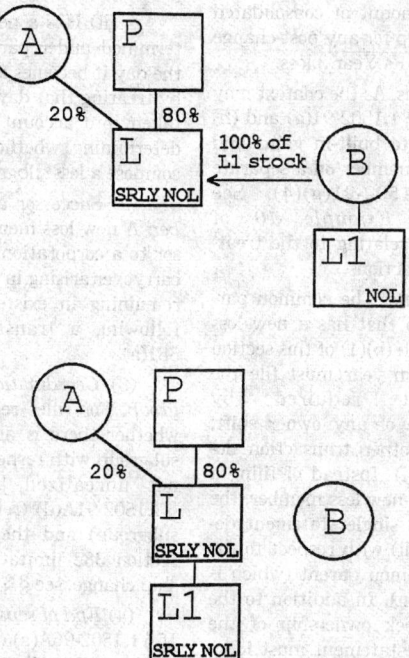

(ii) L1 is a new loss member because it has a net operating loss carryover from Year 3 that arose in a SRLY with respect to the P group and L1 is not a member of a loss subgroup under § 1.1502-91(d)(1).

(iii) L's purchase of all the stock of L1 causes an ownership change of L1 on December 31, Year 6, under section 382 and § 1.382-2T. Accordingly, a section 382 limitation based on the value of the L1 stock immediately before the ownership change limits the amount of consolidated taxable income of the P group for any post-change year that may be offset by L1's loss from Year 3.

(iv) L1's ownership change upon becoming a member of the P group is an ownership change described in § 1.1502-96(a). Thus, starting on January 1, Year 7, the P group no longer separately tracks owner shifts of the stock of L1 with respect to L1's loss from Year 3, and the P group is a loss group because L1's Year 3 loss is treated as a loss described in § 1.1502-91(c).

Example 3. Ownership changes of new loss members. (i) The facts are the same as in *Example 2*, and, on July 30, Year 7, C purchases all the stock of P for cash.

(ii) L is a new loss member on July 30, Year 7, because its Year 1 and Year 2 losses arose in SRLYs with respect to the P group and it is not a member of a loss subgroup under § 1.1502-91(d)(1). The testing period for L commences on August 1, Year 4. C's purchase of all the P stock causes an ownership change of L on July 30, Year 7, under section 382 and § 1.382-2T with respect to its Year 1 and Year 2 losses. Accordingly, a section 382 limitation based on the value of the L stock immediately before the ownership change limits the amount of consolidated taxable income of the P group for any post-change year that may be offset by L's Year 1 and Year 2 losses. See § 1.1502-21(c) for rules relating to an additional limitation.

(iii) The P group is a loss group on July 30, Year 7, because it is entitled to use L1's loss from

Reg. § 1.1502-94(b)(4)

Year 3, and such loss is no longer treated as a loss of a new loss member starting the day after L1's ownership change on December 31, Year 6. See §§ 1.1502-96(a) and 1.1502-91(c)(2). C's purchase of all the P stock causes an ownership change of P, and therefore the P loss group, on July 30, Year 7, with respect to L1's Year 3 loss. Accordingly, a consolidated section 382 limitation based on the value of the P stock immediately before the ownership change limits the amount of consolidated taxable income of the P group for any post-change year that may be offset by L1's Year 3 loss.

(c) *Built-in gains and losses.* As the context may require, the principles of §§ 1.1502-91(g) and (h) and 1.1502-93(c) (relating to built-in gains and losses) apply to a new loss member on a separate entity basis. See § 1.1502-91(g)(4). See § 1.1502-13 (including *Example 10* of § 1.1502-13(c)(7)) for rules relating to the treatment of intercompany transactions.

(d) *Information statements.* The common parent of a consolidated group that has a new loss member subject to paragraph (b)(1) of this section during a consolidated return year must file the information statement required by § 1.382-2T(a)(2)(ii) because of any owner shift, equity structure shift, or other transaction described in § 1.382-2T(a)(2)(i). Instead of filing a separate statement for each new loss member, the common parent may file a single statement described in § 1.382-2T(a)(2)(ii) with respect to the stock ownership of the common parent (which is treated as a loss corporation). In addition to the information concerning stock ownership of the common parent, the single statement must identify each new loss member and state which new loss members, if any, have had ownership changes during the consolidated return year. The new loss member is, however, required to maintain the records necessary to determine if it has an ownership change. This paragraph (d) applies with respect to the attributes of a new loss member until an event occurs which ends separate tracking under § 1.1502-96(a). After that time, the information statement described in § 1.1502-92(e)(1) must be filed with respect to these attributes. [Reg. § 1.1502-94.]

☐ [T.D. 8824, 6-25-99.]

[Reg. § 1.1502-94A]

§ 1.1502-94A. **Coordination with section 382 and the regulations thereunder when a corporation becomes a member of a consolidated group generally applicable for corporations becoming members of a group before June 25, 1999.**—(a) *Scope*—(1) *In general.* This section applies section 382 and the regulations thereunder to a corporation that is a new loss member of a consolidated group. A corporation is a new loss member if it—

(i) Carries over a net operating loss that arose (or is treated under § 1.1502-21(c) or 1.1502-21T(c) in effect prior to June 25, 1999, as contained in 26 CFR part 1 revised April 1, 1999, as applicable as arising) in a SRLY with respect to the current group, and that is not described in § 1.1502-91A(d)(1); or

(ii) Has a net unrealized built-in loss (determined under paragraph (c) of this section on the day it becomes a member of the current group by treating that day as a change date) that is not taken into account under § 1.1502-91A(d)(2) in determining whether two or more corporations compose a loss subgroup.

(2) *Successor corporation as new loss member.* A new loss member also includes any successor to a corporation that has a net operating loss carryover arising in a SRLY and that is treated as remaining in existence under § 1.382-2(a)(1)(ii) following a transaction described in section 381(a).

(3) *Coordination in the case of a loss subgroup.* For rules regarding the determination of whether there is an ownership change of a loss subgroup with respect to a net operating loss or a net unrealized built-in loss described in § 1.1502-91A(d) (relating to the definition of loss subgroup) and the computation of a subgroup section 382 limitation following such an ownership change, see §§ 1.1502-92A and 1.1502-93A.

(4) *End of separate tracking of certain losses.* If § 1.1502-96A(a) (relating to the end of separate tracking of attributes) applies to a new loss member, then, while that member remains a member of the consolidated group, there is an ownership change with respect to its attributes described in § 1.1502-96A(a)(2) only if the consolidated group is a loss group and has an ownership change under § 1.1502-92A(b)(1)(i) (or that member has an ownership change under § 1.1502-96A(b) (relating to ownership changes of subsidiaries)). If, however, the new loss member has had an ownership change before § 1.1502-96A(a) applies, see § 1.1502-96A(c) for the continuing application of the section 382 limitation with respect to the member's pre-change losses.

(5) *Cross-reference.* See section 382(a) and § 1.1502-96A(c) for the continuing effect of an ownership change after a corporation becomes or ceases to be a member.

(b) *Application of section 382 to a new loss member*—(1) *In general.* Section 382 and the regulations thereunder apply to a new loss member to determine, on a separate entity basis, whether and to what extent a section 382 limitation applies to limit the amount of consolidated taxable income that may be offset by the new loss member's pre-change separate attributes. For example, if an ownership change with respect to the new loss member occurs under section 382 and the regulations thereunder, the amount of consolidated taxable income for any post-change year that may be offset by the new loss member's pre-change separate attributes shall not exceed the section 382 limitation as determined separately under section 382(b) with respect to that member for such year. If the post-change year includes the change date, section 382(b)(3)(A) is applied so that the section 382 limitation of the new loss member does not apply to the portion of the taxable income for such year that is allocable to the period in such year on or before the change date. See generally § 1.382-6 (relating to the allocation of income and loss).

(2) *Adjustment to value.* The value of the new loss member is adjusted to the extent necessary to prevent any duplication of the value of the stock of a member. For example, the principles of § 1.382-8T (relating to controlled groups of corporations) apply in determining the value of a new loss member.

(3) *Pre-change separate attribute defined.* A pre-change separate attribute of a new loss member is—

(i) Any net operating loss carryover of the new loss member described in paragraph (a)(1) of this section; and

(ii) Any recognized built-in loss of the new loss member.

(4) *Examples.* The following examples illustrate the principles of this paragraph (b).

Example 1. Basic case. (a) A and P each own 50 percent of the L stock. On December 19, Year 6, P purchases 30 percent of the L stock from A for cash. L has net operating losses arising in Year 1 and Year 2 that it carries over to Year 6 and Year 7. The following is a graphic illustration of these facts:

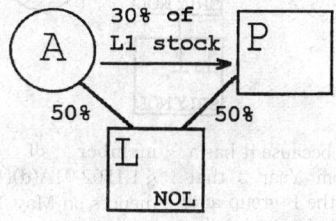

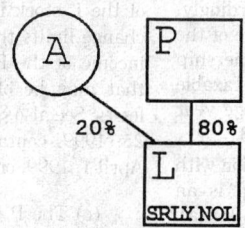

(b) L is a new loss member because it has net operating loss carryovers that arose in a SRLY with respect to the P group and L is not a member of a loss subgroup under § 1.1502-91A(d). Under section 382 and the regulations thereunder, L is a loss corporation on December 19, Year 6, that day is a testing date for L, and the testing period for L commences on December 20, Year 3.

(c) P's purchase of L stock does not cause an ownership change of L on December 19, Year 6, with respect to the net operating loss carryovers from Year 1 and Year 2 under section 382 and § 1.382-2T. The use of the loss carryovers, however, is subject to limitation under § 1.1502-21(c) or 1.1502-21T(c) in effect prior to June 25, 1999, as contained in 26 CFR part 1 revised April 1, 1999, as applicable.

Example 2. Multiple new loss members. (a) The facts are the same as in *Example 1,* and, on December 31, Year 6, L purchases all the stock of L1 from B for cash. L1 has a net operating loss of $40 arising in Year 3 that it carries over to Year

Reg. § 1.1502-94A(b)(4)

7. The following is a graphic illustration of these facts:

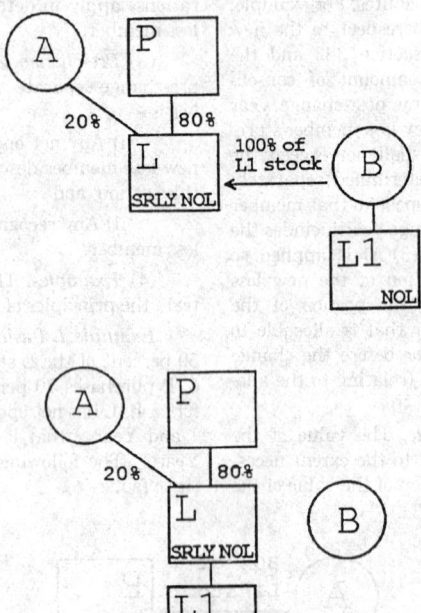

(b) L1 is a new loss member because it has a net operating loss carryover from Year 3 that arose in a SRLY with respect to the P group and L1 is not a member of a loss subgroup under § 1.1502-91A(d)(1).

(c) L's purchase of all the stock of L1 causes an ownership change of L1 on December 31, Year 6, under section 382 and § 1.382-2T. Accordingly, a section 382 limitation based on the value of the L1 stock immediately before the ownership change limits the amount of consolidated taxable income of the P group for any post-change year that may be offset by L1's loss from Year 3.

(d) L1's ownership change in connection with its becoming a member of the P group is an ownership change described in § 1.1502-96A(a). Thus, starting on January 1, Year 7, the P group no longer separately tracks owner shifts of the stock of L1 with respect to L1's loss from Year 3. Instead, the P group is a loss group because of such loss under § 1.1502-91A(c).

Example 3. Ownership changes of new loss members. (a) The facts are the same as in Example 2, and, on April 30, Year 7, C purchases all the stock of P for cash.

(b) L is a new loss member on April 30, Year 7, because its Year 1 and Year 2 losses arose in SRLYs with respect to the P group and it is not a member of a loss subgroup under § 1.1502-91A(d)(1). The testing period for L commences on May 1, Year 4. C's purchase of all the P stock causes an ownership change of L on April 30, Year 7, under section 382 and § 1.382-2T with respect to its Year 1 and Year 2 losses. Accordingly, a section 382 limitation based on the value of the L stock immediately before the ownership change limits the amount of consolidated taxable income of the P group for any post-change year that may be offset by L's Year 1 and Year 2 losses. See also § 1.1502-21T in effect prior to June 25, 1999, contained in 26 CFR Part 1, revised April 1, 1999, or § 1.1502-21, as applicable.

(c) The P group is a loss group on April 30, Year 7, because it is entitled to use L1's loss from Year 3, and such loss is no longer treated as a loss of a new loss member starting the day after L1's ownership change on December 31, Year 6. See §§ 1.1502-96A(a) and 1.1502-91A(c)(2). C's purchase of all the P stock causes an ownership change of P, and therefore the P loss group, on April 30, Year 7, with respect to L1's Year 3 loss. Accordingly, a consolidated section 382 limitation based on the value of the P stock immediately before the ownership change limits the amount of consolidated taxable income of the P group for

Reg. § 1.1502-94A(b)(4)

any post-change year that may be offset by L1's Year 3 loss.

(c) *Built-in gains and losses.* As the context may require, the principles of §§ 1.1502-91A(g) and (h) and 1.1502-93A(c) (relating to built-in gains and losses) apply to a new loss member on a separate entity basis. See § 1.1502-91A(g)(3).

(d) *Information statements.* The common parent of a consolidated group that has a new loss member subject to paragraph (b)(1) of this section during a consolidated return year must file the information statement required by § 1.382-2T(a)(2)(ii) because of any owner shift, equity structure shift, or issuance or transfer of an option with respect to the new loss member. Instead of filing a separate statement for each new loss member the common parent may file a single statement described in § 1.382-2T(a)(2)(ii) with respect to the stock ownership of the common parent (which is treated as a loss corporation). In addition to the information concerning stock ownership of the common parent, the single statement must identify each new loss member and state which new loss members, if any, have had ownership changes during the consolidated return year. The new loss member is, however, required to maintain the records necessary to determine if it has an ownership change. This paragraph (d) applies with respect to the attributes of a new loss member until an event occurs which ends separate tracking under § 1.1502-96A(a). After that time, the information statement described in § 1.1502-92A(e)(1) must be filed with respect to these attributes. [Reg. § 1.1502-94A.]

☐ [T.D. 8678, 6-26-96. Amended by T.D. 8823, 6-25-99 and amended and redesignated by T.D. 8824, 6-25-99.]

[Reg. § 1.1502-95]

§ 1.1502-95. **Rules on ceasing to be a member of a consolidated group (or loss subgroup).**—(a) *In general*—(1) *Consolidated group.* This section provides rules for applying section 382 on or after the day that a member ceases to be a member of a consolidated group (or loss subgroup). The rules concern how to determine whether an ownership change occurs with respect to losses of the member, and how a consolidated section 382 limitation (or subgroup section 382 limitation) and a loss group's (or loss subgroup's) net unrealized built-in gain or loss is apportioned to the member. As the context requires, a reference in this section to a loss group, a member, or a corporation also includes a reference to a loss subgroup, and a reference to a consolidated section 382 limitation also includes a reference to a subgroup section 382 limitation.

(2) *Election by common parent.* Only the common parent (not the loss subgroup parent) may make the election under paragraph (c) of this section to apportion a consolidated section 382 limitation (or subgroup section 382 limitation) or a loss group's (or loss subgroup's) net unrealized built-in gain.

(3) *Coordination with §§ 1.1502-91 through 1.1502-93.* For rules regarding the determination of whether there is an ownership change of a loss subgroup and the computation of a subgroup section 382 limitation following such an ownership change, see §§ 1.1502-91 through 1.1502-93.

(b) *Separate application of section 382 when a member leaves a consolidated group*—(1) *In general.* Except as provided in §§ 1.1502-91 through 1.1502-93 (relating to rules applicable to loss groups and loss subgroups), section 382 and the regulations thereunder apply to a corporation on a separate entity basis after it ceases to be a member of a consolidated group (or loss subgroup). Solely for purposes of determining whether a corporation has an ownership change—

(i) Any portion of a consolidated net operating loss that is apportioned to the corporation under § 1.1502-21(b) is treated as a net operating loss of the corporation beginning on the first day of the taxable year in which the loss arose;

(ii) The testing period may include the period during which (or before which) the corporation was a member of the group (or loss subgroup); and

(iii) Except to the extent provided in § 1.1502-96(d) (relating to reattributed losses), the day it ceases to be a member of a consolidated group is treated as a testing date of the corporation within the meaning of § 1.382-2(a)(4).

(2) *Effect of a prior ownership change of the group.* If a loss group has had an ownership change under § 1.1502-92 before a corporation ceases to be a member of a consolidated group (the former member)—

(i) Any pre-change consolidated attribute that is subject to a consolidated section 382 limitation continues to be treated as a pre-change loss with respect to the former member after it is apportioned to the former member and, if any net unrealized built-in loss is allocated to the former member under paragraph (e) of this section, any recognized built-in loss of the former member is a pre-change loss of the member;

(ii) The section 382 limitation with respect to such pre-change attribute is zero unless the common parent, under paragraph (c) of this section, apportions to the former member all or part of the consolidated section 382 limitation applicable to such attribute. The limitation applicable to a pre-change attribute other than a recognized built-in loss may be increased to the extent that the common parent has apportioned all or part of the loss group's net unrealized built-in gain to the former member, and the former member recognizes built-in gain during the recognition period;

(iii) The testing period for determining a subsequent ownership change with respect to such pre-change attribute (or such net unrealized built-in loss, if any) begins no earlier than the first day following the loss group's most recent change date; and

(iv) As generally provided under section 382, an ownership change of the former member that occurs on or after the day it ceases to be a member of a loss group may result in an additional, lesser limitation amount with respect to such losses.

(3) *Application in the case of a loss subgroup.* If two or more former members are included in the same loss subgroup immediately after they cease to be members of a consolidated group, the principles of paragraphs (b), (c) and (e) of this section apply to the loss subgroup. Therefore, for example, an apportionment by the common parent under paragraph (c) of this section is made to the loss subgroup rather than separately to its members. If the common parent of the consolidated group apportions all or part of a limitation (or net unrealized built-in gain) separately to one or more former members that are included in a loss subgroup because the common parent of the acquiring group makes an election under § 1.1502-91(d)(4) with respect to those members, the aggregate of those separate amounts is treated as the amount apportioned to the loss subgroup. Such separate apportionment may occur, for example, because the election under § 1.1502-91(d)(4) has not been filed at the time that the election of apportionment is made under paragraph (f) of this section.

(4) *Examples.* The following examples illustrate the principles of this paragraph (b):

Example 1. Treatment of departing member as a separate corporation throughout the testing period. (i) A owns all the L stock. L owns all the stock of L1 and L2. The L group has a consolidated net operating loss arising in Year 1 that is carried over to Year 3. On January 12, Year 2, A sells 30 percent of the L stock to B. On February 7, Year 3, L sells 40 percent of the L2 stock to C, and L2 ceases to be a member of the group. A portion of the Year 1 consolidated net operating loss is apportioned to L2 under § 1.1502-21(b) and is carried to L2's first separate return year, which ends December 31, Year 3. The following is a graphic illustration of these facts:

Reg. § 1.1502-95(b)(3)

Consolidated Returns

See p. 20,601 for regulations not amended to reflect law changes

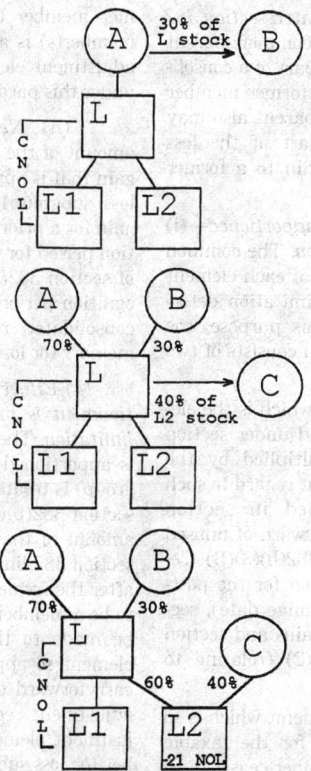

(ii) Under paragraph (b)(1) of this section, L2 is a loss corporation on February 7, Year 3. Under paragraph (b)(1)(iii) of this section, February 7, Year 3, is a testing date. Under paragraph (b)(1)(ii) of this section, the testing period for L2 with respect to this testing date commences on January 1, Year 1, the first day of the taxable year in which the portion of the consolidated net operating loss apportioned to L2 arose. Therefore, in determining whether L2 has an ownership change on February 7, Year 3, B's purchase of 30 percent of the L stock and C's purchase of 40 percent of the L2 stock are each owner shifts. L2 has an ownership change under section 382(g) and §1.382-2T because B and C have increased their ownership interests in L2 by 18 and 40 percentage points, respectively, during the testing period.

Example 2. Effect of prior ownership change of loss group. (i) L owns all the L1 stock and L1 owns all the L2 stock. The L loss group had an ownership change under §1.1502-92 in Year 2 with respect to a consolidated net operating loss arising in Year 1 and carried over to Year 2 and Year 3. The consolidated section 382 limitation computed solely on the basis of the value of the stock of L is $100. On December 31, Year 2, L1 sells 25 percent of the stock of L2 to B. L2 is apportioned a portion of the Year 1 consolidated net operating loss which it carries over to its first separate return year ending after December 31, Year 2. L2's separate section 382 limitation with respect to this loss is zero unless L elects to apportion all or a part of the consolidated section 382 limitation to L2. (See paragraph (c) of this section for rules regarding the apportionment of a consolidated section 382 limitation.) L apportions $50 of the consolidated section 382 limitation to L2, and the remaining $50 of the consolidated section 382 limitation stays with the loss group composed of L and L1.

(ii) On December 31, Year 3, L1 sells its remaining 75 percent stock interest in L2 to C, resulting in an ownership change of L2. L2's section 382 limitation computed on the change date with respect to the value of its stock is $30. Accordingly, L2's section 382 limitation for post-change years ending after December 31, Year 3, with respect to its pre-change losses, including the consolidated net operating losses apportioned to it from the L group, is $30, adjusted for a short taxable year, carryforward of unused limitation, or any other adjustment required under section 382.

Reg. § 1.1502-95(b)(4)

(c) *Apportionment of a consolidated section 382 limitation*—(1) *In general.* The common parent may elect to apportion all or any part of a consolidated section 382 limitation to a former member (or loss subgroup). The common parent also may elect to apportion all or any part of the loss group's net unrealized built-in gain to a former member (or loss subgroup).

(2) *Amount which may be apportioned*—(i) *Consolidated section 382 limitation.* The common parent may apportion all or part of each element of the consolidated section 382 limitation determined under § 1-1502-93. For this purpose, the consolidated section 382 limitation consists of two elements—

(A) The value element, which is the element of the limitation determined under section 382(b)(1) (relating to value multiplied by the long-term tax-exempt rate) without regard to such adjustments as those described in section 382(b)(2) (relating to the carryforward of unused section 382 limitation), section 382(b)(3)(B) (relating to the section 382 limitation for the post-change year that includes the change date), section 382(h) (relating to built-in gains and section 338 gains), and section 382(m)(2) (relating to short taxable years); and

(B) The adjustment element, which is so much (if any) of the limitation for the taxable year during which the former member ceases to be a member of the consolidated group that is attributable to a carryover of unused limitation under section 382(b)(2) or to recognized built-in gains under 382(h).

(ii) *Net unrealized built-in gain.* The aggregate amount of the loss group's net unrealized built-in gain that may be apportioned to one or more former members that cease to be members during the same consolidated return year cannot exceed the loss group's excess, immediately after the close of that year, of net unrealized built-in gain over recognized built-in gain, determined under section 382(h)(1)(A)(ii) (relating to a limitation on recognized built-in gain). For this purpose, net unrealized built-in gain apportioned to former members in prior consolidated return years is treated as recognized built-in gain in those years.

(3) *Effect of apportionment on the consolidated group*—(i) *Consolidated section 382 limitation.* The value element of the consolidated section 382 limitation for any post-change year ending after the day that a former member (or loss subgroup) ceases to be a member(s) is reduced to the extent that it is apportioned under this paragraph (c). The consolidated section 382 limitation for the post-change year in which the former member (or loss subgroup) ceases to be a member(s) is also reduced to the extent that the adjustment element for that year is apportioned under this paragraph (c).

(ii) *Net unrealized built-in gain.* The amount of the loss group's net unrealized built-in gain that is apportioned to the former member (or loss subgroup) is treated as recognized built-in gain for a prior taxable year ending in the recognition period for purposes of applying the limitation of section 382(h)(1)(A)(ii) to the loss group's recognition period taxable years beginning after the consolidated return year in which the former member (or loss subgroup) ceases to be a member.

(4) *Effect on corporations to which an apportionment is made*—(i) *Consolidated section 382 limitation.* The amount of the value element that is apportioned to a former member (or loss subgroup) is treated as the amount determined under section 382(b)(1) for purposes of determining the amount of that corporation's (or loss subgroup's) section 382 limitation for any taxable year ending after the former member (or loss subgroup) ceases to be a member(s). Appropriate adjustments must be made to the limitation based on the value element so apportioned for a short taxable year, carryforward of unused limitation, or any other adjustment required under section 382. The adjustment element apportioned to a former member (or loss subgroup) is treated as an adjustment under section 382(b)(2) or section 382(h), as appropriate, for the first taxable year after the member (or members) ceases to be a member (or members).

(ii) *Net unrealized built-in gain.* For purposes of determining the amount by which the former member's (or loss subgroup's) section 382 limitation for any taxable year beginning after the former member (or loss subgroup), ceases to be a member(s) is increased by its recognized built-in gain—

(A) The amount of net unrealized built-in gain apportioned to a former member (or loss subgroup) is treated as if it were an amount of net unrealized built-in gain determined under section 382(h)(1)(A)(i) (without regard to the threshold of section 382(h)(3)(B)) with respect to such member or loss subgroup, and that amount is not reduced under section 382(h)(1)(A)(ii) by the loss group's recognized built-in gain;

(B) The former member's (or loss subgroup's) 5 year recognition period begins on the loss group's change date;

(C) In applying section 382(h)(1)(A)(ii), the former member (or loss subgroup) takes into account only its prior taxable years that begin

Reg. § 1.1502-95(c)(1)

after it ceases to be a member of the loss group; and

(D) The former member's (or loss subgroup's) recognized built-in gain on the disposition of an asset is determined under section 382(h)(2)(A), treating references to the change date in that section as references to the loss group's change date.

(5) *Deemed apportionment when loss group terminates.* If a loss group terminates, to the extent the consolidated section 382 limitation or net unrealized built-in gain is not apportioned under paragraph (c)(1) of this section, the consolidated section 382 limitation or net unrealized built-in gain is deemed to be apportioned to the loss subgroup that includes the common parent, or, if there is no loss subgroup that includes the common parent immediately after the loss group terminates, to the common parent. A loss group terminates on the first day of the first taxable year that is a separate return year with respect to each member of the former loss group.

(6) *Appropriate adjustments when former member leaves during the year.* Appropriate adjustments are made to the consolidated section 382 limitation for the consolidated return year during which the former member (or loss subgroup) ceases to be a member(s) to reflect the inclusion of the former member in the loss group for a portion of that year.

(7) *Examples.* The following examples illustrate the principles of this paragraph (c):

Example 1. Consequence of apportionment. (i) L owns all the L1 stock and L1 owns all the L2 stock. The L group has a $200 consolidated net operating loss arising in Year 1 that is carried over to Year 2. At the close of December 31, Year 1, the group has an ownership change under § 1.1502-92. The ownership change results in a consolidated section 382 limitation of $10 based on the value of the stock of the group. On August 29, Year 2, L1 sells 30 percent of the stock of L2 to A. L2 is apportioned $90 of the group's $200 consolidated net operating loss under § 1.1502-21(b). L, the common parent, elects to apportion $6 of the consolidated section 382 limitation to L2. The following is a graphic illustration of these facts:

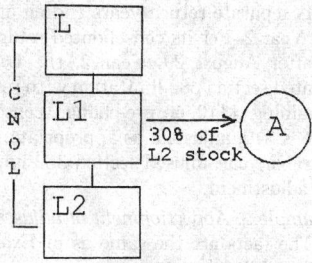

(ii) For its separate return years ending after December 31, Year 2, L2's section 382 limitation with respect to the $90 of the group's net operating loss apportioned to it is $6, adjusted, as appropriate, for any short taxable year, unused section 382 limitation, or other adjustment. For its consolidated return year ending December 31, Year 2 the L group's consolidated section 382 limitation with respect to the remaining $110 of pre-change consolidated attribute is $4 ($10 minus the $6 value element apportioned to L2), adjusted, as appropriate, for any short taxable year, unused section 382 limitation, or other adjustment.

(iii) For the L group's consolidated return year ending December 31, Year 2, the value element of its consolidated section 382 limitation is increased by $4 (rounded to the nearest dollar), to account for the period during which L2 was a member of the L group ($6, the consolidated section 382 limitation apportioned to L2, times 241/365, the ratio of the number of days during Year 2 that L2 is a member of the group to the number of days in the group's consolidated return year). See paragraph (c)(6) of this section. Therefore, the value element of the consolidated section 382 limitation for Year 2 of the L group is $8 (rounded to the nearest dollar).

(iv) The section 382 limitation for L2's short taxable year ending December 31, Year 2, is $2 (rounded to the nearest dollar), which is the amount that bears the same relationship to $6, the value element of the consolidated section 382 limitation apportioned to L2, as the number of days during that short taxable year, 124 days, bears to 365. See § 1.382-5(c).

Example 2. Consequence of no apportionment. The facts are the same as in *Example 1,* except that L does not elect to apportion any portion of the consolidated section 382 limitation to L2. For its separate return years ending after August 29, Year 2, L2's section 382 limitation with respect to the $90 of the group's pre-change consolidated attribute apportioned to L2 is zero under paragraph (b)(2)(ii) of this section. Thus, the $90 consolidated net operating loss apportioned to L2 cannot offset L2's taxable income in

Reg. § 1.1502-95(c)(7)

any of its separate return years ending after August 29, Year 2. For its consolidated return years ending after August 29, Year 2, the L group's consolidated section 382 limitation with respect to the remaining $110 of pre-change consolidated attribute is $10, adjusted, as appropriate, for any short taxable year, unused section 382 limitation, or other adjustment.

Example 3. Apportionment of adjustment element. The facts are the same as in *Example 1*, except that L2 ceases to be a member of the L group on August 29, Year 3, and the L group has a $4 carryforward of an unused consolidated section 382 limitation (under section 382(b)(2)) to the Year 3 consolidated return year. The carryover of unused limitation increases the consolidated section 382 limitation for the Year 3 consolidated return year from $10 to $14. L may elect to apportion all or any portion of the $10 value element and all or any portion of the $4 adjustment element to L2.

(d) *Rules pertaining to ceasing to be a member of a loss subgroup*—(1) *In general.* A corporation ceases to be a member of a loss subgroup on the earlier of—

(i) The first day of the first taxable year for which it files a separate return; or

(ii) The first day that it ceases to bear a relationship described in section 1504(a)(1) to the loss subgroup parent (treating for this purpose the loss subgroup parent as the common parent described in section 1504(a)(1)(A)).

(2) *Exceptions.* Paragraph (d)(1)(ii) of this section does not apply to a member of a loss subgroup while that member remains a member of the current group—

(i) If an election under § 1.1502-91(d)(4)(relating to treating the subgroup parent requirement as satisfied) applies to the members of the loss subgroup;

(ii) Starting on the day after the change date (but not earlier than the date the loss subgroup becomes a member of the group), if there is an ownership change of the loss subgroup within six months before, on, or after becoming members of the group; or

(iii) Starting the day after the period of 5 consecutive years following the day that the loss subgroup become members of the group during which the loss subgroup has not had an ownership change.

(3) *Examples.* The principles of this paragraph (d) are illustrated by the following examples:

Example 1. Basic case. (i) P owns all the L stock, L owns all the L1 stock and L1 owns all the L2 stock. The P group has a consolidated net operating loss arising in Year 1 that is carried over to Year 2. On December 11, Year 2, P sells all the stock of L to corporation M. Each of L, L1, and L2 is apportioned a portion of the Year 1 consolidated net operating loss, and thereafter each joins with M in filing consolidated returns. Under § 1.1502-92, the L loss subgroup has an ownership change on December 11, Year 2. The L loss subgroup has a subgroup section 382 limitation of $100. The following is a graphic illustration of these facts:

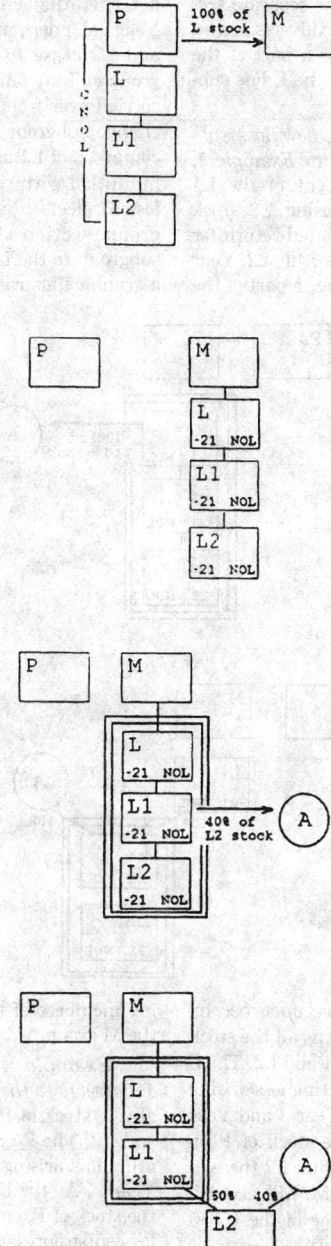

(ii) On May 22, Year 3, L1 sells 40 percent of the L2 stock to A. L2 carries over a portion of the P group's net operating loss from Year 1 to its separate return year ending December 31, Year 3. Under paragraph (d)(1) of this section, L2 ceases to be a member of the L loss subgroup on May 22, Year 3, which is both (1) the first day of the first taxable year for which it files a separate return and (2) the day it ceases to bear a relationship described in section 1504(a)(1) to the loss subgroup parent, L. The net operating loss of L2 that is carried over from the P group is treated as a pre-change loss of L2 for its separate return years ending after May 22, Year 3. Under paragraphs

Reg. § 1.1502-95(d)(3)

(a)(2) and (b)(2) of this section, the separate section 382 limitation with respect to this loss is zero unless M elects to apportion all or a part of the subgroup section 382 limitation of the L loss subgroup to L2.

Example 2. Formation of a new loss subgroup. The facts are the same as in *Example 1,* except that A purchases 40 percent of the L1 stock from L rather than purchasing L2 stock from L1. L1 and L2 file a consolidated return for their first taxable year ending after May 22, Year 3, and each of L1 and L2 carries over a part of the net operating loss of the P group that arose in Year 1. Under paragraph (d)(1) of this section, L1 and L2 cease to be members of the L loss subgroup on May 22, Year 3. The net operating losses carried over from the P group are treated as pre-change subgroup attributes of the loss subgroup composed of L1 and L2. The subgroup section 382 limitation with respect to those losses is zero unless M elects to apportion all or part of the subgroup section 382 limitation of the L loss subgroup to the L1 loss subgroup. The following is a graphic illustration of these facts:

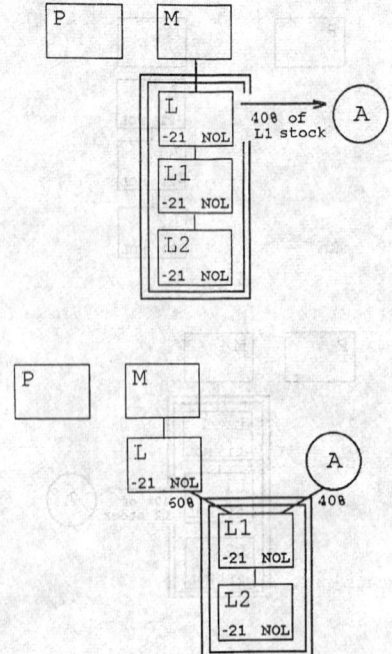

Example 3. Ownership change upon becoming members of the group. (i) A owns all the stock of P, and P owns all the stock of L1 and L2. The P group has a consolidated net operating loss arising in Year 1 that is carried over to Year 3 and Year 4. Corporation M acquires all the stock of P on November 11, Year 3, and P, L1, and L2 thereafter file consolidated returns with M. M's acquisition results in an ownership change of the P loss subgroup under § 1.1502-92(b)(1)(ii).

(ii) P distributes the L2 stock to M on October 7, Year 4, and L2 ceases to bear the relationship described in section 1504(a)(1) to P, the P loss subgroup parent. However, under paragraph (d)(2) of this section, L2 does not cease to be a member of the P loss subgroup because the P loss subgroup had an ownership change upon becoming members of the M group and L2 remains in the M group.

Example 4. Ceasing to bear a section 1504(a)(1) to the loss subgroup parent. (i) A owns all the stock of P, and P owns all the stock of L1 and L2. The P group has a consolidated net operating loss arising in Year 1 that is carried over to Year 7. At the close of Year 2, X acquires all of the stock of P, causing an ownership change of the loss subgroup composed of P, L1 and L2 under § 1.1502-92(b)(1)(ii). In Year 4, M, which is owned by the same person that owns X, acquires all of the stock of P, and the M acquisition does not cause a second ownership change of the P loss subgroup.

(ii) P distributes the L2 stock to M on February 3, Year 6 (less than 5 years after the P loss subgroup became members of the M group) and

Reg. § 1.1502-95(d)(3)

L2 ceases to bear the relationship described in section 1504(a)(1) to P, the loss subgroup parent. Thus, the section 382 limitation from the Year 2 ownership change that applies with respect to the pre-change attributes attributable to L2 is zero except to the extent M elects to apportion all or part of the P loss subgroup section 382 limitation to L2.

Example 5. Relationship through a successor. The facts are the same as in *Example 3*, except that M's acquisition of the P stock does not result in an ownership change of the P loss subgroup, and, instead of P's distributing the stock of L2, L2 merges into L1 on October 7, Year 4. L1 (as successor to L2 in the merger within the meaning of § 1.1502-1(f)(4)) continues to bear a relationship described in section 1504(a)(1) to P, the loss subgroup parent. Thus, L2 does not cease to be a member of the P loss subgroup as a result of the merger.

Example 6. Reattribution of net operating loss carryover under § 1.1502-20(g). The facts are the same as in *Example 3*, except that, instead of distributing the L2 stock to M, P sells that stock to B, and, under § 1.1502-20(g), M reattributes $10 of L2's net operating loss carryover to itself. Under § 1.1502-20(g), M succeeds to the reattributed loss as if the loss were succeeded to in a transaction described in section 381(a). M, as successor to L2, does not cease to be a member of the P loss subgroup.

(e) *Allocation of net unrealized built-in loss*— (1) *In general.* This paragraph (e) provides rules for the allocation of a loss group's (or loss subgroup's) net unrealized built-in loss if a member ceases to be a member of a loss group (or loss subgroup). This paragraph (e) applies if—

(i) A loss group (or loss subgroup) has a net unrealized built-in loss on a change date; and

(ii) Immediately after the close of the consolidated return year in which the departing member ceases to be a member, the amount of the loss group's (or loss subgroup's) excess of net unrealized built-in loss over recognized built-in loss, determined under section 382(h)(1)(B)(ii) (relating to a limitation on recognized built-in loss), is greater than zero. (The amount of such excess is referred to as the remaining NUBIL balance.) In applying section 382(h)(1)(B)(ii) for this purpose, net unrealized built-in loss allocated to departing members in prior consolidated return years is treated as recognized built-in loss in those years.

(2) *Amount of allocation*—(i) *In general.* The amount of net unrealized built-in loss allocated to a departing member is equal to the remaining NUBIL balance, multiplied by a fraction. The numerator of the fraction is the amount of the built-in loss, taken into account on the change date under § 1.1502-91(g), in the assets held by the departing member immediately after the member ceases to be a member of the loss group (or loss subgroup). The denominator of the fraction is the sum of the numerator, plus the amount of the built-in loss, taken into account under § 1.1502-91(g) on the change date, in the assets held by the loss group (or loss subgroup) immediately after the close of the taxable year in which the departing member ceases to be a member. (Fluctuations in value of the assets between the change date and the date that the member ceases to be a member of the group (or loss subgroup), or the close of the taxable year in which the member ceases to be a member of the loss group, are disregarded.) Because the amount of built-in loss on the change date with respect to a departing member's assets is taken into account (rather than that member's separately computed net unrealized built-in loss on the change date), a departing member can be apportioned all or part of the loss group's net unrealized built-in loss, even if the departing member had a separately computed net unrealized built-in gain on the change date. Amounts taken into account under section 382(h)(6)(C) (relating to certain deduction items) are treated as if they were assets in determining the numerator and denominator of the fraction.

(ii) *Transferred basis property and deferred gain or loss.* For purposes of paragraph (b)(2)(i) of this section, assets held by the departing member immediately after it ceases to be a member of the group (or by other members immediately after the close of the taxable year) include—

(A) Assets held at that time that are transferred basis property that was held by any member of the group (or loss subgroup) on the change date; and

(B) Assets held at that time by any member of the consolidated group with respect to which gain or loss of the group member or loss subgroup member at issue has been deferred in an intercompany transaction and has not been taken into account.

(iii) *Assets for which gain or loss has been recognized.* For purposes of paragraph (b)(2)(i) of this section, assets held by the departing member immediately after it ceases to be a member of the group (or by other members immediately after the close of the taxable year) do not include assets with respect to which gain or loss has previously been recognized and taken into account during the recognition period (including gain or loss recognized in an intercompany transaction and taken into account immediately before the mem-

Reg. § 1.1502-95(e)(2)

ber leaves the group). Appropriate adjustments must be made if gain or loss on an asset has been only partially recognized and taken into account.

(iv) *Exchanged basis property.* The rules of § 1.1502-91(h) apply for purposes of this paragraph (e) (disregarding stock received from the departing member or another member that is a member immediately after the close of the taxable year).

(v) *Two or more members depart during the same year.* If two or more members cease to be members during the same consolidated return year, appropriate adjustments must be made to the denominator of the fraction for each departing member by treating the other departing members as if they had not ceased to be members during that year and as if the assets held by those other departing members immediately after they cease to be members of the group (or loss subgroup) are assets held by the group immediately after the close of the taxable year.

(vi) *Anti-abuse rule.* If assets are transferred between members or a member ceases to be a member with a principal purpose of causing or affecting the allocation of amounts under this paragraph (e), appropriate adjustments must be made to eliminate any benefit of such acquisition, disposition, or allocation.

(3) *Effect of allocation on the consolidated group.* The amount of the net unrealized built-in loss that is allocated to the former member is treated as recognized built-in loss for a prior taxable year ending in the recognition period for purposes applying the limitation of section 382(h)(1)(B)(ii) to a loss group's (or loss subgroup's) recognition period taxable years beginning after the consolidated return year in which the former member ceases to be a member.

(4) *Effect on corporations to which the allocation is made.* For purposes of determining the amount of the former member's recognized built-in losses in any taxable year beginning after the former member ceases to be a member—

(i) The amount of the loss group's (or loss subgroup's) net unrealized built-in loss that is allocated to the former member is treated as if it were an amount of net unrealized built-in loss determined under section 382(h)(1)(B)(i)(without regard to the threshold of section 382(h)(3)(B)) with respect to such member or loss subgroup, and that amount is not reduced under section 382(h)(1)(B)(ii) by the loss group's (or loss subgroup's) recognized built-in losses;

(ii) The former member's 5 year recognition period begins on the loss group's (or loss subgroup's) change date;

(iii) In applying section 382(h)(1)(B)(ii), the former member takes into account only its prior taxable years that begin after it ceases to be a member of the loss group (or loss subgroup); and

(iv) The former member's recognized built-in loss on the disposition of an asset is determined under section 382(h)(2)(B), treating references to the change date in that section as references to the loss group's (or loss subgroup's) change date.

(5) *Subgroup principles.* If two or more former members are members of the same consolidated group (the second group) immediately after they cease to be members of the current group, the principles of paragraphs (e)(1), (2) and (4) of this section apply to those former members on an aggregate basis. Thus, for example, the amount of net unrealized built-in loss allocated to those members is based on the assets held by those members immediately after they cease to be members of the current group and the limitation of section 382(h)(1)(B)(ii) on recognized built-in losses is applied by taking into account the aggregate amount of net unrealized built-in loss allocated to the former members and the aggregate recognized losses of those members in taxable years beginning after they cease to be members of the current group. If one or more of such members cease to be members of the second group, the principles of this paragraph (e) are applied with respect to those members to allocate to them all or part of any remaining unrecognized amount of net unrealized built-in loss allocated to the members that became members of the second group.

(6) *Apportionment of consolidated section 382 limitation (or subgroup section 382 limitation)*—(i) *In general.* For rules relating to the apportionment of a consolidated section 382 limitation (or subgroup section 382 limitation) to a former member, see paragraph (c) of this section.

(ii) *Special rule for former members that become members of the same consolidated group.* If recognized built-in losses of one or more former members would be subject to a consolidated section 382 limitation (or subgroup section 382 limitation) if recognized immediately before the member (or members) cease to be members of the group, an apportionment of that limitation may be made, under paragraph (c) of this section, to a loss subgroup that includes such member (or members), and the recognized built-in losses (if any) of that member (or members) will be subject to that apportioned limitation. If two or more of such former members are not included in a loss subgroup immediately after they cease to be members of the group (for example, because they do not have net operating loss carryovers or, in the aggregate, a net unrealized built-in loss), but are members of the same consolidated group, an apportionment of the consolidated section 382 limitation (or subgroup section 382 limitation) may be made to them as if they were a loss subgroup.

(7) *Examples.* The following examples illustrate the principles of this paragraph (e):

Example 1. Basic allocation case. (i) P owns all of the stock of L1 and L2. On September 4, Year 1, A purchases all of the P stock, causing an ownership change of the P group. On that date P has two assets (other than the L1 and L2 stock), asset 1 with an adjusted basis of $40 and a fair market value of $15 and asset 2 with an adjusted basis of $50 and a fair market value of $100. L1 has two assets, asset 3, with a fair market value of $50 and an adjusted basis of $100, and asset 4, with an adjusted basis of $125 and a fair market value of $75. L2 has two assets, asset 5, with a fair market value of $150 and an adjusted basis of $100, and asset 6, with an adjusted basis of $90 and a fair market value of $40. Thus, the P loss group has a net unrealized built-in loss of $75.

(ii) On March 19, Year 3, P sells all of the L2 stock to M. At that time, asset 5, which has appreciated in value, has a fair market value of $250 and an adjusted basis of $100. Asset 6, which has declined in value, has an adjusted basis of $90 and a fair market value of $10.

(iii) On April 8, Year 3, P sells asset 1, and has a recognized built-in loss of $25 that is subject to the P group's section 382 limitation. On November 11, Year 4, L2 sells asset 6 for its then fair market value, $10, recognizing a loss of $80. On June 3, Year 5, L1 sells asset 4, recognizing a loss of $50.

(iv) Immediately after the close of Year 3, the P loss group's remaining NUBIL balance is $50 ($75 net unrealized built-in loss reduced by the $25 recognized built-in loss of P). The portion of the remaining NUBIL balance that is allocated to L2 is $17 (rounded to the nearest dollar). Seventeen dollars is the product obtained by multiplying $50 (the remaining NUBIL balance) by $50/$150. The numerator of the fraction ($50) is the amount of built-in loss in asset 6, taken into account on the change date under § 1.1502-91(g). The denominator ($150) is the sum of the numerator ($50) and the amount of built-in loss in assets 3 and 4, taken into account on the change date under § 1.1502-91(g) ($100). The built-in loss in asset 1 is not included in the denominator of the fraction because it is not held by the P group immediately after the close of Year 3.

(v) Seventeen dollars of L2's $80 loss on the sale of asset 6 is a recognized built-in loss and subject to a section 382 limitation of zero, unless P apportions some or all of the P group's consolidated section 382 limitation to L2 (adjusted for a short taxable year, carryover of unused limitation, or any other adjustment required under section 382).

(vi) Thirty-three dollars of L1's $50 loss on the sale of asset 4 is subject to the P group's consolidated section 382 limitation, reduced by the amount of such limitation apportioned to L2, and adjusted for any short taxable year, a carryforward of unused limitation, or other adjustment. (In applying section 382(h)(1)(B)(ii) with respect to Year 5, the P group's net unrealized built-in loss is reduced by P's $25 recognized built-in loss in Year 3 and the $17 of net unrealized built-in loss allocated to L2, thus limiting the P group's recognized built-in loss in Year 5 to $33.)

Example 2. Two members depart in the same year. The facts are the same as in *Example 1,* except that P sells all of the stock of L1 to C on November 1, Year 3. The amount of net unrealized built-in loss apportioned to L2 (rounded to the nearest dollar) is $17 ($50 remaining NUBIL balance × $50/$150). The amount of net unrealized built-in loss apportioned to L1 (rounded to the nearest dollar) is $33 ($50 remaining NUBIL balance × $100/$150).

(8) *Reporting requirement.* If a net unrealized built-in loss is allocated under this paragraph (e), the common parent must file a statement with its income tax return for the taxable year in which the former member(s) (or a new loss subgroup that includes that member) ceases to be a member. The statement must provide the name and employer identification number (E.I.N.) of the departing member, the amount of remaining NUBIL balance for the taxable year in which the member departs, and the amount of the net unrealized built-in loss allocated to the departing member. The common parent must also deliver a copy of the statement to the former member on or before the day the group files its income tax return for the consolidated return year that the former member ceases to be a member. A copy of the statement must be attached to the first income tax return of the former member (or the first return in which the former member joins) that is filed after the close of the consolidated return year of the group of which the former member (or a new loss subgroup that includes that member) cease to be a member. This paragraph (e)(8) does not apply if the required information (other than the amount of remaining NUBIL balance) is included in a statement of election under paragraph (f) of this section (relating to apportioning a section 382 limitation).

Reg. § 1.1502-95(e)(8)

(f) *Filing the election to apportion the section 382 limitation and net unrealized built-in gain—* (1) *Form of the election to apportion.* An election under paragraph (c) of this section must be made by the common parent. The election must be made in the form of the following statement: "THIS IS AN ELECTION UNDER § 1.1502-95 OF THE INCOME TAX REGULATIONS TO APPORTION ALL OR PART OF THE [insert THE CONSOLIDATED SECTION 382 LIMITATION, THE SUBGROUP SECTION 382 LIMITATION, THE LOSS GROUP'S NET UNREALIZED BUILT-IN GAIN, THE LOSS SUBGROUP'S NET UNREALIZED BUILT-IN GAIN, as appropriate] TO [insert name and E.I.N. of the corporation (or the corporations that compose a new loss subgroup) to which allocation is made]". The declaration must also include the following information, as appropriate—

(i) The date of the ownership change that resulted in the consolidated section 382 limitation (or subgroup section 382 limitation) or the loss group's (or loss subgroup's) net unrealized built-in gain;

(ii) The amount of the departing member's (or loss subgroup's) pre-change net operating loss carryovers and the taxable years in which they arose that will be subject to the limitation that is being apportioned to that member (or loss subgroup);

(iii) The amount of any net unrealized built-in loss allocated to the departing member (or loss subgroup) under paragraph (e) of this section, which, if recognized, can be a pre-change attribute subject to the limitation that is being apportioned;

(iv) If a consolidated section 382 limitation (or subgroup section 382 limitation) is being apportioned, the amount of the consolidated section 382 limitation (or subgroup section 382 limitation) for the taxable year during which the former member (or new loss subgroup) ceases to be a member of the consolidated group (determined without regard to any apportionment under this section);

(v) If any net unrealized built-in gain is being apportioned, the amount of the loss group's (or loss subgroup's) net unrealized built-in gain (as determined under paragraph (c)(2)(ii) of this section) that may be apportioned to members that ceased to be members during the consolidated return year;

(vi) The amount of the value element and adjustment element of the consolidated section 382 limitation (or subgroup section 382 limitation) that is apportioned to the former member (or new loss subgroup) pursuant to paragraph (c) of this section;

(vii) The amount of the loss group's (or loss subgroup's) net unrealized built-in gain that is apportioned to the former member (or new loss subgroup) pursuant to paragraph (c) of this section;

(viii) If the former member is allocated any net unrealized built-in loss under paragraph (e) of this section, the amount of any adjustment element apportioned to the former member that is attributable to recognized built-in gains (determined in a manner that will enable both the group and the former member to apply the principles of § 1.1502-93(c));

(ix) The name and E.I.N. of the common parent making the apportionment.

(2) *Signing of the election.* The election statement must be signed by both the common parent and the former member (or, in the case of a loss subgroup, the common parent and the loss subgroup parent) by persons authorized to sign their respective income tax returns. If the allocation is made to a loss subgroup for which an election under § 1.1502-91(d)(4) is made, and not separately to its members, the election statement under this paragraph (e) must be signed by the common parent and any member of the new loss subgroup by persons authorized to sign their respective income tax returns.

(3) *Filing of the election.* The election statement must be filed by the common parent of the group that is apportioning the consolidated section 382 limitation (or the subgroup section 382 limitation) or the loss group's net unrealized built-in gain (or loss subgroup's net unrealized built-in gain) with its income tax return for the taxable year in which the former member (or new loss subgroup) ceases to be a member. The common parent must also deliver a copy of the statement to the former member (or the members of the new loss subgroup) on or before the day the group files its income tax return for the consolidated return year that the former member (or new loss subgroup) ceases to be a member. A copy of the statement must be attached to the first return of the former member (or the first return in which the members of a new loss subgroup join) that is filed after the close of the consolidated return year of the group of which the former member (or the members of a new loss subgroup) ceases to be a member.

(4) *Revocation of election.* An election statement made under paragraph (c) of this section is revocable only with the consent of the Commissioner. [Reg. § 1.1502-95.]

☐ [T.D. 8824, 6-25-99.]

[Reg. § 1.1502-95A]

§ 1.1502-95A. Rules on ceasing to be a member of a consolidated group generally applicable for corporations ceasing to be members before June 25, 1999.—(a) *In general*—(1) *Consolidated group.* This section provides rules for applying section 382 on or after the day that a member ceases to be a member of a consolidated group (or loss subgroup). The rules concern how to determine whether an ownership change occurs with respect to losses of the member, and how a consolidated section 382 limitation (or subgroup section 382 limitation) is apportioned to the member. As the context requires, a reference in this section to a loss group, a member, or a corporation also includes a reference to a loss subgroup, and a reference to a consolidated section 382 limitation also includes a reference to a subgroup section 382 limitation.

(2) *Election by common parent.* Only the common parent (not the loss subgroup parent) may make the election under paragraph (c) of this section to apportion either a consolidated section 382 limitation or a subgroup section 382 limitation.

(3) *Coordination with §§ 1.1502-91A through 1.1502-93A.* For rules regarding the determination of whether there is an ownership change of a loss subgroup and the computation of a subgroup section 382 limitation following such an ownership change, see §§ 1.1502-91A through 1.1502-93A.

(b) *Separate application of section 382 when a member leaves a consolidated group*—(1) *In general.* Except as provided in §§ 1.1502-91A through 1.1502-93A (relating to rules applicable to loss groups and loss subgroups), section 382 and the regulations thereunder apply to a corporation on a separate entity basis after it ceases to be a member of a consolidated group (or loss subgroup). Solely for purposes of determining whether a corporation has an ownership change—

(i) Any portion of a consolidated net operating loss that is apportioned to the corporation under § 1.1502-21(b) or 1.1502-21T(b) in effect prior to June 25, 1999, as contained in 26 CFR part 1 revised April 1, 1999, as applicable is treated as a net operating loss of the corporation beginning on the first day of the taxable year in which the loss arose;

(ii) The testing period may include the period during which (or before which) the corporation was a member of the group (or loss subgroup); and

(iii) Except to the extent provided in § 1.1502-20(g) (relating to reattributed losses), the day it ceases to be a member of a consolidated group is treated as a testing date of the corporation within the meaning of § 1.382-2(a)(4).

(2) *Effect of a prior ownership change of the group.* If a loss group has had an ownership change under § 1.1502-92A before a corporation ceases to be a member of a consolidated group (the former member)—

(i) Any pre-change consolidated attribute that is subject to a consolidated section 382 limitation continues to be treated as a pre-change loss with respect to the former member after the attribute is apportioned to the former member;

(ii) The former member's section 382 limitation with respect to such attribute is zero except to the extent the common parent apportions under paragraph (c) of this section all or a part of the consolidated section 382 limitation to the former member;

(iii) The testing period for determining a subsequent ownership change with respect to such attribute begins no earlier than the first day following the loss group's most recent change date; and

(iv) As generally provided under section 382, an ownership change of the former member that occurs on or after the day it ceases to be a member of a loss group may result in an additional, lesser limitation amount with respect to such loss.

(3) *Application in the case of a loss subgroup.* If two or more former members are included in the same loss subgroup immediately after they cease to be members of a consolidated group, the principles of paragraphs (b) and (c) of this section apply to the loss subgroup. Therefore, for example, an apportionment by the common parent under paragraph (c) of this section is made to the loss subgroup rather than separately to its members.

(4) *Examples.* The following examples illustrate the principles of this paragraph (b).

Example 1. Treatment of departing member as a separate corporation throughout the testing period. (a) A owns all the L stock. L owns all the stock of L1 and L2. The L group has a consolidated net operating loss arising in Year 1 that is carried over to Year 3. On January 12, Year 2, A sells 30 percent of the L stock to B. On February 7, Year 3, L sells 40 percent of the L2 stock to C, and L2 ceases to be a member of the group. A portion of the Year 1 consolidated net operating loss is apportioned to L2 under § 1.1502-21(b) or 1.1502-21T(b) in effect prior to June 25, 1999, as contained in 26 CFR part 1 revised April 1, 1999, as applicable and is carried to L2's first separate return year, which ends December 31, Year 3.

Reg. § 1.1502-95A(b)(4)

The following is a graphic illustration of these facts:

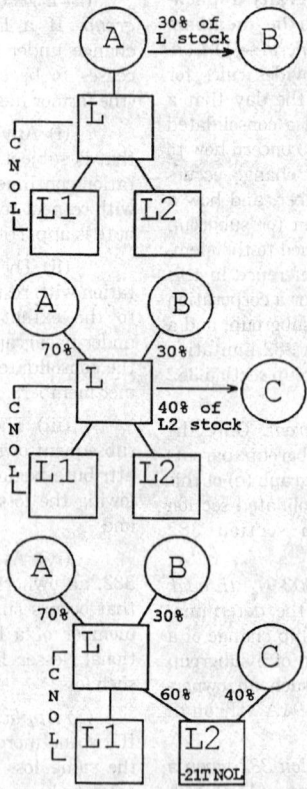

(b) Under paragraph (b)(1) of this section, L2 is a loss corporation on February 7, Year 3. Under paragraph (b)(1)(iii) of this section, February 7, Year 3, is a testing date. Under paragraph (b)(1)(ii) of this section, the testing period for L2 with respect to this testing date commences on January 1, Year 1, the first day of the taxable year in which the portion of the consolidated net operating loss apportioned to L2 arose. Therefore, in determining whether L2 has an ownership change on February 7, Year 3, B's purchase of 30 percent of the L stock and C's purchase of 40 percent of the L2 stock are each owner shifts. L2 has an ownership change under section 382(g) and § 1.382-2T because B and C have increased their ownership interests in L2 by 18 and 40 percentage points, respectively, during the testing period.

Example 2. Effect of prior ownership change of loss group. (a) L owns all the L1 stock and L1 owns all the L2 stock. The L loss group had an ownership change under § 1.1502-92A in Year 2 with respect to a consolidated net operating loss arising in Year 1 and carried over to Year 2 and Year 3. The consolidated section 382 limitation computed solely on the basis of the value of the stock of L is $100. On December 31, Year 2, L1 sells 25 percent of the stock of L2 to B. L2 is apportioned a portion of the Year 1 consolidated net operating loss which it carries over to its first separate return year ending after December 31, Year 2. L2's separate section 382 limitation with respect to this loss is zero unless L elects to apportion all or a part of the consolidated section 382 limitation to L2. (See paragraph (c) of this section for rules regarding the apportionment of a consolidated section 382 limitation.) L apportions $50 of the consolidated section 382 limitation to L2.

(b) On December 31, Year 3, L1 sells its remaining 75 percent stock interest in L2 to C, resulting in an ownership change of L2. L2's section 382 limitation computed on the change date with respect to the value of its stock is $30. Accordingly, L2's section 382 limitation for post-change years ending after December 31, Year 3, with respect to its pre-change losses, including the

Reg. § 1.1502-95A(b)(4)

consolidated net operating losses apportioned to it from the L group, is $30, adjusted as required by section 382 and the regulations thereunder.

(c) *Apportionment of a consolidated section 382 limitation*—(1) *In general.* The common parent may elect to apportion all or any part of a consolidated section 382 limitation to a former member (or loss subgroup). See paragraph (e) of this section for the time and manner of making the election to apportion.

(2) *Amount of apportionment.* The common parent may apportion all or part of each element of the consolidated section 382 limitation determined under § 1.1502-93A. For this purpose, the consolidated section 382 limitation consists of two elements —

(i) The value element, which is the element of the limitation determined under section 382(b)(1) (relating to value multiplied by the long-term tax-exempt rate) without regard to such adjustments as those described in section 382(b)(2) (relating to the carryforward of unused section 382 limitation), section 382(b)(3)(B) (relating to the section 382 limitation for the post-change year that includes the change date), section 382(h) (relating to built-in gains and section 338 gains), and section 382(m)(2) (relating to short taxable years); and

(ii) The adjustment element, which is so much (if any) of the limitation for the taxable year during which the former member ceases to be a member of the consolidated group that is attributable to a carryover of unused limitation under section 382(b)(2) or to recognized built-in gains under 382(h).

(3) *Effect of apportionment on the consolidated section 382 limitation.* The value element of the consolidated section 382 limitation for any post-change year ending after the day that a former member (or loss subgroup) ceases to be a member(s) is reduced to the extent that it is apportioned under this paragraph (c). The consolidated section 382 limitation for the post-change year in which the former member (or loss subgroup) ceases to be a member(s) is also reduced to the extent that the adjustment element for that year is apportioned under this paragraph (c).

(4) *Effect on corporations to which the consolidated section 382 limitation is apportioned.* The amount of the value element that is apportioned to a former member (or loss subgroup) is treated as the amount determined under section 382(b)(1) for purposes of determining the amount of that corporation's (or loss subgroup's) section 382 limitation for any taxable year ending after the former member (or loss subgroup) ceases to be a member(s). Appropriate adjustments must be made to the limitation based on the value element so apportioned for a short taxable year, carryforward of unused limitation, or any other adjustment required under section 382. The adjustment element apportioned to a former member (or loss subgroup) is treated as an adjustment under section 382(b)(2) or section 382(h), as appropriate, for the first taxable year after the member (or members) ceases to be a member (or members).

(5) *Deemed apportionment when loss group terminates.* If a loss group terminates, to the extent the consolidated section 382 limitation is not apportioned under paragraph (c)(1) of this section, the consolidated section 382 limitation is deemed to be apportioned to the loss subgroup that includes the common parent, or, if there is no loss subgroup that includes the common parent immediately after the loss group terminates, to the common parent. A loss group terminates on the first day of the first taxable year that is a separate return year with respect to each member of the former loss group.

(6) *Appropriate adjustments when former member leaves during the year.* Appropriate adjustments are made to the consolidated section 382 limitation for the consolidated return year during which the former member (or loss subgroup) ceases to be a member(s) to reflect the inclusion of the former member in the loss group for a portion of that year.

(7) *Examples.* The following examples illustrate the principles of this paragraph (c).

Example 1. Consequence of apportionment. (a) L owns all the L1 stock and L1 owns all the L2 stock. The L group has a $200 consolidated net operating loss arising in Year 1 that is carried over to Year 2. At the close of December 31, Year 1, the group has an ownership change under § 1.1502-92A. The ownership change results in a consolidated section 382 limitation of $10 based on the value of the stock of the group. On August 29, Year 2, L1 sells 30 percent of the stock of L2 to A. L2 is apportioned $90 of the group's $200 consolidated net operating loss under § 1.1502-21(b) or 1.1502-21T(b) in effect prior to June 25, 1999, as contained in 26 CFR part 1 revised April 1, 1999, as applicable. L, the common parent, elects to apportion $6 of the consolidated section 382 limitation to L2. The following is a graphic illustration of these facts:

Reg. § 1.1502-95A(c)(7)

56,972 Consolidated Returns

See p. 20,601 for regulations not amended to reflect law changes

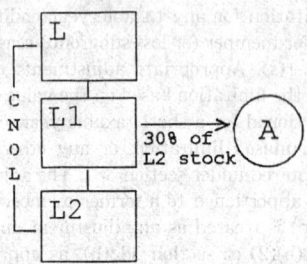

(b) For its separate return years ending after August 29, Year 2 (other than the taxable year ending December 31, Year 2), L2's section 382 limitation with respect to the $90 of the group's net operating loss apportioned to it is $6, adjusted, as appropriate, for any short taxable year, unused section 382 limitation, or other adjustment. For its consolidated return years ending after August 29, Year 2, (other than the year ending December 31, Year 2) the L group's consolidated section 382 limitation with respect to the remaining $110 of pre-change consolidated attribute is $4 ($10 minus the $6 value element apportioned to L2), adjusted, as appropriate, for any short taxable year, unused section 382 limitation, or other adjustment.

(c) For the L group's consolidated return year ending December 31, Year 2, the value element of its consolidated section 382 limitation is increased by $4 (rounded to the nearest dollar), to account for the period during which L2 was a member of the L group ($6, the consolidated section 382 limitation apportioned to L2, times 241/365, the ratio of the number of days during Year 2 that L2 is a member of the group to the number of days in the group's consolidated return year). See paragraph (c)(6) of this section. Therefore, the value element of the consolidated section 382 limitation for Year 2 of the L group is $8 (rounded to the nearest dollar).

(d) The section 382 limitation for L2's short taxable year ending December 31, Year 2, is $2 (rounded to the nearest dollar), which is the amount that bears the same relationship to $6, the value element of the consolidated section 382 limitation apportioned to L2, as the number of days during that short taxable year, 124 days, bears to 365. See § 1.382-4(c).

Example 2. Consequence of no apportionment. The facts are the same as in *Example 1*, except that L does not elect to apportion any portion of the consolidated section 382 limitation to L2. For its separate return years ending after August 29, Year 2, L2's section 382 limitation with respect to the $90 of the group's pre-change consolidated attribute apportioned to L2 is zero under paragraph (b)(2)(ii) of this section. Thus, the $90 consolidated net operating loss apportioned to L2 cannot offset L2's taxable income in any of its separate return years ending after August 29, Year 2. For its consolidated return years ending after August 29, Year 2, the L group's consolidated section 382 limitation with respect to the remaining $110 of pre-change consolidated attribute is $10, adjusted, as appropriate, for any short taxable year, unused section 382 limitation, or other adjustment.

Example 3. Apportionment of adjustment element. The facts are the same as in *Example 1*, except that L2 ceases to be a member of the L group on August 29, Year 3, and the L group has a $4 carryforward of an unused consolidated section 382 limitation (under section 382(b)(2)) to the 1993 consolidated return year. The carryover of unused limitation increases the consolidated section 382 limitation for the Year 3 consolidated return year from $10 to $14. L may elect to apportion all or any portion of the $10 value element and all or any portion of the $4 adjustment element to L2.

(d) *Rules pertaining to ceasing to be a member of a loss subgroup*—(1) *In general.* A corporation ceases to be a member of a loss subgroup—

(i) On the first day of the first taxable year for which it files a separate return; or

(ii) The first day that it ceases to bear a relationship described in section 1504(a)(1) to the loss subgroup parent (treating for this purpose the loss subgroup parent as the common parent described in section 1504(a)(1)(A)).

(2) *Examples.* The principles of this paragraph (d) are illustrated by the following examples.

Example 1. Basic case. (a) P owns all the L stock, L owns all the L1 stock and L1 owns all the L2 stock. The P group has a consolidated net operating loss arising in Year 1 that is carried over to Year 2. On December 11, Year 2, P sells all the stock of L to corporation M. Each of L, L1, and L2 is apportioned a portion of the Year 1 consolidated net operating loss, and thereafter each joins with M in filing consolidated returns. Under § 1.1502-92A, the L loss subgroup has an ownership change on December 11, Year 2. The L loss subgroup has a subgroup section 382 limitation of $100. The following is a graphic illustration of these facts:

Reg. § 1.1502-95A(d)(1)

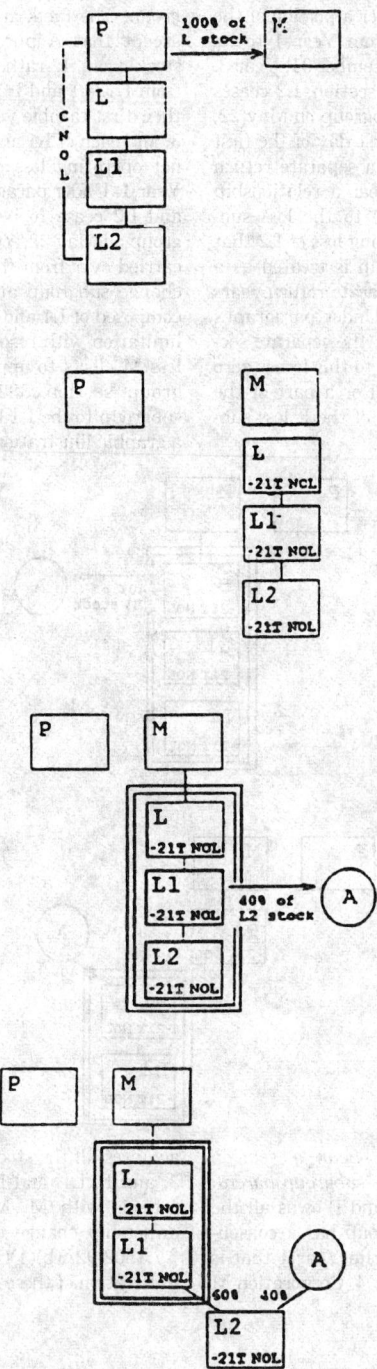

56,974 Consolidated Returns

See p. 20,601 for regulations not amended to reflect law changes

(b) On May 22, Year 3, L1 sells 40 percent of the L2 stock to A. L2 carries over a portion of the P group's net operating loss from Year 1 to its separate return year ending December 31, Year 3. Under paragraph (d)(1) of this section, L2 ceases to be a member of the L loss subgroup on May 22, Year 3, which is both (1) the first day of the first taxable year for which it files a separate return and (2) the day it ceases to bear a relationship described in section 1504(a)(1) to the loss subgroup parent, L. The net operating loss of L2 that is carried over from the P group is treated as a pre-change loss of L2 for its separate return years ending after May 22, Year 3. Under paragraphs (a)(2) and (b)(2) of this section, the separate section 382 limitation with respect to this loss is zero unless M elects to apportion all or a part of the subgroup section 382 limitation of the L loss subgroup to L2.

Example 2. Formation of a new loss subgroup. The facts are the same as in *Example 1*, except that A purchases 40 percent of the L1 stock from L rather than purchasing L2 stock from L1. L1 and L2 file a consolidated return for their first taxable year ending after May 22, Year 3, and each of L1 and L2 carries over a part of the net operating loss of the P group that arose in Year 1. Under paragraph (d)(1) of this section, L1 and L2 cease to be members of the L loss subgroup on May 22, Year 3. The net operating losses carried over from the P group are treated as pre-change subgroup attributes of the loss subgroup composed of L1 and L2. The subgroup section 382 limitation with respect to those losses is zero unless M elects to apportion all or part of the subgroup section 382 limitation of the L loss subgroup to the L1 loss subgroup. The following is a graphic illustration of these facts:

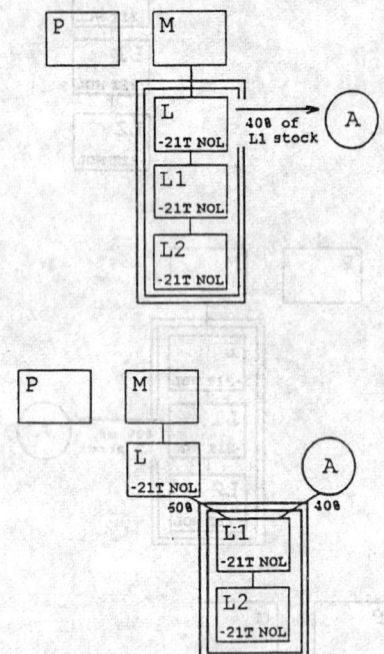

Example 3. Ceasing to bear a section 1504(a)(1) relationship to a loss subgroup parent. (a) A owns all the stock of P, and P owns all the stock of L1 and L2. The P group has a consolidated net operating loss arising in Year 1 that is carried over to Year 3 and Year 4. Corporation M acquires all the stock of P on November 11, Year 3, and P, L1, and L2 thereafter file consolidated returns with M. M's acquisition results in an ownership change of the P loss subgroup under § 1.1502-92A(b)(1)(ii). The following is a graphic illustration of these facts:

Reg. § 1.1502-95A(d)(2)

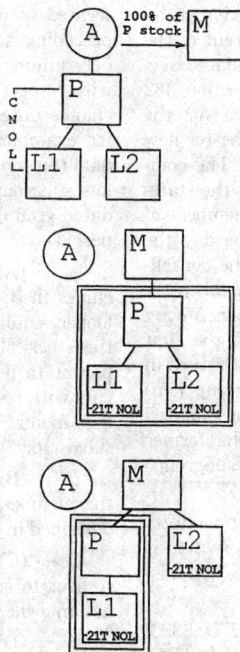

(b) P distributes the L2 stock to M on October 7, Year 4. L2 ceases to be a member of the P loss subgroup on October 7, Year 4, the first day that it ceases to bear the relationship described in section 1504(a)(1) to P, the P loss subgroup parent. See paragraph (d)(1)(ii) of this section. Thus, the section 382 limitation with respect to the pre-change subgroup attributes attributable to L2 is zero except to the extent M elects to apportion all or a part of the subgroup section 382 limitation of the P loss subgroup to L2.

Example 4. Relationship through a successor. The facts are the same as in *Example 3,* except that, instead of P's distributing the stock of L2, L2 merges into L1 on October 7, Year 4. L1 (as successor to L2 in the merger within the meaning of § 1.382-2T(f)(4)) continues to bear a relationship described in section 1504(a)(1) to P, the loss subgroup parent. Thus, L2 does not cease to be a member of the P loss subgroup as a result of the merger.

(e) *Filing the election to apportion*—(1) *Form of the election to apportion.* An election under paragraph (c) of this section must be made by the common parent. The election must be made in the form of the following statement: "THIS IS AN ELECTION UNDER § 1.1502-95A OF THE INCOME TAX REGULATIONS TO APPORTION ALL OR PART OF THE [insert either CONSOLIDATED SECTION 382 LIMITATION or SUBGROUP SECTION 382 LIMITATION, as appropriate] TO [insert name and E.I.N. of the corporation (or the corporations that compose a new loss subgroup) to which allocation is made]. The declaration must also include the following information, as appropriate—

(i) The date of the ownership change that resulted in the consolidated section 382 limitation (or subgroup section 382 limitation);

(ii) The amount of the consolidated section 382 limitation (or subgroup section 382 limitation) for the taxable year during which the former member (or new loss subgroup) ceases to be a member of the consolidated group (determined without regard to any apportionment under this section;

(iii) The amount of the value element and adjustment element of the consolidated section 382 limitation (or subgroup section 382 limitation) that is apportioned to the former member (or new loss subgroup) pursuant to paragraph (c) of this section; and

(iv) The name and E.I.N. of the common parent making the apportionment.

(2) *Signing of the election.* The election statement must be signed by both the common parent and the former member (or, in the case of a loss subgroup, the common parent and the loss subgroup parent) by persons authorized to sign their respective income tax returns.

Reg. § 1.1502-95A(e)(2)

(3) *Filing of the election.* The election statement must be filed by the common parent of the group that is apportioning the consolidated section 382 limitation (or the subgroup section 382 limitation) with its income tax return for the taxable year in which the former member (or new loss subgroup) ceases to be a member. The common parent must also deliver a copy of the statement to the former member (or the members of the new loss subgroup) on or before the day the group files its income tax return for the consolidated return year that the former member (or new loss subgroup) ceases to be a member. A copy of the statement must be attached to the first return of the former member (or the first return in which the members of a new loss subgroup join) that is filed after the close of the consolidated return year of the group of which the former member (or the members of a new loss subgroup) ceases to be a member.

(4) *Revocation of election.* An election statement made under paragraph (c) of this section is revocable only with the consent of the Commissioner. [Reg. § 1.1502-95A.]

☐ [T.D. 8678, 6-26-96. Amended by T.D. 8823, 6-25-99 and amended and redesignated by T.D. 8824, 6-25-99.]

[Reg. § 1.1502-96]

§ 1.1502-96. **Miscellaneous rules.**—(a) *End of separate tracking of losses*—(1) *Application.* This paragraph (a) applies to a member (or a loss subgroup) with a net operating loss carryover that arose (or is treated under § 1.1502-21(c) as arising) in a SRLY, or a member (or loss subgroup) with a net unrealized built-in loss determined at the time that the member (or loss subgroup) becomes a member of the consolidated group if there is—

(i) An ownership change of the member (or loss subgroup) within six months before, on, or after becoming a member of the group; or

(ii) A period of 5 consecutive years following the day that the member (or loss subgroup) becomes a member of a group during which the member (or loss subgroup) has not had an ownership change.

(2) *Effect of end of separate tracking*—(i) *Net operating loss carryovers.* If this paragraph (a) applies with respect to a member (or loss subgroup) with a net operating loss carryover, then, starting on the day after the earlier of the change date (but not earlier than the day the member (or loss subgroup) becomes a member of the consolidated group) or the last day of the 5 consecutive year period described in paragraph (a)(1)(ii) of this section, such loss carryover is treated as described in § 1.1502-91(c)(1)(i). The preceding sentence also applies for purposes of determining whether there is an ownership change with respect to such loss carryover following such change date or 5 consecutive year period. Thus, for example, starting the day after the change date (but not earlier than the day the member (or loss subgroup) becomes a member of the consolidated group) or the end of the 5 consecutive year period—

(A) The consolidated group which includes the new loss member or loss subgroup is no longer required to separately track owner shifts of the stock of the new loss member or subgroup parent to determine if an ownership change occurs with respect to the loss carryover of the new loss member or members included in the loss subgroup;

(B) The group is a loss group because the member's loss carryover is treated as a loss described in § 1.1502-91(c)(1)(i);

(C) There is an ownership change with respect to such loss carryover only if the group has an ownership change; and

(D) If the group has an ownership change, such loss carryover is a pre-change consolidated attribute subject to the loss group's consolidated section 382 limitation.

(ii) *Net unrealized built-in losses.* If this paragraph (a) applies with respect to a new loss member described in § 1.1502-94(a)(1)(ii) (or a loss subgroup described in § 1.1502-91(d)(2)) then, starting on the day after the earlier of the change date (but not earlier than the day the member (or loss subgroup) becomes a member of the group) or the last day of the 5 consecutive year period described in paragraph (a)(1)(ii) of this section, the member (or members of the loss subgroup) are treated, for purposes of applying § 1.1502-91(g)(2)(ii), as if they have been affiliated with the common parent for 5 consecutive years. Starting on that day, the member's (or the members of the loss subgroup's) separately computed net unrealized built-in loss is included in the determination whether the group has a net unrealized built-in loss, and there is an ownership change with respect to the member's separately computed net unrealized built-in loss only if the group (including the member) has a net unrealized built-in loss and has an ownership change. Thus, for example, starting the day after the change date (but not earlier than the day the member (or loss subgroup) becomes a member of the consolidated group), or the end of the 5 consecutive period—

(A) The consolidated group which includes the new loss member or loss subgroup is no longer required to separately track owner shifts of the stock of the new loss member or subgroup parent to determine if an ownership change occurs with respect to the net unrealized built-in loss of the new loss member or members of the loss subgroup;

(B) The group includes the member's (or the loss subgroup members') separately computed net unrealized built-in loss in determining whether it is a loss group under § 1.1502-91(c)(1)(iii);

(C) There is an ownership change with respect to such net unrealized built-in loss only if the group is a loss group and has an ownership change; and

(D) If the group has an ownership change, the member's separately computed net unrealized built-in loss and its assets are taken into account in determining the group's prechange consolidated attributes described in § 1.1502-91(e)(1) (relating to recognized built-in losses) that are subject to the group's consolidated section 382 limitation.

(iii) *Common parent not common parent for five years.* If the common parent has become the common parent of an existing group within the previous 5-year period in a transaction described in § 1.1502-75(d)(2)(ii) or (3), appropriate adjustments must be made in applying paragraphs (a)(2)(ii) and (3) of this section. In such a case, as the context requires, references to the common parent are to the former common parent.

(3) *Continuing effect of end of separate tracking*—(i) *In general.* As the context may require, a current group determines which of its members are included in a loss subgroup on any testing date by taking into account the application of this section in the former group. See the example in § 1.1502-91(f)(2). For this purpose, corporations that are treated under paragraph (a)(2)(ii) of this section as having been affiliated with the common parent of the former group for 5 consecutive years are also treated as having been affiliated with any other members that have been (or are treated as having been) affiliated with the common parent. The corporations are treated as having been affiliated with such other members for the same period of time that those members have been (or are treated as having been) affiliated with the common parent. If two or more corporations become members of the group at the same time, but paragraph (a)(1) of this section does not apply to every such corporation, then immediately after the corporations become members of the group, the corporations to which paragraph (a)(1) of this section applied are treated as not having been previously affiliated, for purposes of applying this paragraph (a)(3), with the corporations to which paragraph (a)(2)(ii) of this section did not apply.

(ii) *Example.* The following example illustrates the principles of this paragraph (a)(3):

Example. (i) L has owned all the stock of L1 for three years. At the close of December 31, Year 1, the M group purchases all the L stock, and L and L1 become members of the M group. Other than the stock of L1, L has one asset (the L loss asset) with a net unrealized built-in loss of $200 on this date. L1 has one asset with a net unrealized built-in gain of $50 (the L1 gain asset). L and L1 do not compose a loss subgroup because they do not meet the five year affiliation requirement of § 1.1502-91(d)(2)(i). L is a new loss member, and M's purchase of L causes an ownership change of L. At the close of December 31, Year 4, at a time when L1 has been affiliated with the M group for three years and has been affiliated with L for six years, the S group purchases all the M stock. On this date, the L loss asset has a net unrealized built-in loss of $300, the L1 gain asset has a net unrealized built-in gain of $80, and M, the common parent of the M group, has one asset with a net unrealized built-in gain of $200.

(ii) Paragraph (a)(1) of this section applies to L because L is a new loss member described in § 1.1502-94(a)(1)(ii) that has an ownership change upon becoming a member of the M group on December 31, Year 1. Accordingly, L is treated as having been affiliated with M for 5 consecutive years, and the L loss asset with a net unrealized built-in loss of $300 is included in the determination whether the M group has a net unrealized built-in loss.

(iii) The S group determines which of its members are included in a loss subgroup by taking into account application of paragraph (a) of this section in the M group. For this purpose, application of paragraph (a) of this section causes L to be treated as having been affiliated with M (or as having been a member of the M group) for 5 consecutive years as of January 1, Year 2. Therefore, the S group includes L in the determination whether the M subgroup acquired by S on December 31, Year 4, has a net unrealized built-in loss.

(iv) Because paragraph (a)(1) of this section applied to L when L became a member of the M group, but did not apply to L1, L is treated as not having been affiliated with L1 before L and L1 joined the M group. Also, L1 is not included in the determination whether the M subgroup has a net unrealized built-in loss because L1 has not been continuously affiliated with members of the M group for the five consecutive year period end-

Reg. § 1.1502-96(a)(3)

ing immediately before they become members of the S group. See § 1.1502-91(g)(2).

(4) *Special rule for testing period.* For purposes of determining the beginning of the testing period for a loss group, the member's (or loss subgroup's) net operating loss carryovers (or net unrealized built-in loss) described in paragraph (a)(2) of this section are considered to arise—

(i) In a case described in paragraph (a)(1)(i) of this section, in a taxable year that begins not earlier than the later of the day following the change date or the day that the member becomes a member of the group; and

(ii) In a case described in paragraph (a)(1)(ii) of this section, in a taxable year that begins 3 years before the end of the 5 consecutive year period.

(5) *Limits on effects of end of separate tracking.* The rule contained in this paragraph (a) applies solely for purposes of §§ 1.1502-91 through 1.1502-95 and this section (other than paragraph (b)(2)(ii)(B) of this section (relating to the definition of pre-change attributes of a subsidiary)) and § 1.1502-98, and not for purposes of other provisions of the consolidated return regulations. However, the rule contained in this paragraph (a) does apply in §§ 1.1502-15(g), 1.1502-21(g) and 1.1502-22(g) for purposes of determining the composition of loss subgroups defined in § 1.1502-91(d). See also paragraph (c) of this section for the continuing effect of an ownership change with respect to pre-change attributes.

(b) *Ownership change of subsidiary*—(1) *Ownership change of a subsidiary because of options or plan or arrangement.* Notwithstanding § 1.1502-92, a subsidiary may have an ownership change for purposes of section 382 with respect to its attributes which a group or loss subgroup includes in making a determination under § 1.1502-91(c)(1) (relating to the definition of loss group) or § 1.1502-91(d) (relating to the definition of loss subgroup). The subsidiary has such an ownership change if it has an ownership change under the principles of § 1.1502-95(b) and section 382 and the regulations thereunder (determined on a separate entity basis by treating the subsidiary as not being a member of a consolidated group) in the event of—

(i) The deemed exercise under § 1.382-4(d) of an option or options (other than an option with respect to stock of the common parent) held by a person (or persons acting pursuant to a plan or arrangement) to acquire more than 20 percent of the stock of the subsidiary; or

(ii) An increase by 1 or more 5-percent shareholders, acting pursuant to a plan or arrangement to avoid an ownership change of a subsidiary, in their percentage ownership interest in the subsidiary by more than 50 percentage points during the testing period of the subsidiary through the acquisition (or deemed acquisition pursuant to § 1.382-4(d)) of ownership interests in the subsidiary and in higher-tier members with respect to the subsidiary.

(2) *Effect of the ownership change*—(i) *In general.* If a subsidiary has an ownership change under paragraph (b)(1) of this section, the amount of consolidated taxable income for any post-change year that may be offset by the pre-change losses of the subsidiary shall not exceed the section 382 limitation for the subsidiary. For purposes of this limitation, the value of the subsidiary is determined solely by reference to the value of the subsidiary's stock.

(ii) *Pre-change losses.* The pre-change losses of a subsidiary are—

(A) Its allocable part of any consolidated net operating loss which is attributable to it under § 1.1502-21(b) (determined on the last day of the consolidated return year that includes the change date) that is not carried back and absorbed in a taxable year prior to the year including the change date;

(B) Its net operating loss carryovers that arose (or are treated under § 1.1502-21(c) as having arisen) in a SRLY; and

(C) Its recognized built-in loss with respect to its separately computed net unrealized built-in loss, if any, determined on the change date.

(3) *Coordination with §§ 1.1502-91, 1.1502-92, and 1.1502-94.* If an increase in percentage ownership interest causes an ownership change with respect to an attribute under this paragraph (b) and under § 1.1502-92 on the same day, the ownership change is considered to occur only under § 1.1502-92 and not under this paragraph (b). See § 1.1502-94 for anti-duplication rules relating to value.

(4) *Example.* The following example illustrates paragraph (b)(1)(ii) of this section:

Example. Plan to avoid an ownership change of a subsidiary. (i) L owns all the stock of L1, L1 owns all the stock of L2, L2 owns all the stock of L3, and L3 owns all the stock of L4. The L group has a consolidated net operating loss arising in Year 1 that is carried over to Year 2. L has assets other than its L1 stock with a value of $900. L1, L2, and L3 own no assets other than their L2, L3, and L4 stock. L4 has assets with a value of $100. During Year 2, A, B, C, and D, acting pursuant to a plan to avoid an ownership change of L4, acquire the following ownership interests in the members of the L loss group: (A) on September 11, Year 2, A acquires 20 percent of the L1 stock from L and B acquires 20 percent of the L2 stock from L1; and (B) on September 20, Year 2, C acquires 20 percent of the stock of L3 from L2 and D acquires 20 percent of the stock of L4 from L3.

(ii) The acquisitions by A, B, C, and D pursuant to the plan have increased their respective percentage ownership interests in L4 by approximately 10, 13, 16, and 20 percentage points, for a total of approximately 59 percentage points during the testing period. This more than 50 percentage point increase in the percentage ownership interest in L4 causes an ownership change of L4 under paragraph (b)(2) of this section.

(c) *Continuing effect of an ownership change.* A loss corporation (or loss subgroup) that is subject to a limitation under section 382 with respect to its pre-change losses continues to be subject to the limitation regardless of whether it becomes a member or ceases to be a member of a consolidated group. See § 1.382-5(d) (relating to successive ownership changes and absorption of a section 382 limitation).

(d) *Losses reattributed under § 1.1502-20(g)*—(1) *In general.* This paragraph (d) contains rules relating to net operating carryovers that are reattributed to the common parent under § 1.1502-20(g). References in this paragraph (d) to a subsidiary are references to the subsidiary (or lower tier subsidiary) whose net operating loss carryover is reattributed to the common parent.

(2) *Deemed section 381(a) transaction.* Under § 1.1502-20(g)(1), the common parent succeeds to the reattributed losses as if the losses were succeeded to in a transaction described in section 381(a). In general, §§ 1.1502-91 through 1.1502-95, this section, and § 1.1502-98 are applied to the reattributed net operating loss carryovers in accordance with that characterization. See generally, § 1.382-2(a)(1)(ii) (relating to distributor or transferor loss corporations in transactions under section 381), § 1.1502-(1)(f)(4) (relating to the definition of predecessor and successor) and § 1.1502-91(j) (relating to predecessor and successor corporations). For example, if the reattributed net operating loss carryover is a pre-change attribute subject to a section 382 limitation, it remains subject to that limitation following the reattribution. In certain cases, the limitation applicable to the reattributed loss is zero unless the common parent apportions all or part of the limitation to itself. (See paragraph (d)(4) of this section.)

(3) *Rules relating to owner shifts*—(i) *In general.* Any owner shift of the subsidiary (including any deemed owner shift resulting from section 382(g)(4)(D) or 382(1)(3)) in connection with the disposition of the stock of the subsidiary is not taken into account in determining whether there is an ownership change with respect to the reattributed net operating loss carryover. However, any owner shift with respect to the successor corporation that is treated as continuing in existence under § 1.382-2(a)(1)(ii) must be taken into account for such purpose if such owner shift is effected by the reattribution and an owner shift of the stock of the subsidiary not held directly or indirectly by the common parent would have been taken into account if such shift had occurred immediately before the reattribution. See paragraph (d)(3)(ii) *Example 2* of this section.

(ii) *Examples.* The following examples illustrate the principles of this paragraph (d)(3):

Example 1. No owner shift for reattributed loss. (i) P, the common parent of a consolidated group, owns 60% of the stock of L, and B owns the remaining 40%. L has a net operating loss carryover of $100 from year 1 that it carries over to Years 2, 3, and 4. At the beginning of Year 2, P purchases 40% of the L stock from B, which does not cause an ownership change of L. On December 31, Year 3, P sells all of the L stock to M. Pursuant to § 1.1502-20(g), P reattributes $10 of L's $100 net operating loss carryover to itself, and L carries $90 of its net operating loss carryover to its Year 4.

(ii) The sale of the L stock to M does not cause an owner shift that is taken into account in determining if there is an ownership change with respect to the $10 reattributed loss. Following the reattribution, § 1.1502-94(b) continues to apply to determine if there is an ownership change with respect to the $10 reattributed loss, until, under paragraph (a) of this section, the loss is treated as described in § 1.1502-91(c)(1)(i). In applying § 1.1502-94(b), the 40 percentage point increase by the P shareholders prior to the reattribution is taken into account. The sale of the L stock to M does cause an ownership change of L with respect to the $90 of its net operating loss that it carries over to Year 4.

Example 2. Owner shift for reattributed loss. The facts are the same as in *Example 1*, except that P only purchases 20% of the L stock from B and sells 80% of the L stock to M. L is a new loss member, and, under § 1.1502-94(b)(1), an owner shift of the stock of L not held directly or indirectly by the common parent (the 20% of L stock still held by B) would have been taken into account if such shift had occurred immediately before the reattribution. Following the reattribution, § 1.1502-94(b) continues to apply to deter-

Reg. § 1.1502-96(d)(3)

mine if there is an ownership change with respect to the $10 reattributed loss, until, under paragraph (a) of this section, the loss is treated as described in § 1.1502-91(c)(1)(i). With respect to the $10 reattributed loss, the P shareholders have increased their percentage ownership interest by 40 percentage points. The P shareholders have increased their ownership interests by 20 percentage points as a result of P's purchase of stock from B, and, under § 1.382-2(a)(1)(ii), are treated as increasing their interests by an additional 20 percentage points as a result of the reattribution. (The acquisition of the L stock by M does not, however, effect an owner shift for the $10 of reattributed loss.) The sale of the L stock to M causes an ownership change of L with respect to the $90 of net operating loss that L carries over to Year 4.

(4) *Rules relating to the section 382 limitation*—(i) *Reattributed loss is a pre-change separate attribute of a new loss member.* If the reattributed net operating loss carryover is a pre-change separate attribute of a new loss member that is subject to a separate section 382 limitation prior to the disposition of subsidiary stock, the common parent's limitation with respect to that loss is zero, except to the extent that the common parent apportions to itself, under paragraph (d)(5) of this section, all or part of such limitation. A separate section 382 limitation is the limitation described in § 1.1502-94(b) that applies to a pre-change separate attribute.

(ii) *Reattributed loss is a pre-change subgroup attribute.* If the reattributed net operating loss carryover is a pre-change subgroup attribute subject to a subgroup section 382 limitation prior to the disposition of subsidiary stock, and, immediately after the reattribution, the common parent is not a member of the loss subgroup, the section 382 limitation with respect to that net operating loss carryover is zero, except to the extent that the common parent apportions to itself, under paragraph (d)(5) of this section, all or part of the subgroup section 382 limitation. See, however, § 1.1502-95(d)(3) Example 6, for an illustration of a case where the common parent, as successor to the subsidiary, is a member of the loss subgroup immediately after the reattribution.

(iii) *Potential application of section 382(l)(1).* In general, the value of the stock of the common parent is used to determine the section 382 limitation for an ownership change with respect to the reattributed net operating loss carryover that occurs at the time of, or after, the reattribution. For example, if the net operating loss carryover is a pre-change consolidated attribute, the value of the stock of the common parent is used to determine the section 382 limitation, and no adjustment to that value is required because of the deemed section 381(a) transaction. However, if the net operating loss carryover is a pre-change separate attribute of a new loss member (or is a pre-change attribute of a loss subgroup member and the common parent was not the loss subgroup parent immediately before the reattribution), the deemed section 381(a) transaction is considered to constitute a capital contribution with respect to the new loss member (or loss subgroup member) for purposes of section 382(l)(1). Accordingly, if that section applies because the deemed capital contribution is (or is considered under section 382(l)(1)(B) to be) part of a plan described in section 382(l)(1)(A), the value of the stock of the common parent after the deemed section 381(a) transaction must be adjusted to reflect the capital contribution. Ordinarily, this will require the value of the stock of the common parent to be reduced to an amount that represents the value of the stock of the subsidiary (or loss subgroup of which the subsidiary was a member) when the reattribution occurred.

(iv) *Duplication or omission of value.* In determining any section 382 limitation with respect to the reattributed net operating loss carryover and with respect to other pre-change losses, appropriate adjustments must be made so that value is not improperly omitted or duplicated as a result of the reattribution. For example, if the subsidiary has an ownership change upon its departure, and the common parent (as successor) has an ownership change with respect to the reattributed pre-change separate attribute upon its reattribution under paragraph (d)(3)(i) of this section, proper adjustments must be made so that the value of the subsidiary is not taken into account more than once in determinining the section 382 limitation for the reattributed loss and the loss that is not reattributed.

(v) *Special rule for continuity of business requirement.* If the reattributed net operating loss carryover is a pre-change attribute of new loss member and the reattribution occurs within the two year period beginning on the change date, then, starting immediately after the reattribution, the continuity of business requirement of section 382(c)(1) is applied with respect to the business enterprise of the common parent. Similar principles apply if the reattributed net operating loss carryover is a pre-change subgroup attribute and, on the day after the reattribution, the common parent is not a member of the loss subgroup.

(5) *Election to reattribute section 382 limitation*—(i) *Effect of election.* The common parent may elect to apportion to itself all or part of any

separate section 382 limitation or subgroup section 382 limitation to which the net operating loss carryover is subject immediately before the reattribution. However, no net unrealized built-in gain of the member (or loss subgroup) whose net operating loss carryover is reattributed can be apportioned to the common parent. The principles of § 1.1502-95(c) apply to the apportionment, treating, as the context requires, references to the former member as references to the common parent, and references to the consolidated section 382 limitation as references to the separate section 382 limitation (or subgroup section 382 limitation) that is being apportioned. Thus, for example, the common parent can reattribute to itself all or part of the value element or adjustment element of the limitation, and any part of such element that is apportioned requires a corresponding reduction in such element of the separate section 382 limitation of the subsidiary whose net operating loss carryover is reattributed (or in the subgroup section 382 limitation if the reattributed loss is a pre-change subgroup attribute). Appropriate adjustments must be made to the separate section 382 limitation (or subgroup section 382 limitation) for the consolidated return year in which the reattribution is made to reflect that the reattributed net operating loss carryover is an attribute acquired by the common parent during the year in a transaction to which section 381(a) applies. The election is made by the common parent as part of the election to reattribute the net operating loss carryover. See § 1.1502-20(g)(4) for the time and manner of making the election.

(ii) *Examples.* The following examples illustrate the principles of this paragraph (d)(5):

Example 1. *Consequence of apportionment.* (i) P, the common parent of a consolidated group, purchases all of the stock of L on December 31, Year 1. L carries over a net operating loss arising in Year 1 to each of the next 5 taxable years. The purchase of the L stock causes an ownership change of L, and results in a separate section 382 limitation of $10 for L's net operating loss carryover based on the value of the L stock. On July 2, Year 3, P sells 30 percent of the L stock to A. Under § 1.1502-20(g), P elects to apportion to itself $110 of L's $200 net operating loss carryover. P also elects to apportion to itself $6 of the $10 value element of the separate section 382 limitation.

(ii) For the consolidated return years ending after December 31, Year 3, P's separate section 382 limitation with respect to the reattributed net operating loss carryover is $6, adjusted as appropriate for any short taxable year, unused section 382 limitation, or other adjustment. For the P group's consolidated return year ending December 31, Year 3, the separate section 382 limitation for L's net operating loss carryover is $8, the sum of $5 and $3. Five dollars of the limitation is the amount that bears the same relationship to $10 as the number of days in the period ending with the deemed section 381(a) transaction, 183 days, bears to 365. Three dollars of the limitation is the amount that bears the same relationship to $6 as the number of days in the period between July 3 and December 31, 182, bears to 365.

(iii) For L's taxable years ending after December 31, Year 3, L's separate section 382 limitation for its $90 of net operating loss carryover that was not reattributed to P is $4, adjusted as appropriate for any short taxable year, unused section 382 limitation, or other adjustment. For L's short taxable year ending December 31, Year 3, the section 382 limitation for its $90 of net operating loss carryover is $2, the amount that bears the same relationship to $4 (the portion of the value element that was not apportioned to P), as the number of days during the short taxable year, 182 days, bears to 365. See § 1.382-5(c).

Example 2. *No apportionment required for consolidated pre-change attribute.* (i) P, the common parent of a consolidated group, forms L. For Year 1, L has an operating loss of $70 that is not absorbed and is included in the group's consolidated net operating loss that is carried over to subsequent years. On January 1 of Year 3, A buys all of the P stock and the P group has an ownership change. The consolidated section 382 limitation based on the value of the P stock is $10.

(ii) On April 13 of Year 4, P sells all of the stock of L to B and, under § 1.1502-20(g), elects to reattribute to itself $45 of L's net operating loss carryover. Following the reattribution, the $45 portion of the Year 1 net operating loss carryover retains its character as a pre-change consolidated attribute, and remains subject to so much of the $10 consolidated section 382 limitation as P does not elect to apportion to L under § 1.1502-95(c).

(e) *Time and manner of making election under § 1.1502-91(d)(4)*—(1) *In general.* This paragraph (e) prescribes the time and manner of making the election under § 1.1502-91(d)(4), relating to treating two or more corporations as treating the section 1504(a)(1) requirement of § 1.1502-91(d)(1)(ii) and (d) (2)(ii) as satisfied.

(2) *Election statement.* An election under § 1.1502-91(d)(4) must be made by the common parent. The election must be made in the form of the following statement: "THIS IS AN ELECTION UNDER § 1.1502-91(d)(4) TO TREAT THE FOLLOWING CORPORATIONS AS

Reg. § 1.1502-96(e)(2)

MEETING THE REQUIREMENTS OF § 1.1502-91(d)(1)(ii) AND (d)(2)(ii) IMMEDIATELY AFTER THEY BECAME MEMBERS OF THE GROUP." [List separately the name of each corporation, its E.I.N., and the date that it became a member of the group]. If separate elections are being made for corporations that became members at different times or that were acquired from different affiliated groups, provide a separate statement and list for each election.

(3) The election statement must be filed by the common parent with its income tax return for the consolidated return year in which the members with respect to which the election is made become members of the group. Such election must be filed on or before the due date for such income tax return, including extensions.

(4) An election made under this paragraph (e) is irrevocable. [Reg. § 1.1502-96.]

☐ [T.D. 8824, 6-25-99.]

[Reg. § 1.1502-96A]

§ 1.1502-96A. **Miscellaneous rules generally applicable for testing dates before June 25, 1999.**—(a) *End of separate tracking of losses*—(1) *Application.* This paragraph (a) applies to a member (or a loss subgroup) with a net operating loss carryover that arose (or is treated under § 1.1502-21(c) or 1.1502-21T(c) in effect prior to June 25, 1999, as contained in 26 CFR part 1 revised April 1, 1999, as applicable as arising) in a SRLY (or a net unrealized built-in gain or loss determined at the time that the member (or loss subgroup) becomes a member of the consolidated group if there is—

(i) An ownership change of the member (or loss subgroup in connection with, or after, becoming a member of the group; or

(ii) A period of 5 consecutive years following the day that the member (or loss subgroup) becomes a member of a group during which the member (or loss subgroup) has not had an ownership change.

(2) *Effect of end of separate tracking.* If this paragraph (a) applies with respect to a member (or loss subgroup), then, starting on the day after the earlier of the change date (but not earlier than the day the member (or loss subgroup) becomes a member of the consolidated group) or the last day of the 5 consecutive year period described in paragraph (a)(1)(ii) of this section, the member's net operating loss carryover that arose (or is treated under § 1.1502-21(c) or 1.1502-21T(c) in effect prior to June 25, 1999, as contained in 26 CFR part 1 revised April 1, 1999, as applicable as arising) in a SRLY, is treated as described in § 1.1502-91A(c)(1)(i). Also, the member's separately computed net unrealized built-in gain or loss is included in the determination whether the group has a net unrealized built-in gain or loss. The preceding sentences also apply for purposes of determining whether there is an ownership change with respect to such attributes following such change date (or earlier day) or 5 consecutive year period. Thus, for example, starting the day after the change date or the end of the 5 consecutive year period—

(i) The consolidated group which includes the new loss member or loss subgroup is no longer required to separately track owner shifts of the stock of the new loss member or loss subgroup parent to determine if an ownership change occurs with respect to the attributes of the new loss member or members included in the loss subgroup;

(ii) The group includes the member's attributes in determining whether it is a loss group under § 1.1502-91A(c);

(iii) There is an ownership change with respect to such attributes only if the group is a loss group and has an ownership change; and

(iv) If the group has an ownership change, such attributes are pre-change consolidated attributes subject to the loss group's consolidated section 382 limitation.

(3) *Continuing effect of end of separate tracking.* As the context may require, a current group determines which of its members are included in a loss subgroup on any testing date by taking into account the application of this section in the former group. See the example in § 1.1502-91A(f)(2).

(4) *Special rule for testing period.* For purposes of determining the beginning of the testing period for a loss group, the member's (or loss subgroup's) net operating loss carryovers (or net unrealized built-in gain or loss) described in paragraph (a)(2) of this section are considered to arise—

(i) in a case described in paragraph (a)(1)(i) of this section, in a taxable year that begins not earlier than the later of the day following the change date or the day that the member becomes a member of the group; and

(ii) in a case described in paragraph (a)(1)(ii) of this section, in a taxable year that begins 3 years before the end of the 5 consecutive year period.

(5) *Limits on effects of end of separate tracking.* The rule contained in this paragraph (a) applies solely for purposes of §§ 1.1502-91A through 1.1502-95A and this section (other than paragraph (b)(2)(ii)(B) of this section (relating to

the definition of pre-change attributes of a subsidiary)) and § 1.1502-98A, and not for purposes of other provisions of the consolidated return regulations, including, for example, §§ 1.1502-15 and 1.1502-21 (or § 1.1502-15T in effect prior to June 25, 1999, as contained in 26 CFR part 1 revised April 1, 1999 and 1.1502-21T in effect prior to June 25, 1999, as contained in 26 CFR part 1 revised April 1, 1999, as applicable) (relating to the consolidated net operating loss deduction). See also paragraph (c) of this section for the continuing effect of an ownership change with respect to pre-change attributes.

(b) *Ownership change of subsidiary*—(1) *Ownership change of a subsidiary because of options or plan or arrangement*. Notwithstanding § 1.1502-92A, a subsidiary may have an ownership change for purposes of section 382 with respect to its attributes which a group or loss subgroup includes in making a determination under § 1.1502-91A(c)(1) (relating to the definition of loss group) or § 1.1502-91A(d) (relating to the definition of loss subgroup). The subsidiary has such an ownership change if it has an ownership change under the principles of § 1.1502-95A(b) and section 382 and the regulations thereunder (determined on a separate entity basis by treating the subsidiary as not being a member of a consolidated group) in the event of—

(i) The deemed exercise under § 1.382-4(d) of an option or options (other than an option with respect to stock of the common parent) held by a person (or persons acting pursuant to a plan or arrangement) to acquire more than 20 percent of the stock of the subsidiary; or

(ii) An increase by 1 or more 5-percent shareholders, acting pursuant to a plan or arrangement to avoid an ownership change of a subsidiary, in their percentage ownership interest in the subsidiary by more than 50 percentage points during the testing period of the subsidiary through the acquisition (or deemed acquisition pursuant to § 1.382-4(d)) of ownership interests in the subsidiary and in higher-tier members with respect to the subsidiary.

(2) *Effect of the ownership change*—(i) *In general*. If a subsidiary has an ownership change under paragraph (b)(1) of this section, the amount of consolidated taxable income for any post-change year that may be offset by the pre-change losses of the subsidiary shall not exceed the section 382 limitation for the subsidiary. For purposes of this limitation, the value of the subsidiary is determined solely by reference to the value of the subsidiary's stock.

(ii) *Pre-change losses*. The pre-change losses of a subsidiary are—

(A) Its allocable part of any consolidated net operating loss which is attributable to it under § 1.1502-21(b) or 1.1502-21T(b) in effect prior to June 25, 1999, as contained in 26 CFR part 1 revised April 1, 1999, as applicable (determined on the last day of the consolidated return year that includes the change date) that is not carried back and absorbed in a taxable year prior to the year including the change date;

(B) Its net operating loss carryovers that arose (or are treated under § 1.1502-21(c) or 1.1502-21T(c) in effect prior to June 25, 1999, as contained in 26 CFR part 1 revised April 1, 1999, as applicable as having arisen) in a SRLY; and

(C) Its recognized built-in loss with respect to its separately computed net unrealized built-in loss, if any, determined on the change date.

(3) *Coordination with §§ 1.1502-91A, 1.1502-92A, and 1.1502-94A*. If an increase in percentage ownership interest causes an ownership change with respect to an attribute under this paragraph (b) and under § 1.1502-92A on the same day, the ownership change is considered to occur only under § 1.1502-92A and not under this paragraph (b). See § 1.1502-94A for anti-duplication rules relating to value.

(4) *Example*. The following example illustrates paragraph (b)(1)(ii) of this section.

Example. Plan to avoid an ownership change of a subsidiary. (a) L owns all the stock of L1, L1 owns all the stock of L2, L2 owns all the stock of L3, and L3 owns all the stock of L4. The L group has a consolidated net operating loss arising in Year 1 that is carried over to Year 2. L has assets other than its L1 stock with a value of $900. L1, L2, and L3 own no assets other than their L2, L3, and L4 stock. L4 has assets with a value of $100. During Year 2, A, B, C, and D, acting pursuant to a plan to avoid an ownership change of L4, acquire the following ownership interests in the members of the L loss group: (A) on September 11, Year 2, A acquires 20 percent of the L1 stock from L and B acquires 20 percent of the L2 stock from L1; and (B) on September 20, Year 2, C acquires 20 percent of the stock of L3 from L2 and D acquires 20 percent of the stock of L4 from L3. The following is a graphic illustration of these facts:

Reg. § 1.1502-96A(b)(4)

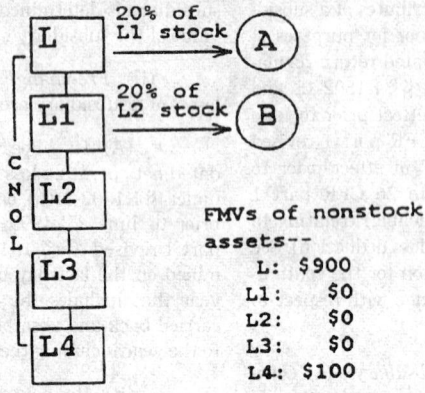

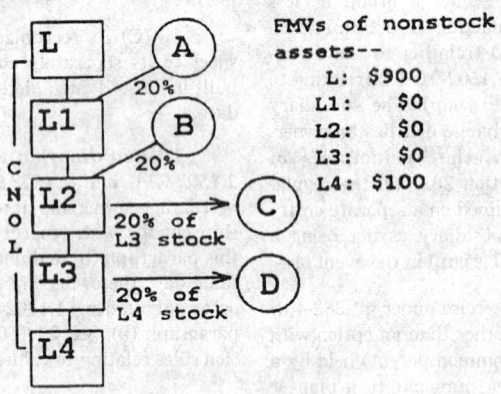

(b) The acquisitions by A, B, C, and D pursuant to the plan have increased their respective percentage ownership interests in L4 by approximately 10, 13, 16, and 20 percentage points, for a total of approximately 59 percentage points during the testing period. This more than 50 percentage point increase in the percentage ownership interest in L4 causes an ownership change of L4 under paragraph (b)(2) of this section.

(c) *Continuing effect of an ownership change.* A loss corporation (or loss subgroup) that is subject to a limitation under section 382 with respect to its pre-change losses continues to be subject to the limitation regardless of whether it becomes a member or ceases to be a member of a consolidated group. See § 1.382-5(d) (relating to successive ownership changes and absorption of a section 382 limitation). [Reg. § 1.1502-96A.]

Reg. § 1.1502-97

☐ [T.D. 8678, 6-26-96. *Amended by T.D. 8823, 6-25-99 and amended and redesignated by T.D. 8824, 6-25-99.*]

[Reg. § 1.1502-97]

§ 1.1502-97. Special rules under section 382 for members under the jurisdiction of a court in a title 11 or similar case.—[Reserved]

☐ [T.D. 8824, 6-25-99.]

[Reg. § 1.1502-97A]

§ 1.1502-97A. Special rules under section 382 for members under the jurisdiction of a court in a title 11 or similar case.— [Reserved]

☐ [T.D. 8678, 6-26-96. *Amended and redesignated by T.D. 8824, 6-25-99.*]

[Reg. § 1.1502-98]

§ 1.1502-98. Coordination with section 383.—The rules contained in §§ 1.1502-91 through 1.1502-96 also apply for purposes of section 383, with appropriate adjustments to reflect that section 383 applies to credits and net capital losses. For example, subgroups with respect to the carryover of general business credits, minimum tax credits, unused foreign tax, and net capital loss are determined by applying the principles of § 1.1502-91(d)(1). Similarly, in the case of net capital losses, general business credits, and excess foreign taxes that are pre-change attributes, § 1.383-1 applies the principles of §§ 1.1502-91 through 1.1502-96. For example, if a loss group has an ownership change under § 1.1502-92 and has a carryover of unused general business credits from a pre-change consolidated return year to a post-change consolidated return year, the amount of the group's regular tax liability for the post-change year that can be offset by the carryover cannot exceed the consolidated section 383 credit limitation for that post-change year, determined by applying the principles of §§ 1.383-1(c)(6) and 1.1502-93 (relating to the computation of the consolidated section 382 limitation). [Reg. § 1.1502-98.]

☐ [T.D. 8824, 6-25-99. Amended by T.D. 8884, 5-24-2000.]

[Reg. § 1.1502-98A]

§ 1.1502-98A. Coordination with section 383 generally applicable for testing dates (or members joining or leaving a group) before June 25, 1999.—The rules contained in §§ 1.1502-91A through 1.1502-96A also apply for purposes of section 383, with appropriate adjustments to reflect that section 383 applies to credits and net capital losses. Similarly, in the case of net capital losses, general business credits, and excess foreign taxes that are pre-change attributes, § 1.383-1 applies the principles of §§ 1.1502-91A through 1.1502-96A. For example, if a loss group has an ownership change under § 1.1502-92A and has a carryover of unused general business credits from a pre-change consolidated return year to a post-change consolidated return year, the amount of the group's regular tax liability for the post-change year that can be offset by the carryover cannot exceed the consolidated section 383 credit limitation for that post-change year, determined by applying the principles of §§ 1.3831(c)(6) and 1.1502-93A (relating to the computation of the consolidated section 382 limitation). [Reg. § 1.1502-98A.]

☐ [T.D. 8678, 6-26-96. Amended and redesignated by T.D. 8824, 6-25-99.]

[Reg. § 1.1502-99]

§ 1.1502-99. Effective dates.—(a) *In general.* Except as provided in paragraphs (b) and (c) of this section, §§ 1.1502-91 through 1.1502-96 and § 1.1502-98 apply to any testing date on or after June 25, 1999. Sections 1.1502-94 through 1.1502-96 also apply to a corporation that becomes a member of a group or ceases to be a member of a group (or loss subgroup) on any date on or after June 25, 1999.

(b) *Special rules*—(1) *Election to treat subgroup parent requirement as satisfied.* Section 1.1502-91(d)(4), § 1.1502-91(d)(7), Example 4, § 1.1502-92(b)(1)(iii), § 1.1502-92(b)(2), Example 5, the last two sentences of § 1.1502-95(b)(3), § 1.1502-95(d)(2)(i), and § 1.1502-96(e)(all of which relate to the election under § 1.1502-91(d)(4) to treat the loss subgroup parent requirement as satisfied) apply to corporations that become members of a consolidated group in taxable years for which the due date of the income tax return (without extensions) is after June 25, 1999.

(2) *Principal purpose of avoiding a limitation.* The third sentence of § 1.1502-91(d)(5) (relating to members excluded from a loss subgroup) applies to corporations that become members of a consolidated group on or after June 25, 1999.

(3) *Ceasing to be a member of a loss subgroup*—(i) *Ownership change of a loss subgroup.* Section 1.1502-95(d)(2)(ii) and § 1.1502-95(d)(3), Example 3 apply to corporations that cease to bear a relationship described in section 1504(a)(1) to a loss subgroup parent in taxable years for which the due date of the income tax return (without extensions) is after June 25, 1999.

(ii) *Expiration of 5-year period.* Section 1.1502-95(d)(2)(iii) applies with respect to the day after the last day of any 5 consecutive year period described in that section that ends in a taxable year for which the due date of the income tax return (without extensions) is after June 25, 1999.

(4) *Reattribution of net operating loss carryovers under § 1.1502-20(g).* Section 1.1502-96(d) applies to reattributions of net operating loss carryovers (or capital loss carryovers) in taxable years for which the due date of the income tax return (without extensions) is after June 25, 1999; except that the election under § 1.1502-96(d)(5) (relating to an election to reattribute section 382 limitation) can be made with any election under § 1.1502-20(g)(4) to reattribute to the common parent a net operating loss or net capital loss that is timely filed on or after June 25, 1999.

(5) *Election to apportion net unrealized built-in gain.* In the case of corporations that cease to be members of a loss group (or loss subgroup) before June 25, 1999 in a taxable year for which the due date of the income tax return

(without extensions) is after June 25, 1999, § 1.1502-95(a), (b), (c), and (f) apply to those corporations if the common parent makes the election described in the second sentence of paragraph (c)(1) of § 1.1502-95 in the time and manner prescribed in paragraph (f) of § 1.1502-95.

(c) *Testing period may include a period beginning before June 25, 1999*—(1) *In general.* A testing period for purposes of §§ 1.1502-91 through 1.1502-96 and 1.1502-98 may include a period beginning before June 25, 1999. Thus, for example, in applying § 1.1502-92(b)(1)(i)(relating to the determination of an ownership change of a loss group), the determination of the lowest percentage of ownership interest of any 5-percent shareholder of the common parent during a testing period ending on a testing date occurring on or after June 25, 1999 takes into account the period beginning before June 25, 1999, except the extent that the period is more than 3 years before the testing date or is otherwise before the beginning of the testing period. See § 1.1502-92(b)(1).

(2) *Transition rule for net unrealized built-in loss.* A loss group (or loss subgroup) that has a net unrealized built-in loss on a testing date on or after June 25, 1999 may apply § 1.1502-91A(g) (and § 1.1502-96A(a) as it relates to § 1.1502-91A(g)) for the period ending on the day before June 25, 1999 to determine under § 1.382-2T(d)(ii)(A) the earliest date that its testing period begins (treating the day before June 25, 1999 as the end of a taxable year.) Thus, for example, if a consolidated group with no net operating losses has a net unrealized built-in loss determined under § 1.1502-91(g) on a testing date after June 25, 1999, but, under § 1.1502-91A(g), does not have a net unrealized built-in loss for the period ending on the day before June 25, 1999, the group's testing period begins no earlier than June 25, 1999. [Reg. § 1.1502-99.]

☐ [*T.D.* 8824, 6-25-99.]

[Reg. § 1.1502-99A]

§ 1.1502-99A. **Effective dates.**—(a) *Effective date*—(1) *In general.* Except as provided in § 1.1502-99(b), §§ 1.1502-91A through 1.1502-96A and 1.1502-98A apply to any testing date on or after January 1, 1997, and before June 25, 1999. Sections 1.1502-94A through 1.1502-96A also apply on any date on or after January 1, 1997, and before June 25, 1999, on which a corporation becomes a member of a group or on which a corporation ceases to be a member of a loss group (or a loss subgroup).

(2) *Anti-duplication rules for recognized built-in gain.* Section 1.1502-93(c)(2) (relating to recognized built-in gain of a loss group or loss subgroup) applies to taxable years for which the due date for income tax returns (without extensions) is after June 25, 1999.

(b) *Testing period may include a period beginning before January 1, 1997.* A testing period for purposes of §§ 1.1502-91A through 1.1502-96A and 1.1502-98A may include a period beginning before January 1, 1997. Thus, for example, in applying § 1.1502-92A(b)(1)(i) (relating to the determination of an ownership change of a loss group), the determination of the lowest percentage ownership interest of any 5-percent shareholder of the common parent during a testing period ending on a testing date occurring on or after January 1, 1997, takes into account the period beginning before January 1, 1997, except to the extent that the period is more than 3 years before the testing date or is otherwise before the beginning of the testing period. See § 1.1502-92A(b)(1).

(c) *Transition rules*—(1) *Methods permitted*—(i) *In general.* For the period ending before January 1, 1997, a consolidated group is permitted to use any method described in paragraph (c)(2) of this section which is consistently applied to determine if an ownership change occurred with respect to a consolidated net operating loss, a net operating loss carryover (including net operating loss carryovers arising in SRLYs), or a net unrealized built-in loss. If an ownership change occurred during that period, the group is also permitted to use any method described in paragraph (c)(2) of this section which is consistently applied to compute the amount of the section 382 limitation that applies to limit the use of taxable income in any post-change year ending before, on, or after January 1, 1997. The preceding sentence does not preclude the imposition of an additional, lesser limitation due to a subsequent ownership change nor, except as provided in paragraph (c)(1)(iii) of this section, does it permit the beginning of a new testing period for the loss group.

(ii) *Adjustments to offset excess limitation.* If an ownership change occurred during the period ending before January 1, 1997, and a method described in paragraph (c)(2) of this section was not used for a post-change year, the members (or group) must reduce the section 382 limitation for post-change years for which an income tax return is filed after January 1, 1997, to offset, as quickly as possible, the effects of any section 382 limitation that members took into account in excess of the amount that would have been allowable under §§ 1.1502-91A through 1.1502-96A and 1.1502-98A.

(iii) *Coordination with effective date.* Notwithstanding that a group may have used a method described in paragraph (c)(2)(ii) or (iii) of this section for the period before January 1, 1997, §§ 1.1502-91A through 1.1502-96A and 1.1502-98A apply to any testing date occurring on or after January 1, 1997, for purposes of determining whether there is an ownership change with respect to any losses and, if so, the collateral consequences. Any ownership change of a member other than the common parent pursuant to a method described in paragraph (c)(2)(ii) or (iii) of this section does not cause a new testing period of the loss group to begin for purposes of applying § 1.1502-92A on or after January 1, 1997.

(2) *Permitted methods.* The methods described in this paragraph (c)(2) are:

(i) A method that does not materially differ from the rules in §§ 1.1502-91A through 1.1502-96A and 1.1502-98A (other than those in § 1.1502-95A(c) and (b)(2)(ii) (relating to the apportionment of a section 382 limitation) as they would apply to a corporation that ceases to be a member of the group before January 1, 1997). As the context requires, the method must treat references to rules in current regulations as references to rules in regulations generally effective for taxable years before January 1, 1997. Thus, for example, the taxpayer must treat a reference to § 1.382-4(d) (relating to options) as a reference to § 1.382-2T(h)(4) for any testing date to which § 1.382-2T(h)(4) applies. Similarly, a reference to § 1.1502-21(c) or 1.1502-21T(c) in effect prior to June 25, 1999, as contained in 26 CFR part 1 revised April 1, 1999, as applicable may be a reference to § 1.1502-21A(c), as appropriate. Furthermore, the method must treat all corporations that were affiliated on January 1, 1987, and continuously thereafter as having met the 5 consecutive year requirement of § 1.1502-91A(d)(2)(i) on any day before January 1, 1992, on which the determination of net unrealized built-in gain or loss of a loss subgroup is made;

(ii) A reasonable application of the rules in section 382 and the regulations thereunder applied to each member on a separate entity basis, treating each member's allocable part of a consolidated net operating loss which is attributable to it under § 1.1502-21(b) or 1.1502-21T(b) in effect prior to June 25, 1999, as contained in 26 CFR part 1 revised April 1, 1999, as applicable as a net operating loss of that member and applying rules similar to § 1.382-8 to avoid duplication of value in computing the section 382 limitation for the member (see § 1.382-8(h) (relating to the effective date and transition rules regarding controlled groups)); or

(iii) A method approved by the Commissioner upon application by the common parent.

(d) *Amended returns.* A group may file an amended return in connection with an ownership change occurring before January 1, 1997, to modify the amount of a section 382 limitation with respect to a consolidated net operating loss, a net operating loss carryover (including net operating loss carryovers arising in SRLYs), or a recognized built-in loss (or gain) only if it files amended returns:

(1) For the earliest taxable year ending after December 31, 1986, in which it had an ownership change, if any, under § 1.1502-92A;

(2) For all subsequent taxable years for which returns have already been filed as of the date of the amended return;

(3) The modification with respect to all members for all taxable years ending in 1987 and thereafter complies with §§ 1.1502-91A through 1.1502-96A and 1.1502-98A; and

(4) The amended return(s) permitted by the applicable statute of limitations is/are filed before March 26, 1997.

(e) *Section 383.* This section also applies for the purposes of section 383, with appropriate adjustments to reflect that section 383 applies to credits and net capital losses. [Reg. § 1.1502-99A.]

☐ [T.D. 8678, 6-26-96. *Amended by T.D.* 8823, 6-25-99 *and amended and redesignated by T.D.* 8824, 6-25-99.]

[Reg. § 1.1502-100]

§ 1.1502-100. **Corporations exempt from tax.**—(a) *In general*—(1) *Computation of tax liability.* The tax liability for a consolidated return year of a group of two or more corporations described in section 1504(e) which are exempt from taxation under section 501 (hereinafter referred to in this section as "exempt group") shall be determined on a consolidated basis by applying the provisions of subchapter F of chapter 1 of the Code in the manner provided in this section. See section 1504(e) for tax-exempt corporations eligible to file a consolidated return.

(2) *Applicability of other consolidated return provisions.* The provisions of § 1.1502-1 through § 1.1502-80 shall be applicable to an exempt group to the extent they are not inconsistent with the provisions of this section or the provisions of subchapter F of chapter 1 of the Code. For purposes of applying the provisions of § 1.1502-1 through § 1.1502-80 to an exempt group, the following substitutions shall be made—

(i) The term "exempt group" shall be substituted for the term "group",

(ii) The terms "unrelated business taxable income", "separate unrelated business taxable income", and "consolidated unrelated business taxable income" shall be substituted for the terms "taxable income", "separate taxable income", and "consolidated taxable income", and

(iii) The term "consolidated liability for tax determined under § 1.1502-2" (or an equivalent term) shall mean the consolidated liability for tax of an exempt group determined under paragraph (b) of this section.

(b) *Consolidated liability for tax.* The tax liability for a consolidated return year of an exempt group is the tax imposed by section 511(a) or section 1201(a) on the consolidated unrelated business taxable income for the year (determined under paragraph (c) of this section), and by allowing the credits and surtax exemption provided in § 1.1502-2.

(c) *Consolidated unrelated business taxable income.* The consolidated unrelated business taxable income for a consolidated return year shall be determined by taking into account—

(1) The separate unrelated business taxable income of each member of the exempt group (determined under paragraph (d) of this section);

(2) Any consolidated net operating loss deduction (determined under § 1.1502-21A or 1.1502-21 (as appropriate)) subject to the limitations provided in section 512(b)(6);

(3) Any consolidated charitable contribution deduction (determined under § 1.1502-24) subject to the limitations provided in section 512(b)(10); and

(4) Any consolidated net gain or net loss from the disposition of debt-financed property (as defined in section 514(b)) taken into account as provided by section 514(a), or from the cutting of timber to which section 631 applies.

(d) *Separate unrelated business taxable income.* The separate unrelated business taxable income of a member of an exempt group shall be computed in accordance with the provisions of section 512 covering the determination of unrelated business taxable income of separate corporations, except that—

(1) The provisions of paragraphs (a) through (k) and (o) of § 1.1502-12 shall apply; and

(2) No charitable contributions deduction shall be taken into account under section 512(b)(10).

See sections 511(c) and 512(a)(3)(C) for special rules applicable to organizations described in section 501(c)(2). [Reg. § 1.1502-100.]

☐ [T.D. 7183, 4-30-72. Amended by T.D. 2-16-79; T.D. 8677, 6-26-96 and T.D. 8823, 6-25-99.]

Reg. § 1.1503-1(a)

[Reg. § 1.1503-1]

§ 1.1503-1. Computation and payment of tax.—(a) *General rule.* In any case in which a consolidated return is filed or required to be filed, the tax shall be determined, computed, assessed, collected, and adjusted in accordance with the regulations prescribed under section 1502 promulgated prior to the last date prescribed by law for the filing of such return.

(b) *Limitation.* If the affiliated group includes one or more Western Hemisphere trade corporations (as defined in section 921) or one or more regulated public utilities (as defined in section 1503(c)) the increase in tax described in section 1503(a) shall be applied in a manner provided in the regulations under section 1502. [Reg. § 1.1503-1.]

☐ [T.D. 6140, 8-29-55. Amended by T.D. 7244, 12-29-72.]

[Reg. § 1.1503-2]

§ 1.1503-2. Dual consolidated loss.—(a) *Purpose and scope.* This section provides rules for the application of section 1503(d), concerning the determination and use of dual consolidated losses. Paragraph (b) of this section provides a general rule prohibiting a dual consolidated loss from offsetting the taxable income of a domestic affiliate. Paragraph (c) of this section provides definitions of the terms used in this section. Paragraph (d) of this section provides rules for calculating the amount of a dual consolidated loss and for adjusting the basis of stock of a dual resident corporation. Paragraph (e) of this section contains an anti-avoidance provision. Paragraph (f) of this section applies the rules of paragraph (d) of this section to the computation of foreign tax credit limitations. Paragraph (g) of this section provides certain exceptions to the limitation rule of paragraph (b) of this section. Finally, paragraph (h) of this section provides the effective date of the regulations and a provision for the retroactive application of the regulations to qualifying taxpayers.

(b) *In general*—(1) *Limitation on the use of a dual consolidated loss to offset income of a domestic affiliate.* Except as otherwise provided in this section, a dual consolidated loss of a dual resident corporation cannot offset the taxable income of any domestic affiliate in the taxable year in which the loss is recognized or in any other taxable year, regardless of whether the loss offsets income of another person under the income tax laws of a foreign country and regardless of whether the income that the loss may offset in the foreign country is, has been, or will be subject to tax in the United States. Pursuant to paragraph (c)(1) and (2) of this section, the same limitation shall apply to a dual consolidated loss of a separate unit of a domestic corporation as if the separate unit were a wholly owned subsidiary of such corporation.

(2) *Limitation on the use of a dual consolidated loss to offset income of a successor-in-interest.* A dual consolidated loss of a dual resident corporation also cannot be used to offset the taxable income of another corporation by means of a transaction in which the other corporation succeeds to the tax attributes of the dual resident corporation under section 381 of the Code. Similarly, a dual consolidated loss of a separate unit of a domestic corporation cannot be used to offset income of the domestic corporation following the termination, liquidation, sale, or other disposition of the separate unit. However, if a dual resident corporation transfers its assets to another corporation in a transaction subject to section 381, and the acquiring corporation is a dual resident corporation of the same foreign country of which the transferor dual resident corporation is a resident, or a domestic corporation that carries on the business activities of the transferor dual resident corporation as a separate unit, then income generated by the transferee dual resident corporation, or separate unit, may be offset by the carryover losses of the transferor dual resident corporation. In addition, if a domestic corporation transfers a separate unit to another domestic corporation in a transaction subject to section 381, the income generated by the separate unit following the transfer may be offset by the carryover losses of the separate unit.

(3) *Application of rules to multiple tiers of separate units.* If a separate unit of a domestic corporation is owned indirectly through another separate unit, the principles of paragraph (b)(1) and (2) of this section shall apply as if the upper-tier separate unit were a subsidiary of the domestic corporation and the lower-tier separate unit were a lower-tier subsidiary.

(4) *Examples.* The following examples illustrate the application of this paragraph (b).

Example 1. P, a domestic corporation, owns all of the outstanding stock of DRC, a domestic corporation. P and DRC file a consolidated U.S. income tax return. DRC is managed and controlled in Country W, a country that determines the tax residence of corporations according to their place of management and control. Therefore, DRC is a dual resident corporation and any net operating loss it incurs is a dual consolidated loss. In Years 1 through 3, DRC incurs dual consolidated losses. Under this paragraph (b), the dual consolidated losses may not be used to offset P's income on the group's consolidated U.S. income tax return. At the end of Year 3, DRC sells all of its assets and discontinues its business operations. DRC is then liquidated into P, pursuant to the provisions of section 332. Normally, under section 381, P would succeed to, and be permitted to utilize, DRC's net operating loss carryovers. However, this paragraph (b) prohibits the dual consolidated losses of DRC from reducing P's income for U.S. tax purposes. Therefore, DRC's net operating loss carryovers will not be available to offset P's income.

Example 2. The facts are the same as in *Example 1*, except that DRC does not sell its assets and, following the liquidation of DRC, P continues to operate DRC's business as a separate unit (*e.g.*, a branch). DRC's loss carryovers are available to offset P's income generated by the assets previously owned by DRC and now held by the separate unit.

(c) *Definitions.* The following definitions shall apply for purposes of this section.

(1) *Domestic corporation.* The term "domestic corporation" has the meaning assigned to it by section 7701(a)(3) and (4). The term also includes any corporation otherwise treated as a domestic corporation by the Code, including, but not limited to, sections 269B, 953(d), and 1504(d). For purposes of this section, any separate unit of a domestic corporation, as defined in paragraph (c)(3) and (4) of this section, shall be treated as a separate domestic corporation.

(2) *Dual resident corporation.* A dual resident corporation is a domestic corporation that is subject to the income tax of a foreign country on its worldwide income or on a residence basis. A corporation is taxed on a residence basis if it is taxed as a resident under the laws of the foreign country. An S corporation, as defined in section 1361, is not a dual resident corporation. For purposes of this section, any separate unit of a domestic corporation, as defined in paragraph (c)(3) and (4) of this section, shall be treated as a dual resident corporation. Unless otherwise indicated, any reference in this section to a dual resident corporation refers also to a separate unit.

(3) *Separate unit*—(i) The term "separate unit" shall mean any of the following:

(A) A foreign branch, as defined in § 1.367(a)-6T(g) (or a successor regulation), that is owned either directly by a domestic corporation or indirectly by a domestic corporation through ownership of a partnership or trust interest (regardless of whether the partnership or trust is a United States person);

(B) an interest in a partnership; or

(C) an interest in a trust.

(ii) If two or more foreign branches located in the same foreign country are owned by a single domestic corporation and the losses of each branch are made available to offset the income of the other branches under the tax laws of the foreign country, within the meaning of paragraph (c)(15)(ii) of this section, then the branches shall be treated as one separate unit.

(4) *Hybrid entity separate unit.* The term "separate unit" includes an interest in an entity that is not taxable as an association for U.S. income tax purposes but is subject to income tax in a foreign country as a corporation (or otherwise at the entity level) either on its worldwide income or on a residence basis.

(5) *Dual consolidated loss*—(i) *In general.* The term "dual consolidated loss" means the net operating loss (as defined in section 172(c) and the regulations thereunder) of a domestic corporation incurred in a year in which the corporation is a dual resident corporation. The dual consolidated loss shall be computed under paragraph (d)(1) of this section. The fact that a particular item taken into account in computing a dual resident corporation's net operating loss is not taken into account in computing income subject to a foreign country's income tax shall not cause such item to be excluded from the calculation of the dual consolidated loss.

(ii) *Exceptions.* A dual consolidated loss shall not include the following—

(A) A net operating loss incurred by a dual resident corporation in a foreign country whose income tax laws—

(*1*) Do not permit the dual resident corporation to use its losses, expenses or deductions to offset the income of any other person that is recognized in the same taxable year in which the losses, expenses or deductions are incurred; and

(*2*) Do not permit the losses, expenses or deductions of the dual resident corporation to be carried over or back to be used, by any means, to offset the income of any other person in other taxable years; or

(B) A net operating loss incurred during that portion of the taxable year prior to the date on which the domestic corporation becomes a dual resident corporation or subsequent to the date on which the domestic corporation ceases to be a dual resident corporation. For purposes of determining the amount of the net operating loss incurred in that portion of the taxable year prior to the date on which the domestic corporation becomes a dual resident corporation or subsequent to the date on which the domestic corporation ceases to be a dual resident corporation, in no event shall more than the aggregate of the equal daily portion of the net operating loss commensurate with the portion of the taxable year during which the domestic corporation was not a dual resident corporation be allocated to that portion of the taxable year in which the domestic corporation was not a dual resident corporation.

(iii) *Dual consolidated losses of separate units that are partnership interests, including interests in hybrid entities.* [Reserved]

(6) *Subject to tax.* For purposes of determining whether a domestic corporation is subject to the income tax of a foreign country on its income, the fact that the corporation has no actual income tax liability to the foreign country for a particular taxable year shall not be taken into account.

(7) *Foreign country.* For purposes of this section, possessions of the United States shall be considered foreign countries.

(8) *Consolidated group.* The term "consolidated group" means an affiliated group, as defined in section 1504(a), with which a dual resident corporation or domestic owner files a consolidated U.S. income tax return.

(9) *Domestic owner.* The term "domestic owner" means a domestic corporation that owns one or more separate units.

(10) *Affiliated dual resident corporation or affiliated domestic owner.* The term "affiliated dual resident corporation" or "affiliated domestic owner" means a dual resident corporation or domestic owner that is a member of a consolidated group.

(11) *Unaffiliated dual resident corporation or unaffiliated domestic owner.* The term "unaffiliated dual resident corporation" or "unaffiliated domestic owner" means a dual resident corporation or domestic owner that is an unaffiliated domestic corporation.

(12) *Successor-in-interest.* The term "successor-in-interest" means an acquiring corporation that succeeds to the tax attributes of an acquired corporation by means of a transaction subject to section 381.

(13) *Domestic affiliate.* The term "domestic affiliate" means any member of an affiliated group, without regard to the exceptions contained in section 1504(b) (other than section 1504(b)(3)) relating to includible corporations.

(14) *Unaffiliated domestic corporation.* The term "unaffiliated domestic corporation" means a domestic corporation that is not a member of an affiliated group.

Reg. § 1.1503-2(c)(4)

(15) *Use of loss to offset income of a domestic affiliate or another person*—(i) A dual consolidated loss shall be deemed to offset income of a domestic affiliate in the year it is included in the computation of the consolidated taxable income of a consolidated group. The fact that no tax benefit results from the inclusion of the dual consolidated loss in the computation of the group's consolidated taxable income in the taxable year shall not be taken into account.

(ii) Except as provided in paragraph (c)(15)(iii) of this section, a loss, expense, or deduction taken into account in computing a dual consolidated loss shall be deemed to offset income of another person under the income tax laws of a foreign country in the year it is made available for such offset. The fact that the other person does not have sufficient income in that year to benefit from such an offset shall not be taken into account. However, where the laws of a foreign country provide an election that would enable a dual resident corporation or separate unit to use its losses, expenses, or deductions to offset income of another person, the losses, expenses, or deductions shall be considered to offset such income only if the election is made.

(iii) The losses, expenses, or deductions taken into account in computing a dual resident corporation's or separate unit's dual consolidated loss shall not be deemed to offset income of another person under the income tax laws of a foreign country for purposes of this section, if under the laws of the foreign country the losses, expenses, or deductions of the dual resident corporation or separate unit are used to offset the income of another dual resident corporation or separate unit within the same consolidated group (or income of another separate unit that is owned by the unaffiliated domestic owner of the first separate unit). If the losses, expenses, or deductions of a dual resident corporation or separate unit are made available under the laws of a foreign country to offset the income of other dual resident corporations or separate units within the same consolidated group (or other separate units owned by the unaffiliated domestic owner of the first separate unit), as well as the income of another person, and the laws of the foreign country do not provide applicable rules for determining which person's income is offset by the losses, expenses, or deductions, then for purposes of this section, the losses, expenses or deductions shall be deemed to offset the income of the other dual resident corporations or separate units, to the extent of such income, before being considered to offset the income of the other person.

(iv) Except to the extent paragraph (g)(1) of this section applies, where the income tax laws of a foreign country deny the use of losses, expenses, or deductions of a dual resident corporation to offset the income of another person because the dual resident corporation is also subject to income taxation by another country on its worldwide income or on a residence basis, the dual resident corporation shall be treated as if it actually had offset its dual consolidated loss against the income of another person in such foreign country.

(16) *Examples.* The following examples illustrate this paragraph (c).

Example 1. X, a member of a consolidated group, conducts business through a branch in Country Y. Under Country Y's income tax laws, the branch is taxed as a permanent establishment and its losses may be used under the Country Y form of consolidation to offset the income of Z, a Country Y affiliate of X. In Year 1, the branch of X incurs an overall loss that would be treated as a net operating loss if the branch were a separate domestic corporation. Under paragraph (c)(3) of this section, the branch of X is treated as a separate domestic corporation and a dual resident corporation. Thus, under paragraph (c)(5), its loss constitutes a dual consolidated loss. Unless X qualifies for an exception under paragraph (g) of this section, paragraph (b) of this section precludes the use of the branch's loss to offset any income of X not derived from the branch operations or any income of a domestic affiliate of X.

Example 2. A and B are members of a consolidated group. FC is a Country X corporation that is wholly owned by B. A and B organize a partnership, P, under the laws of Country X. P conducts business in Country X and its business activity constitutes a foreign branch within the meaning of paragraph (c)(3)(i)(A) of this section. P also earns U.S. source income that is unconnected with the branch operations and, therefore, is not subject to tax by Country X. Under the laws of Country X, the branch can consolidate with FC. The interests in P held by A and B are each treated as a dual resident corporation. The branch is also treated as a separate dual resident corporation. Unless an exception under paragraph (g) of this section applies, any dual consolidated loss incurred by P's branch cannot offset the U.S. source income earned by P or any other income of A or B.

Example 3. X is classified as a partnership for U.S. income tax purposes. A, B and C are the sole partners of X. A and B are domestic corporations and C is a Country Y corporation. For U.S. income tax purposes, each partner has an equal

Reg. § 1.1503-2(c)(16)

interest in each item of partnership profit or loss. Under Country Y's law, X is classified as a corporation and its income and losses may be used under the Country Y form of consolidation to offset the income of companies that are affiliates of X. Under paragraph (c)(3) and (4) of this section, the partnership interests held by A and B are treated as separate domestic corporations and as dual resident corporations. Unless an exception under paragraph (g) of this section applies, losses allocated to A and B can only be used to offset profits of X allocated to A and B, respectively.

Example 4. P, a domestic corporation, files a consolidated U.S. income tax return with its two wholly-owned domestic subsidiaries, DRC1 and DRC2. Each subsidiary is also treated as a Country Y resident for Country Y tax purposes. Thus, DRC1 and DRC2 are dual resident corporations. DRC1 owns FC, a Country Y corporation. Country Y's tax laws permit affiliated resident corporations to file a form of consolidated return. In Year 1, DRC1 incurs a $200 net operating loss for both U.S. and Country Y tax purposes, while DRC2 recognizes $200 of income under the tax laws of each country. FC also earns $200 of income for Country Y tax purposes. DRC1, DRC2, and FC file a Country Y consolidated return. However, Country Y has no applicable rules for determining which income is offset by DRC1's $200 loss. Under paragraph (c)(15)(iii) of this section, the loss shall be treated as offsetting DRC2's $200 of income. Because DRC1 and DRC2 are members of the same consolidated group, for purposes of this section, the offset of DRC1's loss against the income of DRC2 is not considered a use of the loss against the income of another person under the laws of a foreign country.

Example 5. DRC, a domestic corporation, files a consolidated U.S. income tax return with its parent, P. DRC is also subject to tax in Country Y on its worldwide income. Therefore, DRC is a dual resident corporation and any net operating loss incurred by DRC is a dual consolidated loss. Country Y's tax laws permit corporations that are subject to tax on their worldwide income to use the Country Y form of consolidation, thus enabling eligible corporations to use their losses to offset income of affiliates. However, to prevent corporations like DRC from offsetting losses against income of affiliates in Country Y and then again offsetting the losses against income of foreign affiliates under the tax laws of another country, Country Y prevents a corporation that is also subject to the income tax of another country on its worldwide income or on a residence basis from using the Country Y form of consolidation. There is no agreement, as described in paragraph (g)(1) of this section, between the United States and Country Y. Because of Country Y's statute, DRC will be treated as having actually offset its losses against the income of affiliates in Country Y under paragraph (c)(15)(iv) of this section. Therefore, DRC will not be able to file an agreement described in paragraph (g)(2) of this section and offset its losses against the income of P or any other domestic affiliate.

(d) *Special rules for accounting for dual consolidated losses*—(1) *Determination of amount of dual consolidated loss*—(i) *Dual resident corporation that is a member of a consolidated group.* For purposes of determining whether a dual resident corporation that is a member of a consolidated group has a dual consolidated loss for the taxable year, the dual resident corporation shall compute its taxable income (or loss) in accordance with the rules set forth in the regulations under section 1502 governing the computation of consolidated taxable income, taking into account only the dual resident corporation's items of income, gain, deduction, and loss for the year. However, for purposes of this computation, the following items shall not be taken into account:

(A) Any net capital loss of the dual resident corporation; and

(B) Any carryover or carryback losses.

(ii) *Dual resident corporation that is a separate unit of a domestic corporation.* For purposes of determining whether a separate unit has a dual consolidated loss for the taxable year, the separate unit shall compute its taxable income (or loss) as if it were a separate domestic corporation and a dual resident corporation in accordance with the provisions of paragraph (d)(1)(i) of this section, using only those items of income, expense, deduction, and loss that are otherwise attributable to such separate unit.

(2) *Effect of a dual consolidated loss.* For any taxable year in which a dual resident corporation or separate unit has a dual consolidated loss to which paragraph (b) of this section applies, the following rules shall apply.

(i) If the dual resident corporation is a member of a consolidated group, the group shall compute its consolidated taxable income without taking into account the items of income, loss, or deduction taken into account in computing the dual consolidated loss. The dual consolidated loss may be carried over or back for use in other taxable years as a separate net operating loss carryover or carryback of the dual resident corporation arising in the year incurred. It shall be treated as a loss incurred by the dual resident corporation in a separate return limitation year and (without regard to whether the dual resident

Reg. § 1.1503-2(d)(1)

corporation is a common parent) shall be subject to all of the limitations of § 1.1502-21A(c) or 1.1502-21(c), as appropriate (relating to limitations on net operating loss carryovers and carrybacks from separate return limitation years).

(ii) The unaffiliated domestic owner of a separate unit, or the consolidated group of an affiliated domestic owner, shall compute its taxable income without taking into account the items of income, loss or deduction taken into account in computing the separate unit's dual consolidated loss. The dual consolidated loss shall be treated as a loss incurred by a separate corporation and its use shall be subject to all of the limitations of § 1.1502-21A(c) or 1.1502-21(c), as appropriate, as if the separate unit were filing a consolidated return with the unaffiliated domestic owner or with the consolidated group of the affiliated domestic owner.

(3) *Basis adjustments for dual consolidated losses*—(i) *Dual resident corporation that is a member of an affiliated group.* When a dual resident corporation is a member of a consolidated group, each other member owning stock in the dual resident corporation shall adjust the basis of the stock in the following manner.

(A) *Positive adjustments.* Positive adjustments shall be made in accordance with the principles of § 1.1502-32(b)(1), except that there shall be no positive adjustment under § 1.1502-32(b)(1)(ii) for any amount of the dual consolidated loss that is not absorbed as a result of the application of paragraph (b) of this section. In addition, there shall be no positive adjustment for any amount included in income pursuant to paragraph (g)(2)(vii) of this section.

(B) *Negative adjustments.* Negative adjustments shall be made in accordance with the principles of § 1.1502-32(b)(2), except that there shall be no negative adjustment under § 1.1502-32(b)(2)(ii) for the amount of the dual consolidated loss subject to paragraph (b) of this section that is absorbed in a carryover year.

(ii) *Dual resident corporation that is a separate unit arising from an interest in a partnership.* Where a separate unit is an interest in a partnership, the domestic owner shall adjust its basis in the separate unit in accordance with section 705, except that no increase in basis shall be permitted for any amount included as income pursuant to paragraph (g)(2)(vii) of this section.

(4) *Examples.* The following examples illustrate this paragraph (d).

Example 1. (i) P, S1, S2, and T are domestic corporations. P owns all of the stock of S1 and S2. S2 owns all of the stock of T. T is a resident of Country FC for Country FC income tax purposes. Therefore, T is a dual resident corporation. P, S1, S2, and T file a consolidated U.S. income tax return. X and Y are corporations that are not members of the consolidated group.

(ii) At the beginning of Year 1, P has a basis of $1,000 in the stock of S2. S2 has a $500 basis in the stock of T.

(iii) In Year 1, T incurs interest expense in the amount of $100. In addition, T sells a noncapital asset, u, in which it has a basis of $10, to S1 for $50. T also sells a noncapital asset, v, in which it has a basis of $200, to S1 for $100. The sales of u and v are intercompany transactions described in § 1.1502-13. T also sells a capital asset, z, in which it has a basis of $180, to Y for $90. In Year 1, S1 earns $200 of separate taxable income, calculated in accordance with § 1.1502-12, as well as $90 of capital gain from a sale of an asset to X. P and S2 have no items of income, loss, or deduction for Year 1.

(iv) In Year 1, T has a dual consolidated loss of $100 (attributable to its interest expense). T's $90 capital loss is not included in the computation of the dual consolidated loss. Instead, T's capital loss is included in the computation of the consolidated group's capital gain net income under § 1.1502-22(c) and is used to offset S1's $90 capital gain.

(v) No elective agreement, as described in paragraph (g)(1) of this section, exists between the United States and Country FC. For Country FC tax purposes, T's $100 loss is offset against the income of a Country FC affiliate. Therefore, T is not eligible for the exception provided in paragraph (g)(2) of this section.

(vi) Because T has a dual consolidated loss for the year, the consolidated taxable income of the consolidated group is calculated without regard to T's items of income, loss or deduction taken into account in computing the dual consolidated loss. Therefore, the consolidated taxable income of the consolidated group is $200 (the sum of $200 of separate taxable income earned by S1 plus $90 of capital gain earned by S1 minus $90 of capital loss incurred by T). The $40 gain recognized by T upon the sale of item u to S1 and the $100 loss recognized by T upon the sale of Item v to S1 are deferred pursuant to § 1.1502-13(c)(1).

(vii) S2 may not make the positive adjustment provided for in § 1.1502-32(b)(1)(ii) to its basis in the stock of T for the $100 dual consolidated loss incurred by T. In addition, no positive adjustment in the basis of the stock is required for T's $90 capital loss because the loss has been absorbed by the consolidated group. S2, however, must make the negative adjustment provided for in § 1.1502-32(b)(2)(i) for its allocable part of T's

Reg. § 1.1503-2(d)(4)

deficit in earnings and profits for the taxable year attributable to both T's $100 dual consolidated loss and T's $90 capital loss. Thus, as provided in § 1.1502-32(e)(1), S2 must make a $190 net negative adjustment to its basis in the stock of T, reducing its basis to $310. As provided in § 1.1502-33(c)(4)(ii) (a), S2's earnings and profits for Year 1 will reflect S2's decrease in its basis in T stock for the taxable year. Since S2 has no other earnings and profits for the taxable year, S2 has a $190 deficit in earnings and profits for the year. As provided in § 1.1502-32(b)(2)(i), P must make a negative adjustment to its basis in the stock of S2 for its allocable part of S2's deficit in earnings and profits for the taxable year. Thus, P must make a $190 net negative adjustment to its basis in S2 stock, reducing its basis to $810.

Example 2. (i) The facts are the same as in Example 1, except that in Year 2, S1 sells items *u* and *v* to X for no gain or loss. The disposition of items *u* and *v* outside of the consolidated group restores the deferred loss and gain to T. T also incurs $100 of interest expense in Year 2. In addition, T sells a noncapital asset, *r*, in which it has a basis of $100, to Y for $300. P and S2 have no items of income, loss, or deduction for Year 2.

(ii) T has $40 of separate taxable income in Year 2, computed as follows:

($100)	interest expense
($100)	sale of item *v* to S1
$ 40	sale of item *u* to S1
$200	sale of item *r* to Y
$ 40	

Thus, T has no dual consolidated loss for the year.

(iii) Since T does not have a dual consolidated loss for the taxable year, the group's consolidated taxable income is calculated in accordance with the general rule of § 1.1502-11 and not in accordance with paragraph (d)(2) of this section. T is the only member of the consolidated group that has any income or loss for the taxable year. Thus, the consolidated taxable income of the group, computed without regard to T's dual consolidated loss carryover, is $40.

(iv) As provided by § 1.1502-21A(c), the amount of the dual consolidated loss arising in Year 1 that is included in the group's consolidated net operating loss deduction for Year 2 is $40 (that is, the consolidated taxable income computed without regard to the consolidated net operating loss deduction minus such consolidated taxable income recomputed by excluding the items of income and deduction of T). Thus, the group has no consolidated taxable income for the year.

(v) S2 must make the positive adjustment provided for in § 1.1502-32(b)(1)(i) to its basis in T stock for its allocable part of T's undistributed earnings and profits for the taxable year. S2 cannot make the negative adjustment provided for in § 1.1502-32(b)(2)(ii) for the dual consolidated loss of T incurred in Year 1 and absorbed in Year 2. Thus, as provided in § 1.1502-32(e)(2), S2 must make a $40 net positive adjustment to its basis in T stock, increasing its basis to $350. As provided in § 1.1502-33(c)(4)(ii)(a), S2's earnings and profits for Year 2 will reflect S2's increase in its basis in T stock for the taxable year. Since S2 has no other earnings and profits for the taxable year, S2 has $40 of earnings and profits for the year. As provided in § 1.1502-32(b)(1)(i), P must make a positive adjustment to its basis in the stock of S2 for its allocable part of the undistributed earnings and profits of S2 for the taxable year. Thus, P must make a $40 net positive adjustment to its basis in S2 stock, increasing its basis to $850.

(e) *Special rule for use of dual consolidated loss to offset tainted income*—(1) *In general.* The dual consolidated loss of any dual resident corporation that ceases to be a dual resident corporation shall not be used to offset income of such corporation to the extent that such income is tainted income, as defined in paragraph (e)(2) of this section.

(2) *Tainted income defined.* Tainted income is any income derived from tainted assets, as defined in paragraph (e)(3) of this section, beginning on the date such assets are acquired by the dual resident corporation. In the absence of evidence establishing the actual amount of income that is attributable to the tainted assets, the portion of a corporation's income in a particular taxable year that is treated as tainted income shall be an amount equal to the corporation's taxable income for the year multiplied by a fraction, the numerator of which is the fair market value of the tainted asset at the end of the taxable year and the denominator of which is the fair market value of the total assets owned by the corporation at the end of the taxable year. Documentation submitted to establish the actual amount of income that is attributable to the tainted assets must be attached to the consolidated group's or unaffiliated dual resident corporation's timely filed tax return for the taxable year in which the income is recognized.

(3) *Tainted assets defined.* Tainted assets are any assets acquired by a dual resident corporation in a nonrecognition transaction, as defined in section 7701(a)(45), or any assets otherwise transferred to the corporation as a contribution to capital, at any time during the three taxable years immediately preceding the taxable year in which the corporation ceases to be a dual resident corporation or at any time thereafter. Tainted

Reg. § 1.1503-2(e)(1)

assets shall not include assets that were acquired by such dual resident corporation on or before December 31, 1986.

(4) *Exceptions.* Income derived from assets acquired by a dual resident corporation shall not be subject to the limitation described in paragraph (e)(1) of this section, if—

(i) For the taxable year in which the assets were acquired, the corporation did not have a dual consolidated loss (or a carry forward of a dual consolidated loss to such year); or

(ii) The assets were acquired as replacement property in the ordinary course of business.

(f) *Computation of foreign tax credit limitations.* If a dual resident corporation or separate unit is subject to paragraph (d)(2) of this section, the consolidated group or unaffiliated domestic owner shall compute its foreign tax credit limitation by applying the limitations of paragraph (d)(2). Thus, the dual consolidated loss is not taken into account until the year in which it is absorbed.

(g) *Exception*—(1) *Elective agreement in place between the United States and a foreign country.* Paragraph (b) of this section shall not apply to a dual consolidated loss to the extent the dual resident corporation, or domestic owner of a separate unit, elects to deduct the loss in the United States pursuant to an agreement entered into between the United States and a foreign country that puts into place an elective procedure through which losses offset income in only one country.

(2) *Elective relief provision*—(i) *In general.* Paragraph (b) of this section shall not apply to a dual consolidated loss if the consolidated group, unaffiliated dual resident corporation, or unaffiliated domestic owner elects to be bound by the provisions of this paragraph (g)(2). In order to elect relief under this paragraph (g)(2), the consolidated group, unaffiliated dual resident corporation, or unaffiliated domestic owner must attach to its timely filed U.S. income tax return for the taxable year in which the dual consolidated loss is incurred an agreement described in this paragraph (g)(2)(i). The agreement must be signed under penalties of perjury by the person who signs the return and must include the following items, in paragraphs labeled to correspond with the items set forth below:

(A) A statement that the document submitted is an election and an agreement under the provisions of § 1.1503-2(g)(2) of the Income Tax Regulations;

(B) The name, address, identifying number, and place and date of incorporation of the dual resident corporation, and the country or countries that tax the dual resident corporation on its worldwide income or on a residence basis, or, in the case of a separate unit, identification of the separate unit, including the name under which it conducts business, its principal activity, and the country in which its principal place of business is located;

(C) An agreement by the consolidated group, unaffiliated dual resident corporation, or unaffiliated domestic owner to comply with all of the provisions of paragraphs (g)(2)(iii) through (vii) of § 1.1503-2;

(D) A statement of the amount of the dual consolidated loss covered by the agreement;

(E) A certification that no portion of the dual resident corporation's or separate unit's losses, expenses, or deductions taken into account in computing the dual consolidated loss has been, or will be, used to offset the income of any other person under the income tax laws of a foreign country; and

(F) A certification that arrangements have been made to ensure that no portion of the dual consolidated loss will be used to offset the income of another person under the laws of a foreign country and that the consolidated group, unaffiliated dual resident corporation, or unaffiliated domestic owner will be informed of any such foreign use of any portion of the dual consolidated loss.

(ii) *Consistency rule*—(A) If any loss, expense, or deduction taken into account in computing the dual consolidated loss of a dual resident corporation or separate unit is used under the laws of a foreign country to offset the income of another person, then the following other dual consolidated losses (if any) shall be treated as also having been used to offset income of another person under the laws of such foreign country, but only if the income tax laws of the foreign country permit any loss, expense, or deduction taken into account in computing the other dual consolidated loss to be used to offset the income of another person in the same taxable year:

(*1*) Any dual consolidated loss of a dual resident corporation that is a member of the same consolidated group of which the first dual resident corporation or domestic owner is a member, if any loss, expense, or deduction taken into account in computing such dual consolidated loss is recognized under the income tax laws of such country in the same taxable year; and

(*2*) Any dual consolidated loss of a separate unit that is owned by the same domestic owner that owns the first separate unit, or that is owned by any member of the same consolidated group of which the first dual resident corporation or domestic owner is a member, if any loss, expense, or deduction taken into account in computing such dual consolidated loss is recognized under the income tax laws of such country in the same taxable year.

(B) The following examples illustrate the application of this paragraph (g)(2)(ii).

Example 1. P, a domestic corporation, owns A and B, which are domestic corporations, and C, a Country X corporation. A is subject to the income tax laws of Country X on a residence basis and, thus, is a dual resident corporation. B conducts business in Country X through a branch, which is a separate unit under paragraph (c)(3) of this section. The income tax laws of Country X permit branches of foreign corporations to elect to file consolidated returns with Country X affiliates. In Year 1, A incurs a dual consolidated loss, which is used to offset the income of C under the Country X form of consolidation. The branch of B also incurs a net operating loss. However, B elects not to use the loss on a Country X consolidated return to offset the income of foreign affiliates. The use of A's loss to offset the income of C in Country X will cause the separate unit of B to be treated as if it too had used its dual consolidated loss to offset the income of an affiliate in Country X. Therefore, an election and agreement under this paragraph (g)(2) cannot be made with respect to the separate unit's dual consolidated loss.

Example 2. The facts are the same as in Example 1, except that the income tax laws of Country X do not permit branches of foreign corporations to file consolidated income tax returns with Country X affiliates. Therefore, an election and agreement described in this paragraph (g)(2) may be made for the dual consolidated loss incurred by the separate unit of B.

(iii) *Triggering events requiring the recapture of dual consolidated losses*—(A) The consolidated group, unaffiliated dual resident corporation, or unaffiliated domestic owner must agree that, if there is a triggering event described in this paragraph (g)(2)(iii), and no exception applies under paragraph (g)(2)(iv) of this section, the consolidated group, unaffiliated dual resident corporation, or unaffiliated domestic owner will recapture and report as income the amount of the dual consolidated loss provided in paragraph (g)(2)(vii) of this section on its tax return for the taxable year in which the triggering event occurs (or, when the triggering event is a use of the loss for foreign purposes, the taxable year that includes the last day of the foreign tax year during which such use occurs). In addition, the consolidated group, unaffiliated dual resident corporation, or unaffiliated domestic owner must pay any applicable interest charge required by paragraph (g)(2)(vii) of this section. For purposes of this section, any of the following events shall constitute a triggering event:

(*1*) In any taxable year up to and including the 15th taxable year following the year in which the dual consolidated loss that is the subject of the agreement filed under this paragraph (g)(2) was incurred, any portion of the losses, expenses, or deductions taken into account in computing the dual consolidated loss is used by any means to offset the income of any other person under the income tax laws of a foreign country;

(*2*) An affiliated dual resident corporation or affiliated domestic owner ceases to be a member of the consolidated group that filed the election. For purposes of this paragraph (g)(2)(iii)(A)(*2*), a dual resident corporation or domestic owner shall be considered to cease to be a member of the consolidated group if it is no longer a member of the group within the meaning of § 1.1502-1(b), or if the group ceases to exist because the common parent is no longer in existence or is no longer a common parent or the group no longer files on the basis of a consolidated return. Such disaffiliation, however, shall not constitute a triggering event if the taxpayer demonstrates, to the satisfaction of the Commissioner, that the dual resident corporation's or separate unit's losses, expenses, or deductions cannot be used to offset income of another person under the laws of a foreign country at any time after the affiliated dual resident corporation or affiliated domestic owner ceases to be a member of the consolidated group;

(*3*) An unaffiliated dual resident corporation or unaffiliated domestic owner becomes a member of a consolidated group. Such affiliation of the dual resident corporation or domestic owner, however, shall not constitute a triggering event if the taxpayer demonstrates, to the satisfaction of the Commissioner, that the losses, expenses, or deductions of the dual resident corporation or separate unit cannot be used to offset the income of another person under the laws of a foreign country at any time after the dual resident corporation or domestic owner becomes a member of the consolidated group.

(*4*) A dual resident corporation transfers assets in a transaction that results, under the laws of a foreign country, in a carryover of its losses, expenses, or deductions. For purposes of this paragraph (g)(2)(iii) (A)(*4*), a transfer, either in a single transaction or a series of transactions within a twelve-month period, of 50% or more of the dual resident corporation's assets (measured

Reg. § 1.1503-2(g)(2)

by the fair market value of the assets at the time of such transfer (or for multiple transactions, at the time of the first transfer)) shall be deemed a triggering event, unless the taxpayer demonstrates, to the satisfaction of the Commissioner, that the transfer of assets did not result in a carryover under foreign law of the dual resident corporation's losses, expenses, or deductions to the transferee of the assets;

(5) A domestic owner of a separate unit transfers assets of the separate unit in a transaction that results, under the laws of a foreign country, in a carryover of the separate unit's losses, expenses, or deductions. For purposes of this paragraph (g)(2)(iii)(A)(5), a transfer, either in a single transaction or a series of transactions over a twelve-month period, of 50% or more of the separate unit's assets (measured by the fair market value of the assets at the time of the transfer (or for multiple transfers, at the time of the first transfer)), shall be deemed a triggering event, unless the taxpayer demonstrates, to the satisfaction of the Commissioner, that the transfer of assets did not result in a carryover under foreign law of the separate unit's losses, expenses, or deductions to the transferee of the assets;

(6) An unaffiliated dual resident corporation or unaffiliated domestic owner becomes a foreign corporation by means of a transaction (e.g., a reorganization) that, for foreign tax purposes, is not treated as involving a transfer of assets (and carryover of losses) to a new entity. Such a transaction, however, shall not constitute a triggering event if the taxpayer demonstrates, to the satisfaction of the Commissioner, that the dual resident corporation's or separate unit's losses, expenses, or deductions cannot be used to offset income of another person under the laws of the foreign country at any time after the unaffiliated dual resident corporation or unaffiliated domestic owner becomes a foreign corporation.

(7) A domestic owner of a separate unit, either in a single transaction or a series of transactions within a twelve-month period, sells, or otherwise disposes of, 50% or more of the interest in the separate unit (measured by voting power or value) owned by the domestic owner on the last day of the taxable year in which the dual consolidated loss was incurred. For purposes of this paragraph (g)(2)(iii)(A)(7), the domestic owner shall be deemed to have disposed of its entire interest in a hybrid entity separate unit if such hybrid entity becomes classified as a foreign corporation for U.S. tax purposes. The disposition of 50% or more of the interest in a separate unit, however, shall not constitute a triggering event if the taxpayer demonstrates, to the satisfaction of the Commissioner, that the losses, expenses, or deductions of the separate unit cannot be used to offset income of another person under the laws of the foreign country at any time after the disposition of the interest in the separate unit; or

(8) The consolidated group, unaffiliated dual resident corporation, or unaffiliated domestic owner fails to file a certification required under paragraph (g)(2)(vi)(B) of this section.

(B) A taxpayer wishing to rebut the presumption of a triggering event described in paragraphs (g)(2)(iii)(A)(2) through (7) of this section, by demonstrating that the losses, expenses, or deductions of the dual resident corporation or separate unit cannot be carried over or otherwise used under the laws of the foreign country, must attach documents demonstrating such facts to its timely filed U.S. income tax return for the year in which the presumed triggering event occurs.

(C) The following example illustrates this paragraph (g)(2)(iii).

Example. DRC, a domestic corporation, is a member of CG, a consolidated group. DRC is a resident of Country Y for Country Y income tax purposes. Therefore, DRC is a dual resident corporation. In Year 1, DRC incurs a dual consolidated loss of $100. CG files an agreement described in paragraph (g)(2) of this section and, thus, the $100 dual consolidated loss is included in the computation of CG's consolidated taxable income. In Year 6, all of the stock of DRC is sold to P, a domestic corporation that is a member of NG, another consolidated group. The sale of DRC to P is a triggering event under paragraph (g)(2)(iii)(A) of this section, requiring the recapture of the dual consolidated loss. However, the laws of Country Y provide for a five-year carryover period for losses. At the time of DRC's disaffiliation from CG, the losses, expenses and deductions that were included in the computation of the dual consolidated loss had expired for Country Y purposes. Therefore, upon adequate documentation that the losses, expenses, or deductions have expired for Country Y purposes, CG can rebut the presumption that a triggering event has occurred.

(iv) *Exceptions*—(A) *Acquisition by a member of the consolidated group.* The following events shall not constitute triggering events, requiring the recapture of the dual consolidated loss under paragraph (g)(2)(vii) of this section:

(1) An affiliated dual resident corporation or affiliated domestic owner ceases to be a member of a consolidated group solely by reason of a transaction in which a member of the same consolidated group succeeds to the tax attributes

Reg. § 1.1503-2(g)(2)

of the dual resident corporation or domestic owner under the provisions of section 381;

(2) Assets of an affiliated dual resident corporation or assets of a separate unit of an affiliated domestic owner are acquired by a member of its consolidated group in any other transaction; or

(3) An affiliated domestic owner of a separate unit transfers its interest in the separate unit to another member of its consolidated group.

(B) *Acquisition by an unaffiliated domestic corporation or a new consolidated group*— (1) If the requirements of paragraph (g)(2)(iv)(B)(2) of this section are met, the following events shall not constitute triggering events, requiring the recapture of the dual consolidated loss under paragraph (g)(2)(vii) of this section:

(*i*) An affiliated dual resident corporation or affiliated domestic owner becomes an unaffiliated domestic corporation or a member of a new consolidated group;

(*ii*) An unaffiliated dual resident corporation or unaffiliated domestic owner becomes a member of a consolidated group;

(*iii*) Assets of a dual resident corporation or a separate unit are acquired by an unaffiliated domestic corporation or a member of a new consolidated group; or

(*iv*) A domestic owner of a separate unit transfers its interest in the separate unit to an unaffiliated domestic corporation or to a member of a new consolidated group.

(2) If all of the following requirements are satisfied, the events listed in paragraph (g)(2)(iv)(B)(1) of this section shall not constitute triggering events requiring recapture under paragraph (g)(2)(vii) of this section.

(*i*) The consolidated group, unaffiliated dual resident corporation, or unaffiliated domestic owner that filed the agreement under this paragraph (g)(2) and the unaffiliated domestic corporation or new consolidated group must enter into a closing agreement with the Internal Revenue Service providing that the consolidated group, unaffiliated dual resident corporation, or unaffiliated domestic owner and the unaffiliated domestic corporation or new consolidated group will be jointly and severally liable for the total amount of the recapture of dual consolidated loss and interest charge required in paragraph (g)(2)(vii) of this section, if there is a triggering event described in paragraph (g)(2)(iii) of this section;

(*ii*) The unaffiliated domestic corporation or new consolidated group must agree to treat any potential recapture amount under paragraph (g)(2)(vii) of this section as unrealized built-in gain for purposes of section 384(a), subject to any applicable exceptions thereunder;

(*iii*) The unaffiliated domestic corporation or new consolidated group must file an agreement described in paragraph (g)(2)(i) of this section with its timely filed income tax return for the taxable year in which the event described in paragraph (g)(2)(iv)(B)(1) of this section occurs. The agreement must be signed under penalties of perjury by the person who signs the tax return of the unaffiliated domestic corporation or new consolidated group.

(C) *Subsequent triggering events.* Any triggering event described in paragraph (g)(2)(iii) of this section that occurs subsequent to one of the transactions described in paragraph (g)(2)(iv)(A) or (B) of this section and does not fall within the exceptions provided in paragraph (g)(2)(iv)(A) or (B) of this section shall require recapture under paragraph (g)(2)(vii) of this section.

(v) *Ordering rules for determining the foreign use of losses.* If the laws of a foreign country provide for the use of losses of a dual resident corporation to offset the income of another person but do not provide applicable rules for determining the order in which such losses are used to offset the income of another person in a taxable year, then for purposes of this section, the following rules shall govern:

(A) If under the laws of the foreign country the dual resident corporation has losses from different taxable years, the dual resident corporation shall be deemed to use first the losses from the earliest taxable year from which a loss may be carried forward or back for foreign law purposes.

(B) Any net loss, or income, that the dual resident corporation has in a taxable year shall first be used to offset net income, or loss, recognized by affiliates of the dual resident corporation in the same taxable year before any carryover of the dual resident corporation's losses is considered to be used to offset any income from the taxable year.

(C) Where different losses, expenses, or deductions (*e.g.*, capital losses and ordinary losses) of a dual resident corporation incurred in the same taxable year are available to offset the income of another person, the different losses shall be deemed to offset such income on a pro rata basis.

Example. DRC, a domestic corporation, is taxed as a resident under the tax laws of Country Y. Therefore, DRC is a dual resident corporation. FA is a Country Y affiliate of DRC. Country Y's tax laws permit affiliated corporations to file a form of consolidated return. In Year 1, DRC

Reg. § 1.1503-2(g)(2)

incurs a capital loss of $80 which, for Country Y purposes, offsets completely $30 of capital gain recognized by FA. Neither corporation has any other taxable income or loss for the year. In Year 1 (and in other years), DRC recognizes the same amount of income for U.S. purposes as it does for Country Y purposes. Under paragraph (d)(1)(i) of this section, however, DRC's $80 capital loss is not a dual consolidated loss. In Year 2, DRC incurs a net operating loss of $100, while FA incurs a net operating loss of $50. DRC's $100 loss is a dual consolidated loss. Since the dual consolidated loss is not used to offset the income of another person under Country Y law, DRC is permitted to file an agreement described in this paragraph (g)(2). In Year 3, DRC has a net operating loss of $10 and FA has capital gains of $60. For Country Y purposes, DRC's $10 net operating loss is used to offset $10 of FA's $60 capital gain. DRC's $10 loss is a dual consolidated loss. Because the loss is used to offset FA's income, DRC will not be able to file an agreement under this paragraph (g)(2) with respect to the loss. Country Y permits FA's remaining $50 of Year 3 income to be offset by carryover losses. However, Country Y has no applicable rules for determining which carryover losses from Years 1 and 2 are used to offset such income. Under the ordering rules of paragraph (g)(2)(v)(A) of this section, none of DRC's $100 Year 2 loss will be deemed to offset FA's remaining $50 of Year 3 income. Instead, the $50 of capital loss carryover from Year 1 will be considered to offset the income.

(vi) *Reporting requirements*—(A) *In general.* The consolidated group, unaffiliated dual resident corporation, or unaffiliated domestic owner must answer the applicable questions regarding dual consolidated losses on its U.S. income tax return filed for the year in which the dual consolidated loss is incurred and for each of the following fifteen taxable years.

(B) *Annual certification.* Except as provided in paragraph (g)(2)(vi)(C) of this section, until and unless Form 1120 (or the Schedules thereto) contains questions pertaining to dual consolidated losses, the consolidated group, unaffiliated dual resident corporation, or unaffiliated domestic owner must file with its income tax return for each of the 15 taxable years following the taxable year in which the dual consolidated loss is incurred a certification that the losses, expenses, or deductions that make up the dual consolidated loss have not been used to offset the income of another person under the tax laws of a foreign country. The annual certification must be signed under penalties of perjury by a person authorized to sign the agreement described in paragraph (g)(2)(i) of this section. The certification must identify the dual consolidated loss to which it pertains by setting forth the taxpayer's year in which the loss was incurred and the amount of such loss. In addition, the certification must warrant that arrangements have been made to ensure that the loss will not be used to offset the income of another person under the laws of a foreign country and that the taxpayer will be informed of any such foreign use of any portion of the loss. If dual consolidated losses of more than one taxable year are subject to the rules of this paragraph (g)(2)(vi)(B), the certifications for those years may be combined in a single document but each dual consolidated loss must be separately identified.

(C) *Exception.* A consolidated group or unaffiliated domestic owner is not required to file annual certifications under paragraph (g)(2)(vi)(B) of this section with respect to a dual consolidated loss of any separate unit other than a hybrid entity separate unit.

(vii) *Recapture of loss and interest charge*—(A) *Presumptive rule*—(*1*) *Amount of recapture.* Except as otherwise provided in this paragraph (g)(2)(vii), upon the occurrence of a triggering event described in paragraph (g)(2)(iii) of this section, the taxpayer shall recapture and report as gross income the total amount of the dual consolidated loss to which the triggering event applies on its income tax return for the taxable year in which the triggering event occurs (or, when the triggering event is a use of the loss for foreign tax purposes, the taxable year that includes the last day of the foreign tax year during which such use occurs).

(*2*) *Interest charge.* In connection with the recapture, the taxpayer shall pay an interest charge. Except as otherwise provided in this paragraph (g)(2)(vii), such interest shall be determined under the rules of section 6601(a) as if the additional tax owed as a result of the recapture had accrued and been due and owing for the taxable year in which the losses, expenses, or deductions taken into account in computing the dual consolidated loss gave rise to a tax benefit for U.S. income tax purposes. For purposes of this paragraph (g)(2)(vii)(A)(*2*), a tax benefit shall be considered to have arisen in a taxable year in which such losses, expenses or deductions reduced U.S. taxable income.

(B) *Rebuttal of presumptive rule*—(*1*) *Amount of recapture.* The amount of dual consolidated loss that must be recaptured under this paragraph (g)(2)(vii) may be reduced if the taxpayer demonstrates, to the satisfaction of the Commissioner, the offset permitted by this paragraph (g)(2)(vii)(B). The reduction in the amount

Reg. § 1.1503-2(g)(2)

of recapture is the amount by which the dual consolidated loss would have offset other taxable income reported on a timely filed U.S. income tax return for any taxable year up to and including the year of the triggering event if such loss had been subject to the restrictions of paragraph (b) of this section (and therefore had been subject to the separate return limitation year restrictions of § 1.1502-21A(c) or 1.1502-21(c) (as appropriate)) commencing in the taxable year in which the loss was incurred. A taxpayer utilizing this rebuttal rule must attach to its timely filed U.S. income tax return a separate accounting showing that the income for each year that offsets the dual resident corporation's or separate unit's recapture amount is attributable only to the dual resident corporation or separate unit.

(2) *Interest charge.* The interest charge imposed under this paragraph (g)(2)(vii) may be appropriately reduced if the taxpayer demonstrates, to the satisfaction of the Commissioner, that the net interest owed would have been less than that provided in paragraph (g)(2)(vii)(A)(*2*) of this section if the taxpayer had filed an amended return for the year in which the loss was incurred, and for any other affected years up to and including the year of recapture, treating the dual consolidated loss as a loss subject to the restrictions of paragraph (b) of this section (and therefore subject to the separate return limitation year restrictions of § 1.1502-21A(c) or 1.1502-21(c) (as appropriate)). A taxpayer utilizing this rebuttal rule must attach to its timely filed U.S. income tax return a computation demonstrating the reduction in the net interest owed as a result of treating the dual consolidated loss as a loss subject to the restrictions of paragraph (b) of this section.

(C) *Computation of taxable income in year of recapture*—(*1*) *Presumptive rule.* Except as otherwise provided in paragraph (g)(2)(vii)(C)(*2*) of this section, for purposes of computing the taxable income for the year of recapture, no current, carryover or carryback losses of the dual resident corporation or separate unit, of other members of the consolidated group, or of the domestic owner that are not attributable to the separate unit, may offset and absorb the recapture amount.

(2) *Rebuttal of presumptive rule.* The recapture amount included in gross income may be offset and absorbed by that portion of the taxpayer's (consolidated or separate) net operating loss carryover that is attributable to the dual consolidated loss being recaptured, if the taxpayer demonstrates, to the satisfaction of the Commissioner, the amount of such portion of the carryover. A taxpayer utilizing this rebuttal rule must attach to its timely filed U.S. income tax return a computation demonstrating the amount of net operating loss carryover that, under this paragraph (g)(2)(vii)(C)(*2*), may absorb the recapture amount included in gross income.

(D) *Character and source of recapture income.* The amount recaptured under this paragraph (g)(2)(vii) shall be treated as ordinary income in the year of recapture. The amount recaptured shall be treated as income having the same source and falling within the same separate category for purposes of section 904 as the dual consolidated loss being recaptured.

(E) *Reconstituted net operating loss.* Commencing in the taxable year immediately following the year in which the dual consolidated loss is recaptured, the dual resident corporation or separate unit shall be treated as having a net operating loss in an amount equal to the amount actually recaptured under paragraph (g)(2)(vii)(A) or (B) of this section. This reconstituted net operating loss shall be subject to the restrictions of paragraph (b) of this section (and therefore, the separate return limitation year restrictions of §§ 1.1502-21A(c) or 1.1502-21T(c) (as appropriate)). The net operating loss shall be available only for carryover, under section 172(b), to taxable years following the taxable year of recapture. For purposes of determining the remaining carryover period, the loss shall be treated as if it had been recognized in the taxable year in which the dual consolidated loss that is the basis of the recapture amount was incurred.

(F) *Consequences of failing to comply with recapture provisions*—(*1*) *In general.* If the taxpayer fails to comply with the recapture provisions of this paragraph (g)(2)(vii) upon the occurrence of a triggering event, then the dual resident corporation or separate unit that incurred the dual consolidated loss (or a successor-in-interest) shall not be eligible for the relief provided in paragraph (g)(2) of this section with respect to any dual consolidated losses incurred in the five taxable years beginning with the taxable year in which recapture is required.

(2) *Exceptions.* In the case of a triggering event other than a use of the losses, expenses, or deductions taken into account in computing the dual consolidated loss to offset income of another person under the income tax laws of a foreign country, this rule shall not apply in the following circumstances:

(*i*) The failure to recapture is due to reasonable cause; or

(*ii*) A taxpayer seeking to rebut the presumption of a triggering event satisfies the

Reg. § 1.1503-2(g)(2)

filing requirements of paragraph (g)(2)(iii)(B) of this section.

(G) *Examples.* The following examples illustrate this paragraph (g)(2)(vii).

Example 1. P, a domestic corporation, files a consolidated return with DRC, a dual resident corporation. In Year 1, DRC incurs a dual consolidated loss of $100 and P earns $100. P files an agreement under this paragraph (g)(2). Therefore, the consolidated group is permitted to offset P's $100 of income with DRC's $100 loss. In Year 2, DRC earns $30, which is completely offset by a $30 net operating loss incurred by P. In Year 3, DRC earns income of $25 while P recognizes no income or loss. In addition, there is a triggering event in Year 3. Therefore, under the presumptive rule of paragraph (g)(2)(vii)(A) of this section, DRC must recapture $100. However, the $100 recapture amount may be reduced by $25 (the amount by which the dual consolidated loss would have offset other taxable income if it had been subject to the separate return limitation year restrictions from Year 1) upon adequate documentation of such offset under paragraph (g)(2)(vii)(B)(*1*) of this section. Commencing in Year 4, the $100 (or $75) recapture amount is treated as a loss incurred by DRC in a separate return limitation year, subject to the restrictions of § 1.1502-21A(c) or 1.1502-21(c), as appropriate. The carryover period of the loss, for purposes of section 172(b), will start from Year 1, when the dual consolidated loss was incurred.

Example 2. The facts are the same as in *Example 1,* except that in Year 2, DRC earns $75 and P earns $50. In Year 3, DRC earns $25 while P earns $30. A triggering event occurs in Year 3. The $100 presumptive amount of recapture can be reduced to zero by the $75 and $25 earned by DRC in Years 2 and 3, respectively, upon adequate documentation of such offset under paragraph (g)(2)(vii)(B)(*1*) of this section. Nevertheless, an interest charge will be owed. Under the presumptive rule of paragraph (g)(2)(vii)(A)(*2*) of this section, interest will be charged on the additional tax owed on the $100 of recapture income as if the tax had accrued in Year 1 (the year in which the dual consolidated loss reduced the income of P). However, the net interest will be reduced to the amount that would have been owed if the consolidated group had filed amended returns, treating the dual consolidated loss as a loss subject to the separate return limitation year restrictions of § 1.1502-21A(c) or 1.1502-21(c), as appropriate, upon adequate documentation of such reduction of interest under paragraph (g)(2)(vii)(B)(*2*) of this section.

Example 3. P, a domestic corporation, owns DRC, a domestic corporation that is subject to the income tax laws of Country Z on a residence basis. DRC owns FE, a Country Z corporation. In Year 1, DRC incurs a net operating loss for U.S. tax purposes. Under the tax laws of Country Z, the loss is not recognized until Year 3. The Year 1 net operating loss is a dual consolidated loss under paragraph (c)(5) of this section. The consolidated group elects relief under paragraph (g)(2) of this section by filing the appropriate agreement and uses the dual consolidated loss on its U.S. income tax return. In Year 3, the dual consolidated loss is used under the laws of Country Z to offset the income of FE, which is a triggering event under paragraph (g)(2)(iii) of this section. However, the consolidated group does not recapture the dual consolidated loss. The consolidated group's failure to comply with the recapture provisions of this paragraph (g)(2)(vii) prevents DRC from being eligible for the relief provided under paragraph (g)(2) of this section for any dual consolidated losses incurred in Years 3 through 7, inclusive.

(h) *Effective date*—(1) *In general.* These regulations are effective for taxable years beginning on or after October 1, 1992. Section 1.1503-2A is effective for taxable years beginning after December 31, 1986, and before October 1, 1992.

(2) *Taxpayers that have filed for relief under § 1.1503-2A*—(i) *In general.* Except as provided in paragraph (h)(ii)(b) of this section, taxpayers that have filed agreements described in § 1.1503-2A(c)(3) or certifications described in § 1.1503-2A(d)(3) shall continue to be subject to the provisions of such agreements or certifications, including the amended return or recapture requirements applicable in the event of a triggering event, for the remaining term of such agreements or certifications.

(ii) *Special transition rule.* A taxpayer that has filed an agreement described in § 1.1503-2A(c)(3) or a certification described in § 1.1503-2A(d)(3) and that is in compliance with the provisions of § 1.1503-2A may elect to replace such agreement or certification with an agreement described in paragraph (g)(2)(i) of this section. However, a taxpayer making this election must replace all agreements and certifications filed under § 1.1503-2A. If the taxpayer is a consolidated group, the election must be made with respect to all dual resident corporations or separate units within the group. Likewise, if the taxpayer is an unaffiliated domestic owner, the election must be made with respect to all separate units of the domestic owner. The taxpayer must file the replacement agreement with its timely

Reg. § 1.1503-2(h)(2)

filed income tax return for its first taxable year commencing on or after October 1, 1992, stating that such agreement is a replacement for the agreement filed under § 1.1503-2A(c)(3) or the certification filed under § 1.1503-2A(d)(3) and identifying the taxable year for which the original agreement or certification was filed. A single agreement described in paragraph (g)(2)(i) of this section may be filed to replace more than one agreement or certification filed under § 1.1503-2A; however, each dual consolidated loss must be separately identified. A taxpayer may also elect to apply § 1.1503-2 for all open years, with respect to agreements filed under § 1.1503-2A(c)(3) or certifications filed under § 1.1503-2A(d)(3), in cases where the agreement or certification is no longer in effect and the taxpayer has complied with the provisions of § 1.1503-2A. For example, a taxpayer may have had a triggering event under § 1.1503-2A that is not a triggering event under § 1.1503-2. If the taxpayer fully complied with the requirements of the agreement entered into under § 1.1503-2A(c)(3) and filed amended U.S. income tax returns within the time required under § 1.1503-2A(c)(3), the taxpayer may file amended U.S. income tax returns consistent with the position that the earlier triggering event is no longer a triggering event.

(3) *Taxpayers that are in compliance with § 1.1503-2A but have not filed for relief thereunder.* A taxpayer that is in compliance with the provisions of § 1.1503-2A but has not filed an agreement described in § 1.1503-2A(c)(3) or a certification described in § 1.1503-2A(d)(3) may elect to have the provisions of § 1.1503-2 apply for any open year. In particular, a taxpayer may elect to apply the provisions of § 1.1503-2 in a case where the dual consolidated loss has been subjected to the separate return limitation year restrictions of § 1.1502-21A(c) or 1.1502-21(c) (as appropriate) but the losses, expenses, or deductions taken into account in computing the dual consolidated loss have not been used to offset the income of another person for foreign tax purposes. However, if a taxpayer is a consolidated group, the election must be made with respect to all dual resident corporations or separate units within the group. Likewise, if the taxpayer is an unaffiliated domestic owner, the election must be made with respect to all separate units of the domestic owner. [Reg. § 1.1503-2.]

☐ [T.D. 8434, 9-4-92. Amended by T.D. 8597, 7-12-95; T.D. 8677, 6-26-96 and T.D. 8823, 6-25-99.]

[Reg. § 1.1503-2A]

§ 1.1503-2A. Dual consolidated loss.—(a) *In general.* This section applies for purposes of determining whether and to what extent the net operating loss of a dual resident corporation incurred in tax years beginning after December 31, 1986, shall be allowed to reduce the taxable income of any other member of the affiliated group. Except as provided in paragraph (c) of this section, any dual consolidated loss of a domestic corporation incurred in taxable years beginning after December 31, 1986, cannot reduce the taxable income of any affiliate of such domestic corporation for that or any other taxable year, regardless of whether those losses offset income of another corporation under the income tax laws of the foreign country and regardless of whether any of the income of any corporation that the loss may reduce in the foreign country is, has been, or will be subject to tax in the United States. This rule shall also apply to preclude the use of a dual consolidated loss to offset any income of an affiliate (whether or not an election to file a consolidated return has been made) by means of a transaction subject to section 381 of the Code. For purposes of the preceding sentence, an "affiliate" means any member of the affiliated group as determined under section 1504(a) without regard to the exceptions contained in section 1504(b) (other than section 1504(b)(3)) relating to includible corporations. Further, this rule shall also apply to preclude the use of a dual consolidated loss of a separate unit by a domestic corporation upon or as a result of the termination, liquidation, or sale of the separate unit. The following example illustrates the application of this paragraph (a).

Example. P, a domestic corporation, owns all of the outstanding stock of DRC, a domestic corporation. DRC is managed and controlled in Country W, a country which determines the tax residence of corporations according to place of management and control. Therefore, the income of DRC is subject to tax in both the United States and in Country W. There are currently no other corporations in Country W which could use the losses of DRC to offset income under the income tax laws of Country W. P no longer wishes to operate DRC as a separate corporation. Therefore, DRC will be liquidated into P under section 332 of the Code. Normally, P, under section 381, would succeed to and take into account DRC's net operating loss carryovers. However, this paragraph (a) prohibits the net operating loss of DRC from reducing P's income (including income of P generated by assets previously held by DRC) for U.S. tax purposes. Therefore, DRC's net operating loss carryovers will not be available to offset P's

Reg. § 1.1503-2A(a)

income unless one of the exceptions described in paragraph (c) of this section applies.

(b) *Definitions.* The following definitions apply for purposes of this section.

(1) *Domestic corporation.* For purposes of this section, the term "domestic corporation" has the meaning assigned to it by sections 7701(a)(3) and (a)(4) and shall also include any corporation treated as a domestic corporation by the Internal Revenue Code, including, but not limited to, section 269B and section 1504(d). Subject to the rules of paragraph (d) of this section, any separate unit (as defined in paragraph (b)(4) of this section) of a domestic corporation will be treated as a separate domestic corporation (and as a dual resident corporation) for purposes of this section. The following example illustrates the application of this paragraph (b)(1).

Example. A is a domestic corporation with a branch operation in Country X. A is owned by FP, a Country X corporation. Country X allows the Country X branch income and losses of A to be used to offset FP's losses or income. Under paragraph (d) of this section, the branch operations of A in Country X will be treated as a separate domestic corporation and as a dual resident corporation for purposes of this section. See paragraph (d) of this section for the treatment of any dual consolidated loss of the branch operations of A.

(2) *Dual consolidated loss.* The term "dual consolidated loss" means the net operating loss (as defined in section 172(c) and the regulations thereunder) of a domestic corporation incurred in a year in which the corporation is a dual resident corporation. The fact that a particular item taken into account in computing such net operating loss deduction is not taken into account in computing income subject to income tax in a foreign country shall not cause such item to be excluded from the calculation of the dual consolidated loss. A dual consolidated loss shall arise even though no other person, corporation, or entity is permitted, under the income tax laws of the foreign country, to use by any means the losses, expenses or deductions of the dual resident corporation to offset income. A dual consolidated loss shall not include—

(i) The net operating loss incurred during that portion of the taxable year prior to the date on which the domestic corporation becomes a dual resident corporation or subsequent to the date on which the domestic corporation ceases to be a dual resident corporation. For purposes of determining the amount of the net operating loss incurred in that portion of the taxable year prior to the date on which the domestic corporation becomes a dual resident corporation or subsequent to the date on which the domestic corporation ceases to be a dual resident corporation, in no event shall more than a pro rata portion of the net operating loss commensurate with the portion of the taxable year during which the domestic corporation was not a dual resident corporation be allocated to that portion of the taxable year in which the domestic corporation was not a dual resident corporation; or

(ii) Losses incurred in taxable years beginning on or before December 31, 1986.

(3) *Dual resident corporation.* For purposes of this section, a domestic corporation shall be a dual resident corporation if the worldwide income of such corporation is subject to the income tax of a foreign country, or such corporation is subject to the income tax of a foreign country on a residence basis (and not on a source basis).

(4) *Separate unit.* Solely for purposes of this section, the term "separate unit" shall mean any of the following:

(i) a foreign branch as defined in § 1.367(a)-6T(g);

(ii) a partnership interest; or

(iii) a trust interest.

(5) *Subject to tax.* For purposes of determining whether a domestic corporation is subject to the income tax of a foreign country on its income, the fact that the corporation has no actual tax liability to the foreign country for a particular taxable year shall not be taken into consideration.

(c) *Exceptions*—(1) *No ability to use dual consolidated loss under foreign law*—(i) *In general.* Paragraph (a) of this section shall not apply to a dual consolidated loss if—

(A) At no time after December 31, 1986, has there been any other person, corporation, or entity which, under the income tax laws of the foreign country, is permitted to use by any means the losses, expenses, or deductions of the dual resident corporation to offset income; and

(B) Under the income tax laws of the foreign country, the losses, expenses, or deductions of the dual resident corporation incurred in taxable years beginning after December 31, 1986, cannot be carried over or back to be used, by any means, to offset the income of any other person, corporation, or entity in other years.

(ii) *Limitations.* For purposes of paragraph (c)(1)(i) of this section, none of the following circumstances shall constitute a satisfaction of paragraph (c)(1)(i)(A) of this section—

(A) The failure to make use of an election (including, but not limited to, the ability to surrender losses, expenses or deductions) that would enable another person, corporation, or entity to use the losses, expenses, or deductions of

Reg. § 1.1503-2A(c)(1)

the dual resident corporation to offset income under the income tax laws of the foreign country;

(B) The fact that the income tax laws of the foreign country deny the use of losses, expenses, or deductions of its corporate residents that are also residents for tax purposes of another country to offset income of another person, corporation, or entity;

(C) The fact that the other person, corporation, or entity does not have sufficient income to benefit from an offset permitted under the income tax laws of the foreign country for a particular taxable year; or

(D) The fact that the dual resident corporation has no losses, expenses, or deductions during a particular taxable year.

(iii) *Examples.* The following examples illustrate this paragraph (c)(1).

Example (1). DRC, a domestic corporation, is also subject to tax in Country Y on its worldwide income. DRC has been filing a consolidated return for U.S. income tax purposes with DP, its domestic parent. DRC has also been able to use its losses to offset income of its affiliates in Country Y by using Country Y's form of consolidation. In order to prevent companies like DRC from taking losses against income of affiliates under Country Y law and then again using the losses of DRC to offset income of affiliates for U.S. tax purposes, Country Y law prevents a company which is also subject to tax on its worldwide income in another country, or is subject to tax on a residence basis in another country, from using the Country Y form of consolidation. DRC is a dual resident corporation as defined in paragraph (b)(3) of this section. DRC's losses are dual consolidated losses as defined in paragraph (b)(2) of this section which under paragraph (a) of this section may not be used to offset income of any other U.S. affiliate of DRC. The Country Y statute does not cause the exception provided by this paragraph (c)(1) to apply.

Example (2). P, a domestic corporation, owns DRC, a domestic corporation which is also subject to the income tax laws of Country Z on a residence basis, and FS, a Country Z corporation. Under Country Z laws, income or losses of DRC may not be consolidated with income or losses of P or FS. There is, however, a provision under Country Z's law by which DRC's unused losses could be carried forward, acquired, and used by FS if DRC is merged into FS. DRC's dual consolidated loss does not qualify for the exception from application of paragraph (a) provided by this paragraph (c)(1) because of the loss carryforward provisions under Country Z's income tax laws. However, DRC may qualify for an exemption from paragraph (a) of this section under the provisions of paragraph (c)(3) of this section.

Example (3). DRC is a dual resident corporation subject to tax on a residence basis in foreign country Y. Under the income tax laws of Y, DRC could elect to use its losses to offset the income of foreign entity FE on a Country Y consolidated income tax return for the taxable year ending December 31, 1987. Regardless of whether such election is made, DRC fails to satisfy the requirement of paragraph (c)(1)(i)(A) of this section.

Example (4). The same facts apply as in Example (3), except that Country Y changes its income tax law, effective as of January 1, 1987, to prevent the consolidation of losses by dual resident corporations. Under paragraph (c)(1)(ii)(B) of this section, the fact that this Country Y legislation prevents DRC from using its losses to offset the income of FE is disregarded and DRC fails to satisfy the requirement of paragraph (c)(1)(i)(A) of this section.

Example (5). The same facts apply as in Example (4), except that FE has no taxable income in taxable years 1987 through 1989. Moreover, DRC is profitable throughout this period and consequently has no losses which it could share with FE. Under paragraphs (c)(1)(ii)(C) and (D) of this section, the fact that FE would not receive a tax benefit from consolidation with DRC on a Country Y return is disregarded and DRC fails to satisfy the requirement of paragraph (c)(1)(i)(A) of this section. Because DRC does not have a net operating loss during 1987 through 1989, section 1503(d) does not affect the consolidation of DRC on a U.S. return for these years. However, DRC's failure to satisfy paragraph (c)(1)(i)(A) of this section at all times after December 31, 1986 will make it ineligible for the exception described in paragraph (c)(1) of this section with respect to any future taxable year in which it incurs a net operating loss.

Example (6). The same facts apply as in Example (5). In 1990, FE is transferred and is no longer eligible for consolidation on a Country Y return. There are no other entities with which DRC could consolidate under the income tax laws of Y. Nevertheless, since FE and DRC could have consolidated on a Country Y return during the period after December 31, 1986 and before the transfer of FE, DRC fails to satisfy the requirement of paragraph (c)(1)(i)(A) of this section in 1990 and in all future taxable years.

(2) *Elective agreement in place between United States and the foreign country.* Paragraph (a) of this section shall not apply to a dual consolidated loss to the extent such loss is subject to an

Reg. § 1.1503-2A(c)(2)

election by the dual resident corporation to deduct the loss in the United States pursuant to an agreement entered into between the United States and the foreign country which puts into place an elective procedure through which losses would offset income in only one country.

(3) *Agreement to amend returns upon later use of losses, expenses, or deductions of a dual resident corporation*—(i) *In general.* Notwithstanding that, under the income tax laws of the foreign country, the losses, expenses, or deductions of the dual resident corporation can be carried over or back to offset, by some means, the income of any other person, corporation, or entity in other taxable years, paragraph (a) of this section shall not apply to a dual consolidated loss of that dual resident corporation if the requirements described in this paragraph (c)(3)(i) are satisfied.

(A) At no time after December 31, 1986, has there been any other person, corporation, or entity which, under the income tax laws of the foreign country, is permitted to use by any means the losses, expenses, or deductions of the dual resident corporation to offset income. For purposes of the preceding sentence, none of the circumstances described in paragraphs (c)(1)(ii)(A) through (D) of this section shall constitute a satisfaction of this paragraph (c)(3)(i)(A).

(B) The affiliated group or, if there is no affiliated group filing a consolidated return, the dual resident corporation which incurs the loss, files with its U.S. tax return for the taxable year in which the dual consolidated loss arises a binding agreement described in paragraphs (c)(3)(ii) and (iii) of this section. The agreement must be filed under this paragraph (c)(3) even if the only effect of the dual consolidated loss is to increase a net operating loss for U.S. tax purposes.

(ii) *Description of agreement.* Except as otherwise provided in paragraph (c)(3)(viii) of this section, the agreement described in this paragraph (c)(3)(ii) must be attached to, and filed by the due date (including extensions) of, the tax return of the affiliated group or dual resident corporation for the taxable year in which the dual consolidated loss arises. The agreement must be signed under penalties of perjury by the person who signs the tax return of the group or dual resident corporation. The agreement must include the following items, in paragraphs labeled to correspond with the subdivisions set forth below:

(A) The name, address, identifying number, and place and date of incorporation of the dual resident corporation and the country or countries which tax the dual resident corporation on a residence basis or which tax the worldwide income of the dual resident corporation;

(B) A statement that the document submitted constitutes the agreement of the affiliated group or dual resident corporation in accordance with the requirements of § 1.1503-2T(c)(3);

(C) A statement of the amount of the dual consolidated loss to be covered by the agreement and the year in which it arose;

(D) The agreement of the group or dual resident corporation to amend returns, as described in paragraph (c)(3)(iii) of this section;

(E) A waiver of the period of limitations, as described in paragraph (c)(3)(iv) of this section; and

(F) An agreement to file with the tax returns of the group or dual resident corporation for each of the fifteen years following the year the dual consolidated loss arose a waiver of the period of limitation, as described in paragraph (c)(3)(iv) of this section, and a certification as described in paragraph (c)(3)(v) of this section.

(iii) *Terms of agreement.* The affiliated group or dual resident corporation must agree that if there is a "triggering event" described in this paragraph (c)(3)(iii), then, the affiliated group filing a consolidated return, or if there is no affiliated group filing a consolidated return, the dual resident corporation, shall, within 90 days after the date of occurrence of the triggering event, file an amended U.S. income tax return for the taxable year in which the dual consolidated loss arose reporting the dual consolidated loss on the amended return as a loss to which paragraph (a) of this section applies. An amended U.S. income tax return must also be filed for any other taxable year in which the tax liability increases as a result of such applications of paragraph (a) of this section. In addition, upon examination, the group or dual resident corporation must provide to the District Director a schedule of the amended carryforward and carryback losses and credits for each of the group's or dual resident corporation's taxable years for which no amended return is required to be filed pursuant to this paragraph (c)(3)(iii). For purposes of section 6601, the last date prescribed for payment of the additional amount of tax shown on an amended return filed pursuant to this paragraph (c)(3)(iii) shall be the same date as the date prescribed for the payment of tax for the taxable year with respect to which the amended return is filed. Any of the following events shall constitute a "triggering event" for purposes of this section—

(A) There is a failure for any taxable year to file the annual waiver or certification described in paragraphs (c)(3)(iv) and (v) of this section.

Reg. § 1.1503-2A(c)(3)

(B) Prior to the close of the fifteenth taxable year following the taxable year in which the dual consolidated loss arose, any of the following events—

(1) There is a failure to satisfy both the requirement of paragraph (c)(3)(i)(A) of this section and the requirements of paragraph (c)(4) of this section;

(2) Where the agreement is made by an affiliated group filing a consolidated return, the dual resident corporation (or its successor-in-interest) ceases to be a member of the affiliated group;

(3) Where the agreement is made by a dual resident corporation that is not a member of an affiliated group filing a consolidated return, the dual resident corporation is no longer in existence; or

(4) Where the dual resident corporation is a separate unit of a domestic corporation, the domestic corporation sells or transfers the dual resident corporation.

(iv) *Waiver of period of limitation.* The affiliated group or the dual resident corporation (or the successor-in-interest of such group or dual resident corporation) must file, with the agreement to amend returns and with the tax return for each of the fifteen taxable years following the taxable year in which the dual consolidated loss arose, a waiver of the limitation on assessment of any tax resulting from the amendment of any return as described in paragraph (c)(3)(iii) of this section. The waiver shall extend the period for assessment of such tax to a date not earlier than three years after the return is filed for the fifteenth taxable year following the taxable year in which the dual consolidated loss arose. The waiver shall also contain such other terms with respect to assessment as may be considered by the Commissioner to be necessary to insure the assessment and collection of the correct tax liability for each year for which the waiver is required. The waiver must be signed by a person authorized to sign the agreement described in paragraph (c)(3)(ii) of this section. A failure, at any time, to comply with the requirements of this paragraph (c)(3) or with the terms of any agreement filed pursuant to this paragraph (c)(3) shall extend the period of assessment of such tax until three years after the date on which the Internal Revenue Service receives actual notice of the use of or of the ability to use the losses, expenses, or deductions of the dual resident corporation to offset the income of another person, corporation, or entity under the income tax laws of the foreign country.

(v) *Annual certification.* The affiliated group or the dual resident corporation (or the successor-in-interest of such group or dual resident corporation) must file with its income tax return for each of the fifteen taxable years following the taxable year in which the dual consolidated loss arose a certification that the losses, expenses, or deductions of the dual resident corporation were not used or permitted to be used to offset the income of another person, corporation, or entity under the income tax laws of a foreign country. The annual certification pursuant to this paragraph (c)(3)(v) must be signed under penalties of perjury by a person authorized to sign the agreement described in paragraph (c)(3)(ii) of this section. The certification must identify the dual consolidated loss with respect to which it is given by setting forth the taxpayer's year in which the loss arose and the amount of such loss and must warrant that arrangements have been made to insure that the group or dual resident corporation will be informed of any subsequent use of or ability to use the losses, expenses, or deductions of the dual resident corporation to offset the income of another person, corporation, or entity under the income tax laws of the foreign country. If dual consolidated losses of more than one taxable year are subject to the rules of this paragraph (c)(3), the certifications for those years may be combined in a single document, but each dual consolidated loss must be separately identified.

(vi) *Special rules for a succeeding group or a successor-in-interest*—(A) *Ceasing to be a member of the affiliated group.* For purposes of this paragraph (c)(3), and except as otherwise provided in this paragraph (c)(3)(vi), a dual resident corporation shall be deemed to have ceased to be a member of the affiliated group that filed the agreement described in paragraph (c)(3)(ii) of this section if it is no longer a member of that group, as defined in § 1.1502-1(b), or if the group ceases to exist because the common parent is no longer in existence or is no longer a common parent or the group no longer files on the basis of a consolidated return. However, the obligation to file an amended return pursuant to the agreement described in paragraph (c)(3)(ii) of this section shall not apply and the dual resident corporation shall not be deemed to have ceased to be a member of the group for purposes of this paragraph (c)(3) where the dual resident corporation ceases to be a member of the group solely by reason of an acquisition of its assets by a member of the group in a transaction to which section 381(a) applies provided the successor-in-interest of the dual resident corporation continues to be a member of the group.

(B) *Special rules for a succeeding group.* The obligation to file an amended return pursuant to the agreement described in paragraph (c)(3)(ii)

Reg. § 1.1503-2A(c)(3)

of this section shall not apply where the dual resident corporation becomes a member of a succeeding group as a result of an acquisition described in § 1.1502-13(f)(2)(i)(a) or (b) (relating generally to the acquisition of assets of, by, or from a member of the affiliated group in a tax-free reorganization) and the succeeding group attaches to, and files with, its timely filed (including extensions) tax return for the taxable year in which the acquisition takes place a binding agreement—

(1) which sets forth the same terms as are described in paragraph (c)(3)(ii) of this section,

(2) in which the group agrees to be bound by the terms of the agreement previously filed by the terminating group, and

(3) in which the group agrees to all the terms set forth in paragraph (c)(3)(iii) of this section.

The agreement must be signed under penalties of perjury by the person who signs the tax return of the succeeding group.

(C) *Special rules for a successor-in-interest.* In the case of a dual resident corporation that was not a member of an affiliated group filing a consolidated return in the taxable year in which the dual consolidated loss arose and that filed an agreement described in paragraph (c)(3)(ii) of this section, the assets of which are acquired in a transaction described in section 381(a), such corporation shall not be required to file an amended return pursuant to paragraph (c)(3)(iii)(B)(3) of this section provided its successor-in-interest attaches a binding agreement to its timely filed (including extensions) tax return for the taxable year in which the acquisition takes place. The agreement must be signed under penalties of perjury by the person who signs the tax return of the successor-in-interest. The agreement must (1) set forth the same terms as are described in paragraph (c)(3)(ii) of this section, (2) state the agreement of the successor-in-interest to be bound by the terms of the agreement previously filed by the dual resident corporation, and (3) state the agreement of the successor-in-interest to all the terms set forth in paragraph (c)(3)(iii) of this section.

(vii) *Definitions.* For purposes of this section—

(A) The terms "succeeding group" and "terminating group" shall have the same meaning as in § 1.1502-13(f)(2)(i); and

(B) The term "successor-in-interest" shall mean an acquiring corporation that succeeds to the tax attributes of an acquired corporation under the provisions of section 381 by reason of a transaction described in section 381(a).

(viii) *Transition rules.* An affiliated group or a dual resident corporation (or a succeeding group or a successor-in-interest of a dual resident corporation) that meets the eligibility requirements described in paragraph (c)(3)(ix) of this section will be permitted to apply the transition rules in this paragraph (c)(3)(viii) for taxable years ending before December 31, 1989.

(A) The agreement in satisfaction of paragraph (c)(3)(ii) or (vi) of this section may be attached to the timely filed (including extensions) tax return of the affiliated group or of the dual resident corporation (or the succeeding group or the successor-in-interest of such dual resident corporation) for the first taxable year which ends on or after December 31, 1989. The agreement required for each of the taxable years ending before December 31, 1989 and for the first taxable year ending on or after December 31, 1989 may be combined on a single document.

(B) The requirement of paragraphs (c)(3)(iv) and (c)(3)(v) of this section regarding the filing of an annual waiver of the period of limitation and certification shall be satisfied for the taxable years ending before December 31, 1989, and no failure to file shall be deemed to have occurred with respect to such taxable years for purposes of paragraph (c)(3)(iii)(A) of this section if the waivers and certifications required under paragraphs (c)(3)(iv) and (c)(3)(v) of this section are filed with the tax return for the first taxable year ending on or after December 31, 1989.

(ix) *Eligibility for transition rules.* The rules in paragraph (c)(3)(viii) of this section shall apply only if, as of the date of the agreement in satisfaction of paragraph (c)(3)(ii) or (vi) of this section and filed pursuant to paragraph (c)(3)(viii) of this section, none of the triggering events described in paragraph (c)(3)(iii)(B) of this section has occurred.

(4) *No ability to use dual consolidated loss under foreign law after restructuring*—(i) *In general.* Notwithstanding that a dual resident corporation fails to satisfy either paragraph (c)(1)(i)(A) or (c)(3)(i)(A) of this section, paragraph (a) of this section shall not apply to any dual consolidated loss (or portion of a dual consolidated loss) described in paragraph (c)(4)(iii) of this section provided the requirements of either paragraph (c)(1)(i)(B) or (c)(3)(i)(B) of this section are satisfied and a restructuring that meets the requirements of paragraph (c)(4)(ii) of this section has been completed.

Reg. § 1.1503-2A(c)(4)

(ii) *Qualified restructuring.* A restructuring meets the requirements of this paragraph (c)(4)(ii) if it is completed on or before December 31, 1989, in the foreign country so that at all times from the date of such restructuring to the close of the taxable year in which the dual consolidated loss arises, there is no other person, corporation, or entity which, under the income tax laws of the foreign country, is permitted to use by any means the losses, expenses, or deductions of the dual resident corporation to offset income. For purposes of the preceding sentence, none of the circumstances described in paragraphs (c)(1)(ii)(A) through (D) of this section shall constitute a satisfaction of this paragraph (c)(4)(ii).

(iii) *Qualified losses.* Losses to which paragraph (c)(4)(i) of this section applies are the dual consolidated losses of a dual resident corporation that arise in a taxable year beginning after the restructuring described in paragraph (c)(4)(ii) of this section (or the portion of any dual consolidated loss that arises during that portion of the taxable year following the restructuring described in paragraph (c)(4)(ii) of this section). For purposes of determining the amount of the dual consolidated loss which arises in that portion of the taxable year following the restructuring, in no event shall more than a pro rata portion of the dual consolidated loss commensurate with the portion of the taxable year beginning with the date of completion of the restructuring and ending on the last day of that same taxable year be allocated to that portion of the taxable year following the restructuring.

(d) *Special rule for separate units*—(1) *Separate units characterized as corporations under foreign law.* If a separate unit of a domestic corporation consists of an interest in an entity (including a foreign branch) that for U.S. tax purposes is not taxable as an association, but the entity is subject to income tax in a foreign jurisdiction as a corporation either on its worldwide income or on a residence basis (and not on a source basis), then for purposes of this section such separate unit of the domestic corporation will be treated as if it were a dual resident corporation and a wholly-owned domestic subsidiary of the domestic corporation. For purposes of paragraphs (c)(3) and (4) of this section, any agreement, waiver and certification required to be filed with respect to such dual resident corporation shall be filed with the federal income tax return of the domestic corporation owning the separate unit or by the affiliated group with which the domestic corporation files a consolidated return.

(2) *Other separate units.* Except as provided in paragraph (d)(3) of this section, if a separate unit of a domestic corporation (other than a separate unit described in paragraph (d)(1) of this section) is permitted under the income tax laws of a foreign country—

(i) To use its losses, expenses, or deductions to offset the income of any other person, corporation, or entity in the taxable year in which the dual consolidated loss arises; or

(ii) To carry over or back its losses, expenses, or deductions so that they may offset the income of any other person, corporation, or entity in other years,

then such separate unit will be treated for purposes of this section as if it were a dual resident corporation and a wholly-owned domestic subsidiary of the domestic corporation. For purposes of the preceding sentence, none of the circumstances described in paragraphs (c)(1)(ii)(A) through (D) of this section shall preclude a separate unit from being treated as a dual resident corporation and a separate domestic corporation under this paragraph (d)(2). This paragraph (d)(2) applies regardless of whether the domestic corporation is a member of an affiliated group, and, if it is, regardless of whether the group files a consolidated return.

(3) *Certification.* Paragraph (d)(2) of this section shall not apply with respect to any taxable year for which the domestic corporation owning the separate unit (or the affiliated group of which the domestic corporation is a member) files a certification as described in this paragraph (d)(3). The certification must be attached to, and filed by the due date (including extensions) of, the federal income tax return of the domestic corporation owning the separate unit (or the affiliated group with which the domestic corporation files a consolidated return) for the taxable year to which it applies. With respect to returns filed without an attached certification for taxable years ending before December 31, 1989, the certification in satisfaction of this paragraph (d)(3) may be attached to the return for the first taxable year ending on or after December 31, 1989. The certification must be signed under penalties of perjury by the person who signs the return. The certification must include the following items, in paragraphs labeled to correspond with the subdivisions set forth below:

(i) A statement that the document submitted constitutes the certification required under the provisions of § 1.1503-2T(d)(3);

(ii) Identification of the separate unit, including the name under which it conducts business and its principal activity;

Reg. § 1.1503-2A(d)(1)

(iii) Identification of the total losses, expenses, and deductions incurred by the separate unit and included on the tax return for the taxable year;

(iv) Certification that no portion of the separate unit's losses, expenses or deductions identified above has been or will be used to offset the income of any other person, corporation, or entity under the income tax laws of the foreign country; and

(v) An agreement to comply with the recapture and interest charge requirements of paragraph (d)(4) of this section.

If the domestic corporation has more than one separate unit, the certification described above may be made on a single document, but the total losses, expenses, and deductions must be separately identified for each separate unit to which the certification applies.

(4) *Recapture upon subsequent use.* If in any taxable year any portion of the losses, expenses, or deductions of a separate unit which were the subject of a certification filed under paragraph (d)(3) of this section are used by any means to offset the income of any other person, corporation, or entity under the income tax laws of a foreign country, then the total amount of the dual consolidated loss shall be recaptured and reported as income on the tax return of the domestic corporation (or the affiliated group with which the domestic corporation files a consolidated return) for the taxable year that includes the last day of the taxable year for foreign tax purposes during which such use occurred. In addition, the domestic corporation owning the separate unit (or the affiliated group with which the domestic files a consolidated return) shall pay an interest charge on the amount of additional tax owed as a result of the recapture described in the preceding sentence. Such interest shall be determined under the rules of section 6601(a) as if the additional amount of tax had accrued and been due and owing for the taxable year in which the losses, expenses, or deductions giving rise to the recapture gave rise to a tax benefit for U.S. income tax purposes. For purposes of this paragraph (d)(4), a tax benefit will be considered to have arisen in a taxable year in which a loss that would have been considered a dual consolidated loss if paragraph (d)(3) of this section had not applied has reduced the U.S. income tax liability of the domestic corporation or of the affiliated group with which it files a consolidated return.

(5) *Treatment of separate units as separate entities*—(i) *In general.* A separate unit of a domestic corporation will be treated as a separate entity for purposes of determining under this section whether losses of one entity are permitted under the income tax laws of the foreign country to offset the income of another entity.

(ii) *Exception for separate units in same country.* If two or more separate units (not described in paragraph (d)(1) of this section) located in the same foreign country are owned by a single domestic corporation and the income and losses of such units are consolidated on an income tax return in that foreign country, then the separate units will be treated as one separate unit for purposes of paragraph (d)(2) of this section.

(6) *Examples.* The following examples illustrate this paragraph (d).

Example (1). X, a member of a U.S. affiliated group, has a foreign branch (as defined in § 1.367(a)-6T(g)) in Country Y. Under the Country Y income tax laws, the branch will be taxed as a permanent establishment and its income and losses may be used (on an elective basis) in the Country Y form of consolidation to offset the income of Z, an affiliate of X, under Country Y law. The branch of X incurs a net operating loss during the taxable year ending December 31, 1987. The foreign branch of X will be treated as a separate domestic corporation and a dual resident corporation under paragraph (d)(2) of this section, and its net operating loss will constitute a dual consolidated loss. Consequently, under paragraph (a) of this section, the branch's net operating loss may not be used to offset the income of any other U.S. affiliate or any income of X other than income derived from the branch operations. However, the branch will not be treated as a dual resident corporation if X (or the affiliated group of which X is a member) files a certification for the taxable year as described in paragraph (d)(3) of this section that its net operating loss was not in fact used by Z (or any other entity) to offset income under the Country Y income tax laws, and that such loss will be recaptured if it is so used in the future.

Example (2). X is classified as a partnership for U.S. tax purposes under Code section 7701 and applicable regulations. A, B and C are the sole partners of X. A and B are domestic corporations and C is a resident of foreign country Y. Under Country Y's law, X is classified as a corporation and its income and losses may be used in the Country Y form of consolidation to offset the income of the companies that are affiliates of X. X generates net operating losses. The partnership interests held by A and B are each treated as separate domestic corporations and dual resident corporations under paragraph (d)(1) of this section. A's and B's pro rata share of the losses of X are dual consolidated losses as defined in para-

Reg. § 1.1503-2A(d)(6)

graph (b)(2) of this section. Under paragraph (a) of this section, the losses of X may not be used to offset the income of any other U.S. affiliate. A's pro rata share of losses of X may be used by A only to offset A's pro rata share of income of X. However, paragraph (a) of this section shall not apply to A's pro rata share of losses of X if A meets one of the exceptions described in paragraph (c) of this section. The same principles apply to limit the use of losses allocated to B.

Example (3). Domestic corporation W owns two unincorporated business operations in Country Y. The two businesses, A and B, constitute separate foreign branches (as defined in § 1.367(a)-6T(g)). Under the tax laws of Country Y, A is treated as a separate corporation and taxed on a residence basis. Thus, A is a separate unit described in paragraph (d)(1) of this section. B is not a separate unit described in paragraph (d)(1) of this section. W is a calendar year taxpayer for both United States and Country Y purposes. During the calendar year ending December 31, 1987, A operated at a loss and B was profitable. Country Y allows both of W's branches to report their combined operations on a single income tax return. Thus, the losses incurred by A may be used on the 1987 Country Y return to offset the income of B. A will be treated as a dual resident corporation under paragraph (d)(1) of this section. Because A is a separate unit described in paragraph (d)(1) of this section, paragraph (d)(5)(i) of this section treats A and B as separate entities for purposes of determining whether the losses, expenses, or deductions of A may be used to offset the income of another person, corporation, or entity and the exception in paragraph (d)(5)(ii) of this section does not apply. Since the loss incurred by A may be used to offset B's income under foreign tax laws, W will not qualify for the exceptions described in paragraph (c) of this section. Accordingly, W will report the income from B on its 1987 U.S. tax return, but will not be allowed to use the losses from A to offset that income or the income from any source other than from the operations of A.

(e) *Special rule for use of dual consolidated loss to offset tainted income*—(1) *In general.* The dual consolidated loss of any dual resident corporation that ceases to be a dual resident corporation shall not be used to offset income of such corporation to the extent that such income is tainted income as defined in paragraph (e)(2) of this section.

(2) *Tainted income defined.* Tainted income is any income derived from tainted assets (as defined in paragraph (e)(3) of this section), during the period beginning on the date of the transfer or acquisition of tainted assets and ending at the close of the fifteenth taxable year following the taxable year in which the dual resident corporation ceased to be a dual resident corporation.

(3) *Tainted assets defined.* Tainted assets are any assets transferred to or acquired by a dual resident corporation in a non-recognition transaction (as defined in section 7701(a)(45)) at any time during the three taxable years immediately preceding the taxable year in which such dual resident corporation ceased to be a dual resident corporation or at any time during the 15 taxable years immediately following the taxable year in which a dual resident corporation ceased to be a dual resident corporation. Tainted assets shall not include assets that were transferred to or acquired by such dual resident corporation on or before December 31, 1986.

(4) *Exception.* For assets transferred to or acquired by a dual resident corporation prior to the time it ceased to be a dual resident corporation, if it can be shown that, for the year in which assets were transferred to or acquired by such corporation, the corporation did not incur a dual consolidated loss (or carry forward a dual consolidated loss to such year) and that there was a valid business reason for the transfer or acquisition of such assets, the income derived from such assets shall not be subject to the limitation described in paragraph (e)(1) of this section.

(f) *Special rules for accounting for dual consolidated losses*—(1) *Determination of amount of dual consolidated loss*—(i) *Dual resident corporation that is a member of an affiliated group.* For purposes of determining whether a dual resident corporation that is a member of an affiliated group filing a consolidated return has a dual consolidated loss for the taxable year, the dual resident corporation shall compute its taxable income (or loss) in accordance with the provisions of § 1.1502-12 (relating to computation of separate taxable income of a member of an affiliated group filing a consolidated return), determined by taking into account the adjustments provided in § 1.1502-79(a)(3), that is:

(A) The portion of the consolidated dividends received deduction, the consolidated charitable contributions deductions, and the consolidated section 247 deduction, attributable to such member;

(B) Such member's capital gain net income (determined without regard to any net capital loss carryover attributable to such member);

(C) Such member's net capital loss and section 1231 net loss, reduced by the portion of the consolidated net capital loss attributable to such member (as determined under paragraph (b)(2) of § 1.1502-22); and

Reg. § 1.1503-2A(e)(1)

(D) The portion of any consolidated net capital loss carryover attributable to such member which is absorbed in the taxable year.

For purposes of this paragraph (f), any income, gain, or loss of a dual resident corporation shall not be deferred or eliminated under § 1.1502-13(b)(2) or (c), or 1.1502-14. Further, sections 267 and 163(e)(3) shall not apply.

(ii) *Dual resident corporation that is a separate unit of a domestic corporation.* For purposes of determining whether a dual resident corporation that is a separate unit of a domestic corporation has a dual consolidated loss for the taxable year, the dual resident corporation shall compute its taxable income (or loss) as if it were a separate domestic corporation and a dual resident corporation, using only those items of income, expenses, and deductions which are otherwise attributable to such separate unit.

(2) *Effect of dual consolidated loss.* For any taxable year in which a dual resident corporation has a dual consolidated loss to which paragraph (a) of this section applies, the following rules shall apply.

(i) If the dual resident corporation is a member of an affiliated group filing a consolidated return, then such affiliated group shall compute its taxable income without regard to the items of income, loss, or deduction of the dual resident corporation for the taxable year. The amount of taxable loss of the dual resident corporation for the taxable year shall be the amount of dual consolidated loss determined under paragraph (f)(1)(i) of this section. Such loss may be carried over or back for use in other taxable years as a net operating loss deduction by the dual resident corporation to the extent permitted under section 172. However, such loss shall be treated as a loss incurred by the dual resident corporation in a separate return limitation year, and, including in the case of a dual resident corporation that is a common parent, shall be subject to all of the limitations of §§ 1.1502-21A(c)(2) or 1.1502-21(c) (as appropriate) (relating to limitations on net operating loss carryovers and carrybacks from separate return limitation years).

(ii) If the dual resident corporation is a separate unit of a domestic corporation, then such domestic corporation and the affiliated group with which it may file a consolidated return shall compute taxable income for the taxable year without regard to the items of income, loss, or deductions of the dual resident corporation for the current year. Further, the loss of the dual resident corporation (the separate unit of the domestic corporation) shall be treated as a loss incurred by a separate corporation and its use shall be subject to all of the limitations of §§ 1.1502-21A(c)(2) or 1.1502-21(c) (as appropriate) (relating to limitations on net operating loss carryovers and carrybacks from separate return limitation years), as if such dual resident corporation were filing a consolidated return with the domestic corporation or with the affiliated group with which the domestic corporation files a consolidated return.

(3) *Basis adjustments for dual consolidated losses.* When a dual resident corporation is a member of an affiliated group filing a consolidated return, each member owning stock in the dual resident corporation shall adjust the basis of the stock in the manner described in subparagraphs (i) and (ii) of this paragraph (f)(3).

(i) *Positive adjustment.* Adjustments shall be made in accordance with the principles of § 1.1502-32(b)(1), except that there shall be no positive adjustment under § 1.1502-32(b)(1)(ii) for any amount of the dual consolidated loss which is not absorbed. There shall be no positive adjustment for any amount included in income upon the use of a dual consolidated loss in a foreign country under § 1.1503-2T(c)(3).

(ii) *Negative adjustments.* Adjustments shall be made in accordance with the principles of § 1.1502-32(b)(2), except that there shall be no negative adjustment under § 1.1502-32(b)(2)(ii) for the amount of the dual consolidated loss.

(4) *Examples.* The following examples illustrate this paragraph (f).

Example (1). (i) P, S1, S2, and T are domestic corporations. P owns all of the stock of S1 and S2. S2 owns all of the stock of T. T is a dual resident corporation. None of the exceptions described in paragraph (c) apply with respect to T. P, S1, S2, and T have filed and continue to file a consolidated federal income tax return. X, Y, and Bank are corporations which are not members of the affiliated group of which P is the common parent.

(ii) At the beginning of 1989, P had a basis in S2 of $1000. S2 had a basis in T of $500.

(iii) In 1989, T had an interest expense of $100 on a loan from Bank. T sold a noncapital item *u* in which it had a basis of $10 to S1 for $50. T sold noncapital item *v* in which it had a basis of $200 to S1 for $100. The sale of *u* and *v* are deferred intercompany transactions described in § 1.1502-13(a)(2). S1 had separate taxable income calculated in accordance with § 1.1502-12 of $200. In addition, S1 sold item *w* in which it had a basis of $50 to T for $100. The sale of item *w* is a deferred intercompany transaction described in § 1.1502-13(a)(2). P and S2 had no items of income, loss, or deduction for 1989.

Reg. § 1.1503-2A(f)(4)

(iv) For purposes of determining whether T has a dual consolidated loss in 1989 and the amount of such dual consolidated loss, T's taxable income (loss) is calculated under paragraph (f)(1) as follows:

($100)	interest expense to Bank
($100)	sale of item v to S1
$ 40	sale of item u to S1
($160)	

T therefore has a dual consolidated loss of $160 for 1989.

(v) Because T has a dual consolidated loss for the year, the consolidated taxable income of the P affiliated group is calculated without regard to the items of income, loss, or deduction of T. However, T is still a member of the P affiliated group. Therefore, the consolidated taxable income of the P group is $200 (attributable solely to the income of S1). The $50 gain recognized by S1 upon the sale of item w to T is deferred pursuant to § 1.1502-13(c)(1).

(vi) S2 may not make the positive adjustment provided for in § 1.1502-32(b)(1)(ii) to its basis in T for the dual consolidated loss incurred by T. However, S2 must make the negative adjustment provided for in § 1.1502-32(b)(2)(i) for the amount of its allocable part of the deficit in earnings and profits of T for the taxable year. Thus, as provided in § 1.1502-32(e)(1), S2 shall make a net negative adjustment to its basis in T of $160 and S2's basis in T is now $340. As provided in § 1.1502-33(b)(4)(ii)(a), S2's earnings and profits for 1989 must reflect S2's decrease in its basis in T stock for the taxable year. Since S2 has no other earnings and profits for the taxable year, S2 has a deficit in earnings and profits of $160 for the taxable year. As provided in § 1.1502-32(b)(2)(i), P must make a negative adjustment for the amount of its allocable part of the deficit in earnings and profits of S2 for the taxable year. Thus, P must make a net negative adjustment to its basis in S2 of $160 and P's basis in S2 is now $840.

Example (2). (i) The facts are the same as in Example (1), except that in 1990, S1 sold items u and v to X for no gain or loss. T incurred an interest expense of $100 on a loan from Bank. T also sold item q in which it had a basis of $50 to S1 for $100. T also sold item r in which it had a basis of $100 to Y for $300. P and S2 had no items of income, loss, or deduction for 1990.

(ii) For purposes of determining whether T has a dual consolidated loss in 1990 and the amount of such dual consolidated loss, T's taxable income (loss) is:

($100)	interest expense to Bank
$ 50	sale of item q to S1
$200	sale of item r to Y
$150	

T therefore has no dual consolidated loss for 1990.

(iii) Since T does not have a dual consolidated loss for the taxable year, the group's consolidated taxable income is calculated in accordance with the general rule of § 1.1502-11 and not in accordance with the rule of § 1.1503-2T(f)(2). T has separate taxable income calculated in accordance with § 1.1502-12 of $100. On the disposition of items u and v outside the P affiliated group, no gain or loss is restored to income to T in accordance with § 1.1502-13(f)(1)(i) because the gain or loss on these items was not deferred, pursuant to § 1.1503-2T(f)(3). The $50 gain on the sale of item q from T to S1 is an intercompany transaction on which the gain or loss recognized is deferred pursuant to § 1.1502-13(c)(1). The consolidated taxable income of the P affiliated group computed without regard to the consolidated net operating loss deduction is $100.

(iv) As provided by § 1.1502-21A(c)(2) of the regulations, the amount of the dual consolidated loss arising in 1989 which may be absorbed by the P affiliated group in 1990 is $100; that is, the consolidated taxable income computed without regard to the consolidated net operating loss deduction minus such consolidated taxable income recomputed by excluding the items of income and deduction of T. Section 1.1502-21A(c) allows $100 of the dual consolidated loss to be included in the consolidated net operating loss deduction for 1990. The consolidated taxable income of the P group for 1990 is $0.

(v) S2 must make the positive adjustment provided for in § 1.1502-32(b)(1)(i) to its basis in T for the amount of its allocable part of the undistributed earnings and profits of T for the taxable year. S2 can not make the negative adjustment provided for in § 1.1502-32(b)(2)(ii) for the dual consolidated loss of T incurred in 1989 and absorbed in 1990. Thus, as provided in § 1.1502-32(e)(2), S2 shall make a net positive adjustment to its basis in T of $100 and S2's basis in T is now $440. As provided in § 1.1502-33(b)(4)(ii)(a), S2's earnings and profits for 1989 must reflect S2's increase in its basis in T stock for the taxable year. Since S2 has no other earnings and profits for the taxable year, S2 has earnings and profits of $100 for the taxable year. As provided in § 1.1502-32(b)(1)(i), P must make a positive adjustment for the amount of its allocable part of the undistributed earnings and profits of S2 for the taxable year. Thus, P must make a net positive adjustment to its basis in S2 of $100

Reg. § 1.1503-2A(f)(4)

and P's basis in S2 is now $940. [Reg. § 1.1503-2A.]

☐ [T.D. 8261, 9-7-89. Redesignated by T.D. 8434, 9-4-92. Amended by T.D. 8677, 6-26-96 and T.D. 8823, 6-25-99.]

[Reg. § 1.1504-0]

§ 1.1504-0. Outline of provisions.—In order to facilitate the use of §§ 1.1504-1 through 1.1504-4, this section lists the captions contained in §§ 1.1504-1 through 1.1504-4.

§ 1.1504-1. Definitions.

§ 1.1504-2. [Reserved].

§ 1.1504-3. [Reserved].

§ 1.1504-4. Treatment of warrants, options, convertible obligations, and other similar interests.—
(a) Introduction.
  (1) General rule.
  (2) Exceptions.
(b) Options not treated as stock or as exercised.
  (1) General rule.
  (2) Options treated as exercised.
    (i) In general.
    (ii) Aggregation of options.
    (iii) Effect of treating option as exercised.
      (A) In general.
      (B) Cash settlement options, phantom stock, stock appreciation rights, or similar interests.
    (iv) Valuation.
  (3) Example.
(c) Definitions.
  (1) Issuing corporation.
  (2) Related or sequential option.
  (3) Related persons.
  (4) Measurement date.
    (i) General rule.
    (ii) Issuances, transfers, or adjustments not treated as measurement dates.
    (iii) Transactions increasing likelihood of exercise.
    (iv) Measurement date for options issued pursuant to a plan.
    (v) Measurement date for related or sequential options.
    (vi) Example.
  (5) In-the-money.
(d) Options.
  (1) Instruments treated as options.
  (2) Instruments generally not treated as options.
    (i) Options on section 1504(a)(4) stock.
    (ii) Certain publicly traded options.
      (A) General rule.
      (B) Exception.
    (iii) Stock purchase agreements.
    (iv) Escrow, pledge, or other security agreements.
    (v) Compensatory options.
      (A) General rule.
      (B) Exceptions.
    (vi) Options granted in connection with a loan.
    (vii) Options created pursuant to a title 11 or similar case.
    (viii) Convertible preferred stock.
    (ix) Other enumerated instruments.
(e) Elimination of federal income tax liability.
(f) Substantial amount of federal income tax liability.
(g) Reasonable certainty of exercise.
  (1) Generally.
    (i) Purchase price.
    (ii) In-the-money option.
    (iii) Not in-the-money option.
    (iv) Exercise price.
    (v) Time of exercise.
    (vi) Related or sequential options.
    (vii) Stockholder rights.
    (viii) Restrictive covenants.
    (ix) Intention to alter value.
    (x) Contingencies.
  (2) Cash settlement options, phantom stock, stock appreciation rights, or similar interests.
  (3) Safe harbors.
    (i) Options to acquire stock.
    (ii) Options to sell stock.
    (iii) Options exercisable at fair market value.
    (iv) Exceptions.
    (v) Failure to satisfy safe harbor.
(h) Examples.
(i) Effective date.
[Reg. § 1.1504-0.]

☐ [T.D. 8462, 12-28-92.]

[Reg. § 1.1504-1]

§ 1.1504-1. Definitions.—The privilege of filing consolidated returns is extended to all includible corporations constituting affiliated groups as defined in section 1504. See the regulations under

§ 1.1502 for a description of an affiliated group and the corporations which may be considered as includible corporations. [Reg. § 1.1504-1.]

☐ [*T.D. 6140, 8-29-55.*]

[Reg. § 1.1504-2]

§ 1.1504-2. [Reserved].

[Reg. § 1.1504-3]

§ 1.1504-3. [Reserved].

[Reg. § 1.1504-4]

§ 1.1504-4. **Treatment of warrants, options, convertible obligations, and other similar interests.**—(a) *Introduction*—(1) *General rule.* This section provides regulations under section 1504(a)(5)(A) and (B) regarding the circumstances in which warrants, options, obligations convertible into stock, and other similar interests are treated as exercised for purposes of determining whether a corporation is a member of an affiliated group. The fact that an instrument may be treated as an option under these regulations does not prevent such instrument from being treated as stock under general principles of law. Except as provided in paragraph (a)(2) of this section, this section applies to all provisions under the Internal Revenue Code and the regulations to which affiliation within the meaning of section 1504(a) (with or without the exceptions in section 1504(b)) is relevant, including those provisions that refer to section 1504(a)(2) (with or without the exceptions in section 1504(b)) without referring to affiliation, provided that the 80 percent voting power and 80 percent value requirements of section 1504(a)(2) are not modified therein.

(2) *Exceptions.* This section does not apply to sections 163(j), 864(e), or 904(i) or to the regulations thereunder. This section also does not apply to any other provision specified by the Internal Revenue Service in regulations, a revenue ruling, or revenue procedure. See § 601.601(d)(2)(ii)(*b*) of this chapter.

(b) *Options not treated as stock or as exercised*—(1) *General rule.* Except as provided in paragraph (b)(2) of this section, an option is not considered either as stock or as exercised. Thus, options are disregarded in determining whether a corporation is a member of an affiliated group unless they are described in paragraph (b)(2) of this section.

(2) *Options treated as exercised*—(i) *In general.* Solely for purposes of determining whether a corporation is a member of an affiliated group, an option is treated as exercised if, on a measurement date with respect to such option—

(A) It could reasonably be anticipated that, if not for this section, the issuance or transfer of the option in lieu of the issuance, redemption, or transfer of the underlying stock would result in the elimination of a substantial amount of federal income tax liability (as described in paragraphs (e) and (f) of this section); and

(B) It is reasonably certain that the option will be exercised (as described in paragraph (g) of this section).

(ii) *Aggregation of options.* All options with the same measurement date are aggregated in determining whether the issuance or transfer of an option in lieu of the issuance, redemption, or transfer of the underlying stock would result in the elimination of a substantial amount of federal income tax liability.

(iii) *Effect of treating option as exercised*—(A) *In general.* An option that is treated as exercised is treated as exercised for purposes of determining the percentage of the value of stock owned by the holder and other parties, but is not treated as exercised for purposes of determining the percentage of the voting power of stock owned by the holder and other parties.

(B) *Cash settlement options, phantom stock, stock appreciation rights, or similar interests.* If a cash settlement option, phantom stock, stock appreciation right, or similar interest is treated as exercised, the option is treated as having been converted into stock of the issuing corporation. If the amount to be received upon the exercise of such an option is determined by reference to a multiple of the increase in the value of a share of the issuing corporation's stock on the exercise date over the value of a share of the stock on the date the option is issued, the option is treated as converted into a corresponding number of shares of such stock. Appropriate adjustments must be made in any situation in which the amount to be received upon exercise of the option is determined in another manner.

(iv) *Valuation.* For purposes of section 1504(a)(2)(B) and this section, all shares of stock within a single class are considered to have the same value. Thus, control premiums and minority and blockage discounts within a single class are not taken into account.

(3) *Example.* The provisions of paragraph (b)(2) of this section may be illustrated by the following example:

Example. (i) Corporation P owns all 100 shares of the common stock of Corporation S, the only class of S stock outstanding. Each share of S stock has a fair market value of $10 and has one vote. On June 30, 1992, P issues to Corporation X

Reg. § 1.1504-2

an option to acquire 80 shares of the S stock from P.

(ii) If, under the provisions of this section, the option is treated as exercised, then, solely for purposes of determining affiliation, P is treated as owning only 20 percent of the value of the outstanding S stock and X is treated as owing the remaining 80 percent of the value of the S stock. P is still treated as owning all of the voting power of S. Accordingly, because P is treated as owning less than 80 percent of the value of the outstanding S stock, P and S are no longer affiliated. However, because X is not treated as owning any of the voting power of S, X and S are also not affiliated.

(c) *Definitions.* For purposes of this section—

(1) *Issuing corporation.* "Issuing corporation" means the corporation whose stock is subject to an option.

(2) *Related or sequential option.* "Related or sequential option" means an option that is one of a series of options issued to the same or related persons. For purposes of this section, any options issued to the same person or related persons within a two year period are presumed to be part of a series of options. This presumption may be rebutted if the facts and circumstances clearly establish that the options are not part of a series of options. Any options issued to the same person or related persons more than two years apart are presumed not to be part of a series of options. This presumption may be rebutted if the facts and circumstances clearly establish that the options are part of a series of options.

(3) *Related persons.* Persons are related if they are related within the meaning of section 267(b) (without the application of sections 267(c) and 1563(e)(1)) or 707(b)(1), substituting "10 percent" for "50 percent" wherever it appears.

(4) *Measurement date*—(i) *General rule.* "Measurement date" means a date on which an option is issued or transferred or on which the terms of an existing option or the underlying stock are adjusted (including an adjustment pursuant to the terms of the option or the underlying stock).

(ii) *Issuances, transfers, or adjustments not treated as measurement dates.* A measurement date does not include a date on which—

(A) An option is issued or transferred by gift, at death, or between spouses or former spouses under section 1041;

(B) An option is issued or transferred—

(*1*) Between members of an affiliated group (determined with the exceptions in section 1504(b) and without the application of this section); or

(*2*) Between persons none of which is a member of the affiliated group (determined without the exceptions in section 1504(b) and without the application of this section), if any, of which the issuing corporation is a member, unless—

(*i*) Any such person is related to (or acting in concert with) the issuing corporation or any member of its affiliated group; and

(*ii*) The issuance or transfer is pursuant to a plan a principal purpose of which is to avoid the application of section 1504 and this section;

(C) An adjustment occurs in the terms or pursuant to the terms of an option or the underlying stock that does not materially increase the likelihood that the option will be exercised; or

(D) A change occurs in the exercise price of an option or in the number of shares that may be issued or transferred pursuant to the option as determined by a bona fide, reasonable, adjustment formula that has the effect of preventing dilution of the interests of the holders of the options.

(iii) *Transactions increasing likelihood of exercise.* If a change or alteration referred to in this paragraph (c)(4)(iii) is made for a principal purpose of increasing the likelihood that an option will be exercised, a measurement date also includes any date on which—

(A) The capital structure of the issuing corporation is changed; or

(B) The fair market value of the stock of the issuing corporation is altered through a transfer of assets to or from the issuing corporation (other than regular, ordinary dividends) or by any other means.

(iv) *Measurement date for options issued pursuant to a plan.* In the case of options issued pursuant to a plan, a measurement date for any of the options constitutes a measurement date for all options issued pursuant to the plan that are outstanding on the measurement date.

(v) *Measurement date for related or sequential options.* In the case of related or sequential options, a measurement date for any of the options constitutes a measurement date for all related or sequential options that are outstanding on the measurement date.

(vi) *Example.* The provisions of paragraph (c)(4)(v) of this section may be illustrated by the following example.

Example. (i) Corporation P owns all 80 shares of the common stock of Corporation S, the only class of S stock outstanding. On January 1, 1992, S issues a warrant, exercisable within 3

Reg. § 1.1504-4(c)(4)

years, to U, an unrelated corporation, to acquire 10 newly issued shares of S common stock. On July 1, 1992, S issues a second warrant to U to acquire 10 additional newly issued shares of S common stock. On January 1, 1993, S issues a third warrant to T, a wholly owned subsidiary of U, to acquire 10 newly issued shares of S common stock. Assume that the facts and circumstances do not clearly establish that the options are not part of a series of options.

(ii) January 1, 1992, July 1, 1992, and January 1, 1993, constitute measurement dates for the first warrant, the second warrant, and the third warrant, respectively, because the warrants were issued on those dates.

(iii) Because the first and second warrants were issued within two years of each other, and both warrants were issued to U, the warrants constitute related or sequential options. Accordingly, July 1, 1992, constitutes a measurement date for the first warrant as well as for the second warrant.

(iv) Because the first, second, and third warrants were all issued within two years of each other, and were all issued to the same or related persons, the warrants constitute related or sequential options. Accordingly, January 1, 1993, constitutes a measurement date for the first and second warrants, as well as for the third warrant.

(5) *In-the-money.* "In-the-money" means the exercise price of the option is less than (or in the case of an option to sell stock, greater than) the fair market value of the underlying stock.

(d) *Options*—(1) *Instruments treated as options.* For purposes of this section, except to the extent otherwise provided in this paragraph (d), the following are treated as options:

(i) A call option, warrant, convertible obligation, put option, redemption agreement (including a right to cause the redemption of stock), or any other instrument that provides for the right to issue, redeem, or transfer stock (including an option on an option); and

(ii) A cash settlement option, phantom stock, stock appreciation right, or any other similar interest (except for stock).

(2) *Instruments generally not treated as options.* For purposes of this section, the following will not be treated as options:

(i) *Options on section 1504(a)(4) stock.* Options on stock described in section 1504(a)(4);

(ii) *Certain publicly traded options*—(A) *General rule.* Options which on the measurement date are traded on (or subject to the rules of) a qualified board or exchange as defined in section 1256(g)(7), or on any other exchange, board of trade, or market specified by the Internal Revenue Service in regulations, a revenue ruling, or revenue procedure. See § 601.601(d)(2)(ii)(*b*) of this chapter;

(B) *Exception.* Paragraph (d)(2)(ii)(A) of this section does not apply to options issued, transferred, or listed with a principal purpose of avoiding the application of section 1504 and this section. For example, a principal purpose of avoiding the application of section 1504 and this section may exist if warrants, convertible or exchangeable debt instruments, or other similar instruments have an exercise price (or, in the case of convertible or exchangeable instruments, a conversion or exchange premium) that is materially less than, or a term that is materially longer than, those that are customary for publicly traded instruments of their type. A principal purpose may also exist if a large percentage of an issuance of an instrument is placed with one investor (or group of investors) and a very small percentage of the issuance is traded on a qualified board or exchange;

(iii) *Stock purchase agreements.* Stock purchase agreements or similar arrangements whose terms are commercially reasonable and in which the parties' obligations to complete the transaction are subject only to reasonable closing conditions;

(iv) *Escrow, pledge, or other security agreements.* Agreements for holding stock in escrow or under a pledge or other security agreement that are part of a typical commercial transaction and that are subject to customary commercial conditions;

(v) *Compensatory options*—(A) *General rule.* Stock appreciation rights, warrants, stock options, phantom stock, or other similar instruments provided to employees, directors, or independent contractors in connection with the performance of services for the corporation or a related corporation (and that is not excessive by reference to the services performed) and which—

(*1*) Are nontransferable within the meaning of § 1.83-3(d); and

(*2*) Do not have a readily ascertainable fair market value as defined in § 1.83-7(b) on the measurement date;

(B) *Exceptions.* (*1*) Paragraph (d)(2)(v)(A) of this section does not apply to options issued or transferred with a principal purpose of avoiding the application of section 1504 and this section; and

(*2*) Paragraph (d)(2)(v)(A) of this section ceases to apply to options that become transferable;

(vi) *Options granted in connection with a loan.* Options granted in connection with a loan if the lender is actively and regularly engaged in the business of lending and the options are issued in connection with a loan to the issuing corporation that is commercially reasonable. This paragraph (d)(2)(vi) continues to apply if the option is transferred with the loan (or if a portion of the option is transferred with a corresponding portion of the loan). However, if the option is transferred without a corresponding portion of the loan, this paragraph (d)(2)(vi) ceases to apply;

(vii) *Options created pursuant to a title 11 or similar case.* Options created by the solicitation or receipt of acceptances to a plan of reorganization in a title 11 or similar case (within the meaning of section 368(a)(3)(A)), the option created by the confirmation of the plan, and any option created under the plan prior to the time the plan becomes effective;

(viii) *Convertible preferred stock.* Convertible preferred stock, provided the terms of the conversion feature do not permit or require the tender of any consideration other than the stock being converted; and

(ix) *Other enumerated instruments.* Any other instruments specified by the Internal Revenue Service in regulations, a revenue ruling, or revenue procedure. See § 601.601(d)(2)(ii)(*b*) of this chapter.

(e) *Elimination of federal income tax liability.* For purposes of this section, the elimination of federal income tax liability includes the elimination or deferral of federal income tax liability. In determining whether there is an elimination of federal income tax liability, the tax consequences to all involved parties are considered. Examples of elimination of federal income tax liability include the use of a loss or deduction that would not otherwise be utilized, the acceleration of a loss or deduction to a year earlier than the year in which the loss or deduction would otherwise be utilized, the deferral of gain or income to a year later than the year in which the gain or income would otherwise be reported, and the acceleration of gain or income to a year earlier than the year in which the gain or income would otherwise be reported, if such gain or income is offset by a net operating loss or net capital loss that would otherwise expire unused. The elimination of federal income tax liability does not include the deferral of gain with respect to the stock subject to the option that would be recognized if such stock were sold on a measurement date.

(f) *Substantial amount of federal income tax liability.* The determination of what constitutes a substantial amount of federal income tax liability is based on all the facts and circumstances, including the absolute amount of the elimination, the amount of the elimination relative to overall tax liability, and the timing of items of income and deductions, taking into account present value concepts.

(g) *Reasonable certainty of exercise*—(1) *Generally.* The determination of whether, as of a measurement date, an option is reasonably certain to be exercised is based on all the facts and circumstances, including:

(i) *Purchase price.* The purchase price of the option in absolute terms and in relation to the fair market value of the stock or the exercise price of the option;

(ii) *In-the-money option.* Whether and to what extent the option is in-the-money on the measurement date;

(iii) *Not in-the-money option.* If the option is not in-the-money on the measurement date, the amount or percentage by which the exercise price of the option is greater than (or in the case of an option to sell stock, is less than) the fair market value of the underlying stock;

(iv) *Exercise price.* Whether the exercise price of the option is fixed or fluctuates depending on the earnings, value, or other indication of economic performance of the issuing corporation;

(v) *Time of exercise.* The time at which, or the period of time during which, the option can be exercised;

(vi) *Related or sequential options.* Whether the option is one in a series of related or sequential options;

(vii) *Stockholder rights.* The existence of an arrangement (either within the option agreement or in a related agreement) that, directly or indirectly, affords managerial or economic rights in the issuing corporation that ordinarily would be afforded to owners of the issuing corporation's stock (*e.g.*, voting rights, dividend rights, or rights to proceeds on liquidation) to the person who would acquire the stock upon exercise of the option or a person related to such person. For this purpose, managerial or economic rights in the issuing corporation possessed because of actual stock ownership in the issuing corporation are not taken into account;

(viii) *Restrictive covenants.* The existence of restrictive covenants or similar arrangements (either within the option agreement or in a related agreement) that, directly or indirectly, prevent or limit the ability of the issuing corporation to undertake certain activities while the option is outstanding (*e.g.*, covenants limiting the payment of dividends or borrowing of funds);

Reg. § 1.1504-4(g)(1)

(ix) *Intention to alter value.* Whether it was intended that through a change in the capital structure of the issuing corporation or a transfer of assets to or from the issuing corporation (other than regular, ordinary dividends) or by any other means, the fair market value of the stock of the issuing corporation would be altered for a principal purpose of increasing the likelihood that the option would be exercised; and

(x) *Contingencies.* Any contingency (other than the mere passage of time) to which the exercise of the option is subject (*e.g.*, a public offering of the issuing corporation's stock or reaching a certain level of earnings).

(2) *Cash settlement options, phantom stock, stock appreciation rights, or similar interests.* A cash settlement option, phantom stock, stock appreciation right, or similar interest is treated as reasonably certain to be exercised if it is reasonably certain that the option will have value at some time during the period in which the option may be exercised.

(3) *Safe harbors*—(i) *Options to acquire stock.* Except as provided in paragraph (g)(3)(iv) of this section, an option to acquire stock is not considered reasonably certain, as of a measurement date, to be exercised if—

(A) The option may be exercised no more than 24 months after the measurement date and the exercise price is equal to or greater than 90 percent of the fair market value of the underlying stock on the measurement date; or

(B) The terms of the option provide that the exercise price of the option is equal to or greater than the fair market value of the underlying stock on the exercise date.

(ii) *Options to sell stock.* Except as provided in paragraph (g)(3)(iv) of this section, an option to sell stock is not considered reasonably certain, as of a measurement date, to be exercised if—

(A) The option may be exercised no more than 24 months after the measurement date and the exercise price is equal to or less than 110 percent of the fair market value of the underlying stock on the measurement date; or

(B) The terms of the option provide that the exercise price of the option is equal to or less than the fair market value of the underlying stock on the exercise date.

(iii) *Options exercisable at fair market value.* For purposes of paragraphs (g)(3)(i)(B) and (g)(3)(ii)(B) of this section, an option whose exercise price is determined by a formula is considered to have an exercise price equal to the fair market value of the underlying stock on the exercise date if the formula is agreed upon by the parties when the option is issued in a bona fide attempt to arrive at fair market value on the exercise date and is to be applied based upon the facts in existence on the exercise date.

(iv) *Exceptions.* The safe harbors of this paragraph (g)(3) do not apply if—

(A) An arrangement exists that provides the holder or a related party with stockholder rights described in paragraph (g)(1)(vii) of this section (except for rights arising upon a default under the option or a related agreement);

(B) It is intended that through a change in the capital structure of the issuing corporation or a transfer of assets to or from the issuing corporation (other than regular, ordinary dividends) or by any other means, the fair market value of the stock of the issuing corporation will be altered for a principal purpose of increasing the likelihood that the option will be exercised; or

(C) The option is one in a series of related or sequential options, unless all such options satisfy paragraph (g)(3)(i) or (ii) of this section.

(v) *Failure to satisfy safe harbor.* Failure of an option to satisfy one of the safe harbors of this paragraph (g)(3) does not affect the determination of whether an option is treated as reasonably certain to be exercised.

(h) *Examples.* The provisions of this section may be illustrated by the following examples. These examples assume that the measurement dates set forth in the examples are the only measurement dates that have taken place or will take place.

Example 1. (i) P is the common parent of a consolidated group, consisting of P, S, and T. P owns all 100 shares of S's only class of stock, which is voting common stock. P also owns all the stock of T. On June 30, 1992, when the fair market value of the S stock is $40 per share, P sells to U, an unrelated corporation, an option to acquire 40 shares of the S stock that P owns at an exercise price of $30 per share, exercisable at any time within 3 years after the granting of the option. P and T have had substantial losses for 5 consecutive years while S has had substantial income during the same period. Because P, S, and T have been filing consolidated returns, P and T have been able to use all of their losses to offset S's income. It is anticipated that P, S, and T will continue their earnings histories for several more years. On July 31, 1992, S declares and pays a dividend of $1 per share to P.

(ii) If P, S, and T continue to file consolidated returns after June 30, 1992, it could reasonably be anticipated that P, S, and T would eliminate a

Reg. § 1.1504-4(g)(2)

substantial amount of federal income tax liability by using P's and T's future losses to offset S's income in consolidated returns. Furthermore, based on the difference between the exercise price of the option and the fair market value of the S stock, it is reasonably certain, on June 30, 1992, a measurement date, that the option will be exercised. Therefore, the option held by U is treated as exercised. As a result, for purposes of determining whether P and S are affiliated, P is treated as owning only 60 percent of the value of outstanding shares of S stock and U is treated as owning the remaining 40 percent. P is still treated as owning 100 percent of the voting power. Because members of the P group are no longer treated as owning stock possessing 80 percent of the total value of the S stock as of June 30, 1992, S is no longer a member of the P group. Additionally, P is not entitled to a 100 percent dividends received deduction under section 243(a)(3) because P and S are also treated as not affiliated for purposes of section 243. P is only entitled to an 80 percent dividends received deduction under section 243(c).

Example 2. (i) The facts are the same as in *Example 1* except that rather than P issuing an option to acquire 40 shares of S stock to U on June 30, 1992, P, pursuant to a plan, issues an option to U1 on July 1, 1992, to acquire 20 shares of S stock, and issues an option to U2 on July 2, 1992, to acquire 20 shares of S stock.

(ii) Because the options issued to U1 and U2 were issued pursuant to a plan, July 2, 1992, constitutes a measurement date for both options. Therefore, both options are aggregated in determining whether the issuance of the options, rather than the sale of the S stock, would result in the elimination of a substantial amount of federal income tax liability. Accordingly, as in *Example 1,* because the continued affiliation of P, S, and T could reasonably be anticipated to result in the elimination of a substantial amount of federal income tax liability and the options are reasonably certain to be exercised, the options are treated as exercised for purposes of determining whether P and S are affiliated, and P and S are no longer affiliated as of July 2, 1992.

Example 3. (i) The facts are the same as in *Example 1* except that the option gives U the right to acquire all 100 shares of the S stock, and U is the common parent of a consolidated group. The U group has had substantial losses for 5 consecutive years and it is anticipated that the U group will continue its earnings history for several more years.

(ii) If P sold the S stock, in lieu of the option, to U, S would become a member of the U group. Because the U group files consolidated returns, if P sold the S stock to U, U would be able to use its future losses to offset future income of S. When viewing the transaction from the effect on all parties, the sale of the option, in lieu of the underlying S stock, does not result in the elimination of federal income tax liability because S's income would be offset by the losses of members of either the P or U group. Accordingly, the option is disregarded and S remains a member of the P group.

Example 4. (i) P is the common parent of a consolidated group, consisting of P and S. P owns 90 of the 100 outstanding shares of S's only class of stock, which is voting common stock, and U, an unrelated corporation, owns the remaining 10 shares. On August 31, 1992, when the fair market value of the S stock is $100 per share, P sells a call option to U that entitles U to purchase 20 shares of S stock from P, at any time before August 31, 1993, at an exercise price of $115 per share. The call option does not provide U with any voting rights, dividend rights, or any other managerial or economic rights ordinarily afforded to owners of the S stock. There is no intention on August 31, 1992, to alter the value of S to increase the likelihood of the exercise of the call option.

(ii) Because the exercise price of the call option is equal to or greater than 90 percent of the fair market value of the S stock on August 31, 1992, a measurement date, the option may be exercised no more than 24 months after the measurement date, and none of the items described in paragraph (g)(3)(iv) of this section that preclude application of the safe harbor are present, the safe harbor of paragraph (g)(3)(i) of this section applies and the call option is treated as if it is not reasonably certain to be exercised. Therefore, regardless of whether the continued affiliation of P and S would result in the elimination of a substantial amount of federal income tax liability, the call option is disregarded in determining whether S remains a member of the P group.

Example 5. (i) The facts are the same as in *Example 4* except that the call option gives U the right to vote similar to that of a shareholder.

(ii) Under paragraph (g)(3)(iv) of this section, the safe harbor of paragraph (g)(3)(i) of this section does not apply because the call option entitles U to voting rights equivalent to that of a shareholder. Accordingly, all of the facts and circumstances surrounding the sale of the call option must be taken into consideration in determining whether it is reasonably certain that the call option will be exercised.

Example 6. (i) In 1992, two unrelated corporations, X and Y, decide to engage jointly in a new

Reg. § 1.1504-4(h)

business venture. To accomplish this purpose, X organizes a new corporation, S, on September 30, 1992. X acquires 100 shares of the voting common stock of S, which are the only shares of S stock outstanding. Y acquires a debenture of S which is convertible, on September 30, 1995, into 100 shares of S common stock. If the conversion right is not exercised, X will have the right, on September 30, 1995, to put 50 shares of its S stock to Y in exchange for 50 percent of the debenture held by Y. The likelihood of the success of the venture is uncertain. It is anticipated that S will generate substantial losses in its early years of operation. X expects to have substantial taxable income during the three years following the organization of S.

(ii) Under the terms of this arrangement, it is reasonably certain, on September 30, 1992, a measurement date, that on September 30, 1995, either through Y's exercise of its conversion right or X's right to put S stock to Y, that Y will own 50 percent of the S stock. Additionally, it could reasonably be anticipated, on September 30, 1992, a measurement date, that the affiliation of X and S would result in the elimination of a substantial amount of federal income tax liability. Accordingly, for purposes of determining whether X and S are affiliated, X is treated as owning only 50 percent of the value of the S stock as of September 30, 1992, a measurement date, and S is not a member of the X affiliated group.

Example 7. (i) The facts are the same as in *Example 6* except that rather than acquiring 100 percent of the S stock and the right to put S stock to Y, X acquires only 80 percent of the S stock, while S, rather than acquiring a convertible debenture, acquires 20 percent of the S stock, and an option to acquire an additional 30 percent of the S stock. The terms of the option are such that the option will only be exercised if the new business venture succeeds.

(ii) In contrast to *Example 6*, because of the true business risks involved in the start-up of S and whether the business venture will ultimately succeed, along with the fact that X does not have an option to put S stock to Y, it is not reasonably certain on September 30, 1992, a measurement date, that the option will be exercised and that X will only own 50 percent of the S stock on September 30, 1995. Accordingly, the option is disregarded in determining whether S is a member of the X group.

(i) *Effective date.* This section applies, generally, to options with a measurement date on or after February 28, 1992. This section does not apply to options issued prior to February 28, 1992, which have a measurement date on or after February 28, 1992, if the measurement date for the option occurs solely because of an adjustment in the terms of the option pursuant to the terms of the option as it existed on February 28, 1992. Paragraph (b)(2)(iv) of this section applies to stock outstanding on or after February 28, 1992. [Reg. § 1.1504-4.]

☐ [*T.D. 8462, 12-28-92.*]

RELATED RULES

In General

[Reg. § 1.1551-1]

§ 1.1551-1. **Disallowance of surtax exemption and accumulated earnings credit.**—(a) *In general.* If—

(1) Any corporation transfers, on or after January 1, 1951, and before June 13, 1963, all or part of its property (other than money) to a transferee corporation,

(2) Any corporation transfers, directly or indirectly, after June 12, 1963, all or part of its property (other than money) to a transferee corporation, or

(3) Five or fewer individuals are in control of a corporation and one or more of them transfer, directly or indirectly, after June 12, 1963, property (other than money) to a transferee corporation,

and the transferee was created for the purpose of acquiring such property or was not actively engaged in business at the time of such acquisition, and if after such transfer the transferor or transferors are in control of the transferee during any part of the taxable year of the transferee, then for such taxable year of the transferee the Secretary or his delegate may disallow the surtax exemption defined in section 11(d) or the accumulated earnings credit of $150,000 ($100,000 in the case of taxable years beginning before January 1, 1975) provided in paragraph (2) or (3) of section 535(c), unless the transferee establishes by the clear preponderance of the evidence that the securing of such exemption or credit was not a major purpose of the transfer.

(b) *Purpose of section 1551.* The purpose of section 1551 is to prevent avoidance or evasion of the surtax imposed by section 11(c) or of the accumulated earnings tax imposed by section 531. It is not intended, however, that section 1551 be interpreted as delimiting or abrogating any principle of law established by judicial decision, or any existing provisions of the Code, such as sections

In General

See p. 20,601 for regulations not amended to reflect law changes

269 and 482, which have the effect of preventing the avoidance or evasion of income taxes. Such principles of law and such provisions of the Code, including section 1551, are not mutually exclusive, and in appropriate cases they may operate together or they may operate separately.

(c) *Application of section 269(b) to cases covered by section 1551.* The provisions of section 269(b) and the authority of the district director thereunder, to the extent not inconsistent with the provisions of section 1551, are applicable to cases covered by section 1551. Pursuant to the authority provided in section 269(b) the district director may allow to the transferee any part of a surtax exemption or accumulated earnings credit for a taxable year for which such exemption or credit would otherwise be disallowed under section 1551(a); or he may apportion such exemption or credit among the corporations involved. For example, corporation A transfers on January 1, 1955, all of its property to corporations B and C in exchange for all of the stock of such corporations. Immediately thereafter, corporation A is dissolved and its stockholders become the sole stockholders of corporations B and C. Assuming that corporations B and C are unable to establish by the clear preponderance of the evidence that the securing of the surtax exemption defined in section 11(d) or the accumulated earnings credit provided in section 535, or both, was not a major purpose of the transfer, the district director is authorized under sections 1551(c) and 269(b) to allow one such exemption and credit and to apportion such exemption and credit between corporations B and C.

(d) *Actively engaged in business.* For purposes of this section, a corporation maintaining an office for the purpose of preserving its corporate existence is not considered to be "actively engaged in business" even though such corporation may be deemed to be "doing business" for other purposes. Similarly, for purposes of this section, a corporation engaged in winding up its affairs, prior to an acquisition to which section 1551 is applicable, is not considered to be "actively engaged in business."

(e) *Meaning and application of the term "control"*—(1) *In general.* For purposes of this section, the term "control" means—

(i) With respect to a transferee corporation described in paragraph (a)(1) or (2) of this section, the ownership by the transferor corporation, its shareholders, or both, of stock possessing either (*a*) at least 80 percent of the total combined voting power of all classes of stock entitled to vote, or (*b*) at least 80 percent of the total value of shares of all classes of stock.

(ii) With respect to each corporation described in paragraph (a)(3) of this section, the ownership by five or fewer individuals of stock possessing (*a*) at least 80 percent of the total combined voting power of all classes of stock entitled to vote or at least 80 percent of the total value of shares of all classes of the stock of each corporation, and (*b*) more than 50 percent of the total combined voting power of all classes of stock entitled to vote or more than 50 percent of the total value of shares of all classes of stock of each corporation, taking into account the stock ownership of each such individual only to the extent such stock ownership is identical with respect to each such corporation.

(2) *Special rules.* In determining for purposes of this section whether stock possessing at least 80 percent (or more than 50 percent in the case of subparagraph (1)(ii)(*b*) of this paragraph) of the total combined voting power of all classes of stock entitled to vote is owned, all classes of such stock shall be considered together; it is not necessary that at least 80 percent (or more than 50 percent) of each class of voting stock be owned. Likewise, in determining for purposes of this section whether stock possessing at least 80 percent (or more than 50 percent) of the total value of shares of all classes of stock is owned, all classes of stock of the corporation shall be considered together; it is not necessary that at least 80 percent (or more than 50 percent) of the value of shares of each class be owned. The fair market value of a share shall be considered as the value to be used for purposes of this computation. With respect to transfers described in paragraph (a)(2) or (3) of this section, the ownership of stock shall be determined in accordance with the provisions of section 1563(e) and the regulations thereunder. With respect to transfers described in paragraph (a)(1) of this section, the ownership of stock shall be determined in accordance with the provisions of section 544 and the regulations thereunder, except that constructive ownership under section 544(a)(2) shall be determined only with respect to the individual's spouse and minor children. In determining control, no stock shall be excluded because such stock was acquired before January 1, 1951 (the effective date of section 1551(a)(1)), or June 13, 1963 (the effective date of section 1551(a)(2) and (3)).

(3) *Example.* This paragraph may be illustrated by the following example:

Example. On January 1, 1964, individual A, who owns 50 percent of the voting stock of corporation X, and individual B, who owns 30 percent of such voting stock, transfer property (other than money) to corporation Y (newly created for the

Reg. § 1.1551-1(e)(3)

purpose of acquiring such property) in exchange for all of Y's voting stock. After the transfer, A and B own the voting stock of corporations X and Y in the following proportions:

Individual	Corporation X	Corporation Y	Identical Ownership
A.........	50	30	30
B.........	30	50	30
Total.....	80	80	60

The transfer of property by A and B to corporation Y is a transfer described in paragraph (a)(3) of this section since (i) A and B own at least 80 percent of the voting stock of corporations X and Y, and (ii) taking into account each such individual's stock ownership only to the extent such ownership is identical with respect to each such corporation, A and B own more than 50 percent of the voting stock of corporations X and Y.

(f) *Taxable year of allowance or disallowance*—(1) *In general.* The district director's authority with respect to cases covered by section 1551 is not limited to the taxable year of the transferee corporation in which the transfer of property occurs. Such authority extends to the taxable year in which the transfer occurs or any subsequent taxable year of the transferee corporation if, during any part of such year, the transferor or transferors are in control of the transferee.

(2) *Examples.* This paragraph may be illustrated by the following examples:

Example (1). On January 1, 1955, corporation D transfers property (other than money) to corporation E, a corporation not actively engaged in business at the time of the acquisition of such property, in exchange for 60 percent of the voting stock of E. During a later taxable year of E, corporation D acquires an additional 20 percent of such voting stock. As a result of such additional acquisition, D owns 80 percent of the voting stock of E. Accordingly, section 1551(a)(1) is applicable for the taxable year in which the later acquisition of stock occurred and for each taxable year thereafter in which the requisite control continues.

Example (2). On June 20, 1963, individual A, who owns all of the stock of corporation X, transfers property (other than money) to corporation Y, a corporation not actively engaged in business at the time of the acquisition of such property, in exchange for 60 percent of the voting stock of Y. During a later taxable year of Y, A acquires an additional 20 percent of such voting stock. After such acquisition A owns at least 80 percent of the voting stock of corporations X and Y. Accordingly, section 1551(a)(3) is applicable for the taxable year in which the later acquisition of stock occurred and for each taxable year thereafter in which the requisite control continues.

Example (3). Individuals A and B each owns 50 percent of the stock of corporation X. On January 15, 1964, A transfers property (other than money) to corporation Y (newly created by A for the purpose of acquiring such property) in exchange for all the stock of Y. In a subsequent taxable year of Y, individual B buys 50 percent of the stock which A owns in Y (or he transfers money to Y in exchange for its stock, as a result of which he owns 50 percent of Y's stock). Immediately thereafter the stock ownership of A and B in corporation Y is identical to their stock ownership in corporation X. Accordingly, section 1551(a)(3) is applicable for the taxable year in which B acquires stock in corporation Y (see paragraph (g)(3) of this section) and for each taxable year thereafter in which the requisite control continues. Moreover, if B's acquisition of stock in Y is pursuant to a preexisting agreement with A, A's transfer to Y and B's acquisition of Y's stock are considered a single transaction and section 1551(a)(3) also would be applicable for the taxable year in which A's transfer to Y took place and for each taxable year thereafter in which the requisite control continues.

(g) *Nature of transfer.*—(1) *Corporate transfers before June 13, 1963.* A transfer made before June 13, 1963, by any corporation of all or part of its assets, whether or not such transfer qualifies as a reorganization under section 368, is within the scope of section 1551(a)(1), except that section 1551(a)(1) does not apply to a transfer of money only. For example, the transfer of cash for the purpose of expanding the business of the transferor corporation through the formation of a new corporation is not a transfer within the scope of section 1551(a)(1), irrespective of whether the new corporation uses the cash to purchase from the transferor corporation stock in trade or similar property.

(2) *Corporate transfers after June 12, 1963.* A direct or indirect transfer made after June 12, 1963, by any corporation of all or part of its assets to a transferee corporation, whether or not such transfer qualifies as a reorganization under section 368, is within the scope of section 1551(a)(2) except that section 1551(a)(2) does not apply to a transfer of money only. For example, if a transferor corporation transfers property to its shareholders or to a subsidiary, the transfer of that property by the shareholders or the subsidiary to a transferee corporation as part of the same transaction is a transfer of property by the transferor corporation to which section 1551(a)(2) applies. A transfer of property pursuant to a purchase by a

Reg. § 1.1551-1(f)(1)

transferee corporation from a transferor corporation controlling the transferee is within the scope of section 1551(a)(2), whether or not the purchase follows a transfer of cash from the controlling corporation.

(3) *Other transfers after June 12, 1963.* A direct or indirect transfer made after June 12, 1963, by five or fewer individuals to a transferee corporation, whether or not such transfer qualifies under one or more other provisions of the Code (for example, section 351), is within the scope of section 1551(a)(3) except that section 1551(a)(3) does not apply to a transfer of money only. Thus, if one of five or fewer individuals who are in control of a corporation transfers property (other than money) to a controlled transferee corporation, the transfer is within the scope of section 1551(a)(3) notwithstanding that the other individuals transfer nothing or transfer only money.

(4) *Examples.* This paragraph may be illustrated by the following examples:

Example (1). Individuals A and B each owns 50 percent of the voting stock of corporation X. On January 15, 1964, A and B each acquires property (other than money) from X and, as part of the same transaction, each transfers such property to his wholly owned corporation (newly created for the purpose of acquiring such property). A and B retain substantial continuing interests in corporation X. The transfers to the two newly created corporations are within the scope of section 1551(a)(2).

Example (2). Corporation W organizes corporation X, a wholly owned subsidiary, for the purpose of acquiring the properties of corporation Y. Pursuant to a reorganization qualifying under section 368(a)(1)(C), substantially all of the properties of corporation Y are transferred on June 15, 1963, to corporation X solely in exchange for voting stock of corporation W. There is a transfer of property from W to X within the meaning of section 1551(a)(2).

Example (3). Individuals A and B, each owning 50 percent of the voting stock of corporation X, organize corporation Y to which each transfers money only in exchange for 50 percent of the stock of Y. Subsequently, Y uses such money to acquire other property from A and B after June 12, 1963. Such acquisition is within the scope of section 1551(a)(3).

Example (4). Individual A owns 55 percent of the stock of corporation X. Another 25 percent of corporation X's stock is owned in the aggregate by individuals B, C, D, and E. On June 15, 1963, individual A transfers property to corporation Y (newly created for the purpose of acquiring such property) in exchange for 60 percent of the stock of Y, and B, C, and D acquire all of the remaining stock of Y. The transfer is within the scope of section 1551(a)(3).

(h) *Purpose of transfer.* In determining, for purposes of this section, whether the securing of the surtax exemption or accumulated earnings credit constituted "a major purpose" of the transfer, all circumstances relevant to the transfer shall be considered. "A major purpose" will not be inferred from the mere purchase of inventory by a subsidiary from a centralized warehouse maintained by its parent corporation or by another subsidiary of the parent corporation. For disallowance of the surtax exemption and accumulated earnings credit under section 1551, it is not necessary that the obtaining of either such credit or exemption, or both, have been the sole or principal purpose of the transfer of the property. It is sufficient if it appears, in the light of all the facts and circumstances, that the obtaining of such exemption or credit, or both, was one of the major considerations that prompted the transfer. Thus, the securing of the surtax exemption or the accumulated earnings credit may constitute "a major purpose" of the transfer, notwithstanding that such transfer was effected for a valid business purpose and qualified as a reorganization within the meaning of section 368. The taxpayer's burden of establishing by the clear preponderance of the evidence that the securing of either such exemption or credit or both was not "a major purpose" of the transfer may be met, for example, by showing that the obtaining of such exemption, or credit, or both, was not a major factor in relationship to the other consideration or considerations which prompted the transfer. [Reg. § 1.1551-1.]

☐ [T.D. 6140, 8-29-55. *Amended by* T.D. 6377, 5-12-59; T.D. 6412, 9-10-59; T.D. 6911, 2-23-67 and T.D. 7376, 9-15-75.]

[Reg. § 1.1552-1]

§ 1.1552-1. **Earnings and profits.**—(a) *General rule.* For the purpose of determining the earnings and profits of each member of an affiliated group which is required to be included in a consolidated return for such group filed for a taxable year beginning after December 31, 1953, and ending after August 16, 1954, the tax liability of the group shall be allocated among the members of the group in accordance with one of the following methods, pursuant to an election under paragraph (c) of this section:

(1)(i) The tax liability of the group shall be apportioned among the members of the group in accordance with the ratio which that portion of the consolidated taxable income attributable to each member of the group having taxable income bears to the consolidated taxable income.

Reg. § 1.1552-1(a)(1)

(ii) For consolidated return years beginning after December 31, 1965, a member's portion of the tax liability of the group under the method of allocation provided by subdivision (i) of this subparagraph is an amount equal to the tax liability of the group multiplied by a fraction, the numerator of which is the taxable income of such member, and the denominator of which is the sum of the taxable incomes of all the members. For purposes of this subdivision the taxable income of a member shall be the separate taxable income determined under § 1.1502-12, adjusted for the following items taken into account in the computation of consolidated taxable income:

(a) The portion of the consolidated net operating loss deduction, the consolidated charitable contributions deduction, the consolidated dividends received deduction, the consolidated section 247 deduction, the consolidated section 582(c) net loss, and the consolidated section 922 deduction, attributable to such member;

(b) Such member's capital gain net income (net capital gain for taxable years beginning before January 1, 1977) (determined without regard to any net capital loss carryover attributable to such member);

(c) Such member's net capital loss and section 1231 net loss, reduced by the portion of the consolidated net capital loss attributable to such member; and

(d) The portion of any consolidated net capital loss carryover attributable to such member which is absorbed in the taxable year.

If the computation of the taxable income of a member under this subdivision results in an excess of deductions over gross income, then for purposes of this subdivision such member's taxable income shall be zero.

(2)(i) The tax liability of the group shall be allocated to the several members of the group on the basis of the percentage of the total tax which the tax of such member if computed on a separate return would bear to the total amount of the taxes for all members of the group so computed.

(ii) For consolidated return years beginning after December 31, 1965, a member's portion of the tax liability of the group under the method of allocation provided by subdivision (i) of this subparagraph is an amount equal to the tax liability of the group multiplied by a fraction, the numerator of which is the separate return tax liability of such member, and the denominator of which is the sum of the separate return tax liabilities of all the members. For purposes of this subdivision the separate return tax liability of a member is its tax liability computed as if it has filed a separate return for the year except that—

(a) Gains and losses on intercompany transactions shall be taken into account as provided in § 1.1502-13 as if a consolidated return had been filed for the year;

(b) Gains and losses relating to inventory adjustments shall be taken into account as provided in § 1.1502-18 as if a consolidated return had been filed for the year;

(c) Transactions with respect to stock, bonds, or other obligations of members shall be reflected as provided in § 1.1502-13(f) and (g) as if a consolidated return had been filed for the year;

(d) Excess losses shall be included in income as provided in § 1.1502-19 as if a consolidated return had been filed for the year;

(e) In the computation of the deduction under section 167, property shall not lose its character as new property as a result of a transfer from one member to another member during the year;

(f) A dividend distributed by one member to another member during the year shall not be taken into account in computing the deductions under section 243(a)(1), 244(a), 245, or 247 (relating to deductions with respect to dividends received and dividends paid);

(g) Basis shall be determined under §§ 1.1502-31 and 1.1502-32, and earnings and profits shall be determined under § 1.1502-33, as if a consolidated return had been filed for the year;

(h) Subparagraph (2) of § 1.1502-3(f) shall apply as if a consolidated return had been filed for the year; and

(i) For purposes of subtitle A of the Code, the surtax exemption of the member shall be an amount equal to $25,000 ($50,000 in the case of a taxable year ending in 1975), divided by the number of members (or such portion of $25,000 or $50,000 which is apportioned to the member pursuant to a schedule attached to the consolidated return for the taxable year). (However, if for the taxable year some or all of the members are component members of a controlled group of corporations (within the meaning of section 1563) and if there are other such component members which do not join in filing the consolidated return for such year, the amount to be divided among the members filing the consolidated return shall be (in lieu of $25,000 or $50,000) the sum of the amounts apportioned to the component members which join in filing the consolidated return (as determined for taxable years beginning after December 31, 1974, under § 1.1561-2(a)(2) or § 1.1561-3, whichever is appli-

Reg. § 1.1552-1(a)(2)

cable, and for taxable years beginning before January 1, 1975, under § 1.1561-2A(a)(2) or § 1.1561-3A, whichever is applicable).)

If the computation of the separate return tax liability of a member under this subdivision does not result in a positive tax liability, then for purposes of this subdivision such member's separate return tax liability shall be zero.

(3)(i) The tax liability of the group (excluding the tax increases arising from the consolidation) shall be allocated on the basis of the contribution of each member of the group to the consolidated taxable income of the group. Any tax increases arising from the consolidation shall be distributed to the several members in direct proportion to the reduction in tax liability resulting to such members from the filing of the consolidated return as measured by the difference between their tax liabilities determined on a separate return basis and their tax liabilities (determined without regard to the 2-percent increase provided by section 1503(a) and paragraph (a) of § 1.1502-30A (as contained in the 26 C.F.R. edition revised as of April 1, 1996) for taxable years beginning before Jan. 1, 1964) based on their contributions to the consolidated taxable income.

(ii) For consolidated return years beginning after December 31, 1965, a member's portion of the tax liability of the group under the method of allocation provided by subdivision (i) of this subparagraph shall be determined by—

(*a*) Allocating the tax liability of the group in accordance with subparagraph (1)(ii) of this paragraph, but

(*b*) The amount of tax liability allocated to any member shall not exceed the separate return tax liability of such member, determined in accordance with subparagraph (2)(ii) of this paragraph, and

(*c*) The sum of the amounts which would be allocated to the members but for (*b*) of this subdivision (ii) shall be apportioned among the other members in direct proportion to, but limited to, the reduction in tax liability resulting to such other members. Such reduction for any member shall be the excess, if any, of

(*1*) its separate return tax liability determined in accordance with subparagraph (2)(ii) of this paragraph, over

(*2*) the amount allocated to such member under (*a*) of this subdivision (ii).

If any amount remains after being apportioned among members with a reduction in tax liability to the extent of such reduction, as provided in (*c*) of this subdivision (ii), such remaining amount shall, notwithstanding (*b*) of this subdivision (ii),

be allocated to the members in accordance with the fractions determined under subparagraph (1)(ii) of this paragraph.

(4) The tax liability of the group shall be allocated in accordance with any other method selected by the group with the approval of the Commissioner. No method of allocation may be approved under this subparagraph which may result in the allocation of a positive tax liability for a taxable year, among the members who are allocated a positive tax liability for such year, in a total amount which is more or less than the tax liability of the group for such year. (However, see paragraph (d) of § 1.1502-33.)

(b) *Application of rules*—(1) *Tax liability of the group.* For purposes of section 1552 and this section, the tax liability of the group for a taxable year shall consist of the Federal income tax liability of the group for such year determined in accordance with § 1.1502-2 or § 1.1502-30A (as contained in the 26 C.F.R. edition revised as of April 1, 1996), whichever is applicable. Thus, in the case of a carryback of a loss or credit to such year, although the earnings and profits of the members of the group may not be adjusted until the subsequent taxable year from which the loss or credit was carried back, the effect of the carryback, for purposes of this section, shall be determined by allocating the amount of the adjustment as a part of the tax liability of the group for the taxable year to which the loss or credit is carried. For example, if a consolidated net operating loss is carried back from 1969 to 1967, the allocation of the tax liability of the group for 1967 shall be recomputed in accordance with the method of allocation used for 1967, and the changes resulting from such recomputation shall, for accrual method taxpayers, be reflected in the earnings and profits of the appropriate members in 1969.

(2) *Effect of allocation.* The amount of tax liability allocated to a corporation as its share of the tax liability of the group, pursuant to this section, shall (i) result in a decrease in the earnings and profits of such corporation in such amount, and (ii) be treated as a liability of such corporation for such amount. If the full amount of such liability is not paid by such corporation, pursuant to an agreement among the members of the group or otherwise, the amount which is not paid will generally be treated as a distribution with respect to stock, a contribution to capital, or a combination thereof, as the case may be.

(c) *Method of election.* (1) The election under paragraph (a)(1), (2), or (3) of this section shall be made not later than the time prescribed by law for filing the first consolidated return of the group for a taxable year beginning after December 31,

Reg. § 1.1552-1(c)

1953, and ending after August 16, 1954 (including extensions thereof). If the group elects to allocate its tax liability in accordance with the method prescribed in paragraph (a)(1), (2), or (3) of this section, a statement shall be attached to the return stating which method is elected. Such statement shall be made by the common parent corporation and shall be binding upon all members of the group. In the event that the group desires to allocate its tax liability in accordance with any other method pursuant to paragraph (a)(4) of this section, approval of such method by the Commissioner must be obtained within the time prescribed above. If such approval is not obtained in such time, the group shall allocate in accordance with the method prescribed in paragraph (a)(1) of this section. The request shall state fully the method which the group wishes to apply in apportioning the tax liability. Except as provided in subparagraph (2) of this paragraph, an election once made shall be irrevocable and shall be binding upon the group with respect to the year for which made and for all future years for which a consolidated return is filed or required to be filed unless the Commissioner authorizes a change to another method prior to the time prescribed by law for filing the return for the year in which such change is to be effective.

(2) Each group may make a new election to use any one of the methods prescribed in paragraph (a)(1), (2), or (3) of this section for its first consolidated return year beginning after December 31, 1965, or in conjunction with an election under paragraph (d) of § 1.1502-33, or may request the Commissioner's approval of a method under paragraph (a)(4) of this section for its first consolidated return year beginning after December 31, 1965, irrespective of its previous method of allocation under this section. If such new election is not made in conjunction with an election under paragraph (d) of § 1.1502-33, it shall be effective for the first consolidated return year beginning after December 31, 1965, and all succeeding years. (See § 1.1502-33 for the method of making such new election in conjunction with an election under paragraph (d) of § 1.1502-33.) Any other such new election (or request for the Commissioner's approval of a method under paragraph (a)(4) of this section) shall be made within the time prescribed by law for filing the consolidated return for the first taxable year beginning after December 31, 1965 (including extensions thereof), or within 60 days after July 3, 1968, whichever is later. Such new election shall be made by attaching a statement to the consolidated return for the first taxable year beginning after December 31, 1965, or if such election is made within the time prescribed above but after such return is filed, by filing a statement with the internal revenue officer with whom such return was filed.

(d) *Failure to elect.* If a group fails to make an election in its first consolidated return, or any other election, in accordance with paragraph (c) of this section, the method prescribed under paragraph (a)(1) of this section shall be applicable and shall be binding upon the group in the same manner as if an election had been made to so allocate.

(e) *Definitions.* Except as otherwise provided in this section, the terms used in this section shall have the same meaning as provided in the regulations under section 1502.

(f) *Example.* The provisions of this section may be illustrated by the following example:

Example. Corporation P is the common parent owning all of the stock of corporations S1 and S2, members of an affiliated group. A consolidated return is filed for the taxable year ending December 31, 1966, by P, S1, and S2. For 1966 such corporations had the following taxable incomes or losses computed in accordance with paragraph (a)(1)(ii) of this section:

```
P............................... $    0
S1...............................  2,000
S2...............................  (1,000)
```

The group has not made an election under paragraph (c) of this section or paragraph (d) of § 1.1502-33. Accordingly, the method of allocation provided by paragraph (a)(1) of this section is in effect for the group. Assuming that the consolidated taxable income is equal to the sum of the members' taxable income and losses, or $1,000, the tax liability of the group for the year (assuming a 22-percent rate) is $220, all of which is allocated to S1. S1 accordingly reduces its earnings and profits in the amount of $220, irrespective of who actually pays the tax liability. If S1 pays the $220 tax liability there will be no further effect upon the income, earnings and profits, or the basis of stock of any member. If, however, P pays the $220 tax liability (and such payment is not in fact a loan from P to S1), then P shall be treated as having made a contribution to the capital of S1 in the amount of $220. On the other hand, if S2 pays the $220 tax liability (and such payment is not in fact a loan from S2), then S2 shall be treated as having made a distribution with respect to its stock to P in the amount of $220, anshall be treated as having made a contribution to the capital of S1 in the amount of $220. [Reg. § 1.1552-1.]

☐ [*T.D.* 6140, 8-29-55. *Amended by T.D.* 6962, 7-2-68; *T.D.* 7528, 12-27-77; *T.D.* 7728, 10-31-80; *T.D.* 8560, 8-12-94; *T.D.* 8597, 7-12-95 *and T.D.* 8677, 6-26-96.]

Certain Controlled Corporations

[Reg. § 1.1561-0]

§ 1.1561-0. Effective date.—(a) *Taxable years beginning after December 31, 1974.* The provisions of §§ 1.1561-1 through 1.1561-3 apply only to taxable years beginning after December 31, 1974.

(b) *Taxable years beginning before January 1, 1975.* The provisions of §§ 1.1561-1A through 1.1561-3A apply only to taxable years beginning before January 1, 1975. [Reg. § 1.1561-0.]

☐ [T.D. 7528, 12-27-77.]

[Reg. § 1.1561-1]

§ 1.1561-1. Limitations on certain multiple tax benefits in the case of certain controlled corporations.—(a) *In general.* Part II (section 1561 and following), subchapter B, chapter 6 of the Code, provides rules relating to certain controlled corporations. In general, section 1561 provides that the component members of a controlled group of corporations on a December 31, for their taxable years which include such December 31, shall be limited for purposes of subtitle A to

(1) One surtax exemption under section 11(d),

(2) One $150,000 amount for purposes of computing the accumulated earnings credit under section 535(c)(2) and (3), and

(3) One $25,000 amount for purposes of computing the limitation on the small business deduction of life insurance companies under sections 804(a)(4) and 809(d)(10).

For certain definitions (including the definition of a "controlled group of corporations" and a "component member") and special rules for purposes of part II of subchapter B, see section 1563 and the regulations thereunder.

(b) *Tax avoidance.* The provisions of part II, subchapter B, chapter 6 do not delimit or abrogate any principle of law established by judicial decision, or any existing provisions of the Code, such as sections 269, 482, and 1551, which have the effect of preventing the avoidance or evasion of income taxes.

(c) *Special rules.* (1) For purposes of sections 1561 and 1563 and the regulations thereunder, the term "corporation" includes an electing small business corporation (as defined in section 1371(b)). However, for the treatment of an electing small business corporation as an excluded member of a controlled group of corporations, see paragraph (b)(2)(ii) of § 1.1563-1.

(2) In the case of corporations electing a 52-53-week taxable year under section 441(f)(1), the provisions of sections 1561 and 1563 and the regulations thereunder shall be applied in accordance with the special rule of section 441(f)(2)(A). See paragraph (b)(1) of § 1.441-2. [Reg. § 1.1561-1.]

☐ [T.D. 7528, 12-27-77.]

[Reg. § 5.1561-1]

§ 5.1561-1. Taxable years of component members of controlled group of corporations that include December 31, 1978 (Temporary).—(a) *In general.* This section prescribes a regulation for applying sections 301(a) and (b)(19), and 106, of the Revenue Act of 1978 (the Act) in the case of certain taxable years of component members of a controlled group of corporations (as defined in section 1563 of the Internal Revenue Code). The section applies only to taxable years that include December 31, 1978, and only if the taxable year of at least one component member ends in 1979.

(b) *Background.* Section 301(a) of the Act amends section 11 of the Code (relating to tax imposed on corporations) to provide for taxable income brackets that are subject to tax at rates less than the maximum rate of 46 percent. Section 301(b)(19) of the Act amends section 1561(a) of the Code (relating to limitations on certain multiple tax benefits in the case of certain controlled corporations) to limit the component members of a controlled group to an aggregate amount in each bracket which does not exceed the maximum amount in such bracket to which a corporation which is not a component member of a controlled group is entitled. Section 106 of the Act amends section 21 of the Code (relating to effect of changes in rate of tax) to provide that the amendments made by section 301 of the Act shall be treated as a change in a rate of tax. Since the amendments made by section 301 of the Act are effective for taxable years beginning after December 31, 1978, under the amendment to section 21 the effective date of the change in rate of tax is January 1, 1979.

(c) *No apportionment plan in effect.* If no apportionment plan (see § 1.1561-3 of the Income Tax Regulations) is in effect with respect to December 31, 1978, the single $50,000 surtax exemption available before January 1, 1979, and the single bracket amounts available after December 31, 1978, shall be equally divided among the component members of the controlled group on December 31, 1978. In the case of a controlled group which includes component members that join in the filing of a consolidated return and other component members that do not join in the filing of such a return, each component member of the group (including each component member that joins in filing the consolidated return) shall be

Reg. § 5.1561-1(c)

treated as a separate corporation for purposes of equally apportioning the $50,000 surtax exemption in effect before January 1, 1979, and the bracket amounts in effect after December 31, 1978. In such a case, the surtax exemption and bracket amounts of the corporations filing the consolidated return shall be the sum of the amount apportioned to each component member that joins in filing the consolidated return.

(d) *Apportionment plan.* (1) If one or more component members of the controlled group have a calendar taxable year and if an apportionment plan is adopted under § 1.1561-3 apportioning the entire $50,000 surtax exemption available for 1978 to such calendar-year members, then the amount in each taxable income bracket available for fiscal-year members is zero. If only a part of the $50,000 surtax exemption is apportioned to calendar-year members, then a proportionate part of the $25,000 amount in each taxable income bracket is available for the fiscal-year members. For example, if $30,000 (3/5 of $50,000) is apportioned to calendar-year members, 2/5 of the $25,000 amount in each bracket, or $10,000, as well as the remaining 2/5 of the 1978 surtax exemption, is available to the fiscal-year members.

(2) The amount in each taxable income bracket available to fiscal-year members may be apportioned among such members in any manner the controlled group may select. For example, the available amount in the first bracket (subject to a 17-percent rate) may be allocated to one member, the amount in the second bracket (subject to a 20-percent rate) may be allocated to another member, and so on. Moreover, the available amount in each bracket may be divided among the members in any manner the group may select.

(3) In computing 1978 tentative taxes under section 21, the total surtax exemption available to fiscal-year members for 1978 must be divided among such members in the same proportion as the sum of the available amount in each bracket is divided among them. Thus, if the sum of the available bracket amount is $100,000 (i.e., $25,000 in each bracket), and if corporation X is apportioned 30 percent, or $30,000, of this amount (regardless of which brackets corporation X may select), then 30 percent of the surtax exemption available to the fiscal-year members for 1978 (i.e., 30 percent of $50,000, or $15,000) must be apportioned to corporation X.

(e) *Corporations affected.* The provisions of section 1561 may reduce the surtax exemption or bracket amounts of any corporation which is a component member of a controlled group of corporations and which is subject to the tax imposed by section 11, or by any other provision of subtitle A of the Code if the tax under such other provisions is computed by reference to the tax imposed by section 11. Such other provisions include, for example, sections 511(a)(1), 594, 802, 831, 852, 857, 882, 1201, and 1378.

(f) *Example.* This section may be illustrated by the following example:

Example. Corporations X, Y, and Z are component members of a controlled group of corporations on December 31, 1978. X has taxable income of $10,000 for the taxable year ending December 31, 1978. Y has taxable income of $60,000 for the taxable year ending June 30, 1979. Z has taxable income of $90,000 for the taxable year ending September 30, 1979. The group files an apportionment plan under § 1.1561-3 apportioning $10,000 (i.e., 1/5 of $50,000) to X, the calendar-year member. Therefore, 4/5 of the amount in each bracket, or $20,000, is available to Y and Z, the fiscal-year members. Under the plan, Y is apportioned the entire amount in the first bracket and $10,000 of the amount in the second bracket. Z is apportioned $10,000 of the amount in the second bracket and the entire amount in the third and fourth brackets. Therefore, Y is apportioned $30,000, or 3/8 of the total available amounts in the four brackets, and Z is apportioned $50,000, or 5/8 of the total available amount. The tax liabilities of Y and Z for their taxable years ending in 1979 are computed as follows: (Computation of X's tax liability for 1978, using a surtax exemption of $10,000, is not shown.)

1979 Tentative Tax

	Y
Taxable income	$60,000
Tax on amount in first bracket: 17 percent of $20,000	$ 3,400
Tax on amount in second bracket: 20 percent of $10,000	2,000
Tax on remaining income: 46 percent of $30,000	13,800
1979 tentative tax	$19,200

Reg. § 5.1561-1(d)(2)

Certain Controlled Corporations

See p. 20,601 for regulations not amended to reflect law changes

	Z
Taxable income	$90,000

Tax on amount in second bracket:	
20 percent of $10,000	$ 2,000
Tax on amount in third bracket:	
30 percent of $20,000	6,000
Tax on amount in fourth bracket:	
40 percent of $20,000	8,000
Tax on remaining income:	
46 percent of $40,000	18,400
1979 tentative tax	$34,400

1978 Tentative Tax

	Y
Taxable income	$60,000

Normal tax:		
20 percent of $7,500 (3/8 of $20,000)		$ 1,500
22 percent of $52,500		11,550
		$13,050
Surtax:		
Taxable income	$60,000	
Surtax exemption	15,000 (3/8 of $40,000)	
	$45,000 × 26 percent	11,700
1978 tentative tax		$24,750

	Z
Taxable income	$90,000

Normal tax:		
20 percent of $12,500 (5/8 of $20,000)		$ 2,500
22 percent of $77,500		17,050
		$19,500
Surtax:		
Taxable income	$90,000	
Surtax exemption	25,000 (5/8 of $40,000)	
	$65,000 × 26 percent	$16,900
1978 tentative tax		$36,450

The 1978 and 1979 tentative taxes are apportioned as follows:

Corporation Y:

1978—184/365 of $24,750	$12,477
1979—181/365 of $19,200	9,521
Total tax for taxable year	$21,998

Corporation Z:

1978— 92/365 of $36,450	$ 9,187
1979—273/365 of $34,400	25,729
Total tax for taxable year	$34,916

[Temporary Reg. § 5.1561-1.]   ☐ [T.D. 7583, 1-2-79.]

Reg. § 5.1561-1(f)

[Reg. § 1.1561-2]

§ 1.1561-2. Determination of amount of tax benefits.—(a) *Surtax exemption.* (1) If a corporation is a component member of a controlled group of corporations on a December 31, the surtax exemption under section 11(d) of such corporation for the taxable year which includes such December 31 shall be an amount equal to—

(i) $50,000 divided by the number of corporations which are component members of such group on such December 31, or

(ii) If an apportionment plan is adopted under § 1.1561-3 which is effective with respect to such taxable year, such portion of $50,000 as is apportioned to such member in accordance with such plan.

(2) In the case of a controlled group of corporations which includes component members which join in the filing of a consolidated return and other component members which do not join in the filing of such a return, and where there is no apportionment plan effective under § 1.1561-3 apportioning the $50,000 amount among the component members filing the consolidated return and the other component members of the controlled group, each component member of the controlled group (including each component member which joins in filing the consolidated return) shall be treated as a separate corporation for purposes of equally apportioning the $50,000 amount under subparagraph (1)(i) of this paragraph. In such case, the surtax exemption of the corporations filing the consolidated return shall be the sum of the amounts apportioned to each component member which joins in filing the consolidated return.

(3) The provisions of section 1561 may reduce the surtax exemption of any corporation which is a component member of a controlled group of corporations and which is subject to the tax imposed by section 11, or by any other provision of subtitle A of the Code if the tax under such other provisions is computed by reference to the amount of the surtax exemption provided by section 11. Such other provisions include, for example, sections 511(a)(1), 594, 802, 831, 852, 857, 882, 1201, and 1378.

(4) This paragraph (a) shall not apply with respect to any component member of a controlled group of corporations on a December 31 if one or more component members of such controlled group has a taxable year including such December 31 which ends after December 31, 1978. Rules pertaining to the apportionment of the surtax exemption with respect to component members of controlled groups of corporations to which this paragraph does not apply are reserved.

(5) The application of this paragraph may be illustrated by the following examples:

Example (1). Corporations W, X, Y, and Z are component members of a controlled group of corporations on December 31, 1975, and each corporation files its income tax return on the basis of a calendar year. For their taxable years ending on December 31, 1975, W and X each incurs a net operating loss; Y has $5,250 of taxable income; and Z has $30,000 of taxable income. If an apportionment plan is not effective for such taxable years, the surtax exemption under section 11(d) of each corporation determined under subparagraph (1)(i) of this paragraph is $12,500 ($50,000 ÷ 4). However, the four corporations may avoid a pro rata division of the $50,000 amount by filing an apportionment plan in accordance with the provisions of § 1.1561-3 allocating the $50,000 amount in any manner they deem proper.

Example (2). Corporation A files its income tax return on the basis of a calendar year; corporation B files its income tax return on the basis of a fiscal year ending March 31. On December 31, 1975, A and B are the only component members of a controlled group of corporations. Under subparagraph (1)(i) of this paragraph, the surtax exemption of A for 1975, and the surtax exemption of B for its fiscal year ending March 31, 1976, is $25,000 ($50,000 ÷ 2). However, if an apportionment plan is filed in accordance with the provisions of § 1.1561-3, the surtax exemption of each such corporation will be the amount apportioned to the corporation pursuant to the plan.

Example (3). Corporations R, P, and S are component members of a controlled group of corporations on December 31, 1975. P and S file a consolidated return for their fiscal years ending June 30, 1976. R files a separate return for its taxable year ending on December 31, 1975. No apportionment plan is effective with respect to R's, P's, and S's taxable years which include December 31, 1975. Therefore, R, P, and S are each apportioned $16,666.67 ($50,000 ÷ 3) as their surtax exemption under section 11(d) for their taxable years including such date. The surtax exemption of the affiliated group filing a consolidated return (P and S) for the year ending June 30, 1976, is $33,333.34 (i.e., the sum of $16,666.67 amounts apportioned to P and S). However, if an apportionment plan is filed in accordance with the provisions of § 1.1561-3, the surtax exemption of the corporations which are members of the affiliated group filing a consolidated return and of each other corporation which is a component member of the controlled group of corporations will be the amount apportioned to such affiliated group and to each such other corporation pursuant to the plan.

(b) *Allocation of amounts of taxable income subject to normal tax.* (1) In the case of a taxable year of a corporation, if—

(i) The amount of normal tax under section 11(b) is equal to the sum of 20 percent of so much of the taxable income as does not exceed $25,000, plus 22 percent of so much of the taxable income as exceeds $25,000 for a taxable year, and

(ii) The amount of surtax exemption of the corporation is less than $50,000 under paragraph (a)(1)(i) or (ii) of this section,

then for purposes of applying section 11(b), the taxable income subject to taxation at the rate of 20 percent shall be (in lieu of the first $25,000 of taxable income) one-half of the amount of the surtax exemption allocated to such corporation under paragraph (a)(1)(i) or (ii) of this section. In addition, the amount of taxable income subject to taxation at the rate of 22 percent shall be (in lieu of the amount of taxable income in excess of $25,000) the taxable income that exceeds one-half of the amount of the surtax exemption allocated to such corporation under paragraph (a)(1)(i) or (ii) of this section for such year. In the case of an affiliated group of corporations filing a consolidated return for a taxable year, the preceding sentence shall be applied by substituting the term "affiliated group" for the term "corporation" each time it appears.

(2) The provisions of this paragraph may be illustrated by the following example:

Example. Corporations P and S are component members of a controlled group of corporations on December 31, 1975, and each corporation files a separate income tax return on the basis of a calendar year. For the taxable year ending on December 31, 1975, P incurs a net operating loss and S has $25,000 of taxable income. If an apportionment plan is not effective for that taxable year, the surtax exemption under section 11(d) of each corporation (determined under paragraph (a)(1)(i) of this section) is $25,000 ($50,000 ÷ 2). For purposes of applying section 11(b) to determine S's liability for tax for 1975, the amount of taxable income subject to taxation at the rate of 20 percent is limited to $12,500 (i.e., one-half of the amount of the surtax exemption allocated to S under paragraph (a)(1)(i) of this section), and the amount of taxable income subject to taxation at the rate of 22 percent is $12,500 (i.e., the amount of taxable income in excess of one-half of the amount of the surtax exemption). If, on the other hand, an apportionment plan is adopted by P and S effective for such taxable years apportioning the entire $50,000 surtax exemption to S, then, for purposes of applying section 11(b) to determine S's liability for tax for 1975, the amount of taxable income subject to taxation at the rate of 20 percent is $25,000.

(3) If an apportionment plan is adopted under § 1.1561-3 for a December 31, and if paragraph (b)(1) of this section applies to any component member whose taxable year includes such December 31, then the plan shall specify—

(i) The amount subject to taxation at the rate of 20 percent, and

(ii) The amount subject to taxation at the rate of 22 percent

as determined under paragraph (b)(1) of this section for each component member. The information required to be included in a plan by this subparagraph is in addition to the information required under § 1.1561-3(a). Where an existing apportionment plan is effective under § 1.1561-3(a)(3) for such December 31, the additional information required under this subparagraph may be provided in an amendment of the existing plan as provided in § 1.1561-3(c).

(c) *Accumulated earnings credit.* (1) Except as provided in subparagraph (2) of this paragraph, if a corporation is a component member of a controlled group on a December 31, the amount for purposes of computing the accumulated earnings credit under section 535(c)(2) and (3) of such corporation shall be an amount equal to $150,000 divided by the number of corporations which are component members of such group on such December 31. In the case of a controlled group of corporations which includes component members which join in the filing of a consolidated return and other component members which do not join in the filing of such a return, each component member of the controlled group (including each component member which joins in filing the consolidated return) shall be treated as a separate corporation for purposes of equally apportioning the $150,000 amount under this subparagraph. In such case, the amount for purposes of computing the accumulated earnings credit for the component members filing the consolidated return shall be the sum of the amounts apportioned to each component member which joins in filing the consolidated return.

(2) If, with respect to any component member of the controlled group, the amount determined under subparagraph (1) of this paragraph exceeds the sum of (i) such member's accumulated earnings and profits as of the close of the preceding taxable year, plus (ii) such member's earnings and profits for the taxable year which are retained (within the meaning of section 535(c)(1)), then any such excess shall be subtracted from the

Reg. § 1.1561-2(c)(2)

amount determined under subparagraph (1) of this paragraph with respect to such member and shall be divided equally among those remaining component members of the controlled group that do not have such an excess (until no such excess remains to be divided among those remaining members that have not had such an excess). The excess so divided among such remaining members shall be added to the amount determined under subparagraph (1) with respect to such members. If a controlled group of corporations includes component members which join in the filing of a consolidated return and other component members which do not join in filing such return, the component members filing the consolidated return shall be treated as a single corporation for purposes of this subparagraph.

(3) A controlled group may not adopt an apportionment plan, as provided in § 1.1561-3, with respect to the amounts computed under the provisions of this paragraph.

(4) The provisions of this paragraph may be illustrated by the following example:

Example. A controlled group is composed of four component member corporations, W, X, Y, and Z. Each corporation files a separate income tax return on the basis of a calendar year. The sum of the earnings and profits for the taxable year ending December 31, 1975, which are retained plus the sum of the accumulated earnings and profits (as of the close of the preceding taxable year) is $15,000, $75,000, $37,500, and $300,000 for W, X, Y, and Z, respectively. The amounts determined under this paragraph for W, X, Y, and Z for 1975 are $15,000, $48,750, $37,500, and $48,750, respectively, computed as follows:

	Component members			
	W	X	Y	Z
Earnings and profits	$15,000	$75,000	$37,500	$300,000
Amount computed under subparagraph (1)	37,500	37,500	37,500	37,500
Excess	22,500	0	0	0
Allocation of excess		7,500	7,500	7,500
New excess			7,500	
Reallocation of new excess		3,750		3,750
Amount to be used for purposes of section 535(c)(2) and (3)	$15,000	$48,750	$37,500	$ 48,750

(d) *Small business deduction of life insurance companies.* (1) Except as provided in subparagraph (2) of this paragraph, if two or more life insurance companies which are taxable under section 802 are component members of a controlled group of corporations on a December 31, the amount for purposes of computing the limitation on the small business deduction under sections 804(a)(4) and 809(d)(10) of such corporations for their taxable years which include such December 31 shall be an amount equal to $25,000 divided by the number of life insurance companies taxable under section 802 which are component members of such group on such December 31.

(2) If, with respect to any of the component members of the controlled group which are described in subparagraph (1) of this paragraph, the amount determined under such subparagraph exceeds 10 percent of such member's investment yield (as defined in section 804(c)), then any such excess shall be subtracted from the amount determined under subparagraph (1) of this paragraph with respect to such member and shall be divided equally among those remaining life insurance company members of the controlled group that do not have such an excess (until no such excess remains to be divided among those remaining members that have not had such an excess). The excess so divided among such remaining members shall be added to the amount determined under subparagraph (1) with respect to such members.

(3) A controlled group may not adopt an apportionment plan, as provided in § 1.1561-3, with respect to the amounts computed under the provisions of this paragraph.

(e) *Certain short taxable years.* (1) If the return of a corporation is for a short period which does not include a December 31, and such corporation is a component member of a controlled group of corporations with respect to such short period, then for purposes of subtitle A of the Code—

(i) The surtax exemption under section 11(d) of such corporation for such short period shall be an amount equal to $50,000 ($25,000 in the case of certain taxable years), divided by the number of corporations which are component members of such controlled group on the last day of such short period;

(ii) The amount to be used in computing the accumulated earnings credit under section 535(c)(2) and (3) of such corporation for such short period shall be an amount equal to $150,000 divided by the number of corporations which are members of such controlled group on the last day of such short period; and

Reg. § 1.1561-2(c)(3)

(iii) The amount to be used in computing the limitation on the small business deduction of life insurance companies under sections 804(a)(4) and 809(d)(10) of such corporation for such short period shall not exceed an amount equal to $25,000 divided by the number of life insurance companies taxable under section 802 which are component members of the controlled group on the last day of such short period.

For purposes of the preceding sentence, the term "short period" does not include any period if the income for such period is required to be included in a consolidated return under § 1.1502-76. The determination of whether a corporation is a component member of a controlled group of corporations on the last day of a short period is made by applying the definition of "component member" contained in section 1563(b) and § 1.1563-1 as if the last day of such short period were a December 31 occurring after December 31, 1974.

(2) *Examples.* The provisions of this paragraph may be illustrated by the following examples:

Example (1). On January 2, 1975, corporation X transfers cash to newly formed corporation Y (which begins business on that date) and receives all of the stock of Y in return. X also owns all of the stock of corporation Z on each day of 1974 and 1975. X uses the calendar year as its taxable year and Z uses a fiscal year ending on March 31. Y adopts a fiscal year ending on June 30 as its annual accounting period, and, therefore, files a return for the short taxable year beginning on January 2, 1975, and ending on June 30, 1975. On June 30, 1975, Y is a component member of a parent-subsidiary controlled group of corporations of which X, Y, and Z are component members. Accordingly, the surtax exemption of Y for the short taxable year ending on June 30, 1975, is $16,666.67 ($50,000 ÷ 3). On December 31, 1975, X, Y and Z are component members of a parent-subsidiary controlled group of corporations. Accordingly, the surtax exemption of each such corporation for its taxable year including December 31, 1975 (i.e., X's calendar year ending December 31, 1975, Z's fiscal year ending March 31, 1976, and Y's fiscal year ending June 30, 1976) is $16,666.67 ($50,000 ÷ 3), or, if an apportionment plan is filed under § 1.1561-3, the amount apportioned pursuant to such plan.

Example (2). On January 1, 1975, corporation P owns all of the stock of corporations S-1, S-2, and S-3. P, S-1, S-2, and S-3 file separate returns on a calendar year basis. On July 31, 1975, S-1 is liquidated and therefore files a return for the short taxable year beginning on January 1, 1975, and ending on July 31, 1975. On August 31, 1975, S-2 is liquidated and therefore files a return for the short taxable year beginning on January 1, 1975, and ending on August 31, 1975. On July 31, 1975, S-1 is a component member of a parent-subsidiary controlled group of corporations of which P, S-1, S-2, and S-3 are component members. Accordingly, the surtax exemption under section 11(d) of S-1 for the short taxable year ending on July 31, 1975, is $12,500 ($50,000 ÷ 4). On August 31, 1975, S-2 is a component member of a parent-subsidiary controlled group of corporations of which P, S-2, and S-3 are component members. Accordingly, the surtax exemption of S-2 for the short taxable year ending on August 31, 1975, is $16,666.67 ($50,000 ÷ 3). On December 31, 1975, P and S-3 are component members of a parent-subsidiary controlled group of corporations. Accordingly, the surtax exemption of each such corporation for the calendar year 1975 is $25,000 ($50,000 ÷ 2), or, if an apportionment plan is filed under § 1.1561-3, the amount apportioned pursuant to such plan. [Reg. § 1.1561-2.]

☐ [*T.D.* 7528, 12-27-77.]

[Reg. § 1.1561-3]

§ 1.1561-3. Apportionment of surtax exemption.—(a) *In general.* (1) In the case of corporations which are component members of a controlled group of corporations on a December 31, the single $50,000 surtax exemption under section 11(d) may be apportioned among such members (for the taxable year of each such member which includes such December 31) if all such members consent, in the manner provided in paragraph (b) of this section, to an apportionment plan with respect to such December 31. Such plan shall provide for the apportionment of a fixed dollar amount to one or more of such members, but in no event shall the sum of the amounts so apportioned exceed $50,000. An apportionment plan shall not be considered as adopted with respect to a particular December 31 until each component member which is required to consent to the plan under paragraph (b)(1) of this section files the original of a statement described in such paragraph (or, the original of a statement incorporating its consent is filed on its behalf). In the case of a return filed before a plan is adopted, the surtax exemption for purposes of such return shall be equally apportioned in accordance with the rules provided in § 1.1561-2(a)(1)(i). (If a valid apportionment plan is adopted after the return is filed and within the time prescribed by subparagraph (2) of this paragraph, such return should be amended (or a claim for refund should be made) to reflect the change from equal apportionment.)

(2) A controlled group may adopt an apportionment plan with respect to a particular De-

Reg. § 1.1561-3(a)(2)

cember 31 only if, at the time such plan is sought to be adopted, there is at least one year remaining in the statutory period (including any extensions thereof) for the assessment of a deficiency against any corporation the tax liability of which would be increased by the adoption of such plan. If there is less than one year remaining with respect to any such corporation, the director of the service center with which such corporation files its income tax return will ordinarily, upon request, enter into an agreement to extend such statutory period for the limited purpose of assessing any deficiency against such corporation attributable to the adoption of such apportionment plan.

(3)(i) The amount apportioned to a component member of a controlled group of corporations in an apportionment plan adopted with respect to a particular December 31 shall constitute such member's surtax exemption for its taxable year including the particular December 31, and for all taxable years of such members including succeeding December 31's, unless the apportionment plan is amended in accordance with paragraph (c) of this section or is terminated under subdivision (ii) of this subparagraph. Thus, the apportionment plan (including any amendments thereof) has a continuing effect and need not be renewed annually.

(ii) If an apportionment plan is adopted with respect to a particular December 31, such plan shall terminate with respect to a succeeding December 31, if—

(a) The controlled group ceases to remain in existence during the calendar year ending on such succeeding December 31,

(b) Any corporation which was a component member of such group on the particular December 31 is not a component member of such group on such succeeding December 31, or

(c) Any corporation which was not a component member of such group on the particular December 31 is a component member of such group on such succeeding December 31.

An apportionment plan, once terminated with respect to a December 31, is no longer effective. Accordingly, unless a new apportionment plan is adopted, the surtax exemption of the component members of the controlled group for their taxable years which include such December 31 and all December 31's thereafter will be determined in accordance with the rules provided in paragraph (a)(1)(i) of § 1.1561-2.

(iii) For purposes of subdivision (ii)(a)— (a) A parent-subsidiary controlled group of corporations shall be considered as remaining in existence as long as its common parent corporation remains as a common parent.

(b) A brother-sister controlled group of corporations shall be considered as remaining in existence as long as the requirements of paragraph (a)(3)(i) of § 1.1563-1 continue to be satisfied with respect to at least two corporations, taking into account the stock ownership of only those five or fewer persons whose stock ownership was taken into account at the time the apportionment plan adopted by the component members of such group first became effective.

(c) A combined group of corporations shall be considered as remaining in existence as long as the brother-sister controlled group of corporations referred to in paragraph (a)(4)(i) of § 1.1563-1 in respect of such combined group remains in existence (within the meaning of (b) of this subdivision), and at least one such corporation is a common parent of a parent-subsidiary controlled group of corporations referred to in such paragraph (a)(4)(i).

(d) If, by reason of paragraph (a)(5)(i) of § 1.1563-1, two or more insurance companies subject to taxation under section 802 are treated as an insurance group separate from any corporations which are members of a controlled group described in paragraph (a)(2), (3), or (4) of § 1.1563-1, such insurance group shall be considered as remaining in existence as long as the controlled group described in paragraph (a)(2), (3), or (4) of such section, as the case may be, remains in existence (within the meaning of (a), (b), or (c) of this subdivision), and there are at least two insurance companies which satisfy the requirements of paragraph (a)(5)(i) of such section.

(iv) If an apportionment plan is terminated with respect to a particular December 31 by reason of an occurrence described in subdivision (ii)(b) or (c) of this subparagraph, each corporation which is a component member of the controlled group on such particular December 31 should, on or before the date it files its income tax return for the taxable year which includes such particular December 31, notify the service center with which it files such return of such termination. If an apportionment plan is terminated with respect to a particular December 31 by reason of an occurrence described in subdivision (ii)(a) of this subparagraph, each corporation which was a component member of the controlled group on the preceding December 31 should, on or before the date it files its income tax return for the taxable year which includes such particular December 31, notify the service center with which it files such return of such termination.

(b) *Consents to plan.* (1)(i) The consent of a component member (other than a wholly-owned subsidiary) to an apportionment plan with respect to a particular December 31 shall be made by means of a statement, signed by any person who is duly authorized to act on behalf of the consenting member, stating that such member consents to the apportionment plan with respect to such December 31. The statement shall set forth the name, address, taxpayer account number, and taxable year of the consenting component member, the amount apportioned to such member under the plan, and the service center where the original of the statement is to be filed. The consent of more than one component member may be incorporated in a single statement. The original of a statement of consent shall be filed with the service center with which the component member of the group on such December 31 which has the taxable year ending first on or after such date filed its return for such taxable year. (If two or more component members have the same such taxable year, a statement of consent may be filed with the service center with which the return for any such taxable year is filed.) The original of a statement of consent shall have attached thereto information (referred to in this paragraph as "group identification") setting forth the name, address, taxpayer account number, and taxable year of each component member of the controlled group on such December 31 (including wholly-owned subsidiaries) and the amount apportioned to each such member under the plan. If more than one original statement is filed, a statement may incorporate the group identification by reference to the name, address, taxpayer account number, and taxable year of a component member of the group which has attached such group identification to the original of its statement.

(ii) Each component member of the group on such December 31 (other than wholly-owned subsidiaries) should attach a copy of its consent (or a copy of the statement incorporating its consent) to the income tax return, amended return, or claim for refund filed with its service center for the taxable year including such date. Such copy shall either have attached thereto information on group identification or shall incorporate such information by reference to the name, address, taxpayer account number, and taxable year of a component member of the group which has attached such information to its income tax return, amended return, or claim for refund filed with the same service center for the taxable year including such date.

(2)(i) Each component member of a controlled group which is a wholly-owned subsidiary of such group with respect to a December 31 shall be deemed to consent to an apportionment plan with respect to such December 31, provided each component member of the group which is not a wholly-owned subsidiary consents to the plan. For purposes of this section, a component member of a controlled group shall be considered to be a wholly-owned subsidiary of the group with respect to a December 31 if, on each day preceding such date during its taxable year which includes such date, all of its stock is owned directly by one or more corporations which are component members of the group on such December 31.

(ii) Each wholly-owned subsidiary of a controlled group with respect to a December 31 should attach a statement containing the information which is required to be set forth in a statement of consent to an apportionment plan with respect to such December 31 to the income tax return, amended return, or claim for refund filed with its service center for the taxable year which includes such date. Such statement should either have attached thereto information on group identification or incorporate such information by reference to the name, address, taxpayer account number, and taxable year of a component member of the group which has attached such information to its income tax return, amended return, or claim for refund filed with the same service center for the taxable year including such date.

(c) *Amendment of plan.* An apportionment plan adopted with respect to a December 31 by a controlled group of corporations may be amended with respect to such December 31, or with respect to any succeeding December 31 for which the plan is effective under paragraph (a)(3) of this section. An apportionment plan must be amended with respect to a particular December 31 and the amendments to the plan shall be effective only if adopted in accordance with the rules prescribed in this section for the adoption of an original plan with respect to such December 31.

(d) *Component members filing consolidated returns.* If the component members of a controlled group of corporations on a December 31 include corporations which join in the filing of a consolidated return, the corporations filing the consolidated return shall be treated as a single component member for purposes of this section. Thus, for example, only one consent, executed by the common parent, to an apportionment plan filed pursuant to this section is required on behalf of the component members filing the consolidated return. [Reg. § 1.1561-3.]

☐ [T.D. 7528, 12-27-77.]

[Reg. § 1.1563-1]

§ 1.1563-1. **Definition of controlled group of corporations and component members.**—(a) *Controlled group of corporations*—(1) *In general.*

Certain Controlled Corporations

See p. 20,601 for regulations not amended to reflect law changes

For purposes of sections 1561 through 1563 and the regulations thereunder, the term "controlled group of corporations" means any group of corporations which is either a "parent-subsidiary controlled group" (as defined in subparagraph (2) of this paragraph), a "brother-sister controlled group" (as defined in subparagraph (3) of this paragraph), a "combined group" (as defined in subparagraph (4) of this paragraph), or an "insurance group" (as defined in subparagraph (5) of this paragraph). For the exclusion of certain stock for purposes of applying the definitions contained in this paragraph, see section 1563(c) and § 1.1563-2.

(2) *Parent-subsidiary controlled group.* (i) The term "parent-subsidiary controlled group" means one or more chains of corporations connected through stock ownership with a common parent corporation if—

(a) Stock possessing at least 80 percent of the total combined voting power of all classes of stock entitled to vote or at least 80 percent of the total value of shares of all classes of stock of each of the corporations, except the common parent corporation, is owned (directly and with the application of paragraph (b)(1) of § 1.1563-3, relating to options) by one of more of the other corporations; and

(b) The common parent corporation owns (directly and with the application of paragraph (b)(1) of § 1.1563-3, relating to options) stock possessing at least 80 percent of the total combined voting power of all classes of stock entitled to vote or at least 80 percent of the total value of shares of all classes of stock of at least one of the other corporations, excluding, in computing such voting power or value, stock owned directly by such other corporations.

(ii) The definition of a parent-subsidiary controlled group of corporations may be illustrated by the following examples:

Example (1). P Corporation owns stock possessing 80 percent of the total combined voting power of all classes of stock entitled to vote of S Corporation. P is the common parent of a parent-subsidiary controlled group consisting of member corporations P and S.

Example (2). Assume the same facts as in example (1). Assume further that S owns stock possessing 80 percent of the total value of shares of all classes of stock of T Corporation. P is the common parent of a parent-subsidiary controlled group consisting of member corporations P, S, and T. The result would be the same if P, rather than S, owned the T stock.

Example (3). L Corporation owns 80 percent of the only class of stock of M Corporation and M, in turn, owns 40 percent of the only class of stock of O Corporation. L also owns 80 percent of the only class of stock of N Corporation and N, in turn, owns 40 percent of the only class of stock of O. L is the common parent of a parent-subsidiary controlled group consisting of member corporations L, M, N, and O.

Example (4). X Corporation owns 75 percent of the only class of stock of Y and Z Corporations; Y owns all the remaining stock of Z; and Z owns all the remaining stock of Y. Since intercompany stockholdings are excluded (that is, are not treated as outstanding) for purposes of determining whether X owns stock possessing at least 80 percent of the voting power or value of at least one of the other corporations, X is treated as the owner of stock possessing 100 percent of the voting power and value of Y and of Z for purposes of subdivision (i)(b) of this subparagraph. Also, stock possessing 100 percent of the voting power and value of Y and Z is owned by the other corporations in the group within the meaning of subdivision (i)(a) of this subparagraph. (X and Y together own stock possessing 100 percent of the voting power and value of Z, and X and Z together own stock possessing 100 percent of the voting power and value of Y.) Therefore, X is the common parent of a parent-subsidiary controlled group of corporations consisting of member corporations X, Y, and Z.

(3) *Brother-sister controlled group*—(i) The term "brother-sister controlled group" means two or more corporations if the same five or fewer persons who are individuals, estates, or trusts own (directly and with the application of the rules contained in paragraph (b) of § 1.1563-3), stock possessing—

(a) At least 80 percent of the total combined voting power of all classes of stock entitled to vote or at least 80 percent of the total value of shares of all classes of the stock of each corporation; and

(b) More than 50 percent of the total combined voting power of all classes of stock entitled to vote or more than 50 percent of the total value of shares of all classes of stock of each corporation, taking into account the stock ownership of each such person only to the extent such stock ownership is identical with respect to each such corporation.

The five or fewer persons whose stock ownership is considered for purposes of the 80 percent requirement must be the same persons whose stock ownership is considered for purposes of the more-than-50 percent requirement.

(ii) The principles of this subparagraph may be illustrated by the following examples:

Reg. § 1.1563-1(a)(2)

Certain Controlled Corporations

See p. 20,601 for regulations not amended to reflect law changes

Example (1). The outstanding stock of corporations P, Q, R, S, and T, which have only one class of stock outstanding is owned by the following unrelated individuals:

CORPORATIONS

Individuals	P	Q	R	S	T	Identical ownership
A	55%	51%	55%	55%	55%	51%.
B	45%	49%	...	...	...	(45% in P & Q).
C	...	...	45%	...	...	
D	...	...	...	45%	...	
E	...	...	...	...	45%	
Total	100%	100%	100%	100%	100%	

Corporations P and Q are members of a brother-sister controlled group of corporations. Although the more-than-50 percent identical ownership requirement is met for all 5 corporations, corporations R, S, and T are not members because at least 80 percent of the stock of each of those corporations is not owned by the same 5 or fewer persons whose stock ownership is considered for purposes of the more-than-50 percent identical ownership requirement.

Example (2). The outstanding stock of corporations U and V, which have only one class of stock outstanding, is owned by the following unrelated individuals:

Individuals	Corporations	
	U (percent)	V (percent)
A	12	12
B	12	12
C	12	12
D	12	12
E	13	13
F	13	13
G	13	13
H	13	13
Total	100	100

Any group of five of the shareholders will own more than 50 percent of the stock in each corporation, in identical holdings. However, U and V are not members of brother-sister controlled group because at least 80 percent of the stock of each corporation is not owned by the same five or fewer persons.

Example (3). Corporations X and Y each have two classes of stock outstanding, voting common and non-voting common. (None of this stock is excluded from the definition of stock under section 1563(c).) Unrelated individuals A and B own the following percentages of the class of stock entitled to vote (voting) and of the total value of shares of all classes of stock (value) in each of corporations X and Y:

Individuals	Corporations	
	X	Y
A	100% voting, 60% value.	75% voting, 60% value.
B	0% voting, 10% value.	25% voting, 10% value.

No other shareholder of X owns (or is considered to own) any stock in Y. X and Y are a brother-sister controlled group of corporations. The group meets the more-than-50 percent ownership requirements because A and B own more than 50 percent of the total value of shares of all classes of stock of X and Y in identical holdings. (The group also meets the more-than-50 percent ownership requirement because of A's voting stock ownership.) The group meets the 80 percent requirement because A and B own at least 80 percent of the total combined voting power of all classes of stock entitled to vote.

Example (4). Assume the same facts as in example (3) except that the value of the stock owned by A and B is not more than 50 percent of the total value of shares of all classes of stock of each corporation in identical holdings. X and Y are not a brother-sister controlled group of corporations. The group meets the more-than-50 percent ownership requirement because A owns more than 50 percent of the total combined voting power of the voting stock of each corporation. For purposes of the 80 percent requirement, B's voting stock in Y cannot be combined with A's voting stock in Y since B, who does not own any voting stock in X, is not a person whose ownership is considered for purposes of the more-than-50 percent requirement. Because no other shareholder owns stock in both X and Y, these other shareholders' stock ownership is not counted towards meeting either the more-than-50 percent ownership requirement or the 80 percent ownership requirement.

(iii) Paragraph (a)(3) of this section, as amended by T.D. 8179, applies to taxable years ending on or after December 31, 1970. See, how-

Reg. § 1.1563-1(a)(3)

ever, the transitional rule in paragraph (d) of this section.

(4) *Combined group.* (i) The term "combined group" means any group of three or more corporations, if—

(*a*) Each such corporation is a member of either a parent-subsidiary controlled group of corporations or a brother-sister controlled group of corporations, and

(*b*) At least one of such corporations is the common parent of a parent-subsidiary controlled group and also is a member of a brother-sister controlled group.

(ii) The definition of a combined group of corporations may be illustrated by the following examples:

Example (1). Smith, an individual, owns stock possessing 80 percent of the total combined voting power of all classes of the stock of corporations X and Y. Y, in turn, owns stock possessing 80 percent of the total combined voting power of all classes of the stock of corporation Z. Since—

(*a*) X, Y, and Z are each members of either a parent-subsidiary or brother-sister controlled group of corporations, and

(*b*) Y is the common parent of a parent-subsidiary controlled group of corporations consisting of Y and Z, and also is a member of a brother-sister controlled group of corporations consisting of X and Y,

X, Y, and Z are members of the same combined group.

Example (2). Assume the same facts as in example (1), and further assume that corporation X owns 80 percent of the total value of shares of all classes of stock of corporation T. X, Y, Z, and T are members of the same combined group.

(5) *Insurance group.* (i) The term "insurance group" means two or more insurance companies subject to taxation under section 802 each of which is a member of a controlled group of corporations described in subparagraph (2), (3), or (4) of this paragraph. Such insurance companies shall be treated as a controlled group of corporations separate from any other corporations which are members of the controlled group described in such subparagraph (2), (3), or (4). For purposes of this section and § 1.1562-5, the common parent of the controlled group described in subparagraph (2) of this paragraph shall be referred to as the common parent of the insurance group.

(ii) The definition of an insurance group may be illustrated by the following example:

Example. Corporation P owns all the stock of corporation I which, in turn, owns all the stock of corporation X. P also owns all the stock of corporation Y which, in turn, owns all the stock of corporation J. I and J are life insurance companies subject to taxation under section 802 of the Code. Since I and J are members of a parent-subsidiary controlled group of corporations, such companies are treated as members of an insurance group separate from the parent-subsidiary controlled group consisting of P, X, and Y. For purposes of this section and § 1.1562-5, P is referred to as the common parent of the insurance group even though P is not a member of such group.

(6) *Voting power of stock.* For purposes of § 1.1562-5, this section and §§ 1.1563-2, and 1.1563-3, in determining whether the stock owned by a person (or persons) possesses a certain percentage of the total combined voting power of all classes of stock entitled to vote of a corporation, consideration will be given to all the facts and circumstances of each case. A share of stock will generally be considered as possessing the voting power accorded to such share by the corporate charter, by-laws, or share certificate. On the other hand, if there is any agreement, whether express or implied, that a shareholder will not vote his stock in a corporation, the formal voting rights possessed by his stock may be disregarded in determining the percentage of the total combined voting power possessed by the stock owned by other shareholders in the corporation, if the result is that the corporation becomes a component member of a controlled group of corporations. Moreover, if a shareholder agrees to vote his stock in a corporation in the manner specified by another shareholder in the corporation, the voting rights possessed by the stock owned by the first shareholder may be considered to be possessed by the stock owned by such other shareholder if the result is that the corporation becomes a component member of a controlled group of corporations.

(b) *Component members*—(1) *In general.* For purposes of sections 1561 through 1563 and the regulations thereunder, a corporation is a component member of a controlled group of corporations on a December 31 (and with respect to the taxable year which includes such December 31) if such corporation—

(i) Is a member of such controlled group on such December 31 and is not treated as an excluded member under subparagraph (2) of this paragraph, or

(ii) Is not a member of such controlled group on such December 31 but is treated as an additional member under subparagraph (3) of this paragraph.

(2) *Excluded members.* (i) A corporation, which is a member of a controlled group of corpo-

Reg. § 1.1563-1(a)(4)

Certain Controlled Corporations

See p. 20,601 for regulations not amended to reflect law changes

rations on the December 31 included within its taxable year, but was a member of such group for less than one-half of the number of days in such taxable year which precede such December 31, shall be treated as an excluded member of such group on such December 31.

(ii) A corporation which is a member of a controlled group of corporations on any December 31 shall be treated as an excluded member of such group on such date if, for its taxable year including such date, such corporation is—

(a) Exempt from taxation under section 501(a) (except a corporation which has unrelated business taxable income for such taxable year which is subject to tax under section 511) or 521,

(b) A foreign corporation not subject to taxation under section 882(a) for the taxable year,

(c) An electing small business corporation (as defined in section 1371(b)) not subject to the tax imposed by section 1378,

(d) A franchised corporation (as defined in section 1563(f)(4) and § 1.1563-4), or

(e) An insurance company subject to taxation under section 802 or 821, except that an insurance company taxable under section 802 which (without regard to this subdivision) is a component member of an insurance group described in paragraph (a)(5) of this section shall not be treated as an excluded member of such insurance group.

(iii) A corporation which has a taxable year ending on December 31, 1963, shall be treated as an excluded member of a controlled group on such date.

(3) *Additional members.* A corporation which—

(i) Is not a member of a controlled group of corporations on the December 31 included within its taxable year, and

(ii) Is not described, with respect to such taxable year, in subparagraph (2)(ii) (a), (b), (c), (d), or (e), or (2) (iii) of this paragraph, shall be treated as an additional member of such group on such December 31 if it was a member of such group for one-half (or more) of the number of days in such taxable year which precede such December 31.

(4) *Examples.* The provisions of the paragraph may be illustrated by the following examples:

Example (1). Brown, an individual, owns all of the stock of corporations W and X on each day of 1964. W and X each uses the calendar year as its taxable year. On January 1, 1964, Brown also owns all of the stock of corporation Y (a fiscal year corporation with a taxable year beginning on July 1, 1964, and ending on June 30, 1965), which stock he sells on October 15, 1964. On December 1, 1964, Brown purchases all the stock of corporation Z (a fiscal year corporation with a taxable year beginning on September 1, 1964, and ending on August 31, 1965). On December 31, 1964, W, X, and Z are members of the same controlled group. However, the component members of the group on such December 31 are W, X, and Y. Under subparagraph (2)(i) of this paragraph, Z is treated as an excluded member of the group on December 31, 1964, since Z was a member of the group for less than one-half of the number of days (29 out of 121 days) during the period beginning on September 1, 1964 (the first day of its taxable year) and ending on December 30, 1964. Under subparagraph (3) of this paragraph, Y is treated as an additional member of the group on December 31, 1964, since Y was a member of the group for at least one-half of the number of days (107 out of 183 days) during the period beginning on July 1, 1964 (the first day of its taxable year) and ending on December 30, 1964.

Example (2). On January 1, 1964, corporation P owns all the stock of corporation S, which in turn owns all the stock of corporation S-1. On November 1, 1964, P purchases all of the stock of corporation X from the public and sells all of the stock of S to the public. Corporation X owns all the stock of corporation Y during 1964. P, S, S-1, X, and Y file their returns on the basis of the calendar year. On December 31, 1964, P, X, and Y are members of a parent-subsidiary controlled group of corporations; also, corporations S and S-1 are members of a different parent-subsidiary controlled group on such date. However, since X and Y have been members of the parent-subsidiary controlled group of which P is the common parent for less than one-half the number of days during the period January 1 through December 30, 1964, they are not component members of such group on such date. On the other hand, X and Y have been members of a parent-subsidiary controlled group of which X is the common parent for at least one-half the number of days during the period January 1 through December 30, 1964, and therefore they are component members of such group on December 31, 1964. Also since S and S-1 were members of the parent-subsidiary controlled group of which P is the common parent for at least one-half the number of days in the taxable years of each such corporation during the period January 1 through December 30, 1964, P, S, and S-1 are component members of such group on December 31, 1964.

Example (3). Throughout 1964, corporation M owns all the stock of corporation F which, in turn, owns all the stock of corporations L-1, L-2,

Reg. § 1.1563-1(b)(4)

X, and Y. M is a domestic mutual insurance company subject to taxation under section 821, F is a foreign corporation not engaged in trade or business within the United States, L-1 and L-2 are domestic life insurance companies subject to taxation under section 802, and X and Y are domestic corporations subject to tax under section 11 of the Code. Each corporation uses the calendar year as its taxable year. On December 31, 1964, M, F, L-1, L-2, X, and Y are members of a parent-subsidiary controlled group of corporations. However, under subparagraph (2)(ii) of this paragraph, M, F, L-1, and L-2 are treated as excluded members of the group on December 31, 1964. Thus, on December 31, 1964, the component members of the parent-subsidiary controlled group of which M is the common parent include only X and Y. Furthermore, since subparagraph (2)(ii)(e) of this paragraph does not result in L-1 and L-2 being treated as excluded members of an insurance group, L-1 and L-2 are component members of an insurance group on December 31, 1964.

(5) *Application of constructive ownership rules.* For purposes of subparagraphs (2)(i) and (3) of this paragraph, it is necessary to determine whether a corporation was a member of a controlled group of corporations for one-half (or more) of the number of days in its taxable year which precede the December 31 falling within such taxable year. Therefore, the constructive ownership rules contained in paragraph (b) of § 1.1563-3 (to the extent applicable in making such determination) must be applied on a day-by-day basis. For example, if P Corporation owns all the stock of X Corporation on each day of 1964, and on December 30, 1964, acquires an option to purchase all the stock of Y Corporation (a calendar-year taxpayer which has been in existence on each day of 1964), the application of paragraph (b)(1) of § 1.1563-3 on a day-by-day basis results in Y being a member of the brother-sister controlled group on only one day of Y's 1964 year which precedes December 31, 1964. Accordingly, since Y is not a member of such group for one-half or more of the number of days in its 1964 year preceding December 31, 1964, Y is treated as an excluded member of such group on December 31, 1964.

(c) *Overlapping groups*—(1) *In general.* If on a December 31 a corporation is a component member of a controlled group of corporations by reason of ownership of stock possessing at least 80 percent of the total value of shares of all classes of stock of the corporation, and if on such December 31 such corporation is also a component member of another controlled group of corporations by reason of ownership of other stock (that is, stock not used to satisfy the at-least-80-percent total value test) possessing at least 80 percent of the total combined voting power of all classes of stock of the corporation entitled to vote, then such corporation shall be treated as a component member only of the controlled group of which it is a component member by reason of the ownership of at least 80 percent of the total value of its shares.

(2) *Brother-sister controlled groups.* (i) If on a December 31, a corporation would, without application of this subparagraph, be a component member of more than one brother-sister controlled group on such date, such corporation shall be treated as a component member of only one such group on such date. Such a corporation may select which group in which it is to be included by filing an election as provided in this subparagraph. The election shall be in the form of a statement designating the group in which the corporation is to be included. The statement shall provide all the information with respect to stock ownership which is reasonably necessary to satisfy the Internal Revenue officer with whom it is filed that the corporation would, but for the election, be a component member of more than one controlled group. Once filed, the election is irrevocable and effective until such time that a change in the stock ownership of the corporation results in termination of membership in the controlled group in which such corporation has been included.

(ii) Except as provided in subdivision (iii) of this subparagraph, the statement shall be signed by a person duly authorized to act on behalf of such corporation and shall be filed on or before the due date (including extension of time) for the filing of the income tax return of such corporation for the taxable year. However, in the case of an election with respect to December 31, 1970, the statement shall be considered as timely filed if filed on or before December 15, 1971. In the event no election is filed in accordance with the provisions of this subdivision, then the district director with audit jurisdiction of such corporation's return for the taxable year which includes such December 31 shall determine the group in which such corporation is to be included, and such determination shall be binding for all subsequent years unless the corporation files a valid election with respect to any such subsequent year.

(iii) If more than one corporation would, without application of this subparagraph, be a component member of more than one controlled group, a single statement shall be signed by persons duly authorized to act on behalf of each such corporation. Such statement shall designate the group in which each corporation is to be included. The statement shall be attached to the income tax return of the corporation that, among those corporations which would (without the application of this subparagraph) belong to more than one group, has the taxable year including such December 31 which ends on the earliest date. However, in the case of an election with respect to December 31, 1970, the statement may be filed by December 15, 1971, with the service center director with whom such corporation's return is filed for the taxable year which includes such December 31. In the event no election is filed in accordance with the provisions of this subdivision, then the district director with audit jurisdiction of such corporation's return for the taxable year that includes such December 31 shall determine the group in which each corporation is to be included, and such determination shall be binding for all subsequent years unless the corporations file a valid election with respect to any such subsequent year.

(iv) The provisions of this subparagraph may be illustrated by the following examples (in which it is assumed that all the individuals are unrelated):

Example (1). On each day of 1970 all the outstanding stock of corporations M, N, and P is held in the following manner:

Individuals	Corporations		
	M	N	P
A	55%	40%	5%
B	40%	20%	40%
C	5%	40%	55%

Since the more-than-50-percent stock ownership requirement of section 1563(a)(2)(B) is met with respect to corporations M and N and with respect to corporations N and P, but not with respect to corporations M, N, and P, corporation N would, without the application of this subparagraph, be a component member on December 31, 1970, of overlapping groups consisting of M and N and of N and P. If N does not file an election in accordance with subdivision (ii) of this subparagraph, the district director with audit jurisdiction of N's return will determine the group in which N is to be included.

Example (2). On each day of 1970, all the outstanding stock of corporations S, T, W, X, and Z is held in the following manner:

Individuals	Corporations				
	S	T	W	X	Z
D	52%	52%	52%	52%	52%
E	40%	2%	2%	2%	2%
F	2%	40%	2%	2%	2%
G	2%	2%	40%	2%	2%
H	2%	2%	2%	40%	2%
I	2%	2%	2%	2%	40%

On December 31, 1970, the more-than-50-percent stock ownership requirement of section 1563(a)(2)(B) may be met with regard to any combination of the corporations but all five corporations cannot be included as component members of a single controlled group because the inclusion of all the corporations in a single group would be dependent upon taking into account the stock ownership of more than five persons. Therefore, if the corporations do not file a statement in accordance with subdivision (iii) of this subparagraph, the district director with audit jurisdiction of the return of the corporation whose taxable year ends on the earliest date will determine the group in which each corporation is to be included. The corporations or the district director, as the case may be, may designate that three corporations be included in one group and two corporations in another, or that any four corporations be included in one group and that the remaining corporation not be included in any group.

(d) *Transitional rules*—(1) *In general.* Treasury decision 8179 amended paragraph (a)(3) of this section to revise the definition of a brother-sister controlled group of corporations. In general, those amendments are effective for taxable years ending on or after December 31, 1970.

(2) *Limited nonretroactivity.* (i) Under the authority of section 7805(b), the Internal Revenue Service will treat an old group as a brother-sister controlled group of corporations for purposes of applying sections 401, 404(a), 408(k), 409A, 410, 411, 412, 414, 415, and 4971 of the Code and sections 202, 203, 204, and 302 of the Employment Retirement Income Security Act of 1974 (ERISA) in a plan year or taxable year beginning before March 2, 1988. To the extent necessary to prevent an adverse effect on any old member (or any other corporation), or on any plan or other entity described in such sections (including plans, etc., of corporations not part of such old group), that would result solely from the retroactive effect of the amendment to this section by T.D. 8179. An adverse effect includes the disqualification of a plan or the disallowance of a deduction or credit for a contribution to a plan. The Internal Revenue Service, however, will not treat an old member as a member of an old group to the extent that such treatment will have an adverse effect on that old member.

(ii) Section 7805(b) will not be applied pursuant to paragraph (d)(2)(i) of this section to treat an old member of an old group as a member of a brother-sister controlled group to prevent an adverse effect for a taxable year if, for that taxable year, that old member treats or has treated itself as not being a member of that old group for

Reg. § 1.1563-1(d)(2)

purposes of sections 401, 404(a), 408(k), 409A, 410, 411, 412, 414, 415, and 4971 of the Code and sections 202, 203, 204, and 302 and Title IV of ERISA for such taxable year (such as by filing, with respect to such taxable year, a return, amended return, or claim for credit or refund in which the amount of any deduction, credit, limitation, or tax due is determined by treating itself as not being a member of the old group for purposes of those sections).

However, the fact that one or more (but not all) of the old members do not qualify for section 7805(b) treatment because of the preceding sentence will not preclude that old member (or members) from being treated as a member of the old group under paragraph (d)(2)(i) of this section in order to prevent the disallowance of a deduction or credit of another old member (or other corporation) or to prevent the disqualification of, or other adverse effect on, another old member's plan (or other entity) described in the sections of the Code and ERISA enumerated in such paragraph.

(3) *Election of general nonretroactivity.* In the case of a taxable year ending on or after December 31, 1970, and before March 2, 1988. An old group will be treated as a brother-sister controlled group of corporations for all purposes of the Code for such taxable year if—

(i) Each old member files a statement consenting to such treatment for such taxable year with the District Director having audit jurisdiction over its return within six months after March 2, 1988, and

(ii) No old member (A) files or has filed, with respect to such taxable year, a return, amended return, or claim for credit or refund in which the amount of any deduction, credit, limitation, or tax due is determined by treating any old member as not a member of the old group or (B) treats the employees of all members of the old group as not being employed by a single employer for purposes of sections 401, 404(a), 408(k), 409A, 410, 411, 412, 414, 415, and 4971 of the Code and sections 202, 203, 204, and 302 of ERISA for such taxable year.

(4) *Definitions.* For purposes of this paragraph (d) of this section—

(i) An "old group" is a brother-sister controlled group of corporations, determined by applying paragraph (a)(3) of this section as in effect before the amendments made by Treasury decision 8179, that is not a brother-sister controlled group of corporations, determined by applying paragraph (a)(3) of this section as amended by such Treasury decision, and

(ii) An "old member" is any corporation that is a member of an old group.

(5) *Election to choose between membership in more than one controlled group.* If—

(i) An old member has filed an election under paragraph (c)(2) of this section to be treated as a component member of an old group for a December 31 before March 2, 1988, and

(ii) That corporation would (without regard to such paragraph) be a component member of more than one brother-sister controlled group (not including an old group) on the December 31, that corporation may make an election under that paragraph by filing an amended return on or before September 2, 1988. This paragraph (d)(5) does not apply to a corporation that is treated as a member of an old group under paragraph (d)(3) of this section.

(6) *Refunds.* See section 6511(a) for period of limitation on filing claims for credit or refund. [Reg. § 1.1563-1.]

☐ [*T.D.* 6845, 8-4-65. Amended by *T.D.* 6960, 6-24-68, *T.D.* 7181, 4-24-72, *T.D.* 7293, 11-27-73, and *T.D.* 8179, 3-1-88.]

[Reg. § 1.1563-2]

§ 1.1563-2. **Excluded stock.**—(a) *Certain stock excluded.* For purposes of sections 1561 through 1563 and the regulations thereunder, the term "stock" does not include—

(1) Nonvoting stock which is limited and preferred as to dividends, and

(2) Treasury stock.

(b) *Stock treated as excluded stock*—(1) *Parent-subsidiary controlled group.* If a corporation (hereinafter in this paragraph referred to as "parent corporation") owns 50 percent or more of the total combined voting power of all classes of stock entitled to vote or 50 percent or more of the total value of shares of all classes of stock in another corporation (hereinafter in this paragraph referred to as "subsidiary corporation"), the provisions of subparagraph (2) of this paragraph shall apply. For purposes of this subparagraph, stock owned by a corporation means stock owned directly plus stock owned with the application of the constructive ownership rules of paragraph (b)(1) and (4) of § 1.1563-3, relating to options and attribution from corporations. In determining whether the stock owned by a corporation possesses the requisite percentage of the total combined voting power of all classes of stock entitled to vote of another corporation, see paragraph (a)(6) of § 1.1563-1.

(2) *Stock treated as not outstanding.* If the provisions of this subparagraph apply, then for

purposes of determining whether the parent corporation or the subsidiary corporation is a member of a parent-subsidiary controlled group of corporations within the meaning of paragraph (a)(2) of § 1.1563-1, the following stock of the subsidiary corporation shall, except as otherwise provided in paragraph (c) of this section, be treated as if it were not outstanding:

(i) *Plan of deferred compensation.* Stock in the subsidiary corporation held by a trust which is part of a plan of deferred compensation for the benefit of the employees of the parent corporation or the subsidiary corporation. The term "plan of deferred compensation" shall have the same meaning such term has in section 406(a)(3) and the regulations thereunder.

(ii) *Principal stockholders and officers.* Stock in the subsidiary corporation owned (directly and with the application of the rules contained in paragraph (b) of § 1.1563-3) by an individual who is a principal stockholder or officer of the parent corporation. A principal stockholder of the parent corporation is an individual who owns (directly and with the application of the rules contained in paragraph (b) of § 1.1563-3) 5 percent or more of the total combined voting power of all classes of stock entitled to vote or 5 percent or more of the total value of shares of all classes of stock of the parent corporation. An officer of the parent corporation includes the president, vice-presidents, general manager, treasurer, secretary, and comptroller of such corporation, and any other person who performs duties corresponding to those normally performed by persons occupying such positions.

(iii) *Employees.* Stock in the subsidiary corporation owned (directly and with the application of the rules contained in paragraph (b) of § 1.1563-3) by an employee of the subsidiary corporation if such stock is subject to conditions which substantially restrict or limit the employee's right (or if the employee constructively owns such stock, the direct owner's right) to dispose of such stock and which run in favor of the parent or subsidiary corporation. In general, any condition which extends, directly or indirectly, to the parent corporation or the subsidiary corporation preferential rights with respect to the acquisition of the employee's (or direct owner's) stock will be considered to be a condition described in the preceding sentence. It is not necessary, in order for a condition to be considered to be in favor of the parent corporation or the subsidiary corporation, that the parent or subsidiary be extended a discriminatory concession with respect to the price of the stock. For example, a condition whereby the parent corporation is given a right of first refusal with respect to any stock of the subsidiary corporation offered by an employee for sale is a condition which substantially restricts or limits the employee's right to dispose of such stock and runs in favor of the parent corporation. Moreover, any legally enforceable condition which prohibits the employee from disposing of his stock without the consent of the parent (or a subsidiary of the parent) will be considered to be a substantial limitation running in favor of the parent corporation.

(iv) *Controlled exempt organization.* Stock in the subsidiary corporation owned (directly and with the application of the rules contained in paragraph (b) of § 1.1563-3) by an organization (other than the parent corporation)—

(*a*) To which section 501 (relating to certain educational and charitable organizations which are exempt from tax) applies, and

(*b*) Which is controlled directly or indirectly by the parent corporation or subsidiary corporation, by an individual, estate, or trust that is a principal stockholder of the parent corporation, by an officer of the parent corporation, or by any combination thereof.

The terms "principal stockholder of the parent corporation" and "officer of the parent corporation" shall have the same meanings in this subdivision as in subdivision (ii) of this subparagraph. The term "control" as used in this subdivision means control in fact and the determination of whether the control requirement of (*b*) of this subdivision is met will depend upon all the facts and circumstances of each case, without regard to whether such control is legally enforceable and irrespective of the method by which such control is exercised or exercisable.

(3) *Brother-sister controlled group.* If 5 or fewer persons (hereinafter referred to as common owners) who are individuals, estates, or trusts own (directly and with the application of the rules contained in paragraph (b) of § 1.1563-3) stock possessing 50 percent or more of the total combined voting power of all classes of stock entitled to vote or 50 percent or more of the total value of shares of all classes of stock in a corporation, the provisions of subparagraph (4) of this paragraph shall apply. In determining whether the stock owned by such person or persons possesses the requisite percentage of the total combined voting power of all classes of stock entitled to vote of a corporation, see paragraph (a)(6) of § 1.1563-1.

(4) *Stock treated as not outstanding.* If the provisions of this subparagraph apply, then for purposes of determining whether a corporation is a member of a brother-sister controlled group of corporations within the meaning of paragraph

Reg. § 1.1563-2(b)(4)

(a)(3) of § 1.1563-1, the following stock of such corporation shall, except as otherwise provided in paragraph (c) of this section, be treated as if it were not outstanding:

(i) *Exempt employees' trust.* Stock in such corporation held by an employees' trust described in section 401(a) which is exempt from tax under section 501(a), if such trust is for the benefit of the employees of such corporation.

(ii) *Employees.* Stock in such corporation owned (directly and with the application of the rules contained in paragraph (b) of § 1.1563-3) by an employee of such corporation if such stock is subject to conditions which run in favor of a common owner of such corporation (or in favor of such corporation) and which substantially restrict or limit the employee's right (or if the employee constructively owns such stock, the record owner's right) to dispose of such stock. The principles of subparagraph (2)(iii) of this paragraph shall apply in determining whether a condition satisfies the requirements of the preceding sentence. Thus, in general, a condition which extends, directly or indirectly, to a common owner or such corporation preferential rights with respect to the acquisition of the employee's (or record owner's) stock will be considered to be a condition which satisfies such requirements. For purposes of this subdivision, if a condition which restricts or limits an employee's right (or record owner's right) to dispose of his stock also applies to the stock in such corporation held by such common owner pursuant to a bona fide reciprocal stock purchase arrangement, such condition shall not be treated as one which restricts or limits the employee's (or record owner's) right to dispose of such stock. An example of a reciprocal stock purchase arrangement is an agreement whereby a common owner and the employee are given a right of first refusal with respect to stock of the employer corporation owned by the other party. If, however, the agreement also provides that the common owner has the right to purchase the stock of the employer corporation owned by the employee in the event that the corporation should discharge the employee for reasonable cause, the purchase arrangement would not be reciprocal within the meaning of this subdivision.

(iii) *Controlled exempt organization.* Stock in such corporation owned (directly and with the application of the rules contained in paragraph (b) of § 1.1563-3) by an organization—

(a) To which section 501(c)(3) (relating to certain educational and charitable organizations which are exempt from tax) applies, and

(b) Which is controlled directly or indirectly by such corporation, by an individual, estate, or trust that is a principal stockholder of such corporation, by an officer of such corporation, or by any combination thereof. The terms "principal stockholder" and "officer" shall have the same meanings in this subdivision as in subparagraph (2)(ii) of this paragraph. The term "control" as used in this subdivision means control in fact and the determination of whether the control requirement of (b) of this subdivision is met will depend upon all the facts and circumstances of each case, without regard to whether such control is legally enforceable and irrespective of the method by which such control is exercised or exercisable.

(5) *Other controlled groups.* The provisions of subparagraphs (1), (2), (3), and (4) of this paragraph shall apply in determining whether a corporation is a member of a combined group (within the meaning of paragraph (a)(4) of § 1.1563-1) or an insurance group (within the meaning of paragraph (a)(5) of § 1.1563-1). For example, under paragraph (a)(4) of § 1.1563-1, in order for a corporation to be a member of a combined group such corporation must be a member of a parent-subsidiary group or a brother-sister group. Accordingly, the excluded stock rules provided by this paragraph are applicable in determining whether the corporation is a member of such group.

(6) *Meaning of employee.* For purposes of this section, §§ 1.1563-3 and 1.1563-4, the term "employee" has the same meaning such term is given in section 3306(i) of the Code (relating to definitions for purposes of the Federal Unemployment Tax Act). Accordingly, the term employee as used in such sections includes an officer of a corporation.

(7) *Examples.* The provisions of this paragraph may be illustrated by the following examples:

Example (1). Corporation P owns 70 of the 100 shares of the only class of stock of corporation S. The remaining shares of S are owned as follows: 4 shares by Jones (the general manager of P), and 26 shares by Smith (who also owns 5 percent of the total combined voting power of the stock of P). P satisfies the 50 percent stock ownership requirement of subparagraph (1) of this paragraph with respect to S. Since Jones is an officer of P and Smith is a principal stockholder of P, under subparagraph (2)(ii) of this paragraph the S stock owned by Jones and Smith is treated as not outstanding for purposes of determining whether P and S are members of a parent-subsidiary controlled group of corporations within the meaning of paragraph (a)(2) of § 1.1563-1. Thus, P is considered to own stock possessing 100 percent (70 ÷ 70) of the total voting power and value of all the S

Reg. § 1.1563-2(b)(5)

stock. Accordingly, P and S are members of a parent-subsidiary controlled group of corporations.

Example (2). Assume the same facts as in example (1) and further assume that Jones owns 15 shares of the 100 shares of the only class of stock of corporation S-1, and corporation S owns 75 shares of such stock. P satisfies the 50 percent stock ownership requirement of subparagraph (1) of this paragraph with respect to S-1 since P is considered as owning 52.5 percent (70 percent × 75 percent) of the S-1 stock with the application of paragraph (b)(4) of § 1.1563-3. Since Jones is an officer of P, under subparagraph (2)(ii) of this paragraph, the S-1 stock owned by Jones is treated as not outstanding for purposes of determining whether S-1 is a member of the parent-subsidiary controlled group of corporations. Thus, S is considered to own stock possessing 88.2 percent (75 ÷ 85) of the voting power and value of the S-1 stock. Accordingly, P, S, and S-1 are members of a parent-subsidiary controlled group of corporations.

Example (3). Corporation X owns 60 percent of the only class of stock of corporation Y. Davis, the president of Y, owns the remaining 40 percent of the stock of Y. Davis has agreed that if he offers his stock in Y for sale he will first offer the stock to X at a price equal to the fair market value of the stock on the first date the stock is offered for sale. Since Davis is an employee of Y within the meaning of section 3306(i) of the Code, and his stock in Y is subject to a condition which substantially restricts or limits his right to dispose of such stock and runs in favor of X, under subparagraph (2)(iii) of this paragraph such stock is treated as if it were not outstanding for purposes of determining whether X and Y are members of a parent subsidiary controlled group of corporations. Thus, X is considered to own stock possessing 100 percent of the voting power and value of the stock of Y. Accordingly, X and Y are members of a parent-subsidiary controlled group of corporations. The result would be the same if Davis's wife, instead of Davis, owned directly the 40 percent stock interest in Y and such stock was subject to a right of first refusal running in favor of X.

(c) *Exception*—(1) *General.* If stock of a corporation is owned by a person directly or with the application of the rules contained in paragraph (b) of § 1.1563-3 and such ownership results in the corporation being a component member of a controlled group of corporations on a December 31, then the stock shall not be treated as excluded stock under the provisions of paragraph (b) of this section if the result of applying such provisions is that such corporation is not a component member of a controlled group of corporations on such December 31.

(2) *Illustration.* The provisions of this paragraph may be illustrated by the following example:

Example. On each day of 1965, corporation P owns directly 50 of the 100 shares of the only class of stock of corporation S. Jones, an officer of P, owns directly 30 shares of S stock and P has an option to acquire such 30 shares from Jones. The remaining shares of S are owned by unrelated persons. If, pursuant to the provisions of paragraph (b)(2)(ii) of this section, the 30 shares of S stock owned directly by Jones is treated as not outstanding, the result is that P would be treated as owning stock possessing only 71 percent (50 ÷ 70) of the total voting power and value of S stock, and S would not be a component member of a controlled group of corporations on December 31, 1965. However, since P is considered as owning the 30 shares of S stock with the application of paragraph (b)(1) of this section, and such ownership plus the S stock directly owned by P (50 shares) results in S being a component member of a controlled group of corporations on December 31, 1965, the provisions of this paragraph apply. Therefore, the provisions of paragraph (b)(2)(ii) of this section do not apply with respect to the 30 shares of S stock, and on December 31, 1965, S is a component member of a controlled group of corporations consisting of P and S. [Reg. § 1.1563-2.]

☐ [*T.D.* 6845, 8-4-65. *Amended by T.D.* 7181, 4-24-72.]

[Reg. § 1.1563-3]

§ 1.1563-3. Rules for determining stock ownership.—(a) *In general.* In determining stock ownership for purposes of §§ 1.1562-5, 1.1563-1, 1.1563-2, and this section, the constructive ownership rules of paragraph (b) of this section apply to the extent such rules are referred to in such sections. The application of such rules shall be subject to the operating rules and special rules contained in paragraphs (c) and (d) of this section.

(b) *Constructive ownership*—(1) *Options.* If a person has an option to acquire any outstanding stock of a corporation, such stock shall be considered as owned by such person. For purposes of this subparagraph, an option to acquire such an option, and each one of a series of such options, shall be considered as an option to acquire such stock. For example, assume Smith owns an option to purchase 100 shares of the outstanding stock of M Corporation. Under this subparagraph, Smith is

Reg. § 1.1563-3(b)(1)

considered to own such 100 shares. The result would be the same if Smith owned an option to acquire the option (or one of a series of options) to purchase 100 shares of M stock.

(2) *Attribution from partnerships.* (i) Stock owned, directly or indirectly, by or for a partnership shall be considered as owned by any partner having an interest of 5 percent or more in either the capital or profits of the partnership in proportion to his interest in capital or profits, whichever such proportion is the greater.

(ii) The provisions of this subparagraph may be illustrated by the following example:

Example. Green, Jones, and White, unrelated individuals, are partners in the GJW partnership. The partners' interests in the capital and profits of the partnership are as follows:

Partner	Capital	Profits
Green	36%	25%
Jones	60	71
White	4	4

The GJW partnership owns the entire outstanding stock (100 shares) of X Corporation. Under this subparagraph, Green is considered to own the X stock owned by the partnership in proportion to his interest in capital (36 percent) or profits (25 percent), whichever such proportion is the greater. Therefore, Green is considered to own 36 shares of the X stock. However, since Jones has a greater interest in the profits of the partnership, he is considered to own the X stock in proportion to his interest in such profits. Therefore, Jones is considered to own 71 shares of the X stock. Since White does not have an interest of 5 percent or more in either the capital or profits of the partnership, he is not considered to own any shares of the X stock.

(3) *Attribution from estates or trusts.* (i) Stock owned, directly or indirectly, by or for an estate or trust shall be considered as owned by any beneficiary who has an actuarial interest of 5 percent or more in such stock, to the extent of such actuarial interest. For purposes of this subparagraph, the actuarial interest of each beneficiary shall be determined by assuming the maximum exercise of discretion by the fiduciary in favor of such beneficiary and the maximum use of such stock to satisfy his rights as a beneficiary. A beneficiary of an estate or trust who cannot under any circumstances receive any interest in stock held by the estate or trust, including the proceeds from the disposition thereof, or the income therefrom, does not have an actuarial interest in such stock. Thus, where stock owned by a decedent's estate has been specifically bequeathed to certain beneficiaries and the remainder of the estate is bequeathed to other beneficiaries, the stock is attributable only to the beneficiaries to whom it is specifically bequeathed. Similarly, a remainderman of a trust who cannot under any circumstances receive any interest in the stock of a corporation which is a part of the corpus of the trust (including any accumulated income therefrom or the proceeds from a disposition thereof) does not have an actuarial interest in such stock. However, an income beneficiary of a trust does have an actuarial interest in stock if he has any right to the income from such stock even though under the terms of the trust instrument such stock can never be distributed to him. The factors and methods prescribed in § 20.2031-7 of this chapter (Estate Tax Regulations) [Reg. § 20.2031-7 of this chapter is reproduced at ¶ 2391.05.—CCH.] for use in ascertaining the value of an interest in property for estate tax purposes shall be used for purposes of this subdivision in determining a beneficiary's actuarial interest in stock owned directly or indirectly by or for a trust.

(ii) For the purposes of this subparagraph, property of a decedent shall be considered as owned by his estate if such property is subject to administration by the executor or administrator for the purposes of paying claims against the estate and expenses of administration notwithstanding that, under local law, legal title to such property vests in the decedent's heirs, legatees or devisees immediately upon death. With respect to an estate, the term "beneficiary" includes any person entitled to receive property of the decedent pursuant to a will or pursuant to laws of descent and distribution. A person shall no longer be considered a beneficiary of an estate when all the property to which he is entitled has been received by him, when he no longer has a claim against the estate arising out of having been a beneficiary, and when there is only a remote possibility that it will be necessary for the estate to seek the return of property or to seek payment from him by contribution or otherwise to satisfy claims against the estate or expenses of administration. When pursuant to the preceding sentence, a person ceases to be a beneficiary, stock owned by the estate shall not thereafter be considered owned by him.

(iii) Stock owned, directly or indirectly, by or for any portion of a trust of which a person is considered the owner under subpart E, part I, subchapter J of the Code (relating to grantors and others treated as substantial owners) is considered as owned by such person.

(iv) This subparagraph does not apply to stock owned by any employees' trust described in

Reg. § 1.1563-3(b)(2)

section 401(a) which is exempt from tax under section 501(a).

(4) *Attribution from corporations.* (i) Stock owned, directly or indirectly, by or for a corporation shall be considered as owned by any person who owns (within the meaning of section 1563(d)) 5 percent or more in value of its stock in that proportion which the value of the stock which such person so owns bears to the value of all the stock in such corporation.

(ii) The provisions of this subparagraph may be illustrated by the following example:

Example. Brown, an individual, owns 60 shares of the 100 shares of the only class of outstanding stock of corporation P. Smith, an individual, owns 4 shares of the P stock, and corporation X owns 36 shares of the P stock. Corporation P owns, directly and indirectly, 50 shares of the stock of corporation S. Under this subparagraph, Brown is considered to own 30 shares of the S stock (60/100 × 50), and X is considered to own 18 shares of the S stock (36/100 × 50). Since Smith does not own 5 percent or more in value of the P stock, he is not considered as owning any of the S stock owned by P. If, in this example, Smith's wife had owned directly 1 share of the P stock, Smith (and his wife) would each own 5 shares of the P stock, and therefore Smith (and his wife) would be considered as owning 2.5 shares of the S stock (5/100 × 50).

(5) *Spouse.* (i) Except as provided in subdivision (ii) of this subparagraph, an individual shall be considered to own the stock owned, directly or indirectly, by or for his spouse, other than a spouse who is legally separated from the individual under a decree of divorce, whether interlocutory or final, or a decree of separate maintenance.

(ii) An individual shall not be considered to own stock in a corporation owned, directly or indirectly, by or for his spouse on any day of a taxable year of such corporation, provided that each of the following conditions are satisfied with respect to such taxable year:

(*a*) Such individual does not, at any time during such taxable year, own directly any stock in such corporation.

(*b*) Such individual is not a member of the board of directors or an employee of such corporation and does not participate in the management of such corporation at any time during such taxable year.

(*c*) Not more than 50 percent of such corporation's gross income for such taxable year was derived from royalties, rents, dividends, interest, and annuities.

(*d*) Such stock in such corporation is not, at any time during such taxable year, subject to conditions which substantially restrict or limit the spouse's right to dispose of such stock and which run in favor of the individual or his children who have not attained the age of 21 years. The principles of paragraph (b)(2)(iii) of § 1.1563-2 shall apply in determining whether a condition is a condition described in the preceding sentence.

(iii) For purposes of subdivision (ii)(*c*) of this subparagraph, the gross income of a corporation for a taxable year shall be determined under section 61 and the regulations thereunder. The terms "royalties", "rents", "dividends", "interest", and "annuities" shall have the same meanings such terms are given for purposes of section 1244(c). See paragraph (e)(1)(ii), (iii), (iv), (v), and (vi) of § 1.1244(c)-1.

(6) *Children, grandchildren, parents, and grandparents.* (i) An individual shall be considered to own the stock owned, directly or indirectly, by or for his children who have not attained the age of 21 years, and, if the individual has not attained the age of 21 years, the stock owned, directly or indirectly, by or for his parents.

(ii) If an individual owns (directly, and with the application of the rules of this paragraph but without regard to this subdivision) stock possessing more than 50 percent of the total combined voting power of all classes of stock entitled to vote or more than 50 percent of the total value of shares of all classes of stock in a corporation, then such individual shall be considered to own the stock in such corporation owned, directly or indirectly, by or for his parents, grandparents, grandchildren, and children who have attained the age of 21 years. In determining whether the stock owned by an individual possesses the requisite percentage of the total combined voting power of all classes of stock entitled to vote of a corporation, see paragraph (a)(6) of § 1.1563-1.

(iii) For purposes of section 1563, and §§ 1.1563-1 through 1.1563-4, a legally adopted child of an individual shall be treated as a child of such individual by blood.

(iv) The provisions of this subparagraph may be illustrated by the following example:

Example—(*a*) *Facts.* Individual F owns directly 40 shares of the 100 shares of the only class of stock of Z Corporation. His son, M (20 years of age), owns directly 30 shares of such stock, and his son, A (30 years of age), owns directly 20 shares of such stock. The remaining 10 shares of the Z stock are owned by an unrelated person.

Reg. § 1.1563-3(b)(6)

(b) *F's ownership.* Individual F owns 40 shares of the Z stock directly and is considered to own the 30 shares of Z stock owned directly by M. Since, for purposes of the more-than-50-percent stock ownership test contained in subdivision (ii) of this subparagraph, F is treated as owning 70 shares or 70 percent of the total voting power and value of the Z stock, he is also considered as owning the 20 shares owned by his adult son, A. Accordingly, F is considered as owning a total of 90 shares of the Z stock.

(c) *M's ownership.* Minor son, M, owns 30 shares of the Z stock directly, and is considered to own the 40 shares of Z stock owned directly by his father, F. However, M is not considered to own the 20 shares of Z stock owned directly by his brother, A, and constructively by F, because stock constructively owned by F by reason of family attribution is not considered as owned by him for purposes of making another member of his family the constructive owner of such stock. See paragraph (c)(2) of this section. Accordingly, M owns and is considered as owning a total of 70 shares of the Z stock.

(d) *A's ownership.* Adult son, A, owns 20 shares of the Z stock directly. Since, for purposes of the more-than-50-percent stock ownership test contained in subdivision (ii) of this subparagraph, A is treated as owning only the Z stock which he owns directly, he does not satisfy the condition precedent for the attribution of Z stock from his father. Accordingly, A is treated as owning only the 20 shares of Z stock which he owns directly.

(c) *Operating rules and special rules*—(1) *In general.* Except as provided in subparagraph (2) of this paragraph, stock constructively owned by a person by reason of the application of subparagraph (1), (2), (3), (4), (5), or (6) of paragraph (b) of this section shall, for purposes of applying such subparagraphs, be treated as actually owned by such person.

(2) *Members of family.* Stock constructively owned by an individual by reason of the application of subparagraph (5) or (6) of paragraph (b) of this section shall not be treated as owned by him for purposes of again applying such subparagraphs in order to make another the constructive owner of such stock.

(3) *Precedence of option attribution.* For purposes of this section, if stock may be considered as owned by a person under subparagraph (1) of paragraph (b) of this section (relating to option attribution) and under any other subparagraph of such paragraph, such stock shall be considered as owned by such person under subparagraph (1) of such paragraph.

(4) *Examples.* The provisions of this paragraph may be illustrated by the following examples:

Example (1). A, 30 years of age, has a 90 percent interest in the capital and profits of a partnership. The partnership owns all the outstanding stock of corporation X and X owns 60 shares of the 100 outstanding shares of corporation Y. Under subparagraph (1) of this paragraph, the 60 shares of Y constructively owned by the partnership by reason of subparagraph (4) of paragraph (b) of this section is treated as actually owned by the partnership for purposes of applying subparagraph (2) of paragraph (b) of this section. Therefore, A is considered as owning 54 shares of the Y stock (90 percent of 60 shares).

Example (2). Assume the same facts as in example (1). Assume further that B, who is 20 years of age and the brother of A, directly owns 40 shares of Y stock. Although the stock of Y owned by B is considered as owned by C (the father of A and B) under paragraph (b)(6)(i) of this section, under subparagraph (2) of this paragraph such stock may not be treated as owned by C for purposes of applying paragraph (b)(6)(ii) of this section in order to make A the constructive owner of such stock.

Example (3). Assume the same facts assumed for purposes of example (2), and further assume that C has an option to acquire the 40 shares of Y stock owned by his son, B. The rule contained in subparagraph (2) of this paragraph does not prevent the reattribution of such 40 shares to A because, under subparagraph (3) of this paragraph, C is considered as owning the 40 shares by reason of option attribution and not by reason of family attribution. Therefore, since A satisfies the more-than-50-percent stock ownership test contained in paragraph (b)(6)(ii) of this section with respect to Y, the 40 shares of Y stock constructively owned by C are reattributed to A, and A is considered as owning a total of 94 shares of Y stock.

(d) *Special rule of section 1563(f)(3)(B)*—(1) *In general.* If the same stock of a corporation is owned (within the meaning of section 1563(d)) by two or more persons, then such stock shall be treated as owned by the person whose ownership of such stock results in the corporation being a component member of a controlled group on a December 31 which has at least one other component member on such date.

(2) *Component member of more than one group.* (i) If, by reason of subparagraph (1) of this paragraph, a corporation would (but for this subparagraph) become a component member of more than one controlled group on a December 31, such

Reg. § 1.1563-3(c)(1)

corporation shall be treated as a component member of only one such controlled group on such date. The determination as to which group such corporation is treated as a component member of shall be made in accordance with the rules contained in subdivisions (ii), (iii), and (iv) of this subparagraph.

(ii) In any case in which a corporation is a component member of a controlled group of corporations on a December 31 as a result of treating each share of its stock as owned only by the person who owns such share directly, then each such share shall be treated as owned by the person who owns such share directly.

(iii) If the application of subdivision (ii) of this subparagraph does not result in a corporation being treated as a component member of only one controlled group on a December 31, then the stock of such corporation described in subparagraph (1) of this paragraph shall be treated as owned by the one person described in such subparagraph who owns, directly and with the application of the rules contained in paragraph (b)(1), (2), (3), and (4) of this section, the stock possessing the greatest percentage of the total value of shares of all classes of stock of the corporation.

(iv) If the application of subdivision (ii) or (iii) of this subparagraph does not result in a corporation being treated as a component member of only one controlled group of corporations on a December 31, then the determination of that group of which such corporation is to be treated as a component member shall be made by the district director with audit jurisdiction of such corporation's return for the taxable year that includes such December 31 unless such corporation files an election as provided in this subdivision. The election shall be in the form of a statement, signed by a person authorized to act on behalf of such corporation, designating the group in which the corporation has elected to be included. The statement shall provide all the information with respect to stock ownership which is reasonably necessary to satisfy the district director that the corporation would, but for the election, be a component member of more than one controlled group. The statement shall be filed on or before the due date (including extensions of time) for the filing of the income tax return of such corporation for the taxable year. However, in the case of an election with respect to December 31, 1970, the statement shall be considered as timely filed if filed on or before December 15, 1971. Once filed, the election is irrevocable and effective until subdivision (ii) or (iii) of this subparagraph applies or until there is a substantial change in the stock ownership of such corporation.

(3) *Examples.* The provisions of this paragraph may be illustrated by the following examples, in which each corporation referred to uses the calendar year as its taxable year and the stated facts are assumed to exist on each day of 1970 (unless otherwise provided in the example):

Example (1). Jones owns all the stock of corporation X and has an option to purchase from Smith all the outstanding stock of corporation Y. Smith owns all the outstanding stock of corporation Z. Since the Y stock is considered as owned by two or more persons, under subparagraph (2)(ii) of this paragraph the Y stock is treated as owned only by Smith since he has direct ownership of such stock. Therefore, on December 31, 1970, Y and Z are component members of the same brother-sister controlled group. If, however, Smith had owned his stock in corporation Z for less than one-half of the number of days of Z's 1970 taxable year, then under subparagraph (1) of this paragraph the Y stock would be treated as owned only by Jones since his ownership results in Y being a component member of a controlled group on December 31, 1970.

Example (2). Individual H owns directly all the outstanding stock of corporation M. W (the wife of H) owns directly all the outstanding stock of corporation N. Neither spouse is considered as owning the stock directly owned by the other because each of the conditions prescribed in paragraph (b)(5)(ii) of this section is satisfied with respect to each corporation's 1970 taxable year. H owns directly 60 percent of the only class of stock of corporation P and W owns the remaining 40 percent of the P stock. Under subparagraph (2)(iii) of this paragraph, the stock of P is treated as owned only by H since H owns (directly and with the application of the rules contained in paragraph (b)(1), (2), (3), and (4) of this section) the stock possessing the greatest percentage of the total value of shares of all classes of stock of P. Accordingly, on December 31, 1970, P is treated as a component member of a brother-sister group consisting of M and P.

Example (3). Unrelated individuals A and B each own 49 percent of all the outstanding stock of corporation R, which in turn owns 70 percent of the only class of outstanding stock of corporation S. The remaining 30 percent of the stock of corporation S is owned by unrelated individual C. C also owns the remaining 2 percent of the stock of corporation R. Under the attribution rule of paragraph (b)(4) of this section A and B are each considered to own 34.3 percent of the stock of corporation S. Accordingly, since five or fewer persons own at least 80 percent of the stock of corporations R and S and also own more than 50

Reg. § 1.1563-3(d)(3)

percent identically (A's and B's identical ownership each is 34.3 percent, C's identical ownership is 2 percent), on December 31, 1970, corporations R and S are treated as component members of the same brother-sister controlled group. [Reg. § 1.1563-3.]

☐ [T.D. 6845, 8-4-65. Amended by T.D. 7181, 4-24-72, T.D. 7779, 6-1-81 and T.D. 8179, 3-1-88.]

[Reg. § 1.1563-4]

§ 1.1563-4. Franchised corporations.—(a) *In general.* For purposes of paragraph (b)(2)(ii)(*d*) of § 1.1563-1, a member of a controlled group of corporations shall be considered to be a franchised corporation for a taxable year if each of the following conditions is satisfied for one-half (or more) of the number of days preceding the December 31 included within such taxable year (or, if such taxable year does not include a December 31, for one-half or more of the number of days in such taxable year preceding the last day of such year):

(1) Such member is franchised to sell the products of another member, or the common owner, of such controlled group.

(2) More than 50 percent (determined on the basis of cost) of all the goods held by such member primarily for sale to its customers are acquired from members or the common owner of the controlled group, or both.

(3) The stock of such member is to be sold to an employee (or employees) of such member pursuant to a bona fide plan designed to eliminate the stock ownership of the parent corporation (as defined in paragraph (b)(1) of § 1.1563-2) or of the common owner (as defined in paragraph (b)(3) of § 1.1563-2) in such member.

(4) Such employee owns (or such employees in the aggregate own) directly more than 20 percent of the total value of shares of all classes of stock of such member. For purposes of this subparagraph, the determination of whether an employee (or employees) owns the requisite percentage of the total value of the stock of the member shall be made without regard to paragraph (b) of § 1.1563-2, relating to certain stock treated as excluded stock. Furthermore, if the corporation has more than one class of stock outstanding, the relative voting rights as between each such class of stock shall be disregarded in making such determination.

(b) *Plan for elimination of stock ownership.* (1) A plan referred to in paragraph (a)(3) of this section must—

(i) Provide a reasonable selling price for the stock of the member, and

(ii) Require that a portion of the employee's compensation or dividends, or both, from such member be applied to the purchase of such stock (or to the purchase of notes, bonds, debentures, or similar evidences of indebtedness of such member held by the parent corporation or the common owner).

It is not necessary, in order to satisfy the requirements of subdivision (ii) of this subparagraph, that the plan require that a percentage of every dollar of the compensation and dividends be applied to the purchase of the stock (or the indebtedness). The requirements of such subdivision are satisfied if an otherwise qualified plan provides that under certain specified conditions (such as a requirement that the member earn a specified profit) no portion of the compensation and/or dividends need be applied to the purchase of the stock (or indebtedness), provided such conditions are reasonable.

(2) A plan for the elimination of the stock ownership of the parent corporation or of the common owner will satisfy the requirements of paragraph (a)(3) of this section and subparagraph (1) of this paragraph even though it does not require that the stock of the member be sold to an employee (or employees) if it provides for the redemption of the stock of the member held by the parent or common owner and under the plan the amount of such stock to be redeemed during any period is calculated by reference to the profits of such member during such period. [Reg. § 1.1563-4.]

☐ [T.D. 6845, 8-4-65.]

Reg. § 1.1563-4(a)(1)